HANDBOOK OF PERCEPTION AND HUMAN PERFORMANCE

Volume I

HANDBOOK OF PERCEPTION AND HUMAN PERFORMANCE

VOLUME I
Sensory Processes and Perception

Editors:

KENNETH R. BOFF *Armstrong Aerospace Medical Research Laboratory*

LLOYD KAUFMAN *New York University*

JAMES P. THOMAS *University of California at Los Angeles*

A Wiley-Interscience Publication

JOHN WILEY AND SONS

New York • Chichester • Brisbane • Toronto • Singapore

This publication is designed to provide accurate and authoritative information in regard to the subject matter covered. It is sold with the understanding that the publisher is not engaged in rendering legal, accounting, or other professional service. If legal advice or other expert assistance is required, the services of a competent professional person should be sought. *From a Declaration of Principles jointly adopted by a Committee of the American Bar Association and a Committee of Publishers.*

Library of Congress Cataloging in Publication Data:

Main entry under title:

Handbook of perception and human performance.

Also published with different foreword for limited distribution to the U.S. Dept. of Defense.
"A Wiley-Interscience publication."
Includes bibliographical references and indexes.
Contents: v. 1. Sensory processes and perception.
1. Perception. 2. Cognition. 3. Human information processing. 4. Performance. I. Boff, Kenneth R. II. Kaufman, Lloyd. III. Thomas, James P. (James Peringer), 1932– [DNLM: 1. Perception. 2. Psychomotor Performance. BF 311 H2357]

BF311.H3345 1986 153.7 85-20375

ISBN 0-471-88544-4 (v. I)
ISBN 0-471-82956-0 (Two-volume set)

Printed in the United States of America

10 9 8 7 6 5 4 3 2 1

CONTRIBUTORS

STUART ANSTIS, PH.D.
Professor of Psychology
York University
Downsview, Ontario, Canada

ARIES ARDITI, PH.D.
Department of Research
The New York Association for the Blind
and Department of Psychology
New York University
New York, New York

H. G. BARROW, PH.D.
Chief Scientist, Artificial Intelligence
Schlumberger Palo Alto Research
Palo Alto, California

JACKSON BEATTY, PH.D.
Professor of Psychology
University of California at Los Angeles
Los Angeles, California

KENNETH R. BOFF, PH.D.
Senior Scientist
Armstrong Aerospace Medical Research Laboratory
Wright-Patterson Air Force Base, Ohio

SØREN BUUS, PH.D.
Senior Scientist
Northeastern University and Harvard University
Boston and Cambridge, Massachusetts

STUART K. CARD, PH.D.
Research Scientist
Xerox Palo Alto Research Center
Palo Alto, California

THOMAS H. CARR, PH.D.
Associate Professor of Psychology
Michigan State University
East Lansing, Michigan

WILLIAM G. CHASE, PH.D. (*Deceased*)
Professor of Psychology
Carnegie-Mellon University
Pittsburgh, Pennsylvania

ROGER W. CHOLEWIAK, PH.D.
Research Psychologist
Princeton University
Princeton, New Jersey

FRANCIS J. CLARK, PH.D.
Professor of Physiology
University of Nebraska College of Medicine
Omaha, Nebraska

DIANA DEUTSCH, PH.D.
Research Psychologist
University of California at San Diego
La Jolla, California

EMANUEL DONCHIN, PH.D.
Professor of Psychology and Physiology
University of Illinois
Champaign, Illinois

BARBARA ANNE DOSHER, PH.D.
Associate Professor of Psychology
Columbia University
New York, New York

F. THOMAS EGGEMEIER, PH.D.
Assistant Professor of Psychology (WSU)/ Senior Scientist (SRL)
Wright State University/Systems Research Laboratories, Inc.
Dayton, Ohio

J. C. FALMAGNE, PH.D.
Professor of Psychology
New York University
New York, New York

RONALD A. FINKE, PH.D.
Assistant Professor of Psychology
State University of New York at Stony Brook
Stony Brook, New York

MARCIA A. FINKELSTEIN, PH.D.
Assistant Professor of Psychology
University of South Florida
Tampa, Florida

HERBERT FREEMAN, DR.ENG.SC.
Professor of Computer Engineering
Rutgers University
New Brunswick, New Jersey

ARTHUR P. GINSBURG, PH.D.
Director of R&D
Vistech Consultants, Inc.
Dayton, Ohio

DANIEL GOPHER, PH.D.
Associate Professor of Industrial Engineering and Management
Technion-Israel Institute of Technology
Haifa, Israel

PETER E. HALLETT, B.A., M.A., B.SC., B.M. (Oxon)
Professor of Physiology
University of Toronto
Toronto, Ontario, Canada

HAROLD L. HAWKINS, PH.D.
Psychological Sciences Division
Office of Naval Research
Arlington, Virginia

JULIAN HOCHBERG, PH.D.
Centennial Professor of Psychology
Columbia University
New York, New York

G. ROBERT HOCKEY, PH.D.
Department of Psychology
University of Sheffield
Sheffield, England

DONALD C. HOOD, PH.D.
Professor of Psychology
Columbia University
New York, New York

KENNETH W. HORCH, PH.D.
Department of Physiology
University of Utah School of Medicine
Salt Lake City, Utah

ADRIANUS J. M. HOUTSMA, PH.D.
Senior Research Associate
Institute for Perception Research
Technical University, Eindhoven
Eindhoven, The Netherlands

IAN P. HOWARD, PH.D.
Professor of Psychology
York University
Toronto, Ontario, Canada

PETER W. JUSCZYK, PH.D.
Associate Professor of Psychology
University of Oregon
Eugene, Oregon

LLOYD KAUFMAN, PH.D.
Professor of Psychology and Professor of Physiology and Biophysics
New York University
New York, New York

STEVEN W. KEELE, PH.D.
Professor of Psychology
University of Oregon
Eugene, Oregon

MICHAEL KUBOVY, PH.D.
Professor of Psychology
Rutgers University
New Brunswick, New Jersey

SUSAN J. LEDERMAN, PH.D.
Associate Professor of Psychology
Queen's University at Kingston
Kingston, Ontario, Canada

JANET LINCOLN, PH.D.
Research Associate
Department of Psychology
New York University
New York, New York

JACK M. LOOMIS, PH.D.
Associate Professor of Psychology
University of California at Santa Barbara
Santa Barbara, California

ARIEN MACK, PH.D.
Professor of Psychology
New School for Social Research
New York, New York

LEONARD MATIN, PH.D.
Professor of Psychology
Columbia University
New York, New York

THOMAS P. MORAN, PH.D.
Manager, User-System Research Area
Xerox Palo Alto Research Center
Palo Alto, California

NEVILLE MORAY, M.A., D. PHIL. (Oxon)
Professor of Industrial Engineering
University of Toronto
Toronto, Ontario, Canada

ALLEN NEWELL, PH.D.
Professor of Computer Science
Carnegie-Mellon University
Pittsburgh, Pennsylvania

ROBERT D. O'DONNELL, PH.D.
Research Psychologist (Colonel, USAF)
Armstrong Aerospace Medical Research Laboratory
Wright-Patterson Air Force Base, Ohio

LYNN A. OLZAK, PH.D.
Assistant Research Psychologist
University of California at Los Angeles
Los Angeles, California

RAJA PARASURAMAN, PH.D.
Associate Professor of Psychology
Catholic University of America
Washington, D.C.

JOEL POKORNY, PH.D.
Professor of Ophthalmology and Behavioral Sciences
University of Chicago
Chicago, Illinois

JAMES R. POMERANTZ, PH.D.
Professor of Psychology
State University of New York at Buffalo
Buffalo, New York

MICHAEL I. POSNER, PH.D.
Professor of Psychology
University of Oregon
Eugene, Oregon

JOELLE C. PRESSON, PH.D.
Research Associate, Psychology
University of Oregon
Eugene, Oregon

DAVID MARTIN REGAN, PH.D., D.SC.
Professor of Biomedical Engineering
Rutgers University
New Brunswick, New Jersey

I. ROCK, PH.D.
Professor of Psychology
Rutgers University
New Brunswick, New Jersey

BERTRAM SCHARF, PH.D.
Professor of Psychology
Northeastern University
Boston, Massachusetts

H. A. SEDGWICK, PH.D.
Associate Professor of Vision Sciences
State University of New York
College of Optometry
New York, New York

ROGER N. SHEPARD, PH.D.
Professor of Psychology
Stanford University
Stanford, California

CARL E. SHERRICK, PH.D.
Senior Research Psychologist and Lecturer
Princeton University
Princeton, New Jersey

VIVIANNE C. SMITH, PH.D.
Professor of Ophthalmology
University of Chicago
Chicago, Illinois

GEORGE SPERLING, PH.D.
Professor of Psychology
New York University
New York, New York

JAMES J. STASZEWSKI
Research Associate
Carnegie-Mellon University
Pittsburgh, Pennsylvania

J. MARTIN TENENBAUM, PH.D.
Director, Artificial Intelligence Research
Schlumberger Palo Alto Research Computer Aided Systems
Palo Alto, California

JAMES P. THOMAS, PH.D.
Professor of Psychology
University of California at Los Angeles
Los Angeles, California

ANNE TREISMAN, PH.D.
Professor of Psychology
University of British Columbia
Vancouver, British Columbia, Canada

DAVID H. WARREN, PH.D.
Professor of Psychology/Dean, College of Humanities and Social Sciences
University of California at Riverside
Riverside, California

ANDREW B. WATSON, PH.D.
Research Scientist
NASA Ames Research Center
Moffett Field, California

ROBERT B. WELCH, PH.D.
Professor of Psychology
University of Kansas
Lawrence, Kansas

GERALD WESTHEIMER, O.D., PH.D.
Professor of Physiology
University of California at Berkeley
Berkeley, California

CHRISTOPHER D. WICKENS, PH.D.
Professor and Head, Aviation Research Laboratory
University of Illinois Institute of Aviation
Savoy, Illinois

GUNTER WYSZECKI, DR.-ING. (*Deceased*)
Director
Institute of Optics, National Research Council
Ottawa, Ontario, Canada

"Nam et ipsa scientia potestas est"

(In and of itself, knowledge is power.)

From
Francis Bacon's *Meditationes Sacrae*,
1597, De Haeresibus

FOREWORD

Technology forecasts generally agree that our society is becoming one of instant communication of information between people, mediated by complex information systems. The issue of design efficiency of the communications interface remains the central area of concern to designers. Indeed, when not designed well, this interface becomes a major source of system error, thereby leading to customer rejection or, in the worst case, unsafe conditions. Many system designers do not appreciate that a great deal of basic research data germane to this issue exists in the literature of perception and human performance. Until now this information has not been readily available to designers of information systems and, until recent advances in display and information handling technology, was probably not needed in the depth presented in these volumes. Hence a major purpose for development of this Handbook was to critically filter the basic research literature for data and models that would be of practical significance to the human engineering of equipment design. Data spanning 45 topic domains involving more than 60 authors and editors were selected for their potential value to practical application in design. This effort is particularly significant because much of this subject matter has not previously been considered for human engineering applications.

The information found in these volumes was distilled from the open literature by an eminently qualified group of contributors whose emphasis was foremost on producing an accurate and scholarly account of their respective areas of expertise. Without a doubt many omissions have occurred; however, the rigorous in-depth treatment of the subject matter, biased by concern over practical value, commends this Handbook to the practitioner, researcher, or advanced student requiring a comprehensive level of detail outside his or her own technical specialty.

CHARLES BATES, JR.

Director, Human Engineering Division
Armstrong Aerospace Medical Research Laboratory
Wright-Patterson Air Force Base, Ohio

PREFACE

In science, by a fiction as remarkable as any to be found in law, what has once been published, even though it be in the Russian language, is spoken of as known, *and it is too often forgotten that the rediscovery in the library may be a more difficult and uncertain process than the first discovery in the laboratory.*

LORD RAYLEIGH, 1884

The successful acquisition and interpretation of relevant information from primary source literature in perception and human performance can be a formidable task. This is due, in part, to the continuing growth and staggering volume of existing data and the manner in which it is organized topically and distributed physically over a wide number of individual journals and report media. The further removed an investigator's expertise from the objective of search, the more probable that important sources of data will be misinterpreted or missed entirely. Thus the effectiveness of direct access to the literature may be seriously constrained by the selection of appropriate key terms and the investigator's ability to discriminate "hits" from "false alarms" from the volume of potential sources related to the object of search.

Secondary sources, including textbooks, anthologies, and reference handbooks, such as this, provide an alternative basis for access to research data. As such, the worth of any source reference is inextricably tied to the individual user's trust in the author's objectivity and expertise in selecting and interpreting the subject matter. In the basic concept and design of this Handbook we have made a deliberate commitment to honor this trust. It is designed as a professional desk reference for the research psychologist or human factors practitioner in search of pertinent and reliable data on perception and human performance.

In his preface to the 1938 edition of *Experimental Psychology*, R. S. Woodworth reflected on the increasing difficulty of consolidating the burgeoning literature of experimental psychology. In mid-1980, we faced a nearly overwhelming dilemma of selecting the topics to include and exclude in planning the general outline for this Handbook. Numerous existing texts were reviewed for content and format of presentation. A primary consideration weighting our decisions was the potential applicability of the candidate topics to applied research and development. This choice of criterion was motivated by our basic conviction that many sensory, perceptual, and human performance data exist that are potentially useful to the human factors design of system controls and information displays. For various reasons, in part having to do with access and interpretability, these data have been relatively unexploited for purposes of application. We reasoned that the design of effective information displays, irrespective of sensory modality, must systematically take into account the variables that influence the display user's ability to acquire, process, and make control decisions regarding task critical information. Hence in this Handbook we have attempted to systematize and digest what is reliably known of the limits of these variables from the broader set of data resident within experimental psychology.

Although we sought to adhere to the criterion of "potential applicability" in selecting subject areas, many data found in this Handbook may be of questionable applied value. This is true for several reasons: first, we encouraged expanded treatment in some subject areas to provide a necessary perspective context in which applicable data might be interpreted. Conceptual issues that are highly theoretical have been included because of their prospective usefulness to design research and development in its basic phases. Indeed, we often doubted the reliability of our oracular skills and arbitrarily chose to bias selection on the side of inclusion. Section editors and authors were likewise instructed to bias their selection of data toward this notion of applicability in outlining the individual chapters. Nonetheless, we are guilty of excluding some research areas of potential applied value owing to oversight, lack of foresight, or our inability to attract the talents of the appropriate experts.

The problem, then, was to attract support for design of a reference Handbook of these data that we believed would satisfy a need by professional psychologists and provide a sound basis for follow-on data products geared specifically toward human engineering design applications. In December 1980, the Air Force Aerospace Medical Research Laboratory with major support by a consortium of DOD and NASA agencies initiated the Integrated Perceptual Information for Designers (IPID) project. This project was planned to be accomplished in several phases. In the first phase, resulting in this Handbook, we tried to produce a comprehensive though selective consolidation of data from a range of subject domains within experimental psychology. In the second phase, we developed a presentation format for communicating these data to human factors psychologists and engineers for design applications. The product of this phase, the *Engineering Data Compendium: Human Perception and Performance* (to be published in three volumes by the Air Force), draws upon this Handbook for source material on perception and human performance, though it also encompasses a broader set of data drawn from the applied research literature on human/machine interfaces and systems design.

MAJOR FEATURES OF THE HANDBOOK

From the outset of this effort, it has been our view that the architecture of a professional-level reference Handbook must be founded on relatively independent, self-contained units of information that provide a detailed treatment of logical elements of the subject area. The benefit of this approach is that it allows for nondisruptive, in-depth treatment of branching issues that are subordinate to the main sequence logic of a chapter. This should be of significant value to the professional user seeking answers to specific questions, though not to the exclusion of the advanced student who is surveying the field. The accuracy and reliability of the data reported in this Handbook are of paramount concern to us. Each author was requested to carefully screen the data selected for treatment and to specify confidence limits wherever possible. Each chapter was then reviewed a minimum of six times by at least three different editors. In addition, many chapters were subjected to additional reviews by technical peers.

Related material in the Handbook and in other sources can be accessed through the abundant cross references, in-text citations, and reference listings. Those references marked by an asterisk (*) were selected as key sources of information by the authors and editors. Extraordinary efforts were taken to ensure the accuracy of each of these reference citations. In addition to a master table of contents at the beginning of each volume, there is a detailed table of contents at the front of each chapter.

The Handbook is profusely illustrated with data figures, tables, and schematics. Accompanying captions have been designed to be as self-contained as possible to enable basic interpretation by the informed reader without recourse to the text. In the same vein, the text draws upon the figures and captions to substantiate or illustrate the discussion without unnecessary digression to general experimental details. Overall, this has resulted in legends that treat the figures in considerably greater detail than commonly found in related texts. Whenever possible, figure and table captions contain a description of dependent and independent variables, an indication of the data's reliability, a "bottom line" summary of what the data are about, and a reference giving the source of the data. All figures have been plotted or converted and re-plotted using SI (Système International) units. We hope these features will add to the usefulness of the Handbook and the clarity of the in-text discussions.

ORGANIZATION AND SYNOPSIS

The Handbook is organized around seven major topical sections, encompassing 45 chapters and 7 overviews, presented in two volumes. Each major section was produced under the direct editorial supervision of independent section editors. Volume One, "Sensory Processes and Perception," provides a methodological basis for the Handbook followed by a data-oriented treatment of sensitivity in sensory systems and the perception of space and motion. Volume Two, "Cognitive Processes and Performance," deals with empirical issues in cognitive and human information processing followed by a treatment of factors in complex human performance.

Section I, developed as a collaborative editorial effort, provides detailed background on psychophysical theory and methods in a chapter by J. C. Falmagne and one by G. Sperling and B. Dosher. With increasing reliance by experimental psychologists on computer-generated images as stimuli, the chapter by H. Freeman on "Computer Graphics" will be of considerable value to the reader as a methodological resource.

Section II, edited by D. MacLeod and J. Thomas, treats issues of basic visual sensitivity and eye movements. It begins with a chapter by G. Westheimer on the optical formation of the retinal image. The temporal variable is examined in the chapter on "Temporal Sensitivity" by A. Watson, and the spatial variables are the topic of the chapter on "Seeing Spatial Patterns" by L. Olzak and J. Thomas. The role of the wavelength variable is discussed in two chapters: "Colorimetry and Color Discrimination" by J. Pokorny and V. Smith and "Color Appearance" by G. Wyszecki. The chapter by D. Hood and M. Finkelstein on "Sensitivity to Light" also treats the wavelength variable in examining spectral sensitivity. In addition, their chapter treats the phenomena of adaptation, which collectively alter the absolute sensitivity of the visual system and its response properties with respect to temporal and spatial as well as spectral dimensions. The section closes with a compendium on "Eye Movements" by P. Hallett.

Section III, edited by C. Sherrick and R. Cholewiak, deals with sensitivity of hearing and the cutaneous, kinesthetic, and vestibular senses. In-depth treatment of the anatomical, physiological, and psychophysical aspects of these modalities is provided. Separate chapters by B. Scharf and S. Buus and by B. Scharf and A. Houtsma describe the structure, function, and qualitative and quantitative phenomena associated with the hearing sense. A chapter by I. Howard describes the vestibular sense in fine detail. The exquisite sensitivity and responsiveness of the kinesthetic system to varieties of strain and pressure are discussed in the chapter by F. Clark and K. Horch. An integrated treatment of the senses of the skin is provided by C. Sherrick and R. Cholewiak in their chapter on "Cutaneous Sensitivity."

Section IV, edited by H. Sedgwick, deals with the perception of space and motion by human observers. In the first chapter of this section, S. Anstis discusses sensory aspects of motion in the frontal plane. The goal of this chapter is to describe "some of the basic properties of the mechanisms by which motion is registered by the visual system." Higher-order "Perceptual Aspects of Motion in the Frontal Plane" are then systematically explored by A. Mack. Next "The Perception of Posture, Self Motion, and the Visual Vertical" is detailed by I. Howard. Two other important parameters of motion perception are covered by D. Regan, L. Kaufman, and J. Lincoln in their chapter on "Motion in Depth and Visual Acceleration." L. Matin considers the "integration of retinal information with extra-retinal information about the position of the eye" in his chapter on "Visual Localization and Eye Movements." In the following chapter, "Space Perception" H. Sedgwick discusses "how and how well the spatial layout of the environment is perceived." Next, "The Representation of Motion and Space in Video and Cinematic Displays" by J. Hochberg considers how characteristics of visual perception enable compelling representation of three-dimensional motion "from a succession of two-dimensional displays containing no real motion." "Binocular Vision" by A. Arditi reviews the literature on the perceptual integration of information from the inputs of the two eyes. The ability of the observer to adapt in perceptually guided interactions with the environment is surveyed by R. Welch in "Adaptation of Space Perception." The last chapter of this section, by R. Welch and D. Warren, takes up the theme of the relations between the senses.

The chapters selected for Section V, "Information Processing," edited by M. Posner, reflect the information processing approach but do so with emphasis on the human performance of complex tasks. In his Overview, Posner defines the study of human performance as "a branch of experimental psychology that analyzes the skills involved in skilled performance, studies the development of skill, and attempts to identify factors which limit different aspects of performance." The chapter on "Visual Information Processing" by W. Chase stresses the elementary operations of visual codes. The processing of symbolic visual information—that is, "mental operations involved in forming visual, phonological and semantic codes of words and pictures"—is given comprehensive treatment in the chapter "Perceiving Visual Language" by T. Carr. "Auditory Information Processing" by H. Hawkins and J. Presson analyzes the role of attention in guiding the selection of auditory information with emphasis on the ability to sustain and share attention among different auditory levels. The relations between auditory information and speech are treated in P. Jusczyk's chapter on "Speech Perception." In the final chapter of this section, "Motor Control," S. Keele outlines "basic limitations on the speed and accuracy of simple movements" and shows how movements are assembled in memory as complex programs for the execution of tasks.

Section VI, "Perceptual Organization and Cognition," edited by M. Kubovy, addresses the multisensory elements of consciousness and how these affect our perception of form and pattern. The first chapter of this section, "Tactual Perception" by J. Loomis and S. Lederman, is concerned with "the sense of touch as a channel of information about objects and events outside the body." The next chapter, by D. Deutsch, provides an evaluative review of the literature on "Auditory Pattern Recognition." How the auditory system "parses," "groups," and "fuses" complex sounds into acoustic objects and events is the focus of this chapter. In the next chapter, I. Rock develops "The Description and Analysis of Object and Event Perception," providing in effect a Gestalt description of perceptual organization. "Spatial Filtering and Visual Form Perception" by A. Ginsburg follows, in which perceptual phenomena are discussed in terms of multichannel spatial filtering in the visual system. In a following chapter, "Properties, Parts, and Objects," A. Treisman integrates the research dealing with "decomposition of perceptual experience into dimensions and features, and the decomposition of objects and events into parts." "Theoretical Approaches to Perceptual Organization: Simplicity and Likelihood Principles" is the subject of the next chapter by J. Pomerantz and M. Kubovy. It focuses on the question of whether the visual system uses algorithms that maximize "regularity, homogeneity, and symmetry" to enable awareness of "the layout of the world." In the chapter "Visual Functions of Mental Imagery," R. Finke and R. Shepard review evidence for the "hypothesis that imagination and visual perception are functionally equivalent, and that under some conditions visual perception can be facilitated by mental imagery." The last chapter of this section, "Computational Approaches to Vision" by H. Barrow and J. Tenenbaum, provides a comprehensive treatment of methodology, data, and theory underlying concepts of machine vision.

Section VII, "Human Performance," edited by J. Beatty, deals with the measurement and characterization of human performance. This section addresses performance under task and environmental demands with more obvious practical implications for human factors engineering. The first chapter, "Effects of Control Dynamics on Performance" by C. Wickens, provides a lucid account of optimal control theory and measurement of the manual control task. N. Moray then "considers the role of the human operator as a supervisor or monitor rather than a direct controller." Next D. Gopher and E. Donchin provide a basic theoretical introduction to "Workload: An Examination of the Concept." This is followed by a detailed catalog of available "Workload Assessment Methodology" expertly consolidated by R. O'Donnell and T. Eggemeier. Next, theory and data on the maintenance of "Vigilance, Monitoring, and Search" for prolonged periods is treated by R. Parasuraman. This is followed by a review by R. Hockey of the experimental literature of the effects of noise, heat, anxiety, drugs, fatigue, and circadian rhythms on performance. The final chapter of the Handbook, "The Model Human Processor: An Engineering Model of Human Performance," by S. Card, T. Moran, and A. Newell, provides a model of transition between the theories of experimental psychology and the theories of human performance.

In all, there are a number of unifying themes that cross the boundaries of these sections. It would require a special essay to describe how the generalization of Muller's doctrine of specific nerve energies by Helmholtz laid the foundations for modern theories of color vision, and how this same idea, decorated with notions derived from Fourier analysis, led to modern theories of visual pattern perception and detection and shows signs of affecting theories of cutaneous sensitivity. However, such considerations transcend the purpose of this preface, which is designed simply to introduce this work.

KENNETH R. BOFF
LLOYD KAUFMAN
JAMES P. THOMAS

Wright-Patterson Air Force Base, Ohio
New York, New York
Los Angeles, California

March 1986

ACKNOWLEDGMENTS

A most difficult task for a project of this scope is to acknowledge appropriately the contribution and dedication of the many individuals indispensable to its success. This is further complicated by the range of different roles assumed by contributors with respect to fiscal support, management, administration, moral support, and editorial and secretarial stamina. The program was accomplished under Project 71842603 and managed through the offices of the Visual Display Systems Branch of the Human Engineering Division of the Armstrong Aerospace Medical Research Laboratory at Wright-Patterson Air Force Base in Ohio. Dr. Thomas A. Furness III, Branch Chief, and Mr. Charles Bates, Jr., Division Chief, provided encouragement and moral support during the many periods of frustration inevitable in a project this size. Most important, they provided an environment in which novel ideas, such as the one that spawned this Handbook, could be nurtured to maturity and final delivery of a product. The fact that the Handbook now exists is testimony to the success of this management philosophy.

Within the Branch and the Human Engineering Division, much has depended on the attention, dedication, and support provided by the secretarial and administrative staff. In particular, Dena Brooks, former Branch Secretary, carried the burden of typing, filing, and editing mounds of correspondence associated with the project, including more than 400 pages of chapter reviews and contractual documentation. Much gratitude for efficiently following in this effort is offered to the current Branch Secretaries, Tanya Ellifritt and Jeni Blake. Barbara Osman, Executive Secretary for the Human Engineering Division, carefully proofread and prevented many errors in project correspondence. Administrative support was provided by many others in the Division whom we are guilty of not singling out by name.

The idea for this project evolved from a prior Air Force effort for which much inspiration is owed to our colleagues Pat Knoop, Lawrence Reed, Bert Cream, and Don Gum. Belief in this idea and its potential value to the design engineering community spurred Art Doty, Director of Engineering for the Air Force Deputy for Simulators, to agree to provide major sponsorship of this project. The initial support opened doors to subsequent multi-government agency funding that the project has enjoyed and that, in fact, enabled its survival. In particular, special acknowledgment is due to Dr. Edward A. Martin, Air Force Deputy for Engineering, Training Systems Division. Ed graciously gave of his time and made significant conceptual contributions during all phases of this project. Most important, Ed's support has been invaluable to maintaining liaison and rapport with the engineering community, thereby ensuring the relevance of the project to engineering needs. Invaluable suggestions and support were provided by many others of the Wright Field community. Most worthy of mention are Jim Basinger, Richard Heintzman, George Dickison, Tom Kelly, and Bill Curtice.

In addition to the Armstrong Aerospace Medical Research Laboratory, agencies within each of the Armed Services and the National Aeronautics and Space Administration (NASA) provided financial and technical support. The principal individuals from whom this vital support came are Dr. Walter Chambers, Dr. Stanley Collyer, and Dennis Wightman of the Naval Training Equipment Center in Orlando, Florida; Charles Gainer of the Fort Rucker (Alabama) Field Unit of the Army Research Institute; Clarence Fry of the Army Human Engineering Laboratory at Aberdeen Proving Grounds, Maryland; Dr. Thomas Longridge of the Air Force Human Resources Laboratory at Williams Air Force Base in Arizona; Dr. Melvin Montemerlo of NASA Headquarters in Washington D.C.; and Dr. Walter Truskowski of NASA's Goddard Space Flight Center, Maryland.

Drs. Janet Lincoln of New York University and Lynn Olzak of the University of California at Los Angeles made very special contributions to the Handbook. They served as associates to the general editors during the organizational period, when authors were being recruited and were formulating the outlines of the chapters they were to write. Lynn Olzak at UCLA and Janet Lincoln at NYU worked with the editors and authors to achieve the desired coordination, of both content and treatment, among the chapters and sections.

At the outset, administration project management was supported by Drs. Lincoln and Olzak and coordinated through Jill Easterly of the Armstrong Aerospace Medical Research Laboratory. These efforts were ably supported by Leslie Johnson at UCLA. A subsequent reorganization resulting from the growth of the project placed the administrative management of the

Handbook with the University of Dayton Research Institute (UDRI). Words cannot express the debt this project owes to the UD Program Manager, Karen Pettus. Karen's uncommon zeal, high standards, good management sense, and loyalty were the key to the success of this effort. Her willingness to give of herself and her unwillingness to bend to mediocrity are rare and highly sought-after virtues. We simply could not have done this job without her.

To a considerable extent, this spotlight must be shared with another rare individual who has made major contributions and personal sacrifice for this effort, Anita Cochran of UDRI. As senior copy editor Anita has been the primary gatekeeper of the standards we have sought to maintain within this Handbook. This has been a Herculean task requiring the melding of idiosyncratic styles and formats, from more than 50 authors involving over 10,000 pages, into a reference handbook of homogeneous appearance. Her indefatigable energy level, persistent good humor, and single-minded dedication to producing a product of endurable quality have been indispensable to the success of this effort. In accomplishing these functions, Anita was assisted by Ms. Stevie Ann Hardyal and by many University of Dayton students who played a critical and often understated role on the project. These included Nancy Wrobel, Mark Jones, Donna Smith, Phil Masline, Eric Ramsey, Matt Rossano, Lisa Barnes, Carol Van Houten, Michelle Gilkison, and Jeffrey A. Landis. Lawrence Sauer, Carol Messler, and Kirsten Means efficiently oversaw acquisition of figure permissions, which was a massive undertaking involving over 1,500 figures. The UDRI project secretary, Jean Scheer, expertly coordinated voluminous correspondence and contractual communications to all segments of the project management and authors.

UDRI also had responsibility for preparing camera-ready drafting of illustrations and data figures. This major segment of the project owes much of its success to a sequence of able supervisors, Reinhold M. W. Strnat, Kanith L. Stone, and Fred Davis. Computer-aided drafting was enabled by the efforts of Robert Blanchard and Keith Miller. Expert artwork and cosmetic touchup were provided by Margaret Plattenburg, David Levitan, and Joseph Deady. Quality control and the basic composition of figures were efficiently accomplished by the many student contributors to the project. Among these are Dennis Weatherby, Allen L. Barbadora, Stephen J. Cook, Andrew Dejaco, Catherine M. Fuchs, Russell J. Velego, Jolene Boutin, Denise L. McCullum, and Julie Gerdeman.

At New York University, the project benefited from the administrative support of William Salen and Ann Demarais. We thank Sam Williamson for his helpful suggestions and friendship over the duration of this effort.

Each individual manuscript was technically reviewed by at least three different members of the Handbook editorial staff. In addition, many of these manuscripts were also distributed for external peer review. We are eternally grateful for the invaluable commentary provided by a legion of reviewers who so graciously gave of their time. Many of these individuals will remain, by choice, anonymous. Those cited for our sincere appreciation include Robert Eggleston, Sharon Ward, Mark Cannon, Herschel Self, David Post, and Henning Von Gierke of the Armstrong Medical Research Laboratory; Frank Ward, Wright State University; Christopher Arbak, Systems Research Laboratories, Inc.; Ethel Matin, Long Island University; Edward A. Martin, Air Force Deputy for Engineering, Training Systems Division.

We are especially pleased to have had the opportunity to work with and present important contributions by William B. Chase ("Visual Information Processing") and Gunter Wyszecki ("Color Appearance"), both of whom passed away during the course of this project.

We are also grateful for the perseverance and good-natured support of Herb Reich, Senior Project Editor at John Wiley & Sons, New York. Our sincerest thanks are also offered to the many publishers and authors who gave us permission to reprint the myriad of data figures, tables, and illustrations that populate this Handbook.

Finally, this project incurred great sacrifice on the part of those closest to us and to whom this Handbook is dedicated. The good-natured forebearance of Elaine Kaufman was vitally supportive during the many hours devoted to work on this Handbook. Cory Boff was born in the early stages of this effort and was old enough to inquire about "Daddy's" whereabouts by the time the manuscript went to press. Judy Boff simply endured and was a frequently accessed source of comfort and encouragement.

The naiveté and bravado with which we assumed this task cannot be overstated. The relief and gratitude we feel, now that it is completed, have no bounds.

K. R. B.
L. K.
J. P. T.

CONTENTS FOR VOLUME I

CONTENTS FOR VOLUME II

SECTION I

THEORY AND METHODS

LLOYD KAUFMAN

New York University, New York, New York

OVERVIEW

LLOYD KAUFMAN

New York University, New York, New York

The first section of this *Handbook* focuses on conceptual and methodological issues that pertain broadly to the chapters of other sections. Many of the chapters of other sections also contain such material but in a form largely pertinent to the chapters themselves. The three chapters here are concerned with very general methods and techniques and, more important, with the theoretical underpinnings of the methods employed in other chapters. Thus this section examines the often unstated reasons for the methods used in fields as diverse as sensory psychophysics, cognition, and information processing.

The concepts described in the chapters by Falmagne and by Sperling and Dosher apply across virtually all the "boundaries" dividing the sections of this *Handbook*. Even though there are real differences between a study of the sensitivity of a sensory system and of, say, divided attention, scientists in both these areas often employ the same basic assumptions. Similarly, chapters in the section on information processing and those in the section on the perception of pattern and form are closely related to each other because both areas are strongly affected by a common set of conceptual tools.

Many of these conceptual tools are related to the problem of how one is to measure physical stimuli and patterns and relate those measures to the ways in which the organism transforms and responds selectively to attributes of the stimuli and patterns. This problem has a long and honorable history in psychology, and it is dealt with at length in Falmagne's chapter. In its more precise form it is often referred to as *Fechner's problem*, which can be described as the problem of finding a way to transform a scale of physical magnitudes so that they are proportionally related to psychological magnitudes. To understand this problem fully, one must grasp the notion of the *psychometric function*, dealt with at length in this first chapter of the *Handbook*. Falmagne bases his discussion on the theory of measurement and how it may be applied to measuring psychological phenomena. This introduction to measurement theory equips the reader to understand better the psychophysical methods and relationships discussed in later chapters.

Choices about method usually carry with them assumptions about underlying models and processes. For example, a simple forced-choice experiment implies a complex set of processes. The multiplicity and complexity of the models and assumptions entailed defy succinct summary. However, Falmagne's chapter will carry the reader a long way toward a fuller understanding of the implications of each choice about method.

The concepts of *threshold* and of *sensitivity* are given rigorous definitions, as are their relations to the now pervasive theory of signal detection. The latter theory comes to grips with the fact that all psychophysical tasks have cognitive components, and the assumptions we make about the guessing strategy adopted by the subject affect our interpretation of data. Falmagne provides the reader with a basic understanding of the theory of signal detection and the assumptions it entails. This portion of Falmagne's chapter serves as an introduction to the chapter by Sperling and Dosher that follows.

Sperling and Dosher provide a very general treatment of methods and theories designed to deal with the strategies employed by humans performing perceptual and cognitive tasks. The choice and sequencing of mental operations by subjects in the performance of many kinds of tasks may not be directly observable, but strong inferences can often be drawn using the methods and models discussed in the chapter. The authors demonstrate that these methods and theories are closely related to signal detection theory.

The authors choose to examine the application of general principles of decision optimization and resource allocation to mental processes occurring within relatively short periods of time. Signal detection theory is one application of the concepts of optimization to sensory-perceptual tasks. The *receiver operating characteristic* of signal detection theory is shown to be closely related to the *attention operating characteristic* and other *performance operating characteristics*. The authors also discuss how operating characteristics can be used to decide if independent resources are being tapped in a complicated task or if a single resource is being depleted by the several aspects of such a task. The discussion of concurrent and compound tasks in this chapter provides information that is essential to full understanding of the chapters by Welch and Warren, Gopher and Donchin, Wickens, and Moray (among others) in this *Handbook*. Despite the diversity of their substance, these chapters reflect a common need for basic methods, such as those dealt with here.

The chapter by Sperling and Dosher could have been placed in the section on human information processing, and this in fact was the original intention. However, it soon became clear that their message supplemented that of Falmagne and what they had to say was equally important to chapters dealing with topics as diverse as human performance, space perception, and pattern vision. Therefore, it was placed in this first section.

The chapter by Freeman is quite distinct from the other two chapters in this section. It does not address specific psychological or perceptual problems. We chose to include this chapter here because of the central role of the digital computer as a tool for the perception researcher. We recognize that the computer has changed the conduct of psychological inquiry, and it must be given the same type of treatment as is given to the physics of light in books on visual perception. Nearly all workers in perception and cognition employ computers and their graphics capabilities to produce the stimuli of their experiments. This chapter is designed to inform the reader about how computers are used to generate stimuli for perception research. It discusses methods of display and the ways in which lines and curves are generated, and it introduces the complexities of transformations and projections of images, all matters of vital concern to the perceptionist. It is also relevant to more practical matters, for example, the ability of today's computers to simulate scenes, such as those used in flight simulators.

The section of Freeman's chapter on stereoscopic displays is not as detailed as some of the other sections. The reason for this is that the details of stereoscopic display techniques are covered in the chapter by Arditi, and the reader wishing more information is referred to that source.

In conclusion, it should be noted that there was no single editor for this section. D. MacLeod, J. Thomas, M. Posner, K. Boff, H. Sedgwick, and L. Kaufman all contributed to the editorial process.

CHAPTER 1

PSYCHOPHYSICAL MEASUREMENT AND THEORY

J. C. FALMAGNE

New York University, New York, New York

CONTENTS

I am grateful to H. Levitt, M. Gizzi, and especially G. Iverson and M. Pavel for their comments on previous drafts of this material.

Based on *Elements of Psychophysical Theory*, by Jean-Claude Falmagne, copyright 1985, Oxford University Press. Used by arrangement with Oxford University Press.

1. PRELIMINARIES

1.1. Outline of This Chapter

G. T. Fechner, the founder of psychophysics, was originally a professional physicist. At the age of 39, he turned to psychology and set out to apply the methods of experimental physics to the measurement of sensory events. To fully understand the details of Fechner's idea, as well as some of its difficulties, an excursion into physical measurement is necessary.

Section 2 contains a detailed description of the procedures that are the basis for the measurement of fundamental physical quantities, such as length or mass. The reader interested only in the applications of psychophysical models will be tempted to skip this section and may do so without much harm. However, we urge anyone striving for a solid understanding of the foundations of psychophysical measurement to study Section 2 carefully. A comparison between physical and psychophysical measurement is of interest for two major reasons.

First, measurement procedures proposed by Fechner for psychophysical phenomena result from a straightforward transposition of those applicable in physics. In both cases, the procedures are justified by a testable theory, and a detailed comparison of the two theories is instructive. Second, on the background of physical measurement, it is much easier to disentangle substantive from philosophical issues, the confusion of which has been an enduring plague in this field. A number of authors have contributed to a clarification of the foundations of psychophysical measurement, and key references are given in due place. The seminal role of R. D. Luce is recognized here, however.

Section 3 contains a description of Fechner's approach to psychophysics. The basic notion is that of a probability $P_{a,b}$ that stimulus a is perceived as exceeding stimulus b from the viewpoint of some sensory attribute. The theory justifying Fechner's procedure is that this probability only depends on the difference $u(a) - u(b)$, in which u is some unknown sensory scale, a candidate for a measure of "sensation." In symbols, this gives rise to the equation

$$P_{a,b} = F[u(a) - u(b)], \tag{1}$$

with F a strictly increasing continuous function. This equation occupies a central place in psychophysical theory. In fact, it would be only a mild exaggeration to say that a substantial part of psychophysical theory consists in comments on Eq. (1).

Section 4 reviews various discrimination models, many of which turn out to be special cases of Eq. (1). This section contains a discussion of the so-called law of comparative judgment of Thurstone, a particular instance of which (case V) is obtained when the function F in Eq. (1) is the normal integral.

The treatment of psychometric functions given in Section 5 may surprise the knowledgeable reader. It covers in detail a number of important questions often left to the intuition of the psychophysicist. Examples of such questions are, What does it mean to say that two or more psychometric functions are "parallel" or that they can be rendered so by a transformation of the physical scale? What is the relationship between "parallelism" and Eq. (1)? In a two-alternative forced-choice design, the probability $P_{a,b}$ is typically estimated by averaging the frequencies in the two alternatives. What is the theoretical impact, if any, of this standard practice, in particular with respect to Eq. (1)?

Sections 6 and 7 deal with the Weber functions Δ_π, the methods currently in use to estimate those functions experimentally (stochastic approximation, up–down), and a number of models proposed to explain typical data. Various generalizations of Weber's law are considered.

Section 8 is devoted to signal detection theory, which is presented so as to play down the notion that the subject is behaving as a statistician applying some optimal decision procedure. The prominent place usually given to this notion is misleading, in our opinion. However interesting, it is only a case of a general theory justifying a particular analysis of the so-called receiver operating characteristic (ROC) curves.

As suggested by the title of Section 9, the material there is rather mixed, discussing a variety of topics, among which are "probability summation," models for conjoint measurement (deterministic and probabilistic), bisection, and so on.

Finally, Section 10 is devoted to the many issues related to psychophysical scaling.

Although quite extensive, this chapter does not cover all the topics that its title could evoke. Two omissions among others are color theory, which is discussed by Pokorny and Smith, Chapter 8, and by Wyszecki, Chapter 9, and multidimensional scaling, which is also discussed by Wyszecki, Chapter 9.

In writing, we had in mind a reader with a minimal background in mathematics, corresponding to a few calculus courses and a *good* course in probability or statistics. Notions such as random variables, distributions, and expectations are assumed to be solid items of the reader's statistical equipment. A one-semester course in algebra may be helpful at some point but is by no means essential.

It is our firm belief that there has been in psychophysical theory a great deal more controversy than there was reasonable ground for. The attentive reader will notice a deliberate attempt to minimize the disputes and to give a unified presentation.

1.2. Key References

A useful complement to this chapter is a monograph by Gescheider (1976). As described in the preface, it is addressed to advanced undergraduate students with some background in statistics. This treatment differs from ours in that it covers a greater variety of empirical issues but pays less attention to the details of the mathematical aspects of the theories. Moreover, no attempt is made to cast psychophysical measurement in the general framework of measurement theory.

2. CONSTRUCTION OF A PHYSICAL SCALE FOR LENGTH (AN EXAMPLE OF EXTENSIVE MEASUREMENT)

2.1. Outline

By extensive measurement, we mean the measurement of fundamental physical quantities, such as mass or length, using qualitative devices. We shall give a concrete example. Consider a collection of thin rods. The problem at hand is the measurement of their length, but no rulers or other devices are available. A natural way of measuring the length of a given rod would involve the following steps:

1. Pick a particular, fixed rod as a "unit."

2. Count the maximum number of exact copies of this unit which can be placed along the rod to be measured without overlap.

The number so obtained is a measure of the length of the rod. If exact measurement is required, some refinements must be introduced. For the essentials, however, this algorithm is the usual one. The intuition supporting it is so compelling that it is at first difficult to realize (1) that quite a number of assumptions about physical reality are implicitly made and (2) that it involves a considerable amount of arbitrariness.

2.2. Notation

Our discussion of these issues will be facilitated by the adoption of a precise notation and terminology. The algorithm previously outlined can be analyzed into two distinct experimental procedures.

For any two rods a, b a *comparison procedure* is used to decide which of a, b has the greater length. The rods are placed alongside each other, in such a way that they coincide at one end. If they also coincide at the other end, we shall write

$$a \sim b\ .$$

Figure 1.1 illustrates the notions introduced in this subsection. The case where b covers a, but is not covered by it, will be denoted

$$a < b\ .$$

A more compact notation is also useful. Whenever either $a < b$, or $a \sim b$, we write $a \leqslant b$. Thus

$$a \leqslant b$$

simply means that b covers a (whether or not a covers b).

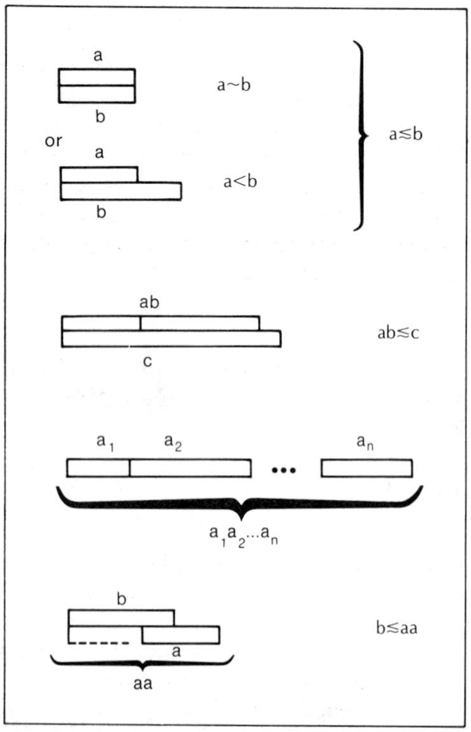

Figure 1.1. Measurement of length. Comparison and concatenation procedures.

The *concatenation procedure* for two rods a, b involves placing a and b end to end along a straight line, forming a new object, which we denote ab. Using the comparison procedure, this new object can be placed along some rod c to yield, for example, $ab \leqslant c$.

When the rods of a sequence $a_1, a_2, \ldots, a_n$ are successively concatenated in the order: a_1 with a_2, then a_1a_2 with a_3, and so on, the result is denoted $a_1a_2 \ldots a_n$. A convenient abbreviation will be used to denote the successive concatenations of a with (exact copies of) itself. We shall write

$$n * a = \underbrace{aa \ldots a}_{n \text{ times}}\ .$$

Thus, in particular, $1 * a = a$, $2 * a = aa$, $b(3 * a) = baaa$, and so on. By convention, we shall admit that $n * a \sim n * a$, for $n = 1, 2, \ldots$. It will be convenient by extension to also refer to objects such as ab, aab, ... as rods. In the sequel, the letters x, y, z, ... will refer either to rods in the original sense or to objects resulting from some concatenation. Two methods for the measurement of the length of rods are described next.

2.3. First Method

Going back to the measurement algorithm proposed in Section 2.1, consider the task of measuring the length of some rod x. We pick arbitrarily some (small) rod y as a unit, and we form the successive concatenation of y with itself, until the following situation obtains

$$n * y \leqslant x < (n + 1) * y\ . \tag{2}$$

(In words: x covers $n * y$ but does not cover $(n + 1) * y$.)

We assign then the number n to x as its value on a scale measuring length, and we proceed similarly with the other rods in the collection. This method seems reasonable but encounters, in fact, a number of difficulties worth serious consideration, since they also occur in psychophysical application of the algorithm.

2.4. Difficulties

First, it is possible that $x < y$. In this case, we could assign the number 0 to x, but this would not be very satisfying. For example, there might be another rod x', such that $x \sim x' < y$, but $y < xx' < 2 * y$. In other words, both x and x' would have a scale value equal to 0, but xx' would have a scale value equal to 1. A very counterintuitive result! This shocking situation results from a general defect of the method; it is not very precise. When measuring the length of a rod by this method, we may commit an error, the size of which is smaller than the length of our unit, which by convention is equal to 1. The reason for this is the following. For any rod x, let us denote its true length by $l(x)$. We assume that, for any two rods z, w we have

$$z \leqslant w \quad \text{iff} \quad l(z) \leqslant l(w)\ .$$

(We write *iff* for *if and only if*.) In the situation symbolized by Eq. (2), we obtain

$$l(n * y) \leqslant l(x) < l[(n + 1) * y]\ . \tag{3}$$

The natural interpretation of the concatenation procedure for rods leads to the requirement that the length of a composite rod zw must be the sum of the length of z and w, that is,

$$l(zw) = l(z) + l(w) .$$

In general, for any sequence of rods $z_1, z_2, ..., z_n$ we must have

$$l(z_1 z_2 \dots z_n) = \sum_{i=1}^{n} l(z_i) .$$

In particular

$$l(n * z) = n\, l(z) . \quad (4)$$

Going back to Eq. (3), this gives

$$n\, l(y) \leqslant l(x) < (n + 1) l(y) ,$$

which implies, since $l(y) = 1$ (y is the unit),

$$n \leqslant l(x) < n + 1 ,$$

that is,

$$l(x) = n + \gamma$$

with $0 \leqslant \gamma < 1$. Consequently, when we assign the number n to x as a scale value, we are making an error γ, the size of which is smaller than 1. Methods minimizing such an error—making it as small as one wishes—are not hard to design. One such method is considered in Section 2.5.

A second difficulty is that we have a priori no certainty that the method will work. Even if $y < x$, how can we be sure that by successively concatenating y with itself, we shall finally obtain Eq. (2) for some integer n? In the particular case analyzed here, considering the empirical interpretation of such expressions as $y < x$, $n * y$, and so on, it seems intuitively obvious that this will be the case. But where does this intuition come from? The answer is that we have learned from experience that the "physical" world around us satisfies a number of constraints, or "laws." An instance of such a law of immediate relevance to our discussion is the following:

Archimedean Axiom. For any rods x,z, we have either $x < z$, or there exists a positive integer n such that

$$n * z \leqslant x < (n + 1) * z .$$

This axiom is called *Archimedean*, since it evokes the so-called Archimedean property of real numbers: for any real numbers s,t with $t > 0$, there exists a positive integer n such that $s \leqslant nt$.

This method is based on the assumption that this law and various others are empirically true. In the sequel, such laws will be referred to as *axioms*. Another example of an axiom, intuitively consistent with the interpretation of the relation $\leqslant$ as meaning "is covered by," is the following:

Monotonicity Axiom. For any rods x,x',z,z', whenever $x \leqslant z$ and $x' \leqslant z'$, then $xx' \leqslant zz'$.

We stress the importance of this last axiom which, in some form or other, is the centerpiece of many axiom systems for extensive measurement. It would be tedious, and probably not very enlightening, to justify each step of the algorithm by the axiom or axioms on which it is based. It is sufficient for our purpose to remember that the algorithm described in Section 2.3, or its refinement, to which we turn in a moment, relies on axioms such as those exemplified here. In general, after a short reflection on their content, these axioms appear to be consistent with the reader's experience of the physical world (so that no experimental verification is required). We emphasize that this obvious character of the axioms will not extend into psychophysical applications of the algorithm.

2.5. Second Method

The precision of the algorithm described in Section 2.3 can be improved, provided that "fractions" of the "unit" can be used for the purpose of measurement. Since the unit is arbitrary, this means that any rod, no matter how small, can be divided more or less at will. A weak form of this notion is embodied in the following axiom.

Solvability Axiom. For any rod z, there exists a rod w such that $ww \leqslant z$.

In other terms, for any rod z, the formula $ww \leqslant z$ can always be solved for some rod w. The method based on this axiom requires more work than the preceding one and is based on a rather subtle idea, the details of which are worth careful study. (As before, our discussion will be heuristic; not all the axioms will be mentioned explicitly.) As a first step, we construct a "distinguished" sequence of shorter and shorter rods, as follows. We choose w_1 arbitrarily. Next, we pick w_2 such that $w_2 w_2 \leqslant w_1$, and so forth. In general, we shall have $w_n w_n \leqslant w_{n-1}$. Thus when n becomes large, w_n becomes shorter and shorter. In particular, if n is large enough, we can achieve $w_n \leqslant x$ and $w_n \leqslant y$, where x and y are, respectively, the rod to be measured and our "unit." Using the Archimedean axiom, we also know that

$$p_n(x) * w_n \leqslant x < [p_n(x) + 1] * w_n ,$$

$$p'_n(x) * w_n \leqslant y < [p'_n(x) + 1] * w_n$$

for some positive integers $p_n(x)$, $p'_n(x)$. (The index n in $p_n(x)$, $p'_n(x)$ is a reminder that these integers depend on the term w_n in the sequence; notice that $p'_n(x)$ does not depend on y, which is fixed.) Considering the (true) length of the rods involved in these expressions, we obtain

$$l(p_n(x) * w_n) \leqslant l(x) < l[(p_n(x) + 1) * w_n]$$

$$l(p'_n(x) * w_n) \leqslant l(y) < l[(p'_n(x) + 1) * w_n] ,$$

which implies, with $l(y) = 1$,

$$p_n(x)\, l(w_n) \leqslant l(x) < [p_n(x) + 1] l(w_n) ,$$

$$p'_n(x)\, l(w_n) \leqslant 1 < [p'_n(x) + 1] l(w_n) .$$

The basic idea is to use these inequalities to approximate the unknown quantity $l(x)$. Given w_n, the integers $p_n(x)$, $p'_n(x)$ are empirically determined (we can "compute" them). A little algebra involving some of the these inequalities permits the elimination of the bothersome quantities $l(w_n)$; we obtain

$$p'_n(x)\ l(x) < p_n(x) + 1 . \tag{5}$$

A similar computation of the remaining inequalities yields

$$p_n(x) < l(x)[p'_n(x) + 1] . \tag{6}$$

Combining Eqs. (5) and (6) and rearranging terms finally gives

$$p_n(x)/[p'_n(x) + 1] < l(x) < [p_n(x) + 1]/p'_n(x) , \tag{7}$$

providing two bounds for $l(x)$. Let us investigate the situation when n becomes large; as indicated earlier, this means that w_n gets shorter and shorter. In turn, $p_n(x)$, $p'_n(x)$ must increase (a greater number of concatenations of w_n with itself are required to exceed x or y). In fact, when $n \to \infty$, we have both $p_n(x) \to \infty$ and $p'_n(x) \to \infty$. At this stage the consequences of this result on the two bounds in Eq. (7) are unclear. Fortunately, it can be shown that under the assumptions (i.e., axioms) underlying our discussion, the ratio $p_n(x)/p'_n(x)$ converges to some limit $\eta(x)$. This means, of course, that the two bounds in Eq. (7) converge to the same limit. That is,

$$p_n(x)/[p'_n(x) + 1] \to \eta(x) , \quad [p_n(x) + 1]/p'_n(x) \to \eta(x) ,$$

implying $l(x) = \eta(x)$. The outcome is that we can take either of the two bounds or $p_n(x)/p'_n(x)$ itself as a scale value of approximately $l(x)$, the approximation becoming increasingly accurate as n gets large. For example, we have

$$l(x) = [p_n(x)/p'_n(x)] + \gamma_{n'} \tag{8}$$

with

$$-[p_n(x)/p'_n(x)] \times [p'_n(x) + 1]^{-1} < \gamma_n < 1/p'_n(x) .$$

(We leave it to the reader to check the algebra.)

Taking $p_n(x)/p'_n(x)$ as a scale value for x involves thus an error γ_n, the absolute value of which can be as small as required by practical or scientific applications.

At this point, the reader probably feels somewhat uneasy about the foundations of these methods. A proof of the key results, such as the convergence of $p_n(x)/p'_n(x)$, requires a more precise apparatus than was given here. In particular, a precise statement of all the axioms would be required. Such technical treatment of our subject is beyond the scope of this chapter, however.

Our aims in discussing these algorithms in such minute detail were as follows. We wanted to illustrate, with a minimum of formalism, the process by which qualitative observations, which are a typical outcome of an experiment, are progressively transformed into numerical statements regarding extensive measurement. This type of measurement is not only the most important example so far provided by science but also the cornerstone of various other types of measurement of interest to the psychologist. In particular, Fechner's enterprise must be regarded as an attempt to apply, in the context of psychophysical experiments, such algorithms to the measurement of sensory phenomena.

2.6. Representation Problem for Extensive Measurement

Reflecting on the position adopted so far in this section, it should be recognized that it is not devoid of obscurities. In particular, we discussed in detail two methods for the construction of a scale for length, without ever making exactly clear which problems such a scale was supposed to solve. At each step of these constructions it was somehow natural or obvious that this was the right course to follow. This approach leaves too many questions unanswered to be satisfying. Examples of puzzling questions are, What justifies the agreement existing in the scientific, as well as in the social, community that the scales obtained by such methods are appropriate? Is the agreement based on practical reasons, theoretical reasons, or both? Could a different scale have been used and, if so, under which conditions?

Here we shall take a more critical viewpoint regarding the methods of scale construction as previously discussed. Our manipulations involve two empirical procedures: the comparison procedure (symbolized by the relation $\preccurlyeq$), and the concatenation procedure (symbolized by writing xy for the two rods x, y). A scale is essentially a device by which the rods are represented by numbers. This suggests asking: *By which notions (operations, relations) of the real number system are we representing the two procedures*? Some hints were given earlier. In Section 2.4 it was argued that a function l defined on the set of rods and representing their true length, should be such that

$$x \preccurlyeq y \quad \text{iff} \quad l(x) \leq l(y) . \tag{9}$$

In the same context, it was also maintained that a natural interpretation of the concatenation procedure for rods would require that the length of xy should be equal to the length of x added to the length of y. Thus

$$l(xy) = l(x) + l(y) . \tag{10}$$

In other words, the comparison procedure is represented by the ordering relation of the real numbers ($\leq$), and the concatenation is represented by the addition of the real numbers (+). Turning the question around leads to the following:

2.6.1. Representation Problem. Under which conditions does there exist a function l, defined on the set of rods and taking its values in the positive reals, such that Eqs. (9) and (10) are satisfied for all rods x,y?

A typical answer to this problem is a list, call it Λ, of conditions or axioms constraining the possible experimental results obtained from applying the two procedures. An example of such a list Λ would contain the monotonicity, Archimedean, and solvability axioms, plus some other conditions. The solution to the representation problem would then be given in the form of a representation theorem:

2.6.2. Representation Theorem. If all the axioms in the list Λ are satisfied, then there exists a function l mapping the set of rods in the positive real numbers, such that Eqs. (9) and (10) are satisfied for all rods x,y.

One proof of such a theorem is based on the following idea. We prove the existence of the function l by constructing it piecewise, so to speak. That is, we define $l(x)$ for every rod x, using essentially the second method described in Section 2.5. (Intuitively, the axioms are shown to imply that in Eq. (8), $p_n(x)/p'_n(x)$ converges and that $\gamma_n \to 0$. We define $l(x) = \lim_{n\to\infty} p_n(x)/$

$p'_n(x)$; thus, in particular, $l(y) = 1$.) Next, we show that the function l, as defined, satisfies Eqs. (9) and (10).

Note that, if *some* function l has been found to satisfy Eqs. (9) and (10), then any function l^* obtained by multiplying l by some constant $\alpha > 0$—that is,

$$l^*(x) = \alpha\, l(x)$$

for all rods x—also satisfies these formulas.

It is natural to ask whether *all* functions satisfying Eqs. (9) and (10) can be generated by this device. This question is of interest, since it corresponds to the situation commonly encountered; all usual scales for length are related by a multiplication, for example (approximately),

$$l_{\text{cm}}(x) = 2.54\, l^*_{\text{inch}}(x) .$$

When the axioms of a list Λ are sufficiently constraining, this situation obtains. The result is then formalized as follows.

2.6.3. Uniqueness Theorem. Suppose that all the axioms in a list Λ are satisfied. Let l, l^* be two functions satisfying Eqs. (9) and (10). Then, necessarily, $l(x) = \alpha\, l^*(x)$ for some constant $\alpha > 0$.

2.7. Summary and Remarks

The adoption of a measurement scale by the scientific community is a complex process, the various aspects of which have to be distinguished sharply. The formalism introduced in this section, with its central piece the representation problem, is standard in measurement theory. Its advantage is to make clear those aspects of the process which are susceptible to empirical verification.

Let us summarize. In the case of the measurement of the length of the rods in a collection, the scale was obtained by a succession of steps.

1. Two empirical procedures, comparison and concatenation, were chosen, more or less arbitrarily (no theoretical justifications were given).
2. A representation of each of these procedures by an entity (relation) of the real number system was adopted. The comparison procedure $\preccurlyeq$ was represented by the inequality ($\leq$) of the real numbers, and the concatenation was represented by the addition (+) of the reals.
3. The representation problem was formulated, involving the search for a positive-valued function l, satisfying for all rods x,y

$$l(x) \leq l(y) \quad \text{iff} \quad x \preccurlyeq y$$

and

$$l(xy) = l(x) + l(y)$$

4. A theory, that is, a list Λ of axioms, was proposed, implying the existence of the required scale l. This theory can be verified empirically. In particular, the validity of the monotonicity axiom:

$$\text{whenever } x \preccurlyeq y \text{ and } x' \preccurlyeq y', \text{ then } xx' \preccurlyeq yy' ,$$

can in principle be checked.

5. A proof of the existence of the scale l was sketched, based on an algorithm (Section 2.5) permitting the construction of the scale within an arbitrarily small error.

At this stage, a scale for the measurement of length is available which, obviously, is the one commonly used. However, it must be realized that, in principle, the fact that steps 1–5 have been taken successfully does not guarantee that the resulting scale will be adopted for scientific or other practices. Other procedures could have been used, leading to a different scale. (An example will follow.) A consensus of the scientific community regarding a scale certainly requires the existence of a sound theoretical foundation, but it is also influenced by other considerations, such as, Is the scale convenient to construct and to use? Does it have the property of rendering the equations of models reasonably simple and intuitive?

Few people realize the extent to which the basic physical scales are arbitrary. As mentioned earlier, length, for example, could be measured by procedures essentially different from those discussed so far in this section, with no other consequences than that of rendering the writing of some physical laws more cumbersome and the actual application of the procedures more painful. We are not suggesting that mathematical or practical convenience is to be taken lightly. Clearly, however, neither of these has a bearing on "physical reality." It is of some importance for a psychophysicist to have a clear understanding of such facts. Ultimately, the measurement of sensation will rely on an agreement in the psychophysical community, based essentially on considerations of convenience. The alternative procedure for measuring length to be discussed, illustrates these remarks. (This example is due to Ellis, 1966.)

The comparison procedure for noncomposite rods is the same as before, but the concatenation differs. We write

$$ab \sim x$$

if the rods a, b, and x can be used to form a right triangle, with x as its hypotenuse, and a, b as the two other sides. Thus to check whether

$$ab \preccurlyeq cde ,$$

one forms, successively (see Figure 1.2),

$$ab \sim x ,$$

$$cd \sim y ,$$

$$ey \sim z .$$

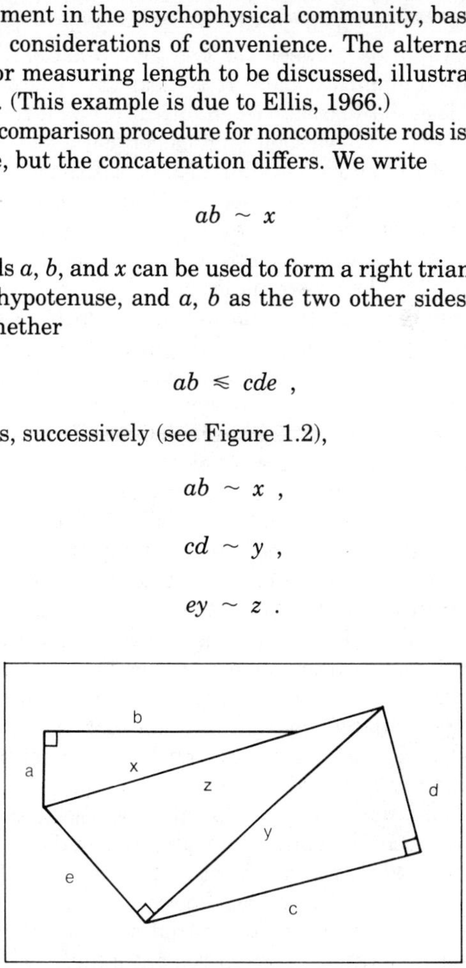

Figure 1.2. Alternative procedures for the measurement of the length of a collection of rods. We have $ab \preccurlyeq cde$, since $x \preccurlyeq z$ with $ab \sim x$, $cd \sim y$ and $ye \sim z$. The rods x, y, and z are hypotenuses of right triangles.

We define then

$$ab \preccurlyeq cde \quad \text{iff} \quad x \leqslant z \; .$$

It is clear that these procedures cannot give rise to the same scale as the usual one. Nevertheless, as it turns out, all the axioms that would be satisfied in the usual case would also be satisfied here. (The reader may be tempted to check that the Archimedean, monotonicity, and solvability axioms are verified, and this may be moderately convincing. The key observation, however, is that for positive real numbers, addition is isomorphic to the operation $(s,t) \rightarrow (s^2 + t^2)^{1/2}$.) We may thus apply the representation theorem, and claim that there is some function f such that for all rods x,y,

$$x \preccurlyeq y \quad \text{iff} \quad f(x) \leqslant f(y)$$

and

$$f(xy) = f(x) + f(y) \; .$$

We emphasize that this concatenation is different from the usual one. We do *not* have $l(xy) = l(x) + l(y)$, where l is the usual scale. (A different notation could have been used to stress the fact that the two concatenations under consideration involve distinct empirical operations. We could have written, for example, $f(x\hat{\ }y) = f(x) + f(y)$.) From the viewpoint of physical reality, f is as defensible as l as a possible scale for length. The choice between l and f, or between the two concatenations, is in no way based on empirical data. It is clear that l is preferable because it is easier to construct empirically, and it renders the writing of physical laws somewhat easier. For a more detailed discussion of this practically minded, or positivistic, attitude toward measurement, the reader is referred to Ellis (1966), where several other empirical examples of extensive measurement will also be found. This raises the question of the relation between l and f. The answer is simple enough: $f(x) = l(x)^2$.

With minor adaptation (the details of which we shall not enter into here), the analysis of the measurement of length given in this section in terms of two empirical procedures (comparison and concatenation) is also applicable to the measurement of mass, using a two-pan, equal-arm balance. In this case, the experimenter has a collection of objects a,b ... and writes ab to signify that the objects a,b have been placed in the same pan of the balance. The experimenter also writes $cde \preccurlyeq ab$ if the pan containing c,d, and e does not stabilize itself at a lower level than the pan containing a,b. An examination of this situation indicates that essentially the same axioms will apply.

The examples of extensive measurement given so far in this section illustrate a type of measurement which is relatively well understood, one in which a measurement theory (a list Λ of axioms) is available, guaranteeing the existence of a representation of the empirical structure into the real number system, with a specified correspondence between the empirical procedures and some numerical relations. In this case, the scientist may feel relatively confident of the interpretation of the role played by a number assigned to an object by a scale, since the interpretation is based on an explicit theory.

Obviously, there are methods that are characteristically different for generating a measurement scale. For the measurement of mass, an example is provided by the spring balance, the readings of which could, in principle, be accepted a priori, without any theoretical justification. In fact, however, the numbers assigned by the spring balance are known, as a consequence of Hooke's law, to be proportional to those obtained through the two-pan, equal-arm balance, so that, indirectly, a measurement theory is available also in the case of the spring balance.

Whether a measurement theory can be dispensed with altogether is unclear. Some, such as S. S. Stevens's followers, would probably argue that this is the case. What cannot be disputed is that a measurement theory is a highly desirable rationale for any measurement scale designed to play an important role in the scientific formulation of the data.

2.8. Key References

Since Helmholtz (1887), various axiom systems for extensive measurement have been proposed. The discussion given here, even though it is only one of many possibilities, is representative of the mainstream of these theories. Generally, the axiom systems differ in the emphasis placed on side conditions or in the details of the representation. In most cases, these axiom systems deal with a deterministic situation. A probabilistic theory for extensive measurement has been presented by Falmagne (1980). A basic reference for this topic is Krantz, Luce, Suppes, and Tversky (1971) or, more recently, Roberts (1979).

3. FECHNER'S APPROACH TO PSYCHOPHYSICS

3.1. Construction of a Fechnerian Scale

Fechner's fundamental idea is that a sensory scale can be constructed by adapting, to a particular kind of sensory data, the standard measurement procedure for the measurement of length in physics. (We assume that, at a minimum, the material in Section 2.1 is familiar to the reader.) This is by no means obvious, and we shall proceed carefully.

Suppose that a, b, c ... are numbers representing, in conventional units, values of some physical magnitude, such as mass (or sound pressure, luminance, etc.). For simplicity, we shall refer to a, b, c ... as stimuli. Let $P_{a,b}$ be the probability that a subject, presented with the pair (a,b) of stimuli in some experimental paradigm, judges a at least as heavy as b. For the time being, consider only the data obtained for pairs (a,b) such that $a \geqslant b$. Let us assume that there exists a psychophysical scale, the properties of which govern important aspects of performance in this paradigm. Thus each stimulus a is mapped to a point $u(a)$ in this scale. We also assume that this mapping is order preserving (that is, $a < b$ iff $u(a) < u(b)$) and that $P_{a,b}$ is strictly increasing with the distance $u(a) - u(b)$ between the points representing a and b.

The following illustrative device is helpful: identify a and b in the pair (a,b) as names given to the two endpoints of a "rod"; a is the right endpoint, b the left endpoint. In fact, to stress the analogy with extensive measurement, the pairs (a,b) themselves, in this section, will be referred to as *rods*. Thus $P_{a,b}$ increases strictly monotonically with the length of the rod (a,b). We write

$$(a,b) \prec (c,d) \quad \text{iff} \quad P_{a,b} < P_{c,d} \; ,$$

$$(a,b) \sim (c,d) \quad \text{iff} \quad P_{a,b} = P_{c,d} \; ,$$

$$(a,b) \preccurlyeq (c,d) \quad \text{iff} \quad P_{a,b} \leqslant P_{c,d} \; .$$

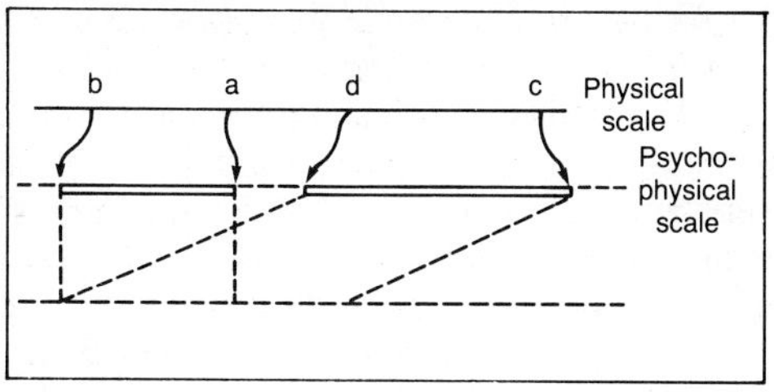

Figure 1.3. In a discrimination experiment, the two pairs of stumuli (a,b), (c,d) considered as rods; $(a,b) < (c,d)$.

Figure 1.3 summarizes the situation. We have thus a collection of rods and a comparison procedure represented by the relation $\preccurlyeq$. This analogy with the extensive measurement of the length of rods discussed in Section 2 also suggests a concatenation procedure. For example, (a,b) concatenated with (b,c) should have a length equal to that of (a,c). We symbolize this fact by the formula

$$(a,b)(b,c) \sim (a,c) .$$

Thus a comparison of $(a,b)(b,c)$ with (d,e) is made possible by a comparison of (a,c) with (d,e). For example, if $(a,c) < (d,e)$, one concludes that

$$(a,b)(b,c) < (d,e) .$$

This, of course, is a special case. Generally, two rods to be concatenated need not have a common endpoint. A discussion of the more general situation, although quite straightforward, involves technical details and will be omitted here.

Let us proceed to construct a scale measuring the length of the rods (keeping in mind that the "length" of (a,b) is the distance between the stimuli a,b on some psychophysical scale). Suppose that we decide to use the method of Section 2.3 to measure the length of some rod (a,a'). We pick some rod (b_0, b_1) as a unit, together with any number of exact copies of that rod;

$$(b_0,b_1) \sim (b_1,b_2) \sim \ldots \sim (b_i,b_{i+1}) \sim \ldots .$$

We have thus by definition of the concatenation operation

$$(b_0,b_1)(b_1,b_2) \ldots (b_{i-1},b_i) \sim (b_0,b_i), \quad i = 1,2, \ldots .$$

The length n will be assigned to (a,a') (n being some positive integer) if

$$(b_0,b_n) \preccurlyeq (a,a') < (b_0,b_{n+1}) ,$$

that is, if correspondingly, the probabilities satisfy the inequalities

$$P_{b_n,b_0} \leqslant P_{a,a'} < P_{b_{n+1},b_0} . \tag{11}$$

The number n is thus a measure of the length of the rod (a,a'), that is, of the distance between a and a' on the psychophysical scale. Let us apply this idea in an example. Suppose that the probabilities for all the pairs of stimuli in a set $\{a_0, a_1, a_2, a_3, a_4\}$ are given by the matrix

$$\begin{array}{c} \\ a_0 \\ a_1 \\ a_2 \\ a_3 \\ a_4 \end{array} \begin{array}{c} \begin{array}{ccccc} a_0 & a_1 & a_2 & a_3 & a_4 \end{array} \\ \begin{bmatrix} .5 & .75 & .80 & .90 & .95 \\ & .5 & .75 & .80 & .90 \\ & & .5 & .75 & .80 \\ & & & .5 & .75 \\ & & & & .5 \end{bmatrix} \end{array} \tag{12}$$

If we take (a_0,a_1) as a unit, this method leads us to assign the values in the matrix below, as measuring the distance between the points:

$$\begin{array}{c} \\ a_0 \\ a_1 \\ a_2 \\ a_3 \\ a_4 \end{array} \begin{array}{c} \begin{array}{ccccc} a_0 & a_1 & a_2 & a_3 & a_4 \end{array} \\ \begin{bmatrix} 0 & 1 & 2 & 3 & 4 \\ & 0 & 1 & 2 & 3 \\ & & 0 & 1 & 2 \\ & & & 0 & 1 \\ & & & & 0 \end{bmatrix} \end{array} . \tag{13}$$

We leave it to the reader to verify this in detail. (The values 0–3 follow from a straightforward application of the criterion represented by Eq. (11). The value 4 would require a refinement of that criterion.) The five stimuli can thus be represented as points on a straight line, say, with a_0 at the point 0, and the distance between a_i and a_{i+1} being constant, equal to 1.

Except for unessential details, this is Fechner's fundamental idea.

3.2. Remarks

In our deliberate emphasis of the relation between Fechner's scaling method and extensive measurement, we were led, for simplicity's sake, to make a somewhat unrealistic assumption. We supposed that any rod (a,b) could be "squeezed" between two rods (b_0,b_n) and (b_0,b_{n+1}), in the sense of Eq. (11). In practice, however, if a,b are far enough apart, the probability $P_{a,b}$ will be equal to 1 (or 0, if $b < a$) and will be unaffected by small changes of the values of a and b. This means of course that Eq. (11) cannot hold. A minor modification of the algorithm takes care of this difficulty, without altering the spirit of the method. We assign the number n to (a,b) if there exists a sequence a_0, a_1, ..., a_{n+1} such that

(i) $a = a_0 < a_1 < \ldots < a_n \leqslant b < a_{n+1}$.
(ii) $P_{a_{i+1},a_i} = .75$ for $0 \leqslant i \leqslant n$.

The distance $a_{i+1} - a_i$ is often referred to as a *just-noticeable difference* (jnd). Unfortunately, this term is used for a variety of closely related, but different, indices. To eliminate confusion, we shall reserve the term for one particular such index, which is defined in Section 7.4.

The Fechnerian method of scale construction described in Section 3.1 is an adaptation of the algorithm for the measurement of the length of rods outlined earlier (see the first method in Section 2.3). We have seen that such an algorithm lacks precision. In fact, it can be shown that a full psychophysical scale, one that would assign a scale value to each stimulus, could not be constructed using this method. A more sophisticated algorithm must be used, similar to the second method described in Section 2.5. This point was made by Luce and Edwards (1958).

Even assuming that an appropriate refinement of the algorithm is used, there is no guarantee that the method will work. The analogy of this method with that used in extensive measurement indicates that some axioms are implicitly assumed. In fact, this analogy even suggests which axioms might be involved. For example, one of the key axioms of extensive measurement is the monotonicity axiom (cf. Section 2.4): for rods x,x', y,y'

$$\text{if } x \leq z \text{ and } x' \leq z', \text{ then } xx' \leq zz' \ .$$

This axiom has a natural translation in the notations of this chapter. Indeed, identifying

x with the rod (a,b)
z with the rod (a',b')
x' with the rod (b,c)
z' with the rod (b',c') we obtain:

$$\text{If } P_{a,b} \leq P_{a',b'} \text{ and } P_{b,c} \leq P_{b',c'}, \text{ then } P_{a,c} \leq P_{a',c'} \ . \qquad (14)$$

(See Figure 1.4.) As we shall see, a weak form of this axiom will play a major role in the axiomatization of Fechner's method.

This condition sets constraints on the results of an experiment intended to provide the basic data for the construction of a Fechnerian scale. A priori there is no reason to believe that this condition would be satisfied experimentally for a given psychophysical continuum. To our knowledge, no direct test of this axiom has ever been made. As can be shown easily, Weber's law—a strong form of it, that is—implies Eq. (14). (Weber's law is discussed in Section 7.) Weber's law itself, however, is not always satisfied experimentally and, in any event, is not necessary for the method to be applicable. (Fechner was well aware of this fact; cf. Fechner, 1860/1966, pp. 54–55.) More generally, two questions are raised here: (1) Which axioms are involved in Fechner's method of scale construction? (2) Are these axioms satisfied experimentally?

Important errors of measurement will unavoidably result from any method based on successive concatenation of rods, possibly a large number of times. The method described in Section 3.1, for example, involves as a first step fixing (b_0, b_1) as a "unit." As a second step, b_2 is estimated such that (approximately) $P_{b_1,b_2} = P_{b_0,b_1}$. Next, b_3 is estimated such that (approximately) $P_{b_0,b_1} = P_{b_2,b_3}$, and so on. Any error made on the estimation of the location of b_2 will affect the estimated location of b_3. In general, the location of b_n will be affected by the accumulated errors made in the location of $b_2, b_3, ..., b_{n-1}$. Fechner realized this difficulty, which he bypassed by solving a functional equation: he did not actually construct the psychophysical scale but simply derived its mathematical form under the constraints

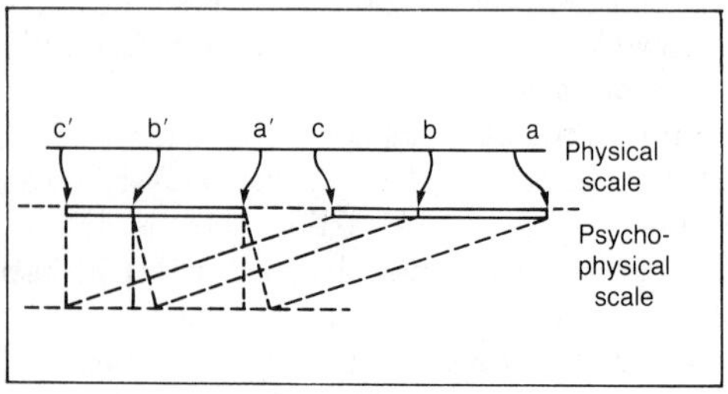

Figure 1.4. Equation 14 and the rod analogy:

If $P_{a,b} \leq P_{a',b'}$ and $P_{b,c} \leq P_{b',c'}$, then $p_{a,c} \leq P_{a',c'}$

(The conventions are as in Figure 1.3).

imposed by Weber's law. We shall go back to these issues later in this chapter.

Finally, the status of the Fechnerian scale obtained by this method is ambiguous. Exactly what problems are we solving by such construction? Why would this particular scale be of central importance in psychophysical theory? Fechner's viewpoint seems to have been that such a scale is adequate as a measure of the magnitude of the sensation evoked by the stimulus. As is well known, this position has been sternly criticized, in particular by a contemporary school of psychophysics which originated with S. S. Stevens (1957). (See also Marks, 1974, and many references in that book. We shall go back to this question in Section 10.)

In the discussion of such issues, it is important to differentiate the factual ones (mathematical or empirical) from the philosophical or semantic ones. Here we are mainly concerned with the mathematical aspects, a suitable framework for which is offered by *Fechner's problem*.

3.3. Fechner's Problem

We begin by tightening up our notation. We shall assume that the physical variable under consideration takes its values in some real interval I. Thus in a weight-lifting experiment, I might contain all weights between 0 and 500 gm, for example. Since the probabilities $P_{a,b}$ are defined for pairs (a,b) of stimuli, P can be regarded as a function of two variables, taking its values in the closed interval [0,1]. (A real interval is called *closed* when it contains its endpoints and *open* when it does not contain its endpoints.) Let C be the domain of the function P, that is, the set of all pairs (a,b) for which $P_{a,b}$ is defined. For reasons that will be made clear in a moment, we do not assume that P is necessarily defined for *all* pairs (a,b) of stimuli. In other words, we do not assume that we have necessarily $C = I \times I$. When $(a,b) \in C$, that is, when $P_{a,b}$ is defined, we shall say that a is *comparable* to b.

From a mathematical standpoint, the problem implicitly proposed by Fechner can be stated as follows.

3.3.1. Problem. Let I be a real interval; let C be a subset of $I \times I$; let P be a mapping of C into the closed interval [0,1]. Find an algorithm for the construction of a real-valued, strictly increasing (continuous) function u on I, such that whenever P is defined, then

$$P_{a,b} = F[u(a) - u(b)] \ , \qquad (15)$$

where F is also strictly increasing (and continuous).

Thus in the rod analogy used in Section 3.1, $u(a) - u(b)$ is the length of the rod (b,a) (when $b < a$). Under a slightly different form, this problem was proposed by Luce and Galanter (1963a) under the name *Fechner's problem*. It immediately suggests the following one.

3.3.2. Representation Problem. Let I,C,P be as in Section 3.3.1. Under which conditions on (I,C,P) does problem F have a solution?

The answer to this last problem would be a list of axioms on (I,C,P) ensuring the existence of a pair (u,F) of functions satisfying Eq. (15).

3.4. Remarks

With suitable refinements (cf. Section 3.2), Fechner's scaling algorithm provides a solution to problem F. This method, however, is applicable only if (I,C,P) satisfies the axioms in a list constituting a solution to the representation problem (Section 3.3.2). There is more than one such solution. For example, we shall see that Weber's law itself is a solution to the representation problem. This solution, however, is only a particular case, and there are many more.

There is, obviously, a degree of arbitrariness in the choice of Eq. (15) to represent the subject's ability to discriminate between adjacent stimuli. In particular, if Eq. (15) holds, then

$$P_{a,b} = H[g(a)/g(b)] \tag{16}$$

also holds with $g(a) = e^{u(a)}$, $H(s) = F(\ln s)$. Instead of differences, we could thus equally well represent pairs of stimuli by ratios. Clearly, Eqs. (15) and (16) are equivalent, in the sense that they impose identical constraints on the choice probabilities. In the sequel, we shall occasionally adopt Eq. (16), rather than Eq. (15), whenever convenient for one reason or other.

The errors of measurement inherent in Fechner's method of scale construction are so severe as to rule out such construction as impractical. One may thus wonder whether the representation problem (Section 3.3.2) is worth investigating. Actually, Fechner's algorithm can be improved. More important, it must be realized that the axioms of a solution to the representation problem constitute a genuine psychophysical theory. If these axioms are found to hold experimentally, this is of importance whether or not a practical method is available to construct the scale.

Equation (15) is sometimes objected to on the grounds that it is too abstract and offers little intuition regarding the mechanisms responsible for the subject's choices. The fundamental importance of Eq. (15) in psychophysical theory, however, is that it characterizes a large family of models, some of which postulate compelling, explicit choice mechanisms. Several examples of such models will be discussed in Section 4.

3.5. Representation Theorem

In view of the central importance of the representation problem (Section 3.3.2) for Fechnerian scaling, two complete solutions will be given here. We proceed by stating first a number of background conditions on the choice probabilities. Some of the conditions 1–5 gathered in the next definition may be puzzling at first reading, in part because the mathematical symbolism may be unfamiliar. To facilitate the reader's approach to these notions, each condition is followed by a verbal paraphrase in parentheses. Some reflection will certainly convince that, in each case, the condition is reasonable from an empirical viewpoint (see the remarks after the definition in Section 3.5.1). The set C in the definition is the set of all pairs (a,b) of stimuli that could be presented to the subject. Note that this set is much larger than the set of pairs actually used in an experiment. This last set is a finite subset of C. We do not assume that all pairs of stimuli could be used, even in an idealized experiment. The reason for this is that some pairs (a,b) of stimuli are uninformative, since the corresponding discrimination probability is 0 or 1 and is unaffected by small changes of the values of a, b. Accordingly, we require the function P to be strictly monotonic in both variables (see axioms 4 and 5 in Section 3.5.1). Statements regarding the "openness" of sets have a technical import and can be overlooked if their meaning is obscure. (They cannot, however, be omitted by this writer since the theorem in Section 3.5.3 would cease to be true.)

3.5.1. Definition. As customary, we write $s \in S$ to signify that some element s belongs to a set S. When a pair (a,b) of stimuli belong to the set C (that is, when $(a,b) \in C$), we shall sometimes say that a is *comparable* to b. Let I be a real, open interval; let $(a,b) \mapsto P_{a,b}$ be a function mapping C into the open interval $(0,1)$. Then (I,C,P) is a *psychophysical discrimination system* iff for all stimuli a, $b \in I$:

1. $(a,a) \in C$ (every pair (a,a) can be presented to the subject for discrimination).
2. $(a,b) \in C$ implies $(b,a) \in C$ (if a is comparable to b, then b is comparable to a).
3. There exists a positive integer n (depending on a,b) and a sequence $a_1, a_2, \ldots, a_n \in I$, such that $a_1 = a$, $a_n = b$ and $(a_i,a_{i+1}) \in C$ for $1 \leq i \leq n-1$ (the stimuli in every pair (a,b) are linked by a sequence $a = a_1, a_2, \ldots, a_n = b$ of successively comparable stimuli).
4. P is strictly increasing in the first variable, strictly decreasing in the second variable, and continuous in both (for every fixed $b \in I$, the two functions p_b and q_b of one variable, defined by $p_b(a) = P_{a,b}$ and $q_b(a) = P_{b,a}$ are continuous; moreover, $a < a'$ iff $p_b(a) < p_b(a')$ iff $q_b(a') < q_b(a)$).
5. The sets $\{c \in I \mid (c,d) \in C\}$ and $\{c \in I \mid (b,c) \in C\}$ are real intervals (for every fixed $b \in I$, the domains of the functions p_b and q_b are real intervals).

A psychophysical discrimination system (I,C,P) is called *balanced* if, in addition,

$$P_{a,b} + P_{b,a} = 1$$

whenever both $(a,b) \in C$ and $(b,a) \in C$.

A few remarks on some of these axioms are in order. The function p_b, introduced in the verbal paraphrase of axiom 4, is the so-called psychometric function with standard stimulus b, a familiar concept in psychophysical practice, which will be discussed in the next section. In terms of this concept, the remaining axioms state that the psychometric functions are strictly increasing and continuous (axiom 4); the domain of any psychometric function is a real interval; and the domains of these psychometric functions overlap, provided that the standard stimuli are close enough. To a reader acquainted with the paradigm analyzed here, these assumptions should appear very natural.

In some cases, the balance condition will hold by virtue of the paradigm or of the mode of data collection. An example is a brightness discrimination experiment (such as Cornsweet & Pinsker, 1965) where the position of two patches of light is varying randomly, over trials, from above to below a fixation point and the data are pooled over position. In other cases, however, such averaging is not legitimate and may mask an important phenomenon. For instance, the order of the stimuli in the notation (a,b) may symbolize the fact that stimulus a is presented first, followed by stimulus b. The balance condition states, in effect, that the order of presentation has no effect on the result of a comparison. This may not be true, for example, for auditory stimuli presented successively. This case is considered in the next section where a more general theory is outlined.

Notice that, taken by themselves, the axioms of a balanced psychophysical discrimination system are not sufficient to ensure that Eq. (15),

$$P_{a,b} = F[u(a) - u(b)] ,$$

holds for some strictly increasing, continuous functions u, F. Indeed, suppose that

$$P_{a,b} = \Phi\left[\frac{a - b}{(a + b)^{1/2}}\right] \tag{17}$$

for all positive real numbers a,b. (As customary, we denote by Φ the distribution function of a standard, normal random variable.) It is easy to check that, as defined by Eq. (17), the probabilities $P_{a,b}$ satisfy all the conditions of a balanced pychophysical discrimination system. (This verification is left to the reader.)

This model, however, is incompatible with Eq. (15). The reason for this is that the (functional) equation

$$P_{a,b} = \Phi\left[\frac{a - b}{(a + b)^{1/2}}\right] = F[u(a) - u(b)]$$

has no solution for the functions u, F. (That is, there are no functions u, F "solving" this equation; cf. Iverson, 1979). Thus additional conditions on the choice probabilities are needed, if Eq. (15) is to hold. Two such conditions are introduced in the next definition.

3.5.2. Definition. A psychophysical discrimination system (I,C,P) is called *Fechnerian* iff the equation $P_{a,b} = F[u(a) - u(b)]$ holds for some strictly increasing continuous functions u, F.

We say that (I,C,P) satisfies the *bicancellation condition* iff whenever $P_{a,b} \leq P_{a',b'}$, $P_{b,c} \leq P_{b',c'}$ and $(a,c),(a',c') \in C$, then $P_{a,c} \leq P_{a',c'}$.

A psychophysical discrimination system (I,C,P) satisfies the *quadruple condition* iff

$$P_{a,b} \leq P_{a',b'} \text{ iff } P_{a,a'} \leq P_{b,b'}$$

whenever all four probabilities are defined. The importance of the bicancellation condition has been emphasized earlier, in connection with a similar condition in extensive measurement (cf. Section 3.2). The relation between the three concepts in this definition is made clear in the theorem in Section 3.5.3.

3.5.3. Representation and Uniqueness Theorem. Let Ψ be a balanced psychophysical discrimination system. Then the following three conditions are equivalent:

(i) Ψ is Fechnerian
(ii) Ψ satisfies bicancellation
(iii) Ψ satisfies the quadruple condition.

Moreover, if any of these conditions is satisfied and (u, F), (u^*, F^*) are two pairs of functions satisfying Eq. (15), then $u^*(a) = \alpha u(a) + \beta$ and $F^*(s) = F(s/\alpha)$ for some constants $\alpha > 0$ and β.

The relation between the functions u and u^* in this theorem is sometimes expressed by stating that "u is an interval scale" (see Section 10 in this connection).

A full proof of this theorem would take many pages and is beyond the scope of this chapter. Some parts of this result are easy to obtain however, for example, the two implications (i) $\Rightarrow$ (ii) and (i) $\Rightarrow$ (iii). Assume, for example, that (i) holds, and let u, F be the two functions satisfying Eq. (15). Successively,

$$\begin{aligned}
P_{a,b} \leq P_{a',b'} &\text{ iff } F[u(a) - u(b)] \leq F[u(a') - u(b')] \\
&\text{ iff } u(a) - u(b) \leq u(a') - u(b') \\
&\text{ iff } u(a) - u(a') \leq u(b) - u(b') \\
&\text{ iff } F[u(a) - u(a')] \leq F[u(b) - u(b')] \\
&\text{ iff } P_{a,a'} \leq P_{b,b'},
\end{aligned}$$

establishing the quadruple condition. The second implication, (i) $\Rightarrow$ (ii), is obtained by a similar method.

Placed on the background of the conditions defining a balanced psychophysical discrimination system, the bicancellation and the quadruple condition each constitutes a complete solution to the representation problem in Section 3.3.2. To put it another way: any model for choice probabilities $P_{a,b}$ satisfying either bicancellation or the quadruple condition can be put in the form of Eq. (15). In principle, these conditions can be tested experimentally. In practice, however, rather delicate statistical issues arise (cf. Iverson & Falmagne, in press).

The importance given in this chapter to Eq. (15) may surprise the reader. Actually, this representation has an impact beyond Fechner's scaling method. Many current models for choice probabilities are Fechnerian (in the sense of the definition in Section 3.5.2). As we shall see, these models differ in the specific assumptions made regarding the mechanisms of choice, which in turn determine the form of the function F in Eq. (15).

The critical issue remains of the status of the scale u, once it has been constructed. Does it make sense, as proposed by Fechner, to consider that such a scale measures the magnitude of the "sensation" evoked by the stimulus? We shall postpone this discussion for the moment (see Section 10).

3.6. Key References

The discussion of Fechner's scaling methods given here, even though perfectly compatible with Fechner's own presentation, was strongly influenced by the developments of measurement theory, as given, for example, in Krantz and colleagues (1971) or Roberts (1979). In this context, Fechner's problem is a case of difference measurement. The notions of a representation problem, representation theorem, and uniqueness theorem are standard in measurement theory.

This modern viewpoint regarding Fechner's enterprise is due to Luce and his collaborators (Luce, 1959a; Luce & Edwards, 1958; Luce & Galanter, 1963). The solution to the representation problem given here is mostly due to Doignon and Falmagne (1974; see also Falmagne, 1971, 1974). Related references are Levine (1971, 1972) and Krantz (1971). Eq. (15) also appears in the general context of choice theory, where it is dubbed the *strong utility model* (Luce & Suppes, 1965). The quadruple condition has been investigated by Marschak (1960) and Debreu (1960).

As indicated, statistical issues regarding the empirical testing of axioms such as bicancellation or the quadruple condition are discussed in Iverson and Falmagne (in press).

4. MODELS OF DISCRIMINATION

In Section 3 we considered a forced-choice paradigm, in which a subject is presented with pairs (a,b) of stimuli (a,b are real numbers, representing the stimulus values on some physical scale). The task is to select one of the two stimuli as exceeding the other, in terms of some subjective attribute, such as loudness or perceived weight, depending on the nature of the stimuli.

The basic theoretical notion was a probability $P_{a,b}$ that the subject chooses a over b. It was assumed that P is strictly increasing in a and strictly decreasing in b. A detailed theoretical analysis was made of the representation

$$P_{a,b} = F[u(a) - u(b)] \tag{18}$$

for these choice probabilities. In this equation, u and F are assumed to be real-valued, continuous, and strictly increasing functions, but are otherwise unspecified. Such a model says little regarding the details of the mechanism of choice. Certainly, the choice of a stimulus is the final stage of a complex process, involving physiological and psychological components. All these aspects are somehow captured by the functions u and F. This rather abstract viewpoint is open to criticisms, in particular regarding the interpretation of the functions u and F. Suppose, for example, that the subject is under time pressure. Say the choice response must be made within t sec after the presentation of the stimuli, with t varying across conditions (e.g., $t = 1, 3, 10$). Assuming that Eq. (18) holds in each condition, will the value of t affect u, F, both of these functions? Without a more explicit model, it is difficult to venture a guess. One could obviously *assume*, for instance, that only F will vary across conditions. However, some may feel uneasy about the (absence of) rationale for such a position. To take another example, suppose that the stimuli a,b ... are pure tones, presented on a background n of noise (say, n is the average sound pressure of a Gaussian noise). The values of n, if their range is chosen appropriately, will certainly affect the choice probabilities. Again, however, the impact of n on u or F is difficult to predict. In turn, one may argue, this uncertainty regarding the role of u and F in these experiments casts some doubt on the interpretation of u as a "sensation scale" (cf. Section 3).

This section is devoted to a discussion of a number of models consistent with Eq. (18). This means that a given model is either a special case of Eq. (18) (its assumptions imply a particular functional form for the function F) or has a special case that takes the form of Eq. (18), with F specified.

4.1. Random Utility Models

Let us assume that to each presented stimulus a, corresponds a random variable $\mathbf{U}_a$ symbolizing the effect of the stimulus on the subject's sensory apparatus. We also assume that a appears at least as intense as some other offered stimulus b if the sampled value of $\mathbf{U}_b$ does not exceed that of $\mathbf{U}_a$; formally

$$P_{a,b} = \text{Prob}\{\mathbf{U}_a \geqslant \mathbf{U}_b\} .$$

The distributions of the random variables $\mathbf{U}_a$ are unspecified.

In the literature of choice theory, this model is often referred to as the *random utility model* (Block & Marschak, 1960; Luce & Suppes, 1965; Marschak, 1960). Since no assumptions are made regarding the joint distribution of the random variables $\mathbf{U}_a$, one may ask whether this model sets any constraint on the data. Actually, it may be shown that if *some* collection of random variables $\mathbf{U}_a$ exists satisfying this model, then (in the case of a balanced system, cf. Section 3.5) we must have

$$1 \leqslant P_{a,b} + P_{b,c} + P_{c,a} \leqslant 2$$

for all stimuli a, b, and c (Block & Marschak, 1960). This is a rather weak condition, but one which can conceivably be rejected for some data.

This general model is consistent with the Fechnerian Eq. (18). In other words, under specific assumptions on the joint distribution of the random variables $\mathbf{U}_a$ and $\mathbf{U}_b$, Eq. (18) will be obtained. An example is given in Section 4.2.

4.2. Thurstone Law of Comparative Judgments

More specifically, suppose that $\mathbf{U}_a$ and $\mathbf{U}_b$ are independent and normally distributed, with respective means and variances $\mu(a)$, $\mu(b)$, $\sigma(a)^2$, $\sigma(b)^2$. Thus $\mathbf{U}_a - \mathbf{U}_b$ is normally distributed, with mean $\mu(a) - \mu(b)$ and variance $\sigma(a)^2 + \sigma(b)^2$. We obtain

$$P_{a,b} = \text{Prob}\{\mathbf{U}_a - \mathbf{U}_b \geqslant 0\} \tag{19}$$

$$= \Phi\{[\mu(a) - \mu(b)]/[\sigma(a)^2 + \sigma(b)^2]^{1/2}\} \tag{20}$$

where Φ is the distribution function of a unit normal random variable (i.e., a normal random variable with a mean equal to 0 and a variance equal to 1). Suppose, moreover, that the random variables have equal variances, say, $\sigma^2(c) = \alpha^2/2$ for all stimuli c. Then dividing by α in both the numerator and the denominator of Eq. (20), and writing $u(c) = \mu(c)/\alpha$, yields

$$P_{a,b} = \Phi[u(a) - u(b)] , \tag{21}$$

a special case of Eq. (18), with $F = \Phi$. The models embodied in Eqs. (20) and (21) are usually referred to as *cases III* and *V*, respectively, of Thurstone's *law of comparative judgment* (Thurstone, 1927a, 1927b; a very complete discussion of Thurstone's theory can be found in Bock & Jones, 1968). Thurstone case V has been given a special interpretation in a psychoacoustic context and has been applied to an impressive body of data by Durlach, Braida, and their coworkers (Braida & Durlach, 1972; Durlach & Braida, 1969; Jesteadt & Bilger, 1974; Jesteadt & Sims, 1975; Lim, Rabinowitz, Braida, & Durlach, 1977; Pynn, Braida, & Durlach, 1972).

4.3. Dropping the Normality Assumption

Notice that the normality assumption is not critical in the above discussion. Suppose that in Eq. (19) the random variables $\mathbf{U}_a$, $\mathbf{U}_b$ are independent and identically distributed except for a "shift" parameter. That is, suppose that for any stimulus c, $\mathbf{U}_c$ has the same distribution as $u(c) + \xi$, where u is a real-valued function and ξ is a fixed random variable. From Eq. (19), we have with ξ, ξ' independent and identically distributed

$$P_{a,b} = \text{Prob}\{u(a) + \xi - [u(b) + \xi'] \geqslant 0\}$$

$$= \text{Prob}\{\xi' - \xi \leqslant u(a) - u(b)\}$$

$$= G[u(a) - u(b)]$$

where G is the distribution function of $\xi' - \xi$. This is a special case of Eq. (18), generalizing case V of the law of comparative judgment.

4.4. Dropping the Constant Variance Assumption

The constant variance assumption used in the two preceding examples is not essential. Suppose that in Eq. (20) μ varies linearly with σ:

$$\mu(c) = \alpha\sigma(c) + \beta , \quad (22)$$

for some constants $\alpha > 0$ and β. Successively, from Eqs. (20) and (22)

$$P_{a,b} = \Phi\{\alpha[\sigma(a) - \sigma(b)]/[\sigma(a)^2 + \sigma(b)^2]^{1/2}\}$$

$$= \Phi\{\alpha[(\sigma(a)/\sigma(b)) - 1]/[(\sigma(a)/\sigma(b))^2 + 1]^{1/2}\} \quad (23)$$

Thus $P_{a,b}$ only depends on the ratio $\sigma(a)/\sigma(b)$. Defining

$$u(a) = \ln \sigma(a) ,$$

we rewrite the ratios $\sigma(a)/\sigma(b)$ in Eq. (23) as differences $u(a) - u(b)$, obtaining

$$P_{a,b} = F[u(a) - u(b)] , \quad (24)$$

where

$$F(s) = \Phi[\alpha(e^s - 1)/(e^{2s} + 1)^{1/2}] . \quad (25)$$

It is easy to check that F is strictly increasing. This model is sometimes referred to as *case VI* of Thurstone's law of comparative judgments (Bock & Jones, 1968; S. S. Stevens, 1959, 1966b). Again, the normality assumption is not essential in the above derivation.

4.5. A Timing Model

The linearity assumption, Eq. (22), linking mean and standard deviation of a random variable $\mathbf{U}_c$ may seem arbitrary. Actually, the above model arises quite naturally in psychoacoustics. Let a and b denote the sound pressure levels of two pure tones of the same frequency, say, 1000 Hz, presented successively and monaurally. Fairly detailed hypotheses will be made regarding the neural coding of physical sound intensity. We assume that a tone of level c applied in the auditory channel gives rise to a homogeneous Poisson process $L_t(c)$ of neural point events, with mean $\lambda(c)$. The interarrival times of these events (the interspike intervals) are thus independent and distributed exponentially, with expectation $\lambda(c)^{-1}$. Along lines explored by Luce and Green (1972, 1974a), suppose that a sample average $\mathbf{S}_{n,c}$ of these interarrival times is used as the basis for loudness discrimination (where n denotes the size of the sample). Stimulus a will be judged at least as loud as stimulus b if $\mathbf{S}_{n,a} \leq \mathbf{S}_{n,b}$; that is,

$$P_{a,b} = \text{Prob}\{\mathbf{S}_{n,a} \leq \mathbf{S}_{n,b}\} .$$

Since n can be assumed to be large ($n > 100$), $\mathbf{S}_{n(c)}$ is distributed very nearly normally, with expectation $\lambda(c)^{-1}$ and variance $\lambda(c)^{-2}/n$. The standard deviation is thus a linear function of the expectation, as in Eq. (22). We obtain

$$P_{a,b} = \Phi\{n^{1/2}[\lambda(b)^{-1} - \lambda(a)^{-1}]/[(\lambda(b)^{-2} + \lambda(a)^{-2}]^{1/2}\}$$

$$= \Phi\{n^{1/2}[(\lambda(a)/\lambda(b)) - 1]/[(\lambda(a)/\lambda(b))^2 + 1]^{1/2}\} ,$$

a special case of Eq. (23). In particular, Eqs. (24) and (25) follow with $u(a) = \ln \lambda(a)$ and $\alpha = n^{1/2}$.

4.6. An Extreme Value Model and the Strict Utility, or Logistic, Model

In the psychoacoustic paradigm used earlier, we suppose with Thompson and Singh (1967) that the neural coding of sound pressure is based on the combined effect of the stimulus on many independent, parallel channels. The sensory effect of a stimulus of level c in channel j, $(1 \leq j \leq n)$, is represented by a random variable $\mathbf{X}_{c,j}$.

We assume that $n(c)$ channels are triggered by stimulus c, the combined effect of which is represented by a random variable

$$\mathbf{U}_c = \max\{\mathbf{X}_{c,1}, \mathbf{X}_{c,2}, \ldots, \mathbf{X}_{c,n(c)}\} .$$

In words, the neural code of a stimulus c is the maximum of the excitation levels in $n(c)$ channels. As a basic equation specifying the choice probabilities, we have

$$P_{a,b} = \text{Prob}\{\mathbf{U}_a \geq \mathbf{U}_b\} .$$

It can be shown that if the random variables $\mathbf{X}_{c,j}$ are, with respect to c and j, independent and identically distributed (thus only the number of channels $n(a)$, $n(b)$ distinguishes the distribution of $\mathbf{U}_a$ from that of $\mathbf{U}_b$) and moreover satisfies some stability property, then we have approximately for large $n(a)$, $n(b)$,

$$P_{a,b} = \frac{n(a)}{n(a) + n(b)}$$

$$= \{1 + e^{-[\ln n(a) - \ln n(b)]}\}^{-1} \quad (26)$$

$$= F[u(a) - u(b)] ,$$

with $u(c) = \ln n(c)$ and

$$F(s) = (1 + e^{-s})^{-1} . \quad (27)$$

Taken by itself, Eq. (26) defines the *strict utility model* (Luce & Suppes, 1965), also called the *BTL* (Bradley-Terry-Luce) *system*, extensively investigated by Bradley (1954a, 1954b, 1955), Bradley and Terry (1952), and Luce (1959a) (cf. Suppes & Zinnes, 1963). Eq. (27) is the defining equation of the distribution function of a standard logistic random variable (Johnson & Kotz, 1970b, Chapter 22). This result, leading to Eq. (26), is due to Thompson and Singh (1967), based on extensive earlier work on the so-called extreme value distributions (Fisher & Tippett, 1928; Frechet, 1927; Gnedenko, 1943; Gumbel, 1958; von Mises, 1939). For some recent applications of these notions in choice theory and psychophysics, the reader is referred to Yellott (1977), and Wandell and Luce (1978), respectively.

4.7. Remarks

The diversity of these examples, which all lead to Eq. (18), justifies the central place given here to this equation. This diversity also carries an important lesson. In each of these examples, a key role is played for each stimulus c, by a basic random variable $\mathbf{U}_c$, formalizing the neural coding of the stimulus. The discrimination probabilities are symbolized by the equation

$$P_{a,b} = \text{Prob}\{\mathbf{U}_a \geqslant \mathbf{U}_b\} . \quad (28)$$

Assuming that such a theoretical device is warranted and that the particular form of (the distribution function of) these random variables is taken seriously, it may seem sensible to assign a fundamental role to a central location index of these random variables. This would suggest adopting $E(\mathbf{U}_c)$—the expectation of the random variable $\mathbf{U}_c$—as a measure of the magnitude of the sensation evoked by the stimulus c. Notice, however, that $E(\mathbf{U}_c)$ does not necessarily coincide with $u(c)$ in Eq. (18). Such coincidence is obtained in Eqs. (20) and (21) but not in (22) and (23) (where we have $u(c) = \ln E(\mathbf{U}_c)$) and not, as we shall see, in our next model.

Thus even though Eq. (18) may play a fundamental role, the theoretical status of the scale u entering in this equation is not necessarily clear.

It is natural to ask, Are there reasonable models incompatible with Eq. (18)? The example in Section 4.8 provides an answer.

There is another lesson to be derived from these examples. Comparing the extreme value model Eq. (24) with the law of comparative judgment, case V, Eq. (20), it must be concluded that the mechanisms postulated are very different. Nevertheless, these models are extremely difficult to distinguish from an empirical viewpoint. The extreme value model predicts that the choice probabilities will satisfy the equation

$$P_{a,b} = F[u(a) - u(b)]$$

where F is the distribution function of a standard logistic random variable, while in Thurstone case V, the same equation is obtained, except that F is replaced by Φ, the distribution function of a standard normal random variable. It turns out that F and Φ are close approximations to each other (see Johnson & Kotz, 1970b, for details on this matter), so close, in fact, that choosing one model over the other by some empirical test is practically hopeless.

The reason for this paradox—drastically different assumptions but indistinguishable predictions—is that these models consist of very elaborate constructions concerning unobservable choice mechanisms for a relatively scarce data base. There are simply not enough data to support the edifice. This is especially true for the extreme value model.

It is certainly tempting to model the unobservable details of the choice mechanisms, and it may even be useful to do so, since this may provide insightful interpretations of the data and suggest useful experiments. The lesson is, however, that such detailed assumptions should probably not be taken too seriously, except in cases in which the data base is much richer, relative to the theoretical construction, than was assumed here.

4.8. A Neural Poisson Counting Model

Now let us consider a neural Poisson counting model incompatible with the equation $P_{a,b} = F[u(a) - u(b)]$. As in the psychoacoustic example in Section 4.6, suppose that a tone of level c generates a homogeneous Poisson process of spike events $L_t(c)$, of mean $\lambda(c)$. Suppose now, however, that intensity discrimination, rather than being based on the average spike intervals as in Section 4.5, relies on a count of the number of spikes during a fixed interval τ. Let $\mathbf{N}_a$, $\mathbf{N}_b$ be two random variables representing the number of spikes counted for each of the two stimuli a, b. Thus $\mathbf{N}_a$, $\mathbf{N}_b$ are two independent Poisson random variables, with expectations $\mu(a) = \lambda(a)\tau$, $\mu(b) = \lambda(b)\tau$, respectively. (We recall the variance of a Poisson random variable is equal to its expectation.) Assume further that

$$P_{a,b} = \text{Prob}\{\mathbf{N}_a \geqslant \mathbf{N}_b\} .$$

For large $\lambda(a)\tau$, $\lambda(b)\tau$, the random variables $\mathbf{N}_a$, $\mathbf{N}_b$ are nearly normal (Cramer, 1963, p. 250), yielding approximately

$$P_{a,b} = \Phi\{[\mu(a) - \mu(b)]/[\mu(a) + \mu(b)]^{1/2}\} .$$

This model, which, as far as we know, was proposed originally by Strackee and van der Gon (1962; see also Luce & Green, 1972, 1974a; McGill & Goldberg, 1968), is incompatible with Eq. (18); there are no (continuous, monotonic) functions μ, u, and F satisfying the equation

$$\Phi\{[\mu(a) - \mu(b)]/[\mu(a) + \mu(b)]^{1/2}\} = F[u(a) - u(b)] . \quad (29)$$

The proof of this fact, based on a result due to Iverson (1979), will not be given here.

4.9. Remark on Statistical Testing

The models discussed in this section can be tested empirically by standard statistical techniques. A likelihood ratio method is sketched below for the logistic model, the principle of which is easily extended to other cases.

According to the logistic model defined by Eqs. (26) and (27), the choice probabilities must satisfy the equation

$$P_{a,b} = (1 + e^{-\theta_{ab}})^{-1} , \quad (30)$$

with

$$\theta_{ab} = u(a) - u(b) . \quad (31)$$

Notice that Eq. (31) implies—in fact, is equivalent to—the condition

$$\theta_{ab} + \theta_{bc} + \theta_{ca} = 0 , \quad (32)$$

for all stimuli a, b, and c. In particular,

$$\theta_{aa} = 0 ,$$

$$\theta_{ba} = -\theta_{ab} .$$

There is a good reason for this reparameterization of the model. The new parameters θ_{ab} have to be estimated from the data, subject to the linear constraint, Eq. (32). This is a standard situation in statistics, which leads naturally to a likelihood ratio procedure. Let n_{ab} be the number of choices of stimulus a observed in the course of $n_{ab} + n_{ba}$ trials. Let Θ be the vector of all the parameters θ_{ab}. Under the usual conditions concerning the independence of trials, the likelihood of the data is the product

$$l(\Theta) = \prod_{(a,b)} (1 + e^{-\theta_{ab}})^{-n_{ab}}(1 + e^{-\theta_{ba}})^{-n_{ba}} . \quad (33)$$

The unconstrained maximum likelihood estimates of the parameters θ_{ab} are given by

$$\hat{\theta}_{ab} = \ln(n_{ab}/n_{ba}) . \quad (34)$$

(This corresponds to estimating the probabilities $P_{a,b}$ by their relative frequencies.) Let l_1 be the value of the likelihood function l in Eq. (33), when the parameters θ_{ab} are replaced by their unconstrained maximum likelihood estimates. Let l_2 be the value of the likelihood function l, when the parameters θ_{ab} are replaced by their maximum likelihood estimates, obtained under the linear constraint, Eq. (32). A classical result is that the ratio

$$-2 \ln(l_1/l_2)$$

is asymptotically (i.e., for a large number of trials) distributed as a chi-square random variable with a degree of freedom equal to the number of independent parameters remaining in l_2 (cf. Wilks, 1962, or any standard statistical text).

This procedure can be applied in principle to any model for binary choices, consistent with the Fechnerian equation

$$P_{a,b} = F[u(a) - u(b)] , \quad (35)$$

in which the function F is specified exactly. This function being strictly increasing, its inverse F^{-1} exists, and Eq. (35) gives immediately

$$F^{-1}(P_{a,b}) + F^{-1}(P_{b,c}) + F^{-1}(P_{c,a}) = 0 , \quad (36)$$

generalizing Eq. (32).

4.10. Key References

Some papers of general interest are Luce and Suppes (1965) and Luce (1977a, 1977b). Even though centered on applications in economics, the review paper by McFadden (1976) is a useful reference, in which special attention is paid to statistical matters. The book by Bock and Jones (1968) contains a very thorough discussion of Thurstone's discrimination models. Gumbel (1958) and Galambos (1978) are introductory texts on extreme value distributions. Other useful titles are listed below, organized by topics.

General Random Utility Models. Marschak (1960); Block and Marschak (1960); McFadden and Richter (1970, 1971), Manski (1977); Falmagne (1978).

Thurstone Law of Comparative Judgment. Thurstone (1927a, 1927b); Braida and Durlach (1972); Durlach and Braida (1969); Jesteadt and Bilger (1974); Jesteadt and Sims (1975); Lim, Rabinowitz, Braida, and Durlach (1977); Pynn, Braida, and Durlach (1972).

Extreme Value Model. Fisher and Tippett (1928); Frechet (1927); Gnedenko (1943); Thompson and Singh (1967); von Mises (1939); Wandell and Luce (1978).

Logistic Model; BTL Systems. Bradley (1954a, 1954b, 1955); Bradley and Terry (1952); Luce (1959a); Suppes and Zinnes (1963); Yellott (1977). (As indicated by its title, this paper of Yellott could also be placed in either of the two above categories.)

Timing and Counting Models. Luce and Green (1972, 1974a); Strackee and van der Gon (1962); McGill and Goldberg (1968).

The complete literature on probabilistic choice theory is huge, and the above list should not be taken as exhaustive. Only references of general interest, or having a potential relevance to psychophysics, were included.

Finally, a generally useful source for facts regarding the distribution function of commonly encountered random variables is Johnson and Kotz (1969, 1970a, 1970b).

5. PSYCHOMETRIC FUNCTIONS

Consider, for a fixed stimulus b, the probability $p_b(a)$ that stimulus a is judged as exceeding b. (Both b and a are in some real interval representing the physical scale.) A somewhat idealized graph of a function p_b, which is consistent in its main features with many data, is displayed in Figure 1.5.

Clearly, regarded as a function of two variables, $(a,b) \mapsto p_b(a)$ is (except for a change of notations) exactly the choice probability function $(a,b) \mapsto P_{a,b}$ analyzed in Sections 3 and 4. As we shall see, however, the change of notation is indicative of a change of viewpoint, which in turn leads to new theoretical insights.

Such a function p_b is traditionally referred to as a *psychometric function*. This term is also used in a different situation, when $p_b(a)$ denotes the probability of detecting a stimulus a embedded in some "noisy" background b. In other words, a and b may be different kinds of physical variables. Occasionally, we encounter the term in an even broader context, when the empirical measure under investigation is not a probability of discrimination or detection but of some other variable, such as a reaction time or a count of a neural spike firing. Our discussion will cover all these cases.

A central topic of this section will be whether the data support the assumption that two or more psychometric functions are "parallel," that is, can be made to coincide by rigid shifts along the horizontal axis. The rationale for this question is that parallelism is a criterion for an important class of model represented by the equation

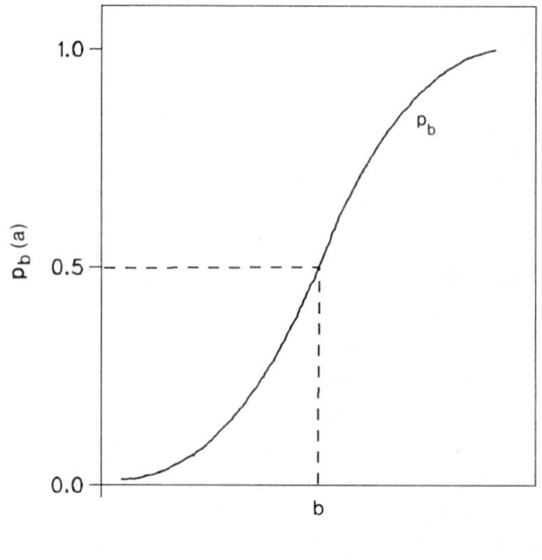

Figure 1.5. Idealized graph of a psychometric function.

$$p_b(a) = F[a - g(b)] , \quad (37)$$

in which the functions F and g depend on the particular model considered. In other words, any model satisfying this equation must predict parallel psychometric functions. The exact correspondence between Eq. (37) and parallelism will be described. A more general situation will also be investigated, corresponding to the equation

$$p_b(a) = F[u(a) - g(b)] . \quad (38)$$

In this case, the psychometric functions are not (necessarily) parallel but may be rendered so by some appropriate transformation u of the physical scale. Obviously, Eq. (38) generalizes the Fechnerian equation

$$P_{a,b} = F[u(a) - u(b)] \quad (39)$$

discussed at length in Sections 3 and 4. The importance of the issue of parallelism in psychophysical theory must be understood. Parallel psychometric functions indicate that the discrimination (or detection) acuity is uniform on the entire stimulus scale, a fact which may lead to adopting this scale as a measure of sensation magnitude.

Other topics are touched upon in this section. For instance, in the so-called two-alternative forced-choice (2AFC) design, the probability $P_{a,b}$ is often estimated by averaging the frequencies of the responses in the two alternatives. The theoretical consequences of this practice will be analyzed. It will be shown, for example, that it may have the unfortunate consequence of forcing nonparallelism.

We begin by considering a few empirical examples, leading to a basic definition.

5.1. Empirical Examples

5.1.1. Example. In an experiment reported by Engen (Kling & Riggs, 1971, p. 24), a subject was required to compare, by inspection, the length of two lines projected successively on a screen. In the course of the experiment, five lines of lengths 61, 62, 63, 64, and 65 mm were to be compared to a fixed line of length 63 mm. Thus in the above notations, $b = 63$ mm and a takes on five values. The pairs (a,b) of stimuli were presented randomly, with 100 trials per pair. On half of the trials, b was presented first. The subject was asked whether the perceived length of the first line exceeded that of the second. No feedback was given. Denote by $f_b(a)$ the relative frequency of the judgment that the perceived length of a exceeds that of b. The values of $f_b(a)$ are displayed in Figure 1.6. Such data are consistent with Figure 1.5 and suggest that p_b is a smooth function, strictly increasing on an interval bracketing b and such that $p_b(b) = .5$. The method employed in this experiment is usually referred to as the method of *constant stimuli*, and the fixed stimulus b is called the standard stimulus.

5.1.2. Example. In an unpublished experiment of Graham and Hartline (1933; reported in Sirovich & Abramov, 1977), the frequency of spike firing of a single fiber in the lateral eye of the horseshoe crab, *Limulus*, was recorded as a function of the intensity of a visual stimulus for various monochromatic lights. The data (frequency of spike firing in the initial portion of the response immediately following the stimulus) are plotted in Figure 1.7, which is reproduced from Sirovich and Abramov

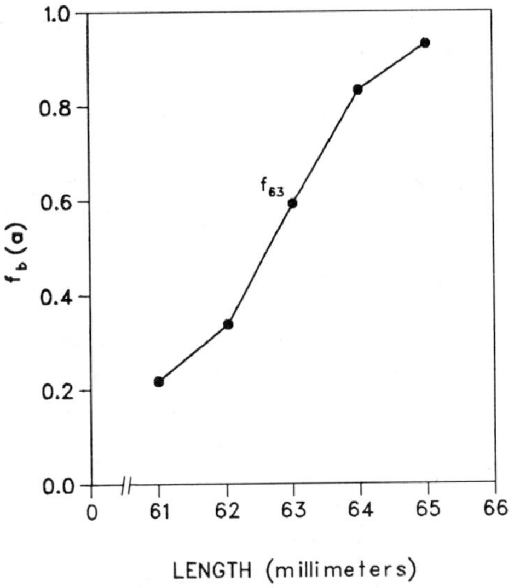

Figure 1.6. Proportion of "longer" judgment as a function of line length obtained with the method of constant stimuli. (From T. Engen, Psychophysics: Discrimination and detection, in J. W. Kling & L. A. Riggs (Eds.), *Experimental psychology* (3rd ed.). Copyright 1938, 1954, 1971 by Holt, Rinehart & Winston, Inc., CBS College Publishing. Reprinted with permission.)

(1977). The wavelength of the monochromatic light (in nm) is the parameter. It is clear that the five curves underlying the data in Figure 1.7 contain essentially the same information as traditional psychometric functions. Notice a difference, however, which concerns the ranges of the frequency of firing functions. As suggested by the data, these are real intervals bounded by, say, 0 and 80. This is easily taken care of. Any of a number of transformations would yield ranges bounded by 0 and 1. For example, with $\Psi_b(a)$ denoting the frequency of spike firing, for

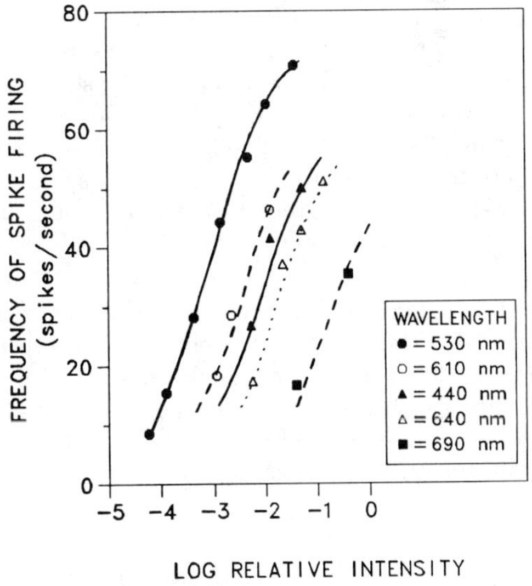

Figure 1.7. Response versus log intensity (quantum basis) functions from a single fiber in the lateral eye of the horseshoe crab, *Limulus*. Stimuli were monochromatic lights; the wavelength is indicated next to each curve. The response measure is frequency of spike firing in the initial portion of the response immediately following light onset. The five fitted curves are identical except for a shift along the abscissa. (From L. Sirovich & I. Abramov, Photopigments and pseudo-pigments, *Vision Research*, *17*. Copyright 1977 by Pergamon. Reprinted with permission.)

a stimulus b of intensity a, either of the two transformations below would be adequate:

$$\Psi_b(a) \mapsto p_b(a) = \Psi_b(a)/80$$

or

$$\Psi_b(a) \mapsto p_b(a) = \frac{\Psi_b(a)}{\Psi_b(a) + k}, \quad (40)$$

where k is a positive constant. Such transformations would not affect an important property suggested by the data of Figure 1.7: the frequency of firing functions appear to be parallel, when plotted as functions of the logarithm of intensity. In fact, this parallelism would not be altered by any transformation

$$\Psi_b(a) \mapsto g[\Psi_b(a)] ,$$

where g is any continuous, strictly increasing function mapping the ranges of the functions Ψ_b into (0,1). For good reasons, much is made of this parallelism by Sirovich and Abramov, who point out that it supports (actually, is essentially equivalent to) the representation

$$\Psi_b(a) = R[a\mu(b)] \quad (41)$$

where μ, R are real-valued functions, with R strictly increasing. The product $a\mu(b)$ is regarded as measuring the number of light quanta absorbed by the photoreceptor (cf. Naka & Rushton, 1966a, 1966b, 1966c). Notice that, with $p_b(a)$ as in Eq. (40) and $F(s) = R(e^s)/[R(e^s) + k$, Eq. (41) can be rewritten as

$$P_b(a) = F\{\ln a - \ln[1/\mu(b)]\} ,$$

a special case of Eq. (38).

In this example, a complete description of the stimulus involves a pair (b,a), where b denotes the wavelength and a the intensity. Thus the role of the standard in the example in Section 5.1.1 is played here by one coordinate of the stimulus. In the sequel, however, *background* will often be used as a generic term denoting the index of a psychometric function. For the sake of consistency, we shall also occasionally speak about the *masking effect* of the background even though such language refers only to particular applications.

5.1.3. Example. In the experiment described, Graham and Hartline also recorded the latency from light onset to first spike (see Figure 1.8). Most of the comments made concerning the example in Section 5.1.2 remain applicable here. To force the (average) latency $l_b(a)$ (where a,b are as in Section 5.1.2) into our theoretical framework, we can, to take an example among many, adopt the transformation

$$l_b(a) \mapsto p_b(a) = \frac{k}{k + l_b(a)}$$

where $k > 0$ is an appropriately chosen constant.

These examples pave the way to a general definition of a family of psychometric functions, in which the background (or index) is assumed to vary in some abstract set I, which may or may not be a real interval.

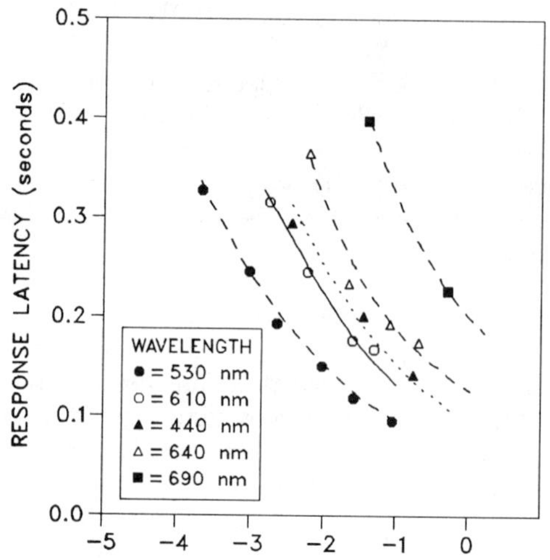

Figure 1.8. Response versus log intensity (quantum basis) functions from a single fiber in the lateral eye of the horseshoe crab, *Limulus*. Stimuli were monochromatic lights; the wavelength is indicated next to each curve. This set of records is identical to that of Figure 1.7, except that the response measure is the latency of the response from light onset to first spike. The five fitted curves are identical except for a shift along the abscissa. (From L. Sirovich & I. Abramov, Photopigments and pseudo-pigments, *Vision Research, 17*. Copyright 1977 by Pergamon. Reprinted with permission.)

5.2. Psychometric Families—Definition

Unless one is interested in modeling their exact mathematical shape, psychometric functions are of little interest considered in isolation. Typically, the psychophysicist wishes to investigate how the shape of a psychometric function is affected by variation of the standard or the background. Accordingly, the definition in Section 5.2.1 is concerned with a *family* of psychometric functions. Notice the switch in notation, from $p_b(a)$ to $p_b(x)$, to emphasize that b, x may belong to different physical domains.

5.2.1. Definition. Let I be a set of backgrounds. For each background b in I, let C_b be a subset of the reals, and let p_b be a real-valued function defined on C_b. Suppose that, for some $b \in I$, the following axioms are satisfied:

1. C_b is an open interval.
2. $0 < p_b < 1$.
3. The function $x \mapsto p_b(x)$ is strictly increasing and continuous in the variable x.

Then p_b is called a *psychometric function*. The index b of a psychometric function p_b will be referred to as the *standard* or the *background*. A set $\{p_b | b \in I\}$ of psychometric functions is called *well linked* iff

4. For all a, $b \in I$ there exists a finite sequence $a_1 = a, a_2, ..., a_n = b$, such that

$$C_{a_i} \cap C_{a_{i+1}} \neq \emptyset, \quad \text{for } 1 \leq i \leq n .$$

A well-linked set of psychometric functions is called a psychometric family. Some comments on these conditions can be found in Section 5.3.

5.3. Remarks

Notice that, as defined in Section 5.2, a psychometric function resembles a distribution function (in the sense of statistics), but does not necessarily satisfy all the properties of this concept. Specifically, we do not require in general that a psychometric function take all the values between 0 and 1. Such property is not essential in most of our developments. More important, it would be a source of difficulty with various kinds of data.

The conditions defining a psychometric family should appear quite acceptable in many empirical situations. Axioms 1 and 2 are straightforward. Axiom 3 states that a psychometric function is strictly increasing and continuous. (This presupposes that the possibly constant upper and lower portions have been deleted.) This seems reasonable. (See, however, Falmagne, 1982.) The role of axiom 4 should be appreciated. This axiom states that any two psychometric functions can be linked by a finite sequence of psychometric functions, such that any two successive psychometric functions in the sequence have overlapping domains. This requirement is very natural from an empirical and especially a theoretical standpoint. A particular psychometric function provides precise but highly local information regarding the detectability (or discriminability) of the stimulus in a neighborhood of the stimulus scale. Axiom 4 ensures that these local informations can be pieced together to provide an overall picture of the subject sensitivity, for example, in the form of a psychophysical scale.

Examples of psychometric families are not difficult to manufacture, for example, by generalizing the models of discrimination discussed in Section 4.

5.4. Parallel Psychometric Families

Two empirical examples of "parallel" psychometric families were provided in Sections 5.1.2 and 5.1.3. Intuitively, a psychometric family is parallel if any two psychometric functions can be made to coincide by a horizontal "rigid" shift of one toward the other. This suggests that given one psychometric function, say, p_a, any other psychometric function p_b is completely characterized by the value of one parameter depending on b, which we denote by $g(b)$, expressing the length and direction of the rigid shift ($g(b)$ may be negative). This intuition is basically sound, but slightly misleading in its details. For instance, one or both of the psychometric functions p_a, p_b may be "truncated," and if both are, their truncation may be of a different kind, so that the coincidence after shift may not be complete (see Figure 1.9). The definition below takes care of this situation and is in fact consistent with a case in which for two particular psychometric functions p_a, p_b, no shift would achieve coincidence because the ranges of p_a, p_b do not overlap.

The concept of parallelism is of importance since it offers an easily testable criterion of the fact that the effects of the stimulus and the background combine "subtractively" (or "additively" as the case may be).

5.4.1. Definition. A psychometric family Ξ is called *parallel* iff for any two psychometric functions $p_a, p_b \in \Xi$,

$$p_a[p_a^{-1}(\pi) + \delta] = p_b[p_b^{-1}(\pi) + \delta] \qquad (42)$$

for all $\pi \in (0,1)$ and $\delta \in$ Re such that both members of the equation are defined. (We recall that we write f^{-1} for the inverse function of a one-to-one function f; Re denotes the set of real numbers.)

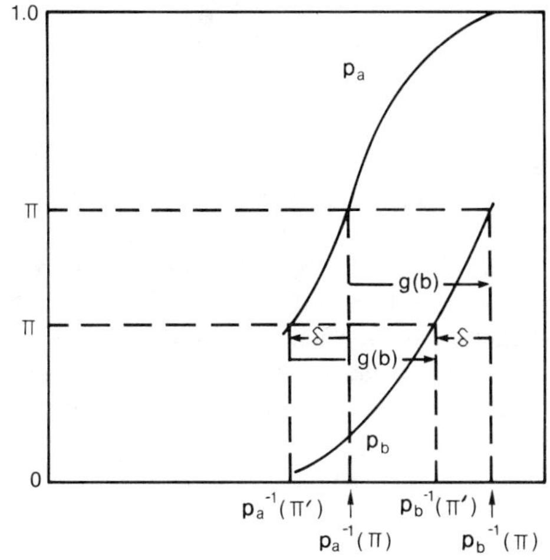

Figure 1.9. Two psychometric functions in a parallel psychometric family. The figure illustrates the notion of truncation, and the concepts of the definition in Section 5.4.1 and the theorem in Section 5.4.2. Notice that $g(b)$ is positive, and δ negative.

The simple result in Section 5.4.2 will help the reader to see the correspondence between this definition and Figure 1.9.

5.4.2. Theorem. A psychometric family Ξ is parallel iff for all $p_a, p_b \in \Xi$,

$$p_a^{-1}(\pi) - p_a^{-1}(\pi') = p_b^{-1}(\pi) - p_b^{-1}(\pi') \qquad (43)$$

whenever all four terms are defined.

This means in particular that if p_a, p_b are distribution functions, they must have the same interquartile range:

$$p_a^{-1}(.75) - p_a^{-1}(.25) = p_b^{-1}(.75) - p_b^{-1}(.25) .$$

We include the proof of this result, which is very simple.

Proof. Suppose that Ξ is parallel, with

$$p_a^{-1}(\pi) - p_a^{-1}(\pi') = \delta, \; p_b^{-1}(\pi) = p_b^{-1}(\pi') = \delta' .$$

This implies

$$\pi = p_a[p_a^{-1}(\pi) + \delta] = p_b[p_b^{-1}(\pi') + \delta']$$

which, since Ξ is parallel, leads easily to $\delta = \delta'$.

Conversely, suppose that Eq. (43) holds whenever its terms are defined, but

$$\pi' = p_a[p_a^{-1}(\pi) + \delta] < p_b[p_b^{-1}(\pi) + \delta] = \pi'' .$$

Suppose also that $\delta \geq 0$. This implies that $\pi =< \pi' < \pi''$. Since the range of p_b is an interval, $p_b^{-1}(\pi')$ is defined, yielding successively

$$\delta = p_a^{-1}(\pi') - p_a^{-1}(\pi)$$

$$= p_b^{-1}(\pi') - p_b^{-1}(\pi)$$

$$< p_b^{-1}(\pi'') - p_b^{-1}(\pi)$$

$$= \delta ,$$

a contradiction.

The argument is similar in the case $\delta < 0$. ∎

As mentioned earlier, the definition of a parallel psychometric family does not preclude the possibility that the ranges of some psychometric functions would not overlap. In a special case where such a situation does not arise, a useful representation of a psychometric family is available: the psychometric functions satisfy the equation

$$p_a(x) = F[x - g(a)] ,$$

for some functions F, g, where F is strictly increasing and continuous. This case is analyzed in the definition and theorem in Sections 5.4.3 and 5.4.4, respectively.

5.4.3. Definition. A psychometric family $\Xi = \{p_a | a \in I\}$ is called *anchored* iff there exists a number $\xi \in (0,1)$ such that:

(i) For all $a \in I$ there is an x satisfying $p_a(x) = \xi$.
(ii) For all $x \in \cup_{a \in I} C_a$, there is an $a \in I$ such that $p_a(x) = \xi$.

(We recall that C_a denotes the domain of the psychometric function p_a.) In words, conditions (i) and (ii) mean that for every background a there is a stimulus x and for every stimulus x there is a background a, such that $p_a(x) = \xi$. A number $\xi \in (0,1)$ satisfying these conditions will be called an *anchor* of Ξ.

These conditions are not very demanding. Suppose, for example, that the psychometric functions are defined from the choice probabilities $P_{a,b}$ of a balanced discrimination system (see Section 3.5.1) by the equation $p_a(b) = P_{a,b}$. It follows easily then that .5 is an anchor. Indeed, $p_a^{-1}(.5) = a$ is the identity function on I.

5.4.4. Theorem. An anchored psychometric family $\Xi = \{p_a | a \in I\}$ is parallel iff it has a representation

$$p_a(x) = F[x - g(a)] ,$$

where F is a continuous, strictly increasing function.

For a proof of this result, see Falmagne (1982). It must be realized that the property of parallelism of a psychometric family depends critically on the scale used to measure the stimulus and would not be preserved under nonlinear transformation of that scale. Consider, for example, an anchored, parallel psychometric family $\Xi = \{p_a | a \in I\}$ admitting a representation

$$p_a(x) = F[x - g(a)]$$

in the sense of the theorem in Section 5.4.4. Let v be a real-valued, strictly increasing, and continuous function defined on the interval of variation of x. Notice that, with $t = v(x)$, the equation $p_a^*(t) = p_a(x)$ defines a new anchored, psychometric family $\Xi^* = \{p_a^* | a \in I\}$. But Ξ^* need not be parallel. In fact, it is easy to show that Ξ^* is parallel if and only if v is a function of the form $v(x) = \mu x + \theta$, where $\mu > 0$ and θ is a constant. In general—that is, when v is not necessarily linear—the transformation of the stimulus scale generates a new psychometric family Ξ^* satisfying a subtractive representation

$$p_a^*(t) = F[u(t) - g(a)] . \quad (44)$$

(Thus $u = v^{-1}$.) This suggests reversing the process. In Section 5.9.1 we ask, Under which conditions on a psychometric family does there exist a transformation of the stimulus scale which renders the psychometric functions parallel? Or in other terms, When does a psychometric family $\Xi^* = \{p_a^*\}$ have a subtractive representation of the form Eq. (44)?

5.5. Subtractive Families

5.5.1. Definition. A psychometric family $\Xi = \{p_a | a \in I\}$ is *subtractive* or a *subtractive family* iff there are three real-valued functions g, u, and F, the latter two being continuous and strictly increasing, such that

$$p_a(x) = F[u(x) - g(a)] \quad (45)$$

for all $a \in I$ and $x \in C_a$. In such a case, we shall occasionally say that (g,u,F) is a *subtractive representation of* Ξ.

A special case of this representation has of course been encountered before, in the framework of a Fechnerian psychophysical discrimination system (definition in Section 3.5.1). It makes sense to adopt here a terminology consistent with the earlier one. Suppose, thus, that the psychometric family Ξ has in fact been obtained from a psychophysical discrimination system (I,C,P), through the equation

$$p_a(b) = P_{b,a} .$$

In this situation, Ξ will be referred to as a *discrimination family*, which will be called *balanced* iff (I,C,P) is balanced, that is, iff

$$p_a(b) + p_b(a) = 1 .$$

Thus when Ξ is a discrimination family, the functions g and u in Eq. (45) have the same domain. In the special case where $g = u$, Ξ will be called Fechnerian, or a Fechner family, and (u,F) will be labeled a Fechnerian representation of Ξ.

5.6. Remarks

A discrimination family $\Xi = \{p_a | a \in I\}$ can be subtractive without being Fechnerian. (Say, Eq. (45) is satisfied but u is not linearly related to g. An example is provided in Section 5.8). If, however, Ξ is a balanced discrimination family, then it is subtractive only if it is Fechnerian. Indeed, for all $a \in I$,

$$p_a(a) = F[u(a) - g(a)] = .5 ,$$

yielding, with $\alpha = F^{-1}(.5)$,

$$u(a) = g(a) + \alpha .$$

Defining $G(s) = F(s + \alpha)$, we obtain

$$p_b(a) = F[u(a) - gb)]$$

$$= G\{u(a) - [g(b) + \alpha]\}$$

$$= G[u(a) - u(b)] .$$

This indicates that our usage of the term Fechnerian is consistent with that in Section 3. (Notice that the above argument only uses the fact that $p_a(a) = .5$.)

5.7. A Remark on the Balancing Condition

Notice that if a discrimination family $\Xi = \{p_b\}$ is unbalanced, it can always be rendered balanced by a normalization such as

$$p_b^{**}(a) = p_b(a)/[p_b(a) + p_a(b)] .$$

More generally, any real-valued continuous function Ψ of two real variables, strictly increasing in the first variable and strictly decreasing in the second, satisfying

$$0 < \Psi < 1 , \tag{46}$$

$$\Psi(s,t) + \Psi(t,s) = 1 \tag{47}$$

achieves a similar normalization. The reader can check that the family $\Xi^{**} = \{p_b^{**}\}$ defined from the family Ξ by the equation

$$p_b^{**}(a) = \Psi[p_b(a),p_a(b)] \tag{48}$$

is indeed a balanced discrimination family. However, as demonstrated by the model in Section 5.8, it is not generally the case that if Ξ is subtractive, then the normalized family Ξ^{**} is subtractive. What is true, and easy to show, is that if Ξ is Fechnerian, then Ξ^{**} is also Fechnerian.

In some experimental situations, the order of presentation of the stimuli has an effect on the (probability of the) response. Such an effect is often of little interest, and the "careful experimenter" sometimes adopts a normalization procedure that suffers from the drawback just mentioned; namely, it does not necessarily preserve the subtractive character of a psychometric family. Let us demonstrate this. Denote by $n[a,(a,b)]$ the number of times stimulus a is chosen in the set $\{a,b\}$ when this set is presented in the order (a,b). Let $N(a,b)$ be the number of times $\{a,b\}$ is presented in the order (a,b). To simplify the argument, we identify probabilities and relative frequencies, in the sense that

$$p_b(a) = n[a,(a,b)]/N(a,b) .$$

The standard normalization is

$$p_b^{**}(a) = \{n[a,(a,b)] + n[a,(b,a)]\}/[N(a,b) + N(b,a)]$$

$$= (1/2)[p_b(a) + 1 - p_a(b)] , \tag{49}$$

which indeed defines a balanced discrimination family $\Xi^{**} = \{p_b^{**}\}$, if $\Xi = \{p_b\}$ is a discrimination family. If we assume that both Ξ and Ξ^{**} are subtractive, then (by the remark in Section 5.6) Ξ^{**} is Fechnerian, and we must have for some continuous, strictly increasing functions u, g, F, h, and H,

$$p_b(a) = F[u(a) - g(b)] ,$$

$$p_b^{**}(a) = H[h(a) - h(b)] ,$$

which, together with Eq. (49), yields an equation of the form

$$F[u(a) - g(b)] - F[u(b) - g(a)] = K[h(a) - h(b)] \tag{50}$$

(where the constants 1/2 and 1 of Eq. (49) have been absorbed in the function K). An equation such as (50) is often referred to in the mathematical literature as a *functional equation*, a term suggesting that the unknowns in the equation are not numbers, as in elementary algebra, but functions (here F, u, g, K, and h). The point is that this equation severely restricts the relation between the functions u, g, and the form of the function F. In general, the normalization is ill-advised since a subtractive model will not survive it. In cases in which F is approximately linear, this normalization may not create difficulties, however.

5.7.1. Definition. In the sequel, any function $(p,p') \to \Psi(p,p')$ defined on the unit square $(0,1) \times (0,1)$, real valued, continuous, strictly increasing in the first variable, strictly decreasing in the second variable, and satisfying Eqs. (46) and (47) will be called a *balancing function.*

5.8. Examples of Subtractive Discrimination Families

Consider the family of functions $\Xi = \{p_b | b > 0\}$, defined by

$$p_b(a) = e^{-(b^\eta/a^\mu)}$$

for each $a > 0$, where $\eta,\mu > 0$ are constants. This expression is closely related to a model frequently encountered in the vision literature (Green & Luce, 1975; Nachmias, 1981; Quick, 1974; see Watson, Chapter 6, and Olzak and Thomas, Chapter 7, in this handbook). It is easily checked that Ξ satisfies all the conditions of an unbalanced discrimination family, which is subtractive, since

$$p_b(a) = \exp[-e^{-(\mu \log a - \eta \log b)}] . \tag{51}$$

Let us balance Ξ. Since for every positive real number s, we have (denoting as usual by Φ the distribution function of a standard, normal random variable)

$$0 < \Phi(\log s) < 1$$

and

$$\Phi(\log s) + \Phi(\log \frac{1}{s}) = 1 ,$$

it follows that the function $(p,p') \to \Phi[\log(p/p')]$ is a balancing function. This yields the balanced family $\Xi^{**} = \{p_b^{**} | b > 0\}$, defined by

$$p_b^{**}(a) = \Phi\left\{\log\left[\frac{p_b(a)}{p_a(b)}\right]\right\} ,$$

that is

$$p_b^{**}(a) = \Phi[(ab)^{-\mu}(a^{\eta+\mu} - b^{\eta+\mu})] .$$

Since Ξ^{**} is balanced, the assumption that it is subtractive would lead (using the remark in Section 5.6), to the equation

$$(ab)^{-\mu}(a^{\eta+\mu} - b^{\eta+\mu}) = \Phi^{-1}\{G[u(a) - u(b)]\} , \tag{52}$$

in which u, G are strictly increasing, continuous functions. It is not difficult to prove that considered as a functional equation with unknown functions u, G, Eq. (52) has no solution (see

Falmagne, 1982). This shows that balancing a subtractive discrimination family does not necessarily yield a Fechnerian family.

5.8.1. Ideal Observer Model. Suppose that the background is a sample of so-called Gaussian noise, with power density b, presented for T units of time, and that the stimulus itself is also a sample of Gaussian noise of the same duration, of power density $x = b + \gamma$, with $\gamma \geq 0$, a constant. Each of the stimuli and the background is then a stochastic process which, to a good approximation (see however Levitt, 1972) admits a Fourier series representation

$$\sum_{k=1}^{WT} [\alpha_k \cos(2\pi kt/T) + \beta_k \sin(2\pi kt/T)]$$

where W is the bandwidth, and α_k, β_k are independent, normal random variables with mean 0, and variance σ_k^2 depending on the signal presented. It can be shown (e.g., Green & Swets, 1974) that in such a case the energy in the stimulus and the background are respectively distributed as

$$Wx\chi^2_{(2WT)},\ Wb\chi^{2'}_{(2WT)}$$

where $\chi^2_{(2WT)}$ and $\chi^{2'}_{(2WT)}$ are two independent chi-square random variables with $2WT$ degrees of freedom. Let us suppose that some (ideal) subject bases the decision on a comparison of the energies in the stimulus and the background. More precisely, we assume that

$$p_b(x) = \text{Prob}\{Wx\chi^2_{(2WT)} \geq Wb\chi^{2'}_{(2WT)}\} .$$

If $2WT$ is large, each of the two chi-square random variables is approximately normally distributed. Since $E(\chi^2_{(n)}) = n$ and $\text{var}(\chi^2_{(n)}) = 2n$, we obtain after simplification

$$p_b(x) = \Phi\{WT(x - b)/[x^2WT + b^2WT]^{1/2}\}$$

$$= \Phi\{(WT)^{1/2}[(x/b) - 1]/[(x/b)^2 + 1]^{1/2}\}$$

$$= G(\log x - \log b) ,$$

with

$$G(s) = \Phi\{(WT)^{1/2}(e^s - 1)/(e^{2s} + 1)^{1/2}\} .$$

Thus $\{p_b\}$ is a subtractive family.

We recall briefly here the examples in Sections 5.1.2 and 5.1.3 concerning the frequency and latency of spike firing of a single fiber in the lateral eye of the horseshoe crab, *Limulus* (Graham & Hartline, 1933; see Sirovich & Abramov, 1977). With the logarithm of intensity in the abscissa, parallel psychometric functions were observed, which gave support to the assumption of a representation

$$p_b(a) = R[a\,\mu(b)]$$

for these psychometric functions (R, $\mu > 0$ are real-valued functions). Clearly, such representation is equivalent to a subtractive one, since it can be rewritten

$$p_b(a) = R\{e^{[\log a - g(b)]}\}$$

$$= F[\log a - g(b)] ,$$

with

$$F(s) = R(e^s) \quad \text{and} \quad g(b) = -\log \mu(b) .$$

In this case, parallel psychometric functions are obtained after a suitable transformation—here logarithmic—of the physical variable measuring the intensity of the stimulation. A generalization of this idea is considered in Section 5.9.

5.9. Representation of Subtractive Psychometric Families

5.9.1. Problem. Under which conditions does a psychometric family $\Xi = \{p_a | a \in I\}$ have a subtractive representation? This problem generalizes Fechner's problem, discussed in Section 3.3. Necessary conditions are not difficult to find; for example, suppose that Ξ is subtractive, with a representation (g,u,F), and that

$$p_a(x) \leq p_{a'}(x') \tag{53}$$

$$p_{a'}(y') \leq p_a(y) \tag{54}$$

$$p_b(y) \leq p_{b'}(y') \tag{55}$$

are simultaneously satisfied. Since the function F in the subtractive representation of Ξ is strictly increasing, this yields

$$u(x) - g(a) \leq u(x') - g(a')$$

$$u(y') - g(a') \leq u(y) - g(a)$$

$$u(y) - g(b) \leq u(y') - g(b') .$$

Adding these inequalities, we obtain

$$u(x) - g(b) \leq u(x') - g(b') ,$$

or equivalently, assuming that $x \in C_b$, $x' \in C_{b'}$,

$$p_b(x) \leq p_{b'}(x') . \tag{56}$$

5.9.2 Definition. A psychometric family $\Xi = \{p_b | b \in I\}$ satisfies *triple cancellation* iff Eqs. (53), (54), and (55) together imply (56) for all a, a', b, $b' \in I$ and $x, y \in C_a \cap C_b$ and $x', y' \in C_{a'} \cap C_{b'}$.

This condition is well known in the measurement literature (cf. Krantz et al., 1971). The above argument shows, thus, that a psychometric family has a subtractive representation only if it satisfies triple cancellation. A set of necessary and sufficient conditions, based on triple cancellation as a central axiom, was obtained by Falmagne (1982). A related result can be found in Narens and Luce (1976).

The scales u and g are usually specified up to a linear transformation. For example, the following uniqueness result follows from a slight strengthening of the conditions defining an anchored psychometric family: if (u,g,F) and (u^*,g^*,F^*) are two subtractive representations of the same psychometric family, then

$$g(t) = \beta_0 g^*(t) + \beta_1 ,$$

$$u(t) = \beta_0 u^*(t) + \beta_1 + \beta_2 ,$$

$$F(t) = F^*\left(\frac{t - \beta_2}{\beta_0}\right),$$

for some constants $\beta_0 > 0$, β_1, and β_2.

5.10. Key References

The material in this section is based largely on a paper by Falmagne (1982), which contains a number of additional results. As far as we know, the term psychometric function is due to Urban (1907), even though the notion was in use since Fechner and Wundt. Despite its importance in psychophysical research, this notion has prompted exceptionally few theoretical investigations. Three papers by Levine (1971, 1972, 1975) deserve to be mentioned. His general approach to the analysis of a family of psychometric functions is similar to that of this section. Rather than focusing on particular models or processes, general conditions are sought that guarantee the existence and uniqueness properties of some abstract (e.g., subtractive) representation. His side conditions are somewhat different from ours, however. In his 1972 paper, Levine analyzes a problem that was not considered here, involving a generalization of the notion of a subtractive representation. In the notation of this section, this representation is symbolized by the equation

$$p_a(x) = F[k(a)u(x) - g(a)] .$$

An introduction to functional equations can be found in Aczél (1966).

6. WEBER FUNCTIONS—PSYCHOPHYSICAL METHODS

What is the smallest increment of a stimulus, on a physical continuum, which is detectable by a subject? In other terms, given a stimulus value equal to a, what is the smallest increment $\Delta(a)$ such that $a + \Delta(a)$ "just noticeably" exceeds a? This was one of the earliest questions raised by psychophysicists. This minimal increment $\Delta(a)$ is often referred to as the *just-noticeable difference* (jnd), or the *difference limen*. A variant—or rather, a special case—of this question is, What is the minimum value of a stimulus which is "just detectable" by a subject? This is called the *absolute threshold*.

Various experimental methods for the determination of $\Delta(a)$ have been designed and are described in this section. Such questions are by no means straightforward, however, since they are ambiguous. For example, what is meant by "just noticeably"? Suppose, for example, that $a + \Delta(a)$ is judged as exceeding a on 65% of the trials. Does that mean that $a + \Delta(a)$ just noticeably exceeds a? An empirical criterion is clearly involved here. In the method of constant stimuli (cf. Section 6.2.2) $\Delta(a)$ is often taken as a correct determination if $a + \Delta(a)$ is judged as exceeding a on 75% of the trials. (We are ignoring statistical issues for the moment.) The arbitrariness of this choice is troubling. This arbitrariness is less apparent, but just as critical, in the method "of limits" or in the method "of adjustments" (see Sections 6.1.1 and 6.1.2). Certainly, one would not want the general pattern of experimental results to depend critically on the choice of the criterion. In fact, as pointed out by Luce and Edwards (1958), there are theoretical difficulties involved in adopting a unique, fixed criterion. Accordingly, there is a trend in contemporary psychophysical research toward varying the value of the criterion across experimental conditions. We shall go back to this point later on.

A basic notion of this section is a function Δ of two variables,

$$(a,\pi) \mapsto \Delta_\pi(a)$$

with π, $0 < \pi < 1$, representing the value of the criterion. Thus in the particular case discussed above, $a + \Delta_{.75}(a)$ is judged as exceeding a on 75% of the trials. Notice that $\Delta_\pi(a)$ may be negative for some values of π: it is natural, for example, to expect that $a + \Delta_{.25}(a) < a$, at least in some experimental situations.

There is an obvious relation between the function of one variable $\pi \mapsto \Delta_\pi(a)$ and the psychometric function p_a, analyzed in Section 5. For instance, suppose that p_a is a psychometric function in a discrimination family Ξ (definition in Section 5.2.1), such that $p_a(a) = .5$. As illustrated in Figure 1.10, we have in such a case

$$\Delta_\pi(a) = p_a^{-1}(\pi) - a . \tag{57}$$

In this situation, the value $p_a^{-1}(.50)$ is sometimes referred to as the *point of subjective equality*. The function Δ contains, thus, exactly the same information as the family Ξ of psychometric functions. The emphasis on this function here is justified, however. In particular, psychophysicists have found out that experimental plots of the functions Δ_π provided very revealing summaries of their data, and they use such plots routinely. Correspondingly, this function is of great theoretical interest, as we shall see in Section 7. An equally important place in our developments will be taken by the function

$$a \mapsto \xi_\pi(a) = p_a^{-1}(\pi)$$

(see Figure 1.10). Actually, it can be argued that ξ is a more central concept than Δ: ξ can always be defined from the psychometric functions, while Δ is only defined if the subtraction $p_a^{-1}(\pi) - a$ makes sense, which it does not if a is an object of a different nature than $p_a^{-1}(\pi)$. For instance, Δ would not be defined in a detection situation in which $p_a^{-1}(\pi) = x$ would specify the intensity x of a stimulus detected with a probability π, over a background of noise a, where a denotes a waveform or a spectral density function (i.e., a possibly infinite dimensional

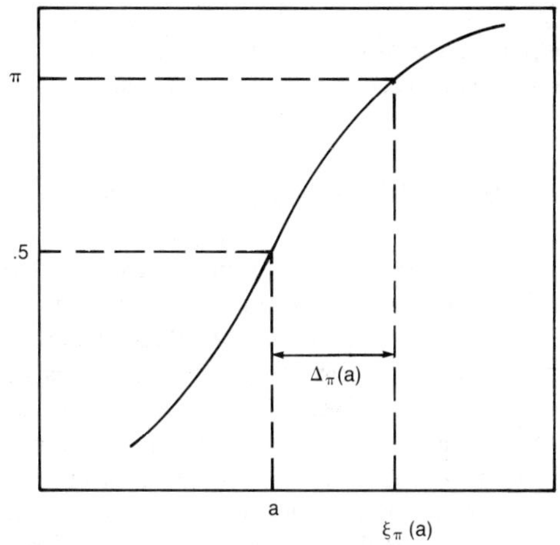

Figure 1.10. The function Δ in a discrimination family $\Xi = \{p_a\}$ satisfying $p_a(a) = .5$. We have $\xi_\pi(a) = p_a^{-1}(\pi)$ and $\Delta_\pi(a) = \xi_\pi(a) - a$.

vector). The functions Δ and ξ will be called, respectively, the *Weber function* and the *sensitivity function*.

Empirical determinations of function ξ or Δ can be achieved by a number of methods, a discussion of which is the topic of this section.

6.1. Traditional Psychophysical Methods

Since the interest of the method of limits and of the method of adjustments is mostly historical, only a brief description will be given. For more details, the reader is referred, for example, to Engen (1971) or Fechner (1860/1966). Each method involves a subject making successive comparisons of a stimulus with a standard or background. (We use the terminology of the preceding section.) In the determination of the absolute threshold, the value of the background is considered negligible.

6.1.1. The Method of Limits. The experimenter varies the value of the stimulus in small ascending or descending steps. At each step the subject reports whether the stimulus appears smaller than, equal to, or larger than the background. The experimenter records the values of the stimulus at which the subject's response shifts from one category to another. This method is used in applied situations, such as audiology, to provide a quick estimate of the point of subjective equality, $p_a^{-1}(.50)$. As pointed out by Levitt (1970), this method has serious defects from the viewpoint of efficiency (the observations may be poorly placed) and validity (the estimates may be substantially biased) (see Anderson, McCarthy, & Tukey, 1946; Brown & Cane, 1959).

6.1.2. The Method of Adjustments. The method of adjustments is similar to the method of limits. The subject adjusts the value of the stimulus, which can be varied continuously (e.g., by turning a dial), and sets it to apparent equality with the standard. Repeated applications of this procedure yield an empirical distribution of stimulus values, the variability of which is used to compute or estimate the jnd.

6.1.3. The Method of Constant Stimuli. The method of constant stimuli, which has been encountered earlier (Section 5.1.1), purports to estimate experimentally a number of suitably located points of some psychometric function p_a. If a particular mathematical expression is assumed for the psychometric functions (derived, for instance, from a mathematical model), then this expression is fitted to the experimental points. (Typically, the mathematical expression of p_a is only specified up to the values of some parameters, which have to be estimated from the data.) Finally, an estimate of the jnd is provided, for example, by Eq. (57).

In the past, a different estimate of the jnd has frequently been used, which corresponds to the equation

$$\text{jnd}(a) = (1/2)[\Delta_{.75}(a) - \Delta_{.25}(a)] \ . \tag{58}$$

The main objection to this procedure is that it is implicitly based on an assumption of symmetry between negative and positive differences, which is closely related to the balancing condition discussed in Section 5. The difficulties with such assumptions have been analyzed in Section 5.7.

If no specific mathematical model is assumed but the psychometric function appears to be approximately linear, say, between the values .20 and .80, then a straight line can be fitted to the experimental points in that interval, replacing the mathematical form used above.

In general, each of these three methods suffers from one or more of the following defects:

1. Absence of control on the criterion (Sections 6.1.1 and 6.1.2).
2. No theoretical justification for important aspects of the procedure (Sections 6.1.1 and 6.1.2).
3. The estimates may be biased (Sections 6.1.1 and 6.1.2).
4. Costs; a large amount of data is often wasted (all three methods).

In computerized laboratories, sophisticated versions of the method in Section 6.1.3 are used routinely, which we now describe. These methods are applicable when the exact mathematical form of the psychometric functions is unknown.

6.2. Adaptive Methods

Consider the problem of finding a point ξ in the domain of a psychometric function p_a, such that $p_a(\xi) = \pi$, where π is chosen arbitrarily in the range of p_a. Notice that the location of ξ depends on both a and π; ξ is thus a function of the two variables a and π. Actually, ξ is the sensitivity function introduced earlier, with $\xi_\pi(a) = p_a^{-1}(\pi)$ (Figure 1.10). In the rest of this section, we assume that the background a is fixed. We thus occasionally simplify our notation and write $\xi_\pi = p^{-1}(\pi)$.

It must be realized that the problem of estimating ξ_π with an acceptable degree of accuracy from the data is not trivial, since the exact mathematical form of the psychometric function may be unknown. A number of practical methods are described below. They differ from the methods decribed in Section 6.1 in that the course of the experiment depends critically on the data: the stimulus presented on trial n depends on the subject's responses on one or more of the preceding trials. At present, none of these methods taken by itself is completely free of defects. As indicated in Section 6.3, however, a suitable combination of methods provides an estimation procedure which seems to be reasonable for empirical applications.

From a theoretical standpoint, the sequence of stimulus–response pairs will be regarded as a stochastic process (Parzen, 1962). For the time being, we assume that the process is stationary. The following notations will be used. The stimulus presented at trial n will be denoted by $\mathbf{X}_n$, a random variable. The subject's responses will be coded:

1	If a is not judged as exceeding $\mathbf{X}_1$
0	Otherwise

Thus 0,1 are the values of a random variable, which we denote by $\mathbf{Z}_n$. We have by definition

$$\text{Prob}\{\mathbf{Z}_n = 1 | \mathbf{X}_n\} = p_a(\mathbf{X}_n) \ .$$

In the methods described below, the succession of stimuli is governed by an equation of the form

$$\mathbf{X}_{n+1} = \mathbf{X}_n + \theta(\pi, n, \mathbf{Z}_n, \mathbf{Z}_{n-1}, \mathbf{X}_{n-1}, \dots) \ , \tag{59}$$

in which θ is a function that may vary with the probability π assigned to the target value $\xi_\pi(a)$, the trial number n, the subject's response on that trial, and possibly some stimulus–response pairs on earlier trials.

6.2.1. Stochastic Approximation. Fix π, $0 < \pi < 1$ and choose a point x_1 arbitrarily, somewhere in the neighborhood of $\xi_\pi(a)$, the point to be estimated. (Since $\xi_\pi(a)$ is unknown, an educated guess has to be made. The accuracy of this guess is not crucial.) Present the pair (x_1, a) to the subject. Determine a second point x_2 by the following rule:

$$x_2 = \begin{cases} x_1 + \frac{c}{2}\pi & \text{if } \mathbf{Z}_1 = 0 \\ x_1 - \frac{c}{2}(1 - \pi) & \text{if } \mathbf{Z}_1 = 1 \,; \end{cases}$$

where $c > 0$ is some constant, the choice of which is of importance, as we shall see. Thus x_2 is a value of the random variable $\mathbf{X}_2$. We have $\mathbf{X}_1 = x_1$ by convention. The above rule can be rewritten compactly as

$$\mathbf{X}_2 = \mathbf{X}_1 - \frac{c}{2}[\mathbf{Z}_1 - \pi] \,.$$

Next, we determine successively $x_3, x_4, \ldots, x_n, \ldots$ using the rule

$$\mathbf{X}_{n+1} = \mathbf{X}_n - \frac{c}{n}(\mathbf{Z}_n - \pi) \,. \tag{60}$$

This yields

$$\theta(\pi, n, \mathbf{Z}_n) = \frac{c}{n}(\pi - \mathbf{Z}_n) \,,$$

in the notation of Eq. (59). The sequence of random variables $\{\mathbf{X}_n\}$ is known as a *Robbins-Monro process*. It can be shown that as n gets large, $\mathbf{X}_n$ tends to a normal random variable, with expectation equal to ξ_π and a vanishing variance. This result holds under general differentiability assumptions regarding the psychometric function p (which seem quite reasonable in the present context) and provided that the constant c is chosen appropriately. For details the reader is referred to Robbins and Monro (1951) or Wasan (1969). In practice, an estimate of ξ_π is provided by a sample value of $\mathbf{X}_n$ for some large n. This method is a substantial improvement over the preceding ones. It is not very economical, however, since a large number of trials are needed, only the last one of which is actually used. Moreover, if the number of trials is not large, the estimate of ξ_π is biased, the size and direction of the bias depending on the curvature of the psychometric function at the point to be estimated. One difficulty is that the convergence of c/n is slow, from the viewpoint of the scale of a psychophysical experiment. As suggested by Kesten (1958) and Pavel (Note 1), the convergence of the estimation process can be speeded up significantly by modifying the constant c *in Eq. (60) as a function of the subject's responses on trials preceding trial n*. For example, the value of c/n in Eq. (60) could fail to decrease in the case of a succession of identical responses. (We refer to this modification of the method as *accelerated stochastic approximation*.) Finally, it must be remembered that there are often practical limitations to the resolution of the apparatus used to generate the stimuli. In psychoacoustics, for instance, the minimum difference between distinct stimuli is often of the order of 0.25 dB or more. Even assuming that an accelerated stochastic approximation method is used, these limitations may suffice to render the estimate unacceptable. Stochastic approximation has nevertheless its use as an early component of an adaptive estimation procedure (see Section 6.3).

6.2.2. Up-Down, or Staircase, Method. This method is probably the most popular one. The essential difference with the stochastic approximation method is that on each trial the value of the stimulus is changed by a constant amount, either positively or negatively. In other terms, in Eq. (59),

$$|\theta(\pi, \mathbf{Z}_n, \mathbf{Z}_{n-1}, \mathbf{X}_{n-1}, \ldots)| = |\mathbf{X}_{n+1} - \mathbf{X}_n|$$

is constant for all trials n, the direction of the change depending on the probability π, on the subject's responses, and so on. The increments by which the stimulus is either increased or decreased are referred to as *steps*. A sequence of steps in one direction, in a realization of this process, is called a *run*. This is illustrated in Figure 1.11, in which the value of the stimulus presented at the first trial is set arbitrarily equal to 0 and the step size is equal to 1. There are eight runs, corresponding to trials 1–2, 2–5, 5–7, and so on. Three variants of the method will be described.

6.2.2.1. Simple Up-Down Method. In the *simple* up-down method, the problem is to estimate $\xi_{.5}$. As in Section 6.2.1, an educated guess is made for the initial value $\mathbf{X}_1$ of the stimulus. The successive remaining values are then obtained by the rule

$$\mathbf{X}_{n+1} = \mathbf{X}_n + \delta(1 - 2\mathbf{Z}_n) \,. \tag{61}$$

In words, δ is the step size, and the stimulus is increased by δ in the case of a negative response ($\mathbf{Z}_n = 0$) and decreased by δ in the case of a positive one ($\mathbf{Z}_n = 1$). In Figure 1.11, the succession of responses is "no, yes, yes, yes, no, ... " and so on. The choice of the step size is obviously important and will be commented on in a moment. Since

$$\text{Prob}\{\mathbf{Z}_n = 1 | \mathbf{X}_n\} = p_a(\mathbf{X}_n) \,,$$

it is apparent that Eq. (61) defines a discrete parameter Markov chain $\{\mathbf{X}_n\}$ with state space $\{x_1 \pm n\delta | n = 1, 2, \ldots\}$. The states are recurrent, with a finite mean recurrent time, which implies (see, e.g., Parzen, 1962, p. 252) that the distribution of $\mathbf{X}_n$ converges as $n \to \infty$. In particular, taking expectations and limits in Eq. (61) and denoting the expectations by E, we obtain after rearranging,

$$0 = \lim_{n\to\infty} E(\mathbf{X}_{n+1}) - \lim_{n\to\infty} E(\mathbf{X}_n) = \delta[1 - \lim_{n\to\infty} E(\mathbf{Z}_n)] \,.$$

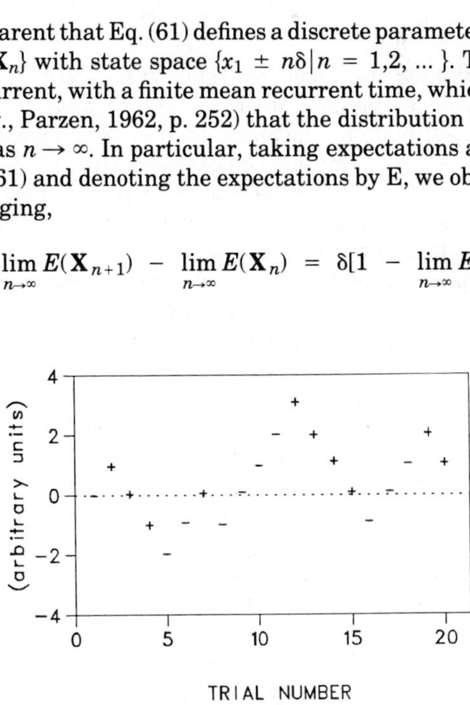

Figure 1.11. Exemplary data for the simple up-down method. The initial value is arbitrarily set at 0. The step size is equal to 1. There are eight runs, corresponding to trials 1–2, 2–5, 5–7, and so on.

Using the fact that p_a is a bounded, continuous function, this gives successively, with obvious notation,

$$.5 = \lim_{n\to\infty} E(\mathbf{Z}_n) = \lim_{n\to\infty} \text{Prob}\{\mathbf{Z}_n = 1\}$$

$$= \lim_{n\to\infty} E[\text{Prob}\{\mathbf{Z}_n|\mathbf{X}_n\}] = \lim_{n\to\infty} E[p_a(\mathbf{X}_n)]$$

$$= E[p_a(\mathbf{X}_\infty)] \approx p_a[E(\mathbf{X}_\infty)] ,$$

in which the approximation holds if we assume either that the psychometric function p_a is approximately linear in the region of concentration of the mass of $\mathbf{X}_\infty$ or that the distribution of $\mathbf{X}_\infty$ is approximately symmetric. (Indeed, in this last case, the expectation of $\mathbf{X}_\infty$ is confounded with its median $M(\mathbf{X}_\infty)$, and for any strictly increasing function f, we have $M[f(\mathbf{X}_\infty)] = f[M(\mathbf{X}_\infty)]$.) In principle, the value $\xi_{.5} \approx E(\mathbf{X}_\infty)$ can be estimated by the statistic

$$\frac{1}{k}\sum_{i=1}^{k} \mathbf{X}_{n+i} ,$$

for n sufficiently large. As pointed out by Wetherill (1963), a practical estimate of $\xi_{.5}$ is provided by averaging the peaks and the valleys in all the runs. As an illustration, the data of Figure 1.11 would yield for this estimate the value

$$\frac{1}{8}(0 + 1 - 2 + 0 - 1 + 3 - 1 + 2 + 1) = 3/8 .$$

It is easy to verify that this method amounts to considering the midpoint of every second run as an estimate of $\xi_{.5}$ and then to compute the average of these midpoints. Thus in Figure 1.11

$$\frac{1}{4}(-.5 - .5 + 1 + 1.5) = 3/8 .$$

These estimates are sometimes referred to as the *midrun estimates*. An even number of runs should be used, to reduce a bias in the estimation. The bias is then small, provided that to a reasonable approximation the psychometric function or the distribution of $\mathbf{X}_n$ satisfies the conditions indicated above. This procedure based on the midrun estimates is known to be fairly efficient. In fact for a small number of trials ($n < 30$), it is more efficient than a maximum likelihood estimate (Wetherill, Chen, & Vasudeva, 1966). There are various problems with this procedure, only some of which will be mentioned here (see Levitt, 1970.)

One problem concerns the choice of the step size δ, the value of which should be small compared to the "spread" of the psychometric function. As a rule of thumb, a good choice is to set δ equal to the slope of the psychometric function at the point to be estimated. (If we assume that the psychometric function is approximately linear in some neighborhood of the target value, then this value of δ can be shown to minimize the variance of the asymptotic distribution of the stimuli presented. See Wetherill, 1963.) Since both locations and spread are typically unknown at the early stage of experimentation, this recommendation is only of heuristic use. A frequently employed, reasonable procedure is to start the first few (say, 10) trials of each experimental session with a large step size, which is then decreased for the useful part of the data.

Another source of difficulty is that the subject may become aware of the systematic character of the stimulus changes. In turn, this may induce a strategy of anticipation of these changes that may be responsible for a bias in the responses. This is easily taken care of by "interleaving" two or more staircase processes (involving different estimates) within each experimental session. This remark also applies, obviously, to the stochastic approximation procedure.

It is clear that, as described here, the staircase procedure is only of limited use, since it only permits the estimation of the point $\xi_{.5}$.

6.2.2.2. ***Estimate of*** ξ. Following Derman (1957), the simple up-down procedure can be adapted to provide, at least in principle, an estimate of ξ_π for any choice of π. The idea is simple enough. From a given psychometric function p_a, let us define a new psychometric function p_a^* by

$$p_a^*(x) = \alpha p_a(x) ,$$

where α is a multiplicative constant, $.5 \leq \alpha \leq 1$, the role of which will be made clear in a moment. An application of the simple up-down method to p_a^* will yield a stimulus value ξ satisfying

$$\alpha p_a(\xi) = p_a^*(\xi) \approx .5$$

Thus

$$p_a(\xi) \approx 1/2\alpha ,$$

and for any π, $.5 \leq \pi < 1$, an appropriate choice of α will yield an estimate of ξ_π. In the style of Eqs. (59) and (61) this amounts to setting

$$\mathbf{X}_{n+1} = \mathbf{X}_n + \delta(1 - 2\mathbf{Z}_n\mathbf{Y}_\pi) ,$$

where $\mathbf{Y}_\pi$ is a random variable taking value 1 with probability $\frac{1}{2}\pi$ and value 0 with probability $1 - \frac{1}{2}\pi$, and independent of the random variables $\mathbf{X}_n$'s. We have thus, clearly,

$$\alpha p_a(\mathbf{X}_n) = p_a^*(\mathbf{X}_n) = \text{Prob}\{\mathbf{Z}_n\mathbf{Y}_\pi = 1\} .$$

A similar method is used in the case of the determination of a point ξ_π with $0 < \pi < .5$. For example, we define a psychometric function

$$p_a^*(x) = (1 - \alpha)p_a(x) + \alpha ,$$

with

$$0 < \alpha = \frac{.5 - \pi}{1 - \pi} < .5 .$$

Again, applying the simple up-down procedure to p_a^* yields the required estimate of ξ_π. An objection to Derman's method is that the slope of p_a^* is smaller than the slope of p_a, a fact which may reduce the efficiency of the procedure.

6.2.2.3. ***Transformed Up-Down Method.*** The impact of this objection is less critical in the so-called transformed up-down method, where the function p_a^* is defined differently, for example, by one of the following expressions:

$$p_a^*(x) = p_a(x)^n ; \qquad n = 2, 3, 4, \ldots \quad (62)$$

$$p_a^*(x) = 1 - [1 - p_a(x)]^n ; \qquad n = 2, 3, 4, \ldots \quad (63)$$

$$p_a^*(x) = [1 - p_a(x)]p_a(x) + p_a(x) . \quad (64)$$

Such transformations have been used by a number of authors (see Levitt, 1970, for some references). As an illustration, we discuss the case $n = 2$ in Eq. (62). We consider the psychometric function $p_a^*(x) = p_a(x)^2$. As in the simple up-down procedure, we search for an estimate of a point ξ satisfying

$$.5 = p_a^*(\xi) = p_a(\xi)^2 ,$$

that is,

$$p_a(\xi) = \sqrt{.5} \approx .707 .$$

The case $n = 2$ in Eq. (62) is thus useful when this particular point of the psychometric function is of interest. The relevant stochastic process is defined as follows. Pick x_1 as usual. Set $x_2 = x_1$ if $\mathbf{Z}_1 = 1$ and $x_2 = x_1 - \delta$ if $\mathbf{Z}_n = 0$. For $n = 3, 4, \ldots$ we use the rule

$$\mathbf{X}_{n+1} = \mathbf{X}_n + \theta(\mathbf{Z}_n, \mathbf{Z}_{n-1}, \mathbf{X}_{n-1}) ,$$

in which the function θ is defined by

$$\theta(\mathbf{Z}_n, \mathbf{Z}_{n-1}, \mathbf{X}_{n-1}) = \begin{cases} \delta & \text{if } \mathbf{Z}_n = 0 ; \\ -\delta & \text{if } \mathbf{Z}_n = \mathbf{Z}_{n-1} = 1 \text{ and } \mathbf{X}_n = \mathbf{X}_{n-1} ; \\ 0 & \text{in all other cases} . \end{cases}$$

An example of realization of such a process is pictured in Figure 1.12(a). The point $\xi_{.5}$ of p_a^*, which is also the point $\xi_{\sqrt{.5}}$ of p_a, can be estimated by the midrun procedure. A slight adaptation of our definition of a run must be introduced however. For the data of Figure 1.12(a) a strict application of this definition leads to a count of four runs between trials 1 and 10, while we mean to have only two runs: 1–5, 5–10, with respective midpoints −1 and 0. The clearest approach is to begin by recoding the data, so as to eliminate the repetitions of a stimulus on consecutive trials. The function of this recoding is made transparent by a comparison of Figures 1.12(a) and 1.12(b). The exact definition given below is somewhat involved however. Let $\{x_n\}$ be a realization of the process $\{\mathbf{X}_n\}$. Consider the largest subsequence $\{x_{n_i}\}$ of $\{x_n\}$, such that $x_{n_i} \neq x_{n_{i+1}}$ for $i = 1, 2, \ldots$. Define $x_i^* = x_{n_i}$, for $i = 1, 2, \ldots$. The sequence $\{x_i^*\}$ will be called the *recoding* of $\{x_n\}$. An illustration of such recoding is given in Figure 1.12(b), starting from the data of Figure 1.12(a). By eliminating the repetitions, the number of trials has been reduced to 19. There are six runs: 1–3, 3–7, 11–15, and so on, with respective midpoints −1, 0, 0, and so on.

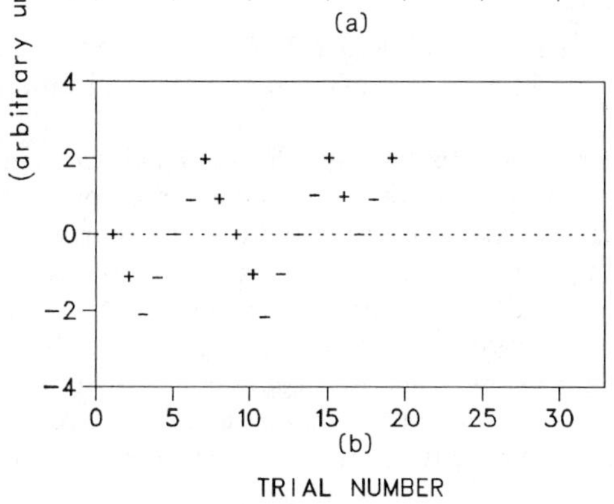

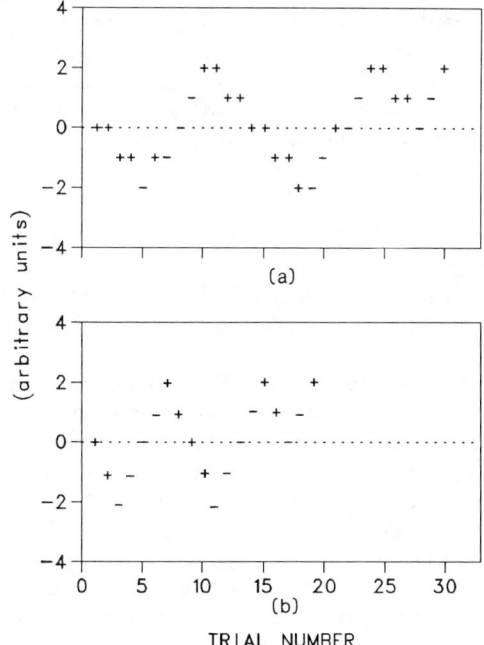

Figure 1.12. (a) Exemplary data for the transformed up-down methods, Eq. (62). The conventions regarding initial value and step size are as in Figure 1.11: $x_1 = 0$ and $\delta = 1$. (b) Recoding of the data of (a), eliminating consecutive repetitions of identical stimulus values. Six runs are obtained, corresponding to trials 1–3, 3–7, 7–10, and so on.

6.2.3. Remark. The assumption that the stochastic process $(\mathbf{X}_n, \mathbf{Z}_n)$ is stationary is critical for the procedures discussed in this section to be applicable. In some situations, the experimenter may have reasons to believe that this assumption is not warranted. An examination of the data generated by the up-down procedure may then reveal a systematic drift over time. If this happens, not only is the adaptive procedure useless for the estimation of ξ_π, but the very notion of psychometric function is of dubious value.

6.3. A Recommended Adaptive Procedure

In practice, it is advisable to adopt a combination of the methods described in Section 6.2. We recommend the following procedure. To estimate a point ξ_π satisfying $p_a(\xi_\pi) = \pi$:

Step 1. Choose $\mathbf{X}_1 = x_1$, the first stimulus to be presented, in a (conjectured) neighborhood of ξ_π.

Step 2. Determine the values of the following stimuli by accelerated stochastic approximation; for example, apply Eq. (60), modified by having c/n remaining constant in the course of a succession of identical responses. Pursue this procedure up to the limit of resolution of the stimulus continuum (e.g, 0.25 dB in psychoacoustic).

Step 3. Suppose that this limit is reached at trial n. On that trial, switch to a suitable up-down procedure, such as in Sections 6.2.2.2 or 6.2.2.3. Use the midrun estimates on the data from trial n onward to compute an estimate of ξ_π.

An example of application of this procedure is given in Figure 1.13 and Table 1.1 for some simulated data. This combined procedure avoids most of the criticisms elicited by other methods discussed in this section. We must point out, however, that it has not been investigated systematically, either from a mathematical or a practical standpoint. The last word is by no means said on the question of designing an optimal adaptive procedure, as indicated by recent activity in this field (Pavel, Note 1; Vorberg, Note 2).

6.4. Key References

A basic paper by Levitt (1970) contains a discussion of adaptive procedures geared toward psychophysical applications. A fairly complete mathematical treatment is available in the monograph by Wasan (1969).

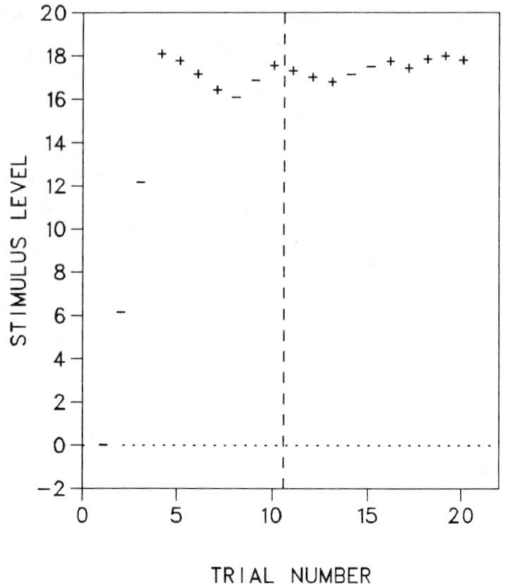

Figure 1.13. Simulated application of the adaptive procedure to estimate $\xi_{.75}$. The vertical dotted line separates the two modes of the procedure. See the Table 1.1 for details.

7. WEBER'S LAW, GENERALIZATIONS AND ALTERNATIVES

The central concept of Section 5 concerned a probability $p_a(\xi) = \pi$ for which a stimulus of intensity ξ is detected over a background denoted by a. In Section 6, the intensity ξ, rather than the probability π, was taken as the independent variable, and several practical procedures were discussed for the empirical determination of ξ, for given π and a. In general, the value of ξ will depend on both π and a; in other terms, ξ is a function of the two variables a and π. Mathematically, the function ξ contains exactly the same information as the psychometric functions of Section 5. The long-standing interest of psychophysicists in this function is well grounded, however. As we shall see, the knowledge of ξ gives a more ready access to the underlying sensory scale, a primary focus of interest for the psychophysicist. This is true at least for the most popular class of models for psychometric function data.

Table 1.1. Simulation of the Adaptive Procedure Recommended in Section 6.3, to Estimate $\xi_{.75}$.

Trial Number	Stimulus Value	Response ($\mathbf{Z}_n$)	$\mathbf{Y}_{.75}$	Computation of x_{n+1}
1	0	0	—	0 − 8(0 − .75) = 6
2	6	0	—	6 − 8(0 − .75) = 12
3	12	0	—	12 − 8(0 − .75) = 18
4	18	1	—	18 − (8/4)(1 − .75) = 17.5
5	17.5	1	—	17.5 − (8/4)(1 − .75) = 17
6	17	1	—	17 − (8/4)(1 − .75) = 16.5
7	16.5	1	—	16.5 − (8/4)(1 − .75) = 16
8	16	0	—	16 − (8/8)(0 − .75) = 16.75
9	16.75	0	—	16.75 − (8/8)(0 − .75) = 17.5
10	17.5	1	—	17.5 − (8/10)(1 − .75) = 17.3
11	17.25	1	—	17.25 + .25(1 − 2) = 17
12	17	1	—	17 + .25(1 − 2) = 16.75
13	16.75	1	0	16.75 + .25(1 − 0) = 17
14	17	0	1	17 + .25(1 − 0) = 17.25
15	17.25	0	1	17.25 + .25(1 − 0) = 17.5
16	17.5	1	1	17.5 + .25(1 −2) = 17.25
17	17.25	1	0	17.25 + .25(1 − 0) = 17.5
18	17.5	1	0	17.5 + .25(1 − 0) = 17.75
19	17.75	1	1	17.75 + .25(1 −2) = 17.5
20	17.50	1	1	17.5 + .25(1 −2) = 17.25

From trial 1 to 10, accelerated stochastic approximation is used, with $x_1 = 0$ and $c = 8$. (The successive values of the stimulus are obtained from Eq. (60), except that c/n does not vary in the course of repetitions of a response.) From trial 11 on, method 6.2.2.2 is used, with $\alpha = .5/.75$. The values of *$Y_{.75}$ are obtained by random sampling with Prob $\{\mathbf{Y}_{.75} = 1\} = \alpha$. The midrun estimate of $\xi_{.75}$ would be obtained by averaging 17, 16.75, 17.5; and so on.*

We consider here a number of models or properties for the function ξ and its close relative, the *Weber function* Δ, the most celebrated of which is the so-called Weber's law.

We begin with a definition recasting these two functions in the general framework of this chapter.

7.1. Basic Notions

7.1.1. Definition. Let $\Xi = \{p_a | a \in I\}$ be a psychometric family (i.e., a family of psychometric functions satisfying certain hypotheses; see the definition in Section 5.2). The *sensitivity function* of Ξ is a function ξ defined for all backgrounds (or standards) a and all probabilities π in the range of a psychometric function p_a, by the equation

$$\xi_\pi(a) = p_a^{-1}(\pi) .$$

(As usual, we write f^{-1} for the inverse of a one-to-one function f.) In words, $\xi_\pi(a)$ is the intensity of the stimulus yielding a response probability π, for the background a; that is, $p_a[\xi_\pi(a)] = \pi$. We recall that the index a in the notation p_a of a psychometric function need not always represent a real number. An example is that of a detection paradigm in which the index may denote a background noise, which in some situations may be represented by a spectral density function, that is, an infinite dimensional vector. (Thus $p_a(x)$ is the probability that the stimulus of intensity x is detected over the background a.) Let us assume that Ξ is anchored at .5 (cf. Section 5.4.3; thus .5 is a possible value for all the psychometric functions in the family). Then the Weber function of Ξ is a function Δ of two variables a and π, defined by

$$\Delta_\pi(a) = \xi_\pi(a) - \xi_{.5}(a) .$$

This was illustrated in Figure 1.10, in the particular case in which a denotes a real number (say, a physical intensity) and $\xi_{.5}(a) = a$.

It is important to distinguish in our notation the concept of Δ from that of Δ_π. The latter is a function of one variable, namely, the background, or standard. In other words, in the notation $\Delta_{.75}$, the probability .75 is implicitly assumed to be fixed. Occasionally, it will nevertheless be convenient, by abuse of language, to refer to the functions Δ_π as the Weber functions of Ξ. A similar convention will apply to the functions ξ_π, which will be called the *sensitivity functions* of Ξ. Psychophysicists often analyze their data in terms of one or more functions

$$a \mapsto \Delta_\pi(a)/a ,$$

in a situation in which division by a is legitimate. Such a function will be called the *π-Weber fraction* of Ξ, or, more simply, when no ambiguity can arise, a *Weber fraction*. Notice that since, in a case where $p_a(a) = .5$ for all intensities a, we have by definition

$$\frac{\Delta_\pi(a)}{a} = \frac{\xi_\pi(a)}{a} - 1 ,$$

any property of a Weber fraction will be almost exactly reflected in the corresponding function $\xi_\pi(a)/a$.

7.1.2. Remark. The change of notation, from $p_a^{-1}(\pi)$ to $\xi_\pi(a)$, symbolizes an important shift of focus in our analysis. The quantity π, the probability of the response, ceases to be the variable of interest and becomes the parameter. Typically, at most a couple of values of π are considered in experimental plots of Weber functions or sensitivity functions. By contrast, the effect on $\Delta_\pi(a)$ or $\xi_\pi(a)$ of the variable a is investigated in minute detail. This is in line with a long tradition in psychophysical research in which the sensory scales uncovered by the analysis of the data are deemed of central importance. This point is critical and should be discussed in some detail.

Suppose, for example, that some psychometric family $\Xi = \{p_a\}$ is subtractive, in the sense of the definition in Section 5.5.1. This means that the following representation holds for the response probabilities:

$$p_a(x) = F[u(x) - g(a)] , \tag{65}$$

in which u and F are continuous and strictly increasing functions. The psychophysicist using such a model typically interprets the functions u, g as representing a rescaling of the physical variables by the sensory mechanisms. As such, these functions are far more important than the function F, which, it is feared, may be plagued by nuisance variables of the "cognitive" type (response bias, motivation, etc.).

Let us transform Eq. (65) in terms of the sensitivity function ξ. Setting $p_a(x) = \pi$ and $F^{-1} = h$, we obtain $\xi_\pi(a) = x$, which together with Eq. (65) yields

$$\xi_\pi(a) = u^{-1}[g(a) + h(\pi)] . \tag{66}$$

Consequently, if the variable π in Eq. (66) is kept constant, the resulting equation in one variable only involves the functions u, g, which for reasons given are the interesting ones.

Such is the strategy of the psychophysicist. It relies heavily on a few assumptions. One is that the sensitivity functions ξ_π can be determined empirically with enough accuracy. A number of methods designed for this purpose have been discussed in the preceding section. Another, more critical assumption is that the rescaling functions u, g in Eqs. (65) and (66) are unaffected by nuisance (i.e., nonsensory) variables. As far as we know, there is little experimental evidence suggesting that this assumption may be invalid.

As a by-product of our discussion, we have, in any event, the following theorem.

7.1.3. Theorem. Let ξ be the sensitivity function of a psychometric family $\Xi = \{p_b | b \in I\}$. Then Ξ is subtractive (that is, Eq. (65) holds) iff there exist three functions h, u, and g, with u and h strictly increasing and continuous, such that

$$\xi_\pi(a) = u^{-1}[g(a) + h(\pi)] .$$

Indeed, we have shown that Eq. (65) implies Eq. (66), and it is clear that the reverse implication also holds. As suggested by this theorem, all the results obtained in Section 5 regarding psychometric functions could be translated in terms of sensitivity functions or, when they are defined, in terms of Weber functions. Following are a few additional examples, which may be skipped at first reading without much loss of continuity. (We omit the proofs of these results, which are easy to obtain.)

7.1.4. Theorem. Let $\Xi = \{p_a | a \in I\}$ be a psychometric family, with sensitivity function ξ. Then the following two conditions are equivalent:

1. Ξ is a parallel family in the sense of the definition in Section 5.5.1.
2. $\xi_\pi(a) - \xi_{\pi'}(a) = \xi_\pi(b) - \xi_{\pi'}(b)$, for all π, π', and a, b such that both members are defined.

This result follows readily from the definitions, as well as from the theorem in Section 5.4.2.

7.1.5. Theorem. If $\Xi = \{p_a | a \in I\}$ is an anchored psychometric family (in the sense of the definition in Section 5.4.3) with a sensitivity function ξ, then Ξ is parallel iff there exist two functions g, h with h strictly increasing and continuous, such that the equation

$$\xi_\pi(a) = g(a) + h(\pi) \tag{67}$$

holds whenever $\xi_\pi(a)$ is defined. In particular, g is defined on I.

This implies that in the situation described in the theorem, the Weber functions $a \mapsto \Delta_\pi(a)$ do not vary with a since

$$\Delta_\pi(a) = h(\pi) - h(.5)$$

for all background a. As suggested by a comparison of Sections 7.1.4 and 7.1.5, the functions g, h do not necessarily exist if the assumption of anchoring is removed.

We consider next the effect of the balancing condition (from the definition in Section 5.5.1)

$$p_a(b) + p_b(a) = 1 ,$$

on the sensitivity function of a discrimination family.

7.1.6. Theorem. A discrimination family $\Xi = \{p_b | b \in I\}$ is balanced iff its sensitivity function ξ satisfies

$$\xi_{1-\pi}[\xi_\pi(a)] = a$$

whenever the left member of this equation is defined.

These few results should suffice to familiarize the reader with the notions of the definition in Section 7.1.1. Further results along these lines can be found in Falmagne (1982).

7.2. Linear Psychometric Families—Weber's Law

So far, no assumptions were made regarding the structure of the set I of backgrounds of a psychometric family $\{p_a | a \in I\}$. Such properties as parallelism or subtractivity could be discussed while assuming that the elements $a \in I$ were just labels for the psychometric functions p_a in the family. Of particular importance in this section is the situation in which I is actually a (subset of a) vector space over the real numbers. For example, $a \in I$ may denote a spectral density function or, in the case of a discrimination family (see Section 5.5.1), a real number representing a physical intensity. What is critical here is that the multiplication

$$\lambda a$$

of a real vector a by a positive real number λ makes sense. From an empirical standpoint, the multiplication λa means that the intensity of the background has been multiplied by the factor λ. (In the case of a spectral density function, a denotes a real-valued function and λa symbolizes the fact that all the intensities of the background have been multiplied by the same constant λ.) When such a situation arises, properties can be investigated in the data, which are both strong and of central interest for psychophysical research.

7.2.1. Definition. A psychometric family $\Xi = \{p_b | b \in I\}$ is called *linear* iff the index set I is a (subset of a) vector space over the real numbers.

A special case of a linear psychometric family arises when the indices of the psychometric function denote physical intensities. This case was referred to in Section 5.5.1 as a discrimination family.

We recall that in a psychometric family $\Xi = \{p_b | b \in I\}$, the notation C_b, for any $b \in I$, refers to the domain of the psychometric function p_b, which is an open interval (see Section 5.2.1). The psychometric family Ξ will be called *positive* iff each interval C_b is positive. (This is a typical case for physical intensities.) Most results in the remainder of this section will be obtained in the framework of linear, positive psychometric families.

The definition in Section 7.2.2 will also be useful in connection with Weber's law and more general forms of this law.

7.2.2. Definition. Let V be a vector space over the real numbers. Let T be a subset of V. Let f be a real-valued function on T. Then f is said to be *homogeneous of degree* β (on T) iff for any real number $\lambda \neq 0$, whenever $a, \lambda a \in T$, then

$$f(\lambda a) = \lambda^{\beta} f(a) .$$

7.2.3. Definition. A linear, positive psychometric family $\Xi = \{p_b | b \in I\}$ satisfies Weber's law iff

$$p_a(x) = p_{\lambda a}(\lambda x) \tag{68}$$

whenever both members of Eq. (68) are defined, with $0 < \lambda < \infty$. In other words, Ξ satisfies Weber's law iff the function p, $(a,x) \mapsto p_a(x)$ is homogeneous of degree 0. Occasionally, Eq. (68) will be referred to as Weber's law.

7.2.4. Remark. In two respects, this definition of Weber's law departs from tradition. Weber's law is usually stated in the special case in which the backgrounds are real numbers. For example, in the context of auditory detection of a stimulus embedded in noise, Weber's law would imply that the probability of a correct detection would not vary when both the stimulus and the noise are increased in intensity by the same number of decibels. We believe, however, that this prediction would apply for a fairly large set of spectral density functions specifying the noise. Such an assumption is made explicit in Section 7.2.3. Another difference is that Weber's law is most often expressed in terms of the Weber functions Δ_π. The equivalence is made clear in the theorem in Section 7.2.6. We have two reasons for adopting Eq. (68) as the defining condition of Weber's law, rather than the more customary form

$$\Delta_\pi(\lambda a) = \lambda \Delta_\pi(a) .$$

One is that Eq. (68) is more general; this equation makes sense in situations in which the Weber functions are not always defined. (The Weber function Δ_π was defined in Section 7.1.1 from the sensitivity function $\xi_{.5}$. There may be cases in which $\xi_{.5}$ is not obtainable.) Another is to stress the fact that in view of the binomial variability of the relative frequencies providing the basic data for Eq. (68), it is more readily amenable to statistical testing. In practice, however, evaluations of Weber's law are mostly based on investigating the empirical behavior of the Weber functions.

Some strengthening of our conditions will be useful for this and later results.

7.2.5. Definition. A linear psychometric family $\Xi = \{p_b | b \in I\}$ is called *solvable* iff for all $a \in I$ and all $x \in C_a$, the equation

$$p_{\lambda a}(\mu x) = p_a(x)$$

is solvable in μ for every λ and is solvable in λ for every μ. We say that Ξ has a *Weberian domain* iff for any $\lambda > 0$, $p_{\lambda a}(\lambda x)$ is defined whenever $p_a(x)$ is defined.

These strengthenings of our assumptions will occasionally be convenient but are hardly innocuous. The reader is invited to reflect on the empirical impact of these two conditions. Both of them practically entail that neither of the two physical domains spanned by the function p is bounded, obviously not a realistic assumption. Neither of these conditions is essential, but they certainly render our developments much easier. In any event, they will be used sparingly in the sequel.

In the theorem in Section 7.2.6, a central result of this section, we consider an important generalization of Weber's law, symbolized by the equation

$$p_{\lambda a}(\lambda^{\beta} x) = p_a(x) ,$$

and we establish the equivalence between this equation and some constraints on sensitivity function and Weber function data. We show that our definition of Weber's law is equivalent to the traditional one. The interpretation of the exponent β is discussed in Section 7.3.1.

7.2.6. Theorem. Let $\Xi = \{p_b | b \in I\}$ be a linear, positive, solvable psychometric family, with sensitivity function ξ. Then the following three conditions are equivalent:

1. Every sensitivity function ξ_π is homogeneous of degree $\beta > 0$:

$$\xi_\pi(\lambda a) = \lambda^{\beta} \xi_\pi(a) .$$

2. There is a constant $\beta > 0$ such that

$$p_{\lambda a}(\lambda^{\beta} x) = p_a(x) ,$$

whenever both members of this equation are defined, with $0 < \lambda < \infty$.

3. There exists a function F and a constant $\beta > 0$ such that

$$p_a(x) = F(a/x^{1/\beta}) .$$

Moreover, if Ξ is anchored at .5, then each condition 1–3 is equivalent to the assumptions that any Weber function Δ_π is homogeneous of degree $\beta > 0$. In particular, Weber's law holds iff

$$\Delta_\pi(\lambda a) = \lambda\, \Delta_\pi(a) \;; \tag{69}$$

that is, the Weber functions Δ_π are homogeneous of degree 1.

Proof. (1) *implies* (2). Suppose that $p_a(x) = \pi$, $p_{\lambda a}(\lambda^\beta x) = \pi'$. Then $\xi_\pi(a) = x$, and successively

$$\xi_{\pi'}(\lambda a) = \lambda^\beta x = \lambda^\beta \xi_\pi(a) = \xi_\pi(\lambda a) \;,$$

since Ξ is solvable, and $\pi = \pi'$ follows by the strict monotonicity of $\xi_\pi(\lambda a)$ in the variable π.

(2) *implies* (3) Setting $\lambda^\beta x = K$, a constant, we obtain $\lambda = (K/x)^{1/\beta}$, yielding

$$p_a(x) = p_{\lambda a}(\lambda^\beta x) = p_{(K/x)^{1/\beta} a}(K) = F(a/x^{1/\beta}) \;,$$

with the function F defined by $F(s) = p_{K^{1/\beta}s}(K)$. In fact, (2) and (3) are equivalent since obviously

$$F(a/x^{1/\beta}) = F[\lambda a/(\lambda^\beta x)^{1/\beta}] \;.$$

(3) *implies* (1). In view of the equivalence between (2) and (3), this is clear since, with

$$\pi = p_{\lambda a}(\lambda^\beta x) = p_a(x) \;,$$

we have

$$\xi_\pi(\lambda a) = \lambda^\beta x = \lambda^\beta \xi_\pi(a) \;.$$

If the Weber function is defined, it follows by substitution that the sensitivity functions are homogeneous of degree $\beta > 0$ iff the Weber functions Δ_π also satisfy this condition. Finally, the equivalence between Weber's law and Eq. (69) is obtained from the case $\beta = 1$ of the equivalence between (1) and (2). ■

7.3. Remarks

We shall see that the homogeneity equation

$$\xi_\pi(\lambda a) = \lambda^\beta \xi_\pi(a)$$

plays an important role in the analysis of data, as a substitute to Weber's law. (This equation is often referred to as the *near-miss to Weber's Law*, cf. McGill & Goldberg, 1968.) The interpretation of the exponent β in this equation must be considered carefully. There seems to be a tendency in the psychophysical community to take this exponent as representing a critical aspect of the neural coding of physical intensity. For a number of reasons, this position is open to challenge. One difficulty is indicated below. Suppose that Ξ is a discrimination family satisfying this condition, together with $\xi_{.5}(a) = a$, for all intensities a. This implies that the Weber functions are also homogeneous of degree β:

$$\Delta_\pi(\lambda a) = \lambda^\beta \Delta_\pi(a) \;. \tag{70}$$

But we have also

$$\Delta_\pi(\lambda a) = \xi_\pi(\lambda a) - \xi_{.5}(\lambda a) = \lambda^\beta \xi_\pi(a) - \lambda a$$

$$= \lambda^\beta[\Delta_\pi(a) + a] - a \;,$$

which together with Eq. (70) implies

$$\lambda^\beta \Delta_\pi(a) = \lambda^\beta[\Delta_\pi(a) + a] - \lambda a \;,$$

that is,

$$a(\lambda^\beta - \lambda) = 0 \;.$$

Since $a > 0$, we must conclude that $\beta = 1$. Thus in the case of a discrimination family satisfying $p_a(a) = .5$, the assumption that the Weber functions are homogeneous of degree β implies in fact Weber's law.

The crux of the argument here is that the condition

$$p_a(a) = .5$$

or the more general balance condition

$$p_a(b) + p_b(a) = 1 \;,$$

which implies it, results from a symmetry of the experimental paradigm which is not necessarily of a sensory nature. We shall go back to this point later in this section.

A special case of the theorem in Section 7.2.6 is of historical interest. If Weber's law holds, then $\beta = 1$ in Eq. (70) and by virtue of Condition (3) in Section 7.2.6, the choice probabilities take the form

$$p_a(x) = F(a/x) = F[e^{-(\log x - \log a)}] \;,$$

yielding

$$p_a(x) = G(\log x - \log a) \;, \tag{71}$$

with $G(s) = F(e^{-s})$, a strictly increasing, continuous function. Equation (71) has sometimes been given the interpretation that "the sensation grows as the logarithm of the excitation," a statement which has been named *Fechner's law*. Such interpretation has been at the center of a long controversy and should not be dismissed or accepted casually. It relies in part on some empirical evidence, Weber's law. (How well Weber's law is supported by the data is considered in Section 7.4.) It also relies on the somewhat arbitrary choice of a particular mathematical representation of such data, namely Eq. (71). Finally, it involves using a philosophically charged label such as "sensation." Each of these factors has contributed its share to the polemical aspects of the debate, a brief account of which can be found in a later section of this chapter (see Section 10.9).

7.4. Examination of the Data

As an empirical prediction, Weber's law holds reasonably well for sensory continua such as loudness discrimination of Gaussian noises, loudness discrimination of pure tones, lifted weights, and visual brightness. As mentioned in Section 7.3, the analysis of the data is sometimes based on the just-noticeable-difference (jnd) function, which can be computed from the sensitivity functions by the equation

$$\mathrm{jnd}(a) = [\xi_{.75}(a) = \xi_{.25}(a)]/2 .$$

The experimenter checks whether the ratio

$$\mathrm{jnd}(a)/a \qquad (72)$$

remains constant, while a varies on a chosen subset of the physical scale. (Thus a takes values in the positive reals.) We have elected to base our developments on the sensitivity function, rather than on the jnd function. For various reasons, which the reader will discover gradually, the sensitivity function is the appropriate notion to use as the cornerstone of the theory. Notice in this connection that Eq. (72) is constant if the functions

$$a \mapsto \xi_\pi(a)/a$$

are constant. More generally, the jnd function is homogeneous of degree β if the sensitivity functions ξ_π are homogeneous of degree β. It is clear that the reverse implication does not necessarily hold. Any one of the psychophysical methods discussed in Section 6 can be employed for the empirical determination of the sensitivity function. Even though these methods differ drastically from an experimental viewpoint, many believe that the overall pattern of empirical results is not seriously affected by which method has been used. This opinion is not universal, however, and we shall be cautious in this respect. (Luce and Green, 1974a, for example, analyze the data of six studies of the Weber fraction $\Delta_\pi(a)/a$ for tone intensities, with considerable discrepancy in the results.)

The experimental evidence favoring Weber's law is exemplified in Figure 1.14. For some sensory continua, the Weber fraction $\Delta_\pi(a)/a$, with $a \in \mathrm{Re}_+$ (the set of positive real numbers), remains indeed constant over a substantial portion of the domain (2–3 log units, for audition and vision), thus supporting Weber's law. A more comprehensive description of the data would emphasize the fact that the Weber fraction is initially decreasing. In fact, for audition and smell, it never increases. Finally, a conjecture which is validated by the data for all five continua in Figure 1.14 is that the Weber fraction is "convex" (i.e., it never "curves downward"). A precise definition of the convexity of a function is given in the definition in Section 7.4.1. The reader should remember these aspects of the data, which will lead to a theoretical analysis in Section 7.5.

The initial decrease of the Weber fraction is sometimes attributed to an absolute threshold of perception, while the late rise of the fraction in some cases is attributed to the sensory mechanisms reaching the limit of their operational range. However legitimate such interpretations might be, they do not necessarily justify an analysis of an empirical Weber fraction into fragments, each requiring a separate model. In this section, only models attempting a comprehensive description of the data are considered.

7.4.1. Definition. Let f be a real-valued function defined on a real interval (s,t). Then f is called *convex* iff

$$f[\lambda x + (1 - \lambda)y] \leqslant \lambda f(x) + (1 - \lambda) f(y)$$

whenever $s < x < t$, $s < y < t$, and $0 < \lambda < 1$. The function f is *strictly convex* iff the above inequality is strict. If $-f$ is convex (respectively, strictly convex), then f is said to be *concave* (respectively, *strictly concave*).

Any linear function is both convex and concave. Examples of strictly convex functions are $x \rightarrow e^x$, $x \rightarrow x^2$, for $-\infty < x < \infty$. The following results are easy consequences of the definition: any convex function is continuous; if g is an increasing, convex function and f is convex, then the composition $s \mapsto g[f(s)]$ is convex (in particular, e^f is convex, in fact, strictly convex); if the second derivative f'' of f exists, then f is convex iff $f'' \geqslant 0$. A geometrical interpretation of convexity is that any segment of a straight line joining two points of the graph of a convex function f lies above or on the graph of f (see Figure 1.15).

It is clear that the Weber fractions depicted in Figure 1.14 are convex in the sense of the definition in Section 7.3.1. A case can be made that these functions are actually strictly convex.

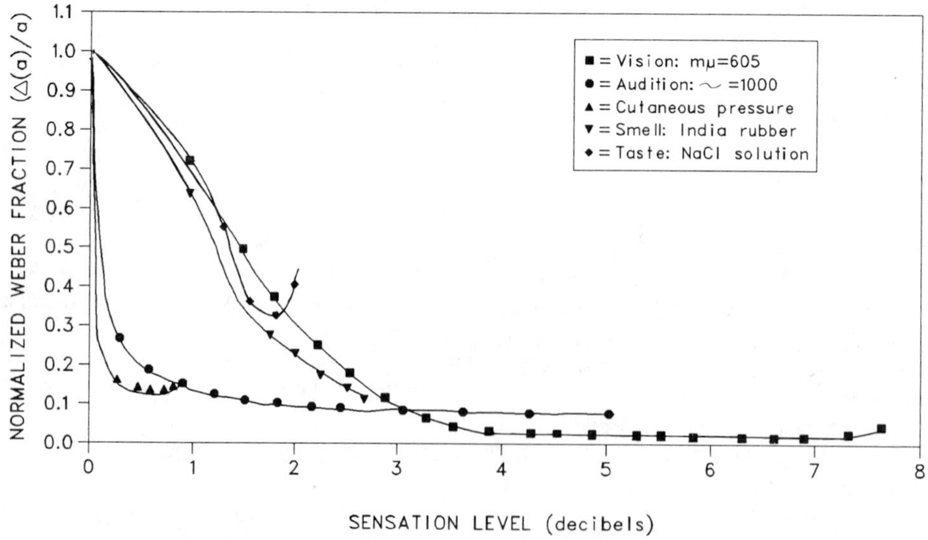

Figure 1.14. Weber fraction data, for various sensory continua. The abscissa is in decibels, sensation level. The Weber fractions have been normalized so as to be unity at threshold. (From R. D. Luce, R. R. Bush, & E. Galanter (Eds.), *Handbook of mathematical psychology*. Copyright 1963 by John Wiley & Sons, Inc. Reprinted with permission.)

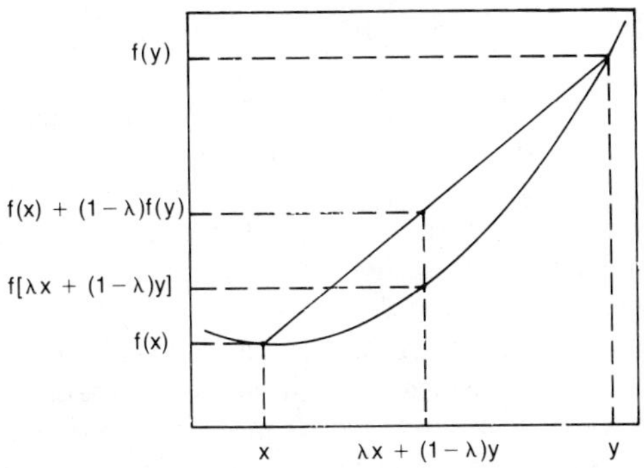

Figure 1.15. Geometrical interpretation of the convexity of a real valued function f: $[\lambda x + (1 - \lambda)y] \leq \lambda f(x) + (1 - \lambda) f(y)$.

The failures of Weber's law illustrated in Figure 1.14 prompted psychophysicists to propose various alternatives.

7.5. Alternatives to Weber's Law

One generalization of Weber's law has been encountered earlier which, in terms of the sensitivity function, is symbolized by the equation

$$\xi_\pi(\lambda a) = \lambda^\beta \xi_\pi(a) \tag{73}$$

for $0 < \lambda < \infty$ and with $\beta > 0$, a constant independent of π. When the Weber function is defined, this is equivalent to

$$\Delta_\pi(\lambda a) = \lambda^\beta \Delta_\pi(a) . \tag{74}$$

This prediction, which is often referred to as the near-miss to Weber's law (McGill & Goldberg, 1968), has been supported experimentally in some situations (Jesteadt, Wier, & Green, 1977; see Figure 1.16). Notice that the data in Figure 1.16 require the exponent β in Eq. (74) to be smaller than 1; the Weber fraction

$$\Delta_\pi(\lambda a)/a = \lambda^{\beta-1}\Delta_\pi(a)$$

must be decreasing. It cannot be assumed, however, that the near-miss to Weber's law holds generally, across experimental paradigms and sensory continua. For one thing, this law would fail to explain most of the data displayed in Figure 1.13. For another, it was pointed out earlier (see Section 7.3) that in the case where $\beta \neq 1$, Eqs. (73) and (74) necessarily imply the existence of some asymmetry in the paradigm: the psychometric functions cannot satisfy the condition, $p_a(a) = .5$. This condition, however, is sometimes inherent to the experimental paradigm (e.g., in a situation in visual psychophysics, where the stimuli to be compared are two spots of light symmetrically positioned

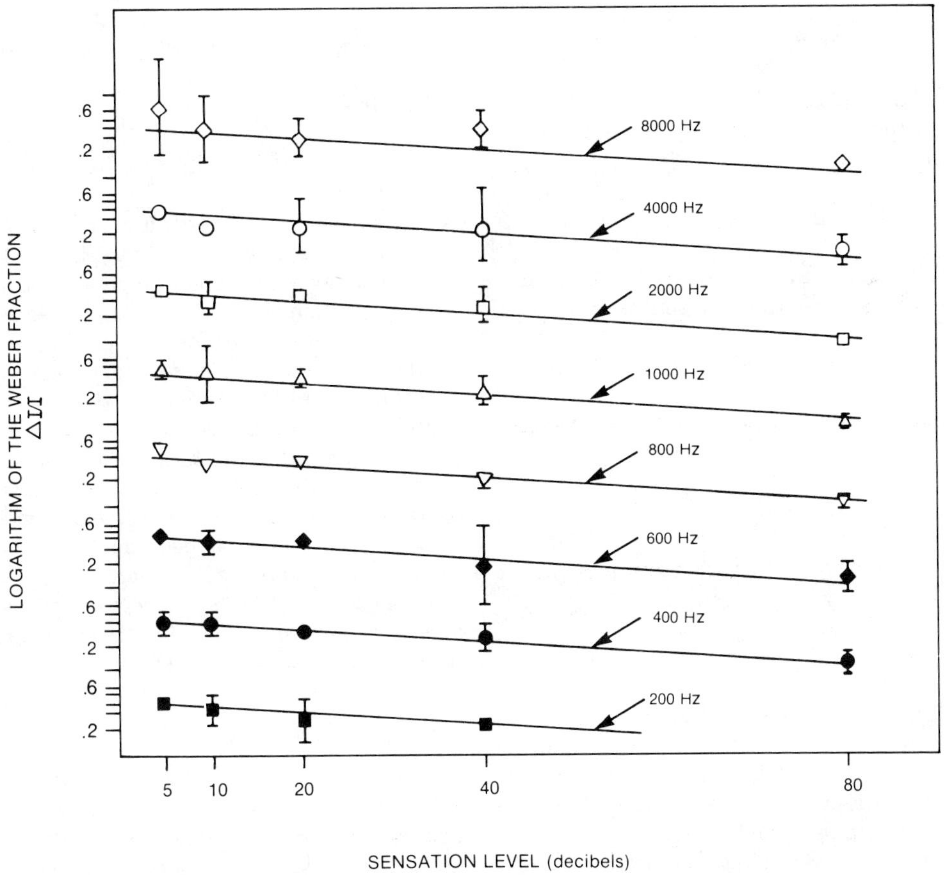

Figure 1.16. Values of the logarithm of the Weber fraction, averaged across subjects and replications, for various intensities and frequencies of pure tones. The abscissa is in decibels, sensation level. The vertical bars indicate ± 3 standard errors. A bar is omitted when its size is exceeded by that of the symbol. The same linear function has been fitted to the eight sets of data. (From W. Jesteadt, C. C. Wier, & D. M. Green, Intensity discrimination as a function of frequency, *Journal of the Acoustical Society of America*, 1977, *61*. Reprinted with permission.)

with respect to a fixation point). It is also possible to ensure that this condition holds by a "normalization" of the data. As argued in Section 5.7, we are certainly not advocating such tampering with the data. The fact is, however, that such normalizations are fairly frequent. In such cases, it is clear that Eq. (74) describes the data only if $\beta = 1$ (that is, Weber's law holds) or, possibly, if β is a function of π. This, however, is not what is intended by the near-miss to Weber's law, at least as we understand it.

In any event, the above discussion suggests a further generalization of Weber's law, which is embodied in the equation

$$\xi_\pi(\lambda a) = \lambda^{\beta(\pi)}\xi_\pi(a) , \tag{75}$$

in which β is a function of π satisfying $\beta(.5) = 1$. (This ensures $p_a(a) = .5$.) The consequences of that assumption deserve some attention. It can be shown in particular that if the balancing condition is satisfied, then the function β must satisfy

$$\beta(\pi)\beta(1 - \pi) = 1 . \tag{76}$$

As far as we know, this condition or, even more generally, the effect of the choice probability π on the estimated value of the exponent β in Eq. (75) has never been investigated from an experimental viewpoint. Other substitutes to Weber's law are of interest. As in the case of the near-miss to Weber's law, each of the examples below is a special case of the representation

$$\xi_\pi(a) = u^{-1}[g(a) + h(\pi)] ,$$

as can be checked without difficulty.

Let the sensitivity function ξ of a discrimination family be defined by the equation

$$\xi_\pi(\lambda a) = \lambda^{\beta}[\xi_\pi(a) - K] + K , \tag{77}$$

where K is a positive constant. In the style of the theorem in Section 7.2.6, this is equivalent to the representation

$$p_a(x) = F[a(x - K)^{-1/\beta}] \tag{78}$$

for the choice probabilities (we assume $x > K$). Provided that $\beta > 1$ and $\xi_\pi(a) > K$, the function

$$\lambda \mapsto \xi_\pi(\lambda a)/\lambda$$

is convex on the positive real numbers, with a minimum at the point

$$\lambda = [K/(\beta - 1)(\xi_\pi(a) - K)]^{1/\beta} .$$

Thus the Weber fractions are also convex in the same conditions, a fact worth noticing in connection with our discussion of the data displayed in Figure 1.14. It is clear that this model generalizes the near-miss to Weber's law. The constant K may be interpreted as a measure of a threshold value.

In the case where Ξ is a discrimination family, we also consider the representation

$$\xi_\pi(a) = [h(\pi) + \delta a^{\beta'}]^{1/\beta} \tag{79}$$

for the sensitivity functions, involving a strictly increasing, continuous function h and three positive constants β, β', and δ. This leads immediately to the representation

$$p_a(x) = F(x^{\beta} - \delta a^{\beta'}) , \tag{80}$$

with $F = h^{-1}$, for the choice probabilities. This model has been discussed by several authors (see, for example, Parker & Schneider, 1980). It is not consistent with Weber's law. However, for appropriately chosen values of the parameters, it would predict the main features (monotonicity, convexity) of data such as that pictured in Figure 1.14.

The late increase of the Weber fraction is often interpreted as resulting from a saturation of the sensory or neuronal mechanisms. In turn, this leads to the postulate that the sensory scale, for example, the function u in Eq. (65), is bounded. An example along these lines is given below. It is assumed that the sensitivity functions satisfy the equation

$$\xi_\pi(a) = K\{h(\pi)f(a)/[1 - h(\pi)f(a)]\}^{1/\beta} , \tag{81}$$

with

$$f(a) = a^{\beta'} + K' ,$$

and $\beta, \beta', K, K' > 0$, constants. Using simple algebra, we obtain for the response probabilities the form

$$p_a(x) = G[x^{\beta}/(x^{\beta} + K^{\beta})f(a)] ,$$

or equivalently, as a difference model,

$$p_a(x) = F\{\ln[x^{\beta}/(x^{\beta} + K^{\beta})] - \ln f(a)\} ,$$

with $F(\ln s) = G(s)$. Thus

$$u(x) = \ln[x^{\beta}/(x^{b} + K)] < 0 .$$

Again, such a model is capable of accommodating typical Weber fraction data (cf. Alpern, Rushton, & Tori, 1970a, 1970b, 1970c).

Other models have been proposed, which differ only in details from one or the other of those discussed in this section. They are not reviewed here. Our purpose in this subsection is not to single out one particular mathematical expression as the appropriate model for the sensitivity function. In fact, it is quite conceivable that the choice of a suitable model (that would provide a good fit to the data, from a statistical viewpoint) may depend not only on the sensory continuum envisaged but also on rather specific details of the experimental paradigm. Accordingly, an effort has been made by some psychophysicists to focus the theoretical developments on aspects of the data that may perhaps be robust to minor changes of the experimental procedure (cf. Falmagne, 1977; Iverson, 1983). The results are too specialized to be included here.

7.6. Key References

Weber fraction data are compiled, for example, in Boring, Langfeld, and Weld (1948, p. 268) and Holway and Pratt (1936, p. 337) for various sensory continua. Luce and Green (1974a; see also Green, 1978, p. 257) review a number of experimental studies of the discrimination of the difference in the amplitudes of a sinusoidal tone. The data are plotted in terms of the Weber fraction. See also the Chapters in Sections II and III of this handbook. In a recent monograph, Laming (1983) gave a theoretical analysis of Weber functions, based on a large collection of data. (Unfortunately, this work came to our attention in the final stage of the writing of this chapter, and no discussion of its content could be included.)

8. SIGNAL DETECTION THEORY

Any psychophysical task has cognitive components, which covers a variety of factors, such as response bias, guessing strategy, motivation, and so on. Thus far in our approach to psychophysical theory, we have implicitly assumed that such factors could be bypassed or controlled by careful experimental design. In fact, we have ignored them. This position is not without its weaknesses. An example will make this clear.

Consider a task in which a subject is required to detect a stimulus embedded in a noisy background. On 50% of the trials the noise is presented alone. Across conditions, the intensity of the stimulus is varied, providing the basic data for a psychometric function. Two kinds of error can be made in such a task, which is often referred to as the yes-no paradigm: (1) the subject may fail to report a stimulus presented (this is called *a miss*) and (2) the subject may report a detection on a noise-alone trial (this is called a *false alarm*, or a *false positive*). A correct detection will be referred to as a *hit*. The remaining case is a *correct rejection*.

A guessing strategy is available to the subject in this situation: when not quite sure that the stimulus was presented on a trial, the subject may nevertheless claim to have detected it. Such strategy would succeed in a situation in which a miss is much more heavily penalized than a false alarm. For example, suppose that the system of rewards and penalties is the one displayed in Table 1.2, where the numbers represent monetary values. Thus each correct detection brings 3 monetary units (μs): each miss costs 3 μs, and so on. Such a table is often referred to as a *payoff matrix*. It is reasonable to suppose that the particular payoff matrix shown above would favor a guessing strategy over a conservative one. (For instance, if the subject reports a detection on every trial, whether or not the stimulus was presented, the average gain per trial is 2 μs, while the opposite strategy of responding "no detection" on every trial results in an average gain of 0 μs.) Obviously, another payoff matrix may evoke a completely different strategy. A naive experimenter may be tempted to believe that if a constant payoff matrix is used across conditions varying in stimulus intensity, the subject strategy will not change, a fact which can be tested by checking that the proportion of false alarms remains constant. Unfortunately, a subject's interpretation of a payoff matrix is largely personal, and this interpretation may change drastically from one condition to another. Needless to say, these remarks also apply when no explicit payoff matrix is used, but the subject strategy is induced by verbal instructions. The problem at hand is thus that of disentangling the purely sensory aspects of the task from those resulting from the subject's strategy.

Table 1.2. System of Rewards and Penalties in Which Numbers Represent Monetary Values

	Responses	
Stimulus	Yes	No
Yes	3 Hit	−3 Miss
No	−1 False Alarm	3 Correct Rejection

This section is devoted to a particular solution to this problem, which is usually discussed under the label *signal detection theory*, even though its applicability extends far beyond the detection of signals. Our presentation is far from exhaustive. It should however be sufficient to acquaint the reader with the most commonly used notions and techniques of signal detection theory. For an extensive treatment of this topic, see Green and Swets (1974).

8.1. Receiver Operating Characteristic (ROC) Graphs and Curves

For simplicity, we shall ignore statistical variability for the moment and identify response frequencies and probabilities.

Let us suppose that for a given stimulus intensity, three payoff matrices have been used, labeled θ_1, θ_2, and θ_3, inducing three different guessing strategies. Let s and n denote the stimulus and the noise, respectively. Let $p_s(\theta_i)$ and $p_n(\theta_i)$, $i = 1, 2, 3$, be the hit and false alarm probabilities. For concreteness, some hypothetical data follow:

	$p_n(\theta_i)$	$p_s(\theta_i)$
θ_1	.10	.35
θ_2	.40	.75
θ_3	.65	.90

A useful graphic representation of such data is often used by psychophysicists, in which each pair of response probabilities $[p_n(\theta_i), p_s(\theta_i)]$ is pictured as a point in the unit square (see Figure 1.17, but ignore the three curves for the moment). There is a consensus in psychophysics that by appropriately choosing the payoff matrix, most types of strategies can be induced in the subject, ranging from the most conservative ones (if the slightest doubt arises, say "no detection") to the most daring guessing. (High false alarm rates, however, are exceptional.) It is also reasonable to suppose that any change in a payoff matrix that would increase the probability of a false alarm would also increase (continuously) the probability of a hit. (This assumption is supported by much data.) In other words, this means that the three points in Figure 1.17 belong to the graph of a continuous function ρ mapping the interval [0,1] into itself. We have thus

$$\rho[p_n(\theta)] = p_s(\theta) ,$$

in which θ ranges in a large set of payoff matrices Θ.

8.1.1. Definition. Let Θ be a collection of payoff matrices; for each $\theta \in \Theta$, let $p_n(\theta)$ and $p_s(\theta)$ be the probabilities of a false alarm and of a hit, respectively. Then the set of points

$$\{[p_n(\theta), p_s(\theta)] | \theta \in \Theta\} ,$$

in the unit square is called a *receiver operating characteristic (ROC) graph* (of (n,s)). When an ROC graph is the graph of a continuous function ρ mapping the closed interval [0,1] into itself, it will be called an *ROC curve*. The function ρ will be referred to as the *ROC function*.

Three examples of ROC curves are displayed in Figure 1.17, in which the functions are increasing. It is reasonable to suppose that any change in a payoff matrix that would increase the probability of a false alarm would also increase (or at least not decrease) the probability of a hit. This assumption is supported by much data. Incidentally, the acronym ROC is borrowed

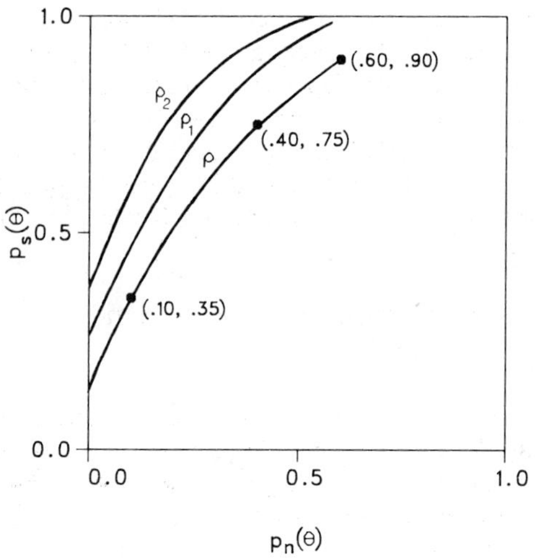

Figure 1.17. Three ROC curves and one ROC graph containing three points.

from signal detection theory in telecommunication (references are given in Section 8.11).

The basic idea of this representation is that the strategy is varying along the ROC curves, while the discriminability is varying across the ROC curves. In this framework, the three ROC curves ρ, ρ_1, and ρ_2 in Figure 1.17 correspond to increasingly detectable stimuli. A particularly illuminating interpretation of the information captured by an ROC curve is offered by the model described in Section 8.2.

8.2. A Random Variable Model for ROC Curves

Suppose that to each stimulus s corresponds a random variable $\mathbf{U}_s$, representing the activation evoked by that stimulus in some critical neural location. Similarly, let $\mathbf{U}_n$ be the activation random variable corresponding to the noise. The random variables $\mathbf{U}_s$ and $\mathbf{U}_n$ are assumed to be independent. As before, let $p_s(\theta)$ and $p_n(\theta)$ be the hit and false alarm probabilities, corresponding to a payoff matrix θ. We assume that on every trial (whether or not the stimulus is presented) a positive response occurs if the momentary (or sample) value of $\mathbf{U}_s$ or $\mathbf{U}_n$ exceeds a criterion λ_θ, the value of which is determined by the payoff matrix θ. In symbols:

$$p_s(\theta) = \text{Prob}\{\mathbf{U}_s > \lambda_\theta\} \tag{82}$$

and

$$p_n(\theta) = \text{Prob}\{\mathbf{U}_n > \lambda_\theta\} . \tag{83}$$

Such a model is in the spirit of the random utility, or Thurstone-type models discussed earlier in this chapter (see Sections 4.2 to 4.8). In the context of ROC curves, it entails a few interesting results. Suppose that

$$p_n(\theta) > p_n(\theta')$$

for some payoff matrices θ and θ'. Using, successively, Eqs. (83) and (82), this implies

$$\lambda_\theta < \lambda_{\theta'} ,$$

yielding

$$p_s(\theta) \geqslant p_s(\theta') .$$

This means that the ROC function $p_n(\theta) \mapsto p_s(\theta)$ must be nondecreasing, a prediction which, as indicated earlier, is consistent with much data. Another basic result is that the area under the ROC curve (the integral of the ROC function from 0 to 1) is equal to the probability that $\mathbf{U}_s$ exceeds $\mathbf{U}_n$:

$$\text{Prob}\{\mathbf{U}_s > \mathbf{U}_n\} .$$

The argument is spelled out below. Using the fact that the random variables in question are independent, we have

$$\text{Prob}\{\mathbf{U}_s > \mathbf{U}_n\} = \int_{-\infty}^{\infty} \text{Prob}\{\mathbf{U}_s > \lambda | \mathbf{U}_n = \lambda\} d\text{Prob}\{\mathbf{U}_n \leqslant \lambda\}$$

$$= \int_{-\infty}^{\infty} \text{Prob}\{\mathbf{U}_s > \lambda\} d\text{Prob}\{\mathbf{U}_n \leqslant \lambda\}. \tag{84}$$

According to this model, the response probabilities $p_s(\theta) = \text{Prob}\{\mathbf{U}_s < \lambda_\theta\}$ and $p_n(\theta) = \text{Prob}\{\mathbf{U}_n < \lambda_\theta\}$ depend on the payoff matrix θ only through the number λ_θ. There is thus no ambiguity in writing $p_s(\lambda)$ for $p_s(\theta)$ and $p_n(\lambda)$ for $p_n(\theta)$, with $\lambda = \lambda_\theta$. Consequently, using ρ to denote the ROC function, Eq. (84) yields

$$\text{Prob}\{\mathbf{U}_s > \mathbf{U}_n\} = \int_{-\infty}^{\infty} p_s(\lambda) d[1 - p_n(\lambda)]$$

$$= -\int_{-\infty}^{\infty} \rho[p_n(\lambda)] dp_n(\lambda)$$

$$= \int_{\infty}^{-\infty} \rho[p_n(\lambda)] dp_n(\lambda) .$$

Changing variables, from λ to $p_n(\lambda) = p$, we obtain finally

$$\text{Prob}\{\mathbf{U}_s > \mathbf{U}_n\} = \int_0^1 \rho(p)\, dp , \tag{85}$$

as asserted.

In the framework of this model, the area below the ROC curve appears as a reasonable measure of the detectability of the stimulus. In practice, it will often be the case that only a few points of the ROC curve have been determined experimentally. The evaluation of the area below the ROC curve may thus be prone to serious errors. One way out of this difficulty is to make specific assumptions concerning the distributions of the random variables $\mathbf{U}_s$ and $\mathbf{U}_n$. Such assumptions would determine (up to the values of a couple of parameters) the exact analytical form of the ROC curve. If the assumptions are valid, a few suitably placed points of the ROC curve will suffice to estimate the parameters of the ROC curve experimentally, and the area under the ROC curve can then be evaluated by integration.

8.3. Remarks

One may be suspicious of such a method and object that the estimated value of the area will be model bound. This objection is not as strong as it may appear. Notice in this connection that Eq. (85) was obtained without making any assumption regarding the distribution of the random variables $\mathbf{U}_s$ and $\mathbf{U}_n$. In fact, the shape of these distributions is arbitrary. For instance, let us assume that Eqs. (82), (83), and (85) hold for some random variables $\mathbf{U}_s$, $\mathbf{U}_n$. For any strictly increasing continuous function g, we have

$$p_s(\theta) = \text{Prob}\{g(\mathbf{U}_s) > g(\lambda_\theta)\} = \text{Prob}\{\mathbf{U}'_s > \lambda'_\theta\}$$

and

$$p_n(\theta) = \text{Prob}\{g(\mathbf{U}_n) > g(\lambda_\theta)\} = \text{Prob}\{\mathbf{U}'_n > \lambda'_\theta\} ,$$

with $\mathbf{U}'_s = g(\mathbf{U}_s)$ and $\mathbf{U}'_n = g(\mathbf{U}_n)$ and $\lambda'_\theta = g(\lambda_\theta)$. It is clear that the representation of the response probabilities provided by the random variables $\mathbf{U}'_s$ and $\mathbf{U}'_n$ is equivalent to that obtained with $\mathbf{U}_s$ and $\mathbf{U}_n$. In particular, the predicted ROC curve is not changed by the transformation.

Later on in this section, we will make precise hypotheses regarding the distributions of the random variables entering into Eqs. (82), (83), and (85). When evaluating these hypotheses, the reader should keep in mind the above remark pointing out the relative arbitrariness of the distributions of $\mathbf{U}_s$ and $\mathbf{U}_n$.

It must be realized that the random variable model discussed here does not necessarily describe a rational strategy. Depending on how optimality is defined and on more specific assumptions on the random variables $\mathbf{U}_s$ and $\mathbf{U}_n$, the decision rule embodied in Eqs. (82) and (83) may or may not be optimal.

To illustrate this point, let π be the probability of a stimulus trial and suppose that for some criterion value λ_o

$$\text{Prob}\{\mathbf{U}_n > \lambda_o\}(1 - \pi) > \text{Prob}\{\mathbf{U}_s > \lambda_o\}\pi . \quad (86)$$

A special case of this assumption is pictured in Figure 1.18, which is by no means unrealistic. Nevertheless, it leads to a somewhat undesirable conclusion. Namely, when reacting to an activation value exceeding λ_o, the subject reports a detection, even though the likelihood of a stimulus trial is then smaller than that of a noise trial. Such a conclusion easily follows from the above inequality. Indeed, denoting by S, as before, the stimulation at a given trial (thus $S = s$ or $S = n$), Eq. (86) holds if and only if (iff) successively

$$\text{Prob}\{\mathbf{U}_S > \lambda_o | S = n\}\text{Prob}\{S = n\} >$$
$$\text{Prob}\{\mathbf{U}_S > \lambda_o | S = s\}\text{Prob}\{S = s\}$$

iff

$$\text{Prob}\{S = n, \mathbf{U}_S > \lambda_o\}/\text{Prob}\{\mathbf{U}_S > \lambda_o\} >$$
$$\text{Prob}\{S = s, \mathbf{U}_S > \lambda_o\}/\text{Prob}\{\mathbf{U}_S > \lambda_o\}$$

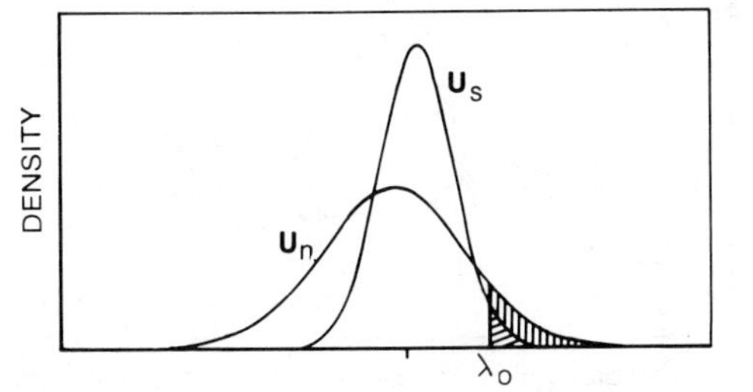

Figure 1.18. Two normal densities of $\mathbf{U}_s$ and $\mathbf{U}_n$ for which Eq. (86) holds, with $\pi = 1 - \pi = .5$.

iff

$$\text{Prob}\{S = n | \mathbf{U}_S > \lambda_o\} > \text{Prob}\{S = s | \mathbf{U}_S > \lambda_o\} .$$

In words, this last inequality means that the conditional probability of a noise trial, when observing the event $\mathbf{U}_S > \lambda_o$, is greater than that of a stimulus trial. However, according to the model, the subject will report a detection. A definition of optimality suggested by that argument would require that such a situation does not arise; that is,

$$\text{Prob}\{\mathbf{U}_s > \lambda\}\pi \geqslant \text{Prob}\{\mathbf{U}_n > \lambda\}(1 - \pi) ,$$

for all criterion values λ. This definition does not take into account the monetary gains or losses resulting from the strategy. Other definitions of optimality are conceivable, one of which will be considered shortly.

8.4. Axioms of the Random Variable Model

For convenient reference, the assumptions of the model are summarized in the following three axioms.

Axiom SD1. To each stimulus s and noise n correspond independent random variables, respectively, $\mathbf{U}_s$ and $\mathbf{U}_n$. The presentation of s evokes a sample value of the random variable $\mathbf{U}_s$. Similarly, the presentation of n evokes a sample value of the random variable $\mathbf{U}_n$.

Axiom SD2. For any payoff matrix $\theta \in \Theta$, the hit and false alarm probabilities satisfy the equation for $S = s,n$,

$$p_S(\theta) = \text{Prob}\{\mathbf{U}_S > \lambda_\theta\} .$$

Occasionally, we shall also assume:

Axiom SD3. The random variables $\mathbf{U}_s$ and $\mathbf{U}_n$ have densities

$$f_s \text{ and } f_n, \text{ with } f_n > 0 .$$

8.5. ROC Analysis and Likelihood Radio

The slope of the ROC curve is susceptible to an interesting interpretation. Let us assume that Axioms SD1–SD3 hold. Thus the random variables $\mathbf{U}_s$ and $\mathbf{U}_n$ have densities f_s and f_n, respectively, with $f_n > 0$. Writing, as before, ρ for the ROC function, we have successively

$$d\rho[p_n(\theta)]/dp_n(\theta) = \frac{d\text{Prob}\{\mathbf{U}_s > \lambda_\theta\}}{d\text{Prob}\{\mathbf{U}_n > \lambda_n\}}$$

$$= \frac{d[1 - \text{Prob}\{\mathbf{U}_s \leqslant \lambda_\theta\}]}{d[1 - \text{Prob}\{\mathbf{U}_n \leqslant \lambda_\theta\}]}$$

$$= \frac{-f_s(\lambda_\theta)}{-f_n(\lambda_\theta)}$$

$$= \frac{f_s(\lambda_\theta)}{f_n(\lambda_\theta)} . \quad (87)$$

In other terms, the slope of the ROC curve evaluated at the point $p_n(\theta)$ is equal to the ratio of the densities at that point.

Notice for further reference the monotonicity relation between the ratio $f_s(\lambda_\theta)/f_n(\lambda_\theta)$ and the slope of the ROC curve. Since as a consequence of Eq. (83), λ_θ decreases as $p_n(\theta)$ increases, a decrease in the slope of the ROC function in some interval corresponds to an increase in the ratio $f_s(\lambda_\theta)/f_n(\lambda_\theta)$, in the corresponding interval of the variable λ_θ. Typical data strongly support the assumption of concave ROC functions—that is, ROC functions with nonincreasing slopes. This suggests that the ratio $f_s(\lambda)/f_n(\lambda)$ should be an increasing function of λ. We shall go back to this point.

In statistical decision theory, a ratio of densities, such as the one appearing in Eq. (87), is often called a *likelihood ratio.* In fact, with a slight strengthening of our assumptions, the random variable model discussed here is consistent with a fundamental rule used in statistical decision theory. To the Axioms SD1–SD3, we shall add the following:

Axiom SD4. The likelihood ratio

$$l(x) = f_s(x)/f_n(x)$$

is a strictly increasing function of x.

One implication of assumptions SD1–SD4 has been indicated above: the slope of the ROC curve must be strictly decreasing. (That is, in terms of the definition in Section 7.4.1, the ROC function must be strictly concave.) Another consequence is of interest, since it suggests a drastically different interpretation of the model. By Axiom SD4, the likelihood function l is strictly increasing, which implies (see Section 8.3)

$$\begin{aligned} p_s(\theta) &= \text{Prob}\{\mathbf{U}_s > \lambda_\theta\} \\ &= \text{Prob}\{l(\mathbf{U}_s) > l(\lambda_\theta)\} \\ &= \text{Prob}\{f_s(\mathbf{U}_s)/f_n(\mathbf{U}_s) > l(\lambda_\theta)\} . \end{aligned}$$

By a similar argument, we also obtain

$$p_n(\theta) = \text{Prob}\{f_s(\mathbf{U}_n)/f_n(\mathbf{U}_n) > l(\lambda_\theta)\} .$$

The last two equations prompt a comparison of the subject's strategy with that of a statistician engaged in a decision task and applying an optimal decision procedure. The successive steps of the procedure are reviewed in Figure 1.19, which is self-explanatory. The statistician receiving a signal of value x must decide in some optimal fashion whether this signal is a sample of $\mathbf{U}_s$ or a sample of $\mathbf{U}_n$. We will suppose that the decision procedure maximizes the expected value of the gain, as determined by the payoff matrix θ. Let $\gamma(\theta)_{ss}$ and $\gamma(\theta)_{nn}$ be the gains resulting from a hit and a correct rejection, respectively; let $\gamma(\theta)_{ns}$ and $\gamma(\theta)_{sn}$ be the costs attached to a false alarm and a miss. Let π be the probability that a stimulus is presented on any trial. The expected value $G(\theta,\pi)$ of the gain is easily computed from the tree diagram in Figure 1.20, which displays the possible paths and their probabilities. We obtain:

$$\begin{aligned} G(\theta,\pi) = \pi\{p_s(\theta)\gamma_{ss}(\theta) - [1 - p_s(\theta)]\gamma_{ns}(\theta)\} \\ + (1 - \pi)\{[1 - p_n(\theta)]\gamma_{nn}(\theta) - p_n(\theta)\gamma_{sn}(\theta)\} , \end{aligned}$$

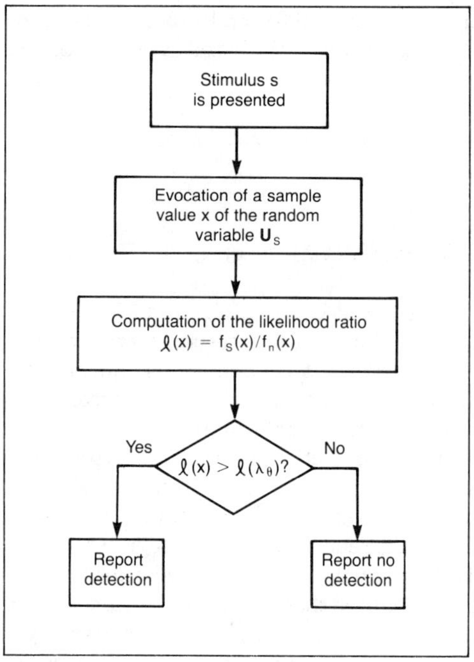

Figure 1.19. Successive stages of the decision process elicited by the presentation of the stimulus, in case of the likelihood ratio model. The diagram is identical in the case of the presentation of the noise n, except that $\mathbf{U}_s$ is replaced by $\mathbf{U}_n$.

which we rewrite

$$G(\theta,\pi) = \pi[\gamma_{ss}(\theta) + \gamma_{ns}(\theta)][p_s(\theta) - p_n(\theta)\beta_\theta] , \quad (88)$$

with

$$\beta_\theta = (1 - \pi)[\gamma_{sn}(\theta) + \gamma_{nn}(\theta)]/\pi[\gamma_{ss}(\theta) + \gamma_{ns}(\theta)] . \quad (89)$$

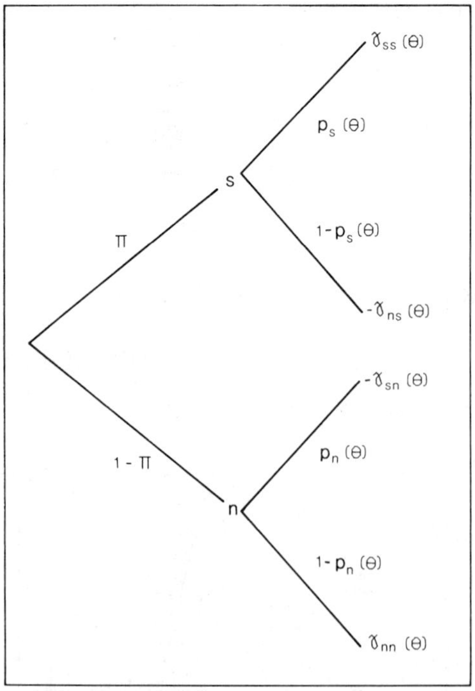

Figure 1.20. Tree diagram of the possible paths in the yes-no paradigm with their probabilities and their outcomes. See text for the definition of symbols.

The statistician decision procedure concerns the response probabilities $p_s(\theta)$ and $p_n(\theta)$, which can be manipulated via the quantity λ_θ in the equations

$$p_s(\theta) = \text{Prob}\{\mathbf{U}_s > \lambda_\theta\}$$

and

$$p_n(\theta) = \text{Prob}\{\mathbf{U}_n > \lambda_\theta\} .$$

Since $\pi[\gamma_{ss}(\theta) + \gamma_{ns}(\theta)]$ is constant, a value of λ_θ maximizes the expected gains $G(\theta,\pi)$ in Eq. (88) iff it maximizes

$$\text{Prob}\{\mathbf{U}_s > \lambda_\theta\} - \text{Prob}\{\mathbf{U}_n > \lambda_\theta\}\beta_\theta .$$

It follows that the required value of λ_θ must satisfy

$$f_s(\lambda_\theta) - f_n(\lambda_\theta)\beta_\theta = 0 ,$$

that is

$$l(\lambda_\theta) = \frac{f_s(\lambda_\theta)}{f_n(\lambda_\theta)} = \beta_\theta .$$

We conclude that the subject strategy is optimal in the sense of a maximization of the expected gain if the response probabilities satisfy the two equations

$$p_s(\theta) = \text{Prob}\{\mathbf{U}_s > l^{-1}(\beta_\theta)\}$$

$$p_n(\theta) = \text{Prob}\{\mathbf{U}_n > l^{-1}(\beta_\theta)\} ,$$

with β_θ defined by Eq. (89).

If precise assumptions are made concerning the distributions of the random variables $\mathbf{U}_s$ and $\mathbf{U}_n$, it can then be checked whether the subject's strategy is optimal in the above sense, by evaluating the fit of the above equation to the data. This comparison of the subject's strategy with that of a statistician engaged in a decision-making task was discussed in some detail, since it is an inherent part of the common wisdom in this field. It must be clear, however, that the analysis of the data in terms of ROC curves is a useful device to disentangle sensory from cognitive components of the task, whether or not the subject's strategy happens to be optimal.

This analysis is also valuable, or at least relevant, in cases of experimental procedures or paradigms somewhat different from those envisaged so far in this section. Two examples are discussed in Sections 8.6 and 8.7.

8.6. ROC Analysis and the Forced-Choice Paradigm

In the two-alternative forced-choice (2AFC) paradigm, the subject's task is to decide on every trial which of two locations, or two intervals of time, contains the stimulus. Even though the effect on performance of guessing strategies is minimized in such paradigms, an ROC analysis will be useful. In particular, the connections between the predictions in the yes-no and the 2AFC paradigms are of interest.

For concreteness, we consider as before an auditory detection situation. On every trial, the subject is presented with two successive intervals of time, of equal duration, one of which containing the stimulus (a click, say) embedded in noise, the other containing only the noise. There are thus two types of trials, depending on whether the stimulus was in the first or the second interval. We shall denote these two cases by (s,n) and (n,s), respectively. Let $p_{1,sn}$ and $p_{2,ns}$ be the corresponding probabilities of a correct response, and let $p_{2,sn}$ and $p_{1,ns}$ be the error probabilities. By design, we must have

$$p_{1,sn} + p_{2,sn} = 1$$

and

$$p_{1,ns} + p_{2,ns} = 1 ,$$

since the subject is forced to choose one of the two intervals on every trial. For the time being, let us suppose that the two probabilities of a correct response are equal,

$$p_{1,sn} = p_{2,ns} .$$

This assumption, which is not always realistic and can be rejected for some data, will be relaxed in a moment. From a purely sensory viewpoint, the 2AFC paradigm differs but little from the yes-no paradigm, and it makes sense to apply the same theoretical analysis. Let us assume that

$$p_{1,sn} = \text{Prob}\{\mathbf{U}_s > \mathbf{U}_n\} = p_{2,ns} , \qquad (90)$$

in which $\mathbf{U}_s$ and $\mathbf{U}_n$ are independent random variables with the same interpretations as in Section 8.2. If we assume that $\mathbf{U}_s$ and $\mathbf{U}_n$ are continuous, we have

$$\text{Prob}\{\mathbf{U}_s = \mathbf{U}_n\} = 0 ,$$

which implies for the probabilities of errors,

$$p_{2,sn} = 1 - p_{1,sn} = \text{Prob}\{\mathbf{U}_n > \mathbf{U}_s\} = p_{1,ns} .$$

The idea is that each of the two intervals provides a sample of one of the random variables $\mathbf{U}_s$ and $\mathbf{U}_n$, and the subject's response is based on a comparison of these samples. In the case of an (s,n) trial, for instance, if x_1 and x_2 are sample values of $\mathbf{U}_s$ and $\mathbf{U}_n$, respectively, the subject will choose interval 1 (the correct one) if $x_1 > x_2$.

Notice that, under Axiom SD4, we have

$$\text{Prob}\{\mathbf{U}_s > \mathbf{U}_n\} = \text{Prob}\{f_s(\mathbf{U}_s)/f_n(\mathbf{U}_s) > f_s(\mathbf{U}_n)/f_n(\mathbf{U}_n)\} .$$

This means that the above interpretation of the subject's decision process as based on a comparison of samples of $\mathbf{U}_s$ and $\mathbf{U}_n$ is equivalent to another, in which the subject would behave as a statistician and compare likelihood ratios.

In any event, the conclusion to be derived from Eqs. (85) and (90) is that the probability of a correct response in the 2AFC paradigm, under the assumption that $p_{1,sn} = p_{2,ns}$, is equal to the area under the ROC curve in the corresponding yes-no paradigm.

As indicated, the assumption that $p_{1,sn} = p_{2,sn}$ may be unrealistic. We shall briefly examine here the possibility that the subject may be biased toward one of the two intervals. A systematic way of inducing such bias would be to assign different probabilities to the events (s,n) and (n,s). Our random variable model for the 2AFC paradigm can be generalized as follows.

Let Θ be a set of bias-inducing conditions; let $p_{1,sn}(\theta)$ and $p_{1,ns}(\theta)$ be the two probabilities of choosing the first interval, in condition θ, for the two cases (s,n) and (n,s). We assume that the effect of a given condition $\theta \in \Theta$ is to transform the distribution of the random variable corresponding to the second interval. Specifically, we assume that the following two equations hold:

$$p_{1,sn}(\theta) = \text{Prob}\{\mathbf{U}_s > g_\theta(\mathbf{U}_n)\}$$

$$p_{1,ns}(\theta) = \text{Prob}\{\mathbf{U}_n > g_\theta(\mathbf{U}_s)\} ,$$

where g_θ is a strictly increasing, continuous function. With obvious notation, the two remaining probabilities are computed from the equations

$$p_{1,sn}(\theta) + p_{2,sn}(\theta) = 1 ,$$

$$p_{1,ns}(\theta) + p_{2,ns}(\theta) = 1 ,$$

which are inherent to the 2AFC paradigm. Let us suppose for a moment that the set of points

$$[p_{1,ns}(\theta), p_{1,sn}(\theta)] ,$$

generated by varying $\theta \in \Theta$, is an ROC curve. Under fairly general properties on the set of transformations $\{g_\theta | \theta \in \Theta\}$, it follows then that this ROC curve must be symmetric with respect to the negative diagonal of the unit square (see Figure 1.21). One such property is that if g_θ is a strictly increasing transformation, then there must be some condition $\theta' \in \Theta$ corresponding to the "opposite" transformation, $g_\theta^{-1} = g_{\theta'}$. Indeed, we have then

$$1 - p_{1,sn}(\theta) = \text{Prob}\{g_\theta(\mathbf{U}_n) > \mathbf{U}_s\}$$

$$= \text{Prob}\{\mathbf{U}_n > g_\theta^{-1}(\mathbf{U}_s)\}$$

$$= \text{Prob}\{\mathbf{U}_n > g_{\theta'}(\mathbf{U}_s)\}$$

$$= p_{1,ns}(\theta') ,$$

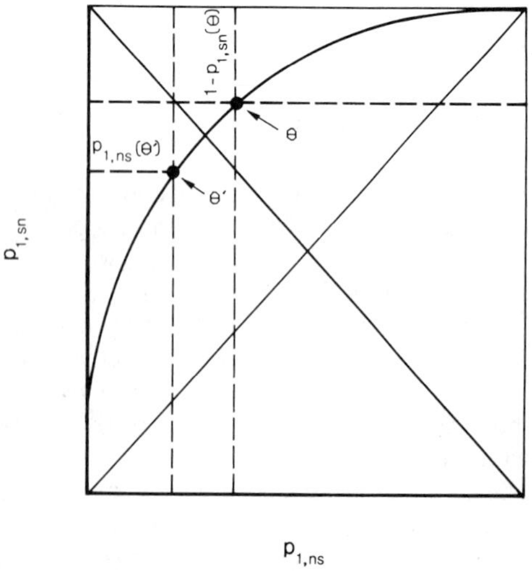

Figure 1.21. Hypothetical ROC curve symmetric with respect to the negative diagonal of the unit square, in the 2AFC paradigm. We have $p_{1,ns}(\theta') = 1 - p_{1,sn}(\theta)$.

and

$$p_{1,sn}(\theta') = \text{Prob}\{\mathbf{U}_s > g_{\theta'}(\mathbf{U}_n)\}$$

$$= \text{Prob}\{\mathbf{U}_s > g_\theta^{-1}(\mathbf{U}_n)\}$$

$$= \text{Prob}\{g_\theta(\mathbf{U}_s) > \mathbf{U}_n\}$$

$$= 1 - p_{1,ns}(\theta) .$$

The two equations,

$$1 - p_{1,sn}(\theta) = p_{1,ns}(\theta') ,$$

$$p_{1,sn}(\theta') = 1 - p_{1,ns}(\theta)$$

express the symmetry property of the ROC curve mentioned above. This situation is illustrated in Figure 1.21.

8.7. ROC Analysis of Rating-Scale Data

In the same experimental situation, consider a procedure in which, rather than giving a yes-no detection response on every trial, the subject is required to quantify the certainty that the stimulus was presented. Suppose, for example, that a six-category rating scale is used, ranging from 0 (certainty that the stimulus was not presented) to 5 (certainty that the stimulus was presented). Some hypothetical but plausible data are given in Table 1.3. Let $\mathbf{R}_s$ and $\mathbf{R}_n$ be two random variables corresponding to the ratings in the two types of trials. (For example, Prob$\{\mathbf{R}_s = 3\}$ is the probability of observing a rating of 3 on a trial when the stimulus was presented.) Since the experimental situation is unchanged except for the subject's responses, it makes sense to suppose that the same underlying activation random variables $\mathbf{U}_s$ and $\mathbf{U}_n$ are responsible for the ratings. The following model seems reasonable: an observed rating will exceed a value i ($i = 0, \ldots, 4$) only if the activation random variable exceeds a criterion λ_i, the value of which depends on the rating value considered. In symbols,

$$\text{Prob}\{\mathbf{R}_s > i\} = \text{Prob}\{\mathbf{U}_s > \lambda_i\} ,$$

$$\text{Prob}\{\mathbf{R}_n > i\} = \text{Prob}\{\mathbf{U}_n > \lambda_i\} .$$

Observe that the right members of these two equations strongly resemble those in Axiom SD2 of the yes-no procedure. This suggests an ROC analysis of the data. It is as if each possible value of the rating (with the exception of the maximal one) would implicitly define a particular payoff matrix and a recoding of the rating data into two yes-no classes. In Table 1.3, the value $i = 3$ leads to the recoding

write "yes" if $i = 4, 5$
write "no" if $i = 1, 2, 3,$

Table 1.3. Hypothetical Rating Data in a Signal Detection Task

	Rating Value					
	0	1	2	3	4	5
Noise trials	.10	.15	.35	.20	.15	.05
Stimulus trials	.05	.10	.30	.20	.25	.10

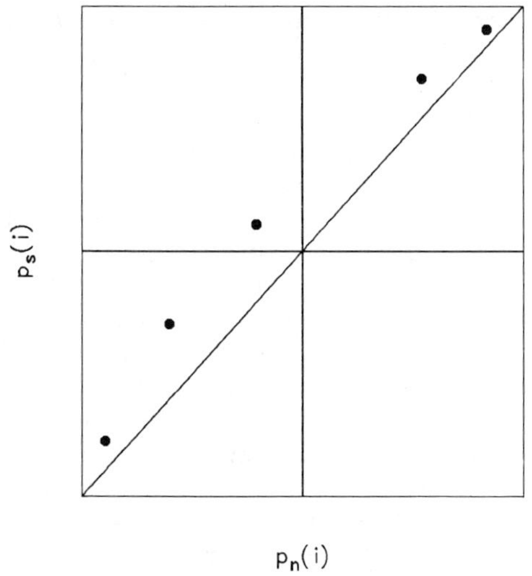

Figure 1.22. ROC graph obtained for the rating scale data.

with

proportion of false alarms	.05 + .15 = .20	
proportion of hits	.10 + .25 = .35.	

The results of this recoding for Table 1.3 are:

	Proportion of Ratings Exceeding i				
i	0	1	2	3	4
n	.90	.75	.40	.20	.05
s	.95	.85	.55	.35	.10

The corresponding ROC graph is displayed in Figure 1.22. In general, the probabilities of hits and false alarms corresponding to each rating value i up to (but not including) the maximal one are given by the equations

$$p_s(i) = \text{Prob}\{\mathbf{R}_s > i\}$$

$$p_n(i) = \text{Prob}\{\mathbf{R}_n > i\} ,$$

with the ROC function $p_n(i) \mapsto p_s(i)$.

An obvious advantage of this method is its efficiency. The subject is required to make more sophisticated responses than in the yes-no procedure, which results in a substantial economy in the collection of data. This was illustrated in our example, in which only one condition, rather than five, had to be run to obtain a five-point ROC graph.

On the negative side, it must be noted that the points of an experimental ROC graph are not independent, which may create difficulties in fitting and evaluating a model.

Finally, data collected by the rating-scale procedure, but analyzed by methods different from those discussed here, may provide a sharp test of some models. We return to this point in Section 8.10.

8.8. Gaussian Assumption

In principle, an ROC analysis is feasible without making any assumptions on the distributions of the random variables $\mathbf{U}_s$ and $\mathbf{U}_n$ (cf. Bramber, 1975). However, the application is greatly facilitated if such assumptions are made. We discuss here the case of Gaussian distributions.

8.8.1. Yes-No Paradigm. In the yes-no paradigm with a payoff matrix θ, we shall assume that

$$p_s(\theta) = \text{Prob}\{\mathbf{U}_s > \lambda_\theta\} = \Phi\left(\frac{\mu_s - \lambda_\theta}{\sigma_s}\right) , \tag{91}$$

$$p_n(\theta) = \text{Prob}\{\mathbf{U}_n > \lambda_\theta\} = \Phi\left(\frac{\mu_n - \lambda_\theta}{\sigma_n}\right) , \tag{92}$$

in which our notations are as in Section 8.2, μ_s, μ_n, and σ_s, σ_n denote the means and standard deviations of the random variables $\mathbf{U}_s$ and $\mathbf{U}_n$, and Φ is the distribution function of a standard normal random variable, that is,

$$\Phi(z) = \frac{1}{\sqrt{2\pi}} \int_{-\infty}^{z} e^{-x^2/2} dx .$$

From Eqs. (91) and (92), it is apparent that the ROC curve is determined by four parameters: the means and the standard deviations of the random variables $\mathbf{U}_s$ and $\mathbf{U}_n$. (In fact, we shall see that only two parameters are necessary.) From a practical viewpoint it will be convenient to rewrite Eqs. (91) and (92) in terms of the so-called z-scores. With

$$z_s(\theta) = \Phi^{-1}[p_s(\theta)] ,$$

$$z_n(\theta) = \Phi^{-1}[p_n(\theta)] ,$$

and dropping θ in the notations, we obtain

$$z_s = \frac{\mu_s - \lambda}{\sigma_s}$$

$$z_n = \frac{\mu_n - \lambda}{\sigma_n} .$$

Eliminating λ in these equations and solving for z_s, yields

$$z_s = z_n\sigma_n/\sigma_s + \frac{\mu_s - \mu_n}{\sigma_s} . \tag{93}$$

In other terms, when the hit and false alarm probabilities are transformed into z-scores, the ROC curve is transformed into a straight line with slope σ_n/σ_s and intercept $(\mu_s - \mu_n)/\sigma_s$. Using linear regression, these two parameters can be estimated from the response frequencies of the data. Notice that the ROC curve only specifies two of the four parameters μ_s, μ_n, σ_s, and σ_n. For example, we can assume without loss of generality, that $\mu_n = 0$ and $\sigma_n = 1$. The area under the ROC curve can be computed from the equations

$$\text{Prob}\{\mathbf{U}_s > \mathbf{U}_n\} = \text{Prob}\{\mathbf{U}_s - \mathbf{U}_n > 0\}$$

$$= \Phi\left[\frac{\mu_s - \mu_n}{(\sigma_s^2 + \sigma_n^2)^{1/2}}\right] . \tag{94}$$

It is easy to show that this model satisfies Axiom SD4 only if $\sigma_s = \sigma_n$. (If we equate the two densities of $\mathbf{U}_s$ and $\mathbf{U}_n$ and take logarithms, a quadratic equation obtains, which has a unique solution only if $\sigma_s = \sigma_n$.) We shall investigate this particular case in some detail.

8.8.2. Equal Variance Assumption. Suppose that

$$\sigma_s = \sigma_n = 1 .$$

Equation (93), which specifies the transformed ROC curve, becomes

$$z_s = z_n + (\mu_s - \mu_n)$$

Thus in the special case where $\mathbf{U}_s$ and $\mathbf{U}_n$ are independent Gaussian random variables with equal variance, the transformed ROC curves are parallel straight lines with a slope equal to 1. Only one parameter remains in the model, which is the difference $\mu_s - \mu_n$. When this model is used, a standard measure of the detectability of the stimulus is

$$d' = (\mu_s - \mu_n)/\sqrt{2} .$$

This choice has some intuitive appeal, since d' is proportional to the difference between the means of the two activation distributions. Moreover, d' is closely related to the other measure, the area under the ROC curve. Indeed, from Eq. (94) we have

$$\mathrm{Prob}\{\mathbf{U}_s > \mathbf{U}_n\} = \Phi(d') .$$

Occasionally, it is convenient to plot the empirical ROC graphs and the theoretical ROC curves on "double-probability" paper (a two-dimensional Cartesian representation in which the coordinates are in units of the normal integral; see Figure 1.23).

8.9. Threshold Theory

A rather different interpretation of an ROC analysis of yes-no detection data is possible, in which the basic, underlying notions are not activation random variables but detection states. A number of such models have been proposed, which differ in particular by the number of (unobservable) states postulated or by the exact relation linking the states to the response probabilities or other observable quantities (e.g., response latencies, ratings). We shall discuss a simple example, due to Luce (1960, 1963a, 1963b).

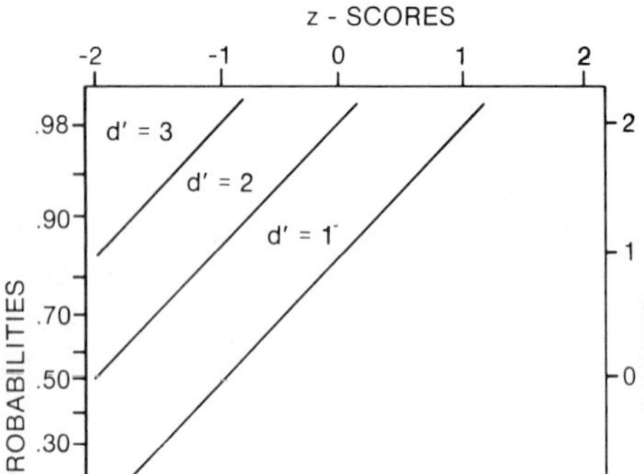

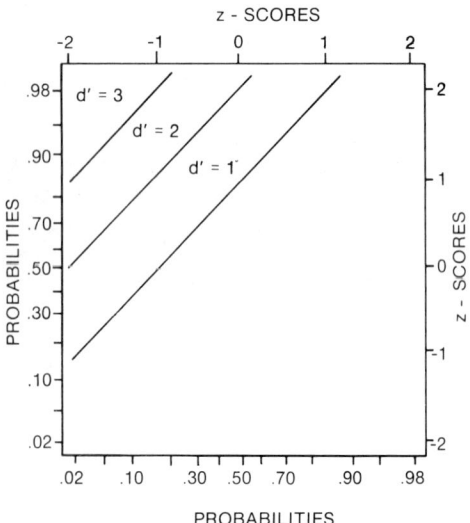

Figure 1.23. In the equal variance case, three ROC curves plotted on "double probability" paper, corresponding to the cases $d' = 1, 2, 3$.

We will assume that the presentation of the stimulus or the noise elicits one of two sensory states in the subject: either a neural threshold has been exceeded or it has not. The event that the threshold is exceeded may lead to a "yes" response (the subject reports a detection) but not necessarily so. We also assume that a given payoff matrix θ may induce one of two opposite response strategies: (1) a *conservative strategy*, in which the subject never says "yes" when the threshold has not been exceeded; when the threshold has been exceeded, the subject only says "yes" with a probability β_θ, depending on the payoff matrix, and (2) a guessing strategy, in which the subject always says "yes" when the threshold has been exceeded; when the threshold has not been exceeded, the subject says "yes" with a probability α_θ, depending on the payoff matrix. This means that the collection Θ of payoff matrices is partitioned into two classes: (1) Θ_c, the set of payoff matrices inducing a conservative strategy, and (2) Θ_g, the set of payoff matrices inducing a guessing strategy. The event that the threshold has been exceeded will be denoted $D = 1$; the complementary event will be denoted $D = 0$. Thus in the framework of a probabilistic model, D is a random variable taking values 0,1. As before, the letter S denotes the stimulation; we have two cases: $S = s$ (the stimulus is presented) and $S = n$ (only the noise is presented). The probability that the stimulation determines a neural event exceeding the threshold ($D = 1$) only depends on S and will be denoted $q(S)$. Notice that we have introduced four numerical parameters: two for the response probabilities, β_θ and α_θ, and two for the probabilities of the states, $q(s)$ and $q(n)$. In the framework of an ROC analysis, however, two of these parameters will be eliminated in the equations, leaving only $q(s)$ and $q(n)$ to be estimated from the data. Finally, we denote by Y_θ and N_θ the two events of a "yes" and a "no" response, respectively.

8.9.1. Axioms for the Threshold Theory. We provide a compact summary of these assumptions in the form of two axioms.

State Axiom T1.

$$\mathrm{Prob}\{D = 1|S\} = q(S) , \qquad \text{for } S = s, n .$$

(The probability that the threshold is exceeded is equal to $q(s)$ if the stimulus is presented and to $q(n)$ if the noise is presented, these probabilities being independent of the payoff matrix.)

Response Axiom T2. For any payoff matrix θ,

$$\mathrm{Prob}\{Y_\theta|S,D\} = \begin{cases} (1 - D)\alpha_\theta + D & \text{if } \theta \in \Theta_g, \\ \beta_\theta D & \text{if } \theta \in \Theta_c, \end{cases}$$

independent of S.

(The probability of a "yes" response to a stimulation only depends on the payoff matrix θ and whether the threshold has been exceeded. If θ is in Θ_g, it is equal to 1 or α_θ, depending on whether $D = 1$ or $D = 0$, respectively. If θ is in Θ_c, this probability is equal β_θ or 0, again depending on whether $D = 1$ or $D = 0$.)

8.9.2. Form of the ROC Curve. As shown by a simple calculation, these axioms predict an ROC curve made of two

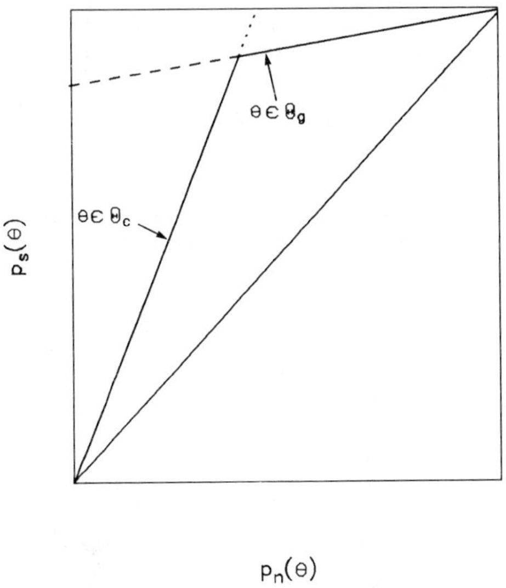

Figure 1.24. An example of an ROC curve in the two-state threshold model. The upper limb of the curve corresponds to Eq. (96), $\theta \in \Theta_g$; the lower limb corresponds to Eq. (97), $\theta \in \Theta_c$.

segments of a straight line (see Figure 1.24). The upper limb describes the guessing strategy and contains the corner (1,1) of the unit square. The points of that segment are generated by varying θ in Θ_g. The lower limb describes the conservative strategy, contains the point (0,0), and is generated by varying θ in Θ_c. Let us demonstrate this.

With our usual notations, $p_s(\theta)$ and $p_n(\theta)$ for the two probabilities of a "yes" response, we have

$$\begin{aligned} p_S(\theta) &= \text{Prob}\{Y_\theta|S\} \\ &= \text{Prob}\{Y_\theta|D = 1,S\}\ \text{Prob}\{D = 1|S\} \\ &\quad + \text{Prob}\{Y_\theta|D = 0,S\}\ \text{Prob}\{D = 0|S\}\ . \end{aligned}$$

Using Axiom T1, this yields

$$\begin{aligned} p_S(\theta) = \text{Prob}\{Y_\theta|D = 1,S\}q(S) + \\ \text{Prob}\{Y_\theta|D = 0\}[1 - q(S)]\ . \end{aligned} \tag{95}$$

8.9.2.1. ***Case $\theta \in \Theta_g$.*** Using Axiom T2, Eq. (95) specializes into

$$p_s(\theta) = q(s) + \alpha_\theta[1 - q(s)]\ ,$$

$$p_n(\theta) = q(n) + \alpha_\theta[1 - q(n)]\ .$$

Eliminating α_θ in these two equations, dropping θ in the notations, and solving for p_s, we obtain

$$\begin{aligned} p_s = p_n[1 - q(s)]/[1 - q(n)] \\ + [q(s) - q(n)]/[1 - q(n)]\ , \end{aligned} \tag{96}$$

a linear function containing the point (1,1). Thus as θ varies in Θ_g, the point of the ROC moves along a segment of a straight line specified by Eq. (96). Notice that in this case, we have $q(n) \leqslant p_n$.

8.9.2.2. ***Case $\theta \in \Theta_c$.*** From Eq. (95) and Axiom T2, we obtain

$$p_s(\theta) = \beta_\theta q(s)\ ,$$

$$p_n(\theta) = \beta_\theta q(n)\ .$$

Eliminating β_θ and dropping θ in the notation yields

$$p_s = p_n q(s)/q(n)\ , \tag{97}$$

the equation of a straight line going through the origin. Here we have $p_n \leqslant q(n)$.

Equations (96) and (97) together specify the class of ROC curves predicted by Luce's two-state threshold theory. This prediction has been shown to hold reasonably well for some data (cf. Luce, 1963a). In other cases, however, the theory is not so successful. For example, Nachmias and Steinman (1963) have shown that in some empirical situations the probability $q(n)$ that the threshold is exceeded on noise trials (as estimated from the data) has to vary with signal strength. Such a fact is obviously difficult to accommodate in the framework of the two-state threshold theory.

8.10. Rating Data and the Threshold Theory

It is natural to inquire about the predictions of the threshold theory concerning data obtained by the rating-scale procedure. Some authors have been quick to point out that rating-scale data characteristically favor an ROC function with a smooth curvature, a fact which may appear to be inconsistent with the two segments of straight lines predicted by the threshold theory (Broadbent & Gregory, 1963; Nachmias & Steinman, 1963; Swets, 1961; Watson, Rilling, & Bourbon, 1964). Actually, as stated above and in the cited papers of Luce, the theory is not relevant to rating data, and no inferences can legitimately be made in this respect. (The only "response axiom" is T2, which concerns itself specifically with the response probabilities in the yes-no paradigm.) If rating-scale data are to be predicted by the theory, a new axiom is required, and there are various candidates, one of which is briefly considered here. Our reasons for including such discussion in this chapter are twofold: (1) to show by a counterexample that the argument against the two-state theory based on the curvature of the ROC curve implied by the data does not apply and (2) to demonstrate the general vulnerability of two-state theories to a particular type of analysis of the data.

We make the reasonable assumption that the rating given by the subject on a trial only depends on the sensory state evoked by the stimulation. However, the exact value of the rating is not determined by the state. To each of the two sensory states, corresponding to the events $D = 1, D = 0$, corresponds a rating random variable, with distribution function G_1, G_0, respectively. In other terms, with $\mathbf{R}_s$ and $\mathbf{R}_n$ as in Eq. (88), we have the following axiom:

Axiom T3. For $S = s, n$ and $D = 0, 1$,

$$\text{Prob}\{\mathbf{R}_S \leqslant i|D\} = G_D(i)\ ,$$

independent of S.

Let us derive the prediction for the ROC curve. For $S = s, n$, we have

$$\begin{aligned}\mathrm{Prob}\{\mathbf{R}_S \le i\} &= \mathrm{Prob}\{\mathbf{R}_S \le i \mid D = 1\}\mathrm{Prob}\{D = 1 \mid S\} \\ &\quad + \mathrm{Prob}\{\mathbf{R}_S \le i \mid D = 0\}\mathrm{Prob}\{D = 0 \mid S\} \\ &= G_1(i)q(S) + G_0(i)[1 - q(S)] \ .\end{aligned}$$

Specializing this equation for the two cases $S = s$ and $S = n$, we obtain

$$\mathrm{Prob}\{\mathbf{R}_s \le i\} = q(s)G_1(i) + [1 - q(s)]G_0(i) \ , \quad (98)$$

$$\mathrm{Prob}\{\mathbf{R}_n \le i\} = q(n)G_1(i) + [1 - q(n)]G_0(i) \ . \quad (99)$$

Eliminating $G_1(i)$ in these two equations and solving for $\mathrm{Prob}\{\mathbf{R}_s > i\}$ yields the following prediction for the ROC curve:

$$\begin{aligned}\mathrm{Prob}\{\mathbf{R}_s > i\} &= \mathrm{Prob}\{\mathbf{R}_n > i\}q(s)/q(n) \\ &\quad - [1 - G_0(i)][q(s) - q(n)]/q(n) \ . \quad (100)\end{aligned}$$

Notice that the ROC function defined by Eq. (100) depends on G_0. This implies that the corresponding ROC curve is not necessarily made of two segments of straight lines. In fact, a cursory investigation suggests that for an appropriate choice of the distribution function G_0, this equation may provide an acceptable fit to ROC data obtained from the rating-scale procedure.

On the other hand, it is doubtful that this particular version of the two-state theory is viable, since it makes extremely strong predictions concerning some other aspect of rating data. Using an argument of Falmagne (1968), Vorberg (Note 3) points out that the observed distributions of ratings should conform to a very constraining fixed-point property, stemming from the fact that, as indicated by Eqs. (98), (99), the distribution of ratings for any stimulus s (or noise n) is a "mixture" of the two latent distributions G_1 and G_0, in proportions $q(s)$ and $1 - q(s)$ (or $q(n)$ and $1 - q(n)$). This property is easily stated in words. Consider the empirical histograms of ratings obtained for s and n in some situation. Suppose that these two histograms "cross" each other at some value j (say, the proportions of ratings j are not significantly different). Then the histogram of ratings obtained for any other stimulus s' should have, except for statistical errors, the same proportion of ratings j (see Figure 1.25). The argument is as follows. Let k_s, k_n, g_0, and g_1 be the densities of $\mathbf{R}_s$, $\mathbf{R}_n$, G_0, and G_1, respectively. Thus these densities idealize the histograms mentioned above. Taking derivatives in Eqs. (98) and (99) gives

$$k_s(i) = q(s)g_1(i) + [1 - q(s)]g_0(i) \quad (101)$$

and

$$k_n(i) = q(n)g_1(i) + [1 - q(n)]g_0(i) \ . \quad (102)$$

Suppose that for some rating value j, we have

$$k_s(j) = k_n(j) \ .$$

From Eqs. (101) and (102) it follows necessarily that

$$g_1(j) = g_0(j) = k_1(j) = k_0(j) \ .$$

Consequently, if s' is some other stimulus, we must have

$$\begin{aligned}k_{s'}(j) &= q(s')g_1(j) + [1 - q(s')]g_0(j) \\ &= g_1(j) \\ &= k_s(j) = k_n(j) \ ,\end{aligned}$$

as predicted.

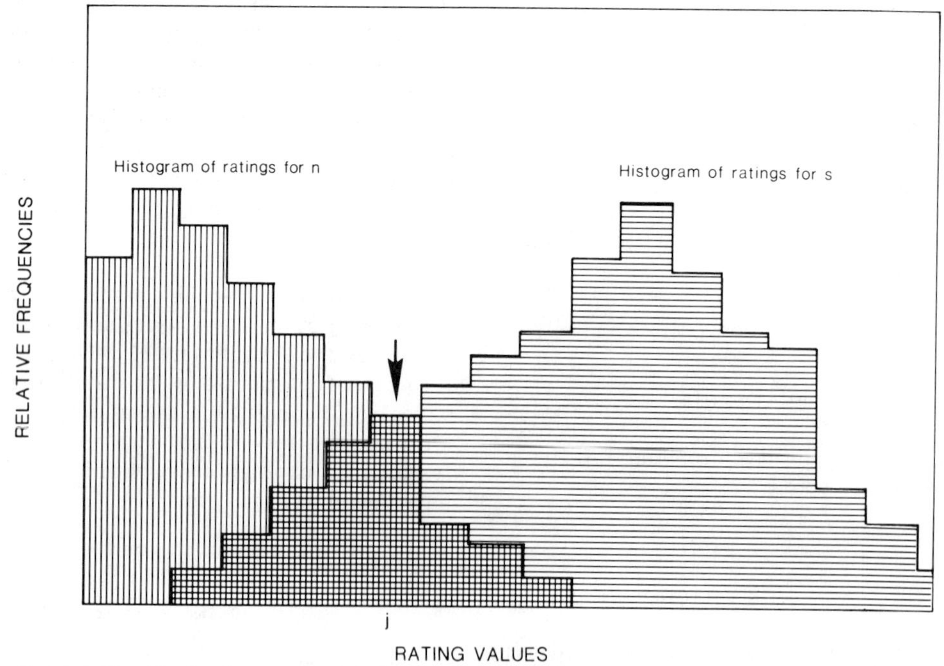

Figure 1.25. The fixed point property of the two-state threshold model applied to hypothetical rating scale data. The two histograms "cross" at the point indicated by the arrow, corresponding to rating j; any other histogram (say, of s') should go through the same point.

8.11. Key References

The notions of signal detection theory discussed in this section were selected, from a vast literature, as being the most central from the viewpoint of the analysis of psychophysical data. This theory, a very detailed account of which can be found in Green and Swets (1974), originated from an adaptation by W. P. Tanner and his coworkers at the University of Michigan, of a number of optimal procedures for the detection of signal in noise (Peterson, Birdsall, & Fox, 1954; van Meter & Middleton, 1954). In turn, these procedures are based on statistical decision theory (Neyman & Pearson, 1933; Wald, 1947, 1950). As emphasized by our presentation, in which the role of optimality is played down, signal detection theory has also a valid claim to the parentage of the law of comparative judgments (Thurstone 1927a, 1927b).

The applications of signal detection theory were first in psychophysics (e.g., Tanner & Swets, 1953, 1954a, 1954b) but were very quickly extended to other fields. The extraordinary success of the theory is evidenced by the number and variety of the papers in which it is used in some form or other. Today, applications can be found, for instance, in learning, memory, medical diagnosis, personality, reaction time, and skills (vigilance). A large sample of the early papers is collected in Swets (1964). Green and Swets (1974), the basic reference on this topic, contains a very extensive bibliography. As indicated in the text, various forms of the theory are obtained depending on specific assumptions made on the distributions of the random variables $\mathbf{U}_s$ and $\mathbf{U}_n$. A discussion of these special cases is provided in Egan (1975). A number of versions of the threshold theory are examined in Krantz (1969).

For applications of the basic notions of signal detection theory to other paradigms, see Sperling and Dosher, Chapter 2.

9. PSYCHOPHYSICS WITH SEVERAL VARIABLES OR CHANNELS

We consider here a number of paradigms and models designed to analyze how a subject integrates the information flowing from different sensory inputs. Examples of how this may arise have been encountered earlier in this chapter. For instance, in the yes-no paradigm discussed in Section 8, the subject had to detect a stimulus s embedded in a masking noise n. The subject's responses were regarded as resulting from some operation combining, on the sensory side, the effect of both s and n on the organism and, on the cognitive side, factors affecting decision making.

Another example, which this section treats in some detail, is offered by an auditory detection situation in which a stimulus is presented binaurally. The intensity in the two auditory channels may be manipulated independently, and the resulting performance may be investigated. This section is devoted to a general study of such situations, various cases of which will be given. Our purpose is not to provide an extensive survey. Rather, our selection of examples aims at familiarizing the reader with a collection of useful tools.

The word *channel* is of standard usage in psychophysics. As far as we know, however, no satisfying, generally accepted definition has been given for this term, even though several have been proposed. Depending on the context, *two channels* may mean that two sensory modalities are involved, or two neurophysiological locations, or two psychophysical variables, or even the same psychophysical variable but with different intensities. For the time being, we urge the reader to use the term intuitively and to check any ambitious drive toward rigor or consistency.

9.1. A General Model for Two-Channel Detection

9.1.1. Detection of Binaural Stimuli. In a version of the yes-no paradigm, the stimulus is a binaural, 1000-Hz tone (a,x) embedded in a masking noise (n,n'). The letters a, x denote the intensities of the stimulus in the left and right auditory channels, respectively; n and n' stand for the intensities of the noise in the two channels. As in the standard yes-no paradigm, the noise is presented alone on some proportion of the trials. To evaluate a possible response bias, the experimenter varies the payoff matrix across conditions. (See Section 8 for a discussion of payoff matrices.) Let us denote by $p_{ax}(\theta)$ and $p_{nn'}(\theta)$ the two probabilities of a "yes" response on a stimulus trial and on a noise trial, respectively, with a payoff matrix θ. (Our notation is slightly misleading. A more explicit but much heavier notation for these response probabilities would be $p_{ax,nn'}(\theta)$, $p_{oo,nn'}(\theta)$.)

This paradigm can obviously be transposed to other experimental situations (e.g., binocular perception as in Arditi, Chapter 23). From a theoretical viewpoint, the problem is to provide an explanation for the typical data: the presentation of the stimulation through two channels results in an improvement of detection performance.

9.1.2. The Model. In a natural extension of the signal detection model discussed in Section 8.2, we assume that the presentation of a stimulus of intensity a in the left auditory channel evokes some activity in a specific neural location, the level of which is represented by a random variable $\mathbf{U}_{1,a}$. Correspondingly, the presentation of x in the other channel generates a sample of a random variable $\mathbf{U}_{2,x}$. On noise trials, samples are taken from two "noise" random variables $\mathbf{V}_{1,n}$ and $\mathbf{V}_{2,n'}$. We assume that $(\mathbf{U}_{1,a},\mathbf{U}_{2,x})$ and $(\mathbf{V}_{1,n},\mathbf{V}_{2,n'})$ are pairs of independent random variables. On a trial where the stimulus (a,x) is presented, the information available to the organism is thus a sample of the pair of random variables $(\mathbf{U}_{1,a},\mathbf{U}_{2,x})$. We suppose that $\mathbf{U}_{1,a}$ and $\mathbf{U}_{2,x}$ are combined or pooled in some way, resulting in a random variable $\mathbf{Q}_{ax}$. The subject reports a detection if $\mathbf{Q}_{ax}$ exceeds a criterion λ_θ, the value of which depends on the payoff matrix θ. In other terms, we assume that there is some function F of two variables, the form of which is left unspecified for the moment, such that

$$\mathbf{Q}_{ax} = F(\mathbf{U}_{1,a},\mathbf{U}_{2,x}) .$$

The subject reports a detection if

$$\mathbf{Q}_{ax} > \lambda_\theta .$$

(See Figure 1.26.) Similar assumptions hold for the noise trials, with the same function F operating on the pair of random variables $(\mathbf{V}_{1,n},\mathbf{V}_{2,n'})$. The model is thus specified by the two equations

$$p_{ax}(\theta) = \text{Prob}\{F(\mathbf{U}_{1,a},\mathbf{U}_{2,x}) > \lambda_\theta\} , \quad (103)$$

$$p_{nn'}(\theta) = \text{Prob}\{F(V_{1,n},\mathbf{V}_{2,n'}) > \lambda_\theta\} . \quad (104)$$

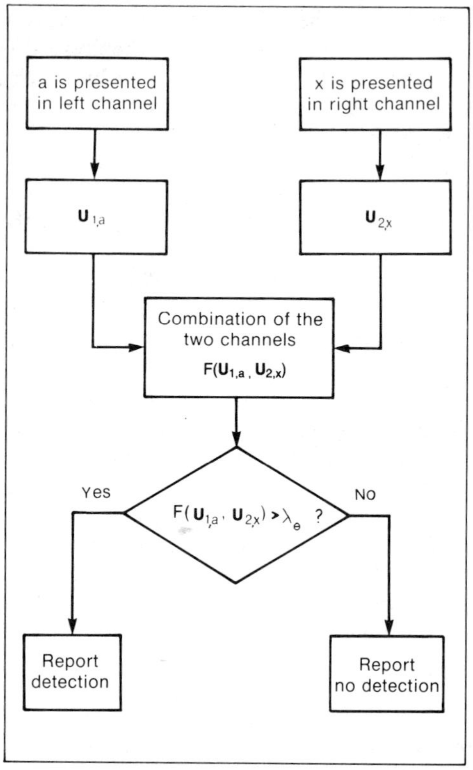

Figure 1.26. A general random variable model for the pooling of information from two sensory channels. Special cases of the model correspond to specifications of the function F.

It is clear that the data collected by varying the payoff matrix θ are amenable to a receiver operating characteristic (ROC) analysis (cf. Section 8). Applying the argument used in Section 8.2, we obtain as a measure of the area under the ROC curve, which, you will recall from Section 8.2, is a measure of performances independent of the effects of response criterion,

$$\text{Prob}\{F(\mathbf{U}_{1,a},\mathbf{U}_{2,x}) > F(\mathbf{V}_{1,n},\mathbf{V}_{2,n'})\} \ . \tag{105}$$

Several particular cases of this model, which is also discussed by Olzak and Thomas in Chapter 7, are considered. These cases correspond to special forms of the function F in Eqs. (103), (104), and (105).

9.2. Probability Summation

Probability summation covers a class of models in which the improvement of performance resulting from having the stimulation delivered to two or more channels is attributed to chance alone. For an analogy, consider a group of $n \geq 2$ observers, watching the same visual display. Suppose that the probability p of detecting a faint stimulus is the same for all observers and that the group reports a detection if at least one of the n observers claims to have detected the stimulus. Assuming that the observers' responses are independent, the detection probability of the group is

$$1 - (1 - p)^n \geq p \ .$$

The application of this idea in psychophysics can be traced back to Pirenne (1943) and plays an important role in current theorizing, especially in visual perception. We shall limit our discussion to a two-channel situation. (For the case of a large number of channels, see Watson, Chapter 6, and Olzak and Thomas, Chapter 7.)

In the framework of the general model discussed in Section 9.1.2, this notion leads to the assumption that the subject reports a detection if at least one of the two activation random variables exceeds the criterion λ_θ. (Sometimes, different criteria are postulated for the two channels. This assumption seems to be more general. See, however, Section 9.3.) This means that the function F has the form

$$F(s,t) = \max\{s,t\} \ ,$$

in which *max* stands for the maximum in the set of numbers $\{s,t\}$. (Thus $\max\{s,t\} = s$ iff $s \geq t$.) Using the assumption of independence of the random variables, we obtain for the stimulus trials,

$$\begin{aligned} p_{ax}(\theta) &= \text{Prob}\{\max\{\mathbf{U}_{1,a},\mathbf{U}_{2,x}\} > \lambda_\theta\} \\ &= 1 - \text{Prob}\{\lambda_\theta \geq \max\{\mathbf{U}_{1,a},\mathbf{U}_{2,x}\}\} \\ &= 1 - \text{Prob}\{\lambda_\theta \geq \mathbf{U}_{1,a},\ \lambda_\theta \geq \mathbf{U}_{2,x}\} \\ &= 1 - \text{Prob}\{\lambda_\theta \geq \mathbf{U}_{1,a}\}\text{Prob}\{\lambda_\theta \geq \mathbf{U}_{2,x}\} \ . \end{aligned} \tag{106}$$

Similarly, for the noise trials,

$$p_{nn'}(\theta) = 1 - \text{Prob}\{\mathbf{V}_{1,n} \leq \lambda_\theta\}\text{Prob}\{\mathbf{V}_{2,n'} \leq \lambda_\theta\} \ . \tag{107}$$

A basic assumption is implicit in Eqs. (106) and (107), a clear statement of which is critical at this point.

9.2.1. Weak Criterion Invariance. Within a yes-no paradigm involving a stimulus (a,x) and a noise (n,n'), the criterion value λ_θ only depends on the payoff matrix θ. (This value is thus the same on stimulus trials and on noise trials.) This assumption is inherent to an ROC analysis and practically inescapable.

At this level of generality, it is not clear that the predictions of the model are sufficiently constraining to be rejected by available data. The negative evidence, some of which is reviewed by Blake and Fox (1973), is mostly circumstantial, by which we mean that it has no direct bearing on the predictions formally derivable from the assumptions. However, for (implicitly) fixed θ, Eq. (106) has been checked by various authors. Some refinements of the assumptions, considered below, lead to useful empirical tests.

9.2.2. Strong Criterion Invariance. Consider the following strengthening of the criterion invariance. The criterion value λ_θ only depends on the payoff matrix θ. In particular, for a given payoff matrix, this value is constant over conditions varying the intensities of the stimulus (a,x) and of the noise (n,n').

This assumption is frequently made (explicitly or not). It lends itself to a straightforward empirical test. For example, consider an application of Eq. (106) to a situation in which two payoff matrices θ_1 and θ_2 have been used, together with four values of the variable a and six values of the variable x. The data consist of $2 \times 4 \times 6 = 48$ empirical frequencies of "yes" responses, to be explained with $2 \times 4 + 2 \times 6 = 20$ parameters. This leads to a standard chi-square (or likelihood ratio) test, with $48 - 20 = 28$ degrees of freedom. In the framework of the strong criterion invariance, this is essentially a test of the independence of the random variables $\mathbf{U}_{1,a}$ and $\mathbf{U}_{2,x}$. To the best of our knowledge, no such test has been performed.

Notice that signal detection theory is not used or even needed here (the data only concern Eq. (106)). In fact, signal detection theory was introduced explicitly to deal with situations in which an assumption such as the strong criterion invariance does not hold.

A rejection of this model could thus be attributed either to a failure of the strong criterion invariance or to a failure of the assumption of independence of the random variables. Dropping the strong criterion invariance, the model can be strengthened in a different way, by making specific assumptions regarding the distributions of the random variables. Obviously, there are numerous possibilities, each of which leads to a specific form of the ROC curves. We shall not enter here the details of such assumptions.

9.3. Remarks

As indicated above, the probability summation model defined by Eqs. (106) and (107) takes different forms depending on specific assumptions regarding the distributions of the activation random variables. The arbitrariness of the choice of the distributions should not be a cause of excessive concern (cf. Section 8.3). Indeed, suppose that a particular version of the model involves the four random variables $\mathbf{U}_{1,a}$, $\mathbf{U}_{2,x}$, $\mathbf{V}_{1,n}$, and $\mathbf{V}_{2,n'}$. Nothing changes in the predictions if these random variables are subjected to a strictly increasing transformation, provided that this transformation is the same for all variables. For example, let g be an arbitrary, strictly increasing function. Starting from Eq. (105), with F as the maximum function, we have

$$\mathrm{Prob}\{\max\{\mathbf{U}_{1,a},\mathbf{U}_{2,x}\} > \max\{\mathbf{V}_{1,n},\mathbf{V}_{2,n'}\}\}$$

$$= \mathrm{Prob}\{g(\max\{\mathbf{U}_{1,a},\mathbf{U}_{2,x}\}) > g(\max\{\mathbf{V}_{1,n},\mathbf{V}_{2,n'}\})\}$$

$$= \mathrm{Prob}\{\max\{g(\mathbf{U}_{1,a}),g(\mathbf{U}_{2,x})\} > \max\{g(\mathbf{V}_{1,n}),g(\mathbf{V}_{2,n'})\}\} \ . \tag{108}$$

Thus the prediction for the area under the ROC curve is unaffected by the transformation g. Notice that this relative "robustness" of the prediction with regard to the particular form of the distributions cannot be extended to other combination rules, that is, when the function F is different from the maximum function. Two examples of such combination rules will be briefly considered in Section 9.4.

As specified by Eqs. (106) and (107), probability summation assumes that the same criterion λ_θ is used for both channels. According to Eq. (106), for instance, a "yes" response occurs following the presentation of a stimulus (a,x) if

$$\text{either } \mathbf{U}_{1,a} > \lambda_\theta \quad \text{or} \quad \mathbf{U}_{2,x} > \lambda_\theta \ . \tag{109}$$

Occasionally (e.g., Nachmias, 1981), a model is used in which Eqs. (106) and (107) are replaced by the forms

$$p_{ax}(\theta) = 1 - \mathrm{Prob}\{\mathbf{U}_{1,a} \leqslant \lambda_{\theta,1}\}\mathrm{Prob}\{\mathbf{U}_{2,x} \leqslant \lambda_{\theta,2}\} \ , \tag{110}$$

$$p_{nn'}(\theta) = 1 - \mathrm{Prob}\{\mathbf{V}_{1,n} \leqslant \lambda_{\theta,1}\}\mathrm{Prob}\{\mathbf{V}_{2,n'} \leqslant \lambda_{\theta,2}\} \ . \tag{111}$$

Thus for a given payoff matrix θ, the criteria $\lambda_{\theta,1}$ and $\lambda_{\theta,2}$ corresponding to each channel may be different. The extra generality is only apparent, however. This must be understood as follows. Let Θ be the set of all payoff matrices. To each payoff matrix θ in Θ correspond two criteria $\lambda_{\theta,1}$ and $\lambda_{\theta,2}$. In other terms, there are two functions $\theta \mapsto \lambda_{\theta,1}$, $\theta \mapsto \lambda_{\theta,2}$, each of which maps Θ onto a real interval. It is reasonable to suppose that even though these functions may be different, they generate the same order on the set Θ of payoff matrices. That is, for any two θ and θ' in Θ, we must have

$$\lambda_{\theta,1} < \lambda_{\theta',1} \quad \text{iff} \quad \lambda_{\theta,2} < \lambda_{\theta',2} \ .$$

By a simple mathematical argument, this means that there exists a continuous, strictly increasing function g, such that $g(\lambda_{\theta,2}) = \lambda_{\theta,1}$. But then Eq. (110) implies

$$p_{ax}(\theta) = 1 - \mathrm{Prob}\{\mathbf{U}_{1,a} \leqslant \lambda_{\theta,1}\}\mathrm{Prob}\{g(\mathbf{U}_{2,x}) < g(\lambda_{\theta,2})\}$$

$$= 1 - \mathrm{Prob}\{\mathbf{U}_{1,a} \leqslant \lambda_{\theta,1}\}\mathrm{Prob}\{g(\mathbf{U}_{2,x}) < \lambda_{\theta,1}\} \ .$$

Similarly Eq. (111) yields

$$p_{nn'}(\theta) = 1 - \mathrm{Prob}\{\mathbf{V}_{1,n} \leqslant \lambda_{\theta,1}\}\mathrm{Prob}\{g(\mathbf{V}_{2,n'}) \leqslant \lambda_{\theta,1}\} \ .$$

Thus after transforming $\mathbf{U}_{2,x}$ into $g(\mathbf{U}_{2,x})$ and $\mathbf{V}_{2,n'}$ into $g(\mathbf{V}_{2,n'})$, the criteria are identical for both channels. We conclude that the two models are equivalent. Obviously, the distributions of the random variables $\mathbf{U}_{2,x}$ and $\mathbf{V}_{2,n'}$ may be modified by the transformation g. For example, if both $\mathbf{U}_{2,x}$ and $\mathbf{V}_{2,n'}$ are normal, $g(\mathbf{U}_{2,x})$ and $g(\mathbf{V}_{2,n'})$ are normal only if g is a linear function. This means that if particular forms of distributions are imposed by the model, the above equivalence does not necessarily hold. The notion of probability summation is often formalized differently (e.g., Nachmias, 1981), in terms of a two-state threshold model in the spirit of Luce (1960, 1963a, 1963b) which we discussed in Section 8.9. This model is defined by the two equations

$$p_{ax}(\theta) = 1 - (1 - p_{1,a})(1 - p_{2,x})[1 - \gamma(\theta)] \tag{112}$$

$$p_{nn'}(\theta) = 1 - (1 - p_{1,n})(1 - p_{2,n'})[1 - \gamma(\theta)] \ . \tag{113}$$

and is sometimes referred to as the *high-threshold model*. In Eq. (112) $p_{1,a}$ and $p_{2,x}$ are two parameters specifying the probabilities, when stimulus (a,x) is presented, that the thresholds are exceeded in channels 1 and 2, respectively. A "yes" response is given if the threshold is exceeded in at least one of the two channels. A "yes" response may also result from a guess, in a case in which neither of the two thresholds is exceeded. The probability of this positive guess is $\gamma(\theta)$, the value of which may vary with the payoff matrix. A similar interpretation holds for Eq. (113), which corresponds to the noise trials and introduces two additional parameters $p_{1,n}$, and $p_{2,n'}$.

The apparent popularity of this model is difficult to justify since it makes the inescapable but unlikely prediction that the ROC curves in the binaural situation are straight lines. For visual contrast detection data, this model was rejected convincingly by Nachmias (1981) in the framework of particular assumptions on the parameters $p_{1,a}$, $p_{2,x}$, $p_{1,n}$, and $p_{2,n'}$.

Further discussion regarding probability summation models can be found in Watson, Chapter 6, and Olzak and Thomas, Chapter 7.

9.4. Two Additive Combination Rules

For the same two-channel paradigm, we consider here two other possibilities for the form of the function F of the general model defined by Eqs. (103) and (104).

9.4.1. An Additive, Equal Variance, Gaussian Model. We assume that F is a binary addition, namely

$$F(s,t) = s + t .$$

The area under the two-channel ROC curve, expressed by Eq. (105), becomes

$$\text{Prob}\{\mathbf{U}_{1,a} + \mathbf{U}_{2,x} > \mathbf{V}_{1,n} + \mathbf{V}_{2,n'}\} . \qquad (114)$$

Let $\mu_{1,a}$, $\mu_{2,x}$, $\mu_{1,n}$, and $\mu_{2,n'}$ be the expectations of the respective random variables, and suppose that their common variance is equal to 1. Assume moreover that all four random variables are normally distributed. From Eq. (114) we obtain

$$\text{Prob}\{\mathbf{U}_{1,a} + \mathbf{U}_{2,x} - \mathbf{V}_{1,n} - \mathbf{V}_{2,n'} > 0\}$$

$$= \Phi[(\mu_{1,a} + \mu_{2,x} - \mu_{1,n} - \mu_{2,n'})/2] = \Phi(d'_{1,2}) .$$

The last equation defines a detectability index $d'_{1,2}$, for the two-channel situation, consistent with that introduced in Section 8.3 for the one-channel situation. Let d'_1 and d'_2 be the detectability indices in the 2 one-channel situations. That is,

$$\text{Prob}\{\mathbf{U}_{1,a} > \mathbf{V}_{1,n}\} = \Phi[(\mu_{1,a} - \mu_{1,n})/\sqrt{2}] ,$$

$$= \Phi(d'_1) ,$$

$$\text{Prob}\{\mathbf{U}_{2,x} > \mathbf{V}_{2,n'}\} = \Phi[(\mu_{2,x} - \mu_{2,n'})/\sqrt{2}]$$

$$= \Phi(d'_2) .$$

By simple algebra, it follows that

$$d'_{1,2} = (d'_1 + d'_2)/\sqrt{2} , \qquad (115)$$

a prediction which can be tested by methods discussed in Section 8.

9.4.2. Integration Model. Let f_{ax} be the joint density of $\mathbf{U}_{1,a}$ and $\mathbf{U}_{2,x}$, and let $f_{nn'}$ be the joint density of $\mathbf{V}_{1,n}$ and $\mathbf{V}_{2,n'}$; let $f_{1,a}$, $f_{2,x}$, $f_{1,n}$, and $f_{2,n'}$ be the densities of $\mathbf{U}_{1,a}$, $\mathbf{U}_{2,x}$, $\mathbf{V}_{1,n}$, and $\mathbf{V}_{2,n'}$, respectively (e.g., Green & Swets, 1974). As in Section 8.5, we suppose that the subject behaves as a statistician and bases the decision on the computation of likelihood ratios. In other terms, we assume that the function F has the form

$$F(s,t) = \frac{f_{ax}(s,t)}{f_{nn'}(s,t)} = f_{1,a}(s)f_{2,x}(t)/f_{1,n}(s)f_{2,n'}(t) , \qquad (116)$$

by the independence of the random variables. Thus when a stimulus (a,x) is presented, the subject reports a detection if

$$f_{1,a}(\mathbf{U}_{1,a})f_{2,x}(\mathbf{U}_{2,x})/f_{1,n}(\mathbf{U}_{1,a})f_{2,n'}(\mathbf{U}_{2,x}) > \lambda_\theta .$$

The same decison rule holds for the noise trials, based on a sample of $(\mathbf{V}_{1,n},\mathbf{V}_{2,n'})$. Green and Swets (1974, p. 271) show that if all four random variables are Gaussian, and in addition

$$\text{Var}(\mathbf{U}_{1,a}) = \text{Var}(\mathbf{V}_{1,n}) ,$$

$$\text{Var}(\mathbf{U}_{2,x}) = \text{Var}(\mathbf{V}_{2,n'}) ,$$

then

$$d'_{1,2} = [(d'_1)^2 + (d'_2)^2]^{1/2} . \qquad (117)$$

Applications of this model to visual perception data are discussed in Kristofferson and Dember (1958) and Green and Swets (1974). Another combination rule

$$d'_{1,2} = d'_1 + d'_2$$

is also considered there.

9.5. Additive Conjoint Measurement

A central notion in a number of models in this chapter is that the sensory system of the subject, when confronted with a multidimensional stimulus, performs a simple arithmetical operation (e.g., addition, multiplication, subtraction). Often, this operation is at the kernel of a process modeling other aspects of the subject's performance (e.g., probabilistic or cognitive), such as in the models introduced in Section 9.4. The analysis of such operations, to the extent that they can model aspects of scientific data, is the concern of measurement theory, a case of which was discussed in Section 2. This subsection is devoted to a discussion of an important special case, in which the effect on the organism of a two-dimensional stimulus (a,x) is captured by an addition of two numbers, $f(a) + g(x)$.

Consider a two-alternative forced-choice (2AFC) paradigm. On each trial, the subject is presented with two stimuli (a,x) and (b,y). For concreteness, suppose that as earlier in this section, these are pure tones presented binaurally. Thus a and b are the intensities of the tone in the left auditory channel, and x and y are the intensities in the right auditory channel. The subject is asked which of (a,x) and (b,y) seems loudest. If (a,x) is chosen, the experimenter writes

$$by < ax ,$$

as the data for the trial. It is assumed that the effect of component a of stimulus (a,x) can be represented by some number, denoted by $f(a)$. Similarly, the effect of component x is represented by a number $g(x)$. These numbers can be interpreted as measuring the intensities of the activations evoked by the stimulus at some neural locations. The model, however, is noncommittal in that respect. The basic assumption is that

$$by < ax \quad \text{iff} \quad f(b) + g(y) < f(a) + g(x) . \qquad (118)$$

This model is in the spirit of those discussed in Section 9.4, except that, somewhat unrealistically, it is deterministic: the presentation of (a,x) always evokes the same number $f(a) + g(x)$. (By comparison, in the model of Section 9.4.1, each presentation of (a,x) determines a sample of a random variable $\mathbf{U}_{1,a} + \mathbf{U}_{2,x}$.) This implies that each presentation of a pair of stimuli (a,x) and (b,y) results in the same choice by the subject, a prediction which may be reasonable for some carefully selected set of stimuli but would certainly not be acceptable in general. It is not assumed that the numbers $f(a)$, $f(b)$, $g(x)$, and so on, are accessible to direct investigation. It may not be immediately clear that this model imposes strong constraints on the data, but it does. Suppose indeed that the experimenter observes

$$bz < ay \quad \text{and} \quad cy < bx \ .$$

According to the model, this can arise only if

$$f(b) + g(z) < f(a) + g(y)$$

and

$$f(c) + g(y) < f(b) + g(x) \ .$$

Adding these two inequalities and canceling appropriately yields

$$f(c) + g(z) < f(a) + g(x) \ ,$$

which in turn predicts that

$$cz < ax \ .$$

Summarizing this argument, we see that the model specified by Eq. (118) holds only if

$$\text{whenever } bz < ay \text{ and } cy < bx, \text{ then } cz < ax \ .$$

In the measurement literature, this is known as the *double-cancellation condition*. It is illustrated thus:

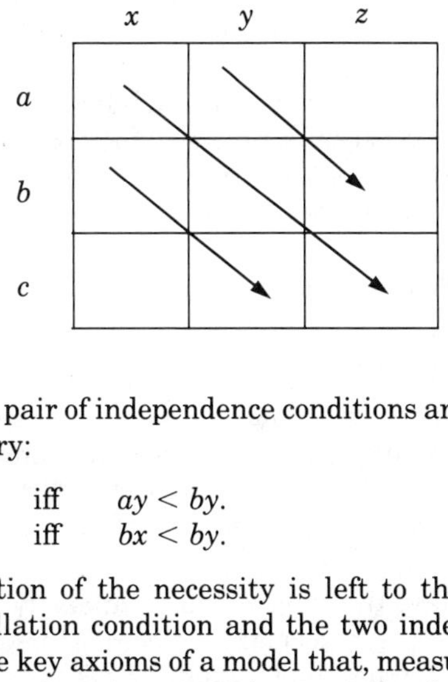

In addition, a pair of independence conditions are easily shown to be necessary:

1. $ax < bx$ iff $ay < by$.
2. $ax < ay$ iff $bx < by$.

(The verification of the necessity is left to the reader.) The double-cancellation condition and the two independence conditions are the key axioms of a model that, measurement theory tells us, implies the existence of the two scales f and g satisfying Eq. (118). We will not go into the details of this model, which are quite technical (see, e.g., Roberts, 1979; or Krantz et al., 1971). It suffices to remember that if the data are to be explained by the additive model specified by Eq. (118), then the double-cancellation condition and the two independence conditions must be satisfied.

An illustration of an experimental test of these conditions, in binaural perception, can be found in a paper by Levelt, Riemersma, and Bunt (1972). However, Levelt and colleagues' positive conclusions have recently (and rightly, in the opinion of this writer) been criticized by Gigerenzer and Strube (1983).

The appeal of measurement models of this kind is that they offer, at least in principle, the possibility of getting at the essential determinants of the subject's performance, from a psychophysical viewpoint: the scale or scales transforming the physical input or inputs, the basic operation or operations performed by the sensory system. A serious weakness of such models is that they are ill-equipped to deal with data variability, which characteristically results from psychophysical experimentation. In Sections 9.6 and 9.7 we discuss some probabilistic versions of the additive conjoint measurement model considered here.

9.6. Random Conjoint Measurement

We begin with a slight modification of the binaural loudness paradigm.

9.6.1. Matching Task. As in the 2AFC paradigm, the subject is first presented with a binaural stimulus (a,x), followed by another stimulus (b,y). The task is to modify the intensity of b (for example, by turning a dial) until, by successive approximations, the two stimuli appear equally loud. This final value of b is recorded. Typically, this value varies across trials (for fixed a, x, and y).

9.6.2. The Model. Let us write $\mathbf{U}_{xy}(a)$, a random variable, for the final value of b yielding a match. This notation seems appropriate since this value depends on a, x, and y. (The reason for the asymmetry in the notation—x, y as indices and a in parentheses—will become clear in a moment.) In the deterministic framework of additive conjoint measurement, (a,x) should appear as loud as (b,y) iff

$$f(a) + g(x) = f(b) + g(y) \ ,$$

or, equivalently,

$$f(b) = g(x) - g(y) + f(a) \ .$$

If b is replaced by the random variable $\mathbf{U}_{xy}(a)$, it seems reasonable to balance the above equation by adding an error term in the right member, which gives

$$f[\mathbf{U}_{xy}(a)] = g(x) - g(y) + f(a) + \boldsymbol{\epsilon}_{xy}(a) \ . \qquad (119)$$

The error term $\boldsymbol{\epsilon}_{xy}(a)$ is assumed to be a random variable with a (uniquely defined) median equal to 0. This model is in the spirit of the additive conjoint measurement model discussed in this section but may be applied to noisy data.

Since the scales f and g are unknown, one may ask, How is Eq. (119) constraining the data? Or, in other terms, under which conditions (necessary or sufficient) do scales f and g exist satisfying Eq. (119)? It turns out that Eq. (119) imposes strong, highly testable constraints on the medians of the random variables $\mathbf{U}_{xy}(a)$. A simple argument demonstrating this fact is given in Section 9.6.3.

9.6.3. Some Necessary Key Conditions. If $\mathbf{T}$ is a random variable having a unique median ν, we write $M(\mathbf{T}) = \nu$. The following fact will be useful: if h is any real, strictly increasing function, then $M[h(\mathbf{T})] = h[M(\mathbf{T})]$. (This follows immediately from the definition of the unique median of $\mathbf{T}$.) For simplicity, we shall adopt the abbreviation

$$m_{xy}(a) = M[\mathbf{U}_{xy}(a)]$$

for the median of the matching random variable $\mathbf{U}_{xy}(a)$. Taking medians on both sides of Eq. (119) yields

$$M\{f[\mathbf{U}_{xy}(a)]\} = f\{M[\mathbf{U}_{xy}(a)]\} = g(x) - g(y) + f(a)$$

or, equivalently,

$$m_{xy}(a) = f^{-1}[g(x) - g(y) + f(a)] , \qquad (120)$$

in which f^{-1} is the inverse of the scale f. From this equation, the following condition is easily derived.

9.6.3.1. ***Cancellation Rule.***

$$m_{xz}(a) = m_{xy}[m_{yz}(a)] ,$$

whenever all three medians are defined.

This condition, which is illustrated in Figure 1.27, is the counterpart in this probabilistic framework of the double-cancellation condition encountered in additive conjoint measurement. It has an elegant, compact expression but appears somewhat abstract at first. A good grasp of this condition requires careful study. To begin with, notice that it only concerns the "observable" medians of the matching random variables (the unknown scales f and g have been eliminated). Let us show how the cancellation rule follows from Eq. (120). Successively,

$$\begin{aligned} f\{m_{xy}[m_{yz}(a)]\} &= g(x) - g(y) + f[m_{yz}(a)] \\ &= g(x) - g(y) + f\{f^{-1}[g(y) \\ &\quad - g(z) + f(a)]\} \\ &= g(x) - g(y) + g(y) - g(z) + f(a) \\ &= f[m_{xz}(a)] . \end{aligned}$$

We conclude that

$$f\{m_{xy}[m_{yz}(a)]\} = f[m_{xz}(a)] ,$$

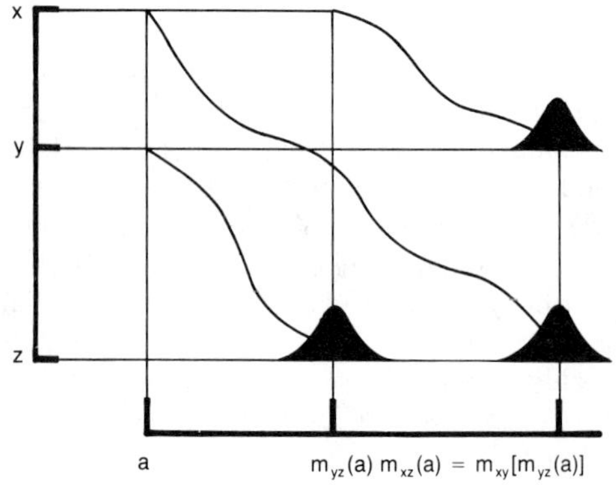

Figure 1.27. Cancellation rule. The three distributions of the figure are those of $\mathbf{U}_{xz}(a)$, $\mathbf{U}_{xy}[m_{yz}(a)]$ and $\mathbf{U}_{yz}(a)$. The three curves are the "isoloudness curves" of (a, x), $[m_{yz}(a), x]$ and (a, y).) (See also section 9.6.4.) (From J. C. Falmagne, Random conjoint measurement and loudness summation, *Psychological Review, 83*. Copyright 1976 by American Psychological Association. Reprinted with permission.)

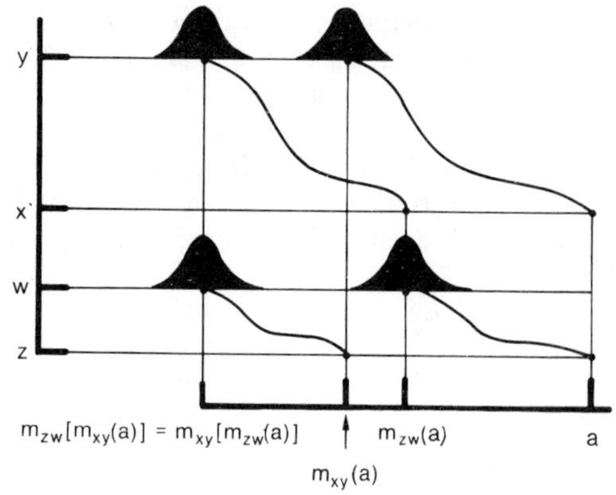

Figure 1.28. Commutativity rule. The conventions are similar to those of Figure 1.27. The four distributions are those of $\mathbf{U}_{xy}(a)$, $\mathbf{U}_{zw}(a)$, $\mathbf{U}_{xy}[m_{zw}(a)]$, and $\mathbf{U}_{zw}[m_{zy}(a)]$. The four curves are the "isoloudness curves" of (a, x), (a, z), $[m_{zw}(a), x]$, and $[m_{xy}(a), w]$.) (From J. C. Falmagne, Random conjoint measurement and loudness summation, *Psychological Review, 83*. Copyright 1976 by American Psychological Association. Reprinted with permission.)

which is equivalent to the cancellation rule, since f is a one-to-one function. A further understanding of this condition will be obtained from a discussion of how it can be tested. (See Section 9.6.4.) Using similar methods, another condition can also be shown to be necessary.

9.6.3.2. ***Commutativity Rule.***

$$m_{xy}[m_{zw}(a)] = m_{zw}[m_{xy}(a)] ,$$

whenever all four medians are defined.

In other terms, if we pick one intensity a in the left channel and four intensities x, y, z, and w in the right channel and take the two medians $M[\mathbf{U}_{zw}(a)] = m_{zw}(a) = b_1$ and $M[\mathbf{U}_{xy}(a)] = m_{xy}(a) = b_2$ and, next, the two medians $M[\mathbf{U}_{xy}(b_1)] = m_{xy}(b_1)$ and $M[\mathbf{U}_{zw}(b_2)] = m_{zw}(b_2)$, then the two medians $m_{xy}(b_1)$ and $m_{zw}(b_2)$ should be equal. The commutativity rule is illustrated in Figure 1.28.

It can be shown that if continuity assumptions are made, then the implication can be reversed: the cancellation rule and the commutativity rule together imply that Eq. (120) holds for some scales f and g. A proof of this fact can be found in Falmagne (1976).

9.6.4. A Test. A test of the cancellation rule could proceed as follows.

Step 1. Choose one intensity a in the left channel and three intensities x, y, and z in the right channel. Have the subject find an intensity b in the left channel, so that (b, z) matches (a, y) in loudness. Repeat $2p$ times. Order these $2p + 1$ values $b_1 \leqslant b_2 \leqslant \ldots \leqslant b_{2p+1}$. Then b_{p+1} is an estimate of $m_{yz}(a)$.

Step 2. Have the subject find an intensity c such that (c, y) matches (b_{p+1}, x) in loudness. Repeat q times. The obtained empirical distribution is denoted by D.

Step 3. Have the subject find an intensity d, such that (d, z) matches (a, x). Repeat k times. The obtained empirical distribution is denoted D'.

Step 4. Test whether $\mathbf{U}_{xy}(b_{p+1})$ and $\mathbf{U}_{xz}(a)$ have the same median, for example, by performing a median test comparing D and D'. (This test is known to be reasonably robust to a difference in the shape of the distributions; cf. Pratt, 1964.)

A similar test can be designed for the cancellation rule. A discussion regarding the soundness of such procedures can be found in Falmagne (1976).

Gigerenzer and Strube (1983) have applied this model to binaural loudness data. The hypothesis that the two auditory channels are additive, in the sense of Eq. (119), is convincingly rejected. The data favor a model in which one channel dominates when its intensity sufficiently exceeds that of the other.

9.7. Probabilistic Conjoint Measurement

As reported in a number of papers, Falmagne and his coworkers have investigated another way of injecting statistical considerations into additive conjoint measurement (Falmagne, 1978, 1979; Falmagne & Iverson, 1979; Falmagne, Iverson, & Marcovici, 1979). Suppose that, in a 2AFC paradigm, the subject must select one of the 2 two-component stimuli (a,x) and (b,y). As before, we assume that a, b, x, and y are numbers denoting physical variables. Let $P_{ax,by}$ be the probability that (a,x) is chosen over (b,y). A general additive model is embodied in the equation

$$P_{ax,by} = F[f(a) + g(x), f(b) + g(y)] , \quad (121)$$

in which the real-valued functions F, f, and g in the right member are unspecified, except for monotonicity and continuity properties: all three functions are continuous, F is strictly increasing in the first variable and strictly decreasing in the second variable, and f and g are strictly increasing. We also assume that the function F in Eq. (121) satisfies the following balance property (see the definition in Section 3.5.1):

$$F(s,t) = .5 \text{ iff } s = t . \quad (122)$$

The connections between this model and that previously discussed under the label *random conjoint measurement* must be appreciated. Consider a situation in which the experimenter, an expert in adaptive methods (see Section 6), fixes the values of a, x, and y in Eq. (121) and has the subject's performance converging over trials—say, using stochastic approximation—to a point β satisfying

$$P_{ax,\beta y} = F[f(a) + g(x), f(\beta) + g(y)] = .5 .$$

The estimated value of β is actually a random variable, the distribution of which depends on a, x, and y. Under reasonable differentiability assumptions (see Section 6.2.1), the asymptotic distribution of this random variable is normal and has an expectation equal to β. Let us denote this asymptotic random variable by $\mathbf{V}_{xy}(a)$. Notice that, using Eq. (122),

$$f(a) + g(x) = f(\beta) + g(y) ,$$

and thus

$$E[\mathbf{V}_{xy}(a)] = f^{-1}[g(x) - g(y) + f(a)] , \quad (123)$$

which is, for all practical purposes, equivalent to Eq. (120) constraining the medians, in our discussion of random conjoint measurement. (Indeed, for normal distributions the expectation and the median are equal.) The model specified by Eq. (121) can thus be tested by checking whether the cancellation and commutativity rules are satisfied empirically by the expectations $E[\mathbf{V}_{xy}(a)]$. A number of special cases of this model are of interest, the defining equations of which are listed below. Note that the function k in Eq. (124) is assumed to be strictly increasing and continuous.

$$P_{ax,by} = F\{k[f(a) + g(x)] - k[f(b) + g(y)]\} . \quad (124)$$

$$P_{ax,by} = F[f(a) + g(x) - f(b) - g(y)] . \quad (125)$$

$$P_{ax,by} = F\{[f(a) + g(x)]/[f(b) + g(x)]\} . \quad (126)$$

$$P_{ax,by} = F[f(a)g(x) - f(b)g(y)] . \quad (127)$$

Diagnostic properties permitting one to sort out these models have been developed (Falmagne, 1979). The behavior of the function $a \mapsto P_{ax,bx}$ is particularly instructive in this respect. Assuming that Eq. (124) holds, it can be shown, for example (Falmagne et al., 1979), that for $a > b$, the function

$$k \text{ is } \left\{\begin{array}{l}\text{linear}\\ \text{strictly convex}\\ \text{strictly concave}\end{array}\right\} \text{iff } P_{ax,bx} \text{ is } \left\{\begin{array}{l}\text{independent of } x;\\ \text{strictly increasing in } x;\\ \text{strictly decreasing in } x.\end{array}\right.$$

(We recall that *strictly convex* means curved upward and *strictly concave* means curved downward; cf. Section 7.4.) Important examples of (strictly) convex and concave functions are the logarithmic and exponential functions. Observe in this connection that each of the Eqs. (125), (126), and (127) follows from Eq. (124) by assuming that k is a linear, a logarithmic, or an exponential function, respectively. (Obviously, a change of notations vis-à-vis functions F, f, and g is taking place between Eqs. (124) and (125), (126), and (127).

These models have been applied by Falmagne and colleagues (1979) to binaural loudness data collected in a series of experiments, using the 2AFC paradigm. A special case of Eq. (126) was found to yield a good fit. (See, however, Gigerenzer & Strube, 1983.) More will be said about this study in Section 9.8.

9.8. Homogeneity Laws

There is a class of empirical laws that deserves serious consideration by the psychophysicist. (Let us avoid both misunderstanding and a philosophical trap. By "law" we mean an important equation purporting to explain a body of data. The equation derives its importance, and thus the label "law," from that of the data to be explained, from the consequences of the equation regarding feasible theories, and possibly also from the simplicity of its form. Scientific usage indicates that complete accuracy of the prediction is not a major requirement, e.g., the failure of Boyle's law at low temperature.) Examples of laws in that class are provided by two forms of Weber's law encountered in Section 7. As defined in Section 7.2.3, it constrains the psychometric functions and takes the form

$$p_{\lambda a}(\lambda x) = p_a(x) . \quad (128)$$

In words, a psychometric function is invariant under multiplication of the intensities of the standard and the stimulus by the same constant $\lambda > 0$. Equivalently (theorem in Section 7.2.6), Weber's law concerns the Weber functions and states that

$$\Delta_{\pi}(\lambda a) = \lambda \Delta_{\pi}(a) . \qquad (129)$$

We recall that a real-valued function h of n real variables is *homogeneous of degree* β iff

$$h(\lambda x_1, \lambda x_2, ..., \lambda x_n) = \lambda^{\beta} h(x_1, x_2, ..., x_n) ,$$

for all $\lambda > 0$ (see Section 7.2.2). Thus Eqs. (128) and (129) mean that the functions p and Δ are homogeneous of degree 0 and 1, respectively.

A couple of additional examples of homogeneity laws will be discussed. They show that such laws are typically easy to verify experimentally and tend to have strong implications on theorization. If Weber's law is any indication, they may have a more durable impact than specific process models, a prospect that justifies the space allocated here to this topic.

No proof of any of the results discussed below will be given. Incidentally, we mention that the arguments used to derive the theoretical consequences of homogeneity laws often appeal to results from a field of mathematics called *functional equations*, an introduction to which the reader can find in Aczél (1966).

9.8.1. The Conjoint Weber Laws. Let us go back to the 2AFC paradigm used by Falmagne and colleagues (1979), in which the subject was required to compare binaural stimuli (a,x) and (b,y). A test of the following generalization of Weber's law was performed:

$$P_{(\lambda a)(\lambda x),(\lambda b)(\lambda y)} = P_{ax,by} .$$

That is, using the decibel scale, the choice probability does not vary when the same number of decibels is added to all four intensities. This prediction, called the *conjoint Weber law*, was found to be well supported by the data, at least for the relatively modest range of stimulus intensities considered in the experiment. The importance of this result from a theoretical standpoint should not be underestimated. Researchers in this field are concerned with the hypothesis that the two auditory channels may be additive. As indicated in Section 9.7, a possible formalization of this notion lies in Eq. (121).

$$P_{ax,by} = F[f(a) + g(x), f(b) + g(y)] ,$$

in which the functions F, f, and g are unspecified, except for continuity and monotonicity properties. Falmagne and Iverson (1979) show that if both the conjoint Weber law and Eq. (121) hold, then the choice probabilities must have one of the following three forms:

$$P_{ax,by} = G[(a^{\beta} + \delta x^{\beta})/(b^{\beta} + \delta y^{\beta})] ; \qquad (130)$$

$$P_{ax,by} = G[a^{\beta} x^{\gamma} / b^{\beta} y^{\gamma}] ; \qquad (131)$$

$$P_{ax,by} = Q[a/x, b/y] , \qquad (132)$$

in which β and γ are constants, G is strictly increasing and continuous, and Q is continuous, strictly increasing in the first variable and strictly decreasing in the second variable. These three equations are easy to discriminate experimentally. For instance, Eq. (132) can be eliminated immediately, as a model for binaural loudness, since it predicts that $P_{ax,by}$ is decreasing in x and increasing in y. A different way of separating these equations leads us to introduce two other homogeneity laws, each of which is a strengthening of the conjoint Weber law:

Strong Conjoint Weber Law Type I (SCWI)

$$P_{ax,by} = P_{(\lambda a)(\lambda x),(\tau b)(\tau y)}$$

Strong Conjoint Weber Law Type II (SCWII)

$$P_{ax,by} = P_{(\lambda a)(\tau x),(\lambda b)(\tau y)} .$$

These equations are assumed to hold for all positive a, b, x, y, λ, and τ. These two laws provide a sharp method to distinguish between Eqs. (130), (131), and (132) from an experimental standpoint. In particular, it is easy to prove that SWCI is equivalent to Eq. (132). It can also be shown that the additive form Eq. (121), together with SCWII, is equivalent to Eq. (131). A useful conclusion follows: if the conjoint Weber law holds, but both SCWI and SCWII fail, then the additive form Eq. (121) has necessarily the form of Eq. (130).

This example shows how the experimental testing of homogeneity laws (with positive or negative outcomes) may result in a considerable strengthening of the hypotheses of a model. Following is another example, along the same lines but with a different motivation and a different paradigm.

9.8.2. Shift Invariance in Loudness Recruitment. A tone embedded in noise does not appear as loud as the same tone in quiet. As the intensity of the tone increases, however, the subjective difference tends to disappear. In psychoacoustics, this phenomenon is known as *loudness recruitment*. Let us denote by $\varphi(x,n)$ the intensity of a tone in quiet matching an intensity x of the same tone embedded in a noise of intensity n. These matching functions were recently investigated by Iverson and Pavel (1981a, 1981b; see also Pavel, 1980), who demonstrated that to an excellent approximation the following property was satisfied by the data: for some $\theta > 0$ and all $\lambda > 0$

$$\varphi(\lambda x, \lambda^{\theta} n) = \lambda \varphi(x,n) . \qquad (133)$$

They investigated the theoretical consequences of this property, which they called *shift invariance*. The choice of this name is justified by a geometrical interpretation of Eq. (133), an illustration of which is given in Figure 1.29. Shift invariance can be seen as a homogeneity property under a slight disguise: defining the function ψ,

$$\psi(x,y) = \varphi(x, y^{\theta}) ,$$

it follows that

$$\psi(\lambda x, \lambda y) = \varphi(\lambda x, \lambda^{\theta} y^{\theta}) = \lambda \varphi(x, y^{\theta}) = \lambda \psi(x,y) .$$

That is, ψ is homogeneous of degree 1.

As in the preceding example, it may be asked whether shift invariance may be assumed in conjunction with some general, reasonable model, with the effect of strengthening the model

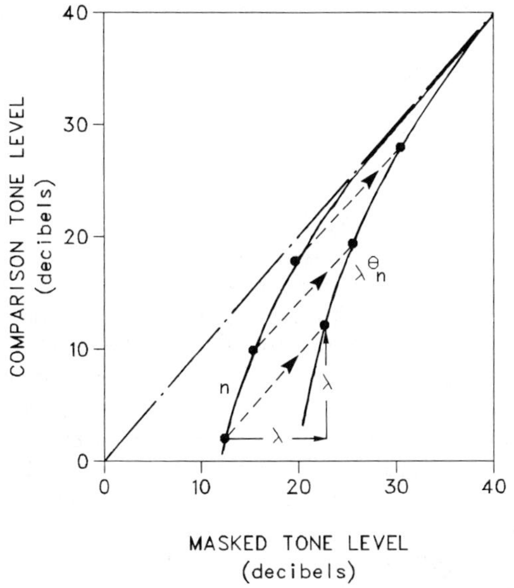

Figure 1.29. The property of shift invariance illustrated by two hypothetical loudness matching curves. The right curve representing loudness matching with noise $\lambda^\theta n$ can be obtained by a rigid shift of the left curve (generated by loudness matches with noise n) along the first bisector. (From M. Pavel, *Homogeneity in complete and partial masking*. Unpublished doctoral dissertation, New York University, 1980.)

in a useful way. Iverson and Pavel (1981a) assume that the matching function ρ satisfies the gain control equation

$$\varphi(x,n) = F\{g(x)/[h(x) + k(n)]\} , \qquad (134)$$

with the functions g, h, k, and F being subjected only to natural monotonicity and continuity conditions. They show then that in the presence of shift invariance Eq. (134) can take only one of two forms:

$$\varphi(x,n) = [Ax^{\alpha}/(x^{\alpha'} + Kn^{\alpha'/\theta})]^{1/(\alpha-\alpha')} \qquad (135)$$

or

$$\varphi(x,n) = A[x^{\alpha}(x^{\alpha'} - Kn^{\alpha'/\theta})]^{1/(\alpha+\alpha')} , \qquad (136)$$

where A, K, α, α', and θ are appropriately chosen constants. Note that a special case of Eq. (136) was proposed by Lochner and Burger (1961) as an extension of the power law (cf. Section 10), incorporating the effects of a masking noise. Objections to Eq. (136) as a possible model for recruitment can be found in Scharf (1978). A plot of a least-square fit of Eq. (135) to some data of Stevens and Guirao (1967) is presented in Figure 1.30.

Another example of homogeneity law arises in our discussion of the bisection method in Section 9.9.

9.9. Bisection

This name refers to a class of paradigms in which, on each trial, a subject is presented with a pair (a,b) of stimuli and is required to "produce" (in a way depending on the experimental conditions) a stimulus appearing "midway" between a and b. As before in this section, a and b are physical intensities. We shall denote by $B(a,b)$ the midway intensity produced by the subject. In some situations, the subject may be asked to adjust a dial; $B(a,b)$ may then be estimated by averaging over trials. In other cases, $B(a,b)$ may be obtained by applying an adaptive procedure (cf. Section 6.2).

A frequently proposed model for the resulting data is formalized by the equation

$$u[B(a,b)] = \frac{u(a) + u(b)}{2} , \qquad (137)$$

in which the function u is assumed to be strictly increasing and continuous but is otherwise arbitrary. The idea behind this representation is that the subject performs the task by computing the arithmetic average of a and b. This computation, however, is not (necessarily) carried out in the physical scale, but may involve instead some unknown psychophysical scale, represented in Eq. (137) by the function u. It may seem that since u is unspecified, Eq. (137) is not saying very much. But this is not so. Equation (137) is telling us that B is an operation which must behave essentially like an arithmetic average. In fact, this model puts severe constraints on the data. A simple example is the *commutativity* equation

$$B(a,b) = B(b,a) , \qquad (138)$$

which immediately results from Eq. (137) by observing that the terms $u(a)$ and $u(b)$ commute in the right member. Equation (137) also implies that B must be *idempotent*; that is, we must have

$$B(a,a) = a \qquad (139)$$

for all stimuli a. This follows from the fact that

$$u[B(a,a)] = [u(a) + u(a)]/2 = u(a)$$

which yields Eq. (139) since u is a one-to-one function. A less obvious consequence of Eq. (137) is the condition

$$B[B(a,b),B(c,d)] = B[B(a,c),B(b,d)] , \qquad (140)$$

which is often referred to as *bisymmetry*. The easy proof that Eq. (137) implies bisymmetry is left to the reader. This implication can be reversed; under general continuity and monoton-

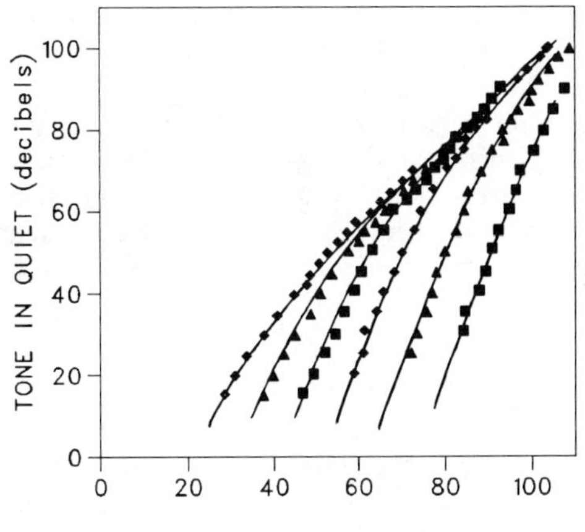

Figure 1.30. Best fit of Eq. (135) to scale data of Stevens and Guirao (1967). (From G. J. Iverson & M. Pavel, On the functional form of partial masking functions in psychoacoustics, *Journal of Mathematical Psychology*, 1981, *24*. Reprinted with permission.)

icity properties of the midway function B, idempotent, commutativity, and bisymmetry together imply the existence of a function u satisfying Eq. (137) (Krantz et al., 1971).

An experimental test of bisymmetry in auditory perception can be found in Cross (1965; cited by Coombs, Dawes, & Tversky, 1970). Bypassing such tests, it is also possible to "search" directly for a function u satisfying Eq. (137). This is done by Weiss (1975) and Anderson (1976, p. 107, 1981, p. 37). A good fit is obtained for a power function $u(a) = \lambda a^{\beta}$. As we shall see in this section, this form of the scale u is of particular interest.

In some cases, commutativity may not hold. Consider a situation in which a and b are two intensities of a pure tone presented monaurally and successively. It is conceivable (in fact, likely) that the produced midway value will depend on which of a and b is presented first: the midway operation has to be performed between two stimuli, one of which is being kept in memory for some time and thus subject to the effects of a possible decay. The idempotent property may also fail. In such cases, Eq. (137) may be generalized as follows. If bisymmetry and idempotent hold, but not (necessarily) commutativity, then the appropriate model is

$$u[B(a,b)] = \alpha u(a) + (1 - \alpha)u(b)$$

with $\alpha > 0$, a constant. If neither idempotent nor commutativity is assumed to hold, but bisymmetry is satisfied, then we have the still more general model

$$u[B(a,b)] = \alpha u(a) + \gamma u(b) + \delta$$

with $\alpha > 0, \gamma > 0$.

Bisection provides an additional example of a homogeneity law. In a classic application of this type of paradigm, Plateau (1872) gave a pair of painted disks, one white and one black, to each of eight artists and instructed them to return to their respective studios and paint a gray disk midway between the two. The resulting gray disks, reported Plateau, were almost identical for all eight artists, in spite of the variation in the illumination conditions under which they were produced. Let us suppose that such results would hold for any pair of gray disks. A possible formalization of this circumstance would be as follows. Let (a,b) denote a pair of gray disks, in a specified viewing condition in Plateau's laboratory. Let a and b denote the luminance of the disks in conventional units. Let $B(a,b)$ denote the midway gray disk in the same viewing condition. The artist, however, has performed the task in a studio, in different illumination conditions, that is, with the pair $(\lambda a,\lambda b)$ (where λ is a positive constant equal to the ratio of the illumination in the artist's studio to that of Plateau's laboratory). By hypothesis, the resulting midway disk is independent of the illumination. As a consequence, the following equation must hold:

$$B(\lambda a,\lambda b) = \lambda B(a,b) . \quad (141)$$

Indeed, this means that the midway disk obtained in Plateau's laboratory is identical to that produced by the artist in the studio, when seen under the same conditions. In other terms, B is homogeneous of degree 1 (cf. Section 7.2.2). But if both the averaging model, Eq. (137), and the homogeneity property, Eq. (141), are assumed to hold, then the possible forms of the function u are very limited; u must be either a power function,

$$u(a) = \alpha a^{\beta} + \gamma ,$$

or a logarithmic function,

$$u(a) = \alpha \log a + \delta$$

(α, β, γ constants). No other forms exist which would satisfy both Eqs. (137) and (141). This was noted by Krantz (Note 3), who also remarked that essentially the same argument applies to the basic equal-spacing principle underlying the construction of the Munsell system (Munsell, 1929). We recall in this connection the results of Weiss (1975) and Anderson (1976, 1981) who, using a different method, also obtained a power function for their bisection data.

The bisection models discussed here are deterministic, which renders their application to data delicate. Fortunately, probabilistic versions of such models can be developed, which are similar in spirit to the models discussed in Sections 9.6 and 9.7 for additive conjoint measurement. For the sake of illustration, one possibility is outlined here.

We begin by replacing the operation yielding a stimulus midway between a and b by a random variable $\mathbf{B}(a,b)$. Eq. (137) becomes

$$u[\mathbf{B}(a,b)] = [u(a) + u(b)]/2 + \boldsymbol{\epsilon}(a,b) , \quad (142)$$

in which $\boldsymbol{\epsilon}(a,b)$ is an error random variable with a unique median equal to 0. Let $m(a,b)$ be the median of the random variable $\mathbf{B}(a,b)$. By a simple argument along the lines of that used in Section 9.6.3, Eq. (142) implies

$$u[m(a,b)] = [u(a) + u(b)]/2 ,$$

an equation which has exactly the form of Eq. (137), with the median m replacing the deterministic operation B. This means that the conditions of idempotency, commutativity, and bisymmetry must be satisfied by the medians. In other terms, we must have

$$m(a,a) = a ,$$

$$m(a,b) = m(b,a) ,$$

$$m[m(a,b),m(c,d)] = m[m(a,c),m(b,d)] .$$

Similarly, the homogeneity condition uncovered in Plateau's experiment is formalized by the equation

$$m(\lambda a,\lambda b) = \lambda m(a,b) .$$

As in the case of the random conjoint measurement model, nonparametric tests can be used to evaluate the empirical validity of these conditions.

9.10. Key References

Preoccupations with the role of chance in the improvement of performance observed in multichannel perception were expressed early (Dawson, 1913). The first explicit formalization of probability summation in the sense of this section is attributed to Pirenne (1943). A review can be found in Blake and Fox (1973). Chapter 9 in Green and Swets (1974) is devoted to models for multichannel perception, including the integration model.

Tests of a specific model of probability summation are described in a recent paper by Nachmias (1981). The applications of probability summation considered in this chapter were limited to a two-channel situation. The ideas developed are easily extended to n-channels. However, when a large number of channels is involved, a new situation arises, in which some convergence theorems of probability theory are applicable. These issues are considered in chapters by Watson; Arditi; Olzak and Thomas; Regan, Kaufman, and Lincoln; Ginsburg; and Treisman in this handbook.

Additive conjoint measurement is a standard topic of measurement theory, a detailed exposition of which is contained in Krantz and colleagues (1971) and Roberts (1979). The introduction of probabilistic models in additive conjoint measurement is in the spirit of the models encountered in probabilistic choice theory (Luce & Suppes, 1965). The models discussed here were developed by Falmagne and his coworkers (Falmagne, 1976, 1978, 1979; Falmagne & Iverson, 1979; Falmagne, Iverson, & Marcovici, 1979).

Implicitly, the study of homogeneity laws has been part of psychophysics since its inception (Weber's law is a homogeneity law). Many psychophysical laws or models are instances of or at least are consistent with some homogeneity law. A systematic investigation of homogeneity laws and their impact on psychophysical theorizing has recently been undertaken by Falmagne, Iverson, and Pavel (Falmagne & Iverson, 1979; Falmagne, Iverson, & Marcovici, 1979; Iverson & Pavel, 1980, 1981a, 1981b; Pavel, 1980). An introduction to the functional equation techniques used in these papers can be found in Aczél (1966).

A treatment of bisection, from the viewpoint of measurement theory, is contained in Krantz and colleagues (1971; see also Pfanzagl, 1968).

There was a substantial amount of arbitrariness in the choice of topics covered in this section. The reader may be surprised, for example, that only a passing reference was made to the work of Anderson and his collaborators (Anderson, 1970a, 1970b, 1974, 1976, 1981]. Actually, the organizing principle for this section was to include multivariable models or techniques only if they were a natural extension of "classical" psychophysics. Scaling models or techniques are covered in Section 10.

10. SCALING

Scaling covers a collection of models, procedures, and empirical analyses, purporting to provide a representation of some data in terms of one or more numerical scales. Such is, of course, also the aim of measurement theory, a field in which, typically, axiom systems are given justifying specific methods of scale construction (cf. Section 2). In the work usually classified under the scaling label, however, acquiring the scales is often regarded as an end in itself, and the theoretical underpinnings are of secondary importance. Objections have deservedly been made to that state of affairs. The uses of a scale without a firm theoretical foundation are restricted. In particular, if the *type* of a scale (see Section 10.1) is unknown, it may be difficult to decide whether a given model or a mathematical expression employing that scale makes sense from a certain logicophilosophical viewpoint (see Section 10.10).

After an introduction to scale types, the most common unidimensional scaling methods and data will be reviewed. Two theoretical approaches will then be considered: the Shepard-Krantz relation theory and the functional measurement procedures, introduced by Norman Anderson. A brief discussion of the issue of the psychophysical scale and the measurement of sensation will follow. Finally, the notion of meaningful psychophysical laws will be brought to the attention of the reader. (Note that the so-called multidimensional scaling techniques are considered by Wyszecki, Chapter 9.)

10.1. Common Types of Scales

In most cases, numerical scales constructed from (and explaining) some empirical data are not defined uniquely. It is usually agreed, for example, that the numerical scale used for the measurement of length is a *ratio scale*, which means that the numerical values assigned to the objects are defined up to a multiplication by a positive constant (e.g., a change of units from centimeter to meter is admissible). In this exemplary case, the exact degree of arbitrariness of the scale is a consequence derivable from a completely axiomatized theory. One assumes that the data satisfy the axioms of the theory, which in turn provides a procedure for the construction of the scale and specifies the degree of arbitrariness of such construction. How this applies in the case of length has been discussed in detail in Section 2. The degree of arbitrariness of the scale is referred to as its *type*. Despite the variety of forms of data, only a few types of scales are actually used in scientific practice. The reasons for this scarcity are not very well understood (see, however, Narens, 1981). The most commonly used types of scales are listed in Table 1.4.

10.2. Overview of (Unidimensional) Scaling Methods

The psychophysical procedures discussed in earlier sections of this chapter (such as that used in the yes-no paradigm) were rather painstaking. In a typical experiment, several hundred observations per point are collected for each subject. By contrast, the methods considered here may use only a few observations per point (sometimes as few as one or two observations per subject). However, the subject's responses tend to be much more elaborate. For example, the subject may be asked to identify the stimulus presented, using a label previously attached to that stimulus (as in the *absolute identification* method) or be required to evaluate the stimulus numerically, according to some rule (as in *magnitude estimation*). There are a number of such scaling methods, and ways of classifying them. In the next four sections, we classify the methods by the type of response required from the subject. Each subsection contains a brief de-

Table 1.4. The Most Commonly Used Types of Scales.

Scale Type	Admissible Transformations	Examples
Absolute	Identity: $x \mapsto \phi(x) = x$	Counting
Ratio	Similarity: $x \mapsto \phi(x) = \alpha x$, with $\alpha > 0$	Length, mass
Interval	Affine: $x \mapsto \phi(x) = \alpha x + \beta$, with $\alpha > 0$	Temperature
Log-interval	$x \mapsto \phi(x) = \alpha x^{\beta}$, with $\alpha > 0$ and $\beta > 0$	Density

Each type is defined by the class of admissible transformations of the scale; for example, the ratio scale type is that defined by all the transformations of the form $x \mapsto \alpha x$, with $\alpha > 0$. The case for density and other fundamental physical quantities to be log-interval scales is made by Krantz, Luce, Suppes, and Tversky (1971).

scription of the procedures and of the typical experimental results.

Under the impetus of S. S. Stevens, an impressive array of experimental results were collected, which generally support the contention that through subjective judgments the sensory continua are related to each other and to the number continuum by power laws (at least to a first approximation). The *power law* was offered by Stevens as a substitute for the logarithmic relation of Fechner (cf. Section 7.3). The merit of this proposal is discussed in Section 10.10. In this connection, the reader should bear in mind that the psychophysical methods discussed in this section were often introduced in a spirit of criticism of the "classical" methods, such as the yes-no paradigm and its close relatives. These were thought to lack realism, to the extent that the data were focusing on "local" effects (e.g., the discrimination of neighboring stimuli), while the natural environment involves the simultaneous apprehension of a large collection of widely distributed stimuli. The terms *local* and *global* are sometimes used to denote the two classes of procedures.

10.3. Absolute Identification

In a preliminary period, the subject is trained to associate one of n labels (say, the numbers from 1 to $n = 10$) to each of n stimuli. During the main phase of the experiment the subject is presented a stimulus on each trial and is required to produce the appropriate label. The subject's response is recorded. The succession of stimuli is random. Occasionally, immediate repetitions are avoided.

A straightforward analysis of the data is in terms of the proportion of correct responses. Another measure of performance, not often used now, is the *average information transmitted by the responses* (cf. Coombs, Dawes, & Tversky, 1970; Garner, 1962; Miller, 1953). More recently, a measure based on the index d' of signal detection theory (cf. Section 8) has been proposed (Luce, Green, & Weber, 1976).

For stimuli varying along one sensory continuum, the main finding is that the maximum number of stimuli that can be identified perfectly by an untrained subject is between five and nine, depending on the continuum, for example, Pollack (1952) and Garner (1953). (See Miller, 1956, for a review of the facts. Obviously, specialists, such as professional musicians for pitch identification, may score much better than that.) This result is regarded as puzzling since it appears to be at variance with the data of local studies. For instance, only stimuli that are very close on the physical scale (say, less than a couple of decibels apart in auditory discrimination) are ever confused in a two-alternative forced-choice (2AFC) paradigm. An extrapolation would lead to predict a perfect identification of several dozen suitably located stimuli in an absolute identification experiment. The discrepancy may be due to the fact that efficient guessing strategies can be used in a 2AFC situation, which are no longer available in absolute identification.

At first, the absolute identification paradigm may seem straightforward. Actually, the data are plagued with a variety of sequential effects and "anchoring" effects that render the analysis extremely difficult. Regarding anchoring, or edge, effects, see, for example, Berliner and Durlach (1973), Berliner, Durlach, and Braida (1977), Braida and Durlach (1972), Durlach and Braida (1969), Gravetter and Lockhead (1973), Lippman, Braida, and Durlach (1976), and Weber, Green, and Luce (1977). Sequential effects in absolute identification have been explored, for example, by Holland and Lockhead (1968), Jesteadt, Luce, and Green (1977), Purks, Callaghan, Braida, and Durlach (1980), Ward (1972), and Ward and Lockhead (1970, 1971).

10.4. Category Rating

As with absolute identification, in *category rating* one stimulus from a sensory continuum is presented at each trial. The subject is instructed to assign each stimulus to one of m-ordered categories, for example, the numbers 1 to m. These categories are assumed to be subjectively "equally spaced"; that is, the subjective distance between category 3 and 4 is identical to that between 10 and 11. The number m of categories is often smaller than the number of stimuli and may vary from a few (5–7) to several dozen.

In variations of this method, pairs of stimuli are presented at each trial, and the subject is required to rate (that is, to assign a category to) subjective "differences" or "ratios" of these stimuli. In a rather extreme version, four stimuli are presented simultaneously, and the subjects are asked to make very sophisticated judgments, such as rating the ratio of differences or the difference of ratios (Birnbaum, 1978).

The most startling result is perhaps that the subjects not only are capable of performing such tasks without major difficulties but also provide surprisingly regular data: the average rating values often appear to vary smoothly with stimulus intensity. The data may be analyzed in various ways. In an exemplary case, the subjects rate subjective differences between stimuli, and it is assumed that the average rating $D_{x,y}$ corresponding to physical intensities x, y satisfies a Fechnerian-type relation

$$D_{x,y} = F[u(x) - u(y)] , \tag{143}$$

in which u and F are strictly increasing functions. In some cases, F is shown to be well approximated by a linear function. Unfortunately, the subject's performance in these tasks varies markedly with the context. For example, the value of $D_{x,y}$ in Eq. (143) strongly depends on the distribution of all the stimuli used in the experiment, specifically, the range, the spacing, and the frequencies of these stimuli. Such facts, which are well documented, may create problems for psychophysical theorizing, depending on the locus of the effects. To pursue our example, a major concern is which of the two functions u, F in the right member of Eq. (143) is affected by the context. The available evidence points out that only F is affected (Parducci, 1963, 1965, 1974; Parducci & Perrett, 1971; see Birnbaum, 1982, for a general discussion and further references). Since the function u is a candidate for the psychophysical scale, the key invariant, this would leave open the possibility of a general theory.

10.5. Magnitude Estimation

In the widely used method of *magnitude estimation*, the main advocate of which was S. S. Stevens, the subject is required to provide "direct" numerical estimates of the magnitude of the sensation evoked by the stimulation. Two variants of the method have been employed.

In one, the subject is initially presented with a stimulus (the standard) and told that the sensory magnitude of that stimulus is assigned a certain value (modulus), say, 100. Other stimuli are then presented in random order, and the subject is instructed to estimate their sensory magnitude so as to preserve ratios. For instance, if the second stimulus presented seems to have a sensory magnitude which is half that of the standard, its sensory magnitude should be estimated to be 50. Typically, only a couple of observations are taken from each subject, and the data of all subjects are combined by computing the median or the geometrical mean.

The second variant has the favor of many investigators. No standard and no modulus are provided. The subject is simply told to assign to any stimulus presented any number that seems suitable as an estimate of the sensation magnitude.

Interestingly, the results are very similar for the two methods. For intensive continua, the mean or median response $\phi(x)$ is approximately a power function of the physical intensity x:

$$\phi(x) = \alpha x^{\beta} . \tag{144}$$

In log–log coordinates, Eq. (144) becomes the equation of a linear function with slope β, which can be fitted to the data by linear regression. As exemplified in Figure 1.31, this prediction holds reasonably well for much data, at least for moderate to large intensities (see Marks, 1974, or S. S. Stevens, 1975, for a presentation of the evidence). A better overall fit may be obtained, at the cost of one extra parameter, by forms such as

$$\phi(x) = \alpha x^{\beta} + \gamma$$

or

$$\phi(x) = \alpha(x - \gamma)^{\beta} ,$$

both of which are capable of handling the data at low intensities (cf. Ekman, 1956, 1961; Fagot, 1963; Galanter & Messick, 1961; Luce, 1959a; S. S. Stevens, 1959a).

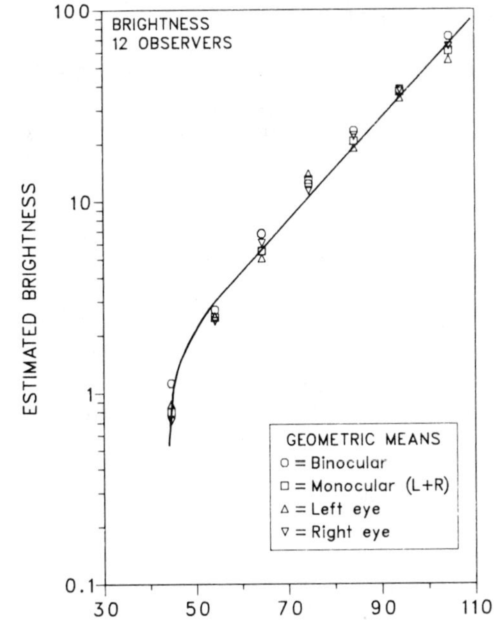

Figure 1.31. Magnitude estimates of brightness. In abscissa, the luminance of the stimuli in decibels re 10^{-6} Lambert. (Adopted from J. C Stevens, Brightness function: Binocular versus monocular stimulation, *Perception and Psychophysics*, 1967, *2*. Reprinted with permission.)

The magnitude estimation procedure is also used in other paradigms. For example, in *ratio estimation*, the observer is asked to evaluate the subjective "ratio" of two stimuli. At least to a first approximation, the experimental results are consistent with those reported for the magnitude estimation of single stimuli. More is said about such consistency in Section 10.7.

It was strongly argued by S. S. Stevens (1957, 1959a, 1961a, 1961b, 1961c) that Eq. (144) should be taken as the fundamental psychophysical law, rather than the logarithmic Fechnerian form derived from Weber's law together with the difference representation for choice probabilities (cf. Section 7.3). Accordingly, serious consideration is given to the estimated value of the exponent β in Eq. (144), which some believe could be a measure of some basic feature of the subject's sensory system. Several dozen sensory continua were investigated by Stevens and others, and the values of the exponent β were tabulated (see, for example, Table 1 in S. S. Stevens, 1975). The claim that the exponent in Eq. (144) is of fundamental importance for psychophysical theory encounters difficulties with various data, however, which indicate that its estimated value strongly depends on the experimental conditions or even on the instructions given to the subject. Among other studies, we mention Teghtsoonian (1971), who shows that the estimated values of β are correlated with the range of the set of stimuli used in the experiment, and Robinson (1976), who demonstrates how the instructions can systematically affect this exponent. A review of some of these effects can be found in Poulton (1968). In the light of available evidence, it is clear that no single, basic sensory factor is responsible for the variations of the exponent. In particular, as argued by Green and Luce (1974), its value may reflect some aspects of the subject's decision-making process.

10.6. Production and Matching Methods

In *production and matching methods*, the subject is requested to react to the stimulation by "producing" a value of a sensory variable, for example, by turning a dial. There are several commonly used procedures, some of which have been encountered earlier in this chapter. The bisection method described in Section 9.9 belongs to that category.

The *magnitude production* reverses the procedure used in magnitude estimation. The subject is given a number and asked to produce a matching intensity. As in magnitude estimation, a power law can be fitted to the data. However, as observed by many investigators, the estimated exponent tends to be larger (see S. S. Stevens & Greenbaum, 1966, for a summary of the data).

In the *ratio production* method, the observer is instructed to adjust the intensity of the stimulus in such a manner that it appears to be a particular multiple or fraction of a standard. (In this last case, the term *fractionation* method is also used.) For example, the subject may be required to produce a tone intensity appearing half as loud as the standard tone of the same frequency. These methods have a long but scattered history and were regarded with some suspicion until Stevens's major contribution to the field. By and large, the data are similar to those obtained with magnitude estimation. (For details, see Marks, 1974 or S. S. Stevens, 1975).

A rather startling prediction may be obtained for the data of the so-called cross-modality matching method. Suppose that for two sensory continua, denoted below as 1 and 2, the magnitude estimation data are adequately summarized by the two power laws

$$\phi_1(x) = \alpha_1 x^{\beta_1} , \qquad \phi_2(y) = \alpha_2 y^{\beta_2} . \qquad (145)$$

For concreteness, suppose that the two sensory continua are loudness and brightness. Imagine now that in a third experiment the subject, rather than matching physical quantities to numbers as in a magnitude estimation experiment, is requested to match the values directly from one sensory continuum to the other, say, from loudness to brightness. At first, this instruction may seem rather bizarre. Actually, not only are the subjects capable of performing such a task without undue hardship, but, once again, they provide reasonably regular data. Assuming that the matching of brightness to loudness is achieved by equating the values of the two psychophysical scales, that is, the two right members in Eq. (145), we obtain

$$\alpha_1 x^{\beta_1} = \alpha_2 y^{\beta_2} .$$

Writing $\phi_{1,2}$ for the cross-modality matching function (thus $\phi_{1,2}(x) = y$) and rearranging, yields

$$\phi_{1,2}(x) = \alpha_{1,2} x^{\beta_{1,2}} , \qquad (146)$$

a power law with

$$\beta_{1,2} = \beta_1/\beta_2 , \qquad (147)$$

and

$$\alpha_{1,2} = \alpha_1/\alpha_2 . \qquad (148)$$

The prediction that the cross-modality matching function is a power law has been verified by several authors, for many continua, and it holds rather well (cf. Figure 1.32). For a number of reasons, the verification of the specific relation linking the exponents in cross-modality matching and magnitude estimation is not as straightforward as it may seem. While S. S. Stevens (1975) and Marks (1974) conclude that Eq. (147) is well supported by the facts, doubt has been expressed by others, based on their analysis of their own data (Baird, Green, & Luce, 1980; Mashour & Hosman, 1968).

10.7. Krantz-Shepard Theory

Despite the limitations, the array of results collected by Stevens and his followers, and summarized in the last two subsections, contains enough regularities to require a systematic explanation.

The *relation theory* outlined below represents the most satisfactory effort made to account for a substantial part of the data. Some seminal ideas were first proposed by Shepard, in an unpublished manuscript, and were then elaborated and axiomatized by Krantz (1972; see also Shepard, 1981). In presenting this theory, we make a number of idealizations. We omit the fact that the data are noisy, are the locus of important contextual and sequential effects, and so forth. To simplify and shorten the exposition, we also specify the theory by properties actually derivable from more abstract axioms in Krantz's paper. (To some extent, our presentation "trivializes" the theory but hopefully renders key notions more transparent.)

The data concern n sensory continua, numbered 1, 2, ..., n. We begin by tightening up the notations. The letters $x, y, \ldots$ (or sometimes $x_i, y_i, \ldots, 1 \leq i \leq n$, to avoid ambiguities) will stand for positive real numbers representing physical intensities of the stimuli (energy level). We denote by:

$N_i(y|x,p)$. The magnitude estimation of stimulus y, with standard x and modulus p, in the sensory continuum i, $1 \leq i \leq n$.

$P_i(x,y)$. The ratio estimation of the pair (x,y) in the sensory continuum i.

$C_{ji}(y_j|x_j,x_i)$. The cross-modality matching value of stimulus y_j from sensory continuum j into sensory continuum i, with modulus (x_j,x_i).

In Krantz's system, the cross-modality matching modulus may be taken to be the stimulus–response pair of the preceding trial. Six axioms, labeled RT1–RT6, specify the theory.

Axiom RT1. For every sensory continuum i, $1 \leq i \leq n$, there is a function $(x,y) \rightarrow l_i(x,y)$ mapping the pairs of stimuli onto a subset of the positive reals (independent of i). These functions

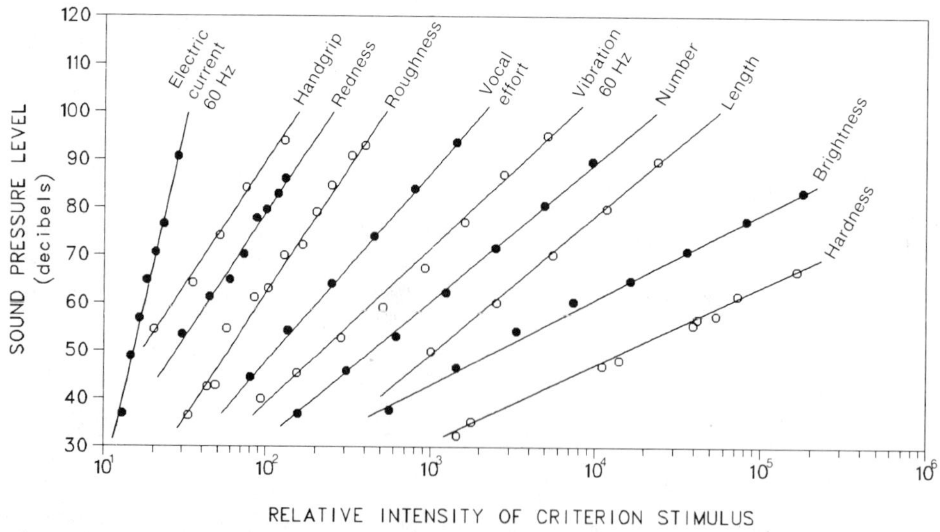

Figure 1.32. Cross-modality matching data between loudness and 10 other sensory continua. (From S. S. Stevens, Matching function between loudness and ten other continua, *Perception and Psychophysics*, 1966, *1*. Reprinted with permission.)

are continuous, strictly increasing in the first variable and strictly decreasing in the second variable. Moreover, the functions l_i are assumed to satisfy the two conditions:

1. $l_i(x,y) \geq l_j(z,w)$ implies $l_j(w,z) \geq l_i(y,x)$.
2. If $l_i(x,y) \geq l_j(x',y')$ and $l_i(y,z) \geq l_j(y',z')$, then $l_i(x,z) \geq l_j(x',z')$.

This is the basic notion. Every pair (x,y) in a sensory continuum i is mapped into a *sensation continuum* by the function l_i. We shall see that the two conditions (1) and (2) ensure that the quantities $l_i(x,y)$, $l_j(z,w)$, ..., and so forth, behave in a certain sense like arithmetical ratios (see Eq. (149)). In the sequel, we shall refer to $l_i(x,y)$ as the *sensation "ratio"* of (x,y). Any estimation or production task is then carried out through the mediation of the sensation "ratios" of the pairs of stimuli involved. Examples are given in the next two axioms.

Axiom RT2. There is a positive-valued, strictly increasing function H such that for every sensory continuum i,

$$P_i(x,y) = H[l_i(x,y)] .$$

In words, the ratio estimates are strictly increasing with the sensation "ratios."

Axiom RT3. For every pair (j,i) of sensory continua,

$$C_{ji}(y_j|x_j,x_i) = y_i \text{ implies } l_j(y_j,x_j) = l_i(y_i,x_i) .$$

In words, with cross-modality matching modulus (x_j,x_i), y_j is matched to y_i only if the sensation "ratios" of (y_j,x_j) and (y_i,x_i) coincide.

The next two axioms emphasize the special role played by one sensory continuum, arbitrarily numbered 1.

Axiom RT4. For the sensory continuum 1,

$$P_1(x,y) \cdot P_1(y,z) = P_1(x,z) .$$

Axiom RT5. If $l_i(y,x) = l_1(z,w)$, then

$$N_i(y|x,p) = p_1^P(z,w) .$$

The special continuum is assumed to be length. Axiom RT4 states essentially that mental estimation of length ratios behaves like physical measurement, an assumption which, Krantz argues, is supported by the fact that the estimated exponents of the power law for judgments of distance are often close to 1. (Some would question that fact. We postpone criticism at this point.) Axiom RT5 is consistent with a mechanism in which magnitude estimation in any sensory continuum i is obtained through computation in the length continuum.

Axiom RT6. For any sensory continuum i and any positive real numbers x, y, and λ,

$$l_i(\lambda x,\lambda y) = l_i(x,y) .$$

Note that this last axiom, which will procure the power law, has the form of Weber's law but applies also to discriminable stimuli. These six axioms have a number of consequences for psychophysical judgments, examples of which follow.

From Axiom RT1 it can be derived that for any sensory continuum i

$$l_i(x,y) = G[f_i(x)/f_i(y)] , \qquad (149)$$

for strictly increasing, continuous functions G and f_i. Combining this result and Axiom RT2, we obtain

$$P_i(x,y) = H\{G[f_i(x)/f_i(y)]\} . \qquad (150)$$

By a standard functional equation argument, applying Eq. (150) and Axiom RT4 results in the function $H[G(s)]$ having the form

$$H[G(s)] = s^\gamma \qquad (151)$$

for some positive constant γ. From Eq. (150) and Axiom RT6, we deduce

$$f_i(\lambda x)/f_i(\lambda y) = f_i(x)/f_i(y) ,$$

a functional equation which (in the conditions of monotonicity or continuity of f_i) has only the solution

$$f_i(x) = \alpha_i x^{\beta_i} ,$$

for some constant α, $\beta > 0$. From Eq. (149), we obtain thus

$$l_i(x,y) = G[(x/y)^{\beta_i}] . \qquad (152)$$

Replacing the sensation magnitudes in Axioms RT2, RT3, and RT5 by their expressions as given by Eq. (152) and using also Eq. (151) gives the expected predictions:

$$P_i(x,y) = (x/y)^{\beta_i\gamma} ;$$

$$N_i(y|x,p) = p(x/y)^{\beta_i\gamma} ;$$

$$C_{ji}(y_j|x_j,x_i) = x_i(y_j/x_j)^{\beta_j/\beta_i} .$$

Notice that the cross-modality matching exponents β_j/β_i can be predicted by the ratio of the magnitude estimation exponents of the preceding equation.

Various criticisms can be made against this theory. In particular, (1) it is deterministic, while the data are highly variable, within or across observers; (2) it omits important sequential and contextual effects, which some believe to be important enough to bias the picture seriously; and (3) the special role of the length continuum can be questioned, specifically the contention that the estimated exponent of the power law is approximately equal to 1 (Baird, 1970).

In our opinion, even though the predictions of relation theory may not be fully supported by the data, they certainly represent useful approximations. If nothing more, relation theory may be taken as a good summary of the way a sizable part of the psychophysical community idealizes data, still a serviceable device.

10.8. Functional Measurement

For some psychophysicists, the data of magnitude estimation and production are hopelessly biased by uncontrollable nuisance effects and such methods should be abandoned. Such is the position of Anderson, who advocates an alternative collection of procedures and models which he calls *functional measurement* (see Anderson 1974, 1976, 1981, for numerous references).

In a typical application of functional measurement, the subject is presented with stimuli varying along several dimensions or aspects, in a factorial design, and is required to produce a rating value, say, on a 20-category rating scale. In one experiment, for example, designed to assess the so-called size–weight illusion, subjects were asked to rate the subjective heaviness of cubical blocks varying in weight and size (Anderson, 1970a). One or more algebraic models are then applied, symbolizing different combination rules for the factors. Let r_{ij} stand for the (average) rating in cell (i,j) of a two-factor design. The most frequently used models are:

The Adding Model $\quad r_{ij} = \alpha_i + \beta_j$;

The Averaging Model $\quad r_{ij} = \dfrac{w_i\alpha_i + w_j\beta_j}{w_i + w_j}$;

The Multiplying Model $\quad r_{ij} = \alpha_i \cdot \beta_j$.

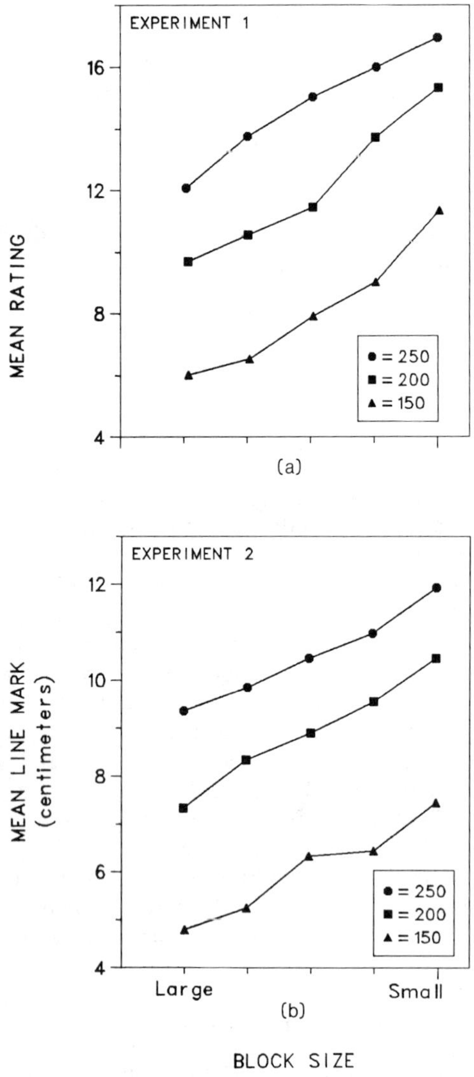

Figure 1.33. Anderson's data for the size-weight illusion. Subjects lift and judge heaviness of cubical blocks in a 3 × 5, gram weight × block size design. Verbal rating response plotted in upper graph (a); graphic rating response in lower graph (b). (From M. H. Anderson, Averaging model applied to the size-weight illusion, *Perception and Psychophysics*, 1970, *8*. Reprinted with permission.)

Assuming appropriate distributions for the variances of the errors, these models can be tested through standard analysis of variance techniques. A graphic plot of the data is also used to validate a model. In the case of the adding model, for instance, since $r_{ik} - r_{jk} = \alpha_i - \beta_j$, independent on k, a check of "parallelism" can be made. This is illustrated in Figure 1.33 for the size–weight illusion experiment mentioned above (Anderson, 1970a, 1981). This analysis favors a model in which subjective heaviness (as evaluated by the ratings) is represented as the sum of subjective weight and appearance.

Occasionally, the standard models cannot be fitted to the rating data. A monotonic rescaling of the ratings is then carried out by numerical techniques. When the fit of a model is taken to be acceptable, the estimated values of the parameters α_i, β_j can be plotted against the corresponding physical measure. The resulting relation is called the *psychophysical law* for that sensory continuum. It is assumed, or hoped, that this relation will hold across situations varying the experimental design, the instructions, and the model but involving the same sensory continuum.

Over the years, Anderson and his followers have applied functional measurement methods to a large body of data in psychophysics and elsewhere and have often succeeded in parsing out the effects of the factors on the ratings, through one or the other of the standard models.

A number of criticisms of Anderson's approach have been made however. The major point of contention concerns the rating response used and, in particular, the status of that response measure with respect to scale type. The mathematical form of the adding and averaging models is invariant under affine transformations (i.e., transformations $x \mapsto \gamma x + \delta$). This property led Anderson to argue that when one such model is found to fit some data, it can be concluded that the rating response and the estimated parameters are interval scales. The objections to this controversial claim are reviewed in Birnbaum (1982).

10.9. Measurement of Sensation

It is impossible in a few pages to do justice to the diversity of positions concerning the measurement of sensation and the form of the "psychophysical scale," that is, the mathematical function relating physical intensity to sensation magnitude. (For a recent sample, see Warren, 1981, and the comments following the article.) These positions go from a rejection of the issue (the measurement of sensation is a hopeless enterprise; e.g., Tumarkin, 1981) to a strongly held opinion that given appropriate experimental control, a particular method yields the desired psychophysical scale (e.g., Anderson, 1981; or S. S. Stevens, 1975). A consensus is not in sight; it has been helpful to distinguish two classes of sensible positions.

1. *Category 1.* Given a large collection of psychophysical data considered important by the psychophysical community, a psychophysical scale should be *adopted* that renders simple or convenient the numerical expression of these data and of the models explaining them. In line with such a position, it is recognized that there is typically a degree of arbitrariness in the choice of a scientific scale and that models and data can usually be recoded if a monotonic rescaling is taking place. Exemplars of this position are Luce and Galanter (1963a), Ellis (1966), and Falmagne (1974). In this connection, we note that there is an overwhelming tendency to plot psychophysical data in logarithmic coordinates and that many models currently in

use have their variables in decibel units or could easily be recast in such terms. From this viewpoint, the Fechnerian logarithmic scale would yet appear—notwithstanding all the attacks—as a reasonable choice for the psychophysical scale.

One objection to this admittedly utilitarian position is that there is no foreseeable agreement regarding what constitutes the bulk of important psychophysical data.

2. *Category 2.* The psychophysicists in this second category consider some particular data to be of primal value in *uncovering* the psychophysical law. The basic idea is that stimulus intensities have a *numerical* representation in the subject's organism, which can be accessed *directly* if the right response is elicited from the subject in the right paradigm. In the same vein, the logarithmic scale is rejected by observing, for example, that pairs of stimuli which are equidistant on the logarithmic scale do not appear to be equidistant subjectively or by showing that this scale differs from that obtained by the selected direct method. Many examples of tenants of such a position may be found among Stevens followers. The belief in the existence, within the organism, of a numerical representation of sensory intensities may perhaps strike a philosopher as a severe case of reification. However, the surprising consistency of the results reported by different laboratories using the same direct method prevents a casual dismissal of the notion. As if some analog device were available to them, the subjects are indeed able to make sense of descriptions of stimuli, such as "half as loud" or "twice as bright," or to provide regular magnitude estimation or rating data.

The difficulty for the advocates of a particular direct method is, again, that there is no agreement in the psychophysical community regarding the choice of such a method. This is both understandable and justified, since the regularity and consistency of the data generated by any direct method (however surprising they may be) are not such that these data could provide the foundation for a scientific scale.

In our opinion, the choice of a psychophysical scale is in part a matter of scientific strategy, with unavoidable political overtones. What should be accomplished with such a scale? It is easily conceivable that no scale could usefully serve the dual purpose of (1) determining a convenient numerical notation of scientific psychophysical facts and models and (2) providing a medium of communication with a naive public on practical questions involving subjective impressions of sensory intensities.

10.10. A Note on Meaningful Psychophysical Laws

One might suppose that the choice of a mathematical formula to represent some data, say, in the form of a scientific law, is solely a matter of goodness of fit. Of course, routine precautions must be taken when evaluating the fit, such as accounting for the number of parameters. This can often be done by standard statistical methods, such as likelihood ratio or minimum chi-square. Granted a proper statistical analysis, the best-fitting formula or model should be chosen, or so it may seem.

Actually, the above scheme is not completely accurate, and considerations of a completely different nature may enter into the selection of a formula. In particular, depending on the type of the scale or scales involved, a given formula may or not be a sensible choice. Suppose, for example, that in an application of the 2AFC paradigm, the binary choice probabilities are represented by the equation

$$P_{a,b} = F\left(\frac{a + 1.83}{b + 1.83}\right), \qquad (153)$$

in which a and b are stimulus intensities expressed in some units of a standard ratio scale (say, sound pressure, weight, or length), F is a strictly increasing continuous function, and 1.83 is a constant. Equation (152) can be objected to on the grounds that it conveys little information if the particular units of the variables a and b are not mentioned. One might ask, Why not mention the units? It turns out that all the scientific laws of importance satisfy the property that they can be quoted without mentioning the units of the scales. Curiously, this is a statement of fact, not a regulation. To illustrate, according to Coulomb's law, "The force in a homogeneous isotropic medium of infinite extent between two point charges is proportional to the product of their magnitude, divided by the square of the distance between them" (Gray, 1957).

Note that this statement of Coulomb's law remains true no matter which units are adopted for the scales entering in the formulation of the law. This statement is thus unambiguous. Numerous similar examples could be given in physics and other fields. By contrast, the form of Eq. (152) is not invariant with admissible transformations of the scales. A better formulation for the lawfulness that Eq. (152) was attempting to capture would be

$$P_{a,b} = F\left(\frac{a + \lambda}{b + \lambda}\right)$$

in which λ is a scale-dependent constant. In the technical jargon, those mathematical formulas having a form invariant of the units of the scales are called *meaningful*. As noted by Falmagne and Narens (1983), the strong liking of scientists for meaningful formulas to represent laws is probably due to a combination of practical and theoretical reasons. From a practical viewpoint, the adoption of nonmeaningful formulas would almost certainly introduce chaos into scientific communication. From a theoretical viewpoint, meaningfulness appears to lead to coherent systems of units (cf., Luce, 1959(b)). Our example involving Eq. (152) may suggest that these matters are relatively trivial and that, with some care, considerations of meaningfulness are easy to apply. Actually, this is only true in the case of very simple mathematical forms.

The space available here only permits us to alert the reader to this question, a full discussion of which would take many rather technical pages. For an introduction to the issue of meaningfulness, see Suppes and Zinnes (1963), Roberts (1979), or Falmagne and Narens (1983). Applications in psychophysics can be found in Luce (1959b).

10.11. Key References

The field of scaling is among those covered regularly in the *Annual Review of Psychology*; for example, Ekman and Sjoberg (1965), Zinnes (1969), Cliff (1973), Carroll and Arabie (1980). The last paper reviews the developments in multidimensional scaling techniques.

The notion of the type of a measurement scale is analyzed in basic measurement papers or books (Ellis, 1966; Krantz et al., 1971; Roberts, 1979; Suppes & Zinnes, 1963).

Techniques, data, and philosophy of direct scaling are discussed in great detail in the books by Marks (1974) or S. S. Stevens (1975).

Introductions to functional measurement procedures are contained in a number of papers and in one book by Anderson (e.g., 1970a, 1970b, 1974, 1976, 1981). An axiomatic analysis of functional measurement, from a measurement standpoint, has been given by Luce (1981).

A recent discussion of some controversial issues in psychological measurement, with a special emphasis on rating scales (including functional measurement methods), can be found in Birnbaum (1982).

Since Fechner, numerous discussions of the issue of measuring sensation have been published, few of which are really enlightening. The last section of Krantz (1972)—although written in a rather terse style—is useful reading in this connection.

Space limitation forced us to consider in detail only two theoretical viewpoints on psychophysical scaling, namely, the Krantz-Shepard relation theory and Anderson's functional measurement procedures, both of which were chosen in view of the amount of data concerned by the theories. This selection may give a distorted view of the field. Among other regrettable omissions, we mention Green and Luce's theory (1974; see also, e.g., Green, Luce, & Duncan, 1977, and Levine, 1974).

REFERENCE NOTES

1. Pavel, M. Personal communication, 1982.
2. Vorberg, D. *Bayesian estimation of arbitrary points on psychometric functions.* Paper presented at the Thirteenth Annual Mathematical Psychology Meeting, University of Wisconsin, August 1980.
3. Krantz, D.H. Personal communication.

REFERENCES

Aczél, J. *Lectures on functional equations and their applications.* New York: Academic Press, 1966.

Alpern, M., Rushton, W. A. H., & Tori, S. The attenuation of rod signals by backgrounds. *Journal of Physiology*, 1970, *206*, 209–227. (a)

Alpern, M., Rushton, W. A. H., & Tori, S. The signals from cones. *Journal of Physiology*, 1970, *207*, 463–475. (b)

Alpern, M., Rushton, W. A. H., & Tori, S. The size of rod signals. *Journal of Physiology*, 1970, *206*, 193–208. (c)

Anderson, N. H. Averaging model applied to the size–weight illusion. *Perception and Psychophysics*, 1970, *8*, 1–4. (a)

Anderson, N. H. Functional measurement and psychophysical judgement. *Psychological Review*, 1970, *77*, 153–170. (b)

Anderson, N. H. Information integration theory: A brief survey. In D. H. Krantz, R. C. Atkinson, R. D. Luce, & P. Suppes (Eds.), *Contemporary developments in mathematical psychology, Vol. 2: Measurement, psychophysics, and neural information processing.* San Francisco: W. H. Freeman, 1974.

Anderson, N. H. Integration theory, functional measurement and the psychophysical law. In H. G. Geissler, & Y. U. M. Zabrodin (Eds.), *Advances in psychophysics.* Berlin: VEB Deutscher Verlag, 1976.

Anderson, N. H. *Foundations of information integration theory.* New York: Academic Press, 1981.

Anderson, T. W., McCarthy, P. I., & Tukey, I. W. Staircase methods of sensitivity testing. *Navord Reports*, 1946, March 21, 46–65.

Baird, J. C. *Psychophysical analysis of visual space.* Oxford: Pergamon Press, 1970.

Baird, J. C., Green, D. M., & Luce, R. D. Variability and sequential effects in cross-modality matching of area and loudness. *Journal of Experimental Psychology: Human Perception and Performance*, 1980, *6*, 277–289.

Berliner, J. E., & Durlach, N. I. Intensity perception IV. Resolution in roving-level discrimination. *Journal of the Acoustical Society of America*, 1973, *53*, 1270–1287.

Berliner, J. E., Durlach, N. I., & Braida, L. D. Intensity perception VII. Further data on roving-level discrimination and the resolution and bias edge effects. *Journal of the Acoustical Society of America*, 1977, *61*, 1577–1585.

Birnbaum, M. H. Differences and ratios in psychological measurement. In F. Restle & N. J. Castellan, Jr. (Eds.), *Cognitive theory* (Vol. 3). Hillsdale, N.J.: Erlbaum, 1978.

Birnbaum, M. H. Controversies in psychological measurement. In B. Wegener (Ed.), *Social attitudes and psychophysical measurement.* Hillsdale, N.J.: Erlbaum, 1982.

Blake, R., & Fox, R. The psychophysical inquiry into binocular summation. *Perception and Psychophysics*, 1973, *14*, 161–185.

Block, H. D., & Marschak, J. Random orderings and stochastic theories of responses. In I. Olkin, S. Ghurye, W. Hoeffding, W. Madow, & H. Mann (Eds.), *Contributions to probability and statistics.* Stanford: Stanford University Press, 1960.

Bock, R. D., & Jones, L. V. *The measurement and prediction of judgement and choice.* San Francisco: Holden-Day, 1968.

Boring, E. G., Langfeld, H. S., & Weld, H. P. *Foundations of psychology.* New York: Wiley, 1948.

Bradley, R. A. Incomplete block rank analysis: On the appropriateness of the model for a method of paired comparisons. *Biometrics, 10*, 1954, 375–390. (a)

Bradley, R. A. Rank analysis of incomplete block designs. II. Additional tables for the method of paired comparisons. *Biometrika, 41*, 1954, 502–537. (b)

Bradley, R. A. Rank analysis of incomplete block designs. III. Some large sample results on estimation and power for a method of paired comparisons. *Biometrika, 42*, 1955, 450–470.

Bradley, R. A., & Terry, M. E. Rank analysis of incomplete block designs. I. The method of paired comparisons. *Biometrika, 39*, 1952, 324–345.

Braida, L. D., & Durlach, N. I. Intensity perception. II. Resolution in one-interval paradigms. *Journal of the Acoustical Society of America*, 1972, *51*, 483–502.

Bramber, D. The area above the ordinal dominance graph and the area below the receiver operating characteristic graph. *Journal of Mathematical Psychology*, 1975, *12*, 387–415.

Broadbent, D. E., & Gregory, M. Vigilance considered as a statistical decision. *British Journal of Psychology*, 1968, *54*, 309–323.

Brown, J., & Cane, V. R. An analysis of the limiting method. *British Journal of Statistical Psychology*, 1959, *12*, 119–126.

Carroll, J. B., & Arabie, P. Multidimensional scaling. *Annual Review of Pscyhology*, 1980, *31*, 607–649.

Cliff, N. Scaling. *Annual Review of Psychology*, 1973, *24*, 473–506.

Coombs, C. H., Dawes, R. M., & Tversky, A. *Mathematical psychology: An elementary introduction.* Englewood Cliffs, N.J.: Prentice-Hall, 1970.

Cornsweet, T. N., & Pinsker, H. M. Luminance discrimination of brief flashes under various conditions of adaptation. *Journal of Physiology*, 1965, *17*(6), 713–719.

Cramer, H. *Mathematical methods of statistics.* Princeton, N.J.: Princeton University Press, 1963.

Cross, D. V. An application of mean value theory to psychological measurement. In *Progress Report No. 6* (Report No. 05613-3-P). Ann Arbor: The Behavioral Analysis Laboratory, University of Michigan, 1965.

Dawson, S. Binocular and uniocular discrimination of brightness. *British Journal of Psychology*, 1913, *6*, 78–108.

Debreu, G. Topological methods in cardinal utility theory. In S. Karlin & P. Suppes (Eds.), *Mathematical methods in the social sciences.* Stanford: Stanford University Press, 1960.

Derman, C. Non-parametric up-and-down experimentation. *Annals of Mathematical Statistics*, 1957, *28*, 795–797.

Doignon, J. P., & Falmagne, J. C. Difference measurement and simple scalability with restricted solvability. *Journal of Mathematical Psychology*, 1974, *11*(4), 473–499.

Durlach, N. I., & Braida, L. D. Intensity perception: I. Preliminary theory of intensity resolution. *Journal of the Acoustical Society of America*, 1969, *46*, 372–383.

Egan, J. P. *Signal detection theory and ROC analysis*. New York: Academic Press, 1975.

Ekman, G. Subjective power functions and the method of fractionation. *Report from the psychological laboratory* (*No. 34*). Stockholm: University of Stockholm, 1956.

Ekman, G. Methodological note on scales of gustatory intensity. *Scandinavian Journal of Psychology*, 1961, *2*, 185–190.

Ekman, G., & Sjoberg, L. Scaling. *Annual Review of Psychology*, 1965, *16*, 451–474.

Ellis, B. *Basic concepts of measurement*. London: Cambridge University Press, 1966.

Engen, T. Psychophysics: Discrimination and detection. In J. W. Kling & L. A. Riggs (Eds.), *Experimental psychology*. New York: Holt, Rinehart & Winston, 1971.

Fagot, R. F. On the psychophysical law and estimation procedures in psychophysical scaling. *Psychometrika*, 1963, *28*, 145–160.

Falmagne, J. C. Note on a simple property of binary mixtures. *British Journal of Mathematical & Statistical Psychology*, 1968, *21*(1), 131–132.

Falmagne, J. C. The generalized Fechner problem and discrimination. *Journal of Mathematical Psychology*, 1971, *8*, 22–43.

Falmagne, J. C. Foundations of Fechnerian psychophysics. In D. H. Krantz, R. C. Atkinson, R. D. Luce, & P. Suppes (Eds.), *Contemporary developments in mathematical psychology, Vol. 2. Measurement psychophysics and neural information processing*. San Francisco: W. H. Freeman, 1974.

Falmagne, J. C. Random conjoint measurement and loudness summation. *Psychological Review*, 1976, *83*, 65–79.

Falmagne, J. C. Note: Weber's inequality and Fechner's problem. *Journal of Mathematical Psychology*, 1977, *16*, 267–271.

Falmagne, J. C. A representation theorem for finite random scales systems. *Journal of Mathematical Psychology*, 1978, *18*, 52–72.

Falmagne, J. C. On a class of probabilistic conjoint measurement models: Some diagnostic properties. *Journal of Mathematical Psychology*, 1979, *19*, 73–88.

Falmagne, J. C. A probabilistic theory of extensive measurement. *Journal of Philosophy of Science*, 1980, *47*(2), 277–296.

Falmagne, J. C. Psychometric functions theory. *Journal of Mathematical Psychology*, 1982, *25*(1), 1–50.

Falmagne, J. C., & Iverson, G. J. Conjoint Weber laws and additivity. *Journal of Mathematical Psychology*, 1979, *20*, 164–183.

Falmagne, J. C., Iverson, G. J., & Marcovici, S. Binaural loudness summation: Probabilistic theory and data. *Psychological Review*, 1979, *86*, 25–43.

Falmagne, J. C., & Narens, L. Scales and meaningfulness of quantitative laws. *Synthese*, 1983, *55*(3), 287–326.

Fechner, G. T. *Elements of psychophysics*. D. H. Howes and E. C. Boring (Eds.), (H. E. Adler, trans.). New York: Holt, Rinehart & Winston, 1966. (Originally published, 1860).

Fisher, R. A., & Tippett, L. H. C. Limiting forms of the frequency distributions of the largest or smallest member of a sample. *Proceedings of the Cambridge Philosophical Society*, 1928, *24*, 180–190.

Fréchet, M. Sur la loi de probabilité de l'écart maximum. *Annales de la Société Polonaise de Mathématiques (Cracow)*, 1927, *6*, 93.

Galambos, J. *The asymptotic theory of extreme order statistics*. New York: Wiley, 1978.

Galanter, E., & Messick, S. The relation between category and magnitude scales of loudness. *Psychological Review*, 1961, *68*, 363–372.

Garner, W. R. An informational analysis of absolute judgements of loudness. *Journal of Experimental Psychology*, 1953, *46*, 373–380.

Garner, W. R. *Uncertainty and structure as psychological concepts*. New York: Wiley, 1962.

Gescheider, G. A. *Psychophysics: Method and theory*. Hillsdale, N.J.: Erlbaum, 1976.

Gigerenzer, G., & Strube, G. Are there limits to binaural additivity of loudness? *Journal of Experimental Psychology: Human Perception and Performance*, 1983, *9*(1), 126–136.

Gnedenko, B. V. Sur la distribution limite tu terme maximum d'une serie aleatoire. *Annals of Mathematics*, 1943, *44*, 423–453.

Gravetter, F., & Lockhead, G. R. Criterial range as a frame of reference for stimulus judgments. *Psychological Review*, 1973, *80*, 203–216.

Gray, D. E. (Ed.). *American Institute of Physics handbook*. New York: McGraw-Hill, 1957.

Green. D. M. *An introduction to hearing*. Hillsdale, N.J.: Erlbaum, 1978.

Green, D. M., & Luce, R. D. Variability of magnitude estimates: A timing theory analysis. *Perception and Psychophysics*, 1974, *15*, 291–300.

Green, D. M., & Swets, J. A. *Signal detection theory and psychophysics*. New York: Krieger, 1974.

Green, D. M., & Luce, R. D. Parallel psychometric functions from a set of independent detectors. *Psychological Bulletin*, 1975, *82*, 483–486.

Green, D. M., Luce, R. D., & Duncan, J. E. Variability and sequential effects in magnitude production and estimation of auditory intensity. *Perception and Psychophysics*, 1977, *22*, 450–456.

Gumbel, E. G. *Statistics of extremes*. New York: Columbia University Press, 1958.

Helmholtz, H. V. Zahlen und Messen erkenntnis-theoretisch betrachtet, Philosophische Aufsutze Eduard Zeller gewidmet, Leipzig, 1887. (Reprinted in Gesammelte Abhandl., 1895, *3*, 356–391. (English translation by C. L. Bryan), *Counting and measuring*. Princeton, N.J.: Van Nostrand, 1930.

Holland, M. K., & Lockhead, G. R. Sequential effects in absolute judgments of loudness. *Perception and Psychophysics*, 1968, *3*, 409–414.

Holway, A. H., & Pratt, C. C. The Weber-ratio for intensive discrimination. *Psychological Review*, 1936, *43*, 322–340.

Iverson, G. J. Note: Conditions under which Thurstone Case III representations for binary choice probabilities are also Fechnerian. *Journal of Mathematical Psychology*, 1979, *20*(3), 263–271.

Iverson, G. J. Weber's inequality and asymptotic representations of binary choice probabilities. Submitted to *Journal of Mathematical Psychology*, 1983.

Iverson, G. J., & Falmagne, J. C. Statistical issues in measurements. *Mathematical Social Sciences*. In press.

Iverson, G. J., & Pavel, M. Invariant properties of masking phenomena in psychoacoustics and their theoretical consequences. *SIAM-AMS Proceedings*, 1980, *13*, 17–24.

Iverson, G. J., & Pavel, M. On the functional form of partial masking functions in psychoacoustics. *Journal of Mathematical Psychology*, 1981, *24*, 1–20. (a)

Iverson, G. J., & Pavel, M. Invariant characteristics of partial masking: Implications for mathematical models. *Journal of the Acoustical Society of America*, 1981, *69*, 1126–1131. (b)

Jesteadt, W., & Bilger, R. C. Intensity and frequency discrimination in one- and two-interval paradigms. *Journal of the Acoustical Society of America*, 1974, *55*, 1266–1276.

Jesteadt, W., Luce, R. D., & Green, D. M. Sequential effects in judgments of loudness. *Journal of Experimental Pscyhology: Human Perception and Performance*, 1977, *3*, 92–104.

Jesteadt, W., & Sims, S. L. Decision processes in frequency discrimination. *Journal of the Acoustical Society of America*, 1975, *57*, 1161–1168.

Jesteadt, W., Wier, C. C., & Green, D. M. Intensity discrimination as a function of frequency and sensation level. *Journal of the Acoustical Society of America*, 1977, *61*, 169–177.

Johnson, N. I., & Kotz, S. *Distributions in statistics: Discrete distributions*. Boston: Houghton Mifflin, 1969.

Johnson, N. I., & Kotz, S. *Distributions in statistics: Continuous univariate distributions* (Vols. 1 & 2). Boston: Houghton Mifflin, 1970. (a)

Johnson, N. I., & Kotz, S. *Distributions in statistics: Continuous multivariate distributions*. New York: Wiley, 1970. (b)

Kesten, H. Accelerated stochastic approximation. *Annals of Mathematical Statistics*, 1958, *29*, 41–59.

Kling, J. W., & Riggs, L. A. *Experimental psychology* (3rd ed.). New York: Holt, Rinehart & Winston, 1971.

Krantz, D. H. Threshold theories of signal detection. *Psychology Review*, 1969, *76*, 308–324.

Krantz, D. H. Integration of just noticeable differences. *Journal of Mathematical Psychology*, 1971, *8*, 591–599.

Krantz, D. H. A theory of magnitude estimation and cross-modality matching. *Journal of Mathematical Psychology*, 1972, *9*, 168–199.

Krantz, D. H., Luce, R. D., Suppes, P., & Tversky, A. *Foundation of measurement* (Vol. 1). New York: Academic Press, 1971.

Kristofferson, A. B., & Dember, W. N. *Detectability of targets consisting of multiple small points of light*. University of Michigan: Vision Research Laboratories, Technical Report No. 2144-298-T, 1958.

Laming, D. R. J. *Sensory analysis*. (Technical report), Department of Experimental Psychology, Cambridge University, 1983.

Levelt, W. J. M., Riemersma, J. B., & Bunt, A. A. Binaural additivity in loudness. *British Journal of Mathematical and Statistical Psychology*, 1972, *25*, 51–68.

Levine, M. V. Transformations that render curves parallel. *Journal of Mathematical Psychology*, 1971, *7*, 410–444.

Levine, M. V. Transforming curves into curves with the same shape. *Journal of Mathematical Psychology*, 1972, *9*, 1.

Levine, M. V. Geometric interpretations of some psychophysical results. In D. H. Krantz, R. C. Atkinson, R. D. Luce, & P. Suppes (Eds.), *Contemporary developments in mathematical psychology, Vol. 2, Measurement, psychophysics, and neural information processing*. San Francisco: W. H. Freeman, 1974.

Levine, M. V. Additive measurement with short segments of curves. *Journal of Mathematical Psychology*, 1975, *12*, 212–224.

Levitt, H. Transformed up-down methods in psychoacoustics. *Journal of the Acoustical Society of America*, 1970, *49*, 467–476.

Levitt, H. Decision theory, signal-dectection theory, and psychophysics. In E. E. David & P. D. Denas (Eds.), *Human communication: A unified view*. New York: McGraw-Hill, 1972.

Lim, J. S., Rabinowitz, W. M., Braida, L. D., & Durlach, N. I. Intensity perception VIII: Loudness comparisons between different types of stimuli. *Journal of the Acoustical Society of America*, 1977, *62*, 1256–1267.

Lippman, R. P., Braida, L. D., & Durlach, N. I. Intensity perception. V. Effect of payoff matrix on absolute indentification. *Journal of the Acoustical Society of America*, 1976, *59*, 121–134.

Lochner, J. P., & Burger, J. F. Form of the loudness function in the presence of masking noise. *Journal of the Acoustical Society of America*, 1961, *33*, 1705–1707.

Luce, R. D. *Individual choice behavior: A theoretical analysis*. New York: Wiley, 1959. (a)

Luce, R. D. On the possible psychophysical laws. *Psychological Review*, 1959, *66*(2), 81–95. (b)

Luce, R. D. Detection thresholds: A problem reconsidered. *Science*, 1960, *132*, 1495.

Luce, R. D. A threshold theory for simple detection experiments. *Psychological Review*, 1963, *70*, 61–69. (a)

Luce, R. D. Detection and Recognition. In R. D. Luce, R. R. Bush, & E. Galanter (Eds.), *Handbook of mathematical psychology* (Vol. 2). New York: Wiley, 1963. (b)

Luce, R. D. The choice axiom after twenty years. *Journal of Mathematical Psychology*, 1977, *15*, 215–233. (a)

Luce, R. D. Thurstone discriminal processes fifty years later. *Psychonometrika*, 1977, *42*(4), 461–498. (b)

Luce, R. D. Axioms for the averaging and adding representations of functional measurement. *Mathematical Social Sciences*, 1981, *1*, 144–139.

Luce, R. D., & Edwards, W. The derivation of subjective scales from just noticeable differences. *Psychological Review*, 1958, *65*(4), 222–237.

Luce, R. D., & Galanter, E. Discrimination. In R. D. Luce, R. R. Bush, & E. Galanter (Eds.), *Handbook of mathematical psychology* (Vol. 1). New York: Wiley, 1963. (a)

Luce, R. D., & Galanter, E. Psychophysical scaling. In R. D. Luce, R. R. Bush, & E. Galanter (Eds.), *Handbook of mathematical psychology*. New York: Wiley, 1963. (b)

Luce, R. D., & Suppes, P. Preference utility and subjective probability. In R. D. Luce, R. R. Bush, & E. Galanter (Eds.), *Handbook of mathematical psychology* (Vol. 3). New York: Wiley, 1965.

Luce, R. D., & Green, D. M. A neural timing theory for response times and the psychophysics of intensity. *Psychological Review*, 1972, *79*, 14–57.

Luce, R. D., & Green, D. M. Neural coding and psychophysical discrimination data. *Journal of the Acoustical Society of America*, 1974, *56*, 1554–1564. (a)

Luce, R. D., & Green, D. M. The response ratio hypothesis for magnitude estimation. *Journal of Mathematical Psychology*, 1974, *11*(1), 1–14. (b)

Luce, R. D., Green, D. M., & Weber, D. M. Attention bands in absolute identification. *Perception and Psychophysics*, 1976, *20*, 49–54.

Manski, C. F. The structure of random utility models. In G. L. Eberlein, W. Kroeber-Reil, W. Leinfellner, & F. Schick (Eds.), *Theory and decision*. Dordrecht, Holland: D. Reidel, 1977.

Marks, L. E. *Sensory processes*. New York: Academic Press, 1974.

Marschak, J. Binary choice constraints on random utility indicators. In K. E. Arrow, S. Karlin, & P. Suppes (Eds.), *Standard symposium on mathematical methods in the social sciences*. Stanford, Calif.: Stanford University Press, 1960.

Mashour, M., & Hosman, J. On the new "psychophysical law": A validation study. *Perception and Psychophysics*, 1968, *3*, 367–375.

McFadden, D., & Richter, M. K. *Revealed stochastic preferences*. Department of Economics, University of California, Berkeley, 1970.

McFadden, D., & Richter, M. K. *On the extension of a set function to a probability on the Boolean algebra generated by a family of events, with applications*. (Working paper No. 14), Mathematical Social Science Board Workshop on the Theory of Markets under Uncertainty, Department of Economics, University of California, Berkeley, unpublished, 1971.

McFadden, D. Quantal choice analysis: A survey. *Annals of Economic and Social Measurement*, 1976, *5*(4), 363–390.

McGill, W. J., & Goldberg, J. P. Pure-tone intensity discrimination and energy detection. *Journal of the Acoustical Society of America*, 1968, *44*, 576–581.

Miller, G. A. What is information measurement? *American Psychologist*, 1953, *8*, 3–11.

Miller, G. A. The magical number seven, plus or minus two: Some limits on our capacity for processing information. *Psychological Review*, 1956, *63*, 81–97.

Mises, R. von. La distribution de la plus grande de n valeurs. *Revue mathématique de l'union interbalkanique*, 1939, *I*(1), 141–160. (Reprinted in *Selected papers II*). American Mathematical Society, Providence, R.I., 1954, pp. 271–294.

Munsell. *Munsell Book of Color*. 1929.

Nachmias, J. On the psychometric function for contrast detection. *Vision search*, 1981, *21*, 215–224.

Nachmias, J., & Steinman, R. M. Study of absolute visual detection by the rating-scale method. *Journal of the Optical Society of America*, 1963, *53*, 1206–1213.

Naka, K. I., & Rushton, W. A. H. S-Potentials from colour units in the retina of fish (*Cyprinidae*). *Journal of Physiology, London*, 1966, *185*, 536–555. (a)

Naka, K. I., & Rushton, W. A. H. An attempt to analyse color perception by electrophysiology. *Journal of Physiology, London*, 1966, *185*, 556–586. (b)

Naka, K. I., & Rushton, W. A. H. S-Potentials from luminosity units in the retina of fish (*Cyprinidae*). *Journal of Physiology, London*, 1966, *185*, 587–599. (c)

Narens, L. On the scales of measurement. *Journal of Mathematical Psychology*, 1981, *24*, 249–275.

Narens, L., & Luce, R. D. The algebra of measurement. *Journal of Pure and Applied Algebra*, 1976, *8*, 197–233.

Neyman, J., & Pearson, E. S. On the problem of the most efficient tests of statistical hypothesis. Royal Society London, Series A, 1933, p. 289.

Parducci, A. Range-frequency compromise in judgment. *Psychological Monographs*, 1963, *77* (2, Whole No. 565).

Parducci, A. Category judgment: A range-frequency model. *Psychological Review*, 1965, *72*, 407–418.

Parducci, A. Contextual effects: A range-frequency analysis. In E. C. Carterette & M. P. Friedman (Eds.), *Handbook of perception* (Vol. 2). New York: Academic Press, 1974.

Parducci, A., & Perrett, L. F. Category rating scales: Effects of relative spacing and frequency of stimulus values. *Journal of Experimental Psychology*, 1971, *89*, 427–452.

Parker, S., & Schneider, B. Loudness and loudness discrimination. *Perception and Psychophysics*, 1980, *28*(5), 398–406.

Parzen, E. *Stochastic processes*. San Francisco, Calif.: Holden-Day, 1962.

Pavel, M. *Homogeneity in complete and partial masking*. Unpublished doctoral dissertation, New York University, 1980.

Peterson, W. W., Birdsall, T. L., & Fox, W. C. The theory of signal detectability. (Trans.) *IRE Prof. Group on Info. Theory*, PGIT-4, 1954, 171–212.

Pfanzagl, J. *Theory of measurement* (2nd ed.). New York: Wiley, 1968, 1971.

Pirenne, M. M. Binocular and uniocular thresholds for vision. *Nature*, 1943, *153*, 698–699.

Plateau, M. J. Sur la mesure des sensations physiques, et sur la loi qui lie l'intensité de ces sensations à l'intensité de la cause excitante. *Bull. Acad. Royale Belge*, 1872, *33*, 376–388.

Pollack, I. Information in elementary auditory displays. *Journal of the Acoustical Society of America*, 1952, *24*, 745–750.

Poulton, E. C. The new psychophysics: Six models for magnitude estimation. *Psychological Bulletin*, 1968, *69*, 1–19.

Pratt, J. W. Robustness of some procedures for the two-sample location problem. *Journal of the American Statistical Association*, 1964, *59*, 665–680.

Purks, S. R., Callaghan, D. J., Braida, L. D., & Durlach, N. I. Intensity perception. X. Effect of preceding stimulus on identification performance. *Journal of the Acoustical Society of America*, 1980, *67*, 634–637.

Pynn, C. T., Braida, L. D., & Durlach, N. I. Intensity perception. III: Resolution in small-range identification. *Journal of the Acoustical Society of America*, 1972, *51*, 559–566.

Quick, R. F. A vector magnitude model of contrast detection. *Kybernetic*, 1974, *16*, 65–67.

Robbins, H., & Monro, S. A stochastic approximation method. *Annals of Mathematical Statistics*, 1951, *22*, 400–407.

Roberts, F. S. Measurement theory. In Gian-Carlo Rota (Ed.), *Encyclopedia of mathematics and its applications* (Vol. 7): *Mathematics and the social sciences*. Reading, Mass.: Addison-Wesley, 1979.

Robinson, G. H. Biasing power law exponents by magnitude estimation instructions. *Perception and Psychophysics*, 1976, *19*, 80–84.

Scharf, B. In E. C. Carterette & M. P. Friedman (Eds.), *Handbook of perception. Vol. 4: Hearing*. New York: Academic Press, 1978, 187–242.

Shepard, R. N. Psychological relations and psychophysical scales: On the status of "direct" psychophysical measurement. *Journal of Mathematical Psychology*, 1981, *24*, 21–57.

Sirovich, L., & Abramov, I. Photopigments and pseudo-pigments. *Vision Research*, 1977, *17*, 5–16.

Stevens, J. C. Brightness function: Binocular versus monocular stimulation. *Perception and Psychophysics*, 1967, *2*, 189–192, 452.

Stevens, S. S. On the psychophysical law. *Psychological Review*, 1957, *64*, 153–181.

Stevens, S. S. Cross-modality validation of subjective scales for loudness, vibration, and electric shock. *Journal of Experimental Psychology*, 1959, *57*, 201–209. (a)

Stevens, S. S. Review of L. L. Thurstone, "The measurement of values." *Contemporary Psychology*, 1959, *4*, 388–389. (b)

Stevens, S. S. Procedure for calculating loudness: Mark VI. *Journal of the Acoustical Society of America*, 1961, *33*, 1577–1585. (a)

Stevens, S. S. The psychophysics of sensory function. In W. A. Rosenblith (Ed.), *Sensory communication*. New York: Wiley, 1961, 1–33. (b)

Stevens, S. S. To honor Fechner and repeal his law. *Science*, 1961, *133*, 80–86 (c)

Stevens, S. S. Matching functions between loudness and ten other continua. *Perception and Psychophysics*, 1966, *1*, 5–8. (a)

Stevens, S. S. A metric for the social consensus. *Science*, 1966, *151*, 530–541. (b)

Stevens, S. S. *Psychophysics: Introduction to its perceptual, neural, and social prospects*. New York: Wiley, 1975.

Stevens, S. S., & Greenbaum, H. B. Regression effect in psychophysical judgment. *Perception and Psychophysics*, 1966, *1*, 439–446.

Stevens, S. S., & Guirao, M. Loudness functions under inhibition. *Perception and Psychophysics*, 1967, *2*, 459–465.

Strackee, G., & van der Gon, J. J. D. The frequency distribution of the difference between two Poisson variables. *Statistica Neerlandica*, 1962, *16*, 17–23.

Suppes, P., & Zinnes, J. L. Basic measurement theory. In *Handbook of mathematical psychology* (Vol. 1). New York: Wiley, 1963.

Swets, J. A. Detection theory and psychophysics: A review. *Psychometrika*, 1961, *26*, 49–63.

Swets, J. A. (Ed.) *Signal detection and recognition by human observers: Contemporary readings*. New York: Wiley, 1964.

Tanner, W. P., Jr., & Swets, J. A. *A new theory of visual detection*. (Technical Report No. 18), University of Michigan: Electric Defense Group, 1953.

Tanner, W. P., Jr., & Swets, J. A. The human use of information: I. Signal detection for the case of the signal known exactly. (Trans.) *IRE Prof. Group on Info. Theory*, PGIT-4, 1954, 213–221. (a)

Tanner, W. P., Jr., & Swets, J. A. A decision-making theory of visual detection. *Psychological Review*, 1954, *61*, 401–409. (b)

Teghtsoonian, R. On the exponents in Stevens' law and the constant in Ekman's law. *Psychological Review*, 1971, *78*, 71–80.

Thompson, W. A., Jr., & Singh, J. The use of limit theorems in paired comparison model-building. *Psychometrika*, 1967, *32*, 255–264.

Thurstone, L. L. A law of comparative judgment. *Psychophysical Review*, 1927, *34*, 273–286. (a)

Thurstone, L. L. Psychophysical analysis. *American Journal of Psychology*, 1927, *38*, 368–389. (b)

Tumarkin, A. A biologist looks at psychoacoustics. A commentary to: Warren, R. M. Measurement of sensory intensity. *The Behavioral and Brain Sciences*, 1981, *4*, 175–223.

Urban, F. M. On the method of just perceptible differences. *Psychological Review*, 1907, *14*, 244–253.

Van Meter, D., & Middleton, D. Modern statistical approaches to reception in communication theory. (Trans.) *IRE Prof. Group on Info. Theory*. PGIT-4, 1954, 119–141.

Wald, A. *Sequential analysis*. New York: Wiley; London: Chapman and Hall, 1947.

Wald, A. *Statistical decision functions*. New York: Wiley, 1950.

Wandell, B., & Luce, R. D. Pooling peripheral information: Average versus extreme values. *Journal of Mathematical Psychology*, 1978, *17*(3), 220–235.

Ward, L. M. Category of judgments of loudness in the absence of an experimenter-induced identification function: Sequential effects of power-function fit. *Journal of Experimental Psychology*, 1972, *94*, 179–184.

Ward, L. M., & Lockhead, G. R. Sequential effects and memory in category judgments. *Journal of Experimental Psychology*, 1970, *84*, 27–34.

Ward, L. M., & Lockhead, G. R. Response system processes in absolute judgment. *Perception and Psychophysics*, 1971, *9*, 73–78.

Warren, R. M. Measurement of sensory intensity. *The Behavioral and Brain Sciences*, 1981, *4*, 175–223.

Wasan, M. T. *Stochastic approximation*. Cambridge: University Press, 1969.

Watson, C. S., Rilling, M. E., & Bourbon, W. T. Receiver-operating characteristics determined by a mechanical analog to the rating scale. *Journal of the Acoustical Society of America*, 1964, *36*, 283–288.

Weber, D. L., Green, D. M., & Luce, R. D. Effects of practice and distribution of auditory signals on absolute identification. *Perception and Psychophysics*, 1977, *22*, 223–231.

Weiss, D. J. Quantifying private events: A functional measurement analysis of equisection. *Perception and Psychophysics*, 1975, *17*, 351–357.

Wetherill, G. B. Sequential estimation of quantal response curves. *Journal of Royal Statistical Society*, 1963, *B25*, 1–48.

Wetherill, G. B., Chen, H., & Vasudeva, R. B. Sequential estimation of quantal response curves: A new method of estimation. *Biometrika*, 1966, *53*, 439–454.

Wilks, S. S. *Mathematical statistics*. New York: Wiley, 1962.

Yellot, J. L., Jr. The relationship between Luce's choice axiom, Thurstone's theory of comparative judgment, and the double exponential distribution. *Journal of Mathematical Psychology*, 1977, *15*, 109–144.

Zinnes, J. L. Scaling. *Annual Review of Psychology*, 1969, *20*, 447–478.

CHAPTER 2

STRATEGY AND OPTIMIZATION IN HUMAN INFORMATION PROCESSING

GEORGE SPERLING

Department of Psychology, New York University, New York, New York

BARBARA ANNE DOSHER

Department of Psychology, Columbia University, New York, New York

CONTENTS

The authors wish to dedicate this chapter to the memory of Marilyn Shaw (1946–1983).

This chapter deals with the recent methods and theories developed to study subjects' strategies in the performance of perceptual and cognitive tasks. *Strategy* refers to the selection and sequencing (by the subject) of mental operations in the performance of a task. In some cases, important components of the strategy are externally observable, as in the sequence of eye movements that a subject makes in searching a display for a target signal. In the cases considered here, the strategy is not directly observable but must be inferred by means of elaborate theories from repeated, indirect observations. A guiding principle in these theories is that the subject chooses a strategy with the intent of optimizing behavior with respect to the external situation, given his or her internal limitations. For example, the sequence of eye movements in search cannot be understood unless we know critical situation-determined facts (such as where the subject expects to find targets and what the payoffs for various outcomes of the search task are) and critical internal constraints (such as the distribution of acuity around the point of fixation and the maximum rate of eye movement).

It is much more difficult to establish the existence and to provide a quantitative description of an unobservable strategy than of a directly observable one. Consequently, this chapter is restricted to relatively simple tasks performed in very brief time periods. Nevertheless, the same general principles of optimization that apply to decision making and resource allocation on a large scale apply to "micro" strategies that govern decision making and mental resource allocation on a millisecond time scale. In psychology, signal detection theory (SDT) introduced the concepts of optimization to the most elementary perceptual tasks, simple detection of threshold signals. In SDT, strategy is restricted to variation of a decision criterion (the bias) to maximize the subject's expected utility. In earlier detection theories, the subject's strategy consisted of selecting a guessing algorithm applied on some fraction of trials, usually those on which the subject had acquired insufficient information for a stimulus-controlled response. In this chapter, the scope of all these theories is expanded. It is assumed that the goal of the subject is to maximize rewards (utility). In SDT, this optimization principle is explicit. Nevertheless, optimization has been obscured by particularizing the optimization principles inherent in SDT to signal detection so that some general properties and problems of optimization, such as iso-utility contours, complex payoff rules, multidimensional strategies, and changeover costs, have been overlooked or neglected.

Subjects' strategies in SDT and, more generally, in compound tasks are *decision* strategies, governed by the same general principles that govern decision making under uncertainty, that is, decision making with partial or inaccurate information. On the other hand, in other multitask, divided-attention situations, such as driving a car and listening to the radio, subjects' strategies deal with the allocation of mental processing resources. Remarkably, the optimization theory underlying resource allocation is largely isomorphic to the theory underlying decision making in detection! This is a powerful argument for considering these two areas of study together.

Reaction-time experiments are another domain in which subjects' performance can only be understood in terms of their unobservable strategy. Strategy manifests itself, for example, in the choice of a particular operating point on a speed–accuracy trade-off; the theory of how this choice is made is an extension of the optimization theory governing detection and resource allocation.

The methods for measuring observable motor responses have been developed to a high degree of precision. New experimental methods allow equally precise measurement of the reaction time of an observer's attention shift. This is the precise characterization of the dynamics of the mental resource allocation involved in strategies. Finally, some classical psychophysical procedures, and some new ones, are analyzed in terms of how they control, or fail to control, subjects' strategies and what this means in terms of choosing experimental procedures appropriate for the subsequent uses of the data.

1. CONCURRENT VERSUS COMPOUND: A TASK TAXONOMY

In the study of signal detection, attention, and performance, one is often interested in the subject's ability to perform several tasks (or to respond to several classes of stimuli) in the same situation. While there are many ways to combine subtasks into a combined task, two kinds of combinations are by far the most common: *concurrent* combinations and *compound* combinations (Sperling, 1984). The exact manner in which the component tasks are combined is critical for interpreting the results and for understanding the subject's strategy. This section contains the formal definitions of a task and of compound and concurrent combinations, with some representative examples. The interpretation of results is considered in Section 4, after the issues of optimization have been considered.

1.1. Task Definition

The discussion here is restricted to *discrete* tasks, tasks which consist of discrete trials, as contrasted to *continuous* tasks. One trial of a discrete task consists of the presentation of a stimulus s and the observation of a response r. For example, a visual search task might present a 5 × 5 array with the digit *1* in one of the 25 locations. The task is to report location. One characterization of this is a 25-element stimulus set and a 25-element response set. The *outcome* of a trial is the s,r pair resulting from that trial. For every outcome, there is assumed to be a utility, which is a real number representing the value of that outcome to the subject.

The description of a discrete task can be made rigorous (Sperling, 1983). The task is a triple (S, R, U), consisting of two sets (*stimuli, responses*) and a function, the utility function. Let S denote the set of alternative stimuli in a task. A particular stimulus is represented as s ($s \in S$, that is, s is an element of S). Let R denote the set of alternative responses, and let r ($r \in R$) denote a particular response. Let the symbol X denote the Cartesian product. Then the utility function U is a mapping of $S X R$ into the real numbers Re, that is, U: $S X R \rightarrow$ Re. Ideally, in carefully controlled procedures, utility is defined explicitly by the experimenter. Commonly, utility is not fully defined by the experimenter, and the subject is assumed to define a utility function implicitly. The utility function may be a simple two-valued function (e.g., 0,1 to represent "wrong," "right"), or it may be a complicated real-valued function that involves, for example, the speed and accuracy of choice reaction times.

1.2. Compound Tasks

A compound task combines two or more component tasks in such a way that each trial consists of a single stimulus drawn randomly from one of the component tasks and a response, also from one of the component tasks. A compound task (S,R,U) is a combination of component tasks (S_i,R_i,U_i) that satisfies certain conditions. Consider a particular component task i. Let S_i represent the set of alternative stimuli in task i; let R_i represent the set of alternative responses; and let the real-valued function $U_i(s_i,r_i)$ represent the utility of a stimulus–response pair (s_i,r_i). (Note that subscripts are used to denote a task; lowercase letters are used to indicate a stimulus within a task; and s_i refers to *any* element of S_i, the stimulus set of task i; i.e., the subscript refers to the task, not to a particular stimulus in the task.)

1.2.1. Definition. The task (S,R,U) is a compound task composed of component tasks (S_i,R_i,U_i), $1 \leq i \leq n$, $n \geq 2$, if and only if the following three conditions hold:

Condition (CP-1)

$$S = \bigcup_{i=1}^{n} S_i ,$$

The notation $\cup_{i=1}^{n} S_i$ means union of S_i; that is, every stimulus that can occur in any task i occurs in the union. The stimulus presented on each trial of the compound task is a selection of one stimulus from any one of the component tasks.

Condition (CP-2)

$$R = \bigcup_{i=1}^{n} R_i ,$$

Any response that can occur in a component task can also occur in the compound task. Note that it is possible for new stimulus–response pairs to occur in the component task, since a stimulus from component task i might elicit a response from component task j. In defining utility $U(s_i,r_j)$, there are two cases. In the first case, the response to a stimulus from task i is a member of R_i. In this case, utility is simply proportional to the utility of that stimulus–response pair within task i alone. The relative importance of task i in the task ensemble is expressed by the positive constant α_i in Condition (CP-3a).

Condition (CP-3a)

$$U(s_i,r_i) = \alpha_i U_i(s_i,r_i), \qquad \alpha_i > 0, \qquad 1 \leq i \leq n .$$

The second case deals with utility when subjects respond to a stimulus s_i from one of the component tasks with a response r_j from another.

Condition (CP-3b). The utility of response r_j to stimulus s_i, $U(s_i,r_j)$, $i \neq j$, is inversely related to the *distance* of response r_j from an optimal response r_i^* to the particular s_i; this utility is expressed as a utility function, $V(r_j,r_i^*)$, defined on two responses. The utility of a wrong response cannot exceed the utility of the optimal response, for example, $U(s_i,r_i^*) \geq V(r_j,r_i^*)$. Alternatively, utility might have been defined by the distance between stimuli.

1.2.2. Examples.

1.2.2.1. Visual Search. Consider the visual search example described in the previous section in which the task consisted of locating the digit *1* in a 5 × 5 array of characters. This task is combined with that of locating a *2* in a 5 × 5 array. Either a *1* or a *2* (but not both) appears unpredictably on each trial. The way to conceptualize the compounding operation is to imagine two urns: Urn 1 contains all possible stimuli consisting of the target "1" and 24 nontarget letters; Urn 2 contains all possible stimuli with target "2" and nontarget letters. A compound task trial consists of selecting a stimulus from either Urn 1 (task 1) or Urn 2 (task 2).

Searching for the location of *1* or *2* is a *compound* task that might be used to study the question of attentional limitations of searching for two characters at the same time. This is a special case of a compound task where the response sets (25 locations) of the two component tasks are identical. In this case, many of the complexities of defining utility are avoided, and Conditions (CP-3a) and (CP-3b) reduce simply to

Condition (CP-4)

$$\text{If } R = R_i = R_j \quad \text{for } 1 \leq i,j \leq n ,$$

$$U(s_i, r) = \alpha_i U_i(s_i, r) \qquad \alpha_i > 0 .$$

1.2.2.2. Signal Detection. Another example of a compound task is a signal detection task in which one of a number of stimuli (i.e., one of four tones of different frequencies) is presented unpredictably on each trial, and the response is saying either "signal" or "noise." The discrimination from noise of each tone separately can be considered to be a component task, so $S_i = (t_i,n)$, $1 \leq i \leq 4$; $R_i = R =$ ("signal," "noise") for all i, and this example is another of the special cases covered by Condition (CP-4).

Signal detection illustrates a potentially confusing aspect of compound tasks. The selection of the stimulus value noise (also called *no signal, null*) from Task 1 produces precisely the same physical stimulus event as the selection of noise from Task 2. Two conceptually different events (presentation of stimuli from Task 1 or Task 2) have the same physical instantiation. This is not a problem unless the subject is required to discriminate them, which obviously was not required in this example. The discrimination problem does manifest itself when the signals in the subtasks (e.g., Tone 1, Tone 2) are not completely discriminable, and we have to explicitly consider separately the tasks of *detection* and of *discrimination at threshold*, a subject about which much has been written.

1.2.2.3. Choice Reaction Time. Finally, consider a choice reaction-time experiment where the subject is presented with one of five lights and must press one of five corresponding keys. This choice task may be thought of as a compound combination of five simple reaction-time tasks.

A simple reaction task consists of a warning tone (which can be regarded as part of the experimental situation, much like the chair the subject sits on) followed, after a variable foreperiod, by a reaction signal. A stimulus, then, consists of a foreperiod and a signal. The response is a reaction *time*. Each component task has associated with it a set of stimuli; the compound task consists of a selection of one stimulus from one of the component tasks, followed by a response. The response to a stimulus from set *i* may be with the finger that is appropriate to component task *j*, the situation to which Condition (CP-3b) applies. The very large observed increase in reaction time with an increase in the number of alternatives points out the importance of uncertainty in the analysis of compound reaction-time tasks. This issue is considered in Section 5.

1.3. Concurrent Tasks

A concurrent task is one that combines two or more tasks in such a way that each component task must be performed on each trial. This is generally exemplified by situations where each component task is performed independently, like driving an automobile while listening to the news on the radio. A concurrent task (S,R,U) is a combination of component tasks (S_i, R_i,U_i) that satisfies the following conditions.

Let S_i represent the set of alternative stimuli in task i, $s_i \in S_i$. Let R_i represent the set of alternative responses, $r_i \in R_i$. Let the utility U_i of a particular stimulus–response pair be a real number defined for every pair (s_i,r_i).

1.3.1. Definition. The task (S,R,U) is a concurrent combination of the n component tasks (S_i,R_i,U_i), $1 \leq i \leq n$, $n \geq 2$, if and only if the following four conditions hold:

Condition (CC-1)

$$S = S_1 X\, S_2 X \ldots X\, S_n$$

Condition (CC-2)

$$R = R_1 X\, R_2 X \ldots X\, R_n$$

Condition (CC-3)

$$U(s,r) = U[(s_1,s_2, \ldots, s_n),(r_1,r_2, \ldots, r_n)]$$

$$= H[U_1(s_1,r_1), U_2(s_2,r_2), \ldots, U_n(s_n,r_n)]$$

where H is strictly increasing in each variable.

Condition (CC-4). The stimulus components s_i from each component task of the concurrent task are chosen independently of each other.

1.3.2. Explanation. We consider first Condition (CC-1). The concurrent stimulus S is regarded as an n-dimensional vector whose components S_i are the stimuli of the component tasks. Suppose i and j are two component tasks of the concurrent combination. Condition (CC-1) means that any stimulus that can occur in task i can occur in combination with any stimulus that can occur in task j. Condition (CC-4) asserts that this co-occurrence is independent.

Condition (CC-2), the possible co-occurrence of any response from task i with any other response from task j, parallels exactly Condition (CC-1) with stimuli.

Condition (CC-3) asserts (1) that the utility mapping for a component task does not change when that task occurs concurrently with other tasks and (2) that the utility of the concurrent combination of tasks is an increasing function of the utility of each component task. The function H is stated in very general form. One commonly used function is a weighted linear combination of component utilities:

Condition (CC-5)

$$H(U_1, U_2, \ldots, U_n) = \sum_{i=1}^{n} \alpha_i U_i, \quad \alpha_i > 0 \ .$$

Given Condition (CC-5), an equal attention combination is one where $\alpha_i = \alpha_j$ for all i, j.

Another common, nonlinear, utility function is the logical product (or intersection) exemplified by a high school curriculum. In this example, a component task is an individual high school course. The examination questions are the stimulus; the student's answers are the response. The utility is 1 if the course is passed, 0 if failed. The concurrent task consists of taking all the courses necessary to graduate. Graduating is possible only if all the component courses are passed. Thus:

Condition (CC-6)

$$H(U_1, U_2, \ldots, U_n) = 1 \text{ iff } \bigcap_{i=1}^{n} U_i = 1$$

$$= 0, \textit{ otherwise} \ .$$

Of course, this particular example is unrealistically simple. However, it illustrates that there is nothing in the definition of a concurrent task that requires the component stimuli to be presented at precisely the same time (though this is the usual case), merely that one stimulus from each task be presented on each trial, even when the trial lasts for years.

1.3.3. Examples. In a numeral detection task, S_1 represents the presence of numeral 1 in some location l_1, $l_1 \in L_1$, and S_2 represents numeral 2 in a location l_2, $l_2 \in L_2$. Concurrency requires that, in the concurrent task, every combination $L_1 X L_2$ of l_1 and l_2 can occur. In particular, consider the case where $L_1 = L_2$, and L_1 represents the locations in a 3×3 array. In the concurrent task, not only must targets 1 and 2 both occur, but by Condition (CC-4) they must also occasionally occur in the same location. This makes psychological sense if the two targets occur at different times (e.g., in successive arrays) but not when they occur in the same location at the same time. However, concurrent search is possible within an array. For example, Sperling and Melchner (1976b, 1978a) described a visual search task in which subjects concurrently detected the location of digit targets in both an outer and an inner array. Since the location sets for these two tasks did not overlap, these two detection tasks occurred concurrently on the same stimulus frame.

Some examples of concurrent tasks that have been studied experimentally are: shadowing one auditory message (repeating it with as little delay as possible) while attempting to listen to and recall another (Glucksberg & Cowen, 1970; Treisman, 1964), shadowing one message while sight-reading and playing a piano score (Allport, Antonis, & Reynolds, 1972), recalling digits heard in the left ear concurrently with digits heard in the right ear (Broadbent, 1954), and reporting concurrently on the presence or absence of three independent near-threshold tones—500, 810, and 1320 Hz (Sorkin, Pohlman, & Woods, 1976) or two independent visual spatial frequencies (Hirsch, Hylton, & Graham, 1982).

1.3.4. Overview. From the formal description of concurrent and compound tasks, it should be clear that both types of task have been used widely in the investigation of signal detection, attention, decision processes, and other aspects of performance, although compound tasks are perhaps the more common. Difficulty in interpreting compound tasks arises because of an inevitable *signal uncertainty* component. An ideal detector would show a loss in a compound task, and a quantitative model of the uncertainty decrement is necessary to determine whether there is an attentional loss (due to an insufficiency of processing resources) in addition to the uncertainty loss. Results of concurrent tasks are interpretable directly as determined by human limitations, but difficulties may occasionally occur in the interpretation of loss in performance of concurrent tasks as due to attentional limitations, reporting bottlenecks, or other limitations. Both kinds of tasks may be required to answer a particular question. The advantages and disadvantages of these paradigms are discussed in subsequent sections.

2. MAXIMIZING UTILITY: AN ATTENDANCE EXAMPLE

This section introduces the classroom attendance example (Sperling, 1984; Sperling & Melchner, 1978a, 1978b), which is a model for resource theories of attention. The concept of an *operating characteristic* is introduced and related to the notions of *utility* and *utility maximization* as a determinate of the subjects' *strategy*.

2.1. Information Densities and the Performance Operating Characteristic

A student wishes to attend two classes, A and B. The classes are offered in adjacent classrooms, so that going from one class to the other requires a negligible amount of time. Once the student leaves a classroom, return to it is not permitted. At the end of the term, the student takes an examination in each class. On the examinations, each instructor asks one question from each lecture. It is assumed that the tested information is distributed uniformly over the lecture period.

The left panels of Figure 2.1 show three examples that differ in the overlap of times at which the classes are offered. Cases (a), (b), and (c) differ in the degree of competition for attendance. The student's only strategic option is the criterion time c at which he moves from class A to class B. Depending on the student's choice of c, he or she can control the performance level in the class A and class B examinations. The joint performance in the two classes (probability correct on examination questions) is plotted on the right panels of Figure 2.1. The joint performance at various switching times c defines the *attendance operating characteristic.* As the class times overlap less and less, it is possible to choose c to result in better and better performance, so that in the case in Figure 2.1(c) the student can perform perfectly in both classes by choosing $c = 3$ o'clock as the switching time. This level of joint performance represents the independence point in Figure 2.1(c); the student performs as well in each of the concurrent tasks as in the isolated component tasks. The independence point is achievable only in the nonoverlapping case, where there is no competition for the student's attending resources.

When class times overlap, it is not possible to achieve a score of 100% in both classes. In case (b), the student can perform

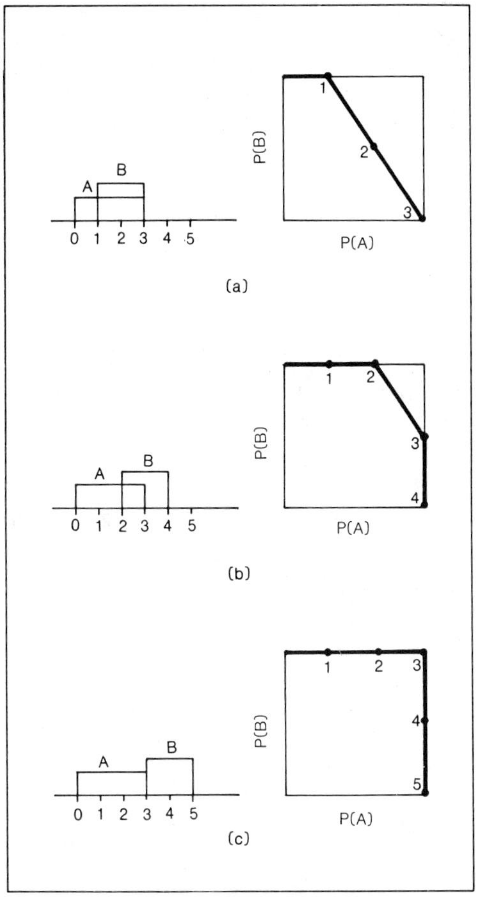

Figure 2.1. Classroom information densities and the corresponding attendance operating characteristics (AOCs). The left panels show hypothetical information densities as a function of time in hours for two classes, *A* and *B*, with different, uniform density functions. The right panels show the resulting AOCs with points indicating several classroom switching times. The axes of the AOCs represent performance (the probability of correct responses on examinations) in the two classes. (a) A case where class *B* overlaps completely with *A*, and the information density per unit time is higher for *B*. (b) An intermediate degree of overlap. The resulting AOC is closer to the upper right corner (the *independence point*) indicating less processing conflict. (c) A case of no overlap and the resulting AOC.

perfectly in class A and 50% in class B, perform perfectly in class B and 66.7% in class A, or do something in between. Or the student could do something perverse, such as sit in classroom B until 2:00 P.M. and then switch to A or not attend either class. Perverse and obviously inferior strategies are not considered in this chapter. The next section examines how the student *should* choose among the reasonable strategies.

2.2. Utility and Strategy Selection

For the student to choose a particular strategy from the set of reasonable strategies, the utility of all the candidate strategies must be determined. The method is illustrated for the situation in Figure 2.1(b).

Suppose that classes A and B contribute equally to the student's overall grade point average (the higher the average, the greater the utility), and no other considerations enter into this computation. The corresponding utility function is

$$u(x_A, x_B) = 50(x_A + x_B) \tag{1}$$

where x_i is the probability of a correct response in class i and $u(x_A, x_B)$ is utility. (Because utility is known only up to an arbitrary, strictly increasing monotonic transformation, scale factors are introduced only to clarify the example.)

The optimal strategy is to attend all of class B and as much of class A as possible, thereby achieving an average of 83.3%. This and other implications of the particular utility function are made intuitively obvious by plotting iso-utility contours together with the operating characteristic, as in Figure 2.2. This iso-utility, or indifference, curve approach, according to Due (1951), was first suggested by Pareto (1909) and later developed by Hicks and Allen (1934).

Given an explicit utility function, the utility of each strategy can be computed directly. That is, utility can be written as a function of the class-switching time c by writing the examination scores as a function of c:

$$u(c) = 50\left[\frac{\min(c,\ 3)}{3} + \frac{\min(4-c,\ 2)}{2}\right], \quad 0 \leqslant c \leqslant 4 \tag{2}$$

where $\min(x,y)$ is defined as the smaller (minimum) of x and y, and c is measured in hours (with noon taken as 0).

The parallel, diagonal lines in Figure 2.2(b) represent *iso-utility contours*. Utility can be computed for every point in the joint performance space (x_A, x_B) whether or not that point is achievable. The parameters used to label iso-utility contours in Figure 2.2(b) indicate their utility. The *attending operating characteristic* crosses iso-utility contours until it touches (is tangent to) the maximum utility contour it can reach. The highest contour reached is 83.3%; this occurs with a class-switching time of 2:00 P.M.; it results from a perfect score in class B and 66.7% in class A. The reason for the relative neglect of class A is that useful information has higher density per unit time in class B than in class A, and therefore the *marginal utility* of attending class B is greater than that of attending class A. The student should exchange time in class A for time in class B whenever possible.

Suppose that the utility of success in class B were only 2/3 that of class A; this would happen if class A were weighted as three credit-hours and class B as two credit-hours. Then

$$u(x_A, x_B) = 60(x_A + 2/3x_B)\ . \tag{3}$$

These iso-utility contours are shown in Figure 2.2(c). In this case, the lower utility of class B exactly offsets its higher-information density, and a switching time anywhere between 2 and 3 will maximize utility as defined by Eq. (3).

In a third case, suppose that what matters is not grade point average but simply passing all the courses. The utility is 1.0 if all courses are passed, 0 otherwise. Figure 2.2(d) illustrates utility graphs for three minimum-required passing grades, 50%, 65%, and 80%. The curves in Figure 2.2(d) are not iso-utility contours as before, but divisions of the graph into two regions: (1) pass both courses and (2) fail one or both courses. For convenience, the three boundaries under consideration are represented on one graph. All the reasonable strategies suffice when the minimum passing grade is 50%; about half of the reasonable strategies are adequate with a minimum passing grade of 65%; only one strategy will achieve 80%, which is the highest grade simultaneously achievable in both courses. To achieve a grade of 80%, the student attends 80% of each class;

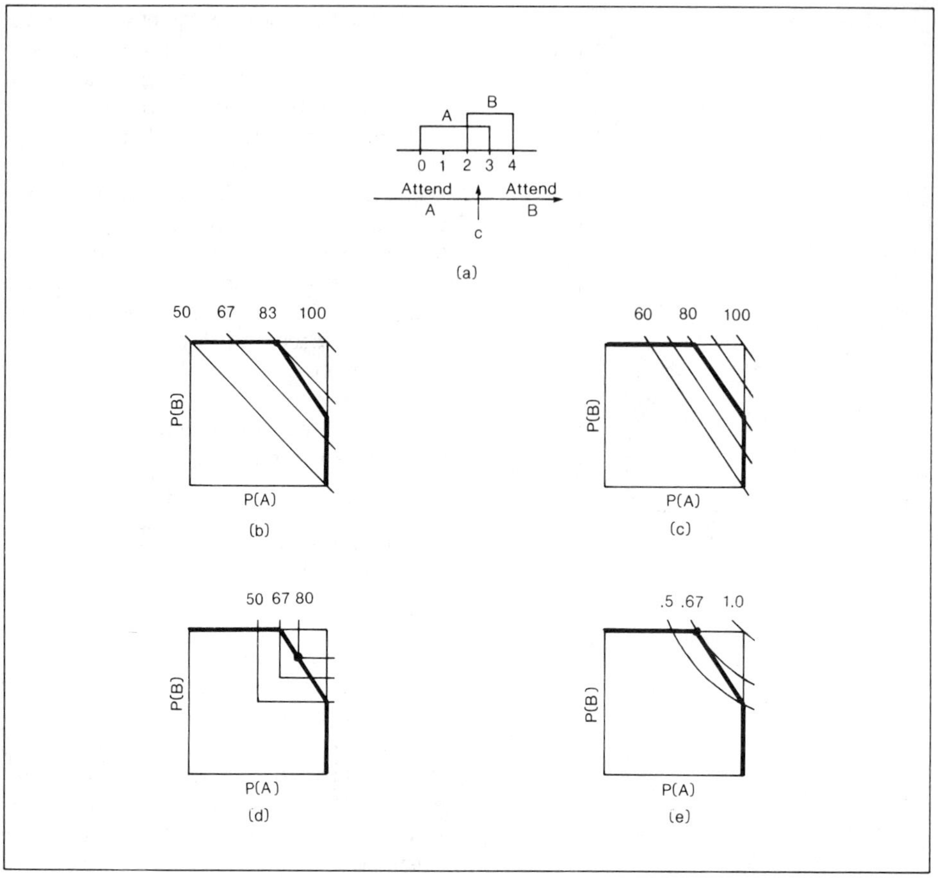

Figure 2.2. A classroom attendance example with four different utility functions. (a) Two partially overlapping class information density functions. (b) The resulting attendance operating characteristics (AOCs) with iso-utility contours for an equal weighting utility function, $u(x_A, x_B) = 50(x_A + x_B)$, where x_i represents performance in class i ($i = A, B$). Several iso-utility contours are shown; the parameter indicates their relative value. Optimal performance occurs where the AOC intersects or is tangent to the highest possible iso-utility contour. The intersection corresponds to a switching time of c = 2.0 in this example. (c) The same AOC with a utility function that weights performance in class A and B directly in accordance with the relative durations of the two classes—a 3:2 ratio: $u(x_A, x_B) = 20(3x_A + 2x_B)$. Because the iso-utility contour coincides with one branch of the AOC, there is an extended range of optimal switching times. Time in class A and class B is precisely equal in value. (d) A pass-fail utility function. The student requires a given score (e.g., 80%) to pass each class and needs to pass each class to graduate. This defines iso-utility *graduation regions* above and to the right of the lines shown, and *fail regions* elsewhere. Performance everywhere in a region is equivalent, since the pass-fail utility rule does not value increments (or decrements) in performance above (or below) the pass-fail criterion, nor does it discriminate between failing one or failing more courses. Criterion c in panel (a) represents the optimal switching time (c = 2.4). The iso-utility contours exhibit the property of diminishing returns to an extreme degree; attendance beyond that required for a passing grade produces no additional return whatsoever. (e) A case with statistical uncertainty in the probability $P(i)$ that a class i will be passed, such that the probability of passing both classes is $P(A\&B) = P(A)P(B)$. Utility is assumed to be directly proportional to $P(A\&B)$. The utility function favors equidistribution of effort; however, in this example it cannot overcome the greater utility of time spent in class B. (d. is from G. Sperling, A unified theory of attention and signal detection, in R. Parasuraman and R. Davies (Eds.), *Varieties of attention*, Academic Press, 1984. Reprinted with permission.)

that is, he or she switches from class A to B after 2.4 hours in class A (at 2:24 P.M.). Ironically, this strategy, which is the only one that will enable the student to pass both courses when a passing grade of 80% is required, is the strategy that would cause the person to *fail* both courses when a passing grade of 80.1% is required.

The iso-utility contours in the pass-fail example reflect the important principle of *diminishing returns*. Attendance up to the point of achieving a passing grade is valuable; additional attendance offers no return whatever.

A different example than simple pass or fail is constructed by assuming that the probability $p(i)$ of passing a course i is simply proportional to the cumulative attendance x_i in the course. As in the previous examples, $p(i) = x_i/\tau_i$, where τ_i is the number of classroom hours. The event that determines utility is passing both courses. The probability, $p(A\&B)$, of passing both class A and B is $p(A\&B) = p(A)p(B)$. Iso-probability contours for $p(A\&B)$ (which also represent iso-utility contours) are shown in Figure 2.2(e).

If it is assumed that utility is directly proportional to $p(A\&B)$, then the iso-utility contours of Figure 2.2(e) do not exhibit diminishing returns. For a fixed value x_B of attendance in class B, an additional minute (Δx_A) of attendance in class A produces precisely the same increment in $p(A\&B)$, independent of the value x_A has already attained. However, this utility function does represent a high value for *equidistribution of effort.* It represents the case where it is advantageous for the student to be well rounded, that is, to have approximately equal scores (as high as possible) in all classes, or the case of the professor who is better off with a reasonable level of knowledge about the subject matter *and* a reasonable level of communicative ability than with a surplus of one and an insufficiency of the other. While this utility for equidistribution of effort would favor actual equal distribution if the marginal utility of time spent in each class were equal, it cannot in this example overcome the greater utility of time spent in class B, and the optimum is the same as in Figure 2.2(b).

2.3. Interpretation of the Classroom Example

The classroom example of Section 2.2 is a model for the case of attention to two *concurrent* tasks. The temporal overlap of the courses is analogous to an overlap in requirements for processing resources (Navon & Gopher, 1979). Processing resources are considered in detail in Sections 3.4 and 3.7. The subject's strategic choice in attentional tasks involves the allocation of mental resources (i.e., attention) between the two tasks.

To avoid confusion, it is very useful to use different words for real-world quantities and for the variables that represent them in a theory or model. "Attention" normally is used as a real-world term; "processing resources" is a mathematical construct in models proposed to account for attentional phenomena. Insofar as a particular model is in one-to-one correspondence with some set of attentional phenomena, there may be (but need not be) an observable or potentially observable quantity, such as "amount of attention," that corresponds to the amount of processing resources. The classroom model is a single-processor model, in which *time* is the resource divided between the processes. However, the classroom model generates performance operating characteristics that describe data perfectly well even when time is not the critical resource, for example, when memory capacity is critical. Thus the hours from noon to 5:00 P.M. could represent five memory slots that could be allocated to storing items either from list A or from list B according to the task demands and conditions. The essential aspect of the classroom model is the computational procedure and not the particularities of the classroom. In the resource analogy to attention, the performance operating characteristic is called the *attention operating characteristic* (Sperling & Melchner, 1978b; see also Sperling, 1984, p. 112). When utility functions are not defined explicitly, the subject performing concurrent tasks is assumed to choose a strategy according to subjective utilities. Because subjective utilities are difficult to discover and because they are likely to be labile, the experimenter should endeavor to make the utility function as explicit as possible.

3. SIGNAL DETECTION THEORY, ATTENTION, AND ECONOMICS

The formal analogy of the classroom attendance example to models of signal detection, attention, and economic production is developed here with special emphasis on the different interpretations of the basic components of the model in these various contexts. The operating characteristics of the classroom example are related to the receiver operating characteristics of signal detection theory, the production possibilities frontiers of economics, and the attention operating characteristics of human information processing. The approaches to optimization in these domains are outlined.

3.1. Attendance Example Generalized

In this section, the logic of the (classroom) attending operating characteristic is reviewed in a more formal way. During class period i and at the moment in time x, let the rate at which an instructor is presenting information be given by $p_i(x)$. The information rate $p_i(x)$ is assumed to be 0 when class is not in session and to be nonnegative while class is in session. The total *amount of information* E_i presented in Class i [$E_i = \int_{start}^{finish} p_i(x)dx$, $i = 1,2$] is assumed to exist and be bounded. For the attending strategy in which a student attends class 1 from its start until time c and then attends class 2 until its finish, the amount of information E_i accumulated in each class is given by:

$$E_1 = \int_{-\infty}^{c} p_1(x)\,dx \quad \text{and} \quad E_2 = \int_{c}^{\infty} p_2(x)\,dx\,. \tag{4}$$

Information accumulates only from the starting time x_0 of the class. However, since $E_1(x)$ is zero for $x < x_0$, it is convenient to write the integral from $-\infty$ to c rather than from x_0; similarly, for class 2. The performance operating characteristic is a graph of E_2 versus E_1 as c varies.

It will be convenient in the following discussion to consider the special case of the classroom attendance example where the information densities are approximately normal (and the class periods are equivalent). Thus instructors take a while to warm up before they reach their maximum exposition rate, and having once reached this rate, they quickly begin to tire, and less information is presented late in the class period. Figure 2.3(a) illustrates the information rates estimated for two instructors, one in a nursing class given from noon until 1:40 P.M., the other in a Spanish class given from 12:20 to 2:00 P.M. Figure 2.3(b) illustrates the attendance operating characteristic for a student who attempts to take both classes. With these normal distribution assumptions, the sharp edges of the previous performance operating characteristics have been rounded to a smooth curve, but the logic remains the same.

3.2. Signal Detection Theory

For simplicity of exposition, consider now a case of signal detection theory (SDT) that is more particular than it needs to be, but which can readily be generalized. An experimenter presents two kinds of trials: those on which only noise N is presented and those on which a signal plus noise $S + N$ is presented. (The notation $S + N$ and S will be used interchangeably when the addition of noise is irrelevant or obvious from context.) The observer's task is to distinguish between these two kinds of trials, that is, to say "signal" or "yes" whenever believing S was presented and to say "noise" or "no" otherwise. The possible outcome of a signal trial is either a correct detection (i.e., hit) or a failure to detect (i.e., miss); the possible outcome of a noise trial is either a correct rejection or a false detection (false alarm).

Signal Detection Theory proposes that any stimulus (either S or N) is represented internally by a real number x along an internal continuum. This real number is regarded as a random variable, with conditional distributions (given N) $p_N(x)$ and (given S) $p_S(x)$ usually assumed to be normally distributed.

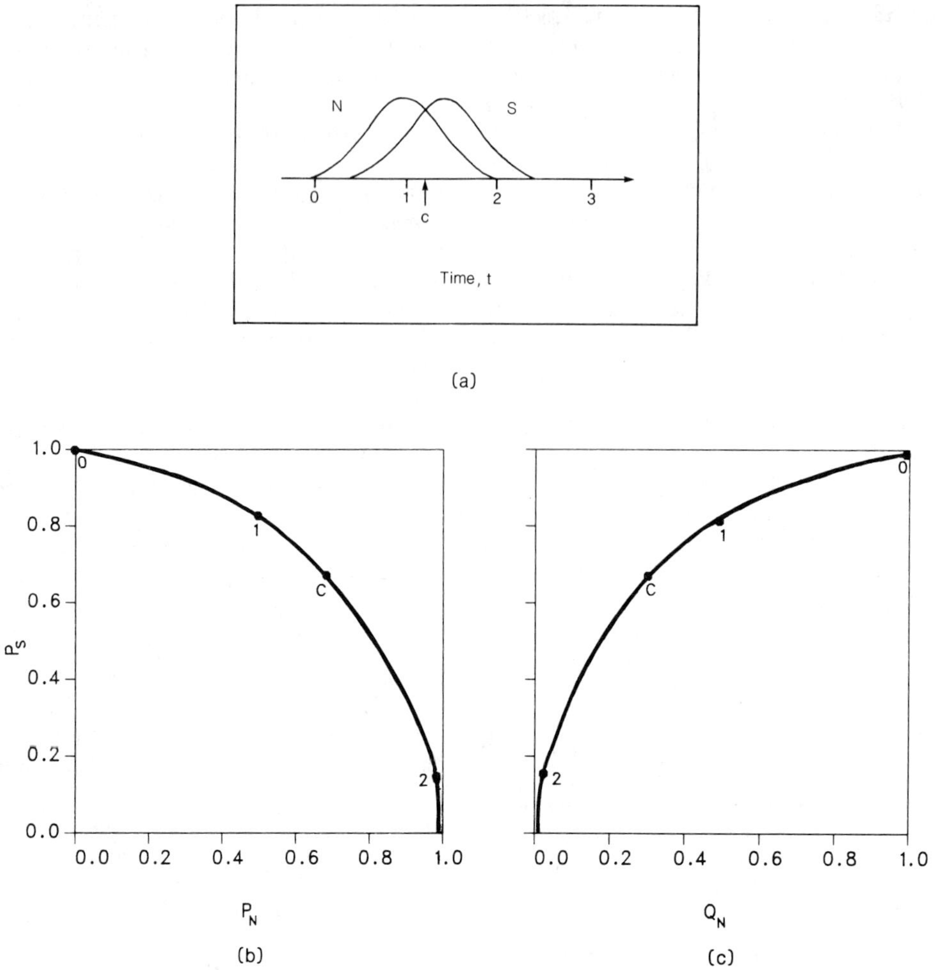

Figure 2.3. (a) A classroom example in which information densities as a function of time in two classes (N, S) are assumed to be normal distributions. The switching time for maximizing the total amount of acquired information is indicated by c. (b) The performance operating characteristic for a student who switches from class N to class S at various times is called an attendance operating characteristic (AOC) in this example. Representative switching times are indicated by points along the AOC. The axes represent the probability of correct responses (P_N and P_S) on examinations in the two classes. (c) When the two distributions in panel (a) are assumed to represent the signal and noise distributions of a signal detection experiment, the POC obtained as the decision criterion is varied is called a Receiver Operating Characteristic (ROC). The abscissa in the ROC graph, $Q_N = 1 - P_N$, is $P(``S''|N)$, the probability of incorrectly saying "signal" when noise is presented; the ordinate, $P_S = P(``S''|S)$, is the probability of correctly saying "signal" when a signal is presented. Alternatively, panel (b) is the mirror image of panel (c) and therefore panel (b) can be interpreted either as a decision operating characteristic (DOC) for a signal detection experiment (the DOC is the mirror image of the ROC), or as a resource allocation operating characteristic for classroom attendance. (From G. Sperling, A unified theory of attention and signal detection, in R. Parasuraman and R. Davies (Eds.), *Varieties of attention*, Academic Press, 1984. Reprinted with permission.)

While psychological interpretation of the random variable as a sensory continuum is not essential to the application of SDT, intuitive interpretations are useful. When the two stimuli consist of a brief burst of noise, or noise to which a faint 1000-Hz tone has been added, then the random variable may be interpreted as the perceived amount of 1000 Hz on any trial. This perceived amount will vary from trial to trial but will tend to be slightly larger on signal trials than on noise trials. In visual experiments, the random variable may be interpreted as perceived intensity or contrast; in memory experiments, it might correspond to perceived familiarity. If in some unusual situation it should happen that the likelihood ratio $[lr(x) = p_S(x)/p_N(x)]$ does not increase monotonically with x, then it is mathematically convenient (but psychologically incorrect) to consider $lr(x)$ (rather than x directly) as the decision variable.

Figure 2.3(a), which we previously interpreted as representing information density, is now interpreted as representing the conditional distributions $[p_N(x); p_S(x)]$ of the random variable on the sensory continuum x, where x represents an amount of 1000 Hz, and so on. On any trial, k, the stimulus produces an effect x_k described by a sample from the appropriate distribution (p_S, p_N) and the observer reports "signal" if $x_k > c$ and "noise" otherwise. The probabilities of a hit P_S and of a false alarm Q_N are given by

$$P_S = \int_c^{\infty} p_S(x)\,dx \quad \text{and} \quad Q_n = \int_c^{\infty} p_N(x)\,dx\,. \tag{5}$$

A graph of P_S versus Q_N, shown in Figure 2.3(c), is called a *receiver operating characteristic*.

3.3. Decision Operating Characteristic

The graphic conventions for receiver operating characteristics (ROCs) produce mirror images of other performance operating characteristics. Compare Figures 2.3(b) and 2.3(c). In fact, the ROC uses a counterintuitive convention: good performance on signal trials (hits) is graphed against bad performance on noise trials (false alarms). The mirror image of an ROC plots correct performance on signal trials versus correct performance on noise trials, or P_S versus $P_N = 1 - Q_N$. The mirror-image ROC is mathematically equivalent to the ROC but follows the more usual convention of graphing good performance up and to the right. Although SDT originally was applied to the discrimination of signals from noise, the formalism of SDT has been applied equally well to many other situations. For example, SDT applies well to discrimination experiments in which an observer's task is to discriminate two stimuli (e.g., tones of 1000 and 1001 Hz) as opposed to discriminating one stimulus from zero. The general case is discrimination (of which discrimination from zero, detection, is a subcase). The graph of $P_S(x)$ versus $P_N(x)$ as x varies is appropriately called a *decision operating characteristic* (Sperling & Melchner, 1978b) or, more generally, a *performance operating characteristic* (Norman & Bobrow, 1975).

3.4. Operating Characteristics in Economics

Economic theory is useful in the attentional framework because it explicitly considers productivity given *limited resources*. Operating characteristics occur throughout economic theory; the relevant trade-off here is called the production possibility frontier (e.g., Samuelson, 1980). Figure 2.4 illustrates a hypothetical production possibility frontier for the strength of the military sector of an economic system measured in units of "swords" and agricultural output measured in "plowshares." The production possibility frontier results from a limited pool of resources, for example, citizens who could be either farmers or warriors, which can be allocated to either goal of the economy or shared between goals in various proportions.

Production possibility frontiers are generally concave toward the origin, as a result of the principle of symmetrically disposed diminishing returns. Diminishing returns mean, for example, that if the society were to increase the fraction of farmers from 0.95 to 1.0, it would increase the number of plowshares by less than when it increased the fraction of farmers from 0.0 to 0.05. Since diminishing returns for plowshares and swords occur on opposite ends of the production possibility frontier, decreasing the fraction of farmers from 1.0 to 0.95 would decrease plowshares by less than the increase in swords (see Figure 2.4(a)). It is assumed that the first persons to change occupations would be among the worst farmers, that is, persons who were relatively more efficient as warriors than as farmers. Similarly, if the fraction of warriors were to increase from 0.95 to 1.0, it would increase the number of swords only slightly, as the very last to join the army would be the least efficient soldiers relative to their efficiency as farmers.

The tendency to concavity toward the origin is a general property of performance operating characteristics that results from *unequal resources*—resources that are not equally interchangeable for all tasks. One way of expressing the inequality of resources is the performance resource function (Norman & Bobrow, 1975), a graph that describes the performance (e.g., agricultural production, plowshares) as a function of resources (e.g., farmers, number of acres, facilities, research) devoted to it. The discussion here is restricted to a single kind of resource, labor. Figure 2.4(b) shows the increase in agricultural production (plowshares) as a function of the number of agricultural laborers; it has a horizontal asymptote indicating that productivity ultimately is absolutely limited by factors other than labor. Figure 2.4(c) shows a graph $X - Y$ of the possible allocations of labor (number of workers) to the two competing sectors, swords and plowshares. The nonlinear performance resource function of Figure 2.4(b), which is the production possibilities frontier of Figure 2.4(a), is embodied in the utility function of Figure 2.4(c), yielding an equivalent description. The description in Figure 2.4(a) almost always is preferable to that in Figure 2.4(c).

In economics, production possibility frontiers, insofar as the two sorts of productivity can be measured, are considered to be objective descriptions. They are computed by the engineers and managers of the society. However, the *utility* of any joint combination of swords and plowshares depends, in principle, on the values and circumstances of the members of the society, although all may not contribute with equal weight. Equal utility contours are generally concave away from the origin because unbalanced combinations (strong military but no food or vast food supplied but no protection) are not as advantageous as balanced ones. The solution for the society, once the utility function is determined, is to find the point along the production possibility frontier where it touches the highest iso-utility contour. For smooth curves, the utility contour and the production possibilities frontier will be tangent to each other and of equal slope at the optimum point. Finding the optimum point along various trade-offs is at the heart of classical economic theory, and specialized branches of mathematics (such as linear programming) have been developed to deal with the problems of optimization. Section 3.5 explores the equivalences between trade-offs and optimization in signal detection, in concurrent attentional tasks, and in economic theory.

3.5. Optimization

3.5.1. Signal Detection Theory. Optimization in SDT traditionally involves the computation of the likelihood ratio lr. If x represents values on the relevant internal decision axis, and the probability distributions over x for Noise and Signal + noise conditions are $p_N(x)$ and $p_S(x)$, respectively, the likelihood ratio, given a particular value of x, is

$$lr(x) = p_S(x)/p_N(x) \ . \qquad (6)$$

Figure 2.5 illustrates $p_S(x)$ and $p_N(x)$ as the equal-variance normal distributions of SDT. The decision criterion c on the x-axis corresponds to a decision criterion of β on the lr-axis, where the optimal β is chosen according to prior probabilities and payoffs (Green & Swets, 1966). The decision operating characteristic (mirror-image receiver operating characteristic) at the upper right of Figure 2.5 represents the joint performance on N trials and S trials as c is varied from $-\infty$ to ∞. The logarithm of the likelihood ratio is illustrated in Figure 2.5, center. The reason for illustrating log lr rather than lr itself is that log lr is symmetric around $lr = 0$, which reflects the actual symmetry of treatment of lr and lr^{-1}, and because log lr occurs in many statistical treatments.

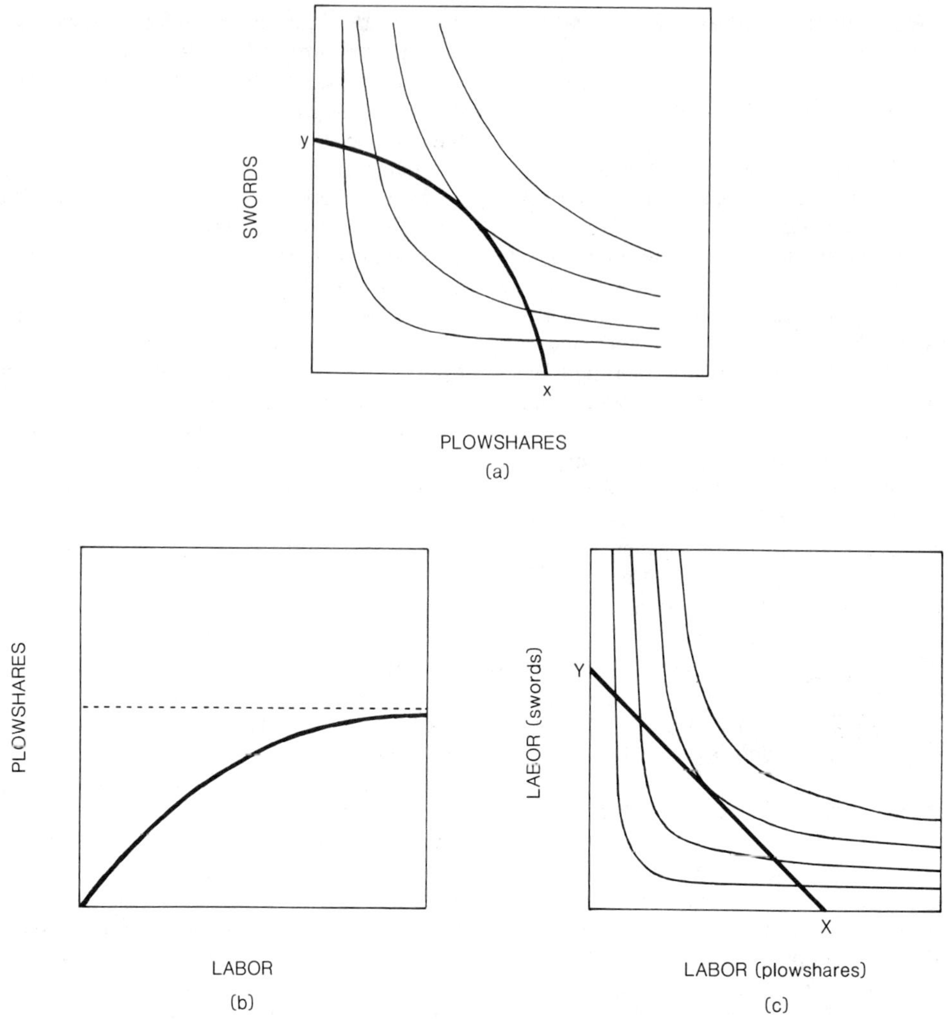

Figure 2.4. (a) A *production possibility frontier* (thick curve *xy*) for a primitive economy capable of producing swords or plowshares. The axes represent the number of plowshares and swords produced. Several iso-utility contours are shown as thin curves. The iso-utility contours are nearly flat on the extreme right because the utility of large changes in surplus plowshares can be compensated by small changes in scarce swords. The almost vertical ends of the iso-utility contours on the upper left represent symmetrically disproportionate marginal utilities for surplus swords. These iso-utility contours represent the principle of diminishing returns. (b) A resource-performance function illustrating agricultural production (plowshares) as a function of the amount of labor devoted to agriculture. (c) An alternative description of the swords-plowshares trade-off; a trade-off function (heavy line *XY*) showing the amount of labor devoted to swords versus labor devoted to plowshares. The thin lines represent iso-utility contours for these labor allocations; these iso-utility contours combine the nonlinear resource-performance function of panel (b). (From G. Sperling, A unified theory of attention and signal detection, in R. Parasuraman and R. Davies (Eds.), *Varieties of attention*, Academic Press, 1984. Reprinted with permission.)

The d' statistic of SDT is the normalized distance between the mean of the N and S density functions; d' summarizes the discriminability of N from S. A more general statistic is the area under the receiver operating characteristic or the decision operating characteristic. The area under the decision operating characteristic, A, is:

$$A = P(x_S > x_N) \ . \tag{7}$$

That is, A is the probability that a random sample x_S from the distribution p_S exceeds a sample x_N from p_N. According to a simple SDT model, A is the probability of a correct choice in a two-alternative forced-choice (2AFC) task (Green & Swets, 1966). More generally, A is a nonparametric measure of the amount by which the S distribution dominates (is to the right of) the N distribution. Statistics for A are given in Bamber (1975). Signal Detection Theory (or decision theory) deals with compound tasks. The remaining cases considered in Figure 2.5 deal with concurrent tasks.

The following sections outline the reinterpretation of the critical concepts of SDT (the decision axis, probability densities, likelihood ratio, and area under the operating characteristic) when a similar optimization theory is applied to the classroom analogy, to economic production, and to attention. These analogies are developed in more detail in Sperling (1984).

3.5.2. Attendance Theory. In the classroom attendance example, two classes are offered during overlapping time periods and compete for the student's attendance. In this example, the

x-axis (decision axis of SDT) represents time, and the conditional distributions represent the usefulness of information offered at time x for each of the classes (N or S). The ratio of the two usefulness functions at any given time x is analogous to the likelihood ratio of SDT. This ratio should be interpreted as the relative usefulness of spending the moment of time x in class S relative to class N. The classroom switching time in the classroom example is analogous to the criterion in SDT. The performance operating characteristic (POC) is generated by varying the classroom-switching time. Finally, the area under the POC has an interesting interpretation. If x_S and x_N are the times at which randomly sampled bits of information occur for class S and class N, then the area A under the POC is $A = P[x_S > x_N]$, the probability that a randomly sampled bit of information in class S is offered later than a bit sampled from class N. This is a measure of the difference in times at which information in the two classes is actually offered.

3.5.3. Economic Production Theory. In economic theory, the SDT decision axis of "observations" (ordered in terms of their likelihood of indicating N or S) is replaced by an ordering of resources (ordered according to their usefulness for the competing production goals of the economy). Let f_1 represent the usefulness (productivity) of a laborer as a farmer, and let f_2 represent his or her usefulness as a warrior. The ratio $x = f_2/f_1$ corresponds to the likelihood ratio of decision theory and can be used to order all the laborers or resources on a *usefulness ratio axis*. Those whose usefulness as farmers (relative to warriors) is greatest would be represented at the left side of the axis; those whose usefulness as warriors is greatest would be represented on the right side; $p(x)$ is the density function that indicates the fraction of laborers whose usefulness ratio is x. The usefulness ratio f_2/f_1, is sometimes called the *objective substitution rate*; in this example, it represents the rate at which swords can be substituted for or converted into plowshares.

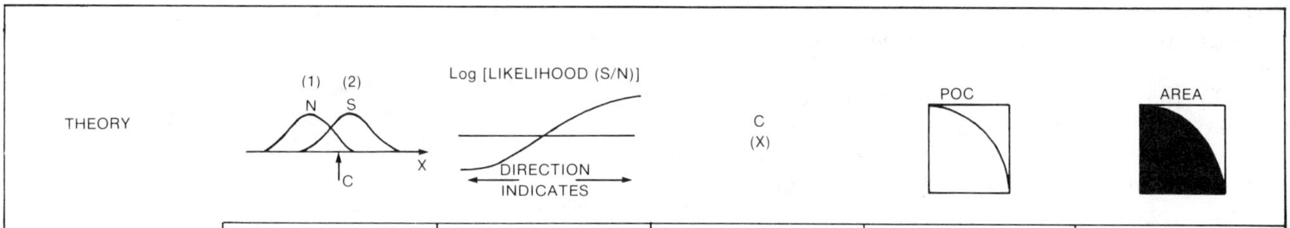

SIGNAL DETECTION SDT	Density function for conditional probability that sensory observation = x, given N, given S	Noise	Signal	Criterion (sensory continuum)	ROC Receiver Operating Characteristic	P ($X_S > X_N$)
DECISION	Density function for conditional probability that sensory observation x, given stimulus 1, given stimulus 2	Stimulus 1	Stimulus 2	Criterion (decision continuum)	DOC Decision Operating Characteristic	P ($X_2 > X_1$)
ATTENDANCE	Density of classroom information, given class 1, given class 2	Usefulness for class 1	Usefulness for class 2	Classroom switching (time)	AOC Attendance Operating Characteristic	P (info in class 2 is offered after info in class 1)
ATTENTION	Net productivity of resources for tasks 1,2	Usefulness for task 1	Usefulness for task 2	Allocation decision (resources)	AOC Attention Operating Characteristic	P (a task 2 resource is more useful for task 2 than a task 1 resource is)
ECONOMIC PRODUCTION	Net productivity of resources for tasks 1, 2	Usefulness for producing product 1 (Objective substitution rate)	Usefulness for producing product 2	Allocation decision (resources)	PF Production Possibilities Frontier	P (a resource used to produce 2 is more efficient in producing 2 than is a resource used to produce 1)

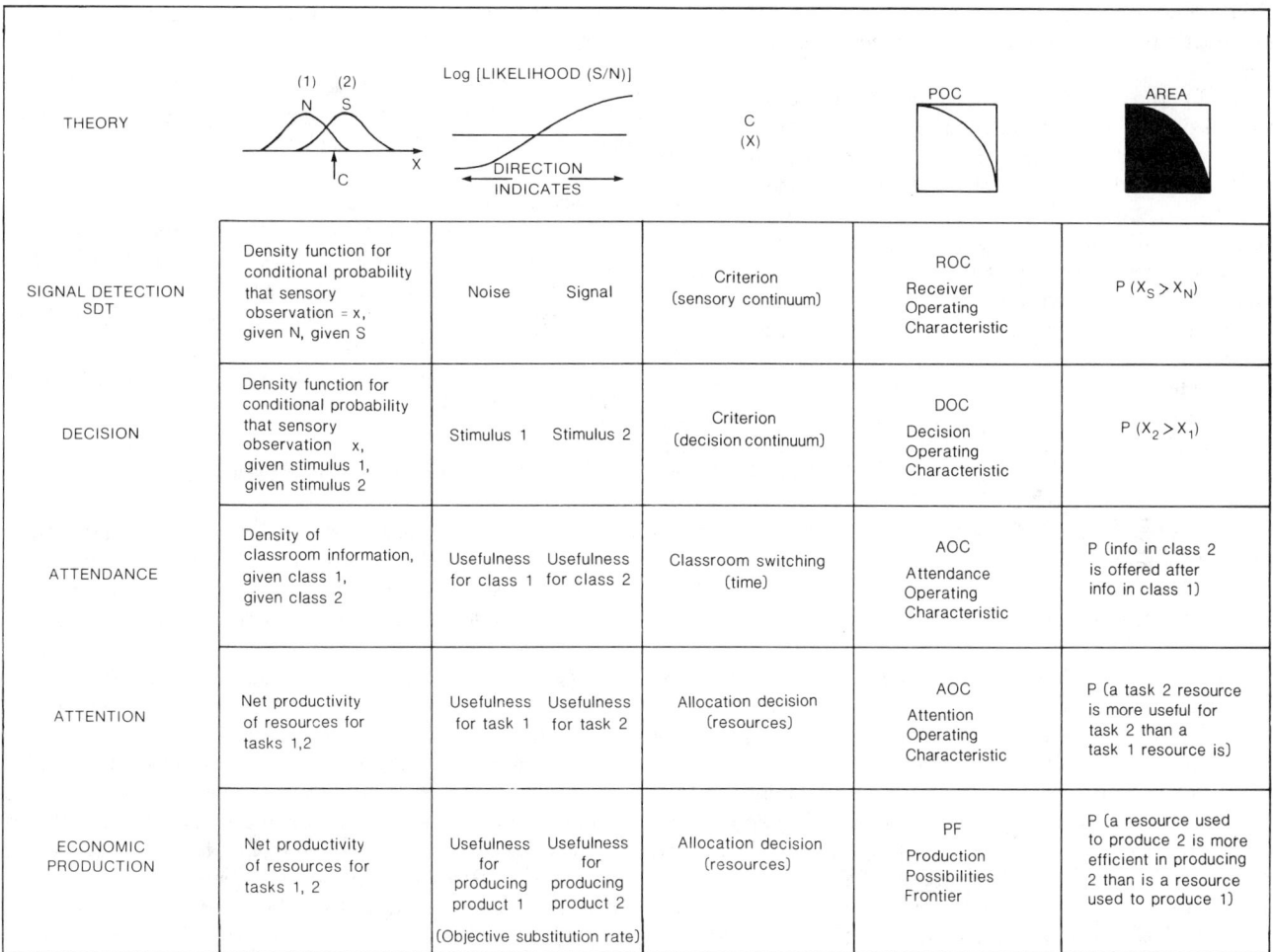

Figure 2.5. A summary of the isomorphisms between five theories: signal detection, decision (compound tasks), attendance, attention (concurrent tasks), and economic production. Density functions are indicated by $N(x)$, $S(x)$. The log likelihood ratio is $\ln[S(x)/N(x)]$; it is a *log usefulness* ratio in the resource theories. The dimensional interpretation of the variable x is indicated by the term in parentheses; c indicates the decision criterion. The performance operating characteristic (POC) is the curve indicated in the graph. The shaded area in the rightmost graph represents the area A under the POC; $A = P(X_2 > X_1)$ represents the probability of the event that a randomly chosen sample from distribution 2 is greater than a randomly chosen sample from distribution 1. The interpretation of each of these quantities in each theory is indicated in the figure. See the text for details. (From G. Sperling, A unified theory of attention and signal detection," in R. Parasuraman and R. Davies (Eds.), *Varieties of attention*, Academic Press, 1984. Reprinted with permission.)

Productivity functions analogous to the density functions $p_N(x)$ and $p_S(x)$ of SDT are derived as follows. The fraction of laborers with usefulness ratio between x and $x + dx$ is $p(x)dx$. The average usefulness for agricultural production of these laborers is $f_1(x)$. The net productivity of this group is $p_1(x)dx = f_1(x)p(x)dx$; $p_1(x)$ is a density function analogous to $p_N(x)$ of SDT. (In order for $p_1(x)$ to represent a density function, $f_1(x)$ has to be appropriately scaled, and there are other technical restrictions that are not central to the discussion here.) The density function $P_1(x)$ represents the net productivity as farmers, $p_1(x)dx$, of all the laborers whose objective substitution rate (or usefulness ratio) is between x and $x + dx$. The function $p_2(x)$, analogously defined, represents the productivity as warriors of this same group. Productivity is measured in normalized units, that is, in terms of the fraction of the maximum capacity for the specified task.

The decision criterion c corresponds to the decision to assign all laborers with usefulness ratio less than c to farming and the remainder to fighting. The decision operating characteristic of SDT, generated as c varies from $-\infty$ to $+\infty$, corresponds to the production possibilities frontier of economic theory, similarly generated.

Finally, the area A under the production possibilities frontier has a similar interpretation to the areas under the decision operating characteristic and the performance operating characteristic: it represents the probability that a randomly chosen sword-resource unit will be more useful for sword production than a randomly chosen plowshare-resource one would be for sword production. A is a measure of the extent to which skills or facilities (e.g., for farming, fighting) are segregated into different people or facilities (nonsubstitutable) as opposed to coexisting in the same person or facility (substitutable). A similar analysis in terms of economic consumption by laboratory animals (where there is only one resource, e.g., time, to allocate to separate appetites) is treated in detail by Rachlin, Battalio, Kagel, and Green (1981) and Sperling (1984). Rachlin, Green, Kagel, and Battalio (1976), Rachlin, Kagel, and Battalio (1980), and Rachlin and Burkhard (1978) give empirical examples of substitutability and interference.

3.6. Attention Theory

3.6.1. Concurrent Tasks. Attentional allocation is closest in interpretation to economic production theory. The allocation of mental resources is assumed to determine the quality of performance of several concurrent cognitive tasks, just as the allocation of economic resources determines the extent to which competing manufacturing goals are achieved. The application of economic theory to attention was proposed by Navon and Gopher (1979). The direct application of the economic analogy is appropriate only for *concurrent* tasks; in compound tasks, the effects of stimulus uncertainty must first be removed.

The critical aspect of attention theory is the interpretation of the decision axis as an ordering of resources—in the case of attention, *mental processing resources*. The units of mental resources are defined analogously to those of production resources. Allocation of any single unit of Task 1 resources to Task 1 will accomplish, say, 1% of the maximum achievable performance for Task 1. Of course, those particular resources may be more or less effective for Task 2. The mental resources whose usefulness ratio x (usefulness for Task 2 divided by usefulness for Task 1) is lowest are represented at the extreme left of the resource axis (Figure 2.5). Thus the resource axis is directly analogous to a likelihood decision axis of SDT. The conditional density function $p_1(x)$ represents the usefulness or productivity for Task 1 of resources as a function of their *usefulness ratio* x; $p_2(x)$ represents the usefulness of resources for Task 2. (More precisely, the area $p_i(x)dx$ under the density function represents the aggregate usefulness of resources whose usefulness ratio lies between x and $x + dx$.) The functions $p_1(x)$, $p_2(x)$ are both normalized relative to the maximum achievable performances. The decision by the subject to allocate mental resources with usefulness ratio less than c to Task 1 and the remainder to Task 2 is analogous to the decision criterion c in SDT. The attention operating characteristic is traced out as c is varied over its range by attentional manipulations (e.g., instructions to attend to Task 1 versus Task 2). The area under the attention operating characteristic represents the probability that a resource unit, chosen at random from all those useful for Task 2, really is more useful for Task 2 than a randomly chosen Task 1 resource unit would have been. It is a nonparametric measure of the extent to which distinct (nonsubstitutable), as opposed to interchangeable (substitutable), resources are involved in performing the two tasks.

3.6.2. Compound Tasks. Attentional manipulations can be interpreted as controlling resource allocation only in concurrent tasks. In compound tasks, because of the effects of stimulus uncertainty, the attentional manipulation must first be viewed as a decision manipulation subject to decision uncertainty (as in signal detection or decision theory, Sperling, 1984). More qualitative arguments along these lines can be found in Duncan (1980). Stimulus uncertainty in compound tasks is treated extensively in Section 5. If, after stimulus uncertainty has been accounted for, there is a residual effect of attention in a compound task, then obviously resource analysis would be appropriate for this residual effect.

3.7. Single and Multiple Resources

3.7.1. Undifferentiated versus Differentiated Attention. Early in the development of attention theory, concurrent task performance was interpreted with respect to an undifferentiated capacity hypothesis (Kahneman, 1973; Moray, 1969). According to this hypothesis, interference between tasks occurs when the total demands exceed the pool of attentional (processing) capacity. This pool is undifferentiated with respect to the specific operations of the particular tasks. Alternatively, Treisman (1969) suggested a structural attention model, where tasks interfere only to the degree that they call upon the same processing "subsystems" or "analyzers." The formal attention theory described here is a differentiated model; the model represents an ordering of processing resources according to the usefulness ratio for two competing tasks. Relative usefulness is a continuous concept and more general than the structural model of Treisman. The undifferentiated capacity model corresponds to the special case in which all resources have precisely the same usefulness ratio for all the competing tasks.

In the language of the classroom analogy, an undifferentiated capacity model could be conceived as follows. The limitation in resources is a maximum number of hours m to be spent in class. Since the capacity is undifferentiated, a subject would be free to arrange two classes to occur in the optimal arrangement within the m hours (i.e., the x-axis is arbitrary), and interference would occur only if even the optimal arrangement involved overlapping class times.

The undifferentiated capacity model makes a strong prediction about the relation to each other of the attention operating characteristics (AOCs) produced by the three binary combinations of three tasks. This situation is outlined in Figure 2.6, which shows some hypothetical arrangements of classes A, B, and C. Under the undifferentiated capacity model, once the AOCs for concurrent tasks (A,B) and for (A,C) have been measured, the AOC for the concurrent tasks (B,C) is completely specified. See Figure 2.6 (a), (b), (c), (d), (g), and (h).

No such prediction is made by the differentiated processing resource model specified in this chapter. Sample configurations of classes for the differentiated processing resource model are shown in Figure 2.6. Two extremes are shown. In case (e)-(f), the classes B and C both partially interfere with A, but they

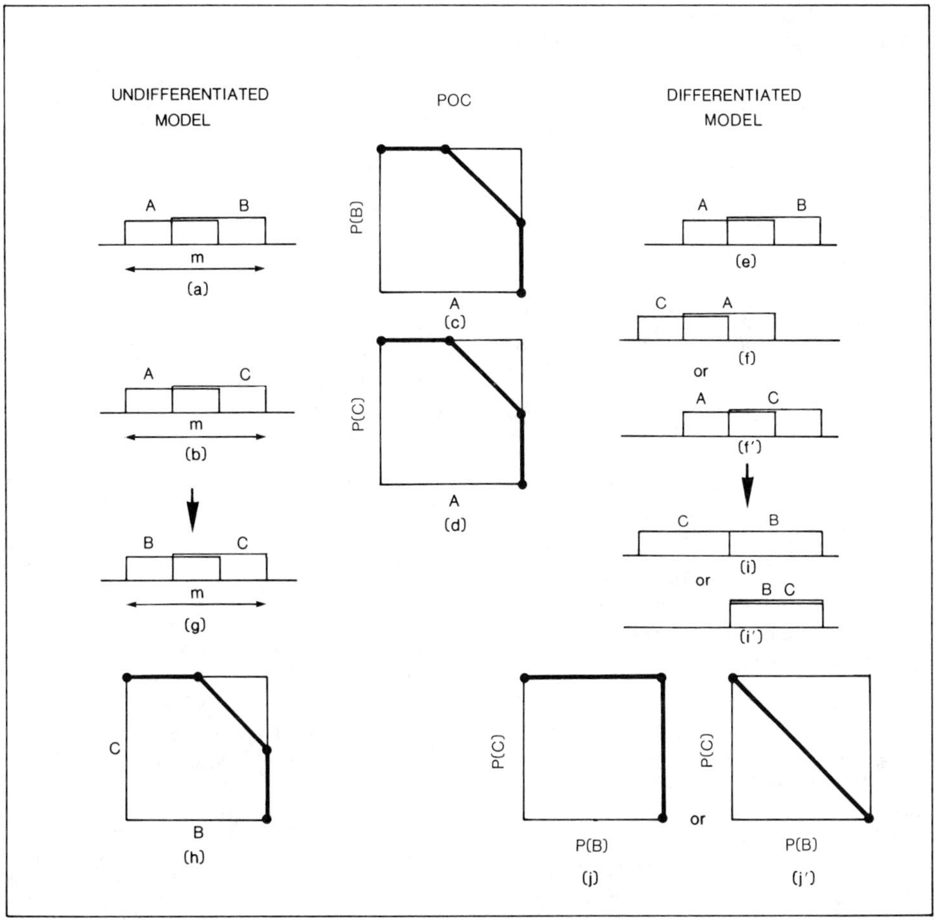

Figure 2.6. The undifferentiated and differentiated attentional models. The *undifferentiated capacity model* assumes that all processing resources are interchangeable, but that there is a limitation in the total amount of resources. These assumptions are embodied in an example of tutorial instruction in which *m* is the capacity limit—the maximum number of student hours available for attending tutorial instruction. Tutorial instruction can be arranged freely (up to a maximum with each tutor) within the *m*-hour limit. Panels (a) and (b) indicate various tutorial schedules a student can arrange involving tutors (*A, B*) and (*A, C*). The performance operating characteristics (POCs) resulting from varying the proportion of *A* in (*A, B*) and (*A, C*) are shown in panels (c) and (d). When task combinations (*A, B*) and (*A, C*) are known to produce the POCs in (c) and (d), then the undifferentiated capacity model first specifies that the tutors (*B, C*) can be scheduled, for example, as shown in panel (g), and second, uniquely specifies that the resulting POC from *any* reasonable schedule is that shown in panel (h). The *differentiated model* assumes that resources can be differentially useful for various classes. Possible classroom information density functions under the differentiated model that would produce the AOCs in panels (c) and (d) are shown in panels (e) and (f or f′), respectively. If panels (e) and (f) describe the overlap of (*A, B*) and (*A, C*), then the overlap of (*B, C*) is shown in panel (i) and the corresponding AOC is shown in panel (j). If, instead, panels (e) and (f′) describe the overlap of (*A, B*) and (*A, C*), then the overlap of (*B, C*) and the corresponding AOC appear in panels (i′) and (j′). The same (*A, B*) and (*A, C*) AOCs yield radically different AOCs for the (*B, C*) class combination. Any AOC between the extremes, shown as panels (j) and (j′), is possible under the differentiated model. However, if classes (*A, B*) and/or classes (*A, C*) overlap more than the examples in panels (e) and (f), the differentiated model constrains the possible (*B, C*) AOCs, in a manner analogous to the constraints on correlations between three random variables (Kendall, 1970). In the limit, if (*A, B*) overlap completely and (*A, C*) overlap completely, then (*B, C*) must overlap completely in both the undifferentiated and the differentiated models.

require different resources, and therefore B and C do not interfere with each other. In case (e)-(f′), B and C partially interfere with A by virtue of requiring identical resources, and therefore they interfere totally with each other.

The usefulness ratio is inherently defined for a particular task combination (A,B). Another task combination (A,C) need not result in the same ordering of processing resources. Both the cases considered for the differentiated model in Figure 2.6 actually assume some similarity in the usefulness-ratio axis for the (A,B) and (A,C) combinations. However, in the general case each task combination reflects the task distribution on a potentially *unique* usefulness-ratio axis. Therefore, knowing the AOC for (A,B) and (A,C) specifies only a limited constraint about the task combination (B,C), which could fall somewhere between the two special cases shown in Figure 2.6. In the special case where classes (A,B) overlap completely and classes (A,C) overlap completely, both the differentiated and the undifferentiated models make the same clear prediction: (B,C) also must overlap completely.

3.7.2 Nature of Mental Resources. What are mental resources? There are two approaches to this question. The first is that it is not necessary to know what mental resources are. Mental resources may have the status of a random variable much like the decision variable of SDT. All the power and prediction of SDT work whether or not the psychological (mental) dimensions of the decision variable are precisely known. All the power of optimization theory is available to predict and describe performance in concurrent tasks even when it is not known precisely where these tasks conflict. However, cognitive psychologists have a special interest in learning precisely what particular mental resources are involved in cognitive functions.

With respect to particular mental resources, the critical resources for which there is competition vary with the task. In the partial-report or concurrent whole-report tasks (Section 7.4.1), the critical resource is short-term memory, it has a limited capacity, and that capacity is allocated to items from one stimulus row or the other according to the task demand. This memory resource seems to be quite interchangeable.

In search tasks (Section 5), the critical resource probably is a processing resource involved in making comparisons. A stimulus item at one location in the visual field *can* be compared to a memory representation of a target at the same time that another item in another part of the field is being compared to a representation of another target. However, the extent to which such comparisons draw on different resources (and therefore can occur simultaneously) and the extent to which they draw from a common pool of resources (and therefore must be made serially) depends on many factors, among the most important of which is the familiarity of the target—the extent to which special resources have been developed for particular targets (Shiffrin & Schneider, 1977). The issue of serial versus parallel processing is a fascinating research problem; for an example of recent theorizing involving queuing theory, see Fisher (1982). Section 8.6 examines a powerful method of determining whether resources from a common pool can be evenly shared by two tasks or whether they are switched in all-or-none fashion from one task to the other on different trials.

3.8. Iso-utility Contours

Iso-utility contours are a powerful heuristic device for studying optimization. They have long been used in economic theory to investigate which of a number of alternative procedures or parameters produces the maximum utility or most preferred outcome. Navon and Gopher (1979) introduced iso-utility contours into the study of attention. They were introduced here in the classroom example of Section 2. Their use in signal detection experiments remains to be specified.

On each trial of a signal detection task, either a signal or a noise stimulus is presented and the subject responds either "S" or "N." The experimenter explicitly or implicitly assigns a utility to each of the four possible outcomes of a trial. This is commonly called the *payoff matrix*, as shown in Table 2.1. Let the fraction of signal trials be α; then the fraction of noise trials is $1 - \alpha$. The subject's probability of saying "S" given S (i.e., detecting the signal when it is presented) denotes $P(\text{"}S\text{"}|S)$; $P(\text{"}N\text{"}|N)$ is analogously defined. Given the payoff matrix in Table 2.1, the expected utility EU of a trial is

$$EU = \alpha[dP(\text{"}S\text{"}|S) + cP(\text{"}N\text{"}|S)] + (1 - \alpha)[bP(\text{"}S\text{"}|N) + aP(\text{"}N\text{"}|N)] \ . \quad (8)$$

Equation (8) gives the expected utility for every possible performance level, $P(\text{"}S\text{"}|S)$ and $P(\text{"}N\text{"}|N)$ for particular values of a, b, c, and d. The limit on achievable performance levels is described by the discrimination operating characteristic, which is a graph of $P(\text{"}S\text{"}|S)$, $P(\text{"}N\text{"}|N)$ pairs obtained as some nonstimulus parameter of the experiment is varied. (The operating characteristic is the "limit of performance" since the subject could follow a nonoptimal decision strategy.)

To illustrate the effect of α on performance, we choose a particular payoff matrix; for example, wrong responses b and c earn zero ($b = c = 0$) and correct responses a and d earn 1 dollar per trial ($a = d = 1$). Figure 2.7(a) illustrates iso-utility contours for $\alpha = 0.25$, and Figure 2.7(b) illustrates iso-utility contours for $\alpha = 0.75$. The parameter on the contours is the expected utility. Expected utility as defined by the payoff matrix and Eq. (8) is computable for all values of $P(\text{"}S\text{"}|S)$, $P(\text{"}N\text{"}|N)$, not just achievable values. The iso-utility contours are straight lines with slope M, where M is

$$M = \left(\frac{b - a}{d - c}\right)\left(\frac{1 - \alpha}{\alpha}\right) \ . \quad (9)$$

Table 2.1. Payoff Matrix for the Four Possible Outcomes of a Trial in a Signal Detection Experiment

		Response: "Noise"	Response: "Signal"
Stimulus	N	a Correct rejection	b False alarm
	S	c Miss	d Hit (correct detection)

Note: a, b, c, d are real numbers that represent the payoffs (utilities).

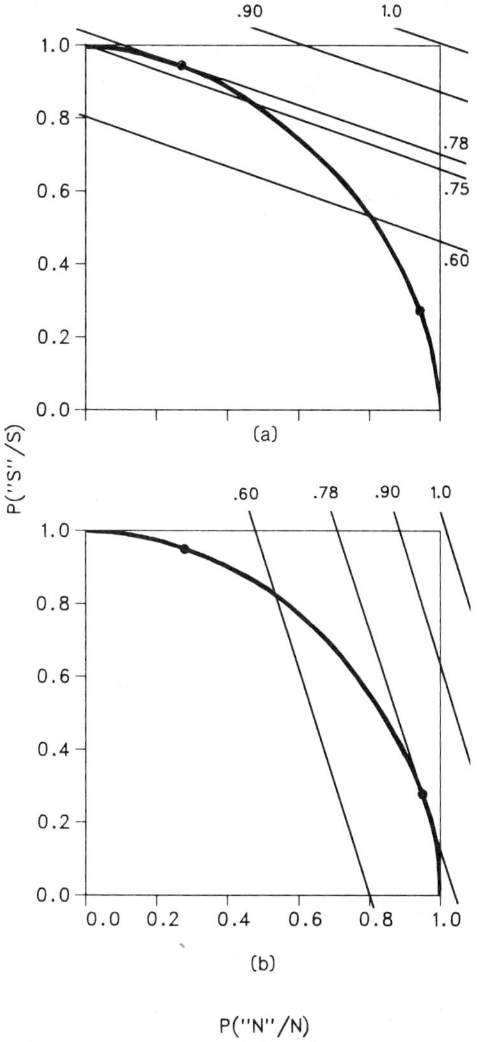

Figure 2.7. The influence of a priori signal probability on performance. Panels (a) and (b) show the same discrimination operating characteristic (DOC) for a signal detection task. The abscissa is the probability of a correct response given a noise stimulus, and the ordinate is the probability of a correct response given a signal stimulus. The DOC shown assumes equal-variance Normal distributions and a d' of 1. In (a), the a priori probability of a signal is 0.75, the utility is 1 for correct responses and 0 for incorrect responses. The iso-utility contours show the expected utility (payoffs). Panel (b) shows the iso-utility contours when the a priori probability of a signal is 0.25. (From G. Sperling, A unified theory of attention and signal detection, in R. Parasuraman and R. Davies (Eds.), *Varieties of attention*, Academic Press, 1984. Reprinted with permission.)

If the outcomes of a trial are symmetrical with respect to S and N for both errors and correct responses, then the iso-utility slope is simply the ratio of the two a priori stimulus probabilities, $-(1 - \alpha)/\alpha$. In the two examples of Figure 2.7, the slopes are -3 and $-1/3$.

A typical decision operation characteristic based on the assumption of equal-variance normal distributions for N, and $S + N$ also, is illustrated in both panels of Figure 2.7. From the graph, it is obvious that the criterion should be adjusted quite differently to achieve the optimal performance with $\alpha = 0.25$ than with $\alpha = 0.75$. The expected utility of each strategy (each criterion value) can also be estimated from the graph. The optimal strategy has an expected utility of 0.78 dollars per trial. This is only marginally better than 0.75, the utility that could be achieved by simply naming the a priori more probable stimulus on each trial without actually observing the stimulus presentation. For normally distributed signal and noise, it always pays to observe the stimulus because the likelihood ratio varies between 0 and ∞. But there are many distributions, such as the logistic distribution, for which the likelihood ratio is bounded. For stimuli characterized by distributions like the logistic, it can be better *not* to observe the stimulus when the a priori probabilities are very asymmetrical, but merely to use the a priori information.

The value of a priori information is the expected value of a trial with this information minus the value of a trial without it. In the example of Figure 2.7, suppose that an observer has no information about the a priori stimulus probabilities and therefore sets the criterion symmetrically (at a likelihood ratio equal to 1.0). The expected probability of a correct response would be 0.69 which, in this example, is also the number of utility units (dollars) the observer would expect to earn on each trial. Note that 0.69 is the highest achievable expected probability of a correct response with equally probable stimuli or with unequally probable stimuli when the probability is unknown. The a priori information that one stimulus is 3 times more probable than the other enables the observer to achieve an expected probability of a correct response of 0.75 without even observing the stimulus and 0.78 if choosing to actually observe it. The a priori information alone is thus worth more (0.75) than the opportunity of viewing the stimulus without a priori information (0.69). Finally, it is obvious that good detection of signal stimuli $P(\text{“}S\text{”}|S) \approx 1$ can be profitably exchanged for good detection of noise stimuli $P(\text{“}N\text{”}|N) \approx 1$ when there are more noise than signal stimuli, and vice versa.

All these properties and relations of variables in signal detection are, of course, derivable algebraically, and they are well known. The concept of utility is central to SDT (Swets, Tanner, & Birdsall, 1961). Furthermore, receiver operating characteristics have been graphed with various performance criteria (Swets, 1973) but not generally with iso-utility contours. (The sole exception is Metz, Starr, Lusted, & Rossman, 1975, Figure 5, p. 420). The aim here is to illustrate the properties of SDT and utility theory in a new way so that previously unobserved similarities between all the various kinds of situations (detection, discimination, attendance, attention, economics, etc.) are made explicit.

4. COMPOUND TASKS: UNCERTAINTY IN DECISION

A compound combination of several subtasks is defined as a task on which the stimulus on any trial is drawn randomly from the set of stimuli of any of the component tasks. Thus uncertainty is introduced in any compound combination. It was asserted earlier that decrements in performance in *compound* tasks can be interpreted as attentional decrements only after discounting the effects of decision uncertainty in an ideal observer. A computational model of uncertainty effects is required for interpretation. This section reviews the uncertainty loss of an ideal observer as it is treated in SDT (Egan, 1975; Swets, 1964). It then examines uncertainty and attentional effects as they apply in several kinds of detection experiments. The concept of uncertainty is extended to classification experiments, in general, and to experiments in visual search.

4.1. Examples of Compound Detection Experiments

4.1.1. Auditory Detection Example. In an auditory signal detection experiment, a 500-Hz tonal signal plus noise or noise alone occurs for 0.5 sec on each trial. The stimuli are $S + N$, N. The responses are "S," "N." This is component Task 1. In component Task 2, the stimuli are 810 Hz + N, N; in component Task 3, 1320 Hz + N, N. In the compound task, the stimuli are 500, 810, or 1320 Hz, each plus noise or noise alone. The responses are "S," "N." That is, the stimulus set is the union of the stimuli of the three component tasks; this is the special case, Condition (CP-4), where the response sets of the compound task and each component task are equal. A more elaborate version of this compound task would require the subject to make the response "S" or "N" and then to "recognize" the signal, that is, say "low," "medium," or "high" pitch.

Uncertainty decrements are almost always observed for frequency mixtures. The question is whether these decrements are "attention" decrements or the result of decision uncertainty. Auditory detection experiments with multiple alternative signals and single-band versus multiple-band interpretations of these experiments are extensively reviewed in Swets (1984). The analogous visual paradigms are considered in this section.

4.1.2. Visual Detection Example. One possible uncertainty experiment in the visual domain compares "S"/"N" detection of sine-wave gratings of various frequencies in "alone" blocks (the component tasks) with "S"/"N" detection in intermixed blocks (the compound experiment). This is analogous to the auditory frequency uncertainty experiment described in Section 4.1.1. In the visual domain, the compound experiments have shown decrements for intermixing of widely separated spatial frequencies and for intermixing of separated spatial positions but not for intermixing of contrast levels (Davis, Kramer, & Graham, 1983).

4.1.3. Location Experiments. This section considers in more detail the case of attending to several spatial locations. Wundt, in his introductory psychology text (1912), described a self-experiment for observing the spatial distribution of attention. The reader was instructed to fixate his or her eyes on a mark at the center of an array of letters and to direct his or her attention to a letter off to the side. Wundt asserted that the letters around the attended peripheral location appeared more vivid than those elsewhere in the array. Unfortunately, Wundt's dependent variable (judged vividness) is problematical; certainly it is not an objective measure of a *performance* that is affected by selective attention.

4.1.3.1. Simple Yes-No Detection. One of the first serious experimental attempts to measure the spread of visual attention to several locations was by Mertens (1956). He required his observers to maintain fixation faithfully on a central fixation mark. He then presented them with very weak flashes of light to be detected. When they detected a flash, they indicated so by pressing a button. In some blocks of trials, the flashes could occur at any of four locations around fixation (northwest, southwest, southeast, or northeast), in others, only one (say, southwest). See Figures 2.8(a) and 2.8(b). Mertens's observers seemed to have slightly lower detection thresholds at an unknown one of four locations than at one predetermined location. He concluded that it was more effective for the subject to allow attention to spread out over four locations than "to stress himself continually not to look in the direction of attention" (p. 1070). Unfortunately, Mertens was unaware of the rudiments of SDT, so there were flaws in his procedure, such as inadequate treatment of false alarms. It is possible that the observer altered his criterion (c in Figure 2.3(a)) between conditions but that d' (the separation between $p_S(x)$ and $p_N(x)$) was not affected (or was even oppositely affected) by the attentional manipulation. Mertens's strange result was replicated once by Schuckman (1963) in an experiment with the same difficulties as Mertens's and by Howarth and Lowe (1966), who found no effect of any kind

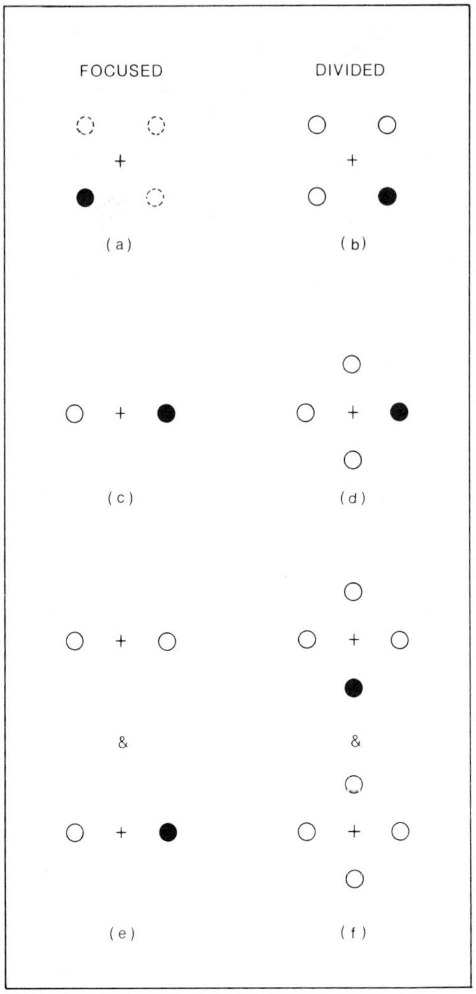

Figure 2.8. Stimulus configurations for visual detection experiments that compare focused with divided attention. Each panel illustrates a particular potential stimulus. A plus sign indicates the visual fixation point; a filled circle indicates a target; an open circle indicates a noise (nontarget) stimulus. (a) *Yes-No detection judgments*: Mertens's stimuli for focused attention. In the focused condition, targets could occur only in the particular location selected by the subject; the dashed open circles indicate that the other locations were displayed nevertheless. The subject's task is to say whether the target occurred on that trial. (b) In Mertens's divided attention condition, the target could occur at an unknown one-of-four possible locations; it is shown here in the southeast location. (c, d) *Forced-location judgments*. The target occurs on every trial in one-of-two locations in panel (c) or in one-of-four in panel (d), and the subject must say *where* it occurred. (e, f) *Two-interval forced-choice procedure*. Two temporal intervals (separated by & in panels) within which the target can occur are defined for the subject, but the target occurs only in one. The subject must identify the interval. (From G. Sperling, A unified theory of attention and signal detection, in R. Parasuraman and R. Davies (Eds.), *Varieties of attention*, Academic Press, 1984. Reprinted with permission.)

of uncertainty, not of stimulus location, size, or time of occurrence. Since then the opposite result has been obtained.

We now consider some contemporary approaches to spatial uncertainty in detection.

4.1.3.2. Forced Location Judgment. Consider first the following Gedanken experiment. In some sessions a flash can occur in either of two locations (east or west); in other sessions it occurs in any of four locations. See Figures 2.8(c) and 2.8(d). The accuracy of naming the target location is measured and found to be higher in two-location than in four-location sessions. Unfortunately, it requires a theory of guessing to estimate the attention effect, since visual detection accuracy is higher in two-location than in four-location stimuli even when the observer's eyes are shut and, for low-intensity stimuli, the guessing effect is predominant. To obviate guessing analysis, a two-alternative forced-choice paradigm may be used (Cohn & Lasley, 1974). All trials are composed of two intervals, and a target always occurs in one or the other of the intervals. In some sessions there are two possible locations in which the target may occur; in others there are four possible locations for the target, as seen in Figures 2.8(e) and 2.8(f). Subjects correctly identify the interval containing the target more frequently in the two-location than in the four-location trials. Since chance guessing is the same in both kinds of trials, this result appears to demonstrate an attentional loss in attempting to monitor four locations. Unfortunately this conclusion is premature, as shown in Section 4.2.

4.2. Signal Detection Theory and the Ideal Observer

In all these examples, the question that must be answered is whether the performance loss in the compound experiment compared to performance in its components is due to a *limitation of attention* or to *uncertainty in the decision process.* Signal Detection Theory predicts a decrement in performance whenever the subject is confronted with a larger number of independent noise samples.

4.2.1. Uncertainty in Location. Consider a detection task in which the target can occur at one of a number of possible locations. Each location i that the subject must monitor is assumed to produce a sample n_i from a noise distribution. At the target location t, the signal is added to noise to produce $n_t + s$. The decision rule for the ideal detector (assuming that the target occurs with equal probability at all locations) is to choose the location with the largest sample. If $n_t + s$ is greater than $n_i, i \neq t$, then a correct location detection would occur. If, however, $n_i > (n_t + s)$ for some $i \neq t$, a false detection would occur. The probability of false detections will increase with the number of locations, even when the quality of information about each location remains the same. Quantitative predictions, of course, depend on the assumed shape of the noise distribution.

Intuitively, an ideal detector makes a mistake when the noise sample at some nontarget location exceeds the sample of signal plus noise at the target location. If the decision rule chooses the location with the largest sample, it is necessary to consider only the largest noise sample. The two-interval (Cohn & Lasley, 1974) paradigm described previously compares the maximum of three noise samples (in the two-interval–two-location case, Figure 2.8(e)), with the maximum of seven noise samples (in the two-interval–four-location case, Figure 2.8(f)). It is known from the general properties of order statistics that the expected value of the maximum of n independent, identically distributed random variables increases as the n increases, and hence the chance of an error in detection increases. In the two-interval paradigms, a response based on a noise sample may be either correct or incorrect, but a response based on the signal will necessarily be correct. The more locations monitored, the larger the number of noise samples, and the larger the number of errors. One advantage of concentrating on the largest noise sample (subject to some technical restrictions; see Gumbel, 1958) is that while the distribution of the noise random variable may be unknown, in the limit as $n \rightarrow \infty$ there are only three possible distributions of maxima (Galambos, 1978; Gumbel, 1958). When the number of monitored locations is large, the distribution of the maximum noise sample may be better known than that of the individual samples.

4.2.2. Distribution-Free Bounds on Location Uncertainty. A special case of the location uncertainty problem has been considered by M. L. Shaw (1980). She derived a distribution-free prediction for the maximum decision (stimulus uncertainty) loss for experiments involving two or M locations in which the subject's task is to name the target's *location.* This computation is valid only when a test of two-location identification indicates that the subject is monitoring both locations to some degree. Let P_2 and P_M, respectively, represent the probabilities of a correct location judgment in 2- and M-location experiments, respectively. If the data from a 2- versus 4-location experiment fall below the distribution-free boundary shown in Figure 2.9 or more generally if $P_M < (P_2)^{M-1}$, then the explanation must involve more than decision uncertainty. Figure 2.9 also illustrates predictions of the stimulus uncertainty loss for the 2- and 4-location cases assuming exponential or normally distributed noise. The exponential and normal computations illustrate the large range of stimulus uncertainty loss possible in compound tasks and the corresponding problems in interpreting data. Although data falling below the distribution-free boundary indicate a performance loss that cannot be due only to stimulus uncertainty (and therefore could be attentional), this is a very weak test. Data falling anywhere between the distribution-free boundary and no loss (Figure 2.9) are ambiguous; they exceed the normative stimulus uncertainty loss under some distributional assumptions but not others.

4.2.3. Uncertainty in Detection of Independent Signals. One approach to the problem of uncertainty in *detection* of one of M *independent* (orthogonal) signals is to make the computations based on the assumptions of equal-variance Normal noise distributions (Nolte & Jaarsma, 1967). Suppose it is known that, on signal trials, only one of M independent signals (plus noise) will be presented, and the problem is to discriminate signal trials from noise trials. Optimally, the observer will construct a likelihood ratio lr that combines the information from each of the M independent samples, or "channels." For noise trials, lr reflects M independent and identically distributed noise samples; for signal trials, $M - 1$ noise samples and the signal-plus-noise sample. Under the assumption of equal-variance Normally distributed noise and signal plus noise, Nolte and Jaarsma (1967) derived receiver operating characteristics for several values of d'_1 for a known signal (the subscript refers to $M = 1$) and for one of M signals, assuming an ideal (optimal) detector. These predicted receiver operating characteristics are shown as solid lines in Figure 2.10 for $d'_1 = 2$ and six values of M, ranging from 1 to ∞. The optimal detector's stimulus uncertainty loss in detection is a graphic illustration with Normally distributed

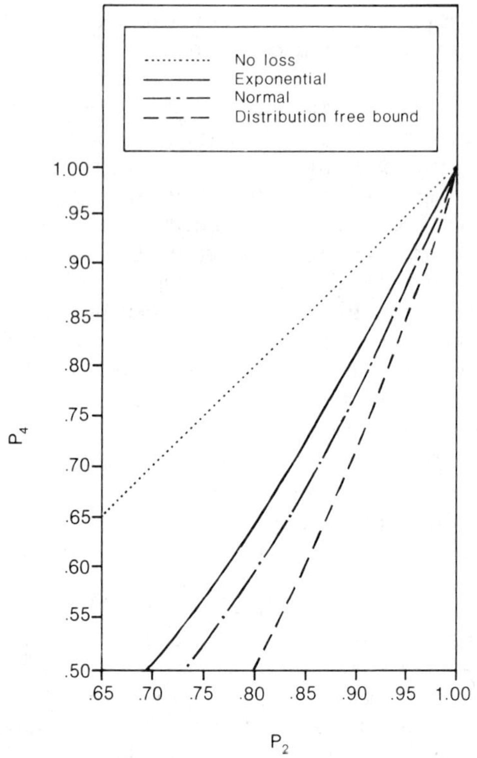

Figure 2.9. Theoretical comparison of two versus four alternatives in location judgments. The ordinate shows the predicted probability of a correct location judgment in a four-location task (P_4); the abscissa shows the probability of a correct location judgment in a two-location task (P_2). The curves illustrate the theoretical accuracy of location judgments of various ideal detectors as the signal-to-noise ratio varies. The curve label indicates the probability density function (*pdf*) assumed for the computation. Values of (P_2, P_4) are shown assuming (1) exponential and (2) normal *pdfs* for both targets and distractors, and (3) a distribution-free bound $[P_4 < (P_2)^3]$ on of the maximum uncertainty loss in comparing a four-location to a two-location task. The difference $(P_2 - P_4)$ is the *uncertainty decrement*. (From M. L. Shaw, Identifying attentional and decision making components in information processing, in R. S. Nickerson (Ed.), *Attention and performance* (Vol. 8), Lawrence Erlbaum, © 1980 by the International Association for the Study of Attention and Performance. Reprinted with permission.)

noise of the general arguments about increasing the number of noise sources given in Section 4.2.1.

Nolte and Jaarsma's (1967) ideal detector, whose performance is illustrated in Figure 2.10, gives equal weight to all channels in forming the likelihood ratio. More generally, when a priori probabilities of signals differ in different channels, or payoffs are unequal across channels, the optimum decision rule requires the likelihood ratio to be based on the appropriately weighted likelihoods in each channel. This is a *weighted decisions* rule, which is considered further in Section 6.2.4. In the optimal decision rule, all the information available from each channel is combined (although the weighting is not necessarily equal) before a decision is made.

Nolte and Jaarsma (1967) were able to show that the optimal likelihood-based receiver operating characteristics could be closely approximated by the behavior of a suboptimum threshold detector that performs a much simpler computation. The threshold detector sets a criterion for each of the M channels separately and responds "signal" when at least one channel or sample exceeds the criterion. When the a priori probabilities and payoffs for the various alternatives are symmetrical, the criterion is taken to be the same in the component channels. Otherwise, different channels have different threshold criteria corresponding to the different weights of the weighted decisions rule. Let $p(\text{"}S\text{"}|E)$ be the probability of a detection response (i.e., criterion exceeded in at least one channel given an input event E), and let $p_j(\text{"}N\text{"}|E)$ be the probability of a nondetection response in channel j, then

$$p(\text{"}S\text{"}|E) = 1 - \prod_{j=1}^{M} p_j(\text{"}N\text{"}|E) \ . \quad (10)$$

A threshold detector following the scheme of Eq. (10) is sometimes called a *pandemonium detector* (the loudest channel is heard if its threshold is exceeded), or a *maximum* rule; it differs from the optimal rule slightly. Section 7.2 considers other situations in which analogous rules—separately categorizing each channel as containing signal or noise before combining the channels to make a decision—are optimal.

Receiver operating characteristics generated by the threshold detector as the channel criterion is varied are shown in Figure 2.10 as dashed lines. The predictions of the likelihood-integrating detector and of the maximum detector are practially

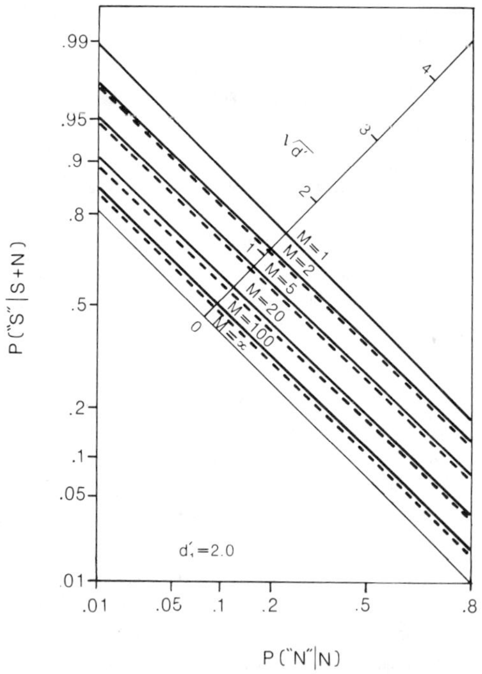

Figure 2.10. The uncertainty decrement of an ideal detector as the number M of different, alternative, independent signals increases in a yes-no detection experiment. The computations assume noise has a normal distribution; the M alternative signals are known exactly and each is detected in its own, ideal "channel"; and the signal-to-noise ratio is such that in the most favorable case ($M = 1$, only one possible signal), $d'_1 = 2.0$. The abscissa represents the probability of correctly responding "N" (no detection response in any channel) on a noise trial; the ordinate represents the probability of a correct detection response "S" when a single signal S_i occurs in channel i. Solid lines assume an optimal (maximum likelihood) detector that operates on the integrated output of the M channels. Dashed lines indicate performance of a nonoptimal decision maker that applies an optimum detection criterion to each channel separately, and responds "Noise" only when all M channels fail to exceed their individual criterion. (From L. W. Nolte & D. Jaarsma, More on the detection of one of m orthogonal signals, *Journal of the Acoustical Society of America*, 1967, *41*. Reprinted with permission.)

indistinguishable in simple stimulus detection paradigms (as opposed to paradigms in which the stimulus is formed by adding together simple stimuli). However, in multiple-look paradigms (where the subject observes several stimulus presentations before making a response), the likelihood and the maximum detectors yield distinct predictions (M. L. Shaw, 1982). And an adding-of-outputs rule is better than the maximum rule for probability summation experiments (Graham, Kramer, & Yager, 1983; Green & Swets, 1966).

4.2.4. Attentional Limitations and Uncertainty. This discussion has focused on the use of compound tasks to investigate attentional *limits* on an observer's ability to perform several tasks (i.e., monitor several locations or frequencies) at once. An attentional limitation would result in poorer information about one or all of the multiple information sources. In the language of SDT, this would be represented by a change in the signal or noise distributions (lower target mean, higher noise variance).

The foregoing discussion reviewed why a loss of accuracy in single-target detection resulting from an increase in the number of locations being monitored is uninterpretable unless one has a theory to determine whether the loss is greater than would be exhibited by an ideal detector. This dependence on a theory (ideal detectors) comes about because the paradigms considered here were exemplars of compound tasks and had more stimulus uncertainty in the compound than in the component tasks, the control conditions. While the complexities of compound tasks may be unavoidable in some real-life situations, they can be avoided in the laboratory by using concurrent tasks which have different, perhaps more tractable, problems. In the case of n locations being monitored, concurrent means that each location has the same probability of containing a target when it is viewed in the context of the other $n - 1$ locations, as it does in isolation. It also means that 0, 1, 2, ..., n targets may occur in a presentation instead of just 0 or 1 as in most compound tasks. Obviously, a large number of targets would pose memory, recognition, and identification problems, as well as detection problems. In multitarget experiments, the occurrence of one target does appear to make the detection of a second target more difficult. These results are described in Section 5.1.1 (see also Gilliom & Sorkin, 1974; Hirsch, Hylton, & Graham, 1982; Pohlmann & Sorkin, 1976; Schneider & Shiffrin, 1977; Sorkin, Pohlmann, & Gilliom, 1973; Sperling & Melchner, 1978b, p. 681). Fortunately, there are paradigms to provide the data to estimate these sources of interference.

Partialing out the effects of stimulus uncertainty from experimental data will affect conclusions about attentional *limitations* on performance that might otherwise have been drawn. In the detection literature, a variety of models (i.e., single band, multiple band, switching single band, etc.) have been discussed extensively (see Swets, 1984, for a review). These "band" models have been called *attention* models in several of the source articles, but they refer to attention in quite a different sense. They do not necessarily reflect *limitations of attention*, but may reflect a *voluntary decision* to weight some sources more heavily and to neglect others. Under appropriate experimental circumstances, electing to sample stimulus information from a narrow-frequency band or from a single location is an optimal strategy to avoid stimulus uncertainty loss, and the neglect of other frequencies or locations does not reflect an attentional limitation. These band models deal with strategic decision processes and not with resource allocation processes. The information from neglected frequency bands or locations may be given less weight (a decision process, e.g., Kinchla, 1977; Kinchla & Collyer, 1974), but the quality of the information (e.g., the signal-to-noise ratio) is not reduced (a resource process).

4.3. Visual Search: A Compound Task

4.3.1. Classical Visual Search Paradigm. In their classical experiments, Neisser and his collaborators (Neisser, 1964; Neisser, Novick, & Lazar, 1963) studied the ability of the subjects to find a particular target character or characters embedded in long lists of randomly chosen characters. Subjects searched lists from top to bottom and made a manual response when they detected the target. Some sample lists are shown in Figure 2.11. The fastest reported search times were on the order of 20 msec per distractor (nontarget) character. For example, if the target were the thousand and first character on the list, it would take the subject about 20 sec longer to discover the target than if it were the first character on the list. Unfortunately, Neisser and colleagues' calculated search times per character or per row were not consistent between lists having different spatial arrangements of characters.

4.3.2. Eye Movements in Visual Search. To investigate the conjecture that eye movements might have been a *limiting factor* in Neisser's visual search, a computer-driven display was devised to enable visual search to proceed without eye movements (Budiansky & Sperling, 1969). In the sequential search procedure, a sequence of briefly flashed letter arrays is presented on a CRT display screen, each new array falling on top of its predecessor. A critical array containing a lone numeral target is embedded somewhere in the middle of the sequence. The target's spatial location (within the array) and its identity are chosen randomly on each trial. The task of the subject is to detect the location and to identify the target (Figure 2.12(a)).

HX	VSWO	VSWOGT
SP	GTXU	XUHXSP
ZP	HXSP	ZPSJXZ
SJ	ZPSJ	PZTPGI
XZ	XZPZ	VSWOXU
PZ	ZPGI	HXSPSJ
ZP	QGOB	XZPZGI
GI	FIVL	QGOBVL
QG	IRDB	IRDBZQ
OB	EQZQ	VLSMHT
FK	VLSM	HWFBWJ
VL	DNHT	DSVEBH
IR	HWFB	LFPKHX
DB	GWWJ	SUWVYR
EQ	DSVE	JBVIWB
ZQ	RCBH	BARGCO
VL	LFPK	CPLBMR
SM	NQHX	PRVNGA
DN	SUWV	XYLZBC
HT	OTYR	CVYNFM
HW	JBVI	WJDVYC
FB	SGWB	QGOBFH
GW	BARG	VLIRDB
WJ	VACO	EQZHVL
DS	DPLA	SMDNHT
VE	CBMR	HWFBGW
LC	PRVN	WJDSVE

Figure 2.11. Sample stimulus arrays of varying configurations for a visual search task like that of Neisser (1963, 1964). The target is "K." Observed search rates (characters per second) vary with display configuration due to eye movements and other factors.

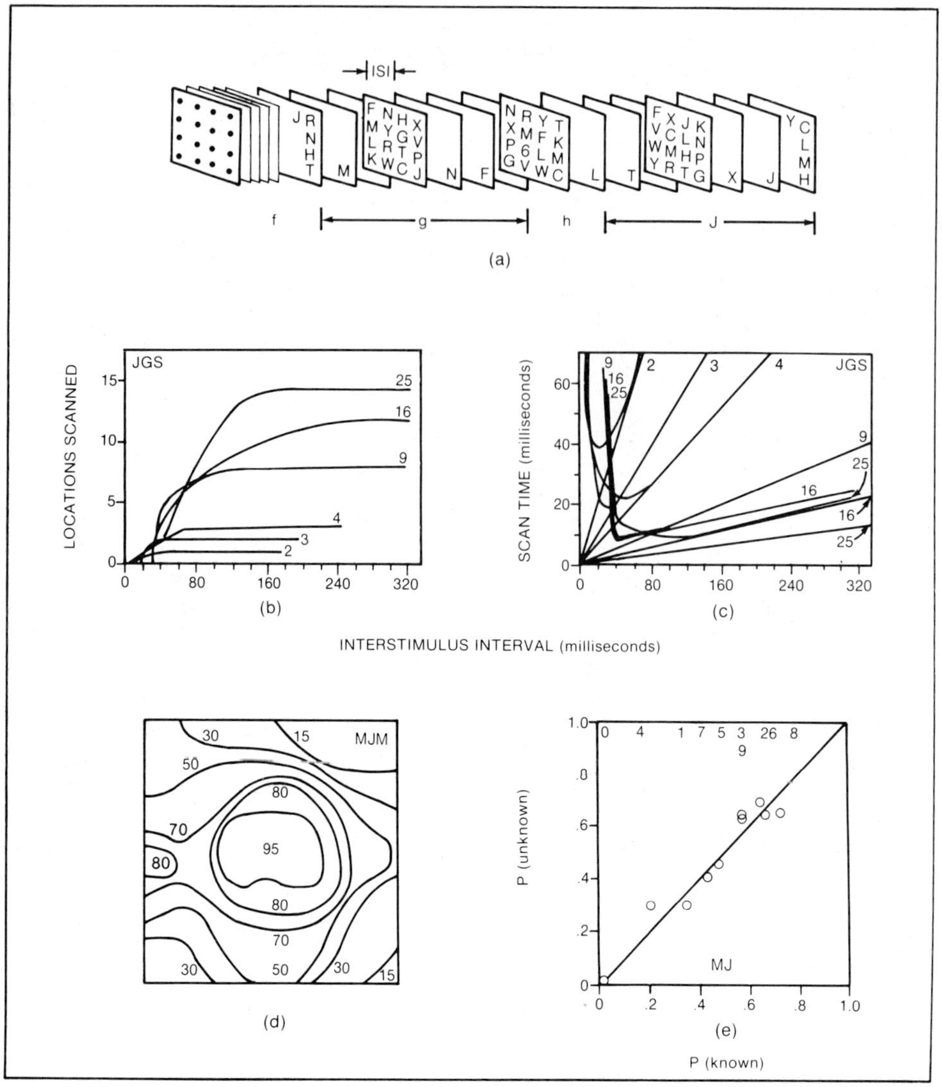

Figure 2.12. Computer-generated displays permit rapid visual search without eye movements. (a) The stimulus fixation (*f*); a random number (6, ..., 12) of displays containing only letters (*g*); critical display containing a numeral target (*h*); 12 more nontarget displays (*j*). (b) Number of locations *L* searched as a function of interstimulus interval *ISI*. *L* is corrected for guessing; the parameter is the number of letters in the display. (c) *T*, the scan time per letter, as a function of *ISI*; $T = ISI/L$ is derived from data in (b). (d) Search field contours describing search accuracy at each location of a 7 × 7 array. The indicated parameter is search accuracy at the contour. (e) Comparison of the probability correct of a location judgment in search for a known numeral target with search for an unknown 1-of-10 numeral targets. Each numeral at the top of (e) indicates the identity of the target for the data point below. The line through the data has slope 1.0; it accounts for 97% of the variance. Panel (d) is based on Sperling and Melchner (1978b). (From G. Sperling, J. Budiansky, J. G. Spivak, & M. C. Johnson, Extremely rapid visual search: The maximum rate of scanning letters for the presence of a numeral, *Science*, 1971, *174*. © 1971 by the American Association for the Advancement of Science. Reprinted with permission.)

In rapid, natural visual search through simple material, the eyes make about four saccadic eye movements per sec, each movement lasting a few tens of msec (depending on the distance traversed) with the eyes relatively motionless between saccades (see Woodworth & Schlosberg, 1954, for a historical review). To approximate this natural search mode, the computer-generated arrays are exposed for durations of 200 msec with brief 40-msec blank periods between arrays. The subjects are instructed to maintain stable eye fixation on the center of the display, and they do (Murphy, 1978; Murphy, Kowler, & Steinman, 1975). The successive arrays displayed to the stationary eye approximate the stimulus sequence ordinarily produced by saccadic eye movements. The exposure parameters are not critical. For example, data obtained with 200-msec exposures followed by 40-msec blank periods are not different from data obtained with 10-msec exposures and 230-msec blank periods (Sperling, 1973; Sperling & Melchner, 1976b, 1978a, p. 676).

The computer-generated sequence has many information processing advantages over the natural sequence. For example, in natural search, when the eyes do not move quite far enough between fixations, some of the same material falls within the eyes' search area in successive fixations and is searched twice, which is wasteful. Even if redundant material on the retina is ignored, the redundant material still usurps space within the search area that could have been occupied by new material. If the eyes move too far between fixations, they leave unsearched lacunae in the stimulus.

In natural search, there are two unknown factors: (1) the eye movement strategy and (2) the attentional field around the eye fixations. Eye movement strategy must be known to determine the attentional factors. In the computer-generated sequence, eye movements are effectively eliminated, so that the attentional field around fixation can be determined.

4.3.3. Maximal Search Rates. In experimental investigations of visual search in computer-driven visual displays, Sperling, Budiansky, Spivak, and Johnson (1971) studied visual search with many different presentation rates in addition to those that most closely approximated natural search. They discovered that the most rapid visual search actually occurred when new arrays were presented every 40 msec, 5 times faster than the fastest possible saccade rate. See Figures 2.12(b) and 2.12(c). At these artificially high presentation rates, search proceeded at a rate of 1 background character per 10 msec, about twice as fast as Neisser's maximum rate and twice as fast as in the 240-msec presentation rate that simulated Neisser's conditions. In fact, there was only a small difference in detection accuracy between interarray times of 120 and 240 per sec, as shown in Figure 2.12(b), suggesting that in some natural searches the motor control of the eye is indeed the limiting factor. In Neisser and colleagues' search task, if their subjects' eyes had executed saccades every 120 msec, search rates might have doubled with little loss of accuracy. The data of Figure 2.12(b) suggest that the second half of many fixation pauses may have been wasted waiting for the eyes to move.

In contrast to Neisser's lists, the computer-generated arrays of different sizes are searched at similar rates (characters per sec). Further, there is a considerable trade-off possible between scanning characters in one array or in several; thus almost as many background characters can be scanned in one array presented for 120 msec (12) as in 3 arrays, each presented for 40 msec (4 per array). This is best seen by looking at the scan times per character in Figure 2.12(c), which dip just below 10 msec per character throughout the 40–120-msec range of interarray times.

The effective search field around fixation is defined by the proportion of targets detected at various points within it. It is illustrated in Figure 2.12(d) for search of 7 × 7 letter arrays. The search field is approximately concentric, centered slightly above fixation. However, locations with fewer neighbors or with adjacent blank space are easier to search (Bouma, 1978; Harris, Shaw, & Bates, 1979; P. Shaw, 1969) so that the measured search field is distorted by the boundaries of the 7 × 7 stimulus. The subject in Figure 2.12(d) tends to concentrate the search more in the left than in the right half of the stimulus. The search field depends on the stimuli used to measure it; extremely rapid presentations or extremely small size characters shrink the search field. However, these parameter variations do not necessarily alter the *shape of the search field* which suggests that, except for a task-dependent monotonic transformation, the search field is an invariant property of the visual system. Obviously, the search field pattern in part reflects perceptual limitations. Later work has shown, however, that the spatial distribution of attention can be voluntarily altered (Sperling & Melchner, 1978a), so that the search field also reflects voluntary, cognitive factors.

4.3.4. Application of Detection Models. Search experiments are variants of the multiple-location detection experiments considered in Section 4.1. Instead of discriminating a low-intensity flash (signal) from background illumination (noise), subjects must discriminate a particular target (e.g., the character 3) from an array of distractors (e.g., C, F, H, R). The underlying decision axis represents "3-ness," where the distractors are drawn from a distribution with a lower mean on this dimension than the target. In Neisser's classical version of the search task, not only is eye movement time the limiting factor in performance but also the functional size of the array and array overlap are unknown. The computer-generated displays solve these problems but cannot solve the theoretical problem of estimating limitations in performance due to various sizes of arrays. Accounting for the effect of array size in visual search is a difficult, incompletely solved problem because at least three factors are usually involved: stimulus uncertainty, retinal nonhomogeneity, and attentional strategy. For theoretical attempts see Fisher (1982), Rumelhart (1970), and Shiffrin and Schneider (1977).

4.3.5. Visual Search for Multiple Targets: A Compound Task without Stimulus Uncertainty Deficit. Among the most interesting questions relating to attention in visual search is whether a subject can search as efficiently for one of several targets, say, any of the numerals 0,1, ..., 9 as for a known target 5. This problem has generally been approached by comparing performance in the known-target conditions (where the subject knows the target will be 5) to the unknown condition. According to the analysis earlier in this chapter, the unknown condition is the compound combination of 10 component tasks (where search for the numeral *1* is Task 1, etc.), since only one of the targets appears on any trial. Neisser (1964; 1966) and Neisser, Novick, and Lazar (1963) claimed that subjects could search as quickly for an unknown as for a known target, but they did not test the hypothesis correctly.

4.3.6. Sequential Search Procedure. A correct test of the hypothesis that search proceeds as quickly for an unknown as for a known target requires comparing performance for the *same* target in known and in unknown conditions. In the sequential search procedure, comparing detection accuracy for known and unknown targets requires comparing accuracy of the location judgments (*where* in the critical array did the target occur?) in the two conditions. A typical numeral-known condition is a block of 100 trials in which only the target 5 occurs. The corresponding numeral-unknown condition is a mixed list of 1000 trials in which the numeral targets 0,1, ..., 9 occur with equal probability. From this mixed list, the subset of 100 trials, on each of which the target 5 occurred, is extracted for comparison with the known condition.

4.3.7. Methodological Refinements. Obviously it would make no sense to compare identification responses between numeral-known and numeral-unknown conditions since the subject knows in advance the identity of the target in the numeral-known condition. However, location judgments can be used to efficiently compare numeral-known and numeral-unknown conditions. A second (but far less efficient) method of comparing detection of known and unknown targets would be to include catch sequences in which no target is present and to determine how well the subject can discriminate catch from target-containing sequences (e.g., compute a d' measure). A third method requires the subject to respond within some brief fixed interval after the critical array to indicate that the target has been detected. Method 3 should be combined with methods 1 and 2, if used. A fourth refinement is to require that the subject give a confidence rating (e.g., "certain," "probable,") of response. This confidence rating can be used to improve the estimate of d' (method 2). Or it can be used to improve the estimate of the probability of a correct location response (method 1). For example, location responses in the lowest-confidence category ("unsure") frequently are found to be statistically independent of the stimulus; that means the subject knows when a response is a guess, and these guesses can be treated differently from other responses.

4.3.8. Results. Location judgments were used by Sperling, Budiansky, Spivak, and Johnson (1971) to compare target-known and target-unknown conditions in a visual search task. Accuracy of location judgments for each of the numerals 0,1,...,9 was measured in target-known and target-unknown blocks; these two measured accuracies were nearly the same and were correlated 0.97, as seen in Figure 2.12(e). This near-perfect correlation is very strong evidence that the same search processes were executed in target-known and target-unknown conditions. If there were any substantial differences in search processes, one would expect a somewhat different ordering of target difficulties in the target-known and target-unknown conditions. That is, a target that is relatively easy in one condition might be relatively hard in another. Since this did not happen, it suggests that the search processes in the two conditions are essentially the same process.

Since the target-unknown condition is a compound task, a decrement in search performance would have been attributable to *either* uncertainty loss *or* attentional limitations, and the conclusions would have depended on an uncertainty model. However, since virtually no performance decrement is observed, it can safely be concluded that there is no attentional decrement associated with this particular task combination. Apparently, the 10 searches for each of the 10 alternative targets can be carried out simultaneously, in parallel, without loss.

4.3.9. Information Overload. What distinguishes the lossless compound search for an unknown 1-of-10 numerals from the many other similar compound detection tasks that do show stimulus uncertainty losses? First and foremost: *overlearning*. Neisser, Novick, and Lazar (1963) and Schneider and Shiffrin (1977) studied the temporal course of learning as a compound search for arbitrary combinations of targets. Both laboratories found that, with thousands of trials of practice, the initially slow compound search becomes as quick as the search for a single target, which also improves substantially. Following LaBerge (1975), Shiffrin and Schneider labeled the practiced search *automatic* search and observed some interesting properties. For example, when paired as a concurrent task with other tasks, automatic search produces little loading (uses few mental processing resources), and when told to ignore previously overlearned targets, the subject is unable to avoid detecting them. However, these explanations deal with the difficulties of compound search from the human's standpoint. Resource limitations do not restrict an ideal detector, and it nevertheless shows a loss in compound tasks. Why do humans not show more of a loss in this compound-search task?

The second significant aspect of Sperling and colleagues' (1971) sequential-search procedure is that it induces an enormous overload of information. For example, the maximum-likelihood detection model, when confronted with Sperling and colleagues' multiple-array stimulus, would have to compute the likelihood of each of the 10 targets at each of 9 stimulus locations in each of the 10 or more arrays in which the target might occur. About 1000 additions (or more, if target identity and location are to be retained) would have to be computed within a second. Clearly, Nolte and Jaarsma's (1967) procedure of setting a threshold in each channel and responding only if any of the thresholds is exceeded is a more practical alternative. Because there are so many locations and arrays to be searched, thresholds have to be set very high to avoid multiple responses—so high that essentially complete target identification is required. A high threshold does not, without further assumptions, explain why the threshold is so little changed between target-known and target-unknown conditions. But it does suggest that processes different from those proposed for detection of weak signals may be predominant. For example, Posner, Snyder, and Davidson (1980) and others have asserted that the signal detection model is not applicable to all tasks involving above-threshold stimuli. Unalloyed SDT does not explain all detection experiments.

4.3.10. Location Uncertainty. When detecting a target, does the subject necessarily know the spatial location where it occurred? A casual examination of the data indicates that the answer is obviously not. Correct identification responses frequently are associated with seemingly random location responses. However, these mislocated detections might have resulted from the subject mistakenly identifying one of the distractors as the target (or from random guessing) and being correct by chance. To separate accidentally correct detection responses from true detections, the refinements of Section 4.3.7 are necessary. Sperling (1984) found that when the identification responses in 5×5 arrays were correct and made with one of the top two (of five) confidence ratings, the overwhelming majority of location responses were correct and, more significantly, when occasional errors did occur, 95% of the incorrect location responses were assigned to a vertically or horizontally (but not diagonally) adjacent cell. In this search task, whenever detection occurs, it is associated with a spatial location. Different results have been reported for other search tasks, and when all the methodological precautions have been taken, it would be interesting to know what distinguishes the two kinds of tasks.

5. RESOURCE SHARING AND CONCURRENT TASKS

A concurrent combination of two or more subtasks requires the subject to perform all subtasks on each trial. While such a procedure is not feasible in all situations, it has the distinct advantage of not requiring a complex computational model of stimulus uncertainty to place a lower bound on optimal performance. The feasibility of the concurrent task combination often can be determined by examining performance in control conditions. This section reviews the resource sharing model of attentional sharing in concurrent task paradigms, treats several examples of concurrent tasks, and then examines concurrent visual search experiments and the attention operating characteristics derived from them.

5.1. Simultaneous Auditory Two-Channel Detection

Consider a typical, compound, auditory detection experiment. In the compound task, any of three possible stimuli occurs within a block of trials: one of two tones differing in frequency or a noise stimulus. The stimuli for component tasks are $(N_1, S_1 + N_1)$ for Task 1 and $(N_2, S_2 + N_2)$ for Task 2. Generally, $N_1 =$

N_2. A trial of the compound task consists of a random selection of a trial from Task 1 *or* Task 2. A performance loss in the mixed block indicates an inability to share attention between different frequency ranges but only if the alternative hypothesis of a statistical *stimulus uncertainty* loss can be excluded.

5.1.1. Concurrent Detection. The concurrent version of the two-tone task presents a stimulus from Task 1 *and* a stimulus from Task 2 on each trial. That is, the appropriate stimulus set for the concurrent task, where the subscript indicates the task, is [N_1 & N_2], [N_1 & ($N_2 + S_2$)], [($N_1 + S_1$) & N_2], [($N_1 + S_1$) & ($N_2 + S_2$)], where S_1 & S_2 indicate joint presentation of S_1 and S_2. The appropriate response set is (N_1 & N_2), (N_1 & S_1), (S_2 & N_2), (S_1 & S_2).

In auditory detection, Pastore and Sorkin (1972), Sorkin and Pastore (1971), Sorkin, Pastore, and Pohlmann (1972), and Sorkin, Pohlmann, and Gilliom (1973) use paradigms that are interpretable as the concurrent task just described. Consider, for example, the experiment of Sorkin, Pohlmann, and Gilliom (1973) that investigated the detection of simultaneously presented auditory signals of different frequency. In one of their conditions, stimuli consisting of either 0, 1, or 2 tones, plus noise, were presented to the left ear. Tone 1 was 630 Hz, Tone 2, 1400 Hz. The subjects responded to each tonal stimulus independently; thus, the response alternatives were [0, 1, 2, 1&2]. Sorkin and colleagues (1973) found an interference effect of the concurrent task; detection of Tone 1 (and of Tone 2) was less accurate in the concurrent condition than in the corresponding isolated control task. Additional analyses showed that concurrent detection performance was especially impaired on trials when both tones were present. Given the fact of these performance deficits in a concurrent task, can they be attributed to an attentional failure (the subject is unable to monitor two channels), to response interference (while the subject is responding to the stimulus in one channel, events in the other channel are forgotten), or to some other kind of interference? Further analysis of the procedure reveals two problems taken up in order: (1) the subjects may not be able to *identify* weak stimuli after they have been detected and (2) the procedure is not truly concurrent.

5.1.2. Discriminability in Concurrent Tasks. Consider the following compound and concurrent Gedanken experiments. In a detection task, on each trial, the subject is presented with one of two tones or with noise. The tonal frequencies are 630.000 and 630.001 Hz. This is a compound experiment in which performance on the compound task (mixed list of two frequencies and noise) is guaranteed to be equal to performance on the component task (pure list of one frequency and noise) because these two "different" tones will not differentially affect any human performance, if indeed the differences could be physically measured in a brief trial interval. Consider the same three signals in a concurrent paradigm. Either 0, 1, or 2 frequencies are presented on a trial, and the subject must answer separately whether each was present. Designating the signals as ("low," "high") and the absence or presence of a stimulus as 0, 1, respectively, there are four possible stimulus combinations on a trial: (0, 0), (0, 1), (1, 0), (1, 1) and the four corresponding responses. In the concurrent task, the subject must be able to identify the stimulus to perform well. Since the subject cannot do this when stimuli are indiscriminable (0, 1), (1, 0), there is a performance deficit in the concurrent task. The conclusion is that a concurrent procedure makes sense only when the subject knows which task he or she is performing, and concurrency becomes problematical when the component tasks are confusable.

Sorkin and colleagues (1973) do not know how discriminable their tonal signals are, and therefore their concurrent procedure by itself is questionable. Their observation that detection of two binaurally presented tones is not better than detection of the same two tones presented monaurally suggests either that the 630- and 1400-Hz tones are quite discriminable at threshold (or merely that routing the threshold tones to different ears does not make them more discriminable than presenting them to the same ear). But *discriminability* can be determined experimentally, for example, in a two-interval forced-choice procedure in which a 630-Hz tone occurs in one interval and 1400-Hz tone in the other. *Attentional limitations* can be measured directly by attentional manipulations (instructions, payoffs, a priori probabilities) that direct attention to one or the other stimulus. *Cross-stimulus interference* can be estimated by varying the strength of concurrent stimulus events. *Response interference* can be measured by varying the order of report, by comparing partial reports with full reports, by varying the numbers of responses required, and so on. The point of this analysis is that one procedure is not sufficient to resolve a difficult issue, such as multiband auditory detection. That requires both a carefully formulated theoretical framework *and* many convergent paradigms.

5.1.3. Noise as an Environmental Feature. A technical point about Sorkin and colleagues' (1973) monaural, concurrent multitone detection task is that the stimuli of component tasks are not ($S_i + N, N$) but (S_i, 0). The noise is a feature of the experimental situation, like the chair and the earphones and, technically, not a stimulus. Regarding noise as a stimulus could lead to the selection of $S_i + N$ from task 1 and N from task 2 to produce $S_1 + 2N$ in the concurrent task, which is obviously much more difficult to detect than $S_i + N$ in the component task. On the other hand, in *dichotic* listening, in which each component task is directed at a different ear, the stimuli of component tasks are ($S_L + N_L, N_L$) and ($S_R + N_R, N_R$) where L,R designate left- and right-ear presentations, respectively. This is not an idle quibble because, in dichotic concurrent tasks, the two noise stimuli are uncorrelated (they are chosen independently), whereas in the monaural concurrent tasks, the noise stimulus for each of the component tasks is the same. Technical issues of this sort often are critical to a theoretical understanding of an experiment, and careful analysis of the paradigm in terms of concurrency and compounding may help the experimenter to resolve them. The question of attentional loss in frequency monitoring is still unresolved.

5.2. Shadowing

One of the most studied concurrent tasks in attentional research is auditory shadowing (Cherry, 1953; Cherry & Taylor, 1954). The typical shadowing task requires a subject to repeat a message heard in one ear while another message is being presented to the other ear (Treisman, 1964). Early single-channel models of attention (Broadbent, 1958; Craik, 1948) were supported by the observation that shadowing a message in one ear prevents a subject from remembering anything about the content of the other ear's message (Glucksberg & Cowen, 1970; Moray, 1959; Mowbray, 1964; Norman, 1968). One explanation of the subjects' recall failures might be that auditory shadowing of a single message requires most or all of the subjects' attention and that *any* competing task suffers severe disruption. Allport, Antonis, and Reynolds (1972) demolished this simplistic notion about attentional capacity in a series of studies that demonstrated adequate performance on *some* tasks but not others, when performed concurrently with auditory shadowing.

The results of Allport and colleagues' (1972) experiments are shown in Figure 2.13. Figure 2.13(a) illustrates data from three pairs of concurrent tasks. Auditory shadowing was a component task in all task pairs; it was paired with three different recognition tasks, recognition of auditorily presented word lists, visually presented word lists, and visually presented picture lists. The recognition items were selected to yield approximately the same accuracy level when tested alone. In the concurrent task, the subject shadowed the auditory message while attempting to remember the recognition items, which were presented concurrently. Recognition was tested afterward. Quite different levels of accuracy resulted for these three different task combinations. Allport and colleagues (1972) suggest that the degree of compatibility in these task pairs depends on the similarity of the recognition tasks to the shadowing task, which is both linguistic and auditory. Picture recognition, which is neither linguistic nor auditory, is near control levels when performed concurrently with shadowing. Recognition of visual words was impaired by concurrent shadowing, and recognition memory for auditory words (presented in the ear opposite the shadowed message) was impossible.

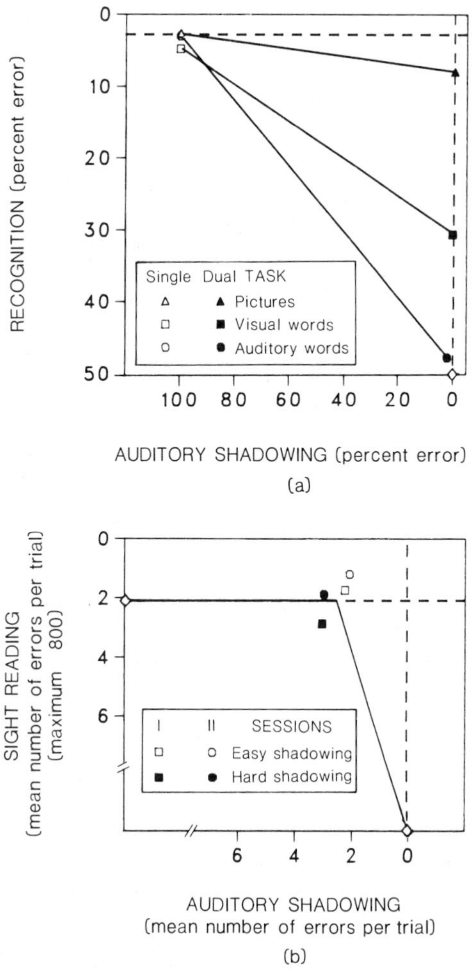

Figure 2.13. Results of the concurrent, auditory shadowing experiments of Allport, Antonis, and Reynolds (1972). (a) Accuracy of shadowing performed concurrently with the study phase of a subsequent test of recognition memory for pictures, for visually displayed words, and for orally presented words. Data are estimated from Allport and colleagues' (1972) bar graphs and graphed in a two-dimensional operating space: percentage errors in recognition versus percentage errors in shadowing. The three recognition memory tasks were calibrated for approximately equal single-task baselines (open symbols) but show large differences in the amount of concurrency loss (closed symbols). The mean single-task baseline for the recognition tasks is shown by the dashed line; baseline performance for shadowing is zero errors. This is a problematical design because the shadowing performance is at ceiling. (b) Errors in shadowing and in concurrently performed sight reading of piano music. Diamond symbols indicate the single-task baseline for piano sight reading and for easy shadowing. Concurrent performance data were estimated as in (a); concurrent sight-reading data are separated by levels of shadowing difficulty and practice. Single-task data for difficult shadowing were unavailable. The performance operating characteristic is the light line drawn through the mean single-task and mean dual-task performances.

Allport and colleagues' (1972) experiment exemplifies a common technical error in concurrent experiments: performance on one of the tasks (shadowing) is at ceiling in both the isolated control and the concurrent conditions. Therefore, Allport concludes that sight-reading does not interfere with shadowing. However, it is impossible to know whether there might have been a performance decrement in a more difficult shadowing task, one in which performance was not already at ceiling. Furthermore, an attention operating characteristic must be determined by more than one joint-performance point.

Figure 2.13(b) shows the levels of concurrent performance of auditory shadowing and piano sight-reading. Although both component tasks are difficult, a high level of concurrent performance was achievable simultaneously by Allport and colleagues' (1972) subjects.

5.3. Concurrent Visual Search

5.3.1. Arrays Matched to Processing Capacity. Compound visual search experiments were reviewed in Section 4.3. These experiments (Sperling et al., 1971) were directed at finding the optimal stimuli for visual search, but the stimuli were restricted to one size of character. What is the optimum size of character for visual search? Many small characters can be presented in the foveal area where acuity is good, but small characters are below the acuity limit of peripheral vision. Conversely, composing an array of large characters that are resolvable in peripheral vision causes central acuity to be squandered; the fovea will be fully occupied by a mere fragment of a character. The obvious solution is to compose an array of characters of different sizes. How should characters of different sizes be arranged to facilitate the scan of the largest possible number of characters? Place small characters in the center ranging to large characters in the periphery, where each size of character is matched to the information processing capacity of the retinal area on which it was imaged. Anstis (1974) developed such displays, which he used for demonstrating letters that are equally above their acuity threshold in different areas of the retina.

5.3.2. Concurrent Search for Large and Small Targets. The investigation of visual search in arrays that are spatially matched to visual information processing capacity was undertaken by Sperling and Melchner (Sperling, 1975; Sperling & Melchner, 1978b). Array sequences were constructed in which only one target numeral occurred in a critical array otherwise composed entirely of letters. Figure 2.12(a) illustrates the procedure. This target might occur at peripheral locations that received large-size targets or central locations that received smaller targets. Figure 2.14 shows one of several array configurations tested. Surprisingly, Melchner was unable to search arrays simultaneously for large and small targets. That Melchner could not search simultaneously for a large and a small target (e.g., a large *9* or a small *9*) in the same array was especially astonishing since, in earlier experiments, he had been able to search simultaneously, without loss, for 10 numeral targets (0,1,...,9) when they were all the same size. Is a large *9* more different from a small *9* than from a large *3* or *4*?

The appropriate search task to test this possibility is a concurrent search for a large and small target numeral. Figure 2.15 illustrates a display consisting of 16 large characters on the outside perimeter and 4 small characters in the center. The character sizes were adjusted to make detection of the small foveal target approximately as difficult as detection of the large peripheral target. The attentional question concerned the subject's ability to search for both a small and a large numeral *concurrently*. Hence the large and small targets both appeared on the same frame in the search task.

5.3.2.1. ***Procedure.*** Sperling and Melchner (1978a, 1978b) presented a long sequence of briefly flashed arrays at a rate of 4 per sec. A critical array embedded in the middle of the sequence contained a randomly chosen numeral target at 1 of the 16 outside locations and another randomly chosen numeral at 1 of the 4 inside locations. In the main experimental conditions, the subjects' task was to detect both targets. The subjects had to state the identity, location, and their confidence level for each of the two targets. The subjects' allocation of attention was explicitly controlled by instruction. In some blocks of trials, they were told to give 90% of their attention to the inside target and 10% to the outside target; in the other blocks the instructions were reversed; and in still other blocks, subjects were instructed to give equal attention to both classes of targets.

5.3.2.2. ***Results.*** Some useful methodological innovations were incorporated in the analysis of these data. Responses on which the lowest confidence was used (zero, "guessing") were found by chi-square tests to indeed be statistically independent of the stimuli. This means the subjects know when they do not know (cf. Sperling & Melchner, 1976a, p. 209). Further, analysis of verifiable location errors showed that more than 95% of the time when a target was mislocated, it was mislocated at an adjacent horizontal or vertical (not diagonal) position. These two additional items of information can be incorporated into a rigorous, tripartite criterion for true identifications, namely, (1) correct identification response, (2) confidence greater than zero, and (3) mislocation not greater than one adjacent position.

The data for concurrent search of large and small characters with various attention instructions are shown in Figure 2.15(a). The abscissa represents the percentage of correct target identifications of the outside targets; the ordinate represents the percentage of correct identifications of inside targets. Each data point represents the average of data collected in several blocks of trials. The data fall along a line of slope approximately −1, indicating that as probability of identifying one class of target increases (according to the instructional demand), it is compensated by an almost exactly equivalent decrease in identification probability for the other class of targets. The locus of all achievable joint performances on the two tasks (approximated by the straight-line segments connecting the data points) is the attention operating characteristic (Sperling & Melchner, 1976b, 1978a). The term was proposed by Kinchla (see Kinchla, 1980, p. 217, and Sperling, 1984, p. 112) following the terminology of signal detection theory (SDT) (Swets, 1964).

If subjects could search for both targets concurrently without loss, then their performance in all experimental conditions would fall on the *independence point*—the point at which subjects identify both large and small targets concurrently as accurately as they do in the corresponding control condition. (This is the upper right point of the square in Figure 2.15(a).) Clearly this point was not achieved; there always was some loss.

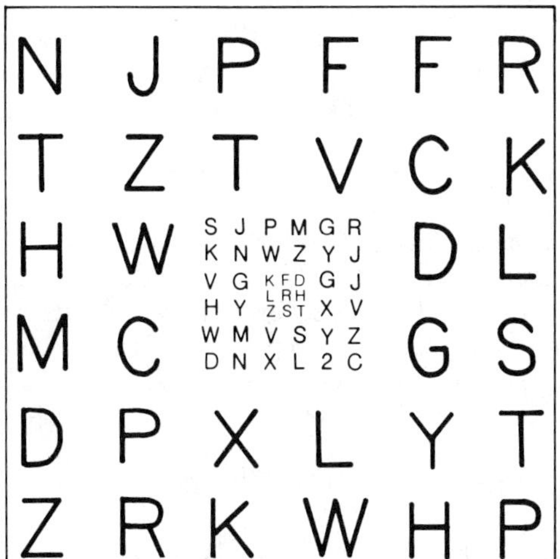

Figure 2.14. A search array in which character size has been approximately matched to the information processing capacity of the visual system. The target is a single numeral. This display does *not* maximize performance because subjects have difficulty searching concurrently among characters of different sizes. (From G. Sperling, A unified theory of Attention and signal detection, in R. Parasuraman & R. Davies (Eds.), *Varieties of attention*, Academic Press, 1984. Reprinted with permission.)

5.3.3. Performance in the Component Tasks and Other Control Conditions

5.3.3.1. ***Control for Memory Overload.*** A series of trials was run in which the letter distractors were replaced by dots. This made target identification trivially easy, and subjects never failed to report both targets correctly. Thus any errors subjects may make in experimental conditions are due to their inability to detect the targets among distractors, not to their inability to report both targets, once detected.

5.3.3.2. ***Component Tasks.*** In some blocks of trials, subjects were instructed to report *only* outside targets and to ignore inside targets, and in other blocks, they received the reverse instruction. These control data are graphed directly on the coordinate axes of Figure 2.15(a). That the probability of report is nearly equal in the two control tasks (inside, outside) is not a coincidence; the character sizes and array sizes were chosen to match the tasks in difficulty.

5.3.4. Three Concurrent Pairs of Search Tasks.

To gauge the amount of loss in concurrent search, it is informative to investigate several related pairs of concurrent tasks. In all, three pairs of tasks were studied. One task in each pair remained precisely the same throughout: detection of a numeral among the outside letters. Three different inside tasks were matched to this task in difficulty: (1) detection-identification of a small inside target; (2) detection-identification of a normal-size inside numeral (where every inside character was obscured by a ran-

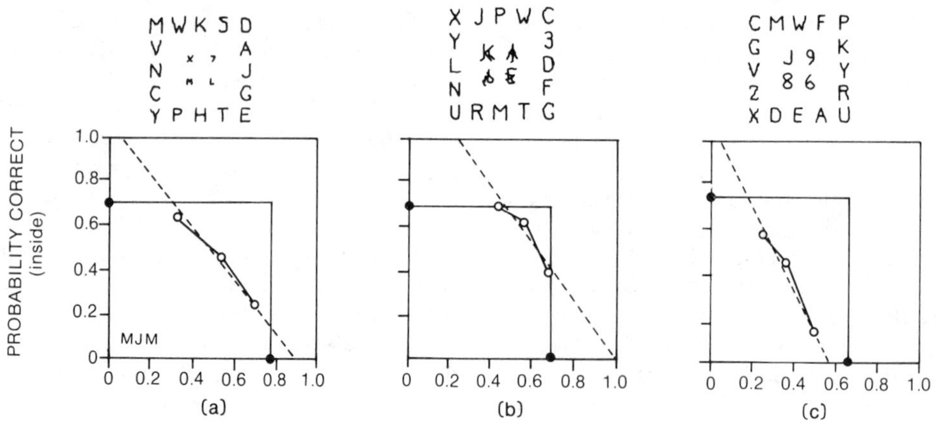

Figure 2.15. Stimulus configurations and the empirical attention operating characteristics (AOCs) for three pairs of concurrent tasks. The trial structure in the experiment was similar to that shown in Figure 2.12(a). (a) A large (outside) and small (inside) numeral target appear concurrently for independent detection. Abscissa and ordinate indicate the percentage of correct identifications of the outside target and inside target, respectively. Isolated control conditions are shown as filled circles on the coordinate axes. The intersection of the perpendiculars drawn through these control points defines the independence point. Concurrent performance is indicated by open circles. Attention conditions, ordered from upper left to lower right, respectively, are 90% to inside, equal, 90% to outside, with each point representing the average of two or three blocks of trials. The heavy line connecting the data points is the empirical AOC. The broken line represents the best-fitting straight line to the data. (b) Same conditions as (a) except the inside task is detection of a noise-obscured numeral target of same size as the outside target. (c) Same conditions as (a) except the concurrent inside task is detection of a letter target among three numeral distractors. These three task combinations show different levels of compatibility, as indicated by the distance of the AOC from the independent point. (From G. Sperling & M. J. Melcher, The attention operating characteristic: Some examples from visual search, *Science*, 1978, *202*. © 1978 by the American Association for the Advancement of Science. Reprinted with permission.)

domly chosen "noise squiggle"); and (3) detection-identification of a single target *letter* among inside numerals.

The same control and experimental conditions as before were conducted with these stimuli. Figure 2.15 shows the attention operating characteristics (AOCs) generated by these three pairs of tasks. The distance of the AOC from the independence point is a measure of the incompatibility of two tasks. As in the classroom example of Figure 2.1(c), perfectly compatible tasks, performed as well concurrently as in isolation, would fall on the independence point.

As an index of compatibility between two tasks, we can take the percentage of *isolated* performance achieved by the *concurrent* performance. Concurrent performance is averaged over the component tasks under conditions of equal attention, that is, at the point where the AOC curve—or surface in higher-dimensional space—crosses the line connecting the origin and the independence point. (Let B represent the percent correct measure; A, the area under the AOC, is a better but more complex measure than B, given approximately—in this example—by $A \approx 1 - 2(1 - B)^2$.) The most incompatible pair of tasks consists of (1) searching for a numeral among letters concurrently with (2) searching for a letter among numerals. These tasks are almost mutually exclusive, average concurrent performance being about 54% of isolated performance. (By doing only one task or the other, never both—even under concurrent instructions—50% of isolated performance would be achieved, by definition.)

The most compatible tasks are (1) searching for a numeral (on the outside) and (2) searching for a numeral of the same size obscured by noise (on the inside). Concurrent performance is about 82% of isolated performance. The original pair of tasks (search for a large and for a small numeral) falls in between with a concurrent performance of 66% of isolated performance. Apparently, searches for a large 9 and a large 3 are more compatible than searches for a large 9 and a small 9. As usual, however, matters are not quite as simple as they first appear to be. When both large and small characters could occur in any of a small number of central locations (rather than being confined to spatially separated areas), Sperling and Harris (Note 1) found no effect of attentional instructions; performance was at the independence point. A similar result was reported by Hoffman and Nelson (1981).

The visual search experiment is perhaps the most complete example of the use of concurrent tasks to investigate attention. The performance levels of each component task (search inside, search outside) were explicitly measured. The concurrent combination was tested under several attention instructions (verbally defined utilities). Appropriate controls were performed to determine that the performance losses were "attentional" and could not be attributed to reporting bottlenecks.

5.4. Attention Operating Characteristics

5.4.1. Determining Entire AOCs versus Determining Single Points. In the analysis of concurrent tasks previously described, there are two processes by which performance may differ. Different task combinations move performance from one AOC to another, and varying attention allocation between two tasks moves performance along a single AOC. To compare the compatibility of two pairs of tasks, it is necessary to obtain the two AOCs, not just single points on the AOCs. The situation is analogous to SDT in which, to compare the detectability of two signals, two receiver operating characteristics (ROCs) are needed, not just one point on each. In two-task concurrent paradigms where only one point per AOC is measured, for example, one point for task A with task B and another for task A with task C (as in the examples of Section 5.2), one cannot be sure that subjects have applied the same implicit attentional allocation in the two concurrent experiments. Generally, one cannot draw quantitative conclusions, and in some cases even qualitative conclusions may be in error.

5.4.2. Secondary-Task Procedure. To illustrate the pitfalls of determining less than a complete AOC, consider the *secondary-task* procedure (Kahneman, 1973), a concurrent paradigm sometimes used to measure attentional requirements of a task. In this procedure, a secondary task *C* is performed concurrently with a primary task *A*. The subject is instructed to optimize performance on the primary task, that is, to hold performance on *A* as close to control levels as possible. It is assumed that the observed level of performance on *C* will provide a measure of the attentional requirements of the primary task *A*. To compare the resource requirements of task *A* to those of task *B*, each of *A* and *B* is paired with *C*, and the corresponding deficits in performance of *C* provide the index for comparison.

The classroom analogy is helpful in conceptualizing the problem in the secondary-task procedure. Examples are shown in Figure 2.16. Subjects are given instructions to operate near 100% of control levels on the primary tasks *A* and *B*. Figure 2.16(a) illustrates a case in which it would be erroneously concluded that these tasks were exactly equivalent in attentional demand characteristics, although they differ substantially. Conversely, in the situation illustrated in Figure 2.16(b), the secondary-task method produces an overestimate of the difference between tasks *A* and *B*. Perhaps these unfavorable hypothetical situations are unlikely. However, as one can safely restrict the number of attentional conditions to be studied only after one knows the AOC and one can know the AOC only by studying several attentional conditions, there seems to be no alternative to measuring AOCs.

6. REACTION TIMES AND SPEED–ACCURACY TRADE-OFF

Many investigations of attention employ reaction-time (RT) paradigms. The same task classifications apply to RT tasks as

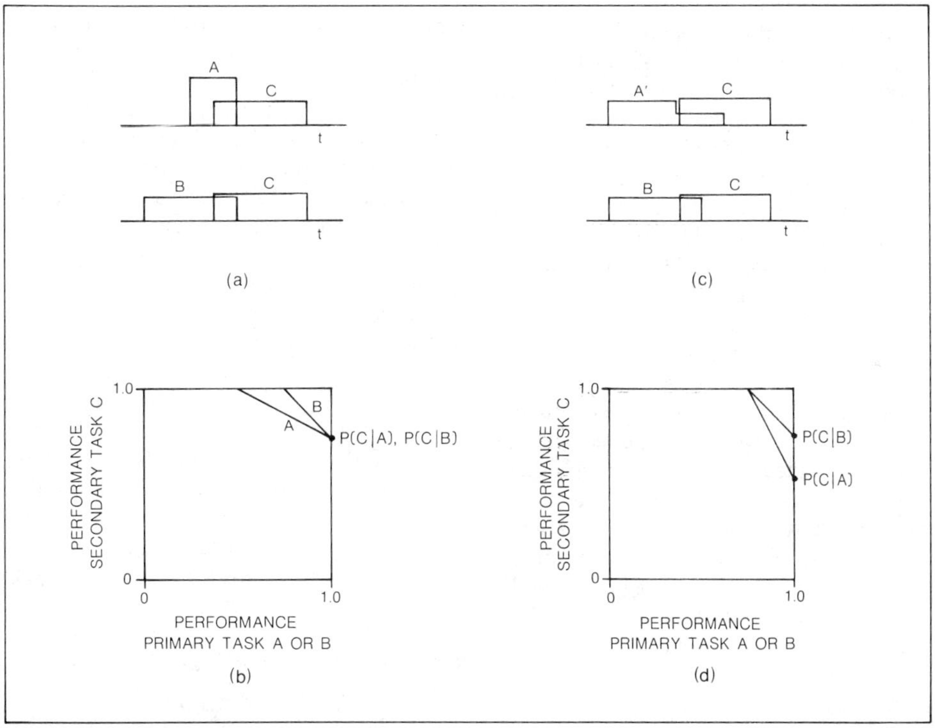

Figure 2.16. Representation of the "secondary task" procedure in classroom examples. (a) Information densities for two primary tasks *A* or *B* (classes) combined with a secondary task (class *C*) to yield secondary task deficits $\Delta(C|A) = 1 - P(C|A)$, and $\Delta(C|B) = 1 - P(C|B)$. (b) The attendance operating characteristics (AOCs) corresponding to the task combinations (A, C) and (B, C) in panel (a). The abscissa is the proportion of single-task performance on the concurrent primary task; the ordinate is the proportion of single-task performance on the concurrent secondary task. These different task combinations yield different AOCs but identical secondary-task deficits [shown by the point $P(C|A) = P(C|B)$] when primary task performance is held near control levels, as per instruction in this paradigm. (c) Alternative information densities for two primary tasks (A', B) and a secondary task (C) to yield a larger secondary task deficit. (d) Operating space as in panel (b); the AOCs correspond to the information densities in panel (c). With these task combinations, a secondary task experiment yields the secondary task deficits shown by the points $P(C|A)$ and $P(C|B)$. Panels (a) and (b) show that different fractions of overlapping resources (of *A* and of *B* with *C*) can lead to identical secondary-task deficits; panels (c) and (d) show that the same fraction of overlapping resources (of *A* and of *B* with *C*) can lead to different secondary-task deficits, illustrating the danger of using a single point from a secondary-task procedure rather than obtaining a full AOC.

to tasks that use only accuracy measures. This section develops a theoretical approach to ideal (lossless) RT performance trade-off, simple RT experiments, choice RT experiments, speed–accuracy trade-offs (SATs), and utility functions for some of these procedures.

6.1. Ideal Performance in Compound Reaction-Time Tasks: Random Walk Model

6.1.1. Definition of Reaction-Time Tasks. In a simple RT task, the subject is presented with a single stimulus and asked to make the designated response as quickly as possible. A choice RT task is the union of k, $k \geq 2$ simple RT tasks. Any of the component stimuli $[s_j, j = 1, \dots k]$ is presented and the subject makes a response, r_i. Only $s_j - r_j$ pairs are "correct" (e.g., utility = 1); others are "wrong" (e.g., utility = 0). A choice RT task requires all stimuli and all responses be different. When all the responses r_j are the same, the compound task is sometimes called a *Donders Type 3* task.

6.1.2. Examples. Consider the following kinds of RT experiments. On each trial, a subject is presented a stimulus which must be classified into one of two (or more) categories as quickly as possible. For example, the subject may be shown a letter string and be asked to press a reaction key with the left hand if it is a word or another key with the right hand if it is not. This is the lexical decision task originally described by Rubenstein, Garfield, and Millikan (1970) and Rubenstein, Lewis, and Rubenstein (1971a, 1971b). Or the subject may be asked to classify a colored patch that has an irrelevant color name written on it, as red or green. When the color of the patch and the color name differ, the subject is slower and less accurate than when the name is omitted. This is called the *Stroop effect* (Kahneman & Treisman, 1984; Stroop, 1935). Or the subject may be asked to classify stimuli by means of a card-sorting task, placing cards as quickly as possible into different piles according to category. All these tasks are compound (not concurrent) tasks; the subject is presented only one of the possible stimuli and makes only one of the alternative responses on any one trial. RT tasks usually do not involve multiple or concurrent responses to concurrent or simultaneous stimuli, although there are exceptions, for example, the double-stimulation paradigm (Karlin & Kestenbaum, 1968; Smith, 1968). For a review of the double-stimulation paradigms, see Kantowitz (1974). To determine whether an attentional loss occurs in a compound RT experiment (as compared to a simple RT control experiment), it is useful to compare performance in compound RT experiments to a model of an ideal (or lossless) processor.

6.1.3. Random Walk Model. The *random walk model* of Link (1975) and Link and Heath (1975) is a simple theory for RT closely related to signal detection theory (SDT). SDT is a model for the perception and decision component in detection tasks. The random walk model is a theory for the perception and response–decision component in RT tasks. (For a review of other possible models, see Green & Luce, 1973.) Without going into full detail, the principle of the random walk model can be summarized as follows: an ideal (lossless) detector accumulates information from the start of a trial, and when the information exceeds a threshold, the appropriate response is made. Each new increment of information is assumed to be somewhat unreliable, so that the cumulative balance of all the information may waiver between the alternatives, that is, execute a random walk. A strategy consists of a choice of *response threshold* (the distance from the starting point to the absorbing boundary) for *each* of the alternative responses. Equivalently, Link's (1975) notation uses the distance between the two boundaries, A, and a bias, or starting point between them, C.

Random walk models are a subclass of the larger class of *sequential decision strategies*, characterized by (1) continuing to make observations until, (2) some function on the sample space of observations is satisfied, and (3) making the decision. There is a wide range of problems for which functions are known that will make a sequential strategy the optimum strategy (Wald, 1950). The random walk model, as outlined, is known to be an ideal detector—that is, an optimum strategy—when the incoming information can be regarded as symmetric between the choice alternatives (Laming, 1968). For example, evidence is like the outcome of a toss of a coin biased 0.55 in favor of one side or the other; a decision in favor of a heads-bias would be made when the number of observed head tosses exceeded the number of tails by a criterion and vice versa for a tails-bias decision.

To optimize its performance with respect to the experimentally defined payoffs, the response threshold of the random walk model is adjusted so that an optimum compromise is made between several incompatible criteria. The response threshold is set high to avoid accidental incorrect responses (due to some randomness in the incoming information) but not so high that the RT is too long. (The higher the threshold, the longer it takes, on the average, to reach it.) These relations are illustrated in Figure 2.17. A priori information that a stimulus is probable will cause the threshold for the corresponding response to be set lower, thereby decreasing RT and increasing the accuracy when that stimulus is presented, and decreasing the accuracy when the other stimulus is presented. A priori information that a stimulus is unlikely forces the response threshold to be raised in order to avoid errors. The response threshold is changed by changing A or C or both together. Several sample random walks are shown in Figure 2.17.

In SDT attentional *limitations* were represented by change in the underlying distributions (lower signal mean or higher noise variance) as a result of an attentional manipulation. In an ideal detector, decrements in performance occur with increasing numbers of potential stimuli; thus corresponding decrements in human performance might still be compatible with a lossless detector. Analogously, in the random walk model, attentional limitations are represented by changes in the *quality* of the accumulating information—the rate of growth of internal d' with time. Changes in expectancies may alter the criteria (response thresholds, biases) in the random walk model, but they do not reflect a limitation in attentional capacity. When the experimental conditions are varied, in the random walk model of choice RT, as in SDT, the issue becomes one of attributing the corresponding performance variations to criterion changes or to sensitivity changes.

6.2. Costs and Benefits in Reaction-Time Tasks

The cost-benefit paradigm is an example of an expectancy manipulation that has been interpreted within an attentional framework. For reviews of experiments, see Audley (1973) and Welford (1980a, 1980b). Consider the following experiment by Posner, Nissen, and Ogden (1978). A subject views a fixation point between two locations, designated "left" and "right," where a light flash may appear on a given trial. Whichever flash ap-

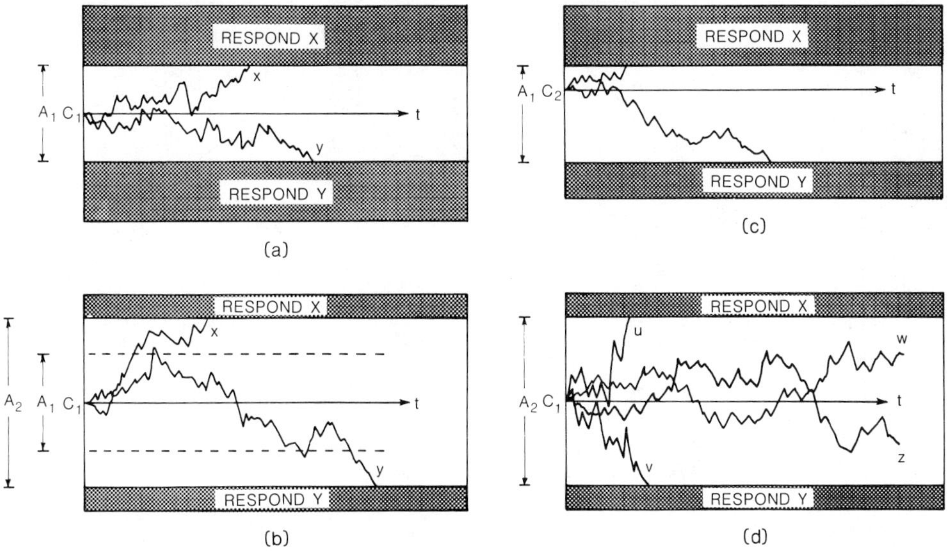

Figure 2.17. Graphic examples of the role of the parameters in Link's (1975) random walk model (RWM). (a) Illustration of a RWM for a choice RT with two alternative stimuli and corresponding responses. The abscissa represents time *t*; the ordinate represents the position (cumulative information value) of the random walk at time *t*. The random walk executed on any given trial is statistically dependent on the stimulus. Sample random walks leading to correct responses *X* and *Y* are labeled with the stimulus value (*x* or *y*). When a random walk reaches the response boundary a RT response is initiated. Expected accuracy and speed of the model are controlled by the sensitivity parameter *A* (the sum of the threshold distances) and the bias parameter *C* (the starting point). The starting point is adjusted to reflect an expectation of stimulus *x* versus stimulus *y*. (b) The same random walk processes as (a) but with greater distance A_2 between response boundaries. This leads to longer expected RTs and higher expected accuracy than for panel (a). The random walk to stimulus *y* would have resulted in an error with response boundaries A_1, but not with response boundaries A_2. (c) Same random walk processes as in panel (a) but with high a priori expectation of stimulus *x*, reflected in a lower threshold for response *X* than response *Y* (shift of starting point C_2 toward boundary *X*). Starting point C_2 toward boundary *X*). Starting point C_2 leads to very fast correct responses to stimulus *X* but also to frequent fast errors when *Y* is presented. (d) The effect of speeding up (*u*,*v*) or slowing down (*w*,*z*) the drift rate of random walks (relative to *x*,*y* in panel (b)) is different than changing threshold parameters *A* or *C*. Speed reflects the *rate* at which information is acquired; *A* and *C* reflect the *accuracy* and *bias* parameters of the decision rule that determines the response, given the available information.

pears, the subject is to respond as quickly as possible by pressing a key. Occasional blank trials (no flash) are introduced to reduce anticipatory responses (responses before the flash). This is a *go/no-go* RT experiment in which the subject must respond ("go") when any stimulus is presented and must not respond ("no-go") on catch trials. The experimental manipulation of concern here is the fraction α of stimulus-containing trials on which the left stimulus appears. Posner and colleagues (1978) investigated three conditions: trials in which α was, respectively, 0.80, 0.50, and 0.20. Trials with different α's traditionally are run in separate blocks. However, in Posner and colleagues' experiment, these conditions are interleaved in a mixed-list design; a warning cue (1 sec before stimulus presentation) informs the subject of α.

Posner and colleagues' experiment is a two-task compound experiment in which the two component tasks are (1) press the key when the "left" flash appears and (2) press the (same) key when the "right" flash appears. One dependent measure in Posner and colleagues' experiment, as in virtually all RT experiments, is *mean* RT. Ignore, for the moment, the other dependent measure, *accuracy*, which, in this experiment, is determined by errors that occur when the observer responds before the stimulus occurs (or within 100 msec of its onset), fails to respond within a reasonable time period, or responds on a catch trial. The observed RTs for each of the two component tasks in each of the three conditions is represented in Figure 2.18(a). [Except for a slowing of RT, Posner et al. (1978) found no important differences between the RTs in this Donders Type 3 RT experiment and in a choice RT experiment in which the subject had to press a left key in response to the left flash and a right key to the right flash.]

The data from Posner and colleagues' experiments also can be graphed in operating space; thus the data of Figure 2.18(a) are graphed as an operating characteristic in Figures 2.18(b), 2.18(c), and 2.18(d). Fast reaction time represents good performance, and in this chapter we maintain the convention of representing good performance up and to the right.

6.2.1. Iso-utility Contours for Reaction Times. What are the utilities in Posner and colleagues' experiment? The authors did not define these explicitly for the subjects. However, suppose that utility varies in direct inverse proportion to the RT: the faster the reaction time, the higher the utility. With this assumption, the expected utility *EU* of any joint performance [*RT*(*left*), *RT*(*right*)] can be computed as a function of α, the proportion of left stimuli and the mean RTs:

$$EU = -[\alpha RT(left) + (1 - \alpha) RT(right)] . \quad (11)$$

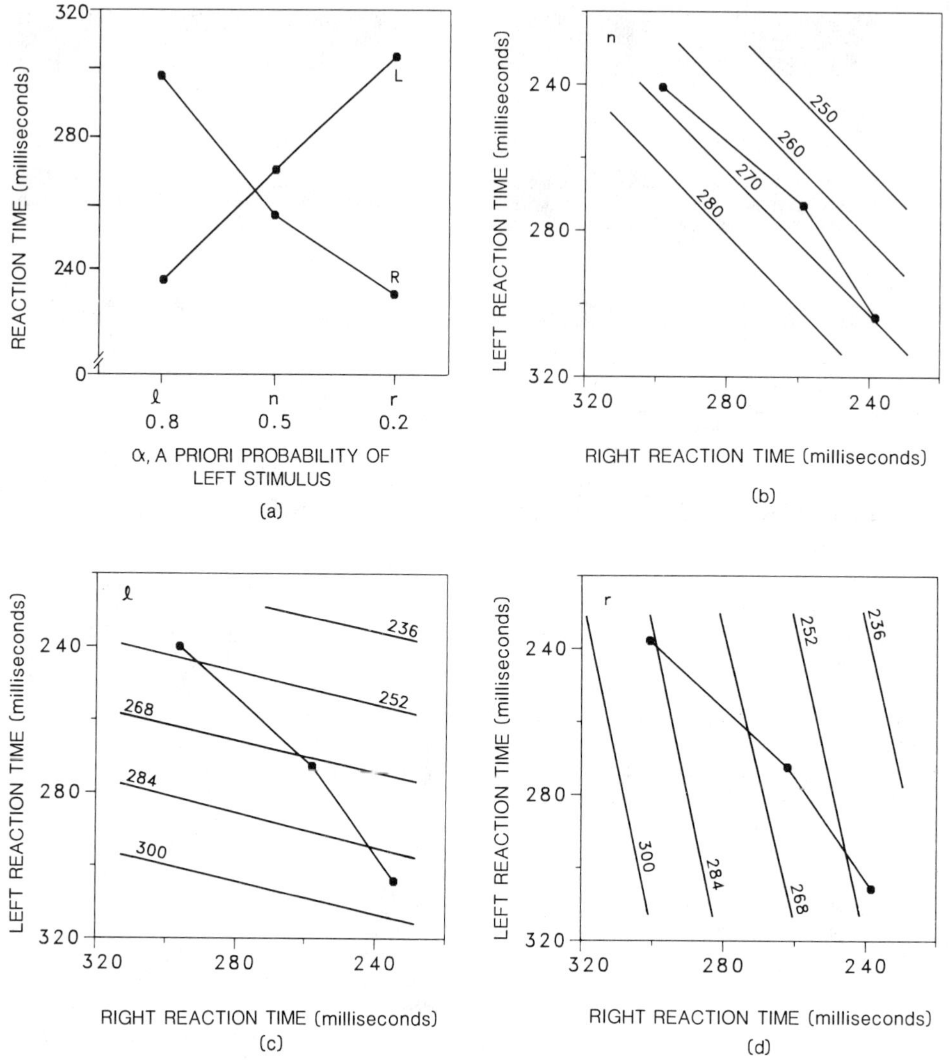

Figure 2.18. Iso-utility contours and trade-offs in RTs to stimuli with different a priori stimulus probabilities. All panels illustrate the same data from an experiment by Posner, Nissen, and Ogden (1978). One of two alternative stimuli (a left *L* or right *R* stimulus light) was presented on each trial; the response (a key press) was the same in either case. Three different probabilities α of the left stimulus were tested; the subject was informed of these probabilities by three warning cues (left *l* for $\alpha = 0.8$, neutral *n* for $\alpha = 0.5$, and right *r* for $\alpha = 0.2$). (a) Conventional representation of reaction times to the two stimuli (*L*, *R*) with the three a priori probabilities α. The ordinate is mean RT in msec. The abscissa is α, the a priori probability of the left stimulus as indicated by the warning cue. In panels (b), (c), and (d), the data of (a) are regraphed as a performance operating characteristic; the panels differ only in the iso-utility contours. The coordinates represent RTs to the left and right stimuli, respectively, and are oriented to show good performance up and to the right. The iso-utility contours in panels (b), (c), and (d) represent the mean RTs indicated on the contour; that is, each point along the contour represents a joint RT performance to left and right stimuli; the overall mean reaction time is the *u* value indicated on the contour, $u = \alpha RT_{\text{left}} + (1 - \alpha) RT_{\text{right}}$. The iso-utility contours represent a weighting of performance appropriate to the stimulus probabilities for the conditions. (b) Neutral cue *n*, $\alpha = 0.5$; (c) Left cue *l*, $\alpha = 0.8$; (d) Right cue *r*, $\alpha = 0.2$. (From G. Sperling, A unified theory of attention and signal detection, in R. Parasuraman and R. Davies (Eds.), *Varieties of attention*, Academic Press, 1984. Reprinted with permission.)

Expected utility happens to be a negative number; it increases (approaches zero) as performance improves (RT becomes faster). Iso-utility functions based on Eq. (11) are illustrated in Figures 2.18(b), 2.18(c), and 2.18(d) for the three values of α for which data are available. Note that the utility functions derived from Eq. (11) are similar to those in typical signal detection tasks, but the data are not, in that the data approximate a straight, rather than a curved, line. Straight-line data in this experiment, as in Sperling and Melchner's (1976b, 1978a, 1978b) attention study, have special significance; they suggest that a mixture of just two states, rather than a continuum of states, is sufficient to account for the data. This point will be taken up in detail later in Sections 8.2, 8.6, and 8.7.

Posner and colleagues' (1978) observers seem to operate sensibly with respect to the utility function Eq. (11), optimizing their performance in each case. See Figures 2.18(b), 2.18(c), and 2.18(d). Knowing α when $\alpha \neq 0.5$ enables the observers to shorten their mean RT substantially over the mean RT when $\alpha = 0.5$. The "benefit" to RT (i.e., the reduction of RT in msec) when the more probable stimulus occurs is about the same as the "cost" (RT increase) when the less probable stimulus occurs. The important point is not that the costs and benefits of an asymmetric a priori stimulus probability $\alpha = 0.8$ happen to be approximately symmetric but that the benefits are available on 80% of the trials, while the costs are incurred on only 20%. Thus the mean RT improves with asymmetric stimulus probabilities in a way completely analogous to the improvement of *S/N* detection accuracy with asymmetric stimulus probabilities, considered in Section 4.2.

A second important point about RT benefits is that, once it is known that a simple reaction time $RT_S(i)$ to a stimulus i is quicker than the reaction time $RT_{CP}(i)$ to the same stimulus embedded in a compound RT task, then RT benefits follow directly as a consequence of the procedure for measuring them. To see this, let α represent the fraction of trials of stimulus i in the compound mixture. Then

$$\lim_{\alpha \to 1} RT_{CP}(i,\alpha) = RT_S(i) \ . \qquad (12)$$

Equation (12) follows because, as $\alpha \to 1$, the *physical* descriptions of the tasks represented by the left and right sides of the equation become identical. In the limit then, as $\alpha \to 1$, the RT benefit approaches the limit set by the previously determined simple RT. The magnitudes of the RT costs for the tasks that occur with probability $1 - \alpha$ remain to be determined empirically.

6.2.2. Random Walk Models of Reaction-Time Paradigms

6.2.2.1. *Choice Reaction Times.* Choice RT is a compound task. In a choice RT task, a left and a right stimulus would each require a corresponding left- or right-hand response, instead of the same response as in the multistimulus go/no-go task. Random walk models for choice RTs were treated in Section 6.1.3 and illustrated in Figure 2.17.

6.2.2.2. *Concurrent Reaction Times.* A concurrent RT task might require a left-hand response to a left stimulus and a right-hand response to a right stimulus, where both stimuli would appear on some trials. In some respects, this would be the ideal test of whether subjects could deal with two stimuli as well as one, but it might involve additional difficulties if conflicts arose in the motor system (Kantowitz, 1974). Assigning the locus of performance loss to attentional processes (versus perceptual or motor processes) can be complicated, but it is solvable (e.g., Sperling & Melchner, 1978b).

6.2.2.3. *What Constitutes Evidence for Loss in Reaction-Time Trade-offs.* The original question in Section 6.2 was whether the subject was able to deal with two possible stimuli as effectively as with one. For a multistimulus go/no-go task to inform us as to whether the subject is unable to deal simultaneously with two possible stimuli (and hence must divide attention between stimuli according to the a priori probabilities), it is necessary to compare performance in the compound task to a model of ideal (lossless) performance. The compound task in which either a left or right signal, or no signal, occurs on each trial is analogous to the compound signal detection experiment where $S_1 + N$, $S_2 + N$, or N appear on each trial. In SDT an ideal observer should show some loss in combining information about the two signals. Furthermore, an ideal detector should respond to changes in a priori signal probabilities or changes in the payoff matrix by changing the criteria but not by changes in the quality of information upon which a judgment is based. Is it possible, in Posner and colleagues' multistimulus go/no-go experiment, that performance varies with instructions and payoffs and yet the quality of perceived information remains invariant? That is, does an observer react more slowly when there are two locations to monitor because information cannot be processed as efficiently from two as from one location, or does the observer's slower reaction reflect the same loss that an ideal detector with no information loss would show in the same situation? As with all compound tasks, a theory is necessary to answer this question.

The random walk model (RWM) is a model of an ideal detector for reaction time; it is necessary to apply an RWM to Posner's task to answer the original question. However, to apply an RWM, it is necessary to choose one from among the many candidate configurations, and the choice-RT RWM does not apply. In a prototypical choice RT task, the problem is to discriminate between two or more clearly above threshold stimuli. The moment of stimulus onset is obvious; the difficulty is in discriminating which of two or more possible stimuli occurred. The random walk in these cases is assumed to begin at the moment of stimulus onset.

6.2.2.4. *Random Walks for Go/No-Go Paradigms.* The go/no-go paradigm differs from the choice RT paradigms in that sampling of information cannot begin at a well-defined point of stimulus onset; it is stimulus onset itself that is to be decided. In the go/no-go case, especially with random foreperiods, the random walk must begin before the stimulus appears. This requires a random walk that begins after the warning signal and fluctuates around the bias point until stimulus onset. Once the stimulus appears, the parameters of the drift become stimulus dependent. On no-go trials, the stimulus never appears, and the observation interval typically ends when the experimenter terminates the trial. Thus, on signal trials, there are two phases to the random walk: (1) a period of fluctuation prior to stimulus onset with an expected value of zero, and (2) a subsequent period in which the drift is dependent on the identity of the stimulus. Analytic solutions for the predictions of an RWM where the characteristics of the drift alter in midtrial are not generally available (but see Ratcliff, 1980). Conceptually, the simple go/no-go walk can be considered to be equivalent to a stimulus-initiated random walk in which prestimulus fluctuations simply contribute to the intertrial variability in the effective starting point (e.g., C_L in Figure 2.19(a)).

For a single location being monitored in a go/no-go RT experiment (the alone or baseline condition), consider an RWM with two boundaries. A near boundary is for the go responses, and another, much farther boundary corresponds to no-go responses. When the near go-boundary is reached by the random walk, a response is initiated. When the no-go boundary is reached, observation ceases on that trial, and preparation is made for the next trial. The no-go boundary has little influence on the simple go/no-go experiment: a distant no-go boundary guarantees there will be few trials where the stimulus appears, but the subject omits the response. The experimenter, not the no-go boundary, typically terminates processing on the catch (no-go) trials. The single-stimulus conditions are shown in Figures 2.19(a) and 2.19(b), with the distance to the go boundaries labeled $A_L(1)$ and $A_R(1)$.

When the subject is asked to monitor two locations simultaneously, this is modeled by two simultaneous go/no-go random

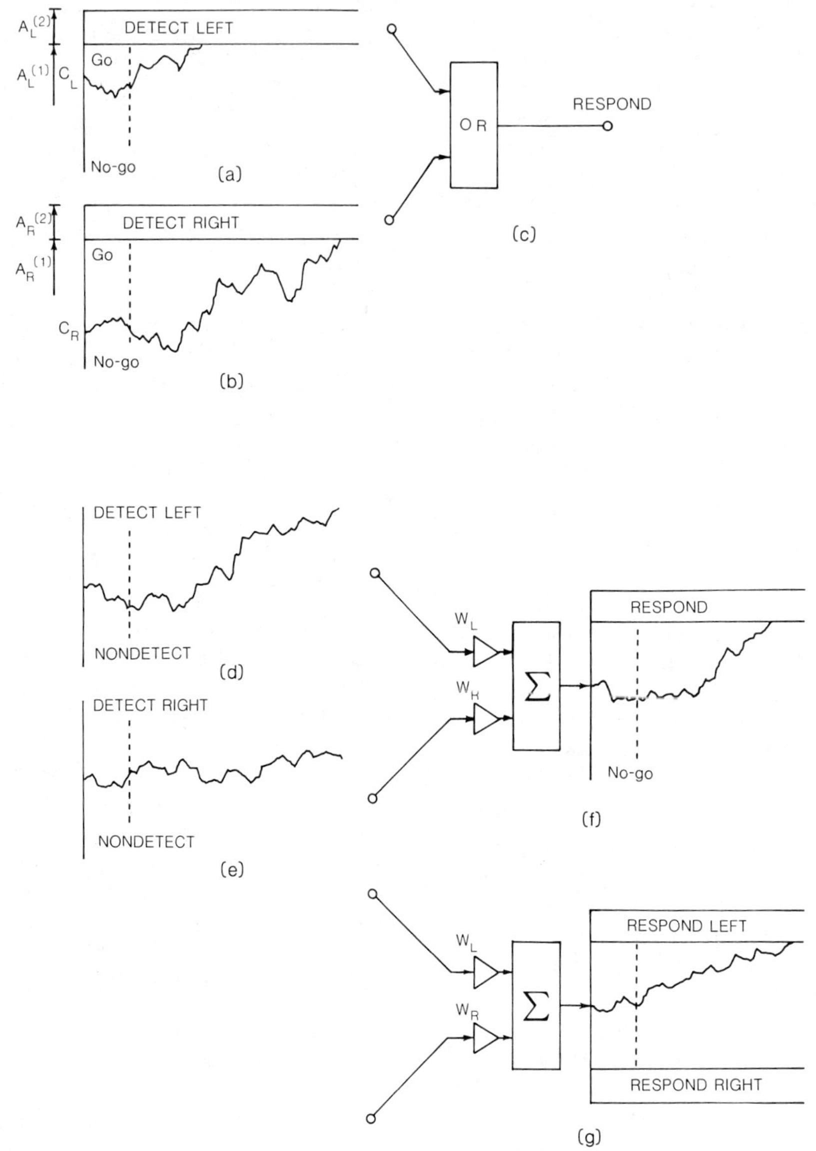

Figure 2.19. Random walk models (RWMs) for reaction-time (RT) experiments. (a) Representation of a RWM for a go/no-go RT experiment with a left stimulus. The coordinates are the value of the random walk and time *t*. The point C_L on the left boundary represents the beginning of the trial; the vertical dashed line represents the onset of the stimulus on go trials. The random walk response boundary $A_L(i)$ is used for go/no-go trials on which there are *i* possible stimulus alternatives. The no-go boundary (for "abandon trial") is not shown. (b) Representation of a RWM for a right stimulus with coordinates as in (a). Performance in a concurrent RT task (independent, concurrent presentation of tasks (a) and (b)) is modeled by the independent operation of random walk processes (a) and (b). (c) The additional apparatus needed to extend the single-stimulus go/no-go RT models to a multistimulus go/no-go task. Components (a) + (b) + (c) together represent a *pandemonium* (or *sensory threshold*) model. When either a left or a right random walk boundary is crossed, the OR component causes a predetermined response to be executed. The a priori probability α of a left stimulus determines the starting points C_L, C_R, shown here for $\alpha > 5$. (d, e, f) A *weighted decision* model for the multistimulus go/no-go task. The random walks (d) and (e), respectively, are equivalent to (a) and (b) except that (d) and (e) do not initiate responses. The current values of the walks in (d) and (e), respectively, are multiplied by positive weighting constants W_R, W_L, respectively, and summed, and the resultant walk initiates a predetermined response when it exceeds its threshold. A priori stimulus probabilities are reflected in constants W_R and W_L. (g) A RWM for choice reaction time that differs for (d, e, f) only in that the stimulus walks are subtracted (right is multiplied by $-W_R$) and in that one of two alternative responses is admissible. (From G. Sperling, A unified theory of attention and signal detection, in R. Parasuraman and R. Davies (Eds.), *Varieties of attention*, Academic Press, 1984. Reprinted with permission.)

walks. Crossing *either* go boundary initiates a response. This is a *pandemonium* model in the sense that all sensory channels shout out their evidence simultaneously; if any one exceeds threshold, a response is initiated. (The pandemonium model is equivalent to the maximum rule of Section 4.2.3.) Obviously, two random walks would produce more false reactions to catch trials than one walk. Since subjects are instructed to avoid errors, they must move the boundaries farther away from the starting point to maintain the same accuracy in performance. This is illustrated in Figures 2.19(a) and 2.19(b) by increasing the distances to the boundaries, that is, by shifting from boundaries labeled $A_L(1)$ and $A_R(1)$ to boundaries $A_L(2)$ and $A_R(2)$. Because of the boundary shift, even in this RWM which has perfect retention of all information received from all channels, monitoring two locations produces slower decisions than monitoring just one.

Figures 2.19(d), 2.19(e), and 2.19(f) outline an alternative RWM for the same multistimulus go/no-go task. This weighted decisions model takes account of a priori stimulus probabilities in the weights W_L and W_R assigned to the sensory evidence being obtained from the left- and right-input channels. A response is initiated when the weighted, cumulated evidence exceeds a threshold.

6.2.2.5. Compatible Models for Choice and for Go/No-Go Reaction-Time Tasks. Both the pandemonium and the weighted decisions RWM models are easily elaborated to deal with choice RTs. The pandemonium model becomes a *race* model; the subject executes a left or right response according to whichever random walk reaches a boundary first. (That is, Figures 2.19(a) and 2.19(b) suffice to describe the race model.) The adaptation to choice RT of the weighted decisions model is illustrated in Figure 2.19(g); it merely involves changing the sign of one of the weights and admitting a second response alternative. An attractive feature of the weighted decisions models in Figures 2.19(f) and 2.19(g) is that they account nicely for the covariation, reported by Posner and colleagues (1978), between RTs in choice and in go/no-go tasks as stimulus probabilities are varied.

Both the race and the weighted decisions RWMs are different from Link's RWM (Section 6.1.3). The mathematical equivalences and differences between these various models have not been worked out. Deciding between such models, experimentally, requires complex paradigms and systematic data collection. Probably, different models will work best in different situations. The purpose of illustrating them here is to show a variety of models that have no internal attentional or memory losses and yet exhibit probability effects such as cost-benefits in RT paradigms.

6.2.3. Random Walk Models and Signal Detection Theory: Bias versus Sensitivity. The explanation of two-location compound RT tasks is exactly analogous to the explanation of the difficulty in searching for two targets ("1" or "2") instead of one target. The concurrent task of searching for ("1" and "2") does not have this problem. Nor would the concurrent task of presenting stimuli independently for responses with the left and right hands. The concurrent RT task is composed of two simple component RT tasks: respond with the left hand if left stimulus, respond with the right hand if right stimulus. The concurrent RT task, in which both left and right stimuli might occur on any given trial, is quite different from the usual disjunctive (choice) RT task, which is a compound time (RT) paradigm in which subjects responded directly to stimuli that were differentiated only by their location. Here we consider a choice RT experiment by M. L. Shaw (1978) in which spatial location and target identity are independently varied. Shaw's subjects were required to search arrays of n locations for a single target (either F or Z) among $n - 1$ distractors (H, J, K, L, N). On each trial the subject reported either "F" or "Z." The probability function, which gives the probability of the target appearing at each location, was held constant over a block of trials (instead of being cued on each trial). Shaw compared RTs for high-probability locations to RTs for low-probability locations. In Shaw's experiment, the location expectancy should not cause a bias to respond "F" or "Z," thus eliminating one of the explanations of the Posner and colleagues (1978) experiment discussed in Section 6.2.2.

M. L. Shaw fit her data with a quantitative attention model adapted from Koopman (1957). It is a model for optimal allocation of a limited search capacity and is discussed in detail in Section 7.3. The capacity-restricted search model, when applied to Shaw's experiment, explicitly assumes a limitation in attentional capacity and fits the data quite well.

Shaw's experiment, when all the complications are stripped away, is a choice RT experiment (respond "F" or "Z" as quickly as possible) and therefore is a *compound* task. The task requires a model for the stimulus uncertainty effect before an attentional loss can be inferred; an appropriate model for stimulus uncertainty in choice RT tasks is the RWM. An RWM for Shaw's data might involve a separate random walk between an F and Z at each location. The value of the random walk for each location might sum together, weighted by a fraction proportional to location probability. This is the random walk analog to the Nolte-Jaarsma optimal rule in SDT.

In the RWM, when a target appears at a low-probability location, the overall random walk to the Z boundary is slowed because of the high weighting of information about distractors at high-probability locations. Such a scheme (see Figure 2.20) exhibits location-dependent reaction time, but this is due to differential *weighting* of information from different locations (a form of bias) and not due to any loss of information. The analogous model applied to detection paradigms has been called a *weighted decisions* model by Green and Swets (1966) and has been studied by M. L. Shaw (1982) and Kinchla and Collyer (1974). A detection paradigm was used by Bashinski and Bacharach (1980).

Both Shaw's model (based on resource allocation), and an elaborated RWM (based on weighted decisions) can fit Shaw's data reasonably well. This is another example of the ambiguity of compound tasks. The main question, Can attention be divided between locations without loss? cannot be answered without reference to a model. Further, the choice between the two contending models must be made on the basis of additional tests. The data may already be available. For example, both the elaborated RWM and especially Shaw's optimal-allocation model implicitly make strong predictions not merely about the RT means of correct and error responses but about the entire distribution of reaction times in the various conditions.

6.3. Speed–Accuracy Trade-offs

In RT tasks subjects traditionally are asked to respond as quickly as possible while making as few mistakes as possible. These are clearly incompatible goals; the subject could go faster by accepting more mistakes or could reduce errors by slowing down RTs. The ambiguity of the fast-and-accurate instruction

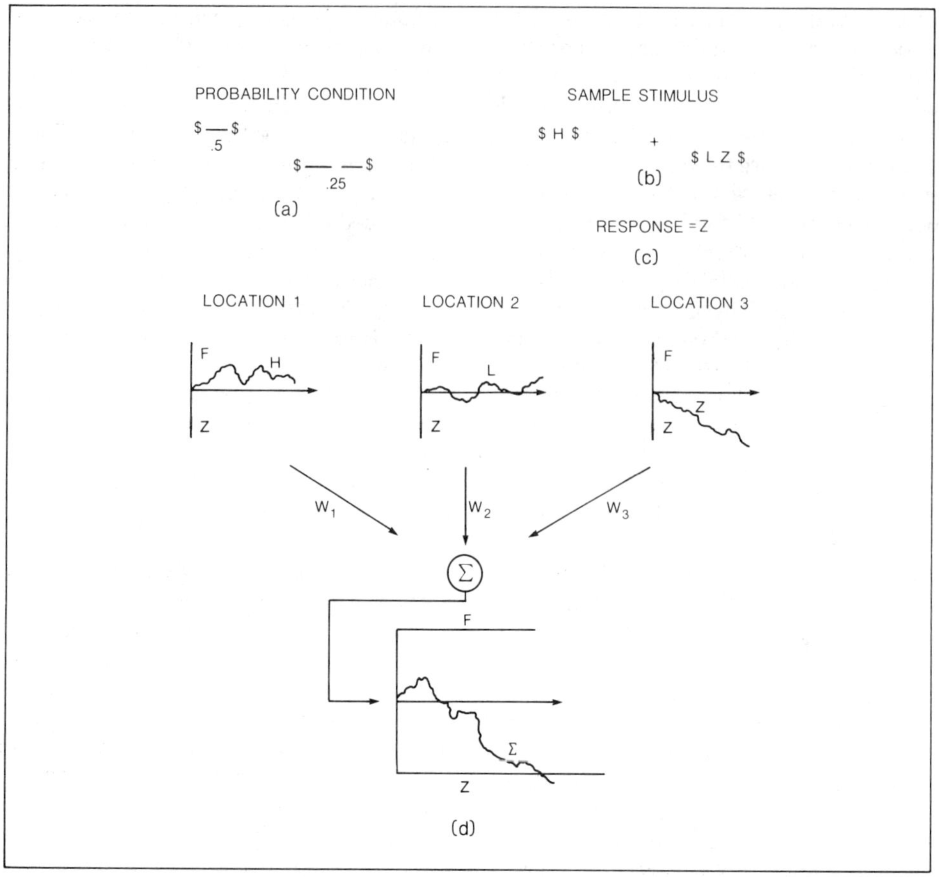

Figure 2.20. Optimization in letter search. (a) One probability condition from M. L. Shaw's (1978) letter search experiments. The subject's task is to identify the target, which is either an *F* or a *Z*. There are three spatial locations indicated by dashes; the number under a location indicates to the subject the probability that the target will appear in that location. (b) A sample stimulus display. The + indicates the fixation mark. (c) The response. (d) A *weighted decision* random walk model to account for the effect of location bias. The coordinates of each random walk (RW) are the value of the walk and time, *t*. A RW is carried out at each of the three locations, and the values are summed with a weighting, W_i, the location bias. The summed RW hits the appropriate boundary more rapidly when the target is in an expected location because it has a larger value of W_i. Shaw interpreted her results in the framework of Koopman's (1957) optimal search model, Figure 2.24.

is well known and, in better-designed contemporary experiments, the subject is rewarded according to a well-specified payoff matrix for quick correct responses and penalized for errors.

This section analyzes the implicit trade-off between speed and accuracy in the classical RT procedure, as well as in two variations. In the *deadline procedure*, the subject is given a time limit (the deadline) within which the response must fall to avoid an explicit penalty (Fitts, 1966). In the *cued-response procedure* (Dosher, 1976, 1981; Reed, 1973; Wickelgren, Corbett, & Dosher, 1980), a "respond-now" cue follows the stimulus with a variable delay. The subject is required to respond within a very brief interval (deadline) following the response cue.

To induce the subject to respond more quickly in the three procedures (classical reaction time, deadline, cued response), the rewards for fast and the penalties for slow responses are increased, the deadline is shortened, or the delay of the response cue is decreased. To induce the subject to be more accurate, the penalty for errors is increased, the response deadline is increased, or the delay of the respond-now cue is increased. Thus, given precisely the same stimuli, we can induce subjects to be either fast and inaccurate or to be slow and accurate. The range of performance of which a subject is capable defines the speed–accuracy trade-off.

6.3.1. Deadline Speed–Accuracy Trade-off and an Analysis. Figure 2.21 illustrates a typical speed–accuracy trade-off. The data are from a two-choice RT experiment by Pachella and Fisher (1972), with deadlines of 300, 400, 700 msec, and infinity (accuracy emphasis). To show the general form of the speed–accuracy trade-off, both accuracy and speed are averaged over all responses. Accuracy is presented as proportion correct, speed as the mean reaction time. To maintain the convention that good performance is represented up and to the right, fast RTs are represented to the right of slow RTs. Graphing the speed–accuracy trade-off in operating space emphasizes its similarity to other operating characteristics (attention operating characteristics, receiver operating characteristics, and production possibilities frontiers) and shows the relation of the speed–accuracy trade-off curve to optimization criteria embodied in utility functions.

Payoffs in speed–accuracy trade-off experiments usually are defined in terms of individual responses. Therefore, to compute the utility of a mean RT and a mean accuracy (averaged

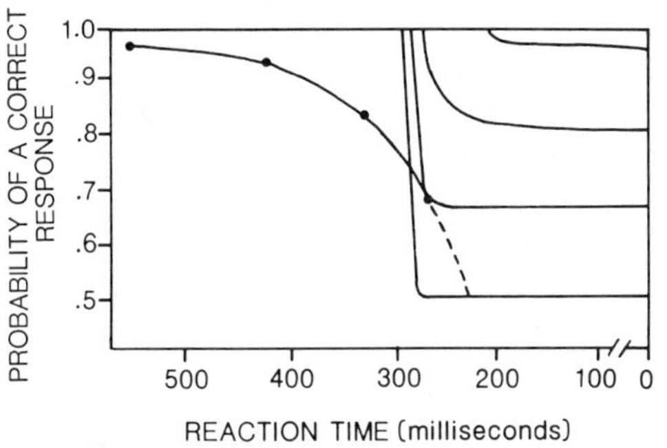

Figure 2.21. An operating characteristic and iso-utility contours for a speed–accuracy trade-off experiment using the deadline method. Data are derived from Pachella and Fisher's (1972) two-alternative reaction-time (RT) experiment. The abscissa is mean RT, with fast RTs at right; the ordinate is the probability of a correct response. Data are computed from Pachella and Fisher, (1972). Iso-utility contours are illustrated for a deadline of 300 msec, corresponding to the right-most data point. (From G. Sperling, A unified theory of attention and signal detection, in R. Parasuraman and R. Davies (Eds.), *Varieties of attention*, Academic Press, 1984. Reprinted with permission.)

over a session, as in Figure 2.21) requires knowledge about the actual distributions of RTs and error rates. The form of the utility function assumed here for deadline and cued response procedures is so simple, however, that it is relatively independent of the distributional details.

Figure 2.21 shows utility functions for a single trial with a 300-msec deadline in Pachella and Fisher's (1972) experiment. Although this experiment did not use an explicit payoff scheme, subjects were instructed to be as accurate as possible but *not* to exceed the response deadline. Utility is assumed to be proportional to the number of correct responses, with a very high penalty for responses that exceed the deadline, so the iso-utility function is vertical at the deadline. Responding much sooner than the deadline is not explicitly rewarded, so the iso-utility function is horizontal over all RTs shorter than the deadline, with higher accuracy having greater utility.

The experimentally defined utility for a single trial, illustrated in Figure 2.21, does not take into account irreducible variability in the subject's RT. For example, if the subject were to attempt to respond with an RT of 299 msec to beat a 300-msec deadline, then, because of RT variability, the RT would exceed the deadline on almost half the trials. To reduce post-deadline responses to a tolerable level, the subject has to aim response well in front of the deadline. Thus the utility function of strategies observed *over a whole session* must incorporate RT variability, and these utility functions are illustrated in Figure 2.21. Points in operating space have a utility corresponding jointly to the explicitly graphed accuracy (the ordinate of Figure 2.21) and to the fraction of postdeadline responses that are implicit in the graphed speed (the abscissa of Figure 2.21).

Quite generally, in nonpathological cases, the performance operating characteristic (POC) is concave down, the iso-utility contour is concave up, and the two curves are tangent to each other at the optimum point. In limiting cases, either the POC or the iso-utility contour may be straight lines. If both are straight lines, the POC and iso-utility contour may be co-linear, and the optimum performance is not uniquely defined. In the deadline and cued-response procedures, however, the "corners" of the iso-utility contours (where the tangent point of the speed–accuracy trade-off and utility function will be) tend to be almost vertically above each other (Figure 2.21), demonstrating the overriding importance of speed relative to accuracy in determining the operating point on the speed–accuracy trade-off.

How is it that subjects accomplish performance under a deadline procedure? One possibility, here designated as *information criteria*, is that an RWM applies, and the boundaries (information criteria) are set so that no more than, say, 5% of the responses exceed the deadline. Since most of the RT distribution must lie before the deadline, the mean RT would be to the right of the deadline. Alternatively, subjects could be *estimating a time interval* slightly shorter than the deadline and responding on the basis of whatever information is available at that time. The question of which strategy (information criterion or time estimation) is actually used is unresolved. Link (1978) has argued that information criteria (horizontal boundaries) adequately account for performance in deadline experiments. Wandell (1977), in a slightly different context, proposes that time estimation may be used under some circumstances.

6.3.2. Cued-Response Speed–Accuracy Trade-off. The purpose of the cued-response speed–accuracy trade-off procedure is to interrupt the subject's stimulus processing at some known time after stimulus presentation. By repeating the procedure with cues at different times, it is possible to determine the amount of processing that has been accomplished as a function of time following stimulus presentation.

In the cued-response speed–accuracy trade-off procedure, at some unpredictable time after stimulus presentation, the subject is cued with a secondary stimulus (tone or light flash) to respond immediately. Subjects are trained not to anticipate the cue, just as subjects in any RT experiment are trained not to respond in advance of the reaction stimulus. Subjects also are trained to respond as quickly as possible following the cue. Cue RTs should not exceed about 275 msec; ideally, mean RTs are under 225 msec, quite comparable to simple RTs to the cue stimulus.

The iso-utility contours in the cued-response procedure are steep U-shaped functions, intended to confine RTs to the interval defined by the *U*. The cued-response procedure constrains responses to a narrower time interval than does the deadline procedure as is obvious from the comparison of the utility functions in Figures 2.21 and 2.22. The deadline procedure is a blocked procedure; the cued-response procedure is a mixed-list procedure. (The implications of the blocked/randomized difference are treated in Section 8.)

A typical cued-response speed–accuracy trade-off function from Dosher (1984) is shown in Figure 2.22. Iso-utility contours are shown for a cue to respond 1.0 sec after stimulus presentation. As with the deadline procedure, the utility contours defined by the experimenter are simply rectangular (respond after the cue and before the deadline). As in Figure 2.21, the rounded shape in Figure 2.22 results from the subject's inability to control response latency perfectly. In principle, it would be advantageous for the subject (1) to aim safely inside the experimenter-defined boundaries and (2) to wait as long as possible to gain the most information. In practice, these options can be virtually removed by careful placement of the boundaries, that is, by the extreme pressure to respond to the cue as quickly as possible.

Information-controlled response strategies cannot account for the increase in accuracy with increasing cue delay in the cued-response paradigm. For example, to account for these increases in accuracy with cue delay, an RWM would have to have delay-dependent boundaries, that is, more distant boundaries for long delays. Because cue delays are randomly intermixed, subjects cannot make their processing strategy contingent upon cue delay (as they might if delays were run in blocks of the same delay). Therefore, the RWM cannot have delay-dependent boundaries, and therefore it cannot account for cued-response performance.

An alternative model for the cued-response procedure is an elaborated RWM with very distant (ignorable) informational boundaries. The subject's response is determined not by the random walk's intersection with a boundary, but by which side of its starting point the random walk happens to be at the moment the cue is presented (Dosher, 1982; Ratcliff, 1978). The RWMs for deadline and cued-response procedures are compared in Figure 2.23. The difference between models for these procedures is that performance in a deadline paradigm is accounted for by an *information-controlled* random walk (Figure 2.23(a)), while performance in a cued-response paradigm is accounted for by a *time-controlled* random walk (Figure 2.23(b)).

Subjects in the cued-response procedure must be trained to allow time-controlled processing. Early in training (in the first 100 trials), subjects have a strong tendency to anticipate the cue on late-cue trials and respond late to early-cue trials. Even with extensive practice, cue RTs (measured from cue onset) are somewhat longer for early cues than for late cues (Dosher, 1976, 1981, 1982; Reed, 1973). These RT patterns rarely depend on the stimulus; they resemble warning functions (Section 8).

Subjects in the deadline procedure also require practice to optimize their performance, especially to minimize the number of trials that exceed the deadline. Optimal setting of information criterion (horizontal) boundaries or time estimation (vertical) boundaries in an RWM requires sophisticated understanding of the RT distributions. Reaction-time distributions are generally more skewed and have a longer tail as mean RT (and accuracy) increase, and the subjects must take this into account in setting response boundaries.

6.3.3. Iso-utility Contours from Reaction Times. According to an optimization theory, even with the ordinary, ambiguous speed-plus-accuracy instruction, the subject operates at the optimal point on the speed–accuracy trade-off; with ambiguous instructions, the optimum is determined by the subject's *implicit* utility function. Insofar as different points on a speed–accuracy trade-off can be measured, the reasoning can be reversed and the tangent relation between the speed–accuracy trade-off and the iso-utility contour may be used to infer the shape of the subject's implicit iso-utility contours.

Finally, it should be noted that multiresponse RT experiments cannot be represented completely by a single speed–accuracy trade-off. For example, the speed and accuracy of particular response alternatives can be varied inversely even as overall performance averaged over alternative responses remains relatively unaffected, the problem to which RWMs are addressed. However, in symmetrical situations, where the difficulty and payoffs for the various alternative responses in the compound task are approximately equal, the speed–accuracy trade-off has interesting and useful properties (see Section 7).

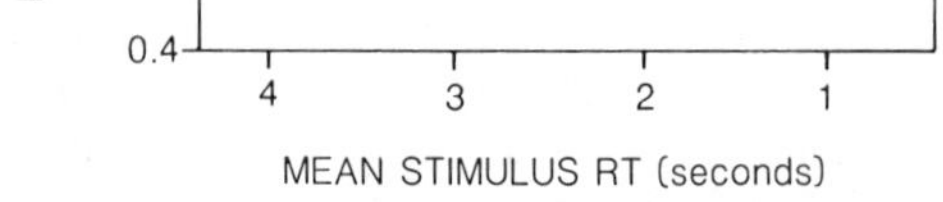

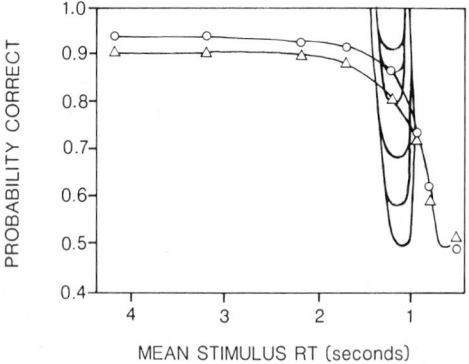

Figure 2.22. Operating characteristics and iso-utility contours for a speed–accuracy trade-off experiment using the cued-response method. The abscissa is the time (in seconds) from the stimulus onset to response (stimulus reaction time (RT)); the ordinate is the probability of a correct response. *Two speed–accuracy trade-off* curves (recognition accuracy for materials studied for 2 or 5 sec) observed under the cued-response procedure (Dosher, 1984) are shown, along with the hypothetical iso-utility contours for a cue to respond at 1.0 sec after test stimulus onset. Subjects are instructed *not* to anticipate the cue but to respond as quickly as possible—within 200 msec *after* the cue. The narrow windows defined by the utility curves of the cued-response procedure constrain the processing time very closely; they strongly penalize anticipations of the cue (fast guesses, cue RT < 100 msec) and slow responses (cue RT > 300 msec).

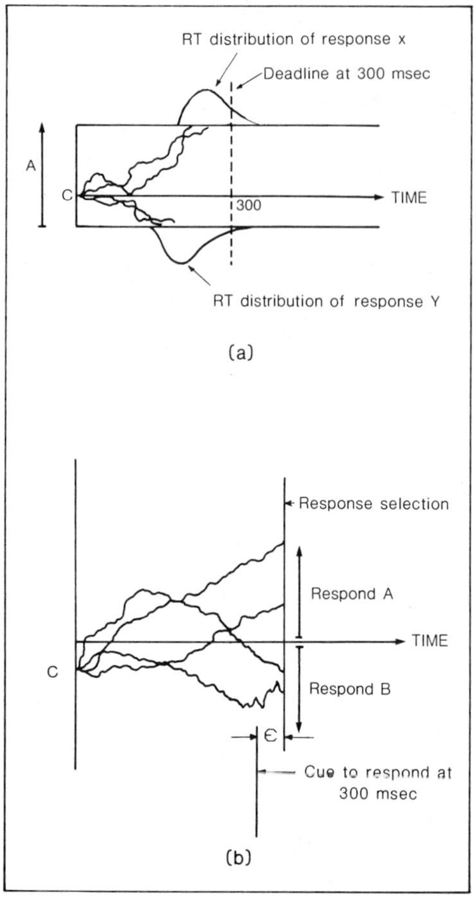

Figure 2.23. Random walk models (RWMs) of two speed–accuracy trade-off (SAT) procedures. For simplicity, in this figure, only decision processes (RWM) are assumed to contribute to overall reaction time. (a) A random walk (RW) interpretation of the *deadline* speed–accuracy trade-off procedure. The abscissa is time *t*, and the ordinate is the value of the RW at each time. Several representative RWs are shown. Stimulus *y* is much more probable than stimulus *x*. The RW boundaries (*A*) and the bias point (C) are set by the subject (after some experience) so that only a small fraction of trials produce RTs beyond the 300 msec deadline. Only RWM contributions to overall reaction time of (b) An RWM of the cued-response speed–accuracy trade-off procedure. A cue to respond is given 300 msec after stimulus onset; ϵ msec later, the subject selects the response. The boundaries *A* are absent, and the position of the RW relative to the ordinate at the time of response selection determines the response.

7. PURE STRATEGIES

A subject's selection of a processing or decision strategy can have a substantial impact on task performance. Pure strategies are considered in this section, strategy mixtures in Section 8. First, optimum strategies for common psychological paradigms are given. Second, the dependence of the subject's strategy on the trial-by-trial structure of the experiment is illustrated with several detailed examples from classical procedures.

7.1. Definitions of Pure Strategy

7.1.1. Unidimensional Strategy. For the purposes of this chapter, a *strategy* is defined as the choice by which a subject arrives at a particular point along a particular performance operating characteristic (POC). The choice may involve several component processes, such as a decision criterion or a resource allocation decision. When only one independent choice is possible (e.g., decision criterion and resource allocation cannot be varied orthogonally), this is called a *simple*, or *unidimensional*, strategy. Varying the strategy parameter moves performance along a line in operating space, the POC. The dimensionality of the operating space itself is equal to the number of independent measures of performance.

7.1.2. Multidimensional Strategy. The definition of a strategy can be extended to multiple-independent choices. For example, when a two-dimensional strategy is varied appropriately and two or more responses are measured, the locus of accessible points is a POC surface (not a line) in multidimensional operating space. Strategy decisions may result in complex patterns on the POC surface. When the higher-dimensional data are projected into two-dimensional operating space, strategy variations (movements on the POC surface) can easily be confused with sensitivity variations (shifts to different POCs). The only multidimensional strategies considered in this chapter occur in reaction-time (RT) models (such as the random walk model) where the subject can choose a different strategy for each response alternative.

Strategy is a real-world term; that is, it refers to something the subject does or is assumed to do. In a model or in theory of performance, a strategy is represented by a decision rule and a single parameter; different strategies are represented by different values of the parameter. To avoid the cumbersome "the subject selected the strategy S_c, which is represented in the model by the decision rule with parameter c," one may say simply "the subject selected c," keeping in mind that data analysts, not subjects, select parameters. In the classroom model, a strategy S_c is represented by the choice of classroom switching time c. In signal detection theory (SDT) a strategy S_c is defined as the value c "chosen" for the decision criterion. In attention or economic theory, a strategy is represented by the parameter that describes the resource allocation choice. In RT tasks, a strategy is the selection of a joint level of speed and accuracy along the speed–accuracy trade-off for each of the response alternatives. In the random walk model, this multidimensional strategy is represented by the values of the response boundaries.

7.2. Optimal Strategies for Psychophysical Paradigms with Two-Stimulus Alternatives

7.2.1. Single-Stimulus Presentation (Yes-No). Signal Detection Theory, unelaborated, deals with the problem of an optimal strategy in the case of a single-stimulus presentation. The stimulus may be either N, or $S + N$, and the subject responds either "N" or "S." In this chapter, the decision rule that has been proposed is the choice of a criterion c on a psychological continuum. That is, from the subjects' point of view, the outcome of observing the stimulus on a trial is the perceived stimulus intensity, which is represented by a real number x. If $x \geqslant c$ the subject responds "S," otherwise, "N." In the case of discriminating stimulus A from stimulus B, the argument is exactly parallel; the continuum represents the ratio of perceived "A-ness" to "B-ness."

The optimum decision rule is correctly expressed not in terms of a sensory variable but in terms of the *a posteriori* likelihood ratio, $aplr = p(S|x)/p(N|x)$, where $p(E|x)$, the likelihood of E given x, is the *a posteriori* probability of the event E having occurred given the observation x. When the utility of a trial is defined in terms of the value of various outcomes of a trial, decision rules that maximize *expected utility* are based on the *a posteriori* likelihood ratio. For example, the optimal decision rule is of the form: respond "S" if $aplr(x) \geqslant c$, otherwise respond "N."

The formulation of optimal decisions in terms of *a posteriori* probabilities is conceptually basic. For computation, the equivalent formulation in terms of *a priori* probabilities is more useful. Thus, if π_i is the *a priori* probability of the event i, the optimal decision rule transposes to: Respond 'S' if the likelihood ratio $lr(x) = p(x/S)/p(x/N) \geqslant \pi_N/\pi_S$. Recall that the decision rule based on a sensory variable is equivalent to the likelihood rule when $lr(x)$ is an increasing monotonic function of x (as it was in the examples of this chapter); otherwise, only the lr rule is optimal. Further, the likelihood-based rule is optimal under much broader definitions of utility, but these considerations are beyond the scope of this chapter.

7.2.2. Two-Stimulus Presentations

7.2.2.1. Two-Alternative Forced Choice. In the two-alternative forced-choice (2AFC) procedure, a subject is presented with two stimuli, A,B (which represent, for example, N, $S + N$). The stimuli may occur in successive intervals, or they may occur in adjacent locations. The subject's task is to state whether the order of presentation was AB or BA. In the case of adjacent presentations, the subject's task is to state whether the target occurred in the left location or in the right location. This procedure grew out of signal detection considerations because when rewards for both kinds of correct responses are equal and penalties of both kinds of errors are equal (symmetric payoffs), it appears to remove the choice of a decision criterion from the task. The optimal decision strategy is simply to compare the observations x_1, x_2 from the two intervals and to report the order as AB if $aplr_{A|B} = p(A|x_1)/p(A|x_2) \geqslant 1$ and report the order BA otherwise.

For the special case of Normally distributed random variables with equal variance, the optimal decision (in asymmetric as well as symmetric cases) can be made on the basis simply of $x_1 - x_2$. Indeed, in the Normal case, the decision variable $(x_1 - x_2)/\sqrt{2}$ in two-alternative forced choice is equivalent to the decision variable x of the yes-no procedure. The discussion here is restricted to symmetric payoffs and equal probabilities of the signal occurring in each interval. For additional assumptions, for treatment of asymmetric situations, and other complexities, see Noreen (1981).

7.2.2.2. Same-Different Paradigm. As in two-interval forced choice, there are two stimulus presentations, A,B, but the correct responses are "same" for presentations of AA or BB and "different" for AB or BA. The optimal decision strategy (derived by Noreen, 1981) requires the subject to make two separate categorizations of the two-stimulus observations x_1, x_2. The procedure is (1) first categorize x_1 as A if $aplr_A(x_1) = p(A|x_1)/p(B|x_1) \geqslant 1$ and otherwise categorize x_1 as B, (2) then categorize x_2, and (3) if x_1 and x_2 have been categorized as A,A or B,B respond "same," otherwise respond "different." Self-evident as the categorize-first rule may be, a sensory different rule (respond "same" if $|x_1 - x_2| < c$, otherwise respond "different") was previously described as the optimal rule (Krueger, 1978; Macmillan, Kaplan, & Creelman, 1977; Vickers, 1979). The advantage of the categorize-first rule is that two events, both of which are very likely to be A, may still differ greatly and be categorized optimally; the sensory-difference rule would miscategorize them. The advantage of the sensory-difference rule is that it is applicable to the case of the "roving standard" or to early stages of practice before categorization boundaries have developed. (The difference rule yields equivalent statistical predictions to the optimal rule in the special case of two-alternative forced choice under the assumption of equal-variance Normal distributions.)

The actual differences that would be observed between the optimal early-categorization and the sensory-difference rules are slight in practical situations. The great interest that the analysis of the same-different paradigm has aroused is due to its incorrect application of sensory-difference rules to the problem of categorical perception (Macmillan et al., 1977). According to the optimal-decision model, same-different discrimination *is* essentially a process of categorization, even though, at first glance, it seems ideally suited for a sensory-difference strategy. Since the predictions of the two decision rules differ slightly, and in some cases not at all, the same-different paradigm does not seem to be an arena in which the issue of categorical versus sensory-difference rules will be decided.

7.2.3. Three-Stimulus Presentations

7.2.3.1. **ABX.** In the most common variant of ABX three-stimulus paradigms, there are only two alternative stimuli A,B. A trial consists of three-stimulus presentations: ABX or BAX, where $X = A$ or B. The subject's task is to state whether the third stimulus is the same as the first ("first") or the same as the second ("second").

According to the decision model, the subject extracts three observations x_1,x_2,x_3 from a trial. The optimum strategy (derived by Noreen, 1981) is an extension of the optimal rules for two presentations. It is (1) categorize x_1 and x_2 as either AB or BA (exactly as in the two-alternative forced-choice paradigm), (2) categorize x_3 as A or B (as in the yes-no paradigm), and (3) respond "first" if the resulting categorizations are ABA or BAB, otherwise, respond "second." A sensory-difference strategy in which $|x_3 - x_1|$ and $|x_3 - x_2|$ are compared is almost optimal in typical situations.

7.2.3.2. **AXA.** In this paradigm, the subject must decide whether the middle one of three presentations is the same or different from the outer two. The possible presentations are AAA, BBB ("same") and ABA, BAB ("different"). Upon decision analysis, this task becomes equivalent to ABX—the two identical stimuli (AA) supplying exactly the same benefit as the two complementary stimuli (AB) in ABX. For analyses of still other paradigms, see Noreen (1981).

7.2.4. Conclusions. The conclusion about optimum strategies in the most common paradigms with multiple presentations are:

1. Compute the likelihood of each stimulus alternative (A,B) for every observation x_i.
2. In two-alternative forced choice, use the likelihood ratio to decide whether the first- or second-stimulus presentation is more likely to have been A. In the other paradigms, categorize each of the observations as the more likely of A or B.
3. Formulate the appropriate response based on the categorizations.
4. An alternative approach is forming *sensory differences*. (e.g., $|x_i - x_j|$) and making decisions based on these. A strategy based on sensory differences is exactly equivalent to the *early categorization* strategy in some paradigms with some distributional assumptions (two-alternative forced-choice, equal-variance Normal distributions) and only slightly inferior in others of the paradigms considered here. The sensory-difference model is nonoptimal because it depends only on *relative* information (how different is x_1 from x_2) and neglects the absolute information that controls the independent categorization of the x_i in the optimal model. The two models differ in their responses when (1) the sensory difference is small but the two observations fall on opposite sides of a criterion or (2) the sensory difference is large but the two observations fall on the same side of a criterion value. Since the difference model and the optimal model would result in the same response on most trials, the quantitative predictions differ only slightly.
5. As in the analysis of n-state threshold versus continuous theories in signal detection, and in Nolte and Jaarsma's (1967) analysis of ideal detection in multichannel listening experiments (Figure 2.10), two apparently quite different strategies can lead to very similar performances. Evidence for the use of one versus another of the decision strategies usually requires consistent data from more than one paradigm.

7.3. Resource Allocation: Optimal-Search Strategy

The concept of an *optimal* performance probably is best known in psychology in the context of SDT. It involves the question of whether subjects can perform (set a criterion in the signal detection model) according to an optimum-decision rule, for example, a maximum-likelihood rule. The notion of optimization (the maximization of utility) applies not only to decision strategies for dealing with incomplete information but also to resource allocation decisions. This section describes an important theory of the optimal *allocation* of search resources.

In the 1950s, Koopman (1956a, 1956b, 1957), the mathematician, derived a theory of search that defined the optimal allocation or distribution of limited resources for searching for the location of a target. This theory was originally developed in the context of military applications, for example, aircraft searching optimally for a submarine, given a limited number of flying hours. The basic assumptions are (1) a fixed, limited search capacity, (2) no cost for sharing search capacity among several locations and no cost for changing the allocation strategy, (3) a known probability density for the target in each location, and (4) a principle of diminishing returns in search efficacy. Koopman's theory can be applied only to compound tasks, since it assumes that the target is in *one* particular location.

Koopman's theory provides an algorithm for defining the amount of search effort that should be allocated to different locations under an optimal-allocation policy. In one dimension, the theory deals with a target located somewhere on a line, the x-axis, on a graph as in Figure 2.24. The y-axis represents the natural logarithm of the probability density function ($\ln p(x)$)

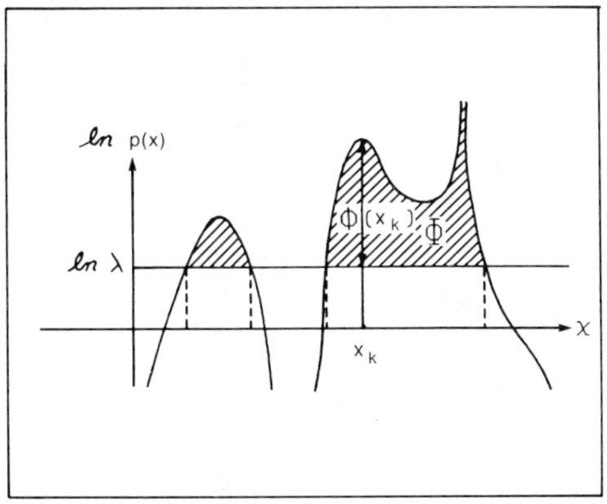

Figure 2.24. The graphic interpretation of Koopman's (1957) solution for determining the optimal distribution of search effort for detecting a single target whose location is unknown. The algorithm assumes that (1) the *probability* $p(x)$ of the target being at any location x is known, (2) there is a limited pool of search effort, and (3) the probability $f(x)$ of detecting a target at location x_k is $f(x_k) = 1 - e^{-\varphi(x_k)}$, an exponential (diminishing returns) function of the search effort $\varphi(x_k)$ allocated to x_k. The graph illustrates the special case where the target appears somewhere on a line. The abscissa represents location x; the ordinate is $\ln p(x)$. To determine the optimal distribution over x of search effort, $\varphi(x)$, first graph $\ln p(x)$. Then draw a horizontal line such that the area between $\ln p(x)$ and the line (shaded area in the graph) is equal to the available search capacity ϕ; this line is labeled $y = \ln\lambda$. Optimal allocation of search effort requires $\varphi(x) = 0$ for all positions where $\ln p(x) < \ln\lambda$, and $\varphi(x) = \ln p(x) - \ln\lambda$ for the remaining (high probability) locations. The area between $p(x)$ and λ on a linear graph (i.e., $\int p(x) - \lambda$, for all x where $p(x) > u/\lambda$) is the probability that the search is successful. (From B. O. Koopman, The theory of search III: The optimum distribution of searching effort, *Operations Research*, 1967, *5*. Reprinted with permission.)

for the target on the axis. To compute the optimal search strategy, the following graphic construction is used. A line parallel to the axis is adjusted in height ($\ln\lambda$) such that the area above the line and below $\ln p(x)$ equals a constant that represents the fixed capacity Φ. Then only those locations where the function $\ln p(x) > \ln\lambda$ are searched, and the amount of effort allocated to the searched locations, $\varphi(x)$, is $\ln p(x) - \ln\lambda$. This is shown graphically in Figure 2.24.

One useful aspect of Koopman's (1957) model is that if more capacity or resources (Φ') become available after some search has been completed on the basis of the original resource commitment (Φ), the algorithm can simply be applied on the a posteriori probabilities. Successive applications of this sort yield the same optimal distribution of resources as if (Φ') had been known originally.

Koopman's theory of optimal-detection search was imported into psychology by M. L. Shaw (1978; M. L. Shaw & P. Shaw, 1977) and applied to the problem of visual search for a target among distractors where the probability of a target at several locations is known. M. L. Shaw and P. Shaw (1977) applied this model directly to an experiment with detection probability as the dependent measure, and M. L. Shaw (1978) extended it to handle RT data. The issue was whether her subjects demonstrated an optimal distribution of attentional capacity. A related model for *optimal localization*, or "whereabouts," search was developed by Tognetti, 1968, Kadane, 1971, and Stone, 1975, and was extended and applied to visual search data by M. L. Shaw, Mulligan, and Stone, 1983.

In a search experiment with just two target locations, one likely target location and one unlikely location, Shaw's adaptation of the optimal-allocation model to RT data uses Koopman's principle of reallocation to predict that subjects should allocate all their search capacity to the higher-probability location until its posterior probability equals the a priori probability of the low-probability location (M. L. Shaw, 1978). Subsequently, the subject should divide capacity equally. The posterior probability of any location diminishes with search capacity already spent because a target in that location would likely have been detected given a reasonable expenditure of search resources. Shaw's data were fit reasonably by this model. The application of Koopman's model to RTs yields an additional strong prediction that apparently was overlooked by Shaw. The RTs for detections at the high-probability locations should be a mixture of two distributions resulting from the two levels of attention allocation and hence should obey the fixed-point property (cf. Falmagne, 1968).

From the psychological point of view, one interesting assumption of Koopman's model is that of no changeover or sharing costs. The "optimal" search allocation would differ from this if it were necessary to include changeover cost in the computations. In particular, changeover cost should lead to perseveration in a given allocation scheme past the point where the a posteriori probabilities would indicate an alteration of allocation. Changeover costs in visual search are considered in Section 9.

7.4. Strategies: Mixed-List and Blocked Designs

Many situational factors may influence a subject's selection of a particular strategy. Previous sections have considered the importance of task instructions, a priori stimulus probabilities, and payoffs in determining attentional allocation, decision criterion, and the speed-versus-accuracy of responding. Another factor, also under experimenter control, is the kind of stimulus mixture: which stimuli are presented in separate blocks and which stimuli are presented within a block. Such experimenter decisions can have a large impact on the strategy employed by the subject and on the interpretation of the data by the experimenter.

A *blocked* experimental design is one in which a set of experimental parameters Ω is kept constant for a block of trials (usually 100 or more) and Ω is varied between blocks. For example, Ω may represent the intensity of a tonal signal in a signal–noise detection task. The corresponding *mixed-list* experimental design (mixed blocks) is one in which all the values of the parameters Ω can occur within any block of trials. In the mixed-list experiment, all the types of trials that have been segregated into separate blocks in the block design are mixed together and presented in random order.

In terms of the compound-concurrent analysis of experimental procedures, the mixed-list procedure is a compound task; the individual blocks of the blocked procedure are the component tasks. Section 4 compared component to compound tasks in terms of *stimulus uncertainty* and outlined procedures for drawing correct inferences from experiments that varied stimulus uncertainty between conditions. This section continues the development of compound tasks in terms of the specific strategies adopted by the subjects.

Practical considerations influence the choice of experimental design. Historically, with manually operated apparatus, it was impractical to vary conditions between trials, so many experiments were run in block designs, not by choice but by necessity. To offset learning, fatigue, and other extraneous changes between blocks, complex, counterbalanced experimental designs were required. These were inefficient procedures because they required a commitment in advance to a particular number of subjects (required for counterbalancing) and an experiment of a particular size (that may have been too small or too large).

With the advent of computer-controlled experimentation in which new stimuli are generated cheaply and quickly, mixed-list designs became not only practical but also preferable. The conditions are mixed together, so the counterbalancing problem is instantly solved. A few subjects can be run for large numbers of trials. If data from a session are lost, it does not spoil the experimental design. Data collection is continued until a stopping criterion (such as a certain level of statistical reliability of estimated parameters) is reached; the amount of data may be different for different subjects. Such sequential statistical procedures are far more efficient than fixed procedures—an instance of optimizing the experimenter's strategy.

To illustrate the often crucial importance of the choice of mixed-list versus block design procedure, two kinds of commonly used paradigms are considered. In the first (exemplified by partial report, Section 7.4.1), a mixed-list design is essential for interpretation, but a block design is usually used; in the other (the method of constant stimuli, Section 7.4.2), the mixed-list design is universally advocated but leads to data that are awkward to interpret whenever SDT is appropriate.

7.4.1. Pure versus Mixed Blocks in Information Processing Experiments. Consider experiments with briefly presented stimuli in which presentation time is a critical parameter. For example, a row of letters is briefly exposed for a duration D. In a recall task, the subject must report as many letters as possible. In a search task, the subject may be required to say whether the stimulus contains the letter q. In these tasks, the experimenter wishes to determine the level of performance as a function of exposure duration. Should the various durations under investigation be run in separate blocks or together in a mixed list? The answer depends on the purpose of the experiment.

7.4.1.1. Equivalent Processing Assumption. Whenever stimulus duration is varied, the *equivalent processing assumption* almost invariably is made implicitly. To illustrate: suppose the following stimulus durations are being experimentally tested: 50, 100, 200, and 500 msec. The theorist assumes that during the first 50 msec of the 100-, 200-, and 500-msec exposures, the subject processes information exactly as in the 50-msec exposure, and only after that time does processing differ. The equivalent processing assumption is especially important in comparing the longer durations, 200 and 500 msec, since they overlap much more.

The equivalent processing assumption is valid only in the mixed-list design. In the block design, the subject may (and usually does) employ different strategies in different blocks. For example, the subject may attend to the center of the display in brief exposures but attempt to process the display from left to right in longer exposures. In very brief exposures, *exposure* duration effectively controls apparent contrast but is ineffective in controlling *processing* duration (because of visual persistence). Since strategies tend not to vary enormously with contrast, the misinterpretations of exposure duration experiments did not become serious until the introduction of postexposure visual noise fields (Sperling, 1963) to interrupt processing. An instructive bad example in which the equivalent processing assumption is made incorrectly is described in Section 7.4.1.2.

7.4.1.2. Equivalent Processing in Whole Reports. Sperling (1967) exposed a row of five letters for various durations, followed by a noise field, and determined the rate at which his subjects acquired information from each of the five letter locations. However, the experiment was run in a block design, so the assumption that the subject viewing long exposures was doing the same initial processing as at short exposures was unwarranted. Such an assumption requires a mixed-list design. In a block design, it is not even necessary that performance increase monotonically with exposure duration at each of the various locations. For example, in a long-exposure duration block, a subject may neglect a location j (in favor of attending to location k) although reporting location j accurately at short-exposure durations. This kind of paradoxical nonmonotonicity is ruled out in mixed lists.

7.4.1.3. Equivalent Processing in Partial Reports. Partial report experiments are a particular trouble area for block designs. In the partial report procedure, a subject is presented with more stimulus information than can be recalled, for example, a brief flash of a 3×3 array of letters. The subject is required to report only one of the three rows. The cue that informs the subject which particular row is required (e.g., a high-, medium-, or low-pitched tone) occurs only after a delay of D msec after the stimulus has been turned off. The logic of this experiment is that the subject cannot report all the letters (because of a recall-memory limitation) but can nevertheless give perfectly accurate partial reports as long as the stimulus is stored in a visual sensory memory. When the cue is delayed, the contents of visual sensory memory have decayed, and partial reports are less accurate. The decay of partial report performance with increased cue delay is assumed to represent the decay of sensory memory with the passage of time.

Partial report is a procedure crying for the delays to be run in mixed lists, yet they are nearly always run in blocks. It is simply wrong to assume that a subject waiting for a cue in a block of 500-msec delays is as passive during the first 150 msec as in a block of 150-msec cues. In blocks of short delays the subject may wait passively for the cue (equal-attention strategy), whereas in long-delay blocks the subject may begin to encode a particular row for response as quickly as possible following stimulus onset (a strategy of guessing which row will be cued). This block-dependent strategy is so obvious that it was described in the original partial-report study. Figure 2.25 exhibits data from a subject who failed to switch soon enough between an equal-attention strategy and a guessing strategy in successive blocks of trials, as the cue delay gradually increased (open circles) or gradually decreased (closed circles) between blocks. The data exhibit classical *Einstellung*, or, as it is often called now, *hysteresis*, where performance on one block of trials depends on the strategy chosen in previous blocks. Without the knowledge or control of the subject's strategy, it is not possible to estimate either the capacity or the duration of sensory storage. For example, the fact that Sperling's subject's performance reached asymptotic accuracy at cue delays of 0.5 sec may mean that the subject switched strategy to guessing in that block, not that the sensory store was empty.

7.4.1.4. Conclusion. The important lesson is that the particular sequence in which trials are presented has an enormous influence on the subject's strategy and, thereby, on responses. In a block design, the subject can choose an optimal strategy for each block. In a mixed list, the subject must choose one strategy (or one mixture of strategies) for all the trials in the list. To be sure that a subject uses the same strategy in different conditions, these conditions must be run together in a mixed list.

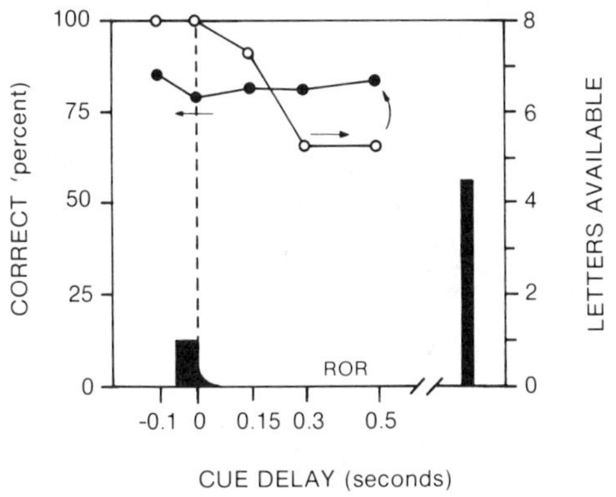

Figure 2.25. Partial report accuracy as a function of cue delay: an example of path dependence (hysteresis) in the selection of attention strategies. Cue delay was varied between 10 blocks of trials in 1 session; the arrows indicate the order of blocks, beginning with the series of increasing delays. The bar at the right shows the accuracy of whole reports. Increasing cue-delay blocks (open circles) correspond to a strategy of equal attention to the two rows of letters in the stimulus; decreasing cue-delay blocks (closed circles) correspond to a strategy of attending primarily to the top row. (Subject ROR from Sperling (1960), Fig. 5.) (From G. Sperling, The information available in brief visual presentations, *Psychological Monographs*, 1960, *74* (11, Whole No. 498). © 1960 by the American Psychological Association. Reprinted by permission.)

7.4.2. Pure versus Mixed Lists in Detection: Method of Constant Stimuli. Consider an experiment in which the subject must detect the presence of a tonal stimulus in noise and the tone occurs at several intensities within a block of trials. Note that the noise stimulus alone (blank, catch trial) must occur at least occasionally within the block; otherwise, the subject could simply report "signal" on all trials without observing the stimulus. Since several stimulus intensities appear randomly within a block, this is a compound task. The probability of a "signal" response as a function of signal intensity is called the *psychometric function* (Figure 2.26). The *method of constant stimuli*, just described, traditionally has been used to yield the psychometric function (Woodworth & Schlosberg, 1954).

The tone-in-noise discrimination task is well described by SDT. The difficulty detecting a tone in noise comes about because the noise contains energy at and near the tonal frequency. For many kinds of noise, including white noise, the amount of this energy is Normally distributed from trial to trial, with mean and variance, μ_N, σ_N^2. On signal trials, the tonal energy is Normally distributed with mean and variance $\mu_N + \mu_S$, σ_N^2. An ideal detector, confronted with the signal-in-noise discrimination task, will compute these energy statistics and use them in exact conformity with psychological SDT. A human observer need not necessarily operate in conformity with SDT, but in situations like tone-in-noise discrimination in which the assumptions of SDT theory are virtually built into the physical stimuli themselves, humans conform quite closely to SDT.

Unfortunately, the method of constant stimuli does not fare well under analysis by SDT. The utter futility of the classical procedure of absolutely prohibiting false alarms (positive responses on noise-alone trials) and the enormous dependence of the psychometric function on the penalty for false alarms have long ago been extensively documented (Green & Swets, 1966) and need not be detailed further here. Payoff manipulations move the psychometric function to the left or right (as it is usually plotted) but leave the monotonicity properties intact; that is, the various psychometric functions obtained with different payoffs do not cross. (For an elaborate analysis of noncrossing psychometric functions, see Kruskal, 1965; Levine, 1971.) The effect of varying trial mixtures is more serious. According to SDT the various psychometric functions generated by block designs do cross (are not monotonically related, do not lie uniformly above or uniformly below) the psychometric functions generated in mixed-list designs. In the following, nonmonotonicity is demonstrated, and various remedies for the lack of a unique or generic psychometric function are considered.

The N and the $S + N$ probability density functions (*pdfs*) that are at the core of the SDT analysis of the tone-in-noise experiment are illustrated in Figure 2.26(a). In the method of constant stimuli, the task is discrimination of noise alone from the compound alternative, the union of the various signal stimuli, which is represented in Figure 2.26(a) by the sum of the various signal density functions (S_1, ..., S_6). The decision criterion is set in accordance with expected utility which depends on the payoff matrix. Even in the traditional method of constant stimuli, in which the instruction is to avoid false alarms absolutely while detecting as many stimuli as possible, the payoffs cannot be defined simply in terms of penalties for false alarms, or the subject would never observe the stimulus but would merely respond "noise" on all trials. Once payoffs are defined, SDT applies and an optimum criterion can be selected. For the usual case of equally likely signal stimuli and the case of symmetrical payoffs for correct and incorrect responses, the optimum criterion (c_1) occurs where the N *pdf* crosses the compound ΣS_i *pdf* in Figure 2.26(a). The psychometric function generated by the SDT parameters corresponding to these experimental conditions is illustrated in Figure 2.26(b). It is generated by considering where each individual stimulus *pdf* lies with respect to the criterion. Provided that the payoff matrix retains positive payoffs for correct and negative payoffs for incorrect responses, changing the payoff matrix only moves the psychometric function to the left or right in Figure 2.26(b) but does not alter its shape. Figures 2.26(a) and 2.26(b) also illustrate the case where the penalty for false alarms (and the reward for correct rejections) is 6 times greater than the penalty for misses and the reward for correct detections. This case of 6 to 1 *payoff ratio* is represented graphically in the same way as a case of equal payoffs in which the *frequency* of noise stimuli is increased sixfold.

The method of constant stimuli can be analyzed as a compound task (or mixed-list experiment) in which the corresponding component tasks (or pure blocks) each contain noise and just one of the stimuli. Let the trials of the mixed block (which contains the noise and six stimuli) be separated out into six pure blocks, each of which contains just one signal intensity and just one-sixth of the noise trials. The pure block experiments are represented in Figure 2.26(c) corresponding to the two different payoffs (or to two different a priori stimulus probabilities) as described for Figure 2.26(a). Given the same payoff matrix as in the method of constant stimuli, the decision criterion differs for each of the pure blocks, and the optimum criterion occurs at the point where the noise *pdf* crosses the signal *pdf*. The corresponding psychometric function for the pure block experiments, curve p in Figure 2.26(d), is flatter than and crosses the function m for mixed blocks. However, a psychometric function is not really appropriate for pure blocks because the criterion varies between blocks. An accuracy function, such as percent correct (from which d' is computable), describes the data better. The overall expected accuracy in the mixed blocks is, inevitably, somewhat lower than in the pure blocks, Figure 2.26(e), illustrating once again that signal uncertainty causes a performance

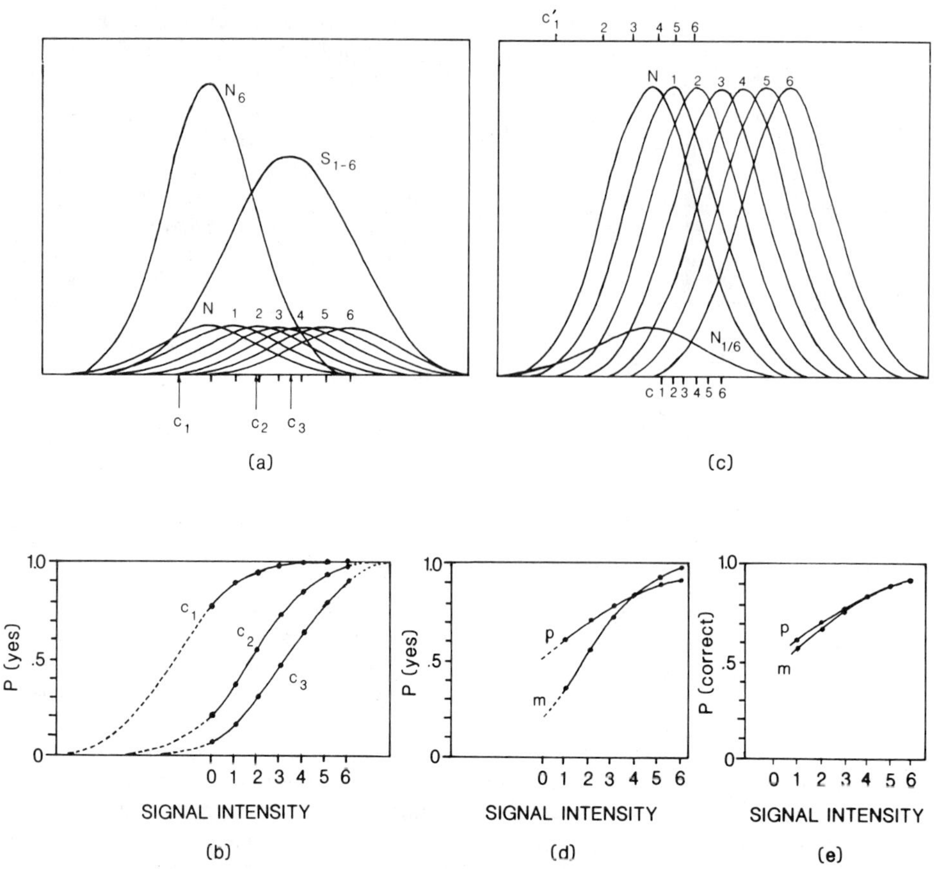

Figure 2.26. Analysis of the method of constant stimuli and the corresponding blocked designs. (a) Probability density functions (*pdf*s) of the assumed internal effects of the stimulus (noise-alone labeled *N*) and six different signal-plus-noise stimuli (signal labeled 1, ..., 6 in order of increasing signal intensity). S_{1-6} is the sum of the six signal distributions and represents the compound *pdf* of the stimulus for correct "yes" responses in the method of constant stimuli. N_6 represents the *pdf* for noise multiplied by a factor of 6 to represent either a penalty 6 times greater for incorrect responses on noise than on signal trials or a sixfold increase in the frequency of noise stimuli. The point c_2 represents the criterion that maximizes expected utility in the discrimination of N_6 versus S_{1-61}. Criterion c_1 maximizes expected utility in the discrimination of *N* versus S_{1-6}—the case of equal probability of occurrence of each stimulus (noise and the six signals) and equal payoffs for correct and incorrect responses to each stimuli. Criterion c_3 restricts errors (false alarms) to exactly 5% when the noise stimulus is presented. (b) Probability of a detection ("yes") response as a function of signal intensity, where zero represents noise-alone. The predicted *p*("yes") for each of the three criteria in (a) are indicated by filled circles connected by heavy lines. (c) Optimal criteria in block designs. The *pdf*s (*N*,1, ..., 6) represent noise and the six signals as in (a). In a block composed of equal numbers of *N* and signal *i* ($i = 1, ..., 6$) trials, with symmetric payoffs, the optimal criterion c_i occurs where the *N* and signal-*i* *pdf*s cross. In the usual method of constant stimuli, however, there are many fewer noise than signal stimuli. The segregation of these stimuli into pure blocks is represented by $N_{1/6}$ and signals 1, ..., 6 such that a block contains *k*/6 noise trials and *k* trials with a signal of a particular intensity *i*. The corresponding optimal criteria are the c'_i. (d) The probability of a detection response ("yes") as a function of signal intensity in typical mixed lists and in typical pure blocks compared: *m* indicates mixed lists (method of constant stimuli) using criterion c_2 as shown in (a) and (b); *p* indicates pure blocks using criteria c_i shown in (c). (e) Expected probability of correct responses in mixed lists and in pure blocks. The conditions are as in (d): *m* indicates the typical mixed case of the method of constant stimuli (higher penalties for false alarms than misses, which is equivalent to equal numbers of noise and signal stimuli, N_6 versus S_{1-6} in (a)); *p* indicates the expected outcome with the equal number of noise and signal stimuli segregated into six pure blocks.

decrement in compound tasks, relative to component tasks, even with an ideal observer (defined in the framework of SDT).

The original, theoretical rationale behind the method of constant stimuli was that the observer could maintain a constant criterion, for example, a criterion that admitted exactly 5% false alarms, independent of the values of the signal stimuli and their proportions relative to noise. In fact, this method of defining payoffs seems not to have been attempted experimentally. When payoffs are defined in terms of the values of hits, misses, false alarms, and correct rejections, the observer's criterion varies widely with the proportion of stimuli and values of outcomes in the experiment. According to SDT analysis, the method of constant stimuli yields not a unique psychometric function but one member of a family of alternative functions depending on the mixture of stimuli and on the payoffs of the experiment. The threshold (which usually is taken as the 50%

or 75% point of the psychometric function) similarly depends on payoffs and context. The threshold is a property of the idiosyncratic experimental situation in which it is measured; it is not an invariant of the sensory system.

7.4.3. General Description of Threshold Events. What is needed is an economical, general method of describing human responses to threshold stimuli. Signal detection theory offers a theory for two stimuli: noise and a signal of a particular intensity. For the case of equal-variance Normal probability density functions (*pdf*s), with ($\sigma^2_{S+N} = \sigma^2_N$), and independent observations, the single parameter d' provides a complete description of the subject's encoded stimulus information. Any possible predictions about detection performance can be made on the basis of d' alone, plus the relevant aspects of the external situation (stimulus probabilities, payoffs, etc.).

When there is more than one near-threshold stimulus, matters are much more complex. One may wish to determine the discriminability of each stimulus s_j from noise, as in the preceding example (Fig. 2.26). This yields a d'_j value for each stimulus. One may ask, "How does d' grow with stimulus intensity?" When d' increases linearly with stimulus intensity (or energy, e), which it must for small ranges of e, the slope of this line, $\partial d'/\partial e$, is a single number from which the results of many experiments can be derived. Underlying this particular formulation is a much more fundamental issue which is considered now.

Is the discriminability d'_{jk} between two stimuli s_j and s_k given by $|(d_{jk} = d'_k - d'_j)|$, where d'_i measures the discriminability of stimulus i from noise and $|\,|$ represents absolute value? This formulation of the question suggests that threshold detection is a special case of discrimination or categorization, a domain that has been extensively studied. In fact, the assumptions made by Thurstone (1947) in Case V of his theory of comparative judgment are equivalent to those of SDT (i.e., stimuli spaced on a single dimension with Normal equal-variance *pdf*s). The general problem is finding a representation of stimuli in a multidimensional space where the distance between pairs of stimuli reflects their psychological distance, that is, their confusability in various experimental settings. Although SDT is concerned with microscopic portions of this space, that is, with stimuli that are very close and highly confusable, the general, cosmic scaling methods developed are applicable to the SDT microcosmos.

To show the close relation between classical psychophysics procedures and multidimensional scaling methods, consider the hypothetical auditory detection experiment described in Figure 2.26(a). The method of constant stimuli was used to generate a psychometric function from stimuli consisting of noise S_0 and six tones ($S_1, S_2, ..., S_6$) ordered in increasing intensity. In the classical method, the observer simply responded "detect" (1) or "nondetect" (0) after each stimulus was presented. In the more efficient modern method, the observer also gives confidence in the response; for example, 0 = definitely noise, 1 = probably noise, 2 = possibly noise, 3 = undecided, 4 = possibly signal, 5 = probably signal, 6 = definitely signal. (The confidence data are extremely useful in discriminating between theories; they can and should be collected, usually, at no extra cost.) From the seven levels of confidence it is a small leap to ask the observer to use the same seven values to identify the stimuli. This procedure (Sperling, 1965) has two great advantages: (1) the response is objectively correct or incorrect, and therefore it can be reinforced and thereby shaped, and (2) it externalizes the internal psychological dimension. That is, when the observer says "2" to a noise stimulus for which the correct (and most frequent) response is "0," it is interpreted to mean that on that particular trial, the noise produced an internal response of the same magnitude as the stimulus S_2 usually does (assuming that S_2 elicits "2" more frequently than other responses).

By a small modification in procedure, the psychophysical method of constant stimuli becomes an experiment in absolute identification in which n stimuli are presented one at a time, and the subject must identify each of them. The resulting $n \times n$ (stimulus $\times$ response) confusion matrix can be analyzed by any of the many scaling methods that have been developed for this purpose. Analysis by Thurstone's Case V (1947) would be equivalent to a generalized SDT. Other such analyses are equivalent to other assumptions (than normal equal-variance *pdf*s) about encoding variability at threshold. For example, various multidimensional scaling methods derive both the *pdf* and the distance metric from stimulus–response matrices.

The application of multidimensional scaling to threshold data is especially interesting when the sensory continuum under study is not simply one dimensional. For example, brief threshold increments and decrement pulses of light are said to appear more similar to each other than to zero—no pulse at all. Sperling (quoted in Levitt, 1972, p. 160) conducted an identification experiment with near-threshold pulses to investigate this sensory continuum experimentally. His confusion data were analyzed by a multidimensional scaling program which revealed that, indeed, this sensory continuum was not a straight line. It was horseshoe shaped, with increment and decrement flashes juxtaposed at opposed ends of the shoe (Figure 2.27).

On the whole, multidimensional scaling methods are ways of representing stimuli in a space independent of the observer's strategy. Strategy affects how the encoded stimulus information is used but not how it is represented in these models. Strategy can appear as a vector of response biases or a vector of weighting factors in the models (Shepard, 1958). On the whole, the decision rules that are necessary to translate a multidimensional representation into behavioral predictions (dependent on situational factors) have not been worked out adequately. Some models, such as INDSCAL (INdividual Differences SCALing, Carroll, 1972), which have been especially adapted for dealing with between-individual differences, are also adaptable to dealing with within-individual differences on occasions where the same individual may be using different strategies. Eventually, these more general scaling methods (with very unrestrictive assumptions) may come to supplement the highly restrictive, specialized threshold theories.

7.4.4. Pure versus Mixed Blocks in Reaction Time

7.4.4.1. Foreperiod Uncertainty. The foreperiod is the interval between a warning stimulus and the reaction stimulus in an RT task. The blocking or mixing of foreperiods has profound effects on RT (Drazin, 1961). The more accurately the subject knows exactly when a stimulus will occur, the quicker the subject can respond to it. When foreperiods are blocked (held constant) over a series of trials, the subject can prepare for the reaction stimulus at a particular moment. Catch trials are necessary in both simple and choice RT procedures to prevent anticipations that indicate the subject is timing the response (from the warning stimulus) to coincide with the end of the foreperiod interval.

There are three main determinants of the effect of foreperiods on RT.

1. When foreperiods are very short, for example, less than about 0.2 sec, the subject may have incompletely processed the

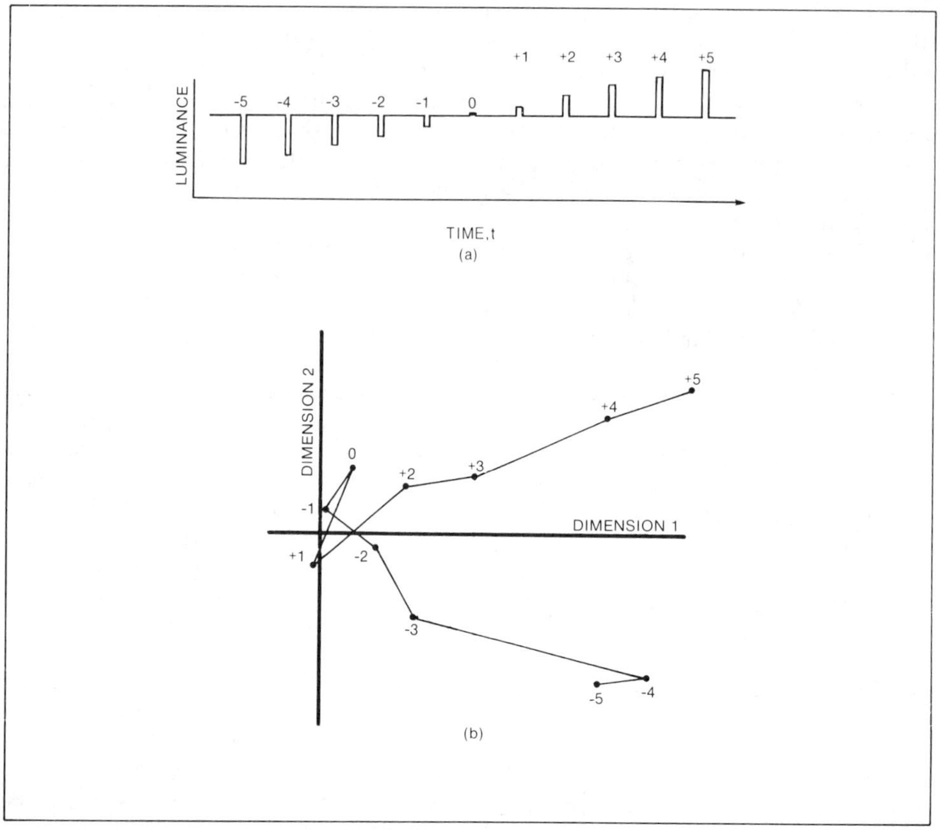

Figure 2.27. Scaling representation of near-threshold increments or decrements in intensity, the stimuli for a visual detection and recognition experiment. (a) The stimuli are shown schematically. The stimuli were brief pulse increments or decrements in a steady background luminance; stimulus intensity took on 11 values from −5 units to +5 units relative to the background. Subjects were required to identify which stimulus occurred on each trial. The confusion matrix resulting from this experiment was analyzed by multidimensional scaling to yield the multidimensional representation shown in (b), where close proximity in the space corresponds to greater confusion frequency. Dimension 1 represents "flashiness," independent of sign; dismension 2 represents black-to-white contrast. Large increment and decrement flashes are much more confusable with each other than can be explained by a one-dimensional (SDT) representation. (From an experiment by G. Sperling described in H. Levitt, Decision theory, signal detection theory, and psychophysics, in E. E. David and P. B. Denes (Eds.), *Human communication: A unified view*, McGraw-Hill, 1972. Reprinted with permission.)

warning stimulus when the reaction stimulus arrives; the subject will be unprepared and will produce long RTs.

2. In block designs, the longer the foreperiod in the block, the less accurately the subject can estimate the interval and, therefore, the longer the resulting RT. Under blocked foreperiods, simple RT is at a minimum when the foreperiod is near 250 msec, the time interval that optimizes the trade-off between preparedness and time uncertainty. There is only a modest increase in RT for longer foreperiods (Bevan, Hardesty, & Avant, 1965).

3. In mixed-list designs with variable foreperiods, uncertainty about when the stimulus will occur is the primary determinant of RT. This uncertainty is a function of the distribution $f(t)$ of foreperiods. The *aging*, or *hazard function*, $a(t)$ describes the probability $a(t)dt$ that the stimulus will occur in the interval $(t, t + dt)$ given that it has not yet occurred:

$$a(t) = \frac{f(t)}{1 - \int_0^t f(t')dt'} \qquad (13)$$

The warning stimulus is assumed to occur at time $t = 0$. Subjects' RT is determined, to a first approximation, by the aging function: readiness depends on expectancies.

Probably the most common distribution of foreperiods is the uniform (rectangular) distribution; its aging function increases monotonically. In the authors' experience, whenever they have used a uniform distribution of foreperiods, the RTs, conditionalized on foreperiod (the *warning* function), have shown a corresponding monotonic decrease throughout the interval. An exponential distribution of foreperiods produces a constant aging function and hence, presumably, a constant expectation of the stimulus as a function of time. In practice, however, unbounded distributions of foreperiods are impractical, so this theoretical perfection is not quite achievable. In fact, the approximately exponential foreperiod distributions that have been tested produce the fastest RTs when the mean foreperiod is about 250 msec. A review of the empirical findings is contained in Brebner and Welford (1980) and Welford (1980a).

The foreperiod effect may not be large in comparison to other stimulus and processing effects, but it is ubiquitous in

RT experiments. Although often overlooked, it should be regarded as a factor in the experimental design because partialing it out (rather than treating it as *error*) allows more sensitive statistical tests of other results. It is another example of how subjects use a priori information, about foreperiod probabilities in this instance, to optimize their performance. When such information is reduced in compound (mixed-list) designs, performance (mean RT) suffers because of the increased stimulus uncertainty.

7.4.4.2. ***Intensity Effects.*** The blocking structure of experiments is also known to alter the effect of stimulus intensity on RT. When simple RT to visual stimuli of high and low intensity is measured in pure blocks, intensity may have little or no effect on mean RT (Grice, 1968; Murray, 1970). When high- and low-intensity stimuli are intermixed in the same block, there is a profound effect of intensity, with the more intense stimuli producing faster RTs. (This is but one example of the effect of experimenter-selected stimulus mixtures on RT.) These

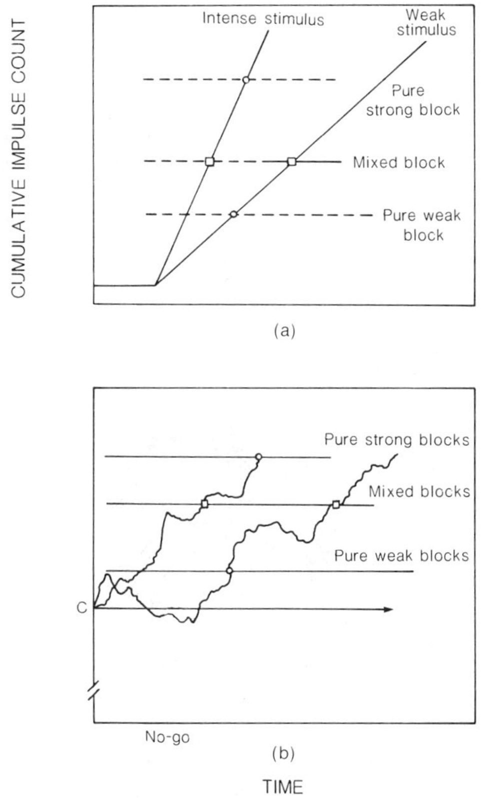

Figure 2.28. A schematic counting model and a random walk model equivalent to account for the effects of pure and mixed block designs on simple reaction time to weak and strong signals. (a) A schematic interpretation of the dependence of simple reaction time (RT) to weak or intense stimuli in pure versus mixed blocks. The axes are time and the cumulative count of neural impulses. Strong stimuli evoke a faster cumulation of neural impulses than weak stimuli, but detection criteria can be set to produce a large effect of intensity on RT in mixed blocks, and no effect in pure block comparisons (From Nissen (1977), Fig. 2.) (b) A random walk interpretation of the same pattern of RT data is similar to counting models that have variability in the interval between counts but differs from such counting models in that it allows negative evidence (negative counts). The axes are time and the cumulative value of the random walk. Hypothetical random walks are shown for an intense and a weak stimulus. The response boundaries are as in (a). (a. is from M. J. Nissen, Stimulus intensity and information processing, *Perception and Psychophysics*, 1977, *22*. Reprinted with permission.)

effects of intensity on RT occur with go/no-go and with variable-foreperiod procedures. The pattern of simple RT to tones of various intensities and the dependence of this pattern on the subject's knowledge have been known since the time of Wundt (1893). He presented tones of two intensities either in a strictly alternating sequence or in a random sequence within a block. These conditions produced results similar to the pure- and mixed-intensity blocks described here.

Figure 2.28(a) schematically illustrates a suggestion by Nissen (1977, after Grice, 1968) to explain RT data from Murray (1970). The subject is assumed to accumulate information from the stimulus at a fixed rate, the rate being faster for high-intensity stimuli. When a criterion amount of information is acquired, a response is initiated. The criteria in the various conditions may be set so that there is no mean RT difference between weak and intense stimuli for pure blocks but a substantial difference for mixed blocks.

The neural-counting model (McGill, 1963) and the neural-timing model (Luce & Green, 1972) are two models of sensory decision making that were designed specifically to account for intensity effects on detection and RT. The neural-timing model assumes that detection occurs with the first neural interarrival time below a criterion. In the neural-counting model, the subject is assumed to count the number of (neural) events in an observation interval, but the criterion number is assumed to be constant. Nissen's (1977) model, Figure 2.28(a), follows the spirit of the counting model but with a criterion that varies between conditions. Figure 2.28(b) schematically illustrates a random walk model which embodies similar principles but which could generate detailed, statistical predictions about RT distributions, error rates, and speed–accuracy trade-offs.

8. STRATEGY MIXTURES

This section examines some of the consequences of, and tests for, strategy mixtures. Mixtures between two strategies lie on a straight line in operating space. Unless the performance operating characteristic also is a straight line, strategy mixtures yield strictly worse performance than appropriately chosen pure strategies. Nevertheless, humans exhibit strategy mixture in many common tasks. Contingency tests for demonstrating strategy mixtures are described in this section. Changeover costs in switching strategies (e.g., in switching attention) lead to *path dependence* and suboptimal performance in strategy selection, a topic discussed in Section 9.

8.1. Definition

Assume that there exist two distinct strategies S_a and S_b and that the resulting performances are represented by points *a* and *b* on a performance operating characteristic, as shown in Figure 2.29. Suppose that a subject uses strategy S_a on a fraction α of trials and S_b on the remaining fraction $1 - \alpha$ of trials. If α is 0 or 1, then we say the subject is using the *pure* strategy, S_b (or S_a). When $0 < \alpha < 1$, then the subject is using a *strategy mixture*. Whenever a strategy mixture is used, the subject's performance falls along the straight line connecting the pure strategies on the performance operating characteristic (POC). The straight-line property of strategy mixtures is obvious, because overall performance is simply an average of performances given S_a and S_b, weighted according to the fractions of trials of each type. More generally, a mixture of a larger number of

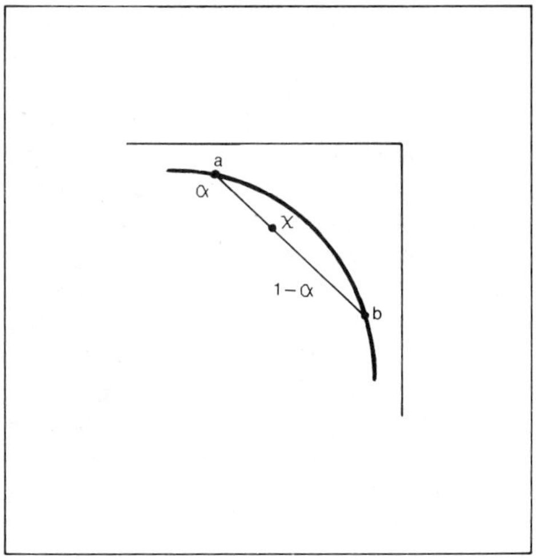

Figure 2.29. Operating characteristics for strategy mixtures. A performance operating characteristic with two pure strategies associated with points *a* and *b* and a strategy mixture at point *x* determined by the probability α of executing strategy *a* and 1 − α of executing strategy *b*. The axes either represent performance on Task 1 versus performance on Task 2 in a concurrent experiment, or they represent two measures of performance (i.e., *P*(Yes|*s*) versus *P*(No/*n*) in a compound experiment. (From G. Sperling, A unified theory of attention and signal detection, in R. Parasuraman and R. Davies (Eds.), *Varieties of attention*, Academic Press, 1984. Reprinted with permission.)

strategies is represented by a point in operating space that lies at the center of gravity of the mixture. Also obvious from Figure 2.29 is that a strategy mixture results in inferior performance relative to some pure (nonpathological) strategy, except when the performance operating characteristic is a straight line, in which case the mixture yields equal performance.

Experimentally, different points along a performance operating characteristic are produced by directly instructing the subjects to change their strategy or by indirectly inducing them to change strategy in response to changes in the reward structure of the experiment. In concurrent attention experiments, the subject may be told to attend more to one or another task; in signal detection, subjects are instructed to be conservative or lax in their decisions; and in reaction-time (RT) tasks, instructions may emphasize speed or accuracy. A priori, one may not know how subjects will respond to these instructions, but one can observe the shape of the operating characteristic.

When the empirical performance operating characteristic (POC) takes the form of a straight line, it is possible that strategy mixtures are accounting for movements along the observed POC. However, this is not a necessary conclusion. Appropriate distributional assumptions can lead to a linear POC, as in the classroom example. Or the true POC may be only slightly curvilinear and hence difficult to discriminate empirically from the linear function that would result from strategy mixtures. For *concurrent tasks* there are some additional statistical tests for strategy mixtures. These are treated in the following sections.

8.2. Strategy Mixture in Signal Detection Experiments

8.2.1. Two-State Threshold Models. Threshold models are the most common source of the (implicit) assertion of strategy mixture in signal detection experiments. *Two-state threshold* models have only two sensory states, a detect state D and a nondetect state $\bar{D}$. A signal detection theory (SDT) interpretation of a threshold model is illustrated in Figure 2.30. Two-state models encounter difficulties when the number of responses (e.g., confidence ratings) is larger than two. In this case, the response rule, given state i, is probabilistic. When the possible response alternatives are confidence ratings, a probabilistic rule means that one of several alternative responses is chosen randomly according to a probability density function (*pdf*). The set of alternative responses, and their probabilities, may be termed a *probability mix* corresponding to state i.

In all previous signal detection examples in this chapter, once the criterion had been chosen, there was a well-defined, optimal response for every possible observation (sensory state, x) on a trial. In classical SDT, a mix of response alternatives results when the criterion is chosen randomly on each trial. When the likelihood ratio $lr(x)$ is strictly monotonic in x, there is one and only one optimum criterion; mixing criteria means

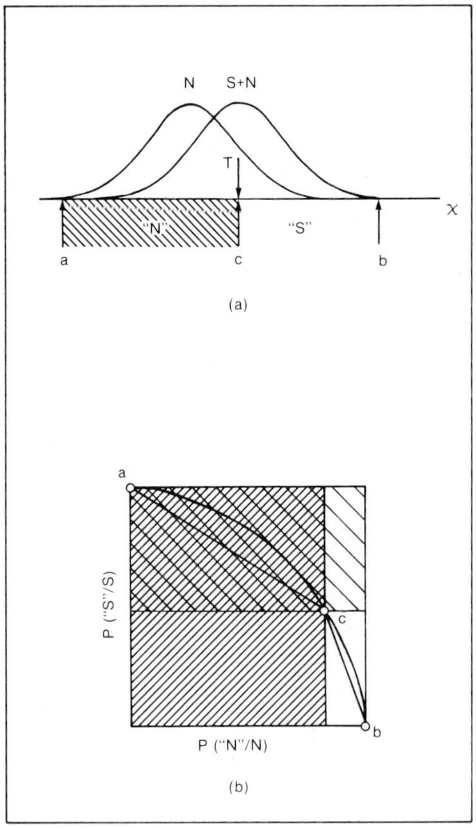

Figure 2.30. Graphical representations of response-threshold theory. (a) Probability density functions (*pdfs*) for noise (*N*) and for signal-plus-noise (*S* + *N*) stimuli on a psychological continuum (*x*). In conventional signal detection theory, the criterion (c) divides the continuum into "N" and "S" response regions. In response-threshold theory, the threshold (*T*) functions similarly, except that it cannot be set lower than some vlaue, resulting in a "forbidden" region, indicated by crosshatching. (b) Decision operating characteristic (DOC) for the *pdfs* in (a). Criteria *a, b, c* in panel (a) generate corresponding points *a, b, c* on the DOC in panel (b). The forbidden region for response thresholds results in a corresponding forbidden region in operating space, indicated by hatching. However, a *mixture* of strategies a and c can produce data along the straight line ac. In the strong form of threshold theory, the threshold can be set only at *T* and not under or above it. The DOC is then additionally constrained to the straight line *cb*. (From G. Sperling, A unified theory of attention and signal detection, in R. Parasuraman and R. Davies (Eds.), *Varieties of attention*, Academic Press, 1984. Reprinted with permission.)

that nonoptimal criteria are used. This kind of strategy mixture inevitably degrades performance (see Figure 2.29). The reason for complicating two-state threshold models with probability mixes of responses is that, without mixes, they cannot deal with data from confidence-rating experiments. Discrete-state models produce an operating characteristic not by varying a criterion along an internal sensory continuum but by varying the probability mix of confidence ratings (or of yes-no when these are the only ratings). Under the strong assumption that the probability mix for different confidence ratings does not overlap for the two states, the two-state model produces a straight-line receiver operating characteristic with a single elbow (Krantz, 1969), and the n-state model could produce up to $n - 1$ elbows.

8.2.2. *n*-State Threshold Models. Because the two-state threshold model with nonoverlapping confidence-rating mixtures, does not give an adequate account of threshold data, two embellishments have been proposed (Krantz, 1969): (1) allow the mixes of ratings to overlap and (2) increase the number of states. Embellishment (1), the introduction of a response-confusion process, results in complex, hybrid models (with both stimulus- and response-confusion processes) that are beyond the scope of this chapter. Embellishment (2), increasing the number of allowable states, obviously can bring a discrete-state model into arbitrarily close agreement with a continuous-state model in dealing with real psychophysical data.

8.2.2.1. Factor-Analytic Approach. The critical question for discrete-state models, is, What is the minimum number of states needed to account for the data? The data are entirely contained in a stimulus–response matrix that gives the probability $p(r_j|s_i)$ of a response rating r_j $(j=1, \ldots, J)$ given presentation of stimulus s_i $(i=1, \ldots, I)$. The question of the number of states reduces to a question of the rank of the $I \times J$ stimulus–response matrix, one of the most studied questions in psychometrics.

The classical approach to the rank of a matrix with imperfect data has been factor analysis (Thurstone, 1947), as developed in the context of test theory. Stimuli in the detection experiment correspond to subjects in the testing situation, and rating probabilities correspond to profiles of scores on tests, except that rating probabilities must sum to 1.0. Varying the stimulus probabilities and payoffs in the detection experiment corresponds to varying the state of the subject between test and retest in the testing situation, for example, by aging, drugs, selective motivation, differential education, and so on. The number of internal states corresponds to the number of factors needed to account for the data.

The output of a factor analysis of a rating experiment is a list of factors (probability-mix profiles), loadings (the amount of each factor in the various experimental conditions), and the percentage of variance accounted for by each factor. Whether a two-factor theory that accounts, for example, for 87% of the variance is adequate or should be supplanted by a three-factor theory that accounts for 95% of the variance is a question to which factor analysis offers no answer; it is a matter of the experimenter's and the reader's judgment. A recent statistical approach to the number-of-internal-states problem that offers significance tests (unavailable in factor analysis) has been developed by Bamber and van Santen (in press; van Santen & Bamber, 1981).

8.2.2.2. Direct Methods. There are at least two alternatives to the ever-more-elaborate indirect methods of discovering whether a subject is using a complex strategy, such as randomly selecting different ratings given the same internal state. The first and always recommended procedure is to ask the subject what strategy he or she is using. A second method (Sperling, 1984) is to contrive a parallel experiment with clearly discriminable suprathreshold stimuli that induce obviously distinct internal states corresponding to the hypothesized internal states induced by the threshold experiment. Then determine whether, with these experimenter-controlled states, subjects can carry out the strategies ascribed to them with threshold stimuli. These and similar direct methods can easily be carried out concurrently with the primary signal detection study, and they may well provide useful or even critical information for the primary data analysis.

8.3. Strategy Mixture in Reaction Time

8.3.1. Fast-Guess Model. The assertion of strategy mixture in speed–accuracy trade-off comes most commonly in the guise of the fast-guess model. This model applies, for example, to two-choice RT experiments, in which the subject is presented on each trial with one of two alternative stimuli and is required to make the corresponding one of two responses as quickly as possible. For example, in Ollman's (1966) and Yellott's (1967, 1971) theory, the subject is asserted to respond to the stimulus with a stimulus-controlled RT on some fraction $(1 - \alpha)$ of the trials, and on the remaining trials α, the subject responds as quickly as possible (simple RT) according to a predetermined guess at what the stimulus might be. On fast-guess trials, the subject is correct with only chance accuracy ($p = .5$) but with very short RTs. On the remaining trials, the subject has longer RTs and a correspondingly higher percentage of correct responses. When the experimenter demands from the subject an even lower average RT, the subject complies by increasing the proportion α of fast guesses.

The fast-guess model is equivalent to the assertion that the speed–accuracy trade-off (SAT) is composed of a straight-line segment whose end points represent the two strategies, the honest strategy and the fast-guess strategy. An alternative hypothesis to fast guess would be that the subject chooses a pure strategy appropriate to each payoff matrix, a process that could be modeled, for example, by boundary changes in a random walk model. This alternative strategy might generate either a curved- or a straight-line speed–accuracy trade-off. As in all the previous cases, it is not efficient to discriminate pure from mixed strategies by close examination of the curvature of the operating characteristic. In the case of the speed–accuracy trade-off, we have associated with each point on the speed–accuracy trade-off not only the mean RT and mean accuracy (which define the point) but also four RT distributions, one for each type of correct response and one for each type of error. The fast-guess model not only requires the speed–accuracy trade-off to be a straight line, but it requires the RT distribution associated with each point to be a mixture of the RT distributions associated with the extreme points. This is a powerful test to discriminate between strategy mixtures and pure strategies and is discussed in Section 8.8.1.3.

8.3.2. Ordered Memory Scanning. In the fast-guess model of choice RT, it is not clear why the subject would choose the fast-guess or observation strategy on any particular trial. Falmagne, Cohen, and Dwivedi (1975) deal with the question of how the strategy on the current trial is determined by local history on preceding trials. They propose a Markov model of choice RT, in which observed mean RTs are interpreted as resulting from mixtures of just two strategies (corresponding to two Markov states). Note that the more general approach of factor analysis (used in Section 8.2.2.1 to disentangle mixtures of confidence ratings) also is applicable here to disengage mixtures of RT distributions.

The subjects in Falmagne and colleagues' experiment were asked to discriminate a left-pointing from a right-pointing isosceles triangle and to respond "left" or "right," respectively. A new stimulus presentation followed the subject's response after only 100 msec, so there were more than 2 trials per sec, a situation designed to maximize sequential trial-to-trial dependencies. Reaction-time data were gathered for a large number of trials per subject to allow the examination of sequential dependencies in stimulus presentation order.

Stimulus presentation history for several trials preceding a critical trial was found to exert substantial effects on both mean RTs and on errors. For example, RT for a right stimulus was faster if it was preceded by several right stimuli. This pattern is shown in Figure 2.31, which displays (mean correct) RT arranged in a tree graph to represent the stimulus histories through trial $n - 3$.

8.3.2.1. Two-State Markov Model. Falmagne and colleagues (1975) propose a two-state (two-strategy) model for their data. They assume that subjects compare the observed stimulus with two internal prototypes corresponding to the left and right stimulus (L_p and R_p) *serially* and with *termination* in either the order (L_p, R_p) or (R_p, L_p). These two strategies are considered as two states of a Markov process, with the transitions between them being probabilistically determined by the stimulus on the previous trial. (Higher-level strategies, not considered here, might consist of the selection by the subject of the *probabilities* of switching from one state to the other.) Each node of the tree in Figure 2.31(a) is represented in the model by a probabilistic mixture of two latency distributions, where the proportions in the mixture are determined by the stimulus history. This simple two-state model was used to represent one subject's data, subject P, illustrated in Figure 2.31(a). For others, such as subject F, whose data are shown in Figure 2.31(b), Falmagne used more complex multistate models.

The data of subject P are graphed in Figure 2.31(c) in a two-dimensional operating space; that is, each point represents the left and right RTs, RT_{Left} *vs.* RT_{Right}, for a particular stimulus history. The dashed line connects the second-order data points; that is, the points are conditional on the stimulus presented on the previous two trials. Data from subject E are shown in Figure 2.31(d). Although Falmagne and colleagues (1975) fit these subjects with different models, the data of the two subjects are quite similar in showing an operating characteristic that is concave *away* from the origin. This apparently pathological operating characteristic results from collapsing onto the two dimensions of the graph data that are actually embedded in a four-dimensional operating space consisting of RTs to the left and right stimuli for various stimulus histories and of the corresponding left and right accuracy levels. A two-dimensional strategy (choices of two operating levels, one on the left and one on the right speed–accuracy trade-off) is projected on the one-dimensional performance operating characteristic shown in Figures 2.31(c) and 2.31(d). In the middle of the performance operating characteristic, the subjects respond slowly and minimize errors. At the extremes of the performance operating characteristic when, because of the trial history, the subjects are willing to guess what the next stimulus will be, they adopt a riskier strategy that yields faster RTs but more errors when the unexpected stimulus occurs. The midpoint strategy is not inferior to a mixture of the end-point strategies; it exceeds the mixture strategy in "accuracy," a dimension not portrayed in the two-dimensional graphs of Figures 2.31(c) and 2.31(d).

Falmagne and colleagues (1975) fit a two-state mixture model to the data of subject P, and the solid line in Figure 2.31(c) is drawn through the second-order values from the model estimates. This is not quite a straight-line mixture here because the model selects separate error rates for left and right conditions, requiring that more errors be made on the less likely stimulus. Thus the probability mixtures from the two latency distributions need not be the same for the left and right conditions. Their two-state Markov model predicts a performance operating characteristic that is concave in the opposite direction from the data. (Falmagne and colleagues' more complex model assumes a mixture of four latency distributions and several error levels and fits the pattern of data reasonably well.)

8.3.2.2. Dimensional Constraints. Falmagne and colleagues' (1975) simple two-state Markov model uses one parameter (the proportion of each state in the RT mixture) to fit all the different operating points on the performance operating characteristics that result from different sequences of prior trials. They use one parameter to describe movement along an operating characteristic that lies in a four-dimensional operating space (two accuracies, two RTs). A one-dimensional model requires the data to lie on a *curve* (not necessarily straight) in four-dimensional operating space. This one-dimensional constraint on the data was not investigated and may or may not have been satisfied. The two-dimensional projections of the data in Figures 2.31(c) and 2.31(d) suggest that the data do lie on a line in two-dimensional space but, unfortunately, not the line required by the Markov model. The random walk model (Link, 1975; Link & Heath, 1975) has two free parameters (two boundaries) and could, in principle, fit data that lie on a two-dimensional *surface* in four-dimensional operating space. There are no standard statistical methods for determining the dimensionality of data that are not describable by a linear model (such as factor analysis), but investigators should attempt to judge the dimensionality of their data by looking at various two-dimensional projections of the data before a commitment is made to a particular model or class of models.

8.3.2.3. Ordered Memory Scanning in Memory-Retrieval Paradigms. Markov models have been proposed for more complex choice RT paradigms. Theios, Smith, Haviland, Trupman, and Moy (1973) use a buffer model (of items in short-term memory) to predict data of memory-search experiments based on Sternberg's (1966) paradigm. In this choice-reaction paradigm, the subject is presented with a single stimulus on each trial. The subject must make either a positive response (e.g., push a button with the right hand when the stimulus is chosen from a set of "positive" items) or a negative response (e.g., push a button with the left hand when the stimulus is chosen from the "negative" pool of items). Theios and colleagues experimentally varied the number and the presentation probabilities of the items in the positive and negative sets. Their model predicts both the memory-scanning data ($\overline{RT}$ is an increasing linear function of the number of memory items) and the effects of stimulus probability for both positive and negative stimuli ($\overline{RT}$ is faster for more probable stimuli).

Theios and colleagues' model consists of a memory buffer that contains a list of all the positive- and negative-stimulus items, each item being paired with its appropriate response.

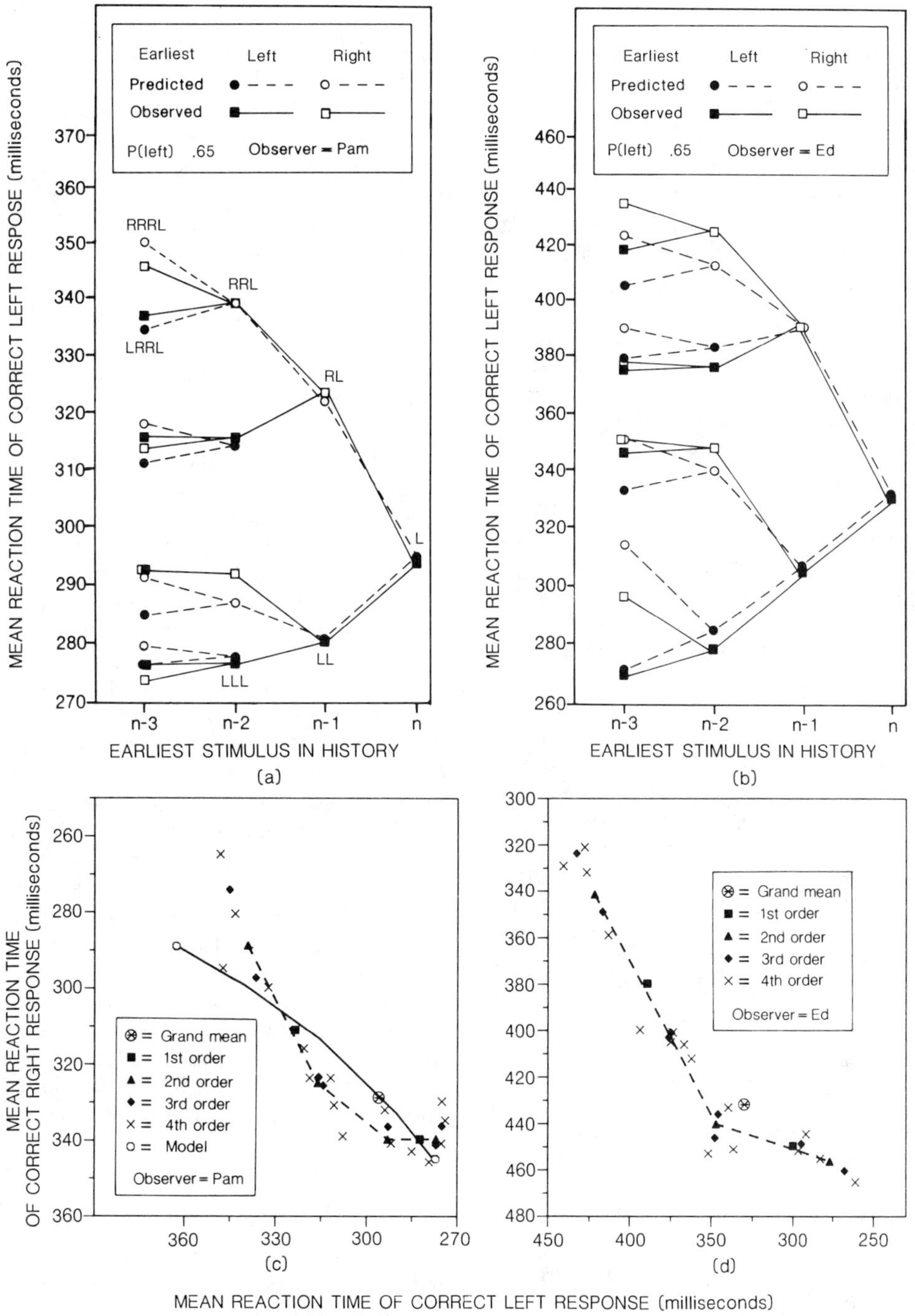

Figure 2.31. Tree-graph and operating-space representations of sequential dependency data from a choice reaction time (RT) experiment by Falmagne, Cohen, and Dwivedi (1975). (a) Tree graph. The abscissa is the number of the earliest preceding trial in the conditional analysis (the current trial is *n*), and the ordinate is the mean RT of a correct left response. Each node on the tree diagram is the mean correct RT conditionalized on the stimulus history of preceding trials, with third-order (three-trial) histories appearing on the left and zero order on the right. The trial history (e.g., RRRL) is indicated for seven representative nodes. Data points are filled if the earliest trial in the history is left and unfilled if it is right. Data for one stimulus, left, and one subject, Pam, are shown. (b) Same conventions and format as (a), but for subject Ed. (c) The data of panel (a), combined with the data for correct right responses, graphed in two-dimensional operating space. The axes are mean correct RT to a right stimulus and mean correct RT to a left stimulus, oriented so that fast performance is up and to the right. The dashed line connects the *empirical* second-order points which are, from top to bottom: (RRL, RRR), (LRL, LRR), (RLL, RLR), (LLL, LLR). The two open circles represent the estimated parameters of the two pure states of Falmagne and colleagues' Markov mixture model; the solid line connecting the two pure states is drawn through the four model-estimated second-order points. (d) Same format as (c), the data of subject Ed. Falmagne and colleagues used a more complex, four-state mixture model (not shown) to predict Ed's data. The "pathological" (concave-up) operating characteristics in (c) and (d) probably result from projecting a convex four-dimensional performance operating characteristic (left and right reaction times, left and right error rates) into two dimensions. (a. and b. from J. C. Falmagne, S. P. Cohen, & A. Dwivedi, Two choice reactions as an ordered memory scanning, *Attention and performance* (Vol. 5). © 1975 by Academic Press. Reprinted with permission.)

When a stimulus is presented, the buffer is scanned from top (beginning) to bottom (end) until the matching item, which contains the information defining the correct response, is found. At this point, the search terminates, and a response process is initiated. (If the matching item is not in the buffer, the subject must search a long-term memory.) This is a *serial, self-terminating* scan. Reaction time predictions are based on the length of time (about 35 msec) that it takes to compare stimulus to memory items. On each trial, there is a certain probability that the subject will change the order of items in the buffer by moving the current stimulus to the top (the most favorable scan position). In this model, each possible ordering of the buffer corresponds to a search strategy or state. (A higher-order strategy would consist of the selection of the *probability* of moving the current item to the top of the buffer and possibly the selection of the buffer length.) Overall RTs to a particular stimulus in Theios and colleagues' (1973) model are the result of a mixture of many possible states that depends on recent presentation history. This dynamic aspect of the buffer corresponds to Falmagne and colleagues' (1975) dynamic two-item buffer and is the basis of the accurate prediction of stimulus probability effects.

Raaijmakers and Shiffrin (1981) propose a model to account for recall of experimentally learned word lists. According to their model, studying a list of words results in a stored matrix of interitem strengths, where general context may also serve as an item. Upon a request to recall, the subject uses any experimenter-provided recall cues (list items and/or the context item) to prompt retrieval from memory, with retrieved items then possibly serving as retrieval cues in the next cycle of list retrieval. Recall is based on a selection of retrieved items that satisfy the recall criteria. The item or items retrieved are probabilistically determined by the stored matrix of interitem strengths and the particular cue set being used.

Raaijmakers and Shiffrin's (1981) model is even more complex than the model of Falmagne and colleagues (1975) or Theios and colleagues (1973). Performance on a given trial depends both on higher-level subject-selected strategies (i.e., number of unsuccessful iterations of the cue-retrieval cycle before stopping and the number of cue-retrieval cycles before changing the retrieval cue) and on the (probabilistic) order in which new items are recalled. Performance over trials consists of a mixture of these strategy-dependent single-trial performances.

8.4. Blocked versus Randomized Procedures in Speed–Accuracy Trade-off

To observe a speed–accuracy trade-off in a classical, choice RT procedure requires a blocked design in which payoffs, deadlines, or speed instructions are varied between blocks of trials. The problem with the blocked design is that strategy also varies between blocks. The experimenter cannot observe the effect of the speed manipulation on a particular strategy because the manipulation itself induces changes in strategy. For example, in a deadline experiment, the subject may use completely different strategies depending on the deadline in force. A fast deadline induces fast guesses or alternative computations, not interrupted long computations. Change of strategy is a probable confounding variable in blocked RT experiments.

The cued-response procedure (Dosher, 1976, 1979, 1981, 1982; Reed, 1973) allows different speed–acuracy trade-off conditions to be conducted in a mixed-list design. It currently is the only procedure available to obtain speed–accuracy trade-offs without the strategy confound. In this respect, it shares the good properties of the mixed-list designs (see Section 7.4) for eliminating strategy confound in partial report and in search paradigms.

However, not all strategy effects are eliminated in mixed-list designs. The memory-search and Falmagne's choice RT experiments used mixed-list designs in which all the conditions of interest are intermixed in one long sequence of trials. Nevertheless, sequential strategy effects, for example, the ordering of items in a memory buffer, were prominent. Strategy varied depending on the recent stimulus history, and these strategy variations presumably also occur in the cued-response procedure.

8.5. Mixed Strategies in Production and Performance

Consider the primitive plowshares-swords economy. Suppose it is decided to devote half the economy to each goal. Does it make any difference whether on every odd-numbered day of the year the whole economy is devoted to agriculture and on every even-numbered day the economy is devoted to defense production (mixed strategy) versus the case where on all days the resources are divided in half and equally devoted to each goal (pure strategy)? Certainly! The pure strategy is far more efficient in terms of the production facilities needed. But even if production facilities were not at issue, only the availability of labor, it would still be more efficient to divide labor equally on every day than to alternate days. The reason is that if even one laborer were more efficient at making plowshares than swords, it would be efficient to assign the person to the task to which he or she is better suited. By similar reasoning, with respect to any resource, a pure strategy is preferable whenever resources are not completely equal and interchangeable, with respect to the economic goals. This is the line of argument used previously to demonstrate that production possibility frontiers are always concave toward the origin. A mixed strategy does not take advantage of the curvature; it always lies closer to the origin and is of lower utility than the corresponding pure strategy. See Figure 2.29 in Section 8.1. There is inherent superiority in a pure strategy—optimal for the situation—over a mixture of less-than-optimal strategies.

Given the economic superiority of pure over mixed strategies, it is reasonable to ask, What limitation in allocation of mental processing resources prevents the utilization of pure strategies in human divided attention tasks? One possible answer is that there is a single processor or process involved in concurrent tasks and that there is a changeover delay incurred in switching this resource from task to task. Switching the resource within a trial produces unacceptable costs. An analogous problem occurs in computer time-sharing systems in switching from one user to another. There is an overhead cost (time and memory) incurred in swapping a second user's program into the central processor unit and the first user's program out into a buffer until it again gains access to the central processor unit. Trying to divide time too finely results in too many swaps per second with a corresponding, disproportionately high overhead cost. In the limit, as time is too finely divided between users, no useful work gets done, only swapping. Changeover costs have some interesting consequences in other systems as well; these are considered in Section 9.

8.6. Contingency Analysis of Strategies

8.6.1. Contingency Analysis: Attendance Example. To explore the properties of strategy mixtures in attention operating characteristics, consider an extreme classroom attendance example. Two courses are offered at precisely overlapping time periods, say noon until 1:00 P.M. See Figure 2.32(b). Suppose a student attends only Course 1 (strategy S_1). This student's performance is perfect on examinations for Class 1, zero for Class 2. Another student who attends only Class 2 (strategy S_2) has perfect performance for Class 2, zero for Class 1. To produce an equal mixture of the strategies, S_{1+2}, a third student (M) flips a fair coin each day before class to determine which class to attend. His performance with S_{1+2} is 50% on examinations for each course. On the other hand, a fourth student (P) attends Class 1 from noon to 12:30 and Class 2 from 12:30 to 1:00, a pure strategy. Student P also scores 50% on each class's examinations. How can we discriminate student M's mixture of strategies from student P's pure strategy?

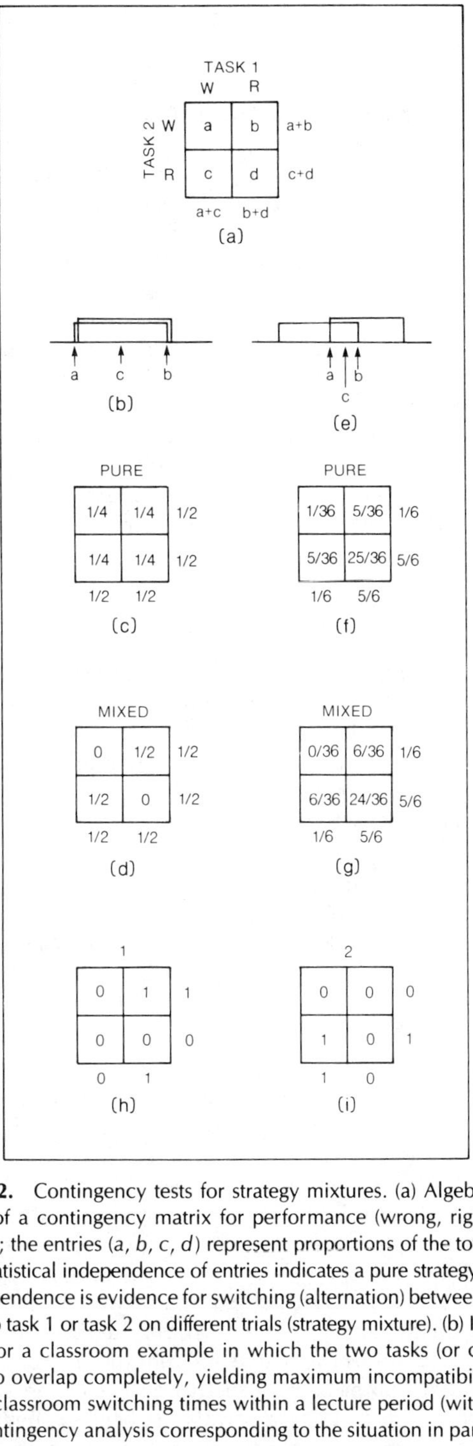

Figure 2.32. Contingency tests for strategy mixtures. (a) Algebraic representation of a contingency matrix for performance (wrong, right) on two tasks (1, 2); the entries (*a*, *b*, *c*, *d*) represent proportions of the total number of trials. Statistical independence of entries indicates a pure strategy; deviation from independence is evidence for switching (alternation) between strategies to attend to task 1 or task 2 on different trials (strategy mixture). (b) Information densities for a classroom example in which the two tasks (or classes) are assumed to overlap completely, yielding maximum incompatibility; *a*, *b*, *c* represent classroom switching times within a lecture period (within a trial). (c) The contingency analysis corresponding to the situation in panel (b) with a pure strategy of changing classes at time c. (d) Contingency analysis corresponding to a 50 to 50% mixture over days of changing classroom at times *a* or *b*. The matrices resulting from the two pure strategies a or *b* are shown in (h) and (i). Panels (e), (f), and (g) correspond to (b), (c), and (d), but show a situation where classes are only partly incompatible. The expected performance difference between the pure strategy (f) and strategy mixture (g) is very small (0.03) in this case.

When a performance operating characteristic (POC) is strictly concave, then a mixture of strategies lies on a straight line away from the curved POC. Insofar as an intermediate point y on a POC lies above the line representing the mixture of its neighbors (a and b), it cannot represent the mixture of strategies that gave rise to a and b but represents a new strategy. This test can be generalized. Suppose it is established that at least n straight-line segments are required to approximate a curved POC. Then there are at least $n + 1$ different strategies. In the limit (for example, in the usual signal detection case with Normal distributions assumed for noise and signal plus noise and with a continuously variable criterion), an infinite number of possible strategies is assumed.

The problem with using the shape of the POC to infer the number, or existence, of possible intermediate strategies is that it is a statistically weak test when the POC is not very curved and it is useless when the POC is straight, as it is in the classroom example. Nevertheless, a strong differentiation between a strategy mixture and an intermediate pure strategy is possible by considering joint performance on the two tasks. For each day, consider the examination questions asked about the material covered on that day in each classroom. For simplicity, it is assumed that just one question is asked by each instructor. There are four possible outcomes of the joint response to these questions: a student can correctly answer both, neither, or one question from either one of the two classes. These outcomes are represented in the 2 × 2 contingency table in Figure 2.32(a). In the mixed strategy, student M attends all of one class or the other. Student M always answers the question from the attended class correctly, always fails the other question, never answers both questions correctly, and never misses both. See Figure 2.32(d) which illustrates performance with the mixed strategy; the performance with the component strategies of the mixture is shown in Figure 2.32(h) and (i). Over the whole examination, with questions asked about many days, student M's performance will average out to 50% in each class, as shown in Figure 2.32(d).

On the other hand, if it is assumed that instructors construct their examination questions independently and that they are equally likely to probe information offered in the first half as in the second half of the class period, then student P, who switches classes halfway through the period, is as likely to answer any examination question as any other. Student P's pure strategy results in a contingency matrix in which all cells have equal probability (see Figure 2.32(c)). Thus the pure strategy results in a contingency matrix in which there is statistical independence components, for example, for the matrices in Figure 2.32, $(d) = \frac{1}{2}(h) + \frac{1}{2}(i)$.

8.7. Strategy Mixture in Attention Operating Characteristics

8.7.1. Visual Search. The attention operating characteristics (see Figure 2.15 in Section 5.3.2) reported by Sperling and Melchner (1978a, 1978b) are nearly straight lines. The extreme strategies are "give 90% of your attention to the inside" and "to the outside," respectively. The equal-attention strategy is near the midpoint of these extremes. One may ask, Can the contingency matrix tell us whether the equal-attention strategy is a pure strategy (attention sharing) or whether it is a mixture of two extreme strategies?

The answers differ little for the three different task combinations in Sperling and Melchner. In no case were the data powerful enough to reject the switching mixture hypothesis (switching attention strategies between trials). However, the sharing hypothesis could be rejected for concurrent search for large and for small targets and for concurrent search for numerals and for letters. For the concurrent search of noise-masked and normal numerals, performance was so close to the independence point (similar to the case shown in Figures 2.32(e), 2.32(f), and 2.32(g)) that the mixed strategy and pure strategy predictions of the equal-attention matrix do not differ enough to make a discrimination feasible. Although mixture cannot be rejected for any individual subject or condition, all the data deviate somewhat from the pure mixture predictions in the direction of sharing. Thus the most likely conclusion is that strategies entering into the mixture in the equal-attention conditions are not quite as extreme as the strategies employed in "give 90% of your attention" conditions. In other words, there are more than two strategies. Equal attention is achieved by probabilistic mixing of strategies that allocate more resources to one or the other class of target, but not such an extreme allocation as is the case with the instruction: "give 90% of your attention" to one class of target.

8.7.2. Switching Attention versus Switching Strategies. There are two uses of the word *switch* that need to be carefully distinguished. In the classroom example, there is the switch from one class to another. This first use refers to a switch within a trial. It denotes a particular allocation of resources, time, produced by allocating time first to Class 1 and then to Class 2.

The second use of *switch* is a change between trials in the allocation of resources—a strategy switch. The contingency analysis dealt with between-trials strategy switching.

An attention switch can refer to either a within- or between-trials shift. Within a trial, an attention shift is analogous to a classroom switch. For example, if a subject always attended to the left half of an array to be searched during the first half of the processing interval and to the right half during the remainder, that would be a pure strategy involving a simple switch of attention. A between-trials switch of attention occurs, for example, when the subject sometimes attends first to the left and other times attends first to the right half of the array. Such strategy alternation represents a strategy switch (or strategy mixture).

All the psychological examples in this chapter have considered only the case of a single switch of resources, as in the classroom example. When multiple switches (e.g., back and forth between classes) are possible, the resulting performance is not *in practice* discriminable from a sharing strategy (standing in the hallway between classrooms) for the examples considered here.

8.8. Contingency Analysis in Speed–Accuracy Trade-off: Microtrade-offs and Conditional Accuracy Functions

Speed–accuracy performance operating characteristics result from compound (not concurrent) tasks. Nevertheless, a type of contingency analysis can be performed on speed–accuracy trade-off data, a contingency analysis examining the extent to which accuracy is related to response time *within* a given speed stress (within a single point on the operating characteristic). There are two methods for performing such an analysis: (1) conditionalizing on correct or error responses and observing mean RT (called *microtrade-off analysis* by Pachella, 1974) and (2) conditionalizing on RT and observing accuracy (called *conditional accuracy functions* by Lapin & Disch, 1972; Woods & Jennings, 1976).

8.8.1. Fast-Guess Model

8.8.1.1. Microtrade-off. The fast-guess model (Section 8.3.1) clearly predicts that within any speed-stress condition, errors should be faster than correct responses, but observing a statistically significant difference requires a condition with reasonably high overall accuracy. This prediction is derived as follows: in the fast-guess model, all error responses are the result of fast guesses; correct responses result from a mix of stimulus-controlled processing and correct guesses. When the proportion α of a fast guess is very high (e.g., 1.0), correct and error reaction times (RTs) will be essentially identical since both arise from the guess RT distribution. As the proportion α of fast guesses declines and overall accuracy improves, the mean RT for correct and error responses should diverge. Yellott (1971) derived a more specific prediction of the fast-guess model. The weighted difference between mean correct and error RT should be linear with $p_c - p_e$.

$$p_c \overline{RT}_c - p_e \overline{RT}_e = k(P_c - p_e) \ . \tag{14}$$

Here p represents probability, $\overline{RT}$ represents mean RT, and the subscripts c and e refer to correct and error responses, respectively. Yellott (1967, 1971) presented data from several choice RT experiments for two highly discriminable stimuli (red and green lights) which met this constraint. Whether the fast-guess model holds in any particular situation must be empirically determined.

8.8.1.2. Conditional Accuracy Functions. Equation (14) describes a microtrade-off relation—mean RT as a function of accuracy. When conditional accuracy functions are measured, the fast-guess model simply predicts that accuracy should be strictly monotonically increasing with RT (Pachella, 1974).

8.8.1.3. Fixed-Point Property. Although it is not a contingency analysis, a second strong test of the fast-guess model exists. Under the fast-guess model, the RT probability density function (*pdf*) for any speed-stress condition is a weighted mixture of two source *pdf*s, the fast-guess *pdf* and the stimulus-controlled *pdf*. Different speed-stresses vary only in the weighting of the two source *pdf*s. When this is true, the various speed-stress *pdf*s must observe the *fixed-point property* (Falmagne, 1968). At the point x^* where the two source *pdfs* cross, the height $h^* = p(x^*)$ of the two *pdf*s is identical. Therefore, no matter what the mixture, the height of the resulting *pdf* at x^* must be h^*. A failure of *pdf*s from different speed-stress conditions to show a fixed point (x^*,h^*) constitutes a rejection of the fast-guess model. This test has generally not been applied to speed–accuracy trade-off data; it is more convenient but less powerful than the factor-analytic approach that has been recommended here for the analysis of mixtures.

8.8.1.4. Conclusion. The microtrade-off prediction (faster errors than correct responses) and the conditional accuracy prediction (monotonic increasing $\overline{RT}(P_c)$) can both be tested within a single condition of speed test. For fast choice RTs to simple sensory stimuli, these predictions obtain, but they do not strongly differentiate, the fast-guess from other models. Equation (14) and the fixed-point property can be tested only between conditions. These predictions have not fared as well.

8.8.2. Other Models. How different are the predictions concerning microtrade-offs for other models of speed–accuracy trade-off? Although discrete-state Markov processes were introduced in Section 8.3.2, the main alternative to the fast-guess model considered in this chapter has been the random walk model. So far it has been necessary to consider random walk models only in a general way. A criterion shift (starting point or boundary) in the random walk model is a shift between pure strategies. It turns out, however, that the form of the predicted microtrade-off for a random walk model depends on the detailed assumptions of those models. The simple discrete random walk model considered by Pachella (1974) predicts equal RTs for correct responses and errors. The more complicated, discrete random walk model developed by Link and Heath (1975) assumes a possibly asymmetric distribution of steps (drift distribution) to allow faster error than correct responses. (Specifically, Link and Heath assume an asymmetric moment generating function so that the step distribution is skewed in the direction of an error.) Alternatively, Pachella noted that if a criterion of a random walk model varies from trial to trial *within* a speed stress or block (i.e., if there is strategy mixture in the random walk), this also produces faster errors than correct response. Finally, Ratcliff (1978) proposed a generalization of a continuous random walk where drift rates for "positive" and "negative" trials are normally distributed and typically overlapping. In his version of the random walk model, errors are primarily the result of the overlapping tails of the drift rate distributions, and tend to have longer RTs. Thus every possible microtrade-off pattern is consistent, at least in a general way, with some version of a random walk model. Discriminating between models requires, as usual, convergent data from many conditions and experiments.

8.9. Summary

The fine-grained analysis of signal detection experiments made possible an accurate and powerful description of the subject's implicit decision strategies. In the case of concurrent detection tasks, the analysis could be extended to the strategies governing the implicit allocation of mental processing resources. A similar analysis in the domain of RT experiments revealed complex, implicit decision processes that molded the subject's performance to the experimentally imposed demands. Section 9.2 demonstrates that it is possible to measure the dynamics of implicit resource allocation strategies with the same precision as one typically measures observable motor responses. Just as in physics, where elementary particles are not directly observable but can be inferred with great precision from their effects, the cognitive strategies involved in processing information are not directly observable but can be inferred and measured with mathematical precision.

9. PATH DEPENDENCE AND THE DYNAMICS OF STRATEGY SWITCHING

The discussion of strategies and strategy mixtures in attention operating characteristics has so far ignored the question of whether one strategy can be traded or changed for another without any changeover costs whatsoever. For example, the optimal-search models of Section 7 incorporated no changeover or sharing costs. The alternative is that a strategy switch (e.g., a switch of attention from one focus to another) entails a changeover cost. This section describes the general phenomena of path dependence that occur whenever there are changeover costs. Path dependence is widespread in studies of performance. Examples are given from partial reports in iconic memory, signal detection, and reaction time (RT) studies. These examples deal with trial-to-trial changes in strategy. Within a trial, the *attention-reaction time procedure* is shown to offer a comprehensive method for measuring the dynamics of shifting attention.

9.1. Path Dependence in Performance Operating Characteristics

9.1.1. Path Dependence in Classroom Attendance

9.1.1.1. Path Dependence within a Single Day. The simplest situation in which to discover effects of changeover costs is the classroom example of Section 2. Suppose that when a student was ready to run from class 1 to class 2, the second class was located not in an adjacent room but in a different building and the trip between classes would consume 5 minutes. Clearly, there would be no point in switching from class 1 to class 2 unless the information being offered in class 2 were so much more valuable that it could compensate for the lost time.

The effect of a changeover cost is to maintain the status quo. The student remains in the present classroom, even when another class would be slightly more useful, because the additional utility is insufficient to compensate for the changeover cost. The student's current classroom reflects not only the current utility of the competing classes but also reflects the past history that brought the student to the present class. A class that was useful in the recent past holds students even after its utility has slipped below that of its competitors. The dependence of the response to the present stimulus on the response to immediately preceding stimulus is called *path dependence*.

The kind of path dependence exemplified by the persistence of previous modes of response is sometimes referred to as *hysteresis*, a reference to the electromagnetic phenomenon in which a magnetic substance tends to retain its previous magnetic orientation even after an oppositely directed external inducing field has been applied. The new field, had the previous magnetic orientation been neutral, would have been sufficient to induce a change. Of course, hysteresis can be overcome; it simply requires a stronger external inducing field. Energy is lost in a hysteresis cycle, related to the amount of path dependence, with no energy being lost when there is no hysteresis. See Figure 2.33(a).

The classroom dilemma is analogous to magnetic hysteresis. Students can be induced to switch classes, provided the required differential benefit is sufficient to overcome the cost. The classroom-switching cost, lost information during changeover, is loosely analogous to lost energy in hysteresis. (A better analogy with magnetic hysteresis is the loss in information due to the student's being in a nonoptimal classroom; see Figure 2.33(b).) When classes are adjacent and there is no changeover delay, there also is no path dependence, no hysteresis, and no lost information; see Figure 2.33(c). The student's strategy at any and every instant of time can be optimal for that instant.

There is an interesting heuristic representation of path-dependent effects in *catastrophe theory* (Thom, 1975; Thom &

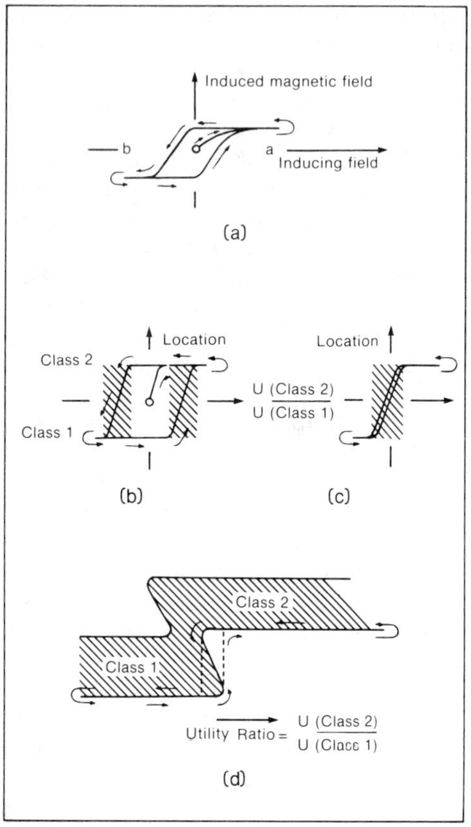

Figure 2.33. Schematic analysis of path dependence in classroom attendance. (a) Hysteresis in a piece of magnetized iron. The inducing field is initially neutral (open circle) and then varies back and forth between *a* and *b*, indicated on the abscissa. The ordinate indicates the induced magnetic orientation of the microcrystals in the iron. The curved arrows indicate the time sequence. (b) Hysteresis in the classroom. Two courses are offered; the ratio of their utilities, *UR* = *U*(*Class* 2)/*U*(*Class* 1) is varied periodically during a long class period. Initially (open circle) the inexperienced student is midway between classes. The information being offered in class 2 is just becoming more valuable than in class 1, so the student runs to class 2 and remains there. Subsequently, class 1 becomes more valuable, so the student runs to it. As the utility of class 1 subsides, the student returns to class 2, and so on. Information is completely lost during transit (heavily shaded area) and partially lost during the time the student lingers in the less informative class (one-half of the clear center rectangle). (c) Classroom strategy of senior student. Being smarter than an iron crystal or an entering student, the person anticipates the future course of events. When in class 2, as its utility diminishes, the student leaves while it is still more valuable than class 1, knowing that by the time he or she has arrived in class 1 the relative utility will have reversed. The person loses information only as a result of transit (shaded area), never by being in the wrong classroom. (d) Catastrophe theory representation of the events in (b). The upper surface represents class 2, the lower surface class 1. The abscissa represents the control parameter, the utility ratio, *UR* = *U*(*Class* 2)/*U*(*Class* 1). When *UR* is varied and the student reaches a fold in the surface, the student jumps to the other surface and continues there. The jump is the "catastrophe" of catastrophe theory. (From G. Sperling, A unified theory of attention and signal detection, In R. Parasuraman and R. Davies (Eds.), *Varieties of attention*, Academic Press, 1984. Reprinted with permission.)

Zeeman, 1975; Zeeman, 1976). The classroom in which we find the student may be thought of as the dependent variable, which is under the control of an independent variable, the utility ratio of the material offered in the two competing classes. As the utility ratio changes, the state changes, as described above and as illustrated in Figure 2.33(d). The catastrophe occurs when the student switches from one surface (classroom) to the other at a fold in the surface. A useful aspect of the catastrophe theory representation is that all possible equilibrium states and the relations between them are clearly shown. A limitation of the catastrophe theory representation is that neither the dynamic aspects of the situation nor the underlying processes are represented. By itself, a catastrophe theory representation is an insufficient description of a dynamic system (Sperling, 1981; Sussman & Zahler, 1978).

9.1.1.2. Path Dependence between Days. The separated classrooms example illustrates how changeover costs (distance between classrooms) can cause a strategy (sitting in a particular classroom) to persist beyond the point at which it would be chosen if there were no changeover costs. A related, and more complex, phenomenon occurs in the student's choice of which classroom to enter on each day. Suppose two sessions of a course, Session 1 and Session 2, are being offered at exactly the same time. Initially, Session 1 is more informative than Session 2. With succeeding days, Session 2 improves and becomes more informative than 1. The student initially attends Session 1 and continues to attend it even after Session 2 has surpassed it. This kind of path dependence between trials has an honorable but intermittent history in the experimental psychology of attention under the pseudonyms of *set* and *Einstellung*. It, too, may be related to changeover costs—the costs to the student of discovering (by sampling the information offered in even the less advantageous session) which session currently is optimal. A related cost apparently is willingly incurred in probability matching (Restle, 1961), a phenomenon in which a subject occasionally chooses less-than-optimal gambles even when the optimal gamble could be chosen on every occasion (see Section 10).

9.1.2. Path Dependence in Partial Report Procedures. The example of path dependence in an iconic memory experiment was discussed in Section 7, and the data were shown in Figure 2.25. These data, which exhibit a textbook case of hysteresis, are from a subject reported in Sperling (1960). In this iconic memory experiment, cue delay was constant within a block; the cue delays were given in ascending, then descending, order for this subject, as indicated by the arrows. The subject gradually shifted from an equal-attention strategy to an attend-top-row strategy over a series of blocks but did not switch strategies soon enough. Thus there was hysteretic path dependence, a perseverance of previously appropriate strategies.

9.1.3. Path Dependence in Signal Detection Procedures. In an adaptive psychophysical procedure, the selection of successive stimuli is determined by the subject's responses to previous stimuli. These methods are sometimes called *up-down* procedures because the intensity of the next stimulus is varied up or down depending on whether the subject has just responded "nondetect" or "detect." The optimal rules for the determination of particular points on the psychometric function have been extensively investigated, and up-down procedures are widely used (Campbell & Lasky, 1968; Hall, 1981; Levitt, 1970; Pentland, 1980; Robbins & Monro, 1951; Taylor & Creelman, 1967).

The corresponding rules that should be adopted by a subject in setting an internal threshold criterion to optimize his or her responses have received somewhat less attention. Clearly the subject uses results of preceding trials to optimize detection parameters for the present trial (path dependence). Kac (1962, 1969) originally proposed a threshold criterion that essentially executed a random walk, adjusting appropriately up or down by a fixed amount whenever an error was made. It now appears that subjects vary their threshold criterion (nonoptimally) even when they have made a correct response and that while they move their threshold criterion in the direction of the optimum criterion (in response to changes in the probability of stimulus events), they do not move it far enough to optimize steady-state performance (Dorfman & Biderman, 1971; Kubovy & Healy, 1977; Schoeffler, 1965).

9.1.4. Path Dependence in Reaction-Time Procedures. In *stack* models of RT tasks, an ordered list of possible stimuli (the stack) is maintained in memory. Each stimulus item on the stack is paired with the appropriate response to be executed (see Section 8.3.2.). The order of the pairs on the stack determines the order in which comparisons of the current stimulus input to memory representations are carried out. Theios, Smith, Haviland, Trupman, and Moy (1973) propose a stack model for probability effects on RTs in memory search, and Falmagne, Cohen, and Dwivedi (1975) propose a stack model for probability effects in simple, choice RTs. In both models, the stack begins with the items in a random order and, with a probability less than 1.0, the current stimulus item causes its memory representation to advance to the head of the stack. Such a stack organizes itself to reflect a priori stimulus probabilities in terms of the mean positions of items in the stack.

As a choice RT experiment grinds inexorably on, a priori stimulus probabilities become quite well determined. The optimal strategy would appear to be to simply arrange the stack items in order of decreasing probability of occurrence and then to leave the stack unchanged until there is significant evidence that the experiment itself has been changed. Clearly this does not happen. Falmagne and colleagues' (1975) subjects change the stack according to the immediately preceding three or four stimuli, oblivious to the evidence provided by thousands of previous trials. While such a stack exhibits some hysteresis, it exhibits far too little; it is far too labile to approach optimality in a stationary environment. As in probability matching, the subject seems to give too much weight to unlikely events, although here the explanation is in terms of a decision strategy (to advance or not to advance an item in the stack) that uses no memory, being based entirely on the most recent event.

In random walk models of RT, strategy manifests itself as the choice of response thresholds for each of the alternative responses. The dynamics of how these choices are achieved have received scant attention. This is unfortunate because the dynamics of strategy choice in RT procedures, with the rich data of time, accuracy, and confidence, seem to be a promising, unexplored avenue of research.

9.2. Dynamics of an Attention Response

A particular state of attention is represented in a model by a particular allocation of mental processing resources; an attention shift is represented by a shift in resource allocation. The attention shift is not directly observable, but it can be inferred from its consequences. The RT of a motor response is the time from the onset of the reaction stimulus to the onset of the required response. Both the stimulus (e.g., a light flash) and the response (e.g., pressing a key) are trivial to measure. In the case of an attention response, the stimulus is easy to measure, but measuring the attention response requires ingenuity.

9.2.1. Measuring Attention Reaction Times. Because the attention response under study here involves "grabbing" an item from a list, the attention RT procedure is introduced by means of an analogous procedure for measuring the RT of a motor grabbing response. Figure 2.34 shows a subject seated adjacent to a conveyer belt, observing a screen upon which stimuli are displayed. The subject's task is to monitor the visual display until a visual target appears and then to reach through a small opening that gives access to the conveyer belt and to grab the first passing ball possible. The balls are numbered consecutively and arranged so that the ball numbered 1 passes the window exactly 0.1 sec after the target, the ball numbered 2 passes the window exactly 0.2 sec after the target, and so on. The subject reports the number of the ball that he or she has grabbed. From the reported number, the precise motor RT of the grabbing response can be inferred. Of course, the subject also knows the RT. To keep the subject honest, numbers on the balls must be scrambled so that, from the number, the experimenter can deduce the grabbing time but the subject can not. As a further refinement, a random one of the numbers could be omitted from all the balls on each trial. If the subject ever reported that number, it would immediately indicate a flaw in the procedure.

The subject reports the number on the ball only several seconds after it was grabbed. From the reported number, the experimenter *infers* the RT of the grabbing response, which actually occurred much earlier. The latency of the verbal report has little to do with the latency of the grabbing response; the content of the verbal report is what reveals the grabbing RT. Obviously, this is an indirect method of measuring a RT. In the case of motor RT, we have a choice of direct or indirect measures of RT. In the case of attention responses, there is no visible

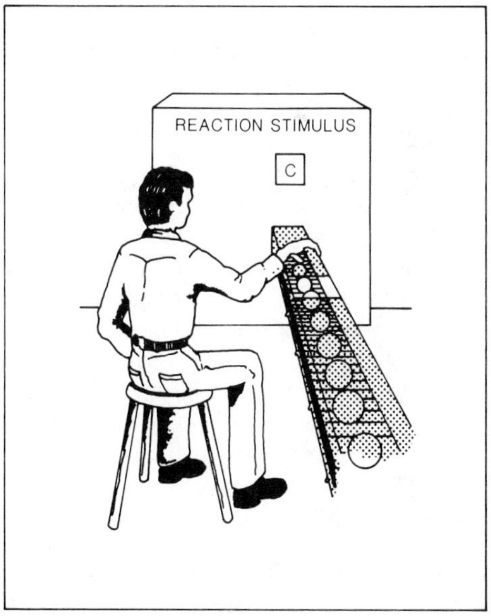

Figure 2.34. Measuring the reaction time (RT) of the "grabbing" response by the indirect method. The subject monitors the screen for the occurrence of the target stimulus. Instead of pressing a key as in traditional RT methods, the subject grabs the earliest possible ball from the conveyor belt. The number on the ball indicates its position in the sequence, thus providing an indirect measure of the RT. This is analogous to the indirect method used by Sperling and Reeves (1980) to measure the RT of an attention response. When a target is detected in one stimulus stream, the subject shifts attention to a stream of numeral stimuli and mentally grabs the earliest available stimulus. The subsequent verbal report of the identity of the numeral stimulus indicates its place in the sequence and, thereby, the attention RT.

response, nothing that can be directly observed; only indirect measures are possible. On the other hand, little is lost in the indirect measurement. Not only the mean but also the variance and, in fact, the whole RT distribution are obtained by the indirect method. The responses are perforce quantized into discrete times—there are balls passing only every 0.1 sec—but this is neither a serious problem nor a necessary aspect of the indirect procedure.

9.2.1.1. Mental Grabbing Response. To measure the reaction of a shift of visual attention, Sperling and Reeves (1976, 1978, 1980) used the following procedure. The subject maintained fixation on a fixation mark throughout a trial (see Sperling & Reeves, 1980, p. 349). To the left of fixation, a target appeared. In one series of experiments, the target was chosen at random from a letter *C*, a letter *U*, or an outline square. The target was embedded in a stream of distractors (consisting of the other letters of the alphabet) which were flashed briefly, one on top of the other, at a rate of 1 character per 110 msec. At the right of fixation, a stream of numerals occurred, one on top of the other, at either a fast rate of from 1 per 75 msec or, in other conditions, at rates as slow as 1 per 240 msec (see Figure 2.35).

The subject's task was to detect the target in the letter stream and then to report the first numeral available from the numeral stream. (In other conditions, the subjects had to report the earliest possible *four* numerals.) The task implicitly requires the subject to attend to the letter stream until the target is detected and then to shift attention to the numeral stream in order to grab the earliest numeral. The identity of the reported numeral is important only insofar as it indicates the numeral's temporal position. The attention RT on a trial is defined as the time from the onset of the target to the onset of the named numeral. From a block of trials, an entire attention RT distribution is obtained.

9.2.1.2. Critical Interval. There are certain important procedural considerations. In the measurement of a simple motor RT, for example, the interval between the warning stimulus, or trial initiation, and the occurrence of the target is varied randomly so that the RT experiment does not degenerate into an experiment in time estimation. Moreover, one cannot simply instruct the subject to "respond as quickly as possible." There must be explicit contingencies so that responses that occur before the target stimulus are punished as premature "anticipations"; responses occurring too late are punished for being "slow." The effect of such restrictions is to define a critical interval within which the response is supposed to occur (e.g., from 100–800 msec after target occurrence) and to reward the subject for responding as early as possible within the critical interval. Similar considerations hold in measuring the attention RT. As with the motor RT procedure, the beginning of the critical interval is placed so early that it cannot be achieved by a legitimate response. In the attention RT procedure, the numerals within the critical interval, as well as the one or two before and after it, are arranged to be all different, so that a report of a numeral's identity unambiguously indicates its position in the stream.

9.2.1.3. Simultaneous Attention and Motor Reaction Times. Using the motor and attention RT methods previously outlined, Reeves (1977) simultaneously measured motor and attention RTs for 3 subjects in 17 conditions, obtaining a total of over 50 pairs of attention and motor RT distributions. A representative pair of motor RT and attention RT distributions is illustrated in Figure 2.35. Although motor RT is measured by a *direct* method and attention RT by an *indirect* method, they are quite comparable in terms of their mean and variance. These data are typical of the attention RT procedure when the numeral stream occurs at a high rate (7 per sec or faster); with slow numeral rates, attention RTs become shorter than motor RTs.

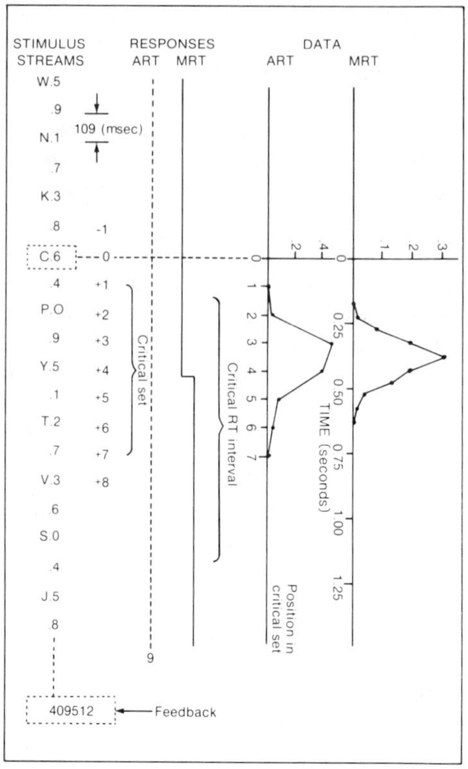

Figure 2.35. The results of measuring the reaction time (RT) of a shift of visual attention by the indirect method. Sample stimulus streams are shown at left. Letters in a stream are displayed one on top of the other in the same location, and the series represents time. The subject monitors the letter stream for the presence of a target, C in this case. The subject then shifts attention to the numeral stream and reports the earliest possible numeral. The seven numerals immediately following the target letter in time define the critical set, and correspond to the critical interval in a motor RT procedure. The attention RT panel shows the actual histogram of attention RTs derived from the position in the critical set of the numeral reported. The right-most panel shows a histogram of the concurrently measured motor RTs. (From G. Sperling & A. Reeves, Measuring the reaction time of an unobservable response, in R. Nickerson (Ed.), *Attention and performance VIII*, Lawrence Erlbaum, 1980. Reprinted with permission of the International Association for the Study of Attention and Performance.)

Attention RTs vary in a way similar to motor RTs with manipulations of target difficulty (both motor and attention RTs get slower for hard-to-detect targets) or target probability (both motor and attention RTs get faster as the likelihood of a target increases). The indirect method yields measures of attention RTs—unobservable responses—that are no less reliable and no more difficult to obtain than directly observable motor RTs. The indirect measurement of the dynamics of a reallocation of mental processing resources depends on the *effect* of the reallocation, on how soon the reallocated resources have an effect on behavior. The indirect method can, in principle, be extended to many other attentional tasks.

9.2.2. Order Properties in the Attention Response. In some blocks of trials, Sperling and Reeves (1980) asked their subjects to report the first four numerals following the target, not just the earliest numerals in the critical interval. The first of the four reported numerals in the report-four procedure was equivalent in all important respects to the only reported numeral in the report-one procedure. The three remaining numerals in the response provide data that are critical for models of attentional dynamics.

There are three main properties of the responses produced under the extended report procedure: *clustering*, *disorder*, and *folding*. The clustering property refers to the fact that the positions of the four numerals reported on any trial are generally clustered around the position of the peak of the attention RT distribution described in the previous section.

To compare the order of report in the four-numeral response to the actual order of the stimulus numerals, it is necessary to define a measure of order. Let i and j represent the stimulus positions of two reported items. Let iBj (read "i before j") represent the report of the item from position i before, earlier in the response than the item from position j. Let $i < j$ (read "i less than j") represent the fact that i occurred earlier than j in the stimulus. A pair of response items is in the correct order if $i < j$ and iBj or if $j < i$ and jBi. A comparison of stimulus and response item pairs shows that, at high numeral rates (13 per sec), almost half the response pairs are in the wrong order, and this is true for all separations of i and j. This represents total disorder in the response. At the slowest rate (4.6 per sec), about 75% of response pairs are in the correct order.

To describe the third response property, folding, it is useful to investigate P_{iBj}, the probability of reporting stimulus item i before item j, irrespective of whether $i < j$ or $j < i$. Graphs of P_{iBj} for all i and j in the critical set are shown in Figure 2.36.

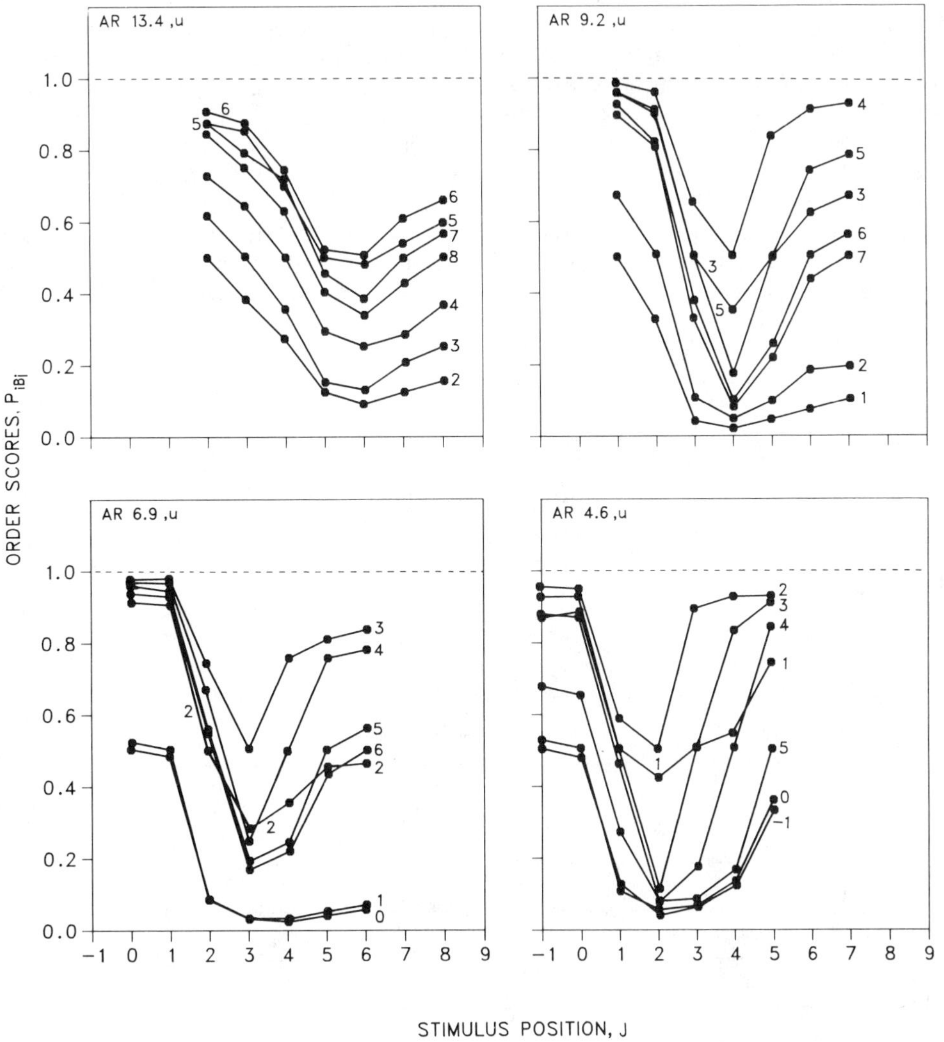

Figure 2.36. Order properties of the report of the first four numerals following a shift of visual attention. The experiment is identical to that outlined in Figure 2.35, except that the subject attempts to report the first four numerals following the target, rather than merely the first numeral following the target. The data shown are from one subject, AR, for four rates of display of the numeral stream (4.6, 6.9, 9.1, and 13.4 per sec) and for detection of the target *U*. The different horizontal placements of the data in various panels results from the different placements of the critical set. The ordinate, P_{iBj}, is the probability that the subject reports the item from stimulus position *i* before the item from stimulus position *j*. The curve parameter is *i*, and the abscissa is *j*. Mostly, the P_{iBj} data exhibit the property of laminarity, indicating that the order of report respects an internal order of strengths (e.g., 6, 5, 7, 8, 4, 3, 2 for 13.4 per sec) that is related to the objective stimulus order (2, 3, 4, 5, 6, 7, 8) by folding at position 6. (From A. Reeves & G. Sperling, Attentional theory of ordering information in short-term visual memory, *Mathematical studies in perception and cognition*, 1983, *83-7*. Reprinted with permission.)

The data exhibit the important property of *laminarity*, that is, the P_{iBj} versus j curves (for different values of i) do not cross each other.

Laminarity in Figure 2.36 is equivalent to the monotonicity property in multidimensional scaling. Provided that some other weak constraints are satisfied, monotonicity means there exists a consistent strength ordering of the stimulus positions (i) with the strongest position tending to be reported first, the next strongest second, and so on, and that all significant properties of the data are derivable from this ordering. The order of these strengths reveals the third property, folding. The strength (subjective order) is related to the objective order by folding. For example, in Figure 2.36, rate 9.2/sec, position 4 is strongest, followed alternately by earlier and later positions, vis-à-vis, 4, 5, 3, 6, 7, 2, 1.

A simple Thurstone Case V strength model accounts for 95% of the variance in Reeves and Sperling's (1983, 1986) data and demonstrates the usefulness of describing response order by examining pairs of items. The P_{iBj} measure makes available the full power of the well-established scaling methods originally developed for pair comparisons.

9.2.3. Gating Model of Attention Switching. A simple *gating model of attention switching* accounts for the complex properties of clustering, disorder, and folding that occur in the report of the first four items following an attention switch. The model assumes that an attention *gate* opens after a delay time τ following target presentation. Here τ represents the time required to detect the target and to initiate an attention response; τ depends on precisely the same factors that influence motor RT: difficulty of detecting the particular target, expectancy, and so on. The attention gate opens and closes as quickly as possible, but even the fastest gate action (which follows the time course illustrated in Figure 2.37) is slow by camera standards.

Items in the numeral string that enter through the attention gate accrue strength depending on the state of the gate. An analogy can be drawn to a snapshot taken with a shutter that opens and closes gradually: the exposure of objects in the snapshot is determined jointly by how long the object is displayed and how wide open the shutter is during the display time. The snapshot is developed, and the subject reports the items from the snapshot in order of their clarity, those items with the greatest exposure being reported first, and so on. This report produces the properties of clustering, disorder, and folding. There is clustering because objects that appear close in time to the moment of maximum gate opening will tend to have maximum strength. There is disorder and folding because objects that occur early during the attention gate have low-attention weighting and are reported intermixed with late-occurring items, after the middle items.

Apart from shifting attention, strategy occurs in the gating model as a stretching out of the duration of a gate opening (beyond the minimum) to admit more items. In fact, for the

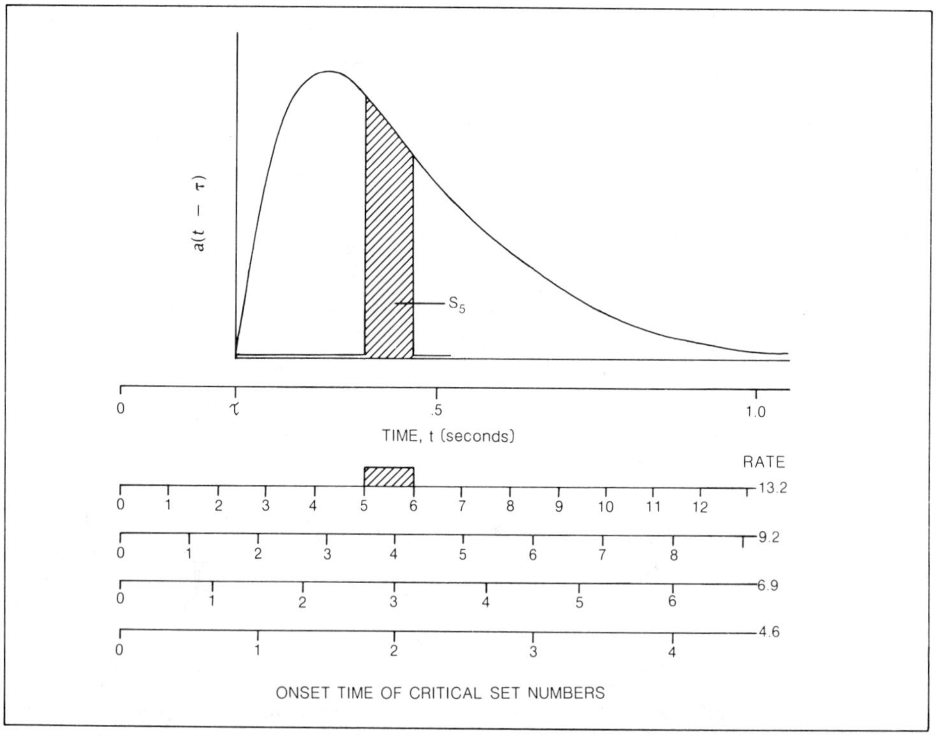

Figure 2.37. The gating model of the shift of visual attention from the letter (target) stream to the numeral stream for the Sperling and Reeves (1980) experiment. The bottom of the figure shows the temporal placement of the numerals at four different display rates; the period of availability of the fifth numeral at a rate of 13.2 per sec is illustrated. The model assumes that an attention gate begins to open at time τ and opens and closes gradually, as shown by the function $a(t)$. The memory strength S_i of item i is $S_i = \int_{t_i}^{t_{i+1}} a(t')dt'$, the total attention received from the onset of the numeral (t_i) to the onset of the following numeral (t_{i+1}), indicated for the +5 numeral by the shaded area S_5. Numerals are then reported in descending order of strength. This model accounts for the data of Figures 2.35 and 2.36. (From A. Reeves & G. Sperling, Attentional theory of ordering information in short-term visual memory, *Mathematical studies in perception and cognition*, 1983, *83-7*. Reprinted with permission.)

item rates (13.6–4.2 per sec) studied by Sperling and Reeves (1980) and analyzed by Reeves and Sperling (1983, 1986), this increase in gate opening did not seem to occur; stretching the moment of attention apparently requires still slower rates. The simple gating model, with only two parameters to describe the course of attention, and several to describe the detection delay τ as a function of stimulus conditions, accurately predicts hundreds of data points representing many different conditions and aspects of the data.

10. OPTIMIZATION?

Is all behavior arranged so as to optimize some utility function? To gain insight into the answer to this question, consider the following Gedanken experiment. A machine (or a computer program) is built so that it will optimize its behavior. Then a part of the machine is broken (or an instruction is perturbed) so that the resulting behavior becomes less than optimal. Perhaps this broken machine still could be described as optimizing a strange utility function, but whether or not this were possible, it obviously would be better described as a faulty machine that behaved nonoptimally in some circumstances.

Testing the hypothesis of optimization versus alternative hypotheses offers the same difficult problems as deciding between models in other domains, in which issues of accuracy, generality, simplicity, and efficiency must be weighed. However, the a priori evidence from considerations of biological evolution and human nature suggests that the hypothesis of optimization should be taken as a null hypothesis, the yardstick against which alternative hypotheses are matched.

For example, in two-alternative forced-choice gambling situations in which one alternative produces a reward on, say, 90% of the trials on which it is chosen and the other on, say, 30% of the trials, the optimal strategy is to always elect the highest-yield choice. Humans and other species do not do this. They occasionally elect the lower-yield choice, typically in the same 1:3 ratio as the reward ratio in this example, one of a large class of phenomena often described as probability matching (Estes, 1976; Herrnstein, 1974; Luce, 1959; Prelec, 1982; Restle, 1961; Thomas, 1975). While probability matching is a nonoptimal strategy under the very narrow constraints of the experimentally defined situation, in natural situations, as well as in encounters with real psychologist-experimenters, things do not always remain the way they seemed at first. In fact, when subjects fail to sample and to notice an alternative that the experimenter has cunningly advanced in relative value, they are convicted of "persistence of set," or *Einstellung* (Section 9.1.1.2). It is prudent to probe the environment to assess the current situation, even when such confirmatory information has a cost, as it does in probability-matching situations.

For optimum performance in choice reaction-time (RT) experiments with two alternatives, subjects should always prepare for the most likely alternative. Falmagne and colleagues (1975) found that their subjects did not do so (Section 8.3.2). The subjects' RTs depended on the stimuli that happened to have been presented in the immediately preceding three or four trials. Overall, the subjects' preparation for one or the other response alternative greatly resembles probability matching as observed in prediction experiments (Restle, 1961, chapter 6).

Falmagne and colleagues propose a two-state Markov model to account for their RT data. The probability matching in the differential response preparation results from the limited memory being used in decision making. The choice of strategy is limited to two alternative strategies (prepare for left, prepare for right) and the choice depends directly only on the last stimulus. All the information the subject may have acquired about stimulus probabilities from the observation of all the previous experimental events is represented by one of only two possible memory states. Here probability matching derives not from wisdom about the world but from meager computation.

Whether simple models (such as the two-state Markov model just described) that ignore optimization constraints in complex situations can adequately describe behavior is an unresolved empirical matter. And whether behavior, even if adequately described, can be understood without reference to optimization constraints is a matter of taste. However, intelligent behavior is seldom simple and seldom remains adequately described by a simple model once it has been intelligently investigated. Models that do not take expectations and uncertainty into account are likely to have as restricted a scope in the laboratory as they do in the real world.

REFERENCE NOTES

1. Sperling, G., & Harris, J. R. Unpublished experiments. Bell Laboratories, Murray Hill, N.J., 1976–1977.
2. Vorberg, D. *Bayesian estimation of arbitrary points on psychometric functions.* Presented at the 13th annual Mathematical Society Meeting, Madison, Wis., 1980.

REFERENCES

* References preceded by an asterisk are "key references."

Allport, D. A., Antonis, B., & Reynolds, P. On the division of attention: A disproof of the single channel hypothesis. *Quarterly Journal of Experimental Psychology*, 1972, *24*, 225–235.

Anstis, S. M. A chart demonstrating variations in acuity with retinal position. *Vision Research*, 1974, *14*, 589–592.

*Audley, R. J. Some observations on theories of choice reaction time: Tutorial review. In S. Kornblum (Ed.), *Attention and performance IV*. New York: Academic Press, 1973.

Bamber, D. The area above the ordinal dominance graph and the area below the receiver operating characteristic graph. *Journal of Mathematical Psychology*, 1975, *12*, 387–415.

Bamber, D., & van Santen, J. P. H. How many parameters can a model have and still be testable? *Journal of Mathematical Psychology*, in press.

Bashinski, H. S., & Bacharach, V. R. Enhancement of perceptual sensitivity as the result of selectively attending to spatial locations. *Perceptions and Psychophysics*, 1980 *28*, 241–248.

Bevan, W., Hardesty, D. L., & Avant, L. L. Response latency with constant and variable interval schedules. *Perceptual and Motor Skills*, 1965, *20*, 969–972.

*Bouma, H. Visual search and reading: Eye movements and functional visual field: A tutorial review. In J. Requin (Ed.), *Attention and performance VII*. Hillsdale, N.J.: Erlbaum, 1978.

Brebner, G. M. T., & Welford, A. T. In A. T. Welford (Ed.), *Reaction times*. New York: Academic Press, 1980.

Broadbent, D. E. The role of auditory localization in attention and memory span. *Journal of Experimental Psychology*, 1954, *47*, 191–196.

Broadbent, D. E. *Perception and communication*. London: Pergamon Press, 1958.

Budiansky, J. T., & Sperling, G. *GSLetters. A general purpose system for producing visual displays in real time and for running psychological experiments on the DDP24 computer.* Unpublished technical memorandum, Bell Laboratories, 1969.

Campbell, R. A., & Lasky, E. Z. Adaptive threshold procedures: BUDTIF. *Journal of the Acoustical Society of America*, 1968, *44*, 537–541.

*Carroll, J. D. Individual differences and multidimensional scaling. In R. N. Shepard, A. K. Romney, & S. Nerlove (Eds.), *Multidimensional scaling: Theory and applications in the behavioral sciences* (Vol. 1). New York: Seminar Press, 1972.

Cherry, E. C. Some experiments on the recognition of speech, with one and with two ears. *Journal of the Acoustical Society of America*, 1953, *25*, 975–979.

Cherry, E. C., & Taylor, W. K. Some further experiments on the recognition of speech with one and two ears. *Journal of the Acoustical Society of America*. 1954, *26*, 554–559.

Cohn, T., & Lasley, D. Detectability of a luminance increment: Effect of spatial uncertainty. *Journal of the Optical Society of America*, 1974, *64*, 1715–1719.

Craik, K. J. W. Theory of the human operation in control systems: II. Man as an element in a control system. *British Journal of Psychology*, 1948, *38*, 142–148.

Davis, F. T., Kramer, P., & Graham, N. Uncertainty about spatial frequency, spatial position, or contrast of visual patterns. *Perception and Psychophysics*, 1983, *33*, 20–28.

Dorfman, D. D., & Biderman, M. A leaning model for a continuum of sensory states. *Journal of Mathematical Psychology*, 1971, *8*, 264–284.

Dosher, B. A. The retrieval of sentences from memory: A speed-accuracy study. *Cognitive Psychology*, 1976, *8*, 291–310.

Dosher, B. A. Empirical approaches to information processing: Speed accuracy tradeoff functions or reaction time. *Acta Psychologica*, 1979, *43*, 347–359.

Dosher, B. A. The effects of delay and interference: A speed-accuracy study. *Cognitive Psychology*, 1981, *13*, 551–582.

Dosher, B. A. Effect of sentence size and network distance on retrieval speed. *Journal of Experimental Psychology: Learning, Memory and Cognition*, 1982, *8*, 173–207.

Dosher, B. A. Degree of learning and retrieval speed: Study time and multiple exposures. *Journal of Experimental Psychology: Learning, Memory and Cognition*, 1984, *10*, 541–574.

Drazin, D. H. Effects of foreperiod, foreperiod variability and probability of stimulus occurrence on simple reaction time. *Journal of Experimental Psychology*, 1961, *62*, 43–50.

Due, J. F. *Intermediate economic analysis*. Chicago: Richard D. Irwin, 1951.

Duncan, J. The demonstration of capacity limitation. *Cognitive Psychology*, 1980, *12*, 75–96.

*Egan, J. P. *Signal detection theory and ROC analysis*. New York: Academic Press, 1975.

Estes, W. K. The cognitive side of probability learning. *Psychological Review*, 1976, *83*, 37–64.

Falmagne, J. C. Note on a simple property of binary mixtures. *British Journal of Mathematical and Statistical Psychology*, 1968, *21*(1), 131–132.

Falmagne, J. C., Cohen, S. P., & Dwivedi, A. Two-choice reactions as an ordered memory scanning process. In P. M. A. Rabbitt & S. Dornic (Eds.), *Attention and performance V*. London: Academic Press, 1975.

Fisher, D. L. Limited-channel models of automatic detection: Capacity and scanning in visual search. *Psychological Review*, 1982, *89*, 662–692.

Fitts, P. M. Cognitive aspects of information processing: III. Set for speed versus accuracy. *Journal of Experimental Psychology*, 1966, *71*, 849–857.

*Galambos, J. *The asymptotic theory of extreme order statistics*. New York: Wiley, 1978.

Gilliom, J. D., & Sorkin, R. D. Sequential versus simultaneous two channel signal detection: More evidence for a high level interrupt theory. *Journal of the Acoustical Society of America*, 1974, *56*, 157–164.

Glucksberg, S., & Cowen, G. N. Memory for nonattended auditory material. *Cognitive Psychology*, 1970, *1*, 149–156.

Graham, N., Kramer, P., & Yager, D. Explaining uncertainty effects and probability summation. *Investigative Ophthalmology and Visual Science*, ARVO Supplement, 1983, *24*, 186.

*Green, D. M., & Luce, R. D. Speed-accuracy tradeoff in auditory detection. In S. Kornblum (Ed.), *Attention and performance IV*. New York: Academic Press, 1973.

*Green, D. M., & Swets, J. A. *Signal detectability and psychophysics*. New York: Wiley, 1966.

Grice, G. R. Stimulus intensity and response evocation. *Psychological Review*, 1968, *75*, 359–373.

*Gumbel, E. J. *Statistics of extremes*. New York: Columbia University Press, 1958.

Hall, J. L. Hybrid adaptive procedure for estimation of psychometric functions. *Journal of the Acoustical Society of America*, 1981, *69*, 1763–1769.

Harris, J. R., Shaw, M. L., & Bates, M. Visual search in multicharacter arrays with and without gaps. *Perception and Psychophysics*, 1979, *26*(1), 69–84.

Herrnstein, R. J. Formal properties of the matching law. *Journal of the Experimental Analysis of Behavior*, 1974, *21*, 159–164.

Hicks, J. R., & Allen, R. G. D. A reconsideration of the theory of value. *Economica*, 1934, *1*, 52–76, 196–219.

Hirsch, J., Hylton, R., & Graham, N. Simultaneous recognition of two spatial-frequency components. *Visison Research*, 1982, *22*, 365–375.

Hoffman, J. E., & Nelson, B. Spatial selectivity in visual search. *Perception and Psycophysics*, 1981, *30*, 283–290.

Howarth, C. I., & Lowe, G. Statistical detection theory of Piper's Law. *Nature*, 1966, *212*, 324–326.

Kac, M. A note on learning signal detection. *IRE Transactions on Information Theory*, 1962, *IT-8*, 126–128.

Kac, M. Some mathematical models in science. *Science*, 1969, *166*, 695–699.

Kadane, J. B. Optimal whereabouts search. *Operations Research*, 1971, *19*, 894–904.

*Kahneman, D. *Attention and effort*. Englewood Cliffs, N.J.: Prentice-Hall, 1973.

Kahneman, D., & Treisman, A. Selection, filtering and automaticity. In R. Parasuraman & D. R. Davies (Eds.), *Varieties of attention*. New York: Academic Press, 1984.

*Kantowitz, B. H. Double stimulation. In B. H. Kantowitz (Ed.), *Human information processing: Tutorial in performance and cognition*. Hillsdale, N.J.: Erlbaum, 1974.

Karlin, I., & Kestenbaum, R. Effects of number of alternatives on the psychological refractory period. *Quarterly Journal of Experimental Psychology*, 1968, *20*, 167–178.

Kendall, M. G. *Rank correlation methods* (4th ed.). London: Griffin, 1970.

Kinchla, R. A. The role of structural redundancy in the detection of visual targets. *Perception and Psychophysics*, 1977, *22*, 19–30.

Kinchla, R. A. The measurement of attention. In R. S. Nickerson (Ed.), *Attention and performance VIII*. Hillsdale, N.J.: Erlbaum, 1980.

Kinchla, R. A., & Collyer, C. E. Detecting a target letter in briefly presented arrays: A confidence rating analysis in terms of a weighted additive effects model. *Perception and Psychophysics*, 1974, *16*, 117–122.

Koopman, B. O. The theory of search: I. Kinematic bases. *Operations Research*, 1956, *4*, 324–346. (a)

Koopman, B. O. The theory of search: II. Target detection. *Operations Research*, 1956, *4*, 503–531. (b)

*Koopman, B. O. The theory of search: III. The optimum distribution of searching effort. *Operations Research*, 1957, *5*, 613–626.

*Krantz, D. H. Threshold theories of signal detection. *Psychological Review*, 1969, *76*, 308–324.

Krueger, L. E. A theory of perceptual matching. *Psychological Review*, 1978, *85*, 278–304.

Kruskal, J. B. Analysis of factorial experiments by estimating monotone transformations of the data. *Journal of the Royal Statistical Society*, Series B, 1965, *27*, 251–263.

Kubovy, M., & Healy, A. F. The decision rule in probabilistic categorization: What it is and how it is learned. *Journal of Experimental Psychology: General*, 1977, *106*, 427–446.

LaBerge, D. Acquisition of automatic processing in perceptual and associative learning. In P. M. A. Rabbitt & S. Dornic (Eds.), *Attention and performance V*. London: Academic Press, 1975.

Laming, D. R. *Information theory of choice-reaction times*. New York: Academic Press, 1968.

Lapin, J. S., & Disch, K. The latency operating characteristic: I. Effect of stimulus probability on choice reaction time. *Journal of Experimental Psychology*, 1972, *92*, 116–427.

Levine, M. V. Transformations that render curves parallel. *Journal of Mathematical Psychology*, 1971, *7*, 410–444.

Levitt, H. Transformed up-down methods in psychoacoustics. *Journal of the Acoustical Society of America*, 1970, *49*, 467–477.

Levitt, H. Decision theory, signal detection theory, and psychophysics. In E. E. David & P. B. Denes (Eds.), *Human communication: A unified view*. New York: McGraw-Hill, 1972.

Link, S. W. The relative judgment theory of two-choice response time. *Journal of Mathematical Psychology*, 1975, *12*, 114–135.

*Link, S. W. New views of reaction time and accuracy. In N. J. Castellan, Jr., & F. Restle (Eds.), *Cognitive theory* (Vol. 3). Hillsdale, N.J.: Erlbaum, 1978.

Link, S. W., & Heath, R. A. A sequential theory of psychological discrimination. *Psychometrika*, 1975, *40*, 77–105.

Luce, R. D. *Individual choice behavior*. New York: Wiley, 1959.

Luce, R. D., & Green, D. M. A neural timing theory for response times and the psychophysics of intensity. *Psychological Review*, 1972, *79*, 14–57.

Macmillan, N. A., Kaplan, H. L., & Creelman, C. D. The psychophysics of categorical perception. *Psychological Review*, 1977, *84*, 452–471.

McGill, W. J. Stochastic latency mechanisms. In R. D. Luce, R. R. Bush, & E. Galanter (Eds.), *Handbook of mathematical psychology* (Vol. 1). New York: Wiley, 1963.

Mertens, J. J. Influence of knowledge of target location upon the probability of observation of peripherally observable test flashes. *Journal of the Optical Society of America*, 1956, *46*, 1069–1070.

Metz, C. E., Starr, S. J., Lusted, L. B., & Rossmann, K. Progress in evaluation of human observer visual detection performance using the ROC curve approach. In C. Raynaud & A. Todd-Pokropek (Eds.), *Information processing in scintigraphy*, Orsay, France: Commissariat a l'Energie Atomique, Departement de Biologie, Service Hospitalier Frederic Joliot, 1975.

Moray, N. Attention in dichotic listening: Affective cues and the influence of instructions. *Quarterly Journal of Experimental Psychology*, 1959, *11*, 56–60.

Moray, N. *Listening and attention*. London: Penguin, 1969.

Mowbray, G. H. Perception and retention of verbal information presented during auditory shadowing. *Journal of the Acoustical Society of America*, 1964, *36*, 1459–1465.

Murphy, B. J. Pattern thresholds for moving and stationary gratings during smooth eye movements. *Vision Research*, 1978, *18*, 521–530.

Murphy, B. J., Kowler, E., & Steinman, R. M. Slow oculomotor control in the presence of moving backgrounds. *Vision Research*, 1975, *15*, 1263–1268.

Murray, H. G. Stimulus intensity and reaction time: Evaluation of a decision theory model. *Journal of Experimental Psychology*, 1970, *84*, 383–391.

*Navon, D., & Gopher, D. On the economy of the human-processing system. *Psychological Review*, 1979, *86*, 214–255.

Neisser, U. Decision time without reaction time: Experiments in visual scanning. *American Journal of Psychology*, 1963, *76*, 376–385.

Neisser, U. Visual search. *Scientific American*, 1964, *210*, 94–102.

*Neisser, U. *Cognitive psychology*. New York: Appleton-Century-Crofts, 1966.

Neisser, U., Novick, R., & Lazar, R. Searching for ten targets simultaneously. *Perceptual and Motor Skills*, 1963, *17*, 955–961.

Nissen, M. J. Stimulus intensity and information processing. *Perception and Psychophysics*, 1977, *22*, 338–352.

Nolte, L. W., & Jaarsma, D. More on the detection of one of *m* orthogonal signals. *Journal of the Acoustical Society of America*, 1967, *41*, 497–505.

Noreen, D. L. Optimal decision rules for some common psychophysical paradigms. In S. Grossberg (Ed.), *Mathematical psychology and psychophysiology*. Providence, R.I.: Society of Industrial and Applied Mathematics—American Mathematical Society (SIAM-AM) Proceedings, *13*, 1981.

Norman, D. A. Toward a theory of memory and attention. *Psychological Review*, 1968, *75*, 522–36.

*Norman, D. A., & Bobrow, D. G. On data-limited and resource-limited processes. *Cognitive Psychology*, 1975, *7*, 44–64.

Ollman, R. Fast guesses in choice reaction time. *Psychonomic Science*, 1966, *6*, 155–156.

*Pachella, R. G. The interpretation of reaction time in information processing research. In B. Kantowitz (Ed.), *Human information processing: Tutorials in performance and cognition*. Potomac, Md.: Erlbaum, 1974.

Pachella, R. G., & Fisher, D. Hick's Law and the speed-accuracy tradeoff in absolute judgment. *Journal of Experimental Psychology*, 1972, *92*, 378–384.

Pareto, V. *Manuel d'economie politique* (A. Bonnet, trans.). Paris: Giard & Briere, 1909.

Pastore, R. E., & Sorkin, R. D. Simultaneous two-channel signal detection: I. Simple binaural stimuli. *Journal of the Acoustical Society of America*, 1972, *51*, 544–551.

Pentland, A. Maximum likelihood estimation: The best PEST. *Perception and Psychophysics*, 1980, *28*, 377–379.

Pohlmann, L. D., & Sorkin, R. D. Simultaneous three-channel signal detection: Performance and criterion as a function of order of report. *Perception and Psychophysics*, 1976, *20*, 179–186.

Posner, M. I., Nissen, M. J., & Ogden, W. C. Attended and unattended processing modes: The role of set for spatial location. In H. I. Pick, Jr., & E. Saltzman (Eds.), *Modes of perceiving and processing information*. Hillsdale, N.J.: Erlbaum, 1978.

Posner, M. I., Snyder, C. R. R., & Davidson, B. J. Attention and the detection of signals. *Journal of Experimental Psychology: General*, 1980, *109*, 160–174.

Prelec, D. Matching, maximizing, and the hyperbolic reinforcement feedback function. *Psychological Review*, 1982, *89*, 189–230.

Raaijmakers, J. G. W., & Shiffrin, R. M. Search of associative memory. *Psychological Review*, 1981, *88*, 93–134.

Rachlin, H., Battalio, R., Kagel, J., & Green, L. Maximization theory in behavioral psychology. *The Behavioral and Brain Sciences*, 1981, *4*, 371–417.

*Rachlin, H., & Burkhard, B. The temporal triangle: Response substitution in instrumental conditioning. *Psychological Review*, 1978, *85*, 22–47.

Rachlin, H., Green, L., Kagel, J. H., & Battalio, R. C. Economic demand theory and psychological studies of choice. In G. Bower (Ed.), *The psychology of learning and motivation* (Vol. 10). New York: Academic Press, 1976.

Rachlin, H., Kagel, J. H., & Battalio, R. C. Substitutability in time allocation. *Psychological Review*, 1980, *87*, 355–374.

*Ratcliff, R. A theory of memory retrieval. *Psychological Review*, 1978, *85*, 59–108.

Ratcliff, R. A note on modeling accumulation of information when the rate of accumulation changes over time. *Journal of Mathematical Psychology*, 1980, *21*, 178–184.

Reed, A. V. Speed-accuracy trade-off in recognition memory. *Science*, 1973, *181*, 574–576.

Reeves, A. *The detection and recall of rapidly displayed letters and digits*. Unpublished doctoral dissertation, City University of New York, 1977.

Reeves, A., & Sperling, G. Attentional theory of order information in short-term visual memory. *Mathematical studies in perception and cognition* (83-7). New York University, Department of Psychology, 1983.

Reeves, A., & Sperling, G. Attentional gating in short-term visual memory. *Psychological Review*, 1986, *92*, in press.

Restle, F. *Psychology of judgment and choice: A theoretical essay*. New York: Wiley, 1961.

Robbins, H., & Monro, S. A stochastic approximation method. *Annals of Mathematical Statistics*, 1951, *22*, 400–407.

Rubenstein, H., Garfield, L., & Millikan, J. A. Homographic entries in the internal lexicon. *Journal of Verbal Learning and Verbal Behavior*, 1970, *9*, 487–494.

Rubenstein, H., Lewis, S. S., & Rubenstein, M. A. Evidence for phonemic recoding in visual word recognition. *Journal of Verbal Learning and Verbal Behavior*, 1971 *10*, 645–657. (a)

Rubenstein, H., Lewis, S. S., & Rubinstein, M. A. Homographic entries in the internal lexicon: Effects of systematicity and relative frequency of meanings. *Journal of Verbal Learning and Verbal Behavior*, 1971, *10*, 57–62. (b)

Rumelhart, D. E. A multicomponent theory of the perception of briefly exposed visual displays. *Journal of Mathematical Psychology*, 1970, *7*, 191–216.

*Samuelson, P. A. *Economics* (11th ed.). New York: McGraw-Hill, 1980.

*Schneider, W., & Shiffrin, R. M. Controlled and automatic human information processing: I. Detection, search, and attention. *Psychological Review*, 1977, *1*, 1–66.

Schoeffler, M. S. Theory for psychophysical learning. *Journal of the Acoustical Society of America*, 1965, *37*, 1124–1133.

Schuckman, H. Attention and visual threshold. *American Journal of Optometry and Archives of the American Academy of Optometry*, 1963, *40*, 284–291.

Shaw, M. L. A capacity allocation model for reaction time. *Journal of Experimental Psychology: Human Perception and Performance*, 1978, *4*, 586–598.

Shaw, M. L. Identifying attentional and decision making components in information processing. In R. S. Nickerson (Ed.), *Attention and performance VIII*. Hillsdale, N.J.: Erlbaum, 1980.

*Shaw, M. L. Attending to multiple sources of information: (1) The integration of information in decision making. *Cognitive Psychology*, 1982, *4*, 353–409.

Shaw, M. L., Mulligan, R. M., & Stone, L. D. Two-state versus continuous-state stimulus representations: A test based on attentional constraints. *Perception and Psychophysics*, 1983, *33*(4), 338–354.

Shaw, M. L., & Shaw, P. Optimal allocation of cognitive resources to spatial locations. *Journal of Experimental Psychology: Human Perception and Performance*, 1977, *3*, 201–211.

Shaw, P. Processing of tachistoscopic displays with controlled order of characters and spaces. *Perception and Psychophysics*, 1969, *6*, 257–266.

Shepard, R. N. Stimulus and response generalization: Tests of a model relating generalization to distance in psychological space. *Journal of Experimental Psychology*, 1958, *55*, 509–523.

*Shiffrin, R. M., & Schneider, W. Controlled and automatic human information processing: II. Perceptual learning, automatic attending, and a general theory. *Psychological Review*, 1977, *84*, 127–189.

*Smith, E. E. Choice reaction time: An analysis of the major theoretical positions. *Psychological Bulletin*, 1968, *69*, 77–110.

Sorkin, R. D., & Pastore, R. E. Stimulus binaural signal detection: Comments on time sharing in auditory perception. *Journal of the Acoustical Society of America*, 1971, *49*, 1319.

Sorkin, R. D., Pastore, R. E., & Pohlman, L. D. Simultaneous two-channel signal detection: II. Correlated and uncorrelated signals. *Journal of the Acoustical Society of America*, 1972, *51*, 1960–1965.

Sorkin, R. D., Pohlmann, L. D., & Gilliom, J. D. Simultaneous two-channel signal detection: III. 630- and 1400-Hz signals. *Journal of the Acoustical Society of America*, 1973, *53*, 1045–1050.

Sorkin, R. D., Pohlmann, L. D., & Woods, D. D. Decision interaction between auditory channels. *Perception and Psychophysics*, 1976, *19*, 290–295.

*Sperling, G. The information available in brief visual presentations. *Psychological Monographs*, 1960, *74*, (11, Whole No. 498).

Sperling, G. A model for visual memory tasks. *Human Factors*, 1963, *5*, 19–31.

*Sperling, G. Temporal and spatial visual masking: I. Masking by impulse flashes. *Journal of the Optical Society of America*, 1965, *55*, 541–559.

Sperling, G. Successive approximations to a model for short-term memory. *Acta Psychologica*, 1967, *27*, 285–292.

Sperling, G. The search for the highest rate of search. *Symposium on Attention and Performance V.*, Stockholm, Sweden: Saltsjobaden, August 1973.

Sperling, G. Multiple detections in a brief visual stimulus: The sharing and switching of attention. *Bulletin of the Psychonomic Society*, 1975, *9*, 427.

Sperling, G. Mathematical models of binocular vision. In S. Grossberg (Ed.), *Mathematical psychology and psychophysiology*. Providence, R.I.: Society of Industrial and Applied Mathematics—American Mathematical Society (SIAM-AM) Proceedings, *13*, 1981.

Sperling, G. Unified theory of attention and signal detection. *Mathematical studies in perception and cognition* (83-3). New York University, Department of Psychology, 1983.

*Sperling, G. A unified theory of attention and signal detection. In R. Parasuraman & D. R. Davies (Eds.), *Varieties of attention*. New York: Academic Press, 1984.

Sperling, G., Budiansky, J., Spivak, J. G., & Johnson, M. C. Extremely rapid visual search: The maximum rate of scanning letters for the presence of a numeral. *Science*, 1971, *174*, 307–311.

Sperling, G., & Melchner, M. J. Estimating item and order information. *Journal of Mathematical Psychology*, 1976, *13*, 192–213. (a)

*Sperling, G., & Melchner, M. J. Visual search and visual attention. In V. D. Glezer (Ed.), *Information processing in visual system*. Proceedings of the Fourth Symposium of Sensory System Physiology. Leningrad, U.S.S.R.: Academy of Sciences, Pavlov Institute of Physiology, 1976. (b)

Sperling, G., & Melchner, M. J. The attention operating characteristic: Some examples from visual search. *Science*, 1978, *202*, 315–318. (a)

Sperling, G., & Melchner, M. J. Visual search, visual attention, and the attention operating characteristic. In J. Requin (Ed.), *Attention and performance VII*. Hillsdale, N.J.: Erlbaum, 1978. (b)

Sperling, G., & Reeves, A. Reaction time of an unobservable response. *Bulletin of the Psychonomic Society*, 1976, *10*, 247.

Sperling, G., & Reeves, A. Measuring the reaction time of a shift of visual attention. *Investigative Ophthalmology and Visual Science*, ARVO Supplement, 1978, *17*, 289.

Sperling, G., & Reeves, A. Measuring the reaction time of an unobservable response: A shift of visual attention. In R. Nickerson (Ed.), *Attention and performance VIII*. Hillsdale, N.J.: Erlbaum, 1980.

Sperling, G., & Reeves, A. Gating model of visual attention. *Bulletin of the Psychonomic Society*, 1983, *17*, 354.

Sternberg, S. High speed scanning in human memory. *Science*, 1966, *153*, 652–654.

*Stone, L. D. *Theory of optimal search*. New York: Academic Press, 1975.

Stroop, J. R. Studies of interference in serial verbal reactions. *Journal of Experimental Psychology*, 1935, *18*, 643–662.

Sussman, H. J., & Zahler, R. S. Catastrophe theory as applied to the social and biological sciences: A critique. *Synthese*, 1978, *37*, 117–216.

*Swets, J. A. (Ed.). *Signal detection and recognition by human observers: Contemporary readings*. New York: Wiley, 1964.

Swets, J. A. The relative operating characteristic in psychology. *Science*, 1973, *182*, 990–1000.

*Swets, J. A. Mathematical models of attention. In R. Parasuraman & D. R. Davies (Eds.), *Varieties of attention*. New York: Academic Press, 1984.

Swets, J. A., Tanner, W. P., & Birdsall, T. G. Decision processes in perception. *Psychological Review*, 1961, *68*, 301–340.

Taylor, M. M., & Creelman, C. D. PEST: Efficient estimates on probability functions. *Journal of the Acoustical Society of America*, 1967, *41*,

782–787.

Theios, J., Smith, P., Haviland, S., Trupman, J., & Moy, M. Memory scanning as a serial self-terminating process. *Journal of Experimental Psychology*, 1973, *97*, 323–336.

Thom, R. *Structural stability and morphogenesis* (D. H. Fowler, trans.). Reading, Mass.: W. A. Benjamin, 1975.

Thom, R., & Zeeman, E. C. Catastrophe theory: Its present state and future perspectives. In A. Manning (Ed)., *Proceedings of a Symposium Held at the University of Warwick 1973/74*. In Dynamical Systems—Warick 1974. Berlin: Springer-Verlag, 1975.

Thomas, E. A. C. Criterion adjustment and probability matching. *Perception and Psychophysics*, 1975, *18*, 158–162.

Thurstone, L. L. *Multiple-factor analysis: A development and expansion of the vectors of mind.* Chicago: Chicago University Press, 1947.

Tognetti, K. P. An optimal strategy for a whereabouts search. *Operations Research*, 1968, *16*, 209–211.

Treisman, A. M. Monitoring and storage of irrelevant messages in selective attention. *Journal of Verbal Learning and Verbal Behavior*. 1964, *3*, 449–459.

Treisman, A. M. Strategies and models of selective attention. *Psychological Review*, 1969, *76*, 282–299.

van Santen, J. P. H., & Bamber, D. Finite and infinite state confusion models. *Journal of Mathematical Psychology*, 1981, *24*, 101–111.

Vickers, D. *Decision processes in visual perception*. New York: Academic Press, 1979.

Wald, A. *Statistical decision functions*. New York: Wiley, 1950.

Wandell, B. A. Speed-accuracy tradeoff in visual detection: Applications of neural counting and timing. *Vision Research*, 1977, *17*, 217–225.

Welford, A. T. (Ed.), *Reaction times*. London: Academic Press, 1980. (a)

Welford, A. T. The single channel hypothesis. In A. T. Welford (Ed.), *Reaction times*. New York: Academic Press, 1980. (b)

Wickelgren, W. A., Corbett, A. T., & Dosher, B. A. Priming and retrieval from short-term memory: A speed accuracy analysis. *Journal of Verbal Learning and Verbal Behavior*, 1980, *19*, 387–404.

Woods, C., & Jennings, J. Speed accuracy tradeoff functions in choice reaction time: Experimental designs and computational procedures. *Perception and Psychophysics*, 1976, *19*, 92–101.

Woodworth, R. S., & Schlosberg, H. *Experimental psychology* (rev. ed.). New York: Holt, 1954.

Wundt, W. *Grundzuge der physilogischen psychologie*. Leipzig: Engelmann, 1893.

Wundt, W. *An introduction to psychology* (R. Pintner, trans.). London: Geroge Allen & Unwin, 1912 (reprinted 1924).

Yellott, J. I. Correction for guessing in choice reaction time. *Psychonomic Science*, 1967, *8*, 321–322.

Yellott, J. I. Correction for fast guessing and the speed-accuracy tradeoff. *Journal of Mathematical Psychology*, 1971, *8*, 159–199.

Zeeman, E. C. Catastrophe theory, *Scientific American*, 1976, *234*, 65–83.

CHAPTER 3

COMPUTER GRAPHICS

HERBERT FREEMAN

Department of Electrical and Computer Engineering, Rutgers University, New Brunswick, New Jersey

CONTENTS

1. DEFINITION AND SCOPE

1.1. What Is Computer Graphics?

Computer graphics is the name commonly applied to the process of synthesizing pictures with the aid of a digital computer. It begins with an idea—a "mental picture"—of what one wants to create and, perhaps together with some given data or specification, proceeds through a sequence of procedures to result eventually in the desired image. The image may be a line drawing, a halftone image, or a full-color picture. It may represent an engineering or architectural design, it may be a graphic representation of some scientific or empirical data, or it may be a piece of purely visual art.

Computer graphics—as most other computer processing—can be either batch mode or interactive. In batch mode a drawing or picture is generated directly from data provided by the application program, without any intervention or modification by the user. The picture is almost always presented on paper or photographic film. Batch-mode graphics plays an important role in graphics production environments—generation of maps, pattern layouts, and computer animation—but it is interactive computer graphics that is of particular importance in the computer-aided design process, in greatly enhacing man–machine communication, and in opening up entirely new vistas for picture generation.

Interactive computer graphics can replace tedious manual drawing. It can permit an artistically unskilled person to create high-quality pictures, as well as pictures of a complexity that would severely challenge even the most skilled draftsman. Finally, and perhaps most importantly, once an image has been created with a computer, the computer contains a structured description of the image in its data base. This description can be saved for future revisions of the image, it can serve as a takeoff point for generating new images, and it can supply the data for an analysis of the depicted scene. It is this last feature that was found to result in the greatest economic benefit when computer graphics was first utilized in engineering and architectural applications.

Computer graphics is potentially useful in all those endeavors in which humans have traditionally employed pictures as an aid in representing and understanding information. These include architecture, engineering, industrial design, map making, graphic design (as in the publishing industry), animated cartoons, visual aids in education and business, the visual arts, the creation of displays for research in visual perception, and the simulation of visual scenes (as in flight simulators, for example).

1.2. Related Disciplines

Closely related disciplines are computer-aided design (where the emphasis is on creating the design for a two- or three-dimensional object), computer image processing (the analysis and manipulation of natural-scene pictures), visual perception and pattern recognition (which are concerned with the "understanding" of an image), and display technology (the engineering aspects of graphics terminals and systems).

Computer graphics should not be confused with computer image processing, which involves recorded or transmitted images of natural scenes, such as photographs, television pictures, and fingerprints. The objective of computer image processing may be enhancement (removing blurriness or other noise), compression (encoding the image information of interest in a compact form), or pattern recognition (interpreting the information contained in the image, that is, understanding it in a higher-level context). (See Chapter 38 by Barrow & Tenenbaum.)

Computer graphics and computer image processing have many features in common. Much of the same equipment tends to be used and many of the algorithms employed in one are of equal value in the other. Nevertheless, because of their fundamentally different objectives, they should be treated as distinct disciplines, each with its own experts, adherents, conferences, and bodies of literature. In this chapter we confine our discussion to computer graphics.

1.3. Major Aspects of Computer Graphics

Computer graphics can be discussed from three different points of view: (1) the specialized equipment required for display of and interaction with an image, (2) the algorithms required for the generation and manipulation of an image, and (3) the software that lets a user create images from data generated by an application program. This chapter deals with all these aspects, placing primary emphasis, however, on the algorithms, for these play the most central role in understanding what computer graphics can do, what its limitations are, and how it can be utilized effectively.

1.4. Historical Perspective and Literature

Although some early attempts to generate pictures with computers can be traced back to the 1950s, computer graphics is generally regarded as having begun in the early 1960s with the work of Sutherland (1963). Although interest in the field developed rapidly, especially in the engineering community, most activities were confined to research investigations. Practical, economically sound applications were few until well into the mid-1970s. The reasons for this were the limitations and relatively high cost of the graphics equipment, the lack of powerful and yet easy-to-use software for image generation and manipulation, and the high cost of the computing power needed to provide effective interaction. Not until the late 1970s did all these barriers suddenly break and permit computer graphics to expand into one of the largest and most rapidly growing fields of computer technology. Of course, time was also in its favor as year after year the cost of graphics equipment kept dropping and the cost of human labor kept increasing. Computer graphics offers enormous possibilities for increased productivity in every activity in which a picture can facilitate understanding, be it the creation of a design, the monitoring of a manufacturing process, or the display of scientific or business data.

Until the late 1960s most of the literature related to computer graphics was confined to the established publications in the computer field: the *IEEE Transactions on Computers*, the *Communications of the ACM*, and the proceedings of the joint computer conferences held in the spring and fall by the American Federation of Information Processing Societies (AFIPS). The first regular journal directly concerned with the field was *Computer Graphics and Image Processing*, published by Academic Press starting in 1970. Other journals that have appeared in recent years are *Computer Graphics*, *Computer Graphics Applications*, *Computer and Graphics*, and the *ACM Transactions on Graphics*.

The books dealing with computer graphics that appeared during the late 1960s and early 1970s either tended to be collections of papers presented at specialized conferences (Faiman & Nievergelt, 1969; Gruenberger, 1967; Parslow, Prowse, & Green, 1969) or dealt with only limited aspects of the field (Fetter, 1965; Parslow, 1971). It was not until 1973 that the first full-fledged textbook appeared, *Principles of Interactive Computer Graphics* by Newman and Sproull. Others that have followed are *Interactive Computer Graphics* (Giloi, 1978), *Fundamentals of Interactive Computer Graphics* (Foley & Van Dam, 1982), and *Applied Concepts in Microcomputer Graphics* (Artwick, 1984). A comprehensive reprint volume that traces the development of the field was published by Freeman (1980). Programming for computer graphics is stressed by Harrington (1983), Enderle, Kansy, and Pfaff (1984), and Hearn and Baker (1983).

2. THE GRAPHICS SYSTEM

The key components of an interactive graphics system are shown in Figure 3.1. The display processor, the display unit, and the interactive controls are frequently referred to collectively as a *graphics terminal*, connected via an appropriate interface (or communication link) to a host computer. The application program resides in the host computer and sends the data for creating the display image to the display processor. The display processor creates a "computer version" of the image called the *display file*. This is stored in a buffer memory and is sent periodically to the display unit for conversion to a visible image. The interactive controls enable the user to modify the displayed image by having the display processor directly alter the display file or, indirectly, by communicating with the host computer to cause changes in the data generated by the application program. For an interactive computer graphics system the display unit

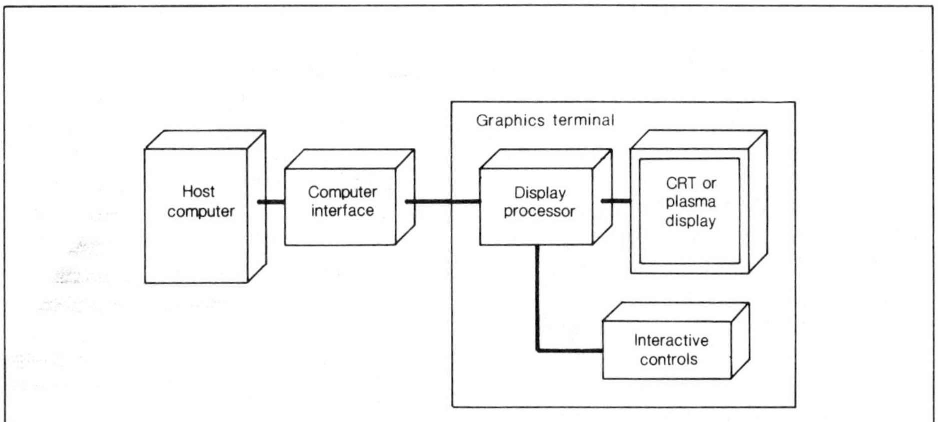

Figure 3.1. The key components of an interactive graphics system. The terminal (sometimes also called work station) consists of a display screen (CRT or plasma panel) on which the generated image appears, a display processor (special-purpose graphics computer), and a set of interactive controls (buttons, levers, dials, etc.) that permit the operator to send commands to the processor. The terminal is connected via a computer interface to a host computer, in which the graphics application computations take place.

must permit the image to be created quickly, displayed for as long as desired, and then erased and replaced by another image. The performance capability of an interactive computer graphics system is to a large extent measured by the rapidity with which one image can be replaced by another.

2.1. Display Device Characteristics

The following characteristics are normally used to compare the quality and performance capabilities of different display devices:

1. Spatial resolution.
2. Intensity resolution.
3. Color capability (monochrome vs. multiple hues).
4. Linearity.
5. Brightness.
6. Writing speed.
7. Selective erasability.
8. Inherent storage.
9. Power requirements.
10. Life.
11. Resistance to shock and vibration.
12. Cost.

The relative importance assigned to the different characteristics depends, of course, on the application and the environment in which the display unit is to be used. Not all the characteristics can be achieved with a particular display device, and a high rating in some characteristics may force a low rating in others. In general, the higher the performance, the greater the cost.

1. *Spatial Resolution.* When a visible image is displayed on an electronic device, the generation of that image is not continuous but discrete; that is, it consists of an array (normally square) of discrete points at which the emanating light can be controlled to take on the desired brightness. The discrete points are called *pels* or *pixels* (for pictures elements). The discreteness of the picture may stem from an inherent discreteness of the display medium, as in an array of light-emitting diodes, or it may be derived from the digital nature of the spatial addressing mechanism. Thus to select a particular spot in the image, one specifies a pair of coordinates (x and y) in the computer. The number of bits available for specifying a coordinate determines the resolution in that coordinate. For example, if 10 bits are available to cover the full range of x, the resolution in x is 1 part in 2^{10}, that is, 1:1024. If the x dimension of the display area is 25 cm, points can be selected to the nearest $25/1024 \sim 0.025$ cm. This applies even for those display devices for which the display medium itself is continuous. Typical resolution values for computer graphics displays range from a low of 1:256 to a high of 1:4096.

2. *Intensity Resolution.* Intensity resolution refers to the identifiable, distinct levels in the brightness of the light emanating from a selected point (pixel) of the display. These may normally range from a minimum of two for a bi-level (black/white) display, to a maximum of 256. High values of intensity resolution are required for gray-tone images; for line drawings it is rare to require more than eight intensity levels.

3. *Color Capability.* Most computer graphics displays are monochrome; that is, the image has only one color, which occurs in various intensities or shades. Such displays are often referred to also as black-and-white displays even though the image may in fact be shown in different shades of some other color (e.g., green or yellow-orange). True color displays permit the user to specify the color desired for a particular displayed entity, out of a set of available colors. Note that color and intensity are not independent quantities. In a full-color graphics display, a large set of colors, defined in terms of hue, saturation, and intensity, can be generated by appropriately mixing red, green, and blue light sources of different intensity. The number of displayable colors depends on the ranges in intensity available for each of the three primary colors. In low-cost displays these may be as few as eight; in high-performance displays they may range into many millions, for example, $(256)^3 = 16{,}777{,}216$.

4. *Linearity.* The linearity of a display can be measured by the precision with which geometric properties are preserved. Thus in a display with high linearity, specifying a horizontal line segment to be twice as long as another segment yields a segment that is indeed twice as long, within a tolerance that does not exceed the resolution of the display. Further, in such displays straight lines (of any orientation) tend to be as straight and as much to the desired slope as the discreteness of the display permits.

5. *Brightness.* The brightness of a display determines the level of ambient light under which the display can be comfortably viewed. It refers to the psychological perception of light intensity and is closely related to luminance, the luminous intensity per unit area, which is a photometric quantity. Also affecting the "visibility" of a display, of course, is contrast, the ratio of the difference between the maximum and minimum luminance to their sum.

6. *Writing Speed.* Writing speed refers to the rate with which pictorial information can be brought up on the display. The parameter is important for two reasons. For interactive graphics to be effective, it is necessary that a request for a new image or a change in an existing image be carried out virtually instantly, or at most with perhaps 1- or 2-sec delay, for otherwise the user finds it difficult to maintain continuity of thought. Further, most cathode-ray tube (CRT) displays are of the refresh type. In these the image decays rapidly after being drawn and must be periodically redrawn (refreshed) to give the viewer the illusion of seeing a steady image. The faster the image can be drawn, the more complex it can be and still be refreshable at a rate that will permit it to appear flicker-free to the viewer. Writing speed is generally measured in centimeters per microsecond of vector drawing, although a number of other, slightly different measures are also in common use.

7. *Selective Erasability.* Most display devices permit any portion of the displayed image to be erased without altering the rest of the image. There are some, however, that do not; to erase a portion of an image, the entire image must first be erased, after which it can be redrawn with the undesired portion omitted. This tends to slow down interaction process and may be objectionable for some applications.

8. *Inherent Storage.* For a display device to present a steady, nonflickering image to the viewer, either the image must be stored in the display medium and kept there until erased, or it must be stored elsewhere (say, in a computer memory) and redrawn on the display sufficiently frequently to appear as a steady image to the viewer. This "refreshing" operation complicates the display electronics. Displays with inherent storage (e.g., plasma panels and direct-view storage tubes) tend, however, to be limited in resolution, brightness, color, or other factors that may make them less desirable.

9. *Power Requirements.* For normal office or laboratory use, the power requirements for virtually all common display

devices are relatively modest and reasonable. The required power can be an important factor if a display is to be portable or to be used in a military or space vehicle. Of the common display devices available, the CRT requires the most power and the plasma panel the least.

10. *Life.* The life expectancy of a display is normally not a serious factor, for most of the devices are capable of performing satisfactorily for many years. Somewhat reduced life is exhibited by the direct-view storage tube, in which the storage capability may degrade with use after about 1–2 years.

11. *Resistance to Shock and Vibration.* The ruggedness of a display is important for display devices that must be used in severe environments (e.g., aircraft, military vehicles). One of the best performers in this regard appears to be the plasma panel.

12. *Cost.* The cost of a display device is influenced mainly by the quantity in which the device is produced. This is controlled by market forces that tend to be affected by other desirable features of the device. Complexity of manufacturing appears to have only a secondary effect.

2.1.1. Cathode-Ray Tubes. In its basic form, a CRT consists of a sealed glass bottle in which a high vacuum has been created, as shown in Figure 3.2. The electron gun at the left consists of a cathode which is heated by a filament to emit electrons. The electrons, which are of a negative potential, are attracted by the positive potential of the anode and are accelerated to move at high speed toward the tube face at the right. In passing through the focusing section of the electron gun the stream of electrons is focused into a narrow beam, which is then deflected by the magnetic deflection coils to impinge at the desired spot on the tube face. A phosphor layer on the inside of the tube face is made to glow by the impinging electron beam, creating a spot that is visible to the viewer.

There are many varieties and sizes of CRTs. In computer graphics we find (1) the vector-refresh CRT, (2) the raster-refresh CRT, and (3) the direct-view storage tube (DVST). CRTs are available in sizes ranging from 2.5 to over 75 cm for the diagonal of the rectangular display area on the CRT's face. The rectangular area has an aspect ratio—ratio of width to height—that generally ranges from about 3:2 to 1:1.

2.1.1.1. Vector-Refresh CRT. A vector-refresh CRT is used in computer graphics for displaying line drawings. It is not suitable for displaying gray-tone images. To draw a line segment the beam is commanded to move to the segment's starting point and then to trace out the line segment until its end point is reached. Normally, the beam is controlled to draw every line segment and character in the image once and then to repeat the entire process. If the image is redrawn 30 or more times per second, it appears as a steady picture to the viewer. When some portion of a line drawing is to be deleted, this portion is simply not redrawn on the next refresh cycle. The brightness of the line segments and characters can be varied by varying the beam current.

The requirement that the image be refreshed at least 30 times per second imposes an upper limit on the complexity of the image that can be displayed. If the CRT beam can be moved at the rate of 2 $cm \cdot msec^{-1}$, total beam movement per refresh cycle (whether tracing out a segment or merely moving from one point to another) cannot exceed $2 \times 10^6/30 = 66{,}666$ cm. Although this is sufficient for many applications, there are situations where a greater image complexity is needed. This can then be achieved only at the cost of tolerating some flicker (i.e., refreshing at, say, only 20 times per second).

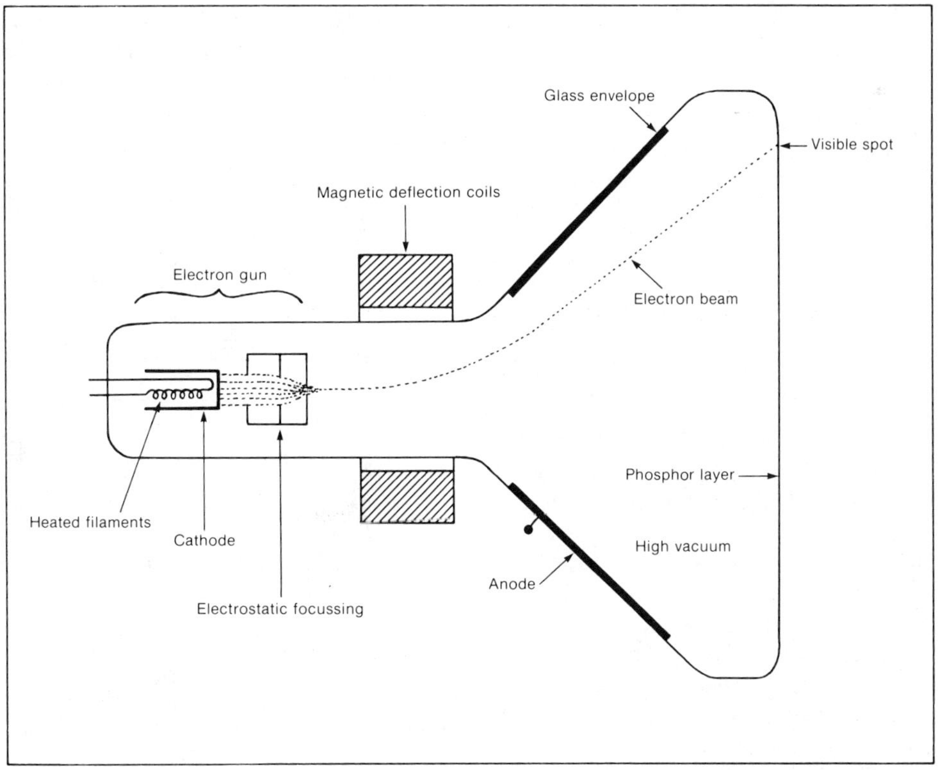

Figure 3.2. Cross-section view of a CRT with electrostatic focusing and electromagnetic deflection. The electron beam generated by the electron gun can be deflected vertically and horizontally (with the magnetic deflection coils) to cause it to impinge on the phosphor layer and thereby generate a visible spot of light at any selected point.

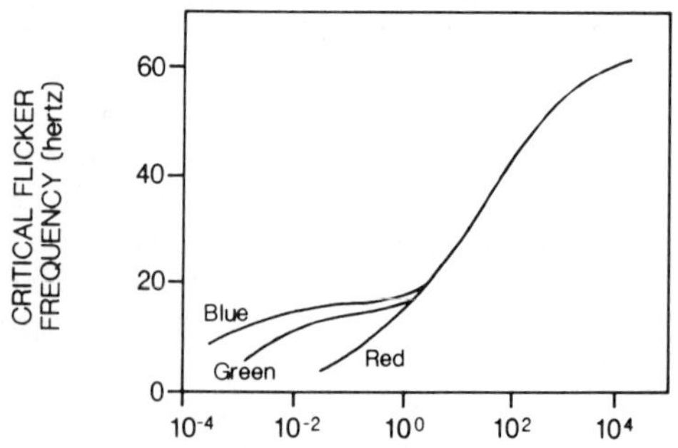

Figure 3.3. Minimum flicker-free refresh rate as a function of display luminance. Note that for high luminance levels flicker can be detected at refresh rates up to 60 Hz. (See Chapter 6 by Watson.) (From Conrac Corp., *Raster Graphics Handbook*, Van Nostrand Reinhold Company, Inc., 1980. Reprinted with permission.)

A refresh rate of 30 frames per second is normally adequate to create a flicker-free image for the viewer. This is due to the persistence of the viewer's visual system and does not depend on the persistence of the image itself. With a low-persistence phosphor, the glow on the face of the tube is gone within 1 msec or less after the beam has passed that area. The reaction time of the human visual systems depends on the brightness and color of the display. For very high levels of brightness, flicker may be perceived even when an image is displayed at 60 frames per second, as is illustrated in Figure 3.3. If the image complexity and line-drawing rate are such as to preclude refreshing at 30 or more frames per second, one scheme for avoiding undesirable flicker is to use a CRT with a longer-persistence phosphor. Some phosphors continue to glow for an appreciable amount of time—from a few milliseconds up to a couple of seconds—after having been excited by the electron beam. Unfortunately, for the longer-persistence phosphors the persisting glow is not of uniform brightness and does not provide as pleasing a display as a higher refresh rate. Also, use of long-persistence phosphor makes the display unsuitable for showing images in motion. However, for displaying static images, a long-persistence phosphor can make it possible to display flicker-free images of acceptable quality at refresh rates as low as 20 or perhaps even 10 frames per second.

Although vector-refresh CRT displays are monochrome, limited color capability is available through use of a phosphor penetration-type tube. In the latter, the phosphor on the inside of the tube face consists of two layers, each giving off a different color when excited (typically green and red). By varying the speed with which the electrons impinge on the phosphor, the beam may excite only the first or, if moving faster, may penetrate through to the second layer. Thus by appropriately controlling the speed, a limited set of different colors can be achieved.

2.1.1.2. Raster-Refresh CRT. The raster-refresh CRT display is essentially identical to a home television monitor, except that instead of receiving the image data via a television signal receiver, it obtains the image data from the image buffer memory via the image display system. A digital version of the image is stored in the memory and then read out and sent to the display monitor at the rate of 30 frames per second. To minimize the perception of flicker by the viewer, the image is commonly read out in the form of two interlaced half-frames, one each 1/60 sec. In the U.S. television transmission, the display consists of 480 displayed raster lines. (The frame interval actually spans 525 raster lines but some of the "lines" are not used for the visible portion of the display.) For a typical good-quality graphics raster display, 1024 lines, each consisting of 1024 discrete pixels, are used. If one 8-bit byte is set aside for each pixel, a total of 256 different shades of gray or different colors can be displayed, and a buffer memory capacity of 1024 × 1024 = 1,048,576 bytes is required. The buffer memory is frequently also referred to as the "refresh memory" because it stores the data from which the image is continually redisplayed ("refreshed") on the monitor at the rate of 30 times per second.

In a raster-type display, the electron beam of the CRT is made to trace out successive lines on the face of the tube from left to right. When a line is completed, the beam "flies back" at high speed to the left and moves down slightly to commence tracing out the next line. When the bottom line has been drawn, the beam returns to the top left to repeat the entire process. In noninterlaced rasters, all the lines are drawn in succession to make up one frame, typically in 1/60 sec. In the more common interlaced raster displays, lines 1, 3, 5, 7, ... are drawn first. When all the odd-numbered lines have been drawn (in 1/60 sec), the beam returns to draw lines 2, 4, 6, 8, ... In this way drawing of a full raster (odd and even lines) takes 1/30 sec, yet because of the interlacing, no objectionable flicker is observed. The reduced drawing speed permits use of lower-cost electronic circuitry in the display monitor and also reduces the transmission rate (bandwidth) required for sending the image data from the buffer memory to the monitor. For a 512 × 512 pixel interlaced display with 1 byte per pixel, the required transmission rate is 7,864,320 bytes·sec^{-1}. For a 1024 × 1024 × 1 byte display it is 31,457,280 bytes·sec^{-1}. For a noninterlaced display these values would be doubled.

A visible image is generated in a raster display by modulating the intensity of the beam. The beam is "off" during both line and frame retrace. To display a binary (two-level) image, the beam is turned on and off during each line trace, as required to generate the image. This is illustrated in Figure 3.4 for a simple line-drawing-type image. To achieve a multilevel, gray-tone image, the intensity of the beam is controlled according

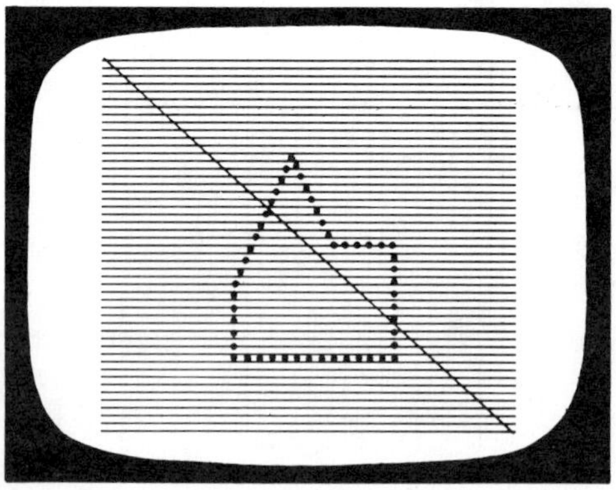

Figure 3.4. Display of a simple line drawing on a raster display. The electron beam traces out the raster pattern from left to right, top to bottom, "flying back" to the beginning of the next line whenever one line has been traced out. After tracing out the last line it returns to the beginning of the first line. (To prevent cluttering the picture, the line retraces are omitted.) A line drawing is displayed by intensifying the beam at the points on each raster line that lie on a line segment. For so-called interlaced displays, the beam alternately traces out only the odd-numbered raster lines (i.e., 1, 3, 5, . . .) or the even-numbered raster lines (i.e., 2, 4, . . .). By alternately drawing only half the raster lines, less costly display terminals can be utilized than if the full raster were refreshed at 50 or 60 Hz (though at some reduction in image quality).

to the stored pixel values to yield the proportional image intensity values on the face to the CRT.

It should be noted that if the raster display uses a buffer memory in which there is one memory cell for each pixel in the raster, the buffer memory must be quite large. For gray-tone images 1 byte may be required for each pixel. This implies a buffer memory of 1,048,576 bytes for a 1024 × 1024 pixel raster.

Until the late 1970s a memory of this size could not compete economically with a fast vector-refresh CRT. However, this is no longer the case, and raster displays are becoming more and more common, replacing vector-refresh displays in many applications.

2.1.1.3. Direct-View Storage Tube. To overcome the image-complexity limitation of the vector-refresh CRT and avoid the high memory cost of a raster display, the DVST display was developed. This display uses a CRT in which the writing electron beam causes a positive charge pattern to be placed on an insulated screen just inside the tube face. The deposited charge then attracts slowly moving electrons from a continuous flooding beam and causes these to strike the phosphor layer, thereby creating a visible image in correspondence with the stored charge pattern (Newman & Sproull, 1979; Sherr, 1970). A cross-section schematic of such a display tube is shown in Figure 3.5.

Because the image is automatically retained by the stored charge in the tube itself, there is no need for periodic refreshing. Nor, however, is there now the possibility for selective erasure or for showing images in motion. To erase any part, the entire screen must be erased and the desired image redrawn. Image complexity is virtually unlimited, and the associated electronics is simple and of low cost.

Direct-view storage tubes offered an excellent choice for a low-cost graphics terminal until the late 1970s, when low-cost raster terminals (which are also virtually unlimited in image complexity) became available. Although DVSTs are capable of considerably higher resolution than are raster terminals, they are expected to fade from use because of (1) their inability to handle selective erasure or moving images, and (2) their inherent limitation to monochrome images.

2.1.1.4. Comparative Features of CRT Displays. Of the three major kinds of CRTs, the raster-refresh CRT is the most versatile and is expected to predominate in the future as the cost of the buffer memory continues to drop and the demand for color increases. A comparison of the three kinds of CRT displays is shown in Table 3.1.

2.1.2. Plasma Panels. A plasma panel is in effect an array of closely spaced cells containing a gas such as neon that ionizes and glows when a moderately high voltage is applied across it. The gas (i.e., plasma) continues to glow even when the voltage is reduced to a much lower value, and is extinguished only at very low voltage. Plasma panels have been constructed with a resolution of 1024 × 1024 cells and densities of 100 cells per linear inch. (In practice, the "cells" are, in fact, not distinct but are merely localized areas in a thin layer of gas between two glass plates; this is irrelevant, though, from a functional point of view.)

A cell once lit remains lit until explicitly extinguished, or until the power is turned off. Plasma panels (or "gas panels," as they are also called) thus have inherent image storage and do not require any refreshing as long as the power is not turned off. Selective erasure is possible on a cell-by-cell basis. Color and variable-intensity monochrome are not available, but some color or gray-tone capability can be achieved by building multiple-layer panels.

The main advantages of the plasma panel are (1) that the panel is flat and thin, (2) that it can be made transparent, permitting it to serve as an overlay display for other images,

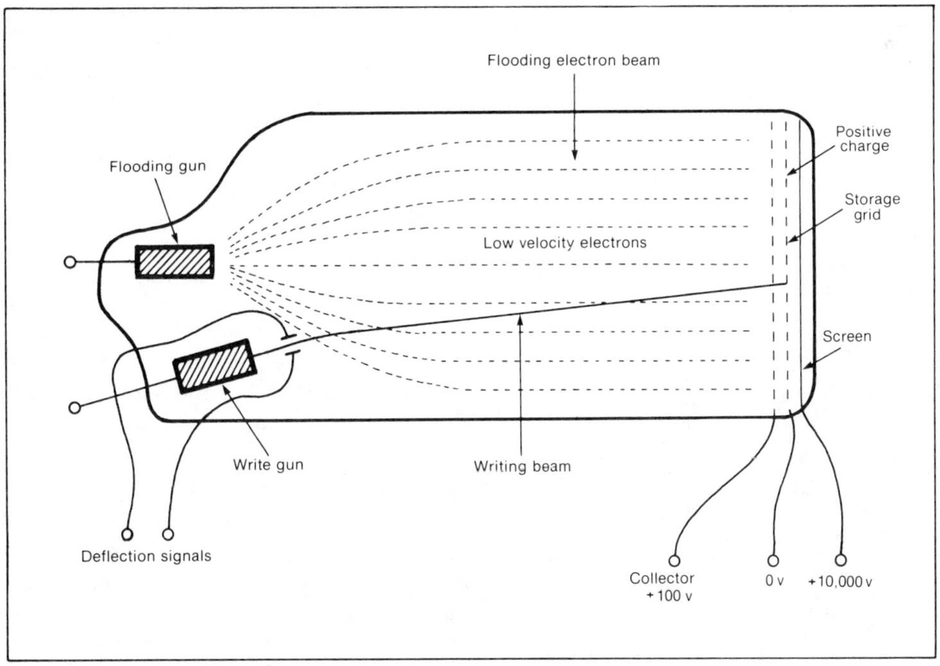

Figure 3.5. Cross-section schematic of a DVST. The tube contains two electron guns, one for generating a continuous low-velocity flooding beam that is distributed over the entire tube width, and one that generates a focused beam that can be deflected as in a conventional CRT. The latter is used to deposit a positive charge (corresponding to the desired image) on the storage grid. The flooding beam supplies the electrons that, upon being attracted by the stored positive charge, cause a visible image to appear on the screen's phosphor layer.

Table 3.1. Comparison of the Three Major Types of CRT Graphic Displays

Feature	Vector-Refresh CRT	Raster-Refresh CRT	DVST
Primary Suitability	Line drawings	Gray-tone or color images	Line drawings
Availability of color	Limited color range & costly	Excellent color range & economical	No color
Resolution	High (to 4096 square), economical	High resolution available but costly	Moderately high, economical
Variable intensity	Yes	Yes	No
Capability to display moving images	Yes	Yes	No
Brightness	High	High	Low
Life	Long	Long	1–2 years of steady use
Cost	Moderate	Moderate, except for very high resolution	Low

(3) that no high voltages are required, (4) that it is rugged (highly resistant to shock and vibration), and (5) that it is characterized by excellent spatial linearity and repeatability.

Its disadvantages are (1) the need for relatively complex addressing electronics, (2) a high manufacturing cost (relative to CRT) until now, (3) the difficulty of providing variable intensity or multiple colors, and (4) the inherent resolution limitation.

2.1.3. Continuous versus Discrete Displays. On a vector-refresh display a line segment is displayed by having the beam trace out the segment on the CRT's phosphor layer. The resulting segment is smooth and continuous. However, on a raster display—or a plasma panel—the line segment is composed of a series of small illuminated dots (or pixels, for "picture elements"). These dots are located at the nodes of a fine square grid. As a result, straight-line segments—except for those that are purely vertical, horizontal, or diagonal—must necessarily appear with a kind of "staircase" pattern, as illustrated in Figure 3.6. This effect, which is especially noticeable in low-resolution raster displays or panels, can be quite annoying to the viewer. We shall show below that for gray-tone or color raster displays this effect can be at least partially overcome through a so-called "anti-aliasing" technique.

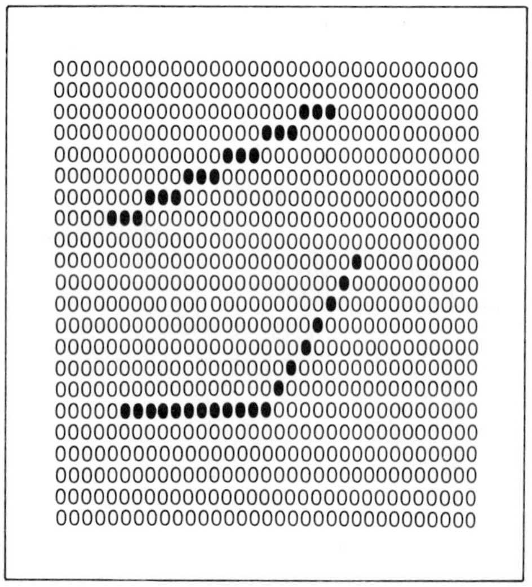

Figure 3.6. Discrete-cell type display. When a plasma panel or similar "cell" type display is used, a display image consists of individual points. For a line segment, the spacing between points is different at a 45° slope than when the line is vertical or horizontal. For line segments having slopes other than multiples of 45°, a staircase-type representation is unavoidable.

2.2. Hard-Copy Output Devices

Hard-copy devices fall into two major categories, depending on whether the hard-copy medium is paper or photographic film. Devices that record on paper are referred to as plotters; those that record on film, as cameras. Plotters come in two varieties: pen plotters and raster plotters. Cameras divide primarily according to whether they permit fast output of moderate-resolution CRT images, usually in full color, or whether they yield high-resolution images and are intended primarily for the printing industry.

2.2.1. Pen Plotters. Pen plotters consist of a pen holder that is guided over the paper to generate a line drawing. The pen holder may contain one or more pens, which can be selected under program control to achieve multiple-color capability. In some plotters of recent manufacture, there is a pen storage area where, under program control, the holder selects a pen from a set of up to eight available pens. The pens may contain different-color inks or may draw in different line widths, or be intended for different media (e.g., plastic instead of paper).

In the so-called flat-bed plotters, the pen holder is guided in two dimensions (x and y) over the paper. In the drum plotters, the pen holder is moved parallel to one axis while movement parallel to the other axis is achieved by moving the paper itself.

Pen plotters come in different sizes, permitting drawings ranging in size from about 28 × 42 cm to as large as 2 m wide by virtually unlimited length. They can make drawings with resolutions as fine as 0.025 mm and with drawing speeds up to 30 cm·sec^{-1}. Most plotters now contain microprocessors to enhance their capabilities and facilitate their use. Virtually all contain a character generator that permits characters of different sizes and orientations (and often even of different fonts) to be drawn on command.

2.2.2. Raster Plotters. Unlike pen plotters, which imitate the manner in which a person creates a line drawing, raster plotters deposit all the drawing's information in a single horizontal line simultaneously, on vertically moving paper. The drawings thus inherently consist of discrete dots; however, the dots are spaced closely (and may even be overlapping) so as to create the visual appearance of solid lines or areas. Densities of 8 dots·mm^{-1} are common; higher densities are available for special applications.

To display line-drawing data on a raster plotter, vector-to-raster scan conversion must be performed. Gray-tone images can be displayed by using a pseudo-halftone technique in which the density of the displayed dots is chosen to create the desired

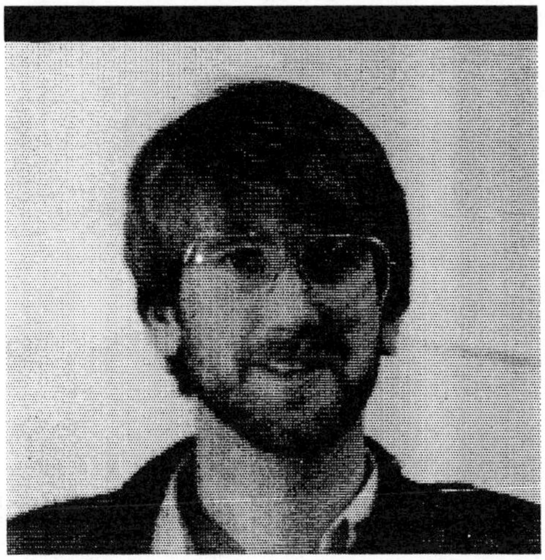

Figure 3.7. Bi-level display of a gray-tone image on a raster plotter. The gray-tone effect is achieved by varying the average density of the uniform-size black dots.

average gray level. A number of techniques exist that yield good-quality images in this way (Jarvis, Judice, & Ninke, 1976). An illustration of a gray-tone image displayed on a bi-level (black/white) raster plotter using the so-called ordered-dither technique is shown in Figure 3.7.

On a raster plotter, the time required to generate a plot is independent of the complexity of the line-drawing or gray-tone image and depends only on the image length (and for some plotters, also on image width). Typically, these plotters produce plots at a rate of about 12 cm of paper length per second.

2.2.2.1. ***Electrostatic Plotters.*** The most common type of raster plotter is the electrostatic plotter. This plotter uses specially coated paper. A row of closely spaced metallic nibs (typically spaced about 0.125 mm apart) can be used to deposit an electric charge pattern on the paper. The paper then passes through a toner ("ink") bath, where toner is picked up for any spot that is holding a charge. The paper is relatively inexpensive and is dry within seconds of coming out of the plotter. Color can be made available by using multiple, colored toners, but at considerably increased cost. Plotting time is independent of image width.

2.2.2.2. ***Ink-Jet Plotters.*** Ink-jet plotters utilize fine droplets of colored ink that are deposited on the paper from a horizontally moving carriage. The droplets are electrostatically propelled to achieve the desired pattern on the paper. Relatively low-cost, full-color ink-jet plotters have recently come on the market. Resolutions range from 4 to 6 dots·mm^{-1}. Plotting time for a 15 × 20-cm color picture is about 1½ min (considerably longer than for an electrostatic plotter but at much lower cost).

2.2.3. Cameras. Although it is possible to photograph directly the image displayed on a display monitor, the results thus obtained tend not to be very good. Monitors intended for direct viewing normally have slightly curved surfaces, the images commonly exhibit some "barrel"-type distortion, and the colors recorded on film may differ significantly from those seen on the monitor.

The preferred manner of recording computer-generated images on film (whether in monochrome or in color) is by using one of the special CRT cameras. These utilize a special flat-face, white-phosphor CRT, a filter wheel which contains red, green, and blue filters, a film-holding mechanism, and a microprocessor control unit. The input signals are the same as those that cause an image to be displayed on a conventional CRT monitor. However, instead of displaying the red, green, and blue image components for simultaneous viewing, they are displayed sequentially on the black-and-white CRT with the appropriate color filter interposed between CRT and color film. Exposure for each color is controlled by the microprocessor to take into account the different sensitivities of the film for each of the colors. High-quality, high-resolution images can be obtained in this manner. A schematic diagram of such a CRT camera is shown in Figure 3.8.

2.3. The Display Processor

The display processor (see Fig. 3.1) is a special-purpose computer that creates a digital version of the image to be displayed. In the case of a raster display system, this is then stored in a buffer memory and sent continually to the display unit to refresh the displayed image (usually at a rate of 30–40 frames per second). As new image data are sent to the buffer, old image data are automatically overwritten. During such image updating, the display shows for awhile a raster image consisting of both old data and incoming new data, which may be objectionable to the viewer. This can be avoided by blanking the display during the updating process. A better (but more costly) method is to use two buffer memories, one for holding the current image data and one for storing the incoming new image data. When the update is complete (which may take a few seconds), the display is then simply switched from one buffer to the other.

The display processor receives structured image data from the host computer, or, if the display processor is sufficiently powerful, runs the appropriate applications software to create the structured image data itself. In the case of a vector-type refresh display, the display processor stores a vector list and continually sends the coordinates of the vector end points to a hardware vector generator. The latter then causes the CRT beam to be deflected to trace out the desired series of vectors (line segments).

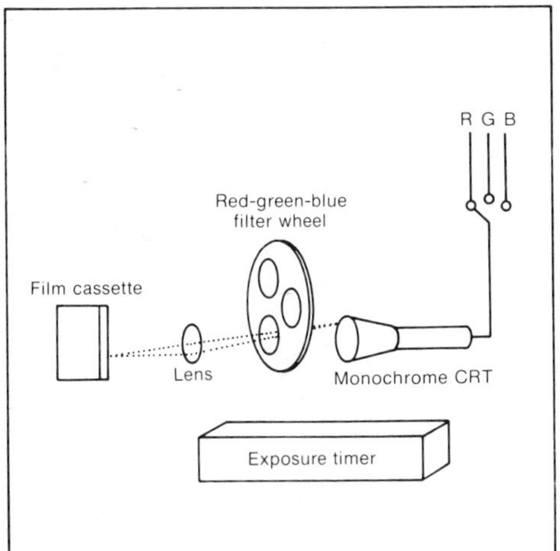

Figure 3.8. Schematic diagram of a CRT color camera. The camera employs a monochrome (black-and-white) CRT on which the three primary color components of the color image are displayed one at a time and then photographed through a color filter wheel to create the superposed color images on the film.

The display processor may be very simple, thereby placing more computational burden on its host computer, or it may be highly sophisticated and be capable of operating without any host computer. Typically, it contains hardware to generate all the intermediate points for a line segment given only the segment's end points, to scale, translate, and perhaps even rotate a line-drawing picture, to generate characters, to link different subpictures to form the displayed image, and to handle interrupts from the interactive devices.

3. LINE AND CURVE GENERATION

When we generate a curve with a digital computer, we do so in a discrete domain that normally is a uniform square lattice; that is, the curve is formed over a set of discrete points that are the nodes of such a lattice. This is illustrated in Figure 3.9 for both a straight-line segment and a circular arc; both the ideal curves and the corresponding digital approximations are shown. If the lattice is of very fine spacing, the digital approximation is indistinguishable from the ideal curve.

Although we may not be aware of the existence of the lattice, it is, in fact, always present. The use of finite-length digital numbers for both the x and y coordinates of a point implies the existence of such a lattice: points whose coordinates would require longer digital numbers are not defined and are not available to us. A 1-bit change in the least-significant position of either the x or y coordinate causes us to jump from one lattice node to a neighboring node.

The actual generation of digital line segments or curves can be carried out in either hardware or software. Most graphics display systems generate digital line segments in hardware and leave the generation of curves to software.

In considering the algorithms for line or curve generation, it is convenient to organize them into three groups: (1) algorithms for generating straight-line segments, (2) algorithms for generating digital approximations to mathematically defined curves (of which the circular arc is the most ubiquitous), and (3) digital approximations to so-called free-form curves, that is, curves that are defined only by a sketch or empirical data and that cannot readily be described in a mathematical sense. Examples of the last-named are the silhouette of a person's face and the cross-section outline of a ship's hull.

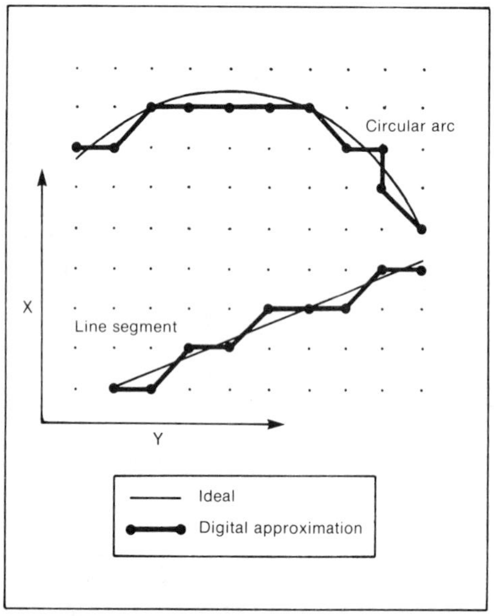

Figure 3.9. Representation of a line segment and a circular arc on a digital plotter. The approximations consist of sequences of short straight-line segments. The segments can assume only eight possible directions in moving from one defined point to the next.

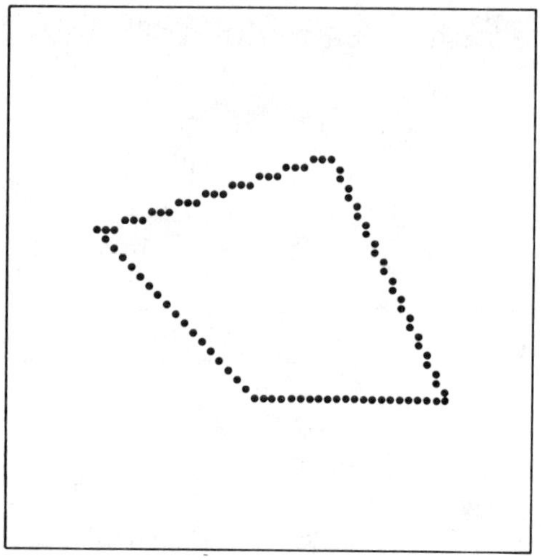

Figure 3.10. The "staircase" effect for line segments on a raster display. The raster points can lie on a true straight line only when the line segment is oriented at a multiple of 45° relative to the horizontal. For line segments oriented at arbitrary angles, the points exhibit the staircase effect shown in the top and right segments. Also note that the spacing between points varies, depending on the slope of the line. The latter causes the line to be perceived with varying brightness.

3.1. Digital Line Generation

A line segment is specified by the coordinates of its end points. To display a line segment on a vector-refresh display, the end point coordinates are supplied to a vector generator which, utilizing a hardware algorithm, computes all the intermediate points to move the beam on the screen so that the line segment is displayed. Because the beam is digitally "steered," it cannot in general trace out a true straight-line segment but only a digital approximation thereto. Note how in Figure 3.9 the approximation to the straight-line segment takes on a broken-line form and consists of tiny segments connecting adjacent nodes on a uniform square lattice. For a good-quality vector-refresh display, however, the lattice spacing is so small that the digital approximation appears as a smooth line segment to the viewer. (Note: In the early days of computer graphics only vector-refresh displays were used and the vector generators were all of the analog, that is, continuous-electric-signal, type. The vectors generated were thus true stepless straight-line segments. Now digital vector generators are used, but because of their high resolution, the viewer is normally unable to detect any staircase effects in a vector-refresh display image.)

On a raster display, the lattice is normally fairly coarse, with the spacing between adjacent raster points (i.e., the lattice spacing) being generally large enough to be discernible by the viewer (e.g., 0.5 mm). Hence a straight-line segment on a raster display appears as a noticeable "staircase" unless oriented at 0, 45, 90, or 135° relative to the horizontal. This staircase effect is illustrated in Figure 3.10.

3.1.1. DDA Algorithm. The algorithm most commonly employed in hardware vector generators is the DDA algorithm.

We describe it only for the first octant, that is, for line segments whose slope makes an angle between 0 and 45° with the positive x-axis. Suppose we wish to find the digital approximation of the line segment from a point (x_1, y_1) to point (x_2, y_2). Clearly, in the first octant, the slope of the line segments will range from 0 to at most 1. This implies that the digital line (i.e., the approximation) will advance by unity in the x direction at every step; the only question for the algorithm to answer is whether there should be an advance of 1 in the y direction. (There will never be an advance in y for a slope of 0 and there will always be such an advance for a slope of 1. For slopes between 0 and 1 there will be occasional advances, which depend on the actual slope.) (Note: The letters DDA stand for "digital differential analyzer" and refer to a special computer architecture popular for awhile in the early 1950s. The algorithm is patterned after algorithms used in those computers.)

Let $t = (y_2 - y_1)/(x_2 - x_1)$. Clearly,

$$x(0) = x_1$$

$$y(0) = y_1$$

$$x(i) = x(i - 1) + 1$$

$$w(i) = w(i - 1) + t$$

$$y(i) = \text{INTEGER VALUE OF } [w(i) + 0.5] .$$

The digital line segment is defined by the sequence $x(i)$, $y(i)$ for $i = 0, 1, ..., x_2 - x_1$.

The reader will note that in this algorithm t represents the slope of the line, and the w_i are the y-coordinates of points that lie on the line. The digital-point coordinates, y_i, are obtained simply by rounding the w_i to an integer value.

The DDA algorithm is readily extended to the other octants either by interchanging x and y or by making the required sign changes, as appropriate.

3.1.2. Bresenham Algorithm. The following algorithm, developed by Bresenham, will generate a digital line, given the coordinates of the end points (Bresenham, 1965). The algorithm, originally developed for digital plotters, is equally applicable to vector or raster CRT displays. Its main attraction is that it uses only integer arithmetic and is particularly easy to implement in either hardware or software.

As in the DDA algorithm, we concern ourselves only with the first octant, where the line slope must lie between 0 and 1. Given are end points (x_1, y_1) and (x_2, y_2), with the latter located in the first octant relative to the former.

Assume that the lattice spacing is taken as 1. Let

$$m = x_2 - x_1$$

$$n = y_2 - y_1$$

$$m > n > 0 .$$

Then

$$\Delta x = 1$$

and

$$\Delta y = 0 \text{ or } 1$$

depending on whether a *decision criterion* $d(i)$ is less than 0, or equal to or greater than 0. For the initial point (x_1, y_1),

$$d(1) = 2n - m .$$

Subsequently, if $d(i) \geqslant 0$,

$$y(i) = y(i - 1) + 1 \quad \text{and}$$

$$d(i + 1) = d(i) + 2n - 2m ;$$

if $d(i) < 0$,

$$y(i) = y(i - 1) \text{ and } d(i + 1) = d(i) + 2n ,$$

$$i = 2, 3, ..., m .$$

The algorithm is extended to any octant by either interchanging x and y or making the required sign changes, as appropriate. The digital line segment in Figure 3.9 was generated using this algorithm.

3.2. Circle Generation

A large variety of circle generation algorithms exist, differing in precision, convenience of use, and computational speed (Chung, 1977; McIlroy, 1984). The one described here is conceptually simple, but computationally some others are faster. It was first described by Fulton (1974) and can be understood with the aid of Figure 3.11.

The algorithm starts with a point where the circle intersects the x axis, that is, at a distance equal to the radius from the center. A step back in the x direction is then taken and the largest y value is computed that will give a point on or just inside the circle. This point will be part of the digital circle, and the process is repeated until the circle's x component has been reduced to 0.

Because a digital circle has four axes of symmetry (i.e., about the vertical, horizontal, and both diagonal axes), whenever

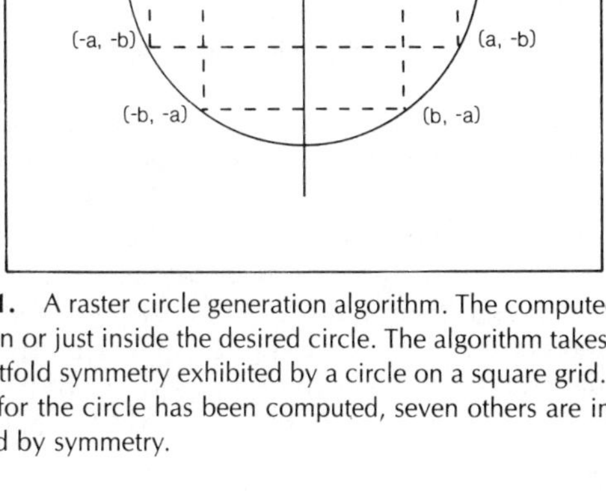

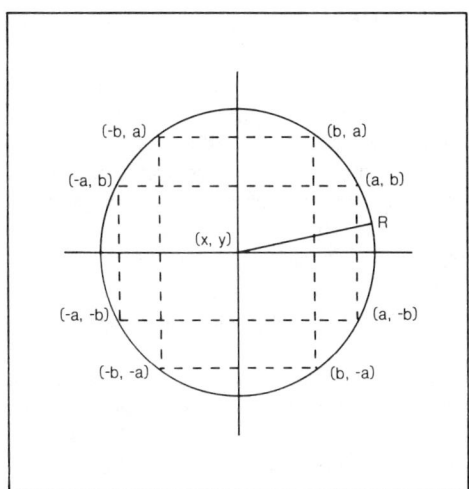

Figure 3.11. A raster circle generation algorithm. The computed points all lie either on or just inside the desired circle. The algorithm takes advantage of the eightfold symmetry exhibited by a circle on a square grid. Thus once one point for the circle has been computed, seven others are immediately determined by symmetry.

one point's coordinates have been found, the coordinates of seven additional points can be gotten immediately by symmetry.

The details of the algorithm are as follows, where the origin of the circle is at (x_0, y_0) and the radius is equal to R:

1. Let $DX = R, DY = 0$.
2. Replace DX by $DX - 1$.
3. Select largest integer DY such that

$$DX^2 + DY^2 \leqslant R^2 .$$

4. Generate the eight points on the circle:

$$(x_0 + DX, y_0 + DY) ,$$

$$(x_0 - DX, y_0 + DY) ,$$

$$(x_0 + DX, y_0 - DY) ,$$

$$(x_0 - DX, y_0 - DY) ,$$

$$(x_0 + DY, y_0 + DX) ,$$

$$(x_0 - DY, y_0 + DX) ,$$

$$(x_0 + DY, y_0 - DX) ,$$

$$(X_0 - DY, y_0 - DX) .$$

5. If $DX = 0$, stop. Otherwise repeat from step (2).

Although it may appear at first glance that the algorithm could be terminated when $DX < DY$, it is, in fact, necessary to continue until $DX = 0$. While the range $0 < DX < DY$ is traversed, new points are obtained that fill in gaps between some of the points previously computed. When DX reaches zero, all gaps will have been filled.

The algorithm works well for raster displays; however, it is quite unsuitable for vector displays because the circle points are not computed optimally for line-segment approximation. A more suitable algorithm for a vector display is given by Denert (1973).

3.3. Display of Mathematically Defined Curves

A variety of algorithms has been developed for displaying curves defined by a mathematical expression (Faux & Pratt, 1979; Jordan, Lennon, & Holm, 1973; Rogers & Adams, 1976). One of the simplest of these is the following. Suppose we wish to plot the curve $f(x, y) = 0$, where $f(x, y)$ is some particular mathematical expression. By the curve corresponding to a mathematical expression we mean the *locus* of all points (x, y) for which the equation $f(x, y) = 0$ holds, that is, all x, y-pair values that when substituted in $f(x, y)$ cause that expression to equal 0.

For a large class of mathematical expressions that have a locus of points for which the expression goes to zero we find further that the expression takes on a positive value to one side of the curve and a negative value to the other side. For curves of this kind (which fortunately includes most of the common curves we are likely to encounter), the following algorithm can be used effectively to generate a digital approximation.

Consider the curve shown in Figure 3.12. As indicated, the expression $f(x, y)$ takes on positive values to the left of the curve

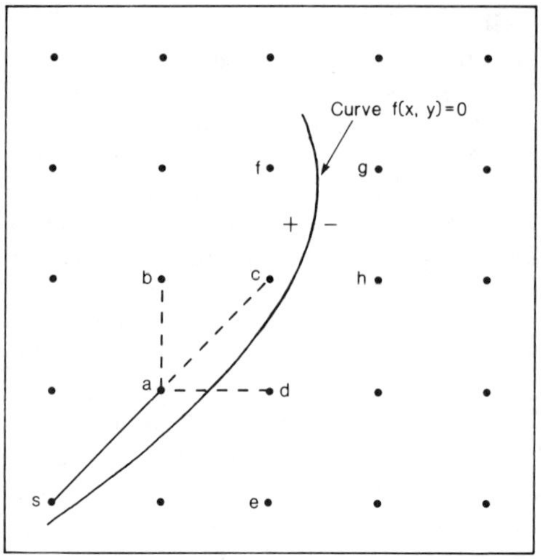

Figure 3.12. Algorithm for the selection of optimum lattice nodes for mathematical curve approximation. The algorithm proceeds to trace out the curve by testing for a pair of adjacent points such that the error is positive for one and negative for the other. This indicates that the curve passes between these two points. The point for which the error magnitude is smallest is then selected as the best approximation. Here the line segment *sa* is continued with a segment *ac* as point *c* is found to yield a smaller error than point *d*. The curve is known to pass between points *c* and *d* because the error is positive on one side of the curve and negative on the other. By first testing the points that lie in the same direction as the preceding pair, it is often necessary to evaluate only two points at each step.

and negative values to the right of the curve. Let us assume that it has already been determined that the line segment *sa* is the best digital approximation to the curve in that region. The question to be answered now is whether the next segment should be *ab*, *ac*, or *ad*. We proceed as follows.

We first evaluate $f(c)$ because c lies on the line *sa*; that is, we substitute the x, y coordinates of the point c in the expression. If the expression goes to zero, it means we were fortunate to find a point on the curve and we of course select it as our next lattice node and draw the segment *ac*. If, as in the case shown in Figure 3.12, c lies to the left of the curve, the value is positive. We next select the neighboring nodes to either side of c, that is, b and d, and evaluate $f(x, y)$ for these. For the curve shown, we find that $f(b)$ is also positive but $f(d)$ is negative, indicating that in going from c to d we have crossed over the curve.

When we have found two nodes that are neighbors of the last-used node as well as neighbors of each other, and which yield values of opposite sign when substituted in $f(x, y)$, we know that we have "straddled" the curve and that no other eligible nodes lie between. We then compare the magnitudes of the two values thus obtained and select the node that yields the smaller value. The reason for this is based on the assumption that the value at a node increases with distance from the curve. Thus in Figure 3.12, if $|f(c)| \leqslant |f(d)|$, we would select c as the next node and draw the segment *ac*. The process would then be repeated, using c as the starting node and evaluating nodes f, g, and h. In summary:

1. Starting from the current node, look for two neighboring nodes, c and d, that are also neighbors of each other and such that $f(c)$ and $f(d)$ are of opposite sign.
2. When such a pair has been found, select as the next approximation node

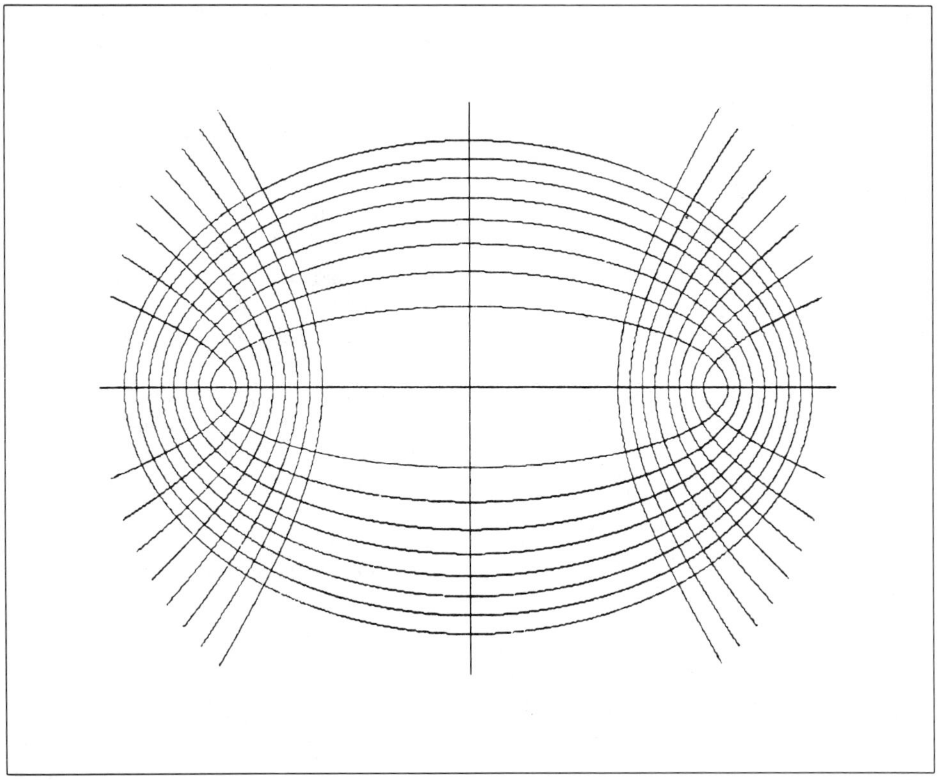

Figure 3.13. A series of digital ellipses and hyperbolas generated with the optimum lattice node selection algorithm of Section 3.3. The algorithm utilizes the quadratic equation $f(x, y) = (x/a)^2 \pm (y/b)^2 - c^2$, with the plus sign yielding the ellipses and the minus sign, the hyperbolas. The different curves of each kind are obtained by using different values of c. (Illustration by P. Woon, unpublished.)

$$c \text{ if } |f(c)| \leq |f(d)|$$

$$d \text{ if } |f(c)| > |f(d)| \text{ .}$$

3. Using the node thus found, repeat the process until the end of the curve is reached (or some specified termination criterion is satisfied).

The reader should note that because the expression $f(x, y)$ is successively evaluated for x, y pairs that differ only slightly, the evaluation can often be carried out in an incremental fashion, that is, by using the preceding value and computing only the adjustment required because of the small change in x or y.

A series of curves drawn with a digital plotter using this algorithm is shown in Figure 3.13.

3.4. Display of Free-Form Curves

In the preceding section an algorithm was described for displaying a mathematically defined curve, such as an ellipse or a cubic. We now describe a scheme for generating a curve that is only intuitively described; that is, the curve may be described in terms of a hand-drawn sketch plus some verbal description about its "fairness." The scheme is interactive; that is, the user can make an initial specification of the curve in terms of a series of control points and then request that the curve be displayed. If the initial curve does not meet objectives, the user can now change the location of one or more of the control points and repeat the process. The scheme described here was developed by Chaikin (1974). It is one of many such free-form curve generation algorithms (Barnhill & Riesenfeld, 1974) that have been developed in the past two decades.

Consider the sketched curve shown in Figure 3.14. It may be the complete curve we desire or merely a section of it. Let us suppose that we want the curve to pass through the points 0 and 3, and that we want the tangent to the curve (slope) at

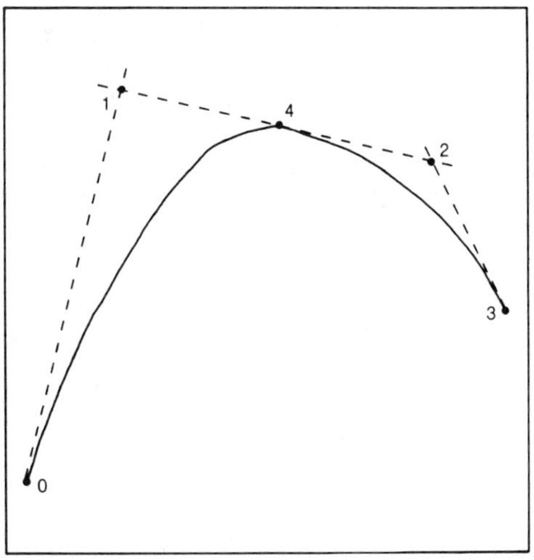

Figure 3.14. A rough, free-hand curve for which a smooth computer-drawn curve is to be obtained by means of the Chaikin algorithm. Points 0 and 3 are the curve's end points. Points 1 and 2 are chosen so that the lines 0–1 and 2–3 are tangent to the curve at 0 and 3, respectively, and so that the midpoint 4 of line segment 1–2 is also tangent to the curve.

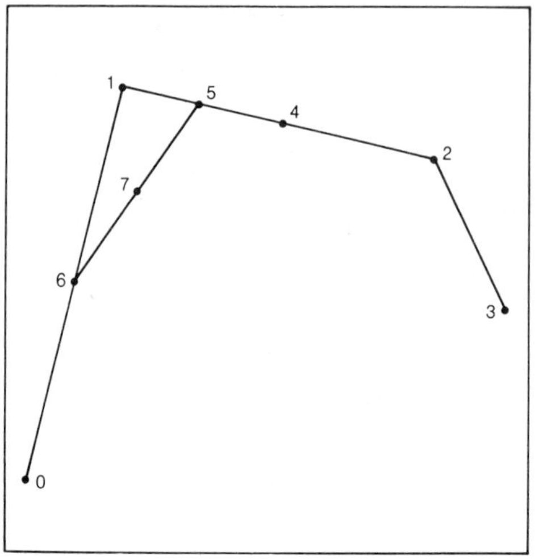

Figure 3.15. Successive midpoint determination in the Chaikin algorithm. Point 4 is the midpoint of segment 1–2, 5 is the midpoint of segment 1–4, 6 is the midpoint of segment 0–1, and 7 is the midpoint of 6–5.

these points to be as indicated by the dashed lines. We introduce two control points, 1 and 2, positioned on the two tangent lines so that the line segment joining them will also be tangent to the curve at its midpoint; this is the line so shown in Figure 3.14.

The actual algorithm now is as follows: Starting with the points 0, 1, 2, and 3, one finds the midpoint 4 of line segment 1–2. Next one finds the midpoints 5 and 6 of line segments 1–4 and 0–1, respectively, and connects these with a straight line, as shown in Figure 3.15. The set of points 0, 6, 5, 4 is now treated as a "new" set of four points (replacing 0, 1, 2, and 3) and the entire process is repeated. This continues until the distance between the first and last points of such a set of four falls below a specified threshold. When that occurs, the line segment corresponding to those points is drawn, the initial point is shifted to the end of the segment just drawn, and the process is repeated using points previously stored. The algorithm is described in detail in the flow chart of Figure 3.16. An example making use of the notation of the flow chart is given in Figure 3.17.

The control points for a curve are normally selected either (1) by making a rough sketch of the desired curve on a sheet of graph paper and reading off the points' x, y coordinates, or (2) by entering them with a data tablet on a graphics display. In the latter case, a suitable interactive graphics input program is required to "read" the data tablet values, display the points, and then pass the points' coordinates to the curve generation program. (See Section 5 of this chapter.)

Note that if a curve is more complex than can be modeled with the four control points, then additional points, beyond the initial four, must be used. The additional points are simply stored initially and then retrieved, three new points at a time, when one curve section has been completed and the next one is to be started. The last point of one four-point set always serves as the first point of the next set.

It is advisable to use a relatively large value initially for the threshold T to speed the process while the shape of the curve is being refined to suit the user's goals; once the desired shape has been achieved, the algorithm is run once more with a much smaller value of T to obtain a plot with the desired smoothness. The curve of Figure 3.18 was drawn with $T = 5$; the same curve is shown with $T = 2$ in Figure 3.19. Figure 3.20 shows a curve for a different set of control points; the value used for the threshold was $T = 2$.

3.5. The Chain Coding Scheme

In Section 3.1 it was pointed out that any line or curve segment on a digital display must necessarily be constituted of a sequence of points (or tiny line segments connecting these) that are neighboring nodes on a square lattice. The spacing of the lattice corresponds to the resolution of the display. When the resolution is very high, the lattice spacing may be so small that a viewer is unable to perceive it with the naked eye. Nevertheless such a lattice is in fact present, whether apparent or implied. This is as true for a CRT or plasma panel as it is for a pen plotter, where the lattice spacing may be as small as 0.01 mm.

As a digital curve (i.e., the digital approximations to a mathematical or otherwise-defined curve) moves from one lattice node to the next, it must select one of the eight nodes that surround the present node, as is clear from an examination of

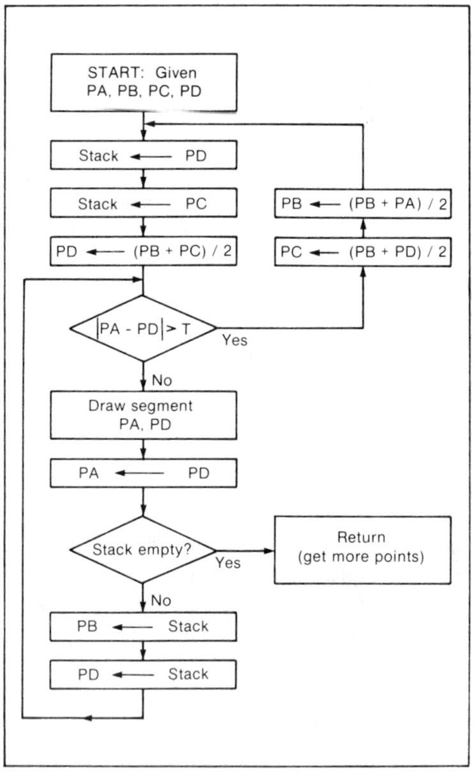

Figure 3.16. Flow chart of Chaikin algorithm. PA, PB, PC, and PD are software registers into which the x, y coordinates of the control points 0, 1, 2, and 3 are initially loaded. During the computation, the values in these registers change as more and more intermediate control points are computed (e.g., the points 5 and 6 in Fig. 3.15). The "stack" is a last-in, first-out storage area. The arrow "←" indicates that the value to its right (obtained by evaluating the indicated expression or by retrieving it from the top of the stack) is placed into the register (or top-of-stack position) at the left. The diamond-shaped box in the center indicates a decision step. When the distance between the points whose coordinates are currently stored in registers PA and PD is no longer greater than a specified threshold T, then a straight-line segment is drawn between these points and forms part of the straight-line approximation for the desired curve. The algorithm continues to generate such straight-line segments, starting from point 0, until the stack is empty (when point 3 will have been reached).

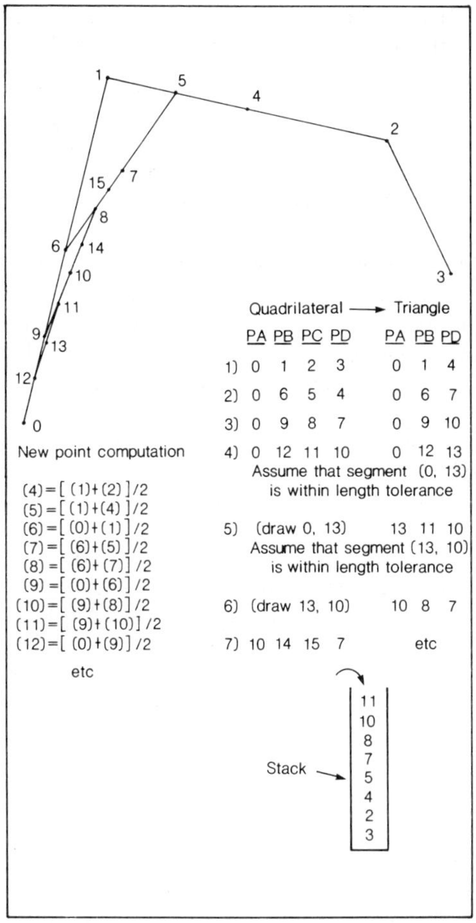

Figure 3.17. Example of use of Chaikin algorithm, using the notation of the flow chart of Figure 3.16. The resulting curve is shown in the next two figures. A total of seven iterations are shown at the right. The column at left shows the successive midpoint calculations. The points placed in the stack are shown at the bottom right.

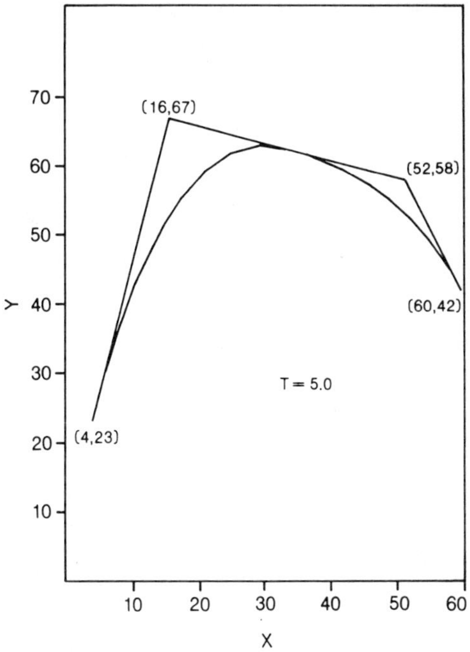

Figure 3.18. Digital curve generated with the Chaikin algorithm. A relatively coarse threshold of $T = 5$ is used.

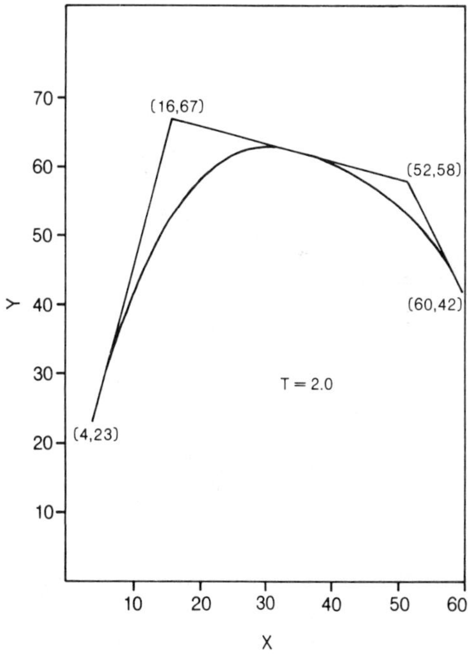

Figure 3.19. The same digital curve as that of Figure 3.18 but with a threshold value of $T = 2$ instead of 5. The result is a smoother curve, but at the expense of considerably longer computation time.

Figure 3.9. This suggests that the path of the curve can be coded in terms of a sequence of octal digits (0 through 7), where each digit indicates a node-to-node transition. This is illustrated in Figure 3.21. The given curve is shown with its digital approximation, which is encoded with the number sequence 1 2 1 1 1 0 1 0 0 1 2 3 4 4 4 5 4 4 5, using the octal coding scheme shown in the lower right. This particular curve coding scheme is known as *chain coding* (Freeman, 1974). Note that the sequence (i.e., the *chain*) uniquely defines the digital curve on the lattice (except for the coordinates of the starting point, for which the precise x, y coordinates must be specified).

3.5.1. Properties of the Chain Code

3.5.1.1. Link Length. A chain is a concatenation of octal digits (the chain's *links*) that describe a curve on a square lattice. The links make an angle of $m45°$ with the positive x axis, where m is the link value. Accordingly, all even-valued links (0, 2, 4, 6) have a length of 1, and all odd-valued links (1, 3, 5, 7) have a length of $\sqrt{2}$ times the lattice spacing h (which can be set to unity when its actual dimension is of no interest).

3.5.1.2. Length of a Chain. The length L of a chain is given by

$$L = n_e + n_o\sqrt{2}$$

where n_e and n_o are the total numbers of even-valued links and odd-valued links, respectively. For example, the length of the chain 1 1 2 1 2 1 2 3 is equal to $3 + 5\sqrt{2}$.

3.5.1.3. Inverse Links. Each chain link may be regarded as a short vector of length 1 or $\sqrt{2}$ and direction $m45°$. Two links are *inverses* of each other if they are directed in the opposite sense, for example, 1 and 5. Inspection of the code matrix in

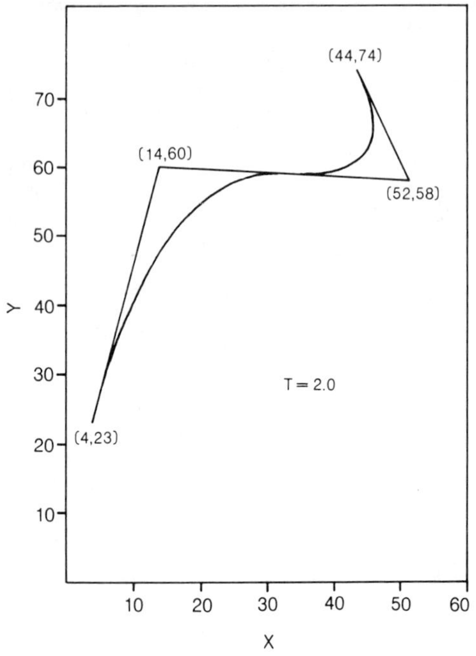

Figure 3.20. Another example of a digital curve generated with the Chaikin algorithm. A threshold of $T = 2$ is used.

Figure 3.21 indicates that we can obtain the inverse a_i^{-1} of a link a_i by modulo-8 addition of 4 to the link value:

$$a_i^{-1} = a_i \dot{+} 4$$

The dot over the plus sign denotes modulo-8 addition, that is, the sum must also be an octal digit (0 through 7); if ordinary addition yields a value greater than 7, 8 is subtracted as many times as necessary to bring the sum into the range 0 to 7.

3.5.1.4. Inverse Chains. A chain has a sense of direction, from a starting node to an end node. This means that a curve (which has no sense of direction) can be described in either of two ways, depending on which end is taken as the start node. The two chains are referred to as being *inverses* of each other. An examination of Figure 3.21 shows that the inverse of a chain can be obtained by replacing each chain link by its inverse and then rearranging these inverses in reverse order; that is, given a chain

$$A = a_1 a_2 a_3 \cdots a_n ,$$

its inverse is given by

$$A^{-1} = a_n^{-1} a_{n-1}^{-1} \cdots a_2^{-1} a_1^{-1} .$$

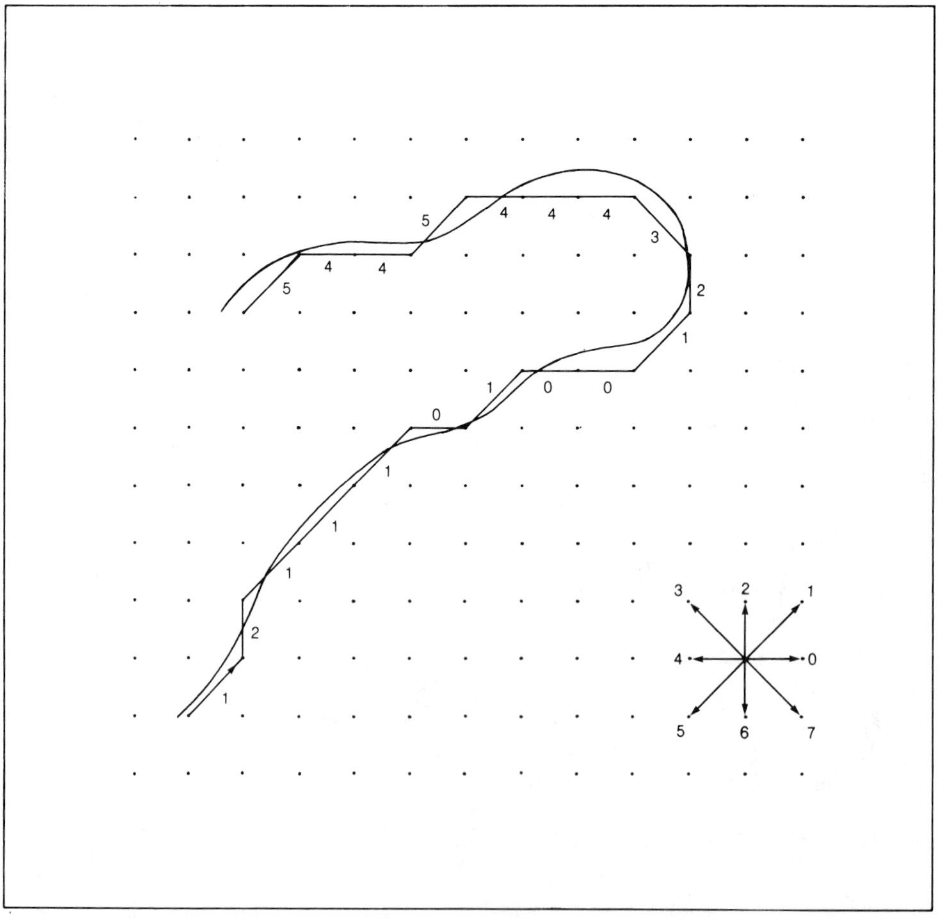

Figure 3.21. A curve and its chain (digital approximation). The coding matrix is shown in the lower right. The chain code is given by the sequence of digits along the chain, assuming a starting point in the lower left. Observe that if the chain were traced out in the opposite sense, the inverse chain would be obtained, given by 1 0 0 1 0 0 0 7 6 5 4 4 5 4 5 5 5 6 5.

Thus the inverse of the chain 1 2 1 1 1 0 1 0 0 1 2 3 4 4 4 5 4 4 5 is the chain 1 0 0 1 0 0 0 7 6 5 4 4 5 4 5 5 5 6 5.

3.5.1.5. Link Components. Because the links are really small vectors, they can be individually resolved into their x and y components, as follows:

a_i	a_i	a_{iy}
0	1	0
1	1	1
2	0	1
3	−1	1
4	−1	0
5	−1	−1
6	0	−1
7	1	−1

3.5.1.6. Width and Height of a Chain. The width of chain is the difference between its maximum and minimum x coordinate values. These can be readily found by keeping a running tally of the maximum and minimum values of the sum of the links' x components. Thus let

$$X_j = \sum_{i=0}^{j} a_{ix} \qquad \text{where } a_{0x} = 0 \ .$$

Then

$$\text{width} = \max_j X_j - \min_j X_j \ .$$

Similarly, for

$$Y_j = \sum_{i=0}^{j} a_{iy} \qquad \text{where } a_{0y} = 0 \ ,$$

$$\text{height} = \max_j Y_j - \min_j Y_j \ .$$

3.5.1.7. Test for a Closed Chain. A chain is closed if and only if its end point coincides with its start point. In terms of its links, a chain is closed if and only if

$$\sum_{i=1}^{n} a_{ix} = \sum_{i=1}^{n} a_{iy} = 0 \ .$$

The preceding paragraphs illustrate the ease with which chain coded curve data can be processed to extract information of interest. A comprehensive set of algorithms has been accumulated over the years for processing chain data. Included are algorithms for obtaining the area of a closed chain, the first and second moments of a chain about a specified axis, the distance between two points connected by a chain, and the minimum distance between a chain and a point or line, as well as for testing whether a chain is symmetrical about a specified axis and for determining the degree to which two chains match in shape, with or without regard to orientation or scale (Freeman, 1974, 1978).

3.5.2. Chain Control Codes. To make effective use of the chain coding scheme, it is necessary to provide for control codes

Table 3.2. Chain Control Codes

Octal Code Number[a]	Message
0400	End of chain
0401	Invisible links follow
0402	Visible links follow
0404	Valid 04 sequence
0405XYZ	Marker number XYZ_8
0407UV	Serial number, UV_8 digits long
0411	Nonchain data follows (e.g., "comments")
04127777	End of nonchain data
0413UWXYZ	Node number $WXYZ_8$ (U branches)
0417UXYZ	Link U is repeated XYZ_8 times
0420UN	Link U is repeated, next N + 4 digits specify number
0422U	Color U follows
0425U	Check code, modulo 8
0426ABCDE	X coordinate value $ABCDE_8$
0427ABCDE	Y coordinate value $ABCDE_8$

[a] The letters denote octal digits that the user must specify.

in the chain. The control codes are all identified by the link-pair 04. Because this is an inverse pair, it is not likely to occur naturally in a chain. A list of the most common chain control codes is given in Table 3.2.

Particularly noteworthy are the codes 0401 and 0402. The control code 0401 indicates that the subsequent chain links are to be regarded as being "invisible." When plotting a chain on a pen plotter the effect of this control code is to lift the pen up. The code 0402 negates the effect of the 0401 code and in the case of a pen plotter, would be equivalent to a "pen-down" command. Use of these "invisible" and "visible" control codes is illustrated in Figure 3.22, where the chains A and B are kept in the proper position relative to each other by the "invisible" chain C.

3.5.3. Application of the Chain Coding Scheme. The chain coding scheme is particularly useful for the representation of

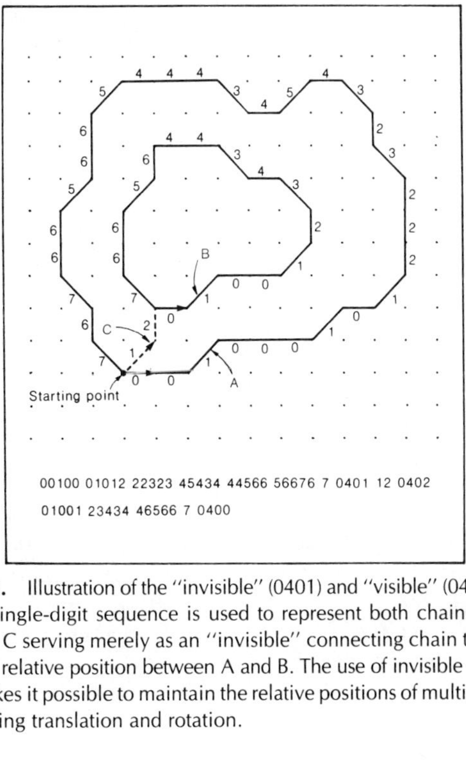

Figure 3.22. Illustration of the "invisible" (0401) and "visible" (0402) control codes. A single-digit sequence is used to represent both chains A and B, with chain C serving merely as an "invisible" connecting chain to maintain the correct relative position between A and B. The use of invisible connecting chains makes it possible to maintain the relative positions of multiple disjoint curves during translation and rotation.

irregular line drawings, such as, for example, the elevation contour lines in a topographic map. As shown in Section 3.5.1, the chain representation has many useful properties for chain manipulation and analysis. The chain code representation can, of course, also be used for regular line drawings containing any long straight-line segments; however, the simple polygonal representation is then more efficient.

Algorithms exist for generating the chain code for mathematically defined curves, for extracting the chain code of curves directly from the raster scan data of automatically digitized curves, and for rotating and scaling chains (Freeman, 1974). The chain representation scheme is most effective when the data are to be subjected to extensive computer processing in addition to display. Its primary application has been in map data processing and cartography, in the processing of line-drawing data extracted from medical imagery, and in a variety of pattern recognition applications (Freeman, 1974; Pavlidis, 1982; Sklansky, 1973).

4. TRANSFORMATIONS

Of great importance to users of interactive computer graphics is the ability to subject their graphic design—including any portions of it—to simple linear transformations: translation, scaling, and rotation. Techniques have been developed to perform these operations efficiently through the use of vector algebra (Rogers & Adams, 1976; Foley & Van Dam, 1982).

The building blocks of computer graphics are the point, the line segment, and the polygon; however, the real primitive is the point because a line segment is the shortest distance connecting two points, and a polygon is a connected sequence of line segments lying in one plane. Thus transformations need be performed only on points. To transform a line segment we transform its end points; to transform a polygon we transform its line segments.

4.1. Vector and Matrix Notation

For the point (x, y) in two-dimensional space, we shall use the vector notation

$$\begin{bmatrix} x \\ y \end{bmatrix}$$

and, correspondingly, for a point (x, y, z) in three-dimensional space,

$$\begin{bmatrix} x \\ y \\ z \end{bmatrix} .$$

Vectors can be multiplied by matrices to obtain a transformed vector. The only condition on a pre-multiplying matrix (i.e., a matrix placed to the *left* of the vector it multiplies) is that the number of its columns be equal to the number of rows of the (column) vector. The new vector has as many rows as the matrix. Thus

$$\begin{bmatrix} u_1 \\ u_2 \\ \cdot \\ \cdot \\ \cdot \\ u_m \end{bmatrix} = \begin{bmatrix} a_{11} & a_{12} & \cdots & a_{1n} \\ a_{21} & a_{22} & \cdots & \\ \cdot & & & \cdot \\ \cdot & & & \cdot \\ \cdot & & & \cdot \\ a_{m1} & \cdot & \cdots & a_{mn} \end{bmatrix} \begin{bmatrix} v_1 \\ v_2 \\ \cdot \\ \cdot \\ \cdot \\ v_n \end{bmatrix}$$

where the value of each component u_i of the new vector is given by

$$u_i = \sum_{k=1}^{n} a_{ik} v_k \qquad \text{for all } 1 \leq i \leq m .$$

For the type of matrix operations encountered in computer graphics, the matrices are virtually always square and do not exceed a dimension of 4; that is, $m = n \leq 4$.

Occasionally we find it necessary to take the product of two $m \times m$ matrices. The resulting product matrix is another $m \times m$ matrix whose elements w_{ij} can be expressed in terms of the elements of the multiplying matrices, a_{ij} and b_{ij}, by

$$w_{ij} = \sum_{k=1}^{m} a_{ik} b_{kj} ,$$

where both i and j range from 1 to m. For example, for two 3×3 matrices **A** and **B**, the element w_{12} of the 3×3 product matrix **W** is

$$w_{12} = \sum_{k=1}^{3} a_{1k}\, b_{k2}$$

$$= a_{11}\, b_{12} + a_{12}\, b_{22} + a_{13}\, b_{32} .$$

The reader should note that throughout this chapter we are pre-multiplying column vectors by matrices to obtain other column vectors. An equally acceptable scheme, sometimes seen in other books, is to post-multiply row vectors by matrices to obtain other row vectors. (In post-multiplication, the matrix is placed to the *right* of the vector it multiplies.) The matrices in the latter case differ from those in the first even though the same transformation (e.g., rotation) is accomplished; specifically, the rows and columns have their roles interchanged, causing element a_{ij} to be replaced by element a_{ji} for all i and j.

Finally, care must be taken with regard to the *order* in which matrices multiply a vector, that is, $\mathbf{M} \times \mathbf{N}\,\mathbf{v}$ is not equal to $\mathbf{N} \times \mathbf{M}\,\mathbf{v}$ (except in special cases).

4.2. Translation

Translation of the point (x_1, y_1) by DX and DY, respectively, in the x and y directions yields the new point (x_2, y_2), as shown in Figure 3.23:

$$x_2 = x_1 + DX$$

$$y_2 = y_1 + DY$$

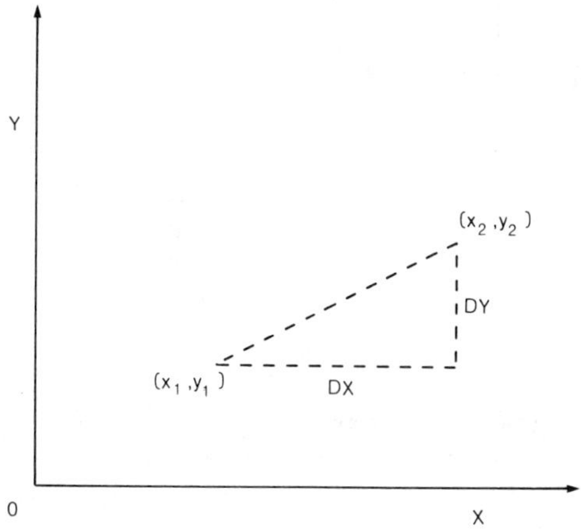

Figure 3.23. Translation of a point. The given point (x_1, y_1) is translated by amounts DX and DY, respectively, in the x and y directions.

or, in vector notation,

$$\begin{bmatrix} x_2 \\ y_2 \end{bmatrix} = \begin{bmatrix} x_1 \\ y_1 \end{bmatrix} + \begin{bmatrix} DX \\ DY \end{bmatrix} .$$

4.3. Rotation

To rotate the point (x_1, y_1) counterclockwise about the origin by an angle θ, we use the equations

$$x_2 = x_1 \cos\theta - y_1 \sin\theta$$

$$y_2 = x_1 \sin\theta + y_1 \cos\theta$$

or, in vector notation,

$$\begin{bmatrix} x_2 \\ y_2 \end{bmatrix} = \begin{bmatrix} \cos\theta & -\sin\theta \\ \sin\theta & \cos\theta \end{bmatrix} \begin{bmatrix} x_1 \\ y_1 \end{bmatrix} = \mathbf{M} \begin{bmatrix} x_1 \\ y_1 \end{bmatrix}$$

where **M** is the rotation matrix. This is illustrated in Figure 3.24.

4.4. Scaling

To expand the scale of a point by a factor k_x in the x direction and a factor k_y in the y direction, as shown in Figure 3.25, we use the equation

$$x_2 = k_x x_1$$

$$y_2 = k_y y_1$$

or, in vector notation,

$$\begin{bmatrix} x_2 \\ y_2 \end{bmatrix} = \begin{bmatrix} k_x & 0 \\ 0 & k_y \end{bmatrix} \begin{bmatrix} x_1 \\ y_1 \end{bmatrix} .$$

Clearly, if $k_x = k_y = k$, the scale factor is uniform in all directions.

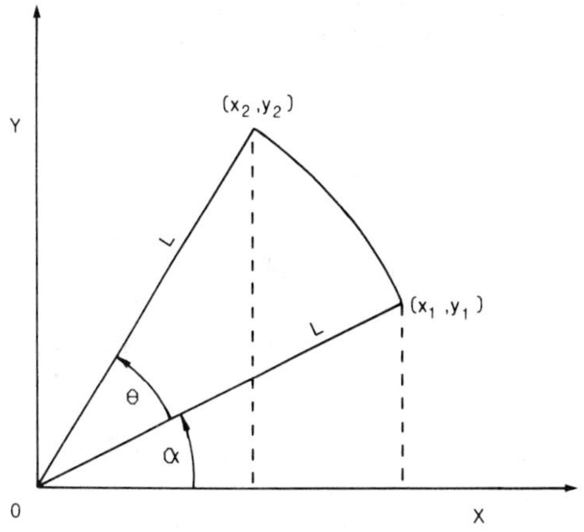

Figure 3.24. Rotation of a point about the origin. The given point (x_1, y_1) is rotated by an angle θ about the origin to (x_2, y_2). If the vector from the origin to (x_1, y_1) makes an angle of α with the positive x axis, after rotation its angle with this axis is $\alpha + \theta$. Note that $x_1 = L\cos\alpha$, $y_1 = L\sin\alpha$, $x_2 = L\cos(\alpha + \theta)$ and $y_2 = L\sin(\alpha + \theta)$. Thus from the formulas for the sine and cosine of the sum of two angles,

$$x_2 = L(\cos\alpha\cos\theta - \sin\alpha\sin\theta) = x_1\cos\theta - y_1\sin\theta$$

$$y_2 = L(\cos\alpha\sin\theta + \sin\alpha\cos\theta) = x_1\sin\theta + y_1\cos\theta .$$

4.5. Homogeneous Coordinates

It is apparent from Sections 4.2–4.4 that translation of a point can be achieved by means of vector addition, whereas both rotation and scaling are achieved through a matrix multiplication. Because all three kinds of transformations occur frequently in interactive computer graphics, it is considered desirable that all three operations be identical in form and be able to be combined into a single, composite transformation. This can be accomplished through use of so-called *homogeneous coordinates* (Rogers & Adams, 1976), which, by adding an extra dimension, permit translation as well as rotation and scaling to be represented by a matrix multiplication.

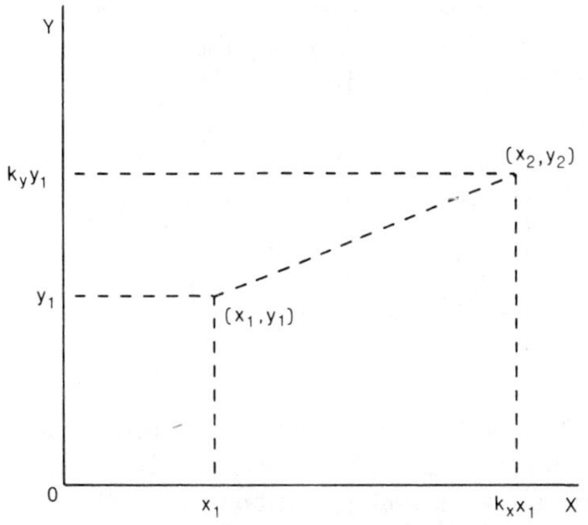

Figure 3.25. Illustration of scaling by k_x and k_y, respectively, in the x and y directions. Observe that the scaling is with respect to the origin. If $k_x = k_y$, we have uniform scaling, which is the more common case.

A point (x_1, y_1) in two-dimensional space is represented in homogeneous coordinates by the (three-dimensional) vector

$$\begin{bmatrix} x_1 \\ y_1 \\ 1 \end{bmatrix}$$

and a point (x_1, y_1, z_1) in three-dimensional space by the (four-dimensional) vector

$$\begin{bmatrix} x_1 \\ y_1 \\ z_1 \\ 1 \end{bmatrix}.$$

Note that the last component for both vectors is simply unity.

The homogeneous-coordinate matrices for translation, rotation, and scaling, given in Sections 4.5.1, 4.5.2, and 4.5.3, respectively, represent the same equations as those given in Section 4.2–4.4.

4.5.1. Translation in Homogeneous Coordinates. Translation of the point (x_1, y_1) by (DX, DY) can be expressed in homogeneous coordinates by the matrix multiplication

$$\begin{bmatrix} x_2 \\ y_2 \\ 1 \end{bmatrix} = \begin{bmatrix} 1 & 0 & DX \\ 0 & 1 & DY \\ 0 & 0 & 1 \end{bmatrix} \begin{bmatrix} x_1 \\ y_1 \\ 1 \end{bmatrix}.$$

4.5.2. Rotation in Homogeneous Coordinates. Counterclockwise rotation by an angle θ in homogeneous coordinates is expressed by the matrix multiplication

$$\begin{bmatrix} x_2 \\ y_2 \\ 1 \end{bmatrix} = \begin{bmatrix} \cos\theta & -\sin\theta & 0 \\ \sin\theta & \cos\theta & 0 \\ 0 & 0 & 1 \end{bmatrix} \begin{bmatrix} x_1 \\ y_1 \\ 1 \end{bmatrix}.$$

4.5.3. Scaling in Homogeneous Coordinates. In homogeneous coordinates, the scaling of a point (x_1, y_1) by k_x in the x direction and k_y in the y direction, relative to the origin, is expressed by

$$\begin{bmatrix} x_2 \\ y_2 \\ 1 \end{bmatrix} = \begin{bmatrix} k_x & 0 & 0 \\ 0 & k_y & 0 \\ 0 & 0 & 1 \end{bmatrix} \begin{bmatrix} x_1 \\ y_1 \\ 1 \end{bmatrix}.$$

4.5.4. Composite Transformations. Because the product of two 3×3 matrices is another 3×3 matrix, one can combine any number of translations, rotations, and scale changes into a *single matrix multiplication*. It is this ability of combining any number of transformations into a single matrix multiplication that is the justification for the use of homogeneous coordinates. Thus

$$\begin{bmatrix} x_2 \\ y_2 \\ 1 \end{bmatrix} = \begin{bmatrix} 1 & 0 & DX \\ 0 & 1 & DY \\ 0 & 0 & 1 \end{bmatrix} \begin{bmatrix} \cos\theta & -\sin\theta & 0 \\ \sin\theta & \cos\theta & 0 \\ 0 & 0 & 1 \end{bmatrix} \begin{bmatrix} x_1 \\ y_1 \\ 1 \end{bmatrix}$$

$$= \begin{bmatrix} \cos\theta & -\sin\theta & DY \\ \sin\theta & \cos\theta & DY \\ 0 & 0 & 1 \end{bmatrix} \begin{bmatrix} x_1 \\ y_1 \\ 1 \end{bmatrix}$$

represents rotation of the point (x_1, y_1) about the origin by an angle θ, followed by a translation (DX, DY).

Observe that the *order* of the transformations is important. Thus if the point (x_1, y_1) is first translated and then rotated, a different result is obtained:

$$\begin{bmatrix} x_2 \\ y_2 \\ 1 \end{bmatrix} = \begin{bmatrix} \cos\theta & -\sin\theta & 0 \\ \sin\theta & \cos\theta & 0 \\ 0 & 0 & 1 \end{bmatrix} \begin{bmatrix} 1 & 0 & DX \\ 0 & 1 & DY \\ 0 & 0 & 1 \end{bmatrix} \begin{bmatrix} x_1 \\ y_1 \\ 1 \end{bmatrix}$$

$$= \begin{bmatrix} \cos\theta & -\sin\theta & (DX\cos\theta - DY\sin\theta) \\ \sin\theta & \cos\theta & (DX\sin\theta + DY\cos\theta) \\ 0 & 0 & 1 \end{bmatrix} \begin{bmatrix} x_1 \\ y_1 \\ 1 \end{bmatrix}.$$

As another example, the composite transformation, consisting of a rotation, a scale change, and finally a translation, would appear as follows:

$$\begin{bmatrix} x_2 \\ y_2 \\ 1 \end{bmatrix} = \begin{bmatrix} k_x\cos\theta & -k_y\sin\theta & DX \\ k_y\sin\theta & k_y\cos\theta & DY \\ 0 & 0 & 1 \end{bmatrix} \begin{bmatrix} x_1 \\ y_1 \\ 1 \end{bmatrix}.$$

4.5.5. Rotation about a Point Other than Origin. The rotation transformation causes a point to be rotated counterclockwise about the origin. Sometimes it is desired to rotate a point (x_1, y_1) about another point (x_3, y_3), as illustrated in Figure 3.26. We accomplish this by first translating the origin of the coordinate system to (x_3, y_3). Then we perform the rotation (about the translated origin) and, when done, translate the origin back to its original position. In homogeneous coordinates,

$$\begin{bmatrix} x_2 \\ y_2 \\ 1 \end{bmatrix} =$$

$$\begin{bmatrix} 1 & 0 & x_3 \\ 0 & 1 & y_3 \\ 0 & 0 & 1 \end{bmatrix} \begin{bmatrix} \cos\theta & -\sin\theta & 0 \\ \sin\theta & \cos\theta & 0 \\ 0 & 0 & 1 \end{bmatrix} \begin{bmatrix} 1 & 0 & -x_3 \\ 0 & 1 & -y_3 \\ 0 & 0 & 1 \end{bmatrix} \begin{bmatrix} x_1 \\ y_1 \\ 1 \end{bmatrix}.$$

(The reader should carefully note the right-to-left order of the transformation matrices.)

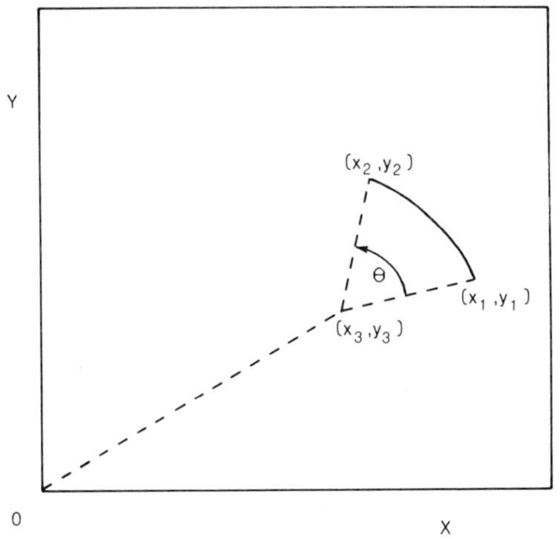

Figure 3.26. Rotation about a point other than the origin. To rotate the point (x_1, y_1) about the point (x_3, y_3), one temporarily shifts the origin to (x_3, y_3), performs the rotation, and then shifts the origin back to its original position.

4.6. Transformations in Three Dimensions

Translation and scaling in three dimensions are identical in form as for two dimensions; rotation is, however, more complex because instead of a simple rotation in the plane, as many as three separate rotations may be involved. The matrix formulas given apply to counterclockwise rotation about the axis specified, as seen by an observer looking inward along the positive portion of the axis, toward the origin. All are given in homogeneous coordinates. The three rotations are illustrated in Figure 3.27.

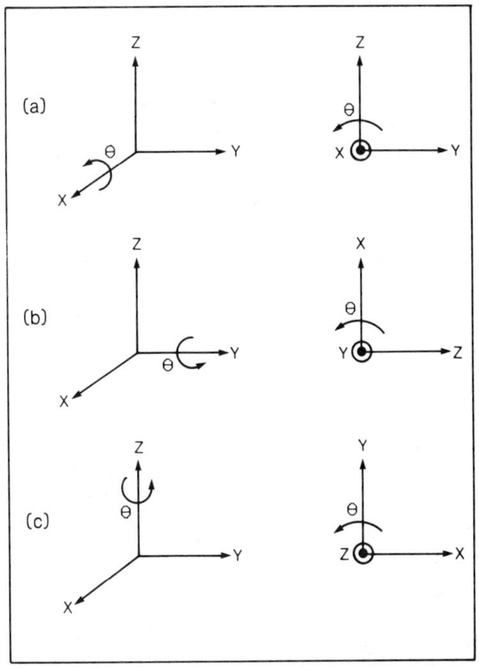

Figure 3.27. Rotation about an axis in three-dimensional space: (a) about x-axis, (b) about y-axis, and (c) about z-axis. The coordinate axis pictures at the right each show one axis pointed directly at the observer (out of the paper); these notations are preferable to the ones at the left because the latter are subject to ambiguous interpretation (e.g., in the bottom left figure, does the x-axis come out of the paper or go into the paper?).

4.6.1. Rotation about *x*-Axis. Figure 3.27(a).

$$\begin{bmatrix} x_2 \\ y_2 \\ z_2 \\ 1 \end{bmatrix} = \begin{bmatrix} 1 & 0 & 0 & 0 \\ 0 & \cos\theta & \sin\theta & 0 \\ 0 & \sin\theta & \cos\theta & 0 \\ 0 & 0 & 0 & 1 \end{bmatrix} \begin{bmatrix} x_1 \\ y_1 \\ z_1 \\ 1 \end{bmatrix}.$$

4.6.2. Rotation about *y*-Axis. Figure 3.27(b).

$$\begin{bmatrix} x_2 \\ y_2 \\ z_2 \\ 1 \end{bmatrix} = \begin{bmatrix} \cos\theta & 0 & \sin\theta & 0 \\ 0 & 1 & 0 & 0 \\ -\sin\theta & 0 & \cos\theta & 0 \\ 0 & 0 & 0 & 1 \end{bmatrix} \begin{bmatrix} x_1 \\ y_1 \\ z_1 \\ 1 \end{bmatrix}.$$

4.6.3. Rotation about *z*-Axis. Figure 3.27(c).

$$\begin{bmatrix} x_2 \\ y_2 \\ z_2 \\ 1 \end{bmatrix} = \begin{bmatrix} \cos\theta & -\sin\theta & 0 & 0 \\ \sin\theta & \cos\theta & 0 & 0 \\ 0 & 0 & 1 & 0 \\ 0 & 0 & 0 & 1 \end{bmatrix} \begin{bmatrix} x_1 \\ y_1 \\ z_1 \\ 1 \end{bmatrix}.$$

4.6.4. Composite Transformations in Three-Dimensional Space. As shown in Section 4.5.4, successive transformations can be combined by simply multiplying the appropriate matrices, in the proper order. The result is a single 4 × 4 matrix, which can combine within it the effect of any sequence of translations, scale changes, and rotations about any of the axes.

4.6.5. Rotation about an Arbitrary Axis. Sections 4.6.1–4.6.3 dealt with rotations about each of the three Cartesian-coordinate axes. We now describe the procedure that will permit us to rotate a point by an angle about any arbitrarily oriented line. (Note that rotating a line segment, a polygon, or a polyhedron about a line consists simply of rotating all the object's vertices about the line by the same amount.)

We consider the configuration shown in Figure 3.28, where the point P is to be rotated about the line w through (x_1, y_1, z_1) and (x_2, y_2, z_2). The approach taken is to transform both the point and the line, through a translation and series of rotations, so that the line will be aligned with the z-axis. The desired rotation of P about the line is then identical with rotation about the z-axis, for which we already have a matrix. The rotation is performed, after which the line and the rotated point are taken through the same transformations in reverse, restoring the line to its original position. The point P then has been rotated by the desired amount about the indicated line. The following describes the actual steps of this procedure.

1. The line and point are translated so that the line passes through the coordinate system's origin. This is done by translating (x_1, y_1, z_1) to the origin. The transformation for this is

$$\mathbf{T}_1 = \begin{bmatrix} 1 & 0 & 0 & -x_1 \\ 0 & 1 & 0 & -y_1 \\ 0 & 0 & 1 & -z_1 \\ 0 & 0 & 0 & 1 \end{bmatrix}.$$

2. The line and point are next rotated counterclockwise about the x-axis to place the line into the x–z plane, as shown in Figure 3.29(a). (The new orientation of the line w is now indicated by w^1. The rotation is given by

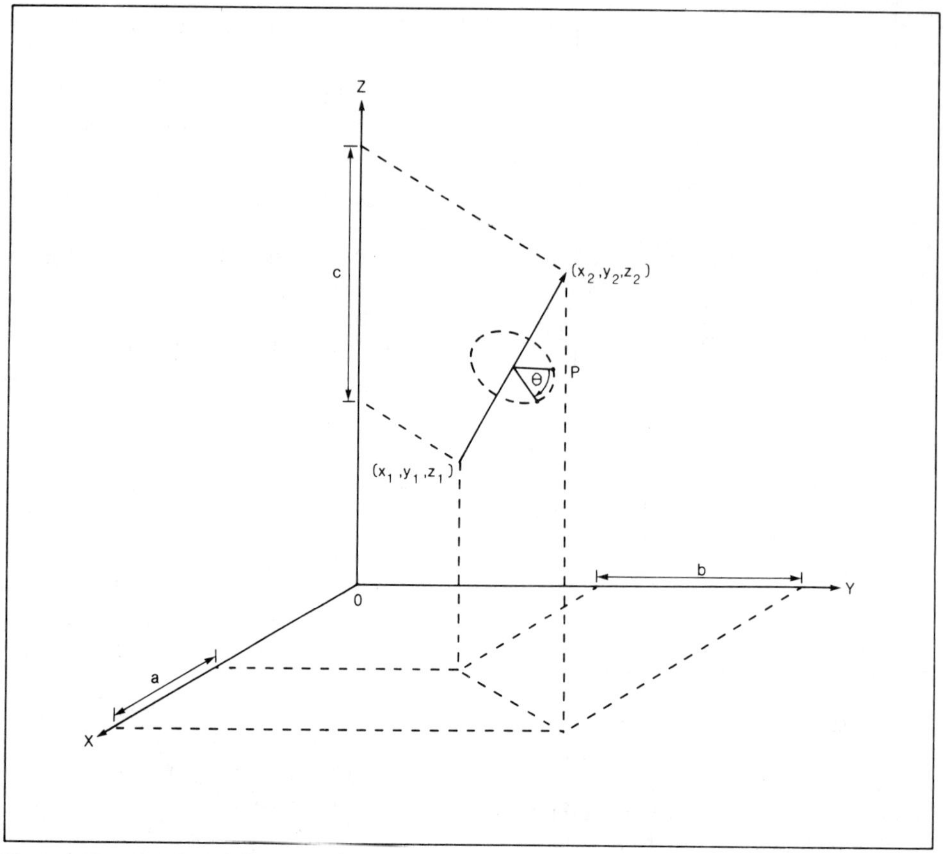

Figure 3.28. Rotation of the point P by an angle θ about the arbitrary line in space passing through the points (x_1, y_1, z_1) and (x_2, y_2, z_2). The rotation is achieved by translating (x_1, y_1, z_1) to the origin, then rotating the line segment first about the x-axis and then about the y-axis until the segment is *aligned* with the positive z-axis. Then rotating P about the z-axis is equivalent to rotating P about the line segment. The various steps are then reversed to restore the line segment to its original position. The desired rotation of P about the line segment has been achieved and P is in its proper new position in three-dimensional space. The detailed steps are illustrated in Figure 3.29.

$$\mathbf{R}_1 = \begin{bmatrix} 1 & 0 & 0 & 0 \\ 0 & \cos\phi & -\sin\phi & 0 \\ 0 & \sin\phi & \cos\phi & 0 \\ 0 & 0 & 0 & 1 \end{bmatrix}$$

where

$$\cos\phi = \frac{c}{\sqrt{b^2 + c^2}}$$

$$\sin\phi = \frac{b}{\sqrt{b^2 + c^2}}$$

and

$$a = x_2 - x_1, \quad b = y_2 - y_1, \quad c = z_2 - z_1 .$$

3. A clockwise rotation about the y-axis now aligns the line with the positive z-axis. This is shown in Figure 3.29(b), where the new line orientation is w^{11}. The applicable rotation is

$$\mathbf{R}_2 = \begin{bmatrix} \cos\psi & 0 & -\sin\psi & 0 \\ 0 & 1 & 0 & 0 \\ \sin\psi & 0 & \cos\psi & 0 \\ 0 & 0 & 0 & 1 \end{bmatrix}$$

where

$$\cos\psi = \frac{\sqrt{b^2 + c^2}}{\sqrt{a^2 + b^2 + c^2}}$$

$$\sin\psi = \frac{a}{\sqrt{a^2 + b^2 + c^2}} .$$

4. With the line oriented along the z-axis the rotation of P by an angle θ about the line can now take place. The rotation matrix is the one for any rotation about the z-axis:

$$\mathbf{R}_3 = \begin{bmatrix} \cos\theta & -\sin\theta & 0 & 0 \\ \sin\theta & \cos\theta & 0 & 0 \\ 0 & 0 & 1 & 0 \\ 0 & 0 & 0 & 1 \end{bmatrix} .$$

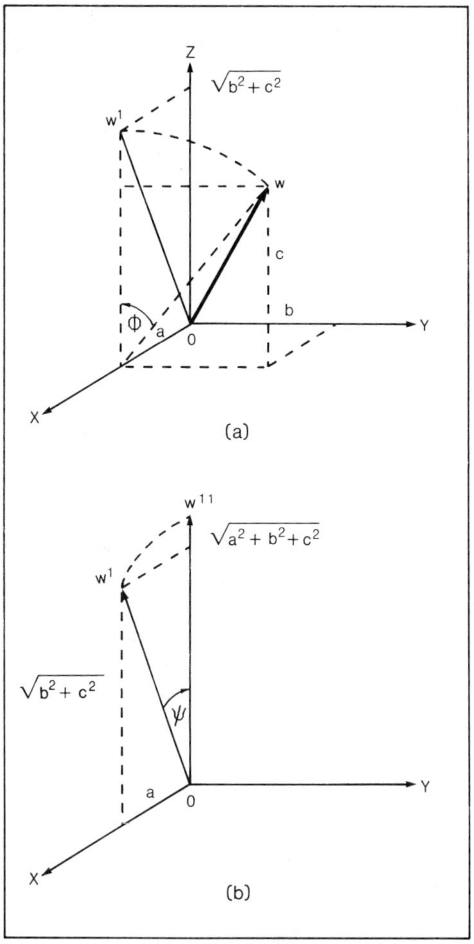

Figure 3.29. Intermediate steps in computing the rotation of point P by an angle θ about the specified line segment. In (a) point 1—whose original coordinates were (x_1, y_1, z_1)—has been translated to the origin and the line segment rotated about the positive x-axis by an angle ϕ to place point 2—with original coordinates (x_2, y_2, z_2)—at location w^1. The rotation of point 2 takes place in the plane $x = a$. The sine and cosine of the rotation angle ϕ in this plane are simply the ratios of opposite and adjacent line segments to the hypotenuse, respectively. In (b) the line segment has been rotated about the y-axis by an angle ψ (in the negative sense, i.e., clockwise) to place point 2 at location w^{11}. Rotating P about the line segment by the angle θ now is equivalent to rotating P by the angle θ about the z-axis, for which a simple formula exists. Once this rotation is accomplished, the series of transformations (rotations by ϕ and ψ) are reversed, and point 2 is translated back to its original position. The desired rotation about the arbitrarily oriented line segment has been achieved.

5. Now the transformation process must be reversed, using rotations $\mathbf{R}_2^{-1}$, $\mathbf{R}_1^{-1}$, and $\mathbf{T}^{-1}$, in that order, where the superscripts "-1" indicate use of the *inverse matrix* or, what is equivalent, rotation by an equal or opposite angle. That is, we use $-\psi$ and $-\phi$ for $\mathbf{R}_2$ and $\mathbf{R}_1$, respectively. Similarly, for $\mathbf{T}^{-1}$ we translate by the negatives of the amounts used originally for $\mathbf{T}$. The complete transformation then is represented by

$$\mathbf{T}_0 = \mathbf{T}^{-1}\mathbf{R}_1^{-1}\mathbf{R}_2^{-1}\mathbf{R}_3\mathbf{R}_2\mathbf{R}_1\mathbf{T} \; ,$$

which can be expressed as a single 4×4 matrix. Note that where we are rotating an entire object, consisting perhaps of thousands of vertices, about an arbitrary line, all we need do

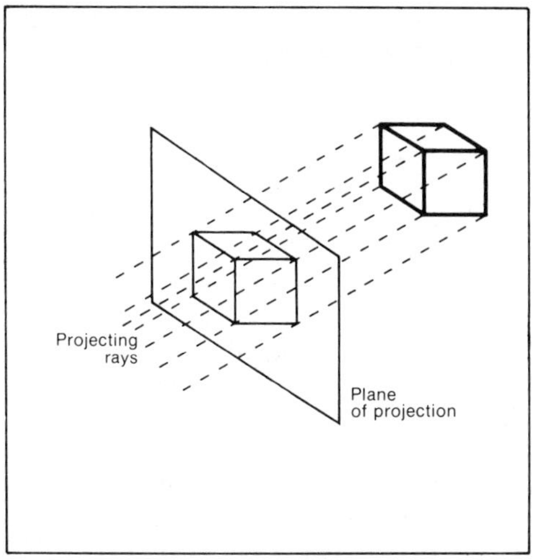

Figure 3.30. Illustration of a parallel projection. The projecting rays are all parallel.

is compute $\mathbf{T}_0$ and then apply this transformation to all the vertices of the object.

4.7. Projections

Computer graphics, like all graphics, is by definition two-dimensional; that is, it involves the display of a picture on a two-dimensional surface. When we use the words "three-dimensional object" in graphics we are referring to the two-dimensional picture of what is purported to be a three-dimensional (solid) object. Such a picture is a *projection* of the object; the projection is performed automatically by the human eye (or photographic camera) when "viewing" an object in the three-dimensional world. In computer graphics we must see computational techniques to generate the two-dimensional display, that is, projection, of a (computer-modeled) three-dimensional object.

There are two principal types of projections from three to two dimensions: *parallel projections*, in which the projecting rays are all parallel to each other, and *central projections*, in which the projecting rays converge to a point (the so-called *center of projection* or *vantage point*). The latter type is commonly also referred to as *perspective projection* and is the projection that describes the image formation process of the human eye. The two types of projection are shown in Figures 3.30 and 3.31,

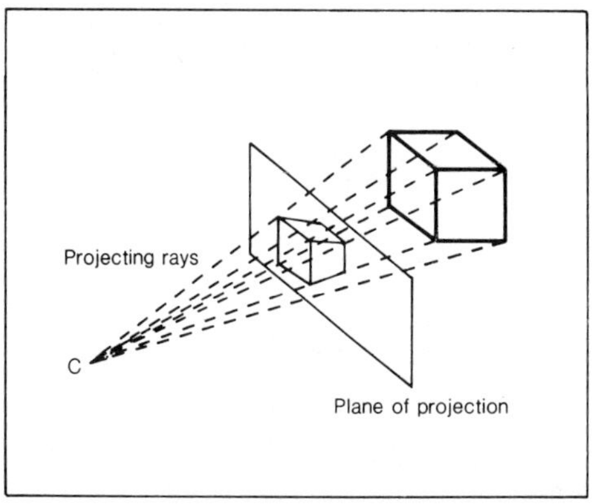

Figure 3.31. Illustration of a perspective projection. The center of projection is at C. Because the projecting rays converge at C, the size of the projection depends directly on the location of the plane of projection.

respectively (Carlbom & Paciorek, 1978). See Chapter 21 by Sedgwick concerning the uses of parallel and perspective projections in studying perception.

An *orthographic projection* is a parallel projection in which the plane of projection is perpendicular to the projecting rays. This is the most common form of parallel projection used.

The perspective (or parallel) projection of a solid object as rendered on a vector-type display consists of the projection of *all* of the object's edges, without regard to the question as to whether the edges are actually visible from the vantage point. In effect, the solid object is regarded as being transparent but having clearly discernible edges. The problem of determining the projection of only those edges, or parts of edges, that are actually visible from the vantage point is referred to as the *hidden-line* problem. For a raster-type display, where we show surface areas, the corresponding problem is called the *hidden-surface* problem. Both problems are dealt with in Section 7.

4.7.1. Orthographic Projection. The computation of the orthographic projection of a three-dimensional object is remarkably simple. One rotates the object in 3-space until the desired plane of projection is parallel to the x–y plane. (This is the plane for which $z = 0$ everywhere.) The projection is then obtained by taking all the (x, y, z) coordinates of the object's points and eliminating the z coordinate. For example, the x,y-plane projection of the object point (x_1, y_1, z_1) in three-dimensional space is simply the point (x_1, y_1) in two-dimensional space.

4.7.2. Perspective Projection. As is apparent from Figure 3.31, a perspective projection depends on the distance of the projection plane from the object. This is not true for a parallel projection. Accordingly, the computation of a perspective projection is more complicated.

Consider the configuration of Figure 3.32. The perspective projection PA, of a point A in 3-space is computed by determining the intersection of the projecting ray VA with the projection plane. The coordinates of a moving point P, which travels on the line VA between V and A, can be expressed by the three equations:

$$P_x = V_x + s(A_x - V_x)$$

$$P_y = V_y + s(A_y - V_y)$$

$$P_z = V_z + s(A_z - V_z)$$

where s is a parameter that represents the fractional distance along VA at which the projection plane is located. Clearly, for the configuration shown, s must lie between 0 and 1. When $s = 0$, P is at V; when $s = 1$, P is at A. In Figure 3.32 the projection plane is coplanar with the plane $z = 0$. Hence for the projection of A in this plane, the moving point P's z coordinate must be 0; that is $P_z = 0$. This permits us to solve for s:

$$0 = V_z + s_0(A_z - V_z)$$

$$s_0 = \frac{V_z}{V_z - A_z} .$$

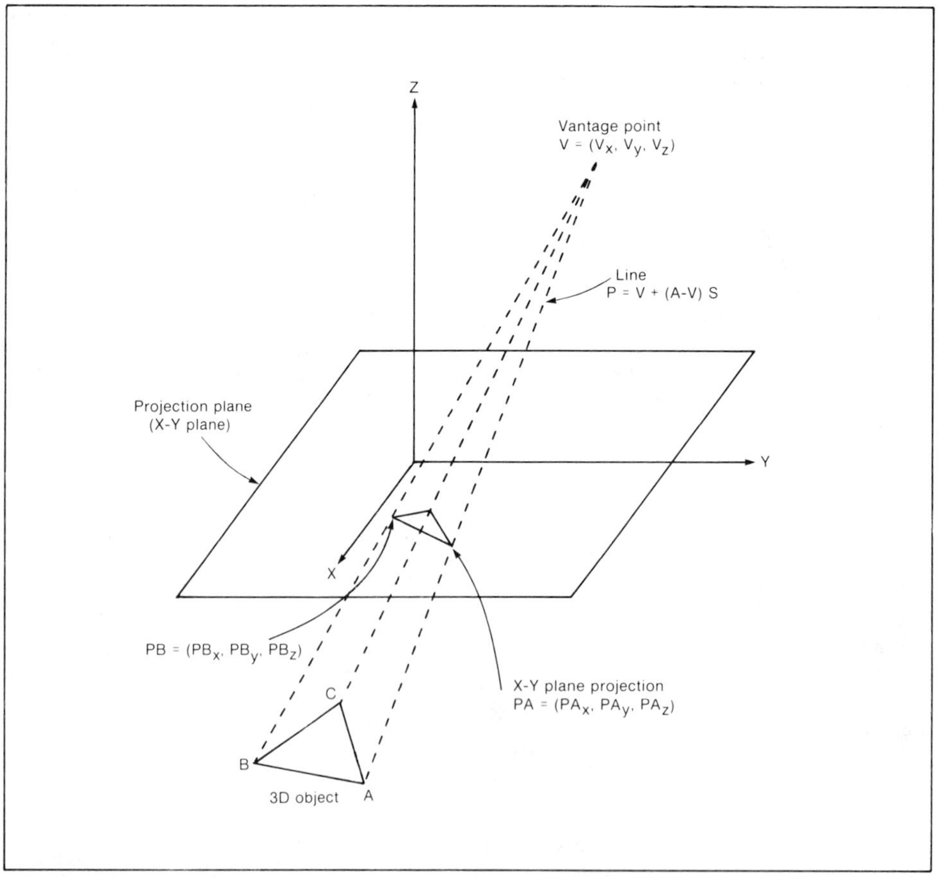

Figure 3.32. Geometry for the computation of the perspective projection. The center of projection is equivalent to the vantage point (location of the observer). *P* is a moving point, which, as *s* varies from 0 to 1, moves from the vantage point *V* to the object vertex *A*. *PA* is the projection of *A* in the *x*–*y* plane.

Substituting this in the other two equations yields the x and y projections of A:

$$PA_x = V_x + \frac{V_z}{V_z - A_z}(A_x - V_x)$$

$$PA_y = V_y + \frac{V_z}{V_z - A_z}(A_y - V_y) .$$

But if we now shift the coordinate system in the x and y directions so that the point V lies on the z-axis, then $V_x = V_y = 0$, and hence

$$PA_x = \frac{V_z}{V_z - A_z} A_x$$

$$PA_y = \frac{V_z}{V_z - A_z} A_y .$$

Similarly, for the point B,

$$PB_x = \frac{V_z}{V_z - B_z} B_x$$

$$PB_y = \frac{V_z}{V_z - B_z} B_y .$$

Because a line segment is fully determined by its end points, knowing the coordinates of the two projection points PA and PB also establishes the projection of the line segment AB in the projection plane. Observe that the determination of a point's perspective projection involves a division by a term that includes the point's z coordinate (or, more precisely, the distance from the point to the vantage point).

The perspective transformation of a point in homogeneous coordinates can also be represented as a matrix multiplication (and thus combined with other transformation matrices). For the point A above,

$$\begin{bmatrix} PA_x \\ PA_y \\ 0 \\ 1 \end{bmatrix} = \left(\frac{1}{V_z - A_z}\right) \begin{bmatrix} V_z & 0 & 0 & 0 \\ 0 & V_z & 0 & 0 \\ 0 & 0 & 0 & 0 \\ 0 & 0 & -1 & V_z \end{bmatrix} \begin{bmatrix} A_x \\ A_y \\ A_z \\ 1 \end{bmatrix} .$$

That matrix itself is the same for all points being projected; however, the division term is different for points with different z coordinates.

4.7.3. Stereo Projections. Stereoscopic displays may be generated by a computer graphics system that provides disparate images for the two eyes. Means for presenting such displays are described in Chapter 23 by Arditi.

4.8. Windowing and Clipping

When working interactively with a created picture we often want to display only a portion of this image. The reason for this may be that the entire image is very complex and, to perceive clearly a particular portion of the image, we must "zoom in" on this portion, discarding the rest of the image. This process is known as *windowing*. One specifies a *window* in the image space and then displays only that portion of the image that lies within the window.

When an image (or a selected window in the image space) is displayed, it may be desirable not to use the entire display area. This makes it possible, for example, to display more than one image simultaneously on the display device. This process of selecting a subspace of the available display area is referred to as *viewporting*, and the actual subarea on the device is referred to as a *viewport*.

The use of windows and viewports is illustrated in Figure 3.33. Note how the portion of the image lying inside the window is displayed in the selected viewport.

The process of windowing requires that the image data be clipped to the window boundaries; only what lies inside is then transformed (scaled and translated as required) to permit its display in the viewport.

When clipping an image to determine the portion that lies in a window, we must test each line segment as to whether it lies inside the window or intersects the window boundaries. We do this by checking each line segment's end points. There are three cases, as illustrated in Figure 3.34:

1. *Both End Points Are Inside the Window.* The entire line segment then lies inside and must be displayed.
2. *One End Point Is Inside and One Is Outside the Window.* We must determine the point of intersection between the segment and the window boundary, and then display only the interior portion of the segment.
3. *Both End Points Lie Outside the Window.* In this case we do not know whether the line segment is entirely outside or cuts across the window. (This case is illustrated by segments EF and GH in Figure 3.34.)

Cases 1 and 2 pose no problem. Case 3 can be resolved in the following manner. Because a window is presumed always to be rectangular, with sides parallel to the coordinate axes, we can classify each end point in case 3 as to whether it is above, to the right, below, or to the left of the window. This is easily established by comparing the point's x, y coordinates with those of the window boundary lines.

If both end points have a common property, that is, both are below or both are to the right, of the window, and so forth, then the entire line segment connecting these points is outside the window. However, if the two end points do not have a property in common, the matter is still unresolved. We then compute the coordinates of the midpoint of the segment:

$$x_m = \frac{x_1 + x_2}{2}$$

$$y_m = \frac{y_1 + y_2}{2}$$

and form two segments, one from each end point to the midpoint. The process is then repeated for the two line segments separately. A number of iterations may be required until either a newly computed midpoint is found to lie inside the window (case 2) or the end points of the line segments are found to have a property in common, establishing that the segment is entirely exterior to the window. The validity of the foregoing scheme is

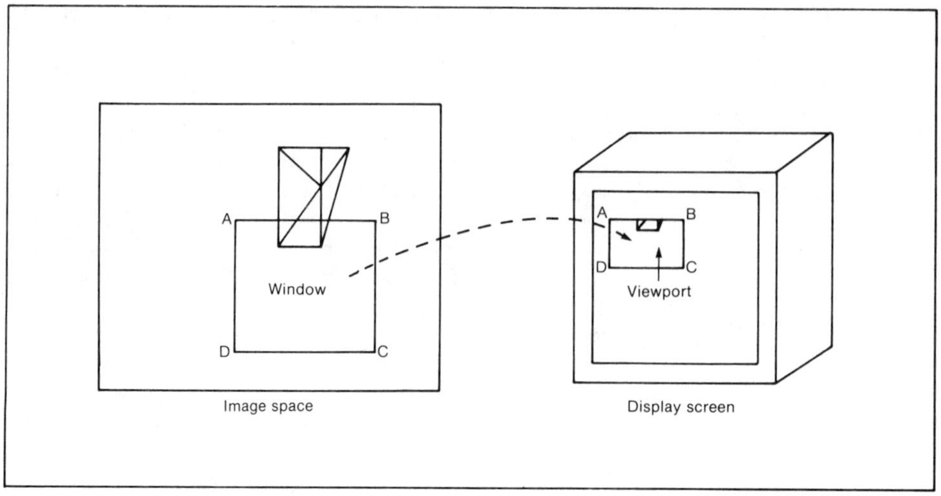

Figure 3.33. Illustrations of the window and viewport concepts. A window is a rectangular area in the image space that is currently to be displayed in the viewport, a rectangular area on the display screen. The length-to-width ratios of the window and viewport need not be the same, in which case the portion of the image space selected by the window is nonuniformly scaled in the x and y directions. The window can be any area within the image space, or be equal to the entire image space. Similarly, the viewport can be the entire screen or any portion of it. Windows permit the user to select only that portion of the image space that is currently of interest. Viewports permit the user to display multiple pictures—derived from different image spaces or different portions of the same image space—on a screen simultaneously.

quite apparent from an examination of Figure 3.34 (Foley & Van Dam, 1982).

5. GRAPHICS PROGRAMMING

When taken in its simplest form, computer graphics is merely the process of creating pictures with the aid of a computer. Early in its development it was realized, however, that computer graphics can be more than merely a drawing aid. If we think more carefully about what is really involved when we create a picture, we realize that there are two distinct task environments involved in this process—the object environment (object space or "scene") and the display environment. In effect, we first create for ourselves a mental picture of a scene, involving one or more objects, and then map this mental picture onto a display. If the scene is three-dimensional, this mapping process includes a three-to-two-dimensional projection. The usefulness of computer graphics is enhanced if we let it encompass the entire process—the modeling in the object space as well as the creation of the visible display thereof. In fact, it is not uncommon to find applications of computer graphics in which there is more emphasis on the modeling of the objects in the scene than on the actual display generation. This is reflected also in the computer software associated with computer graphics. It typically divides itself into application programs that deal with the scene modeling in object space (often also referred to as the "world") and a graphics system program which then generates the desired display of the scene (Harrington, 1983; Nake & Rosenfeld, 1972).

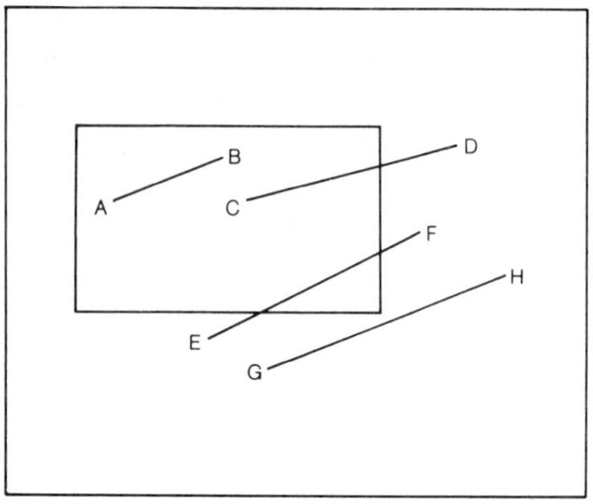

Figure 3.34. The different situations encountered when clipping a line segment against a window or viewport boundary. A difficulty occurs when both endpoints of a segment lie outside of the rectangular area, as for segments *EF* and *GH*. In that case the segment may either lie entirely outside the area or cut across the area. The so-called clipping algorithm is used to resolve this situation.

5.1. Graphics Commands

It is common in computer graphics to describe objects in terms of points and line segments, defined in an application-oriented, so-called *world-coordinate system* (WCS). The reason for this is, at least in part, that prior to the arrival of computer graphics, virtually all design graphics was in terms of line drawings, even when these were subsequently filled in with paint to create a color picture. With the availability of computers, other possibilities for graphics primitives can be considered; however, these are still very much in the novelty stage at this time (Requicha & Voelker, 1982).

A line segment is defined by the coordinates of its end points. Because frequently the end point of one line segment serves also as the initial point of another line segment, it has been found convenient in computer graphics to think of line segments in the manner in which they might be drawn sequentially by a pen plotter and to introduce the concept of *current pen (or beam) position* (or, simply, *current position*) as a moving point having the coordinates of the last segment drawn, or the last position to which the pen (or beam) was moved. This makes it possible then to generate a line drawing by means of simple MOVE and LINE commands. A MOVE merely changes the coordinates of the current position (CP); a LINE causes a line segment to be drawn from the current CP to the new value of the CP. Thus the sequence of commands

MOVE (3,2)
LINE (3,5)
LINE (6,5)
LINE (6,2)
LINE (3,2)

causes a square to be drawn, three units on a side, as shown in Figure 3.35.

Sometimes we wish to mark a point with a predefined symbol. This can be done with the command MARK, which causes the CP to be moved and the desired symbol to be displayed at the specified coordinates.

The three commands MOVE, LINE, and MARK all change the CP to the new coordinates in absolute terms. It is useful also to permit *relative* changes in the CP location. This can be done with the three commands:

RMOVE (dx, dy)
RLINE (dx, dy)
RMARK (dx, dy)

(read "relative MOVE", etc.) which cause the CP to be changed by an amount dx in x and dy in y, respectively. The square of Figure 3.35 can then be drawn equally well with the command sequence

MOVE (3,2)
RLINE (0,3)
RLINE (3,0)
RLINE (0,−3)
RLINE (−3,0)

Finally we must have the capability to insert text. For this we introduce the command TEXT ("string"), which causes the specified string to be displayed starting at the CP.

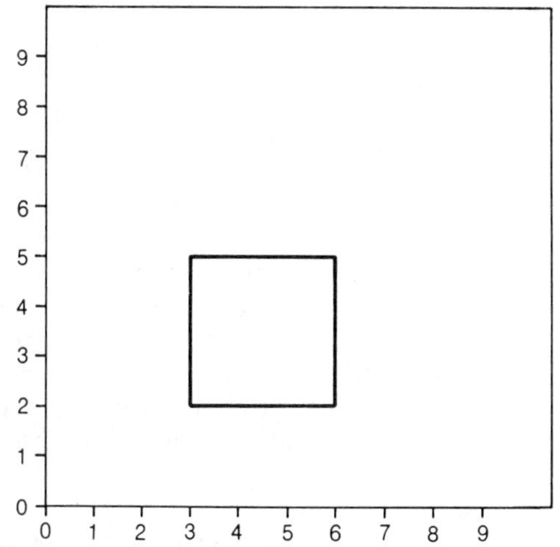

Figure 3.35. A simple computer-drawn square. The program begins with the corner in the lower left and draws the square in a clockwise sense, one line segment at a time.

Because we often deal with polygons, we may want to add the command

POLYGON (x-array, y-array)

which causes a closed polygon to be generated, using corresponding x and y values from the given arrays. The command automatically closes the polygon by providing a line segment from the last specified x, y pair to the first. The square of Figure 3.35 thus could also have been drawn with the single command:

POLYGON (XA,YA)

where the arrays are

XA = (3,3,6,6)
YA = (2,5,5,2)

For raster terminals we want a command with which we can fill the entire area enclosed by a polygon with a specified color. To accomplish this we provide two new commands:

COLOR (value)

which sets the color for all subsequent commands, until changed by another color command, and

FPOLYGON (x-array, y-array)

which is similar to POLYGON except that it fills in the area enclosed by the polygon, assuming that the *interior lies to the right*. Thus

COLOR (black)
FPOLYGON (XA,YA)

where XA and YA are the previously given arrays, will generate a solid black (filled-in) square, as shown in Figure 3.36(a). The sequence

COLOR (black)
FPOLYGON (XB,YB)

where

XB = (3,6,6,3)
YB = (2,2,5,5)

will yield the result shown in Figure 3.36(b) because the *interior* (defined as lying to the right of the polygon's edges as these are traversed) here surrounds the square. All the commands described thus far, except for COLOR, are called graphics primitives because they result directly in the display of some graphic component. The command COLOR is called an *attribute command* rather than a graphic primitive because it merely changes the manner in which the subsequent graphic primitives are displayed. Other attribute commands are

LINETYPE (style)

which is used to set the width and type of all subsequent lines (e.g., thin, thick, solid, short dashes, dash-dot-dash),

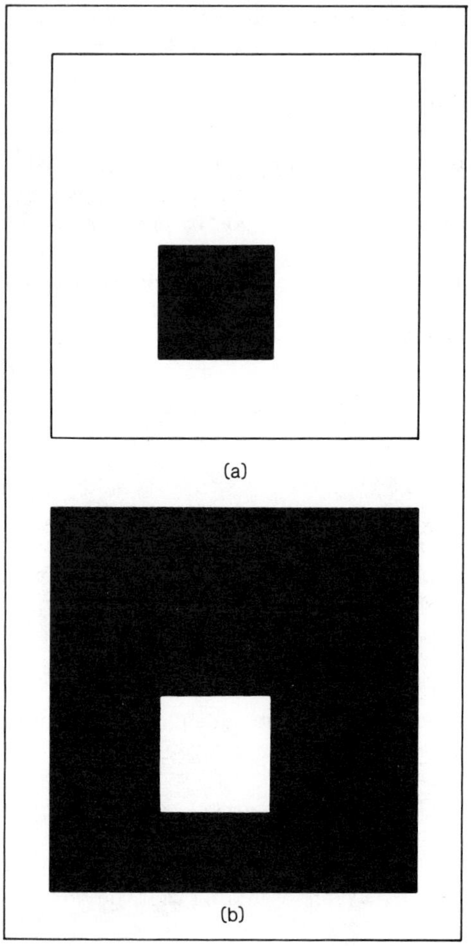

Figure 3.36. Two filled-in polygons (interior defined to lie to the right of the bounding line segments). In (a), the square is drawn in a clockwise sense, causing the interior to be filled. In (b) the square is drawn in the counter-clockwise sense, causing the exterior to be filled instead. (In a sense, the computer regards the square's exterior now to be its interior!)

MARKTYPE (style)

which lets one select one of a number of predefined symbols for marking points (e.g., small square, circle, solid dot, star), and

TEXTTYPE (font, size)

which is used to choose a font and character size for all subsequent text strings.

For raster-type displays it is useful to add two more graphic primitives:

RECT (X,Y)
RRECT (*dx*, *dy*)

RECT (X,Y) causes a filled-in rectangle to be drawn parallel to the coordinate axes, with the CP and the point (x, y) as diagonal corner points. RRECT (*dx*, *dy*) is similar except that the new CP is displaced by *dx*, *dy* from the original CP (and the rectangle will be of width *dx* and height *dy*).

5.2. Simple Program Example

Through use of the commands just described it is possible to generate virtually any picture on any of the displays commonly used in computer graphics, whether they are of the vector-drawing or raster-display type, or whether they continuously refresh the display (as the normal CRT) or are of the storage type (as a DVST or plasma panel). The picture shown in Figure 3.37 can be generated with the following program. A color raster-refresh display is assumed, 512 × 512 in spatial resolution and with 16 possible color values (0–15) for each pixel.

Step	Program Command	Operation Executed
01	COLOR (0)	Sets color to black
02	MOVE (0,0)	Moves CP to origin
03	RECT (511,511)	Makes entire screen black
04	MOVE (1,1)	Moves CP to (1,1)
05	COLOR (15)	Sets color to white
06	RECT (510,510)	Fills in black rectangle leaving only black border one pixel wide
07	COLOR (0)	Sets color to black
08	MOVE (100,100)	Sets CP to (100,100)
09	RDRAW (0,200)	Line segment to (100,300)
10	RDRAW (150,100)	Line segment to (250,400)
11	RDRAW (150, −100)	Line segment to (400,300)
12	RDRAW (0, −200)	Line segment to (400,100)
13	RDRAW (−300,0)	Line segment to (100,100)
14	RMOVE (50,75)	Sets CP to (150,175)
15	RRECT (60,40)	Draws filled-in window (black)
16	RMOVE (−59, −39)	Sets CP to (151,176)
17	COLOR (15)	Sets color to white
18	RRECT (58,38)	Makes rectangle interior white
19	COLOR (0)	Sets color to black
20	MOVE (290,175)	Moves CP to (290,175)
21	RRECT (60,40)	Draws filled-in black rectangle
22	RMOVE (−59, −39)	Sets CP to (291,176)
23	COLOR (15)	Sets color to white
24	RRECT (58,38)	Leaves boundary of rectangle black but makes inside white
25	COLOR (0)	Sets color to black
26	MOVE (350,450)	Sets CP to (350,450)
27	TEXT ('HOUSE')	Plots text, starting at current CP

The display processor, running under the graphics system software, would interpret each of the commands in the above program. Scan conversion would be performed and the raster buffer memory (512 × 512 × 4 bits) would be filled with the appropriate pixel data. To display the picture on a raster-refresh CRT, the stored pixel data would be read out, scanline-by-scanline, for one full scan every 1/30 sec.

If a vector-refresh display were used, the RECT command would not be available and all line segments would be generated with LINE, RLINE, or POLYGON. Because there would be no need for scan conversion, the buffer memory would contain the actual program commands, and the display processor would cycle through this program, say, once every 1/30 sec. (Refresh

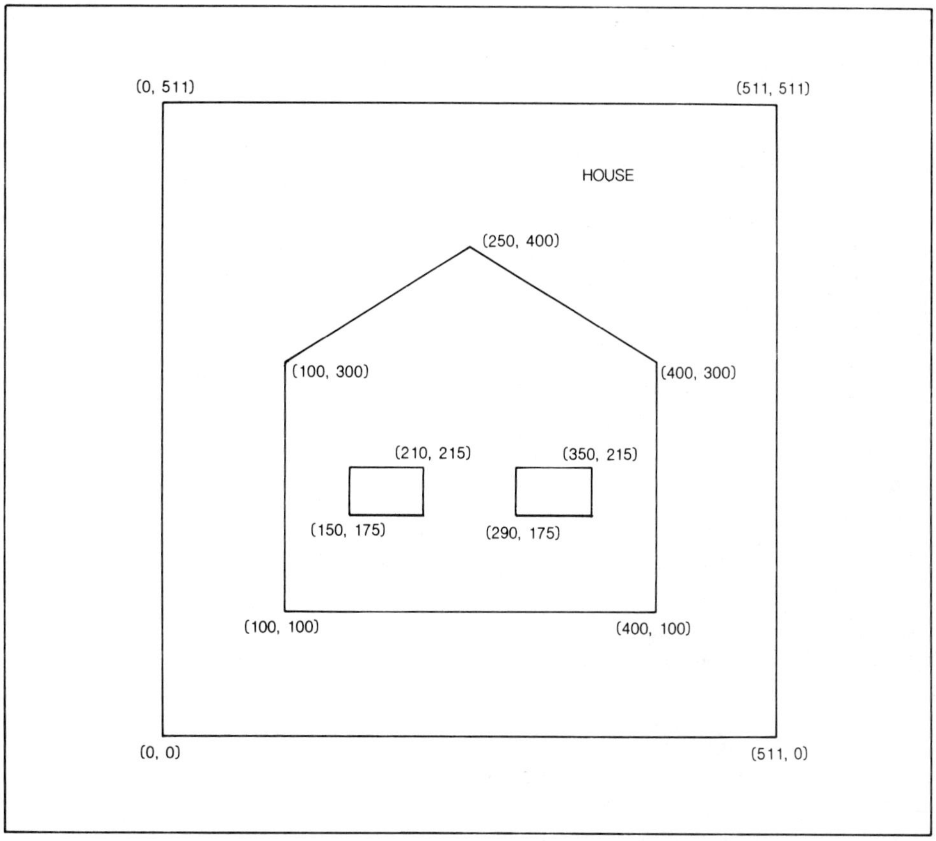

Figure 3.37. Display generated by the sample program of Section 5.2. The coordinate values are shown for ease of understanding; they are not part of the generated image. The word "HOUSE" is a text string displayed by the program.

rates slower than 1/30 sec result in objectionable flicker.) A frame-time command would have to be inserted at the end of the program to check whether the 1/30 sec has elapsed and refresh should commence; otherwise the processor waits. This feature is necessary for vector-refresh displays (but not raster displays) to prevent screen burnout when very simple pictures are displayed (which could be refreshed in much faster time than the selected 1/30 sec and might thus cause too much energy to be transferred into the screen's phosphor coating).

A variety of graphic programming languages has been designed to go along with the equipment offered by various manufacturers. Some of the languages are graphics extensions to conventional programming languages such as Fortran and Pascal. Although they may differ in detail, in terms of their key features they are generally not much different from the language described here. Efforts to adopt a standard programming language for graphics to facilitate software portability, such as through the CORE and GKS system, have thus far met with only limited success (Bergeron, Bono, & Foley, 1978; Enderle, Kansy, & Pfaff, 1984; Hopgood, Duce, Gallop & Sutcliffe, 1983).

5.3. Program Interaction

Program interaction can be achieved by providing some additional commands in a graphic system which can be used "to ask questions" as follows:

1. LOCATOR (x,y). This command, when inserted into a program, causes the display controller to sample a designated interactive device and return the coordinate pair (x,y) indicated by the device at that moment. Common devices used as locators are data tablets, joysticks, light pens together with a displayed tracking cross, and track balls.
2. VALUATOR (n,v). This command samples single-variable device number n and returns its current value as v. Suitable for this are dials, track balls, light pens with displayed pseudodials, as well as data tablets. The command is used by an operator to insert a specific data value into a program during an interactive session.
3. PICK (object). This command is used to answer the question "what?". When the user points (normally, by positioning a cursor on the screen) to a particular displayed object, the pick command will be able to identify the object by the segment of code that describes it. The segment or object name is returned to the program.
4. CHOICE (t,n). Most graphics display systems provide a set of buttons (real or simulated) which the user can activate to request a particular action. The choice is of the on-off type. The parameter n selects the particular choice device; the parameter t indicates a maximum waiting time during which the action must be taken; or the program proceeds with the assumption that no action was intended.
5. KEYBOARD $(t,k,$text$)$. This command causes the program to listen to the keyboard for a string of k characters, which are returned as "text." The time parameter t sets a maximum time, after which the program accepts no further characters and proceeds to the next command.

In writing a graphics program for interactive use, the user would insert one or more of these interaction commands, as appropriate, into the program. During program execution, the display controller samples the interactive devices (or accepts interrupts from them, as the case may be) and makes the indicated data available to the program.

6. THREE-DIMENSIONAL OBJECT MODELING

Computer graphics is concerned with the synthesis of images. These images are either two-dimensional representations of something we perceive as being also two-dimensional, such as a highway map or the floor plan of an office, or they may be two-dimensional representations of some object we perceive as being three-dimensional, such as pictures of a house. When computer graphics is used to depict three-dimensional objects, it is often also referred to as "three-dimensional graphics"; this is especially true when the activity involves first modeling the object in three-dimensional space, subjecting it to one or more transformations, and ultimately projecting it onto a two-dimensional surface for display.

The reader should take note of the distinction between creating the two-dimensional picture of a house and creating a three-dimensional model of a house and then displaying a projection of that model. Although the results may appear identical for a particular view of the house, there is an important difference. In the first case, an entirely new image would have to be created whenever a different view is desired; in the second case it is necessary merely to transform the model and generate a new projection, something that a computer can do very well with a minimum of human interaction. In addition, in the second case there exists a three-dimensional model that can now be used to determine other, nonimage properties of the house, such as the interior volume and total surface area. Because much of computer graphics is, in fact, concerned with the display of pictures of three-dimensional objects (especially in computer-aided design), the process of modeling such objects deserves particular attention.

The most common way of modeling a three-dimensional object is by describing its exterior surface. This can be done by representing the surface in terms of (1) polygons, (2) quadric-surface sections, or (3) bicubic patches. An alternate method for modeling a three-dimensional object is to use a set of primitive solids. This method, known as *solid modeling*, is of great potential value in computer-aided design. Its inclusion here, however, would be beyond the scope of this chapter (Requicha & Voelker, 1982).

6.1. Representation Using Polygons

If the surface of a three-dimensional object consists of many planar faces, representation in terms of polygons is the obvious choice. One makes a list of all the *vertices* (points where three or more polygons intersect), all the *edges* (line segments formed by two intersecting polygons), and all the *polygons*. This is illustrated in Figure 3.38 where such a description is shown for a simple four-sided object (a tetrahedron). Note that by listing the vertices around a polygon in fixed order (always clockwise or always counterclockwise), the edge list can be omitted and the polygon list given directly in terms of the (ordered) vertices, as also shown in Figure 3.38.

One may ask whether a planar-faced object can be uniquely described by the vertex and edge lists alone. Although this is true for the object of Figure 3.38, it is not true in general. An example for which it is *not* true is shown in Figure 3.39. This

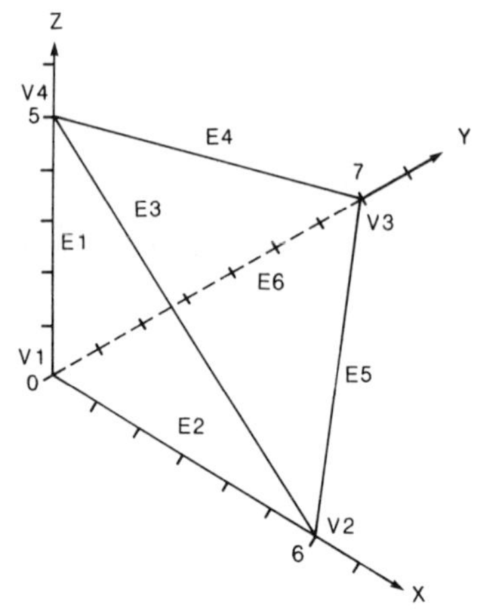

VERTEX LIST	EDGE LIST
V1 = (0,0,0)	E1 = V1,V4
V2 = (6,0,0)	E2 = V1,V2
V3 = (0,7,0)	E3 = V2,V4
V4 = (0,0,5)	E4 = V3,V4
	E5 = V2,V3
	E6 = V1,V3

POLYGON LIST	ALTERNATE POLYGON LIST
F1 = E1,E3,E2	F1 = V1,V4,V2
F2 = E3,E4,E5	F2 = V2,V4,V3
F3 = E1,E6,E4	F3 = V1,V3,V4
F4 = E2,E5,E6	F4 = V1,V2,V3

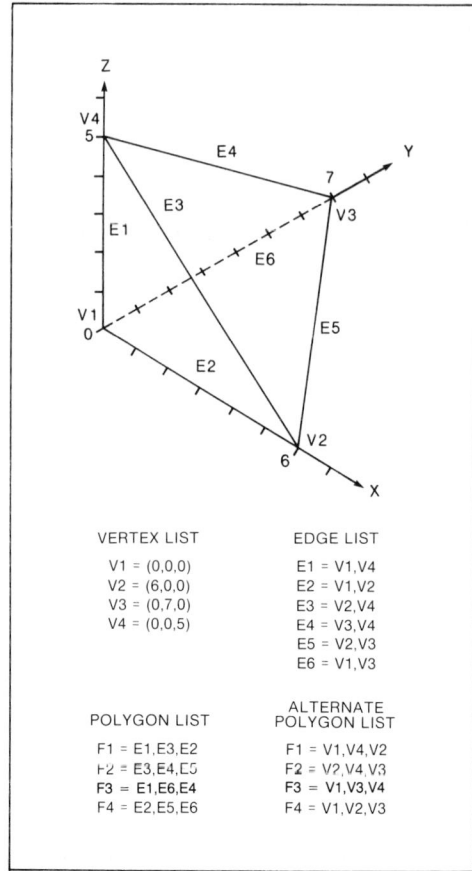

Figure 3.38. A planar-faced solid, represented in terms of its vertices, edges, and polygons. The object shown is a tetrahedron (a four-sided polyhedron). The dashed edge (E6) is a hidden edge. Although for the figure shown, the vertex and edge lists would be sufficient to provide a unique description of the polyhedron, this is not the case in general. The polygon list, which is needed to provide an unambiguous object description, can be given in either of the two forms shown (i.e., either by means of edge-defined faces or by means of vertex-defined faces).

"wire-frame" object has three possible interpretations as a solid body, as shown in Figure 3.40 (where now only the visible edges in each case are displayed).

The polygon-type surface description of a three-dimensional object is ideally suited for use in computer graphics. An object defined this way can be easily translated, scaled, or rotated by applying the appropriate transformations to the object's vertex list. No change need be made in the edge or polygon lists. A particular two-dimensional projection is thus easily generated. The polygon description also lends itself to *rendering* the object in terms of its edges on a vector-refresh display. The picture of the tetrahedron in Figure 3.38 is, in fact, such a rendering in which the dashed edge (E6) is presented as being a "hidden" edge. Such edge-line representations of planar-faced objects have long been used in engineering and architecture.

Because of the convenience of the polygon-surface representation method, it is often also applied to curved-surface objects, for which it is, of course, now only an approximation. Where this approximation is acceptable, the handling of curved objects is then no different from that of planar-faced objects. The approximation can be made arbitrarily precise by using sufficiently small polygons; the cost of this, however, is that the vertex list and polygon list become very large, requiring both large amounts of memory and long processing times. An

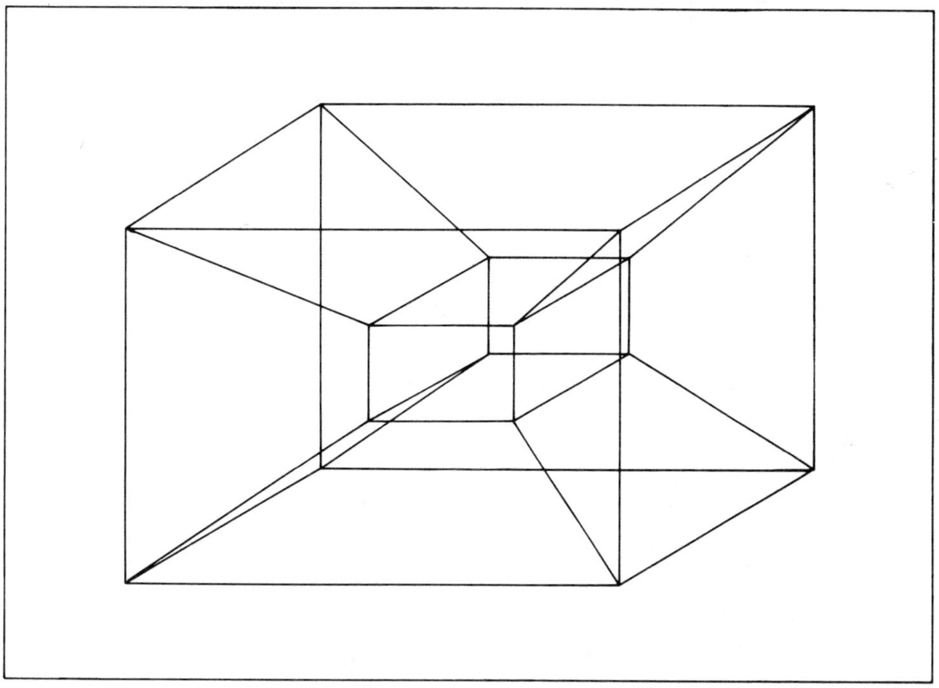

Figure 3.39. Example of an object for which the vertex and edge lists are insufficient to provide an unambiguous description. There are three equally valid solid-object interpretations of the edge-only projection shown. The rectangular hole in the center of the object can be from front to back, from top to bottom, or from left to right, depending on which edge sequences bound actual object faces. See Figure 3.40.

example of two intersecting cylinders modeled in terms of polygons is shown in Figure 3.41.

6.2. Representation Using Quadric-Surface Sections

Among man-made curved-surface objects, one finds many that have surface parts that are cylindrical, spherical, or conical. The reason for this is that these surfaces have rotational symmetry about an axis and are relatively easy to manufacture. These surfaces belong to the class of *quadric* surfaces (Levin, 1979; Woon & Freeman, 1972), which includes also ellipsoids, paraboloids, hyperboloids, and parabolic hyperboloids ("saddle-shaped" surfaces), and are governed by the equation

$$Ax^2 + By^2 + Cz^2 + Dxy + Eyz + Fzx + Gx + Hy + Kz + L = 0 \, .$$

Although much more complicated to process than polygons, quadric surfaces do permit precise modeling of objects (or parts of objects) whose surfaces are of this type. They can be rendered in projection either as line drawings, in which case only intersection curves and silhouette curves are drawn, or as shaded surfaces on suitable raster displays, in which case realistic-looking images can be displayed. Examples of both these kinds of displays are shown in Figure 3.42.

6.3. Representation Using Bicubic Surface Patches

The third important scheme for representing solid objects in terms of their boundary surfaces is by means of bicubic patches. This scheme is especially appropriate for representing so-called free-form objects, that is, objects whose form cannot be readily identified with simple geometric shapes. Examples of such objects are airplane wings, automobile fenders, boat hulls, and turbine blades.

In this scheme, the object must be described in terms of the (x, y, z) coordinates of sample points on the object's surface. The sample points must be sufficiently close together to permit the rest of the surface to be derived from these points by the process of bicubic interpolation (i.e., cubic interpolation in two orthogonal directions). A bicubic polynomial has two independent variables and 16 coefficients. It thus requires 16 points to be uniquely determined. Let us describe this in more detail. Given an object's description in terms of a set of surface sample points, one divides the points into sets of 16, arranged in 4×4 fashion as shown in Figure 3.43. One then fits bicubic polynomials to these of the type

$$\begin{aligned} x(s, t) = {} & a_{11}s^3t^3 + a_{12}s^3t^2 + a_{13}s^3t + a_{14}s^3 \\ & + a_{21}s^2t^3 + a_{22}s^2t^2 + a_{23}s^2t + a_{24}s^2 \\ & + a_{31}st^3 + a_{32}st^2 + a_{33}st + a_{34}s \\ & + a_{41}t^3 + a_{42}t^2 + a_{43}t + a_{44} \, . \end{aligned}$$

This is a parametric equation in the two parameters s and t for the surface's x coordinate. The 16 coefficients can be determined by substituting the $x(s, t)$ values for the 16 selected points and then solving the resulting 16 simultaneous equations. Equations of identical form (but with different coefficients a_{ij} would be

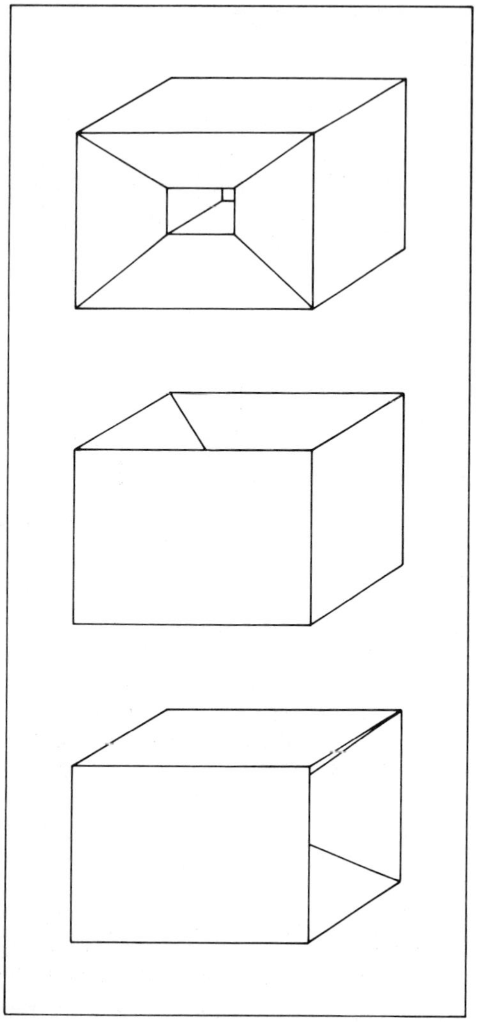

Figure 3.40. Three solid objects, all of which can have the identical vertex and edge list description and be consistent with the "wire-frame" object of Figure 3.39. The threefold ambiguity associated with Figure 3.39 is resolved here by showing only those edges that are visible from the same vantage point in each case.

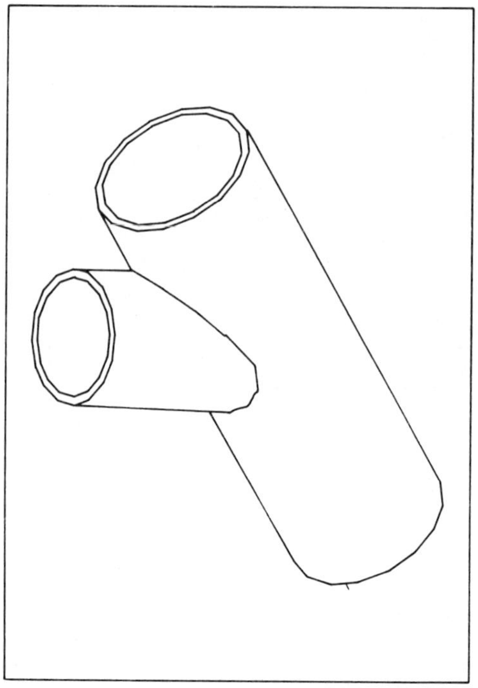

Figure 3.41. Two intersecting "cylinders" modeled as multifaceted planar-faced columns. The facet lines have been deleted; however, they would be present in the data structure, as would all the vertices. The main drawback of this type of representation is that to achieve a good-quality "cylinder," an inordinately large number of vertices and facet lines is required, consuming an excessive amount of computer memory and computation time.

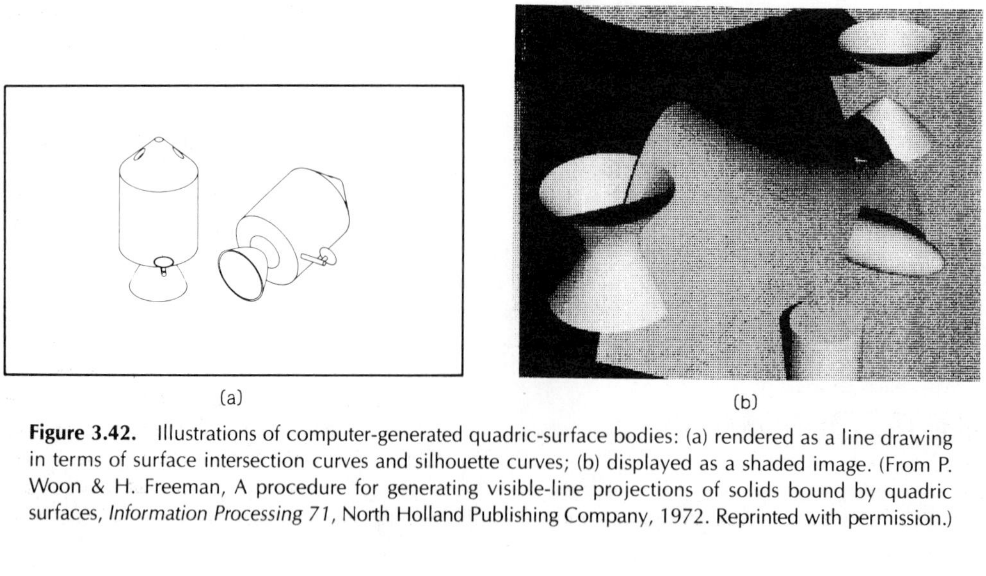

(a) (b)

Figure 3.42. Illustrations of computer-generated quadric-surface bodies: (a) rendered as a line drawing in terms of surface intersection curves and silhouette curves; (b) displayed as a shaded image. (From P. Woon & H. Freeman, A procedure for generating visible-line projections of solids bound by quadric surfaces, *Information Processing 71*, North Holland Publishing Company, 1972. Reprinted with permission.)

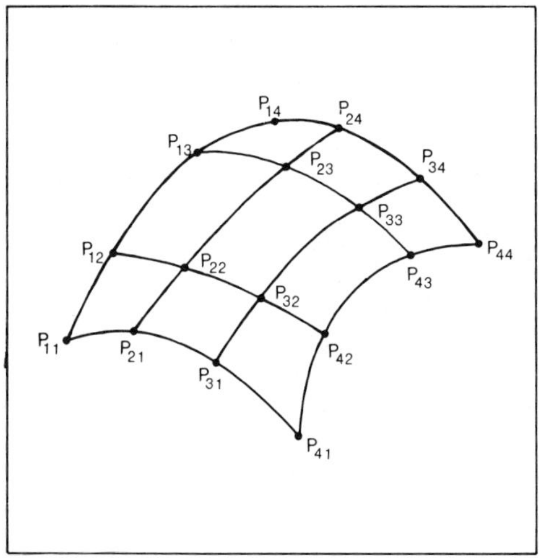

Figure 3.43. A surface defined in terms of bicubic interpolation over 16 sample points of the surface. The interpolation is cubic in two orthogonal directions and will pass through the 16 defining points.

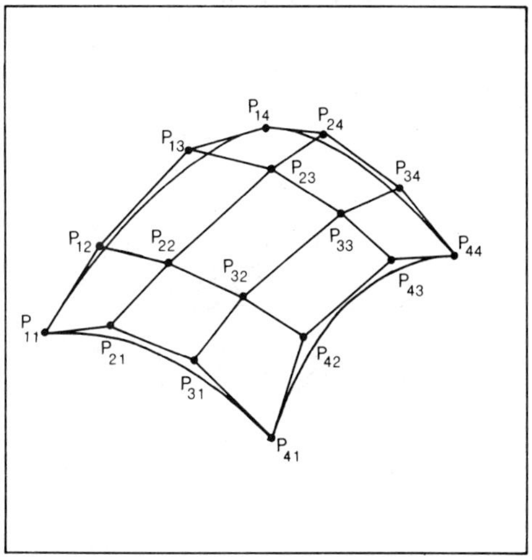

Figure 3.45. Illustration of the Bezier surface definition method. Intermediate, off-surface control points are used to control the surface shape. The method is more amenable to interactive surface modeling than the bicubic scheme shown in Figure 3.43. Bezier surface patches can be smoothly assembled into large free-form surfaces by setting up appropriate relationships between the control points of adjacent patches (Bezier, 1972).

required for the y and z coordinates. (Note that the surface "patch" is called "bicubic" because it is a cubic in the two parameters.) In practice, tedious simultaneous-equation solving is not required. The same result can be obtained by means of straightforward matrix multiplication methods (Faux & Pratt, 1979; Foley & Van Dam, 1982; Rogers & Adams, 1976).

A number of variations exist on this scheme. In one, the actual sample surface points are specified and the design of each patch is carried out to ensure continuity of the first derivative (slope) between adjacent patches to avoid "edges" from appearing. This is illustrated in Figure 3.44.

In a second variation, not all the points are prespecified but instead the surface tangents (slopes) as well as the (x, y, z) coordinates of only the corner points of each patch are given (Faux & Pratt, 1979).

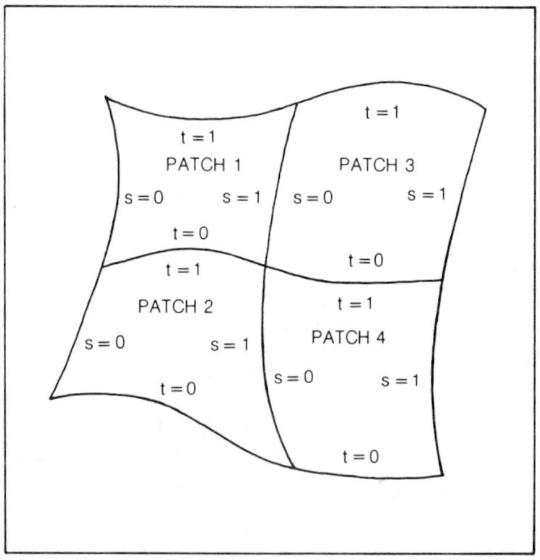

Figure 3.44. Illustration of the manner in which a large free-form surface can be constructed by piecing together patches of the type shown in Figure 3.43. To achieve smoothness, continuity of the first derivative—and possibly even the second derivative—must be maintained across adjacent patch boundaries. Arbitrarily large free-form surfaces can be constructed in this manner. The parameters s and t each vary from 0 to 1 as one moves over a patch from left to right or top to bottom, respectively. At the lower boundary curves of each patch one of the variables, s or t, ranges from 0 to 1, and the other is fixed at either 0 or 1.

In another variation (Bezier, 1972) the patch corner points are specified and then additional "control points" are given through which the surface will not pass but which act as "magnets" to "pull" the surface toward them. This is illustrated in Figure 3.45. This variation has been found especially convenient for interactively modifying surface designs. One lays out the corner points of a patch and then positions the control points in a way that one hopes will give the desired surface. The actual surface can then be computed and displayed as a fine-mesh "fishnet." If the result is not as desired, one repositions one or more of the control points and repeats the process until the desired surface patch is obtained, and then proceeds to do this for all the surface patches of the object.

Although this scheme is mathematically somewhat complicated, the results obtainable with it can be impressive. High-precision air foils can be designed with comparative ease and with accurate control over the slope and curvature that will result.

7. THE HIDDEN-LINE AND HIDDEN-SURFACE PROBLEMS

When a solid opaque object is viewed in real life, observers see only those portions of the object's surface that are pointed toward them and are not obscured by other parts of the object or by another object. When we model a solid object in a computer and then wish to compute the visible projection as it would be seen from a specified vantage point, we face a complex problem. The computer must determine for us which parts of the model's surface will be visible and which will be invisible from the vantage point. If we are rendering the object as a line drawing on a vector display, we must eliminate the hidden edges (or hidden parts of edges); this is called the *hidden-line problem* and is probably the single most complex problem in computer graphics (Sutherland, Sproull, & Schumacker, 1974). If the object's projection is to be rendered on a raster display, possibly in gray tone or color, the problem is one of removing the hidden

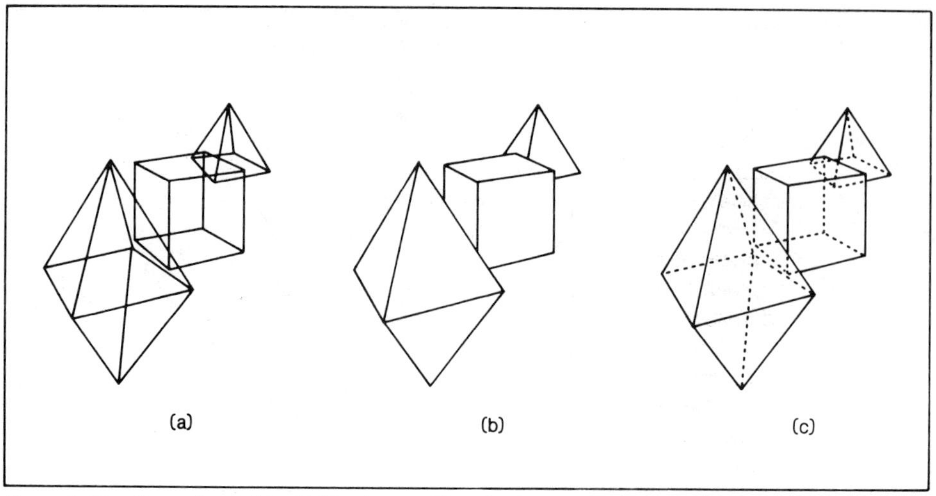

Figure 3.46. Illustrations of the hidden-line problem for three simple polyhedra: (a) all lines shown, (b) visible lines shown only, and (c) hidden lines shown dashed. The problem is to determine which line segments or parts of line segments are hidden by one or more faces of an object.

surface parts; it is referred to as the *hidden-surface problem* and is somewhat more tractable than the hidden-line problem.

7.1. The Hidden-Line Problem

The hidden-line problem is illustrated in Figure 3.46, where some objects are shown with all lines visible in (*a*), with the hidden lines deleted in (*b*), and with the hidden lines shown dashed in (*c*). Of course, once we have determined which line segments are visible and which are not, it is trivial to delete the invisible ones or to display them as dashed line segments. Let us examine the two objects shown in Figure 3.47, in which the hidden lines are shown dashed. Some appreciation for the problem is obtained by noting that there are four different kinds of edges (each formed by the intersection of two faces) designated H_1 through H_4:

1. H_1 edges are formed by the intersection of two back faces, that is, faces whose outsides are pointed *away* from the observer, such as faces F_A and F_B in Figure 3.47(a).
2. H_2 edges are formed by the intersection of two front faces, where a front face is one that is pointing *toward* the observer, such as F_C and F_D in Figure 3.47(b).
3. H_3 edges are formed by the intersection of a back face and a front face, where the front face is closer to the observer than the back face (such as faces F_D and F_E).
4. H_4 edges are formed by the intersection of a back face and a front face, where the back face is closer to the observer than the front face (such as F_E and F_F).

Simple reasoning now shows clearly that H_1 and H_4 edges will always be hidden, but that H_2 and H_3 edges will be visible, unless they are hidden by another part of the same object or by a different solid object. Note that it is easier to establish that an edge is invisible than that it is visible. A seemingly visible edge may be occluded by some other object and we may not realize this until we have checked the relative positions of all the faces of all objects in a scene against the location of the vantage point. In contrast, once an edge is determined as being invisible, nothing discovered later can cause this designation to change.

The general hidden-line determination problem is one of the most complex problems in computational geometry; however, for many objects, it is possible to determine which lines are visible and which are not by means of relatively straightforward algorithms, though the user must realize that these algorithms may give incorrect results (or no results at all) when presented with a particularly complicated object configuration.

Among the simplest cases is that of a single convex object. (An object is convex if the line connecting any two of its surface

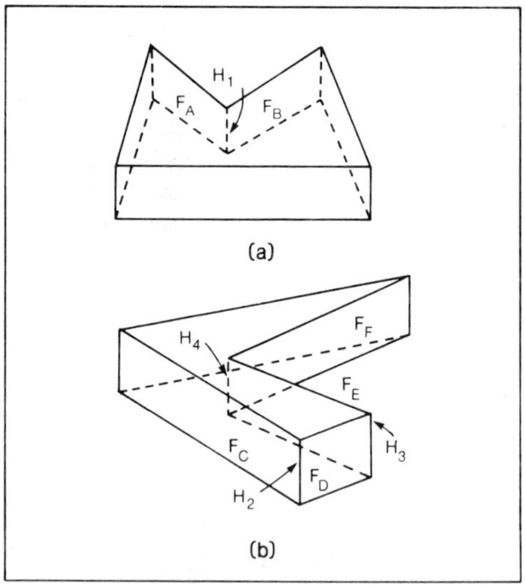

Figure 3.47. The four types of face intersections (edges) to be considered in hidden-line determination of a solid body. In (a), the faces F_A and F_B are back faces, that is, faces whose outside surfaces are oriented *away* from the observer. Their intersection is an H_1 edge, which is always invisible. In (b), F_C, F_D, and F_F are front faces, that is, faces whose outsides are oriented *toward* the observer. F_E is a back face. The intersection between the two front faces F_C and F_D is an H_2 edge; such an edge is visible unless it is blocked from view by one or more other front faces. The same is true for the intersection between a front face and a back face *if the front face is closer to the observer than the back face*, as in the case of F_D and F_E. Such an edge is referred to as an H_3 edge. However, the intersection between a front face and a back face *where the front face lies farther from the observer than the back face* will always be invisible. It is denoted an an H_4 edge and is exemplified here by F_E and F_F.

points lies either on the object's surface or entirely inside the object.) Such an object can exhibit only H_1, H_2, and H_3 edges. Because there is no other object to hide any part of the object, all H_2 and H_3 edges are fully visible.

When there are two or more convex objects (as in Fig. 3.46), one may hide edges or parts of edges of another. In most cases, this situation can be handled by sorting the objects according to their distance from the observer. The closest object will have all its H_2 and H_3 edges fully visible. For the more distant objects, one takes them one at a time (in order of increasing distance from the observer) and checks whether each is overlapped (i.e., "shadowed") by the polygon or polygons representing the combined two-dimensional projection of all previously considered objects. If there is complete overlap, the object is fully hidden; if there is no overlap, the object is fully visible; if there is partial overlap, the intersections between the object edges and the overlap polygons must be determined. Those edges or parts of edges overlapped will be hidden and those not overlapped will be visible. The overlap polygon or polygons are then augmented by the two-dimensional projection of this object to obtain the overlap polygons for the next object test. Note that whenever there is no overlap, an additional new overlap polygon is created, which must be tested against when the next, more distant, object is considered (Harrington, 1983; Hearn & Baker, 1983).

The foregoing procedure fails when we are unable to sort objects according to their distance from the observer, as is the case, for example, when object A is partially in front of object B, object B is partially in front of object C, and object C is partially in front of object A, a perfectly possible situation! Also, the complexity increases if we must deal with nonconvex objects. One possible solution in these cases is *to segment* the objects into components, all of which are convex and can be sorted according to distance. Alternatively, one may then want to invoke one of the general-purpose hidden-line determination algorithms that are applicable in all cases.

In the general case, the process of determining the hidden edges (or parts of edges) involves establishing which faces of the object are front faces and which are back faces, determining the intersections involving at least one front face, classifying the intersections, and performing a series of visibility tests. These visibility tests will have to be made only at points where an edge of type H_2 and H_3 intersects an edge of type H_3 in the wire-frame projection of the three-dimensional objects (that is, in projections such as the one shown in Fig. 3.39), for it is only at such intersections that the status of an H_2 or H_3 edge can change from being visible to being invisible, or vice versa. Line segments of types H_1 and H_4 are *always* invisible and need not be considered any further. They can have no effect on the visibility or invisibility of an H_2 or H_3 edge (or any part of such an edge). The full details of the available techniques for hidden-line determination are beyond the scope of this chapter. The interested reader will find detailed descriptions in the literature (Foley & Van Dam, 1982; Giloi, 1978; Loutrel, 1970; Newman & Sproull, 1979; Potmesil & Freeman, 1980). An example of a three-dimensional modeled object, displayed with hidden lines deleted, is shown in Figure 3.48.

7.2. The Hidden-Surface Problem

The problem of displaying only what can truly be seen of an object from a specified vantage point is somewhat easier when we display the object in terms of its surface on a raster display rather than using an edge-line rendering. A large variety of suitable algorithms has been developed over the years (Foley & Van Dam, 1982; Hamlin & Gear, 1977) but we describe only two of the best-known here.

7.2.1. The *z*-Buffer Algorithm. An extremely simple algorithm for displaying only the visible projection of an object on a raster display is the following. Suppose that in addition to the refresh buffer, in which we store the $m \times n$ pixel data for display on the $m \times n$-resolution raster display, we also have an $m \times n$ buffer (called the "z buffer") for storing the $m \times n$ depth values associated with each pixel, as shown in Figure 3.49. Let us use an x, y, z-coordinate system in which the projection plane corresponds to $z = 0$ and depth values (corresponding to distances away from the observer) are measured in increasing z values. (Such a coordinate system is referred to as a left-handed Cartesian-coordinate system because the positive z direction is opposite to conventional notation.) The configuration is illustrated in Figure 3.50.

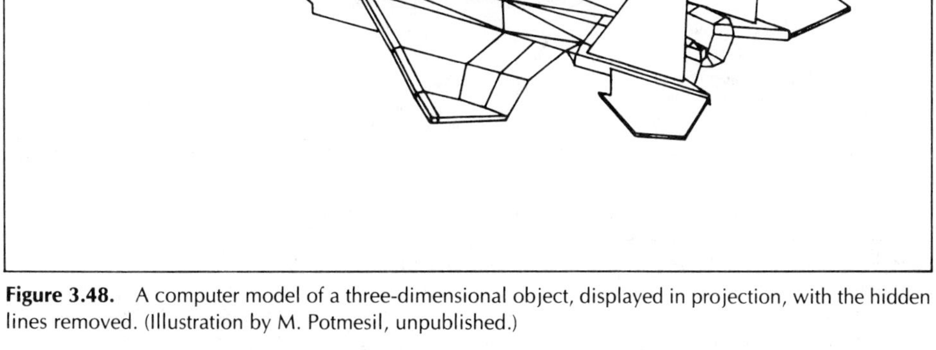

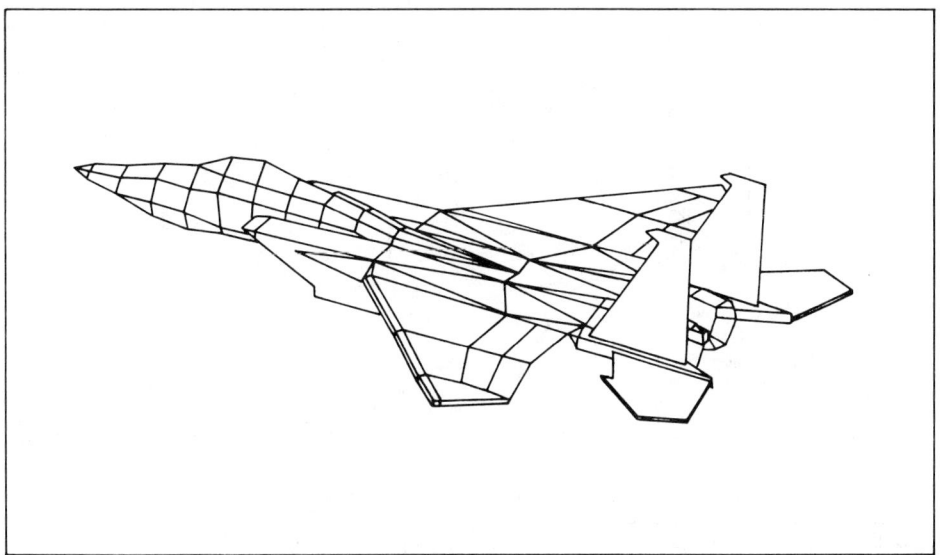

Figure 3.48. A computer model of a three-dimensional object, displayed in projection, with the hidden lines removed. (Illustration by M. Potmesil, unpublished.)

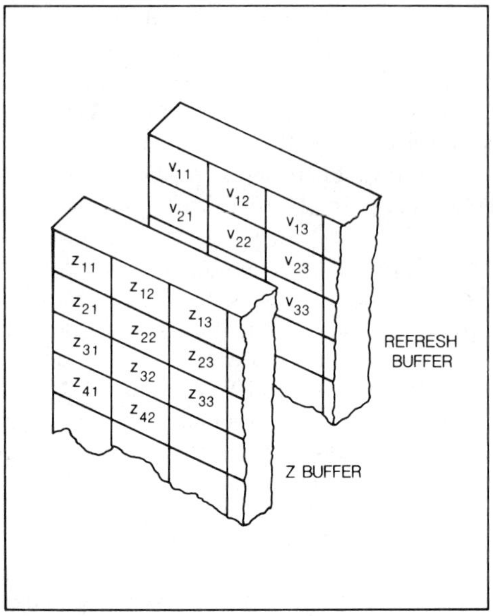

Figure 3.49. Illustration of the z-buffer concept. For each pixel in the refresh buffer, a corresponding depth value is stored in the z buffer, representing the distance between the surface area associated with the pixel and the observer. A displayable image is created by taking each surface section of the object to be displayed (i.e., each face polygon or surface patch) and for each pixel computing the distance between the corresponding point on the surface and the observer. This distance is compared against the value stored in the z buffer for that pixel. If it is less, the pixel's color and intensity values are entered in the refresh buffer and its distance value replaces the preceding value in the corresponding z-buffer location. If the distance is greater than the stored value, the pixel data is ignored. If this is done for all surface sections of all the objects in the scene, the image data finally retained in the refresh buffer is the true visible projection of the objects in the scene.

At the start we set all the pixel values in the refresh buffer to the background color and all the depth values in the z buffer to the greatest allowable depth. For each of the object's surface polygons, we compute the depth $z(x, y)$ for each point (x, y) spanned by the polygon's projection. If for a particular x, y location, the z value obtained from a polygon is less than the value currently stored in the z buffer at that location, this new value replaces the old value in the z buffer and, in addition, the polygon's color value is entered in the refresh buffer at that location. If the polygon z value is greater than the value in the z buffer, no change is made and the next x, y location is examined. This continues until all x, y values for all the object's polygons have been thus examined. The data then contained in the refresh buffer will correspond to the actual visible-surface projection of the object and can be displayed without any further processing.

In effect, the foregoing algorithm works by comparing the polygons' pixel values according to their distances from the observer and retaining only those pixel values that are closest. When all comparisons have been made, what remains in the refresh buffer is then the actual visible projection. The only undesirable aspect of this algorithm is that it requires the extra memory for the z buffer. In terms of performance it is competitive with other hidden-surface elimination algorithms; its implementation is particularly simple (Sutherland et al., 1974). Note that the z-buffer algorithm can be easily applied also to objects having curved surfaces.

7.2.2. Depth-Sort Algorithm. An algorithm that is similar in principle to the z-buffer algorithm but does not require a large amount of extra memory is the depth-sort algorithm. In this algorithm, the projection polygons of all of an object's surface polygons are determined and then sorted according to their distance from the observer. To facilitate the sorting, all projection

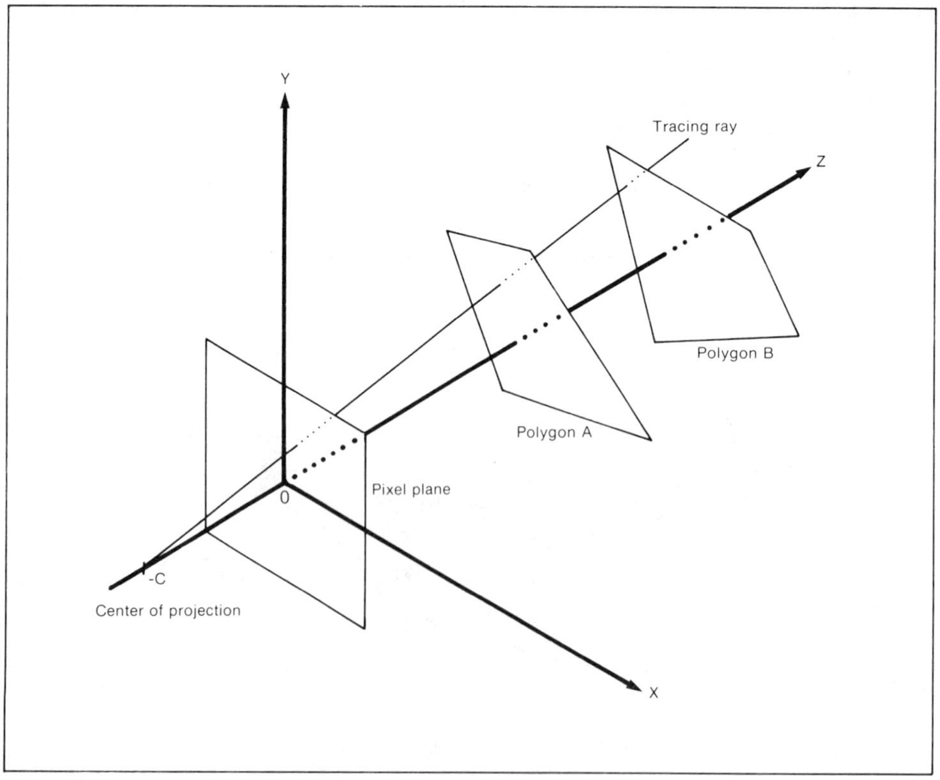

Figure 3.50. Illustration of the use of a left-handed Cartesian-coordinate system (the positive z direction is opposite to the conventional one) in connection with depth determination for the z-buffer hidden-surface scheme. As shown here, the projection plane (pixel plane) is placed at z = 0. The associated z buffer stores the z value of the closest (smallest z value) polygon point that projects into the pixel.

polygons are made convex by dividing them into triangles and treating each triangle separately. (This avoids having to deal with the case where two projection triangles mutually hide each other in part. Special multiple-interaction hiding effects are resolved by subdividing larger triangles into smaller ones.)

After all polygons have been sorted according to their z values, each polygon is "drawn" into the refresh buffer, beginning with the most distant one. As successive projection polygons are drawn, they will draw over those drawn previously (in those areas where they overlap in the display space). After the last polygon has been drawn, the visible-surface projection of the object is contained in the refresh buffer, ready for immediate display (Newell, Newell, & Sancha, 1972).

8. SHADING AND COLORING

To achieve a high degree of realism in the display of a three-dimensional object, the object's surface should appear *shaded*, that is, possess a light intensity distribution that resembles the light intensity distribution that a real object would exhibit. In a real three-dimensional scene, the shading of an object depends, of course, on the sources of light that illuminate the object (their intensity and location), on the orientation of the object's surface relative to the light sources and to the observer, and on the reflection characteristics of the object's surface. To obtain a realistic-looking display of a three-dimensional object, all these factors must be taken into account. The treatment of both shading and coloring here is kept quite brief because much of the relevant material is covered in Chapter 8 by Pokorny and Smith and Chapter 9 by Wyszecki.

8.1. Surface Reflection

It has been found convenient to classify the reflection properties of surfaces into two types, specular and diffuse. A particular surface may exhibit one or the other type of reflection, or both types may be simultaneously present in different proportions, depending entirely on the physical nature of the surface (i.e., its "texture").

8.1.1. Specular Reflection. Specular reflection is the type of reflection that characterizes a mirror. In its perfect form it is governed by Snell's law, according to which the angle of reflection is equal to the angle of incidence. This is illustrated in Figure 3.51, where **n** is the surface normal (perpendicular), $\mathbf{I}_0$ is the incidence vector, and **R** is the reflection vector. Under perfect specular reflection, a point source of light along $\mathbf{I}_0$ would be visible in reflection from the surface only along the vector **R**. In practice, we do not have perfect specular reflection and hence the light along $\mathbf{I}_0$ would be visible also in an area around the vector **R**, though its brightness would be attenuated sharply as we deviate from the direction **R**. In practice it has been found that the actual reflection to the viewer along **V** can be approximated by $\cos^m\phi$, where ϕ is the angle between **R** and the vector **V**, and **m** is some moderately large integer (e.g., 80) (Phong, 1975). The larger the value of m, the more perfectly specular the reflection will appear. Because the fraction of light reflected depends also on the physical properties of the surface, we introduce a reflection coefficient k_s. This gives us the equation

$$I_{sr} = k_s I_0 \cos^m \phi \qquad (1)$$

for the amount of specularly reflected light seen by an observer along **V**, with a point source intensity of I_0.

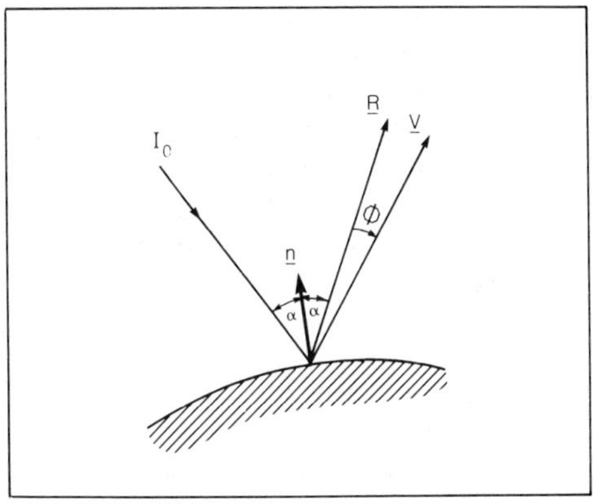

Figure 3.51. The geometry of specular reflection. The angle of perfect reflection, α, is equal to the angle of incidence of the light-source vector I_0. In practice, the reflected light along a view vector V, oriented at a different angle, is much reduced but not zero.

8.1.2. Diffuse Reflection. Surfaces that have a dull or matte finish do not reflect light according to Snell's law but distribute it more or less uniformly in all directions. The amount of light illuminating a particular surface point depends only on the cosine of the angle between the incident light ray $\mathbf{I}_0$ and the surface normal **n**, as shown in Figure 3.52. The amount of light reflected in that case depends on the absorption properties of the surface; we use the diffuse reflection coefficient k_d to let us model this. Although, just as in the case of specular reflection, in practice diffuse reflection (also called Lambertian reflection) is never ideal, we can satisfactorily describe it by the equation

$$I_{dr} = k_d I_0 \cos \alpha \qquad (2)$$

where α is the angle between the surface normal **n** and the incident light ray $\mathbf{I}_0$.

8.1.3. Ambient Light and Distance Effects. Thus far we have considered only the fractions of light reflected by a surface under either specular or diffuse reflection. The light actually detected at the vantage point clearly depends on the distance v between the point of reflection and the vantage point. Although good arguments can be made that the amount of light actually received by the viewer should decrease with the square of the distance, that is, as $1/v^2$, experimentation has shown that a decrease by $1/(v + b)$ yields more realistic and pleasing results

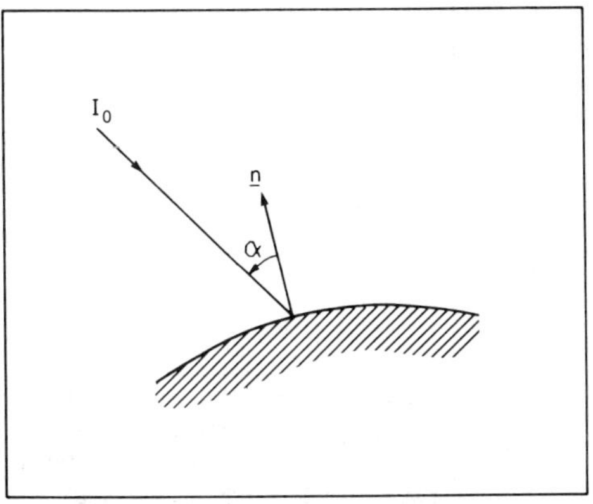

Figure 3.52. The geometry of diffuse (Lambertian) reflection. The amount of light reflected depends only on the cosine of the angle of incidence (the angle between the light-source vector I_0 and the surface normal N) and is uniform in all directions.

in practice, where b is an experimentally determined constant (Blinn, 1977).

In addition to illumination from point sources of light we must also provide for so-called ambient illumination. We denote this by I_a and use the coefficient k_a to denote the fraction that is reflected. If we then combine specular, diffuse, and ambient light reflection in a single expression, we obtain for J distinct point sources of light

$$I_r = k_a I_a + \frac{1}{v + b} \sum_{j=1}^{J} I_j (k_d \cos \alpha_j + k_s \cos^m \phi_j) . \quad (3)$$

8.2. Image Formation by Ray Tracing

A method for forming images of computer-modeled scenes that has the potential for achieving an exceptionally high degree of realism is the so-called *ray-tracing* method. In this method rays of light are traced (backward) from the vantage point, through each pixel of the image, to an object surface point, and from there by either reflection or refraction to other surface points until finally a point source of light is reached, as illustrated in Figure 3.53. By considering multiple-surface reflections, and refractions, one can realistically model image reflections (where one object is reflected as an image in another object), shadows, transparency effects, and highlights.

Let us look more closely at the situation depicted in Figure 3.53. We select a hypothetical vantage point (the intended position of our eye) and place an image plane at a "comfortable" distance from it. The image plane corresponds to the location of the raster display screen where the computer-generated image will appear. However, for the purpose of computation, we pretend that the image plane contains a window through which we can see the actual three-dimensional scene, as illuminated by one or more light sources (as shown in Fig. 3.53).

Next we divide the image window into pixels, using horizontal and vertical resolutions that are identical to those of our raster display. To calculate each of the pixel values for our raster display, we pretend to trace out rays from our eye through each pixel in the image window into the actual three-dimensional scene. If no object of the scene is encountered, our ray eventually impinges on the scene background, in which case the pixel is assigned the color values of the background. (If no background has been specified, we can let the ray vanish into outer space and simply color the pixel black.)

If the ray does strike an object, we proceed to determine the amount of light emanating from that point. The light coming from that point may be due to (1) light generation, where the point is, in fact, a *source* of light (such as a CRT display, an incandescent bulb, or a candle); (2) diffuse light reflected at that point; (3) specularly reflected light coming from a source whose angle with the surface normal at that point does not differ very much from the angle our ray makes with that normal (and lies in the same plane), as discussed in Section 8.1.1; (4) transmitted light, which passes through the object surface at that point and is refracted (bent); and (5) ambient light.

We now continue the ray tracing by following the reflected and refracted light component vectors away from that point to their sources, using the appropriate angles for reflection and refraction. These sources now may be actual light sources or they may be other object surface points from which reflected and refracted light emanates. The process is continued until all light vectors terminate on actual light sources, where the

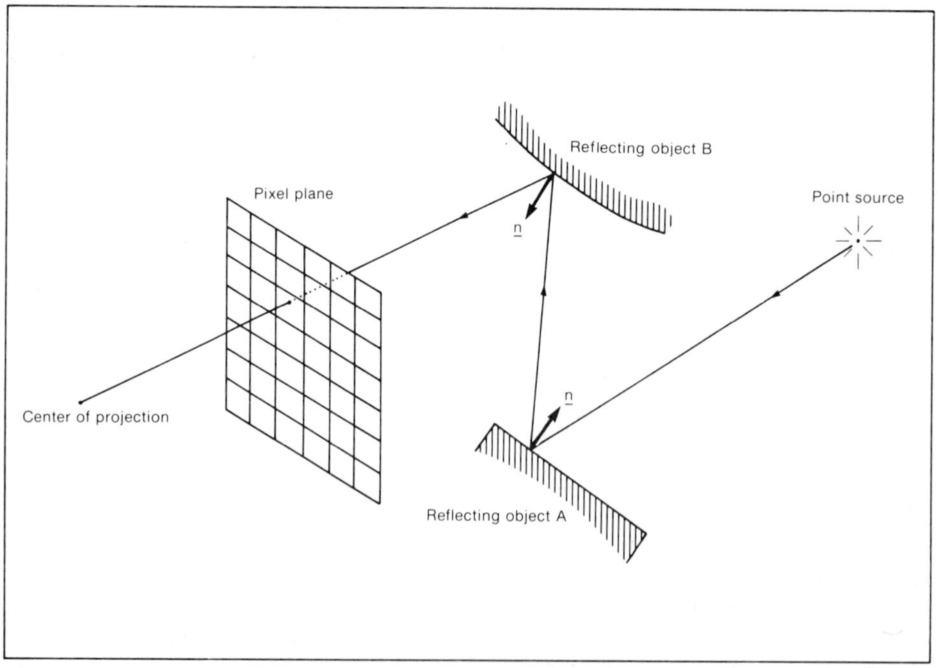

Figure 3.53. Ray tracing. The intensity value of a pixel is determined by tracing back from the center of projection, through the pixel, to either an object or the background. If an object is encountered, the light reflected at that point is computed, using the specular and Lambertian reflection formulas. Note that the light vector illuminating the point may itself be a reflection from another object. Also, though not shown here, light may also be transmitted through a surface and refracted (direction altered) at a point and contribute to the total amount of light emanating from that point. If the proportion of transmitted light is large compared to the amount of reflected light, the surface appears quasi-transparent in the display.

originating red, green, and blue light intensities can now be determined. (The tracing must be done separately for each of the three primary light components, for their reflection and transmission coefficients are likely to be different at each surface.) When completed, the red, green, and blue intensity values of the selected pixel in the image place will have been determined and can be stored in the refresh buffer.

The calculation must be repeated for each pixel in the scene, for example, more than one million times for a 1024 × 1024 image. As a result, ray tracing is a computation-intensive process, although it is unrivaled in the degree of realism that can be achieved with it (Potmesil & Chakravarty, 1981; Smith, 1984; Whitted, 1980).

8.3. Polygon Shading

If the object to be displayed can be satisfactorily modeled in terms of surface polygons, we can make use of a method for creating a shaded image of the object that is much simpler than the ray-tracing scheme. If we assume that the light source (or sources) as well as the vantage point are sufficiently distant from the object, the light reflected to the observer can be taken as being uniform over each projection polygon. Thus Eq. (3) need be evaluated only once for each polygon (instead of once for each pixel). Good shaded images of polyhedral objects can be obtained this way with very modest computations, after the hidden surfaces have been eliminated by either of the methods described in Section 7.2 (Blinn, 1977; Gouraud, 1971).

This method can also be extended to curved-surface objects. The surfaces are first approximated by polygonal faces and the surface normals are then computed. To prevent false edges (with mach bands) to appear in the supposedly curved surfaces, averages of illumination are computed across the polygon edges and linear interpolation is used to provide smooth transitions. The results tend to be quite good and to give satisfactory renderings of continuously curving surfaces, though not of the quality attainable with ray tracing (Catmull, 1975).

8.4. Color Image Display

8.4.1. Color Image Generation. The generation of multicolor images as projections of three-dimensional objects is only slightly more complicated than the generation of monochrome images. Typically such images are displayed on a color television monitor, which requires intensity modulation signals for each of its three electron guns—one each for red, green, and blue—as the raster is being traversed by the three-component electron beam. In effect, to generate a color image one really generates three component images, in red, green, and blue, and lets the eye fuse them into the desired color. For the ray-tracing method of Section 8.2 or the polygon-shading method of Section 8.3, this means that the computations must be performed three times, once for each of the primary colors. Note that the reflection coefficients k_a, k_d, and k_s are normally different for each component color, as is also the point source light intensity I_0.

In generating color images, most computer graphics designers tend to work with the additive primary colors, red, green, and blue (the RGB system). It is perfectly possible, however, to work also with colors in a different coordinate system, such as the HLS (hue, lightness, saturation) system. The latter may be intuitively easier to utilize for specific color effects. In any case, simple linear transformations are available for converting from RGB to HLS or vice versa, as well as to some of the other color models available (Foley & Van Dam, 1982).

8.4.2. Color Image Display System. A block diagram of a representative color image display system is shown in Figure 3.54. The system differs from an ordinary monochrome system in the use of so-called color lookup tables (sometimes also called intensity transformations tables). These tables, one for each color channel, can be used to modify the color intensity value stored in the refresh buffer before applying it to the appropriate gun of the color CRT. This makes it possible to modify the color mix without changing the stored image data. The three color values stored for each pixel serve as the *addresses* to the color lookup tables. Thus if for a particular pixel a blue color value of 157 is stored, the table would be accessed at address 157 and the actual value stored there (which could be any other number) would then be passed on to the digital-to-analog converters to control the intensity of the "blue" gun of the CRT.

A video lookup table has a "length" (number of entries) equal to the range covered by the pixel values in the refresh buffer. Thus if, for example, 4 bits are allocated for the color blue in the refresh buffer, then the table must have $2^4 = 16$ entries; for 8 bits, the number of entries would be $2^8 = 256$. The number of entries determines the maximum number of distinct intensities of the particular primary color that can be selected.

The "width" of a color lookup table is the size (in bits) of the numbers that can be *stored* in the table. The width may be the same as the length, or it may be much larger. The width of a table determines what is referred to as the "color palette," that is, the actual color intensity variations that can be obtained on the CRT face. If a color lookup table has a length of 4 bits and a width of 8 bits (that is, if it has 16 entry points, at each of which an 8-bit number can be stored), then it is possible to select any 16 color intensities out of an *available* set of 256. The actual different color combinations of hue, lightness, and saturation that can be obtained in the display will be equal to the product of the widths of the three color lookup tables. Thus for pixels that are stored as 12 bits in the refresh buffer, with 4 bits assigned to each of red, green, and blue, and color lookup tables each of width 8, it is possible to display $2^{12} = 4096$ distinct colors, selected from a palette of $2^{24} = 16,777,216$!

The color lookup tables are easily (and rapidly) changed because they involve much less data than the refresh buffer; thus it is even possible to change the colors in a display at high speed, that is, from one frame time to the next. Although the main purpose of the color lookup tables is to adjust interactively the colors in a displayed color image, important other uses are compensation for color variations among different display systems and compensation for nonlinearities in film sensitivities prior to recording displayed images on photographic film.

9. ANIMATION AND REAL-TIME MOTION DISPLAY

One application area in which computer graphics can have an enormous impact is in the generation of moving-image displays. Such displays divide into two categories, depending on whether the moving images are or are not displayed in real time. We shall refer to them as computer animation or real-time motion display, respectively.

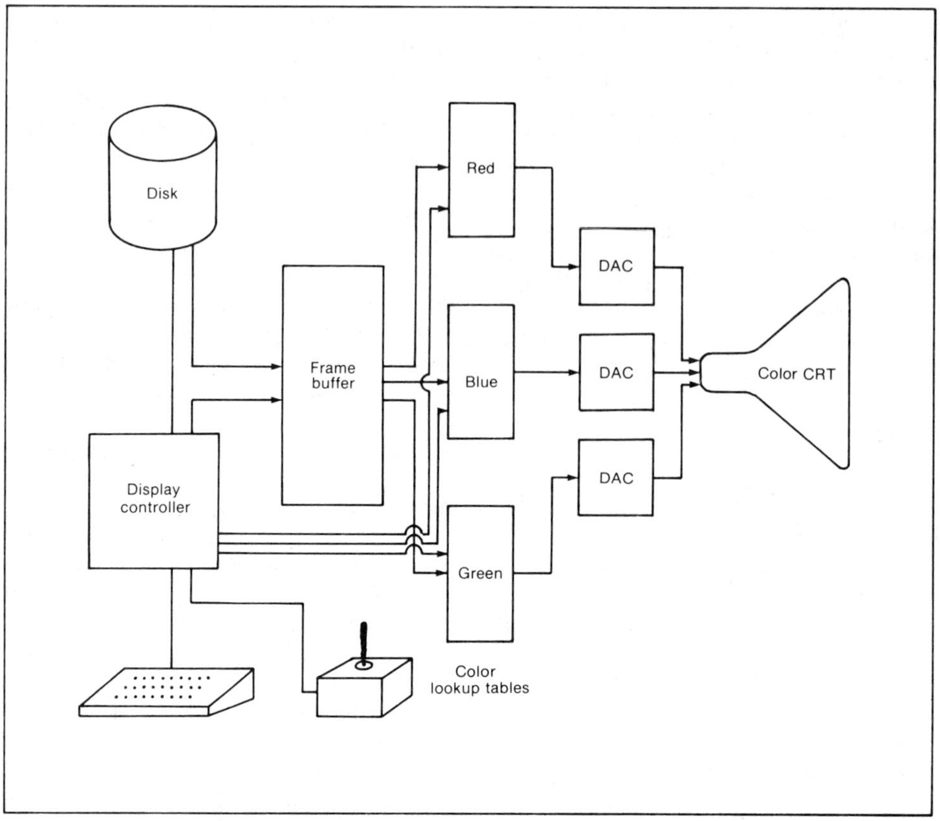

Figure 3.54. Color image display system, showing the frame buffer (refresh memory), the three color lookup tables, the digital-to-analog converters (DAC), the color CRT, and the display controller. No other computer is shown; it is to be assumed here that the display controller also serves as the computer for the system and handles any required application computations.

9.1. Computer Animation

In computer animation, image sequences are generated and recorded one frame at a time on either film or videotape. They are then played back at high speed to achieve a moving-image display. Computer graphics is an ideal tool for computer animation because it can enormously reduce the effort required over manual or animation-stand techniques and make possible the creation of a variety of special effects that can be easily implemented via computer programs but are prohibitively costly—if not impossible—to accomplish by manual methods.

For computer animation one simply creates a series of static images (frames) such that when these are shown in rapid sequence (typically, at from 16 to 24 frames per second) a moving-image effect is created. The images can be as complex and elaborate as desired, with only the cost of computation and the production time as factors that need be considered. Because, for example, a 5-min film sequence at 24 frames per second requires a total of 7200 frames, the production of even relatively short films can consume a large number of hours (or days!).

9.2. Real-Time Motion Display

In contrast to computer animation, real-time motion display requires that successive frames in the image sequence be generated at high speed so that smooth, flicker-free motion is obtained. This is a challenging task for a raster image generation system, for which only partially successful solutions exist at this time.

When motion is displayed in real time somewhat lower spatial resolution is generally satisfactory over what would be required for a static image (say, 512 × 512 instead of 1024 × 1024). However, even at a resolution of only 512 × 512, it is extremely difficult to perform the necessary object transformations, hidden-surface elimination, and shading for realistic motion display in a single frame time.

One possibility for achieving limited real-time motion display consists of utilizing the color lookup tables. Consider the simple example of displaying a bouncing ball against a uniform-color background in real time. If a new position of the ball were to be computed from one display frame to the next (say, in 1/30 sec), the computation for even as simple an object as this might be difficult to achieve in the available time. What can be done, however, is to compute the entire sequence of ball positions in advance and store it as a single image in the refresh buffer. Different pixel color values are now assigned for each different position of the ball. The color table is then loaded so as to cause the ball in the initial position to be displayed; the balls in all subsequent positions are made invisible by having the color lookup table assign a color to them that is identical to that of the background. One or two frame times later, the color table is modified so that the ball in the initial position is given the background color, the ball in the second position is given a distinctive color, and all other balls are still assigned the background color. By thus giving a distinctive color to one ball and assigning the background color to all other balls, display of a single ball in real-time motion can be accomplished. This process of motion display is referred to as *color table animation*

(Shoup, 1979). Some remarkable animation effects have been achieved with it. It is, however, limited in that successive moving-object locations may not overlap, and that the complexity of objects and background are limited by the number of entries in the color lookup table (i.e., by the "length" of the table).

For real-time motion of complex scenes color-table animation is inadequate. The only solution is to resort to special high-speed hardware that will permit fast image generation. In recent years, specialized graphics processors have been developed that permit high-speed, real-time transformation of raster images (three-dimensional rotation, translation, scaling and perspective), as well as hidden-surface removal and shading (Clark, 1982). The cost of these systems is quite high, often two or three times the cost of a conventional graphics system. The quality of the resulting images also tends to be somewhat less, a compromise necessary to achieve real-time motion capability.

One of the most demanding applications of real-time motion display is found in flight simulators, driver-education trainers, and other interactive training devices. In these the problem is to display to the users a realistic view of a scene, often on a large-scale, surrounding-type display screen. The scene must change smoothly in response to user actions that would in a real-life environment cause the vantage point orientation and position to change (e.g., as a pilot banks an aircraft for a turn). The necessary high-speed computation that permits real-time image generation under such conditions can be obtained only through the use of highly specialized parallel-processing types of computer architectures. The cost of such systems tends to be extremely high, ranging into many millions of dollars for some of the systems currently available for aircraft pilot training.

REFERENCES

*References preceded by an asterisk are "key references."

Artwick, B. A. *Applied concepts in microcomputer graphics*. Englewood Cliffs, N.J.: Prentice-Hall, 1984.

Barnhill, R. E., & Riesenfeld, R. F. *Computer aided geometric design*. New York: Academic Press, 1974.

Bergeron, R. D., Bono, P., & Foley, J. D. Graphics programming using the CORE system. *Computing Surveys*, 1978, *10*(4), 389–443.

Bezier, P. E. *Numerical control—Mathematics and applications*. London: Wiley, 1972.

Blinn, J. F. Models of light reflection for computer synthesized pictures. *Computer Graphics*, 1977, *11*(2), 192–198.

Bresenham, J. E. Algorithm for computer control of a digital plotter. *IBM Systems Journal*, 1965, *4*(1), 25–30.

Carlbom, I., & Paciorek, J. Planar geometric projections and viewing transformations. *Computing Surveys*, 1978, *10*(4), 465–502.

Catmull, E. Computer display of curved surfaces. *Proceedings of Conference on Computer Graphics, Pattern Recognition, and Data Structures, IEEE*, 975, 11–17.

Chaikin, G. M. An algorithm for high speed curve generation. *Computer Graphics and Image Processing*, 1974, *3*(4), 346–349.

Chung, W. L. On circle generation algorithms. *Computer Graphics and Image Processing*, 1977, *6*(2), 196–198.

Clark, J. The geometry engine: A VLSI geometry system for graphics. *Computer Graphics*, 1982, *16*(3), 127–133.

Denert, E. A method for computing points of a circle using only integers. *Computer Graphics and Image Processing*, 1973, *2*(1), 83–91.

Enderle, G., Kansy, K., & Pfaff, G. *Computer Graphics Programming*. New York: Springer-Verlag, 1984.

Faiman, M., & Nievergelt, J. (Eds.). *Pertinent concepts in computer graphics*. Urbana, Ill.: University of Illinois Press, 1969.

Faux, I. D., & Pratt, M. J. *Computational geometry for design and manufacture*. New York: Wiley, 1979.

Fetter, W. A. *Computer graphics in communication*. New York: McGraw-Hill, 1965.

*Foley, J. D., & Van Dam, A. *Fundamentals of interactive computer graphics*. Reading, Mass.: Addison-Wesley, 1982.

Freeman, H. Computer processing of line-drawing images. *Computing Surveys*, 1974, *6*(1), 57–97.

Freeman, H. Shape description via the use of critical points. *Pattern Recognition*, 1978, *10*(3), 159–166.

Freeman, H. (Ed.). *Interactive computer graphics*. Piscataway, N.J.: IEEE Computer Society Press, 1980.

Fulton, D. L. A plasma-panel interactive graphics system. *Proceedings of the Society for Information Display*, 1974, *15*(2).

Giloi, W. K. *Interactive computer graphics*. Englewood Cliffs, N.J.: Prentice-Hall, 1978.

Gouraud, H. Continuous shading of curved surfaces. *IEEE Transactions on Computers*, 1971, *C-20*(6), 623–628.

Gruenberger, F. (Ed.). *Computer graphics*. Washington, D.C.: Thompson, 1967.

Hamlin, G., & Gear, W. Raster-scan hidden surface algorithm techniques. *Computer Graphics*, 1977, *11*(2), 206–213.

*Harrington, S. *Computer graphics—A programming approach*. New York: McGraw-Hill, 1983.

*Hearn, D., & Baker, M. P. *Microcomputer graphics*. Englewood Cliffs, N.J.: Prentice-Hall, 1983.

Hopgood, F. R. A., Duce, D. A., Gallop, J. R., & Sutcliffe, D. C. *Introduction to the Graphical Kernel System (GKS)*. New York: Academic Press, 1983.

Jarvis, J. F., Judice, C. N., & Ninke, W. H. A survey of techniques for the display of continuous tone pictures on bilevel displays. *Computer Graphics and Image Processing*, 1976, *5*(1), 13–40.

Jordan, B. W., Lennon, W. J., & Holm, B. D. An improved algorithm for the generation of nonparametric curves. *IEEE Transactions on Computers*, 1973, *C-22*(12), 1052–1060.

Levin, J. Mathematical models for determining the intersections of quadric surfaces. *Computer Graphics and Image Processing*, 1979, *11*(1), 73–87.

Loutrel, P. A solution to the hidden-line problem for computer-drawn polyhedra. *IEEE Transactions on Computers*, 1970, *C-19*(3), 205–213.

McIlroy, M. D. Best approximate circles on integer grids. *ACM Transactions on Graphics*, 1984, *2*(4), 237–263.

Nake, F., & Rosenfeld, A. (Eds.). *Graphic languages*. Amsterdam: North-Holland, 1972.

Newell, M. E., Newell, R. G., & Sancha, T. L. A solution to the hidden surface problem. *Proceedings of the ACM National Meeting*, 1972, 443–450.

*Newman, W., & Sproull, R. F. *Principles of interactive computer graphics* (2nd ed.). New York: McGraw-Hill, 1979.

Parslow, R. D., Prowse, R. W., & Green, R. E. (Eds.). *Computer graphics*. London: Plenum Press, 1969.

Parslow, R. D., & Green, R. E. (Eds.). *Computer graphics in medical research and hospital administration*. London: Plenum Press, 1971.

Pavlidis, T. *Algorithms for graphics and image processing*. Rockville, MD: Computer Science Press, 1982.

Phong, B. T. Illumination for computer-generated pictures. *Communications of the ACM*, 1975, *18*(6), 311–317.

Potmesil, M., & Chakravarty, I. A lens and aperture camera model for synthetic image generation. *Computer Graphics*, 1981, *15*(3), 297–305.

Potmesil, M., & Freeman, H. Implementation of two hidden-line algorithms. *Computers and Graphics*, 1980, *5*, 31–40.

Requicha, A. A. G., & Voelker, H. B. Solid modeling: a historical summary and contemporary assessment. *Computer Graphics and Applications*, 1982, *2*(2), 9–24.

*Rogers, D. F., & Adams, A. J. *Mathematical elements for computer graphics*. New York: McGraw-Hill, 1976.

Sherr, S. *Fundamentals of display system design.* New York: Wiley, 1970.

Shoup, R. G. Color table animation. *Computer Graphics*, 1979, *13*(2), 8–13.

Sklansky, J. (Ed.). *Pattern recognition: Introduction and foundations.* Stroudsburg, Pa.: Dowden, Hutchinson & Ross, 1973.

Smith, A. R. Plants, fractals, and formal languages. *Computer Graphics*, 1984, *18*(3), 1–10.

Sutherland, I. E. Sketchpad—A man-machine graphical communication system. *Spring Joint Computer Conference.* Arlington, Va.: AFIPS Press, 1963.

Sutherland, I. E., Sproull, R. F., & Schumacker, R. A. A characterization of ten hidden-surface algorithms. *Computing Surveys*, 1974, *6*(1), 1–55.

Whitted, T. An improved illumination model for shared display. *Communications of the ACM*, 1980, *23*(6), 343–349.

Woon, P., & Freeman, H. A procedure for generating visible-line projections of solids bounded by quadric surfaces. *Information Processing 71.* Amsterdam: North-Holland, 1972, 1120–1125.

SECTION II

BASIC SENSORY PROCESSES I

DONALD I. A. MACLEOD

Department of Psychology, University of California at San Diego, La Jolla, California

JAMES P. THOMAS

Department of Psychology, University of California at Los Angeles, Los Angeles, California

OVERVIEW

JAMES P. THOMAS

Department of Psychology, University of California at Los Angeles, Los Angeles, California

1. THE ORGANIZATION OF THE SECTION

The immediate stimulus for vision is the retinal image, in which light is distributed as a function of four variables: wavelength, time, and two spatial dimensions. Historically, the study of visual perception has been similarly structured. Most research has asked how the perception of an object depends upon the spectral, temporal, and spatial properties of the object. Individual research projects have usually focused on the influence of single variables, with other variables held constant or treated as parameters. In the same vein, the study of eye movements, which modify both the spatial and temporal properties of the image, has been a largely separate line of investigation.

This section has been divided into chapters along similar lines, not only because of historical precedent, but also because the organization suits one of the major goals of the *Handbook*. That goal is to summarize basic laboratory research in a form that facilitates application to problems outside the laboratory. Such problems are often defined in terms of the tasks to be performed and the environment in which the tasks are set. That is, they are defined in terms of the stimuli that must be perceived and processed and in terms of the stimulus environment. Thus the organization of the section by stimulus variables is appropriate to this goal.

The section opens with a chapter by Westheimer on the formation of the retinal image itself. The temporal variable is examined in the chapter on temporal sensitivity by Watson; and the spatial variables are the topic of the chapter on seeing spatial patterns, by Olzak and Thomas. The role of the wavelength variable is discussed in two chapters, one on colorimetry and color discrimination by Pokorny and Smith, and the other on color appearance by Wyszecki. The chapter by Hood and Finkelstein on sensitivity to light also treats the wavelength variable in examining spectral sensitivity. In addition, their chapter treats the phenomena of adaptation, which collectively alter the absolute sensitivity of the visual system and its response properties with respect to temporal and spatial as well as spectral dimensions. The section closes with a separate chapter on eye movements by Hallett.

2. UNDERLYING MECHANISMS

The driving force in research is the attempt to identify and describe underlying mechanisms. Although this section has been divided into chapters according to stimulus variables, there is within each chapter a central concern with the underlying visual mechanisms. This emphasis is also appropriate to the goals of the *Handbook*, as well as to the goals of science. The application of laboratory findings always entails some degree of extrapolation and interpolation, and these extensions of the data are most accurate when guided by sound understanding of the underlying mechanisms.

The visual system may be thought of as divided into a number of intersecting sets of subsystems or mechanisms. The best established set consists of the scotopic and photopic systems, which differ from each other in absolute sensitivity, spectral sensitivity, receptor distribution, and properties of spatial and temporal integration. Another established set of subsystems contains the different color mechanisms of normal trichromatic vision, which differ most prominently in spectral sensitivity. Other sets have also been proposed, containing mechanisms that differ in sensitivity with respect to such stimulus properties as direction of motion, orientation, and temporal and spatial frequency. The sets are intersecting in the sense that a given pathway may be a member of several of these conceptual sets. For example, a given cortical cell can be tuned with respect to orientation, direction of motion, spatial and temporal frequency, and color, and thus be a member of many sets at once. (For an illustration, see the methods and results sections of Thorell, DeValois, & Albrecht, 1984.)

The enterprise of studying these mechanisms psychophysically and relating them to visual perception is challenging, to say the least. In a very general sense, visual perception is an envelope function in which the contributions of individual mechanisms are run together. It is necessary to break through the envelope and isolate individual mechanisms in order to study their properties and how their contributions meld together to determine visual performance. Fortunately, the relative importance of each mechanism is not fixed, but shifts as stimulus conditions change. By appropriately manipulating the stimulus conditions, a given mechanism can be made dominant and at least a portion of its response properties studied. The basic concepts and techniques of this approach were developed to isolate and study the scotopic and photopic subsystems. The chapter on sensitivity to light by Hood and Finkelstein is a superb primer on these concepts and techniques. Variations of the same approach, using many of the same concepts and techniques, have been applied to isolate and study the various color, temporal, and spatial mechanisms. The results of these efforts are described in other chapters of this section.

3. SOME THINGS FALL THROUGH THE CRACKS

The traditional structure lets some things escape notice. In particular, certain properties and phenomena emerge only when variables are examined in combination. For example, the chapter by Olzak and Thomas discusses the spatial tuning of individual pathways in the visual system and the role of spatial tuning in both detecting and recognizing objects. The chapter by Watson discusses the temporal tuning of these same pathways. What these treatments do not bring out is that, when spatial and temporal tuning are considered together, a new property emerges: the same pathways have the potential to detect and encode motion (Adelson & Bergen, 1985; Watson & Ahumada, 1985).

Another example involves the spatial and wavelength variables. Perception of spatial patterns has traditionally been investigated with patterns created by varying luminance (effective intensity) only, in a fashion akin to black and white photographs. However, a few investigators have used wavelength variations to create patterns, holding luminance constant, with some surprising results. One such result is that a luminance pattern (uniform wavelength) may be more strongly masked by a wavelength pattern (uniform luminance) than by another luminance pattern (DeValois & Switkes, 1983).

Happily, the trend toward examining variables in combination is increasing and more such results can be expected.

REFERENCES

Adelson, E. H., & Bergen, J. R. Spatio-temporal energy models for the perception of motion. *Journal of the Optical Society of America A*, 1985, *2*, 284–299.

DeValois, K. K., & Switkes, E. Simultaneous masking interactions between chromatic and luminance gratings. *Journal of the Optical Society of America*, 1983, *73*, 11–18.

Thorell, L. G., DeValois, R. L., & Albrecht, D. C. Spatial mapping of monkey V1 cells with pure color and luminance stimuli. *Vision Research*, 1984, *24*, 751–769.

Watson, A. B., & Ahumada, A. J. Model of human visual-motion sensing. *Journal of the Optical Society of America A*, 1985, *2*, 322–342.

CHAPTER 4

THE EYE AS AN OPTICAL INSTRUMENT

GERALD WESTHEIMER

Department of Physiology-Anatomy, University of California, Berkeley, California

CONTENTS

Visual stimuli go through a mandatory transformation before they become available to the neural transduction apparatus at the retinal level. This chapter delineates the salient characteristics of this transformation process, making apparent what differences between the actual and the perceived visual objects can be ascribed to it. Because the optical and neural structures subserving vision have evolved together, building on each other's strength and compensating for each other's weakness, it is not always profitable to differentiate between them, especially where higher perceptual mechanisms are concerned. However, a number of simple discrimination tasks are confined by the limitations of the optical imaging apparatus of the eye; they can be understood and coped with once the optical properties of the eye have been charted.

Fortunately, the eyes of young adults selected for normal visual function differ little from one another and it is thus possible to formulate general statements with excellent applicability to all members of this population. The exception—simple errors of refraction—can be corrected without loss of validity of the remaining principles.

The confounding of the various stages of transformation of the visual stimulus, which often makes it unprofitable to pursue its dissection into constituent factors, is illustrated by the search for the particular pattern that an observer will regard as a perfect checkerboard (Helmholtz, 1962). Even if the type of barrel-shaped or pincushion distortion of the eye were known in detail, one could not assume that such distortion had not already been corrected by a suitable compaction or expansion operation in the anatomical projection of the visual pathway. Whether the pattern in Figure 4.1 satisfies the condition of being seen as a perfect checkerboard is therefore best left to experimental verification rather than to analysis of optical parameters of the eye.

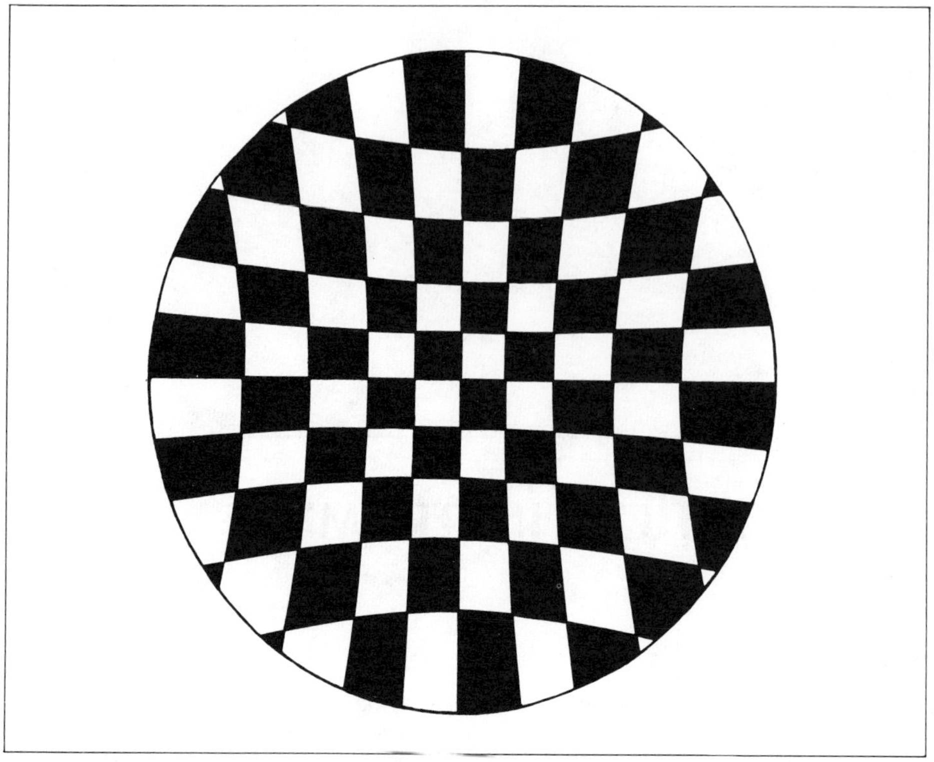

Figure 4.1. Checkerboard pattern. When viewed at a distance of 7.5 cm this pattern is seen by many subjects as a rectangular checkerboard. A variety of factors contribute to the object-sided "distortion" needed for the perception of a perfect checkerboard. They include perspective distortions, pincushion aberration of the eye, and innate and acquired remapping of the visual field. In a complex task of this kind, sifting the geometrical and optical components from the perceptual ones is very difficult, and a phenomenological approach is usually the most efficient.

The anatomical structure of the eye and the retina has an occasional modifying influence on vision. The photochemical and neural transformation of the optical image takes place after passage through all of the retina. This means that the retinal vasculature, especially the large vessels near the optic disk (Fig. 4.2), can obscure light from reaching the receptors. The optic nerve head produces the blind spot. Behind the retinal receptors are the pigment epithelium and the richly vascular choroid. The light they reflect back to the receptors is predominantly of long wavelength. This accounts for the red appearance of the fundus and also for more stray light at long wavelengths. On the other hand, lightly pigmented eyes may have intraocular scatter over a wider wavelength band.

The retina has a radially differentiated structure outward from the fovea, where the concentration of cones is highest and where there is a total absence of rods (Fig. 4.3). For most purposes it may be assumed that the structure is circularly organized,

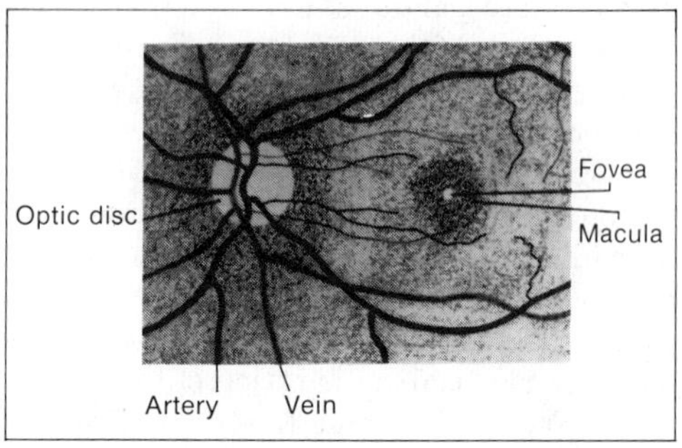

Figure 4.2. Retina of a left eye as seen with an ophthalmoscope. Features visible include the arterial and venous vascular tree, the optic disk, and the central visual area, which includes the fovea. The scale may be inferred from the size of the optic disk, which extends about 7.5° vertically and 5° horizontally in the visual field. (From R. W. Ditchburn, *Eye movements and visual perception*, Clarendon Press, 1973. Reprinted with permission.)

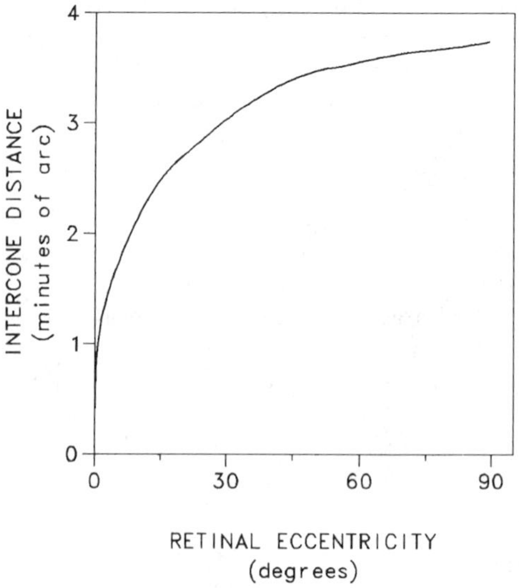

Figure 4.3. Intercone distance as a function of retinal eccentricity (after Polyak, 1941). This figure gives an indication of how the grain of the retina, as far as spatial resolution is concerned, changes going from the fovea outward.

but this is only approximately the case. For example, visual acuity is better along the lower field than along the upper (Millodot & Lamont, 1974).

1. BASIC CONCEPTS

The best reference framework for the following discussion is the eye itself. Operational definitions are possible for most of the concepts involved. Because the most likely application of the material in this chapter is the alert human subject, we begin by asking the subject to look at a point target (the fixation point). A constant and repeatable relationship will then have been established between the eye and the world of targets being imaged on the retina, the object space. (Movements of the eye and the head must be dealt with separately; they are the subject of detailed treatment; see Hallett, Chapter 10) A three-dimensional coordinate system is now set up, as shown in Figure 4.4, using the eye's entrance pupil as origin (for reasons to be explained later) and the line joining the center of the entrance pupil with the fixation point as the z-axis. This line is known as the primary line of sight. Horizontal and vertical meridians of the eye will serve to define the x- and y-axes.

1.1. Polar Coordinates in the Visual Field

Although it might seem natural to specify the location of targets by means of the x, y, and z coordinates thus defined, this is not usually done. Instead, a polar system of coordinates is preferred because it has a closer affinity to the anatomical organization of the eye. The primary line of sight becomes the principal line, that is, the radius vector in its centered position. Planes containing this axis are called meridians making angles ϕ with the horizontal meridian. In accord with the nomenclature employed in the specification of the axis of astigmatism in ophthalmic optics, the 0 meridian is to the right of each eye, looking at the eye; the 90° meridian is up, the 180° meridian left, and so on. The angle of eccentricity of the radius vector, that is, the angle between the primary line of sight and the line joining the target point with the center of the entrance pupil, is the third coordinate (Fig. 4.5). The relationship between x, y, and z rectangular coordinates and r, ϕ, and θ polar coordinates is given in Eq. (1), where θ is the angle of eccentricity and ϕ defines the meridian.

$$\theta = \tan^{-1}\left(\frac{y}{z}\right)$$

$$\phi = \tan^{-1}\left[\frac{(x^2 + y^2)^{1/2}}{z}\right] \tag{1}$$

$$r = (x^2 + y^2 + z^2)^{-1/2} .$$

1.2. Reciprocal of Target Distance—The Diopter

The distance of the target from the eye is on many occasions calculated not in terms of the actual value of r, but of its reciprocal. When r is in meters, the unit of its reciprocal has been designated the diopter. Table 4.1 shows values for these two variables for some typical target positions. In particular, a target at infinity corresponds to 0 diopters. It is also important to recognize that the reciprocity between target distances in meters and their dioptric equivalents does not allow immediate transfer of differences. For example, the half diopter step from 1 to 1.5 diopters represents a distance of 0.33 m, that from 2 to 2.5 diopters, 0.1 m, and that from 5 to 5.5 diopters, 0.02 m.

Consider first the situation in which a completely normal eye is presented with a point object at infinity, placed on the primary line of sight. The beginning approach is that of first-order geometrical optics, which postulates that each object point is represented in the image plane by a perfect point. The meaning of an optically normal eye—an emmetropic eye, as it is called—is that within the framework of geometrical optics there is indeed such a mapping of a point object at infinity into a point image. The advantage of our definition of the primary line of sight is that this image will now be formed in the center of the fovea and hence be available to the most highly elaborated neural processing mechanisms. Section 2 identifies and characterizes the various factors that mitigate against the application

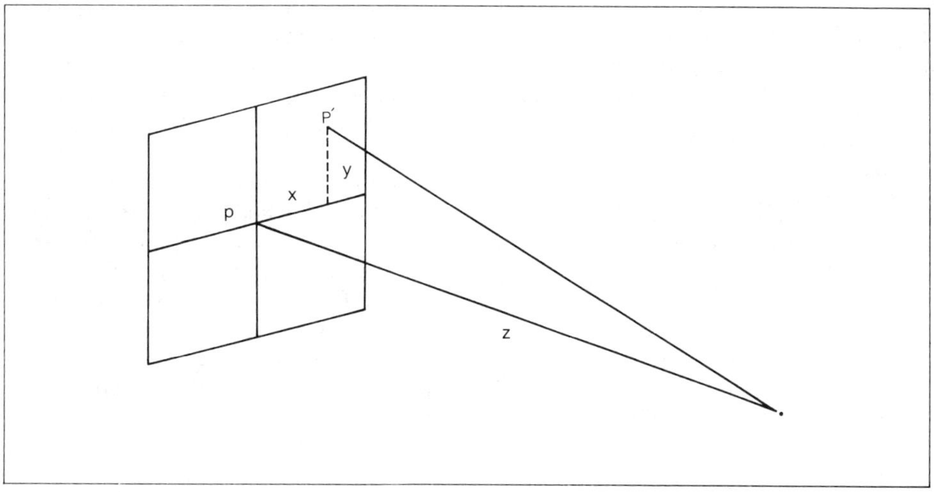

Figure 4.4. Rectangular coordinate system identifying the location of a point P' with respect to the center of the eye's entrance pupil in terms of the three Cartesian coordinates x, y, and z. The point P with coordinates (0, 0, z) is the fixation point, joined to the center of the entrance pupil by the primary line of sight.

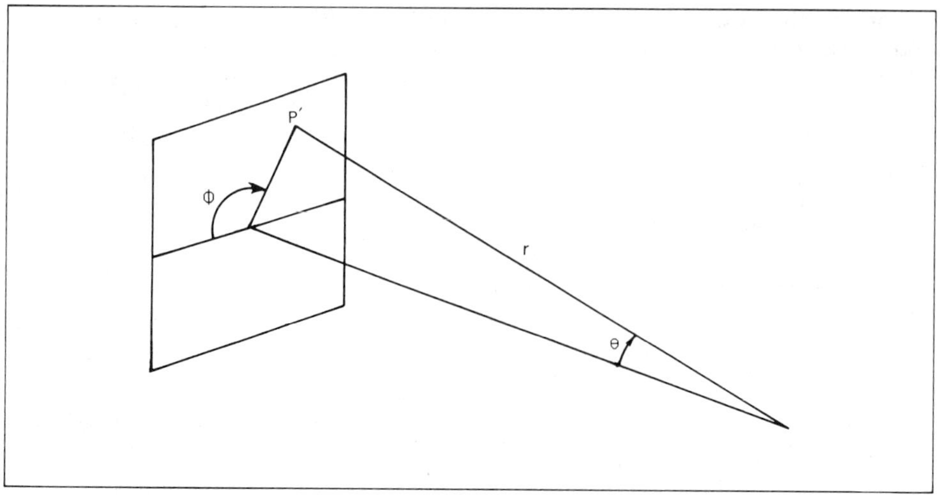

Figure 4.5. Polar system of coordinates to specify the location of point P' with respect to the center of the eye's entrance pupil and the primary line of sight. Any plane containing the primary line of sight is called a meridian. Point P' lies in a meridian making an angle ϕ with the horizontal. θ is the angle of eccentricity. The relationship between coordinates ϕ, θ, and r in this figure and corresponding coordinates x, y, and z of Figure 4.4 is given in Eq. (1).

of first-order geometrical optics in a real-life situation and make clear how different from a point the image really is. There are, however, still some aspects of optical imaging by the eye that allow satisfactory analysis by this simple approach.

1.3. Entrance Pupil and Primary Line of Sight

Figure 4.6 illustrates some details of the way the eye, acting as a first-order optical system, accepts a bundle of rays issuing from a point object at infinity and converts it into a conical bundle of rays converging to the retinal point image. All rays from such an object are parallel. The entrance pupil of the eye is, by definition, the delimiter in object space of those rays that will be allowed by the real aperture stop, the pupil, to enter the eye's image space and participate in the creation of the image. In the image space there is the homolog of the entrance pupil, the exit pupil. For the full characterization of first-order imagery, it suffices to know the positions of the entrance and exit pupils, their relative sizes, and the position of the secondary focal plane, that is, the plane in which infinitely far images are focused. These parameters are, of course, derived from the optical constants of the eye, that is, from the positions and radii of curvature of the various surfaces and the index of refraction of the ocular media. For the actual derivations and subsequent construction of the particular model eye, the reader is referred to specialized texts (Emsley, 1939; Westheimer, 1972). The schema in Figure 4.6 suffices for the purposes of this discussion. In particular, it illustrates the significance of the line from the object point to the center of the entrance pupil and its image-sided counterpart, the line joining the center of the exit pupil with the geometrical point image. This line, also known as the chief ray, as seen in the figure, is the most representative of all the rays making up the bundle because it is its core.

Table 4.1. Relationship between Focus Point and Target Distance in Front of the Eye

Focus Point (diopters)	Target Distance (m)
0	∞
0.25	4
0.5	2
1	1
1.5	0.67
2	0.5
2.5	0.4
3	0.33
4	0.25
5	0.2
5.5	0.18

A slight extension of the example will demonstrate the utility of the approach. Suppose a second point object is now added, as would occur, for instance, when an observer fixates one star in the sky and a second star becomes visible. For purposes of simplicity let the second star be situated in the meridian represented by the plane of the paper and let the chief ray from the second star make an angle θ with that from the first star (Fig. 4.7). The image-sided chief rays emerge into the image space making an angle 0.82θ, the factor 0.82 being a consequence of the geometry of the eye and the fact that light on the image side travels in the vitreous humor, a medium with refractive index approximately equal to that of water. The distance between the exit pupil and the retina is also known, 20.3 mm in the schematic eye used as our model. We are now in a position to calculate the retinal distance separating the images of the two stars. It is $y = 20.3 \tan \theta$ mm. For example, if θ is equal to $0.60°$, that is, 36 min arc, $y = 0.218$ mm. In the fovea, cones are about 0.003 mm apart, so that the images will have about 70 cones between their centers.

The dimensions associated with the structure of the eye, in particular the distance between the exit pupil and the retina, and the angular magnification ratio of the chief rays (0.82), will remain the same for all situations in any one eye. They will also differ little from one typical normal eye to another. As a consequence, we can accept, to a good approximation, that there is a fixed relationship between the angular separation of the chief rays of objects and the positions on the retina of their images. It can be concluded that for the specification of retinal

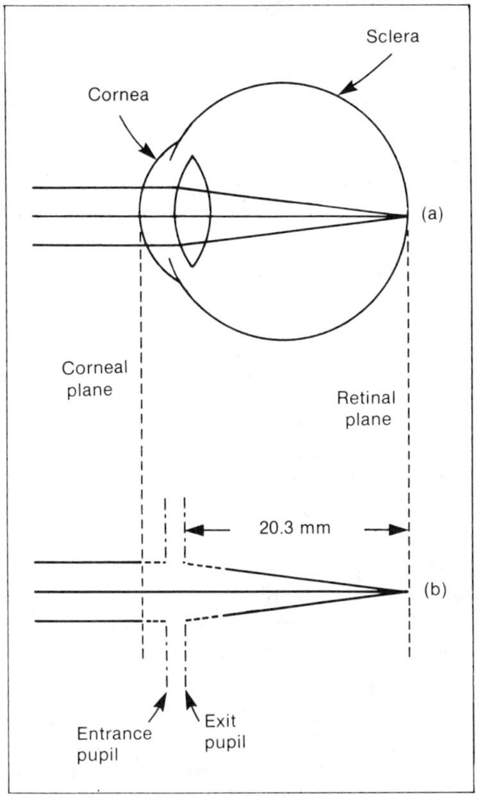

Figure 4.6. Schematic of the eye's optics. (a) Outline of the human eye showing how the light from a fixation point at infinity (parallel bundle of incident rays) is refracted to come to a focus on the retina. Only those rays admitted by the eye's pupil reach the image plane. (b) Schematic diagram of the passage of the rays in (a). The entrance pupil belongs to the object space. There is a fixed relationship between the eye's pupil, entrance pupil, and exit pupil, and it therefore suffices to specify the characteristics of visual targets in terms of their relationship to the entrance pupil.

image positions of objects, it suffices to know the chief rays in object space. What goes on inside the eye can then be taken for granted without further calculation.

1.4. Target Size Expressed in Terms of Visual Angle

The convention of expressing the size of visual features in terms of their angular subtense at the eye's entrance pupil in the eye's object space is so universal that it is worthwhile to identify a few typical values. See Table 4.2.

It can be noted that both visual targets and retinal structures have an identical kind of measure applied to them: the size of the anatomical feature is expressed in terms of the angular subtense of an object whose geometrical image would just cover it. In ophthalmic practice it is customary to quote the position and size of scotomas, for example, or the extent of the visual field, in angular measure for reasons that have been given; namely, the intraocular structure is not easily accessible for direct measurement and, in any case, visual angles bear a constant relationship to retinal distances in any one eye and are highly comparable from one eye to the next.

It is possible, though not usually practicable, to find the exact relationship between retinal distances and visual angle in an intact eye. X-rays penetrating the orbital walls are not subjected to optical changes by the media of the eye, yet they stimulate the retina and can be perceived by a subject as a localized phosphene. In the method of Goldmann and Hagen (1942), for example, two sheets of x-rays, whose lateral separation is accurately known, are directed to the retina while the subject adjusts a pair of visual targets so that their images are superimposed on the x-ray phosphenes (Fig. 4.8). It is then possible to find the object-sided entrance pupil angle in degrees that correspond in that particular eye to a given retinal distance in millimeters.

This formulation used so far to specify retinal images can be extended even to cases where the objects are not at infinity. Figure 4.9 shows the bundle of rays when the target has been moved inward from infinity without any concomitant refractive changes in the eye. The image bundle would converge to a point behind the retina were it not intercepted by the latter, forming a blur patch whose size is directly proportional to the pupil

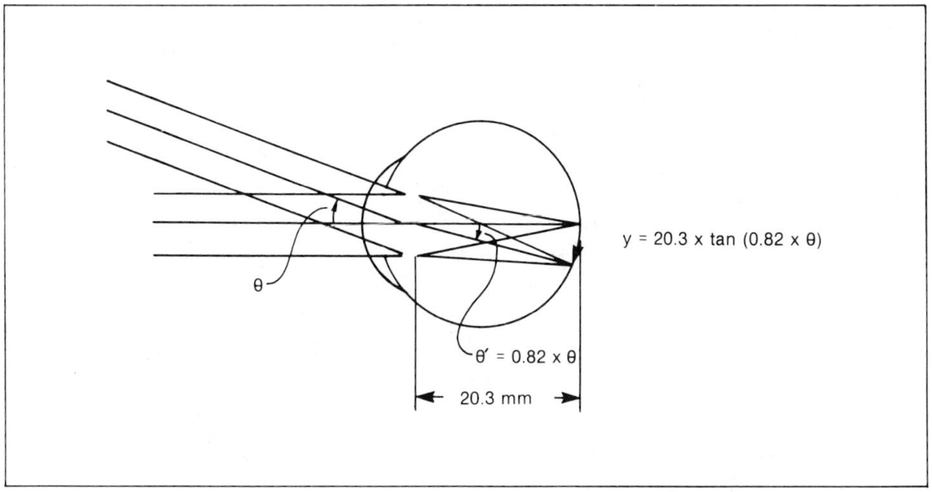

Figure 4.7. How two point sources at infinity separated by an angle θ give rise to two bundles of rays in the eye's image space. The image-sided chief rays are inclined at an angle of 0.82θ. The two bundles converge to image points on the retina separated by a linear distance given by $y = 20.3 \tan(0.82\theta)$.

Table 4.2. Visual Angle Associated with Some Typical Objects and Ocular Structures

Object	Visual angle
Alphanumeric character on CRT screen at 50 cm	17 min arc
Diameter of moon	36 min arc
5-cm-diameter gauge at 50 cm	5.7°
Diameter of fovea	30 min arc
Diameter of foveal retinal receptor	0.5 min arc
Position of inner edge of blind spot	12° from fovea
Size of blind spot	7.5° (vertical) 5° (horizontal)

diameter and the focus defect. The diagram, moreover, illustrates that the center of the blur patch is defined by the chief ray. This leads to an important generalization: the chief ray can be used to define image position regardless of whether the image is a hypothetical point image or a blur patch, provided we are willing to accept the position of the center of the blur patch as representative of the image. This applies also when the blur is due to factors other than just defocus.

1.5. Accommodation

A target not at infinity need not always generate the type of imagery shown in Figure 4.9. Normal eyes have the facility to change focus in response to close-up targets; they can accommodate. This means that, provided the focus deficit is accurately assessed, the optical power of the eye is changed and the theoretical point-object point-image relationship reestablished; that is, the retina is again made conjugate to the object.

Accommodation is accomplished by contraction of an intraocular muscle, the ciliary muscle. This entrains a series of mechanical changes resulting in an altered configuration of the crystalline lens and, consequently, a different optical power of the whole eye. Because the retinal position remains unaffected by this maneuver, its conjugate target distance is changed by accommodation. The amount of accommodation can therefore be expressed by the reciprocal of the new focus distance, that is, in diopters.

The structural changes in the eye during accommodation are confined in the main to the anterior portions of the crystalline lens. Calculation on optical schemata of the eye in the unaccommodated and accommodated states (Emsley, 1939) shows little change in the position of the principal points and the entrance pupil under these two conditions and that it is therefore justifiable in practice to use the same quantitative procedure for retinal image calculation in all states of accommodation. It follows that there is no essential difference in position and angular magnification of the chief rays between the accommodated and the unaccommodated eye. We thus have yet a further generalization concerning the chief-ray method of specifying retinal image position. Not only does it hold for targets at infinity as well as close up, but it also holds regardless of the accommodative state of the eye. Extremely high levels of accommodation can, however, cause mechanical changes at the retinal level (Blank, Provine, & Enoch, 1975).

The maximum amount of accommodation that a subject can exert is called the amplitude of accommodation. It is a function of age, as illustrated in Figure 4.10. Most subjects cannot, however, comfortably maintain more than about one-third of their accommodative amplitude for any length of time.

The time course of accommodation has been determined by measurement on normal young adults (Campbell & Westheimer, 1960). The reaction time for a reponse to a visual stimulus is of the order of 0.3 sec and the movement is essentially complete approximately 0.9 sec after the stimulus onset (see Fig. 4.11).

The ciliary muscle is somewhat anomalous among muscles. It is a smooth muscle with typical parasympathetic autonomic characteristics, yet it is under good voluntary control and its normal mode of operation involves responses to visual stimuli that are usually associated with cortical functions: detailed visual discriminations, sophisticated distinctions between targets, rapid learning, and so forth (Campbell & Westheimer, 1959). The accommodative stance in a young subject with active accommodation cannot be assumed to be steady. There are oscillations with an amplitude that can exceed 0.5 diopters, in a frequency band centered on 2 Hz (Campbell, Robson, & Westheimer, 1959). When the visual scene is devoid of details, as in complete darkness or in a Ganzfeld, the resting state of accom-

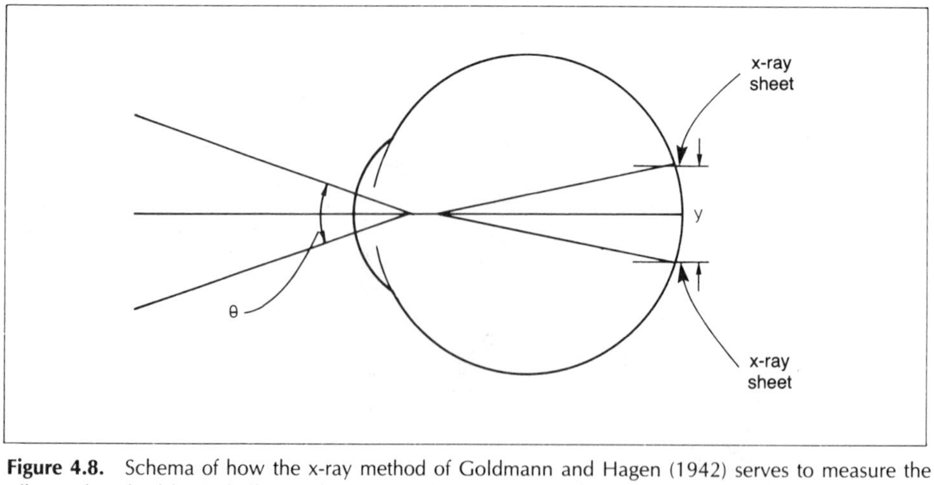

Figure 4.8. Schema of how the x-ray method of Goldmann and Hagen (1942) serves to measure the effective length of the eyeball. Two thin parallel sheets of x-rays, normal to the plane of the paper, intersect the retina, and are visible to the subject as lines. Their linear separation is known; the subject is given the task of placing two targets in the visual field to coincide with the x-ray phosphenes. This enables a subjectively determined visual angle to be correlated with the associated retinal distance.

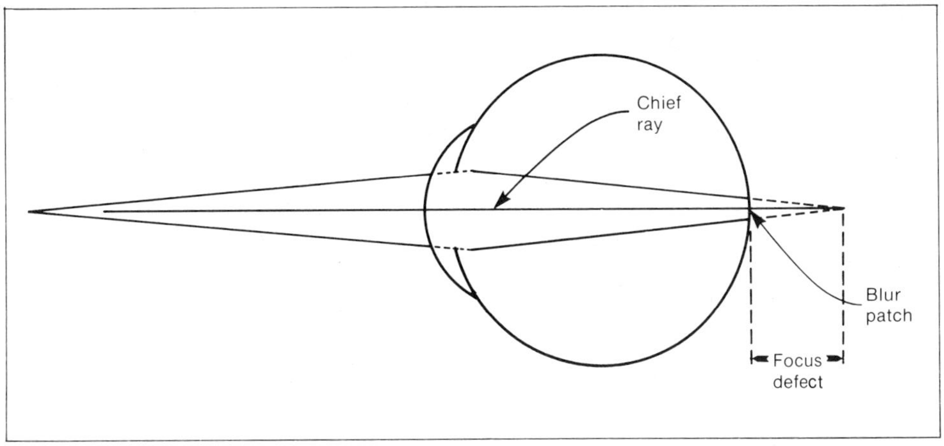

Figure 4.9. Passage of rays from a point object that is not conjugate to retina. Image-sided bundle intersects the retina in a blur patch, which is centered on the chief ray and whose diameter is proportional to the pupil diameter and the focus defect.

modation is not zero. Although it has usually been taught that a representative value for this "empty field myopia" is about 0.75 diopters (Borish, 1970), more extensive recent studies, using 220 college-age observers, have given a mean and standard deviation of 1.52 and 0.77 diopters (Leibowitz & Owens, 1978).

Although an individual's accommodation response cannot be foretold accurately, some general rules are represented graphically in Figure 4.12. On the whole, the best match between stimulus and steady-state accommodative response occurs when the target is detailed and situated within arm's reach and when the luminance is high. On the other hand, unstructured fields, low luminance and targets that are very far or very near represent situations in which the focus errors are likely to be highest. Contour delineated by only chromatic differences also does not yield accurate accommodation responses (Wolfe & Owens, 1981). Specific measurements relating the accommodative response to the spatial frequency of sinusoidal patterns have been reported by Charman and Tucker (1977). They were extended into the

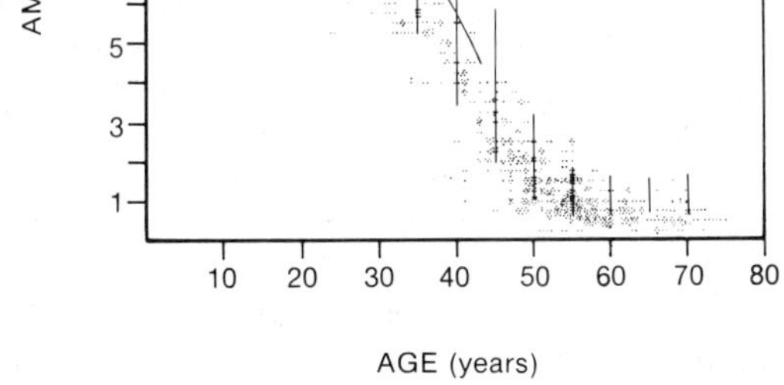

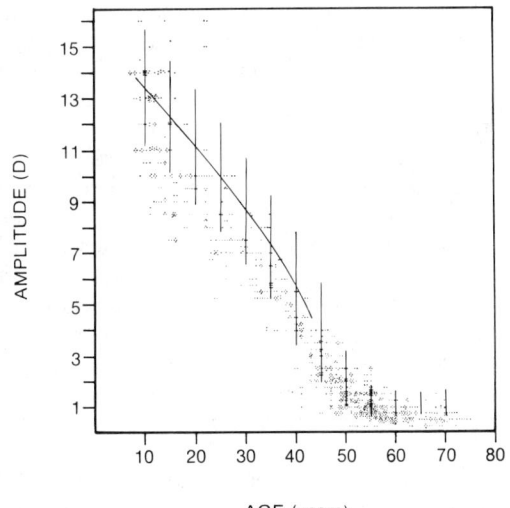

Figure 4.10. Amplitude of accommodation, determined by the standard clinical procedure, as a function of age, measured in 1000 eyes. Solid line and vertical brackets indicate the accepted clinical norms (from Turner, 1958).

low spatial frequency region (0.5 cycle per degree) by Owens (1980). In a field containing only a very low spatial frequency pattern, accommodation responses are not accurate. Depending on the situation, there may also be some inaccuracy when only very high spatial frequency gratings are shown, but this is not seen universally. The situation here is complicated by the possibility of spurious resolution. In any case, a field filled with a high spatial frequency grating must not be confused with one containing small detailed targets.

1.6. Refractive Errors

It has so far been assumed that the observer is emmetropic; that is, that within the standards of geometrical optics the retina is conjugate to infinity, and this pertains to a good portion of a selected young adult population. But many focus defects are capable of correction, making the eye then indistinguishable, for many visual purposes, from an emmetropic one. Leaving aside for a moment astigmatic defects, where there are focus differences in different meridians of the eye, we have two classes of nonemmetropic (or, as they are called, ametropic) eyes: those manifesting myopia and those manifesting hyperopia. A myopic eye has its retina conjugate not to infinity, but to a real plane in front of the subject. The scale used is the diopter. Thus a 3-diopter myope is in perfect focus without accommodation at a distance ⅓ m or 33 cm in front of the eyes, a point called the far point. By bringing accommodation into play, such a myope can bring the focus closer. For example, a 3-diopter myope exerting 2 diopters accommodation will be in focus for a distance of 20 cm. But a myope without correction cannot be in focus for targets beyond the far point. However, when the appropriate lens is placed in front of the eye, such an observer will have a visual performance, in terms of focusing ability, that is for most purposes indistinguishable from that of an emmetrope. This correction can be worn in the form of either contact lenses or spectacles.

Hyperopia is another class of ametropia. In this condition, the optical apparatus of the eye does not have enough power to bring objects even at infinity to a focus on the retina. Because ocular accommodation is in effect a process of adding optical power to the eye—used by the emmetrope to increase refractive

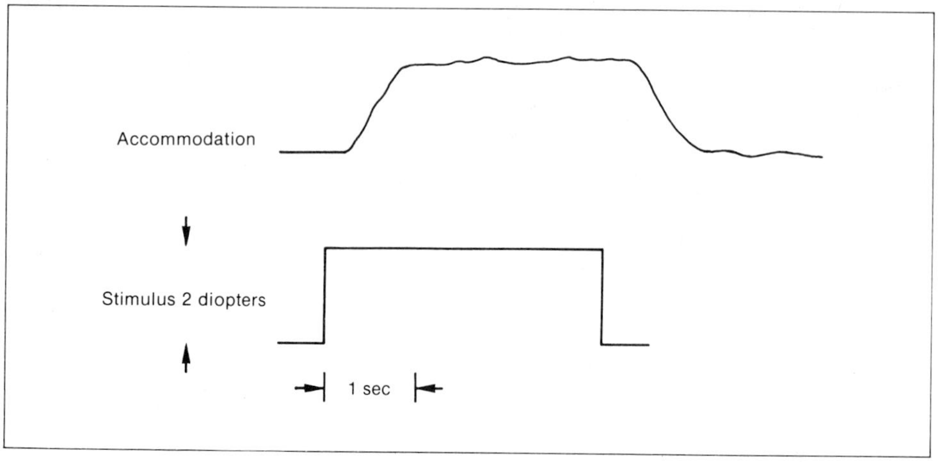

Figure 4.11. Time course of response of accommodation to step-focused stimuli in a young subject. The latency is about 0.3 sec and total time elapsed between stimulus onset and reaching of final response level is nearly 1 sec. There are many small oscillatory changes when active accommodation is being maintained (after Campbell & Westheimer, 1960).

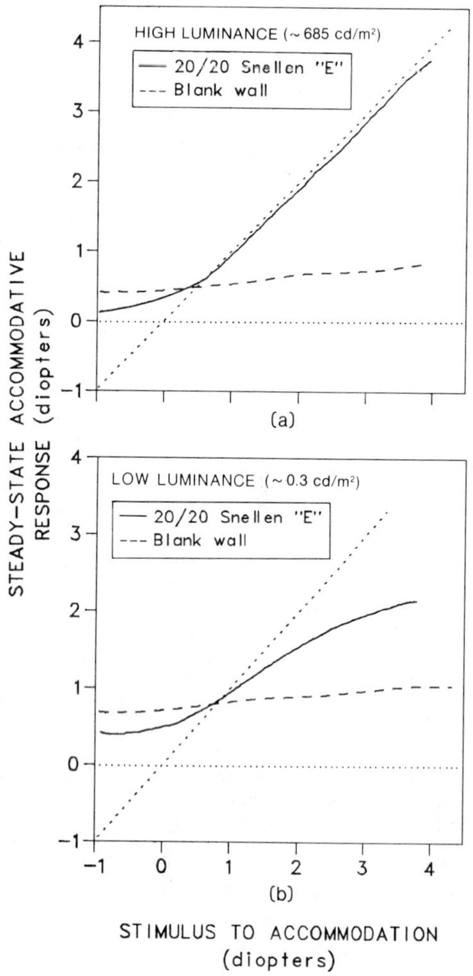

Figure 4.12. Levels of accommodation when viewing detailed (solid line) and unstructured (dashed line) visual stimuli at two luminance levels. Dotted oblique line shows hypothetical perfect response. Schematic summary of data from Nadell and Knoll (1956). (a) Photopic vision (685 $cd{\cdot}m^{-2}$). (b) Low luminance (0.3 $cd{\cdot}m^{-2}$). Only for detailed targets under good lighting conditions does the eye's focus setting consistently approach the optical demand. By definition, accommodation does not go negative.

power and bring targets to a focus that are nearer than infinity—the hyperope without correction can use it to focus at infinity and, if there is enough residual accommodation, even at a close distance. A 3-diopter hyperope without correction needs 3 diopters of accommodation to focus at infinity. If a total of 10 diopters of accommodation is available, such a hyperope can then manage to see objects clearly in up to 7 diopters, that is, 14 cm. In many practical situations a hyperope of low degree with enough accommodative power is therefore capable of functioning as an emmetrope.

The error of refraction known as astigmatism has a somewhat different character from myopia and hyperopia, the so-called spherical refractive errors. In astigmatism there is a difference in refractive state in different meridians of one eye. Fortunately, most cases of astigmatism resolve themselves into the simple situation called regular astigmatism, which can be characterized by a single refractive state in each of just two meridians at right angles. The full specification of the refractive error of such eyes then demands the ametropia in each of these so-called principal meridians as well as their orientations. It is usual to state this in terms of the spherical refractive error in one of the meridians, plus the difference in refractive errors between the two meridians and the orientation of the meridian with the lesser ametropia. The bundle of rays from a point object at infinity passes through a series of complex configurations as it traverses the image space on its way to the retina. Consequently there is no plane in which such an astigmatic bundle can produce a point image, even under the laws of geometrical optics. An uncorrected astigmat, therefore, unless the astigmatism is of a trivial degree (say, less than ½ diopter) cannot achieve perfect imagery, either by exerting accommodation, like the uncorrected hyperope, or for images at or nearer than the far point, like the uncorrected myope with accommodation.

The significant aspect of the above three kinds of refractive error—myopia, hyperopia, astigmatism—is that they are capable of correction by relatively simple lenses. There are eyes in which more complex defects occur, for example, severe spherical aberration or irregular astigmatism, but such instances are quite rare. It is thus feasible to restore almost perfect optical performance in most ametropic eyes, by one of the two classes of therapy, contact lenses or spectacles. It should be pointed out that under special conditions of optical stimulation it is quite simple to counteract spherical refractive errors. For example, focus adjustments in binoculars and microscopes allow the target to be imaged by the instrument at the observer's far point just as easily as at infinity, as would be required for an emmetropic observer without accommodation. In fact, there is the recognized syndrome of instrument myopia, referring to the prevalent tendency of young emmetropes to accommodate when confronted with the view of a target through an instrument. They then act for the time being as myopes and need a corresponding focus adjustment. To the extent that any target view is not direct but is mediated by one or more optical imaging stages capable of focus adjustment, spherical refractive errors may not present any problem.

For ordinary viewing, refractive errors can be corrected either by contact lenses or by spectacles. Contact lens corrections present a series of clinical problems beyond the scope of this chapter. Once these have been surmounted, contact lenses provide optically the most satisfactory correction of ametropia for two reasons. First, the inevitable magnification changes that occur when any correcting lens is placed in front of an eye (see below) are minimized, for the effective location of a contact lens is quite close to the eye's entrance pupil. Second, contact lenses move with the eye and avoid a number of problems associated with viewing the visual world through large curved surfaces, such as aberrations of lenses away from their optical centers, changes in the field of view, and vignetting near the edge of the lens.

1.7. Magnification Properties of Visual Aids

The design of spectacle lenses to minimize aberrations is complicated by the need to compromise between a variety of competing requirements. Even when this has been resolved optimally, there remain substantial differences between the retinal image with and without the spectacle lens (apart from the fundamental difference that one image is clear and the other blurred). They center on the fact that the objects viewed through the lens are seen with an altered magnification. That is, the angle subtended at the eye's entrance pupil of an object is different with and without the lens. Even though an object may appear blurred without the lens, the difference in its size or position when seen through the lens may cause misjudgments of spatial relationships. A point target situated on the optical axis of the spectacle lens will be seen in the original direction (if the axis of the spectacle lens is aligned with a line of sight). For other object positions, the relationship will be that diagramed in Figure 4.13. With the object at infinity, its relative magnification with the lens in place is given by Eq. (2) involving h, the distance between the lens and the center of the entrance pupil of the eye (in meters), and F, the power of the lens in diopters.

$$m = \frac{1}{1 - hF} \tag{2}$$

See Figure 4.13 for an illustration. The value of h is usually about 0.017 m. A 6-diopter lens will therefore cause a 10% change in image size, minification for negative lenses (i.e., in myopia) and magnification for positive lenses (i.e., in hyperopia).

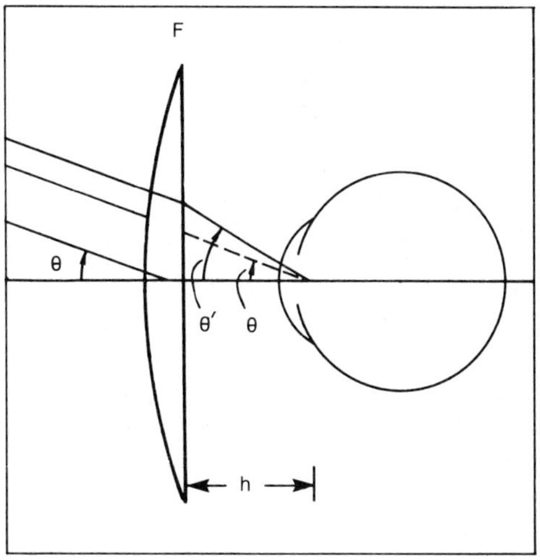

Figure 4.13. A target at infinity, subtending an angle θ at the eye will, when seen through a lens of power F, appear to subtend an angle θ′. The relationship between $m = \theta'/\theta$ and the power of the lens F (diopters) and the distance between the lens and the eye, h (m), is given by Eq. (2).

When the target is not situated at infinity but at a finite distance (meters) in front of the eye, Eq. (2) assumes the form of Eq. (3),

$$m = \frac{l}{l(1 - hF) + h^2F} \tag{3}$$

where l (meters) is the distance of the target in front of the eye. As l goes to infinity, this expression becomes equal to m in Eq. (2).

These equations apply directly to the size of the retinal image of an object seen with the lens (as compared to the same object at the same distance without the lens) and, because they are derived for chief rays, that is, they use the center of the eye's entrance pupil as the reference point, they retain their validity regardless of the presence or absence of image blur.

The equations also apply to the specification of the location of an extra-axial object point in angular measure. Suppose a target point is situated such that a line joining it with the center of the eye's entrance pupil makes an angle θ with the optical axis of the lens (assumed also to pass through the center of the eye's entrance pupil). As seen through the lens, the target now makes an angle $m\theta$. With a slight modification, the same arguments and equations also apply to the angle through which the eye has to be moved to bring the fovea to a peripheral target. All it needs is the substitution of the center of rotation of the eye (see Hallett, Chapter 10) for the center of the entrance pupil of the eye. The former is about 10 mm behind the latter, so that the effects become more prominent when related to the changes that a spectacle lens introduces in the eye movement necessary to fixate an eccentric target point.

1.8. Magnification of Astigmatic Corrections and the Declination Error

The best approach for dealing with astigmatic corrections is to carry through the calculations separately in the two principal meridians. Because the values of F differ in the two meridians although those of the other variables remain the same, all magnification factors will differ and, as a consequence, a circle will be imaged as an ellipse and a square aligned with the principal

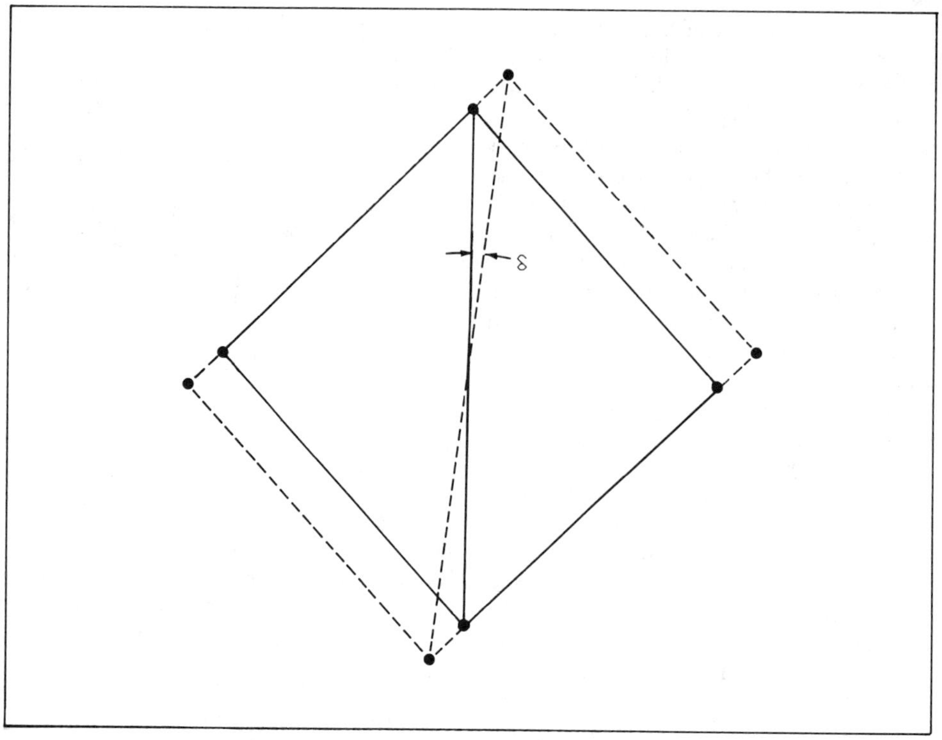

Figure 4.14. Inclination of the objective vertical by an oblique astigmatic lens. If a subject wearing a compound astigmatic spectacle lens views a square aligned with the principal axes of astigmatism, it will appear as a rectangle, magnified in each principal meridian by the ratio given in each case by Eq. (2) or Eq. (3). A line in the frontoparallel plane that is not in one of the principal meridians will appear rotated through an angle δ, called the declination error.

meridians will emerge as a rectangle. This latter effect serves to introduce an important complication brought about by astigmatic corrections.

Suppose one is looking through an astigmatic lens whose magnification for the particular observation distance is m in one principal meridian and m' in the other principal meridian. The target is a square that, to simplify the case, is aligned with the principal axes of the lens. The square will be imaged as a rectangle with one side $m' - m$ times longer than the other (Fig. 4.14). That means that the diagonal of the original square will still join the two opposite corners, but it will no longer be at 45° from the principal meridians, but at an angle whose tangent is equal to m'/m. This is the so-called declination error, treated in detail in textbooks (e.g., Ogle, 1950). Its importance lies not only in the orientation differences that astigmatic lenses can bring about when viewing lines, but also in the serious distortion of binocular depth effects when a subject wears unequal astigmatic spectacle corrections in the two eyes.

1.9. Depth of Focus

So far the discussion has been kept within the frame of first-order geometrical optics. One further aspect of image formation in the eye can be quite adequately covered by such an analysis. We have seen in Figure 4.9 how a point object that is not at infinity produces a blur patch on the retina of an emmetropic eye. Simple geometric optical considerations make it clear that there is a reciprocal relationship between the diameter of the entrance pupil and the focus error in diopters, that is, the distance in diopters between the plane for which the eye is in focus and the plane in which the target is situated. Thus a given blur patch diameter can be maintained by simultaneously doubling the focus defect (in diopters) and halving the pupil diameter. It happens that the performance of an emmetropic eye in focus for infinity will not suffer until a certain blur patch size is exceeded, that is, until for a given pupil diameter there is a certain focus defect. This is known as depth of focus. A typical value for a 3-mm pupil may be 0.25 diopters. The reciprocal relationship between focus defect and pupil diameter then leads to the conclusion that with a 1.75-mm pupil diameter the depth of focus may be expected to be 0.50 diopters and with a 6-mm pupil diameter, 0.12 diopters. The former expectation is fulfilled in practice (Campbell, 1957), but the latter may not be fulfilled where photopic vision is concerned. The reason for this is the Stiles-Crawford effect (see Section 3.5).

1.10. Axial Chromatic Aberration of the Eye

Although the whole problem of aberrations of the eye will be dealt with under the heading of the point-spread function, one kind of chromatic aberration is quite easily understood in terms of focus defect. Without doing an injustice to the complex molecular structure of the cornea and the crystalline lens, to a first approximation the eye may be regarded as being constituted of water so far as its longitudinal chromatic aberration is concerned. This means that the focus difference for various wavelengths is determined by the difference in refractive index of water for these wavelengths. Figure 4.15 shows the expected difference in focus across the visible spectrum. For a point source radiating a mixture of wavelengths, only one of these can be in focus. The remainder will be imaged in blur patches whose sizes follow the rule given in Section 1.9. A telling demonstration

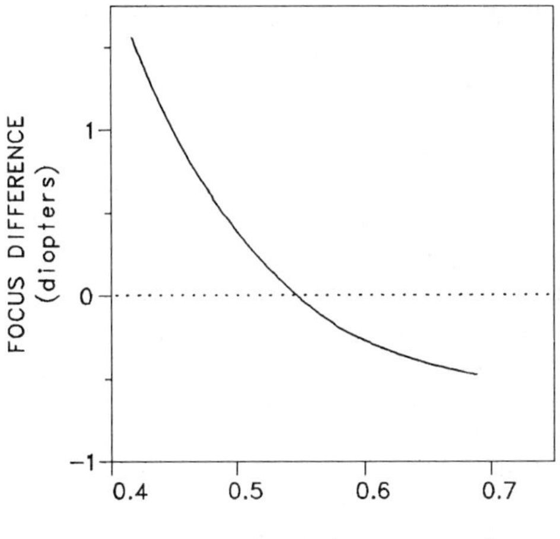

Figure 4.15. Axial chromatic aberration of the eye. The graph shows the expected focus position for targets composed of monochromatic light of the indicated wavelength. The wavelength at which the photopic luminosity peaks is used as a reference: relative to it, the eye is myopic for blue light and hyperopic for red. Chromatic aberration of the eye is close to what may be expected of a system whose changes in refractive index with wavelength are those of water.

of this phenomenon is afforded by viewing a point source of white light through a piece of cobalt glass, which passes only the extreme red and violet ends of the spectrum; depending on the state of focus, one sees either a red point in a violet disk or a violet point in a red disk. The disk diameter varies with the pupil size.

1.11. Optical and Pupillary Axes of the Eye

The schema of the eye used so far has been built around two significant simplifications: that the eye is made of a system of optical surfaces with a common axis of symmetry, and that the fixation point lies on this axis. If the surfaces were spherical, this would mean that their centers of curvature lie on a single line, the optical axis, which would also pass through the center of the fovea. There are practical methods of demonstrating whether these conditions are met in any one case.

The optical axis of a centered optical system is found by using a point source of light, sighting along the beam, and moving it until the reflections from all surfaces coincide. Under this condition, the beam would be normal to all surfaces, which by definition meets the requirement for the optical axis. When this is done with the eye of a subject, it is advisable to provide a separate fixation target to ensure that the eye remains still during the test. Once the optical axis has been determined, the subject can be instructed to fixate the light point, and it can be ascertained whether the reflections from the principal optical surfaces of the eye still appear superposed. Usually this is no longer the case.

Identification of the eye's optical axis is not easy because the reflections from the intraocular surfaces are quite faint. Also, as we have seen, the entrance pupil of the eye plays an important part in imagery and it is not covered by the above definitions. It is therefore customary to seek a landmark line in the eye that involves the entrance pupil. This is the pupillary axis, defined as the line joining the center of the entrance pupil of the eye and the center of curvature of the anterior surface of the cornea. In practice, the pupillary axis is found by placing a point source of light in front of the eye, sighting along it, and moving it around until the image of the source formed by reflection in the anterior surface of the cornea appears to lie in the center of the pupil. (This image is easily identified because it is by far the brightest of the reflected images one sees looking into the eye.) This should be done while the subject is keeping the eye steady by fixating a suitable target. The line joining the center of the entrance pupil with this fixation target is the primary line of sight and in general this does not coincide with the pupillary axis, a situation that manifests itself to the examiner by the fact that the point source used to define the pupillary axis has to be placed somewhat temporal to the fixation point. Or, to put it differently, if a subject is shown a small light source and asked to fixate it, an observer whose eye is behind the light source will find that the corneal reflex of the light source does not lie in the center of the subject's pupil, but is rather somewhat nasal to it. Typically, the primary line of sight and the pupillary axis form an angle of 5°. This discrepancy must be taken into account when using the corneal reflex to check whether a subject is accurately fixating a target.

None of the procedures described guarantees that the fixation point is, in fact, imaged in the center of the fovea, because the act of fixation is voluntary on the part of the subject. In some pathological conditions, the center of the fovea is not the preferred retinal fixation region. The best way to diagnose such a deviation of fixation is by an ophthalmoscopic view of the fundus during the process of voluntary fixation.

The fact that the fovea does not usually lie on the optic axis of the eye gives rise to a widely noticed phenomenon relating to depth localization of colored targets. Looking at a red and a green light source situated in the same plane, most observers report that the red light appears nearer to them than the green one. This is called chromastereopsis. If the primary line of sight of the eye were also the optical axis, light of all wavelengths from the fixation point would enter the eye undeviated because it would be normal to all surfaces. To the extent that this is not the case, there is deviation owing to refraction in an amount proportional to the refractive index of the eye media for the wavelength. The consequence is that green light is subjected to more deviation by refraction than red light is. The anatomical angular displacements of the optical axes of a subject's two eyes being symmetrical, that is, outward, the red and green images on the two retinas will have a binocular disparity as if they originated from two different object planes (see Arditi, Chapter 23).

1.12. Pupil Diameter

Although the diameter of the pupil affects a variety of visual functions, it is controlled only loosely by the visual system. The relationship between the luminance of the visual field and steady-state pupil diameter in normal observers under typical viewing conditions is shown in Figure 4.16.

Among the factors influencing pupil sizes is the state of adaptation. Immediately following a rhodopsin bleach (see Hood & Finkelstein, Chapter 5) the pupil assumes a contracted diameter and gradually dilates pari passu with rhodopsin regeneration even though the eye is in the dark (Fig. 4.17). The dynamics of step pupillary responses are similar to those for accommodation (Fig. 4.11).

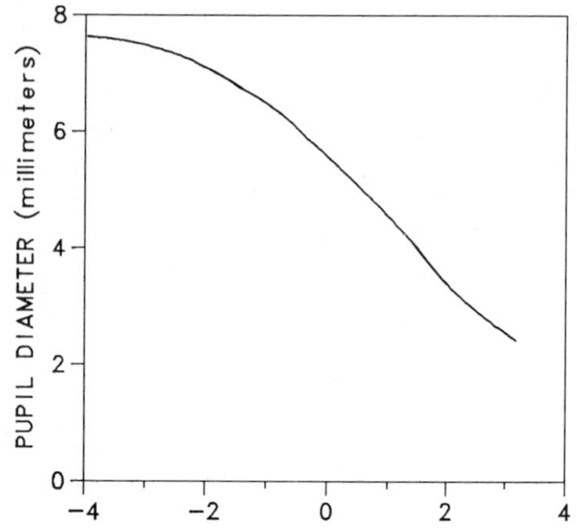

Figure 4.16. Pupil diameter in a normal young observer as a function of the prevailing field luminance (after Reeves, 1920). This applies to a steady, nonstructured full field. Light transients have a much steeper gain. Illumination of only a small part of the visual field is not as effective in constricting the pupil.

2. IMAGE QUALITY OF THE TYPICAL HUMAN EYE

Not all optical aspects of the human eye can, however, be adequately dealt with on the assumption that a point object would end up as a point image on the retina. This is the framework used so far and it has merit in that it allows a good treatment of such phenomena as image position and size, blur patches due to focus defects, and simple changes in imagery due to longitudinal and lateral chromatic aberration.

2.1. Point-Spread Function

Under no circumstances are point objects ever actually imaged as points; a variety of physical and geometrical optical factors prevent this. As a result, a point object gives rise to a retinal light distribution that is bell-shaped in cross-section. It is called the point-spread function and has fundamental significance not only when the object is a point but whenever it is necessary to know the light distribution for a target more complex than a point source of light. The reason is that it is possible to think of any visual object as made of points. Its retinal image, then, consists of the superposition of the light distributions from all the points constituting the object. This procedure is not only of general theoretical value, but it has direct and immediate application in such situations as cathode-ray tube displays composed of individual lines or points.

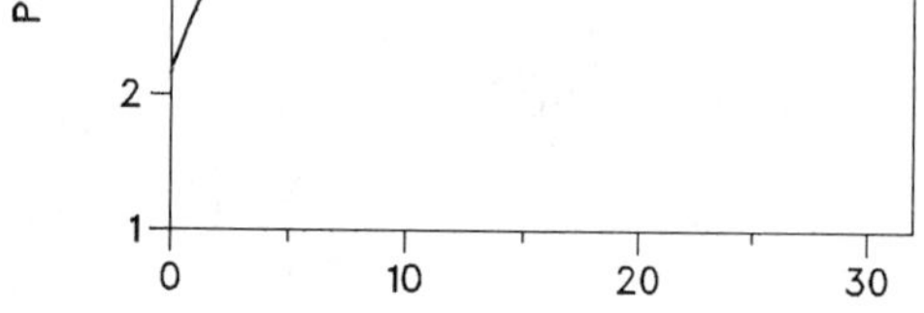

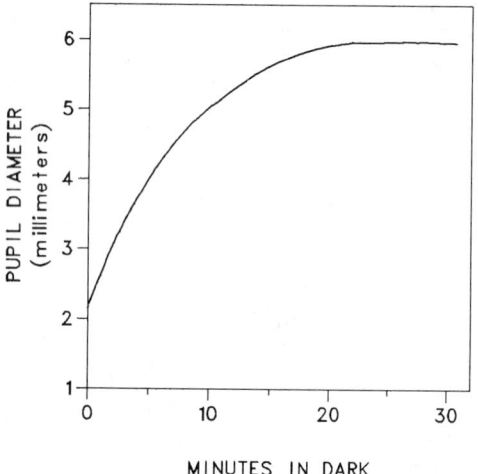

Figure 4.17. Pupil diameter in the dark as a function of time following extinction of a bright field (after Alpern & Campbell, 1962). The time course of recovery to the usual pupil diameter in darkness (see Fig. 4.16) matches the time course of rhodopsin regeneration (see Hood & Finkelstein, Chapter 5).

There is a substantially equivalent way of formulating the problem by way of Fourier transforms of objects, or by way of image and point-spread functions. If calculations have to be carried out without a computer, the Fourier domain has an advantage because the laborious process of convolution then becomes mere multiplication and, of course, if the targets are the basic functions of the Fourier domain, namely, spatial sine-wave gratings, the Fourier approach is the obvious choice. But the anatomical and functional organization of the retina and visual pathways does not fit the template of sine-wave gratings, so it is in general advantageous to describe the spatial proximal stimulus for vision in terms of the retinal light distribution. There will be occasions, as in delving into the events inside the individual retinal receptors, when an even more localized approach is needed, namely, the number of photons actually being absorbed in a receptor in a given time, and then it is necessary to distinguish between photons arriving at the retina and photons being absorbed.

2.2. Diffraction

Of the various factors that contribute to spreading the light from a point object beyond a single point image, one has a deep and well-known origin and deserves separate description. It is called diffraction and is a cornerstone of both the wave and photon theories of light. In the latter formulation its basis is the uncertainty proposition, according to which there are limits to the simultaneous identification of the direction of travel and the position of a photon. To the extent that a photon passes through the pupil of the eye, that is, has its position delimited, its direction (that is, its point of absorption in the retina) is less certain. In other words, there is a reciprocal relationship between the pupil diameter of an eye and the point-spread function which, in this formulation, is looked at as the probability distribution of the absorption of a single photon. A large number of photons arriving from a single point source will produce a heap of absorptions, centered on the geometrical point image and having the outline of the point-spread function. Diffraction theory (see, e.g., Born & Wolf, 1959) leads to similar results.

If no other effects are at play except diffraction, the following equations are operative. Let a be the pupil diameter in the meridian under consideration and λ be the wavelength of light. Then the point-spread function in that meridian is given by Eqs. (4) and (5).

$$I(\rho) = \left[\frac{J_1(\pi a \rho/\lambda)}{\pi a \rho/\lambda}\right]^2 \tag{4}$$

Equation (4) gives the Fraunhofer diffraction pattern for a circular aperture, where I is the light intensity in the image (a function of ρ, the radial distance from the geometrical point image), a is the diameter of the entrance pupil, and λ is the wavelength of light. J_1 is the first-order Bessel function; a and λ are measured in the same units; and ρ is the visual angle in radians.

$$I(\alpha) = \left[\frac{\sin(2\pi a\alpha/\lambda)}{2\pi a\alpha/\lambda}\right]^2 \quad (5)$$

Equation (5) gives the Fraunhofer diffraction pattern for a rectangular aperture, where I is a function of α, the distance from the geometrical image point. Both α and a are measured in the same meridian, which must be a principal meridian of the rectangular aperture. α is a visual angle in radians; a and λ should be expressed in the same units, for example, meters.

The function for a circular pupil [Eq. (4)] is illustrated in Figure 4.18. The abscissa is scaled in relative units. The central patch between the first 0 on either side of the center is called Airy's disk and its radius, expressed in minutes of arc visual angle for a wavelength of 555 nm, is tabulated as a function of pupil diameter in Table 4.3. To a first approximation, the two-point resolution of an optical system (Olzak & Thomas, Chapter 7) is equal to the radius of the Airy disk, and the data in Table 4.3 may thus serve as an indication of the minimum angle of resolution of the eye as an optical system, were diffraction its only limit.

As will be seen in Section 2.4, the eye is diffraction-limited only under certain conditions and the theoretically derived equation for the point-spread function does not necessarily apply in the general case.

2.3. Point-Spread Function and Line-Spread Function

Before we turn to the point-spread function of a typical eye, it will be convenient to extend the discussion somewhat. A line may be considered as being made up of a string of points. The image of a line object is therefore actually the superposition on the images of a row of finely spaced points, and it can be arrived at by relatively simple calculation, which derives the so-called line-spread function, the intensity distribution in the direction normal to the length of the image of a long line target. For a radially symmetrical point-spread function $s(\rho)$, the corresponding line-spread function $A(\alpha)$ can be found through the use of Eq. (6), where both α and ρ are visual angles, α a measure of distance from the geometrical image of the line in a direction normal to the line, and ρ the radial distance from the center of the geometrical point image.

$$A(\alpha) = 2\int_{\alpha}^{\infty} s(\rho)(\rho^2 - \alpha^2)^{-1/2}\rho \, d\rho \quad (6)$$

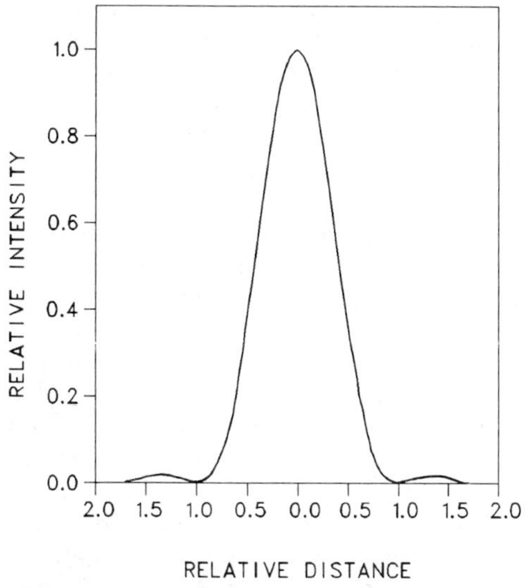

Figure 4.18. Fraunhofer diffraction pattern for an optical system with a round pupil. The light distribution is given by Eq. (4). Ordinates are in relative units. Position of the first zero defines the radius of Airy's disk. See Table 4.3 for values of Airy's disk radius in terms of visual angle, as a function of pupil diameter. This figure depicts the inescapable spread of light in the image of a point source due to diffraction; actual light spread (see Fig. 4.19) is usually wider.

Table 4.3. Relationship between the Diameter of the Eye's Entrance Pupil and Radius of Airy's Disk for Light of Wavelength 555 nm

Diameter of Entrance Pupil (mm)	Radius of Airy's Disk (min arc)
0.5	4.66
1	2.33
1.5	1.56
2	1.16
2.5	0.94

Note: Airy's disk is the central patch of the Fraunhofer diffraction pattern for a circular pupil. It is the distance between the first 0 on either side of the center in the light distribution illustrated in Figure 4.18. Beyond 2–2.5-mm pupil diameters, the eye no longer acts as a diffraction-limited device, and the actual retinal point-spread function does not become proportionally smaller as would be the case if only diffraction were involved.

2.4. Current Best Estimate of Eye's Line-Spread Function

Early attempts to describe the eye's point-spread function (Helmholtz, 1962; Fry & Cobb, 1935; DeMott & Boynton, 1958) were superseded by the method introduced by Flamant (1955). As improved by Westheimer and Campbell (1962), Krauskopf (1962), and Gubisch (1967), this technique has now made available a description of ocular imagery that is practically useful. The approach eschews the dissection of imagery into the various categories of aberrations, and instead characterizes the overall shape of the point-spread function, illustrated in Figure 4.19. Equation (7) is an empirical expression for this curve, where ρ, the distance from the center of the geometrical image, is in minutes of arc visual angle. Figure 4.20 and Eq. (8) give corresponding data for the line-spread function, where α, the distance from the geometrical image of the line in a direction normal to the line, is in minutes of arc.

$$Q(\rho) = 0.952\exp(-2.59|\rho|^{1.36}) + 0.048\exp(-2.43|\rho|^{1.74}) \quad (7)$$

$$A(\alpha) = 0.47\exp(-3.3\alpha^2) + 0.53\exp(-0.93|\alpha|) \quad (8)$$

The data in Figures 4.19 and 4.20 (also provided in tabular form in Table 4.4) apply to standard viewing conditions of white

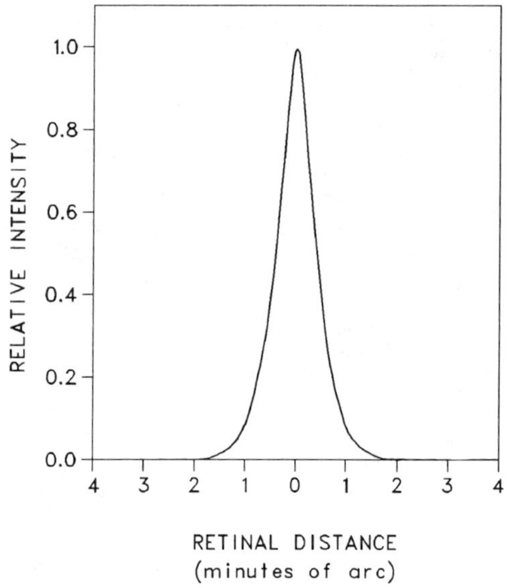

Figure 4.19. Point-spread function of the human eye under good focus conditions, medium pupil diameter and white light. An empirical expression for this light distribution is given in Eq. (7).

targets with pupil diameter in the vicinity of 3 mm and should be accepted only as an approximate guide. These data are directly applicable in many situations, but some important exceptions must be pointed out:

1. *Pupil Size.* According to theory [e.g., Eq. (4)] and practice (Leibowitz, 1952), the eye's resolution limit varies with pupil diameter. When the pupil is small (less than about 2.5 mm in diameter), optical imagery in the eye can be accepted to be purely diffraction limited. The point-spread function then is more or less identical with that calculated on the basis of diffraction theory. When the pupil in a normal subject exceeds about 5 mm, the point-spread function widens owing to the aberrations of the eye. A good guide would be the assumption of an approximate doubling of the effective point-spread function for a dark-adapted normal subject and scotopic viewing conditions.

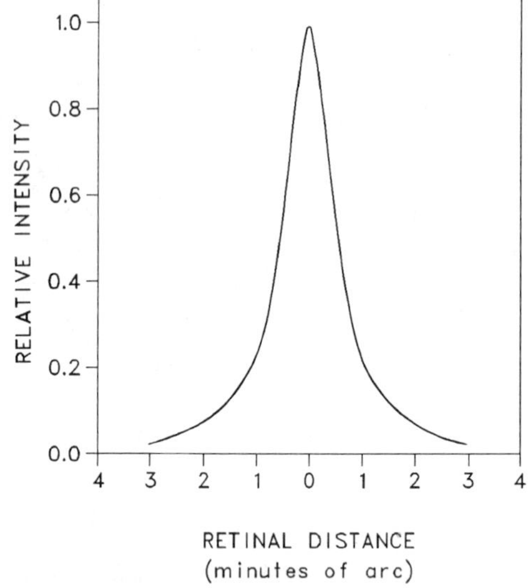

Figure 4.20. Line-spread function of the human eye in good focus. An empirical expression for this light distribution is given in Eq. (8).

Table 4.4. Tabulation of Point and Line Spreads According to Eqs. (7) and (8) and Figures 4.19 and 4.20

Distance from Center (min arc)	Relative Height of Function	
	Point Spread	Line Spread
0.0	1.000	1.000
0.2	0.754	0.852
0.4	0.481	0.643
0.6	0.279	0.447
0.8	0.150	0.309
1.0	0.076	0.226
1.2	0.036	0.178
1.4	0.017	0.145
1.6	0.007	0.120
1.8	0.003	0.099
2.0	0.001	0.083
2.2	0.000	0.069
2.4	0.000	0.057
2.6	0.000	0.047
2.8	0.000	0.039
3.0	0.000	0.033
3.2	0.000	0.027
3.4	0.000	0.022
3.6	0.000	0.019
3.8	0.000	0.015
4.0	0.000	0.013
4.2	0.000	0.011
4.4	0.000	0.009
4.6	0.000	0.007
4.8	0.000	0.006
5.0	0.000	0.005

2. *Chromatic Aberrations* (see Fig. 4.15). These introduce defocusing (see Section 2.5 and Fig. 4.26). On occasions when the spectral characteristics of the fixation and stimulus patterns are accurately known, this fact may be taken into account in estimating the image spread for a specific target.

3. *Retinal Periphery.* Although the grain of the retina changes rapidly as one goes from the fovea to the periphery (Fig. 4.2) and there is therefore progressively less call for ideal imagery with increasing eccentricity, the image quality falls off surprisingly little away from the fovea. Figure 4.21 deals with two parameters of concern when off-fovea images are characterized in comparison with foveal ones: the width of the line-spread function and the best state of focus. Considerable intersubject variability may be expected here; nevertheless the figure gives a guide to the relatively mild defocusing and image-degradation for the near periphery of the retina.

4. The point-spread function relates only to the distribution of light available at the level of the retina, as would be measured by a very small photocell scanning the image. (This has actually been accomplished in the cat; see Robson & Enroth-Cugell, 1978.) The visual process is, however, triggered initially by absorption of photons by molecules of visual pigment. Complexities introduced by any intervening stages, for example, funneling in receptors, the Stiles-Crawford effect (see Section 3.5), and so forth, may make the spatial pattern of intrareceptoral photon absorptions differ from the estimates here provided.

2.5. Fourier Description of the Eye's Imaging Property

All optical imaging devices, including the eye, have a point-spread function whose size is at best that given by the diffraction

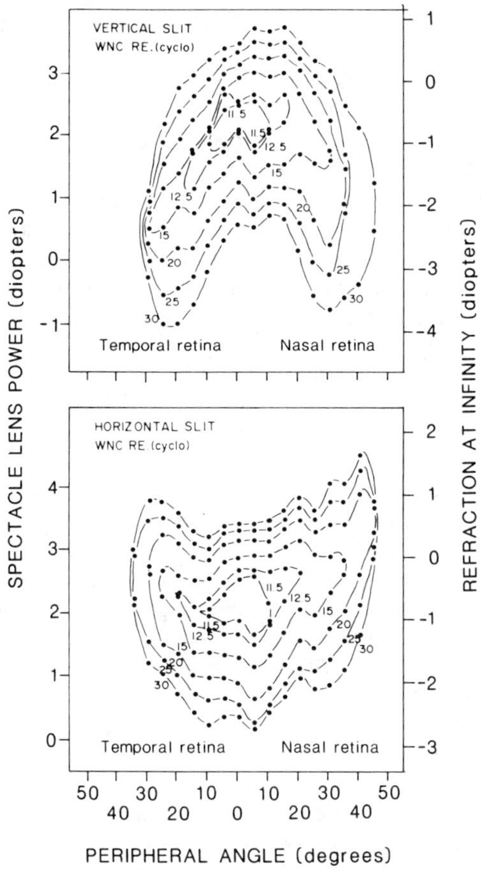

Figure 4.21. Image quality and focus setting for targets presented to the peripheral retina for vertical (upper) and horizontal (lower) line targets in the eye of one observer when the accommodation has been paralyzed by a cycloplegic. Contours join points of equal external line-spread function halfwidths; numbers refer to halfwidth in minutes of arc. There is a central zone of about 20° diameter in which the focus setting and image quality are good, but beyond 10° from the fovea there may be considerable defocus and the image quality deteriorates. Compare, however, the change of cone density with retinal eccentricity (Fig. 4.3). (From J. A. M. Jennings & W. N. Charman, Off-axis quality in the human eye, *Vision Research, 21*. Copyright 1981 by Pergamon Press, Ltd. Reprinted with permission.)

equations for the pupil aperture and the wavelength of light; that is, they are at best diffraction-limited. It is therefore profitable to examine the properties of such systems from other useful points of view. Diffraction equations happen to have the mathematical form of Fourier transforms, and consequently the whole methodology of systems analysis by sinusoidal basis functions is rigorously applicable when considering the way an image is created by an optical system. The reservations that have to be expressed about a full description of image processing by the whole visual apparatus in terms of transfer functions (see Olzak & Thomas, Chapter 7) can therefore be dropped so long as the discussion is restricted to the relationship between the object light distribution and its coordinated retinal image. In fact, the Fourier view of vision had its origin in an attempt by Schade (1956) to match the description of visual processing to that used for television picture and transmission specification.

In Figure 4.22 is laid out a schema interrelating four different descriptors of the image-forming properties of a typical optical device, which would include the eye. The basic information is contained in the aperture function, which describes the deformation and/or attenuation that the wave front from a point source suffers in being transferred from the object to the image space. Because the aperture is always limited, the least that can happen is a circumscription of the wave front to the pupil shape. This is the simplest case of diffraction; when the object and image planes are conjugate and there are no aberrations, the emerging wave front is spherical and centered on the image point. The situation is called Fraunhofer diffraction. Equations (4) and (5) refer to this reduction case.

Fourier transformation of the aperture function yields the amplitude and phase distribution of electromagnetic radiation in the image of a point source. Autocorrelation of the aperture function yields the optical transfer function of the system and its Fourier transform is the intensity point-spread function. The latter can also be obtained by multiplying the amplitude point-spread function by its complex conjugate.

A special form of the optical transfer function, which leaves out phase information, is the modulation transfer function of an optical instrument. It specifies the changes in modulation that (theoretical) infinite sinusoidal grating patterns undergo

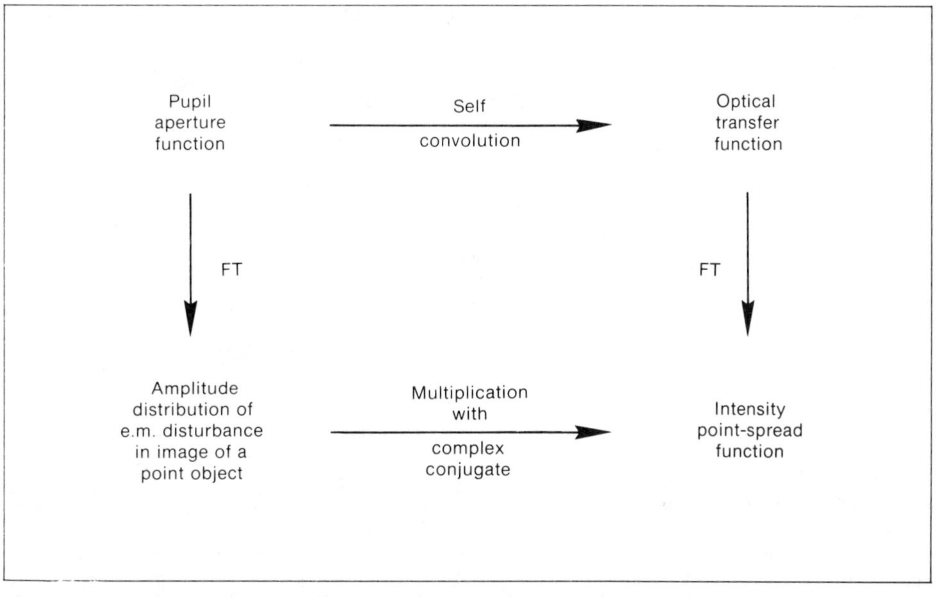

Figure 4.22. Schema relating pupil aperture function of an optical system, the optical transfer function, the amplitude distribution of electromagnetic disturbance in the image of a point object, and the intensity point-spread function. FT is Fourier transformation.

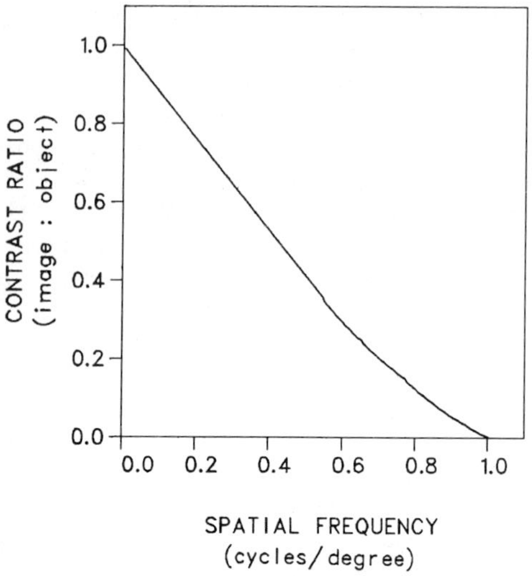

Figure 4.23. Modulation transfer function of an optical system like the eye's without aberrations, for monochromatic light, and a round pupil. Abscissa axis is scaled in spatial frequency referred to cutoff spatial frequency, which is the spatial frequency at and beyond which no components are represented in the image. Table 4.5 gives the relationship between cutoff spatial frequency and pupil diameter for an optical system like the eye's.

in their transfer from being objects to becoming images. This descriptor is in the Fourier domain; that is, it deals with the spatial frequency description of objects and images rather than the description in terms of their intensity distribution in real space. Typical units of spatial frequency are cycles per millimeter or cycles per degree of visual angle. Where the modulation transfer function goes negative, this means a contrast reversal, which is equivalent to a 180° phase shift. Figure 4.23 gives the modulation transfer function of a diffraction-limited optical system with circular pupil. It should be noted that the curve goes to zero at a defined value, called the cutoff spatial frequency. Only in this context is there a sharp distinction between optical systems and most mechanical and electrical systems. The latter may have severe reductions in performance at higher frequency, but there is in general no defined cutoff frequency beyond which there is absolutely no response. Units of the abscissa in Figure 4.23 have been left in parametric form. Table 4.5 can be used

Table 4.5. Relationship between Cutoff Spatial Frequency of the Eye's Optical Transfer Function and the Pupil Diameter for Light of Wavelength 555 nm

Pupil Diameter (mm)	Cutoff Spatial Frequency (cycles/degree)
0.5	15.6
1	31.3
1.5	48.0
2	62.6
3	[a]
4	[a]
5	[a]
6	[a]

Note: The cutoff spatial frequencies shown are calculated from the diffraction limit of an optical system of the given pupil diameter. For pupil diameter larger than 2–2.5 mm, the theoretical cutoff spatial frequency increases in direct proportion to the pupil diameter, but actually the eye cannot perform at the theoretical limit due to aberrations.

[a] No longer diffraction limited.

to convert them to the specific values for a given situation of pupil size and wavelength.

Although the different ways of describing the image-forming property of optical systems are equivalent, the modulation transfer function has some distinct advantages in practical situations. It must be stressed that the following treatment applies only where the objects are incoherent emitters of light. Examples of coherent modes of illumination, where the equations given below cannot be used, are patterns illuminated by a single point source of monochromatic light or a laser. It is in fact quite difficult to produce coherent light from standard light sources (the source has to be imaged on a pinhole less than 0.1 mm in diameter and the radiation must be highly monochromatic), but laser light, which is coherent, is now widely available. When light is incoherent, it is possible to regard any object as being made up of point sources, each imaged separately, and one can then reconstruct the total image light distribution by simply superposing the point-spread functions of all appropriately placed point images. Object points whose light is derived from a single coherent source, however, emit radiation that is capable of interfering. Superposition of the image light intensity distributions of such points will not yield the correct result; the calculation has to be carried out with due regard for the phase of the electromagnetic radiation, allowing interference effects to occur. Computations involving purely coherent light can still be handled without very much trouble, but when an object is partially coherent the problem often becomes very complicated.

The modulation transfer function derives its utility from the mathematical principle that sets as equivalent two different operations, whose interrelation is shown schematically in Figure 4.24.

1. The dissection of each object light distribution into individual light points, the imaging of each of these points into its own appropriately placed and properly scaled point-spread function, and the summation of light in all (usually partially superposed) point spreads to yield the final image light distribution are together known as convolution; this operation is expressed in rectangular image coordinates α, β in Eq. (9), where $I(\alpha,\beta)$ is the total image spread and $s(\alpha_0,\beta_0)$ is the spread function in rectangular coordinates. The image without any spreading would be expressed by the function $O(\alpha_0,\beta_0)$. All calculations remain in the domain of light intensity as a function of position in object or image space. Convolution used to be an awkward computational procedure in the days before computers,

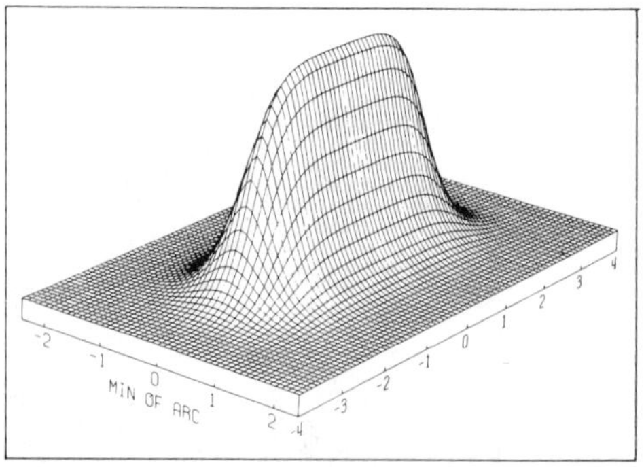

Figure 4.24. Retinal light distribution of a line segment 4 min arc long. The line was created by a row of 25 points 10 sec arc apart. The image light distribution was calculated by convoluting the object pattern with the eye's point-spread function shown in Figure 4.19. (From G. Westheimer, The spatial sense of the eye, *Investigative Ophthalmology and Visual Science*, 1979, *18*. Reprinted with permission.)

and this accounts in part for the popularity of the other approach, which involves only multiplication.

$$I(\alpha, \beta) = \iint_{\text{object}} O(\alpha - \alpha_0, \beta - \beta_0)\, s(\alpha_0, \beta_0)\, d\alpha_0\, d\beta_0 \tag{9}$$

2. Multiplication of the Fourier transform of the object light distribution by the modulation transfer function gives the Fourier transform of the image light distribution. Here the calculations are carried out in the Fourier domain, and the units are not retinal distance in minutes or degrees of visual angle as in paragraph 1, but spatial frequency in cycles per degree of visual angle. There are occasions on which it may be convenient to leave the process entirely in the Fourier domain, but usually the visual object is a locally defined pattern and the interest is in the coordinated locally defined image pattern. In such cases it is necessary to carry out the transformation from object light distribution into the Fourier domain and, after multiplication by the modulation transfer function, back into image light distribution.

$$I(\alpha, \beta) = \iint_{-\infty}^{\infty} O(\omega_\alpha, \omega_\beta)\, e^{-2\pi(\alpha\omega_\alpha + \beta\omega_\beta)}\, t(\omega_\alpha, \omega_\beta)\, d\omega_\alpha\, d\omega_\beta \tag{10}$$

$$I(\rho) = 2\pi \int_0^\infty O(\omega) \cdot J_o(2\pi\rho\omega)t(\omega)\rho\, d\omega \tag{11}$$

Equation (10) would be used to carry out the calculation, where $O(\omega_\alpha, \omega_\beta)$ is the Fourier transform of the object, $t(\omega_\alpha, \omega_\beta)$ is the optical transfer function, α and β are rectangular coordinates in the image plane, expressed in visual angle, and ω_α and ω_β are spatial frequency coordinates in the same two directions. The Fourier transform of the object light distribution and the optical transfer function must be known; one ends up arriving at the light distribution in the image plane. Equation (11) is a special form of Eq. (10) to be used when the light distribution is circularly symmetrical, as in the case of a disk or an annulus. Here I is a function of ρ, the radial distance from the center of the geometrical image. It is important to note that complete Fourier transformation always involves the specification of amplitude and phase spectra. Only when both object and point-spread functions have even-order symmetry can the phase calculation be omitted.

The two procedures are fully equivalent, and the selection of one over the other is a matter of convenience in any individual case. The reader is reminded that the modulation transfer function refers to the optical changes introduced in the process of imaging by the eye; the term modulation sensitivity function is reserved for psychophysical response functions to sinusoidal grating targets. Use of the eye's modulation transfer function for optical calculations is free from some of the conceptual problems associated with using linear systems theory for the whole visual process.

The following examples illustrate the application of the above object/image calculation.

A short line, 4 min arc in length, is imaged by the eye. The line is created on an oscilloscope by placing small points in a row, 10 sec arc apart. The oscilloscope's point-spread function is small compared to that of the eye; that is, at the observation distance, the diameter of a point is less than ½ min arc of visual angle. Convoluting this object pattern with the eye's point-spread function (Fig. 4.19) yields the image light distribution shown in Figure 4.24.

To test the proposition that hyperacuity processing involves the localization of the centroid of a light distribution (Westheimer & McKee, 1977), a particular "ribbon" pattern is created on a vector oscilloscope. It consists of ten long parallel lines. Nine of these are placed at regular intervals, 18 sec arc apart, and the tenth is 20 sec to one side of the center of the "ribbon." Figure 4.25 shows schematically the object and what the cross-sectional light distribution of the retinal image looks like after the whole object pattern has been convoluted with eye's line-spread function (Fig. 4.20).

So far it has been assumed that the eye remains in perfect focus. Some indication of the effect of defocusing can be obtained from the sketch of the theoretical modulation transfer function of an optical system like the eye's for various extents of dioptric refractive errors (Fig. 4.26). The exact modulation transfer coefficients depend critically on the pupil diameter as well as the wavelength of light used. The data were generated without regard to any possible aberrations of the eye, but that is a fair assumption because the significant effects occur for even quite low spatial frequencies. Important aspects of these curves are the negative values of the modulation transfer coefficients in

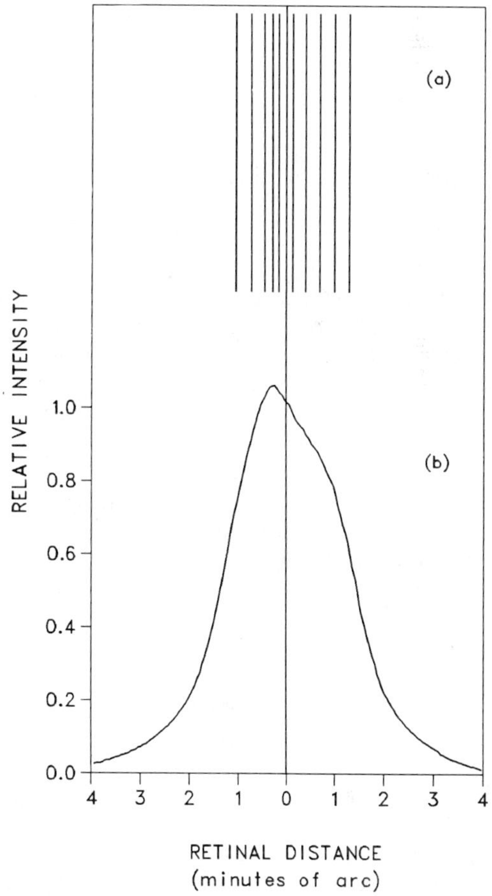

Figure 4.25. An example illustrating the use of the convolution procedure to provide retinal light distribution for a complex object pattern. (a) Object pattern consisting of a series of 10 long lines on a CRT, arranged as shown. (b) Retinal light distribution in a slice through the middle of the image, calculated by convoluting the object pattern with the eye's line-spread function, shown in Figure 4.20. This shows how basic knowledge of the eye's line-spread function, when combined with details and specification of the target, can spell out fine structure of the image pattern available to the photoreceptors.

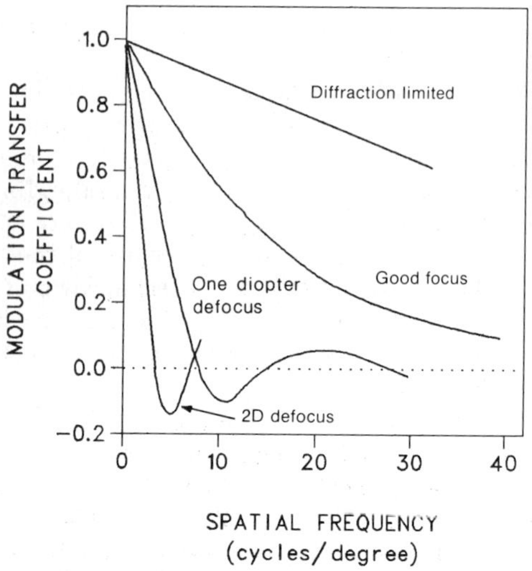

Figure 4.26. Modulation transfer function for defocused imagery. Diffraction limited: theoretical modulation transfer function of an eye in perfect focus without aberrations when the pupil diameter is 3 mm, monochromatic light of a median photopic wavelength. Good focus: best current estimate of the actual modulation transfer function of a good normal eye under similar conditions. 1 and 2 diopter defocus: sketches of the theoretical transfer functions of a normal eye with a 3-mm pupil defocused, respectively, by 1 and 2 diopters. Note that when the transfer coefficients first reach zero at relatively low spatial frequencies these are not the cutoff spatial frequencies. The coefficients then become negative and may cross the axis more than once before remaining strictly zero beyond the cutoff spatial frequency, which is determined by the pupil diameter of the eye and the wavelength of light. A negative transfer coefficient means that a sinusoidal target is imaged with reversed contrast. (From G. Westheimer & S. P. McKee, Stereoscopic acuity with defocused and spatially filtered retinal images, *Journal of the Optical Society of America*, 1980, *70*. Reprinted with permission.)

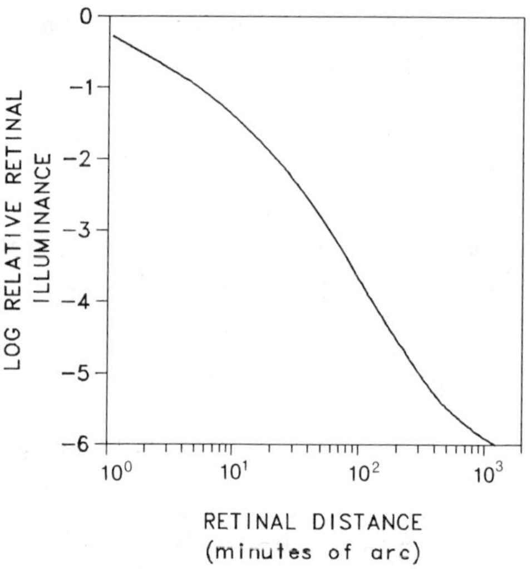

Figure 4.27. Scatter of light from a small glare source onto unilluminated retina. Ordinate, log relative intensity; abscissa, distance along retina, minutes of arc on logarithmic scale (after Flamant, 1955).

some spatial frequency regions. They mean that sinusoidal grating targets at those spatial frequencies are imaged on the retina in reversed contrast, that is, a place in which the object grating has a maximum is represented in the image by minimum. Inspection of Figure 4.26 also reveals that the modulation transfer function under defocus blur undergoes oscillatory changes after it first approaches zero and before it reaches the cutoff spatial frequency. This means that some information about the whole spatial frequency spectrum inside the cutoff spatial frequency is contained in the image, even though it may be quite blurred.

2.6. Other Factors

In the treatment of image light distributions, the emphasis so far has been on the spread in the close vicinity of the geometrical image. There is, however, some scattering of light in the passage through the ocular media that has the effect of introducing small quantities of radiation at distances from the image point that are quite large compared to the point-spread function. It is not easy to measure this stray light, which may be as little as 1/1000 of the intensity of the focal image. Also, considerable interindividual differences may be expected. In contact lens wearers, for example, scattering may occur in the cornea; in older subjects the origin is the lens of the eye, which becomes compacted with age. The best estimate of the distribution of this scattered light in a typical eye comes from Flamant (1955) and is shown in Figure 4.27. It is seen that enough stray light falls at distances of tens of degrees that the most sensitive visual functions can readily be affected.

The ocular media are not uniformly transparent over the visual spectrum (see Pokorny and Smith, Chapter 8). Absorption and scatter remove differing proportions of light at various wavelengths. Figure 4.28 depicts the best current estimate of the transmissivity of the ocular media as a function of wavelength. Depending on the use to be made of the information, a distinction may have to be made between direct transmittance of the media and total transmittance (Boettner & Wolter, 1962). Direct transmittance refers to the relative proportion of light of the various wavelengths that make up the focal image. Because scattering is a function of wavelength, the light in the focal image may have a different wavelength composition from the total quantity of light that reaches all of the retina. Here, such factors as the reflectance of the fundus also enter. There

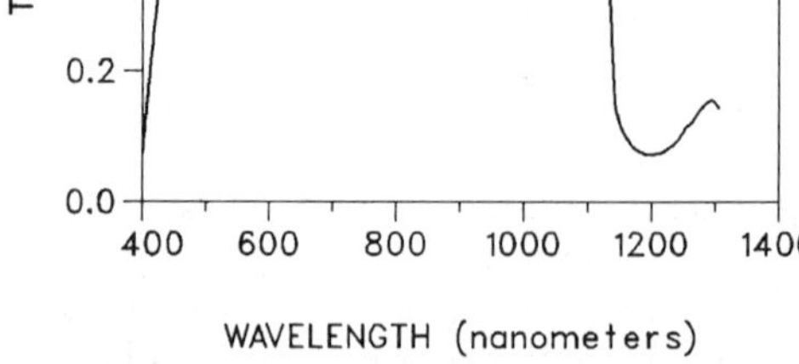

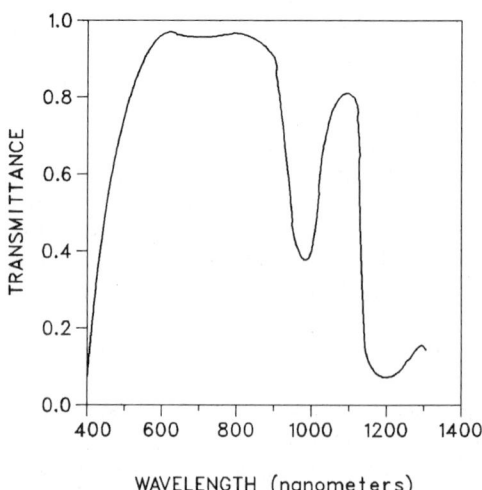

Figure 4.28. Estimate of the transmissivity of the ocular media. (From W. T. Ham, H. A. Mueller, & J. J. Ruffolo, Retinal effects of blue light exposure, *Ocular Effects of Non-Ionizing Radiation*, 1980, *SPIE 229*. Reprinted with permission.)

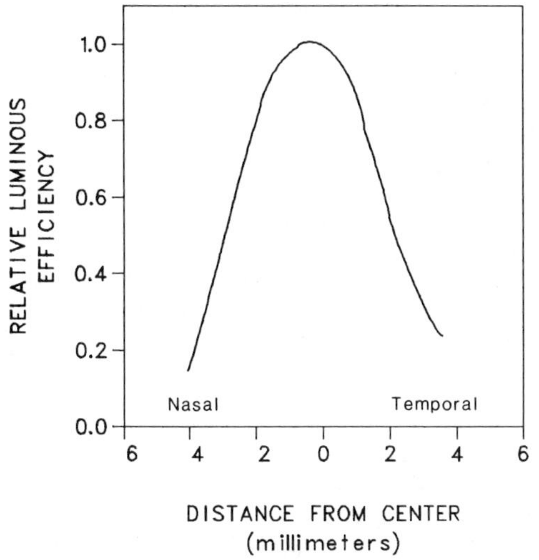

Figure 4.29. Typical Stiles-Crawford effect for foveal light reception. A narrow bundle of light rays entering the eye in positions away from the center of the pupil leads to a visual signal of lower luminous efficiency according to this curve (Stiles and Crawford, 1933). Similar functions apply to other meridia.

are also certain to be individual differences, particularly as a function of age.

As pointed out before, it cannot be taken for granted that the light distribution due to a given object created by the eye's optics will be immediately able to stimulate the photopigments. For example, the retina is known to introduce polarization effects (Bone, 1980; Hochheimer & Kuehn, 1982). In some retinal regions in and adjoining the fovea there is a minus blue pigment, called macular pigment, which must be taken into account when dealing with spatial differences in color perception.

Finally, there is the Stiles-Crawford effect. It can be demonstrated in isolation by showing that a narrow beam entering the eye near the edge of the pupil is less efficient in eliciting a visual response in the photopic system than a similar beam passing through the center of the pupil (Fig. 4.29). It has its origin in the structure of the receptor cells, but a really satisfactory account of its physical mechanism is still lacking (Enoch & Bedell, 1981). The full visual implications of the Stiles-Crawford effect have yet to be explored. It is known to be differentially effective as far as color vision is concerned. Although it has been suggested that it may be taken care of in diffraction calculations by regarding it as an apodization phenomenon, that is, a gradual reduction in amplitude transmission of the pupil, this is by no means certain and it remains to be seen whether such formulations are successful in predicting visual responses when partially occluded and annular pupils are involved.

3. KEY REFERENCES

Two previous articles (Fry, 1959; Westheimer, 1972) are devoted to overviews of the eye as an optical instrument. Because they are addressed to different audiences, they treat the subject from somewhat different perspectives. A more formal account of visual optics is contained in the textbooks by Emsley (1939; also later editions) and LeGrand (1955). Borish (1970) contains a wealth of reference material, assembled somewhat uncritically.

REFERENCES

Alpern, M., & Campbell, F. W. The behavior of the pupil during dark adpatation. *Journal of Physiology*, 1962, *165*, 5.

Blank, K., Provine, R. R., & Enoch, J. M. Shift in the peak of the photopic Stiles-Crawford function with marked accommodation. *Vision Research*, 1975, *15*, 499–507.

Boettner, E. A., & Wolter, J. R. Transmission of the ocular media. *Investigative Ophthalmology*, 1962, *1*, 776–783.

Bone, R. A. The role of macular pigment in the detection of polarized light. *Vision Research*, 1980, *20*, 213–220.

Borish, T. M. *Clinical refraction* (3rd ed.). Chicago: Professional Press, 1970.

Born, M., & Wolf, E. *Principles of optics*. New York: Pergamon Press, 1959.

Campbell, F. W. The depth of field of the human eye. *Optica Acta*, 1957, *4*, 157–164.

Campbell, F. W., Robson, J. G., & Westheimer, G. Fluctuations of accommodation during steady viewing conditions. *Journal of Physiology*, 1959, *145*, 579–594.

Campbell, F. W., & Westheimer, G. Factors influencing accommodation responses in the human eye. *Journal of the Optical Society of America*, 1959, *49*, 568–571.

Campbell, F. W., & Westheimer, G. Dynamics of accommodation responses in the human eye. *Journal of Physiology*, 1960, *151*, 285–295.

Charman, W. N., & Tucker, J. Dependence of accommodation responses on the spatial frequency spectrum of the observed object. *Vision Research*, 1977, *17*, 129–140.

De Mott, D. W., & Boynton, R. M. Retinal distribution of entopic stray light. *Journal of the Optical Society of America*, 1958, *48*, 13–21.

Ditchburn, R. W. *Eye movements and visual perception*. Oxford: Clarendon Press, 1973.

Emsley, H. H. *Visual optics* (2nd ed.). London: Hatton Press, 1939.

Enoch, J. M., & Bedell, H. E. The Stiles-Crawford effects. In J. M. Enoch & F. L. Tobey (Eds.), *Vertebrate photoreceptor optics*. Berlin: Springer-Verlag, 1981.

Flamant, F. Etude de la repartition de lumiere dans l'image retinienne d'une fente. *Revue d'optique*, 1955, *34*, 433–459.

Fry, G. A. The image-forming mechanism of the eye. In J. Field (Ed.), *Handbook of physiology* (Section I, Vol. I). Washington, D.C.: American Physiological Society, 1959.

Fry, G. E., & Cobb, P. W. A new method for determining the blurredness of the retinal image. *Transactions of the American Academy of Ophthalmology and Otolaryngology*, 1935, *40*, 423–438.

Goldmann, H., & Hagen, R. Zur direkten Messung der Totalbrechkraft des lebenden menschlichen Auges. *Ophthalmologica*, 1942, *104*, 15–22.

Gubisch, R. W. Optical performance of the human eye. *Journal of the Optical Society of America*, 1967, *57*, 407–415.

Ham, W. T., Mueller, H. A., & Ruffolo, J. J. Retinal effects of blue light exposure. *Society of Photo-optical Instrumentation and Engineering*, 1980, *229*, 46–50.

Helmholtz, H. *Treatise on physiological optics*. (J. P. Southall, Ed. and trans.). New York: Dover, 1962.

Hochheimer, B. F., & Kuehn, H. A. Retinal polarization effects. *Applied Optics*, 1982, *21*, 3811–3818.

Jennings, J. A. M., & Charman, W. N. Off-axis quality in the human eye. *Vision Research*, 1981, *21*, 445–456.

Krauskopf, J. Light distribution in human retinal images. *Journal of the Optical Society of America*, 1962, *52*, 1046–1050.

LeGrand, Y. *Optique physiologique* (Vol. III). Paris: Revue d'Optique, 1955.

Leibowitz, H. The effect of pupil size on visual acuity for photometrically equated test fields at various levels of luminance. *Journal of the Optical Society of America*, 1952, *42*, 416–422.

Leibowitz, H., & Owens, D. A. New evidence for the intermediate position of relaxed accommodation. *Documenta Ophthalmologica*, 1978, *46*, 133–147.

Millodot, M., & Lamont, A. Peripheral visual acuity in the vertical plane. *Vision Research*, 1974, *14*, 1497–1498.

Nadell, M. C., & Knoll, H. A. The effect of luminance, target configuration, and lenses upon the refractive state of the eye. *American Journal of Optometry and Archives of American Academy of Optometry*, 1956, *33*, 24–42.

Ogle, K. N. *Researches in binocular vision*. Philadelphia: Saunders, 1950.

Owens, D. A. A comparison of accommodative responsiveness and contrast sensitivity for sinusoidal gratings. *Vision Research*, 1980, *20*, 159–167.

Polyak, S. L. *The retina*. Chicago: University of Chicago Press, 1941.

Reeves, P. The response of the average pupil to various intensities of light. *Journal of the Optical Society of America*, 1920, *4*, 35–40.

Robson, J. G., & Enroth-Cugell, C. Light distribution in the cat's retinal image. *Vision Research*, 1978, *18*, 159–174.

Schade, O. H. Optical and photoelectric analog of the eye. *Journal of the Optical Society of America*, 1956, *46*, 721–739.

Stiles, W. S., & Crawford, B. H. The luminous efficiency of rays entering the eye pupil at different points. *Proceedings of the Royal Society of London*, 1933, *B112*, 428–450.

Turner, M. J. Observations on the normal subjective amplitude of accommodation. *British Journal of Physiological Optics*, 1958, *15*, 70–100.

Westheimer, G. Optical properties of vertebrate eyes. In M. G. F. Fuortes (Ed.), *Physiology of photoreceptor organs: Handbook of sensory physiology* (Vol. VII/2). Berlin: Springer-Verlag, 1972.

Westheimer, G. The spatial sense of the eye. Proctor Lecture. *Investigative Ophthalmology and Visual Science*, 1979, *18*, 893–912.

Westheimer, G., & Campbell, F. W. Light distribution in the image formed by the living human eye. *Journal of the Optical Society of America*, 1962, *52*, 1040–1044.

Westheimer, G., & McKee, S. P. Integration regions for visual hyperacuity. *Vision Research*, 1977, *17*, 89–93.

Westheimer, G., & McKee, S. P. Stereoscopic acuity with defocused and spatially filtered retinal images. *Journal of the Optical Society of America*, 1980, *70*, 772–778.

Wolfe, J. M., & Owens, D. A. Is accommodation colorblind? Focusing chromatic contours. *Perception*, 1981, *10*, 53–62.

CHAPTER 5

SENSITIVITY TO LIGHT

DONALD C. HOOD

Department of Psychology, Columbia University, New York, New York

MARCIA A. FINKELSTEIN

Department of Psychology, University of South Florida, Tampa, Florida

CONTENTS

The term *sensitivity to light* refers to an observer's ability to detect a change in visual stimulation. An observer's sensitivity may be measured to a change in a variety of physical aspects of the stimulus, such as its wavelength or its spatial or temporal configuration. In this chapter, we are concerned with the ability to detect changes in intensity. Therefore, sensitivity is defined here as the amount of light (expressed as number of quanta or quantal flux) a stimulus must deliver to the eye for detection to occur. The following two sections examine sensitivity as a function of the wavelength, size, duration, and retinal eccentricity of aperiodic stimuli. The remaining sections explore the adjustments in sensitivity due to changes in ambient illumination.

The problem of adjusting sensitivity (or *adapting*) to increases and decreases in illumination is best understood by considering the variety of situations confronting the human visual system. The human observer experiences a range of naturally occurring ambient light levels of more than 10^8 and must be able to discriminate objects in the environment over this entire range. However, the differences in intensity reflected by those objects at any single light level are very small (spanning a factor of 20, or 100 if shadows are included). The question that models of adaptation must answer is how the visual system remains sensitive to such small differences over such a wide ambient range.

The extent of the range is illustrated in Table 5.1. The intensities or *luminances* over which the visual system functions

Table 5.1. The Dynamic Range of the Visual System

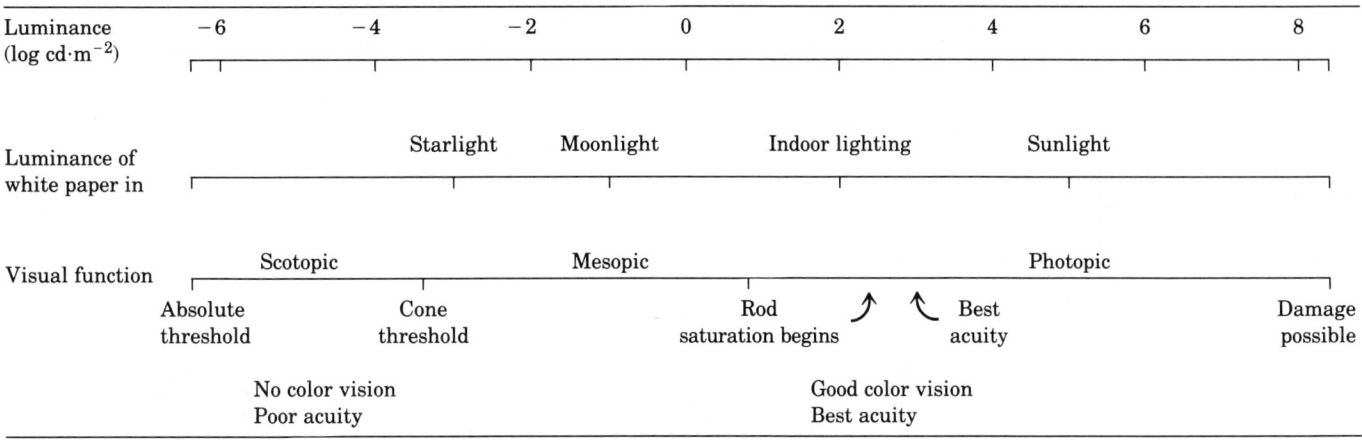

Luminance ($\log cd{\cdot}m^{-2}$)	−6	−4	−2	0	2	4	6	8
Luminance of white paper in		Starlight	Moonlight		Indoor lighting	Sunlight		
Visual function	Scotopic		Mesopic			Photopic		
	Absolute threshold	Cone threshold		Rod saturation begins		Best acuity		Damage possible
	No color vision Poor acuity				Good color vision Best acuity			

Note: Row 1 expresses the range in units of luminance, log candles per meter squared ($cd{\cdot}m^{-2}$). The luminances extend from the minimum required for detection to levels at which damage to the visual system is possible. The second row relates these values to the luminance of white paper under a variety of viewing conditions, and the bottom row expresses the operating range in terms of visual functions. These extend from scotopic (rod-mediated) viewing through mesopic (rod plus cone) and photopic (cone-mediated) vision.

are indicated along the top row. (See Section 1 for a discussion of terminology used to specify amount of light.) The luminances extend from the minimum required for detection to levels at which damage to the visual system is possible. The second row relates the luminances to familiar viewing conditions by indicating the luminance of a white paper under illumination from starlight to sunlight. Finally, the bottom row links the physical stimulus to a variety of visual functions. These functions are explored in detail in the following section.

1. SENSITIVITY AND WAVELENGTH

1.1. The Visible Spectrum

Light is electromagnetic radiation that can be seen. A beam of light consists of individual packets of energy called *quanta*; quanta of light are also referred to as *photons*. Individual quanta have wave properties as well as the properties of discrete particles. This chapter emphasizes the particulate nature of light as it is emitted by a source, reflected from an object, or absorbed by the eye.

Every quantum of light has a characteristic frequency of vibration, ν, which is proportional to its energy, E:

$$E = h\nu \tag{1}$$

where h is Planck's constant and is equal to 6.6×10^{-27} erg · sec. The frequency of a quantum of light is inversely proportional to its wavelength, λ:

$$\lambda = \frac{v}{\nu} \tag{2}$$

where v is the speed of light and equals $3 \times 10^8 m{\cdot}sec^{-1}$ in vacuo. It is the wavelength of quanta that is the physical dimension most closely related to their perceived color. Within a given medium all quanta of the same wavelength or frequency are identical. When a quantum undergoes a change of medium, its frequency and energy remain invariant, but its speed and consequently its wavelength change. The *refractive index* of a medium, η_m, specifies the decrease in each that occurs when a quantum enters that medium from a vacuum:

$$\eta_m = \frac{c}{v_m} = \frac{\lambda}{\lambda_m} \tag{3}$$

where c is the speed of light in vacuo; v_m and λ_m are its speed and wavelength, respectively, in the particular medium. The refractive index of air is only slightly greater than 1.0; the refractive index of the eye is approximately 1.3.

Thus the wavelength of a quantum of light shortens as it enters the eye from the air. Frequency, however, is independent of speed and does not change. Although frequency is therefore the more fundamental property, quanta are more often described in terms of wavelength. Alternatively, identification by *wave number*, the reciprocal of wavelength, is not uncommon. (Wave number scales are usually specified in units of $1/\lambda \times 10^7$). Wave number and frequency are linearly related; both qualities are inversely proportional to wavelength [see Eq. (2)]. Figure 5.1 shows the relation between wavelength, wave number, frequency, and the characteristics of the electromagnetic spectrum as well as apparent color for the visible spectrum. Note the very narrow range of the electromagnetic spectrum, from approximately 400 to 700 nm, that constitutes light. The color names are those most often associated with each spectral region. Color is a property not of the light but of the visual system (see Pokorny & Smith, Chapter 8.)

1.2. Sensitivity Defined

This section examines the effect of the wavelength of light on visual sensitivity. In the psychophysical data used here, the term *sensitivity* is defined as the reciprocal number of quanta required to detect a light on some percent of trials. The psychophysical *spectral sensitivities* will be compared to the *absorption spectra* of the underlying photopigments. Sensitivity in this case refers to a constant rate or number of quantal absorptions. We emphasize quantal values of sensitivity rather than energy values because it is the rate at which quanta are absorbed, and not their energy per se, that determines a receptor's response (and thus the ability of an observer to detect a

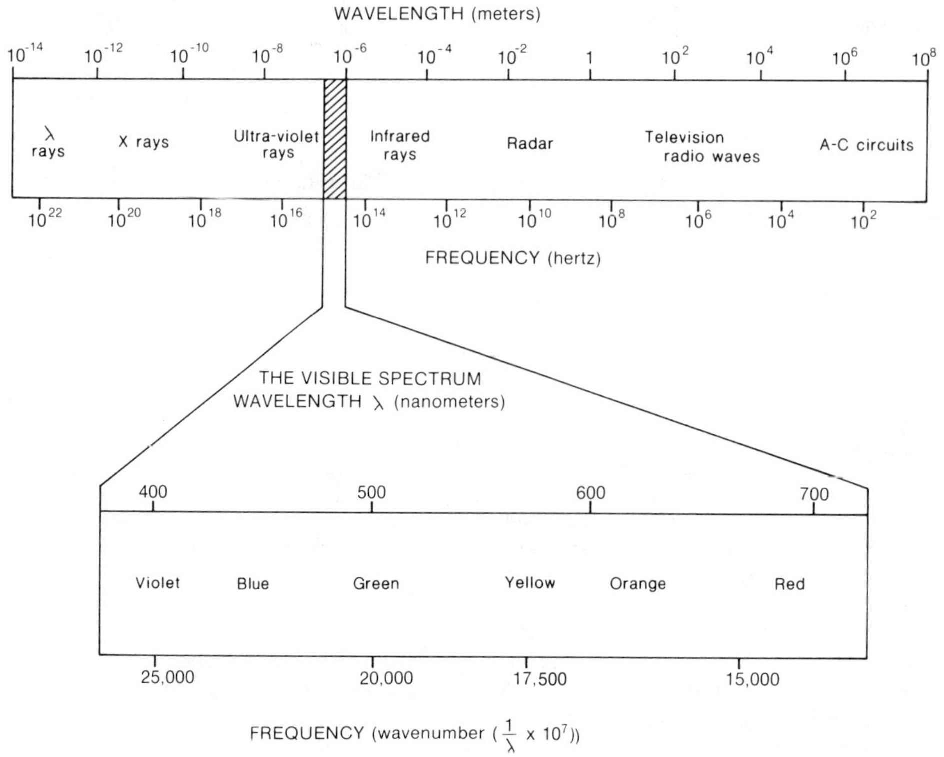

Figure 5.1. The electromagnetic spectrum. The hatched area delineates the narrow band of electromagnetic energy that constitutes light. An expanded view of this region is shown below. The visible spectrum includes roughly the wavelengths from 400 to 700 nm (1 nm = 10^{-9} m). The frequencies corresponding to the wavelengths, and the colors most often associated with each portion of the visible spectrum, are also indicated. (See Chapter 9 for a detailed discussion of the determinants of perceived hue.) (From I. Abramov & J. Gordon, Vision, in E. C. Carterette & M. P. Friedman (Eds.), *Handbook of perception* (Vol. 3), Academic Press, Inc., 1973. Reprinted with permission.)

light). Recall that the energy of a quantum is inversely proportional to its wavelength [Eqs. (1) and (2)]. This means that if lights of different wavelengths must produce the same amount of energy to be detected, then the shorter-wavelength light produces fewer quantal absorptions.

1.3. The Visual Receptors and Their Pigments

1.3.1. The Receptor Types. The first step in the visual process is the absorption of quanta of light by the receptors of the eye. The *duplex retina* of the human eye contains two types of receptors, *rods* and *cones*. They are so named because of the characteristic shapes of the outer tips (outer segments) of the receptors in lower animals (e.g., frogs). Figure 5.2 shows a human rod and two human cones, one from the fovea and one from the periphery. Note that although the rod looks somewhat rodlike, and the peripheral cone like a cone, the foveal cone has much the same shape as the rod. From the standpoint of this chapter the functional differences between rods and cones are more important than their anatomical differences.

The functional differences between rods and cones constitute the basis of *duplicity theory*. The theory holds that vision is mediated by two receptor systems (rod and cone), their respective properties evident in a variety of visual functions. The cone system subserves detection at high intensities and is responsible for color vision and for detection of fine detail. The rod system is more sensitive at low light levels, is poor at discriminating details, and does not provide color discrimination. We emphasize the term *system* in the present discussion because the visual

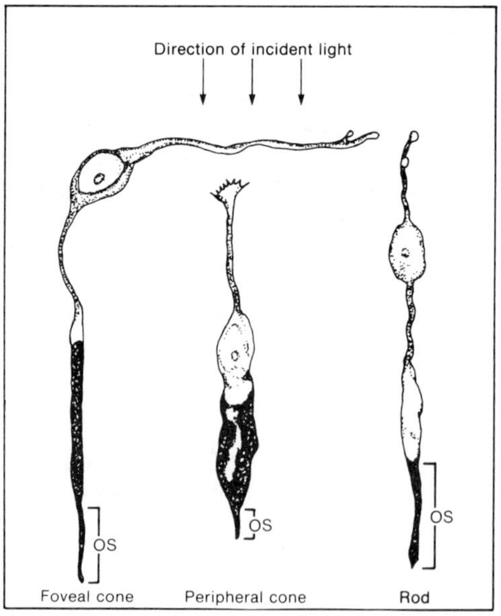

Figure 5.2. A comparative illustration of a foveal cone, peripheral cone, and rod. Light is absorbed by photopigment molecules contained in the receptor outer segment (OS). All rods contain the pigment rhodopsin, whereas an individual cone contains one of the three other photopigments. The rods and cones were named for the shapes of their outer segments in lower animals; the human foveal cone is actually more rodlike than conelike in appearance. Note that the outer segments face away from the incoming light. (From T. N. Cornsweet, *Visual perception*, Academic Press, Inc., 1970. Reprinted with permission.)

functions to be examined reflect not the response of a single receptor, but the overall output of a collection of cells from receptor to cortex. (See Walls, 1942, for a discussion of the history of duplicity theory and its relation to anatomical differences in the animal kingdom.)

1.3.2. Retinal Distribution. The human retina contains many more rods than cones: approximately 120 million rods to 6.5 million cones. Rods and cones are also distributed differently across the retina as shown in Figure 5.3. Panel (a) is a view of the left eye as seen from above. Below is a receptor count for a horizontal section through the eye. (The count is from Osterberg (1935) for a single human retina.) In panel (b) the number of rods and cones per square millimeter of retina is shown as a function of distance in visual angle from the fovea.

The fovea is the region of the central retina where images fall when an observer fixates. It is usually assumed to contain no rods. (There are, however, few human anatomical data to either confirm or reject this assumption.) The fovea extends roughly 1.5–2° in diameter; the cone population is at its most dense within this region. Cone density falls sharply outside the fovea, reaching a minimum around 10° eccentricity. Beyond this point the retina contains a (very thin) uniform distribution

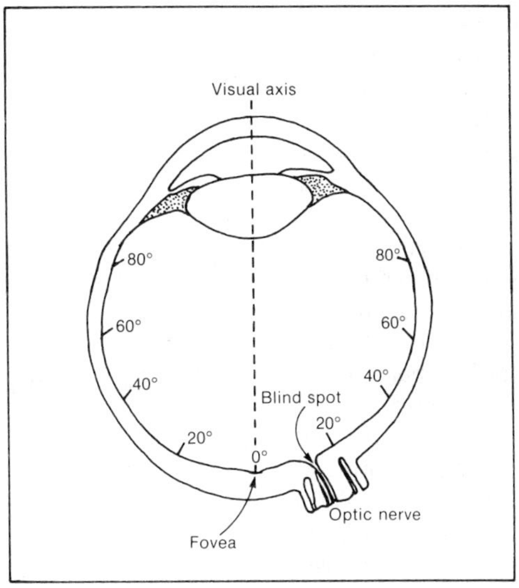

(a)

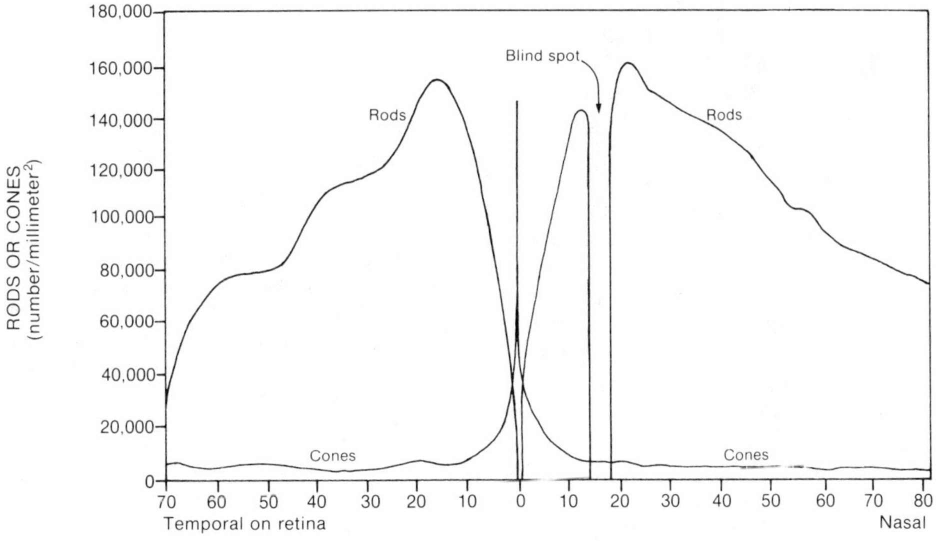

(b)

Figure 5.3. (a) Schematic of a horizontal section through the left eye. Light traveling along the visual axis is imaged on the fovea (0°); distance from the fovea along the retina is labeled in degrees. The "blind spot" is the region of the retina where the optic nerve leaves the eye and contains no photoreceptors. (b) Rod and cone densities as a function of eccentricity along the horizontal meridian (according to Osterberg, 1935). Cone density is greatest in the fovea and falls rapidly to a minimum by 10° eccentricity. Beyond 10°, the retina contains a thin, uniform distribution of cones. The rods are absent in the fovea and increase sharply in number out to 18°. Rod density declines with further increases in eccentricity but remains much greater than cone density. (From M. H. Pirenne, *Vision and the eye* (2nd ed.), Methuen and Company, 1967. Reprinted with permission.)

of cones. Thus cones are found at all eccentricities but have sparse density beyond 10°.

Rod density increases with eccentricity up to about 18° and then gradually declines; however, the density of rods remains much greater than cone density in the far periphery. The "*blind spot*," located at 15° along the nasal retina, is the region where the optic nerve leaves the eye. It is so named because as it contains no photoreceptors, one cannot see an object centered entirely within it.

1.3.3. Pigments. The receptors for vision contain photosensitive pigments in their outer segments (see Figure 5.2). These pigments serve to transduce electromagnetic energy into the electrochemical signals of the nervous system. A pigment molecule consists of a protein (an *opsin*) bonded to a *chromophore*, the light-sensitive portion of the molecule. The chromophore is retinal, a derivation of Vitamin A. It is generally assumed that the human retina contains four photopigments, each with a different absorption spectrum. One pigment is found in the rods, and three in the cones; a single cone contains only one of the three types of photopigment. The data on the visual pigments come from a variety of techniques, both behavioral and physical (see Boynton, 1979; Pokorny & Smith, Chapter 8 for references and discussion). Recent studies suggest that the differences among pigments are in the locations of negative charges along the opsin. The location of these charges determines the way in which the opsin binds to the retinal. This in turn determines the chromophore's absorption spectrum (Honig, Dinur, Nakanishi, Balagh-Nair, Gawinowicz, Arnaboldi, & Motto, 1979).

All photopigments absorb quanta of all wavelengths in the visible spectrum. Photopigments are not, however, equally sensitive to light of all wavelengths. Figure 5.4 shows current estimates of the absorption spectra of the rod and cone pigments. The graphs plot log (relative quantal sensitivity) at the cornea as a function of wavelength. To convert these spectra to true pigment absorption spectra (i.e., the percentage of light absorbed) requires adjustments, including corrections for the selective absorption and scattering of light by the ocular media and macular pigment and for the density of the photopigment (see Section 1.4).

The rods are maximally sensitive to quanta of 500 nm; that is, quanta of wavelength near 500 nm have the greatest probability of absorption. The three cone pigments are maximally sensitive to quanta around 440, 535–540, and 560–565 nm, respectively. The cones are sometimes referred to by the wavelength of peak sensitivity and sometimes by the colors they are assumed to signal in Helmholtz's trichromatic theory (blue, green, and red). We shall use the labels of short-wavelength, middle-wavelength, and long-wavelength sensitive cones to refer to the three cone types.

The probability that a pigment molecule will absorb a given quantum of light depends on the wavelength of that quantum. Once a quantum is absorbed, its effect is thought to be independent of wavelength. Quantal absorption causes a characteristic change in shape, or isomerization, of the pigment molecule. The isomerization per se preserves no information about the properties of the absorbed quanta. Consequently, wavelength cannot be deduced from the response of a single receptor. The only information in the receptor response is the rate at which quanta are being absorbed. The idea that a receptor responds in only one way regardless of the characteristics of the incident light has been called the *principle of univariance* (Naka & Rushton, 1966). The univariance assumption does occasionally come under question. However, if it is wrong, it is in ways that are minor for our purposes.

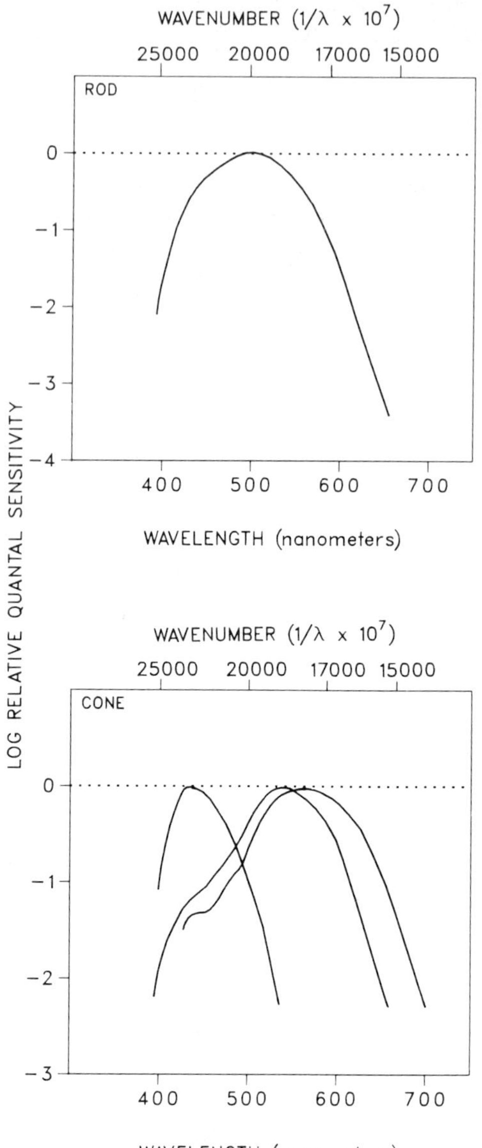

Figure 5.4. Estimates of the absorption spectra of the rod (top) and cone (bottom) photopigments. These are theoretical curves derived in large part from psychophysical data (see Smith & Pokorny, 1975). The curves show log (relative quantal sensitivity) as a function of the wavelength of the quanta. To convert these to true pigment absorption spectra requires corrections for the selective absorption and scattering of light by the ocular media and macular pigment (see Section 2.4). All pigments absorb light of all wavelengths but differ in their relative sensitivities across the visible spectrum. The rod pigment is maximally sensitive to (i.e., shows the greatest probability of absorption of) 500 nm light. The three cone pigments are maximally sensitive to 440 nm (short-wavelength cones), 535–540 nm (middle-wavelength cones), and 560–565 nm (long-wavelength cones), respectively. All curves are normalized to their own maxima.

1.4. Correcting for Pre-Receptoral Light Loss

What we call "light" is one small portion of the electromagnetic spectrum, from about 400 to 700 nm (Fig. 5.1). In the human visual system, sensitivity to long wavelengths is limited by the sensitivity of the photopigments, which do not readily absorb quanta of very long wavelengths (very low frequencies). The eye can, however, detect lights well into the infrared (above 1000 nm) if they are sufficiently intense (e.g., Griffin, Hubbard, & Wald, 1947). The insensitivity to short-wavelength light, on the other hand, is due largely to absorption, mainly by the lens, before light reaches the receptors. Again, extremely intense radiation can extend visibility into the ultraviolet.

The present section examines the selective transmission of the lens and of the macular pigment, which also serves selectively to depress sensitivity to short-wavelength light. In the sections that follow, we shall see the influence of these factors on psychophysically measured spectral sensitivities. For more complete discussions of light loss in the ocular media and macular pigment, see Wyszecki and Stiles (1982), Ruddock (1972), and Westheimer, Chapter 4.

1.4.1. The Lens. The lens of the human eye contains a yellowish pigment; it appears yellow because it selectively absorbs short-wavelength light. Absorption by the lens is the greatest source of pre-retinal short-wavelength light loss. The spectral transmission of the lens has been estimated from direct measurements of excised eyes and by comparisons of normal and aphakic (lensless) observers' sensitivity to short-wavelength light. Figure 5.5 shows results obtained by both methods (from Pokorny, Smith, & Verriest, 1979). The figure shows the optical density (left-hand ordinate) of the lens relative to that at 546 nm. The right-hand ordinate expresses this in terms of transmittance relative to 546 nm. Notice that optical density increases sharply below about 440 nm. The lens transmits more than 1000 times more light at 546 nm than at 360 nm.

The curve is only an approximation of the relative transmittance (or absorbance) of the lens for any individual. There will be large differences between young and old observers. Lens pigmentation increases with age, causing substantial increases in absorption of short-wavelength light.

1.4.2. Macular Pigment. The most important source of light loss in the retina is the *macular pigment*, a nonphotosensitive pigment found in the central 5–10° of the retina. It appears to be distributed over an elliptical area with the major axis horizontal. The pigment is mainly concentrated in the central 2° of the retina, falling to an almost negligible level by 4° (see Le Grand, 1968; U. Stabell & B. Stabell, 1980). The yellow pigment has been identified as xanthophyll, a carotenoid pigment. Measurements of its density spectrum in the fovea, as obtained via several different psychophysical techniques, are given in Figure 5.6 (from Wyszecki & Stiles, 1982). Estimates of the optical density at 460 nm, the wavelength of maximum density, in general range from 0.35 to 0.50; the pigment absorbs between 55 and 68% of the light at 460 nm. Optical density falls to 0 above 530 nm.

We will see below that the macular pigment influences the spectral sensitivity of the fovea and accounts for some foveal-parafoveal differences. Its influence on sensitivity varies widely among observers because of individual differences in the density of the pigment. Bone and Sparrock (1971) divided subjects into high-, medium-, and low-density groups. The high-density subjects had a maximum pigment density greater than 0.60; low-density observers showed a maximum of less than 0.45. Individual differences in density were attributed to variations in pigment concentration and/or the thickness of the absorbing layer. A psychophysical estimate of the density of an individual's macular pigment can be obtained and applied to that observer's data (e.g., U. Stabell & B. Stabell, 1980). Note, however, that

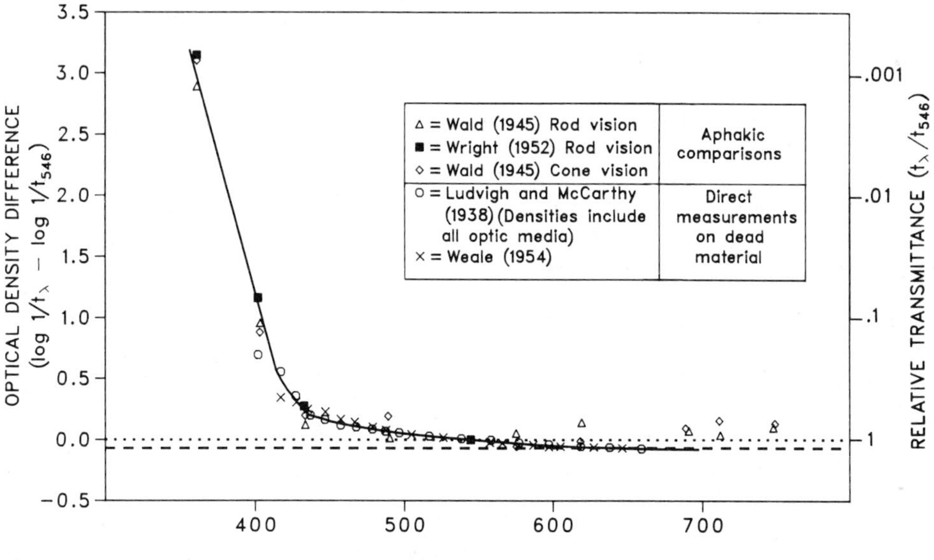

Figure 5.5. The relative transmittance of the lens. Transmittance is plotted relative to that at 546 nm (right-hand ordinate). Transmittance at any wavelength is the ratio of flux transmitted by the lens to the flux incident on the lens. The left-hand ordinate is the difference in optical density at any given wavelength and at 546 nm. Optical density, or absorbance, is the difference between the log (flux incident on the lens) and the log (flux transmitted). The data include both direct measurements of excised material and psychophysical comparisons of the spectral sensitivities of normal and aphakic (lensless) observers. Note the sharp increase in optical density for wavelengths below 440 nm. The lens absorbs more than 1000 times more light at 360 nm than at 546 nm. (From J. Wyszecki & W. S. Stiles, *Color science*. Copyright 1982 by John Wiley & Sons, Inc. Reprinted with permission.)

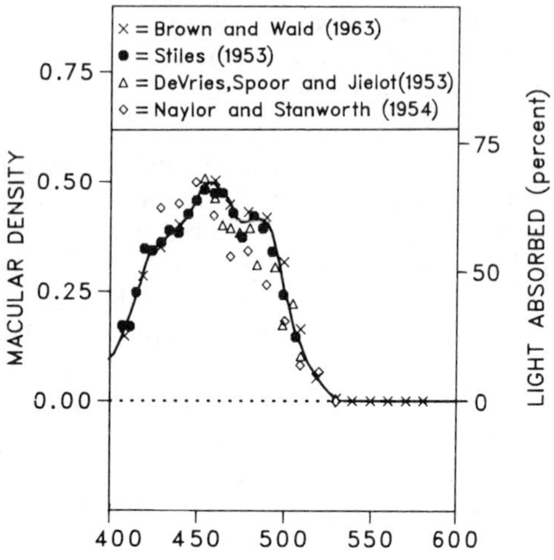

Figure 5.6. The density spectrum of the macular pigment. Measurements were made in the fovea with a variety of psychophysical techniques. The nonphotosensitive macular pigment is concentrated mainly in the central 2° of the retina. It constitutes the major source of light loss in the retina. Estimates of its optical density at the wavelength of maximum absorbance, 460 nm, in general range from 0.35 to 0.50; 55–68% of the incident light is absorbed. Density falls to 0.0 above 530 nm. The macular pigment has been identified from its density spectrum as the carotenoid pigment, xanthophyll. (From J. Wyszecki & W. S. Stiles, *Color science*. Copyright 1982 by John Wiley & Sons, Inc. Reprinted with permission.)

not all changes in relative sensitivity between macular and nonmacular regions of the retina can be attributed to the macular pigment (see Section 1.5.1.2).

1.5. Spectral Sensitivity

The human observer, like the underlying photopigments, is not equally sensitive to lights of all wavelengths. Equal numbers of quanta of different wavelengths differ greatly in brightness and in detectability. Furthermore, the visual system's relative sensitivity to lights of different wavelengths is not constant. The wavelength that is brightest or most easily seen depends on a number of factors, especially the ambient illumination. The classic observations of Purkyně (1825; see Le Grand, 1968) provide a real-world illustration of the change in relative effectiveness of lights with changes in ambient radiance. Purkyně noticed that signposts painted in blue and red looked somewhat different at different times of day. Although the two colors appeared equally bright during the day, the blue was brighter than the red at dawn. Purkyně's observations are consistent with duplicity theory, which assumes one set of receptors (cones) for detection at high intensities and another set (rods) at low intensities.

The relative sensitivity of the visual system across the visible spectrum is studied routinely in the lab. Sensitivity is measured in a number of ways, the detection paradigm being the most straightforward. The intensity needed to detect a stimulus of a given wavelength on a certain proportion of presentations (e.g., 50%) is defined as the threshold intensity. Intensities in this chapter are expressed in terms of relative numbers of quanta per second per degree incident at the cornea. See Westheimer, Chapter 4, for a discussion of visual angle. Sensitivity is defined as the reciprocal of this intensity. A spectral sensitivity function relates sensitivity to the wavelength of the light. This chapter emphasizes detection data. Other procedures for estimating spectral sensitivity are mentioned below.

When a spectral sensitivity is measured in the laboratory, the size and duration of the test stimulus are usually held constant. The stimulus is presented on a background of fixed intensity and to a fixed part of the retina. One purpose of this chapter is to examine how these parameters affect relative spectral sensitivity. We shall attempt to relate changes in spectral sensitivity to changes in the relative sensitivities of the rods and cones. By spectral sensitivity, we mean the relative *detectability* of lights of different wavelengths. Those interested in the appearance of suprathreshold lights (e.g., brightness) should refer to Pokorny and Smith, Chapter 8, and Wyszecki, Chapter 9.

The fact that the spectral sensitivity of the human eye changes has both theoretical and practical implications. One attempt to solve the practical issue is seen in the adoption by the CIE (Commission International de l'Eclairage) of two standard relative *luminous efficiency* (spectral sensitivity) functions. The two functions specify the relative spectral sensitivity of the visual system under scotopic (nighttime) and photopic (daytime) conditions. They are usually expressed in energy terms. We show them in Figure 5.7 in terms of quantal sensitivity, with each curve normalized to a maximum log (relative quantal sensitivity) of 0.0. The scotopic function (solid curve) is assumed to represent the spectral sensitivity of the rod system, the photopic function (dashed curve), the cone system. These are theoretical curves based on psychophysical data obtained from a number of laboratories with a variety of procedures (see Boynton, 1979 for references).

The scotopic and photopic luminosity functions (also called V'_λ and V_λ) can be used to construct a model of visual sensitivity.

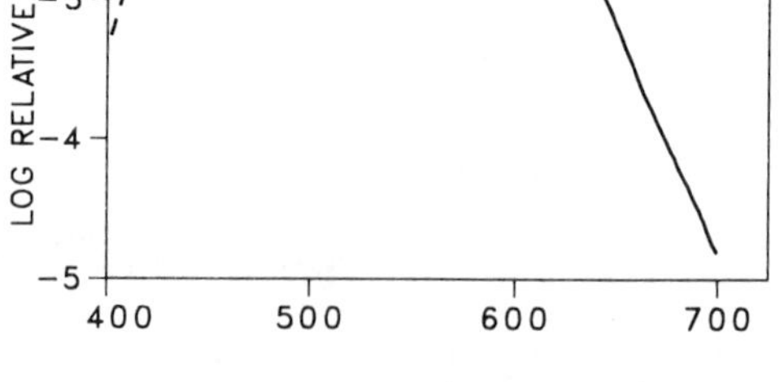

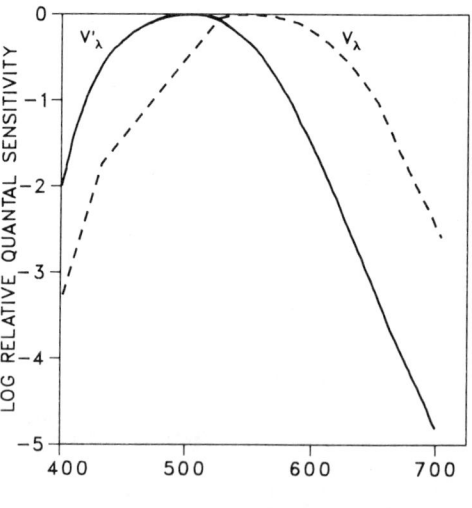

Figure 5.7. The CIE relative luminous efficiency, or luminosity, functions. The curves specify relative (quantal) spectral sensitivity under scotopic (nighttime) and photopic (daytime) conditions. Each curve is normalized to its own maximum. The scotopic luminosity function (solid curve, V'_λ) describes the rod system. The photopic function (dashed curve, V_λ) is assumed to describe cone system sensitivity; it can be fitted by a weighted sum of the (psychophysically measured) long- and middle-wavelength cone absorption spectra. The luminosity functions are based on a variety of psychophysical data and represent a theoretical "standard observer." It is generally agreed that V_λ underestimates relative sensitivity in the short wavelengths; Judd (1951) presents a photopic correction for wavelengths below 460 nm (see dashed curve, Fig. 5.11.)

This model is an oversimplified description of the visual system, but it does describe spectral sensitivity data obtained under a number of test and adapting conditions. We present here a brief summary of the model's main assumptions. We then present the empirical findings and evaluate the model's ability to account for them.

In accordance with duplicity theory, what we will call the "duplicity model" assumes two separate detection systems, a rod system and a cone system. The former is responsible for detection at low light levels and is most sensitive in the rod-dominated periphery. The cone system, on the other hand, is more sensitive at higher intensities and predominates in the rod-free fovea. In the strongest version of this model, each system is assumed to have an *invariant* relative spectral sensitivity, given by V'_λ and V_λ, respectively. Changes in parameters such as adapting intensity or the retinal position of the stimulus change the absolute sensitivity of a system but not its relative sensitivity to lights of different wavelengths.

The systems are also assumed to be *independent*; the sensitivity of one system is unaffected by stimulation of the other. The system more sensitive to a particular test determines the overall sensitivity of the visual system to that test. The independence assumption leads to the prediction that the overall spectral sensitivity will approximate an envelope of the component rod and cone system sensitivities. Changes in the shape of the overall sensitivity curve that occur with variations in stimulus parameters reflect changes in relative sensitivity between systems, never within systems. Graphically, this corresponds to a differential shifting of the scotopic and photopic functions vertically along the log (sensitivity) axis.

Consider, for example, the hypothetical spectral sensitivities of Figure 5.8. In panel (a), the rod system is the more sensitive at all wavelengths and alone determines overall sensitivity. The reverse is seen in panel (c), where the sensitivity of the cone system exceeds that of the rod system over the entire spectrum. Panel (b) shows an intermediate situation. The rod system controls sensitivity to wavelengths shorter than 590 nm, whereas the cone system is more sensitive at longer wavelengths. The spectral sensitivity of the eye should be the envelope of the underlying rod and cone sensitivities.

Keeping this model in mind, we turn now to the data the model is meant to describe. We shall see below that different stimulus conditions can produce spectral sensitivities similar to the three schematized in Figure 5.8. For example, the sensitivity of the dark-adapted peripheral retina resembles panel (a). Increasing the size of the test to include the fovea gives a combined rod-and-cone sensitivity like that in panel (b). By adding an adapting background, a spectral sensitivity similar to the one in panel (c) is produced. For a wide range of test and adapting conditions, sensitivity is consistent with the assumption of independent, spectrally invariant rod and cone systems and the assumption that detection is subserved by whichever system is the more sensitive. We shall also see conditions, particularly at high adapting intensities, under which this simple model breaks down.

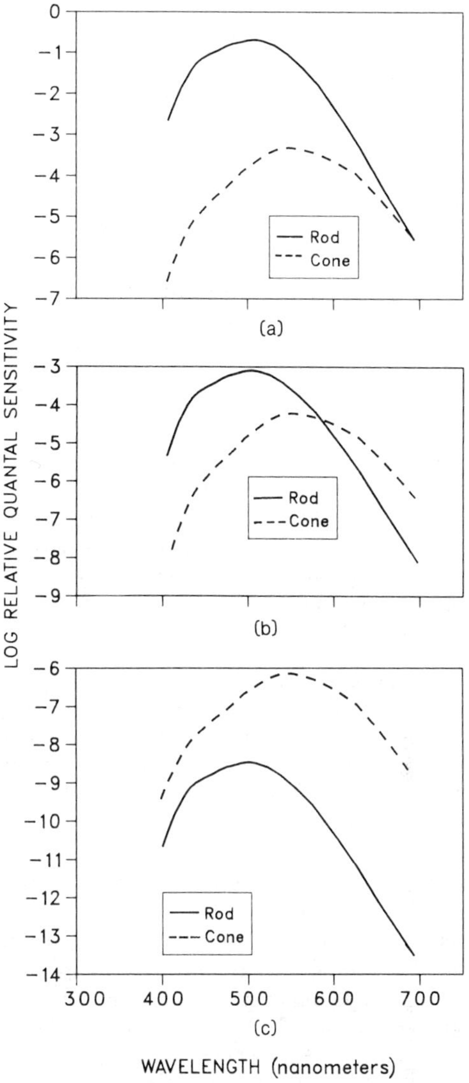

Figure 5.8. A duplicity model of detection. The model assumes independent rod and cone systems, each with an invariant relative spectral sensitivity (the solid and dashed curves, respectively). Detection at any wavelength is served by the more sensitive system, and the overall spectral sensitivity approximates an envelope of the rod and cone curves. Changes in the shape of the overall function reflect changes in relative sensitivity between systems, never within systems. Panels (a)–(c) show the effect of changes in conditions that progressively favor the cone system (e.g., increased adapting intensity). (a) The rod system is more sensitive at all wavelengths and alone determines detection. (b) The rod system serves detection below 590 nm; the cone system takes over for longer wavelengths. (c) The cone system is responsible for detection across the entire spectrum.

1.5.1. Dark-Adapted Eye

1.5.1.1. Rod System: Dark-Adapted Periphery. To isolate the spectral sensitivity of the rod system without cone influence, thresholds are measured under conditions that favor the rods: stimulation of the periphery of the dark-adapted eye. Figure 5.9 shows two sets of spectral sensitivity data obtained under such conditions. The triangles are data obtained by Wald (1945) for detection of a 1°, 40-msec test light presented 8° above the fovea; the plot is the average data of 22 observers. The circles (from Crawford, 1949) are the averages of the thresholds obtained for "a few observers" using a 10°, 1-sec test centered 10° below the fovea.

The solid curve through the data is the scotopic luminosity function, V'_λ. The function, representing the relative spectral sensitivity of the rod system, was derived from the Wald and Crawford data. The psychophysical results are affected by the selective absorption of short-wavelength light by the lens. Figure 5.10 contains Wald's results from Figure 5.9 and the results obtained for a group of 24 aphakic (lensless) observers. Again, the solid curve is V'_λ. Note the increased relative sensitivity to

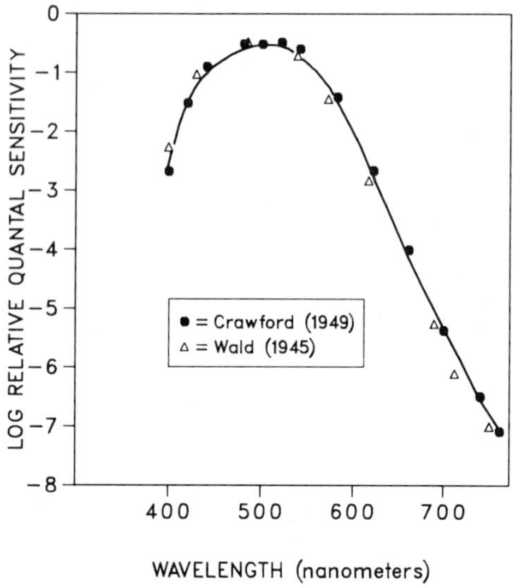

Figure 5.9. Relative spectral sensitivity of the rod system. Thresholds were measured in the dark-adapted peripheral retina. The figure plots log (relative quantal sensitivity) at the cornea for two sets of "young" observers (under 30 years). The data are from the two studies on which the CIE scotopic luminosity function is based. Triangles: data for a 1°, 40-msec test centered 8° above the fovea. Each point is the average of the results from 22 observers. The test appeared colorless at all wavelengths (from Wald, 1945, Table 1). Circles: data for a 10°, 1-sec test centered 10° below the fovea; average results of "a few" observers (from Crawford, 1949, Table 6). The two sets of data are shifted arbitrarily along the ordinate to aid comparison. The rod system is maximally sensitive to wavelengths around 500 nm.

short wavelengths in the aphakic data. Because the selective absorption of the lens has been eliminated, the aphakic curve provides a close match to the absorption spectrum of rhodopsin in vivo. The Wald and Crawford data presented in Figure 5.9 were obtained from young observers (under 30 years). The differences between aphakic and normal relative spectral sensitivities would be even greater for older observers owing to the progressive yellowing of the lens with age.

1.5.1.2. Cone System: Dark-Adapted Fovea. By restricting stimulation to the fovea, it is generally expected that a pure-cone spectral sensitivity will be obtained. Figure 5.11 plots spectral sensitivities for the dark-adapted fovea from four different studies (Dillon & Zegers, 1958; Hsia & Graham, 1957; Sperling & Hsia, 1957; Wald, 1945). In each study, the test stimulus was confined to, but filled, most of the fovea (about 1°). The solid curve is V_λ positioned for best fit to the middle of the spectrum. Despite differences in stimulus parameters (see figure caption), the four sets of data are remarkably similar. All are considerably broader than the photopic curve in the short wavelengths. It is generally agreed that V_λ underestimates relative sensitivity in the short wavelengths. Judd (1951) reviewed the available literature and proposed a correction for wavelengths below 460 nm. The dashed curve is Judd's correction and provides a much closer fit to the data.

Although the assumption of a rod-free fovea serves as a viable working hypothesis, there are reports of rod intrusions on foveally measured sensitivities (see, e.g., Stiles, 1946). Whether these intrusions are due to the existence of a few foveal rods in some observers, to interactions between foveal cones and parafoveal rods, or to some other aspect of the experimental situation, such as unsteady fixation, is not clear. We suspect that failure to maintain proper fixation accounts for at least some of the apparent rod intrusion.

The effects of unsteady fixation are illustrated quite dramatically in Figure 5.12. The filled circles show a dark-adapted spectral sensitivity obtained from an experienced psychophysical observer. The stimuli were presented in the center of a 2° square patch outlined by four small fixation points (see figure caption for details). The observer was instructed to fixate the center of the field. The data do not resemble the spectral sensitivity of the foveal cone system. In fact, they provide a good fit to the spectral sensitivity of the rod system (V'_λ, solid curve). The open circles show the results obtained when a fixation point was positioned in the center of the stimulus. These data resemble the foveal spectral sensitivity of the normal observer (V_λ, dashed curve). It is clear that under the first set of viewing conditions, the observer was unknowingly moving her eyes to bring the target onto the more sensitive peripheral retina.

The spectral sensitivity of the central fovea measured with a very small spot is quite close to V_λ. Figure 5.13 shows dark-adapted spectral sensitivities obtained for three observers with a 3-min arc, 100-msec test (Sperling & Hsia, 1957). The curve V_λ provides a much better fit to these data. In contrast to the large-spot data of Figure 5.11, the results for two observers actually fall slightly below the standard curve in the short wavelengths. It has been suggested that the reduced short-wavelength sensitivity obtained with small spots reflects the absence of short-wavelength cones in the central fovea (e.g., Sperling & Hsia, 1957; Wald, 1967; Williams, MacLeod, & Hayhoe, 1981a, 1981b). Estimates of the area lacking in short wavelength cones vary from 7 to 25 min arc (cf. Wald, 1967; Williams et al., 1981a).

1.5.1.3. Effects of Retinal Position: Rod and Cone Systems. The spectral sensitivity of the eye depends on the part of the retina stimulated. There are two main sources for the variation of spectral sensitivity with eccentricity. First is the change in

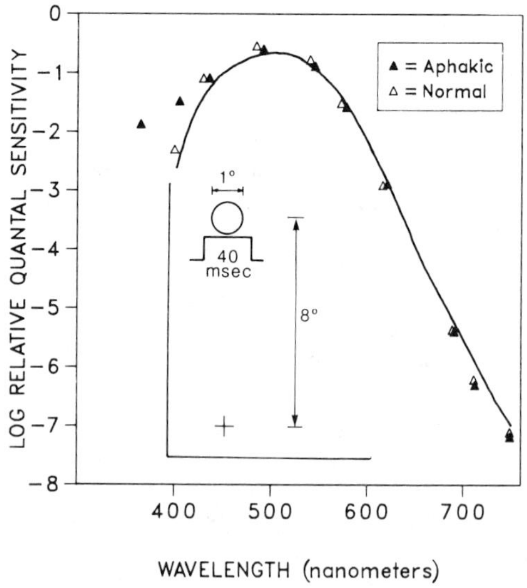

Figure 5.10. Comparison of rod system spectral sensitivities for normal and aphakic (lensless) observers. Open triangles: dark-adapted (normal) spectral sensitivity replotted from Figure 5.9. Filled triangles: spectral sensitivity measured under the same conditions for 24 aphakic observers. The data are shifted arbitrarily along the ordinate to aid comparison; the curve is the scotopic luminosity function. The difference in log (relative sensitivity) between normals and aphakics gives an estimate of the density spectrum of the lens. Because the lens selectively absorbs short-wavelength light, the aphakic measures more closely approximate the rhodopsin absorption spectrum. (From Wald, 1945, Table 1.)

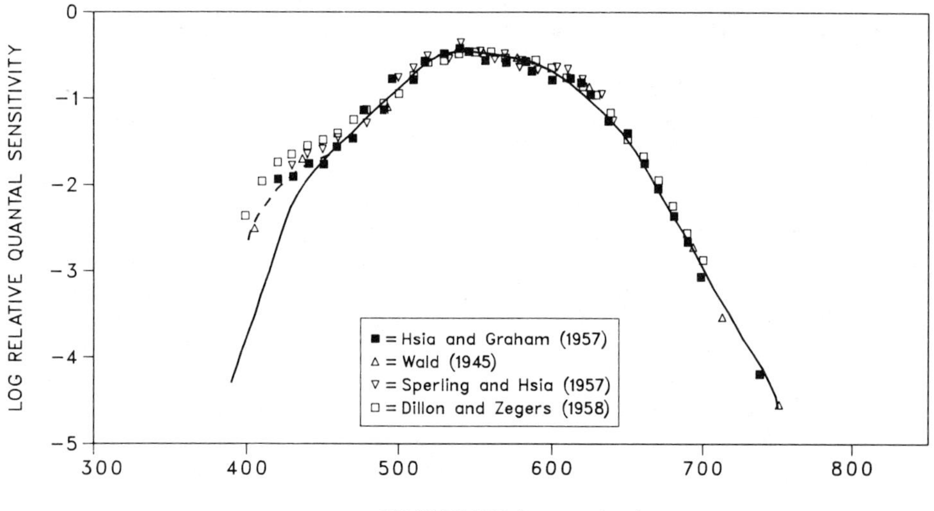

Figure 5.11. Dark-adapted spectral sensitivities for large foveal tests; data from four studies. Open triangles: spectral sensitivity for a 1°, 40-msec test. Average data of 22 observers, mean age 20 years. (From Wald, 1945, Table 1.) Filled squares: data for a 42°, 4-msec test. Average data of seven observers, three sessions per observer. (From Hsia & Graham, 1957, Table 1.) Inverted triangles: spectral sensitivity for a 42-min arc, 4-msec test; average data of four observers. Variability (±1 SEM) overall, 0.08; below 500 nm, 0.15; above 500 nm, 0.04. (From Sperling & Hsia, 1957, Table 1.) Squares: data for a 1°, 50-msec test. Averages of five observers, age 21–45. Variability (±1 SEM): 0.02. (From Dillon & Zegers, 1958, Table 1.) The four sets of data are shifted vertically to aid comparison. Under these conditions, the photopic system shows peak sensitivity around 560 nm. The solid curve is the CIE photopic luminosity function positioned for best fit to the data in the middle of the spectrum. The function predicts a more rapid falloff in sensitivity at short wavelengths than the data indicate. The dashed curve shows Judd's (1951) corrected luminosity function for wavelengths below 460 nm.

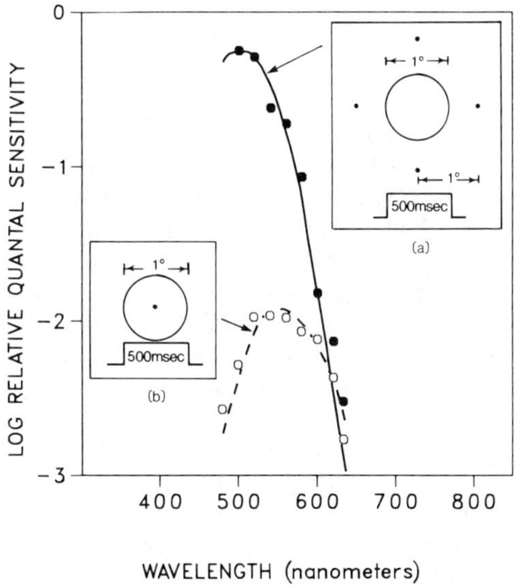

Figure 5.12. The effect of unsteady fixation on spectral sensitivity. Foveal dark-adapted thresholds were measured for large (1°), long-duration (500-msec) test lights. (a) The observer, highly experienced in psychophysical observation, was instructed to fixate the center of a 2° square formed by four small "red" lights; the stimuli were presented in the center of the square (see inset). The resulting data (filled circles) show a clear failure to maintain central fixation. The solid curve through the data is the relative spectral sensitivity of the rod system (V'_λ). The close fit indicates that the observer was unknowingly moving her eye to bring the target onto the more sensitive peripheral retina. (b) Fixation was aided by centering the target upon one small "red" light (see inset). The open circles show the spectral sensitivity obtained for the same observer under the same adapting and test conditions. The dashed curve, the photopic luminosity function (V_λ), provides a good fit to these data, indicating that central fixation was maintained. (Finkelstein, Note 1.)

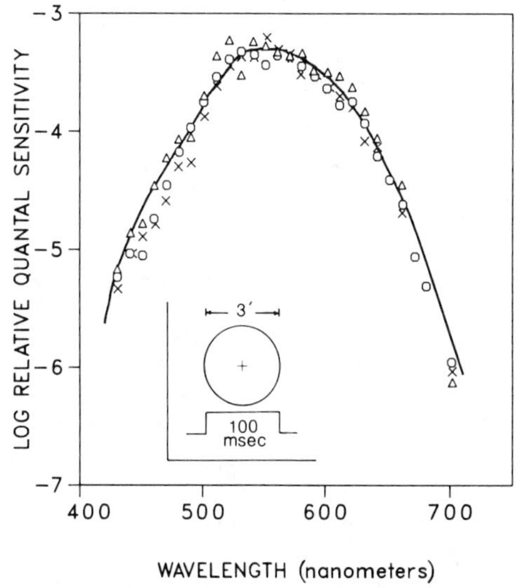

Figure 5.13. Dark-adapted spectral sensitivities for a small foveal target. The stimulus was 3 min arc in diameter and 100 msec in duration (see inset). Each symbol shows the data for one observer. The curve is the photopic luminosity function positioned to coincide with the data in the middle of the spectrum. The theoretical curve provides a good fit to the data even in the short wavelengths (cf. Fig. 5.11). (From Sperling & Hsia, 1957, Table 1.)

the relative distributions of the different photopigments, both between the rod and cone systems and within the cone system. Recall that the strong version of the duplicity model does not allow changes within a system. We shall see, however, that some data suggest a weaker version of the model that allows for changes in relative sensitivity among (but not within) the different classes of cones. The second source of changes in relative sensitivity from fovea to periphery is the change in the density of the inert macular pigment.

Neither of the above factors exerts a substantial effect on the spectral sensitivity of the rod system. There is only one rod pigment, and its absorption spectrum is assumed to remain invariant with eccentricity. There should be some small change in relative spectral sensitivity to short wavelengths owing to changes in the density of macular pigment. However, the density is thought to be quite low by 3–4° eccentricity. Consequently, at almost all retinal locations at which a rod spectral sensitivity can be measured, the macular pigment exerts a negligible effect. We would therefore predict, in accordance with the duplicity model, that the relative spectral sensitivity of the rod system will remain invariant with retinal eccentricity.

The data shown in Figure 5.14, from B. Stabell and U. Stabell (1981), support this prediction. The figure summarizes dark-adapted spectral sensitivity data collected at eccentricities from 6 to 65°. The open circles show the spectral sensitivity obtained 17° extrafoveally, the region of greatest rod sensitivity. The filled circles are the data obtained at the most extreme eccentricity, 65°, where sensitivity was lowest. The solid curve through the data is the scotopic luminosity function, V'_λ. At every eccentricity, V'_λ was found to provide a close fit to the spectral sensitivity data. Varying eccentricity varied only the

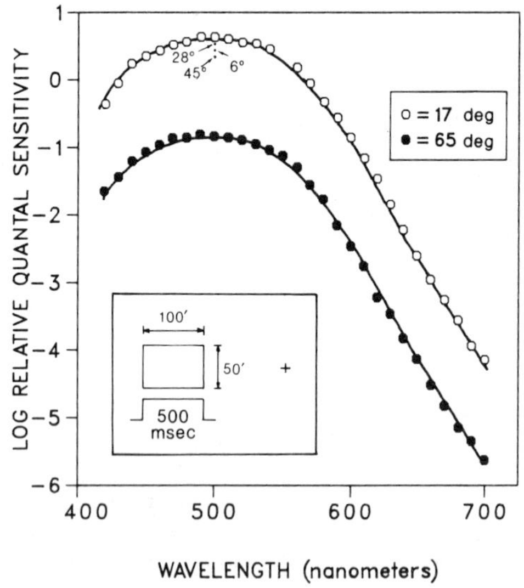

Figure 5.14. Dark-adapted spectral sensitivities for five locations along the temporal retina. Each point is the average of six measurements made on a single observer. The test subtended 50 min arc × 100 min arc and was 500 msec in duration (see inset). The open circles were obtained at 17° eccentricity, the filled circles at 65°. For clarity, only the point of maximum sensitivity is plotted for eccentricities of 6, 28, and 45°. In every case, the data are well fitted by the scotopic luminosity function (solid curves). The variation in absolute sensitivity with retinal position is similar to the variation in the number of rods. Both sensitivity and rod density reach a maximum around 17° and decline with further increases in eccentricity. (From B. Stabell & U. Stabell, Absolute spectral sensitivity at different eccentricities, *Journal of the Optical Society of America*, 1981, *71*. Reprinted with permission.)

absolute sensitivity of the rod system. The three dots mark the maximum sensitivity obtained at the other eccentricities investigated. Note that the changes in absolute sensitivity occurring with retinal position are at least qualitatively consistent with the distribution of the rods across the retina. Thus sensitivity is greatest at 17°, near the region of maximum rod density (see also Section 2).

Studying the effects of retinal position on the spectral sensitivity of the dark-adapted cone system is much more difficult. The problem is to avoid intrusions from the more sensitive rod system. One solution involves taking advantage of the more rapid rate of dark adaptation of the cone system. (Dark adaptation is discussed in detail in Section 4.) Briefly, the eye is adapted to some intensity of "white" light. The adapting background is then removed, and the recovery of sensitivity over time is monitored. Recovery is at first attributable to the increased sensitivity of the cone system. After several minutes, sensitivity reaches a plateau, representing the dark-adapted sensitivity of the cone system. If, to a first approximation, sensitivity up to the "cone plateau" is uninfluenced by rod activity, then thresholds measured at the cone plateau will reflect the dark-adapted sensitivity of peripheral cones. (See Section 4 for a discussion of this assumption.)

In contrast to the rod system, the relative spectral sensitivity of the cone system does change with eccentricity. Figure 5.15 (from B. Stabell & U. Stabell, 1981) illustrates the sorts of changes that occur. The top six sets of data show the spectral sensitivity of the dark-adapted cone system at the indicated eccentricities. Each set of points is connected by a solid curve. The top set of data is the most sensitive rod spectral sensitivity (17° eccentricity) replotted from Figure 5.14 for comparison. The foveal (0°) cone data resemble the photopic luminosity function. However, relative sensitivity to wavelengths below about 460 nm increases extrafoveally, reaching a maximum around 28° from the fovea (see also Wooten, Fuld, & Spillman, 1975). The enhanced short-wavelength sensitivity is mainly due to two factors. One is the almost complete absence of the short-wavelength-absorbing macular pigment beyond an eccentricity of 6°. The second is the increased number (or sensitivity) of short-wavelength cones outside the central fovea. The change in relative sensitivity constitutes a violation of the invariance assumption underlying the duplicity model of detection. It is important to note that this is a relatively minor variation. Over most of the spectrum (above 520 nm) the cone curves all have the same shape, and we can accept V_λ as the spectral sensitivity of the peripheral retina.

Note also the changes in absolute sensitivity that occur with eccentricity. For wavelengths below 460 nm, sensitivity increases slightly between 0 and 17°. Above 460 nm, sensitivity declines monotonically with distance from the fovea. (These changes in absolute sensitivity are discussed in detail in Section 2.)

1.5.1.4. The Combined System: Predicting Dark-Adapted Spectral Sensitivities. The data of Figures 5.14 and 5.15, along with the duplicity model, can be used with minor modification to predict the dark-adapted spectral sensitivity of the visual system under a variety of conditions. First consider sensitivity in a localized retinal region. Figure 5.16 (from Metz & Brown, 1970) shows dark-adapted spectral sensitivities for a 1°, 16-msec test centered 1.5° from the fovea. The filled and open circles give the results for two observers. The data of Figures 5.14 and 5.15 suggest that at this eccentricity, rod sensitivity

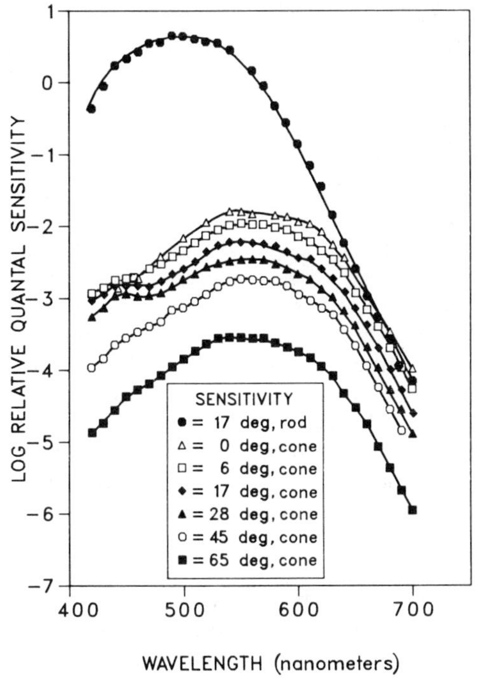

Figure 5.15. Spectral sensitivities for the dark-adapted cone system at various retinal locations. Eccentricity (from 0 to 65° along the temporal retina) is indicated beside each set of data, with each set connected by a solid curve. The (one) observer preadapted for 3 min to a 5 log td "white" (2800° K) field 75° in diameter and centered on the eccentricity at which the tests would be delivered. Spectral sensitivities for the 50 min arc × 100 min arc, 500-msec test were then measured at the cone plateau of the dark adaptation functions. The data show increased relative sensitivity to short wavelengths with increased eccentricity up to 28°. The top set of data replots the most sensitive rod spectral sensitivity (17°) from Figure 5.14. Note that the absolute sensitivity of the foveal cone system exceeds that of the rod system at the longest wavelengths. (From B. Stabell & U. Stabell, Absolute spectral sensitivity at different eccentricities, *Journal of the Optical Society of America*, 1981, *71*. Reprinted with permission.)

will far exceed cone sensitivity at all but the longest wavelengths. The data presented here are consistent with that suggestion. The solid curve fit to the shorter wavelengths is the scotopic luminosity function, V'_λ; the dashed curve is the photopic function, V_λ. The data are fit quite well by an envelope of the two functions. Relative sensitivity in the short and middle wavelengths resembles V'_λ, with V_λ describing the results above 600 nm. The duplicity model fits these data.

We can also predict the shape of the spectral sensitivity curve when the observer is allowed to use the most sensitive part of the retina. Detection under optimal viewing conditions can be measured by using a very large stimulus that encompasses the most sensitive retinal area, or a very small stimulus for which the observer is free to search. To a first approximation, these spectral sensitivities should be an envelope of the most sensitive rod and cone curves. In Figure 5.15, at all but the longest wavelengths, the absolute sensitivity of the rod system exceeds that of the cone system. At wavelengths above about 650 nm, the foveal cones are most sensitive. We would therefore expect the rod system to mediate detection over most of the spectrum, its sensitivity falling below that of the cone system at long wavelengths.

In general, we suspect that dark-adapted functions will follow such an envelope of the rod and cone system sensitivities. Some changes in the relative sensitivities of the two systems would be required for very small, or very brief, stimuli. These fail to take advantage of the greater areal and temporal summation of the rod and give relative advantage to the cones.

1.5.2. Light-Adapted Eye. As ambient illumination increases, the cone system becomes progressively more sensitive relative to the rod system. Over a range of ambient intensities, the variation in the relative rod and cone system sensitivities can be described by the simple duplicity model shown in Figure 5.8. The progression from panel (a) to panel (c) illustrates the effect of increased illumination: a shift from a rod-dominated to a cone-dominated spectral sensitivity. This shift is manifested psychophysically as a change in the shape of the overall spectral sensitivity curve. The region of maximum sensitivity gradually moves from about 500 nm, the peak of the scotopic luminosity function, to 560 nm, the peak of the photopic function. Under these conditions, an observer would be approximately three times more sensitive to 560 nm than to 500 nm light. The shift in the region of greatest sensitivity that occurs with changes in adapting intensity is known as the *Purkyně shift*. Its perceptual consequences are seen as changes in the relative brightnesses of objects of different colors at different times of day (e.g., blue paint appears relatively brighter than red at night).

This section examines the effect of ambient illumination on the spectral sensitivity function. In the laboratory monochromatic lights are presented upon a background or adapting field of different intensities. The section begins with a look at sensitivity within the cone system where, at very high adapting intensities, the duplicity model no longer holds. Adapting levels

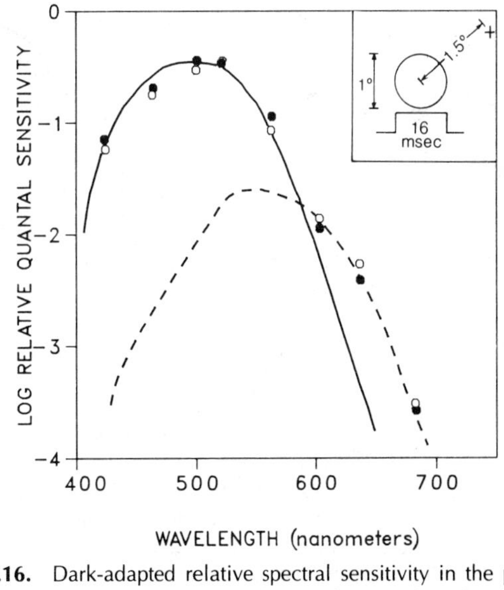

Figure 5.16. Dark-adapted relative spectral sensitivity in the parafovea. The 1°, 16-msec test light was centered 1.5° inferior and nasal to the fixation point along a 45° diagonal (see inset). The filled and open circles are data for two observers; each is positioned arbitrarily along the ordinate to aid comparison. The solid and dashed curves through the data are the scotopic and photopic luminosity functions (V'_λ and V_λ), respectively. Relative sensitivity below 590 nm is described by the scotopic (rod) curve, and above 590 nm by the photopic (cone) curve. Thus the dark-adapted spectral sensitivity in the near periphery is well fitted by an envelope of the rod and cone curves. (From J. W. Metz & J. L. Brown, *Integration of responses between different types of cones and between rods and cones* (Tech. Rep. #11), Kansas State University, Department of Psychology, 1970. Reprinted with permission.)

at which both the rods and cones contribute to detection are then discussed. The changes in relative spectral sensitivity that occur with decreased adapting intensity can be related to changes in the relative brightness of real-world objects at different times of day (e.g., Purkyně's blue and red signposts).

1.5.2.1. Photopic Spectral Sensitivity: Fovea. By restricting stimulation to the fovea, the cone system can be studied more or less in isolation. The effects of adapting intensity on foveal spectral sensitivity are examined below. We are concerned here only with adaptation to lights with a broad spectral distribution as normally encountered outside the laboratory (e.g., daylight; tungsten or fluorescent lights). Monochromatic adaptation is discussed further in Section 3 of this chapter and in Pokorny and Smith, Chapter 8.

Foveal spectral sensitivities obtained at low to moderate adapting intensities (2 log td) resemble the dark-adapted curves of Figure 5.11 (cf. Hurvich & Jameson, 1957; King-Smith & Carden, 1976; Sperling & Harwerth, 1971). The data are similar in shape to the photopic luminosity function, indicating a pure-cone spectral sensitivity.

Relative spectral sensitivity at high intensities depends largely on the size and duration of the test stimulus. Figure 5.17 shows two sets of detection data both obtained on a 4.0 log td adapting field. At the top are the sensitivities obtained with a large (49-min arc-diameter), long-duration (500-msec) test (Finkelstein & Hood, 1984); below are the results for a small (10-min arc-diameter), brief (40-msec) test (from Finkelstein & Hood, 1982). Note that the spectral sensitivities for a small,

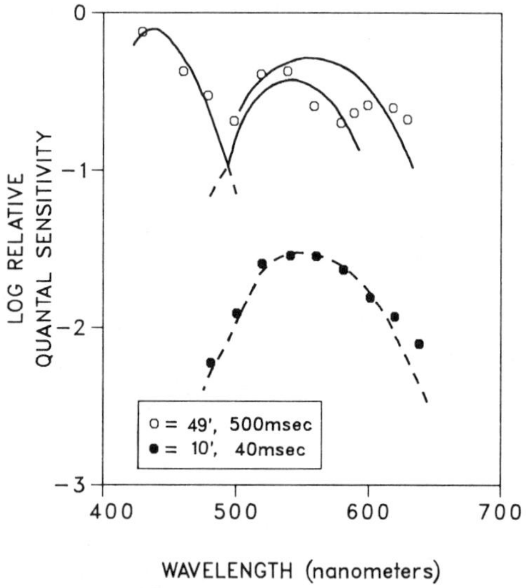

Figure 5.17. Foveal spectral sensitivities measured under intense achromatic adaptation. The stimuli were presented in the center of a 4.0 log td unfiltered tungsten adapting field. Each point is the mean of the thresholds obtained from at least three sessions. Top: spectral sensitivity for a large (49-min arc), long-duration (500-msec) test. The data show narrow peaks around 430, 540, and 600 nm. The solid curves are the three cone absorption spectra positioned for best fit to the data in the short, middle, and long wavelengths, respectively. The two longer-wavelength lobes in the data are narrower than the corresponding receptor absorption spectra, suggesting subtractive interactions between classes of cones. (After Finkelstein & Hood, 1984, Fig. 1.) Bottom: spectral sensitivity for a small (10-min arc), brief (40-msec) test. The data are approximately fitted at all but the longest wavelengths by the broad-band photopic luminosity function (dashed curve). (From M. A. Finkelstein & D. C. Hood, Opponent-colored cells can influence the detection of small, brief lights, *Vision Research, 22*. Copyright 1982 by Pergamon Press, Ltd. Reprinted with permission.)

brief test, like the sensitivities obtained at lower adapting intensities, approximate the photopic function, V_λ (dashed curve). The data are consistent with the duplicity model (but see Hood & Finkelstein, 1983).

The data for the large spot clearly cannot be fit by V_λ. Instead of the single broad peak, we now see narrow peaks around 540 and 600 nm and a third peak in the short wavelengths. The effect of increased adapting intensity is not simply a change in the absolute sensitivity of an invariant cone system as depicted in Figure 5.8. Even a somewhat weaker model that allows for changes with adapting intensity in the relative weights of the three cone classes cannot account for these data. In fact, the data cannot be modeled as a change in the absolute sensitivity of any summation (or envelope) of cone absorption spectra. The short-, middle-, and long-wavelength receptor absorption spectra from Figure 5.4 have been drawn through the data (solid curves). Although the short-wavelength cone sensitivity provides a good fit, the two longer-wavelength sensitivities are much too broad. The narrow and shifted peaks in the data (relative to the receptor absorption spectra) indicate subtractive interactions at some stage between the outputs of the middle- and long-wavelength receptors. Thus adaptation involves changes in sensitivity not only at the receptor stage, but also at a post-receptoral subtractive or "opponent" stage. Data such as those in Figure 5.17 have in recent years been fitted by models that assume an opponent stage (e.g., Guth, Massof, & Benzschawel, 1980; Ingling & Tsou, 1977; Kranda & King-Smith, 1979; Sperling & Harwerth, 1971). (For a detailed discussion of opponent interactions and modern color theory, see Pokorny & Smith, Chapter 8.)

1.5.2.2. Photopic Spectral Sensitivity: Effects of Retinal Position. For moderate levels of light adaptation, the changes in relative sensitivity that occur with eccentricity are analogous to those observed for the dark-adapted cone system. Relative sensitivity to short wavelengths increases extrafoveally up to about 10° (B. V. Graham, Holland, & Sparks, 1975). At high adapting intensities, evidence of opponent mechanisms in detection again emerges. Large, long-duration lights yield spectral sensitivities with narrow peaks around 450, 540, and 600 nm. However, the test size required to produce these narrow peaks increases as eccentricity is increased. Thus at 20° eccentricity, a 4° test is needed to produce a relative spectral sensitivity like that obtained for a 1° foveal test (Kuyk, 1982).

1.5.2.3. Mesopic Spectral Sensitivity: The Combined Systems. Adapting levels intermediate to the rod-dominated scotopic, and cone-dominated photopic, levels are referred to as *mesopic*. If the test lights are large, or if the eye is free to move, then detection at mesopic levels involves both the rod and cone systems. Sensitivity under these conditions is reasonably well described by the duplicity model, as illustrated by the data of Figure 5.18 (from Siegel, Graham, Ripps, & Hsia, 1966). These are spectral sensitivity data obtained 7° extrafoveally at a mesopic adapting intensity. The data are fitted quite well by an envelope of the scotopic and photopic luminosity functions (the solid and dashed curves, respectively). The photopic (cone) function is the more sensitive over most of the spectrum, whereas the scotopic (rod) function describes the data in the short wavelengths. The mesopic data provide a sharp contrast to spectral sensitivities obtained in the periphery of the dark-adapted eye (Figure 5.9). In the absence of any adapting field, relative sensitivity resembles the scotopic curve over the entire spectrum.

The changes in relative sensitivity within the cone system that violate the duplicity model (see Section 1.5.2.1) occur only

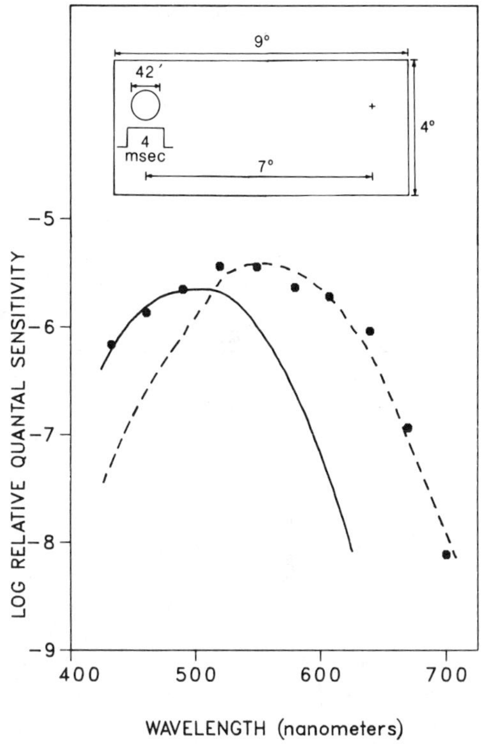

Figure 5.18. Spectral sensitivity measured in the near periphery under mesopic conditions; data for one observer. The tests were presented 7° nasal to the fovea upon a 1.75 cd·m^{-2} "white" (5000° K) adapting field (see inset). They were 42 min arc in diameter and 4 msec in duration. The data are well fitted by an envelope of the scotopic and photopic (i.e., rod system and cone system) luminosity functions (solid and dashed curves, respectively). (From I. M. Siegel, C. H. Graham, H. Ripps, & Y. Hsia, Analysis of photopic and scotopic function in an incomplete achromat, *Journal of the Optical Society of America*, 1966, *56*. Reprinted with permission.)

at photopic intensities, where the rods are no longer contributing to detection. Interactions between the rod and cone systems also violate the model (see Section 4). However, the effects of the interactions on spectral sensitivity are small and are apparent only under conditions of approximately equal rod and cone sensitivity. (When rod and cone sensitivities to a test light are nearly equal, sensitivity is actually slightly greater than their envelope. The increased detectability is due partly to physiological summation between the rod and cone systems (Benimoff, Schneider, & Hood, 1982; Ikeda & Urakubo, 1969). Excitatory interactions between the rod and cone systems clearly serve to increase sensitivity, and the increase is most apparent when the two systems are equally sensitive. Yet even with completely independent systems, there will be some probability "summation." This refers to the added sensitivity that accompanies additions in the number of systems capable of detecting a stimulus on a given trial.)

1.5.3. Other Measurement Procedures. The preceding discussion of spectral sensitivity is based on the results of threshold experiments. Spectral sensitivities are also measured with suprathreshold procedures. These procedures are of practical interest because they provide a measure of the relative effectiveness of lights as they appear outside the laboratory. Sensitivity in these cases is not a measure of the detectability of a light, but a measure, for example, of its relative brightness. The spectral sensitivity curve shows the reciprocal intensity needed to satisfy some brightness criterion.

The two most common ways of obtaining an equal brightness spectrum are via the brightness matching and the minimum flicker procedures. Of these, brightness matching is conceptually the more direct method. The observer adjusts the intensity of a monochromatic test until it matches in brightness a standard of fixed wavelength and intensity. Sensitivity is the reciprocal of the test intensity required for a brightness match. The minimum flicker method involves alternating a test light and a standard at a rate of typically between 10 and 20 Hz. The rate is too rapid for the observer to see alternations in hue; alternations in brightness are seen, however, and are apparent as flicker. The observer's task is to adjust the intensity of the test to minimize the apparent flicker. Sensitivity is the reciprocal of the test intensity that yields minimum flicker.

The spectral sensitivity of the rod system has been measured with both detection and brightness matching procedures. In fact, the scotopic luminosity function is based mainly on brightness matching results. Any procedure used to measure the relative spectral sensitivity of the rod system should yield the same result because the system includes only a single photopigment with an invariant absorption spectrum. Indeed, there is excellent agreement among procedures (cf. Crawford, 1949; Kinney, 1955).

The procedure used is a more important consideration when measuring the spectral sensitivity of the cone system. There are differences in the response properties of the different cone mechanisms, and these differences can substantially affect the results. For example, the short-wavelength mechanism makes little or no contribution to spectral sensitivities obtained with the minimum flicker method (e.g., Eisner & MacLeod, 1980). Flicker sensitivity therefore declines somewhat more rapidly in the short wavelengths than brightness matching or detection sensitivity (e.g., U. Stabell & B. Stabell, 1980; Wagner & Boynton, 1972). The photopic luminosity function is derived largely from flicker data.

1.6. Photometric Measurement

1.6.1. Luminance. We have seen that the visual system is not equally sensitive to lights of all wavelengths. For lights that differ in wavelength, equal numbers of quanta do not imply equal detectability or equal brightness. Neither are the differences in detectability constant under different adapting conditions. Thus simply specifying the amount of electromagnetic energy in a stimulus gives no information about the ability of that stimulus to elicit a visual response. The measurement of quantity of electromagnetic energy is the domain of *radiometry*. A second measurement system has been developed to specify electromagnetic energy in terms of its effectiveness for vision. This is the system of *photometry*. Photometry involves a mathematical conversion from units of *radiant intensity* to *luminous intensity* or units of *luminance*. The conversion is a weighting of a light's radiance by the relative sensitivity of the visual system to that light.

The practical importance of specifying the effectiveness of lights for vision led the CIE to adopt two spectral sensitivity functions for photometric conversions. One function specifies relative sensitivity under scotopic conditions, the other under photopic conditions (see Table 5.1). These are the luminosity functions of Figure 5.7, which are being used in this chapter to represent the spectral sensitivities of the rod and cone systems, respectively. (Note: There is no standard mesopic luminosity function.) The purpose of these standard functions is to enable one to determine the relative effectiveness of any light or mixture of lights. To specify a light in terms of its scotopic or photopic luminance, the radiant energy in the light is weighted by its relative scotopic or photopic luminous efficiency. A light of wavelength λ and radiance I has a scotopic luminance L' of

$$L' = K'_m I_\lambda V'_\lambda \tag{4a}$$

where K' is a constant (defined below) and V'_λ is the light's scotopic relative luminous efficiency. Luminances are by definition additive so that for a source with a continuous spectral distribution:

$$L' = K'_m \int I_\lambda V'_\lambda \, d\lambda \tag{4b}$$

where the limits of the integral are the ends of the visible spectrum. Analogously, for the photopic system, a light has a photopic luminance L of

$$L = K_m I_\lambda V_\lambda \tag{5a}$$

where V_λ is the photopic luminosity coefficient. For a continuous spectrum,

$$L = K_m \int I_\lambda V_\lambda \, d\lambda \; . \tag{5b}$$

From 1948 to 1979, the standard for photometric measurement was defined as the luminance of a blackbody radiator at the temperature of freezing platinum (T = 2042°K). The standard was assigned a photopic luminance of 60 (photopic) cd·m^{-2}; its scotopic luminance was 60 (scotopic) cd·m^{-2}. The values of K_m and K'_m derived from this definition were 680 and 1745 lm·W^{-1}, respectively. In 1979 the candle was redefined as the luminance of a light of 555 nm (in air) at a radiant energy of 1/683 W·sr^{-1} (see Wyszecki & Stiles, 1982 for details). The values of K_m and K'_m are slightly altered: 683 and 1700 lm·W^{-1}, respectively.

1.6.2. Retinal Illuminance: The Troland. The intensity of light incident on the cornea of the eye is not the same as the intensity at the retina. The amount of light arriving at the retina depends on a number of factors, among them the size of the pupil. The larger the pupil, the more light enters the eye. A unit of retinal illuminance, the troland (td), is based on the fact that the light passing into the eye is proportional to the area of the pupil. The troland is defined as the retinal stimulation provided by a source of 1 cd·m^{-2} viewed through a pupil of 1 mm^2: the troland value for the stimulus is given by

$$\text{td} = L\,(\text{cd·m}^{-2}) \times A\,(\text{mm}^2) \; . \tag{6}$$

Two categories of trolands are specified, photopic trolands based on V_λ and scotopic trolands based on V'_λ. Luminances are usually expressed in photopic terms, but the conversion to scotopic units is quite simple. Recall that

$$L \text{ (photopic)} = K_m I_\lambda V_\lambda$$

$$L' \text{ (scotopic)} = K'_m I_\lambda V'_\lambda$$

where K_m = 683 and K'_m = 1700. Then

$$\frac{L'}{L} = \frac{1700 I_\lambda V'_\lambda}{683 I_\lambda V_\lambda}$$

or

$$L' = 2.49 \frac{V'_\lambda}{V_\lambda} L \; .$$

Wyszecki and Stiles (1982, p. 104) provide a table for converting from photopic to scotopic trolands. In this chapter, whenever we express intensity in trolands, we shall be referring to photopic trolands. When pupil size is reported, we shall specify intensities of nonmonochromatic lights in terms of photopic trolands.

Although the troland takes pupil size into account, it neglects other variables that influence the effectiveness of the light reaching the retina. First, the measure implies that quanta entering all parts of the pupil are equally effective. However, it has been shown for the cones that luminous efficiency is greater for quanta entering the center of the pupil than entering the periphery. This is the Stiles-Crawford effect. Second, there are extensive absorption and scattering of light by the ocular media. Much of the light that enters the pupil never reaches the retina. In addition, pre-retinal light loss is not uniform across the spectrum but is greater at shorter wavelengths.

Table 5.2 shows the relation between luminance and retinal illuminance for situations in which pupil size is free to vary. Row 1, taken from Table 5.1, gives luminance values. The second row shows the average pupil size corresponding to the above intensities for full field illumination; pupil size is larger for small intense fields. In row 3, the measures of luminance and pupil size have been used to obtain retinal illuminance in trolands. The bottom two lines are again replotted from Table 5.1 and show the relation between the above photometric quantities and some familiar stimuli and visual functions (rows 4 and 5, respectively).

2. ABSOLUTE SENSITIVITY

The visual system reaches its maximum sensitivity after 30 or more min in the dark (see Section 4). *Absolute* sensitivity refers to the sensitivity of the dark-adapted eye. The detectability of a *change* of intensity (e.g., the detectability of a light presented upon a background) is a measure of *incremental* sensitivity and is discussed in Section 3. This section consists of two major parts. The first examines the influence on absolute sensitivity of several parameters of stimulation, specifically test size, duration, and retinal location. Test wavelength also has a profound influence on measures of sensitivity; this parameter is the topic of Section 2.1. Section 2.2 examines the absolute sensitivity of the rod and cone systems under optimal conditions. The amount of light needed to produce a visual sensation is considered.

2.1. Spatial and Temporal Factors

The visual system sums the effects of light over space and time. This section examines the relation between the size and duration of a stimulus and visual sensitivity. When lights are small and brief, the visual system shows complete summation. Lights of equal energy (or equal numbers of quanta) are equally detectable. Beyond a certain area and duration, there is no further summation. Figure 5.19 illustrates the general relationship. The

Table 5.2. The Relation between Luminance and Retinal Illuminance

Luminance (log cd·m^{-2})	−6	−4	−2	0	2	4	6	8
Pupil diameter (mm)	7.1	6.6	5.5	4.0	2.4	2.0	2.0	2.0
Retinal illuminance (log td)	−4.4	−2.5	−.62	1.1	2.6	4.5	6.5	8.5

Luminance of white paper in: Starlight — Moonlight — Indoor lighting — Sunlight

Visual function: Scotopic — Mesopic — Photopic

Absolute threshold — Cone threshold — Rod saturation begins — Best acuity — Damage possible

No color vision, Poor acuity — Good color vision, Best acuity

Note: Row 1 expresses the operating range of the visual system in units of log luminance (cd·m^{-2}). The second row shows the decrease in diameter of the natural pupil with increases in ambient light levels. In row 3, the values of luminance and pupil size have been used to obtain retinal illuminance in trolands: td = L (cd·m^{-2}) × A (mm^2). Rows 4 and 5 are redrawn from Table 5.1.

figure represents a hypothetical threshold versus area or threshold versus duration function.

Consider first the relation between threshold intensity and stimulus size in Figure 5.19(a). In this case, the abscissa is log (area), the ordinate log (threshold intensity). Larger tests require less light to be detected. For small stimuli, there is an inverse relation between area and the intensity required for detection; the data fall along a line of slope −1.0. Specifically,

$$\log I = -\log A + \log k_A \quad (7a)$$

$$I = \frac{k_A}{A} \quad \text{or} \quad I \times A = k_A \quad (7b)$$

where I = intensity in quanta per unit retinal area per unit time, A = area, and k_A is a constant. The relationship between area and total quantal flux ($I \times A$) at threshold is shown in Figure 5.19(b). The data for small areas follow a line of zero slope. Visual effectiveness is determined by the total number of quanta regardless of their spatial distribution. The complete summation of quanta over space as specified in Eq. (7) is known as Ricco's law of areal summation (Ricco, 1877).

For large lights, threshold intensity is independent of the area of the test, and the data of Figure 5.19(a) are fit by a horizontal line. In other words, increases in area are accompanied by a proportional increase in the number of quanta at threshold. This is indicated in Figure 5.19(b) by the slope of 1.0.

The relationship between stimulus duration and threshold is similar to the area-threshold relationship. In this case, the abscissas in Figure 5.19(a) and (b) indicates log (stimulus duration). With brief lights, the visual system shows complete temporal summation:

$$\log I = -\log t + \log k_t \quad (8a)$$

$$I = \frac{K_t}{t} \quad \text{or} \quad I \times t = k_t \quad (8b)$$

where t = duration and k is a constant. This relationship, which is known as Bloch's law (Bloch, 1885), is actually an extension of the Bunsen-Roscoe law of photochemistry. When applied to human vision, it states that equal energies or equal numbers of quanta are equally detectable. With long-duration lights there is no summation, and equal *intensities* are equally detectable.

In actuality, whether spatial or temporal summation is being examined, data are rarely as neat as the solid curves in Figure 5.19. One seldom observes an abrupt shift from complete summation to no summation. Instead there is usually a region of partial summation as indicated by the dashed curves in Figure 5.19(a) and (b). Within this region, increases in area (or duration) require decreased intensity for a constant visual effect, but that decrease is less than expected from total summation of energy. The point at which data begin to deviate from complete spatial summation is known as the *critical area* or *Ricco area.* The point at which data begin to deviate from complete temporal summation is known as the *critical duration.* Some psychophysicists have proposed that the intermediate regions follow a slope of −0.5 ($I \propto A^{-1/2}, I \propto t^{-1/2}$). These relationships have theoretical importance and are known as Piper's law (Piper, 1903) in the spatial domain and the inverse-square law (van der Velden, 1944) in the temporal domain. However, these "laws" apply under very restricted conditions, and many maintain that the data are too irregular to be simply fitted by three straight lines.

The following discussion examines spatial and temporal summation in the rod and cone systems. We look at the effects on summation of retinal eccentricity and, in the cone system, wavelength. Further, we see that areal summation depends on stimulus duration and temporal summation on stimulus size. Summation is typically studied with either of two basic para-

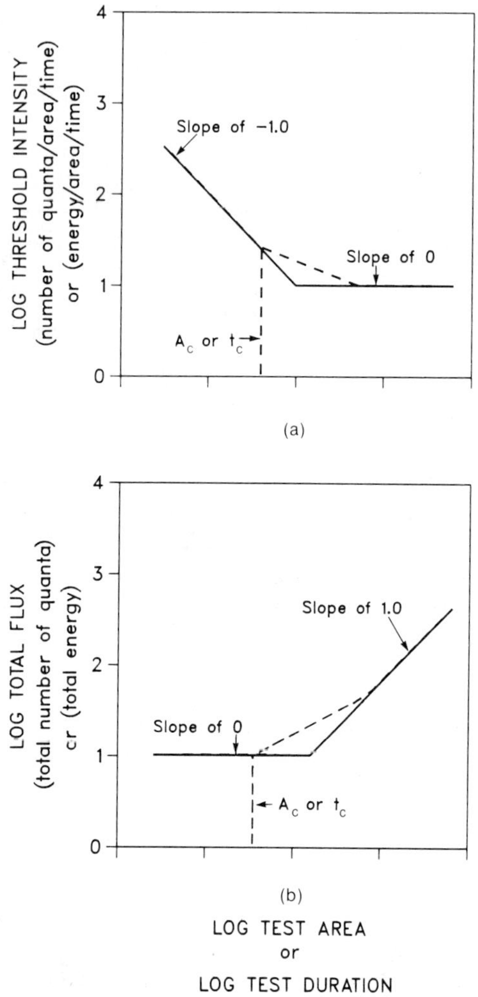

Figure 5.19. Schematic representation of spatial and temporal summation. (a) Log (threshold intensity) as a function of the log (area) or log (duration) of a light. For small areas and short durations, there is complete summation of energy over space and time. That is, $I \times A = k_A$ (Ricco's law) and $I \times t = k_t$ (Bloch's law). Threshold intensity varies inversely with changes in either parameter, and the data follow a slope of −1.0. With very large areas and long durations, further increases in size and duration produce no further summation, and threshold intensity is constant (slope of 0.0). Between the regions of complete and no summation is a region of partial summation. Here increasing size or duration improves sensitivity, but the improvement is less than expected from total energy integration. The point at which the data begin to deviate from complete summation is known as the critical area, or Ricco's area, in the spatial domain and the critical duration in the temporal domain (A_c and t_c, respectively). (b) The function in panel (a) replotted in terms of the total energy required at threshold. Note the regions of complete summation (slope of 0.0), no summation (slope of 1.0), and partial summation (intermediate region).

digms. The more common involves measuring thresholds for a single circular test flash of varying area or duration. Another approach uses two test lights separated over space and/or time. The threshold for detecting the pair is measured as a function of the separation between the two lights. We deal predominantly with data from experiments employing single lights but reference two-spot data where appropriate. In general, spatial summation is greater with a single uniform test spot, whereas temporal summation is less affected by the stimulus configuration.

2.1.1. Rod System

2.1.1.1. Spatial Summation. Figure 5.20 shows the data of a prototypical study of spatial summation in the rod system (from C. H. Graham & Bartlett, 1939). The stimulus parameters (see inset) were chosen to maximize rod system sensitivity relative to the cone system. A short-wavelength test was presented to a region of maximum rod sensitivity, 15° nasal to the fovea in the dark-adapted eye. The triangles and circles are the results for two observers. The lines through each set of data have slopes of −1.0. If the data fall on the line, complete spatial summation is taking place; a constant number of quanta are required at threshold.

The observer's data given by the triangles show complete summation for areas up to about .55 log degree^2 (diameter 2.1°). Larger stimuli produce very little improvement in sensitivity. The data given by the circles indicate complete summation up to 0.0 log degree^2 (diameter 1.1°) but substantial improvement with increases in diameter up to 2.1°. The general finding is that the area of complete summation extends to between 30 min arc and 1°. (See Hallett, 1963 for references. Hallett reports a few studies in which critical area is only 10–20 min arc and attributes the difference to the existence of two classes of observers.)

(a) Effect of Eccentricity. Within the rod system, spatial summation increases with retinal eccentricity. Figure 5.21 (from Scholtes & Bouman, 1977) shows the total energy needed to detect tests of four sizes at different retinal eccentricities. Ignore temporarily the small (7 min arc) target data. At 4° eccentricity, the energy required at threshold increases with stimulus size. However, by 39° eccentricity, the three energy thresholds are nearly equal. That is, at the most peripheral location, there is complete summation up to a diameter of at least 4.7°. Based on a review of the literature, Hallett (1963) concluded that, in general, spatial summation increases with eccentricity. Critical diameters increase from about 0.5° at 5° from the fovea to 2° for lights 35° from the fovea.

The small-spot data of Figure 5.21 are inconsistent with the model of spatial summation represented by Figure 5.19. At eccentricities of 15° and beyond, the 7-min arc test requires

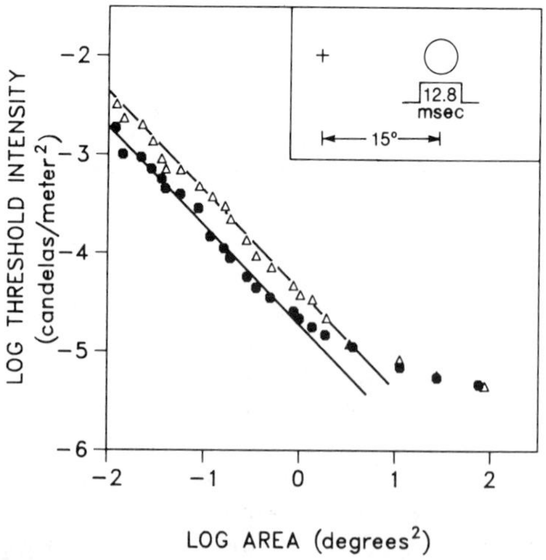

Figure 5.20. Spatial summation in the dark-adapted rod system. The figure shows log (threshold intensity) as a function of the log (area) of a 12.8-msec, 445 nm (Wratten #76) test. The test flashes were presented 15° nasal to the fovea. Four complete sets of data were obtained for each observer, and the results for two observers are given by the triangles and circles. The lines through each set of results have slopes of −1.0 and signify complete energy summation. The data show complete summation for diameters up to 1–2°. (From Graham & Bartlett, 1939, Table II.)

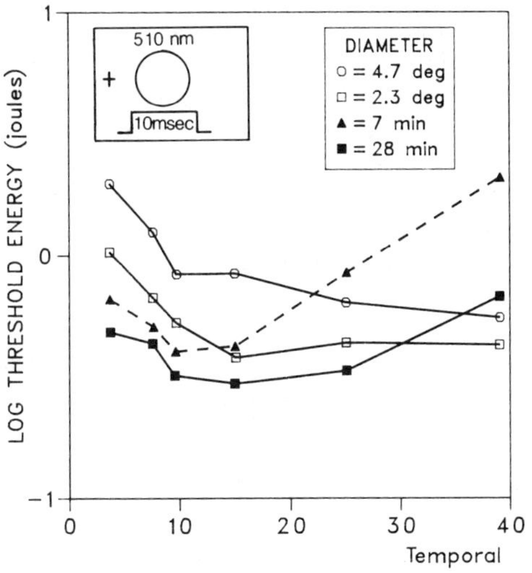

Figure 5.21. Effect of retinal eccentricity on rod system spatial summation. The figure shows the variation in log (threshold energy) with eccentricity for tests of four diameters: 7 min arc (triangles); 28 min arc (filled squares); 2.3° (open squares); and 4.7° (circles). Test duration was 10 msec, test wavelength 510 nm. Spatial summation improves with distance from the fovea. Between 4 and 25° extrafoveally, critical diameter is less than 2.3°; increasing test size from 28 min arc to 2.3° increases the energy required for detection. The differences in energy requirements for the different test diameters diminish with increased eccentricity until, by 39° extrafoveally, the rod system shows complete summation for diameters up to at least 4.7°. The 7-min arc diameter data present problems for explanations of spatial summation based on a simple addition of energy (quanta). At the more peripheral retinal locations, more quanta are required when they are compressed into 7 min arc than when they are spread out over more than 2°. (From A. M. Scholtes & M. A. Bouman, Psychophysical experiments on spatial summation at threshold level of the human peripheral retina, *Vision Research, 17*. Copyright 1977 by Pergamon Press, Ltd. Reprinted with permission.)

more total energy than larger tests. More quanta are required for detection when they are compressed into 7 min arc than when they are spread out over more than 2°. Also at odds with the model of Figure 5.19 are the data of Sakitt (1971). She found higher thresholds for two square tests separated by 3.4–56 min arc than for single test squares subtending the same total area. Scholtes and Bouman offer one possible explanation of both their and Sakitt's results. They propose that detection requires the activation of a minimum number of receptors, not simply the absorption of a minimum number of quanta. Whatever the appropriate explanation of spatial summation, the above studies demonstrate that it must involve more than a simple addition of quanta, even within Ricco's area.

(b) EFFECT OF STIMULUS DURATION. Spatial summation also varies with stimulus duration and tends to be greater for briefer stimuli. Figure 5.22 (from Barlow, 1958a) compares threshold versus area curves for two test durations. The short-wavelength test was centered 6.5° extrafoveally (see inset). Each set of data has been fitted by a line of slope −1.0. The 8.5-msec test produces complete summation up to diameters of almost 1° (about −.15 log degree^2). Increasing test duration to 930 msec decreases the critical diameter to about 32 min arc (−.65 log degree^2). Note also that the brief test elicits a greater range of partial summation, with thresholds continuing to fall fairly rapidly for all test sizes examined.

2.1.1.2. Temporal Summation. Figure 5.23(a) shows data from a study by C. H. Graham and Margaria (1935) of temporal summation within the rod system. Log (threshold intensity) is plotted against log (test duration) for four test sizes; the tests were presented 15° extrafoveally (see inset). The lines fitted to each set of data have slopes of −1.0. Consider first the small-spot (2 min arc) data. Temporal summation is complete (the data obey Bloch's law) for durations up to about 100 msec. Threshold intensity then begins to asymptote with further increases in duration.

Just as increasing stimulus duration has been shown to decrease spatial summation (Fig. 5.22), the data of C. H. Graham and Margaria are often cited as evidence that increasing stimulus size affects temporal summation. Although their data in Figure 5.23(a) do show a clear negative relationship between area and critical duration, *total* temporal summation is independent of stimulus size. As diameter is increased from 2 min arc to 3°, critical duration falls about 1 log unit. There is, however, substantially more partial summation for the larger tests. Consequently, increasing duration from 1 to 500 msec produces the same improvement in sensitivity for a 3° test as for a 2-min arc test (about 2 log units).

Baumgardt and Hillman (1961) also found that total improvement in sensitivity due to duration was independent of area. Moreover, they did not find an effect of stimulus size on the critical duration. Figure 5.23(b) shows data obtained for tests of three sizes presented 20° extrafoveally. Each plot shows the data for two observers; all data are fitted at short durations with lines of slope −1.0. The small-spot data resemble those of Figure 5.23(a). Bloch's law is obeyed for durations up to 100 msec, and there is substantial summation up to at least 1 sec. Unlike the data of Figure 5.23(a), increases in diameter up to 7.8° produce no change in the shape of the curves. From an

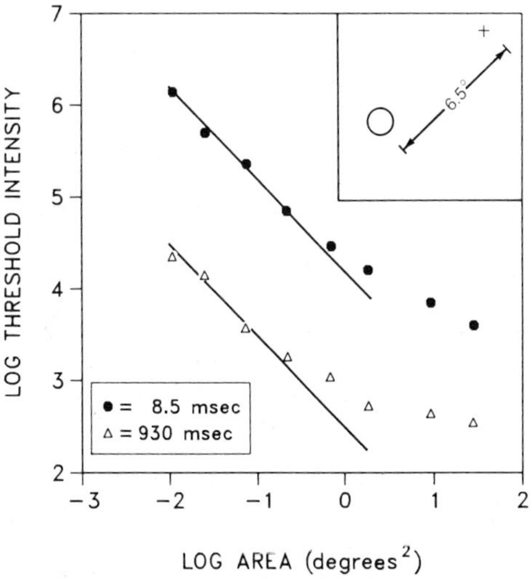

Figure 5.22. Effect of stimulus duration on rod system spatial summation. The figure shows the relationship between log area and log threshold for tests of two durations: 8.5 msec (circles) and 930 msec (triangles). Thresholds are expressed as number of quanta (507 nm) per second per square degree. The 497 nm (Ilford 603) tests were delivered 6.5° from the fovea in the inferior nasal quadrant. Each point is the mean of two threshold measures obtained in a single session. The solid lines through each set of points have slopes of −1.0 and delineate the areas over which complete energy summation occurs. Increasing the test duration decreases the critical area approximately 0.5 log unit from −0.15 log degree^2 (diameter 1°) to −0.65 log degree^2 (diameter 32 min arc). (From H. B. Barlow, Temporal and spatial summation in human vision at different background intensities, *Journal of Physiology* (London), 1958, *141*. Reprinted with permission.)

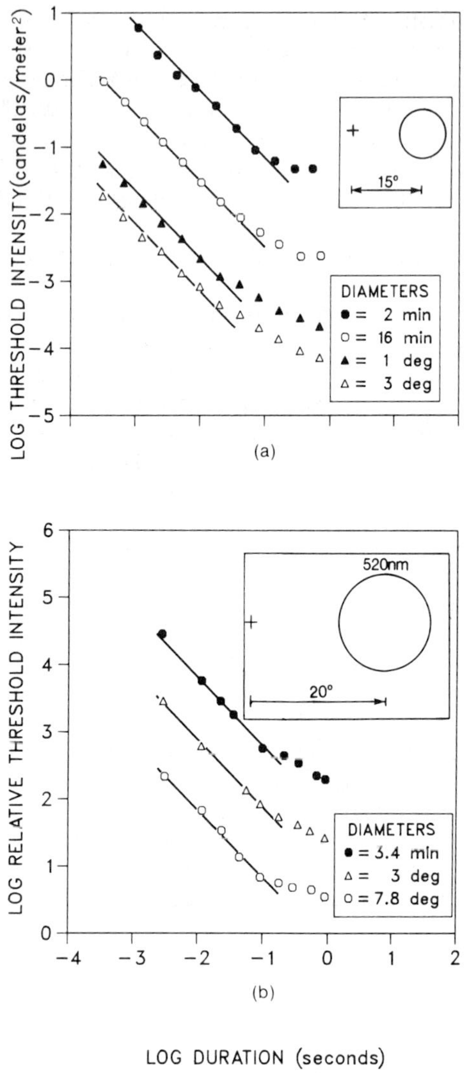

Figure 5.23. The effect of test size on rod system temporal summation. The figure shows the relation between log threshold intensity and log duration for tests of various diameters. The lines of slope −1.0 through each set of data delineate the durations over which complete energy integration occurs. (a) Data for test diameters of 2 min arc (filled circles), 16 min arc (open circles), 1° (filled triangles), and 3° (open triangles). The "white" (unfiltered tungsten) light was presented 15° nasal to the fovea. As test size is increased, the critical duration decreases, falling 1 log unit (from 100 to 10 msec) between 10 min arc and 3°. The total amount of temporal summation is unaffected by the changes in size because partial summation increases with stimulus area. (From Graham & Margaria, 1935, Table I.) (b) Data for three test diameters: 3.4 min arc (filled circles), 3° (triangles), and 7.8° (open circles). The test was 520 nm and was presented 20° from the point of fixation. The curves are positioned arbitrarily along the log threshold intensity ordinate; the units of threshold are unspecified by the authors. All three curves have the same shape, indicating no effect of area on temporal summation. (After Baumgardt & Hillman, 1961, Fig. 2.)

engineering standpoint, the exact shape of the threshold versus duration function is unimportant. What is important is that the duration is sufficient to take full advantage of the system's summing abilities, both complete and partial.

Barlow (1958a) reported data that, in contrast to the above studies, suggest a negative relationship between size and total temporal summation. Like Baumgardt and Hillman, he measured critical durations of approximately 100 msec for tests of both 7 min arc and 6°. Unlike Baumgardt and Hillman (and C. H. Graham & Margaria), he found almost no partial summation with the large test. Thresholds between 10 msec and 1 sec fell approximately 1.8 log units with the 7-min arc test and only 1.1 log units with the 6° test.

Barlow's finding of reduced summation for large tests may be due to the fact that the stimuli were encroaching on the fovea. His measurements were made only 6.5° extrafoveally with tests as large as 6° in diameter. In studying temporal summation at long test durations, it is difficult to be certain at any retinal location that a single detection mechanism has been isolated. There may be contributions from multiple mechanisms integrated over time.

Several studies suggest that Bloch's law may be a more accurate description of temporal summation at short durations than Ricco's law is for spatial summation with small tests. First, in contrast to the Scholtes and Bouman (1977) data (Figure 5.21), temporal summation shows no lower limit (see Baumgardt, 1972 for references). Second, within the time over which Bloch's law holds, threshold is in fact independent of the distribution of quanta over time; multiple pulses are as detectable as a single pulse (e.g., Davy, 1952; Long, 1951). These data are consistent with a single detection mechanism that linearly sums the effects of quanta over time; the spatial data require a more complicated detection hypothesis (see Section 2.1.1.1).

Because there is a single rod pigment, the wavelength of the stimulus does not affect temporal (or spatial) summation within the rod system. This is illustrated for the temporal domain by the data of Figure 5.24(a)–(c) (from Sperling & Jolliffe, 1965). Each panel shows threshold versus duration curves for tests of three sizes and two wavelengths: 450 nm (filled circles) and 650 nm (open circles). The two wavelengths produce no systematic differences in temporal summation. Conversely, as the following section shows, there is a clear effect of wavelength on cone system temporal summation.

2.1.2. Cone System: Fovea

2.1.2.1. Temporal Summation: Effect of Area. Karn (1936) examined the effects of test size on temporal summation in the dark-adapted fovea. Data for four test sizes are presented in Figure 5.25(a)–(c). Each panel shows the data for one observer. The solid lines through the points have slopes of −1.0. The results for all three observers are quite similar. Consider first the 1-min arc-diameter data. Critical duration approximates that obtained for the rod system and falls between 100 and 200 msec. Further increases in duration produce little improvement in sensitivity.

Increasing test size decreases the critical duration. For lights 20 min arc in diameter, Bloch's law fails for durations longer than 50 msec. However, there is more partial summation than with the smaller test lights; increasing the duration from 50 to 500 msec decreases threshold intensity by more than a factor of 2. The finding of reduced critical duration and more shallow threshold versus duration functions with larger tests is qualitatively similar to the Graham and Margaria data for the rod system.

Sperling and Jolliffe (1965), using monochromatic stimuli, also found shorter critical durations for larger tests. Figure 5.26(a)–(c) shows data for three observers and test diameters of 4.5 min arc and 45 min arc. Each panel presents data for test wavelengths of 450 nm (filled circles) and 650 nm (open circles); the results for both wavelengths are pinned at log (threshold) = 2.55. As in Karn's study, the small-spot data obey Bloch's law up to 100–200 msec, the large-spot data up to only 50 msec.

2.1.2.2. ***Temporal Summation: Effect of Wavelength.*** The 45-min arc-test data of Figure 5.26 also reveal an influence of wavelength on temporal summation in the fovea. Increasing the duration of the test improves sensitivity more when the test is 450 nm than when it is 650 nm. The 4.5-min arc data show no such wavelength effect. These findings can be understood from other psychophysical data that suggest that (1) the central fovea lacks short-wavelength cones (see Section 1) and (2) the short-wavelength cone system shows longer integration times than the two longer wavelength cone systems (see Boynton, 1979 for discussion and references). Thus as the 450 nm test is enlarged, it encroaches on areas of greater short-wavelength cone sensitivity and increases temporal summation.

We might expect a large, broadband (e.g., "white") foveal test, which stimulates multiple cone mechanisms, to produce a relatively shallow threshold versus duration curve. The curve would approximate the envelope of the short- and longer-wavelength cone threshold versus duration functions. The effect of wavelength on cone system temporal summation underscores the problem of intrusion from multiple mechanisms with large test spots.

2.1.2.3. ***Spatial Summation.*** Unlike the rod system, the cone system is very poor at summing the effects of quanta over space. Figure 5.27 (from C. H. Graham & Bartlett, 1939) shows areal summation as measured for two observers in the dark-adapted fovea. Note the very small Ricco areas (or Ricco diameters) indicated by these data; critical diameters are approximately 6 min arc.

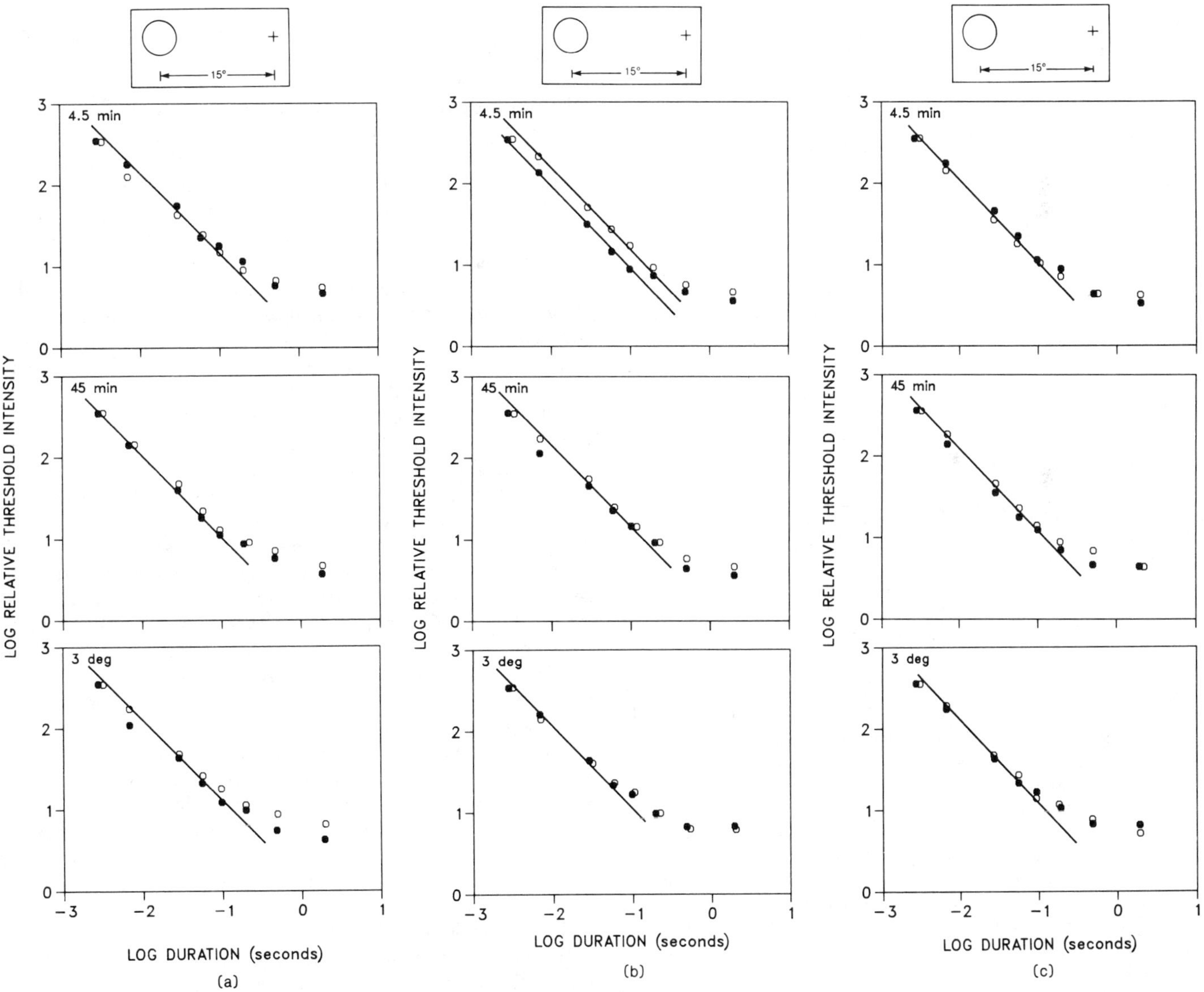

Figure 5.24. The effect of wavelength on rod system temporal summation. Threshold versus duration curves were measured 15° nasal to the fovea for tests of 450 nm (filled circles) and 650 nm (open circles). Each panel shows the data for one observer and three test sizes, 4.5 min arc, 45 min arc, and 3°. The results for the two wavelengths are translated vertically and pinned at log relative threshold intensity = 2.55; the units for the ordinate are unspecified by the authors. The two test wavelengths produce no systematic differences in temporal summation. (From Sperling & Jolliffe, 1965, Table II.)

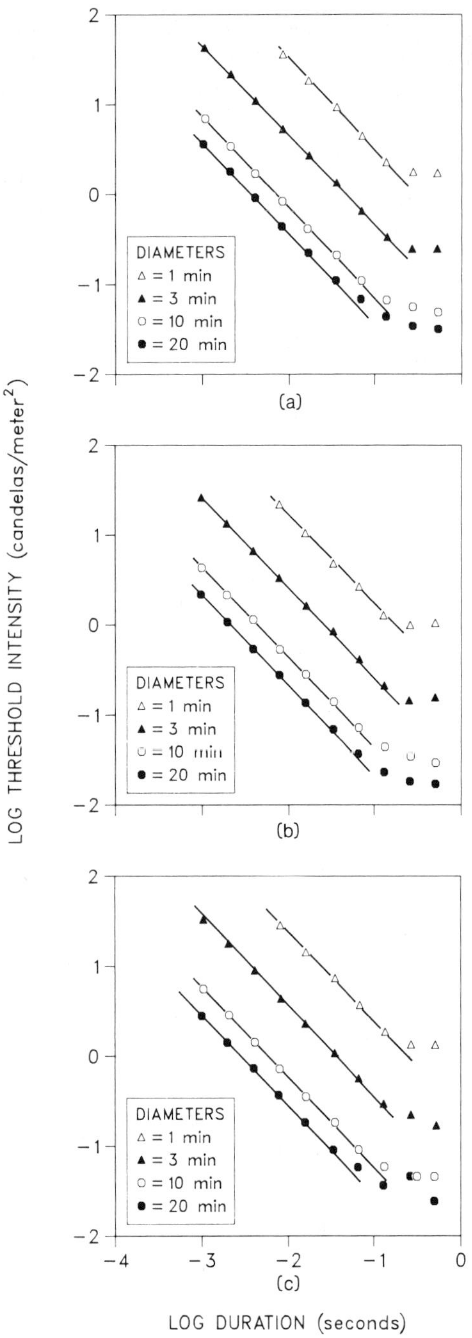

Figure 5.25. The effect of test size on temporal summation in the dark-adapted fovea. The relation between log (threshold intensity) and log (duration) is shown for tests of four diameters: 1 min arc (open triangles), 3 min arc (filled triangles), 10 min arc (open circles), 20 min arc (filled circles). Each panel shows the data for one observer. The lines of slope −1.0 indicate the range of durations over which complete summation holds. For all observers, critical duration decreases with increased test size. Deviations from Bloch's law begin between 100 and 200 msec with the 1-min arc test and around 50 msec with the 20-min arc test. Partial summation, however, increases with stimulus size, producing a shallower threshold versus duration function. (From Karn, 1936, Table I.)

The finding of little spatial integration in the fovea is not surprising given that the region is designed for maximum spatial discrimination. In fact, estimates of Ricco's area for the fovea are typically so small (between 2 and 8 min arc; see Baumgardt, 1972; Brindley, 1970 for references) that the existence of a true spatial summation by the foveal retina has been questioned (e.g., Brindley, 1970). It is possible that the apparent summation is simply a manifestation of optical blur. If stimuli are sufficiently small (several minutes of arc), Ricco's law must hold because further decreases in the size of the physical stimulus do not decrease the size of the retinal image.

There is also the possibility, in attempting to measure spatial summation in the fovea, of confounding the degree of summation with the effect of retinal eccentricity. The proportion of rods to cones increases sharply within several degrees of the fovea. What may appear to be spatial summation within the dark-adapted cone system may actually be the progressive intrusion of the more sensitive rod system. Finally, as in the rod system, the foveal data suggest that summation depends not only on the size of the test, but also on its spatial configuration (cf. R. H. Brown & Niven, 1944; Cohn & Lasley, 1975; Lamar, Hecht, Shlaer, & Hendley, 1947).

2.2. Sensitivity and Eccentricity

The preceding discussion dealt with the influence on absolute sensitivity of three stimulus parameters: wavelength, size, and duration. Also important is the retinal location to which the stimulus is delivered. This section examines the effect of retinal eccentricity on absolute sensitivity. Changes in sensitivity will be considered in the context of concurrent changes in the proportions, and absolute numbers, of rods and cones.

It is crucial in measuring sensitivity as a function of eccentricity to ensure that a light is indeed being detected by mechanisms in the region of interest and not by the mechanisms of more sensitive retinal regions. For this reason, the test light should be relatively small and brief, and fixation must be carefully controlled. When these conditions are met, detection in the completely dark-adapted eye is served by the cone system in the fovea and by the rod system outside the fovea.

The contributions of the two systems to detection are evident in the data of Figure 5.28 (from Crozier & Holway, 1939). Detection thresholds were measured along the horizontal meridian from 10° outside the fovea in the nasal retina to 32° temporal. Data for three observers are shown.

Notice the sharp increase in sensitivity as the test is moved in either direction from the fovea. Beyond about 4° eccentricity, sensitivity increases more gradually, reaching a maximum between 10 and 20°. (Hence it is observed that a dim light in the dark, for example, a dim star, may be more easily detected by looking away from it than directly at it; see Section 2.3.1.3.) With further increases in eccentricity, sensitivity remained relatively constant. Although the shapes of the sensitivity versus eccentricity curves are similar among observers, there are sizable differences in absolute sensitivity, as much as a log unit in the peripheral retina (note squares and triangles in Figure 5.28).

One issue that remains unresolved is whether the variations in absolute sensitivity with eccentricity are accounted for by variations in rod density. Data such as Crozier and Holway's are sometimes cited as refuting a simple link between sensitivity and receptor density, because they do not show a sharp peak in the region of maximum rod density (around 16° in the temporal retina). However, if we plot rod densities on a logarithmic scale, the receptor distribution looks much like the threshold data; density between 16 and 30° temporal falls only 0.13 log unit. The solid curves through each set of data in Figure 5.28 show log (rod density) replotted from Figure 5.3. The curves are positioned to coincide with the threshold data in the region of maximum rod density. In general, the rod curves provide a good fit to the behavioral data for eccentricities beyond about 5°.

The fit is not perfect even beyond this region, but the largest deviations occur near the fovea. Sensitivity toward the fovea drops much more rapidly than the corresponding rod count.

A more gradual decline in sensitivity toward the fovea can be seen in the data of Riopelle and Bevan (1953). They measured sensitivity versus eccentricity functions for eight retinal meridia. Figure 5.29 shows the results for three meridia. The data are the averages of the thresholds obtained for eight relatively inexperienced observers.

The shapes of the threshold functions are similar across meridia. As the test is moved into the periphery, sensitivity increases, reaching a maximum between 12 and 22° from the fovea. Beyond 32° (the most extreme eccentricity in Crozier & Holway's study), sensitivity again begins to decline. Of the eight meridia examined, the horizontal (filled circles) showed the greatest sensitivity, particularly along the temporal retina. Sensitivity was lowest in the inferior retina. [Threshold out to 56° eccentricity remains lower than the foveal threshold. The values plotted in Figure 5.29 must be corrected for the decrease in apparent pupil size produced by increasingly oblique angles of view. The changes in pupil area have been systematically examined by Spring and Stiles (1948). Their study looked only at pupils along the horizontal meridian, but to a first approximation, the corrections can be applied to other meridia. The decrease in area is less than 0.10 log unit within 40° of the fovea. At 48°, effective pupil area is roughly 0.15 log unit less than the effective area with central fixation; at 56°, the correction is approximately 0.20 log unit.]

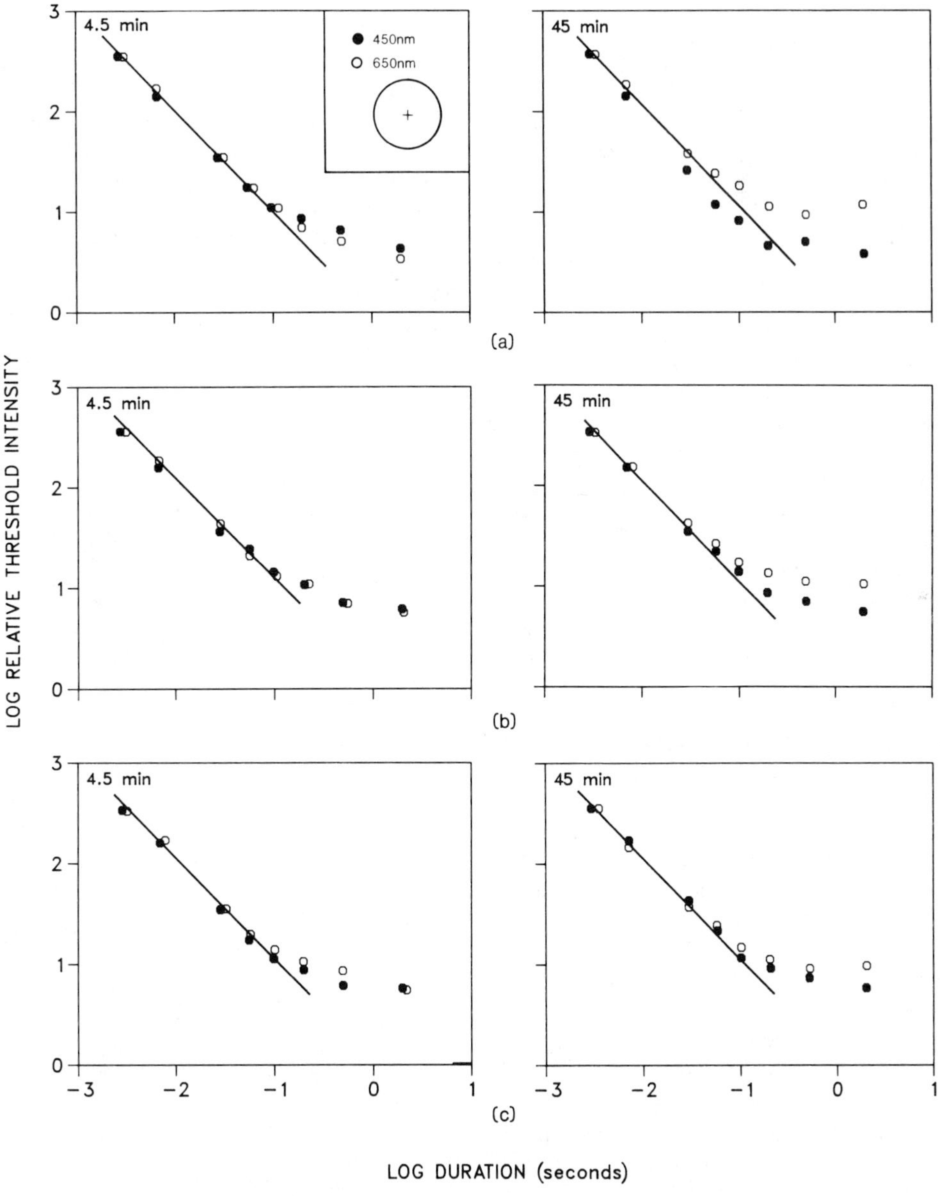

Figure 5.26. The effect of wavelength on temporal summation in the dark-adapted fovea. Threshold versus duration curves were measured for tests of 450 nm (filled circles) and 650 nm (open circles). Each panel shows the data for one observer and two test diameters, 4.5 and 45 min arc. The results for both wavelengths are pinned at log relative threshold intensity = 2.55 to aid comparison; the threshold units are unspecified by the authors. With small spots, temporal summation is independent of wavelength. Increasing test size decreases summation only for the 650 nm test. The advantage acquired by the 450 nm test is that the larger stimulus encroaches on areas of increasing short-wavelength cone sensitivity and hence longer summation times. (From Sperling & Jolliffe, 1965, Table I.)

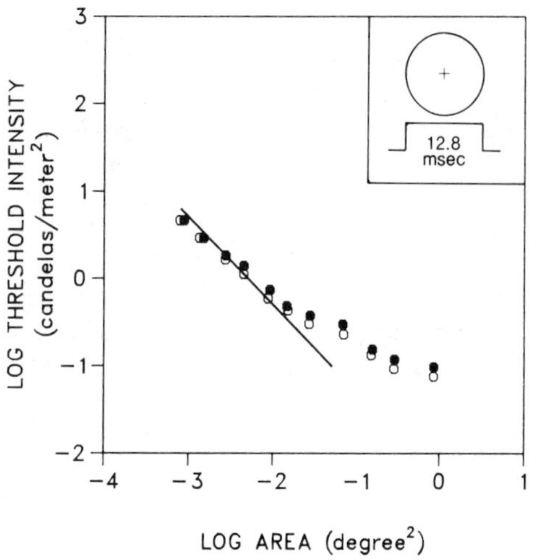

Figure 5.27. Spatial summation in the dark-adapted fovea. Threshold versus area curves were measured for a 12.8-msec, 680 nm (Wratten 70) test. The observers viewed the stimuli through a dark aperture 1.5° in diameter located in the center of a dimly illuminated (.06 cd·m^{-2}) "white" cardboard screen. Data for two observers are given by the open and filled circles. The line of slope −1.0 delineates the very small area over which complete summation occurs: approximately −2.0 log degree^2 (diameter 6–7 min arc). (From Graham & Bartlett, 1939, Table I.)

The solid curve through the data gives log (number of rods) versus eccentricity for the horizontal meridian (the only meridian for which Osterberg made a complete receptor count). Like detection sensitivity, the number of rods increases steadily to a maximum and then slowly falls. The maximum is located about 20° from the fovea in the nasal retina and 16° in the temporal. Although the threshold and receptor density data are qualitatively similar, the correspondence between the two is imperfect. The deviations occur because of the disproportionately high sensitivity of the temporal and superior retinas relative to the nasal and inferior retinas, respectively.

2.3. Minimum Absolute Threshold: Rod and Cone Systems

How sensitive is the visual system? The answer to this question depends on whether it refers to how little light *intensity* is required for detection or how little *energy* or total number of quanta are required. The answer to the first has practical consequences, while the answer to the second has important theoretical implications. In this section, we examine the answers to both questions for the rod system and the foveal cone system. Because the rod system is the more sensitive, the minimum threshold for this system will be the minimum threshold for the visual system as a whole.

2.3.1. Minimum Energy Threshold

2.3.1.1. ***Rod System.*** To answer the question of how little light is needed for detection, the light must be smaller in size than Ricco's area and briefer than the critical duration (see Figure 5.23). It should consist of quanta near 500 nm, the peak of the scotopic luminosity function (see Figure 5.9), and the light should be presented to the most sensitive part of the peripheral retina (see Figure 5.29). Since at least 1889, many attempts have been made to determine the minimum energy threshold of the visual system. The best known study is the classic Hecht, Shlaer, and Pirenne experiment (1942). They delivered a small (10-min arc-diameter), brief (1-msec), 510 nm light 20° temporal to the point of fixation [see inset, Fig. 5.30(a)]. The observer dark-adapted at least 30 min before measurements were made. For seven observers, the minimum amount of light needed to see the test on 60% of the trials varied between 54 and 148 quanta (or 2.1 and 5.7 × 10^{-10} ergs), with a mean of 92. The mean value of 92 quanta lies within a factor of 2 of the values obtained in the more carefully conducted earlier studies. This includes an estimation based on various assumptions made by Von Kries and Eyster (1907). Baumgardt's (1972) review in the *Handbook of Sensory Physiology* remains the best summary of this literature. He concludes that for the rod system, most studies find that the mean for a group of observers is between 50 and 100 quanta. This is a reasonable estimate of the minimum threshold for the rod system and, consequently, for the entire visual system. (See also the review by Pirenne & Marriott, 1959.)

2.3.1.2. ***Cone System.*** For the cone system, the minimum energy threshold is about six to ten times higher. The cone system is most sensitive in the central fovea. Marriott (1963) used a small (1-min arc), brief (1.2-msec), foveal light of 550 nm, a wavelength near the peak of the photopic luminosity function (see Fig. 5.7). For nine observers, the number of quanta required for 50% detection ranged from 494 to 879 with a mean of 606. An average of 600 quanta of 555 nm light represents a reasonable estimate of the minimum energy threshold for the fovea and consequently for the cone system. (See Baumgardt, 1972 for references.)

2.3.1.3. ***Detecting Small "White" Lights: Rod System versus Cone System Sensitivity.*** Most visual stimulation outside the laboratory is not monochromatic. The relative sensitivities of

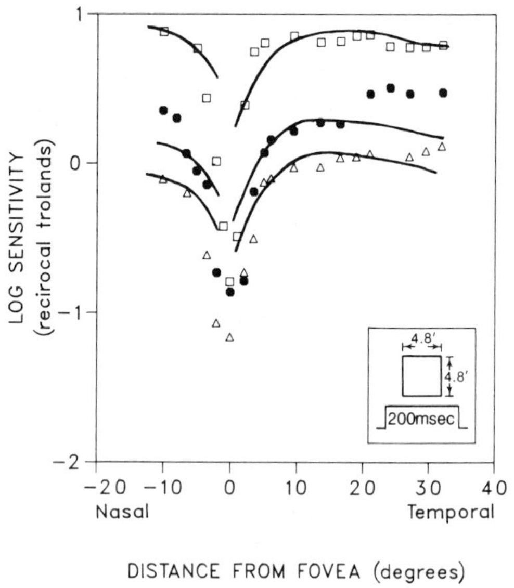

Figure 5.28. The relation between absolute sensitivity and eccentricity along the horizontal meridian. The "white" (2050° K) square test light was 4.8 min arc on a side and 200 msec in duration. Each symbol shows the data for one observer; note the large interobserver differences in sensitivity at any given eccentricity. A cosine correction for pupil size has been applied to the data (see Section 3.3). Each point is the mean of the measurements obtained in a single session. Sensitivity increases with distance from the fovea, reaching a maximum between 10 and 20° and remaining fairly constant with further increases in eccentricity. The solid curves trace log (rod density) as a function of eccentricity; the variation in sensitivity across the retina corresponds closely to the variation in the number of rods. The largest discrepancy between the two functions occurs toward the fovea, where sensitivity declines more rapidly than rod density. (From Crozier & Holway, 1939, Table I.)

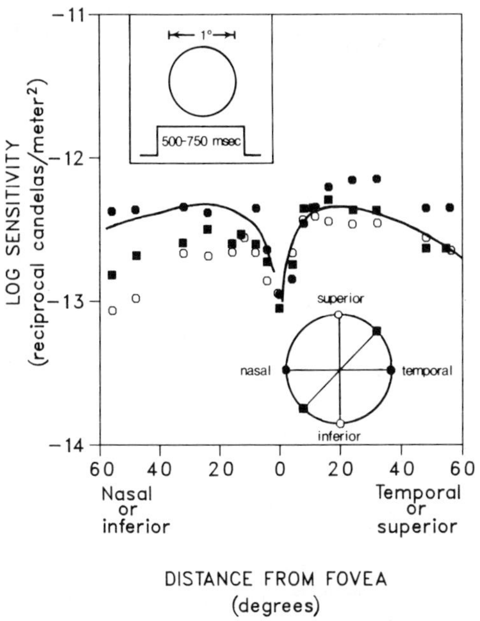

Figure 5.29. The relation between absolute sensitivity and retinal eccentricity for three meridia: horizontal (filled circles), vertical (open circles), and the meridian lying 45° between these two and extending from the inferior nasal to superior temporal retina (squares—see inset). The "white" test was 1° in diameter and varied in duration between 500 and 750 msec. The data are the average thresholds of eight relatively inexperienced observers, one session per observer. Data are uncorrected for changes in apparent pupil size with eccentricity (see Section 3.3). The shapes of the functions are similar for all three meridia and resemble the distribution of rods (solid curves). Sensitivity increases between 0 and 12–22°, remains fairly constant to 32°, and begins to fall with further increases in eccentricity. Absolute sensitivity is greatest along the horizontal meridian, particularly the temporal retina. Sensitivity is lowest in the inferior retina. (From Riopelle & Bevan, 1953, Table I.)

the rod and cone systems to a broadband stimulus depend, of course, on the spectral distribution of the stimulus. In general, however, the rod system is more sensitive to "white" lights. The greater sensitivity of the rod system is the explanation behind the "astronomer's trick." The trick refers to the fact that one may more easily see a dim star at night by looking slightly away from it than by fixating it directly. Consequently, the star is imaged on the rod-dominated peripheral retina rather than the less sensitive fovea.

The rod system advantage in detecting small "white" lights can be reduced by presenting the light continuously and maintaining careful fixation. Rod thresholds increase due to local fatigue; the result is analogous to the Troxler effect in which suprathreshold stimuli fade with prolonged fixation. This and other factors probably contributed to Arden and Weale's (1954) erroneous conclusion that the rod and cone systems are equally sensitive to small "white" lights.

2.3.1.4. Threshold Variability: Frequency-of-Seeing Functions. The values of minimum threshold given above are the number of quanta necessary for detection on approximately half the presentations. The actual values vary somewhat with psychophysical procedure. The same light is detected on some trials and not on others. Thus threshold is not a discrete boundary between seeing and not seeing, but is a probabilistic concept. Figure 5.30(a) and (b) shows the frequency of detection varies with light energy in the two studies discussed above. Panel (a) shows the Hecht, Shlaer, and Pirenne (1942) data for the rod system, panel (b) the Marriott data for the foveal cone system. To a first approximation, twice the threshold energy (the energy for 50% seeing) is detected on more than 95% of the trials; half the threshold energy brings detection below 5%. The frequency-of-seeing function is steeper for the fovea than for the periphery and steepens slightly with light adaptation.

The role played by quantal fluctuations and other sources of variability is discussed in Section 3.2.7. It is interesting to note that if one had to set a light such that observers were convinced they were "seeing it," threshold would probably correspond to the value at the 90% frequency-of-seeing level.

2.3.2. Minimum Intensity Threshold. To obtain a minimum intensity threshold for the rod system requires a large, long-duration light that takes advantage of the system's integrating capabilities [see Fig. 5.19(a)]. The intensity (quanta or energy per unit area per unit time) a light must provide to be detected can be reduced tremendously by increasing its spatial and temporal extent. Size and duration should be chosen such that any further increase in the magnitude of either parameter produces no further improvement in sensitivity. In principle, there is no upper limit to the values that each of these parameters can take. In practice, however, an intermittent light is easier to detect than a steady light.

Pirenne, Marriott, and O'Doherty (1957) measured intensity thresholds for 22 young observers using a 47°, 15-sec, "white" (2400°K) test light. The test was viewed with both eyes and the natural pupil. The mean threshold was 0.75×10^{-6} cd·m^{-2} and the range was 0.4×10^{-6} to 2×10^{-6} cd·m^{-2}, a factor of 5. Compare the threshold intensity of 10^{-6} cd·m^{-2} to the intensity required by Hecht et al. (1942). Their small (10-min arc), brief (1-msec) test, although delivering only 92 quanta to the eye at threshold, had an intensity of 0.58 cd·m^{-2}, almost 6 log units above the minimum intensity threshold.

The substantial effect of area and duration on the light intensity required for detection can also be predicted from the Hecht et al. (1942) data and the discussion above of rod system spatial and temporal summation. If we take the minimum threshold energy to be 100 quanta of 500 nm light, the effective critical duration to be 100 msec, and the effective critical diameter to be 1° and assume a fully dilated (8 mm) pupil, then the calculated threshold intensity is 7×10^{-6} cd·m^{-2}. This is in good agreement with the Pirenne et al. (1957) results.

3. LIGHT ADAPTATION: CHANGES IN SENSITIVITY

In our environment, we experience a wide range of ambient light levels. The illumination provided by the noon sun is on the order of 10^8 times the illumination provided by the moon. The visual system functions at both levels to allow us to successfully navigate our environment. However, the way in which we process visual stimuli, and consequently our visual world, is very different. Under dim illumination, the eye exhibits exquisite absolute sensitivity to light; substantially more light is required for detection at higher ambient intensities. For example, whereas a light that supplies as little as 100 quanta may be seen against a totally dark background, the same light presented against a white paper illuminated by the noon sun would need to supply millions of quanta to the eye.

By considering only thresholds, one might conclude that the visual system does not function well at high intensities. This is, of course, not true. Only under intense illumination can we see fine details and appreciate small differences in the

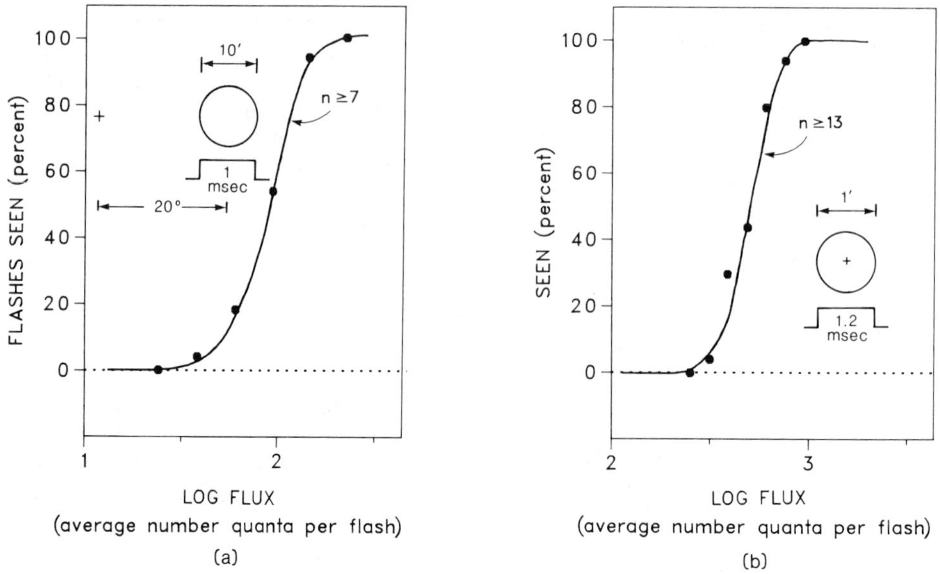

Figure 5.30. Frequency-of-seeing functions showing the relationship between the average number of quanta in a flash and the percentage of flashes detected. (a) Data for the dark-adapted rod system. Test lights 10 min arc in diameter and 1 msec in duration were presented 20° temporal to the fovea; wavelength was 510 nm. The solid curve is a cumulative Poisson probability distribution. It shows the relation between the average energy in a test flash and the probability of the rods absorbing at least *n* quanta from that flash:

$$p_{na} = 1 - e^{-a}\left(1 + a + \frac{a^2}{2!} + \frac{a^3}{3!} + \cdots + \frac{a^{n-1}}{(n-1)!}\right)$$

where a is the average flash energy, *n* is the number of quantal absorptions needed for detection (set here to 7), and p_{na} is the probability of 7 or more quantal absorptions occurring. The close fit of the curve to the data suggests that the observer detects the test flash whenever 7 or more quanta are absorbed. (From Hecht et al., 1942, Table V.) (b) Data for the dark-adapted foveal cone system. A 1-min arc-diameter, 1.2-msec, 550 nm test was used. The solid curve is the Poisson probability distribution for $n = 13$. Its correspondence to the data suggests that a flash is detected whenever 13 or more quanta are absorbed. (Panel (b) from F. H. C. Marriott, The foveal absolute thresholds for short flashes and small fields, *Journal of Physiology*, 1963, *169*. Reprinted with permission.)

color of the objects around us. Objects are distinguished by the visual system based on very small differences in the light they reflect. Small differences in the intensity of the light reflected are seen as different lightnesses or brightnesses. (Small differences in spectral reflectance are seen as different hues. See Wyszecki, Chapter 9.) Imagine a series of achromatic objects from white (reflecting at most 80% of the incident light) to black (reflecting about 5%). The total range of reflected intensities under any given illumination is 16. With increasing illumination, sensitivity is lost, but discrimination of intensity differences within this range improves. To relate these changes to everyday experience, consider the changes taking place during sunrise. As the prevailing illumination increases, the visual system becomes less sensitive to light. The moon, the street lights, and the stars all appear dimmer and may even disappear. At the same time, the black print on a page becomes discernible from the white background. The changes in sensitivity to light and sensitivity to contrast are the subject of this section.

3.1. Measuring Changes in Intensity Discrimination

3.1.1. Case Study. An experiment by Blackwell (1946) can be used to introduce the measurement of intensity discrimination. The experiment, conducted during World War II, was designed to combine the precise control of the laboratory with conditions more closely approximating the outside world than those usually found in the laboratory. (The differences between his conditions and those used in the laboratory today will be considered.) Blackwell's observers viewed an evenly illuminated wall about 65 m from where they were seated. The wall subtended a visual angle of approximately 10°. The observers' task was to detect the presence of a circular test light projected upon the wall. The light could appear in any of eight positions around the orientation point [see inset in Fig. 5.31(a)]. The test duration of 6 sec was sufficient to enable the observer to scan ". . . at a rate comparable to that employed by lookouts in the military service . . ." (Blackwell, 1946, p. 632). Illumination of both the test and wall was provided by unfiltered incandescent bulbs; the broad spectral distribution gave the test light and the wall an achromatic appearance.

Blackwell asked, how does the level of illumination of the wall affect the amount of light needed to detect the test? Figure 5.31(a) shows one way of presenting the answer. For nine observers, the average test intensity needed for detection is plotted as a function of the luminance of the wall. Each curve shows the results for a different test diameter. For all diameters, considerably more light is needed to see the test against the more highly illuminated walls. The plot in Figure 5.31(a) emphasizes the large loss in sensitivity that accompanies increases in the ambient light level.

Figure 5.31(b) presents the same data in another way. The figure plots the average contrast needed for detection as a function of the illuminance of the wall. The contrast between the test and wall is defined as

$$C = \frac{I_t}{I_A}, \qquad (9)$$

where I_t is the incremental intensity added by the test and I_A is the adapting intensity of the wall. This figure emphasizes the *improvement* in intensity discrimination that accompanies increases in the ambient light level. Consider the data for the largest test (121 min arc). Notice that contrast threshold decreases from greater than 1.0 at the lowest background intensity to less than .01 at the highest. That is, when the wall is most intensely illuminated, a local spot can be detected when it is only 1% greater in intensity.

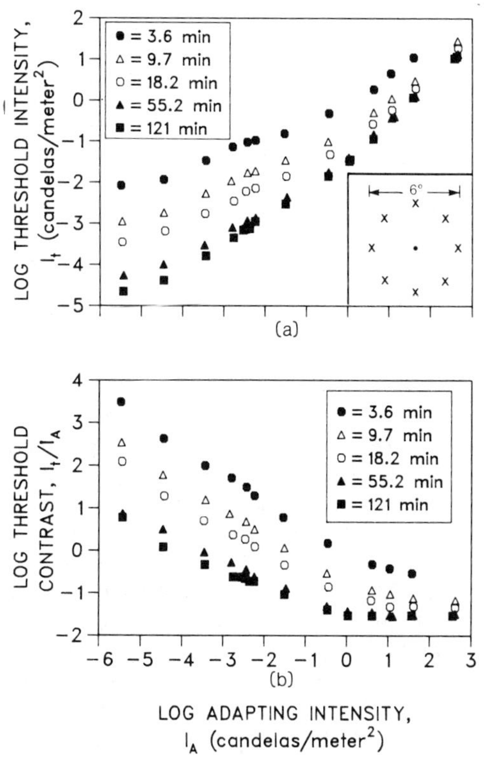

Figure 5.31. (a) Threshold versus intensity (t.v.i.) curves for test lights of five sizes: 3.6 min arc (filled circles); 9.7 min arc (open triangles); 18.2 min arc (open circles); 55.2 min arc (filled triangles); and 121 min arc (squares). The "white" tests were presented for 6 sec upon a "white" adapting screen 10° on a side. A stimulus was delivered to any of eight positions describing a circle of diameter 6° centered around an orientation point (see inset). A free viewing procedure was used, and the observer's task was to signal the position of the test light. Threshold was defined as the intensity required for 50% correct response (adjusted for guessing). Data are the average thresholds obtained over a 4-month period for nine observers, ages 19–26. All observers were extensively trained in psychophysical observation. For all test sizes, the intensity required for detection increases monotonically with increases in the ambient illumination. The decrease in threshold with increased test size is attributable both to areal summation and to the stimulation of more sensitive retinal regions. Confidence intervals calculated for the group data measured ±8% at the 99% confidence level and ±2% at the 50% confidence level. (b) Data of part (a) replotted as contrast versus intensity (c.v.i.) functions. Contrast is defined as I_t/I_A where I_t is threshold intensity and I_A is adapting intensity. Note the steady improvement in contrast sensitivity with increases in ambient illumination up to about 1 cd·m^{-2}. Beyond this level (for the three larger tests), contrast sensitivity is relatively constant, $I_t/I_A = k$ (Weber-Fechner law). (From Blackwell, 1946, Table II.)

Several important features of the curves in Figure 5.31 will be considered in detail. First, note that contrast threshold is relatively constant at high illumination levels. This is particularly evident for larger tests, where contrast threshold is constant for background levels greater than 1.0 cd·m^{-2}. This is the so-called Weber-Fechner law, usually expressed as $I_t/I_A = k$, where k equals a constant. Displayed as in Figure 5.31(a), the Weber-Fechner law is represented by a line of slope 1.0 ($\log I_t = \log I_A + \log k$). Second, there is a hint of a discontinuity around −2.5 log cd·m^{-2}, especially for the small-spot data. Blackwell noted that his observers reported a change in fixation strategy around this intensity. For higher background intensities, the observers attempted to fixate the targets with their foveas; below this intensity the parafovea was used. The transition from parafoveal to foveal fixation is related to rod-cone differences below. Third, the curves for different test diameters do not have the same shape. The size of the test influences absolute and relative changes in sensitivity with illumination level.

3.1.2. Typical Laboratory Conditions and Terminology. Blackwell's conditions are quite different from those typically used in the laboratory. The observer in the laboratory usually peers directly into an optical system rather than viewing the light reflected off a distant wall. However, only two differences between his study and laboratory studies are likely to affect the results. In the Blackwell study, pupil size was free to vary, and fixation was not controlled. In the laboratory, fixation is carefully controlled so that the test light is presented to a specifiable part of the retina. Also, an image of the light source is focused in the plane of the pupil. This so-called Maxwellian view allows high levels of retinal illumination that are independent of pupil size if the image of the source is small (less than about 2 mm).

Figure 5.32 shows various stimulus configurations used in laboratory studies. The configuration in Figure 5.32(c) is closest to Blackwell's and is the one most commonly used today. Unless specified otherwise, the studies below employ this paradigm. A spot of light, the test, is presented upon a larger, homogeneous patch of light, the adapting field or adapting light. (The test is variously referred to as the test spot, target, increment, or probe; the adapting field is also the conditioning field or background.) The test is generally presented for less than 1 sec and is confined to a specific retinal area with the use of a fixation point. As is discussed below, the spectral distributions of the test and adapting light are often manipulated to test some theoretical notion. In fact, conditions, paradigms, and terminology have all evolved as the questions, both theoretical and practical, have changed. Below we emphasize those studies that use broadband ("white") illumination.

The data from intensity discrimination experiments are usually plotted in either of the two forms shown in Figure 5.31(a), which is a threshold versus intensity (t.v.i.) curve (also known as increment threshold functions). Figure 5.31(b) is a contrast versus intensity (c.v.i.) function. Occasionally the reciprocals of threshold or contrast are plotted, in which case we speak of sensitivity and contrast sensitivity, respectively.

3.2. Increment Threshold Curves for the Rod and Cone Systems

As the ambient light level increases, visual function shifts from domination by the rod system to domination by the cone system (see Section 1). In the dark, the threshold for detecting an in-

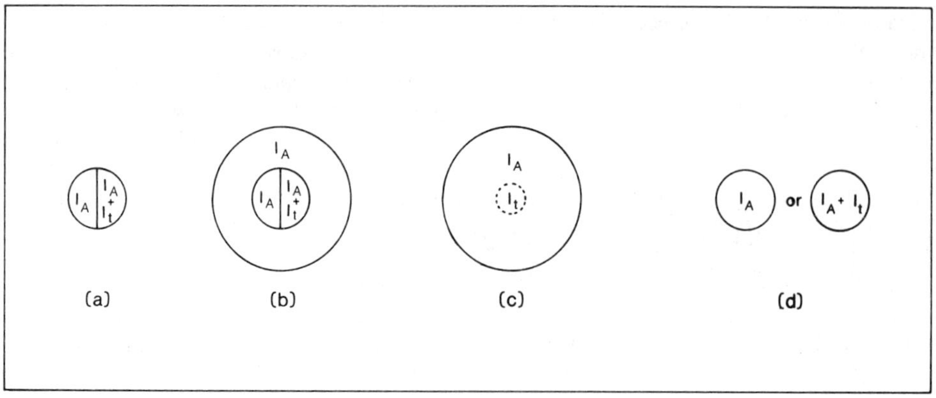

Figure 5.32. Four spatial configurations used to measure intensity discrimination. Each arrangement consists of a stimulus field of intensity, I_A, and a field of variable intensity, $(I_A + I_t)$. The observer increases the intensity of the variable field until it is just discriminable from the fixed field. I_t is the increment in intensity that must be added to I_A to produce a difference in appearance. Generally, the stimuli are confined to a specific retinal area with the use of a fixation point. (a) A bipartite field is presented to the dark-adapted eye. The observer adjusts the intensity of the variable hemifield (on the right) until it is just discriminable from the fixed-intensity hemifield (left). (b) The bipartite field is superposed on a surround of intensity, I_A. (c) The incremental light is presented upon a homogeneous adapting field of intensity, I_A. The observer adjusts the intensity of the small patch until it is distinguishable from the surround. This is the configuration most commonly used. Often the surround is presented continuously, while the increment is delivered as a brief flash. (d) The observer is presented with a two-alternative forced-choice task. On each trial a stimulus of either intensity I_A or intensity $(I_A + I_t)$ is delivered, and the observer must signal the correct stimulus. (Adapted from Pirenne, 1962, Fig. 1)

cremental light of almost any wavelength is determined by the rod system. On relatively intense adapting fields, the cone system controls detection independent of the wavelength of the test. Between these extremes, the spectral distribution of the light and various parameters of the test and adapting fields determine which system is the more sensitive. The transition from rod to cone vision is largely due to desensitization of the rod system by relatively weak lights that leave cone system sensitivity unaffected. Under most conditions a dual-branched t.v.i. function such as in Figure 5.31 results. When broadband ("white") light comprises both the test and the adapting field, it is not always easy to see the transition from rod to cone vision. Before examining t.v.i. functions under conditions where both rods and cones contribute, we shall consider experimental conditions designed to isolate a single system.

3.2.1. Intensity Discrimination by the Foveal Cone System. Restricting the test to the fovea isolates the cone system. Figure 5.33 (from Mueller, 1951) shows t.v.i. and c.v.i. functions for "white" test and adapting lights. Stimulation of the fovea was ensured by having the observer fixate the region where a brief (20-msec) test would be presented. The resulting t.v.i. curve shows three distinct regions. At low adapting intensities (white lights below −1 to −5 log td), threshold is unaffected by changes in the adapting level; the data fall along a slope of 0.0. At high intensities, threshold intensity is proportional to the adapting intensity (slope of 1.0); this relationship continues no matter how intense the field is made. Between these two regions threshold is increasing with increasing slope.

Although the t.v.i. curves approach a slope of 1.0, the c.v.i. curve [Fig. 5.33(b)] approaches a slope of 0.0. At high adapting levels, *contrast* threshold is constant; that is, the Weber-Fechner law holds. Notice that in Mueller's experiment, contrast threshold asymptotes at about 6%. Under optimal conditions, the foveal cone system can discriminate lights that differ by less than 1%. The precise shapes of the t.v.i. and c.v.i. functions, and the actual threshold and contrast values, depend on the size and duration of the test.

3.2.1.1. Test Duration and the Foveal Threshold versus Intensity Function. The duration of the test affects threshold and the shape of the foveal t.v.i. curve. For brief exposure durations, threshold decreases with increasing duration owing to the cone system's ability to sum light over time (see Section 2). The duration over which temporal summation occurs shortens as the adapting level is raised. Therefore, increasing the exposure duration affects threshold more at lower adapting intensities than at high. Figure 5.34 (from Keller, 1941) illustrates this point with t.v.i. functions for test durations of 30 msec (circles) and 200 msec (triangles). At the lowest adapting intensity (−0.68 log td), threshold for the 30-msec test exceeds that for the 200-msec test by a factor of roughly 3.5. The advantage of the large exposure duration diminishes as the adapting intensity is increased until, at the highest intensities, the thresholds for the two test durations coincide. The effect on t.v.i. curves of such changes in temporal summation can even be seen at the level of the receptor (e.g., Hood & Grover, 1974; Hood & Hock, 1975).

Exposure duration also affects the appearances of lights near threshold, especially at higher adapting intensities. With very brief exposures (below the critical duration), the test appears as a speck or streak of light. At longer durations, a larger part, including edges, of the target is seen (Hood, 1973).

3.2.1.2. Test Area and the Foveal Threshold versus Intensity Function. Increasing the size of the test also lowers the threshold obtained and can affect the shape of the t.v.i. function. Figure 5.35 (from Geisler, 1979) shows t.v.i. curves for three test diameters. Threshold intensity decreases with increased diameter, and the extent of that decrease is slightly larger at low adapting levels. The difference between small- and large-target thresholds is about 1.5–2 times greater at low adapting intensities than at high. Thus the decrease in areal summation with adapting

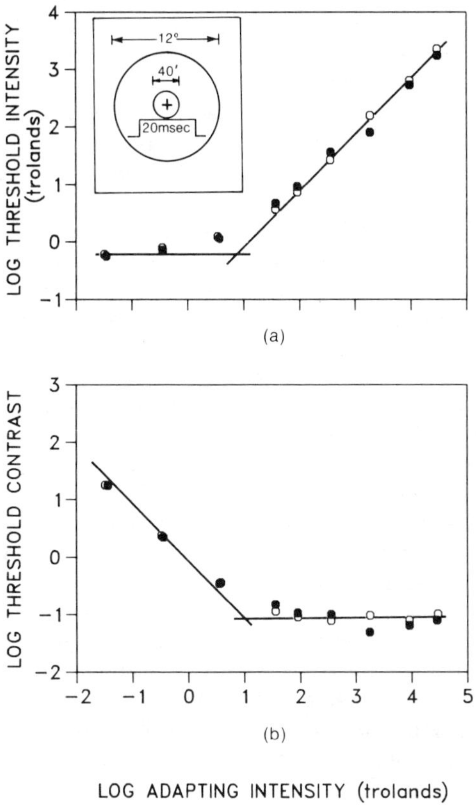

Figure 5.33. (a) Threshold versus intensity (t.v.i.) function for the foveal cone system. The test light, 40 min arc in diameter and 20 msec in duration, was presented in the center of a 12° circular adapting field (see inset); test and adapting lights were "white." Threshold intensity was calculated from frequency-of-seeing data and was defined as the intensity detected on 60% of the presentations. Data are shown for two observers and represent a total of 23 experimental sessions. The t.v.i. functions show three distinct regions, as indicated by the solid lines through the data. The lowest adapting intensities have no effect on threshold, and the data fall along a slope of 0.0. At high intensities, the increase in threshold is proportional to the increase in adapting intensity; the data follow a slope of 1.0 in accordance with the Weber-Fechner law: $I_t = k \cdot I_A$. This relationship holds no matter how intense the background is made. Between these two regions (roughly from −0.5 to 1.5 log td) threshold increases at an accelerating rate. (b) The data of panel (a) replotted as contrast versus intensity (c.v.i.) functions. These show three regions described by lines of slope −1.0 at low adapting intensities, 0.0 at high intensities, and an intermediate segment of decelerating slope. Thus *contrast* sensitivity improves (I_t/I_A decreases) with increased adapting intensity up to the level at which the Weber-Fechner law ($I_t/I_A = k$) holds. (From Mueller, 1951, Table I.)

intensity is less than the decrease in temporal summation (cf. Figs. 5.34 and 5.35). The small change in areal summation may not be due to a modification of the retina's ability to sum light (see Section 2.1.2.3).

Figure 5.36 (from Barlow, 1958b) shows foveal increment threshold curves for tests of two sizes and durations. The open circles are thresholds for a small, brief test; the filled circles are for a large, long-duration light. The two curves differ markedly in shape. As adapting intensity increases, the small, brief-test thresholds show a gradual transition in slope from 0.0 to 0.5. Thresholds for the large, long test increase more steeply and follow a slope of 1.0 at the higher intensities. Thus the separation between the two t.v.i. curves diminishes as adapting intensity increases. The advantage of the large size and longer test diminishes with increased adapting intensity and is about 0.8 log unit (six times) smaller at the high adapting levels than at the low. This difference is quantitatively consistent with the changes in temporal and spatial summation reported by Keller and Geisler, respectively (see Figs. 5.34 and 5.35). Temporal summation decreases about 0.5 log unit (threefold) from low to high adapting levels and spatial summation decreases approximately 0.3 log unit (twofold).

3.2.2. Intensity Discrimination by the Rod System. There is no cone-free area, analogous to the fovea, where the rod system can be studied in isolation. To examine intensity discrimination within the rod system, conditions must be manipulated to minimize cone intrusion. Aguilar and Stiles (1954) carefully chose stimulus parameters such that the adapting light favored detection by the rod system. The "red" adapting light stimulated the cone system more than the rods, keeping it less sensitive. The "blue-green" test light was chosen from the part of the spectrum most effective for rod stimulation. It was large (9°) and positioned in a retinal area rich in rods (9° parafoveal). In addition, the test light entered the periphery of the pupil to take advantage of the Stiles-Crawford effect (see Section 1.6.2). The t.v.i. curves for four observers are presented in Figure 5.37(a). Aguilar and Stiles were successful in isolating the rod t.v.i. function over a wide range of adapting intensities. A loss in sensitivity of more than a factor of a million occurs before the cone system finally intrudes (see arrow).

For a large range of adapting intensities, the rod t.v.i. curve resembles the cone t.v.i. function of Figure 5.31(a). At low intensities is a portion of slope 0.0, in which threshold is not affected by the adapting light. After a short transition, there

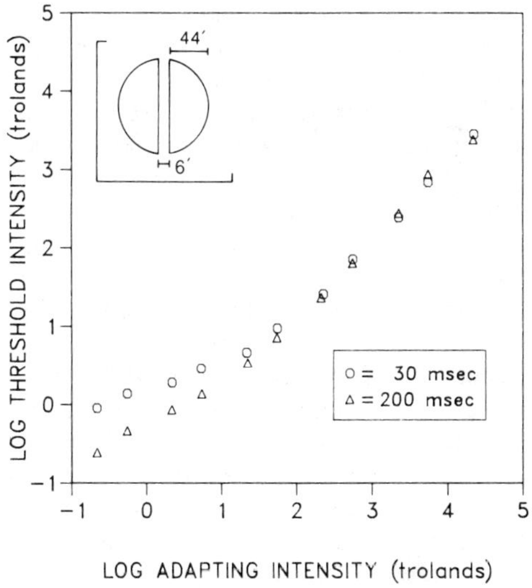

Figure 5.34. Foveal t.v.i. (threshold versus intensity) functions for two test durations: 30 msec (circles) and 200 msec (triangles). The stimulus configuration consisted of two semicircular patches, each of radius 44 min arc, separated by a 6-min arc gap (see inset). The intensities of both patches were set at the appropriate adapting intensity, and the incremental flashes were presented upon the left-hand semicircle. All stimuli were "white." Each point is the mean of the thresholds obtained for two observers, four measurements (in a single session) per observer. Increasing test duration improves sensitivity at low to moderate adapting intensities. The advantage of increased duration (i.e., temporal summation) decreases as the adapting level is raised, until the two t.v.i. functions coincide (above 1.5–2.0 log td). The discontinuity apparent in the data near the lowest adapting levels is often seen in foveal data and may indicate rod intrusions resulting from errors in fixation. (From Keller, 1941, Table I.)

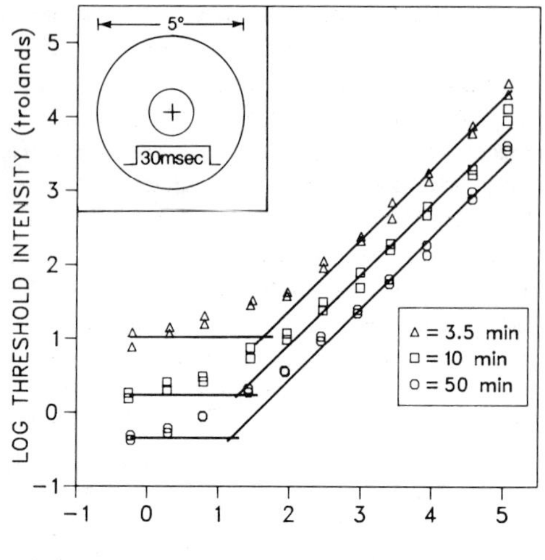

Figure 5.35. Foveal increment thresholds measured for three test diameters: 3.5 min arc (triangles); 10 min arc (squares); and 50 min arc (circles). Test flashes were presented for 30 msec in the center of a 5° adapting field (see inset); both test and adapting lights were "white." Data are shown for one observer from two experimental sessions. Increasing test size reduces threshold intensity (areal summation). The amount of summation is similar at all adapting intensities. The solid curves drawn through the data aid comparison of the three t.v.i. functions. The difference between the smallest- and largest-test thresholds is about 1.5–2.0 times greater at low adapting intensities than at high. Note that some investigators question the existence of true areal summation in the fovea. (From W. S. Geisler, Evidence for the equivalent-background hypothesis in cones, *Vision Research, 19*. Copyright 1979 by Pergamon Press, Ltd. Reprinted with permission.)

is a large region within which threshold increases with a slope of 1.0; the Weber-Fechner law holds for the rod system over approximately 4 log units of adapting intensity. The corresponding segments in the c.v.i. functions are apparent in Figure 5.37(b). Notice that the contrast threshold is constant for the rods over about a 4-log-unit change in adapting intensity. Note, however, that the rod system is much worse than the cone system at discriminating small differences in intensity. The cone system can discriminate intensities that differ by as little as 2%; the rod system requires changes of 20% or more.

Above about 100 scotopic td, but before the cones intrude, the rod system exhibits a large and rapid loss in sensitivity with small increases in adapting intensity. This phenomenon has been called rod saturation because the rod system is assumed to be maximally stimulated or saturated. According to this view, the rods reach their maximum response just above 2.0 log scotopic td. By about 2,000 scotopic td, the rod system is incapable of discriminating between two lights that differ in intensity by as much as a factor of 100. This should make the rod system incapable of discriminating nearly all naturally occurring contrasts at ambient illuminations above about 120 $cd \cdot m^{-2}$. Indeed, individuals exist called rod monochromats who lack a cone system and who are functionally blind at moderate levels of illumination.

The cone system never saturates in the presence of large, steady adapting fields no matter how intense they are made. Saturation of the cone system can be observed, however, if a brief adapting flash is used (see Sections 3.2.4.2 and 3.2.6.2). Section 3.2.6 contains a discussion of the mechanisms involved in protecting the cone system from saturation in the presence of steady lights.

Increasing the area or duration of the test light decreases threshold intensity and improves contrast sensitivity. In Sections 2 and 4 we discuss some of the problems of separating temporal and areal summation from changes in sensitivity due to retinal position. Large areas and long durations mainly serve to allow the observer to use the most sensitive part of the retina. It is clear that increasing test duration up to 100 msec does decrease threshold intensity for the rod system (see Fig. 5.23). Beyond 100 msec, sensitivity improves more slowly with further increases in duration. The extent of this improvement depends on other stimulus conditions, including adapting intensity. Over the range of adapting levels normally encountered, temporal summation is greater for the rod system than for the cone system.

The case for changes in areal summation with adapting intensity is much clearer for the rod system than for the foveal cone system (e.g., Barlow, 1958a; Van den Brink & Bouman, 1954). It is more difficult, however, to follow the desensitization of the rod system with increased adapting intensity because, in the normal observer, the cone system becomes more sensitive at higher adapting levels. Figure 5.38 (from Blakemore & Rushton, 1965a) shows t.v.i. data for a rod monochromat. Data were obtained for two test sizes, 5 min arc (filled circles) and 6° (open circles). Note that for both large and small targets, the monochromat's rod system exhibits the saturation seen in Figure 5.37. At all adapting intensities, threshold intensity is lower for the 6° test than for the 5-min arc target. However, keep in mind that increasing test size may lower threshold, not only because of areal summation, but also because the larger light may stimulate a more sensitive retinal region.

To assess summation per se, one can examine the *change* in areal summation that occurs with adapting intensity. In the

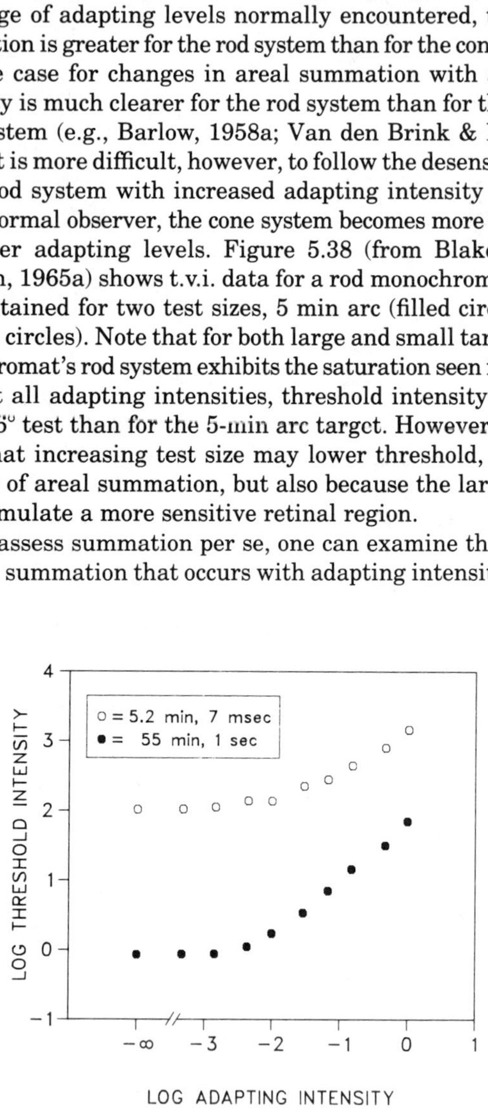

Figure 5.36. Foveal threshold versus intensity functions for a small, brief test (5.2-min arc diameter, 7 msec) and a large, long-duration test (55-min arc diameter, 1 sec). Data are given by the open and filled circles, respectively. The test light was "green," the adapting field "red." Changing test size and duration changes the shape of the t.v.i. function. Threshold for the larger, longer test is lower at all adapting intensities, but the separation between the two curves diminishes (i.e., the large-test thresholds increase more rapidly) as the adapting level is raised. The advantage of increased size and duration is about 0.8 log unit (six times) greater at the low adapting intensities than at the high. Most of the advantage of the larger, longer test at any adapting intensity is that it contains more total energy than the small, brief light; the brief test falls well within the integration time for foveal targets in the dark. (From H. B. Barlow, Dark and light adaptation: Psychophysics, *Handbook of sensory physiology* (Vol. 7/4), Springer-Verlag, Inc., 1972. Reprinted with permission.)

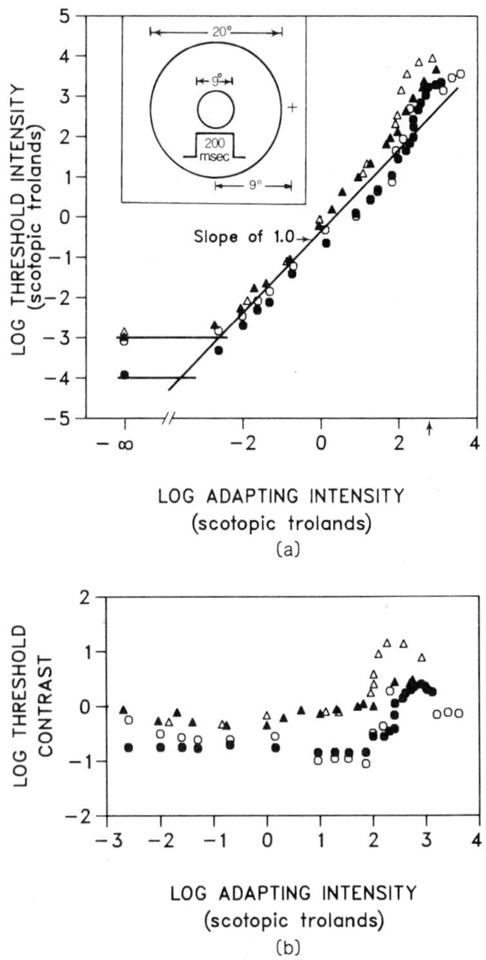

Figure 5.37. Threshold versus intensity functions for the rod system. Data are presented for four observers (ages 20–30 years). Test and adapting field parameters were chosen to favor the rods relative to the cones. The test was large (9°), long-duration (200 msec), and short wavelength ("blue-green" broad-band filter). It was presented 9° extrafoveally in the center of a "red" adapting field 20° in diameter (see inset). The test stimulus entered the edge of the pupil to take advantage of the Stiles-Crawford effect. Each data point is the mean of the thresholds obtained from at least three sessions. Thresholds at the lowest adapting intensities are unaffected by the background light (slope of 0.0). This is followed by a 4-log unit range of intensities over which the Weber-Fechner law holds ($I_t/I_A = k$), and the data fit a slope of 1.0. Above 2 log scotopic td, thresholds rise sharply with further increases in adapting intensity. This is the phenomenon of "rod saturation" and is assumed to correspond to a maximum response, or saturation, of the rod receptors. The subsequent decrease in slope at the highest adapting intensities (see arrow) indicates intrusion from the cone system. At this point, subjects reported a change in the appearance of the test from white or colorless to green. (b) The data of one observer [bottom curve, Fig. part (a)] replotted as contrast versus intensity (c.v.i.) functions. Note again the almost 4-log unit range over which Weber's law holds ($I_t/I_A = k$). The rod system shows a constant contrast threshold of about 20% within this range. (From M. Aguilar & W. S. Stiles, Saturation of the rod mechanism of the retina at high levels of stimulation, *Optica Acta*, 1954, *1*. Reprinted with permission.)

rod data of Figure 5.38, the threshold advantage of the 6° test diminishes from more than 2.5 log units in the dark to less than 1.5 log units at 2 log td (i.e., a reduction of more than a factor of 10). We will see in Section 3.2.3.2 that in the normal observer, the cone system has already taken over detection at this adapting intensity. To summarize, increasing test area and duration improves contrast sensitivity, produces large decreases in rod-mediated thresholds, and changes the shape of the t.v.i. function.

3.2.3. Combined Rod and Cone Function. Over a wide range of ambient light levels, both our rod and cone systems contribute to the detection of changes in the visual world. The system that dominates depends upon a variety of factors including the spectral composition of the test and adapting fields as well as the retinal locus of stimulation. These factors are considered in this section.

3.2.3.1. Retinal Location. Retinal position exerts a large influence on the relative sensitivity of the rod and cone systems. Cone system sensitivity is greatest in the fovea. The rod system is most sensitive around 20° eccentricity and loses sensitivity toward the fovea and far periphery (see Section 2). Figure 5.39 (from Crawford, 1937) shows t.v.i. functions obtained at three retinal eccentricities. The test, a 0.46°, 50-msec, "white" light, was presented at one of three retinal positions. There is no indication of a rod contribution to detection in the fovea (0°). At 5 and 14°, rod system sensitivity exceeds that of the foveal cone system for adapting intensities up to about −1.8 log $cd{\cdot}m^{-2}$. An important implication can be drawn from these data; intensity discrimination is best in the fovea at all higher ambient light levels. Over a large range of ambient light levels, you will do best by looking at what you want to see.

A study by Pöppel and Harvey (1973) nicely illustrates the advantage of the fovea at higher levels of illumination. Contrast sensitivity across the horizontal meridian was measured for a 10-min arc, 200-msec "white" test light. Each curve in Figure 5.40 shows the sensitivity profile for a different adapting intensity. For adapting intensities equal to or exceeding −2.6 log

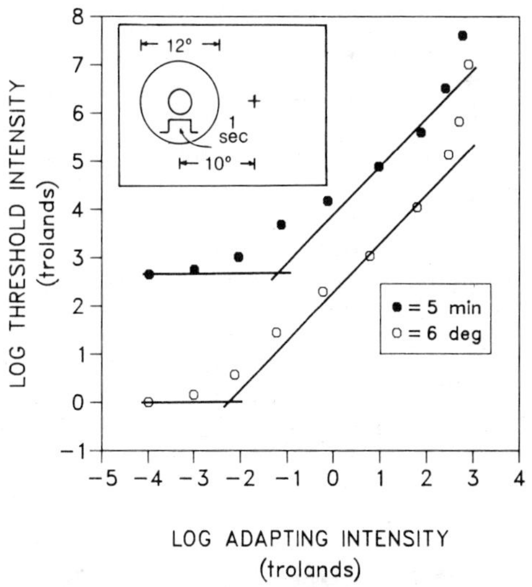

Figure 5.38. Rod system threshold versus intensity functions for "white" tests of two sizes: 5 min arc (filled circles) and 6° (open circles). They were presented for 1 sec upon a 12° "white" adapting field. The observer was a rod monochromat, age 28. The retinal region used to detect the test flashes was chosen by the observer and was approximately 10° parafoveal. Increasing test size improves sensitivity at all adapting intensities, but the advantage of the larger test diminishes from more than 2.5 log units in the dark to less than 1.5 log units at 100 td. In the normal observer, the cone system has already taken over detection by this point. Note the "rod saturation" (the sharp rise in threshold above about 2.0 log td). (From C. B. Blakemore & W. A. Rushton, Adaptation and increment threshold in a rod monochromat, *Journal of Physiology*, 1965, *181*. Reprinted with permission.)

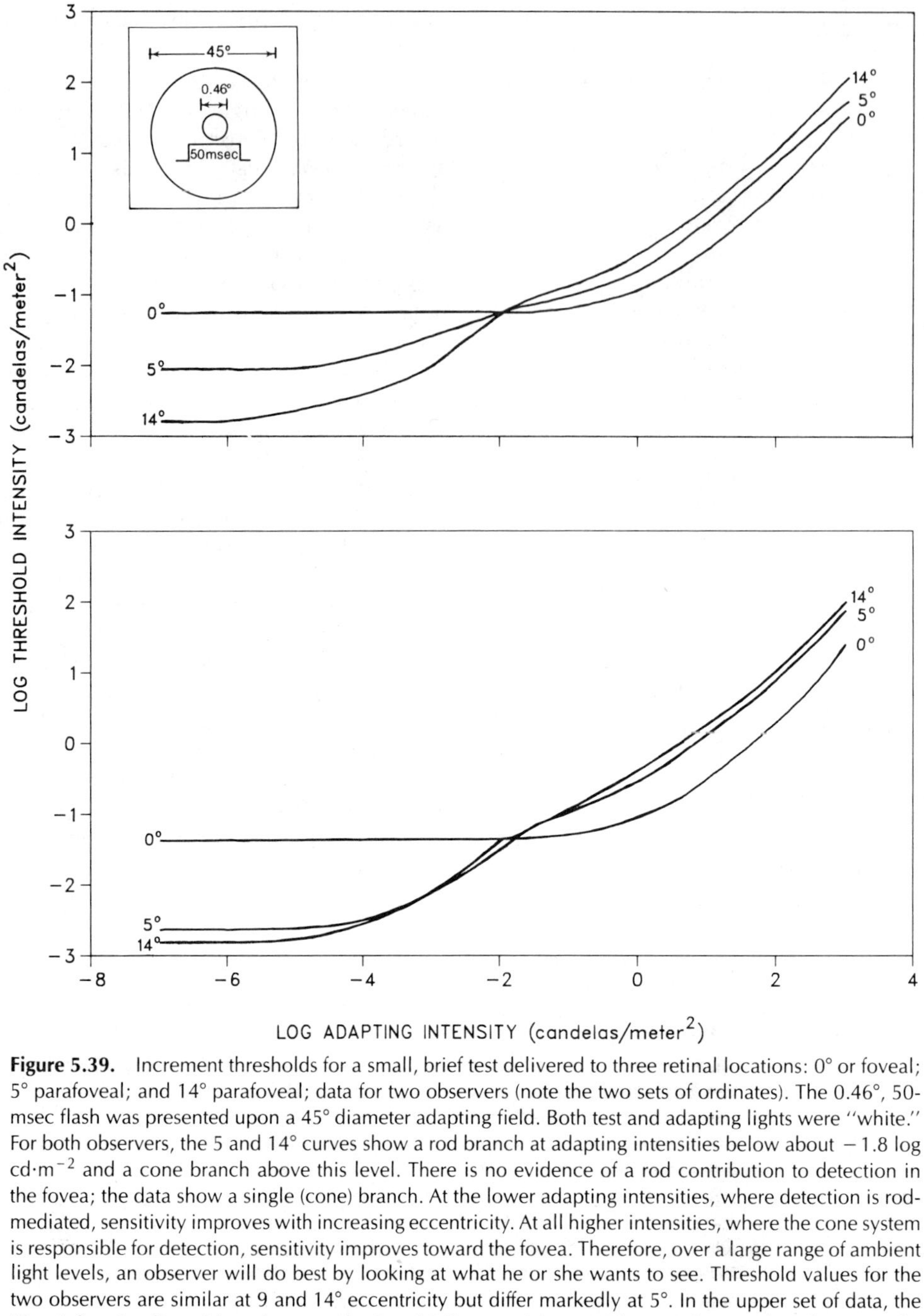

Figure 5.39. Increment thresholds for a small, brief test delivered to three retinal locations: 0° or foveal; 5° parafoveal; and 14° parafoveal; data for two observers (note the two sets of ordinates). The 0.46°, 50-msec flash was presented upon a 45° diameter adapting field. Both test and adapting lights were "white." For both observers, the 5 and 14° curves show a rod branch at adapting intensities below about −1.8 log $cd \cdot m^{-2}$ and a cone branch above this level. There is no evidence of a rod contribution to detection in the fovea; the data show a single (cone) branch. At the lower adapting intensities, where detection is rod-mediated, sensitivity improves with increasing eccentricity. At all higher intensities, where the cone system is responsible for detection, sensitivity improves toward the fovea. Therefore, over a large range of ambient light levels, an observer will do best by looking at what he or she wants to see. Threshold values for the two observers are similar at 9 and 14° eccentricity but differ markedly at 5°. In the upper set of data, the 5° t.v.i. function lies midway between the 0 and 14° curves (about 0.7 log unit from each), whereas in the lower set, the 5 and 14° thresholds differ by less than 0.2 log unit. (From B. H. Crawford, The change of visual sensitivity with time, *Proceedings of the Royal Society of London*, 1937, *123B*. Reprinted with permission.)

$cd \cdot m^{-2}$, contrast sensitivity is greatest in the fovea. This foveal advantage is less marked for larger test lights (see Section 2).

3.2.3.2. ***Understanding Blackwell's Data.*** We are now in a position to better understand the functions in Figure 5.31. Recall that Blackwell's observers were not required to maintain steady fixation and had 6 sec in which to locate and detect the test. Because the fovea shows greater contrast sensitivity than the periphery under higher levels of illumination [e.g., Fig. 5.37(b)] an optimal strategy would be to search for, and look at, the light to be detected. At lower light levels, where the rod system is more sensitive, fixating the orientation point or looking away from the target would increase the probability of detection. The reports of observers of a change in fixation strategy at about −2.5 log $cd \cdot m^{-2}$ suggest just such optimizing behavior.

If the observers actually used such a strategy, then the t.v.i. functions of Figure 5.31 should contain a lower limb attributable to rod vision and a higher limb where the cone system is responsible for detection. With "white" test lights, the rod-cone transition is not always easily seen. The 3.6-min arc- and 121-min arc-test data of Figure 5.31(a) are replotted in Figure 5.41. We have added hypothetical rod (solid curves) and cone (dashed curves) t.v.i. functions. For both receptor systems, the data have been fitted with lines of slope 0, 0.5, and 1.0. The point at which Blackwell's data suggest the switch from rod to cone vision is approximately the place where his observers reported the change in fixation strategy. We have used this point as an estimate of the dark-adapted cone threshold. Given the differences between Blackwell's study and the studies discussed here, exact agreement in t.v.i. curves should not be expected. In spite of these differences, however, the shapes of the rod and cone curves are in general agreement with the shapes of the t.v.i. functions in Figures 5.33–5.38. Rod saturation is not seen in these data because detection shifts to the cone system around -2.5 log cd·m^{-2}. In fact, notice how little of the range of rod vision studied by Aguilar and Stiles (Fig. 5.37) or Blakemore and Rushton (Fig. 5.38) is used in this situation. Outside the laboratory, we actually utilize only a small portion of our rod t.v.i. function. The cone system takes over detection long before there is a danger of saturating the rod system.

The same qualitative effects of test size as those seen in the foveal cone and rod data of Geisler (Fig. 5.35) and Blakemore and Rushton (Fig. 5.38) can be seen in Figure 5.41. Increasing test size lowers threshold for both receptor systems (i.e., there is spatial summation) but also causes thresholds to increase more rapidly (i.e., there is less spatial summation at higher adapting intensities).

Also in agreement with the data of Figures 5.35 and 5.38, increasing test size improves sensitivity more for the rod system than for the cones. Consequently, at lower adapting intensities, the rod portion of the t.v.i. function becomes more pronounced. Larger lights favor the rod system in two ways. They take advantage of the system's areal summation, and they enable the observer to bring the target onto the more sensitive peripheral retina. Under conditions of prolonged viewing, it is likely that the observer will move his or her eye to optimize contrast sensitivity. Indeed, the contrast threshold of 1% in Blackwell's study is about the best reported in the literature, better than the approximate 6% seen in Figures 5.34 and 5.35. This is most likely due to the observers moving their eyes to bring the edge of the target into the fovea. If more time were allowed, presumably lower rod branches would also have resulted; 6 sec is not long enough to allow the observers to use the most sensitive part of their peripheral retinas. Blackwell reports that for the particular spatial configuration used, exposure durations as long as 60 sec were not sufficient for optimal "looking strategies."

We can also use the rod and cone t.v.i. functions of the preceding figures to try to make quantitative predictions about

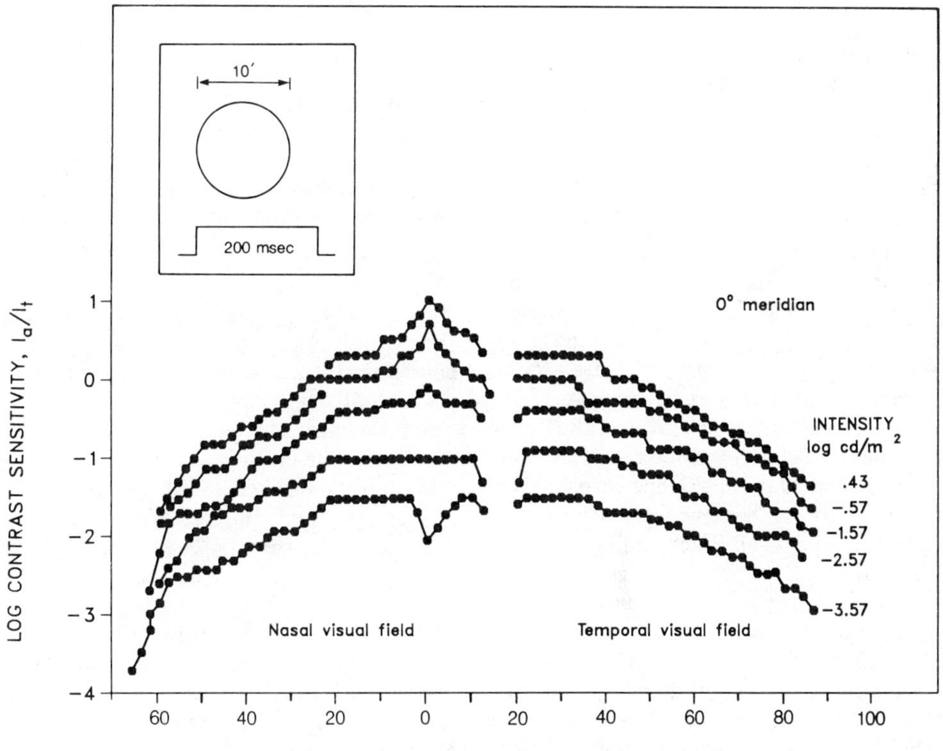

Figure 5.40. Contrast sensitivity (I_A/I_t) as a function of retinal eccentricity. Data are presented for the horizontal (0°) meridian of the right eye (one observer). Measurements were made at five adapting intensities: .43, $-.57$, -1.57, -2.57, and -3.57 log cd·m^{-2}. The test flash was 10 min arc in diameter and 200 msec in duration. Both test and background were "white" (unfiltered tungsten) lights. As adapting intensity is decreased, contrast sensitivity decreases. This is seen at all eccentricities but is more pronounced toward the fovea (0°). In other words, decreasing the ambient intensity hurts the cone system relative to the rods. For the three highest adapting levels, contrast sensitivity is highest in the fovea (0°) and decreases monotonically with distance from it. By -2.57 log cd·m^{-2}, the region of maximum sensitivity extends from 20° nasal to 35° temporal. At the lowest intensity, contrast sensitivity is higher in the fovea than in this surrounding region. (From E. Pöppel & L. O. Harvey Jr., Eight-difference threshold and subjective brightness in the periphery of the visual field, *Psychologische Forschung*, 1973, *36*. Reprinted with permission.)

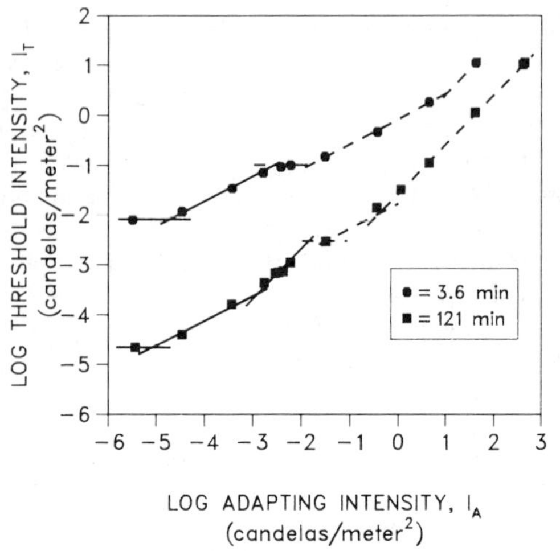

Figure 5.41. Threshold versus intensity functions replotted from Figure 5.31 for two test sizes: 3.6 min arc (circles) and 121 min arc (squares). The solid and dashed curves through the data separate the rod and cone portions of the functions, respectively. For both receptor systems, thresholds increase from 0 slope, first along a slope of 0.5, then along the Weber-Fechner line (slope of 1.0). Neither saturation nor much of the slope of 1.0 is seen in the rod data since detection switched to the cone system around −2.5 log cd·m^{-2}. The point at which the t.v.i. functions suggest a shift from rod to cone vision coincides with reports by observers of a change in viewing strategy from parafoveal to foveal fixation. The increase in test size from 3.6 min arc to 121 min arc improves sensitivity more for the rod system than for the cones so that, at lower adapting intensities, a more pronounced rod branch is seen. Large lights favor the rod system by taking advantage of its spatial summation and by enabling the observer to bring the target onto the more sensitive peripheral retina. One can see more clearly in the cone data the decrease in spatial summation that accompanies increases in adapting intensity. (From Blackwell, 1946, Table II.)

Blackwell's data. There is strong agreement between his rod data and those of Blakemore and Rushton (Fig. 5.38). Rod thresholds for the large test begin increasing near the same adapting field intensity (−4.5 log cd·m^{-2}, which is approximately equal to −3 log td) and reach a slope of 1.0 about 2 log units higher. With the small test, thresholds also start to rise around the same adapting intensity but do not reach a slope of 1.0 before (in the normal observer) the cone system takes over detection. Comparing Blackwell's data to cone t.v.i. functions is much more difficult. It is not clear where cone threshold is, and changes in pupil diameter must be considered. Remember that the two major differences between Blackwell's conditions and those of the others include his use of the natural pupil and of a free viewing situation. There is more reasonable agreement between the measurements in Figure 5.41 (Blackwell) and the t.v.i. data in Figure 5.34 (Keller) and Figure 5.35 (Geisler) if adjustments are made for changes in pupil diameter. Quantitative disagreements still exist, and it is not clear how much of these are due to the differences in stimulus presentation. Before we are happy with applying either the Blackwell data or more conventional t.v.i. data from the laboratory to nonlaboratory situations, further work is needed.

3.2.4. Spectral Composition of Test and Adapting Lights. Thus far we have been concerned largely with achromatic ("white") test and adapting lights. Manipulation of the spectral composition of either will differentially affect the sensitivity of the rod and cone systems and thus change the shape of the overall t.v.i. function. Recall that the rod system is most sensitive around 500 nm and is extremely insensitive to long-wavelength light. The relative spectral sensitivity of the rod system does not vary with adapting intensity; the effect on sensitivity of a given change in wavelength is the same at all adapting intensities. The spectral tuning of the cone system can be affected by a number of factors but, in general, shows a maximum around 560 nm. To a first approximation, except at reasonably high adapting intensities (see Section 1), the relative spectral sensitivity of the cone system is also constant. (We assume here achromatic adaptation.)

The rod and cone t.v.i. functions are most easily isolated by choosing stimulus parameters (including wavelength) that favor detection by one system. Thus Aguilar and Stiles used a short-wavelength test light and long-wavelength adapting field in order to obtain increment thresholds for the rod system (Fig. 5.37). We can predict intensity discrimination even in relatively complicated situations if we know the shapes of the rod and cone t.v.i. functions and the parameters of the test and adapting lights. Next we examine the effects of test and adapting wavelength on combined rod and cone t.v.i. data.

3.2.4.1. Wavelength and a Model of Independent Receptor Systems. The duplicity model introduced in Section 1 provides a framework for understanding the effect of wavelength on the t.v.i. function. The model assumed two detection systems (rod and cone), each with a unique and invariant relative spectral sensitivity. These are given by the CIE scotopic and photopic luminosity functions, respectively (see Section 1.5 and Fig. 5.7). The model further assumed that the rod and cone systems respond independently to a test stimulus; an observer's detection threshold corresponds to the threshold of the more sensitive system. To extend the model to deal with t.v.i. data, we add the assumption that the two systems adapt independently (Stiles, 1959). That is, the sensitivity changes effected in one system by an adapting field do not affect the other. Using this model, and holding constant the spatiotemporal parameters of the test, the combined t.v.i. curves of the rod and cone systems can be estimated for any pair of test and adapting wavelengths.

(a) TEST WAVELENGTH. Figure 5.42(a) illustrates the effect on the overall t.v.i. curve of a change in test wavelength. The data points are increment thresholds for a 580 nm test presented 5° parafoveally on a 500 nm adapting field (from Stiles, 1959). The solid curves through these data are the rod and cone t.v.i. functions. The lower branch is the rod system t.v.i. function; at low adapting intensities, the rod system is more sensitive than the cone system to the test. With increasing adapting intensity, the rod system thresholds increase, and detection shifts to the cone system (i.e., this system becomes the more sensitive one to the test).

From the absolute thresholds of the rod and cone systems to the 580 nm test, one can extrapolate the sensitivities of the two systems to all test wavelengths. Based on the 580 nm absolute threshold of the rod and cone systems (open circles) the relative sensitivity of the rod and cone systems (V'_λ and V_λ, respectively), can be estimated and the combined t.v.i. function for any test wavelength determined. For example, the dashed curves show the t.v.i. curves predicted for a 500 nm test. Note that the effect of a change in test wavelength is to shift the t.v.i. curve for each system vertically along the ordinate without a change in shape. In other words, a change in wavelength is equivalent to a change in the effective intensity of the test for each receptor system. The rod system is about 1 log unit more sensitive to 500 nm than to 580 nm light. Consequently, the rod t.v.i. curve shifts downward 1 log unit; the detection thresholds at every adapting intensity are 1 log unit lower.

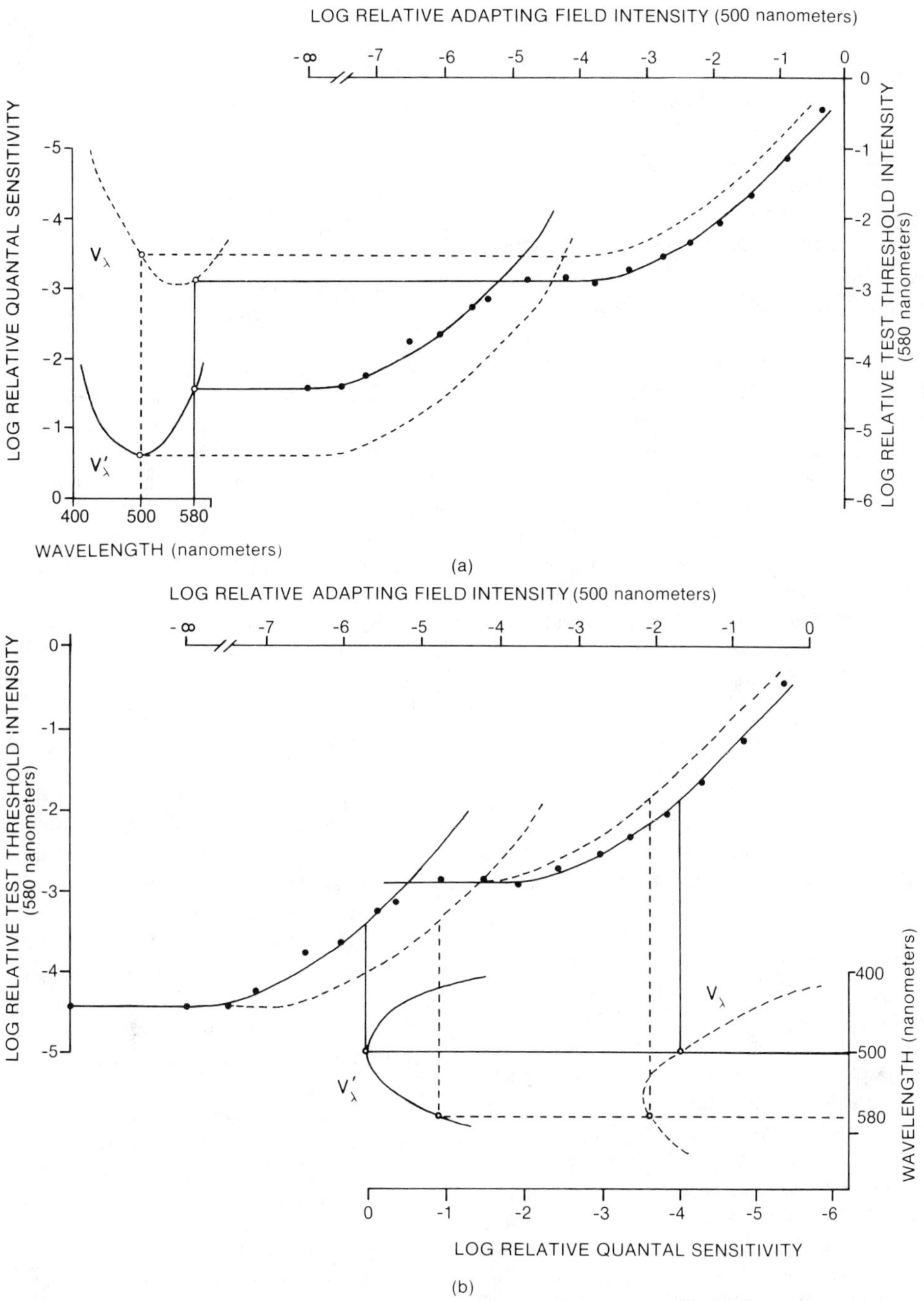

Figure 5.42. (a) Predictions of a duplicity model of light adaptation. The model assumes independent rod and cone systems. The shape of the t.v.i. function for each system is assumed to be fixed by the adapting conditions. Changes in the parameters of the test affect the absolute sensitivity of a system but not the way in which sensitivity varies as a function of adapting intensity. The figure illustrates the effect of a change in test wavelength on the combined rod-cone t.v.i. function. The circles and solid curves are increment thresholds for a 580 nm test presented 5° parafoveally upon a 500 nm field (Stiles, 1959). The data show a rod branch at low adapting intensities and a cone branch at high intensities; the overall threshold function approximates an envelope of the two branches. The dashed curves illustrate the effect of a decrease in test wavelength to 500 nm. The absolute sensitivity of the rod system increases; cone system sensitivity decreases. The individual t.v.i. functions are shifted along the log (threshold) ordinate according to the relative spectral sensitivity of the rod and cone systems (curves labeled V'_λ and V_λ, respectively). A change in test wavelength is thus equivalent to a change in the effective intensity of the test for each receptor system. The differential shifting of the rod and cone curves changes the shape of the overall t.v.i. function; the rod branch is more pronounced at 500 than at 580 nm. (b) The effect on the combined rod-cone t.v.i. function of a change in the wavelength of the adapting field. The circles and solid curves replot the 580 nm test/500 nm adapting field data from panel (a). The dashed curves are the results predicted for an increase in the adapting wavelength to 580 nm. The results are again determined by the relative spectral sensitivities of the rod and cone systems. The change in wavelength is equivalent to a change in the effective intensity of the adapting light, and the rod and cone functions shift along the log (adapting intensity) axis without a change in the shape. The 580 nm field is less effective than the 500 nm background at desensitizing the rod system and more effective at desensitizing the cones, thereby resulting in a more pronounced rod branch.

Conversely, cone system sensitivity *decreases* approximately 0.40 log unit with the shift to a 500 nm test. The cone t.v.i. curve is displaced 0.40 log unit upward. The ultimate effect of the change in wavelength is to increase the range of adapting intensities over which the rod system subserves detection by about 1.3 log units. The shape of the overall t.v.i. curve has changed, but this is due to changes in relative sensitivity *between* systems, not within systems.

(b) ADAPTING WAVELENGTH. The effect on the combined rod and cone t.v.i. function of a change in adapting wavelength can also be predicted from the spectral sensitivities of the two systems. The data of Figure 5.42(a) are replotted in Figure 5.42(b) (circles). The dashed curves show the t.v.i. function predicted for an adapting wavelength of 580 nm. The prediction is made from the spectral sensitivities of the rod and cone systems (at the bottom of the figure). The change in wavelength is equivalent to a change in the effective intensity of the adapting light. Thus the rod and cone t.v.i. functions shift horizontally along the log (adapting intensity) abscissa without changing shape. The amount and direction of the shift are determined by the relative sensitivity of each system to the 500 and 580 nm fields.

Thus the rod curve is shifted 1 log unit to the right; the threshold-raising ability of a given field intensity is decreased by this factor. On the other hand, the 580 nm field is more effective than the 500 nm background at reducing the sensitivity of the cone system, and the cone t.v.i. function shifts 0.40 log unit to the left. Again, the result is a change in the shape of the *overall* t.v.i. curve and an increase in the range of adapting intensities over which the rod system is responsible for detection.

3.2.4.2. Limitations of the Model. The duplicity model of light adaptation outlined above assumes two independent detection systems, each with an invariant relative spectral sensitivity. Knowing the spectral sensitivities of the two systems thus allows one to estimate a t.v.i. function for any spectral distribution of test and adaptation lights. Although the duplicity model appears to hold (to a first approximation) under some stimulus conditions, other conditions indicate that it is not a theoretically viable model of light adaptation. First, the relative spectral sensitivity of the cone system is not invariant. The relative contribution to detection of the short-wavelength cones increases outside the fovea (Section 1.5), and post-receptoral opponent interactions influence spectral sensitivities at the high adapting intensities (Section 1.5). In addition, interactions between the rod and cone systems do occur. Nonetheless, the model is potentially useful to provide crude estimates of how detectability changes with test and adapting wavelength. The deviations from the model attributable to rod-cone interactions are reasonably small upon steady adapting fields. If intense backgrounds and short-wavelength test lights are avoided, the deviations attributable to changes in the relative spectral sensitivity of the cone system, although not minor, can be minimized.

Stiles (1959) attempted to salvage an independent-mechanisms model by assuming three cone systems in addition to the rod system. He found, however, that to describe t.v.i. curves under all conditions, including higher adapting intensities, required *seven* cone mechanisms (see also reviews by Pirenne, 1962, and Enoch, 1972). Current detection models generally include four systems, one rod and three cone systems. Two of the cone systems are called "opponent" and involve subtractive interactions among different classes of cones. These models would probably prove cumbersome for practical applications, particularly since the relative spectral sensitivities of the systems change with stimulus parameters and retinal position. We do not know of anyone who has compared the predictive value of the current models and the duplicity model in practical situations.

3.2.5. Variations in the Adapting Field. The characteristics of the adapting field also affect t.v.i. functions. Here we examine two parameters of the adapting field, its size and duration, or, more specifically, the spatial and temporal relationship between test and adapting lights.

3.2.5.1. Spatial Relationship of Test to Adapting Field. Thus far, we have considered adapting fields that are much larger than the test lights. Suppose the test is superimposed on an adapting field that is close in size. The result is that more light is needed to detect the test on the smaller field (cf. Crawford, 1940; Westheimer, 1967).

Figure 5.43 shows what has become known as the sensitization or Westheimer effect. The conditions in Figure 5.43(a) were selected to favor the rod system. Each curve was obtained for a different adapting intensity. At all four levels of adapting field intensity, enlarging the adapting field up to a diameter of about 40 min arc increases threshold. Further increases in diameter result in a decrease in threshold at all but the lowest adapting intensity. A very similar phenomenon is seen for the cone system in Figure 5.43(b). Here light has been restricted to the fovea. Take careful note of the abscissa. The adapting field producing the greatest increase in threshold is considerably smaller for the cone system than for the rod system, about 5 min arc in diameter as compared to 40 min arc.

One can infer from Figure 5.43 that the size of the adapting field can affect the shapes of the t.v.i. functions. If we assume that a test is smaller than the diameter of the field producing maximal desensitization of the system (d_m), then Figure 5.44 (page 5-38) shows how rod or cone t.v.i. functions will depend on the area of the adapting field. The t.v.i. curves are schematized for fields of diameter d_m and d_l (a very large adapting field). The point is that rod and cone t.v.i. functions are not necessarily invariant with changes in the size of the adapting field relative to the test field. (This finding has important implications for the equivalent background principle; see Section 5.)

3.2.5.2. Time Course of Adaptation. Visual sensitivity does not adjust instantaneously to the addition of an adapting light. Figure 5.45, on page 5-38, (from Baker, 1949) shows how threshold for the foveal cone system varies after the onset of an adapting field. Data are presented for four adapting intensities. The thresholds, which are highest immediately at the onset of the field, decrease with prolonged exposure, although not strictly monotonically (see the 5000-td condition). The adjustment in sensitivity can be very rapid after weak adapting fields but can require more than 10 min to reach steady state for the more intense fields. For all adapting levels, most of the change in sensitivity occurs within the first several seconds after the onset of the field (see also Crawford, 1947).

Measurements of the time course of adaptation of the rod system indicate a similar recovery function. Figure 5.46, (page 5-39) from a study by Adelson (1982), shows rod thresholds after the onset of a 0.5-log td field. The two panels present the same data on different time scales. Sensitivity recovers rapidly immediately after the onset of the background; this is followed by a more gradual improvement which lasts approximately through the first minute of adaptation. (See C. H. Graham, 1965 for additional references for both rod and cone systems.)

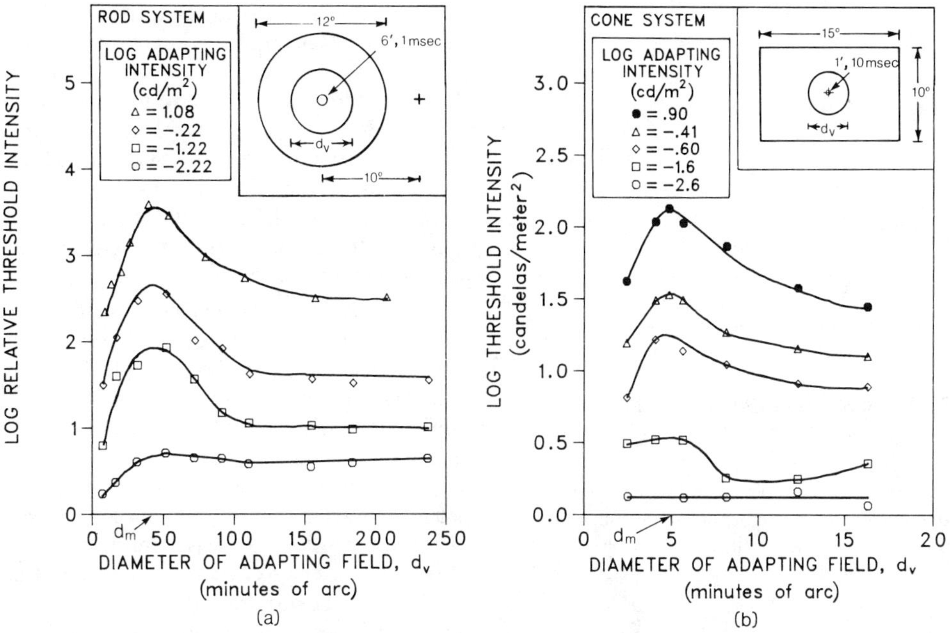

Figure 5.43. (a) Rod system thresholds as a function of size (in degrees) of the adapting field. The 500 nm test lights were 6 min arc in diameter and less than 1 msec in duration. They were presented 10° parafoveally upon a "red" adapting field of variable size (d_v). The parameter in the figure is the intensity of the adapting field in log cd · m^{-2}: 1.08 (triangles), −0.22 (diamonds), −1.22 (squares), −2.22 (circles). The test and adapting lights were in turn superposed on a 12° surround whose intensity was always 1 log unit less than that of the adapting background (see inset). The purpose of the surround was to mask any stray light from the test that might fall outside the adapting field. At all adapting field intensities, enlarging the field up to a diameter of 40 min arc (d_m in figure) increases contrast threshold. Further increases in diameter decrease the threshold, particularly at the higher adapting intensities. (From Westheimer, 1965, Fig. 4.) (b) Detection threshold as a function of the size of the adapting field (d_v) for the foveal cone system. Five adapting intensities were examined: 0.90, −0.41, −0.60, −1.6, and −2.6 log cd · m^{-2}. Both the small (1 min arc), brief (10 msec) test and the adapting field were superposed on a large surround approximately 10 × 15° (see inset); surround intensity was 1.5 log units below that of the adapting field. All stimuli were "white." The data are qualitatively similar to those obtained for the rod system. With the exception of the lowest adapting intensity, enlarging the adapting field up to 5 min arc diameter (d_m) increases detection thresholds, whereas further increases in size lead to a decrease in threshold. Thus the most effective adapting field is considerably smaller for the cone system than for the rod system. (From G. Westheimer, Spatial interaction in human cone vision, *Journal of Physiology*, 1967, *190*. Reprinted with permission.)

3.2.5.3. Brief Adapting Fields. Figures 5.47 (page 5-40) and 5.48 (page 5-41) compare the relative effectiveness of a brief (500-msec) and prolonged adapting field. Consider Figure 5.47(a) (from Geisler, 1979) which contains t.v.i. curves for the rod system. The 50-msec test light was presented simultaneously with the onset of a 500-msec flashed field or upon the same field after prolonged viewing. The 500-msec field is more effective in raising threshold than the steady background, particularly at the higher adapting intensities. A similar result, also for the rod system, is presented in Figure 5.47(b) (from Adelson, 1982). Here a 400-msec background light is more effective than a continuously presented light at raising threshold. (It is interesting that brief fields that coterminate with the test are less effective than fields slightly longer in duration; see Geisler, 1979.)

The same phenomena can be seen for the cone system. Steady adapting fields are less effective than brief ones (cf. Brindley, 1959; Cornsweet & Pinsker, 1965; Geisler, 1978a; Hood, Ilves, Maurer, Wandell, & Buckingham, 1978). Figure 5.48 (from Finkelstein & Hood, 1981) compares the relative effectiveness of a steady versus a flashed field for the foveal cone system. It also reveals a striking effect of field duration on the shape of the increment threshold function. Thresholds for a 10-msec test were measured on a field that was continuously presented (filled circles) or flashed for 500 msec (triangles). At moderate to high adapting intensities, the steady-field t.v.i. function follows a slope of 1.0, much like the cone functions of Figures 5.33–5.36. Thresholds on the flashed field are much higher and increase much more steeply with adapting intensity. This sharp loss in sensitivity is reminiscent of the rod saturation seen in response to steady fields (see Fig. 5.37). In fact, the finding has been called "cone saturation" (Alpern, Rushton, & Torii, 1970). It is better labeled cone *system* saturation because it is clear that part of the so-called saturation can take place at a stage of processing beyond the receptors (Finkelstein & Hood, 1981).

3.2.6. Mechanisms of Light Adaptation In the preceding section, we examined various aspects of the sensitivity loss accompanying increased ambient light levels. Here we consider some of the factors that cause the decrease in sensitivity as well as factors that operate to *maintain* sensitivity in the light-adapted eye.

3.2.6.1. Pigment Depletion. The presence of a steady light decreases the number of pigment molecules in the receptors capable of absorbing light. This depletion of pigment must contribute to the loss in sensitivity with increased adapting field

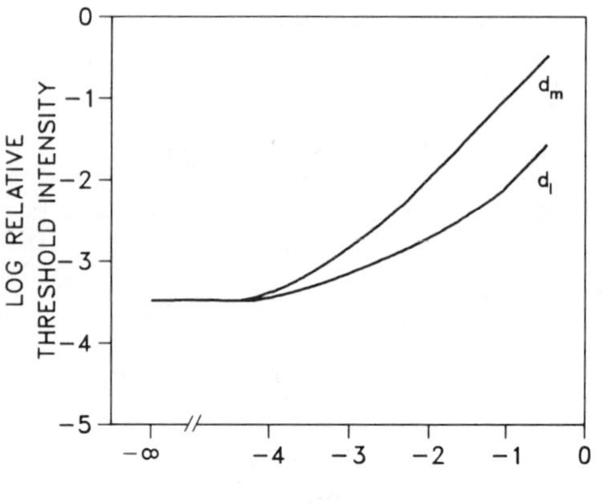

Figure 5.44. Schematic of the effect of adapting field size on the shape of rod or cone t.v.i. functions. Hypothetical functions are shown for fields of two sizes. d_m is the diameter that produces maximal desensitization of the system; d_l is a very large-diameter field. The shapes of the rod and cone t.v.i. functions do not necessarily remain invariant with changes in the size of the adapting field.

intensity. Section 4.5 details the nature of the changes in pigment content with changes in light intensity. The reader may want to read that section before continuing. Alternatively, one can accept that the dashed curves at the bottom of Figure 5.49 (page 5-42) indicate the proportion of (rod or cone) pigment present at any given intensity of a steady adapting field. The proportion of molecules available to absorb light decreases monotonically as intensity is increased.

Figure 5.49(a) presents an analysis of the effects of bleaching on the sensitivity of the rod system. The solid curve is Aguilar and Stiles's (1954) t.v.i. function from Figure 5.37. The dotted curve shows the predicted increase in threshold intensity due solely to the depletion of pigment molecules. In the steady state, the increase in threshold should be inversely proportional to pigment content. Thus, for example, halving the number of available molecules would double the threshold intensity (see Section 4.5.3 for a detailed discussion of sensitivity and pigment). Clearly the decrease in quantal absorption due to pigment depletion contributes remarkably little to the large loss in sensitivity of the rod system. Notice that the rod system has lost 5–6 log units of sensitivity and has become saturated before the pigment content is decreased by even a few percent.

For the cone system, pigment depletion makes an insignificant contribution to sensitivity loss at low background intensities but a substantial contribution at higher intensities. The solid curve in Figure 5.49(b) is a foveal t.v.i. function derived from the data of Figure 5.33; from the dotted curve is the function calculated based on pigment depletion. Below about 4 log td, pigment depletion has little effect on threshold. This means that within the range of lights normally encountered (see Table 5.1), pigment depletion plays a small role in cone system adaptation. In contrast, above about 5 log td, pigment depletion accounts for virtually *all* the loss in sensitivity. For a given adapting intensity, I_A, and assuming low pigment density, the proportion of pigment present at equilibrium, $p_e = I_0/(I_0 + I_A)$ where I_0 is a constant (4.5 log td for the cone system; see Section 4.5.1.2). When I_A is very large relative to I_0, $p_e = I_0/I_A$; p_e and I_A are inversely proportional. This means, for example, that a tenfold increase in the rate at which quanta are delivered to the eye (I_A) reduces the number of pigment molecules available to absorb those quanta (p_e) by a factor of 10. Thus the *effective* intensity of the adapting light is constant. Pigment depletion in effect protects the cone system from further increases in adapting intensity. Because $p_e \cdot I_t$ (threshold intensity) therefore remains constant, I_t increases in proportion to I_A, and thresholds follow the Weber line. For example, increasing the adapting intensity from 5.0 to 6.0 log td increases cone system thresholds by 1 log unit. The loss in available pigment predicts an increase in threshold of 0.9 log unit; pigment depletion plays a large role. However, this still leaves the lower range of cone system sensitivity loss to be explained.

3.2.6.2. Physical Noise: Quantal Fluctuations. Quantal emission from a source of light is a probabilistic event. The number of quanta in a test light varies from presentation to presentation. Suppose a test light of fixed intensity and duration delivers, on an average, n quanta to the cornea. On some trials there will be more than n quanta and on others, fewer than n quanta. The frequency distribution of the number of quanta per presentation will be Poisson with a mean of n and a standard deviation of $n^{1/2}$. The fluctuation in the number of quanta is a physical fact; the extent to which these fluctuations affect our ability to discriminate lights is open to experimental investigation and theoretical calculation. There is evidence that quantal fluctuations are one form of noise limiting the accuracy with

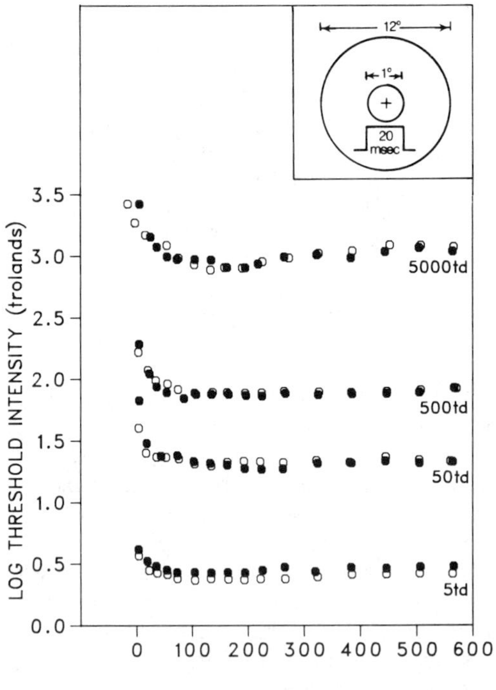

Figure 5.45. Foveal increment thresholds as a function of the duration (in seconds) of adaptation. The four sets of points show the results for the adapting intensities indicated to the right: 5000, 500, 50, and 5 td. The test light, 1° in diameter and 20 msec in duration, was presented in the center of a 12° adapting field (see inset). Open and filled circles show data for two observers, eight sessions per observer. Thresholds are highest immediately after the onset of the adapting field and decrease with continued exposure. They reach a minimum after approximately 3 min and then rise slightly (particularly at the highest adapting intensity), reaching their final level within 10 min after the onset of the field. For all adapting intensities, most of the changes in sensitivity occur within the first several seconds after the onset of the field. (From Baker, 1949, Tables I and II.)

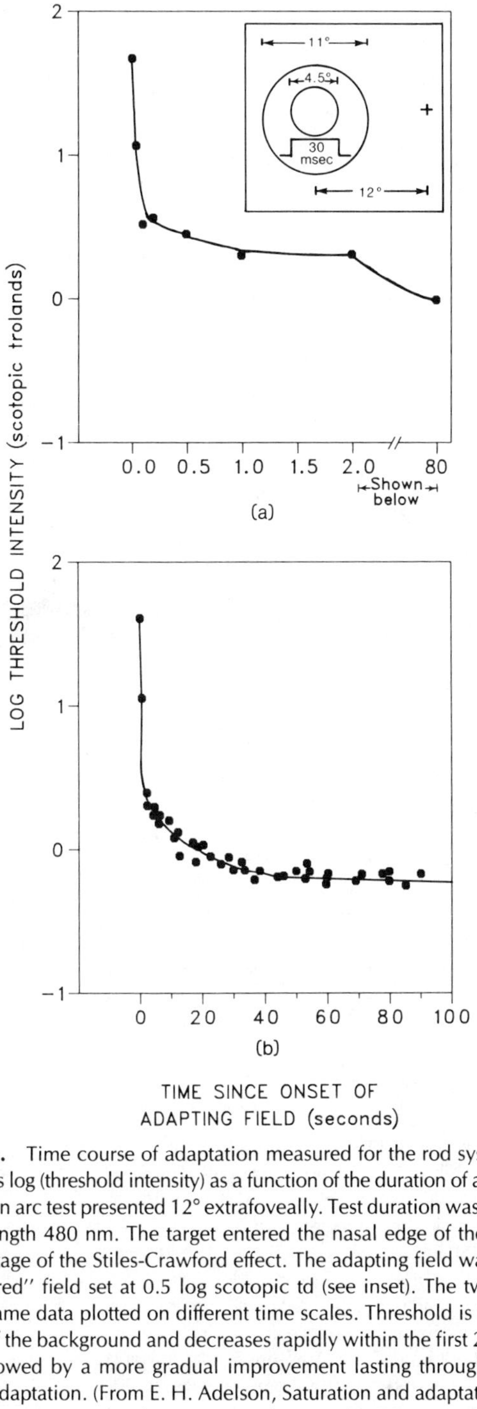

Figure 5.46. Time course of adaptation measured for the rod system. The figure shows log (threshold intensity) as a function of the duration of adaptation for a 4.5-min arc test presented 12° extrafoveally. Test duration was 30 msec, test wavelength 480 nm. The target entered the nasal edge of the pupil to take advantage of the Stiles-Crawford effect. The adapting field was an 11°-diameter "red" field set at 0.5 log scotopic td (see inset). The two graphs show the same data plotted on different time scales. Threshold is highest at the onset of the background and decreases rapidly within the first 200 msec. This is followed by a more gradual improvement lasting through the first minute of adaptation. (From E. H. Adelson, Saturation and adaptation in the rod system, *Vision Research, 22*. Copyright 1982 by Pergamon Press, Ltd. Reprinted with permission.)

which we detect lights in the dark. As intensity levels are increased, the role of this so-called noise in the physical stimulus diminishes, although it may be important in some situations. The evidence for these statements is briefly reviewed below. See also Barlow (1964), Baumgardt (1972), Cornsweet & Hayhoe (in press), and Nachmias (1972).

(a) Quantal Fluctuations and Dark-Adapted Thresholds. Threshold intensity is a statistically defined quantity. An observer's ability to detect a given light varies from trial to trial. This is illustrated in the frequency-of-seeing curves of Figure 5.30. Threshold intensity is usually defined as that intensity which is detected on some criterion percentage of the trials, typically 50–75%. To assess the role of quantal variation in detection, the variability in human performance can be compared to the variability in the stimulus. The smooth curves in Figure 5.30 are the best-fitting cumulative Poisson distributions. For the rods [panel (a)], these curves are fit by assuming an average of between 5 and 7 quanta per trial, depending on the observer. If at detection threshold 5–7 quanta are absorbed the observer's variability can be attributed strictly to the variability in the stimulus.

Using a different line of argument, Hecht et al. (1942) also calculated that 5–14 quanta were *absorbed* by the receptors. They arrived at this value by estimating the number of quanta reaching and being absorbed by the rods. The calculation included a number of estimations, such as the percentage of quanta incident at the cornea that are absorbed or scattered by preretinal structures. The two estimates of threshold intensity, one from the best-fitting curve to the frequency-of-seeing data, and one from the estimate of actual quanta absorbed, were close; Hecht et al. concluded that quantal fluctuations limit the accuracy of detection of single flashes of light by the dark-adapted eye. We shall see below that Hecht et al. may have attributed too much of our variability to physical noise; biological noise must be considered.

It is less clear whether the variability in detection by the dark-adapted fovea is also limited by quantal fluctuations. However, as in the case of the rods, the accuracy of detection is probably influenced, but not entirely limited, by quantal fluctuations. (Baumgardt, 1972; Cohn, 1976.)

(b) Quantal Fluctuations and Intensity Discrimination. Quantal fluctuations do play a part in limiting the accuracy of detection of lights presented in the dark. Most of the preceding sections have dealt with the detectability of one light (the test) presented upon a second, the adapting field. We briefly review the role of quantal fluctuations in the loss of sensitivity with increased adapting intensity. The review is brief because, in general, quantal fluctuations do not play a major role, except perhaps under very limited conditions. For more comprehensive reviews, see the references mentioned earlier in this section.

To examine the role of quantal fluctuations, the visual system is usually compared to a theoretical construct, an ideal detector. The ideal detector can "count" each absorbed quantum and is limited only by the noise due to quantal fluctuations in the stimulus. The ideal detector is also the ideal decision maker, capable of choosing the stimulus with the highest quantal count. (In the case of a brief test light presented upon a steady adapting field, assumptions must be made about the time and area over which the ideal device is counting.) For any combination of test and adapting intensities, an ideal detector will be wrong on some percentage of the trials. Owing to fluctuations in the physical stimulus, the light containing the increment is not necessarily the one with the higher quantal count. If we specify the level of false alarms (mistakes), then t.v.i. curves can be calculated.

What would the t.v.i. curve look like for an ideal detector limited only by quantal noise? Because the variability in quanta increases with the number of quanta absorbed (with increased adapting intensity), threshold intensity would increase with adapting intensity. In fact, the increase in threshold should be proportional to the square root of the adapting intensity since, as intensity increases, the fluctuation (standard deviation) increases in proportion to the square root of intensity. On a log-

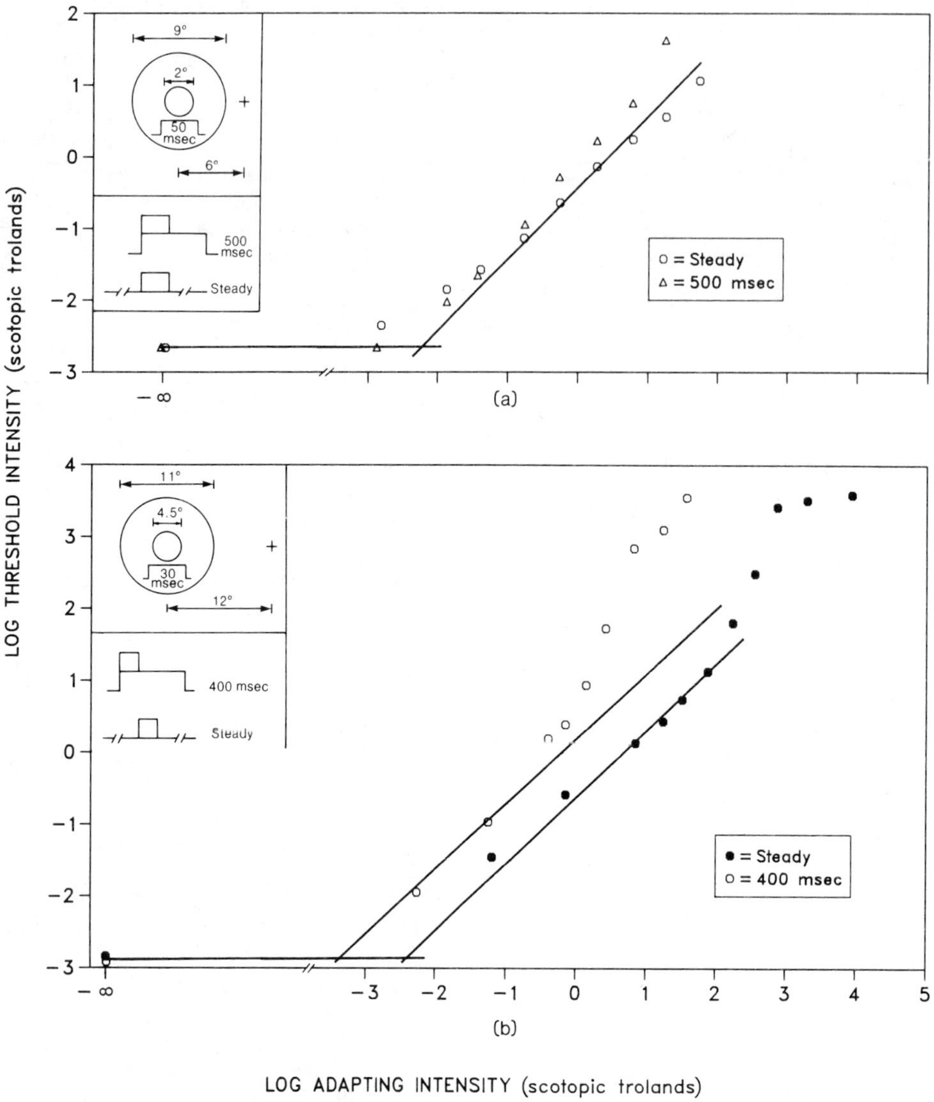

Figure 5.47. (a) Rod system t.v.i. functions for two durations of adaptation: 500 msec (triangles), and steady-state (circles). A 2°, 50-msec test flash was presented 6° extrafoveally in the center of a 9° adapting field; the onset of the flashed adapting field was simultaneous with that of the test (see inset). The 500-msec field is more effective than the steady background at desensitizing the rod system, particularly at higher adapting intensities. (After Geisler, 1979, Fig. 2.) (b) Rod system increment thresholds obtained with a steady adapting background (filled circles) and 400-msec background (open circles). The 480 nm test was presented 12° extrafoveally upon the "red" adapting fields; test and flashed-field onsets were simultaneous. Mean data from two sessions, one observer. The brief adapting light is much more effective than the steady field at raising threshold. (Panel (a) from W. S. Geisler, Evidence for the equivalent-background hypothesis in cones, *Vision Research, 19*. Panel (b) from E. H. Adelson, Saturation and adaptation in the rod system, *Vision Research, 22*. Copyright 1979 and 1982 by Pergamon Press, Ltd. Reprinted with permission.)

log plot, the t.v.i. curves for the ideal detector should follow a slope of 0.5. This means that all psychophysical data which obey Weber's law (slope of 1.0 in Fig. 5.37) are incompatible with detection by an ideal detector. Further, a particularly damaging observation to any approach that considers only stimulus variability is the change in spatial and temporal summation discussed in Sections 3.2.1 and 3.2.2.

Thus the human eye is not an ideal detector. Under most conditions we can reject quantal fluctuations as a limiting factor in visual discrimination (cf. Aguilar & Stiles, 1954; Cornsweet & Pinsker, 1965; Rose, 1948). Only detection of brief, small tests on steady adapting fields produces t.v.i. functions with the requisite slope of one-half (Barlow, 1957, 1958b). However, even under these conditions, noise intrinsic to the visual system must be added to explain the shapes of the curves. In addition, there are a sufficient number of assumptions involved in applying an ideal detector to the steady t.v.i. curve to warrant a degree of skepticism (see Cornsweet & Pinsker, 1965).

To summarize, there is variability in the stimulus, and this factor cannot be ignored in any complete model of the visual system. The physical noise, however, limits the visual system's performance at most under very restricted conditions. Noise in the visual system also affects detectability. This is considered in the next section.

*3.2.6.3. **Intrinsic or Biological Noise.*** The force of the arguments made by Hecht et al. (1942) convinced many that quantal fluctuations limit dark-adapted sensitivity. H. B. Barlow was not among those convinced. Because neural tissue is inherently variable, he reasoned that noise intrinsic to the observer must affect the sensitivity of the visual system much the same way that noise within a physical instrument sets the limit of the instrument's sensitivity. For Barlow, intrinsic noise helped explain why more than 1 quantum of light must be absorbed for detection to occur, even though a single quantum can excite a single rod. Biological or intrinsic noise does exist and probably has numerous sources including the spontaneous isomerization of pigment molecules, variability in neural tissue of the optic nerve, and cortical inefficiencies (Barlow, 1980).

(a) Dark-Adapted Sensitivity. How is the presence of biological noise to be reconciled with the Hecht et al. study? Hecht et al. reached their conclusions via two lines of reasoning, one based on estimates of the number of quanta reaching and being absorbed by the receptors and the other based on the shape of the frequency-of-seeing curves. There are uncertainties involved in both approaches. For example, the argument based on the estimate of quantal absorptions rests on the conclusion that less than 10% of the quanta incident at the cornea are absorbed by the visual pigment. Recent calculations suggest that this estimate is too low, perhaps by as much as a factor of 3 (Barlow, 1980). Further, frequency-of-seeing data are variable, and estimates from them are unreliable. Barlow (1956) and more recently, Teich, Prucnal, Vannucci, Breton, McGill, & Kelly (1982) showed that frequency-of-seeing data such as those in Figure 5.30 can be quantitatively accounted for with combined quantal and intrinsic noise sources. Although the issue has yet to be resolved, the recent data plus clear physiological evidence of intrinsic noise make it likely that intrinsic noise, in part, sets the limit of detectability in the dark (see Barlow, 1980, and Cornsweet & Hayhoe, in press, for further discussion).

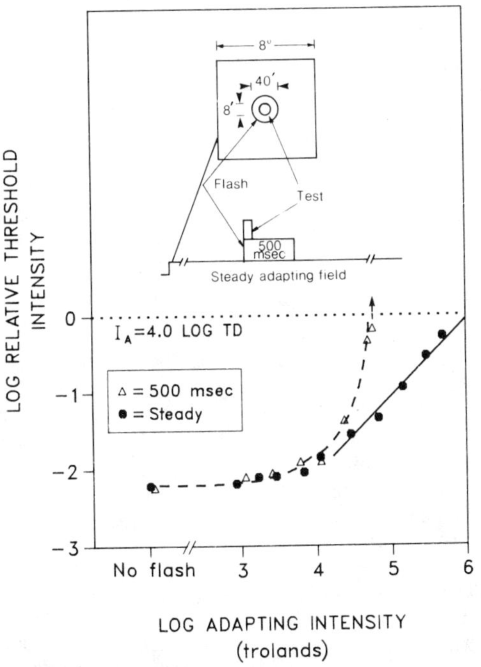

Figure 5.48. Foveal threshold versus intensity functions measured on steady and flashed adapting fields. An 8-min arc, 10-msec test light was presented in the center of a 40-min arc adapting field; the field was presented either continuously (circles) or for 500 msec (triangles). The onset of the test was simultaneous with that of the 500 msec field (SOA = 0). Both the test and adapting lights were superposed on a large steady background of 4.0 log td (see inset). Thresholds on the steady field follow a slope of 1.0 (Weber-Fechner law) at moderate to high adapting intensities. Thresholds on the flashed field are much higher and rise much more steeply. This sharp rise in the threshold function observed with flashed backgrounds is known as "cone system saturation." To obtain saturation, the test must be shorter in duration than the flashed field. (From M. A. Finkelstein & D. C. Hood, Cone system saturation: More than one stage of sensitivity loss, *Vision Research, 21*. Copyright 1981 by Pergamon Press, Ltd. Reprinted with permission.)

(b) Intrinsic Noise and Intensity Discrimination. Barlow related his analysis of intrinsic noise to intensity discrimination, in particular to the t.v.i. function. By assuming that intrinsic noise is also Poisson in nature, he derived t.v.i. functions in much the same way that Rose (1948) did, based on physical noise (see Section 3.2.6.2). Consequently, under all conditions in which the t.v.i. function shows a slope of 1.0, the data are inconsistent with Barlow's model. Perhaps models with intrinsic noise can be generated to deal with the extensive set of conditions showing t.v.i. functions with a slope of 1.0. However, the physiological and psychophysical data suggest that such models would need to consider other factors, such as gain changes induced by the adapting light. These other factors are discussed next.

*3.2.6.4. **Response Compression.*** The cells of the visual system have a limited response range. In the dark, flashes of moderate intensity produce maximum or saturating responses rendering the cells virtually unresponsive to further increases in intensity. This is illustrated in Figure 5.50(a), on page 5-44, in the form of a response-intensity function for a hypothetical cell. The amplitude or size of the response is displayed on the ordinate. The abscissa shows the intensity of the flash of light. For the lower range of flash intensities, response amplitude increases rapidly (linearly) with increases in intensity. For the upper range of intensities, response amplitude increases more slowly and eventually reaches a maximum. Further increases in intensity do not produce further increases in response. This function illustrates what is often called *response compression*.

The response function in Figure 5.50(a) describes the response-intensity relationship of our dark-adapted visual system. Psychophysical data suggest that the cells of the human visual system, like those of lower organisms studied physiologically, have response functions similar to that in Figure 5.50(a) (e.g., Alpern, Rushton, & Torii, 1970; Geisler, 1978b; Hood & Finkelstein, 1979). Figure 5.50(b) can be used to illustrate the dramatic effect that response compression would have on our sensitivity to increments upon adapting fields. The filled circles mark the response of the system to lights of five intensities. Note that the presence of a field of one of the higher intensities would leave very little of the response function available for further increases in intensity.

Figure 5.50(b) illustrates the effect of response compression by plotting the responses to incremental flashes of light upon each of the five adapting intensities. The lowest intensity shown has little effect on the size of the response to incremental lights. However, as adapting intensity is increased, the response to incremental lights diminishes. Note that at the higher adapting intensities, the superimposed flashes produce very small responses. If an adapting field did not lead to a modification of these response-intensity functions, then adapting lights of moderate intensity would leave the visual system blind to incremental changes. This is illustrated in the form of a t.v.i. function in Figure 5.51 (on page 5-45). The solid curves labeled

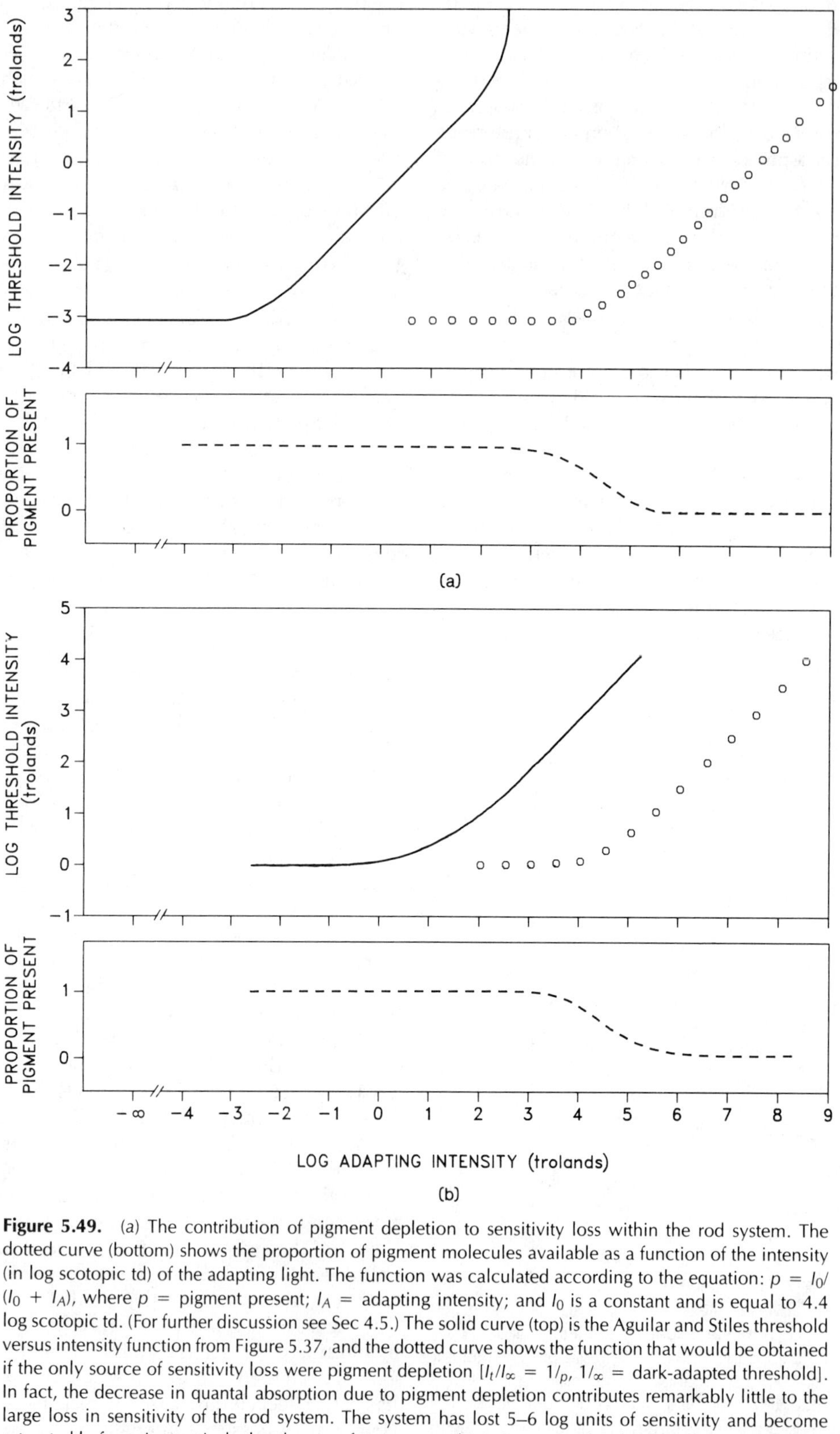

Figure 5.49. (*a*) The contribution of pigment depletion to sensitivity loss within the rod system. The dotted curve (bottom) shows the proportion of pigment molecules available as a function of the intensity (in log scotopic td) of the adapting light. The function was calculated according to the equation: $p = I_0/(I_0 + I_A)$, where p = pigment present; I_A = adapting intensity; and I_0 is a constant and is equal to 4.4 log scotopic td. (For further discussion see Sec 4.5.) The solid curve (top) is the Aguilar and Stiles threshold versus intensity function from Figure 5.37, and the dotted curve shows the function that would be obtained if the only source of sensitivity loss were pigment depletion [$I_t/I_\infty = 1/_p$, $1/_\infty$ = dark-adapted threshold]. In fact, the decrease in quantal absorption due to pigment depletion contributes remarkably little to the large loss in sensitivity of the rod system. The system has lost 5–6 log units of sensitivity and become saturated before pigment is depleted even a few percent. (b) As in part (a), but for the cone system. Again the dashed curve shows the proportion of pigment molecules available; I_0 = 4.5 log (photopic) td. The solid curve is the foveal t.v.i. function derived from Figure 5.33. Below about 4.0 log td (and hence within the range of intensities normally encountered) pigment depletion plays a small role in cone system adaptation. Above 5.0 log td, pigment depletion accounts for all the loss in sensitivity: $p \times I_A$, the effective intensity of the adapting light, is approximately constant. (Modified from Stiles, 1961, Figs. 6 and 7.)

t.v.i. are the rod [panel (a)] and cone [panel (b)] t.v.i. functions from Figure 5.49; the leftmost curve labeled "response compression" shows the t.v.i. function that would result from the response-intensity functions of Figure 5.50(b). According to this simple model, based on response compression, moderate adapting lights drastically desensitize the system. To account for the difference between the observed t.v.i. function and that predicted by response compression, we must consider other mechanisms of adaptation. Unlike the effects of response compression, which are instantaneous, these mechanisms develop with time after the onset of the fields of light. Although the curves labeled response compression in Figure 5.51 are derived from the hypothetical functions in Figure 5.50(b), they resemble the psychophysical data obtained with brief adapting fields (see Section 3.2.5.3). Flashed lights are very effective in raising threshold because there is insufficient time for adaptation to take place; steady lights modify the response intensity function of Figure 5.50(b) and return some of the sensitivity lost to response compression. Next we consider two classes of mechanisms that help maintain sensitivity at high adapting levels.

3.2.6.5. Multiplicative Adaptation. Mechanisms of adaptation are defined by some as factors that decrease the sensitivity of the visual system. By this definition, response compression is one such mechanism. We prefer to define mechanisms of adaptation as those that keep the system responsive at higher adapting intensities, rather than mechanisms that simply decrease sensitivity. Response compression is a necessary evil, the consequence of a system that sets its response range to maximize sensitivity to changes in the ambient light levels. One way to protect the visual system from response compression is to decrease the effective intensity of a flash of light. A number of mechanisms act as if they scale the intensity of light by a multiplicative constant. That is, the change produced by the steady adapting field acts to decrease all intensities by some multiplicative constant. Figure 5.52 (page 5-46) illustrates how multiplicative adaptation alone affects the response-intensity function. Notice that the response-intensity function is moved parallel on a log intensity axis. Although less responsive to lower intensities, the response functions modified in this way allow the system to remain responsive to high intensities. The visual system has a number of mechanisms that produce multiplicative adaptation. For example, pupil constriction at higher ambient light levels decreases the intensity arriving at the retina. At higher light levels, the pupil is about 25% its dark-adapted diameter (1/16 the area). Thus the intensity of the light reaching the retina is 1/16 its dark-adapted value. Pigment depletion, discussed above, is another example of multiplicative adaptation. Steady lights decrease the number of pigment molecules available to absorb quanta of light and consequently decrease the effectiveness of all intensities. Although in principle pigment depletion is very effective, in practice it only affects the t.v.i. function for the cone system, and even there, only at high ambient light levels (see Figure 5.49).

Another factor that may act like a multiplicative change in intensity is the reduction in areal and temporal summation that accompanies increased ambient light levels. By increasing ambient intensity, the effectiveness of large, long lights is decreased (see Sections 4.3.2 and 4.3.3). The visual system has mechanisms, sometimes called automatic gain control mechanisms, that can act as multiplicative changes in intensity. Steady adapting fields decrease the gain and decrease the size of the response. Here we use "gain" to describe adaptive mechanisms not included in the examples above. Models exist that incorporate automatic gain changes with changes in areal and temporal summation (e.g., Fuortes & Hodgkin, 1964; Matin, 1968). Together, pupil changes, pigment depletion, changes in summation, and other multiplicative mechanisms keep the system responsive. Figure 5.50(c) shows the response-intensity functions of Figure 5.50(b) after multiplicative adaptation. Response compression still takes its toll on incremental sensitivity; higher test intensities are needed to produce the same increment in response. However, although lights are less effective, the visual system now remains responsive at higher adapting intensities. The dashed curves in Figure 5.51 show the effect on threshold of adding multiplicative adaptation. Notice that the thresholds, although lower than those predicted from the response compression curve, lie above the observed t.v.i. functions. We need at least one additional mechanism to bring the system to the sensitivity shown by the empirically determined t.v.i. function. That mechanism is response or intensity subtraction.

3.2.6.6. Subtractive Adaptation. Subtractive adaptation was first suggested to explain the color *appearance* of incremental lights (Jameson & Hurvich, 1964). Remarkably, the presence of a large adapting field has little effect on the appearance of a small incremental light. For example, a green patch of light on a larger, relatively intense red field is only slightly altered in hue by the presence of the red field. A large red light combined with the same large green patch would render the patch yellow or orange. When the green patch is smaller, it is as if the adapting field is discounted or subtracted from response to the increment (Jameson & Hurvich, 1964; Shevell, 1978; Walraven, 1976).

To explain our ability to adapt to ambient lights, a similar subtractive mechanism is needed (cf. Adelson, 1982; Geisler, 1981). As Figure 5.50(a) shows, adapting fields produce devastating desensitization by using up most of the response range. Fortunately, a mechanism exists to subtract the response of the adapting field and restore most of this response range. The evidence (e.g., Geisler, 1981) suggests that the subtractive mechanism is very effective at eliminating 80–90% of the effects of the adapting intensity. Like the multiplicative changes, time is required to bring this mechanism into play. Figure 5.50(d) shows the combined results of multiplicative and subtractive changes on the response-intensity functions. The subtractive mechanism of adaptation restores some of the sensitivity lost to response compression. The effects of this mechanism account for the differences between the dashed and solid (empirical) t.v.i. curves in Figure 5.51.

3.2.6.7. Increment Threshold. The mechanisms discussed—physical noise, biological noise, response compression, changes in areal and temporal summation, pigment bleaching, and other multiplicative and subtractive mechanisms—all contribute to the increase in threshold with adapting intensity as described by t.v.i. functions. A complete model of adaptation has yet to be formed, but Figures 5.49 and 5.51 show to a first approximation how multiplicative adaptation, subtractive adaptation, pigment depletion, and response compression contribute to the visual system's sensitivity as defined by the t.v.i. function.

The simplified model outlined here supplies an answer to why rods saturate in the presence of steady backgrounds but cones do not. Suppose that the same model with similar multiplicative and subtractive changes describes both the rod and cone systems. In fact, assume further that the only difference between the systems is their absolute sensitivity. Although this is obviously an oversimplification, to a first approximation

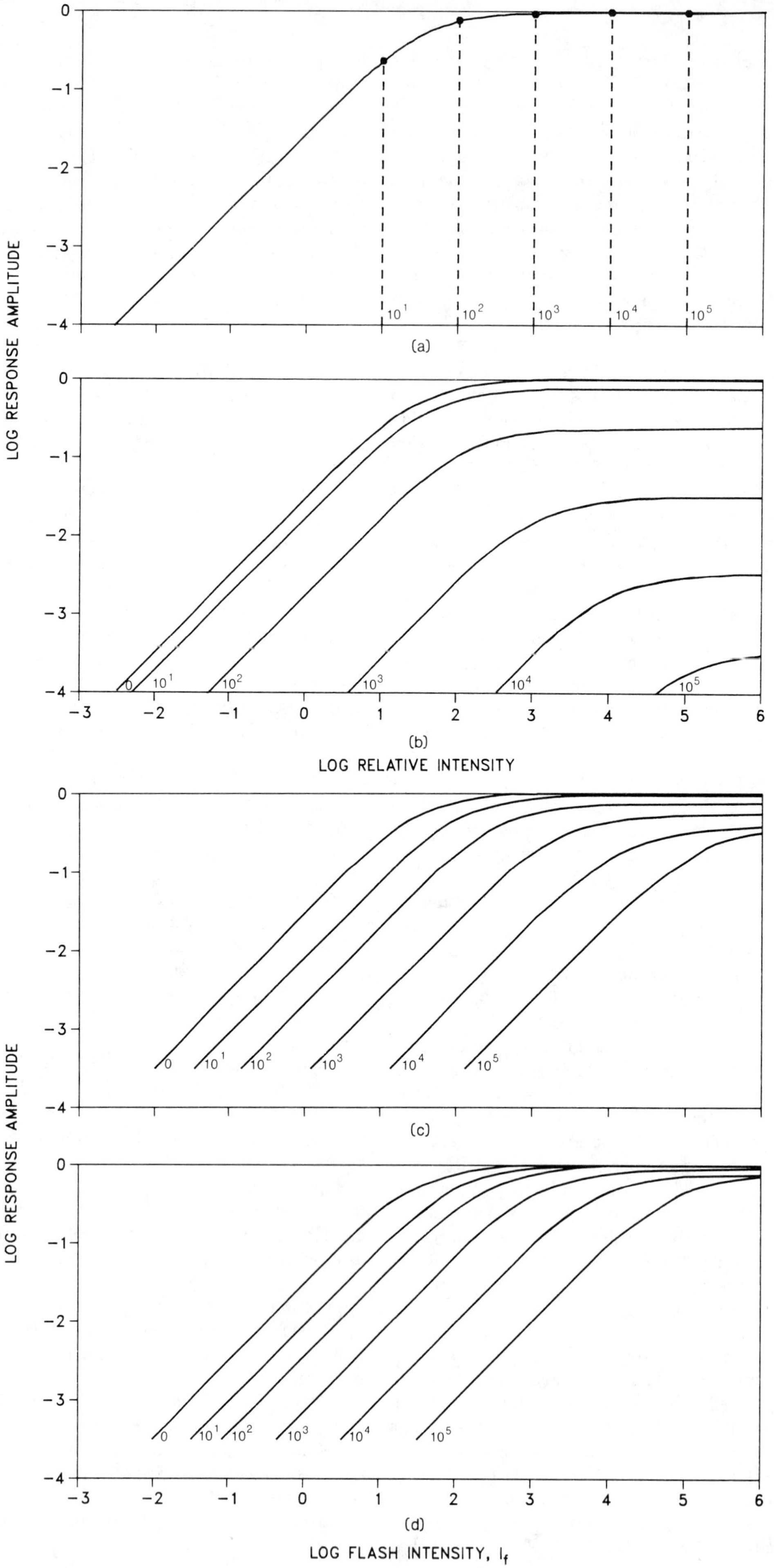
LOG RESPONSE AMPLITUDE
0
−1
−2
−3
−4
10^1
10^2
10^3
10^4
10^5
(a)
0
10^1
10^2
10^3
10^4
10^5
−3
−2
−1
0
1
2
3
4
5
6
(b)
LOG RELATIVE INTENSITY
LOG RESPONSE AMPLITUDE
0
10^1
10^2
10^3
10^4
10^5
(c)
0
10^1
10^2
10^3
10^4
10^5
(d)
LOG FLASH INTENSITY, I_f

the t.v.i. functions for the rod and cone systems are similar. (In fact, they are also similar at the level of the receptor; see Hood & Hock, 1975). The rod system begins to saturate in the presence of backgrounds that are about 5 log units above its threshold. The cone system avoids saturation by being less sensitive. Adapting levels that are 5 log units above the cone threshold deplete sufficient pigment to protect the cone system from saturation. The low sensitivity of the cone system allows pigment depletion to play this protective role.

4. DARK ADAPTATION

After a decrease in the ambient illumination, the sensitivity of the visual system increases. This recovery of sensitivity takes time and can last from a few seconds to tens of minutes. The process of recovery is called dark adaptation. It is most noticeable following extreme changes in ambient light levels. For example, after a person walks from the sunlit outdoors into a darkened movie theater, it may take 30 min or more to detect the weakest lights inside. Upon leaving a well-lit mountain cabin at night, one might not obtain maximum appreciation of the dimmer stars for many minutes. There are also many situations in which the visual system regains sensitivity, but one is unaware of the process. The sensitivity changes may be small, taking place quickly, or large, but taking place very slowly. A glance at the headlights of an oncoming car only transiently affects the ability to see details at night. On the other hand, large changes in sensitivity take place as the sun sets and the ambient illumination passes from daylight through twilight to night. Because these changes occur slowly, one is not aware of them. All these different situations can be approximated in a laboratory, and the recovery of sensitivity can be carefully and quantitatively measured. The result is the dark adaptation function.

4.1. The Dark Adaptation Function

4.1.1. Measuring a Dark Adaptation Function. An experiment by Haig (1941) can be used to introduce the dark adap-

Figure 5.50. The effects of various mechanisms of adaptation on response-intensity and increment threshold functions. (a) Response-intensity function for the dark-adapted visual system. The figure shows response amplitude as a function of the intensity of a flash of light and illustrates the response compression that characterizes the cells of the visual system. The saturating function shown here was calculated from the equation $R(I) = I/(I + \sigma)$, where R is the response amplitude elicited by a flash of intensity, I, and σ is a constant. At low light levels, the response of the system increases linearly with flash intensity (slope of 1.0 on a log-log plot). With further increases in intensity, response amplitude increases more slowly and eventually reaches a maximum, or saturates. The figure also illustrates the problem the visual system confronts in detecting increments in the light adapted state. The filled circles mark the response of the system to five potential adapting intensities. Note that the responses to the adapting lights leave very little of the response function available for further increases in intensity. (b) The effect of response compression on the response-intensity function of the light adapted eye. The curves show the response of the visual system to *incremental flashes* of light (I_F) presented upon adapting fields of five intensities (I_A) and in the dark. The curves are of the form $R(I_F, I_A) = R(I_F + I_A) - R(I_A)$, where $R(I)$ is given by the equation in Figure 5.50(a). The lowest adapting intensity has little effect on the response to incremental stimuli; at higher adapting levels, the superimposed flashes produce very small responses. (c) The effect of multiplicative adaptation on the response-intensity function of panel (b). This class of adaptive mechanism serves to decrease the effective intensity of a light by some constant fraction. It is incorporated into the general response compression equation as a change in σ with adapting intensity: $R(I) = I/[I + \sigma(I_A)]$. Response compression still operates to reduce incremental sensitivity; progressively larger increments in intensity are required to produce the same increment in response. However the visual system remains responsive at higher adapting intensities. (d) The combined effects of multiplicative and subtractive adaptation on the response-intensity functions of panel (b). Subtractive mechanisms discount or subtract out much of the response of the adapting field from the response to the increment, thus restoring some of the sensitivity lost to response compression. That is,

$$R(I_F, I_A) = R[I_F + I_A - f(I_A)] - R[I_A - f(I_A)]$$

where $f(I_A)$ is a function such that $[I_A - f(I_A)] = kI_A$, $k < 1$. In this figure, $k = 0.2$.

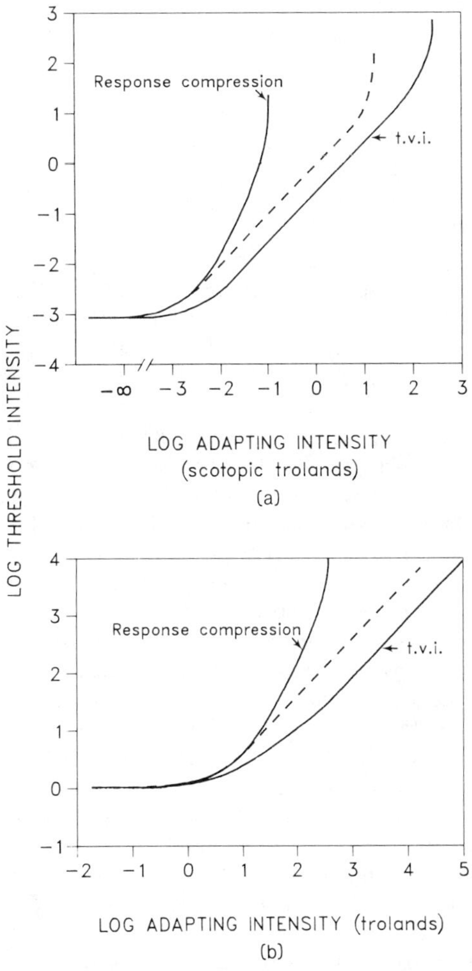

Figure 5.51. A comparison of incremental sensitivity curves derived from models of response compression and multiplicative adaptation with empirically determined t.v.i. curves. Panels (a) and (b) represent the rod and cone systems, respectively. The solid curves labeled "t.v.i." are the empirical functions replotted from Figure 5.49. The curves labeled "response compression" are the increment threshold predicted from the compressive response function of Figure 5.50(b). According to this simple model, lights of moderate intensity should drastically desensitize the visual system. Combining multiplicative adaptation with response compression [as in Fig. 5.50(c)] yields the increment thresholds given by the dashed curves. To bring these thresholds into line with those actually obtained requires a subtractive mechanism, one that assumes either response or intensity subtraction.

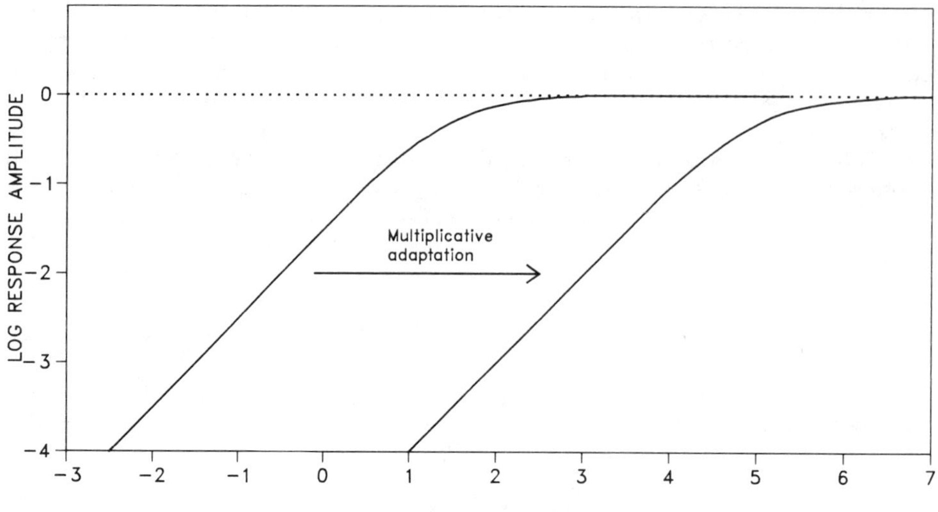

Figure 5.52. The effect of multiplicative adaptation on the response-intensity function. The two curves shown were calculated according to the response compression equation of Figure 5.50(a), $R = I/(I + \sigma)$ with σ increasing from $10^{1.5}$ (left) to 10^5 (right). Because $I/(I + \sigma) = (I/\sigma)/[I/\sigma + 1]$ an increase in σ is equivalent to a decrease in intensity by some constant factor, and the response function is shifted parallel along the log intensity axis. Mechanisms such as pupil constriction, pigment depletion, and changes in areal and temporal summation act to decrease the effective intensity of all lights by some multiplicative constant. Although less responsive to lower intensities, response functions modified in this way allow the system to remain responsive at higher light levels.

tation function. In Haig's experiment, the observers sat in the dark for over 30 min before the experiment began. This assured a relatively stable level of sensitivity. The observer then stared through a 2-mm hole (artificial pupil) at a fixation point and a large adapting light (about 30°). The artificial pupil ensured that measurements would not be affected by changes in pupil size. The adapting light was presented for 4 min. Following its cessation, the observer had to detect a test light or target that was 3° in diameter, 200 msec in duration, and situated 7° from the fixation point (see inset to Fig. 5.53). His ability to detect the test was monitored over time.

The test intensity required for detection is called the threshold intensity or simply "threshold." Figure 5.53 plots log (threshold) for one observer as a function of time in the dark. Each curve shows the results for a different intensity of the adapting field (see figure caption). Notice that at the lowest illumination level (40 td), sensitivity recovers in about 5 min; threshold is within twice (0.3 log unit) the value of the dark-adapted threshold in less than 1.5 min. For the highest adapting level (47,000 td), more than 20 min elapse before threshold falls to within twice the dark adapted value; more than 30 min are needed for complete recovery. The results for intermediate adapting levels fall between these two curves. The adapting fields in Figure 5.53 are analogous to the prevailing illumination in the above examples and in Table 5.2. Recovery of sensitivity upon leaving a well-lit cabin would be described by the function between the lower two in Figure 5.53. Upon entering a movie theater one's dark adaptation function would be best described by one between the top two in Figure 5.53.

4.1.2. The Combined System: Rod and Cone Branches. The dark adaptation curves of Figure 5.53 reflect the combined action of the rod and cone systems. Dark adaptation of the cone system is shown by the dashed lines, and the recovery of the rod system by the solid lines. Both rod and cone branches are evident after adaptation to the highest light intensities; at lower intensities, only a rod branch is seen. Note that the cone system recovers sensitivity much more quickly than does the rod system, but the absolute sensitivity of the rod system is much greater. Unless lights are restricted to the rod-free fovea, rod branches are always present in dark adaptation curves.

The test stimulus used in Haig's experiment was chosen to favor the rod system. It was short-wavelength light, to which the rod system is relatively more sensitive than the cone system; it was positioned 7° in the periphery where the rods are more numerous (see Fig. 5.3); and it was large and long in duration, favoring the greater areal and temporal summation of the rod system (see Section 1.3). In the following sections we examine the effects of a variety of test and adapting parameters on dark adaptation within the rod and cone systems.

4.1.3. Cone System Adaptation. The cone system adapts so quickly under most conditions that the existence of dark adaptation in the cone system was once questioned (see Hecht, 1921 for a discussion). The cone system does take time to return to dark-adapted sensitivity following reasonably intense light, and this can be easily studied by restricting the test light to the rod-free fovea. Figure 5.54(a) shows the recovery of the foveal sensitivity following four levels of adapting light. These data are from a study by Mote and Riopelle (1951). The test light was 1° in diameter and 200 msec in duration. The test was of long-wavelength light (red filter) and centrally fixated, ensuring that the cone system would be isolated. Notice that even at the highest illumination level, which is more than 5 log td, recovery is complete within 10 min and thresholds within twice the dark-adapted value within 5 min. At the lower level used, threshold is returned to dark-adapted values well within 4 min. Compare this to the rod recovery seen in Figure 5.53 for approximately the same adapting illumination (open squares) where 15 min elapsed before threshold was within a factor of 2 from dark-adapted levels.

For lower levels of adaptation, the cone system returns to its absolute sensitivity even more quickly. Nonetheless, these very fast changes in sensitivity have been measured, and they

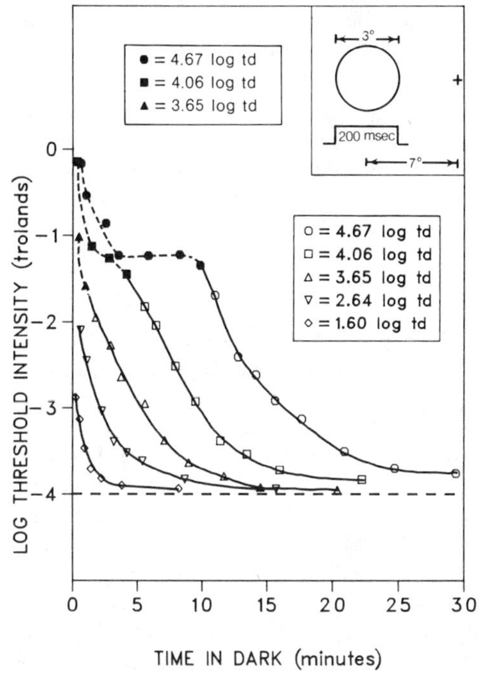

Figure 5.53. Dark adaptation functions following 4 min of adaptation to various intensities of "white" light: 4.67 log td (circles); 4.06 log td (squares); 3.65 log td (triangles); 2.64 log td (inverted triangles); 1.60 log td (diamonds). The figure shows threshold for test lights as a function of time in the dark. Data are for one observer from a single session. The test was a "violet" light (Corning No. 511) 3° in diameter and 200 msec in duration. It was delivered 7° nasal to the fovea (see inset). The filled symbols indicate that the test appeared violet at threshold. The dashed curves through these points presumably delineate the cone-mediated portion of the function; the rod-mediated thresholds are connected by the solid curves. Both rod and cone dark adaptation are evident after adaptation to the highest light intensities. At lower intensities, only a rod branch is seen. The cone system recovers sensitivity more quickly than the rod system, but the absolute sensitivity of the rod system is greater. (From Haig, 1941, Table 3.)

are not instantaneous (Baker, 1953; Crawford, 1937, 1947). Figure 5.54(b) shows Crawford's (1937) measurements after prolonged adaptation (5 min or more) to relatively dim lights. The data points marked by the infinity symbol are the incremental measurements upon the adapting field. Notice that the time axis is in log (sec) and the first measurement is at about 200 msec. Following the offset of the weakest adapting field (about 17 cd·m^{-2}), sensitivity returns within 10 sec. Of course, sensitivity of the fovea recovers even more quickly following weaker lights. For most naturally occurring situations (compare Table 5.2 to Fig. 5.54), the sensitivity of the foveal cone system recovers very quickly in the dark.

4.1.4. Predicting Rod and Cone Dark Adaptation. The dark adaptation functions obtained for the rod and cone systems are affected by the parameters of both the test light and the adapting field. Each function changes with changes in the wavelength, the size, and the duration of the test, as well as its retinal position. Similarly, variations in the conditions of adaptation, such as the area, duration, and intensity of the adapting field, affect the recovery of each system. Below we examine the influence of each of these parameters on dark adaptation within the rod and cone systems.

4.2. Variations in the Test Light

4.2.1. Theory: A Duplicity Model. The shape of the dark adaptation function changes with test light parameters. Many of these changes can be understood by assuming independent rod and cone systems and considering how each individual system is affected by the particular stimulus conditions. We can construct a model much like that used to describe spectral sensitivity data (see Section 1.2). We will assume, in accordance with duplicity theory, that the cone system subserves color vision and discrimination of fine detail, mediates detection at high intensities, and dark adapts relatively quickly. Conversely, the rod system does not have the capacity for color vision or for the

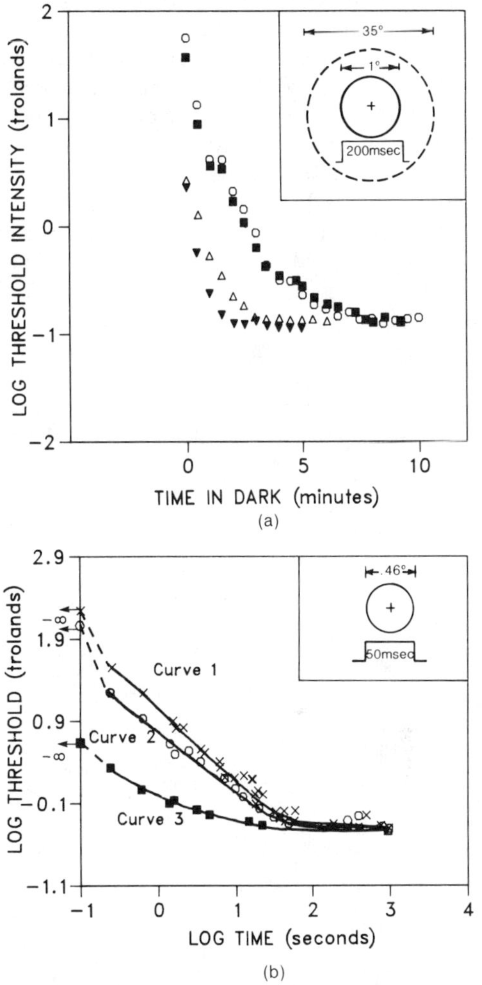

Figure 5.54. (a) Foveal dark adaptation following 300 sec of adaptation to various intensities of "white" light: 5.05 log td (circles); 4.75 log td (squares); 4.05 log td (triangles); 3.75 log td (inverted triangles). Threshold (in log td) is shown as a function of time in the dark. Each point is the mean of the thresholds obtained for one observer from five sessions. The "red" test was 1° in diameter and 200 msec in duration; the preadapting field subtended 35° (see inset). Even at the highest preadapting intensity, the cone system recovers sensitivity completely within 10 min; threshold is less than twice the dark-adapted threshold within 5 min. At the lowest adapting intensity, threshold returns to the dark-adapted value well within 4 min. (From Mote & Riopelle, 1951, Tables 1-4.) (b) Foveal dark adaptation following adaptation to fields of three intensities: 3.2 log cd·m^{-2} (curve 1); 2.9 log cd·m^{-2} (curve 2); and 1.2 log cd·m^{-2} (curve 3). Test flashes were 0.46° in diameter and 50 msec in duration. The points marked by the infinity symbol are the increment threshold upon the adapting background. Sensitivity recovers quickest following adaptation to the weakest background and in all cases returns to the fully dark adapted level within 1–2 min. (From B. H. Crawford, The change of visual sensitivity with time, *Proceedings of the Royal Society of London*, 1937, *123B*. Reprinted with permission.)

resolution of details; it has greater absolute sensitivity than the cone system and it dark adapts slowly.

Figure 5.55(a) presents a set of hypothetical dark adaptation curves measured following some fixed set of adapting conditions. The dashed curves represent cone system adaptation, the solid curves, rod system adaptation. Assume that for each system, if the adapting conditions are held constant, the shape of the dark adaptation function is invariant with variations in stimulus conditions. Changes in parameters such as the wavelength of the test change the absolute sensitivity of a system but not the way in which the system recovers sensitivity over time. Assume, too, that the rod and cone systems are independent; the sensitivity of one system is not affected by the level of activity in the other. The independence assumption predicts that the overall dark adaptation function will approximate an envelope of the rod and cone functions. We refer to the above assumptions collectively as comprising a "duplicity model" of dark adaptation.

For example, suppose that the two sets of curves in Figure 5.55 each represent dark adaptation for a test of a different wavelength. Each cone curve is identical in shape; the different cone curves are positioned vertically according to the spectral sensitivity of the cone system [dashed curve, Fig. 5.55(b)]. Similarly, the rod dark adaptation function has a single shape, and the separations between the rod curves indicate that system's sensitivity [solid curve, Fig. 5.55(b)]. According to this model, if we change some other parameter, for example, the size of the test light, only the absolute sensitivities of the individual systems will change. The shape of the dark adaptation function for a given system remains constant, as does the shape of its spectral sensitivity. We assume that only the relative sensitivity *between* systems changes. Just as this model was shown to alter the shape of the overall spectral sensitivity function (see Section 1.5), it will alter the shape of the overall dark adaptation curve. The duplicity model is used below to predict changes in the dark adaptation function with test parameters. We shall see that some variations in the test can be handled by the model, whereas others cannot.

4.2.2. Wavelength of the Test

4.2.2.1. Support for the Model. By varying the wavelength of a test light, results similar to those schematized in Figure 5.55 can be produced. The data presented in Figure 5.56 are from a study by Auerbach and Wald (1954). The test light, a 1° circular target of either 621 or 436 nm, was positioned 6° in the periphery. With the 621 nm light, the data resemble the foveal cone function (Fig. 5.54) until well over 30 min into dark adaptation. At this point the rods become more sensitive and a rod branch is evident. The data for the 436 nm test resemble those in Figure 5.53, which were also collected with a violet light. There is a brief cone branch followed by a slowly falling rod branch. If the rod and cone systems are independent and the dark adaptation functions are invariant with wavelength, then the rod and cone branches in Figure 5.56 should be the same shape and displaced vertically by the difference in sen-

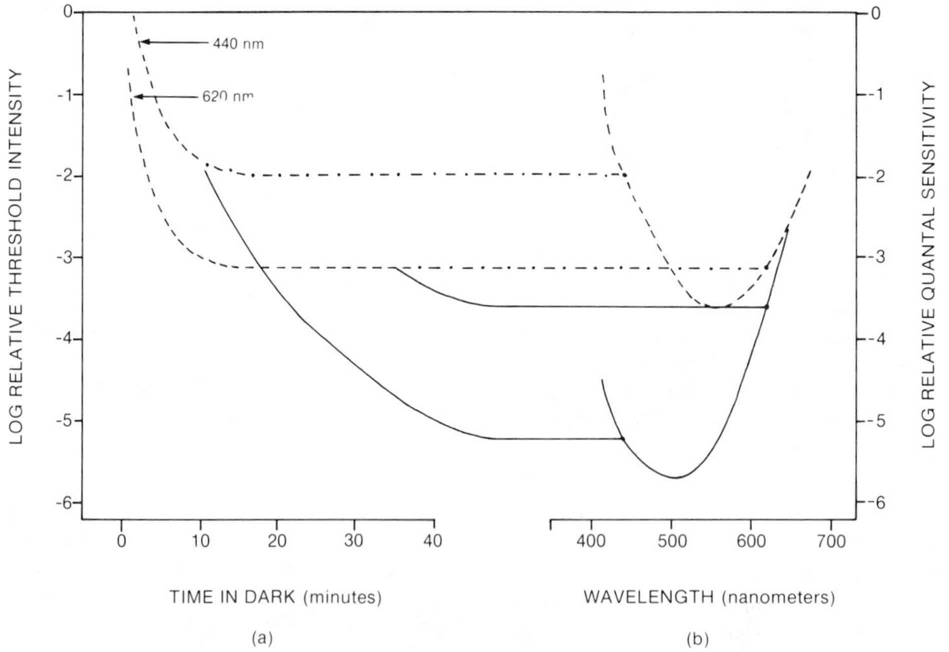

Figure 5.55. Predictions of a duplicity model of dark adaptation. The model assumes independent rod and cone systems. (a) Hypothetical dark adaptation functions for the rod system (solid curves) and cone system (dashed curves). The cone system recovers sensitivity relatively quickly and mediates detection early in dark adaptation. The rod system dark-adapts slowly but shows a greater absolute sensitivity than the cone system. The shape of the dark adaptation function for each system is assumed to be fixed for a fixed set of adapting conditions. Changes in the parameters of the test change the absolute sensitivity of a system but not the way in which the system recovers sensitivity over time. The overall dark adaptation function approximates an envelope of the rod and cone functions. The figure illustrates the effect of an increase in test wavelength from 440 to 620 nm. The absolute sensitivity of the cone system increases; rod system sensitivity decreases. The individual dark adaptation functions are shifted along the ordinate according to the relative spectral sensitivity of each receptor system [indicated in part (b)]. The differential shifting of the rod and cone curves changes the shape of the overall dark adaptation function; the cone branch is much more pronounced at 620 than at 440 nm.

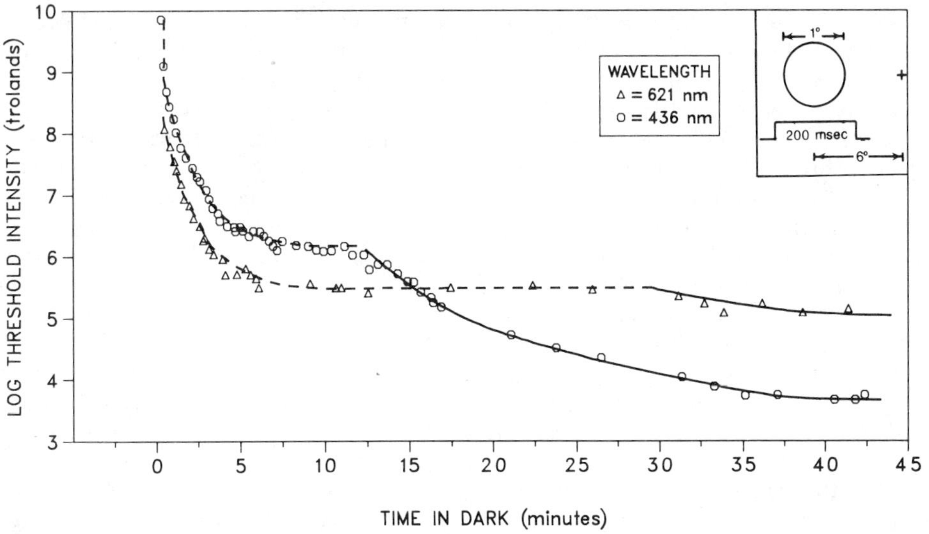

Figure 5.56. Dark adaptation functions for tests of two wavelengths: 436 nm (circles) and 621 nm (triangles); data for one observer. The observer preadapted for 5 min to a 6.2 log cd·m^{-2} "white" light. The test flash, 1° in diameter and 200 msec in duration, was presented 6° extrafoveally (see inset). The dashed curve is a template derived from the 621 nm cone system data and shifted to fit the 436 nm thresholds. The solid curve is a rod system template fit to the 436 nm data and shifted to coincide with the 621 nm points. The fit of the templates indicates that the shape of the dark adaptation function for each receptor system remains invariant with changes in test wavelength. (From E. Auerbach & G. Wald, Identification of a violet receptor in human color vision, *Science, 120*. Copyright 1954 by the American Association for the Advancement of Science. Reprinted with permission.)

sitivity of the rod and cone systems to the test lights. The dashed curve through the 436 nm data is the dashed curve through the 621 nm data shifted vertically. Likewise we have fit the solid rod curve through the 436 nm data and shifted it vertically to fit the 621 nm data. To a first approximation the assumptions appear reasonable. Other studies in which the wavelength of the test was varied and rod and cone branches examined produced similar results (cf. Chapanis, 1947; Hecht, Haig, & Chase, 1937).

4.2.2.2. Limitations of the Model: Cone System Dark Adaptation. The rod dark adaptation function has the same shape independent of wavelength. The cone system dark adaptation function, however, can be shown to change with wavelength. In fact, the data from Figure 5.56 were collected by Auerbach and Wald (1954) as part of a study of multiple cone branches. Auerbach and Wald suggested that a close examination of the cone branch for the 436 nm test light reveals evidence of two or three separate cone branches. By varying the wavelength of intense adapting fields, multiple cone branches can be more easily seen (e.g., Auerbach & Wald, 1954; Das, 1964; DuCroz & Rushton, 1966). These multiple branches do not lend themselves to a simple extension of the duplicity model with three or so independent cone mechanisms, each with invariant curves (cf. Das, 1964; DuCroz & Rushton, 1966). Fortunately, following a white adapting light, a single cone branch is a reasonable description of the data (see references above and Mandelbaum & Mintz, 1941; Stiles, 1949).

According to the duplicity theory of dark adaptation, the cone plateau should provide a measure of the dark-adapted cone threshold. However, notice the data for the two highest adapting intensities in Figure 5.53. There is a suggestion that the cone plateau is lower for the lower adapting intensity. If, as assumed, we are dealing with an independent, invariant cone system, its absolute threshold should be independent of the preceding adapting conditions. Wolf and Zigler (1954) claim that varying the duration of the adapting light does not affect the cone plateau, but varying the intensity does. Their observer's task was to detect the presence of a grating, and this task may affect the shape of the dark adaptation functions (see Section 4.3.5). The conditions under which the cone plateau remains invariant are still being debated (cf. Drum, 1980; Wooten, Fuld, & Spillman, 1975).

Another problem for the model apparent in Figure 5.53 concerns the appearance of the test light. Recall that we have assumed independent rod and cone systems, the cone system alone providing color vision. The filled symbols in the figure indicate that the test appeared colored at threshold. Notice that at lower adapting intensities, the threshold for color is lower than the cone plateaus seen at higher adapting intensities. Mote and Riopelle (1953) also observed that, following low-intensity adapting lights, a violet test appeared colored at intensities up to 2 log units below the cone plateau obtained after intense adapting lights.

The appearance of color below the cone plateau, and the variation in the level of the cone plateau, suggest that either the rods are contributing to color vision, or the rod and cone systems are not independent. Actually, there is evidence that both assumptions should be questioned. A number of studies report that the rod system can contribute to the appearance of color (e.g., McCann, 1972; B. Stabell & U. Stabell, 1976a, 1976b). Other studies suggest violations of rod–cone independence during dark adaptation. We believe that the variation in the level of the cone plateau and the appearance of color at very low intensities are probably two separate phenomena. Our working hypothesis is that test lights that appear colored below the cone plateau are probably examples of rod-mediated color vision and in some cases rod–cone summation. On the other hand, clear cone plateaus that fall at different levels are probably examples of forms of rod–cone interaction.

4.2.3. Spatial Variation of the Test. Varying the size of the test light can affect the dark adaptation function. It is important to distinguish between effects due to changes in areal summation within the rod and cone systems and effects due to the retinal location of the test.

4.2.3.1. ***Changes in Areal Summation.*** The spatial summing ability of the visual system changes during dark adaptation; the dark adaptation functions are not invariant with changes in test size. Some of the data relating to changes in summation are considered in more detail when we discuss the equivalent background concept (see Section 5). For now, Figure 5.57 can be taken as a summary of a number of studies. The two curves are hypothetical dark adaptation functions for different test areas (or durations). The arguments to be made here for changes in area also apply to small changes in duration. With time in the dark the curves for small, brief targets diverge from those obtained with larger, longer-duration targets. Early in dark adaptation there is less of an advantage (less summation) in using a large or long test than there is late into dark adaptation. The changes in areal summation by the rod system are large and take place slowly during dark adaptation (e.g., Arden & Weale, 1954; Blakemore & Rushton, 1965; Craik & Vernon, 1941; and see Fig. 5.68(a) in Section 5 from Crawford, 1947). Changes in areal summation by the cone system are relatively small and take place within 100 sec or so (see Geisler, 1978a; Rinalducci, Higgins, & Cramer, 1970).

Although the evidence is clear that changes in summation take place during dark adaptation, it is important to be careful not to attribute all changes in shape to changes within homogeneous populations of cells. Increasing the area (or even the duration) of a test target can bring into play different populations of cells. (For example, if the short-wave cone system sums light over a larger test area than do the other cone systems, then under some conditions larger test areas may be detected by different populations of cells at different times during dark adaptation.)

4.2.3.2. ***Large Changes in Area.*** For test lights larger than the limit of areal summation, the dark adaptation functions

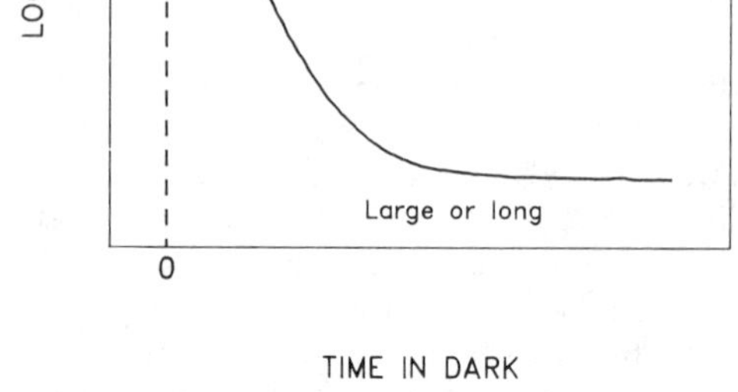

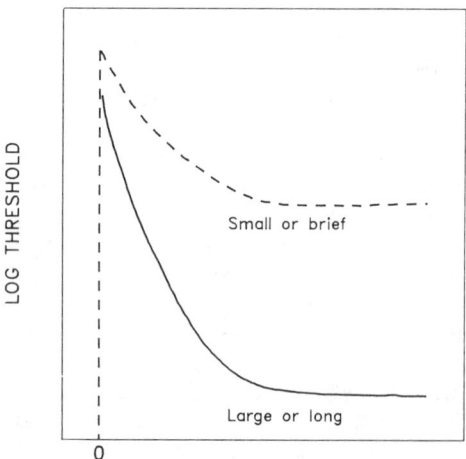

Figure 5.57. The effect of areal and temporal summation on the dark adaptation function. The curves are hypothetical functions showing the recovery of sensitivity over time for tests of two sizes or durations: small or brief (dashed curve) and large or long-duration (solid curve). The ability of the visual system to integrate light over space and time increases during dark adaptation. With increasing time in the dark, the curve for a small (or brief) target and that for a larger (or longer) target diverge.

are not identical. Hecht, Haig, and Wald (1935) measured dark adaptation functions with test lights centered in the fovea and ranging in size from 2 to 20°. Their data in Figure 5.58 show clear rod and cone branches for all tests except the 2° target, the target falling in the relatively rod-free fovea. We have drawn a solid curve through the data for the 20° target. To allow comparison of rod branches, this curve has been shifted vertically to fit the last two data points for the 10, 5, and 3° targets (these are the dashed curves). To a first approximation, the rod branch does not change shape as the target is decreased in size. These data are consistent with the invariance assumptions of the duplicity model (Section 4.2.1). Simply assuming a change in the absolute sensitivity of the rod system describes these data.

The rod system is more sensitive to the larger targets in part because they fall in the more sensitive peripheral retina. However, some other aspect of the larger target, such as the larger circumference, may also be involved. Unlike the rod system, the cone system's branch does change shape with increased size. This change in shape may be due to the involvement of different receptor types.

4.2.4. Temporal Variation of the Test. Varying the duration of the test light produces changes in the dark adaptation function that are analogous to those produced by changes in the size of the test light. Prolonged viewing without fixation allows the observer to use the most sensitive part of the retina for detection. Smaller changes in exposure duration (under 1 sec) produce changes in the dark adaptation function similar to those shown in Figure 5.57. The ability of the visual system to integrate light energy over time increases quickly during dark adaptation. For example, the evidence suggests that critical duration (see Section 2.1) following moderately intense backgrounds can change from about 30–40 msec early in dark adaptation to about 100–200 msec after complete dark adaptation (Crawford, 1937; Montellese, Brown, & Sharpe, 1979; Stewart, 1972). Over half of the change takes place within 10 sec after the offset of the adapting field. (See Fig. 5.69 in Section 5.1.2 from Crawford, 1937; Montellese et al., 1978; Stewart, 1972).

4.2.5. Nonhomogeneous Tests. This chapter has been restricted largely to test lights that are spatially homogeneous and are presented for a fixed, continuous duration. Dark adaptation has been measured for a variety of test targets including airplane silhouettes (Miles, 1943) and pictures of Hamburg Harbor (Crawford, 1947). Two variations of the test light of particular interest are periodic variations in space or time. Some investigators have measured the threshold intensity needed to distinguish between a spatially or temporally varied light and a homogeneous light (e.g., J. L. Brown, Graham, Leibowitz, & Ranken, 1953; Lythgoe & Tansley, 1929). Although these variations are dealt with explicitly in other chapters (Olzak & Thomas, Chapter 7, Pokorny & Smith, Chapter 8, and Watson, Chapter 6), one study of particular interest will be described here. J. L. Brown et al. measured dark adaptation functions using gratings of different bar widths. The observer had to detect the correct orientation of the grating. The curves in Figure 5.59 show the threshold intensities needed as a function of time in the dark. Notice that for the coarser gratings, the dark adaptation function shows both rod and cone branches. For finer gratings, however, only a cone branch is seen.

These data nicely illustrate the difference in resolving ability of the rod and cone systems. Recall that duplicity theory proposes the cone system as the system involved in detailed discriminations. In the experiment summarized in Figure 5.59 when

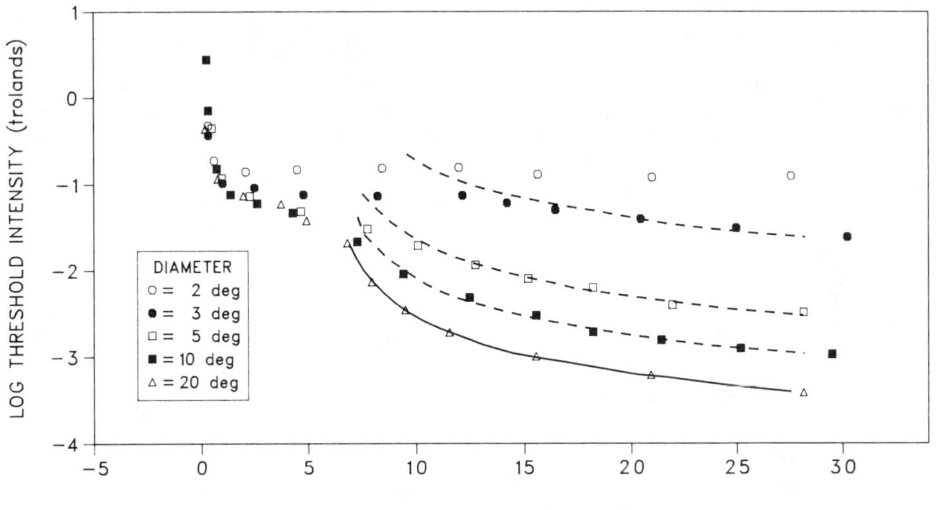

Figure 5.58. Dark adaptation functions for centrally fixated tests of various diameters: 2° (open circles); 3° (filled circles); 5° (open squares); 10° (filled squares); and 20° (triangles). The curves plot threshold (in log td) as a function of time in the dark (in minutes). Data are the means of the thresholds obtained for one observer from at least three sessions. (Data for a second observer were virtually identical whereas the thresholds for a third subject were identical for the 10 and 20° tests but fell 0.3–0.7 log unit below the others for the smaller targets.) The observer preadapted for 2 min to a 3.8 log td "white" light. The functions show clear rod and cone branches for all but the 2° test which falls in the relatively rod-free fovea. The solid curve fitted to the 20° data has been shifted up to fit the final two points in the 10, 5, and 2° data (dashed curves). To a first approximation, the rod branch does not change shape as test size is decreased. The data are described by simply assuming a decrease in the absolute sensitivity of the rod system. The cone branch, however, does change shape as test size is changed. (From Hecht, Haig, & Wald, 1935, Table 1.)

the finest gratings are used (bar widths between 1 and 4 min arc), the sensitivity of the rod system never reaches that of the cone system at any point during dark adaptation. The data are also of practical importance. They show clearly that time in the dark to obtain maximum sensitivity depends on the task. It is pointless for an observer to dark-adapt for 30 min if the task requires enough light to detect fine details. Similar conclusions emerge from studies in which the test is temporally varied.

4.3. Variations in the Adapting Field

4.3.1. Intensity of Adaptation. The effects of adapting intensity on the subsequent dark adaptation function were illustrated in Figure 5.53. Increasing the adapting intensity has two obvious consequences. First, whereas only a rod branch is seen at low intensities, a cone branch emerges early in dark adaptation at high intensities. The rod system shows the greater absolute sensitivity. Only following intense adaptation is the rod system sufficiently desensitized for the cone system to determine the detection threshold. Second, with increased adapting intensity, dark adaptation is prolonged. The rod and cone branches shift rightward along the time axis and change shape. This shape change can be readily seen in the rod functions, which become shallower with increased adapting intensity. We return to the issue of shape change when we discuss theoretical attempts to describe the dark adaptation function (see Section 4.5.3).

4.3.2. Duration of Adaptation. Increasing the duration of an adapting light increases its effectiveness. Figure 5.60, from a study by Baker (1955), nicely illustrates the effect. A 50,000-td adapting field was turned on for periods of time ranging up to about 800 sec. After the appropriate adapting duration (indicated by the arrows) the field was dimmed to 5 td and the resulting changes in sensitivity tracked over time. The data at the top of the figure (open circles) show the increment thresholds obtained on the high-intensity field; the data at the bottom show the recovery of sensitivity following the decrease in adapting intensity. Notice that with increases in the duration of adaptation the rod and cone thresholds take longer to return to base line. Increasing the duration of the adapting light has qualitatively similar effects to increasing the adapting intensity (see Fig. 5.53). Next we examine the effects of adapting duration on the rod and cone systems. Special attention is given to equal-energy adapting lights.

4.3.2.1. Rod System. Over a wide range of intensities and durations, increasing the duration of the adapting light is equivalent to increasing its intensity. Figure 5.61 (from Haig, 1941) shows dark adaptation functions obtained after adaptation to each of five durations of a 3.65-log-td light. Note that increases in duration of up to 4 min or more prolong the time course of dark adaptation. A question of both practical and theoretical significance is, over what combination of intensity and time will a constant amount of energy ($I \times T$ = constant) produce equivalent rod dark adaptation functions? The general answer is that, excluding the earliest part of dark adaptation, equal-energy adapting fields of up to 60 sec or more produce essentially identical dark adaptation functions. This includes adapting lights as brief as 600 msec and as intense as 7.3 log td · sec (Pugh, 1975b). For the first 10–60 sec of the dark adaptation function, increasing the adapting intensity can raise threshold more than increasing its duration (see Crawford, 1946; Mote & Riopelle, 1953; Rushton & Powell, 1972b).

Increasing the duration of a constant-intensity adapting light beyond the 60 sec during which intensity and time trade-off increases its effectiveness. In fact, Figure 5.61 suggests that

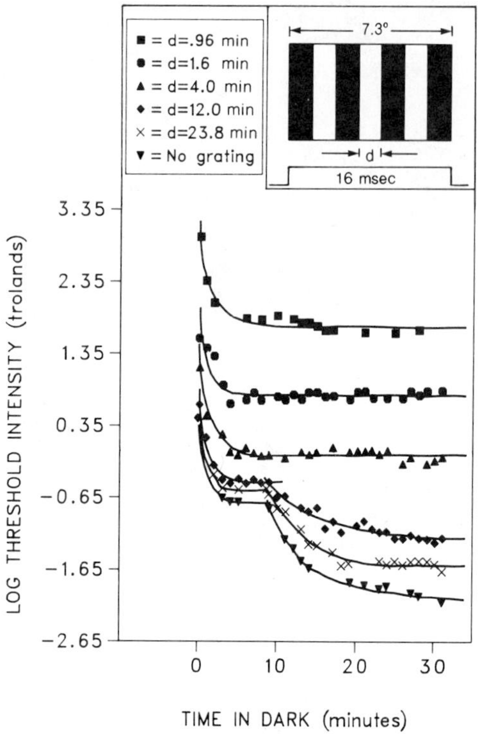

Figure 5.59. Thresholds for resolution of detail during dark adaptation. The observer's task was to detect the orientation of square-wave gratings of various bar widths as indicated beside each curve. The total test field subtended 7.3°; test duration was 16 msec (see inset). All stimuli were presented centrally. Also included is a "no grating" condition showing the dark adaptation function for a 7.3° homogeneous test stimulus. Measurements were made following 5 min of adaptation to a 3.7 log cd·m^{-2} "white" light. With the homogeneous test and the coarser gratings (bar widths of 23.8 and 12.0 min arc), the dark adaptation functions show both rod and cone branches. With finer gratings, only the rapidly adapting cone branch is seen. The data are consistent with the notion that the cone system is responsible for detailed discriminations. (From J. H. Brown, C. H. Graham, H. Leibowitz, & H. B. Rankin, Luminance thresholds for the resolution of visual detail during dark adaptation, *Journal of the Optical Society of America*, 1953, *43*. Reprinted with permission.)

prolonging adapting lights for 4 min or more increases their effectiveness in delaying complete dark adaptation. (See also Wald & Clark, 1937.)

4.3.2.2. Cone System. Increasing the duration of the adapting light also affects the dark adaptation function of the cone system. Figures 5.54 and 5.62 are from the same study. Compare the changes in adapting intensity [Fig. 5.54(a)] to those in adapting duration (Fig. 5.62). Figure 5.62 shows dark adaptation following four durations of light adaptation. Notice that there are clear increases in the effectiveness of the adapting field for increases in duration of at least 150 sec. It is a mistake to conclude from Figure 5.62 that adaptation durations beyond 150 sec are not more effective even though the 150- and 300-sec curves are similar. In this range of intensities, doubling the intensity of the adapting light has a small effect [see Fig. 5.54(a)]. It might therefore be expected that doubling the duration would have a similarly small effect. The dark adaptation curves of the cone system can likely be affected by increasing duration beyond 2 min, but probably not to the extent that rod curves are affected.

Although increases in intensity and time appear to have similar effects in Figure 5.54 and 5.62, adapting lights of equal energy actually produce equivalent cone functions under very restricted conditions. Figure 5.63 is from Crawford's (1946) classic study. Each panel contains dark adaptation functions obtained after adaptation to a field of constant energy. Note that the time axis is logged. The picture is not simple. In general, the curves agree only for high intensities and for times in the dark exceeding 30 sec. Early in dark adaptation, the more intense the adapting field, the more the threshold is elevated. Though longer duration lights are less effective at early times in the dark, they are often more effective late in dark adaptation. (This finding is consistent with data to be discussed that show that recovery can be slower after longer adapting lights that are equated for the amount of pigment bleached.)

4.3.3. Spatial Variation of the Adapting Field. A number of studies have varied the spatial relationship between test and adapting field and measured the course of dark adaptation. Most of these studies were conducted to test one or another theoretical notion and are mentioned again below. In general, if the adapting light is larger than the test, then the dark adaptation functions of the rod system are independent of the area of the adapting light (Teller & Gestrin, 1969; Westheimer, 1968). These findings do not mean that the effect of the adapting light acts locally. It is clear that the effect of an adapting light spreads far beyond its boundaries and further than predicted by stray light (at least for the rods). This desensitization effect is graded with distance from an edge and is not as extensive as originally

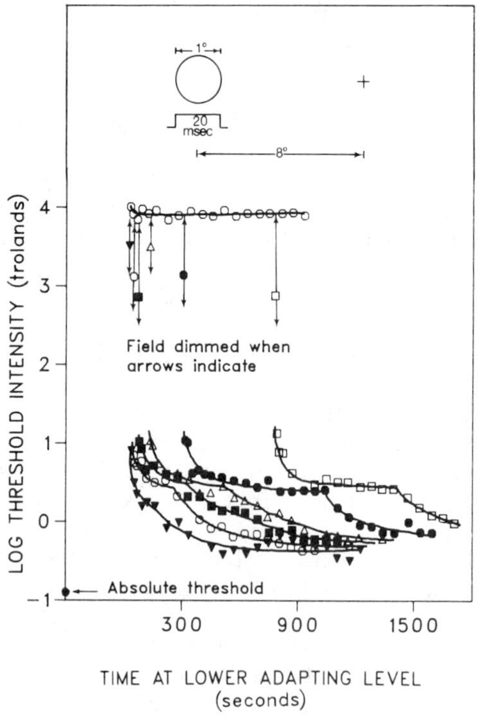

Figure 5.60. Dark adaptation functions obtained 8° parafoveally after various durations of adaptation to a 50,000 td field. At the points in time indicated by the arrows, the field was dimmed to 5 td. The open circles at the top of the figure show the increment thresholds for a 1°, 20 msec, "white" test measured on the high-intensity background. The data below show the recovery of sensitivity following the decrease in intensity; each symbol plots the data for a different duration of adaptation. Increasing the duration of adaptation increases the time required for the rod and cone system thresholds to return to their steady-state values. (From H. D. Baker, Some direct comparisons between light and dark adaptations. *Journal of the Optical Society of America*, 1955, *45*. Reprinted with permission.)

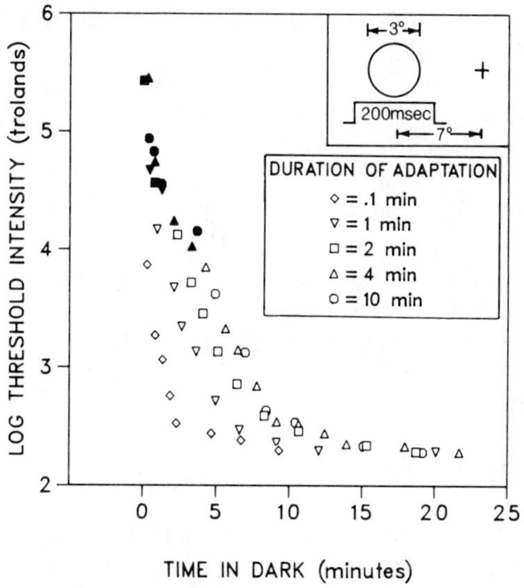

Figure 5.61. Dark adaptation following adaptation to a 3.65 log td "white" field for each of five durations: 0.1 min (diamonds); 1 min (inverted triangles); 2 min (squares); 4 min (triangles); 10 min (circles). The 3°, 200-msec test was delivered 7° nasal to the fovea. A Corning No. 511 filter was placed in the test channel; filled symbols indicate that the light appeared violet at threshold. Increasing the duration of light adaptation up to at least 4 min prolongs the time course of recovery in the dark. (From Haig, 1941, Table 1.)

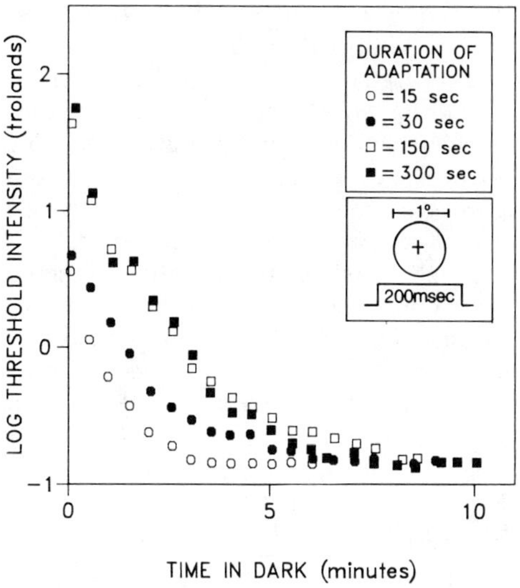

Figure 5.62. Foveal dark adaptation following adaptation to a 5.0 log td "white" field for each of four durations: 15 sec (open circles); 30 sec (filled circles); 150 sec (open squares); 300 sec (filled squares). Each point is the mean of five threshold measurements obtained for one observer. The "red" test patch was 1° in diameter and 200 msec in duration. Increasing duration up to at least 150 sec increases the effectiveness of the adapting field; the time course of recovery of the cone system becomes increasingly prolonged. (From Mote & Riopelle, 1951, Table 1.)

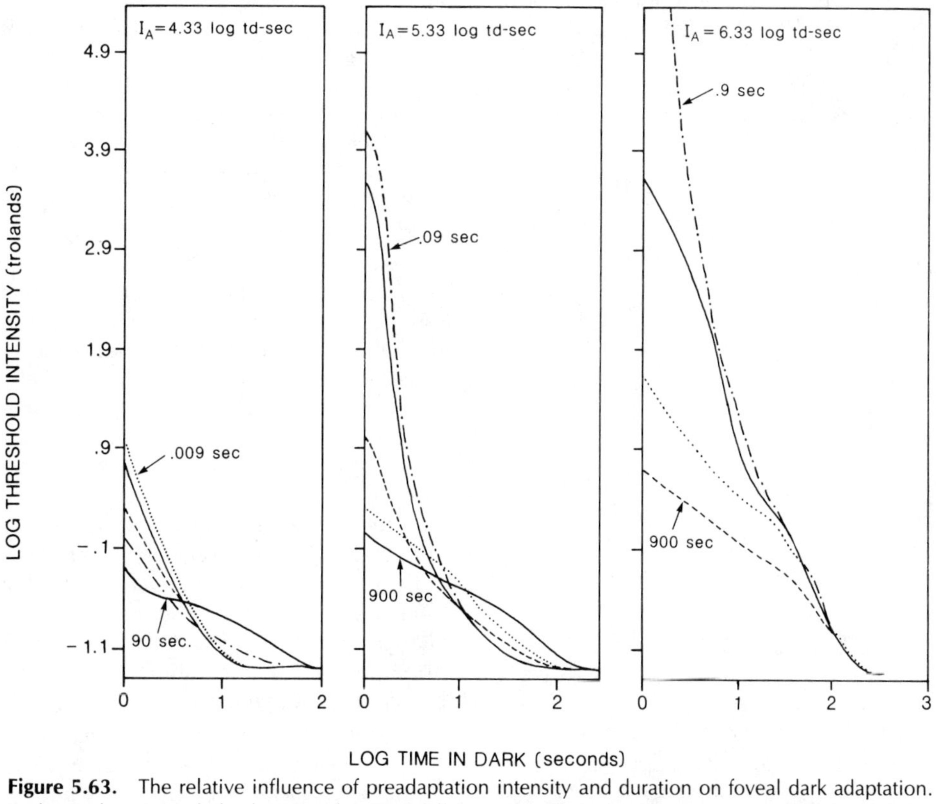

Figure 5.63. The relative influence of preadaptation intensity and duration on foveal dark adaptation. Each panel contains dark adaptation functions following the offset of a constant-energy conditioning field. The duration of the field is increased by a factor of 10 (and intensity is decreased by a factor of 10) in each successive curve (reading from top to bottom as the curves fall at the beginning of dark adaptation). The "white" test light was 30 min arc in diameter, the conditioning field (also "white"), 12°. The stimuli were presented in Maxwellian view, and pupil diameter was 3mm. Equal-energy fields do not have identical effects on dark adaptation. In general, the curves in each panel only coincide for high adapting intensities and for times in the dark exceding 30 sec (1.5 log sec). Early in dark adaptation, high-intensity fields elevate threshold more than long-duration fields, whereas the reverse is often true late in dark adaptation. (From B. H. Crawford, Photochemical laws and visual phenomena, *Proceedings of the Royal Society of London*, 1946, *133B*. Reprinted with permission.)

thought (cf. Andrews & Butcher, 1971; Barlow & Andrews, 1973; Rushton & Westheimer, 1962).

For the cone system, there are conditions under which the area of the adapting field greatly influences the course of dark adaptation. In particular, if the test and adapting field are very small or about the same size, dark adaptation can be much slower. Figure 5.64 (from Hayhoe, 1979) shows dark adaptation functions for a 3-min arc test after bleaching by a 27-min arc-diameter field (open circles) and an equal-luminance 115-min arc field. Decreasing the area of the field elevates threshold throughout most of the duration of dark adaptation. The first measurable thresholds for the small field (around 70 sec) are more than 1700 times those for the larger field. They approximate the large-field values at about 150 sec, but by this time, thresholds are already within 0.2 log unit of the dark-adapted value.

4.4. Pupil Size

In most of the experiments discussed above, the effective size of the pupil was fixed by the use of an artificial pupil. The natural pupil changes size with changes in ambient intensity. As the amount of ambient light is decreased, pupil diameter increases. These changes can affect the time course of dark adaptation. The change in the diameter of the pupil takes time, as can be seen in the data of Figure 5.65 (from Reeves, 1920; reprinted in Wyszecki & Stiles, 1982). The figure tracks the increase in pupil diameter during the dark adaptation which follows adaptation to a "white" light of 2.5 log cd·m^{-2}. The pupil diameter is just under 3 mm in the light. The diameter slowly increases during dark adaptation, reaching its maximum size of 8 mm after about 3 min. Following intense adapting lights, the pupil may take almost 40 min to fully dilate (Alpern & Campbell, 1962).

The maximum change in the area of the pupil that occurs from darkness to very intense illumination, and thus the maximum change in the intensity of light entering the eye, is on the order of 1 log unit.

Dark adaptation with the natural pupil is clearly affected by changes in pupil area. As the pupil dilates, more light is available to the retina. However, the full range of pupil diameters (see Table 5.2) changes the intensity of the light entering the eye on the order of one log unit. The pupil is clearly only one *small* part of the process that controls sensitivity during dark adaptation.

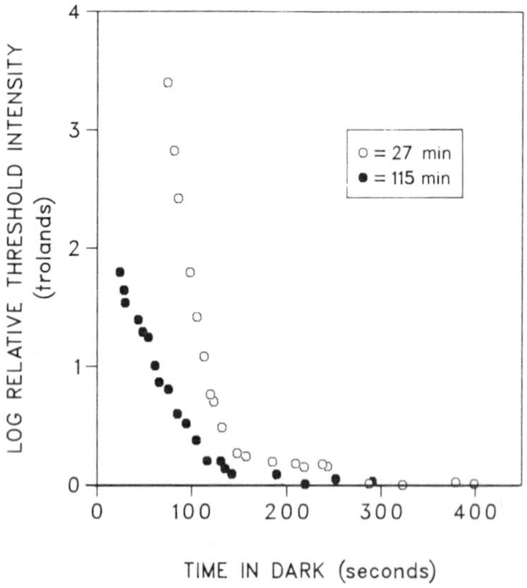

Figure 5.64. Foveal dark adaptation following flash bleaches by lights of two sizes: 27 min arc (open circles) and 115 min arc (filled circles). The energy of both "white" bleaching lights was 6.7 log td · sec. The "red" test spot, 3 min arc in diameter and 20 msec in duration, was presented in the center of the bleached patch. Decreasing the area of the bleaching light elevates threshold throughout most of dark adaptation. The first measurable thresholds following the small-field bleach (around 70 sec) are more than 1700 times those for the larger field. The small-field thresholds fall rapidly and approximate the large-field values at about 150 sec. By this time, the sensitivity of the foveal cone system is already within 0.2 log unit of its fully dark-adapted value. (From M. M. Hayhoe, After-effects of small adapting fields, *Journal of Physiology*, 1979, *296*. Reprinted with permission.)

4.5. Pigment Content and Sensitivity

Vision is initiated by the absorption of quanta by photopigments in the receptors. After a prolonged stay in the dark the receptors have a full complement of visual pigment. A light presented to the dark-adapted eye is said to "bleach" pigment. The term "bleach" comes from the nineteenth-century observation of the frog eye. Boll (1876) observed that a freshly dissected frog retina appeared reddish. As it remained in the light, it turned orange, then yellow, then white (or clear); it was bleached. Kühne (1878) showed that this process could be reversed in the dark. We now know that this "bleaching" of the retina is due to conformational changes of the visual pigment molecule. The only direct effect of light is to change the shape of, or isomerize, the chromophore of the pigment molecule from one form (11-cis) to another (all-trans). Once having absorbed the quantum of light, the individual molecule goes through a series of conformational changes called photoproducts (see Dartnall, 1972 and Wald, 1968 for reviews). These structural changes alter the absorption spectrum of this molecule, thus providing an explanation for the color changes of the frog retina. It is important to remember that a pigment molecule that has absorbed a quantum of light must be "regenerated" back to its dark-adapted state before it can again initiate a visual response. This regeneration takes time.

Once the photochemical nature of vision was established in the late nineteenth century, a debate began about the relationship between the amount of pigment bleached and the changes in our sensitivity to light. Qualitatively, various aspects of the data presented above can be related to pigment changes. Relatively long recovery times in the dark, the differences in the rates of recovery of rod and cone sensitivity, and the intensity-time tradeoffs over reasonably long periods of time can be traced to the photochemical nature of vision. Attempts have been made quantitatively to relate changes in sensitivity in the dark to changes in pigment content. Before reviewing the most successful attempt we must first summarize what is known about pigment bleaching and regeneration.

4.5.1. Pigment Kinetics: Bleaching or Photolysis. The knowledge gained of human pigment kinetics over the past 20 years stands as one of the most important events in visual science. Owing to the development of the reflection densitometer we have considerable information about the kinetics of human rod and cone pigment. In this section we briefly review the kinetics of pigment regeneration and bleaching. Some of the disagreements in the literature, both present and past, are bypassed here in the interest of trying to present a "best guess" at the current state of knowledge.

Because the term "bleaching" is so widely used in secondary and primary sources, it is used here to describe the photoisom-

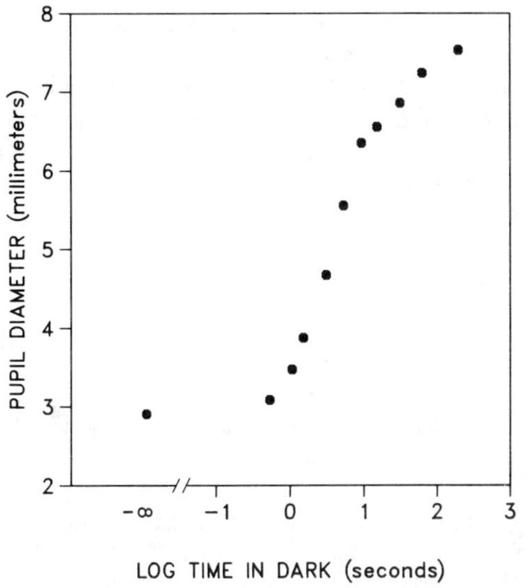

Figure 5.65. Pupil diameter as a function of time in the dark following adaptation to a 2.5 log cd·m^{-2} "white" field. Pupil size recovers from about 3 to 8 mm in 3 min of dark adaptation. (From Wyszecki & Stiles, 1982, Table 1 (2.4.5).)

erization of a pigment molecule. The more general term is "photolysis." Besides lacking technical specificity, the term bleaching is inappropriate because it has not been determined that the cone pigments are literally bleached in situ, that is, that cone pigment molecules decay to photoproducts that do not absorb in the visual spectrum.

More intense lights bleach more pigment molecules. The rate of bleaching is actually proportional to the rate at which quanta are absorbed. The rate of quantal absorption depends upon both the intensity of the light and the amount of pigment present to absorb the quanta. Therefore, the rate of bleaching is given by

$$\frac{dp}{dt} = \frac{I \times p}{Q_e} \tag{10}$$

where I is the intensity of the light, p is the proportion of pigment content, and Q_e^{-1} is photosensitivity. Note that the rate of bleaching is proportional to $I \times p$, the quantal catch.

4.5.1.1. Brief Adapting Lights. When a light is presented to the dark-adapted eye, pigment bleaching is described by Eq. (10). At the same time, some of the pigment is regenerated. However, if the adapting light is brief relative to the rate of regeneration then the amount of pigment bleached can be determined from Eq. (10). If the eye is totally dark adapted, then $p = 1.0$ and the solution of Eq. (10) is

$$p = \frac{e^{-(I \times t)}}{Q_e} . \tag{11}$$

Therefore, if the duration of the adapting light, t, is short relative to the regeneration rate, then p depends upon the total energy in the light and Eq. (11) can be used to calculate the amount of pigment bleached. For the rods Eq. (11), with Q_e equal to about 6.9 log td·sec, holds if t is less than 45 sec (Ripps & Weale, 1969; Rushton, 1956; Rushton & Powell, 1972a). Notice that a light of about 6.7 log td·sec bleaches 50% of the rod pigment. For the cones Q_e is equal to 3.5×10^6, and Eq. (11) describes the amount of pigment bleached for adapting lights up to at least 10 sec in duration (Rushton, 1958; Rushton & Baker, 1963; Rushton & Henry, 1968). When we say "cone pigment" here, and in the following discussion, we mean both middle- and long-wave pigments. These pigments appear to have similar kinetics (Rushton, 1968). No one has successfully measured the kinetics of the short-wave cone using reflection densitometry.

In humans, intense flashes have been estimated to bleach less than 60% of the cone (e.g., Rushton & Baker, 1963) and 60–75% of the rod pigment (Alpern, 1971; Hagins, 1955; Pugh, 1975a; Ripps & Weale, 1969). The exact amount of pigment bleached depends on a number of factors.

4.5.1.2. Longer Lights: Bleaching and Regeneration. For longer lights, the regeneration taking place during the exposure must be considered. Under a variety of conditions bleaching and regeneration aproximate the first-order pigment kinetics of monomolecular photochemical reaction. That is,

$$\frac{dp}{dt} = \frac{I \times p}{Q_e} - \frac{1 - p}{t_0} . \tag{12}$$

The first term in Eq. (12) is Eq. (10), the rate of bleaching of pigment, and the second describes the regeneration of pigment. Note that the rate of regeneration is proportional to the proportion of bleached pigment molecules $(1 - p)$ and inversely proportional to the time constant t_0. There are a number of reasons to expect that visual pigment should deviate from a simple monomolecular photochemical reaction and consequently, Eq. (12). Surprisingly, this equation describes a variety of conditions for the human rods and cones. These conditions as well as the limitations of the equation will be discussed.

One case of practical interest is the effect of prolonged light adaptation on pigment content. The proportion of pigment bleached can be calculated from Eq. (12). The proportion present at equilibrium is obtained by setting Eq. (12) to 0, since at equilibrium the rate of regeneration will equal the rate of bleaching. The solution is

$$p_e = \frac{I_0}{I_0 + I} \tag{13}$$

where $I_0 = Q_e/t_0$. The constant I_0 is the value of the adapting intensity that will produce an equilibrium bleach of 50% of the pigment. Equation (13) describes equilibrium pigment content for both rods and cones. This is a particularly important equation because it allows the estimate of the proportion of pigment bleached by ambient lights of different intensities. If the intensity is specified in terms of retinal illuminance, then typical values of I_0 are 4.4 log scotopic td for the rods and about 4.5 log photopic td for the cones.

There will be times when we are interested in the changes in pigment content during the presentation of a light. The proportion of pigment present at any time can also be estimated from Eq. (12). Specifically, the proportion, p, of pigment present at time, t, after exposure to light of intensity, I, is

$$p = p_e + (P_0 - p_e)e^{-t/t_0 p_e} \tag{14}$$

where p_e is the equilibrium pigment content at $t = \infty$ [see Eq. (13)] and p_0 is the pigment content at $t = 0$. A number of studies suggest that Eq. (14) can be used to describe the bleaching of both rod and cone pigments when the adapting light is increased from one intensity to another (e.g., Alpern, 1971; Rushton, 1958;

Rushton & Henry, 1968). Therefore, if t_0 and I_0 are known, the pigment content can be estimated for lights of any duration, with the same limitation on intense flashes mentioned.

4.5.2. Recovery of Pigment. When an adapting light is extinguished or decreased in intensity, pigment content recovers. If we assume that first-order kinetics holds, then Eqs. (12) and (14) can be used to estimate the recovery of pigment with time. A specific case is the transition into darkness where the portion of pigment present is given by

$$p = 1 - (1 - p_0)e^{-t/t_0} . \qquad (15)$$

Equation (15) describes the recovery of human rod pigment under all conditions studied. Estimates of t_0 for prolonged bleaches range between 3 and 10 min, although there is some consensus that 400 sec is a reasonable figure (Alpern, 1971). The value of t_0 has been found to be the same for all adapting conditions except following flash bleaches when it is about one half, or 165 sec (Alpern, 1971).

For the cones, Eq. (15) describes the recovery after prolonged adapting lights. For longer adapting lights, t_0 is about 110 sec, but Hollins and Alpern believe that individuals may vary on the order of 20%. For shorter bleaching lights t_0 is a function of the duration of the bleaching light. Pigment recovers faster after shorter lights. For brief flashes t_0 is in the neighborhood of 64 sec (Hollins & Alpern, 1973; Rushton & Baker, 1963).

In summary, pigment content recovers exponentially according to Eq. (15) for both rods and cones. For the cones t_0 is a function of the duration of the adapting light.

4.5.3. Sensitivity and Pigment. The nature of the kinetics of human rod and cone pigment supplies a qualitative explanation for various aspects of dark adaptation. For example, both pigment content and psychophysically measured sensitivity recover slowly and follow (roughly) an exponential time course. The question remaining is how quantitatively to relate sensitivity to pigment content during dark adaptation. There have been various attempts to specify this relationship. Of the two discussed here, one is attributed to Hecht, and the other is a more recent attempt by Rushton and Dowling.

As part of his comprehensive photochemical theory of vision, Hecht suggested that the return of sensitivity in the dark might be linearly related to the increased probability of quantal absorption which is in turn proportional to the increase in pigment content. That is,

$$\frac{I_t}{I_\infty} = \frac{1}{p} \qquad (16)$$

where I_t is the threshold intensity at time t after the offset of the adapting light and I_∞ is the steady-state dark-adapted threshold. Thus if an adapting light decreases the pigment content by one half ($p = 0.5$) then threshold intensity must be doubled. As p returns to the dark-adapted value of 1.0, threshold recovers. No one, including Hecht, ever expected nature to be this simple (see Hecht et al., 1937; Lythgoe, 1940). However, until pigment content was actually measured, no one expected how deviant the quantitative predictions of this simple model would be. For example, using Eqs. (13) and (15), we estimate that at the rod–cone break in Figure 5.53 close to 90% of the rod pigment is left unbleached, $p = 0.9$. Instead of the Hechtian increase in threshold of about 1.1, threshold is 500 times the dark-adapted value. How is one to explain the relatively good qualitative agreement between the time course of recovery of sensitivity and pigment and this drastic quantitative mismatch between sensitivity and change in quantal absorption?

An answer to this question was proposed in the early 1960s. Dowling (1960) and Rushton (1961) suggested that the log of the sensitivity change is proportional to the pigment content. This log-linear relationship has become known as the Dowling-Rushton equation. It takes the form of

$$\log \frac{I_t}{I_\infty} = \alpha(1 - p) \qquad (17)$$

where α is a constant. Rushton supplied evidence that the log threshold in the dark returns after an extensive bleach with the same time course as does pigment content, p. Dowling and his colleagues showed that various manipulations of p in animal models produced data consistent with Eq. (17). The combined effect of this work was to elevate Eq. (17) to a "fact" of vision at least at the level of the secondary textbooks. We will not summarize here the various sources of physiological evidence for and against Eq. (17). For more information, see Gordon & Hood (1976) and Schneider, Hood, Cohen, & Stampfer (1977).

It could be very useful, as well as theoretically interesting, if Eq. (17) were to describe even approximately most changes in sensitivity. Before examining the conditions under which Eq. (17) holds, let us first consider the conditions under which it fails.

Equation (17) does not adequately describe the changes in sensitivity if the adapting light bleaches *less* than 10% of the pigment. Two relatively recent studies can be used to illustrate this point. For the rods, Rushton and Powell (1972a) measured both the pigment content and sensitivity changes in the same observer under the same conditions. The test stimuli (see inset, Fig. 5.66) were chosen to favor the rod system. The adapting fields were 40 sec in duration and were chosen to bleach from 0.1% to 99% of the rod pigment (i.e., $p = 0.999$–0.01). The data points are the psychophysical measures; the curves describe the physically measured changes in p. Take careful note of the ordinates. The psychophysical ordinate (leftmost) is log threshold. The pigment ordinate is percentage of pigment remaining bleached, plotted linearly. The pigment ordinates are scaled so that Eq. (17) describes the data points for the highest bleaches. Notice that the pigment ordinate includes only amounts remaining bleached of 10% and less. The reason for this is that the cone-to-rod break in the psychophysical data occurs after all but 7% of the rod pigment has regenerated. The relationship between rod pigment content and rod system threshold can be studied only beyond this point.

Note that the Dowling-Rushton equation describes very little of the data for bleaches of 7% and less. The psychophysical threshold is much higher than one would predict based on Eq. (17).

For bleaches of 13% or more, Eq. (17) does describe the recovery of sensitivity. In each case, recovery of the last 2.5 log units of sensitivity follows the pigment recovery curve; log sensitivity is linearly related to pigment content. Even under these conditions, however, the fit of the Dowling-Rushton equation is limited. There is no evidence in these data for an agreement with the equation for the first 4 min of dark adaptation or while pigment content is still less than 93%. By making use of an observer without a cone system (monochromat) Rushton has been able to extend this agreement to earlier parts of dark

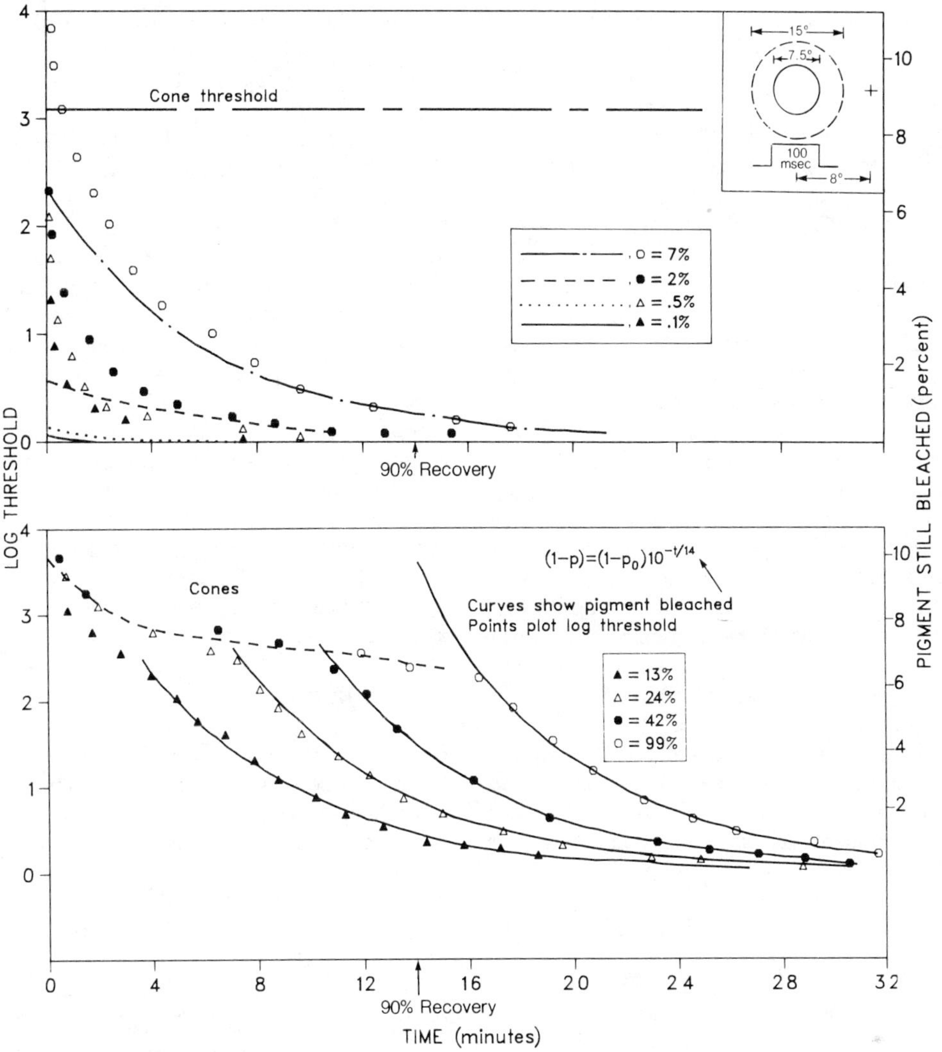

Figure 5.66. The relation between the recovery of sensitivity and the regeneration of rhodopsin in the dark. Dark adaptation functions are shown for a range of adapting intensities chosen to bleach from 0.1 to 99% of the rhodopsin; the percentage bleached is indicated beside each curve. The "white" bleaching lights were 15° in diameter and 40 sec in duration. They were centered 8° from the point of fixation. The test was a 7.5°, 100-msec, "blue" light also centered 8° extrafoveally (see inset). The data points and left-hand ordinate give the psychophysically measured thresholds (log scale). The solid curves and right-hand ordinate indicate percentage of pigment bleached (linear scale). According to the Dowling-Rushton equation $[\log(I_t/I_\infty) = \alpha\ (1 - p)]$ the thresholds and pigment curves should coincide; the log of the sensitivity change should be proportional to the pigment content. Instead the equation describes very little of the data for bleaches of 7% or less. The psychophysical threshold is much higher than predicted by the Dowling-Rushton equation. (From W. A. H. Rushton & D. S. Powell, The phase of dark adaptation, *Vision Research, 12*. Copyright 1972 by Pergamon Press, Ltd. Reprinted with permission.)

adaptation when more than 50% of the pigment remained bleached (see also Alpern, 1971). However, Pugh (1975b) has found that the time constant of his dark adaptation curves was not constant but increased with increasing proportion bleached. In fact, for extensive bleaches the constant was greater than 11 min, far greater than those measured for the rod pigment. Pugh's explanation for the discrepancy between his time constants and others is that previous studies (including Rushton & Powell, 1972a) did not allow time for complete recovery of sensitivity; therefore, they did not get an accurate estimate of the time constant following extensive bleaches. Complete recovery may take an hour or more, and the last few tenths of a log unit recovered during the last 30 min drastically affects the estimate of the time constant.

The Rushton and Powell (1972a) study was not the first to demonstrate that sensitivity during dark adaptation is not as simply related to pigment content as suggested by Eq. (17). It has long been appreciated that if pigment regeneration followed first-order kinetics, and if a given threshold elevation (sensitivity) was always related to a single variable, pigment content, then a single curve should describe the relationship of sensitivity to pigment content following all adapting lights. The dark adaptation curves following different adapting lights should all have the same shape but be shifted horizontally on a linear time axis (see Alpern, 1971; Lythgoe, 1940; Yellott, Wandell, & Cornsweet, 1984 for a discussion). A number of early dark adaptation studies showed that recovery is faster after weak adapting lights (for example, see Fig. 1 in Hecht et al., 1937;

Winsor & Clark, 1936). Consequently, since the 1930s, we knew either that Eq. (15) did not describe pigment kinetics in the dark or that sensitivity was not related to pigment content by a single variable function. When it became clear in the 1960s that pigment recovery after prolonged bleaches was approximated by first-order kinetics, the inescapable conclusion was that a simple relationship between pigment and sensitivity would fail, at least for weak bleaches (cf. Alpern, 1971; Rushton, 1961).

Cone system sensitivity does not conform to the Dowling-Rushton equation either if the adapting light bleaches less than 10% of the pigment. Hollins and Alpern (1973) measured psychophysical thresholds and pigment content in the same observer. The psychophysical data were obtained using a 675 nm light, restricting the study to the long-wave sensitive cone mechanism. These data are shown as symbols in Figure 5.67. Like Figure 5.66, this figure shows the recovery of threshold following various adapting lights. The individual curves have been shifted to the right; time zero for each condition is shown above each set of data. As mentioned, cone dark adaptation is fast, recovering within 10 min even after intense lights that bleached nearly all the pigment. A smooth curve shows the predicted curve based on Eq. (17) and $\alpha = 2.9$. The values of p were estimated from Eq. (15) which was validated in the same situation using the observer's time constant of 105 sec. [Actually value I_t in Eq. (17) was replaced by $p \times I_t$ to correct the changes in probability of quantal absorption. The correction is theoretically important if one is interested in the relationship between threshold elevation and pigment molecules in the bleached stage because there will be an elevation due to a decreased number of molecules available for bleaching. Geisler (1978a) notes the correction is important only above 80%. Those data can be equally well fitted with Eq. (17) and $\alpha = 3.3$.]

For the cone system, Eq. (17) does not fit the early part of the dark adaptation function unless there is substantial pigment bleaching; it fits little of the dark adaptation function for bleaches of less than 10%. On the other hand, a particularly impressive agreement was observed when the duration of the bleaching light was varied. Decreasing the duration of the lights that bleach 30% or more of the pigment decreases the time constant of recovery of both pigment and sensitivity. Both time constants agree, supporting Eq. (17), except under conditions of an intense 1-msec flash.

Another striking violation of Eq. (17) can be observed when a xenon flash (less than 1 msec) is used to bleach the rod or cone pigment. Pigment recovery proceeds about twice as fast as after a prolonged light, but sensitivity proceeds along a course that, compared to the course after a prolonged light, is at least as slow for the rod system (Alpern, 1971; Rushton, 1963) and slower for the cone system (Hollins & Alpern, 1973; Rushton & Baker, 1963).

4.6. Summary

How good a description is the Dowling-Rushton equation of the recovery of sensitivity in the dark? The answer to this question depends upon what is meant to be described. We can differentiate between how useful it is as a theoretical statement versus how

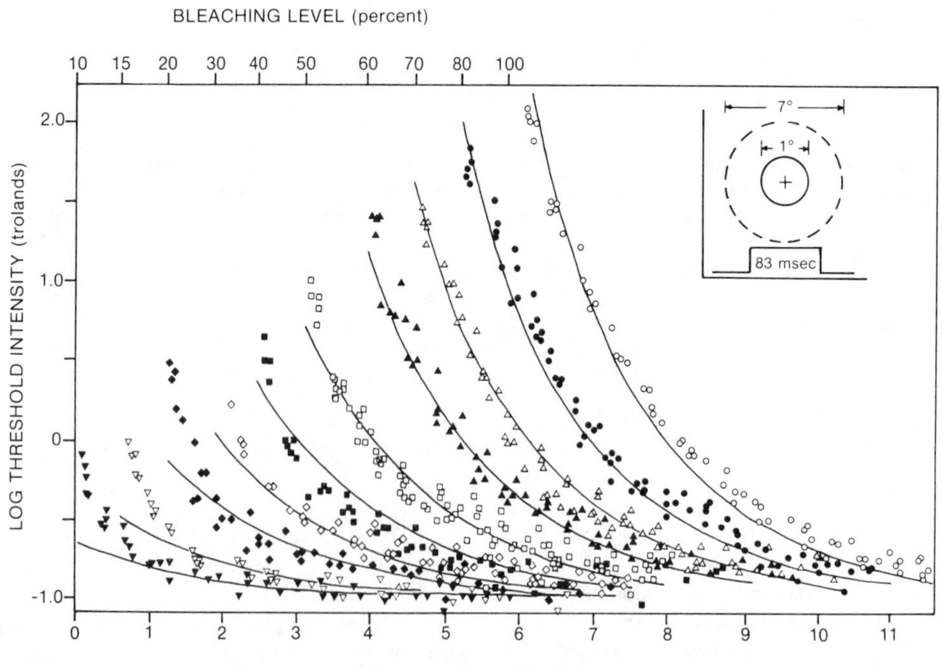

Figure 5.67. Foveal dark adaptation functions following prolonged adaptation (10 sec of a brighter light followed by 1 min at the intensity which at equilibrium held the bleaching level at the value indicated above each function). Data for different strength bleaches are shifted horizontally for clarity; time zero for each condition is marked along the top of the figure. The test was a 1°, 83-msec, 675 nm light (see inset). The smooth curves show the predicted dark adaptation function based on the Dowling-Rushton equation, $\log I_t/I_\infty = \alpha(1 - p)$, for $\alpha = 2.9$. The log-linear relation does not describe the early part of the dark adaptation function unless there has been substantial pigment bleaching. (From M. Hollins & M. Alpern, reproduced from the *Journal of General Physiology*, 62. Copyright 1973 by Rockefeller University Press. Reprinted with permission.)

useful it would be from a practical point of view—as an empirical description of sensitivity. Fortunately our job in this chapter is mainly empirical; the answer to this question is easier. As an empirical description of practical significance it is almost useless. At best Eq. (17) describes dark adaptation functions following adapting lights that bleach greater than 10%. Therefore the best we could expect would be to describe most of the sensitivity changes following steady adapting fields of greater than about 4 log td. However, even under these conditions, there is evidence that Eq. (17) is of limited usefulness. First, the time constants differ for different observers. Second, the value of α in Eq. (17) varies from observer to observer and from one stimulus situation to another. These variations can be quite large. So, for example, for the rod visual system, values of α of 12–40 have been reported (see Rushton & Powell, 1972a).

From a theoretical point of view it is still important if Eq. (17) accounts for dark adaptation after prolonged extensive bleaches. However, there are reasons to believe it may fail. Pugh (1975b) suggests that the time constant may increase with increased pigment bleached. If true, we must abandon Eq. (15) or (17). For the cones, the Hollins and Alpern study suggests that Eq. (17) does much better.

Further, it has long been appreciated, but occasionally forgotten, that the shape of the dark adaptation function changes with test parameters and that these changes reflect some kind of reorganization beyond the receptors (Lythgoe, 1940). Rushton (1961) noted that Eq. (17) could not be thought of as a simple description of sensitivity changes independent of test parameters. Instead, he argued that bleached rhodopsin affects the visual system like a steady background of some equivalent intensity (Blakemore & Rushton, 1965a, 1965b; Rushton, 1965). The usefulness of Eq. (17) became tied to the concept of an equivalent background, a generalization that, like Eq. (17), holds under a limited set of conditions (see Section 5).

The Dowling-Rushton equation will stand as a landmark in our attempt to understand the photochemical nature of vision, even though, in detail, it is probably more wrong than right. When it became clear in the 1940s that Hecht's simple formulation would not work, it encouraged speculation about nonpigment (sometimes called neural) factors determining sensitivity. That such factors exist cannot be debated. However, what we have learned in the last 20 years is that it makes sense to think about the relationship between pigment and sensitivity. Much of the work discussed here suggests that some relationship exists. Or more accurately, some relationships exist. The slow recovery of sensitivity, various rod-cone differences, the long summation times for adapting lights, all point to the involvement of a photochemical process. The nature of the process and its relationship to sensitivity are yet to be understood.

5. EQUIVALENT BACKGROUND

The concept of an equivalent background brightness was developed as an answer to a practical question. The question was, how does the glare from an unshielded source of light (e.g., headlights, streetlights) affect foveal vision? Holladay (1926, 1927) specified the effects of a glare source in terms of the intensity of a steady background (the equivalent background) that produced an elevation of foveal threshold equivalent to that produced by the glare source. Stiles (1929) further quantified the effects of glare sources by relating the size and intensity of the glare source, its position in the field of view, and the prevailing background light all to an equivalent background intensity. The goal was to be able, given the parameters of the glare situation, to calculate an equivalent background intensity. Thus the effects on visual performance of an infinitely large assortment of glare situations could be determined by studying the effects of a simple range of steady background intensities. The potential practical and theoretical significance of this approach lay far beyond the questions of glare. In its most ambitious forms, the equivalent background notion was a way to specify the altered state of the visual system due to numerous factors that affect sensitivity. Theoretically, the goal was to specify the adaptive state of a retinal area by a single variable, the equivalent background intensity. [Stiles & Crawford (1932) pointed out that if the concept was to be of general use, it must also include situations in which the spectral composition of the background was varied. They suspected that three or four variables would be needed to specify the adaptive state of the hypothesized rod and three cone mechanisms. In Section 3.2.6, we considered the problems associated with assuming four separate independent mechanisms. For now we will be content, as were the earlier workers, to restrict ourselves to situations where the spectral composition of the background is held constant.]

Interest in the equivalent background notion was revived in the 1960s by Rushton (Blakemore & Rushton, 1965a, 1965b; Rushton, 1965). Rushton sought to reconcile the seemingly simple relationship between the recovery of sensitivity in the dark and pigment content with the fact that shape of the dark adaptation curve depended upon the area of the test (see Section 4.2.3). Perhaps the course of dark adaptation is equivalent to the presentation of progressively weaker background lights, he reasoned. The equivalent background notion seemed a natural way to link a single variable (the proportion of pigment present) to the adaptive state of the retina. Most of the recent work on the topic of equivalent backgrounds has been concerned with the sensitivity changes during dark adaptation. Some of this work is reviewed here.

5.1. The Equivalent Background Principle and the Detection of Lights during Dark Adaptation

Stiles and Crawford (1932) argued that if the equivalent background notion was to have either theoretical or practical significance, then the equivalent background intensity must be independent of both the parameters of the test light and the task set for the observer. They called this hypothesis the "equivalent background principle." In this section we consider the empirical evidence for and against the equivalent background principle.

5.1.1. Variation in Test Area. Although Crawford's 1947 study is often credited with the first test of this principle for sensitivity changes in dark adaptation, at least two tests preceded it (Crawford, 1937; Stiles & Crawford, 1932). Figure 5.68 is the often-reproduced figure from the Crawford study. The experiment, part of a war-related research project, examined the recovery of sensitivity following a brief light meant to simulate a gun flash. The adapting light was a 100-msec flash of 5.7 log $cd \cdot m^{-2}$. Six different sizes of test light were used, ranging from 0.18 to 5.7°. The observer was free to fixate wherever he wanted. Panel (a) of Figure 5.68 shows the dark adaptation curves obtained for the various test lights. Panel (b) contains the t.v.i. curves for the same test lights upon steady adapting fields.

Notice that the size of the test affects the shape of the curves in both panels. The equivalent background function is

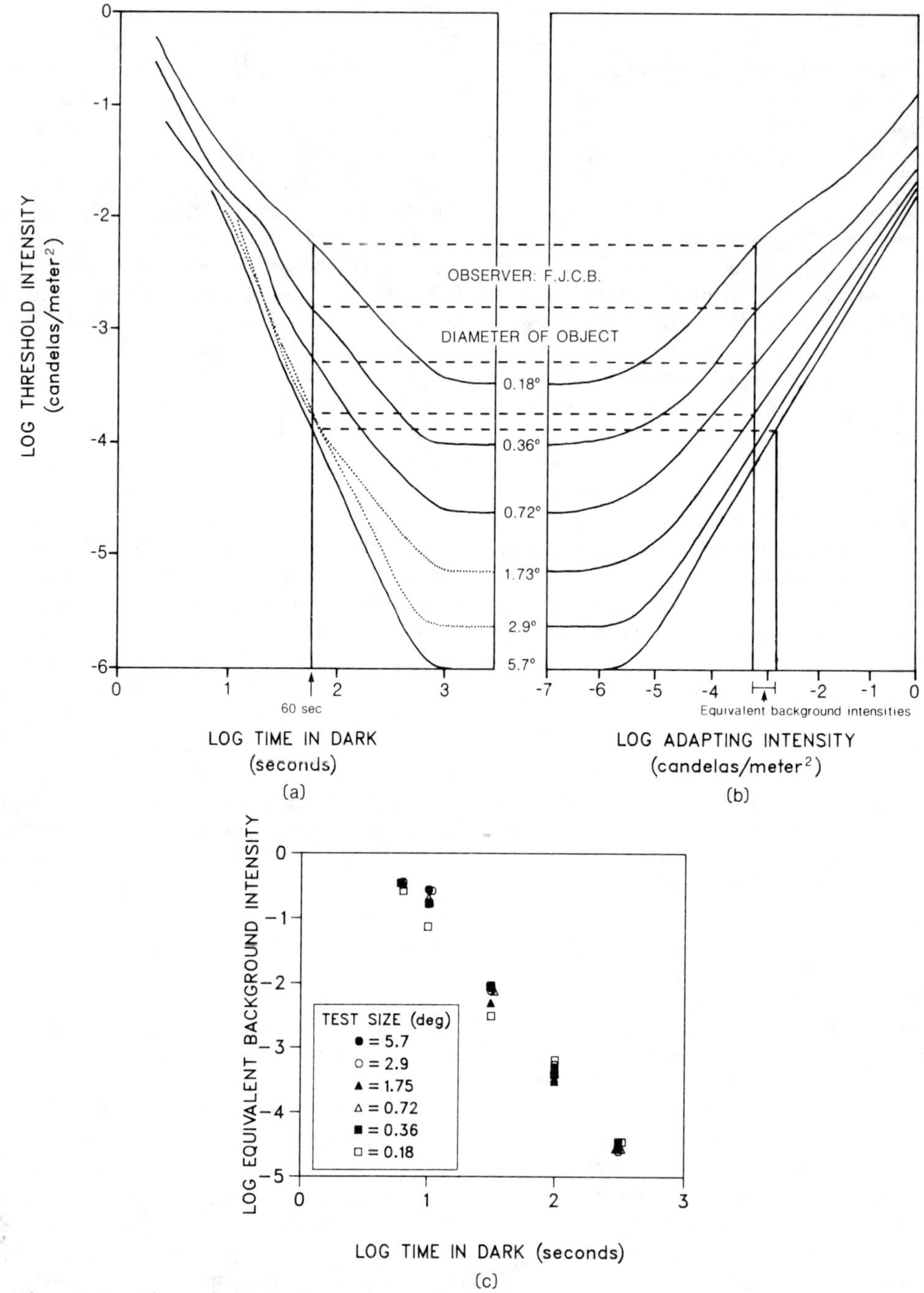

Figure 5.68. The equivalent background principle applied to the time course of dark adaptation. (a) Dark adaptation functions for test lights of six sizes (as labeled in figure). The curves plot log threshold versus log time for a 10-msec test following exposure to a brief adapting light meant to simulate a gun flash. Adapting duration was approximately 100 msec, adapting energy 5.7 log cd·m^{-2}. (b) Threshold versus intensity functions for the six test lights upon a steady adapting field. In both procedures, the observer was free to vary his fixation. The size of the test affects the shapes of both the dark and light adaptation functions, but it affects them in similar ways. If the equivalent background principle holds, then for *all* test sizes, threshold at any given time in the dark will be specifiable in terms of the single adapting intensity (the equivalent background intensity) that elevates threshold the same amount above the dark-adapted level. The figure shows how equivalent background intensities can be measured for the six targets at 60 sec into dark adaptation. The vertical line (a) indicates, for each dark adaptation function, the threshold after 60 sec. The dashed lines mark these same threshold intensities on the corresponding t.v.i. curves. The adapting intensity which yields the specified threshold is the equivalent background intensity for a given test light. As the lines extending from the thresholds to the log adapting intensity axis show, the equivalent background intensities are not all the same. The intensities for the smallest and largest tests differ by more than 0.3 log unit. (c) The test of the equivalent background principle. The figure plots equivalent background intensity as a function of time in the dark for the six test sizes. If the principle holds, then the points at any given time should coincide, that is, the equivalent background intensity should be independent of test size. After prolonged dark adaptation, the points must agree. The differences at shorter times between the small (0.18°) and large (5.7°) targets are probably real. (From B. H. Crawford, Visual adaptation in relation to brief conditioning stimuli, *Proceedings of the Royal Society of London*, 1947, *134B*. Reprinted with permission.)

defined as a function that relates the equivalent background intensity to some parameter affecting sensitivity. For the Crawford experiment, the parameter is time after the offset of the conditioning field. (To estimate the equivalent background function we measure the equivalent background intensity at different times in the dark.) The equivalent background intensity for any time in the dark is the intensity of a steady field that would elevate the threshold the same amount above the dark-adapted level. The dashed lines show how the equivalent background intensities can be measured for the various targets at 60 sec into dark adaptation. According to the equivalent background principle, all these equivalent background intensities should be the same; equivalent background should be independent of the size of the test light. In the case of 60 sec into dark adaptation, the equivalent background intensities vary by about 0.3 log unit. Figure 5.68(c) is a plot of the equivalent background intensity versus time in the dark for the various test lights. For any time in the dark, the estimated equivalent background should be the same for all targets. The data points for different targets should coincide. After prolonged dark adaptation the points must agree. In the limit, all thresholds return to the dark-adapted value. There are reasonably large differences at shorter times. This study supplies less support for the equivalent background principle than is generally accepted.

Surprisingly few investigators have attempted to replicate this important study. Crawford studied only one adapting field intensity. Further, his conditions are not easy to relate to others because fixation was not controlled, and the dark adaptation functions probably reflect mixed cone and rod activity. For the rod systems the strongest evidence in favor of the principle is probably the study by Blakemore and Rushton (1965b). By using a rod monochromat as the subject, they were able to follow the recovery of rod sensitivity over a 6.5 log unit range following an intense bleaching light. Dark adaptation curves were obtained for two circular test lights, 5 min arc and 6° in diameter. The data strongly supported the equivalent background principle. Although the Crawford and the Blakemore and Rushton studies together are often presented as overwhelming evidence in favor of the equivalent background principle, we are uncomfortable concluding that the equivalent background principle holds for the human rod system without more data for a range of test areas and adapting intensities.

For the cone system, Rinalducci, Higgins, and Cramer (1970) found that the equivalent background principle did not hold during foveal dark adaptation. They used two test sizes, 0.13 and 0.33°, and a 5-min adapting light of 4.18 log td. Geisler (1979), on the other hand, found that the equivalent background hypothesis held if a more intense adapting light (6.0 log td for 2 min), which bleached nearly all the pigment, was used. Unfortunately this study does not supply a very strong test of the equivalent background principle. In the extreme, if there are no changes in areal summation during either dark adaptation or steady-state light adaptation, then the dark adaptation functions for different test lights will be parallel and the equivalent background hypothesis will have to hold. Changes in areal summation are small for the fovea (see Sections 3.2.2.2 and 4.2.3.1). Therefore, there is little of theoretical interest to be explained by an equivalent background concept.

5.1.2. Variation in Test Duration. Few studies have tested the equivalent background principle by varying the duration of the test light. Figure 5.69 is from a 1937 study by Crawford. The lower curves show dark adaptation functions obtained for 50- and 400-msec tests. The upper curves show the resulting

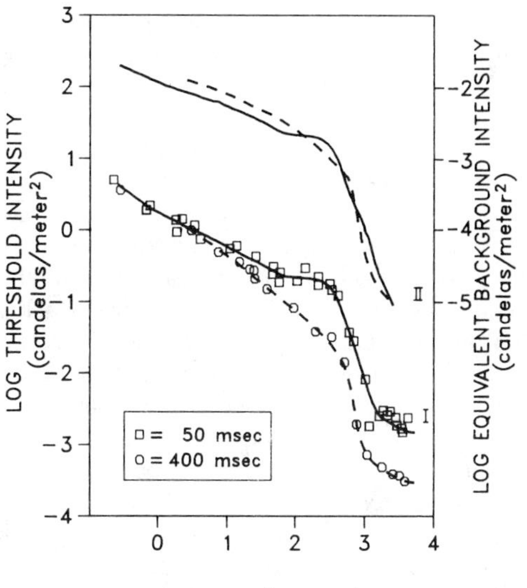

Figure 5.69. A test of the equivalent background principle for test lights of two durations. The two lower curves (labeled I) are dark adaptation functions for a 0.46° test following the removal of a 79 cd·ft^2-adapting field. Test duration was either 50 msec (squares and solid curve) or 400 msec (circles and dashed curve). The upper curves (labeled II) plot equivalent background intensity versus time in the dark for the two tests. The curves do not agree for times less than about 10 min. That they agree beyond 10 min may simply reflect the fact that the tests, in both the light- and dark-adapted conditions, fall within areal and temporal summation. If so, then an equivalent background principle must hold. (From B. H. Crawford, The change of visual sensitivity with time, *Proceedings of the Royal Society of London*, 1937, *123B*. Reprinted with permission.)

equivalent background versus time in the dark derived from the dark adaptation functions. The curves do not agree for times in the dark shorter than 10 min or so. Beyond 10 min the curves are very close. Stewart's (1972) data for different test durations discussed in Section 4.2.4 show the same violation of an equivalent background hypothesis early in dark adaptation.

The deviations from the equivalent background principle are small in both the Crawford and Stewart data. However, the dark adaptation curves and t.v.i. curves are reasonably parallel; that is, there is probably little change in temporal summation over this range. Therefore, there must be agreement between the equivalent backgrounds for the different durations. This is an important point that was alluded to above in reference to the Geisler study and probably bears repeating here. If test lights are within the limits of areal and temporal summation under all conditions (light and dark), then an equivalent background principle must hold.

5.2. Other Tasks

If a retinal area is truly in a state of adaptation equivalent to that produced by the steady equivalent background intensity, then this equivalence should hold for any task set for the observer, not simply for detection. Equivalent background curves, such as those in Figure 5.68, should be the same for different tasks. We know of three experiments that conclude that equivalence holds for nondetection tasks. Blakemore and Rushton (1965a) used conditions similar to those described above; about 50% of the pigment of a rod monochromat was bleached. The task was resolution of an acuity target; the acuity targets used were square-wave gratings with bar widths of 7 and 11 min arc. The equivalent background principle was found to hold. Barlow and Sparrock (1964) measured the brightness of the afterimages during dark adaptation following an intense bleach and found this brightness to be equal to the brightness of the stabilized equivalent background determined from detection data. A study by Alpern and Ohba (1972), which measured changes in pupil diameter during dark adaptation, is sometimes taken as evidence for the equivalent background principle.

At least two studies have shown that the equivalent background principle does not hold when the observer's task is varied. Ernst (1968) measured temporal resolution for a constant-intensity test and the threshold for this test following a 30-sec adapting light of 7 log td. Both temporal resolution and threshold decrease during dark adaptation and with decreases in steady adapting intensity. But the equivalent background principle did not hold; the equivalent background intensities were not the same for the two tasks over most of the range of threshold and temporal resolution measurements. Bowen and Hood (1983) examined changes in foveal visual performance immediately after a "Crawford-like" conditioning impulse. At the offset of the conditioning pulse, threshold is elevated, but temporal resolution and brightness discrimination are improved. These changes are qualitatively but not quantitatively similar to those produced by increasing the steady adapting field intensity. They also reject the equivalent background principle for their conditions.

5.3. Spatial Variations in Steady Backgrounds

The size of the adapting field can affect the shape of the t.v.i. curve. For example, a small steady background can elevate threshold more than a large one (see Westheimer, 1965; Section 3.2.5.1). When these backgrounds are used as bleaching lights, the rod dark adaptation functions are not affected (Rushton, 1965; Tachibana, 1977; Teller & Gestrin, 1969; Westheimer, 1968). Westheimer (1968) showed that the small and large adapting fields that produced very different rod t.v.i. functions produced identical rod dark adaptation curves (see also Teller & Gestrin, 1969). By themselves these observations are not damaging to the equivalent background principle. (The studies do speak to whether the so-called dark light is really equivalent to the presence of a real light.) The equivalent background intensity was originally specified as the intensity of a uniform white light filling the *whole* visual field. The fact that changing the size of the field affects incremental threshold measurements, but not dark adaptation, is not necessarily relevant to this principle. It does, however, provide problems for the more general notion of specifying the adaptive state of a given retinal area by a single variable, the intensity of an equivalent background. On the other hand, a study by Buss, Hayhoe, and Stromeyer (1982) is more troublesome. Hayhoe (1979) reported that the size of the adapting field affected cone dark adaptation functions (see Fig. 5.63). Buss et al. (1982) compared t.v.i. and dark adaptation curves for small and large adapting fields. The equivalent background functions depended on the size of the adapting field. At best, a different equivalent background function is needed for different spatial relationships between the test and adapting light. Again, the hypothesis of a single variable specifying the adaptation of a retinal area is rejected.

5.4. Summary

In summarizing the current status of the equivalent background principle, it is useful for us to keep separate the possible practical significance from its possible theoretical import. As mentioned, the equivalent background principle has been successfully applied to threshold elevations due to glare sources and should be of practical use. However, this example is of little theoretical interest because the effects of glare under most conditions are largely due to scattered light inside the eye, that is, to a real background. We do not know of many attempts to apply the equivalent background to problems that are likely to be practical. Crawford (1947) found that an equivalent background analysis was useful in eliminating the large individual variations in dark adaptation functions. Likewise, Crawford (1937) examined dark adaptation functions and increment threshold functions for different retinal positions. Based on our discussion, we might expect this would be a situation where the equivalent background notion would hold. However, Crawford found real and consistent deviations in his equivalent background functions. He concluded, "From the point of view of practical applications, however, sufficient accuracy for most purposes would be attained by the use of a single (equivalent background brightness, time) curve for all retinal test areas" (Crawford, 1937, p. 83). This represents a reasonable summary of our view. Under a variety of conditions, many of potential practical concern, we expect that equivalent background functions for different test parameters will be similar but not identical. Whether they will be close enough for practical applications remains to be assessed.

Theoretically, the equivalent background notion has not reached the status that its proponents had expected of it. We were surprised by the paucity of experimental tests of the equivalent background notion. Given the high percentage of those tests that have failed, we suspect that on further testing the equivalent background hypothesis will be of extremely limited use, applicable, if at all, only under very restricted conditions.

ACKNOWLEDGMENT

We are indebted to a number of our colleagues for reading portions of this chapter in draft. Ken Boff, Mary Hayhoe, Don MacLeod, Joel Pokorny, Ed Pugh, Vivianne Smith, and especially Jim Thomas deserve our deepest appreciation.

REFERENCE NOTE

1. Finkelstein, M. Unpublished experiment, Columbia University, 1980.

REFERENCES

Abramov, I., & Gordon, J. Vision. In E. C. Carterette & M. P. Friedman (Eds.), *Handbook of perception* (Vol. 3). New York: Academic Press, 1973.

Adelson, E. H. Saturation and adaptation in the rod system. *Vision Research*, 1982, *22*, 1299–1312.

Aguilar, M., & Stiles, W. S. Saturation of the rod mechanism of the retina at high levels of stimulation. *Optica Acta*, 1954, *1*, 59–65.

Alpern, M. Rhodopsin kinetics in the human eye. *Journal of Physiology*, 1971, *217*, 447–471.

Alpern, M., & Campbell, F. W. The behavior of the pupil during dark-adaptation. *Journal of Physiology* (London), 1962, *165*(1), 5–7.

Alpern, M., & Ohba, N. The effect of bleaching and backgrounds on pupil size. *Vision Research*, 1972, *12*, 943–951.

Alpern, M., Rushton, W. A. H., & Torii, S. Signals from cones. *Journal of Physiology*, 1970, *207*, 463–475.

Andrews, D. P., & Butcher, A. K. Rod threshold and patterned rhodopsin bleaching; The pigment epithelium as an adaptation pool. *Vision Research*, 1971, *2*, 761–785.

Arden, G. B., & Weale, R. A. Nervous mechanisms and dark adaptation. *Journal of Physiology*, 1954, *125*, 417–426.

Auerbach, E., & Wald, G. Identification of a violet receptor in human color vision. *Science*, 1954, *120*, 401–405.

Baker, H. D. The course of foveal light adaptation measured by the threshold intensity increment. *Journal of the Optical Society of America*, 1949, *39*, 172–179.

Baker, H. D. Instantaneous thresholds and early dark adaptation. *Journal of the Optical Society of America*, 1953, *43*, 798–803.

Baker, H. D. Some direct comparisons between light and dark adaptation. *Journal of the Optical Society of America*, 1955, *45*, 839–844.

Barlow, H. B. Retinal noise and absolute threshold. *Journal of the Optical Society of America*, 1956, *46*, 634–639.

Barlow, H. B. Increment thresholds at low intensities considered as signal/noise discrimination. *Journal of Physiology*, 1957, *136*, 469–488.

Barlow, H. B. Intrinsic noise of cones. In *Visual problems of colour* (Vol. 2). London: Her Majesty's Stationery Office, 1958. (a)

Barlow, H. B. Temporal and spatial summation in human vision at different background intensities. *Journal of Physiology* (London), 1958, *141*, 337–350. (b)

Barlow, H. B. The physical limits of visual discrimination. In A. C. Giese (Ed.), *Photophysiology* (Vol. 2). New York: Academic Press, 1964.

Barlow, H. B. Dark and light adaptation: Psychophysics. In D. Jameson & L. M. Hurvich (Eds.), *Handbook of sensory physiology* (Vol. 7/4). New York: Springer-Verlag, 1972.

Barlow, H. B. Retinal and central factors in human vision limited by noise. In H. B. Barlow & P. Fatt (Eds.), *Vertebrate photoreception*. New York: Academic Press, 1980.

Barlow, H. B., & Andrews, D. P. The site at which rhodopsin bleaching raises scotopic threshold. *Vision Research*, 1973, *13*, 903–908.

Barlow, H. B., & Sparrock, J. M. B. The role of after-images in dark adaptation. *Science*, 1964, *144*, 1309–1314.

Baumgardt, E. Threshold quantal problems. In D. Jameson & L. M. Hurvich (Eds.), *Handbook of sensory physiology* (Vol. 7/4). New York: Springer-Verlag, 1972.

Baumgardt, E., & Hillman, B. Duration and size as determinants of peripheral retinal response. *Journal of the Optical Society of America*, 1961, *51*, 340–344.

Benimoff, N. I., Schneider, S., & Hood, D. C. Interactions between rod and cone channels above threshold: A test of various models. *Vision Research*, 1982, *22*, 1133–1140.

Blackwell, H. R. Contrast thresholds of the human eye. *Journal of the Optical Society of America*, 1946, *36*, 624–643.

Blakemore, C. B., & Rushton, W. A. H. Adaptation and increment threshold in a rod monochromat. *Journal of Physiology*, 1965, *181*, 612–628. (a)

Blakemore, C. B., & Rushton, W. A. H. The rod increment threshold during dark adaptation in normal and rod monochromat. *Journal of Physiology*, 1965, *181*, 629–640. (b)

Bloch, A. M. Experiences sur la vision. *Société de Biologie* (Paris), 1885, *37*, 493–495.

Boll, F. Zur anatomie und physiologie der retina. *Monatsberichte der Preussisch Academie de Wissenschatten zu Berlin*, 1876, 783–787.

Bone, R. A., & Sparrock, J. M. B. Comparison of macular pigment densities in human eyes. *Vision Research*, 1971, *11*, 1057–1064.

Bowen, R. W., & Hood, D. C. Improvements in visual performance following a pulsed field of light: A test of the equivalent-background principle. *Journal of the Optical Society of America*, 1983, *73*, 1551–1556.

Boynton, R. M. *Human color vision*. New York: Holt, Rinehart & Winston, 1979.

Brindley, G. S. The discrimination of after-images. *Journal of Physiology*, 1959, *147*, 194–203.

Brindley, G. S. *Physiology of the retina and visual pathway*. Baltimore: Williams & Wilkins, 1970.

Brown, J. L., Graham, C. H., Leibowitz, H., & Ranken, H. B. Luminance thresholds for the resolution of visual detail during dark adaptation. *Journal of the Optical Society of America*, 1953, *43*, 197–202.

Brown, R. H., & Niven, J. I. The relation between the foveal intensity threshold and length of an illuminated slit. *Journal of Experimental Psychology*, 1944, *34*, 464–476.

Buss, C. M., Hayhoe, M. M., & Stromeyer, C. F. Lateral interactions in the control of visual sensitivity. *Vision Research*, 1982, *22*, 693–709.

Chapanis, A. The dark adaptation of the color anomalous measured with lights of different hues. *Journal of General Physiology*, 1947, *30*, 423–437.

Cohn, T. E. Quantum fluctuation limit in foveal vision. *Vision Research*, 1976, *16*, 573–579.

Cohn, T. E., & Lasley, D. J. Spatial summation of foveal increments and decrements. *Vision Research*, 1975, *15*, 389–399.

Cornsweet, T. N. *Visual perception*. New York: Academic Press, Inc., 1970.

Cornsweet, T. N., & Hayhoe, M. M. *Visual perception*. New York: Academic Press, in press.

Cornsweet, T. N., & Pinsker, H. M. Luminance discrimination of brief flashes under various conditions of adaptation. *Journal of Physiology* (London), 1965, *176*, 294–310.

Craik, K., & Vernon, M. The nature of dark adaptation. *British Journal of Psychology*, 1941, *32*, 62–81.

Crawford, B. H. The change of visual sensitivity with time. *Proceedings of the Royal Society*, 1937, *B123*, 69–89.

Crawford, B. H. The effect of field size and pattern on the change of visual sensitivity with time. *Proceedings of the Royal Society*, 1940, *B129*, 94–106.

Crawford, B. H. Photochemical laws and visual phenomena. *Proceedings of the Royal Society*, 1946, *B133*, 63–75.

Crawford, B. H. Visual adaptation in relation to brief conditioning stimuli. *Proceedings of the Royal Society*, 1947, *B134*, 283–302.

Crawford, B. H. The scotopic visibility function. *Physics Society Proceedings*, 1949, *62*, 321–334.

Crozier, W. J., & Holway, A. H. Theory and measurement of visual mechanisms. I. A visual discriminometer. II. Threshold stimulus intensity and retinal position. *Journal of General Physiology*, 1939, *22*, 341–364.

Dartnall, H. J. A. Photosensitivity. In H. J. A. Dartnall (Ed.), *Handbook of sensory physiology* (Vol. 7/1). New York: Springer-Verlag, 1972.

Das, S. R. Foveal increment thresholds in dark adaptation. *Journal of the Optical Society of America*, 1964, *54*, 541–546.

Davy, E. The intensity-time relation for multiple flashes of light in the peripheral retina. *Journal of the Optical Society of America*, 1952, *42*, 937–941.

Dillon, D. J., & Zegers, R. T. Quantal determination and statistical evaluation of absolute foveal luminosity thresholds and of threshold variability. *Journal of the Optical Society of America*, 1958, *48*, 877–883.

Dowling, J. E. Chemistry of visual adaptation in the rat. *Nature*, 1960, *188*, 114–118.

Drum, B. Relation of brightness to threshold for light-adapted and dark-adapted rods and cones: Effects of retinal eccentricity and target size. *Perception*, 1980, *9*, 633–650.

Du Croz, J. J., & Rushton, W. A. H. The separation of cone mechanisms in dark adaptation. *Journal of Physiology* (London), 1966, *183*, 481–496.

Eisner, A., & MacLeod, D. I. A. Blue-sensitive cones do not contribute to luminance. *Journal of the Optical Society of America*, 1980, *70*, 121–123.

Enoch, J. M. The two-color threshold technique of Stiles and derived component color mechanisms. In D. Jameson & L. M. Hurvich (Eds.), *Handbook of sensory physiology* (Vol. 7/4). New York: Springer-Verlag, 1972.

Ernst, W. The dependence of critical flicker frequency and the rod threshold on the state of adaptation of the eye. *Vision Research*, 1968, *8*, 889–900.

Finkelstein, M. A., & Hood, D. C. Cone system saturation: More than one stage of sensitivity loss. *Vision Research*, 1981, *21*, 319–328.

Finkelstein, M. A., & Hood, D. C. Opponent-colored cells can influence the detection of small, brief lights. *Vision Research*, 1982, *22*, 89–96.

Finkelstein, M. A., & Hood, D. C. Detection and discrimination of small, brief lights: Variable tuning of opponent channels. *Vision Research*, 1984, *24*, 175–181.

Fuortes, M. G. F., & Hodgkin, A. L. Changes in time scale and sensitivity in the ommatidia of *Limulus*. *Journal of Physiology*, 1964, *172*, 239–263.

Geisler, W. S. Adaptation, afterimages, and cone saturation. *Vision Research*, 1978, *18*, 279–289. (a)

Geisler, W. S. The effects of photopigment depletion on brightness and threshold. *Vision Research*, 1978, *18*, 269–278. (b)

Geisler, W. S. Evidence for the equivalent-background hypothesis in cones. *Vision Research*, 1979, *19*, 799–805.

Geisler, W. S. Effects of bleaching and backgrounds on the flash response of the cone system. *Journal of Physiology*, 1981, *312*, 413–434.

Gordon, J. G., & Hood, D. C. Anatomy and physiology of the frog retina. In K. V. Fite (Ed.), *The Amphibian visual system: A multidisciplinary approach*. New York: Academic Press, 1976.

Graham, B. V., Holland, R., & Sparks, D. L. Letter to the editors. Relative spectral sensitivity to short wavelength light in the peripheral visual field. *Vision Research*, 1975, *15*, 313–316.

Graham, C. H. (Ed.). *Vision and visual perception*. New York: Wiley, 1965.

Graham, C. H., & Bartlett, N. R. The relation of size of stimulus and intensity in the human eye. Intensity thresholds for red and violet light. *Journal of Experimental Psychology*, 1939, *24*, 574–587.

Graham, C. H., & Margaria, R. Area and the intensity-time relation in the peripheral retina. *American Journal of Physiology*, 1935, *113*, 299–305.

Griffin, D. R., Hubbard, R., & Wald, G. The sensitivity of the human eye to infrared radiation. *Journal of the Optical Society of America*, 1947, *37*, 546–554.

Guth, S. L., Massof, R. W., & Benzschawel, T. Vector model for normal and dichromatic color vision. *Journal of the Optical Society of America*, 1980, *70*, 197–212.

Hagins, W. A. The quantum efficiency of bleaching rhodopsin. *Journal of Physiology* (London), 1955, *129*, 22–23.

Haig, C. The course of rod dark adaptation as influenced by the intensity and duration of preadaptation to light. *Journal of General Physiology*, 1941, *24*, 735–751.

Hallett, P. E. Spatial summation. *Vision Research*, 1963, *3*, 9–24.

Hayhoe, M. M. After-effects of small adapting fields. *Journal of Physiology*, 1979, *296*, 141–158.

Hecht, S. The nature of foveal dark adaptation. *Journal of General Physiology*, 1921, *4*, 113–139.

Hecht, S., Haig, C., & Chase, A. M. The influence of light adaptation on the subsequent dark adaptation of the eye. *Journal of General Physiology*, 1937, *20*, 831–850.

Hecht, S., Haig, C., & Wald, G. The dark adaptation of retinal fields of different size and location. *Journal of General Physiology*, 1935, *19*, 321–337.

Hecht, S., Shlaer, S., & Pirenne, M. H. Energy, quanta, and vision. *Journal of General Physiology*, 1942, *25*, 819–840.

Holladay, L. L. The fundamentals of glare and visibility. *Journal of the Optical Society of America*, 1926, *12*, 271–319.

Holladay, L. L. Action of a light-source in the field of view in lowering visibility. *Journal of the Optical Society of America*, 1927, *14*, 1–15.

Hollins, M., & Alpern, M. Dark adaptation and pigment regeneration in human cones. *Journal of General Physiology*, 1973, *62*, 430–447.

Honig, B., Dinur, V., Nakanishi, K., Balagh-Nair, V., Gawinowicz, M. A., Arnaboldi, M., & Motto, M. G. An external point-charge model for wavelength regulation in visual pigment. *Journal of the American Chemical Society*, 1979, *101*, 7084–7086.

Hood, D. C. The effects of edge sharpness and exposure duration on detection threshold. *Vision Research*, 1973, *13*, 759–766.

Hood, D. C., & Finkelstein, M. A. Comparison of changes in sensitivity and sensation: Implications for the response-intensity function of the human photopic system. *Journal of Experimental Psychology: Human Perception and Performance*, 1979, *5*, 391–405.

Hood, D. C., & Finkelstein, M. A. A case for the revision of textbook models of color vision: The detection and appearance of small, brief lights. In J. D. Mollon & L. T. Sharpe (Eds.), *Colour vision: Physiology and psychophysics*. London: Academic Press, 1983.

Hood, D. C., Finkelstein, M. A., & Buckingham, E. Psychophysical tests of models of the response function. *Vision Research*, 1979, *19*, 401–406.

Hood, D. C., & Grover, B. G. Temporal summation of light by a vertebrate visual receptor. *Science*, 1974, *184*, 1003–1005.

Hood, D. C., & Hock, P. A. Light adaptation of the receptors: Increment threshold functions for the frog's rods and cones. *Vision Research*, 1975, *15*, 545–553.

Hood, D. C., Ilves, T., Maurer, E., Wandell, B., & Buckingham, E. Human cone saturation as a function of ambient intensity: A test of models of shifts in the dynamic range. *Vision Research*, 1978, *18*, 983–993.

Hsia, Y., & Graham, C. H. Spectral luminosity curves of protanopic, deuteranopic, and normal subjects. *Proceedings of the National Academy of Science*, 1957, *43*, 1011–1019.

Hurvich, L. M., & Jameson, D. An opponent-process theory of color vision. *Psychological Review*, 1957, *64*, 384–404.

Ikeda, M., & Urakubo, M. Rod-cone interrelation. *Journal of the Optical Society of America*, 1969, *59*, 217–222.

Ingling, C. R., Jr., & Tsou, B. H. P. Orthogonal combination of the three visual channels. *Vision Research*, 1977, *17*, 1075–1982.

Jameson, D., & Hurvich, L. M. Theory of brightness and color contrast in human vision. *Vision Research*, 1964, *4*, 135–154.

Judd, D. B. Basic correlates of the visual stimulus. In S. S. Stevens (Ed.), *Handbook of experimental psychology*. New York: Wiley, 1951.

Karn, H. W. Area and the intensity-time relation in the fovea. *Journal of General Physiology*, 1936, *14*, 360–369.

Keller, M. The relation between the critical duration and intensity in brightness discrimination. *Journal of Experimental Psychology*, 1941, *28*, 407–418.

King-Smith, P. E., & Carden, D. Luminance and the opponent-color contributions to visual detection and adaptation and to temporal and spatial integration. *Journal of the Optical Society of America*, 1976, *66*, 709–717.

Kinney, J. A. S. Sensitivity of the eye to spectral radiation at the scotopic and mesopic intensity levels. *Journal of the Optical Society of America*, 1955, *45*, 507–514.

Kranda, K., & King-Smith, P. E. Detection of coloured stimuli by independent linear systems. *Vision Research*, 1979, *19*, 733–745.

Kühne, W. *On the photochemistry of the retina and on visual purple*. New York: Macmillan, 1878.

Kuyk, T. K. Spectral sensitivity of the peripheral retina to large and small stimuli. *Vision Research*, 1982, *22*, 1293–1298.

Lamar, E. S., Hecht, S., Shlaer, S., & Hendley, C. D. Size, shape and contrast in detection of targets by daylight vision. Data and analytical description. *Journal of the Optical Society of America*, 1947, *37*, 531–545.

Le Grand, Y. *Light, colour and vision* (2nd ed.). R. W. G. Hunt, J. W. T. Walsh, & F. R. W. Hunt (trans.). Somerset, N.J.: Halsted Press, 1968.

Long, G. E. The effect of duration of onset and cessation of light flash on the intensity-time relation in the peripheral retina. *Journal of the Optical Society of America*, 1951, *41*, 743–747.

Lythgoe, R. J. The mechanism of dark adaptation: A critical resume. *British Journal of Ophthalmology*, 1940, *24*, 21–43.

Lythgoe, R. J., & Tansley, K. The relation of the critical frequency to the adaptation of the eye. *Proceedings of the Royal Society*, 1929, *105-B*, 60–92.

Mandelbaum, J., & Mintz, E. The sensitivities of the color receptors as measured by dark adaptation. *American Journal of Ophthalmology*, 1941, *24*, 1241–1254.

Marriott, F. H. C. The foveal absolute thresholds for shorts flashes and small fields. *Journal of Physiology*, 1963, *169*, 416–423.

Matin, L. Critical duration, the differential luminance threshold, critical flicker frequency, and visual adaptation: A theoretical treatment. *Journal of the Optical Society of America*, 1968, *58*, 404–415.

McCann, J. J. Rod-cone interactions: Different color sensations from identical stimuli. *Science*, 1972, *176*, 1255–1257.

Metz, J. W., & Brown, J. L. *Integration of responses between different types of cones and between rods and cones* (Tech. Rep. #11). Lawrence, Kansas: Kansas State University, Department of Psychology, 1970.

Miles, W. R. Red goggles for producing dark adaptation. *Federal Proceedings of the Federation of American Societies for Experimental Biology*, 1943, *2*, 109–115.

Montellese, S., Brown, J. L., & Sharpe, L. T. Changes in critical duration during dark adaptation. *Vision Research*, 1979, *10*, 1147–1153.

Mote, F. A., & Riopelle, A. J. The effect of varying the intensity and the duration of pre-exposure upon foveal dark adaptation in the human eye. *Journal of General Physiology*, 1951, *34*, 657–674.

Mote, F. A., & Riopelle, A. J. The effect of varying the intensity and the duration of pre-exposure upon subsequent dark adaptation in the human eye. *Journal of Comparative Physiology and Psychology*, 1953, *461*, 49–55.

Mueller, C. G. Frequency of seeing functions for intensity discrimination at various levels of adapting intensity. *Journal of General Physiology*, 1951, *34*, 463–474.

Nachmias, J. Signal detection theory and its application to problems in vision. In D. Jameson & L. M. Hurvich (Eds.), *Handbook of sensory physiology* (Vol. 7/4). New York: Springer-Verlag, 1972.

Naka, K. I., & Rushton, W. A. H. S-potentials from colour units in the retina of fish (*Cyprinidae*). *Journal of Physiology*, 1966, *185*, 536–555.

Osterberg, G. Topography of the layer of rods and cones in the human retina. *Acta Ophthalmologica Supplement*, 1935, *6*, 1–102.

Piper, H. Uber die Abhangigkeit des Reizwertes buchtender Objekte von ihrer Flachen-bezw. *Zeitschrift fur psychologie und physiologie der sinnesorgane*, 1903, *32*, 98–112.

Pirenne, M. H. Luminal brightness increments. In H. Davson (Ed.), *The eye—the visual process* (Vol. 2). New York: Academic Press Inc., 1962.

Pirenne, M. H. *Vision and the eye* (2nd ed.). New York: Methuen, 1967.

Pirenne, M. H., & Marriott, F. H. C. The quantum theory of light and the psychophysiology of vision. In S. Koch (Ed.), *Psychology: A study of a science* (Vol. 1). New York: McGraw-Hill, 1959.

Pirenne, M. H., Marriott, F. H. C., & O'Doherty, E. F. *Individual differences in night vision efficiency* (Special Report Series of the Medical Research Council, #294). London: 1957.

Pokorny, J., Smith, V. C., & Verriest, G. Physiological and theoretical bases of normal color vision. In J. Pokorny, V. C. Smith, G. Verriest, & A. J. L. G. Princherse (Eds.), *Congenital and acquired color vision defects*. New York: Grune & Stratton, 1979.

Pöppel, E., & Harvey, L. O., Jr. Eight-difference threshold and subjective brightness in the periphery of the visual field. *Psychologische Forschung*, 1973, *36*, 145–161.

Pugh, E. N., Jr. Rhodopsin flash photolysis in man. *Journal of Physiology*, 1975, *248*, 393–412. (a)

Pugh, E. N., Jr. Rushton's paradox: Rod dark adaptation after flash photolysis. *Journal of Physiology*, 1975, *248*, 413–431. (b)

Purkyně, J. E. *Boebachtungen und Versuche zur Physiologie der Sinne* (Vols. 1 & 2). Berlin: G. Reimer, 1825.

Reeves, P. The response of the average pupil to various intensities of light. *Journal of the Optical Society of America*, 1920, *4*, 35–43.

Ricco, A. Relazione fra il minimo angolo visuale e l'intensita luminosa. *Annali di Ottalmologia*, 1877, *6*, 373–479.

Rinalducci, E. G., Higgins, K. E., & Cramer, J. A. Nonequivalence of backgrounds during photopic dark adaptation. *Journal of the Optical Society of America*, 1970, *60*, 1518–1524.

Riopelle, A. J., & Bevan, W., Jr. The distribution of scotopic sensitivity in human vision. *American Journal of Psychology*, 1953, *66*, 73–80.

Ripps, H., & Weale, R. A. Flash bleaching of rhodopsin in the human retina. *Journal of Physiology*, 1969, *200*, 151–159.

Rose, A. The sensitivity performance of the eye on an absolute scale. *Journal of the Optical Society of America*, 1948, *38*, 196–208.

Ruddock, K. H. Light transmission through the ocular media and macular pigment and its significance for psychophysical investigation. In D. Jameson & L. M. Hurvich (Eds.), *Handbook of sensory physiology* (Vol. 7/4). New York: Springer-Verlag, 1972.

Rushton, W. A. H. The difference spectrum and the photosensitivity of rhodopsin in living human eye. *Journal of Physiology*, 1956, *134*, 11–39.

Rushton, W. A. H. Kinetics of cone pigments measured objectively on the living human fovea. *Annals of the New York Academy of Science*, 1958, *74*, 291–304.

Rushton, W. A. H. Dark adaptation and the regeneration of rhodopsin. *Journal of Physiology*, 1961, *156*, 166–178.

Rushton, W. A. H. Cone pigment kinetics in the protanope. *Journal of Physiology* (London), 1963, *168*, 374–388.

Rushton, W. A. H. The Ferrier lecture: Visual adaptation. *Proceedings of the Royal Society of London*, 1965, *B162*, 20–46.

Rushton, W. A. H. Rod/cone rivalry in pigment regeneration. *Journal of Physiology*, 1968, *198*, 219–236.

Rushton, W. A. H., & Baker, H. D. Effect of a very bright flash on cone vision and cone pigments in man. *Nature*, 1963, *200*, 421–423.

Rushton, W. A. H., & Henry, J. H. Bleaching and regeneration of cone pigments in man. *Vision Research*, 1968, *8*, 617–631.

Rushton, W. A. H., & Powell, D. S. The early phase of dark adaptation. *Vision Research*, 1972, *12*, 1083–1094. (a)

Rushton, W. A. H., & Powell, D. S. The rhodopsin content and the visual threshold of human rods. *Vision Research*, 1972, *12*, 1073–1082. (b)

Rushton, W. A. H., & Westheimer, G. The effect upon rod threshold of bleaching neighboring rods. *Journal of Physiology*, 1962, *164*, 318–329.

Sakitt, B. Configuration dependence of scotopic spatial summation. *Journal of Physiology*, 1971, *216*, 513–529.

Schneider, B., Hood, D. C., Cohen, H., & Stampfer, M. Behavioral threshold and rhodopsin content as a function of vitamin A deprivation in the rat. *Vision Research*, 1977, *17*, 799–806.

Scholtes, A. M. W., & Bouman, M. A. Psychophysical experiments on spatial summation at threshold level of the human peripheral retina. *Vision Research*, 1977, *17*, 867–873.

Shevell, S. S. The dual role of chromatic backgrounds in color perception. *Vision Research*, 1978, *18*, 1649–1661.

Siegel, I. M., Graham, C. H., Ripps, H., & Hsia, Y. Analysis of photopic and scotopic function in an incomplete achromat. *Journal of the Optical Society of America*, 1966, *56*, 699–704.

Smith, V. C., & Porkorny, J. Spectral sensitivity of the foveal cone photopigments between 400 and 500 nm. *Vision Research*, 1975, *15*, 161–171.

Sperling, H. G., & Harwerth, R. S. Red-green cone interactions in the increment threshold spectral sensitivity of primates. *Science*, 1971, *172*, 180–184.

Sperling, H. G., & Hsia, Y. Some comparisons among spectral sensitivity data obtained in different retinal locations with two sizes of foveal stimulus. *Journal of the Optical Society of America*, 1957, *47*, 707–713.

Sperling, H. G., & Jolliffe, C. L. Intensity-time relationship at threshold for spectral stimuli in human vision. *Journal of the Optical Society of America*, 1965, *55*, 191–199.

Spring, K. H., & Stiles, W. S. Apparent shape and size of the pupil viewed obliquely. *British Journal of Ophthalmology*, 1948, *32*, 347–354.

Stabell, B., & Stabell, U. Effects of rod activity on color threshold. *Vision Research*, 1976, *16*, 1105–1110. (a)

Stabell, B., & Stabell, U. Rod and cone contributions to peripheral colour vision. *Vision Research*, 1976, *16*, 1099–1104. (b)

Stabell, B., & Stabell, U. Absolute spectral sensitivity at different eccentricities. *Journal of the Optical Society of America*, 1981, *71*, 836–840.

Stabell, U., & Stabell, B. Variation in density of macular pigmentation and in short-wave cone sensitivity with eccentricity. *Journal of the Optical Society of America*, 1980, *70*, 706–711.

Stewart, B. R. Temporal summation during dark adaptation. *Journal of the Optical Society of America*, 1972, *62*, 449–457.

Stiles, W. S. The effect of glare on brightness difference threshold. *Proceedings of the Royal Society of London*, 1929, *1043*, 322–351.

Stiles, W. S. A modified Helmholtz line element in brightness colour space. *Proceedings of the Physics Society*, 1946, *58*, 41–65.

Stiles, W. S. Increment thresholds and the mechanisms of colour vision. *Documented Ophthalmology*, 1949, *3*, 138–163.

Stiles, W. S. Colour vision: The approach through increment-threshold sensitivity. *Proceedings of the National Academy of Science*, 1959, *45*, 100–114.

Stiles, W. S. Adaptation, chromatic adaptation, colour transformation. (Madrid Annales of) *Sociedad espanole de fisica y quimica* (series A), 1961, *57*, 149.

Stiles, W. S., & Crawford, B. H. *Equivalent adaptation levels in localized retinal areas* (Report of Discussions of the Vision Physiology Society of London #194). London: 1932.

Tachibana, M. Threshold changes near the light-dark border: A comparison of real and equivalent background lights. *Vision Research*, 1977, *17*, 117–122.

Teich, M. C., Prucnal, P. R., Vannucci, G., Breton, M. E., McGill, W. J., & Kelly, D. H. Multiplication noise in the human visual system at threshold: Quantum fluctuations and minimum detectable energy. *Journal of the Optical Society of America*, 1982, *72*, 419–431.

Teller, D. Y., & Gestrin, P. J. Sensitization by annular surrounds: Sensitization and dark adaptation. *Vision Research*, 1969, *9*, 1481–1490.

Van den Brink, G., & Bouman, M. A. Variation of integrative actions in the retinal system: An adaptational phenomenon. *Journal of the Optical Society of America*, 1954, *44*, 616–620.

Velden, H. A. van der. Over het aantal lichtquanta dat voor een lochtprikkel bij het menselijk oog. *Physica*, 1944, *11*, 179–189.

Von Kries, J., & Eyster, J. A. E. Uber die zur Erregung des Sehorgans erforderlichen Energiemenzen. *Zeitschift fur Sinnesphysiologie*, 1907, *41*, 394.

Wagner, G., & Boynton, R. M. Comparison of four methods of heterochromatic photometry. *Journal of the Optical Society of America*, 1972, *62*, 1508–1575.

Wald, G. Human vision and the spectrum. *Science*, 1945, *101*, 653–658.

Wald, G. Blue-blindness in the normal fovea. *Journal of the Optical Society of America*, 1967, *57*, 1289–1301.

Wald, G. The molecular basis of visual excitation. *Nature*, 1968, *219*, 800–807.

Wald, G., & Clark, A. B. Visual adaptation and chemistry of the rods. *Journal of General Physiology*, 1937, *21*, 93–105.

Walls, G. L. *The vertebrate eye and its adaptive radiation*. Bloomfield Hills, Mich.: Cranbrook Institute of Science, 1942.

Walraven, J. Discounting the background, the missing link in the explanation of chromatic induction. *Vision Research*, 1976, *16*, 289–295.

Westheimer, G. Spatial interaction in the human retina during scotopic vision. *Journal of Physiology*, 1965, *181*, 881–894.

Westheimer, G. Spatial interaction in human cone vision. *Journal of Physiology*, 1967, *190*, 139–154.

Westheimer, G. Bleached rhodopsin and retinal interaction. *Journal of Physiology*, 1968, *195*, 97–105.

Williams, D. R., MacLeod, D. I. A., & Hayhoe, M. M. Foveal tritanopia. *Vision Research*, 1981, *21*, 1341–1356. (a)

Williams, D. R., MacLeod, D. I. A., & Hayhoe, M. M. Punctate sensitivity of the blue-sensitive mechanism. *Vision Research*, 1981, *21*, 1357–1376. (b)

Winsor, C. P., & Clark, A. B. Dark adaptation after varying degrees of light adaptation. *Proceedings of the National Academy of Science*, 1936, *22*, 400–404.

Wolf, E., & Zigler, M. J. Location of the break in the dark adaptation curve in relation to pre-exposure brightness and pre-exposure time. *Journal of the Optical Society of America*, 1954, *44*, 875–879.

Wooten, B. R., Fuld, K., & Spillman, L. Photopic spectral sensitivity of the peripheral retina. *Journal of the Optical Society of America*, 1975, *65*, 334–342.

Wyszecki, G., & Stiles, W. S. *Color science*. New York: Wiley, 1982.

Yellott, J. I., Wandell, B. A., & Cornsweet, T. N. The beginnings of visual perception: The retinal image and its initial encoding. In I. Darien-Smith (Ed.), *Handbook of physiology* (Vol. 1). Baltimore: Williams & Wilkins, 1984.

CHAPTER 6

TEMPORAL SENSITIVITY

ANDREW B. WATSON

NASA Ames Research Center, Moffett Field, California

CONTENTS

The stimulus for vision is light distributed over space, time, and wavelength. The distribution in each of these dimensions influences our visual experience. This chapter focuses upon the temporal dimension. The time course of the stimulus affects our experience in two ways: it affects our sensitivity to the stimulus, for example, whether we see it or not, and it affects the appearance of the stimuli that are seen, for example, by controlling the apparent time course of the sensation. Both are important, but this chapter deals primarily with the first sort of effect, which is called *temporal sensitivity*.

This chapter begins with a brief description of the stimuli that are used to measure temporal sensitivity. A set of terms is introduced that serves to describe in a consistent way a wide variety of possible configurations. Some mathematical notation is specified for luminous stimuli distributed over space and time.

The study of temporal sensitivity has always made extensive use of mathematics, primarily Linear Systems Theory. Models of sensitivity and of the underlying mechanisms are frequently couched in these terms. To provide a point of reference, a brief survey of Linear Systems Theory is provided.

Because so many of the phenomena of temporal sensitivity can be explained by a simple generic model, and because this model has appeared piecemeal in the work of a number of authors, a "working model" is given concrete form in Section 4. A working model is one that provides a reasonable quantitative account of the available data, but whose mathematical structure is somewhat arbitrary and whose details are subject to change in the light of new evidence. Wherever possible in the remainder of the chapter, empirical results are compared to the predictions of the working model.

Sections 5–8 review empirical and theoretical analyses of the visibility of a number of particular temporal wave forms: sinusoids, pulses, and pairs of pulses. These wave forms are selected because they have received the bulk of experimental attention, and because they reveal important aspects of temporal sensitivity.

As will be evident, the temporal dimension of a stimulus cannot be studied entirely in isolation from the other dimensions. For example, statements regarding temporal sensitivity can rarely be made independently of the spatial distribution of the stimulus. This interdependence is acknowledged throughout the chapter, and is addressed directly in Section 10.

In natural imagery, as distinct from the artificial stimulus creations of the laboratory, temporal variation arises primarily through image motion, whether through motion of the observer, of the eyes, or of the objects viewed. Image motion is a special sort of temporal variation in which the time wave form is a function of spatial position. In Section 11, the temporal variations induced by image motion are considered, and some basic results on sensitivity to moving patterns are reviewed. The relation of temporal sensitivity to motion sensitivity is also discussed.

As the ambient level of illumination is raised, the eye exchanges sensitivity for temporal resolution. Overall sensitivity is reduced, but the ability to see rapid fluctuations is relatively enhanced. Section 12 reviews the empirical effects of light adaptation upon temporal sensitivity, and considers some theoretical models for these effects.

1. THE TEMPORAL STIMULUS

At its most general, the stimulus for vision includes anything that influences our visual sensations and reactions. This might include our state of light adaptation, our distance from a viewed object, what we had for lunch, and to whom we last spoke. In order to draw the line at a point that will best serve the purpose of this chapter, the stimulus is considered to be a distribution of light lying in a plane orthogonal to the line of sight and in front of the observer. This *image* covers some portion of the visual field and endures for some finite amount of time.

1.1. Intensity

Because we are only rarely concerned with variations in the wavelength of light, it is sufficient to specify the *intensity* of the light at each point in the image. This intensity distribution can be written $I\ (x,\ y,\ t)$, where x and y are horizontal and vertical coordinates of the image measured in degrees of visual angle (degrees), and t is time. Three measures of intensity are used here. The first is *luminance*, expressed in units of candelas per square meter. The precise definition of luminance is quite complicated (Wyszecki & Stiles, 1967). But given our earlier definition of an image, luminance is then the amount of light emitted or reflected toward the eye per unit area of the source, weighted by the photopic luminous efficiency function. The optics of the eye transform the image luminance distribution into a distribution of light upon the retina. This transformation involves many factors, including spatial blurring, chromatic aberration, and attenuation by the pupil. The last effect is taken into account by a second measure, the so-called *retinal illuminance.* It is defined as the luminance ($cd{\cdot}m^{-2}$) multiplied by the area of the pupil (mm^2), and is given in units of *trolands* (td). This measure is used when the precise level of illumination on the retina is important, as in investigations of light adaptation. A third measure, most commonly used in studies of color vision, specifies image intensity in quanta per square degree per second at some particular wavelength or at each wavelength in a spectrally extended source. The troland value can be determined from this measure by way of formulas given by Wyszecki and Stiles (1967) (see also Chapter 5 by Hood & Finkelstein and Chapter 8 by Pokorny & Smith).

1.2. Spatial Configuration and Contrast

The spatial configuration of the stimulus has important effects upon temporal sensitivity. As noted above, our general description of an image is its complete three-dimensional intensity distribution, $I(x,\ y,\ t)$. However, the stimuli used in the majority of laboratory experiments can be described in less general but simpler form. Figure 6.1 illustrates this discussion.

An area of intensity I_B is designated as the *background.* A larger area, extending outward from the limit of the background and with intensity I_S, is called the *surround.* Surround intensity is most often set equal to background intensity, or is absent altogether. Authors rarely specify lighting conditions beyond the borders of the surround.

Superposed on and coextensive with the background is the *target* with an intensity given by the function $I_T(x,\ y,\ t)$. We allow the target intensity to have negative values, as when light is subtracted from the background, but of course the sum of target and background must be positive. *Contrast* is defined as the ratio of target intensity to background intensity,

$$C(x,y,t) \quad = \quad \frac{I_T(x,y,t)}{I_B} \ . \qquad (1)$$

Note that contrast may have negative as well as positive values, though it may never be less than -1. Combining background and target, the intensity within the target area is given by

$$I(x,y,t) \ = \ I_B \ + \ I_T(x,y,t) \ = \ I_B[1 \ + \ C(x,y,t)] \ . \qquad (2)$$

The segregation of the stimulus into contrast and background terms is a tradition that arose from the observation that sensitivity is more nearly invariant with respect to contrast than with respect to intensity. The background intensity must be specified, however, for it controls the state of adaptation which in turn governs sensitivity. Various definitions of background intensity are used, among them the unvarying level upon which the target is superposed, the space-average intensity of the image, the space-time average, or the average of the maximum and minimum intensities in the image. Each of these may be appropriate in some circumstance, but it is important that the expression for contrast be correct relative to the definition of background used.

1.3. Separability

In many experimental situations, the spatial contrast distribution does not vary over time, and likewise the temporal distribution is the same at all points in the image. In this case the spatial and temporal dimensions of the stimulus are said to be *separable* and the overall distribution can be written as a product:

$$C(x,y,t) \ = \ C_{x,y}(x,y)C_t(t) \ . \qquad (3)$$

This condition holds, for example, for a disk target that is flashed on briefly, or for a spatial grating that is counterphase modulated

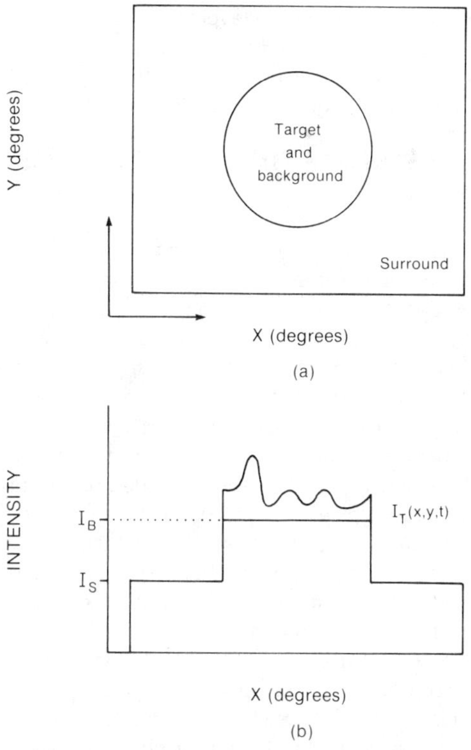

Figure 6.1. Some terms used to describe visual stimuli. (a) The spatial configuration of the image. The target and background are superposed on some specified area, shown here as a disk. The surround lies outside the target and background. (b) A horizontal cross-section through the intensity distribution $I\ (x,y,t)$ of the image. The surround has intensity I_S, the background I_B, and the target $I_T\ (x,y,t)$. Target contrast is the ratio I_T/I_B.

in time. It does not hold for one important class of stimuli, namely, patterns in motion. In spite of this exception, most work on temporal sensitivity has been confined to separable stimuli, and for this reason we focus upon the time wave form $C_t(t)$, abbreviated $C(t)$. If $C(t)$ is to continue to express contrast as defined above, then $C_{x,y}(x, y)$ must be normalized so as to have an overall contrast of 1. This convention has been adopted throughout this chapter. Where intensity rather than contrast is considered, we will specify the intensity wave form $I(t)$.

In reducing the description of the stimulus to the temporal wave form $C(t)$, it must be borne in mind that both background intensity and spatial distribution (which are no longer reflected in the wave form) can have important effects upon temporal sensitivity. These effects are discussed in Sections 9 and 11.

1.4. Temporal Wave Forms

A wide range of temporal wave forms has been studied for their effects upon visual sensitivity. For various reasons, not all entirely sensible, certain wave forms have received most of the attention. These are rectangular incremental pulses, decremental pulses, pulse pairs, square waves, and sinusoids. Sensitivity to each of these wave forms is considered, and they are sketched in Figure 6.2. A useful distinction among these wave forms is that the sinusoid and the square wave are *periodic*, whereas the others are *aperiodic*. A periodic wave form is one that repeats itself forever. Formally, it is a wave form $I(t)$ such that

$$I(t) = I(t - T) \quad \text{for all } t , \tag{4}$$

where T is the *period* of the wave form. No visual stimulus goes on forever, but if the number of cycles in the wave form is large enough so that adding more does not alter sensitivity, then it is reasonable to treat the wave form as periodic.

2. LINEAR SYSTEMS THEORY IN THE TIME DOMAIN

Linear Systems Theory (LST) is an important mathematical tool in the analysis of human temporal sensitivity. Bracewell (1978) provides an excellent introduction to this branch of mathematics. The purpose of this section is to provide a brief, intuitive overview of LST and to note a number of the important results so that they may be referred to in the text.

The experimental analysis of a physical system often consists of applying various inputs and measuring the resulting outputs. The inputs we consider here are real-valued functions of time, $f(t)$. This function typically describes the luminance or contrast of a visual stimulus over time (see Section 1). The output, or response, is also some real-valued function of time, $r(t)$. This function might represent some internal state of excitation, for example, the momentary discharge frequency of a visual neuron. More often it is a purely hypothetical quantity, whose value can be deduced from psychophysical responses only with the aid of additional assumptions. These assumptions are considered here. The *system* is that collection of physical processes that intervenes between the input and the response. In the example above, the system would include all those events between stimulus and neural response, including optical imaging, transduction, and transmission from neuron to neuron.

A complete empirical characterization of the system would consist of a description of the output resulting from any input. When the number of possible inputs is infinite, as is true in the case of temporal wave forms, a purely experimental approach would require an infinite number of measurements. If the system is *linear*, however, LST provides a way of characterizing the system by measuring the response to a single input. LST also supplies a set of mathematical tools for predicting, from this characterization, the response to an arbitrary input.

2.1. Superposition

It is useful to denote the action of the system mathematically by an operator, L. Just as a function $f(t)$ maps values of t to values of $f(t)$, so the operator maps the input *function* $f(t)$ into the output function $r(t)$. We write this mapping in the form

$$L[f(t)] = r(t) . \tag{5}$$

Where it is possible to do so without confusion, we omit the function arguments and write f for $f(t)$.

A system is linear if it obeys the principle of superposition. This principle states that for any two inputs f_1 and f_2, and any constant a,

$$L[af_1] = aL[f_1] \tag{6}$$

$$L[f_1 + f_2] = L[f_1] + L[f_2] . \tag{7}$$

Thus superposition entails two properties, homogeneity and additivity. The system is homogeneous when multiplying an input multiplies the output by the same amount. The system is additive when the response to the sum of two inputs is the sum of the responses to the individual inputs.

2.2. Time Invariance

Let $r(t) = L[f(t)]$. The system is *time invariant* if

$$L[f(t - \tau)] = r(t - \tau) . \tag{8}$$

Note that $f(t - \tau)$ is the input $f(t)$ delayed by τ; likewise $r(t - \tau)$ is the response $r(t)$ delayed by τ. Equation (8) states that delaying the input by τ delays the output by τ but leaves it otherwise unaltered. This means that the properties of the system do not change over time.

2.3. Orthogonal Basis Functions

Two functions $b_1(t)$ and $b_2(t)$ are *orthogonal* if their *inner product* is zero:

$$b_1(t) \cdot b_2(t) = \int_{-\infty}^{\infty} b_1(t) b_2(t) dt = 0 . \tag{9}$$

A *basis* is a set of functions that *spans* some set of functions; that is, any member of the latter set can be constructed from a linear combination of the basis functions. If we have a set of orthogonal basis functions $\{b_j(t)\}$ which span the set of real-valued functions $\{f(t)\}$, then for any function f,

$$f(t) = \sum_{j=-\infty}^{j=\infty} a_j b_j(t) , \tag{10}$$

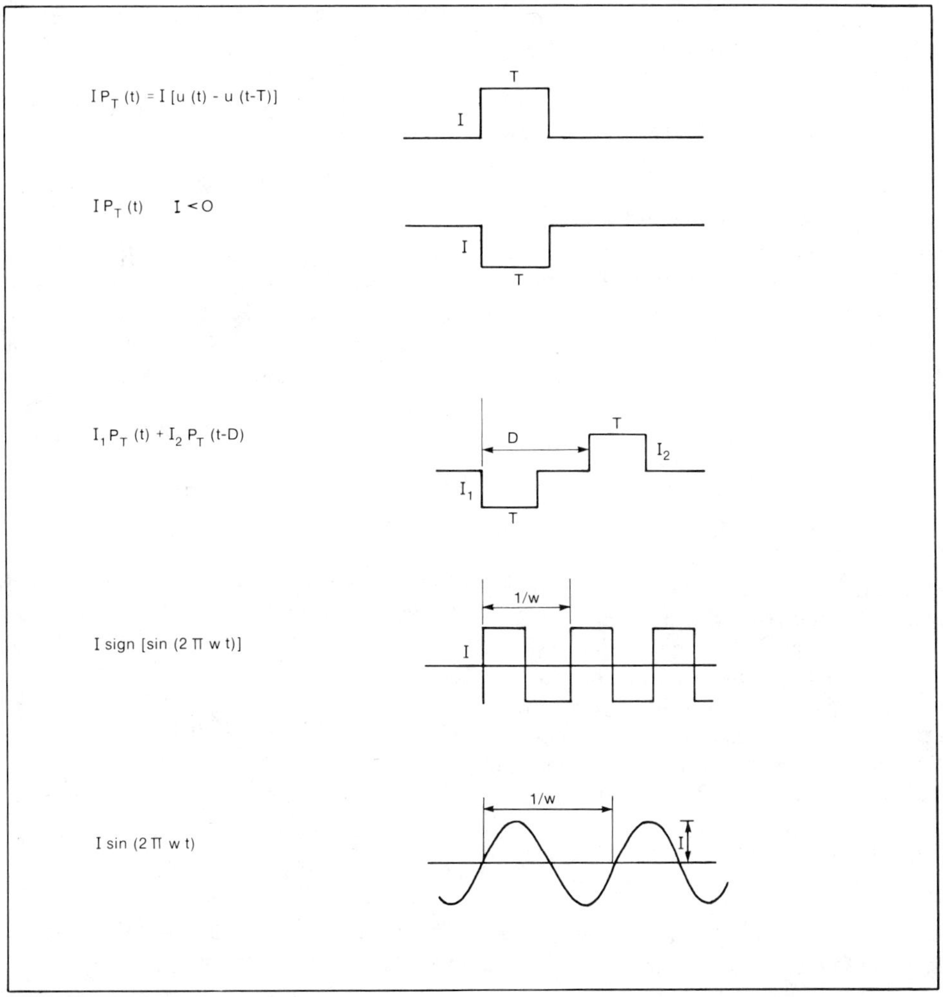

Figure 6.2. Some wave forms used to study visual temporal sensitivity. Each wave form specifies the target intensity as a function of time. An equation defining each wave form is given on the left. From top to bottom the wave forms are a rectangular pulse increment of intensity I and duration T; a pulse decrement of intensity I and duration T; a pulse pair with durations T, intensities I_1 and I_2, and delay between pulses of D; a square wave of intensity I and frequency w; and a sinusoid of intensity I and frequency w. Intensity may be a quantity such as luminance, retinal illuminance, or quanta·degree^{-2}·sec^{-1} at some wavelength. Because light cannot have negative intensity, each wave form must be added to a background more intense than the largest negative excursion in the wave form.

where the a_j are the coefficients of the linear combination, and where both a and b may be complex. Because the basis is orthogonal, the set of coefficients a_j that go to make up a particular f are unique and easily determined.

Now we let f be the input to a linear system. Applying the principle of superposition to Eq. (10), we see that the response to f will be

$$L[f] = \sum_{j=-\infty}^{j=\infty} a_j L[b_j] \ . \tag{11}$$

Thus if we knew the response to each basis function ($L[b_j]$), we could calculate the response to any arbitrary input. The procedure would be as follows: (1) evaluate the coefficients a_j required to represent the input f, (2) multiply each basis response $L[b_j]$ by the coefficient a_j, and (3) add them up to produce the response $L[f]$.

2.4. Impulse and Impulse Response

One natural set of orthogonal basis functions is the set of *impulses* located at different points in time. An impulse $\delta(t)$ is a pulse with infinite height, infinitesimal width, and unit area, located at $t = 0$. The input is easily represented in terms of shifted and scaled impulses,

$$f(t) = \int_{-\infty}^{\infty} f(\tau)\delta(t - \tau)\, d\tau = f(t) * \delta(t) \tag{12}$$

where $*$ indicates convolution. Note that this equation is the continuous version of Eq. (10), with $f(\tau)$ playing the role of the coefficients a_j. Let the response of the system to an impulse be $h(t)$, the *impulse response*. We write

$$h(t) = L[\delta(t)] \ . \tag{13}$$

We can now follow the procedure above to determine the response to $f(t)$. Combining the preceding three equations, and applying the principles of superposition and time invariance, we get

$$r(t) = \int_{-\infty}^{\infty} f(\tau)h(t - \tau)\, d\tau = f(t) * h(t) \ . \qquad (14)$$

Thus the response is equal to the convolution of the input and the impulse response. If the impulse response is known, the response to an arbitrary input can be calculated. Thus the impulse response completely characterizes the system.

2.5. Eigenfunctions

An alternative derivation of $r(t)$ is possible if each basis function is an *eigenfunction*, satisfying the condition

$$L[b_j(t)] = c_j b_j(t) \ . \qquad (15)$$

The response to an eigenfunction is the function itself, multiplied by some complex constant c_j, known as the *eigenvalue*. Fortunately, for a linear, time-invariant system there exists a set of eigenfunctions that are also orthogonal basis functions for the set of real-valued functions $\{f(t)\}$. They are the *complex exponentials*, $e^{i2\pi wt}$ with frequency w. The function f is synthesized from these exponentials in the manner described in Section 2.3, as a linear combination with complex coefficients $F(w)$,

$$f(t) = \int_{-\infty}^{\infty} F(w)e^{i2\pi wt}\, dw \ . \qquad (16)$$

Because the complex exponentials are eigenfunctions, the response of the linear system to f is easily determined:

$$r(t) = \int_{-\infty}^{\infty} H(w)F(w)e^{i2\pi wt}\, dw \ . \qquad (17)$$

The *system function* $H(w)$ (also called the *transfer function*) specifies the complex constant (eigenvalue) by which the complex exponential of frequency w is multiplied as it passes through the system. Note that $H(w)$, like the impulse response, completely specifies the behavior of the system. All we need now are methods for evaluating $F(w)$ and $H(w)$.

2.6. Fourier Transforms

The coefficients $F(w)$ that are required to construct $f(t)$ from complex exponentials are obtained by the *Fourier transform*

$$F(w) = FT[f(t)] = \int_{-\infty}^{\infty} f(t)e^{-i2\pi wt}\, dt \ . \qquad (18)$$

There is also an inverse transform, by which the original wave form is reconstituted from component exponentials with coefficients $F(w)$,

$$f(t) = FT^{-}[F(w)] = \int_{-\infty}^{\infty} F(w)e^{i2\pi wt}\, dw \ . \qquad (19)$$

Fourier transforms are treated extensively by Bracewell (1978).

2.7. The Convolution Theorem

A particularly valuable property of the Fourier transform is that if $f_1(t)$ and $f_2(t)$ are two functions, and $F_1(w)$ and $F_2(w)$ are their transforms, then

$$f_1(t) * f_2(t) = FT^{-}[F_1(w)F_2(w)] \ . \qquad (20)$$

Thus the complicated convolution operation is converted to the simple multiplication operation in the frequency domain. As an example, Eq. (14) shows that the response of a linear system is the convolution of the input and the impulse response. Applying the convolution theorem,

$$r(t) = FT^{-}[F(w)FT[h(t)]] \qquad (21)$$

$$= \int_{-\infty}^{\infty} F(w)FT[h(t)]e^{i2\pi wt}\, dw \ . \qquad (22)$$

Comparison of this result with Eq. (17) shows that the transform of the impulse response is the system function,

$$FT[h(t)] = H(w) \ . \qquad (23)$$

A linear, time-invariant system can therefore be completely described by either its impulse response or its system function, which are Fourier transforms of each other.

2.8. Amplitude and Phase

The complex system function $H(w)$ may be represented as the sum of real and imaginary parts

$$H = R + iI \qquad (24)$$

where $i = (-1)^{1/2}$. Each value of this function is a point in the complex plane at a distance $|H|$ from the origin and at an angle $< H$ from the positive real axis, where

$$|H| = (R^2 + I^2)^{1/2} \qquad (25)$$

$$< H = \tan^{-1} \frac{I}{R} \ . \qquad (26)$$

Application of Euler's theorem shows that

$$H = |H|\, e^{i<H} \ . \qquad (27)$$

The advantage of this last expression is that the response to an eigenfunction $e^{i2\pi wt}$ is now simply

$$L[e^{i2\pi wt}] = |H(w)| \exp\{i[2\pi wt + <H(w)]\} \ . \qquad (28)$$

With a more familiar real input of $\cos 2\pi wt$, we see that the output of the system is

$$L[\cos 2\pi wt] = |H(w)| \cos [2\pi wt + <H(w)] \ . \qquad (29)$$

In other words, the response is also a cosine of the same frequency but altered in amplitude by the factor $|H|$ and in phase by an amount $<H$. Thus $|H|$, the *amplitude response* of the system, describes the gain with which each frequency passes through the system, and $<H$, the *phase response*, describes how much each frequency is advanced or delayed.

2.9. Causality

In a passive physical system operating in the time domain, the response never precedes the input, and the system is said to be *causal*. Formally,

$$H(t) = 0 \qquad \text{for } t < 0 \ . \tag{30}$$

This has various consequences. Most important here is that amplitude and phase responses are even and odd functions, respectively. Accordingly, these functions need only be determined or specified for positive frequencies.

2.10. Some Simple System Functions

The system function of a linear combination of independent systems is the linear combination of their separate system functions. The cascade of two systems yields a system function equal to the product of their individual system functions. By means of these two rules, rather complicated systems can be assembled from simple components. In the following sections some simple systems are considered. For each, impulse response, system function, amplitude response, and phase response are noted in Table 6.1.

2.10.1. Multiplication by a Constant. If a signal is multiplied by a constant k, but not otherwise altered, the transfer function is a constant k. In electrical terms, this would be the action of an ideal amplifier with a gain of k.

2.10.2. Delay. If the signal is delayed by a time τ, but not otherwise altered, the amplitude response is equal to 1, and the phase response to $2\pi w\tau$.

2.10.3. Differentiator. Differentiation of a signal with respect to time is a linear operation, and may be represented by an impulse response that is the derivative of the impulse function, $\delta'(t)$. More generally, the nth time derivative may be represented by an impulse response that is the nth derivative of the impulse. The transfer function is $(i2\pi w)^n$.

2.10.4. Integrator. Integration over the interval $[-\infty, t]$ is equivalent to convolution with the unit step function, $u(t)$. Its system function is therefore the Fourier transform of the step function, $[\delta(w) - i/(\pi w)]/2$. Note that, except at 0, its action is precisely the inverse of that of the differentiator. This is logical, because except for their action on constants, differentiation and integration are inverse operations.

2.10.5. Leaky Integrator. Rather than performing a perfect integration, like that described in Section 2.10.4, many physical devices integrate the input but leak at a rate proportional to the amount accumulated. If the constant of proportionality is $1/\tau$, then the impulse response is

$$h(t) = u(t)e^{-t/\tau} \tag{31}$$

where $u(t)$ is the unit step function. If n identical leaky integrators are cascaded, then

$$h(t) = u(t)\frac{\tau^{n-1}}{(n - 1)!}(t/\tau)^{n-1}e^{-t/\tau} \tag{32}$$

and

$$H(w) = \tau^n(i2\pi w\tau + 1)^{-n} \ . \tag{33}$$

Amplitude and phase responses are

$$|H(w)| = \tau^n[(2\pi w\tau)^2 + 1)^{-n/2} \tag{34}$$

$$<H(w) = -n \tan^{-1}(2\pi w\tau) \ . \tag{35}$$

These functions are drawn in Figure 6.3. Note that the system acts as a low-pass filter. Beyond a frequency of $(2\pi\tau)^{-1}$, the amplitude approaches an asymptote of $(2\pi w)^{-n}$, whereas below $(2\pi\tau)^{-1}$ it asymptotes at τ^n. In log-log coordinates, the lower limb is flat whereas the upper limb falls with an asymptotic slope of $-n$. This is sometimes called a resistance-capacitance filter, by analogy to an electrical circuit composed of a resistor and a capacitor.

Table 6.1. Some Simple Linear Systems

System	Impulse Response, $h(t)$	System Function, $H(w)$	Amplitude Response, $\lvert H(w)\rvert$	Phase Response, $<H(w)$
Cascade	$h_1 * h_2$	H_1H_2	$\lvert H_1\rvert \lvert H_2\rvert$	$<H_1 + <H_2$
Sum	$h_1 + h_2$	$H_1 + H_2$	$\lvert H_1 + H_2\rvert$	$<[H_1 + H_2]$
Constant	$k\ \delta(t)$	k	$\lvert k\rvert$	0
Delay	$\delta(t - \tau)$	$e^{-i2\pi w\pi}$	1	$-2\pi w\tau$
nth derivative	$\delta^{(n)}(t)$	$(i2\pi w)^n$	$(2\pi\lvert w\rvert)^n$	$n\ \mathrm{sgn}(w)\pi/2$
$\int_{-\infty}^{t}$	$u(t)$	$[\delta(w) - i/(\pi w)]$	$[\delta(w) + 1/(\pi\lvert w\rvert)]$	$-\mathrm{sgn}(w)\pi/2$
Low-pass filter	$\frac{u(t)t^{n-1}e^{-t/\tau}}{(n - 1)!}$	$\frac{\tau^n}{(i2\pi w\tau + 1)^n}$	$\frac{\tau^n}{[(2\pi w\tau)^2 + 1]^{n/2}}$	$-n \tan^{-1}(2\pi w\tau)$

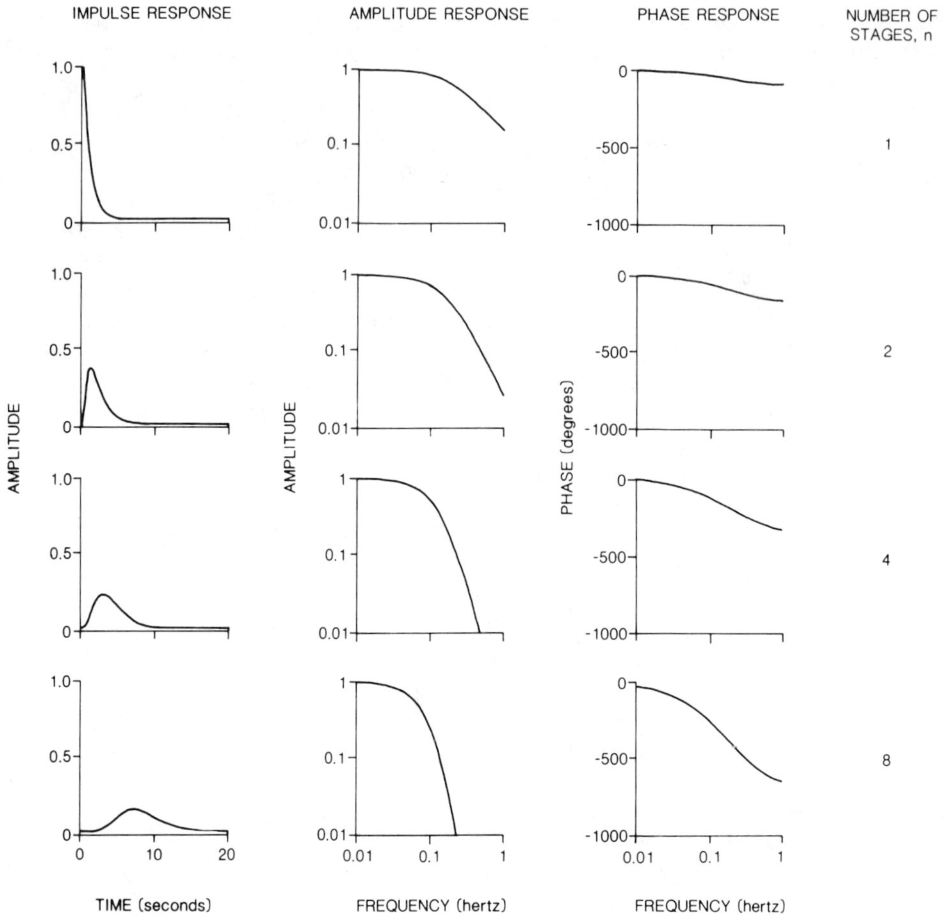

Figure 6.3. Responses of an n-stage low-pass filter with time constant $\tau = 1$. The columns show respectively the impulse response, the amplitude response, and the phase response. Different rows are for different numbers of stages (n), as indicated. With increasing stages, the impulse response becomes longer, lower, more symmetrical, and its peak occurs later in time. All the impulse responses have the same integral (area) of 1. The falling limb of the amplitude response has an asymptotic log-log slope of $-n$. At a given frequency, the phase response is proportional to n.

3. BASIC THEORETICAL CONCEPTS

This section introduces a number of concepts that are used frequently in discussions of temporal sensitivity.

3.1. Time-Invariant Linear Filter

Definitions of linear filters and time invariance are given in Section 2. A time-invariant linear filter often plays the role of the first element in models of the pathway between visual stimulus and psychophysical response. The filter input is the temporal wave form of intensity or contrast, and the output is some hypothetical internal response. Because the observer's psychophysical response is usually discrete rather than time varying (for example, the press of a button), it is necessary to assume some additional, usually nonlinear process between filter output and psychophysical response. Several examples are given here. The properties of the linear filter inferred from psychophysical data depend upon the the final response rule assumed.

Temporal models are often expressed in terms of integration or differentiation with respect to time. These operations may also be represented as linear filters, as described in Section 2. Occasionally integration over some epoch τ is considered. This is equivalent to a filter whose impulse response is a rectangle of height $1/\tau$ between times 0 and τ.

3.2. Threshold Mechanisms

The simplest link between filter output and observer response is some sort of threshold mechanism. Commonly it is assumed that an excursion of the response that exceeds some threshold value leads to a "correct" or "yes, I see it" response from the observer. Depending on the model in question, the threshold may be either a fixed property of the detection apparatus or a statistical criterion, which may be adjusted by the observer to satisfy certain objectives. Because decrements as well as increments can be detected, a threshold for negative excursions of the filter output must also be assumed.

3.3. Probability Summation Over Time

Both the visual stimulus and the physical mechanisms that mediate detection are subject to random perturbations. If the internal response is subject to noise, one cannot be certain which point in the response, if any, will exceed threshold. Accordingly, the probability that each point exceeds threshold must be considered.

A simple treatment of this situation is as follows. Suppose that a response of some duration may be broken into a sequence of n brief intervals, and that within each interval the response is essentially a constant r_i. Assume the probability that the response exceeds threshold in interval i, written p_i, is independent of all other intervals. Assume the signal is detected whenever the response in at least one interval exceeds threshold. The probability of detection will then be

$$p = 1 - \prod_{i=1}^{n} (1 - p_i) \ . \tag{36}$$

Quantitative predictions of sensitivity from this relation depend upon the assumed relationship between p_i and the value of the response r_i. One convenient and plausible assumption is that

$$p_i = 1 - e^{-|r_i|^\beta} \tag{37}$$

where r_i is the value of the internal response within interval i. If this response is linear, r_i is proportional to stimulus strength. The probability of detection is then

$$p = 1 - e^{-\Sigma|r_i|^\beta} \ . \tag{38}$$

Thus for all stimuli at threshold (defined as some fixed value of p)

$$1 = \sum_{i=1}^{n} |r_i|^\beta \ . \tag{39}$$

Note that this expression defines the amplitude scale of the internal response. If the relationship between the stimulus and the internal response sequence r_i is known (for example, if we know the transfer function of an internal linear filter), then this expression provides a method of calculating the effects of probability summation over time.

A successful experimental test of predictions from this analysis was provided by Watson (1979). Additional information on this subject is contained in Sections 4.2, 5.6, and 6.5.2. Other theoretical treatments of probability summation are possible. Nachmias (1981) has shown that details of this analysis (in particular the threshold assumption) are probably incorrect. But this treatment has the virtue of simplicity and is undoubtedly more correct than neglecting probabilistic effects altogether.

3.4. Nonlinear Mechanisms

The threshold mechanism and probability summation are examples of nonlinear operations in the chain of events between stimulus and psychophysical response. Many other nonlinear elements figure in models of temporal sensitivity. These may be loosely divided into three types. The first, such as thresholds and probability summation, are *output* nonlinearities, lying between some internal response and the psychophysical response. Rashbass's early model provides another example. There the linear response is squared, integrated over some epoch, and thresholded (Rashbass, 1970).

The second sort of nonlinearities are adaptive processes. Adaptation is inherently nonlinear, because by definition it violates the principle of superposition. Thus a linear model may be adequate for small signals in a fixed state of adaptation, but a nonlinear mechanism is required to alter the system properties with changes in adaptive state. These frequently appear as feedforward or feedback mechanisms that control the parameters of a linear filter (Fourtes & Hodgkin, 1964).

A third, less frequently considered nonlinearity occurs when signals may pass through any of several independent detection pathways. Examples are so-called *sustained* and *transient* pathways. Even if each pathway is linear, the system is nonlinear, because signals that travel through different pathways violate superposition. This notion is considered further in Section 9.4.

3.5. Detectors and Channels

It is sometimes useful to consider the collection of elements up to and including a threshold device as a single unit, which we call a *detector*. A single stimulus may excite many detectors, and each detector is subject to noise, so a stimulus may from trial to trial be detected by any one of a set of detectors. We call this set of detectors a *channel*.

When a "high threshold" interpretation of the detection process is employed, the channel is that set of detectors in which the response has a nonzero probability of exceeding threshold. If the observer is viewed as applying a more sophisticated computation to the detector outputs, the channel is those detectors entering into the computation.

3.6. Labeled Detectors

If an observer is asked to make some judgment about the appearance of stimuli, then the model must contain some mechanism for the coding of sensory quality. A simple assumption is that the response of each detector can be distinguished from that of all other detectors. This is called a *labeled detector*. Application of this concept is discussed in Section 9.4.1.3.

3.7. Fast, Slow, Transient, and Sustained

In the literature on temporal aspects of vision a number of terms are used whose meanings are not well defined. To avoid confusion, the following clarifications are proposed.

3.7.1. Fast and Slow. The term "fast" has been used to describe either a rapidly developing response, as might lead to a brief reaction time, for example, or the system's ability to follow rapid variation, as reflected in a high fusion frequency. In a linear system, these two properties may be governed by two quite different aspects of the system function. For example, it is quite possible for a high fusion frequency to be associated with a long reaction time, because the latter could be accomplished by an arbitrary delay that does not alter the amplitude response. Unless some other meaning is made explicit, it seems wise to reserve the terms "fast" and "slow" to describe changes in the time scale of the response. In this sense, a faster response shows both of the effects noted.

3.7.2. Transient and Sustained. These terms were used originally by Cleland, Dubin, and Levick (1971) to describe two classes of visual neurons in the cat. The feature of the sustained cell's response that presumably evoked this label was its sustained response to a steady stimulus, whereas a transient cell responded only at onset and offset. Subsequently, the terms have been applied to a wide range of phenomena and hypothetical mechanisms, many of which have little to do with the form of the temporal response. Thus transient mechanisms are frequently presumed to be nonlinear and relatively more sensitive at low spatial frequencies. It seems important, therefore, to distinguish between the use of these terms as adjectives to describe a characteristic property of the temporal response, and their use as names of hypothetical mechanisms.

We consider below the evidence for distinct mechanisms called by these names. Outside of that context, we reserve the terms to describe a property of the temporal response of a linear filter. A *transient* system is one in which the response to a step input vanishes beyond some time T. Because the response to a step is the convolution of step and impulse response, which is in turn the integral of the impulse response from 0 to t, it is evident that a transient impulse response has an integral of 0 and is briefer than T. It is simple to show that the amplitude response of a transient system vanishes at 0 frequency; thus transience implies attenuation of low frequencies.

The *sustained* system response to a step grows monotonically, eventually reaching an asymptote. Thus the integral of the impulse response is also monotonic, from which we see that the impulse response is always of the same sign. The amplitude response of a sustained system is easily shown to have a maximum at 0 frequency.

Many systems are neither entirely transient nor sustained, in which case the terms may be used in a relative sense. Thus of two systems, that with the greater attenuation at low frequencies would be described as more transient.

Occasionally the term "transient" is taken to imply a higher fusion frequency, or higher sensitivity at high temporal frequencies. The definition given here does not include this implication, which does not in any case agree with the common sense meaning of the word.

4. A WORKING MODEL OF TEMPORAL SENSITIVITY

Many aspects of temporal sensitivity can be understood in the context of a working model, which we introduce here. The model has three important features: (1) a linear filter, (2) probability summation over time, and (3) asymmetric thresholds for increments and decrements.

Aspects of the working model have been suggested by numerous authors. The notion of the eye as a linear temporal filter was first developed by Ives (1922) and later in more detail by de Lange (1952). It has been pursued with great energy by Kelly (1961b) and Roufs (1972b). The idea of probability summation over time has appeared in the work of Blackwell (1963), Ikeda (1965), Roufs (1974b), and many others. The specific computational form used here is given in part by Watson and Nachmias (1977), Rashbass (1976), and Watson (1979) and is introduced in Section 3.3.

4.1. The Linear Filter

The first component in the model is a causal, time-invariant linear filter with impulse response

$$h_1(t) = u(t)[\tau(n_1 - 1)!]^{-1}(t/\tau)^{n_1-1}e^{-t/\tau} , \qquad (40)$$

where $u(t)$ is the unit step function. (The impulse response, system function, and amplitude response are defined in Section 2.) This is the impulse response of a cascade of n_1 identical low-pass stages, each with time constant τ (the low-pass filter is described in Section 2.10.5). It has been normalized so that it has unit area. The maximum occurs at $\tau(n_1 - 1)$ and is equal to $[(n_1 - 1)e^{-1}]^{n_1-1}/\tau(n_1 - 1)!$.

The next component is a second filter identical to the first except that it has time constant $\kappa\tau$, n_2 stages, and is multiplied by a factor ζ. The linear filter of the working model is the difference of these two filters, multiplied by a factor ξ. The impulse response of the working model is then

$$h(t) = \xi[h_1(t) - \zeta h_2(t)] . \qquad (41)$$

The parameter ξ is a sensitivity factor or gain that scales the impulse response and amplitude response up or down in amplitude. The parameter ζ is the "transience factor." When ζ is 0, only the first positive component (h_1) remains, and the impulse response is "sustained" in the sense that the response to a step input rises to a maximum and stays there indefinitely. When ζ is 1, the response is "transient" in the sense that the step response rises to a peak and then declines and vanishes. Examples of the impulse response with various transience factors are shown in Figure 6.4. The system response of the working model is easily derived by noting that

$$H_1(w) = (i2\pi w\tau + 1)^{-n_1} \qquad (42)$$

where w is temporal frequency in hertz and $i = \sqrt{-1}$. This system response can be decomposed into the amplitude response

$$|H_1(w)| = [(2\pi w\tau)^2 + 1]^{-n_1/2} \qquad (43)$$

and the phase response

$$<H_1(w) = -n_1 \tan^{-1}(2\pi w\tau) . \qquad (44)$$

From the linearity of the Fourier transform,

$$H(w) = \xi[H_1(w) + \zeta H_2(w)] . \qquad (45)$$

It is then simple to show that the amplitude response of the linear filter of the working model is

$$|H| = \xi[|H_1|^2 + \zeta^2|H_2|^2 - 2\zeta|H_1||H_2|\cos(<H_1 - <H_2)]^{1/2} \qquad (46)$$

and the phase,

$$<H = \tan^{-1}\left\{\frac{|H_1|\sin<H_1 - \zeta|H_2|\sin<H_2}{|H_1|\cos<H_1 - \zeta|H_2|\cos<H_2}\right\} . \qquad (47)$$

Examples of the impulse, amplitude, and phase responses of the working model are shown in Figure 6.4, along with the corresponding impulse responses. Note that when the transience index is 0, the amplitude response reaches a maximum of unity at 0 Hz, whereas when the index is 1, the amplitude response goes to 0 at 0 Hz.

This particular formulation of the impulse response has been chosen because it is a good approximation to empirical results and for mathematical convenience. For example, the degree of low-frequency attenuation is easily varied by means

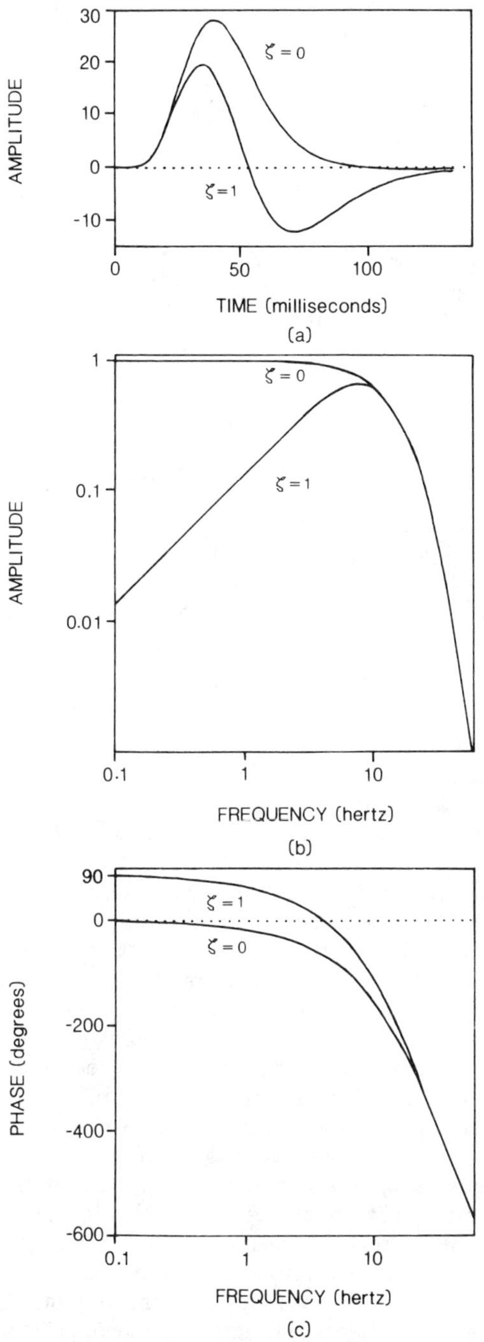

Figure 6.4. The linear filter of a working model of human temporal sensitivity. (a) Impulse responses. (b) Amplitude responses. (c) Phase responses. Responses are shown for the two extreme values of the transience parameter, $\zeta = 0$ and $\zeta = 1$. The other parameters of the filter are time constant $\tau = 4.94$ msec, time constant ratio $\kappa = 1.33$, number of stages in excitatory mechanism $n_1 = 9$ and in inhibitory mechanism $n_2 = 10$, and sensitivity $\xi = 1$. The time constants and number of stages are roughly appropriate for a human observer at high background luminance.

of the transience parameter, the horizontal scale is easily controlled by the time constant τ, and the slope of the high-frequency limb can be controlled by means of κ, n_1, and n_2. By suitable choice of these five parameters, a version of this filter can be found that agrees reasonably well with empirical results. This agreement is illustrated in Figure 6.5. Other models might fit these data equally well. The purpose here is to find a realistic and mathematically convenient form that we can use to illustrate the general properties of temporal sensitivity.

The response to an arbitrary input is the convolution of the input and the impulse response. It is convenient to express the input contrast wave form $C(t)$ as the product of a normalized wave form with unit amplitude, $f(t)$, and a positive constant C equal to the peak contrast of the wave form. The response is then

$$r(t) = Cf(t) * h(t) \tag{48}$$

where $*$ indicates convolution. To compute values of the response it is often necessary to approximate the convolution by a finite sum,

$$r_i = C\Delta t \sum_j f_j h_{i-j} \tag{49}$$

where Δt is the time interval between samples and i and j run over the support of each function. The interval Δt must be made sufficiently small that it can capture the most rapid fluctuations in the response; calculations in this chapter use a value of 5 msec.

4.2. Probability Summation Over Time

The concept of probability summation over time was introduced in Section 3. It is described by the following equation, which states a condition met by all stimuli at threshold:

$$1 = \sum_i |r_i|^\beta \tag{50}$$

where r_i is the value of the response in time interval i and β is the slope of the psychometric function. Combining Eqs. (49) and (50), and rearranging terms so as to leave us with an expression for the contrast at threshold, we get

$$C = \Delta t^{-1} \left[\sum_i \Big| \sum_j f_j h_{i-j} \Big|^\beta \right]^{-1/\beta} . \tag{51}$$

This equation predicts threshold for an arbitrary temporal wave form, given the parameters of the model. Note that the comparisons between model and data shown in Figure 6.5 do not take probability summation into account. In the experiments involved, the duration of the stimulus was not controlled so that a calculation of Eq. (51) cannot be performed. Had probability summation been included, the sensitivity factor ξ would be reduced by a small amount.

4.3. Asymmetric Thresholds

It has been assumed thus far that the model is equally sensitive to positive and negative excursions of the response; the absolute value operation in Eq. (51) ensures that positive and negative response values contribute equally to the probability of detection. Under many circumstances, this is an accurate assumption. In other cases, the system is more sensitive to decrements than to increments (see Section 8). This situation is incorporated into the working model by assuming a higher threshold for increments than for decrements. Computationally, it is done by weighting positive increments by a parameter ρ. Then we can replace Eq. (50) by

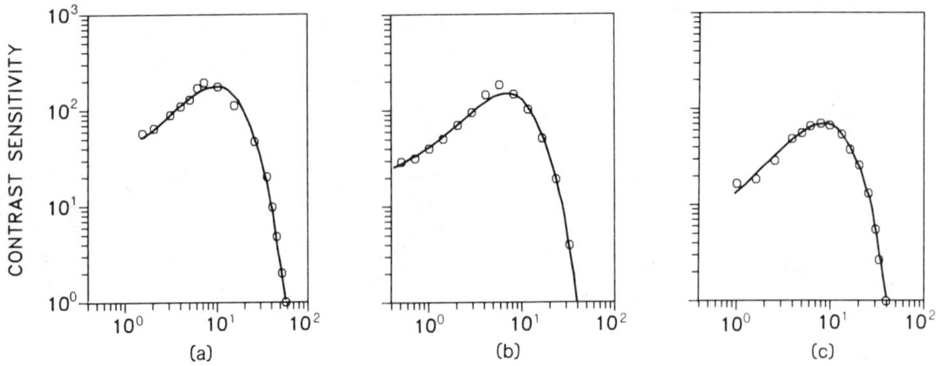

Figure 6.5. Temporal contrast sensitivity functions of the working model (curves) and of human observers (points). All thresholds collected by method of adjustment. Standard deviations probably about 0.05 log unit. Curves are the amplitude response of the linear filter of the working model, with parameters adjusted to approximately match the data. Model parameters common to all curves: $\kappa = 1.33$, $n_1 = 9$, $n_2 = 10$. (a) Data from de Lange (1958), observer V, 2° disk, background and surround 1000 td. Model parameters: $\tau = 4.3$ msec, $\zeta = 0.9$, $\xi = 269$. (b) Data from Robson (1966), 0.5 cycles·degree^{-1} grating, background and surround 20 cd·m^{-2} (≈200 td). Model parameters: $\tau = 6.22$ msec, $\zeta = 0.9$, $\xi = 214$. (c) Data from Roufs and Blommaert (1981), observer JAJR, 1° disk, background 1200 td, no surround. Model parameters: $\tau = 4.94$ msec, $\zeta = 1$, $\xi = 200$.

$$1 = \sum_i \begin{cases} (\rho r_i)^\beta & r_i \geqslant 0 \\ (-r_i)^\beta & r_i < 0 \end{cases} . \qquad (52)$$

When $\rho = 0$, only negative excursions are effective; when $\rho = 1$, positive and negative excursions are equally effective; and when $\rho > 1$, positive excursions are more effective than negative.

4.4. Summary of Parameters of the Working Model

The eight parameters of the working model are the time constant τ, the ratio of time constants κ, the stage numbers n_1 and n_2, the sensitivity factor ξ, the transience factor ζ, the exponent β, and the asymmetry factor ρ.

5. SENSITIVITY TO SINUSOIDS

5.1. Background

Although they appear to give off a steady, constant illumination, many light sources in our world (fluorescent lamps, television, and movies are commonplace examples) in fact produce an amount of light that varies rapidly in time. The effort to understand this insensitivity of the eye to rapid fluctuations has generated a prodigious amount of research, a great deal of it concerned with the *critical flicker frequency* (CFF) for periodic wave forms. A periodic wave form, of which the examples given are instances, repeats itself once each period of T sec. Limited means of controlling light intensity confined early studies to wave forms alternating between "on" and "off." By increasing the frequency of alternation, a light could be made to pass from "flicker" (perceptible variation in intensity) to "fusion" (steady appearance of a fluctuating light). The CFF marked the border between flicker and fusion. These early experiments were concerned primarily with the effects of wave form (the particular shape of the function during one period), with the wave form amplitude, and with the brightness of a periodic stimulus beyond the fusion limit. Some progress was made on the latter two issues: CFF was found to rise linearly with the log of time-average background intensity (the *Ferry-Porter law*: Ferry, 1892; Porter, 1902), and a fused stimulus was found to be as bright as a steady stimulus of the same time-average intensity (the *Talbolt-Plateau law*). The first law is only approximate (as can be seen in Figure 6.28 in Section 11), and has been amended by Kelly (1964).

In the early 1950s, and culminating in his papers of 1954 and 1958, de Lange developed a novel approach that so altered the experimental and theoretical perspective on this problem that much of the earlier work was rendered obsolete (de Lange 1954, 1958). Three aspects of de Lange's work were remarkable. First, he provided independent control of background and target luminance. In previous experiments in which the light alternated only between on and off, a change in the amplitude of the wave form inevitably resulted in a change in the time-average background intensity, and consequently in the adaptive state of the eye. De Lange adopted a procedure whereby wave form amplitude might be changed without alteration of the time-average background. This in turn allowed production of wave forms with equal time-average background, but differing contrast.

This technical innovation paved the way for de Lange's second advance. By generating a wave form of unit contrast and adjusting frequency until flicker gave way to fusion, he could measure the conventional CFF. But by setting contrast to values less than unity and repeating the procedure, he could also measure the more complete function relating fusion frequency to contrast. Several examples of this function, obtained with various wave forms on various backgrounds, are shown in Figure 6.6.

De Lange's third and most important innovation was his use of linear systems theory to provide a coherent interpretation of data like those in Figure 6.6. To illustrate his approach, consider the uppermost wave form in the inset to Figure 6.6. It is reproduced in Figure 6.7, along with its *amplitude spectrum*, the function specifying the amplitudes of sinusoids into which the wave form may be decomposed. In the case of the 10-Hz square wave illustrated here, the spectrum contains odd *harmonics* of frequencies 10, 30, and 50 Hz, and so on, with amplitudes of $I(4/\pi)$, $I(4/3\pi)$, $I(4/5\pi)$, and so on.

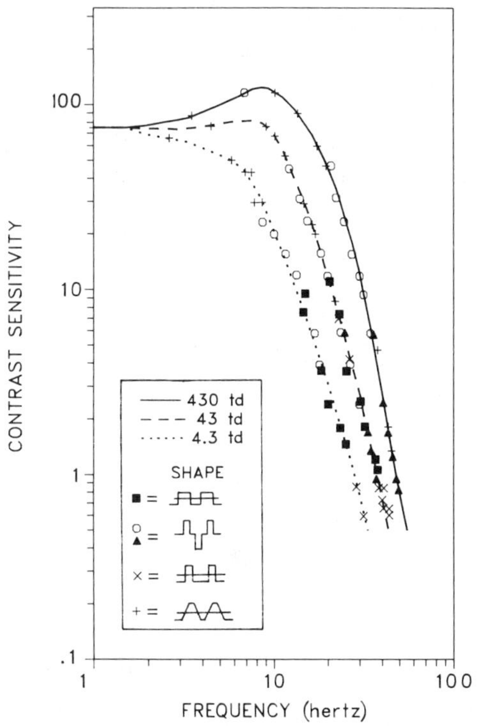

Figure 6.6. Contrast sensitivity for several periodic wave forms as a function of temporal frequency. The wave forms are shown in the inset. Sensitivity is plotted as the inverse of the contrast of the fundamental sinusoidal component in each wave form. Thresholds are the same for all wave forms above 10 Hz, as predicted by a linear model. Target was a 2° foveal disk with a large surround. Data for three background luminances are shown. (From H. de Lange, Relationship between critical flicker frequency and a set of low-frequency characteristics of the eye, *Journal of the Optical Society of America*, 1954, *44*. Reprinted with permission.)

If the visual system responds linearly to perturbations near the threshold of visibility, then its behavior can be characterized by a *transfer function*, specifying the amplitude and phase with which various frequencies are passed through the system (see Section 2). Suppose that the amplitude component of this function is given by the curves in Figure 6.6, at least above 10 Hz. To determine the amplitude spectrum of the response to a square wave of 10 Hz, we simply multiply the input spectrum by the function describing de Lange's data. The result, shown in Figure 6.7, is very nearly a pure sinusoid of 10 Hz. The higher harmonics have been almost entirely filtered out. This suggests that at 10 Hz the contrast threshold for a square wave should be the same as that for a sinusoid of equal fundamental amplitude. This rule should hold even more precisely for frequencies above 10 Hz, because the higher harmonics will be still more severely attenuated.

This rule also applies to any periodic wave form in which the higher harmonics, after multiplication by the amplitude response function, are much smaller than the fundamental. This includes most simple periodic wave forms with fundamentals above 10 Hz. The various symbols in Figure 6.6 show the success of this analysis. Thresholds for all four wave forms used by de Lange fall upon a common curve above 10 Hz, as the linear hypothesis predicts.

The first consequence of this observation was to bring to an end more than a century of investigation of wave form *per se* as a determinant of sensitivity. Beyond those experiments required to document the premise of linearity, empirical measurements of sensitivity to various wave forms were no longer required. The second consequence was to initiate a quarter century of vigorous pursuit of the many ramifications of the linear theory. A third consequence was to confer special status (perhaps too special) upon the sinusoid as a temporal stimulus. The following section reviews some of the fundamental aspects of thresholds for sinusoidal modulation. Table 6.2 notes some of the more important contributions in this area. An interesting view of the subject of "flicker" at an early and active stage in its development is given by the symposium papers in Henkes and van der Tweel (1964). The classic review is by Kelly (1972b).

5.2. The Temporal Contrast Sensitivity Function

When the contrast of a target is varied sinusoidally at some frequency, sufficiently small amplitudes are invisible; that is, they are not distinguishable from a target with zero contrast. The oscillation is said to have "fused." As the amplitude is raised, the target may become visible. The transition to visibility is called the *contrast threshold*, and its inverse, *contrast sensitivity*. A plot of contrast sensitivity versus temporal frequency is called a *temporal contrast sensitivity function* (TCSF).

In the experiments shown in Figure 6.6, de Lange was unable to generate true sinusoids, although his trapezoidal wave form was quite close. In 1958, however, he published extensive measurements of the TCSF for two observers at a number of background intensities. Some of these classic results are reproduced in Figure 6.8. They illustrate several general features of the TCSF. At the higher luminances, a peak in sensitivity of about 200 (a threshold contrast of about 0.005) occurs at about 8 Hz. Above this frequency, sensitivity falls precipitously. In log-log coordinates, the curve appears to accelerate downward. For a sinusoid, the CFF is the highest frequency at which contrast sensitivity is equal to 1. Following the curve downward, the CFF is reached at a frequency of between 50 and 70 Hz. Sensitivity also declines at low frequencies, but the drop is less rapid and stops at a sensitivity of about 50.

It should be emphasized that the TCSF is not a single invariant function. Rather, the form of the TCSF is subject to large alterations, depending primarily upon the background intensity, the spatial configuration of target and surround, the observer, and the method by which the thresholds are obtained. Several authors have noted that the TCSF may be viewed as a slice through a many-dimensioned surface (Kelly, 1972a; Koenderink & van Doorn, 1979). This perspective is often useful in appreciating the interaction between temporal frequency and some other variable, but is obviously limited to two variables at a time.

Before considering the many variations to which the TCSF is subject, it may be worth noting certain general properties of these effects. First, many experimental manipulations appear to have different consequences for those frequencies above the right-hand shoulder of the curve and for those below it. In the traditional log-log coordinates that we use, the high-frequency limb tends only to translate horizontally or vertically. These motions correspond to scaling operations on frequency or sensitivity (equivalent to changes in the time scale τ and sensitivity parameter ξ of the working model). Effects on the low-frequency limb of the curve are more complex, but generally consist of changes in the degree to which the curve drops at low frequencies (equivalent to changes in the transience parameter ζ of the working model). These are simplifications, and should not blind the reader to more subtle features of the TCSF. They are meant

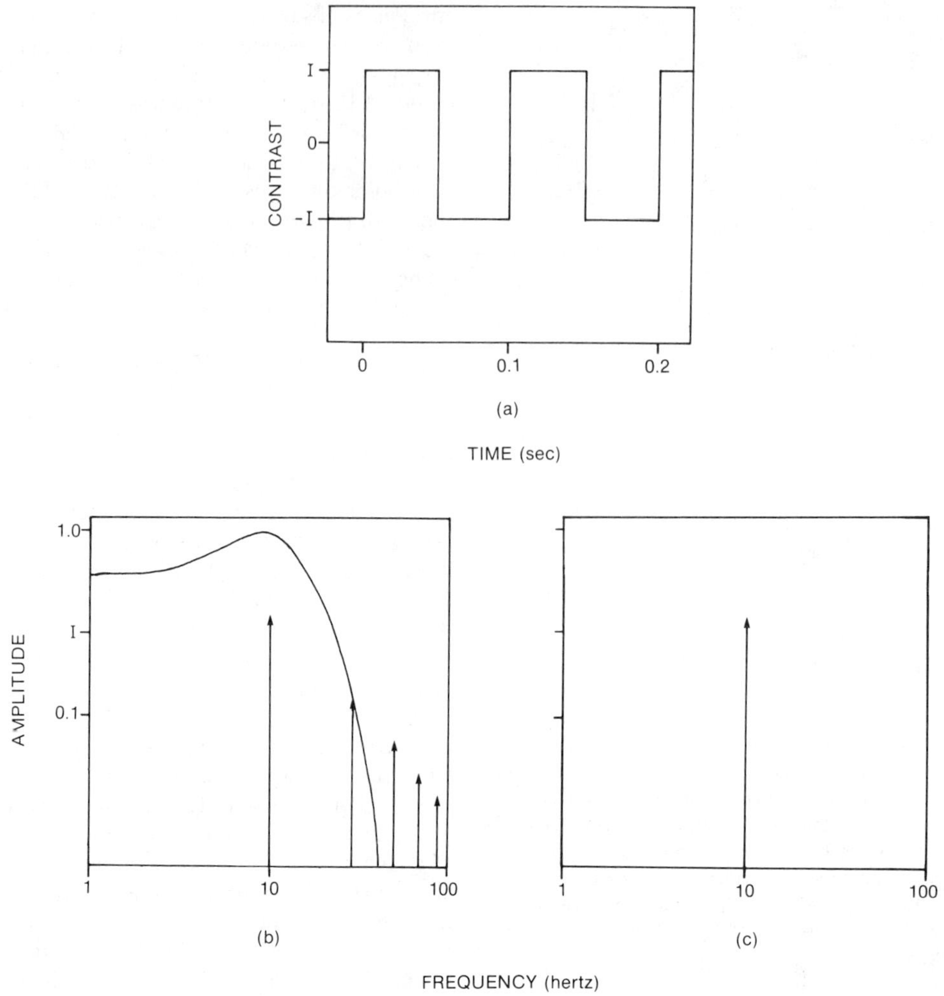

Figure 6.7. An explanation of why thresholds for a square wave and a sine wave are equal at high temporal frequencies. (a) The square wave of frequency 10 Hz and intensity I. (b) The amplitude spectrum of the square wave. The height of each impulse indicates the intensity of the component at the corresponding temporal frequency. The impulse at 10 Hz is the fundamental. Also shown is the amplitude response of a hypothetical linear filter, adapted from de Lange's data in Figure 6.6. (c) The result of multiplying the amplitude spectrum of the square wave by the amplitude response of the filter. Only the fundamental remains, hence thresholds for the square wave and its fundamental are the same.

only to help guide the eye over the results in the following sections.

5.3. The Working Model

To predict empirical thresholds for sinusoidal wave forms from the working model we must know the duration of each stimulus, because probability summation over time causes threshold to decline for as long as the stimulus is exposed. However, when thresholds are collected by method of adjustment (as has most often been the case for sinusoidal wave forms), the duration is unspecified. But if we assume that probability summation over time affects all frequencies equally, then we can compare the amplitude response of the linear filter of the model directly to the empirical TCSF. This is done for three selected data sets in Figure 6.5 in Section 4. The figure illustrates that the model gives a good account of the TCSF under these conditions. The changes in model parameters in the three cases are small and confined to the overall sensitivity ξ, the time constant τ, and the transience ζ. These changes are due to differences in background intensity and spatial configuration. Larger changes in spatial configuration often produce more substantial changes in model parameters.

5.4. Effects of Spatial Configuration

The effects of spatial configuration upon temporal sensitivity are dealt with in Section 9. A summary of those effects is that the form of the high-frequency limb of the TCSF is largely unaffected by spatial configuration, but that the low-frequency limb is raised by the presence of edges, high spatial frequencies, or a surround. Taken together, these results are consistent with the idea that effective high spatial frequencies in the stimulus result in a more "sustained" TCSF. This effect is lessened at low background intensities, all spatial targets then giving a more or less "sustained" result.

5.5. Effects of Background Intensity

This subject is examined in detail in Section 11. In general, as background intensity is raised, luminance thresholds increase. However, the increase is less rapid at high temporal frequencies

Table 6.2. Selected Studies of Sinusoidal Flicker

Reference	Spatial Stimulus	Variables
de Lange, 1954	2° disk with surround	Wave form, background intensity
de Lange, 1958	2° disk with surround	Background intensity
Kelly, 1959	2, 4, 60° disks with & w/o surround	Target size, surround
Kelly, 1961a	60° disk, blurred edges	Background intensity
Robson, 1966	Sinusoidal grating	Spatial frequency
van Nes, Koenderink, Nas, & Bouman, 1967	Drifting grating surround	Background intensity, threshold criteria
Keesey, 1972	1° × 4 min bar, surround	Threshold criteria
Kelly, 1972a	Sinusoidal gratings	Spatial frequency, background intensity
Roufs, 1972a	1° disk with & w/o surround	Background intensity
Kulikowski & Tolhurst, 1973	Sinusoidal gratings	Threshold criteria, spatial frequency
Roufs, 1974b	1° disk w/o surround	Duration
Koenderink, Bouman, Bueno de Mesquita, & Slappendel, 1978	Sinusoidal grating no surround	Eccentricity, background intensity
Koenderink & van Doorn, 1979	Sinusoidal gratings	Spatial frequency
Watson, 1979	Sinusoidal gratings	Duration
Virsu, Rovamo, Laurinen, & Nasanen, 1982	Patch of grating	Eccentricity, spatial frequency

than at low. Expressed in contrast terms, sensitivity increases more rapidly at high temporal frequencies than at low as the background is raised. As a consequence, the low-frequency limb of the TCSF drops as background intensity is increased, as shown by de Lange's data in Figure 6.5. This figure also shows that raising background intensity also shifts the TCSF to higher frequencies. In terms of the working model, these two effects can be accommodated by lowering the time constant τ and increasing the transience ζ as background intensity is raised.

5.6. Effects of Duration

If the duration of a sinusoidal wave form is brief, its spectrum extends above and below its nominal frequency, and sensitivity depends in a complex way upon frequency, duration, and the TCSF. Similarly, if the onset and offset of the sinusoid are abrupt, higher frequencies are introduced that may influence sensitivity. If the duration is substantial (greater than 100 msec) and if the onset and offset are gradual, these problems are largely eliminated, yet duration still has a small but significant effect upon sensitivity. When a gradual onset and offset are accomplished by means of a Gaussian gating function, sensitivity increases approximately as the ¼ power of duration (Watson, 1979). Roufs (1974b), using a slightly different gating function, has obtained comparable results.

Roufs (1974b) and Watson (1979), using somewhat different assumptions, have shown that this is predicted by probability summation over time (see Sections 3.3 and 4.2). In essence, each moment of the presentation provides an independent opportunity to detect the stimulus; as the duration is extended, the number of opportunities grows, and the overall probability of detection is increased. In Watson's formulation, sensitivity should increase with duration at a log-log slope of $1/\beta$, where β is the slope of the psychometric function. The observed slope of ¼ corresponds well to observed psychometric function slopes of about 4 for these conditions (Watson, 1979).

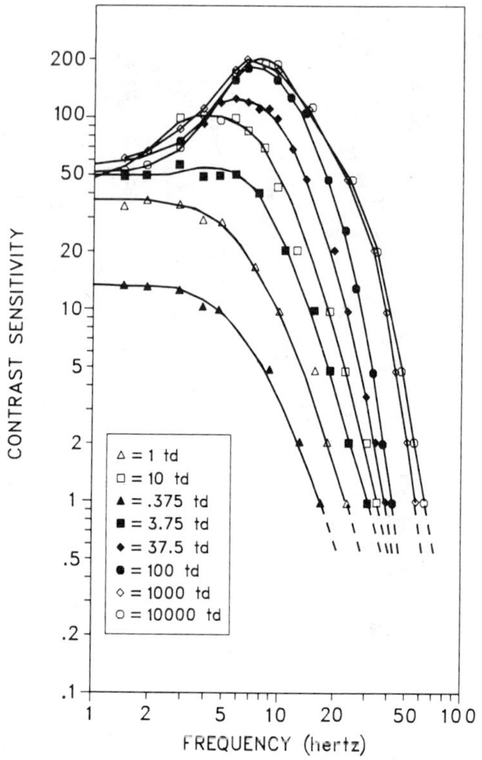

Figure 6.8. The temporal contrast sensitivity function at several background intensities. The temporal wave form was sinusoidal; target was a 2° disk with a large surround. Curves are drawn by eye. On a bright background, sensitivity increases with temporal frequency from about 50 to a peak of about 200 at around 8 Hz, then falls to a CFF of about 60 Hz. The ordinate is extended to sensitivities of 0.5 (contrast = 2.0) because although sinusoids with contrast of 2.0 cannot be constructed, wave forms with a fundamental this large can be produced (data from observer V of de Lange, 1958).

5.7. Effect of Eccentricity

Rather little is known about how the TCSF depends upon the location of the target within the visual field. Sharpe (1974) measured temporal contrast sensitivity for gratings of 0.8, 1.5, 3.5, and 5.5 cycles·degree^{-1}, centered 10° into the left temporal visual field, drifting at various velocities. His results resemble those of Robson (1966) (Figure 6.20 in Section 9) in showing more transience at low spatial frequencies. Apart from the expected decline in spatial resolution, there is little systematic change from the foveal results.

Koenderink, Bouman, Bueno de Mesquita, and Slappendel (1978) have published results that show little variation in the shape of the TCSF when measured with a 0.5 × 0.5°, 4 cycles·degree^{-1} grating target with dark surround at locations of 1, 2, 4, 6, and 8°. With a 4 × 4 °, 0.5 cycles·degree^{-1} target, slightly more relative attenuation is evident at the fovea than at locations of 6, 12, 21, 32, and 50°. The lack of surround and small target size (2 cycles of the grating) make these results somewhat difficult to compare to other data.

One recent result suggests that the temporal properties of the retina are homogeneous, and that all variations with eccentricity are due to spatial inhomogeneity. Virsu, Rovamo, Laurinen, and Nasanen (1982) found that sensitivity to foveal targets was approximately the same as that to peripheral targets that had been magnified so as to occupy an equal cortical projection area. This is consistent with the idea that spatial processing is homogeneous across the retina except for a change in spatial scale. They also found that this result held equally well at temporal frequencies of 0, 1, 4, and 18 Hz. This strongly suggests that the temporal processing is also homogeneous across the retina. In this view, the variations in temporal behavior with eccentricity reported elsewhere are consequences of the change of spatial scale, rather than of temporal processing.

5.8. Effect of Threshold Criteria

In his 1958 report, de Lange noted a difference in the nature of the flicker perception depending on "frequency." This observation has been echoed by many subsequent authors: at high temporal frequencies, stimuli near threshold appear to "flicker," whereas at low temporal frequencies the percept is of a more gradual variation (aptly termed "swell" by Roufs, 1972a). When an adjustment method is used, it may be difficult to equate criteria in the two frequency ranges.

Van Nes, Koenderink, Nas, and Bouman (1967) made a further distinction. With drifting gratings as targets, they reported that as contrast was reduced, the spatial variations in brightness disappeared before temporal variations, so that separate "flicker" and "pattern" thresholds could be observed. Similar suggestions were made by Rashbass (1968), Watanabe, Mori, Nagata, and Hiwatashi (1968), Pantle (1970), and Richards (1971).

Keesey (1972), noting a similar distinction among judgments for a narrow bar whose contrast was modulated sinusoidally in time, measured each of the two thresholds separately at temporal frequencies between 0.4 and 30 Hz. The two temporal sensitivity functions did not differ by a constant factor, and the flicker threshold was not invariably below the pattern threshold.

With grating targets of various spatial frequencies, Kulikowski and Tolhurst (1973) obtained temporal sensitivity functions using both flicker and pattern criteria (see Fig. 6.24 in Section 9). In agreement with Keesey's data, flicker sensitivity declines at low temporal frequencies, but pattern sensitivity does not. The two curves intersect at an intermediate temporal frequency, so that at high temporal frequencies, flicker sensitivity is greater than pattern, whereas at low temporal frequencies the reverse is true. Their interpretation was essentially that of Keesey: each criterion was attributed to a different mechanism, as though the two curves described the temporal contrast sensitivities of distinct flicker and pattern detectors. As further evidence for this idea, they noted that the two curves moved independently with changes in spatial frequency. An increase in spatial frequency lowered the sensitivity curve of the flicker mechanism much more than it lowered the curve of the pattern mechanism.

By analogy to retinal cells of the same name (Cleland et al., 1971), and because the flicker curve showed low-frequency attenuation whereas the pattern curve did not, these two sorts of detectors were called *transient* and *sustained* mechanisms, respectively. Section 9.4 contains a review of the theory of sustained and transient detectors.

5.9. Effect of Eye Movements

When a stimulus contains both temporal and spatial variations, movements of the eye influence the temporal distribution of the stimulus. The TCSF is ordinarily measured with the eye fixating a mark, but it is well known that various eye movements occur during fixation (Riggs, Armington, & Ratliff, 1954).

Therefore the effect of these fixational eye movements upon the TCSF must be considered.

One method of assessing the effects of eye movements is to remove them by stabilizing the image upon the retina. Kelly (1979) and Tulunay-Keesey and Jones (1980) have shown that prolonged viewing of high-contrast, stationary, stabilized gratings leads to very large reductions in sensitivity. This reduction may be 1 log unit or more at the lower spatial frequencies. It appears that these conditions give rise to a strong afterimage, which profoundly alters the properties of the contrast-detecting mechanisms (Burbeck & Kelly, 1982; Kelly, 1982).

However, when brief (7-sec) presentations at contrasts near to threshold are used, the difference between stabilized and unstabilized thresholds is always less than 0.3 log units (Tulunay-Keesey & Jones, 1980; Tulunay-Keesey, 1982). These differences were obtained with a temporal presentation (Gaussian with duration of 7 sec) that is essentially a measure of sensitivity to 0 Hz. Because we would expect higher temporal frequencies to reduce the difference between stabilized and unstabilized thresholds, we may conjecture that the TCSF measured with brief, fixated, unstabilized presentations of near-threshold contrast would differ from the equivalent stabilized data by less than 0.3 log units. This would imply that the TCSF is adequately measured with unstabilized viewing. But, remarkably, no data have been published that directly compare stabilized and unstabilized TCSFs under these conditions. Kelly (1977) has published comparisons of stabilized and unstabilized TCSFs, but these thresholds were collected following prolonged viewing (and hence adaptation), and thus do not reflect purely the contribution of fixational eye movements to the TCSF. Nevertheless, they show that most of the effect of stabilization is absent when the temporal frequency is 0.1 Hz or above.

5.10. Combinations of Frequencies

Much of the theoretical value of the TCSF rests upon the assumption that thresholds are governed by a linear filtering process. One possible test of this assumption is to examine thresholds for combinations of several frequencies. A nonlinearity of particular interest is that introduced by multiple independent channels selective for temporal frequency. Summation between different frequencies is an appropriate test for the existence of such pathways. However, we shall see that the predictions of the linear model in this context depend rather strongly on the nature of the assumed output nonlinearity.

J. Z. Levinson (1960) measured thresholds for compound wave forms made by adding together sinusoids of 10 and 20, or 20 and 40 Hz. The two components had "equal sensation levels"; that is, each was added in proportion to its individual threshold. The wave forms controlled the contrast of a 1° disk target (background = 685 $cd \cdot m^{-2}$, surround = 130 $cd \cdot m^{-2}$). Levinson noted that threshold for the compound, expressed as fraction of threshold for either component alone, varied according to the relative phase of the two components, as shown in Figure 6.9. Levinson pointed out that the compound wave form inverts itself with every 180° change in relative phase, but the threshold minima occur only every 360°. He suggested that this might be explained by a detector with a higher threshold for excursions of one sign than of the other, and demonstrated the principle with an analog model (J. Z. Levinson & Harmon, 1961).

Asymmetric thresholds can be introduced into the working model by weighting positive excursions by a factor ρ, as noted in Section 4.3. When ρ = 1, positive and negative excursions are equally effective; when ρ = 0, only negative excursions are effective. Recall that probability summation may be modeled with β = 3.5, and the absence of probability summation with β = 50. Some predictions of this model are shown in Figure 6.9. The data seem to refute any version that lacks probability summation, both because they show too little summation (the prediction is generally below the data), and because the data show only a modest dependence on phase. Likewise the data reject a model with probability summation but with no asymmetry, because it predicts no dependence upon phase. The data seem reasonably well fitted by the probability summation model if ρ is set to 0.65 and a phase difference of about 45° is assumed between 20 and 10 Hz. The curve must also be displaced upward by about 1 standard deviation, as might occur if the normalizing threshold for the single component were overestimated by this much.

A threshold asymmetry might be encouraged by Levinson's adjustment method. For example, the observer might adjust until a certain criterion darkness was seen, and ignore the

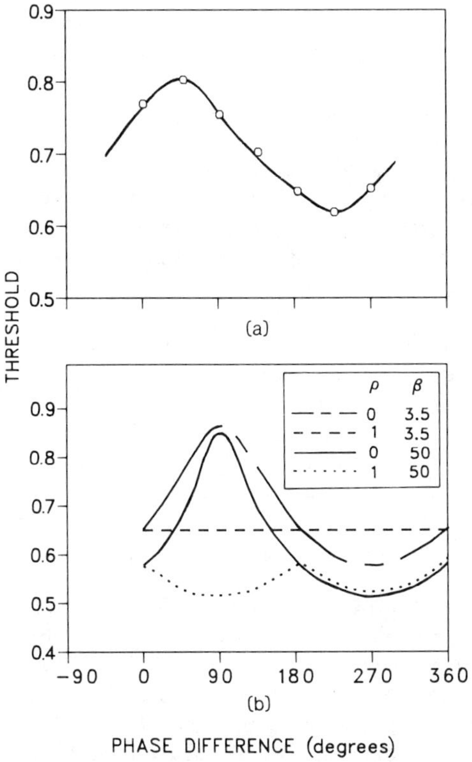

Figure 6.9. Threshold for the sum of two different temporal frequencies as a function of the phase difference between the two components. (a) Data from J. Z. Levinson (1960). The frequencies were 10 and 20 Hz, and the contrast of each component was an equal fraction of its threshold. The phase difference is the lag of the high-frequency component. Thresholds are plotted as fractions of the single-component thresholds (sensation magnitudes). The smooth curve is the fit of the working model with a threshold asymmetry factor (ρ) of 0.65, a β of 3.5, and a phase difference between component responses of about 45°. The curve has also been shifted upward by 0.05. (b) Predictions of the working model for various values of β and ρ. A β of 3.5 simulates probability summation; a value of 50 simulates no probability summation. A ρ value of 0 means that positive excursions of the filter output are invisible; a value of 1 means that positive and negative excursions are equally effective. The model fits best when the phase response at 10 Hz is about 45° greater than that at 20 Hz, when there is probability summation, and when decrements in the filter response are considerably more effective than increments.

bright phases. It would certainly be of interest to repeat these experiments with a forced-choice method, both to reexamine the evidence for threshold asymmetry, and because they may constitute the only known method of estimating the phase response of the linear model.

Using spatially sinusoidal grating targets, Watson (1977) examined thresholds for combinations of a wide range of temporal frequencies. The general finding was that for spatial frequencies of 2, 4, and 10 cycles·degree^{-1} and temporal frequencies of between 1 and 20 Hz, with pairs separated by as much as 8 Hz, only modest departures were observed from the predictions of a linear model with probability summation. The departures were never of the size predicted by narrow band (less than 8 Hz) temporal frequency tuned channels. The data, however, could not rule out the existence of two independent pathways, one moderately selective for high temporal frequencies, the other moderately selective for low.

5.11. Theory

Landis (1953) provides an annotated bibliography of the profusion of experimental work, and some theory, done on periodic wave forms of various kinds during the years 1740–1952. The earliest explicit model of flicker sensitivity was given by Ives (1922), who proposed a log transform followed by diffusion, leaky transmission, and peak detection. De Lange (1952, 1954, 1958) explicitly introduced the application of Linear Systems Theory to temporal sensitivity, and showed how treating the eye as a linear filter could rationalize the great mass of data on flickering periodic wave forms. He also argued that the Talbolt-Plateau law (brightness above fusion is equal to time-average brightness) implied that any nonlinear elements should follow rather than precede the linear filter. His model of the filter consisted of 10 resistance-capacitance filters in cascade (see Section 2.10.5), together with an induction element to attenuate at low frequencies. J. Z. Levinson (1966) has noted that the n low-pass stages in de Lange's model are mimicked by a one-stage statistical process, so the n-stage model need not imply n physical stages.

Kelly (1961b) proposed a two-stage model to account for the pronounced attenuation at low frequencies found with large targets, and the effects of light adaptation. The first stage is a linear filter with both differentiating and integrating components. The second stage is a "pulse encoder" that acts as a nonlinear low-pass filter whose bandwidth is controlled by the background luminance.

Fourtes and Hodgkin (1964) noted that changes in background intensity have a much greater effect on sensitivity than upon the CFF (see Fig. 6.30 in Section 11.4). They observed that this was consistent with an n-stage low-pass filter with time constant τ, because sensitivity is proportional to τ^{n-1}, whereas CFF varies in inverse proportion to τ. They extended de Lange's model to a range of background intensities by introducing feedback stages controlling the time constants in each stage. Sperling and Sondhi (1968) and Matin (1968) have proposed more elaborate but similar models.

Departing from the custom of following the linear filter with a simple threshold mechanism, Rashbass (1970) proposed that the filter output was squared and integrated over an epoch of about 200 msec, and that this signal was then thresholded. Subsequent work has shown that this model, though an elegant solution to the problem it addressed, is not consistent with other results (Watson, 1979), but is a special case of a more general model (essentially the working model of Section 4).

Kelly (1969a) has proposed a diffusion model that gives a good account of the high-frequency asymptote of the TCSF collected at various background intensities (see Fig. 6.29 in Section 11.4). More recently Kelly and Wilson (1978) have partitioned this diffusion process into two stages, which they attribute to first- and second-order neurons. The diffusion process describes only the high-frequency portion of the TCSF. To account for the low-frequency performance Kelly (1971a, 1971b) has appended an inhibitory feedback loop whose parameters are controlled by the background intensity and spatial configuration.

Noting that certain pulse and pulse-pair thresholds call for more low-frequency attenuation than is evident in the TCSF, Roufs (1974a) has proposed that the TCSF is the envelope of two underlying functions, one band pass and sensitive to middle and high frequencies, the other low pass and sensitive only at the lower frequencies. Though based on quite different evidence, this theory closely resembles Kulikowski and Tolhurst's (1973) conjecture of separate "transient" and "sustained" channels (see Section 9.4). The two sets of authors agree in attributing distinct threshold sensations ("agitation" and "swell" in Roufs' terms) to the two filters.

6. SENSITIVITY TO RECTANGULAR PULSES

6.1. Background

A rectangular pulse target with duration T may be written

$$I(t) = Ip_T(t) = I[u(t) - u(t - T)] \qquad (53)$$

where $p_T(t)$ is a pulse of unit height and duration T that starts at $t = 0$, I is the intensity of the pulse, and $u(t)$ is the unit step function. The pulse has a value of I within the interval $(0, T)$ and a value of 0 elsewhere (see Figs. 6.2 and 6.10). Dividing $I(t)$ by the background intensity I_B gives the target contrast wave form $C(t)$. Experimental studies of sensitivity to pulses typically consist of measuring threshold intensity at various durations. A plot of threshold as a function of duration, conventionally on log-log coordinates, is called a *threshold-duration function*.

There have been numerous studies of this function since Bloch (1885). In most of the classical work, targets were circular disks, and principal variables investigated were stimulus size and background intensity. More recently, motivated by evidence that contrast detectors are selective for spatial frequency (see Chapter 7 by Olzak and Thomas), spatial grating targets have also been used.

In early work the threshold-duration function was explained largely in terms of "temporal summation," or integration over some interval of time. More recent explanations appeal to the integrative properties of a more general class of linear filters. Recognition of the stochastic nature of the detection process has led to additional improvements in our understanding of the threshold-duration function, particularly for pulses of long duration. Table 6.3 summarizes some of the published studies, indicating the spatial configuration of the target and the principal variables investigated.

Table 6.3. Selected Studies of Sensitivity to Pulses

Reference	Spatial Target	Variables
Arend, 1976	Sine grating	
Barlow, 1958	Foveal disk	Size, background intensity
Baumgardt & Hillmann, 1961	Peripheral disk	Size
Bouman, 1950	Peripheral disk	Size, background intensity
Breitmeyer & Ganz, 1977	Sine grating	Spatial frequency
Brindley, 1952	Foveal disk	brief durations
C. H. Graham & Kemp, 1938	Foveal hemidisk	Background intensity
C. H. Graham & Margaria, 1935	Peripheral disk	Size
Herrick, 1956	Foveal disk	Background intensity
Keller, 1941	1° hemidisk	Background intensity
Krauskopf & Mollon, 1971	Foveal disk	Background intensity, background wavelength
Legge, 1978	Sine grating	Spatial frequency
Nachmias, 1967	Square grating	Spatial frequency
Owen, 1972	Peripheral disk	Size, background intensity
Rashbass, 1970	17° foveal disk	
Roufs, 1972a	Foveal disk	Size, background intensity
Schober & Hilz, 1965	Square grating	Spatial frequency
Tolhurst, 1975a	Sine grating	Spatial frequency
Tulunay-Keesey & Jones, 1976	Sine grating	Stabilization, spatial frequency

6.2. The Threshold-Duration Function

A classical formula relating sensitivity to duration is that, where conditions are otherwise fixed, a pulse briefer than some *critical duration* will be at threshold when the product of its duration and intensity (the product of contrast and background intensity) equals a constant. This is *Bloch's law* (Bloch, 1885). In units of intensity it may be written

$$IT = I_c T_c \quad \text{for } T \leqslant T_c , \tag{54}$$

where T_c is the critical duration and I_c is the *critical intensity* given by the threshold intensity at the critical duration. For pulses longer than the critical duration, the classical formula states that threshold amplitude is constant,

$$I = I_c \quad \text{for } T > T_c . \tag{55}$$

By dividing target intensity by background intensity, these rules can be restated in terms of contrast, $CT = C_c T_c$ below the critical duration, and $C = C_c$ above it.

These rules are sketched in Figure 6.10. In log-log coordinates, Bloch's law [Eq. (54)] describes a line with a slope of −1. The second formula [Eq. (55)] is described by a horizontal line. These are the "two limbs" of the threshold-duration function. Actual data rarely conform precisely to this template, but it nevertheless serves as a useful model from which departures are readily described.

There seems little doubt that whatever the other dimensions of the stimulus and whatever the background conditions, there exists a critical duration below which Bloch's law is upheld. Such a range has been demonstrated for foveal and peripheral viewing, for disk targets with radii from 0.0059 to 17°, for targets with and without a surrounding background, for sinusoidal gratings between 0.3 and 10 cycles·degree^{-1} and for background intensities ranging from 0 to 6500 td (Arend, 1976; Barlow, 1958; Herrick, 1956; Rashbass, 1970; Roufs, 1972a). Brindley (1952) has shown that the range extends down to at least 400 nsec. There are several reports of initial slopes more gradual than prescribed by Bloch's law, but it seems most likely that they arise from the ambiguities inherent in fitting straight lines to a function whose slope changes gradually (Legge, 1978; Nachmias, 1967; Owen, 1972). If the fitting is confined to durations less than 20 msec, then there are no published instances

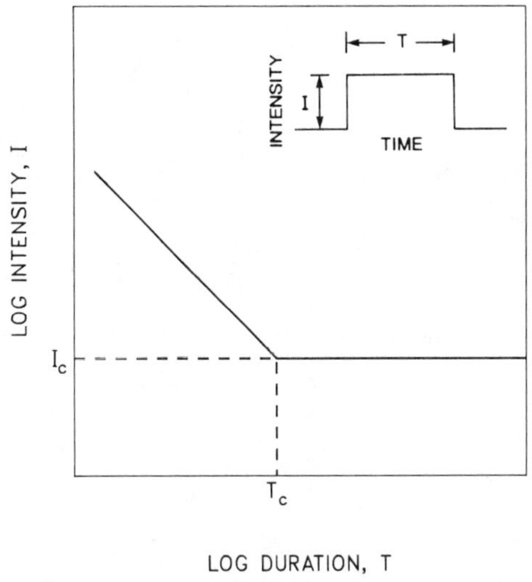

Figure 6.10. An idealized threshold-duration function. The function describes thresholds for rectangular pulses as a function of duration. In log-log coordinates, the left limb of the curve has a slope of −1 (Bloch's law); the right limb has a slope of 0. The transition between the two limbs occurs at the critical duration T_c and the critical intensity I_c. The inset shows the wave form of a rectangular pulse with duration T and intensity I.

of a significant violation of Bloch's law. As will be discussed, there are theoretical reasons for expecting reciprocity between amplitude and duration for some range of brief durations.

Outside of Bloch's regime, thresholds decline less rapidly with increasing duration. There is considerable variety in the actual pattern of decline, but two general trends are evident. For relatively large or low spatial frequency targets, there is a rapid transition to a slope of 0, consistent with Eq. (55), indicating a threshold that is independent of duration. This pattern is evident in Barlow's data shown in Figure 6.11, as well as in Herrick's (1956) and Roufs' (1972a) data for 1° foveal disks, in Nachmias's (1967) data for 0.7° square-wave gratings and in Legge's (1978) data for sine gratings of 0.75 cycles·degree^{-1} and below. For small or high spatial frequency targets, the departure from Bloch's law is more gradual, and does not necessarily resolve to a straight line in log-log coordinates. Barlow's data in Figure 6.11 for small peripheral targets provide good examples, as do Owen's data for small peripheral targets.

These two trends may be roughly characterized by the slope of the second limb of the threshold-duration function: for large targets the slope approaches 0, for small targets it is between 0 and −1. Legge (1978) estimated the slope of this second limb for targets of various spatial frequency. At 0.75 and 0.375 cycles·degree^{-1} the slope was about −0.02; for frequencies between 1.5 and 12 cycles·degree^{-1} it averaged about −0.29.

Higher background intensities also tend to reduce the slope of the second limb of the threshold-duration function, as may be seen in Barlow's data for small targets in Figure 6.11. The influence of both spatial configuration and background intensity upon this slope may be given a common theoretical interpretation, as discussed below.

6.3. Critical Duration

When data conform to the template in Figure 6.10, there is little ambiguity to the definition of critical duration. When, however, the departure from Bloch's law is gradual, and when the subsequent slope is not zero, critical duration is difficult both to define and to measure. Although a conservative definition, and that adopted here, is the duration at which the data first depart from Bloch's law, some authors have defined it as the point in the data at which the slope first changes (Breitmeyer & Ganz, 1977; Legge, 1978). Elsewhere, it has been operationally defined as the ratio of thresholds for short and long pulses, times the duration of the short pulse (Krauskopf & Mollon, 1971). These different methods can give quite different estimates of the critical duration.

In light of these difficulties, we may doubt whether the critical duration, however defined, is a useful or robust measure of the temporal properties of the visual system. For large or low spatial frequency targets on backgrounds of high intensity, T_c and I_c do adequately characterize threshold as a function of duration. For many other targets, they do not. Furthermore, as will be discussed in Section 6.5.5, threshold-duration functions are inherently incapable of providing a complete characterization of the temporal response.

6.4. Effects of Background Intensity

The effects of light adaptation upon temporal sensitivity are discussed in Section 11. Both critical duration and critical intensity vary systematically with background intensity. Critical duration declines monotonically with background illuminance,

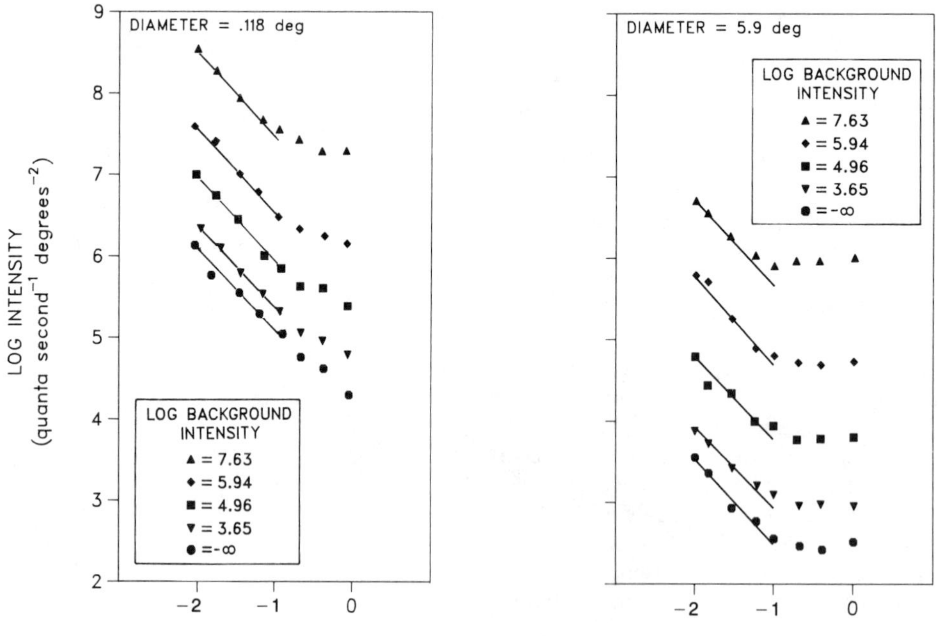

Figure 6.11. Threshold for a rectangular pulse as a function of duration. Target was a disk with diameter of 0.118° (7.1 min), in the left panel, or 5.9°, on the right. Different curves are for different background intensities. The straight lines have a slope of −1 (Bloch's law). Target was centered 6.5° from the fovea in the right eye upon a 13° surround. Intensities are expressed as the number of quanta at 507 nm that would yield an equivalent luminance. Method of adjustment and a 2-mm artificial pupil were used. (From H. B. Barlow, Temporal and spatial summation in human vision at different background intensities, *Journal of Physiology*, 1958, *141*. Reprinted with permission.)

from a value of about 100 msec at 0 log td to about 25 msec at 4 log td, as illustrated in Figure 6.31, Section 11.5.

Critical intensity increases monotonically with background intensity. Beyond about 10 td, the slope of the curve is about −0.91, close to the value of −1 prescribed by Weber's law (Roufs, 1972a). This scaling of sensitivity is comparable to that seen with thresholds for sinusoids and other wave forms. (See also the discussion of temporal summation in Chapter 5 by Hood & Finkelstein.)

6.5. Theory

6.5.1. Bloch's Law. The most widespread interpretation of Bloch's law is that the eye integrates perfectly over a time interval equal to the critical duration. According to this theory, it does not matter how the signal is distributed within the critical duration, provided that its integral equals a criterion value. That this interpretation is wrong may be clearly seen in an experiment of Rashbass (1970). He first measured the threshold-duration function for a 17° radius disk on a 700-td background. Critical duration was about 16 msec. He then measured threshold for a pair of 2-msec pulses, one positive and one negative, their onsets separated by 10 msec. The integral of this stimulus, all of which falls within the critical duration, is 0. If threshold is governed by this integral, the stimulus should be invisible. In fact, Rashbass found it required an amplitude only about 1.85 times that for a single pulse.

A determined advocate of the complete integration theory might counter that there are many possible intervals of 16 msec over which the integral might be taken, many of which would not give a 0 value. Presumably, then, the observer would use the interval with the largest integral, one containing just one of the pulses. But then why is the threshold 1.85 times that for a single pulse?

Rather than pursue the various theoretical dodges that might preserve some variant of the perfect integrator, we consider the more general class of causal, time-invariant linear filters, of which the perfect integrator is but one. First we consider the properties of the perfect integrator as a filter. Its impulse response is a pulse of duration τ, equal to the epoch of integration. This is rather implausible, if only because discontinuities are rarely found in biology. The amplitude response is proportional to $|\sin(\pi w \tau)/\pi w|$, which does not resemble very much the temporal amplitude sensitivity function of the human observer. In short, although the perfect integrator may predict Bloch's law, it is quite firmly refuted on other grounds.

In fact, Bloch's law is an inevitable consequence of any linear filter that passes only frequencies below some cutoff. This is most easily seen by considering the response in the frequency domain. The amplitude spectrum of a pulse of intensity I and duration T is given by

$$I\left|\frac{\sin(\pi T w)}{\pi w}\right| . \tag{56}$$

The peak amplitude of this spectrum is IT and hence any two durations for which reciprocity holds (for which IT are equal) have amplitude spectra with equal peak values. Let us define the unit of intensity as the threshold for a 1-msec pulse. Then two pulses, of durations 10 and 20 msec and amplitudes 1/10 and 1/20, will each be at threshold. Their amplitude spectra are sketched in Figure 6.12.

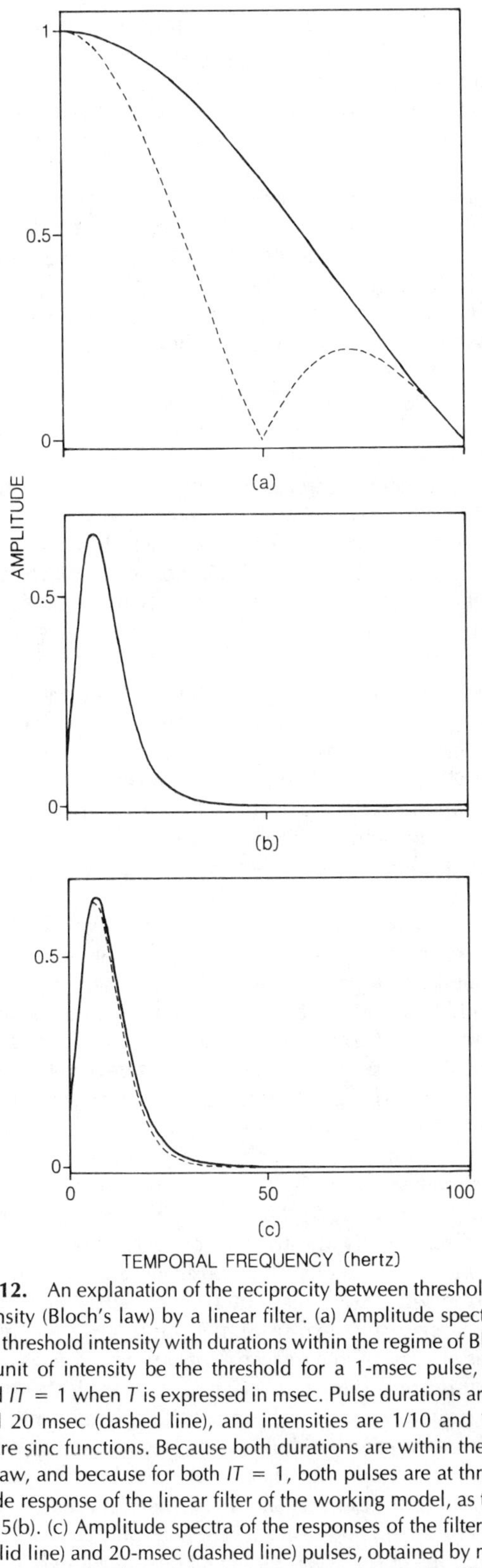

Figure 6.12. An explanation of the reciprocity between threshold duration and intensity (Bloch's law) by a linear filter. (a) Amplitude spectra for two pulses of threshold intensity with durations within the regime of Bloch's law. Let the unit of intensity be the threshold for a 1-msec pulse, so that at threshold $IT = 1$ when T is expressed in msec. Pulse durations are 10 (solid line) and 20 msec (dashed line), and intensities are 1/10 and 1/20. Both spectra are sinc functions. Because both durations are within the regime of Bloch's law, and because for both $IT = 1$, both pulses are at threshold. (b) Amplitude response of the linear filter of the working model, as taken from Figure 6.5(b). (c) Amplitude spectra of the responses of the filter to the 10-msec (solid line) and 20-msec (dashed line) pulses, obtained by multiplying the spectra in (a) by the amplitude response shown in (b). The resulting spectra are nearly identical; hence the stimuli should be equally visible.

If the visual response to these signals is linear, then the amplitude spectrum of the response is the product of amplitude spectra of signal and visual filter. The latter may be approximated for conditions like Rashbass's by the linear filter of the working model as fit to Robson's (1966) data [see Fig. 6.5(b)]. These are drawn in Figure 6.12. The resulting products, which are the amplitude spectra of the responses to 10- and 20-msec pulses, are almost identical, as shown.

This argument is incomplete, because it says only that the amplitude spectra of pulses briefer than the critical duration are identical. The phase spectra of the two responses are in fact different, but as we shall show, they differ in a way not likely to affect threshold. The phase spectrum of a pulse centered at 0 is 0 at all frequencies. To begin the pulse at time 0, as our convention for inputs to a causal system requires, we delay the pulse by half its duration. Table 6.1 shows that a delay of $T/2$ results in a phase shift of $-\pi T w$ at each frequency w. The phase spectrum of the response is obtained by simply adding, at each frequency, the phase response of the visual filter. This function is not easily estimated (see Section 5.10). But the *difference* in the phase of the response to two pulses of durations T_1 and T_2 is $\pi w(T_1 - T_2)$, regardless of the phase response of the visual filter. This difference is just that which would result from shifting the response by an amount $(T_1 - T_2)/2$. So we see that two pulses with durations less than the critical duration result in responses that are identical except for a shift in time equal to half the difference in their durations. Because absolute position in time does not usually influence sensitivity, we conclude that the two pulses are equally visible.

6.5.2. Sensitivity at Long Durations. With increasing duration beyond the critical duration, pulse thresholds either become independent of duration or decline at a more gradual rate than prescribed by Bloch's law. The second limb of the threshold-duration function is steeper at low background intensities and for small or high spatial frequency targets. The spatial effects are somewhat more potent, as may be seen in Barlow's data in Figure 6.11.

It is likely that these effects are due to variations in the degree of attenuation of low temporal frequencies, in combination with probability summation over time (Legge, 1978; Tolhurst, 1975a). All three manipulations—raising target spatial frequency, reducing target size, and lowering background intensity—elevate relative sensitivity to low temporal frequencies. In terms of the working model developed in Section 4, these manipulations reduce the *transience* of the underlying linear filter. In the case of background intensity, this change is probably due to parametric change in the filter. When the spatial stimulus is varied, it may occur because of a shift from one detector to another. This issue is discussed in Section 9.4.

In a purely transient filter, a response occurs only at the onset and offset of the pulse. In a purely sustained filter, the response persists for the duration of the pulse or longer. These properties of sustained and transient pulse responses are illustrated in Figure 6.13. As duration is increased, the sustained response provides a greater number of opportunities to detect the stimulus; hence threshold is reduced by probability summation. For the transient response, the number of opportunities remains constant, and threshold does not decline.

The two threshold-duration functions plotted in Figure 6.13 are predictions of the working model developed in Section 4. It consists of a linear filter whose output is perturbed by noise followed by a threshold mechanism. The two curves are for purely sustained (transience = 0) and purely transient (transience = 1) filters. The figure shows that a good qualitative account of the continuing improvement in sensitivity at long durations is provided by a sustained filter followed by probability summation.

The predictions of the working model depend somewhat upon the parameter β, which reflects the slope of the psychometric function. In particular, for the sustained detector the asymptotic slope of the threshold-duration function is $1/\beta$ in log-log coordinates. The predictions in Figure 6.13 employ a β of 3.5, typical of values found in many contrast detection experiments. The lowest reported values for β are around 1.5; hence the steepest asymptotic slope should be around -0.67, and should be encountered with small targets in dark-adapted conditions. This agrees with Barlow's data for a small target at absolute threshold (Fig. 6.11).

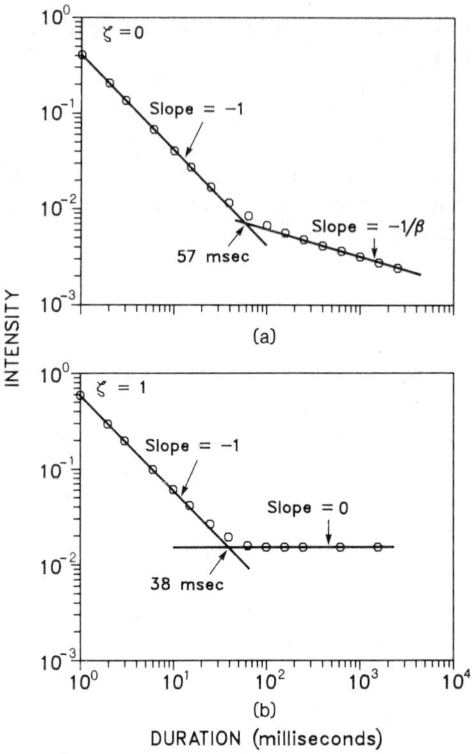

Figure 6.13. Threshold-duration functions predicted by the working model for two values of transience. Points are model predictions; curves are fitted by eye. Panel (a) shows that when the model behaves in a sustained fashion (transience parameter $\zeta = 0$), threshold continues to improve beyond the critical duration and the second limb of the function has a slope of $-1/\beta$ in log-log coordinates, where β governs the slope of the psychometric function of the model. When the model is transient ($\zeta = 1$) as shown in panel (b), the function is flat beyond the critical duration. Other parameters of the model used here are $\tau = 6.25$ msec, $\kappa = 1.33$, $n_1 = 9$, $n_2 = 10$, $\rho = 1.0$, $\beta = 3.5$.

6.5.3. Effects of Background Intensity on Critical Duration. As shown earlier, a threshold duration function may be easily calculated for any particular linear filter, once its transfer function is known. An estimate of the critical duration can then be taken from this curve. We have seen that as background intensity is raised, the amplitude response of the hypothetical filter, as reflected in flicker thresholds, is altered in characteristic ways. From these changes in the amplitude response (and provided some phase assumption is made) changes in critical duration with background intensity can be predicted. This direct prediction of T_c from flicker data has not yet been attempted, but the simpler qualitative prediction that follows suggests that it would succeed.

The explanation of Bloch's law (Fig. 6.12) shows the relationship between the critical duration and the high-frequency falloff of the amplitude sensitivity function. A pulse disobeys Bloch's law when its spectrum is narrow relative to this falloff.

The width of the spectrum of a pulse is inversely related to its duration, so the condition for reciprocity may be stated

$$\frac{K}{T} \leqslant F_c \ , \tag{57}$$

where F_c is some *critical frequency* and where K is some constant. The critical frequency specifies the location of the high-frequency falloff, and is defined as the frequency at which the amplitude response has fallen by some criterion amount from its maximum. The precise value of K depends on this criterion and the shape of the falloff, but so long as they are fixed, we may write

$$T_cF_c = K \ . \tag{58}$$

Any condition that alters F_c should therefore produce an inverse effect upon T_c.

Increases in background intensity increase the value of F_c without markedly changing the shape of the high-frequency falloff (see Section 11). These background increases should therefore result in decreases in T_c, of a size predicted by Eq. (58). Making a similar argument, Roufs (1972a, 1972b) has made extensive measurements of F_c-and T_c for backgrounds between $-\infty$ and 4.4 log td, and has found that Eq. (58) is obeyed reasonably well (compare Figs. 6.30 and 6.31 in Section 11). It seems then that the variation in critical duration with background intensity may be explained by the same processes required to account for the adaptive variations in the amplitude sensitivity function. These processes are considered in more detail in Section 11.

6.5.4. Relation Between Pulse and Flicker Data. A traditional test of any model of temporal sensitivity is its ability to account for sensitivity to both periodic and transient wave forms. Models embodying a linear filter and threshold device, however, invariably overestimate sensitivity to rectangular pulses relative to that for sinusoidal flicker (Roufs, 1972a, 1972b; Sperling & Sondhi, 1968). It seems quite likely that this discrepancy may be removed by introducing probability summation into the model. For example, in Roufs's experiments, observers were allowed unlimited time to judge the presence of sinusoidal signals, whereas the time available to detect a pulse is limited to its duration. This procedure enhances sensitivity to periodic stimuli relative to that for transients.

Predictions from the working model (which includes probability summation) can only be made for wave forms with finite duration. This is a problem for the traditional test noted earlier, because true sinusoids go on forever. Turning a sinusoid on and off abruptly gives it a finite duration, but also introduces a wide range of other frequencies. A practical solution is to use as flicker wave forms sinusoids windowed in time by a Gaussian function. These signals contain a narrow band of frequencies, and hence more or less directly define the amplitude response of the filter, yet they also have finite duration. Examples of the use of these signals to estimate the amplitude response of the filter of the working model may be found in Watson (1977, 1981).

6.5.5. Is the Threshold-Duration Function Informative? Despite their long history of use in visual theory, we may question whether the threshold-duration function and the critical duration are useful measures of temporal sensitivity. We have already noted the variety of forms that the curve may take, and the difficulty of estimating the critical duration. Even when it can be estimated with confidence, it does not give a generally useful description of the temporal response. For a linear system, this description would be provided by the impulse response or by the system function (see Section 3). Neither the critical duration nor the threshold-duration function is capable of defining these functions (Norman & Gallistel, 1978). It should be clear from the argument of Figure 6.12, for example, that the critical duration and critical intensity are insensitive to changes in the low-frequency end of the system function. Likewise they are insensitive to the phase response of the system (unfortunately, so are most other psychophysical measures). In certain simple cases, the critical duration may indicate some useful feature of the impulse response. For example, in the n-stage filter discussed earlier (Sections 3 and 4) the critical duration will be $\tau(n - 1)![e/(n - 1)]^{n-1}$ (Sperling, 1979). More generally, if the time scale of the impulse response is multiplied by some constant k, or equivalently the frequency scale of the system function is divided by k, then the critical duration is multiplied by k. This sensitivity of the critical duration to the time scale of the impulse response is what has recommended its use as a measure of the effects of light adaptation. But as we have seen, background intensity changes not only the time scale and sensitivity of the system, but also its degree of transience. These two effects cannot be separately assessed by a single measure of critical duration.

7. SENSITIVITY TO PULSE PAIRS

7.1. Background

A pulse pair is a wave form consisting of the sum of two pulses of equal duration T, intensities I_1 and I_2, separated by a delay D. The target intensity wave form can be written

$$I(t) = I_1p_T(t) + I_2p_T(t - D) \tag{59}$$

where $p_T(t)$ is a pulse of unit height and width T. The intensities I_1 and I_2 may be either positive (an intensity increment) or negative (a decrement). Dividing by the background intensity gives the contrast wave form $C(t)$. An example of a pulse pair is shown in Figure 6.14.

The pulse pair has most often been used to study the form of the temporal response. Intuitively, the first pulse evokes a response which may be probed by the second pulse. However, to draw strong influences from the data we must know (or assume) how the two overlapping responses are combined, and how the resulting quantity determines threshold.

A useful format in which to represent the results of a pulse-pair experiment is sketched in Figure 6.14 (Rashbass, 1970). Following Boynton, Ikeda, and Stiles (1964), we define S_1 as the intensity (or contrast) of the first pulse, divided by threshold for the first pulse, and S_2 as the intensity (or contrast) of the second pulse divided by its threshold. Quantities scaled by threshold in this way are sometimes called "sensation magnitudes." Now we construct a plot in which the abscissa expresses S_1 and the ordinate, S_2. Threshold for any particular pulse pair can be represented as a point in this space. Several examples are shown in Figure 6.14. A common experimental procedure is to fix the ratio S_2/S_1 and then to measure threshold for the pair. This consists of moving along a ray at an angle of $\tan^{-1}(S_2/S_1)$ in the summation diagram. For example, an experiment using only positive pulses of equal amplitude would be confined to a ray at 45°. When the experiment is repeated

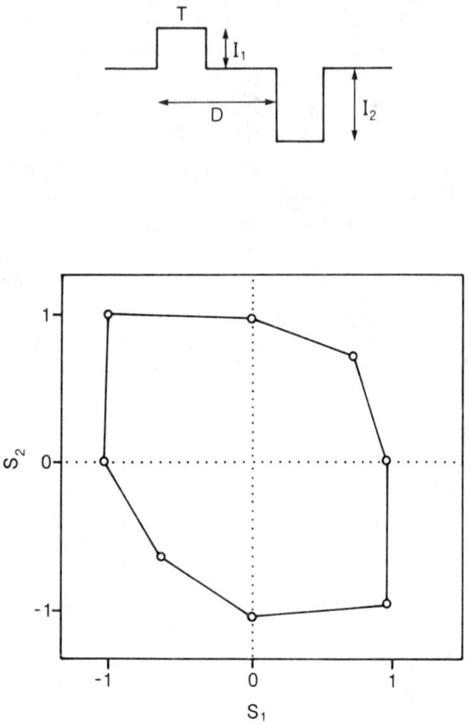

Figure 6.14. Schematic of a summation plot of thresholds for pulse pairs. The abscissa and ordinate indicate S_1 and S_2, sensation magnitudes of first and second pulses (intensities scaled by respective thresholds). Each point in the plot represents a pulse pair at threshold. Points on the axes represent thresholds for single pulses. The collection of all points in the plot is called the threshold locus. The locus may be thought of as separating subthreshold and suprathreshold stimulus regions. The shape of the locus depends upon the delay between pulses, as well as other variables. The inset shows the time wave form of a pulse pair. It consists of two pulses of intensities I_1 and I_2, each of duration T, separated by a delay D. This plot is a useful summary of summation between two pulses.

at a number of angles the threshold points may be connected to form a *threshold locus*.

Thresholds for pulse pairs frequently show one of the following forms of interaction: summation, partial summation, probability summation, partial cancellation, and cancellation. These outcomes lie at progressively greater distances from the origin.

Early studies of pulse-pair sensitivity were made by Granit and Davis (1931), Bouman and van den Brink (1952), and Blackwell (1963), all using two increments of equal size. They found summation at the briefest durations, partial summation at intermediate delays, and probability summation at the longest delays. Blackwell's data also showed partial cancellation at intermediate delays. Ikeda (1965) made extensive measurements with a variety of amplitude ratios, including both increments and decrements. Like Blackwell, he found intermediate delays at which like-signed pairs showed partial cancellation, and speculated that such results might be due to a biphasic internal response, with two lobes of opposite sign. Cancellation between like-signed pairs would occur when the negative phase of the second response overlapped the positive phase of the first response.

Subsequent work has confirmed this result, and has refined Ikeda's insight in the context of a linear filter followed by a nonlinear detection process (Rashbass, 1970, 1976; Roufs, 1973, 1974a; Watson & Nachmias, 1977). The effects of background intensity (Ikeda, 1965; Roufs, 1973, 1974a; Uetsuki & Ikeda, 1970) and spatial configuration of the target (Watson & Nachmias, 1977) have also been investigated. These developments have generally shown that the pulse-pair results can be understood in terms of the same model used to explain visibility of other waveforms such as sinusoids and single pulses.

7.2. Data

Figure 6.15 shows thresholds collected by Rashbass (1970). These data closely resemble those of Ikeda (1965) for a 30-min disk target on a 6° surround. The threshold plotted is the scaled contrast of the first pulse (S_1).

For like-signed pulses (filled symbols) the thresholds show progressively less summation with increasing delay, reaching a minimum of about 1 at around 60 msec. At this delay, the pair has the same threshold as either pulse alone. If the response to the two pulses did not interact, probability summation should result, and the thresholds at the longest delay are consistent with this condition ($S_1 \approx 0.84$). The minimum at 60 msec shows *less* than probability summation, and is therefore consistent with partial cancellation.

Thresholds for opposite-signed pairs (open symbols) show progressively less cancellation with increasing delay, reaching a minimum at about 60 msec, then rising again to a value consistent with probability summation. At short delays, the pairs partially cancel ($S_1 > 1$), but at intermediate delays they show partial summation ($S_1 = 0.53$). In other words, a pair of pulses of opposite sign is considerably more visible than a single pulse alone, or than a like-signed pair at the same delay. Roufs's data for like-signed (Roufs, 1973) and opposite-signed pairs (Roufs, 1974a) show a similar pattern. He used a 1° disk target and no surround. Qualitatively, this behavior agrees with Ikeda's hypothesis: at a delay of about 60 msec, like-signed pairs cancel because opposite-signed phases of the responses overlap; opposite-

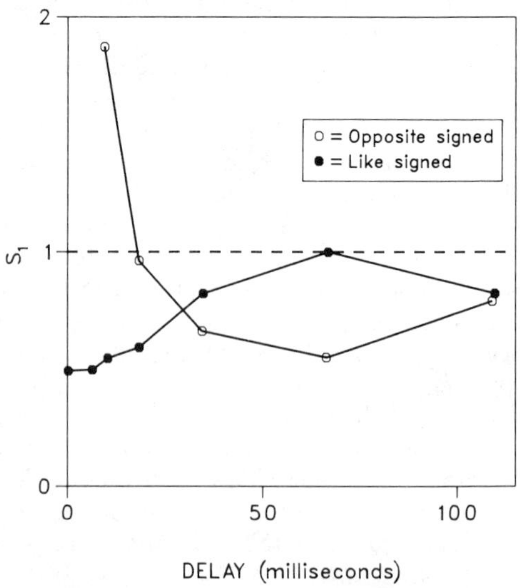

Figure 6.15. Sensitivity to pulse pairs as a function of delay between pulses. The ordinate indicates the intensity of the first pulse divided by its threshold (S_1). Both pulses were equal in intensity and 2 msec in duration. Filled symbols indicate like-signed pulse pairs (both increments or both decrements), and open symbols, opposite-signed. The target was a 17° disk; background was 700 td. Data from Rashbass (1970). Like-signed pairs summate best with 0 delay, and show a slight cancellation at about 65-msec delay. Opposite-signed pairs summate best at about 65-msec delay.

signed pulses summate because like-signed phases of the responses overlap.

The cases pictured in Figure 6.15 correspond to rays lying at 45° (like-signed pairs) and 135° (opposite-signed pairs) in the summation diagram of Figure 6.14. More complete threshold contours are shown in Figure 6.16. The curve in each figure is an ellipse centered at the origin with axes along the diagonals whose equation is

$$1 = S_1^2 + S_2^2 + 2S_1S_2L_D \qquad (60)$$

where L_D is a constant at each delay D. An ellipse leaning to the left has a positive value of L_D; a lean to the right has a negative value. Apart from its possible theoretical meaning, the reasonable fit of the ellipse recommends L_D as a summary measure of pulse-pair summation. The variation of L_D with delay from Rashbass's experiments is shown in Figure 6.17.

Several authors have examined the effect of background intensity on pulse-pair thresholds. All report a change in the time scale of the results, so that, for example, the minimum threshold for opposite-signed pulses moves to longer delays as the background is reduced. The data of Uetsuki and Ikeda (1970) also show less cancellation between like-signed pulses at lower backgrounds.

Watson and Nachmias (1977) and Breitmeyer and Ganz (1977) have used pulse pairs to examine the temporal response to gratings. Figure 6.18 shows the variation in L_D with spatial frequency at four selected delays. In each case, L_D increases with spatial frequency. At the three longer delays, values go from negative to positive, indicating that the negative lobe of the function disappears as spatial frequency increases.

7.3. Theory

Theoretical concerns relating to pulse-pair data focus on models that can account for (1) the elliptical threshold locus and (2) the form of L_D (or some comparable measure of summation versus delay). Most treatments assume an initial linear filter, but differ on the nature of the nonlinear detection stage.

Rashbass (1970) proposed that visual transients are filtered by an impulse response $h(t)$, then squared and integrated over an epoch E of about 200 msec. The stimulus was seen whenever the result was greater than one. At threshold,

$$\int_0^E [C(t) * h(t)]^2 \, dt = 1 . \qquad (61)$$

This model predicts elliptical threshold loci, and leads elegantly to the conclusion that L_D is the inverse Fourier transform of the amplitude response $|H(w)|$ (the autocorrelation function) of the filter. In support of this model, the transform of L_D does resemble qualitatively the TCSF, though no quantitative comparison of the two functions under the same conditions has been made. When transformed, the negative lobe of L_D will result in attenuation at low temporal frequencies (transience). Because transience as reflected in the TCSF is reduced when background intensity is reduced or spatial frequency raised, these manipulations should also reduce the size of the negative lobe of L_D, and they do (Broekhuijsen, Rashbass, & Veringa, 1976; Watson & Nachmias, 1977; Fig. 6.18).

An alternative is the working model developed in Section 4. A stimulus is seen whenever the noise-perturbed output of a linear filter exceeds a criterion. At threshold,

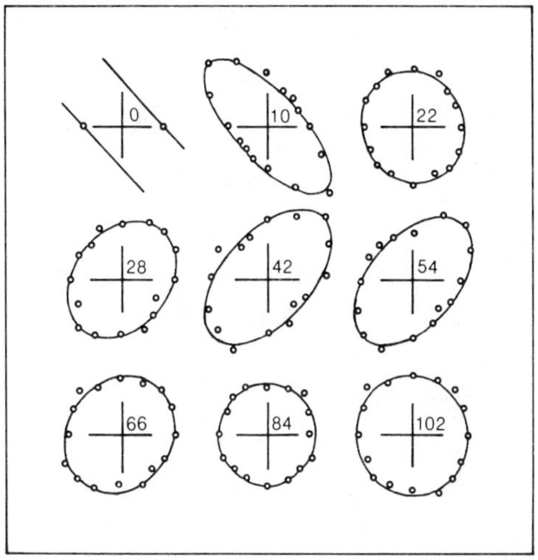

Figure 6.16. Summation between pulses at various delays. The pulses were 2-msec changes in the intensity of a 700-td, 17° disk with no surround. The abscissa and ordinate in each figure indicate S_1 and S_2, respectively, as explained in Figure 6.14. The delay between pulses in msec is indicated near the origin of each plot. The curves are ellipses of the form $1 = S_1^2 + S_2^2 + 2S_1S_2L_D$. The eccentricity of the ellipse, parameterized by L_D, varies as a function of delay. The elliptical threshold contours are predicted by the model of Rashbass. (From C. Rashbass, The visibility of transient changes of luminance, *Journal of Physiology*, 1970, *210*. Reprinted with permission.)

$$\int_a^b |C(t) * h(t)|^\beta \, dt = 1 . \qquad (62)$$

Here a and b are the time limits of the stimulus and β is a parameter determined by the slope of the psychometric function which typically has a value of between 3 and 6 (Nachmias, 1981; Watson, 1979). This model, when associated with a plausible impulse response, also predicts elliptical threshold loci (Rashbass, 1976; Roufs, 1974a; Watson & Nachmias, 1977).

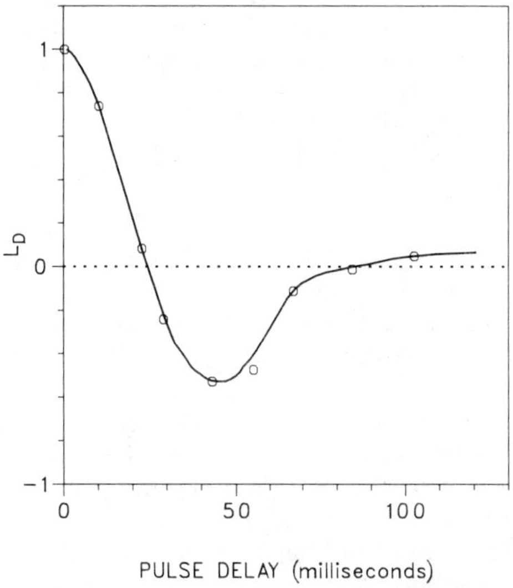

Figure 6.17. Variation in summation between pulse pairs as a function of delay. The quantity plotted is the eccentricity parameter L_D from the ellipses in Figure 6.16. When L_D is positive, like-signed pulses summate and opposite-signed pulses cancel; when it is negative, like-signed pulses cancel and opposite-signed pulses summate. According to Rashbass's model, this function is the Fourier transform of the amplitude spectrum of an underlying linear filter. (From C. Rashbass, The visibility of transient changes of luminance, *Journal of Physiology*, 1970, *210*. Reprinted with permission.)

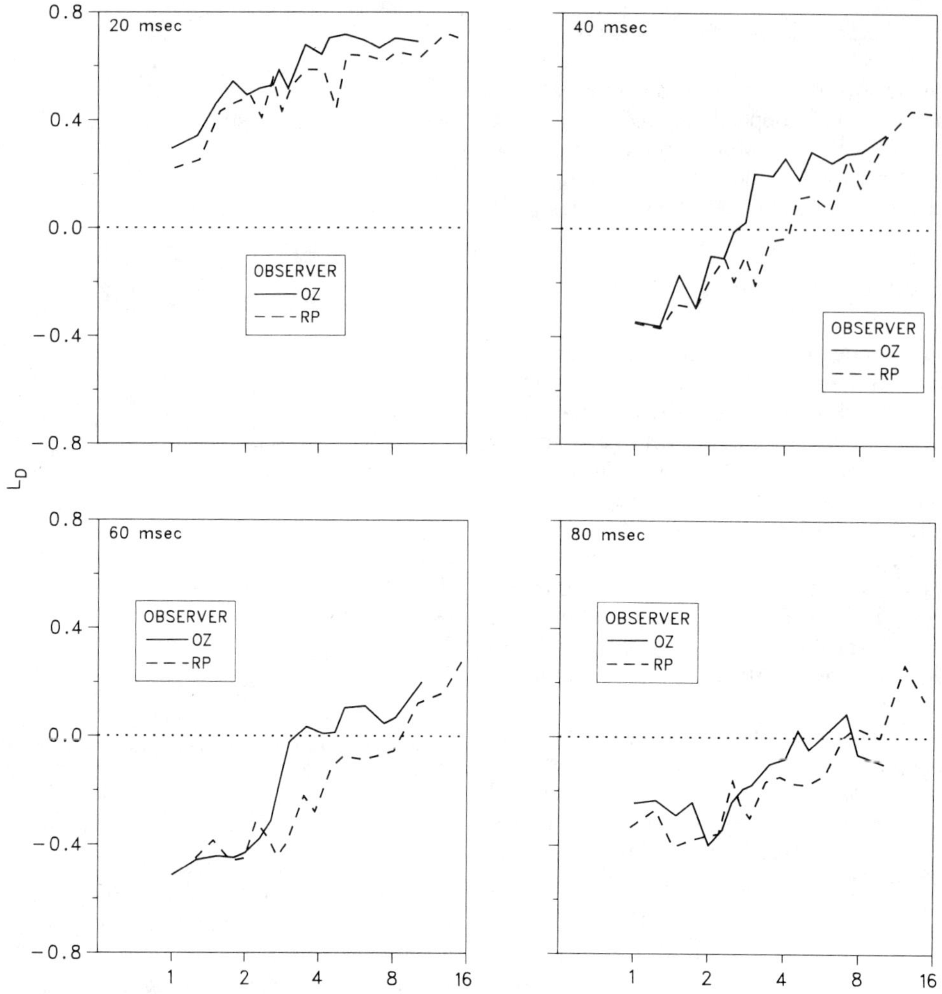

Figure 6.18. Summation between pulses as a function of the spatial frequency of the target. Delay between pulses was 20, 40, 60, or 80 msec. The value plotted is L_D, the parameter of an ellipse fitted to pulse-pair thresholds. Positive values of L_D indicate summation between like-signed pulses and cancellation between opposite-signed pulses; negative values indicate the opposite. L_D increases with spatial frequency at all four delays, so that at the highest spatial frequencies no negative values are obtained. This shows that the system becomes more sustained at higher spatial frequencies. Because the stimuli are briefly exposed, the change in L_D with spatial frequency is unlikely to be due to eye movements. Target was 2 × 1.5° with a 6° diameter surround. Background and surround luminance were about 15 cd·m^{-2}. (a) Observer OZ, (b) observer RP (from Watson, Note 1).

Unlike Rashbass's model, it can predict threshold for stimuli of long durations. For example, it correctly predicts that when the delay between pulses is very long, the contour will be a square with rounded corners, not an ellipse (Watson & Nachmias, 1977).

The defining equations of the two models are quite similar; only the exponent and limits of integration differ. Indeed a third model, a linear filter not followed by probability summation, can also be represented by Eq. (62), by setting the exponent to infinity. This allows a test among these models. Equation (62) predicts that sensitivity to a sinusoid will increase as the β^{-1} power of duration. Estimates of β obtained in this way are between 3 and 6, in agreement with the predictions of the working model (Watson, 1979).

The assumptions made about the final detection stage of the model can have considerable effect upon the interpretation of experimental results. For example, Roufs and Blommaert (1981) assume a deterministic threshold (effectively a β of ∞), and estimate the complete impulse response from pulse-pair data. However, when a more realistic model is assumed (β between 2 and 6) the interpretation of the data is quite different (Watson, 1982). As Rashbass has pointed out, when $\beta = 2$ all phase information is lost and the complete impulse response cannot be recovered (Rashbass, 1970, 1976). Conversely, when $\beta = \infty$ the complete impulse response can be recovered quite directly from pulse-pair data (Roufs & Blommaert, 1981). Because it appears that β is nearer 3 or 4, it is possible that the impulse response might be recovered from pulse-pair data, though probably not in a simple or elegant way. More likely, a brute-force fitting procedure will be required.

8. SENSITIVITY TO INCREMENTS AND DECREMENTS

8.1. Background

A decrement in light intensity can serve as a stimulus for vision, as these dark letters on this white page attest. Therefore, the relative visibility of increments and decrements of light is a matter of practical and theoretical interest. The practical interest arises from the question of whether positive or negative contrast (e.g., bright or dark letters) provides the better visual signal. Our theoretical interest begins with the observation that a simple linear model of temporal sensitivity predicts equality of increments and decrements, because they should produce internal responses equal in magnitude but opposite in sign.

Thresholds for both increments and decrements have been measured by numerous authors. Wherever substantial or consistent differences are found, the threshold for a decrement is lower than for an increment. But the reliability of these differences, between subjects and across conditions, is less than might be desired.

8.2. Data

Using a red, 10-min increment or decrement upon a 10°, 10,400-td largely green surround, Boynton, Ikeda, and Stiles (1964) found a decrement threshold 0.17 log unit lower than an increment. Patel and Jones (1968) used disks of several sizes and durations 7° from the fovea upon a 14° surround at various backgrounds. They reported a decrement advantage of about 0.3 log units for a 15-min, 50-msec target on a 6.1 quanta·degree^{-2}·sec^{-1} background. The advantage declined for larger targets, longer durations, and higher backgrounds.

Short (1966) also showed consistently greater visibility of decrements. He used a 57-min disk, 100 msec long, positioned 15° into the nasal visual field, upon a large surround, and found a difference averaging about 0.24 log unit at low backgrounds (below about 1 td) almost vanishing at higher backgrounds. There were, however, sizable differences among the three observers.

Herrick (1956), using a 1° target, no surround, various durations, and backgrounds between about −1 and 4 td, and Rashbass (1970), using a 17° target, no surround, various durations, and a background of 700 td, found little difference in results for increments and decrements, but neither author directly compared the two thresholds under the same conditions. Using conditions very similar to those of Herrick, Roufs (1974a) found little consistent difference in increment and decrement thresholds. However, Roufs's observers used a threshold criterion ("agitation") that may measure thresholds different from those of other authors (see Sections 5.11 and 9.4.1.4). Contrary to the finding of Patel and Jones (1968), neither Herrick's nor Roufs's data show any systematic effect of duration.

Some explanation of this variability of results may be in order. First, it should be noted that no two of these reports have employed the same conditions. Second, without exception, the authors used methods such as yes/no and method of adjustment, which permit the observer to use different criteria for increments and decrements. Some of the differences reported are larger than might be expected to arise from criterion variations, but in general we cannot be certain what portion of the difference, if any, we should attribute to this source. It would be useful to compare the two thresholds with a method, such as two-alternative forced-choice, which is not subject to this objection.

The reports cited used spatial targets (disks) that are all of one sign. When a spatial target is used, such as a sinusoidal grating, that has positive and negative excursions of equal sign, then it is more appropriate to speak of a comparison between thresholds for positive and negative contrast. These can differ only if the local position of the spatial increments and decrements (e.g., the bright and dark bars) is relevant. This might be the case for very low spatial frequencies, but is unlikely in most other situations. Thus it is not surprising that Watson (1977) found equal thresholds for positive and negative contrast grating targets of 3.5 cycles·degrees^{-1}.

8.3. Theory

A difference between thresholds for positive and negative contrast can be included in the working model by introducing different thresholds for positive and negative excursions of the internal response (Kelly & Savoie, 1973). Thus we assume that detection occurs whenever a positive excursion exceeds 1, or a negative excursion is less than $-\rho$. The parameter ρ is the *asymmetry factor* of the model [see Section 4.3 and Eq. (52)]. Data are best described by the model when ρ is set equal to the ratio of increment and decrement thresholds. This asymmetry factor is also able to account for some aspects of the thresholds for combinations of different temporal frequencies (Section 5.10) and threshold as a function of duration (Section 6.5).

Explanations for the difference between increment and decrement thresholds have generally appealed to physiological mechanisms such as "on-center" and "off-center" cells. Cohn (1974) has offered an interesting alternative, based on the observation that the distributions of quanta absorbed during increments and decrements are different in form when the number absorbed from the background is small. But this hypothesis predicts differences over a much smaller range of backgrounds than found by Short (1966) and Patel and Jones (1968). It is difficult to judge any theory without knowing what proportion of the effect is due to different criteria for increments and decrements.

9. SPATIAL EFFECTS

9.1. Background

Though it is convenient to consider the temporal wave form in isolation from the other dimensions of the visual stimulus, sensitivity is unavoidably governed by all the dimensions in concert. In some cases, the effects of two dimensions are *separable*. Sensitivity is separable along two dimensions if it is given by the product of sensitivity along the individual dimensions. For example, if the function that describes sensitivity as a function of spatial frequency (u) and temporal frequency (w) were separable, it could be written

$$s(u,w) = s_u(u)s_w(w) \tag{63}$$

where $s_u(u)$ is a spatial contrast sensitivity function and $s_w(w)$ is a temporal contrast sensitivity function like that described in Section 5. In this case, a change in spatial configuration would only scale the results up or down by a constant factor, and we could reasonably exclude consideration of $s_u(u)$ from this chapter. In human vision, however, spatial and temporal sensitivity are not separable. Instead, the temporal response depends upon the spatial configuration of the stimulus. This dependence is evident in the full range of temporal phenomena: in sensitivity to various wave forms, in reaction times, and in discriminability of various stimuli.

Theoretical interest in this area has focused upon incorporating spatial effects into models of temporal sensitivity. This has been done either by allowing the spatial configuration to control the parameters of a single temporal filter (Burbeck & Kelly, 1980; Kelly, 1972b; Robson, 1966) or by allowing the spatial configuration to determine the pathway in which the stimulus will be detected, different pathways having different temporal properties. The latter notion is generally associated with the idea of separate "sustained" and "transient" pathways for visual signals (Kulikowski & Tolhurst, 1973).

9.2. Spatial Effects upon Temporal Sensitivity

Four distinct aspects of the spatial configuration have been shown to influence temporal sensitivity: size, the surround, edges, and spatial frequency. These effects are evident in the threshold-duration function, as well as the TCSF, though we shall focus upon the latter.

9.2.1. Size. Enlarging a disk target lowers sensitivity at low temporal frequencies without much altering sensitivity at high frequencies. When changes do occur at high frequencies they take the form of a vertical shift of the high-frequency limb of the TCSF. These changes are illustrated in Figure 6.19. The open squares show sensitivity to a 2° disk on a large, 60° surround; the open circles are for a 65° disk with blurred edges.

9.2.2. Effects of the Surround. The filled symbols in Figure 6.19 show sensitivity to a 4° disk without a surround. Between the 2° disk and these data there is a profound loss in sensitivity at low temporal frequencies. It is not clear whether this loss is due to doubling the size of the target or removing the surround. Roufs (1972a) has shown that removing the surround from a 1° disk target has little effect upon high temporal frequencies,

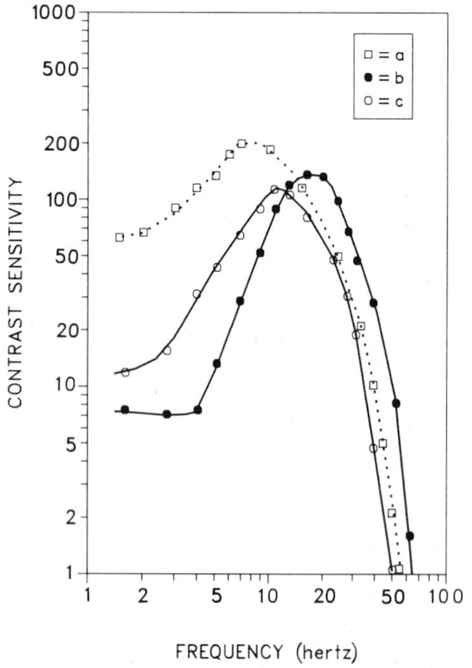

Figure 6.19. The effect of target size and surround upon temporal contrast sensitivity. Temporal wave form was sinusoidal and background intensity was 1000 td. (a) Open square: 2° disk, 60° surround, observer V (de Lange, 1958). (b) Filled circles: 4° disk, no surround (Kelly, 1959). (c) Open circles: 65° disk, blurred edges, no surround, observer P (Kelly, 1959). Enlarging the target and removing the surround reduce sensitivity at low temporal frequencies, thus making the system more transient. (From D. H. Kelly, Effects of sharp edges in a flickering field, *Journal of the Optical Society of America*, 1959, *49*. Reprinted with permission.)

but reduces sensitivity by about 0.5 log units at low frequencies. This suggests that much of the difference between the open squares and filled circles in Figure 6.19 is due to the surround. Harvey (1970), Kelly (1969b), Keesey (1970), Teller (1971), and Westheimer (1967) also provide evidence on the effect of the surround on temporal sensitivity.

Data collected without a surround are subject to other difficulties of interpretation, because the state of light adaptation in the vicinity of the border is somewhat ambiguous. For detectors whose receptive fields lie within the borders of the target, we may be fairly confident that their state of adaptation is governed by the background, regardless of the presence of the surround. But some targets may be detected by mechanisms whose receptive fields span the border of the target, and their adaptive states are much less easily determined when a surround is absent.

9.2.3. Edges. Visually effective edges in the target elevate sensitivity to low temporal frequencies. For example, Kelly (1969b) showed that blurring a 3° disk on a 16° surround reduced sensitivity by about half at low temporal frequencies but had no effect at high temporal frequencies. Very similar results were obtained by blurring the central edge of a counterphase modulated 8 × 16° bipartite field.

Enlarging a disk target moves its edges to regions of the retina of lower spatial resolution, and thus renders them less effective. Thus much of the effect of disk size may be due to this reduction in the visual effectiveness of target edges. This may also partially explain the action of the surround. Without a surround, any visual mechanism sensitive to the edge would be massively stimulated, even in the absence of the target. Presentation of the target would change its response by only a fraction. Thus removing the surround may effectively desensitize the observer to the edges at the border of the target.

9.2.4. Spatial Frequency. Robson (1966) measured the TCSF with sinusoidal gratings of four different spatial frequencies. As shown in Figure 6.20, the two highest spatial frequencies exhibit no decline in sensitivity at low temporal frequencies, whereas at the lowest spatial frequency, a very large low-frequency decline was observed. Similar results have been obtained by van Nes et al. (1967), Koenderink and van Doorn (1979), and Kelly (1972a).

Robson also noted that the shape of the TCSF at high temporal frequencies was invariant with spatial frequency, as shown by the curves superposed on the data, which are the same except for a vertical shift. A change in spatial frequency merely shifted the high-frequency limb up or down in sensitivity. Furthermore, at high spatial frequencies, the spatial contrast sensitivity function is invariant with temporal frequency, apart from a vertical shift. A summary statement of these invariances is that at high spatial and temporal frequencies, spatial and temporal contrast sensitivities are *separable* [see Section 9.1 and Eq. (63)]. This means that at these frequencies, the spatiotemporal contrast sensitivity function is simply the product of the spatial contrast sensitivity function, which describes sensitivity as a function of spatial frequency, and the TCSF. At low spatial or temporal frequencies, the two functions are clearly not separable. These interactions are easily seen in a view of the spatiotemporal contrast sensitivity function such as that provided by Koenderink and van Doorn (1979). Reproduced in Figure 6.21, their figure shows isosensitivity curves for gratings of various spatial and temporal frequencies. Separability of temporal and spatial contrast sensitivity functions is reflected by

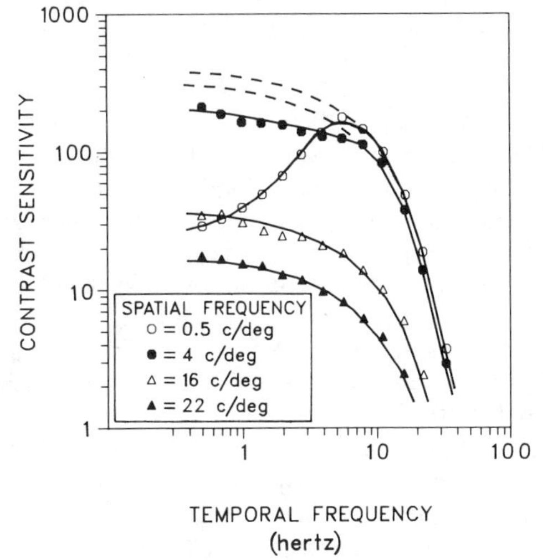

Figure 6.20. The effect of spatial frequency upon the temporal contrast sensitivity function. The target was a sinusoidal grating with a spatial frequency of 0.5, 4, 16, or 22 cycles·degree^{-1}. Background luminance was 20 cd·m^{-2}, target was 2.5 × 2.5°, surround was 10 × 10°, viewing was binocular with natural pupils from 2 m. Points are averages of four adjustment thresholds. The curves (including dashed sections) differ only in vertical position. Spatial and temporal sensitivity are separable at high temporal and spatial frequencies, but at low spatial frequencies sensitivity at low temporal frequencies is reduced. (From J. G. Robson, Spatial and temporal contrast sensitivity functions of the visual system, *Journal of the Optical Society of America*, 1966, *56*. Reprinted with permission.)

the roughly parallel contours beyond 10 Hz and 10 cycles· degree^{-1}. The valley near the origin confirms Robson's earlier observation that a decline in sensitivity at low temporal frequencies occurs only when the spatial frequency is low.

There is a qualitative agreement among the effects of disk size, edges, surrounds, and spatial frequency. It was suggested that the effects of disk size and surround upon the low temporal frequencies are mediated by the visually effective edges in the target. Edges are the repositories of high spatial frequencies. When they are removed by blurring, or made less visually effective by moving them into the periphery, the effective spatial frequency of the target is reduced and we should expect temporal sensitivity to resemble more that obtained with low spatial frequencies; that is, we should observe a more severe attenuation at low temporal frequencies. Thus enlarging a target, blurring its edges, removing its surround, or lowering its spatial frequency should all selectively lower sensitivity at low temporal frequencies, and this does occur.

9.2.5. Miscellaneous Spatial Effects upon Sensitivity. Many other experiments give a similar result through less direct means. Kulikowski and Tolhurst (1973) found that sensitivity to a grating with a square-wave temporal wave form was about twice that for a grating turned on for half a period, then off for half a period, provided the spatial frequency was low. The spectrum of the on–off wave form is equal to half the amplitude of the square-wave spectrum, plus a component at 0 Hz. If low spatial frequency detectors are purely transient they will not respond to the 0-Hz term, and the response to the square wave will be twice that to on–off, as observed. At higher spatial frequencies the system becomes more sustained and the 0-Hz term becomes more effective, reducing the difference in sensitivity between the two wave forms. Tolhurst (1975b) has shown that the detection of a brief increment upon an extended subthreshold pedestal is influenced only near the onset and offset of the pedestal when a low spatial frequency is used. For higher spatial frequencies, detection is enhanced for the duration of the subthreshold grating. Breitmeyer and Julesz (1975) demonstrated that abrupt onsets enhanced visibility relative to gradual onsets at low spatial frequencies but not at high. This is consistent with a reduced sensitivity at low temporal and spatial frequencies, because abrupt transients contain higher frequencies than do gradual transients. They also showed that of the abrupt onset and offset of a pulse, only the onset was effective in enhancing sensitivity. They provided no explanation of this effect, but in fact it is expected in a linear system that is not purely transient. The onset response transient is the step response of the system, but the offset response transient is the step response subtracted from the sustained portion of the response and thus usually has a smaller peak value. Furthermore Stromeyer, Zeevi, and Klein (1979) found that offsets and onsets enhanced visibility by about the same amount when somewhat different background intensities, and spatial and temporal wave forms were used. This discrepancy is not surprising because all of these variables will influence the degree of transience.

Legge (1978) has shown that at high spatial frequencies thresholds continue to decline as duration increases beyond the critical duration, whereas at low spatial frequencies no further improvement is found. He found in addition that brief masking pulses at the start and end of a test pulse had the same effect regardless of test duration for low spatial frequencies, but at high spatial frequencies the effects declined as duration increased. Evidently, only the start and end of the pulse are effective in the first case, whereas in the second case all parts of the signal are effective.

9.3. Spatial Effects upon Reaction Times

Reaction times to sinusoidal gratings increase with the spatial frequency of the grating (Breitmeyer, 1975; Harwerth & Levi, 1978; Lupp, Hauske, & Wolf, 1976; Vassilev & Mitov, 1976).

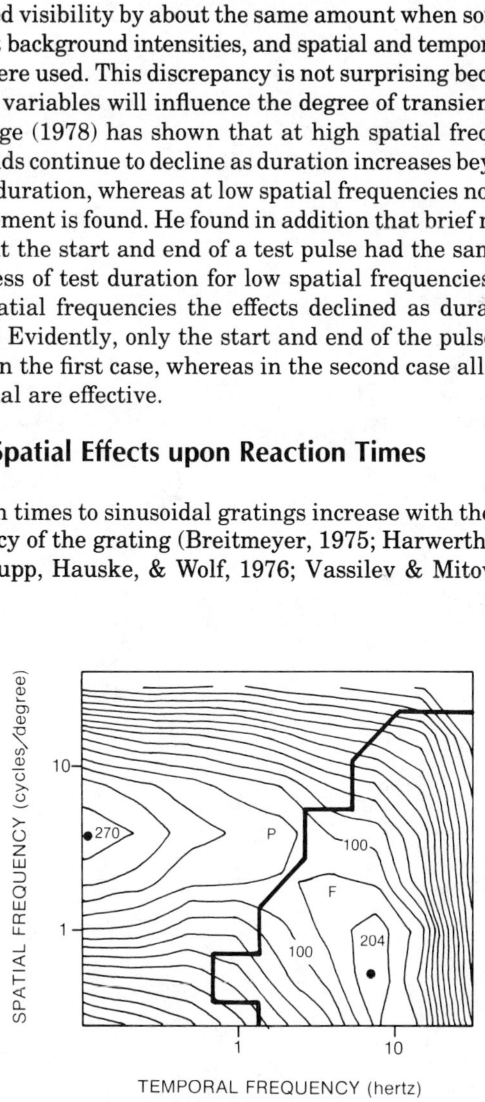

Figure 6.21. Isosensitivity curves for targets that are sinusoidal in both space and time. Each curve connects points of equal sensitivity obtained by linear interpolation from data like those in Figure 6.20. The spacing between lines is 0.1 log unit, corresponding approximately to a standard deviation. The contour at sensitivity = 100, and the peaks at 270 and 204 are marked. The heavy line separates regions the observer judged as giving sensations of "flicker" or "pattern" (see Section 9.4.1.4). Sensitivity falls when either spatial and temporal frequency are high, or when both are low. (From J. J. Koenderink & A. J. van Doorn, Spatiotemporal contrast detection threshold surface is bimodal, *Optic Letters*, 1979, *4*. Reprinted with permission.)

The differences persist when the contrast at each spatial frequency is set to equal apparent contrast (Breitmeyer, 1975) or to a fixed number of threshold units (Lupp, Hauske, & Wolf, 1976; Vassilev & Mitov, 1976). As shown in Figure 6.22, the difference between reaction times to 1 and 16 cycles·degree^{-1} is about 90 msec, and this figure is the same whether the targets are three or six times above threshold. These figures are slightly larger than those found by Breitmeyer (1975). These results have sometimes been explained in terms of the different latencies of X- and Y-type retinal ganglion cells, but as Lennie (1980a) points out, the differences in conduction times are orders of magnitude too small, and the latencies to near-threshold lights may not differ at all (Lennie, 1980b).

Tolhurst (1975a) examined the distributions of reaction times to near-threshold high and low spatial frequency gratings at various durations. The distribution was unimodal to a high spatial frequency (3.5 cycles·degree^{-1}), but bimodal to low. This outcome is consistent with the low-frequency grating being detected only at its onset or offset, as would be the case for a transient mechanism. This view is reinforced by Tolhurst's observation that the position of the second mode of the distribution is always about 250 msec after the offset of the target.

9.4. Sustained and Transient Mechanisms

To characterize the dynamic behavior of some visual cells, Cleland et al. (1971) adopted the terms *sustained*, indicating a response extending for the duration of the stimulus, and *transient*, indicating a response primarily at stimulus onset and offset. Watson and Nachmias (1977) have proposed formal definitions for these terms. Transient behavior is indicated by an impulse response whose integral is 0, for example, a biphasic response with positive and negative lobes of equal area. The transient amplitude response has severe attenuation at low temporal frequencies, reaching 0 at 0 Hz. In a sustained system the impulse response is all of one sign, and the amplitude response has a maximum at 0 Hz. A system intermediate between these extremes may be relatively sustained or transient. In the working model (Section 4) the degree of transience has been captured by a single parameter that governs the amplitude of a second, negative lobe in the impulse response. Further discussion of these terms was given in Section 3.

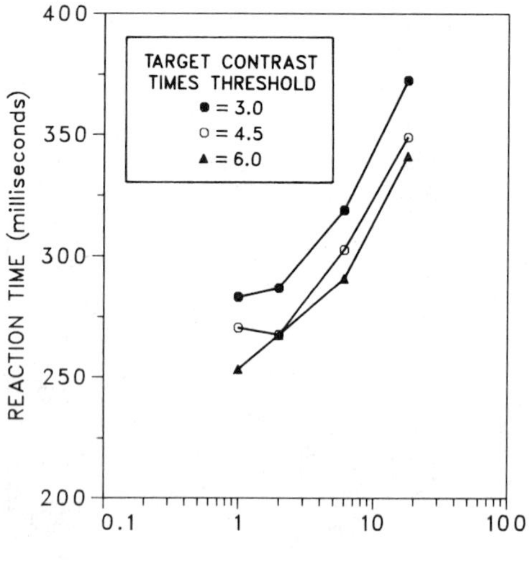

Figure 6.22. Reaction time as a function of spatial frequency. The three curves indicate target contrasts of 3, 4.5, or 6 times threshold. Thresholds were estimated as the 50% point of a yes/no frequency-of-seeing curve. Targets were 5.3 × 3.8° gratings with no surround. Background intensity was 23 cd·m^{-2}. A 2.3-mm diameter artificial pupil was used. Reaction times increase by about 90 msec between spatial frequencies of 1 and 16 cycles·degree^{-1}. (From U. Lupp, G. Hauske, & W. Wolf, Perceptual latencies to sinusoidal gratings, *Vision Research, 16*. Copyright 1976 by Pergamon Press, Ltd. Reprinted with permission.)

The evidence in Sections 9.2 and 9.3 cited above indicates that the higher the effective spatial frequency of the target, the more sustained the temporal response. These and other results led Tolhurst (1973) and Kulikowski and Tolhurst (1973) to propose the existence of two classes of visual mechanisms: transient and sustained. This hypothesis has considerable implications for models of temporal sensitivity, and has found wide acceptance, so it deserves critical examination.

Mild and strong versions of this theory can be distinguished. The mild version only asserts a relationship between spatial configuration and the temporal properties of the detecting mechanism; the strong version proposes the existence of two distinct classes of mechanisms that respond in parallel to a visual stimulus. By analogy to physiology, the mild version imagines the same cells to be capable of either sustained or transient behavior depending upon stimulus conditions, whereas the strong theory assumes separate populations of sustained and transient cells acting in parallel. Examples of the mild theory are provided by Robson (1966) and Burbeck and Kelly (1980), who attribute these effects to differing spatial and temporal properties of the center and surround of retinal units. Proponents of the strong version are Kulikowski and Tolhurst (1973) and Roufs (1974a).

All the data cited to this point are consistent with either mild or strong theories. In the absence of further evidence, the mild theory would be preferred because it is more parsimonious. The strong theory would be called for by evidence of two sorts. The first would show that both sustained and transient mechanisms exist at one spatial frequency. The second would show that mechanisms operating in the two regimes are functionally distinct.

9.4.1. Evidence for Parallel Operation

9.4.1.1. Subthreshold Summation. The most direct test for parallel operation of sustained and transient mechanisms is subthreshold summation between different temporal frequencies. Sustained mechanisms are generally thought to be more sensitive at low temporal frequencies, and transient mechanisms at high. The strong theory therefore predicts that low and high temporal frequencies will excite different mechanisms, and will show little subthreshold summation. The mild theory on the other hand predicts that summation between the two frequencies will be consistent with a single pathway. Using this technique, Watson (1977) found only modest departures from the predictions of a single linear pathway with probability summation over time. However, the data could not rule out the existence of two independent pathways, one moderately selective for high temporal frequencies, the other for low. In these experiments the separation between frequency was never larger than 8 Hz; more convincing evidence of two pathways might have been provided by a larger separation.

9.4.1.2. Adaptation. If sustained and transient mechanisms respond in parallel to the same spatial target, as the strong theory supposes, then it might be possible to adapt selectively one of the two. For example, if transient mechanisms are more sensitive at high temporal frequencies, then adapting to a high temporal frequency might reduce their sensitivity and produce a selective reduction in sensitivity at the high frequencies. More quantitative predictions have not been made, and would require assumptions regarding the temporal sensitivity of each mechanism, the manner of adaptation, and how thresholds are determined when both mechanisms are active.

Evidence for temporal frequency selective adaptation has been sought by numerous authors (Green, 1981; Nilsson, Richmond, & Nelson, 1975; Pantle, 1971; Pantle & Sekuler, 1968; Smith, 1970, 1971). Despite the variety of techniques used, these experiments are unanimous in showing very little selective adaptation. In addition, the experiments have not generally avoided various sources of artifact, such as adapting stimuli of equal contrast rather than equal "sensation magnitude," and testing and adapting stimuli with different average intensity. We may also question whether selective adaptation is compelling evidence for parallel operation of independent pathways. A single pathway may contain elements that are frequency selective and adaptable, yet do not themselves constitute a "mechanism." This issue is discussed by Watson (1977).

Tolhurst (1973) has shown that following adaptation to a stationary grating, different patterns of threshold elevation are found depending upon whether the test pattern moves or is stationary. He proposed that the stationary test revealed the adaptation of the sustained system, the moving test that of the transient system.

9.4.1.3. Discrimination at Threshold. If sustained and transient mechanisms are "separate labeled" pathways (see Section 3.6), then a stimulus that at threshold exclusively excites the transient mechanism should be perfectly discriminated from a stimulus which exclusively excites the sustained mechanism. In agreement with this prediction, Watson and Robson (1981) found that a low and a high temporal frequency were perfectly discriminated. Some of their data are shown in Figure 6.23.

9.4.1.4. Threshold Sensations. In his 1958 report, de Lange noted a difference in the nature of the flicker perception depending on "frequency" (p. 782). This observation has been echoed by numerous authors. At detection threshold a spatial pattern that is modulated sinusoidally in time may appear as primarily a spatial or a temporal variation. These two threshold sensations, called "pattern," and "flicker," "swell," and "agitation," as well as other names, have been described by van Nes et al. (1967), Rashbass (1968), Watanabe et al. (1968), Richards (1971), Keesey (1972), Kulikowski and Tolhurst (1973), and Roufs (1974a). The threshold sensation of pattern predominates at low temporal and high spatial frequencies, whereas flicker predominates at high temporal and low spatial frequencies. Figure 6.21 shows the approximate extent of these two regimes.

Van Nes et al. (1967) noted that thresholds for both sensations could be measured for the same stimulus. At detection threshold either pattern or flicker is evident; at some higher contrast the other sensation emerges. Keesey (1972) had observers adjust the contrast of a thin bar to each threshold at a number of temporal frequencies, thus tracing out TCSFs for each of the two criteria. The two curves differed in shape, and Keesey proposed that the two thresholds were due to different mechanisms with different temporal properties. Kulikowski and Tolhurst (1973) used the same technique with spatial grating targets, with the results shown in Figure 6.24. The two curves intersect at an intermediate temporal frequency, so that at high temporal frequencies, flicker sensitivity is greater than pattern, whereas at low temporal frequencies the reverse is true. Their interpretation was essentially that of Keesey: each criterion was attributed to a different mechanism, as though the two curves described the temporal contrast sensitivities of distinct flicker and pattern detectors. As further evidence for

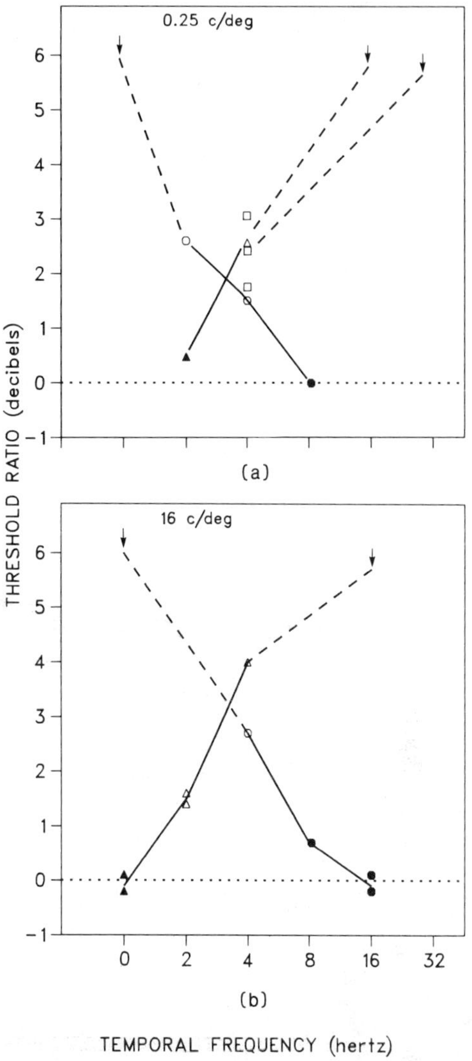

Figure 6.23. Ratio of identification and detection thresholds for different temporal frequencies. The stimuli were patches of spatial grating modulated sinusoidally in time. The spatial envelope was a Gaussian in both horizontal and vertical dimensions, with width between 1/e points of 12° (a), and 3/16° (b). Background intensity was 340 cd·m^{-2}, viewing was binocular with natural pupils. In each experiment two temporal frequencies were used, one indicated by the arrow, the other by the horizontal position of the data point. On each trial the observer tried to detect and identify the stimulus, and separate thresholds for detection and identification were estimated from the same data. When the ratio of these two thresholds is 1 (0 dB), the two frequencies are discriminated as well as they are detected. The filled symbols show cases in which a statistical test indicated that the two stimuli were discriminated as well as they were detected. This occurs only when one temporal frequency is very high and the other very low. These results are consistent with two labeled pathways, one selective for high temporal frequencies, the other for low. Similar results are obtained at both low (a) and high (b) spatial frequencies. (From A. B. Watson & J. G. Robson, Discrimination at threshold: Labelled detectors in human vision, *Vision Research, 21*. Copyright 1981 by Pergamon Press, Ltd. Reprinted with permission.)

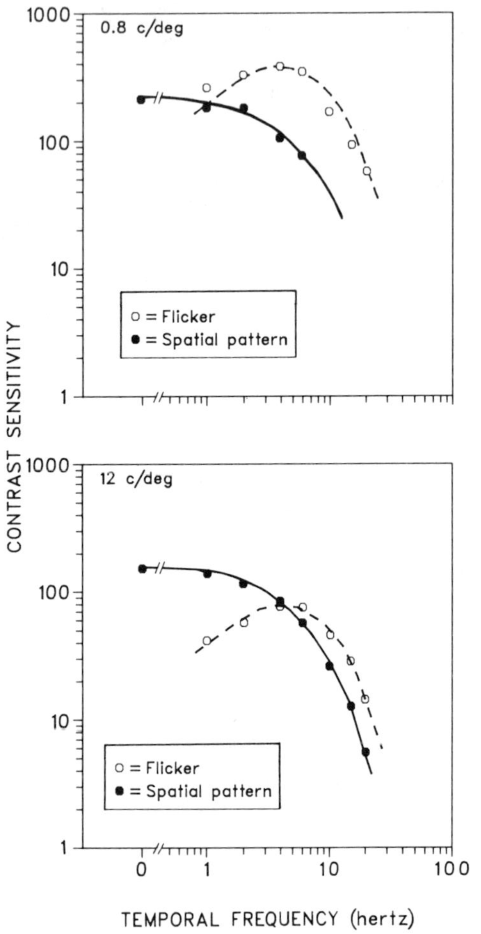

Figure 6.24. Temporal contrast sensitivity functions measured with flicker and pattern criteria. The spatial target was a sinusoidal grating of 0.8 (upper graph) or 12 cycles·degree^{-1} (lower graph). Temporal wave form was sinusoidal. Open symbols result when the observer is instructed to adjust contrast until the stimulus appears to "flicker"; filled symbols result when contrast is adjusted until "spatial pattern" is evident. The curves in the lower graph are the same as those in the upper graph but shifted vertically by different amounts. Flicker and pattern thresholds have different temporal contrast sensitivity functions which move independently with changes in spatial frequency. Flicker sensitivity is high at low spatial and high temporal frequencies; pattern sensitivity is high at high spatial and low temporal frequencies. (From J. J. Kulikowski & D. J. Tolhurst, Psychophysical evidence for sustained and transient mechanisms in human vision, *Journal of Physiology*, 1973, *232*. Reprinted with permission.)

this idea, they noted that a change in spatial frequency shifted each curve vertically, but did not change its shape. This meant that within each pathway, spatial and temporal sensitivities were separable. Furthermore, the vertical shifts were different for the two criteria, implying that the two mechanisms had different spatial sensitivities, the flicker mechanism being relatively more sensitive at low spatial frequencies and the pattern mechanism at high, in agreement with Figure 6.21.

King-Smith and Kulikowski (1975) used flicker and pattern criteria and the technique of subthreshold summation to examine the spatial selectivity of sustained and transient mechanisms. The receptive fields they inferred from their data were two to four times wider for the flicker than for the pattern criterion. This agrees with the generally higher spatial acuity of the pattern criterion (see Fig. 6.21).

Although the two sensations discussed are robust and vivid, a compelling argument that they are due to parallel independent mechanisms has not yet been provided. Furthermore, various results suggest that observers are not very good at describing their own threshold criteria, and that at threshold in the flicker regime observers retain some information about pattern, whereas in the pattern regime they retain information about temporal attributes.

Nachmias (1967) found "sustained" and "transient" threshold-duration functions at high and low spatial frequencies, respectively, even though he used forced choice between orthogonal orientations to measure threshold. If only sustained mechanisms convey pattern information, only sustained threshold duration curves should have been observed. Similarly, Derrington and Henning (1981) have shown that at both high and low rates of temporal modulation, thresholds for forced-choice discrimination between orientations of 0 and 90° are similar to thresholds for simple detection measured with a two-interval forced-choice method. When the rate of temporal modulation is high (10 Hz), the orientation thresholds show little decline in sensitivity at low spatial frequencies. If the mechanisms that detect low spatial, high temporal frequency stimuli conveyed no information about spatial pattern, they would be incapable of distinguishing between gratings at right angles, and threshold for this discrimination would be higher than for detection. As Derrington and Henning note, this result casts doubt upon the ability of the observer to describe the information present in a threshold stimulus, because their observers were unaware of spatial information in stimuli whose orientations they judged correctly.

Watson and Robson (1981) looked at discrimination at detection threshold between gratings of various spatial frequencies. Even when they were well within the transient regime (16 Hz), observers could discriminate perfectly between very different spatial frequencies. Again this suggests that if there are distinct transient mechanisms, they are not entirely without spatial selectivity.

9.4.2. Other Differences between Sustained and Transient Regimes. Although the experiments cited in Section 9.4.1.3 clearly indicate spatial selectivity in the mechanisms that operate in the transient regime, they do not imply that the spatial selectivity is the same as that in the "sustained" regime. For example, Derrington and Henning (1981) only examined discrimination between orthogonal gratings, and not between gratings at smaller angles. Sharpe and Tolhurst (1973) found that spatial adaptation had a considerably broader orientation bandwidth (22°) when the gratings drifted than when they were stationary (13°). Pantle (1973) examined summation between gratings an octave apart in spatial frequency and found more summation when the compound pattern moved than when it was stationary. Watson and Robson (1981) compared the relative discriminability of spatial frequency at threshold for gratings modulated at high and at low spatial frequencies. They found that discrimination was much poorer at high temporal frequencies; only an octave difference in spatial frequency was required for perfect discrimination at 0 Hz, but 2–3 octaves was required at 16 Hz. To summarize, the mechanisms that detect patterns at high temporal frequencies do not appear to be completely without spatial selectivity, but do seem to be less selective for spatial frequency and orientation than are the mechanisms that detect stationary or slowly moving patterns.

Another difference in the selectivities of the mechanisms that serve the "sustained" and "transient" regimes is that the latter are selective for direction of motion, whereas the former are not. E. Levinson and Sekuler (1975) showed that the sum of two gratings drifting in opposite directions (equal to a counterphase grating of twice the contrast) was little more visible than either component alone, as though each was detected by a separate direction-selective mechanism (see Section 10). Watson, Thompson, Murphy, and Nachmias (1980) showed that this result held only when the spatial frequency was low or the temporal frequency was high, that is, when the velocity was above about $1°\cdot sec^{-1}$. This corresponds closely to the "transient" regime as reflected by "flicker" sensations (see Figure 6.21). Watson et al. (1980) also showed that the observers were able to discriminate the direction of motion at detection threshold in the "transient" regime but not in the sustained regime. This is again consistent with the idea that the transient mechanisms respond selectively to motion, and signal motion to the observer.

10. IMAGE MOTION AND TEMPORAL SENSITIVITY

Much of the temporal variation in light intensity in natural visual experience arises from motions of objects or of the eye. In this section, we consider briefly some relationships between temporal sensitivity and sensitivity to image motion. The theory of motion sensing is dealt with at greater length in Watson and Ahumada (1983a, 1983b, 1985).

10.1. Moving Images

Consider an image as defined in Section 2 with a contrast distribution $C(x, y, t)$. Let the image be moved at a rate of $r°\cdot sec^{-1}$ in direction θ. The speed in the horizontal direction is $r_x = r \cos \theta$, and in the vertical direction, $r_y = r \sin \theta$. The contrast distribution in the moving image is then

$$C_{r,\theta}(x,y,t) = C(x - r_x t, y - r_y t, t) \ . \quad (64)$$

The three-dimensional Fourier transform of the original image can be written $\tilde{C}(u, v, w)$, where u and v are horizontal and vertical spatial frequency in cycles·degree^{-1} and w is temporal frequency in hertz. This (complex) transform describes the spatial and temporal frequencies that make up the image. The transform of the moving image is then

$$\tilde{C}_{r,\theta}(u,v,w) = \tilde{C}(u, v, w + r_x u + r_y v) \ . \quad (65)$$

Thus moving an image does not introduce new spatial frequencies, but rather alters the temporal frequency associated with each spatial frequency component. For example, if the original image is constant in time ($w = 0$ Hz for all u,v), then movement imparts to each spatial frequency a temporal frequency equal to the inner product of velocity (r_x, r_y) and spatial frequency (u, v), that is, $r_x u + y_y v$. This is equivalent to the product of the spatial frequency and the component of the velocity in the direction of the spatial frequency. In the simple case of a vertical sinusoidal grating of frequency u cycles·degree^{-1} moving horizontally at speed $r°\cdot sec^{-1}$, the resulting temporal frequency is ru. This is the rate at which contrast will vary over time at any point in the image.

Equation (65) states the fundamental relationship between the velocity of an image and its temporal frequency components. It forms a general basis for understanding the relationship between sensitivity to temporal fluctuations and to moving patterns.

10.2. Direction Selectivity

A mechanism is *direction selective* if it responds primarily or exclusively to movement of a pattern in one direction but not in another. In view of the eye's evolutionary adaptation to its environment, we might expect it to be optimized for the analysis of motion, and hence to contain direction-selective mechanisms. A review of the literature on direction selectivity is given by Sekuler (1975). Evidence for direction selectivity is of three sorts: subthreshold summation, adaptation, and discrimination at threshold.

10.2.1. Subthreshold Summation. E. Levinson and Sekuler (1975) noted that a sinusoidal grating modulated sinusoidally in time is equal to the sum of two gratings with half as much contrast moving in opposite directions,

$$\cos(2\pi ux)\cos(2\pi rut) = {}^1\!/_2\{\cos[2\pi u(x - rt)] + \cos[2\pi u(x + rt)]\} \ , \quad (66)$$

where r is the speed of motion. A direction-selective mechanism would respond to only one or the other of the two moving components. Thus if the counterphase grating is detected by a direction-selective mechanism, it should have a threshold about twice that for either of the drifting components. Their data were largely consistent with this direction-selective prediction.

Using a forced-choice method, Watson et al. (1980) tested this prediction at a wider range of spatial and temporal frequencies. They found it held only when the velocity was above about $1°\cdot sec^{-1}$. At lower velocities, moving and counterphase thresholds were more nearly equal. They proposed that within this latter range the stimuli were detected by nondirection-selective mechanisms. These two regimes correspond roughly to the sustained and transient regimes discussed in Section 9.4, which supports a suggestion of E. Levinson and Sekuler (1975) that the direction-selective mechanisms are part of the transient system.

These important results further constrain any model of temporal sensitivity. It must acknowledge that temporal fluctuations with a "velocity" above 1 cycle·degree^{-1} are detected by direction-selective mechanisms. This is a further nonlinearity in the detection pathway, because in a direction-selective system, response to left and rightward moving stimuli will fail to add. This is so even though each direction-selective mechanism by itself may be linear. A model of a linear direction-selective mechanism is given in Section 10.3.

10.2.2. Discrimination at Threshold. If two stimuli are detected by different labeled mechanisms, they should be discriminated as well as they are detected (see Section 3.6). By this logic, if gratings are detected by direction-selective mechanisms, two gratings that drift in opposite directions should be identified as well as they are detected. Watson et al. (1980) tested this prediction by measuring separate thresholds for detecting and identifying the direction of a grating moving in either of two opposite directions. As shown in Figure 6.25, thresholds for detecting and for identifying the direction are about equal at 2 cycles·degree^{-1} regardless of the temporal frequency, and at 8 cycles·degree^{-1} when the temporal frequency is high. These are roughly the same conditions in which subthreshold summation shows direction-selective results. These

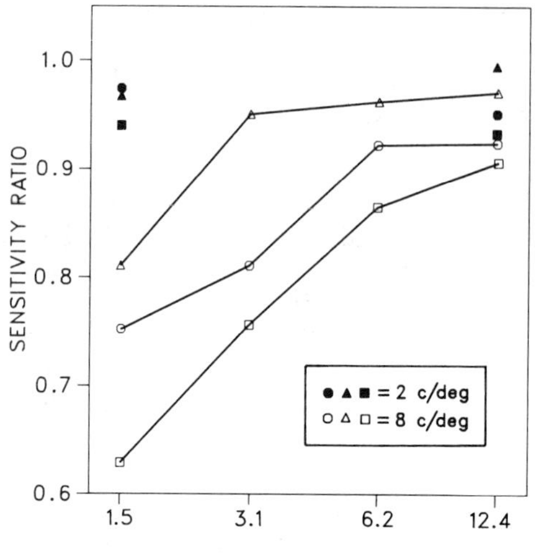

Figure 6.25. Ratio of thresholds for detecting and for identifying the direction of a moving grating. Each trial consisted of two intervals; in one a grating moved either to the left or the right. The observer reported the interval containing the grating, and the grating direction. Detection thresholds were estimated from interval judgments, identification thresholds from direction judgments. Open symbols are for 8 cycles·degree^{-1}, filled symbols are for 2 cycles·degree^{-1}. Different symbols are for three different observers. Detection and identification thresholds are about equal except when the spatial frequency is high and the temporal frequency is low, that is, at low velocities. (From A. B. Watson, P. G. Thompson, B. J. Murphy, & J. Nachmias, Summation of gratings moving in opposite directions, *Vision Research, 20*. Copyright 1980 by Pergamon Press, Ltd. Reprinted with permission.)

results are consistent with the existence of direction-selective mechanisms at medium to high velocities and nondirection-selective mechanisms at low. However, when the velocity is low, the retinal velocity of the target may be due more to eye movements than to motions of the target, thus preventing correct identification of direction. This possibility has been excluded by Mansfield and Nachmias (1981), who showed that the results of Watson et al. (1980) are essentially unaltered by image stabilization.

10.2.3. Adaptation. Following adaptation to a leftward moving grating, threshold is elevated more for a leftward-moving grating than for a rightward-moving grating (Pantle & Sekuler, 1969; Sekuler & Ganz, 1963; Tolhurst, 1973). This is consistent with the idea that the leftward-moving grating selectively excites, and adapts, a mechanism selective for leftward motion. The smaller threshold elevation in the unadapted direction is usually attributed to a nondirection-selective element in the pathway prior to the direction-selective stage (E. Levinson & Sekuler, 1975).

10.2.4. Summary. For grating stimuli, detection in one regime appears to be direction selective, and in the other regime, nondirection selective. These two regimes correspond roughly to the "transient" and "sustained" regimes, respectively. In light of the evidence that many, perhaps all, stimuli are detected by the same mechanisms that detect gratings (N. Graham, 1977), this suggests that many of the stimuli used to study temporal sensitivity are detected by direction-selective mechanisms. This view is not inconsistent with the working model used throughout this chapter, because the nonlinearity implicit in direction selectivity can be part of the threshold process. However, it does require that models of temporal sensitivity take on an explicitly spatiotemporal character when they wish to explain the visibility of targets that move. Section 10.3 shows how this may be done.

10.3. Model of a Motion Sensor

To answer the need for an explicit theory of sensitivity to moving stimuli, Watson and Ahumada (1983a, 1983b, 1985) have constructed a model of a direction-selective motion sensor. The sensor is a linear spatiotemporal filter with a temporal amplitude response equal to that of the working model described in Section 4. The spatial amplitude response is a Gaussian, centered on a frequency of u, v, with a bandwidth of 1 octave. The impulse response is approximately a patch of sinusoidal grating moving briefly in a direction orthogonal to its bars. The sensor is selective for direction, but also for spatial frequency, orientation, and location. Each sensor is a discrete entity located at a point, and the visual field is imagined to be covered by sensors at different locations, orientations, and spatial frequencies.

When stimulated by targets that are separable in space and time, this sensor behaves identically to the linear filter of the working model. The motion sensor may be regarded as a version of the working model in which selectivity for direction and for spatial frequency have been made explicit.

A second, nonlinear stage of the model uses the output of the linear sensors to estimate the two-dimensional velocity of image components localized in space and spatial frequency (Watson & Ahumada, 1985). However, the spatial and temporal sensitivities of the model are governed by the first stage, so that the second stage is beyond the scope of this chapter.

10.4. Stroboscopic Apparent Motion

Stroboscopic apparent motion is the illusion of smooth motion produced by a rapid sequence of static views of an object in motion, as in movies and television. Recently, this phenomenon has been reexamined (Morgan 1980; Watson & Ahumada, 1982; Watson, Ahumada, & Farrell, 1983). Watson and colleagues have explained the relationship between this illusion and the spatial and temporal sensitivity of the eye. They note that in a plot of the spatiotemporal frequency domain, with u running horizontally and w vertically, the spectrum of a line moving to the left with velocity r is a line impulse passing through the origin with slope $-r$. The spectrum of stroboscopic motion is the same, with the addition of parallel replicas at intervals of the strobe frequency (Crick, Marr, & Poggio, 1981, made the same observation). They reason that these replicas will be ineffective, and smooth and stroboscopic motion will appear identical, when the replicas lie outside the region of spatial and temporal frequency to which the eye is sensitive. They note that to a first approximation, this region is a rectangle with halfwidth of $\hat{w}$ Hz and halfheight of $\hat{u}$ cycles·degree^{-1} (see Fig. 6.21). This leads to the prediction that, for smooth and strobed lines to appear identical, the strobe rate must be greater than or equal to $\hat{w} + \hat{u}r$. Figure 6.26 shows the success of these predictions for two observers. For both observers, the temporal frequency limit is about 30 Hz, which is a good estimate of the CFF under their conditions. The spatial limits are 13 cycles·degree^{-1} (ABW) and 6 cycles·degree^{-1} (JEF), which are low but not unreasonable, given the brief exposure, low contrast, and other masking components. In conclusion, stroboscopic apparent motion can be qualitatively explained in terms of the known temporal and spatial filtering action of the eye. From a practical point of view, this explanation provides a formula

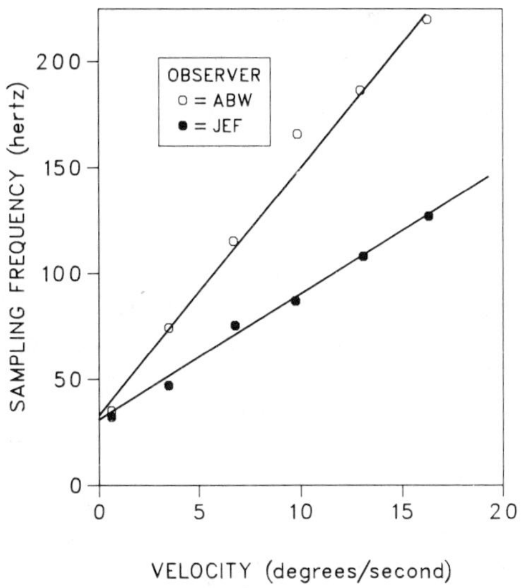

Figure 6.26. Critical temporal sampling frequency as a function of velocity for a moving line. Critical sampling frequency is the lowest rate at which the image can be time-sampled (strobed) keeping smooth and strobed motion indistinguishable. Critical sampling frequency was measured by means of a forced-choice task in which the observer selected which of two presentations he or she believed to be strobed. The stimulus was a vertical line 50 min in length and 0.65 min wide which moved horizontally at the specified velocity (r). Observers fixated a point in the center of the path of travel. The distance traveled was $\sqrt{r}$ 5/4° and the duration $5/(4\sqrt{r})$ sec. Background intensity was 50 cd·m^{-2}. The straight lines are fitted by eye, and are consistent with the hypothesis that stroboscopic apparent motion is due to spatial and temporal filtering by the visual system. The slope and intercept of the line are estimates of the spatial and temporal frequency limits of the filter. For both observers, the intercept is about 30 Hz; the slopes are 6 cycles· degree^{-1} (JEF) and 13 cycles·degree^{-1} (ABW). (From Watson, Ahumada, & Farrell, 1983.)

that can be used to specify the temporal strobe rate required to display any particular moving image.

11. LIGHT ADAPTATION AND TEMPORAL SENSITIVITY

11.1. Background

The sensitivity of the eye declines as the average level of illumination increases, and this phenomenon is referred to as *light adaptation.* A comprehensive discussion of light adaptation is provided by Barlow (1972) (also see Hood & Finkelstein, Chapter 5, and Pokorny & Smith, Chapter 8). The degree of adaptation is not the same for all stimuli, and this has made the subject a matter of continuing interest in all areas of vision research. This is certainly true in the area of temporal sensitivity, in which the amount of adaptation depends upon the temporal wave form of the stimulus. For example, light adaptation has a greater effect on low temporal frequencies than on high, and on long pulses than on short. The following sections document some of these results, and show that they may have a common interpretation in terms of a linear model whose parameters depend upon background intensity.

11.2. Intensity and Contrast Thresholds

Recall that target contrast is defined as target intensity divided by background intensity. This creates a possible source of confusion in discussing light adaptation, because contrast and intensity thresholds change at different rates as a function of background intensity. For example, if intensity thresholds rise in proportion to background, contrast thresholds remain constant, whereas if intensity thresholds remain constant, contrast thresholds decline in proportion to background intensity. In general, if the slope of the relation between log intensity threshold and log background is S, then that between log contrast threshold and log background is $S - 1$. Similar rules apply for sensitivity, defined as the inverse of threshold. For example, the slope relating log intensity sensitivity and log background would be $-S$, and that between log contrast sensitivity and log background would be $1 - S$.

11.3. Weber, de Vries-Rose, and Linear Laws

As background intensity is raised from zero, thresholds usually pass in sequence through three regimes. In the first, threshold intensity is unaltered by background intensity. This regime is called *linear*, because the principle of superposition, as applied to target and background, is upheld. The second regime, which has considerable theoretical importance but few empirical instances, is the *de Vries-Rose law*, in which the intensity threshold rises as the square root of background intensity (de Vries, 1942; Rose, 1942). This is the behavior expected of an ideal detector limited only by quantum fluctuations (though it may also be generated by quite different processes). Note that de Vries-Rose behavior may be exhibited by a detector whose responses, prior to the decision stage, are linear. Thus the "linear" designation applied to the previous regime should not be taken too literally. In the third regime, intensity thresholds rise in proportion to the background intensity. This is the well-known *Weber law.* In a plot of log threshold intensity versus log background intensity, these three laws are straight lines with slopes of 0, ½, and 1, respectively. In a plot of log contrast sensitivity, they are transformed into straight lines of slope 1, ½, and 0. These three sorts of adaptation behaviors are sketched in the insets to Figure 6.27. As with most sensory "laws," these rules should be regarded only as prototypes, which approximate the data within some regime.

11.4. Sinusoidal Wave Forms

Figure 6.27 illustrates some general properties of the effect of background intensity upon temporal sensitivity. (1) Intensity thresholds rise with increasing background intensity. (2) The rate of rise increases as background increases. This rate of rise is approximately consistent with the linear law at the lowest backgrounds, with the de Vries-Rose law at intermediate backgrounds, and with the Weber law at the highest backgrounds. (3) The rate of rise is greater at low temporal frequencies than at high. Consequently, the Weber regime begins at a lower background for lower temporal frequencies.

There is a lower limit to the background intensity that may be used to measure thresholds for sinusoidal targets, reached when background intensity and threshold intensity are equal. The linear region, when it is present, extends from this lowest usable background up no farther than 1.5 log units. The de Vries-Rose law appears only as a brief transition between linear and Weber regions.

Another perspective on the relations among contrast sensitivity, temporal frequency, and background intensity is provided in Figure 6.28. Each curve links points of equal contrast

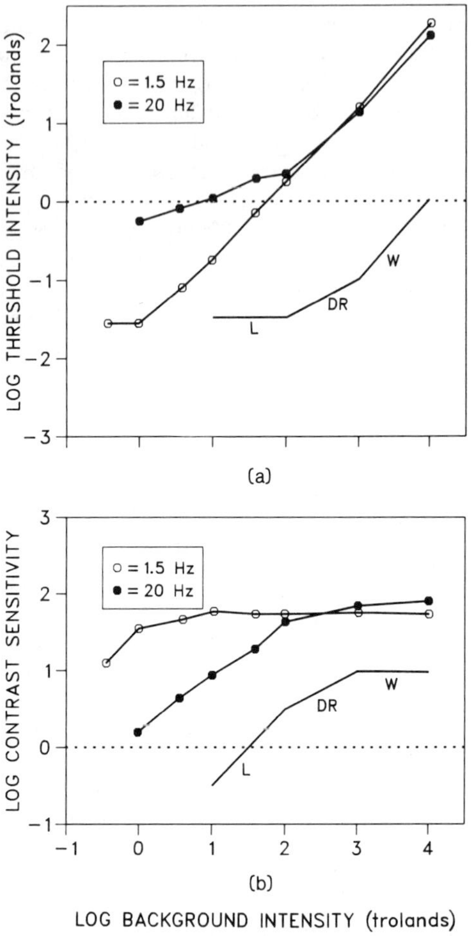

Figure 6.27. Threshold as a function of background intensity. The temporal wave form was sinusoidal at 1.5 or 20 Hz. The spatial target was a 2° disk with no surround. Thresholds were measured by adjustment. The same data are plotted both as intensity thresholds (a) and contrast sensitivities (b). The small insets show the log-log slopes corresponding to linear (L), de Vries-Rose (DR), and Weber (W) laws. The data pass in sequence through each of the laws. At the lower temporal frequency adaptation is more pronounced and the Weber law regime is entered at a lower background intensity (data from de Lange, 1958).

sensitivity. The outermost curve, for a sensitivity of 1, represents the CFF. It grows roughly in proportion to log background intensity, as prescribed by the Ferry-Porter law. This figure also illustrates the relative insensitivity of low frequencies to background intensity, and the enlarged bandwidth at higher backgrounds.

Because light adaptation affects each temporal frequency differently, the TCSF changes shape as background intensity is altered. This is evident in Figures 6.7, 6.28, and 6.29. At the lowest backgrounds, it is "low-pass" in form, showing relative attenuation only at high frequencies. As background intensity is increased, low temporal frequencies move quickly into the Weber regime and show no further improvement in contrast sensitivity. The high frequencies, on the other hand, continue to gain in sensitivity so that the relative attenuation at low frequencies becomes pronounced, and a clear peak in sensitivity emerges at a middle frequency. Furthermore, as backgrounds become more intense, higher frequencies show greater gains in contrast sensitivity. One by one the lower frequencies reach their Weber regime and cease to improve, whereas higher frequencies continue to accrue sensitivity. As a result, the peak in sensitivity increases and moves to higher and higher frequencies, the high-frequency limb moves progressively rightward, and the overall bandwidth of the TCSF is enlarged. These effects agree with the common observation that the light-adapted eye is "faster" and more "transient." In terms of the working model, these changes correspond to a decrease in the time constant (τ), an increase in the transience parameter (ζ), and an increase in sensitivity (ξ) as background is increased.

An alternative view of data like those in Figure 6.28 is given in Figure 6.29. The data in panel (a) of this figure are the same as those in Figure 6.7, but are plotted here as intensity sensitivities rather than contrast sensitivities, achieved by simply dividing each contrast sensitivity by the corresponding background intensity. In log-log coordinates, these divisions correspond to vertical shifts. Despite substantial differences in experimental conditions, and differing behavior at the low frequencies, all three experiments show that, as noted by Kelly (1961a) and J. Z. Levinson and Harmon (1961), above about 1 td all the data appear to approach a common curve. Where

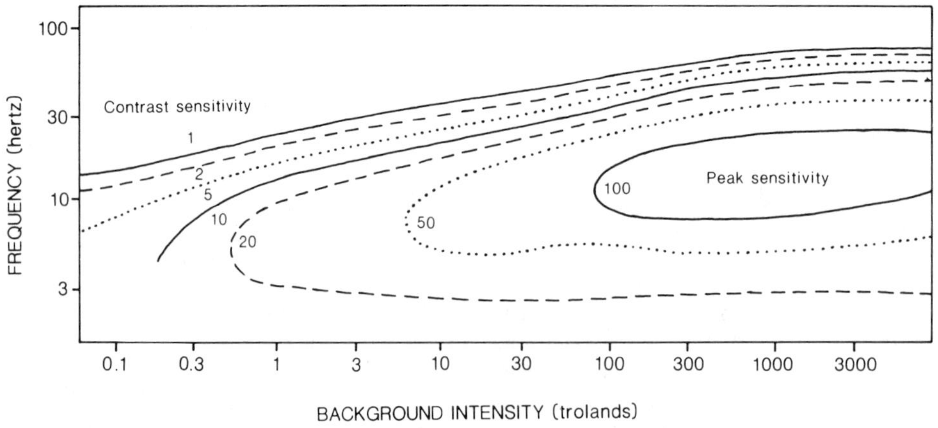

Figure 6.28. Temporal contrast sensitivity as a function of frequency and background intensity. Each line is an isosensitivity curve, obtained by interpolation from data of Figure 6.29, joining points of equal contrast sensitivity. The contrast sensitivity associated with each curve is indicated on the figure. Target was a 60° disk with no surround, modulated sinusoidally. Monocular viewing with a 1.55-mm-diameter artificial pupil. The CFF is indicated by the outermost curve labeled "1." As background intensity increases, peak sensitivity and the CFF move to higher frequencies; sensitivity at low temporal frequencies remains more or less constant. (From D. H. Kelly, Visual responses to time-dependent stimuli, *Journal of the Optical Society of America, 1961, 51*. Reprinted with permission.)

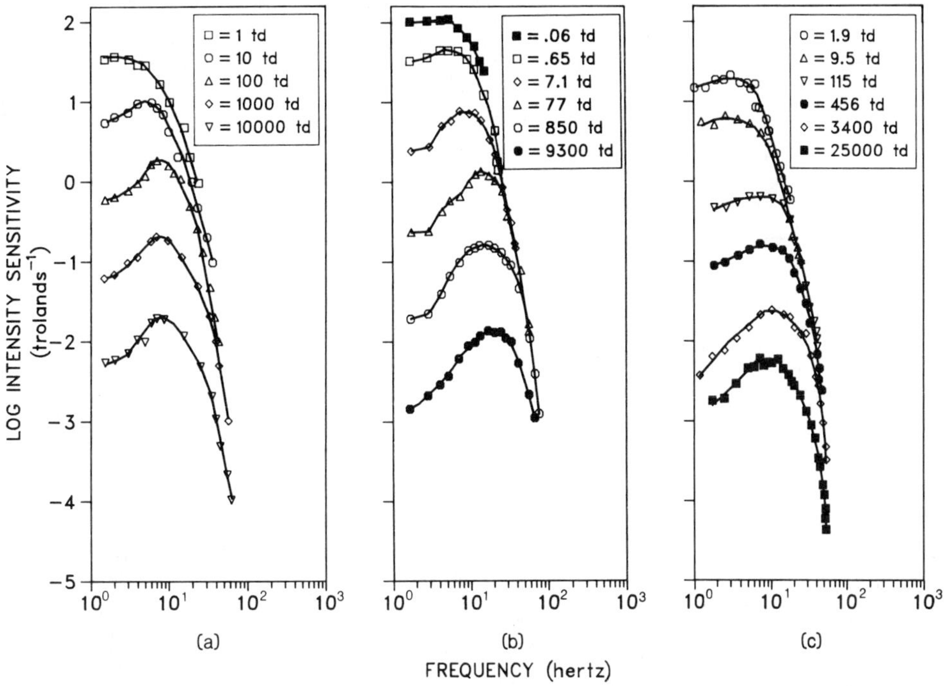

Figure 6.29. Intensity sensitivity as a function of temporal frequency at various background intensities. (a) de Lange (1958), observer V, 2° disk, no surround; (b) Kelly (1961a), 60° disk, no surround; (c) Roufs (1972a), observer HJM, 1° disk, no surround. Increasing background intensity reduces intensity sensitivity at all except the highest frequencies. At the highest temporal frequencies, the curves for different background intensities approach a common curve. This illustrates that at the very highest temporal frequencies, the system approaches linear adaptation behavior.

curves for two adaptation levels coincide, then over that region of frequency and background intensity, thresholds obey the linear rule (Kelly, 1961a). Note, however, that at any given frequency, the linear rule extends, if at all, only over a small range of backgrounds from the lowest upon which it is visible up by 1 log unit or less. Beyond that point, sensitivity moves towards the Weber law. Likewise, at any given background, only a very small range of frequencies will be included in the linear regime, extending down from the CFF. Kelly (1969a) and Kelly and Wilson (1978) have attributed this linear high-frequency asymptote to a diffusion process (see Section 5.11).

Because a large part of the effect of light adaptation takes the form of vertical and horizontal shifts of the high-frequency limb of the TCSF, we might expect that suitable scaling of frequency and sensitivity (equivalent to horizontal and vertical displacements in log-log coordinates) would approximately superimpose the TCSFs measured at different background intensities. Roufs has attempted this exercise, with the results shown in Figure 6.30. The curves agree only to within a factor of about 5, the largest discrepancies being at the lower temporal frequencies. Furthermore, Roufs used a small target and no surround. Use of a surround and/or a larger target (as in the data of de Lange and Kelly in Fig. 6.29), would produce still larger discrepancies at low frequencies. The scaling does not work well at low temporal frequencies because, as we have seen, the TCSF becomes more transient at high backgrounds, and this change is not included in the scaling operations performed in Figure 6.30. Nevertheless this scaling procedure provides a useful condensation of at least the high-frequency data, and Roufs has shown how it provides a qualitative explanation of the luminance dependence of pulse thresholds (see Section 6.5.3).

11.5. Pulse Wave Forms

As shown in Section 6, the function relating threshold to duration for a rectangular pulse (the threshold-duration curve) has an initial segment that falls with a slope of −1, and a second segment that falls at a more gradual rate. The transition between these two segments occurs at the critical duration T_c with intensity threshold I_c (the critical intensity). A rough summary of the effect of light adaptation upon pulse thresholds can therefore be obtained from plots of T_c and I_c as functions of background intensity. These are seen in Figure 6.31, which shows that critical duration declines as background intensity is raised, going from about 100 msec at 0 log td to about 25 msec at 4 log td. The figure also shows the differences that may be expected between observers in the same or different laboratories, and the degree of precision with which statements may be made about critical duration. Because both are measures of the time scale of the temporal response, we might expect a simple relation between the critical duration and the corner frequency of the TCSF. In particular, Section 6.5.3 gives theoretical reasons why these two quantities should be inversely related. Roufs (1972a) has shown that they are, and this may be appreciated by comparison of Figures 6.30 and 6.31.

Just as the adaptational changes in the TCSF cannot be captured completely by scaling of sensitivity and corner frequency, so too changes in the threshold-duration curve are not completely characterized by changes in critical duration and critical intensity. In both cases, the missing parameter is the transience, which also increases with background intensity. As noted in Section 6.5.2, a transient system shows little or no improvement in sensitivity beyond the critical duration, whereas

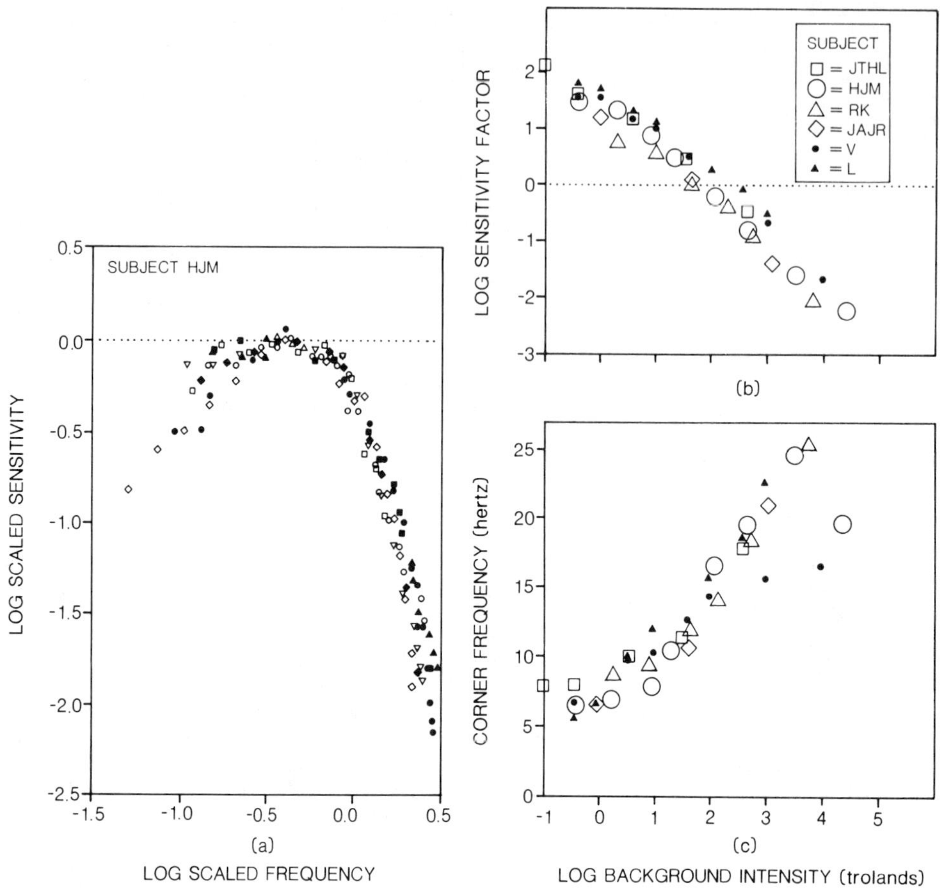

Figure 6.30. Temporal contrast sensitivity functions at different background intensities shifted so as to approximately superpose. (a) Log-scaled sensitivity as a function of log-scaled temporal frequency. Scaled sensitivity is intensity sensitivity divided by a sensitivity factor; scaled temporal frequency is frequency divided by a corner frequency. The sensitivity factor is determined by shifting the curve for each background intensity vertically until it has a peak sensitivity of 1; corner frequency was determined by then shifting each curve horizontally until it had a sensitivity of 0.5 at a frequency of 1. Different symbols are for different background intensities. The curves superimpose reasonably well at high temporal frequencies, but poorly at low. Data from observer HJM. (b) Sensitivity factor as a function of background intensity. (c) Corner frequency as a function of background intensity. (b) and (c) include data of four observers from Roufs (1972a) and two from de Lange (1958). Circles are derived from (a). This figure illustrates that much of the change in the TCSF with background intensity may be expressed as a change in overall sensitivity (a vertical shift) and a change in the corner frequency (an horizontal shift). Sensitivity declines and the corner frequency increases as background increases. (From J. A. J. Roufs, Dynamic properties of vision—I. Experimental relationships between flicker and flash thresholds, *Vision Research, 12*. Copyright 1972 by Pergamon Press, Ltd. Reprinted with permission.)

a sustained system continues to improve at a rate of about 0.25 in log-log coordinates. Thus we expect the second limb of the threshold-duration curve to be somewhat flatter at higher background intensities than at low. This trend is evident in Barlow's data shown in Figure 6.11.

11.6. Other Wave Forms

At very low background intensities (below 1 td) some authors have found that the threshold for a decrement may be as much as 0.3 log unit less than for an increment. This difference tends to disappear at more intense backgrounds.

Pulse-pair thresholds (see Section 7) show the effect of light adaptation in two ways. First, as background intensity increases, the time scale of the results is compressed so that, for example, the delay, at which threshold for an opposite-signed pair is least, moves from about 50 msec at 328 td to about 70 msec at 61.2 td (Ikeda, 1965; Uetsuki & Ikeda, 1970). Second, on less intense backgrounds, the second, negative lobe of the L_D function is reduced or absent. This effect is evident in data of Uetsuki and Ikeda (1970). Because this second lobe is associated with the transience of the linear model, this result is consistent with an increasing degree of transience as background level is raised. This result agrees with observations made with sinusoids and pulses. Roufs (1974a) has also studied the effects of light adaptation upon pulse-pair thresholds.

11.7. Spatial Effects

As noted in Section 9, temporal contrast sensitivity is not separable from the spatial configuration of target and surround. Likewise, the effects of adaptation upon temporal sensitivity

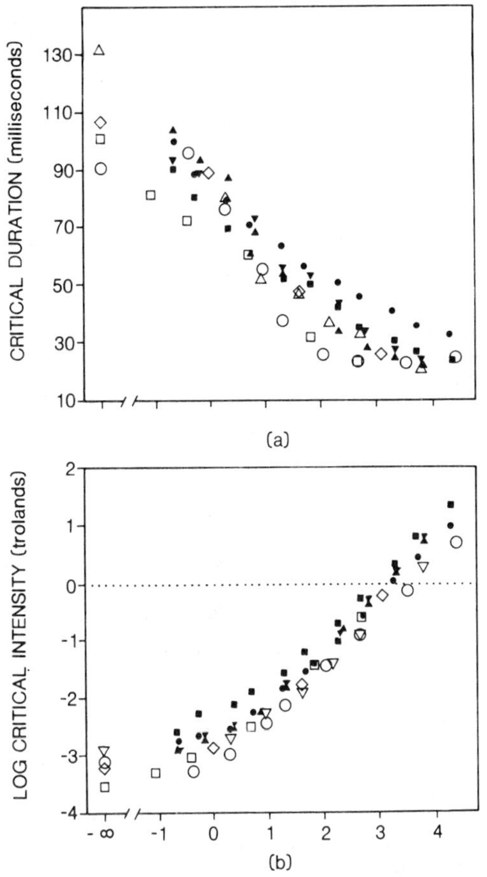

Figure 6.31. Critical duration T_c (a) and critical intensity I_c (b) as functions of background intensity. Critical duration is the longest duration of a rectangular pulse for which reciprocity holds between intensity and duration (Bloch's law). The critical intensity is the threshold intensity at the critical duration. Filled circles are averages of eight subjects of C. H. Graham and Kemp (1938), filled square are average of two subjects of Keller (1941), filled triangles are two subjects of Herrick (1956), open symbols are subjects from Roufs (1972a). Target was a 1° hemidisk (C. H. Graham & Kemp, 1938; Keller, 1941) or a 1° disk (Herrick, 1956; Roufs, 1972a). Critical duration declines from about 100 msec at 0 log td to about 25 msec at 4 log td. Critical intensity increases with background intensity, entering a Weber regime at the more intense backgrounds. (From J. A. J. Roufs, Dynamic properties of vision—I. Experimental relationships between flicker and flash thresholds, *Vision Research, 12*. Copyright 1972 by Pergamon Press, Ltd. Reprinted with permission.)

depend upon spatial configuration. I have suggested that many of the complex spatial effects may be understood by considering the visually effective spatial frequency of the target. To this point, only disk targets have been considered. For a disk target, this frequency is generally low, and may be lowered by enlarging the disk or removing the surround. Consequently, we might expect that data for low spatial frequency grating targets would resemble thresholds for disks.

The first experiments to consider the different effects of background intensity on the TCSF at low and high spatial frequencies were conducted by van Nes et al. (1967). Their measurements were made with drifting, rather than sinusoidally modulated gratings, but as noted in Section 10, thresholds for these two stimuli agree to within a factor of 2. As expected, at a low spatial frequency (0.64 cycles·degree^{-1}) their data show a progressively stronger attenuation at low temporal frequencies as background level is raised. At 11 cycles·degree^{-1}, however, this feature is absent. Above about 1 td, background intensity merely shifts the curve vertically and horizontally with little change in shape. Data from Kelly (1972a), some of which are shown in Figure 6.32, confirm these observations. One way of describing the interaction between spatial configuration and light adaptation is that if the effective spatial frequency is low, the transience increases with background intensity; if the effective spatial frequency is high, the system is sustained at all background intensities.

Kelly's data also show that at low spatial frequencies, as with disk targets, the adaptive response proceeds from a Weber law at low temporal frequencies to a linear rule near to the CFF, passing through an intermediate regime at middle frequencies. Kelly's data suggest that at higher spatial frequencies the intermediate de Vries-Rose regime is enlarged, so that the linear regime may be absent altogether and the Weber regime present only at the highest backgrounds.

11.8. Summary

The following is a summary of the effects of background intensity on temporal contrast sensitivity. The "strength" of adaptation can be characterized by the slope of the relation between log threshold intensity and log background. This is equivalent to the exponent of a power law relating these two quantities. As we have seen, this slope is bounded by values of 0 (linear regime) and 1 (Weber regime). We note the following trends in the strength of adaptation:

1. As background intensity increases, strength increases.
2. As temporal frequency increases, strength decreases.
3. As spatial frequency increases, strength decreases.

Regarding the form of the TCSF, as background intensity is increased, the following occur:

1. Contrast sensitivity increases.
2. Corner frequency increases.
3. Transience increases.

12. SUMMARY

This chapter reviews a small part of the very large literature on human visual temporal sensitivity. An effort has been made to show that the visibility of many different wave forms, both periodic and aperiodic, can be understood in the context of a rather simple model of temporal sensitivity. Some of the effects of spatial configuration and background intensity upon temporal sensitivity have also been examined.

Much of experimental and theoretical effort in this area has been spent finding ever better mathematical representations of the relation between the stimulus temporal wave form $I(t)$ and threshold, and of including ever more refined parametric effects of spatial wave form and background intensity. This endeavor now seems largely complete. A model like the one proposed in Section 4 seems likely to provide a fairly complete quantitative account of the visibility of arbitrary temporal wave forms.

However, a major task for the future will be the integration of models of temporal sensitivity with models of spatial and chromatic sensitivity. We may expect future theoretical developments also to include physiological explanations of temporal

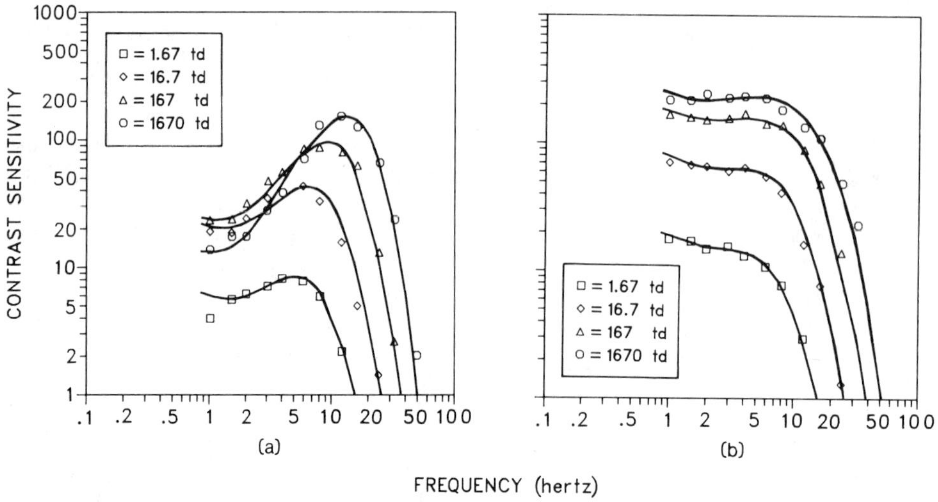

Figure 6.32. The temporal contrast sensitivity function for a uniform field (a) and a 3 cycles·degree^{-1} grating (b) at various background intensities. Data for the uniform field show increasing attenuation at low temporal frequencies as background intensity increases, but data for 3 cycles·degree^{-1} do not. This illustrates that the changes in shape of the TCSF due to adaptation occur primarily at low spatial frequencies. At a low temporal frequency, the adaptation effect is stronger for low spatial frequencies than for high. Background intensities were 1.67 (squares), 16.7 (diamonds), 167 (triangles), and 1670 td (circles). Monocular viewing, 7° circular target, 2.3-mm artificial pupil. Solid lines are from a model proposed by Kelly (1971b). (From D. H. Kelly, Adaptation effects on spatio-temporal sine-wave thresholds, *Vision Research, 12*. Copyright 1972 by Pergamon Press, Ltd. Reprinted with permission.)

sensitivity (which cells do what, and why?). We may hope for a better understanding of sustained and transient channels in human vision. Do they exist, what are their roles, and how are they involved in the processing of temporal, spatial, motion, and chromatic information? An area largely untouched in this chapter that seems likely to receive more attention in the future is the relation between wavelength and temporal sensitivity. This includes the wavelength distribution when it is constant (separable from the temporal wave form) and when it changes as a function of time. Another challenge is the effect of temporal wave form upon color discrimination.

Finally, we are likely to see less emphasis upon sensitivity per se and more upon visual information processing of suprathreshold temporal and spatiotemporal stimuli. A prime example is the study of how we deduce the speed and direction of motion of objects from the spatiotemporal intensity distribution I (*x, y, t*) (Fahle & Poggio, 1981; Watson & Ahumada, 1983a, 1983b, 1985).

REFERENCE NOTE

1. Watson, A. B. Unpublished observations on summation between pulse pairs as a function of delay and spatial frequency.

REFERENCES

Arend, L. E. Response of the human eye to spatially sinusoidal gratings at various exposure durations. *Vision Research*, 1976, *16*, 1311–1317.

Barlow, H. B. Temporal and spatial summation in human vision at different background intensities. *Journal of Physiology*, 1958, *141*, 337–350.

Barlow, H. B. Dark and light adaptation: Psychophysics. In L. Hurvich & D. Jameson (Eds.), *Handbook of sensory physiology*. New York: Springer-Verlag, 1972.

Baumgardt, E., & Hillman, B. Duration and size as determinants of peripheral retinal response. *Journal of the Optical Society of America*, 1961, *51*, 340–344.

Blackwell, H. R. Neural theories of simple visual discrimination. *Journal of the Optical Society of America*, 1963, *53*, 129–160.

Bloch, A. M. Experience sur la vision. *Comptes Rendus de la Société de Biologie (Paris)*, 1885, *37*, 493–495.

Bouman, M. A. Peripheral contrast thresholds of the human eye. *Journal of the Optical Society of America*, 1950, *40*, 825–832.

Bouman, M. A., & van den Brink, G. On the integrative capacity in time and space of the human peripheral retina. *Journal of the Optical Society of America*, 1952, *42*, 617–620.

Boynton, R. M., Ikeda, M., & Stiles, W. S. Interactions among chromatic mechanisms as inferred from positive and negative increment thresholds. *Vision Research*, 1964, *4*, 87–117.

Bracewell, R. *The Fourier transform and its applications*. New York: McGraw-Hill, 1978.

Breitmeyer, B. G. Simple reaction time as a measure of the temporal response properties of transient and sustained channels. *Vision Research*, 1975, *15*, 1411–1412.

Breitmeyer, B. G., & Ganz, L. Temporal studies with flashed gratings: Inference about human transient and sustained channels. *Vision Research*, 1977, *17*, 861–865.

Breitmeyer, B. G., & Julesz, B. The role of on and off transients in determining the psychophysical spatial frequency response. *Vision Research*, 1975, *15*, 411–415.

Brindley, G. S. The Bunsen-Roscoe law for the human eye for very short durations. *Journal of Physiology*, 1952, *118*, 135–139.

Broekhuijsen, M., Rashbass, C., & Veringa, F. The threshold of visual transients. *Vision Research*, 1976, *16*, 1285–1289.

Burbeck, C., & Kelly, D. H. Spatiotemporal characteristics of visual mechanisms: Excitatory-inhibitory model. *Journal of the Optical Society of America*, 1980, *70*, 1121–1126.

Burbeck, C., & Kelly, D. H. A mechanism in the distal retina that accounts for the fading of stabilized images. *Supplement to Investigative Ophthalmology & Visual Science*, 1982, *22*, 50.

Cleland, B. G., Dubin, M. W., & Levick, W. R. Sustained and transient neurones in the cat's retina and lateral geniculate nucleus. *Journal of Physiology*, 1971, *217*, 473–496.

Cohn, T. E. A new hypothesis to explain why the increment threshold exceeds the decrement threshold. *Vision Research*, 1974, *14*, 1277–1279.

Crick, F. H. C., Marr, D. C., & Poggio, T. An information processing approach to understanding the visual cortex. In F. O. Schmitt, F. G. Worden, G. Adelman, & S. G. Dennis (Eds.), *The organization of the cerebral cortex*. Cambridge: MIT Press, 1981.

de Lange, H. Experiments on flicker and some calculations on an electrical analogue of the foveal systems. *Physica*, 1952, *18*, 935–950.

de Lange, H. Relationship between critical flicker frequency and a set of low frequency characteristics of the eye. *Journal of the Optical Society of America*, 1954, *44*, 380–389.

de Lange, H. Research into the dynamic nature of the human fovea-cortex systems with intermittent and modulated light. I. Attenuation characteristics with white and colored light. *Journal of the Optical Society of America*, 1958, *48*, 777–784.

Derrington, A. M., & Henning, G. B. Pattern discrimination with flickering stimuli. *Vision Research*, 1981, *21*, 597–602.

de Vries, H. The quantum character of light and its bearing upon the threshold of vision, the differential sensitivity and visual acuity of the eye. *Physica*, 1942, *10*, 553.

Fahle, M., & Poggio, T. Visual hyperacuity: Spatiotemporal interpolation in human vision. *Proceedings of the Royal Society of London*, 1981, *B213*, 451–477.

Ferry, E. S. Persistence of vision. *American Journal of Science*, 1892, *44*, 192–207.

Fourtes, M. G. F., & Hodgkin, A. L. Changes in the time scale and sensitivity in the omatidia of Limulus. *Journal of Physiology*, 1964, *172*, 239–263.

Graham, C. H., & Kemp, E. H. Brightness discrimination as a function for the duration of the increment intensity. *Journal of General Physiology*, 1938, *21*, 635–650.

Graham, C. H., & Margaria, R. Area and intensity-time relation in the peripheral retina. *Journal of Physiology*, 1935, *113*, 299–305.

Graham, N. Visual detection of aperiodic spatial stimuli by probability summation among narrowband detectors. *Vision Research*, 1977, *17*, 37–652.

Granit, R., & Davis, W. A. Comparative studies of the peripheral and central retina. *Journal of Physiology*, 1931, *98*, 644–653.

Green, M. Psychophysical relationships among mechanisms sensitive to pattern, motion, and flicker. *Vision Research*, 1981, *21*, 971–983.

Harvey, L. O. Flicker sensitivity and apparent brightness as a function of surround luminance. *Journal of the Optical Society of America*, 1970, *60*, 860–864.

Harwerth, R. S., & Levi, D. M. Reaction time as a measure of suprathreshold grating detection. *Vision Research*, 1978, *18*, 1579–1586.

Henkes, H. E., & van der Tweel, L. H. (Eds.). *Flicker*. The Hague: W. Junk, 1964.

Herrick, R. M. Foveal luminance discrimination as a function of the duration of the decrement or increment in luminance. *Journal of Comparative Physiology and Psychology*, 1956, *49*, 437–443.

Ikeda, M. Temporal summation of positive and negative flashes in the visual system. *Journal of the Optical Society of America*, 1965, *55*, 527–534.

Ives, H. E. A theory of intermittent vision. *Journal of the Optical Society of America*, 1922, *6*, 343–361.

Keesey, U. T. Variables determining flicker sensitivity in small fields. *Journal of the Optical Society of America*, 1970, *60*, 390–398.

Keesey, U. T. Flicker and pattern detection: A comparison of thresholds. *Journal of the Optical Society of America*, 1972, *62*, 446–448.

Keller, M. The relation between the critical duration and intensity in brightness discrimination. *Journal of Experimental Psychology*, 1941, *28*, 407–418.

Kelly, D. H. Effects of sharp edges in a flickering field. *Journal of the Optical Society of America*, 1959, *49*, 730–732.

Kelly, D. H. Visual responses to time-dependent stimuli. I. Amplitude sensitivity measurements. *Journal of the Optical Society of America*, 1961, *51*, 422–429. (a)

Kelly, D. H. Visual responses to time-dependent stimuli. II. Single-channel model of the photopic visual system. *Journal of the Optical Society of America*, 1961, *51*, 747–754. (b)

Kelly, D. H. Sine waves and flicker fusion. *Documenta Ophthalmologica*, 1964, *18*, 16–35.

Kelly, D. H. Diffusion model of linear flicker responses. *Journal of the Optical Society of America*, 1969, *59*, 1665–1670. (a)

Kelly, D. H. Flickering patterns and lateral inhibition. *Journal of the Optical Society of America*, 1969, *59*, 1361–1370. (b)

Kelly, D. H. Theory of flicker and transient responses, I. Uniform fields. *Journal of the Optical Society of America*, 1971, *61*, 537–546. (a)

Kelly, D. H. Theory of flicker and transient responses, II. Counterphase gratings. *Journal of the Optical Society of America*, 1971, *61*, 632–640. (b)

Kelly, D. H. Adaptation effects on spatio-temporal sine-wave thresholds. *Vision Research*, 1972, *12*, 89–101. (a)

Kelly, D. H. Flicker. In L. Hurvich & D. Jameson (Eds.), *Handbook of sensory physiology*. New York: Springer-Verlag, 1972. (b)

Kelly, D. H. Visual contrast sensitivity. *Optica Acta*, 1977, *24*, 107–129.

Kelly, D. H. Motion and vision. I. Stabilized images of stationary gratings. *Journal of the Optical Society of America*, 1979, *69*, 1266–1274.

Kelly, D. H. Motion and vision. IV. Isotropic and anisotropic spatial responses. *Journal of the Optical Society of America*, 1982, *72*, 432–439.

Kelly, D. H., & Savoie, R. E. A study of sine-wave contrast sensitivity by two psychophysical methods. *Perception & Psychophysics*, 1973, *14*, 313–318.

Kelly, D. H., & Wilson, H. R. Human flicker sensitivity: Two stages of retinal diffusion. *Science*, 1978, *202*, 896–899.

King-Smith, P. E., & Kulikowski, J. J. Pattern and flicker detection analysed by subthreshold summation. *Journal of Physiology*, 1975, *249*, 519–548.

Koenderink, J. J., Bouman, M. A., Bueno de Mesquita, A. E., & Slappendel, S. Perimetry of contrast detection thresholds of moving spatial sine wave patterns. I. The near peripheral visual field (eccentricity 0°–8°). *Journal of the Optical Society of America*, 1978, *68*, 845–849.

Koenderink, J. J., & van Doorn, A. J. Spatiotemporal contrast detection threshold surface is bimodal. *Optics Letters*, 1979, *4*, 32–34.

Krauskopf, J., & Mollon, J. D. The independence of the temporal integration properties of the individual chromatic mechanisms in the human eye. *Journal of Physiology*, 1971, *219*, 611–623.

Kulikowski, J. J., & Tolhurst, D. J. Psychophysical evidence for sustained and transient mechanisms in human vision. *Journal of Physiology*, 1973, *232*, 149–163.

Landis, C. *An annotated bibliography of flicker fusion phenomena*. Armed Forces National Research Council Vision Committee Secretariat. Ann Arbor, Mich., 1953.

Legge, G. E. Sustained and transient mechanisms in human vision: Temporal and spatial properties. *Vision Research*, 1978, *18*, 69–81.

Lennie, P. Parallel visual pathways: A review. *Vision Research*, 1980, *20*, 561–594. (a)

Lennie, P. Perceptual signs of parallel pathways. *Philosophical Transactions of the Royal Society*, 1980, *B290*, 23–37. (b)

Levinson, E., & Sekuler, R. The independence of channels in human vision selective for direction of movement. *Journal of Physiology*, 1975, *250*, 347–366.

Levinson, J. Z. Fusion of complex flicker II. *Science*, 1960, *131*, 1438–1440.

Levinson, J. Z. One stage model for visual temporal integration. *Journal of the Optical Society of America*, 1966, *56*, 95–97.

Levinson, J. Z., & Harmon, L. D. Studies with artificial neurons—III. Mechanisms of flicker fusion. *Kybernetic*, 1961, *1*, 19–29.

Lupp, U., Hauske, G., & Wolf, W. Perceptual latencies to sinusoidal gratings. *Vision Research*, 1976, *16*, 969–972.

Mansfield, R. J. W., & Nachmias, J. Perceived direction of motion under retinal image stabilization. *Vision Research*, 1981, *21*, 1423–1425.

Matin, L. Critical duration, the differential luminance threshold, critical flicker frequency and visual adaptation, a theoretical treatment. *Journal of the Optical Society of America*, 1968, *58*, 404–415.

Morgan, M. J. Spatiotemporal filtering and the interpolation effect in apparent motion. *Perception*, 1980, *9*, 161–174.

Nachmias, J. Effect of exposure duration on visual contrast sensitivity with square-wave gratings. *Journal of the Optical Society of America*, 1967, *57*, 421–427.

Nachmias, J. On the psychometric function for contrast detection. *Vision Research*, 1981, *21*, 215–223.

Nilsson, T. H., Richmond, C. F., & Nelson, T. M. Flicker adaptation shows evidence of many visual channels selectively sensitive to temporal frequency. *Vision Research*, 1975, *15*, 621–624.

Norman, M. F., & Gallistel, C. R. What can one learn from a strength-duration experiment? *Journal of Mathematical Psychology*, 1978, *18*, 1–24.

Owen, W. G. Spatiotemporal integration in the human peripheral retina. *Vision Research*, 1972, *12*, 1011–1026.

Pantle, A. Adaptation to pattern spatial frequency: Effects on visual movement sensitivity in humans. *Journal of the Optical Society of America*, 1970, *60*, 1120–1124.

Pantle, A. Flicker adaptation—I. Effect on visual sensitivity to temporal fluctuations of light intensity. *Vision Research*, 1971, *11*, 943–952.

Pantle, A. Visual effects of sinusoidal components of complex gratings: Independent or additive? *Vision Research*, 1973, *13*, 2195–2204.

Pantle, A., & Sekuler, R. W. Velocity sensitive elements in human vision: Initial psychophysical evidence. *Vision Research*, 1968, *8*, 445–450.

Pantle, A., & Sekuler, R. W. Contrast response of human visual mechanisms sensitive to orientation and direction of motion. *Vision Research*, 1969, *9*, 397–406.

Patel, A. S., & Jones, R. W. Incremental and decremental visual thresholds. *Journal of the Optical Society of America*, 1968, *58*, 696–699.

Porter, T. C. Contributions to the study of flicker: II. *Proceedings of the Royal Society of London*, 1902, *70A*, 313–329.

Rashbass, C. Spatio-temporal interaction in visual resolution. *Journal of Physiology*, 1968, *196*, 102–103.

Rashbass, C. The visibility of transient changes of luminance. *Journal of Physiology*, 1970, *210*, 165–186.

Rashbass, C. Unification of two contrasting models of the visual increment threshold. *Vision Research*, 1976, *16*, 1281–1283.

Richards, W. Motion perception in man and other animals. *Brain, Behavior, and Evolution*, 1971, *4*, 162–181.

Riggs, L. A., Armington, J. C., & Ratliff, F. Motions of the retinal image during fixation. *Journal of the Optical Society of America*, 1954, *44*, 315–321.

Robson, J. G. Spatial and temporal contrast sensitivity functions of the visual system. *Journal of the Optical Society of America*, 1966, *56*, 1141–1142.

Rose, A. The relative sensitivities of television pick-up tubes, photographic film, and the human eye. *Proceedings of the Institute of Radio Engineers*, 1942, *30*, 295–300.

Roufs, J. A. J. Dynamic properties of vision—I. Experimental relationships between flicker and flash thresholds. *Vision Research*, 1972, *12*, 261–278. (a)

Roufs, J. A. J. Dynamic properties of vision—II. Theoretical relationships between flicker and flash thresholds. *Vision Research*, 1972, *12*, 279–292. (b)

Roufs, J. A. J. Dynamic properties of vision—III. Twin flashes, single flashes and flicker fusion. *Vision Research*, 1973, *13*, 309–323.

Roufs, J. A. J. Dynamic properties of vision—IV. Thresholds of decremental flashes, incremental flashes and doublets in relation to flicker fusion. *Vision Research*, 1974, *14*, 831–851. (a)

Roufs, J. A. J. Dynamic properties of vision—VI. Stochastic threshold fluctuations and their effect on flash-to-flicker sensitivity ratio. *Vision Research*, 1974, *14*, 871–888. (b)

Roufs, J. A. J., & Blommaert, F. J. J. Temporal impulse and step responses of the human eye obtained psychophysically by means of a drift-correcting perturbation technique. *Vision Research*, 1981, *21*, 1203–1221.

Schober, H. A. W., & Hilz, R. Contrast sensitivity of the human eye for square-wave gratings. *Journal of the Optical Society of America*, 1965, *55*, 1086–1091.

Sekuler, R. Visual motion perception. In E. C. Carterette & M. P. Friedman (Eds.), *Handbook of perception V: Seeing*. New York: Academic Press, 1975.

Sekuler, R., & Ganz, L. Aftereffect of seen motion with a stabilized retinal image. *Science*, 1963, *139*, 419–420.

Sharpe, C. R. The contrast sensitivity of the peripheral visual field to drifting sinusoidal gratings. *Vision Research*, 1974, *14*, 905–906.

Sharpe, C. R., & Tolhurst, D. J. The effects of temporal modulation on the orientation channels of the human visual system. *Perception*, 1973, *2*, 23–29.

Short, A. D. Decremental and incremental visual thresholds. *Journal of Physiology*, 1966, *185*, 646–654.

Smith, R. A. Adaptation of visual contrast sensitivity to specific temporal frequencies. *Vision Research*, 1970, *10*, 275–279.

Smith, R. A. Studies of temporal frequency adaptation in visual contrast sensitivity. *Journal of Physiology*, 1971, *216*, 531–552.

Sperling, G. Critical duration, supersummation, and the narrow domain of strength-duration experiments. *The Behavioral and Brain Sciences*, 1979, *2*, 279–282.

Sperling, G., & Sondhi, M. M. Model for visual luminance discrimination and flicker detection. *Journal of the Optical Society of America*, 1968, *58*, 1133–1145.

Stromeyer, C. F., III, Zeevi, Y. Y., & Klein, S. Response of visual mechanisms to stimulus onsets and offsets. *Journal of the Optical Society of America*, 1979, *69*, 1350–1354.

Teller, D. Y. Sensitization by annular surrounds: Temporal (masking) properties. *Vision Research*, 1971, *11*, 1325–1335.

Tolhurst, D. J. Separate channels for the analysis of the shape and the movement of a moving visual stimulus. *Journal of Physiology*, 1973, *231*, 385–402.

Tolhurst, D. J. Reaction times in the detection of gratings by human observers: A probabilistic mechanism. *Vision Research*, 1975, *15*, 1143–1149. (a)

Tolhurst, D. J. Sustained and transient channels in human vision. *Vision Research*, 1975, *15*, 1151–1155. (b)

Tulunay-Keesey, U. Contrast thresholds with stabilized and unstabilized targets. *Journal of the Optical Society of America*, 1982, *72*, 1284–1286.

Tulunay-Keesey, U., & Jones, R. M. The effect of micromovements of the eye and exposure duration on contrast sensitivity. *Vision Research*, 1976, *16*, 481–488.

Tulunay-Keesey, U., & Jones, R. M. Contrast sensitivity measures and accuracy of image stabilization systems. *Journal of the Optical Society of America*, 1980, *70*, 1306–1310.

Uetsuki, T., & Ikeda, M. Study of the temporal response by the summation index. *Journal of the Optical Society of America*, 1970, *60*, 377–381.

van Nes, F. L., Koenderink, J. J., Nas, H., & Bouman, M. A. Spatiotemporal modulation transfer in the human eye. *Journal of the Optical Society of America*, 1967, *57*, 1082–1088.

Vassilev, A., & Mitov, D. Perception time and spatial frequency. *Vision Research*, 1976, *16*, 89–92.

Virsu, V., Rovamo, J., Laurinen, P., & Nasanen, R. Temporal contrast sensitivity and cortical magnification. *Vision Research*, 1982, *22*, 1211–1217.

Watanabe, A., Mori, T., Nagata, S., & Hiwatashi, K. Spatial sine wave responses of the human visual system. *Vision Research*, 1968, *8*, 1245–1263.

Watson, A. B. The visibility of temporal modulations of a spatial pattern.

Doctoral dissertation, University of Pennsylvania. 1977.

Watson, A. B. Probability summation over time. *Vision Research*, 1979, *19*, 515–522.

Watson, A. B. A single-channel model does not predict visibility of asynchronous gratings. *Vision Research*, 1981, *21*, 1799–1800.

Watson, A. B. Derivation of the impulse response: Comments on the method of Roufs and Blommaert. *Vision Research*, 1982, *22*, 1335–1337.

Watson, A. B., & Ahumada, A. J., Jr. A theory of apparently real motion. *Investigative Ophthalmology and Visual Science*, 1982, *22*(Suppl.), 143.

Watson, A. B., & Ahumada, A. J., Jr. *A look at motion in the frequency domain* (NASA Technical Memorandum 84352). Washington, D.C.: U.S. Government Printing Office, 1983. (a)

Watson, A. B., & Ahumada, A. J., Jr. A model of the human motion sensor. *Journal of the Optical Society of America*, 1983, *73*, 1862. (b)

Watson, A. B., & Ahumada, A. J., Jr. A model of human visual motion sensing. *Journal of the Optical Society of America*, 1985, *2*, 322–342.

Watson, A. B., Ahumada, A. J., Jr., & Farrell, J. *The window of visibility: A psychophysical theory of fidelity in time-sampled visual motion displays* (NASA Technical Paper 2211). Washington, D.C.: U.S. Government Printing Office, 1983.

Watson, A. B., & Nachmias, J. Patterns of temporal interaction in the detection of gratings. *Vision Research*, 1977, *17*, 893–902.

Watson, A. B., & Robson, J. G. Discrimination at threshold: Labelled detectors in human vision. *Vision Research*, 1981, *21*, 1115–1122.

Watson, A. B., Thompson, P. G., Murphy, B. J., & Nachmias, J. Summation and discrimination of gratings moving in opposite directions. *Vision Research*, 1980, *20*, 341–347.

Westheimer, G. Spatial interaction in human cone vision. *Journal of Physiology*, 1967, *190*, 139–154.

Wyszecki, G., & Stiles, W. S. *Color science*. New York: Wiley, 1967.

CHAPTER 7

SEEING SPATIAL PATTERNS

LYNN A. OLZAK
and
JAMES P. THOMAS
University of California, Los Angeles, California

CONTENTS

This chapter concerns the visual perception of two-dimensional spatial patterns. Examples of such patterns are gratings, bars, lines, disks and squares of light, and the letters used in acuity testing. The goal of the chapter is to summarize information from laboratory studies that is potentially useful to those who design equipment and environments to be used by human viewers. This information includes laboratory findings, generalizations and models that can be used to apply the findings, and hypotheses about the mechanisms which mediate the perception of spatial patterns. For the most part, the presentation is organized according to the types of visual tasks the observer performs and the variables affecting performance. However, theoretical issues, particularly questions about the properties of the underlying visual mechanisms, are considered throughout.

The chapter is divided into four major sections. Section 1 summarizes conceptual and methodological information needed as a background for the findings and models presented in the later sections. Section 2 discusses tasks in which the observer must simply decide whether or not a pattern is present. Findings are presented about the factors that determine how accurately the tasks are performed and about the probable mechanisms involved. Formal models of these mechanisms and their operation are also described. Section 3 concerns tasks in which the observer must distinguish between different patterns, usually identifying which of two possible alternatives has been presented. Again, the information includes findings about factors affecting performance, the probable mechanisms involved, and formal models. Section 4 concerns the assessment of visual capacities in applied settings. For the most part, it discusses procedures for measuring visual acuity and factors affecting acuity.

1. OVERVIEW OF BACKGROUND INFORMATION

This section summarizes conceptual and methodological information, which forms a background for the presentation of empirical findings in Sections 2, 3, and 4. Section 1.1 is a theoretical overview. It discusses spatial tuning, a concept dominating contemporary research. Spatial tuning is defined, and the evidence for it is summarized. Section 1.2 summarizes relevant methodology, including how stimuli are described, the kinds of visual tasks studied, how performance is measured, and the use of masking and adaptation paradigms. Section 1.3 discusses three factors which influence performance in a wide variety of tasks: mean luminance, retinal location, and stimulus uncertainty.

1.1. Theoretical Overview: Spatially Tuned Pathways

Since the pioneering physiological studies of Hubel and Wiesel (1962, 1968) and Enroth-Cugell and Robson (1966), the study of spatial pattern vision has been increasingly dominated by the concept of multiple, spatially tuned pathways acting in parallel. This section provides an introduction to the concept. Spatial tuning is defined and methods for describing tuning and obtaining evidence of tuning are discussed. Then the evidence itself is summarized. The section is intended to serve as a theoretical background and context for the more detailed descriptions of experimental findings contained in Sections 2 and 3.

1.1.1. The Concept of Spatial Tuning. The process of perception begins when an optical image of the stimulus is formed on the mosaic of photoreceptors in the retina. The receptors, in turn, activate many neural pathways which act in parallel to process the visual information. Each pathway is a complex structure consisting of an ascending series of synaptically linked neurons and extending from the retinal photoreceptors to the visual cortex and beyond. Although each pathway can be thought of as acting separately, there is abundant interaction between pathways at all levels.

Each pathway is spatially tuned in the sense that whether the pathway responds to a given stimulus depends on the spatial characteristics of the stimulus. One important characteristic is the location of the stimulus in the visual field and, thus, the location of its image on the retina. Each pathway is driven, directly and indirectly, by a limited population of receptors grouped together in one region of the retina, the receptive field for that pathway. The pathway responds directly only to those stimuli imaged in its receptive field. The receptive fields of different pathways are located in different parts of the retina, and the pathways, accordingly, respond to stimuli at different locations in the visual field. Conversely, stimuli in different parts of the visual field activate different groups of pathways. This kind of selectivity, which can be called *location tuning*, is discussed in greater detail in Section 1.1.5.1.

Other kinds of spatial tuning are superimposed upon location tuning. Thus a given pathway may not respond to a particular stimulus, even though that stimulus is imaged in the receptive field of the pathway. For example, the pathway may respond only if the pattern contains contours or other linear elements that lie at or near a particular orientation with respect to the vertical. Other pathways, with similarly located receptive fields, respond to stimulus elements at other orientations. This kind of selectivity is called *orientation tuning*. There may be many additional kinds of tuning such as this. However, recent psychophysical research has been concentrated on tuning with respect to two particular spatial properties: the orientation of stimulus elements and the spatial frequency content of the stimulus. These kinds of tuning are described at greater length in Section 1.1.5.

An important question concerns how spatial tuning contributes to the perception of spatial patterns. An obvious possibility is that information about the spatial properties of the stimulus is encoded by which pathways are activated, different combinations of pathways representing different combinations of stimulus properties. Elements of this question are discussed throughout this chapter. Systematic consideration is presented in Sections 2.3 and 3.4, which discuss models of the detection and identification of spatial patterns, respectively.

1.1.2. Descriptions of Spatial Tuning. What is the best way to specify the spatial characteristics that determine which pathways respond to a particular stimulus? Or, conversely, what is the best way to describe the tuning properties of a particular pathway? At some point in the study of visual perception, it is necessary to relate the responses of the individual pathways to perceptual features, such as edges, bars, or even letters of the alphabet. However, the research described in this chapter has generally been directed toward more abstract methods of description. For the most part, two complementary approaches have been followed in describing the spatial tuning of individual pathways: (1) description in the space domain and (2) description in the Fourier domain.

Description in the space domain is the older approach and dates back to the classical paper of C. H. Graham, Brown, and Mote (1939). In this approach, the attempt is to define a spatial sensitivity map for each pathway, that is, a map of the relevant portion of the retina or visual field in which each elemental area is characterized according to whether stimulation of that area tends to increase or decrease the activity of the pathway. The characterization may be qualitative, as in the case of physiological receptive field maps which simply divide the receptive field into antagonistic on- and off-response areas. Or the map may be quantitative, in which case each area is given a signed number. The sign indicates whether stimulation in the elemental area tends to increase or decrease activity, and the magnitude of the number reflects the relationship between the strength of the stimulation and the magnitude of the change in the response of the pathway. The usefulness of this type of description depends on the extent to which the response properties of the pathway exhibit certain kinds of linearity. Given those linearities, the sensitivity function is analogous to the impulse response function of linear systems analysis and can be used to predict the response of the pathway to many different kinds of stimuli. The nature and use of these functions is discussed further in Section 2.3.

The second method is to describe each pathway in terms of its sensitivity to different Fourier, or spatial frequency, components. In this approach, the tuning properties of a pathway are defined by examining the response of the pathway to sinusoidal grating patterns. Such patterns consist of alternating light and dark strips such that the intensity of the light varies as a sinusoidal function of distance across the grating. Grating patterns can differ along four orthogonal dimensions: contrast (the intensity difference between light and dark strips); orientation (the orientation of the strips with respect to the vertical); spatial frequency (the number of light–dark pairs, or cycles, per degree of visual angle); and phase (the phase of the grating with respect to its light–dark cycle at a reference point in space). These four stimulus properties are discussed at greater length in Section 1.2. The tuning characteristics of a pathway are described by indicating which combinations of these four properties are required to activate the pathway. In many cases, the pathway can be described as responding to a single range or band of orientations and/or a single band of spatial frequencies. Considerable effort has been directed toward defining the widths of these bands, that is, the bandwidths of the pathways with respect to orientation and spatial frequency.

Grating stimuli have proved extremely useful in describing and differentiating between pathways. However, the primary reason for their use is that each is an approximate realization of a Fourier or spatial frequency component. Mathematically, any visual pattern is equivalent to a particular combination of Fourier components, each component being characterized by its contrast, orientation, spatial frequency, and phase. To the extent that the pathway exhibits certain kinds of linearity, it responds to a given Fourier component in the same fashion regardless of whether the component is presented alone, as in the case of a grating stimulus, or combined with other components, as in the case of more complex stimuli. Thus the possibility exists that the knowledge of how a pathway responds to gratings can be used to predict its response to many other kinds of stimuli. The linearity issues are discussed further in Section 2.3, which describes detection models. Further information about Fourier analysis and its application to the study of vision may be found in Chapter 34 by Ginsburg and in the Friedenwald Lecture of Enroth-Cugell and Robson (1984).

The two methods of describing the tuning characteristics of a pathway may be viewed as complementary to one another. Indeed, to the extent that the pathway exhibits the required linear properties, the space domain and frequency domain descriptions contain the same information and can be derived from one another by Fourier transforms. In the latter case, the choice between the methods becomes a matter of convenience. Additional discussions of the relationship between these two types of description are contained in Chapter 34 by Ginsburg, Chapter 6 by Watson, and Chapter 4 by Westheimer.

1.1.3. The Relationship between Neurons and Psychophysically Defined Pathways. The tuning characteristics of a single neuron can be estimated rather directly: The response of the neuron is recorded with a microelectrode as various diagnostic stimuli are presented in the visual field. However, most of the estimates presented in this chapter are derived from psychophysical experiments and should be treated as characterizing a hypothetical entity that may be called a *psychophysically defined pathway*. This pathway differs from any single neuron. At the least, the psychophysical pathway is intended to represent an entire neural chain extending from receptor to cortex. The pathway is treated as having a single set of tuning characteristics, whereas the neural chain has characteristics which evolve from one neuron to the next. For example, the psychophysical pathway is often treated as being tuned with respect to orientation; in the neural chain, this tuning property emerges only at the cortical level (Hubel & Wiesel, 1962, 1968). Similarly, the psychophysical pathway is often considered to have a single bandwidth with respect to spatial frequency; in the neural chain, the bandwidth changes from one link to another, being narrower at the cortex than at the retina (Robson, 1975). Sometimes, the pathway is conceptualized as having the properties of the ultimate member of the neural chain, usually taken as the cortical cell (e.g., Wilson & Bergen, 1979). However, even this analogy should be accepted with caution. The information about a pathway that is derived from a psychophysical experiment rests on an explicit or implicit model of how the pathway functions as a whole and how responses from different pathways are combined to yield the perceptual judgment. Such models, and the manner in which they are used to estimate tuning properties, are discussed in Section 2.3. It should be noted, however, that the models are simplified and idealized, as well as fallible, representations of the visual process. Consequently, the tuning properties derived from psychophysical data are likely to be simpler than those that characterize any single neuron and should be treated as rather idealized approximations.

1.1.4. The Kinds of Evidence about Spatial Tuning. The evidence about spatial tuning comes from both physiological and psychophysical experiments. The physiological evidence provides rather direct estimates of the tuning characteristics of individual neurons. These estimates are important for two reasons. First, they are primary evidence of the existence of spatial tuning within the visual system. Second, they complement, confirm, and constrain estimates derived from psychophysical studies. The estimates of tuning properties of cortical cells are of particular interest since they may correspond most closely to the properties of psychophysically defined pathways.

Psychophysical evidence about the spatial tuning of the pathways comes from two types of studies: (1) studies of interaction phenomena, such as summation at threshold, masking, and pattern-selective adaptation, and (2) studies of discrimination between stimuli which are at or near the detection threshold.

Interaction phenomena involve the perception of two or more stimuli or stimulus components. An interaction is said to occur when the perception of the combination differs from what would be expected if each component were perceived independently of the other. In the case of summation at threshold, summation occurs when the detection threshold for a compound stimulus formed by superimposing two components is higher or lower than the threshold for either component presented alone. In evaluating summation effects, allowance is made for probability summation: The fact that the probability of either or both of two independent events occurring is greater than the probability of either event taken alone. Masking occurs when the detection threshold for the test stimulus per se is altered by the presence of a second stimulus. Masking usually, but not always, raises the threshold of the test stimulus by an amount directly related to the contrast of the second stimulus. Pattern-selective adaptation occurs when the threshold for the test stimulus is changed by adaptation to a second stimulus of suprathreshold contrast. The effect is called *selective* because it occurs only if the two stimuli are similar with respect to certain spatial characteristics. As in the case of masking, the usual effect is a rise in threshold; however, threshold can decrease when test and adapting stimuli differ widely on one dimension (K. K. DeValois, 1977).

These three kinds of interaction are assumed to occur only if the two stimuli affect at least some pathways in common. Thus if an interaction occurs, both stimuli are considered to lie within the response domain of at least one common pathway. In some cases, the stronger assumption is made that interaction occurs if and only if the stimuli activate common pathways. Given this assumption, the absence of an interaction indicates that the stimuli activate completely separate groups of pathways. If the two stimuli differ on only one spatial dimension, they are considered to be separated by at least one bandwidth on that dimension. Quantitative models of summation and masking have been proposed that permit more precise description of the spatial properties of the pathways. The latest summation models (N. Graham, 1977; King-Smith & Kulikowski, 1975; Sachs, Nachmias, & Robson, 1971; Wilson & Bergen, 1979) allow for the effects of probability summation. Earlier models did not allow for these effects (Blackwell, 1963; C. H. Graham, Brown, & Mote, 1939; Thomas, 1970). Legge and Foley (1980), Henning, Hertz, and Hinton (1981), and Wilson, McFarlane, and Phillips (1983) have described quantitative models of masking. Section 2.3 discusses some of these models at greater length.

The second source of evidence is studies of the ability to discriminate between stimuli that are at or near the detection threshold. In this case, the reasoning is that two stimuli that activate completely different sets of pathways will be distinguished with the same accuracy with which they are detected. The method of comparing detection and identification performance must be chosen carefully to ensure that the measures are comparable (Olzak & Thomas, 1981). The most common method is the 2-by-2 simultaneous detection and identification task in which one of two low-contrast test stimuli is presented on each trial. The observer must identify both the stimulus and the interval of presentation. If the stimuli activate completely different groups of pathways, the probabilities of correct responses are the same for both judgments (Nachmias & Weber, 1975; Thomas & Gille, 1979; Thomas, Gille, & Barker, 1982; Tolhurst & Dealy, 1975; Watson & Robson, 1981). Thus if the identification judgment is less accurate than the interval judgment, it can be concluded that the two test stimuli activate some pathways in common. Additional assumptions permit more precise definition of the response domains of the pathways (Thomas & Gille, 1979; Thomas, Gille, & Barker, 1982).

1.1.5. Evidence for Spatial Tuning. Physiological and psychophysical evidence indicates that pathways are selectively sensitive or tuned with respect to several spatial dimensions. This section summarizes the evidence for tuning with respect to location in the visual field, orientation, and spatial frequency content. Pathways are also tuned with respect to nonspatial properties, such as temporal variation and color. Tuning for these properties is described in Chapter 6 by Watson and Chapter 8 by Pokorny and Smith.

1.1.5.1. Tuning with Respect to Location in the Visual Field. Tuning with respect to location in the visual field has been established the longest. The physiological evidence is that each cell in the primary visual system responds to stimulation in only a restricted portion of the visual field, the receptive field for that cell (Barlow, 1953; Hartline, 1938; Hubel & Wiesel, 1962, 1968). Receptive fields are smallest in the fovea and increase in size as a function of their distance from the fovea (Hubel & Wiesel, 1974b). The psychophysical evidence for location tuning is that substantial summation, masking, and adaptation effects occur only if the stimuli are spatially superimposed or adjacent. Further, stimuli delivered to well-separated regions of the visual field are distinguished whenever detected, and correct identification can be used as the measure of detection (Blackwell, 1953). This last fact is the basis for spatial forced-choice procedures.

There is abundant physiological evidence that spatial order is maintained in the neural projection from retina to cortex (Daniel & Whitteridge, 1961; Talbot & Marshall, 1941; Tootell, Silverman, Switkes, & DeValois, 1982). The maintenance of spatial order is called *retinotopic projection*. To a first approximation, the pattern of neural activity at the cortex is spatially isomorphic with the pattern of excitation at the retina and with the visual pattern (Tootell, Silverman, Switkes, & DeValois, 1982). At one time, this isomorphism played a dominant role in theories of pattern vision, particularly Gestalt theories (Kohler, 1940; Kohler & Wallach, 1944). Gestalt theorists postulated that the cortical pattern was, in turn, spatially isomorphic with the pattern perceived by the observer. As will be seen in Sections 2.3 and 3.4, contemporary models of detection and identification stress the roles of other types of tuning, as well as the role of retinotopic projection.

1.1.5.2. Tuning with Respect to Orientation. Orientation is the second spatial dimension to which pathways are selectively tuned. The physiological evidence for tuning comes from studies of single cells in the visual cortex. Most cells are selective with respect to orientation (R. L. DeValois, Yund, & Hepler, 1982; Hubel & Wiesel, 1962; 1968; 1974a; Schiller, Finlay, & Volman, 1976a). That is, a given cell responds best when the stimulus contains elements lying within a restricted range of orientations and responds less or not at all to elements at other orientations. Among the cells serving a given small region of the visual field, the preferred orientation varies systematically from cell to cell over the entire range of orientations. Cells are organized in columns or slabs which run perpendicular to the surface of the cortex. The cells within a given column have the same preferred orientation, which changes progressively from one column to the next in steps of 5–10° (Hubel & Wiesel, 1974a).

The psychophysical evidence for tuning with respect to orientation is that stimuli, such as bars or gratings, that differ substantially in orientation do not interact and can be distinguished with the same accuracy with which they are detected. Summation at threshold occurs only when stimuli differ in orientation by less than 10° (Kulikowski, Abadi, & King-Smith, 1973; Thomas & Shimamura, 1975). However, Thomas and Shimamura found evidence of inhibitory interaction between line stimuli differing by 15–25°; that is, the detection threshold for the compound was higher than for the more visible component presented alone. Masking and selective adaptation effects also occur only when stimuli are similar in orientation (Blakemore & Nachmias, 1971; Campbell & Kulikowski, 1966; Sekuler, 1965). Campbell and Kulikowski found that the masking effect of one grating on another was reduced to half the maximum value when the gratings differed in orientation by 12–15°. Selective adaptation between grating stimuli falls to half the maximum value when the gratings differ by about 7° (Blakemore & Nachmias, 1971). Differently oriented line or grating stimuli are distinguished with the same accuracy with which they are detected when the difference in orientation is 10–20°, depending on the observer (Thomas & Gille, 1979).

To summarize, evidence indicates that stimuli that differ in orientation by 15–20° or more activate few, if any, pathways in common. Thus 15–20° can be taken as a rough estimate of the bandwidth of tuning for orientation.

1.1.5.3. Tuning with Respect to Spatial Frequency. The third dimension of tuning is spatial frequency content. The primary physiological evidence is that when tested with grating stimuli, single cells in the visual cortex respond to limited ranges of spatial frequencies (R. L. DeValois, Albrecht, & Thorell, 1982; Schiller, Finlay, & Volman, 1976b). The range of frequencies to which the cell responds varies from cell to cell. There is some evidence that cells are organized in a columnar fashion analogous to that found for orientation, all cells in a given column responding to the same range of frequencies (Tootell, Silverman, & DeValois, 1981).

With respect to the psychophysical evidence, masking and selective adaptation occur only if the stimuli share common or similar spatial frequency components. Using gratings for both test and adapting stimuli, Blakemore and Campbell (1969) found that adaptation effects fell to half the maximum value when the stimuli differed in spatial frequency by 0.5 octave and were essentially zero when the spatial frequency of the test grating was more than an octave above or 2 octaves below the frequency of the adapting grating. (An *octave* is a 2:1 ratio of spatial frequencies.) Small increases in sensitivity to the test grating occur when the test and adapting frequencies are even more widely separated (K. K. DeValois, 1977). Stromeyer and Julesz (1972) and Henning, Hertz, and Hinton (1981) measured masking using gratings as test stimuli and filtered noise patterns as masks. They found that the masking effect was half its maximum value when the frequencies of the grating and the nearest noise component differed by 0.5–0.75 octave. Legge and Foley (1980) obtained similar results using gratings for both test and masking stimuli. To summarize, substantial adaptation and masking effects occur only if the stimuli are separated by less than an octave on the dimension of spatial frequency.

The results for summation at threshold are more complex. When grating stimuli are used, only probability summation is observed when the frequencies are separated by a factor of 2 or more (N. Graham & Nachmias, 1971; Sachs, Nachmias, & Robson, 1971). When the frequencies are very different, there is even some evidence of inhibition (Hirsch, Hylton, & Graham, 1982; Olzak, 1981; Olzak & Thomas, 1981). On the other hand, when the frequencies differ by less than a factor of 2, summation exceeds that expected on probabilistic grounds alone. When extended gratings are used as stimuli, the amount of summation observed is a nonmonotonic function of the frequency difference (Bacon, 1976). Stromeyer and Klein (1975) and King-Smith and Kulikowski (1975) have suggested that this complex relationship results from the variations in local contrasts, or beats, which are produced when gratings of different frequencies are combined. Production of beats can be avoided by using component stimuli that contain narrow bands of frequencies, rather than gratings which approximate a single frequency. Watson (1982) combined truncated gratings, each of which contained a half-octave band of frequencies. He found that summation decreased monotonically as the difference between the center frequencies of the bands increased. He observed little summation when the center frequencies differed by a factor of 2. Mostafavi and Sakrison (1976) found only slight summation when narrow bands of noise, centered on 4.5 and 6 cycles per degree were combined. To summarize, little or no summation occurs when the stimuli differ in spatial frequency by more than an octave. Summation does occur at smaller separations and, when spatial beats are avoided, is monotonically related to the difference in frequency.

Additional evidence of selectivity with respect to spatial frequency comes from studies of identification of low-contrast gratings. Such gratings are distinguished with the same accuracy with which they are detected if their spatial frequencies differ by a factor of 2 or more (Furchner, Thomas, & Campbell, 1977; Nachmias & Weber, 1975; Thomas, Gille, & Barker, 1982).

Taken together, the results of the foregoing psychophysical studies indicate that stimuli with similar spatial frequency content activate at least some pathways in common. There is little evidence of shared pathways if spatial frequencies differ by a factor of 2 or more. Accordingly, 1 octave may be taken as a rough estimate of the bandwidth of tuning with respect to spatial frequency, or at least as a lower bound for bandwidth. There is some evidence of inhibitory interaction between pathways that respond to spatial frequencies separated by a factor of 3 or more.

The property of size has sometimes been considered as a dimension of tuning. Thomas (1970) proposed a matrix of pathways that were selective with respect to size, as well as spatial location. He proposed that for a given pathway the response to an aperiodic stimulus was best when the stimulus was optimally located and optimal in size. Weaker responses were given to either larger or smaller stimuli. Optimal size was presumed to vary from one pathway to another. The model was stimulated by physiological findings that the optimal spot of light for activating ganglion cells varies in diameter from cell to cell (Barlow, 1953; Wiesel, 1960). The model was supported by psychophysical experiments on summation (summarized in Thomas, 1970), pattern-selective adaption (Bagrash, 1973; Kerr & Thomas, 1972), and discrimination at threshold (Thomas & Shimamura, 1974). However, it must be emphasized that the size-tuned pathways proposed by Thomas also have band-pass selectivity with respect to spatial frequency. The same is true for the mechanisms more recently proposed by Wilson and Bergen (1979) and Wilson and Gelb (1984). As far as these models are concerned, tuning with respect to size and spatial frequency are merely two aspects of the same underlying selectivity.

1.1.5.4. Summary. Both physiological and psychophysical evidence indicate that pattern vision is mediated by parallel pathways that are tuned with respect to properties of spatial location, orientation, and spatial frequency content. The psychophysical results cited can be used as rough estimates of the bandwidths of the individual pathways, or at least of the lower bounds of those bandwidths. More precise estimates can be derived through application of explicit models. Kulikowski, Abaadi, and King-Smith (1973) and Thomas and Gille (1979) have used such models to estimate bandwidths for orientation, although the former does not allow for probability summation. N. Graham (1977), Wilson and Bergen (1979), Legge and Foley (1980), Henning, Hertz, and Hinton (1981), and Wilson, McFarlane, and Phillips (1983) have used their respective models to estimate bandwidths for spatial frequency content.

Each pathway is conceived as selective with respect to all three dimensions: location, orientation, and spatial frequency content. The physiological evidence is that single cells in the visual cortex are so tuned (R. L. DeValois, Albrecht, & Thorell, 1982). Figure 7.1 provides an example of this evidence. On the psychophysical side, two stimuli interact or are confused at threshold only if they are similar with respect to all three properties. Tuning on the three different dimensions may not be separable (Daugman, 1980). That is, selectivity with respect to spatial frequency content may not be the same at all orientations and vice versa.

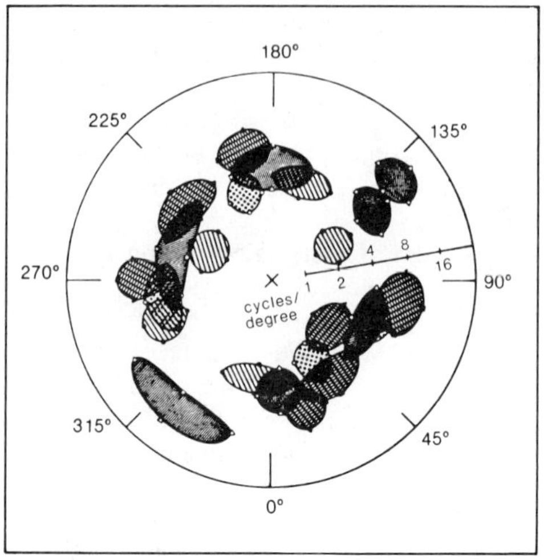

Figure 7.1. Tuning of cortical cells with respect to both orientation and spatial frequency. The figure is based on recordings from single cells in macaque visual cortex. The stimuli were sine wave gratings, which varied in orientation and spatial frequency. Orientation is indicated around the circumference of the figure, and spatial frequency is shown along the radius. Spatial frequency increases with distance from the center. Each shaded area represents data from a single cell and indicates the combinations of orientations and spatial frequencies to which the cell responds. The receptive fields of the cells were located about 1° from the fovea. Each cell responds to only limited bands of orientations and spatial frequencies. Different cells respond to different bands. (From R. L. DeValois, D. G. Albrecht, & L. G. Thorell, Spatial frequency selectivity of cells in macaque visual cortex, *Vision Research, 22*. Copyright 1982 by Pergamon Press, Ltd. Reprinted with permission.)

1.2. Methodological Overview

This section gives a brief summary of the more common methods and procedures used to obtain the experimental results presented in Sections 2, 3, and 4. Specifically, the section discusses the techniques to describe stimulus patterns, the different tasks which have been investigated, and the measures used to describe the performance of the observer.

1.2.1. Description of Stimulus Patterns. The spatial dimensions of the stimulus patterns are generally specified in degrees of visual angle. See Figure 7.2. The immediate stimulus for vision is the image formed on the retina, and it is the dimensions of this image that are of prime importance. However, they are not directly measurable. The advantage of visual angle is that it is directly proportional to distance on the retina. For practical purposes, the ratio of proportionality can be taken as constant for a given eye over all viewing conditions. For more imformation about visual angle and its relationship to distance on the retina, see Chapter 4 by Westheimer.

The basic measure of stimulus intensity is luminance, which is expressed in candelas per square meter (cd/m^2). A candela is a measure of the luminous flux that the stimulus emits or reflects in the direction of the viewer or measuring instrument. One candela represents one lumen per unit solid angle (steradian). The area of the stimulus is measured as projected onto a plane which is perpendicular to the line of sight of the observer or measuring instrument.

Many stimuli used in the laboratory, and most stimuli encountered outside the laboratory, vary in intensity from point to point. Thus it is useful to talk about the luminance at a point or the luminance of an elemental region. For this purpose, the following definition of luminance is useful:

$$L = \frac{dI}{dA} , \tag{1}$$

as dA is decreased toward zero. The unit I is cd and the unit A is m^2. For a fuller treatment of these measures, see Chapter 8 by Pokorny and Smith.

The intensity of the retinal image depends on the size of the pupil, as well as on the luminance of the stimulus pattern. As the pupil increases in diameter, more light enters the eye and the image becomes more intense. The *troland* is a measure which takes pupil size into account:

$$T = LS , \tag{2}$$

where T is the intensity in trolands, L is the luminance of the stimulus in cd/m^2, and S is the area of the pupil in mm^2. The troland has been used extensively to describe stimuli presented in Maxwellian view, an optical technique which was once standard and is still widely used. Westheimer (1966) has written a good introduction to the Maxwellian view, including procedures for calculating trolands.

In many viewing situations, the most important variable is the variation in luminance within the pattern itself. Contrast is a measure of this variation, expressed in relative terms. In the case of a repetitive pattern consisting of symmetrical deviations above and below a mean value, Michelson contrast is generally used:

$$\text{Contrast} = \frac{L(\max) - L(\min)}{L(\max) + L(\min)} \tag{3}$$

where L(max) is the maximum luminance in the pattern and L(min) is the minimum luminance. See Figure 7.3 for examples. This contrast measure can be applied to other types of patterns as well. However, when the pattern consists of a single increment or single decrement to the background luminance, the following contrast ratio is often used:

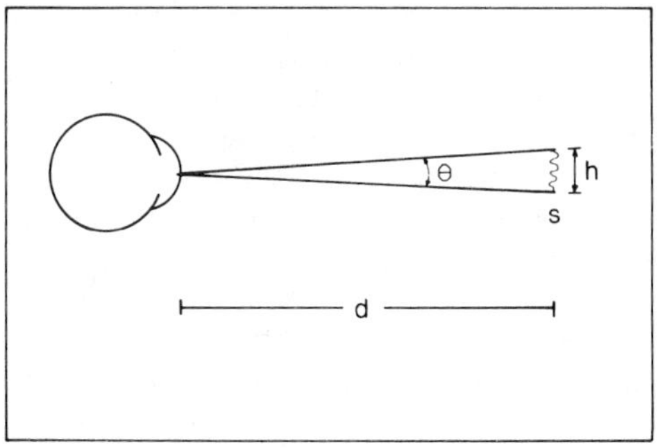

Figure 7.2. Definition of visual angle. The stimulus element *s*, shown on the right, subtends the visual angle Θ, which is related to the spatial extent of the stimulus element *h* and the viewing distance *d* by the following equation:

$$\tan(\Theta/2) = h/2d ,$$

where Θ is measured in degrees; *s* and *h* can be measured in any unit, but the same unit must be used for both; and *d* is measured from the front surface of the cornea. When Θ is small, the following approximation is useful:

$$\Theta = 57.3\ h/d .$$

The second equation overestimates Θ by about 1% when the true value of Θ is 10°.

$$\text{Contrast ratio} = \frac{\Delta L}{L(\text{background})} , \tag{4}$$

where ΔL is the increment or decrement and L(background) is the luminance of the background. See Figure 7.3 for an example.

When the stimulus consists of a few areas of uniform luminance, the pattern can be described by listing the spatial dimensions and the luminances of the areas. In other cases, a luminance profile is useful. The luminance profile plots luminance as a function of spatial position. Figure 7.3 contains examples of one-dimensional luminance profiles, that is, plots of the luminance variations across one dimension of the stimulus. The algebraic representation of the luminance profile is $L(x,y)$, where x and y represent the two spatial dimensions of the pattern.

The temporal properties of the stimulus pattern are also important. As is detailed in Section 2 and in Chapter 6 by Watson, there is a strong dependency between the temporal properties of the stimulus and the characteristics of spatial tuning and spatial interaction that are observed. For this reason, experimenters devote considerable effort to controlling and describing the temporal properties of the stimuli. In general, the best practice is to expand the luminance profile to include the dimension of time, that is, $L(x,y,t)$, where t represents time. In many cases, the temporal variation is accomplished by multiplying the spatial pattern of the stimulus by a factor which varies over time, such that at any given instant each point in the pattern is multiplied by the same factor. In this case, the luminance profile $L(x,y,t)$ can be factored into separate functions, $L(x,y)$ and $f(t)$, which represent the spatial pattern and the temporal variation, respectively. Gaussian or sinusoidal functions are frequently used for the temporal variation.

The metrics of Fourier or spatial frequency analysis are increasingly used to describe the performance of the visual system as a whole and the tuning characteristics of individual pathways. (See Section 1.1.2 for discussion of the latter.) Consequently, stimulus patterns are often described in terms of their Fourier or spatial frequency components. The following paragraphs discuss this method of description in simple and intuitive fashion. Chapter 34 by Ginsburg contains a longer and more formal treatment of this topic. For a full presentation, the reader should consult Bracewell (1965), a source widely used by researchers in visual pattern perception.

Mathematically, each stimulus pattern is equivalent to a uniform field modulated by the linear sum of a set of simple, sinusoidal patterns. Each simple pattern is of indefinite extent and consists of alternating light and dark stripes. Specifically, each component has the following luminance profile:

$$L(x,y) = L_0\{1 + m\sin[2\pi f(x\cos\theta + y\sin\theta) + \phi]\} , \tag{5}$$

where L_0 is the luminance of the uniform field; m is the amplitude or relative contrast of the pattern; f is the spatial frequency of the pattern, expressed as the number of light–dark pairs or cycles per degree of visual angle, measured along an axis perpendicular to the stripes; θ defines the orientation of the stripes relative to the axes x and y; and ϕ describes the phase of the light–dark cycle with respect to a reference point in space.

When θ is zero, the stripes are perpendicular to the x axis and the expression simplifies to

$$L(x,y) = L_0\{1 + m\sin[(2\pi fx) + \phi]\} . \tag{6}$$

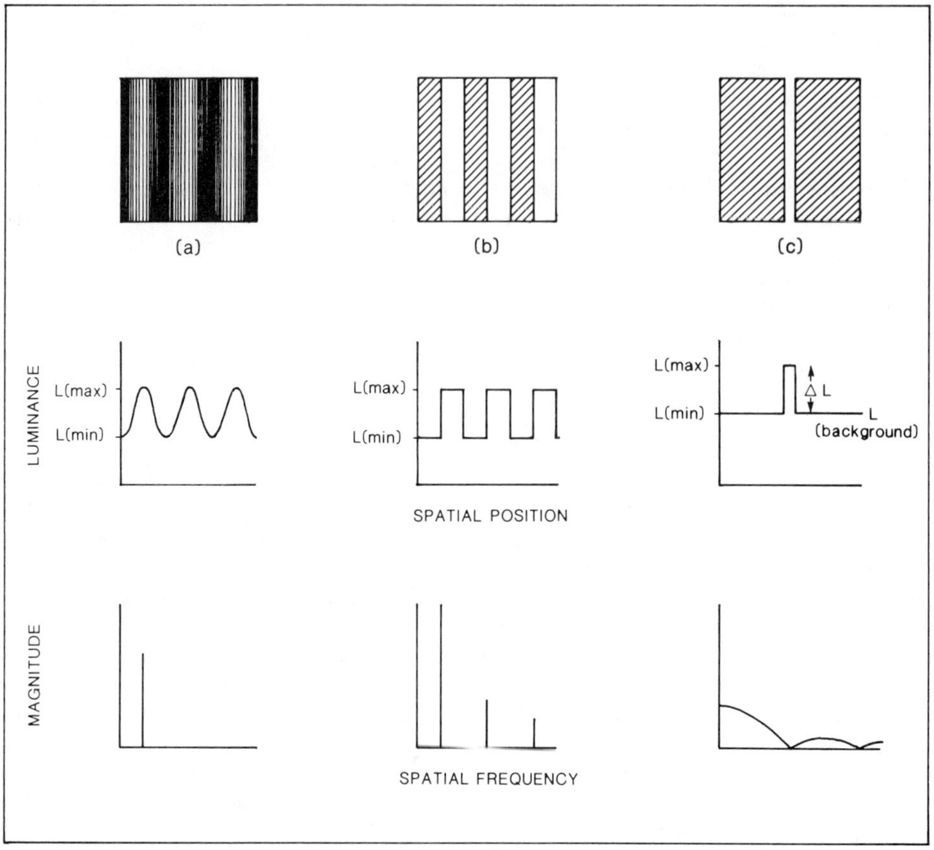

Figure 7.3. Methods of describing spatial patterns. The top row shows three different patterns: (a) a sine wave grating, (b) a square wave grating, and (c) a single narrow bar. The second row contains luminance profiles of the stimuli and illustrates the definitions of L(max), L(min), ΔL, and background luminance. The third row gives the spatial frequency spectra of the stimuli.

The sinusoidal grating pattern in Figure 7.3 is an approximate realization of a single Fourier component with θ equal to zero. It is only an approximation because it is finite in extent.

A full description of the Fourier components of a stimulus pattern involves specifying the amplitude, spatial frequency, orientation, and phase of each member of the set. However, simplified and idealized descriptions are often encountered. Phase information is frequently omitted. Also, the additional components introduced when the stimulus is truncated are often ignored. Such truncation can involve only one dimension (such as a bar which is not infinitely long) or both dimensions (such as a grating which does not extend indefinitely in both directions).

The Fourier or spatial frequency spectra included in Figure 7.3 are examples of such idealized descriptions. Each spectrum shows the relative magnitude of each component contained in the stimulus as a function of the spatial frequency of the component. In this idealized form, the sine wave grating pattern contains only a single spatial frequency component. The square wave grating contains a harmonic series of components, the spatial frequencies all being integer multiples of the lowest or fundamental spatial frequency. Harmonically related components are often referred to as f (the fundamental component), $2f$ (the component with spatial frequency twice that of the fundamental), and so forth. The single narrow bar has a continuous spectrum. In general, repetitive patterns, such as gratings, have discrete spectra composed of harmonically related components; nonrepetitive patterns, such as single lines and bars, have continuous spectra.

The goal of many experiments is to examine the visual response to a restricted band of Fourier components. Figure 7.4 illustrates a stimulus pattern particularly useful for these purposes. The pattern consists of a sine wave grating that is truncated along the axis perpendicular to the stripes by multiplication with a Gaussian function. The spatial-frequency content of the pattern is restricted to a band of frequencies centered on the frequency of the grating. The width of the band is inversely proportional to the space constant of the Gaussian function, that is, the half-width of the function measured at $1/e$ of its peak magnitude. A large space constant yields a pattern that stimulates a wide patch of retina but contains a narrow band of frequencies; a small space constant yields a pattern that stimulates a narrow patch of retina but contains a broad band of frequencies. Thus the most appropriate balance between spatial extent and spatial frequency content can be obtained by using the appropriate space constant.

Patterns of this type are sometimes called *Gabor packets*, after the man who explored their mathematical properties (Gabor, 1946). Gaussian truncation can also be used on the axis parallel to the stripes. Daugman (1980) has discussed the usefulness of such two-dimensional Gabor packets.

1.2.2. Definition of the Observer's Tasks: Detection and Identification. The research presented in this chapter concerns the ability of observers to make judgments about spatial patterns.

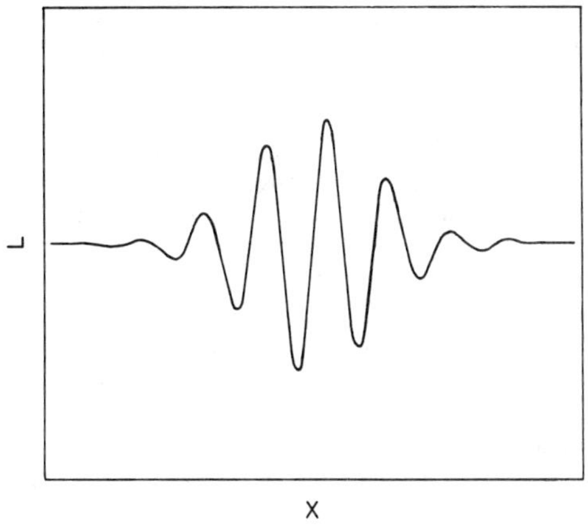

Figure 7.4. Luminance profile of a sine wave grating truncated by multiplication with a Gaussian function. The graph shows $L(x)$, the variation in luminance along the horizontal axis of the stimulus.

$$L(x) = L_0\{[\mathrm{EXP}(-x^2/w^2)\, m \sin(2\pi f x)] + 1\},$$

where x is distance along the horizontal axis, measured from the center of the pattern; w is the space constant of the Gaussian function, that is, the value of x at which the function falls to $1/e$ of the peak value; m is the amplitude of the sine wave grating; and f is the frequency of the grating expressed in cycles per degree. The Fourier components of this pattern lie within a single band, on the spatial-frequency axis, centered on f. The width of the band is inversely proportional to w. For further information, consult Gabor (1946) or Marcelja (1980). (From N. Graham, J. G. Robson, & J. Nachmias, Grating summation in fovea and periphery, *Vision Research, 18*. Copyright 1978 by Pergamon Press, Ltd. Reprinted with permission.)

In one class of experiments, the judgment is whether any pattern is present at all. That is, the observer is asked to distinguish between a field of uniform luminance, on the one hand, and a field on which a target stimulus has been superimposed or which has been modulated by the presence of a pattern, on the other hand. These tasks are called *detection tasks* in this chapter. Low-contrast patterns are used in detection studies. The goal is often to determine the lowest contrast at which each pattern can be distinguished from a uniform field. That contrast is taken as an inverse measure of the observer's sensitivity to the pattern. Section 2 is devoted to detection studies and their theoretical interpretation.

Another class of experiments examines the ability of observers to distinguish between patterns. In some cases, the observer is shown two patterns and simply asked to judge the patterns as the same or different. This task is called *discrimination* in this chapter. More often, particularly in recent years, the observer is shown one of a set of two or more possible patterns and is asked to identify which it is. This task is called *identification*. High-contrast patterns are often used in these studies to maximize performance. However, there have been a number of studies of identification of low-contrast patterns and of how performance improves as contrast increases. Section 3 presents studies of discrimination and identification and their interpretation.

1.2.3. Measures of Performance. The basic measure of performance is an estimate of the probability that the observer will detect or correctly identify the target pattern. When the task is detection, it may either be the probability that the observer reports seeing the pattern, if a yes-no procedure is used, or it may be the probability that the observer correctly identifies the time or place of presentation if a forced-choice procedure is used. If the methods of signal detection theory are used, the basic measure is d'. (Signal detection theory, d', and related measures are discussed in Chapter 1 by Falmagne and in Chapter 2 by Sperling and Dosher.)

Most experiments seek to establish the conditions that limit performance of detection and identification tasks. Therefore, they examine performance as a function of variation in one or more properties of the stimulus. The contrast of the target is the property most often varied. The purpose often is to estimate the "threshold" contrast for the particular task, that is, the lowest contrast at which the probability of detection or identification exceeds a criterion value.

When the task is detection, the reciprocal of threshold contrast is called *contrast sensitivity*. Contrast sensitivity is the most widely used measure of the sensitivity of the visual system to the target stimulus. Basic sensitivity data generally take the form of contrast sensitivity functions in which contrast sensitivity is plotted as a function of one or more stimulus properties, such as spatial frequency, orientation, or location in the visual field.

When the task is detection, and the observer simply reports "seen" or "not seen," the convention is to use a probability of .5 as the criterion for threshold. When detection is measured by a forced-choice procedure, in which the observer indicates in which of two or more spatial positions or time intervals the stimulus is presented, the criterion is generally halfway between chance performance and perfect performance. For example, in a two-alternative forced-choice procedure in which the probability of chance success is .5, the criterion is usually set at .75.

The functions relating probability of detection or identification to contrast are called *psychometric functions*. Figure 7.5 presents examples of psychometric functions and illustrates the estimation of threshold contrast.

In some detection experiments, the contrast threshold is estimated by having the observer adjust the contrast of the target to the point at which the observer just barely perceives the target. Several such adjustments are made during a single session and averaged to obtain an estimate of the threshold contrast. Estimates must be obtained from several different sessions to assess the repeatability of the measures. This method, called *method of adjustment*, is widely used because it is rapid and typically yields highly repeatable results for a given observer and a given set of experimental conditions. However, the method has some limitations. One is the fact that the criterion for "barely perceived" is not well controlled and may vary from observer to observer and even from one experimental condition to another within an observer. Another limitation is that only one point on the psychometric function is estimated.

In another class of experiments, contrast is held constant, usually at a high value, and other properties of the target are varied. For example, the observer may be required to identify which of two gratings has the higher spatial frequency. The difference in spatial frequency is manipulated to produce a psychometric function which shows the relationship between the probability of correct identification and the difference in frequency. Acuity experiments provide another example. In these experiments, the size of a critical detail of a high-contrast target is varied. The threshold size is estimated, that is, the minimum size at which the probability that the detail is detected or identified exceeds a criterion value. Acuity is defined as the reciprocal of this minimum size. Figure 7.32(c), in Section 3, illustrates the psychometric function for this type of experiment.

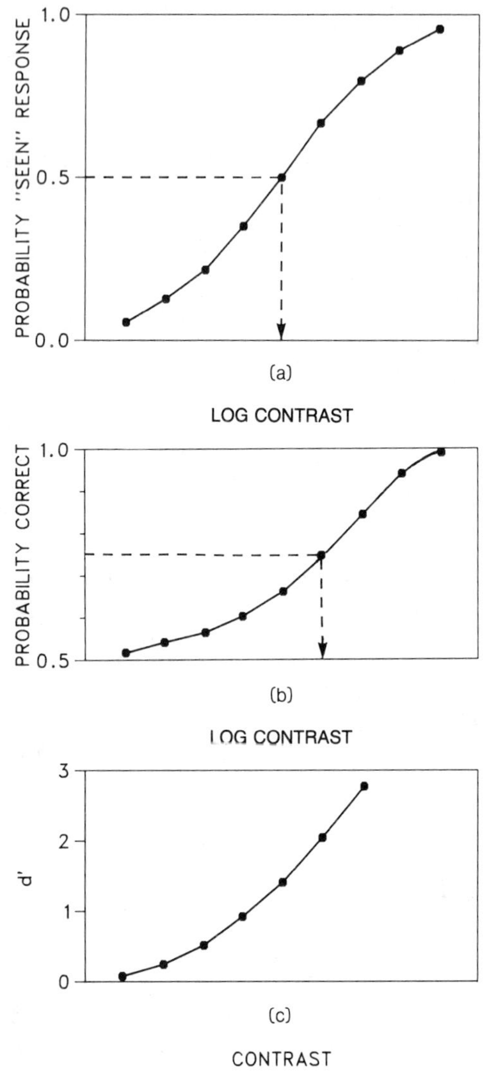

Figure 7.5. Examples of psychometric functions. (a) Psychometric function for a detection experiment in which the observer reports "seen" or "not seen" at the end of each trial. The horizontal axis gives the logarithm of the contrast of the target. The vertical axis gives the estimated probability of a "seen" response. Each data point represents the probability estimated from a large number of stimulus presentations at the contrast shown. In this type of procedure, presentations at the various contrasts are randomly intermixed, not blocked. The broken lines illustrate threshold contrast, defined as the contrast at which $p(\text{seen}) = 0.5$. When the logarithm of contrast is used, as shown here, the psychometric functions for the detection of most stimuli are similar in shape and slope and differ primarily in horizontal location. Thus the differences between stimuli can be summarized by a single variable: the contrast threshold (or its reciprocal, contrast sensitivity). Estimation of the threshold is aided by fitting a smooth curve to the data. The cumulative normal function is most often used. Alternatively, the following function can be used:

$$p(\text{seen}) = 1 - 2^{-(cs)^{\alpha}},$$

where c is the contrast of the stimulus, s is a measure of contrast sensitivity, and α determines the slope of the function. This function is particularly useful when analyses involving probability summation are to be performed. For discussions of this function, see Quick (1974) and Nachmias (1981). (b) Psychometric function for the detection of a target in a two-alternative temporal forced-choice procedure. The horizontal axis shows the logarithm of the contrast of the stimulus. The vertical axis shows the probability that the observer correctly identifies the temporal interval in which the stimulus is presented. Each data point shows the probability estimated from a large number of presentations of the target at the contrast indicated. In forced-choice procedures, the various contrast levels can either be blocked or randomly intermixed. The broken lines show estimation of the threshold contrast, defined as $p(\text{correct}) = 0.75$. Chance is 0.50. (c) Psychometric function using d' as the measure of detection performance. The horizontal axis shows the contrast of the stimulus in linear coordinates. The vertical axis shows d'. Each point shows the value of d' estimated from many trials on which the target, when presented, had the contrast shown. The positive acceleration is typical of detection data and of identification data at low contrasts (Nachmias & Kocher, 1970; Stromeyer & Klein, 1974). Similar acceleration is seen with forced-choice data when the standard normal deviate corresponding to $p(\text{correct})$ is plotted against linear contrast.

1.2.4. Masking. The visibility of a pattern is often reduced by the presentation of a second pattern. When the interference occurs more or less immediately on presentation of the second stimulus, the effect is called *masking*. When the interference builds up over many seconds, it is called *adaptation*. This section describes experimental procedures for measuring masking. Adaptation procedures are described in Section 1.2.5.

Masking refers to an interference in the perception of one stimulus (target) by the presence of a second stimulus (mask) that is nearby in time and space. Masking is distinguished from other visual interactions by its restricted time course; both target and mask are briefly presented, and it is the immediate effect which is measured. Because mutual interactions often occur, the stimulus designated "mask" is usually configured so as to exert the greater influence and is manipulated as the independent variable. Near threshold, the magnitude of the masking effect is measured by the increase in contrast or brightness needed to detect the test stimulus. Above threshold, masking effects are assessed by changes in apparent contrast or brightness using matching techniques or by changes in identification performance.

The large number of spatial and temporal combinations possible in masking paradigms and the dependence of results on the particular combination have led to the emergence of a number of standardized procedures. For example, target and mask can be presented to a single eye (monoptic) or to separate eyes (dichoptic). Masking effects that cannot be obtained dichoptically are assumed to reflect interactions which occur peripherally in the visual system prior to the locus of binocular interactions. Effects obtained with dichoptic presentation are assumed to occur more centrally.

The mask can appear before, after, or simultaneously with the target. These temporal sequences are respectively termed *forward*, *backward*, and *simultaneous* masking and, most commonly, are measured by the stimulus onset asynchrony (SOA). The SOA is the difference in time between the onsets of the target and mask. By convention, SOA is negative in forward-masking paradigms, positive in backward masking, and equal to zero in simultaneous masking. An alternative measurement is the interstimulus interval (ISI), the difference between the offset of the first stimulus and the onset of the second. Figure 7.6 illustrates these temporal configurations.

In the spatial domain, the mask can be a homogeneous light flash, spatially localized contours, or a repetitive pattern, such as a grating. Two terms are reserved for the special masking paradigms in which both target and mask are suprathreshold and near one another but do not overlap retinal areas. *Metacontrast* describes this paradigm for backward masking, whereas *paracontrast* refers to the forward-masking version (Stigler, 1910). Masking by overlapping contours is often referred to as a nonmetacontrast configuration or, simply, masking. When the overlapping mask consists of spatially random elements, the technique is called masking by noise (Kinsbourne & Warrington, 1962); if the mask shares spatial structure with the target, it is known as masking by structure.

The effect of a mask is determined by the temporal sequence of exposure, the spatial relationship between target and mask, and the relative luminances of target and mask. In addition, results may be dependent on the psychophysical task used to measure the degree of masking. Thus an enormous number of studies have emerged, often with apparently contradictory results. This complexity reflects the fact that the masking paradigm taps many types of visual interactions, located at different processing stages. A number of comprehensive and excellent reviews of the literature are currently available (e.g., Alpern, 1952; Boynton, 1972; Fox, 1978; Ganz, 1975; Kahneman, 1968; Lefton, 1973; Raab, 1963; and Weisstein, 1972). Specific findings on the effects of masking on detection and identification of visual patterns are presented in Sections 2 and 3.

1.2.5. Pattern-Selective Adaptation. Adaptation is a procedure similar to masking, differing primarily in time course. Typically, a high-contrast adapting pattern is viewed for a prolonged period of time (up to several minutes) just prior to presentation of the test stimulus. The prolonged viewing permits the adaptation effects to build up over time. The adaptation pattern is then removed (to eliminate masking effects), and the test pattern is presented. When the test pattern is at threshold, the effect of the adapting stimulus is measured by a rise in the contrast threshold for detection of the test stimulus or by an altered ability to discriminate between two stimuli that differ along some dimension. At suprathreshold levels, adaptation is measured by decreases in apparent contrast or by apparent changes in other properties of the test stimulus, such as orientation (Blakemore & Nachmias, 1971; Vernon, 1934) or spatial frequency (Blakemore, Nachmias, & Sutton, 1970; Blakemore & Sutton, 1969).

The magnitude of the adaptation effect is related to the contrast of the adapting pattern, becoming larger as the adapting contrast increases. The buildup of the effect can be measured by varying the length of time that the adapting pattern is viewed before presentation of the test pattern. Typically, the effect approaches its maximum strength after about 1 min of adaptation, regardless of adapting intensity (e.g., Blakemore & Campbell, 1969). The decay of the adaptation effect can be measured by varying the time between removing the adapting stimulus and presenting the test stimulus. Most of the effect is lost within a minute (Blakemore & Campbell, 1969). The rapid decay of the effect poses problems for its measurement. The usual strategy is to have the observer view the adapting pattern for 2 or 3 min and then intermix brief presentations of the test stimulus with short periods of readaptation. Contingent aftereffects, such as the McCollough (1965) effect, build up and decay much more slowly.

Threshold elevation effects produced by adaptation closely parallel those found with masking studies: the largest effect is

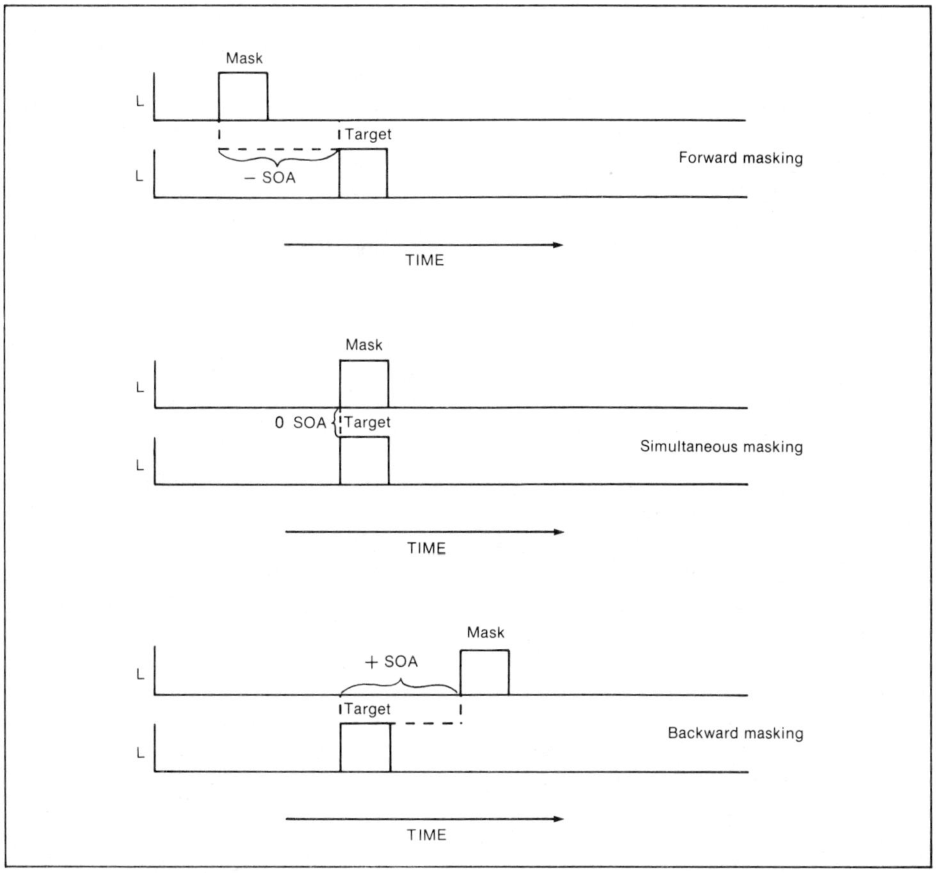

Figure 7.6. Temporal relationships in masking paradigms: forward masking, simultaneous masking, backward masking.

found when both adapting and test stimuli are similar and, presumably, affect common spatially tuned mechanisms. As indicated in Section 1.1, a major use of adaptation experiments has been to estimate tuning properties. Specific findings on the effects of pattern adaptation on the visibility and appearance of visual patterns are presented in Sections 2 and 3.

1.3. Parameters Which Affect Performance

The accuracy with which a pattern is perceived depends both on the properties of the pattern itself and on the properties of the situation in which the pattern is viewed. The latter can be considered parameters because they influence the functions which relate visual performance to the properties of the target stimulus. This section summarizes the effects of three such parameters: mean luminance, retinal location, and stimulus uncertainty. The functions they affect are presented in Sections 2 and 3.

1.3.1. Mean Luminance. Performance of most visual tasks improves as the average luminance of the visual scene increases over a wide range. This section discusses the improvement and its possible causes.

The space–average luminance (i.e., ratio of total flux to total area) is easily specified for most experimental displays. In some experiments, the stimuli are generated by modulating the luminance of an otherwise uniform field in such a fashion that the space–average luminance is unchanged. Experiments using sine wave gratings are an example of this technique. If a surround is used, it has the same luminance as the field. In these experiments, the mean luminance is the luminance of the uniform field and the surround. In other experiments, the stimuli are luminance increments or decrements on an otherwise uniform field. Strictly speaking, they alter the space–average luminance of the display. However, the stimuli are generally small relative to the field and are often presented intermittently. Accordingly, they are treated as having a negligible effect, and the luminance of the field is taken as the mean luminance.

Both contrast sensitivity and acuity improve as mean luminance increases. Figure 7.11 illustrates the effect on contrast sensitivity, and Figure 7.45 describes the effect on acuity. In both tasks, most of the improvement occurs at low and moderate luminances. There is little or no improvement as luminance increases above 300 cd/m^2.

Several factors probably contribute to improved performance, including the following three: improved image quality, improved signal-to-noise ratios, and changes in the visual system itself.

In normal viewing, pupil diameter decreases as scene luminance increases, which improves the quality of the retinal image by reducing aberrations and increasing depth of field. (See Chapter 4 by Westheimer for a discussion of the relationship between pupil diameter and image quality.) However, this factor is of limited importance since large changes in performance occur even when pupil size is effectively held constant. For example, a 2-mm artificial pupil was used in gathering all the data shown in Figure 7.11 and Figure 7.45.

Another factor is improved signal-to-noise ratio. Both the light stimulus and the neural response to it are perturbed by noise. Such noise must constrain performance of detection and identification tasks. As illumination becomes more intense, the signal-to-noise ratios increase, permitting better performance.

In the case of light itself, the quantum fluctuations are such that the ratio of the mean number of quanta absorbed by the photoreceptors to the standard deviation of the quantal fluctuations increases as the square root of the mean. (This relationship holds only as long as other sources of noise in the physical display follow the same relationship or are small relative to the inherent quantal fluctuations.) To the extent that performance is limited by quantum noise, performance should improve as the square root of mean luminance (DeVries, 1943; Rose, 1948). This relationship, called the *DeVries-Rose law*, is an accurate approximation for some tasks at low luminances but breaks down at higher luminances. The luminance at which the relationship breaks down depends on spatial and temporal properties of the stimuli. For example, when the task is detection of a sinusoidal grating, the luminance at which the relationship breaks down is lower for gratings of low spatial frequency than it is for high-frequency gratings. (Figure 7.11 illustrates this point.) This kind of dependency is difficult to explain on the basis of quantal fluctuations alone and indicates the importance of other factors, even at low luminances.

A variety of phenomena suggest that properties of the visual system itself change as mean luminance increases. For example, the contrast sensitivity function changes shape and the location of the peak shifts to higher spatial frequencies as luminance increases. Figure 7.11 illustrates this point. Other experiments have shown that spatial and temporal summations occur over shorter distances and durations as luminance level increases (Barlow, 1958; Blackwell, 1946). (Section 2 presents a further discussion of the effect of mean luminance on spatial and temporal summation.) As a final example, the magnitude and spatial parameters of the Westheimer sensitization effect, which is described in Section 2.2.3, change as a function of background luminance (Westheimer, 1965, 1967). These various phenomena imply that the parameters of spatial and temporal interaction in the visual system change as a function of mean luminance level.

One major change that occurs is the transition from scotopic to photopic vision. At the least, this transition involves a change in receptor distribution and, therefore, in the relative effectiveness of foveal and parafoveal vision. Further, many functions, such as the plot of acuity against mean luminance (Shlaer, 1937), have distinct rod and cone segments. However, the change from rod to cone vision is only part of the story. Acuity increases as illumination increases over all of the scotopic range and over much of the photopic range. Similarly, the contrast sensitivity function changes continuously as illumination increases, stabilizing only at the highest levels. Thus the changes occur within the scotopic and photopic ranges, as well as at the transition from one to the other.

Chapter 5 by Hood and Finkelstein discusses at length the relationship between changes in detection performance and changes in both quantal and neural noise and in spatial and temporal summation.

1.3.2. Retinal Location. The accuracy with which spatial patterns are detected and identified is affected by their location in the visual field. In the case of photopic vision, the accuracy with which a given target is perceived decreases as a monotonic function of the distance of the target from fixation. This section presents an overview of the effect of retinal location. Details about the effect on performance of specific tasks are presented in Sections 2 and 4. Section 2.1.5 discusses the effect of retinal location on the detection of aperiodic targets and gratings, and Section 4.3.3 discusses the effect on performance of acuity tasks.

The major reason for decreased performance in peripheral vision is that the visual system allots fewer resources to the periphery than to the center of the visual field. The density of cone receptors decreases sharply as a function of distance from the center of the fovea (Woodson, 1954). In addition, the relative size of the cortical representation decreases as a function of eccentricity (Daniel & Whitteridge, 1961; Hubel & Wiesel, 1974b). On the other hand, the quality of the retinal image plays little or no role in the difference between central and peripheral vision. Image quality appears to limit performance only in central vision (Jennings & Charman, 1981; Millodot, Johnson, Lamont, & Leibowitz, 1975).

In scotopic vision the effect of retinal location is somewhat different. Because rod receptors are absent from the fovea, there is a central blind spot. Estimates of the diameter of the rod-free area vary from 30 to 100 min of visual angle (LeGrand, 1968). Outside of this region, the density of the rods first increases and then decreases as a function of eccentricity, peaking at about 20° (Woodson, 1954). However, visual performance, as measured by acuity, is greatest at about 4° and decreases at greater eccentricities (Mandelbaum & Sloan, 1947).

In photopic vision and when eccentricity is less than 20°, performance on a number of tasks approximates a linear function of eccentricity, provided that performance is measured by minimum angle (Anstis, 1974; Weymouth, 1958). Minimum angle is the size, in visual angle, of the smallest critical detail that can be resolved or correctly judged. For these eccentricities and tasks, performance can be described by the following equation:

$$\mathrm{MA}(E) = \mathrm{MA}(0)(1 + aE) \ , \tag{7}$$

where E is the eccentricity, $\mathrm{MA}(E)$ is the minimum angle at that eccentricity, MA(0) is the minimum angle at fixation, and a is a parameter which varies from one task to another, from one observer to another, and with illumination level. Figure 7.7 illustrates the linear relationship for two tasks, grating resolution, and two-dot vernier acuity. The figure also illustrates how the value of a varies with task and observer.

At eccentricities greater than 20°, the linear relationship gives way to one in which the minimum angle increases as a positively accelerating function of eccentricity. The rate of acceleration is different for different tasks (Millodot, Johnson, Lamont, & Leibowitz, 1975). Figure 7.46 illustrates the positively accelerated function obtained for acuity tasks.

Some authors have suggested that the difference between central and peripheral vision is primarily one of scale (Koenderink, Bouman, Bueno de Mesquita, & Slappendel, 1978a, 1978b, 1978c; Rovamo, Virsu, & Nasanen, 1978). Specifically, the suggestion is that much of the difference between central and peripheral vision can be eliminated by multiplying the spatial dimensions of each peripheral target by a factor that increases as a monotonic function of the distance of the target from fixation. One version of this hypothesis is that equal performance occurs when the cortical representations of the stimuli are equal in size (Rovamo, Virsu, & Nasanen, 1978).

For the hypothesis to be strictly true, the value of a in Eq. (7) would have to be independent of task. Figure 7.7 illustrates the failure of this strict interpretation. Indeed, for the two-dot acuity task, the two critical dimensions of the same stimulus pattern (minimum angle and optimal vertical separation) increase at different rates as eccentricity increases. Despite this limitation, the hypothesis is useful to describe a fairly large body of data on stationary, drifting, and flickering gratings (Koenderink et al., 1978a, 1978b, 1978c; Rovamo, Virsu, & Nasanen, 1978; Virsu, Rovamo, Laurinen, & Nasanen, 1982).

1.3.3. Stimulus Uncertainty. Detection performance suffers when the observer is uncertain about one or more properties of the target. Figure 7.8(a,b) illustrates the problem. In (a), the observer must detect a low-contrast, high-spatial-frequency grating. Performance is worse when the grating can occur in any 1 of 16 possible positions (indicated by the broken circles) than when the observer knows the position in which it will appear. There are two reasons for the deficit. First, because of its high spatial frequency, the grating can be resolved only if centrally viewed. Thus performance will suffer unless the observer happens to be looking in the right place. If the target is present long enough to permit visual search, detection will be delayed as the observer searches the possible positions. This example illustrates one possible reason why uncertainty reduces detection performance: the observer cannot fully attend to all possible stimulus conditions at once. In this particular example, the act of attending has a well-defined, concrete meaning: moving the eyes to fixate a particular location.

The second reason why uncertainty reduces detection performance is related to noise. As each location is fixated, the observer must decide whether the concomitant activity in the visual system represents the target or whether it is merely noise. The more positions to be examined, the greater the possibility of mistaking noise for the representation of the target. As the number of possible positions increases, the observer will either make more false alarms (mistaking noise for target) or adopt a more stringent criterion and miss more presentations of the target.

Figure 7.8(b) presents a more abstract example of the problem. The target is still a grating. However, in this case it appears at only one position but may have any one of three widely separated spatial frequencies. In other words, this is a case of uncertainty with respect to spatial frequency. An attentional limitation exists if the observer cannot attend fully to mechanisms tuned to all spatial frequencies at once. In this case, detection performance will suffer if the observer happens to be attending to the wrong band of spatial frequencies, or detection will be delayed while the observer surveys the responses of mechanisms tuned to different spatial frequency ranges. As will be seen below, it is not yet established that such an attentional limitation with respect to spatial frequency actually exists. The noise problem occurs because the observer must decide for each mechanism which might possibly represent the stimulus whether activity in that mechanism represents the stimulus or is merely noise. The more mechanisms to be considered, the greater the possibility of error.

Chapter 2 by Sperling and Dosher discusses at length the theoretical and experimental analysis of uncertainty effects arising from both noise and attentional limitations. Green and Birdsall (1978) have written an excellent theoretical introduction to the analysis of effects related to noise. The reader is referred to these sources for additional information about models and theory. Sections 1.3.3.1 and 1.3.3.2 describe empirical findings with respect to the effect of uncertainty on the detection and identification of visual stimuli.

1.3.3.1. Detection of 1-of-m Signals. In one class of experiments, the observer is required to detect 1 of m possible signals. The different signals represent the possible values of the dimension for which uncertainty exists. For example, they could represent m different spatial locations, m different time intervals, or m different spatial frequencies. In nearly all cases, the signals are orthogonal, that is, different enough to be processed independently in the visual system. The task of the ob-

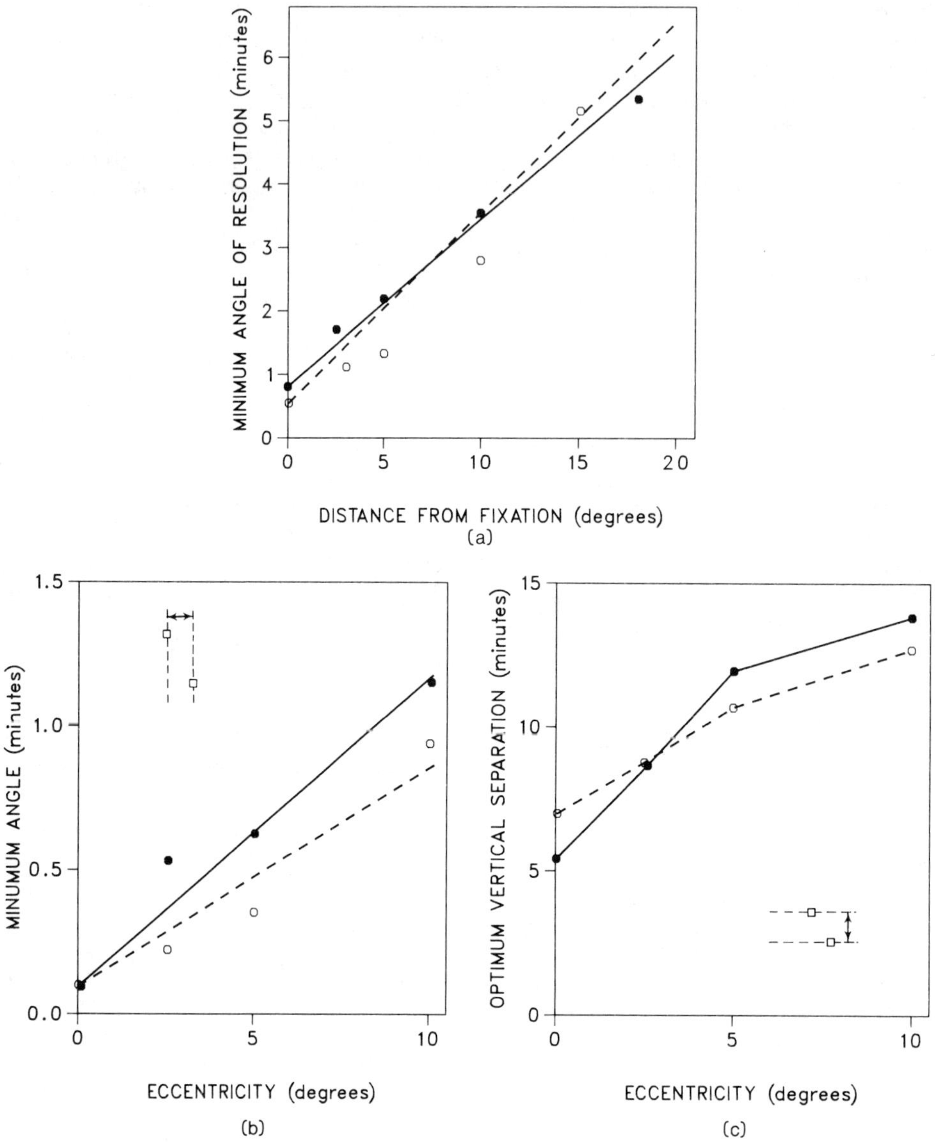

Figure 7.7. Minimum angle as a linear function of retinal eccentricity. (a) Grating resolution. The target was a square patch of rectangular wave grating. The square was six periods on a side. Mean luminance 64–80 cd/m^2, contrast high but indeterminate. Eccentricity is the distance, in degrees of visual angle, between the center of the target and fixation. The minimum angle is half the period, in minutes of visual angle, of the finest grating resolved. Resolution was defined as 75% correct identification of the orientation of the bars (vertical or horizontal). Each data point represents the results for one observer. The straight lines represent the equation $MA(E) = MA(0)[1 + ae]$. The value of a is 0.33 for one observer and 0.55 for the other. Over this range of eccentricities, minimum angle increases as an approximately linear function of eccentricity. Data from Westheimer (1979b). (b) Two-dot vernier acuity. The target consisted of two dots, one above the other. Dot luminance was 160 cd/m^2. The upper dot was placed a variable distance either to the left or to the right of the lower dot. The task of the observer was to identify whether the dot was to the left or right. Minimum angle is the smallest distance, in minutes of visual angle, which is correctly identified 75% of the time. The vertical distance between the dots varied with eccentricity, as shown in (c). The straight lines represent the equation given in (a). The value of a is 1.08 for one observer and 0.77 for the other. Over this range of eccentricities, minimum angle increases as an approximately linear function of eccentricity. However, the rate of increase, as indexed by the value of a, is double that for grating resolution. (c) Optimal dot separation for the two-dot vernier task as a function of eccentricity. Optimal vertical separation is the separation at which the minimum angle is smallest. Although optimal separation increases as a function of eccentricity, the rate of percentage increase is much smaller than the rate for minimum angle. ((b) and (c) from G. Westheimer, The spatial grain of the perifoveal visual field, *Vision Research*, *22*. Copyright 1982 by Pergamon Press, Ltd. Reprinted with permission.)

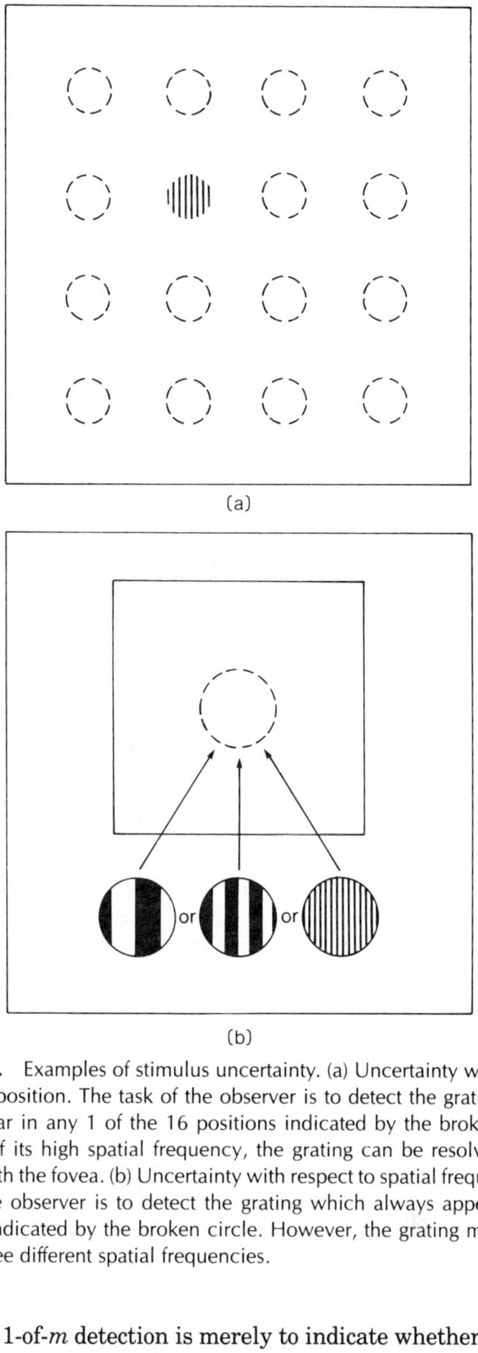

Figure 7.8. Examples of stimulus uncertainty. (a) Uncertainty with respect to spatial position. The task of the observer is to detect the grating, which may appear in any 1 of the 16 positions indicated by the broken circles. Because of its high spatial frequency, the grating can be resolved only if viewed with the fovea. (b) Uncertainty with respect to spatial frequency. The task of the observer is to detect the grating which always appears in the location indicated by the broken circle. However, the grating may be any one of three different spatial frequencies.

server in 1-of-m detection is merely to indicate whether a signal has occurred. The signal is not identified.

Performance decrements have been observed in the 1-of-m detection situation when there was uncertainty about spatial position or about spatial frequency. Cohn and Lasley (1974) found decrements when the target could occupy any one of four positions in the fovea. The design of the study eliminated visual search as a factor. Swensson and Judy (1981) also found spatial uncertainty effects. Their targets were imbedded in visual noise. Observers in their study were given unlimited time to search the display, but search time was not reflected in the performance measure. Thus both studies were so designed as to exclude the effect of time required for visual search. Nevertheless, uncertainty effects were observed. The magnitudes of the decrements were consistent with predictions based on noise effects only.

Davis, Kramer, and Graham (1983) used patches of gratings as stimuli. They found that performance was reduced by uncertainty about either the location of the patch in the visual field or the spatial frequency of the grating. The uncertainty effects disappeared when the observer was given an auditory cue just before each trial to indicate the location or frequency of the stimulus to be presented. Graham, Robson, and Nachmias (1978) and Davis and Graham (1981) also found that performance was reduced by uncertainty about spatial frequency. In all these studies, the magnitudes of the effects were consistent with predictions based only on noise. At present, there is no evidence of an attentional limitation with respect to spatial frequency.

Uncertainty about the contrast of the stimulus has little or no effect on detection performance (Davis, Kramer, & Graham, 1983; Thomas, 1983). This finding is consistent with the notion that each visual pathway is tuned with respect to spatial position and spatial frequency but responds to a broad range of contrasts. Thus uncertainty about position or spatial frequency but not about contrast requires the observer to poll more pathways and encounter more sources of noise.

1.3.3.2. Detection and Recognition. Sometimes the observer must not only detect the occurrence of a target but must also identify which of the m possible targets it is. This task is called *detection and recognition.* (The task is *detection and identification* in the terminology used in this chapter.) Starr, Metz, Lusted, and Goodenough (1975) have provided the most widely used analysis of the task. Their theorem permits the accuracy of the identification judgment to be predicted from the accuracy of the detection judgment. The soundness of the theorem has been confirmed for detection and identification of targets in radiographic images (Starr et al., 1975) and targets imbedded in visual noise (Swensson & Judy, 1981). Green and Birdsall (1978) provide an excellent discussion of the theorem.

A related task is the 2-by-2 simultaneous detection and identification task which is often used in the laboratory. On each trial, one of two possible targets is presented in one of two possible observation intervals (either temporal or spatial). The observer identifies both the interval of presentation (the detection judgment) and the target (the identification judgment). The detection judgment is affected by uncertainty because the observer does not know which of the two stimuli is to be presented on a given trial; the identification judgment is also affected because the observer does not know which interval contains the stimulus. Thomas, Gille, and Barker (1982) have analyzed the uncertainty effects presented by this paradigm. Their analysis is noteworthy because it does not assume that the stimuli are orthogonal. The analysis is designed to be applied when the stimuli are similar enough that they activate overlapping sets of pathways.

2. DETECTION

Much of our current knowledge of spatial pattern perception comes from studies of the detection task. The detection task itself and related performance measures were described in Sections 1.2.2 and 1.2.3, respectively. In this section, empirical results from detection studies and models based on the detection task are presented. Results presented in Section 2.1 focus on basic sensitivity data, illustrating how detection thresholds vary with changes in the spatial parameters of the stimulus; temporal parameters are briefly considered in this section, but Chapter 6 by Watson should be consulted for a fuller treatment. Section 2.2 concentrates on interaction phenomena. Results presented in that section illustrate how the detection threshold is affected by a second stimulus, as a function of similarity along one or more stimulus dimensions. Studies of interaction phenomena are primarily used to estimate the tuning characteristics of detecting mechanisms. The rationale underlying studies of this type was discussed in Section 1.1.4. Finally, Section 2.3 provides a theoretical discussion of current detection models.

2.1 Parameters of Detection Sensitivity

Two types of targets have been used to determine basic detection sensitivity. Historically, the visibility of spatially localized, aperiodic targets, such as spots of light or lines, has been measured. The basic data which describe sensitivity to spatially localized stimuli are spatial summation curves, which relate the luminance threshold (cd/m^2) to stimulus size. More recently, repetitive grating patterns have been widely adopted as stimuli. Basic sensitivity to these repetitive patterns is described by contrast sensitivity curves, which plot the reciprocal of the contrast threshold as a function of the spatial frequency of the grating pattern. Sections 2.1.1 and 2.1.2, respectively, describe areal summation and contrast sensitivity curves.

Sensitivity to either aperiodic or periodic patterns is affected in parallel ways by some additional stimulus parameters: mean luminance level, the orientation of the pattern, and the location of the pattern in the visual field. Temporal parameters of stimulation also affect the visibility of both target types, but the results are not always directly comparable. The effects of these parameters are discussed in Sections 2.1.3 through 2.1.6. Two other stimulus properties, each pertaining only to one target type, are discussed in conjunction with the basic detection curves. For spatially localized targets, the effect of shape on spatial summation is considered in Section 2.1.1. For grating patterns, the effect of the number of visible cycles on contrast sensitivity curves is described in Section 2.1.2.

2.1.1. Spatial Summation. It has long been established that the detectability of a spatially localized stimulus varies with its size. The basic data describing this variation in the space domain are spatial summation curves. Each curve in Figure 7.9 illustrates the contrast threshold for circular spots of light as a function of stimulus size. The parameter is mean luminance level, discussed in Section 2.1.3. In each curve, the contrast threshold is lower for larger stimuli than for small, reflecting the property termed *spatial* or *areal summation*.

Each curve can be characterized in terms of three segments. For small stimuli, threshold is determined by total flux, regardless of its spatial distribution. Such complete summation is described by Ricco's law, which characterizes integration across space as the linear sum of the light within a stimulus. This linear relationship breaks down for larger stimulus sizes. For circular stimuli, the point at which Ricco's law breaks down is characterized by the stimulus diameter, a measure termed the *critical diameter*. Beyond the critical diameter, each curve shows a transition region. In this segment of the curve, the threshold contrast decreases more slowly than Ricco's law predicts, indicating only partial summation across space. The transition region gives way to the final segment of each curve, which is nearly flat. For these larger stimuli, detection is nearly independent of size.

Detectability is not simply determined by target area. It is also affected by the shape of the stimulus. For example, the range over which spatial summation occurs depends in part on the shape of the stimulus (Lamar, Hecht, Shlaer, & Hendley, 1947; Thomas, 1978). For rectangular stimuli, spatial summation occurs over a greater range when the longer dimension of the stimulus is varied than when the shorter dimension is varied, as can be seen in Figure 7.10. The effect occurs regardless of the orientation of the rectangle. One interpretation of these results is that they reflect the asymmetrical organization of cortical receptive fields (Thomas, 1978).

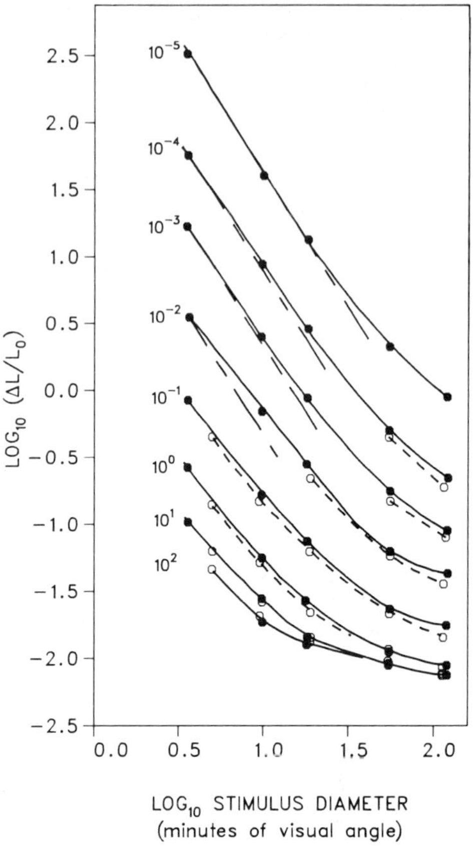

Figure 7.9. Spatial summation as a function of target size and adaptation level. Log-increment (solid lines) and log-decrement (dashed lines) thresholds $\Delta L/L_0$ plotted as a function of log stimulus diameter for several adaptation levels. Complete summation (Ricco's law) is given by a slope of −2. The area of complete summation decreases as mean luminance level increases. The test stimulus was a variable diameter circle (3.6–121.0 min) presented for 6 sec on a 10° background. Adaptation level, L_0, ranged from 10^{-5} to 10^2 cd/m^2. Observers were 19 young women, 19–26 years old, with normal vision. Each freely scanned the background from a distance of 18.2 m, so that viewing was probably parafoveal for the three lowest adaptation levels. The test spot could appear at one of eight positions projected on the circumference of an imaginary 3° radius circle, and a spatial forced-choice detection task was used to estimate threshold. Threshold was taken to be the point at which the probability of a correct detection was 0.5, corrected for chance. Data from Blackwell (1946).

The original interpretation of spatial summation curves obtained with aperiodic stimuli was that they reflected integration across space within a single, broadly tuned mechanism (Blackwell, 1963). Predictions on the basis of this approach, however, inadequately account for a number of pattern-specific effects. Interactions between two stimuli in subthreshold summation, masking, and adaptation paradigms depend on the similarity of the stimuli, with respect to size, shape, orientation, and contours. Because of these phenomena (discussed in Section 2.2), spatial summation curves have been reinterpreted. Rather than reflecting a single mechanism, each curve is considered to be the envelope of the summation functions of a number of differently tuned mechanisms (Thomas, 1970).

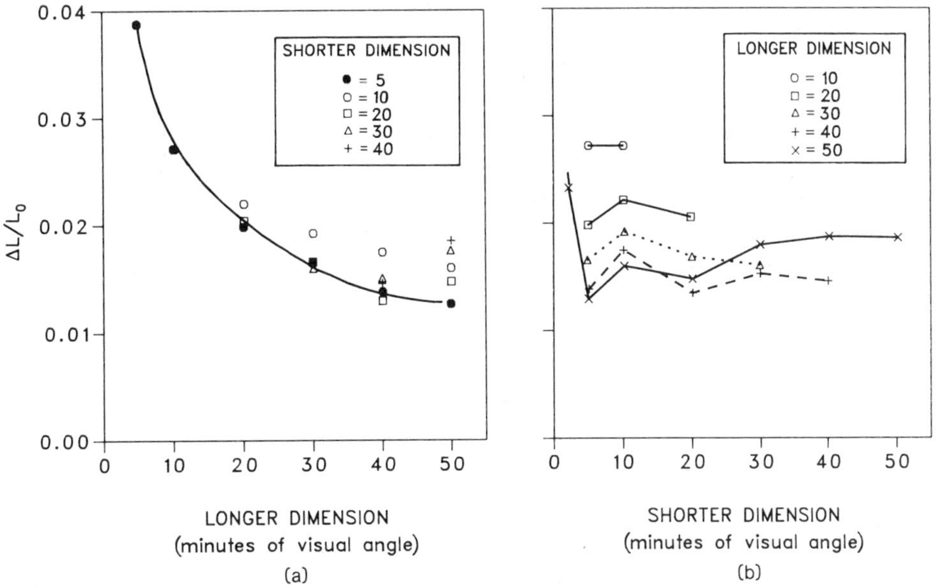

Figure 7.10. Visibility ($\Delta L/L_0$) as a function of (a) longer dimension and (b) shorter dimension. The long and short dimensions (0–50 min) of rectangular stimuli were independently varied to obtain detection thresholds. All stimuli were presented for 1 sec against a continuous background (L_0 = 320 cd/m^2), 5° high by 10° wide. Stimuli were viewed monocularly in a Maxwellian view through a 2-mm artificial pupil. Detection thresholds were measured in a signal detection rating procedure, from which the area under the receiver operating characteristic was calculated. Visibility was defined as the luminance which yielded an area of 0.8 (comparable to 80% visibility in a two-alternative forced-choice procedure). Visibility increased as the longer dimension was increased up to 40 or 50 min. Increases in the short dimension produced systematic increases in visibility only from 0 to 5 min. Data from Thomas (1978).

2.1.2. Contrast Sensitivity. Recently, contrast sensitivity curves obtained with sinusoidal gratings have been used to describe variations in detection sensitivity. The basic measure is variation in contrast sensitivity with the spatial frequency of the grating, as shown in Figure 7.11. Each curve plots the reciprocal contrast needed to detect a sinusoidal grating as a function of the spatial frequency of the grating. The general shape of each curve is that of a band-pass filter, characterized by a peak in the middle-frequency range with lower sensitivity to frequencies on either side. The frequency at which peak sensitivity occurs depends upon mean luminance, but generally occurs in the range of 4–8 cycles/degree. When contrast is maximal, the highest frequency grating which can be detected is about 60 cycles/degree at high luminance levels. This high-frequency cutoff is a measure of acuity.

The shape of the curve as a whole depends on mean luminance, the parameter in Figure 7.11. Contrast sensitivity also depends on the orientation of the grating and on its location in the visual field. Sensitivity to low frequencies further depends on temporal parameters. These effects are discussed in Sections 2.1.3 through 2.1.6.

One additional parameter affects the low-frequency portion of the contrast sensitivity curve as it is usually measured, which is the number of visible cycles. Below a critical number, the visibility of sinusoidal gratings increases with an increase in the number of cycles visible to the observer (Campbell & Robson, 1968; Hoekstra, van der Gott, van den Brink, & Bilsen, 1974; Savoy & McCann, 1975). The magnitude of the effect does not depend on spatial frequency. However, the critical number of cycles increases with increases in mean luminance. This effect is shown in Figure 7.12 for a 2 cycles/degree grating.

Because contrast sensitivity curves are normally measured under fixed-aperture viewing conditions, the effect of visible cycles is only evident at low spatial frequencies. When corrected for this effect, the shape of the contrast sensitivity curve is low pass, rather than band pass. A contrast sensitivity curve corrected for number of visible cycles is presented in Figure 7.13.

Contrast sensitivity curves obtained with grating patterns are interpreted as tracing the envelope over a number of more narrowly tuned mechanisms. Like the similar interpretation of spatial summation curves, the evidence supporting multiple mechanisms is based primarily upon the pattern-specific results of interaction studies. Grating stimuli interact in spatial summation, adaptation, and masking studies only if both patterns are similar in spatial frequency and orientation. Such pattern-specific interactions can only be explained on the basis of multiple mechanisms. The results of interaction studies obtained with grating stimuli are discussed in Section 2.2.

2.1.3. Mean Luminance. Contrast sensitivity for any pattern increases as mean luminance, or adaptation level, increases. The multiple curves in Figures 7.9 and 7.11 illustrate the magnitude of this increase for spatially localized spots of light and for grating patterns, respectively. A second change occurring with increases in mean luminance is that the resolution capabilities of the visual system increase. In Figure 7.9, this increased ability is reflected by the decreasing critical diameters of the test spots (Barlow, 1958; Blackwell, 1946) as mean luminance increases. For grating stimuli, the high-frequency cutoff (acuity) occurs at higher spatial frequencies (Campbell & Robson, 1968). This result is clearly seen in Figure 7.11.

Contrast sensitivity curves obtained with grating stimuli show a third effect of increasing mean luminance, also evident in Figure 7.11. The shape of the curve changes from low pass to band pass, and the frequency at which peak sensitivity occurs

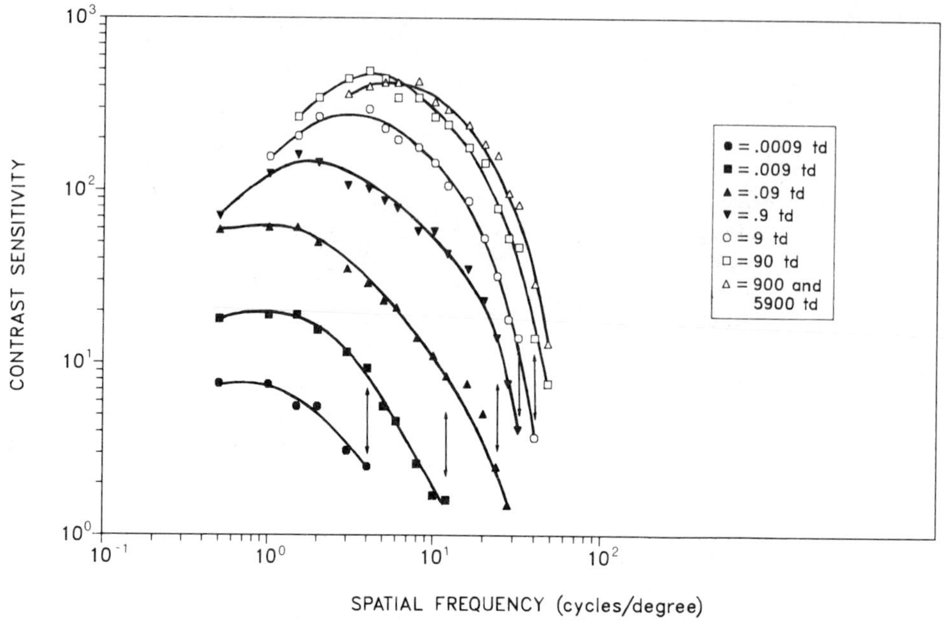

Figure 7.11. Contrast sensitivity as a function of spatial frequency. The target was a sine wave grating, 4.5° wide by 8.25° high, formed by transilluminating a transparency with monochromatic light of 525 nm. The target was seen in Maxwellian view through a 2-mm artificial pupil. The surround was dark. The independent variable is the spatial frequency of the grating. The dependent variable is contrast sensitivity, the reciprocal of contrast at the detection threshold. The parameter is the mean luminance of the grating expressed in trolands (trolands = cd/m^2 multiplied by the area of the artificial pupil). The data are from a single observer. The heights of such curves are known to vary somewhat from one observer to another and from one psychophysical procedure to another. The exact shapes of the curves and the locations of the peaks depend on the width of the grating and the temporal parameters of each exposure. However, three features of the data are commonly observed: (1) contrast sensitivity increases as mean luminance increases and approaches an asymptote as mean luminance nears 1000 trolands (or approximately 300 cd/m^2); (2) as mean luminance increases, the shape of the contrast sensitivity function changes from low pass to band pass; and (3) as mean luminance increases, the peaks of the functions shift to higher spatial frequencies. The arrows indicate the magnitude of the displacement between successive curves required by the DeVries-Rose square-root law. For clarity, the arrows are omitted from the upper curves, where the relationship breaks down. (From F. L. Van Nes & M. A. Bouman, Spatial modulation transfer in the human eye, *Journal of the Optical Society of America*, 1967, *57*. Reprinted with permission.)

shifts to the right. One feature of a band-pass shape is that a low-frequency falloff occurs, and sensitivity is lower at low frequencies than at intermediate frequencies. Part of the reduced sensitivity commonly observed at higher luminance levels may be related to the fact that less than the critical number of cycles is visible. This effect becomes more pronounced at higher luminance levels because, as noted in Section 2.1.2, the critical number of cycles increases with increases in mean luminance.

2.1.4. Orientation. The detectability of a stimulus varies as a function of orientation. Visibility is highest for targets oriented vertically or horizontally and is reduced at oblique orientations (Appelle, 1972; Camisa, Blake, & Lema, 1977; Higgins & Stultz, 1948; Ogilvie & Taylor, 1958). The effect is similar for both spatially localized targets and for grating stimuli and is termed the *oblique* effect. When grating stimuli are used, it has been found that the effect is not constant for all spatial frequencies; visibility at oblique orientations is more severely degraded for high spatial frequencies. Campbell, Kulikowski, and Levinson (1966) describe this relationship, illustrated in Figure 7.14, by the equation:

$$S(f) = A^{-akf},$$

where $S(f)$ is the contrast sensitivity, A is a constant which depends on intensity and focal state, a represents the slope of the function for the most visible orientation when plotted on semilog coordinates (as in Figure 7.14), k is a coefficient which depends upon orientation, and f is spatial frequency.

Optical astigmatism can produce a spatial-frequency–dependent effect similar to the oblique effect, when the axis of the astigmatism is such that oblique lines are blurred. However, the oblique effect occurs in the absence of such astigmatism. Furthermore, the effect is evident when the optics of the eye are bypassed entirely by imaging interference fringes directly on the retina (Campbell, Kulikowski, & Levinson, 1966). Thus it is likely that the origin of the oblique effect is neural in nature. Physiological evidence also suggests that the origin of the effect is cortical. No anisotropy is found in electrical activity at the retina, but the effect appears in evoked cortical potentials (Maffei & Campbell, 1970).

Noting that the oblique effect is more pronounced at high spatial frequencies, Quinn and Lehmkuhle (1983) recently suggested that the oblique effect may in part be the result of superior spatial pooling along the primary axes in mechanisms responding selectively to higher frequencies. (*Spatial pooling* refers to the putative integration of information from pathways tuned to different spatial locations. It is distinct from spatial summation, which presumably includes integration within individual pathways. See Section 2.3 for a further discussion of pooling.) Quinn and Lehmkuhle reported that the effect of in-

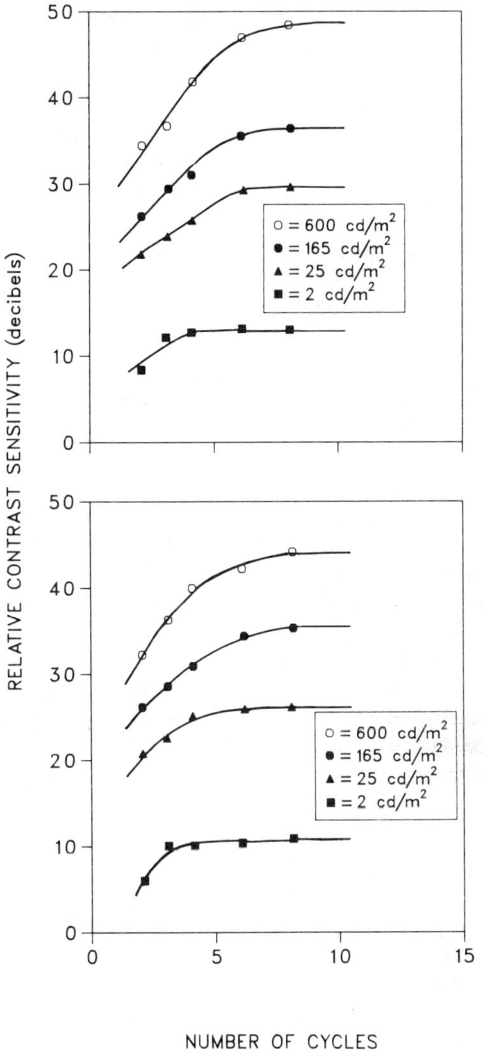

Figure 7.12. Relative contrast sensitivity as a function of number of cycles visible, at four mean luminance levels. Relative sensitivity is expressed in decibels. The test stimulus was a 2 cycles/degree sinusoidal grating, presented in vertical orientation on a TV monitor. The number of visible cycles was controlled by varying the aperture size of the display with masks, which were never less than 1° in height. Observers freely scanned the display, but other procedural details of data collection were not reported. The two figures represent results from two different observers. At each of the mean luminance values tested, a critical number of cycles were found. Above this critical number, threshold was independent of the number of visible cycles. Below this critical value, threshold decreased as fewer cycles were visible. The critical number increased with increasing mean luminance. Although the results presented here are for a single spatial frequency, virtually identical results were found for gratings up to 7 cycles/degree when tested at the two highest luminance levels. This result suggests that the effect of visible cycles is independent of spatial frequency, at least for frequencies below 8 cycles/degree. (From J. Hoekstra, D. P. A. van der Goot, G. van den Brink, & F. A. Bilsen, The influence of the number of cycles upon the visual contrast threshold for spatial sine wave patterns, *Vision Research, 14*. Copyright 1974 by Pergamon Press, Ltd. Reprinted with permission.)

creasing the number of visible cycles on contrast sensitivity depended on both spatial frequency and orientation. For sinusoidal grating patterns of 3, 10.5, and 13.5 cycles/degree, visibility increased for all stimuli with an increase in the visible number of cycles, and vertical gratings were more visible than those oriented obliquely. However, at the two highest spatial frequencies, visibility increased more rapidly for gratings oriented vertically than for those oriented along the oblique axis. This result suggests that for mechanisms responding to these higher spatial frequencies, spatial pooling is superior along the vertical axis. For the 3 cycles/degree gratings, the effect of increasing the number of visible cycles was identical for vertical and oblique orientations.

The magnitude of the oblique effect may depend in part on other factors. For example, the effect can be reduced in adults by experience with oblique angles (Fiorentini, Ghez, & Maffei, 1972a, 1972b), and criterion effects may account for a portion of the psychophysical results (Weitzman, Smith, & Karasik, 1972).

2.1.5. Retinal Location. The ability to detect a pattern depends on retinal location, generally decreasing as eccentricity increases (Millodot, 1966; Wilson & Giese, 1977). However, the functions obtained depend both on spatial and temporal properties of the stimulus.

The rate at which sensitivity decreases with eccentricity depends on size or spatial frequency. Figure 7.15 clearly illustrates this dependency in the spatial frequency domain. Sensitivity to all frequencies is highest at the fixation point, decreasing as a function of eccentricity. However, sensitivity to high spatial frequencies decreases much more rapidly than sensitivity to lower frequencies.

With aperiodic stimuli, the area over which spatial summation occurs is larger in the periphery than in the fovea (C. H. Graham, Brown, & Mote, 1939), perhaps reflecting larger receptive fields found peripherally (Hubel & Wiesel, 1974b). However, the critical diameter found at any retinal location also depends on temporal parameters of the stimulus (Barlow, 1958; Zuidema, Verschuure, Bouman, & Koenderink, 1981).

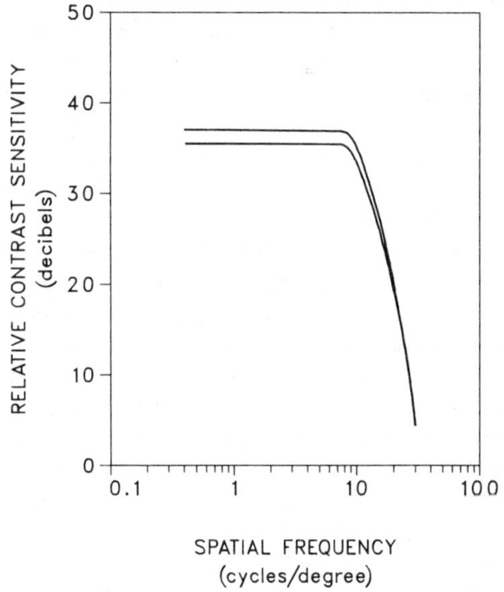

Figure 7.13. Contrast sensitivity function corrected for number of visible cycles. Relative sensitivity is shown, expressed in decibels. The theoretical curves depicted here were constructed on the basis of the results presented in Figure 7.12. Curves are shown for two subjects at a mean luminance of 165 cd/m². When corrected for the number of visible cycles, the low-frequency dropoff in sensitivity disappears; contrast sensitivity is constant for all spatial frequencies below about 8 cycles/degree. (From J. Hoekstra, D. P. A. van der Goot, G. van den Brink, & F. A. Bilsen, The influence of the number of cycles upon the visual contrast threshold for spatial sine wave patterns, *Vision Research, 14*. Copyright 1974 by Pergamon Press, Ltd. Reprinted with permission.)

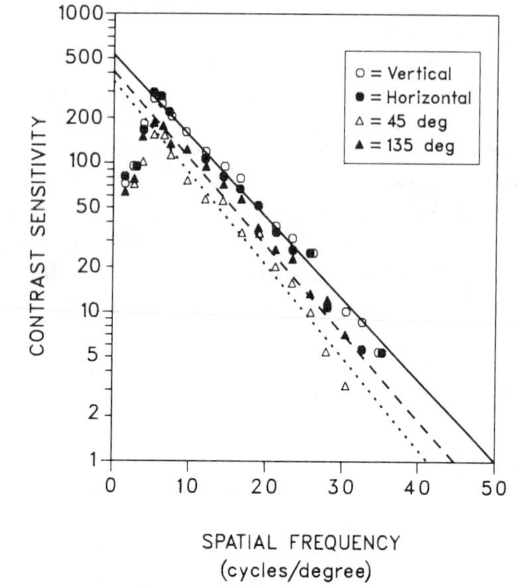

Figure 7.14. Effect of orientation on contrast sensitivity functions. Sinusoidal gratings at a mean luminance of 170 cd/m^2 were presented. Log contrast sensitivity is plotted against spatial frequency for gratings presented at four orientations. Vertical and horizontal orientations are given by open and filled circles; oblique angles of 45° and 135° are represented by open and filled triangles. Straight lines are drawn by eye. Relative grating acuities as a function of orientation are shown by the relative positions at which these lines cross the frequency axis. (From D. E. Mitchell & F. Wilkinson, The effect of early astigmatism on the visual resolution of gratings, *Journal of Physiology*, 1974, *243*. Reprinted with permission.)

These effects are discussed further in Chapter 5 by Hood and Finkelstein. The interpretation of interactions between stimulus size, temporal parameters, and retinal location is further complicated by recent evidence that rapid, spatially selective adaptation effects may contaminate measured thresholds (Frome, MacLeod, Buck, & Williams, 1981; Zuidema et al., 1981).

It was pointed out in Section 1.3.2 that performance degradation in the periphery can be in part accounted for by decreased receptor density and cortical representation, but such an explanation cannot fully account for the changes in spatiotemporal characteristics found at different retinal eccentricities.

2.1.6. Temporal Parameters. The visibility of a pattern depends in part on the temporal parameters of stimulation. The visual system integrates light not only over space but also over time. The two kinds of integration are interdependent, and the relationship varies in complex ways with retinal eccentricity. A detailed discussion of temporal factors is provided in Chapter 6 by Watson.

The primary finding with spatially localized stimuli is that spatial and temporal factors are separable with small, briefly presented stimuli but interact in complex ways when stimuli are extended either in time or space. When small spatially localized stimuli are briefly presented to the fovea, threshold luminance is inversely proportional to stimulus duration (Barlow, 1958; Zuidema et al., 1981). This simple relationship breaks down at longer durations or when large stimuli are presented. At eccentricities beyond about 15°, no simple relationship is found for any size-duration combination. These issues are discussed at length in Chapter 5 by Hood and Finkelstein.

Parallel results are found with grating stimuli. The effect of temporal modulation on contrast sensitivity is shown in Figure 7.16. At high temporal frequencies, the effect of modulation is independent of spatial frequency; the entire contrast sensitivity function is simply translated vertically. At low temporal frequencies, sensitivity to low spatial frequencies is selectively reduced. As pointed out in Chapter 6 by Watson, these results indicate that the relationship between temporal modulation and spatial frequency is separable at high spatial and temporal frequencies but more complex and not separable at lower frequencies in either the time- or spatial-frequency domains (Koenderink & van Doorn, 1980; Robson, 1966).

2.2. Interaction Phenomena

Subthreshold summation, masking, and adaptation paradigms have been widely used to determine the tuning characteristics of spatial mechanisms involved in the detection process. The focus of these studies is to determine the extent to which the detection threshold for one stimulus is affected by a second stimulus. In some cases, the detectability of a compound stimulus is compared to the detectability of each component in isolation. The presence of an interaction, signaled by a change in threshold, is taken as evidence that the two stimuli share at least some processing pathways. Conversely, the absence of an interaction is taken as evidence that the stimuli are processed by separate and, in some cases, independent neural pathways. A more detailed discussion of the rationale and assumptions underlying interaction phenomena can be found in Section 1.1.4.

The two major questions addressed by studies of interaction phenomena are (1) What are the dimensions along which stimuli

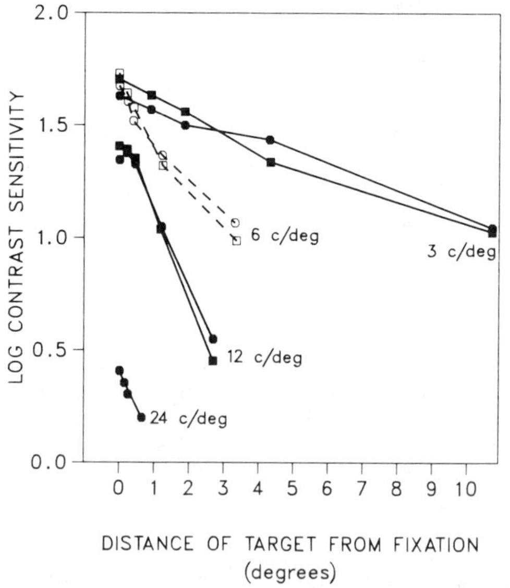

Figure 7.15. Contrast sensitivity as a function of eccentricity. The target was a patch of sine wave grating. The height and width of the patch each were equal to four periods of the grating. Thus the patch contained four cycles. The patch was presented either above or below fixation, bars oriented horizontally. Mean luminance was 500 cd/m^2. Eccentricity is the distance, in degrees of visual arc, between the fixation point and the center of the patch. Contrast sensitivity is the reciprocal of contrast at the detection threshold. Each point represents the results for one observer, averaged over placements both above and below fixation. Contrast sensitivity decreases with eccentricity for all spatial frequencies measured. However, the rate of decrease increases as the spatial frequency increases. (From J. G. Robson & N. Graham, Probability summation and regional variation in contrast sensitivity across the visual field, *Vision Research*, *21*. Copyright 1981 by Pergamon Press, Ltd. Reprinted with permission.)

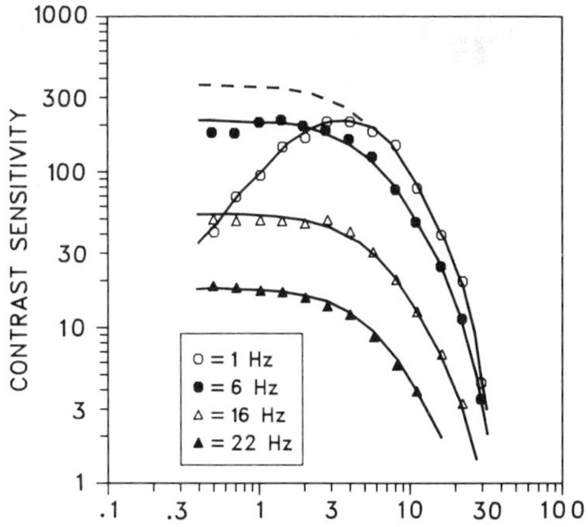

Figure 7.16. Spatial contrast sensitivity function for several temporal modulations. Sinusoidal grating patterns subtending 2.5° were viewed binocularly at a distance of 2 m. The patterns were displayed in the center of a 10° surround and temporally modulated around a mean luminance of 20 cd/m^2. Each point represents the mean of four measurements (method not given): open circles, 1 Hz; closed circles, 6 Hz; open triangles, 16 Hz; closed triangles, 22 Hz. (From J. G. Robson, Spatial and temporal contrast sensitivity functions of the visual system, *Journal of the Optical Society of America*, 1966, *56*. Reprinted with permission.)

interact and (2) Along any one dimension, what is the range of the interaction? In answer to the first question, the general finding of relevance to this chapter is that the detection threshold for a target is affected by a second stimulus to the greatest extent when the stimuli share certain spatial characteristics. For spatially extended grating patterns, interactions occur when the stimuli are similar in spatial frequency and orientation. For spatially localized stimuli, threshold is affected when the stimuli share the characteristics of size, shape or contour, location in the visual field, and orientation.

As the two stimuli increasingly differ along any of these dimensions, the magnitude of the interaction generally decreases. When plotted as a function of the difference between the stimuli, the magnitude of the interaction traces a tuning curve that reflects the response range of the shared neural pathways. The response range is generally measured as twice the difference at which the effect reaches half its maximum value in either direction, termed the *half-amplitude, full bandwidth*. The magnitude of the interaction continues to fall as the difference between the stimuli increases, until at some difference no interaction is observed. This result is often interpreted as an indication that stimuli that differ at least to this extent are processed by separate and independent mechanisms. The assumption of independence, however, has recently been called into question. Along a number of dimensions, stimuli that differ beyond the point of apparent independence may also interact. The nature of the interaction for these widely differing stimuli is opposite in polarity to that found when the stimuli are similar.

In this section, the evidence for tuning along each of the relevant dimensions is summarized. Tuning functions obtained by the various interaction techniques are presented and compared wherever possible. All empirically determined bandwidths reported in this section should be distinguished from the theoretical bandwidths discussed in Section 2.3. Theoretically determined bandwidths are based on models which assume a single processing stage. The tuning functions revealed by studies of subthreshold summation, masking, and adaptation may reflect interactions occurring at any stage of processing. To clearly distinguish between these two types of bandwidths, the estimates empirically determined by studies of interaction phenomena will be referred to as *interaction bandwidths*.

2.2.1. Spatial Frequency. There is considerable evidence that spatial frequency components that differ by more than 1 octave are processed by separate neural pathways. For a variety of complex repetitive patterns (square, rectangular, and sawtooth waveforms), visibility is not determined by the amplitude of the pattern as a whole. Instead, the pattern is detected when the contrast of the fundamental component reaches its own independent threshold (Campbell & Robson, 1968). For these patterns, the fundamental frequency component has the highest physical amplitude and differs from the next highest component by at least a factor of 2. However, a similar result is found when a compound grating is formed by superimposing two well-separated frequency components and the contrasts of the components are independently manipulated. The compound grating is not detected until one frequency component reaches its own independent threshold. In addition, the relative phase of the two component sinusoids has no effect on the detectability of the pattern, although the amplitude of the complex waveform varies markedly (N. Graham & Nachmias, 1971). Figure 7.17 illustrates these results for several component-frequency combinations. A final result that suggests multiple-frequency-tuned pathways is that unless frequency components in a complex waveform differ by less than a factor of 2, psychometric functions for complex waveforms are well predicted by a model that assumes independent detection of the components (Sachs, Nachmias, & Robson, 1971).

When frequency components differ by less than an octave, interactions do occur. Adaptation to a grating pattern of one spatial frequency elevates the detection threshold for patterns of a similar frequency by as much as a factor of 5 (Blakemore & Campbell, 1969; Pantle & Sekuler, 1968). The peak effect occurs at the adapting frequency, decreasing as test and adapting frequencies increasingly differ. Tuning functions estimated by adaptation are illustrated in Figure 7.18 for five adapting frequencies. At each frequency, the adaptation effect is reduced by half at frequency separations of about 0.5 octave. Frequency-dependent adaptation effects are orientation specific (Blakemore & Nachmias, 1971; Gilinsky, 1968) and show interocular transfer (Blakemore & Campbell, 1969).

Masking paradigms yield tuning curves and interaction bandwidth estimates similar to those obtained by selective adaptation. For both grating and filtered noise masks, threshold for grating stimuli is maximally elevated when the mask contains the same frequency component as the test stimulus. Interaction bandwidths estimated by masking are similar to those estimated by adaptation methods; the effect is reduced by half when the mask and test differ by 0.5–0.75 octave (Henning, Hertz, & Hinton, 1981; Legge & Foley, 1980; Stromeyer & Julesz, 1972).

These data collectively provide strong evidence that spatial frequency components that differ by more than an octave are detected by separate neural pathways. At separations of about 1 octave, the data suggest that the pathways operate independently. However, for pathways tuned to widely separated frequencies, the assumption of independence has been challenged by the results of other summation (Hirsch, Hylton, & Graham, 1982; Olzak, 1981; Olzak & Thomas, 1981), adaptation (K. K. DeValois, 1977; Nachmias, Sansbury, Vassilev, & Weber, 1973;

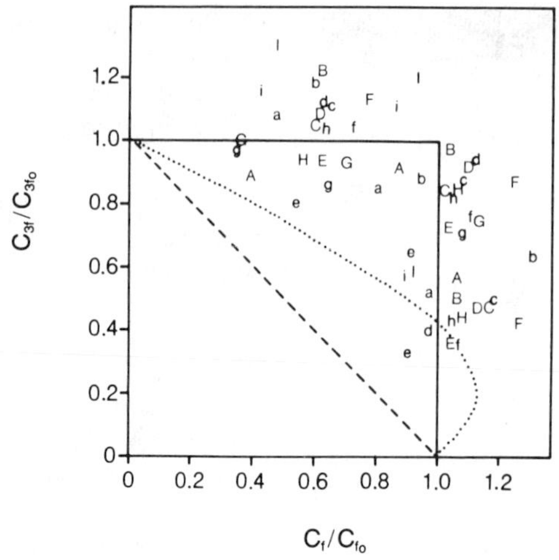

Figure 7.17. Contrast thresholds for compound gratings, relative to thresholds for their sinusoidal components. The detectability of four types of grating patterns was determined by two procedures: the method of adjustment and a temporal forced-choice staircase. All patterns were composed of vertically oriented sinusoidal components, displayed on a cathode-ray tube (CRT) and viewed monocularly through a 1.5-mm-diameter artificial pupil from a distance of 103 cm. For most conditions, the display subtended 4.8 × 4.4° of visual angle, and patterns were presented at a mean luminance of 3 ftL. Two of the pattern types were compound gratings whose components were in the ratio of 3:1 (*f* and 3*f*). The components were added in either peaks-add or peaks-subtract phase. The remaining two pattern types were simple gratings, composed of just the *f* or the 3*f* component alone. The lower frequencies *f* are listed in the table below. Each symbol plots the contrast needed to just detect the compound grating relative to the contrast thresholds for each component alone (C_{3f}/C_{3f_0} and C_f/C_{f_0}). Each letter depicts a different absolute combination of spatial frequency components and/or method of data collection, as shown in the list below. Results obtained when components were added in peaks-add phase are shown in capital letters; those obtained for the peaks-subtract phase are depicted by lowercase letters. Predictions based on a single-channel model are shown by the dashed diagonal line for the peaks-add patterns and by the dotted curve for the peaks-subtract patterns. A single-channel model assumes that the visibility of the compound pattern depends on the summed effects of both components, leading to the expectations that (1) the compound will be detectable even when both components are below their own independent thresholds and (2) threshold for the compound depends on the phase relationship between the components. It is clear that the data do not support this model. Predictions based on a multiple-channel model, which assumes independent detection of *f* and 3*f* components, are shown by the solid lines. Each line represents the prediction for both phase relationships. This model predicts that (1) the compound will be detected only when at least one component reaches its own independent threshold and (2) since detection of the components is independent, the phase relationship between them will not be a factor. The data support both predictions. (From N. Graham & J. Nachmias, Detection of grating patterns containing two spatial frequencies: A comparison of single-channel and multiple-channel models, *Vision Research, 11*. Copyright 1971 by Pergamon Press, Ltd. Reprinted with permission.)

Key to Symbols

Symbols	Lower Frequency	Method	Number of Determinations
A, *a*	0.9	Staircase	6
B, *b*	1.8	Staircase	6
C, *c*	2.7	Staircase	7
D, *d*	0.9	Adjustment	9
E, *e*	3.6	Staircase	6
F, *f*	3.6	Adjustment	10
G, *g*	4.5	Adjustment	12
H, *h*	5.4	Adjustment	10
I, *i*	6.3	Adjustment	12

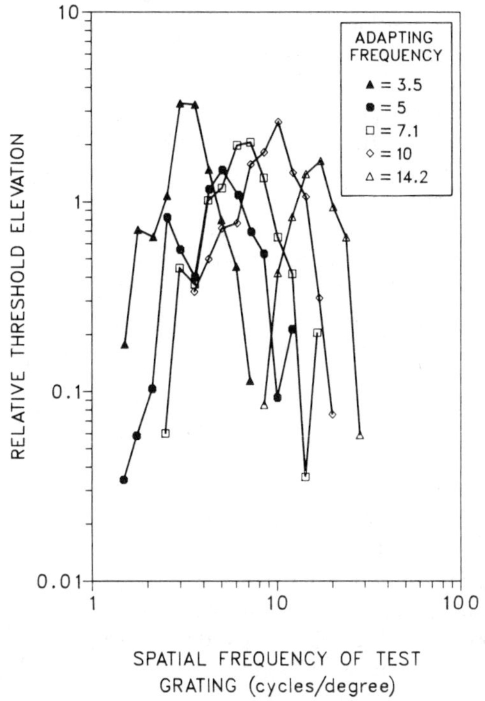

Figure 7.18. Spatial-frequency selective adaptation curves. Contrast thresholds for a series of sinusoidal grating patterns which differed in spatial frequency were determined prior to, and following adaptation to, a high-contrast grating. Mean luminance was held constant at 100 cd/m^2. The observer freely scanned an oscilloscope display, which subtended 1.5° of visual arc at a viewing distance of 2.9 m. The pattern was displayed twice per second, and contrast was adjusted by the observer to threshold. In the adaptation condition, the observer adapted for 60 sec to a high-contrast (1.5 log units above threshold) pattern of either 3.5, 5, 7.1, 10, or 14.2 cycles/degree. Immediately following the adaptation period, threshold was determined for a low-contrast test grating, which varied in spatial frequency from trial to trial. The ratio of the contrast threshold after adaptation to the threshold before adaptation is plotted for each adapting frequency as a function of the test frequency. A constant of 1.0 has been subtracted for convenience, so that no difference is indicated by a 0 threshold elevation. The adapting effect was found to be maximal at the adapting frequency, declining as test and adapting frequencies differed. The curves are very similar across adapting frequencies, each showing a similar magnitude and shape. The half-amplitude bandwidth determined by adaptation was found to be just over 1 octave. (From C. Blakemore & F. W. Campbell, On the existence of neurons in the human visual system selectively sensitive to the orientation and size of retinal images, *Journal of Physiology*, 1969, *203*. Reprinted with permission.)

Stetcher, Sigel, & Lange, 1973; Tolhurst, 1972; Tolhurst & Barfield, 1978), and masking studies (Barfield & Tolhurst, 1975; Nachmias & Weber, 1975; Stromeyer & Klein, 1974; Tolhurst & Barfield, 1978). The evidence from these studies suggests that such pathways exhibit small but consistent interactions. Unfortunately, the exact nature of the interactions, and the conditions under which they are found, is not yet entirely clear.

The results obtained in adaptation paradigms suggest the existence of mutual, tonic inhibition between mechanisms that respond to widely separated frequency. When the difference between adapting and test frequencies is extended beyond the point of apparent independence, adaptation increases contrast sensitivity for frequencies up to 3 octaves away (K. K. DeValois, 1977; Tolhurst & Barfield, 1978). On the assumption that mechanisms excited by a narrow range of frequencies also tonically inhibit mechanisms sensitive to other frequency ranges, these authors suggest that adaptation at one frequency not only reduces sensitivity to nearby frequencies but also reduces the inhibitory effect at more removed frequencies.

Other results support the notion of inhibition between mechanisms that respond to widely separated frequencies but suggest that the effect is not mutually symmetric. The detectability of a 3–5 cycles/degree sinusoidal grating is reduced when a threshold-level grating 3 to 4 times higher in frequency is superimposed spatially and temporally (Hirsch, Hylton, & Graham, 1982; Olzak, 1981). A similar effect was reported for very low spatial frequencies by Furchner, Thomas, and Campbell (1977). For these frequency combinations, no reduction in visibility is found for the higher frequency grating (Hirsch, Hylton, & Graham, 1982; Olzak, 1981). Olzak (1981), in fact, reported a slight increase in sensitivity to the higher-frequency component. These results reject the possibility of independence between mechanisms that respond to widely separated spatial frequencies. Instead, they suggest that mechanisms that respond to one range of frequencies inhibit other mechanisms that respond preferentially to lower frequencies.

Asymmetric interactions are also found in masking paradigms, but it is unclear how these results relate to other interaction results. When the mask and tést frequencies are separated by at least 0.5 octave, masking increases sensitivity to test components up to 3 octaves away (Barfield & Tolhurst, 1975; Nachmias & Weber, 1975; Stromeyer & Klein, 1974; Tolhurst & Barfield, 1978). The functions obtained are similar in shape to those obtained following adaptation, with one exception. Unlike the adaptation functions, the masking effect is asymmetric with respect to spatial frequency. With masking, a greater increase in sensitivity is found for test frequencies higher than the masking frequency. Figure 7.19 illustrates the asymmetric effect of masking.

2.2.2. Orientation. There is considerable evidence that detection of stimuli which differ in orientation by 15–20° is mediated by separate neural pathways. The effects of two or more near-threshold stimuli summate only if they are similar in orientation (Blakemore & Nachmias, 1971; Kulikowski, Abadi, & King-Smith, 1973; Thomas & Shimamura, 1975). Similarly, the effects of adaptation (Fidell, 1970; Gilinsky, 1968; McCollough, 1965) and masking (Campbell & Kulikowski, 1966; Parlee, 1969; Sekuler, 1965) are specific with respect to orientation. Estimates of interaction bandwidths, however, differ considerably depending on the technique used in the estimation procedure. Estimates obtained from subthreshold summation, adaptation, and masking studies are compared in Figure 7.20.

Subthreshold summation techniques yield the narrowest bandwidth estimates of orientation selectivity. For both periodic gratings and fine lines, sensitivity is increased by the addition of a subthreshold grating that is similar in orientation. This effect decreases as orientation differences increase; half-amplitude half-bandwidths are estimated to be about 3°, and no increase in sensitivity is found when stimuli differ by 10° (Kulikowski, Abadi, & King-Smith, 1973). However, at separations of 15–25°, Thomas and Shimamura (1975) reported that threshold for two lines was higher than for either stimulus alone. This result was interpreted as evidence for inhibitory interactions between orientation-tuned mechanisms.

Prior adaptation to or the simultaneous presence of a suprathreshold (masking) grating increases the contrast threshold for a test grating by an amount that is a function of the difference in orientation of the suprathreshold grating. Estimates of half-amplitude half-bandwidth are wider for masking (12–15°; Campbell & Kulikowski, 1966) than for adaptation (6–7°;

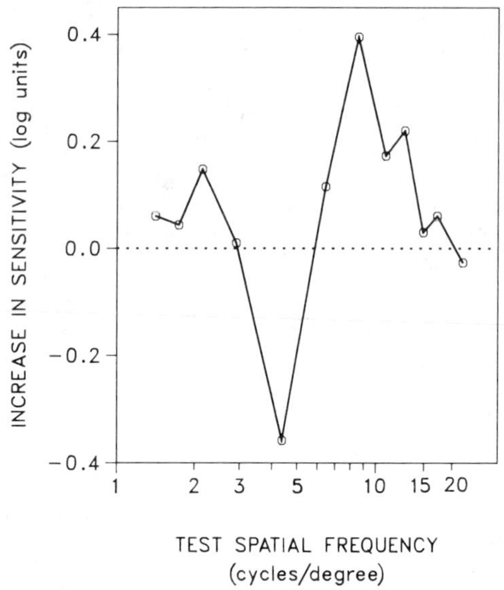

Figure 7.19. Masking as a function of test frequency. Stimuli were presented on a square cathrode-ray tube (CRT) display which subtended 5° of visual angle at a viewing distance of 228 cm. The mean luminance was 300 cd/m^2. Thresholds were determined for test gratings which differed in spatial frequency in a two-alternative forced-choice procedure and remeasured in the presence of a masking grating. In the masking condition, the mask, a 4.25 cycles/degree grating with a fixed contrast of 0.026, was presented in both intervals. In one interval, the test grating was also presented. Gratings were summed in cosine phase. The contrast at which the observer correctly identified the test plus mask interval on 75% of the trials was taken as threshold. Sensitivity was defined as the reciprocal of threshold contrast. The data plotted represent the difference between log sensitivities for several test gratings when measured with and without the mask. Data below the horizontal line indicate the usual masking effect of a decrease in sensitivity at frequencies near the mask. When the target and mask differ by about 1 octave, the effect reverses in polarity; the presence of a mask facilitates detection of test gratings. Facilitation is greater when the test grating is of a higher frequency than the mask. (From D. J. Tolhurst & L. P. Barfield, Interactions between spatial frequency channels, *Vision Research, 18*. Copyright 1978 by Pergamon Press, Ltd. Reprinted with permission.)

Blakemore & Nachmias, 1971; Gilinsky, 1968). Temporal differences between the two techniques may in part account for the differences in estimated interaction bandwidths (Kulikowski, Abadi, & King-Smith, 1973) by tapping two different populations of orientation-selective mechanisms. The results suggest that mechanisms that respond to transient stimuli are less selective to orientation than those fatigued by the more sustained adaptation paradigm.

2.2.3. Size. Size has sometimes been considered a dimension along which the visual system exhibits properties of tuning. As noted in Section 1.1.2, size- and spatial-frequency selectivity may simply be two manifestations of the same underlying processes. To the extent that this is true, the choice of the space or the spatial-frequency domain is a matter of convenience. The studies of interaction phenomena described in this section have employed spatially localized, aperiodic stimuli. Except in special cases, such stimuli have complex spatial-frequency spectra and are more easily characterized in the space domain. For this reason, selectivity with respect to size will be treated separately from spatial frequency.

One line of evidence for selectivity with respect to size is based on size-selective adaptation effects. Prior adaptation to a spatially localized stimulus will cause a decrease in the detectability of another target only when the two are similar in size. The peak effect occurs when the test diameter or width is equal to the adapting diameter or width; the effect decreases as the size difference between adapting and test stimuli increases (Bagrash, 1973; Gilinsky, 1968; Westheimer, 1967). When the adaptation and test diameter differ by a large amount, a weak facilitation effect can occur. In Figure 7.21, the selectivity of adaptation with respect to size is illustrated for two observers. The shift in the peak effect to coincide with the adapting size suggests that different, size-selective mechanisms are fatigued by the adapting stimulus in each case. An additional result which suggests the existence of multiple mechanisms is the size-dependent effect of adapting stimulus intensity. Although adaptation increases with intensity for all adapting sizes, the exact functions obtained depend on the size of the adapting stimulus (Bagrash, 1973).

In Figure 7.22, the functions from Figure 7.21 are superimposed for each observer to show how adaptation decreases as a function of the difference between test and adapting diameters. For the range of diameters examined, the function is similar for all adapting stimuli; the magnitude of the effect falls to 50% when the adapting and test stimuli differ by about 12–15 min of visual arc (Bagrash, 1973).

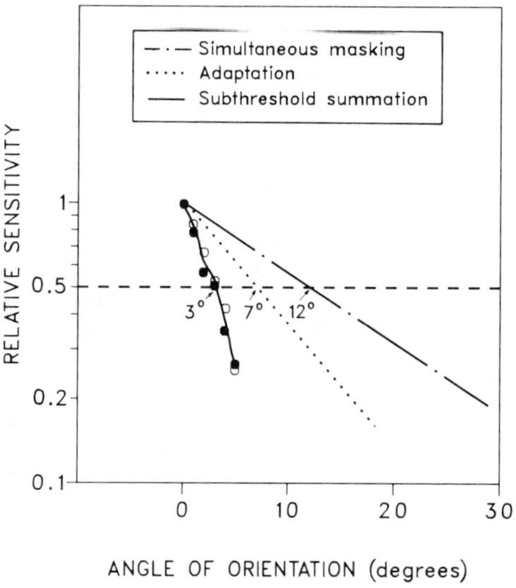

Figure 7.20. Relative orientation selectivity for grating patterns derived from three procedures: simultaneous masking (dash-dotted line, Campbell & Kulikowski, 1966), adaptation (dotted line, Blakemore & Nachmias, 1971), and subthreshold summation (solid line, Kulikowski, Abadi, & King-Smith, 1973). In each procedure, the relative effectiveness of one pattern in changing sensitivity to another is measured as a function of the relative tilt of the two patterns. The test pattern was 10 cycles/degree in the masking and subthreshold summation studies and 8.4 cycles/degree in the adaptation experiment. The narrowest bandwidth estimate (3° at half-amplitude) is found with the subthreshold summation procedure, in which threshold to a pattern is determined in the presence and absence of a second subthreshold pattern that varies in tilt relative to the test grating. A medium-bandwidth estimate (7° at half-amplitude) is found with the adaptation paradigm when the change in threshold or the apparent periodicity is measured following adaptation to patterns of various tilts. The widest-bandwidth estimate (12° at half-amplitude) results from the masking paradigm, in which the change in threshold is measured when a high-contrast pattern is briefly presented concurrently with the test, at various rotation angles. (From J. J. Kulikowski, R. Abadi, & P. E. King-Smith, Orientational selectivity of grating and line detectors in human vision, *Vision Research, 13*. Copyright 1973 by Pergamon Press, Ltd. Reprinted with permission.)

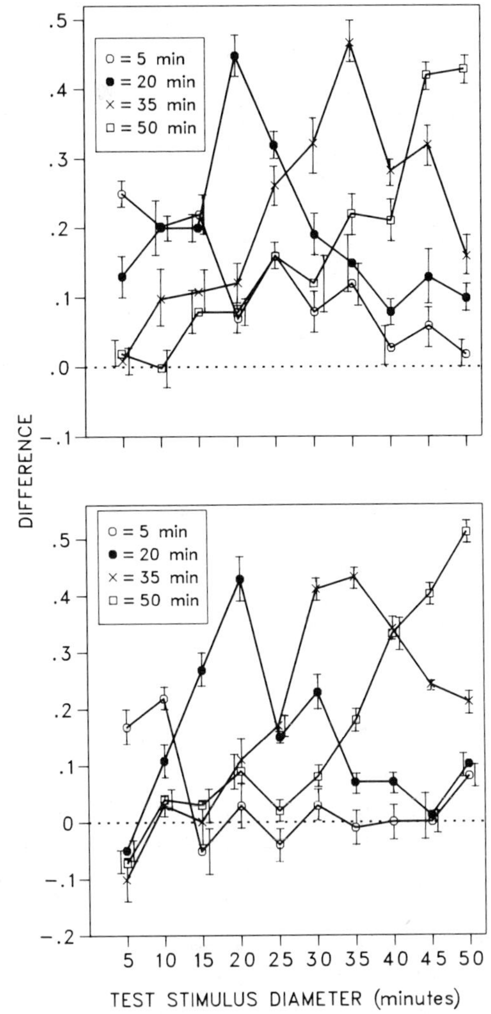

Figure 7.21. Adaptation as a function of test-stimulus diameter. The difference between log visibility with and without prior adaptation is plotted for four adapting conditions: 5, 20, 35, and 50 min. Error bars represent ± one standard error of the difference. Data shown are for two observers. Test discs (diameter range: 5–50 min in 5-min increments) were presented monocularly in Maxwellian view on a 15° background (72 cd/m^2) for 1 sec. Visibility for each test disc alone was measured in a signal detection rating procedure, and threshold taken as the luminance required to obtain an area under the receiver operating characteristic of 0.8. In adapting conditions, observers adapted to a uniform disc 1.0 log unit above its own threshold for 3 min prior to a block of 100 trials, and each trial was preceded by a 2-sec presentation of the adapting disc. Peak effect generally occurs at adapting size, decreasing as test diameter differs. (From F. M. Bagrash, Size-selective adaptation: Psychophysical evidence for size-tuning and the effects of stimulus contour and adapting flux, *Vision Research, 13*. Copyright 1973 by Pergamon Press, Ltd. Reprinted with permission.)

A second line of evidence supporting the concept of size tuning comes from masking studies. The results obtained in masking paradigms are complex, however, depending on both spatial and temporal parameters. When the degree of masking is plotted as a function of stimulus onset asynchrony (SOA), one of two functions is typically obtained. Type A functions decrease monotonically; type B functions are nonmonotonic and U shaped (Kohlers, 1962). It has been assumed (e.g., Weisstein, 1972) that these functions reflect different underlying visual processes. Although much work has been devoted to isolating the spatial conditions under which each function is obtained, the results have not yet been fully integrated. For a more comprehensive review than is possible here, the reader should consult Weisstein (1972) and others (Eriksen, 1966; Fehrer, 1966; Frumkes & Sturr, 1968; Kohlers, 1968; Schiller & Smith, 1966; Sperling, 1963; Weisstein & Haber, 1965).

One general result related to size is that when the stimuli are spatially superimposed and of the same shape, masking is most effective when the mask and the test are equal in size, declining monotonically as target and mask become increasingly dissimilar (Battersby & Wagman, 1964; Frumkes & Sturr, 1968). For these masking conditions, the functions obtained closely resemble those obtained following adaptation. However, the degree of masking depends not only on area but also upon shape (Uttal, 1970), retinal proximity (Alpern, 1953), and the presence of edges (Growney, 1976).

A third result which suggests the existence of size-tuned mechanisms concerns spatial summation within compound stimuli. When two small (< 1°) rectangles of light are superimposed, the detection threshold for the compound stimulus is generally lower than the threshold for either component alone. Sensitivity increases as the width of the smaller component approaches that of the larger component, reflecting spatial summation within the area of the compound stimulus. However, the spatial summation function observed is not constant but depends on the width of the larger component (Thomas, Padilla, & Rourke, 1969). These results have been interpreted in terms of a comprehensive model by Thomas (1970), who suggested that the different functions reflect spatial summation within separate, size-tuned mechanisms.

One phenomenon likely to be related to size tuning in the visual system combines aspects of both masking and adaptation. Threshold for a small spot of light superimposed on a larger background varies with the size of the background. As background size increases, threshold for the probe first increases and then falls (Westheimer, 1967). The increase in sensitivity found with large backgrounds is referred to as *Westheimer sensitization*. The effect decreases with decreasing background luminance, as shown in Figure 7.23. As retinal eccentricity increases, the maximal effect obtained occurs for larger background sizes. This effect can be seen in Figure 7.24. Westheimer sensitization and related phenomena are discussed at length in Chapter 5 by Hood and Finkelstein.

2.2.4. Location in the Visual Field. Substantial pattern-specific interactions between two stimuli only occur when the images fall on the same, nearby, or (in the case of interocular effects) corresponding retinal areas. For example, masking effects show a high degree of spatial localization. When the distance between the target and mask increases, masking effects decline rapidly, essentially disappearing at separations of 1–3° of visual angle (Alpern, 1953; Weisstein & Growney, 1969). Similarly, pattern adaptation depends on the adapting and test stimuli being imaged on the same retinal location throughout the adapting and test periods, respectively. Scanning the adapting stimulus reduces the adaptation effect and abolishes its pattern-specificity (Sullivan, Georgeson, & Oatley, 1972; Thomas & Kerr, 1971). All these results suggest that the mechanisms involved in the detection of spatially localized stimuli are narrowly tuned with respect to location.

2.2.5. Edge Effects. A number of investigators have emphasized the role of sharp luminance gradients, or edges, in interaction phenomena. The presence of edges in the visual field can reduce the visibility of a nearby target, and the effect

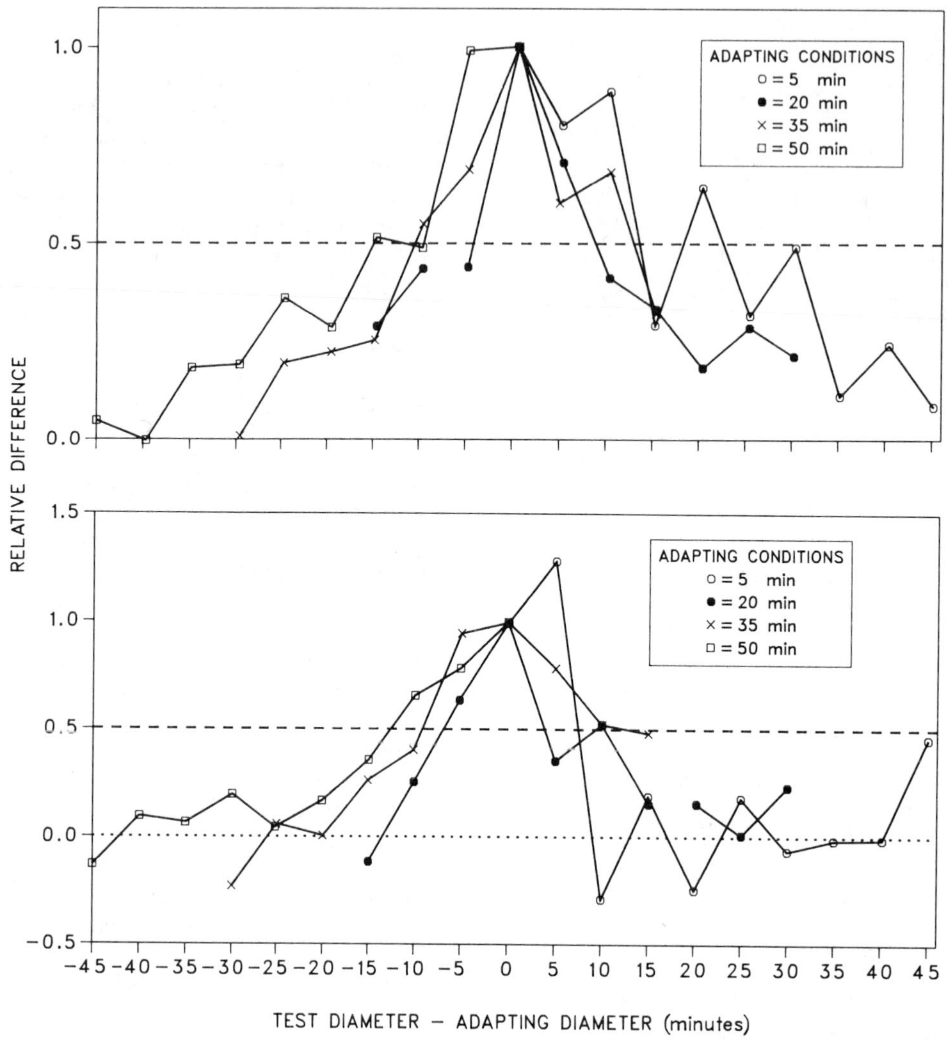

Figure 7.22. Size-selective adaptation curves plotted as a function of the difference between test- and adapting-stimulus diameters. The data from Figure 7.21 are replotted to compare the magnitude and range of the adapting effect across all adapting sizes. For all adapting sizes, adaptation falls to half its maximum value when the adapting and test stimuli differ by 10–15 min of visual arc. The data of the observer plotted in the lower panel show a small facilitation effect when test and adapting stimuli are very different in diameter. (From F. M. Bagrash, Size-selective adaptation: Psychophysical evidence for size-tuning and the effects of stimulus contour and adapting flux, *Vision Research, 13*. Copyright 1973 by Pergamon Press, Ltd. Reprinted with permission.)

is particularly striking when the stimuli share the property of shape. For example, effects obtained in metacontrast (masking by contour) paradigms are maximal when mask contours are sharply defined and similar to test contours; masking is reduced when the mask edges are blurred (Growney, 1976) or when mask and test contours differ. Near a vertical edge, greater threshold elevation is found for narrow line stimuli than for disk stimuli (Lukas, Tulunay-Keesey, & Limb, 1980; Vassilev, 1973). Sharp edges or contours alone can produce significant pattern-selective adaptation effects. For example, size-selective adaptation effects can be obtained by adapting to an annulus, as long as the adapting stimulus shares the same outer diameter as a test spot (Bagrash, 1973). Edge effects are spatially localized; an aperiodic target is less detectable if it is located near the sharp edge of a background than if it is more centrally located (Fiorentini, Jeanne, & Toraldi di Francia, 1955; Fiorentini & Zoli, 1966; Matthews, 1966).

These results can be understood if one considers the populations of mechanisms involved in each of the interaction effects. A contour can be characterized in terms of its spatial frequency, orientation, and retinal location properties—the three dimensions of tuning in the visual system. Two stimuli will interact maximally when they are identical along all three dimensions and, to a lesser extent, as they differ along any one dimension. A sharp edge contains a large number of spatial frequency components, which will stimulate all frequency-selective mechanisms at a given orientation and retinal location. Blurring the edge effectively removes high-spatial-frequency components, reducing the number of activated mechanisms. It is not surprising that such a stimulus is less effective at masking another sharp contour. Similarly, interactions are reduced when the edges of two stimuli differ in contour (the dimensions of orientation and spatial location) or when the two are physically separated (the dimension of spatial location).

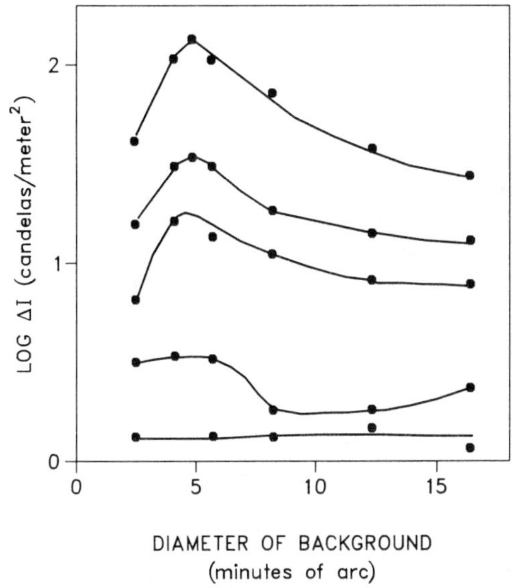

Figure 7.23. Log increment thresholds as a function of background diameter for five background luminance levels. The increment threshold was measured for a small (1-min diameter), brief (10 msec) test flash presented once a second against a background which varied in diameter but remained at constant luminance. The observer viewed the stimulus monocularly. Each curve shows thresholds measured for a given background luminance. From bottom to top curves, the luminances were 0.0025, 0.025, 0.25, 0.4, and 8.0 cd/m^2. At the three highest luminance levels illustrated here, threshold first rises with increasing background diameter, then falls. At low photopic levels, the measure was not sensitive to the effect; however, Westheimer determined (by the method described in Figure 7.24) that although the effect is reduced at low photopic levels, it does not disappear. (From G. Westheimer, Spatial interaction in human cone vision, *Journal of Physiology*, 1967, *190*. Reprinted with permission.)

2.3. Detection Models

Contemporary models of detection assume that perception of the target is mediated by a mosaic of differently tuned pathways, acting in parallel. The evidence for this assumption is summarized in Section 1.1. Given this position, the two major questions to be asked are: (1) How does each pathway respond to the target? and (2) How are the responses from different pathways combined? Nearly all models assume that the response of each pathway is initiated by a linear filter stage. The models diverge beyond this stage and can be grouped into two main categories: threshold models and continuous models. The paragraphs which follow discuss, in order, the linear filter stage, threshold models, and continuous models. The section closes with a discussion of how the models have been used to estimate the response ranges, or bandwidths, of the linear filters.

2.3.1. Linear Filter Stage. The linear filter stage has characterized detection models for many years (Blackwell, 1963; C. H. Graham, Brown, & Mote, 1939; N. Graham, 1977; Henning, Hertz, & Hinton, 1981; King-Smith & Kulikowski, 1975; Kulikowski & King-Smith, 1973; Legge & Foley, 1980; Sachs, Nachmias, & Robson, 1971; Thomas, 1970; Wilson & Bergen, 1979). The expected output of this stage is given by the convolution of the luminance distribution of the stimulus with the sensitivity function of the pathway. Specifically,

$$F_i = \int_{-\infty}^{+\infty}\int_{-\infty}^{+\infty}\int_{-\infty}^{+\infty} L(x,y,t)\ S_i\,(x,y,t)\ dx\ dy\ dt\ , \qquad (8)$$

where F_i is the expected output of the filter stage: $L(x,y,t)$ is the luminance distribution of the stimulus pattern in the two spatial dimensions x and y and in time t; and $S_i(x,y,t)$ is the sensitivity function of pathway i. The sensitivity function describes how the response of the pathway to an element of stimulation varies as a function of the spatial and temporal position of the element.

Alternatively, the luminance distribution and the pathway's sensitivity may be specified in Fourier terms, that is, as functions of spatial and temporal frequency. In this latter case,

$$F_i = \iiint \theta(u,v,w)\ \mathrm{T}(u,v,w)\ du\ dv\ dw\ , \qquad (9)$$

where $\theta(u,v,w)$ is the Fourier transform of $L(x,y,t)$ and $\mathrm{T}(u,v,w)$ is the Fourier transform of $S(x,y,t)$.

Figure 7.25 illustrates the kind of function often proposed for the linear filter stage. The function produces selective sensitivity with respect to orientation and to spatial frequency or size.

2.3.2. Threshold Models. Contemporary threshold models have a structure proposed by Sachs, Nachmias, and Robson (1971). Noise is added to the output of each filter stage, and

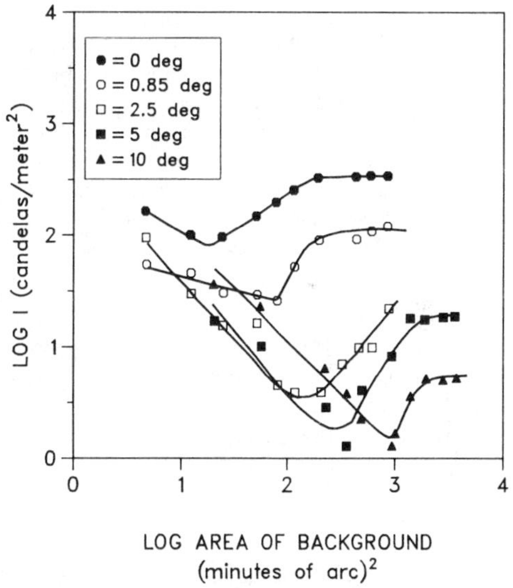

Figure 7.24. Log background luminance as a function of log background area needed to just detect a fixed-luminance test probe for five retinal locations. An alternative measure of Westheimer sensitization that is more sensitive to the effect at low luminance levels is to measure the background luminance needed to just cause a probe of fixed luminance to disappear, as a function of background area. This figure illustrates the results obtained for a 2-min test probe, at five retinal locations. In other respects, the stimuli were identical to those described in Figure 7.23. At any retinal eccentricity, increasing the area of a background first decreases the luminance needed to detect the probe. This indicates that to maintain a constant state of adaptation, a reciprocal relation exists between area and intensity, up to some critical area. For larger backgrounds, background-luminance requirements are increased to maintain a state of constant adaptation. This reversal is expected if the data are interpreted in terms of center–surround receptive fields. As eccentricity of retinal stimulation is increased, the curves obtained are similar in shape, but the critical area (minimal luminance required) occurs at progressively larger background areas. This result is consistent with increasing receptive field size at more eccentric retinal locations. (From G. Westheimer, Spatial interaction in human cone vision, *Journal of Physiology*, 1967, *190*. Reprinted with permission.)

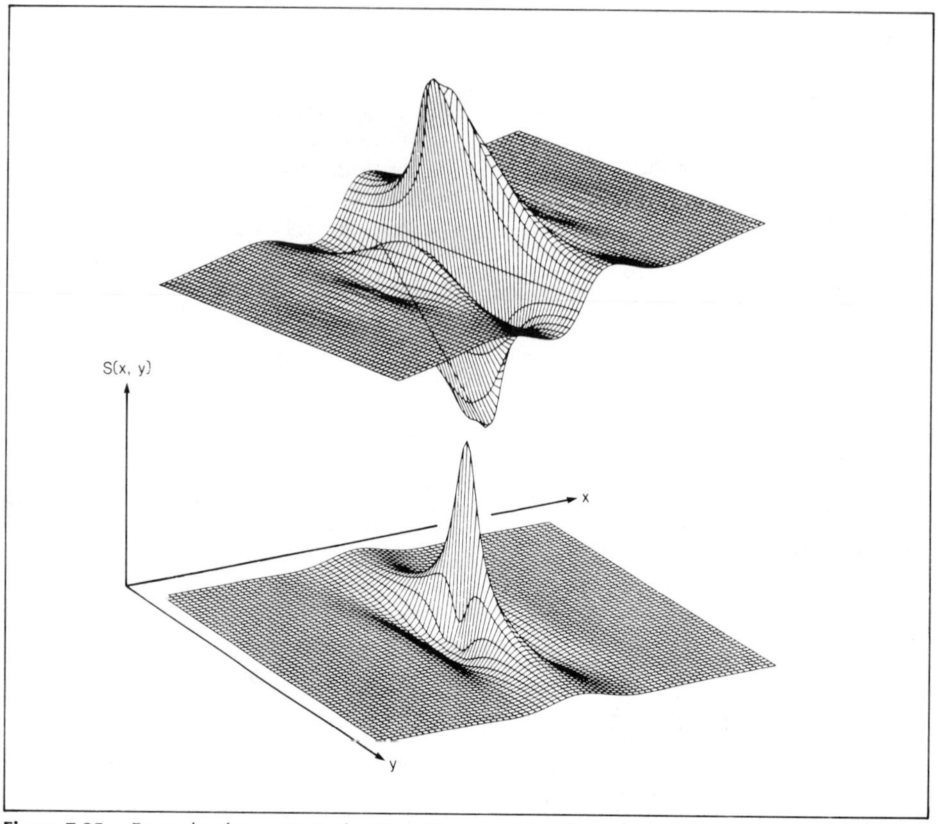

Figure 7.25. Example of a sensitivity function. Two representations of the sensitivity function $S(x,y)$. The vertical axis shows sensitivity, which takes both positive and negative values. The two other axes show the two spatial dimensions x and y. The top function has odd symmetry, the bottom one even symmetry. In the Fourier domain, both functions have a full bandwidth at half-amplitude of 1.8 octaves with respect to spatial frequency and 20° with respect to orientation. The functions were derived from experiments with filtered noise patterns. (From H. Mostafavi & D. J. Sakrison, Structure and properties of a single channel in the human visual system, *Vision Research, 16*. Copyright 1976 by Pergamon Press, Ltd. Reprinted with permission.)

the sum is passed through a threshold device. Detection occurs if the sum exceeds threshold in one or more pathways. Figure 7.26 illustrates the model.

The response of each pathway may be formally specified by

$$r_i = T_i(F_i + e_i) , \qquad (10)$$

where F_i is the expected output of the filter stage defined above. The quantity e_i is a random noise component; its variations are generally assumed to be independent from one pathway to another; T_i is a threshold function which is 1 when $(F_i + e_i)$ exceeds a critical value and is otherwise 0; and r_i is the response of pathway i. Because of the added noise, a given pathway may respond to a particular stimulus on one occasion but not on another. Thus a basic measure is $p_i(r_i = 1)$, the probability that pathway i responds to the stimulus.

The responses of the different pathways are combined by probability summation. The probability that a stimulus is detected on a particular presentation is simply the probability that activity in one or more pathways exceeds threshold. Provided that the noise fluctuations are independent from one pathway to another,

$$p(\text{detect}) = 1 - \prod_{i=1}^{n} [1 - p_i(r_i = 1)] , \qquad (11)$$

where Π indicates multiplication over the n pathways.

Quick (1974) suggested an approximation to probability summation, which several authors have employed. According to this formulation,

$$p(\text{detect}) = 1 - 2^{-F^{\alpha}} , \qquad (12)$$

where

$$F = \left[\sum_{i=1}^{n} F_i^{\alpha} \right]^{1/\alpha} . \qquad (13)$$

The constant α is estimated from the slope of the psychometric function, that is from the slope of the function relating p(detect) to the contrast of the test stimulus. For examples of how this approximation has been used, see Graham (1977) and Wilson and Bergen (1979). Nachmias (1981) has provided an empirical and theoretical evaluation of this approximation to probability summation.

Sachs, Nachmias, and Robson (1971) conceptualized each pathway as a channel that responds to the entire spatial extent of the target stimulus but to only a limited range of spatial-frequency components. Thus their pathways differ from one another only with respect to the range of frequencies to which each responds. In later adaptations of the model, each pathway has been treated as responding to only a limited spatial region, as well as to only a limited range of spatial frequencies or sizes (King-Smith & Kulikowski, 1975; Watson & Robson, 1981;

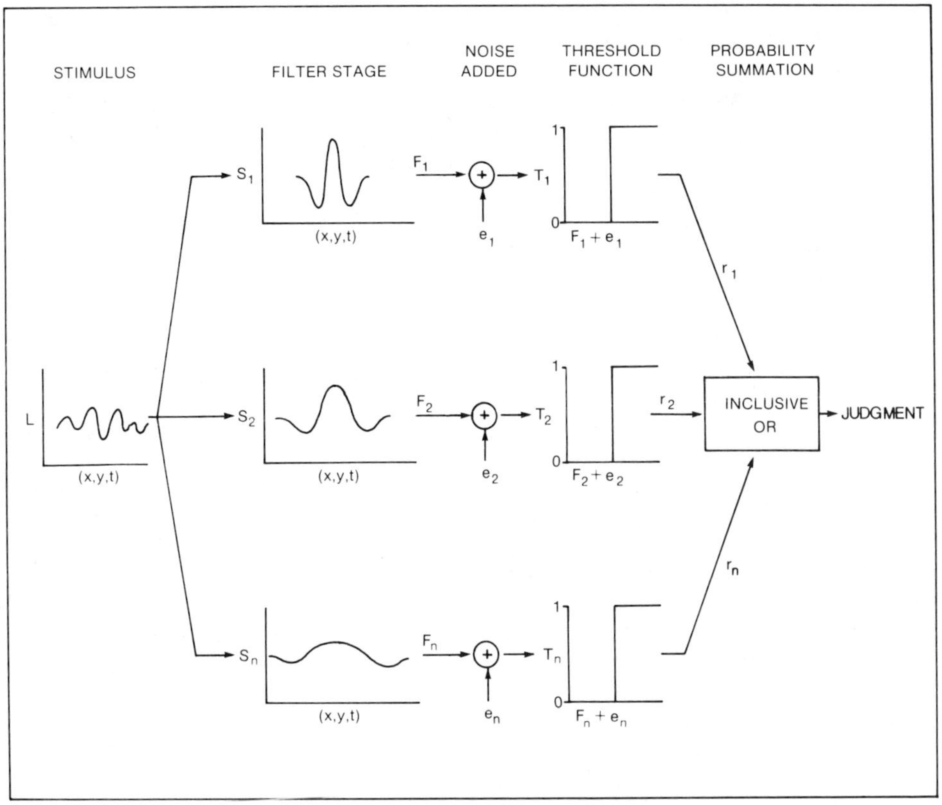

Figure 7.26. Threshold model for detection. The stimulus is represented at the extreme left. It is specified by the luminance function $L(x,y,t)$. It is processed by n pathways that act in parallel. The linear filter is the first stage of processing in each pathway. The expected output of the filter F_i is given by Eq. (8). Independent noise is added, and the sum is passed through the threshold function T. The output of the threshold device is r_i, which takes the value 0 or 1. Detection occurs if $r_i = 1$ for one or more pathways. One pathway differs from another only with respect to the sensitivity function of the filter, $S_i(x,y,t)$. This type of model was introduced by Sachs, Nachmias, and Robson (1971), and this figure is an adaptation of their model.

Wilson & Bergen, 1979). In these adaptations, the pathways differ from one another with respect to the spatial locations of their sensitive areas, as well as the spatial frequencies to which they respond. In the cases of the Wilson and Bergen and the Watson and Robson models, the pathways also differ in temporal properties. Presumably, the pathways also have different response domains with respect to orientation, at the same time that they differ with respect to the other dimensions.

The major application of the model has been to the detection of stimuli containing more than one Fourier component. The most straightforward application is to the detection of a compound grating formed by superimposing two orthogonal sinusoidal gratings, that is, gratings so different that they activate completely different sets of pathways. The model predicts the relationship between the probability of detecting the compound and the probabilities of detecting the two components when they are viewed individually. The prediction has been tested using components that differ in spatial frequency. It is accurate when the spatial frequencies of the components differ by a factor of 2 for frequencies above 2 cycles/degree or 3 for lower frequencies (Furchner, Thomas, & Campbell, 1977; Sachs, Nachmias, & Robson, 1971).

Application of the model is more difficult when the stimulus contains nonorthogonal components. Two examples of such stimuli are compound gratings, which contain components with similar spatial frequencies, and aperiodic stimuli, which contain continuous bands of frequencies. To apply the model to these stimuli, such parameters must be estimated as the number of pathways, the sensitivity functions, and the function relating $p_i(r_i = 1)$ to F_i. For examples of such treatments, see N. Graham (1977), Wilson and Bergen (1979), and Bergen, Wilson, and Cowan (1979).

Threshold models can also be applied to masking and adaptation phenomena by assuming that these effects occur only within pathways. That is, it is assumed that masking or adaptation effects will occur between two stimuli only if the stimuli activate one or more pathways in common. Williams, Wilson, and Cowan (1982) and Williams and Wilson (1983) carried out a more extensive application of the threshold model to adaptation phenomena. They concluded that adaptation has two major effects. The first is to reduce the sensitivity of the linear filter stage of each affected pathway, that is, to multiply the sensitivity function by a number less than 1. This multiplier varies from one pathway to another. The second effect of adaptation is to steepen the psychometric function and reduce the effect of probability summation. This effect is modeled by increasing the value of alpha in Eqs. (12) and (13).

Threshold models also yield some predictions about how well threshold stimuli can be discriminated from one another. If the observer can identify which pathway is above threshold, then orthogonal stimuli should be discriminated with the same accuracy with which they are detected. This prediction has been validated for a wide variety of stimuli (Furchner, Thomas, & Campbell, 1977; King-Smith & Kulikowski, 1981; Nachmias & Weber, 1975; Thomas & Gille, 1979; Tolhurst & Dealy, 1975; Watson & Robson, 1981).

2.3.3. Continuous Models. In continuous models, the threshold function is replaced by a continuous response function, and probability summation is replaced by other ways of combining the responses of the different pathways. A good example is the model suggested by Legge and Foley (1980), which Figure 7.27 illustrates.

In the Legge and Foley model, the response of each pathway is determined by

$$r_i = G_i(F_i) + e_i , \qquad (14)$$

where G_i is the response function and the other terms are as defined in connection with Eq. (10). Note that noise is added after the filter output is transformed by the response function.

There is much psychophysical evidence that the response function is positively accelerated at low contrasts (Foley & Legge, 1981; Nachmias & Kocher, 1970; Nachmias & Sansbury, 1974; Stromeyer & Klein, 1974; Thomas, 1983). Legge and Foley assume that the function is positively accelerated at low contrasts and negatively accelerated at higher contrasts. They also assume that the variance of the added noise e_i is constant across pathways and is independent of contrast. Thomas (1983) has proposed an alternative in which the response function is positively accelerated over all contrasts but the variance of the noise increases as contrast increases. There is some evidence that the variance does increase with contrast, but the evidence is limited to low contrasts (Foley & Legge, 1981; Nachmias & Kocher, 1970; Olzak, 1981).

It is of some interest to consider physiological evidence that may be relevant to the nature of the response function. Albrecht and Hamilton (1982) found that the response function of most cells in the visual cortex is described by the hyperbolic ratio

$$\text{Response frequency} = R_{\max}\,[C^n/(C^n + C_{0.5}{}^n)] , \qquad (15)$$

where $R_{\max}$ is the maximum response frequency to the particular stimulus; C is the contrast of the stimulus; and $C_{0.5}$ is the contrast at which response frequency is half the maximum. Albrecht and Hamilton found that the value of the exponent n was usually greater than 1. In these cases, the response functions of the single cortical cells were positively accelerated at low contrasts and negatively accelerated at high contrasts. In other words, the response functions of these cells had the same form as that assumed for the function G_i by Legge and Foley (1980) and by Wilson and Gelb (1984). However, Albrecht and Hamilton also found considerable variation between the cells with respect to both the form of the response functions and the dynamic range (the range of contrasts over which response rises from minimum to maximum). The center of the dynamic range varied, from cell to cell, from less than 0.1 contrast to more than 0.3.

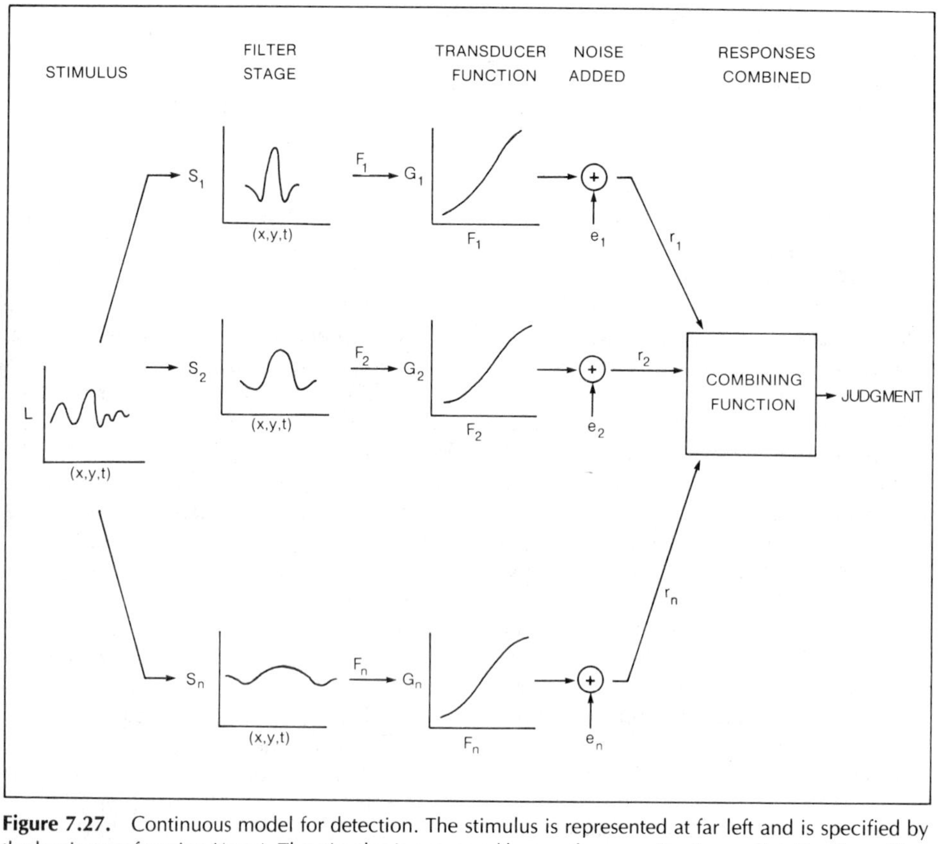

Figure 7.27. Continuous model for detection. The stimulus is represented at far left and is specified by the luminance function $L(x,y,t)$. The stimulus is processed by n pathways acting in parallel. The linear filter is the first stage of processing in each pathway. The output of the filter F_i is transformed by the response function G_i. Independent noise e_i is added to yield the response of the pathway r_i. The responses are combined by a combining function, such as the one given in Eq. (16). The model illustrated is adapted from Legge and Foley (1980).

Returning to the psychophysical models, a variety of rules for combining the responses of different pathways has been proposed. Legge and Foley suggest a dual mechanism: at low contrasts the observer monitors all pathways but uses only the largest individual response and at high contrasts only the most sensitive pathway is monitored. A more general rule is

$$r = \left[\sum_{i=1}^{n} (a_i r_i)^p \right]^{1/p} , \quad (16)$$

where r is the combined response, and a_i is a weight assigned to pathway i. The value of a_i is determined a priori and weights the response of each pathway according to its expected usefulness. The exponent p, on the other hand, weights each response according to its magnitude on the particular occasion. As p grows larger, more weight is given to the largest responses. The low-contrast rule of Legge and Foley is a special case in which a_i is the same for all pathways and p is indefinitely large. Their high-contrast rule is a special case in which a_i is 1 for one pathway and 0 for all others. An important special case is when $p = 1$ and

$$a_i = R_i / \sigma_i^2 = G_i(F_i)/\sigma_i^2 , \quad (17)$$

where R_i is the expected response of pathway i and σ_i^2 is the variance of the added noise. Given certain common assumptions, this case is equivalent to multiplying likelihood ratios and is, according to signal detection theory, the optimal combining rule (Green & Swets, 1974).

It is often convenient to apply an analogous general rule to the expected responses, rather than deal with the individual responses to each presentation:

$$R = \left[\sum_{i=1}^{n} R_i^P \right]^{1/P}$$

$$= \left[\sum_{i=1}^{n} (G_i \cdot (F_i))^P \right]^{1/P} , \quad (18)$$

where R is the expected combined response. It is important to note that the exponents have different meanings in this case. For example, when P is indefinitely large, Eq. (18) mimics the high-contrast rule of Legge and Foley. As Quick (1974) noted, when G_i is a linear function and P takes an intermediate value, the rule mimics probability summation. When $P = 2$ and certain common assumptions are met, the rule expresses the optimal integration model of signal detection theory (Green & Swets, 1974).

No continuous model is complete without a specification of the relationship between the combined response and detection performance. The nature of the specification depends on the task and the psychophysical method. For example, the model might specify that on each trial in a two-alternative temporal forced-choice procedure, the observer selects the interval yielding the larger value of r in Eq. (16). The probability that the detection judgment is correct is the probability that the larger value of r comes from the interval containing the signal. For actual examples, see Henning, Hertz, and Hinton (1981), Legge and Foley (1980), Quick (1974), Thomas (1983), Thomas and Gille (1979), and Thomas, Gille, and Barker (1982).

Continuous models have been used to analyze masking phenomena (Henning, Hertz, & Hinton, 1981; Legge & Foley, 1980; Wilson, McFarlane, & Phillips, 1983), detection of compound stimuli (Olzak & Thomas, 1981; Thomas & Shimamura, 1975), and the relationship between the abilities to detect and identify low-contrast stimuli (Olzak & Thomas, 1981; Thomas & Gille, 1979; Thomas, Gille, & Barker, 1982). Quantitatively, continuous models and threshold models fit the data with much the same accuracy. The major advantage of the continuous models of detection is that they are special cases of more general models applicable to detection, discrimination, and identification tasks at all contrast levels.

2.3.4. Bandwidths of the Filter Functions. One major application of detection models has been to derive the sensitivity characteristics of the linear filter stages, particularly with respect to the dimensions of spatial frequency and orientation. The results of the interaction studies summarized in Sections 1.1 and 2.2 suggest that each spatially tuned pathway responds to a single, limited band of spatial frequencies and a similarly limited band of orientations. The common goal of the studies discussed in this section has been to estimate the widths of these bands.

The bandwidth of the individual filter function should be distinguished from what may be called the *interaction bandwidth*. As summarized in Sections 1.1 and 2.2, no interaction is observed between two grating stimuli unless they differ by less-than-critical amounts with respect to spatial frequency and orientation. These critical amounts are the interaction bandwidths. Given the assumption that two stimuli will interact only if they activate some tuned pathways in common, the occurrence of an interaction implies that the two stimuli lie within the bandwidth of at least one pathway. However, the absence of a measurable interaction does not necessarily imply that no pathways are stimulated in common, that is, that the two stimuli are separated by more than the bandwidth of any pathway. Thus the interaction bandwidth should be treated as a lower bound for the bandwidth of a single filter stage. The filter bandwidth may be either equal to or greater than the interaction bandwidth.

The task of deriving the bandwidths of individual filters from psychophysical data is complicated by several factors. One is that each judgment is mediated by the combined responses of a number of pathways, even if the combination is only probabilistic. Another difficulty is that changes in the stimulus properties (such as the spatial frequency of the test grating) generally change the relative contributions of the different pathways to the combined response. Finally, the response of each pathway is probably a nonlinear function of the output of the linear filter stage. Analytic derivations of bandwidths are possible only by making strong simplifying assumptions, such as that only a single pathway mediates each judgment. (For examples, see Henning, Hertz, & Hinton, 1981; Kulikowski & King-Smith, 1973; Mostafavi & Sakrison, 1976; Thomas, 1970.) The alternative is numerical analysis, in which different combinations of filter functions, response functions, and combining rules are examined to find the combination that strikes the best balance between parsimony and goodness of fit to the psychophysical data. The papers by Wilson and his colleagues illustrate this type of approach (Wilson & Bergen, 1979; Wilson & Gelb, 1984; Wilson, McFarlane, & Phillips, 1983).

Table 7.1 summarizes the bandwidth estimates from several studies. There is significant variation in the estimates, at least part of which reflects the different modeling assumptions used

Table 7.1. Estimates of Bandwidths with Respect to Spatial Frequency and Orientation

Study	Bandwidth for Spatial Frequency (in Octaves)	Orientation (in Degrees)
Henning, Hertz, and Hinton (1981)[a]	1.15 or 2.30	—
Legge and Foley (1980)[b]	1.0	—
Mostafavi and Sakrison (1976)[c]	1.8	20
Thomas and Gille (1979)[d]	—	10–20 or 6–12
Watson (1982)[e]	<1.0	—
Wilson, McFarlane, and Phillips (1983)[f]	2.0–2.5 and 1.25–1.50	—

Estimates of the bandwidths of the sensitivity functions of the linear filter stages of individual spatially tuned pathways. Bandwidth is defined as the full width of the sensitivity function measured at one-half maximum sensitivity. Although there is considerable variation from one study to another, the estimates are on the order of 1–2 octaves for spatial frequency and 10–20° for orientation.

[a] Estimate derived from the masking effect of filtered noise on detection of a grating pattern. Test gratings of 1, 3, and 6 cycles/degree were used. Estimated bandwidth was 1.15 or 2.30 octaves, depending on which of two decision rules the observer was assumed to adopt.
[b] Estimate derived from the masking effect of a grating pattern on detection of a test grating. Spatial frequency of the test grating was 2 cycles/degree.
[c] Estimates derived from summation studies using filtered noise. Bandwidth of the noise was varied with respect to both spatial frequency and orientation. Bandwidths estimated for a single pathway centered on 4.5 cycles/degree and vertical orientation.
[d] Estimates derived from comparison of performance in simultaneous detection and identification tasks. Stimuli were narrow lines or 5 cycles/degree gratings, which differed only in orientation. Bandwidth was estimated for pathways centered on vertical, but data gathered at an oblique orientation did not differ consistently from the vertical data. Bandwidth varied between 10 and 20°, depending on the observer. When allowance is made for the effects of stimulus uncertainty, these values are reduced to 6–12° (Thomas, Gille, & Barker, 1982).
[e] Estimate derived from summation studies. Stimuli were Gabor packets (vertical sine gratings truncated by multiplication with a two-dimensional Gaussian weighting function). Both low-frequency (between 1 and 3 cycles/degree) and high-frequency (between 16 and 32 cycles/degree) gratings were used. Watson concluded that bandwidth was nearly constant on an octave scale and was less than 1 octave.
[f] Estimates derived from masking experiments. The test stimulus was a vertically oriented, spatially localized pattern generated by taking the sixth spatial derivative of a Gaussian pattern. The Fourier transform has a bandwidth of 1 octave. The visual appearance is a small number of bright and dark stripes. The masking stimuli were cosine gratings oriented 14.5° from vertical. The authors concluded that spatial vision is served by six different spatially tuned pathways. Two low-frequency pathways, centered on 0.75 and 1.5 cycles/degree, have bandwidths between 2.0 and 2.5 octaves. The remaining pathways are centered on 2.8, 4.4, 8.0, and 16.0 cycles/degree and have bandwidths between 1.25 and 1.5 octaves.

to derive the estimates from the data. For explicit examples of how different assumptions affect the estimates, see the papers by Henning, Hertz, and Hinton (1981) and Thomas and Gille (1979).

Despite the variations seen in Table 7.1., some common conclusions emerge. Considering only pathways tuned to the vertical orientation, central vision appears to be served by at least six different spatially tuned pathways (Watson & Robson, 1981; Wilson, McFarlane, & Phillips, 1983). However, the number in effective operation may depend on the temporal properties of the stimulus, perhaps only three being effective at high temporal frequencies (Watson & Robson, 1981). The estimates of the bandwidths of the pathways, with respect to spatial frequency, range from less than 1.0 to 2.5 octaves. Most estimates lie between 1 and 2 octaves. Mechanisms tuned to high temporal frequencies appear to have wider bandwidths than pathways tuned to lower temporal frequencies (Watson & Robson, 1981; Wilson & Bergen, 1979). In the case of orientation, bandwidth estimates vary between 6 and 20° of rotation. Part of this variation reflects different modeling assumptions. However, there are also substantial differences between observers (Thomas & Gille, 1979).

It is generally agreed that pathways spatially centered away from fixation have tuning functions that are shifted to lower spatial frequencies. One assumption is that the center frequency of each type of pathway decreases as a linear function of distance from fixation but that the bandwidth stays the same on an octave scale (Watson, 1983; Wilson & Bergen, 1979). This assumption has not been rigorously tested, however.

3. IDENTIFICATION

This section discusses performance in discrimination and identification tasks. The term *discrimination* is used when the observer judges whether two patterns appear different; the term *identification* is used when the observer must indicate which of two or more patterns has been presented. Section 3.1 describes performance of these tasks when the stimuli differ from one another along only one dimension, and Section 3.2 describes how performance is affected by masking. Section 3.3 discusses how the appearance of stimuli, with respect to such variables as spatial frequency or orientation, is changed by adaptation and by changes in stimulus contrast. Section 3.4 describes some formal models of identification.

3.1. Identification of Stimuli Which Differ on a Single Dimension

This section discusses the ability of observers to discriminate between or identify spatial patterns which differ from one another on only a single dimension. The dimensions considered are contrast, spatial frequency and size, orientation, phase, and spatial position.

3.1.1. Stimuli Which Differ in Contrast. This section examines the ability to distinguish between spatial patterns which differ only in contrast. One of the patterns is treated as the reference or base stimulus. This task may also be considered as a special case of masking in which the target to be detected consists of an increment in the contrast of the mask. The task differs from traditional brightness discrimination, in which the observer detects a luminance increment superimposed on a larger, uniform field. The traditional task is treated in Section 2. (See also Chapter 5 by Hood and Finkelstein.)

The basic measure is the *contrast difference threshold*, the smallest difference in contrast that permits two stimuli to be distinguished. In general, the difference threshold is not fixed but varies as a function of the contrast of the reference stimulus. This relationship is represented by plotting the difference threshold ΔC against the contrast C of whichever stimulus is designated as the reference. See Figure 7.28(a) for an example. Over most of the contrast range, ΔC increases as C increases. However, over the lowest contrasts, ΔC actually decreases as C increases; in this range, ΔC is lower than the simple detection threshold in the absence of a mask. As C increases further, the relationship changes and ΔC increases as C increases throughout the rest of the contrast range.

The negative slope, or *dip*, of the function at low contrasts occurs for both grating stimuli and aperiodic stimuli. (For examples of grating stimuli, see Campbell & Kulikowski, 1966; Foley & Legge, 1981; Legge & Foley, 1980; Nachmias & Sansbury, 1974; Stromeyer & Klein, 1974; and for examples of aperiodic stimuli, see Barlow, 1962; Legge & Kersten, 1983; Nachmias & Kocher, 1970.) The dip is usually interpreted as meaning that the magnitude of the response of the visual system increases as a positively accelerated function of contrast at low contrasts. However, the dip can also be interpreted as resulting from uncertainty by the observer, at low contrasts, about some of the properties of the stimuli (Lasley & Cohn, 1981).

Over most of the contrast range, ΔC increases as a positive function of C. Generally, ΔC increases at a slower rate than C. When the relationship is plotted in log-log coordinates, as in Figure 7.28(a), the slower rate of increase is manifested as a slope less than 1. The slopes that have been reported range from about 0.5–0.7 (Legge, 1979, 1981; Legge & Foley, 1980; Legge & Kersten, 1983; Nachmias & Sansbury, 1974; Pantle, 1974, 1977; Tolhurst & Barfield, 1978). One exception is a study by Cornsweet and Pinsker (1965), who obtained a slope of 1. However, they used a markedly different stimulus display: the two stimuli to be distinguished were disks of light that were always flashed against a totally dark background.

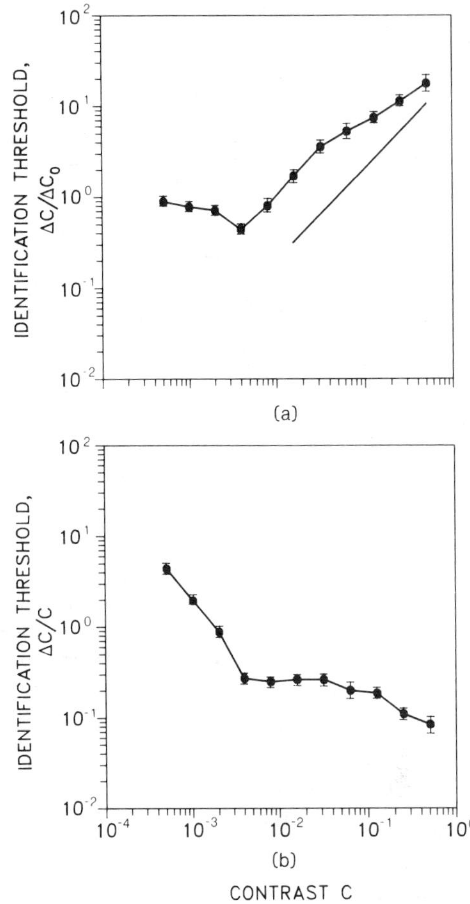

Figure 7.28. Contrast identification thresholds. The stimulus was a 2 cycles/degree sine wave grating with mean luminance of 200 cd /m^2. The task of the observer was to distinguish between a grating of contrast C and a grating of slightly higher contrast. The identification threshold ΔC is the contrast increment which yielded correct identification on 79% of the trials, and ΔC_0 is the increment required when $C = 0$; that is, it is the detection threshold. The data are the means for three observers and the vertical bars are ± one standard error of the mean. (a) The identification threshold expressed as a multiple of the detection threshold ($\Delta C/\Delta C_0$) changes as a function of C: $\Delta C/\Delta C_0$ decreases as C increases from 0 to 0.005, then increases with further increases in C. The heavy diagonal line shows the rate of increase required by Weber's law. (b) The Weber fraction $\Delta C/C$ decreases as a function of C. The fraction is less than 0.3 over most of the contrast range and is less than 0.1 at the highest contrasts. (From G. E. Legge & J. M. Foley, Contrast masking in human vision, *Journal of the Optical Society of America*, 1980, *70*. Reprinted with permission.)

The fact that the slope of the function is less than 1 means that the Weber fraction $\Delta C/C$ continues to decrease as C increases, as shown in Figure 7.28(b). Thus Weber's law never holds strictly for this particular task.

3.1.2. Stimuli Which Differ in Spatial Frequency or in Size. In spatial-frequency identification, the observer distinguishes between gratings which differ only in spatial frequency. Accuracy is dependent on contrast, particularly at low contrasts (Thomas, 1983). As shown in Figure 7.29, performance improves as contrast increases up to a point but is independent of further increases in contrast. The contrast at which performance levels off depends on the spatial frequencies of the gratings. When the frequencies lie between 4 and 5 cycles/degree, there is little

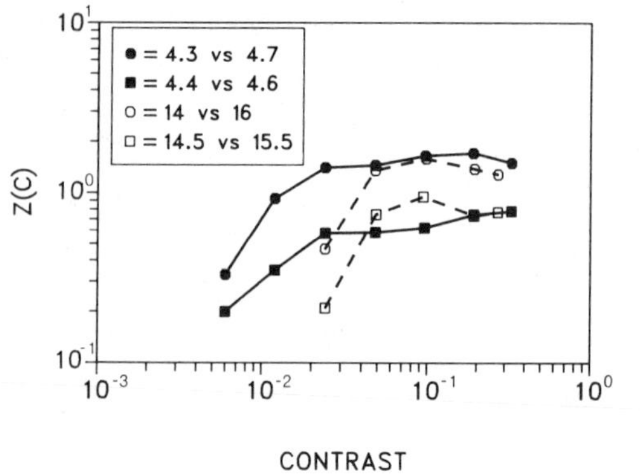

Figure 7.29. Spatial-frequency identification as a function of contrast. The stimuli were pairs of sinusoidal gratings that differed slightly in spatial frequency. The task of the observer was to identify which member of the pair was presented on each trial. The measure of performance Z(C) is the standard normal deviate corresponding to percentage correct. Note that logarithmic spacing is used on both the contrast and performance axes. The four different curves are for four different pairs of stimuli: two centered on 4.5 cycles/degree (filled symbols, solid lines); and two centered on 15 cycles/degree (open symbols, broken lines). The data are from a single subject, but other subjects give like results (Thomas, 1983). As contrast increases, performance improves and then stabilizes at a level which depends on the difficulty of the task. For the particular spatial frequencies shown here, increasing contrast above 0.05 produces little or no improvement in performance. However, different results would be obtained with higher frequencies because their curves would be shifted to the right. In the log-log coordinates used here, differences in contrast sensitivity are represented by shifts along the horizontal axis. That is, the data for the pairs of gratings centered on 15 cycles/degree are shifted to the right from the data for the pairs centered on 4.5 cycles/degree. On the other hand, differences in task difficulty are manifested as shifts along the vertical axis. For example, the curve for the 4.4- versus 4.6-cycles/degree identification is shifted down from the curve for 4.3 versus 4.7 cycles/degree.

or no improvement as contrast increases above 0.03. The curves for higher frequencies level off at higher contrasts. The difference presumably reflects differences in contrast sensitivity. Accuracy is also affected by the number of cycles which the grating contains (Hirsch & Hylton, 1982; Thomas, Gille, & Barker, 1982). Hirsch and Hylton found that performance is reduced when there are fewer than three cycles, but is independent of the number of cycles when there are more than three.

A basic measure is the *difference threshold*, the smallest difference in spatial frequency which permits two gratings to be distinguished. When grating contrast is high enough to yield maximum performance at all spatial frequencies, the difference threshold increases in approximate proportion to the spatial frequency of whichever grating is used as the reference. That is, the ratio of the difference threshold Δf to the reference frequency f is roughly constant (Campbell, Nachmias, & Jukes, 1970; Hirsch & Hylton, 1982). Hirsch and Hylton measured the ratio for reference frequencies between 1 and 15 cycles/degree and found that the ratio fluctuated between 0.02 and 0.04. Their results are shown in Figure 7.30. Campbell, Nachmias, and Jukes obtained generally comparable results for reference frequencies as high as 32 cycles/degree. The proportional relationship between the difference threshold and reference frequency is also found at low contrasts provided that contrasts are adjusted to make all gratings equally visible (Thomas, Gille, & Barker, 1982; Watson & Robson, 1981). As indicated, performance is highly dependent on visibility at low contrasts.

Hirsch and Hylton (1982) noted that the fluctuations in their data were not random but appeared to be periodic with respect to the reference frequency. They suggested that these regular variations result from properties of the foveal receptor mosaic. The periodic variations are not apparent in the data of Campbell, Nachmias, and Jukes (1970), but those authors measured at more widely spaced points along the reference-frequency axis.

In size identification, the observer distinguishes between aperiodic stimuli which differ only in one dimension, such as width or radius. At low contrasts, performance is strongly dependent on the contrast or visibility of the stimuli (Thomas, 1978; Thomas & Shimamura, 1974). It has not been established whether this dependence extends over the entire contrast range or is limited to low contrasts, as is the case for spatial-frequency identification. Accuracy is also affected by the shape of the stimuli at low contrasts. When stimuli are equated for visibility, a given difference in size is more accurately discriminated if it is associated with the shorter dimension of the stimulus. For example, two rectangular stimuli will be more accurately discriminated if their dimensions are, in minutes of visual angle, 20 by 50 and 30 by 50 than if the dimensions are 5 by 20 and 5 by 30 (Thomas, 1978).

Studies of size identification at low contrasts indicate that for targets small enough to be imaged within the fovea, the difference threshold increases as the reference size increases (Thomas & Shimamura, 1974). This conclusion is also supported by related studies at high contrast of the identification of spatial intervals (Westheimer & McKee, 1977b). However, the latter studies indicate that this relationship breaks down when the reference width is less than about 3 min of visual angle. The minimum difference threshold, which is about 6 sec of visual angle, is obtained with a reference width of 3 min. Narrower reference stimuli yield larger difference thresholds. (These studies are discussed in greater detail in Section 3.1.5 and in Figure 7.35.)

Distinguishing between two grating patterns that differ in spatial frequency can also be thought of as a size discrimination, since the width of each bar in a grating is the reciprocal of the grating's frequency. However, the difference threshold for size is larger in the case of a single bar than in the case of a bar included in an extended grating (Hirsch & Hylton, 1982; Thomas, Gille, & Barker, 1982). Apparently the repetitiveness of the grating contributes to the accuracy of the judgment. One reason for this effect is that the extended grating has a narrower spatial-frequency spectrum than the single bar and, accordingly, is more selective in activating spatially tuned mechanisms at a given retinal location. However, the periodic character of the grating may contribute to performance in another way as well. The spatial frequency or periodicity of the grating may be partially represented by the spatial locations of the pathways that respond to the peaks, valleys, and zero crossings of the grating (Gelb & Wilson, 1983; Thomas, Gille, & Barker, 1982). In other words, location tuning may also play a role. This source of information is reduced in the case of a single bar. Whatever the mechanisms, only a portion of the grating is critical; performance improves as the number of cycles in the grating increases up to about three cycles but is independent of further increases in the number of cycles.

There is some reason to suspect that the greater accuracy in identifying grating stimuli may be frequency dependent. Studies of hyperacuity have shown that, when small spatial dimensions are involved, performance is reduced by the presence

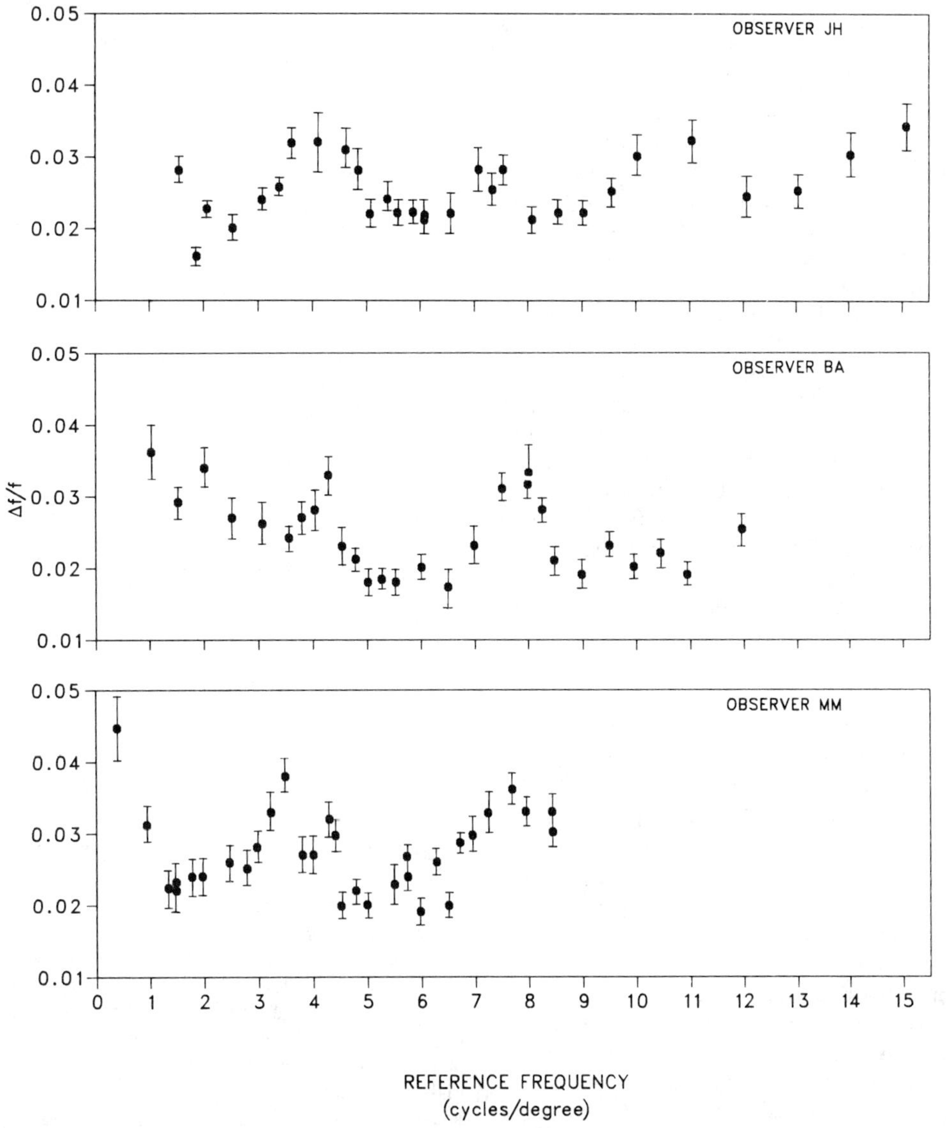

Figure 7.30. Identification thresholds for spatial frequency. The stimuli were sinusoidal gratings with mean luminance of 20 cd/m^2. The task of the observer was to discriminate between a grating having a fixed spatial frequency, the reference grating, and a grating of slightly higher or lower spatial frequency. Contrast of the reference grating was 0.30, and the contrasts of the other gratings were individually adjusted to match the apparent contrast of the reference grating. The difference in frequency which yielded correct identification on 75% of the trials is Δf, and the frequency of the reference grating is f. The Weber fraction $\Delta f/f$ is a function of f. Each panel shows the data of a single observer. Except at the lowest spatial frequencies examined, the value of the Weber fraction fluctuates between 0.02 and 0.04. Hirsch and Hylton (1982) noted that the fluctuation appears to be periodic and suggested that the periodicity is related to the properties of the receptor mosaic. (From J. Hirsch & R. Hylton, Limits of spatial frequency discrimination as evidence of neural interpolation, *Journal of the Optical Society of America*, 1982, *72*. Reprinted with permission.)

of nearby stimuli (Westheimer & Hauske, 1975; Westheimer, Shimamura, & McKee, 1976). Similar lateral masking effects have been reported for letter recognition tasks (Monti, 1973; Taylor & Brown, 1972). Thus at high spatial frequencies the presence of flanking bars may reduce the accuracy with which the width of any single bar in a grating is identified. If so, the repetitive character of the grating may act to both increase and decrease the accuracy of spatial-frequency judgments, with the net effect varying as a function of spatial frequency.

3.1.3. Stimuli Which Differ in Orientation. In orientation identification, the observer distinguishes between spatial patterns which differ only in the orientation of their linear components, that is, in the orientations of their Fourier components. As in other tasks, accuracy depends on contrast when contrast is low (Thomas & Gille, 1979). It has not been determined whether this dependence extends throughout the contrast range or whether performance becomes independent of contrast at some point.

Performance also depends on the length of the elements that are judged. Westheimer (1981) reports that the difference threshold for the orientation of a single high-contrast line decreases as the length of the line increases from zero to approximately 20 min of visual angle. Further increases in line length have little effect on performance. The same finding has also been reported for low-contrast lines (Vassilev, Simeonova, & Zlatkova, 1981).

The difference threshold is the angle of rotation from the reference orientation which is correctly identified 75% of the time, for example, the angle of rotation from vertical which is correctly identified as tilted left or right. For lines and gratings at the contrast detection threshold, and of optimal length, the difference threshold is between 5 and 10° (Thomas & Gille, 1979). For high-contrast lines, of optimal length, threshold is between 10 and 20 min (Westheimer, 1981).

There is some evidence that orientation judgments are less precise when the reference orientation is oblique, rather than vertical or horizontal (Andrews, 1967a, 1967b; Bouman & Andriessen, 1968; Matin & Drivas, 1979). Matin and Drivas report difference thresholds (each taken as the difference in orientation which yields a criterion value of d') that are 25–60% smaller when the reference is vertical or horizontal than when the reference is oblique. However, other studies have failed to show a consistent effect of this nature (Thomas & Gille, 1979; Thomas & Shimamura, 1975). One difference between the two groups of studies is that the former used high-contrast stimuli, while the latter used low-contrast stimuli equated for visibility. (See Section 2.1.4 for the effect of orientation on visibility.) However, the studies differed in other important ways as well, and it cannot be concluded that the difference in findings results from the differences in stimulus contrast.

3.1.4. Stimuli Which Differ in Phase. In phase identification, the observer distinguishes between patterns which differ only in the phase relationships of their Fourier components. As in other kinds of identification, accuracy increases as the contrasts of the components increase (Burr, 1980; Burton & Moorhead, 1981; Caelli & Bevan, 1982).

Burr (1980) measured phase identification with compound gratings that contained two sinusoidal components. His results are presented in Figure 7.31. The difference threshold was defined as the just noticeable change in the phase of the higher-frequency component, relative to the lower-frequency component. He found that the difference threshold depended on the contrasts of the components, the spatial frequencies of the components, and the particular phase relationship used as the reference pattern. At high contrasts, the difference threshold varies between 20 and 35° for components with spatial frequencies between 1 and 20 cycles/degree. The difference threshold was too large to be measured when the spatial frequency of the higher component was 30 cycles/degree.

Burton and Moorhead (1981) investigated phase discrimination using stimuli with more complex spatial-frequency spectra. They altered the phases of Fourier components within a limited band of spatial frequencies. They manipulated the width of the band, the frequency on which it was centered, and the maximum change in phase within the band. The difference threshold was defined as the change in phase (maximum change within the band) which produced a just noticeable change in the appearance of the stimulus. They obtained the lowest thresholds when the contrast of the stimulus was high and the band of shifted components was 0.8 octave wide and centered on a spatial frequency of about 5 cycles/degree. Increasing the central frequency of the band increased the threshold, although the rate of increase depended on the spatial-frequency content of the stimulus. The rate of increase was slower for a stimulus containing more energy at high frequencies.

Caelli and Bevan (1982) examined sensitivity to phase distortions in two-dimensional patterns. They quantized the phase relationships by allowing them to vary only in discrete steps, rather than continuously. They found that for briefly exposed patterns, with contrasts less than 0.30, the steps could be as large as 45° without producing noticeable distortions in appearance.

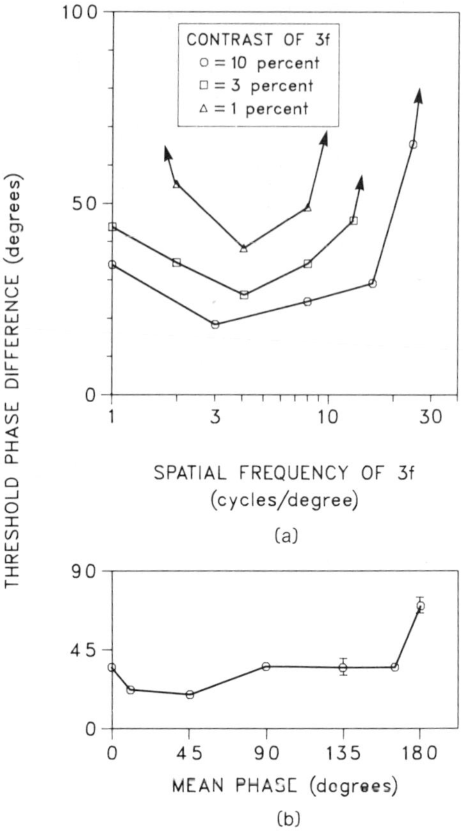

Figure 7.31. Thresholds for the identification of relative phase. The stimuli were compound gratings formed by superimposing two sinusoids. The spatial frequencies of the components, termed f and 3f, always stood in a 1:3 ratio. The contrast of the 3f component was always ⅓ that of the f component. Mean luminance was 200 cd/m^2. Data are for one observer. (a) The observer distinguished between a reference pattern, in which the phases of the components were set in peaks-subtract or square wave relationship, and a pattern in which the phases differed from the reference relationship. The threshold-phase difference is the difference that was correctly identified on 82% of the trials and is expressed as the phase shift of the *3f* component. The threshold-phase difference is plotted as a function of the spatial frequency of the *3f* component. The three different curves are for three different contrasts of the *3f* component (contrast of the *f* component was always 3 times higher). At the highest contrast, the phase-difference threshold lies between 20 and 40° for spatial frequencies up 15 cycles/degree but increases abruptly at higher frequencies. At 30 cycles/degree, even a 180 degree phase shift was not discriminated. At lower contrasts, threshold was higher, and successful performance was limited to narrower ranges of spatial frequencies. Limited data gathered with mean luminance reduced to 1 cd/m^2 appeared similar, except shifted to the left along the spatial-frequency axis. (b) The threshold-phase difference is a function of the mean-phase relationship of the components in the two patterns to be distinguished. The spatial frequencies of the components were 2 and 6 cycles/degree, and their contrasts were 0.10 and 0.033. When mean phase was 0, the *3f* components of the two patterns were shifted symmetrically from a peaks-subtract or square wave relationship. The threshold-phase difference varies between 20 and 40° over a wide range of phase relationships but is higher for phase relationships centered on 180° (peaks add). (From D. C. Burr, Sensitivity to spatial phase, *Vision Research, 20.* Copyright 1980 by Pergamon Press, Ltd. Reprinted with permission.)

3.1.5. Identification of Relative Spatial Position. This section discusses tasks in which the observer identifies the spatial position of the target relative to an explicit or implicit standard. Figure 7.32 provides examples of these tasks. With foveal viewing and high luminance levels, differences in position of only a few seconds of visual angle are correctly identified. Because these differences are small relative to the size and spacing of the foveal cones, as well as to the optical spread function of the eye, these are often called *hyperacuity tasks* (Westheimer, 1975).

Vernier acuity is the most widely studied of these tasks. Figure 7.32(a,b,c) illustrates this task. Under optimal conditions, misalignments on the order of 5 sec of visual angle are correctly identified on 75% of the trials (Berry, 1948; Westheimer & Hauske, 1975; Westheimer & McKee, 1977b).

Several features affect performance. One is the vertical separation of the targets, as is illustrated in Figure 7.33. The

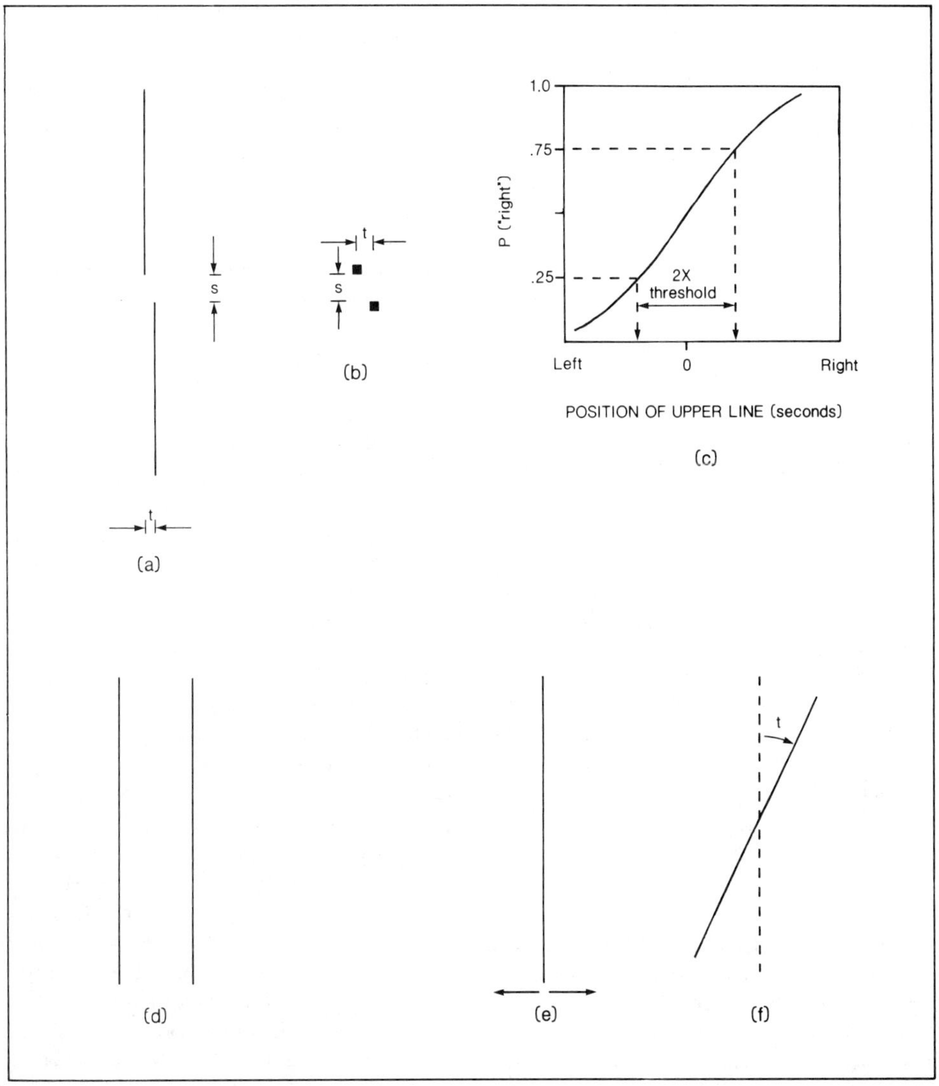

Figure 7.32. Examples of identifying relative spatial position. (a) Vernier acuity. The upper line segment is placed to the left, as shown, or to the right of the lower segment. The magnitude of the misalignment, as well as the direction, is varied from trial to trial. At the end of each trial, the observer responds "left" or "right." The measure of performance is the threshold misalignment *t* measured in seconds of visual angle. Performance depends on the vertical separation *s*. (b) Two-dot vernier acuity. Same as in (a) except that lines are shortened until only two dots remain. (c) Determination of the threshold. The probability that the observer will respond "right" is plotted as a function of the position of the upper line segment or dot. Threshold is defined as half the distance between the positions corresponding to probabilities of 0.25 and 0.75. An equivalent definition is half the distance between the two positions for which the probability of correct identification, left or right, is 0.75. (d) Judgment of spatial extent. The distance between the two lines is varied from trial to trial. On some trials the distance is greater than a standard separation *s*, and on some trials it is less. After each trial, the observer indicates whether the distance was less or more than the standard distance. Threshold *t* is half the difference between the two widths that are correctly identified, as less or more than the standard, 75% of the time. (e) Identification of a spatial displacement. During each trial, the target line is displaced to the left or to the right by a variable distance. At the end of the trial, the observer indicates the direction of displacement. Threshold is defined as the displacement which is correctly identified 75% of the time. (f) The orientation of the target line is randomly varied from trial to trial. At the end of each trial, the observer indicates whether the line was rotated clockwise or counterclockwise from vertical. Threshold is the rotation which is correctly identified on 75% of the trials.

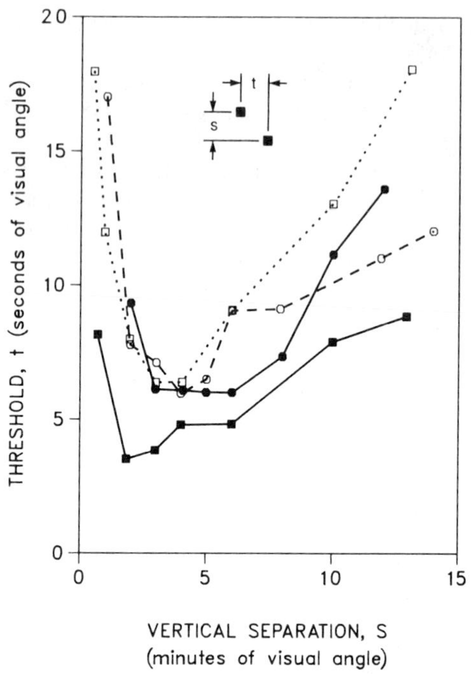

Figure 7.33. Two-dot vernier acuity as a function of the vertical separation of the dots. The stimuli were bright dots (160 cd/m^2) on a dimmer background. The independent and dependent variables are defined in Figure. 7.32(b), (c). Note that vertical separation is measured in minutes of visual angle, whereas threshold misalignment is measured in seconds of visual angle. The four curves are for different observers and are taken from two different studies. Threshold is lowest when the vertical separation is between 2 and 4 min, although the optimum separation differs somewhat from one observer to another. Threshold is higher for vertical separations that are either smaller or larger than the optimal. When the target consists of line segments, rather than dots, the results coincide with those shown when vertical separation is optimal or greater than optimal. However, the threshold for line targets does not increase at smaller vertical separations. (Filled and open circles from G. Westheimer, The spatial grain of the perifoveal visual field, *Vision Research, 22*. Filled and open squares from G. Westheimer & S. P. McKee, Spatial configurations for visual hyperacuity, *Vision Research, 17*. Copyright 1982 and 1977, respectively, by Pergamon Press, Ltd. Reprinted with permission.)

threshold is smallest when the vertical separation is in the range of 3–5 min of visual angle. The threshold rises if the vertical separation is greater than 5 min, regardless of whether the targets are dots or lines. If the targets are dots, the threshold also increases if the vertical separation is less than 3 min. However, this increase does not occur if the targets are lines more than 5 min long. Except when the vertical separation is less than 3 min, performance is independent of the length of the target line. That is, performance is as good when the targets are two dots as when the targets are two lines. When the vertical separation is 0, however, performance improves as the length of the target lines increases up to about 5 min (Westheimer & McKee, 1977b).

Optimal performance depends on both members of the target pattern being present at the same time. Threshold rises by an order of magnitude when an interval of 0.5 sec separates the presentations of the two parts of the target (Westheimer & Hauske, 1975). This fact underscores that the judgment is one of relative, rather than absolute, position.

Vernier acuity is degraded by the presence of other stimuli nearby. Figure 7.34 illustrates this kind of spatial interference. Horizontal masks produce similar interference, so the effect appears to be independent of the orientation of the masking stimuli (Westheimer & Hauske, 1975).

Vernier acuity is not affected by small amounts of target motion. Westheimer and McKee (1975), using exposures that were too short to permit the initiation of tracking movements, found little or no change in threshold when the target moved laterally across the field of view. They examined target velocities from 0.0 to 3.5 degree/sec. Westheimer and McKee (1978) also found little or no change when the target moved in depth by small amounts.

Vernier thresholds are subtantially higher in peripheral vision than in central vision. Figure 7.7 illustrates the effect of position in the visual field.

A second task in this category is identification of a spatial interval, which is illustrated in Figure 7.32(d). On each trial, the observer sees a single interval (defined by the distance between two parallel lines, for example) and must categorize it as wider or narrower than a standard interval. The observer receives feedback, that is, is told whether each judgment is correct or incorrect. The task is particularly interesting because the standard interval is never explicitly identified, although it is one of the several intervals presented. The standard is defined for the observer only by the feedback and by the fact that it is the mean of the distribution of intervals presented for judgment. As seen in Figure 7.35, the judgment can be very accurate, yielding thresholds as small as those observed in vernier acuity tasks. Threshold is smallest when the standard separation is between 1 and 6 min of visual angle. Equivalent results have been reported for spatial intervals defined by bright lines, dark lines, bright and dark edges, and an edge and a line (Westheimer & McKee, 1977b).

A third type of task is judgment of the orientation of the target. Figure 7.32(f) illustrates this task. When target contrast is high, the smallest identifiable deviation from vertical is about 20–30 min of rotation (Westheimer, Shimamura, & McKee, 1976). Threshold is much larger when target contrast is very low, although the orientation of the target can be identified to within 10–20° even at the detection threshold (Thomas & Gille, 1979). As in the case of vernier acuity, the accuracy of orientation judgments is reduced by the presence of nearby stimuli. Figure 7.34 illustrates this interference.

A fourth task in this group is identification of a step translation of the target that occurs during the time the target is exposed. Figure 7.32(e) illustrates the task. When the target is either an isolated line or a sinusoidal grating, the threshold displacement is about 10 sec of visual angle (Westheimer, 1978, 1979a). Placing a second, stationary stimulus a few minutes to one side of the target nearly halves the threshold (Westheimer, 1979a). In the latter case, threshold is about the same as for identification of a spatial interval.

As Westheimer (1979a) has noted, none of the laws of physical optics governing resolution is violated by the fact that hyperacuity thresholds are small relative to the dimensions of the receptor mosaic and relative to the optical spread function. What does seem to be implied is that the visual system is sophisticated enough to calculate the spatial *center of gravity* and other parameters of the retinal image with a precision finer than the spacing of the sample points. Further, the implication is that the visual system uses small changes in these parameters to identify small differences in spatial position. Indeed, Westheimer and McKee (1977a) have demonstrated hyperacuity with stimuli in which spatial position is defined by the center of gravity of the light distribution, rather than by contours. To some extent, spatial hyperacuity is analogous to identifying differences in wavelength (i.e., spectral position) of monochromatic lights. Differences can be identified which are tiny relative

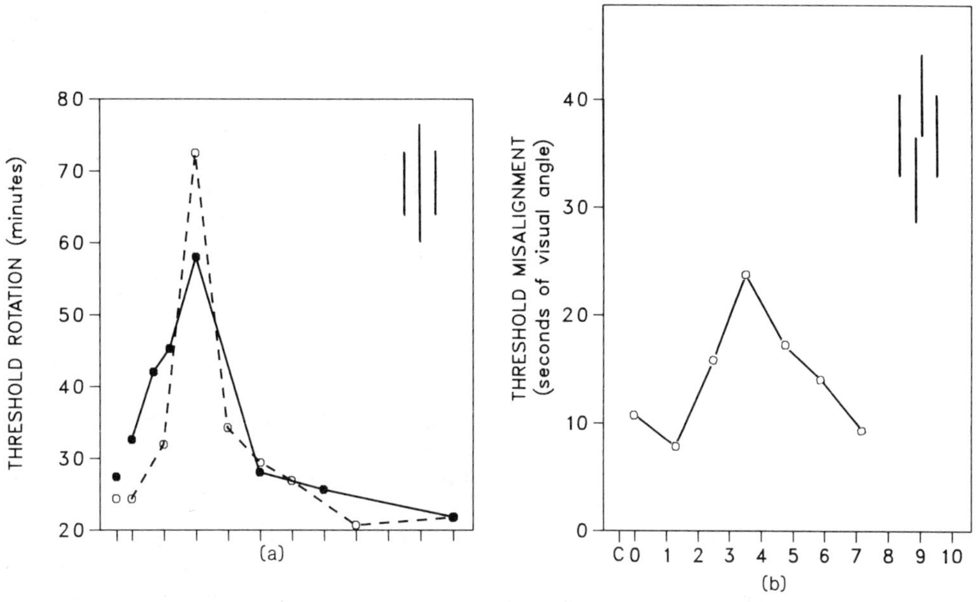

Figure 7.34. Interference with spatial judgments by adjacent stimuli. (a) Interference with judgments of orientation. The target was a single line, 30 min long by 15 sec wide, which was flanked by two vertical masking lines, each 15 min long. Luminance of the lines was about 160 cd/m^2. The orientation of the target was randomly varied from trial to trial. The task of the observer was to identify whether the orientation on each trial was rotated clockwise or counterclockwise from vertical. The masking lines were always vertical. The independent variable is the distance between the target and each mask, measured in minutes of visual angle. No masks were present in the control condition, labeled C. The dependent variable is the magnitude of the rotation from vertical, measured in minutes of angular rotation, which was correctly identified on 75% of the trials. Each data point is based on at least 300 trials and has a standard error of 10–15%. The two curves are for two different observers. Threshold rotation is between 20 and 30 min when no masks are present. Interference with the judgment is greatest when the masks are at a distance of 2 min of visual angle. (From G. Westheimer, K. Shimamura, & S. P. McKee, Interference with line-orientation sensitivity, *Journal of the Optical Society of America*, 1976, 66. Reprinted with permission.) (b) Interference with vernier acuity. The vernier target consisted of two line segements, each 6.4 min of visual angle long, flanked by two masking lines, each 3.2 min long. The luminance of the lines was about 320 cd/m^2. The task of the observer was to identify whether the top target line was to the left or right of the bottom target line. The independent variable is the distance between the center of the vernier target and each mask, measured in minutes of visual angle. The dependent variable is the magnitude of the misalignment that was correctly identified on 75% of the trials, measured in seconds of visual angle. Each data point is based on at least 300 trials and has a standard error of about 10%. The data are for one observer. Interference is greatest when the masks are 3 to 4 min from the center of the vernier target. (From G. Westheimer & G. Hauske, Temporal and spatial interference with vernier acuity, *Vision Research*, *15*. Copyright 1975 by Pergamon Press, Ltd. Reprinted with permission.)

to the bandwidths (spectral spread functions) of the photopigments. In the case of wavelength discrimination, this capacity is generally taken to mean that the visual system compares activities (e.g., takes ratios) of responses in receptors containing different photopigments. Hyperacuity implies that analogous comparisons are made between the responses of receptors at different spatial locations.

3.2. Stimulus Appearance: Interaction Phenomena

The apparent spatial characteristics of a stimulus can be altered by the simultaneous presence of other patterns in the visual field. Section 3.2.1 presents one elegant demonstration of a suprathreshold masking effect and its dependency on spatial frequency. A number of other suprathreshold effects are readily observed in the many visual illusions reprinted in textbooks. Among other characteristics, perceptions of size, length, orientation, and parallelism can be greatly influenced by the spatial context in which they are presented. To the extent that these effects are perceptual, rather than cognitive, the change in appearance implies interactions between mechanisms sensitive to these dimensions. Unfortunately, most of these illusions still resist explanation.

In some cases, prolonged inspection of a variety of contours and stimulus configurations affects the appearance of subsequently viewed patterns. Demonstrations of complex figural aftereffects are available in most introductory perception texts. While many of these aftereffects are visually interesting, the number and complexity of the configurations have perhaps obscured, rather than clarified, the processes involved. These numerous aftereffects are almost universally explained, with varying degrees of success, by selective fatigue of particular neuronal populations. Adaptation aftereffects are discussed in Section 3.2.2.

3.2.1. Masking. Just as masking interferes with the ability to detect a low-contrast pattern, the ability to identify a high-contrast stimulus can be impaired by the presence of a masking pattern. An illustration of this phenomenon was provided by Harmon and Julesz (1973), reproduced in Figure 7.36.

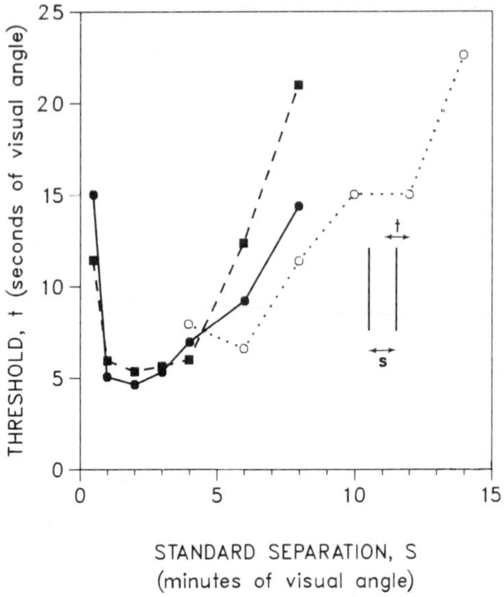

Figure 7.35. Identification of a spatial extent. The task and independent and dependent variables are described in Figure 7.32(d). The stimuli were bright lines (about 300 cd/m^2) on a dimmer background. Each line (closed and open symbols, respectively) was less than 1 min wide and was 12.8 or 30 min of visual angle long. Note that threshold is measured in seconds of visual angle, whereas the standard separation is measured in minutes of visual angle. The three curves are for different observers. The standard error of each threshold is about 15%. Threshold deviation is 5–7 sec of visual angle when the standard separation is optimal and increases for standard separations which are either smaller or larger. The optimal range is 1–6 min of separation, although some individual differences are apparent in the data. Like results are obtained when the spatial extent is defined by dark lines, by bright or dark edges, or by a combination of a line and an edge. (Data shown by closed symbols are from G. Westheimer, The spatial sense of the eye, *Investigative Ophthalmology*, 1979, *18*. Reprinted with permission. Open symbols are from G. Westheimer & S. P. McKee, Spatial configurations for visual hyperactivity, *Vision Research*, *17*. Copyright 1977 by Pergamon Press, Ltd. Reprinted with permission.)

A photograph of Abraham Lincoln was divided into 300 square patches (15 × 20). Each square was replaced with an area of uniform luminance which matched the mean of the original patch. Thus in the vertical dimension, the upper limit of the picture spectrum was 10 cycles. However, the quantization procedure introduced a series of high spatial frequencies into the image (comprising the edges of each square) which rendered the photograph virtually unrecognizable, as can be seen in Figure 7.36(a).

By selectively filtering out coarsely restricted bands of spatial-frequency components, Harmon and Julesz determined that the masking effect evident in Figure 7.36(a) was primarily caused by spatial-frequency components within 2 octaves above the upper limit of the picture spectrum. This range is in reasonable agreement with the range of masking effects found at threshold levels. Masking by these frequency components is shown in Figure 7.36(d). Panels (b) and (c) show much less noticeable masking effect when the critical frequency band is removed.

3.2.2. Adaptation

3.2.2.1. ***Apparent Spatial-Frequency Shift.*** Adaptation to a grating of a particular spatial frequency leads to a shift in the apparent spatial frequency of a subsequently viewed grating. The shift is away from that of the adapting grating. Test gratings of higher frequencies are seen as higher than they are in reality, whereas lower test frequencies are perceived as even lower (Blakemore & Nachmias, 1971; Blakemore, Nachmias, & Sutton, 1970; Blakemore & Sutton, 1969). These results are shown in Figure 7.37, and a model that accounts for this shift in perceived frequency by selective fatigue of spatial frequency or size-tuned mechanisms is shown in Figure 7.38.

The effect is specific to the portion of the retina which is adapted, as can be shown in the demonstration of Figure 7.39. The effect is also orientation specific; adaptation to a vertical grating has no effect on the apparent frequency of a horizontal test grating (Blakemore & Nachmias, 1971; Blakemore, Nachmias, & Sutton, 1970; Pantle & Sekuler, 1968). In fact, changing the orientation of a grating produces results virtually identical to reducing the contrast of the adapting grating (Blakemore, Nachmias, & Sutton, 1970). The magnitude of the spatial frequency shift decreases to half either by tilting the test grating 6.75° or by reducing the adaptation contrast by a factor of 2 (Blakemore & Nachmias, 1971). This result provides evidence for a common neural origin underlying both the threshold elevation and the suprathreshold frequency shift found following adaptation, implying that the same pathways are involved in both detection and identification of gratings.

3.2.2.2. ***Orientation: The Tilt Aftereffect.*** A second suprathreshold consequence of adaptation is the *tilt aftereffect.* Adaptation to a stimulus oriented to a particular direction causes a subsequently viewed stimulus to appear tilted in the opposite direction (Gibson & Radner, 1937). The effect is easily demonstrated, as shown in Figure 7.40. There is evidence that this aftereffect shares a common neural origin with the tilt illusion, in which vertical lines surrounded by lines tilted in one direction appear to be tilted in the opposite direction (O'Toole & Wenderoth, 1977; Tolhurst & Thompson, 1975). Both effects occur when contours are formed by luminance gradients or by color differences alone (Elsner, 1978), and both effects show an interaction between color selectivity and spatial frequency. At low spatial frequencies (around 3 cycles/degree), no difference is found in the magnitude of the effects when adapting and test gratings differ in color. At higher spatial frequencies (around 8 cycles/degree) this color difference greatly reduces the magnitude of the effect (Lovegrove & Badcock, 1981).

At first glance, the tilt aftereffect seems to parallel the perceived frequency shift. That is, it might be seen as a suprathreshold manifestation of selective adaptation in orientation-specific mechanisms. However, there is some disagreement among researchers as to the properties which characterize this effect and the degree to which these properties are consistent with threshold elevation properties. With gratings, some investigators report that the tilt aftereffect was found to be frequency specific (Ware & Mitchell, 1974), whereas others have not found such selectivity (Campbell & Maffei, 1971; Parker, 1972). Similarly, the effect has been reported to occur with oblique adapting stimuli (Lennie, 1972) or only with horizontal and vertical orientations (Campbell & Maffei, 1971). Finally, the degree of interocular transfer of the effect remains an issue (Campbell & Maffei, 1971; Coltheart, 1974; Ware & Mitchell, 1974). Thus unlike the perceived frequency shift, no simple interpretation of the tilt aftereffect currently exists.

3.3. Other Factors Affecting Stimulus Appearance

The apparent size or spatial frequency of a stimulus may vary with contrast. For sinusoidal gratings, the perceived spatial frequency is higher for low-contrast patterns (Georgeson, 1980; Kulikowski, 1975), although the effect is not always obtained (Tynan & Sekuler, 1974; Virsu & Nyman, 1974). For spatially

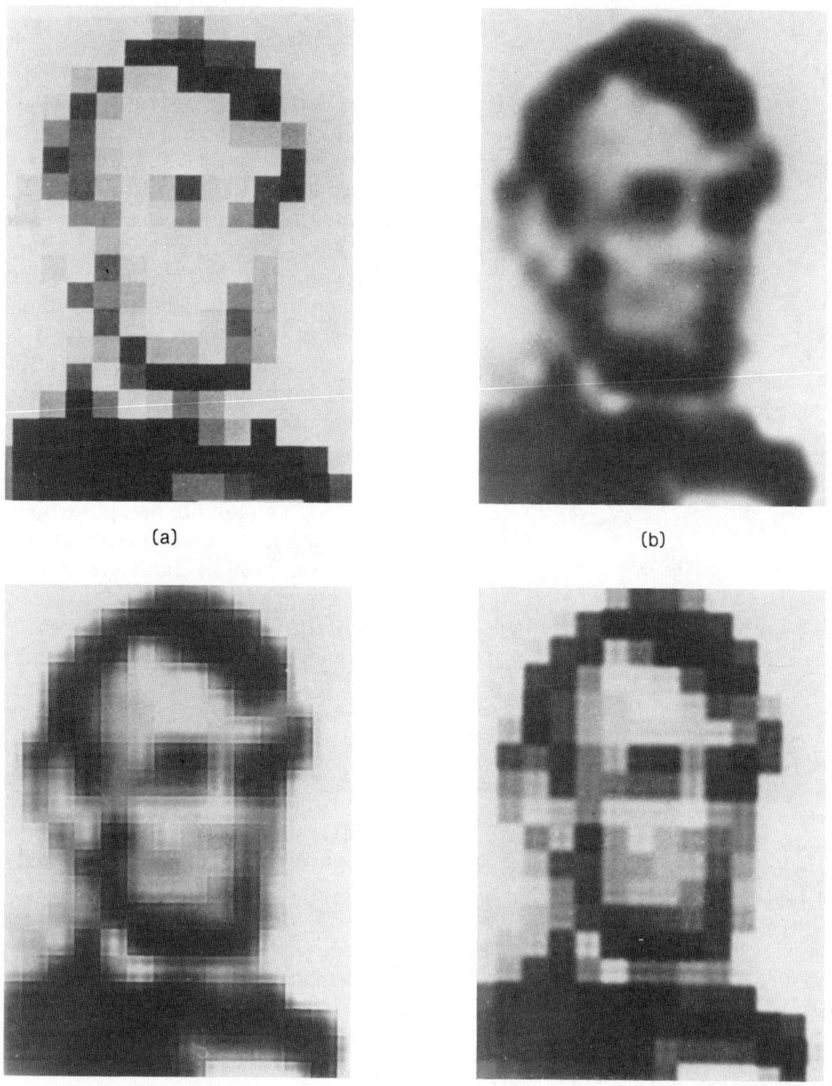

Figure 7.36. Effect of spatially selective filtering on facial appearance. A photograph of Abraham Lincoln was processed through a low-pass filter and divided into 300 square sections. Each square was replaced with an unvarying block equal to the mean luminance of that section, resulting in the image shown in (a). The upper limit of the picture spectrum, *W*, was 10 cycles per vertical dimension. The portrait is difficult to identify. In (b), the image shown in (a) was low-pass-filtered by removing all frequencies higher than 1.2*w*. The result of removing higher frequencies is a blurry but identifiable facial image, suggesting that the presence of the higher frequencies masked the components necessary for facial identification. In (c), intermediate frequencies (between 1.22*w* and 3.94*w*) have been removed. The remaining high frequencies do not interfere with the appearance of the face to as great an extent as in (d), in which only frequencies above 4.06*w* were removed. (From L. D. Harmon & B. Julesz, Masking in visual recognition: Effects of two-dimensional filtered noise, *Science*, *180*. Copyright 1973 by the American Association for the Advancement of Science. Reprinted with permission.)

localized stimuli, reports also conflict. Georgeson (1980) found that localized bars appeared to be of higher frequency at low contrasts. Thomas and Kerr (1969) reported no general change in perceived size with ramp stimuli, although all their observers saw a small increase in perceived size with their smallest stimuli (10 min).

Gelb and Wilson (1983) suggested that the discrepancies among these findings may be due to the particular sizes chosen as stimuli. They measured perceived size as a function of contrast with localized difference of Gaussian (DOG) stimuli ranging from 0.5 to 10 cycles/degree, finding an effect much larger than previously reported. In general, low-contrast patterns were perceived as smaller than high-contrast patterns, although one observer showed reversals at middle frequencies. The effect was most pronounced for small stimuli and under transient temporal conditions.

Temporal parameters may also affect perceived size, but different results are obtained for repetitive and spatially localized patterns. For grating patterns, as presentation becomes more transient, perceived spatial frequency increases, but this effect is limited to low spatial frequencies, below 4 cycles/degree (Gelb & Wilson, 1983; Kulikowski, 1975; Tynan & Sekuler, 1974;

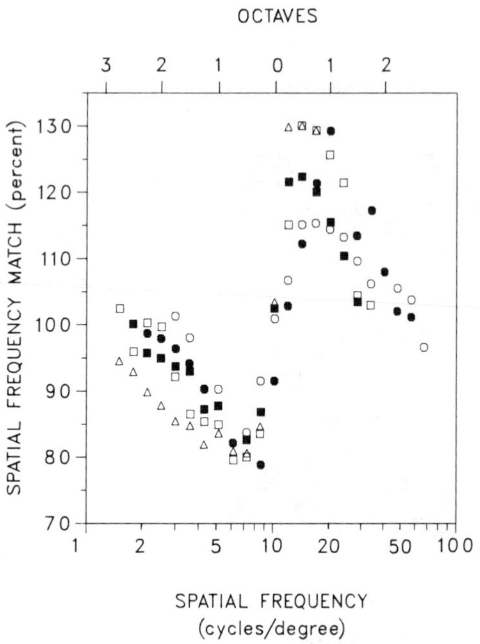

Figure 7.37. Perceived spatial-frequency shift. Observers fixated a bar between two oscilloscopes placed 0.5° apart, from a distance of 2.9 m. The observer adapted to a high-contrast grating (1.5 log units above threshold) on the upper screen for 3 min. During adaptation, the lower screen was a blank field of the same space-average luminance as the upper. A test grating then appeared on both the upper and lower screens. Using a potentiometer, the observer quickly adjusted the spatial frequency of the lower pattern to match the apparent frequency of the upper grating. A 10-sec period of readaptation occurred between test trials. The results for five adapting frequencies between 3.5 and 14.2 cycles/degree are shown for a number of test gratings. These data are superimposed at 10 cycles/degree to facilitate comparison across the adapting frequencies. The ordinate plots the ratio of the matched spatial frequency following adaptation to the matched spatial frequency without adaptation, multiplied by 100. A value of 100 indicates a perfect match, whereas values above and below 100 indicate that following adaptation, the upper grating appeared to be of higher or lower frequency, respectively. (From C. B. Blakemore & P. Sutton, Size adaptation: A new aftereffect, *Science, 166*. Copyright 1969 by the American Association for the Advancement of Science. Reprinted with permission.)

Virsu & Nyman, 1974; Virsu, Nyman, & Lehtio, 1974). Above 3 or 4 cycles/degree there is either no effect or the perceived spatial frequency is lower under transient conditions.

With spatially localized targets, patterns appear smaller at all sizes under transient conditions, but the effect is most prominent for small targets, corresponding to high spatial frequencies (Gelb & Wilson, 1983). The authors suggest that the differences between spatially extensive and localized effects are due to mechanisms whose receptive fields are in the periphery of the retina. They suggest that retinally peripheral mechanisms play a role in size perception, and input from such mechanisms would occur only in the case of repetitive stimuli.

3.4. Identification Models

Contemporary models of identification, like detection models, assume that perception of the target is mediated by a mosaic of differently tuned pathways acting in parallel. The same basic questions must be answered: (1) How does each pathway respond to the target? and (2) How are the responses from different pathways combined and used to arrive at an identification judgment? In general, it is assumed that the same mosaic of pathways mediates both detection and identification and that the response properties of each individual pathway are the same, that is, the response is determined by the properties of the stimulus and not the task. Thus the hypotheses proposed in answer to the first basic question are the same for both detection and identification models, and they will not be repeated here. The reader should refer to Section 2.3 for a discussion of these hypotheses. The answer to the second basic question, on the other hand, is assumed to differ depending on whether the task is detection or identification. Thus the major topic of this section is the manner in which the individual responses are combined to yield an identification judgment.

In the simplest case, the stimuli to be identified are distinguished from one another by orthogonal components, that is, components so different in spatial frequency content or orientation that they activate completely different groups of pathways. Correct identification occurs whenever the contrast of the stimulus is high enough to bring the distinctive components above threshold. The first demonstration of this fact was by Campbell and Robson (1968). Their observers distinguished between a sine wave grating and a square wave grating of the same fundamental frequency. The sine wave contained only the single, fundamental spatial frequency, whereas the square wave contained the fundamental frequency, plus all odd harmonics in progressively diminishing amounts. Of the harmonics, the third is generally the most visible and is sufficiently different from the fundamental to be treated as orthogonal. Campbell and Robson showed that the square wave was correctly identified whenever contrast was high enough to bring the third harmonic above its own, independently established, threshold. (See also Furchner, Thomas, & Campbell, 1977.) Another demonstration of this principle is the fact that orthogonal stimuli, such as gratings that differ widely in spatial frequency or orientation, are identified with the same accuracy with which they are detected; that is, they are correctly identified whenever they are above threshold (Furchner, Thomas, & Campbell, 1977; King-Smith & Kulikowski, 1981; Nachmias & Weber, 1975; Thomas & Gille, 1979; Thomas, Gille, & Barker, 1982; Tolhurst & Dealy; 1975; Watson & Robson, 1981).

In the more general case, the stimuli to be identified are considered to activate broadly overlapping groups of pathways. The stimuli can be identified because each produces a distinctive pattern of activity within the population of pathways. The profile of level of activity across pathways is different for different stimuli. The theoretical question is how the different patterns are distinguished. An early hypothesis was that the identification judgment is made by selecting the pathway giving the largest response (Blakemore & Nachmias, 1971; Thomas, 1970). According to this hypothesis, the stimulus selected by the observer is the stimulus to which the selected pathway is most sensitive. The problem with this hypothesis is that it implies a separate pathway for each discriminable stimulus. An unreasonably large number of pathways must be postulated to account for the extremely fine discriminations of spatial position (Westheimer, 1981), orientation (Westheimer, Shimamura, & McKee, 1976), and spatial frequency (Hirsch & Hylton, 1982) that are made at high contrasts.

More recent treatments propose that the identification judgment is based on a quantitative comparison among the magnitudes of the responses of the pathways. In principle, such a comparison can yield many more discriminations than there are pathways. The number of discriminations that can be made

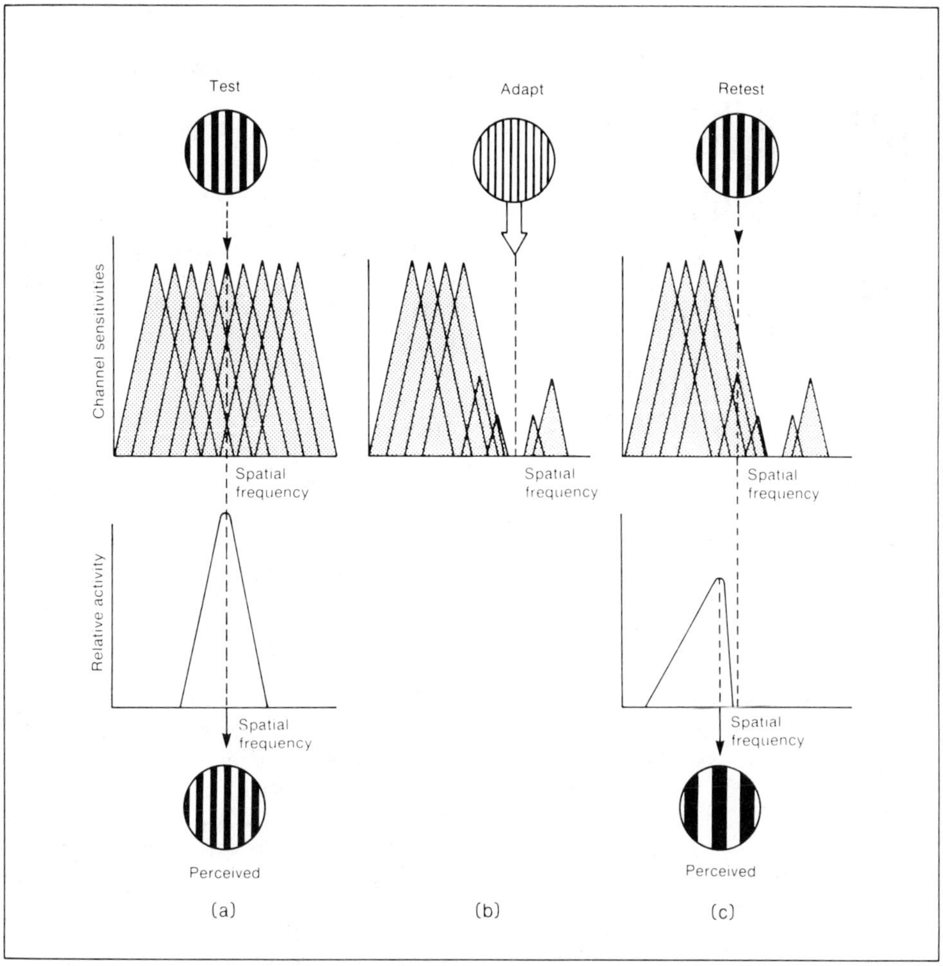

Figure 7.38. Illustrative model for apparent frequency shift following adaptation. (a) Sensitivity of multiple pathways, each selective to a small but overlapping range of spatial frequencies, is shown prior to adaptation (sensitivities are arbitrarily made equal only for the purpose of illustration). It is assumed that the appearance of a stimulus is determined by the tuning characteristics of the most active channel. Prior to adaptation, the most active channel corresponds to that which is optimally tuned to the frequency presented, resulting in an accurate perception of the test grating frequency. (b) Adaptation to a grating of a different frequency selectively depresses activity in those mechanisms sensitive to the pattern. The magnitude of the depression is greatest at the channel tuned to the adapting grating and is symmetrically less for channels tuned to nearby frequencies. If the adapting pattern is presented as a test, no frequency shift is perceived; the symmetric pattern of depression still peaks at the "correct" frequency. (c) When a nearby test frequency is presented following adaptation, peak activity is shifted (in this case to a channel tuned to lower frequencies). In general, higher test frequencies will appear still higher, lower test frequencies lower. (From O. J. Braddick, F. W. Campbell, & J. Atkinson, Channels in vision: Basic aspects, in R. Held, H. Leibowitz, & H. L. Teuber (Eds.), *Handbook of sensory physiology* (Vol. 8): *Perception*, Springer-Verlag, 1978. Reprinted with permission.)

is limited by random variability in the system, rather than by the number of pathways.

In one such treatment, each pathway is identified with a stimulus correlate, such as a particular spatial frequency or width. The identification judgment is based on the weighted mean of the stimulus correlates of the active pathways:

$$c = \sum_{i=1}^{n} r_i c_i / \sum_{i=1}^{n} r_i , \tag{19}$$

where c_i is the stimulus correlate identified with pathway i; r_i is the response of that pathway; and c is the weighted mean on which the identification judgment is based. This approach has been applied to the identification of spatial frequency (Klein, Stromeyer, & Ganz, 1974; Georgeson, 1980) and size (Gelb & Wilson, 1983).

Vector space models have also been proposed (Thomas, 1983; Thomas & Gille, 1979; Thomas, Gille, & Barker, 1982; Wilson & Gelb, 1984). In these models, the visual response to each stimulus is represented as a vector in a multidimensional space. Each axis of the space represents the response of a single tuned pathway. The direction and length of the vector depend on the pattern of responses in the pathways and provide the comparative information required for an identification judgment. In the typical identification or discrimination task the observer must distinguish between two stimuli. The stimuli are represented by vectors which, in turn, define a difference vector. Performance

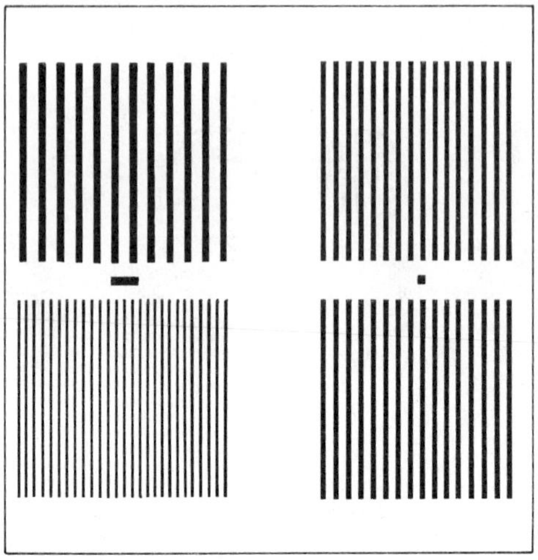

Figure 7.39. Demonstration of spatial-frequency shift following adaptation. The test gratings illustrated on the right side are identical in spatial frequency. On the left side, the top grating is of a lower frequency, whereas the lower grating is a higher frequency than the test gratings. Following adaptation to the left-hand gratings by scanning the center fixation bar for at least 1 min, the test gratings will appear to differ in spatial frequency when the right-hand center bar is fixated. The top grating will appear to be of higher spatial frequency, showing a shift away from the wider bars of the upper adapting grating. Similarly, the lower test grating will appear to be of lower spatial frequency. (From C. B. Blakemore & P. Sutton, Size adaptation: A new aftereffect, *Science, 166*. Copyright 1969 by the American Association for the Advancement of Science. Reprinted with permission.)

of the task is assumed to be a monotonically increasing function of the expected length of the difference vector, although the variability of the responses must also be considered. Wilson and Gelb call the difference vector a *line-element*, a term taken from the color vision literature.

In the model proposed by Thomas and his coworkers, the observer divides the space into sections, each of which represents one of the categories into which the stimuli are to be sorted. For example, if the identification task is to indicate which of six different orientations has been presented, the space is divided into six sections, each of which represents a different orientation. On each presentation of a stimulus, the judgment is based on which section contains the vector encoding that stimulus presentation. This approach differs from the previous one in that stimulus correlates, such as particular spatial frequencies or widths, are assigned to the sections and their boundaries, rather than to individual pathways. Further, the sections and boundaries are set on the basis of the task to be performed.

To date, the primary application of vector models has been to tasks in which equally visible stimuli must be classified into two categories, such as two different spatial frequencies or two different orientations. Figure 7.41 illustrates this application. Points A, B, and N represent the expected responses to stimulus A, stimulus B, and a uniform field, respectively. Similarly, the vectors **NA** and **NB** represent the expected responses to stimuli A and B. The vectors are equal in length because the stimuli have been equated for visibility. Because of noise in the system, the vector generated on each presentation deviates from the expected vector. This variability is symbolized by the irregular contours. The broken line represents the decision boundary adopted by the observer. Each presentation of a stimulus is judged to be A or B, according to which side of the boundary the vector for that presentation falls. The accuracy with which the stimuli are classified depends on the angle formed by the vectors, the lengths of the vectors, and the amount of random variation.

Quantitative application of the model is eased by making some simplifying assumptions and by restricting the treatment to stimuli equated for visibility. The simplifying assumptions are that the variation is multivariate normal, with a standard deviation σ_V on every radius, and that the decision boundary bisects and is normal to the difference vector **AB**. It is presumed that σ_V varies as a function of stimulus contrast and/or vector length. Because the stimuli are equated for visibility, the vectors are taken as having equal expected lengths.

Given these conditions, the accuracy with which the stimuli are classified

$$z(C) = AB/2\sigma_V$$

$$= \sin^{-1}(\Phi/2) \cdot V/\sigma_V \,, \qquad (20)$$

where $z(C)$ is the standard normal deviate corresponding to the probability of a correct classification; AB is the expected length of the difference vector **AB**; Φ is the angle formed by the two expected vectors; and V is the expected length of the vectors representing the stimuli (i.e., the expected length of **NA** and **NB**). Thus predicting performance requires knowledge of the angle Φ and the ratio V/σ_V. Some estimates of these quantities are available for foveally viewed sinusoidal grating stimuli.

The angle Φ varies as a function of the difference between the stimuli with respect to orientation and spatial frequency. Functions relating Φ to these variables have been derived from simultaneous detection and identification data and are presented in Figure 7.42. Φ appears to be relatively independent of contrast, at least over the range of stimulus conditions relevant to studies of discrimination and identification (Thomas, 1983; Thomas & Gille, 1979). The ratio V/σ_V increases as a function of stimulus contrast. Figure 7.43 presents the functions that have been obtained for grating stimuli.

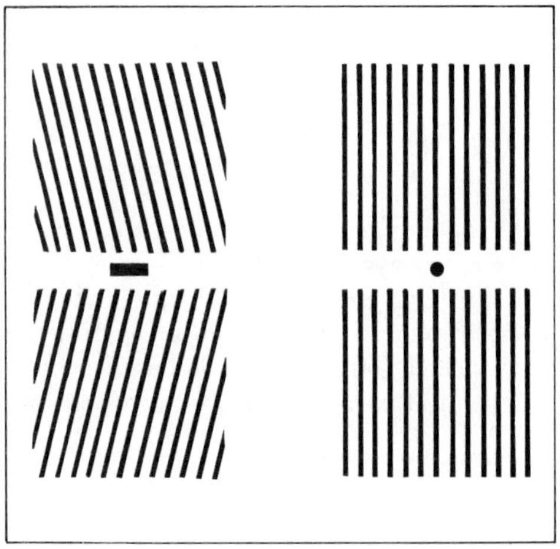

Figure 7.40. Demonstration of the tilt aftereffect. Following prolonged fixation of the tilted grating on the left, the vertical grating on the right appears to be tilted in the opposite direction. (From H. R. Schiffman, *Sensation and perception* (2nd ed.), Wiley, 1982. Reprinted with permission.)

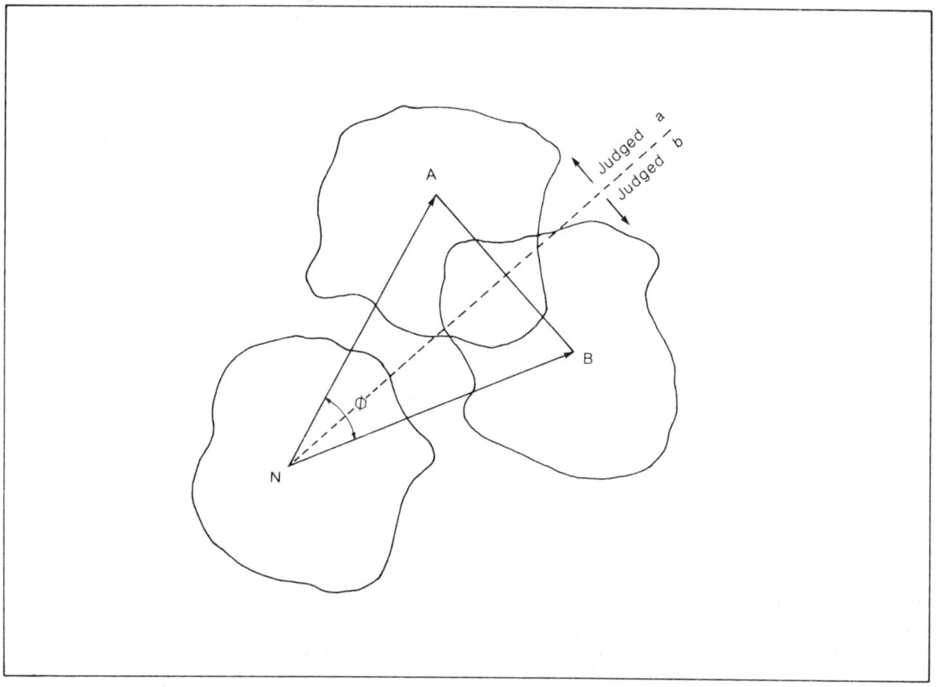

Figure 7.41. Vector model applied to identification of two stimuli *a* and *b*. The response of the visual system to each presentation of a stimulus is presented by a point in a multidimensional space. Each dimension of the space represents the response of one spatially tuned pathway. Because of noise, the response to a given stimulus varies from one presentation to another. Thus over many actual and/or potential presentations, the stimulus is represented by a distribution of points centered on the expected response. The irregular enclosures symbolize these distributions, and *A*, *B*, and *N* represent the expected responses to the stimuli *a*, *b*, and to a uniform field, respectively. The model proposes that the observer establishes a decision plane. The broken line represents the intersection of this plane with the plane containing *A*, *B*, and *N*. All responses which lie to the left of the plane are judged by the observer to represent stimulus a, all responses to the right to represent stimulus *b*. The probability that the judgment will be correct depends on how much the distributions centered on *A* and *B* overlap. That is, performance is directly related to the length of the difference vector **AB** and inversely related to the dispersion of the distributions. The length of the difference vector, in turn, depends on the lengths of the vectors **NA** and **NB** and on the angle ϕ which the vectors form.

4. APPLIED MEASUREMENT OF SPATIAL VISION

Quantifiable and comparable measures of spatial vision capabilities are necessary in many practical and clinical situations. Such capabilities can be determined by a variety of methods, which fall into two major classes: traditional acuity measures and contrast sensitivity measures. Acuity measures the resolution capabilities of the visual system in terms of the smallest high-contrast detail to be perceived at a given distance. It should be noted that this is analogous to measuring a single point on the contrast sensitivity function—the high-frequency cutoff. The ease with which acuity tests can be administered has led to their widespread use as the standard assessment procedure for visual capability. The main focus of this section is on acuity measures and factors affecting acuity. The tasks and targets (optotypes) commonly used in clinical examinations and industrial screening situations are discussed in Section 4.2. Factors affecting acuity are presented in Section 4.3.

Contrast sensitivity has been extensively measured in experimental situations but has not been widely used in clinical or industrial settings. However, recent advances in technology and technique (Sekuler & Tynan, 1977) have increased the feasibility of measuring contrast sensitivity quickly in a nonlaboratory setting. The measurement of contrast sensitivity and many of the factors affecting contrast sensitivity were discussed in Sections 1 and 2 and are not repeated here. The discussion of contrast sensitivity in this section is limited to findings of clinical or industrial importance. A discussion of the relative merits of assessing visual capabilities via acuity measures versus contrast sensitivity measures is provided in Section 4.4.

4.1. Acuity

The ability to clearly perceive spatial detail is termed *visual acuity*. Limits on acuity may either be optical or neural in nature; one or the other may dominate in any given situation. Optical limits lead to a degraded retinal image, which can often be improved by the introduction of corrective lenses. Such limits can be imposed by pupil size, limited accommodation, or corneal and lens imperfections. Neural limits are imposed by the coarseness of the retinal mosaic and inherent sensitivity limits of noisy neural pathways. Acuity is typically measured at both far (20 ft or 6 m) and near (0.4 m) viewing distances, as the factors which limit resolution can differ in these two cases.

To assess acuity, high-contrast patterns of various sizes are presented to the observer from a fixed distance. The smallest pattern (or critical detail of a pattern) to be detected or identified (depending on the task) is taken as the threshold value, expressed

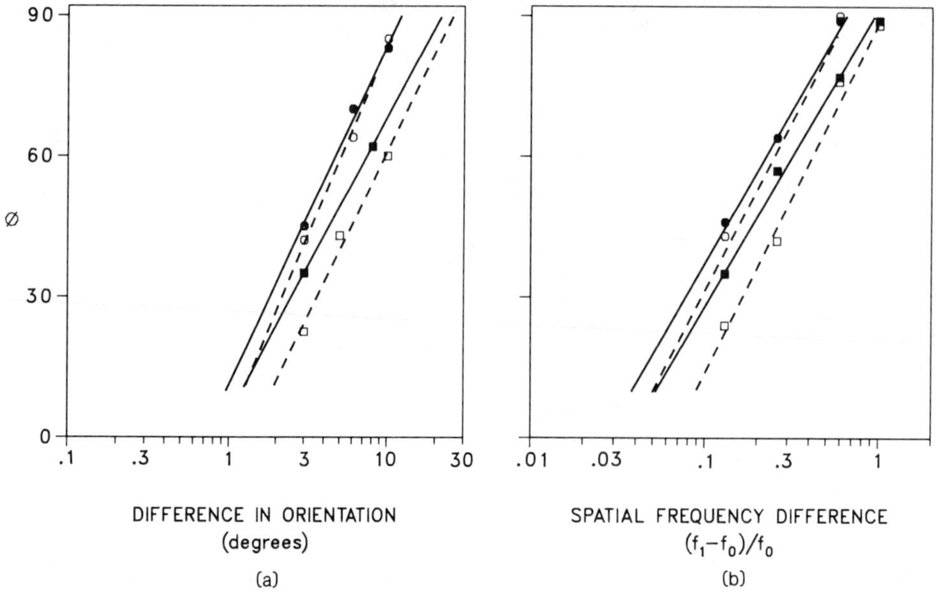

Figure 7.42. Vector model of identification: ϕ, the angle formed by the vectors, as a function of differences in orientation and spatial frequency. The target was a circular patch of a sine wave grating, 3° in diameter, viewed foveally with both eyes. The mean luminance was 60 cd/m². The left-hand panel shows ϕ as a function of the difference in orientation to be discriminated. Note that difference in orientation is plotted in logarithmic coordinates. The data are for four practiced observers. The right panel shows ϕ as a function of the difference in spatial frequency to be discriminated. Note that the difference in frequency is defined as a Weber fraction $(f_1 - f_0)/f_0$, where f_0 is the lower frequency and f_1 is the higher frequency. This fraction is plotted in logarithmic coordinates. The data are for four practiced observers. For these data, the frequencies to be distinguished were centered on 3 cycles/degree. Two observers were also tested with frequencies centered on 15 cycles/degree and gave essentially the same results. However, results by Hirsch and Hylton (1982) indicate that the data for a given observer can oscillate along the horizontal axis as a function of small differences in the f_0. (See Section 3.1.2.) Data reported by Olzak (1982), but not shown, indicate that ϕ slightly exceeds 90° when the stimuli are gratings that differ in spatial frequency by a factor of 3 or 4. (From J. P. Thomas, J. Gille, & R. A Barker, Simultaneous detection and identification: Theory and data, *Journal of the Optical Society of America*, 1982, 72. Reprinted with permission.)

in minutes of visual arc. Visual acuity is expressed as the reciprocal of the resolution threshold. Normal acuity is assumed to be limited by the coarseness of the retinal mosaic. On the basis of intercone spacing, it is assumed that an observer should be able to resolve a detail which subtends about 0.5 min of visual arc, or a grating pattern of 60 cycles/degree given a perfectly focused image. However, depending on the task, the optotype, and the observer, acuities much higher than this normative value are observed. The most commonly used optotypes (Landolt ring and Snellen or Sloan letters) yield resolution thresholds on the order of 0.5–1 min.

Several expressions of visual acuity are in common use. When the reciprocal of threshold in minutes of arc is expressed in terms of a decimal, it is termed *decimal acuity*. Normal acuity in decimal notation is 1. Acuity can also be expressed as a Snellen fraction. The denominator of the fraction is the distance at which the optotype critical detail subtends 1-min arc. The numerator of the fraction is the actual distance from the observer to the optotype. Test charts calibrated for different test distances are available, the most common calibrated for 20 ft, 6 m, and 4 m for distance acuity and 40 cm for near acuity. Normal acuity, expressed as a Snellen fraction, is 20/20, 6/6, 4/4, and 40/40 for these distances, respectively.

In practice, testing environments vary widely along dimensions which can affect acuity, such as illumination, the spectral composition of illumination, and the particular optotypes with their associated assessment tasks. The National Academy of Sciences (1980) has provided a set of recommended standards for use in acuity assessment.

4.2. Acuity Targets and Tasks

In this section, common targets and tasks used to assess acuity are discussed. Examples of the test targets are shown in Figure 7.44.

4.2.1. Minimum Visible. The pattern to be resolved in the minimum-visible task is a single dark line whose length subtends several degrees of arc, superimposed on a bright background. The critical detail measured is the width of the line at threshold. This task provides a measure of the ability to make absolute or relative intensity discriminations (Hartridge, 1922) and yields the highest acuity estimates under optimal conditions. Estimates of threshold width under these conditions are about 0.5-sec arc, for a decimal acuity of 120 (Hecht & Mintz, 1939).

4.2.2. Vernier Acuity. The pattern in vernier acuity consists of two line segments that can be offset from one another by a variable amount. Threshold is determined by the minimum misalignment that can be detected. This task measures the ability to discriminate small displacements in space. Resolution for this task is also much higher than would be predicted on the basis of the retinal mosaic; estimates range from 1- to 2-sec-arc misalignment, for a decimal equivalent of 30 to 60 (Berry, 1948). Factors affecting performance of this task are discussed in Section 3.1.5.

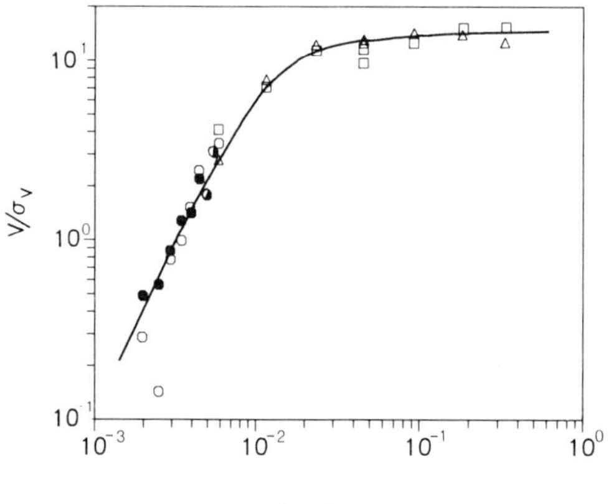

Figure 7.43. Vector model of identification: V/σ_V as a function of stimulus contrast, with σ_V the standard deviation of the distribution representing the stimulus and V the length of the vector representing the expected response to the stimulus. The target was a circular patch of a sine wave grating, viewed foveally with both eyes. The mean luminance was 60 cd/m^2. The data are for a single practiced observer. The filled data points are derived from a detection task. The open data points are derived from identification tasks in which the observer distinguished between gratings of different spatial frequencies. The frequencies were centered on 4.5 cycles/degree. The smooth function fitted to the data has the following form:

$$V/\sigma_V = (S\,c)^2 / [1 + \beta\,(S\,c)^2]\ ,$$

where c is stimulus contrast, expressed as a proportion; S may be interpreted as contrast sensitivity; and β determines the asymptote of the function. For the data shown, $S = 324$ and $\beta = 0.067$. For a group of four practiced observers, S varied from 230 to 421, with a mean of 335, and β varied from 0.045 to 0.141, with a mean of 0.087. Varying the center frequency shifts the function laterally on the log contrast axis and may also affect the initial slope of the function. (From J. P. Thomas, Underlying spatial function for detecting gratings and identifying spatial frequency, *Journal of the Optical Society of America*, 1983, *79*. Reprinted with permission.)

4.2.3. Resolution Tasks

4.2.3.1. Minimum Angle of Resolution. A number of patterns are available to measure the ability to discriminate separations in space, or the minimum angle of resolution (MAR). One such pattern consists of two black lines or points separated by a gap of variable width. The line or point widths are equal to the intervening gap. Threshold is measured as the minimum separation at which the lines or points are perceived as two. Other patterns used to measure MAR are more extensive spatially, such as square-wave gratings, grids, or checkerboards. In these cases, the task is to discriminate the pattern from a uniform field of the same mean luminance. Under optimal conditions, the MAR has been estimated at about 30-sec arc, for a decimal equivalent of 2.0 (Craik, 1939; Shlaer, 1937).

4.2.3.2. Landolt Ring. The Landolt ring (or Landolt C) target is a black ring on a white background, with a gap that can typically appear in one of four positions. The widths of the ring and of the gap vary with the diameter of the ring, each equal to a fifth of the ring diameter. Threshold is taken to be the smallest gap that can be correctly located. With this target, gaps of less than 30 sec can be located, corresponding to a decimal acuity of about 2.5 (Shlaer, 1937; Shlaer, Smith, & Chase, 1942). The Landolt ring has been adopted by the National Academy of Sciences-National Research Council Committee on Vision as the primary optotype.

4.2.3.3. Letters. The ability to read the letters of a chart from a standard distance is the most commonly assessed visual capability in clinical settings. The stimuli are a series of solid-black alphabet letters, which vary in size, printed at high contrast on a white background. Several standard versions of the chart are available, which vary in their calibrated test distance and in the letters used. The task is to correctly name the smallest possible letter. Sloan letters (C, D, H, K, N, O, R, S, V, Z) yield acuity estimates similar to the Landolt ring.

4.3. Factors Which Affect Acuity

Many of the factors which affect contrast sensitivity to intermediate and high spatial frequencies similarly affect acuity. Acuity does not appear to be related to sensitivity for low spatial frequencies, below 2 cycles/degree (Owsley, Sekuler, & Siemsen, 1983), which is not surprising if stimuli of very different sizes are processed through separate neural pathways. Variables which affect acuity are presented in the following.

4.3.1. Luminance Level. For dark targets superimposed on bright backgrounds, acuity improves as the background luminance increases (Baker, 1949; Craik, 1939; Hecht & Mintz, 1939; Shlaer, 1937). For grating targets, both acuity and contrast sensitivity improve as the mean luminance of the pattern increases (Patel, 1966; Shlaer, 1937), approaching an asymptote at about 1000 trolands (a luminance level of about 100 cd/m^2). This relationship is shown in Figure 7.45. In practice, the source of retinal illumination must be considered. Ambient illumination can exert a veiling influence, reducing contrast of target stimuli. The recommended luminance standard for acuity measurements is 85 cd/m^2, and it should not reduce target contrast below 0.85, where contrast is defined as in Eq. (4).

4.3.2. Spectral Composition of Illumination. Acuity measures are normally taken under white light, in which a large number of wavelengths are present. Under such conditions, chromatic aberration may significantly degrade the retinal image. This has been found to be an important factor in the minimum-visible and vernier acuity tasks; acuity improves for these

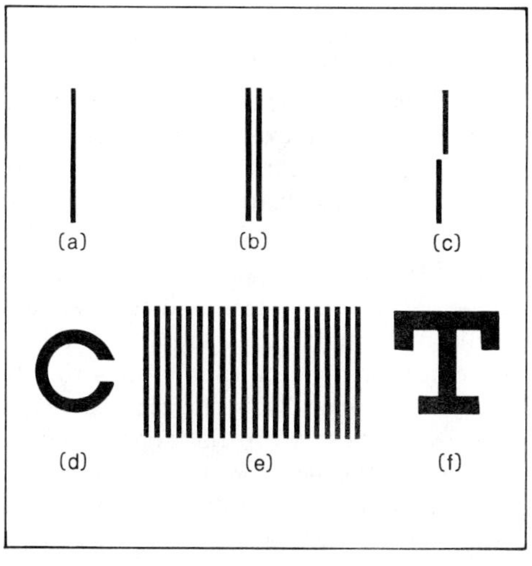

Figure 7.44. Examples of test targets commonly used to assess acuity. (a) Minimum visible. (b) Minimum separable. (c) Vernier. (d) Landolt ring. (e) Grating. (f) Snellen letter. (From J. P. Thomas, Spatial resolution and spatial interaction, in E. Carterette & M. Friedman (Eds.), *Handbook of perception* (Vol. 5), Academic Press, 1975. Reprinted with permission.)

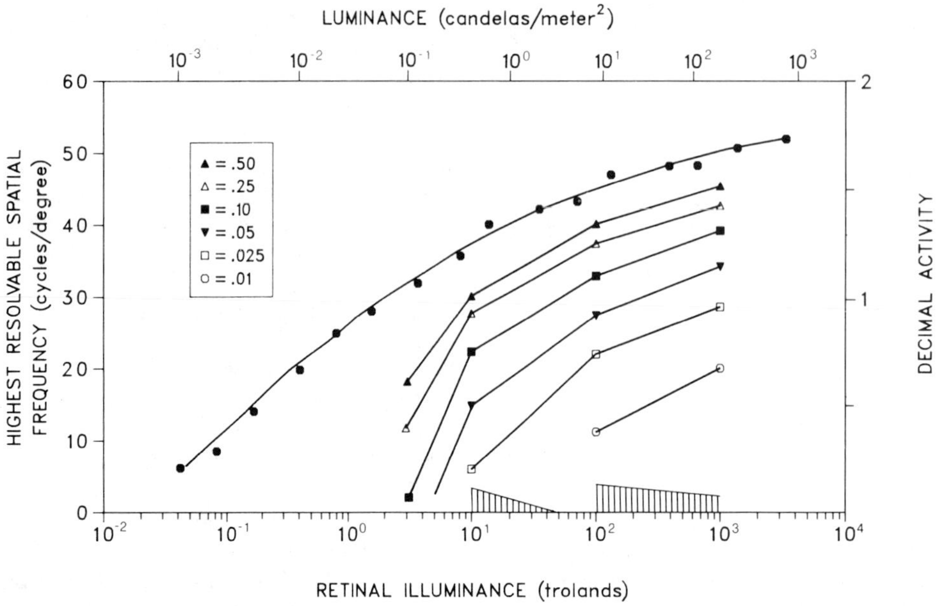

Figure 7.45. Acuity as a function of mean luminance. The filled circles show standard grating acuity. The target was a circular patch, 4° in diameter, of a square wave grating of contrast 1.0. The target was seen in Maxwellian view through a 2-mm artificial pupil. A 30° surround matched the target in mean luminance. The independent variable is the mean retinal illuminance, expressed on the bottom scale in trolands. The top scale gives the mean luminance in cd/m^2. The dependent variable is the finest resolvable grating. The left scale gives the spatial frequency of the finest resolvable grating, and the right scale gives the corresponding acuity value. Data are for one subject and are averaged over four orientations (vertical, horizontal, and two oblique). (Data from Shlaer, 1937.) The open circles also show the finest resolvable grating but with grating contrast as a parameter. In this case, the target was a circular patch, 2° in diameter, of a sine wave grating generated on a cathrode-ray tube (CRT). A 30° surround matched the target in luminance and hue. The independent and dependent variables are the same as for the filled circles. The hatched areas represent low frequencies that cannot be resolved at the two lowest contrast levels; that is, they fall below the lower cutoff frequency of the band-pass function. The data are for one subject and are from Patel (1966). Both sets of data illustrate that acuity increases with mean luminance, approaching an asymptote as retinal illuminance approaches 1000 trolands (or as luminance approaches 100 cd/m^2).

tasks when they are performed under narrow-band illumination (Baker, 1949; Shlaer, Smith, & Chase, 1942). Schober and Wittmann (1938) reported a similar effect with the Landolt ring for illumination levels up to 4000 meter-candles, but others have not observed this result (Baker, 1949; Shlaer, Smith, & Chase, 1942).

Under narrow-band illumination and for a moderate pupil size, wavelength is generally not a factor which affects acuity, provided that (1) illumination levels are above asymptotic levels or (2) at lower illumination levels, compensation is made for relative sensitivities to different wavelengths. With pupil sizes made artificially small (less than 1 mm), acuity is higher for shorter wavelengths.

4.3.3 Retinal Locus of Stimulation. The highest resolution is obtained under photopic levels of illumination when the target is viewed foveally. As the target is displaced toward the periphery of the retina, acuity rapidly decreases, even within the foveal area (Ludvigh, 1941; Sloan, 1968). At scotopic levels of illumination, acuity is highest when the target is offset approximately 4° from the fixation point (Mandelbaum & Sloan, 1947). The effect of retinal location on acuity is shown in Figure 7.46.

4.3.4. Pupil Size. The highest grating acuity is observed when the natural pupil is an intermediate diameter, about 2–5 mm (Leibowitz, 1952). Contrast sensitivity is also maximal with an intermediate pupil diameter (Campbell & Green, 1965). At very small pupil diameters, acuity can be reduced by low retinal illumination and diffraction effects, which degrade the retinal image. As pupil size increases, acuity initially improves from increased retinal illumination and minimization of diffraction effects. At very large pupil sizes, however, the sensitivity resulting from increased retinal illumination and reduced diffraction effects is outweighed by the increasing effects of spherical and chromatic aberration, which degrade the quality of the retinal image.

4.3.5. Viewing Distance, Accommodation, and Optical Blur. When the resolving power of the visual system is expressed in terms of visual angle, it is assumed that viewing distance has no effect on acuity. In practice, however, acuity is found to change with viewing distance, and the effect is associated with the optics of the system (Cavonious & Hilz, 1973; Hennessy & Richards, 1975). Johnson (1976) has demonstrated that this effect can be attributed to errors in accommodation.

As viewing distance decreases, the lens of the eye changes shape in order to properly focus the retinal image (accommodation). This change in the refracting power of the lens is measured in diopters, the reciprocal of the focal distance in meters. Errors of accommodation result in a blurred retinal image, which degrades both acuity and contrast sensitivity. Optical blur resulting from accommodation errors affects the visibility of high spatial frequencies more than low (Campbell, Kulikowski, & Levinson, 1966; Mitchell & Wilkinson, 1974). These results are shown in Figure 7.47. Note that the effect of blur on acuity can be seen by comparing the relative high-frequency cutoff positions of the contrast sensitivity functions.

Accommodation errors are more pronounced at low luminance levels and under other reduced visibility conditions and

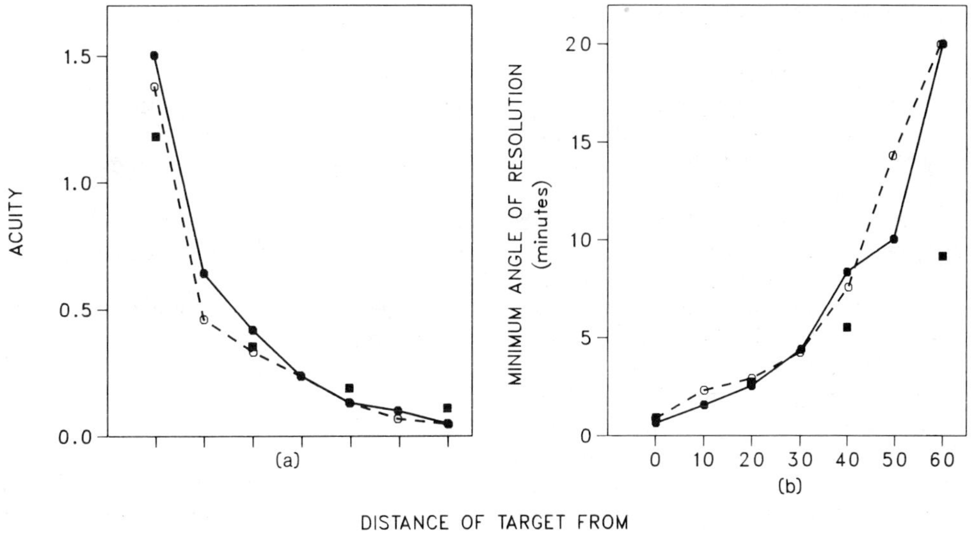

Figure 7.46. Effect of retinal location on acuity. (a) Acuity as a function of eccentricity. Three different targets were used: closed circles (Landolt ring, contrast = 0.65, background luminance = 245 cd/m^2); open circles (same target but with background luminance = 2.45 cd/m^2); squares (circular patch of sine wave grating, diameter = 2°, contrast = 0.66, mean luminance = 1118 cd/m^2). Refractive errors were corrected for each observer at each eccentricity. Eccentricity is the distance between the center of the target and fixation. For the Landolt ring, acuity is the reciprocal of the width, measured in minutes of visual angle, of the smallest gap that can be localized. For the grating, acuity is the reciprocal of the width, measured in minutes, of one bar (or half-period) of the finest grating that can be detected. For the Landolt ring, each data point is the mean for three observers; for the grating, each point is the mean for four observers. For this particular group of observers, the standard deviation is about 25% of the mean. For all targets, acuity decreases sharply as eccentricity increases. However, the exact shape of the function depends on the nature of the target and the luminance level. Grating acuity changes less than Landolt ring acuity, and the curves for the two types of targets cross at an eccentricity of about 20°. The difference between Landolt ring acuity at fixation and in the periphery is greater at the high luminance than at the low luminance. Data from Millodot, Johnson, Lamont, and Leibowitz (1975). (b) Minimum angle of resolution as a function of eccentricity. The same data as (a) except that the reciprocal of acuity is plotted. That is, the width of the smallest gap localized or narrowest bar detected is plotted.

show a consistent pattern of overaccommodation to far stimuli and underaccommodation to others (see Toates, 1972, for a review of this extensive literature). These errors contribute to the decreased acuity and contrast sensitivity observed under such conditions, but the loss is not eliminated when errors are corrected (Johnson, 1976).

4.3.6. Age. Spatial vision capabilities change considerably over the life span of an individual. At photopic luminance levels, infants show both degraded acuity (Dobson & Teller, 1978; Mayer & Dobson, 1982) and contrast sensitivity (Atkinson, Braddick, & Moar, 1977) relative to adult abilities. At scotopic levels of luminance, Hamer and Schenck (1984) have demonstrated that spatial summation areas in infants are considerably larger (a factor of 12 at four weeks) than those found in adults. These reduced capabilities can in part be accounted for by optical factors, such as accommodation errors and smaller optical components in an infant's eye. However, both the psychophysical results and physiological evidence from primates (Blakemore & Vital-Durand, 1979; Dobson & Teller, 1978) suggest that the neural organization of the infant visual system is different from that of adults.

Over the first few years of life, spatial abilities increase to more closely resemble the abilities of an adult. Acuity increases during the first 60 months of age. Nominal adult acuity of 1-min arc is approached at 36 months of age but continues to improve up to 0.75-min arc during the first five years of life (Mayer & Dobson, 1982). Young adults in their twenties show

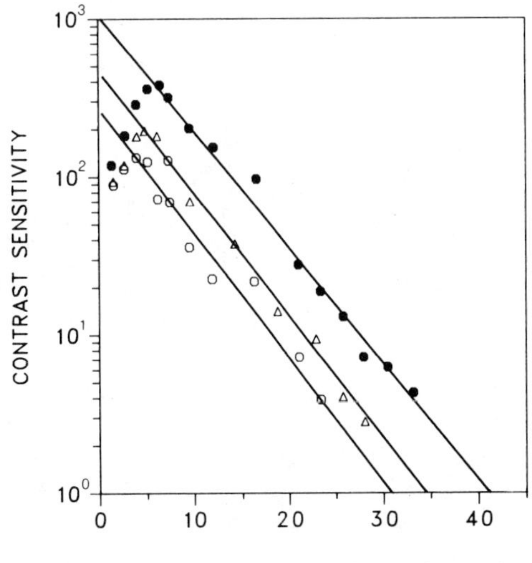

Figure 7.47. Effect of accommodation errors on contrast sensitivity. The stimuli were sine wave gratings presented at a mean luminance of 170 cd/m^2. Accommodation was paralyzed by homatropine, and measurements were taken with either focused or blurred gratings. Contrast sensitivity is plotted on a log scale against linear spatial frequency. Filled circles indicate sensitivity when the eye is in focus. Open triangles and circles represent defocused conditions of 0.75 and 1.0 diopters, respectively. (From D. E. Mitchell & F. Wilkinson, The effect of early astigmatism on the visual resolution of gratings, *Journal of Physiology*, 1974, *243*. Reprinted with permission.)

acuity and contrast sensitivity similar to children older than about five years of age (Owsley, Sekuler, & Siemsen, 1983). Beyond the twenties, both acuity and contrast sensitivity for intermediate and high spatial frequencies decreases, even when optimal optical corrections are used (Gunkel & Gouras, 1963; Owsley, Sekuler, & Siemsen, 1983). The decline in acuity as a function of age is shown in Figure 7.48. Note that "normal" acuity of 1.0 does not represent younger adults but is more characteristic of best corrected acuity at 50 years.

When spatial abilities are assessed with sinusoidal grating patterns, it has been found that contrast sensitivity for intermediate and high spatial frequencies also declines with age, as shown in Figure 7.49. Below 2 cycles/degree, age has little effect on contrast sensitivity. For higher frequencies, the decline is generally more severe for older observers, and the peak of the contrast sensitivity function shifts toward a lower frequency.

Unlike the significant neural component thought to be associated with poor spatial capabilities in infants, the effects contributing to the decreases in acuity and contrast sensitivity with advancing age are currently thought to be largely optical in nature (Dressler & Rassow, 1981; Owsley, Sekuler, & Siemsen, 1983). However, the research on possible neural contributions is not yet complete. At least one major factor contributing to reduced sensitivity in older observers is lowered retinal illuminance, which selectively decreases sensitivity to higher spatial frequencies (Kelly, 1972; Owsley, Sekuler, & Siemsen, 1983). The amount of light transmitted is reduced by ⅔ in a 60-year-old eye because of decreased pupil size (senile miosis) and increased density of the lens (Weale, 1963).

4.4. Acuity Measures versus Contrast Sensitivity

Both acuity and contrast sensitivity measures have advantages and disadvantages in practical application. Acuity tasks are quickly and easily administered to nontrained individuals. The equipment needed to administer and evaluate the results of such tests is inexpensive and widely available in standard formats, and standardized population norms have been established for most of the widely used acuity tasks. As is demonstrated by their wide acceptance in clinical practice, acuity tests adequately assess the ability to perceive spatial detail. The major disadvantage of acuity measures is that they provide information only about a limited portion of spatial perception capabilities: the ability to perceive fine detail at high contrasts.

Although acuity is related to the ability to perceive intermediate and high spatial frequencies, it is not related to the ability to perceive low contrast, low spatial frequencies (Owsley, Sekuler, & Siemsen, 1983), such as might be encountered at night or under other low-visibility conditions. This is not surprising given the now ample evidence, presented throughout this chapter, that low and high spatial frequencies (or large- and small-sized stimuli) are processed through separate neural pathways. In at least one clinical report, Regan, Silver, and Murray (1977) demonstrated that a multiple sclerosis patient who had normal acuity showed a decreased ability to perceive larger objects, a deficit which could be of great consequence. Contrast sensitivity to intermediate and low spatial frequencies has been shown to be of importance in a number of performance tasks, such as facial recognition (Harmon & Julesz, 1973), the range at which targets can be detected (Ginsburg, Evans, Sekuler, & Harp, 1982), or the visibility of stop signs at night (Evans & Ginsburg, 1982).

In summary, the prime advantage of contrast sensitivity measures is that they provide a comprehensive assessment of spatial abilities. A prime disadvantage is the not yet fully understood relationship between contrast sensitivity and everyday pattern perception. Contrast sensitivity measures remain more expensive and more time consuming to administer relative

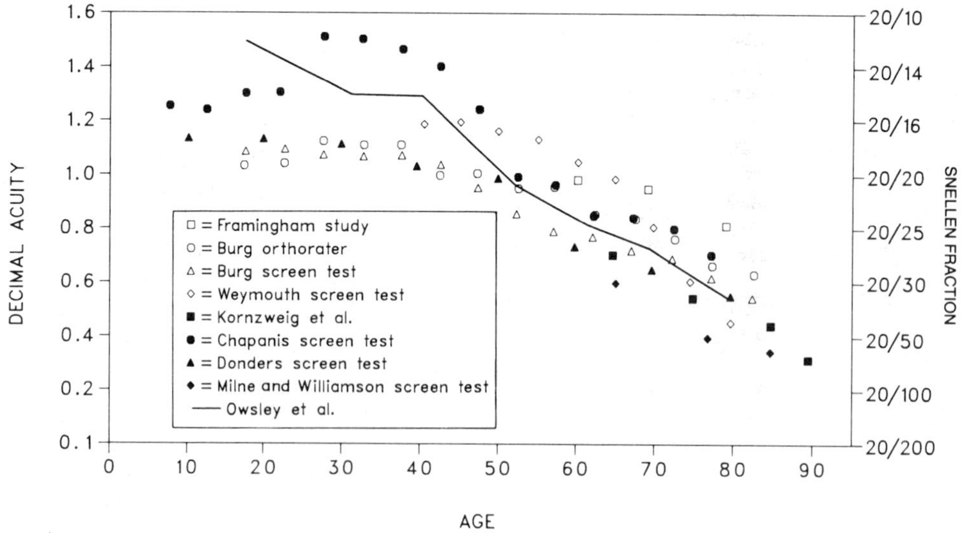

Figure 7.48. Acuity as a function of age. The results of several studies relating acuity to age are presented. Decimal acuity is shown on the left ordinate, with the equivalent Snellen fraction on the right. Data forming the solid line were gathered in the following procedure. Acuity was measured for 100 observers whose ages ranged from 19 to 87 years. All observers were corrected as well as possible for the testing distance of 3 m. Acuity was measured for one eye with Sloan letters at a mean luminance of 87 cd/m^2 at a contrast of 0.90. Results from the other studies are given in Pitts (1982). (From D. G. Pitts, The effects of aging on selected visual functions: Dark adaptation, visual acuity, stereopsis, and brightness contrast, in R. Sekular, D. Kline, & K. Dismukes (Eds.), *Aging and human visual function*, A. R. Liss, 1982. Reprinted with permission.)

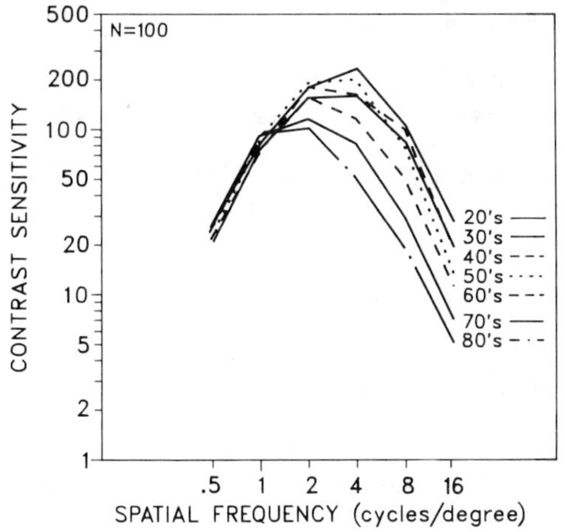

Figure 7.49. Contrast sensitivity as a function of age. Contrast sensitivity was measured for 100 observers whose ages ranged from 19 to 87 years. Stimuli were static sine wave gratings of 0.5, 1, 2, 4, 8, and 16 cycles/degree, presented on a display at a mean luminance of 103 cd/m^2. The display subtended 4.2- × 5.5-deg arc at a test distance of 3 m. Monocular thresholds were determined by a tracking procedure. (From C. Owsley, R. Sekuler, & P. Siemsen, Contrast sensitivity throughout adulthood, *Vision Research, 23.* Copyright 1983 by Pergamon Press. Reprinted with permission.)

to acuity measures, although recent technological developments have made contrast sensitivity measurements feasible in a nonlaboratory situation (Sekuler & Tynan, 1977). Nevertheless, contrast sensitivity functions are increasingly reported in the clinical literature (Bodis-Wollner & Camisa, 1980; Michaels, 1980).

REFERENCES

Albrecht, D. G., & Hamilton, D. B. Striate cortex of monkeys and cat: Contrast response functions. *Journal of Neurophysiology*, 1982, *48*, 217–237.

Alpern, M. Metacontrast: Historical introduction. *American Journal of Optometry*, 1952, *29*, 631–646.

Alpern, M. Metacontrast. *Journal of the Optical Society of America*, 1953, *43*, 648–657.

Andrews, D. Perception of contour orientation in the central fovea. I. Short lines. *Vision Research*, 1967, *7*, 975–979. (a)

Andrews, D. Perception of contour orientation in the central fovea. II. Spatial integration. *Vision Research*, 1967, *7*, 999–1013. (b)

Anstis, S. M. A chart demonstrating variations in acuity with retinal position. *Vision Research*, 1974, *14*, 589–592.

Appelle, S. Perception and discrimination as a function of stimulus orientation: The "oblique effect" in man and animals. *Psychological Bulletin*, 1972, *78*, 266–278.

Atkinson, J., Braddick, O., & Moar, K. Development of contrast sensitivity over the first three months of life in the human infant. *Vision Research*, 1977, *17*, 1037–1044.

Bacon, J. H. The interaction of dichoptically presented spatial gratings. *Vision Research*, 1976, *16*, 337–344.

Bagrash, F. M. Size-selective adaptation: Psychophysical evidence for size-tuning and the effects of stimulus contour and adapting flux. *Vision Research*, 1973, *13*, 575–598.

Baker, K. E. Some variables influencing vernier acuity. I. Illumination and exposure time. II. Wavelength of illumination. *Journal of the Optical Society of America*, 1949, *39*, 567–576.

Barfield, L., & Tolhurst, D. The detection of complex gratings by the human visual system. *Journal of Physiology*, 1975, *248*, 37–38.

Barlow, H. B. Summation and inhibition in the frog's retina. *Journal of Physiology*, 1953, *119*, 69–88.

Barlow, H. B. Temporal and spatial summation in human vision at different background intensities. *Journal of Physiology*, 1958, *141*, 337–350.

Barlow, H. B. Measurement of the quantum efficiency of discrimination in human vision. *Journal of Physiology*, 1962, *160*, 169–188.

Battersby, W. S., & Wagman, I. H. Light adaptation kinetics: The influence of spatial factors. *Science*, 1964, *143*, 1029–1031.

Bergen, J. R., Wilson, H. R., & Cowan, J. D. Further evidence for four mechanisms mediating vision at threshold: Sensitivities to complex gratings and aperiodic stimuli. *Journal of the Optical Society of America*, 1979, *69*, 1580–1587.

Berry, R. N. Quantitative relations among vernier, real depth and stereoscopic depth acuities. *Journal of Experimental Psychology*, 1948, *38*, 708–721.

Blackwell, H. R. Contrast thresholds of the human eye. *Journal of the Optical Society of America*, 1946, *36*, 624–643.

Blackwell, H. R. Psychophysical thresholds: Experimental studies of methods of measurements. *Bulletin Engineering Research Institute of Michigan*, 1953, No. 36.

Blackwell, H. R. Neural theories of simple visual discriminations. *Journal of the Optical Society of America*, 1963, *53*, 129–160.

Blakemore, C., & Campbell, F. W. On the existence of neurons in the human visual system selectively sensitive to the orientation and size of retinal images. *Journal of Physiology*, 1969, *203*, 237–260.

Blakemore, C. B., & Nachmias, J. The orientation specificity of two visual after-effects. *Journal of Physiology*, 1971, *213*, 157–174.

Blakemore, C. B., Nachmias, J., & Sutton, P. The perceived spatial frequency shift: Evidence for frequency selectivity neurons in the human brain. *Journal of Physiology*, 1970, *210*, 727–750.

Blakemore, C. B., & Sutton, P. Size adaptation: A new after-effect. *Science*, 1969, *166*, 245–247.

Blakemore, C. & Vital-Durand, F. Development of the neural basis in monkeys: Speculation on the origins of deprivation amblyopia. *Transactions of the Ophthalmological Society of the United Kingdom*, 1979, *99*, 363–368.

Bodis-Wollner, I., & Camisa, J. Contrast sensitivity measurement in clinical diagnosis. In S. Lessell and J. T. W. Van Dalen (Eds.) *Neuroophthalmology*. Amsterdam: Excerpta Medica, 1980.

Bouma, H., & Andriessen, J. J. Perceived orientation of isolated line segments. *Vision Research*, 1968, *8*, 493–507.

Boynton, R. M. Discrimination of homogenous double pulses of light. In D. Jameson & L. Hurvich (Eds.), *Handbook of sensory physiology* (Vol. 7). Berlin: Springer, 1972.

Bracewell, R. *The Fourier transform and its applications*. New York: McGraw-Hill, 1965.

Braddick, O. J., Campbell, F. W., & Atkinson, J. Channels in vision: Basic aspects. In R. Held, H. Leibowitz, & H. L. Teuber (Eds.), *Handbook of sensory physiology* (Vol. 8). Heidelberg: Springer-Verlag, 1978.

Burr, D. C. Sensitivity to spatial phase. *Vision Research*, 1980, *20*, 391–396.

Burton, G. J., & Moorhead, I. R. Visual form perception and the spatial phase transfer function. *Journal of the Optical Society of America*, 1981, *71*, 1056–1063.

Caelli, T., & Bevan, P. Visual sensitivity to two-dimensional spatial phase. *Journal of the Optical Society of America*, 1982, *72*, 1375–1381.

Camisa, J. M., Blake, R., & Lema, S. The effects of temporal modulation on the oblique effect in humans. *Perception*, 1977, *6*, 165–171.

Campbell, F. W., & Green, D. G. Optical and retinal factors affecting visual resolution. *Journal of Physiology*, 1965, *181*, 576–593.

Campbell, F. W., & Kulikowski, J. J. Orientational selectivity of the human visual system. *Journal of Physiology*, 1966, *187*, 437–445.

Campbell, F. W., Kulikowski, J. J., & Levinson, J. The effect of orientation on the visual resolution of gratings. *Journal of Physiology*, 1966, *187*, 427–436.

Campbell, F. W., & Maffei, L. The tilt after-effect: A fresh look. *Vision Research*, 1971, *11*, 833–840.

Campbell, F. W., Nachmias, J., & Jukes, J. Spatial-frequency discrimination in human vision. *Journal of the Optical Society of America*, 1970, *60*, 555–566.

Campbell, F. W., & Robson, J. G. Application of Fourier analysis to the visibility of gratings. *Journal of Physiology*, 1968, *197*, 551–566.

Cavonious, C. R., & Hilz, R. Invariance of visual receptive field size and visual acuity with viewing distance. *Journal of the Optical Society of America*, 1973, *63*, 929–933.

Cohn, T. E., & Lasley, D. J. Detectability of a luminance increment: Effect of spatial uncertainty. *Journal of the Optical Society of America*, 1974, *64*, 1715–1719.

Coltheart, M. Review of *Annual review of psychology*, *Quarterly Journal of Experimental Psychology*, 1974, *26*, 661–662.

Cornsweet, T. N., & Pinsker, H. M. Luminance discrimination of brief flashes under various conditions of adaptation. *Journal of Physiology*, 1965, *176*, 294–310.

Craik, K. J. W. The effect of adaptation on visual acuity. *British Journal of Psychology*, 1939, *29*, 252–266.

Daniel, P. M., & Whitteridge, D. The representation of the visual field on the cerebral cortex in monkeys. *Journal of Physiology*, 1961, *159*, 203–221.

Daugman, J. G. Two-dimensional spectral analysis of cortical receptive field profiles. *Vision Research*, 1980, *20*, 847–856.

Davis, E. T., & Graham, N. Spatial frequency uncertainty effects in the detection of sinusoidal gratings. *Vision Research*, 1981, *21*, 705–712.

Davis, E. T., Kramer, P., & Graham, N. Uncertainty about spatial frequency, spatial position, or contrast of visual patterns. *Perception and Psychophysics*, 1983, *33*, 20–28.

DeValois, K. K. Spatial frequency adaptation can enhance contrast sensitivity. *Vision Research*, 1977, *17*, 1057–1065.

DeValois, R. L., Albrecht, D. G., & Thorell, L. G. Spatial frequency selectivity of cells in macaque visual cortex. *Vision Research*, 1982, *22*, 545–559.

DeValois, R. L., Yund, E. W., & Hepler, N. The orientation and direction selectivity of cells in macaque visual cortex. *Vision Research*, 1982, *22*, 531–544.

DeVries, H. The quantum character of light and its bearing upon the threshold of vision, the differential sensitivity and acuity of the eye. *Physica*, 1943, *10*, 533–564.

Dobson, V., & Teller, D. Y. Visual acuity in human infants: A review and comparison of behavioral and electrophysiological studies. *Vision Research*, 1978, *18*, 1469–1483.

Dressler, M., & Rassow, B. Neural contrast sensitivity measurements with a laser interference system for clinical screening application. *Investigative Ophthalmology and Visual Science*, 1981, *21*, 737–744.

Elsner, A. Hue difference contours can be used in processing orientation information. *Perception and Psychophysics*, 1978, *24*, 451–456.

Enroth-Cugell, C., & Robson, J. G. The contrast sensitivity of retinal ganglion cells of the cat. *Journal of Physiology*, 1966, *258*, 517–552.

Enroth-Cugell, C., & Robson, J. G. Functional characteristics and diversity of cat retinal ganglion cells. *Investigative Ophthalmology and Visual Science*, 1984, *25*, 250–267.

Eriksen, C. W. Temporal luminance summation effects of backward and forward masking. *Perception and Psychophysics*, 1966, *1*, 87–92.

Evans, D. W., & Ginsburg, A. P. Predicting age-related differences in discriminating road signs using contrast sensitivity. *Journal of the Optical Society of America*, 1982, *72*, 1785–1786. (Abstract)

Fehrer, E. Effect of stimulus similarity on retroactive masking. *Journal of Experimental Psychology*, 1966, *71*, 612–615.

Fidell, L. S. Orientation specificity in chromatic adaptation of human "edge detectors." *Perception and Psychophysics*, 1970, *8*, 235–237.

Fiorentini, A., Ghez, C., & Maffei, L. Physiological correlates of adaptation to a rotated visual field. *Brain Research*, 1972, *42*, 544–545. (a)

Fiorentini, A., Ghez, C., & Maffei, L. Physiological correlates of adaptation to a rotated visual field. *Journal of Physiology*, 1972, *227*, 313–322. (b)

Fiorentini, A., Jeanne, M., & Toraldi di Francia, G. Measures photometriques visuelles sur une champ a d'éclairement variable. *Optica Acta*, 1955, *1*, 192–193.

Fiorentini, A., & Zoli, M. Detection of a target superimposed to a step pattern of illumination. *Atti Fondazione Giorgio Ronchi*, 1966, *21*, 338–356.

Foley, J. M., & Legge, G. E. Contrast detection and near-threshold discrimination in human vision. *Vision Research*, 1981, *21*, 1041–1053.

Fox, R. Visual masking. In R. Held, H. W. Leibowitz, & H. L. Teuber (Eds.), *Handbook of sensory physiology* (Vol. 8): *Perception*. Heidelberg: Springer-Verlag, 1978.

Frome, F. S., MacLeod, D. I. A., Buck, S. L., & Williams, D. R. Large loss of visual sensitivity to flashed peripheral targets. *Vision Research*, 1981, *21*, 1323–1328.

Frumkes, T. E., & Sturr, J. F. Spatial and luminance factors determining visual excitability. *Journal of the Optical Society of America*, 1968, *58*, 1657–1662.

Furchner, C. S., Thomas, J. P., & Campbell, F. W. Detection and discrimination of simple and complex patterns at low spatial frequencies. *Vision Research*, 1977, *17*, 827–836.

Gabor, D. Theory of communication. *Journal of the Institute of Electrical Engineers* (London), 1946, *93*, 429–457.

Ganz, L. Temporal factors in visual perception. In E. Carterette & M. Friedman (Eds.), *Handbook of perception* (Vol. 5). New York: Academic Press, 1975.

Gelb, D. J., & Wilson, H. R. Shifts in perceived size as a function of contrast and temporal modulation. *Vision Research*, 1983, *23*, 71–82.

Georgeson, M. A. Spatial frequency analysis in early visual processing. *Philosophical Transactions of the Royal Society*, 1980, *Series B 290*, 11–22.

Gibson, J. J., & Radner, M. Adaptation, after-effect and contrast in the perception of tilted lines. I. Quantitative studies. *Journal of Experimental Psychology*, 1937, *20*, 453–467.

Gilinsky, A. S. Orientation-specific effects of patterns of adapting light on visual acuity. *Journal of the Optical Society of America*, 1968, *58*, 13–18.

Ginsburg, A., Evans, D., Sekuler, R., & Harp, S. Contrast sensitivity predicts pilots' performance in aircraft simulators. *American Journal of Optometry and Physiological Optics*, 1982, *59*, 105–109.

Graham, C. H., Brown, R. H., & Mote, F. A. The relation of size of stimulus and intensity in the human eye. I. Intensity thresholds for white light. *Journal of Experimental Psychology*, 1939, *24*, 555–573.

Graham, N. Visual detection of aperiodic spatial stimuli by probability summation among narrowband channels. *Vision Research*, 1977, *17*, 637–652.

Graham, N., & Nachmias, J. Detection of grating patterns containing two spatial frequencies: A comparison of single-channel and multiple-channel models. *Vision Research*, 1971, *11*, 251–259.

Graham, N., Robson, J. G., & Nachmias, J. Grating summation in fovea and periphery. *Vision Research*, 1978, *18*, 815–826.

Green, D. M., & Birdsall, T. G. Detection and recognition. *Psychological Review*, 1978, *85*, 192–206.

Green, D. M., & Swets, J. A. *Signal detection theory and psychophysics*. New York: Kreiger, 1974.

Growney, R. The function of contour in metacontrast. *Vision Research*, 1976, *16*, 253–261.

Gunkel, R. D., & Gouras, P. Changes in the scotopic visibility with age. *Archives of Ophthalmology*, 1963, *69*, 4–9.

Hamer, R. D., & Schenck, M. E. Spatial summation in dark-adapted human infants. *Vision Research*, 1984, *24*, 77–85.

Harmon, L. D., & Julesz, B. Masking in visual recognition: Effects of two dimensional filtered noise. *Science*, 1973, *180*, 1194–1197.

Hartline, H. K. The response of single optic nerve fibers of the vertebrate eye to illumination of the retina. *American Journal of Physiology*, 1938, *121*, 400–415.

Hartridge, H. Visual acuity and the resolving power of the eye. *Journal of Physiology*, 1922, *57*, 52–67.

Hecht, S., & Mintz, E. U. The visibility of single lines at various illuminations and the retinal basis of visual resolution. *Journal of General Physiology*, 1939, *22*, 593–612.

Hennessy, R. T., & Richards, W. Contrast sensitivity and viewing distance. *Journal of the Optical Society of America*, 1975, *65*, 97–98.

Henning, G. B., Hertz, B. G., & Hinton, J. L. Effects of different hypothetical detection mechanisms on the shape of spatial-frequency filters inferred from masking experiments: I. Noise masks. *Journal of the Optical Society of America*, 1981, *71*, 574–581.

Higgins, G. C., & Stultz, K. Visual acuity as measured with various orientations of a parallel line test target. *Journal of the Optical Society of America*, 1948, *38*, 766–768.

Hirsch, J., & Hylton, R. Limits of spatial frequency discrimination as evidence of neural interpolation. *Journal of the Optical Society of America*, 1982, *72*, 1367–1374.

Hirsch, J., Hylton, R., & Graham, N. Simultaneous recognition of two spatial frequency components. *Vision Research*, 1982, *22*, 365–375.

Hoekstra, J., van der Goot, D. P. A., van den Brink, G., & Bilsen, F. A. The influence of the number of cycles upon the visual contrast threshold for spatial sine wave patterns. *Vision Research*, 1974, *14*, 365–368.

Hubel, D. H., & Wiesel, T. N. Receptive fields, binocular interaction and functional architecture in the cat's striate cortex. *Journal of Physiology*, 1962, *160*, 106–154.

Hubel, D. H., & Wiesel, T. N. Receptive fields and functional architecture of monkey striate cortex. *Journal of Physiology*, 1968, *195*, 215–243.

Hubel, D. H., & Wiesel, T. N. Sequence regularity and geometry of orientation columns in the monkey striate cortex. *Journal of Comparative Neurology*, 1974, *158*, 267–294. (a)

Hubel, D. H., & Wiesel, T. N. Uniformity of monkey striate cortex: A parallel relationship between field size, scatter, and magnification factor. *Journal of Comparative Neurology*, 1974, *158*, 295–305. (b)

Jennings, J. A. M., & Charman, W. N. Off-axis image quality in the human eye. *Vision Research*, 1981, *21*, 445–456.

Johnson, C. A. Effects of luminance and stimulus distance on accommodation and visual resolution. *Journal of the Optical Society of America*, 1976, *66*, 138–142.

Kahneman, D. Method, findings and theory in studies of visual masking. *Psychological Bulletin*, 1968, *69*, 404–425.

Kelly, D. H. Adaptation effects on spatio-temporal sine-wave thresholds. *Vision Research*, 1972, *12*, 89–101.

Kerr, L. G., & Thomas, J. P. Effect of selective adaptation on detection of simple and compound parafoveal stimuli. *Vision Research*, 1972, *12*, 1367–1379.

King-Smith, P. E., & Kulikowski, J. J. The detection of gratings by independent activation of line detectors. *Journal of Physiology*, 1975, *247*, 237–271.

King-Smith, P. E., & Kulikowski, J. J. The detection and recognition of two lines. *Vision Research*, 1981, *21*, 235–250.

Kinsbourne, M., & Warrington, E. K. The effect of an aftercoming random pattern on the perception of brief visual stimuli. *Quarterly Journal of Experimental Psychology*, 1962, *14*, 223–234.

Klein, S., Stromeyer, C. F., & Ganz, L. The simultaneous spatial frequency shift: A disassociation between the detection and perception of gratings. *Vision Research*, 1974, *14*, 1421–1432.

Koenderink, J. J., Bouman, M. A., Bueno de Mesquita, A. E., & Slappendel, S. Perimetry of contrast detection thresholds of moving spatial sine wave patterns. I. The near peripheral visual field (eccentricity 0–8 deg). *Journal of the Optical Society of America*, 1978, *68*, 845–849. (a)

Koenderink, J. J., Bouman, M. A., Bueno de Mesquita, A. E., & Slappendel, S. Perimetry of contrast detection thresholds of moving spatial sine wave patterns. II. The far peripheral visual field (eccentricity 0–50 deg). *Journal of the Optical Society of America*, 1978, *68*, 850–854. (b)

Koenderink, J. J., Bouman, M. A., Bueno de Mesquita, A. E., & Slappendel, S. Perimetry of contrast detection thresholds of moving spatial sine wave patterns. III. The target extent as a sensitivity controlling parameter. *Journal of the Optical Society of America*, 1978, *68*, 854–860. (c)

Koenderink, J. J., & van Doorn, A. J. Spatial summation for complex bar patterns. *Vision Research*, 1980, *20*, 169–176.

Kohler, W. *Dynamics in psychology*. New York: Liveright, 1940.

Kohler, W., & Wallach, H. Figural after-effects, an investigation of visual processes. *Proceedings of the American Philosophical Society*, 1944, *88*, 269–357.

Kohlers, P. A. Intensity and contour effects in visual masking. *Vision Research*, 1962, *2*, 277–294.

Kohlers, P. A. Some psychological aspects of pattern recognition. In P. A. Kohlers & M. Eden (Eds.), *Recognizing patterns: Studies in living and automatic systems*. Cambridge: MIT Press, 1968.

Kulikowski, J. J. Apparent fineness of briefly presented gratings: Balance between movement and pattern channels. *Vision Research*, 1975, *15*, 673–680.

Kulikowski, J. J., Abadi, R., & King-Smith, P. E. Orientational selectivity of grating and line detectors in human vision. *Vision Research*, 1973, *13*, 1479–1486.

Kulikowski, J. J., & King-Smith, P. E. Spatial arrangement of line, edge, and grating detectors revealed by subthreshold summation. *Vision Research*, 1973, *13*, 1455–1478.

Lamar, E., Hecht, S., Shlaer, S., & Hendley, C. Size, shape, and contrast detection of targets by daylight vision. I. Data and analytical description. *Journal of the Optical Society of America*, 1947, *37*, 531–545.

Lasley, D. J., & Cohn, T. E. Why luminance discrimination may be better than detection. *Vision Research*, 1981, *21*, 273–278.

Lefton, L. A. Metacontrast: A review. *Perception and Psychophysics*, 1973, *13*, 161–171.

Legge, G. A power law for contrast discrimination. *Vision Research*, 1981, *21*, 457–467.

Legge, G. E. Spatial frequency masking in human vision: Binocular interactions. *Journal of the Optical Society of America*, 1979, *69*, 838–847.

Legge, G. E., & Foley, J. M. Contrast masking in human vision. *Journal of the Optical Society of America*, 1980, *70*, 1458–1471.

Legge, G. E., & Kersten, D. Light and dark bars: Contrast discrimination. *Vision Research*, 1983, *23*, 473–483.

LeGrand, Y. *Light, colour, and vision* (2nd ed.). London: Chapman & Hall, 1968.

Leibowitz, H. The effect of pupil size on visual acuity for photometrically equated test fields at various levels of luminance. *Journal of the Optical Society of America*, 1952, *42*, 416–422.

Lennie, P. *Mechanisms underlying the perception of orientation*. Unpublished doctoral dissertation, University of Cambridge, 1972.

Lovegrove, W., & Badcock, D. The effect of spatial frequency on color selectivity in the tilt illusion. *Vision Research*, 1981, *21*, 1235–1237.

Ludvigh, E. Extrafoveal visual acuity as measured with Snellen test-letters. *American Journal of Ophthalmology*, 1941, *24*, 303–310.

Lukas, X., Tulunay-Keesey, U., & Limb, J. Thresholds at luminance edges under stabilized viewing conditions. *Journal of the Optical Society of America*, 1980, *70*, 418–419.

Maffei, L., & Campbell, F. W. Neurophysiological localization of the vertical and horizontal visual coordinates in man. *Science*, 1970, *167*, 386–387.

Mandelbaum, J., & Sloan, L. L. Peripheral visual acuity. *American Journal of Ophthalmology*, 1947, *30*, 581–588.

Marcelja, S. Mathematical description of the responses of simple cortical cells. *Journal of the Optical Society of America*, 1980, *70*, 1297–1300.

Matin, E., & Drivas, A. Acuity for orientation measured with a sequential recognition task and signal detection methods. *Perception and Psychophysics*, 1979, *25*, 161–168.

Matthews, M. L. Appearance of mach bands for short durations and at sharply focused contours. *Journal of the Optical Society of America*, 1966, *56*, 1401–1402.

Mayer, D. L., & Dobson, V. Visual acuity development in infants and young children assessed by operant preferred looking. *Vision Research*, 1982, *22*, 1141–1151.

McCollough, C. Color adaptation of edge-detectors in the human visual system. *Science*, 1965, *149*, 1115–1116.

Michaels, D. D. *Visual optics and refraction: A clinical approach* (2nd ed.). St. Louis: C. V. Mosby, 1980.

Millodot, M. Foveal and extra-foveal acuity with and without stabilized retinal images. *British Journal of Physiological Optics*, 1966, *23*, 75–106.

Millodot, M., Johnson, C. A., Lamont, A., & Leibowitz, H. A. Effect of dioptrics on peripheral visual acuity. *Vision Research*, 1975, *15*, 1357–1362.

Mitchell, D. E., & Wilkinson, F. The effect of early astigmatism on the visual resolution of gratings. *Journal of Physiology*, 1974, *243*, 739–756.

Monti, P. Lateral masking of end elements by inner elements in tachistoscopic pattern perception. *Perception and Motor Skills*, 1973, *36*, 777–778.

Mostafavi, H., & Sakrison, D. J. Structure and properties of a single channel in the human visual system. *Vision Research*, 1976, *16*, 957 968.

Nachmias, J. On the psychometric function for contrast detection. *Vision Research*, 1981, *21*, 215–223.

Nachmias, J., & Kocher, E. C. Visual detection and discrimination of luminance increments. *Journal of the Optical Society of America*, 1970, *60*, 382–389.

Nachmias, J., & Sansbury, R. V. Grating contrast: Discrimination may be better than detection. *Vision Research*, 1974, *14*, 1039–1042.

Nachmias, J., Sansbury, R., Vassilev, A., & Weber, A. Adaptation to square wave gratings: In search of the elusive third harmonic. *Vision Research*, 1973, *13*, 1335–1342.

Nachmias, J., & Weber, A. Discrimination of simple and complex gratings. *Vision Research*, 1975, *15*, 217–223.

National Academy of Sciences. Recommended standard procedures for the clinical measurement and specification of visual acuity. Report of Working Group 39, Committee on Vision. *Adventures in Ophthalmology*, 1980, *41*, 103–148.

Ogilvie, J. C., & Taylor, M. M. Effect of orientation on the visibility of fine wires. *Journal of the Optical Society of America*, 1958, *48*, 628–629.

Olzak, L. Inhibition and stochastic interactions in spatial pattern perception. (Doctoral dissertation, University of California, Los Angeles, 1981) *Dissertation Abstracts International*, 1981, *42*, 1651B. (University Microfilm No. 8121021)

Olzak, L. Inhibition: Effects on grating detection and identification. *Investigative Ophthalmology and Visual Science*, 1982, *22*, (Suppl.), 206.

Olzak, L., & Thomas, J. P. Gratings: Why frequency discrimination is sometimes better than detection. *Journal of the Optical Society of America*, 1981, *71*, 64–70.

O'Toole, B., & Wenderoth, P. The tilt illusion: Repulsion and attraction effects in the oblique meridian. *Vision Research*, 1977, *17*, 367–374.

Owsley, C., Sekuler, R., & Siemsen, D. Contrast sensitivity throughout adulthood. *Vision Research*, 1983, *23*, 689–699.

Pantle, A. *Visual information processing of complex imagery* (Report No. AMRL-TR-74-33). Wright-Patterson Air Force Base, Ohio: Aerospace Medical Research Laboratory, 1974.

Pantle, A. Simultaneous masking of one spatial sine wave by another. *Investigative Ophthalmology and Visual Science*, 1977, *16* (Suppl.), 47.

Pantle, A., & Sekuler, R. Size detecting mechanisms in human vision. *Science*, 1968, *162*, 1146–1148.

Parker, D. M. Contrast and size variables and the tilt after-effect. *Quarterly Journal of Experimental Psychology*, 1972, *24*, 1–7.

Parlee, M. B. Visual backward masking of a single line by a single line. *Vision Research*, 1969, *9*, 199–205.

Patel, A. S. Spatial resolution by the human visual system. The effect of mean retinal illuminance. *Journal of the Optical Society of America*, 1966, *56*, 689–694.

Pitts, D. G. The effects of aging on selected visual functions: Dark adaptation, visual acuity, stereopsis and brightness contrast. In R. Sekuler, D. W. Kline, & K. Dismulkes (Eds.), *Aging in human visual functions*. New York: A. R. Liss, 1982.

Quick, R. F. A vector magnitude model of contrast detection. *Kybernetic*, 1974, *16*, 65–67.

Quinn, P. C., & Lehmkuhle, S. An oblique effect of spatial summation. *Vision Research*, 1983, *23*, 655–658.

Raab, D. Backward masking. *Psychological Bulletin*, 1963, *60*, 118–129.

Regan, D., Silver, R., & Murray, T. J. Visual acuity and contrast sensitivity in multiple sclerosis–Hidden visual loss. *Brain*, 1977, *100*, 563–579.

Robson, J. G. Spatial and temporal contrast sensitivity functions of the visual system. *Journal of the Optical Society of America*, 1966, *56*, 1141–1142.

Robson, J. G. Receptive fields: Neural representation of the spatial and intensive attributes of the visual image. In E. C. Carterette & M. P. Friedman (Eds.), *Handbook of perception* (Vol. 5). New York: Academic Press, 1975.

Robson, J. G., & Graham, N. Probability summation and regional variation in contrast sensitivity across the visual field. *Vision Research*, 1981, *21*, 409–418.

Rose, A. The sensitivity performance of the human eye on an absolute scale. *Journal of the Optical Society of America*, 1948, *38*, 196–208.

Rovamo, J., Virsu, V., & Nasanen, R. Cortical magnification factor predicts the photopic contrast sensitivity of peripheral vision. *Nature*, 1978, *271*, 54–56.

Sachs, M. B., Nachmias, J., & Robson, J. G. Spatial-frequency channels in human vision. *Journal of the Optical Society of America*, 1971, *61*, 1176–1186.

Savoy, R. L., & McCann, J. J. Visibility of low-spatial-frequency sine-wave targets: Dependence on number of cycles. *Journal of the Optical Society of America*, 1975, *65*, 343–350.

Schiffman, H. R. *Sensation and perception* (2nd ed.). New York: Wiley, 1982.

Schiller, P. H., Finlay, B. L., & Volman, S. F. Quantitative studies of single cell properties in monkey striate cortex. II. Orientation specificity and ocular dominance. *Journal of Neurophysiology*, 1976, *39*, 1320–1333. (a)

Schiller, P. H., Finlay, B. L., & Volman, S. F. Quantitative studies of single cell properties in monkey striate cortex. III. Spatial frequency. *Journal of Neurophysiology*, 1976, *39*, 1334–1351. (b)

Schiller, P. H., & Smith, M. Detection in metacontrast. *Journal of Experimental Psychology*, 1966, *71*, 32–39.

Schober, H., & Wittman, K. Untersuchungen über die Sehscharfe bei verschieden für bigen Licht. *Das Licht: Z praktische Leucht-u. Baleuchtungs-Aufgab*, 1938, *8*, 199–201.

Sekuler, R. W. Spatial and temporal determinants of visual backward masking. *Journal of Experimental Psychology*, 1965, *70*, 401–406.

Sekuler, R., & Tynan, P. Rapid measurement of contrast sensitivity functions. *American Journal of Optometry and Physiological Optics*, 1977, *54*, 573–575.

Shlaer, S. The relation between visual acuity and illumination. *Journal of General Physiology*, 1937, *21*, 165–188.

Shlaer, S., Smith, E. L., & Chase, A. M. Visual acuity and illumination in different spectral regions. *Journal of General Physiology*, 1942, *25*, 553–569.

Sloan, L. L. The photopic acuity-luminance function with special reference to parafoveal vision. *Vision Research*, 1968, *8*, 901–911.

Sperling, G. A model for visual memory tasks. *Human Factors*, 1963, *5*, 19–31.

Starr, S. J., Metz, C. J., Lusted, L. R., & Goodenough, D. J. Visual detection and localization of radiographic images. *Radiology*, 1975, *116*, 533–538.

Stecher, S., Sigel, C., & Lange, R. Composite adaptation and spatial frequency interaction. *Vision Research*, 1973, *13*, 2527–2531.

Stigler, R. Chronophotische studien uber der umgebungskontrast. *Pflugers Archiv fur die Gesamte Physiologie*, 1910, *134*, 365–435.

Stromeyer, C. F., & Julesz, B. Spatial frequency masking in vision: Critical bands and spread of masking. *Journal of the Optical Society of America*, 1972, *62*, 1221–1232.

Stromeyer, C. F., & Klein, S. Spatial frequency channels in human vision as asymmetric (edge) mechanisms. *Vision Research*, 1974, *14*, 1409–1420.

Stromeyer, C. F., & Klein, S. Evidence against narrow-band spatial frequency channels in human vision: The detectability of frequency modulated gratings. *Vision Research*, 1975, *15*, 889–910.

Sullivan, G. D., Georgeson, M. A., & Oatley, K. Channels for spatial frequency selection and the detection of single bars by the human visual system. *Vision Research*, 1972, *12*, 383–394.

Swensson, R. G., & Judy, P. F. Detection of noisy visual targets: Models for the effects of spatial uncertainty and signal-to-noise ratio. *Perception and Psychophysics*, 1981, *29*, 521–534.

Talbot, S. A., & Marshall, W. H. Physiological studies on neural mechanisms of visual localization and discrimination. *American Journal of Ophthalmology*, 1941, *24*, 1255–1264.

Taylor, S. G., & Brown, D. R. Lateral visual masking: Supraretinal effects when viewing linear arrays with unlimited viewing time. *Perception and Psychophysics*, 1972, *12*, 97–99.

Thomas, J. P. Model of the function of receptive fields in human vision. *Psychological Review*, 1970, *77*, 121–134.

Thomas, J. P. Spatial resolution and spatial interaction. In E. C. Carterette & M. P. Friedman (Eds.), *Handbook of perception* (Vol. 5). New York: Academic Press, 1975.

Thomas, J. P. Spatial summation in the fovea: Asymmetrical effects of longer and shorter dimensions. *Vision Research*, 1978, *18*, 1023–1029.

Thomas, J. P. Underlying psychometric function for detecting gratings and identifying spatial frequency. *Journal of the Optical Society of America*, 1983, *73*, 751–758.

Thomas, J. P., & Gille, J. Bandwidths of orientation channels in human vision. *Journal of the Optical Society of America*, 1979, *69*, 652–660.

Thomas, J. P., Gille, J., & Barker, R. A. Simultaneous detection and identification: Theory and data. *Journal of the Optical Society of America*, 1982, *72*, 1642–1651.

Thomas, J. P., & Kerr, L. Effect of ramp-like contours upon perceived size and detection threshold. *Perception and Psychophysics*, 1969, *5*, 381–384.

Thomas, J. P., & Kerr, L. G. Evidence of role of size-tuned mechanisms in increment threshold task. *Vision Research*, 1971, *11*, 647–655.

Thomas, J. P., Padilla, G. J., & Rourke, D. L. Spatial interactions in identification and detection of compound visual stimuli. *Vision Research*, 1969, *9*, 283–292.

Thomas, J. P., & Shimamura, K. K. Perception of size at the detection threshold: Its accuracy and possible mechanisms. *Vision Research*, 1974, *14*, 535–543.

Thomas, J. P., & Shimamura, K. K. Inhibitory interaction between visual pathways tuned to different orientations. *Vision Research*, 1975, *15*, 1373–1380.

Toates, F. M. Accommodation function of the human eye. *Physiological Review*, 1972, *52*, 828–863.

Tolhurst, D. J. Adaptation to square-wave gratings: Inhibition between spatial frequency channels in human visual system. *Journal of Physiology*, 1972, *226*, 231–248.

Tolhurst, D. J., & Barfield, L. P. Interactions between spatial frequency channels. *Vision Research*, 1978, *18*, 951–958.

Tolhurst, D. J., & Dealy, R. S. The detection and identification of lines and edges. *Vision Research*, 1975, *15*, 1367–1372.

Tolhurst, D. J., & Thompson, P. G. Orientation illusions and aftereffects: Inhibition between channels. *Vision Research*, 1975, *15*, 967–972.

Tootell, R. B., Silverman, M. S., & DeValois, R. L. Spatial frequency columns in primary visual cortex. *Science*, 1981, *214*, 813–815.

Tootell, R. B., Silverman, M. S., Switkes, E., & DeValois, R. L. Deoxyglucose analysis of retinotopic organization in primate striate cortex. *Science*, 1982, *218*, 902–904.

Tynan, P., & Sekuler, R. Perceived spatial frequency varies with stimulus duration. *Journal of the Optical Society of America*, 1974, *64*, 1251–1255.

Uttal, W. R. On the physiological basis of masking with dotted visual noise. *Perception and Psychophysics*, 1970, *7*, 321–327.

Van Nes, F. L., & Bouman, M. A. Spatial modulation transfer in the human eye. *Journal of the Optical Society of America*, 1967, *57*, 401–406.

Vassilev, A. Contrast sensitivity near borders: Significance of test stimulus form, size, and duration. *Vision Research*, 1973, *13*, 719–730.

Vassilev, A., Simeonova, B., & Zlatkova, M. Orientation acuity at the detection threshold. *Proceedings of the Fourth European Conference on Visual Perception*, 1981, 17.

Vernon, M. D. The perception of inclined lines. *British Journal of Psychology*, 1934, *25*, 186–196.

Virsu, V., & Nyman, G. Monophasic temporal modulation increases apparent spatial frequency. *Perception*, 1974, *3*, 337–353.

Virsu, V., Nyman, G., & Lehtio, P. Diphasic and polyphasic temporal modulations multiply apparent spatial frequency. *Perception*, 1974, *3*, 323–326.

Virsu, V., Rovamo, J., Laurinen, P., & Nasanen, R. Temporal contrast sensitivity and cortical magnification. *Vision Research*, 1982, *22*, 1211–1217.

Ware, C., & Mitchell, D. E. The spatial selectivity of the tilt aftereffect. *Vision Research*, 1974, *14*, 735–737.

Watson, A. B. Summation of grating patches indicates many types of detectors in one retinal location. *Vision Research*, 1982, *22*, 17–25.

Watson, A. B. *Detection and recognition of simple spatial forms.* In O. J. Braddick & A. C. Slade (Eds.), *Physical and biological processing of images.* Berlin: Springer-Verlag, 1983.

Watson, A. B., & Robson, J. G. Discrimination at threshold: Labelled detectors in human vision. *Vision Research*, 1981, *21*, 1115–1122.

Weale, R. *The aging eye.* London: H. K. Lewis, 1963.

Weisstein, N. Metacontrast. In D. Jameson & L. Hurvich (Eds.), *Handbook of sensory physiology* (Vol. 7). Berlin: Springer, 1972.

Weisstein, N., & Growney, R. L. Apparent movement and metacontrast: A note on Kahneman's formulation. *Perception and Psychophysics*, 1969, *5*, 321–328.

Weisstein, N., & Haber, R. N. An U-shaped masking function in vision. *Psychonomic Science*, 1965, *2*, 75–76.

Weitzman, D. O., Smith, J. M., & Karasik, R. Signal detection analysis of meridional variations to vertical and horizontal gratings. *Vision Research*, 1972, *12*, 1755–1758.

Westheimer, G. Spatial interaction in the human retina during scotopic vision. *Journal of Physiology*, 1965, *181*, 881–894.

Westheimer, G. The Maxwellian view. *Vision Research*, 1966, *6*, 669–682.

Westheimer, G. Spatial interaction in human cone vision. *Journal of Physiology*, 1967, *190*, 139–154.

Westheimer, G. Visual acuity and hyperacuity. *Investigative Ophthalmology*, 1975, *14*, 570–572.

Westheimer, G. Spatial phase sensitivity for sinusoidal grating targets. *Vision Research*, 1978, *18*, 1073–1074.

Westheimer, G. Scaling of visual acuity measurements. *Archives of Ophthalmology*, 1979, *97*, 327–330. (a)

Westheimer, G. The spatial sense of the eye. *Investigative Ophthalmology and Visual Science*, 1979, *18*, 893–912. (b)

Westheimer, G. Visual hyperacuity. *Progress in Sensory Physiology*, 1981, *1*, 1–30.

Westheimer, G. The spatial grain of the perifoveal visual field. *Vision*

Research, 1982, *22*, 157–162.

Westheimer, G., & Hauske, G. Temporal and spatial interference with vernier acuity. *Vision Research*, 1975, *15*, 1137–1141.

Westheimer, G., & McKee, S. Visual acuity in the presence of retinal motion. *Journal of the Optical Society of America*, 1975, *65*, 847–850.

Westheimer, G., & McKee, S. P. Integration regions for visual hyperacuity. *Vision Research*, 1977, *17*, 89–93. (a)

Westheimer, G., & McKee, S. P. Spatial configurations for visual hyperacuity. *Vision Research*, 1977, *17*, 941–947. (b)

Westheimer, G., & McKee, S. P. Stereoscopic acuity with moving retinal images. *Journal of the Optical Society of America*, 1978, *68*, 450–455.

Westheimer, G., Shimamura, K., & McKee, S. P. Interference with line-orientation sensitivity. *Journal of the Optical Society of America*, 1976, *66*, 332–338.

Weymouth, F. W. Visual sensory units and the minimum angle of resolution. *American Journal of Ophthalmology*, 1958, *46*, 102–113.

Wiesel, T. N. Receptive fields of ganglion cells in the cat's retina. *Journal of Physiology*, 1960, *153*, 583–594.

Williams, D. W., & Wilson, H. R. Spatial-frequency adaptation affects spatial-probability summation. *Journal of the Optical Society of America*, 1983, *73*, 1367–1371.

Williams, D. W., Wilson, H. R., & Cowan, J. D. Localized effects of spatial-frequency adaptation. *Journal of the Optical Society of America*, 1982, *72*, 878–887.

Wilson, H. R., & Bergen, J. R. A four mechanism model for threshold spatial vision. *Vision Research*, 1979, *19*, 19–32.

Wilson, H. R., & Gelb, D. J. Modified line element theory for spatial-frequency and width discrimination. *Journal of the Optical Society of America A*, 1984, *1*, 124–131.

Wilson, H. R., & Giese, S. C. Threshold visibility of frequency gradient patterns. *Vision Research*, 1977, *17*, 1177–1190.

Wilson, H. R., McFarlane, D. K., & Phillips, G. C. Spatial frequency tuning of orientation selective units estimated by oblique masking. *Vision Research*, 1983, *23*, 873–882.

Woodson, W. E. *Human engineering guide for equipment designs*. Los Angeles: University of California Press, 1954.

Zuidema, P., Verschuure, H., Bouman, M., & Koenderink, J. Spatial and temporal summation in the dark-adapted retina. *Journal of the Optical Society of America*, 1981, *71*, 1472–1480.

CHAPTER 8

COLORIMETRY AND COLOR DISCRIMINATION

JOEL POKORNY and VIVIANNE C. SMITH

Eye Research Laboratories, The University of Chicago, Chicago, Illinois

CONTENTS

Some of the research and theoretical analyses reported in this chapter were supported in part by USPH NIH Grants EY 00901 (Pokorny) and EY01876 (Smith).

1. SPECIFICATION OF THE STIMULUS

1.1. Physical Specification of Light

The Commission Internationale de l'Eclairage (CIE) defined light as "any radiation capable of causing a visual sensation directly" or as "radiation capable of stimulating the organ of vision," that is, electromagnetic radiation in the wavelength range of 360–830 nm (Wyszecki & Stiles, 1982). Our natural source of electromagnetic radiation is the sun, and as Figure 8.1 (Henderson, 1977) shows, the wavelength region 360–830 nm is well within its major radiation band. Artificial sources

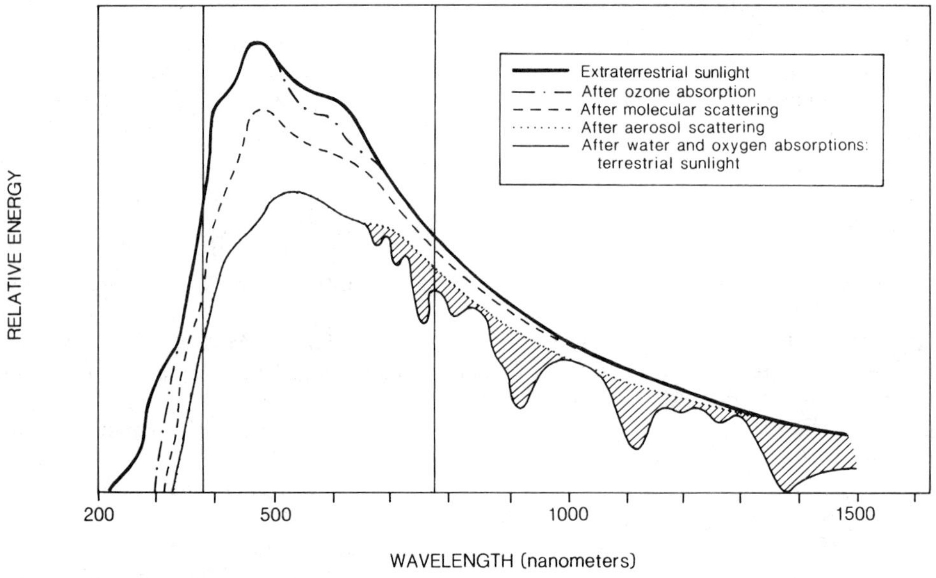

Figure 8.1. The spectral distribution of sunlight as it enters the earth's atmosphere and its modification by scattering and absorption. The vertical lines enclose the spectral region to which the visual system is most sensitive. (From S. T. Henderson, *Daylight and its spectrum* (2nd ed.), Adam Hilger, Ltd., 1977. Reprinted with permission.)

of electromagnetic radiation include tungsten or fluorescent illuminants.

Color stimuli are produced when a broad or narrow portion of the visible electromagnetic spectrum is isolated. Color filters, diffraction gratings, and prisms can all be used to separate or select narrow bands of visible radiation from a broadband illuminant. Some light sources have their output confined to a few wavelengths called *line spectra* (e.g., gas discharge lamps and lasers) or confined to a wavelength band (e.g., light-emitting diodes). The physical causes of both source and object color are diverse. Nassau (1983) describes some 15 physical principles for generation or selective reflection of light. A wide diversity of sources have been employed in color vision research, and useful properties are summarized by a number of authors (Carlson & Clark, 1965; Eby & Levin, 1979; Kaufman, 1981; Wyszecki & Stiles, 1982). Raster displays are suitable for some applications, offering a convenient means of displaying chromatic stimuli (Conrac, 1980; Sproson, 1983), and some attention has been paid to attaining adequate stimulus control (Cowan, 1983; Rodieck, 1983).

1.2. Specification of Visual Stimuli

1.2.1. Spectral Emittance. Radiant emittance is the amount of radiant flux emitted by a source per unit of its area. The spectral emittance of any arbitrary radiation source may be measured using a device called a *spectroradiometer*. Figure 8.2 shows relative spectral emittance for some common broadband sources. The high-pressure xenon arc has approximately constant output in the visible spectrum; the zirconium arc has a continuous output that increases with wavelength and contains occasional line spectra; fluorescent lights show line spectra superimposed on a continuous spectrum.

Incandescent sources emit radiation as a function of their temperature. At low temperatures the rate of radiation is low and concentrated at long wavelengths. As the temperature is increased, the rate of radiation increases and is spread over an increasingly wider band of wavelengths. The relative spectral emittance of an incandescent source will depend on both the emissivity property of the metal and on the operating temperature.

1.2.2. Color Temperature. An incandescent source is usually specified by means of its color temperature (K). The color temperature of the source is the operating temperature of an ideal radiator whose spectral output matches or closely approximates that of the source. The spectral output of an ideal radiator depends only on its temperature. Tabulations of the relative spectral output of ideal radiators are available (Moon, 1961; Wyszecki & Stiles, 1982). Figure 8.3 shows both absolute and relative spectral emittance of an ideal radiator or blackbody source. The color temperature of tungsten sources is usually between 2400 and 3000 K. The output of tungsten sources increases with wavelength, being relatively low at short wavelengths. Tungsten-halogen lamps have higher color temperatures typically in the 3000–3400 K range.

The concept of color temperature may also be extended to describe discontinuous or arc sources or filtered incandescent light sources. The term *correlated color temperature* is used for sources of similar appearance to the blackbody source but whose spectral output does not conform to the blackbody. The correlated color temperature is a specification of the perceptually most similar blackbody radiation (see Wyszecki & Stiles, 1982, for a more extensive discussion).

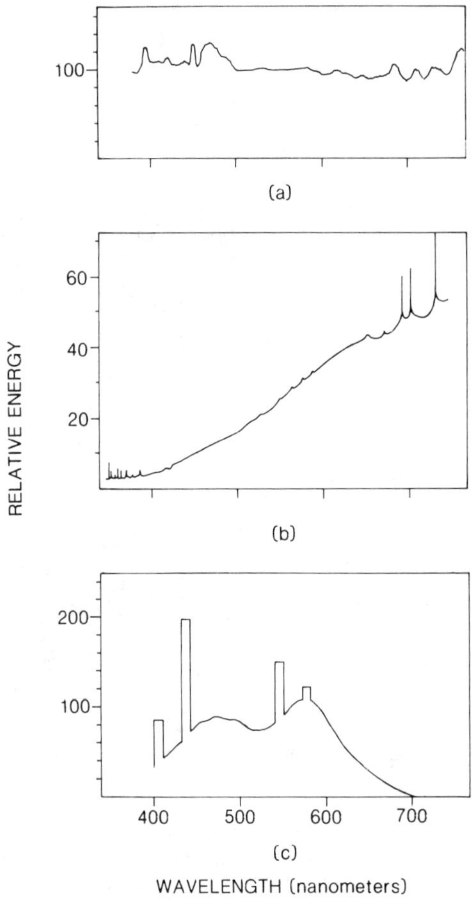

Figure 8.2. Spectral energy distribution of some electrical discharge lights. (a) High-pressure xenon. (b) Zirconium. (c) Conventional "daylight" fluorescent lamp. (From G. Wyszecki & W. S. Stiles, *Color science—Concepts and methods, quantitative data and formulae*. Copyright 1967 by John Wiley & Sons, Inc. Reprinted with permission.)

1.2.3. Standard Illuminants. Several working standards for "white" lights have been specified by the CIE (Wyszecki & Stiles, 1982) and are called *standard illuminants*. These illuminants provide standards for calibration of colored filters and papers. They provide important nonspectral references for colorimetry (see Section 3.4). The relative spectral distribution of four such standards is shown in Figure 8.4 (on page 8-5) and in Table 8.1 (on page 8-6).

Source A is realized directly by operating an incandescent lamp at a color temperature of 2854 K. Sources B and C are obtained by modifying the spectral distribution of source A with precisely specified liquid filters. Source D_{65} is one of a group of sources that represents various phases of daylight; each is characterized by the letter D and a subscript representing the first two digits of the color temperature. Specification of illuminant D includes near ultraviolet, as well as visible light.

1.2.4. Reciprocal Color Temperature. The reciprocal color temperature R (expressed in reciprocal megakelvins) is an alternative specification of color temperature. Reciprocal color temperature is a desirable metric because it has two important properties: a given change in reciprocal color temperature—delta R is approximately an equal perceptible step for a wide range of color temperatures (Judd, 1933a)—and a given color temperature conversion filter will cause the same change in R over a wide range of actual color temperature. Color temperature conversion filters (or color-correcting filters) are designed to

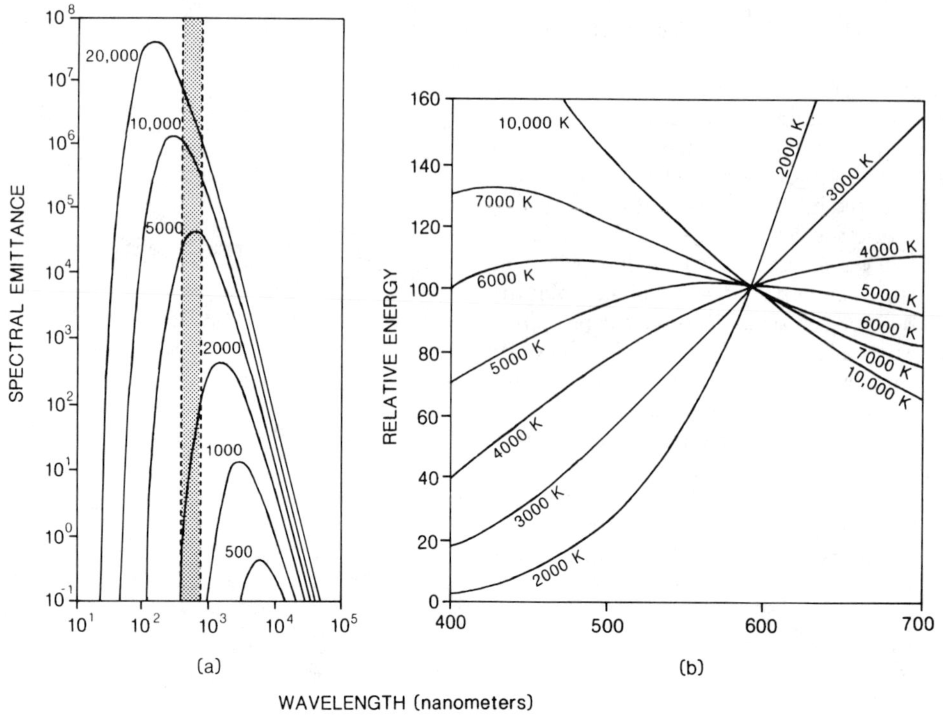

Figure 8.3. Spectral energy distribution of a blackbody as a function of temperature. (a) Spectral emittance as a function of wavelength for selected blackbody temperatures. Spectral emittance increases with increasing color temperature. The band indicates the range of visible radiation. (b) The relative energy in the visible region of the spectrum as a function of color temperature. The heights of the curves have been adjusted so that the energy at 590 nm is equal to 100. With increasing color temperature, the relative energy distribution shifts to include more short wavelength radiation. (From J. Pokorny & V. C. Smith, Color vision, in A. M. Potts (Ed.), *The assessment of visual function*, C. V. Mosby Company, 1972. Reprinted with permission.)

alter the color temperature of a hypothetical blackbody source while maintaining its conformation to a blackbody source. Many filter manufacturers specify a color temperature conversion filter in terms of its R shift value (called *mired shift* in many catalogs). The color temperature is achieved by use of such a filter with a blackbody source is predicted by

$$K_{(\text{source } + \text{ filter})} = \frac{10^6}{(R_{\text{source}} + R_{\text{filter}})} \tag{1}$$

yellow-appearing filters, which lower color temperature, have positive R shifts; blue-appearing filters, which raise color temperature, have negative R shifts. Table 8.2 (on page 8-6) shows filters that may be used to convert conventional tungsten lamps to approximate one of the four CIE standard illuminants.

1.2.5. Specification of Narrow-Band Stimuli. The color properties of a transparent object such as a glass filter are determined primarily by its spectral transmittance; the color properties of an opaque object such as colored paper are primarily determined by its spectral reflectance.

Measurement of spectral transmittance (τ_λ) or spectral reflectance (ρ_λ) is made by spectrophotometers which compare the incident with the transmitted or the reflected light. Reflectance measurements are made relative to the reflectance of a spectrally uniform reflecting surface (see Wyszecki & Stiles, 1982). Characteristic transmission tabulations for glass filters are published in many manufacturers' catalogs; such tabulations approximate an individual filter's transmittance. A transmission function for a given filter, such as an interference filter, is often available for a small fee at the time of purchase.

Filters may transmit only a limited portion of the visible spectrum (band-pass filters) or may preferentially transmit light above or below a given wavelength (pass filters). Description of the transmission characteristics of a filter showing a single peak in the visible spectrum includes (1) the wavelength and peak transmission at maximum output and (2) the half-width (also called half-height bandwidth or half-height band-pass). This specification may be supplemented by other characteristics (Scharf, 1965). The half-width is obtained by finding the wavelength difference between the two wavelengths having half the maximum transmittance. Pass filters (also called cut-on or cutoff filters) are specified by (1) the cut-on wavelength, usually the wavelength having 5% transmission and (2) the slope, calculated as the difference in nanometers between the cut-on wavelength and the wavelength of 70% transmission (Scharf, 1965). Other values of transmission may be used to specify the cut-on wavelength and to calculate the slope; further, the slope may be expressed as a percentage of the wavelength difference relative to the cut-on wavelength.

When a color filter is used in an experimental application, the relative spectral emittance is of interest:

$$Se_\lambda = H_\lambda T_\lambda \; , \tag{2}$$

where SE_λ is the relative spectral emittance, H_λ is the spectral emission of the source, and T_λ is the transmittance of the filter.

1.3. Wavelength and Frequency

In the study of color vision the most usual metric is wavelength λ, expressed in nanometers. In the study of the spectral response of the visual photopigment, many researchers prefer the wave number m^{-1}:

$$m^{-1} = \frac{\nu}{c} = 10^7/\lambda \ , \qquad (3)$$

where ν is the frequency. This preference reflects the fact that for the visual photopigment, it is quantal absorptions that count. Each quantum has a characteristic energy proportional to its frequency:

$$E = h\nu = hc/\lambda \ , \qquad (4)$$

where h is the Planck constant, approximately $6.624940 \cdot 10^{-34}$ J·sec, c is the speed of light *in vacuo*, $3 \cdot 10^8$ m·s^{-1}, and λ is expressed in meters. Further, when light enters a medium, its speed is reduced. Its frequency is constant, but the wavelength is changed by the factor $1/n$, where n, the index of refraction, is the ratio of the speed of light *in vacuo* to that in the medium. Table 8.3 (on page 8-7) gives the wavelengths corresponding to fixed wave-number steps, together with the relative quantal energy referred to 14,000 m^{-1} and the wave numbers corresponding to fixed wavelength steps together with the relative quantal energy referred to 700 nm.

2. MEASUREMENT OF LIGHT

2.1. Measurement of Radiant Energy

Measurement of the quantity of radiant energy may be accomplished by determining the rise in temperature of a blackened surface as it absorbs radiation. Such instruments as thermocouples and thermopiles (devices consisting of a junction or junctions of dissimilar materials across which an electric potential exists which varies with temperature) or bolometers (devices in which absorbed energy varies the resistance of a blackened metal or semiconductor strip) measure the total energy emitted at all wavelengths. In the case of a complex radiation, it is often convenient to consider this as the sum of several monochromatic radiations.

There are three fundamental types of energy measurement: the total energy emitted from a point in a given direction (radiant intensity), the energy incident on a surface at some distance from a source (irradiance), and the energy emitted from a unit area of a surface (radiance); see Table 8.4 (on page 8-8).

2.1.1. Radiant Intensity. When electric power is supplied to a lamp, radiation is emitted. The radiant energy P_e, emitted per unit of time, is measured in watts.

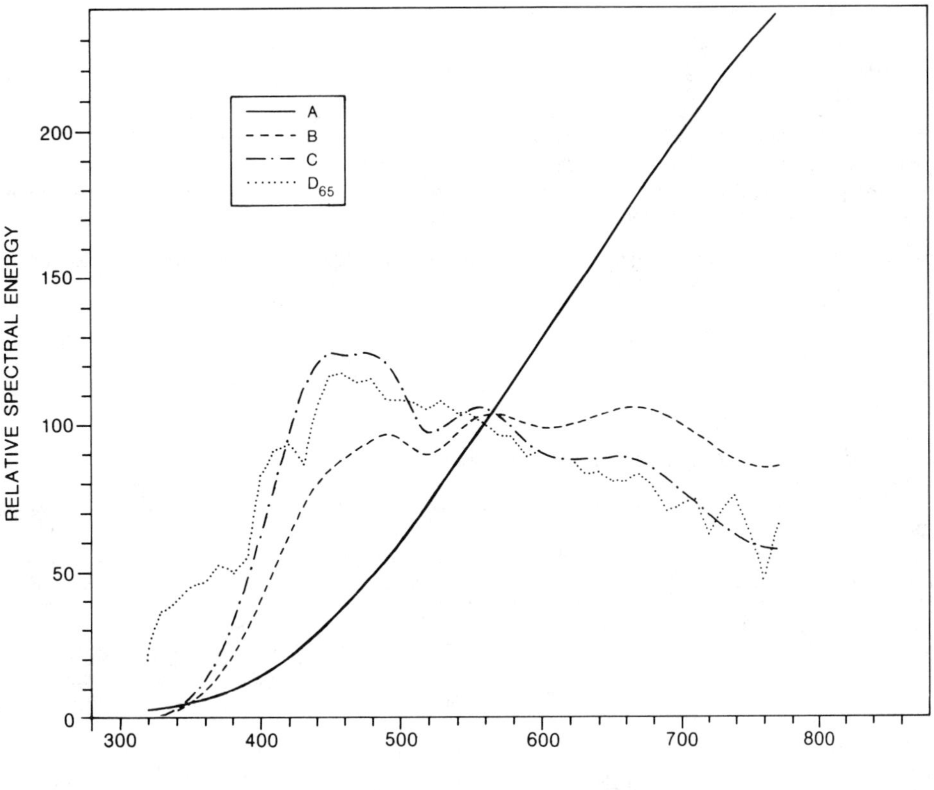

Figure 8.4. Specified illuminants. Spectral energy distribution of the CIE illuminants *A*, *B*, *C*, and D_{65}. They are representative of the following types of radiant energy distribution: standard illuminant *A*: incandescent lamp light at color temperature of 2854 K; standard illuminant *B*: direct sunlight with a correlated color temperature of 4874 K; standard illuminant C: light of the overcast sky (northern for northern hemisphere) with a correlated color temperature of 6774 K; standard illuminant D_{65}: daylight with a correlated color temperature of 6504 K.

Table 8.1. Relative Spectral Radiant Power Distributions of CIE Standard Illuminants *A, B, C,* and D_{65}

nm	$A, S(\lambda)$	$B, S(\lambda)$	$C, S(\lambda)$	$D_{65}, S(\lambda)$	nm	$A, S(\lambda)$	$B, S(\lambda)$	$C, S(\lambda)$	$D_{65}, S(\lambda)$
300	0.93			0.03	600	129.04	98.00	89.70	90.00
310	1.36			3.30	610	136.35	98.50	88.40	89.60
320	1.93	0.02	0.01	20.20	620	143.62	99.70	88.10	87.70
330	2.66	0.50	0.40	37.10	630	150.84	101.00	88.00	83.30
340	3.59	2.40	2.70	39.90	640	157.98	102.20	87.80	83.70
350	4.74	5.60	7.00	44.90	650	165.03	103.90	88.20	80.00
360	6.14	9.60	12.90	46.60	660	171.96	105.00	87.90	80.20
370	7.82	15.20	21.40	52.10	670	178.77	104.90	86.30	82.30
380	9.80	22.40	33.00	50.00	680	185.43	103.90	84.00	78.30
390	12.09	31.30	47.40	54.60	690	191.93	101.60	80.20	69.70
400	14.71	41.30	63.30	82.80	700	198.26	99.10	76.30	71.60
410	17.68	52.10	80.60	91.50	710	204.41	96.20	72.40	74.30
420	20.99	63.20	98.10	93.40	720	210.36	92.90	68.30	61.60
430	24.67	73.10	112.40	86.70	730	216.12	89.40	64.40	69.90
440	28.70	80.80	121.50	104.90	740	221.67	86.90	61.50	75.10
450	33.09	85.40	124.00	117.00	750	227.00	85.20	59.20	63.60
460	37.81	88.30	123.10	117.80	760	232.12	84.70	58.10	46.40
470	42.87	92.00	123.80	114.90	770	237.01	85.40	58.20	66.80
480	48.24	95.20	123.90	115.90	780	241.68			63.40
490	53.91	96.50	120.70	108.80	790	246.12			64.30
500	59.86	94.20	112.10	109.40	800	250.33			59.50
510	66.06	90.70	102.30	107.80	810	254.31			52.00
520	72.50	89.50	96.90	104.80	820	258.07			57.40
530	79.13	92.20	98.00	107.70	830	261.60			60.30
540	85.95	96.90	102.10	104.40					
550	92.91	101.00	105.20	104.00					
560	100.00	102.80	105.30	100.00					
570	107.18	102.60	102.30	96.30					
580	114.44	101.00	97.80	95.80					
590	121.73	99.20	93.20	88.70					

The relative spectral radiant power S(λ) is tabulated for the four standard illuminants as a function of wavelength. The illuminants are representative of the following types of radiant energy distribution: Standard illuminant A: incandescent lamp light at a color temperature of 2854 K. Standard illuminant B: direct sunlight with a correlated color temperature of 4874 K. Standard illuminant C: light of the overcast sky (northern for northern hemisphere) with a correlated color temperature of 6774 K. Standard illuminant D_{65}: daylight with a correlated color temperature of 6504 K.

Source: From G. Wyszecki & W. S. Stiles, *Color science: Concepts and methods, quantitative data and formulae* (2nd ed.). Copyright 1982, John Wiley & Sons, Inc. Reprinted with permission.

Table 8.2. Differences in Reciprocal Color Temperature between Tungsten Illuminants and the CIE Standard Illuminants

Tungsten Color Temperature	Reciprocal mK	*A* 2854 350	*B* 4874 205	D_{65} 6504 154	*C* 6774 148
2400	417	−67	−210	−263	−269
		82C + 82A	80A + 80C	80A + 80A	80A + 80A
2600	385	−35	−180	−231	−237
		82B	80A + 82C	80A + 80B	80A + 80B
2800	357	−7	−152	−203	−209
		82	80A + 82A	80A + 80C	80A + 80C
3000	333	+17	−128	−179	−185
		80A	80A	80A + 82C	80A + 80D
3200	312	+38	−107	−158	−164
		81C	80B	80B + 82C	80A + 82B

The data are expressed in reciprocal megakelvins and below are given the single or pair of Kodak color-compensating filters which adjust (approximately) the tungsten sources to the CIE standard illuminants. For example, to obtain standard illuminant C from a tungsten illuminant of 2800 K, an R of − 209 is required. This value is approximated by the Kodak color-compensating filters 80A + 80C.

Table 8.3. Conversion from Wave number to Wavelength and Vice Versa

Wave Number	Lambda	$Q/Q_{14,000}$	Lambda	Wave Number	Q_{700}/Q
25,000	400	1.78571	400	25,000	1.75
24,750	404	1.76786	410	24,390	1.70732
24,500	408	1.75	420	23,809	1.66667
24,250	412	1.73214	430	23,255	1.62791
24,000	416	1.71429	440	22,727	1.59091
23,750	421	1.69643	450	22,222	1.55556
23,500	425	1.67857	460	21,739	1.52174
23,250	430	1.66071	470	21,276	1.48936
23,000	434	1.64286	480	20,833	1.45833
22,750	439	1.625	490	20,408	1.42857
22,500	444	1.60714	500	20,000	1.4
22,250	449	1.58929	510	19,607	1.37255
22,000	454	1.57143	520	19,230	1.34615
21,750	459	1.55357	530	18,867	1.32075
21,500	465	1.53571	540	18,518	1.2963
21,250	470	1.51786	550	18,181	1.27273
21,000	476	1.5	560	17,857	1.25
20,750	481	1.48214	570	17,543	1.22807
20,500	487	1.46429	580	17,241	1.2069
20,250	493	1.44643	590	16,949	1.18644
20,000	500	1.42857	600	16,666	1.16667
19,750	506	1.41071	610	16,393	1.14754
19,500	512	1.39286	620	16,129	1.12903
19,250	519	1.375	630	15,873	1.11111
19,000	526	1.35714	640	15,625	1.09375
18,750	533	1.33929	650	15,384	1.07692
18,500	540	1.32143	660	15,151	1.06061
18,250	547	1.30357	670	14,925	1.04478
18,000	555	1.28571	680	14,705	1.02941
17,750	563	1.26786	690	14,492	1.01449
17,500	571	1.25	700	14,286	1.0
17,250	579	1.23214			
17,000	588	1.21429			
16,750	597	1.19643			
16,500	606	1.17857			
16,250	615	1.16071			
16,000	625	1.14286			
15,750	634	1.125			
15,500	645	1.10714			
15,250	655	1.08929			
15,000	666	1.07143			
14,750	677	1.05357			
14,500	689	1.03571			
14,250	701	1.01786			
14,000	714	1.0			

A set of lines radiating from a point defines a solid angle at that point (Figure 8.5(a)). With this point as center and with any distance r, as radius, a spherical surface may be constructed. The set of lines emanating from the center of the sphere defines an area A on the surface of the sphere. The steradian (sr) measure of the solid angle ω is the ratio $\omega = A/r^2$. The solid angle is one sr, when $A = r^2$. Since the total area of a sphere is $4\pi r^2$, the total solid angle subtended at the point is

$$\omega_{(\text{total})} = \frac{4\pi r^2}{r^2} = 4\pi \text{ srs} . \quad (5)$$

The radiant intensity I_e of a point source with radiant flux P_e is the radiant flux per solid angle

$$I_e = P_e/\omega , \quad (6)$$

expressed in units of W·sr^{-1}. A point source emitting at 5 W will have a radiant intensity of $5/4\pi$ W·sr^{-1}, or approximately 0.4 W·sr^{-1}. Artificial sources typically do not radiate uniformly in all directions. In this case radiant energy intensity is specified with respect to a specific direction.

2.1.2. Irradiance. When radiant flux is incident on a surface, the surface is said to be *irradiated*. Let P_e be that radiant

Table 8.4. Radiometric Terms, Symbols and Units

Term	Symbol	Units
Radiant flux	P_e	watts (W)
Radiant intensity	I_e	$W{\cdot}sr^{-1}$
Irradiance	E_e	$W{\cdot}m^{-2}$
Radiance	L_e	$W{\cdot}m^{-2}{\cdot}sr^{-1}$

flux incident on the interior surface of a sphere of radius r. The total area of the sphere is $4\pi r^2$. The irradiance E_e is the radiant flux from a point source falling on a unit area of this surface:

$$E_e = \frac{P_e}{\omega r^2} . \tag{7}$$

Irradiance is radiant flux incident per unit area, expressed in $W{\cdot}m^{-2}$.

The irradiance E_e is usually expressed in terms of the radiant intensity I_e by substituting the terms $P_e = \omega I_e$ into Eq. (7). Irradiance is related to radiant intensity I_e by the expression

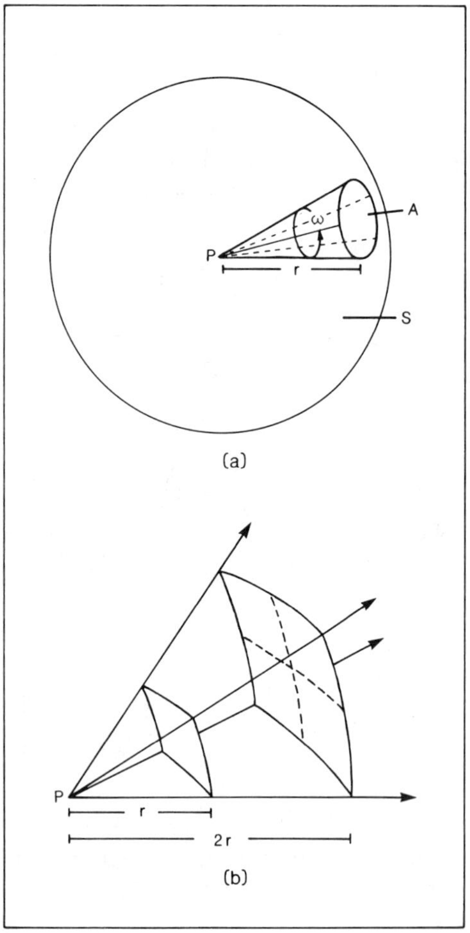

Figure 8.5. Definition of solid angle ω and the inverse-square law. (a) Point P lies at the center of sphere S with radius r. A set of lines of radius r emanating from P defines an area A on the surface of S. The steradian measure of solid angle ω is the ratio $\omega = A/r^2$. (b) The radiant flux emitted by point source P irradiates a larger area as the distance r from the source increases. The irradiance varies inversely with the square of the distance r. Thus at distance $2r$ the irradiance is ¼ that at distance r. (From J. Pokorny, V. C. Smith, G. Verriest, & A. J. S. C. Pinckers, *Congenital and acquired color defects*, Grune & Stratton, 1979. Reprinted with permission.)

$$E_e = \frac{I_e}{r^2} . \tag{8}$$

Thus a point source emitting at 5 W will produce an irradiance on the interior surface of a sphere of 100-cm radius of approximately $0.4{\cdot}10^2\ W{\cdot}m^{-2}$.

The radiant flux emitted by a point source falls on a successively greater area as the distance from the source increases (Figure 8.5(b)). As noted in Eq. (8), the irradiance E_e varies inversely with the square of the distance r from the source P_e. This relation is called the *inverse square law*.

Suppose the surface is a flat screen, rather than a spherical surface (Figure 8.6(a)). Two important changes occur as α, the angle from the normal, increases. First, the distance to the surface C is greater than r by the factor 1/cosα, and in accord with the inverse square law, the irradiance will be reduced by a factor of $\cos^2\alpha$. Second, since the area of the surface is irradiatd at angle α, rather than perpendicularly, the radiant flux contained in a narrow solid angle ω will be spread over a larger area. For example, in Figure 8.6(a), the object lies in plane C and is thus at angle α to the normal plane A; the irradiated area in plane C is 1/cosα times the area at A with perpendicular irradiance. The irradiance is therefore reduced by a factor of cosα in comparison to perpendicular incidence. The total irradiance on C at angle α is given by

$$E_e = \left(I_e \cos^2 \frac{\alpha}{r^2} \right) (\cos\alpha) = I_e \cos^3 \frac{\alpha}{r^2} \tag{9}$$

Thus on a flat surface, irradiance from a point source decreases with the $\cos^3$ of the angle from the normal.

The definition of irradiance and the operation of the inverse square law are valid only for a point source of light. Few physical light sources approximate a point source. Examples of natural point sources are stars. For practical purposes of measurement, the inverse square law will operate with an error less than 1% provided the maximal dimension of the source is smaller than or equal to ¹⁄₁₀ the distance at which irradiance is measured (Teele, 1965).

2.1.3. Radiance. The majority of light sources do have finite dimensions and are called *extended sources*. Radiance L_e is used to describe the radiant flux per unit of solid angle of an extended source measured in a given direction per unit area of the source when projected in that direction. Radiance refers to the areal density of radiant intensity either leaving a source or arriving at the surface of an object. In the measurement of radiance (Figure 8.6(b)) of an extended source in a direction normal to the surface, L_e is given by I_e/A, where A is the area of an infinitesimal surface element of the source. With measurement at angle θ to the normal, only the projected surface, A' of A is sampled. The projected area A' is given by A cosθ. Radiance is expressed as

$$L_e = \frac{I_e}{A} \cos\theta = \frac{P_e}{\omega A} \cos\theta \tag{10}$$

in $W{\cdot}sr^{-1}{\cdot}m^{-2}$, where A is the area of the surface of the source and θ is the angle between the normal from the surface and the direction of measurement.

Many extended sources have emission characteristics which follow or approximate Lambert's law:

$$I\theta = I_0 \cos\theta , \tag{11}$$

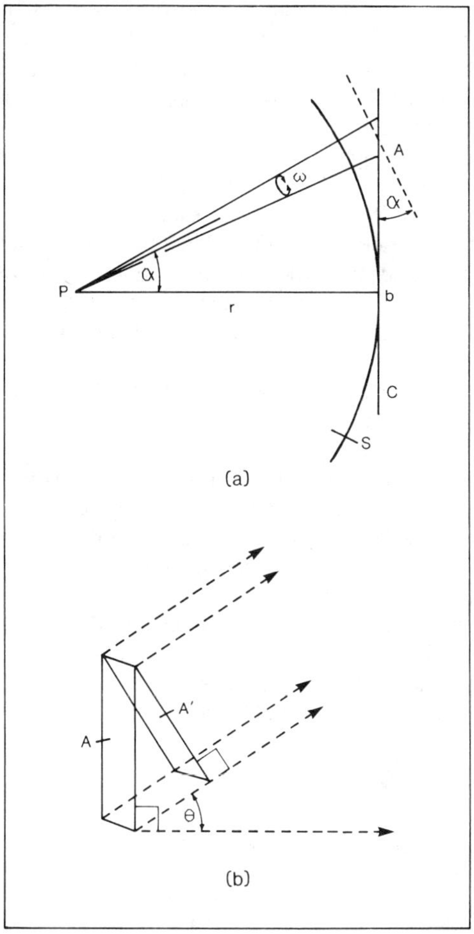

Figure 8.6. Definition of irradiance and radiance at an angle. (a) The irradiated surface *C* is a flat screen tangent to sphere *S* only at point *b*. As α, the angle from the normal to *C*, increases, the distance from source *P* to the surface of *C* increases by the factor 1/cos α. In addition, since the irradiating beam striking *C* deviates from the perpendicular by angle α, the radiant flux contained in a narrow solid angle incident perpendicularly on surface *A* will cover a larger area on surface *C* (by a factor of 1/cos α). (b) The horizontal dashed line shows the perpendicular measurement of the radiance of surface element *A* of an extended source. If the direction of measurement varies from the perpendicular by angle θ, only the projected area *A*′ is sampled, and the area of *A*′ is less than that of *A* by a factor of cos θ. (From J. Pokorny, V. C. Smith, G. Verriest, & A. J. L. C. Pinckers, *Congenital and acquired color defects*, Grune & Stratton, 1979. Reprinted with permission.)

in which the radiant intensity in $W \cdot sr^{-1}$ decreases as the angle θ from the normal to the surface of the source increases. Thus L_e decreases by the factor cosθ. But since measurements of radiance are made in a plane normal to the direction of radiation and the area of the projected surface of the source A' also decreases exactly with cosθ (Figure 8.6(b)), the measured radiance of a Lambertian emitter remains constant. Lambertian surfaces are equally radiant from whatever angle or distance they are viewed.

For a perfect Lambertian emitter it is possible to derive the radiant flux per unit area by calculating the total power radiated into a hemisphere by a Lambertian emitter. It is found that for a perfect Lambertian emitter of surface area A and radiant intensity I, in $W \cdot sr^{-1}$, the total power radiated into the hemisphere is πIA W. Thus radiation per unit area of source into the hemisphere is $\pi I \ W \cdot m^{-2}$.

2.2. Spectral Luminous Efficiency Function

Radiometric units have a purely physical specification. However the definition of light includes reference to the human observer. The CIE has defined *luminous flux* as the radiant flux weighted by the spectral luminous efficiency function of the eye. This function describes the relative sensitivity of the eye to different wavelengths. It is defined for both photopic (bright, light-adapted, or cone-dominated) and scotopic (dim, dark-adapted, or rod-dominated) adaptation levels.

The relative sensitivity of the light-adapted eye varies both with psychophysical technique and stimulus conditions, including retinal area, stimulus size, and luminance level. Three major techniques of historical importance to photopic photometry (Section 2.3) are brightness matching, flicker photometry, and minimally distinct border measured for a 2° foveal field. Other techniques, such as absolute (foveal) or increment threshold, and criterion studies, such as constant critical flicker frequency (CFF) or visual acuity, have been used less frequently; the data are reviewed in a CIE (1978) report.

The relative sensitivity of the dark-adapted eye measured with extrafoveal stimuli does not vary with psychophysical technique. The absolute threshold method and brightness matching have been used.

The relative sensitivity of the eye in mesopic (twilight) mixed cone-rod function adaptation is more variable than for light-adapted conditions. Mesopic luminous efficiency depends on field size and radiance level. Mesopic luminous efficiency is usually assessed by heterochromatic brightness matching.

2.2.1. Heterochromatic Flicker Photometry. In heterochromatic flicker photometry (HFP), a fixed radiance reference light of known luminance is alternated in time with a coextensive wavelength comparison light. The observer adjusts the radiance of the comparison light to eliminate or minimize the sensation of flicker. The alternation rate at which flicker is minimized depends upon the wavelength of the comparison light and the radiance and field size of the reference light.

2.2.2. Heterochromatic Brightness Matching. In heterochromatic brightness matching, a fixed radiance reference light of known luminance is presented adjacent to a variable wavelength comparison field. The observer adjusts the radiance of the comparison field until both appear of equivalent brightness. For foveal fields at photopic levels, the match is made with high precision, provided the two fields are of identical hue (homochromatic brightness matching). If the two fields are of different hue, the observer may be instructed to ignore the hue difference. However, it is recognized that many observers have conceptual problems with the task. At mesopic levels, a series of functions is obtained showing a gradual change reflecting the change from dark (rod-dominated) to light (cone-dominated) adaptation (Ikeda & Shimozono, 1981; Kokoschka, 1972; Walters & Wright, 1943).

2.2.3. Step-by-Step Brightness Matching. Step-by-step brightness matching is a variant of photopic heterochromatic brightness matching. A number of reference lights are used so that the color differences between reference and comparison lights are never large. Some observers find this task easier to perform than heterochromatic brightness matching.

2.2.4. Minimally Distinct Border. In the minimally distinct border (MDB) technique, the reference and comparison fields are presented side by side as in brightness matching but with a precisely juxtaposed border. The observer sets the radiance of the comparison field to minimize the contrast of the border. The MDB procedure is as reliable as HFP.

2.2.5. Comparison of Data. A comparison (Wagner & Boynton, 1972) of the relative sensitivity functions obtained by the four techniques is shown in Table 8.5, and the logarithms are plotted in Figure 8.7 These data represent averages of four observers. The broadest function is obtained for heterochromatic brightness matching, the narrowest for the HFP and MDB techniques. The step-by-step method gives an intermediate function. The Kokoschka (1972) data for brightness matching using a 9.5° field at five mesopic levels is shown in Figure 8.8 (on page 8-12).

2.2.6. Abney's Law. In radiometry the energy of a complex radiation is equivalent to the summed effects of the component monochromatic radiations. In defining photometry, this principle of additivity is formalized as *Abney's law*. Abney's law states that the total luminance contributed by a complex radiation is equal to the sum of the luminances of the component monochromatic radiations.

Luminances estimated by heterochromatic flicker photometry and minimally distinct border obey the principle of additivity, at least for the usual conditions of measurement where the standard field is a specified white 2° field of approximately 100 td retinal illuminance. Formal demonstrations of additivity for lights evaluated via heterochromatic flicker photometry were made by Dresler (1953); Eisner and MacLeod (1981); Richards and Luria (1964); and Sperling (1961); and for MDB by Wagner and Boynton (1972). The spectral sensitivity functions obtained by HFP and MDB techniques give similar results (Figure 8.7). In comparison, brightness matching is not additive (Burns, Smith, Pokorny, & Elsner, 1982; Guth, Donley, & Marrocco, 1969; Kaiser & Wyszecki, 1978; Piéron, 1942). The spectral sensitivity function derived from brightness matching shows reliable differences from the sensitivity functions obtained using heterochromatic flicker photometry or minimally distinct border (CIE, 1978; Ikeda, Yaguchi, & Sagawa, 1982; Wagner & Boynton, 1972).

Other methods of assessing spectral sensitivity functions fall into two general categories: (1) those that yield sensitivity functions resembling HFP (and probably obeying Abney's law) and (2) those resembling brightness matching (and showing additivity failures). Functions resembling HFP are obtained from detection of acuity targets both for Landolt Cs (Ives, 1912; Schwarz, 1956) and grating targets (Brown, Phares, & Fletcher, 1960; Pokorny, Graham, & Lanson, 1968). Additivity for Landolt Cs was confirmed by Graham and Guth (1970) and by Myers, Ingling, and Drum (1973) for grating targets. Constant critical flicker fusion criteria have been used to derive spectral sensitivity functions. At intermediate photopic luminances, functions re-

Table 8.5. The Luminous Efficiency Function Obtained by Different Techniques

Wavelength	HFP	MDB	Step-by-Step	Brightness Matching
400	0.0128	0.0144	0.0470	0.0202
410	0.0222	0.0236	0.0538	0.0436
420	0.0301	0.0329	0.0748	0.0800
430	0.0361	0.0402	0.1010	0.0941
440	0.0410	0.0505	0.1250	0.1555
450	0.0525	0.0616	0.1445	0.1650
460	0.0681	0.0817	0.1920	0.1870
470	0.0985	0.1145	0.2400	0.2370
480	0.1518	0.1715	0.3010	0.3285
490	0.1950	0.2280	0.3420	0.3530
500	0.2782	0.3470	0.4630	0.4500
510	0.4550	0.5330	0.6320	0.5870
520	0.6790	0.7500	0.8450	0.8080
530	0.8315	0.8880	0.9540	1.0000
540	0.9410	0.9750	1.0000	1.0000
550	0.9891	0.9970	0.9200	0.9420
560	1.0100	0.9880	0.8360	0.8530
570	0.9670	0.9390	0.6980	0.8310
580	0.8935	0.9060	0.6200	0.8710
590	0.8035	0.8560	0.5360	0.9130
600	0.6450	0.6930	0.4970	0.8600
610	0.5200	0.5950	0.4170	0.7920
620	0.3880	0.4640	0.3200	0.6880
630	0.2945	0.3340	0.2570	0.5550
640	0.1890	0.2340	0.1760	0.3490
650	0.1082	0.1295	0.0925	0.1825
660	0.0615	0.0678	0.0550	0.0765
670	0.0321	0.0358	0.0299	0.0431

A comparison of the relative sensitivity functions obtained by the methods of heterochromatic flicker photometry (HFP), minimally distinct border (MDB), step-by-step brightness matching, and heterochromatic brightness matching. The data represent the averages of four observers.

Source: Data supplied by Wagner and Boynton, 1972.

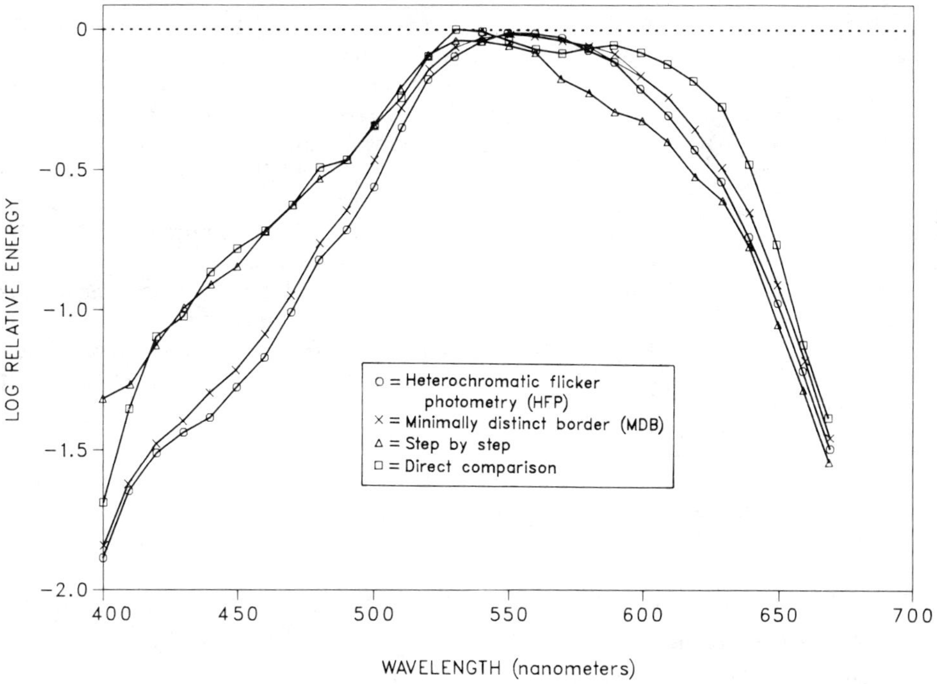

Figure 8.7. Logarithm of foveal spectral sensitivities for a 1° 40′ field. Data are average of four color-normal observers. The four techniques are heterochromatic flicker photometry (HFP), minimally distinct border (MDB), step-by-step brightness matching, and direct comparison brightness matching. The heterochromatic flicker photometric and minimally distinct border techniques yield similar spectral sensitivities. The two brightness-matching techniques yield spectral sensitivity functions which differ from each other and from those obtained by the HFP and MDB techniques. (From G. Wagner & R. M. Boynton, Comparison of four methods of heterochromatic photometry. *Journal of the Optical Society of America*, 1972, *65*. Reprinted with permission.)

sembling HFP are obtained (Bornstein & Marks, 1972; Ives, 1912). At higher luminance levels, the CFF functions become narrower than the HFP function (Bornstein & Marks, 1972). A technique based on minimizing apparent motion has been described by Anstis and Cavanagh (1983). Criterion reaction times have been used to estimate spectral sensitivity and yield functions resembling the HFP function (Lit, Young, & Shaffer, 1971; Pollack, 1968). Absolute threshold spectral sensitivities are broader than the HFP function, generally resembling brightness matching spectral sensitivities (CIE, 1978; Hsia & Graham, 1952; Sheppard, 1968). Threshold measures of spectral sensitivity are not additive (Guth, 1965; Guth, Donley, & Marrocco, 1969; Ikeda, 1963).

2.3. Photometry

2.3.1. Standard Spectral Luminous Efficiency Functions. In 1924 the Commission Internationale de l'Eclairage (CIE, 1926) adopted a standard luminous efficiency function, $V(\lambda)$. This function was based on averaged data from seven laboratories, primarily HFP data but also some step-by-step brightness matching data. Subsequently, it has been suggested that the standard luminous efficiency function underestimated true luminous efficiency at short wavelengths. Judd (1951b) proposed a revision of the $V(\lambda)$ function. The Judd revision does not have official status; the 1924 $V(\lambda)$ function remains the standard for photometry. However, the Judd function is widely used by theoreticians in color vision models.

In 1951 the CIE (1951) adopted a standard luminous efficiency function $V'(\lambda)$ for scotopic (dark-adapted) vision. This function was based on brightness matching and absolute threshold for the periphery of the dark-adapted eye of young observers. Table 8.6 shows tabulations of the two standard luminous efficiency functions $V(\lambda)$ and $V'(\lambda)$ adopted by the CIE, and Figure 8.9 (on page 8-13) shows logarithmic plots.

The $V(\lambda)$ function and Judd's (1951b) revision are characteristic of a field of 2° but are applicable for fields of less than 4°. In its study of the 10° color-matching functions (see Section 3), the CIE adopted a function representative of the luminous efficiency function for a 10° field. This function has never been officially adopted as a large-field standard observer for photometry but is a useful function in color modeling work. Table 8.7 (on page 8-13) includes values of the Judd revision and the CIE 10° luminous efficiency function; heterochromatic brightness functions are shown in Table 8.8 (on page 8-14).

2.3.2. The Photometric Units. Section 2.1 described the units used to specify radiant energy. Parallel sets of units used to specify luminous energy are called *photometric units*. Photometric energy is radiant energy modified by the luminous efficiency function of the standard observer. Corresponding to the quantities of radiant intensity, irradiance and radiance are the photometric quantities luminous intensity, illuminance, and luminance (Table 8.9, page 8-15).

With defined luminous efficiency functions $V(\lambda)$ and $V'(\lambda)$ for the standard observer, the luminous energy F_v (lumen) is related to the radiant energy P_e by two equations:

$$F_v = K_m \int P_e(\lambda) V(\lambda) d\lambda \ , \tag{12}$$

$$F_v' = K'_m \int P_e(\lambda) V'(\lambda) d\lambda \ , \tag{13}$$

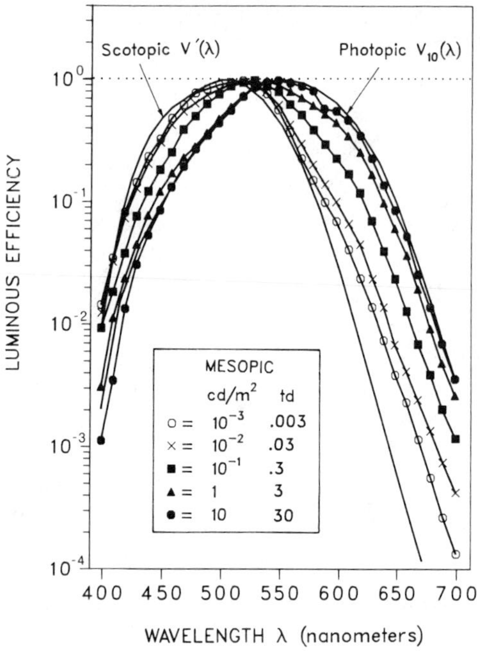

Figure 8.8. Mean mesopic luminous efficiency functions obtained by Kokoschka (1972) for three observers (aged 27 to 32) in a 9.5° bipartite field centrally viewed. The observers made direct heterochromatic brightness matches between quasi-monochromatic test stimuli and a 530-nm reference stimulus whose luminance was set at 10^{-3}, 10^{-2}, 10^{-1}, 1, and 10 $cd \cdot m^{-2}$ seen through a 3-mm artificial pupil. The heavy lines represent the standard scotopic luminous efficiency function $V'(\lambda)$ and the photopic $V_{10}(\lambda)$ function. With decreases in luminance, the spectral sensitivity function gradually shifts from the photopic to the scotopic function. (From G. Wyszecki & W. S. Stiles, *Color science: Concepts and methods, quantitative data and formulae* (2nd ed.), Copyright 1982 by John Wiley & Sons, Inc. Reprinted with permission.)

where K_m and K'_m are constants that relate (photopic and scotopic) lumens to watts. Equation (12) is applicable for photopic conditions of vision, Eq. (13) for scotopic levels of vision.

The unit of luminous intensity I_v (lumens · sr^{-1}) is called the *candela* (cd); that of illuminance E_v ($lm \cdot m^{-2}$) is called the *lux*; and that of luminance L_v ($lm \cdot m^{-2} sr^{-1}$) is called the candela per square meter ($cd \cdot m^{-2}$). Table 8.9 summarizes the relations between the radiometric and photometric quantities.

2.3.3. Obsolete Units. The need for photometry developed simultaneously in a variety of disciplines and in a number of nations. Photometric quantities in England and the United States were defined using the foot as the unit of measurement for distance. In continental Europe, photometric quantities were based on both the centimeter and the meter.

A further complication was that some units of luminance (e.g., the $cd \cdot m^{-2}$ and stilb) were derived in terms of candelas per unit area, while others (e.g., the lambert, millilambert, footlambert, and apostilb) were defined in terms of lumens per unit area. Conversion to lumens per unit area was obtained using the concept of the perfect lambertian emitter; it is possible to calculate the flux per unit area of a perfect lambertian emitter of known intensity. A perfect lambertian emitter with a luminous intensity of I candelas will have a luminous flux of πI lumens. The lambert, millilambert, footlambert, and apostilb all contain the factor $1/\pi$ in their definition.

Given the consideration that luminance is the areal density of luminous intensity, the unit of $cd \cdot m^{-2}$ ($lm \cdot sr^{-1} \cdot m^{-2}$) is the one which parallels luminous intensity of a point source measured in $lm \cdot sr^{-1}$ (Teele, 1965). The rationale for the conversion to the form of $lm \cdot m^{-2}$ was to relate illuminance to luminance (Teele, 1965). A perfectly diffusing and transmitting surface receiving illumination of 1 lux will have a luminance of $1/\pi$ $cd \cdot m^{-2}$ (or 1 apostilb in the old notation). Similarly, a perfectly diffusing and transmitting surface receiving illuminance of 1 footcandle will have a luminance of $1/\pi$ $cd \cdot f^{-2}$ (or 1 footlambert in the old notation).

An array of terms for expressing luminance was developed, and photometric instruments were calibrated in these units. Table 8.10 (on page 8-15) provides conversion factors with which to convert from obsolete to accepted SI units.

Table 8.6. Spectral Luminous Efficiencies for the CIE Standard Observers

	Relative Efficiency		Log Relative Efficiency	
Wavelength	$V(\lambda)$	$V'(\lambda)$	$V(\lambda)$	$V'(\lambda)$
380	0.000039	0.000589	−4.41	−3.23
390	0.000120	0.00221	−3.92	−2.66
400	0.000396	0.00929	−3.40	−2.03
410	0.00121	0.0348	−2.92	−1.46
420	0.00400	0.0966	−2.40	−1.01
430	0.0116	0.1998	−1.93	−0.79
440	0.023	0.328	−1.64	−0.48
450	0.038	0.455	−1.42	−0.34
460	0.060	0.567	−1.22	−0.25
470	0.091	0.676	−1.04	−0.17
480	0.129	0.793	−0.89	−0.17
490	0.208	0.904	−0.68	−0.04
500	0.323	0.982	−0.49	−0.01
510	0.503	0.997	−0.30	−0.00
520	0.710	0.935	−0.15	−0.03
530	0.862	0.811	−0.06	−0.09
540	0.954	0.650	−0.02	−0.19
550	0.995	0.481	−0.00	−0.32
560	0.995	0.329	−0.00	−0.48
570	0.952	0.208	−0.02	−0.68
580	0.870	0.121	−0.06	−0.92
590	0.757	0.0655	−0.12	−1.18
600	0.631	0.0332	−0.20	−1.48
610	0.503	0.0159	−0.30	−1.80
620	0.381	0.00737	−0.42	−2.13
630	0.265	0.00334	−0.57	−2.48
640	0.175	0.00150	−0.76	−2.82
650	0.107	0.000677	−0.97	−3.17
660	0.061	0.000313	−1.21	−3.50
670	0.032	0.000148	−1.49	−3.83
680	0.017	0.0000715	−1.77	−4.15
690	0.00821	0.0000353	−2.09	−4.45
700	0.00410	0.0000178	−2.39	−4.75

The V(λ) function represents the spectral luminous efficiency of the standard observer for phototopic vision. The function was based on averaged data from seven laboratories and was primarily based on HFP data. The V′(λ) function represents the spectral luminous efficiency of the standard observer for scotopic vision. The function was based on brightness matching and absolute threshold for the periphery of the dark-adapted eye of young observers. The tables list luminous efficiency values (both arithmetic and logarithmic) between 380 and 700 in 10-nm steps. Complete values in 1-nm steps are available in Wyszecki and Stiles, 1982.

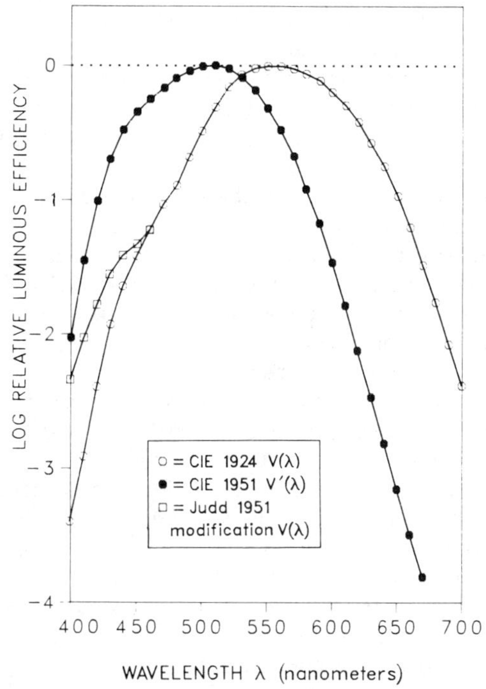

Figure 8.9. Luminous efficiency functions of CIE 1924 standard observer $V(\lambda)$ for photopic vision, CIE 1951 standard observer $V'(\lambda)$ for scotopic vision, and Judd's (1951b) modification of the CIE 1924 $V(\lambda)$ function in the blue end of the spectrum. The CIE 1924 $V(\lambda)$ and Judd 1951 modified $V(\lambda)$ are for a 2° foveally fixated field. The CIE 1951 $V'(\lambda)$ is for a completely dark-adapted observer under the age of 30.

2.3.4. Retinal Illuminance. The photometric units are derived by weighting the radiant units by the standard luminous efficiency function. However, the amount of light arriving at the retina of a human observer is dependent not only on the luminance of the viewed object but also on characteristics of the observer such as the diameter of the pupil.

The concept of retinal illuminance was introduced to take account of the effective illumination on the retina. The troland (td) T is the standard unit of retinal illuminance:

$$T = L_v \cdot A , \tag{14}$$

where L_v is the luminance in cd·m^{-2} and A is the area of the pupil in mm^2. For example, a 100 cd·m^{-2} surface viewed through a 2-mm-diameter pupil would have a retinal illuminance of 314 td. Frequently, an artificial pupil is placed in front of a subject's eye to maintain a constant specifiable retinal illuminance. In some optical systems (e.g., Maxwellian view), other techniques may be used to limit the size of the effective entrance pupil. When the natural pupil is used, an approximate value for retinal illuminance can be made by estimating the size of the pupil for the luminance level employed (see Chapter 5 by Hood and Finkelstein).

Several techniques for calibration of Maxwellian view optical systems have been described (Graham & Landis, 1959; Nygaard & Frumkes, 1982; Westheimer, 1966). One method (Nygaard & Frumkes, 1982; Westheimer, 1966) uses illuminance rather than luminance. The troland value is calculated from the equation

$$T_d = (E_v d^2) 10^6 , \tag{15}$$

where E_v is the illuminance in lux and d, measured in meters, is the distance from the exit aperture to the photometer surface. It is important that the photometer surface is totally illuminated and that the distance of the photometer from the exit aperture is at least 10 times the diameter of the exit aperture.

Another factor affecting the total effective retinal illuminance is the directional sensitivity of the cone photoreceptors (the Stiles-Crawford effect). The luminous efficiency of a light beam is reduced by 50% when the light rays are directed through the pupillary aperture at ±2.5 mm from the optic axis. The calculation of retinal illuminance by Eq. (14) is thus in error for pupil sizes greater than 2 mm. Equations to calculate effective retinal illuminance, called the *effective troland*, for large natural or dilated pupils have been derived (de Groot & Gebhard, 1952; Le Grand, 1948, 1968) for a range of luminance levels.

Table 8.7. Spectral Luminous Efficiencies for the CIE Supplementary Observer (10°)

	Relative Efficiency		Log Relative Efficiency	
Wavelength	Judd 2°	10°	Judd 2°	10°
380	0.0004	0.000014	−2.40	−4.85
390	0.0015	0.000283	−2.82	−3.55
400	0.0045	0.0020	−2.35	−2.70
410	0.0093	0.0088	−2.03	−2.06
420	0.0175	0.0214	−1.76	−1.67
430	0.0273	0.0387	−1.56	−1.41
440	0.0379	0.0621	−1.42	−1.21
450	0.0468	0.0895	−1.33	−1.05
460	0.060	0.1282	−1.22	−0.89
470	0.091	0.1852	−1.04	−0.73
480	0.129	0.2536	−0.89	−0.60
490	0.208	0.3391	−0.68	−0.47
500	0.323	0.4608	−0.49	−0.34
510	0.503	0.6067	−0.30	−0.22
520	0.710	0.7618	−0.15	−0.12
530	0.862	0.8752	−0.06	−0.06
540	0.954	0.9620	−0.02	−0.02
550	0.995	0.9918	−0.00	−0.00
560	0.995	0.9973	−0.00	−0.00
570	0.952	0.9556	−0.02	−0.02
580	0.870	0.8689	−0.06	−0.06
590	0.757	0.7774	−0.12	−1.11
600	0.631	0.6583	−0.20	−0.18
610	0.503	0.5280	−0.30	−0.28
620	0.381	0.3981	−0.42	−0.40
630	0.265	0.2835	−0.57	−0.55
640	0.175	0.1798	−0.76	−0.75
650	0.107	0.1076	−0.97	−0.97
660	0.061	0.0603	−1.21	−1.22
670	0.032	0.0318	−1.49	−1.50
680	0.017	0.0159	−1.77	−1.80
690	0.00821	0.0077	−2.09	−2.11
700	0.00410	0.00372	−2.39	−2.43

The Judd function is a revision of the CIE standard observer (Table 8.6) and incorporates corrections to wavelengths below 460 nm based on additional data reviewed by Judd (1951b). The CIE supplementary observer is based on large field color matching and is representative of luminous efficiency for photopic vision for a 10° field.

Source: Data supplied by Wyszecki and Stiles, 1982.

Table 8.8. Spectral Luminous Efficiency for Brightness Matching

	Relative Efficiency		Log Relative Efficiency	
Wavelength	CIE (1978)	Ikeda et al. (1982)	CIE (1978)	Ikeda et al. (1982)
400	0.019	0.0085113	−1.72	−2.07
410	0.032	0.0194984	−1.49	−1.71
420	0.042	0.0398107	−1.38	−1.40
430	0.076	0.0602559	−1.12	−1.22
440	0.103	0.0851138	−0.99	−1.07
450	0.135	0.1047128	−0.87	−0.98
460	0.166	0.1318256	−0.78	−0.88
470	0.214		−0.67	−0.73
480	0.294	0.2511886	−0.53	−0.60
490	0.359	0.3162277	−0.44	−0.50
500	0.523	0.4570881	−0.28	−0.34
510	0.698	0.7079457	−0.16	−0.15
520	0.987	0.9772372	−0.01	−0.01
530	1.103	1.1481536	−0.04	−0.06
540	1.200	1.2302687	−0.08	−0.09
550	1.179	1.2302687	−0.07	−0.09
560	1.075	1.1220184	−0.03	−0.05
570	1.000	1.0000000	−0.00	−0.00
580	0.967	0.9772372	−0.01	−0.01
590	0.965	0.9549925	−0.01	−0.02
600	0.895	0.8709635	−0.05	−0.06
610	0.782	0.7413102	−0.11	−0.13
620	0.651	0.6025595	−0.19	−0.22
630	0.494	0.4466835	−0.31	−0.35
640	0.357		−0.45	−0.51
650	0.184	0.1862087	−0.73	−0.73
660	0.093	0.1071519	−1.03	−0.97
670	0.049	0.0588843	−1.31	−1.23
680	0.028	0.0316227	−1.55	−1.50
690	0.014	0.0147910	−1.85	−1.83
700	0.007	0.0083176	−2.15	−2.08

The functions represent brightness matching for photopic vision and are broader in shape than the CIE standard observer (Table 8.6). The CIE (1978) function is the averaged data of several laboratories; Ikeda, Yaguchi, and Sagawa (1982) is more recent.

It is also possible to derive the number of trolands N from knowledge of the rate R of quanta emanating within a fixed area (see Boynton, 1979):

$$N(\text{td}) = \left[\frac{(8 \times 10^{-7})}{V(\lambda)}\right] \cdot R(\text{photons} \cdot \text{sec}^{-1} \cdot \text{deg}^{-2}) \ . \quad (16)$$

At a wavelength of 555 nm, the energy of one photon is 3.58×10^{-19} J (see Eq. (4)).

2.4. Current Problems in Photometry

A visual photometer contains a comparison field, and measurement is accomplished by making a direct brightness match between the comparison and the field to be measured. For measurement of illuminance, the match is made to a test plate of known spectral reflectance. For precise measurement, the comparison light is itself calibrated against a working standard traceable to a national standards laboratory (e.g., in the United States, the National Bureau of Standards). The comparison light contained within the photometer is usually an incandescent lamp run at a specified current. Its appearance is yellowish-white but, in some instruments, may be modified by color filters.

In a photoelectric device, current is generated when light is incident on a photosensitive surface. The spectral response of the photosensitive surface is corrected, by combinations of filters, to approximate that of the CIE standard observer.

When two photometric fields are identical in spectral emittance and thus in visual appearance (homochromatic), a visual match may be made with an error of less than 1%. Problems arise in photometry because measurements are not purely physical. The definition of light and luminance encompasses the visual system and is essentially circular. The types of situations causing problems include (1) measurement of narrow band sources, (2) measurement of fields larger than 2°, (3) measurement at mesopic levels of illumination (between 10^{-3} and 3 cd·m^{-2}). A subcommittee of the CIE recently made recommendations useful in daily application (CIE, 1978). Briefly summarized, difficulties arise because the CIE 1924 standard luminous efficiency function $V(\lambda)$ has errors, notably at short wavelengths, the CIE 1924 standard luminous efficiency function may be used inappropriately, and the assumption of Abney's law may not always be appropriate.

2.4.1. Brightness of Narrow-Band Sources.

The luminance of a narrow-band illuminant can be assessed using IIFP or MDB followed by photometry of the white standard. Filter characteristics of photoelectric photometers should be carefully checked before a direct photoelectric measurement of a narrow-band field is attempted. It should be noted that the luminance obtained will not predict the apparent brightness of the narrow-band light. If brightness is the measurement of interest, it is necessary either to correct the measurement by the difference in brightness matching and HFP (see Table 8.5) or to use equations derived from color vision models (CIE, 1978). Guth and colleagues (Guth, Donley, & Marrocco, 1969; Guth & Lodge, 1973) proposed one such formula to predict brightness at threshold L^{**}:

$$L^{**} = (A^2 + T^2 + D^2)^{1/2} \ , \quad (17)$$

where

$$A(\lambda) = .954\bar{y}(\lambda) + 0.010\bar{z}(\lambda) \ , \quad (18)$$

$$T(\lambda) = .799\bar{x}(\lambda) + 0.646\bar{y}(\lambda) - 0.167\bar{z}(\lambda) \ , \quad (19)$$

$$D(\lambda) = - 0.058\bar{y}(\lambda) + 0.030\bar{z}(\lambda) \ . \quad (20)$$

In these equations $\bar{x}(\lambda)$, $\bar{y}(\lambda)$, and $\bar{z}(\lambda)$ are the color-matching functions of the CIE standard colorimetric observer (see Section 3). The Guth theory is discussed further in Section 5. Ikeda, Yaguchi, and Sagawa (1982) have proposed a formula:

$$\left[\int\left(\frac{L_{e\lambda}}{L_b}\right)\bar{a}_\lambda d\lambda\right]^2 + \left[\int\left(\frac{L_{e\lambda}}{b}\right)\bar{c}_{1\lambda} d\lambda\right]^{1.28} + \left[\int\left(\frac{L_{e\lambda}}{L_b}\right)\bar{c}_{2\lambda} d\lambda\right]^{.72} = 1 \ , \quad (21)$$

where $L_{e\lambda}$ is the spectral distribution of the light, L_b is its brightness, and

Table 8.9. Photometric Terms Corresponding to the Radiometric Terms

Radiometric Term	Photometric Term	Symbol	Unit
Radiant flux	Luminous flux	F_v	lumen (lm)
Radiant intensity	Luminous intensity	I_v	candela (cd) = $1\text{m}\cdot\text{sr}^{-1}$
Irradiance	Illuminance	E_v	lux ($\text{m}\cdot\text{m}^{-2}$)
Radiance	Luminance	L_v	candela per square meter ($\text{cd}\cdot\text{m}^{-2}$) = $\text{lm}\cdot\text{sr}^{-2}\cdot\text{m}^{-2}$

$$\bar{a}(\lambda) = 1.000\,\bar{y}_j(\lambda)\,, \tag{22}$$

$$\bar{c}_1(\lambda) = 0.758\bar{x}_j(\lambda) - 0.736\bar{y}_j(\lambda) - 0.156\bar{z}_j(\lambda)\,, \tag{23}$$

$$\bar{c}_2(\lambda) = 0.024\bar{y}_j(\lambda) - 0.029\bar{z}_j(\lambda)\,, \tag{24}$$

where $\bar{x}$, $\bar{y}$, and $\bar{z}$ are the Judd (1951b) color-matching functions (Section 3.4).

In the case of equienergy monochromatic lights, the equation reduces to

$$\left[\frac{\bar{a}(\lambda)}{L_b}\right]^2 + \left[\frac{\bar{c}_1(\lambda)}{L_b}\right]^{1.28} + \left[\frac{\bar{c}_2(\lambda)}{L_b}\right]^{.72} = 1\,. \tag{25}$$

This formula is similar to the Guth formulation in that brightness represents a sum of a luminance term $\bar{a}(\lambda)$ and two chromatic terms $\bar{c}_1(\lambda)$ and $\bar{c}_2(\lambda)$. However, the chromatic terms are not squared. The Ikeda, Yaguchi, and Sagawa (1982) formulation provides a good fit to their data.

2.4.2. Measurement of Large Fields. The CIE has never officially adopted a large-field photometric system. However, the luminosity function $Y_{10}(\lambda)$ does exist in the large-field colorimetric system. Even if this $Y_{10}(\lambda)$ is used, there are the same problems of measurement that exist for small fields. Spectral sensitivities of 10° for brightness matching have recently been published (Ikeda, Yaguchi, & Sagawa, 1982; Palmer, 1985).

2.4.3. Mesopic Photometry. Photometry at mesopic levels of illumination offers a continuing challenge. Data are available for brightness matching (Ikeda & Shimozono, 1981; Kinney, 1955, 1958, 1964; Palmer, 1967, 1968; Walters & Wright, 1943) and a grating acuity criterion (Brown, Phares, & Fletcher, 1960). One computational procedure provisionally recommended by the CIE (1972) was based on data and analysis of Palmer (1967, 1968). This technique assesses scotopic S and photopic P lu-

Table 8.10. Conversion Factors to Obtain SI Units

Conversion Factors for Illuminance

Unit	Geometry	Conversion Factor to Give Lux
Lux	$1\ \text{lm}\cdot\text{m}^{-2}$	1
Phot	$1\ \text{lm}\cdot\text{cm}^{-2}$	10,000
Milliphot	$10^{-3}\ \text{lm}\cdot\text{cm}^{-2}$	10
Footcandle	$1\ \text{lm}\cdot\text{ft}^{-2}$	10.76

Conversion Factors for Luminance

Unit	Geometry	Conversion Factor to Give $\text{cd}\cdot\text{m}^{-2}$
Candela per square meter (nit or meter-candle)	$1\ \text{cd}\cdot\text{m}^{-2}$	1
Lambert	$(1/\pi)\ \text{cd}\cdot\text{cm}^{-2}$	3,183
Millilambert	$10^{-3}\ (1/\pi)\ \text{cd}\cdot\text{cm}^{-2}$	3.183
Stilb	$1\ \text{cd}\cdot\text{cm}^{-2}$	10,000
Apostilb	$(1/\pi)\ \text{cd}\cdot\text{m}^{-2}$	0.3183
Footlambert	$(1/\pi)\ \text{cd}\cdot\text{ft}^{-2}$	3.426

Conversion factors are given to obtain SI units from obsolete units. The quantity of obsolete units is multiplied by the conversion factor listed in the right-hand column. For example, supposing a measurement yielded a value of 20 millilamberts, this quantity would be multiplied by 3.183 to give 63.66 $\text{cd}\cdot\text{m}^{-2}$. The table can also be used to convert between different obsolete units. To derive the conversion factors for two units listed in the left-hand column: 3.426 × footlambert = 1 $\text{cd}\cdot\text{m}^{-2}$ = 3.183 × millilambert, or 1 millilambert = 3.426/3.183 × footlambert = 1.076 × footlambert.

Source: From J. Pokorny, V. C. Smith, G. Verriest, and A. J. L. C. Pinckers, *Congenital and acquired color defects*, Grune & Stratton, 1979. Reprinted with permission.

minances independently using $V'(\lambda)$ and $V_{10}(\lambda)$. These values are combined to predict L_v, the mesopic brightness, by the formula

$$L_v = \frac{(0.06S + P^2)}{(0.06 + P)} \text{ cd}\cdot\text{m}^{-2} . \qquad (26)$$

This formula is adequate for low and moderate mesopic levels. Other formulations are available (Ikeda & Shimozono, 1981; Kokoschka, 1972), but there is no recommended technique for mesopic photometry at present. The Ikeda and Shimozono (1981) formula is

$$\frac{L_v}{10^{Mv}} = \left[\left(\frac{S_s}{10^{Mr}}\right)^a\right]\left[\left(\frac{S_p}{10^{Mp}}\right)^b\right], \qquad (27)$$

where L_v is the brightness-matching function, S_s is the (rod) brightness-matching function obtained at 0.01 td, and S_p is the (cone) brightness-matching function at 100 td. The values Mv, Mr, and Mp are the means of the respective sensitivity curves calculated in logarithms. Values for a and b were found by least squares. The original data are shown in Figure 8.10, together with the fits of Eq. (27) and the variation in coefficients a and b as a function of log retinal illuminance. It is of note that Ikeda and Shimozono (1981) chose to fit their data with a product of the photopic and scotopic functions. In threshold studies it is usual to sum sensitivities.

3. COLOR MIXTURE

A human observer looking at a colored object has no way of knowing from its appearance the spectral composition of the

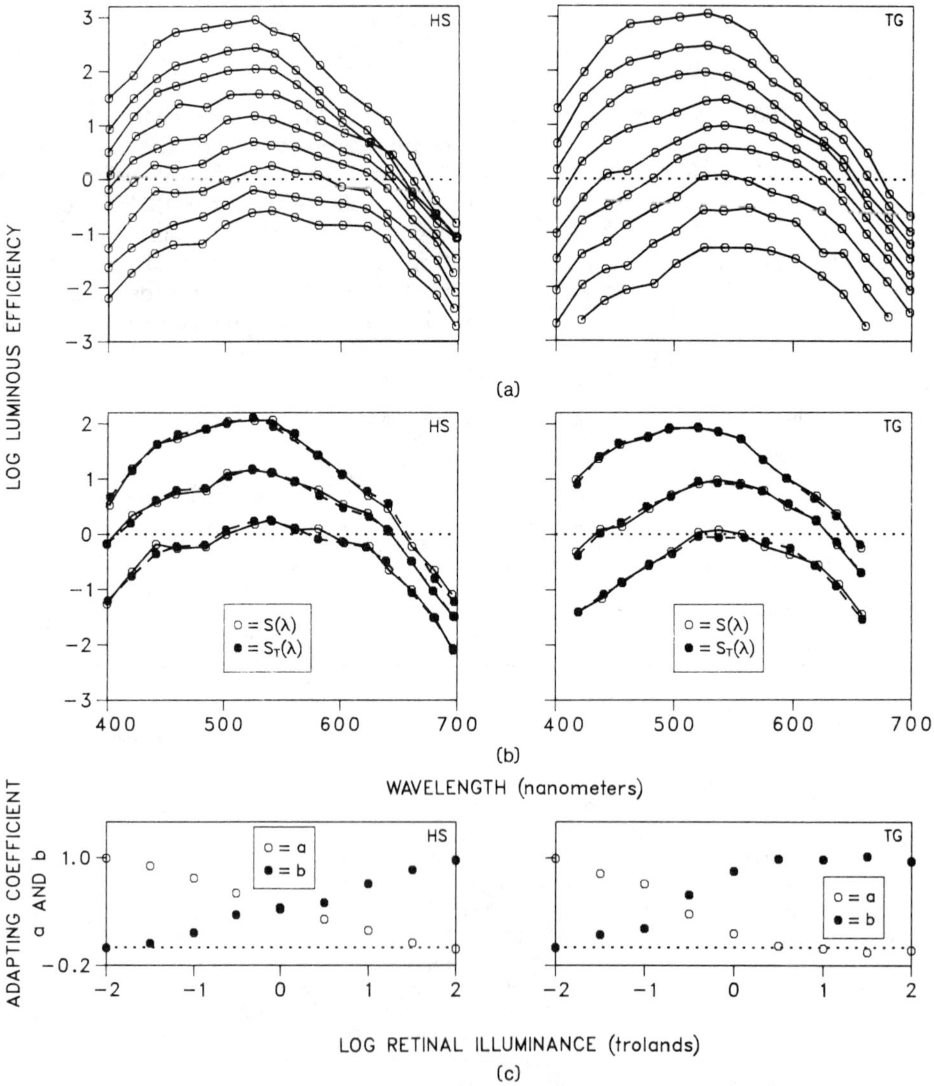

Figure 8.10. Experimental and theoretical mesopic luminous efficiency functions. (a) Luminous efficiency functions at nine retinal illuminance levels between 0.01 (top curve) and 100 (bottom curve) photopic trolands. Left, subject HS; right, subject TG. The data are brightness matches to a white reference for a 10° bipartite field. (b) Comparison of the experimental luminous efficiency functions $S(\lambda)$ with the theoretical luminous efficiency function $S_T(\lambda)$, defined by Eq. (26), at three retinal illuminance levels, 0.1, 1, and 10 photopic trolands. Left, subject HS; right, subject TG. (c) Adapting coefficients a and b as a function of the retinal illuminance level from subjects HS and TG. (From M. Ikeda & H. Shimozono, Mesopic luminous-efficiency functions, *Journal of the Optical Society of America*, 1981, *71*. Reprinted with permission.)

physical stimulus. In fact, identical-appearing stimuli may have radically different spectral content. Colorimetry is an experimental technique that involves simultaneous viewing of two fields, with experimental control over the spectral content of each. The observer's task is to make two fields appear identical. The aim of colorimetry is to provide an economical system of color measurement and specification based on the concept of equivalent-appearing stimuli.

3.1. Principles and Procedures

3.1.1. Metamers. In a typical color-matching experiment (Section 3.1.3) the two halves of the bipartite field contain dissimilar spectral radiations which are nevertheless seen as the same by the observer; they are called *metameric lights*. Isomeric lights, a subset of metamers, are equivalent-appearing lights of identical spectral composition. Metamers have three important properties that allow treatment of color mixture as a linear system, usually attributed to Grassmann (1854):

1. *The Additive Property.* When a radiation is identically added to both sides of a color mixture field, the metamerism is unchanged.
2. *The Scalar Property.* When both sides of the color mixture field are increased or decreased in radiance, metamerism is unchanged.
3. *The Associative Property.* A metameric mixture may be substituted for a field without changing the metameric property of the color fields. Thus if a spectral yellow is metameric to a mixture of spectral red and green, the mixture may be interchanged in any match that contains the spectral yellow.

From these properties it is deduced that a color match is invariant under a variety of experimental conditions that may alter the appearance of the matching fields. If an observer looks at a metameric match to white after preexposure to a moderately bright green field, the two halves of the field will appear the same reddish hue. Likewise, if a chromatic surround is placed around the matching fields, they both will change in appearance, but the metamerism still holds.

3.1.2. Trichromacy. A fundamental property of normal human color vision is that it is possible to find a metamer for any color by variation of only three primary colors. The terms *trichromat* (i.e., a three-color mixer) and *trichromacy* come from this property of normal vision. The importance of trichromacy is not in prediction of hue appearance but in prediction of equivalent hues.

There is wide freedom in the choice of primaries. For spectral colors, the primaries and the spectral hue will be arranged pairwise in the bipartite field so that a mixture of the spectral hue and one primary match a mixture of the two other primaries. A formal requirement is that one primary cannot be metameric to a mixture of the other two. In practice, it is desirable that the primaries be spectrally separated as much as possible. Apart from these considerations, the choice of primaries is dictated largely by experimental convenience. Primaries may or may not themselves be spectral.

3.1.3. The Color-Matching Experiment. Basic color-matching data were reported by Wright (1929, 1946), Guild (1931), and Stiles (1955). Wright (1929) used a 2° foveal bipartite field and spectral primaries at 650 (R), 530 (G), and 460 nm (B). The spectral wavelengths were scanned in 10- or 20-nm steps between 410 and 700 nm. At each step, the test and primary lights were arranged pairwise, the primary amounts were adjusted to obtain a color match, and the amounts of each primary at the match were recorded. These mixtures are represented as linear equations. Taking 490 nm as an example:

$$a_{490}490 \ + \ a_R R \ \equiv \ a_G G \ + \ a_B B \ , \tag{28}$$

where $\equiv$ reads matches and $+$ means mixture. This equation may be rewritten as an algebraic equation in terms only of the variable wavelength:

$$a_{490}490 \ \equiv \ -a_R R \ + \ a_G G \ + \ a_B B \ , \tag{29}$$

where a_R, a_G, and a_B represent the amount of the primaries R, G, and B and are called the tristimulus values. Every spectral wavelength can be specified in terms of the three primaries, with one of the three being negative or zero.

3.2. Representation of Data

There are many ways to specify the unit of measurement for the primaries. For example, both radiometric units (Stiles, 1955; Stiles & Burch, 1959) and photometric units (Wright, 1946) have been used. In the most usual method, the units for the primaries are normalized at the match to white. In this case, the amounts necessary for the three primaries (all together on one side of the colorimetric field) to match a specified white are taken as unit amounts of primary. This normalization may be thought of as reflecting the relative "coloring power" of each primary in rendering the match to white.

The amounts of the primary units (tristimulus values) which match each spectral wavelength are usually plotted for an equal-energy spectrum (i.e., equal energy of each test wavelength). The tristimulus values define a set of functions called color-matching functions. For a set of three primaries, identified as P_1, P_2, and P_3, the color-matching functions are identified as $\bar{p}_1(\lambda)$, $\bar{p}_2(\lambda)$, and $\bar{p}_3(\lambda)$. A variety of other terms have been used in the past (see Graham, 1965). Figure 8.11 shows the Wright (1929) color-matching functions normalized to his source S (a white of color temperature 4800 K) and plotted for the equal-energy spectrum. Note that P_1 is the 650-nm primary, P_2 the 530-nm primary, and P_3 the 460-nm primary.

3.2.1. Color Spaces. The data of a color-matching experiment can be expressed in terms of vectors in a three-dimensional space (Schrödinger, 1920). For simplicity let us consider representation of the Wright (1929) data in a Cartesian coordinate system. In Figure 8.12 the coordinates are rectangular; that is, they are mutually perpendicular. Quantities of each of the primaries are represented by distances from the origin O. The location of a mixture of the three primaries is represented by the point P. This location is calculated by first calculating the vector $\mathbf{V}'$ from a_r, a_g in the P_{650}, P_{530} plane and then calculating the vector $\mathbf{V}$ between $\mathbf{V}'$ and the orthogonally located a_b. In a like manner, the results of all physically realizable mixtures of the three primaries may be calculated. Figure 8.13 (on page 8-19) shows the Wright (1929) color mixture data plotted in a Cartesian coordinate system with the units of the three primary vectors expressed in terms of the normalization to white. Other conventions sometimes used to display chromaticity spaces utilize oblique, rather than right, angles.

3.2.2. Color Planes (Chromaticity Diagrams). Color planes are two-dimensional representations of the results of a color mixture experiment. In the three-dimensional color space, we

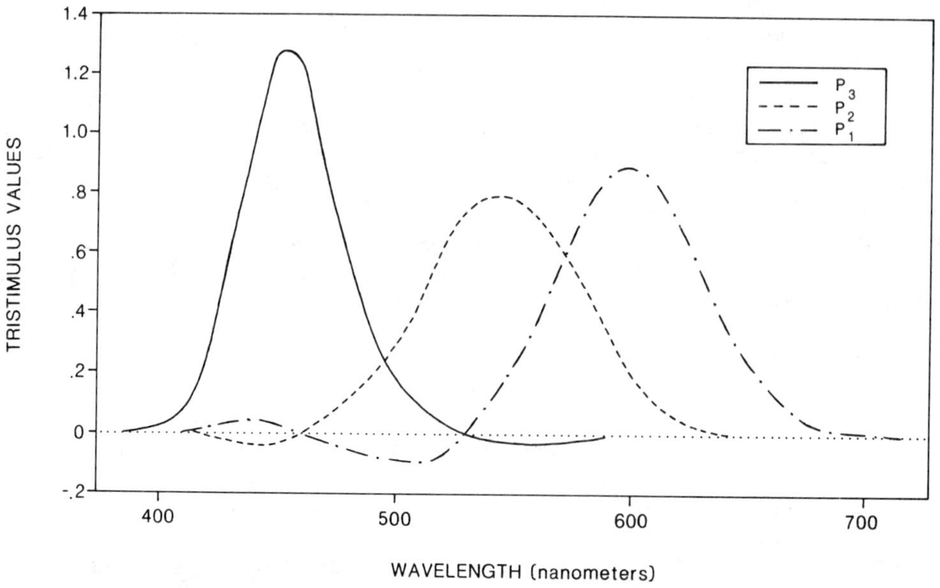

Figure 8.11. Tristimulus values for the equal-energy spectrum, using primaries of 650 (P_1), 530 (P_2), and 460 (P_3) nm. The primaries are normalized so that equal amounts of P_1, P_2, and P_3 match a specified white (Wright's source *S*, a white with a color temperature of 4800 K). The graph shows the amounts of each of the three primaries required to match equal-energy spectral stimuli. (From W. D. Wright, *Research on normal and defective colour vision*, Kimpton Medical Publishers, 1946. Reprinted with permission.)

defined the result of a color mixture by the units a_r, a_g, and a_b. From Grassmann's second law (scalar property), it is the ratio of the primaries that determines the direction of the vector in color space. If we wish to express color mixture in a plane, it is the proportional lengths and directions of vectors that need to be preserved. This is accomplished by converting the tristimulus values into a form where the sum of the three always equals unity:

$$p_1(\lambda) = \frac{\overline{p}_1(\lambda)}{\overline{p}_1(\lambda) + \overline{p}_2(\lambda) + \overline{p}_3(\lambda)]}, \quad (30)$$

$$p_2(\lambda) = \frac{\overline{p}_2(\lambda)}{\overline{p}_1(\lambda) + \overline{p}_2(\lambda) + \overline{p}_3(\lambda)]}, \quad (31)$$

$$p_3(\lambda) = \frac{\overline{p}_3(\lambda)}{\overline{p}_1(\lambda) + \overline{p}_2(\lambda) + \overline{p}_3(\lambda)]}. \quad (32)$$

For the color-matching functions, $\overline{p}_1(\lambda)$, $\overline{p}_2(\lambda)$, and $\overline{p}_3(\lambda)$, the coefficients p_1, p_2, and p_3 are called the *chromaticity coordinates* (or *trichromatic coefficients*). If p_1 is plotted against p_2 on Cartesian axes, the values of the spectral wavelength fall on a horseshoe-shaped curve called the *spectrum locus*. Figure 8.14 (on page 8-20) shows the Wright (1929) average data plotted in this manner.

3.2.3. WDW Normalization. W. D. Wright devised an important method of normalization now termed the *WDW system.* Two wavelengths, one in the yellow (Wright, 1929, used 582.5 nm) and one in the blue-green (Wright, 1929, used 494 nm), are chosen as normalizing wavelengths. The amount of the P_1 primary is set equal to the P_2 primary at the first normalizing wavelength, and the amount of the P_3 primary is set equal to the P_2 primary at the second. This normalization can be achieved physically in the apparatus (by either adjusting slits or adding filters to P_1 and P_3). Alternatively, the normalization is performed algebraically by weighting the various P_1 primary amounts by the factor $\overline{p}_2/\overline{p}_1$ at 582.5 nm and the various P_3 primary amounts by the factor $\overline{p}_2/\overline{p}_3$ at 494 nm and recomputing trichromatic coefficients. Figure 8.15 (on page 8-21) shows the coefficients and chromaticity diagrams for the Wright (1929) observers. The ranges of the coefficients for the 10 observers are constricted at the normalization wavelengths and at the primaries but spread out at other wavelengths. In the chromaticity diagram, the coefficients for the 4800 K white are now spread out for the different observers. In comparison, the coefficients of Figure 8.14 are all normalized to the white, and all subjects occupy the same locus for "white."

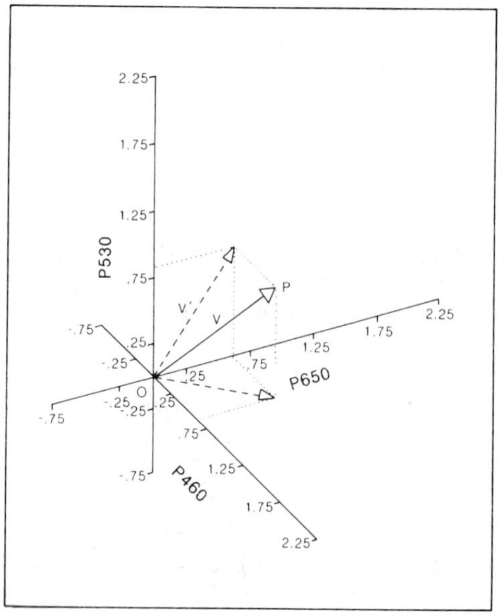

Figure 8.12. Representation of color mixture in a rectangular coordinate system. The three primaries form the three axes and the color *P* is represented by the vector **V**.

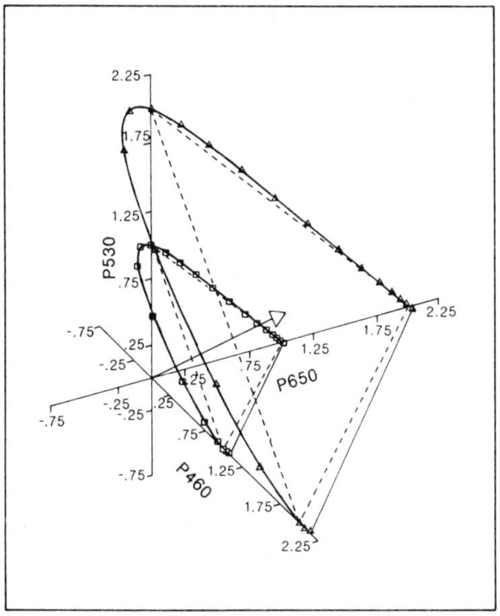

Figure 8.13. The spectrum locus represented in a rectangular coordinate system. Wright's (1929) color mixture data have been normalized so that equal amounts of P_{460}, P_{530}, and P_{650} match 4800 K white. The two planes represent two different radiance levels. The dashed lines enclose the region of color space that can be realized by summing various proportions of the primaries. The horseshoe-shaped curves represent the spectrum locus. Experimentally, this is realized by adding one of the primaries to the spectral light to be matched (Section 3.1.3). The arrowhead of the white vector is in the higher-radiance chromaticity plane.

The importance of the WDW normalization is that it separates interobserver variance caused by receptor variation from variance caused by prereceptor variation. It may be shown algebraically that in this system interobserver variation greater than experimental error must be attributed to interobserver differences in the spectral absorption characteristics of the visual photoreceptors. Individual variation in the lens and macular pigment shows its effect in the distribution of the coefficients for white (Wright, 1946; Wyszecki & Stiles, 1982).

3.3. Linear Transformation of Color-Matching Data

The observation (Grassmann, 1854) that color mixture data have the associative property allows expression of a set of data in sets of primaries other than those used in a particular experiment. For example, if we wished to substitute 490 nm for 460 nm as the blue primary for the Wright (1929) data set, we can rearrange Eq. (28) to read:

$$a_B B \equiv a490 + a_R R - a_G G . \tag{33}$$

If we substitute the right side of Eq. (33) for $a_B B$ in the color mixture equations, the derived tristimulus values would all be expressed in terms of R, G, and 490 nm. More generally, we can specify a transformation from one set of primaries to another by a general homogeneous linear transformation

$$R' = a_{11}R + a_{12}G + a_{13}B , \tag{34}$$

$$G' = a_{21}R + a_{22}G + a_{23}B , \tag{35}$$

$$B' = a_{31}R + a_{32}G + a_{33}B . \tag{36}$$

The only constraint is that the determinant d must differ from zero.

$$d = \begin{vmatrix} a_{11} & a_{12} & a_{13} \\ a_{21} & a_{22} & a_{23} \\ a_{31} & a_{32} & a_{33} \end{vmatrix} \neq 0 . \tag{37}$$

If this condition is fulfilled, then we can find the inverse transformation of Eqs. (34) to (36):

$$R = b_{11}R' + b_{12}G' + b_{13}B' , \tag{38}$$

$$G = b_{21}R' + b_{22}G' + b_{23}B' . \tag{39}$$

$$B = b_{31}R' + b_{32}G' + b_{33}B' . \tag{40}$$

Any point in the RGB space is represented in the $R'G'B'$ space and conversely. The properties of a homogeneous linear transformation (also called an *affine transformation*) include straight lines remain straight after transformation, parallel lines remain parallel; and plane surfaces remain plane surfaces.

A color plane derived from a color space automatically includes the properties of that space. However, the transformation is projective, rather than affine. Straight lines remain straight, but parallel lines need not remain parallel.

As can be seen from Eqs. (34) to (36), nine constants completely determine the transformation of color mixture data. In the color space, six determine the new axes, three the units along the three axes. Such transformations have been used for widely diverse purposes including (1) comparison of data sets, (2) derivation of an expression of color mixture data in a coordinate system in which the primaries represent the cone spectral sensitivities, (3) attempts to derive color planes in which equal vector lengths represent equal steps in discriminability, and (4) derivation of color planes to represent the relevant direction of the physiological transformation from receptor sensitivities to opponent channel sensitivities.

3.4. CIE Standard Colorimetric Observers

3.4.1. *RGB* and *XYZ* Systems. The value of a standard observer for colorimetry was recognized as it had been for photometry. A CIE standard observer for colorimetry was defined in 1931 (CIE, 1932); the RGB and XYZ systems of units are two equivalent statements of the color-matching behavior of the 1931 CIE standard observer. The systems incorporate both colorimetric and photometric behavior. To obtain the RGB system, the chromaticity coordinates of Wright (1929) and Guild (1931) were combined and transformed into a primary system based on primaries R, G, and B of 700, 546.1, and 435.8 nm, respectively. Normalization was to the equal-energy white. The $r(\lambda)$, $g(\lambda)$, and $b(\lambda)$ coefficients were then converted to color-matching functions $\bar{r}(\lambda)$, $\bar{g}(\lambda)$, and $\bar{b}(\lambda)$ using a technique described by Wright (1929) incorporating the $V(\lambda)$ of the 1924 CIE standard observer for photometry as the luminosity function. Color-matching functions and chromaticity coordinates for the RGB system are tabulated in Wyszecki and Stiles (1982).

The XYZ system was derived by a linear transformation of the RGB system. A third and important new property was introduced; the transformation was defined so that the color-matching function $\bar{y}(\lambda)$ was equivalent to $V(\lambda)$ (the CIE photopic luminous efficiency function for the standard observer). Thus

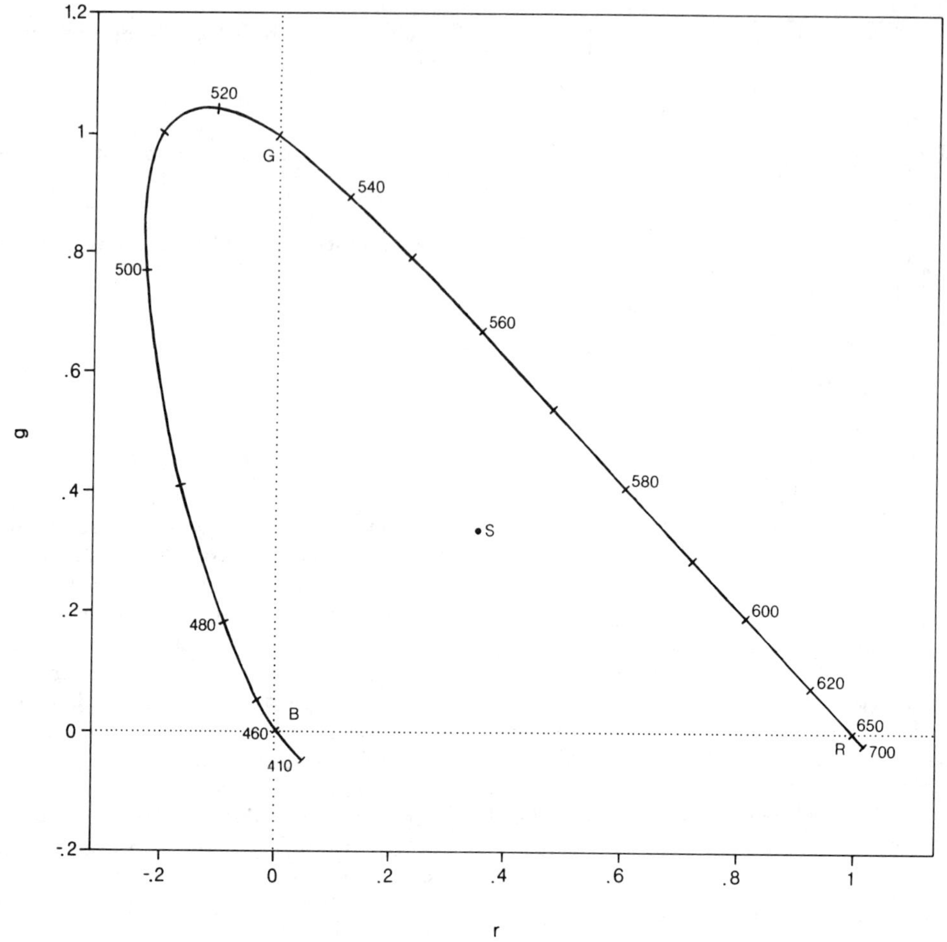

Figure 8.14. The spectrum locus in the chromaticity diagram for primaries 650, 530, and 460 nm. Normalization is to 4800 K white. (From W. D. Wright, *Research on normal and defective colour vision*, Kimpton Medical Publishers, 1946. Reprinted with permission.)

photometric quantities can be computed using $\bar{y}(\lambda)$. The *XYZ* system is more widely used than the *RGB* system. Table 8.11 (on page 8-22) shows chromaticity coordinates and color-matching functions at 10-nm intervals.

3.4.2. Judd's Modification of the 2° Observer. For work in color vision theory the Judd (1951b) modification of the 1931 CIE observer is frequently used. The Judd modification at short wavelengths affected not only the $\bar{y}(\lambda)$ function but also the $\bar{z}(\lambda)$ function and the short-wavelength spectrum locus in the chromaticity chart. Table 8.12 (on page 8-23) shows chromaticity coordinates and color-matching functions for the Judd modified observer. Smith, Pokorny, and Zaidi (1983) have noted that the Judd modified observer is characterized by less lens but more macular pigmentation (see Section 5.2) than the CIE 2° observer.

3.4.3. The 10° Observer. In 1963 the CIE defined a supplementary standard observer (CIE, 1964) based on the large-field color-matching data from the laboratories of Speranskaya (1959, 1961) and Stiles and Burch (1959).

The CIE transformed the data into an all-positive system with properties similar to those of the 1931 *XYZ* system. The 1964 supplementary standard observer is specified by a set $[\bar{x}_{10}(\lambda), \bar{y}_{10}(\lambda)$, and $\bar{z}_{10}(\lambda)]$ of color-matching functions and a (x_{10}, y_{10}) chromaticity diagram. The $\bar{y}_{10}(\lambda)$ represents the relative spectral luminous efficiency function of the supplementary standard observer. The chromaticity coordinates and color-matching functions of the CIE (1964) observer are shown in Table 8.13 (on page 8-24) at 10-nm intervals for the spectrum. The characteristics of the large-field observer are recommended for visual stimuli whose extent exceeds 4°.

3.5. Properties of the Chromaticity Diagram

In the *XYZ* system, an isosceles right triangle completely encloses the experimentally determined chromaticity diagram. In the chromaticity diagram, spectral hues and whites are represented as loci on the perimeter and the center, respectively. The abscissa ($y = 0$) has no luminance by definition and is called the *alychne* ("without light," Schrödinger, 1925). The line connecting the coordinates for 380 and 700 nm is identified as the line of nonspectral purples.

A color Q whose chromaticity coordinates are known may be specified by its dominant wavelength, λ_d, and excitation purity p_e (Figure 8.16, page 8-25). The dominant wavelength of a sample of chromaticity Q for a source C is the wavelength occurring at the intersection of the spectrum locus and a line extending from the locus of C through Q. Both dominant wavelength and excitation purity are frequently estimated graphically. Computation of dominant wavelength is nontrivial. Judd (1933b) gave examples of such computation for CIE chromaticity coordinates and illuminants A, B, and C. If Q occurs in a region

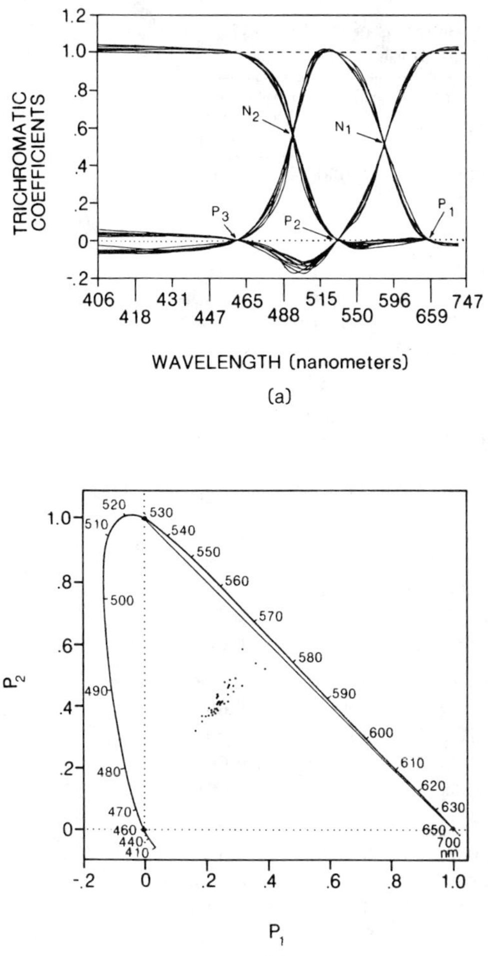

Figure 8.15. The WDW normalization of color mixture data. (a) Superimposed trichromatic coefficient curves for 10 observers; N_1 and N_2 are wavelengths 582.5 and 494 nm, respectively. (b) Chromaticity diagram showing the spectrum locus derived from the mean coefficient curves for the 10 observers. White chromaticity points of matches to a standard for 36 observers are shown as dots. The chromaticity diagram is plotted in terms of the matching primaries 650, 530, and 460 nm with units based on matches of 582.5 and 494 nm. The color temperature of the white stimulus was 4800 K. (From W. D. Wright, *Research on normal and defective colour vision*, Kimpton Medical Publishers, 1946. Reprinted with permission.)

of the diagram for which the line extending from C to Q has no intersection on the spectrum locus, then the complementary wavelength may be used and should be noted by $-\lambda_d$ or λ_c. The hue of dominant wavelength λ_d or λ_c may be loosely considered as indicating the predominant hue quality of the color Q under neutral adaptation. The excitation purity is the ratio of the distance from C to Q and the distance from C to $_d$:

$$p_e = \frac{(x_Q - x_C)}{(x_{\lambda dC} - x_C)} = \frac{(y_Q - y_C)}{(y_{\lambda d} - y_C)} . \tag{41}$$

In the case of a color whose dominant wavelength is $-\lambda_d$, the intersection with the purple line is used. Excitation purity is zero when C and Q coincide and unity when Q and λ_d coincide. The purity gives an approximate idea of the apparent relative saturation of a color Q on a scale from white to the dominant wavelength (or purple).

All physically realizable colors are represented in the x,y diagram; chromaticity coordinates (x,y) may be calculated for any color surface whose reflectance $\rho(\lambda)$ is known. Suppose there is a pigment sample of spectral reflectance $\rho(\lambda)$ viewed under an illumination of spectral distribution $H(\lambda)\Delta\lambda$. The object color Q may be thought of as a continuous sum of varying amounts of spectral wavelengths. The tristimulus values of Q are given by

$$X = K\sum \rho(\lambda)H(\lambda)\bar{x}(\lambda)\Delta\lambda , \tag{42}$$

$$Y = K\sum \rho(\lambda)H(\lambda)\bar{y}(\lambda)\Delta\lambda , \tag{43}$$

$$Z = K\sum \rho(\lambda)H(\lambda)\bar{z}(\lambda)\Delta\lambda , \tag{44}$$

where K is a normalizing factor usually set at $100/\Sigma H(\lambda)\bar{y}(\lambda)\Delta\lambda$. The chromaticity of Q is given by computing the proportions of x and y.

$$x = \frac{X}{(X + Y + Z)} , \tag{45}$$

$$y = \frac{Y}{(X + Y + Z)} . \tag{46}$$

These calculations may be made using the color-matching functions of the 1931 CIE standard observer or the 1964 CIE large-field standard observer.

With K set at $100/\Sigma H(\lambda)\bar{y}(\lambda)\Delta\lambda$, Y has the value of 100 $\Sigma[\rho(\lambda)H(\lambda)\bar{y}(\lambda)\Delta\lambda]/\Sigma[H(\lambda)\bar{y}(\lambda)\Delta\lambda]$. For a chromatic filter, the spectral transmission $\tau(\lambda)$ replaces the term $\rho(\lambda)$ for spectral reflectance. Figure 8.17 (on page 8-26) illustrates the necessary calculations for a Wratten gelatin filter (#78) and standard illuminant A. If the object is a perfectly diffusing surface, with $\rho(\lambda) = 1.0$ for all wavelengths, or a perfectly transmitting object, with $\tau(\lambda) = 1.0$ for all wavelengths, Y has the value 100. Thus Y may be interpreted as the percentage luminous reflectance or percentage luminous transmittance. Calculation of the percentage luminous reflectance or transmittance is appropriate only for the 1931 CIE colorimetric standard observer (Wyszecki & Stiles, 1982), since the standard luminous efficiency function $V(\lambda)$ corresponds to the 1931 $\bar{y}(\lambda)$ function.

3.6. Experimental Variables Affecting Color Matching

The Wright (1929) and Guild (1931) data were based on a 2° field viewed with foveal fixation. The effects of field size, retinal illuminance, and fixation are important in color-matching experiments.

3.6.1. Effect of Field Size. Color matches depend on the field of view; for example, color-matching functions based on a 1.5° field show systematic differences from the 2° data (Fridrikh, 1957). A match for a 2° field will not hold for a larger or a smaller field. There is a continuous change in the amounts of the primaries required for the color match as field size is changed (Pokorny & Smith, 1976).

Stiles (1955; Stiles & Burch, 1959) and Speranskaya (1959, 1961) measured the color-matching functions using a 10° field. Two experimental problems became evident in the measurement of these functions. First, for many fields a Maxwell spot appeared

Table 8.11. Chromaticity Coordinates and Color-Matching Functions of the CIE 1931 Standard Colorimetric System, for λ Equals 380–780 nm at 10-nm Intervals

Chromaticity Coordinates			Wavelength	Color-Matching Functions		
$x(\lambda)$	$y(\lambda)$	$z(\lambda)$	(nm)	$\bar{x}(\lambda)$	$\bar{y}(\lambda)$	$\bar{z}(\lambda)$
0.1741	0.0050	0.8209	380	0.0014	0.0000	0.0065
0.1738	0.0049	0.8213	390	0.0042	0.0001	0.0201
0.1733	0.0048	0.8219	400	0.0143	0.0004	0.0679
0.1726	0.0048	0.8226	410	0.0435	0.0012	0.2074
0.1714	0.0051	0.8235	420	0.1344	0.0040	0.6456
0.1689	0.0069	0.8242	430	0.2839	0.0116	1.3856
0.1644	0.0109	0.8247	440	0.3483	0.0230	1.7471
0.1566	0.0177	0.8257	450	0.3362	0.0380	1.7721
0.1440	0.0297	0.8263	460	0.2908	0.0600	1.6692
0.1241	0.0578	0.8181	470	0.1954	0.0910	1.2876
0.0913	0.1327	0.7760	480	0.0956	0.1390	0.8130
0.0454	0.2950	0.6596	490	0.0320	0.2080	0.4652
0.0082	0.5384	0.4534	500	0.0049	0.3230	0.2720
0.0139	0.7502	0.2359	510	0.0093	0.5030	0.1582
0.0743	0.8338	0.0919	520	0.0633	0.7100	0.0782
0.1547	0.8059	0.0394	530	0.1655	0.8620	0.0422
0.2296	0.7543	0.0161	540	0.2904	0.9540	0.0203
0.3016	0.6923	0.0061	550	0.4334	0.9950	0.0087
0.3731	0.6245	0.0024	560	0.5945	0.9950	0.0039
0.4441	0.5547	0.0012	570	0.7621	0.9520	0.0021
0.5125	0.4866	0.0009	580	0.9163	0.8700	0.0017
0.5752	0.4242	0.0006	590	1.0263	0.7570	0.0011
0.6270	0.3725	0.0005	600	1.0622	0.6310	0.0008
0.6658	0.3340	0.0002	610	1.0026	0.5030	0.0003
0.6915	0.3083	0.0002	620	0.8544	0.3810	0.0002
0.7079	0.2920	0.0001	630	0.6424	0.2650	0.0000
0.7190	0.2809	0.0001	640	0.4479	0.1750	0.0000
0.7260	0.2740	0.0000	650	0.2835	0.1070	0.0000
0.7300	0.2700	0.0000	660	0.1649	0.0610	0.0000
0.7320	0.2680	0.0000	670	0.0874	0.0320	0.0000
0.7334	0.2666	0.0000	680	0.0468	0.0170	0.0000
0.7344	0.2656	0.0000	690	0.0227	0.0082	0.0000
0.7347	0.2653	0.0000	700	0.0114	0.0041	0.0000
0.7347	0.2653	0.0000	710	0.0058	0.0021	0.0000
0.7347	0.2653	0.0000	720	0.0029	0.0010	0.0000
0.7347	0.2653	0.0000	730	0.0014	0.0005	0.0000
0.7347	0.2653	0.0000	740	0.0007	0.0003	0.0000
0.7347	0.2653	0.0000	750	0.0003	0.0001	0.0000
0.7347	0.2653	0.0000	760	0.0002	0.0001	0.0000
0.7347	0.2653	0.0000	770	0.0001	0.0000	0.0000
0.7347	0.2653	0.0000	780	0.0000	0.0000	0.0000
			Totals	10.6836	10.6857	10.6770

The chromaticity coordinates and color-matching functions are shown for the XYZ system of units with normalization to the equal-energy white. These functions represent the standard observer for colorimetry for photopic vision and visual fields of less than 4° in extent. The $\bar{y}(\lambda)$ function is identical to the CIE standard observer for photometry (Table 8.6).

at the area of fixation. The *Maxwell spot* is a color inhomogeneity that appears as an ill-defined ellipse with major axis horizontal, extending 1° or 2°. The spot follows fixation and is best observed by switching rapidly from one half of the bipartite field to the other. In 10° trichromatic matching, the observer must ignore the Maxwell spot (e.g., Stiles & Burch, 1959). Speranskaya (1959, 1961) used a 10° annulus with the central part blocked. The Maxwell spot is usually attributed to higher density of macular pigment in the central 1–2° of the fovea. Trezona (1970) has suggested that the Maxwell spot might be a rod contrast color. This conclusion was based on her studies of 10° color matching using a tetrachromatic technique. A fourth primary was added to the mixture field to allow the observer to balance the rods in a dark-adapted state. By repeating the matching procedure in light- and dark-adapted states, a match is eventually obtained that holds in both states. This "tetrachromatic"

Table 8.12. Chromaticity Coordinates and Color-Matching Functions of the CIE 1931 Standard Colorimetric System, as Modified by Judd (1951b), for λ Equals 370–770 nm at 10-nm Intervals

Chromaticity Coordinates			Wavelength	Color-Matching Functions		
$\bar{x}(\lambda)$	$\bar{y}(\lambda)$	$\bar{z}(\lambda)$	(nm)	$\bar{x}(\lambda)$	$\bar{y}(\lambda)$	$\bar{z}(\lambda)$
0.1776	0.0132	0.8092	370	0.0008	0.0001	0.0046
0.1775	0.0132	0.8093	380	0.0045	0.0004	0.0224
0.1772	0.0131	0.8097	390	0.0201	0.0015	0.0925
0.1767	0.0130	0.8103	400	0.0611	0.0045	0.2799
0.1760	0.0131	0.8109	410	0.1267	0.0093	0.5835
0.1748	0.0133	0.8119	420	0.2285	0.0175	1.0622
0.1723	0.0153	0.8124	430	0.3081	0.0273	1.4526
0.1677	0.0192	0.8131	440	0.3312	0.0379	1.6064
0.1598	0.0259	0.8143	450	0.2888	0.0468	1.4717
0.1470	0.0380	0.8150	460	0.2323	0.0600	1.2880
0.1266	0.0660	0.8074	470	0.1745	0.0910	1.1133
0.0933	0.1409	0.7658	480	0.0920	0.1390	0.7552
0.0463	0.3033	0.6504	490	0.0318	0.2080	0.4461
0.0082	0.5454	0.4464	500	0.0048	0.3230	0.2644
0.0140	0.7546	0.2314	510	0.0093	0.5030	0.1541
0.0750	0.8351	0.0899	520	0.0636	0.7100	0.0763
0.1599	0.8057	0.0384	530	0.1668	0.8620	0.0412
0.2310	0.7533	0.0157	540	0.2926	0.9540	0.0200
0.3030	0.6909	0.0061	550	0.4364	0.9950	0.0088
0.3741	0.6235	0.0024	560	0.5970	0.9950	0.0039
0.4447	0.5541	0.0012	570	0.7642	0.9520	0.0020
0.5124	0.4867	0.0009	580	0.9159	0.8700	0.0016
0.5742	0.4252	0.0006	590	1.0225	0.7570	0.0011
0.6254	0.3742	0.0004	600	1.0544	0.6310	0.0007
0.6634	0.3364	0.0002	610	0.9922	0.5030	0.0003
0.6886	0.3112	0.0001	620	0.8432	0.3810	0.0002
0.7046	0.2953	0.0001	630	0.6327	0.2650	0.0001
0.7156	0.2843	0.0000	640	0.4404	0.1750	0.0000
0.7225	0.2775	0.0000	650	0.2787	0.1070	0.0000
0.7264	0.2736	0.0000	660	0.1619	0.0610	0.0000
0.7284	0.2716	0.0000	670	0.0858	0.0320	0.0000
0.7298	0.2702	0.0000	680	0.0459	0.0170	0.0000
0.7308	0.2692	0.0000	690	0.0222	0.0082	0.0000
0.7311	0.2689	0.000	700	0.0113	0.0041	0.0000
0.7311	0.2689	0.000	710	0.0057	0.0021	0.0000
0.7311	0.2689	0.000	720	0.0028	0.0011	0.0000
0.7311	0.2689	0.000	730	0.0015	0.0005	0.0000
0.7311	0.2689	0.000	740	0.0005	0.0002	0.0000
0.7311	0.2689	0.000	750	0.0003	0.0001	0.0000
0.7311	0.2689	0.000	760	0.0002	0.0001	0.0000
0.7311	0.2689	0.000	770	0.0001	0.0000	0.0000
			Totals	10.7533	10.7526	10.7531

The Judd (1951b) modification incorporated the changes made to improve the luminosity function $\bar{y}(\lambda)$ at short-wavelengths Table 8.7. The modifications affected also the $\bar{z}(\lambda)$ function and the chromaticity coordinates at short wavelengths. The Judd revision is widely used for work in color theory.

match does not show a Maxwell spot. Explanation of the Maxwell spot remains controversial. A second problem evident in 10° color matching is rod intrusion (changes in color matches caused by rod activity). Since photopic color-matching functions were desired, Stiles and Burch (1959) made mathematical corrections to the data using a theoretical expectation of the nature of rod intrusion (see also Wyszecki & Stiles, 1982).

When the color mixture field is reduced below 30 min of arc, there is a severe loss of discrimination. With stable fixation, if the field subtends 15 or 20 min and is viewed either foveally or at 20 or 40 min from the fovea, the normal trichromatic observer becomes dichromatic, requiring only two primaries for full-spectrum color matching (Thomson & Wright, 1947). The color matches resemble those of the congenital color defect *tritanopia*.

3.6.2. Effect of Retinal Illuminance. The scalar property states that metamers hold for all levels of retinal illumination; however, the range for which the 2° trichromatic metamers

Table 8.13. Chromaticity Coordinates and Color-Matching Functions of the CIE 1964 Supplementary Standard Colorimetric System, for λ Equals 380–780 nm at 10-nm Intervals (10° or large field)

Chromaticity Coordinates			Wavelength	Color-Matching Functions		
$x(\lambda)$	$y(\lambda)$	$z(\lambda)$	(nm)	$\bar{x}(\lambda)$	$\bar{y}(\lambda)$	$\bar{z}(\lambda)$
0.1813	0.0197	0.7990	380	0.0002	0.0000	0.0007
0.1803	0.0194	0.8003	390	0.0024	0.0003	0.0105
0.1784	0.0187	0.8029	400	0.0191	0.0020	0.0860
0.1755	0.0181	0.8064	410	0.0847	0.0088	0.3894
0.1706	0.0179	0.8115	420	0.2045	0.0214	0.9725
0.1650	0.0203	0.8147	430	0.3147	0.0387	1.5535
0.1590	0.0257	0.8153	440	0.3837	0.0621	1.9673
0.1510	0.0364	0.8126	450	0.3707	0.0895	1.9948
0.1389	0.0589	0.8022	460	0.3023	0.1282	1.7454
0.1152	0.1090	0.7758	470	0.1956	0.1852	1.3176
0.0728	0.2292	0.6980	480	0.0805	0.2536	0.7721
0.0210	0.4401	0.5389	490	0.0162	0.3391	0.4153
0.0056	0.6745	0.3199	500	0.0038	0.4608	0.2185
0.0495	0.8023	0.1482	510	0.0375	0.6067	0.1120
0.1252	0.8102	0.0646	520	0.1177	0.7618	0.0607
0.2071	0.7663	0.0267	530	0.2365	0.8752	0.0305
0.2786	0.7113	0.0101	540	0.3768	0.9620	0.0137
0.3473	0.6501	0.0026	550	0.5298	0.9918	0.0040
0.4142	0.5858	0.0000	560	0.7052	0.9973	0.0000
0.4790	0.5210	0.0000	570	0.8787	0.9555	0.0000
0.5386	0.4614	0.0000	580	1.0142	0.8689	0.0000
0.5900	0.4120	0.0000	590	1.1185	0.7774	0.0000
0.6306	0.3694	0.0000	600	1.1240	0.6583	0.0000
0.6612	0.3388	0.0000	610	1.0305	0.5280	0.0000
0.6827	0.3173	0.0000	620	0.8563	0.3981	0.0000
0.6955	0.3045	0.0000	630	0.6475	0.2835	0.0000
0.7059	0.2941	0.0000	640	0.4316	0.1798	0.0000
0.7137	0.2863	0.0000	650	0.2683	0.1076	0.0000
0.7168	0.2832	0.0000	660	0.1526	0.0603	0.0000
0.7187	0.2813	0.0000	670	0.0813	0.0318	0.0000
0.7198	0.2802	0.0000	680	0.0409	0.0159	0.0000
0.7202	0.2798	0.0000	690	0.0199	0.0077	0.0000
0.7204	0.2796	0.0000	700	0.0096	0.0037	0.0000
0.7202	0.2798	0.0000	710	0.0046	0.0018	0.0000
0.7199	0.2801	0.0000	720	0.0022	0.0008	0.0000
0.7195	0.2806	0.0000	730	0.0010	0.0004	0.0000
0.7189	0.2811	0.0000	740	0.0005	0.0002	0.0000
0.7183	0.2817	0.0000	750	0.0003	0.0001	0.0000
0.7176	0.2824	0.0000	760	0.0001	0.0000	0.0000
0.7169	0.2831	0.0000	770	0.0001	0.0000	0.0000
0.7161	0.2839	0.0000	780	0.0000	0.0000	0.0000
			Total	11.6646	11.6643	11.6645

The chromaticity coordinates and color-matching functions are shown for the XYZ system of units with normalization to the equal-energy white. These functions represent the standard observer for colorimetry for photopic vision and visual fields of greater than 4° in extent.

hold is limited to about 1–8000 td. Chromatic discrimination is optimal in a similar range of retinal illuminance.

With reduction in retinal illuminance, color matches continue to hold as low as 1 td. With further reduction in luminance, rod intrusion becomes evident (Richards & Luria, 1964). Whether this is due to rod function in a foveal 2° area or to changes in fixation with decreases in luminance is unknown. Estévez (1979) suggested that the Wright (1929), Guild (1931), and Stiles (1955) 2° data have a small rod contribution.

Pokorny and Smith (1981) and Pokorny, Smith, and Went (1981) noted rod contribution in color-defective individuals for 50-td fields as small as 1°. Rod intrusion is more easily seen in the color-defective observer whose cone-dominated color vision is compromised.

Another effect of reduction in retinal illuminance is discrimination loss, especially of the blueness-yellowness content of the stimuli. The effect is similar to that of small-field tritanopia (Grigorovici & Aricescu-Savopol, 1958).

When the retinal illuminance exceeds 5000–10,000 td, lights that were metamers are no longer perceived as such (Alpern, 1979; Brindley, 1953; Burns & Eisner, 1985; Terstiege, 1967; Wyszecki & Stiles, 1980). For example, in the match of spectral yellow to a mixture of red and green primaries, more red is required. While the change in match is a failure of the scalar property, the matches remain trichromatic. The effect and its explanation are described further in Section 5.2.3

3.6.3. Peripheral Color Matching. Color matching may also be performed using the parafoveal or peripheral retina. With the dark-adapted eye and a scotopic illuminance, the normal observer is monochromatic, using the rod mechanism for color matching. At mesopic and photopic levels, parafoveal and peripheral color matching is trichromatic.

Color-matching data that allow the description of peripheral color matches in terms of foveal color vision have been described by Moreland and Cruz (1959). For a spectral test field of 40 × 80-min viewed by the periphery and a 40 × 80-min mixture field viewed by the fovea with WDW normalization (Section 3.2.3) at the foveal match, Moreland and Cruz (1959) determined the proportions of foveal red and green primaries necessary to match various peripherally viewed stimuli. These chromaticity coefficients were all within the spectrum locus for the Wright (1929) 2° foveal data, indicating that a spectral radiation of fixed size viewed in the peripheral retina is desaturated in appearance compared with its appearance at the fovea. Abramov and Gordon (1977) have emphasized that a peripheral stimulus must be larger than a foveal stimulus in order to appear colored.

Stabell and Stabell (1976) used the Moreland and Cruz paradigm to evaluate rod contribution to color matching by taking measurements during the cone-plateau period following intense light adaptation. Rod participation produces changes in hue and substantial desaturation.

3.7. Some Relevant Sampling Directions in Chromaticity Space: A Theoretical Preview

Modern theories of the human color vision mechanism include a first stage consisting of three classes of photoreceptors with three visual photopigments exhibiting overlapping absorption spectra. The three cone types are frequently denoted by the relative positions of their absorption spectra on a wavelength axis; long-wavelength sensitive (LWS), middle-wavelength sensitive (MWS) and short-wavelength sensitive (SWS). A second

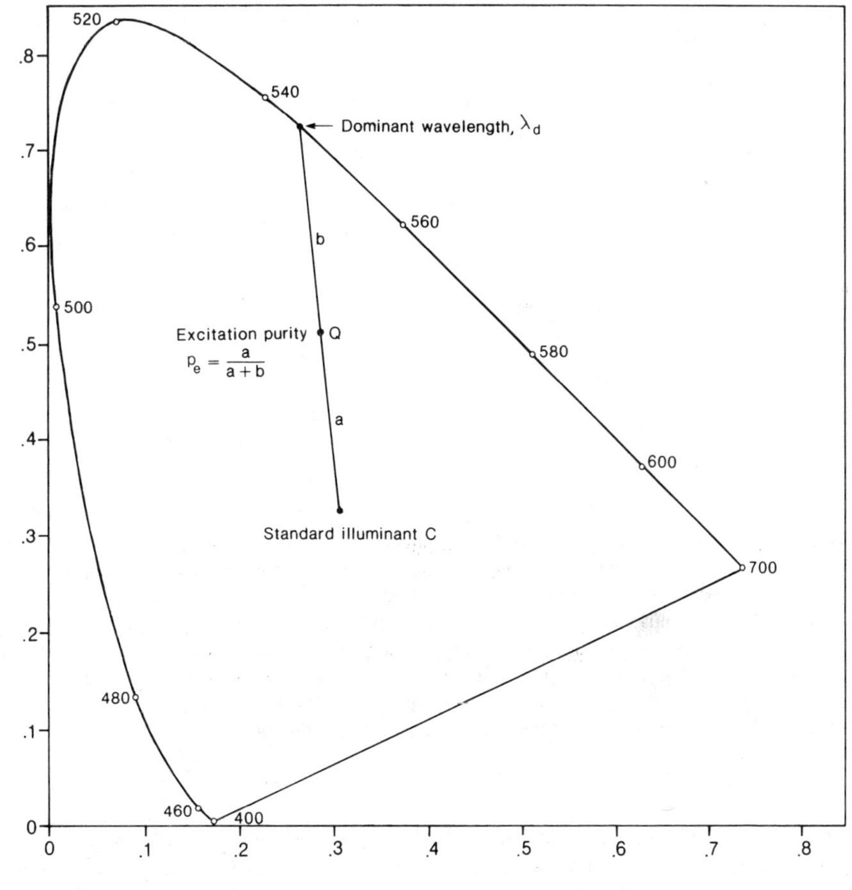

Figure 8.16. Specification of dominant wavelength and excitation purity in the CIE 1931 (x, y) chromaticity diagram. A chromaticity Q can be expressed by its dominant wavelength, λ_d, and its excitation purity, p_e, relative to a specified white (in this case, standard illuminant C). (From J. Pokorny, V. C. Smith, G. Verriest, & A. J. L. C. Pinckers, *Congenital and acquired color defects*, Grune & Stratton, 1979. Reprinted with permission.)

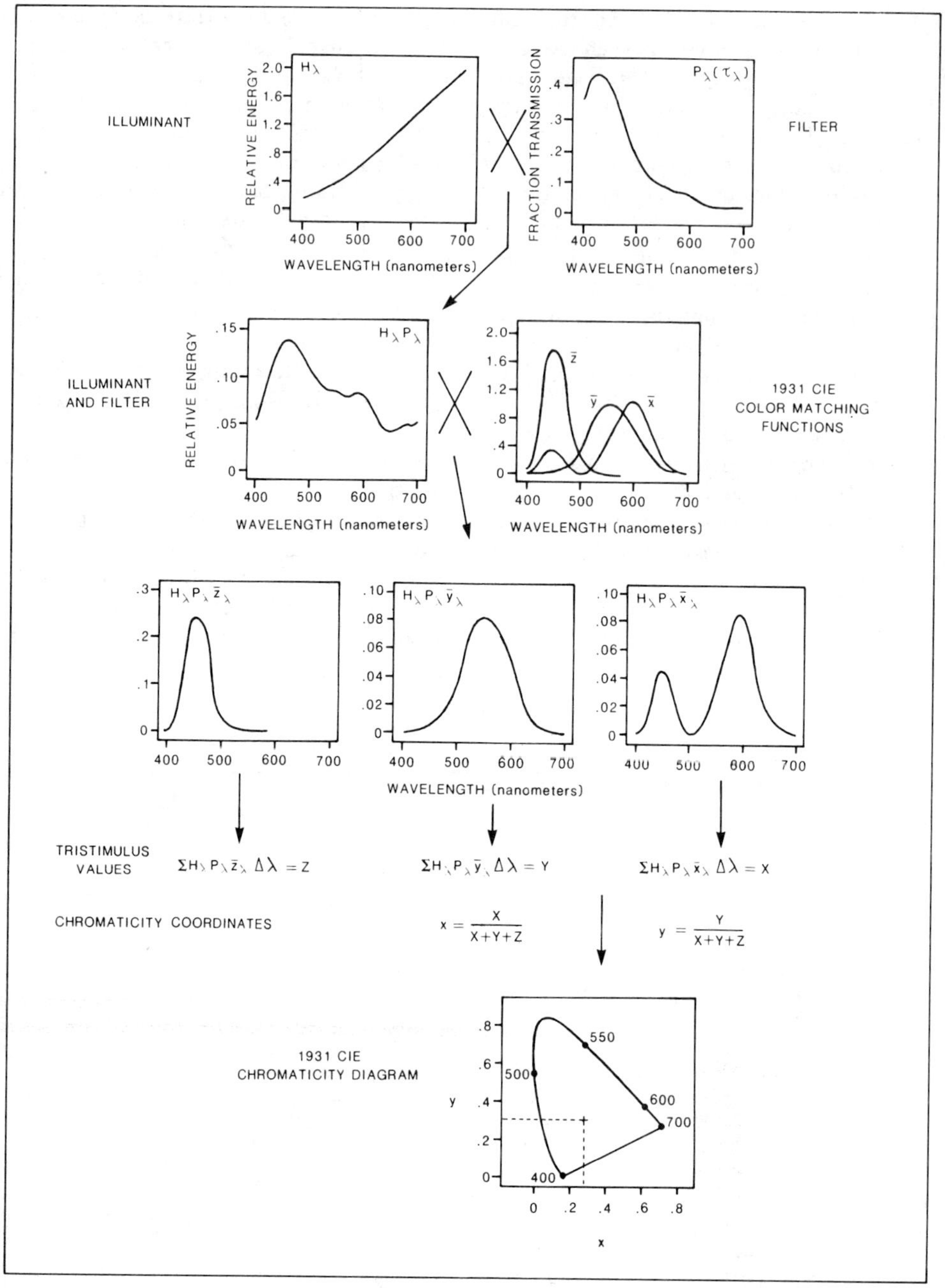

Figure 8.17. Calculation of chromaticity coordinated (x,y) for a Wratten gelatin filter (#78) and standard illuminant *A*. The CIE tristimulus values *X*, *Y*, and *Z* of a color are obtained by multiplying together the relative energy of CIE standard illuminant *A*, the transmittance $t(\lambda)$ of the filter, and then weighting the result by the tristimulus values of the equal-energy spectrum colors $\bar{x}(\lambda)$, $\bar{y}(\lambda)$, and $\bar{z}(\lambda)$, respectively. The three sets of products are summed for all the wavelengths in the visible spectrum to give the tristimulus values as indicated in the diagram and by Eqs. (42)–(44). The chromaticity coordinates (*x*,*y*) are found using Eqs. (45) and (46). (From J. Pokorny, V. C. Smith, G. Verriest, & A. J. L. C. Pinckers, *Congenital and acquired color defects*, Grune & Stratton, 1979. Reprinted with permission.)

stage, representing activity in higher-order neurons, is characterized by color opponent channels, derived (to a first approximation) by sums and differences of the receptor outputs.

The absorption spectra of three classes of photoreceptors can be shown to be linearly related to color mixture data. This interpretation reflects the following reasoning: A perceptual difference across an isomeric bipartite field can occur only if the quantal flux is made different between the two halves (i.e., two fields of identical spectral distribution but differing flux). For each active visual photopigment, the quantal catch is similarly different. The signals generated by the photoreceptors reflect these differences, giving rise to the perception of a brightness or lightness difference. When the quantal flux and hence the quantal catch rate is equivalent for each visual photopigment, a uniform circular field is seen. In the metameric field, the same principle holds; when the quantal catch is equivalent on both halves for each visual photopigment, the two halves will appear identical. Achieving this identity is, however, a more complicated process, since the different spectral radiations on the two halves cause different quantal catch rates in the three photopigments. An adjustment in the total quantal flux of the one half-field can equalize the quantal catch only for one of the photopigments. The requirement that three primaries are needed for color matching reflects the fact that three adjustments will be necessary to balance the quantal catch rates for each of three photopigments and achieve the perception of uniform hue in the bipartite field. This requirement of simultaneous balance of each active photopigment can be expressed by means of three simultaneous equations, one for each photopigment.

Expressing the quantal catch as the absorption sensitivity S weighted by the radiance at tristimulus values a, b, c, and d for test wavelength 490 nm and primaries 650, 530, and 460 nm, respectively, we find

$$\text{SWS: } aS_{\text{SWS}}(490) + bS_{\text{SWS}}(650) = cS_{\text{SWS}}(530) + dS_{\text{SWS}}(460)\,, \quad (47)$$

$$\text{MWS: } aS_{\text{MWS}}(490) + bS_{\text{MWS}}(650) = cS_{\text{MWS}}(530) + dS_{\text{MWS}}(460)\,, \quad (48)$$

$$\text{LWS: } aS_{\text{LWS}}(490) + bS_{\text{LWS}}(650) = cS_{\text{LWS}}(530) + dS_{\text{LWS}}(460)\,. \quad (49)$$

Neither a spectrally shape-invariant change in sensitivity of one or more photopigments nor a change in radiance will change the color match, since multiplying any one of the equations by a constant factor will not alter the relative values of a, b, c, or d. Similarly, color matches do not depend on the relative cone populations; color matches depend only on the shapes of the absorption spectra.

According to this interpretation, a linear transformation of color-matching data can yield the spectral sensitivities of the cone visual photopigments. However, there are infinitely many transformations of color mixture data; each requires solving sets of equations for nine unknowns. A major analytical advance was the König and Dieterici (1886, 1893) suggestion of incorporating data from certain types of color-defective observers (called *dichromats*) to restrict the number of arbitrary choices (Section 5.1.1). Dichromats are observers who, under appropriate experimental conditions, need two, rather than three, primaries to find a metamer for any color (Section 3.1.2). The three classes of dichromats are assumed to each have one nonfunctional class of photoreceptor. Specifically, protanopes are presumed to lack LWS cone function; deuteranopes, MWS cone function; and tritanopes, SWS cone function. Dichromatic color mixture data can be plotted on the CIE chromaticity diagram (a description of the procedure is given in Pokorny, Smith, Verriest, & Pinckers, 1979, pp. 186–191). A dichromat's color matches plot as a series of lines in the trichromat's space (Figure 8.18). These lines are called *isochromatic* or *confusion lines.* In principle, with suitable adjustment of radiance, all colors lying along an isochromatic line will appear metameric to the dichromat. For a color-normal observer, two spectral distributions representing two points along an isochromatic line can be adjusted in radiance so that only one cone system (the nonfunctional one for the class of dichromat from which the isochromatic line is derived) is differentially stimulated. This technique, commonly termed *silent substitution* (Estévez & Spekreijse, 1982), has been employed to explore the properties of isolated receptor mechanisms.

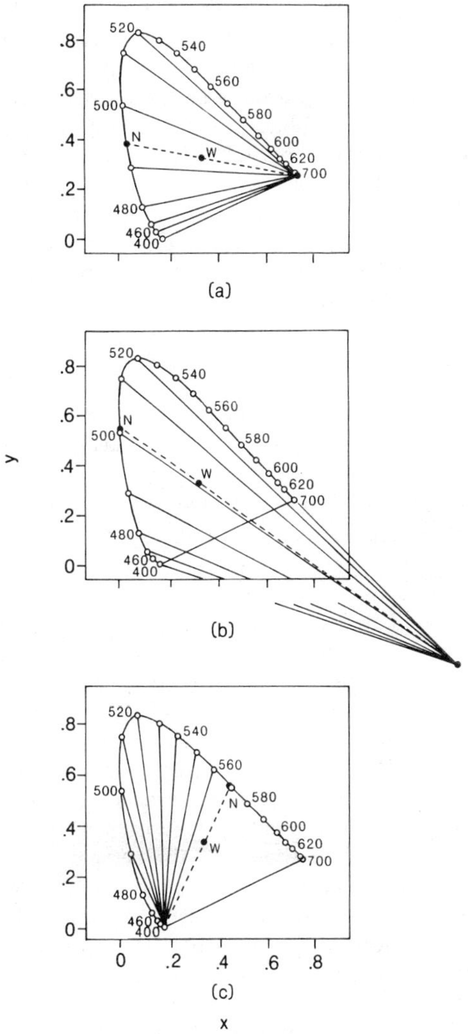

Figure 8.18. Isochromatic lines for dichromats plotted on the Judd (1951b) modified chromaticity diagram for (a) protanope, (b) deuteranope, and (c) tritanope. Also shown are the neutral points *N*, those spectral wavelengths confused with equal-energy white *W* for each class of color-defective observer. With suitable adjustment of radiance, chromaticities on a given isochromatic line will appear metameric to the dichromat. The color-normal observer can distinguish these chromaticities by activity of only one cone system (the nonfunctional one for the class of dichromat from which the isochromatic line is derived). (Based on Smith & Pokorny, 1975.)

4. CHROMATIC DISCRIMINATION

When viewing two patches of light, an observer may discriminate between them on the basis of a difference in chromaticity, a difference in luminance, or a joint difference in luminance and chromaticity. Thresholds measured while keeping luminance constant are called *chromatic thresholds*. The colors being compared can be specified in physical terms (Section 3.1) or by their dominant wavelengths and excitation or colorimetric purities (Section 3.3). Alternatively, chromaticities can be specified by their chromaticity coordinates (Section 3.3). Other methods for expressing discrimination data involve transformations of the data into color spaces, defined by assumed receptor sensitivities or assumed chromatic opponent-response functions.

When a luminous difference between two fields exists, detection is said to be mediated by the incremental difference, and the threshold value is called the *incremental* (or *increment*) *threshold*. If the two fields are of identical spectral composition, this is called a *homochromatic* (or *isomeric*) incremental threshold or a *luminance* increment threshold. If the two fields differ in spectral composition, the resulting measurements are referred to as *two-color thresholds*.

4.1. Wavelength Discrimination

Wavelength discrimination refers to the ability of an observer to detect chromatic differences along the spectrum locus. In a typical wavelength discrimination experiment, the observer views two fields—one filled with light of a standard wavelength, that is, a narrow spectral band of light, and the other with light of a comparison wavelength, again a narrow band. Both fields can be varied in dominant wavelength and radiance. Usually, monochromators are used to control the wavelength composition of the fields. A common procedure is the step-by-step method in which both fields initially have identical spectral composition and radiance (isomeric fields). The wavelength of the comparison field is changed in small steps (one nanometer or less), and the observer adjusts the radiance of the comparison field following each step. Discrimination threshold is reached when the observer reports that the fields cannot be made to appear identical based on adjustment of the radiance of the comparison field. The wavelength discrimination step is expressed in terms of the difference in wavelength $\Delta\lambda$ between the standard and comparison fields. The procedure is repeated for a series of standard wavelengths throughout the visible spectrum. Data are reported either as the $\Delta\lambda$ in one direction, for example, toward longer wavelengths, or as the average of $\Delta\lambda$ for comparison lights both longer and shorter than the standard. In an alternative technique, the standard deviation of a repeated series of color matches is taken as being proportional to the discrimination step. In such a procedure, the experimenter initially sets the two fields to be different in wavelength. The observer is asked to adjust the wavelength and radiance of the comparison field until it appears to be the same as the standard. The procedure is repeated many times to determine the standard deviation of the comparison field settings. In terms of experimental convenience, the step-by-step method is more rapid, but it requires absolute calibration of wavelength for both the standard and the comparison fields. The standard deviation procedure is time consuming but may be more accurate as it shows less dependence on criterion changes of the observer. Figure 8.19 shows representative wavelength discrimination data from several laboratories. The MacAdam (1942) standard deviation data appear to be approximately one-fifth of the discrimination thresholds measured by step-by-step procedures.

There are systematic variations among wavelength discrimination functions of color-normal observers. Figure 8.20 shows individual data for the five observers of Wright and Pitt (1934) (the average of these observers is plotted as triangles in Figure 8.19). Averaging tends to smooth out the details of the individual curves, particularly in the short-wavelength region where a local region of higher discrimination occurs for four of the five observers at slightly different spectral locations.

Although wavelength discrimination data are typically expressed on a wavelength scale, there have been suggestions that frequency, rather than wavelength, may be the appropriate metric for the spectrum (Wald, 1965). This point is particularly important with respect to wavelength discrimination data since the conversion to frequency involves a nonlinear transformation of both the dependent and independent variables. When expressed in frequency, the discrimination steps are increasingly compressed as frequency decreases (Hailman, 1967).

4.2. Colorimetric Purity Discrimination

A threshold for detection of a purity difference can be defined for spectral light added to one half of a bipartite isomeric white field. Results of such measurements are typically expressed in terms of colorimetric purity p_c:

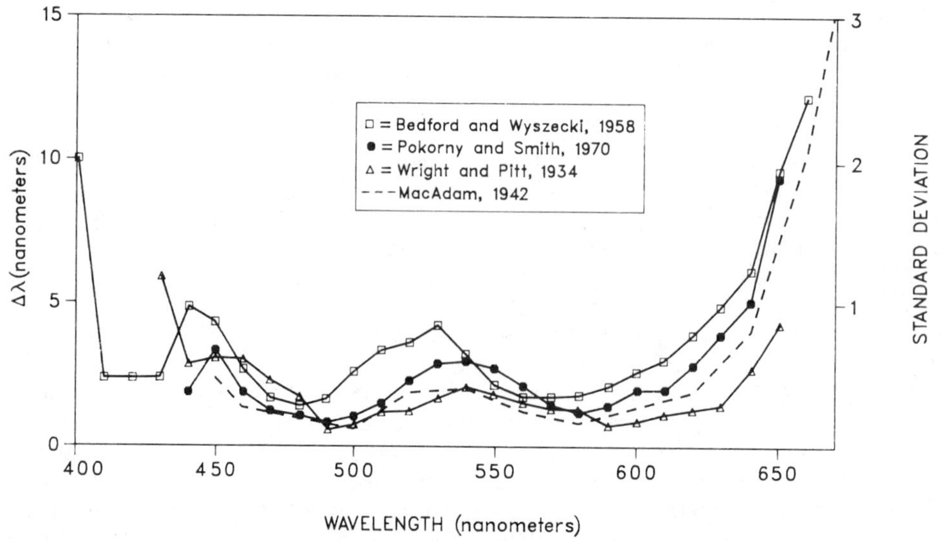

Figure 8.19. Comparison of average step-by-step wavelength discrimination data (Bedford & Wyszecki, 1958; Pokorny & Smith, 1970; Wright & Pitt, 1934) and standard deviation data (MacAdam, 1942). A JND step is equivalent to about five standard deviations of repeated color matches.

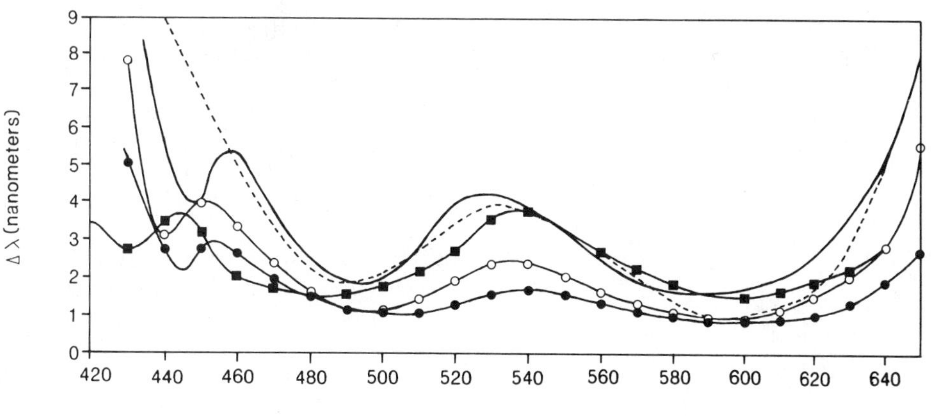

Figure 8.20. Wavelength discrimination curves for five normal observers. Note that although all observers show the same general shape for this function, there are individual differences in the location and size of the maxima and minima. (From W. D. Wright & F. H. G. Pitt, Hue discrimination in normal color vision, *Proceedings of the Physical Society* (London), 1934, *46*. Reprinted with permission.)

$$p_c = \frac{L_\lambda}{(L_w + L_\lambda)}, \tag{50}$$

where L_λ is the luminance of the spectral color and L_w is the luminance of the white. Colorimetric purity is related to excitation purity (Section 3.5) by

$$p_c = \left(\frac{Y_\lambda}{Y_Q}\right) p_e . \tag{51}$$

Colorimetric purity discrimination typically refers to measurements of the least colorimetric purity: Δp_c, the minimum amount of spectral light that allows a mixture of spectral light and white to be distinguished from a specified white. It is possible to measure just-noticeable differences (JNDs) in purity. The first JND is the step from white. Successive JNDs can then be measured stepping from white to the spectrum (Jones & Lowry, 1926; Martin, Warburton, & Morgan, 1933). The number of measurable steps varies with wavelength, being least near 570 and most at the spectral extremes.

Saturation is a perceptual correlate of purity and is usually taken as the reciprocal of least colorimetric purity; that is, the lower the colorimetric purity, the higher the apparent saturation of the spectral light. The number of JNDs measured from white to the spectrum is another estimate of saturation. It is also possible to scale saturation directly by asking an observer to estimate the apparent saturation of a light. Finally, the size of the standard deviations of color matches made to white (e.g., MacAdam, 1942) can also be taken as an index of saturation. Figure 8.21 (on page 8-30) shows a comparison of these various techniques for estimating saturation discrimination, including data from the variability of color matches and scaling procedures where saturation was directly estimated. The results of these various procedures are in general agreement, showing a minimum in saturation in the 570–580-nm region and increasing saturation at the spectral extremes.

If purity is estimated by determining colorimetric purity thresholds for white added to spectral lights, the results in the literature are rather more ambiguous. A number of investigators (Jones & Lowry, 1926; Martin, Warburton, & Morgan, 1933; Wright & Pitt, 1937) observed little wavelength dependence for the first steps from spectral lights. Kaiser, Comerford, and Bodinger (1976) obtained functions that resembled colorimetric purity discriminations from white but were more compressed.

4.3. Systematic Evaluation of Chromaticity Discrimination of Lights of Equal Luminance

In Sections 4.1 and 4.2 two special cases of chromaticity discrimination were described, discriminations along the spectrum locus and discrimination along axes between white and the spectrum locus. It is possible to sample discrimination systematically in all directions starting with any arbitrary chromaticity. Data from such a procedure are typically represented in a chromaticity diagram, such as the 1931 CIE chromaticity diagram. The discrimination step in any arbitrary direction may be represented by a line segment with the length of the line being proportionaltothephysicaldifferencerequiredfordiscrimination to occur. Figure 8.22 (on page 8-31) shows data from Wright's laboratory on wavelength discrimination and the number of steps from white plotted on the 1931 CIE chromaticity diagram. As is evident from this figure, the line segments assume different lengths in different regions of chromaticity space. Thus distances on the 1931 CIE chromaticity diagram are not proportional to discriminability. A number of investigators have done more systematic sampling of chromaticity space than just the wavelength discrimination step and the number of chromaticity steps from white. Figure 8.23 (on page 8-32) shows data from Wright (1941) in which he systematically sampled a whole variety of lines through chromaticity space. A somewhat different approach was taken by MacAdam (1942). He took the standard deviation of color matches as representing chromaticity discrimination and, starting at a number of reference points in chromaticity space, derived a series of discrimination ellipses which represent the discriminable distance in a wide number of directions from each point. Figure 8.24 (on page 8-33) shows the MacAdam data plotted in the 1931 chromaticity diagram with each of the ellipses representing 10 times the measured standard deviations. Brown and MacAdam (1949) and Wyszecki and Fielder (1971) have made extensive experimental evaluations of color-matching ellipses and confirm the general character of those originally measured by MacAdam.

Boynton and Kambe (1980) performed a systematic sampling of chromaticity space in a constant luminance plane with

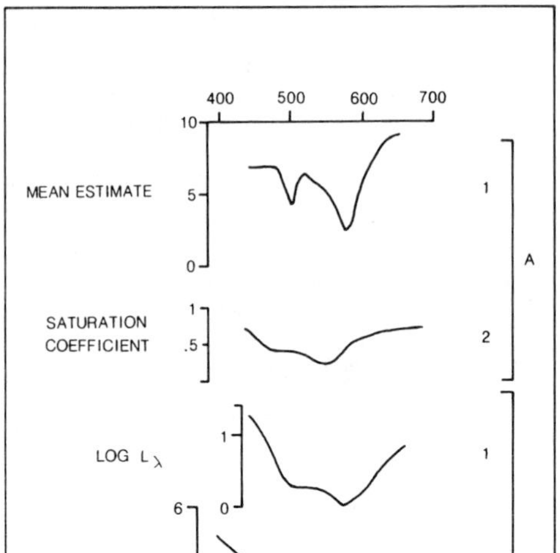

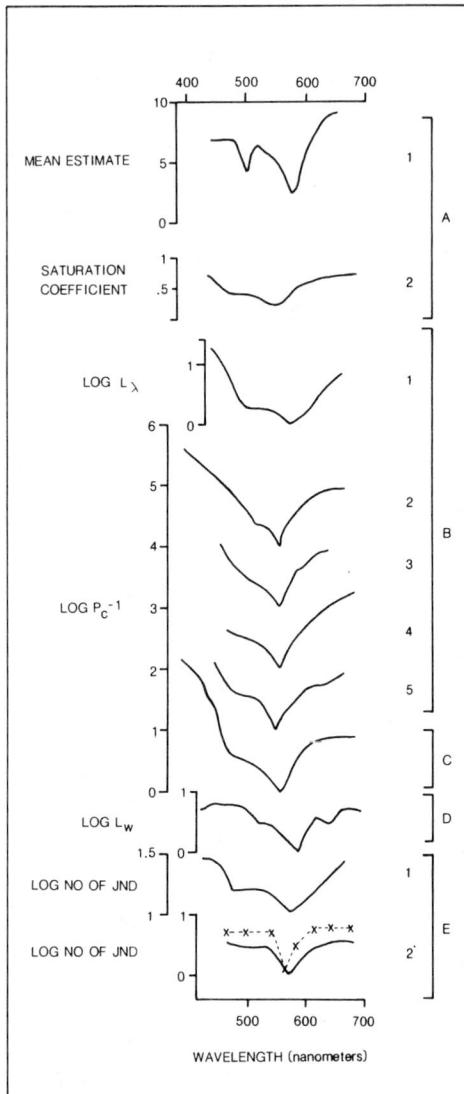

Figure 8.21. Summary of experimental data on purity discrimination. Group A: direct scaling of spectral lights (1, Jacobs; 2, Jameson & Hurvich) group B: saturation discrimination near white (1, Purdy; 2, Priest & Brickwedde; 3, Wright & Pitt; 4, Nelson; 5, Martin, Warburton & Morgan); group C: MacAdam's calculation from data on color matching near white; group D: Troland's data using constant critical-flicker frequency; group E: indirect scaling of spectral lights (1, Jones & Lowry; 2, Martin, Warburton, & Morgan, for two observers). (From P. K. Kaiser, J. P. Comerford, & D. M. Bodinger, Saturation of spectral lights, *Journal of the Optical Society of America*, 1976, 66. Reprinted with permission.)

several notable differences from the earlier studies. The first major difference was methodological. The two halves of the bipartite field were initially matched. The observer initiated a trial, and after an unpredictable delay, one of the test fields began to change in one of the two possible directions. The subject terminated the trial when he or she saw a difference between the two halves of the field large enough for the direction of change to be identified. This yielded discrimination steps rather larger than would be expected on the basis of the MacAdam (1942) standard deviations. The Boynton and Kambe discrimination steps are equivalent to approximately 13 of the MacAdam standard deviations. The second major difference was that discrimination was measured along two theoretically critical axes. One axis involved a constant amount of SWS cone stimulation and varying amounts of LWS to MWS cone stimulation (see Section 3.7). A series of different levels of SWS cone stimulation were evaluated. On a second axis, constant LWS, MWS cone ratios were maintained, and discrimination was evaluated in terms of the SWS cone distribution. The data show general agreement with the MacAdam results. Analysis indicated that SWS cone axis discriminations are affected only by the amount of SWS cone excitation and are independent of the red-green component of the color. On the other hand, red-green discriminations are affected by the level of SWS cone excitation.

4.4. Effects of Stimulus Manipulation

Chromatic discrimination varies with variation in the luminance, spatial structure, temporal presentation, retinal position, and state of chromatic adaptation. Chromatic discrimination deteriorates at low levels of retinal illuminance, particularly discrimination based on SWS cones (Brown, 1951; Clarke, 1967; Farnsworth, 1955; Siegel & Siegel, 1972; Verriest, Buyssens, & Vanderdonck, 1963; but see McCree, 1960a; Stabell & Stabell, 1977; Weale, 1951). Discrimination functions show little change over a range of retinal illuminance of 100–3500 td (Bedford & Wyszecki, 1958; Cornu & Harlay, 1969).

Chromatic discriminations are possible for circular bipartite fields as small as 3 min (MacAdam, 1959). Steady fixation of small fields (20 min or less) leads to a deterioration of discrimination mediated by the SWS cones (small-field tritanopia, Clarke, 1967; Farnsworth, 1955; König, 1894; Thomson & Wright, 1947; Willmer & Wright, 1945). The small-field tritanopic effect also occurs with steady fixation of parafoveal fields (Hartridge, 1945; Thomson & Wright, 1947). It can be reduced or eliminated by employing a scanning or glance technique in which the observer looks away from the field after 5–10 sec of viewing (Bedford & Wyszecki, 1958; McCree, 1960b). There is a strong interaction between field size and luminance, with the deterioration of SWS cone discrimination from reduction in either one being cumulative (Clarke, 1967; Farnsworth, 1955; Yonemura & Kasuya, 1969).

Increasing field size from 2 to 10° or larger improves discrimination (Brown, 1951; Wyszecki & Stiles, 1982) by a factor of about two. The improvement is independent of the sampling direction in chromaticity space.

Boynton, Hayhoe, and MacLeod (1977) describe the effects of increasing the spatial separation of the two halves of a bipartite field. Luminance discrimination was impaired, but chromatic discriminations were relatively unaffected for red-green discriminations and actually were improved for discriminations based on SWS cones. Sharpe and Wyszecki (1976), working with larger separations between the fields, also observed that luminance discrimination was degraded more than chromatic discrimination by field separation.

Wavelength discrimination improves with increasing exposure duration, but there is little agreement in the literature as to the optimal exposure. Siegel (1965) showed that chromatic discrimination at 575 nm continued to improve up to a 5-sec exposure time (the longest duration evaluated) although the improvement is a decelerating function beyond 200 msec. Hita, Romero, Jiménez del Barco, and Martinez (1982) found that discrimination improved with exposures up to 1 sec and then approached a slightly poorer value (at 9 sec) asymptotically. Regan and Tyler (1971) found that discrimination asymptoted at 100 msec for 400 and 580 nm and at 200 msec for 527 and

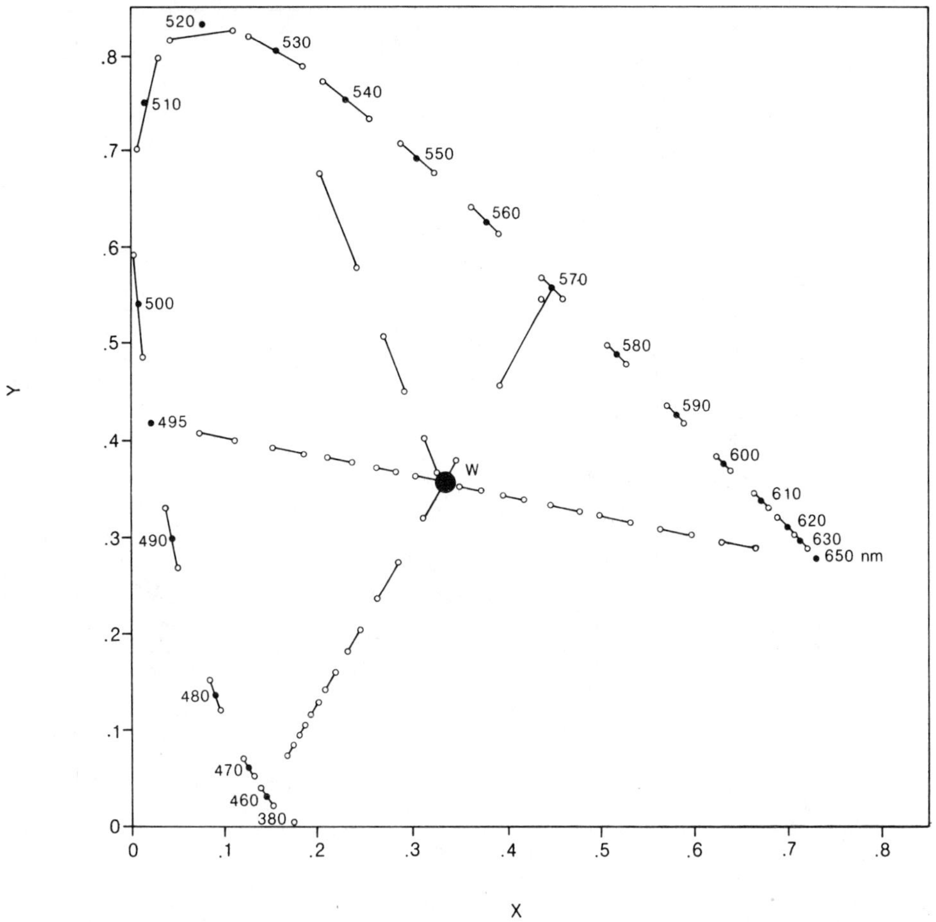

Figure 8.22. Chromatic discrimination represented in a color plane. The graph shows mean wavelength and purity discrimination steps for four observers plotted in the CIE chart. Discrimination steps are indicated by the straight lines with the length of the lines representing about three JNDs in chromaticities for a 2° field. Wavelength discrimination data plot along the spectrum locus, purity discrimination along axes intersecting the standard white. (Data from Wright, 1941).

480 nm. Farnsworth (1961) presented data from Torrey that show that improvements in blue discrimination are less than those for red-green discrimination as stimulus duration increases from 200 msec to 2 sec. Finally, Smith, Bowen, and Pokorny (1984) found threshold colorimetric purity as a function of stimulus duration to be independent of wavelength with asymptotic discrimination at 320–640 msec.

Discrimination deteriorates if stimuli are presented successively, rather than simultaneously. Uchikawa and Ikeda (1981) measured spectral chromatic discrimination as a function of stimulus onset asynchrony (SOA) between two brief (110 msec) presentations of the two halves of a bipartite field. Chromatic discrimination was equivalent to that for simultaneous presentation for SOAs up to 60 msec, then gradually worsened to 190 msec, and remained a constant at 1.5 to 3 times worse to 5 sec (the longest SOA evaluated). Uchikawa (1983) extended these measurements to include a systematic sampling of chromaticity space and confirmed the spectral observations.

Peripheral location of the fields leads to a marked reduction of discrimination particularly in the 490–530-nm region (Gilbert, 1950; Moreland, 1972; Stabell & Stabell, 1977; Weale, 1951). Stabell and Stabell (1977) present data implicating rods as the source of degradation of discrimination (see also Lythgoe, 1931; Stabell & Stabell, 1982). Wavelength discrimination functions for a 1.8 by 3° bipartite field (with a 20-min gap) were similar at the fovea and at 2.5 and 7.5° eccentricities if measurements were made following light adaptation sufficient to render the rods insensitive (see Chapter 5 by Hood and Finkelstein). On the other hand, discrimination functions at 7.5° eccentricity following dark adaptation showed poor discrimination in the 520-nm region for moderately low photopic luminances (3 and 10 td), resembling previous data from the literature.

4.5. Effects of Chromatic Adaptation

Discrimination is affected by chromatic adaptation. Chromatic adaptation has been manipulated either by use of continuously present surrounds or by successive presentation of adapting and discrimination fields. Brown (1952) noted that standard deviations of 2° bipartite field color matches were smallest with a surround of similar chromaticity to the discrimination field. When the surround was of very different chromaticity, discrimination deteriorated. A similar observation was made by Hurvich and Jameson (1961). Brown further noted that if the bipartite field was made large, 12° in diameter, the presence of a surround or its chromaticity had little or no effect. Pointer (1974) extended and confirmed these observations using 1.6° circular fields whose edges were separated by 1.5°. All these data are consistent with

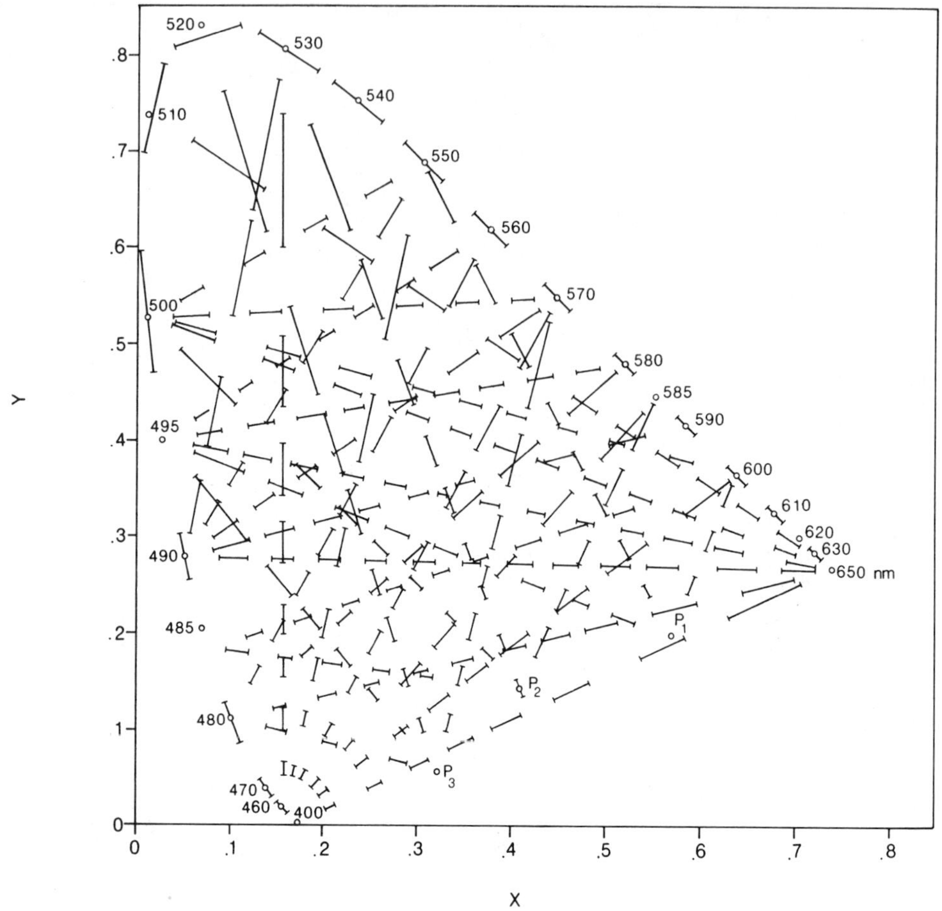

Figure 8.23. Subjectively equal color steps plotted in the CIE chromaticity chart. The lines represent a color difference about 3 times greater than the JNDs for a 2° field. The graph shows discrimination along a large number of color axes. (From W. D. Wright, *Research on normal and defective colour vision*, Kimpton Medical Publishers, 1946. Reprinted with permission.)

the Hurvich and Jameson (1961) analysis in terms of opponent-colors mechanisms. Using a successive adaptation paradigm, Wright (1946) and Loomis and Berger (1979) also noted that discrimination was best when the chromatic discrimination field was of similar chromaticity to a successively presented adaptation field. Loomis and Berger (1979) measured red-green discrimination with the discrimination field presented for 2 sec once every 10 sec. If the adaptation field was flickered at 5 Hz, the deleterious effects of chromatic adaptation were significantly reduced. Krauskopf, Williams, and Healy (1982) measured discrimination from a white in a number of directions in color space following 30 sec of adaptation to a field varying sinusoidally in chromaticity at 1 Hz modulation. They found highly selective chromatic effects with an adaptation field that was modulated in a red-green direction. Red-green discrimination was impaired, but discrimination along an SWS cone line was unaffected. Conversely, modulation along an SWS cone axis affected yellowish-bluish discrimination but not red-green discriminations. In control conditions in which chromaticity was modulated in a direction intermediate between red-green and tritan, thresholds were fairly uniformly elevated in all directions around the white. Luminance modulation had little effect on chromatic thresholds. Chromatic modulation had little effect on luminance thresholds.

Watson (1911) and Tyndall (1933) investigated the effects of adding white light to discrimination fields composed of spectral lights. For wavelengths greater than 490 nm they observed that discrimination deteriorates by a factor of about 1.5 when an equal amount of white and chromatic light are present and by a factor of 3.5 when the white light is 5 times greater in luminance than the spectral discrimination lights. Tyndall (1933) extended these observations into the short-wavelength region of the spectrum and found rather striking results. For 455-nm fields there was little change in discrimination with increases in the luminance of the white light of 1–1.5 times. With further increases in the white, discrimination actually improved and was optimal when the white light was 4–10 times higher in luminance than the spectral discrimination lights. Stiles (1955) observed that the precision of color matches in the short-wavelength region of the spectrum was improved by desaturating the fields with green primary (526 nm). Polden and Mollon (1980) have observed the same phenomenon in a somewhat different context and have coined the term *combinative euchromatopsia* to describe the enhanced sensitivity to hue differences.

4.6. Systematic Sampling of Discrimination of Lights Which Vary in Both Chromaticity and Luminance

Thus far, we have restricted ourselves to analysis of data that involve discriminations in which the luminance of the two fields has been adjusted so that discriminations are based solely on chromaticity. It is also possible to evaluate the joint effects of chromaticity and luminance in determining discrimination steps. Brown and MacAdam (1949) presented 2° bipartite field discrimination ellipsoids for 39 points in chromaticity space; Noorlander, Heuts, and Koenderink (1980) presented data for yellow test fields varying in visual subtense from ¼–1°; and Noorlander, Heuts, and Koenderink (1981) investigated spatio-temporal square-wave modulation of a yellow field. Stromeyer, Cole, and Kronauer (1985) and Wandell (1985) explore some consequences of temporal and chromatic manipulation.

4.7. Spatial and Temporal Chromatic Modulation Transfer Functions

Modulation transfer functions have been measured for equiluminous chromatic alternation in space (DeValois & Switkes, 1983; Granger & Heurtley, 1973; Hilz & Cavonius, 1970; van der Horst, 1969b; van der Horst, de Weert, & Bouman, 1967; Mullen, 1985), time (van der Horst, 1969a; Kelly & van Norren, 1977; De Lange, 1958; Wisowaty, 1981), and joint variation of space and time (van der Horst & Bouman, 1969). A number of techniques have been used to assess the temporal and spatial characteristics of isolated receptor mechanisms. In general, the LWS and MWS cone mechanisms have similar spatial (Brindley, 1954; Cavonius & Estévez, 1975; Green, 1968; but see Kelly, 1974, 1976) and temporal properties (Brindley, du Croz, & Rushton, 1966; Cavonius & Estévez, 1975; Estévez & Cavonius, 1975; Green, 1969; but see Kelly, 1974, 1976). The SWS mechanism exhibits lower spatial (Brindley, 1954; Green, 1968; Stiles, 1949) and temporal (Brindley, du Croz, & Rushton, 1966; Green, 1969; Kelly, 1974; Wisowaty & Boynton, 1980) resolution. It has been suggested that the relatively poor temporal resolution of the SWS mechanism is postreceptoral, rather than receptoral, in origin (Smith, Bowen, & Pokorny, 1984).

5. THEORETICAL DESCRIPTION OF COLOR VISION

Historically, two major ideas dominated attempts to provide a theoretical description of color vision, the Young-Helmholtz trichromatic theory and the Hering opponent-colors theory. Zone or stage theories (Judd, 1949, 1951a) combine an initial trichromatic stage with a subsequent opponent-process stage.

A typical theoretical approach is exemplified by a theory such as that of Hurvich and Jameson (1955), which attempts to describe known psychophysical phenomena in terms of receptors and opponent processes. The theory hypothesizes three classes of photoreceptors with three visual photopigments ex-

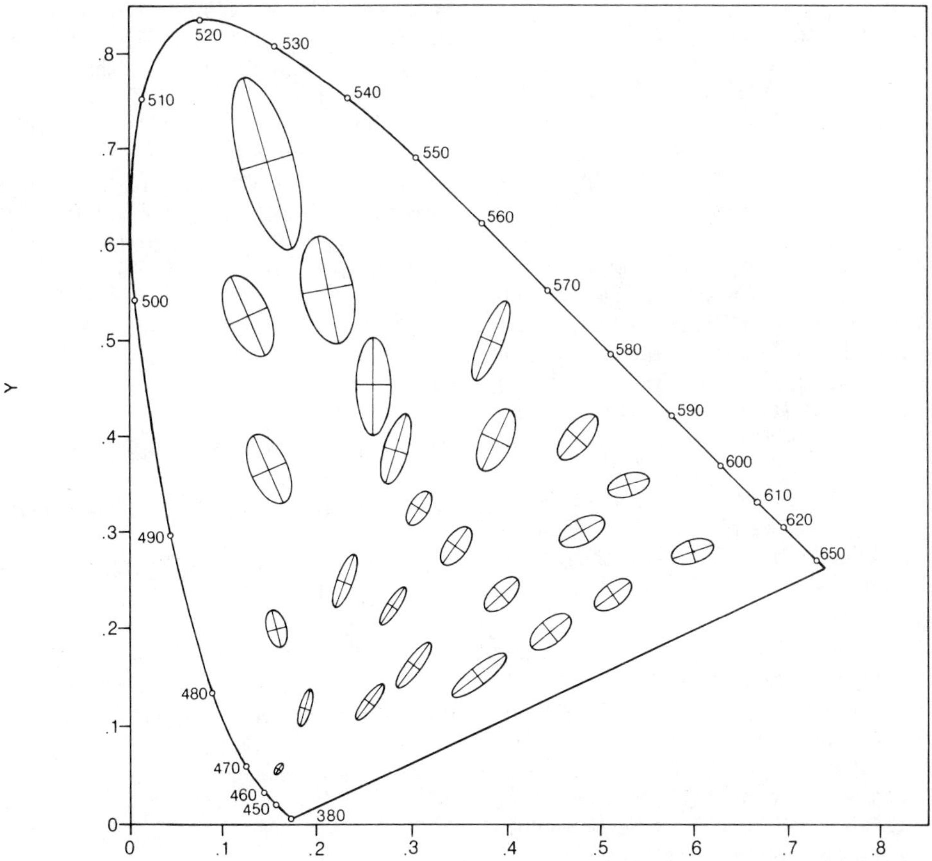

Figure 8.24. Standard deviations of color matches from indicated standards, represented 10 times actual scale in CIE chromaticity diagram. Note that the major axes of the ellipses generally correspond to the axes of poor discrimination in Figure 8.23. (From D. L. MacAdam, Visual sensitivity to color differences in daylight, *Journal of the Optical Society of America*, 1942, *32*. Reprinted with permission.)

hibiting overlapping absorption spectra. The outputs of these receptors (directly or indirectly) may be either excitatory or inhibitory in their effects on higher-order neurons, thus allowing for mutually antagonistic responses. The postulated psychophysical equivalents of these neural substrates are an achromatic channel and two opponent chromatic channels. Proponents of descriptive models have optimized sets of constants to fit selected sets of data. The value of such models lies in their economy of description or in their predictive power but is limited by the arbitrary nature of the constants and the problem that it is difficult to predict accurately results which will be obtained under stimulus conditions other than that for which the model was fitted.

A different approach to a descriptive theory is the *line-element* theory (see Section 5.5). The starting point is the definition of threshold behavior over a radiance range. The model predicts the receptor outputs, which can then be combined. The predictions of psychophysical data, such as wavelength discrimination, are quite complicated (Schrödinger, 1920; Stiles, 1946; Vos, 1979). Since threshold behavior is approximately linear (Massof & Bird, 1978), the line-element approach works well for describing the results from many types of threshold studies. It is not clear that line-element theories are useful for describing above-threshold behavior, for example, large-scale color differences. Line elements are attractive because of their predictive power although some authors have pointed out limitations (Boynton, Nagy, & Olsen, 1983; Noorlander, 1981; Wandell, 1982, 1985).

Some theorists do not attempt a descriptive theory but prefer to evaluate axioms that can be derived from basic postulates (e.g., Bird & Massof, 1978; Krantz, 1975; Massof & Bird, 1978; Zaidi, 1984).

5.1. Trichromatic Stage

Thomas Young (1802) suggested that the eye required only three independent modes of excitation, with each of these being differentially sensitive in the visible spectrum and having peak sensitivities in different regions of the spectrum (a number of authors have summarized the history of trichromatic theory: Balaraman, 1962; Brindley, 1970; Halbertsma, 1949; Sherman, 1981; Weale, 1957). Recent theoretical interpretations of trichromacy (e.g., Estévez, 1979; Pokorny, Smith, & Starr, 1976; Smith & Pokorny, 1972; Smith, Pokorny, & Starr, 1976; Vos & Walraven, 1971) suggest that the physiological substrate mediating foveal color-matching performance lies in the number and shapes of the absorption spectra of the cone visual photopigments.

5.1.1. König Fundamentals and Spaces. If color matching is performed in a retinal area where only cone photopigments are active and provided Grassmann's laws hold, it may be assumed that the color match occurs when the quantal catches are balanced simultaneously in all three cone visual photopigments (Brindley, 1970). For the long-wavelength sensitive (LWS), middle-wavelength sensitive (MWS), and short-wavelength sensitive (SWS) cone visual photopigment, the quantal catch is the product of the amount of primary light and the cone relative sensitivity at the primary or test wavelength (Section 3.7). The color-matching equations can be rewritten

$$\text{LWS}: a_\lambda S_{1\lambda} + a_1 S_{11} = a_2 S_{12} + a_3 S_{13} , \quad (52)$$

$$\text{MWS}: a_\lambda S_{2\lambda} + a_1 S_{21} = a_2 S_{22} + a_3 S_{23} , \quad (53)$$

$$\text{SWS}: a_\lambda S_{3\lambda} + a_1 S_{31} = a_2 S_{32} + a_3 S_{33} , \quad (54)$$

where a_j are the amounts of the primary lights and S_{ij} are the relative sensitivities of the cone visual photopigments. It follows that a linear transformation of color-matching data will yield the relative cone sensitivities (also called *fundamentals*). Cone fundamentals have been described since König (1897). The transformation requires, of course, the setting of nine unknowns. One method is to use data of congenital color defectives assuming that observers with selected types of color vision defects are lacking one of the three normal fundamentals. Fundamentals derived in this way are called *König fundamentals*. Modern sets are those of Estévez (1979), Smith and Pokorny (1972, 1975), Vos (1978), Vos and Walraven (1971), and Walraven (1974). The terminology used by Vos and Walraven (1971) is to call the fundamental of the LWS cone photopigment S_R, that for the MWS, S_G, and that for the SWS, S_B. These transformations are shown in Table 8.14. The Vos and Walraven (1971) fundamentals are based on the Vos (1978) continuous interpolation of the Judd (1951b) observer and also a revision by Walraven (1974) incorporating the original Vos and Walraven (1971) equations. The Smith and Pokorny (1975) fundamentals are based on the Judd observer. The coefficients for S_B were unspecified by their transformation. In Table 8.14 S_B is set to unity at its maximum. The Estévez (1979) transformation is based on the Stiles (1955) 2° pilot color-matching data. Finally, the Smith and Pokorny (1975) fundamentals, all adusted to unity at their maximum, also can be derived in the Stiles primary system (Smith, Pokorny, & Zaidi, 1983). Table 8.15 (on page 8-36) shows the Smith and Pokorny (1975) fundamentals as a function of wavelength.

Boynton and Wisowaty (1980) have provided equations to solve for the Smith and Pokorny (1975) fundamentals in terms of wavelength. For the S_G fundamental they used an equation of the form

$$S_G = (a^n + b^n)^{1/n} , \quad (55)$$

where

$$a = \text{antilog}\,(a_4\lambda^4 + a_3\lambda^3 + a_2\lambda^2 + a_1\lambda + a_0) , \quad (56)$$

$$b = \text{antilog}\,(b_4\lambda^4 + b_3\lambda^3 + b_2\lambda^2 + b_1\lambda + b_0) . \quad (57)$$

For the S_B and S_R fundamentals a more complicated expression was required.

$$Q = [(a^{n1} + b^{n1})^{n2/n1} + c^{n2}]^{1/n2} . \quad (58)$$

For these cases, frequency rather than wavelength was used:

$$a = \text{antilog}\,(a_3\nu^3 + a_2\nu^2 + a_1\nu + a_0) , \quad (59)$$

$$b = \text{antilog}\,(b_3\nu^3 + b_2\nu^2 + b_1\nu + b_0) , \quad (60)$$

$$c = \text{antilog}\,(c_3\nu^3 + c_2\nu^2 + c_1\nu + c_0) . \quad (61)$$

Then S_R and S_B are obtained using the relation

$$S = Q(\lambda)/Q(555) . \quad (62)$$

Table 8.14. Equations for König Fundamentals Derived for the Judd (1951b) and the Stiles (1955) Color-Matching Functions

Vos and Walraven Transformation (Judd, 1951b)

$$\begin{matrix} S_R\colon \bar{r}(\lambda) \\ S_G\colon \bar{g}(\lambda) \\ S_B\colon \bar{b}(\lambda) \end{matrix} = \begin{bmatrix} 0.1551646 & 0.5430763 & -0.0370161 \\ -0.1551646 & 0.4569237 & 0.0296946 \\ 0.0000000 & 0.0000000 & 0.0073315 \end{bmatrix} \begin{bmatrix} \bar{x}'(\lambda) \\ \bar{y}'(\lambda) \\ \bar{z}'(\lambda) \end{bmatrix}$$

Smith and Pokorny Transformation (Judd, 1951b)

$$\begin{matrix} S_R\colon \bar{r}(\lambda) \\ S_G\colon \bar{g}(\lambda) \\ S_B\colon \bar{b}(\lambda) \end{matrix} = \begin{bmatrix} 0.15514 & 0.54312 & -0.03286 \\ -0.15514 & 0.45684 & 0.03286 \\ 0.00000 & 0.00000 & 0.01608 \end{bmatrix} \begin{bmatrix} \bar{x}'(\lambda) \\ \bar{y}'(\lambda) \\ \bar{z}'(\lambda) \end{bmatrix}$$

(S_B is scaled to an arbitrary height.)

Estévez Transformation (Stiles, 1955)

$$\begin{matrix} S_{Rm}\colon \rho(m) \\ S_{Gm}\colon \gamma(m) \\ S_{Bm}\colon \beta(m) \end{matrix} = \begin{bmatrix} 0.3845 & 1.0062 & 0.0512 \\ 0.0538 & 1.4412 & 0.1183 \\ 0.0000 & 0.0305 & 1.551 \end{bmatrix} \begin{bmatrix} \bar{p}_1(m) \\ \bar{p}_2(m) \\ \bar{p}_3(m) \end{bmatrix}$$

Smith and Pokorny Transformation (Stiles, 1955)

$$\begin{matrix} S_{Rm}\colon \bar{r}(m) \\ S_{Gm}\colon \bar{g}(m) \\ S_{Bm}\colon \bar{b}(m) \end{matrix} = \begin{bmatrix} 0.2034 & 0.7239 & 0.0332 \\ 0.0205 & 0.9022 & 0.0531 \\ 0.0000 & 0.0293 & 1.000 \end{bmatrix} \begin{bmatrix} \bar{p}_1(m) \\ \bar{p}_2(m) \\ \bar{p}_3(m) \end{bmatrix}$$

(Normalized to unity.)

Four sets of equations are shown, each of which will allow derivation of König fundamentals from published sets of color-matching functions. The first is the Vos and Walraven transformation of the Judd (1951b) modified observer. The second is the Smith and Pokorny transformation of the same color-matching data. The color-matching functions $\bar{x}(\lambda)$, $\bar{y}(\lambda)$, and $\bar{z}(\lambda)$ are a function of wavelength. Both these transformations have the property that the luminosity function is represented by a sum of the fundamentals. For Vos and Walraven all three fundamentals sum to the Judd luminosity function; for Smith and Pokorny S_R and S_G sum to the Judd luminosity function, while S_B is scaled so that $S_B/(S_R + S_G)$ is equal to unity at 400 nm (cf. MacLeod & Boynton, 1979). The third set of equations is the Estévez transformation of the Stiles (1955) color-matching data. The fourth set is the Smith and Pokorny transformation expressed in terms of the Stiles (1955) color-matching data. The color-matching functions $\bar{p}_1(m)$, $\bar{p}_2$, and $\bar{p}_3(m)$ are a function of wave number. The heights of the fundamentals based on Stiles (1955) are set to unity.

The values of n, a, b, and c are summarized in Table 8.16 (on page 8-37). The purpose of deriving these rather complicated equations was to provide smooth, continuously differentiable functions for use in color-modeling work.

5.1.2. Cone Chromaticity Space. MacLeod and Boynton (1979) suggested that a useful chromaticity chart would be a constant luminance plane of a diagram in which the three cone receptor sensitivities formed the rectangular axes. They suggested the chromaticity diagram formed by

$$r = \frac{S_R}{(S_R + S_G)}, \tag{63}$$

$$g = \frac{S_G}{(S_R + S_G)}, \tag{64}$$

$$b = \frac{S_B}{(S_R + S_G)}, \tag{65}$$

in which b is plotted against r. The functions S_R, S_G, and S_B are cone receptor sensitivities for which the Smith and Pokorny (1975) fundamentals were used. The values of r, g, and b are shown in Table 8.17 (on page 8-38), and the diagram is shown in Figure 8.25 (on page 8-38). The scaling of the b coordinate is essentially arbitrary but was chosen so that $0 \leqslant b \leqslant 1$. The advantages of such a diagram include ease of computation for certain types of colorimetric or discrimination problems (MacLeod & Boynton, 1979). In the space, equal excitations of SWS cones occur on horizontal lines.

The concept of an equal cone excitation space may be extended to include rods. A three-dimensional diagram results for an arbitrary scaling of $V'(\lambda)$ and is shown in Figure 8.26 (on page 8-39). Such a diagram may be useful to investigators who wish to know the relative rod stimulation for a given pair of cone metamers (cf. Rodieck, 1973; Wyszecki & Stiles, 1982). For example, let R be a color formed by either of two pairs of cone metamers p_1,p_2 and q_1,q_2. Then R_p is the rod stimulation for the cone pair (p_1,p_2), and R_q is the rod stimulation for cone pair (q_1,q_2). When (p_1,p_2) and (q_1,q_2) are exchanged, the rod stimulation ratio would be R_p/R_q.

5.1.3. Comparison of König Fundamentals with Cone Sensitivity Estimates Derived from Other Techniques. An alternative approach to deriving the fundamental receptor curves of trichromatic theory depends on the partial-bleaching procedure. Spectral sensitivity curves of the receptors are derived in psychophysical procedures that isolate one or another cone pho-

Table 8.15. König Fundamentals Derived by Smith and Pokorny (1975)

Wavelength (nm)	Sensitivity		
	S_R	S_G	S_B
400	0.00273	0.00177	0.00450
410	0.00553	0.00377	0.00938
420	0.01005	0.00745	0.01708
430	0.01489	0.01241	0.02336
440	0.01918	0.01872	0.02583
450	0.02186	0.02494	0.02366
460	0.02630	0.03370	0.02071
470	0.03991	0.05108	0.01790
480	0.06495	0.07404	0.01214
490	0.1032	0.1047	0.00717
500	0.1675	0.1555	0.00425
510	0.2696	0.2334	0.00248
520	0.3930	0.3170	0.00123
530	0.4926	0.3694	0.00066
540	0.5629	0.3911	0.00032
550	0.6078	0.3871	0.00014
560	0.6329	0.3621	0.00006
570	0.6355	0.3164	0.00003
580	0.6146	0.2554	0.00002
590	0.5697	0.1872	0.00002
600	0.5063	0.1247	0.00001
610	0.4271	0.07586	0.00000
620	0.3377	0.04322	0.00000
630	0.2421	0.02289	0.00000
640	0.1634	0.01160	0.00000
650	0.1014	0.00564	0.00000
660	0.05820	0.00280	0.00000
670	0.03068	0.00132	0.00000
680	0.01634	0.00065	0.00000
690	0.00790	0.00031	0.00000
700	0.00395	0.00015	0.00000

The sensitivities of S_R, S_G, and S_B derived from the equations shown in Table 8.14 are tabulated as a function of wavelength at 10-nm intervals. At each wavelength, the values of S_R and S_G sum to give the relative spectral luminous efficiency V(λ), and S_B, given an arbitrary scaling $S_B/(S_R + S_G)$, is unity at 400 nm, as used by MacLeod and Boynton (1979).

toreceptor class. For example, the observer may be adapted to an intense spectral light, following which matching equations or relative spectral sensitivity thresholds are obtained (Brindley, 1953). Alternatively, thresholds may be measured on steady backgrounds (Stiles, 1939, 1959; Wald, 1964). If, for example, a 650-nm light is used for a bleaching or adapting field, it is hypothesized that the long-wavelength receptor mechanism is adapted more than the middle- or short-wavelength receptor mechanisms. Thus the observer's matches or thresholds after red adaptation should reflect primarily the activities of the middle- or short-wavelength receptors.

Stiles defined a total of seven foveal mechanisms using the threshold versus radiance (tvr) technique (see Chapter 5 by Hood and Finkelstein) to give field sensitivities. Three (π_1, π_2, and π_3) have sensitivity peaks in the short-wavelength region of the spectrum, two in the middle-wavelength region (π_4, π_4'), and two in the long-wavelength region (π_5, π_5') (Stiles, 1959). Figure 8.27 shows the relative field sensitivities of the π_1, π_3, π_4, and π_5 mechanisms plotted in terms of the logarithm of quantal energy as a function of wave number.

The Wald (1964) selective chromatic adaptation technique using 40-msec test flashes in the normal trichromat yielded test sensitivities of three overlapping functions with peaks near 442, 546, and 571 nm. These were termed "blue," "green," and "red" receptor mechanisms. These receptor mechanisms were assumed to be the corneal sensitivities (i.e., cone sensitivity modified by prereceptoral absorption) associated with the absorption spectra of three cone visual photopigments. These adaptation techniques (described in Figure 8.27, page 8-39) have limitations, since the receptor sensitivities overlap and the majority of adapting lights tend to adapt more than one class of receptor (Walraven, 1976). As one result, more sophisticated techniques have been developed, for example, silent substitution, cone saturation, or afterimage matching, as well as a refinement of technique, for example, use of critical flicker frequency or flicker photometry in conjunction with adaptation fields.

There are small but consistent differences between proposed spectral sensitivities of cone photopigments derived from sensitivity data of color-defective observers (or, for that matter, from color mixture data using König's assumptions) and the spectral sensitivities derived using the Stiles adaptation techniques (Boynton, 1963).

The mechanisms are to a first approximation independent, but analysis (Boynton, 1963) suggests that the π mechanisms demonstrated by field sensitivities may not represent the spectral sensitivities of isolated cone receptors. Considerable research activity suggests multiple cone classes contributing to π_1 (Pugh, 1976; Pugh & Mollon, 1979), π_4 (Boynton, Das, & Gardiner, 1966; Reeves, 1982b; Sigel & Brousseau, 1982; Walraven, 1981), and π_5 (Boynton, Das, & Gardiner, 1966; Ikeda, Uetsuki, & Stiles, 1970; Reeves, 1982a; Sternheim, Gorinson, & Markovitz, 1977; Walraven, 1981). A wealth of experimental evidence points to postreceptoral contribution in the spectral sensitivity of π_1, π_4, and π_5. Additivity failures have been shown for π_1 (Pugh, 1976; Pugh & Mollon, 1979), but why the displacement principle works for the original measurement conditions for π_4 and π_5 is an intriguing question. Use of short duration (40 msec or less) test flashes or flickering repetitive stimulation (10 Hz or higher) yields functions which show additivity (Ikeda, 1963; Ingling & Martinez, 1981; Ingling & Tsou, 1977; Reeves, 1982a, 1982b; Sternheim, Stromeyer, & Khoo, 1979; Wandell & Pugh, 1980).

Below 500 nm, π_1 is of the same spectral shape as the SWS cone spectra but shifted a minor amount on the wavelength axis (Smith & Pokorny, 1972); π_4 is considerably broader than MWS (Boynton, 1979; Mollon, 1982); and π_5 is slightly broader than LWS (Boynton, 1979; Mollon, 1982; Ingling & Martinez, 1981; Ingling & Tsou, 1977).

A necessary (but not sufficient) requirement of a candidate set of cone fundamentals is that they be a linear transformation of color mixture data. Estévez and Cavonius (1977) and Pugh and Sigel (1978) found agreement within experimental error between π_1, π_4, and π_5 and linear transformations of color-matching functions.

There are psychophysical data from normal trichromats for which the estimated cone sensitivities are closely similar to those measured on color-defective observers.

1. Brindley (1953) and Stromeyer, Cole, and Kronauer (1985) measured threshold spectral sensitivities and color matches

Table 8.16. Values of the Exponents and the Coefficients Used by Boynton and Wisowaty (1980)

S_R		S_G		S_B	
		Exponents			
n_1 =	2.25	n =	1.45	n_1 =	8.00
n_2 =	8.50			n_2 =	5.00
		Coefficients			
a_3 =	−0.024665	a_4 =	−27957.778	a_3 =	0.687704
a_2 =	−0.555382	a_3 =	52266.5676	a_2 =	−16.192047
a_1	10.561284	a_2 =	−36597.4256	a_1 =	124.940404
a_0 =	−40.000518	a_1 =	11391.0474	a_0 =	−316.796601
		a_0 =	−1332.9406		
b_3 =	0.581813	b_4 =	−1706.1298	b_3 =	−0.391274
b_2 =	−11.340332	b_3 =	493.3857	b_2 =	5.620650
b_1 =	71.653893	b_2 =	−5379.6535	b_1 =	−23.031819
b_0 =	−148.063220	b_1 =	2570.9049	b_0 =	19.863510
		b_0 =	−453.4387		
c_3 =	0.660176			c_3 =	−11.050549
c_2 =	−12.357251			c_2 =	162.285878
c_1 =	74.990768			c_1 =	−790.820409
c_0 =	−148.863364			c_0 =	1275.061864

The values of the exponents and the coefficients suggested by Boynton and Wisowaty to produce continuously differentiable König fundamentals similar to those of Smith and Pokorny (1975). The center column shows the exponents and coefficients for S_G to be used in Eqs. 55–57; these are coefficients of wavelength. The left column shows exponents and coefficients for S_R, the right column for S_B. These are to be used in Eqs. 58–61 and are coefficients of frequency $\nu = 2.998/\lambda$.

Source: From R. M. Boynton and J. S. Wisowaty, Equations for chromatic discrimination models, *Journal of the Optical Society of America*, 1980, *70*. Reprinted with permission.

following intense spectral light adaptation (artificial monochromacy).

2. Wald (1964) measured test sensitivities for 40-msec test flashes on bright chromatic background fields.
3. King-Smith and Webb (1974) used a flashed field to saturate two of the cone systems and measured the test sensitivity of the third.
4. Mitchell and Rushton (1971), Rushton, Powell, and White (1973), Hollins and Montabana (1973), and Piantanida, Bruch, Latch, and Varner (1976) measured spectral sensitivities under conditions of "silent substitution" (Estévez & Spekreijse, 1974, 1982), in which pairs of lights are adjusted so that the quantal catch for one cone type is equivalent for the members of the pair.
5. Williams and MacLeod (1979) used afterimage matching on chromatic backgrounds following chromatic bleaches.
6. Eisner and MacLeod (1981) measured flicker photometric spectral sensitivities on chromatic backgrounds (see also Ikeda & Urakubo, 1968).
7. Eisner (1982) measured critical flicker threshold spectral sensitivities on chromatic backgrounds.

5.2. Physiological Factors: The Visual Photopigments

Fundamental sensitivity curves derived either from color-matching or from partial-bleaching studies are presumed to reflect the spectrum of the cone visual photopigment measured for an equal-energy spectrum at the corneal surface. For comparison with a postulated photopigment, the data must be converted to an equal quantal spectrum and corrected for prereceptoral absorption losses of lens and macular pigment. The corrected sensitivity curve can then be compared to a fractional absorption spectrum for a photopigment of some effective optical density.

5.2.1. The Lens and Macular Pigment. The lens does not transmit equally all wavelengths of light incident upon it. The lens absorbs strongly at short wavelengths, having high optical density (about 1.2) at 400 nm. The optical density function decreases rapidly above 450 nm, and the lens transmits over 90% of incident light for wavelengths longer than 580 nm. Table 8.18 (on page 8-40) shows the optical density of the lens for a 32-year-old human observer, relative to the value at 700 nm. Wyszecki and Stiles (1982) and van Norren and Vos (1974) have reviewed experimental studies of the lens density function. During life, physiologic changes in the lens are accompanied by increases in the optical density function of the lens (Ripps & Weale, 1976). The lens enlarges with age, and the pupil is smaller in older individuals. As a result, mean path length through the lens becomes longer (Weale, 1961). To a first approximation, the spectral density function of an old lens can be predicted as a linear (Said & Weale, 1959; Werner, 1982) or polynomial (Coren & Girgus, 1972) function of the spectral density function for a young lens (see also Moreland, 1978); that is, the change in the lens absorption function represents normal maturational events occurring in the lens from youth. These

Table 8.17. Coefficients for the MacLeod-Boynton Cone Excitation Diagram

Wavelength (nm)	*r*	*g*	*b*
400	0.6000	0.4000	0.9914
410	0.5914	0.4086	1.0000
420	0.5771	0.4229	0.9674
430	0.5458	0.4542	0.8481
440	0.5066	0.4934	0.6756
450	0.4679	0.5321	0.5012
460	0.4383	0.5617	0.3421
470	0.4385	0.5615	0.1950
480	0.4676	0.5324	0.0866
490	0.4961	0.5039	0.0342
500	0.5186	0.4814	0.0130
510	0.5360	0.4640	0.0049
520	0.5535	0.4465	0.0017
530	0.5715	0.4285	0.0008
540	0.5900	0.4100	0.0003
550	0.6371	0.3629	0.0001
560	0.6361	0.3639	0.00006
570	0.6675	0.3325	0.00003
580	0.7064	0.2936	0.00003
590	0.7526	0.2474	0.00002
600	0.8024	0.1976	0.00002
610	0.8491	0.1509	0.00001
620	0.8864	0.1136	0.00001
630	0.9136	0.0864	0.00001
640	0.9337	0.0663	
650	0.9477	0.0523	
660	0.9541	0.0459	
670	0.9594	0.0406	
680	0.9647	0.0353	
690	0.9634	0.0366	
700	0.9756	0.0244	
White	0.6645	0.3355	0.0158

The coefficients r, g, *and* b *derived from Eqs. 63–65 are shown as a function of wavelength. These coefficients are derived from König fundamentals expressed relative to their luminosity. The scaling of the* b *coefficients is arbitrary and in this table differs slightly from that of Tables 8.14 and 8.15 in that the coefficient* b *is set to unity at 410 nm, rather than 400 nm.*

calculations are only an approximation, since the possibility that pigments not present at birth can accumulate in the lens during life (e.g., Tan, 1971) is ignored.

The macular pigment is a substance in the fundus whose appearance in an ophthalmoscope is of darkening around the foveal area. It has variously been described as lying around the fibers of Henle (Segal, 1950), primarily in the outer plexiform layers (Gass, 1973) or through layers 4 to 9 of the retina (Polyak, 1941). Marshall, Hamilton, and Bird (1974) used intraretinal absorption of argon laser irradiation to localize this pigment in the fiber layer of Henle at the fovea and in the inner nuclear and inner plexiform layers at eccentricities of 2° and 3° of visual angle, respectively. This distribution has been confirmed by microspectrophotometric measurement (Snodderly, Brown, Delori, & Auran, 1984). Neither the spatial extent nor the optical density of the macular pigment is precisely known, and both may vary substantially from individual to individual. Measurements of the optical density of the pigment at different retinal eccentricities indicate that the density decreases from a maximum at the fovea to zero at about 4–8° away from the fovea (Gilbert, 1950; Ruddock, 1963; Snodderly, Auran, & Delori, 1984; Stabell & Stabell, 1980; Viénot, 1983; Wright, 1946). Individuals may vary in the amount of psychophysically measurable macular pigment with optical density ranging from 0 to greater than 1 (Bone & Sparrock, 1971). For a 2° field, the average observer's eye is usually assumed to have an optical density of 0.35–0.5 at 460 nm, the wavelength of maximal density (Stiles, 1953; Vos, 1972; Wald, 1945).

The density spectrum of the macular pigment has been measured by a variety of techniques, including psychophysical, reflection, photographic, and polarization. Vos (1972) reviewed these studies and showed that there is general agreement on the absorption spectrum estimated by Wyszecki and Stiles (1982), which is tabulated in Table 8.19 (on page 8-40) for a value of 0.5 for maximal optical density. Wald (1945) observed that the spectrum has the spectral characteristics of xanthophyll, a carotenoid pigment. Although there have been occasional reports of increases in macular pigment density with age, studies that separated lens effects from macular pigment effects suggest that macular pigment changes little (Stiles & Burch, 1959) or not at all (Kelly, 1961; Ruddock, 1965; Verriest, 1974) with age.

5.2.2. The Quantal Energy Spectrum. Each absorbed quantum bleaches a single unit of visual photopigment; this event may then initiate a visual response in a manner only partially understood. The quantal flux, rather than radiant energy, is important in the study of visual photopigment. The energy E of a quantum is proportional to its frequency ν:

$$E = h\nu = hc/\lambda , \quad (66)$$

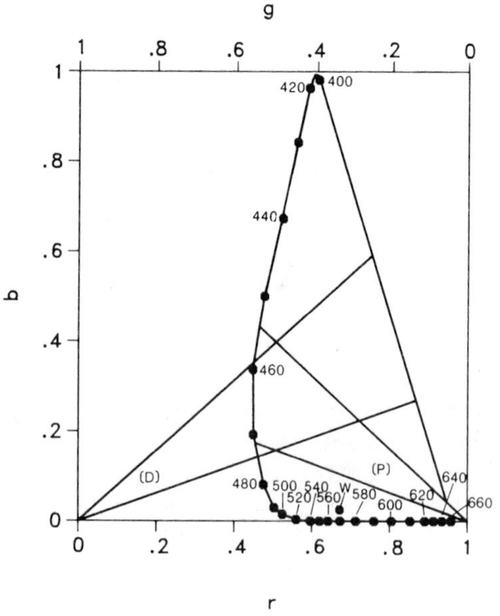

Figure 8.25. Cone excitation diagram of chromaticity. The SWS, or *b*, cone excitation is plotted against *r*, the proportion of LWS cone stimulation from equiluminant stimuli. The isochromatic lines for protanopes *P* and deuteranopes *D* converge at *r* = 1 (point representing LWS) and *g* = 1 (point representing MWS), respectively. Tritanopic isochromatic lines plot as parallel lines orthogonal to the ordinate. (From D. I. A. Macleod & R. M. Boynton, Chromaticity diagram showing cone excitation by stimuli of equal luminance, *Journal of the Optical Society of America*, 1979, 69. Reprinted with permission.)

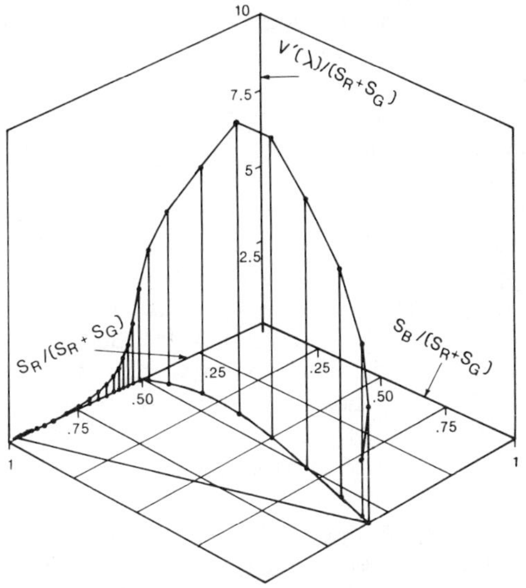

Figure 8.26. A cone-rod excitation diagram of chromaticity. This is a three-dimensional diagram in which the cone excitation diagram of figure 8.25 is plotted in the horizontal plane. On the vertical axis is plotted the rod excitation. In the horizontal plane, SWS cone excitation relative to luminance and scaled, that is, $kS_B/(S_R+S_G)$, is plotted against the proportion of LWS cone stimulation relative to luminance, that is, $S_R/(S_R+S_G)$. The vertical axis shows $V'(\lambda)/(S_R+S_G)$; S_B, S_R, and S_G are from Table 8.15, and $V'(\lambda)$ is from Table 8.6. Points in the space that have the same projection in the horizontal plane are cone metamers that have different rod excitation values.

where h is the Planck constant (approximately $6.624940 \cdot 10^{-34}$ J·sec), c is the speed of light (approximately $3 \cdot 10^8$ m·sec *in vacuo*), and λ is the wavelength in meters. To convert a psychophysical sensitivity function from a radiant energy base to a quantal energy base, it is necessary to multiply by K/λ, where K is a normalizing constant that can be set at any convenient quantity, for example, 1 or 700. If the relative sensitivity is in logarithms, add $\log(K/\lambda)$.

5.2.3. The Absorption Spectrum. Light must be absorbed to be seen. The absorbed light is that portion that was neither transmitted nor reflected. Assuming that the reflected light is negligible, the fraction of light absorbed $F(\lambda)$ is

$$F(\lambda) = 1 - \tau(\lambda)\,, \tag{67}$$

where $\tau(\lambda)$ is the transmittance. Optical density (OD) is defined as the negative decadic logarithm of transmittance, that is,

$$OD = -\log T \quad \text{or} \quad T = 10^{(-OD)}\,. \tag{68}$$

In this equation $A(\lambda)$ is the product

$$A(\lambda) = cl\epsilon(\lambda)\,, \tag{70}$$

where c is the concentration of the pigment, l is the path length traversed through the photopigment, and $\epsilon(\lambda)$ is the (decadic) molar absorptivity spectrum, a characteristic of the pigment (Rodieck, 1973). Absorption spectra are sometimes called *fractional* or *partial absorption spectra.*

An important property of the relative fractional absorption spectrum $F(\lambda)/F(\lambda_{max})$, given by

$$\frac{F(\lambda)}{F(\lambda_{max})} = \frac{1 - 10^{-A(\lambda)}}{1 - 10^{-A(\lambda_{max})}}\,, \tag{71}$$

is that its shape depends on the absorbance $A(\lambda)$ of the pigment. The greater the absorbance, the broader the shape of the fractional absorption spectrum. In comparison, the relative absorbance spectrum $A(\lambda)/A(\lambda_{max})$ reduces to $\epsilon(\lambda)/\epsilon(\lambda_{max})$ and is independent of concentration or path length (Dartnall, 1957). As concentration or path length decrease to a minimal value, $A(\lambda)$ approaches $10^{-A(\lambda)}$; therefore, the relative absorption spectrum, $F(\lambda)/F(\lambda_{max})$, will approach the relative absorbance spectrum $\epsilon(\lambda)/\epsilon(\lambda_{max})$, as shown in Figure 8.28 (on page 8-41). When a psychophysical experiment is designed to derive an estimate of the spectral response of a photoreceptor or to calculate the effect of a bleaching light, the psychophysical functions must be referred to fractional absorption spectra of appropriate optical density. Alternatively, an effective optical density may be ascribed to the psychophysical function, and the hypothetical density spectrum may be derived.

Color matches depend on the effective optical density of the underlying visual photopigments. The optical density of a single photoreceptor for incident light parallel to its long axis is calculated as the peak absorptivity per unit length multiplied by the length of the outer segment. The highest optical densities are calculated for the long cylindrical photoreceptors of the central foveal. Parafoveal and peripheral photoreceptors have lower optical densities. In a psychophysical experiment many cones are stimulated, and the stimulus field will be characterized by an effective optical density representing some average function of the individual photoreceptors. Differences in color matches made in a 2 or 10° field may be partly attributed to differences in the effective optical densities characterizing these fields (Burns & Elsner, 1985; Pokorny & Smith, 1976; Pokorny, Smith, & Starr, 1976).

Foveal color matches are *not* affected by changes in radiance as long as there is no substantial bleaching of the cone visual photopigments (Alpern, 1979; Terstiege, 1967; Wyszecki & Stiles, 1980). At sufficiently high levels of radiance, a proportion of visual photopigment is bleached. The effective optical density is reduced, and the effective absorption spectra are narrower. In a color match of red plus green to yellow, more red is required

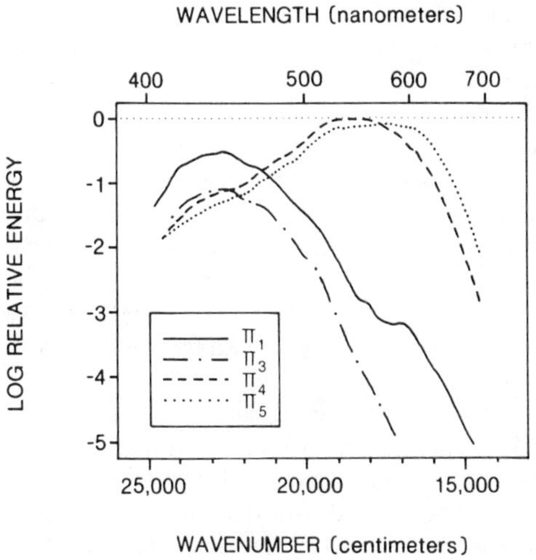

Figure 8.27. Log relative quantal field sensitivities of the Stiles π mechanisms plotted as a function of wave number. The π_5 and π_4 mechanisms show maximal sensitivity in the long- and middle-wavelength regions of the spectrum respectively. The π_1 and π_3 mechanisms show maximal sensitivity in the short-wavelength region. (From J. Pokorny, V. C. Smith, G. Verriest, & A. J. L. C. Pinckers, *Congenital and acquired color defects*, Grune & Stratton, 1979. Reprinted with permission.)

Table 8.18. Optical Density of the Lens Transmission Function T_L for an Average 32-Year-Old Observer

Wavelength	Optical Density	Wavelength	Optical Density
400	1.600	550	0.093
410	1.093	560	0.080
420	0.733	570	0.067
430	0.493	580	0.053
440	0.360	590	0.040
450	0.300	600	0.033
460	0.267	610	0.027
470	0.233	620	0.020
480	0.207	630	0.013
490	0.187	640	0.007
500	0.167	650	0.000
510	0.147	660	0.000
520	0.133	670	0.000
530	0.120	680	0.000
540	0.107	690	0.000
		700	0.000

The optical density (Section 5.2.3) of the lens is tabulated as a function of wavelength. The data represent expected densities for a 32-year-old observer (Smith & Pokorny, 1975) and represent a 1.333 scaling of the data in Wyszecki and Stiles (1982).

(Brindley, 1953, 1955, 1970). This effect, sometimes called *self-screening*, was measured quantitatively by Brindley (1953, 1955) who correctly deduced that the cause was reduction in effective optical density. The complete explanation is complicated and involves understanding of the wave-guide nature of light propagation in the inner and outer segments of the photoreceptors (Starr, 1977). (See Chapter 5 by Hood and Finkelstein for further discussion of photopigment bleaching.)

5.2.4. Comparison of König Fundamentals with Visual Photopigment Spectra. Primate cone visual photopigment absorption spectra were first measured using the technique of microspectrophotometry (Brown & Wald, 1964; Marks, Dobelle, & MacNichol, 1964). Advances in technology (Knowles & Dartnall, 1977; Liebman, 1972) have improved the technique. Modern investigations of primate cone spectra were published by Bowmaker and Dartnall (1980), Bowmaker, Dartnall, and Mollon (1980), and Bowmaker, Dartnall, Lythgoe, and Mollon (1978). The Bowmaker and Dartnall relative density spectra for human cones (tabulated in Wyszecki & Stiles, 1982) are broader than relative density spectra based on König fundamentals. This phenomenon occurs also in comparisons of the primate rhodopsin spectra with the $V'(\lambda)$ curve (Bowmaker & Dartnall, 1980; Bowmaker, Dartnall, & Mollon, 1980; Bowmaker et al., 1978) as emphasized by Ingling and Martinez (1981). The wavelengths of maximal sensitivity do agree both for the rhodopsin spectrum and the cone pigment spectra.

The most recent advance is the technique described by Nunn and Baylor (1983) in which individual monkey rod outer segments are drawn into a suction electrode. Their spectral sensitivity may be measured over 6 log units and agree well with the $V'(\lambda)$. Furthermore LWS and MWS monkey cones indicate good agreement with König fundamentals (Nunn, Schnapf, & Baylor, 1984, 1985).

5.3. Opponent-Process Stage

Chromatic discriminative ability, as in judgments of hue differences, is currently thought to reflect two major dimensions of perceptual color space: judgments of redness-greenness and judgments of blueness-yellowness. A normal observer can abstract these qualities separately from a colored surface. Many theorists postulate that the neural substrates of such perceptual phenomena are a set of independent neural processing channels.

Hering (1878/1964) proposed an opponent-process theory to account for color perception. Based on the complementary nature of blue and yellow and of red and green, Hering suggested that these four colors, together with black and white, form three pairs of unique sensory qualities. Further, since the members of each pair are never simultaneously perceived in a single hue percept, the two are considered mutually exclusive, or opponent sensory qualities. Jameson and Hurvich (1955) and Hurvich and Jameson (1955) revised Hering's notions with the publication of a modern quantitative opponent-process theory.

5.3.1. Psychophysical Evidence for Opponent Processes. Guth and coworkers (Guth & Lodge, 1973, and earlier papers referenced therein) measured the threshold of visibility of monochromatic lights and of bichromatic mixtures. Whenever dissimilar wavelengths were added, more radiance was required for threshold than would be predicted by the individual thresholds of the components. For colors adjacent in the spectrum (e.g., red and yellow), the deviation is small. The greatest effect is observed for complementary colors. A green light of sufficient radiance to be just above threshold by itself is rendered invisible by the addition of a small amount of red light. Kranda and King-Smith (1979) observed similar behavior for detection on a 1000-td white background. Thornton and Pugh (1983) state that blurring the stimulus in space and time enhances subadditivity. They further show that the perception of yellow can be linked to a local minimum in the spectral sensitivity defined by the threshold determinations. Other evidence of suprathreshold color opponency is found in the data of Hood and Finkelstein (1983) and Shevell and Handte (1983).

Table 8.19. Optical Density of the Macular Pigment as a Function of Wavelength

Wavelength	Optical Density	Wavelength	Optical Density
400	0.085	475	0.410
405	0.120	480	0.415
410	0.160	485	0.420
415	0.225	490	0.410
420	0.300	495	0.360
425	0.345	500	0.275
430	0.365	505	0.195
435	0.380	510	0.130
440	0.400	515	0.085
445	0.425	520	0.050
450	0.460	525	0.025
455	0.490	530	0.010
460	0.495	535	0.000
465	0.470	540	0.000
470	0.445	545	0.000
		700	0.000

The optical density (see Section 5.2.3) of the macular pigment is tabulated as a function of wavelength and given an arbitrary maximum of 0.50. These densities are representative of an observer viewing a foveal field of 1–2° in extent and are taken from Wyszecki and Stiles (1982).

Source: From G. Wyszecki and W. S. Stiles, *Color science—Concepts and methods, quantitative data and formulae* (2nd ed.). Copyright 1982, John Wiley & Sons, Inc. Reprinted with permission.

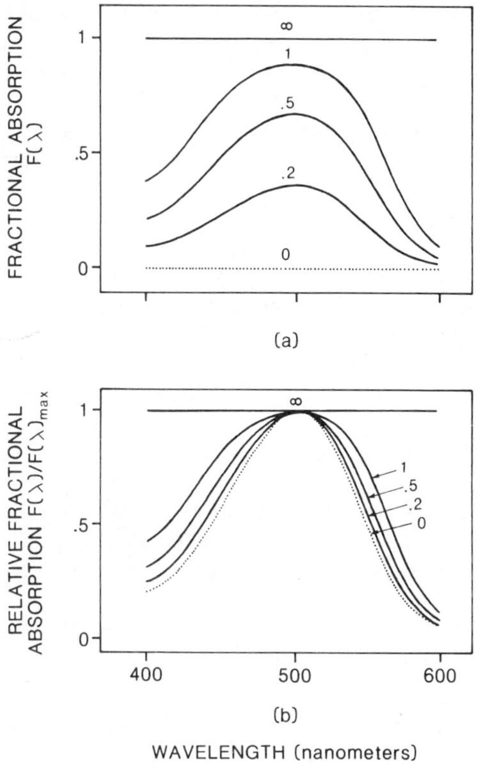

Figure 8.28. Changes in fractional absorption spectrum with changes in pigment concentration. (a) Fractional absorption spectral for different concentrations of the same visual pigment. The numbers describing the individual curves indicate the optical density of the photopigment at the wavelength of peak absorbance. (b) The same curves plotted relative to their maximum values. Note the broadening of these curves as the pigment concentration increases. (From H. J. A. Dartnall, *The visual pigment*, Methuen & Co., 1957. Reprinted with permission.)

5.3.2. Hurvich and Jameson Version of the Opponent-Process Theory. The Hurvich and Jameson version of the opponent-process theory was based on experimental studies of hue cancellation. In hue cancellation, a light, for example, a long-wavelength red, is added to a spectral blue-green; the mixture then appears as a desaturated bluish color tinged with either redness or greenness. A measure is taken of the amount of red necessary to cancel exactly the "greenness" of the blue-green light. This measure gives the strength of the greenness component of the blue-green light. The data are plotted as valences of redness-greenness and blueness-yellowness. It was noted that the experimental data could be approximately fitted by a linear transformation of CIE data previously described by Judd (1951a):

$$(b-y) = 0.4[\bar{y}(\lambda) - \bar{z}(\lambda)] , \qquad (72)$$

$$(r-g) = 1.0[\bar{x}(\lambda) - \bar{y}(\lambda)] . \qquad (73)$$

According to the current theory (Jameson, 1972), signals generated by absorptions in the three cone visual photopigments are recorded in the nervous system to give three new and different quality coding channels V_1, V_2, and V_3: V_1, representing a summation of cone inputs, signals whiteness or brightness; V_2, representing a summing and differencing of cone inputs, signals redness for positive values and greenness for negative values; and V_3, also representing a summing and differencing of cone inputs, signals blueness for negative values and yellowness for positive values. The channels V_2 and V_3 are usually called *chromatic* (or *color*) *opponent channels*. The equations for these channels are little changed from those derived by Judd (1951a).

$$V_1 = \bar{y}(\lambda) , \qquad (74)$$

$$V_2 = 1.0065\bar{x}(\lambda) - 1.0006\bar{y}(\lambda) - 0.0051\bar{z}(\lambda) , \qquad (75)$$

$$V_3 = -0.0039\bar{x}(\lambda) + 0.3998\bar{y}(\lambda) - 0.3999\bar{z}(\lambda) . \qquad (76)$$

These three neural processing channels are used to predict psychophysical functions obtained at a fixed average photopic luminance under conditions of neutral adaptation. For computational examples, see Hurvich and Jameson (1957); Graham (1965); Wyszecki and Stiles (1982). Constant multipliers may be used to change the weightings of the V_i functions for other luminance levels. A more complicated system of weights (see, for example, Wyszecki & Stiles, 1982) is used to predict the effect of nonneutral adaptation.

5.3.3. Opponent-Process Theory Based on Threshold Data. Guth and coworkers presented an opponent-process theory based on threshold behavior. Guth, Massof, and Benzschawel (1980) began with a König transformation based on Smith and Pokorny (1975) fundamentals given by

$$\bar{r}(\lambda) = 0.2435\bar{x}(\lambda) + 0.8524\bar{y}(\lambda) - 0.0516\bar{z}(\lambda) , \qquad (77)$$

$$\bar{g}(\lambda) = -0.3954\bar{x}(\lambda) + 1.1642\bar{y}(\lambda) + 0.0837\bar{z}(\lambda) , \qquad (78)$$

$$\bar{b}(\lambda) = 0.6225\bar{z}(\lambda) . \qquad (79)$$

The second opponent stage obtained gives a nonopponent (achromatic) channel A and two opponent (chromatic) channels T (tritan) and D (deutan).

$$A(\lambda) = M_A[0.5967\bar{r}(\lambda) + 0.3654\bar{g}(\lambda)] , \qquad (80)$$

$$T(\lambda) = M_T[0.9553\bar{r}(\lambda) - 1.2836\bar{g}(\lambda)] , \qquad (81)$$

$$D(\lambda) = M_D[-0.0248\bar{r}(\lambda) + 0.0483\bar{b}(\lambda)] , \qquad (82)$$

where $\bar{r}(\lambda)$, $\bar{g}(\lambda)$, and $\bar{b}(\lambda)$ are as Eqs. (77)–(79) and M_A, M_T, and M_D are weighting factors, set at unity at threshold. When the model is used above threshold, M_D increases, M_A decreases, and M_T is unchanged. Suprathreshold functions are fit with ad hoc manipulation of the "M" weights.

Various psychophysical predictions can be made from the model (see Wyszecki & Stiles, 1982). One important concept is that brightness, called $V^{**}(\lambda)$, is derived as the vector sum of the A, T, and D channels.

$$V^{**}(\lambda) = [A(\lambda)^2 + T(\lambda)^2 + D(\lambda)^2]^{1/2} \qquad (83)$$

Thus the Guth theory predicts that a brightness function will br broader than the pure achromatic function typified by the CIE $V(\lambda)$ (see Section 3).

Deficiencies of the approach include the fact that the model does not predict a difference between blue and violet or the perceived "redness" of violets. Further, it is not precisely specified how to work with this model above threshold.

5.4. Physiological Basis of Opponent-Process Behavior

The concept that retinal processing may show opponency dates from the studies of Svaetichin (reviewed by Svaetichin, Negichi, & Fatehchand, 1965). Studies demonstrating opponency in retinal ganglion and lateral geniculate cells of macaque monkeys are reviewed by DeValois (1971), DeValois and DeValois (1975), and Rodieck (1973).

Spectral response studies were expanded by Wiesel and Hubel (1966) to include spatial properties and by Gouras (1968, 1969) to include both spatial and temporal properties of macaque retinal ganglion cells. Gouras (1968, 1969) found a basic two-part distinction; he classified cells as either *phasic* or *tonic*. Some properties of phasic and tonic cells were summarized by Ingling (1978). Phasic cells have a broadband spectral response (compared with the DeValois, Abramov, & Jacobs, 1966, non-opponent cells) and respond to rapid temporal stimulation but do not have good spatial resolution. Their occurrence is infrequent near the fovea and increases rapidly outside the fovea. The tonic cells have a spectral opponent response similar to that of DeValois, Abramov, and Jacobs (1966) red-green opponent cells. These cells respond continuously to steady light and have relatively poorer temporal resolution but good spatial resolution. These cells appear to be most numerous at the fovea, their numbers decreasing outside the fovea. Currently, the electrophysiology seems more complicated than the original phasic–tonic distinction (reviewed by Lennie, 1980; MacLeod, 1978), but the general two-part classification seems a valid generalization. This dual processing of visual information has analogues in other vertebrates (the *X–Y* dichotomy first described by Enroth-Cugell & Robson, 1966, for the cat). In the primate, from the ganglion cell level to the visual cortex, there are parallel systems—one system (tonic system) that one might speculate is specialized for form and color vision with maximal representation at the fovea and the other (phasic system) specialized for detecting temporal changes.

5.4.1. Comparison of Psychophysical with Physiological Studies of Opponent-Process Behavior. It is possible (although speculative) to view the Hurvich and Jameson three quality coding channels, the achromatic V_1 and the two chromatic V_2 and V_3, as the psychophysical correlates of a phasic and two tonic neural channels similar to those described by Gouras (1968). This type of approach was made specific by Ingling and Drum (1973). Ingling and his coworkers further attempted to derive the sensory coding channels directly from absorption spectra of visual photopigments (Ingling, 1977; Ingling & Tsou, 1977). Since the initial reports of DeValois and colleagues in the 1960s, many investigators have looked at color-opponent neurons in the retina and at geniculate nuclei of primates. It is becoming clear that classification of the color-opponent neurons by suspected cone input is not simple, nor is there a simple correlation between psychophysical opponent color channels and the measured opponent neurons.

5.4.2. Comparison with Other Psychophysical Studies. The Hurvich-Jameson opponent-process models are based on color perception. The models assume that the opponent stage is a linear transformation of the photoreceptor stage and therefore, a linear transformation of the CIE data. Although Larimer, Krantz, and Cicerone (1974) present data indicating that the redness-greenness valence fulfills the requirements for being a linear transform of color-matching functions, Burns, Elsner, Pokorny, and Smith (1984) using a broader range of chromatic stimuli show a substantial nonlinearity. The blueness-yellowness valence also exhibits nonlinearities (Burns et al., 1984; Ikeda & Ayama, 1980; Larimer, Krantz, & Cicerone, 1975; Werner & Wooten, 1979). Pokorny, Smith, Burns, Elsner, and Zaidi (1981) discuss some constraints on the nature of the nonlinearity.

5.5. Line-Element Theories

Line-element theories developed from the idea of Helmholtz (1896) that a threshold change in sensation, ΔS, can be described as the weighted quadratic sum of the cone responses:

$$(\Delta S)^2 = (W_R \Delta R)^2 + (W_G \Delta G)^2 + W_B \Delta B)^2 , \quad (84)$$

where ΔR, ΔG, and ΔB are computed from cone sensitivity functions, such as König fundamentals, and W_R, W_G, and W_B represent a set of weights. Helmholtz suggested that the response of each cone sensitivity function to a small change in stimulation obeyed Weber's law, for example,

$$\frac{dR}{R} = C . \quad (85)$$

With the further assumption that the Weber fractions of the three cone mechanisms are equal, the Helmholtz line element is derived by

$$(dS) = \left[\left(\frac{dR}{R} \right)^2 + \left(\frac{dG}{G} \right)^2 + \left(\frac{dB}{B} \right)^2 \right]^{1/2} . \quad (86)$$

Wyszecki and Stiles (1982) discuss some problems associated with applying a line element to a space represented by color-matching data. A revision of the Helmholtz line-element theory was presented by Schrödinger (1920). Alpern and Torii (1968a, 1968b) applied the Schrödinger line element to predict brightness matching.

5.5.1. Stiles Line Element. Stiles revised the Helmholtz line element to incorporate the results of his two-color threshold studies (Stiles, 1946). Stiles noted that increment thresholds, ΔI as a function of I, followed a template curve $\xi(I)$ of the general form:

$$\xi(I) = \frac{9}{(1 + 9I)} . \quad (87)$$

Stiles further noted that the limiting Weber fractions of the cone mechanisms are not identical. The Stiles line element has the form

$$(dS) = [\{\xi(R) dR/\rho\}^2 + \{\xi(G) dG/\gamma\}^2 + \{\xi(B) dB/\beta\}^2]^{1/2} , \quad (88)$$

where the limiting Weber fractions are given by ρ at 1.28, γ at 1.65, and β at 7.25. At high radiances where $\xi(I) = 1/I$, the expression reduces to

$$(dS)^2 = \left(\frac{dR}{\rho R} \right)^2 + \left(\frac{dG}{\gamma G} \right)^2 + \left(\frac{dB}{\beta B} \right)^2 . \quad (89)$$

Wyszecki and Stiles (1982) review the type of prediction that can be made by the Stiles line element.

5.5.2. Vos and Walraven Line Element. The Vos and Walraven (1972a, 1972b) line element is a revision and expansion of the Walraven and Bouman (1966) line element for low luminances. At low luminances, intensity discrimination follows a square-root law:

$$\frac{dI}{\sqrt{I}} = C \ . \tag{90}$$

The line element is thus

$$(dS)^2 = \left(\frac{dR}{\sqrt{R}}\right)^2 + \left(\frac{dG}{\sqrt{G}}\right)^2 + \left(\frac{dB}{\sqrt{B}}\right)^2 . \tag{91}$$

Vos and Walraven expanded this to include terms that describe discrimination as square-root limited at low luminances, logarithmic (Weber's law) in the Weber range, and saturation limited at high luminances.

Then the line element is

$$(dS)^2 = \left\{\frac{dR}{\left[R\left(1+\frac{R}{R_0}+\frac{R^2}{(R_1)^2}\right)\right]^{1/2}}\right\}^2 + \left\{\frac{dG}{\left[G\left(1+\frac{G}{G_0}+\frac{G^2}{(G_1)^2}\right)\right]^{1/2}}\right\}^2 + \left\{\frac{dB}{\left[B\left(1+\frac{B}{B_0}+\frac{B^2}{(B_1)^2}\right)\right]^{1/2}}\right\}^2 . \tag{92}$$

The constants R_0, G_0, B_0 and R_1, G_1, B_1 are in the same proportions, given by the presumed ratios of R, G, and B receptors:

$$R_0{:}G_0{:}B_0 = R_1{:}G_1{:}B_1 = 32{:}16{:}1 \ . \tag{93}$$

The ratios of R_1/R_0, G_1/G_0, and B_1/B_0 are 2:1. In the Weber range, the effect is that the receptor contributions are proportional to their limiting Weber ratios, as in the Stiles model. The Vos-Walraven is further complicated by a subsequent opponent stage. Vos (1979) gives a clear description of the Vos and Walraven (1972a, 1972b) line element.

6. CONGENITAL COLOR DEFECTS

6.1. Classification of Color Defect

Color defects may be classified by performance or by the presumed mechanism or cause of the defect.

6.1.1. Classification by Performance. Observers may be classified by their color-matching performance or by two aspects of chromatic discriminative ability, one qualitative and the other quantitative. The nomenclature is derived from the color-matching performance of the observer. An observer who needs three primaries for full-spectrum color matching is defined as a trichromat; an observer who needs only two primaries for full-spectrum color matching is defined as a dichromat; and an observer who needs only one primary for full-spectrum color matching is defined as a monochromat. Both a qualitative and a quantitative aspect of chromatic discriminative ability may also be classified. A qualitative assessment of the axis (red-green or violet-yellow) of major chromatic discriminative loss may be made. In addition, the extent of the defect may be assessed on an ordinal scale using terms such as "mild," "moderate," and "severe."

6.1.2. Classification by Mechanism. Defective color vision, as shown by von Kries (1897), can be subdivided according to features of color matches that allow prediction of the mechanism of the defect. It is possible to recognize an absorption defect, an alteration defect, and a reduction defect.

In an absorption defect, some color matches differ from those of normal color vision. However, color matches reported with WDW normalization agree with those of normal trichromats. An absorption defect is caused by abnormal prereceptoral filtering.

In an alteration defect, color matches also differ from those of normal color vision; in addition, color matches reported with WDW normalization will still differ from those of normal trichromats. An alteration defect occurs when one (or more) of the visual photopigments differs from those of normal trichromats. An alteration defect is primary evidence of an abnormality or change in the photopigment absorption spectra.

A reduction defect is characterized by the fact that normal color matches are accepted by the color-defective observer, allowing for normal variation in prereceptoral absorption and normal receptoral variations. Additional matches are also accepted by the color-defective observer. A reduction defect occurs either when one of the normal receptor mechanisms is nonfunctional (called a *König mechanism*) or when two receptor mechanisms are fused (called a *Leber-Fick* or *Aitken-Leber-Fick mechanism*). A König mechanism is usually attributed to loss of function of one class of photoreceptors; a Leber-Fick mechanism is usually considered postreceptoral.

6.2. Congenital Color Defects

The most common congenital defects are the X-chromosome-linked red-green defects, which occur in 8% of the European male and 0.43% of the European female population (4–5% of the total European population). The tritan defect is rarer, occurring equally in both sexes. The frequency has been variously estimated at 1 in 13,000 to 1 in 65,000 (Wright, 1952) or 1 in 1000 (van Heel, Went, & van Norren, 1980) of the population. The tritan defect has autosomal dominant inheritance. The inheritance, incidence, and classification of these defects are summarized in Table 8.20.

6.2.1. The Red-Green Defects. Observers with red-green color defects have normal visual acuity but an abnormality of color vision. Two qualitatively different forms of defects are recognized. The protan defects include a dichromatic form, *protanopia*, and a trichromatic form, *protanomaly* (protanomalous trichromacy). Color confusions of protanopes and protanomalous trichromats are qualitatively similar, justifying the inclusive term *protan* (Farnsworth, 1947). Deutan defects include a di-

Table 8.20. Inheritance and Incidence of Congenital Color Vision Defects

Type	Inheritance	Incidence (%)	Classification
Red-green defects	X-chromosome linked	8–10% (males) <1% (females)	
Protanopia	recessive	1% (males)	Dichromatic
Deuteranopia		1% (males)	Dichromatic
Protanomaly		1% (males)	Trichromatic
Deuteranomaly		5% (males)	Trichromatic
Violet-yellow defects			
Tritan defect	Autosomal dominant	0.002–0.007 (males and females)	Dichromatic and trichromatic

The inheritance, incidence, and classification of the congenital color vision defects. X-chromosome-linked recessive color vision defects are the common red-green defects seen in the United States. They are further subdivided into dichromatic and trichromatic forms. The tritan color vision defect is autosomal dominant in inheritance and has no subclassification.

chromatic form, *deuteranopia*, and a trichromatic form, *deuteranomaly* (deuteranomalous trichromacy). Color confusions of deuteranopes and deuteranomalous trichromats are qualitatively similar, justifying the inclusive term *deutan* (Farnsworth, 1947). Full-spectrum colorimetry, spectral sensitivity, and wavelength and colorimetric purity discrimination functions all have been described in the literature (summarized by Boynton, 1979; Hsia & Graham, 1965; Pokorny, Smith, Verriest, & Pinckers, 1979; and others). Some major features of red-green color deficiency are summarized in Table 8.21. The red-green defects have X-chromosome-linked heredity and are attributed to the activity of two sets of alleles, one governing a protan series of defects and one governing a deutan series of defects. Two-degree color matching (using a clinical instrument called the anomaloscope) to measure the Rayleigh match (546 nm + 670 nm = 589 nm) allows differentiation of the various defects (NAS-NRC, 1981; Pokorny, Smith, Verriest, & Pinckers, 1979). When larger-field sizes are used, dichromatic observers become trichromatic, with color-matching behavior consistent with the third receptor mechanism being either rods (Smith & Pokorny, 1977) or anomalous cones (Breton & Cowan, 1981; Nagy, 1980; Nagy, Purl, & Houston, 1985) depending on adaptational state.

6.2.2. Tritan Defects. For small fields (<2°) the tritan defect is characterized by a lack of function of the mechanism that allows normals to discriminate colors that differ by the amount of SWS cone stimulation. Red-green discriminations are normal. For large fields a majority of tritan observers show color-matching behavior consistent with normal SWS cone function (Pokorny, Smith, & Went, 1981).

The existence of tritanomalous defect analogous to the red-green anomalies has been questioned. Pokorny, Smith, and Went (1981) found color-matching behavior of affected members of autosomal-dominant pedigrees who were trichromatic to be consistent with rods being the third receptor mechanism, rather than an anomalous SWS cone pigment.

6.2.3. Mechanisms of Color Defect in Congenital Red-Green Defect. The observation that anomalous trichromacy may be classified as an alteration defect leads to the view that the allele sequence determines the absorption spectra of the visual photopigments. Figure 8.29 shows the expected visual photopigments according to a simple reduction and alteration hypothesis. Comprehensive coverage of the data and theory of color defect may be found in Boynton (1979), Hsia and Graham

Table 8.21. Characteristics of Defective Color Vision

Characteristic	Normal	Protan	Deutan	Tritan
Number of primaries used in color mixture	3	2(*P*) 3(*PA*)	2(*D*) 3(*DA*)	2 or 3
Neutral point (dichromats only)		494 nm	499 nm	570 nm
Copunctal point (dichromats only)		$x_p = 0.7635$ $y_p = 0.2365$	$x_D = 1.4000$ $y_D = -0.400$	$x_T = 0.1748$ $y_T = 0.0000$
λ max of luminosity	555 nm	540 nm	560 nm	555 nm
Minimum delta λ (best wavelength discrimination)	590 nm	490 nm	495 nm	590 nm
Minimum P_c (worst purity discrimination)	570 nm	494 nm	499 nm	570 nm

A summary of characteristic behavior of different types of color-defective individual, based on material in Pokorny, Smith, Verriest, and Pinckers (1979). The symbols P, D, and T refer to protanopes, deuteranopes, and tritanopes respectively; PA and DA refer to protanomalous and deuteranomalous trichromats.

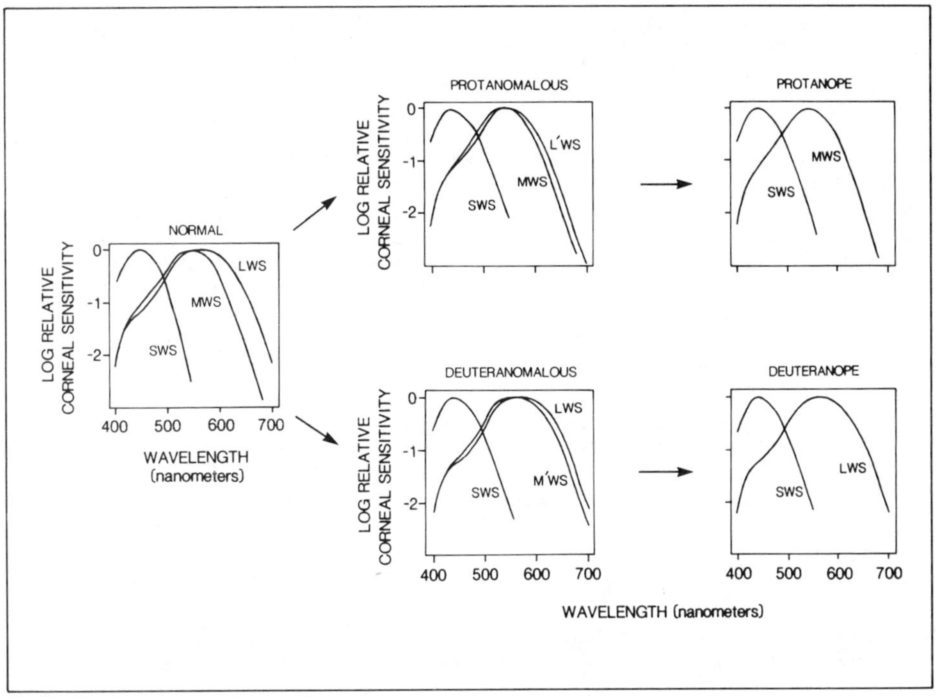

Figure 8.29. Log relative spectral sensitivities of the visual photopigments hypothesized to be active in a 2° color matching of normal trichromats, *X*-linked anomalous trichromats, and *X*-linked dichromats. The normal photopigment absorption spectra are designated as LWS, MWS, and SWS, representing photopigments where maximal sensitivity occurs in the long-, middle-, and short-wavelength regions of the spectrum. For the anomalous trichromats, abnormal photopigments L'WS and M'WS are hypothesized for protanomalous and deuteranomalous observers, respectively. (From J. Pokorny & V. C. Smith, New observations concerning red-green color defects, *Color research and application*. Copyright 1982 by John Wiley & Sons, Inc. Reprinted with permission.)

(1965), Hurvich (1972), Pokorny, Smith, Verriest, and Pinckers (1979), and Wright (1946).

REFERENCES

Abramov, I., & Gordon, J. Color vision in the peripheral retina. I. Spectral Sensitivity. *Journal of the Optical Society of America*, 1977, *67*, 195–202.

Alpern, M. Lack of uniformity in colour matching. *Journal of Physiology (London)*, 1979, *288*, 85–105.

Alpern, M., & Torii, S. Prereceptor colour vision distortions in protanomalous trichromacy. *Journal of Physiology (London)*, 1968, *198*, 549–560. (a)

Alpern, M., & Torii, S. The luminosity curve of the protanomalous fovea. *Journal of General Physiology*, 1968, *52*, 717–737. (b)

Anstis, S., & Cavanagh, P. A minimum motion technique for judging equiluminance. In J. D. Mollon & L. T. Sharp (Eds.), *Colour vision*. London: Academic Press, 1983.

Balaram, S. Color vision research and the trichromatic theory: A historical review. *Psychological Bulletin*, 1962, *59*, 434–448.

Bedford, R. E., & Wyszecki, G. W. Wavelength discrimination for point sources. *Journal of the Optical Society of America*, 1958, *48*, 129–135.

Bird, J. F., & Massof, R. W. A general zone theory of color and brightness vision. II. The space-time field. *Journal of the Optical Society of America*, 1978, *68*, 1471–1490.

Bone, R. A., & Sparrock, J. M. B. Comparison of macular pigment densities in human eyes. *Vision Research*, 1971, *11*, 1057–1064.

Bornstein, M. N., & Marks, L. E. Photopic luminosity measured by the method of critical frequency. *Vision Research*, 1972, *12*, 2023–2034.

Bowmaker, J. K., & Dartnall, H. J. A. Visual pigments of rods and cones in a human retina. *Journal of Physiology*, 1980, *298*, 501–511.

Bowmaker, J. K., Dartnall, H. J. A., Lythgoe, J. N., & Mollon, J. D. The visual pigments of rods and cones in the rhesus monkey, *macaca mulatta*. *Journal of Physiology*, 1978, *274*, 329–348.

Bowmaker, J. K., Dartnall, H. J. A., & Mollon, J. D. Microspectrophotometric demonstration of four classes of photoreceptor in an old world primate, *macaca fascicularis*. *Journal of Physiology*, 1980, *298*, 131–143.

Boynton, R. M. Contributions of threshold measurements to color-discrimination theory. *Journal of the Optical Society of America*, 1963, *53*, 165–178.

Boynton, R. M. *Human color vision*. New York: Holt, Rinehart & Winston, 1979.

Boynton, R. M., Das, S. R., & Gardiner, J. Interactions between photopic visual mechanisms revealed by mixing conditioning fields. *Journal of the Optical Society of America*, 1966, *56*, 1775–1780.

Boynton, R. M., Hayhoe, M. M., & MacLeod, D. I. A. The gap effect: Chromatic and achromatic visual discrimination as affected by field separation. *Optica Acta*, 1977, *24*, 159–177.

Boynton, R. M., & Kambe, N. Chromatic difference steps of moderate size measured along theoretically critical axes. *Color Research & Applications*, 1980, *5*, 13–23.

Boynton, R. M., Nagy, A. L., & Olson, C. A flaw in equations for predicting chromatic differences. *Color Research & Applications*, 1983, *8*, 69–74.

Boynton, R. M., & Wisowaty, J. J. Equations for chromatic discrimination models. *Journal of the Optical Society of America*, 1980, *70*, 1471–1476.

Breton, M. E., & Cowan, W. B. Deuteranomalous color matching in the deuteranopic eye. *Journal of the Optical Society of America*, 1981, *71*, 1220–1223.

Brindley, G. S. The effects on colour vision of adaptation to very bright lights. *Journal of Physiology (London)*, 1953, *122*, 332.

Brindley, G. S. The summation areas of human colour-receptive mechanisms at increment threshold. *Journal of Physiology (London)*, 1954, *124*, 400–408.

Brindley, G. S. A photochemcial reaction in the human retina. *Proceedings of the Physical Society*, 1955, *68B*, 862–870.

Brindley, G. S. *Physiology of the retina and the visual pathway* (2nd ed.). Baltimore: Williams & Wilkins, 1970.

Brindley, G. S., du Croz, J. J., & Rushton, W. A. H. The flicker fusion frequency of the blue-sensitive mechanism of colour vision. *Journal of Physiology (London)*, 1966, *183*, 497–500.

Brown, J. L., Phares, L., & Fletcher, D. E. Spectral energy thresholds for the resolution of acuity targets. *Journal of the Optical Society of America*, 1960, *50*, 950–960.

Brown, P. K., & Wald, G. Visual pigments in single rods and cones of the human retina. *Science*, 1964, *144*, 45–52.

Brown, W. R. J. The influence of luminance level on visual sensitivity to color differences. *Journal of the Optical Society of America*, 1951, *41*, 684–688.

Brown, W. R. J. The effect of field size and chromatic surroundings on color discrimination. *Journal of the Optical Society of America*, 1952, *42*, 837–844.

Brown, W. R. J., & MacAdam, D. L. Visual sensitivities to combined chromaticity and luminance differences. *Journal of the Optical Society of America*, 1949, *39*, 808–834.

Burns, S. A., & Elsner, A. E. Color matching at high illuminances: The color-match area effect and photopigment bleaching. *Journal of the Optical Society of America* A, 1985, *2*, 698–704.

Burns, S. A., Elsner, A. E., Pokorny, J., & Smith, V. C. The Abney effect: Chromaticity coordinates of unique and other constant hues. *Vision Research*, 1984, *24*, 479–489.

Burns, S. A., Smith, V. C., Pokorny, J., & Elsner, A. E. Brightness of equal-luminance lights. *Journal of the Optical Society of America*, 1982, *72*, 1225–1231.

Carlson, F. E., & Clark, C. N. Light sources for optical devices. In R. Kingslake (Ed.), *Applied optics and optical engineering* (Vol. 1). New York: Academic Press, 1965.

Cavonius, C. R., & Estévez, O. Sensitivity of human color mechanisms to gratings and flicker. *Journal of the Optical Society of America*, 1975, *65*, 966–968.

Clarke, F. J. J. The effect of field-element size on chromaticity discrimination. *Proceedings of the Symposium on Colour Measurement in Industry*. London: The Colour Group, April 1967.

Commission Internationale de l'Eclairage. *CIE Proceedings 1924*. Cambridge, England: Cambridge University Press, 1926.

Commission Internationale de l'Eclairage. *CIE Proceedings 1931*. Cambridge, England: Cambridge University Press, 1932.

Commission Internationale de l'Eclairage. *CIE Proceedings 1951* (Vol. 3). Paris: Bureau Central de la CIE, 1951.

Commission Internationale de l'Eclairage. *CIE Proceedings 1963* (Vol. B). Paris: Bureau Central de la CIE, 1964.

Commission Internationale de l'Eclairage. *CIE Compte Rendu 1971*. Paris: Bureau Central de la CIE, 1972.

Commission Internationale de l'Eclairage. *Light as a true visual quantity: Principles of measurement*. Paris: Bureau Central de la CIE, 1978.

Conrac Corporation. *Raster graphics handbook*. Covina, Calif.: Author, 1980.

Coren, S., & Girus, J. S. Density of human lens pigmentation: In vivo measurements over an extended age range. *Vision Research*, 1972, *12*, 343–346.

Cornu, L., & Harlay, F. Modifications de la discrimination chromatique en fonction de l'éclairement. *Vision Research*, 1969, *9*, 1273–1287.

Cowan, W. B. Discreteness artifacts in Raster Display Systems. In J. D. Molon & L. T. Sharpe (Eds.), *Colour vision*. New York: Academic Press, 1983.

Dartnall, H. J. A. *The visual pigments*. London: Methuen, 1957.

de Groot, S. G., & Gebhard, J. W. Pupil size as determined by adapting luminance. *Journal of the Optical Society of America*, 1952, *42*, 492–495.

De Lange, H. Research into the dynamic nature of the human fovea-cortex systems with intermittent and modulated light. *Journal of the Optical Society of America*, 1958, *48*, 779–789.

DeValois, K. K., & Switkes, E. Simultaneous masking interactions between chromatic and luminance gratings. *Journal of the Optical Society of America*, 1983, *73*, 11–18.

DeValois, R. L. Physiological basis of color vision. *Die Farbe*, 1971, *20*, 151–169.

DeValois, R. L., Abramov, I., & Jacobs, G. H. Analysis of response patterns of LGN cells. *Journal of the Optical Society of America*, 1966, *56*, 966–977.

DeValois, R. L., & DeValois, K. K. Neural coding of color. In E. D. Carterette & M. P. Friedman (Eds.), *Handbook of perception* (Vol. 5). New York: Academic Press, 1975.

Dresler, A. The non-additivity of heterochromatic brightness. *Transactions of the Illuminating Engineering Society* (London), 1953, *18*, 141–165.

Eby, J. E., & Levin, R. E. Incoherent light sources. In R. R. Shannon & J. C. Wyatt (Eds.), *Applied optics and optical engineering* (Vol. 7). New York: Academic Press, 1979.

Eisner, A. Comparison of flicker-photometric and flicker-threshold spectral sensitivities while the eye is adapted to colored backgrounds. *Journal of the Optical Society of America*, 1982, *72*, 517–518.

Eisner, A., & MacLeod, D. I. A. Flicker photometric study of chromatic adaptation: Selective suppression of cone inputs by colored backgrounds. *Journal of the Optical Society of America*, 1981, *71*, 705–717.

Enroth-Cugell, C., & Robson, J. G. The contrast sensitivity of retinal ganglion cells of the cat. *Journal of Physiology (London)*, 1966, *187*, 517–552.

Estévez, O. *On the fundamental data-base of normal and dichromatic color vision*. Doctoral dissertation. Amsterdam: Krips Repro Meppel, 1979.

Estévez, O., & Cavonius, C. R. Flicker sensitivity of the human red and green color mechanisms. *Vision Research*, 1975, *15*, 879–881.

Estévez, O., & Cavonius, C. R. Human color perception and Stiles' π mechanisms. *Vision Research*, 1977, *17*, 417–422.

Estévez, O., & Spekreijse, H. A spectral compensation method for determining the flicker characteristics of the human colour mechanisms. *Vision Research*, 1974, *14*, 823–830.

Estévez, O., & Spekreijse, H. The "silent substitution" method in visual research. *Vision Research*, 1982, *22*, 681–691.

Farnsworth, D. *The Farnsworth dichotomous test for color blindness—Panel D-15*. New York: Psychological Corp., 1947.

Farnswsorth, D. Tritanomalous vision as a threshold function. *Die Farbe*, 1955, *4*, 185–197.

Farnsworth, D. A temporal factor in colour discrimination. *National Physical Laboratory Symposium on the Visual Problems of Colour* (Vol. 2). New York: Chemical Publishing, 1961.

Fridrikh, L. Colour-combination curves for normal trichromats determined by direct energy measurements. *Biophysics*, 1957, *2*, 129–132. (Translation of *Biofizika*, 1957, *2*, 129–132.)

Gass, J. D. M. Nicotinic acid maculopathy. *American Journal of Ophthalmology*, 1973, *76*, 500–510.

Gilbert, M. Colour perception in parafoveal vision. *Proceedings of the Physical Society* (London), 1950, *63B*, 83–89.

Gouras, P. Identification of cone mechanisms in monkey ganglion cells. *Journal of Physiology (London)*, 1968, *199*, 533–547.

Gouras, P. Antidromic responses of orthodromically identified ganglion cells in monkey retina. *Journal of Physiology (London)*, 1969, *204*, 407–419.

Graham, B. V., & Guth, S. L. Red-plus-green heterochromatic additivity as applied to the acuity response. *Journal of the Optical Society of America*, 1970, *60*, 1573.

Graham, C. H. Color mixture and color systems. In C. H. Graham (Ed.), *Vision and vision perception.* New York: Wiley, 1965.

Graham, C. H., & Landis, C. Effect of striated fields on critical flicker frequency. *Journal of the Optical Society of America*, 1959, *49*, 580–585.

Granger, E. M., & Heurtley, J. C. Visual chromaticity-modulation transfer function. *Journal of the Optical Society of America*, 1973, *63*, 1173–1174.

Grassmann, H. Zür Theorie der Farbenmischung. *Annalen der Physik und Chemie*, 1853, *89*, 60–84. (English translation, *Philosophical Magazine*, 1854, *7*, 254–264.)

Green, D. G. The contrast sensitivity of the colour mechanisms of the human eye. *Journal of Physiology*, 1968, *196*, 415–429.

Green, D. G. Sinusoidal flicker characteristics of the color-sensitive mechanisms of the eye. *Vision Research*, 1969, *9*, 591–601.

Grigorovici, R., & Aricescu-Savopol, I. Luminosity and chromaticity in the mesopic range. *Journal of the Optical Society of America*, 1958, *48*, 891–898.

Guild, J. The colorimetric properties of the spectrum. *Philosophical Transactions of the Royal Society of London*, 1931, *230A*, 149–187.

Guth, S. L. Luminance addition: General considerations and some results at foveal threshold. *Journal of the Optical Society of America*, 1965, *55*, 718–722.

Guth, S. L., Donley, N. J., & Marrocco, R. T. On luminance additivity and related topics. *Vision Research*, 1969, *9*, 537–575.

Guth, S. L., & Lodge, H. R. Heterochromatic additivity, foveal spectral sensitivity and a new color model. *Journal of the Optical Society of America*, 1973, *63*, 450–462.

Guth, S. L., Massof, R. W., & Benzschawel, T. Vector model for normal and dichromatic color vision. *Journal of the Optical Society of America*, 1980, *70*, 197–212.

Hailman, J. P. Spectral discrimination: An important correction. *Journal of the Optical Society of America*, 1967, *57*, 281–282.

Halbertsma, K. T. A. *A history of the theory of colour.* Amsterdam: Swets & Zeitlinger, 1949.

Hartridge, H. The change from trichromatic to dichromatic vision in the human retina. *Nature*, 1945, *155*, 657–662.

Helmholtz, H. von. *Handbuch der physiologischen optik* (2nd ed.). Hamburg, Germany: Voss, 1896.

Henderson, S. T. *Daylight and its spectrum* (2nd ed.). Bristol, England: Hilger, 1977.

Hering, E. [*Outlines of a theory of the light sense*] (L. M. Hurvich & D. Jameson, Eds. & trans.). Cambridge, Mass.: Harvard University Press, 1964.

Hilz, R., & Cavonius, C. R. Wavelength discrimination measured with square-wave gratings. *Journal of the Optical Society of America*, 1970, *60*, 273–277.

Hita, E., Romero, J., Jimenez del Barco, L., & Martinez, R. Temporal aspects of color discrimination. *Journal of the Optical Society of America*, 1982, *72*, 578–582.

Hollins, M., & Montabana, D. J. Spectral sensitivity of the foveal blue-sensitive mechanism determined by color mixture. *Vision Research*, 1973, *13*, 1391–1393.

Hood, D. C., & Finkelstein, M. A. A case for the revision of textbook models of color vision: The detection and appearance of small brief lights. In J. D. Mollon & L. T. Sharpe (Eds.), *Colour vision.* New York: Academic Press, 1983.

Hsia, Y., & Graham, C. H. Spectral sensitivity of the cones in the dark adapted eye. *Proceedings of the National Academy of Science*, 1952, *38*, 80–85.

Hsia, Y., & Graham, C. H. Color blindness. In C. H. Graham (Ed.), *Vision and visual perception.* New York: Wiley, 1965.

Hurvich, L. M. Color vision deficiencies. In D. Jameson & L. M. Hurvich (Eds.), *Handbook of sensory physiology* (Vol. VII/4): *Visual psychophysics.* Berlin: Springer, 1972.

Hurvich, L. M., & Jameson, D. Some quantitative aspects of an opponent-colors theory. II. Brightness, saturation, and hue in normal and dichromatic vision. *Journal of the Optical Society of America*, 1955, *45*, 602–616.

Hurvich, L. M., & Jameson, D. An opponent-process theory of color vision. *Psychological Review*, 1957, *64*, 384–404.

Hurvich, L. M., & Jameson, D. Opponent chromatic induction and wavelength discrimination. In R. Jung & H. Kornhuber (Eds.), *The visual system: Neurophysiology and psychophysics.* Berlin: Springer, 1961.

Ikeda, M. Study of interrelations between mechanisms at threshold. *Journal of the Optical Society of America*, 1963, *53*, 1305–1313.

Ikeda, M., & Ayama, M. Additivity of opponent chromatic valence. *Vision Research*, 1980, *20*, 995–999.

Ikeda, M., & Shimozono, H. Mesopic luminous-efficiency functions. *Journal of the Optical Society of America*, 1981, *71*, 280–284.

Ikeda, M., Uetsuki, T., & Stiles, W. S. Interrelations among Stiles π mechanisms. *Journal of the Optical Society of America*, 1970, *60*, 406–415.

Ikeda, M., & Urakubo, M. Flicker HTRF as test of color vision. *Journal of the Optical Society of America*, 1968, *58*, 27–31.

Ikeda, M., Yaguchi, H., & Sagawa, K. Brightness luminous-efficiency functions for 2° and 10° fields. *Journal of the Optical Society of America*, 1982, *72*, 1660–1665.

Ingling, C. R., Jr., The spectral sensitivity of the opponent-color channels. *Vision Research*, 1977, *17*, 1083–1090.

Ingling, C. R., Jr., Luminance and opponent color contributions to visual detection and to temporal and spatial integration: Comment. *Journal of the Optical Society of America*, 1978, *68*, 1143–1146.

Ingling, C. R., Jr., & Drum, B. A. Retinal receptive fields: Correlations between psychophysics and electrophysiology. *Vision Research*, 1973, *13*, 1151–1163.

Ingling, C. R., Jr., & Martinez, E. Stiles π_5 mechanism: Failure to show univariance is caused by opponent-channel input. *Journal of the Optical Society of America*, 1981, *71*, 1134–1137.

Ingling, C. R., Jr., & Tsou, B. H.-P. Orthogonal combination of the three visual channels. *Vision Research*, 1977, *17*, 1075–1082.

Ives, H. E. On heterochromatic photometry. *Philosophical Magazine*, 1912, *24*, 845–853.

Jameson, D. Theoretical issues of color vision. In D. Jameson & L. M. Hurvich (Eds.), *Visual psychophysics.* Berlin: Springer, 1972.

Jameson, D., & Hurvich, L. M. Some quantitative aspects of an opponent-colors theory. I. Chromatic responses and spectral saturation. *Journal of the Optical Society of America*, 1955, *45*, 546–552.

Jones, L. A., & Lowry, E. M. Retinal sensibility to saturation differences. *Journal of the Optical Society of America*, 1926, *13*, 25–34.

Judd, D. B. Sensibility to color-temperature change as a function of temperature. *Journal of the Optical Society of America*, 1933, *23*, 7–14. (a)

Judd, D. B. The 1931 I.C.I. standard observer and coordinate system for colorimetry. *Journal of the Optical Society of America*, 1933, *23*, 359–374. (b)

Judd, D. B. Response functions for types of vision according to the Mueller theory. *Journal of Research of the National Bureau of Standards*, 1949, *42*, 1–16.

Judd, D. B. Basic correlates of the visual stimulus. In S. S. Stevens (Ed.), *Handbook of experimental psychology.* New York: Wiley, 1951. (a)

Judd, D. B. *Colorimetry and artificial daylight.* In Technical Committee No. 7, International Commission on Illumination, 12th Session, Stockholm, 1951, 1–60. (b)

Kaiser, P. K., Comerford, J. P., & Bodinger, D. M. Saturation of spectral lights. *Journal of the Optical Society of America*, 1976, *66*, 818–826.

Kaiser, P. K., & Wyszecki, G. Additivity failures in heterochromatic brightness matching. *Color Research & Applications*, 1978, *3*, 177–182.

Kaufman, J. E. *IES lighting handbook.* New York: Illuminating Engineering Society of North America, 1981.

Kelly, D. H. Spatio-temporal frequency characteristics of color-vision mechanisms. *Journal of the Optical Society of America*, 1974, *64*, 983–990.

Kelly, D. H. Spatio-temporal frequency characteristics of mechanism characteristics: Interaction or artifact? *Journal of the Optical Society of America*, 1976, *66*, 1430–1435.

Kelly, D. H., & Van Norren, D. Two-band model of heterochromatic flicker. *Journal of the Optical Society of America*, 1977, *67*, 1081–1091.

Kelly, K. L. Observer differences in colour-mixture functions studied by means of a pair of metameric grays. In *National Physical Laboratory Symposium on the Visual Problems of Colour* (Vol. 1). New York: Chemical Publishing, 1961

King-Smith, P. E., & Webb, J. R. The use of photopic saturation in determining the fundamental spectral sensitivity curves. *Vision Research*, 1974, *14*, 421–429.

Kinney, J. A. S. Sensitivity of the eye to spectral radiation at scotopic and mesopic intensity levels. *Journal of the Optical Society of America*, 1955, *45*, 507–514.

Kinney, J. A. S. Comparison of scotopic, mesopic, and photopic spectral sensitivity curves. *Journal of the Optical Society of America*, 1958, *48*, 185–190.

Kinney, J. A. S. Effect of field size and position on mesopic spectral sensitivity. *Journal of the Optical Society of America*, 1964, *54*, 671–677.

Knowles, A., & Dartnall, H. J. A. The photobiology of vision. In H. Davson (Ed.), *The eye* (Vol. IIB). New York: Academic Press, 1977.

Kokoschka, S. Untersuchungen zur mesopischen Strahlensbewertung. *Die Farbe*, 1972, *21*, 39–112.

König, A. Uber den menschlichen Sehpurpur und seine Bedeutung fur das Sehen. *Sitz Akad Wiss* (Berlin), 1894, 577–598.

König, A. Ueber Blaublindheit. *Sitz Akad Wiss* (Berlin), 1897, 718–731.

König, A., & Dieterici, C. Die Grundempfindungen und ihre Intensitats-Vertheilung im Spectrum. *Sitz Akad Wiss* (Berlin), 1886, 805–829.

König, A., & Dieterici, C. Die Grundempfindungen in normalen und anomalen Farben Systemen und ihre Intensitats-Vertheilung im Spectrum. *Zeitschrist fur Psychologie und Physiologie der Sinnesorgane*, 1893, *4*, 241–347.

Kranda, K., & King-Smith, P. E. Detection of coloured stimuli by independent linear systems. *Vision Research*, 1979, *19*, 733–745.

Krantz, D. H. Color measurement and color theory: I. Representation theorem for Grassmann structures. *Journal of Mathematical Psychology*, 1975, *12*, 283–303.

Krauskopf, J., Williams, D. R., & Heeley, D. W. Cardinal directions of color space. *Vision Research*, 1982, *22*, 1123–1131.

Larimer, J., Krantz, D. H., & Cicerone, C. M. Opponent-process additivity: I. Red/green equilibria. *Vision Research*, 1974, *14*, 1127–1140.

Larimer, J., Krantz, D. H., & Cicerone, C. M. Opponent-process additivity: II. Yellow/blue equilibria and non-linear models. *Vision Research*, 1975, *15*, 723–731.

Le Grand, Y. *Optique physiologique. Tome 2. Lumière et couleurs*. Paris: Editions de la "Revue d'optique," 1948.

Le Grand, Y. [*Light, colour, and vision.*] (2nd ed.) (R. W. G. Hunt, J. W. T. Walsh, & F. R. W. Hunt, Eds. & trans.). London: Chapman & Hall, 1968. (Originally published 1948.)

Lennie, P. Parallel visual pathways: A review. *Vision Research*, 1980, *20*, 561–594.

Liebman, P. A. Microspectrophotometry. In H. J. A. Dartnall (Ed.), *Photochemistry of vision*. Berlin: Springer, 1972.

Lit, A., Young, R. H., & Shaffer, M. Simple time reaction as a function of luminance for various wavelengths. *Perception and Psychophysics*, 1971, *10*, 397–399.

Loomis, J. M., & Berger, T. Effects of chromatic adaptation on color discrimination and color appearance. *Vision Research*, 1979, *19*, 891–901.

Lythgoe, R. Dark-adaptation and the peripheral colour sensations of normal subjects. *British Journal of Ophthalmology*, 1931, *15*, 193–210.

MacAdam, D. L. Visual sensitivities to color differences in daylight. *Journal of the Optical Society of America*, 1942, *32*, 247–274.

MacAdam, D. L. Small-field chromaticity discrimination. *Journal of the Optical Society of America*, 1959, *49*, 1143–1146.

MacLeod, D. I. A. Visual sensitivity. *Annual Review of Psychology*, 1978, *29*, 613–645.

MacLeod, D. I. A., & Boynton, R. M. Chromaticity diagram showing cone excitation by stimuli of equal luminance. *Journal of the Optical Society of America*, 1979, *69*, 1183–1186.

Marks, W. B., Dobelle, W. H., & MacNichol, E. F. Visual pigments of single primate cones. *Science*, 1964, 143, 1181–1183.

Marshall, J., Hamilton, A. M., & Bird, A. C. Intra-retinal absorption of argon laser irradiation in human and monkey retinae. *Experientia*, 1974, *30*, 1335–1337.

Martin, L. C., Warburton, F. L., & Morgan, W. J. The determination of sensitivities of the eye to differences in the saturation of colours. *Special Report Series of the Medical Research Council* (London), 1933, No. 188, 5–24.

Massof, R. W., & Bird, J. F. A general zone theory of color and brightness vision. I. Basic formulation. *Journal of the Optical Society of America*, 1978, *68*, 1465–1471.

McCree, K. J. Colour confusion produced by voluntary fixation. *Optica Acta*, 1960, *7*, 281–291. (a)

McCree, K. J. Small-field tritanopia and the effects of voluntary fixation. *Optica Acta*, 1960, *7*, 317–323. (b)

Mitchell, D. E., & Rushton, W. A. H. The red/green pigments of normal vision. *Vision Research*, 1971, *11*, 1045–1056.

Mollon, J. D. Color vision. *Annual Review of Psychology*, 1982, *33*, 41–85.

Moon, P. *The scientific basis of illuminating engineering*. New York: Dover, 1961.

Moreland, J. D. Peripheral colour vision. In D. Jameson & L. M. Hurvich (Eds.), *Handbook of sensory physiology* (Volume VII/4): *Visual psychophysics*. New York: Springer, 1972.

Moreland, J. D. Temporal variations in anomaloscope equations. *Modern Problems in Ophthalmology*, 1978, *19*, 167–172.

Moreland, J. D., & Cruz, A. Colour perception with the peripheral retina. *Optica Acta*, 1959, *6*, 117–151.

Mullen, K. T. The contrast sensitivity of human colour vision to red-green and blue-yellow chromatic gratings. *Journal of Physiology*, 1985, *359*, 381–400.

Myers, K. J., Ingling, C. R., Jr., & Drum, B. A. Brightness additivity for a grating target. *Vision Research*, 1973, *13*, 1165–1173.

National Academy of Science–National Research Council Committee on Vision. *Procedures for testing color vision*. Washington, D.C.: National Academy Press, 1981.

Nagy, A. L. Large-field substitution Rayleigh matches of dichromats. *Journal of the Optical Society of America*, 1980, *70*, 778–784.

Nagy, A. L., Purl, K. F., & Houston, J. S. Cone mechanisms underlying the color discrimination of deutan color deficients. *Vision Research*, 1985, *25*, 661–669.

Nassau, K. *The physics and chemistry of color*. New York: Wiley, 1983.

Noorlander, C. *The spatiotemporal line element in colour space*. Doctoral dissertation. Utrecht: Drukkerij Elinkwijk BV, 1981.

Noorlander, C., Heuts, M. J. G., & Koenderink, J. J. Influence of the target size on the detection threshold for luminance and chromaticity contrast. *Journal of the Optical Society of America*, 1980, *70*, 1116–1121.

Noorlander, C., Heuts, M. J. G., & Koenderink, J. J. Sensitivity to spatiotemporal combined luminance and chromaticity contrast. *Journal of the Optical Society of America*, 1981, *71*, 453–459.

Nunn, B. J. Schnapf, J. L., & Baylor, D. A. Spectral sensitivity of single cones in the retina of *macaca fascicularis*. *Nature*, 1984, *309*, 264–266.

Nunn, B. J., Schnapf, J. L. & Baylor, D. A. The action spectra of rods and red- and green-sensitive cones of the monkey *macaca fascicularis*. In D. Ottoson and S. Zecki (Eds.). *Central and peripheral mechanisms of colour vision*. Basingstoke: Macmillan, 1985, 139–149.

Nunn, B., & Baylor, D. Visual transduction in single photoreceptors of the monkey, *macaca fascicularis*. In J. D. Mollon & L. T. Sharpe (Eds.), *Colour vision*. New York: Academic Press, 1983.

Nygaard, R. W., & Frumkes, T. E. Calibration of the retinal illuminance provided by Maxwellian views. *Vision Research*, 1982, *22*, 433–434.

Palmer, D. A. The definition of a standard observer for mesopic vision. *Vision Research*, 1967, *7*, 619–628.

Palmer, D. A. Standard observer for large-field photometry at any level. *Journal of the Optical Society of America*, 1968, *58*, 1296–1299.

Palmer, D. A., Visibility curves by direct comparison in a 10° field at 1000 Td. *Journal of the Optical Society of America* A, 1985, *2*, 578–583.

Piantanida, T. P., Bruch, T. A., Latch, M., & Varner, F. D. Detection of quantum flux modulation by single photopigments in human observers. *Vision Research*, 1976, *16*, 1029–1034.

Piéron, H. Recherches sur la validité de la loi d'Abney. *Année Psychologie*, 1942, *40*, 52–83.

Pointer, M. R. Color discrimination as a function of observer adaptation. *Journal of the Optical Society of America*, 1974, *64*, 750–759.

Pokorny, J., Graham, C. H., & Lanson, R. N. Effect of wavelength on foveal grating acuity. *Journal of the Optical Society of America*, 1968, *58*, 1410–1414.

Pokorny, J., & Smith, V. C. Wavelength discrimination in the presence of added chromatic fields. *Journal of the Optical Society of America*, 1970, *69*, 562–569.

Pokorny, J., & Smith, V. C. Color vision. In A. M. Potts (Ed.), *The assessment of visual function*. St. Louis: Mosby, 1972.

Pokorny, J., & Smith, V. C. Effect of field size on red-green color mixture equations. *Journal of the Optical Society of America*, 1976, *66*, 705–708.

Pokorny, J., & Smith, V. C. A variant of red-green color defect. *Vision Research*, 1981, *21*, 311–317.

Pokorny, J., & Smith, V. C. New observations concerning red-green color defects. *Color Research & Applications*, 1982, *7*, 159–164.

Pokorny, J., Smith, V. C., Burns, S. A., Elsner, A. E., & Zaidi, Q. Modeling blue-yellow opponency. In M. Richter (Ed.), *Proceedings of the 4th International Congress of the Color Association*, 1981.

Pokorny, J., Smith, V. C., & Starr, S. J. Variability of color mixture data: II. The effect of viewing field size on the unit coordinates. *Vision Research*, 1976, *16*, 1095–1098.

Pokorny, J., Smith, V. C., Verriest, G., & Pinckers, A. J. L. G. *Congenital and acquired color defects*. New York: Grune & Stratton, 1979.

Pokorny, J., Smith, V. C., & Went, L. N. Color matching in autosomal domnant tritan defect. *Journal of the Optical Society of America*, 1981, *71*, 1327–1334.

Polden, P. G., & Mollon, J. D. Reversed effect of adapting stimuli on visual sensitivity. *Proceedings of the Research Society of London*, 1980, *210*, 235–272.

Pollack, J. D., Reaction time to different wavelengths at various luminances. *Perception & Psychophysics*, 1968, *3*, 17–24.

Polyak, S. L. *The retina*. Chicago: University of Chicago, 1941.

Pugh, E. N. The nature of the π_1 mechanism of W. S. Stiles. *Journal of Physiology*, 1976, *257*, 713–747.

Pugh, E. N., & Mollon, J. D. A theory of the π_1 and π_3 colour mechanisms of Stiles. *Vision Research*, 1979, *19*, 293–312.

Pugh, E. N., Jr., & Sigel, C. Evaluation of the candidacy of the π-mechanisms of Stiles for color-matching fundamentals. *Vision Research*, 1978, *18*, 317–330.

Reeves, A. Exchange thresholds for long-wavelength incremental flashes. *Journal of the Optical Society of America*, 1982, *72*, 565–570. (a)

Reeves, A. Exchange thresholds for green tests. *Vision Research*, 1982, *22*, 961–966. (b)

Regan, D., & Tyler, C. W. Temporal summation and its limit for wavelength changes: An analog of Bloch's law for color vision. *Journal of the Optical Society of America*, 1971, *61*, 1414–1421.

Richards, W., & Luria, S. M. Color-mixture functions at low luminance levels. *Vision Research*, 1964, *4*, 281–313.

Ripps, H., & Weale, R. A. The visual stimulus. In M. Davson (Ed.), *The eye* (Vol. 2A). London: Academic Press, 1976.

Rodieck, R. W. Ganglion cells: Receptive fields. In R. W. Rodieck (Ed.), *The vertebrate retina, Principles of structure and function*. San Francisco: Freeman, 1973.

Rodieck, R. W. Raster-based colour stimulators. In J. D. Mollon & L. T. Sharpe (Eds.), *Colour vision*. New York: Academic Press, 1983.

Ruddock, K. H. Evidence for macular pigmentation from colour matching data. *Vision Research*, 1963, *3*, 417–429.

Ruddock, K. H. The effect of age upon colour vision. II. Changes with age in light transmission of the ocular media. *Vision Research*, 1965, *11*, 143–156.

Rushton, W. A. H., Powell, D. S., & White, K. D. The spectral sensitivity of "red" and "green" cones in the normal eye. *Vision Research*, 1973, *13*, 2003–2015.

Said, F. S., & Weale, R. A. The variation with age of the spectral transmissivity of the living human crystalline lens. *Gerontologia*, 1959, *3*, 213–231.

Scharf, P. T. Filters. In R. Kingslake (Ed.), *Applied optics and optical engineering* (Vol. 1). New York: Academic Press, 1965.

Schrödinger, E. Grundlinien einer Theorie der Farbenmetrik im Tagessehen. *Annual der Physik*, 1920, *63*, 481. (English translation, Outline of a theory of color measurement for daylight vision. In D. L. MacLeod (Ed. & trans.), *Sources of color science*. Cambridge, Mass.: MIT Press, 1970.)

Schrödinger, E. Uber das Verhaltnis der Vierfarben-zur Driefarbentheorie. *Sitzungsberichte der Akademie Wien Wissenchaft und Mathematic-naturwiss, Abt. 2A*, 1925, *134*, 471–490.

Schwarz, R. von. Weitere Untersuchungen über den Einfluss der Farbe Auf Sehscharfe und Sehleistung. *von Graefes Archiv fur Ophthalmologie*, 1956, *157*, 534–539.

Segal, J. Localisation du pigment maculaire de la retine. *Comptes Rendus des Séances de la Société de Biologie*, 1950, *144*, 1630–1631.

Sharpe, L. T., & Wyszecki, G. Proximity factor in color-difference evaluations. *Journal of the Optical Society of America*, 1976, *66*, 40–49.

Sheppard, J. J., Jr. *Human color perception. A critical study of the experimental foundation*. New York: American Elsevier, 1968.

Sherman, P. D. *Colour vision in the nineteenth century*. Bristol, England: Hilger, 1981.

Shevell, S. K., & Handte, J. P. Postreceptoral adaptation in suprathreshold color perception. In J. D. Mollon & L. T. Sharpe (Eds.), *Colour vision*. New York: Academic Press, 1983.

Siegel, M. H. Color discrimination as a function of exposure time. *Journal of the Optical Society of America*, 1965, *55*, 566–568.

Siegel, M. H., & Siegel, A. B. Hue discrimination as a function of stimulus luminance. *Perception & Psychopysics*, 1972, *12*, 295–299.

Sigel, C., & Brousseau, L. Pi-4: Adaptation of more than one class of cone. *Journal of the Optical Society of America*, 1982, *72*, 237–246.

Smith, V. C., Bowen, R. W., & Pokorny, J. Threshold temporal integration of chromatic stimuli. *Vision Research*, 1984, *24*, 653–660.

Smith, V. C., & Pokorny, J. Spectral sensitivity of color-blind observers and the cone photopigments. *Vision Research*, 1972, *12*, 2059–2071.

Smith, V. C., & Pokorny, J. Spectral sensitivity of the foveal cone photopigments between 400 and 500 nm. *Vision Research*, 1975, *15*, 161–171.

Smith, V. C., & Pokorny, J. Large-field trichromacy in protanopes and deuteranopes. *Journal of the Optical Society of America*, 1977, *67*, 213–220.

Smith, V. C., Pokorny, J., & Starr, S. J. Variability of color mixture data: I. Interobserver variability in the unit coordinates. *Vision Research*, 1976, *16*, 1087–1094.

Smith, V. C., Pokorny, J., & Zaidi, Q. How do sets of color-matching functions differ? In J. D. Mollon & L. T. Sharpe (Eds.), *Colour vision*. London: Academic Press, 1983.

Snodderly, D. M., Auran, J. D., & Delori, F. C. The macula pigment. II. Spatial distribution in primate retinas. *Investigative Ophthalmology and Visual Science*, 1984, *25*, 674–685.

Snodderly, D. M., Brown, P. K., Delori, F. C., & Auran, J. D. The macular pigment. I. Absorbance spectra, localization, and discrimination from other yellow pigments in primate retinas. *Investigative Ophthalmology and Visual Science*, 1984, *25*, 660–673.

Speranskaya, M. I. Determination of spectrum color coordinates for twenty-seven normal observers. *Optics & Spectroscopy*, 1959, *7*, 424–428.

Speranskaya, N. I. Methods of determination of the coordinates of spectrum colours. In *National Physical Laboratory Symposium on the Visual Problems of Colour* (Vol. 1). New York: Chemical Publishing, 1961.

Sperling, H. G. An experimental investigation of the relationship between colour mixture and luminous efficiency. In *National Physical Laboratory Symposium on the Visual Problems of Colour* (Vol. 1). New York: Chemical Publishing, 1961.

Sproson, W. N. *Colour science in television and display systems*. Bristol, England: Hilger, 1983.

Stabell, B., & Stabell, U. Rod and cone contributions to peripheral colour vision. *Vision Research*, 1976, *16*, 1099–1104.

Stabell, U., & Stabell, B. Wavelength discrimination of peripheral cones and its change with rod intrusion. *Vision Research*, 1977, *17*, 423–426.

Stabell, U., & Stabell, B. Variation in density of macular pigmentation and in short-wave cone sensitivity with eccentricity. *Journal of the Optical Society of America*, 1980, *70*, 706–711.

Stabell, U., & Stabell, B. Color vision in the peripheral retina under photopic conditions. *Vision Research*, 1982, *22*, 839–844.

Starr, S. J. *Effect of luminance and wavelength on the Stiles-Crawford effect in dichromats*. Unpublished doctoral dissertation, University of Chicago, 1977.

Sternheim, C. E., Gorinson, R., & Markovitz, N. Visual sensitivity during successive chromatic contrast: Evidence for interactions between photopic mechanisms. *Vision Research*, 1977, *17*, 45–49.

Sternheim, C. E., Stromeyer, C. F., III, & Khoo, M. C. K. Visibility of chromatic flicker upon spectrally mixed adapting fields. *Vision Research*, 1979, *19*, 175–183.

Stiles, W. S. The directional sensitivity of the retina and the spectral sensitivities of the rods and cones. *Proceedings of the Royal Society of London*, 1939, *127*, 64–105.

Stiles, W. S. A modified Helmholtz line-element in brightness-colour space. *Proceedings of the Physical Society* (London), 1946, *58*, 41–65.

Stiles, W. S. Increment thresholds and the mechanisms of colour vision. *Documenta Ophthalmologica*, 1949, *3*, 138–163.

Stiles, W. S. Further studies of visual mechanisms by the two-colour threshold method. *Cologuio Sobre Problemas Opticas de la Vision, Madrid*. International Union of Pure & Applied Physics, 1953, *1*, 65103.

Stiles, W. S. Interim report to the Commission Internationale de l'Eclairage, Zurich, 1955, on the National Physical Laboratory's investigation of color-matching (1955) with an appendix by W. S. Stiles & J. M. Burch. *Optica Acta*, 1955, *2*, 168–181.

Stiles, W. S. Color vision: The approach through increment threshold sensitivity. *Proceedings of the National Academy of Science*, 1959, *45*, 100–114.

Stiles, W. S., & Burch, J. M. NPL colour-matching investigation: Final report. *Optica Acta*, 1959, *6*, 1–26.

Stromeyer, C. F., III, Cole, G. R., & Kronauer, R. E. Second-site adaptation in the red-green chromatic pathways. *Vision Research*, 1985, *25*, 219–239.

Svaetichin, G., Negichi, K., & Fatehchand, R. Cellular mechanisms of Young-Hering visual system. In A. V. S. De Rouck & J. Knight (Eds.), *CIBA Foundation Symposium: Colour Vision*. Boston: Little, Brown, 1965.

Tan, K. E. W. P. *Vision in the ultraviolet*. Doctoral dissertation. Utrecht: Drukkerij Elinkwijk BV, 1971.

Teele, R. P. Photometry. In R. Kingslake (Ed.), *Applied optics and optical engineering* (Vol. 1). New York: Academic Press, 1965.

Terstiege, H. Untersuchungen zum Persistenz-und Koeffizientensatz. *Die Farbe*, 1967, *16*, 1–120.

Thomson, L. C., & Wright, W. D. The colour sensitivity of the retina within the central fovea of man. *Journal of Physiology (London)*, 1947, *105*, 316–331.

Thornton, J. E., & Pugh, E. N., Jr. Red/green color opponency at detection threshold. *Science*, 1983, *219*, 191–193.

Trezona, P. W. Rod participation in the "blue" mechanism and its effect on colour matching. *Vision Research*, 1970, *10*, 317–332.

Tyndall, E. P. T. Chromaticity sensibility to wave-length difference as a function of purity. *Journal of the Optical Society of America*, 1933, *23*, 15–24.

Uchikawa, K. Purity discrimination: Successive vs. simultaneous comparison method. *Vision Research*, 1983, *23*, 53–58.

Uchikawa, K., & Ikeda, M. Temporal deterioration of wavelength discrimination with successive comparison method. *Vision Research*, 1981, *21*, 591–595.

van der Horst, G. J. C., & Bouman, M. A. Spatiotemporal chromaticity discrimination. *Journal of the Optical Society of America*, 1969, *59*, 1482–1488.

van der Horst, G. J. C. Chromatic flicker. *Journal of the Optical Society of America*, 1969, *59*, 1213–1217. (a)

van der Horst, G. J. C. Fourier analysis and color discrimination. *Journal of the Optical Society of America*, 1969, *59*, 1670–1676. (b)

van der Horst, G. J. C., de Weert, C. M. M., & Bouman, M. A. Transfer of spatial chromaticity contrast at threshold in the human eye. *Journal of the Optical Society of America*, 1967, *57*, 1260–1267.

van Heel, L., Went, L. M., van Norren, D. Frequency of tritan disturbances in a population study. In G. Verriest (Ed.), *Colour vision deficiencies* (Vol. 5). Bristol, England: Hilger, 1980.

von Kries, J. Uber Farbensysteme. *Zeitschrift fur Psychologie und Physiologie der Sinnesorgane*, 1897, *13*, 241–324.

van Norren, D. V., & Vos, J. J. Spectral transmission of the human ocular media. *Vision Research*, 1974, *14*, 1237–1244.

Verriest, G. Recent advances in the study of the acquired deficiencies of colour vision. *Atti della Fondazione Giorgio Ronchi XXIV*. Florence, Italy: Baccini & Chiappi, 1974.

Verriest, G., Buyssens, A., & Vanderdonck, R. Etude quantitative de l'effet qu'exerce sur les resultats de quelques tests de la discrimination chromatique une diminution non selective du niveau d'un éclairage C. *Revue d'Optique*, 1963, *3*, 105–110.

Vienot, F. Can variation in macular pigment account for the variation of colour matches with retinal position? In J. D. Mollon & L. T. Sharpe (Eds.), *Colour vision*. New York: Academic Press, 1983.

Vos, J. J. *Literature review of human macular absorption in the visible and its consequences for the cone receptor primaries* (TNO Report 1972-17). Soesterberg, Netherlands: Institute for Perception, 1972.

Vos, J. J. Colorimetric and photometric properties of a 2° fundamental observer. *Color Research & Applications*, 1978, *3*, 125.

Vos, J. J. Line elements and physiological models for color vision. *Color Research & Applications*, 1979, *4*, 208–216.

Vos, J. J., & Walraven, P. L. On the derivation of the foveal receptor primaries. *Vision Research*, 1971, *11*, 799–818.

Vos, J. J., & Walraven, P. L. An analytical description of the line element in the zone-fluctuation model of colour vision. I. Basic concepts. *Vision Research*, 1972, *12*, 1327–1344. (a)

Vos, J. J., & Walraven, P. L. An analytical description of the line element in the zone-fluctuation model of colour vision. II. The derivation of the line element. *Vision Research*, 1972, *12*, 1245–1365. (b)

Wagner, G., & Boynton, R. M. Comparison of four methods of heterochromatic photometry. *Journal of the Optical Society of America*, 1972, *62*, 1508–1515.

Wald, G. Human vision and spectrum. *Science*, 1945, *101*, 653–658.

Wald, G. The receptors of human color vision. *Science*, 1964, *145*, 1007–1017.

Wald, G. Frequency or wavelength? *Science*, 1965, *150*, 1239–1240.

Walraven, J. Perceived colour under conditions of chromatic adaptation: Evidence for gain control by π mechanisms. *Vision Research*, 1981, *21*, 611–620.

Walraven, P. L. A closer look at the tritanopic convergence point. *Vision Research*, 1974, *14*, 1339–1343.

Walraven, P. L. Basic mechanisms of defective color vision. *Modern Problems in Ophthalmology*, 1976, *17*, 2–16.

Walraven, P. L., & Bouman, M. A. Fluctuation theory of colour discrimination of normal thrichromats. *Vision Research*, 1966, *6*, 567–586.

Walters, H. V., & Wright, W. D. The spectral sensitivity of the fovea and extrafovea in the Purkinje range. *Proceedings of the Royal Society of London*, 1943, *131B*, 340–361.

Wandell, B. A. Measurement of small color differences. *Psychological Review*, 1982, *89*, 281–302.

Wandell, B. A. Color measurement and discrimination. *Journal of the Optical Society of America* A, 1985, *2*, 62–71.

Wandell, B. A., & Pugh, E. M. A field-additive pathway detects brief-duration, long-wavelength incremental flashes. *Vision Research*, 1980, *20*, 613–624.

Watson, W. Note on the sensibility of the eye to variations of wavelength. *Proceedings of the Royal Society of London*, 1911, *84B*, 118–121.

Weale, R. A. Hue-discrimination in para-central parts of the human retina measured at different luminance levels. *Journal of Physiology*, 1951, *113*, 115–122.

Weale, R. A. Trichromatic ideas in the seventeenth and eighteenth centuries. *Nature*, 1957, *179*, 648–651.

Weale, R. A. Notes on the photometric significance of the human crystalline lens. *Vision Research*, 1961, *1*, 183–191.

Werner, J. S. Development of scotopic spectral sensitivity and the absorption spectrum of the human ocular media. *Journal of the Optical Society of America*, 1982, *72*, 247–258.

Werner, J. S., & Wooten, B. R. Opponent chromatic mechanisms: Relation to photopigments and hue naming. *Journal of the Optical Society of America*, 1979, *69*, 422–434.

Westheimer, G. The Maxwellian view. *Vision Research*, 1966, *6*, 699–682.

Wiesel, T., & Hubel, D. H. Spatial and chromatic interactions in the lateral geniculate body of the rhesus monkey. *Journal of Neurophysiology*, 1966, *29*, 1115–1156.

Williams, D. R., & MacLeod, D. I. A. Interchangeable backgrounds for cone afterimages. *Vision Research*, 1979, *19*, 867–877.

Willmer, E. N., & Wright, W. D. Colour sensitivity of the fovea centralis. *Nature*, 1945, *156*, 119–121.

Wisowaty, J. J. Estimates for the temporal response characteristics of chromatic pathways. *Journal of the Optical Society of America*, 1981, *71*, 970–977.

Wisowaty, J. J., & Boynton, R. M. Temporal modulation sensitivity of the blue mechanism: Measurements made without chromatic adaptation. *Vision Research*, 1980, *20*, 895–909.

Wright, W. D. A re-determination of the trichromatic coefficients of the spectral colours. *Transactions of the Optical Society*, 1929, *30*, 141–164.

Wright, W. D. The sensitivity of the eye to small colour differences. *Proceedings of the Physical Society* (London), 1941, *53*, 93–112.

Wright, W. D. *Researches on normal and defective colour vision*. London: Henry Kimpton, 1946.

Wright, W. D. The characteristics of tritanopia. *Journal of the Optical Society of America*, 1952, *42*, 509–520.

Wright, W. D., & Pitt, F. H. G. Hue-discrimination in normal colour-vision. *Proceedings of the Physical Society* (London), 1934, *45*, 459–473.

Wright, W. D., & Pitt, F. H. G. The saturation-discrimination of two trichromats. *Proceedings of the Physical Society* (London), 1937, *49*, 329–331.

Wyszecki, G., & Fielder, G. H. New color-matching ellipses. *Journal of the Optical Society of America*, 1971, *61*, 1135–1152.

Wyszecki, G., & Stiles, W. S. High-level trichromatic color matching and the pigment-bleaching hypothesis. *Vision Research*, 1980, *20*, 23–37.

Wyszecki, G., & Stiles, W. S. *Color science: Concepts and methods, quantitative data and formulae*. New York: Wiley, 1967.

Wyszecki, G., & Stiles, W. S. *Color science: Concepts and methods, quantitative data and formulae* (2nd ed.). New York: Wiley, 1982.

Yonemura, G. T., & Kasuya, M. Color discrimination under reduced angular subtense and luminance. *Journal of the Optical Society of America*, 1969, *59*, 131–135.

Young, T. On the theory of light and colours. *Philosophical Transactions of London*, 1802, *92*, 12–48.

Zaidi, Q. *A nonlinearity in color vision*. Unpublished doctoral dissertation, University of Chicago, 1984.

CHAPTER 9

COLOR APPEARANCE

GUNTER WYSZECKI

National Research Council, Ottawa, Canada

CONTENTS

Dr. Gunter Wyszecki died in June 1985. The editors wish to thank Dr. William Cowan for compiling the Index for this chapter, and Drs. Joel Pokorny and Vivian Smith for assisting with the proofreading.

The experimental data and theoretical considerations of this chapter deal with color-vision phenomena that play an important role in the assessment of color appearance. In the sense adopted here, *color appearance* refers to that aspect of visual perception by which an observer is able to assign perceptual attributes, such as hue, saturation, and brightness, to a given visual stimulus displayed in the observer's field of view. The visual stimulus presented to the observer as the test stimulus and all other stimuli making up the visual field are specifiable by physical means giving appropriate details of their spatial properties (size, shape, and location in visual field), temporal properties (steady state, moving, pulsing), and their spectral radiant power distributions measured at the pupil of the observer's eye.

An observer's judgment of the perceived color appearance of a visual stimulus rests on the subjective impressions experienced when viewing the stimulus display. In general, the judgment varies greatly with the viewing conditions and the kind of stimuli presented. Thus its precision compares poorly with that of complete color matching employed in the experimental procedure on which conventional colorimetry is based (see Chapter 8 by Pokorny and Smith).

The complex nature of color appearance is not as yet fully understood, and the mathematical models designed to make predictions of color appearance under a variety of observing conditions are not giving entirely satisfactory results. In particular, at the present time there does not exist an internationally adopted system of color-appearance specification equivalent in usefulness to the system standardized by the Commission Internationale de l'Eclairage (CIE) for the purpose of specifying color stimuli in terms of tristimulus values and chromaticity coordinates (see Chapter 8 by Pokorny and Smith). Two color stimuli of different spectral radiant power distributions but identical sets of CIE tristimulus values will be seen by the average observer with normal color vision as having identical colors. The stimuli will be said to match in color. However, the CIE system does not provide any quantitative measure of the color appearance of the stimuli. A different system, or a substantially expanded CIE system, has yet to be developed that can provide quantitative measures of color appearance that are useful to a wide range of applications in science and industry. The interest and need for a standardized system of color-appearance specification is clearly in evidence, and appropriate CIE technical committees have taken steps toward the development of such a system. The rapidly increasing demand for computer-interfaced video-display devices has put some urgency on further research that would enhance our understanding of human visual performance in relation to such devices. The study of color appearance and the development of appropriate models capable of making predictions of color appearance are clearly needed.

1. BASIC ATTRIBUTES OF COLOR APPEARANCE

A selection has been made of the concepts, terms, and definitions regarded as basic and of most value to a general discussion of color appearance. In the following discussion these concepts are given, their terms and definitions being substantially those adopted by the CIE in its *International Lighting Vocabulary* (CIE, 1970). Other publications that have influenced the formulation of the terms and definitions are those of Burnham, Hanes, and Bartleson (1963), Hunt (1978), and Wyszecki and Stiles (1982).

Although the concepts, terms, and their definitions given in Sections 1.1–1.5 are, at present, regarded as basic and of most value to a general discussion of color appearance, they must not be considered as forming a comprehensive set for such a discussion; nor must they be considered, individually or as a set, as having reached a final development stage.

1.1. Color

A widely accepted definition of color is the following: *color* is that aspect of visual perception by which an observer may distinguish differences between two structure-free fields of view of the same spatial and temporal properties, such as may be caused by differences in the spectral composition of the radiant energy concerned in the observation.

In this definition, color is considered an aspect of visual experience apart from spatial and temporal aspects. The spectral composition of the radiant energy entering the observer's eye and stimulating the visual mechanism to produce a color response is the basic physical parameter governing the visual experience. The color response can be described by such names as "yellow," "orange," "brown," "red," "pink," "green," "blue," "purple," and so forth, and by such names as "white," "gray," or "black," possibly modified by intensive adjectives, such as "bright," "dim," "light," "dark," or by forming appropriate combinations of such names (e.g., bright greenish yellow, and dark bluish gray). It is often convenient to distinguish between *chromatic colors*, that is, color stimuli perceived to possess hue (see Section 1.3), and *achromatic colors*, that is, color stimuli perceived to be devoid of hue.

The spectral radiant energy distribution entering the observer's eye is usually referred to as the *visual stimulus* or *color stimulus* and is expressed in terms of an appropriate radiometric quantity and its unit, for example, radiant power measured in watts (W) or radiance measured in watts per square meter per steradian ($W \cdot m^{-2} \cdot sr^{-1}$).

Although color is defined as an aspect of visual experience apart from spatial and temporal aspects, it is immediately noted that spatial and temporal aspects provide key parameters that influence color. In fact, a major concern in color science is to study those experimental and theoretical issues of color vision that reveal the effects of spatial and temporal properties of color stimuli on the color appearance of these stimuli. Typical spatial parameters are size and shape of each color stimulus displayed in the visual field and their location relative to one another. Texture, transparency, and other surface-structure properties of the visual field are further examples of spatial parameters. Typical temporal parameters characterize motion, flicker, and pulsing of color stimuli. In addition to spatial and temporal parameters, the observer's awareness, which includes attention, memory, motivation, and emotion, is sometimes an important parameter with a measurable effect on the observer's judgment of color appearance.

In exploring color and discussing color-vision phenomena, it is often convenient to distinguish between two different color-appearance modes, referred to as *related color* and *unrelated color*. Figure 9.1 illustrates schematically typical visual field configurations used in studying color vision with related and unrelated colors. By far the most often used field configurations in color-vision research have been of the laboratory-arrangement type, that is, a circular test stimulus displayed in a large surround stimulus, or a bipartite-field configuration. Such visual field configurations have proved to be particularly useful in studying basic visual functions, such as color-matching functions, increment-threshold sensitivity functions, luminous efficiency functions, wavelength discrimination functions, and chromatic-response functions (see, for example, Boynton, 1979; Wyszecki & Stiles, 1982). Experimental data of this kind form our *psychophysical* basis on which we rest, to a considerable extent, our present understanding of color vision. In recent years, however, complex visual field configurations, including gratings, checkerboard displays, and landscape scenes, are being used to bring out important additional characteristics of color vision. Spatial and temporal variations in the visual field have been found to affect strongly the response characteristics of our visual mechanism. The use of landscape scenes may lead us directly to models predicting visual performance related to practical tasks, such as those one might encounter in nature or in video displays. Normal daylight viewing of the object world around us clearly deals with related colors.

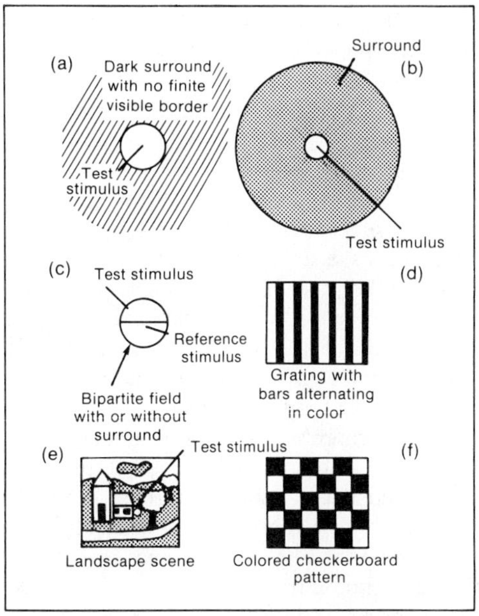

Figure 9.1. Typical visual field configurations used in studying color vision. Field configuration (a) provides an "unrelated" color, that is, a color seen in isolation from other colors. All other field configurations (b–f) provide "related" colors, that is, colors seen in direct relation to other colors in the field. Field configurations (b) and (c) are examples of classical laboratory arrangements; (d), (e), and (f) are examples of field configurations used frequently in more recent experiments. All field configurations may include temporal variations (e.g., pulsed or flicker presentation) of the color stimuli.

Sometimes, the appearance mode of related color is given specific and more limited meaning by the use of such terms as:

Object Color. Color perceived as belonging to an object.

Surface Color. Color perceived as belonging to a surface from which the light appears to be diffusely reflected or radiated.

Illuminant Color. Color perceived as belonging to an area that appears to be emitting light as a primary light source.

An *unrelated color* is a color perceived to belong to an area seen in isolation from other colors. Figure 9.1(a) is the typical field configuration used to generate an unrelated color. A special situation is given by the *Ganzfeld* mode, in which the color stimulus occupies uniformly the entire visual field of the observer.

1.2. Brightness and Lightness

Brightness is the attribute of a visual perception according to which a given visual stimulus appears to be more or less intense or according to which the area in which the visual stimulus is presented appears to emit more or less light. Variations in brightness range from very bright (dazzling) to very dim (dark). Brightness is an attribute that is perceived as belonging to visual stimuli regardless of their appearance mode. In particular, brightness can be judged in situations governed by related colors as well as in situations governed by unrelated colors.

In the case of related colors judging the attribute of lightness is often more appropriate or desirable than judging brightness.

Lightness is the attribute of a visual perception according to which the area in which the visual stimulus is presented appears to emit more or less light in proportion to that emitted by another area in the field of view perceived as a "white" stimulus. In this sense, lightness may be referred to as relative brightness. Variations in lightness range from very light (white) to very dark (black).

These definitions of brightness and lightness are probably the most widely accepted formulations available, and the CIE (1970) encourages their use. However, the reader must be advised that a significant portion of the past and present literature dealing with the concept of brightness or lightness uses the terms brightness and lightness in different senses. Sometimes no distinction is made between the two, sometimes brightness is used as an equivalent term for luminance (a well-defined term used in legal photometry), and sometimes lightness is applied only to surfaces eliciting achromatic perceptions described as grays ranging from black to white. In most cases no definition is offered for either brightness or lightness, and it becomes difficult, if not impossible, to form a clear understanding of the basic concepts underlying the particular study. In the case of experiments with paper chips painted in shades of gray ranging from black to white, the term *perceived reflectance* is also used but left undefined. It is not clear whether the term perceived reflectance can also be given meaning to surfaces coated with spectrally selective paints (nongrays) as opposed to strictly nonselective paints (grays). What is clear, though, is that the term perceived reflectance, to be at all meaningful in a given experimental situation, assumes that the observer perceives surfaces illuminated by one or more light sources.

1.3. Hue

Hue is the attribute of a color perception that can be described by such names as "blue," "green," "yellow," "orange," "red," and "purple" and combinations of such names, for example, bluish purple, yellowish green. Of particular importance are the unique hues. A *unique hue* (also called *unitary hue*) is a hue that cannot be further described by the use of hue names other than its own. There are four unique hues, each of which shows no perceptual similarity to any of the other three; they are described as red, green, yellow, and blue.

A color stimulus perceived to be *unique red* is judged to be neither yellow nor blue, *unique yellow* is judged to be neither green nor red, *unique green* is judged to be neither blue nor yellow, *unique blue* is judged to be neither red nor green.

The *hueness* of a color stimulus can be described as combinations of two unique hues; for example, orange is yellowish red and reddish yellow. Sometimes nonunique hues, such as orange, are referred to as *binary hues.*

1.4. Chroma and Saturation

Chroma is the attribute of a color perception that permits a judgment to be made of the degree to which a chromatic color differs from an achromatic color of the same lightness. The attribute of chroma is particularly useful in displays of color stimuli whose luminance factors, that is, CIE Y-tristimulus values, are the same. The *Munsell Book of Color* (see Section 7.1) provides, in good approximation, examples of what is meant by chroma. Each page of colors of constant Munsell hue contains a rectangular array of paint chips varying in Munsell value V (a function of luminance factor Y) in the vertical direction and in Munsell chroma C in the horizontal direction. Each column of paint chips on such a page of constant Munsell hue displays colors of constant Munsell chroma. Along each row of paint chips Munsell value, and thus luminance factor Y, is constant and Munsell chroma increases in equal perceptual steps when moving away from the inside margin of the page where the Munsell gray chips (with $C = 0$) are placed.

Munsell chroma does not precisely conform with the definition of chroma as given previously. Whereas in the definition, the chromatic color under consideration is judged relative to an achromatic color (gray) of the same lightness, in the *Munsell Book of Color* the judgment is made relative to a gray of the same luminance factor Y. Colors of the same Y value do not necessarily have the same lightness. In general, the lightness of such colors increases with increasing chroma.

Changing the illuminance E (formerly called illumination) on a display does not change the luminance factors Y of the color chips constituting the display. This invariance is not surprising as it is directly embedded in the definition of the photometric quantity Y. However, it is essential that changing the illuminance E must not be accompanied by any change in the relative spectral irradiance distribution $E(\lambda)$ provided by the source illuminating the display. The desired change in E must be accomplished by changing $E(\lambda)$ by a constant factor applicable to every wavelength of the $E(\lambda)$ distribution. The change in E will, of course, change the luminances L of the color stimuli emerging from the display; L will increase by the same factor as E. This is a simple consequence of the definition of the photometric quantity L.

Now suppose one raises the illuminance E of a display of color chips whose luminance factors Y are the same. Pages from the *Munsell Book of Color* may serve as good demonstration material. Photometric tests will then show that the Y value of the color chips will not have changed, but the luminance L will have increased by the same factor as E was raised. The important *visual observation* that will be made is that chroma values of the perceived colors in the display will tend to remain the same. This observation is not too surprising and has its origin in the well-known color-appearance phenomena of color constancy and lightness constancy applied to the restricted case of changing only the illuminance E on the display without changing the spectral distribution of the incident light other than by a constant factor.

Saturation is the attribute of a color perception that permits a judgment to be made of the degree to which a chromatic color differs from an achromatic color regardless of their lightness. The difference between saturation and chroma may be demonstrated by considering color chips whose spectral radiance factors $\beta(\lambda)$, or spectral reflectance curves, differ from one chip to another by only a constant factor. That is, the $\beta_i(\lambda)$ curve of the ith chip precisely matches at every wavelength λ the $\beta_{i+1}(\lambda)$ curve of the $(i+1)$ chip if all values of $\beta_i(\lambda)$ are multiplied by an appropriate constant factor $a_i \lesssim 1$. Color chips with such reflecting properties have the same chromaticity (CIE x,y chromaticity coordinates) but differ in luminance factor Y. With appropriately chosen differences between the Y values of the chips, a so-called shadow series can be displayed, showing the color chips in uniformly increasing lightness steps ranging from dark to light. The colors of such a shadow series are perceived to have (approximately) the same saturation. The visual judgment of the degree to which the chromatic colors differ from an achromatic color is made without taking reference to the lightness of the colors. However, the perceived attribute of chroma decreases with decreasing lightness of the members of the shadow series. The visual judgment of the degree to which the chromatic colors differ from an achromatic color is made, for each color, with specific reference to the achromatic color having the same lightness as the color under consideration.

In the real world of three-dimensional solid objects seen under lighting conditions that are partly directional and partly diffuse, a set of grays ranging from black to white may not be available for direct judgments of the chroma values of the various surfaces of the objects. In such situations chroma becomes a less evident attribute than saturation, and hence saturation may be the more dominant attribute of the two. The color appearance would then be described in terms of brightness (or lightness), hue, and saturation. Lightness is most likely chosen over brightness, particularly if a white surface is part of the real-world display. The white surface would then serve as the necessary reference stimulus with respect to which the lightness of any other stimulus is judged.

The concepts, terms, and definitions of chroma and saturation are perhaps the most controversial in the literature of color appearance. The need for further development of these concepts is clearly indicated, and recent efforts, particularly those made by Hunt (1977a, 1977b, 1979), are intriguing but left to the interested reader to pursue in detail. He proposes a new concept of *colorfulness*. Hunt (1977a) defines it as the "attribute of a visual sensation according to which an area appears to exhibit more or less chromatic color" (pp. 58, 59). He then defines chroma and saturation as two different types of "relative colorfulness." Hunt's main argument for his proposal rests on the observation that as the level of illuminance in a room (e.g., a living room) increases, the objects in it appear to become brighter and more colorful. Similarly, a scene on a color photographic print becomes brighter and more colorful when the level of illuminance on the print is raised. Observations of this kind are readily verified and apply to the full range of photopic levels of illuminance normally encountered in practical situations.

1.5. Color-Perception Space

The basic attributes of color appearance are often considered the dimensions of color perception and, as such, are used to generate the concept of color-perception space. Color-perception space is visualized as a three-dimensional geometrical model in which a given point represents a perceived color completely described by an appropriate set of three basic color attributes.

In the case of related colors, by far the more important of the two modes of color appearance, several geometrical models may be conceived to illustrate color-perception space. Figure 9.2 shows examples of three often-used models.

In Figure 9.2(a) the three dimensions of perceived color are hue, chroma, and lightness taken in accordance with their definitions given previously. The hue of colors of constant lightness and chroma, whose range includes red, orange, yellow, green, blue, violet, purple, and red, is shown as a circle, sometimes referred to as the *hue circuit*. Colors of increasing chroma lie on concentric circles of increasing radius. When lightness is allowed to vary from black to white, colors of constant chroma are represented by coaxial cylinders, their common axis being the series of achromatic colors or grays. Any point P in this model defined by cylindrical coordinates represents a unique color perception described in terms of hue h, chroma c, and lightness l.

In Figure 9.2(b), the three dimensions of perceived color are hue, saturation, and lightness. Again, hue circuits are shown for colors of constant lightness and saturation. However, colors of constant saturation and varying lightness are now represented by coaxial cones with a common apex in the point representing black. Note that the conceptual difference between saturation and chroma is appropriately reflected by the choice of coaxial cones and coaxial cylinders, respectively. In this presentation it becomes clear also that chroma and saturation can be made to have equal values and with no apparent conceptual difference between the two attributes if the paint chips include a gray chip and all chips are perceived to have the same lightness.

In Figure 9.2(c), the three dimensions of perceived color are hueness, described in terms of two unique hues and lightness. This model is built on a Cartesian coordinate system. In a plane of colors of constant lightness, a point P represents a color that can vary in two principal directions corresponding to the two unique hues appropriate to that part of the space. For the example shown, P can vary in redness r and blueness b.

Color-perception space has a boundary, a limiting surface beyond which there is no point to which a perceived color may be assigned. The geometrical concept of the boundary surface corresponds to the empirical fact that lightness has both a lower (black) and upper (white) limit, and chroma (or saturation) has not only a lower limit in an achromatic color but also an upper limit. Positioning the boundary surface in color-perception space requires the introduction of distance in color-perception space, which calls on the notion of the line element of color space (Wyszecki & Stiles, 1982). It is also noted that the boundary surface traced in an actual experiment depends to a large extent on the particular observing conditions that govern the experiment; but an optimal boundary may be conceived representing the extreme perceptions of lightness and chroma (or saturation) that can be generated. This optimal boundary may be considered the envelope of all boundaries obtained by appropriate experiments involving all possible sets of observing conditions (Wyszecki, 1981).

These geometrical models of color-perception space discussed have limitations with regard to their usefulness in illustrating other color-appearance attributes, attributes generally not considered basic but often readily observable and of importance in certain situations. A simple experiment can be used as an example.

Suppose we have in an otherwise dark visual field, a small (1°) circular test stimulus surrounded by a large (10°) concentric stimulus (Evans, 1974); see Figure 9.3. The test stimulus is chromatic, in fact, monochromatic of wavelength 700 nm, and its luminance can be varied independently of that of the surround stimulus. The surround stimulus is achromatic and of constant luminance (1000 $cd \cdot cm^{-2}$). In fact, the size of the surround stimulus relative to that of the test stimulus and the luminance of the surround stimulus relative to that of the test stimulus are such that the surround stimulus is always perceived to be achromatic throughout the experiment. The objective of the experiment is to describe the perceptions of the observer viewing the test stimulus at different luminances.

When the test stimulus has a very low luminance relative to the surround, for example, less than 1/1000 of that of the surround, the test stimulus appears black regardless of its wavelength (or chromaticity). Increasing the luminance of the test stimulus does not change its appearance at first; that is, black persists until a luminance level is reached at which the test stimulus appears to have a just-perceptible hue (reddish,

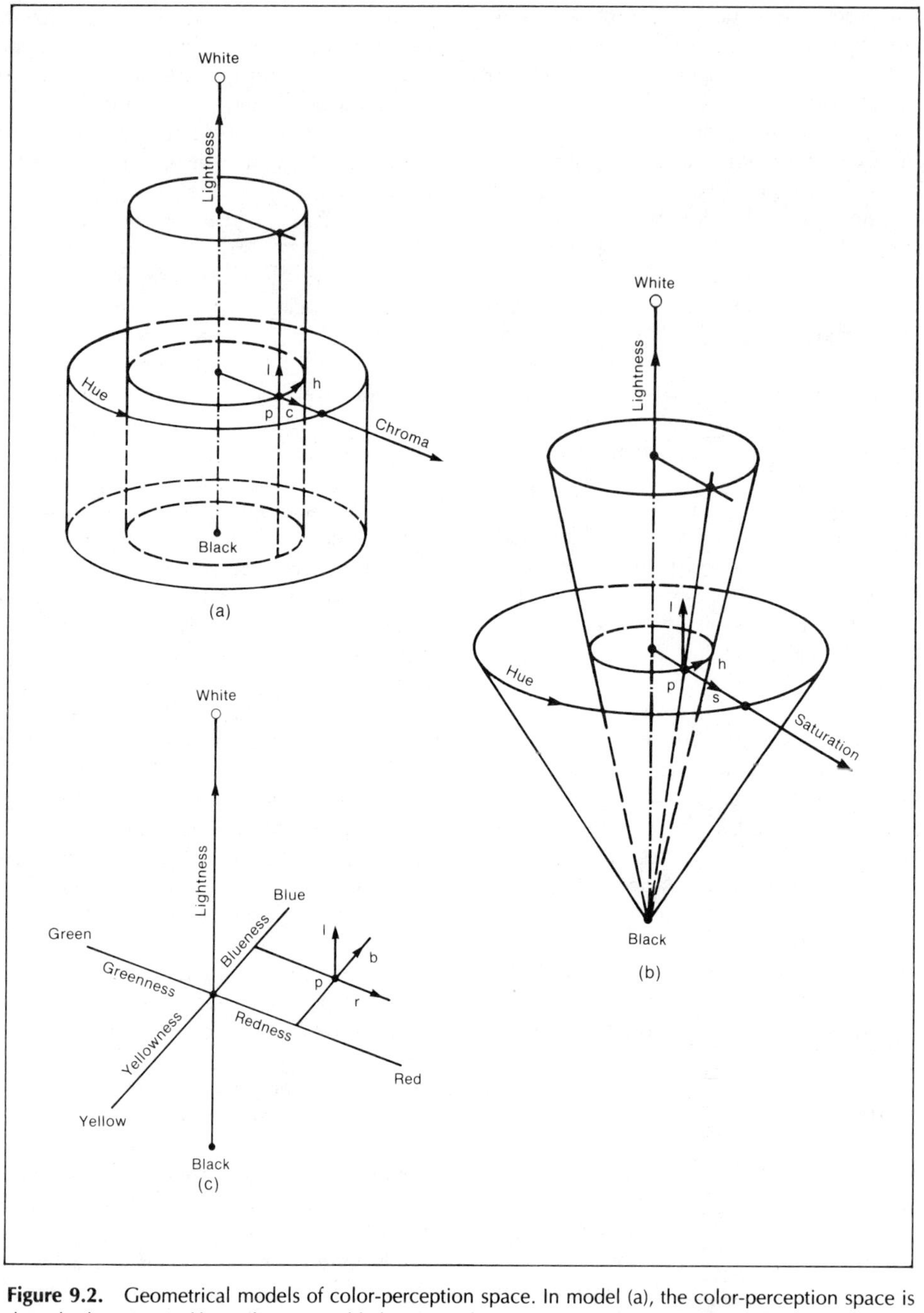

Figure 9.2. Geometrical models of color-perception space. In model (a), the color-perception space is described in terms of hue, chroma, and lightness. Color stimuli perceived to have the same hue lie on a vertical plane; color stimuli perceived to have the same chroma lie on a cylinder; and color stimuli perceived to have the same lightness lie on a horizontal plane. In model (b), the color perception space is described in terms of hue, saturation, and lightness. In this case, the cylindrical surfaces, representing constant chroma in model (a), become conical surfaces representing constant saturation. In model (c), the color perception space is described in terms of hueness (blueness or yellowness, and redness or greenness) and lightness. These perceptual attributes form a Cartesian coordinate system along three mutually perpendicular axes. (From D. B. Judd & G. Wyszecki, *Color in business, science, and industry*, 3rd ed. Copyright 1975 by John Wiley & Sons, Inc. Reprinted with permission.)

if the wavelength of the monochromatic test stimulus is 700 nm). The test stimulus appears to show both blackness and a reddish hue and may be described as reddish black. As the luminance, and thus lightness, is further increased, the hue component of the test stimulus becomes stronger while blackness simultaneously decreases. In fact, soon it becomes more descriptive to call the blackness component grayness, and the appearance of the test stimulus is appropriately given as grayish red. This trend continues with increasing luminance until a point is reached at which grayness has disappeared. For the test stimulus of wavelength 700 nm zero grayness is found at a luminance of approximately 1/10 of that of the surround (Evans, 1974). Zero grayness can be determined with good precision also for other chromatic test stimuli, and Evans denotes zero gray by the letter G_0. In color-perception space, the locus of G_0 points defines a surface containing the white point.

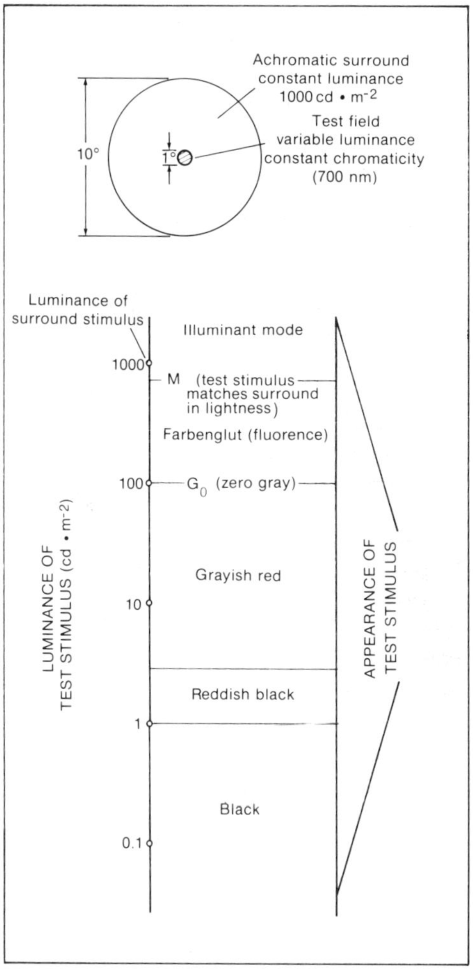

Figure 9.3. The appearance of a monochromatic (700-nm) test stimulus (1° angular subtense) surrounded by an achromatic (white) stimulus (10° angular subtense). The luminance of the test stimulus changes from 0.1 to over 1000 cd·m^{-2} while the luminance of the surrounding stimulus is kept constant at 1000 cd·m^{-2}.

Further increases in luminance increase the lightness of the test stimulus, of course, but another attribute is perceived which Evans (1959) called *fluorence*. This attribute actually seems to be linked with the *Helmholtz–Kohlrausch* effect described in the early German literature as *Farbenglut* (color glow). The zero-gray content G_0 thus constitutes a perceptual threshold obtained at a particular luminance of the test stimulus relative to that of the surround stimulus, below which the test stimulus is perceived to contain gray and above which it is perceived to glow, or to be fluorent.

When the luminance is further increased, both the perceived lightness and the fluorence increase and a lightness match, though often imprecise, is obtained between the test stimulus and the surround at a certain luminance of the test stimulus—not necessarily equal to that of the surround luminance. With increases in luminance beyond the lightness-match point, fluorence continues to be observed, at least within a certain range of luminance, but soon the test stimulus takes on the illuminant mode, and its brightness can become a dominant, attention-drawing feature in the display with the surround stimulus now being the darker element in the display.

The geometrical models of color-perception space illustrated in Figure 9.2 are clearly not equally applicable or useful to the different types of color-perception attributes. They are most useful in illustrating surface-color perceptions, typically elicited by displays of paint chips that do not include fluorescent paints or other specifically brightness-enhanced surfaces. In such a display, the important reference stimulus is either a white chip, another achromatic surface, or recourse is taken to the much less definite notion of the "average lightness" (sometimes "perceived average reflectance") that the display appears to have. The models shown in Figure 9.2(a) and (b) have, most likely, been specifically devised to explain geometrically the attributes of hue, chroma, saturation, and lightness. The third model, shown in Figure 9.2(c), is based on different perceptual attributes, except for lightness. However, the model's usefulness for illustrating surface-color perceptions is readily recognized. The construction of the model and its principal axes are based, of course, on the opponent-colors theory of color vision.

The geometrical models apply also to object-color perceptions elicited by displays of solid (three-dimensional) objects. However, when studying object-color perceptions, special precautions must be made because spatial parameters can readily affect the observer's perceptions. The position of the light source illuminating the display, generating a multitude of shadows and highlights, and suppressing or enhancing edges and textures becomes a particularly critical parameter that must be carefully controlled before meaningful experimental data can be obtained and illustrated in the model.

These three models are not applicable for illustrating illuminant-color–perception space, that is, a space representing colors perceived as belonging to an area that appears to be emitting light as a primary source. The concepts of chroma and saturation, in the sense in which they have been defined, must be revised to apply. In the new definitions for the two, lightness would have to be replaced by brightness. The lightness axis in the revised models must be replaced by a brightness axis. Scale values of brightness would be a nonlinear function of luminance (cd·m^{-2}). There would be no requirement for a change to the concept of hue. The demand for a model of illuminant-color space has been small or nonexistent. However, the interest may increase particularly in research with computer-interfaced video displays which can readily generate illuminant colors of practical importance. A problem may arise when in a particular viewing situation perceptions of both illuminant colors and surface colors are elicited by the display. Judgments of brightness, as well as lightness, may be required to obtain a complete perceptual description of the various color stimuli exhibited in the display. Further research seems to be required to develop an adequate solution of such a problem.

2. COLOR-APPEARANCE PHENOMENA

Color-appearance phenomena arise when the physical characteristics (i.e., spatial, temporal, and spectral properties) of one or more color stimuli in a display are changed. Many color-appearance phenomena, some visually striking, others more subtle, have been reported and studied in the literature. Few, if any, have been fully explained in terms of a complete model of color vision capable of making satisfactory quantitative predictions of the experimental results.

2.1. Abney Effect

The hue of a color stimulus is in general modified if, starting from a monochromatic stimulus or a purple, an achromatic stimulus is added to it to decrease progressively the colorimetric purity. The effect, called the *Abney effect* (Abney, 1910), is manifest in the choice of color samples in color-appearance systems, particularly the Munsell color system (Section 7.1). In a CIE chromaticity diagram showing the chromaticities of the Munsell color samples of constant Munsell value, the chromaticity loci of Munsell colors to which the system assigns the same hue are (for most hues) curved lines joining the achromatic point to a point on the spectrum locus or the line of purples. Figure 9.4 illustrates a number of loci of constant hue in the CIE chromaticity diagram. For a particular yellow at about 570 nm and a particular bluish purple ($x = 0.240, y = 0.035$, approximately), the corresponding hue loci are straight lines, indicating zero Abney effects in these cases.

Other examples of experimentally determined loci of constant hue in the chromaticity diagram have been provided by MacAdam (1950, 1951), Wilson and Brocklebank (1955), and Robertson (1970).

2.2. Bezold–Brücke Effect

The hue perception elicited by a color stimulus of fixed chromaticity generally changes noticeably when substantial increases or decreases are made to the luminance of the stimulus. This effect of luminance on hue is known as the *Bezold–Brücke effect*. Direct measurements by Purdy (1931) make clear the direction and approximate magnitude of the effect for monochromatic stimuli. Purdy's measurements were hue matches (in a 3° bipartite field) between a monochromatic stimulus of fixed wavelength and luminance and a second monochromatic stimulus whose wavelength was varied, the luminance being kept at a constant value considerably lower than for the first

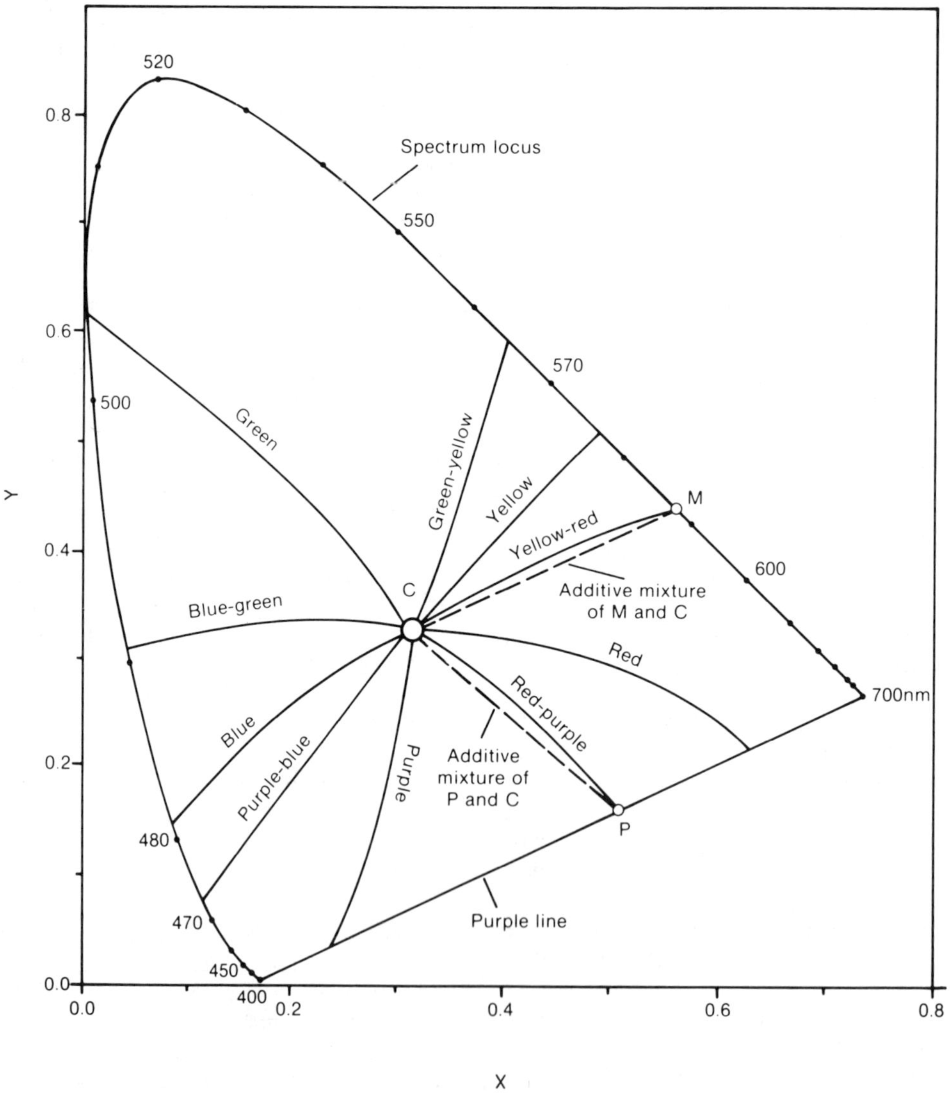

Figure 9.4. Abney effect. Examples of loci of constant hue in the CIE 1931 (*x,y*) chromaticity diagram. These loci, taken from the *Munsell Book of Color* data described in Section 7.1, are, in general, curved lines. This empirical fact is consistent with the Abney effect, which states that the hue of a color stimulus changes if, starting from a monochromatic stimulus *M* or a purple *P*, and achromatic stimulus *C* is added to it to decrease progressively its colorimetric purity. Such additive mixtures would be straight lines in the chromaticity diagram connecting the achromatic chromaticity point *C* ($x = 0.310$, $y = 0.316$) with the chromaticity point of the monochromatic *M* or purple *P* stimulus.

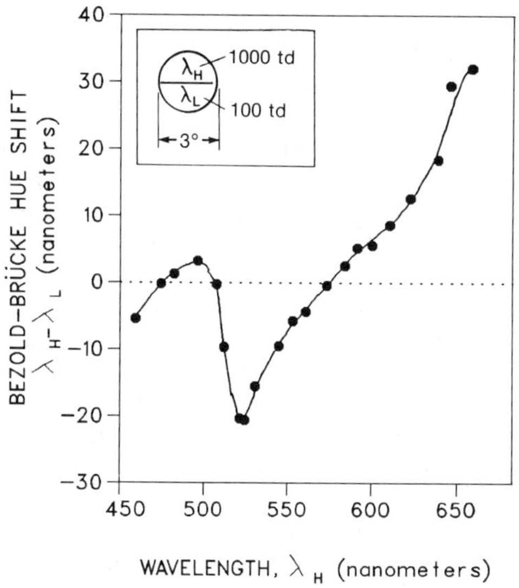

Figure 9.5. Bezold–Brücke effect. Change of hue of monochromatic stimuli corresponding to a reduction in retinal illuminance from 1000 to 100 td. The data shown are extracted from Purdy's (1931) hue-matching experiment in a 3° bipartite field. The stimulus of a fixed wavelength λ_H and a luminance providing 1000 td matches in hue the stimulus of variable wavelength λ_L and luminance providing 100 td. The observed Bezold–Brücke shift ($\lambda_H - \lambda_L$) is plotted against λ_H. (From G. Wyszecki & W. S. Stiles, *Color science*, 2nd ed. Copyright 1982 by John Wiley & Sons, Inc. Reprinted with permission.)

stimulus. The excess of the wavelength λ_H of the higher-luminance field over that of the lower-luminance field λ_L, when the perceived hues were as nearly as possible the same, defined the *Bezold–Brücke hue shift* ($\lambda_H - \lambda_L$). The values obtained for the luminance pair, yielding a ratio of retinal illuminance of 1000/100 td, are shown in Figure 9.5. In addition to the three spectral hues showing no Bezold–Brücke shift, Purdy determined a fourth reddish purple hue with the same property.

Boynton and Gordon (1965) repeated Purdy's (1931) experiment of direct hue matching in a steady-state (continuously exposed) bipartite field and added two other experimental procedures. The first of their additional experiments was a modification of Purdy's procedure in which the observer was asked to make hue matches on the basis of 300-msec pulses of the bipartite field with 9-sec dark intervals. In the second experiment, a color-naming method was used employing a 3° circular field centrally fixated, superimposed upon a tiny fixation point. The monochromatic stimuli were presented in 300-msec pulses providing either 1000 or 100 td, with dark intervals of 12 sec. The observer named the hues in terms of four color names, red (R), yellow (Y), green (G), and blue (B), and was allowed to assign intermediate hue names, such as yellow-red (YR) or red-yellow (RY), with Y being the predominant cardinal hue in YR and R the predominant cardinal hue in RY. Thus the observer had 12 possible choices of naming a hue: BR, B, BG, GB, G, GY, YG, Y, YR, RY, R, RB. Each judgment made by the observer was assigned an arbitrary score value of 3. When the judgment was described by a cardinal-hue name, such as R, the entire score value of 3 was assigned to it. When intermediate-hue names were used, such as RY, a value of 2 was assigned to the first R and a value of 1 to the second Y name. For each level (1000 and 100 td), every monochromatic stimulus of wavelength λ was judged a total of 25 times in a randomized presentation cycle, providing a total score value of 75 distributed among the four cardinal-hue names.

The mean results obtained by Boynton and Gordon (1965) for three observers determining Bezold–Brücke hue shifts by three different experimental methods are illustrated in Figure 9.6. The data obtained by the steady-state hue-matching method are directly comparable with those obtained by Purdy (1931), shown in Figure 9.5. The agreement between the two sets of data is quite good. When the experimental procedure is changed, differences in the results are noted, which Boynton and Gordon (1965) attribute to simultaneous contrast effects whose impor-

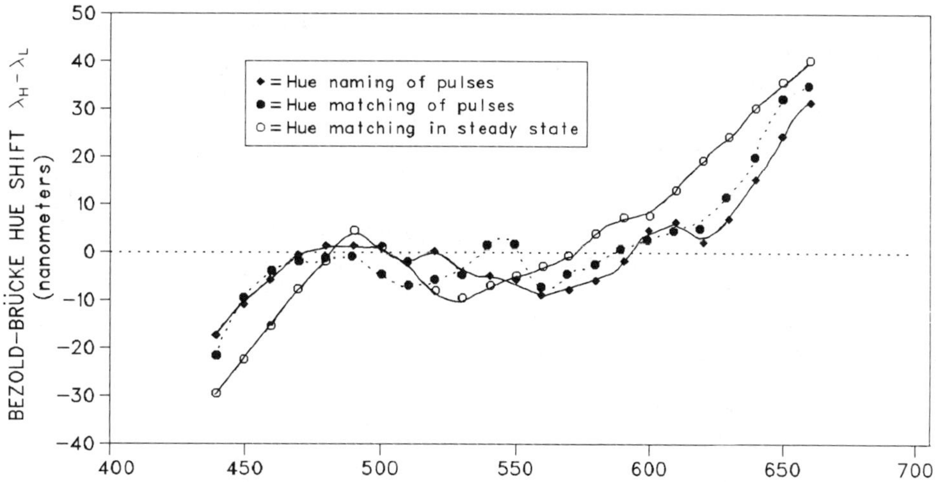

Figure 9.6. Bezold–Brücke effect. Change of hue of monochromatic stimuli corresponding to a reduction in retinal illuminance from 1000 to 100 trolands, determined by Boynton and Gordon (1965) for three observers and three different experimental procedures. The mean Bezold-Brücke hue shift ($\lambda_H - \lambda_L$) for the three observers is plotted against λ_H, for each of the three experimental procedures. There is general agreement between the experimental data of Boynton and Gordon (1965) shown in this figure and those of Purdy (1931) shown in Figure 9.5. (From G. Wyszecki & W. S. Stiles, *Color science*, 2nd ed. Copyright 1982 by John Wiley & Sons, Inc. Reprinted with permission.)

tance varies with the presentation time of the stimuli. The authors also discuss possible connections between stimuli for which zero shifts of hue are observed, that is, $\lambda_H - \lambda_L = 0$, and stimuli that have been found in other studies to exhibit the psychologically "unique hues" red, yellow, green, and blue.

In a later study be Larimer, Krantz, and Cicerone (1974), in which the Bezold–Brücke effect was explored further, it was suggested that the hue-naming data of Boynton and Gordon are likely to have been biased somewhat by the scoring method used. In particular, a bias toward a shorter wavelength of the unique blue was considered possible. The same authors also concluded from their experimental data that monochromatic unique yellow (approximately 578 nm) and monochromatic unique blue (approximately 478 nm) showed either no variation or virtually insignificant variation over a luminance range of 1–2 log units; within that range, these stimuli yield invariant hues relative to the Bezold–Brücke shift. In a subsequent paper, Larimer, Krantz, and Cicerone (1975) found that the monochromatic unique green (approximately 500 nm) stimulus yields an invariant hue. Unique red was obtained for nonmonochromatic stimuli consisting of additive mixtures of the shortwave and longwave ends of the visible spectrum. The additive mixture required for the stimulus to remain unique red must be varied with luminance; otherwise, a stimulus perceived to be unique red at a low luminance level turns bluish red when the luminance is increased.

The study by Nagy and Zacks (1977) dealt with the zero shifts of hue and the measurement procedure used to assess Bezold–Brücke hue shifts. These authors concluded that the stimulus presentation time was an important variable in accounting for the differences between different procedures of measurement.

There are several other studies of the Bezold–Brücke effect, of which the following are of particular interest: P. L. Walraven (1961), Coren and Keith (1970), Yager and Taylor (1970), Cohen (1971), Savoie (1973), and Nagy (1980).

According to the opponent-colors theory, the independent red-green and yellow-blue chromatic-response systems are functions of luminance and exhibit differential response rates consistent with the observed Bezold–Brücke hue shifts (Hurvich, 1981; Hurvich & Jameson, 1955). In particular, it is hypothesized that blueness and yellowness responses increase with luminance more rapidly than do redness and greenness responses. However, under certain observing conditions (stimuli presented at very short pulses), this explanation may not be valid (Nagy, 1980).

2.3. The Color Appearance of the Spectrum: Brindley Isochromes

The appearance of the monochromatic stimuli λ of a continuous spectrum, for example, the spectrum obtained by dispersing white light, varies continuously from one end ($\lambda = 400$ nm) of the spectrum to the other ($\lambda = 700$ nm) in all three color-appearance attributes: hue, saturation, and brightness. Hue varies from violet to blue, blue-green, green, yellow, orange, and red. Saturation is first high, drops to a low in the middle (approximately 570 nm) of the spectrum, and rises again at the longwave end. Brightness is zero at both ends of the spectrum, whose wavelengths depend to some degree on the spectral radiant power emitted by the source. The spectrum tends to contract for weak sources. However, regardless of how high the spectral radiant power is, barring levels unsafe to the eye, the visual mechanism will not respond to stimuli of wavelengths lower than about 350 nm and higher than about 900 nm. Outside the spectral range 350–900 nm the stimuli are perceived to have zero brightness. The spectral range 350–900 nm may be called the *extreme* visible spectral range. The color-matching functions for both the CIE 1931 and CIE 1964 standard colorimetric observers (see Chapter 8 by Pokorny and Smith) have been defined for the range 360–830 nm. For many visual experiments, the range 400–700 nm suffices. The brightness perceived for monochromatic stimuli within the visible spectrum depends, in the first instance, on the spectral radiant power distribution of the source, which may vary greatly from one wavelength to the next. But with constant radiant power at all wavelengths, the brightness increases smoothly and monotonically from zero to a maximum at about 555 nm and decreases smoothly and monotonically to zero at the other end of the spectrum.

An interesting phenomenon occurs with regard to the perception of hue in the far end (beyond 700 nm) of the spectrum. The stimuli in that spectral range begin to appear as red, red-orange, and orange with increasing wavelengths, that is, begin to match in hue stimuli of wavelengths below 700 nm. Pairs of wavelengths that show the same hue are called *Brindley isochromes* in accordance with observations made by Brindley (1955) using a 4° visual field. Table 9.1 identifies some of these isochromes. The CIE 1964 large-field color-matching data (see Chapter 8 by Pokorny and Smith) in the longwave end of the spectrum substantially confirm Brindley's results. The points on the longwave end of the spectrum locus in the CIE 1964 (x_{10}, y_{10}) chromaticity diagram move with increasing wavelength first toward the lower-right corner of the diagram but then reverse their direction for the very long wavelengths.

One implication of the hue reversal is that in a plot of the logarithm of the spectral sensitivity (expressed on a quantum basis) against wave number, the gradients of the curves for the red and green cone mechanisms do not tend to the same constant value as the wavelength is moved deep into the red. A theoretical interpretation of this deviation from the simpler behavior commonly assumed has been advanced by Lewis (1955).

2.4. Stiles–Crawford Effect

The term *directional sensitivity* is now commonly used, in a visual context, to denote variations in visual sensitivity that are observed not when stimuli arrive from different directions in the visual field to be imaged on *different* retinal areas but when stimuli enter the eye through different parts of the pupil and are imaged on the *same* retinal area. Both brightness-matching and increment-threshold methods yield quantitative measurements of directional sensitivity. The value of the directional sensitivity at a pupil point of entry P may be defined as the ratio

$$\eta = \frac{S_O}{S_P}, \tag{1}$$

Table 9.1. Examples of Pairs of Monochromatic Stimuli in the Red End of the Spectrum That Can Be Made to Completely Match in Color

	Pairs of Stimuli That Match in Color				
Shortwave stimulus (nm)	641	652	674	679	688
Longwave stimulus (nm)	887	850	786	749	711

Pairs with this property are called Brindley isochromes; they have the same hue.

where S_P and S_O are the magnitudes producing the same visual effect on the given retinal area when entry is, respectively, at P and at a fixed reference point of entry P_O. Experimentation shows the following:

1. For most eyes studied, the response of a foveal rod-free area is maximal when P is at or near the pupil center and is reduced to about a quarter when P approaches the pupil edge.
2. For extrafoveal (parafoveal) retinal areas the directional sensitivity resembles that for foveal vision, provided the conditions are such that the visual response measured is a cone response. However, when the measured response is attributable to the rod mechanism, the directional changes are very much reduced and the response may be regarded as nearly nondirectional.

The following empirical formula was introduced by Stiles and Crawford (1933) to represent the variation of η with the distance r in mm between P and P_0 (taken to be the point of entry for maximal η):

$$\eta = 10^{pr^2} , \tag{2}$$

where the constant p is a convenient measure of the directional effect. For foveal vision, p has a value in the neighborhood of 0.05. Few data on the variation of p with the wavelength of the stimulus are available, but p appears to be rather larger in the blue and red than in the green, yellow, or orange (Stiles, 1939). The effect characterized by η is commonly referred to as *Stiles–Crawford effect of the first kind.*

Stimuli entering the pupil at points displaced from the center (strictly, displaced from point P_0) appear of slightly different color and not merely of reduced brightness. This is commonly referred to as the *Stiles–Crawford effect of the second kind.* The magnitude of the color changes is illustrated by the data of Figure 9.7, which show the changes in stimuli when the point of entry is shifted from P_0 to a point 3.5 mm temporal (Enoch & Stiles, 1961). There are a hue shift with a characteristic variation through the spectrum (inset) and an increase in saturation in the blue-green.

Directional sensitivity is predominantly retinal in origin; that is, it corresponds to changes in the visual response of a retinal area as the retinal angle of incidence of the stimulus is altered; but differential light losses in the optic media experienced by rays entering through different points of the pupil may modify the effect observed in the intact eye. As emphasized by Weale (1961), the lens with its diminishing thickness from center to edge and its high absorption (or scattering) at short wavelengths must be expected to have a considerable effect on the observed directional sensitivity for spectral stimuli in the

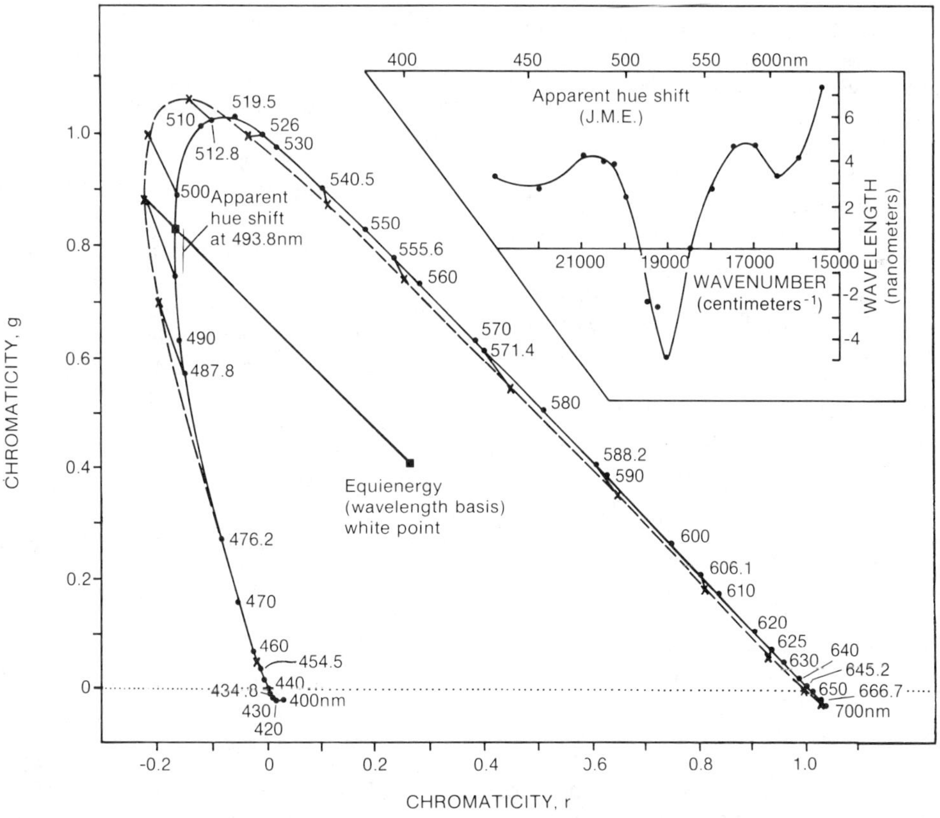

Figure 9.7. Stiles–Crawford effect of the second kind. Change of color of monochromatic stimuli with change in the angle of incidence of the stimulus on the foveal retina. In the (*r,g*) chromaticity diagram, governing the color-matching experiment with monochromatic (red, green, blue) primary stimuli at 444.4, 526.3, 645.2 nm, the solid dots represent chromaticities for normal incidence, and the lines joining the dots to the cross points show the observed chromaticity shifts for oblique incidence (about 10° angle). Except in the blue-green (480–520 nm), where oblique incidence increases saturation, the color shifts are nearly along the spectrum locus and are more clearly shown in the inset figure. The apparent hue shift is determined as illustrated for wavelength 493.8 nm. (From J. M. Enoch & W. S. Stiles, The colour change of monochromatic light with retinal angle of incidence, *Optica Acta*, 1961, *8*. Reprinted with permission.)

blue and violet. The modification is in the sense of a smaller observed variation of sensitivity than would be expected from the purely retinal effect.

Reviews of work on directional sensitivity and attempts to explain the phenomenon by means of an appropriate physiological model have been published by Vos (1960), Stiles (1962), Enoch (1963), Crawford (1972), and Snyder and Pask (1973).

2.5. Constancy of Object-Color Appearance

In real-world visual fields constituting displays of two- and three-dimensional objects, the colors perceived to belong to the objects have the remarkable property of approximate invariance under a considerable range of lighting conditions. Both the level of illuminance on the display provided by the incident light and the light's spectral radiant power distribution can be changed considerably without greatly upsetting the constancy of object-color appearance.

The following example describes a typical situation. When the observer passes from natural daylight into a room illuminated by incandescent-lamp light, the observer notices immediately that the color of the light reflected from the objects in the room have changed. Objects that reflect green light in daylight now appear to reflect yellow-green light; if the object reflects purple light in daylight, it now appears to reflect a more reddish kind of light. This immediate change in perceived color, however, does not seem to the observer to apply to the object. That is, the observer recognizes that the color of the incident light is reddish yellow and perceives the object color relative to this: green, much as it was in daylight; hence the term *object-color constancy*. The observer's ability to recognize and cope with the level and spectral quality of the new incident light (in this case, incandescent-lamp light) has long been thought of as a key factor in attempts to explain object-color constancy and is often referred to as "discounting the illuminant." Gradually, the observer's visual mechanism becomes accustomed to the new quality of illumination; that is, the visual mechanism adapts, and after 5 min or so even the light reflected from the object is perceived to have approximately the same color as that reflected from the same object illuminated by daylight. The yellow-green patch of light seen at the first moment reflected from the object illuminated by the reddish yellow tungsten-lamp light changes back to green. Similarly, a purple that changed toward red will change back toward purple. Unfortunately, the (gradual) adaptive change is usually not complete. In general, there remains a residual, often of significant size, between the color originally perceived in daylight and that perceived in tungsten light. For example, the purple will not lose all the red content it gained in the transition from daylight to tungsten light.

The *resultant color shift* perceived after the observer is adapted to the chromatic illumination of tungsten light is a combination of a *colorimetric shift* and an *adaptive color shift*. The colorimetric shift is simply due to the changed spectral distribution of radiant power leaving the object when illuminated by tungsten light instead of daylight. The change results in a change of the chromaticity and luminance factor of the object-color stimulus and corresponds to what the observer sees at the first instant when entering the room illuminated by tungsten light. This colorimetric shift can be calculated by standard colorimetric procedures (see Chapter 8 by Pokorny and Smith). The adaptive color shift is caused solely by *chromatic adaptation* of the visual mechanism and generally tends toward the original color perceived in daylight. Its precise prediction has been the subject matter of research for many years and is discussed in Section 4.

Early theories and experimental procedures commonly used in studying object-color constancy are thoroughly described in standard textbooks on experimental psychology (see, for example, Kling & Riggs, 1971). Aspects of object-color constancy also arise in studies on achromatic and chromatic induction which seek explanations for such phenomena as lightness (or brightness) contrast, lightness constancy, and color contrast. Some of these items will be discussed in Section 3.

3. ACHROMATIC AND CHROMATIC INDUCTION

Achromatic or chromatic induction is a visual process that occurs when two color stimuli (of any spectral radiance distribution) are viewed side by side; each stimulus alters the color (chromatic or achromatic) appearance of the other. The change in appearance may be confined to a change in only one attribute of color perception, that is, either lightness, hue, or chroma or it may take the form of color shifts in any combination of these attributes.

The effect of achromatic and/or chromatic induction is usually referred to as *simultaneous contrast*, or *spatial contrast*, and is virtually instantaneous. For simultaneous contrast to be visible there must exist in the neural organization of the color-vision mechanisms a substantial interdependence between the neural activities in neighboring parts of the retina and their associated neural pathways, and the signals transmitted to the cortex must be strong enough so that differences between them can be differentiated and be given appropriate interpretations.

3.1. Lightness Constancy and Lightness Contrast

Displays of achromatic stimuli, gray objects or arrays of gray paint chips, give rise to achromatic induction, and its effects of lightness constancy and lightness contrast are of particular interest. In basic quantitative studies of these effects, a very simple display configuration may be used, as illustrated in Figure 9.8. Two fields, the test field and the inducing field, are uniformly illuminated. The light reflected from these two fields provides the test and inducing stimuli. The inducing stimulus may increase or decrease the lightness of the test stimulus or have no effect, depending on the relative luminances of the two stimuli and geometric parameters of the fields (sizes, shapes, and separation). The test stimulus may have, of course, also an inducing effect on the inducing stimulus, but this effect can be reduced greatly by making the test field much smaller than the inducing field.

In a display, such as that illustrated in Figure 9.8, the following qualitative observations are readily made:

1. The test field of fixed reflectance appears to increase in lightness when the reflectance of the inducing field is decreased. Similarly, the test field of fixed reflectance becomes darker when the reflectance of the inducing field is increased.
2. When the illuminance level on the entire display of test and inducing fields, as well as the background, is changed (either increased or decreased), the observer perceives a corresponding change (increase or decrease) in *brightness* (more or less light appears to be emitted from the different fields of the display), but the *lightness* of the test field appears to remain approximately the same.

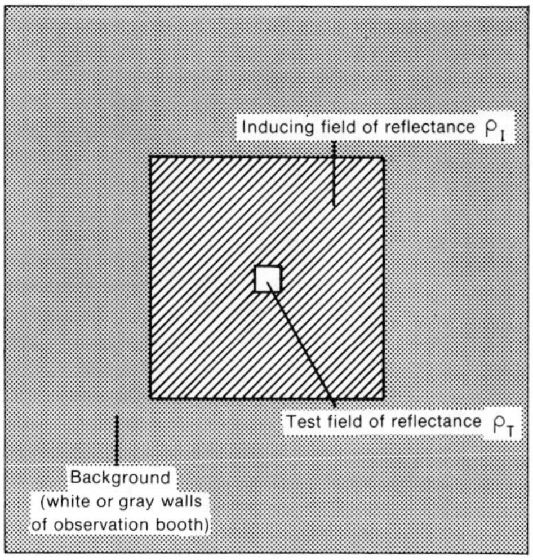

Figure 9.8. Example of visual field configuration used in achromatic induction experiments. A small test field is surrounded by a large inducing field. The two fields are gray paint chips of different reflectances and illuminated uniformly in an observation booth with white or gray walls. The test field of fixed reflectance appears to increase (decrease) in lightness when the reflectance of the inducing field is decreased (increased). This observation is referred to as lightness contrast. When the illuminance level on the entire display is changed (either increased or decreased), the observer perceives a corresponding change (increase or decrease) in *brightness*, but the *lightness* of the test field appears to remain approximately the same. This observation is referred to as lightness constancy.

The observations described under (1) are generally referred to a as *lightness (or brightness) contrast.* In that context, contrast refers to the apparent enhancement of the lightness (or brightness) difference between the two fields in the display. It is important to note that the term contrast is also used in a different sense, referring to the ratio of the luminances of two adjacent stimuli (achromatic or chromatic), and care must be taken to avoid possible confusion.

The observations described under (2) are generally referred to as *lightness constancy.* Both lightness constancy and lightness contrast have been the subject of research for many decades. Informative reviews of the earlier work are those of Graham and Brown (1965), Hurvich and Jameson (1966), Hochberg (1971), and Beck (1972).

Quantitative data of induction effects are often based on lightness matching. Lightness matches are obtained by adding to the display of Figure 9.8 a comparison field, generally of the same shape and size as the test field and often with its own separate surround. Figure 9.9 illustrates a typical field arrangement. To provide versatility of experimentation, the field arrangement shown in Figure 9.9 is often accomplished by sophisticated optical-mechanical devices so as to be able to change by measurable amounts and independent of one another the luminances of all the achromatic fields in the display. For given luminances of the two inducing fields and the test field, the luminance of the comparison field is adjusted by the observer until both the test and the comparison fields appear to match in lightness. One of the earliest experiments of this kind was made by Hess and Pretori (1894) and repeated in a multitude of experimental variants by many workers since that time, notably Wallach (1948), Leibowitz, Mote, and Thurlow (1953), Diamond (1953, 1955, 1962), Fry and Alpern (1953), Heinemann (1955), S. S. Stevens and J. C. Stevens (1960), Jameson and Hurvich (1961a), and Horeman (1963).

For the purpose of illustrating the kinds of results one obtains in such experiments, a brief description of those obtained by Heinemann (1955) may suffice. Heinemann used a display configuration consisting of a circular (28-min) test field surrounded by an annulus-inducing field with a 55-min outside diameter; a circular (28-min) comparison field was placed to the right of the test field at a distance, from center to center, of 104 min. The display had a dark background. Haploscopic viewing was used: the left eye saw the test field and its surrounding inducing field, the right eye the comparison field. Figure 9.10 illustrates in schematic fashion the features of some of Heinemann's results of lightness-matching the comparison field with the test field.

For a given luminance L_T of the test field, the functional relationship between the luminance L_I of the inducing field and the luminance L_C of the comparison field reveals itself as a smooth curve with the following features regardless of the given luminance L_T for the test field. At zero luminance of the inducing field ($L_I = 0$), the luminance L_C of the comparison field is set, as expected, equal to the luminance L_T of the test field. When L_I is gradually increased, the required settings of L_C increase slightly, indicating a small but noticeable increase in the perceived lightness (or brightness) of the test field. At L_I approximately one-half the value of L_T, the value of L_C begins to drop. With further increases in L_I, L_C drops more sharply, and at approximately $L_I = L_T$, even very small increases in L_I make it necessary to decrease L_C drastically if a lightness match between the test and comparison fields is to be retained. Quickly it becomes apparent that with any further increase in L_I, even a setting of L_C equal to zero does not result in a completely satisfactory match; the induced "blackness" in the test field cannot be matched by the comparison field. To obtain a match, it becomes necessary to introduce an inducing field of nonzero luminance around the comparison field.

With the same display configuration, as shown in the inset of Figure 9.10, Heinemann (1955) also determined lightness matches between the test field and the comparison field by holding the luminance L_C of the comparison field at some fixed

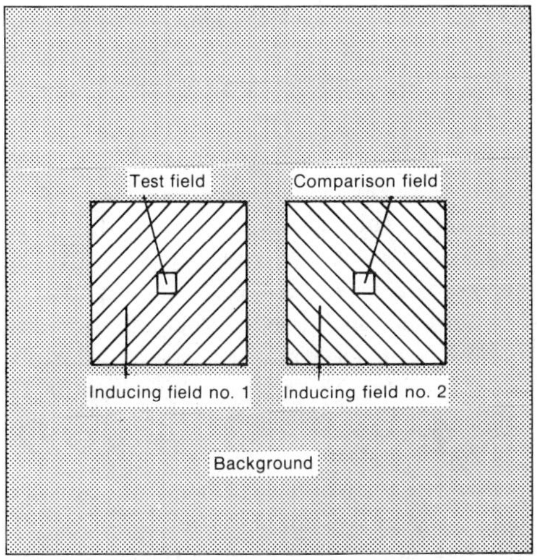

Figure 9.9. Example of visual field configuration used in achromatic induction experiments. To the simple configuration, shown in Figure 9.8, consisting of a test field surrounded by an inducing field, is added a comparison field surrounded by another inducing field. This arrangement allows the observer to make lightness matches between the test and comparison field by manipulating the reflectances (or luminances) of the comparison field.

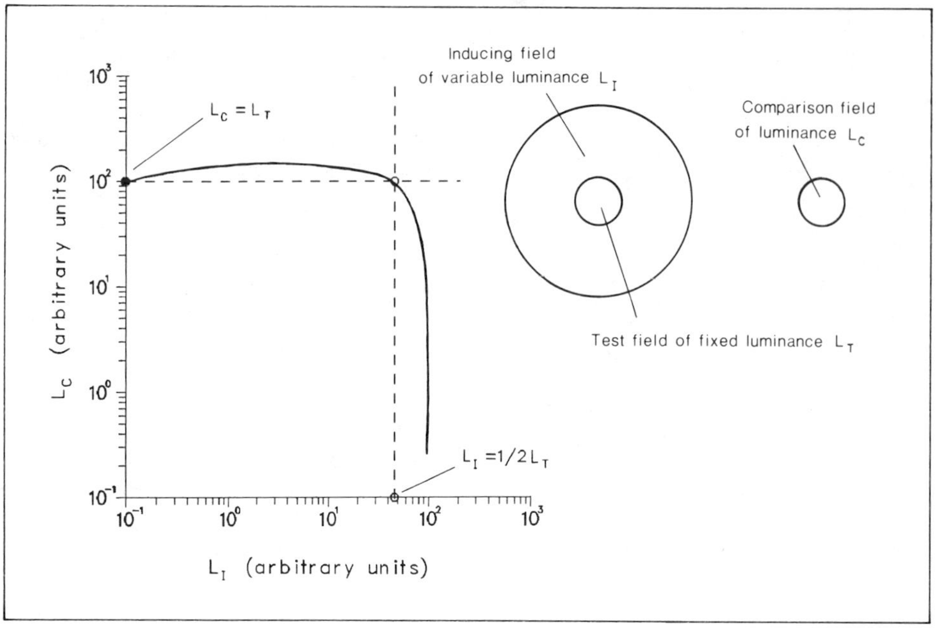

Figure 9.10. Summary of results obtained by Heinemann (1955) in achromatic induction experiments. The inset at the upper-right-hand side shows the visual field configuration. The curve illustrates the main features of the experimental results obtained for an observer whose task it is to match the lightness between the test field and the comparison field by making an appropriate adjustment to the luminance L_C of the comparison field. While the luminance L_T of the test field is kept constant throughout the experiment, the luminance L_I of the inducing field is set at different values ranging from zero to a high value. All luminance values are specified in terms of some convenient units, such as $cd \cdot m^{-2}$. For every given luminance value of L_I (plotted along the abscissa), there is an experimentally determined luminance value of L_C (plotted along the ordinate). The resulting functional relationship between L_C and L_I is represented by the curve. The shape of the curve is typical for such experiments and does not change significantly for other values of the luminance L_T of the test field.

level but varying the luminance L_I of the inducing field. The values of L_T required for the test field to match the lightness of the comparison field trace in the L_I, L_T graph a curve that is appropriately called a *constant lightness* (or *brightness*) *contour*. Figure 9.11 shows a constant lightness contour exhibiting schematically the essential features of the curves obtained by Heinemann (1955). With the comparison field in a dark surround and the luminance L_I of the inducing field, surrounding the test field, set equal to zero, L_T is set by the observer equal to the given value of L_C: the lightness match is produced by a luminance match. When L_I is given increasing values, the lightness of the test field is depressed and the observer must raise L_T to maintain the lightness match with the comparison field. The required increase in L_T is, at first, quite modest compared to the increase in L_I. But with further increases in L_I, the required increases in L_T begin to equal those made in L_I, and the constant lightness contour tends to become a straight line with a slope near 1.0. This indicates that lightness constancy of the test field is at least approximately ensured if the luminance ratio L_T/L_I is kept constant.

The review literature cited earlier in connection with lightness constancy quotes ample evidence of results similar to those shown in Figure 9.11. However, they also include results (see, particularly, Jameson & Hurvich, 1961a) that stress the *approximate* nature of lightness constancy.

Actual experimental data may deviate to some extent from the curves given in Figures 9.10 and 9.11, mainly because variations in the observing conditions can have measurable effects. Heinemann (1972) has reviewed a number of such effects and given examples of actual data obtained by different investigators.

One of the prominent parameters in display configurations used in induction experiments is the size of the inducing field relative to that of the test field. It is not unexpected that, for example, in the case of an annulus-type inducing field, the induction effect decreases with decreasing width of the annulus. However, under virtually all conditions, the lightness of the test field is depressed by inducing fields whose luminance is about equal to that of the test field or higher (Figure 9.10), but the rate at which the lightness-matching luminance L_C decreases (right tail of curve in Figure 9.10) with increasing inducing luminance L_I is greater for large inducing fields than for small ones.

Another important parameter in display configurations is the distance between test and inducing fields. Again, not unexpectedly, the effect of an inducing field of a given luminance on the lightness of the test field diminishes with increasing separation between inducing and test fields. Also, the rate at which the luminance of the test field must be increased to maintain constant lightness with increased luminance of the inducing field is smaller for larger separations. The major changes due to separation occur for relatively small separations. Further increases in separation do not yield significant further changes.

Still other parameters in display configurations are those of the size of the test field, the relative position of a test field inside a larger inducing field, duration of presentation of the display or part of it to the observer, and uniformity of luminance

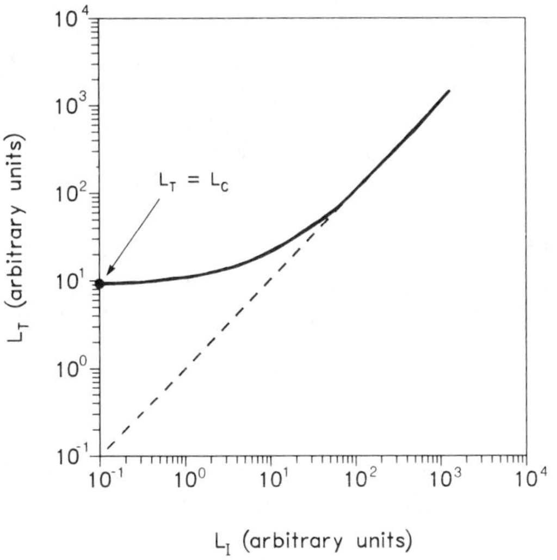

Figure 9.11. Typical result of an achromatic induction experiment leading to a curve representing a constant lightness contour. The experimental arrangement is similar to that illustrated in the inset of Figure 9.10. However, in this case, the observer produces lightness matches between the test field and the comparison field by holding the luminance L_C of the comparison field at some fixed level, but varying the luminance L_I of the inducing field. The luminance L_I is plotted as the abscissa, the luminance L_T as the ordinate; both quantities are given in terms of arbitrary units. The resulting curve gradually becomes a straight line of constant slope (1.0). This means that lightness constancy is obtained when the luminance ratio L_T/L_I is kept constant.

across the test or inducing fields. These parameters have all been studied to some extent (Heinemann, 1972), and a variety of experimental data provides some insight into the importance of such parameters.

A widely accepted explanation of lightness constancy and lightness contrast, as observed in the experiments described in this section, rests on the assumption that lateral inhibition phenomena govern the physiological responses generated by the different stimuli in the retina. Take the classical demonstration involving two chips of identical gray paper placed and illuminated uniformly on adjacent white and black backgrounds, respectively. Although the gray chips provide stimuli of the same luminance, the one on the white background appears darker than the one on the black background. Lightness contrast is observed. Retinal receptors stimulated by light coming from the two physically identical gray chips are equally excited and, if the two backgrounds were also the same, would yield equal levels of neural activity in the form of equal neural-firing rates. However, one of the two backgrounds is white, and receptors receiving light from that background are strongly stimulated resulting in a neural activity that is capable of inhibiting the firing of the neurons connected with those receptors stimulated by the gray chip surrounded by the same background. Thus the gray chip on the white background appears darker than the chip on the black background that does not provide any inhibitory action.

This simple physiological model is extended to explain the case of lightness constancy, which is observed when the level of illuminance on a given display (e.g., a gray paint chip on a white background) is increased or decreased. Raising the level of illuminance, and thus the luminance of every object in the display, does not result in an increased neural-firing rate because the tendency toward an increased level of excitation of a given neural cell is canceled by a virtually equally increased level of lateral inhibition caused on each such cell by its neighbors. The degree to which the increase in excitation cancels the increase in lateral inhibition determines the degree of approximation to which lightness constancy is observed.

Recent studies, notably those of Gilchrist (1977, 1979, 1980) and Gilchrist, Delman, and Jacobsen (1983) have brought out the importance of spatial arrangement and type of edges in a display, parameters that can significantly affect judgments of lightness contrast. In fact, these studies have given rise to alternative explanations of lightness perception and lightness constancy. Central to the argument that the simple physiological model given here is inadequate is the observation that the lightness and, in extension, the color of an object is extracted from the change of light at all edges in the field of view (see also Land & McCann, 1971). An "integration process" of edge information is envisaged to be functioning when the observer views the display. An important additional requirement of the visual system is to be able to distinguish between different types of edges, notably between an edge that is the boundary between two physically different surfaces (e.g., two surfaces of different reflectance characteristics) and an edge created by a difference in illuminance (shadow boundary) cast across a given surface.

Gilchrist (1979) proposes a three-process model that rests on the notion of processing edge information. Specifically, Gilchrist's model consists of the following processes:

1. The *extraction* process gathers information about relative luminances (luminance factors) and color (in the sense of chromaticity) of adjacent parts of the display as it is scanned by the eye, making the display image move across the retina.
2. The *classification* process decides, for each edge in the retinal image, whether it is the image of a physical boundary (reflectance edge) between two different surfaces or an edge generated in the display by a difference in illuminance level (illumination edge).
3. The *integration* process integrates separately the information from reflectance edges and that from illumination edges, generating two representations of the display, one for object color and one for the pattern of illumination.

Gilchrist's three-process model provides intriguing, though qualitative, explanations of the phenomena of achromatic, as well as chromatic, inductions, and further work along these lines might be fruitful. For related studies, the reader is referred to Arend (1973), Barrow and Tenenbaum (1978), Bergström (1977), and Gilchrist, Delman, and Jacobsen (1983).

3.2. Chromatic Induction in Simple Field Configurations

Many experiments on chromatic induction use the simple visual field configuration of a large (e.g., 10°) circular field surrounding a small (e.g., 1°) circular test field. Because of the difference in size between the surrounding and test fields, chromatic induction is usually observable only in the test field, and the inducing effect of the test field on the surrounding field is negligible. The direction and magnitude of the perceived color shift induced by the surrounding field in the color of the test field is measured relative to the colors of both fields seen in isolation.

When the two fields have the same hue and chroma and differ only in lightness, the inducing effect is in the form of an apparent lightness shift in the test field. A surrounding field that is darker than the test field increases the lightness of the

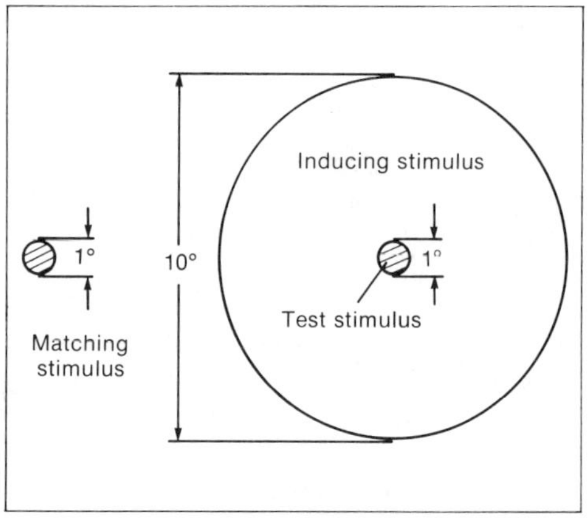

Figure 9.12. Visual field configuration commonly used in chromatic induction experiments. The observer adjusts the color of the matching stimulus (shown in a dark surround) until a complete match in appearance is obtained with the test stimulus of fixed color shown in a surround of another fixed color.

test field. Similarly, a surrounding field that is lighter than the test field decreases the lightness of the test field. In either case, the lightness difference between the two fields is increased due to induction, or, as we say, the lightness contrast is enhanced. The special case of both inducing and test fields being achromatic stimuli, that is, having no hue, has already been treated separately in Section 3.1.

When there ia a color difference between the surrounding and test fields, composed of differences in lightness, hue, and chroma, the direction and magnitude of chromatic induction is more difficult to predict, but in simple field configurations, such as the one at hand, the general rule is for the color of the test field to shift farther away from the inducing color of the surrounding field. For example, a yellow test field shifts toward red when seen in a green surrounding field and shifts toward a higher chroma (more saturated) yellow when seen surrounded by blue. Similarly, a blue test field surrounded by red shifts toward green, whereas the same blue field surrounded by yellow shifts toward a higher chroma blue. In these cases, contrast enhancement is observed. For examples of good demonstration material see Chevreul (1967) and Hurvich (1981).

To quantify the color shifts caused by chromatic induction, an asymmetric color-matching technique is often used. The visual field presented to the observer consists of a test stimulus (e.g., circular of 1°) surrounded by the inducing stimulus (e.g., circular of 10°) and of a spatially separate matching stimulus (e.g., circular of 1°). Figure 9.12 illustrates the configuration. The observer adjusts the matching stimulus to make it identical in color appearance to the test stimulus for a variety of given test and inducing stimuli (Hasegawa, 1977; Kinney, 1962, 1965; Valberg, 1974).

Another experimental procedure does not employ the matching stimulus. Instead, the observer adjusts the test stimulus to some unique hue, typically yellow, in the presence of a variety of inducing stimuli (Akita, Graham, & Hsia, 1964; Eichengreen, 1976; Oyama & Hsia, 1966; Wooten, 1970).

In a more recent study by Ware and Cowan (1982), the visual field configuration shown in Figure 9.13 was used, involving a striped pattern of inducing and test stimuli. Fifteen test stimuli of different chromaticity and approximately equal liminance were observed with each of five different inducing stimuli (red, yellow, green, blue, and white). In preliminary observations it became evident that the axial chromatic aberration of the eye viewing the pattern had a considerable effect, particularly with blue inducing stimuli, on the color appearance of the stripes, but this could be reduced, if not eliminated, by an appropriate achromatizing lens (Bedford & Wyszecki, 1957). With a correction for chromatic aberration, the color shifts obtained by Ware and Cowan generally follow a chromaticity-shift pattern that is in good agreement with the findings of other investigators, and thus they agree with the general rule pronounced in this section. The study of Ware and Cowan provides, for two observers, data sets that are more comprehensive with regard to the number of different test and inducing stimuli than any of the previous chromatic-induction studies. Figure 9.14 illustrates some of the main results obtained by Ware and Cowan.

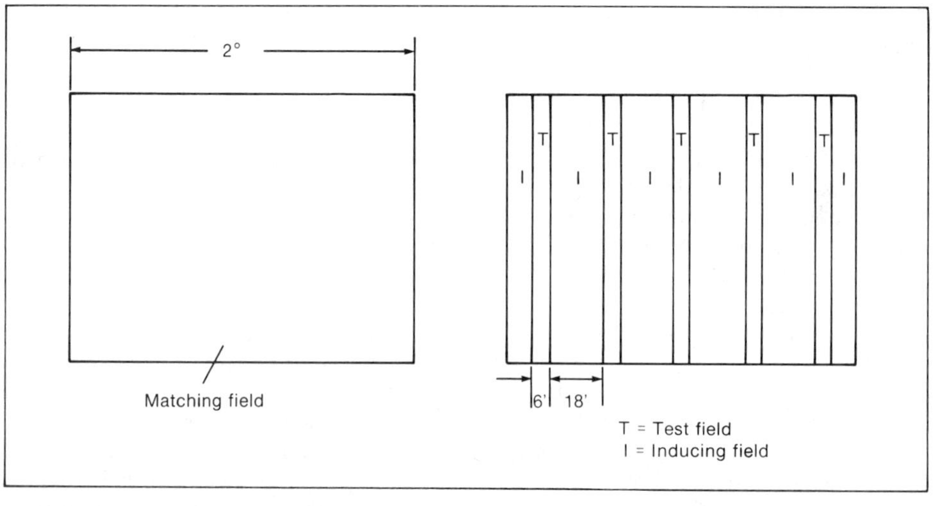

Figure 9.13. Visual field configuration used by Ware and Cowan (1982) in their chromatic induction experiment. Test and inducing fields form a striped pattern. For given test and inducing colors, the observer matches the test color in the neighboring matching field by producing in that field an appropriate mixture of three primary colors provided by a colorimeter not shown in this figure.

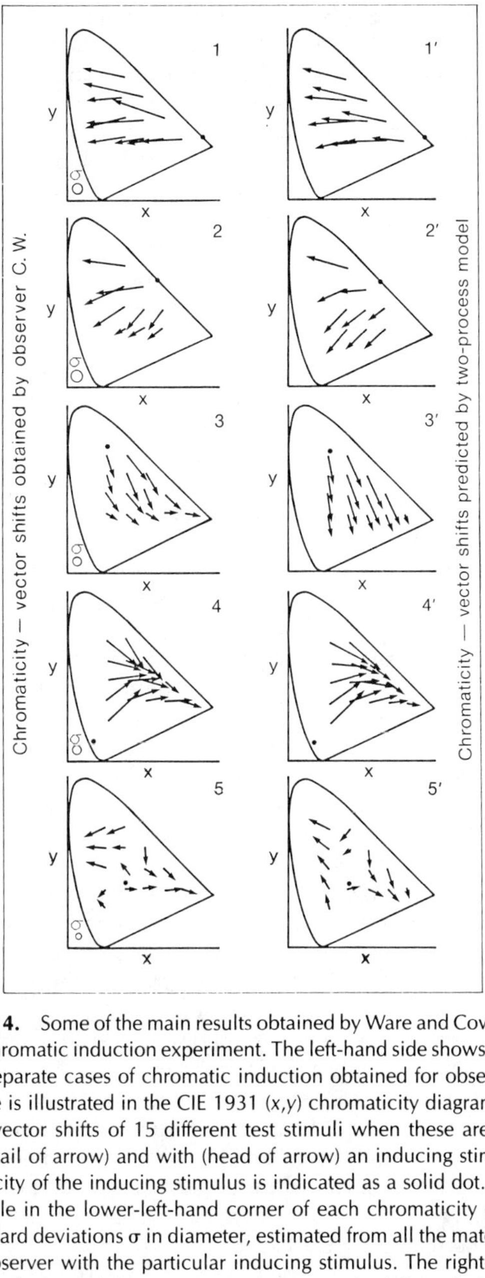

Figure 9.14. Some of the main results obtained by Ware and Cowan (1982) in their chromatic induction experiment. The left-hand side shows the results for five separate cases of chromatic induction obtained for observer C. W. Each case is illustrated in the CIE 1931 (x,y) chromaticity diagram by chromaticity-vector shifts of 15 different test stimuli when these are observed without (tail of arrow) and with (head of arrow) an inducing stimulus. The chromaticity of the inducing stimulus is indicated as a solid dot. The small open circle in the lower-left-hand corner of each chromaticity diagram is two standard deviations σ in diameter, estimated from all the matches made by the observer with the particular inducing stimulus. The right-hand side shows predictions of the experimental data on the left made by a color-vision model that involves both receptor channels and opponent-color channels. A fairly good agreement is obtained between prediction and observation, particularly noteworthy in the case of the blue inducing stimulus which yields a strongly curved chromaticity-vector pattern. (From C. Ware & W. B. Cowan, Changes in perceived color due to chromatic interactions, *Vision Research, 22*. Copyright 1982 by Pergamon Press, Ltd. Reprinted with permission.)

Ware and Cowan (1982) supplement their extensive experimental study with an attempt to interpret their data using a number of different color-vision models proposed in the literature. The analysis shows that the chromatic-induction data cannot be accounted for by a receptor model or by an opponent-channel model, if these are taken separately. This is attributed specifically to the experimental data taken with the blue inducing stimulus that yielded a strongly curved chromaticity-vector pattern, instead of a radial vector pattern that these models predict. Color-vision models that combine changes at both the receptor and the opponent-channel levels yield more satisfactory predictions, but such models may need to be rather complex in their mathematical structure (see Section 4.4).

3.3. Chromatic Induction in Complex Field Configurations

3.3.1. Color Assimilation. In more complex field configurations, chromatic induction does not necessarily lead to contrast enhancement. Instead, the opposite effect may be observed, that is, a reduction in contrast, often referred to as *color spreading*, or *color assimilation*. This effect is best demonstrated in repetitive patterns, such as stripes of one color superimposed on a background of another color. If the stripes are yellow and the background red, the red clearly shifts toward yellow, reducing the color contrast between stripes and background. Black stripes make the background appear darker, and white stripes make it lighter. The color-spreading effect is not the same as an additive mixture of color stimuli, because the alternating stripe–background pattern remains distinct when color spreading occurs. Examples of good demonstrations have been published by Evans (1948), Burnham, Hanes, and Bartleson (1963), and Hurvich (1981). A noteworthy study providing a quantitative insight into the assimilation phenomenon is that of Helson (1963), employing achromatic stripe patterns.

Helson's (1963) display configuration consisted of a gray card (17.5 × 27.5 cm), one half ruled with white lines and the other half ruled with black lines. The observers, placed 3 m from the card, judged the lightness of the intervening gray areas of the two halves by a combination of methods of paired comparisons and limits. The judgments were reported in terms of a category scale ranging from "very, very much lighter" through "equal," to "very, very much darker," with numerals from 1 to 9 assigned them for purposes of computation with "5" standing for "equal," numerals above "5" for contrast, and those below "5" for assimilation. The experimental parameters were line width w, line separation s, and background (gray card) reflectance p. The results show that assimilation depends on both the absolute and relative values of w, s, as well as on p. Moreover there is a continuum from assimilation to regular contrast with an interval in which neither assimilation nor contrast occurs. With a background reflectance of $p \approx 36\%$, assimilation occurs with line widths of s up to 10 mm after which contrast is observed. With background reflectances of $p = 80\%$ and $p = 14\%$, assimilation occurs when w and s are each as wide as 29 mm.

3.3.2. Phantom Colors. In certain displays, an area may appear to be chromatic but actually is not. Such perceptions are referred to as *phantom colors* or *illusory colors*. Kanizsa's (1955) triangle figures with appropriate-colored additions (Varin, 1971; Ware 1980) provide good demonstrations of the effect usually attributed to color assimilation (see Section 3.3.1). Figure 9.15 illustrates the idea. If the shaded portions of the line configuration were colored, the illusory triangle, or phantom image, would be perceived with a color of the same hue but lighter and of less chroma. For example, if the shaded portions of the line configuration were red, the phantom image would be pink.

3.3.3. Land's Experiments. The experiments of Land (1959a, 1959b, 1962, 1964) involve a complex stimulus pattern containing a wide range of different chromatic and achromatic stimuli with sharp or graded boundaries and often representing actual meaningful scenes. The observer's eyes are allowed to

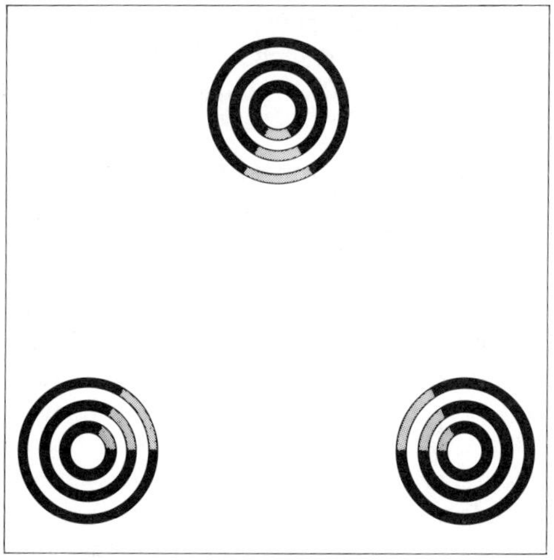

Figure 9.15. An example of a display configuration that generates an illusory triangle. If the shaded sectors of the rings were red, the whole illusory triangle would appear pinkish.

range over the pattern, and the observer's color perceptions are recorded in terms of the color nomenclature of everyday life.

The original striking demonstrations (Land, 1959b) were pictures, mainly elaborate still lifes, produced by projecting in exact register two black and white positives obtained originally by using, in turn, red and green filters over the camera lens. The two projectors emit lights of different color (e.g., white and red), and Land established, among other things, that pictures of complex scenes could be produced in this way, showing a remarkable variety and richness of color and comparable in some cases with three-color projections. This could be done even if monochromatic projector sources were used, provided their wavelengths were not too close; in the yellow region the separation need be no more than about 20 nm. Land rejects explanations of the colors seen in terms of the accepted concepts of trichromatic theory and chromatic induction or adaptation and elaborates a set of principles of color perception in complex scenes coordinating his observations. These principles are difficult to summarize, and reference must be made to Land's (1959a, 1959b, 1962) own explanations. In subsequent work, Land (1964, 1974) has introduced the term *retinex* to characterize a retinal-cerebral system believed to underlie the phenomena that he has described. Further work along the lines of Land's ideas has been produced by Land and McCann (1971), McCann, McKee, and Taylor (1976), McKee, McCann, and Benton (1977), and others. The centers of attention in this work have been complex displays, most of them in the form of a "Mondrian" consisting of rectangular patches attached to a large board that can be illuminated in various ways. Basic to the retinex theory is the propositon that in arriving at the perception of the color of a surface, the human visual system separates the effects of surface reflectance from the effects of the illuminant. The spectral reflectance characteristics of a surface are the predominant physical parameters affecting color perception and not variations in illuminance (mainly shadows) caused by the illuminant. Changes in the illumination of the display are, in general, gradual and are perceived as smooth illumination gradients. Changes in reflectance occur in passing from one surface to another, and these changes are usually physically and perceptually sharp. So-called retinex computations (Land & McCann, 1971; but also see Horn, 1974) simulate the visual process assumed to be responsible for separating reflectance changes from illumination changes. Three independent component processes are postulated, operating in three separate channels, the red, green, and blue channels. The reflectance and illumination changes occurring in the long-wavelength region of the spectrum are analyzed in the red channel, those in the middle-wavelength region in the green channel, and those in the short-wavelength region in the blue channel. Essentially, the display is scanned separately by each of the three channels, each tracing an "intensity record" along each path, thus revealing slow intensity changes interspersed with sudden and often large intensity changes. By applying a gradient threshold, the slow changes, which are attributed to illumination changes, can be removed from further consideration, and the sudden changes, attributed to reflectance changes, are retained. The results obtained for each of the three channels are combined to give a percept of color that rests in the first instance on the surface reflectance characteristics and, to some extent, on the spectral characteristics of the illuminant but ignores changes in illuminance level and gradient in agreement with the observed visual phenomenon of (approximate) constancy of the appearance of object colors. In combining the signals of the three channels, a different weight is assigned to each to allow for an appropriate normalization of the resultant color percept. Land and McCann suggest that this is accomplished by defining the brightest spot in the display as being "white."

Some of Land's phenomena are covered in earlier work (Evans, 1943; Judd, 1940). Judd (1960) gave more traditional explanations of many of Land's observations, using his own fairly elaborate formulas for perceived color, developed in 1940. The main element in these explanations is contained in a simple discussion by Woolfson (1959), who used approximate methods to determine, in effect, the possible range (three dimensional) of the tristimulus vectors corresponding to small areas in the Land projection of a complex picture produced by a particular pair of monochromatic projector sources.

Woolfson's (1959) basic assumption corresponds very nearly to a conception going back to Helmholtz; that is, in judging the color of objects in a real scene, we make an allowance for the color of the illuminant. An interpretation in terms of meaning would postulate that the observer knows certain objects in the picture ought to appear white under normal conditions of illumination, and the observer's eye and brain effect an inevitable and unconscious color transformation that makes this true or nearly true. Against Woolfson's basic assumption is that when the picture consists of a meaningless assembly of patches in a sufficiently random arrangement, the range of colors perceived is at least comparable with that in a meaningful picture, the parts of which provide a set of stimulus vectors (untransformed) similar in range to that of the patches. Perhaps involuntary color transformation is provided not by the internal content of the picture but by side clues. For example, light scattered from the projector beams may be visible and thus reveal the illuminant color that the observer then allows for.

The other extreme of interpretation makes no appeal to "meaning" and attributes the wide range of colors perceived in a random arrangement of patches or in a display generated by the inevitable juxtaposition of areas with markedly different tristimulus vectors. It is certainly true, as shown by Land and others, that in an ordered arrangement of patches in which the tristimulus vectors (untransformed) vary in a simple progressive way by small steps on any line across the picture, and especially in a picture where there is a progressive continuous variation on any line, the range of perceived colors is greatly curtailed.

Whereas the instantaneous chromatic induction would be the principal element in the explanation of the wide differences of perceived color, the more slowly developing component of chromatic adaptation would contribute to determining the average perceived color of the picture. It is, however, difficult to maintain an extreme interpretation that "meaning" is not a factor. In some experiments (see, for example, Judd 1940), observers report that they can change the color they perceive by consciously altering their conception of what it is they are viewing.

3.4. Contour Effects

3.4.1. Sharpness of Contour. The contour, or border, of a given colored area in a display usually affects the color appearance of that area. A colored area with a sharp contour and given lightness, hue, and chroma, displayed on a white background, appears to become lighter and of lower chroma when the sharpness of its border is reduced (for a good demonstration, see Evans, 1971). Figure 9.16 illustrates the idea.

3.4.2. Distinctness of Border. In their pioneering work on the perception of borders in colored displays, Boynton and his coworkers (for a review, see Boynton, 1979) used three methods for estimating the distinctness of the border between juxtaposed areas. In the first method, two juxtaposed areas of uniform chromaticity are presented slightly above, but clearly separated from, two other juxtaposed chromatic areas. The observer adjusts the radiance of one of the two upper areas until perceiving a border that is as distinct as the border seen between the two areas below. In the second method, only one pair of juxtaposed areas is used. The observer first establishes the *minimally distinct border* between the two areas by making an appropriate adjustment of the radiance of one area. The observer then judges the distinctness of the border in terms of an 8-point rating scale ("0" meaning no border at all, "8" meaning a very strong border). In the third method, the observer steadily fixates the border between two juxtaposed areas for a certain period of time, for example, 5 min, and the tendency of the border to fade is then measured in terms of the percentage of time that a border is not seen.

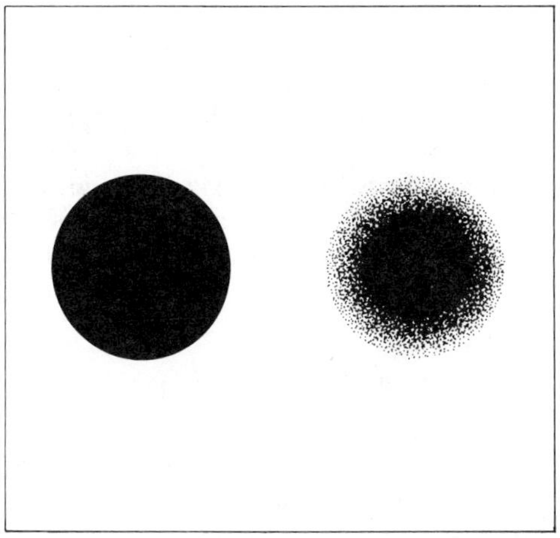

Figure 9.16. Sharpness-of-contour effect. The two circular areas are printed with the same ink. Physically they differ only in the sharpness with which their borders are delineated. When the sharpness of the border is reduced, as is the case on the right, a colored area would retain its hue but increase in lightness and decrease in chroma, as compared to the sharply bordered area on the left.

All three methods yield comparable results of border distinctness and provide a measure of the equivalent amount of achromatic contrast that produces the same "strength of border" as that produced by a purely chromatic difference. One or the other method has been used to study a number of visual response characteristics (Boynton, 1973; Boynton & Kaiser, 1968, 1978; Kaiser, Herzberg, & Boynton, 1971; Tansley & Boynton, 1976, 1978; Valberg & Tansley, 1977).

Luminous efficiency functions (see Chapter 5 by Hood and Finkelstein and Chapter 8 by Pokorny and Smith) have been determined with the minimally distinct border criterion and found to be in close agreement with the $V(\lambda)$ curve obtained by the conventional minimum-flicker technique (Wagner & Boynton, 1972).

When the equivalent achromatic contrast was determined as a function of wavelength for monochromatic stimuli paired with a white stimulus, the resultant curve closely resembled that of the colorimetric purity (saturation) discrimination curve (Boynton, 1973; Kaiser, Herzberg, & Boynton, 1971).

3.4.3. Mach Bands. Mach bands (Mach, 1865) are other border effects. They are light or dark narrow bands perceived near the border of two juxtaposed areas, one area being darker than the other. Figure 9.17 illustrates schematically a typical case showing the spatial luminance distribution across the border and the corresponding spatial distribution of lightness perceived by the observer.

Mach bands have been studied extensively, and the interested reader may find the reviews by Ratliff (1965) and Fiorentini (1972) useful starting points for more detailed information. The phenomenon in all its complexities is not fully understood, but it is generally agreed that lateral interactions in the neural network of the visual system account for it. It is assumed that the function that characterizes the response of each element of the neural network has an excitatory component, which depends on the luminance of the stimulus eliciting a response in that element, and an inhibitory component, which depends on the luminance of the stimulus (or stimuli) eliciting responses in the elements surrounding the first element. The magnitude of the inhibitory effect of each surrounding element on the first element depends on the distance between the two elements.

The experimental evidence of particular interest to color vision is that Mach bands are not always found near chromatic borders when the two juxtaposed fields have no luminance variation but differ only in chromaticity, including possibly a graded transition from the chromaticity of one field to the chromaticity of the other (Pease, 1978). An extensive study by Ware and Cowan (Note 1) clearly demonstrates the existence of chromatic Mach bands in a variety of purely chromatic gradients, but different observers may vary greatly in their chromatic responses to such visual stimulus configurations.

3.5. Models of Achromatic and Chromatic Induction

3.5.1. A Model of Lightness Contrast. A quantitative treatment of lightness contrast as an achromatic induction phenomenon has been given by Jameson and Hurvich (1964). The model rests on the following propositions:

1. In the focal area f containing the test stimulus S_f, the net visual response R_f is proportional to S_f raised to a power n, plus an induced response I_f in f.

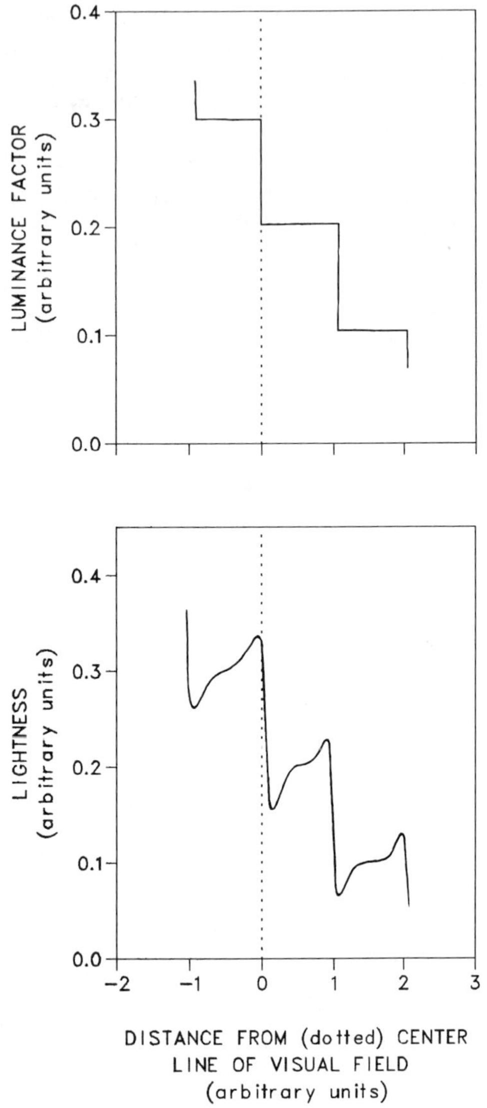

Figure 9.17. Luminance factor and lightness profiles of a visual field consisting of a series of adjacent gray stripes. The stripe on the left has a high-luminance factor (light gray), the one on the right a low-luminance factor (dark gray); stripes in between have intermediate values. At the borders of the stripes abrupt changes in luminance factor occur (upper graph). Right next to these borders, light and dark Mach bands are perceived with a lightness profile sketched in the lower graph. When the gray stripe pattern is replaced by a chromatic pattern whose stripes change, for example, from red to green in a staircase fashion that keeps the luminance factor of the stripes constant and changes only their chromaticity, the Mach bands near the borders are seen, by many observers, as chromatic bands with perceived increased and decreased red-green ratios, respectively.

2. In the surrounding area s containing the surround stimulus S_s, the net visual response R_s proportional to S_s raised to a power n, plus an induced response I_s in s.

These propositions are expressed mathematically as follows:

$$R_f = cS_f^n + I_f \quad \text{and} \quad R_s = cS_s^n + I_s \,. \tag{3}$$

The induced responses I_f and I_s are assumed to be of opposite sign but otherwise proportional to the visual responses R_s and R_f elicited by the stimuli in areas s and f, respectively, thus

$$I_f = -kR_s \quad \text{and} \quad I_s = -kR_f \,. \tag{4}$$

Equations (3) and (4) combine to the two expressions

$$R_f = cS_f^n - kR_s \text{ and } R_s = cS_s^n - kR_f \,, \tag{5}$$

or to the single expression

$$R_f = \frac{c(S_f^n - kS_s^n)}{1 - k^2} \,. \tag{6}$$

The constant c is a scaling factor of appropriate magnitude and dimension to account for the particular unit used to specify the stimulus. The factor k relates to the strength of the induction process and depends on the particular spatial configuration used in the experiment.

In a lightness-matching experiment, as described in Section 3.1, a comparison field f', possibly with its own surround s', is placed side by side with the test field f and its surround s. For the (f', s') field configuration, Eq. (6) becomes

$$R_{f'} = \frac{c(S_{f'}^n - kS_{s'}^n)}{1-k^2} \,. \tag{7}$$

A lightness match is obtained if R_f equals $R_{f'}$; thus

$$s_f^n - kS_s^n = S_{f'}^n - kS_{s'}^n \,. \tag{8}$$

The induction factor k may be determined for a particular lightness match for which the four stimulus values ($S_f = S_{of}$, $S_s = S_{os}$, $S_{f'} = S_{of'}$, $S_{s'} = S_{os'}$) are obtained. It follows that

$$k = \frac{S_{of}^n - S_{of'}^n}{S_{os}^n - S_{os'}^n} \,. \tag{9}$$

By means of Eqs. (8) and (9), it is then possible to predict experimental lightness matches under the condition that any three of the four stimulus values (S_f, S_s, $S_{f'}$, $S_{s'}$) are given, for example, in terms of luminance. A typical case would be to find S_f (stimulus required in test field f) when S_s (surrounds), $S_{f'}$ (comparison stimulus in f'), and $S_{s'}$ (surround s') are fixed.

Jameson and Hurvich (1964) apply their model to the classical data of Hess and Pretori (1894), Diamond (1953, 1955), and Leibowitz, Mote, and Thurlow (1953) with remarkable success. Whether the model of Jameson and Hurvich can be made to apply to field configurations that include shadow patterns, such as those studied by Gilchrist (1979) (see Section 3.1) needs further exploration.

In studies of lightness constancy and lightness contrast, the *Brunswik ratio* has been used as an index of constancy or an index measuring the degree of contrast. The Brunswik ratio b, named after its originator (Brunswik, 1929), is defined by

$$b = \frac{\beta_C - \beta_T'}{\beta_T - \beta_T'} \,, \tag{10}$$

whose quantities are conveniently explained by reference to a typical experiment. A gray paint sample of reflectance β_T is displayed in area A under an illuminant providing an illuminance E. A wheel on which gray paint samples of different reflectances are mounted is displayed in an adjoining area A' under an illuminant providing an illuminance $E'(\neq E)$. By turning the wheel, the observer can view one paint sample at a time. The observer's task is to select a sample on the wheel that matches in lightness the given sample in area A. The reflectance of the sample selected by the observer is denoted by β_c. The wheel also contains a sample of reflectance β_T' making the luminance L' of that sample equal to the luminance L of the given sample of reflectant β_T in area A, that is, $\beta_T \cdot E = \beta_T' \cdot E'$. Perfect lightness constancy ($b = 1.0$) is observed if the observer selects a sample on the wheel whose reflectance β_c equals the reflectance β_T of the given sample in area A. Zero lightness constancy is observed if the observer selects the sample on the wheel whose reflectance is β_T'

A variant of the Brunswik ratio is the *Thouless ratio t*, (Thouless, 1931) in which the reflectances β of Eq. (10) are replaced by the logarithm of the reflectances of test and comparison fields; thus

$$t = \frac{\log \beta_c - \log \beta'}{\log \beta_T - \log \beta_T'} \, . \tag{11}$$

Other variants of the Brunswik ratio involve the luminances of the test and comparison fields instead of their reflectances.

In studies of *color constancy*, the Brunswik ratio has been extended to a set of three ratios, one based on hue differences, one on chroma differences, and one on lightness differences. Hue, chroma, and lightness are specified in terms of Munsell hue, Munsell chroma, and Munsell value, respectively, and in Eq. (10) take the place of reflectance (Newhall, Burnham, & Evans, 1958, 1959).

3.5.2. Models of Chromatic Induction. Most color-vision models now considered in the literature may be classified as two-process (or two-stage) models, illustrated schematically in Figure 9.18. In the initial process (or first stage), the color stimulus is absorbed in the photopigments of the three types of cone, generating three cone-mechanism responses that are characteristic of the spectral radiant power distribution of the color stimulus. In the second process (or second stage), the responses of the cone mechanisms are combined linearly to generate in three separate channels three neural signals whose characteristics correlate with the color perceived to belong to the stimulus. The three neural channels consist of one "luminance channel" (or "white/black neural system") and two "opponent-color channels." One opponent-color channel is referred to as the "red/green neural system," the other as the "yellow/blue neural system."

In using the mathematical notation and closely following the recent exposition of Ware and Cowan (1982) (see Section 3.2), we may write

$$C_j = \sum_i \Gamma_{ji} V_i \, , \tag{12}$$

where

V_i (i = 1,2,3) = response of ith cone mechanism,

C_j (j = 1,2,3) = signal in jth neural channel,

Γ_{ji} = linear coefficients derived from other experiments.

The coefficients are constrained to some extent to allow the resulting neural channels to be interpreted in terms of a luminance channel and two opponent-color channels. For examples of sets of such coefficients, see Hurvich (1981), Boynton (1979),

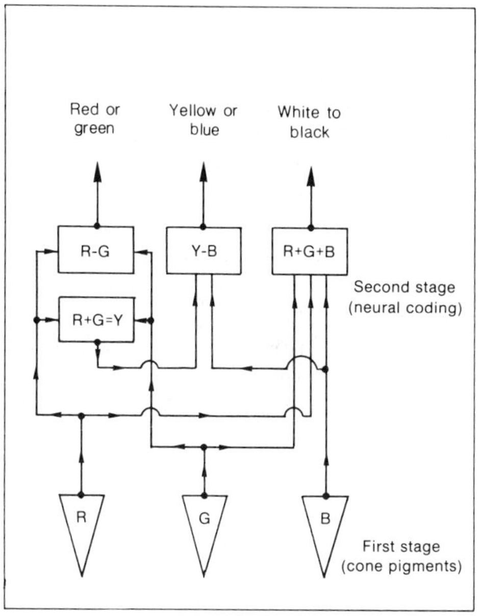

Figure 9.18. Schematic diagram of a two-stage color-vision model commonly used in attempts to explain color-vision phenomena. The first stage is also called the photoreceptor stage, containing three types of cone receptors (R,G,B). In the second stage, the responses generated in the first stage are combined linearly to generate three separate channels: a luminance channel (R+G+B) and two opponent-color channels (R–G and Y–B). The signals produced in the luminance channel elicit "white to black" responses, the two opponent-color channels elicit "red or green" responses and "blue or yellow" responses, respectively.

and Guth, Massof, and Benzschawel (1980). In the present analysis, which is intended to test classes of two-process models and their general properties in relation to the experimental evidence of chromatic induction, any of the published sets of Γ_{ji} coefficients may serve equally well and Ware and Cowan (1982) employed those given by Guth and coworkers (1980).

In most present models, chromatic induction is assumed to be an additive or a multiplicative process. Thus we may write

$$V_i = v_i(A) V_i + \nu_i(A) \, , \tag{13}$$

$$C_j = c_j(A) C_j + \gamma_i(A) \, , \tag{14}$$

where the induction coefficients $v_i(A)$, $\nu_i(A)$, $c_j(A)$, $\gamma_i(A)$ depend on the spectral power distribution of the inducing color stimulus A. An immediate boundary condition can be assumed for the induction coefficients when no inducing stimulus is used, that is, when $A = 0$:

$$\nu_i(A = 0) = \gamma_j(A = 0) = 0 \, ,$$

$$v_i(A = 0) = c_j(A = 0) = 1 \, . \tag{15}$$

By inserting Eqs. (13) and (14) into Eq. (12), we obtain the following channel signals when the inducing color stimulus A is used:

$$C_j(A) = c_j(A) \sum_i \Gamma_{ji} \, [v_i(A) V_i + \nu_i(A)] + \gamma_i(A) \, . \tag{16}$$

This is the most general form of a model of chromatic induction in which simple additive and multiplicative induction processes are assumed. Several models in the literature are special cases of the above general model. This includes models of chromatic adaptation, which, in general, is assumed to be governed by visual processes similar to those operating for chromatic induction. Section 4 deals with chromatic adaptation, and specific models used for predicting chromatic adaptation effects are given in that section.

As color stimuli used in an experiment on chromatic induction are often specified in terms of tristimulus values, such as CIE X, Y, Z tristimulus values, it is convenient to express Eq. (16) in terms of tristimulus values. Basic to all color-vision models is the experimentally well-founded assumption that the tristimulus values of a given color stimulus, obtained by color matching of the color stimulus by an appropriate additive mixture of three given primary stimuli, are linearly related to the three responses of the cone mechanisms. Thus the following relation exists:

$$V_i = \sum_k B_{ik} X_k \tag{17}$$

where V_i ($i = 1,2,3$) are the cone responses, X_k ($X_1 \equiv X$, $X_2 \equiv Y$, $X_3 \equiv Z$) are the tristimulus values, and B_{ik} is an appropriate 3×3 transformation matrix.

In a chromatic induction experiment, X_k may denote the tristimulus values of the test stimulus and X'_k may denote the corresponding tristimulus values of the matching stimulus. Then if the perceptual identity between test and matching stimuli is taken to mean equal signals from the three neural channels, we have, by inserting Eq. (17) into Eqs. (12) and (16), the following:

$$\sum_i \Gamma_{ji}\left[\sum_k B_{ik} X'_k\right] = \gamma_j(A) + c_j(A)\sum_i \Gamma_{ji}\left[v_i(A)\sum_k B_{ik} X_k + \nu_i(A)\right]. \tag{18}$$

This equation can be written in a form that expresses explicitly the tristimulus values of the matching stimulus in terms of the tristimulus values of the test stimulus. We obtain

$$X'_n = \sum_m [B^{-1}]_{nm} \sum_j [\Gamma^{-1}]_{mj} \{c_j(A) \sum_i \Gamma_{ji}[v_i(A)\sum_k B_{ik} X_k + \nu_i(A)] + \gamma_j(A)\} \tag{19}$$

where $[B^{-1}]_{nm}$ and $[\Gamma^{-1}]_{mj}$ are matrices inverse to B_{ik} and Γ_{ji}, respectively. For a given inducing color stimulus A, the above equation has $4 \times 3 = 12$ coefficients, whose complete determination requires a large number of experimental data, not as yet available. However, Ware and Cowan (1982) have analyzed six special cases that are described.

For the matrices Γ_{ji} and B_{ik}, Ware and Cowan adopted the values used by Guth and coworkers (1980). In particular Γ_{ji} relates cone responses V_i, governed by the photopigment-absorption curves proposed by Smith and Pokorny (1972, 1975), to channel signals C_j in accordance with Eq. (12). The matrix B_{ik} of Eq. (17) relates the cone responses to the Judd-modified tristimulus values, which deviate somewhat from the CIE 1931 tristimulus values but are considered preferable in analyzing data of real observers (Vos, 1978; Wyszecki & Stiles, 1982).

3.5.2.1. ***Special Case 1: Additive Receptor Model.*** In this rather simple case, it is assumed that the effect of chromatic induction is equivalent to adding to (or subtracting from) the cone responses, elicited by the test stimulus, quantities depending only on cone responses generated by the inducing stimulus. Thus with

$$\gamma_j(A) = 0 \quad \text{and} \quad v_i(A) = c_j(A) = 1 ,$$

Eq. (19), which defines the general case for additive and multiplicative models of induction processes, reduces to the strictly additive model given by

$$X'_n = X_n + \sum_i [B^{-1}]_{ni} \nu_i(A) . \tag{20}$$

For a given inducing stimulus A, the difference $(X'_n - X_n)$ of tristimulus values of any pair of matching and test stimuli is a constant, which, in tristimulus space, yields a constant vector. In chromaticity space, defined by the chromaticity coordinates

$$x = \frac{X_1}{(X_1 + X_2 + X_3)} \quad \text{and} \quad y = \frac{X_2}{(X_1 + X_2 + X_3)} ,$$

the constant vectors of the tristimulus space convert to radial vectors emanating from a single chromaticity point. The experimental data on chromatic induction plotted in the chromaticity diagram reject the additive receptor model given by Eq. (20). This is clearly evident from Figure 9.14, which shows that in each case studied by Ware and Cowan, the chromaticity vectors do not emanate from a single chromaticity point.

3.5.2.2. ***Special Case 2: Multiplicative Receptor Model.*** In this case, it is assumed that the effect of chromatic induction is equivalent to multiplying the cone responses, elicited by the test stimulus, by quantities depending only on cone responses generated by the inducing stimulus. Thus with

$$\nu_i(A) = \gamma_j(A) = 0 \quad \text{and} \quad c_j(A) = 1 ,$$

it follows from Eq. (18) that the multiplicative model is defined by

$$\sum_k B_{ik} X'_k = v_i(A) \sum B_{ik} X_k$$

or

$$V'_i = v_i(A) V_i . \tag{21}$$

This equation describes what is usually referred to as the *von Kries coefficient law* of chromatic adaptation (see also Section 4). For a given inducing stimulus A, the model predicts that for any pair of matching and test stimuli the corresponding cone responses are in a constant ratio, that is,

$$\frac{V'_i}{V_i} = \text{constant} = v_i(A) .$$

When they apply this model to their own experimental data, Ware and Cowan (1982) find this ratio not to be constant but varying by a factor of 3. Thus the multiplicative receptor model is rejected.

3.5.2.3. ***Special Case 3: Additive Linear Opponent Model.*** Jameson and Hurvich (1961b) proposed an opponent model in which the effect of chromatic induction is assumed to be equivalent to adding to (or subtracting from) the signals of the neural channels, elicited by the test stimulus, quantities depending only on the inducing stimulus. This constrains the conditions defined by Eqs. (13) and (14) to

$$\nu_i(A) = 0 \text{ and } \upsilon_i(A) = c_j(A) = 1 ,$$

and Eq. (19) reduces to

$$X'_n = X_n + \sum_i [B^{-1}]_{ni} \sum_j [\Gamma^{-1}]_{ij} \gamma_j(A) . \qquad (22)$$

This expression makes the same predictions as Eq. (20) which defined the additive receptor model (Section 3.5.2.1). In fact, any model with an arbitrary number of additive chromatic induction processes and linear neural channel combinations yields predictions of a radial vector pattern of chromaticity shifts in the chromaticity diagram. This class of model includes the two-process model characterized by the conditions

$$\upsilon_j(A) = c_j(A) = 1 .$$

A radial vector pattern in the chromaticity diagram has not been found in chromatic induction experiments, and thus the above models must be rejected.

3.5.2.4. ***Special Case 4: Multiplicative Linear Opponent Model.*** In this model, it is assumed that the effect of chromatic induction is equivalent to multiplying the signals of the neural channels, elicited by the test stimulus, by quantities depending only on the inducing stimulus. The constraints to Eqs. (13) and (14) are given by

$$\nu_i(A) = \gamma_j(A) = 0 \text{ and } \upsilon_i(A) = 1 .$$

The actual application of this class of model to the experimental data of Ware and Cowan (1982) presented difficulties. Instead, Ware and Cowan studied a specific example of such a model as proposed by Guth and coworkers (1980). The multiplicative coefficients of the Guth and coworkers' model were manipulated in an attempt to fit the experimental data of Ware and Cowan. No satisfactory fit was found. Indeed, the only effects Ware and Cowan were able to produce were those of expansion and contraction about the axes defined in the chromaticity diagram by the neural opponent channels. These changes were always in opposite directions on either side of the achromatic point, and it was therefore impossible to produce the overall chromaticity shifts across the diagram, as obtained by experiment and illustrated earlier in Figure 9.14.

3.5.2.5. ***Special Case 5: Multiplicative Receptor, Additive Linear Opponent Model.*** This and the last model (given in Section 3.5.2.6) are generalizations of the theoretical framework established to a large extent by Jameson and Hurvich (Hurvich, 1981) in their search for adequate prediction models of chromatic induction and chromatic adaptation.

Shevell (1980) proposed a two-process model for chromatic induction in which first the cone responses, elicited by the test stimulus, are multiplied by quantities depending only on the inducing stimulus and second to the signals of the neural channels are added quantities depending again only on the inducing stimulus. Such two-process models fulfill the conditions

$$\nu_i(A) = 0 \text{ and } c_j(A) = 1 .$$

The resulting equation of this model has six parameters that can be used to fit the chromaticity-shift pattern given by the experimental data. Fair agreement is obtained between the Shevell-type model (see also J. Walraven, 1980) and the actual observations made by observer C. W. shown in Figure 9.14.

3.5.2.6. ***Special Case 6: Multiplicative Receptor, Multiplicative Linear Opponent Model.*** This case is exemplified by the model of Guth and coworkers (1980), which differs from special case 5 in that, at the neural channels, the channel signals are multiplied, instead of added, by quantities depending only on the inducing stimulus. Thus

$$\nu_i(A) = \gamma_j(A) = 0 .$$

Computer manipulation of the coefficients of this two-process model, designed to fit the experimental data of observer C. W., resulted in fairly good agreement between observation and calculation, as shown in Figure 9.14. Note, in particular, the good agreement of the experimental case 4 involving the blue inducing stimulus that yields a strongly curved chromaticity-vector pattern, a pattern that single-process chromatic induction models fail to predict.

4. CHROMATIC ADAPTATION

The term *chromatic adaptation* is applied to modifications of the visual response, particularly the response to chromatic test stimuli, brought about by chromatic conditioning (adapting) stimuli that are surrounding or preexposed. Chromatic adaptation develops slowly in the visual system and in that sense differs from chromatic induction, which is considered a virtually instantaneous process. However, both chromatic adaptation and chromatic induction are usually modeled under the assumption that similar neural activities in the visual system serve both processes; thus the discussion on models for chromatic induction, in Section 3.5.2, is equally applicable to experimental data on chromatic adaptation.

The response characteristics of the visual system under different states of chromatic adaptation may be studied by determining discrimination or increment thresholds, but quantitative investigations have been concerned predominantly with measurements of luminance and chromaticity by asymmetric matching. Despite much observational material obtained under diverse conditions, few general principles of chromatic adaptation have emerged. The following notes discuss the salient points of the work done by a number of investigators and sketch some of the specific models that have been proposed to predict chromatic adaptation data. Useful, more extensive reviews of the subject matter have been given by Jameson and Hurvich (1972), Bartleson (1978), and Wyszecki and Stiles (1982).

4.1. Some Basic Concepts of Chromatic Adaptation

The phenomena of chromatic adaptation are in full play when the test stimuli are imaged on the foveal, rod-free area of the retina. It is a simplification, adopted in most experimental work, to deal only with this case. The basic concepts that underlie such experiments have been formulated by Stiles (1961).

Two stimuli, with spectral radiant power distributions $\{P_\lambda d\lambda\}$ *and* $\{P'_\lambda d\lambda\}$, *applied to foveal areas O* and O' whose luminance and chromaticity are to be compared under different adapting conditions are then specified by their tristimulus values

$$X = \int P_\lambda \bar{x}(\lambda)d\lambda \qquad X' = \int P'_\lambda \bar{x}'(\lambda)d\lambda ,$$

$$Y = \int P_\lambda \bar{y}(\lambda)d\lambda \qquad Y' = \int P'_\lambda \bar{y}'(\lambda)d\lambda ,$$

$$Z = \int P_\lambda \bar{z}(\lambda)d\lambda \qquad Z' = \int P'_\lambda \bar{z}'(\lambda)d\lambda , \tag{23}$$

where the sets of color-matching functions $\bar{x}(\lambda)$ $\bar{y}(\lambda)$, $\bar{z}(\lambda)$, and $\bar{x}'(\lambda)$, $\bar{y}'(\lambda)$, $\bar{z}'(\lambda)$, which in binocular asymmetric matching refer to stimuli imaged on foveal areas of the left and right eyes, respectively, may be different. In fact, they may be different even if only as a result of prereceptor ocular pigment differences, and thus they are not transformable one into the other by a linear transformation. Although in some applications the differences may be unimportant, the possible distinction between the sets of color-matching functions is retained in this discussion.

The various investigations of chromatic adaptation indicate that the matching of the stimuli in differently adapted retinal areas is three dimensional in the sense that for a great many stimuli $\{P'_\lambda d\lambda\}$, whose tristimulus values correspond to points filling a considerable domain of the (X', Y', Z') space, a satisfactory match can be made with a comparison stimulus $\{P_\lambda d\lambda\}$ consisting of a mixture in suitable proportions of three well-chosen fixed primaries of high saturation, whereas the use of just two primaries will not serve.

It may be assumed therefore that there are three matching conditions which may be written in the following functional forms:

$$\psi_1(X,Y,Z;A) = \psi_1(X',Y',Z';A') ,$$

$$\psi_2(X,Y,Z;A) = \psi_2(X',Y',Z';A') ,$$

$$\psi_3(X,Y,Z;A) = \psi_3(X',Y',Z';A') , \tag{24}$$

where A and A' represent, respectively, for O and O', the values of all the variables that may contribute to determining the adaptation of the stimulus area. However, it must be emphasized that, with widely different adaptations A and A', the number of stimuli that cannot be matched with a given three-primary mixture may be very great; their tristimulus points may occupy an extensive domain in the (X', Y', Z') space. Superficially, this resembles the impossibility of matching certain too saturated stimuli in ordinary symmetric matching. However, the unmatchable stimuli in asymmetric matching are not necessarily well described by the expression "too saturated," and the indirect method of deriving a match by desaturating the test color with quantities of one or two of the matching primaries is questionable because it assumes that matching is additive. Moreover, an important difference from symmetric matching is that some test stimuli $\{P'_\lambda d\lambda\}$ may not only be unmatchable by any comparison mixture of three fixed primaries but also by a comparison stimulus $\{P_\lambda d\lambda\}$ of any spectral composition whatever. Striking examples of these points have been brought out in the work of Hunt (1953) and Bartleson (1977, 1978).

The conditioning variables (A or A') for a test area (O or O') must include the tristimulus values for the test area (X,Y,Z or X',Y',Z') and all the parameters of surround and preexposed stimuli applied to the retina in which the test area is located. They may also have to include the tristimulus values and adaptation parameters for the other test area. At this point, the different methods of asymmetric matching must be distinguished.

The crudest procedure, a form of color naming or memory method, was applied in studies of chromatic adaptation by Bouma and Kruithof (1947) and Helson, Judd, and Warren (1952). The observer, in preliminary training, first memorized the appearance of the samples of a color atlas, the *Munsell Book of Color*, exposed under adaptation conditions A. In the main experiments then, the observer had to name, by long-term memory, the sample corresponding to the perceived color of the test object exposed under the test conditions A'. This method is a more systematic application of the purely descriptive procedure used in many demonstrations of chromatic adaptation. In asymmetric matching of the kind just described, the stimuli $\{P_\lambda d\lambda\}$ and $\{P'_\lambda d\lambda\}$ are applied to the same retinal area ($O = O'$) but on entirely distinct occasions; A and A' are the two sets of values assumed on these occasions by a single set of conditioning variables. In these circumstances, asymmetric matching is *transitive*; that is, if stimulus (X,Y,Z) presented under conditions A matches (X',Y',Z') presented under conditions A', and if (X',Y',Z') under A' matches (X'',Y'',Z'') and A'', then (X'',Y'',Z'') under A'' matches (X,Y,Z) under A.

In binocular color matching, as pioneered by Wright (1934, 1946), on the other hand, the response to (X,Y,Z) in area O in the left eye could depend not only on the adapting stimuli applied to the left eye but also on all the stimuli applied to the right eye; in effect, A would represent a double set of parameters. Fortunately for this method, the evidence is that such interference of stimuli in one eye on the response in the other eye is slight. However, in monocular matching in a bipartite field with differential adaptation of the two halves, as used by MacAdam (1956), it is questionable whether a preexposed adapting stimulus applied to one half (retinal area O) has a negligible effect on the condition of the juxtaposed half (retinal area O'). To the extent that this occurs, the matches made represent the hybrid effects of two adapting stimuli on perception in each of the half-fields, and further interpretation is made more difficult. In any study of chromatic adaptation by asymmetric matching, tests of the transivity principle should show whether there is transfer to one matching area of the effects of stimuli used to adapt the other.

The important linearity laws (proportionality and additivity) are not generally true for asymmetric matching, although within the limits of some investigations confined to certain pairs of conditioning stimuli they have been found to be approximately valid. A full discussion of asymmetric comparison and matching and associated basic laws has been given, in more general terms, by Wyszecki and Stiles (1982).

The implications of obedience to the linearity laws for asymmetric matching have played a vital part in the study of chromatic adaptation. If they hold for adaptations A and A', the tristimulus values X,Y,Z and X',Y',Z' at match are related by a constant linear transformation of the following form:

$$X = a_{11}X' + a_{12}Y' + a_{13}Z' ,$$
$$Y = a_{21}X' + a_{22}Y' + a_{23}Z' ,$$
$$Z = a_{31}X' + a_{32}Y' + a_{33}Z' . \tag{25}$$

The nine coefficients $a_{11}, a_{12}, \ldots, a_{33}$ can be determined in principle by making just three asymmetric matches between independent pairs of stimuli. In more recent work, a larger group of matching pairs has been used, and the best values of the nine coefficients are determined by a least-squares method.

For convenience, Eq. (25) is rewritten in matrix notation, and the discussion that follows will make use of such a notation. Thus Eq. (25) is now rewritten as

$$\begin{pmatrix} X \\ Y \\ Z \end{pmatrix} = T_{AA'} \begin{pmatrix} X' \\ Y' \\ Z' \end{pmatrix} , \tag{26}$$

where $T_{AA'}$ denotes the 3×3 matrix whose elements are the a_{ik} coefficients ($i,k = 1,2,3$) shown explicitly in Eq. (25). The $T_{AA'}$ matrix is defined by

$$T_{AA'} = \begin{pmatrix} a_{11} & a_{12} & a_{13} \\ a_{21} & a_{22} & a_{23} \\ a_{31} & a_{32} & a_{33} \end{pmatrix} .$$

If the matching process with different pairs of adapting conditions is transitive, the corresponding matrices satisfy the matrix equation

$$T_{AA''} = T_{AA'} T_{A'A''} . \tag{27}$$

A celebrated hypothesis on chromatic adaptation originating in a *law of coefficients* put forward by von Kries (1904) would lead under certain conditions to asymmetric matching that is linear and transitive. The von Kries *hypothesis* (see also Section 3.5.2) assumes that different adaptations of a particular retinal area modify the overall sensitivities of three cone-response mechanisms, whose relative spectral sensitivities $\bar{r}(\lambda)$, $\bar{g}(\lambda)$, $\bar{b}(\lambda)$ are a particular fixed set of the color-matching functions applicable to the area in question. Thus $\bar{r}(\lambda)$, $\bar{g}(\lambda)$, $\bar{b}(\lambda)$ are related by a linear transformation with matrix M (of nonzero determinant) to the color-matching functions $\bar{x}(\lambda)$, $\bar{y}(\lambda)$, $\bar{z}(\lambda)$. The latter are expressed with respect to any convenient set of primaries without reference to visual theory. The cone responses $V_1 \equiv R$, $V_2 \equiv G$, $V_3 \equiv B$ of a stimulus $\{P_\lambda d\lambda\}$ are then related to X, Y, Z by the same matrix M, that is,

$$\begin{pmatrix} R \\ G \\ B \end{pmatrix} = M \begin{pmatrix} X' \\ Y' \\ Z' \end{pmatrix} . \tag{28}$$

If the two test areas O and O' in an asymmetric matching process have the same color-matching functions [$\bar{x}(\lambda) \equiv \bar{x}'(\lambda)$, etc.] and the same cone-response mechanisms, the same matrix M will be applicable, and this is commonly assumed. According to the hypothesis, the asymmetric match between $\{P_\lambda d\lambda\}$ and $\{P'_\lambda d\lambda\}$. corresponds to equating the absolute responses of the respective cone responses to give

$$K_{AR}R = K_{A'R}R' ,$$
$$K_{AG}G = K_{A'G}G' , \tag{29}$$
$$K_{AB}B = K_{A'B}B' ,$$

where the coefficients K_{AR}, K_{AG}, K_{AB} and $K_{A'R}, K_{A'G}, K_{A'B}$ are completely determined by the surround and preexposed stimuli contributing to the adaptation of areas O and O', respectively, but are independent of the actual test stimuli with spectral radiant power distributions $\{P_\lambda d\lambda\}$ and $\{P'_\lambda d\lambda\}$.

There are obvious objections to conceding that adaptation is unaffected by the test stimuli, but accepting the hypothesis as a whole, Eq. (29) implies that

$$\begin{pmatrix} K_{AR} & \cdot & \cdot \\ \cdot & K_{AG} & \cdot \\ \cdot & \cdot & K_{AB} \end{pmatrix} M \begin{pmatrix} X \\ Y \\ Z \end{pmatrix} = \begin{pmatrix} K_{A'R} & \cdot & \cdot \\ \cdot & K_{A'G} & \cdot \\ \cdot & \cdot & K_{A'B} \end{pmatrix} M \begin{pmatrix} X' \\ Y' \\ Z' \end{pmatrix}$$

or

$$\begin{pmatrix} X \\ Y \\ Z \end{pmatrix} = T_{AA'} \begin{pmatrix} X' \\ Y' \\ Z' \end{pmatrix}$$

where

$$T_{AA'} = M^{-1}DM \tag{30}$$

or

$$MT_{AA'}M^{-1} = D$$

and D is the diagonal matrix

$$D \equiv \begin{pmatrix} K_{AR}/K_{A'R} & \cdot & \cdot \\ \cdot & K_{AG}/K_{A'G} & \cdot \\ \cdot & \cdot & K_{AB}/K_{A'B} \end{pmatrix}$$

whose three elements are often referred to as the von Kries coefficients.

With a valid von Kries coefficient law, the problem of chromatic adaptation would reduce to determining the way the coefficients K_{AR}, K_{AG}, K_{AB} depend on the surround and preexposure stimuli in various adaptation situations. However, several quantitative studies on chromatic adaptation have shown the von Kries scheme to be imperfect in one or more ways (see also Section 3.5.2.2), and alternative models of the visual system have been proposed to yield better predictions. Some of these are of the type discussed in Sections 3.5.2.5 and 3.5.2.6; others, more complex in their mathematical structure, are given in Section 4.2.

4.2. Examples of Chromatic Adaptation Experiments

To demonstrate some of the basic concepts involved in chromatic adaptation, a few examples have been selected from a rather large list of studies made over the last several decades. For a more comprehensive review, see, for example, Wyszecki and Stiles (1982).

4.2.1. Chromatic Adaptation Experiment by Helson, Judd, and Warren. Helson, Judd, and Warren (1952) used a memory method. The observer first learned how to describe the colors of painted chips, presented in daylight, in terms of hue, lightness, and chroma, conveniently making use of Munsell color chips and their notations, Munsell hue, Munsell value, and Munsell chroma (Section 7.1). After sufficient practice, which might take eight hours or so, the observer had memorized hue, lightness, and chroma scales so as to be able to describe with reasonable precision the color of any object in the field of view. The trained observer was then requested to look at the objects in chromatic light, such as tungsten light. After the observer's eyes had adapted to the new illumination, the observer described the color perceptions in terms of the memorized color scales.

Figure 9.19 illustrates some typical results obtained by Helson and coworkers (1952) for six observers judging Munsell samples under CIE standard sources C (average daylight) and A (tungsten light) against a white background. Only the resultant shifts in hue and chroma are shown in the figure, and these are indicated by arrows. Each arrow starts at the point corresponding to the hue and chroma judged to belong to the Munsell sample in daylight (source C) and ends at the point corresponding to the hue and chroma judged to belong to the same sample in tungsten light. The judgment in daylight was made after complete adaptation to daylight; similarly the judgment in tungsten light was made after complete adaptation to tungsten light. The investigators noted that when they changed the background from white to middle gray and to black, the

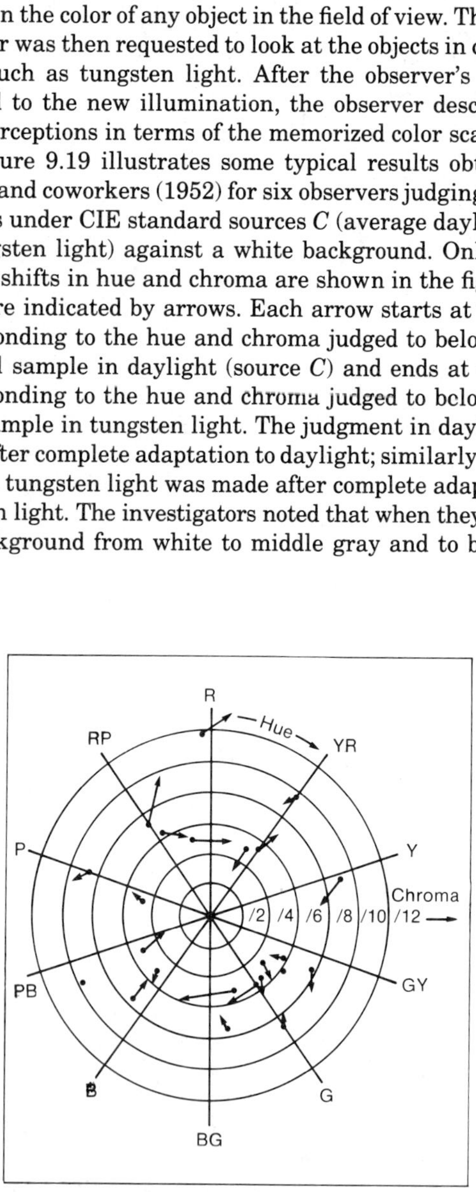

Figure 9.19. Changes in hue and chroma of a number of colored test samples when the state of chromatic adaptation of the observer's eyes is changed from daylight (CIE source C) to tungsten-light (CIE source A) adaptation. The data shown are representative of those obtained by Helson, Judd, and Warren (1952) who used a memory method to determine the color shifts. The color samples were Munsell samples of medium Munsell value in daylight, displayed on a white background. The resultant color shifts (changes in hue and chroma) can be predicted with reasonable success by means of the von Kries transformation for chromatic adaptation. (From D. B. Judd & G. Wyszecki, *Color in business, science, and industry*, 3rd ed. Copyright 1975, John Wiley & Sons, Inc. Reprinted with permission.)

color shifts observed under the white background often changed noticeably. They attributed this observation to previous findings by Helson (1938), which showed that hue and chroma of an object depend importantly on the relation of the object's reflectance to "adaptation reflectance." According to Helson (1938), adaptation reflectance is defined as a weighted mean of the reflectance of all objects in the field of view, but in many cases, such as the one discussed here, the weighted mean is largely determined by the background (Judd, 1940). Helson and coworkers (1952) do not pursue the background effect in this chromatic adaptation study any further.

The analysis that Helson and coworkers (1952) apply to their experimental data is consistent with the von Kries hypothesis, and the transformation equations governing the hypothesis are those outlined in Section 4.2. The predictions made are in fair agreement with the experimental data. Specifically, the average difference between theoretical estimates and observers' estimates of chroma is 1.12 for the white background data with a t value of 5.71, indicating a significant departure of theory from observation. Actually, the differences between the theoretical and observed chromas are small for the most part, amounting to less than one step in the 0–10 scale of chroma employed by the observers. However, because the predicted chromas tend to be greater than the observed chromas nearly consistently, even this small difference proves to be statistically significant.

A similar statistical analysis of the differences between the theoretical and observed hues indicates that the discrepancies are not statistically significant. The average difference between theoretical and observed hues is 0.54 hue steps on a 100-point Munsell hue circuit for the white background.

4.2.2. Chromatic Adaptation Experiment by Sobagaki, Yamanaka, Takahama, and Nayatani. Sobagaki, Yamanaka, Takahama, and Nayatani (1974) use a scaling method, known as *magnitude estimation* (see Section 6.1; also see Chapter 1 by Falmagne). The method aims at assessing the strength of an observer's color perceptions in terms of numbers selected by the observer in proportion to the magnitudes of those perceptions. Hue, chroma, and lightness were scaled in that way for 95 colored chips, selected from the *Munsell Book of Colors* (Section 7.1), which the observer viewed one at a time and in random order under a daylight source (a fluorescent lamp simulating CIE standard illuminant D_{65}) and under a tungsten source (simulating CIE standard illuminant A). Thirteen observers took part in the investigation.

Hues were estimated in terms of the *unique hues*: red R, yellow Y, green G, and blue B. Between neighboring unique hues, the observer had 100 steps available to assign an appropriate scale value to the hue of a given colored chip. For example, to an orange chip, the observer might assign the value 80R/20Y which corresponds to a judgment that the chip appears to have 80% redness and 20% yellowness. A chip of achromatic appearance was assigned the value of zero.

Chroma was estimated on a scale from 0 to 100, 0 being an achromatic perception, 100 being maximum chroma. For studies of the effect of using different methods of estimating chroma, see Sobagaki, Takahama, and Nayatani (1976) and Takahama, Sobagaki, and Nayatani (1978). Lightness was similarly estimated on a scale from 0 to 100, 0 being "no lightness" and 100 being maximum lightness.

The analysis of the experimental data in terms of the von Kries coefficient law led to difficulties. Least-squares fitting procedures called for cone-response functions that were untenable from the physiological point of view. The validity of the von Kries coefficient law was considered questionable.

In two subsequent studies, Nayatani, Takahama, and Sobagaki (1981a, 1981b), developed a nonlinear model of chromatic adaptation designed to predict more adequately various experimental data. The mathematically complex model is a two-process model. The first process operates in accordance with a multiplicative receptor type of model (Section 3.5.2.2) involving a von Kries type of transformation. The second process operates in accordance with a nonlinear transformation, a power function, which describes a response compression assumed to take place in each cone-receptor mechanism.

4.2.3. Chromatic Adaptation Experiment by Bartleson. Bartleson's (1977, 1978, 1979a, 1979b) extensive investigation on chromatic adaptation provides, apart from a detailed review of earlier work, new experimental data, an intercomparison of data from different investigators, and a proposal of predicting the effect of chromatic adaptation.

Bartleson's experimental work involved methods of direct scaling (for the main part, magnitude estimation) applied to a set of 24 test stimuli of different chromaticities seen under different states of adaptation. Each test stimulus (1° diameter) was viewed centrally in a surround (15.2° diameter) of high (near nonselective) reflectance illuminated by one of three sources which provided (x,y) chromaticities of the surround closely representing those of CIE standard illuminant A (2856 K), CIE standard illuminant D_{65} (6504 K), and of an illuminant D_{50} with an intermediate correlated color temperature 5003 K. The test stimulus was presented for periods of 2 sec at intervals of 10 sec. This was accomplished by a shutter made of the same material as the surround and placed right behind the opening in the surround. When the shutter was in its closed position, the entire visual field appeared virtually uniform.

Each of the seven observers, ages 20 to 53, who took part in the experiment, was adapted for 20 min before the start of an experimental session to the uniform visual field with a luminance not less than 200 $cd{\cdot}m^{-2}$. This ensured sufficiently complete adaptation to the conditioning stimulus provided by the surround, making the surround appear perfectly white (that is, a hueless area with no trace of gray), regardless of which source was used to illuminate it. The luminance of 200 $cd{\cdot}m^{-2}$ was found to be the minimum level that could be used to obtain the appearance of white for the surround.

The experimental conditions were varied not only with regard to the correlated color temperature of the sources used to illuminate the surround but also with regard to the luminance of the surround and the luminance of the test stimuli.

At this point, it is useful to recall two luminance-related terms, luminance factor and illuminance, which figure in Bartleson's experiment. *Luminance factor* is defined as the ratio of the luminance of the test stimulus to the luminance of the surround. It is a term commonly used for object-color stimuli as found in everyday life and as simulated in Bartleson's experiment. *Illuminance* is defined as the luminous flux per unit area incident on a surface, measured in terms of $lm{\cdot}m^{-2}$. In the present case, this term applies to the field of view as a whole (surround and test area). By varying both the luminance of the surround and the luminance of the test stimulus by the same factor, the illuminance of the field of view changes by the same factor, but the luminance factor of the test stimulus remains constant. With real objects, such as colored chips from the *Munsell Book of Color* presented on a white background, varying the illuminance means varying the incident radiant flux emitted by the light source without altering its relative spectral distribution.

Bartleson's results led him to the following general conclusions:

1. The *perceived hue* of a given test stimulus, expressed as proportions of neighboring unique hues (red, yellow, green, and blue) varies with the chromaticity (correlated color temperature) of the adapting stimulus (surround) but does not vary significantly with the luminance factor of the test stimulus or the illuminance of the field of view.
2. The *chroma* of a given test stimulus varies with the chromaticity (correlated color temperature) of the adapting stimulus (surround) and the luminance factor of the test stimulus. Changes in the illuminance of the field of view have virtually no effect on chroma.
3. The *lightness* of a given test stimulus varies with the luminance factor of the test stimulus but is essentially invariant to changes in the chromaticity (correlated color temperature) of the adapting stimulus (surround) and the illuminance of the field of view.
4. The color-appearance data obtained for daylight adaptation D_{65} are highly correlated with the Munsell renotation specifications (Section 7.1).

Bartleson's main experimental results are summarized in Figures 9.20–9.23. Figure 9.20 shows (u',v') chromaticity points of the 24 test stimuli used in the experiment. Figure 9.21 shows the shifts in color appearances of the 24 test stimuli when adaptation is changed from daylight D_{65} to tungsten light A for a surround luminance of 1000 $cd{\cdot}m^{-2}$ and a luminance of the test stimuli fixed at 200 $cd{\cdot}m^{-2}$, making the luminance factor β of the test stimuli equal to 0.2. The data given in Figure 9.21 allow the construction of a polar-coordinate system of color appearance for adaptation to A in terms of color appearances for adaptation to D_{65}. Figure 9.22 shows the A-adaptation diagram superimposed on the D_{65}-adaptation diagram. For the benefit of colorimetric applications, it is useful to present the data in a CIE standard chromaticity diagram. This has been done in Figure 9.23. One application of Figure 9.23 is to determine colorimetric specifications for corresponding color stimuli as obtained, for example, by an asymmetric color match involving daylight and tungsten-light adaptations. First, the chromaticity point for one adaptation condition, D_{65}, for example, is located in the appropriate diagram in which its color-appearance specification is determined by interpolation in the grid overlay. Then the just determined color-appearance specification is transferred to the grid for the other (A) adaptation condition given in the other diagram. This yields the chromaticity point of the desired corresponding color stimulus.

To predict his experimental data by means of a suitable mathematical model, Bartleson (1979b) adopted the von Kries hypothesis to which he added a nonlinear compression of the response of the blue cone mechanism. In some ways, Bartleson's model is a simplified version of that proposed by Takahama, Sobagaki, and Nayatani (1978) and Nayatani, Takahama, and Sobagaki (1981b) referred to in Section 4.2.2. In particular, Bartleson chooses cone-response functions $\bar{r}(\lambda)$, $\bar{g}(\lambda)$, $\bar{b}(\lambda)$ that are linearly related to the CIE 1931 standard color-matching functions $\bar{x}(\lambda)$, $\bar{y}(\lambda)$, $\bar{z}(\lambda)$ by the matrix

$$M = \begin{pmatrix} 0.0713 & 0.\ 9625 & -0.0147 \\ -0.3952 & 1.1668 & 0.0815 \\ 0 & 0 & 0.5610 \end{pmatrix}. \qquad (31)$$

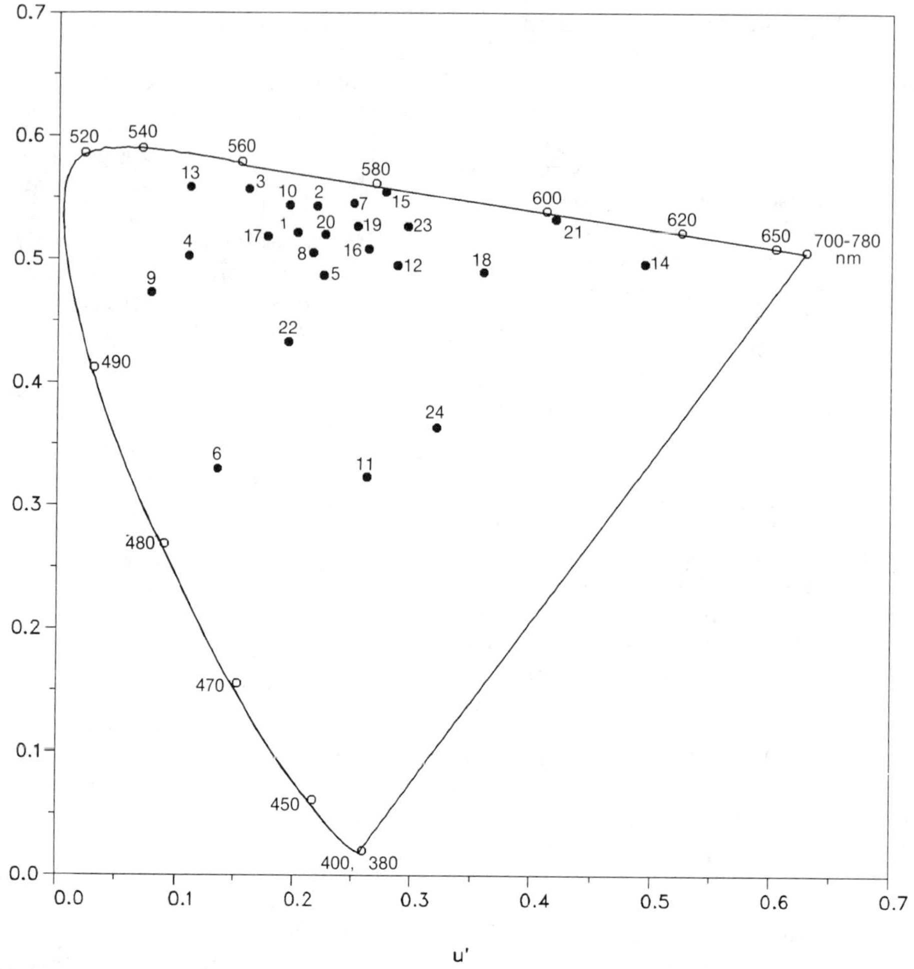

Figure 9.20. Chromaticity points of 24 test stimuli plotted in the 1976 (u',v') chromaticity diagram. These stimuli were used by Bartleson (1977, 1979a) in his study on chromatic adaptation. The observer used a magnitude estimation technique to describe the color appearance of each given stimulus in terms of hue, lightness, and chroma when the stimulus was presented with a white surround, first under daylight D_{65} illumination and then under tungsten light (CIE illuminant A) illumination. The two illumination modes provided two separate states of chromatic adaptation. By going from the first state (D_{65}) to the second state of adaptation, the appearance of the given test stimulus changes, and the objective of the experiment is to determine these changes. (From C. J. Bartleson, *Factors effecting color appearance and measurement by psychophysical methods*. Unpublished doctoral dissertation, The City University of London, 1977. Reprinted with permission.)

The same matrix converts the (X,Y,Z) CIE tristimulus values to (R,G,B) cone responses for any given stimulus of known spectral radiant power distribution, that is,

$$\begin{pmatrix} R \\ G \\ B \end{pmatrix} = M \begin{pmatrix} X \\ Y \\ Z \end{pmatrix} . \tag{32}$$

Stimuli of spectral radiant power distributions $\{P_\lambda d\lambda\}$ and $\{P_\lambda' d\lambda\}$, which elicit identical color perceptions, equate the absolute responses of the respective cone mechanisms as follows:

$$R' = \alpha R ,$$

$$G' = \beta G ,$$

$$B' = k(\gamma B)^p , \tag{33}$$

where α, β, γ are von Kries coefficients that are completely determinable from the fundamental tristimulus values of the two conditioning stimuli that control the two states of adaptation A and A' ($A \equiv$ daylight D_{65}, $A' \equiv$ tungsten light A, in Bartleson's case). The exponent p in Eq. (33) that compresses the response of the blue cone mechanism, interpretable as a postreceptor neural activity, is obtained from the empirical expression

$$p = 0.326\,\alpha^{27.45} + 0.325\,\beta^{-3.91} + 0.340\,\gamma^{-0.45} . \tag{34}$$

The coefficient k is given by

$$k = \gamma B_A / (\gamma B_A)^p , \tag{35}$$

where B_A is the blue cone response for the stimulus providing adaptation condition A ($\equiv$ daylight D_{65} adaptation, in Bartleson's case).

From the calculated cone responses (R', G', B'), the CIE tristimulus values (X', Y', Z') are obtained from

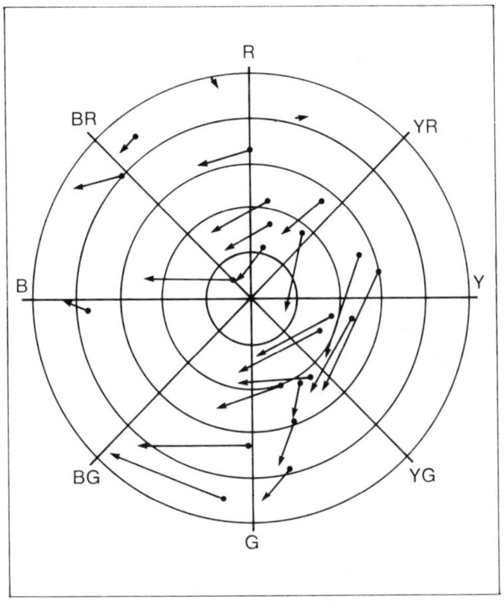

Figure 9.21. Color-appearance diagram. Lines of constant hue are radii originating at the center, and lines of constant chroma are concentric circles; the greater the radius of the circle, the higher the chroma of the test stimulus. Neighboring unique hues (*R*, *Y*, *G*, *B*) are at right angles. Shown in this diagram are the observed shifts in color appearance of the 24 test stimuli (see Figure 9.20) used by Bartleson (1977, 1979a) when the observers' state of adaptation is changed from daylight D_{65} adaptation to tungsten-light *A* adaptation. Direct scaling by the method of magnitude estimation was employed. The white surround, which controlled the adaptation, had a luminance of 1000 $cd{\cdot}m^{-2}$; the test stimuli were kept at a luminance of 200 $cd{\cdot}m^{-2}$, giving them a luminance factor $\beta = 0.2$. Arrow heads are for adaptation to *A*, tails for D_{65}. The observed changes in chromatic adaptation are, in general, quite pronounced and established with a high degree of reliability. (From C. J. Bartleson, *Factors effecting color appearance and measurement by psychophysical methods*. Unpublished doctoral dissertation, The City University of London, 1977. Reprinted with permission.)

$$\begin{pmatrix} X' \\ Y' \\ Z' \end{pmatrix} = M^{-1} \begin{pmatrix} R' \\ G' \\ B' \end{pmatrix}, \qquad (36)$$

with

$$M^{-1} = \begin{pmatrix} 2.5170 & -2.0763 & 0.3676 \\ 0.8525 & 0.1538 & 0 \\ 0 & 0 & 1.7825 \end{pmatrix}.$$

Figure 9.24 illustrates the agreement Bartleson obtains between his observed and predicted data. The diagram shows observed (solid) lines and predicted (dashed) lines of constant hue and chroma for the mean observer whose state of adaptation was changed from daylight D_{65} to tungsten light *A*. The agreement is considered reasonable.

Bartleson (1979b) applied his formulae also to experimental data gathered by other investigators, notably Burnham, Evans, and Newhall (1957), Wassef (1959), MacAdam (1963), and Helson, Judd, and Warren (1952). The agreement between his predictions and the observed data varies from one data set to the other from fair to reasonable and is, in general, comparable with the agreement other investigators had obtained by applying their own formulas to their own data.

4.3. Special Color-Appearance Phenomena Involving Chromatic Adaptation

4.3.1. Afterimages. The existence of adaptation processes including chromatic adaptation is demonstrated by afterimages. Afterimages can vary in hue, lightness, and chroma. They are characteristically less objective and compelling than the perception elicited by the original stimulus and are generally transient and filmy. They drift and move with the eyes.

Afterimages may be classified into different types (see, for example, Burnham, Hanes, & Bartleson, 1963). Commonly observed types are the complementary and homochromatic afterimages. A complementary afterimage is generated after prolonged exposure of the retina, or part of it, to a chromatic field followed by viewing an achromatic (white) field. If the chromatic field is red, the afterimage of that field will appear greenish. A homochromatic afterimage is generated when the eye first focuses for a few seconds on the center of a white field surrounded by a chromatic field and then shifts its fixation to a point in the surrounding chromatic field. If the surrounding chromatic field is red, the afterimage of the white field will be seen as a darker red. Effective demonstrations of afterimages can be found in Evans (1948), Burnham and coworkers (1963), and Hurvich (1981). A useful review of studies of afterimages, including some demonstrations, has been given by Brown (1965).

4.3.2. Ganzfeld. A *Ganzfeld* is a visual field of infinite extent filled with a single, spatially uniform, structureless visual stimulus of a given spectral radiant power distribution. The visual system confronted with a Ganzfeld loses its efficiency quickly, often within seconds. In fact, a complete loss of visual

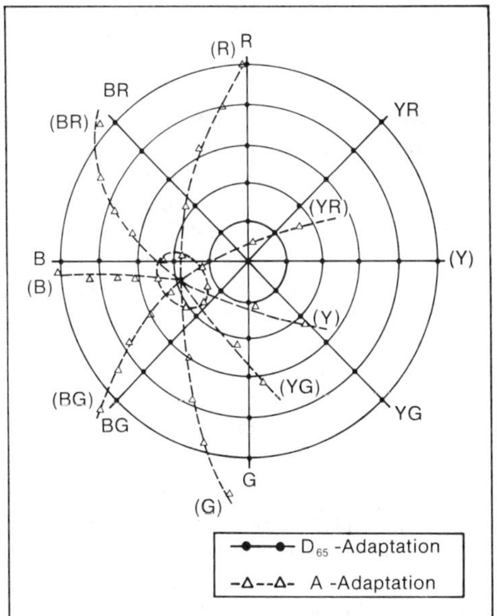

Figure 9.22. Superimposed color-appearance diagrams for D_{65} adaptation (solid dots) and for *A* adaptation (open triangles), derived from data given in Figure 9.21. A triangle in the *A*-adaptation diagram indicates the color appearance of a test stimulus viewed under D_{65} adaptation that, under *A* adaptation, would have the same color appearance as the corresponding solid dot in the D_{65}-adaptation diagram. (From C. J. Bartleson, *Factors effecting color appearance and measurement by psychophysical methods*. Unpublished doctoral dissertation, The City University of London, 1977. Reprinted with permission.)

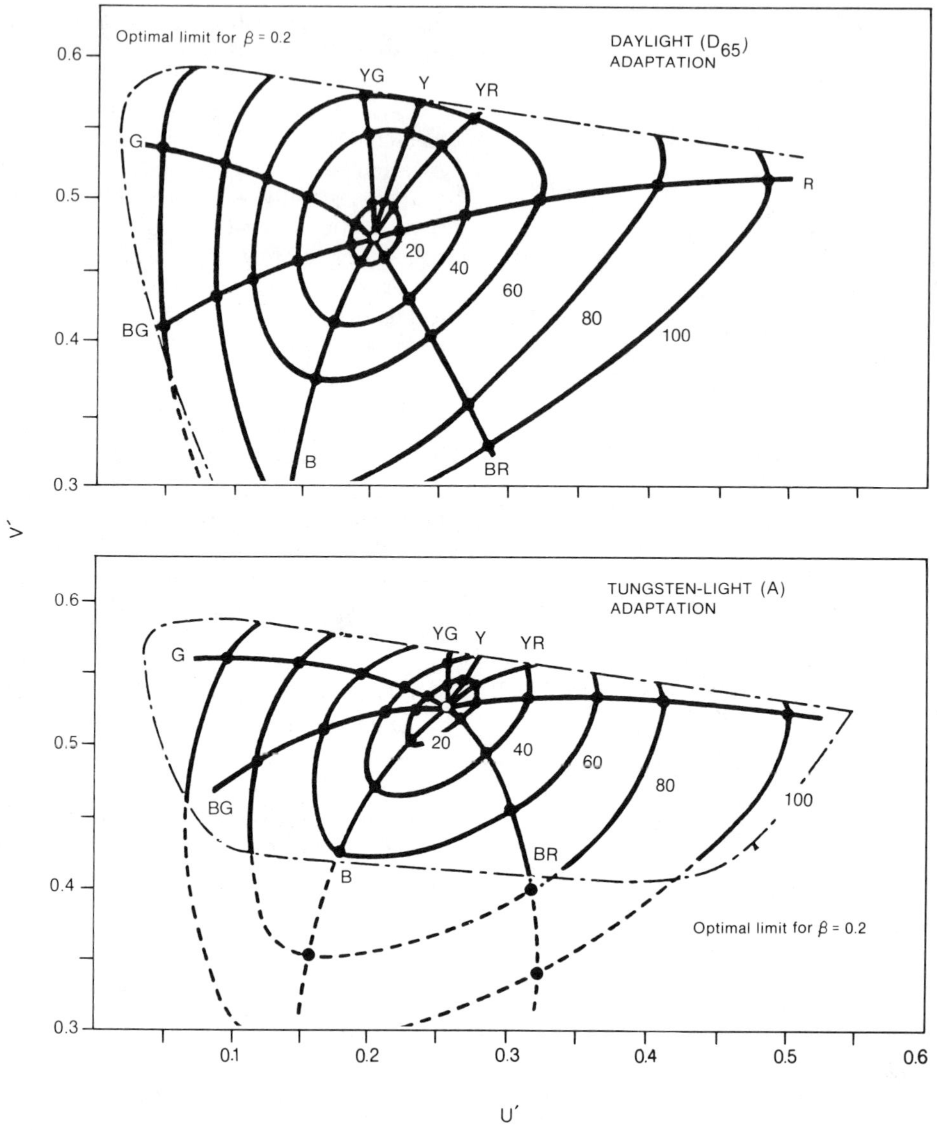

Figure 9.23. Portion of CIE 1976 (u',v') chromaticity diagram showing lines of constant hue and constant chroma for adaptation to daylight D_{65} and for adaptation to tungsten light A. The curved lines are mean and smoothed data obtained by Bartleson (1977, 1979a) for seven observers taking part in a direct-scaling experiment involving the 24 test stimuli specified in Figure 9.20. The 1° test stimuli had a luminance of 200 $cd{\cdot}m^{-2}$ and were presented in a 15.2° white surround with a luminance of 1000 $cd{\cdot}m^{-2}$; the luminance factor of the test stimuli thus being $\beta = 0.2$. The optimal limit beyond which there are no object-color stimuli with $\beta \geqslant 0.2$ is shown by a dot-dash locus. The hue and chroma lines change drastically when the state of chromatic adaptation is changed from D_{65} to A. (From C. J. Bartleson, *Factors effecting color appearance and measurement by psychophysical methods*. Unpublished doctoral dissertation, The City University of London, 1977. Reprinted with permission.)

perception has been reported by some investigators (see reviews by Avant, 1965, and Ditchburn, 1973). Ganzfeld (or empty visual field) situations arise to a close approximation in the sky at high-altitude flights (Whiteside, 1957) and in the arctic whiteout (Wyszecki, 1956). Fair experimental approximations can be obtained by holding the halves of a ping-pong ball over the eyes.

4.3.3. McCollough Effect. Afterimages of an unusual kind are obtained with striped fields in slow alternation. A celebrated demonstration uses a pattern of vertical red and black bars and a pattern of horizontal green and black bars, both of which are looked at for 5–10 min with alternating fixations on each for 10 sec (Figure 9.25). After the 5–10-min period, another pattern is viewed, consisting, in one half, of horizontal black and white bars and, in the other half, of vertical black and white bars. Usually, weak pale greens are perceived in the pattern of the vertical bars and weak pinks in the pattern of the horizontal bars. The effect is called the *McCollough effect* after its discoverer (McCollough, 1965).

To generate the effect, strict fixation of the striped patterns is not required, which is contrary to the condition normally required in generating ordinary afterimages of the type described in Section 4.3.1. It has also been found that the McCollough effect can last much longer (hours or days) than ordinary afterimages. In a monograph on the McCollough effect, Shute (1979) refers to it as an indicator of central neurotransmitter activity and discusses such aspects as strength, decay time, and

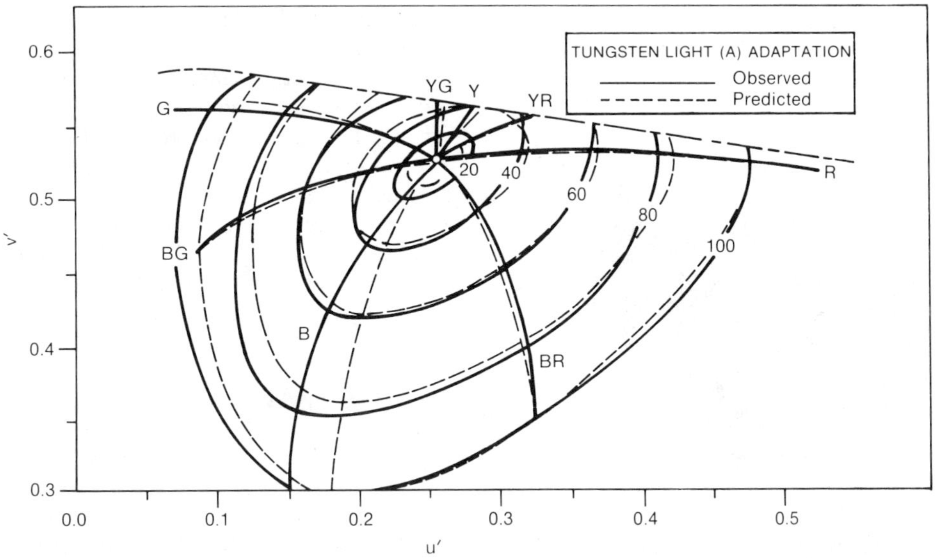

Figure 9.24. Observed and predicted lines of constant hue and constant chroma for the mean of the observers whose state of adaptation was changed from daylight D_{65} to tungsten light *A* in Bartleson's (1977, 1979b) experiment, summarized in Figure 9.23. The predictions were made by means of a simple nonlinear model with coefficients determined empirically. The agreement between predicted and observed data is considered reasonable. (From C. J. Bartleson, *Color research and applications*. Copyright 1979 by John Wiley & Sons, Inc. Reprinted with permission.)

effect of drugs. Fully satisfactory explanations of the McCollough effect have yet to be developed (Strohmeyer, 1978). In most attempts to account for the intriguing effect, the existence of neural analyzers is proposed that are specific to both color and orientation (McCollough, 1965) and, in some cases, to other features, such as movement direction (Hepler, 1968), curvature (Riggs, 1973), and spatial frequency (Strohmeyer, 1972). Other attempts to explain the effect suggest that cognitive factors must be included for a complete explanation (Jenkins & Ross, 1977; Uhlarik, Pringle, & Brigell, 1977); however, these explanations must also be regarded as tentative (Milewski, Iaccino, & Smith, 1980).

4.3.4. Benham Disk. The *Benham disk*, with a black and white pattern as shown in Figure 9.26, produces perceptions of desaturated colors when slowly rotating (5–15 revolutions/sec). These phantom or illusory colors appear along the curved lines. Clockwise rotation generates red inner rings and blue outer rings. Anticlockwise rotation generates blue inner rings and red outer rings (Benham, 1894). The theoretical explanation of the phenomenon, and others similar in design, varies a great deal between different investigators. Useful summaries of such explanations have been given by Campenhausen (1968) and Jameson (1972).

Among earlier researchers, the prevalent view was that the different hue sensations rise and fall at different rates and that periodic light stimulation causes the different hue components, as well as their momentary aftereffects, to separate. A more recent explanation, specifically that put forward by Campenhausen (1968), postulates three initial excitatory activities generated in the three types of cone mechanism. The temporal characteristics of these excitatory activities are then modified in special neural centers, possibly located in the *hor-*

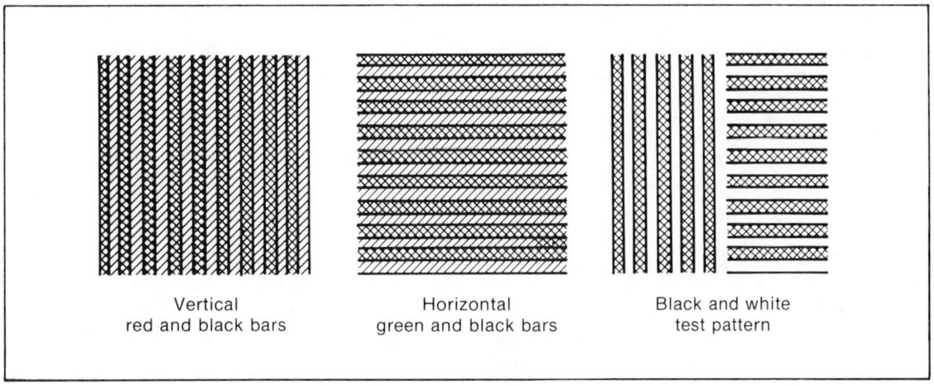

Figure 9.25. Visual field configuration used to demonstrate the McCollough effect. The pattern of vertical red and black bars and the pattern of horizontal green and black bars are first looked at for 5–10 min with alternating fixations on each for 10 sec. After the 5–10-min period, the black and white test pattern on the right is viewed. Weak pale greens are perceived in the pattern of the vertical bars and weak pinks in the pattern of the horizontal bars.

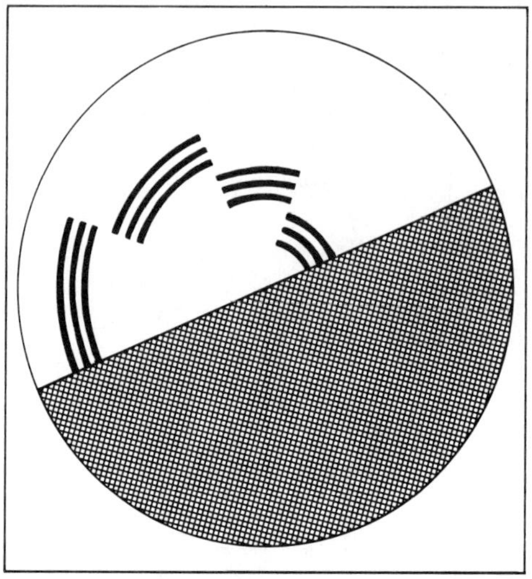

Figure 9.26. Benham disk. The black and white pattern making up the face of the disk produces perceptions of desaturated colors when the disk is slowly rotating (5–15 revolutions per second). The phantom, or illusory, colors appear along the curved lines.

izontal cells, that act as "kinetic fibers," each with its own specific temporal properties. In addition, lateral inhibition mechanisms are postulated, which function through lateral connections between neighboring excitatory signal channels, resulting in a depression of the excitatory flow of signals. Particular temporal patterns of stimulation have a modulating effect on both the excitatory and lateral inhibitory signals. The phase relations between the two types of signal determine the net excitatory signal output. Because the temporal characteristics of the three spectrally selective cone-mechanism channels are not identical, the inhibitory modulation is such as to selectively suppress or favor one or another cone-mechanism channel; hence the appearance of the perception of color on the Benham disk.

4.3.5. Chromatic Flicker. Many experimental data on chromatic and brightness flicker that are relevant to the subject matter of color appearance and explanations of such phenomena have been given by, among others, van der Horst (1969), van der Horst and Bouman (1969), Estévez and Spekreijse (1974), Estévez and Cavonius (1975), Boynton and Baron (1975), Kelly, Boynton, and Baron (1976), Boynton (1979), and Wisowaty and Boynton (1980). A detailed account of flicker phenomena has also been given elsewhere in this book (see Pokorny and Smith, Chapter 8, and Watson, Chapter 6), and thus this note can be very brief. Chromatic flicker may be generated by presenting two stimuli of different colors in a periodically alternating mode. The appearance of the visual field will depend—apart from size, retinal location, no-flickering–conditioning stimuli, and luminance level—on the two colors of the stimuli seen under the steady-state condition and the rate of alternation. At a very low rate of alternation, the observer will see a distinct repetitive change from the first color to the second and back to the first. With an increasing rate of alternation, the observer begins to see not only the two original colors but also colors of intermediate hue, saturation, and brightness; and when the rate is further increased, the two colors will fuse to a single color which is the color of the additive mixture of the two component stimuli.

At the point at which *chromatic fusion* occurs—that is, *critical chromatic flicker frequency* (CCFF) is reached—there may still remain a perceptual brightness flicker. Complete fusion of flicker is reached after a further increase of alternation, this point being called the *critical flicker frequency* (CFF). For a given pair of color stimuli, the observed CCFF is highest when the luminances of the steady-state component stimuli are the same; it decreases with increasing luminance difference between the two stimuli (Truss, 1957). The CCFF also depends on the chromatic differences of the flickering component stimuli (van der Horst, 1969). The difference between CCFF and CFF can be minimized or eliminated if the phase relation of the two component stimuli is appropriately altered (de Lange, 1958a, 1958b; Walraven & Leebeek, 1964).

5. CHROMATIC-RESPONSE FUNCTIONS

5.1. The Data of Jameson and Hurvich

Jameson and Hurvich (1955) put the opponent-colors theory on a quantitative basis by determining experimentally, using a *hue-cancellation technique*, the spectral distributions of the opponent-hue responses which are often referred to as the *chromatic-response functions* (or *chromatic-valence functions*). The data Jameson and Hurvich obtained for their own vision are illustrated in Figure 9.27.

A 1° test stimulus was presented repeatedly for several seconds in a 37° diameter white surround (luminance 32 $\mathrm{cd \cdot m^{-2}}$) and consisted of a mixture of a monochromatic test stimulus of wavelength λ (luminance 32 $\mathrm{cd \cdot m^{-2}}$) with an adjustable amount of one of four so-called cancellation stimuli of fixed wavelength: 467, 490, 588, 700 nm (observer H); 475, 500, 580, 700 nm (observer J). The first three of these were chosen as the monochromatic stimuli evoking for each observer "perceptually unique" blue, green, and yellow hues, while the fourth (700 nm) evoked a predominantly red hue, the unique red being normally extraspectral. Jameson and Hurvich remark that there is nothing critical about using perceptually unique stimuli but that the analysis is simplified by doing so. By repeated adjustments of the radiance $L_e(\lambda_c)$ of the cancellation stimulus, the condition is reached when its mixture with the monochromatic test stimulus of radiance $L_e(\lambda)$ satisfies the criterion (*YB*)—*neutral as between blueness and yellowness*—or the criterion (*RG*)—*neutral as between redness and greenness*. The setting made (by observer H) may be expressed formally as follows:

(i) For $\lambda > 490$ nm and $\lambda_c = 467$ nm :

$L_e(\lambda) + L_e(467)$ satisfies (YB) ;

$$\eta_Y(\lambda) = \sigma_Y \frac{L_e(467)}{L_e(\lambda)} \tag{37}$$

(ii) For $\lambda < 490$ nm and $\lambda_c = 588$ nm :

$L_e(\lambda) + L_e(588)$ satisfies (YB) ;

$$-\eta_B(\lambda) = \sigma_B \frac{L_e(588)}{L_e(\lambda)} \tag{38}$$

(iii) For $\lambda > 588$ nm or $\lambda < 467$ nm, and $\lambda_c = 490$ nm ;

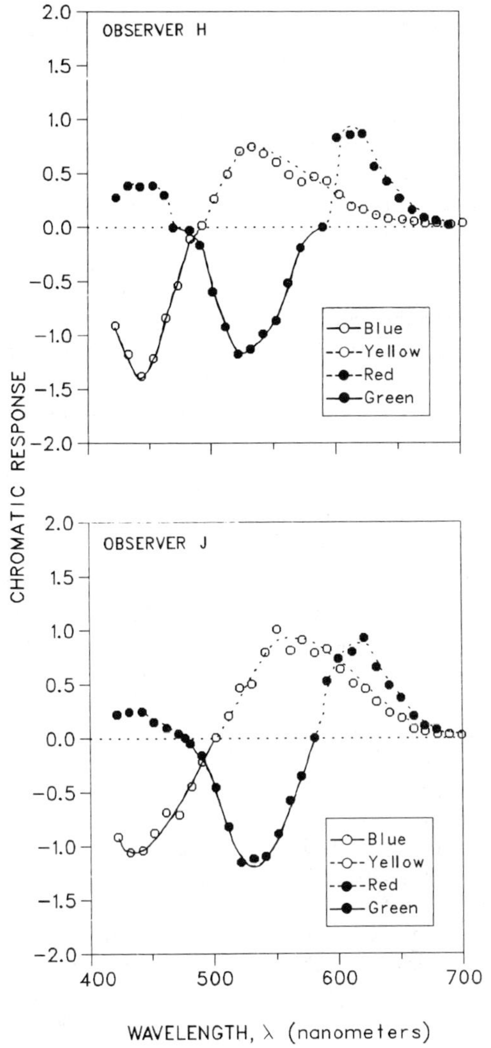

Figure 9.27. The chromatic-response functions determined experimentally by Jameson and Hurvich (1955) by a hue-cancellation technique for two observers. A 1° test stimulus, presented repeatedly for several seconds in a 37° diameter white surround of luminance 32 cd·m^{-2}, consisted of a mixture of a monochromatic test stimulus of wavelength λ and luminance 32 cd·m^{-2} with an adjustable amount of one of four cancellation stimuli of fixed wavelength: 467, 490, 588, 700 nm for observer H and 475, 500, 580, 700 nm for observer J. (From L. M. Hurvich & D. Jameson, Some quantitative aspects of an opponent-colors theory. II. Brightness, saturation, and hue in normal and dichromatic vision, *Journal of the Optical Society of America*, 1955, 45. Reprinted with permission.)

$L_e(\lambda) + L_e(490)$ satisfies (RG) ;

$$\eta_R(\lambda) = \sigma_R \frac{L_e(490)}{L_e(\lambda)} \qquad (39)$$

(iv) For 467 nm $< \lambda <$ 588 nm and λ_c = 700 nm ;

$L_e(\lambda) + L_e(700)$ satisfies (RG) ;

$$-\eta_G(\lambda) = \sigma_G \frac{L_e(700)}{L_e(\lambda)} . \qquad (40)$$

Here $\eta_Y(\lambda)$ and $\eta_B(\lambda)$ define, in their respective spectral regions, the chromatic-response function relevant to the opponent-hue pair yellow-blue, σ_Y and σ_B being suitably chosen constant factors. Similarly, $\eta_R(\lambda)$ and $\eta_G(\lambda)$ define the other chromatic-response function. The relative values of σ_Y and σ_B are determined by postulating that when two monochromatic stimuli of wavelengths λ_1, λ_2, respectively greater than and less than 490 nm, are mixed in such radiance proportions $L_e(\lambda_1)$:$L_e(\lambda_2)$ that the (YB) criterion is satisfied, the yellowness $\eta_Y(\lambda_1)L_e(\lambda_1)$ of the first stimulus equals with opposite sign the blueness $\eta_Y(\lambda_2)L_e(\lambda_2)$ of the second stimulus. By application of this postulate to the special case, λ_1 = 588 nm, λ_2 = 467 nm, it is readily shown that

$$\frac{\sigma_Y}{\sigma_B} = \frac{L_e(588)}{L_e(467)} . \qquad (41)$$

Thus each chromatic-response curve is completely determined in its relative spectral values. It can also be inferred from the postulate that for a mixture of two wavelengths λ_1 and λ_2 with

$$\lambda_1 > 490 \text{ nm} \quad \text{and} \quad \lambda_2 < 490 \text{ nm}$$

$$\lambda_1 \neq 588 \text{ nm} \quad \text{and} \quad \lambda_2 \neq 467 \text{ nm}$$

to be neutral (YB), the radiances $L_e(\lambda_1)$ and $L_e(\lambda_2)$ must be given by

$$\frac{L_e(\lambda_1)}{L_e(\lambda_2)} = \frac{-\eta_B(\lambda_2)}{\eta_Y(\lambda_1)} , \qquad (42)$$

the right-hand side being determined completely once σ_Y/σ_B has been fixed. Because this information is not part of the actual experimental data contained in Figure 9.27, the postulate goes beyond a mere normalizing convention. The ratio σ_G/σ_R is similarly obtained as

$$\frac{\sigma_G}{\sigma_R} = \frac{L_e(490)}{L_e(700)} , \qquad (43)$$

where the mixture of the two stimuli of wavelengths 490 and 700 nm is neutral (RG).

The values of the factors (σ_Y,σ_B) for one chromatic-response curve relative to those of the other factors (σ_G,σ_R) are determined by subjective estimates of the monochromatic stimuli for which the hue sensation appears to partake equally of two qualities belonging to different opponent pairs, for example, equal redness and yellowness, equal greenness and yellowness. When the ordinates of the two chromatic-response curves are made equal (in absolute magnitude), or nearly so, at such estimated wavelengths, the curves are completely determined except for an arbitrary overall factor applied to both.

Romeskie (1976) repeated, for two observers, the hue cancellation experiment, and her results agree closely with those of Jameson and Hurvich shown in Figure 9.27.

5.2. Linearity Laws for Opponent-Hue Cancellation

The generality and hence the usefulness of the chromatic-response functions as a data base for making quantitative predictions of other experimental data, such as wavelength discrimination and chromatic adaptation, rests to a large extent on the assumption that the *linearity laws* for opponent-hue cancellation, which comprise the linear operations of *proportionality* and *additivity*, are strictly valid. The work by Jameson and Hurvich, well summarized by Hurvich (1981), appears to support that assumption. On the other hand, direct experimental tests of the linearity laws, made by Larimer, Krantz, and Cicerone (1974, 1975), Cicerone, Krantz, and Larimer (1975), and Ikeda and Ayama (1980) have brought out certain failures of these laws.

The work of Krantz and his colleagues centers on proportionality and additivity tests of stimuli that are perceived to be in (red/green) and in (yellow/blue) equilibrium. A (red/green)-equilibrium stimulus is defined as a stimulus that appears neither reddish nor greenish, that is, one perceived as having either the unique hue of yellow or the unique hue of blue or is perceived as being achromatic (neutral). Similarly, a (yellow/blue)-equilibrium stimulus is a stimulus that appears neither yellowish nor bluish, that is, one that is perceived as having either the unique hue of red or the unique hue of green or is perceived as being achromatic (neutral).

In denoting the set of all stimuli in (red/green) equilibrium by S_1 and the set in (yellow/blue) equilibrium by S_2, the linearity laws may be formulated as follows:

Proportionality Law. If the stimulus A is in S_i, then the stimulus αA is also in S_i ($i = 1,2$), where α is any positive factor by which the radiance of the stimulus is increased or reduced while its relative spectral distribution is kept the same.

Additivity Law. If stimulus A is in S_i, then stimulus B is also in S_i if, and only if, the additive mixture of the two stimuli, that is, $A + B$, is in S_i ($i = 1,2$).

For a mathematically formal and detailed exposition of the linearity laws in the context of the opponent-colors theory, see Krantz (1975).

The tests of the linearity laws conducted by Larimer and coworkers (1974, 1975) and Cicerone and coworkers (1975) consisted first of the determination, at several luminance levels, of the monochromatic equilibrium stimuli (unique blue, green, and yellow) and the extraspectral equilibrium stimulus (unique red). Then the results of adding the equilibrium stimuli yellow and blue or the equilibrium stimuli red and green were studied.

The Abney and Bezold-Brücke effects (Sections 2.1 and 2.2) are obviously related to the question of the validity of the linearity laws. The proportionality law demands that the equilibrium stimuli are invariant and thus show no Bezold-Brücke hue shift with increasing or decreasing luminance. The additivity law demands that the equilibrium stimuli are invariant and thus show no Abney hue shift when they are desaturated by means of other equilibrium stimuli, in particular, by means of an equilibrium white stimulus.

The results obtained by Larimer and coworkers (1974, 1975) in their linearity tests may be summarized as follows:

1. The wavelengths of the monochromatic equilibrium stimuli perceived as unique yellow ($\approx$ 578 nm), green ($\approx$ 500 nm), and blue ($\approx$ 478 nm) were invariant, or virtually so, with luminance changes ranging over 2 log units. Zero Bezold-Brücke hue shifts were observed for these three stimuli.
2. For the equilibrium stimulus perceived as unique red, which is an extraspectral stimulus, that is, one that cannot be represented by a point on the spectrum locus, invariance with luminance did not hold. When the equilibrium stimulus was produced by an appropriate mixture of a monochromatic stimulus of long wavelength and a monochromatic stimulus of short wavelength, the real equilibrium stimulus turned bluish red when the luminance was increased while keeping its wavelength composition constant.
3. The additive mixture of the monochromatic equilibrium stimuli perceived as unique yellow and blue, in any luminance ratio, is again an equilibrium stimulus. Unique yellow and blue are found to be complementary hues relative to an equilibrium white. No Abney hue shift was observed when a yellow equilibrium stimulus or a blue equilibrium stimulus was desaturated with the equilibrium white stimulus. Additive mixtures of red and green equilibrium stimuli are again equilibrium stimuli, that is, neither yellowish nor bluish stimuli.

From the above experimental results, Larimer and coworkers (1974, 1975) drew the following conclusions.

1. The set of red/green equilibria, that is, stimuli that appear neither reddish nor greenish, obeys the linearity laws (proportionality and additivity). Thus the red/green chromatic-response function, such as that measured by Jameson and Hurvich by the method of hue cancellation (Figure 9.27), is a linear function of the observer's color-matching functions.
2. The set of yellow/blue equilibria, that is, stimuli that appear neither yellowish nor bluish, does not strictly obey the linearity laws. The observed nonlinearities are assumed to be associated only with the responses of the long-wavelength (red) cone mechanism that contributes to the perception of yellowness but via a compressive function of luminance. Thus the relative values of the yellow/blue chromatic-response function of Figure 9.27, determined for an equal-energy spectrum, must vary somewhat with the radiance level.

In a subsequent paper by the same authors (Cicerone, Krantz, & Larimer, 1975), the linearity laws are studied for moderate changes in the observer's state of chromatic adaptation caused by conditioning stimuli of unique blue, green, and yellow and by a (nonunique) monochromatic red stimulus of 650 nm, varying in luminances that provided retinal illuminances from 40 to 2000 td. The main results of this study indicate that adaptation to blue or green stimuli did not introduce significant failures of additivity of red/green equilibria; but adaptation to yellow stimuli of 900 td or more resulted in failures of proportionality and thus additivity. A small proportionality failure was also observed for red-conditioning stimuli at 40 td. The yellow/blue equilibria exhibited nonlinearities under chromatic adaptation that were of similar kind to those observed in the previous experiments, described here, which applied to conditions of dark adaptation.

Ingling and his coworkers (Ingling, Russell, Rea, & Tsou, 1978), tested the validity of the hue-cancellation method by determining the spectral response functions of the opponent channels by means of a hue-matching method that does not desaturate the test stimuli. They found that their method yields closely the same spectral response functions as the hue-cancellation method used by Jameson and Hurvich (1955) except in the violet region of the spectrum from about 400 to 480 nm. In that region the cancellation method indicates that there is about 30 times more redness than indicated by the hue-matching method. These results complicate the application of the spectral response functions to predictions of color-appearance phenomena. More experimental and theoretical work is needed to clarify the problem that has been revealed by Ingling and coworkers.

5.3. Application of Chromatic-Response Functions

In the application of chromatic-response functions to a wide range of color-vision problems, Hurvich and Jameson (1955) (see also Hurvich, 1981) assume for their own experimentally determined functions that the linearity laws hold strictly. This assumption permits them to replace their chromatic-response functions by others constructed from appropriate linear combinations of the CIE 1931 standard color-matching functions $\bar{x}(\lambda), \bar{y}(\lambda), \bar{z}(\lambda)$. The new chromatic-response functions are then regarded as applicable to the CIE 1931 standard observer. Figure 9.28 illustrates the chromatic-response functions postulated for the CIE 1931 standard observer by Hurvich and Jameson (1955) (see also Judd, 1951). For the luminance level (32 $cd{\cdot}m^{-2}$) of the stimuli used in their experiment, they put

$$y(\lambda) - b(\lambda) = 0.4\ \bar{y}(\lambda) - 0.4\ \bar{z}(\lambda)\ , \tag{44}$$

$$r(\lambda) - g(\lambda) = 1.0\ \bar{x}(\lambda) - 1.0\ \bar{y}(\lambda)\ , \tag{45}$$

where the quantities $y(\lambda) - b(\lambda)$ and $r(\lambda) - g(\lambda)$ are the yellow/blue and red/green chromatic-response functions represented in Eqs. (37) to (40) by $[\eta_Y(\lambda), \eta_B(\lambda)]$ and $[\eta_R(\lambda), \eta_G(\lambda)]$, respectively.

The chromatic-response functions characterizing two opponent processes in the visual system are supplemented by an achromatic-response function that characterizes the white/black-nonopponent process. The achromatic-response function is commonly identified as the luminous efficiency function obtained by the minimum-flicker method. The CIE 1924 standard luminous efficiency function $V(\lambda)$, which is by definition identical to $\bar{y}(\lambda)$, may be used for the purpose of numerical exercises; thus

$$w(\lambda) = 1.0\ \bar{y}(\lambda) \tag{46}$$

where $w(\lambda)$ denotes the white/black-nonopponent process.

A color stimulus with a relative spectral power distribution $P(\lambda)$, seen by an observer whose color-matching functions are those of the CIE 1931 standard colorimetric observer $\bar{x}(\lambda), \bar{y}(\lambda), \bar{z}(\lambda)$, elicits in the visual system of that observer chromatic and achromatic responses that can be calculated from:

[Yellow–Blue] Response

$$[J-B] = k\int_\lambda P(\lambda)[a_y\bar{y}(\lambda) - a_z\bar{z}(\lambda)]d\lambda\ ,$$

[Red–Green] Response

$$[R-G] = k\int_\lambda P(\lambda)[b_x\bar{x}(\lambda) - b_y\bar{y}(\lambda)]d\lambda\ ,$$

Achromatic [White] Response

$$[W] = kc_y\int_\lambda P(\lambda)\bar{y}(\lambda)d\lambda\ , \tag{47}$$

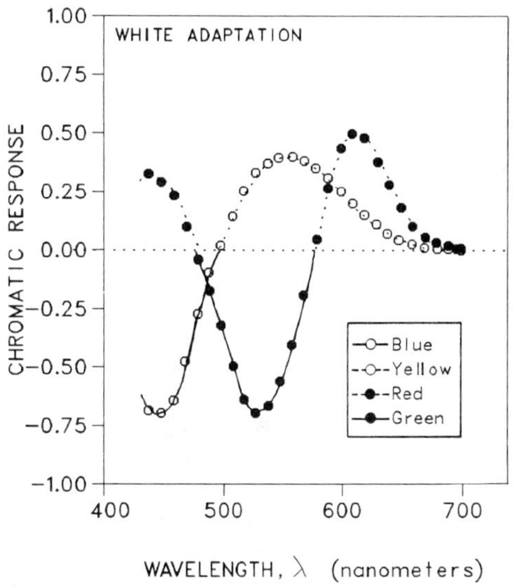

Figure 9.28. Chromatic-response functions postulated for the CIE 1931 standard observer. These functions are linear transformations of the CIE 1931 color-matching functions $\bar{x}(\lambda)$, $\bar{y}(\lambda)$, $\bar{z}(\lambda)$ and resemble the experimentally determined chromatic-response functions shown in Figure 9.27. (From L. M. Hurvich & D. Jameson, Some quantitative aspects of an opponent-colors theory. II. Brightness, saturation, and hue in normal and dichromatic vision, *Journal of the Optical Society of America*, 1955, *45*. Reprinted with permission.)

with k being a normalizing factor. The coefficients a_y, a_z, b_x, b_y, c_y depend on the observing conditions determining the state of adaptation of the observer's visual system and on the luminance of the given test stimulus $P(\lambda)$. For a test stimulus of about 30 $cd{\cdot}m^{-2}$, presented in a 1° circular field surrounded by a white conditioning stimulus (37°) of the same luminance, the coefficients given in Eqs. (44) to (46) apply; that is,

$$a_y = a_z = 0.4\ ,\quad b_x = b_y = c_y = 1.0\ .$$

When the state of adaptation of the observer's visual system changes, for example, due to a change in the conditioning stimulus presented in the surround, the chromatic-response functions change in a way that has yet to be established in quantitative terms (see the discussion of the problem of modeling chromatic induction and chromatic adaptation in Sections 3.5.2, 4.1, and 4.2). Furthermore, when the luminance level of the test stimulus is raised or lowered, the coefficients of Eq. (47) change to different values. These changes are assumed to be caused by changes in the relative rates of rise of the chromatic and achromatic responses with an increase in the luminance level (Hurvich, 1981). The Bezold-Brücke effect (Section 2.2) provides experimental evidence consistent with such differential changes.

The constraints on the coefficients in Eq. (47) put, so it seems, severe limitations on the applicability of these equations to color-engineering problems that involve observing conditions deviating substantially from those used in the determination of the chromatic-response functions. However, if one ignores these constraints, the algorithm implied in Eq. (47) can be pushed a little further by recalling that

$$X = k\int_\lambda P(\lambda)\bar{x}(\lambda)d\lambda\ ,$$

$$Y = k\int_\lambda P(\lambda)\bar{y}(\lambda)d\lambda\ ,$$

$$Z = k\int_{\lambda} P(\lambda)\bar{z}(\lambda)d\lambda \ , \quad (48)$$

are the tristimulus values of the test stimulus (see Chapter 8 by Pokorny and Smith), which allow us to rewrite Eq. (47) as follows:

$$[J-B] = a_y Y - a_z Z$$

$$[R-G] = b_x X - b_y Y$$

$$[W] = Y \ . \quad (49)$$

The positive or negative sign obtained for the J–B and R–G responses determines which part of the unique hues enters in the description of the hueness of the test stimulus. Table 9.2 shows the underlying scheme in accordance with the positive and negative lobes of the chromatic-response functions shown in Figure 9.28. For example, a positive value for J–B and negative value for R–G signifies a yellow-green, that is, a J–G test stimulus.

Hue coefficients can be calculated by forming the ratio of the absolute value of each of the two hue responses just obtained, over the sum of the absolute values of the two hue responses. For example, for a J–G test stimulus, the hue coefficients are obtained from

$$\frac{|J|}{|J| + |G|} \quad \text{and} \quad \frac{|G|}{|J| + |G|}$$

A *saturation coefficient* is obtained by forming the ratio of the total chromatic response (which equals the sum of the absolute values of the J–B and R–G responses) over the sum of the total chromatic response and the achromatic response (which equals the sum of absolute values of J–B, R–G, and W). For the previous example we would calculate the ratio

$$\frac{|J| + |G|}{|J| + |G| + |W|} \ .$$

6. UNIFORM COLOR SCALES

The experimental data and theoretical considerations underlying uniform color scales deal with the ability of the eye to judge differences in the basic attributes of color appearance, such as lightness, hue, and chroma.

A typical experimental situation is provided by a fixed illuminant (daylight, for example) under which material color samples (painted chips, colored papers, etc.) are exposed against a background surface, the latter being usually nonselectively reflecting but with an assigned reflectance that may range from high to low. All the color stimuli are then object-color stimuli whose CIE (X,Y,Z) tristimulus values define representative points contained in the object-color solid appropriate to the relative spectral radiant power distribution of the illuminant being used. Also, points in the object-color solid that mark out the graduations of any derived color scale are realizable, at least in principle, by actual samples. On the other hand, color scales can be constructed and formulated in terms that do not imply the foregoing object-color situation.

The usual judgments being made by observers often go beyond mere matching; the observers assess differences or equalities in certain attributes of their perception of the color stimuli presented to them, attributes which they themselves isolate subjectively. The attributes are initially undefined in any quantitative or numerical sense, and their scaling has to be constructed from the subjective judgments of a group of observers, obtained in extended studies.

An observer's judgment of the relative magnitude of two color differences rests on the subjective impressions the observer experiences when perceiving the two pairs of color stimuli. The judgment varies greatly with the viewing conditions and the kind of stimuli (samples) presented, and, in general, its precision compares poorly with that of complete color matching. The difficulty of making such judgments is reduced if the object-color perceptions are closely similar in one or two of the three basic attributes of color perception, such as hue, chroma, and lightness. Thus judgments of the relative sizes of lightness differences are readily made and with good precision if the stimuli viewed yield at least approximately the same hue and chroma. Similarly, judgments of differences in either hue or chroma, if the stimuli yield the same lightness, are not generally found difficult.

As the lightness, hue, and chroma differences to be judged become large, the observer finds it increasingly hard to assess their magnitude. There is also very little practical value in judging extremely large color differences. Of principal interest is the study of small differences and, in the limit, of differences which the observer finds to be *just noticeable* or to be on the *threshold*. Just noticeable or threshold differences may be considered as the natural units for measuring larger differences. However, the phenomena and concepts associated with threshold judgments differ in various ways from those involved in the assessment of small but clearly perceived color differences and are clearly beyond the scope of this chapter.

Also beyond the scope of this chapter is a detailed theoretical exposition of types of scales and scaling methods, but a brief account of the basic concepts and terms involved is given in Section 6.1. The reader is also referred to Chapter 1 by Falmagne and the excellent expositions given by Torgerson (1958), Krantz, Luce, Suppes, and Tversky (1971), Krantz (1972), Falmagne (1974), S. S. Stevens (1975), and Gescheider (1976).

Table 9.2. Scheme of Assigning the Percepts Yellow (*J*), Blue (*B*), Red (*R*), and Green (*G*) in Accordance with Positive (+) or Negative (−) Values Obtained by Calculation for the Opponent Responses *J*–*B* and *R*–*G*

	+	−
J–B	Yellow J	Blue B
R–G	Red R	Green G

Note: Yellow is denoted here by the letter J instead of the commonly used letter Y. The letter Y is used here to denote the CIE tristimulus value Y in Eq. (48) and (49).

6.1. Types of Scales

In recent years the fundamental concepts of scaling psychological and psychophysical attributes have been clarified greatly, and methods of scaling have been developed which, when combined with appropriate statistical techniques, provide powerful tools for the psychologist and psychophysicist. The application of these methods to the scaling of the attributes of color perception and to quantifying color discrimination is well established. The following notes are intended to bring together the basic concepts and terms often used in the development and application of color scales.

A *color scale* is a series of ordered numbers that represents observable gradations of a given attribute or gradations of a combination of attributes of color perception.

Different types of color scales can be established in accordance with different operations that can be performed on numbers. In following the exposition of Torgerson (1958), the following four types of scales may be used for *one-dimensional* attributes:

1. Ordinal scale
2. Ordinal scale with natural origin
3. Interval scale
4. Ratio scale

In the *ordinal scale*, the numbers y are assigned to the magnitudes x of the attribute, so that the order of the numbers corresponds to the order of these magnitudes. An ordinal scale is thus represented by a *monotonic function*, $y = f(x)$. Any other function $y = \phi(x)$ will also serve provided that $\phi(x)$ is related to $f(x)$ by a monotonic, that is, an order-preserving transformation.

With appropriately chosen sets of color stimuli, ordinal scales can be established readily for the perceptual attributes of lightness and of chroma. Consider, for example, a set of colored paint chips picked at random from the *Munsell Book of Color* (Section 7.1), illuminated by daylight, and displayed randomly in front of the observer. The observer will have little or no difficulty in ordering the chips in accordance with what the particular observer perceives their lightnesses to be under the given observing conditions. In fact, the only difficulty that the observer may have is one of conceptual nature concerning the term *lightness*. The observer's idea of what is meant by lightness may differ from that of the experimenter, particularly when the colored chips do not only vary in lightness but also in hue and chroma. However, in the case of lightness, such conceptual difficulties are rare and different observers agree remarkably well with each other's ordinal scales of lightness generated with a given set of colored paint chips.

Ordinal scales of chroma can also be established fairly readily, though the conceptual difficulties associated in this case are often more pronounced than in the case of lightness. In fact, other attributes have been identified that are related to chroma or to a combination of chroma and lightness. The attribute of *saturation* is the most prominent example of such another attribute (see also Section 1.4).

The attribute of hue perceived by the observer when viewing color stimuli does not present, in general, any conceptual difficulties as to what is meant by the term hue. It is also clear what is meant by ordering magnitudes of four attributes of *hueness*: redness, yellowness, greenness, and blueness. The four attributes are directly associated with the unique hues of red, yellow, green, and blue (Sections 1.3 and 5.1).

Although ordinal scales exist that have no natural origin, the most common attributes of color perception all have a *natural origin*; that is, there exists a point on the scale to which the number zero is assigned when the magnitude of the attribute considered is, in fact, perceived to be nil. Lightness, brightness, saturation, chroma, redness, yellowness, greenness, and blueness can each be characterized by an ordinal scale with a natural origin.

The basic property of an ordinal scale, that is, its monotonicity, is retained for ordinal scales with a natural origin within order-preserving (monotonic) transformations that include preserving the natural origin.

An *interval scale* is, in the first instance, an ordinal scale and as such fulfills all the requirements (postulates or axioms) of an ordinal scale. However, two additional requirements must be added:

1. Differences between different magnitudes can indeed be determined.
2. Numbers can be assigned to these magnitude differences so that the differences between numbers characterize the sizes of the corresponding observed magnitude differences of the attribute.

In scaling of psychological attributes, it has often been useful to introduce the notion of *distance*, that is, to identify an observed magnitude difference of the attribute by the distance (interval), say x, and then to represent x by a number y. The number y increases or decreases in direct proportion to an observed increase or decrease in distance x. It follows that in an interval scale the numbers are determined to within a linear transformation of the form

$$y = f(x) = mx + y_0 , \tag{50}$$

where m is any positive number and y_0 is any finite number.

A *ratio scale* is an interval scale with a natural origin. The invariance characteristics of an interval scale given by Eq. (50) are retained in the ratio scale except that now only one number, instead of two, may be assigned arbitrarily and the linear transformation within which the ratio scale remains invariant takes on the reduced form

$$y = f(x) = mx , \tag{51}$$

which leaves the natural origin of the ratio scale unchanged.

Both interval and ratio scales are by far the most useful scales in efforts of quantifying attributes of color perception. In the particular case in which adjacent intervals x (distances $x_1, x_2, x_3, \ldots$) are assigned the same number y ($y_1, y_2, y_3, \ldots$) throughout the domain of the attribute, we have an interval scale of equal spacing, which in the context of this chapter is referred to as a (one-dimensional) *uniform color scale*.

For a detailed formal treatment of the systems of axioms that govern ordinal and interval scales, the reader is referred to the book by Krantz, Luce, Suppes, and Tversky (1971), *Foundations of Measurement*.

6.2. Scaling Methods

Scaling methods are procedures that attempt to give quantitative descriptions of perceptual attributes. Different scaling methods have been used (for summaries see, for example, Gescheider, 1976, Krantz, 1972, S. S. Stevens, 1975, Torgerson, 1958; also see Chapter 1 by Falmagne), and the following have been selected from those most applicable to scaling the attributes of color perception.

6.2.1. Confusability Scaling. Confusability scaling refers to a procedure in which the observer is required to discriminate between color stimuli that evoke only slight differences in visual sensation. Typically, the stimulus confusions are defined by the *just noticeable difference* (jnd), or *just perceptible difference* (jpd), which serves as a unit of sensation difference. The definition of the jnd is usually linked with the numerical value of the *probability of confusion* or with some other *discriminability index*. The jnd concept is directly associated with the concept of threshold. The number of jnds is then counted to establish the desired scale, which is an *interval scale.*

A good example is obtained by considering an interval scale of brightness in which a stimulus of fixed relative spectral radiant power distribution is arbitrarily adjusted to luminance x providing the zero point of the scale. If y_1 denotes a slightly higher luminance of the same stimulus that is perceived as just noticeably brighter than x, then y_1 is assigned a brightness value of 1; if the luminance of the stimulus is raised to y_2, perceived as just noticeably brighter than y_1, and thus two jnds above x, y_2 is given the brightness value 2; and so forth.

For the interval scale constructed in this way to be useful, it is essential that the scale remains invariant, within a linear transform (Eq. (50)), when (1) the method by which discrimination is tested is changed and (2) another discriminability index is used to define the jnd. A discussion of the invariance of confusability (jnd) scales, when these two changes are introduced, has been given by Krantz (1972). A mathematically formal exposition of a theory of discrimination has been given by Falmagne (1974).

The *Weber law* and the *Fechner law* play key roles in the basic concepts of confusability scaling.

There is considerable evidence that shows when jnds are determined for a number of stimuli which differ with respect to the perceptual attribute (e.g., brightness), the size of the jnd, measured in physical or psychophysical units (e.g., radiance or luminance), for the given attribute depends on the magnitude of the stimuli involved. In general, it is found that the greater the magnitude of the stimuli, the greater the size of the jnd. This empirical fact is mathematically stated in Weber's law, that is,

$$\Delta x = k(x + x_0) , \tag{52}$$

where Δx is the increment that must be added to the magnitude x of the given stimulus to be just noticeable in accordance with some specified value of the discrimination index. The quantity x_0 is a constant, independent of the specified value of the discrimination index, and is often interpreted as internal noise in the visual mechanism. The proportionality constant k is called the *Weber fraction.*

Postulating that jnds are equal increments Δs in sensation magnitude at all stimulus magnitudes and assuming that the empirical Weber law is valid, it follows that

$$\Delta s = k' \frac{\Delta x}{x + x_0} , \tag{53}$$

with k' being a constant factor specifying an appropriate unit of the sensation-magnitude increment. By treating Δs and Δx as differentials ds and dx, respectively, Eq. (53) can be integrated

$$s(x) = \int ds = k' \int \frac{dx}{x + x_0} ,$$

which leads to the expression of the form

$$s(x) = a + b \log(x + x_0) , \tag{54}$$

relating by a logarithmic function the stimulus magnitude x, measured in terms of a physical or psychophysical unit, to the sensation magnitude s. The quantities a and b are constants. The relation expressed by Eq. (54) is known as the Fechner law.

Another important concept in confusability scaling is the *law of comparative judgment* derived by Thurstone (1927).

Thurstone (1927) postulates that each stimulus, when presented to an observer, has a variable effect on a hypothetical continuum of sensation magnitude. The variability is described by a normally distributed random variable, called a *discriminable process.* The mean and standard deviation of the normal distribution associated with each given stimulus are taken as its scale value and discriminal dispersion, respectively.

For example, if we are required to judge which of two given stimuli, one of luminance x and the other of luminance y, we perceive as being the brighter of the two, we sample randomly from the bivariate normal distribution defined by the two discriminal processes and choose whichever value is the higher. If we then denote the means of the two discriminal processes by $S(x)$ and $S(y)$ and their standard deviations by $\sigma(x)$ and $\sigma(y)$, respectively, with $\rho(x, y)$ being the correlation coefficient, the probability, $P(y,x)$, that y is perceived brighter than x is then simply the probability that the difference between the sampled sensation magnitude evoked by y and the sampled sensation magnitude evoked by x is positive. This sample difference is normally distributed and has a mean value equal to the difference $S(\lambda) - S(x)$ of the means of the two-dimensional processes with a standard deviation $\sigma(y,x)$ given by

$$\sigma(y,x) = [\sigma^2(y) + \sigma^2(x) - 2\rho(y,x)\sigma(y)\sigma(x)]^{1/2} . \tag{55}$$

It follows that

$$P(y,x) = f^{-1}\left[\frac{S(y) - S(x)}{\sigma(y,x)}\right] , \tag{56}$$

where f^{-1} denotes the familiar cumulative normal distribution function, that is,

$$f^{-1}(t) = \frac{1}{\sqrt{2\pi}} \int_{-\infty}^{t} \exp\,[\exp - \omega^2/2]\,d\omega .$$

The special case in which both $\sigma(x)$ and $\rho(y,x)$ are constant, and thus, in accordance with Eq. (55),

$$\sigma(y,x) = \text{constant} , \tag{57}$$

is known as *Thurstone's Case V*. Krantz (1972), whose exposition we have followed here, notes that in this case Fechner's law of sensation would be justified.

If Thurstone's Case V does not apply, that is,

$$\sigma(y,x) \neq \text{constant} ,$$

and, in particular, if nonconstancy of $\sigma(y,x)$ is caused by $\rho(y,x)$ being some function of the discriminability defined by $P(y,x)$, it can be shown (Krantz, 1972) that the standard deviation of the discriminal process is a linear function of its mean and that the sensation magnitude follows a *power law.* Thus

$$S(x) = a + b(x + x_0)^P$$

and

$$\sigma(x) = c(x + x_0)^P \qquad (58)$$

or

$$\sigma(x) = \left(\frac{c}{b}\right) [S(x) - a] \; .$$

S. S. Stevens (1959) has referred to the above case as *Thurstone's Case VI* and the power function, given in a slightly different form, is called the *Stevens law*, though it is usually based on direct estimation and not on confusability scaling (Gescheider, 1976) (see also Section 6.2.2).

The *method of paired comparisons* readily follows from the law of comparative judgment under the condition characterizing Thurstone's Case V. From Eqs. (56) and (57) we deduce

$$S(y) - S(x) = \sigma f[P(y,x)] \; , \qquad (59)$$

where σ is a constant and can be set equal to unity. The difference between the scale values $S(y)$ and $S(x)$ of the two given stimuli (y and x) is then given as the inverse normal transform f of the probability $P(y, x)$.

For n given stimuli, denoted by $x_1, x_2, \ldots, x_n$, there exist $n(n-1)/2$ pairs of stimuli. Each pair is presented to the observer who is required to indicate which member of the pair appears greater with respect to the perceptual attribute to be scaled (e.g., brightness). The observer must designate one member of the pair as greater; no equality judgments are allowed. To make adequate estimates of the proportion of greater, a large number of comparisons must be made for each pair of stimuli. This may be accomplished by (1) having a single observer judge each stimulus pair many times, (2) having each of many observers judge each pair just once, and (3) having each of several observers judge each pair several times. The particular method (1, 2, or 3) to be used depends on the aim of the experiment and the type of stimuli involved. Details of the numerical procedures commonly used in analyzing paired comparisons are given, for example, by Torgerson (1958).

6.2.2. Scaling by Direct Estimation. Methods of direct estimation of the magnitude of a given perceptual attribute may be grouped into *partition scaling* and *ratio scaling*.

Partition scaling yields an equal-interval scale of the perceptual attribute with boundaries identified by specific stimuli. In the equisection method, the observer is required to choose from a large number of stimuli, representing the perceptual attribute over a certain range of magnitudes, those stimuli that result in a specified number of perceptually equal differences. In the method of equal-appearing intervals, a common form of category scaling, the observer is required to assign all stimuli of the large set of given stimuli to a specified number of categories. In this technique, it is assumed that the observer is capable of keeping the intervals between the boundaries of the categories perceptually equal as the observer assigns stimuli to the various categories. The experimenter then treats the category value assigned to a particular stimulus as a value on the interval scale.

Ratio scaling yields an equal-interval scale of the perceptual attribute that includes a natural origin; that is, it yields a ratio scale. The specific techniques used in ratio scaling are often referred to as *ratio production, ratio estimation, magnitude estimation*, and *magnitude production*. In each case, the observer is required to judge the ratio between two magnitudes of the perceptual attribute under study.

In ratio production, also known as *fractionation*, the observer adjusts a variable stimulus while observing a reference stimulus. Prescribed magnitude (e.g., brightness) ratios between test and reference stimuli are produced by the observer.

In ratio estimation, the observer estimates the magnitude ratio between the given test and reference stimuli; no adjustment by the observer of either the test or the reference stimulus is made.

In magnitude estimation, the observer makes direct estimates of the perceived magnitudes of given stimuli and assigns appropriate numbers to the estimates. Of the four techniques used in ratio scaling, the one referred to as magnitude estimation is the most commonly used in color-perception studies. A commonly used form of instruction (S. S. Stevens, 1975) given to the observer is the following:

> You will be presented with a series of stimuli in irregular order. Your task is to tell how intense (bright, saturated, etc.) they seem by assigning numbers to them. Call the first stimulus any number that seems appropriate to you. Then assign successive numbers in such a way that they reflect your subjective impression. There is no limit to the range of numbers that you may use. You may use whole numbers, decimals, or fractions. Try to make each number match the intensity (brightness, saturation, etc.) as you perceive it. (p. 30)

In magnitude production, the observer adjusts a variable stimulus to produce a perceived magnitude whose numerical value seems to match that of the magnitude of some given stimulus.

It is important to note that all so-called direct-estimation methods of scaling imply that the observer makes comparative judgments of at least two pairs of stimuli. The number assigned to the perceived magnitude of a given stimulus must be in proportion to the magnitude of at least one previous stimulus, presented earlier in the particular experiment or remembered by the observer from the observer's bank of experience with color stimuli. Thus direct estimation of the magnitude of a given perceptual attribute cannot, strictly speaking, be an *absolute measure* of the attribute's magnitude.

A great deal of experimental evidence exists that for many one-dimensional continua, not only those experienced in color perception, the mean estimate $\psi(x)$ of the magnitude of a given attribute increases approximately as a power function of the intensity x of the stimulus exhibiting that attribute; that is,

$$\psi(\lambda) = bx^p \; . \qquad (60)$$

In this *power law*, S. S. Stevens (1975) considers the exponent p the parameter that characterizes the perceptual continuum (loudness, $p = 0.67$; brightness, $p = 0.33$; taste, e.g., salt, $p = 1.4$; smell, $p = 0.6$; heaviness, $p = 1.45$). In each case, p may vary somewhat with individuals and with stimulating conditions (e.g., state of adaptation), but nonetheless a representative value of p seems to exist for each of many perceptual continua. The exponent p is generally estimated from the slope of the power function in log-log coordinates, that is, from

$$\log \psi(x) = \log b + p \log x \; . \qquad (61)$$

When the variable x has low values, a better agreement between magnitude estimation and power function is obtained by introducing a constant in Eq. (60). Three different forms have been used:

$$\psi(x) = b\,(x - x_0)^p \;, \tag{62}$$

$$\psi(x) = bx^p - \psi_0 \;, \tag{63}$$

$$\psi(x) = b\,[(x + x_0)^p - x_0{}^p] \;. \tag{64}$$

In Eq. (62), the constant x_0 is sometimes interpreted as the stimulus intensity at which absolute threshold is observed. Thus the constant shifts the stimulus scale so that its zero point corresponds to the zero point on the perceptual scale (Ekman, 1956; J. C. Stevens & S. S. Stevens, 1963). However, the connection between x_0 and the concept of threshold in the conventional sense of a statistical quantity is not made clear. In Eq. (63), the subtractive constant ψ_0 is used, which Jameson and Hurvich (1964) introduced to account for simultaneous contrast effects. In Eq. (64) the constant x_0 is chosen to represent a special case of the earlier expressions, given as Eq. (58), which arose from the combination of the Weber law and the law of comparative judgment of Thurstone (Krantz, 1972).

The three variants of the power law given by Eqs. (62), (63), and (64) exhibit an asymptotic slope p when log $\psi(x)$ is plotted against log x. In the case of $0 < p < 1$, the slopes for small x values are steeper than p; this correlates well with most experimental data.

6.2.3. Multidimensional Scaling. The scales considered in Section 6.2.2 are one-dimensional scales; that is, they quantify attributes whose perceived magnitudes or magnitude differences form a one-dimensional series of numbers. In that context, the attribute itself is considered a one-dimensional continuum that can be represented geometrically by a straight line. When taking "color" as the attribute to be scaled, instead of just one of its component attributes (e.g., lightness, hue, or chroma), it is immediately obvious that the scaling problem is more complex and the magnitude differences that one may wish to scale may form a *multidimensional series* with its geometrical representation in a *multidimensional space*. Each observed magnitude difference is, in effect, assigned a *set* of numbers which, in terms of a specified geometrical system, characterizes the relations between the various observed magnitude differences, each of which is represented by a *point* in the multidimensional space. The number of numbers assigned to each observed magnitude difference specifies the dimensionality of the space and thus the dimensionality of the attribute.

There are different spaces, each characterized by a different *metric*, that can be employed as the underlying geometrical model for multidimensional scaling. The Euclidean metric is the one most commonly used, but other metrics and even *nonmetric* multidimensional-scaling procedures have been developed. An excellent introductory booklet on multidimensional scaling has been written by Kruskal and Wish (1978) in which the reader will find many worked examples of multidimensional scaling demonstrating different analysis procedures and data interpretations. Details of computational procedures, all of which require a computer, have been given, for example, by Kruskal (1976). Also the books by Shepard, Romney, and Nerlove (1972) and by Schiffman, Reynolds, and Young (1981) contain useful information.

Multidimensional scaling is an indirect method for determining the number of the component attributes that are evoked by a given set of color stimuli. It also offers the possibility of extracting the internal structure of the given observational data that may offer useful insights into the visual mechanism itself. In following Shepard's (1962) method, which is widely used in practice, for each pair of stimuli some proximity measure is first obtained. Then one looks for a configuration of points in Euclidean space, one point corresponding to the observed magnitude of the attribute associated with each stimulus, such that the ordering of magnitude proximities between stimuli is reproduced as closely as possible by the ordering of the inverse distances between the corresponding points. The aim is to generate a reproduction of the proximity ordering in as small a number of dimensions of the Euclidean space as possible. In general, the computational procedure provides a good fit for a dimensionality $> n$, but the goodness of the fit seems to collapse abruptly for dimensionality $n-1$. When this occurs, it is concluded that the proximities are based on variations in n independent perceptual component attributes. Often, an attempt is also made to draw inferences on the nature of the component attributes, but this is difficult because the principal axes that the analysis provides are only unique within an arbitrary rotation and translation in the given space model. However, a kind of informal principal-axes analysis can sometimes lead to a useful insight into the nature of the component attributes.

In color perception, the dimensionality problem is, in general, of lesser concern to the researcher than it is in other fields of behavioral or social study. There is overwhelming evidence, originating from psychophysical experiments, that perceived color is a three-dimensional attribute, whose most commonly isolated component attributes are hue, chroma, and lightness. In fact, the three-dimensionality of perceived color is considered so well founded that it is often used as a criterion for the validity of a particular multidimensional analysis.

Multidimensional color scaling has been used in many studies. The following is a selection of such studies: Carroll and Wish (1974), Helm (1964), Indow (1963), Shepard (1962), and Torgerson (1958).

6.3 Brightness and Lightness Scales

6.3.1. Achromatic and Homochromatic Brightness Scales. *Brightness* is defined as the attribute of a visual sensation according to which a given visual stimulus appears to be more or less intense or according to which the area in which the visual stimulus is presented appears to emit more or less light. The magnitude of brightness can be estimated for *unrelated* visual stimuli as well as for *related* visual stimuli (Section 1.1).

Brightness scales have been determined for a variety of observing conditions by several investigators, notably by S. S. Stevens and his collaborators (Aiba & S. S. Stevens, 1964; J. C. Stevens & S. S. Stevens, 1963; S. S. Stevens & Diamond, 1965), Jameson and Hurvich (1964), Bartleson and Breneman (1967), Jameson, (1970), and Bodmann, Haubner, and Marsden, (1980). A power law is generally found to provide a satisfactory fit to the experimental data. Recent studies, particularly those by Bodmann, Haubner, and Marsden (1980), provide a convincing case that the power law in the form of

$$B = a\,L^p - B_0 \tag{65}$$

is to be preferred over other forms favored by other investigators, for example, by S. S. Stevens and his collaborators. In Eq. (65),

B denotes a measure of the brightness estimated by an observer presented with a stimulus of luminance L under specified conditions of observation. The exponent p has a value of approximately ⅓; Bodmann and colleagues (1980) find $p = 0.31 \pm 0.03$ for a variety of experimental conditions and different observers. The values of a and B_0 depend on the observing conditions (such as field size of test stimulus, luminance of surround) and include an arbitrary scaling factor. The term B_0 has been given a plausible physiological interpretation by Jameson and Hurvich (1964) (see also Jameson, 1970) who see it as a response correction caused by the neural process of *induction* when the test stimulus is viewed in a surround of nonzero luminance. Haubner (1977) has advanced this idea further.

Figure 9.29 illustrates typical results of brightness-scaling experiments. The two curves were drawn from data obtained by Bodmann and coworkers (1980). They refer to brightness scaling made with a dark surround (0 cd·m^{-2}) and with a surround of luminance 300 cd·m^{-2}. In both cases of observing conditions, interval scaling (bisection method) and ratio scaling (magnitude estimation) were used to derive the corresponding brightness scales. The test stimuli had an angular subtense of 2° and the surround was 180°. Both test and surround stimuli were achromatic. Contrary to work by S. S. Stevens and his collaborators, Bodmann and coworkers find that brightness scales obtained by bisection are *linearly* related to those obtained by magnitude estimation.

Homochromatic brightness scales are obtained when the test stimulus is chromatic, that is, has a given chromaticity eliciting a hue response. The functional relationship between the observed brightness measure B and the luminance L of the test stimulus is expected to be the same as that given in Eq. (65), but detailed experimental data do not seem to be available.

6.3.2. Achromatic and Homochromatic Lightness Scales. *Lightness* is defined as the attribute of a visual sensation according to which the area in which the visual stimulus is presented appears to emit more or less light in proportion to that emitted by a similarly illuminated area perceived as a "white" stimulus. Lightness is thus an attribute of visual sensation

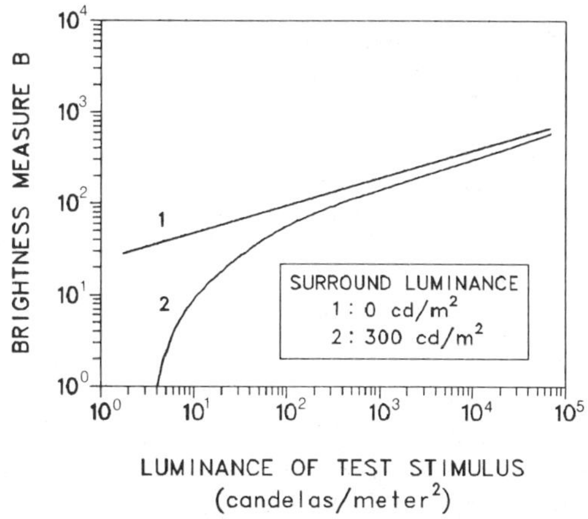

Figure 9.29. Functional relationship between brightness and luminance for two different surround luminances. Both the test (2°) and the surround (180°) stimuli are achromatic. In the case of the nonzero surround (curve 2), the brightness measure B decreases sharply for test stimuli whose luminances are less than the luminance of the surround. This decrease in brightness measure is caused by induction. (After Bodmann, Haubner, & Marsden, 1980.)

that has meaning only for related visual stimuli. As lightness is judged with reference to the brightness of a white stimulus, it may be considered a special form of brightness measure that could be referred to as *relative brightness*.

Perhaps the largest body of existing data on uniform color scales is the one dealing with the establishment of uniform lightness scales for a variety of conditions of observation. These data refer to homochromatic samples that have approximately the same hue and chroma and that differ only in lightness. Most of the investigations are subject to the restriction that they deal with *achromatic* stimuli only, and the lightness scales then developed are often called *gray scales*.

One way of developing a gray scale is by the method of bisection, which leads to an interval scale. The observer is given a black chip, a white chip, and a number of different gray chips and is asked to select a gray that appears about as different from white as it does from black. Then the interval between the black and midgray is halved by the same procedure and also that between white and midgray, resulting in a gray scale extending from black to white by four steps perceived to be equal. The uniform subdivision can be continued, following the same procedure, and a multiple-step gray scale is then obtained.

The results of such experiments are conveniently represented in a graph where the ordinate is the number of lightness steps V between black and each gray and the abscissa is the luminance factor Y of the corresponding chip. The relationship between V and Y can be expressed by an empirical formula, which in more recent investigations has commonly taken the form of a power function, in accordance with the notion of the power law defined by Eq. (65). Table 9.3 lists a number of formulas reported by different investigators and Figure 9.30 shows the corresponding graphical relations between V and Y.

There are important differences between some of the curves, which mean that the spacing of the lightness scales, represented by the curves, is different. For example, the luminance factor of the middle gray ($V = 5$) for curve 5 corresponds to that for the third step ($V = 3$) for curve 1. These differences are generally attributed to the differences in the observing conditions to which the different lightness scales are intended to apply. In particular, the luminance factor of the background is considered the most important parameter influencing the spacing of a lightness scale. The background essentially controls the induction and adaptation processes in the observer's eyes, particularly when the scale samples are relatively small.

Studies of the influence of achromatic induction and adaptation on lightness and its uniform scaling have been made for quite some time. Notable examples of early studies are those by Adams and Cobb (1922) and Judd (1940). But it was only in recent years that a much clearer picture has emerged. The studies by Kaneko (1964), Takasaki (1966), and Semmelroth (1970, 1971) are of particular interest to lightness scaling. Wyszecki and Stiles (1982) have reviewed these studies.

In homochromatic lightness scales the test stimuli have a constant hue and chroma, usually fixed (approximately) by keeping the chromaticity constant. The functional relationship between the observed lightness measure V and the luminance factor Y is the same as the one applicable to a gray scale, typically a power law of the form of Eq. (65), but the coefficients may take on different values.

6.3.3. Heterochromatic Brightness and Lightness Scales. Heterochromatic brightness matching is one of several criteria used to arrive at luminous efficiency functions (see Chapter 8

Table 9.3. Selected Formulae for Calculating Lightness-Scale Values V from Luminance Factors Y of Gray Paint Chips

1. Priest, Gibson, and McNicholas (1920):

$$V = 10Y^{1/2}$$

Used in connection with the original Munsell system. Applies best to observations with a white background (Godlove, 1933; Munsell, Sloan, & Godlove, 1933).

2. Munsell, Sloan, and Godlove (1933); Godlove (1933):

$$V = (1.474\,Y - 0.00474\,Y^2)^{1/2}$$

A modified version of (1); applies best to observations with a middle-gray background of luminance factor $Y_b = 19.1$.

3. Newhall, Nickerson, and Judd (1943):

$$\frac{100\,Y}{Y_{MgO}} = 1.2219V - 0.23111V^2 + 0.23951V^3 - 0.021009V^4 + 0.0008404V^5$$

Used in connection with the Munsell renotation system (Section 7.1). Applies best to observations with a middle-gray background ($Y_b \approx 20$). Defines Munsell value in the Munsell renotation system. The luminance factor Y is relative to magnesium oxide taken as 97.5%; this gives a value of $Y = 102.568$ for $V = 10$.

4. CIE (1976):

$$V = 25\left(\frac{100\,Y}{Y_o}\right)^{1/3} - 16$$

CIE (1976) lightness function $L^*(\equiv V)$. The luminance factor Y_0 refers to the nominally white object-color stimulus; usually $Y_0 = 100$.

5. Foss, Nickerson, and Granville (1944):

$$V = 0.25 + 5\log_{10}Y$$

Defines the gray scale of *Color Harmony Manual* and is based on Weber's law. Note that $V = 0$ corresponds to a good pigment black ($Y = 0.009$); $V = 10$ corresponds to a good pigment white ($Y = 0.891$). Applies best to observations with a gray background whose luminance factor is close to that of the gray chips being compared for their lightness difference.

6. Richter (1953):

$$V = 6.1723\log(40.7Y + 1)$$

Used in connection with the gray scale of the DIN color chart and is based on a modified Delboeuff formula. Applies best to observations with a gray background of luminance $Y_b \approx 50\%$.

by Pokorny and Smith). In a typical experimental procedure the monochromatic test stimulus of wavelength λ is matched in brightness against a fixed reference stimulus usually of a white appearance. Test and reference stimuli are presented in a centrally viewed bipartite field of given angular subtense, for example, 2°. Such an experiment is a special case of the general visual task of making direct heterochromatic brightness matches of test stimuli of arbitrary spectral radiant power distributions (not restricted to a single wavelength) against a given reference stimulus. The general case is of particular interest to practical photometry of colored lights, such as navigational signals and video displays.

When a test stimulus of complex spectral radiant power distribution has been matched in brightness against a fixed white reference stimulus, it is generally found that the luminance of the chromatic test stimulus is lower than the luminance of the reference stimulus. Or, stating it another way, a chromatic stimulus of the same luminance as the white reference stimulus will, in general, appear brighter than the reference stimulus. To many observers the chromatic stimulus appears to "glow" (or appears to exhibit "Farbenglut"). The effect is sometimes referred to as the *Helmholtz-Kohlrausch effect* (see, for example, Judd, 1958; Kohlrausch, 1935; König, 1947).

If the luminance of the reference stimulus is denoted by $L_R \equiv B$ and that of the test stimulus by $L_T \equiv L$, the ratio B/L is, in general, greater than unity and increases with increasing saturation (or excitation purity) of the test stimulus when the reference stimulus has zero saturation, that is, has an achromatic appearance. An exception to this rule is often reported for yellow stimuli for which B/L remains close to unity even at maximum saturation.

In deriving the B/L ratio for the brightness-matched reference and test stimuli, the basic equation of photometry is used, that is,

$$L\ (\text{or } B) = K_m \int_\lambda L_{e\lambda} V(\lambda)\, d\lambda\ , \qquad (66)$$

where $L_{e\lambda}$ is the spectral concentration of radiance of the stimulus (either test or reference), $V(\lambda)$ is the CIE 1924 standard photopic luminous efficiency at wavelength λ, and K_m is a constant fixed at 683 $lm \cdot W^{-1}$. This equation implies that the basic laws of brightness matching, particularly the proportionality and additivity laws, often referred to as *Abney's laws*, hold strictly.

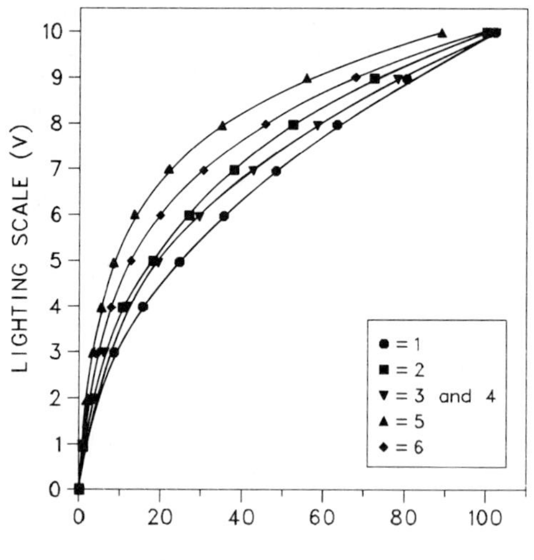

Figure 9.30. Relationship between lightness-scale value V and luminance factor Y plotted in accordance with different formulae (see Table 9.3). (1) Priest, Gibson, and McNicholas (1920); (2) Godlove (1933); Munsell, Sloan, and Godlove (1933); (3) Newhall, Nickerson, and Judd (1943) (also known as the Munsell renotation-value scale); (4) CIE (1976) lightness scale (plotting $V = L^*/10$); (5) Foss, Nickerson, and Granville (1944) (gray scale of the *Color Harmony Manual*); (6) Richter (1953) (gray scale of the German *DIN Color Chart*), (plotting $V = 10 - D$). (From G. Wyszecki & W. S. Stiles, *Color science*, 2nd ed. Copyright 1982 by John Wiley & Sons, Inc. Reprinted with permission.)

Deviations from unity of the B/L ratios for brightness-matched reference and test stimulus can be caused by any of the following:

1. The use of the wrong $V(\lambda)$ function in Eq. (66)
2. The failure of Abney's laws
3. Both (1) and (2) simultaneously

The experimental evidence is that another $V(\lambda)$ function, such as Judd's modified $V(\lambda)$ function or one based on direct heterochromatic brightness matching, if used in place of the CIE standard $V(\lambda)$ function in Eq. (66), does not yield B/L ratios of unity for chromatic test stimuli, each of which is brightness-matched against a given white reference stimulus. Abney's additivity law is not valid for the general case of direct heterochromatic brightness matching.

There are several experimental studies on heterochromatic brightness matching of stimuli of complex spectral radiant power distributions. Of particular interest are the studies of Chapanis and Halsey (1955), Sanders and Wyszecki (1957, 1958, 1964), Wyszecki and Sanders (1957), Breneman (1958), Wyszecki (1967), Kaiser and Smith (1972), and Alman (1977). The paper by Dresler (1953) summarizes the more important studies on the subject matter available up to 1952.

Two sets of experimental data have been selected to illustrate the general trend found by most investigators. The first set has been taken from the paper by Sanders and Wyszecki (1964). Twenty observers with normal color vision made direct heterochromatic brightness matches of 95 test stimuli of different chromaticities against a white reference stimulus of a fixed chromaticity. A 10° bipartite visual field was used surrounded by a white field of approximately 40° × 40° angular subtense.

Each observer viewed the visual field with both eyes; strict fixation was avoided by encouraging frequent direct views of the white surround for the purpose of controlling to some extent the state of adaptation of the observer's eyes. The test stimuli presented in one half of the bipartite field were kept at a constant luminance $L = 20\ \text{cd}\cdot\text{m}^{-2}$, while the luminance B of the white reference stimulus was changed by the observer until equality of brightness between the two halves was perceived. The luminances L and B were calculated in accordance with Eq. (66) but using the $\bar{y}_{10}(\lambda)$ function as the luminous efficiency function $V(\lambda)$.

From the results of such observations curved lines of constant values of the B/L ratio can be plotted in the chromaticity diagram to illustrate how brightness changes with the chromaticity of test stimuli of constant ($20\ \text{cd}\cdot\text{m}^{-2}$) luminance. Figure 9.31 illustrates such a set of contour lines. The further the chromaticity point of the test stimulus is from that of the white reference stimulus, the brighter the test stimulus appears against the white reference stimulus of the same luminance.

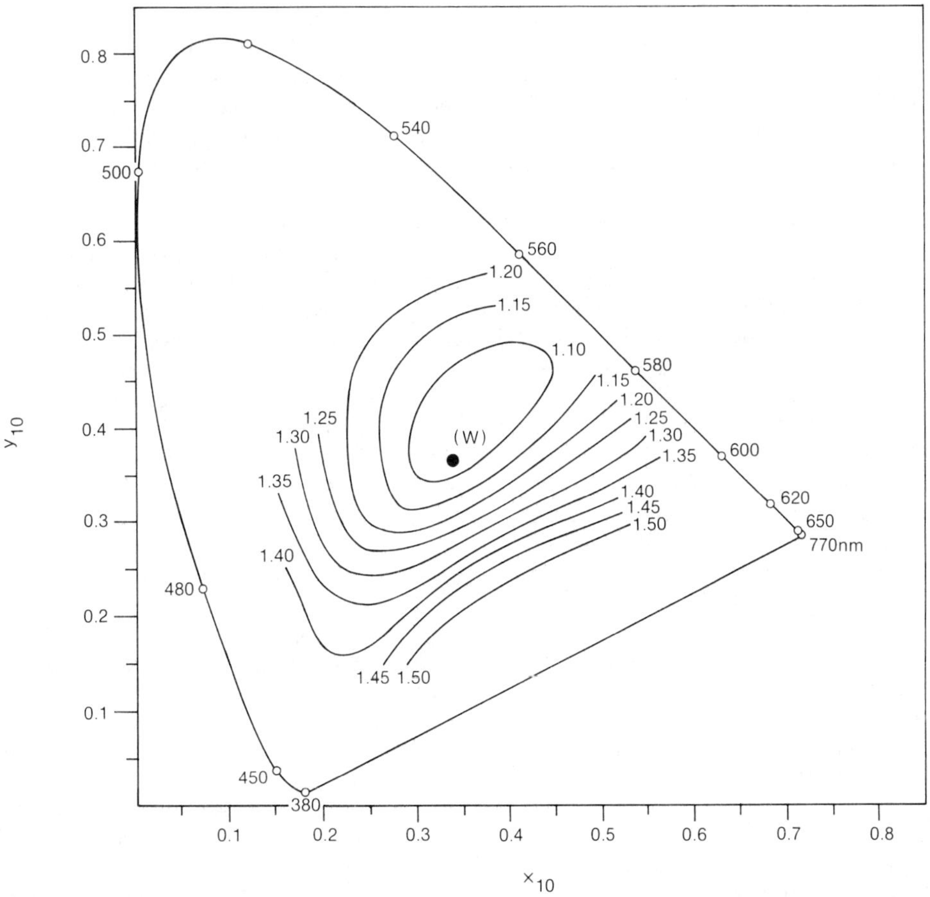

Figure 9.31. CIE 1964 (x_{10},y_{10}) chromaticity diagram showing mean and smoothed loci of constant values of observed B/L ratios for a group of 20 observers making heterochromatic brightness matches. In order to make a test stimulus of given (x_{10},y_{10}) chromaticity coordinates and luminance $20\ \text{cd}\cdot\text{m}^{-2}$ match in brightness with the given reference stimulus W, the luminance of the test stimulus must be reduced by dividing it by the value of B/L applicable to the chromaticity point of the test stimulus. (From G. Wyszecki & W. S. Stiles, *Color science*, 2nd ed. Copyright 1982 by John Wiley & Sons, Inc. Reprinted with permission.)

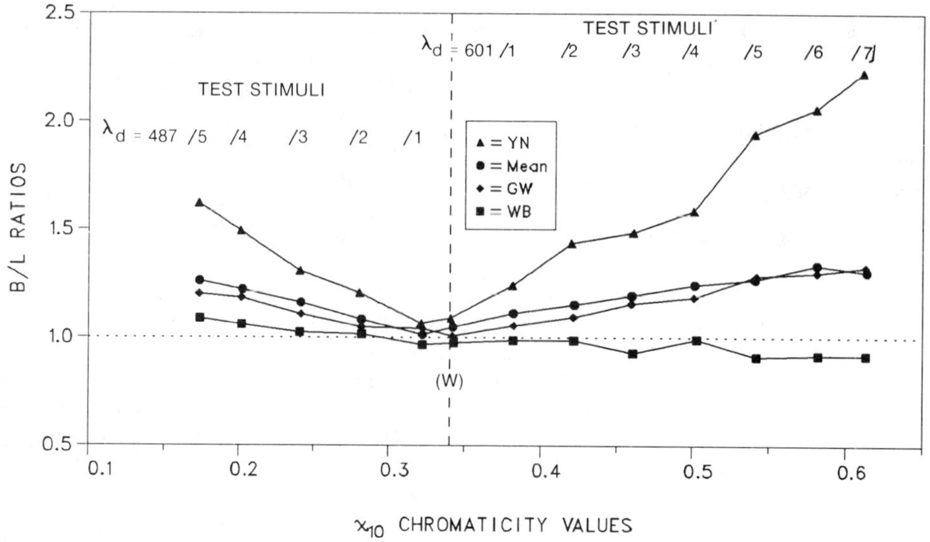

Figure 9.32. Examples of the variation of *B*/*L* ratios between different observers. Diagram shows *B*/*L* ratios for observers YN, GW, and WB in comparison with the mean ratios of a group of 20 observers. Note that YN represents an observer with very high ratios, GW is one with average ratios, and WB is one with unusually low ratios. The test stimuli are of constant dominant wavelength λ_d = 601 nm and λ_d = 487 nm; their x_{10} chromaticity values are plotted along the abscissa of the diagram. (From G. Wyszecki & W. S. Stiles, *Color science*, 2nd ed. Copyright 1982 by John Wiley & Sons, Inc. Reprinted with permission.)

To make the white reference stimulus appear equally bright to the test stimulus of 20 $cd{\cdot}m^{-2}$, its luminance must be raised by a factor equal to the *B*/*L* ratio determined for that test stimulus. Similarly, it follows that for a test stimulus to be equally bright to a white reference stimulus of constant luminance (20 $cd{\cdot}m^{-2}$), the luminance of the test stimulus must be lowered by the factor *L*/*B*.

The variation of *B*/*L* ratios between different observers is fairly large. An example is given in Figure 9.32.

The second set of experimental data has been taken from a paper by Wyszecki (1967), which reports on an experiment conducted by the Committee on Uniform Color Scales of the Optical Society of America (see also Section 7.2). In this experiment, the 43 object-color stimuli used were made up of colored ceramic tiles illuminated by either natural daylight or an equivalent artificial daylight source.

A total of 76 observers located in different laboratories in the United States and Canada took part in the experiment. Each colored tile was compared in lightness with a set of 10 gray tiles, which provided a scale of known luminous reflectances ranging from Y_{N_1} = 28.12 to $Y_{N_{10}}$ = 52.46 in perceptual intervals approximately equal in size. The observer was asked to find, for each chromatic tile, the gray tile that he or she perceived as being of the same lightness as the given chromatic tile. If necessary, the observer interpolated between two neighboring gray tiles. The luminance factor Y_N of the gray tile that matched in lightness the given chromatic tile of luminance factor Y was then used to form the ratio Y_N/Y.

As for the previous set of experimental data, the results can be illustrated effectively by means of loci of constant values of Y_N/Y ratio in the CIE 1931 (x,y) chromaticity diagram. A family of such loci is shown in Figure 9.33. The chromaticity gamut provided by the daylight-illuminated colored tiles is somewhat smaller than that available on the colorimeter used in the first experiment, but in the region where the two gamuts overlap, the two families of loci shown in Figures 9.31 and 9.33, respectively, exhibit similar features. A quantitative comparison between the two sets of data is, however, difficult and has not been attempted because of the marked differences in the observing conditions used in the two experiments and possibly other, yet unspecified, parameters. The experimental data base available in the literature appears inadequate to permit the establishment of satisfactory standard heterochromatic brightness or lightness scales at this time. The lack of adequate experimental data makes it also difficult to construct a satisfactory color-vision model of heterochromatic brightness matching, though several attempts have been made (see, for example, Guth, Massof, & Benzschawel, 1980).

The failure of the additivity law of brightness matching is assumed to be at the root of the problem, and several studies of this law have been made. More recent work in this field includes that of Boynton and Kaiser (1968), Guth, Donley, and Marrocco (1969), Guth (1970), Guth and Lodge (1973), Wagner and Boynton (1972), and Kaiser and Wyszecki (1978).

6.4. Color Scales of Constant Lightness

Uniform scaling of the lightness of object-color stimuli perceived to have approximately the same hue and chroma is a specially simple case because a single variable only is involved. With more than one variable, the possibility of uniform scaling depends on the observer's judgments satisfying a further requirement. Consider all object-color stimuli having a particular fixed lightness; their representative points defined in terms of tristimulus values, in the object-color solid, will generate a surface that is not necessarily contained in a plane. Two pairs of stimuli belonging to this surface that are judged by observers to present the same color difference will not generally be represented by pairs of points separated by the same distance, whether this distance is taken as the length of the straight line joining the two points of the pair or as the length of the shortest joining line lying wholly in the surface (geodesic). The question is

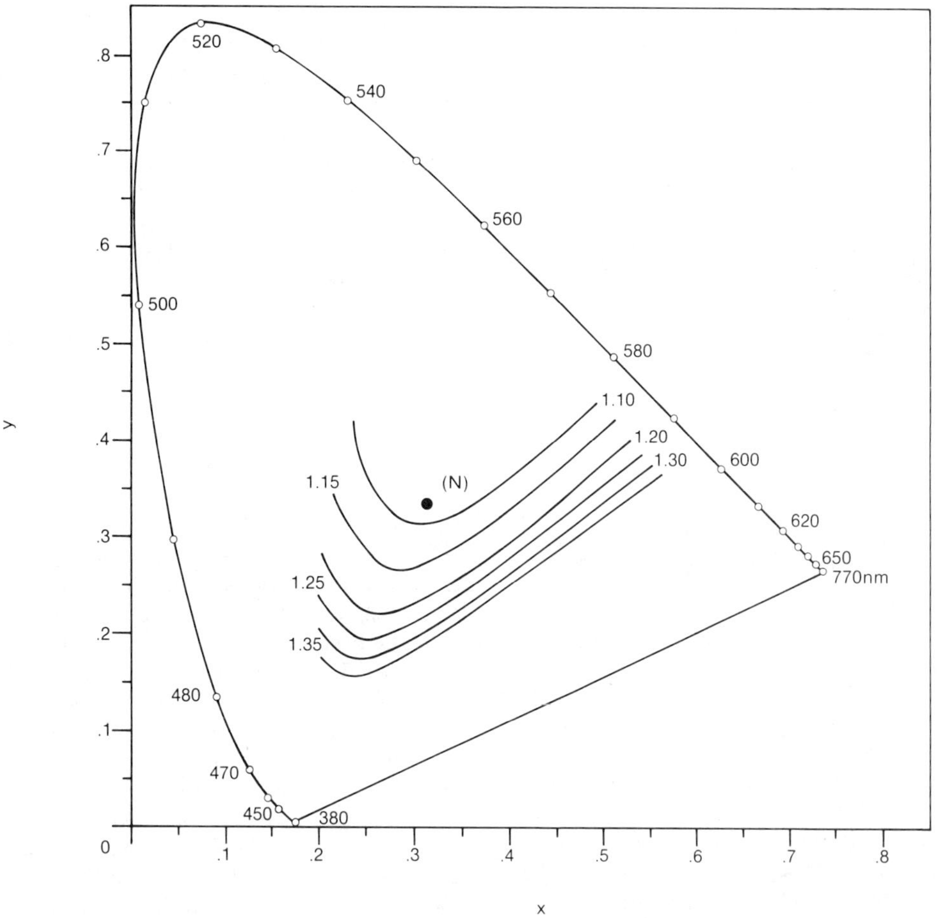

Figure 9.33. CIE 1931 (x,y) chromaticity diagram showing mean and smoothed loci of constant values of Y_N/Y ratios obtained for a group of 76 observers making lightness matches between colored tiles of luminance factors Y and gray tiles of luminance factors Y_N. The chromaticity coordinates of the colored tiles cover the central domain of the diagram; those of the gray tiles are located at the point N. For a colored tile of given chromaticity point (x,y) and given luminance factor Y to appear equally light to a gray tile, the luminance factor of the gray tile must be equal to that of the colored tile multiplied by the Y_N/Y ratio applicable to the chromaticity point of the colored tile. (From G. Wyszecki, Correlate for brightness in terms of CIE chromaticity coordinates and luminous reflectance, *Journal of the Optical Society of America*, 1967, *57*. Reprinted with permission.)

whether by a systematic distortion of the tristimulus space, that is, by a one–one but not necessarily linear transformation, the separation in the transformed space of all pairs of points in the equilightness surface representing object-color stimuli judged to show a given fixed color difference can be made the same. If this can be done at all, then the transformed equilightness surface can be made a plane covered by a network of equilateral triangles, each lattice point of the network representing a stimulus showing the same apparent color difference with each of its six nearest neighbors, as illustrated in Figure 9.34. The set of lattice-point stimuli then provides an ideal uniform scaling of the equilightness system. Present evidence is that observers' judgments of the color difference do not satisfy accurately the requirements for constructing such ideal uniform scaling systems; the geometry of color-appearance space is not Euclidean. However, the failure of the Euclidean property is not so serious as to rule out practically useful approximations of uniform scaling. The color-order system developed by the Committee on Uniform Color Scales of the Optical Society of America (see Section 7.2) provides examples of good approximations to uniform color scales of object-color stimuli of constant lightness.

Another representation of color scales of constant lightness is in terms of loci of constant hue and constant chroma on a surface of constant lightness; these loci form a polar-coordinate system as shown in Figure 9.35. The central point represents a gray; points on a circle represent object-color stimuli of constant chroma. All circles are centered at the gray and evenly spaced corresponding to uniform steps in chroma. Points on a radial line starting at the center represent stimuli of the same hue. Equal angles between these radial lines correspond ideally to equal steps in hue. A complete color solid is constructed from color scales of this kind at different lightness levels ranging from black to white. An example of such a color solid is provided by the Munsell color system (see Section 7.1).

When an approximate uniform scaling of hue and chroma has been set up by selecting, on the basis of observer judgments or otherwise, the particular material color samples that realize the scale graduations, the CIE 1931 tristimulus values of these samples, under the assigned illuminant, can be determined.

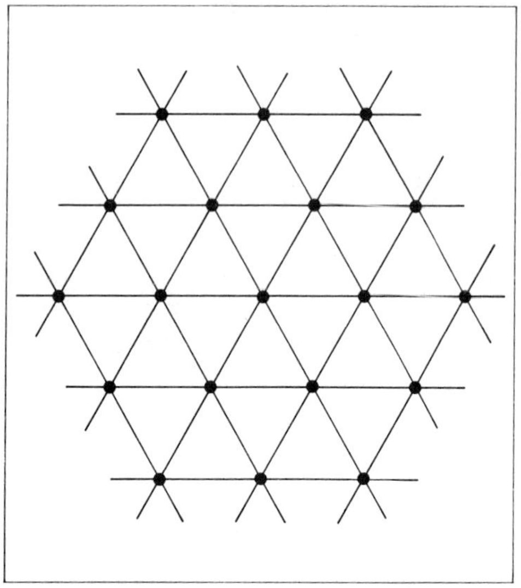

Figure 9.34. Triangular lattice used for uniform scaling of colors of constant lightness.

Analytical expressions can then be sought that transform (nonlinear transformations must be allowed) CIE tristimulus values to three new variables that, used as rectangular coordinates, define the required distorted space. This is the space in which equilightness samples occupy a common plane, and a given color difference between any two samples in an equilightness plane corresponds to the same distance separation of their representative points. With the Munsell system taken as basis, a number of attempts at acceptable but fairly analytical transformations have been made. These attempts have been reviewed, for example, by Wyszecki and Stiles (1982).

6.5. Uniform-Chromaticity-Scale Diagrams

In a slightly different approach to uniform scaling are considered all those color stimuli, not necessarily object-color stimuli, which

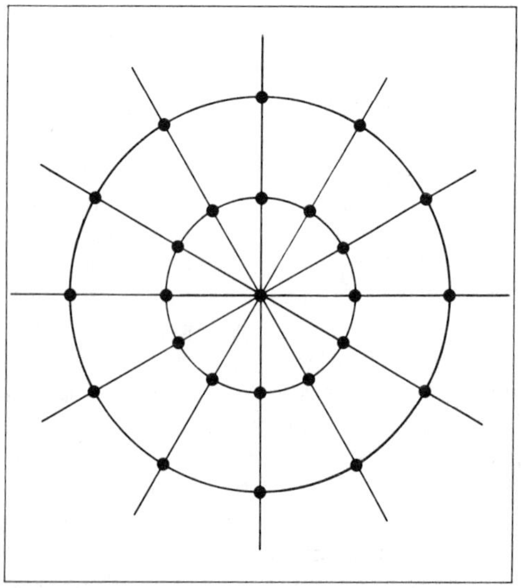

Figure 9.35. Polar-coordinate system. Points on a circle represent object-color stimuli of constant chroma; points on a radial line represent object-color stimuli of the same hue. The center point represents achromatic (gray) color stimuli.

lie in a plane of constant luminance of the CIE 1931 tristimulus space. Only linear transformations of the CIE space are allowed, corresponding to projective transformations of the CIE 1931 (x, y) chromaticity diagram, and it is sought to make equal displacements in the transformed chromaticity diagram correspond to perceptually equal color differences. This objective is known to be impossible in any strict sense, but the simplicity of linear or projective transformations makes even a crude approximation of practical value. The general form of the transformation is as follows:

$$x' = \frac{a_{11}x + a_{12}y + a_{13}}{a_{31}x + a_{32}y + a_{33}},$$

$$y' = \frac{a_{21}x + a_{22}y + a_{23}}{a_{31}x + a_{32}y + a_{33}}, \qquad (67)$$

where x, y are the CIE 1931 chromaticity coordinates and x', y' the coordinates of the new chromaticity diagram which is called a *uniform-chromaticity-scale* (UCS) *diagram* when the coefficients a_{ik} are properly chosen.

The first attempt to develop a UCS diagram was made by Judd (1935), who made his choice of the coefficients a_{ik} on the basis of a variety of data on chromaticity spacing, published prior to the Munsell data. The usefulness of a UCS diagram led several other investigators to try either improvements on Judd's UCS diagram or new UCS diagrams based on different experimental evidence (for a review, see Wyszecki and Stiles, 1982). MacAdam's (1937) diagram was adopted by the CIE in 1960 as a standard UCS diagram, referred to as the *CIE 1960 UCS diagram*, whose coordinates were given the designations u and v. However, on the basis of more recent experimental evidence, the CIE in 1976 modified its 1960 UCS diagram to a slightly improved version with coordinates

$$u' = u \quad \text{and} \quad v' = 1.5\,v\,,$$

thus leading to the following transformation:

$$u' = \frac{4x}{-2x + 12y + 3}$$

$$v' = \frac{9y}{-2x + 12y + 3}\,. \qquad (68)$$

Figure 9.36 illustrates the CIE 1976 (u', v') UCS diagram.

6.6. Three-Dimensional Color Scales

6.6.1. Principles of Construction. In many industrial color-control problems, the color differences being judged are a combination of differences in lightness, hue, and chroma; to assess these, a uniform three-dimensional color scale is needed. The logical extension of the regular triangular lattice arrangement in the plane, shown in Figure 9.34, is to a *regular rhombohedral lattice* arrangement in space (Wyszecki, 1954). In a regular rhombohedral lattice sampling of the color space, each color is surrounded by its 12 nearest neighbors, all equally distant. The 12 points representing these colors form a polyhedron called a *cuboctahedron*, for it is obtained by cutting off the eight corners of the cube by planes through the midpoints of each three concurrent edges. Figure 9.37 illustrates a cuboctahedron.

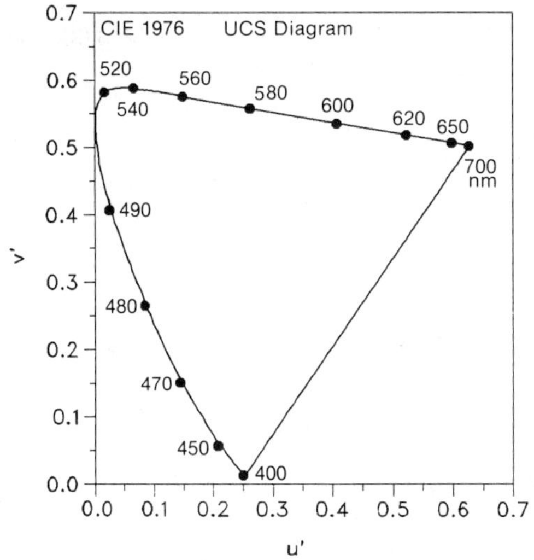

Figure 9.36. The CIE (1976) (u',v') UCS diagram intended to yield perceptual spacing of chromaticity more nearly uniform than that of the CIE 1931 (x,y) chromaticity diagram. The (u',v') diagram is related to the (x,y) diagram by a simple projective transformation.

The regular rhombohedral lattice arrangement provides not only a regular array of colors but also the most closely packed arrangement. The lattice can be resolved into a series of parallel plane lattices in seven different ways. In four of these, the meshes of the plane lattice are equilateral triangles, and in the remaining three, they are squares. A direct determination of a regular rhombohedral lattice in color space has been made by the Committee on Uniform Color Scales of the Optical Society of America. The results of this work is discussed briefly in Section 7.2.

The traditional way of deriving formulas for three-dimensional color scales has been by choosing a chromaticity diagram with approximately uniform spacing for equilightness (or equiluminance) color stimuli and by adding to it some function of luminance factor that gives approximately uniform lightness spacing for color stimuli of the same chromaticity. Suitable scaling factors for both the chromaticity scale and the lightness scale are selected to make the unit of chromaticity difference closely equivalent to the unit of lightness difference. Wyszecki and Stiles (1982) have collected the formulas that have been used in practice. Special weight attaches to the two CIE uniform color spaces, known as the CIE 1976 $(L^*u^*v^*)$ space and the CIE 1976 $(L^*a^*b^*)$ space. These two spaces, recommended by the CIE for practical applications involving object-color stimuli, are defined below. Typical practical applications, which the CIE Colorimetry Committee had in mind when developing the two spaces, are those encountered in the textile and paint industries. All color stimuli are object-color stimuli, consisting of virtually opaque objects illuminated by a light source of given spectral radiant power distribution. Two objects of the same size and shape, whose color difference is to be evaluated, are envisaged to be viewed in juxtaposition in an achromatic surround. All objects are assumed to be made of nonfluorescent materials. The color differences range perceptually from "just noticeable" to "moderate." An example of a moderate difference might be a Munsell chroma step in the *Munsell Book of Color* (Section 7.1) between two Munsell paint chips having the same Munsell value and the same Munsell hue. The CIE has yet to address the problem of uniform scaling of self-luminous color stimuli, seen as unrelated or related colors. Also the measurement of color differences ranging from small to very large, and assessed in chromatic surrounds, has yet to be developed. Some urgency in pursuing these problems is indicated particularly with regard to applications in the computer-graphics industry.

6.6.2. CIE 1976 ($L^*u^*v^*$) Space. The first approximately uniform object-color space is produced by plotting in rectangular coordinates the quantities L^*, u^*, v^* defined by:

$$L^* = 116(Y/Y_n)^{1/3} - 16 \,,$$

$$u^* = 13\,L^*(u' - u'_n) \,,$$

$$v^* = 13\,L^*(v' - v'_n) \,, \qquad (69)$$

with the constraint that $Y/Y_n > 0.008856$. If values of Y/Y_n equal to or less than 0.008856 occur, a somewhat modified procedure is recommended for calculating L^*. The following L^*_m formula is then used:

$$L^*_m = 903.3\,(Y/Y) \quad \text{for } Y/Y_n \leqslant 0.008856 \;.$$

In Eq. (69), the quantities u', v' and u'_n, v'_n are calculated from

$$u' = \frac{4X}{X + 15Y + 3Z}$$

$$v' = \frac{9Y}{X + 15Y + 3Z}$$

$$u'_n = \frac{4X_n}{X_n + 15Y_n + 3Z_n}$$

$$v'_n = \frac{9Y_n}{X_n + 15Y_n + 3Z_n} \,. \qquad (70)$$

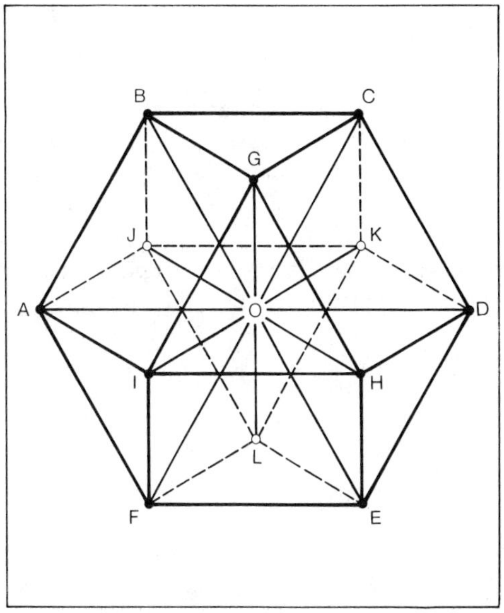

Figure 9.37. Cuboctahedron. The 12 corners *A* to *K* of the cuboctahedron are equally distant from the center *O*.

These equations are equivalent to Eq. (68), which gives u',v' in terms of (x,y) chromaticity coordinates instead of tristimulus values (X,Y,Z).

The tristimulus values X_n, Y_n, Z_n are those of the nominally white object-color stimulus. Usually, the white object-color stimulus is given by the spectral radiant power of one of the CIE standard illuminants, for example, D_{65} or A, reflected into the observer's eye by the perfect reflecting diffuser. Under these conditions, X_n, Y_n, Z_n are the tristimulus values of the standard illuminant with Y_n equal to 100.

The total color difference ΔE^*_{uv} between two color stimuli, each given in terms of L^*, u^*, v^*, is calculated from

$$\Delta E^*_{uv} = [(\Delta L^*)^2 + (\Delta u^*)^2 + (\Delta v^*)^2]^{1/2} . \quad (71)$$

The values of the coefficients of the equations defining the CIE 1976 $(L^*u^*v^*)$ space and its associated color-difference formula are intended to apply to the observing conditions normally found in practice involving object-color stimuli. However, there is evidence that, in certain situations, different values for the coefficients may be more appropriate. In particular, the weight of the perceived lightness difference between two given object-color stimuli relative to the perceived chromatic difference between the same two stimuli may, under certain observing conditions, require different coefficients. No procedures have been standardized that would predict quantitatively the required new coefficients when, for example, the field size and/or the physical separation between the two object-color stimuli is changed. However, an earlier color-difference formula, known as ΔE_{NBS}, defining the now out-of-date National Bureau of Standards (NBS) unit of color difference, includes appropriate parameters to account for certain changes in observing conditions (see, for example, Judd & Wyszecki, 1975). Other relevant work is that by Sharp and Wyszecki (1976) and Boynton, Hayhoe, and MacLeod (1977).

The color space, defined by Eq. (69), is called the *CIE 1976 $(L^*u^*v^*)$ space*. The color-difference formula, defined by Eq. (71), is called the *CIE 1976 $(L^*u^*v^*)$ color-difference formula*. The letters "CIELUV" are often used as an abbreviation.

If v^* is plotted against u^*, the points in the resulting (u^*,v^*) diagram are not uniquely related to chromaticity because their position depends on the value of L^*. However, if L^* is constant, straight lines in the CIE 1931 (x,y) chromaticity diagram or in the CIE 1976 UCS diagram remain straight in the (u^*,v^*) diagram. Except for a constant factor, the (u^*,v^*) diagram becomes the CIE 1976 (u',v') diagram (Figure 9.36). This feature is considered important in cases where color stimuli are mixed additively.

6.6.3. CIE 1976 $(L^*a^*b^*)$ Space. The second approximately uniform object-color space is produced by plotting in rectangular coordinates the quantities L^*, a^*, b^*, defined by

$$L^* = 116(Y/Y_n)^{1/3} - 16 ,$$

$$a^* = 500(X/X_n)^{1/3} - (Y/Y_n)^{1/3} ,$$

$$b^* = 200(Y/Y_n)^{1/3} - (Z/Z_n)^{1/3} , \quad (72)$$

with the constraint that X/X_n, Y/Y_n, $Z/Z_n > 0.008856$.

In calculating L^*, a^*, and b^*, values of X/X_n, Y/Y_n, Z/Z_n, equal to or less than 0.008856, may be included if the normal formulae are replaced by the following modified formulae:

$$L^*_m = 903.3\left(\frac{Y}{Y_n}\right) \quad \text{for } \frac{Y}{Y_n} \leq 0.008856$$

and

$$a^*_m = 500\left[f\left(\frac{X}{X_n}\right) - f\left(\frac{Y}{Y_n}\right)\right] ,$$

$$b^*_m = 200\left[f\left(\frac{Y}{Y_N}\right) - f\left(\frac{Z}{Z_n}\right)\right] , \quad (73)$$

where

$$f\left(\frac{X}{X_n}\right) = \left(\frac{X}{X_n}\right)^{1/3} \qquad \frac{X}{X_n} > 0.008856 ,$$

$$f\left(\frac{X}{X_n}\right) = 7.787\left(\frac{X}{X_n}\right) + \frac{16}{116} \qquad \frac{X}{X_n} \leq 0.008856 ,$$

$$f\left(\frac{Y}{Y_n}\right) = \left(\frac{Y}{Y_n}\right)^{1/3} \qquad \frac{Y}{Y_n} > 0.008856 ,$$

$$f\left(\frac{Y}{Y_n}\right) = 7.787\left(\frac{Y}{Y_n}\right) + \frac{16}{116} \qquad \frac{Y}{Y_n} \leq 0.008856 ,$$

$$f\left(\frac{Z}{Z_n}\right) = \left(\frac{Z}{Z_n}\right)^{1/3} \qquad \frac{Z}{Z_n} > 0.008856 ,$$

$$f\left(\frac{Z}{Z_n}\right) = 7.787\left(\frac{Z}{Z_n}\right) + \frac{16}{116} \qquad \frac{Z}{Z_n} \leq 0.008856 .$$

The tristimulus values X_n, Y_n, Z_n are those of the nominally white object-color stimulus. Usually, the white object-color stimulus is given by the spectral radiant power of one of the CIE standard illuminants, for example, D_{65} or A, reflected into the observer's eye by the perfect reflecting diffuser. Under these conditions, X_n, Y_n, Z_n are the tristimulus values of the standard illuminant with Y_n equal to 100.

The total color difference ΔE^*_{ab} between two color stimuli, each given in terms of L^*, a^*, b^*, is calculated from

$$\Delta E^*_{ab} = [(\Delta L^*)^2 + (\Delta a^*)^2 + (\Delta b^*)^2]^{1/2} . \quad (74)$$

The values of the coefficients of the equations defining the CIE 1976 $(L^*a^*b^*)$ space and its associated color-difference formula are intended to apply to the observing conditions normally found in practice involving object-color stimuli. For specific comments on the values of the coefficients, see Section 6.6.2.

The color space defined by Eq. (72) is called the *CIE 1976* $(L^*a^*b^*)$ space. The color-difference formula, defined by Eq. (74) is called the *CIE 1976 $(L^*a^*b^*)$* color-difference formula. The letters "CIELAB" are used as an abbreviation.

The L^* function defining the lightness measure in the CIE 1976 $(L^*a^*b^*)$ space is identical to the L^* function of the CIE 1976 $(L^*u^*v^*)$ space. No simple relation exists between the scales a^*,b^* of the CIE 1976 $(L^*a^*b^*)$ space and u^*,v^* of the CIE 1976 $(L^*u^*v^*)$ space. If b^* is plotted against a^*, the points in the resulting (a^*,b^*) diagram are not uniquely related to chromaticity because their position depends on the value of L^*. If L^* is constant, straight lines in the CIE 1931 (x, y) chromaticity diagram or in the CIE 1976 UCS diagram become, in general, curved lines in the (a^*, b^*) diagram.

6.6.4. CIE 1976 Measures of Color-Appearance Attributes. The CIE 1976 uniform color spaces and associated color-difference formulas can be used to define measures of the basic color-appearance attributes, lightness, chroma (saturation), and hue. These measures are intended for engineering use where a numerical specification of color-appearance attributes is important but where a high correlation with actual visual perception is not required.

The quantity L^*, given in Eqs. (69) and (72) serves as the measure of *lightness*, that is,

$$L^* = 116 \left(\frac{Y}{Y_n} \right)^{1/3} - 16 \; . \qquad (75)$$

The quantities C^*_{uv} and C^*_{ab}, defined by

$$C^*_{uv} = [(u^*)^2 + (v^*)^2]^{1/3} \; ,$$

$$C^*_{ab} = [(a^*)^2 + (b^*)^2]^{1/2} \; , \qquad (76)$$

serve as measures of *chroma*.

The quantity

$$s^*_{uv} = \frac{C^*_{uv}}{L^*} \qquad (77)$$

derived from C^*_{uv} and L^* in the CIE 1976 $(L^*u^*v^*)$ space can be used as a measure for *saturation*. In a series of object-color stimuli of constant chromaticity, but increasing (or decreasing) luminance factor, s^*_{uv} remains constant with corresponding increases (or decreases) in C^*_{uv}. An equivalent relation for s^*_{uv} is

$$s^*_{uv} = 13 \left[(u' - u'_n)^2 + (v' - v'_n)^2 \right]^{1/2} \; . \qquad (78)$$

A similar measure of saturation cannot be given for the CIE 1976 $(L^*a^*b^*)$ space.

The quantities h_{uv} and h_{ab}, defined by

$$h_{uv} = \arctan \left(\frac{v^*}{u^*} \right) , \quad h_{ab} = \arctan \left(\frac{b^*}{a^*} \right) , \qquad (79)$$

define *hue angles*, which are useful quantities in specifying hue numerically. The angles are given in degrees using the following conventions:

$$0^\circ < h_{uv} < 90^\circ \; , \quad \text{if } u^* > 0, v^* > 0$$

$$90^\circ < h_{uv} < 180^\circ \; , \quad \text{if } u^* < 0, v^* > 0$$

$$180^\circ < h_{uv} < 270^\circ \; , \quad \text{if } u^* < 0, v^* < 0$$

$$270^\circ < h_{uv} < 360^\circ \; , \quad \text{if } u^* > 0, v^* < 0$$

and similarly for h_{ab} using a^*, b^*.

The quantities ΔH^*_{uv} and ΔH^*_{ab}, defined by

$$\Delta H^*_{uv} = [(\Delta E^*_{uv})^2 - (\Delta L^*)^2 - (\Delta C^*_{uv})^2]^{1/2}$$

and

$$\Delta H^*_{ab} = [(\Delta E^*_{ab})^2 - (\Delta L^*)^2 - (\Delta C^*_{ab})^2]^{1/2} \; , \qquad (80)$$

specify *hue differences*. A quantity of hue difference is useful to describe a total color difference ΔE^* in terms of its three components: ΔL^*, ΔC^*, and ΔH^*.

For a small color difference between two color stimuli, both of which are sufficiently different in color from the achromatic stimulus, the hue difference can be calculated from

$$\Delta H^*_{uv} = C^*_{uv} \, \Delta h_{uv} \left(\frac{\pi}{180} \right)$$

$$\Delta H^*_{ab} = C^*_{ab} \, \Delta h_{ab} \left(\frac{\pi}{180} \right) . \qquad (81)$$

The hue difference is given a positive sign when the hue angle h increases and a negative sign when h decreases.

7. COLOR-ORDER SYSTEMS

A color-order system is a rational method or plan of ordering and specifying all object colors or all within a limited domain by means of a set of material standards selected and displayed to represent adequately the whole set of object colors under consideration.

Of the many conceivable color-order systems, a number have been developed and are used. Fairly detailed accounts of the more important systems are given by Judd and Wyszecki (1975) and Wyszecki (1960).

All color-order systems fall broadly into three major groups. Those in the first group are based primarily on the principles of additive mixtures of color stimuli. Systematic variations of the settings of, for example, a Maxwell disk can be used to generate color scales that, in turn, can be duplicated by actual material standards. The classical example is the Ostwald color system (see, for example, Foss, Nickerson, & Granville, 1944).

The principles of colorant mixtures provide the basis for color-order systems of the second group. The desired colored objects are developed by compounding a limited number of pigments of dyes in systematically varied proportions. By application of the screen-plate process of printing and by varying the screening systematically, color-order systems are obtained intermediate in character to those based on additive mixtures and those based on colorant mixtures. With modern printing technology it is relatively easy to produce such color-order systems, and indeed there are several such systems on the market.

The third group of color-order systems is based on principles of color appearance. Material standards are selected to represent scales of constant hue, chroma, and lightness, each one spaced uniformly in accordance with the perceptions of an observer with normal color vision. Color-order systems of this group are called *color-appearance systems*. The outstanding example of such a system is the *Munsell color system*.

When uniformity of color difference is the primary concern in the construction of a color-order system, a regular rhombohedral lattice array of colors serves the purpose as exemplified in the uniform color system of the Optical Society of America (OSA). The Munsell and the OSA color systems are described in Sections 7.1 and 7.2, respectively.

7.1. The Munsell Color System

The Munsell color system has been materialized in the *Munsell Book of Color*, available through the Munsell Color Company. There are different editions of the *Munsell Book of Color* exhibiting different numbers of samples, different sample sizes, and different finishes (glossy or mat). For example, the glossy finish collection displays 1450 glossy color paint chips inserted in slots on 40 constant-hue charts arranged on facing pages. An 18-step gray scale is also included. Each color chip may be removed from the chart. The chart size is 10 by 12 in, the chip size 11/16 by 13/16 in; the whole collection comes in two volumes (13 × 12 × 2 in each).

On each constant-hue chart the chips are arranged in rows and columns. It was intended that the chips in any one row should be perceived to have equally light colors under ordinary viewing conditions (daylight illumination, middle-gray to white surroundings) and that the chips in any one column should be perceived to have colors of equal chroma. The colors progress from very light at the top of each chart to very dark at the bottom by steps intended to be perceptually equal; and they progress from achromatic colors, black, gray, or white, at the inside edge of the chart to chromatic colors at the outside edge of the chart by steps also intended to be perceptually equal.

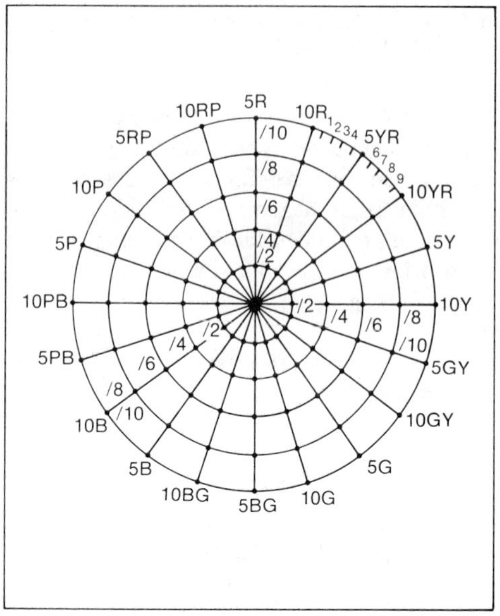

Figure 9.39. Organization of the colors of constant Munsell value in the *Munsell Book of Color*. In this Munsell constant-value chart the colors are represented by solid dots. The colors vary in Munsell hue around the circle and in Munsell chroma along radial lines with the center being gray. Munsell hue ranges from red (5R) to yellow (5Y), green (5G), blue-green (5BG), blue (5B), purple-blue (5PB), purple (5P), red-purple (5RP), and back to red (5R). The hue circuit contains 100 equally spaced colors. Munsell chroma changes in two-chroma steps, from 0 (gray) at the center to the highest possible value (/10 in this chart) at the periphery. Concentric circles are lines of constant Munsell chroma; radial lines are lines of constant Munsell hue. (From D. B. Judd & G. Wyszecki, *Color in business, science, and industry*. Copyright 1975 by John Wiley & Sons, Inc. Reprinted with permission.)

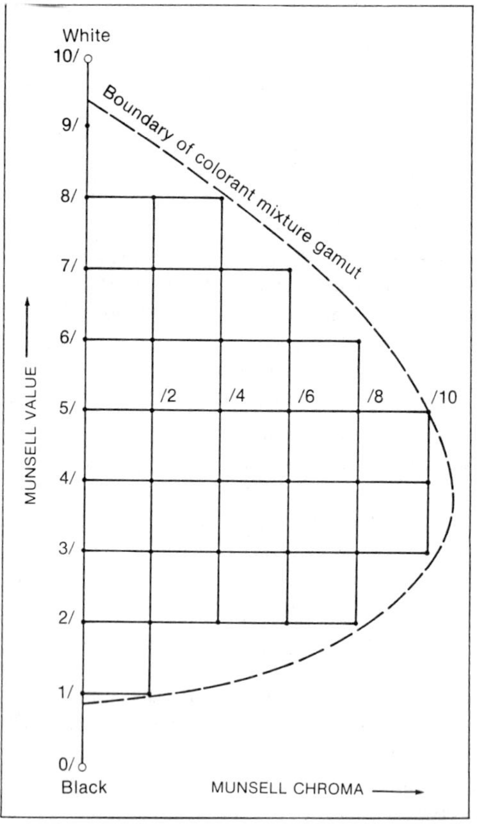

Figure 9.38. Organization of the colors of constant Munsell hue in the *Munsell Book of Color*. In this Munsell constant-hue chart, the colors are represented by solid dots. The colors vary in Munsell chroma and in Munsell value. Munsell chroma ranges from 0 chroma (gray), on the left, to a high chroma (maximum of /10 in this chart), on the right, in two-chroma steps. Munsell value ranges from 0/ (black) to 10/ (white). The dashed line represents the boundary of the colorant-mixture gamut beyond which Munsell color chips cannot be produced by mixtures of chromatic pigments with black and white pigments. (From D. B. Judd & G. Wyszecki, *Color in business, science, and industry*. Copyright 1975 by John Wiley & Sons, Inc. Reprinted with permission.)

Each chip is identified by three symbols: the first indicates *Munsell hue*, the second *Munsell value*, and the third *Munsell chroma*. For example, 2.5 YR 5/10 indicates a Munsell hue of 2.5 YR, a Munsell chroma of /10 steps away from the gray (N 5/) of the same Munsell value 5. Because it is based on nearly uniformly spaced scales of color, the notation of the Munsell system is a useful tool for the formulation and solution of many colorimetric problems.

A Munsell constant-hue chart is laid out as shown in Figure 9.38. The lightness scale is represented by the Munsell value scale with black denoted by 0/ and white by 10/. There are 9 grays placed uniformly in between. Colors of constant chroma are placed on the vertical lines parallel to the Munsell value scale. Munsell chroma increases in steps of 2 (/2, /4, . . ., /10). Colors placed on the horizontal lines have constant Munsell value. The gamut of the colors in the Munsell constant-hue chart is limited. Mixtures of chromatic pigments with black and white pigments yield a color gamut whose boundary is represented by the dashed curve in Figure 9.38. Each row of colors of constant value is extended until the next interval of two chroma steps would extend beyond the boundary of the colorant-mixture gamut.

Figure 9.39 shows the organization of the Munsell constant-value charts that can be built up from the constant-hue charts. The 100-point Munsell hue scale and notation are shown around the outer circle. Colors of constant Munsell hue are shown by the radial lines intersecting at the center representing gray, or chroma /0. The hue scale is built up to 10 segments of 10 hues each, such as the segment from 1 YR to 10 YR, and the fifth hue of each of these segments is alternatively notated by the letters alone; thus 5 YR is often written simply YR. The Munsell chroma scale up to chroma /10 is shown along any radial line in Figure 9.39, and the colors of constant Munsell chroma are shown by each of the 5 concentric circles. It will be noted that the sampling of the color solid near the black–white axis (chroma /0) is, by this plan of development, much denser than that of the high-chroma colors represented far from the axis. This is a necessary defect of any collection of color chips organized on the radial plan. The *Munsell Book of Color* does not show all 100 Munsell hues on the scale of Figure 9.39, but only 40 of them: 2.5 YR, 5 YR, 7.5 Yr, 10 YR, 2.5 Y, . . ., 10 R.

Figure 9.40 is an oblique projection of the Munsell color solid illustrating the arrangement of planes of constant Munsell hue and constant Munsell value; constant Munsell chroma is represented by cylinders with the gray scale as common axis.

The color chips in the *Munsell Book of Color* have CIE tristimulus values in close agreement with the specifications laid down in the "Final Report of the OSA Subcommittee on the Spacing of Munsell Colors" (Newhall, Nickerson, & Judd, 1943). The 1943 report gives a revised spacing of the Munsell system represented in the earlier editions of the *Munsell Book of Color*. This system is commonly referred to as the *Munsell renotation system*. The editions of the *Munsell Book of Color* currently issued by the Munsell Color Company or by the Japan Color Research Institute are intended to conform with the renotation system of 1943. Figure 9.41 shows the CIE (x, y) chromaticity diagram with Munsell hue and chroma lines of the Munsell value plane 5/, that is, for colors of constant luminance factor $Y = 19.8$. A complete set of such graphs and the tables of (x, y, Y) coordinates on which these graphs are based can be found in the final report by Newhall and coworkers (1943) and in Wyszecki and Stiles (1982). The graphs and tables can be used for graphical or numerical interpolations.

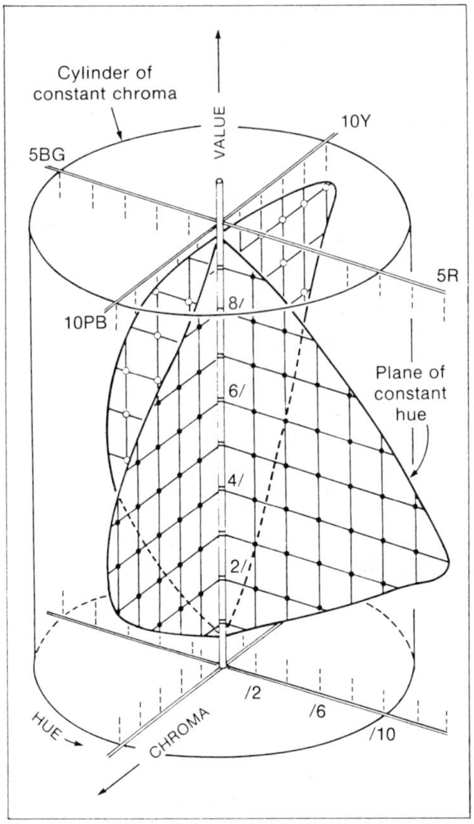

Figure 9.40. Schematic diagram of the Munsell color solid showing four planes of constant Munsell hue (5R, 10Y, 5BG, 10PB) and a cylinder representing constant Munsell chroma (/10). Planes of constant hue intersect each other at the Munsell value axis, which also is the common axis of all cylinders of constant Munsell chroma. Planes of constant Munsell value are horizontal planes intersecting the axis perpendicularly. (From D. B. Judd & G. Wyszecki, *Color in business, science, and industry*. Copyright 1975 by John Wiley & Sons, Inc., Reprinted with permission.)

7.2. OSA Color System

The OSA color system is a color-appearance system that exemplifies uniform color spacing by means of the regular rhombohedral lattice arrangement of color samples (see Section 6.6.1). In this system each color (not lying on the boundary of the object-color solid) is surrounded by 12 neighboring colors, all perceptually equally distant from the given color (Figure 9.37). The arrangement is such that any given color appears in six entirely different series of equally spaced colors, with each series traversing the color solid.

The OSA color system, developed by the Committee on Uniform Color Scales of the Optical Society of America between 1947 and 1974, is available in atlas form from the Optical Society of America in Washington, D.C. The paint chips contained in the atlas closely represent, when viewed under daylight D_{65} illumination and on a middle-gray surround (30% reflectance), the colors of the OSA color system, specified by the OSA Committee in terms of CIE 1964 (x_{10}, y_{10}, Y_{10}) coordinates (MacAdam 1974; Wyszecki & Stiles, 1982). Square lattices are obtained for planes of constant OSA lightness which is denoted by the letter L ranging from -7 to $+5$. All colors of medium lightness are represented by points on the plane square lattice $L = 0$. The planes parallel to and above $L = 0$ are denoted by $L = 1, 2 \ldots$; those below are denoted by $L = -1, -2, \ldots$. Few or no points on the planes $L = 6$, $L = -7$ or beyond represent colors that are producible by stable paint mixtures. Figure 9.42 shows a portion of the CIE 1964 (x_{10}, y_{10}) chromaticity diagram with the square-lattice points of the OSA system when $L = 0$.

In each plane of constant lightness L, lattice coordinates (j, g) are used to identify the lattice points. Both j and g are zero for grays. Positive values of j, with zero values of g, indicate yellow or brownish colors; negative values of j, with zero values of g, indicate blues; positive values of g, with zero values of j, indicate greens; and negative values of g, with zero values of j, indicate reddish purples. It is important to note that colors of constant L are intended to be of constant lightness. This means that the luminance factor Y of such colors varies with chromaticity, usually decreasing with distance from gray. In particular, the OSA committee adopted the following formula:

$$L = \frac{(L' - 14.4)}{\sqrt{2}}, \tag{82}$$

where

$$L' = 5.9\left[\bar{Y}_{10}^{1/3} - \frac{2}{3} + 0.042\ (\bar{Y}_{10} - 30)^{1/3}\right].$$

The quantity $\bar{Y}_{10}$ in Eq. (82) is obtained from a modified formula proposed by Wyszecki and Sanders (1957):

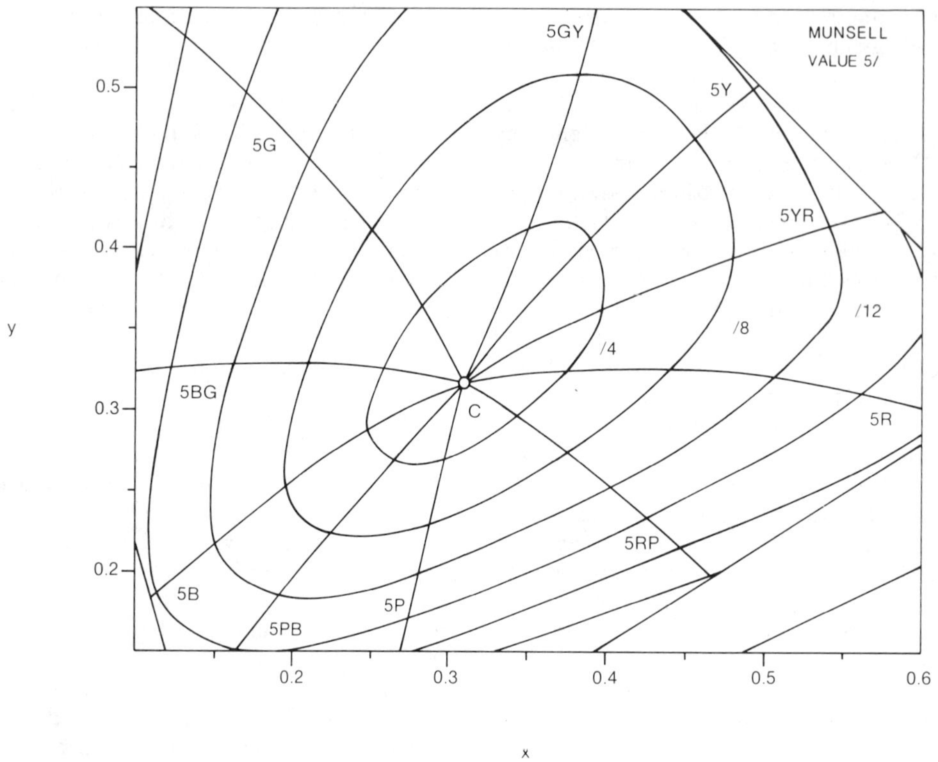

Figure 9.41. CIE 1931 (x,y) chromaticity diagram showing the main loci of constant hue and constant chroma at value 5/ of the Munsell renotation system. (From S. M. Newhall, D. Nickerson, & D. B. Judd, Final report of the O.S.A. subcommittee on spacing of the Munsell colors, *Journal of the Optical Society of America*, 1943, *33*. Reprinted with permission.)

$$\bar{Y}_{10} = Y_{10}\,(4.4934\,x_{10}^2 + 4.3034\,y_{10}^2 - 4.276\,x_{10}y_{10} - 1.3744\,x_{10} - 2.5643\,y_{10} + 1.8103)\,, \qquad (83)$$

where Y_{10}, x_{10}, y_{10} are the CIE 1964 color specifications of a given object-color stimulus. The calculated value of $\bar{Y}_{10}$ is the luminance factor of the gray object-color stimulus that appears equally light to the given object-color stimulus (Y_{10}, x_{10}, y_{10}). The perfect reflecting diffuser illuminated by CIE standard illuminant D_{65} yields the white object-color stimulus with $\bar{Y}_{10} = 100$.

Further aspects of the OSA color system have been treated in detail in a number of recent publications, a selection of which includes MacAdam (1974, 1978), Nickerson (1975, 1977, 1978), Davidson (1978), and Foss (1978).

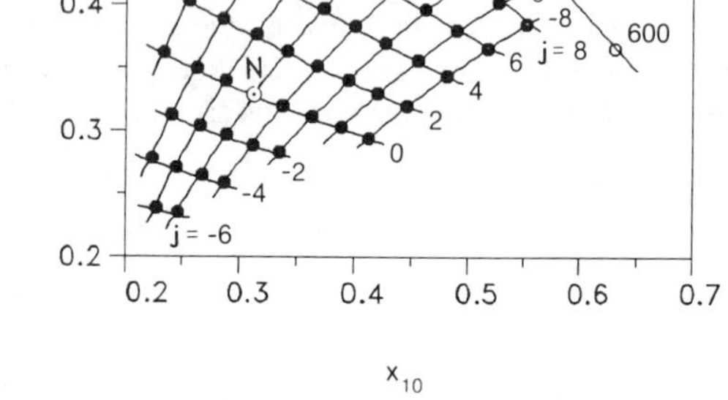

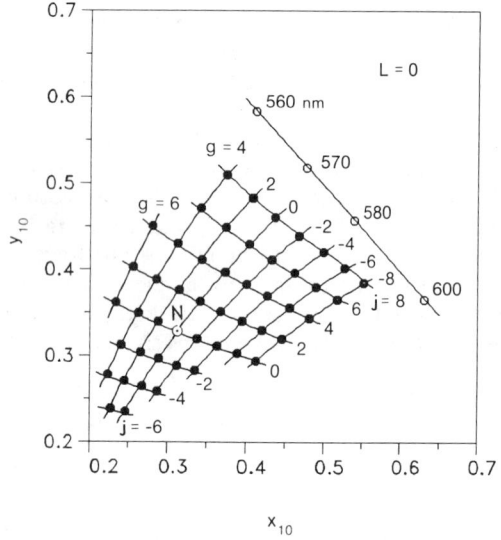

Figure 9.42. CIE 1964 (x_{10},y_{10}) chromaticity diagram showing the square lattice of chromaticity points (*j*,*g*) of the colors of the OSA system for lightness level $L = 0$. The chromaticity point *N* is that of the nominal gray D_{65} in the system. (From G. Wyszecki & W. S. Stiles, *Color science*, 2nd ed. Copyright 1982 by John Wiley & Sons, Inc. Reprinted with permission.)

REFERENCE NOTE

1. Ware, C., & Cowan, W. B. *Chromatic Mach bands: Behavioural evidence for lateral inhibition in color vision.* Manuscript submitted for publication, 1982.

REFERENCES

* References preceded by an asterisk are "key references."

Abney, W. de W. On the change in hue of spectrum colours by dilution with white light. *Proceedings of the Royal Society of London*, 1910, *A83*, 120–127.

Adams, E. Q., & Cobb, P. W. The effect on foveal vision of bright (and dark) surroundings. *Journal of Experimental Psychology*, 1922, *5*, 39.

Aiba, T. S., & Stevens, S. S. Relation of brightness and luminance under light- and dark-adaptation. *Vision Research*, 1964, *4*, 391–401.

Akita, M., Graham, G. H., & Hsia, Y. Maintaining an absolute hue in the presence of different background colors. *Vision Research*, 1964, *4*, 539–556.

Alman, D. H. Errors of the standard photometric system when measuring the brightness of general illumination light sources. *Journal of the Illuminating Engineering Society*, 1977, *7*, 55.

Arend, L. E. Spatial differential and integral operations in human vision: Implications of stabilized retinal image fading. *Psychological Review*, 1973, *80*, 374–395.

Avant, L. L. Vision in the Ganzfeld. *Psychological Bulletin*, 1965, *64*, 246–258.

Barrow, H. G., & Tenenbaum, J. M. Recovering intrinsic scene characteristics from images. In A. Hansen & E. Riseman (Eds.), *Computer vision systems*. New York: Academic Press, 1978.

*Bartleson, C. J. *Factors affecting color appearance and measurement by psychophysical methods*. Unpublished doctoral dissertation, The City University of London, 1977.

Bartleson, C. J. A. A review of chromatic adaptation. In F. W. Billmeyer, Jr. & G. Wyszecki (Eds.), *Color 77*. Bristol, England: Adam Hilger, 1978.

Bartleson, C. J. Changes in color appearance with variations in chromatic adaption. *Color Research and Application*, 1979, *4*, 119–138. (a)

Bartleson, C. J. Changes in color appearance with variations in chromatic adaptation. *Color Research and Application*, 1979, *4*, 143–155. (b)

Bartleson, C. J., & Breneman, E. J. Brightness reproduction in the photographic process. *Photographic Science and Engineering*, 1967, *11*, 254–262.

Beck, J. *Surface color perception*. Ithaca, N.Y.: Cornell University Press, 1972.

Bedford, R. E., & Wyszecki, G. Axial chromatic aberration of the human eye. *Journal of the Optical Society of America*, 1957, *47*, 564–565.

Benham, C. E. Notes. *Nature*, 1894, *51*, 113–114.

Bergström, S. S. Common and relative components of reflected light as information about the illumination, color and three-dimensional form of objects. *Scandinavian Journal of Psychology*, 1977, *8*, 129–136.

*Bodmann, H. W., Haubner, P., & Marsden, A. M. A unified relationship between brightness and luminance. In *Proceedings of 19th Session of the Commission Internationale de l'Eclairage*, Tokyo, 1979. Paris: CIE Central Bureau, 1980.

Bouma, P. J., & Kruithof, A. A. Die chromatische Anpassumg des Auges. *Philips Technical Review*, 1947, *9*, 257.

Boynton, R. M. Implications of the minimally distinct border. *Journal of the Optical Society of America*, 1973, *63*, 1037–1043.

*Boynton, R. M. *Human color vision*. New York: Holt, Rinehart & Winston, 1979.

Boynton, R. M., & Baron, W. S. Sinusoidal flicker characteristics of primate cones in response to heterochromatic stimuli. *Journal of the Optical Society of America*, 1975, *65*, 1091–1100.

Boynton, R. M., & Gordon, J. Bezold-Brücke hue shift measured by color-naming technique. *Journal of the Optical Society of America*, 1965, *55*, 78–86.

Boynton, R. M., Hayhoe, M. M., & MacLeod, D. I. A. The gap effect: Chromatic and achromatic visual discrimination as affected by field separation. *Optica Acta*, 1977, *24*, 159–177.

Boynton, R. M., & Kaiser, P. K. Vision: The additivity law made to work for heterochromatic photometry with bipartite fields. *Science*, 1968, *161*, 366.

Boynton, R. M., & Kaiser, P. K. Temporal analog of the minimally-distinct border. *Vision Research*, 1978, *18*, 111–113.

Breneman, E. Dependence of luminance required for constant brightness upon chromaticity and chromatic adaptation. *Journal of the Optical Society of America*, 1958, *48*, 228–232.

Brindley, G. S. The colour of light of very long wavelength. *Journal of Physiology*, 1955, *130*, 35.

Brown, J. L. Afterimages. In C. H. Graham (Ed.), *Vision and Visual Perception*. New York: Wiley, 1965.

Brunswik, E. Zur Entwicklung der Albedowahrnehmung. *Zeitschrift für Psychologie*, 1929, *109*, 40–115.

Burnham, R. W., Evans, R. M., & Newhall, S. M. Prediction of color appearance with different adaptation illuminations. *Journal of the Optical Society of America*, 1957, *47*, 35–42 (p. 443).

*Burnham, R. W., Hanes, R. M., & Bartleson, C. J. *Color: A guide to basic facts and concepts*. New York: Wiley, 1963.

Campenhausen, C. von. Uber die Farben der Benhamschen Scheibe. *Zeitschrift für vergleichende Physiologie*, 1968, *60*, 351–374.

Carroll, J. D., & Wish, M. Models and methods for three-way multidimensional scaling. In D. H. Krantz, R. C. Atkins, R. D. Luce, & P. Suppes (Eds.), *Measurement, psychophysics, and neural information processing*. San Francisco: Freeman & Company, 1974.

Chapanis, A., & Halsey, R. M. Luminance of equally bright colors. *Journal of the Optical Society of America*, 1955, *45*, 1–6.

Chevreul, M. E. *The principles of harmony and contrast of colors and their applications to the arts*. New York: Reinhold, 1967.

Cicerone, C. M., Krantz, D. H., & Larimer, J. Opponent-process additivity—III. Effect of moderate chromatic adaptation. *Vision Research*, 1975, *15*, 1125–1135.

Cohen, J. D. *Temporal independence of the Bezold-Brücke hue shift*. Unpublished doctoral dissertation, University of Pennsylvania, 1971.

*Commission Internationale de l'Eclairage (CIE). *International lighting vocabulary* (3rd ed.). Paris: CIE Central Bureau, 1970.

*Commission Internationale de l'Eclairage (CIE). *Recommendations on uniform color spaces, color-difference equations, psychometric color terms* (Supplement No. 2 of CIE Publication No. 15, E-1.3.1, 1971). Paris: CIE Central Bureau, 1978. (*Note*: This publication describes CIE recommendations made in 1976.)

Coren, S., & Keith, B. Bezold-Brücke effect: Pigment or neural locus. *Journal of the Optical Society of America*, 1970, *60*, 559–562.

Crawford, B. H. The Stiles-Crawford effects and their significance in vision. In D. Jameson & L. M. Hurvich (Eds.), *Visual psychophysics*. New York: Springer-Verlag, 1972.

Davidson, H. R. Preparation of the OSA Uniform Color Scales Committee samples. *Journal of the Optical Society of America*, 1978, *68*, 1141–1142.

Diamond, A. L. Foveal simultaneous brightness contrast as a function of inducing- and test-field luminances. *Journal of Experimental Psychology*, 1953, *45*, 304–314.

Diamond, A. L. Foveal simultaneous contrast as a function of inducing field area. *Journal of Experimental Psychology*, 1955, *50*, 144–152.

Diamond, A. L. Simultaneous contrast as a function of test-field area. *Journal of Experimental Psychology*, 1962, *64*, 336–345.

*Ditchburn, R. W. *Eye movements and visual perception*. Oxford: Clarendon Press, 1973.

Dresler, A. The non-additivity of heterochromatic brightness. *Transactions of the Illuminating Engineering Society*, 1953, *18*, 141.

Eichengreen, J. M. Unique hue loci: Induced shifts with complimentary surrounds. *Vision Research*, 1976, *16*, 199–203.

Ekman, G. *Subjective power functions and the method of fractionation* (Report No. 34). University of Stockholm, Psychological Laboratory, 1956.

Enoch, J. M. Optical properties of the retinal receptors. *Journal of the Optical Society of America*, 1963, *53*, 71–85.

Enoch, J. M., & Stiles, W. S. The colour change of monochromatic light with retinal angle of incidence. *Optica Acta*, 1961, *8*, 329–358.

Estévez, O., & Cavonius, C. R. Flicker sensitivity of the human red and green color mechanism. *Vision Research*, 1975, *15*, 879–881.

Estévez, O., & Spekreijse, H. A spectral compensation method for determining the flicker characteristics of the human colour systems. *Vision Research*, 1974, *14*, 823–830.

Evans, R. M. Visual processes and color photography. *Journal of the Optical Society of America*, 1943, *33*, 579–614.

*Evans, R. M. *An introduction to color*. New York: Wiley, 1948.

Evans, R. M. Fluorescence and gray content of surface colors. *Journal of the Optical Society of America*, 1959, *49*, 1049–1059.

Evans, R. M. The perception of color. In *Industrial color technology* (Advances in Chemistry Series No. 107). Washington, D.C.: American Chemical Society, 1971.

*Evans, R. M. *The perception of color*. New York: Wiley, 1974.

Falmagne, J. C. Foundations of Fechnerian psychophysics. In D. H. Krantz, R. C. Atkinson, R. D. Luce, & P. Suppes (Eds.), *Measurement, psychophysics, and neural information processing*. San Francisco: Freeman & Company, 1974.

Fiorentini, A. Mach band phenomena. In D. Jameson & L. M. Hurvich (Eds.), *Visual psychophysics*. New York: Springer-Verlag, 1972.

Foss, C. E. Space lattice used to sample the color space of the Committee on Uniform Color Scales of the Optical Society of America. *Journal of the Optical Society of America*, 1978, *68*, 1616–1619.

Foss, C. E., Nickerson, D., & Granville, W. C. Analysis of the Ostwald color system. *Journal of the Optical Society of America*, 1944, *34*, 361–381.

Fry, G. A., & Alpern, M. The effect of a peripheral glare source upon the apparent brightness of an object. *Journal of the Optical Society of America*, 1953, *43*, 189–195.

Gescheider, G. A. *Psychophysics, methods and theory*. Hillsdale, N.J.: Lawrence Erlbaum, 1976.

Gilchrist, A. L. Perceived lightness depends on perceived spatial arrangement. *Science*, 1977, *195*, 185–187.

Gilchrist, A. L. The perception of surface blacks and whites. *Scientific American*, 1979, *240*, 112–124.

Gilchrist, A. L. When does perceived lightness depend on perceived spatial arrangement? *Perception and Psychophysics*, 1980, *28*, 527–538.

*Gilchrist, A. L., Delman, S., & Jacobsen, A. The classification and integration of edges as critical to the perception of reflectance and illumination. *Perception and Psychophysics*, 1983, *33*, 425–436.

Godlove, I. H. Neutral value scales, II. A comparison of results and equations describing value scales. *Journal of the Optical Society of America*, 1933, *23*, 419.

*Graham, C. H., & Brown, J. L. Color contrast and color apperances: Brightness constancy and color constancy. In C. H. Graham (Ed.), *Vision and visual perception*. New York: Wiley, 1965.

Guth, S. L. Photometric and colorimetric additivity at various intensities. In M. Richter (Ed.), *Color 69*. Göttingen: Musterschmidt-Verlag, 1970.

*Guth, S. L., Donley, N. V., & Marrocco, R. T. On luminance additivity and related topics. *Vision Research*, 1969, *9*, 537–575.

Guth, S. L., & Lodge, H. R. Heterochromatic additivity, foveal spectral sensitivity, and a new color model. *Journal of the Optical Society of America*, 1973, *63*, 450–462.

*Guth, S. L., Massof, R. W., & Benzschawel, T. Vector model for normal and dichromatic color vision. *Journal of the Optical Society of America*, 1980, *70*, 197–212.

Hasegawa, T. Simultaneous color contrast: Deviations of the induced colors from directions of complementary colors. In F. W. Billmeyer & G. Wyszecki (Eds.), *Color 77*. Bristol, England: Adam Hilger, 1977.

*Haubner, P. *Zur Helligkeitsbewertung quasi-achromatischer Reize*. Unpublished doctoral dissertation, Universität Karlsruhe, 1977.

*Heinemann, E. G. Simultaneous brightness induction as a function of inducing- and test-field luminances. *Journal of Experimental Psychology*, 1955, *50*, 89–96.

Heinemann, E. G. Simultaneous brightness induction. In D. Jameson & L. M. Hurvich (Eds.), *Visual psychophysics*. New York: Springer-Verlag, 1972.

Helm, C. E. Multidimensional ratio scaling analysis of perceived color relations. *Journal of the Optical Society of America*, 1964, *54*, 256–262.

*Helson, H. Fundamental problems in color vision. I. The principle governing changes in hue, saturation, and lightness of nonselective samples in chromatic illumination. *Journal of Experimental Psychology*, 1938, *23*, 439–476.

*Helson, H. Studies of anomalous contrast and assimilation. *Journal of the Optical Society of America*, 1963, *53*, 179–184.

Helson, H., Judd, D. B., & Warren, M. H. Object-color changes from daylight to incandescent filament illumination. *Illuminating Engineering*, 1952, *47*, 221–233.

Hepler, N. K. A motion-contingent aftereffect. *Science*, 1968, *162*, 376–377.

Hess, C., & Pretori, H. Messende Untersuchungen über die Gesetzmässigkeit des simultanen Helligkeitsconstrastes. *Albrecht von Graefes Archiv für klinische und experimentelle Ophthalmologie*, 1894, *40*, 1–24.

*Hochberg, J. Perception. I. Color and shape. In J. W. Kling & L. A. Riggs (Eds.), *Woodworth & Schlosberg's experimental psychology* (3rd ed.). New York: Holt, Rinehart & Winston, 1971.

Horeman, H. W. Inductive brightness depression as influenced by configurational conditions. *Vision Research*, 1963, *3*, 121–130.

Horn, B. K. P. Determining lightness from an image. *Computer Graphics and Image Processing*, 1974, *3*, 277–299.

van der Horst, G. J. C. Chromatic flicker. *Journal of the Optical Society of America*, 1969, *59*, 1213–1217.

van der Horst, G. J. C., & Bouman, M. A. Spatiotemporal chromaticity discrimination. *Journal of the Optical Society of America*, 1969, *59*, 1482–1488.

Hunt, R. W. G. The perception of color in 1° fields for different states of adaptation. *Journal of the Optical Society of America*, 1953, *43*, 479–484.

*Hunt, R. W. G. The specification of colour appearance. I. Concepts and terms. *Color Research and Application*, 1977, *2*, 55–68. (a)

*Hunt, R. W. G. The specification of colour appearance. II. Effects of changes in viewing conditions. *Color Research and Application*, 1977, *2*, 109–120. (b)

Hunt, R. W. G. Color terminology. *Color Research and Application*, 1978, *3*, 79–87.

Hunt, R. W. G. Measures of colour appearance in colour reproduction. *Color Research and Application*, 1979, *4*, 39–43.

*Hurvich, L. M. *Color vision*. Sunderland, Mass.: Sinauer Associates, 1981.

Hurvich, L. M., & Jameson, D. Some quantitative aspects of an opponent-colors theory. II. Brightness, saturation, and hue in normal and dichromatic vision. *Journal of the Optical Society of America*, 1955, *45*, 602–616.

Hurvich, L. M., & Jameson, D. *The perception of brightness and darkness*. Boston: Allyn and Bacon, 1966.

Ikeda, M., & Ayama, M. Additivity of opponent chromatic valence. *Vision Research*, 1980, *20*, 995–999.

Indow, T. Two kinds of multidimensional scaling methods as tools for investigating color space from the macroscopic point of view. *Acta Chromatica*, 1963, *1*, 60–71.

Ingling, Jr., C. R., Russell, P. W., Rea, M. S., & Tsou, B. H. Red-green opponent spectral sensitivity: Disparity between cancellation and direct matching methods. *Science*, 1978, *201*, 1221–1223.

Jameson, D. Brightness scales and their interpretation. In M. Richter (Ed.), *Color 69*. Göttingen: Musterschmidt-Verlag, 1970.

Jameson, D. Theoretical issues of color vision. In D. Jameson & L. M. Hurvich (Eds.), *Visual psychophysics*. New York: Springer-Verlag, 1972.

*Jameson, D., & Hurvich, L. M. Some quantitative aspects of an opponent-colors theory. I. Chromatic responses and spectral saturation. *Journal of the Optical Society of America*, 1955, *45*, 546–552.

Jameson, D., & Hurvich, L. M. Complexities of perceived brightness. *Science*, 1961, *133*, 174–179. (a)

*Jameson, D., & Hurvich, L. M. Opponent chromatic inductions: Experimental evaluation and theoretical account. *Journal of the Optical Society of America*, 1961, *51*, 46–53. (b)

Jameson, D., & Hurvich, L. M. Theory of brightness and color contrast in human vision. *Vision Research*, 1964, *4*, 135–154.

*Jameson, D., & Hurvich, L. M. Color adaptation: Sensitivity, contrast, after-images. In D. Jameson & L. M. Hurvich (Eds.), *Visual psychophysics*. New York: Springer-Verlag, 1972.

Jenkins, B., & Ross, J. McCollough effect depends upon perceived organization. *Perception*, 1977, *6*, 399–400.

Judd, D. B. A Maxwell triangle yielding uniform chromaticity scales. *Journal of the Optical Society of America*, 1935, *25*, 24.

*Judd, D. B. Hue, saturation, and lightness of surface colors with chromatic illumination. *Journal of the Optical Society of America*, 1940, *30*, 2.

Judd, D. B. Basic correlates of the visual stimulus. In S. S. Stevens

(Ed.), *Handbook of experimental psychology*. New York: W

Judd, D. B. A new look at the measurement of light a
minating Engineering, 1958, *53*, 61–71.

*Judd, D. B. Appraisal of Land's work on two-primar
Journal of the Optical Society of America, 19

*Judd, D. B. & Wyszecki, G. *Color in business*
(3rd ed.). New York: Wiley, 1975.

Kaiser, P. K., Herzberg, P. A., & Boynton ... omatic border distinctness and its relation to satura ... *ision Research*, 1971, *11*, 953–968.

Kaiser, P. K., & Smith, P. W. The lum inance of equally bright colors. In *Proceedings of the 17th Session of the Commission Internationale de l'Eclairage*, Barcelona, 1971 (Vol. 21A, p. 143). Paris: CIE Central Bureau, 1972.

Kaiser, P. K., & Wyszecki, G. Additivity failures in heterochromatic brightness matching. *Color Research and Application*, 1978, *3*, 177–182.

Kaneko, T. A reconsideration of the Cobb-Judd lightness function. *Acta Chromatica*, 1964, *1*, 103–110.

Kanizsa, G. Margini quasi-percettivi in campi con stimolazione omogenea. *Rivista di Psicologia*, 1955, *49*, 7–30.

Kelly, D. H., Boynton, R. M., & Baron, W. S. Primate flicker sensitivity: Psychophysics and electrophysiology. *Science*, 1976, *194*, 1077–1079.

Kinney, J. A. S. Factors affecting induced color. *Vision Research*, 1962, *2*, 503–525.

Kinney, J. A. S. Effect of exposure time on induced color. *Journal of the Optical Society of America*, 1965, *55*, 731–736.

*Kling, J. W., & Riggs, L. A. (Eds.). *Woodworth & Schlosberg's experimental psychology* (3rd ed.). New York: Holt, Rinehart & Winston, 1971.

Kohlrausch, V. A. Zür Photometrie farbiger Lichter. *Das Licht*, 1935, *5*, 259–275.

König, H. *Der Begriff der Helligkeit*. Neuchatel, Switzerland: Griffin, 1947.

*Krantz, D. H. Visual scaling. In D. Jameson and L. M. Hurvich (Eds.), *Visual psychophysics*. New York: Springer-Verlag, 1972.

Krantz, D. H. Color measurement and color theory: II. Opponent-colors theory. *Journal of Mathematical Psychology*, 1975, *12*, 304–327.

Krantz, D. H., Luce, R. D., Suppes, P., & Tversky, A. *Foundations of measurement*, Vol. 1. *Additive and polynomial representations*. New York: Academic Press, 1971.

von Kries, J. Die Gesichtsempfindungen. *Nagel's Handbuch der Physiologie des Menschen*, 1904, *3*, 211.

Kruskal, J. B. Multidimensional scaling and other methods for discovering structure. In K. Enslein, A. Ralston, & H. F. Wilf (Eds.), *Statistical methods for digital computers*. New York: Wiley, 1976.

*Kruskal, J. B., & Wish, M. *Multidimensional scaling*. Beverly Hills: Sage, 1978 (Sage University Paper Series on Quantitative Applications in the Social Sciences. No. 07-011).

Land, E. H. Color vision and the natural image, Part I and II. *Proceedings of the National Academy of Sciences*, 1959, *45*, 115, 636. (a)

Land, E. H. Experiments in color vision. *Scientific American*, 1959, *200*, 84. (b)

Land, E. H. Colour in the natural image. *Proceedings of the Royal Institution of Great Britain*, 1962, *39*, 1.

Land, E. H. The retinex. *American Scientist*, 1964, *52*, 247.

*Land, E. H. The retinex theory of color vision. *Proceedings of the Royal Institution of Great Britain*, 1974, *47*, 23–58.

*Land, E. H., & McCann, J. J. Lightness and retinex theory. *Journal of the Optical Society of America*, 1971, *61*, 1–11.

de Lange, H. Research into the dynamic nature of the human fovea → cortex systems with intermittent and modulated light: I. Attenuation characteristics with white and colored light. *Journal of the Optical Society of America*, 1958, *48*, 777–784. (a)

de Lange, H. Research into the dynamic nature of the human fovea → cortex systems with intermittent and modulated light: II. Phase shift in brightness and delay in color perception. *Journal of the Optical Society of America*, 1958, *48*, 784–789. (b)

...r, J., Krantz, D. H., & Cicerone, C. M. Opponent-process additivity. I. Red/green equilibria. *Vision Research*, 1974, *14*, 1127–1140.

Larimer, J., Krantz, D. H., & Cicerone, C. M. Opponent-process additivity. II. Yellow/blue equilibria and nonlinear models. *Vision Research*, 1975, *18*, 723–731.

Leibowitz, H., Mote, F. A., & Thurlow, W. R. Simultaneous contrast as a function of separation between test and inducing fields. *Journal of Experimental Psychology*, 1953, *46*, 453–456.

Lewis, P. R. A theoretical interpretation of spectral sensitivity curves at long wavelengths. *Journal of Physiology*, 1955, *130*, 45.

MacAdam, D. L. Projective transformations of ICI color specifications. *Journal of the Optical Society of America*, 1937, *27*, 294.

MacAdam, D. L. Loci of constant hue and brightness determined with various surrounding colors. *Journal of the Optical Society of America*, 1950, *40*, 589–594.

MacAdam, D. L. Influence of visual adaptation on loci of constant hue and saturation. *Journal of the Optical Society of America*, 1951, *41*, 615–619.

MacAdam, D. L. Chromatic adaptation. *Journal of the Optical Society of America*, 1956, *46*, 500–513.

MacAdam, D. L. Chromatic adaptation. II. Nonlinear hypothesis. *Journal of the Optical Society of America*, 1963, *53*, 1441–1445.

*MacAdam, D. L. Uniform color scales. *Journal of the Optical Society of America*, 1974, *64*, 1691–1702.

MacAdam, D. L. Colorimetric data for samples of OSA uniform color scales. *Journal of the Optical Society of America*, 1978, *68*, 121–130.

Mach, E. Uber die Wirkung der räumlichen Vertheilung des Lichtreizes auf die Netzhaut. *Akademie der Wissenschaften, Wien, mathematisch-naturwissenschaftliche Klasse*, 1865, *52*, 303–322.

*McCann, J. J., McKee, S. P., & Taylor, T. Quantitative studies in retinex theory: The "color Mondrian" experiments. *Vision Research*, 1976, *16*, 445–458.

McCollough, C. Color adaptation of edge-detectors in the human visual system. *Science*, 1965, *149*, 1115–1116.

McKee, S. P., McCann, J. J., & Benton, J. L. Color vision from rod and long-wave cone interactions: Conditions in which rods contribute to multicolored images. *Vision Research*, 1977, *17*, 175–185.

Milewski, A. E., Iaccino, J., & Smith, D. Checkerboard-specific color aftereffects: A failure to find effects of perceptual organization. *Perception and Psychophysics*, 1980, *28*, 329–336.

Munsell, A. E. O., Sloan, L. L., & Godlove, I. H. Neutral value scales, I. Munsell neutral value scale. *Journal of the Optical Society of America*, 1933, *23*, 394.

Nagy, A. L. Short-flash Bezold-Brücke hue shifts. *Vision Research*, 1980, *20*, 361–368.

Nagy, A. L., & Zacks, J. L. The effects of psychophysical procedure and stimulus duration in the measurement of the Bezold-Brücke hue shifts. *Vision Research*, 1977, *17*, 193–200.

*Nayatani, Y., Takahama, K., & Sobagaki, H. Formulation of a nonlinear model of chromatic adaptation. *Color Research and Application*, 1981, *6*, 161–171. (a)

Nayatani, Y., Takahama, K., & Sobagaki, H. A nonlinear model of chromatic adaptation. *Die Farbe*, 1981, *29*, 109–126. (b)

Newhall, S. M., Burnham, R. W., & Evans, R. M. Color constancy in shadows. *Journal of the Optical Society of America*, 1958, *48*, 976–984.

Newhall, S. M., Burnham, R. W., & Evans, R. M. Influence of shadow quality on color appearance. *Journal of the Optical Society of America*, 1959, *49*, 909–917.

*Newhall, S. M., Nickerson, D., & Judd, D. B. Final report of the O.S.A. subcommittee on spacing of the Munsell colors. *Journal of the Optical Society of America*, 1943, *33*, 385–418.

Nickerson, D. Uniform color scales: Munsell conversion of OSA Committee selection. *Journal of the Optical Society of America*, 1975, *65*, 205–207.

Nickerson, D. History of the OSA Committee on Uniform Color Scales. *Optics News*, Winter 1977.

Nickerson, D. Munsell renotations for samples of OSA uniform color scales. *Journal of the Optical Society of America*, 1978, *68*, 1343–1347.

Oyama, T., & Hsia, Y. Compensatory hue shift in simultaneous color contrast as a function of separation between inducing and test fields. *Journal of Experimental Psychology*, 1966, *71*, 403–413.

Pease, P. L. On color Mach bands. *Vision Research*, 1978, *18*, 751–755.

Priest, I. G., Gibson, K. S., & McNicholas, H. J. *An examination of the Munsell color system, I. Spectral and total reflection and the Munsell scale of value* (U.S. National Bureau of Standards Technical Paper 167). Washington, D.C.: U.S. National Bureau of Standards, 1920.

Purdy, D. McL. Spectral hue as a function of intensity. *American Journal of Psychology*, 1931, *43*, 541.

*Ratliff, F. *Mach bands: Quantitative studies on neural networks in the retina*. San Francisco: Holden-Day, 1965.

Richter, M. Das System der DIN-Farbenkarte. *Die Farbe*, 1953, *1*, 85–98.

Riggs, L. A. Curvature as a feature of pattern vision. *Science*, 1973, *181*, 1070–1072.

Robertson, A. R. A new determination of lines of constant hue. In M. Richter (Ed.), *Color 69*. Göttingen: Musterschmidt-Verlag, 1970.

Romeski, M. I. *Chromatic opponent-response functions of anomalous trichromats*. Unpublished doctoral dissertation, Brown University, 1976.

Sanders, C. L., & Wyszecki, G. Correlate for lightness in terms of CIE-tristimulus values. Part I. *Journal of the Optical Society of America*, 1957, *47*, 398–404.

Sanders, C. L., & Wyszecki, G. L/Y ratios in terms of CIE-chromaticity coordinates. *Journal of the Optical Society of America*, 1958, *48*, 389–392.

*Sanders, C. L., & Wyszecki, G. Correlate for brightness in terms of CIE color matching data. In *Proceedings of the 15th Session of the Commission Internationale de l'Eclairage*, Vienna, 1963. Paris: CIE Central Bureau, 1964.

Savoie, R. S. Bezold-Brücke effect and visual nonlinearity. *Journal of the Optical Society of America*, 1973, *63*, 1253–1261.

Schiffman, S. S., Reynolds, M. L., & Young, F. W. *Introduction to multidimensional scaling theory, methods, and applications*. New York: Academic Press, 1981.

*Semmelroth, C. C. Prediction of lightness and brightness on different backgrounds. *Journal of the Optical Society of America*, 1970, *60*, 1685–1689.

Semmelroth, C. C. Adjustment of the Munsell value and *W**-scale to uniform lightness steps for various background reflectances. *Applied Optics*, 1971, *10*, 14–18.

Sharp, L. T., & Wyszecki, G. Proximity factor in color-difference evaluations. *Journal of the Optical Society of America*, 1976, *66*, 40–49.

Shepard, R. N. The analysis of proximities: Multidimensional scaling with an unknown distance function. *Psychometrica*, 1962, *27*, 125–140; 219–246.

Shepard, R. N., Romney, A. K., & Nerlove, S. B. (Eds.), *Multidimensional scaling*, Vol. 1, *Theory*. New York: Seminar Press, 1972.

Shevell, S. K. Unambiguous evidence for the additive effect in chromatic adaptation. *Vision Research*, 1980, *20*, 637–639.

Shute, C. C. D. *The McCollough effect*. Cambridge: Cambridge University Press, 1979.

Smith, V. C., & Pokorny, J. Spectral sensitivity of color-blind observers and the cone photopigments. *Vision Research*, 1972, *12*, 2059–2071.

Smith, V. C., & Pokorny, J. Spectral sensitivity of the foveal cone photopigments between 400 and 500 nm. *Vision Research*, 1975, *15*, 161–171.

Snyder, A. W., & Pask, C. The Stiles-Crawford effect—explanation and consequences. *Vision Research*, 1973, *13*, 1115–1137.

Sobagaki, H., Yamanaka, T., Takahama, K., & Nayatani, Y. Chromatic-adaptation study by subjective-estimation method. *Journal of the Optical Society of America*, 1974, *64*, 743–749.

Sobagaki, H., Takahama, K., & Nayatani, Y. Effect of using different methods of saturation estimation on prediction of chromatic adaptation. *Acta Chromatica*, 1976, *3*, 35–45.

Stevens, J. C., & Stevens, S. S. Brightness function: Effects of adaptation. *Journal of the Optical Society of America*, 1963, *53*, 375–385.

Stevens, S. S. Review of L. L. Thurstone. The measurement of values. *Contemporary Psychology*, 1959, *4*, 388–389.

*Stevens, S. S. *Psychophysics*. New York: Wiley, 1975.

Stevens, S. S., & Diamond, A. L. Effect of the glare angle on the brightness function for a small target. *Vision Research*, 1965, *5*, 649–659.

Stevens, S. S., & Stevens, J. C. *The dynamics of visual brightness* (Psychophysical Project Report No. PPR-246). Harvard University, 1960.

Stiles, W. S. The directional sensitivity of the retina and the spectral sensitivities of the rods and cones. *Proceedings of the Royal Society of London*, 1939, *B127*, 64–105.

Stiles, W. S. Adaptation, chromatic adaptation, colour transformation. *Anales de la Real Sociedad Española de Fisica y Quimica*, 1961, *57*, 149–175.

Stiles, W. S. The directional sensitivity of the retina. *Annals of the Royal College of Surgeons of England*, 1962, *30*, 73–101.

*Stiles, W. S., & Crawford, B. H. The luminous efficiency of rays entering the pupil at different points. *Proceedings of the Royal Society of London*, 1933, *B112*, 428.

Strohmeyer, C. F. Edge-contingent color aftereffects: Spatial frequency specificity. *Vision Research*, 1972, *12*, 717–733.

Strohmeyer, C. F. Form-color aftereffects in human vision. In R. Herschel, H. W. Leibowitz, & H. L. Teuber (Eds.), *Perception*. New York: Springer-Verlag, 1978.

Takahama, K., Sobagaki, H., & Nayatani, Y. Chromatic-adaptation effects and color appearance at various illuminance levels. *Acta Chromatica*, 1978, *3*, 93–102.

*Takasaki, H. Lightness change of grays induced by change in reflectance of gray background. *Journal of the Optical Society of America*, 1966, *56*, 504–509.

Tansley, B. W., & Boynton, R. M. A line, not a space, represents visual distinctness of borders formed by different colors. *Science*, 1976, *191*, 954–957.

Tansley, B. W., & Boynton, R. M. Chromatic border perception: The role of red- and green-sensitive cones. *Vision Research*, 1978, *18*, 683–697.

Thouless, R. H. Phenomenal regression to the real object, I. *British Journal of Psychology*, 1931, *21*, 339–359.

Thurstone, L. L. A law of comparative judgment. *Psychological Review*, 1927, *34*, 273–286.

*Torgerson, W. S. *Theory and methods of scaling*. New York: Wiley, 1958.

Truss, C. V. Chromatic flicker fusion frequency as a function of chromaticity difference. *Journal of the Optical Society of America*, 1957, *47*, 1130–1134.

Uhlarik, J., Pringle, R., & Brigell, M. Color aftereffects contingent on perceptual organization. *Perception and Psychophysics*, 1977, *22*, 506–510.

Valberg, A. Color induction: Dependence on luminance, purity and dominant or complementary wavelength of inducing stimuli. *Journal of the Optical Society of America*, 1974, *64*, 1531–1540.

Valberg, A., & Tansley, B. W. Tritanopic purity-difference function to describe the properties of visually distinct borders. *Journal of the Optical Society of America*, 1977, *67*, 1330–1336.

Varin, D. Fenomini di contrasto e diffusione chromatica nell'organizzazione spaziale del campo percettivo. *Rivista di Psicologia*, 1971, *65*, 101–128.

Vos, J. J. Twenty-five years Stiles-Crawford effect. *Advances in Ophthalmology*, 1960, *10*, 32–48.

Vos, J. J. Colorimetric and photometric properties of a 2 deg fundamental observer. *Color Research and Application*, 1978, *3*, 125–128.

Wagner, G., & Boynton, R. M. Comparison of four methods of heterochromatic photometry. *Journal of the Optical Society of America*, 1972, *62*, 1508–1515.

Wallach, H. Brightness constancy and the nature of achromatic colors. *Journal of Experimental Psychology*, 1948, *38*, 310–324.

Walraven, J. No additive effect of background in chromatic induction. *Vision Research*, 1980, *19*, 1061–1063.

Walraven, P. L. On the Bezold-Brücke phenomenon. *Journal of the Optical Society of America*, 1961, *51*, 1113–1116.

Walraven, P. L., & Leebeek, H. J. Phase shift of alternating coloured stimuli. In H. E. Henkes & L. H. van der Tweel (Eds.), *Flicker*. The Hague: Dr. W. Junk Publications, 1964.

Ware, C. Coloured illusory triangles due to assimilation. *Perception*, 1980, *9*, 103–107.

*Ware, C., & Cowan, W. B. Changes in perceived color due to chromatic interactions. *Vision Research*, 1982, *22*, 1353–1362.

Wassef, E. G. T. Linearity of the relationship between the tristimulus values of corresponding colours seen under different conditions of chromatic adaptation. *Optica Acta*, 1959, *6*, 378.

Weale, R. A. Notes on the photometric significance of the human crystalline lens. *Vision Research*, 1961, *1*, 183–191.

Whiteside, T. C. D. *The problems of vision in flight at high altitude*. London: Pergamon Press, 1957.

Wilson, M. H., & Brocklebank, R. W. Complementary hues of afterimages. *Journal of the Optical Society of America*, 1955, *45*, 293–299.

Wisowaty, J. J., & Boynton, R. M. Temporal modulation sensitivity of the blue mechanism: Measurements made without chromatic adaptation. *Vision Research*, 1980, *20*, 895–909.

Woolfson, M. M. Some new aspects of color perception. *IBM Journal of Research*, 1959, *3*, 313.

Wooten, B. R. *The effects of simultaneous and successive contrast on spectral hue*. Unpublished doctoral dissertation, Brown University, 1970.

Wright, W. D. The measurement and analysis of colour adaptation phenomena. *Proceedings of the Royal Society of London*, 1934, *115B*, 49.

Wright, W. D. *Researches on normal and defective colour vision*. London: Henry Kimpton, 1946.

Wyszecki, G. A regular rhombohedral lattice sampling of Munsell renotation space. *Journal of the Optical Society of America*, 1954, *44*, 725–734.

Wyszecki, G. Theoretical investigation of colored lenses for snow goggles. *Journal of the Optical Society of America*, 1956, *46*, 1071–1074.

Wyszecki, G. *Farbsysteme*. Göttingen: Musterschmidt-Verlag, 1960.

*Wyszecki, G. Correlate for brightness in terms of CIE chromaticity coordinates and luminous reflectance. *Journal of the Optical Society of America*, 1967, *57*, 254–257.

Wyszecki, G. Color-order systems. In M. Richter (Ed.), *Color 81*. Berlin: Deutscher Verband Farbe, 1981.

Wyszecki, G., & Sanders, C. L. Correlate for lightness in terms of CIE-tristimulus values. Part II. *Journal of the Optical Society of America*, 1957, *47*, 840–842.

*Wyszecki, G., & Stiles, W. S. *Color science* (2nd ed.). New York: Wiley, 1982.

Yager, D., & Taylor, E. Experimental measures and theoretical account of hue scaling as a function of luminance. *Perception and Psychophysics*, 1970, *7*, 360–364.

CHAPTER 10

EYE MOVEMENTS

PETER E. HALLETT
University of Toronto, Toronto, Canada

CONTENTS

This chapter is divided into three main parts. Section 1 is background and deals with the geometric aspects of the orientation of stationary eyes to the complex three-dimensional world; this section largely stands alone and is not a prerequisite to the other sections. The arrangement of the remaining parts is a response to the problem of how usefully to review and integrate a diverse body of knowledge without excessive omission. Section 2 therefore offers an overview of the basic concepts that appear to summarize eye movements in general and the various forms of eye movement in particular. There is an emphasis on *principles* rather than on detailed models because principles are felt to be both practical and prerequisite to useful models. Section 2 is an essential prerequisite to Section 3 for newcomers to the field of eye movements. To pursue a chapter organization based on forms of eye movement (e.g., saccades, vergence) might be advantageous to those specially interested in motor performance and motor mechanisms, but most behavioral scientists or human factors engineers will have a particular laboratory or environmental situation in mind. I have therefore organized the experimental data of Section 3 by the nature of the stimulus and the instructions given to the subject. Section 3 is intended for reference, but its arrangement also helps integrate diverse knowledge, in the sense that one needs to consider alternative possible movements or mixtures of movements, as in the complex circumstances of everyday life on and around this planet. The Table of Contents and the arrangement of the chapter should help the reader to browse and sample at will.

A pleasant introduction to the study of vision is that by Pirenne (1946/1967). Useful reviews of the literature on human eye movements are given by Alpern (1969); Carpenter (1977); Coakley (1983); B. Cohen (1981); Ditchburn (1973); Henn, Cohen, and Young, (1980); Howard (1981); Robinson (1968); and Wilson and Melvill Jones (1979). Useful collections of papers are to be found in Bach-y-Rita, Collins, and Hyde (1971); Brooks and Bajandas (1977); Dichgans and Bizzi (1972); Fisher, Monty, and Senders (1981); Fuchs and Becker (1981); Groner, Menz, Fisher, and Monty (1983); Kommerell (1978); Lennerstrand and Bach-y-Rita (1975); Monty and Senders (1976); Senders, Fisher, and Monty (1978); and Zuber (1981). Useful reviews of visual physiology include those by Brindley (1970) and Hallett (1971).

1. BACKGROUND: THE EYE VIS-À-VIS THE STIMULUS

Section 1 provides useful background but is not a prerequisite to Sections 2 and 3. Current basic research is mainly on eye movements in the horizontal plane. This section deals with eye movements in all directions, and therefore touches on spherical geometry, three-dimensional aspects of the anatomy and movements, and cartography as a means of handling such three-dimensional problems.

1.1. Geometric Aspects

1.1.1. Some Geometric Concepts. Spherical geometry and conic sections provide a basis for the study of eye movements and the visual field. Great circles are the largest circles that can be drawn on a sphere, and their planes intersect along diameters of the sphere. The equator and the meridians of our planet are great circles. In visual problems the sphere is usually a remote visual surface concentric with the eyeball, or sometimes the idealized eyeball itself. The center of the *visual sphere* is either the eye's center of rotation or the optical nodal point; the two are only slightly separate (Howard, 1981). The center of rotation is about 13 mm, and the nodal points about 7.2 mm, behind the cornea (Southall, 1937/1961). *The line of sight*, defined as the line projecting the fovea via the center of rotation and nodal points to the current point of fixation, is a radius of the visual sphere. The angles between the planes of three intersecting great circles on the sphere form the corner angles of an important Euler spherical triangle. The apices of this triangle are typically the origin of the coordinate system, the current point of fixation, and some target which will be the future point of fixation. See Figure 10.1. The sides of the triangle are typically given in angular measure because they are arcs of great circles. An unknown side or angle can be evaluated from the cosine rule (a relation between the sides and an angle), the cosine rule for angles (a relation between the three angles), or the sine rule (a relation between the ratios of the sides and the ratios of the angles), depending on the nature of the problem (Gellert, 1975).

If the line of sight rotates through a given angle around a fixed axis of revolution, such as that formed by the actions of the extraocular muscles, then it sweeps out a cone that intersects a fixed plane in a circle, ellipse, parabola, or hyberbola, depending on the relation of the cone to the plane. See Figure 10.2.

The eye has three degrees of rotational freedom, if we ignore the slight translational movements of the eye in its socket and consider only rotations around a hypothetical center, although only two degrees need be considered for most purposes. Two degrees of freedom specify the magnitude (or eccentricity) and the direction (or meridian) of the deviation of the line of sight

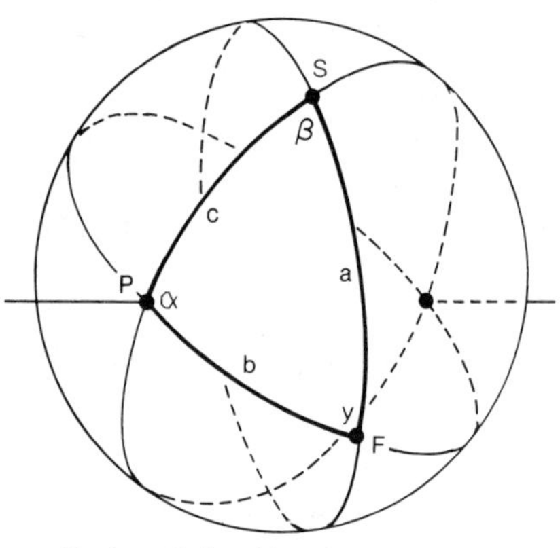

Cosine rule for sides

$\cos a = \cos b \cos c + \sin b \sin c \cos \alpha$

Cosine rule for angles

$\cos \alpha = -\cos \beta \cos y + \sin \beta \sin y \cos a$

Sine rule

$\frac{\sin a}{\sin \alpha} = \frac{\sin b}{\sin \beta} = \frac{\sin c}{\sin y}$

Figure 10.1. Spherical trigonometry relevant to eye movements. The eye (not shown) is at the center of the visual sphere, which is illustrated from an arbitrary viewpoint. The spherical triangle *PSF* on the surface of the visual sphere is bounded by the arcs of great circles. *P* is the pole of the reference system, *S* is the stimulus object, and *F* is the point on which the eye is currently fixed. The sides of the triangle *abc* are measured by their angular subtense at the eye at the center of the sphere; thus *a* is the visual angle of the stimulus from the current point of fixation, *b* is the visual angle between the reference pole and the point of fixation, and c is the visual angle between the reference pole and the stimulus. The corner angles of the triangle (α, β, y) are the angles between the planes of the three intersecting great circles. Angular distance *a* is particularly important because it equals the eccentricity of the retinal image of *S* from the fovea, which is related to rod-cone ratio, ganglion cell density, visual acuity, detectability of signals at night, retinal illumination, and many other aspects of perception and visual performance.

from some chosen reference axis. The third degree (rolling, spin, or torsion about the line of sight) is usually a function of the other two, and is particularly sensitive to the choice of the reference coordinate system. There is thus a useful truth in the humorous remark that "the rolling of the eyes is a subject that depends very much upon your point of view." We consider three reference systems based on the three mutually perpendicular axes, because they have different advantages. The angles in different coordinate systems are sometimes distinguished by different terms, such as elevation and azimuth, latitude and longitude, meridian and eccentricity, and so forth, but it is simpler to use the terms longitude and latitude for all three systems, for these terms have very clear meanings. Similarly, the simple term "rolling" is reserved for any rotation *about* the line of sight, in place of more technical terms, such as torsion, false torsion, and cyclorotation. Whatever the system, we first specify longitude, then latitude, then rolling, and identify each by subscripts 1–3. It is also assumed in most of this section that the head is fixed and erect, and that the lines of sight are initially straight ahead and parallel, as if fixating a point on the horizon. This initial position of the eye defines the *primary position*.

1.1.2. Listing System of Axes. In the Listing coordinate system the polar axis is horizontal and coincides with the line of sight when the eye is in the primary position. In this familiar system (Fig. 10.3) the meridians specify the directions, and the circles of latitude the eccentricities, of stimulus objects that may attract the eye. According to *Listing's law*, when the eye moves from the primary position or pole to a secondary position it can be deemed to do so in three successive operations: (1) selection of a meridian L_1, (2) movement along that meridian to a latitude L_2, and (3) rolling around the line of sight by an amount L_3, *which is generally zero* for normal subjects and movements of less than about 25°. Thus if the line of sight moves away from the primary position along a Listing meridian, afterimages or anatomical features on the eye do not change their orientation *relative to that meridian*, within the limits of Listing's law. In fact, the features can be seen to roll relative to that meridian, but only toward the very extremes of gaze, or if an extraocular muscle is weakened by disease, or if the fixation point is very near (Boeder, 1957; Quereau, 1955). The advantage of Listing coordinates is that the normal range of eye positions can often be described by the two parameters L_1 and L_2, because L_3 is nearly 0. The gaze can be directed in this coordinate system, relative to some fixed optical apparatus, by means of a fixation point sliding along a conventional perimeter arc (Fig. 10.4), though the arrangement is not very convenient as the polar and optical axes coincide, and so the pivots of the perimeter arc may interfere with optical apparatus.

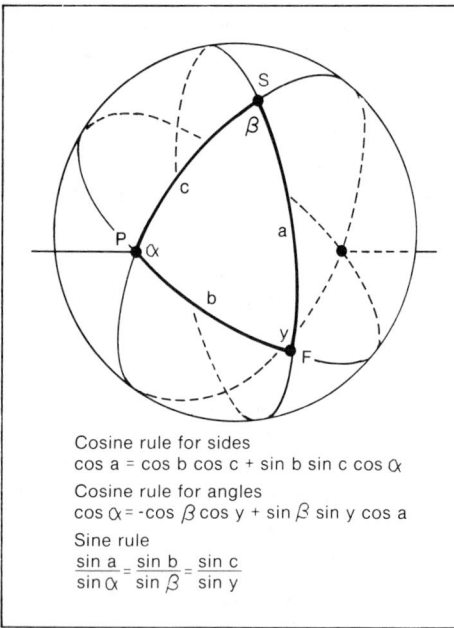

1.1.3. Fick System of Axes. In the Fick coordinate system, the polar axis through the eye is vertical, as we often visualize the poles of our planet, and so the equatorial plane of the reference system is horizontal, whereas the planes of the meridians of longitude are vertical planes. The virtue of the Fick system is that it contains these very important planes through the eye. See Figure 10.5. The line of sight can be deemed to leave the primary position and arrive at a secondary position by the three successive operations of (1) rotating through an angle F_1 in the horizontal equatorial plane to a new meridian, (2) elevating along the meridian of longitude to a particular latitude F_2, and (3) undergoing rolling F_3, which is a function of F_1 and F_2. When the eye looks upward and outward, the top of an initially

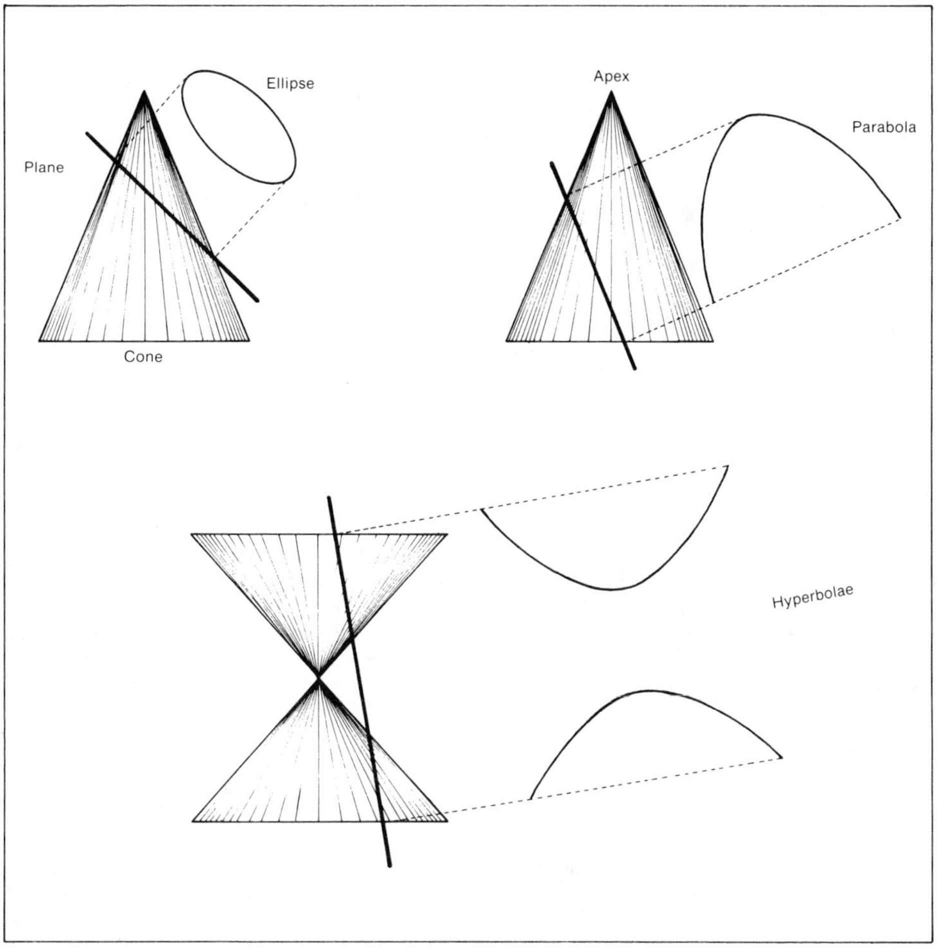

Figure 10.2. Conic sections generated by eye movements. If the eye is at the apex of a cone, the surface of the cone can be imagined to be generated by the line of sight as it tracks around a circular object. The projections of the cone on a plane have different shapes depending on the orientation of the cone and the plane. By line of sight is meant the line projecting the fovea, via the optical nodal points of the eye, to the current point of fixation. The nodal points are actually several millimeters anterior to the center of rotation of the eye, but this separation is so small relative to usual object distances that it is ignored in the rest of this chapter.

vertical linear afterimage, impressed on the fovea when the eye was in the primary position, is rolled outward from the vertical (*extorsion*) and is no longer in the plane of the longitude circle. If one wishes to direct the eye according to Fick coordinates, this is easily done by means of a fixation point attached to a vertical jointed and pivoting parallelogram. See Figure 10.6.

1.1.4. Helmholtz System of Axes. In the Helmholtz coordinate system the polar axis is horizontal and it passes through both eyes. The *plane of regard* is defined as the plane that includes this axis and the lines of sight of both eyes. The plane of the zero meridian in this system corresponds to the horizontal plane of regard, and the planes of the other meridian circles correspond to various elevations of the plane of regard. See Figure 10.7 (page 10-8). The line of sight can be deemed to leave the primary position and arrive at some other position by three successive operations: (1) elevation through an angle H_1 in the equatorial plane to a new meridian, (2) moving along the meridian to a new latitude H_2, and (3) rolling through an angle H_3, which is a function of H_1 and H_2. When the eye looks upward and outward, the outer end of an initially horizontal afterimage is rotated upward and inward relative to a horizontal line that is the projection of the current plane of regard (*intorsion*). The eye can be directed in this system, relative to some fixed optical apparatus, by means of a fixation point that slides along a semicircular arc pivoted at its ends, so as to rotate about the horizontal polar axis through the two eyes (Fig. 10.8, page 10-9). The advantage of the Helmholtz system is that it contains the planes of regard. In addition, it is easy to correct H_1 by simple addition or subtraction, if the initial estimate of the horizontal plane of regard is in error when setting up the subject. A similar correction of F_1 involves trigonometry.

1.1.5. Interconversions. Relations between the angles and coordinate systems are given in Figure 10.9 (page 10-9) but in applications the reader will need to check consistency in the origins and positive directions for measuring the various angles. Fry (1968) gives nomograms for interconversions. For a general mathematical treatment see Westheimer (1957), Alpern (1969), and Bechai and Hallett (1977).

1.1.6. Physiological Implications. With these three systems in mind it is easy to approach otherwise difficult questions. For example, a patch of photoreceptors, which is initially vertical

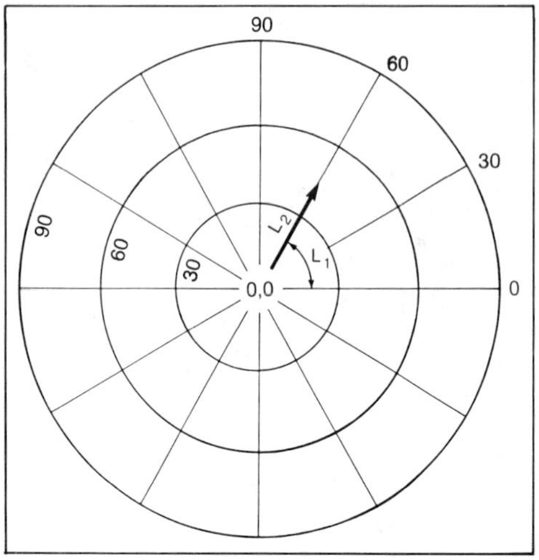

Figure 10.3. The Listing coordinate system for eye movements illustrated by the easily drawn zenithal equidistant projection. The orientation of the eye is specified by moving $L_2°$ along a chosen meridian L_1 away from the pole (0, 0) or primary. There is usually no rolling L_3 around the line of sight (Fick's law). This projection is important (1) because L_3 is nearly 0, and (2) for showing movements of the eyes away from the primary position (0, 0). The plot also reflects the crudely circular distribution of visual functions about the retinal fovea.

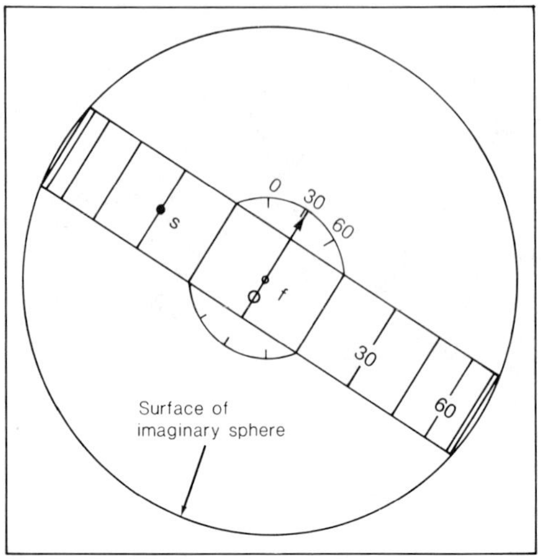

Figure 10.4. Apparatus for Listing system measurements. Presentation of stimulus *s* while the subject fixates point *f* at the origin of a conventional perimeter arc calibrated in Listing coordinates.

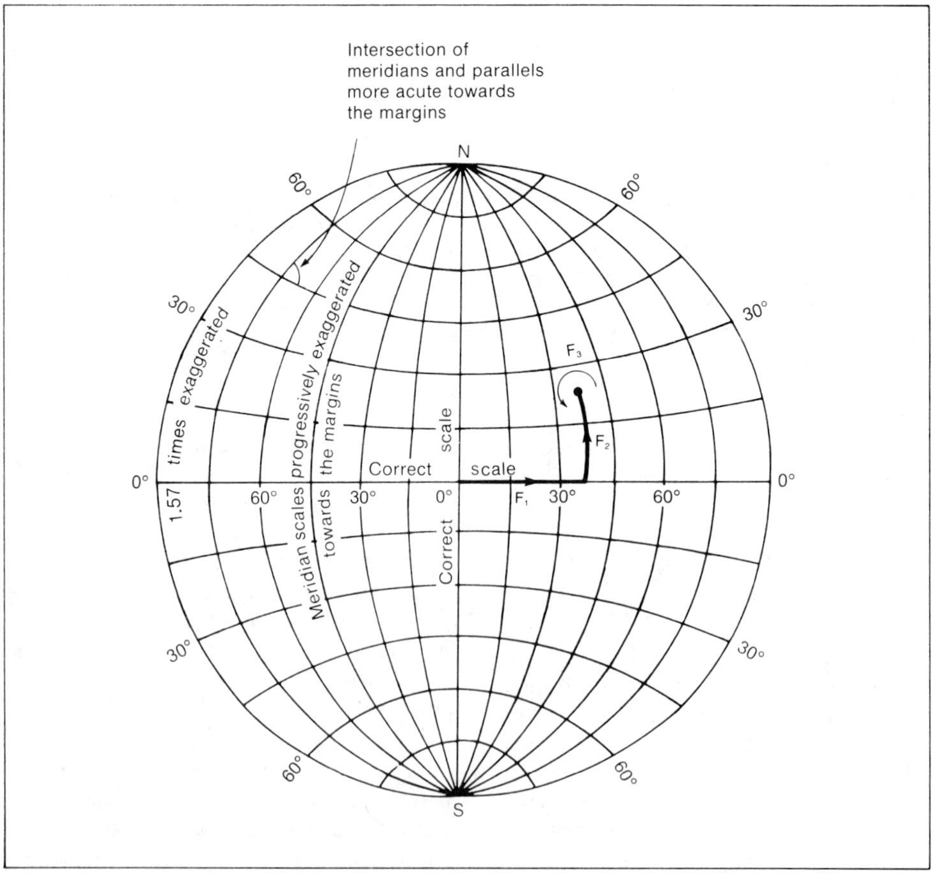

Figure 10.5. The Fick coordinate system for eye movements illustrated by a zenithal equidistant projection. The polar axis is vertical in this system. Some problems with this nonperspective projection are noted on the diagram. The point 0, 0 is the straight-ahead or primary position of the line of sight. The static orientation of the eye at some other position is specified by moving $F_1°$ horizontally along the equator to a meridian, ascending to latitude F_2, and rolling around the line of sight by $F_3°$. Although the nonzero values of F_3 are inconvenient, this projection is important because the meridians correspond to vertical planes through the eye.

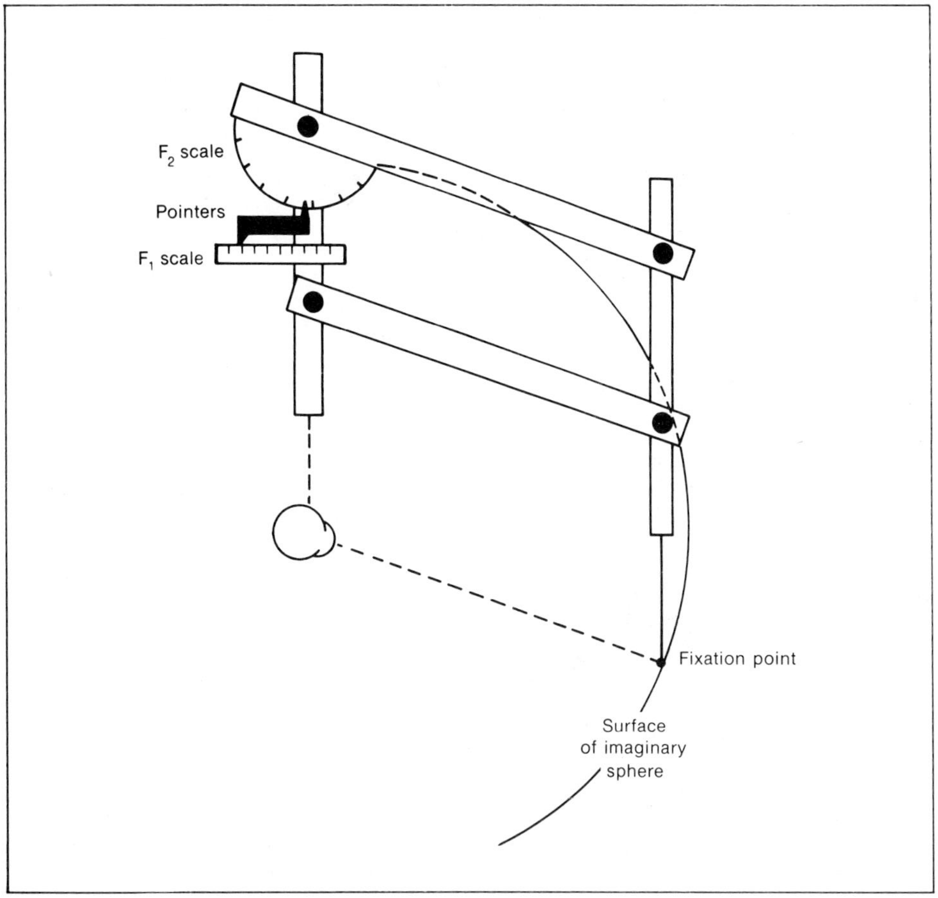

Figure 10.6. Apparatus for Fick system measurements. Method of moving a fixation point over the surface of a sphere by means of a jointed and pivoted parallelogram with scales that read Fick coordinates (author's laboratory).

when the eye is in the primary position, is extorted by about $F_3 = 10°$ relative to the Fick vertical, after an eye movement of magnitude $L_2 = 25°$ obliquely upward and outward ($L_1 = 45°$). An initially horizontal patch of photoreceptors intorts relative to the Helmholtz plane of regard by an exactly opposite amount ($H_3 = -10°$). Thus the projection of these two orthogonal patches on a flat screen or camera directly ahead of the subject is a scissors shape owing to the geometric perspective. See Figure 10.10 (page 10-10). Many clinicians refer to normal values of F_3 or H_3 (i.e., $L_3 = 0$) as "false torsion" and reserve the term "cyclorotation" for deviations from these values due to disease or special stimulus conditions. For a more extensive discussion, see Southall (1937/1961), Alpern (1969), and Helmholtz (1910/1926).

Rolling relative to the vertical (F_3) or the plane of regard (H_3) is never very large, and so a line-detecting neuron in the visual cortex which responds to, say, vertical stripes in the primary position should function in most other comfortable directions of gaze. Listing's law (i.e., $L_3 = 0$) is a special case of the *law of Donders*, which simply says that the eye has a particular reproducible orientation for every possible position. This strongly implies that there is a unique neural discharge to the eye muscles for every possible eye position (Westheimer, 1973), and so the eye should go to whatever orbital address is commanded, irrespective of current position, in the fashion of a stepping motor. This raises the question, "How many possible eye positions are there?" If there were only one nerve fiber per muscle, the number of statistically different firing patterns would be severely limited, and thus the number of possible eye positions finite. Actually, there are thousands of nerve fibers, and so this limitation is unlikely.

Failure of the brain to allow for torsion could lead to defective sensing of the vertical if everyday cues are lacking. When subjects fixate in different directions, their settings for the vertical are found to lie midway between veridicality and the direction of the normally vertical meridian of the eye, as predicted by Listing's law or observable from the projections of an initially vertical afterimage. Evidently the brain may contain signals indicating rolling of the eyes (Nakayama & Balliet, 1977).

The "reason" for Listing's law tantalizes. Extreme torsion would stress the optic nerve or conjunctivas and lead to damage and pain. Helmholtz believed that an object is more easily recognized if it is always tracked and approached with the retina in the same orientation, and he used integral calculus to show that Listing's law minimizes the sum of the squared errors that arise from ocular rolling as the eye searches its usual field of view. Fick and Wundt, however, viewed Listing's law as reducing muscular exertion (Helmholtz, 1910/1926). Westheimer (1981) notes that, given the approximate nature of Listing's law, it is hard to be sure whether it derives from efficient feedback regulation or is largely circumstantial.

1.2. Cartographic Aspects

A major part of the science of vision can be epitomized as "how the real world maps into the brain, and how the activity of the

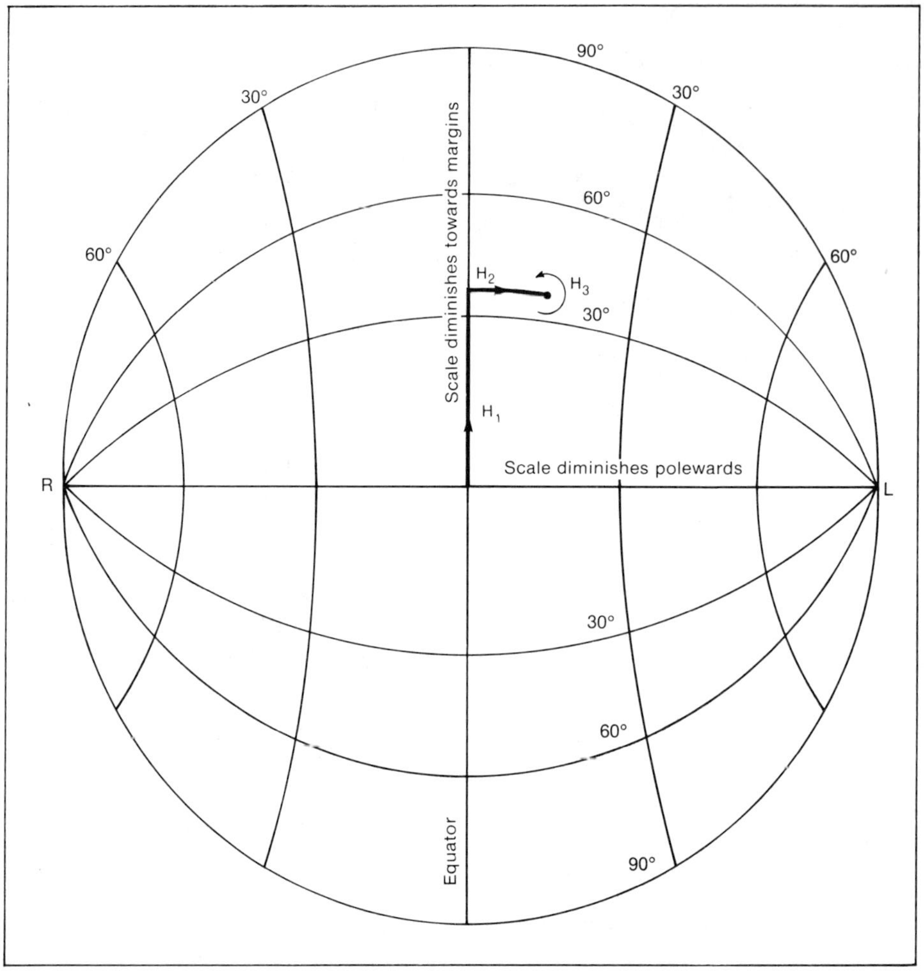

Figure 10.7. The Helmholtz coordinate system for eye movements illustrated by Lambert's zenithal equal-area projection. The polar axis is horizontal in this system. An arbitrary position of the line of sight can be specified by ascending the equator by $H_1°$, moving outward $H_2°$ along a meridian, and then rolling $H_3°$ around the line of sight. Although the nonzero values of H_3 are inconvenient, the importance of this projection is that meridians correspond to various elevations of the plane of regard.

brain maps into the movements of the body and its parts," but cartography is as yet little exploited by visual scientists. This may change with greater use of two-dimensional eye tracking and complex visual stimulus arrays.

1.2.1. Zenithal Gnomonic Projections

1.2.1.1. Relation to Stimulus Design. Figure 10.11 (top), on page 10-10, illustrates the projection of the meridians and parallels of a sphere of radius r onto a flat plane, as seen by an eye at the center of the sphere. This zenithal (= onto a flat plane) gnomic (= central) projection is the natural or perspective map of Listing's coordinate system (Fig. 10.3) and has several practical applications. The map may be used to direct fixation if one wishes to dispense with the sphere or perimeter arc. The distance of a parallel from the pole, $r \tan L_2$, provides a rule for shaping flat stimulus objects to replace objects that would otherwise be mounted on the sphere or perimeter arc. Such shaping may not be necessary for ordinary eccentricities ($L_2 <$ 30°). The map is also useful for plotting eye movements, because direction from the pole is correct and any straight line is the shortest distance between two points.

Referring again to Figure 10.1, if P is the pole, F is the current point of fixation (angular coordinates L_1, L_2), and S is the current angular position of a stimulus object (coordinate L_1', L_2'), then $b = L_2$, $c = L_2'$, and $\alpha = L_1 - L_1'$, whence the shortest angular distance $a°$ between stimulus and fixation can be found from the cosine rule for sides. (Listing coordinates are used merely as an example; the pole P could equally well be the Fick or Helmholtz pole.) The value of the eccentricity a has an obvious bearing on visual acuity, retinal illumination, and other parameters relevant to perception and performance.

1.2.1.2. Relation to Retinal Illumination. There is general agreement about how to calculate retinal illumination only when the eye looks directly ($a = 0$) at a small object, because the Gaussian optical approximation then applies, and area magnification is inversely proportional to the square of the posterior nodal distance (Le Grand, 1957). The magnification factors are not established for peripheral vision. The peripheral retinal surface is obliquely oriented to the exit pupil within the eye, but is closer to the pupil than the foveal region, and the photoreceptors are oblique to the surface so as to be directed at the pupil, which optimizes energy capture. It is best to monitor the angle a in critical situations, until the issue of retinal illumination in the periphery is settled.

1.2.1.3. Relation to Systems of Axes. Figure 10.11 showed the zenithal gnomonic projection of the Listing system. Figure

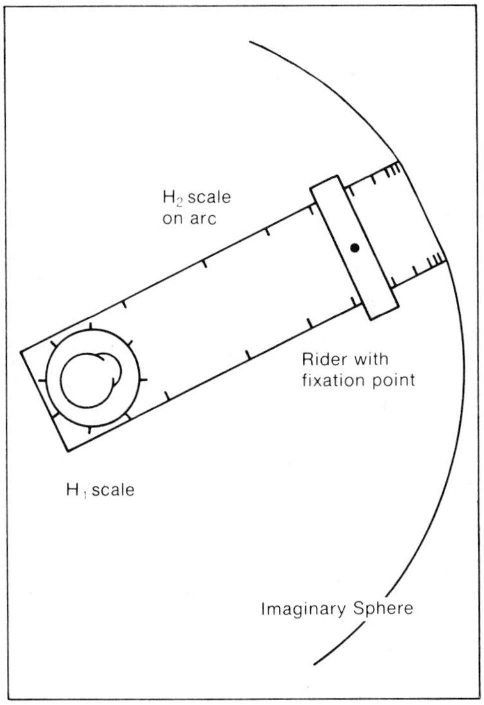

Figure 10.8. Apparatus for Helmholtz system of measurements. Method of moving a fixation point along a horizontally pivotted arc and thus realizing the Helmholtz coordinate system. The horizontal axis passes through the two eyes.

10.12 shows that of the Fick system, or of the Helmholtz system rotated by 90°. Area and shape are badly distorted at large enough eccentricities.

1.2.2. Zenithal Equidistant Projections. The polar equidistant projection is commonly used, and is easily drawn because the parallels are equally spaced. Distance and direction from the center of the map are correct, and shape is satisfactory for distances of less than 30°. See Figure 10.3 for the polar projection, and Figure 10.5 for the equatorial.

1.2.3. Zenithal Stereographic Projections. Figure 10.13 illustrates the projection of the meridians and parallels by a light at a point opposite to Listing's pole. This point is called the "occipital point" in the eye movement literature. Any circle on the sphere that passes through this point is called a "direction circle" and projects as a straight line on the map in the upper part of the figure. The projection is orthomorphic; that is, angles are correct.

The relation between the stereographic projection and the kinematics of eye movements can be developed with the aid of Figure 10.14. This represents a stereographic map of the projection of a cross-shaped foveal afterimage which moves with the eye and translates along a series of arcs, leaving the primary position (0, 0) and arriving at position *f* by a number of different routes. Orientation remains constant, as required by Listing's law. The major question, "Along which arcs does the eye move?" was answered at length by Helmholtz (1910/1926). The short answer is along those arcs that become straight lines in a stereographic map, that is, along the arcs of direction circles. The eye can track from the primary position to *f* either directly along the arc of a single direction circle (in this case a Listing meridian) or indirectly along a series of arcs of different direction circles. There is no need to track along an actual direction circle drawn on the surface of a physical sphere; the central (gnomonic) projection of the direction circle on a plane will suffice. Figure 10.15 illustrates the method of projection, whereas Figure 10.10 shows examples of the projections or direction hyperbolas. There are actually infinities of direction circles at all possible orientations through the occipital point, and consequently there are infinities of axes around which the eye can rotate and satisfy

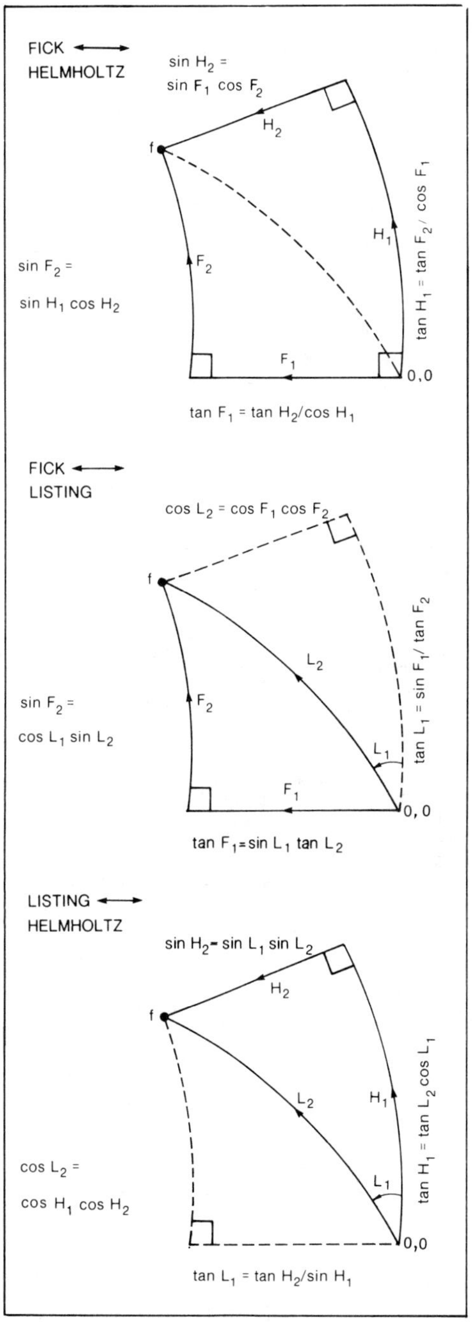

Figure 10.9. Interconversions between the Fick, Helmholtz, and Listing coordinate systems for recording eye movements. The three diagrams show part of the surface of the visual sphere within which the eye is centered, the lines being the arcs of great circles. Point (0, 0) is the straight-ahead or primary position of the line of sight, and point *f* is the new point of fixation. The coordinates of *f* are (F_1, F_2) or (H_1, H_2) or (l_1, L_2), according to the reference system chosen. If one prefers to measure the angle of the Listing meridian from the horizontal (l_1), rather than from the vertical, as here, then substitute $\sin l_1 = \cos L_1$, $\cos l_1 = \sin L_1$, and $\tan l_1 = 1/\tan L_1$.

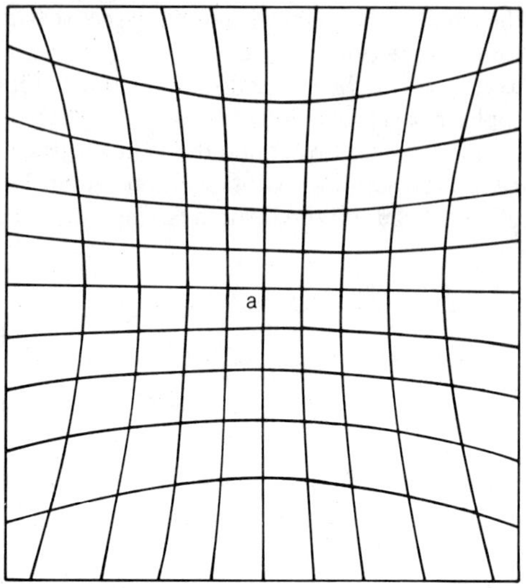

Figure 10.10. To illustrate the projections of afterimages and direction circles in the plane of fixation. The curved lines are called direction hyperbolas. If the afterimage of a vertical cross is formed while fixating point *a* then, on shifting fixation obliquely outward, the projection of the initially vertical and horizontal limbs of the cross become angled (scissors-shaped) and the limbs are *tangent* to the intersecting direction hyperbolas shown. Direction hyperbolas are the central (gnomonic) projections of direction circles in the plane of fixation. The direction hyperbolas shown here are not the only possible ones; there are many other orientations. The eye always tracks along a direction hyperbola when it moves according to Listing's law. (From H. Helmholtz, in J. P. C. Southall (Ed. & trans.), *Physiological Optics*, Dover, 1926. Reprinted with permission.)

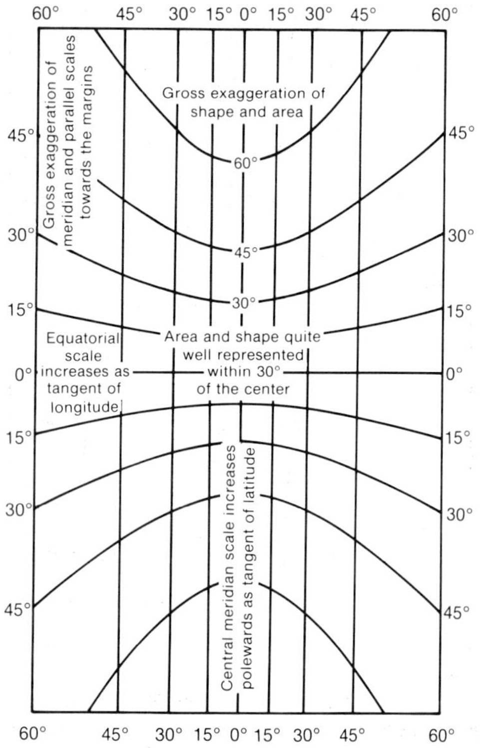

Figure 10.12. Zenithal gnomonic projection of the Fick coordinate system for eye movements (or of the Helmholtz system if the diagram is rotated 90°). This projection is useful for positioning stimuli on a flat surface.

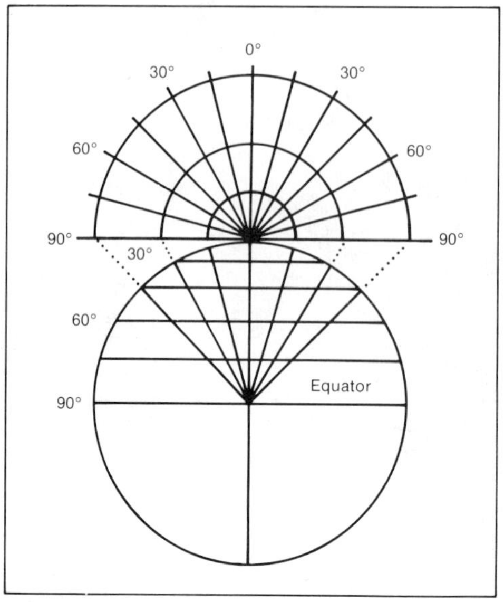

Figure 10.11. Zenithal gnomonic projection of the Listing coordinate system for eye movements. This projection is useful for placing stimuli on a flat surface.

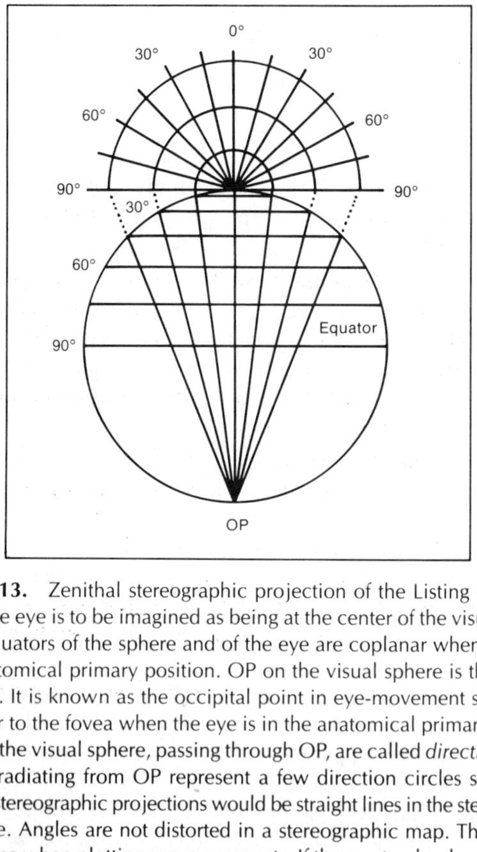

Figure 10.13. Zenithal stereographic projection of the Listing coordinate system. The eye is to be imagined as being at the center of the visual sphere, and the equators of the sphere and of the eye are coplanar when the eye is in the anatomical primary position. OP on the visual sphere is the point of projection. It is known as the occipital point in eye-movement studies and is posterior to the fovea when the eye is in the anatomical primary position. Circles on the visual sphere, passing through OP, are called *direction circles*. The lines radiating from OP represent a few direction circles seen "edge on"; their stereographic projections would be straight lines in the stereographic map above. Angles are not distorted in a stereographic map. The map has a special use when plotting eye movements. If the eye tracks along a straight line on a stereographic map, then the eye obeys Listing's law, and is rotating about a fixed axis perpendicular to the plane of a direction circle.

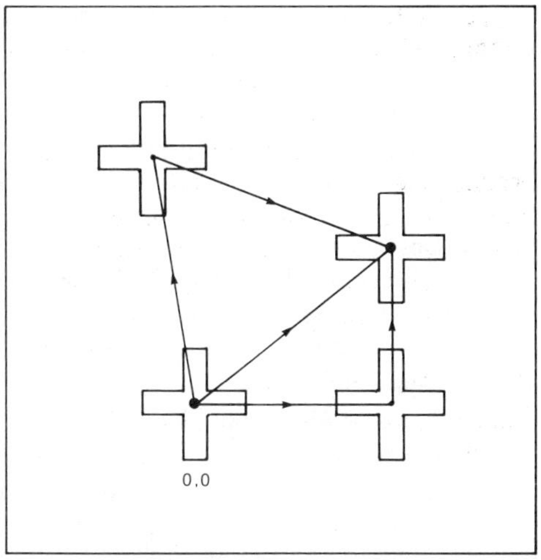

Figure 10.14. Tracking along direction circles as the basis of Listing's law. The map illustrates the projection of an afterimage cross at the fovea, which translates along straight lines, without any change of orientation, from the primary position (0, 0) to the current point of fixation *f*, via direct or indirect routes. Angles are undistorted if the map is a stereographic map. Direction circles project as straight lines in this map. Movements that do not change the orientation of the eye are therefore along the arcs of direction circles.

Listing's law, each axis passing through the center of rotation of the eye and the center of the direction circle (Fig. 10.15). These axes do not all lie in a single plane. Some axes do lie in a single frontal plane (so-called Listing's plane) through the center of rotation of the eye, but only those axes that allow the eye to move directly to and fro in the primary position along the Listing meridians. If an eye movement were to be a curved arc when plotted on a stereographic map, Listing's law would be invalid, although it might be possible to regard the axis of rotation as continuously shifting. The present use of the stereographic projection was anticipated by Boeder (1957).

1.3. Anatomical and Mechanical Aspects

1.3.1. Rotational Axes of Muscle Pairs. Boeder's (1961) study of the cooperation of the extraocular muscles is an interesting application of Listing's law and classical nineteenth-century data. His approach is a useful stepping-stone to the modern position. He begins by defining an individual muscle's plane of action as the plane through the center of rotation of the eye and the effective insertion and origin of the muscle; its axis of rotation is perpendicular to this. Five of the six eye muscles—the vertical and horizontal rectus pairs and the superior oblique—actually originate posteriorly and slightly *medially* at the optic foramen, although the superior oblique runs around the trochlea or pulley at the front of the orbit and consequently has an effectively anterior superior and medial origin. The remaining muscle, the inferior oblique, originates anteriorly, inferiorly, and medially. The tendinous parts of the muscles are wrapped around the globe of the eye for 20–80°, depending on the muscle. The insertions into the sclera are rather broad, so that when the eye rotates, the six axes of rotation do not shift as much as one might expect, even though the insertions may move as much as 6 mm during contraction or relaxation. However, the axes *do* shift!

The individual axes of the opposing superior and inferior rectus muscles (SR and IR, or the vertical rectus pair) are not parallel but are at angles to each other, and move considerably when the eye is *abducted* toward the temple or *adducted* toward the nose by the medial and lateral rectus muscles (also called the horizontal recti). Nevertheless, the common axis of the vertical rectus pair remains effectively fixed in the horizontal plane, as in Figure 10.16(a). The eye therefore rotates around this fixed axis when one vertical rectus muscle contracts and the other reciprocally extends. The movement of the line of sight, however, hinges upon the *initial position* of the eye, varying between the extremes of pure elevation-depression if the eye is initially abducted 23°, and pure rolling if the eye could be initially adducted 67° [Fig. 10.16(b)]. The effect of the muscle pairs when the initial position is the primary position is also shown in Figure 10.16(c). Hypothetically, *cocontraction* of any muscle pair can also rotate the eye in appropriate circumstances, but cocontraction or corelaxation has never been demonstrated electromyographically, and retraction or protrusion of the healthy eye is never more than a few hundred microns (Enright, 1980). In the case of the oblique muscle pair the common axis of rotation is not quite in the horizontal plane, and Boeder claims that the common axis swings outward (from $F_1 = -20$ to $-55°$) as the eye abducts. This axis shift may simplify sensory and perceptual analysis, because if the common axis were fixed, as is commonly assumed [Fig. 10.16(a)], then extreme abduction of the line of sight beyond the oblique axis would automatically reverse the mechanical actions of the two eye muscles, and would thus complicate sensory-motor integration. The common axis of rotation of the medial and lateral rectus muscles (horizontal recti) is commonly taken to be vertical, so that the actions of the horizontal rectus pair are visually thought to be the particularly simple ones of abduction-adduction, whereas Boeder argues that this axis tilts backward and forward by $\pm 5°$ when other muscles elevate and depress the eye.

1.3.2. Extraocular Muscles and Semicircular Canals. A scheme showing the muscles and canals excited by yaw, pitch, and roll of the head is given in Figure 10.17. The connections between canals and muscles in the "same plane" (i.e., in parallel or almost parallel planes) are behaviorally adaptive. A turn to

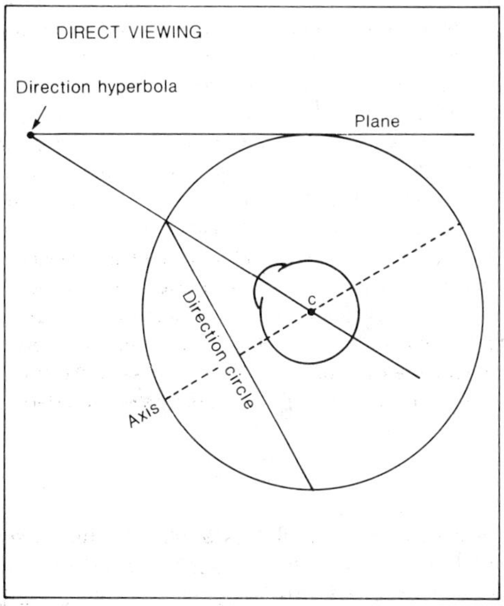

Figure 10.15. Direction circles and hyperbolas. The diagram shows the eye at the center of the visual sphere. The eye obeys Listing's law and is tracking along a direction circle on the sphere or its central projection ("direction hyperbola") on a flat plane.

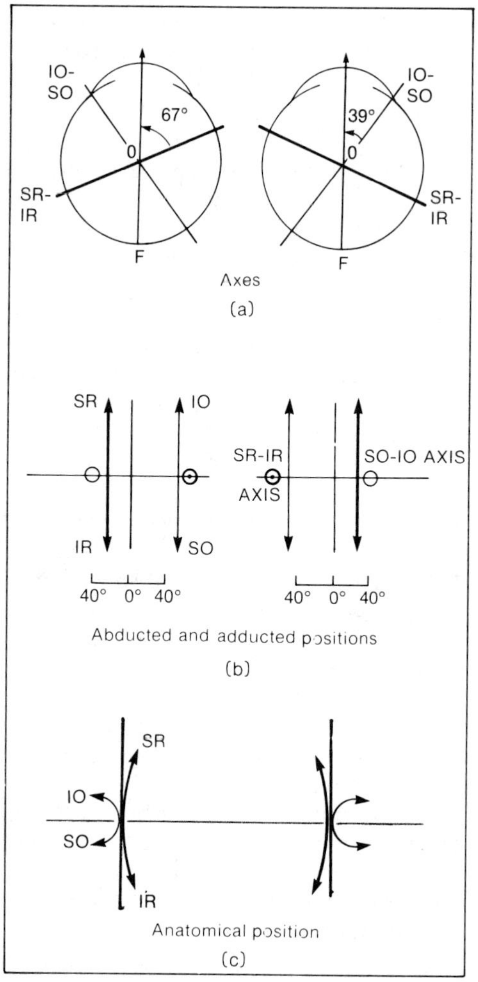

Figure 10.16. Actions of the individual extraocular muscles. (a) Rotations of an eye by its three pairs of muscles are simplified to rotations about three *fixed* axes. IO-SO is the common axis of the inferior and superior oblique muscles. SR-IR is the common axis of the vertical recti (the superior and inferior recti). The common vertical axis of the horizontal recti (the lateral and medial recti) is seen end-on at the intersection of these two axes. F is the fovea with its projected line of sight. The effect of any muscle on the line of sight depends on the initial position of the eye. The two eyes are shown here in the primary position, but for clinical testing they are often directed left or right for convenience, because the axes can be considered to be fixed. (b) Plot represents field of view of each eye; the intersection of the orthogonal reference axes is the primary position. From the top diagram it follows that the vertical recti (SR, IR) are pure elevator-depressors if the line of sight is initially abducted by 90 − 67 = 23°, and pure rollers if adducted 67°. Similarly, the oblique muscles (IO, SO) are pure elevator-depressors if the eye is adducted 90 − 39 = 51° and pure rollers if abducted 39°. (c) Plot represents fields of view of each eye, but now the line of sight is initially in the straight-ahead or primary anatomical position. This leads to the statements that the *primary* actions of the vertical recti are elevation-depression with *secondary* torsion and adduction, whereas the primary actions of the oblique pair are torsion with secondary elevation-depression and abduction.

the right about the vertical yaw axis, for example, excites the mechanoreceptors of the right horizontal canal and thus produces, after only very few milliseconds, a smooth contraction of the right medial and left lateral recti that tends to maintain "eye position" (i.e., direction) in space. Such movements are often known as the *slow phase* of nystagmus. See the caption to Figure 10.17 for details.

The mutual relations of the eye muscles and semicircular canals in frontal and lateral-eyed animals have been reexamined by Simpson and Graf (1981), who confirm Ohm in the following: (1) An approximate relation of the planes of actions of the muscle pairs (assuming fixed axes) and the planes of corresponding canals is recognizable across species. This is supported by electrical stimulation of the canals. (2) Changes in the insertions and planes of action of the vertical muscles suffice to explain why head roll evokes compensatory rolling in frontal-eyed man and compensatory elevation and depression in the lateral-eyed rabbit. There is no need to invoke major changes in the mechanics of the canals or in the neural paths.

1.3.3. Interactions of All Six Muscles. Boeder (1961) calculated the shifts in the insertions of the six muscles when the eye rotates according to Listing's law. One interesting result is that all muscles, not just the horizontal rectus pair, must be active even in the "simple" movement of abduction and adduction, if only to "take up and let out slack" and thus stabilize the eye. Another result is that very many eye positions can be uniquely coded by the ratio of activity across only three "channels" or muscle pairs (see Fig. 14 of Boeder, 1961). The ratio of activity across the three muscle pairs codes direction (L_1), whereas magnitude (L_2) can be coded by a single scale factor that converts the ratio to actual discharge rates. Ratio-coding across parallel motor channels explains why the "*cancellation*" of a saccade or its "*amplitude modification*" is a separate operation in the saccadic system: the direction of a saccade is likely cancelled in an all-or-none manner, because the ratio of activity across the various motor nuclei is established in a complex manner at a higher motor level; but the amplitude of a saccade can be continuously graded, because this need only involve a common increase or decrease of neural excitability in all oculomotor nuclei.

The computer model of Robinson (1975b) goes beyond Boeder's analysis to consider not only Volkman's data for the coordinates of the muscle insertions and origins, but also the length-tension curves, the passive elasticity of the orbital contents, the variable path taken by a muscle across the globe when the globe is in a different position, the twisting of the tendons and sideslipping of the muscles, and thus the variable point at which a muscle makes contact and exerts force. Only part of a muscle's force is counter to that of its antagonist; other parts are expended against the passive tissues of the orbit and wasted in cross-coupling effects by the muscles fighting among themselves. These actions change in complex ways and a computer solution is nearly always necessary. In addition, one must distinguish between the innervation and the mechanical response.

"*Innervation*" is a parameter that reflects the motor neuron discharge frequencies. Innervation is relevant to the sensory physiologist who is interested in "*efference copy*" and the perceptual localization of objects in space. Efference copy is a copy of the neural motor outflow to the eye muscles that is used by the brain as an indication of eye position. Retinal-image position plus eye position localize the stimulus relative to the head. "Innervation" is measured in practice as the isometric tension produced by a muscle when its eye is clamped in the anatomical primary position while the other eye fixates in various directions. Figures 10.18–10.20 show Robinson's estimates of muscle innervation for all six muscles in Fick coordinates. The lines are iso-innervation contours. Equal shifts in fixation require unequal changes in innervation. When the eye is in the primary position, each muscle exerts roughly 10 g of tension (Fig. 10.18). Cursory

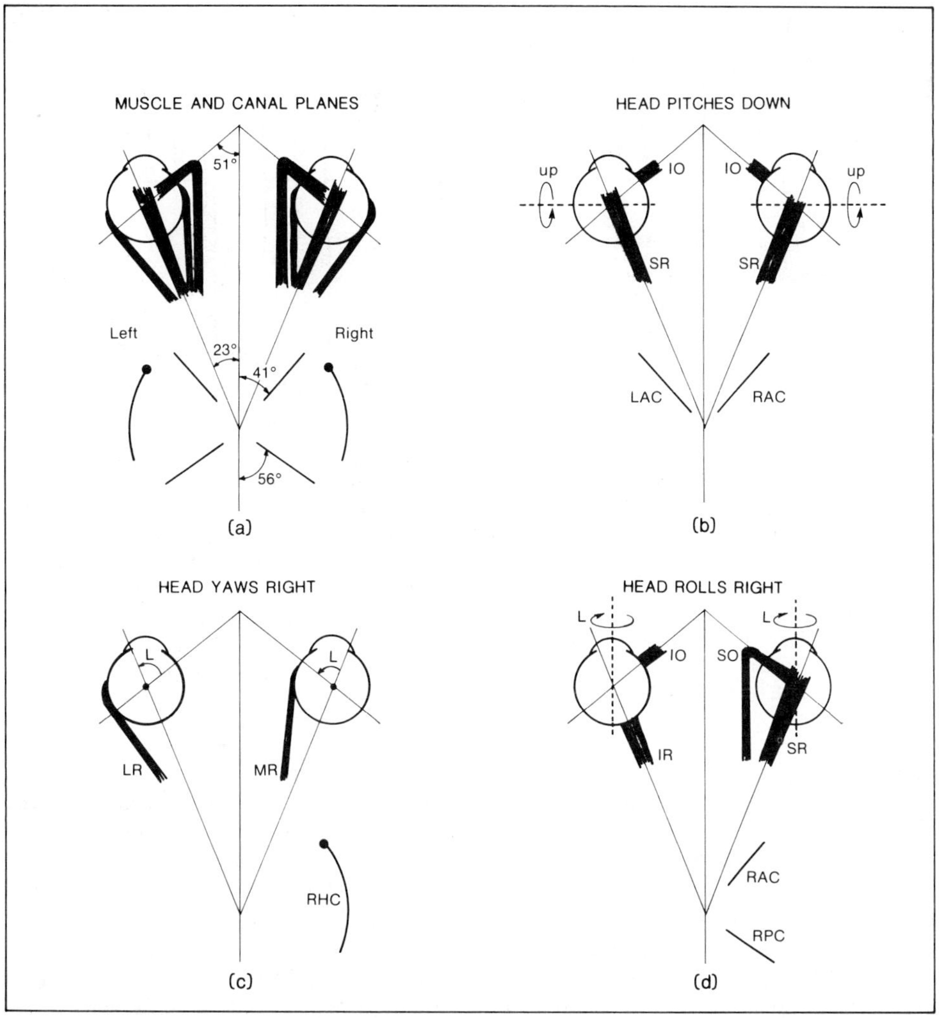

Figure 10.17. Scheme showing the semicircular canals and eye muscles activated by yaw, pitch, and roll movements of the head. (a) The muscles and canals are shown from above. Geometry and electrical stimulation show an association between each of the six extraocular muscles and the six semicircular canals. (The anterior canal excites the ipsilateral superior rectus and contralateral inferior oblique; the posterior canal excites the ipsilateral superior oblique and contralateral inferior rectus; the horizontal canal excites the ipsilateral medial rectus and contralateral lateral rectus.) Actually the so-called "horizontal" canals are horizontal only if the head is pitched 15° downward. (b, c, d) The principally excited (agonist) muscles and canals are shown for particular head movements. The small arrows near the axes show the direction of the compensatory ocular countermovements. Yaw left, pitch up, and roll left would evoke the complementary responses to the cases illustrated. LR, MR, SR, IR = lateral, medial, superior, and inferior rectus muscles. IO, SO = inferior and superior oblique muscles. RHC, LHC = right, left horizontal canal. RAC, LAC = right, left anterior canal. RPC, LPC = right, left posterior canal.

inspection might seem to suggest that a 15° abduction requires 30 g of lateral rectus tension to overcome the elastic forces of the passive orbital tissues and other muscles, including 1.5 g of medial rectus tension. This is too simple because the Figures show innervation or isometric forces, rather than mechanical consequences of movement. Actually, a 15° abduction needs *momentary* lateral and medial rectus forces of 24 and 5 g, respectively, to overcome viscoelastic drag, and the muscles are balanced in the new position of equilibrium at a maintained tension of about 13 g each, other passive forces being sufficiently weak in this instance (about 3 g) to be disregarded. Thus change of fixation in the important ±15° range of vision may be associated with quite small changes in maintained tension, because of the length-tension properties of muscle. Although a 15° abduction involves an effort of will, that is, a persistent change in innervation, at the mechanical level it is almost as if the orbit is "plastic" and has simply been reset.

An interesting aspect of Robinson's study is that it is often difficult to provide answers to general questions, such as, "Do the superior rectus and inferior oblique contribute equally to elevation from all positions of horizontal gaze?" An answer in terms of innervation may not be the same as the answer in terms of a mechanical parameter. The best general answer to this particular question seems to be the innervational answer that the two muscles actually participate about equally. The answer to the more specific question, "In abduction can the patient elevate further if the inferior oblique is paralyzed rather than the superior rectus?" is an innervational and mechanical "yes," which agrees with common clinical experience.

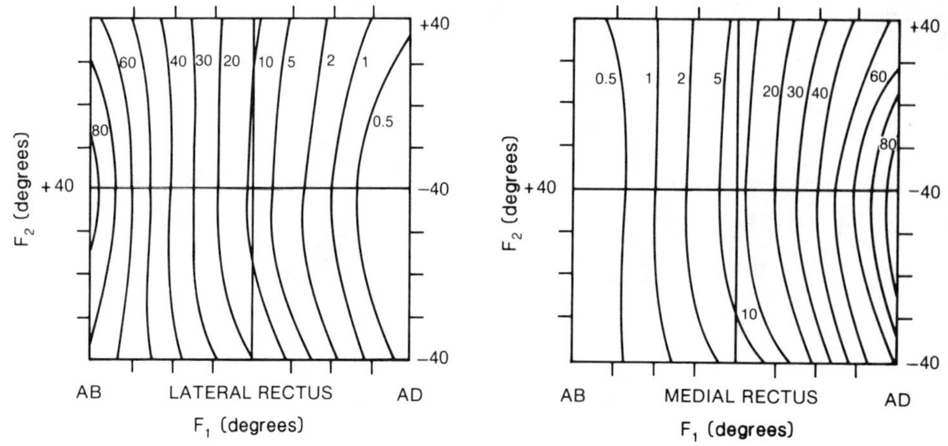

Figure 10.18. Combined actions of extraocular muscles at different fixation positions. Estimated innervation of the horizontal rectus pair as a function of eye position. Muscle innervation is expressed as the isometric tension (in grains) that would be developed if the eye were clamped in the anatomical primary or straight-ahead position. The contours are equi-innervation lines marked in grams. The plot is the field of gaze. Ordinate is the vertical Fick coordinate F_2 of gaze (range $\pm 40°$). Abscissa is the horizontal Fick coordinate F_1 (range $\pm 40°$; AB = abduction, AD = adduction). The intersection of axes in the center is the primary position. The plots in this and the next two figures may be relevant to perceptual questions that assume the neural discharge patterns at different fixation positions. (From D. A. Robinson, A quantitative analysis of extraocular muscle cooperation and squint, *Investigative Ophthalmology and Visual Science*, 1975, *14*. Reprinted with permission.)

More recently, important in situ data have been supplied by adding tension transducers to a pair of clinical forceps (Collins, Carlson, Scott, & Jampolski, 1981). The active force of a contracting muscle can be measured if its tendon is grasped with the forceps, through the anesthetized conjunctivas, while the other eye tracks to and fro through known angles. Passive loading can be measured by smoothly moving the eye with the forceps while the other eye fixates. If a subject is *orthophoric*, that is, if his eyes are naturally straight without overt strabismus or latent squint, then the active force and passive load must balance at every position; if not, the eye will turn in or out until there is a balance. Figure 10.21 shows that these active and passive forces are precisely balanced in the orthophoric subject, as explained in the legend. The passive load on the medial rectus proves to be larger than that on the lateral rectus, but this might have been anticipated as the medial rectus is larger and more powerful. Also, the forces in the $\pm 15°$ region prove to be somewhat larger than expected for the "plastic and resettable orbit" postulated above.

1.3.4. Failure of Donders' and Listing's Laws. These laws were considered in Section 1.1.6 as embodying the concept that there is a unique orientation of the eye at every eye position, no matter how the eye reached that position. The laws are most accurately approximated for static eye positions when the object of fixation is infinitely distant and the subject is normally sighted (emmetropic)—in which case, deviation from Listing's law ($L_3 = 0$) is typically less than 1° over wide ranges of movement. Significantly, these small errors do not accumulate if the eye tracks several times around a loop (Nakayama, 1975).

Various violations of Listing's law were known in the time of Helmholtz. For instance, the law can be invalid dynamically

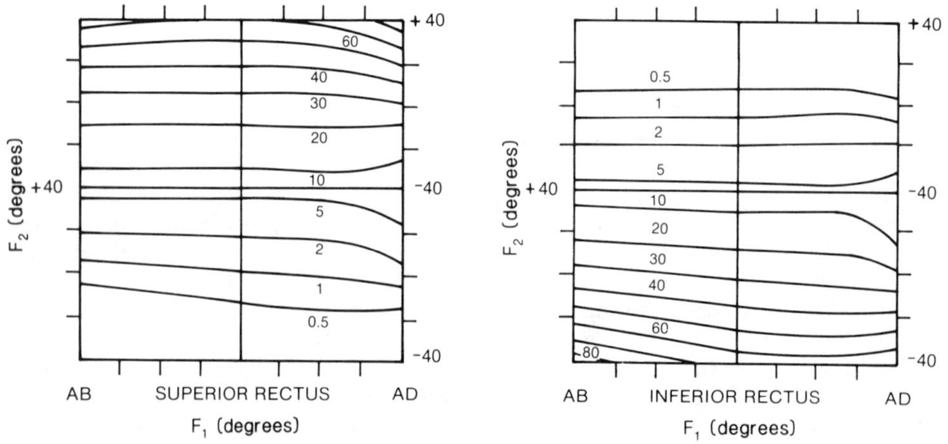

Figure 10.19. Combined actions of extraocular muscles. Estimated innervation of the oblique muscles as a function of the fixation position in Fick coordinates (F_1, F_2; AB = abduction, AD = adduction). (From D. A. Robinson, A quantitative analysis of extraocular muscle cooperation and squint, *Investigative Ophthalmology and Visual Science*, 1975, *14*. Reprinted with permission.)

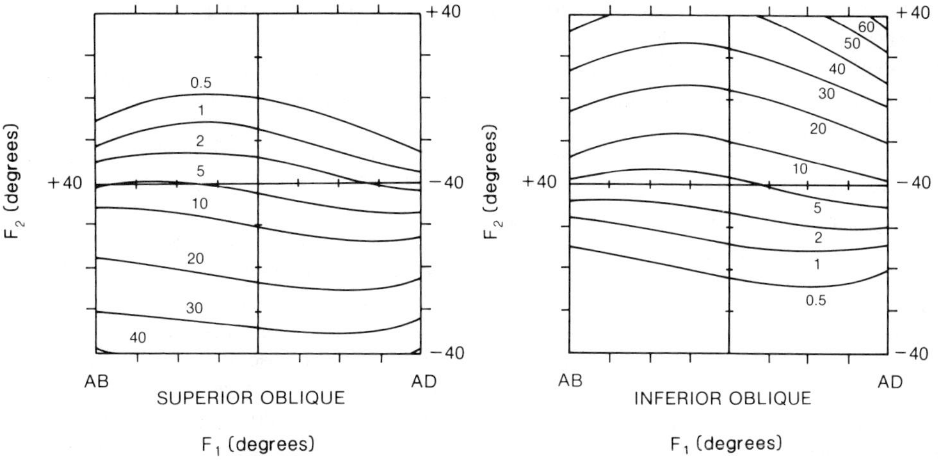

Figure 10.20. Combined actions of extraocular muscles. Estimated innervation for the vertical rectus pair as a function of the fixation position in Fick coordinates (F_1, F_2; AB = abduction, AD = adduction). (From D. A. Robinson, A quantitative analysis of extraocular muscle cooperation and squint, *Investigative Ophthalmology and Visual Science*, 1975, *14*. Reprinted with permission.)

(because an afterimage may take a little time to settle into its customary orientation after an eye movement, and the tops of initially vertical patches of photoreceptors may rotate slightly outward on convergence of the two eyes). There are also important variations between subjects. One of the more intriguing failures occurs during smooth-pursuit eye movements (Westheimer & McKee, 1973). The orientation of the eye, for a particular position of gaze, deviated systematically from the Listing law prediction by 0.9° (0–2.3) of rolling about the line of sight when the eye pursued a target through the specified position from different points in the visual field.

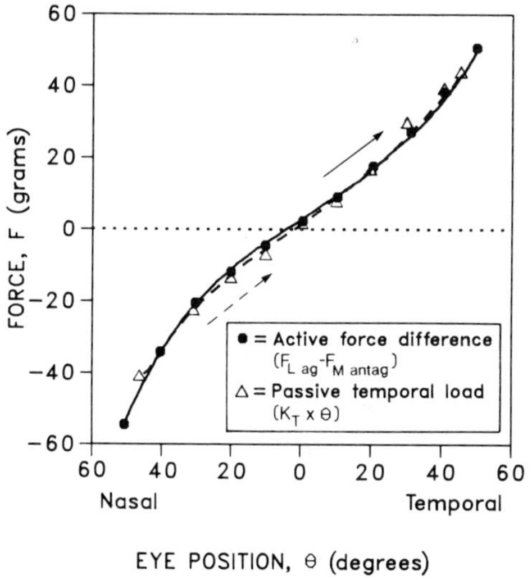

Figure 10.21. Extraocular muscle forces as a function of fixation position. To show the close match between active contractile and passive loading forces as the left eye abducts in an orthophoric subject. The right eye is tracking the stimulus, while the left eye is manipulated. Active force in the agonist of the left eye (left lateral rectus) is measured by holding the left eye adducted with the length-tension forceps (thus slackening the medial rectus) during right eye tracking to the left. The corresponding force in the antagonist (left medial rectus) is measured in a similar manner by holding the eye abducted. The difference between these two forces (agonist minus antagonist) is the active force rotating the eye left, and is shown by a continuous line in the figure. Passive force is measured by moving the left eye to different positions with the forceps while the right eye fixates; this yields the dotted line. The small differences between the left eye active and passive forces at a given right eye position, divided by the current spring stiffness (in degrees per gram), gives the difference in the equilibrium angle of the two eyes, which in this case is nearly 0, that is orthophoria. (From C. C. Collins, M. R. Carlson, A. B. Scott, & A. Jampolski, Extraocular muscle forces in normal human subjects, *Investigative Ophthalmology and Visual Science*, 1981, *20*. Reprinted with permission.)

Deviations from Donders' and Listing's laws when the gaze is static have received most attention. Quereau (1955) plotted the projection of the blind spot on a hemisphere marked in Listing coordinates for eight subjects. He believed Listing's law to be acceptably true. As the eye moves away from the primary position along a Listing meridian the orientation of the line linking the fovea and the blind spot does not shift relative to that meridian, that is, $L_3 = 0$, and the eye assumes the same orientation if it arrives at this new position from some other direction. A failure of Listing's law, amounting to $L_3 = 3$–$5°$, was seen at the extremes of gaze: outward when looking obliquely up and out, and inward for obliquely down and out. Allen and Carter (1967) photographed a piece of thread placed on the topically anesthetized "nonmoving eye" when the subject changed his binocular fixation from a far to a near object on the line of sight of the "nonmoving" eye. Of 17 successfully studied subjects, 16 showed a small outward rolling of the "nonmoving" eye of about 2 ± 2°, as the other eye made a large vergence movement.

More recently Enright (1980) occluded one eye and photographed the seeing eye as it fixated a nearer object on its line of sight: (1) the eye shifted laterally without rotation by about 120 μm (−67 to 225 μm for 12 subjects), (2) the cornea moved forward by about 70 μm (−16 to 142 μm for four subjects), and (3) rolled inward or outward by −1.6 to 2.1°, depending on the individual (nine subjects). The first of these effects is absent when the eye is not in the primary position and is inferred to be translation rather than rotation, because the equivalent rotation would be large enough to affect acuity and thus be sensed subjectively; but there is some room for doubt as the largest of the movements is equivalent to only 1°. Alpern (1969) has reviewed older experiments on how initially aligned objects become misaligned after a shift of fixation. These data suggest both translational and corkscrew movements.

In summary, the mechanisms of eye movements are remarkably simple, considering the light weight and soft consistency of the anatomical parts. There is no true center of rotation, and two degrees of rotational freedom are too few for very exact work. Some deviations from the ideal may originate in unbalanced cocontractions or corelaxations of muscles that are synergistic (supportive) to the major muscles involved. We must also remember that the brain always develops with the ability to control two eyes. It must therefore be rather rare for an experimenter successfully to simplify behavior by arranging the stimulus conditions to "exclude one eye."

1.3.5. Hering's Law. The two eyeballs and their 12 muscles form a system that is very complex anatomically and mechanically. The planes of action of the horizontal rectus pairs of the left and right eyes are parallel, but the muscle planes or axes of cooperating vertical muscles are not. For example, an object like an elevator, ascending and descending to the left of straight ahead, is tracked binocularly by the cooperative effort of the vertical rectus pair in the left eye and the oblique muscle pair in the right eye, the muscle planes being at an angle of $67 - 39 = 28°$, according to Figure 10.16. *Hering's law*, in its broadest form, states that the muscle pairs of the two orbits are precisely *yoked* through innate and acquired neural mechanisms, so as to facilitate binocular single vision (Westheimer, 1981). Thus the eyes remain parallel to within a fraction of a degree when tracking, despite the anatomical complexities, and the eyes move together even if one eye is blind from birth. Although there is general agreement on the law as a principle, how it should be best postulated in terms of angular measures of eye movement (e.g., the angles of "version" and "vergence") is not finally resolved (Sections 2.1.1 and 3.4).

2. MAJOR CONCEPTS

2.1. Physiological Principles Underlying the Different Types of Eye Movement

It is hoped that the following principles will prove useful in orienting the beginning reader to the large subject of human eye movements. Principles are pointers to the truth and not the truth itself. Principles are prerequisites for models. Relatively few references are given, because the data are presented in Section 3 (Experimental Results).

2.1.1. A Few More or Less Distinct Forms of Eye Movement. Eye movements can be unambiguously and easily divided into (1) abrupt and (2) smooth movements as in Figure 10.22 (Fuchs, 1971; Robinson, 1968; Young, 1971). These types are further distinguished by fundamental differences in the muscular forces (Robinson, 1964, 1965).

2.1.1.1. Abrupt Movements. The short-duration movements of the two eyes are always in the same direction (i.e., are conjugate), but are not always of exactly similar amplitude. The heavy viscoelastic damping of the eye by the orbital tissues is overcome by the agonist (active) muscles applying an excessive force for a brief period of time (preemphasis). The resulting pattern of force is called "pulse step." The antagonist muscles are completely relaxed during the agonist pulse owing to central inhibitions. There are two forms of abrupt conjugate eye movement.

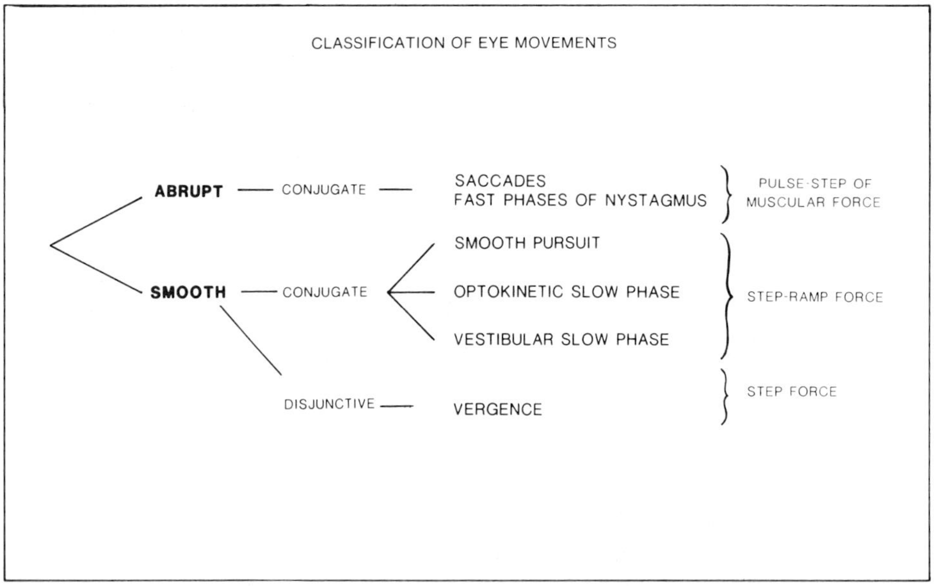

Figure 10.22. Classification of eye movements. *Abrupt*: most saccades are around 50-msec duration (20–150 msec), being of longer duration when larger, usually less than 15° in amplitude (3min arc to 70°), of simultaneous onset (e.g., ±5 msec or better), and similarly directed (i.e., conjugate) in the two eyes. Fast phases of nystagmus are believed to be very similar. Viscoelastic damping of the eye is overcome for abrupt movements by preemphasis, that is, by a pulse of muscular force, followed by a step force to hold the eye in position. *Smooth*: smooth movements are easily separated into those similarly directed (conjugate) and those oppositely directed (disjunctive). Otherwise all smooth movements are similar and relative contributions can only be estimated by changing the viewing conditions and instructions. Classically, vestibular movements are studied by rotating the head or body in the dark about an appropriate axis, or by irrigating the ears with hot or cold water; optokinetic movements by rotating the entire visual scene around the static subject; smooth pursuit by asking the static subject to track a small smoothly moving object; and disjunctive or vergence movements by asking the static subject to track a stimulus that moves in depth. Viscoelastic damping is overcome for the conjugate smooth movements by preemphasis, in this case by a stepramp of force. In the case of the disjunctive movements there is believed to be no preemphasis, the force being a simple step function.

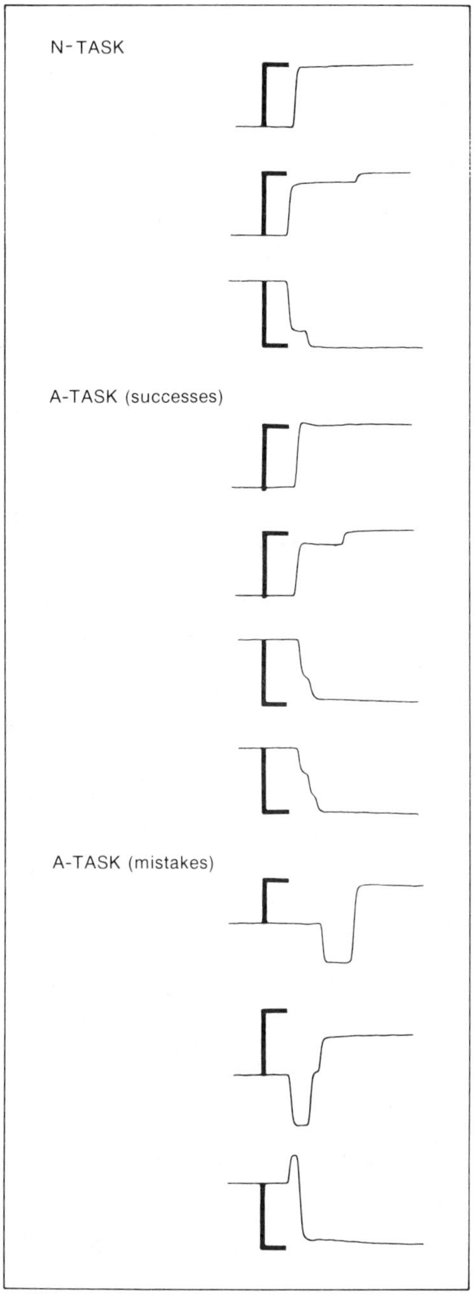

Figure 10.23. Primary and secondary saccades to a single step displacement of the stimulus. In each trial the L-shaped mark illustrates the step of the *goal* (not necessarily the stimulus) to positions 7.7 or 11.5° left or right, plus a 200-msec time bar; the stimulus remained continuously lit. *N-task*: normal foveating task—the goal is the stimulus and the subject is asked to track. The three records respectively show no secondary, a smaller later secondary, and a larger earlier secondary. Secondaries, except for a few earlier ones, depend on visual feedback as to the effect of the primary. *A-task, successes*: successful attempts at the "anti" task, in which the subject is asked to look away from the stimulus by an equal and opposite amount. The *goal* is thus opposite to the stimulus. The primary saccade is away from the stimulus and toward the instructed goal. The four records respectively show no secondary, a large later secondary, a large earlier secondary, and a primary-secondary-tertiary triplet. Secondaries are large (> 1.4°) and nonvisual in this task. *A-task, mistakes*: Mistake trials at the "anti" task in which the first saccade is toward the stimulus with nearly normal mean latency [+10 msec (−20 to +40) relative to N-task latency, eight subjects]. The three records show increasingly shorter saccadic intervals between the direction-error or foveating primary saccade and the large corrective secondary or "anti" saccade. Note the attenuated amplitude of the direction error saccade in the bottom record ("amplitude modification"). (Adapted from Adams, Note 1.) In another subject, blanking the stimulus showed that the large corrective secondary does not use visual feedback as to the effect of the direction-error saccade (Doma, Note 2).

(a) SACCADES. The form of prime importance to most psychologists or human factor engineers is the short-duration, high-velocity movement known as the *saccade* (e.g., 20–100 msec duration, 20–600°·sec^{-1} peak velocity). The latencies of onset for the two eyes are within 5 msec (Williams & Fender, 1977). See Figure 10.23 for examples. Saccades may be highly voluntary, in the sense that saccades can be aimed or suppressed according to instructions (e.g., Hallett, 1978; Steinman, Haddad, Skavenski, & Wyman, 1973). In other instances, the organizational level is somewhat lower, as saccades occur automatically as "idle search" during a great part of the waking state. Also, some saccades cannot be easily suppressed, despite an effort of the will (e.g., the shorter latency correction saccades that refine the aim when the eyes track a single step of the fixation target, Adams, Note 1). The actual saccadic movements are essentially all of one type at the motor level. This is shown in the so-called "main sequence" relationship between saccade amplitude, velocity, and duration (Bahill, Brockenbrough, & Troost, 1981), or in any other analysis that reflects the underlying pulse-step driving force common to all saccades (Robinson, 1964; Section 3.7.1.3). Important minor variations occur for different viewing conditions and tasks, so sensory and central levels are also relevant (e.g., Hallett, 1978; Sharpe, Troost, Dell'Osso, & Daroff, 1975).

Saccades can be classified or categorized in a number of ways: (1) by nature of the *stimulus* (e.g., target step, ramp, or roll motion), (2) by nature of the *instruction* (e.g., "normal" for the usual foveating task, and "anti" for a task that involves looking away from the stimulus), (3) by nature of the *accompanying eye* or head movements in "mixed mode" responses (e.g., microsaccades of fixational eye movements, "catch-up" saccades that supplement smooth pursuit of a laterally moving target, saccades that intersperse the convergence/divergence movements of the two eyes tracking an object that moves in depth), (4) by use of *sensory feedback* as to the angular error to be corrected (e.g., visual/nonvisual), (5) by *latency* (e.g., premature/normal/late), (6) by *ordinal number* (e.g., primary/secondary/etc.), (7) by *action* on the retinal image of the target (e.g., foveating/peripheralizing), (8) by *efficacy* as to correcting the angle error left by previous saccades (e.g., corrective/noncorrective), and (9) by *amplitude* (e.g., hypometric/normometric/hypermetric). These terms are used frequently in the sections following; for example, *microsaccades* are small amplitude responses (e.g., 5 arc min) with large dynamic overshoot, seen when attempting to fixate accurately in the laboratory (Section 3.1). *Catch-up saccades* accompanying smooth pursuit are discussed in Section 3.3, and saccades accompanying vergence in Section 3.4. The terms "primary" and "secondary" are usually restricted to the first and second saccades to a single-step displacement of the target, a common laboratory task treated in Section 3.7. The remaining terms also appear frequently in Section 3.7, though the clinical terms describing amplitude accuracy (hypometric/normometric/hypermetric) are generally expressed as "undershooting," "normally accurate," and "overshooting," respectively.

(b) Fast Phases. The other form of abrupt conjugate movement is the *fast or "quick" phase* of nystagmus. *Nystagmus* means a pattern of alternating and opposite abrupt ("fast phase") and smooth ("slow phase") movement. Nystagmus may be congenital, and is seen often in disease under conditions of little or no stress, or in health when the retina, vestibular apparatus, or skeletal joints are submitted to prolonged or repetitive unidirectional stimulation (thus *optokinetic, vestibular*, and *arthrokinetic* nystagmus); see Sections 3.1.1.3, 3.2.1, and 3.5.1. Fast phases and saccades may show common amplitude-velocity characteristics, which suggests that they use the same or similar final motor circuits (e.g., Ron, Robinson, & Skavenski, 1972). But fast phases and voluntary saccades are differentially affected by congenital blindness (Leigh & Zee, 1980) and interact differently with smooth movements (e.g., Jürgens, Becker, & Rieger, 1981), so they must be different or separate at the penultimate or higher motor levels.

2.1.1.2. Smooth Movements. These are typically of much longer duration and considerably lower velocity than saccades (e.g., durations of longer than 100 msec, and velocities of up to $30–100° \cdot sec^{-1}$), so there is rarely any difficulty in distinguishing the two; however, vestibular slow phases can exceed the peak velocities of smaller saccades. Smooth movements may be similarly directed in the two eyes (*conjugate smooth movements*) or oppositely directed (*disjunctive movements*). These two patterns of movement arise from distinctly different uses of retinal information and eye muscles. Smooth movements are also called "*smooth version*" if the eyes turn *equally* in the same direction, or "*slow vergence*" if the eyes move *equally* but oppositely. "Smooth version" is appropriate for following a translating stimulus at a constant distance, whereas "slow vergence" would track a stimulus moving in depth to or fro along a collision course aimed midway between the eyes; but equality of movement is only approximate (90–95%), even in these two special situations. Unequal movements, whether conjugate or disjunctive, can be arithmetically resolved into a sum of smooth "version" and "vergence" by defining "version" and "vergence" in the above manner, as equal and similar or equal and opposite movements, respectively. That "version" and "vergence" are true components at the motor or neural level, are correctly defined, and are additive, constitutes three propositions into which Hering's law or hypothesis can be separated (Hering, 1868/1977; Ono, 1980; Section 1.3.5). Some authors also use the terms version and vergence merely as synonyms for conjugate and disjunctive movements.

(a) Vergence or Disjunctive Movements. These rarely exceed velocities of $10° \cdot sec^{-1}$ and are usually subdivided into *disparity-evoked vergence* (triggered by disparate retinal-image positions in the two eyes) and so-called "*accommodative*" *vergence* (triggered by optical blur, whether in young or presbyopic subjects), depending on the stimulus conditions selected. However, vergence is also triggered by discrepant images of very different forms in the two eyes (Westheimer & Mitchell, 1969), and is possibly influenced by a variety of relatively unstudied cues as to depth (Section 3.4). Vergence is initiated by a step increase of agonist muscular force and, as a consequence of the heavy viscoelastic damping of the eye, the final position is approached with exponentially decreasing speed (Robinson, 1968).

(b) Conjugate Smooth Movements. These can be further subdivided in humans by careful manipulation of stimulus conditions and instructions, but no purely motor criteria allow direct separation of a single record of smooth movement into components. For example, if both head and stimulus move, then one cannot directly resolve the smooth movement into an arithmetic sum of the motor components that are well established by behavioral and electrophysiological experimentation. However, accessory experiments with modified conditions may permit the researcher to estimate indirectly the contribution of vestibular or optokinetic movement, smooth pursuit, or even vergence (Section 3.3). The agonist muscular force is believed to be step ramp, which leads to the rapid development of eye velocity, (Robinson, 1965).

Vestibular smooth movement (or vestibular slow phase) is the term applied to smooth version elicited by rotating the head in the dark; latency is less than 15 msec and velocity can be very high under appropriate circumstances (e.g., up to $500° \cdot sec^{-1}$: Pulaski, Zee, & Robinson, 1981; Sections 3.2.1.3, 3.4.1.4, 3.5.1, 3.6.1.2). Vestibular movement is due to a short reflex arc of three neurons (vestibular afferent, vestibular neuron, ocular motoneuron), driven by the mechanical velocity transducers in the ampullae of the three pairs of semicircular canals, and overlaid by influences from higher neural levels. The otolith organs of the utricle and saccules also make contributions in appropriate circumstances. Vestibular movement is not stereotyped, because of the intrusion of many higher modifying influences (e.g., Wilson & Melvill Jones, 1979). For example, vestibular movement can be canceled by a special mechanism that is not simply equal and opposite smooth pursuit (Tomlinson & Robinson, 1981).

Optokinetic smooth movement (or optokinetic slow phase) is the term applied to involuntary smooth movements of up to $80° \cdot sec^{-1}$ that are produced by rotating very *large* stimuli around the stationary subject, who is instructed to stare ahead and not track (Collewijn, 1981; Honrubia, Downey, Mitchell, & Ward, 1968). In lower animals the optokinetic response is mediated by the accessory branches of the optic nerve with their appropriate terminal nuclei, and also by particular types of retinal ganglion cell. Optokinetic and vestibular smooth movements are both elicited by head rotation in normally lit surroundings, and are combined at the level of the vestibular nucleus (Dichgans, 1977; Waespe, Henn, & Miles, 1977). Their peculiarities and imperfections often balance, yielding biologically adaptive responses over a wide range of rotational conditions (Sections 3.3.3 and 3.5.2).

Smooth pursuit is the term applied to voluntary tracking of a *small* stimulus, any background being ignored (Sections 3.3, 3.5.4, 3.6.2, and 3.7.5). See Figure 10.24 for an example. Maximum velocity is usually said to be $20–30° \cdot sec^{-1}$ (e.g., Westheimer, 1954); however, a recent study suggests that motivated subjects can pursue at very high velocities when some inaccuracy is allowed (Lisberger, Evinger, Johanson, & Fuchs, 1981). The control of smooth pursuit probably involves many regions of the brain. In humans, it is difficult to distinguish between optokinetic and voluntary smooth pursuit. A lesion in a given part of the brain of man or animal will abolish both reactions, both are most effectively driven from the fovea, both are influenced by selective attention, and both give rise to "after-nystagmus" in the original direction of motion when a prolonged stimulation is stopped (e.g., Henn et al., 1980). Smooth pursuit is sensitive to numerous factors, including age and medications (Sharpe & Sylvester, 1978). See Section 3.3.

2.1.2. "Movement Begins and Ends in Posture." This dictum of Sherrington (1906/1947, 1915)—"Posture follows movement like a shadow; every movement begins in posture and

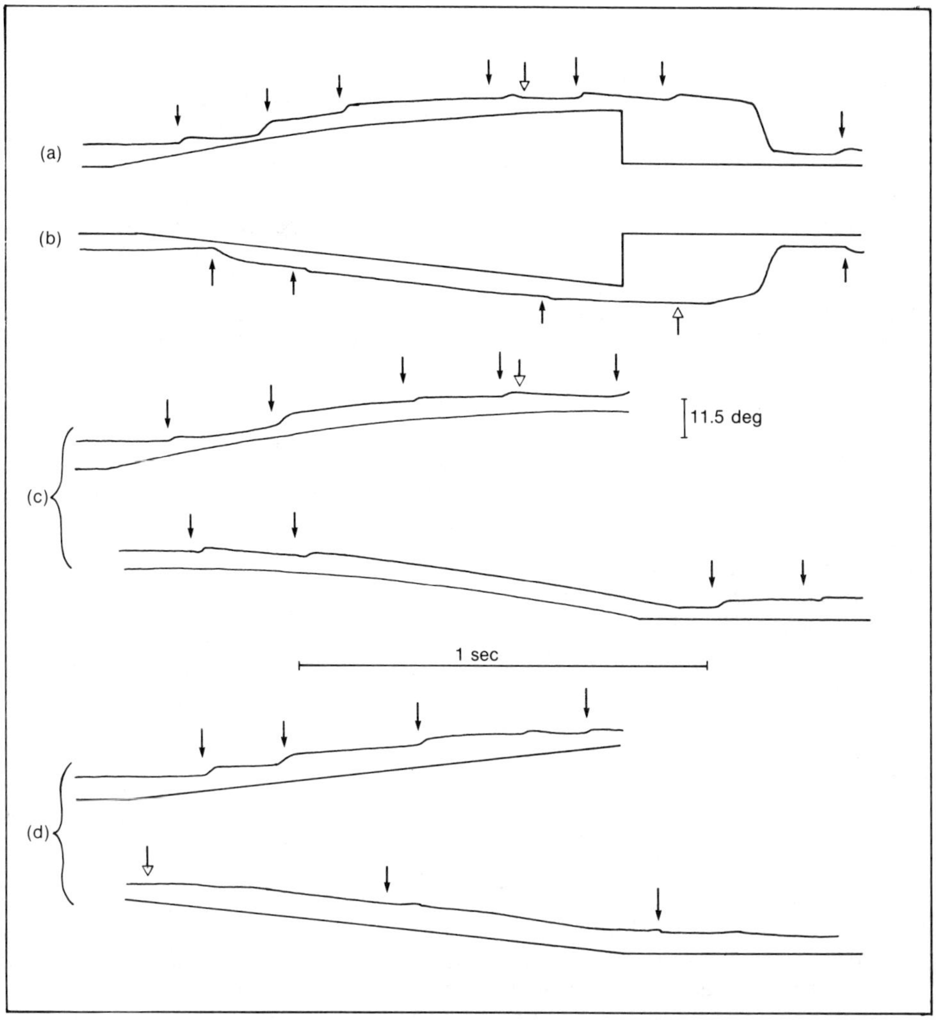

Figure 10.24 Smooth pursuit eye movements, showing under-pursuit, premature reversal, and catch-up saccades. Ordinate is horizontal amplitude of eye movement when tracking randomly chosen single-shot wave forms which reach 15° deviation from center in 1.24 sec. Upward is movement to the right. A 1-sec time mark is shown. Initial velocities of ramps and sinusoids are 12 and 18° · sec^{-1} respectively. Eye traces displaced 5.7° · sec^{-1} above stimulus traces for ease of illustration. Catch-up saccades are marked by filled arrows and velocity reversal points by empty arrows. (a) Quarter cycle of sine motion followed by step return to center. (b) Quarter cycle of triangle motion followed by a step return. (c) Half cycle of sine, record chopped in two at peak for convenience. (d) Half cycle of triangle motion, record chopped in two. 100-times foveal threshold, small blue-green stimulus in darkness. Pupil monitor, data for one experienced subject. Underpursuit (i.e., eye velocity less than target velocity) and premature reversal are seen mainly for the sinusoidal wave forms. Afterpursuit is seen at the ends of records (c) and (d). (After Lightstone, 1973.)

ends in posture"—is as applicable to the motor control of the eyes as it is to the control of the body and limbs. There are several points.

1. The homeostatic or *postural* group of mechanisms, such as vestibular, optokinetic, and fixational smooth movements, and tonic convergence of the eyes, preserve the status quo. They maintain a relatively unperturbed orientation of the eyes in *space*, which is particularly appropriate for the perceptual resolution of the low and medium spatial frequencies in the scene. The higher frequencies, being more easily blurred by retinal slip or poor focus, are often of less behavioral significance. Retinal-image stability should not be too perfect, otherwise perception will suffer, the whole scene fading to invisibility in the extreme case. Fading is evident in everyday life, as the naturally stabilized shadows of one's retinal blood vessels are rarely observed. Fading of the scene is also noted by paralyzed subjects who cannot move their eyes (e.g., Stevens, Emerson, Gerstein, Kallos, Neufeld, Nichols, & Rosenquist, 1976).

2. Visual search or *exploratory* mechanisms shift the eyes to a new position of fixation and relative rest. These mechanisms include saccades, smooth pursuit, and phasic vergence movements.

3. Maintained posture and exploration alternate. Stability of gaze requires visual sensing of retinal image slip and vestibular sensing of head slip in space (e.g., Melvill Jones & Milsum, 1965; Wilson & Melvill Jones, 1979), and no doubt also monitoring of outflow and inflow eye-position signals (e.g., Skavenski, 1976). Exploration presumably occurs whenever some particular spatial feature in the scene becomes the tem-

porary goal for foveation, as a result of novelty, memory, habit, or change.

4. In a stressful environment it is possible that the postural and exploratory actions cooperate. For example, if a given fixed spatial point is continually selected for foveation, saccades could presumably supplement a failing vestibular drive when the head is rotating very rapidly.

5. In almost normal or abnormal subjects temporary fixational stability may not exist. The saccadic system may help preserve useful foveal vision by continually counteracting ocular drift, thus providing a wide variety of sawtooth nystagmus patterns, consisting of drift (slow phase) and counter saccades (quick phases).

2.1.3. Eye Movements Often Underreact. There is a general tendency for the eyes to maintain the status quo and to underreact. Thus saccades are of substantial latency and generally undershoot, or are often canceled in favor of temporary inaction; smooth pursuit, vergence, and the vestibular and optokinetic smooth movements are often too slow to completely stabilize the retinal image. Underreaction is compatible with the fovea providing only a small part of the useful field of view in many tasks, so that accurate fixation is not always essential. Underreaction may be a consequence of the extensive connectivity of the brain, any action being a compromise that meets many opposed demands. Any urgency for shifting fixation is reduced by the disturbed perceptual processing associated with retinal image smear by saccades in a structured field. Incomplete image stabilization is consistent with the more easily blurred, higher spatial frequencies being a lesser source of information in some tasks.

2.1.4. Eye Movements Are Usually, but Not Always, Biologically Adaptive. Under tranquil conditions, underreaction does not dangerously degrade performance. Most eye movements are under 15° amplitude, so that an undershoot of about 10% with the head clamped leaves the stimulus close to the fovea. Furthermore, retinal slip during smooth pursuit is often slow enough to be corrected adequately by small pursuit saccades every 200 msec or so, without the stimulus slipping beyond the foveal edge. In the demanding circumstances of a spinning aircraft, however, there are occasions when the vestibulo-ocular reflex may be worse than useless, because post-rotatory nystagmus may further disorient the pilot after the plane has recovered by virtue of its intrinsic aerodynamics (Melvill Jones, 1965).

In general, it is unwise to assume that all aspects of eye movements are efficient. In the laboratory, oculomotor behavior may be maladaptive in several ways. (1) It is perplexing that saccadic latencies are so very much longer than the saccade itself in the task of tracking a small bright spot against darkness (Carpenter, 1981). In richer visual environments, long latency reduces masking of the target by too-frequent retinal-image motion, but there is no significant masking if the background is dark and the stimulus is bright (Brooks & Fuchs, 1975; Hallett & Lightstone, 1976a). Perhaps oculomotor procrastination is a habit. (2) When a stimulus is just below foveal perceptual threshold, subjects repeatedly allow the stimulus to drift into the night-blind fovea while trying to fixate eccentrically with a more sensitive part of the retina (Steinman & Cunitz, 1968). (3) The ability to look away at will from a conspicuous stimulus is essential for exploratory behavior, but such eye movements are imperfectly executed. For example, subjects can shift their gaze in a direction opposite that of a stimulus that undergoes a step displacement, usually on the first or second attempt at the task. However, latency and absolute error are somewhat worse than normal and scarcely change with several hundred trials practice. There is no visual feedback as to the effect of the first or primary saccade, although corrective secondary saccades do occur (Hallett, 1978). Curiously, direction mistakes (foveating responses) in this task are more common for dimmer stimuli, even though looking away from a dim stimulus is advantageous for perception (Doma, Note 2). Also, subjects can fixate a static target eccentrically, but they cannot shift eccentric fixation to follow a stepping target without first foveating (Zeevi & Peli, 1979).

2.1.5. Two Types of Vision and Associated Eye Movements. The division of eye movements into homeostatic and exploratory kinds can be associated with two different arrangements of optics, retina, and central connections (e.g., Hughes, 1977; Land, 1981). This principle is somewhat idealized but it serves for later debate.

The ideal high-sensitivity panoramic eye is short relative to its pupil diameter. This confers high retinal illumination, and the detector elements (e.g., retinal ganglion cell receptive fields) are relatively few and large, so that the quantal flux per detector is high. The panoramic eye is illustrated by the afoveate laterally placed eyes of the rabbit, rat, and mouse in which the distribution of retinal ganglion cells is relatively uniform and the optics are not specialized for on-axis or central vision. The optic nerve or blind spot may even lie on or near the optical axis. With panoramic vision there is no particular need to track. The stability of the relatively fixed gaze is ensured by the vestibular and optokinetic homeostatic reflexes. Neural organization in afoveate animals may also favor the detection of moving objects by a relatively motionless retina characterized by many amacrine synapses and motion-sensing ganglion cells. In the forward-focusing eyes of primates, panoramic vision for the frontal half of space is supplied by the peripheral retina.

By contrast, the ideal high-resolution type of eye is elongated relative to its pupil diameter, and the retinal region close to the optic axis has a high density of neural elements and a massive representation in the brain. This confers high resolution within a limited part of the field of view. [Intriguingly, in a number of invertebrates and some deep-sea fish, high resolution and panoramic eyes are anatomically separated (Land, 1981; Locket, 1980).] Retinal processing in primates is simpler than in many lower animals. There is a more direct transfer of information, without extensive modification by retina, directly to a larger and more complex brain. This allows integration of the two eyes, permitting depth vision and better isolation of objects from background, and correlation of the current retinal image with the neural residua of older images. More protracted development of the brain after birth, plus social communication and language, allow the elaboration of perception, cognitive mechanisms, and strategies. A penalty of specializing for vision close to the optic axis is the necessity of saccadic search and vergence mechanisms for finding an object of interest, plus smooth pursuit and an adaptable vestibulo-ocular reflex for keeping the image relatively stable and close to the fovea (e.g., Robinson, 1968, 1976).

One limitation of the principle that eyes and eye movements show dual arrangements is that mammalian eyes are structurally varied and are not always easily correlated with ecology and behavior. Also, the distinction between central foveal vision and peripheral vision should not be exaggerated, because most visual functions are continuously graded across the retina. As an example, studies by Aubert, Wertheim, and Bourdon at the end of the nineteenth century showed that angular visual acuity and sensitivity to angular motion decline in a hyperbolic manner with retinal eccentricity; this may provide an appropriate match between vision and the centrifugal flow patterns created in the scene by bodily movement toward a goal (Hughes, 1977). As the body advances, the angular distance from the goal of a point in the scene increases with increasing speed. Thus the effect of the gradient in visual thresholds is that weak flow near the goal is just as visible to the fovea as faster more remote flow is to the retinal periphery. (For further discussions of the differences between central and peripheral vision, see Hood & Finkelstein, Chapter 5, and Olzak & Thomas, Chapter 7).

2.1.6. A Given Situation May Evoke More than One Form of Eye Movement. Most natural activities involve combinations of the different types of eye movements, and the reader may be able to make intelligent guesses as to the movements involved in quiet reading, needlework, walking and observing, playing baseball, etc. (e.g., Nagle, Bridgeman, & Stark, 1980; Winterson & Collewijn, 1976; Bahill, Brendel, Maskarinec, Digioia, McDonald, & Friedman, Note 3). Many responses are "mixed mode," that is, combinations of smooth pursuit and saccades that track a smoothly swinging target, and combinations of saccades and slow disjunctive movement that track in depth. The combinations may vary from person to person. Relatively small changes in viewing conditions may matter. For instance, a target that moves in depth may be tracked by slow disjunctive movement and a single saccade, but a small change in viewing conditions may favor successive unequal conjugate saccades which, by alternating in direction, leave a net change in vergence without any version (Section 3.4). Similarly, a step translation of the target normally evokes saccades, but smooth movements occur in some circumstances (Lightstone, 1973). Persistent fixation may be an important option in some athletic tasks. For example, when teeing off at golf, fixating the ball stabilizes the head and coordinates the swing.

2.1.7. A Given Eye Movement May Have a Number of Possible Origins. If behavior is adaptable, it should be capable of initiation by a variety of sensory or internal stimuli. Several examples can be offered. The stability of fixation is changed very little, if at all, by changes in the shape or color of the fixation object (e.g., Steinman, 1976). This is compatible with fixation using any of several parallel sensory channels. The gain of the vestibulo-ocular reflex is altered by instructions (e.g., Wilson & Melvill Jones, 1979), so the operation of the low-level three-neuron arc can be strikingly modified by cerebral influences. Some primary saccades anticipate a stimulus displacement whereas others track (e.g., Findlay, 1981a). A secondary saccade may or may not use visual feedback as to the success of the primary saccade, depending on the magnitude of the end-primary error and the subject's instructions (Becker, 1972; Hallett, 1978). Smooth pursuit may slavishly track the stimulus in some situations or deviate badly in others as if taking "shortcuts" (Lightstone, 1973). Smooth pursuit may match the physical or the perceived path of the stimulus depending on the circumstances (Holtzman, Sedgwick, & Festinger, 1978; Mack, Fendrich, & Wong, 1982; Steinbach, 1976). All of these examples point to an eye movement having a number of alternative or parallel neural drives, some sensory, others more cognitive. Differences in the selection or weighting of drives may be a source of individual variation and adaptability. If so, it may be appropriate to report individual data, rather than averaging across subjects as is commonly done.

2.1.8. Eye Movements Are Relatively Independent of Nonspatial Stimulus Parameters. If eye movements are biologically adapted to orientation, search, and analysis in different directions at different distances, then eye movements should be insensitive to the remaining parameters of the stimulus. Thus, with clearly visible stimuli, it has been found that: (1) smooth pursuit is not much affected by spectral wavelength (e.g., Goodwin, 1973; Steinman, 1976), (2) the accuracy and latency of primary saccades to stimulus steps are not affected by stimulus duration (Hallett & Lightstone, 1976b), (3) smooth pursuit is not sensitive to contrast (Haegerstrom-Portnoy & Brown, 1979), and (4) vergence movements are initiated by a wide variety of binocular stimuli that are discordant in shape or illumination (Westheimer & Mitchell, 1969). These findings are not surprising. Changes in wavelength, texture, shape (for small shapes), and contrast do not involve changes in spatial position. Primary saccades need not be sensitive to stimulus duration if they are triggered by a sensory mechanism with "transient" characteristics (Hallett, 1978). The initial vergence response may simply attempt to increase the spatial correlation between the images in the two eyes, irrespective of the actual content of the images. Change in luminance does, however, have a profound effect on the latency of saccadic tracking and smooth pursuit (Wheeless, Cohen, & Boynton, 1967; Winterson & Steinman, 1978; Doma, Note 2). This must arise from the necessity of waiting longer to catch sufficient light quanta for the sensory processes of the retina and afferent pathways. Also, a flickering background disrupts the stability of fixation (Haddad & Winterson, 1975), which may again imply a role for transient sensory mechanisms in movements.

2.1.9. Eye Movements Are Relatively Independent of the Perception of Space. Motor responses must conform to physical space in a direct manner to be successful; thus any internal model of visual space must be accurate if it is to drive useful eye movements. This need not be the case for perception. Perceptions should map to physical space but editing or distortion may be allowed as a means of emphasizing salient features.

"Pursuing the perceptual" is pointless if it conflicts with maintaining fixation on the physical object. Fixation in a dark room is stable despite the strong illusion that the stationary fixation point is moving (autokinetic illusion, Winterson & Steinman, 1979), or is apparently moving because of the relative motion of a surrounding frame, or is apparently moving because of a motion aftereffect (e.g., Mack et al., 1982). Also, a transversely moving object is accurately tracked in the transverse plane, despite an imposed difference of retinal illumination in the two eyes, though if not tracked it appears to swing in depth (Pulfrich illusion, Rogers, Steinbach, & Ono, 1974).

Similarly, it would be inappropriate for perceptual illusion to disturb a shift to a new fixation target. Subjects can make an accurate saccade to switch smooth pursuit from one moving stimulus to a second with a horizontal component of motion in the same direction as the first; yet the spatial motion of the second target is *misperceived* while the first target is pursued because of inadequate allowance for eye movement (physical position = retinal-image position + eye position). The subject continues to track the usual *physical* path of the second stimulus, even if it is artificially stabilized on the fovea immediately after the switching saccade; so the subject must have formed an accurate model of the physical motion of the second stimulus at the time when it was perceived moving elsewhere in space (Holtzman et al., 1978). Although small flashed targets before, during, or after saccades are spatially mislocated, primary saccades are of normal latency and accuracy and hammer blows are accurate (Hallett & Lightstone, 1976a, 1976b; Hansen & Skavenski, 1977; Matin, 1976). Similarly, the perceived direction of a more distant object may be badly mislocated when the eyes are converged on a nearer one, but the saccade to the far object is accurate (Ono & Nakamizo, 1977).

Perception can be the major drive for pursuit eye movements in some circumstances (Heywood, 1973b; Steinbach, 1976; Wyatt & Pola, 1979; Yasui & Young, 1976), though some of these examples, such as the tracking of afterimages or of the hidden tip of an object, or of the center of a rolling wheel that can be identified in the dark only by two lit points on its rim, may have other explanations (see Section 3.3.4). An unambiguous example is the switch of smooth pursuit, by means of a saccade, from one moving target to another with an *opposite* horizontal component of motion: tracking resumes along the illusory *perceived* path of the second target (Holtzman et al., 1978). Perhaps no internal physical model of the second target can be elaborated to drive eye movements in this case. In another example, a partly exposed object oscillating behind a fixed slit is perceived in its entirety and is pursued, though poorly, perhaps because of the conflicting necessity of viewing through the slit (Mack et al., 1982; Steinbach, 1976).

2.1.10. Eye Movements Usually Depend on Attention. In nonthreatening situations it is possible for a subject to make eye movements by attending to only one sensory modality when a stimulus activates several modalities (e.g., vision, sound, ground vibration, wind on the face). Also, within the visual modality it is often possible to make satisfactory eye movements to a special object identified by some specified color, size, brightness, contrast, shape, or texture, despite the presence of other objects. Cognitive processes can thus indirectly affect the selection of the spatial goal of the future eye movement. The role presumably varies with the degree of rehearsal, the number of prearranged stimuli, the cognitive difficulty of the task, and so forth. Thus the contribution of attention to a simple latency task, such as "look left on a red light and right on a blue light," is presumably slight compared to the role of attention in more general visual search, where recognition of the "unexpected" hinges on concepts of *a priori* possibilities. To give three other examples of attention: (1) the gain of the vestibulo-ocular reflex is considerably altered if the subject visualizes a real or imaginary object either rotating with him or fixed to the wall (e.g., Barr, Schultheis, & Robinson, 1976), whereas Parkinson's disease of the basal ganglia impairs this normal adaptability (White, Note 4); (2) with complex optokinetic stimuli, slow phase gain may be altered by directing the subject's attention to the periphery of the field (Dubois & Collewijn, 1979); (3) high stability when fixating the center of a large empty annulus (Rattle, 1969) may depend on attention to holding eye velocity very low, though there must also be some contribution from peripheral vision.

On the other hand, novel or threatening stimuli are likely to evoke saccadic eye movements and head turning, regardless of what instructions are given to the subject. It seems that there is a low-level mechanism involved in orientation in such cases. Some investigators are interested in how size, shape, and contrast determine the *salience* of the stimulus, and they have tried to find pairs of shapes that attract saccadic eye movements equally when one shape is presented to the left and the other to the right of the point of fixation (e.g., Findlay, 1981a; Levy-Schoen, 1974). The provisional finding is that salience is determined by temporal onset, proximity to the fovea, and size, whereas fine structure is unimportant. Given the normality of saccadic latency and accuracy to briefly flashed targets (Hallett & Lightstone, 1976b), it has been suggested that transients of illumination initiate saccades by activating a "transient mechanism" (Hallett, 1978) or a coarse acuity mechanism (Findlay, 1981a) that is insensitive to details.

2.1.11. Eye Movements Variably Depend on Eye-Position Signals. It has been traditionally assumed that eye movements are *planned* only on the basis of retinal error, that is, the distance of the retinal image from the fovea (e.g., Robinson, 1973; Young & Stark, 1963). More recently, it has been appreciated that eye movements are *executed* in spatial coordinates (i.e., eye direction relative to the head), which requires both retinal-image position and eye-position signals (Hallett & Lightstone, 1976a, 1976b; Mays & Sparks, 1980, 1981; Robinson, 1975a). The present hypothesis is that good eye-position signals exist at low motor levels, but the role of eye-position signals in the high-level *planning* of eye movements is variable, depending on the nature of the task and the extent of the subject's attention to eye position or velocity.

2.1.11.1. Normal Viewing Conditions. Under normal viewing conditions in lit surroundings, using only retinal information for planning is reasonable. The quality of the optics and the high density of the photoreceptor array allow precise spatial judgments, particularly if the eye is initially stationary. In such cases tracking would not be improved by adding a moderately precise eye-position signal (e.g., ± 20 min arc) to precise (e.g., ± 1 min arc) retinal-image information in order to form a model of target direction relative to the head. If, however, perception is illusory, as when observing a moving target while tracking elsewhere, then forming an oculomotor model of the physical path of the target may hinge entirely on the availability of eye-position signals to the half-brain executing the task.

2.1.11.2. Darkness. Lack of vision favors attention to eye-position signals. In complete darkness, an accurate saccade to the location of a briefly exposed target is possible only if allowance is made for any eye movement intervening between the target stimulus and the eventual response, retinal information alone being insufficient. Experimentally, it is found that a saccade to a briefly lit target presented before, during, or after a prior saccade has means and standard deviations of accuracy and latency similar to those of a saccade made to a continuously lit target (Hallett & Lightstone, 1976a, 1976b; Lightstone, 1973). However, the subject may "fail safe" and forgo a saccade for certain briefly lit spatial patterns of target movement. Related observations have been made by Gresty and Leech (1976) with a less precise method for a wider variety of targets and backgrounds. Also, inspection of records had independently suggested that the second of two closely successive but oppositely directed saccades was adjusted for the size and direction of the first, even though there was insufficient time for visual feedback of angular error (Becker & Jürgens, 1975; Levy-Schoen & Blanc-Garin, 1974). Two hypothetical mechanisms have been suggested (Hallett, 1976).

2.1.11.3. Hypothesis 1: Precise Correlation of Signals. A neural copy of target position relative to the head is obtained by moment-to-moment correlation of retinal position with precise eye position information, and the eye is then driven saccadically to the appropriate orbital position (the head being fixed). The accuracy of such a mechanism might be expected to suffer during the high transient velocities of saccades unless the mechanism is simple and direct, with very short neural delays. Hypothesis 1 appears to be essentially true at the *lower motor levels*, as Robinson and others have argued. For example, saccades resume their flight to the target if momentarily halted by collicular or brainstem stimulation (e.g., Mays & Sparks, 1980; Schiller & Sandell, 1983; Sparks & Mays, 1983), so saccades are executed in spatial coordinates. It is probable that local feedback of eye position at the brainstem level quenches the burst neurons when the eye reaches its targeted position, the eye then halting because of its heavy viscoelastic damping (e.g., Fuchs & Kaneko, 1981; Jürgens, Becker, & Kornhuber, 1981; Robinson, 1975a; Zee & Robinson, 1979). There are also electrophysiological indications that useful eye position signals occur at high brainstem levels, for example, thalamus and superior colliculus (Peck, Schlag-Rey, & Schlag, 1980; Sparks & Porter, 1983).

2.1.11.4. Hypothesis 2: Imperfect Correlation of Signals plus Other Factors. Alternatively, less precise knowledge of eye position may frequently allow a correct association of the briefly exposed stimulus with one of the set of known stimulus positions. For example, a target briefly flashed near the peak velocity of a saccade may perhaps be discriminated as temporally halfway through the duration of the saccade, and thus the required eye position is halfway between the pre- and post-saccadic eye positions. If the error is too high, the subject can always "fail safe" and forgo a saccade. Hypothesis 2 is obviously compatible with less perfect eye-position signals than is hypothesis 1.

2.1.11.5. Implications of Moderately Precise Eye-Control Signals. Good evidence for moderately precise (± 20 min arc) eye-control signals comes from studies of the stability of fixation in the dark in the absence of a fixation point. The short-term standard deviation of eye position is about 29 min arc (e.g., Matin, Matin, & Pearce, 1970; Skavenski, 1971, 1976; Skavenski & Steinman, 1970). Also, a subject can hold the eye steady against an imposed load in the dark (Skavenski, 1972). Both eye *position* and eye *velocity* control signals are plausible, given the existence of two main kinds of eye movement, namely, changes in eye position (via saccade, quick phase, or vergence) and changes in eye velocity (the conjugate smooth movements). If so, a subject "fixating" in the dark and monitoring eye velocity in an effort to keep the eye still would accumulate an increasing position error with time until the position error is large enough to be corrected by saccades. Something like this is observed (Section 3.2.1). Again, a subject would be able to "fixate" a spot, electronically controlled by eye position (at a high negative gain, e.g., Robinson, 1964), without breaking into unstable oscillations if he were to give rather more attention or weight to holding eye velocity very low than to visually tracking the spot. Also, a static subject inside of a rotating optokinetic drum could achieve some success in "staring straight ahead" by attentively holding eye velocity low and thus reducing pursuit of the drum walls (Section 3.3.3). Or a subject could pursue a small moving stimulus, but at a deliberately reduced speed, by similarly holding eye velocity low (Section 3.3.2.1).

Obviously if position and velocity signals are available for planning, then a great deal may depend on the task and other conditions. One engineering requirement is that the retinal and eye-position (or velocity) signals must be *equally* delayed if they are to be correlated with target motion, despite variation in latency due to task difficulty or stimulus intensity. The plausibility of useful correlation is therefore reduced the longer the neural delay, because it is likely that longer delays are more variable. In short, the more cognitive tasks are unlikely to be based on accurate eye-position information.

2.1.11.6. Summary. Precise eye-position signals are almost certainly used at the level of the brainstem "saccade generator" for the execution of the eye movements. Such signals probably do not contribute much to the *planning* of saccades in the light. Similarly, it is known that perceptual localization in the light is based wholly on retinal image position (Matin, 1981). In darkness, it seems safest to assume that planning uses relatively coarse ($\pm 1°$) and intermittent eye-position information rather than precise, continuously available, signals. The correlation of retinal image and eye-position information is probably poorer, the more cognitive the task and the longer the reaction time. In this connection, it is known that perceptual localization in the dark uses imperfect eye-position signals (Matin, 1981), whereas saccadic localization is precise (Hallett, 1976). An important possibility is that subjects may increase stability or flexibility of oculomotor response in certain situations by attending to eye velocity so as to keep the eyes relatively still, but more facts are needed.

2.1.12. Eye Movements Can Be Planned in Parallel. A single eye movement is rare. More often there is a sequence of saccades, or a combination of different types of eye movements or eye and head movements. The question arises as to how these movements are coordinated. Are they jointly planned from an early stage or are the movements independently assembled (parallel planning) with some "last-minute" adjustments to avoid inappropriate responses? Parallel planning can occur in a sequence of saccades (Täumer, 1975) and regularly occurs for joint eye and head saccades (Bizzi, 1974). In the case of a combination of eye movements, parallel planning need not present any problem if eye movements are spatially coded at the brainstem level, for which there is neurophysiological evidence (e.g., Mays & Sparks, 1980). If there is spatial coding, then several independent commands for the eyes to go to the same specified point in space will cause no confusion, no matter what the current position of the eye (whereas in a nonspatially coded system, independent requests to deviate by 10° would yield various end positions, depending on the starting points and the number of requests). In the case of the human saccadic system, saccades are made to spatial goals, and there are mechanisms for canceling or modifying latent saccades that are unsuited to the most recent inputs or decisions (Sections 3.7.2–3.7.4). In the case of small head and eye movements, it is believed that independent head and eye saccades are programmed to the same spatial goal, the vestibulo-ocular reflex modifying the saccade during execution to allow for head movement (Bizzi, 1974). The process for large head and eye movements is not so well understood.

The neural basis of parallel planning is most likely the relatively independent activity of different regions of cerebral cortex and superior colliculus. It is easy to imagine that more than one basic area can be activated, because a given visual stimulus may activate a number of visual sensory areas, and there may be other visual stimuli, accompanying sounds, instructions, or memories. Electroencephalography suggests frontal and occipital varieties of saccades (Kurtzberg & Vaughan, 1980). Neurosurgical ablations show that the frontal cortex is necessary for suppressing foveation of the stimulus in favor of a saccade away from the stimulus (Guitton, Buchtel, & Douglas, 1982). This chapter emphasizes parallel planning in the sections that deal with modeling (Sections 2.3.3–2.3.5, 3.7.1.6, 3.7.2.5, and 3.7.3.2).

2.1.13. Eye Movements Are Plastic and Adaptable. Partly on the basis of animal experiments, it is believed that the human visual system does not develop normally unless it is exposed from birth to a normally diverse visual environment. Patients blind since birth, because of damage to the anterior visual pathways, show an unstable eye position with a variable but persistent jerk nystagmus; the vestibulo-ocular reflex is reduced or absent, although quick phases may be well preserved. Eye movements are more normal if there is limited vision or childhood visual experience followed by lengthy adult blindness. The vestibulo-ocular reflex is retained and can be suppressed, and there is some ability to make pursuit movements or large saccades when tracking the hands (Leigh & Zee, 1980). However, the saccadic eye movements are not entirely normal; they show a tendency toward "gaze paretic" nystagmus with glissades (see Section 2.3.2).

Although it seems that the development of adult eye-movement patterns is protracted (e.g., pilot studies on children by Kowler & Facchiano, 1982), it is unlikely that established adult eye-movement patterns can be permanently extinguished by unusual environments (Leigh & Zee, 1980). Growth, aging, fatigue, and injury place a premium on adaptability and continued "retuning"; consequently, most physiologists now emphasize the longer lasting effects of sensory feedback. Much common motor activity is certainly triggered by immediate input, but is otherwise executed "open loop" in highly familiar environments. Although visual feedback may be too late to correct the current error, it can improve the execution of future movements. A notable example of such parametric feedback is the vestibulo-ocular reflex. Basically a three-neuron reflex arc, the gain can be reduced or even reversed if the subject wears reversing goggles (e.g., Gonshor & Melvill Jones, 1976a; Melvill Jones & Gonshor, 1982), or increased or decreased to compensate for magnifying goggles (Gauthier & Robinson, 1975). This modifiability is natural, for the reflex must change its gain if the spatial region of interest moves with the head (as for a hand-held object), or if the distance of binocular convergence changes (e.g., Section 3.4.1). A clinical example of parametric feedback would be the shift in eye position that restores single binocular vision if a prism is placed in front of that eye. Another example is the shortening of a saccade that rapidly develops if the stimulus moves opposite the eye during the saccade on repeated trials, or the oblique direction of eye movement that tends to develop if the experimenter arranges that the intended target is driven vertically by a horizontal head rotation or by a horizontal saccade (Hay, 1968; Mack, Fendrich, & Pleune, 1978; McLaughlin, 1967). In a sense, strategy and prediction arise when a narrowly variable visual environment forces the oculomotor system's parameters in one direction.

Plasticity, adaptability, strategy, and prediction complicate the researcher's task. Highly predictable stimuli elicit optimal performance as long as interest can be maintained; highly randomized stimuli give the worst measures of performance, but may help elucidate the underlying mechanism and maintain the subject's interest and arousal. In giving feedback as to performance the experimenter risks getting what is wanted, but without feedback there is the risk that the system may assume unusual parameters.

2.1.14. Eye Movements Can Be Influenced by Expectations and "Strategies." Randomization in experimental design helps to reduce undesirable effects of a subject's expectations, strategies, or tactics. However, randomization is never complete, so that there is always some information available to the subject about what will happen next. The following studies exemplify (1) when stimulus timing was not randomized, subjects made very low velocity anticipatory smooth movements away from the stimulus before it moved in an unpredictable direction (Kowler & Steinman, 1979a, 1979b, 1981); (2) when a stimulus stepped left or right at random, and then back to center, subjects responded to the more predictable return steps with a proportion of anticipatory (<120 msec) saccades (e.g., Findlay, 1980); (3) in this laboratory, anticipatory saccades are not seen when a stimulus steps randomly left or right after a random delay of about 1.5–2.2 sec, but a proportion of anticipatory saccades appear when the degree of temporal randomization is effectively reduced by forewarning the stimulus step with a 0.05–0.2 sec dark period (Kalesnykas, Note 5).

Some responses may not use all the information available in the stimulus. One possibility is that the onset and direction of the stimulus displacement trigger a response to a rehearsed location; that is, the amplitude of the stimulus step is assumed, with possible latency saving. This may be termed a "triggered rehearsed response." In a series of experiments four subjects were required to look toward the stimulus and foveate when it stepped to one of two positions at 10° left or right in the "normal" task, and to look away from the stimulus by an equal and opposite amount in the "anti" task (Doma, Note 2). After a number of such "two-goal" sessions at different stimulus luminances, a control experiment was performed with the stimulus stepping to one of six positions in the range 11.5° left or right. In the normal task, angular error (between eye and stimulus at the end of the primary saccade) for the 10° stimulus fell between the errors for the 7.7 and 11.5° control stimuli for all four subjects, as one might expect if foveating responses are always essentially new responses that are both triggered and aimed by the stimulus step. In the "anti" task, however, there was evidence of triggered rehearsed responses. End-primary error at the end of the "anti" saccade for the sessions with a 10° step was *less* than the error for smaller steps in the "six-goal" control session. Three subjects had to increase their "anti" saccade latencies to match the various sizes of step in the control session. The other subject made "anti" saccades with his usual latency and amplitude in the control session as if he were still responding to a 10° target, even though the stimulus was now 3.8–11.5°. Thus the subjects differed in the degree to which they were willing to abandon latency-saving strategies or habits in the control session.

Delay is always a potential option in saccadic tracking tasks. In this laboratory, we try to encourage a fast response by starting a gentle tone on the stimulus step that is terminated by the start of the primary saccade; also, one of the conditions for a "reward" pattern on the visual display at the end of the trial is a less-than-250-msec primary latency (Hallett, 1978). Nevertheless, it is still hypothetically possible that subjects delay for many saccadic tasks, and that visually forewarning the time of the stimulus step in a variety of ways (L. Ross & S. Ross, 1980) achieves a sometimes dramatic shortening of latency (0–80 msec) by eliminating this unnecessary delay. When the task in a saccadic tracking experiment includes not only trials in which the stimulus steps twice, but also trials in which the stimulus steps once, the single-step latency is found to be inflated by 20 msec (Becker & Jürgens, 1979). This suggests that subjects delay their responses to step 1 so as to cope with a possible second step. Presumably this inflation of single-step latency could be avoided by identifying single-step trials by a prearranged tone, light, or verbal comment. In smooth-pursuit tasks with a harmonically swinging target, variable delay offers the option of undertracking on the swing out; the subject is then ahead of the target on the swing back and in a better position to track (Lightstone, 1973).

When a response involves two or more eye movements, the subject has the option of variably distributing accuracy and speed of response between the two movements. Possible cases are mixed-mode tracking, such as mixed saccadic and smooth pursuit of a translating target, and mixed saccadic and slow disjunctive tracking of a stimulus moving in depth, but I am not aware of pertinent data. There are also "non-mixed-mode" possibilities. In certain circumstances a subject might sacrifice the accuracy of the primary saccade to gain short latency, deferring accuracy until the secondary saccade. Indeed, this has been reported or suggested (Festinger, 1971; Leushina, 1965; Robinson, 1973). If this is a common strategy it might be revealed by suitable plots of primary latency against end-primary error, but we have generally failed to detect convincing "latency-accuracy tradeoff" in this laboratory. For example, two of eight subjects made primary saccades ("anti" saccades) of roughly constant "middling" size when asked to look away by an equal and opposite amount from various sizes of stimulus step of 3.8–11.5° amplitude ("anti" task); accuracy was deferred to the large forward or backshooting secondary saccade (Hallett, 1978; Hallett & Adams, 1980). By contrast, the other six subjects made primaries that were graded in amplitude to match the goal. However, the primary latencies of all eight subjects conformed to the same experimental law, so the two different strategies did not differ in latency.

In summary, there are cases where predictable aspects of the stimulus are unconsciously exploited by subjects. (The term "strategy" does not therefore have a strongly cognitive sense.) It is prudent to randomize stimuli and even instructions appropriately within the same session, to complete data collection while the subject is still performing consistently, to converse with subjects in a uniform and guarded manner, and to use a computer to ensure the consistency of experimental protocol. With this approach our experience is that subjects generally behave in a repeatable automatic manner.

2.2. Methods for Measuring Eye Movements

2.2.1. General Considerations. Eye movements are angular rotations of the eyes that orient the eyes for different directions and distances of space. Any translational movement (i.e., movement of the eye through distance) must not be mismeasured as angular rotation.

An ideal instrument would do the following:

1. Offer an unobstructed field of view with good access to the face and head.
2. Make no contact with the subject.
3. Meet the practical challenge of being capable of artificially stabilizing the retinal image if necessary.
4. Possess an *accuracy* of at least 1% or a few minutes of arc, that is, not give a 10° reading when truly 9° (accuracy is limited by the cumulative effects of nonlinearity, distortion, noise, lag, and all other sources of error).
5. Offer a *resolution* of 1 min arc or 1 min arc$\cdot$sec^{-1}, and thus be capable of detecting the smallest changes in eye position (resolution is limited only by instrumental noise).
6. Offer a wide dynamic range of 1 min to 45° (= 3000-fold) for eye position and 1 min arc$\cdot$sec^{-1} to 800°$\cdot$sec^{-1} (= 50,000-fold) for eye velocity.
7. Offer good temporal dynamics and speed of response (e.g., good gain and small phase shift to 100 Hz, or a good step response).
8. Possess a real-time response (to allow physiological maneuvers).
9. Measure all three degrees of angular rotation and be insensitive to ocular translation.
10. Be easily extended to binocular recording.
11. Be compatible with head and body recording.
12. Be easy to use on a variety of subjects.

In considering different methods it is useful to note that 10° is about a hand's breadth at arm's length, and that the larger eye movements (saccades) are usually less than 15° in tranquil strolling and walking (Bahill, Adler, & Stark, 1975; Lancaster, 1941). The subtense of the human rod-free fovea is usually taken to be about 1° (= 0.291 mm of the retina), which also corresponds to the angular height of an average man at 100 m. The cone spacing in the fovea is often taken to be about 0.6 min arc (= 2.5 μm at the retina). It is apparent that a translational movement of 0.1 mm would contribute appreciable inaccuracy if registered as rotation.

Angular resolution and temporal bandwidth are two parameters commonly used in the description of performance; records may look poor even though resolution and bandwidth are high. Many authors specify "resolution," which is easily established from the noise level of the instrument, but few quote "accuracy," which includes all sources of error and is hard to estimate without comparison against an ideal (and nonexistent) instrument. A usual measure of accuracy is the linearity of the plot of registered eye position versus assumed eye position, usually stated in the form that the calibrations did not deviate from linearity by more than 5–10%. A 10% error for a 10° eye movement does, of course, leave doubt as to whether the apparent point of fixation is actually foveated. Linearity can be improved for otherwise high-quality data by scaling the data in a nonlinear manner, provided one can assume that the different calibration targets are fixated with the same retinal point. Presumably the accuracy of good techniques (e.g., the search-coil contact lens method) is such that experimenters have excluded the possibility that the subject under-responds during fixation (e.g., to a rightward calibration target by fixating it with the left edge of the fovea), but I am unaware of any studies showing that subjects fixate differently positioned targets with exactly the same retinal region.

Methods can be listed according to the anatomically anterior-posterior location of the monitored component, as follows. For a review, see Young and Sheena (1975).

2.2.2. Surface Features. Simple photography or video records of the eyes allow determination of all three degrees of rotational freedom, though usually with a low precision and at the expense of some labor. Scleral blood vessels, the corneal reflections, or the pupillary center may be measured, depending on the circumstances (e.g., Llewellyn Thomas, 1968; Mackworth & Llewellyn Thomas, 1962; Sheena, 1976). A useful two-dimensional binocular eye tracker, for laboratory and clinic, monitors the center of gravity of the surface features of the eye (range ±15°, resolution <5 arc min, linearity 5%, frequency response 85 Hz). It is manufactured by Dr. Bouis (Straubenhardt, F.R. Germany).

Rotation can be measured without the contamination of translation, by appropriately measuring two features at different depths in the eye, for example, the corneal reflex relative to the pupillary center (Lambert, Monty, & Hall, 1974; Merchant, Morisette, & Porterfield, 1974). The Gulf Western device, for example, allows head movement within a 30-cm cube with a resolution of about 30 min arc for eye movements.

2.2.3. Contact Lens. Within the limits of their recording systems, contact lens methods provide the most technically satisfactory means of recording ocular rotations uncontaminated by translational artifacts, this advantage being largely offset by the unpleasantness and risks arising from direct contact with the eye. Optical contact lens methods (e.g., Ditchburn, 1973; Fender, 1964a; Heckenmueller, 1965; Matin, 1964; Matin & Pearce, 1964) best meet the technical challenge of stabilizing an image relative to the retina, but optical systems require head restraint and may obstruct access to the face and head.

All three degrees of rotational freedom of the contact lens may be sensed in a variety of nonoptical ways, an embedded search coil being most in vogue, despite the attached leads. In the search-coil method the subject, who needs no head restraint, is placed in an oscillating electromagnetic field and the total flux through the coil (Robinson, 1963), or the phase angle of the flux (Steinman & Collewijn, 1980), is appropriately processed. The former method requires calibration for offset (i.e., what signal equals "straight ahead"?) and gain (i.e., what change in signal corresponds to a ±10° swing?); the latter method needs only the offset adjusted. If necessary, calibrations can be done directly on the lens detached from the subject. The total experimental time must be less than 20 min to avoid small but hazardous corneal or conjunctival ulcerations, and the offset calibration may suffer if the movements are larger than 5–10° because of slippage of the lens on the eye. The method is highly suited to short clinical studies, allowing full access to the face and head, but in basic research the difficulty of obtaining willing subjects may lead to the experiments being restricted to one or two experiments or authors. This is at times inappropriate, given the role of cognitive factors in the planning of eye movements in some experimental situations.

There are several other optical and electromagnetic methods of monitoring a contact lens (Bechai & Hallett, 1977; Reulen & Bakker, 1982; Zeevi & Ish-Shalom, 1982).

2.2.4. Cornea. With a sensitive recording technique, the motion of a light beam reflected from the cornea (the "corneal reflex" or first Purkinje image) is capable of revealing all the details of tremor, drift, and microsaccades that one associates with contact lens recordings, but without the disadvantage of contact (Figs. 10.25, 10.26). In one such technique the corneal reflex covers a few of the phototransistors in a linear array; the center of gravity of the image is determined to within 0.004 of the detector spacing by scanning the array, summing a stereotyped biphasic wave form from each detector (whose amplitude is proportional to radiance), and determining the zero-crossing point of the accumulated signal. The mathematics for this process has been given and a digital device built (Eizenman, Frecker, & Hallett, 1984; Eizenman, Frecker, Joy, & Hallett, 1980). Noise level is 30 arc sec, dynamic range is 30 arc sec to ±18°, linearity is 2%, and sampling rate is 1000 Hz, which gives a velocity resolution of $2°\cdot sec^{-1}$ for a velocity bandwidth of 125 Hz. This method is potentially sensitive to head or eye translatory movements, and the head must be stabilized with a dental impression.

2.2.5. Pupil. The center of gravity of the pupil can be determined by a video technique (e.g., Sheena, 1976, for the Whittaker device), but response is limited to 15 Hz by the usual 30-Hz sampling rate. If the black pupil is imaged on two slits arranged end-to-end (i.e., a single slit, followed by a dividing prism) then an appropriately weighted difference between the radiant fluxes through the two slits varies as the sine of the angle of rotation. Because sine and angle deviate by only 1% for a 15° excursion, the output is effectively linear, and can be shown theoretically and practically to be insensitive to vertical movement of the eye or to change in pupil size (Hallett & Lightstone, 1976b; Lightstone, 1973). The device as implemented by F. G. Oakham in this laboratory could be refined further, peak-to-peak noise being equivalent to 4–6 min arc and linearity 5% for ±10 or ±15° horizontal excursions, depending on the subject, and the corner frequency is currently 15–20 Hz. The quality of published records of saccades is good because the linear phase characteristic optimizes the response to steps. Increasing the bandwidth to about 80 Hz increases noise, but does not noticeably improve the fidelity of recordings of saccades.

Both the Whittaker and Lightstone-Oakham devices are potentially sensitive to translational artifact, but a deep dental impression, good posture, and avoidance of breathing during a short trial of about 1 sec permit the trained subject to keep his head still to very few minutes of arc (Lightstone, 1973). Both devices fail to exploit the full information present in the shape of the pupil. It has been shown theoretically that three horizontal chords across the pupil (e.g., three equally spaced video sweeps) allow both the direction and magnitude of eye rotation to be

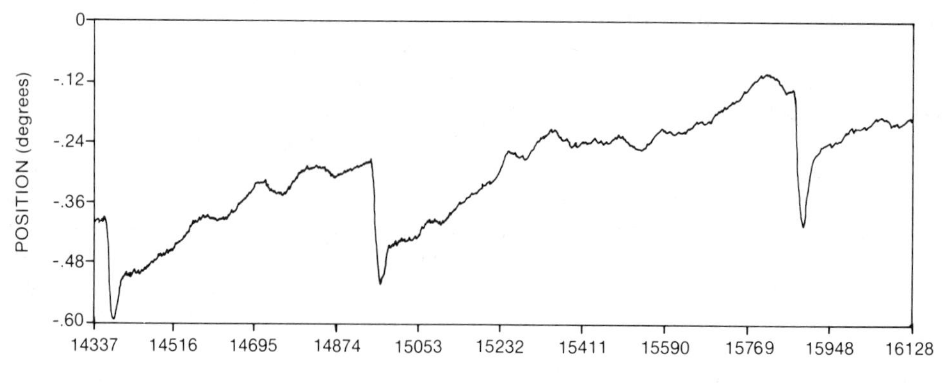

Figure 10.25. Residual eye movements of fixation measured by monitoring the corneal reflex with a precise method. Note microsaccades with large dynamic overshoot, irregular drift, and microtremor. No additional electronic filtering. (Method of Eizenman, Frecker, Joy, & Hallett, 1980.)

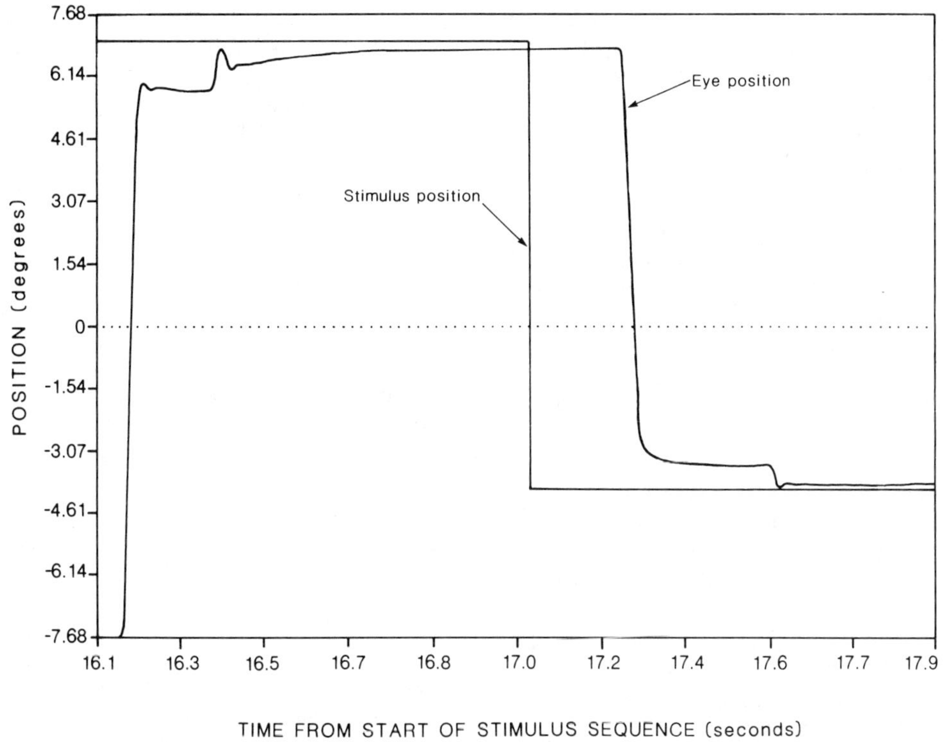

Figure 10.26. Saccadic tracking of a stepping stimulus. Note the large primary and smaller secondary saccades. The saccades at the left of the record show double dynamic overshoot or saccadic oscillations. The large saccade at the right may show dynamic undershoot. The nature of the processing eliminates any possibility that the saccade-like overshoots are due to dynamic artifacts of the recording system. The time scale is in units of 179 msec, the abscissal values are rounded. (Method of Eizenman, Frecker, Joy, & Hallett, 1980.)

found after simple computations, independently of translation (Bechai & Hallett, 1977). The principle here is that the projection of the ideal pupil on a plane changes from a circle to a tilted ellipse as the eye rotates. The pupil or an equivalent contact lens must have a very regular edge for reasonable accuracy, but there are low-accuracy applications.

2.2.6. Iris. The iris shows distinct radial structure. Consequently, if two consecutive video images are digitized and scanned along a circular path centered on the pupil, then cross-correlation will give the roll of the eye in the interval between the two video frames. A real-time system can be implemented with a resolution of up to 4 arc min, temporal response depending on the video frame rate. If the algorithms are extended to track the center of the pupil, roll can be measured in the presence of $\pm 13°$ of pitch and yaw (Hatamian & Anderson, 1983).

2.2.7. Limbus. The edges of the iris-sclera junction (corneo-scleral junction or limbus) can be monitored with a pair of detectors (Young & Sheena, 1975). Commercial instruments are available in which the infrared source and detectors are mounted on spectacle frames (e.g., Biometrics). The spectacle frames are very convenient and there are few if any hazards. The limbus boundary is not as well defined as the iris-pupil boundary; change of contrast in the infrared across the former is almost absent in most subjects with dark irises, as can be established with a video camera of similar spectral sensitivity to the detectors (Hallett & Lightstone, 1976b). Published records suggest that linearity and overall performance are often poorer than in the foregoing methods. Recording over a very wide band of temporal frequencies (e.g., up to 500 Hz) is not a cure for these defects.

2.2.8. Purkinje Images. The anterior and especially the posterior surfaces of the crystalline lens of the eye give rise to "reflexes" of incident light that rotate during eye movements, much as the corneal reflex does. Consequently, if a detector could be (virtually) rotated about the eye, so that corneal and lens reflexes are once more sensed to be aligned, then pure ocular rotation would be measured independently of any lateral or vertical ocular translation. Such an instrument has been developed, using moving mirrors, with an optional optometer for measuring the ocular accommodation for distance (Cornsweet & Crane, 1973). It is commercially available from Stanford Research Institute. In selected subjects, precision, linearity, and range are highly acceptable for studies of reading with fixed head. Although performance is less good than that of the contact lens methods, there is the major advantage of no contact with the eye. In principle, the method could be implemented without moving mirrors by using a static detector like that of Eizenman et al. (1984), but it might be better to monitor the pupil rather than the fourth Purkinje image, because the former is always visible, whereas the latter is always faint and impossible to track when the pupil is small.

2.2.9. Blood Vessels or Optic Nerve Head. Blood vessels in the sclera, or retina, or the optic disk move with the eye and can be tracked automatically (e.g., Kelly & Crane, 1968), though this is not usually done for technical reasons.

2.2.10. Macular Pigment. The molecules of the yellow (= blue-absorbing) macular pigment are oriented relative to the fibers leaving the fovea, and so the pigment can be subjectively visualized in space (rather like an afterimage) by exploiting the dichroic properties of the pigment, or its differential filtering of two metameric colorimetric hemifields (e.g., Brindley, 1970; Wyszecki & Stiles, 1967). The definition of the entoptic image of the macular pigment is less exact than that of a well-formed afterimage, and so the macular image is of less use for precisely assessing shifts in fixation. The macular image may, however, be more acceptable to some subjects than afterimage methods (Richards & Kaufman, 1969).

2.2.11. Afterimage. The afterimage of a linear or cross-shaped light provides a precise useful method for assessing the orientation of the eye or a change in fixation. The afterimage can be restored by flickering the background. This is the only well-tried method, apart from suitable photographic or contact lens techniques, that can measure roll of the eye about the line of sight. A resolution of 1–2 min arc is possible for yaw or pitch eye movements and a degree or so for roll (e.g., Balliet & Nakayama, 1978).

2.2.12. Electro-Oculogram. A DC potential is generated across the anterior and posterior poles of the eye by the pigment epithelium which lines the back of the retina and iris. Provided light-adaptation is kept constant, pitch and yaw eye movements can be measured to 0.5–1° over a wide range, and the experimenter has good access to the subject's face and head (Hood, 1968; Shackel, 1967). An electrical contact to slightly abraded skin near the eyes is needed. The method is suitable for clinical and human factors research, but not for measuring the correction saccades to stimulus steps of less than 15° (although this is sometimes done) because a good proportion will be missed.

2.3. Introduction to Models

Models should provide a useful summary and interpretation of current facts, and should invite critical experiments that allow the possibility that the model will be rejected. This section provides only an introduction to models because the present stress is on underlying principles, and because some current models are due for revision. Some ideas of my own are given to fill gaps in our current thinking about combinations of saccades.

2.3.1. Basic Servomechanistic Diagram. The simple servomechanism in Figure 10.27 makes useful points. A system with a steady-state gain (g) and pure time delay (T) is surrounded by an instantaneous, unity-gain, negative-feedback path. Following the signal from left to right across the forward path allows one to immediately write an equation for the steady state; when this is rearranged, output (θ_o) is seen to approach the input level (θ_i), and the effect of uncontrolled disturbance (θ_d) is greatly attenuated, if gain $g >> 1$. Quite complicated circuits can often be reduced to a simplicity comparable to Figure 10.27. For example, Figure 10.28 is formally similar to Figure 10.27, as can be seen by writing $g = g_1 + g_2$ or by folding Figure 10.28 on itself about a horizontal line. Because the oculomotor system tends to underreact slightly, it is tempting to assume that Figure 10.27 is a fair model, with g of the order of 5 (2–10). This corresponds to the output being 0.8 (0.7–0.9) of the desired value. If one now considers the response of the circuit to a step change in input θ_i (Fig. 10.29), and sketches the signal patterns as the disturbance propagates through the relevant parts of the circuit, the response is seen to be highly unsatisfactory, even when g is as low as 1, and is even more wildly oscillating with waxing positive and negative swings if $g > 1$. Much the same will be true if the circuit includes dynamic components. The conclusion is that the real eye-movement system must either be intermittently *refractory* to the destabilizing aspects of delayed feedback, or else it must be spared those effects in some way.

2.3.2. Simple Servomechanism for Generating Saccades. A particular solution to the destabilizing effects of delayed feedback is shown in Figure 10.30 for the saccadic system. Working from left to right, we see that target position relative to the head (θ_i) and eye position (θ_o) are combined by the optics of the eye to give the potentially destabilizing error (or retinal image position θ_r), which drives the brain in the foveating mode. If, however, anticipated eye position ($\hat{\theta}_o$) is also fed back internally, with the same sign and delay ("= A") as that due to the afferent pathways (A), then the destabilizing effect of the optical feedback path is neutralized and a model of target position ($\hat{\theta}_i$) is available to drive the rest of the oculomotor pathway in an effectively

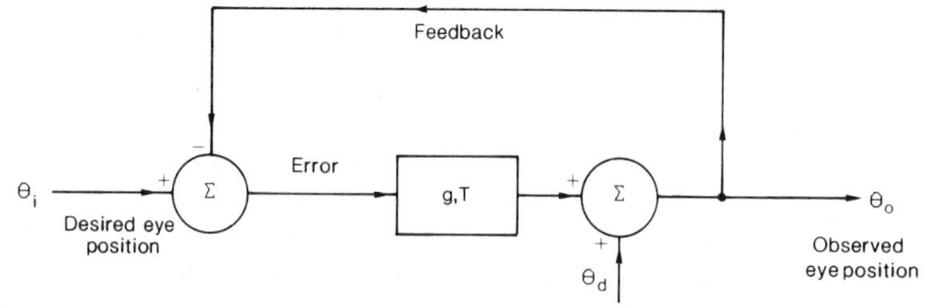

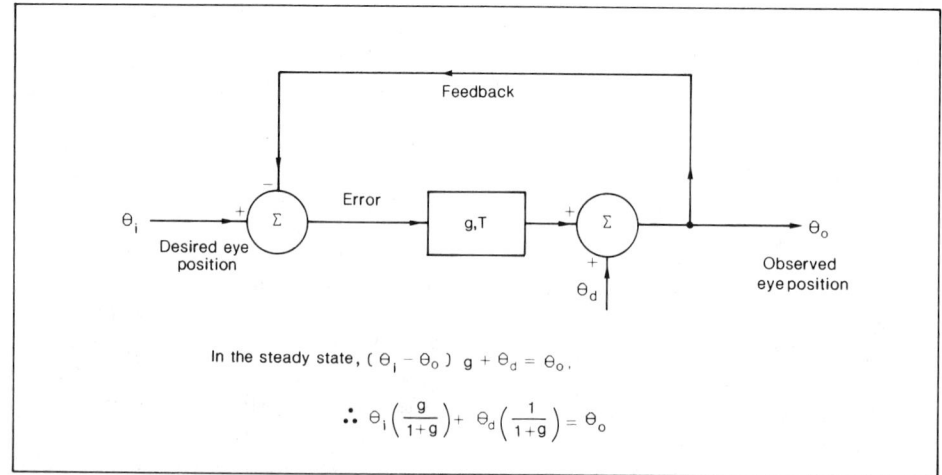

In the steady state, $(\theta_i - \theta_o)\, g + \theta_d = \theta_o$.

$$\therefore\ \theta_i\left(\frac{g}{1+g}\right) + \theta_d\left(\frac{1}{1+g}\right) = \theta_o$$

Figure 10.27. Hypothetical servomechanism utilizing negative feedback to control observed (or output) eye position θ_o close to the desired (or input) level θ_i, despite an uncontrolled disturbance θ_d. Σ denotes summing points where signals interact with positive or negative signs. The feedforward path is described by a steady-state gain g and a pure time delay T without any dynamic components. The steady-state solution is derived. If $g >> 1$, then θ_o is close to θ_i and the effect of the disturbance is minimized.

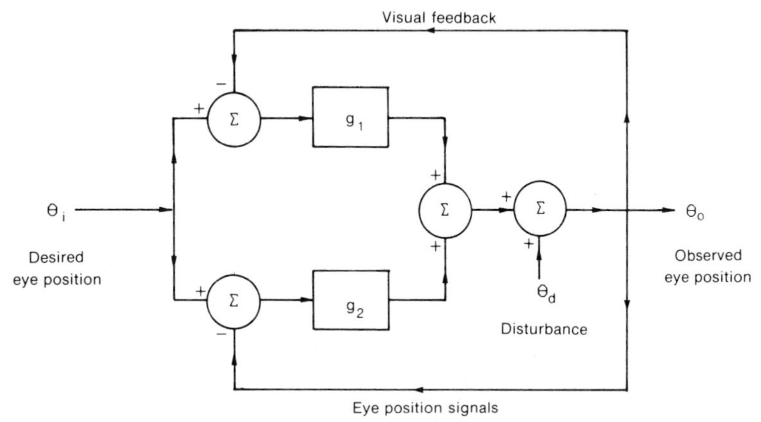

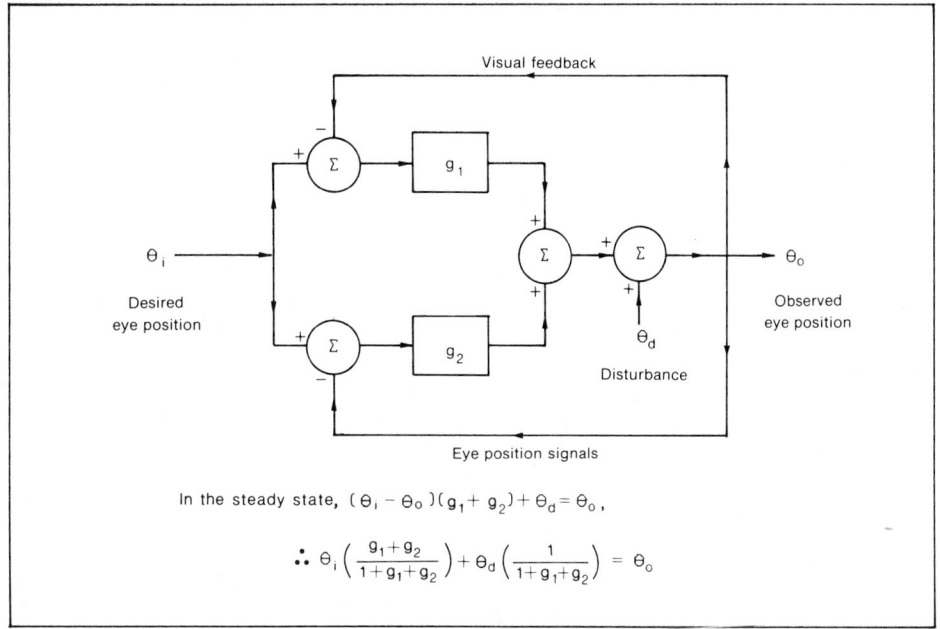

In the steady state, $(\theta_i - \theta_o)(g_1 + g_2) + \theta_d = \theta_o$,

$$\therefore \theta_i\left(\frac{g_1+g_2}{1+g_1+g_2}\right) + \theta_d\left(\frac{1}{1+g_1+g_2}\right) = \theta_o$$

Figure 10.28. Additive control by two parallel feedback paths. θ_i is desired eye position in the skull, θ_o is observed position, θ_d is a disturbance, and g_1 and g_2 are the gains of the visual control and eye position control loops, respectively. If the gains are appreciable (>>1) then the disturbance θ_d is reduced by the sum of the gains. If loss of the g_1 loop in the dark increases the observed noise in θ_o by sixfold (say), then the estimated gain ratio is g_1:g_2 as 5:1.

open-loop manner. The symbolism "= *A*" reminds us that equality with the visual afferent delay *A* must be maintained, even if *A* should prove to be increased at low light levels or in complex tasks.

Saccadic eye movements have many voluntary aspects and many potential goals, and so central delay **C** in Figure 10.30 is intended to provide time for a decision about the spatial goal (θ_g) of the saccade, which decision may vary with the task and instructions. Initially, any decision is revocable, that is, new retinal events or decisions can cancel a saccade if the central process has not elapsed (Becker & Jürgens, 1979; Hallett & Adams, 1980; Hou & Fender, 1979). Efferent delay *E* allows a limited time for compromises as to amplitude once the decision to act is irrevocable. When the brainstem saccade generator is triggered, the motor neurons fire at high or maximum frequency until the local error (θ_1) is 0. The eye then stops more or less abruptly, with little or no dynamic overshoot, because of the viscoelastic damping of the globe. The motor neuron discharge (or muscle force) is described as "pulse step" and can be resolved into two components: a high-frequency (or high-tension) pulse lasting almost as long as the saccade, which drives the eye at high velocity against the viscous damping of the orbit, and the "step," or maintained clock-like discharge that holds the eye against the elastic restoring forces (Fuchs & Kaneko, 1981; J. E. Miller, 1958; Robinson, 1964, 1981). See Figure 10.31(a). Because the pulse step is generated in a consistent manner, and because the mechanical properties of the "load" (i.e., eye and orbit) are fixed, most saccadic eye movements are generated in a stereotyped manner and show a definite relation between peak velocity, amplitude, and duration known as the "main sequence" (Bahill, Clark, & Stark, 1975c; Baloh, Sills, Kumley, & Honrubia, 1975; Boghen, Troost, Dell'Osso, & Birkett, 1974; Zuber, Stark, & Cook, 1965). In certain circumstances saccades deviate from this stereotype; for example, the pulse may be multiple rather than single (Hallett, 1978; Hallett & Adams, 1980). In states of fatigue or inattention (e.g., Bahill & Stark, 1975; Fuchs & Binder, 1983), or in clinical situations, quasi-normal or abnormal forms are frequently encountered. As Figure 10.31(b) shows, one clinical extreme is provided by "pulseless" saccades, in which the eye glides into position with roughly exponentially decaying velocity, as if responding to a step force.

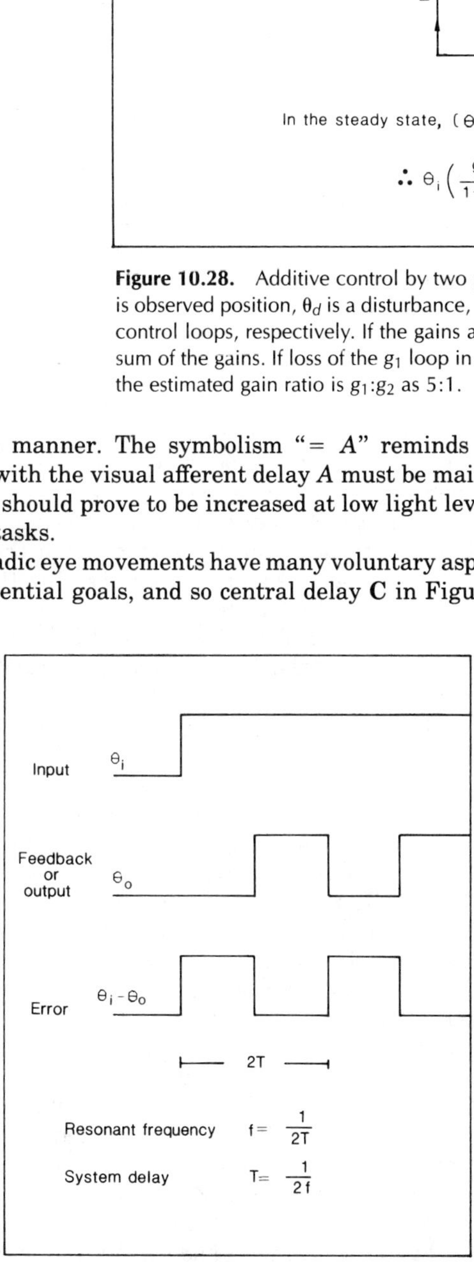

Figure 10.29. The response of the servomechanism in Figure 10.27 to a transient change in the input θ_i, or the response of more complicated systems, can be found by pencil-and-paper methods; let time progress in small increments and trace out the signal levels in all relevant parts of the circuit. In the present example gain g is assumed to be 1, and so the output θ_o intermittently equals either θ_i or 0, periodicity depending on the total delay in the loop (which is T in this example, because feedback is instantaneous).

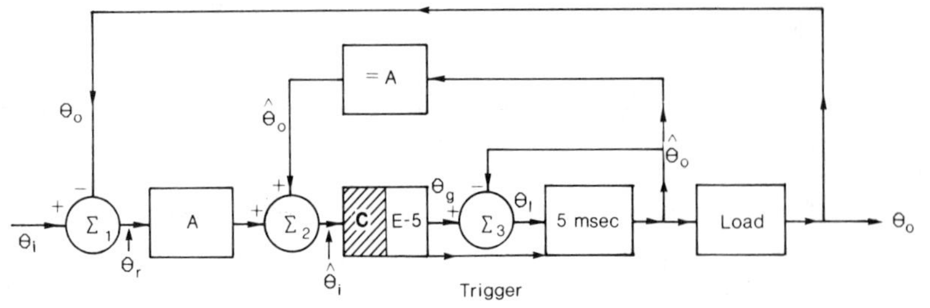

Figure 10.30. A simple servomechanism for generating saccades. Target direction θ_i, relative to the head, interacts with eye position θ_o at the optical summing point Σ_1, yielding retinal image position θ_r. After an afferent delay (*A* msec), θ_r is added at the neural summing point Σ_2 to a similarly delayed (= *A* msec) analog $\hat{\theta}_o$ of θ_o so that θ_i is reconstructed as the internal signal $\hat{\theta}_i$ and potential instability due to feedback delays is averted. Central delay **C** determines the spatial goal for the future saccade. Efferent delay *E* allows compromise as to the amplitude of the saccade in the light of newer stimuli or internal decisions. The saccade generator is the last 5 msec or so of this delay. When the saccade generator is triggered, burst neurons in the brainstem fire at very high frequency. The burst neurons cease firing when the eye position analog $\hat{\theta}_o$ equals the current spatial goal θ_g and local error θ_l is 0. This leaves the motoneurons at the output firing at a new clocklike rate. Thus the motoneuron firing pattern is a pulse step: the pulse component corresponds to the saccade and mainly serves to overcome the viscous drag on the globe; the step component holds the eye against elastic spring forces in the orbit, and is roughly proportional to eye position θ_o. (Adapted from the model of Robinson, 1975a.)

Intermediate are a variety of saccadic *glissades* in which the pulse is too short or too long relative to the height of the step, so that the eye drifts forward or backward with decaying velocity after the saccadic component terminates. At the other clinical extreme is "total gaze paresis," where the step in the pulse step is missing, and, after a saccade, the eyes drift back to center with exponentially slowing velocity (Feldon, Hoyt, & Stark, 1980). For reviews of central eye movement disorders, see Dell'Osso and Daroff (1981) and Sharpe (1981).

The most precise physiological studies of the pulse-step theory are from trained primates, in which good recordings of eye position and velocity can be correlated with the neural control signals (e.g., van Gisbergen, Robinson, & Gielen, 1981). If the pulse of the pulse step is too large by only a few nerve impulses, control shifts to the other half brainstem. When this occurs, the microsaccade or saccade is followed by an *immediate* saccadic reversal (known as "dynamic overshoot"). Sometimes the reversal is even followed by another reversal, so that the eyes "chatter" to and fro in the orbit at a microscopic scale. For records in man, see Eizenman et al. (1984). The pulse-step model for saccades has been extended to nystagmic eye movements by Abel, Dell'Osso, and Daroff (1978).

2.3.3. Combinations of Saccades. Servomechanistic diagrams like Figure 10.30 become complicated when one wishes to discuss the hierarchy of decision processes that must be involved when the saccadic system faces conflicts owing to the target changing direction or new targets appearing. One such circuit has been sketched recently (Becker & Jürgens, 1979). It is perhaps more useful here to demonstrate an alternative method of modeling where the diagram shows not the physical elements of the circuit (as in Fig. 10.30), but the subdivision of time into various operations. Such *timing diagrams* are useful for modeling the saccadic system because it is reasonable, as a first approximation, to represent the operations between a stimulus and its saccade as a sequence of *time delays*; dynamics are important only for the last few milliseconds of the latent period when the brainstem saccade generator is active (e.g., Zee & Robinson, 1979). Figure 10.32 shows timing diagrams for the *ACE* scheme as an introduction to this method of modeling. The upper long rectangle at the top of Figure 10.32 shows the latent period between a step motion of the stimulus and the saccade to that step. Time flows from left to right. Delay *A* is the afferent and retinal delay that precedes a variable central **C** delay for the decision as to the goal. Delay **C** is followed by an efferent delay *E* that allows compromise as to the amplitude of the future saccade. The final few milliseconds of delay *E* are occupied by the saccade generator. Delay **C** is shown cross-hatched in the diagram to stress the temporal variability of this higher-level process relative to the other delays. Parts (a)–(c) of Figure 10.32 illustrate saccadic latent periods in different cases of interest. In part (a), two latent periods are planned in parallel as the eye attempts to track a stimulus which steps rapidly from one side of the midline to the other. In part (b) two latent periods are successive; in this example the link is the altered visual feedback caused by the primary saccade. In part (c) one central delay **C** is associated with the decision not to foveate the stimulus and a second with the decision to look away. Shown in part (d) of Figure 10.32 by double- and single-headed arrows are times of onset of hypothetical neural discharges that may cancel or modify any other latent saccades, as will be explored further in Section 3.7.

The ingredients of the *ACE* scheme in Figure 10.32 are two forms of planning (parallel and successive), three types of delay (*A*, **C**, and *E*), and three types of interaction (cancellation, modification of amplitude, and internal triggering). These postulates are not radical. (1) Parallel and successive planning are old concepts in psychology and apply to saccades (Täumer, 1975). (2) The classification of delays as afferent, central, and efferent is conventional. (3) "Internal triggering" may be considered to be a feature of voluntary behavior. The concepts of cancellation

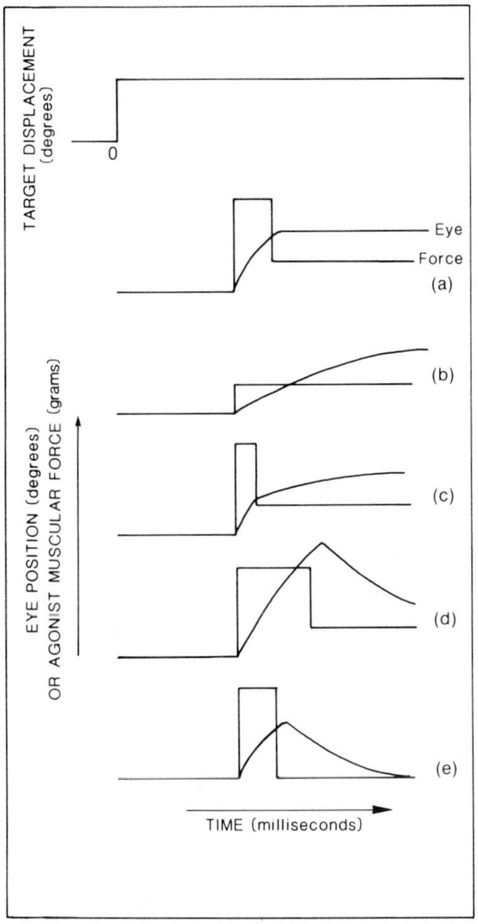

Figure 10.31. Diagram to show that saccadic eye movements are affected by the relative balance of the pulse and step components of the muscular driving force. (a) An "ideal" saccade due to a normal pulse step of force in the agonist muscle. (b) Same, but pulse missing. (c) Pulse too short. (d) Pulse too long. (e) Step missing. Scheme is simplified, because pulse height varies for small saccades, and because some situations probably involve multiple or superimposed pulses in agonist and antagonist muscles. Actual saccades may terminate in multiple overshoots or oscillations that imply a sequence of opposite pulse forces in the agonist and antagonist muscles (e.g., Bahill, Clark & Stark, 1975a; Robinson, 1981; Zee & Robinson, 1979).

and amplitude compromise apply to saccades (Becker & Jürgens, 1979; Hallett & Adams, 1980; Hou & Fender, 1979). (4) A rationale for separate cancellation and compromise operations was given in Section 1.3.3. It is of theoretical interest that very complex behavior can follow from these few postulates. This would still be so if one were to substitute the alternative concept of three types of reaction time (one for initiating a saccade, one for canceling it, and one for modifying its amplitude) for the above delay and interaction postulates.

2.3.4. Combined Head and Eye Saccades. In most experiments described in this chapter, the head is restrained to simplify measurement or analysis. The natural response to a novel object in the peripheral field, or to an abrupt movement of the object of regard, is a combined abrupt movement of both head and eyes toward the object, the head saccade and eye saccade beginning at about the same time. Analysis shows that the head and eye movements are independently planned, that is, are in parallel, so that either movement can accomplish the required shift of gaze in the absence of the other. The vestibulo-ocular reflex functions as a hard-wired peripheral processor that modifies the eye response on the basis of any head response; so the combined actions of head and eye give the required shift of gaze and not twice what is needed. Because the head has the greater inertia, the initial mechanical response is largely the eye saccade (Fig. 10.33), but as head movement becomes appreciable the vestibulo-ocular counterrotation "robs" saccadic eye velocity, and eye velocity eventually reverses (e.g., Bizzi, Kalil, & Morasso, 1972; Lanman, Bizzi, & Allum, 1978; Morasso, Bizzi, & Dichgans, 1973). The net result is a movement of appropriate size. The process is more complicated, and less understood, when the head and eye movements are large.

Figure 10.34 (page 10-34) represents this example of parallel planning as a signal network. At the left, target position θ_t interacts at the optical summing point 1 with eye position in space (i.e., gaze $= \theta_g$) to give retinal image position θ_r. This is applied to two parallel pulse-step controllers, one for the head saccade and one for the eye saccade. At the right, the vestibulo-ocular reflex modifies eye position to compensate for any change in head position; head position in space θ_h and eye position in the head θ_e add physically to give gaze θ_g. Given that one eye saccade can modify a "parallel" saccade, it would not be surprising if the oculomotor system should also modify the head system in appropriate circumstances, as indicated speculatively by the heavy arrow in Figure 10.34. In fact, when the target is continually lit, head movement is too small, so that the eyes remain deviated in their orbits at the end of the total gaze shift [Fig. 10.33(b)]. If the target is briefly flashed, however, the head movement approximates the required gaze shift [Fig. 10.33(c)], and the eye saccade is completely "undone" by the vestibulo-ocular reflex (Gresty, 1974). This leaves the eyes centered in their orbits, which may be biologically adaptive, as the centered position allows visual search in any direction for traces of the vanished target.

2.3.5. Combined Smooth Movements of Head and Eye. Head rotation elicits reflex countermovements of the eyes mediated by mechanoreceptors in the semicircular canals of the vestibules of the inner ears. These movements counter head velocity so that eye velocity in space, and thus retinal-image velocity, is nearly 0. Latency is only 10–15 msec, and the mechanoreceptors are best stimulated by relatively large-amplitude, fast-velocity, or high-frequency head movements. Ocular responses to small, slow, and low-frequency head rotations, or to persistent (>10 sec) head rotation at constant velocity, are mediated by the visual system, which is extremely sensitive to retinal-image slip, though much longer in latency.

Figure 10.35 (page 10-34) summarizes ideas as to how the parallel vestibular and visual signals are integrated to facilitate clear vision. Whereas the saccade model (Fig. 10.30, $\hat{\theta}_o$) postulates positive internal feedback of eye position, the smooth-movement model (Fig. 10.35) postulates positive internal feedback of eye velocity. Various gains, delays, and dynamic elements are omitted for simplicity; see the comments on a model by Robinson elsewhere (Henn et al., 1980; see also Wyatt & Pola, 1983). The angular velocities of the surrounding visual world $\dot{W}$ and of the eyes in space (gaze velocity $\dot{G}$) interact via the optics of the eyes (summing point 1) to give retinal-image-slip velocity $\dot{R}$. At summing point 2, addition of an appropriately delayed and scaled internal estimate of eye velocity ($\dot{E}$, relative to the head) yields an estimate of world velocity ($\dot{W}'_h$, relative to the head). The negative of $\dot{W}'_h$ is visually estimated head velocity relative to the world ($\dot{H}'_v$). In many situations the world is static ($\dot{W}$ is 0), and so visually estimated head velocity is a valid estimate of head velocity in space; but an estimate that is low-pass filtered

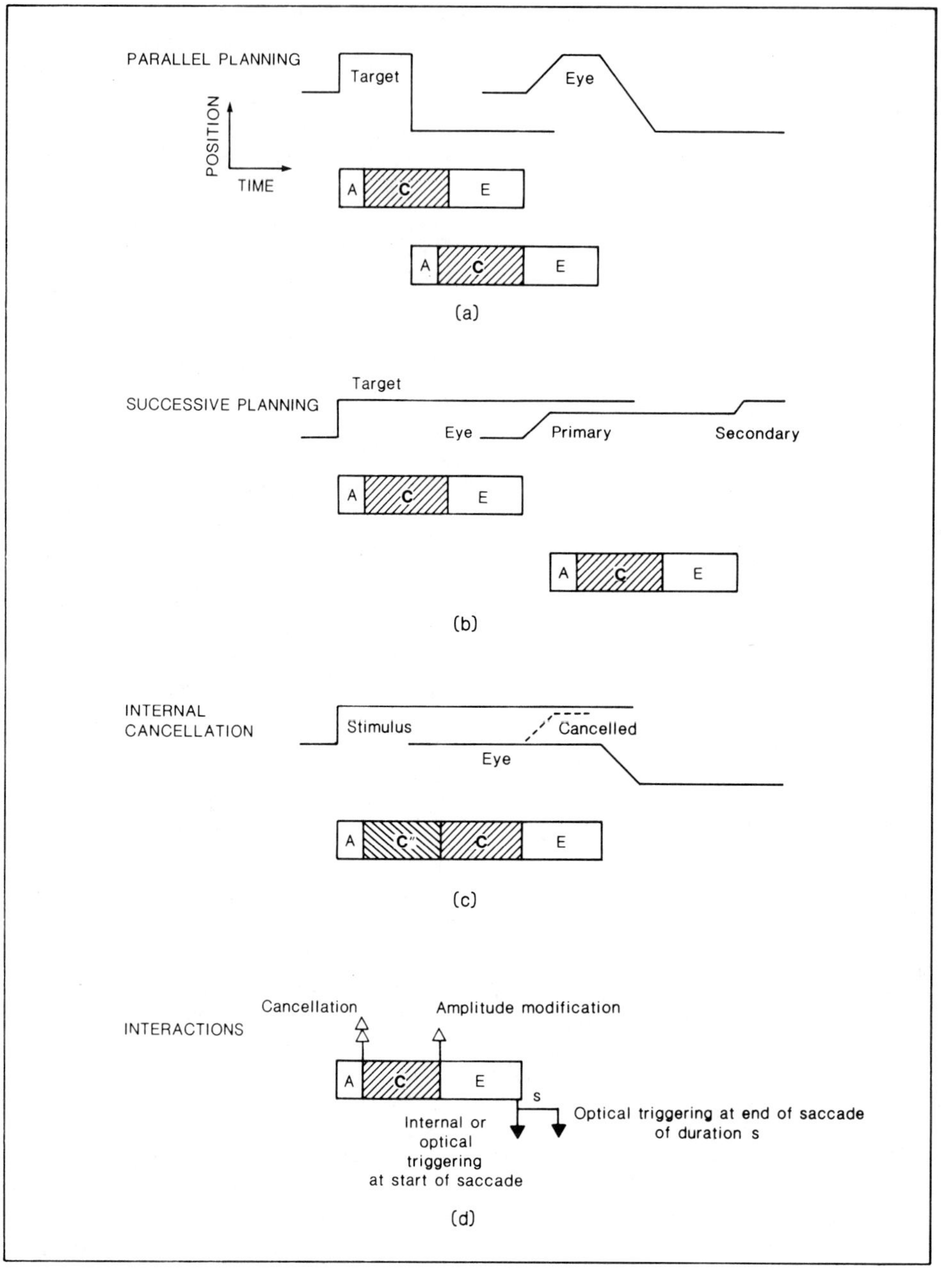

Figure 10.32. Diagrams to illustrate hypotheses about the planning of saccadic eye movements. *Parallel planning*: the upper traces show the displacements of the target and of the eye in a "two-step tracking task." This type of response is called "type-I" because the first saccade is toward step 1. The long rectangles in the timing diagram below show the overlapping latent periods of the saccades and the components of the latent period. *A*-afferent delay, **C**-variable central delay, *E*-efferent delay. *Successive planning*: the upper traces show the primary and secondary saccades to a single step displacement of the stimulus. The timing diagrams below show that the second latent period is initiated by retinal stimulation at the end of the primary saccade, in this example, and is normal in duration. Other diagrams are given below to illustrate other types of secondary saccade. *Internal cancellation*: in the "anti" task, the subject is commonly able to look away from the stimulus. The timing diagram illustrates the hypothesis that the central delay is repeated in this outcome. *Interactions*: different neural discharges are assumed to be possible in the latent period preceding a saccade. The earliest possibility is that the sensory or central processing of the saccade terminate in a discharge (double-headed arrow) that may cancel another latent saccade if the timing is right. Modification of the amplitude of another latent saccade is also possible (single-headed arrow), but this takes more time. Finally, a saccade may trigger another saccade (solid arrowhead) by an internal discharge or by optical feedback.

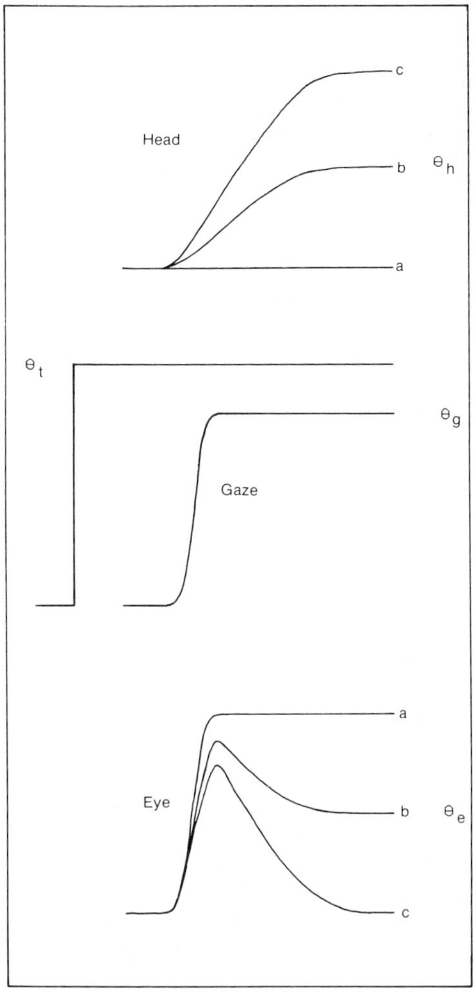

Figure 10.33. Idealized scheme, showing interaction of moderate-sized head and eye saccades. The same change in gaze angle in space ($\theta_g = \theta_h + \theta_e$) occurs whether head movement θ_h is (a) absent, (b) moderate, as when the target is continuously lit, or (c) large, as when the target is briefly flashed. This is because of the modification of eye position θ_e by the vestibulo-ocular reflex. Secondary saccades are omitted for simplicity.

because of the failure of vision to respond to the higher frequencies of oscillatory motion. This is satisfactory, because the semicircular canals provide an independent estimate of head velocity in space, $\dot{H}_{cs}$, which is deficient in the *lower* frequencies (because of the mechanical characteristics of the canals). Combination of the two signals at the level of the vestibular nucleus ("summing point" 3) gives a "best estimate" of head velocity in space which is valid over a wide dynamic range if $\dot{W} = 0$. This best estimate drives eye velocity $\dot{E}$ oppositely to $\dot{H}$, and gives $\dot{G} = 0$ at summing point 4.

The model is applicable to circumstances where $\dot{W}$ is nonzero. In Figure 10.35, heavy arrow 1 allows for variable interactions between the visual and semicircular canal estimates of head velocity $\dot{H}$ in "conflict" situations where the two sources of feedback are at variance. Examples are when the subject is within a heaving ship's cabin, or is seated within an optokinetic drum, or is viewing the world through magnifying goggles with normal head movements. In these cases $\dot{R}$, or perhaps some percept, eventually suppresses or rescales the semicircular canals' estimate of $\dot{H}$, providing biological adaptation. Heavy arrow 2 indicates a role for cognitive factors in more tranquil circumstances. When this factor is absent, visual input is *"global,"* and the estimate $\dot{W}'_h$ (world movement relative to the head) supplements the vestibular stabilization of gaze, as discussed. If vision is more *"focal,"* as when attending to a selected detail of the scene, $\dot{W}'_h$ expresses *target* velocity relative to the head. This is a suitable signal for driving voluntary smooth pursuit.

With appropriate dynamic elements for the processing of the visual and semicircular canal signals, it is possible to treat the dynamics of compensatory eye movements more elegantly than Figure 10.35 (Henn et al., 1980), both when the system responds to some new stress and when it recovers from temporary overload. For example, *afternystagmus* develops after prolonged unidirectional rotation of an optokinetic drum, or of the body, ceases. Optokinetic nystagmus is in the direction of the original stimulus, whereas vestibular nystagmus is opposite. Consequently, the two tend to cancel in most natural circumstances (except, perhaps, for rotations about the roll axis). This usually speeds recovery following a prolonged spin. Flexibility in more advanced models is gained by subtracting the canal signal at one point in the circuit and adding it at another, so that the vestibulo-ocular reflex and voluntary smooth pursuit are not in conflict. Finally, one may note that the more primitive vestibulo-ocular mechanism has, as it were, been captured and subordinated by the visual system. Retinal-slip velocity $\dot{R}$ or its higher manifestations can modify the contributions of the canals, whereas attention may allow one small part of the scene to control the gaze. Global inputs to eye control may be from the whole retina directly to the colliculus and other brainstem nuclei; focal inputs may arise from cerebral-collicular interactions "enhancing" the response of the oculomotor pathways to certain items in the scene (e.g., Wurtz & Albano, 1980).

3. EXPERIMENTAL RESULTS: EYE MOVEMENTS IN DIFFERENT CIRCUMSTANCES

Section 3 is organized into major sections by the *nature of the target.* These are subdivided by the *nature of the instructions* to the human subject; further subdivisions provide convenient *topics*. The table of contents for this chapter facilitates quick reference. Theoretical comment is brief, because the main concepts are listed and discussed in Section 2.

3.1. Eye Movements with a Fixed Visual Target

This section deals largely with the eye movements of steady fixation when the head is relatively static. The initial discussion of head movements serves to alert the reader to the artificial nature of much laboratory experimentation, but it is convenient to defer a fuller discussion of head movements and the vestibulo-ocular reflex to Sections 3.2.1.3 and 3.4.1.4. This is reasonable because the vestibulo-ocular reflex is frequently studied in darkness, and most aspects of the reflex are qualitatively similar in light or in darkness, if the subject is properly instructed.

When the head is relatively fixed, the principal eye movements to a spatially fixed stimulus are the residual smooth movements of fixation, sometimes rhetorically regarded as "smooth pursuit of a zero velocity stimulus," and saccades. Vestibular and optokinetic eye movements partly compensate for any residual head motion, whereas errors in the alignment of the eyes could be deemed to be "vergence movements." Substantial smooth movements may occur if the stimulus is fixed

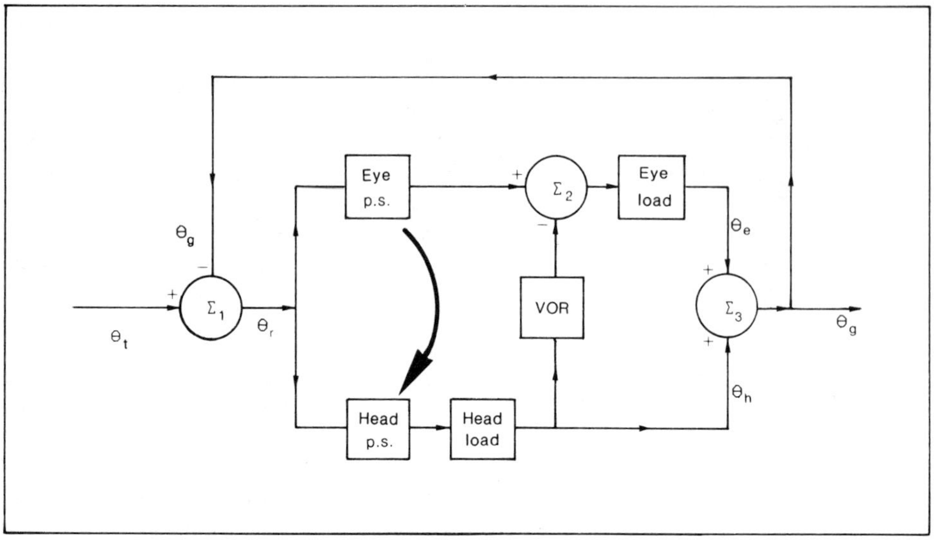

Figure 10.34. Simple circuit for interactions of head and eye saccades. Target direction θ_t and gaze θ_g determine retinal error θ_r, which is applied to two parallel controllers. The eye "pulse-step generator" (eye p.s.) drives the eye load, giving eye position θ_e, and the head pulse-step generator (head p.s.) drives the head load, giving head position θ_h. Head position θ_h adds physically to eye position to give gaze in space θ_g, but is also subtracted from eye position, via the action of the vestibulo-occular reflex VOR. Thus shift in gaze is correct whether the head moves or not. The large arrow indicates possible modification of the head system by the visual system.

relative to the retina. The questionable influence of cognitive styles on eye position is not discussed here (Saring & von Cramon, 1980; Thomason, Arbuckle, & Cady, 1980; Tomer & Mintz, 1980).

3.1.1. Instruction: Fixate the Static Fixation Point. Unless specially qualified, a fixation point means a small object, usually of a few minutes of arc, which is fixed relative to the earth.

3.1.1.1. Head Movements. When a subject attempts to sit as still as possible, looking at a small fixation light in darkness, the head drifts with a speed of about 30 min arc · sec^{-1} around its mean position, with a standard deviation of about 25 min arc or a mean deviation of 1°. There is prominent oscillation below 2 Hz frequency, with peaks at 3.5, 5, and 6.5 Hz

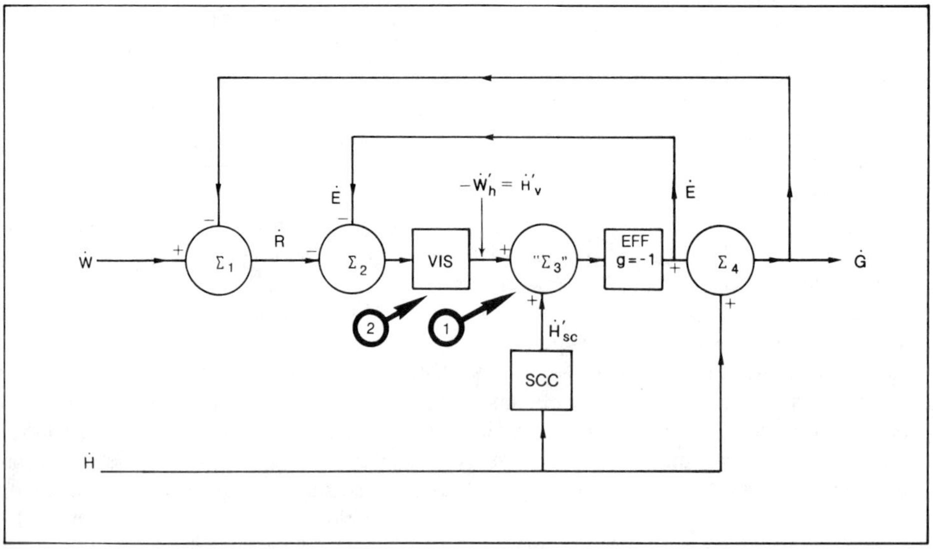

Figure 10.35. Scheme showing how head angular velocity $\dot{H}$ and movement of the visual world $\dot{W}$ determine gaze velocity in space $\dot{G}$. Usually the world is stationary. ($\dot{W} = 0$). Combination of $\dot{W}$ and $\dot{G}$ gives retinal image velocity $\dot{R}$. This combines with eye velocity relative to the head $\dot{E}$ to yield a visual estimate (VIS) of world velocity relative to the head $\dot{W}'_h$. Apart from sign, $\dot{W}'_h$ also equals head velocity relative to the visual world $\dot{H}'_v$, and thus, if $\dot{W} = 0$, head velocity relative to space. The visual estimate of head velocity $\dot{W}'_h$ is supplemented in an appropriate manner by an estimate $\dot{H}'_{sc}$ of $\dot{H}$ from the semicircular canals (SCC). The combined head velocity signal drives the efferent pathway (EFF), so that eye velocity $\dot{E}$ is opposite to $\dot{H}$, which maintains $\dot{G} = 0$, despite variation in $\dot{H}$ over a wide range of frequencies. In other situations $\dot{W}$ is nonzero and optokinetic pursuit or smooth pursuit occurs. The broad numbered arrows indicate the sites of action of influences which modify use of the semicircular canal signal $\dot{H}'_{sc}$ in "conflict" situations (arrow 1), or allow smooth pursuit of a selected target to overrule stabilization of the gaze by stationary world structures (arrow 2).

(Skavenski, Hansen, Steinman, & Winterson, 1979; Steinman, 1976). Standing increases the speed of head drift to 40–60 min arc · $sec.^{-1}$ Because compensation by the vestibulo-ocular and allied reflexes is imperfect for these relatively small motions, *eye* velocity in space is appreciably high (20–40 min arc · sec^{-1} during sitting and standing) and increases to more than 3° · sec^{-1} when the head is shaken from side to side in a normal manner (Steinman & Collewijn, 1980). Given the short- and medium-term modifiability of the gain of the vestibulo-ocular reflex by an effort of visual imagination (e.g., Barr, Schultheis, & Robinson, 1976) or by adaptation to magnifying or reversing spectacles (Gauthier & Robinson, 1975; Gonshor & Melvill Jones, 1976b), it seems plausible that the gains of the ocular stabilizing reflexes are modified to preserve optimal vision: by allowing some retinal motion and preventing visual fading when the head is relatively still, or by reducing retinal slip when visual acuity is impaired by the larger and more rapid head motions.

When the head is locked to a bite board, the residual eye movements of fixation are too slight to preserve peripheral vision for more than a few seconds. Fading is particularly fast if the peripheral stimulus is dim or of low contrast (e.g., Clarke & Belcher, 1962). Central vision is lost in addition when the retinal image is artificially stabilized against both head and eye movements. Optimal visual acuity or contrast sensitivity requires an imposed smooth image motion which is rather faster than the natural drifting movements of the eyes alone, as one might expect if head movement normally contributes to preserving vision. It is especially easy to restore visibility for the lower spatial frequencies with imposed image motion (see references in Kowler & Steinman, 1980). On the other hand, retinal-image motion in excess of 100 min arc · sec^{-1} leads to a deterioration of visual acuity, particularly for the higher spatial frequencies (Murphy, 1978; Westheimer & McKee, 1975); that is, there is reduced perceptual performance at velocities that remove the image from the central fovea after roughly one reaction time (about 0.2 sec).

3.1.1.2. Monocular Fixation. Because of technical difficulties, the residual eye movements of fixation are usually studied with the head stabilized by having the subject bite into a deep dental impression. The residual movements of fixation are extremely small. During 400 msec of viewing the retinal image may show a standard deviation as small as 0.25 min arc; that is, the displacement for 65% of the time may be less than a foveal cone's width (Barlow, 1952). The actual distribution of retinal-image positions on the retina is roughly elliptical, often with the vertical extent greater than the horizontal, and with a slight tilt (e.g., Bennet-Clark, 1964; Boyce, 1967b; Nachmias, 1959, 1960; St. Cyr & Fender, 1969a), but for most purposes it suffices to discuss only the horizontal component of motion (Fig. 10.36). Three types of residual movement are usually recognized: microtremor, drift, and microsaccades (Fig. 10.37).

(a) MICROTREMOR. This is generally discounted as being of any visual relevance, because of its high frequency (30–100 Hz) relative to the usual visual integration times, and small amplitude (18 sec arc or less than 1 min arc) relative to the dimensions of photoreceptors (Ditchburn & Foley-Fisher, 1967; Ditchburn & Ginsberg, 1953; Findlay, 1971; Ratliff & Riggs, 1950). The origins of microtremor are unknown. There is a resonant peak at 37 Hz in the ocular response to imposed sinusoidal forces which could represent some extremely weak mechanical tuning (Thomas, 1969). A very weak peak at 50–100 Hz conceivably reflects the clock-like firing patterns of the innervating motoneurons (Bengi & Thomas, 1968). If so, this tremor frequency should be modified by fixation away from the straight-ahead direction. Torsional tremor is about 45 sec arc and 35 Hz (Fender, 1955).

(b) MICROSACCADES. Microsaccadic movements abruptly displace the visual axis by about 5 (2–28) min arc and occur at a very variable rate, such as one or two per second. Most, but not all, normal subjects are easily instructed to fixate with high accuracy by means of drift movements alone (e.g., Murphy, Kowler, & Steinman, 1975). Microsaccades do not improve visibility, because of visual masking effects (Beeler, 1967), although image-stabilization experiments allow that microsaccades may help maintain retinal stimulation in the unlikely event that head and eye drift are too small (Ditchburn & Drysdale, 1977; King-Smith & Riggs, 1978). Microsaccades are reduced in frequency in a vernier acuity task (Rattle & Foley-Fisher, 1968), in a perceptual task akin to judging whether a needle will be threaded (Bridgeman & Palca, 1980), or when the subject actively threads a needle (Winterson & Collewijn, 1976). Microsaccades are of no value in counting points in a small field, unless the field is appropriately large and the points perceptually clustered (Kowler & Steinman, 1979c). The possibility that microsaccades are essential for certain tasks, such as preserving the border between two different hues of equal luminance (Ditchburn, 1980), has not been adequately tested. But neither is the currently accepted notion that microsaccades represent "busywork" or unnecessary fussing (Steinman et al., 1973) yet supported by studies of the subjects' motivations. Could microsaccades be the attenuated remnants of the large visual search saccades that occur normally in the absence of the instruction to fixate?

(c) SQUARE-WAVE JERKS (SWJ). These are horizontal conjugate saccades of about 1° (0.5–3.0) in extent, which take the eye away from the fixation point and are corrected by a foveating saccade about 200 msec later. This phenomenon has escaped the attention of contact lens workers, and it has been suggested that SWJ are normal only when present under closed lids (e.g., Dell'Osso, Abel, & Daroff, 1977; Feldon & Laneston, 1977). However, relatively insensitive recording methods show SWJ to be present in a substantial proportion of normal subjects (24%) and to increase with age (Herishanu & Sharpe, 1981); see Figure 10.38. One recommendation is that a frequency of more than nine per minute should be taken as the upper limit for normality.

(d) VISUALLY CONTROLLED DRIFT. The most important movement of fixation seems to be visually controlled drift, called "slow control" by some authors. Attention to eye-velocity signals could also play an important synergistic role, though this is not certain (Sections 2.1.11 and 3.2.1). Intersaccadic drifts are usually about 2.5 min, with a speed of about 4 min arc · sec^{-1} (Ditchburn & Foley-Fisher, 1967). When microsaccades are suppressed by instruction, or are naturally scarce, the accuracy of fixation is usually as good as, if not better than, fixation with frequent microsaccades, such as a horizontal or vertical standard deviation of 2–3 versus 4–6 min arc (Steinman et al., 1973). However, a few apparently normal subjects lack effective slow control and drift in one direction at 2–11 min arc · sec^{-1}, because a small fixation point does not provide adequate visual feedback (Murphy et al., 1975); see Figure 10.39(a) on page 10-38. Saccades are presumably useful for very accurate fixation in these subjects. Other subjects attract the interest of clinicians because their ocular instability and its repetitive correction give rise to regular oscillations called nystagmus.

(e) CONGENITAL NYSTAGMUS. Congenital nystagmus persists through life (Daroff, Troost, & Dell'Osso, 1978; Dell'Osso, Gau-

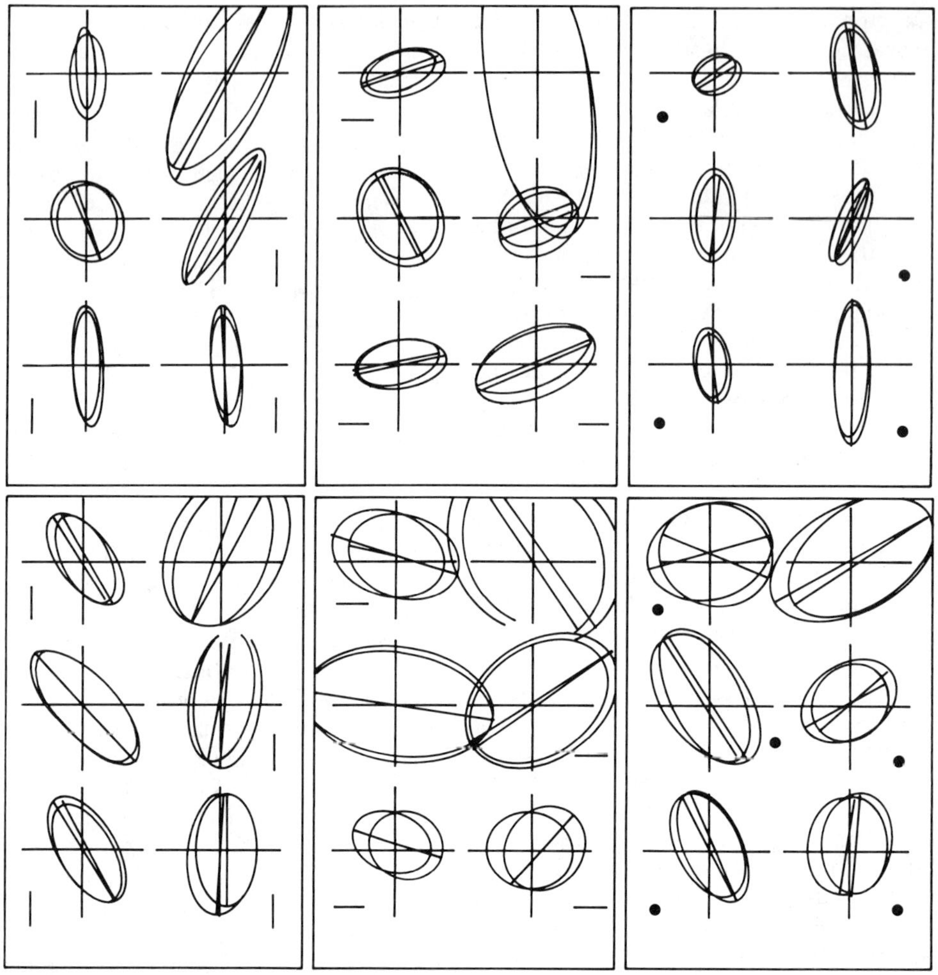

Figure 10.36. Spatial distribution of fixation positions for fixed head. The equiprobability ellipses contain 75% of eye positions before and after microsaccades. Horizontal axes represent 22.5 min arc. The left and right columns within each panel correspond to the left and right eyes. The stimulus is present in the left eye only, or the right eye only, or in both, in the different rows of each panel. Shape of fixation stimulus (bar or dot) is shown, but not to scale, near each pair of left and right eye records. Left, middle, and right pairs of panels correspond to different-shaped targets. Upper and lower sets of panels correspond to two separate subjects. Contact lens data. Fixation is generally better for binocular stimulation and may be sensitive to target shape. Fixation is extremely stable within fixation trials, but it has not been established if the same small retinal area is used after the eye has settled after large saccades. (From G. J. St. Cyr & D. H. Fender, The interplay of drifts and flicks in binocular fixation, *Vision Research*, 9. Copyright 1969 by Pergamon Press, Ltd. Reprinted with permission.)

thier, Liberman, & Stark, 1972). It can be regarded as a high-gain instability of the slow eye-movement system, which drives the eyes conjugately and equally at *increasing* velocity away from the intended object of fixation, until restored by an opposite slow movement or a saccade or both. The variety of resulting nystagmoid wave forms is considerable, but all can be regarded as developmental attempts to preserve an adequate period of stable foveation, and thus clear acute vision (e.g., Fig. 10.40, page 10-39). It is intriguing that the head also oscillates in these subjects, apparently to counter the eye motion and thus preserve gaze stability in space; this is particularly marked when the nystagmus is increased by an effort of fixation. Such compensatory head movements require that the gain of the vestibulo-ocular reflex be 0; otherwise the eyes would make additional movements that would counteract the compensatory head movement. If the vestibulo-ocular reflex is modified, one would expect the associated supporting optokinetic reflexes to be modified also, and in fact their gain is reduced or even reversed. The head may also be carried at a particular angle to exploit an eye position in the orbit for which nystagmus is least. The persistent nystagmus in one direction (e.g., horizontal) may lead to permanently reduced vision for appropriately oriented targets (e.g., vertical), even when these are presented as brief flashes; that is, there may be orientational amblyopia (Abadi & King-Smith, 1979).

(f) Latent Nystagmus. This nystagmus is also congenital, and is intriguing because it is associated with the intention of fixating with one eye (van Vliet, 1973). In these subjects the shift to monocular viewing is evidently associated with a step change in the steady discharge to the ocular muscles, because the eyes drift conjugately to their new position with *decreasing* velocity, in contrast to the increasing velocity of congenital nystagmus. One possibility is that monocular viewing in these subjects shifts the apparent spatial position of the target, driving the

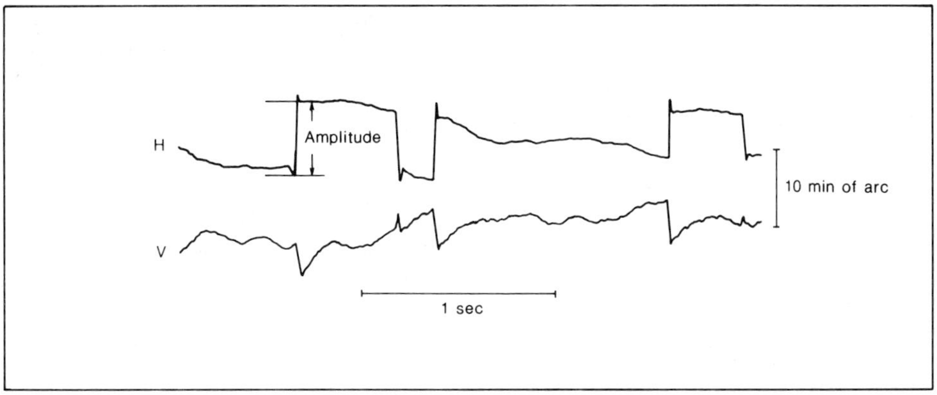

Figure 10.37. Residual eye movements of fixation. Horizontal (*H*) and vertical (*V*) components of micro-tremor, drift, and micro-saccades. Note how horizontal amplitude is measured. Contact lens record. Residual movements are very small. (From K. Gaarder, Mechanisms in fixation saccadic eye movements, *British Journal of Physiological Optics*, 1967, *24*. Reprinted with permission.)

eye at decreasing velocity away from the fixation point until retinal error feedback restores fixation. The condition is also present in some patients with amblyopia or strabismus and alternating fixation.

(g) Fixation when Movement Is Expected. An additional source of instability during fixation is the expectation that the visible fixation point will move (Kowler & Steinman, 1979a, 1979b, 1981). Contact lens experiments and data averaging techniques show that these drifts (or smooth movements) of 2–30 min arc $\cdot$ sec^{-1} are very variable, but are faster than the drift seen in the experiments reviewed in paragraph (d) above, where the subject knows that the fixation point will always be stationary. If there are several unpredictable possibilities for the direction of the anticipated stimulus movement, speeds are more modest. Speeds increase and the directions become highly appropriate when the subject is able to deduce the future stimulus direction, or is told. Velocities also increase as the anticipated stimulus motion becomes imminent. The anticipatory smooth eye movement is replaced by the subject's usual pattern of drift in darkness if the stimulus is blanked prior to its anticipated movement. Anticipatory smooth movements are not seen prior to expected commands (auditory tones) to shift fixation along a line of visible points; that is, the anticipatory smooth movements are not related to the expectation of making a saccade. The movements are reduced slightly by a textured background.

The significance or importance of anticipatory smooth movements is not yet clear. Most of the data are for the two authors themselves, although some of the effects have been replicated on naive subjects. All the target motions were temporally fixed and thus potentially predictable. In the case of a low-velocity target, anticipation may improve the promptness of pursuit and reduce tracking error (Fig. 10.41, page 10-40), but in general the amplitude of anticipatory motion during an ordinary reaction time is extremely small. It is uncertain if

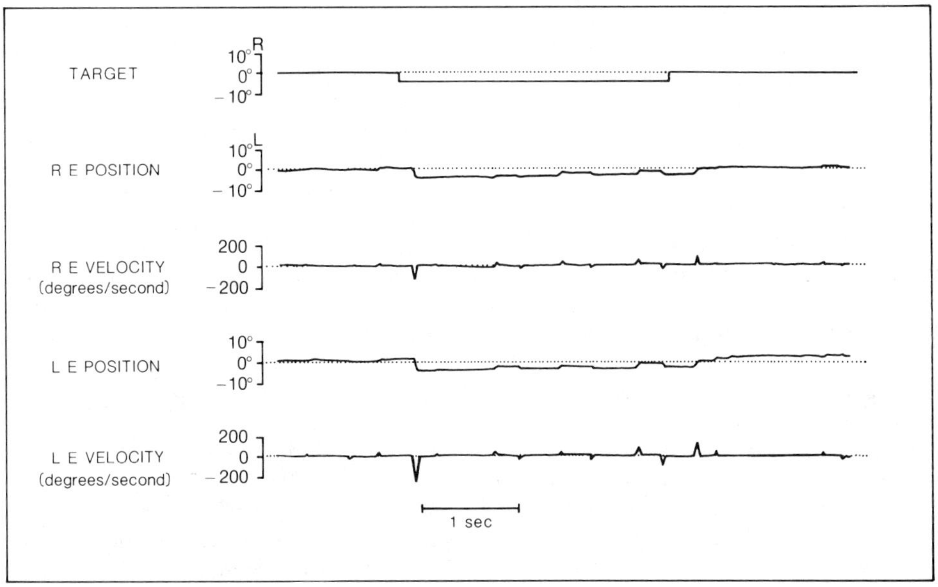

Figure 10.38. Square-wave jerks. Eye position and velocity recordings of unusually frequent square-wave jerks, during fixation of a target at midposition and at 5° left, in a normal subject. These movements are said to be reasonably common in normal subjects, but should not occur at a frequency of more than nine per minute. Limbus monitor. (From Y. O. Herishanu & J. A. Sharpe, Normal square wave jerks, *Investigative Ophthalmology and Visual Science*, 1981, *20*. Reprinted with permission.)

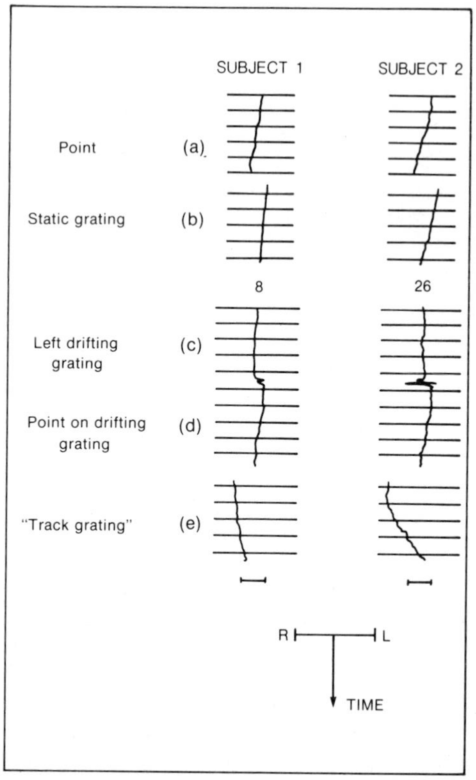

Figure 10.39. Slow control of eye position and selective attention. Representative records of horizontal eye movements in different situations, for two subjects who are unusual in persistently drifting (to the right) if they attempt to fixate without using microsaccades. Horizontal lines are 1-sec time marks and bottom calibration is 1°. Contact lens record. (a) Attempted fixation of a point on a stationary 4° field of black and white bars (1.25 cycles per degree). (b) Same, but point removed and grating stationary. (c) Point removed and grating drifting left at 8 min arc·sec^{-1} for GH and 26 min arc·sec^{-1} for PM. This counters subjects' natural drifts to right. (d) Point visible, grating moving—record now shows drift to right, similar to (a) or (b). (e) Response to instruction to track grating. Thus subjects can easily switch attention from fixation to tracking, and when fixating they show their characteristic residual eye movement patterns, whether the background is moving or not. (From B. J. Murphy, E. Kowler, & R. M. Steinman, Slow oculomotor control in the presence of moving backgrounds, *Vision Research, 15*. Copyright 1975 by Pergamon Press, Ltd. Reprinted with permission.)

there is a relation to mental guessing, as anticipatory movements persist during distracting mental arithmetic.

(h) Fixation During Real or Illusory Movement. Perceptual analysis of scenes is made possible by the ability of subjects to selectively fixate one part of the scene, and ignore other parts that are moving. Two experienced subjects, who could fixate without saccades, were able to fixate a small point in a 4° field that contained a well-lit grating moving at various speeds (1.25 cycles per degree high-contrast square wave at 5, 48, or 480 min arc · sec^{-1}). The moving background increased the probability of the eye drifting in the direction of the grating, but the highest velocity in the direction of the grating was only 3 min arc · sec^{-1} (Murphy et al., 1975). This small effect could be largely eliminated by using a 26-min arc circle as a fixation mark. Two other subjects who drifted at a fairly fast rate (less than 12 min arc · sec^{-1}) when attempting to fixate without saccades were otherwise similar to the experienced subjects in being able to select the fixation point and ignore the moving grating (Fig. 10.39).

Such selective attention does not eliminate simultaneous attention elsewhere; for example, peripheral perceptual thresholds are very low in terms of numbers of quanta, despite the presence of the fixation point (Hallett, 1969; Hecht, Shlaer, & Pirenne, 1941). Similarly, a subject can fixate a steady point and then saccade to a nearby oscillating target (±3° amplitude of motion in various directions), which is at a mean distance of 4° from the steady fixation point. If the target is now stabilized electronically on the fovea during the saccade, smooth tracking continues along the original physical path of the target, as if the brain has acquired an internal model of the target's motion during the earlier fixation phase (Holtzman et al., 1978). See also Section 3.3.5.

Illusory motion does not disturb fixation on a landmark. A troublesome illusion, particularly in laboratory experiments, is that a visible fixation point in darkness may appear to drift, and in some cases there is associated vertigo; however, the small residual eye movements of fixation are not obviously changed during this autokinetic illusion (Barlow, 1952; Crone & Verduyn Lunel, 1969; Matin & MacKinnon, 1964; Winterson & Steinman, 1979). Nor does the eye drift appreciably when the fixation point appears to move because of a slow shift of its physical frame of reference at 2–30 min arc · sec^{-1} (Mack et al., 1979; Mack et al., 1982). Another illusion, which can be disturbing when wading in fast-flowing rivers, is the motion aftereffect: stationary objects appear to "flow" (i.e., to have velocity) without undergoing any actual positional displacement. However, the motion aftereffect due to staring for 1 min at a moving grating has no effect on subsequent fixation of the stationary grating (0.7 cycles per degree high-contrast squarewave grating, moving to the left or right at about 3° · sec^{-1}; Mack et al., 1982).

(i) Fixation on an Afterimage. The fixation point can be stabilized on the retina in the form of its afterimage. If there are no visual landmarks, there is no negative feedback via retinal-image slip to stabilize the gaze, and extremely variable movements result. The nature of the movements depends on several factors, for example, aspects of the image, the subject, instructions, and so forth.

If the afterimage is centered on the fovea, microsaccades are inhibited, and the subject may produce small amplitude (1°) oscillations at roughly 0.5–1 Hz (e.g., ten Doesschate, 1954; Steinbach & Pearce, 1972). Although there are several possibilities, I wonder if the instability may arise from the subject selectively attending to eye position in order to stay within instrumental limitations, and having a dead-time of 0.5–1 sec. If the subject is not under special constraints, or is instructed to follow the afterimage if it moves, the oscillations may be slower, with a suggestion of a dominant direction of drift that is counteracted by saccades (Heywood & Churcher, 1971). When the eccentricity of the 1° afterimage is up to 2–3° from the fovea, there is apparent "pursuit" in the direction of the afterimage, which perceptually swings away from the subject (e.g., Heywood & Churcher, 1972; Steinbach & Pearce, 1972). See Figure 10.42 (page 10-41). The instruction to follow does not alter the "smooth pursuit" very much, and the variability of "pursuit" is presumably related to the rather variable salience of the afterimage. The instruction does, however, change the pattern of saccades toward fewer saccades in the direction of movement of the afterimage. "Pursuit" is less marked for an afterimage at a larger (15°) eccentricity. At low eccentricities "pursuit" may begin with a fairly sudden but smooth acceleration of drift about 150 msec after the offset of the fixation point (Fig. 10.42); it is not initiated by a microsaccade and is probably not an artifact of

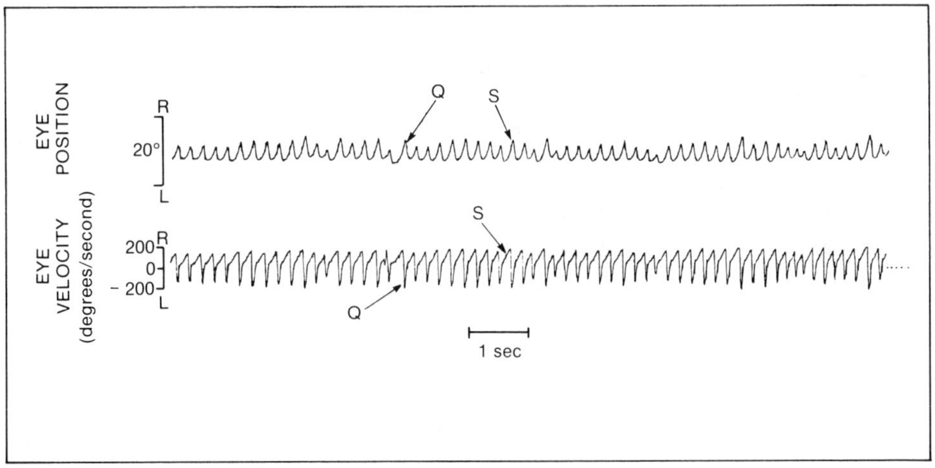

Figure 10.40. Congenital jerk nystagmus beating left, with increasing velocity slow phase to right. Q = quick or fast phase, S = slow phase. There are many types of nystagmus, some quasi-normal, others ominous. Visibility may be reduced, there may be compensatory head movements, and the vestibulo-ocular reflex may be modified. (Unpublished record by J. A. Sharpe, 1982.)

vergence (Steinbach & Pearce, 1972). Although the "pursuit" is determined by the direction of the afterimage from the fovea, it is more prominent for some directions than for others, which may reflect natural directions for drift in that subject. The effect of afterimage size has not been much investigated.

The above data raise the possibility that selective attention is an uncontrolled variable; indeed it has been asserted that a 5° circular afterimage centered on the fovea may be pursued left or right by paying attention to left or right edges (Robinson, 1976, citing Kommerell & Klein, 1971). The suggestion is tentative, however, and the role of attention has yet to be clearly demonstrated. It is also possible that the so-called "pursuit" is simply instability due to the direct effect of disturbed optical feedback on a low-level oculomotor system, any correlation with attention being weak (ten Doesschate, 1954; Hedlun & White, 1959).

(j) Fixation When the Otherwise Static Fixation Point Is Driven by Eye Movements. The fixation point can be very accurately stabilized on the retina by driving it via purely optical contact lens techniques. The contact lens is not likely to slip between blinks if suction is applied (Ditchburn, 1973). Equipment that uses electrical or mechanical signal processing introduces extra noise into the image motion, and may be less satisfactory in some cases.

In some studies the fixation target is a test pattern for purely perceptual measurements. Artificial stimulus motion can be introduced to evaluate the contribution of different residual eye movements to perception, or directly to study perception with retinal motions that are not modified by residual eye movements (King-Smith & Riggs, 1978; Tulunay-Keesey, 1976; Tulunay-Keesey & Riggs, 1962).

If a 1.5° diameter target is approximately stabilized on the fovea, and a surrounding nonstabilized 27 × 22° frame is oscillated to and fro by 5–60° at 0.5 Hz, there is highly variable small amplitude (±1°) oscillatory pursuit at 2–8° · sec^{-1} which is opposite to the frame motion, and therefore possibly related to perceptually induced motion of the small target (Pola & Wyatt, 1980). No effect, however, was observed for technically better stabilization conditions, when a smaller 3 × 0.5° frame was moved at 0.5° · sec^{-1} relative to the retinally stabilized fixation point (Mack et al., 1982). See also Section 3.3.1.4.

If the movements of the eye are processed electrically, it is easy to amplify, invert, and use the eye-movement signal to destabilize the otherwise stationary fixation point. When the external gain is +1, the retinal image is stabilized against eye movement, as in the cases just discussed. At external gains more negative than −1, any substantial amplitude of residual drift, or a microsaccade, causes a large opposite movement of the fixation point which provokes a return movement of the eye, and so on, so that saccadic oscillations develop (Robinson, 1965; Young & Stark, 1963). For example, at external gains of −4 growing saccadic oscillations at 2–2.5 Hz soon place the fixation point beyond the apparatus limits before the subject can gain control (Robinson, 1965). Less negative gains, however, are rapidly adapted to, the intelligent subject reducing the amplitude of any inevitable saccade toward the stimulus (Fleming, Vossius, Bowman, & Johnson, 1969; Vossius, 1972; author's observations).

It is curious that these responses are almost entirely saccadic, because a common rhetoric is that the residual drifting eye movements of fixation are "smooth pursuit of a stationary stimulus," and so one might expect to see large smooth movements owing to feedback of smooth drift. To examine this point, the external eye-movement feedback loop can be altered so that amplification and sign change are followed by filtering out of any saccades. This procedure should selectively destabilize the smooth eye-movement system by feeding back only smooth movements, but in fact it strikingly fails to do so, even at an external gain as negative as −7 (Robinson, 1965). I wonder if the maneuver fails because the subject is not fully trying to pursue a stationary stimulus during fixation, but is also attempting to hold internal eye-velocity signals near zero. If the electrical feedback to the fixation point is now supplemented by an independent external signal, the subject has no choice but to abandon attention to eye position or velocity and pursue. As expected, this pursuit is now oscillatory as soon as the external gain is more negative than −1 (Robinson, 1965).

(k) Nature of the Fixation Point. The physical parameters of clearly visible fixation points generally affect very slightly the accuracy of fixation. Some statistically significant effects can be detected by high-resolution contact lens techniques, but the magnitudes are so small or inconsistent that they can be ignored in most applications. Steinman (1965) examined fixation point

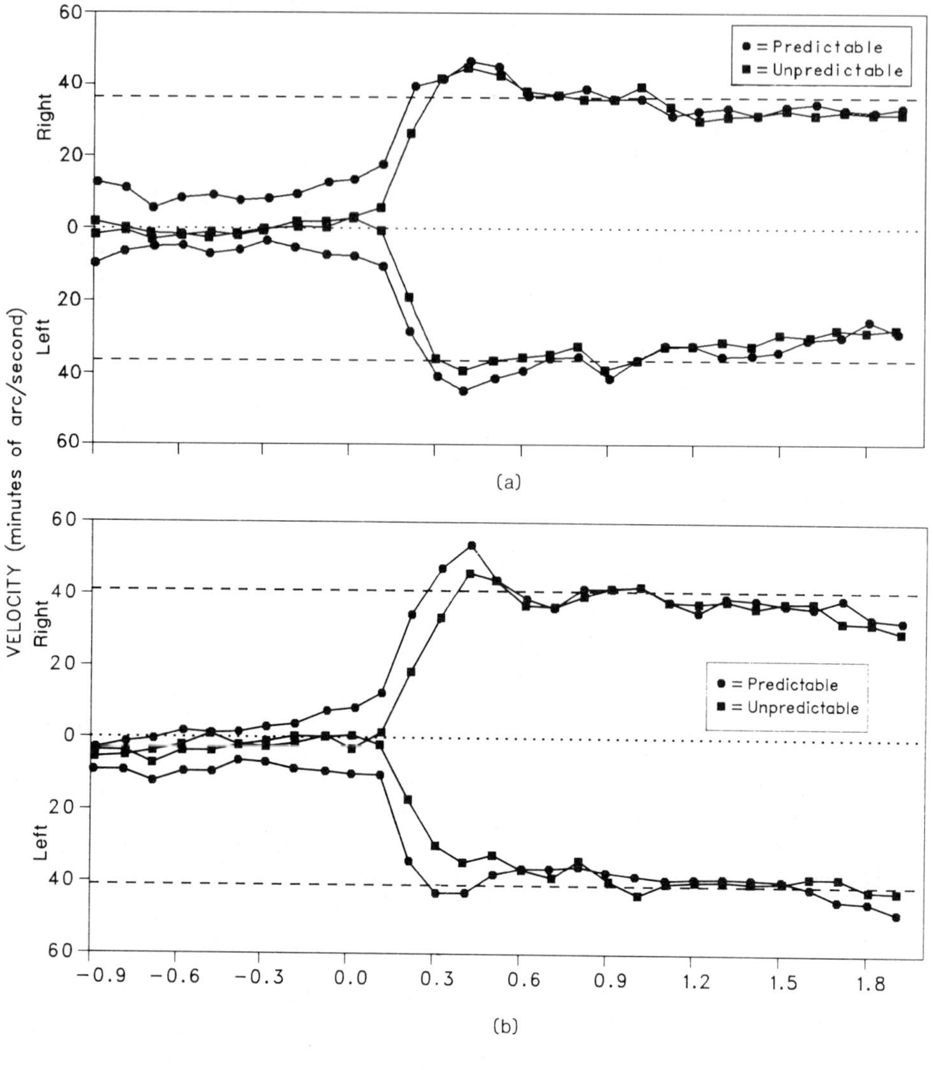

Figure 10.41. Anticipatory smooth eye movement. The ordinate shows velocity (min arc·sec^{-1}) as a function of time relative to the onset of the 41 min arc · sec^{-1} ramp motion at time 0 on the abscissa. The eye drifts slowly before the ramp onset, but more quickly when the direction of the ramp is predictable. Predictability generally improves the tracking of the ramp. Data are shown for two similar subjects. Each point is the mean of about 70 100-msec samples; contact lens data. Anticipation improves tracking. (From E. Kowler & R. M. Steinman, The effect of expectations on slow oculomotor control—II. Single target displacements, *Vision Research, 19*. Copyright 1979 by Pergamon Press, Ltd. Reprinted with permission.)

size, color, and luminance (9–68 cd · m^{-2}), and Boyce (1967a) examined color and luminance (27–2744 cd · m^{-2}), but mean fixation position, intersaccadic interval, and magnitudes of drift scarcely changed in these situations. Probably the ideal fixation mark is a clearly visible small shape, such as a 25-min diameter ring, particularly if a potential disturbance such as moving background is present (Murphy et al., 1975).

If the fixation point is not clearly visible, effects on fixation are to be expected. The influence of contrast has not been examined. If fixation can be regarded as pursuit of a stationary target, one may infer from the lack of effect of contrast on smooth pursuit of predictable targets that fixation statistics should be stable if the fixation mark is above its contrast threshold (Haegerstrom-Portnoy & Brown, 1979).

A peculiar pattern of cyclic fixation behavior can arise for dim white and red stimuli (Steinman & Cunitz, 1968). Visual thresholds were not measured, but it is likely that the white stimuli of 0.06–0.3 cd · m^{-2} were just below the subjects' foveal thresholds. These stimuli were fixated about 20–80 min arc eccentric to the mean fixation position for bright targets, which is not unexpected, given the relative insensitivity of the dark-adapted fovea. But what is surprising was the strong maladaptive tendency for the eye to drift and shift the retinal image into the night-blind fovea. Visibility was restored by means of a peripheralizing saccade, and then the cycle was repeated; see Figure 10.43. Drift cycles were idiosyncratic and apparently not modifiable. Thus, if the drift cycle was diagonally up and right, asking the subject to restore visibility by making a saccade down or left, and so on, created a new type of cycle that was primarily saccadic, the stimulus being returned now to the night-blind region by saccades rather than by drift. Similar patterns were *not* observed for equivalently visible red targets; these disappeared at positions quite widely scattered about the fixation point for a bright target. This is perhaps related to the

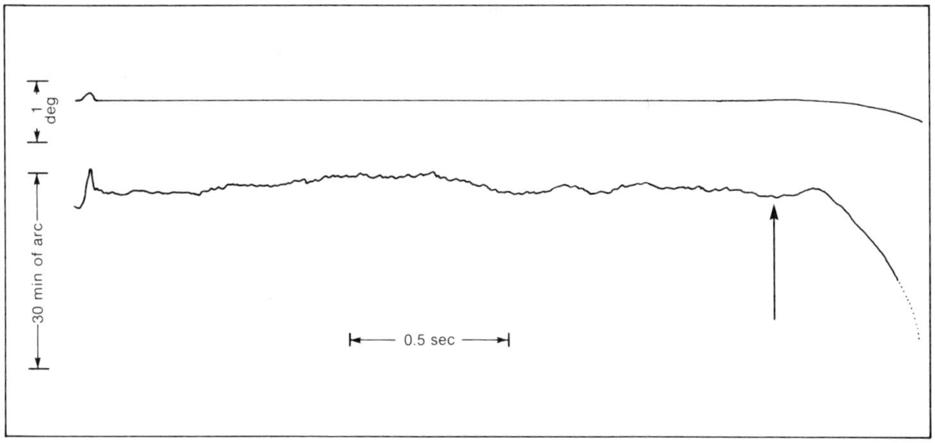

Figure 10.42. Smooth pursuit of afterimages. 1° circular afterimage with left edge at point of fixation. Left part of record shows no pursuit of afterimage in presence of fixation point. Note absence of microsaccades except at extreme left, 2 sec before offset of fixation point at arrow. On some trials, the afterimage was sustained by stroboscopically flashing the background at 10 Hz. Upper record is at lower gain. Contact lens record. Whether tracking is smooth or saccadic depends on retinal position of the afterimage and, perhaps, on the instructions. (From M. J. Steinbach & D. G. Pearce, Release of pursuit eye movements using after images, *Vision Research, 12*. Copyright 1972 by Pergamon Press, Ltd. Reprinted with permission.)

threshold for red light being comparatively uniform over wide retinal regions (Kishto & Saunders, 1970), disappearance being due to the Troxler fading effect (Clarke & Belcher, 1962; Pirenne, 1967). The peculiar behavior of white targets may be related to the very small eccentricity of fixation at the chosen intensities in these experiments. Given the ability of subjects to pursue smoothly a stimulus at the scotopic threshold whenever it is visible (Winterson & Steinman, 1978), one may weakly infer that dimmer white targets than those of Steinman and Cunitz (1968) may be fairly well fixated at large eccentricities, if visible.

3.1.1.3. Binocular Fixation

(a) NORMAL SUBJECTS, HEAD MOVEMENTS. The residual eye movements of binocular fixation are not completely conjugate, and appreciable differences can occur in the sizes of the saccades in the two eyes; that is, there is a partial failure of Hering's hypothesis that version movements are of equal amplitude (Krauskopf, Cornsweet, & Riggs, 1960). The situation is worse when the head is free or is shaken in a fairly ordinary manner [Fig. 10.44(a)]. Imperfection in the vestibulo-ocular and visual-holding responses is shown by vergence velocities in the range of 0–5° · sec^{-1}, or even larger in some subjects [Fig. 10.44(b)]. In addition, saccades are often unequal (Collewijn, Martins, & Steinman, 1981; Steinman & Collewijn, 1980). Subjectively, vision is said to be clear, so subjects are either quite mistaken about this or are basing their perceptions on the coarser spatial frequencies; or internal visual processing monitors self-generated motion so as to stabilize perception. Duwaer (1982) measured eye movements with an afterimage technique and claims lesser effects of head movement on retinal image stability.

(b) STRABISMUS, VOLUNTARY NYSTAGMUS. Strabismus, commonly referred to as squint, is a binocular disorder of fixation in which the seeing eye foveates while the weaker eye deviates, so that the image of the fixation point is displaced from the fovea in that eye. In esotropia the weak eye deviates nasally and foveal vision is frequently impaired (amblyopia). In exotropia the eye deviates laterally and foveal vision is suppressed; in many exotropic patients the eyes alternate and take turns at fixation, suppression switching from one eye to the other at the onset of the conjugate saccadic movement that drives the currently deviating eye toward the fixation point and the currently fixating eye away (Steinbach, 1981). Vertical and torsional (cyclic) disorders also occur, as in Burian and von Noorden (1974). It is interesting that small deviations of a few degrees can be as troublesome in their reduction of perception as larger ones.

In about 5% of the population, convergence on a near target evokes bursts of high-frequency (20-Hz) conjugate oscillations, called voluntary nystagmus (Sharpe, Hoyt, & Rosenberg, 1975). These smooth movements are really superimposed saccades (Shults, Stark, Hoyt, & Ochs, 1977), and are accompanied by apparent quivering of the visual scene, called oscillopsia (e.g., Nagle, Bridgeman, & Stark, 1980). See also Section 3.7.1.3.

3.1.2. Instruction: Fixate Part of an Object.

Fixation stability is largely independent of the nature of the target (e.g., Steinman, 1976). For instance, the standard deviation of fixation is increased by a factor of less than 2, relative to fixation on a point, when the subject fixates either the empty center of a 4° circle or the midpoint between two black dots nearly 4° apart (Rattle, 1969). Peripheral perceptual acuity may not be the most relevant factor here; more relevant to eccentric fixation would be data on the ability of the retinal periphery to detect changes in eye position, via image motion, plus more information on ability to attend to eye-position signals. It has been suggested that there is a tendency to fixate near the center of gravity of simple patterns of less than 5° extent (Richards & Kaufman, 1969). Contours and corners may receive more attention if the object is larger, but even then the tendency is to fixate the brighter sides of the contour, rather than the contour itself (Kaufman & Richards, 1969). These findings may not agree with more detailed data showing that subjects can fixate on any point that they choose within simple 1° line objects, with very high constant accuracy (Murphy, Haddad, & Steinman, 1974). However, most workers would agree that shift of fixation is not necessary for viewing small objects because visual attention can be shifted by an appreciable extent without eye movements (e.g., Pritchard, 1961).

Shift of attention from one grating to another superposed crossed grating (monocular rivalry) is also said to occur without eye movements (Crassini & Broerse, 1982).

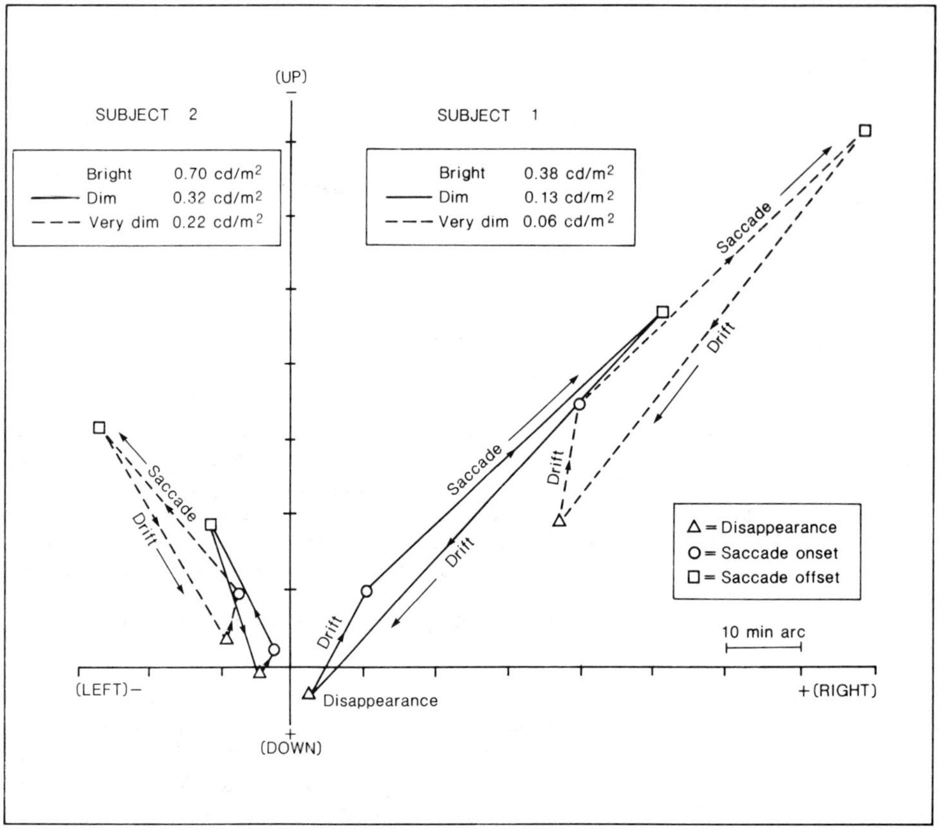

Figure 10.43. Eccentric fixation of dim targets. The plot represents the visual field and the origin is the fixation locus for a bright stimulus, that is, the foveal center. Plotted are cycles of drift toward the fovea, disappearance of the stimulus within the nocturnal scotoma, and peripheralizing saccades. Contact lens data; means for two subjects eccentrically fixating a 5 min arc, near foveal-threshold white stimulus. The dimmer cycles are more eccentric, no doubt because of the larger nocturnal scotoma. Cyclic movement of the retinal image is not necessarily maladaptive, because neural on and off responses may enhance the visibility of a stimulus moving over the retina. It is hard, however, to see the advantage of shifting the stimulus into a blind region! (From R. M. Steinman & R. J. Cunitz, Fixation of targets near the absolute foveal threshold, *Vision Research*, *8*. Copyright 1968 by Pergamon Press, Ltd. Reprinted with permission.)

3.1.3. Instruction: Look To and Fro Between Two Lit Points

3.1.3.1. Saccadic Eye Movements. Some workers would probably equate looking to and fro between two lit points with tracking a single point when it steps, but the former task may be more difficult (Festinger, 1971).

When fine eye movements were assessed by means of an afterimage technique, 7 of 27 subjects needed about 10 sec (*sic*) to shift fixation between two points 7.5 min arc apart, the other 20 subjects needing about 1.5 sec (0.5–5). Less time was needed at larger separations, but extrapolation to infinite time for two particular subjects suggested that 5–10 min arc separation was the minimum to which they could respond (Bennet-Clark, 1964). Of course, failure to shift fixation through such a small distance is not likely to compromise perceptual performance in most tasks because of the ability to shift attention. Note that the saccadic dead zone of 5–10 min arc, inferred for Bennet-Clark's two-point task, is larger than that revealed in later *single-step* experiments, where a step of 3 min arc was responded to with high probability by two subjects (Wyman & Steinman, 1973b). See also Section 3.7.1.1.

It may be hard to release fixation of a current stimulus to fixate elsewhere. In Saslow's "overlap" task, latency of saccades to a 4 or 8° laterally displaced target was greater when the initial fixation point remained lit, and two stimuli were seen, than when the initial point was extinguished and relit elsewhere, as if a single point were stepping laterally (Saslow, 1967a). Perhaps the overlap task involves two central decision delays, one decision to "let go" and one to "choose a new goal" (Hallett & Adams, 1980).

Henson (1978) has commented on the higher frequency of overshooting saccadic errors in the two-point experiments of Weber and Daroff (1971), relative to his own single-step study where undershoots were common. This difference was confirmed by a control experiment, in which the subject fixated on one of two points for 0.7 sec until the fixation point was extinguished; overshoots to the second point (10° horizontally from the first) were increased relative to the single-step situation. Both the single-step and the control experiments were tolerably consistent with the view that subjects were maintaining overshoots at a constant low frequency, with the intention of keeping the stimulus within the same hemifield of vision.

When a subject wore a contact lens of high positive power and viewed two stimulus spots separated by 20–30° through a negative spectacle lens, visual feedback was changed so that the normal 2–3° undershoot in saccade amplitude for a 25–30° target interval was now more or less what was required for accurate foveation (Henson, 1978). Although the method of eye-movement recording was not very sensitive, the three subjects immediately responded by increasing the frequency of undershoots and reducing the frequency of accurate and overshooting secondaries. The interpretation was that the subjects were once more failing to foveate accurately the stimulus. This behavior is probably not restricted to two-point targets, and the result is an interesting one, given the suggestion that undershoots are a deliberate "self-calibration" strategy; perhaps the cerebellum checks for inappropriate gain of retinal-image motion relative to intended eye motion by assessing the magnitude of deliberate undershoots (Optican, 1982).

3.1.3.2. Smooth Eye Movements. Some subjects can make moderately rapid (3-Hz) smooth horizontal eye movements between two fixed points 30° apart (Westheimer & Conover, 1954). It is not clear that two points are essential in this task, and one wonders if these movements are slowed saccades rather than pursuit movements.

3.1.4. Instruction: Scan the Target. A common assumption in various types of perceptual experiment is that free scanning of an adapting pattern will average out retinal illumination, so that any measured effects are definitely due to adaptation of pattern-sensing neurons, and are not due to patterned luminance adaptation of the photoreceptors. There are good reasons for believing that this assumption is wrong (Arend & Skavenski, 1979). Three subjects scanned 4 × 5.3° gratings of 1, 2, or 4 cycles per degree and 0.6 contrast (14 lm/m^2) for 1–4 min. Figure 10.45 shows the results for the intermediate subject of the three: despite clear-cut instructions, fixation was not evenly distributed over the 5.3° horizontal extent of the grating, although fixation was more evenly distributed across spatial phase. Nevertheless, any small nonuniformity in spatial phase distribution will lead to some nonuniformity in the total integrated exposure, and calculation shows this to be so. The contrast of the integrated exposure pattern is, of course, considerably reduced from the original 0.6 value to 0.07 (0.02–0.15). However, this contrast is still 12–25 times the contrast threshold, and is potentially strong enough to cause afterimages, because a 0.15-contrast grating causes strong afterimages when *fixated*. Curiously, subjects do not report seeing afterimages after scanning (nor do subjects report afterimages of everyday high-contrast scenes), presumably because the saccadic eye movements of free scanning interfere with the perception of afterimages.

A related effect occurs when attempting to fixate the arrow points of the Müller-Lyer illusion (Boyce & West, 1967). Three subjects fixated the points of the figure with inward pointing heads as if it were about 9 arc min (7–10) longer than the figure

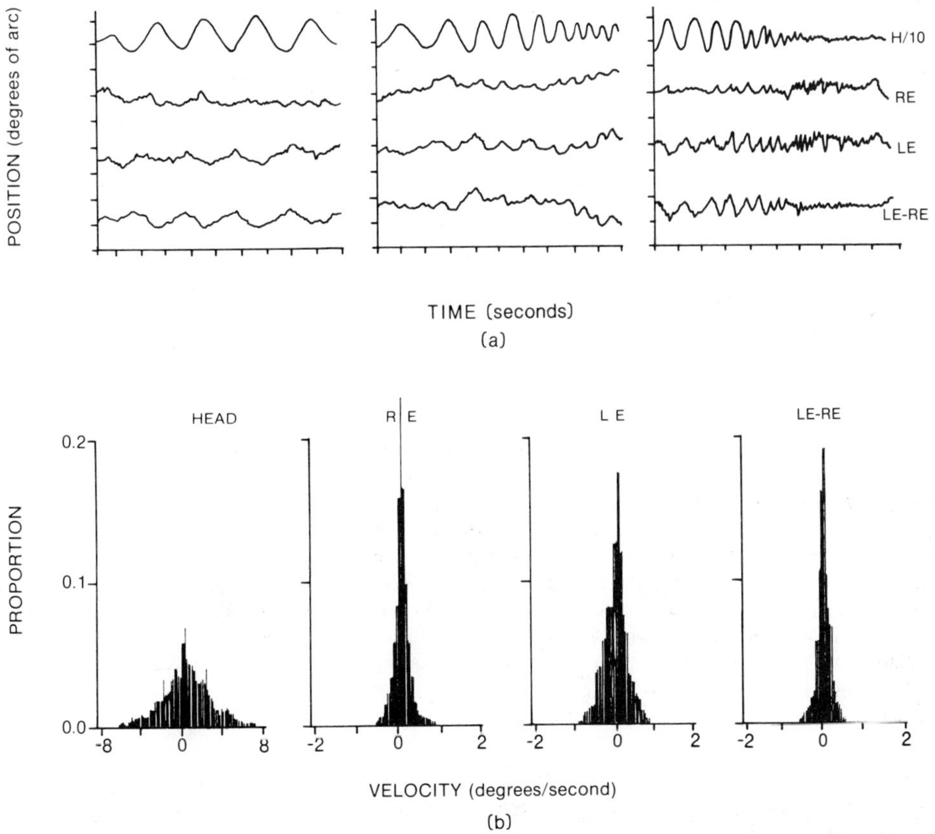

Figure 10.44. Effect of head motion on ocular stability. (a) Three representative records of binocular fixation on a distant object when the best of four subjects shakes his head from side to side at various rates. The four traces in each record are head position in space (scaled down 10 times), right and left eye position in space (right movements upward), and vergence (which is the difference between the horizontal positions of the eyes; convergence upward). Time is in seconds. (b) Frequency histograms of eye velocity over 100-msec periods, head velocity in 4°·sec^{-1} bins, right eye, left eye, and vergence velocities in 1°·sec^{-1} bins. Contact lens records. Note that eye velocity with the head stabilized on a dental impression would be less than 10 min arc·sec^{-1}, so natural head motion substantially destabilizes the retinal image. (From R. M. Steinman & H. Collewijn, Binocular image motion during active head rotation, *Vision Research*, *20*. Copyright 1980 by Pergamon Press, Ltd. Reprinted with permission.)

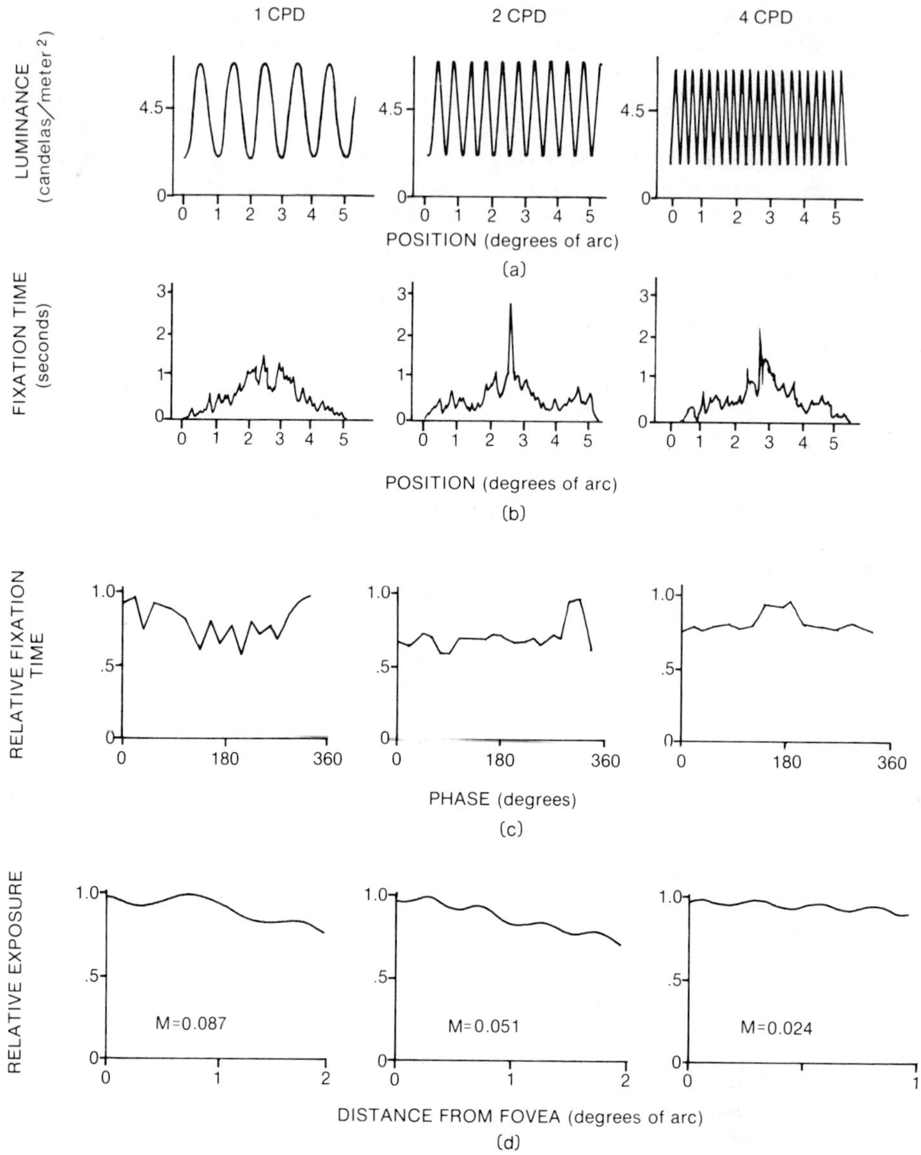

Figure 10.45. Eye movements during scanning of a luminance grating pattern. Subject KD attempts to scan evenly the 4° × 5.3° vertical sinusoidal grating for 4 min. Grating contrast is 0.6. Contact lens method. (a) Luminance distributions of 1, 2, and 4-cycles-per-degree gratings (mean luminance = 4.5 $cd \cdot m^{-2}$). (b) Fixation time in seconds as a function of horizontal position in degrees. (c) Similar, but for spatial phase. (d) Integrated exposure at different retinal eccentricities. Parameter *M* is approximate contrast. The periodicity in the data is that of the adapting grating. The gradual fall in integrated exposure with eccentricity from the fovea is due to the dark surround of the grating. Note that it may be very difficult to achieve a uniform retinal exposure. (From L. E. Arend, Jr. & A. A. Skavenski, Free scanning of gratings produces patterned retinal exposure, *Vision Research, 19*. Copyright 1979 by Pergamon Press, Ltd. Reprinted with permission.)

with outward pointing heads (horizontal Müller-Lyer figures; actual distance between heads 40 arc min in both cases; 1000 $cd \cdot m^{-2}$ background luminance).

Evidently, "even scanning" is an unreliable means of either eliminating or programming patterned photoreceptor adaptation. There may be no general solution. If one pursues a moving point across a grating at $10° \cdot sec^{-1}$, the pattern is effectively averaged by a 1.3° aperture, if peripheral integration time is as long as 0.08 sec; this may be adequate for eliminating spatial frequencies of more than 0.8 cycles per degree. Alternatively, one may fixate during counterphase 13-Hz flicker, but flickering light can cause oscillatory eye movements (Section 3.6), which might in some circumstances reinforce adaptation if eye-movement amplitude and temporal period were appropriately related to the periodicity of the counterphase grating. A mathematical treatment is given by Greenwood (1972).

When subjects view random-dot stereograms in a stereoscope, neither eye sees any meaningful pattern. Subjects can, however, make a saccade from one end to the other of the triangular target which is seen binocularly floating at a different depth to the background (Dimitrov, Yakimoff, Mateef, Mitrani, Radil-Weiss, & Bozkov, 1976). The angle of convergence affects the perceptual size of the target, but not the angular amplitude of the saccadic eye movements. The saccades are normal, as judged by the relations between saccadic amplitude, duration, and peak velocity. Also, the primary saccade undershoots in the usual manner, and is followed by the usual corrective secondary saccade.

3.1.5. Instruction: Search for the Target. This topic is difficult, because both saccadic eye movements and shifts of attention are involved. (For some references to the literature, see Boynton & Bush, 1956; Bozkov, Bohdanecky, Radil-Weiss, Mitrani, & Yakimoff, 1982; Brown & Monk, 1975; Green & Anderson, 1956; Luria & Strauss, 1973; Monk & Brown, 1975). Engel introduced the conspicuity task as a simplification of visual search (e.g., Engel, 1977; Jenkins & Cole, 1982). The conspicuity task requires that subjects fixate, and search by shifting only their attention. Interestingly, a target disk embedded among similar disks of a slightly different size on a video screen can attract the attention of the fixating eye when several degrees from the fovea. A momentary disruption of fixation (a small saccade of about 0.7° toward the target) occurs about 300 msec before the perception is registered by pushing a button (Engel, 1977); perhaps the saccade marks the shift of attention, whereas the subsequent button push marks recognition.

For references to visual search of pictures and printed words, see Kolers (1976); Levy-Schoen (1981); McConkie and Rayner (1975); O'Regan (1979); Rayner (1979); Stark and Ellis (1981); Yarbus (1967). An important issue in reading is whether the lengths of saccades and durations of pauses indicate an automatic scanning mechanism (which is slowed in more difficult passages) or movements that are controlled by either visual features or linguistic content of the text near the current point of fixation.

3.2. Eye Movements in Complete Darkness

If the head is fixed, eye movements in darkness consist mainly of conjugate drift and saccades, although disjunctive movements also occur. Rotation of the head elicits the so-called "vestibulo-ocular reflex" which is usually heavily overlaid by higher-level influences. Eye movements to afterimages are discussed in Section 3.1.1.2.

3.2.1. Instruction: Fixate Remembered or Imagined Position

3.2.1.1. Body Stationary. The eyes drift in a very irregular manner in darkness after the fixation point is extinguished, even when the head is stabilized by the subject biting a good dental impression and making an effort to hold the eye still. Spontaneous microsaccades are reduced in favor of occasional large saccades of several degrees. This is in marked contrast to what is seen in the light. When the fixation point is lit, drift or "slow control" suffices in most subjects to hold the eye with a standard deviation (SD) of 4–5 min arc in the absence of saccades. But in the dark, short-term stability is immediately and persistently reduced by a factor of about 6 (SD 25–30 min arc for a 7.6-sec sample); see Figure 10.46. In addition, the mean fixation position wanders increasingly over long periods of time, unless large saccades return the eye to within ±4° of the target (Skavenski, 1971; Skavenski & Steinman, 1970).

The suggestion that drift is the same for a visible target as in the dark (Cornsweet, 1956) is discounted by Nachmias (1961), who found that the dark drift is roughly twice that in the light. The tendency for an individual to drift in particular directions is modified when the initial fixation point is placed in different directions relative to the orbit. This may reflect instability in particular eye muscles (Nachmias, 1961), but that

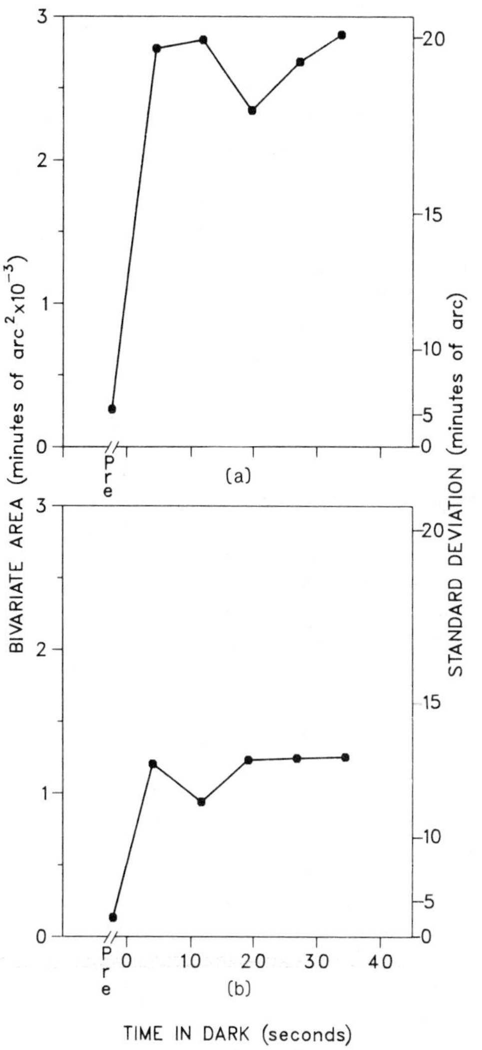

Figure 10.46. Fixation in dark. Panels (a) and (b) show contact lens data for two subjects. Other analyses showed that *mean* eye position in the dark deviated slowly from the initial fixation point; average deviations were 30–34 min arc after 38 sec in the dark. The figure shows fixation stability during consecutive 7.6-sec periods for the two subjects. "Pre" indicates a measurement made with the light on, before the light was extinguished at time 0. Left ordinate is the area (in min arc^2) that contains 68% of eye positions during a 7.6-sec period. Right ordinate is an estimate of the corresponding horizontal standard deviation about the mean eye position in a 7.6-sec period. Note that short-term fixation stability decreases immediately after the fixation light is extinguished, but is stable thereafter. Data are consistent with the loss in darkness of retinal control signals (which leads to increased variability shown here), and with progressive loss of memory for the position of the extinguished fixation light (which leads to the drift in mean eye position in the other analyses). (From A. A. Skavenski & R. M. Steinman, Control of eye position in the dark, *Vision Research, 10*. Copyright 1970 by Pergamon Press, Ltd. Reprinted with permission.)

remains to be shown. It is hard to capture so variable a phenomenon in statistics, but the various studies are in fair agreement, particularly if one allows that the statistics may be affected by the *duration* of the data record. Monocular dark drift averages about 13 min arc·sec^{-1} during several seconds in the horizontal direction (Cornsweet, 1956) or about 12 ± 5 min·sec^{-1} for many 200-msec periods, depending on the direction of drift and the subject (Nachmias, 1961). The short-term standard deviation of eye position during periods of about 0.5 sec is smaller than

20 min arc (Matin et al., 1970; Skavenski & Steinman, 1970). Mean signed horizontal eye position during a 3-sec period changes by only 0–35 min arc (i.e., 0–12 min arc·sec^{-1}), but the mean absolute change in eye position is naturally larger (30–45 min arc); the standard deviation about the mean position is 20–40 min arc (Matin et al., 1970). During a period of 21 sec in the dark, mean two-dimensional eye position changes by 1–2° and the horizontal and vertical standard deviations are 20–60 min arc, depending on the subject and experience (Hansen & Skavenski, 1977). After 7.5 min in the dark, mean errors are about 4°, which is probably a limiting value for highly motivated subjects (Skavenski, 1971).

Subjects could maintain eye position in the dark to within about 2° against 10–14-g loads applied to the contact lens, whichis only possible if proprioceptive feedback exists and is used (Skavenski, 1972). The source of the proprioception was not conjunctivas or lids because these were anesthetized.

After making a vriety of large saccades after the fixation light was extinguished, the subject was still able to return the eye to within about 1–2° of the unlit fixation point (Skavenski & Steinman, 1970). The eyes can similarly be returned to the original orbital position after being displaced 15–35° by rotating the head and body in the dark (Hansen & Skavenski, 1977). Error in fixating in a remembered direction is within 4°, even if the subject leaves the darkroom for 15 min of more normal visual experience (Skavenski, 1971). Poorer performance inreturning to a previously lit target in the primary position (3.3–5.3°) was found for naive subjects with the EOG technique (Heywood, 1973a). Errors were larger still for returning to a previously lit target 15° left or right of the primary position (4.5–9.5°). The pattern of the data suggested that right-handers return best from the right and left-handers from the left. Although this fits the classical neurological concept that the left hemisphere specifies eye movements to the right in right-handed subjects, the neurophysiological basis of eye control involves at least a partial bilateral representation. The issue may be worth pursuing in subjects with agenesis of the corpus callosum.

Clearly, visual feedback is important for eye control under normal circumstances. Equally clearly human performance is not so poor as in the "uninstructed" rabbit, where dark drift is more substantial (1°·sec^{-1}) and amplitudes are larger (20°), as is appropriate for noise in a retinal-image velocity-servo that normally assists the vestibulo-ocular reflex to stabilize the gaze (Collewijn & van der Mark, 1972). The alert cooperative human subject may be attending to additional control loops in the dark. Unfortunately, the nature of these loops is not known. One may speculate that the short-term positional instability of 25–30 min arc (SD) is the remnant of some visual-vestibular disturbance minimized by a high-gain, nonvisual, negative feedback loop that keeps the eye *velocity* near 0, whereas the saccadic returns to within ±4° (or better) of the target may represent intermittent nonvisual correction of *position* error, a correction that will obviously be limited by eroding memory for the target position. Finally, the simple scheme in Figure 10.28 makes the point that, if an injected disturbance is controlled by two additive feedback loops, the effects of the disturbance are reduced by the sum of the gains. If gain reflects the usefulness of the control loop, the simple conclusion is that any nonvisual eye-velocity control loop is roughly 20% as useful as visual control, relatively speaking.

3.2.1.2. Limbs Moved Passively. If the arm or leg is passively rotated in the dark, while the seated subject looks ahead, a perception of whole body rotation (circular vection) develops, together with "arthrokinetic" nystagmus. When the stimulation is eventually stopped there may be a prolonged reversed afternystagmus. If the limb rotates to the right (say), the slow phase is to the right, but at a lesser velocity, and the fast phases are to the left (Brandt & Buchelle, 1977). Presumably this is also the pattern of eye movement that stabilizes gaze in space when the body rotates left, while the arm holds some rigid body for support. See Figure 10.47.

3.2.1.3. Active or Passive Head Rotation About the Yaw Axis. Eye movements in the vestibulo-ocular reflex consist of two components: slow phases that stabilize the retinal image by contrasting head rotation, and fast or "quick" phases that negate the slow phases. The net effect is that gaze velocity in space remains close to 0, and the eyes remain reasonably centered in their orbits. The two phases are easily discriminated. The gain of the reflex is calculated from the velocity of the slow phase relative to head velocity. Introductions to the vestibulo-ocular reflex were given in Sections 1.3.2, 2.1.1, 2.3.4, and 2.3.5.

(a) SLOW PHASES. The vestibulo-ocular reflex is typically studied by rotating the body and head through fairly large amplitudes, either in the dark or with the eyelids closed (Baloh, Sills, & Honrubia, 1979; Barnes, 1979; Barnes, Benson, & Prior, 1978; Benson & Barnes, 1978; Hannen, Kabrisky, Replogle, Hartzler, & Roccaforte, 1966; Paige, 1983). For an example, see Figure 10.48(a). The compensatory smooth or slow phases are opposite to the direction of head rotation, and thus tend to stabilize the direction of gaze in space. The gain of the reflex is defined by the ratio of slow-phase velocity to head angular velocity. Instructions and arousal are important. For repetitive side-to-side sinusoidal oscillations, while the 12 subjects performed mental arithmetic, gain fell from 1 to 0.7 when the fixation light was turned out (oscillations of 0.1–0.9 Hz at ±40° amplitude; Barr et al., 1976). Gain rose to 0.95 on imagining a target light fixed to the wall. Gain fell to 0.3–0.5, which is toward that for a light fixed to the rotating chair (0.1), when imagining such a light (Fig. 10.49, page 10-49). Similar data were obtained for single high-velocity oscillations of the head [Figs. 10.48(b) and 10.49, far right]. The vestibulo-ocular reflex continues to compensate for head velocities up to at least 350°·sec^{-1}, whether the subject turns the head voluntarily or is bodily oscillated, provided that there is an effort to visualize a real or imagined stationary object in space (Fig. 10.50, page 10-50). Compensation is increasingly poorer at the higher head velocities, and the reflex gradually saturates (Pulaski et al., 1981); see Figure 10.50. Slow phase velocities can reach 500°·sec^{-1}, which is faster than saccadic eye movements of less than 10° amplitude. It is therefore not unexpected that slow phases can at times be faster than "fast phases" (Fig. 10.51, page 10-51). The equivalence of active head movements and passive whole-body rotations in these studies supports the traditional view that there is no major cervico-ocular reflex in man.

Note that the majority of vestibulo-ocular studies employ predictable sinusoidal oscillations, and that tracking is a good deal poorer at low frequencies (<2 – 3 Hz) when the motion is random and not predictable (Hyden, Istl, & Schwarz, 1982). In fact, it is highly advantageous in clinical investigations (e.g.) of long-standing unilateral labyrinthine disease) to use wide-frequency-band random oscillations, and the same will probably prove to be the case in physiological research (Schwarz & Tom linson, 1979). The better performance for predictable sinusoids allows the possibility that subjects can supplement the low

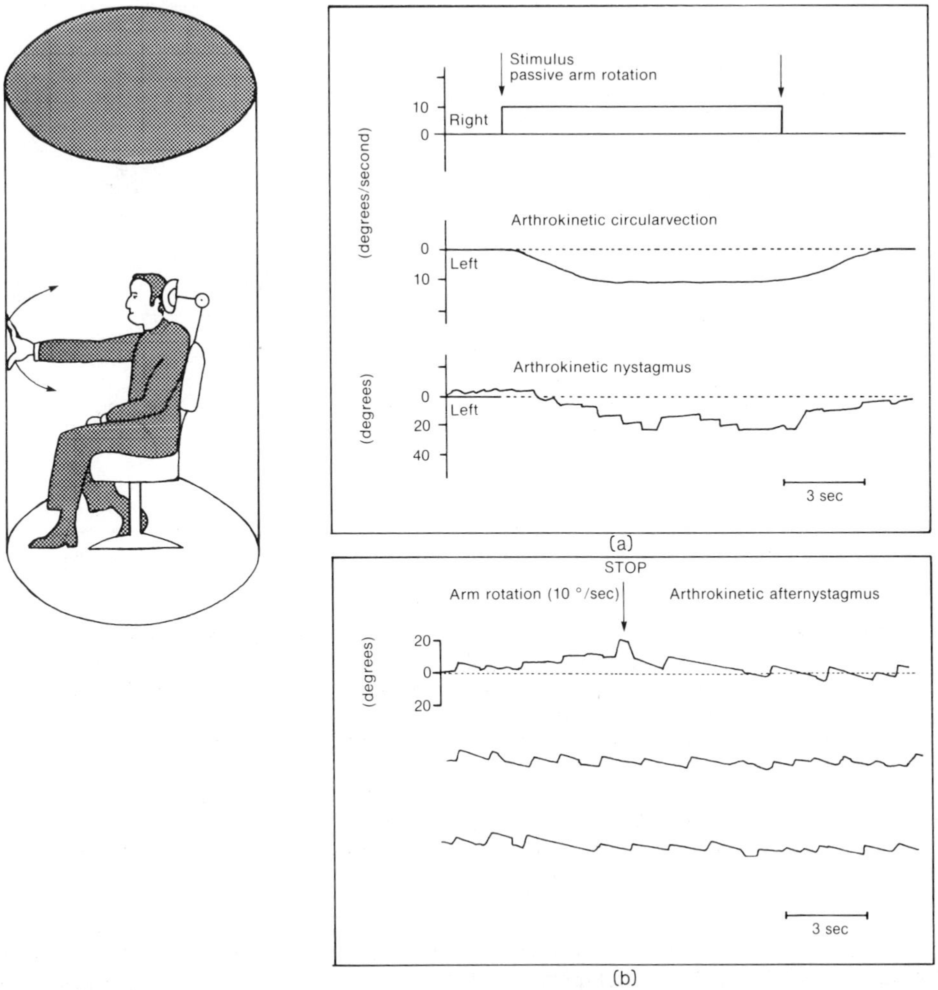

Figure 10.47. Arthrokinetic nystagmus and afternystagmus. Drawing shows passive rotation of subject's arm in the dark. (a) From above down: slow arm rotation to right at $10° \cdot sec^{-1}$, sense of self-rotation to left, slow phase of about $5° \cdot sec^{-1}$ to right with opposite fast phases. (b) After 100° or 10 sec of rotation, arm is stopped at time of arrow, and a reversed afternystagmus occurs which is prolonged for many seconds. Faster passive arm rotation of $90° \cdot sec^{-1}$ would elicit a slow phase of around $10 \pm 5° \cdot sec^{-1}$. EOG technique. One implication is that eye position in practical situations is not determined by retinal and vestibular factors alone. (From T. Brandt & W. Buchelle, Arthrokinetic nystagmus by passive arm or leg rotation, in G. Kommerell (Ed.), *Disorders of ocular motility*, Bergmann Verlag, 1977. Reprinted with permission.)

level vestibulo-ocular reflex by consciously monitoring low-frequency head rotation.

Note also that most studies imply that active head turning, and passive head and body rotation en bloc, are equivalent. At high frequencies of oscillation en bloc (>3 − 4 Hz), vestibulo-ocular gain for sinusoidal stimuli exceeds unity in the dark (Benson, 1970). A more recent study, however, shows that the high gain at high frequencies is missing in man when the body is stationary and the head is turned actively; also, responses to low frequencies are improved, so that gain is close to unity over a wide range, from 0.5 to 5 Hz. This suggests that motor programs can modify the vestibulo-ocular reflex (Tomlinson, Saunders, & Schwarz, 1980).

Data from monkeys for sinusoidal stimuli suggest that low gain at low frequencies in the dark, and high gain at high frequencies, are supplemented in the light by good optokinetic and pursuit responses at low frequencies and poor ones at high frequencies; the final result is unity gain with little or no phase shift for a wide range of oscillations (e.g., Keller, 1978). In more general situations, however, the interaction of vestibular slow phases with voluntary smooth pursuit is not well understood. For example, cancellation of the vestibulo-ocular reflex in darkness, as when imagining a light rotating with the chair, can scarcely be attributed to opposing smooth pursuit movements, because smooth pursuit is usually defined as needing a real target. On the other hand, cancellation when fixating a real light moving with the chair could (in principle) be due to opposing smooth pursuit: as the head rotates the eyes counterrotate, which causes retinal slip of the image of the fixation light, which initiates smooth pursuit. Unfortunately, the behavior of neurons that can carry both vestibular and smooth pursuit signals does not support this appealing notion (Tomlinson & Robinson, 1981). Thus cancellation and smooth pursuit are probably separate mechanisms; once again, one wonders if subjects monitor internal eye position or velocity signals in an effort to keep the eyes stationary (Section 2.1.11).

Head movements under natural sedentary conditions are rather small, and the gain of the vestibulo-ocular reflex is low, despite the subjects trying to imagine stationary lights on the walls (e.g., gains of 0.25 − 0.75 for 0.05 − 2.5° excursions

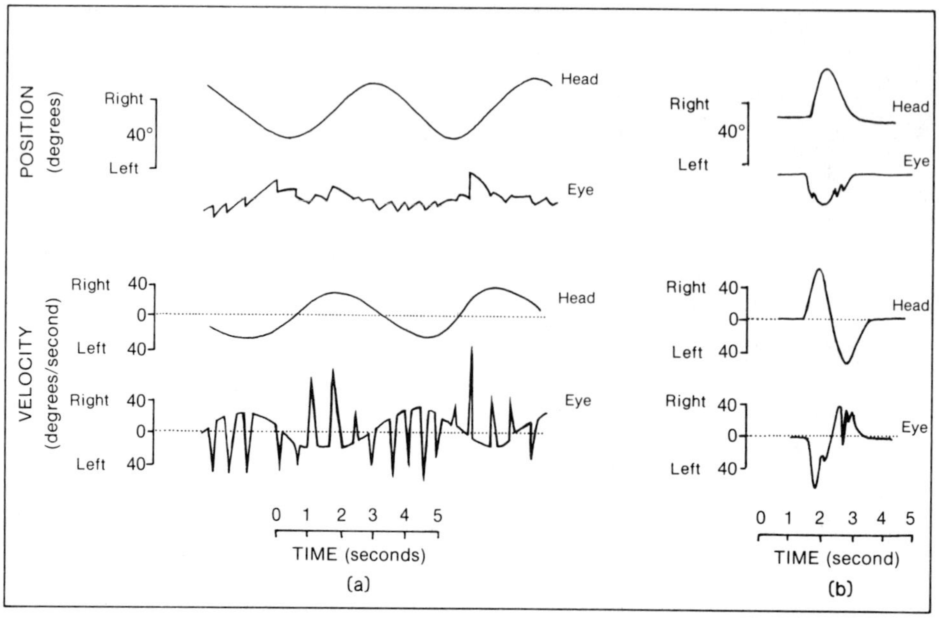

Figure 10.48. Vestibulo-ocular reflex in the dark during mental arithmetic. The eye movements in the vestibulo-ocular reflex consist of slow phases that stabilize the retinal image against head rotation and opposite fast or "quick" phases that approximately recenter the eye in the orbit. (a) Horizontal head position in space and eye position in the orbit in degrees during whole body oscillation, and the respective velocities in degrees per second. Frequency of imposed horizontal oscillation is slow (0.2 Hz) and amplitude is large (ca. ±20°). (b) Similar records for a single transient displacement of the head and body to the right. EOG records. Note that the smooth movement counteracts only about 0.6 of head motion. Fast phases reset eye position in the orbit. (From C. C. Barr, L. W. Schultheis, & D. A. Robinson, Voluntary non-visual control of the human vestibulo-ocular reflex, *Acta Otolaryngologica*, 1976, *81*. Reprinted with permission.)

at 0.1 – 15 Hz; Skavenski et al., 1979). The low gain is in keeping with other evidence that small head motions are incompletely compensated, so as to prevent fading of the retinal image (Section 3.1.1.1.). The reflex adaptively matches the phase of head motions up to high frequencies (8 Hz) in the dark. Horizontal binocular movements are usually worse in the dark than in the light. When the head is voluntarily shaken from side to side in the dark, both left and right eye velocity in space and convergence-divergence velocities are increased (e.g., head oscillations of 0.25 – 5 Hz over a range of 15 min arc to 30°, Steinman & Collewijn, 1980).

If the body and head are rotated en bloc *unidirectionally* at a constant velocity, the vestibulo-ocular response dies away after several seconds in the dark, because of the hydrodynamic characteristics of the semicircular canals (e.g., Wilson & Melvill Jones, 1979). Imagining a light fixed on the wall has no effect on gain in this case. In fully lit surroundings nystagmus continues indefinitely, because the vestibulo-ocular response is replaced by optokinetic nystagmus.

(b) Fast Phases and Saccades. The fast phases of nystagmus are in the same direction as head rotation; indeed, clinicians name the direction of nystagmus by the direction of the fast or "quick" phases. The question arises as to how quick phases interact with slow phases, and whether quick phases and saccades are the result of the same basic mechanism. A study with horizontal head velocities of less than $120°\cdot sec^{-1}$ suggests that there are two aspects to the interaction of slow and quick phases: (1) *Offset*: Vestibular quick phases are about $60°\cdot sec^{-1}$ slower than voluntary saccades of the same amplitude in darkness; (2) *Slope*: Quick-phase velocity is independent of slow-phase velocity (zero slope), both for the vestibular reflex proper and for the post-rotatory (reversed) nystagmus that follows cessation of a prolonged rotation in the dark (Jürgens et al., 1981). The offset effect implies an action of slow phases on quick phases, whereas the zero slope shows that the slow phase is actually shut off during the quick phase at these head velocities. See Figure 10.52 (a) and (b). The interaction of vestibular slow phase with voluntary saccades to acoustic targets in the dark is quite different from the interaction with quick phases [Fig. 10.52(d)]. Offset is now positive (which is consistent with oscillation improving saccadic velocity) and slope is now somewhat less than unity (which shows that some compensatory slow phase is present during voluntary saccades, though not at full strength). Evidently the neural paths of quick phases and voluntary saccades are not identical, even though both presumably use the same saccade generators.

Rather different effects are obtained at high head velocities ($>200°\cdot sec^{-1}$) when attempting to visualize a real or imaginary target. The quick or fast phases can be recognized by being in the same direction as the head; they progressively slow as head velocity increases above $200°\cdot sec^{-1}$, until "quick-phase" velocity is a mere $30–40°\cdot sec^{-1}$, or one-tenth of the corresponding "slow-phase" velocity. See Figure 10.51. [This situation is counter to the relation at lower velocities in Figure 10.52(a), on page 10-52, where there is no progressive effect of slow-phase velocity on the fast phase]. At high head velocities the durations of fast phases are prolonged to 200 or even 500 msec to compensate for their slowness (Fig. 10.51). This is compatible with a spatially coded quick-phase generator (e.g., Zee & Robinson, 1979), which uses local feedback to control the duration of the pulse force, so that the eye eventually reaches the specified direction in space.

The remainder of Figure 10.52 properly belongs to other sections dealing with lit targets. It is convenient to note here that the interaction of acoustically evoked saccades with vestibular movement [Fig. 10.52(d), Section 3.7.1.8] is comparable to that of visually guided saccades with vestibular movement [Fig. 10.52(e), Section 3.7.1.10] or of catch-up saccades to a smoothly moving target with smooth pursuit [Fig. 10.52(f), Section 3.3.2]. Also, the fast phases of optokinetic nystagmus are not influenced by slow-phase velocity, and the slow phase seems to be shut off during the quick phases [Fig. 10.52(c), Section 3.3.3].

(c) Adaptive Plasticity. Rotation in the dark provides an important means of testing for alterations in the neural coupling of the semicircular canals to the eye muscles; such changes can be produced by adapting over a period of minutes or days to normally lit surroundings seen through various types of goggles or spectacles. Normally, if the head is rotated to the right, the smooth-phase movement to the left helps to stabilize the retinal image of the surroundings. If reversing prisms are worn for several days during activity in a lit, structured environment, the slow-phase gain is reduced and may even be reversed when tested by rotation in the dark. Similarly, the gain of the vestibulo-ocular reflex is appropriately increased if magnifying glasses are worn during activity in the lit surroundings, or reduced if minifying glasses are worn. See Gonshor and Melvill Jones (1976a, 1976b), Melvill Jones and Gonshor (1982), Melvill Jones and Mandl (1979), F. A. Miles and Eighmy (1980), F. A. Miles and Fuller (1974), and F. A. Miles and Lisberger (1981).

3.2.1.4. Head Tilt About the Pitch Axis. In the "doll reflex," the eyes counter-roll vertically about the pitch axis when the head is given a static forward or backward tilt. The response is attributed to the otolith organs in the utricles of the vestibular organs, but there has been some doubt about whether the reflex exists, given the obscuring effect of voluntary vertical eye movements. Subjects in darkness were confronted with a vertical arc of about 170 luminous points at 1° intervals as a means of reducing wandering movements of the eyes without providing any definite point of fixation about the pitch axis. The instruction was to look straight ahead (i.e., perpendicular to the frontal or coronal plane), while the head and body were tilted backward en bloc. A maximum ocular depression of about 7° (20 subjects) was observed at 60° backward tilt. This maximum is consistent with the utricular macules being tilted 30° backward when the head is in the erect anatomical position (Ebenholtz & Shebilske, 1975). Most authors would interpret the small ocular depression as an unmodified reflex response. If this view is correct, it implies a weak and relatively useless role for the utriculo-ocular reflex, which is surprising, given considerable human ability to maintain the upright posture or estimate the horizontal. The more "biologically adaptive" hypothesis, I suggest, is that the subject monitors his/her oculomotor outflow in an attempt to keep the eye stationary in the orbit, and so to "look ahead" as instructed. But the subject fails to completely overcome the reflex, because of a limited loop gain g (e.g., Fig. 10.27). If $g = 8$, say, in the above experiments the maximum reflex drive to the eye muscles in the absence of the instruction to look ahead should be $7° \times (1 + 8) = 63°$; this would almost exactly counteract the 60° head tilt in the absence of the "look ahead" instruction.

A strong otolith signal could also supplement the semicircular canal response to low-frequency *oscillation* about the pitch axis. This supplement would be useful because any optokinetic supplement is likely to be weak for rotations about the pitch axis, because the optokinetic system does not necessarily respond well to vertically moving stimuli (Tomlinson, Note 6).

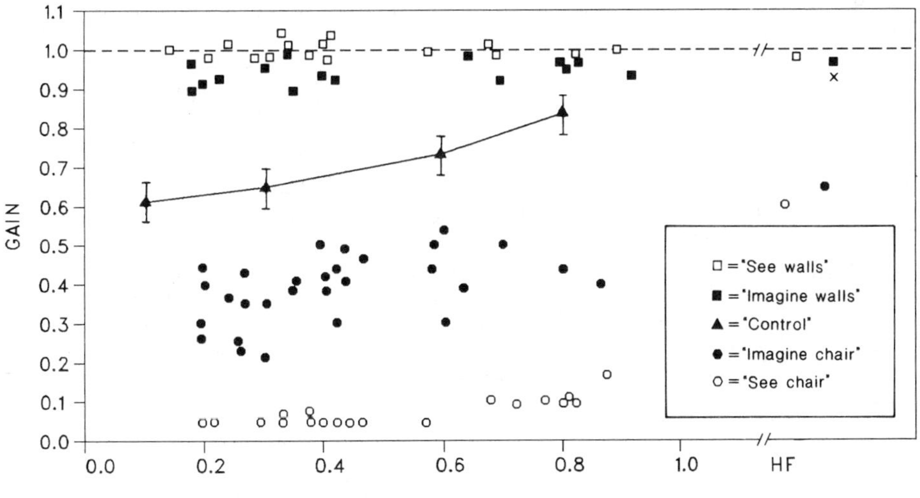

Figure 10.49. Effect of instructions and attention on vestibulo-ocular reflex gain. Gain is ratio of peak slow phase velocity to head velocity. Frequency refers to the motion imposed on the head and body. From above down. "See walls" (open squares) shows gain of almost unity when room lights are on. "Imagine walls" (black squares) in the dark is almost as effective. "Control" (solid triangles) is gain in dark during mental arithmetic with means and standard deviations for the population of 12 subjects shown. "Imagine chair" (solid circles) shows that gain is reduced if the subject imagines a light attached to the chair and rotating with him. "See chair" (open circles) shows virtual absence of overt reflex when a visible light is attached to chair. *HF* at end of abscissas refers to gains for a single high-velocity oscillation. EOG data. Clearly, attention matters. (From C. C. Barr, L. W. Schultheis, & D. A. Robinson, Voluntary non-visual control of the human vestibulo-ocular reflex, *Acta Otolaryngologica*, 1976, *81*. Reprinted with permission.)

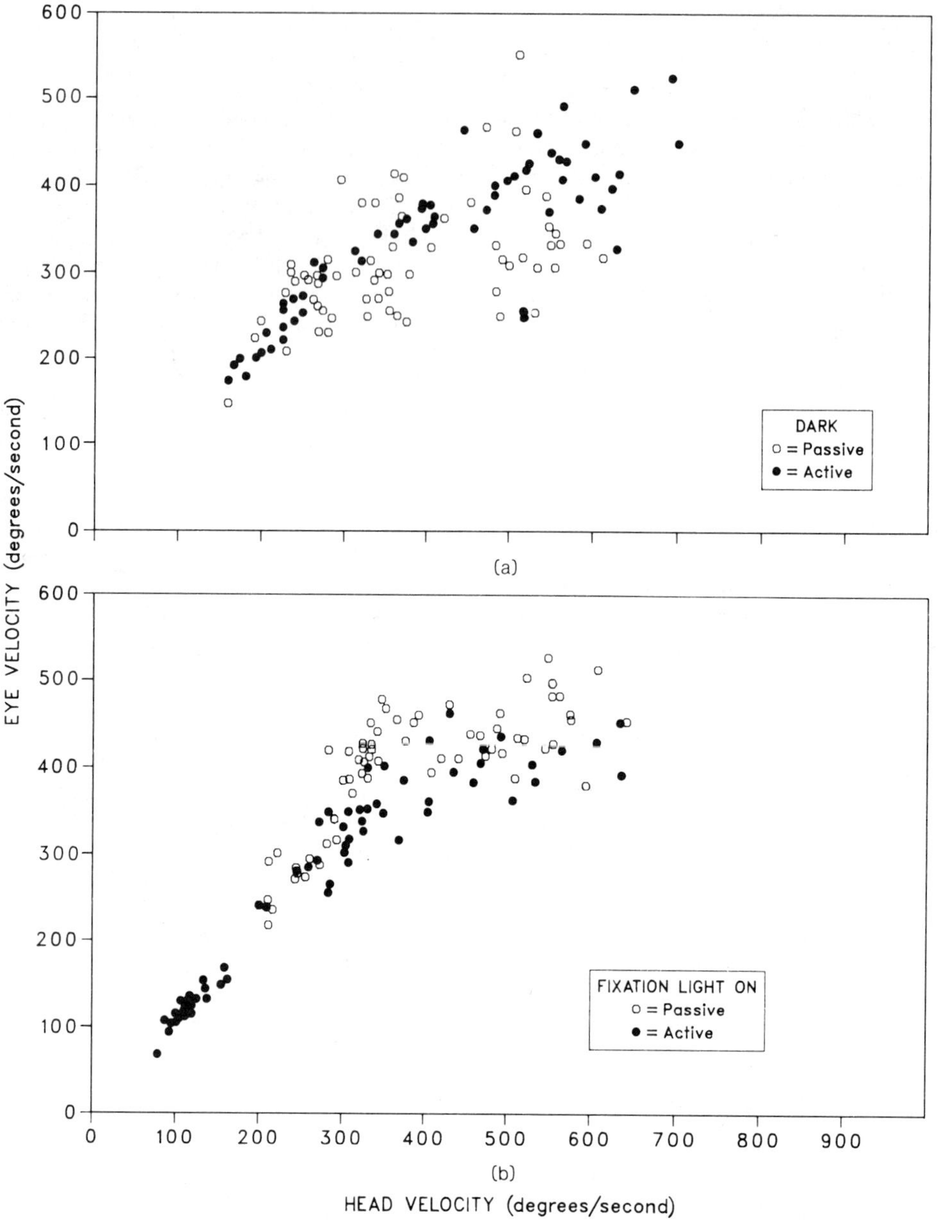

Figure 10.50. Vestibulo-ocular reflex at high head velocities. (a) Darkness. Peak slow-phase velocities versus peak head velocity in degrees per second, during passive (whole body) and active head movements in the dark while the subject imagines the location of a stationary target. Open symbols: passive rotation. Filled symbols: active rotation. (b) Fixation light is on. Results are very similar. EOG recording technique; data for one of three subjects is shown. Note that vestibulo-ocular reflex is approximately compensatory up to 350–400° · sec^{-1}; thereafter eye velocity begins to saturate and becomes more variable. (From P. D. Pulaski, D. S. Zee, & D. A. Robinson, The behavior of the vestibulo-ocular reflex at high velocities of head rotation, *Brain Research*, 1981, *222*. Reprinted with permission.)

3.2.1.5. The Imagined Hand as the Target. The accuracy of fixating the unseen stationary finger with fixed head is about ±1.5° (Gibbs & Logan, 1965; Merton, 1961), and is the same whether the finger is moved actively or passively into position (Steinbach, 1970). This is comparable to the long-term accuracy of holding the eye in the dark (e.g., Skavenski, 1976).

3.2.2 Instruction: Pursue Imagined Moving Object or Hand. It is generally true that smooth eye movements are not possible at will or in darkness; however, it is said that subjects trained on a flickering stimulus can eventually be brought to track for a few seconds in the dark (Whittaker & Eaholtz, 1982). Slow movements behind closed lids were possible in eight of ten subjects when they imagined the motion of a 0.5-Hz and 30° amplitude pendulum that they had just previously tracked in the light (Deckert, 1964); it is not clear whether these movements were true smooth movements or highly damped saccades. One subject could make smooth movements in the dark with eyelids open, without special training, but not with lids closed (Heywood, 1972). A foveal afterimage did not improve smooth movement, as it usually does for most subjects, nor did an afterimage 3° from the fovea elicit saccades. Perhaps the subject favored smooth pursuit movements by canceling saccades.

Although there have been reports that subjects can track their smoothly moving hands in darkness, Steinbach's (1969) impression is that this only applies to about one in three subjects. Jordan (1970) observed variable smooth tracking in six of nine subjects for about 50% (20–95) of the time. An afterimage of the hand greatly improved pursuit of the hand, and active and passive hand movements were equally effective for the rather slow speeds and infrequent reversals used ($\pm 30°$ at <0.5 Hz).

3.2.3. Instruction: Look To and Fro Between Remembered Fixation Points. When horizontal saccades are made between a pair of remembered fixation lights at 40° separation, saccade duration is about 19 $\pm$ 7 msec longer, and peak velocity about 16% lower, than for similar-sized saccades between lit points (Becker & Fuchs, 1969). This effect develops after 1 sec in the dark. Subjects prefer to make horizontal saccades of about 50–60° amplitude in the dark, most probably because this amplitude is not physically uncomfortable and they feel confident that they are making saccades between two very distinct positions (Becker & Klein, 1973). If the subject is requested to make smaller or larger saccades, saccade size increases or decreases toward about 50°. The eyes drift conjugately at the end of each saccade, toward a position near the straight-ahead or primary position, with a velocity roughly proportional to the angle of gaze, that is, with a gaze-dependent drift of about 3 (1–5) min arc $\cdot$ sec^{-1} per degree of gaze. The rate of drift is not usually equal and opposite for symmetrical left and right gaze positions, because drift is often nonzero in the anatomical primary position [at 35 (3–57) min arc $\cdot$ sec^{-1}], being zero at some other position. Drift is corrected (1) subconsciously and immediately by secondary saccades of 0.5–7° amplitude and 130-msec average latency; (2) by drift-correcting saccades of 1–3° amplitude and frequency of up to one per second, depending on drift velocity; (3) consciously by large saccades at long intervals. See Figure 10.53. The drift may arise from "leakiness" in the "neural integrator" that determines eye position by integrating the velocity signals from the semicircular canals, the integrator having a time constant of 10–50 sec, rather than the ideal value of infinity. Drift in the primary position would thus represent an inequality in the resting discharge from the left and right vestibular organs, which differs from one individual to another. It should be noted that the values for drift in the primary position represent persistent unidirectional drift, and are a little higher in this EOG study than reported above for contact lens studies in which the subject attempts to "fixate" in darkness (e.g., 35 here versus 12 min arc $\cdot$ sec^{-1} above). These differences may reflect measuring technique, or may arise from most contact lens studies being based on self-selected subjects who are highly practiced at fixating.

A related experiment involved naive subjects and the more accurate Purkinje-image-tracking technique (Komoda, Festinger, & Sherry, 1977). Three discriminable targets were simultaneously presented at random in a 12 $\times$ 12° display; the saccade to target 1 extinguished all targets in 50% of trials. Subjects were urged to take their time and be accurate. Performance was moderately impaired during 1.5 sec of darkness. Mean ab-

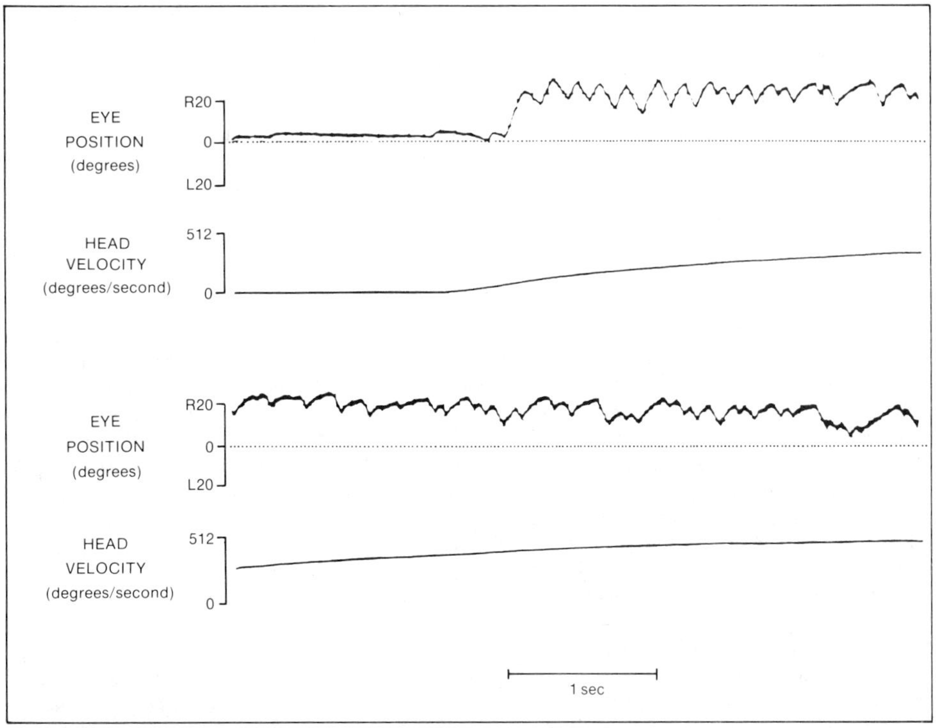

Figure 10.51. Vestibulo-ocular nystagmus at high head velocities. Head and body rotated passively *en bloc* to right in darkness. Upper and lower records are continuous. EOG record. Fast phase is in same direction as head movement and is thus always upward in diagram. Note that as head and "slow-phase" velocities increase, "fast" phases of comparable amplitudes have lower velocities and longer durations. "Fast-phase" velocity is even less than "slow-phase" at times. (From P. D. Pulaski, D. S. Zee, & D. A. Robinson, The behavior of the vestibulo-ocular reflex at high velocities of head rotation, *Brain Research*, 1981, *222*. Reprinted with permission.)

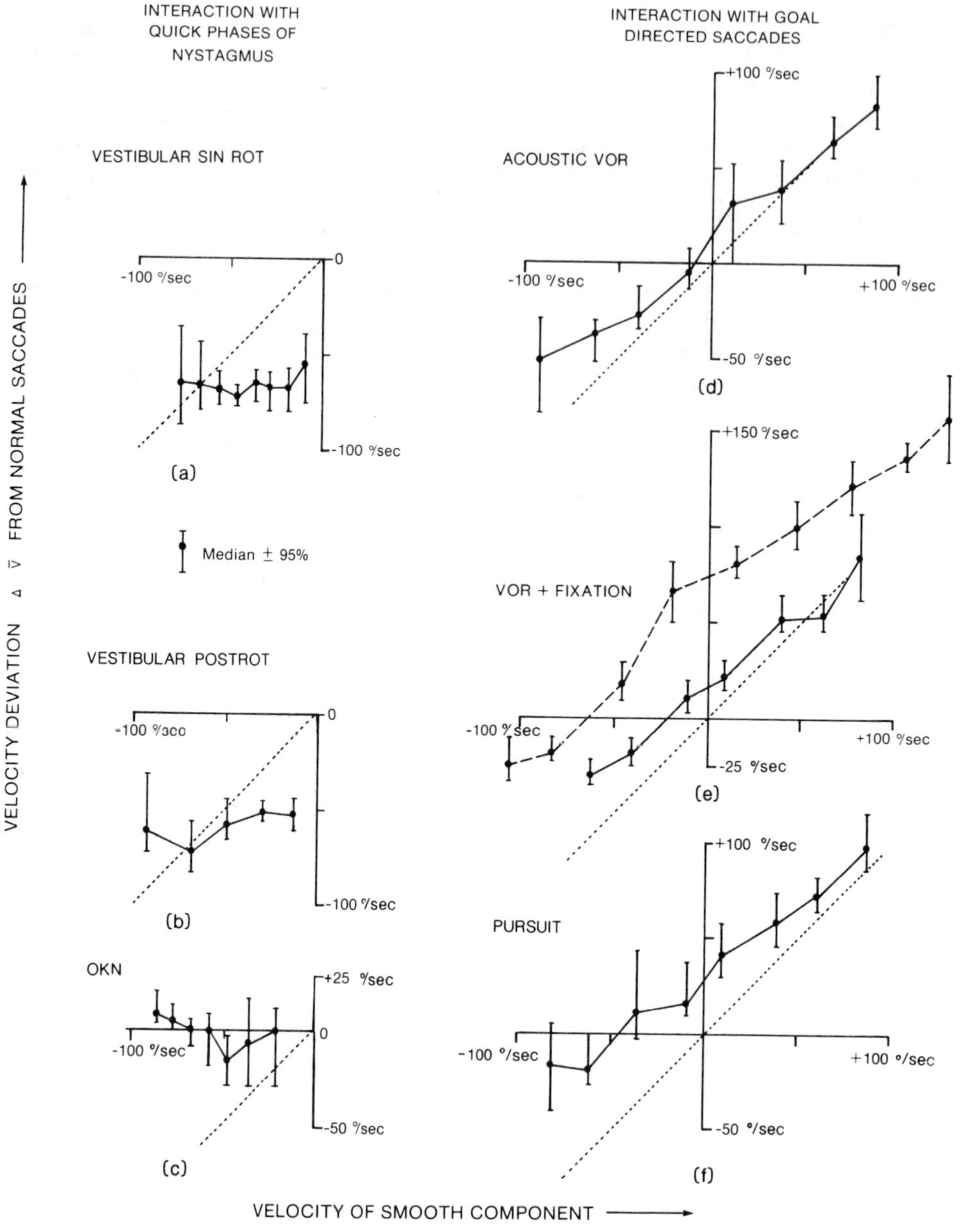

Figure 10.52. Interaction of fast or "quick" phases and voluntary saccades with smooth movements. Ordinates are change in average velocity of saccade, or quick phase, relative to normal saccade velocity in the dark, *versus* velocity of slow phase or smooth movement as abscissas, both in degrees per second. Thus the positive quadrant is for quick phases or saccades in the same direction as the smooth movement, whereas the negative quadrant is for opposed abrupt and smooth movements. The diagonal line corresponds to smooth velocity adding to saccade or quick phase velocity. (a–c) When quick phases show negative offset, this indicates that quick phases are uniformly slower than control saccades. Zero slope shows that the slow phase is shut down during the quick phase, so there is no summation of velocities. (a) Quick phases of vestibular nystagmus during sinusoidal rotation in dark. (b) Quick phases during (reversed) post-rotatory vestibular nystagmus in the dark. (c) Quick phases during optokinetic nystagmus. Thus slow phase is shut down by quick phases in all three examples on the left, and vestibular slow phase reduces quick phase velocity. (d–f) Voluntary saccades show two effects. The positive offset shows that saccadic velocities are uniformly increased by smooth movement, even when smooth movement is temporarily stationary at the reversal point of the oscillating rotation. In addition, saccadic velocity is increased or reduced, depending on the direction of the smooth movement, by about 70% of smooth velocity. (d) Saccades to acoustic signals during rotation *en bloc* in the dark. (e) Saccades to a small red light stepping within the range of 45° in 11° steps, during rotations of $125° \cdot sec^{-1}$ (dashed line) and $75° \cdot sec^{-1}$ (full line). (f) Catch-up saccades during smooth pursuit eye movements with fixed head. The data in each panel are medians and 95% limits, with 4–13 subjects in each panel. (From R. Jürgens, W. Becker, & P. Rieger, Different effects involved in the interaction of saccades and the vestibulo-ocular reflex, *Annals of the New York Academy of Science*, 1981, *374*. Reprinted with permission.)

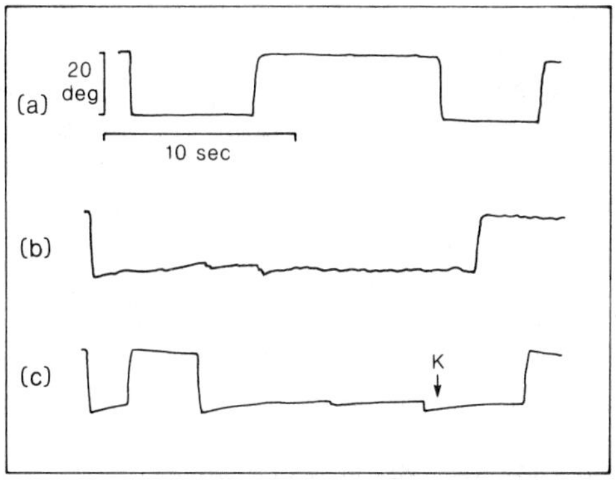

Figure 10.53. Search saccades, smooth drift, and counter saccades in the dark. After the subject practiced 16 saccades between two dimly lit fixation points, the points were extinguished and the subject attempted to reproduce the movements in darkness. EOG records. From the top: (a) Eye movements and fixation during the learning period. (b, c) Large search saccades, followed by drift toward center and small counter saccades that oppose the drift. Point K marks the subject having sensed one of the larger saccades that counter drift. Such experiments demonstrate that subjects prefer to make fairly large search saccades of approximately constant amplitude, though amplitude is erratic if the initial fixation points are close, for example, 5° apart. (From W. Becker & H. M. Klein, Accuracy of saccadic eye movements and maintenance of eccentric eye positions in the dark, *Vision Research, 13*. Copyright 1973 by Pergamon Press, Ltd. Reprinted with permission.)

solute errors, for targets 2 and 3, were about four times as large in the dark as when the targets were lit, that is, about 2.1° (SD 1.2). The saccades from target 2 to target 3 were more variable in size and direction than those from target 1 to target 2. This variability may reflect compensations, because the mean fixation error for target 3 was only 10% greater than for target 2. These results are consistent with absolute spatial codes for the three targets; performance in the dark would then be limited mainly by memory, whereas errors would accumulate from one saccade to the next if the coding used the relative spatial position or retinal positions of the targets. It would be interesting to know how accuracy deteriorates with increasing numbers of targets, up to the point at which memory fails.

3.2.4. Instruction: Look Toward the Acoustic Tone. Auditory feedback improves fixation of a target in the dark (W. M. Smith, 1964). See also Figure 10.52(d) and Section 3.7.1.8.

3.3. Eye Movements to Smooth Pitch and Yaw Motions of the Target

If the targets are imagined to be on the walls of a very large sphere centered on the subject's stationary head, the target motions to be considered here involve rotation of the sphere about axes in the subject's transverse or coronal or Listing plane, for example, yaw about the vertical axis of Fick, or pitch about the transverse horizontal axis of Helmholtz. The corresponding eye movements include voluntary smooth pursuit, assisted by catch-up sacades, and involuntary optokinetic nystagmus, comprising smooth optokinetic movement and fast phases. For interactions with the moving head, see Section 3.2.1.3.

If the object is relatively near, large-amplitude yaw motions of the sphere may require unequal conjugate movements of the two eyes, and may thus include (at least hypothetically) a component of Hering vergence (see Section 3.4.1.4).

3.3.1. Instruction: Pursue the Small Stimulus for Several Seconds

3.3.1.1. Simple Motion in One Dimension

(a) Foveal Tracking. A number of studies have examined tracking performance when the subject is in a steady state, after transient reactions to the initial stimulus motion have settled down. The usual assumption is that the subject necessarily strives to foveate the target and match its velocity, but casual observation suggests that simple luminous targets in darkness are well seen, even if the eyes do not track. If the point target is moving horizontally from side to side with a sinusoidal motion, the amplitude of tracking is generally less than unity and the phase slightly advanced (e.g., gain of 0.6–1 and 5–10° lead for low stimulus frequencies at less than 1.5 Hz). Above a corner frequency of 1–1.5 Hz, performance deteriorates rapidly and ceases at 2.5–3 Hz (Dallos & Jones, 1963; Fender, 1964b; Fender & Nye, 1961; Michael & Melvill Jones, 1966; Stark, Vossius, & Young, 1962). Given variable and less than unity gains, even for predictable sinusoidal motion (Fig. 10.54), it is surprising that stress has been laid on the pursuit system being able to match target velocity. Doubtless the word "match" means "approximately match," because in more precise experiments highly practiced subjects cannot consistently match the velocity of slowly moving targets (2.4 and 5.4° · sec^{-1}), which require very accurate fixation for resolution. Pursuit velocity is rather variable, but near-unity velocity gains (0.97, SD 0.1) are observed for well-rehearsed tracking of slow targets without saccades (Kowler, Murphy, & Steinman, 1978).

A subject does not behave like the linear servomechanism of Section 2.3.5 when tracking predictable motion; the observed lags are nearly always smaller than predicted from amplitude or gain, using the minimum phase condition of servomechanics. Tracking must be controlled, not by the target, but by some internal model of the target, which is time-advanced relative to the target and relatively independent of the subjective appearance of the target (brightness, color, etc.). Undertracking, with premature reversal of eye velocity before the stimulus reaches the extremity of its motion, may contribute to phase lead (Lightstone, 1973). Aftertracking, tracking along the target path for 1–2 sec after target extinction, also points to a learned model (Whittaker & Eaholtz, 1982). Not surprisingly, tracking deteriorates in amplitude and phase when the stimulus motion is made unpredictable by combining several nonharmonically related sinusoids (St. Cyr & Fender, 1969b, 1969c; Stark et al., 1962). The quality of tracking ought also to deteriorate as the amplitude of sinusoidal stimulus motion is increased, because target velocity and acceleration become excessively high (Rashbass, 1961; Robinson, 1965; Westheimer, 1954). Experiments on the relation between eye acceleration and retinal-image velocity during unsuccessful high-velocity pursuit suggest that the limiting factor in pursuit is eye acceleration, which also depends on stimulus predictability (Lisberger et al., 1981).

In the above studies, the head and body are directed parallel to the optic axis of the visual stimulator, so that the eyes are initially centered in the orbits. In the experiments of Yee, Goldberg, Jones, Baloh, and Honrubia (1983) the head and body are at 30° to the stimulator axis, so that the eyes start smooth pursuit from an eccentric position. Amplitude of motion of the bright red dot was 20° and peak velocity was between 6 and 79° · sec^{-1}, depending on the frequency of horizontal sinusoidal oscillation. Pursuit gain was reduced when the eyes moved more eccentrically in the orbits, and increased when the eyes

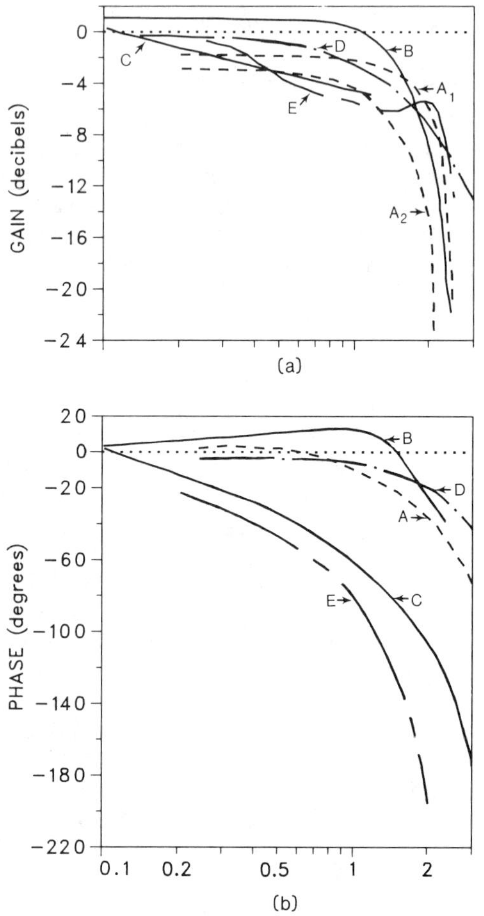

Figure 10.54. Gain and phase of the oculomotor system. (a) Gain in decibels (power units) is the square of the amplitude ratio of response/stimulus motion. In many studies it is the amplitude ratio, unless otherwise defined. (b) Phase lead is positive. (A_1 and A_2) Single sinusoids of 1.1 and 3.4° amplitude (Fender and Nye, 1961). (B) Single sinusoids of about 4–10° amplitude (Stark, Vossius, & Young, 1962). (C) Sums of 4–9 sinusoids (Stark, Vossius, & Young, 1962). (D) Single sinusoids (Dallos & Jones, 1963). (E) Band-limited Gaussian random motion (Dallos & Jones, 1963). Tracking deteriorates above 1.5 Hz. The relative contributions of smooth pursuit and saccades are not distinguished, but it can be assumed that smooth pursuit dominates, although saccades may improve gain at 1.6–2 Hz in some instances. Photopic stimulus. (From G. J. St. Cyr & D. H. Fender, Non-linearity of the human oculomotor system: Gain, *Vision Research*, 9. Copyright 1969 by Pergamon Press, Ltd. Reprinted with permission.)

moved back to orbital center. These effects are traceable to elastic restoring forces and are more marked at high target velocities. (The interaction of smooth-pursuit velocity and the velocities of catch-up saccades is briefly treated in the part of Section 3.2.1.3 that deals with Fig. 10.52).

(b) Low-Stimulus Luminance and Eccentric Tracking. Performance at tracking predictable motions is relatively insensitive to the nature of the stimulus and the task, as one might expect if the subject is responding to an internal model.

Figure 10.55(a), from contact lens experiments (Winterson & Steinman, 1978), shows gain and phase as a function of frequency when the subject directly pursued the stimulus without using saccades (amplitude of stimulus motion 2.2°). Reducing the luminance of the green stimulus, from 1.5 to 0.5 log above foveal threshold did not systematically reduce gain for the two subjects studied. Reducing luminance tended to increase phase lags, but phase leads as low as 0–10° were still observed at low frequencies. Altering the instruction to use saccades freely did not change gain and phase very much, whether this was computed for the smooth-pursuit component alone [Fig. 10.55(b)] or for the total eye movement. More dramatically, there was very little change in performance in a separate experiment where the subjects tracked with their line of sight 5–7° above the stimulus. The stimulus was either 1.5 log above foveal threshold, and seen as distinct and green, or else 0.5 log above scotopic threshold, and seen as diffuse and colorless. The two subjects could eccentrically track on the first attempt; indeed, smooth pursuit is possible near the absolute scotopic threshold in the periods when the stimulus is visible. Gains for eccentric pursuit [Fig. 10.55(c)] were a little lower than for foveal tracking and phase lags and leads were a little larger. Eccentric pursuit, like foveal pursuit, is little altered by low luminance, although there is a tendency toward a slight phase lag. Of course, performance at scotopic luminances can be poor in appropriate circumstances. For example, the subject may attempt to track the stimulus with a night-blind fovea (Wheeless, 1965); or instrumental constraints may encourage a self-selected subject to pursue the stimulus eccentrically, but with a horizontal offset which switches intermittently from nasal to temporal (author's observations).

Data for tracking simple sinusoidal motion and sums of sinusoids at different luminances are also given by Wheeless (1965), who found rather more marked effects of luminance. Perhaps his subject was less well trained and the internal model less well developed.

(c) Interaction of Target and Background. Smooth pursuit of a horizontally oscillating target (constant velocities of 5–60° · sec^{-1}) is affected by the nature of the background. Pursuit velocity is reduced if the stationary background is vertically striped, like the inside of a large optokinetic drum, rather than uniform. If the drum rotates at 30° · sec^{-1}, smooth pursuit is faster when the pursuit target goes with the drum and slower when against. The smooth pursuit and optokinetic slow-phase movements are not fully additive (Yee, Daniels, Jones, Baloh, & Honrubia, 1983).

3.3.1.2. Random One-Dimensional Motion. Horizontally oscillating targets, driven by narrow-bandwidth Gaussian noise, give similar results to mixtures of nonharmonically related sinusoidal motions (Dallos & Jones, 1963; Michael & Melvill Jones, 1966; Stark et al., 1962). Average amplitudes of motion were several degrees. Michael and Melvill Jones (1966) found that phase lag is relatively constant at 15–25° up to a test frequency of 0.7–1.5 Hz, beyond which lag increases very rapidly. The cutoff occurs at lower frequencies for the more random and noisier stimuli (Fig. 10.56). For sensory analyses, phase lag is not as attractive a measure as retinal-image position. However, visual acuity remains adequate, despite some fall in the amplitude of tracking, if phase shift is slight, because a nearly stationary retinal image occurs twice per cycle. Mixtures of sinusoids of about ±10° amplitude are difficult to track without making many saccades. A less confusing wave form is a constant velocity or ramp stimulus, which changes velocity randomly at the middle and end points of the display (Bahill, Iandolo, & Troost, 1980). An even simpler alternative is to instruct subjects not to make catch-up saccades (Puckett & Steinman, 1969), and to reinforce any failure with immediate behavior-modifying feedback.

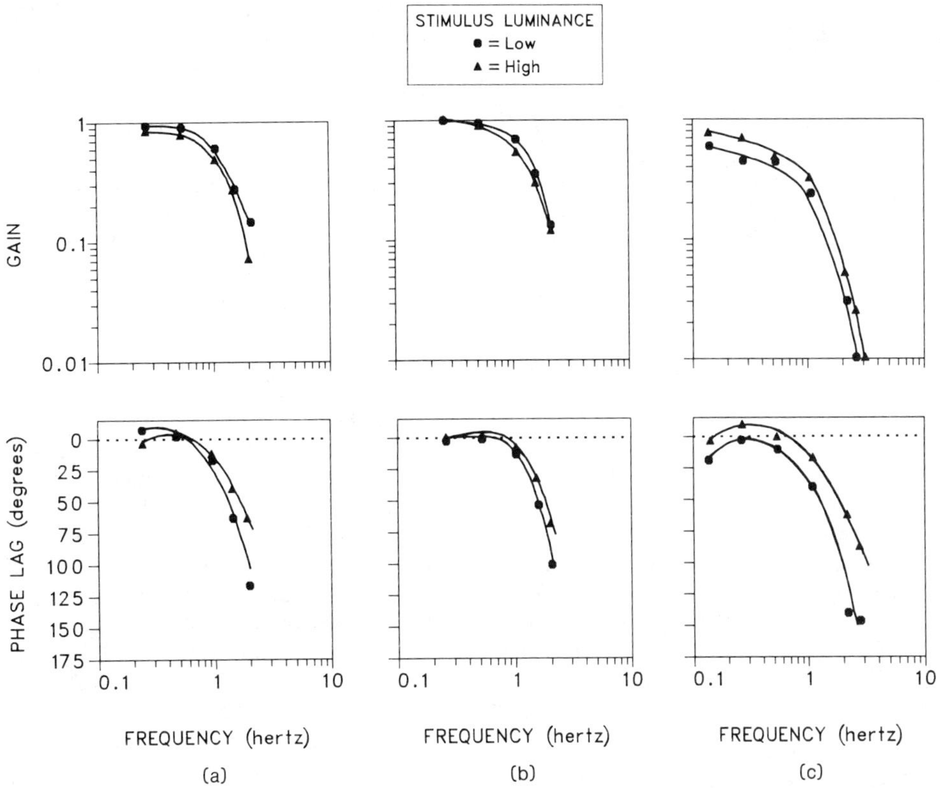

Figure 10.55. Tracking of predictable sine motion at high- and low-stimulus luminances. Gain is the amplitude ratio of smooth movement/stimulus motion. Phase lag is positive. Triangles show the higher, and circles the lower, of two stimulus luminances. Instructions and tasks vary as follows. (a) Smooth foveal pursuit without saccades, stimulus luminance 1.5 or 0.5 log above foveal threshold. (b) Smooth foveal pursuit with saccades, luminances as before. (c) Smooth eccentric pursuit with stimulus held 5–7° below foveal line of sight. Stimulus luminance 1.85 log above foveal threshold or 0.5 log above scotopic threshold. Point stimulus with a motion of 2.2° amplitude at 0.1 to 5 Hz. Two subjects studied, one subject's data shown. Contact lens data. Low luminance has little effect, except an increase in phase lag when stimulus is predictable. Eccentric tracking of predictable stimuli generally resembles foveal tracking. (From B. J. Winterson & R. M. Steinman, The effect of luminance on human smooth pursuit of perifoveal and foveal targets, *Vision Research, 18*. Copyright 1978 by Pergamon Press, Ltd. Reprinted with permission.)

3.3.1.3. Random Two-Dimensional Motion. St. Cyr and Fender (1969b) extended the servo-analytic approach to two-dimensional target motions, using sums of incommensurate sinusoids for the horizontal component. In a related experiment, one orthogonal component was a 1-Hz sinusoid, and the other was a low-pass filtered Gaussian noise with a different high-frequency cutoff in the region of 0.5–7 Hz (Goodwin & Fender, 1973). The field of view was 3°. Both studies show that the vertical component of eye movement may be slightly affected by the horizontal component of the stimulus or eye movement, or vice versa. For example, power may appear in vertical recordings at frequencies that occur only in the horizontal stimulus motion. It is not clear whether this cross-coupling occurs at sensory, motor, or mechanical levels (Fig. 10.57). If the cross-coupling of power were mainly horizontal to vertical (St. Cyr & Fender, 1969a), this would be consistent with a detailed model of orbital mechanics (Robinson, 1975b). Another type of cross-coupling is almost certainly neural; it involves an increase from 10 to 40 msec in the time delay for tracking a 1-Hz sinusoid, when an orthogonal noisy motion is present. The delay for tracking the noisy motion itself is naturally much longer (140–160 msec). Other indications of less than "ideal" performance are frequencies that are occasionally in the eye motion without being present in the stimulus. Also, conjugacy of the eyes is only approximate.

Promising results have been obtained when tracking mixtures of sinusoids that are close in frequency (St. Cyr & Fender, 1969a, 1969b). The overall data for the different frequency bands show the usual fall in gain for frequencies above 0.3–0.5 Hz, which is to be expected for unpredictable wave forms. But within each narrow band the contrary applies and the amplitude *rises* for the faster frequencies. This is biologically adaptive, in the sense that there is an active attempt to minimize the faster shifts of the retinal image that are most deleterious for clear vision, whereas slower drifts are tolerated. It proves useful to examine the time delay in tracking and the rate of information flow between stimulus and response. The former is obtained as the time shift that minimizes the root-mean-square difference between stimulus and eye motion; the latter comes from a power spectra analysis. The results imply a minimum delay of about 65 msec as the minimal transit time between photoreceptors and motoneurons, plus a variable delay that reflects the complexity of the motion. The variable delay is the time required for the retinal image to travel over sufficient receptors to produce adequate excitation for a smooth tracking movement. This variable time ought therefore to be influenced by manipulation

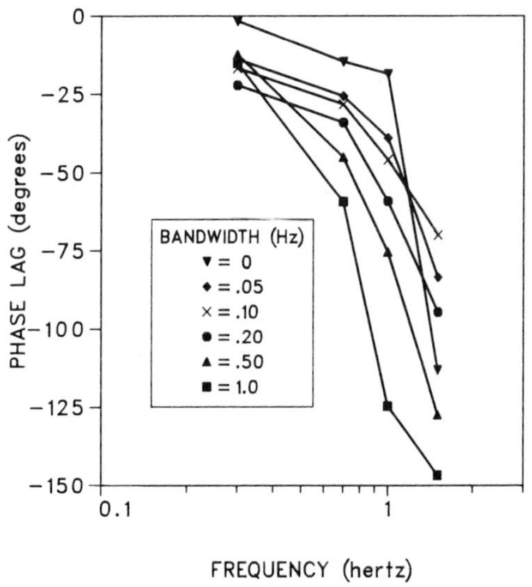

Figure 10.56. Phase lag of smooth pursuit eye movements and its dependence on stimulus predictability. The ordinate is the effective phase lag of eye tracking, obtained from the correlation coefficients between stimulus and response. The abscissa is the central frequency of the horizontal stimulus motion of several degrees of amplitude. Bandwidth in hertz is the parameter (condition 1 is a pure sinusoid). Means for 10 subjects. EOG data. At the lowest frequency the points cluster, indicating no variation of smooth pursuit with predictability. The two intermediate frequencies show increasing lag with increasing bandwidth. Data at the highest frequency are less orderly, possibly due to contributions of saccades. (From J. A. Michael & G. Melvill Jones, Dependence of visual tracking capability upon stimulus predictability, *Vision Research*, 6. Copyright 1966 by Pergamon Press, Ltd. Reprinted with permission.)

of stimulus luminance and contrast. Time delays were not affected (±15 msec), however, by wavelength changes in the range 470–630 nm (Goodwin, 1973). An additional suggestion is that the system can respond when only 60% certain as to the direction of the complexly moving stimulus.

These studies of Fender and colleagues deserve extension, partly because of the novel nature of the analyses, and partly because it is not completely certain whether the movements are pure smooth pursuit (which is likely, given the small amplitude and slow frequencies of stimulus motion) or a mixture of very small saccades and pursuit (so-called "mixed mode tracking"). The physics-based ideas about adaptive control should be compatible with behavioral approaches to the dependence of smooth pursuit on stimulus characteristics, internal models, and expectations.

3.3.1.4. One-Dimensional Motion Controlled by Subject

(a) HAND-DRIVEN STIMULUS. The quality of smooth pursuit is improved if the subject actively controls the moving stimulus (Steinbach, 1969; Steinbach & Held, 1968). Subjects track a target on their moving fingers (moving at about 1–2 Hz and 20° amplitude) with a median delay of 30 msec. If the subject controls the target with a lever, so that target and hand movements are linearly related, smooth pursuit is good, with only about 14 pursuit saccades in 10 sec. If hand and lever are moved passively, the quality of smooth tracking deteriorates, and there are more (about 25) pursuit saccades in the same period of time (Steinbach, 1969). Presumably, active tracking allows anticipation of rapid hand reversals, whereas passive movement does not. (Records are very similar to Fig. 10.83, Sec. 3.6.2.2.)

(b) STIMULUS MOTION SUPPLEMENTED BY DRIVE FROM EYE MOVEMENTS. Using electrical techniques, eye movement can be sensed (e.g., with a contact lens), amplified and inverted, processed to remove saccades, and added to the signal that drives the fixation target. This procedure supplements the fixation target's motion with a smooth motion that is larger than, and opposite to, that of the eye; it should therefore attract the eye toward the stimulus and thus set up smooth oscillatory eye movements. As already noted (Section 3.1.1.2), this maneuver fails when the subject is fixating an otherwise static target, even at an external gain as negative as −7 (Robinson, 1965), perhaps because the subject is attending to internal eye-velocity signals in an attempt to hold the eye still. When the fixation target is displaced horizontally at constant velocity (ramp motion), the subject has no choice but to "let go" and pursue; the eye and target immediately acquire an additional oscillatory motion, even at quite low (−1) external feedback gains (Robinson, 1965). At low negative gains the oscillations end quite suddenly, as if the subject is varying his oculomotor time delay and gain to prevent oscillation (Fleming et al., 1969; Vossius, 1972). Artificially introduced time delays are, however, very hard to cope with (Smith, Putz, & Molitor, 1969). Strategy may also explain why the frequency of oscillation varies somewhat with the gain. The smooth-pursuit resonant frequency (f) of 3.3 Hz is substantially higher than that of the saccadic system (2–2.5 Hz). If one uses the rule that the system delay is $1/2f$, these values are consistent with the observed latencies of about 150 msec for smooth pursuit and 200–250 msec for saccades (Fig. 10.29; Robinson, 1965).

(c) RETINALLY STABILIZED IMAGE MOTION WITH UNSTABILIZED MOTION OF FRAME OF REFERENCE. When the external gain is +1, the basic stimulus motion (e.g., a horizontal sinusoidal oscillation) is supplemented by a motion exactly equal to the eye movement, and so the basic stimulus motion is imposed directly on the retina, independently of eye movements. (This allows measurement of the "open-loop" responses of the smooth pursuit system: Robinson, 1965; Wyatt & Pola, 1983.) Given the considerable evidence that eye movements are usually adapted to the physical world, it is of interest that illusory perception of the open-loop stimulus motion does not reliably affect smooth pursuit. Two recent studies used a large frame (about 20° square), composed of two parallel horizontal strips oscillating horizontally by several degrees (e.g., 15°), to induce increased motion perception (Duncker illusion) of a small retinally stabilized stimulus moving in counterphase through ±1–2° relative to the retina. In the study with the apparently larger Duncker illusion, smooth pursuit was increased by about 25 (15–60)% (Wyatt & Pola, 1979); whereas in the study with the apparently modest illusion (in degrees amplitude), and better image stabilization technique, pursuit was *reduced* by a factor of 4–5 (Mack et al., 1982). See also Sections 3.3.4 and 3.3.5.

3.3.2. Instruction: Pursue the Briefly Active Small Target

3.3.2.1. Overpursuit and Underpursuit. The initial ocular responses to stimulus motion are complex and not extensively studied. Pursuit latency is usually regarded as being shorter than saccadic latency. In the typical response to the onset of a $10° \cdot sec^{-1}$ horizontal stimulus motion, smooth movement does little to reduce position error prior to the first saccade. Total smooth movement and the velocity of the smooth movement reach only about 0.4° and $6° \cdot sec^{-1}$, respectively, by the time of the first saccade. At the end of the saccade, position error is small (0.7°) and smooth velocity high (overpursuit: $12° \cdot sec^{-1}$), so that position error is rapidly reduced, and eye velocity then slackens to match the target (Robinson, 1965).

In view of the practical importance of mixed-mode tracking of briefly active targets, it is appropriate to consider target

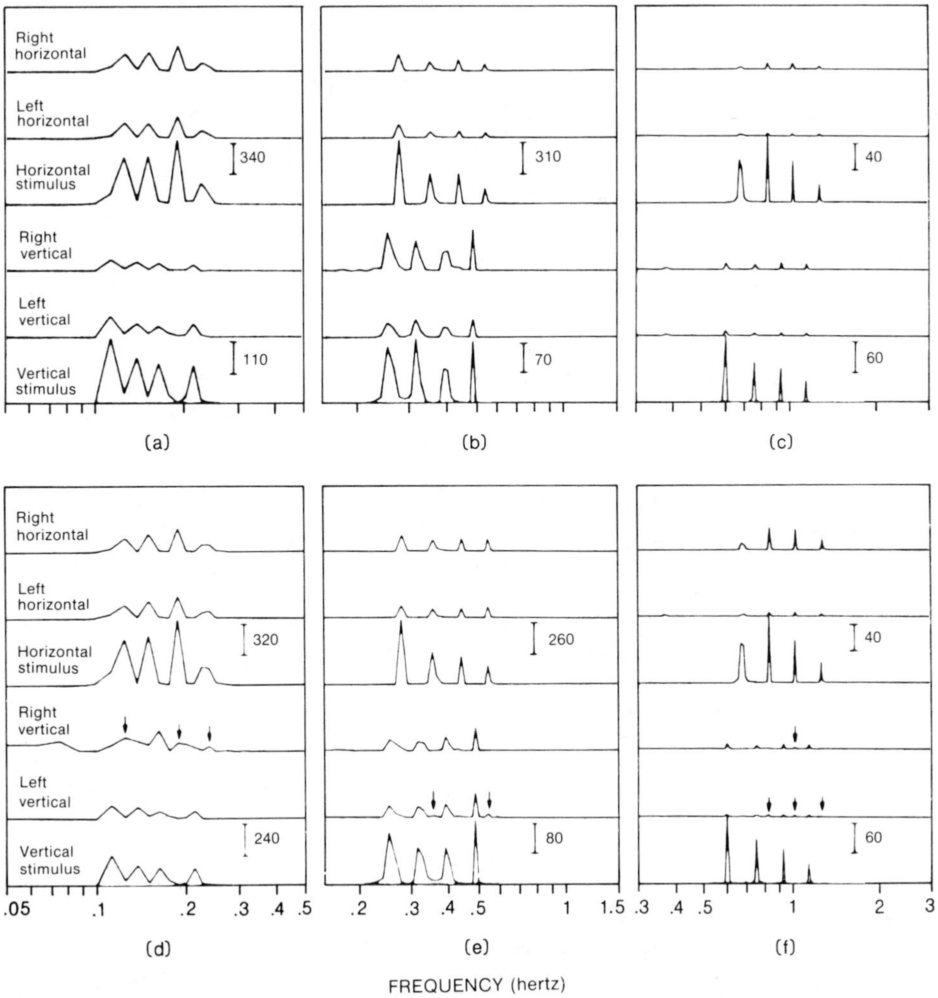

Figure 10.57. Cross talk between horizontal and vertical components of eye movements during tracking of small-amplitude stimulus motions. Power spectra of eye tracking when tracking a mixture of incommensurate sinusoidal motions—four horizontal and four vertical frequencies. From the top down: right and left horizontal tracking power (min arc squared as shown by calibration bars), horizontal stimulus power, right and left vertical tracking power, and vertical stimulus power. The three pairs of vertical panels correspond to frequencies ranging (a) from 0.11 to 0.23 Hz, (b) from 0.26 to 0.55 Hz, and (c) from 0.61 to 1.28 Hz. Upper and lower sets of panels correspond to two different subjects. Contact lens records. Arrows indicate horizontal to vertical cross talk. Thus vertical tracking can be affected by frequencies present only in the horizontal stimulus or horizontal eye motion. This could be due to mechanical cross-coupling between the horizontal and vertical recti in the orbit. (From G. J. St. Cyr & D. H. Fender, The interplay of drifts and flicks in binocular fixation, *Vision Research*, 9. Copyright 1969 by Pergamon Press, Ltd. Reprinted with permission.)

motions studied by Lightstone (1973) and the present author. See Figure 10.24 for typical records. The stimulus was randomly chosen on each trial from four varieties of left- or right-going stimuli: half cycles of triangular or sinusoidal motion, in which the stimulus moves from center in an unpredictable direction at an unpredictable time, and then back to center [Fig. 10.24 (c) and (d)]; the corresponding truncated wave forms where the stimulus steps back to center when the extremity of motion is reached [Fig. 10.24 (a) and (b)]. Stimulus amplitude was 15° and time to peak 1.24 sec. Tracking was monocular. Four aspects of the response are described: (1) underpursuit, including premature reversal, (2) catch-up saccades, (3) afterpursuit, and (4) an unusual saccade in response to the step back to center.

1. There is a tendency to underpursue, particularly in the sinusoidal cases, that is, to stay behind the stimulus on the swing away from center and ahead on the swing back. If it were not for the catch-up saccades, the retinal image would persistently remain somewhat nasal of foveal center. Smooth-pursuit latency is longer than reported by Robinson (means of 200 versus 125 msec), and thus somewhat nearer the subject's typical saccadic latency (263 versus 237 msec in Robinson's study). Smooth velocity increases to match target velocity, on the swing away from center, by the time of the second pursuit saccade. Thereafter eye velocity slackens and reverses prematurely before the stimulus reverses in 55% of half-sines and 5% of half-triangles. The open-headed arrows in Figure 10.24 show that reversal is premature for half-sines (mean −20 msec, range −360 to +180), and tardy for half-triangles (mean +135 msec, range −20 to +200).

2. Catch-up saccades generally oppose undertracking, which is particularly severe in the half-sine trials. During the

return swing to center catch-up saccades (about 1° amplitude) are mostly *away* from center as if preventing a premature return to center.

3. Afterpursuit is eye movement after the stimulus has stopped. Smooth pursuit stops on average about 1° too late when the target returns to center, being canceled about 150 msec (55–225) after the half-sine target stops and about 115 msec (0–205) after the half-triangle stops. In the case of the truncated wave forms, pursuit continues after the target steps back to center; this swings the eye 1.7° (0–4.2) back toward center for both the truncated sine and the truncated triangle.

4. The large return saccade to center position for truncated wave forms is accurate on average (error of 7 arc min), and thus overshoots the target on about half of trials; this is unusual because the subjects typically undershoot.

A simple explanation of Lightstone's data is that underpursuit and premature reversal, afterpursuit, and the large return saccade are driven by an internal model or strategy. Catch-up saccades correct position error between the eye and the target due to the internal model or strategy.

Underpursuit, with the fovea increasingly lagging the stimulus on its swing away from center, is probably a common mode of response. If saccades are forbidden, and the stimulus moves steadily away from center at an unpredictable speed (velocity 1–15° $\cdot$ sec^{-1} and 3° amplitude), velocity matching is poor and variable for even the slower targets (48–83% for 1–2° $\cdot$ sec^{-1} targets). Velocities were not much improved in these experiments when saccades were allowed, but saccades did keep position errors below 1° (Puckett & Steinman, 1969). In related experiments, subjects found it *easy* to track stimulus motion away from the origin at reduced eye velocity, although they did not necessarily track at the exact fractions of stimulus velocity specified by the experimenter. The subjects could not accurately match or smoothly exceed stimulus velocity at any velocity in the range 0.5–11° $\cdot$ sec^{-1}. The instruction to go "twice as fast" produced underpursuit and saccades (Fig. 10.58; Steinman, Skavenski, & Sansbury, 1969). The instruction to underpursue may directly attenuate the gain of a slightly inadequate retinal-slip servo, or the subject may attend to the output of the smooth-pursuit system in an effort to keep eye velocity low, or retinal-image slip may feed a model of target motion within a generally underreactive or lazy system.

3.3.2.2. ***Afterpursuit.*** Periods and amplitudes of afterpursuit longer than the 115–150-msec 1° value just given have been observed for a stimulus that appears and disappears suddenly while moving from left to right at about 10° $\cdot$ sec^{-1} (called overpursuit by Mitrani & Dimitrov, 1978). Afterpursuit lasts about 0.6 sec if the stimulus disappears *early* after 0.4-sec exposure, and only about 0.3 sec if the stimulus disappears after 2 sec or longer. The longer value for early disappearance is attributed to serial processing, retinally initiated cancellation of pursuit by the disappearance being delayed while the internal model of stimulus motion is formulated at the beginning of the trial. In related experiments with 9 and 19° $\cdot$ sec^{-1} targets, afterpursuit was about 4 and 7°, respectively, when the target disappeared 3–20° after the start. The afterpursuit was terminated by one or more saccades back toward the place of target disappearance, which were cumulatively about 2 or 3° too small for exact accuracy (Mitrani, Dimitrov, Yakimoff, & Mateef, 1979). Afterpursuit and saccadic error were relatively independent of where the target disappeared in the range 3–20° along its track, in contrast to the perceptual mislocation of target disappearance relative to a visible scale. These findings support the principle that oculomotor and perceptual processing need not be closely related.

3.3.2.3. ***Modified Ramp Motion.*** Catch-up saccades to a smooth target motion show a tendency to occur in oppositely directed, short latency, pairs (e.g., Hamann, 1977). The interval between the end of one catch-up saccade and the beginning of another can range from 0 to 200 msec, and the typical interval between the beginnings is 60 msec (Lightstone, 1973). Short-latency pairs are relatively frequent (10%), just after the corner

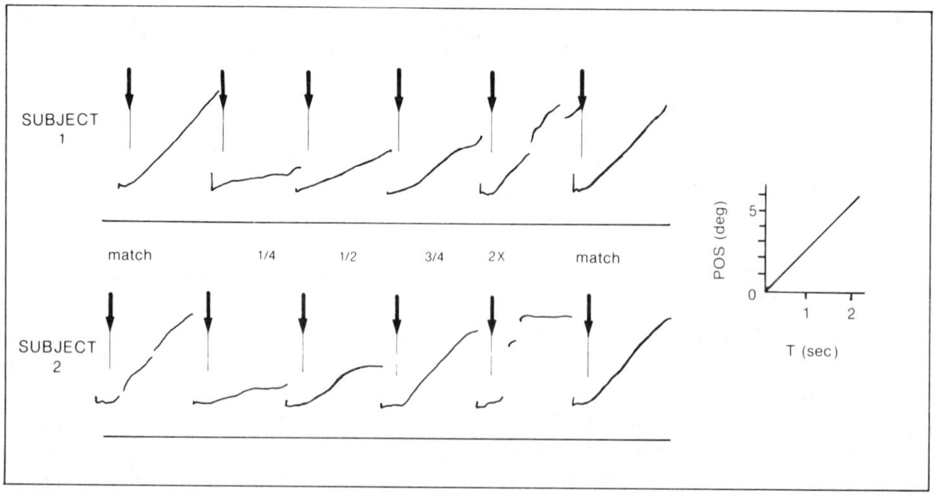

Figure 10.58. Effect of instructions on smooth tracking velocity. Eye position versus time for two different subjects. Records show consecutive trials as subjects attempt to first match stimulus velocity, then attempt to pursue at ¼, ½, ¾ and twice speed, and then finally once again attempt to match. Arrows mark time at which stimulus moves at 2.7° $\cdot$ sec^{-1} through 6° amplitude. Contact lens record. Voluntary underpursuit is easy, though subjects do not necessarily track at the requested speeds. Matching of stimulus velocity or overpursuit is more rarely observed in the range 0.5–11 deg $\cdot$ sec^{-1}. (From R. M. Steinman, A. A. Skavenski, & R. V. Sansbury, Voluntary control of smooth pursuit velocity, *Vision Research*, 9. Copyright 1969 by Pergamon Press, Ltd. Reprinted with permission.)

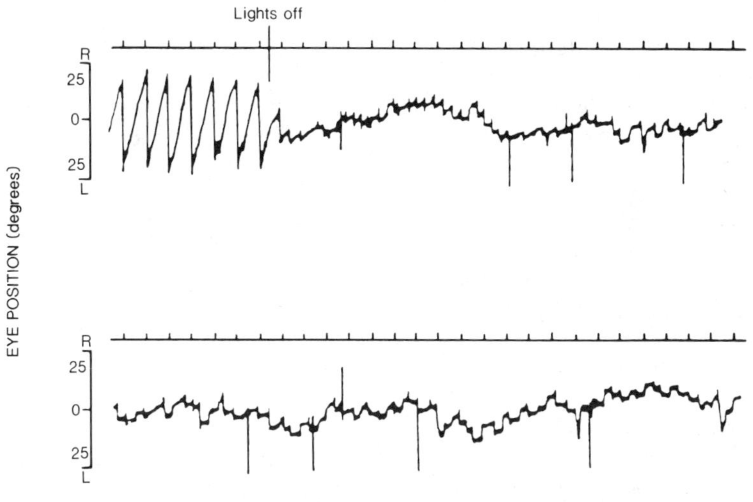

Figure 10.59. Pursuit afternystagmus. Horizontal eye movements during and after smoothly tracking a small target that moves in a sawtooth fashion on a dark background, through 50° in 1 sec. Time marks are 1-sec intervals. The records show about 48 sec of afternystagmus. If any long tails of velocity are excluded, then the typical time constant of decay is about 6 sec for five subjects. Bottom EOG record is continuation of top record. Small spikes at beginning of some saccades are artifacts. Slow component of afternystagmus is in the same direction as the original smooth pursuit. Smooth pursuit and optokinetic pursuit have features in common, including afterpursuit in the direction of the original smooth pursuit. (From R. Muratore & D. S. Zee, Pursuit after-nystagmus, *Vision Research, 19*. Copyright 1979 by Pergamon Press, Ltd. Reprinted with permission.)

of a triangular wave form. The following maneuvers failed to increase the frequency of short-latency pairs: (1) adding to the stimulus ramp ($11.5° \cdot sec^{-1}$) one cycle of a 2° 200-msec duration sinusoidal wobble at a random time, (2) adding a 2° 200-msec square pulse at random, or (3) arranging for catch-up saccades to increase the velocity of the ramp by 20-fold for 10 msec or to reduce velocity for 100 msec (Lightstone, 1973). Wyatt and Pola (1981) have stabilized the retinal image, but only during catch-up saccades, when tracking a $10° \cdot sec^{-1}$ ramp. The resultant stimulus is a ramp with added saccadic jumps. When the added jumps are equal or twice the amplitude of the initiating saccades, there is a tendency for pursuit to be slightly faster (20–40%) than when there are no added jumps frustrating saccadic tracking.

3.3.2.4. ***Stimulus Contrast.*** Tracking velocity is somewhat variable across subjects at about 75–95% of target velocity, and is largely independent of contrast when target velocity is predictable (0.5-sec exposure of a constant velocity 5-min arc stimulus of $5–40° \cdot sec^{-1}$ on a $12\text{-cd} \cdot m^{-2}$ background). Tracking is a little poorer (60–75%) when velocity is not predictable. Retinal errors of a few degrees accumulate for the faster targets (Haegerstrom-Portnoy & Brown, 1979). Presumably the eye can be driven by an internal model of stimulus motion or by retinal error, provided contrast is sufficiently high (>0.1) for the direction of the stimulus motion to be detected.

3.3.3. Instruction: Pursue, Look, Stare, or Watch the Repetitive Unidirectional Motion

3.3.3.1. ***Small Target.*** It is not easy to make behavioral distinctions between smooth and optokinetic pursuit (Section 2.1.1). Subjects pursued a $50° \cdot sec^{-1}$ small spot, which moved horizontally with a sawtooth motion (amplitude of 50°) against darkness or against a large striped background (Muratore & Zee, 1979). Tracking velocities exceeded $40° \cdot sec^{-1}$. After 2 min the stimulus was extinguished, and in 8 out of 11 subjects a nystagmus with slow phase in the original direction was observed to decay with time in the dark (Fig. 10.59). In direction and mean time constant (5.7 sec, range 4–10), pursuit afternystagmus (PAN) resembled the optokinetic afternystagmus (OKAN) generated by a large multicolored plaid drum which oscillated around the subject. The amplitude of the OKAN was larger, however, and the two time constants were often dissimilar in a given subject, so PAN and OKAN *may* be mediated by different mechanisms. PAN is presumably similar to the afterpursuit seen for shorter target exposures (Section 3.3.2.2).

A "velocity-only" stimulus is provided by an endless string of small identical bright dots, stepping through a fixed field aperture of 7° width (Williams & Fender, 1979). The 1-min stepping angle and 1–2-min inter-dot spacing eliminated position clues, and so saccadic tracking of a single dot was scarcely possible and was not observed. Target velocity was only $1.5–2.1° \cdot sec^{-1}$, but binocular smooth pursuit was poor for the three subjects; velocity matching of eyes and target was rarely observed. The eyes were rather independent, the nasally moving eye often exceeding stimulus velocity and the other lagging behind. This is somewhat against Hering's hypothesis that version movements are equal. A possible issue is whether the stimulus was adequate for steady convergence (Howard, 1981).

3.3.3.2. ***Extended Stimulus.*** A 1.25-cycle-per-degree high contrast grating is tracked, even when it moves as slowly as 5 $\text{min arc} \cdot sec^{-1}$ (Murphy et al., 1975). Such low tracking velocities are within the range of drift velocities during fixation, but smooth or optokinetic pursuit is recognized by being more prolonged and unidirectional.

In a standard procedure for evoking horizontal optokinetic nystagmus, subjects are seated and stationary inside the walls of a large cloth drum rotating about a vertical axis. In one example, the black drum bore 12 vertical 1° white stripes (Honrubia et al., 1968). When the subjects are instructed to "look" at a stripe, they do so with long stretches of uninterrupted smooth movement (50 ± 10° in amplitude), which are at about 0.9 of drum velocity over the range 10–60° · sec^{-1}. Oppositely directed fast phases are relatively few, and their frequency is close to the number of stripes passing per second. Some subjects adopt the "look" strategy in the absence of instructions, whereas others stare ahead. When subjects are staring spontaneously, or are instructed to stare, slow-phase smooth movement is more frequently interrupted. Velocity of smooth movement varies around 0.7 of stripe velocity, and amplitude is reduced by the more frequent fast phases (see Fig. 10.60). Nystagmus rate (the rate of fast phases) is always greater than 1 Hz.

Field size and edges provide complications when "stare" nystagmus is studied with more highly specified optical stimulators with restricted fields. Horizontal or vertical sinusoidal or square-wave gratings (10 cd · m^{-2} and 80% contrast) were presented to one eye, and slow-phase gain was studied as a function of target velocity, spatial frequency, and field size (Schor & Narayan, 1981). The schema in Figure 10.61 illustrates the combinations of spatial frequency and velocity that elicit "stare" nystagmus, defined by a nystagmus rate of at least 1 Hz, with a fairly high slow-phase gain of 0.7 or more.

Two of the five boundaries (i–v) of the spatiotemporal stimulus space for stare nystagmus in Figure 10.61 are independent of field size: (i) The lower horizontal border is at a spatial frequency of 0.5 cycles per degree. (ii) The diagonal border shows that the moving bars of the grating must generate a flicker rate of less than 24 Hz (±1 octave) to be effective. This is close to the perceptual flicker-fusion limit (30 Hz) for moving gratings in the same apparatus. The remaining boundaries (iii–v) depend on the configuration of the stimulus field. (iii) The upper horizontal spatial-frequency border may be determined by resolution of the purely physical interaction between the grating bars and the field edges. This limit is higher for smaller fields. The horizontal width of the spatiotemporal region is limited to about 3 octaves, but the left and right boundaries are influenced by field size. (iv) The left or low-velocity border is shifted to lower velocities for smaller fields. This may correlate with enhanced apparent motion of bars seen in smaller fields. (v) The right or high-velocity border apparently represents the tendency of the edges of the field, or of other introduced edges, to provide stable landmarks that oppose the moving grating as a stimulus for the optokinetic system.

Overall, the diagram implies that the higher spatial frequencies are less important for optokinetic nystagmus. Accordingly, it is not surprising that adding higher spatial harmonics (as in a square-wave grating) or deleting them (as in optical blurring) has little effect. Figure 10.61 is for the "stare" or >1 Hz form of optokinetic nystagmus. Whether the "stare" and "look" forms of optokinetic nystagmus are separate mechanisms, involving involuntary or subcortical routes and voluntary or cortical routes, respectively, is not yet settled (Robinson, 1976; Ter Braak, 1962; Yee, Baloh, & Honrubia, 1981). My suggestion is that the subject attends to eye velocity under the "stare" instruction, in an attempt to hold the eye still against reflex drives, and attends to the spatial position of the stripes under the "look" instruction in order to pursue well. If so, normal "stare" and "look" nystagmus *both* depend on routes from the fovea via visual cortex and from the whole retina via the accessory optic pathways (Yee et al., 1981).

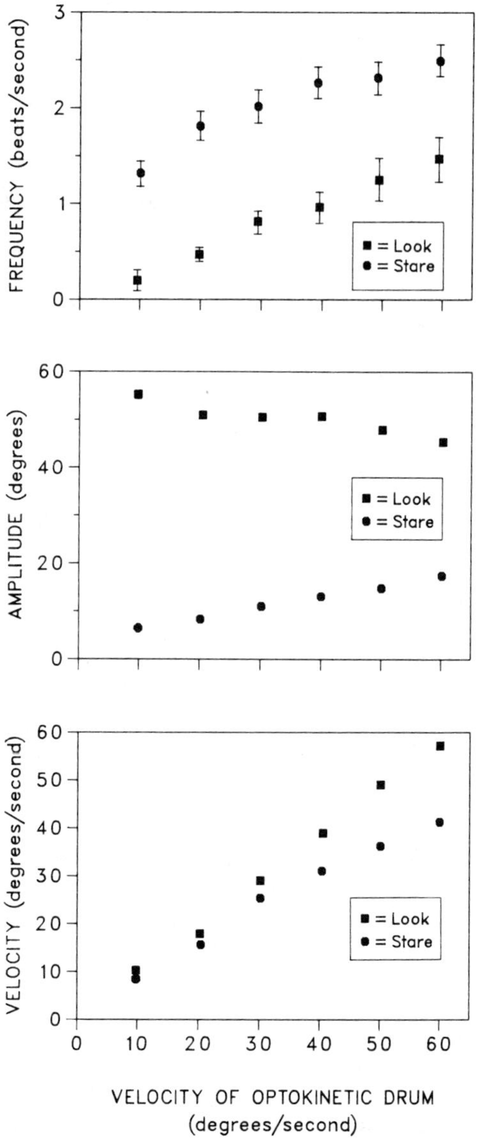

Figure 10.60. Optokinetic nystagmus. Subjects sat within the walls of a large drum, with twelve 1° stripes on its black walls, and either stared ahead or looked at a passing stripe. The three panels show frequency of the nystagmus (as fast phases per second), mean amplitude of smooth movement between fast saccades, and velocity of smooth movement as a function of drum angular velocity. Means based on around 20 (14–33) subjects. Bars at left are standard deviations. EOG data. In comparison with "look" nystagmus, "stare" nystagmus is of small amplitude, comparatively low velocity, and more frequently interrupted by fast saccades. "Look" nystagmus is often regarded as being more voluntary and "stare" nystagmus as more reflex, but this is not certain. (From V. Honrubia, W. L. Downey, D. P. Mitchell, & P. H. Ward. Experimental studies on optokinetic nystagmus. II. Normal humans, *Acta Otolaryngologica*, 1968, 65. Reprinted with permission.)

The fast phases of optokinetic nystagmus exhibit remarkable rhythmic properties (Cheng & Outerbridge, 1974). When the velocity of the optokinetic stimulus is fairly high (40–50° · sec^{-1}), the histogram of time intervals between fast phases is monomodal and symmetrical with a basic mode near 0.3 sec. At progressively lower velocities the histogram becomes asymmetric and may finally change to a multimodal form with modes at multiples of the basic mode. One question raised by these

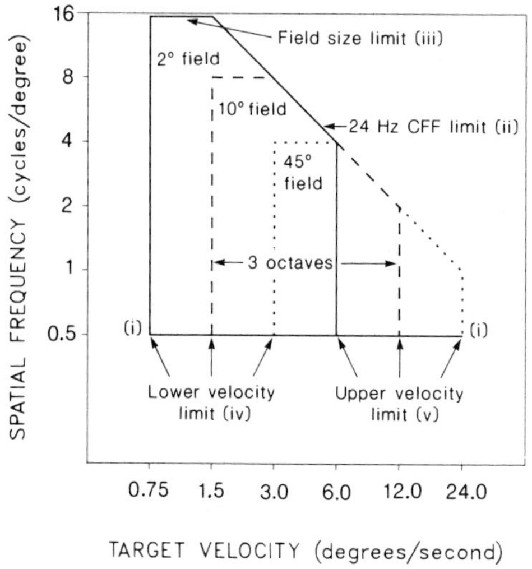

Figure 10.61. Suggested spatiotemporal stimulus space for the "stare" form of optokinetic nystagmus. Three subjects examined a horizontal drifting sine-wave grating on an oscilloscope. Spatial frequency of the drifting sine-wave grating is the ordinate and velocity of the drifting bars is the abscissa. The roughly triangular space of 3 octave width changes with experimental parameters, but in all cases it represents those combinations of bar size and bar velocity that elicit a nystagmus rate of >1 Hz, and a slow phase velocity at 0.7 or more of bar velocity. Using these criteria the lower (i) and diagonal boundaries (ii) are fixed, the latter being close to the flicker limit (= spatial frequency × velocity). The upper (iii) and left (iv) boundaries are set by field size, and the right boundary (v) by the edges of the field. 10 cd·m^{-2} field at 80% contrast. Monocular viewing and limbus or pupil monitor. According to the authors, a 1-Hz nystagmus represents an involuntary as distinct from a voluntary mechanism. The present speculation is that "stare" or >1 Hz nystagmus is reflex drive checked by attention to eye position or velocity, whereas "look" nystagmus *could* be the same drive without such constraint. (From C. Schor & V. Narayan, The influence of field size upon the spatial frequency response of optokinetic nystagmus, *Vision Research, 21*. Copyright 1981 by Pergamon Press, Ltd. Reprinted with permission.)

observations is whether saccadic tracking of stepping targets may also have some sort of periodic basis (Section 3.7). (The interaction of fast and slow phases of optokinetic nystagmus is briefly treated in the part of Section 3.1.1.3 that deals with Fig. 10.52.)

3.3.3.3. Retinally Stabilized Motion. The problems presented by the edges of the display can be eliminated by stabilizing the display on the retina, so that the edges cannot act as landmarks that will stabilize the eye. Subjects may be told to "watch" the stabilized stimulus, but must also be under some restraint to keep their gaze within the limits of the apparatus. Under normal closed-loop viewing conditions, movements of the pattern evoke compensatory eye movements and leave very little retinal slip. Under stabilized open-loop conditions, it is to be expected that small retinal image motions will drive large eye movements, the more so the higher the gain of the oculomotor system. Stabilized image experiments on several subjects, using the search-coil technique and monocular viewing of a high-contrast square-wave grating (7.5 cycles per degree) or a fine random-dot pattern (0.4° dots), reveal very high gain [Fig. 10.62(a); Dubois & Collewijn, 1979]. This is contrary to older work with spatially coarser stimuli (Hood, 1975). Open-loop gains range from 1 to nearly 100, being highest at the lowest retinal image velocities (0.04° · sec^{-1}). The high gain is largely due to the foveal region, because there is little improvement in gain for fields of more than 5–6° subtense. Similarly, blocking out an 8° foveal area in a 15° stimulus lowers gain, unless the subject switches his attention to the moving peripheral part of the stimulus [Fig. 10.62(b)]. Stimulus motion away from the fovea elicits a more powerful tracking response than stimulus motion toward the fovea, for all directions and subjects tested. This may be biologically adaptive. The preference for centrifugal pursuit is equivalent to the statement that a right-going response is best elicited by a right-going stimulus in the right visual hemifields. This may imply that the left cerebral hemisphere is involved in rightward pursuit, but the clinical evidence from hemispherectomy patients is less straightforward (Troost, Daroff, Weber, & Dell'Osso, 1972). An intriguing aspect of Dubois and Collewijn's experiments is that the observed nystagmus rate of >1 Hz indicates involuntary nystagmus by the criterion of Schor and Narayan (1981) and others; nevertheless the subject is able to voluntarily attend to different parts of the visual field. One may wonder if optokinetic slow phase differs in any substantial way in normal subjects from voluntary smooth pursuit of an extended stimulus.

An open-loop analysis of optokinetic tracking is also possible by stimulating the retina of a paralyzed eye and observing the movement of the other normal eye (Leigh, Newman, Zee, & Miller, 1982).

3.3.3.4. Binocular Aspects. In lateral-eyed animals, monocular tracking of targets moving nasally is stronger than for targets moving temporally. This asymmetry in the optokinetic response is not usually present in frontal-eyed animals, where the nasal response is driven by lower levels, while the equal or nearly equal temporal response depends on a new route via visual cortex (e.g., Trevarthen, 1968; Van Hof-Van Duin, 1975). A similar asymmetry of optokinetic nystagmus, reported for patients with disorders of binocular vision, provides support for a cerebral component in human optokinetic nystagmus (Schor & Levi, 1980). Intriguing evidence for a role of cortex is obtained when opposite optokinetic stimuli are presented separately to the two eyes. Subjectively, the stimuli show binocular rivalry, whereas objectively the nystagmus remains conjugate, but reverses its direction from time to time according to which eye is currently dominant in perceiving the stimulus (Enoksson, 1963; Fox, Todd, & Bettinger, 1975).

Optokinetic pursuit (defined by a nystagmus rate of >1 Hz) is also produced by laterally moving, vertical stereoscopic contours (Fox, Lehmkuhle, & Leguire, 1978). The stimuli are random patterns of dots, red for one eye and green for the other, that individually contain no contours; the contours are perceptual. When the patterns are adjusted to eliminate stereoscopic contours (zero disparity, see Section 3.4), there is no tracking. When the stereoscopic contours are present, tracking is almost normal, except that the slow phases are slightly longer, and the nystagmus rate slightly lower, than for real contours. For similar results, involving strobed patterns, see Section 3.6.2.2. Such data scarcely encourage much distinction between optokinetic and voluntary pursuit of extended stimuli.

3.3.4. Instruction: Pursue the Small Target even if Its Motion Is Misperceived. Smooth pursuit is determined by physical position when this is in conflict with perception. A number of examples can be offered. A small stimulus, moving at 3 min arc · sec^{-1}, is well tracked, even though it does not appear to move, the threshold for perception of movement in the absence of landmarks being 9 min arc · sec^{-1} (Mack et al., 1979). A target moving at 1° · sec^{-1} is tracked in the same way, whether it is seen veridically in a stationary surrounding frame or appears to move in reverse because of frame motion in the target direction

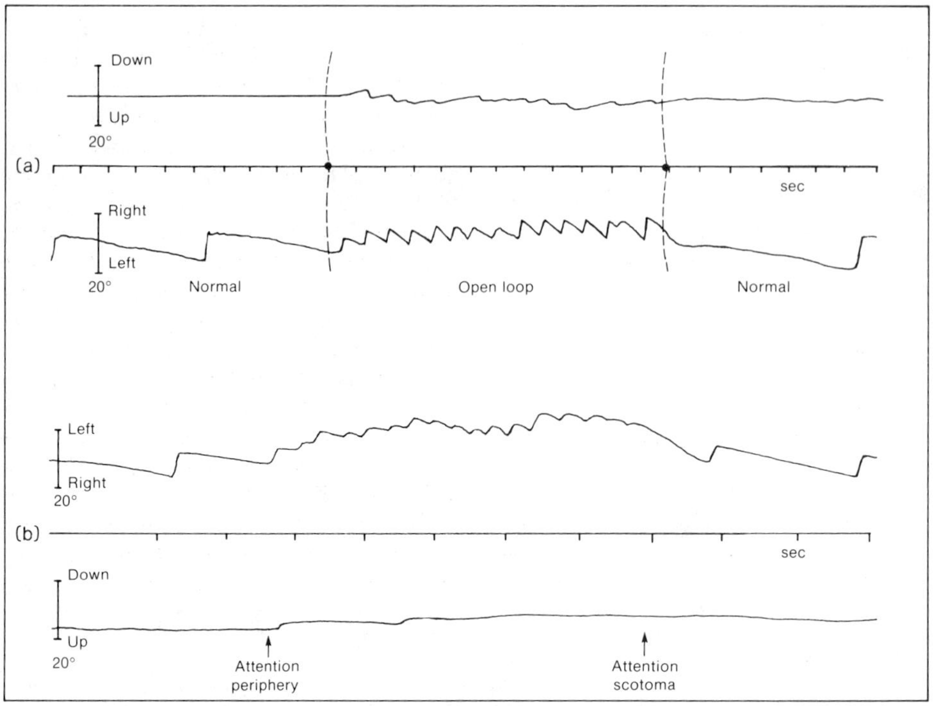

Figure 10.62. Effect of attention on optokinetic nystagmus to normal or stabilized patterns. Contact lens records. (a) Circular aperture (diameter 10°), viewed normally or stabilized on retina, within which is a random dot pattern moving to left at 1.6° · sec^{-1}. From above down, vertical eye position as a control, time marks in seconds, and horizontal position of one eye. Under normal viewing, smooth optokinetic motion is relatively slow and resetting fast phases are infrequent. When pattern is stabilized on the retina against eye movements (open loop) smooth velocity is much faster and fast phases more frequent. (b) Stabilized pattern of 2 cycles per degree high-contrast square waves, moving at 1.6° · sec^{-1} to the right within the stabilized aperture, the central 4° of the aperture being featureless (a "scotoma"). Attention to pattern produces vigorous though variable nystagmus, whereas attention to the scotoma produces a slower response. (From M. F. W. Dubois & H. Collewijn, Optokinetic reactions in man elicited by localized retinal motion stimuli, *Vision Research, 19*. Copyright 1979 by Pergamon Press, Ltd. Reprinted with permission.)

at 2° · sec^{-1}. This also points to the role of attention, because the frame is not tracked. See also Section 3.3.1.4.

The Pulfrich illusion of movement in depth arises from a perceptual latency difference when the stimulus is of unequal brightness in the two eyes. When the eyes fixate a steady point, another sideways-moving point appears to swing in depth if it is brighter to one eye, but when the moving stimulus is tracked, contact lens measurements show only conjugate pursuit movements without vergence, and the illusion disappears (Rogers et al., 1974).

3.3.5. Instruction: Pursue the Perception. Subjects pursue a variety of "stimuli" that, in a sense, are present only perceptually (Steinbach, 1976). If a diamond-shaped card is moved to and fro, with one corner hidden behind a horizontal edge, one has a powerful impression of where the point is, and appropriate pursuit movements occur. Also, a pair of lights on the diameter of a rolling wheel in the dark convey a strong impression of the path of the wheel's hub, which can be pursued. These responses do not prove that perception drives pursuit, because the body of the moving card may be tracked by the peripheral retina, and one can conjecture that the resultant of separately tracking the cycloid motions of the two lights might be equivalent to tracking the hub. More convincing is tracking an object moved horizontally to and fro behind a vertical slit. The percept is of a horizontally moving figure and it is the perceived figure that is tracked, not the parts visible within the fixed slit. A more recent study with a higher resolution technique shows that smooth pursuit is poor in this case (Mack et al., 1982), being only a fraction (about 25%) of the amplitude required to track the full figure, and badly interrupted by frequent saccades.

3.3.6. Instruction: Pursue One of Two Targets Prior to Looking at the Other. Tracking a smoothly moving target does not preclude attention to other targets. One experiment included a task that required pursuit of the target and then a saccade back to a briefly marked point on the target's track. Subjects made return saccades with zero mean error (1.5° SD) when they fixated a steady point (briefly marked with a 50-msec duration circle) prior to tracking a single outward swing of the point. The error in return to the mark was 1°, however, when the subjects started by pursuing four swings of the point for 6 sec, before it was briefly marked and they pursued its last swing (J. M. Miller, 1980). The amplitudes of eye motion would appear to have ranged around 8° in this experiment. Perhaps the slightly poorer performance in the four-swings case is due to tracking an internal model, and not critically attending to the spatial position of the stimulus. Another experiment requires that the subject track a horizontally oscillating target for a few 6° swings, and saccade at an appropriate moment to a second target, which also swings in phase with the first, but at an angle to the horizontal (Holtzman et al., 1978). The path of the second target is misperceived, because the subject is aware of its retinal path but makes no allowance for eye movement. On some trials, the instrumentation stabilized the image of target two on the fovea immediately after the required saccade. But the subject did not notice this and continued to track along what would otherwise have been the *physical* path of target two, even reversing at approximately the appropriate time [Fig. 10.63(a)]. This is consistent with the principle that the eye usually tracks realities, or models of reality, even under illusory conditions. However, eye movements, like perceptions, may not always have access to all the necessary information. In the above experiment, if the two targets were out of phase, in the sense that their horizontal components of motion were opposite, pursuit after the saccade shifted to match the *perceived* path of target two [Fig. 10.63(b)].

3.3.7. Instruction: Pursue the Acoustic Tone. Sinusoidal or ramp motion of a loudspeaker in the dark normally evokes saccadic pursuit, but a small amount of smooth pursuit occurs when the velocity is low ($5° \cdot sec^{-1}$) and the motion predictable and repeated (Zambarbieri, Schmid, Prablanc, & Magenes, 1981).

3.4. Eye Movements to Approaching or Receding Targets

3.4.1. Instruction: Track the Object Seen Binocularly

3.4.1.1. Object Path. If a small distant object is binocularly fixated, the retinal images fall in the centers of the two foveas. If the object is not tracked as it approaches, the two retinal images in general move away from the foveal centers at different velocities and become blurred and loom larger (Regan & Beverley, 1978). Also, the object's projection changes and its color values may alter somewhat, depending on the optical characteristics of the intervening atmosphere (imposed by dust, water vapor, etc.). These cues are potential inputs to the neural tracking mechanisms for objects moving in depth, though only disparate retinal-image motion and blurring have been examined to any extent.

The nature and consequences of the various combinations of binocular retinal image velocities depend on the object's path relative to the subject. As Figure 10.64 shows, irrespective of the orientations of the eyes, there are two major classes of stimulus conditions: (1) if the object is aimed to hit the head between the eyes the two retinal images move oppositely, and tracking in general requires opposite and unequal movements of the eyes; (2) if the object's course is set to pass the head, the retinal images both move in the same direction, at unequal speeds, and tracking requires that the two eyes move in the same direction at different speeds through unequal angles; (3) in the intermediate case, if an object is on a grazing collision course with the head, or is aimed at one eye, the retinal image in the eye at risk remains fairly stationary, so tracking ideally requires that this eye move very little once the object is foveated. More or less corresponding to the extreme viewing conditions (1) and (2) are two classes of eye movement: slow disjunctive eye movements in which the eyes move oppositely and perhaps unequally, and slow (smooth pursuit) or fast (saccadic) conjugate movements in which the eyes move in the same direction, though perhaps unequally. In viewing conditions (1) and (3), disjunctive movements may be combined with saccades from which they are easily distinguished by their longer time courses. Note that the eyes may converge or diverge during either disjunctive or conjugate movements. To take one of the less obvious possibilities, a single "asymmetric" saccade (i.e., one unequal in the left and right eyes) provides one means of changing both the depth and direction of binocular fixation, whereas a second, oppositely directed, asymmetric saccade leaves only a depth change if the successive changes in direction balance.

3.4.1.2. Hering Vergence and Version, Disparity. The terms *vergence* and *version* are variably used in the literature, either as synonyms of disjunctive and conjugate movement (as in accommodative vergence which involves asymmetric binocular movements) or, in a special sense, as ideal components into which a movement can be resolved. Because it is difficult to avoid using these words as synonyms, I shall define the terms "Hering vergence" (calculated from the difference in the angular position of the two eyes) to mean the component that is equal and opposite in the two eyes, and "Hering version" (calculated from the arithmetic mean of the positions of the two eyes) to mean the component that is equal and similarly directed in the two eyes. The acknowledgment to Hering disregards the prior discoveries of Wells in 1792 (Ono, 1980), but is consistent with current usage.

Let us return to the stimulus conditions; at a given instant the distances of the two retinal images from the fovea are determined by object position and eye position. The angular discrepancy between the retinal-image positions in the two eyes is called the *disparity*. Disparity is an important cue for stereopsis, and is also hallowed as a cue for disjunctive movements, (e.g., Alpern, 1969). We restrict our attention from now on to the horizontal plane of regard; then Figure 10.65(a), on page 10-66, shows the ideal horizontal horopter or Vieth-Müller circle. This is a circle through the optical nodal points, and is the loci of objects that have zero disparity when the eyes fixate any point A on the circle. The Vieth-Müller circles are also the loci of points with constant Hering vergence, and the Hillebrand hyperbolas are the loci of points of constant Hering version [Fig. 10.65(b)]. Hering's hypothesis can be usefully stated as three propositions (Ono, 1980, 1983): (1) version and vergence are as defined above; (2) version and vergence actually exist, at some neural or innervational level at least; (3) vergence and version combine additively with due regard for sign. Unequal vestibulo-ocular compensation (Steinman & Collewijn, 1980), unequal smooth pursuit (Williams & Fender, 1979), and unequal saccades (Kenyon, Ciuffreda, & Stark, 1980; Ono, Nakamizo, & Steinbach, 1978) may or may not be compatible with Hering's hypothesis, but given recent evidence of nonadditive combination it seems that Hering's hypothesis only has merit as a useful approximation (e.g., Miller, Ono, & Steinbach, 1980; Ono & Nakamizo, 1978; Ono et al., 1978).

3.4.1.3. Phoria, Tropia, Amblyopia. Tracking in depth is complicated by conspicuous differences between subjects. The angle of vergence is rarely zero when at rest, even when accommodation and disparity cues are defeated by placing dissimilar unfocusable objects before the eyes (e.g., as in the clinical Maddox rod test or its variants). If the angle is small enough to be eliminated by compensatory movements when normal visual cues are present, the angle is called *phoria*, and is present in most subjects; if the control mechanisms are inadequate, the angle is called *tropia*, and *strabismus* is said to be present (see also Section 3.1.1.3). Breakdown of compensation with double vision or *diplopia* occurs in many subjects when they are exhausted or intoxicated. Strabismus in early childhood leads to the suppression of vision or *amblyopia* in the deviated eye. *Esophoria* and *esotropia* refer to convergent tendencies, and *exophoria* and *exotropia* to divergent ones (Burian & von Noorden, 1974).

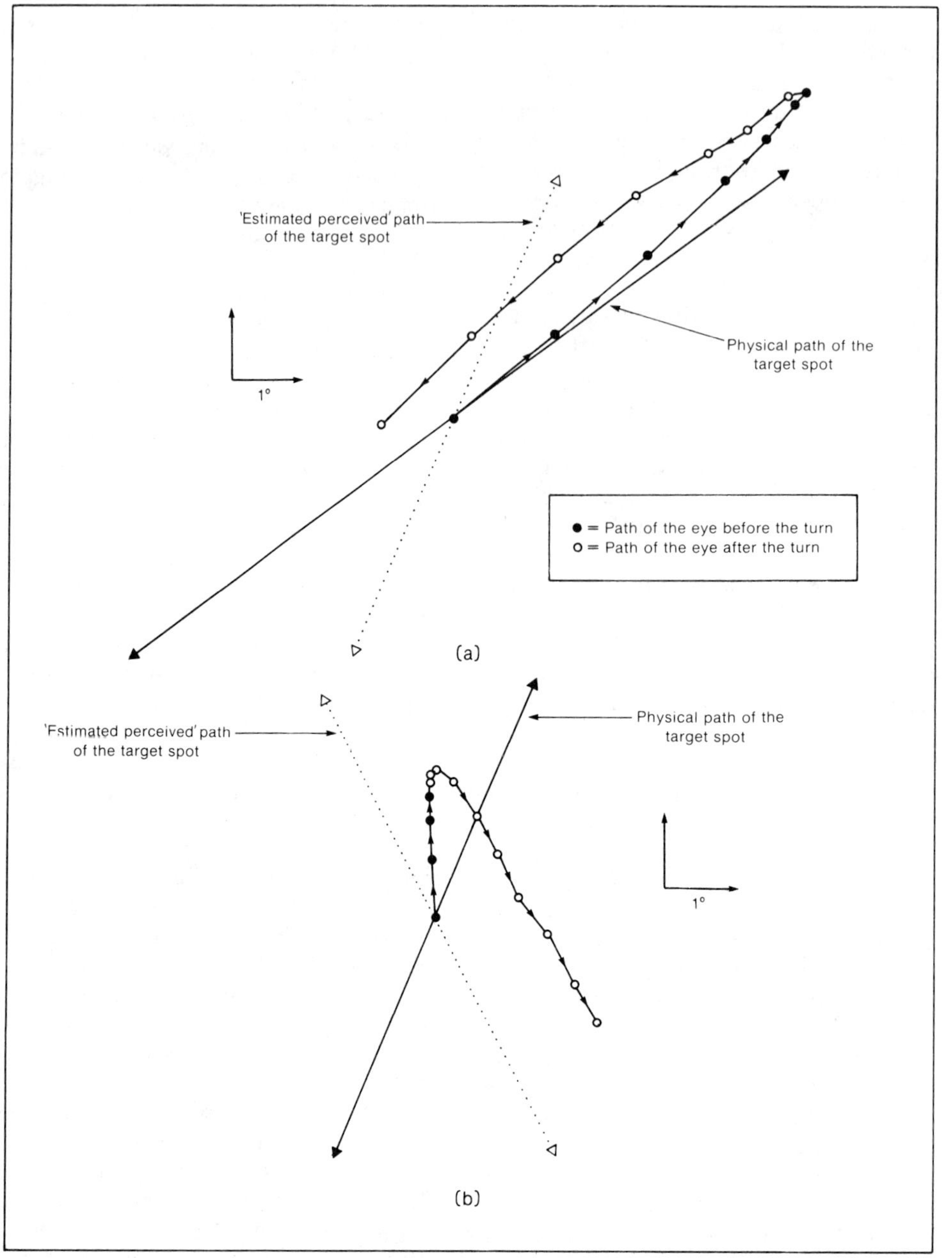

Figure 10.63. Switch of smooth pursuit from one smoothly moving target to another. The reference axes show the vertical and horizontal meridians of the field of view. The subject tracks a horizontally oscillating target (not shown) for a few cycles while observing target 2, which is moving obliquely; oblique direction changes each trial. On control trials the subject makes a saccade to target 2 and tracks it; at the same time target 1 is turned off. The oblique lines show the physical and perceived paths of target 2. Purkinje image eye monitor. (a) Situation when horizontal component of target 2 is in phase (in the same direction) with target 1. On a test trial, target 2 is stabilized on the fovea after the saccade, yet tracking continues along what would have been the physical path of target 2, and even reverses appropriately. (b) Situation when the horizontal component of target 2 is opposite to target 1. On a test trial tracking eventually follows the perceived path of target 2. The upper data imply that a model of target 2 motion is established while tracking target 1, and provides the drive for tracking in the stabilized image case when optical feedback of target 2 motion is not available. The lower data are consistent with the necessary information (eye position or velocity) not being available in all circumstances. (From J. D. Holtzman, H. A. Sedgwick, & L. Festinger, Interaction of perceptually monitored and unmonitored efferent commands for smooth pursuit eye movements, *Vision Research, 18*. Copyright 1978 by Pergamon Press, Ltd. Reprinted with permission.)

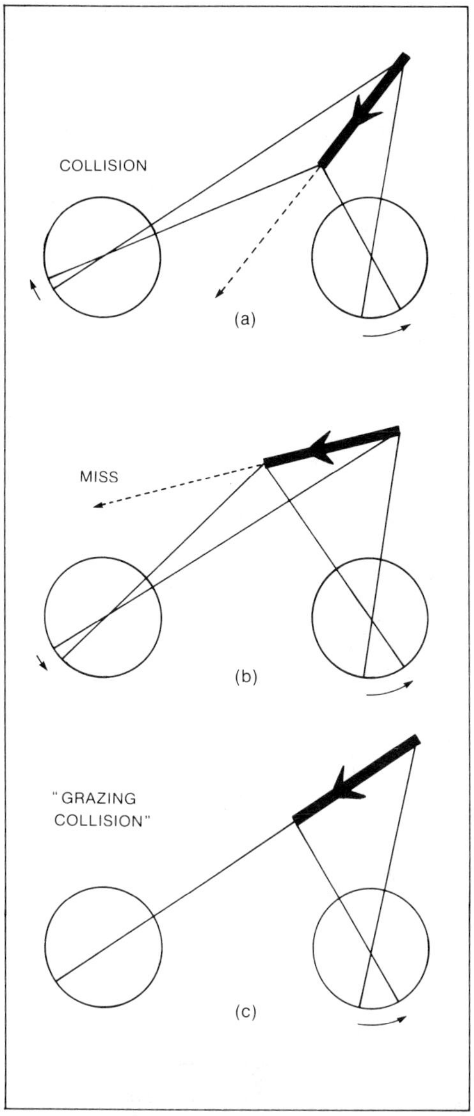

Figure 10.64. Binocular retinal image motion for three classes of object motion. These motions are independent of the point of binocular fixation and so the eyes are drawn simply, without showing the corneas or foveas. (a) Oppositely moving retinal images occur when object approaches or recedes along a collision course aimed between the two eyes. (b) Images move in same direction if trajectory will clear the head. The more equal the speeds, the less threatening the object. (c) One image is relatively stationary if the trajectory grazes the head or is aimed at one eye. The three cases generally elicit different eye and body movements. The figure illustrates only one plane of regard, but the same principle applies to other plane through the centers of eyes.

Disparity-driven vergence is lost in strabismus and amblyopia (Kenyon et al., 1981).

3.4.1.4. ***Head Rotation.*** Tracking of lights moving in depth is more complicated if the head oscillates about the yaw axis, because the centers of rotation of the head and eyes are separated. Figure 10.66 (page 10-67) shows a single eye before and after rotation. A vestibulo-ocular compensation (slow phase) of $-F°$ is required if the head rotates $F°$ while viewing a distant object, and increasingly larger responses are required as the object approaches. Increased vestibulo-ocular gains of about 1.12 have been observed for subjects whose heads are oscillated at high velocities (up to $300° \cdot \sec^{-1}$) while they endeavor to visualize a real or imagined target at 80 cm distance (Pulaski et al., 1981). See also Post and Leibowitz (1982). The effect of head roll on tracking in depth is discussed in Section 3.5.1; otherwise this discussion assumes a relatively static head.

3.4.1.5. ***Real Objects.*** A small light can be made to step in depth and direction in darkness, by extinguishing a near light and simultaneously lighting a far one, or vice versa. Authors may report the left or right eye positions, or Hering version and Hering vergence.

If the near and far objects are aligned on the axis of the right eye, and the initial fixation is "at near," the direction of the far target is misperceived in accordance with Hering's principles of visual direction (Ono & Nakamizo, 1977). The mechanism for perception does not concern us here, but if the reader has normal binocular vision, and aligns the two forefingers carefully on the right eye, the direction of the far finger will be seen to change to its correct location on switching fixation from the near to the far finger. The eye movements conform, however, to the principle that eye movements are generally matched to the physical positions of objects, and in this particular case they also conform to Hering's hypothesis about vergence and version. The classic response (Fig. 10.67, page 10-67) shows initial, approximately equal and opposite, divergence that shifts the point of fixation from N to a, a symmetrical version saccade ab that captures the direction of the target, and a final, approximately equal and opposite divergence from b to F. Actually, in this experiment the drive to accommodative vergence is ambiguous, because the near stimulus occludes the right eye's view of the far stimulus, and so the apparent far target is optically near to the right eye and far from the left eye. The approximation to Hering's law becomes *worse* when the two lights are given a slight vertical separation so that both eyes can view the near and far targets in a more natural manner (Ono & Nakamizo, 1978). In fact, the classic response is not usual for viewing conditions in general; more commonly, disjunctive and conjugate movements are *asymmetric* in the two eyes.

Viewing conditions similar to those in Figure 10.67 have been widely interpreted as providing reasonable support for the spirit of Hering's hypothesis (e.g., Hering, 1868/1977; Riggs & Niehl, 1960; Westheimer & Mitchell, 1956; Yarbus, 1967). Some variation is acknowledged for the relative latencies of the vergence and saccadic movements in different subjects, as well as some variation in the relative contribution of the two eyes to disjunctive movement and saccades (e.g., Kenyon et al., 1980; Ono et al., 1978). However, it is better to emphasize that the classical picture is restricted to target trajectories approaching or receding from one eye (Ono & Tam, 1981), particularly in situations where focusing and thus accommodative vergence play a minor role (Ono & Nakamizo, 1978). If a target approaches or recedes on a collision course aimed between the eyes (the 0 and 3° condition of Ono & Tam, 1981), it is tracked either by unequal slow disjunctive movements, or by oppositely directed pairs of asymmetric saccades that produce little or no net version. If the target trajectory will graze the head (the authors' 9° condition), tracking involves successive similarly directed saccades, as well as slower movements. The biological advantages of these different responses are not obvious.

As just discussed, stepping a binocularly viewed target along the axis of one eye yields approximately symmetrical disjunctive and saccadic movements in the two eyes of normal subjects. When strabismic subjects and some amblyopes are tested in this manner, tracking is like that of normal subjects responding with the off-axis eye covered (Section 3.4.2). That is, monocular

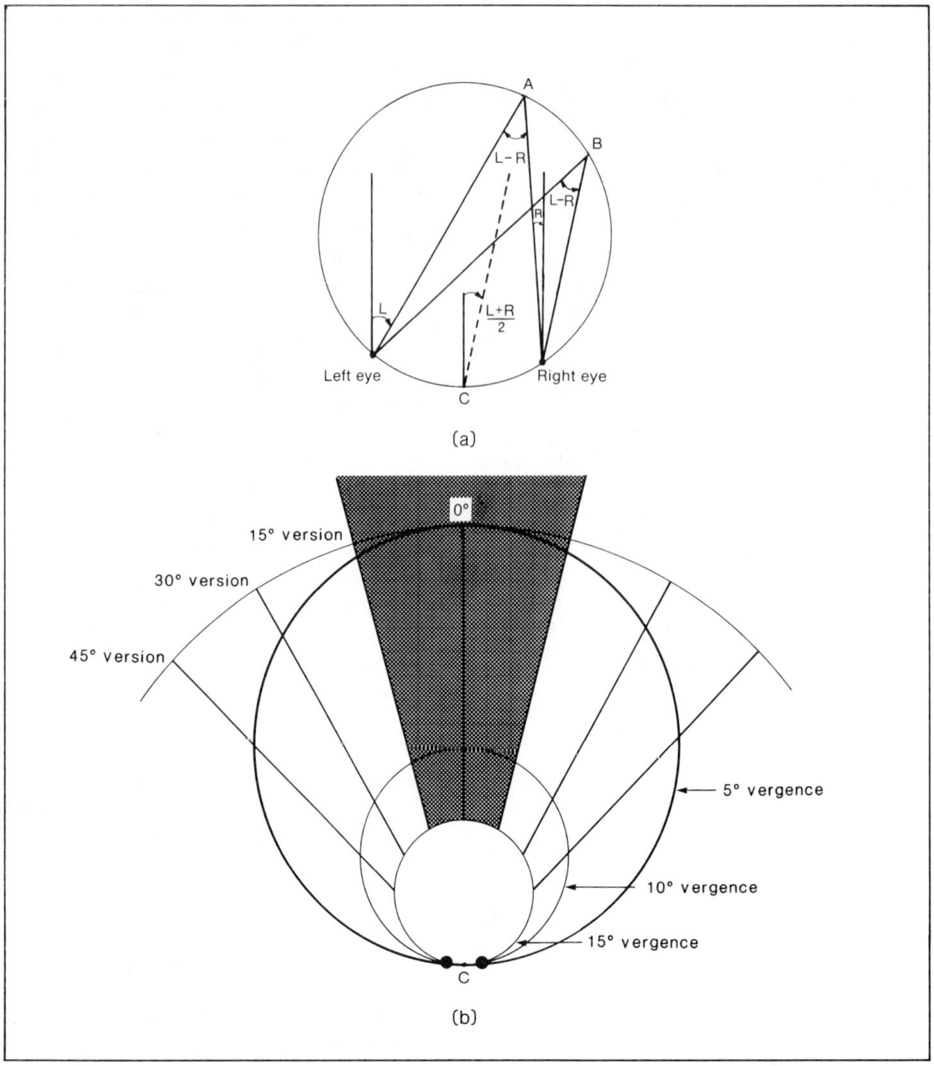

Figure 10.65. Vergence, version, and disparity. Hering's hypothesis defines vergence as equal and opposite eye movement, whence the angle of vergence is the difference in angular directions of the two eyes. Hering version is defined as equal and similarly directed movements, whence the angle of version is half the sum of the angles of the two eyes. Disparity is a measure of depth relative to the current surface of binocular fixation, and is the angular difference between the binocular retinal image positions of a single object point. (a) Example of the Vieth-Müller horopter. The optical nodal points are assumed to coincide with the center of ocular rotation, rather than being a few millimeters anterior. If A is the initial binocular fixation point, then by definition point B on the same horopter is imaged with 0 disparity (i.e., its retinal images are at corresponding retinal points which are the same distance from the fovea in each eye). If point B is now fixated the angle of Hering vergence $L - R$ does not change. Thus disparity is also the change in vergence angle in going from the current horopter of fixation to the horopter of the target. (b) The linear parts of the Hillebrand hyperbolas are shown here as radiating lines of constant version from the interocular midpoint C, which is the position of the "cyclopean eye" of psychologists. Note that the angle of version approximates the subjective direction of an object. The angle of vergence poorly correlates with linear distance. For example, if a small object moves around a semicircular arc centered on point C, then less vergence is required for binocular fixation at the extremes of gaze. However, eye movements are usually restricted to the stippled region, if the head is fixed, and in that region vergence angle is acceptably correlated with optical distance in diopters (m^{-1}).

accommodative vergence (asymmetric in the two eyes) and asymmetric conjugate saccades keep, or place, the dominant eye on target (Kenyon et al., 1980, 1981). Disparity no longer drives the eye movements, and it is as if the subjects have lost retinal-image-position information from the nondominant eye. Movements may not be restored to normal, even after visual acuity is restored by successful orthoptics treatment, but more subjects must be studied, preferably with contact lens methods.

3.4.1.6. Disparity Stimuli. Responses to disparity are often termed "fusional vergence" because the disparity is reduced to within 0.5 min arc so that central stimuli fall within the Panum's area for single binocular vision (Riggs & Niehl, 1960). This permits the two images to be fused into a single percept.

For technical convenience, many commonly used stimulus displays in binocular eye-movement studies are of the stereoscope kind, in which two identical laterally movable targets are pre-

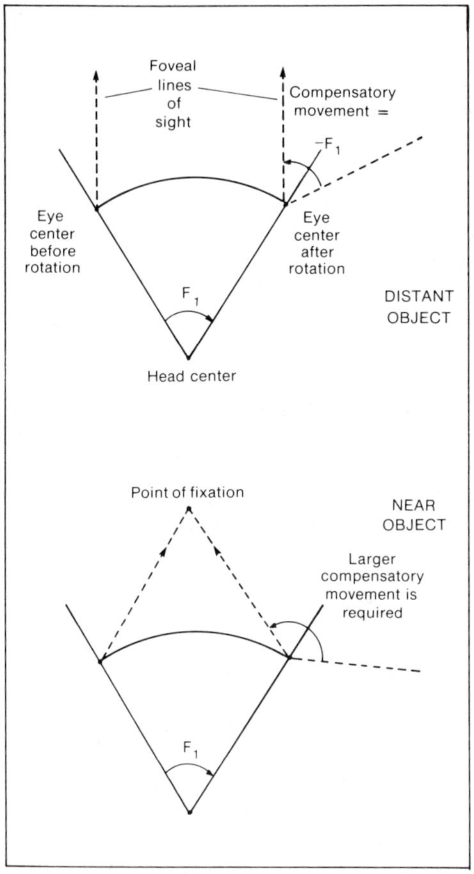

Figure 10.66. Necessity of changing the gain of the vestibulo-ocular reflex for a near target. Diagram refers to only one eye, and shows the centers of rotation of the head and eye before and after the head rotation of $F°$ about the yaw axis. *Distant object*: In this case, the required compensatory conjugate movement (vestibulo-ocular slow phase) is equal and opposite to the head rotation. *Near object*: The magnitude of the compensatory movement must appreciably exceed the angle of the head rotation for objects nearer than 1–2 m.

sented at a fixed distance, one to each eye. Some optical device (e.g., Polaroid, mirrors, baffles) is needed to restrict each eye to its own target. Because accommodative vergence plays no role, there is a tolerable approximation to Hering's hypothesis, disjunctive and conjugate movements being fairly symmetrical in the two eyes (Ono & Nakamizo, 1978). The stimuli are seen as a single object that may be moved in depth without any change in real size or focus; however, the object may appear to enlarge as it recedes because of its fixed angular subtense at the eye. If each eye's stimulus is presented in the visual field nasal to the current point of fixation, the eyes eventually converge nasally as if to a near object, or diverge if the presentation is temporal. No real object can produce divergence if the eyes are already parallel, unless it is viewed through a noncollimating or prismatic optical system.

The ability of subjects to tolerate prisms before one eye is not pursued in this chapter, but it is very relevant to perception (e.g., Howard, 1981; see also Welch, Chapter 24), and to clinical diagnosis and treatment of strabismus and eye strain (e.g., Burian & von Noorden, 1974). Typical tolerances, measured by the ability to see the pattern in a disparity-only stimulus (random-dot stereogram), are 2–4 diopters of vertical prism, either base-up or base-down, or 6-diopter base-in to 22-diopter base-out horizontal prism (e.g., Boltz, Smith, Bennett, & Harwerth, 1980). A prism diopter is defined as a deviation of 1 cm at 1 m distance, that is, 0.01 rad or 34 min arc.

If the disparate retinal images of an object point lie sufficiently binasally or bitemporally, the redistribution of optic-nerve fibers at the optic chiasma leads to the two images being processed in separate half-brains. The correlation of function in this case should depend on the corpus callosum, which is a massive fiber tract linking the two cerebral hemispheres in general, and the various neural representations of the vertical meridian in particular. One subject was unable to converge or diverge in response to bitemporal or binasal retinal images after the callosum was cut (Westheimer, 1971).

3.4.1.7. Servo-Analytical Approaches. An important issue is the extent to which vergence movements are intelligent or mechanical. Rashbass and Westheimer (1961a) demonstrated that steps, ramps, pulses, and up to 0.7-Hz sinusoidal oscillations of disparity (about $\pm 3°$ amplitude) invoke matching slow vergence movements. When these motions were imposed directly on the retina (open loop) by electronic techniques that thwarted the effects of eye movements, many aspects of the movements could be described by a neural integrator, eye velocity being proportional to the disparity that existed one reaction time earlier (e.g., $7\text{–}10° \cdot \sec^{-1}$ velocity per degree disparity 160 msec earlier). However, the phase lag of tracking (40–90°) was less than predicted, as if the system used the direction and

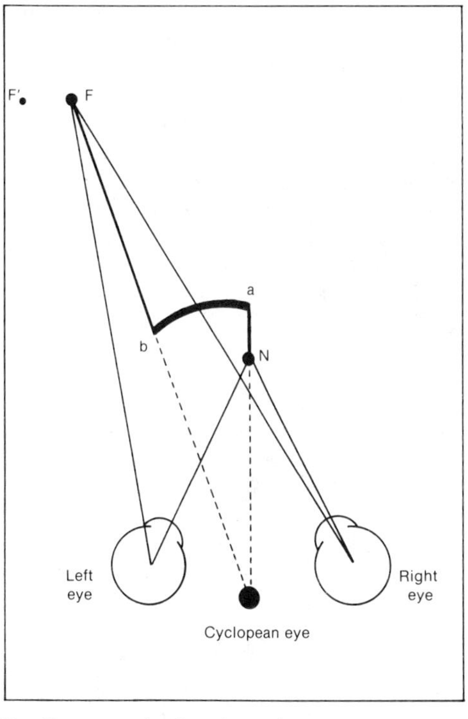

Figure 10.67. One example of version and vergence eye movements when an object steps in depth. Object is displaced from N to F. Eye movements approximate Hering's concepts of vergence and version in this case. The heavy lines show the path of the binocular point of fixation; slow symmetrical divergence from N to a, symmetrical saccade (version) from a to b, and slow symmetrical divergence from b to F. Eye movements track the physical position of the fixation point, and not its initially perceived position at F'. Actually, points N and F are aligned on one eye, so that point N occludes point F; more common target trajectories are tracked with quite different combinations of eye movements. (From H. Ono & S. Nakamizo, Saccadic eye movements during changes of fixation to stimuli at different distances, *Vision Research*, *17*. Copyright 1977 by Pergamon Press, Ltd. Reprinted with permission.)

speed of disparity change, and other stimulus characteristics, to reduce its response time. Note that the stimuli were presented for only 1 or 2 sec. One of the problems with disjunctive movements, apart from asymmetry as to the strengths of divergent and convergent responses, is that exposure to disparity alters the characteristics of the system, as when clinically assessing tolerance to prisms (e.g., Alpern, 1969; Burian & von Noorden, 1974; Ogle, 1964). This is shown in Figure 10.68. Convergence relaxes briskly after a 5-sec exposure of a disparity stimulus, but not after a 60-sec exposure (Schor, 1979). Effects may persist for hours after long exposure. This suggests that disparity-induced vergence may be mediated by two neural integrators in parallel. The fast integrator gives the immediate response, and the slower one relieves the fast one, thus preserving the fast mechanism's full dynamic range.

A slightly different point of view from that of Rashbass and Westheimer (1961a) has been stated by other systems analysts (Zuber, 1971). Figure 10.69 shows gain and phase lag for tracking a disparity stimulus. "Predictability" appears at first sight to be a major factor.However, the better performance (i.e., smaller phase lag) for predictable targets may be due to an input-amplitude-dependent nonlinearity, and not to prediction, because reducing the amplitude of the unpredictable wave form in other experiments gives data more similar to those labeled "predictable." Rashbass and Westheimer (1961a) had suggested, for stimuli that were stabilized against retinal motion, that prediction may explain why open-loop phase lags are smaller than expected, given the gain data and the minimum phase principle of servomechanics. But Zuber and Stark (1968) did not find any difference between predictable and unpredictable stimuli in the open-loop case. When Zuber and Stark altered external-feedback gain, so as to drive the system into oscillation, the frequency of spontaneous oscillation was 2.5 Hz; this is expected for a nonpredictive system, given a 180° phase shift at 2.3 Hz in the open-loop data. By contrast, the smooth pursuit system oscillates rather variably when external-feedback gain is increased, as if this system changes its time delay and other characteristics to prevent oscillation (Robinson, 1965).

3.4.1.8. Stimulus Parameters. The above findings do not encourage the view that disparity-induced disjunctive movements are due to a wide variety of neural drives, as are other types of eye movement. In fact, a low-level neural mechanism might explain why disjunctive movements are triggered by a wide variety of stimuli (Fig. 10.70). Identical stimuli, such as short vertical luminous lines 0.75° long, elicit vergence movements when the horizontal disparities of the images in the two eyes are as large as 5–10°. Such stimuli are seen as double stimuli lying appropriately in front or behind the current point of fixation. More strikingly, pairs of *dissimilar* stimuli are effective when presented one to each eye, although the movements do not usually go to completion. Such pairs include a dot and a line; short vertical or horizontal lines, with vertical separations of up to 4°, as well as horizontal disparities of 1–5°; a vertical and a horizontal line, with or without vertical separation; a cross and a circle; two stimuli that differ by 1.6 log in luminance, so that the dimmer one is scarcely visible; two lines of opposite contrast, one white on black, the other black on white, and so on (Mitchell, 1970; Westheimer & Mitchell, 1969). The stimuli in these experiments were 200-msec flashes, but in additional trials with shorter flashes, disparate stimuli were still effective when presented with an asynchrony of 75–125 msec. The short exposures substantially eliminate visual feedback as to movement, and the small amplitude (about 1°) of these short-lived responses accounts for the subjects' being unaware of them (Fig. 10.71, page 10-70). Curiously, when the subject has the opportunity of fusing a vertical curved arc in one eye with one of a pair of vertical curved arcs in the other eye, there is no preference for fusing with the similarly shaped arc [Fig. 10.70 K; Jones & Kerr, 1972]; so the internal model must be very undiscriminating.

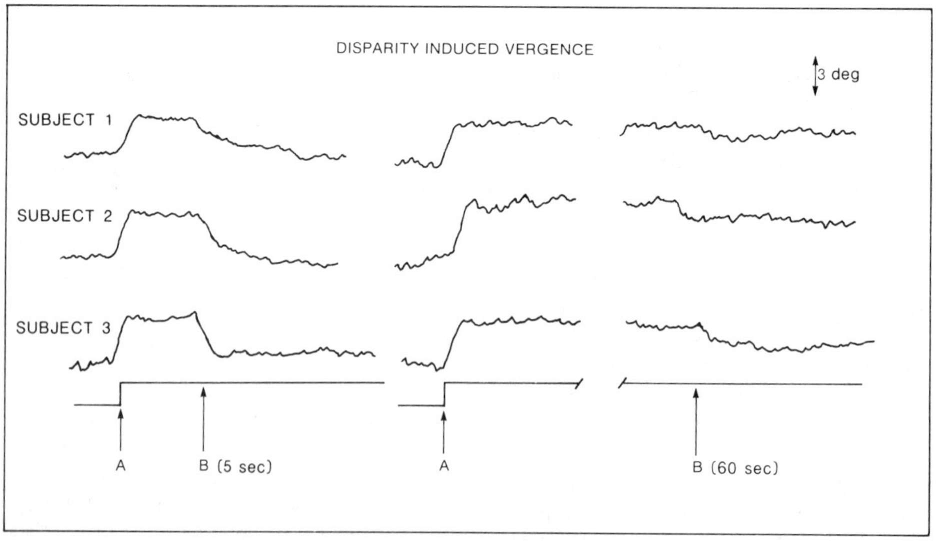

Figure 10.68. Disparity induced disjunctive movement and its variable relaxation. A stereoscopic system, with separate images for each eye, simulates a small object undergoing step displacement in depth. *Left*: Traces for three subjects show convergence at onset of 5 sec of disparity stimulus at A, and prompt relaxation at B when one eye is occluded. *Right*: Record is interrupted. Prompt convergence at onset of a 60-sec stimulus, but very slow and incomplete relaxation after the stimulus is withdrawn at B. (From C. M. Schor, The relationship between fusional vergence eye movements and fixation disparity, *Vision Research*, *19*. Copyright 1979 by Pergamon Press, Ltd. Reprinted with permission.)

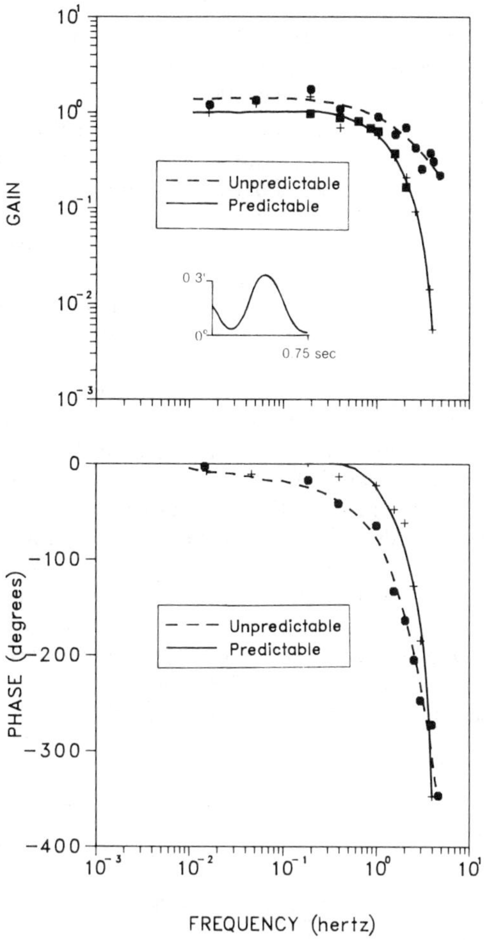

Figure 10.69. Bode plots of gain and phase for tracking disparity stimuli. A stereoscopic system, with separate images for each eye, simulates a small target oscillating continuously in depth from the subject. Stimulus disparity expresses target depth relative to the *mean* plane of fixation; actual retinal disparity will be nearly 0 if vergence tracking is accurate. Gain is amplitude ratio of vergence eye movement to stimulus disparity. Phase is phase lag of Hering vergence relative to stimulus disparity. *Predictable*: Sinusoidal oscillations of stimulus disparity at a single frequency. Data from Zuber and Stark (1968) and Yoshida and Watanabe (1963). *Unpredictable*: The stimulus disparity oscillation is the sum of several sinusoids at different frequencies. Data of Zuber and Stark (1968). *Inset*: Averaged vergence response to a sinusoidal input of 2 Hz and ±1.7° amplitude. Note that bandwidth is hard to estimate, given the effects of stimulus composition. It is not yet settled whether the problem is predictability as such, or an input-amplitude dependent nonlinearity. (From B. L. Zuber, Control of vergence movements. In P. Bach-y-Rita, C. C. Collins, & J. Hyde (Eds.), *The control of eye movements*, Academic Press, Inc., 1971. Reprinted with permission.)

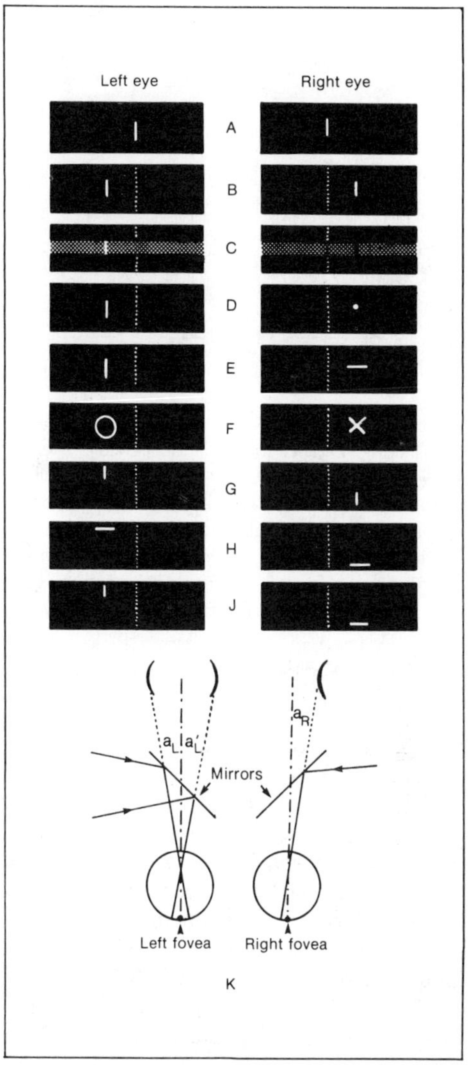

Figure 10.70. Pairs of binocular stimuli that initiate horizontal disjunctive movements. (A) Initial fixation target. This is shown by dotted lines for the stimulus pairs below. Disparate stimuli B–J presented for 200 msec, K for 500 msec. (B) Vertical line stimuli; difference in luminance can be several log units provided each is above threshold. (C) Stimuli of opposite contrast. (D) Unequally long line stimuli. (E) Lines at different orientations. (F) Dissimilar shapes. (G, H) Up to 4° vertical disparity as well horizontal disparity. (J) Vertical disparity as well as orientation difference. (A–J after Westheimer & Mitchell, 1969, Fig. 2.) (K) Example of a stimulus pair presented at various disparities. Two subjects responded by convergence or divergence, and two other subjects always converged, but in all cases shape was not a cue. (After Fig. 1 of Jones & Kerr, 1972, Fig. 1.) Limbus eye monitors. Clearly, vergence can be *initiated* by an uncritical mechanism that accepts almost any two disparate images as being potentially due to a single target. (From G. Westheimer & D. E. Mitchell, The sensory stimulus for disjunctive eye movements, *Vision Research*, 9. Copyright 1969 by Pergamon Press, Ltd.; and from R. Jones & K. E. Kerr, Vergence eye movements to pairs of disparity stimuli with shape selection cues, *Vision Research*, 12. Copyright 1972 by Pergamon Press, Ltd. Reprinted with permission.)

The possibility that subjects' idiosyncratic vergence patterns (e.g., convergence stronger than divergence) form a series of grades deserves examination, as various grades of stereopsis have been recognized (e.g., Jones, 1977; Richards, 1971). However, stereopsis usually involves extremely small disparities of the order of a minute of arc, and may be better correlated with the mechanisms that *maintain* tonic vergence during fixation, rather than with the large disparity mechanisms that *initiate* disjunctive movements.

Although eye movements are generally insensitive to stimulus lighting, color, and shape, it is possible that vergence is slower at low stimulus luminances (Mitchell, 1970). The spatial-frequency structure of the stimulus may also have a minor effect, with vergence to spatially filtered random-dot stereograms being slightly slower at the higher spatial frequencies (Frisby & Mayhew, 1980).

3.4.1.9. Vertical Disparities. The mechanism correcting vertical disparity in the central 4° of visual field appears to be very sensitive, because disparities as small as 0.5 min arc are

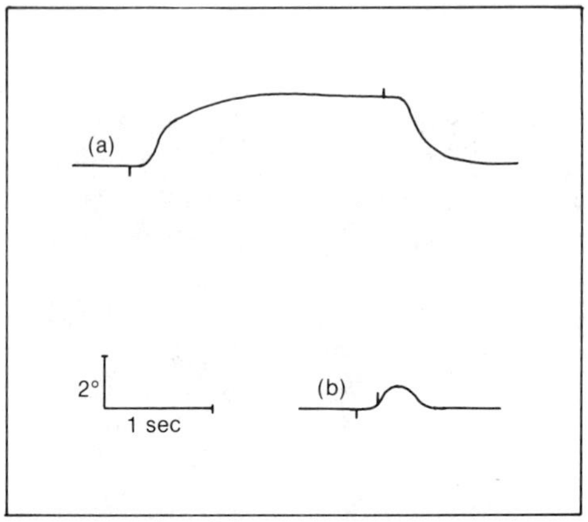

Figure 10.71. Hering vergence (binocular difference in eye position) elicited by a sudden 2.75° disparity stimulus. (a) Long-duration stimulus. (b) Stimulus of 200-msec duration. Eye movement is too late to be modified by altered disparity feedback because stimulus has already disappeared. Beginnings and ends of stimulus marked on records. Limbus eye monitor. The exponentially declining wave form is consistent with a step change in muscle force. (From G. Westheimer & D. E. Mitchell, The sensory stimulus for disjunctive eye movements, *Vision Research*, 9. Copyright 1969 by Pergamon Press, Ltd. Reprinted with permission.)

corrected; these are much too small to cause double vision (Duwaer & van den Brink, 1981).

Vertical disparities of 0.5–1° between 8.5° horizontal lines are corrected about eight times more slowly than similar horizontal disparities between vertical lines. Vertical disjunctive movements show serious deviations from Hering's hypothesis, as the left and right eye responses are different in both amplitude and dynamics (Perlmutter & Kertesz, 1978). Comparable horizontal disjunctive movements show only minor deviations, depending on the subject, for example, small oscillations in one eye (Rashbass & Westheimer, 1961a, 1961b). Horizontal disparities of 2.8° did not initiate movements in the experiments of Figure 10.70 when vertical disparities exceeded 2–4° (Mitchell, 1970). This does not exclude an important role for the extrafoveal retina, because two short vertical lines 40 min arc long, and at 2.8° horizontal and 0° vertical disparity, were effective stimuli as far as 4–6° above the foveas.

3.4.1.10. Peripheral Retina. A major role for the extrafoveal retina in correcting horizontal (yaw), vertical (pitch), and cyclic (roll) disparities is demonstrated by responses to stripes or textured stimuli which cover a large (57°) region of the visual field (Kertesz & Hampton, 1981). Two mesopic patterns (3 cd · m^{-2}, blue-green) were presented, one to each eye, the left eye being provided with a fixation point and the complete pattern, while the central 10° about the right fovea was blanked electronically. The disjunctive responses to 1.5° steps in horizontal convergent or divergent disparity, or to 0.4° steps in vertical disparity, eliminated about 70% (40–77%) of disparity. Responses were complex, the two eyes typically responding asymmetrically, often with faster and slower components (Fig. 10.72). For roll disparities see Section 3.5.1.5.

3.4.1.11. Accommodative Stimuli. The existence of separate disparity and accommodation controllers of disjunctive movements is suggested by Figure 10.73. When the optical distance, but not the disparity, of a binocularly viewed stimulus is suddenly shortened, the initial reaction of accommodative convergence is inappropriate, and is subsequently eliminated by disparity-induced divergence (Semmlow & Venkiteswaran, 1976). The velocity of binocular accommodative vergence is only half of what can be produced in the monocular situation, because of the opposing disparity drive.

3.4.2. Instruction: Track the Object Seen Monocularly. A blurred stimulus in one eye elicits disjunctive movements (the other eye being covered), but as the seeing eye is required to fixate the stimulus, only the covered eye turns inward to any appreciable extent. The small movement of the seeing eye is opposed by small binocular saccades (which may be up to 20% smaller in the seeing eye), or by smooth movements, or by both—a variety of patterns being seen in different subjects (Kenyon et al., 1978). The effect of these compensations is that the stimulus does not stray beyond the edge of the rod-free fovea; this helps preserve sharp imagery by optimally stimulating the accommodative reflex (e.g., Campbell, 1954; Campbell & Westheimer, 1959). The usual amplitude of monocular accommodative vergence (AC) is around 2.3° · diopter^{-1} of accommodative stimulus (A)—the "stimulus AC/A ratio" of the clinicians—but the value varies with the subjects and conditions (e.g., Alpern, 1969; Morgan, 1944, 1968). Accommodative focusing increasingly weakens with age, especially after the age of 40; accommodative vergence does not. Accommodative focusing and increased depth of focus from pupillary constriction both tend to eliminate blur, and would thus reduce the convergence

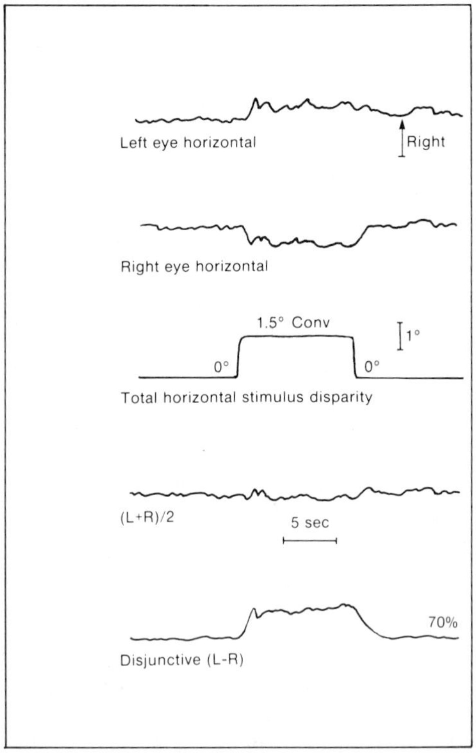

Figure 10.72. Role of extrafoveal retina in disjunctive eye movement. Records from above down: Horizontal eye position for left and right eyes, horizontal convergent disparity stimulus, Hering version, and Hering vergence components. Right eye views 57° subtense vertical grating pattern, and left eye initially views similar pattern but with central 10° about fovea electronically blanked. Both stimuli displaced equally in opposite directions at time of disparity step. Average of 10 contact lens records. The asymmetric responses of the two eyes eliminate most of the disparity. Asymmetry in this instance is largely due to the artificial scotoma (From A. E. Kertesz & D. R. Hampton. Fusional response to extrafoveal stimulation, *Investigative Ophthalmology and Visual Science*, 1981, *21*. Reprinted with permission.)

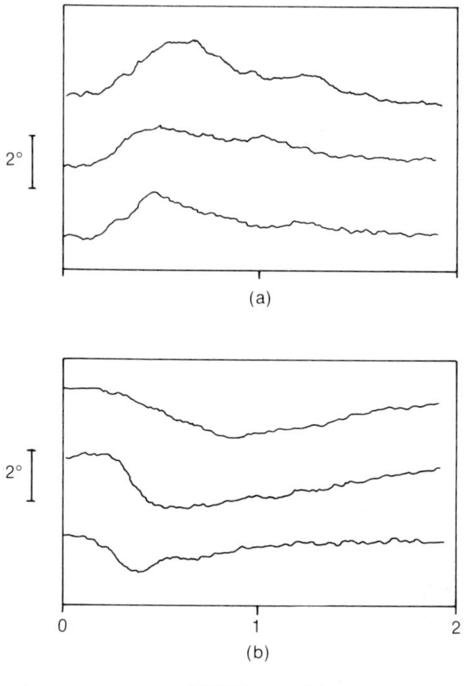

Figure 10.73. Binocular accommodative vergence. Three pairs of records for three subjects. (a) Transient convergence to optical approach of stimulus from 1 to 4 diopters at time 0. (b) Transient movement due to optical recession of stimulus from 4 to 1 diopter at time 0. Optical distance in diopters is reciprocal distance in meters. Averaged records of right eye position. Limbus eye monitor. The transience of the response is due to optical blur stimulating accommodative vergence, which causes disparity, which in turn elicits disparity-reducing vergence. (From J. Semmlow & N. Venkiteswaran, Dynamic accommodative vergence components in binocular vision, *Vision Research*, *16*. Copyright 1976 by Pergamon Press, Ltd. Reprinted with permission.)

response to a near object, were it not for the neural cross-coupling between the neural mechanisms subserving optical accommodation, pupillary constriction, and convergence. These three actions are grouped clinically as the "near triad" by way of reminding us of the biologically adaptive value of the mutually supportive responses to approaching or receding objects (Campbell, 1957; Rashbass, 1981; Semmlow, 1981).

Cross-coupling also applies to occasional mistakes seen in tracking in depth. Such mistakes are apparently never seen when tracking disparity stimuli (Westheimer & Mitchell, 1969), presumably because the "hard-wired" mapping of retina to brain areas via many parallel lines makes mistakes as to retinal position unlikely. However, judging the direction of defocusing is more difficult and may involve learned strategies. Figure 10.74 shows a record where a step reduction of optical distance at the left of the trace led to an inappropriate increase in accommodation and highly asymmetric convergence, as if the subject perceived the object as approaching rather than receding. The mistake was corrected immediately by divergence and relaxation of accommodation. Subsequent changes in focus were correctly tracked (Wilson, 1973a). Such mistakes are believed to be due to the neural drive for optical accommodation driving convergence. The mean latency for accommodative vergence in these experiments ranged from 202 to 327 msec in the four subjects (SD 24–64 msec), which is longer than the frequently cited value of 160 msec for disparity tracking from Rashbass and Westheimer (1961a). The latency for optical accommodation is usually an additional 110–130 msec longer in mean, with relaxation from near to far having a longer latency than far to near. Wilson attributes this asymmetry to the ciliary being a smooth muscle. Other data on latencies appear in Campbell and Westheimer (1960) and O'Neill and Stark (1968). The velocities of both monocular accommodative vergence and disparity-induced vergence decline as the responses progress; the accommodative responses may be a little slower (e.g., with an average time constant of 0.4 sec relative to 0.3 sec for disparity), but there is variation with subject and with direction (Alpern, 1969). The extreme slowness of disjunctive responses relative to their latent period reflects the muscular force being a simple step function of time rather than a driving force with preemphasis (see Sections 2.1.1 and 2.3.2).

Optical accommodation fluctuates noisily by a fraction of a diopter, so noise is to be expected in the disjunctive movement also, if this is driven by accommodation (Campbell, Robson, & Westheimer, 1959). In fact, accommodative noise and convergence noise are roughly proportional. Although accommodation may show power at high frequencies that are not present in vergence, it is plausible that the higher frequencies are simply more attenuated in the neural pathways to vergence (Wilson, 1973b). In monocular viewing, prolonged accommodation does not change the properties of the accommodative vergence system. This is shown by vergence recovering as rapidly after 60 sec accommodation as it does after 5 sec (Schor, 1979). This contrasts with the effects of exposure to disparity (See Section 3.4.1.7).

Accommodative vergence decreases with increasing distance of the stimulus from the fovea, as expected, because visual resolution also declines (Semmlow & Tinor, 1978).

3.5. Eye Movements to Rolling Targets

Roll of the stimulus or scene, relative to the current line of sight, evokes small rolling movements (torsion) of the eyes that are of considerable practical importance, though hard to measure. Similarly directed eye movements occur when the two eyes view the same rolling stimulus (conjugate cycloversion) and opposite movements when the eyes are oppositely stimulated (disjunctive cyclovergence). Optokinetic, smooth pursuit, and saccadic movements have been described, suggesting that torsion differs from horizontal and vertical movements only in axis and magnitude.

3.5.1. Instruction: Fixate the Straight-Ahead Object

3.5.1.1. Fixed Stimulus, Tilting or Rolling Head. Rolling of a fixed stimulus about the longitudinal or Listing axis, relative to the eyes, occurs when the head is tilted toward one shoulder. Self-inspection in a mirror or a number of early studies (e.g., Belcher, 1964; Udo De Haes, 1970) correctly show that the net ocular counterrolling is a sine function of head roll and is quite slight (e.g., a maximum of 4–11° eye roll at 60–70° head tilt). This has led to the idea that ocular compensation for roll is seriously inadequate. The following analysis of the dynamics suggests, on the contrary, that the counterrolling may be just as effective as other visuovestibulo-ocular compensations when the tilt is small.

Figure 10.75(a) shows the two eyes from above, with fixation on point F intermediate in depth between the collinear points A and B. Figure 10.75(b) shows the retinas from behind, with point F foveated, the nearer point A imaged temporally and the further point B nasally. If the head is now tilted, physiological problems arise that require conflicting corrections. Retinal-image

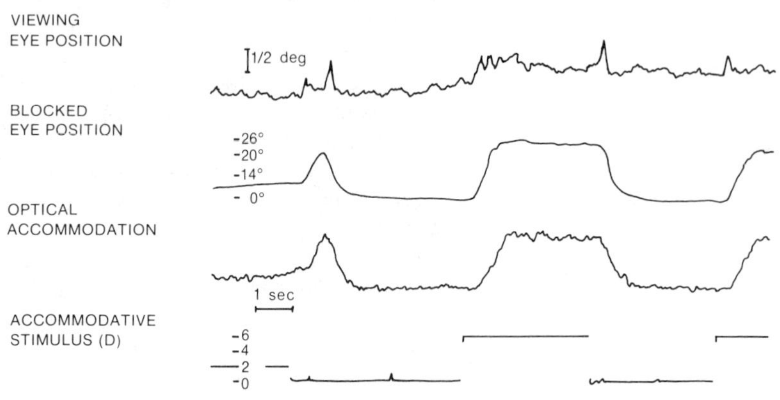

Figure 10.74. Erroneous and "correct" disjunctive responses to monocular accommodative stimulus. Traces from above. *Viewing eye position*: horizontal position of optically stimulated fixating eye. *Blocked eye position*: horizontal position of optically blocked eye. *Optical accommodation*: optical accommodation of seeing eye. *Accommodative stimulus*: optical distance of accommodative stimulus in diopters. At the beginning of the record, optical recession of target evokes erroneous accommodation and accommodative convergence (the initial upswing in the third and second traces), the convergence being mainly adduction of the blocked eye. The remainder of record shows correctly directed accommodation and accommodative vergence. Pupillary eye movement monitor. Optical blur is one cue for convergent or divergent eye movements to secure binocular single vision of a target moving in depth. (From D. Wilson, A centre for accommodative vergence motor control, *Vision Research, 13*. Copyright 1973 by Pergamon Press, Ltd. Reprinted with permission.)

slip reduces the visibility of the finer spatial frequencies, unless the eyes counterroll in the head at an equal and opposite speed, so as to keep the horizontal retinal meridian fixed in space, as in Figure 10.75(c). However, compensation for retinal-image slip introduces vertical disparity for objects before or behind the horizontal horopter. The image of the nearer point A now lies above the horizontal meridian of one eye and below in the other, and vice versa for the further point B. The disparity can be fully corrected by stepping the eyes in the direction of tilt, so that they resume their initial positions in the orbits [Fig. 10.75(d)]. This tilts the plane of the horopter to match the plane of regard. The head roll and the two types of eye movement *in space*, are shown in Figure 10.76(a) as a function of time (Petrov & Zenkin, 1973). The head tilts at about $10° \cdot sec^{-1}$ toward one shoulder and back again, while the subject fixates a small lit point 1.2 m distant in the dark. Slow counterrolling eye movements ($0.5–8° \cdot sec^{-1}$), reduce ocular roll in space and thus reduce retinal-image slip; intermittent rolling saccades restore eye position in the head. As a result, there is a net counterrolling of 12° maximum. The reason why saccadic roll does not restore the eyes completely to their original orbital position is plausibly much as in the "doll reflex" (Section 3.2.1.4). Even if the saccadic system monitors the entire motor outflow, the gain of the control loop may be inadequate to completely reduce the disturbance by smooth rolling to zero. Thus counterrolling is probably the product of an effective visuosaccular reflex, rather than marginally useless behavior.

The effect of head tilt toward the shoulder is different in the dark. Counterrolling smooth movements are often less marked, and saccades are largely absent [Fig. 10.76(b)]. This suggests that rolling pursuit or optokinetic movements supplement the neural drives from the otolith and vestibular canals under lit conditions, as is usual for movements around other axes. Given the modifiability of the vestibulo-ocular reflexes in those other cases, depending on the subject's tasks and visual imagery (see Section 3.2.1.3), it would be interesting to know whether rolling eye movements are trainable or modifiable in pilots and others who depend on good compensations for roll.

Tilting of the head toward one shoulder places very little strain on the compensatory mechanisms compared to acrobatic and other violent activity. A pilot in an aerodynamic spin is subjected to violent roll, yaw, and even pitch movements, of about $20–100° \cdot sec^{-1}$ (e.g., Melvill Jones, 1965). Although vision is initially clear, it deteriorates as vestibulo-ocular compensation decays with time constants of 16 sec in yaw and 5 sec in pitch and roll. This decay is due to the hydrodynamics of the semicircular canals. When the aircraft recovers from the spin, the mechanical inertia of the semicircular canals causes the vestibular drives to reverse. Reversal is minimized for pitch and yaw, because optokinetic afternystagmus is always oppositely directed to vestibular afternystagmus, and so the two tend to cancel. Compensation for violent roll is doubly poor, as the recordings in Figure 10.77 show, because of rapid decay of compensation at the start of the spin, and because of largely unopposed post-rotary vestibular aftereffect (about $50° \cdot sec^{-1}$) at the end of the spin. This aftereffect may encourage the pilot to initiate a new, more disastrous maneuver. An analysis of a similar sequence of eye movements is given in Figure 10.78 (page 10-75). In conclusion, it is argued that visuovestibular compensations are useful and adequate for small-amplitude slow rolls, whereas compensation for greater stresses is very inadequate.

3.5.1.2. Rolling Stimulus, Tilted Head. The net counterrolling eye movements in this situation are easily measured

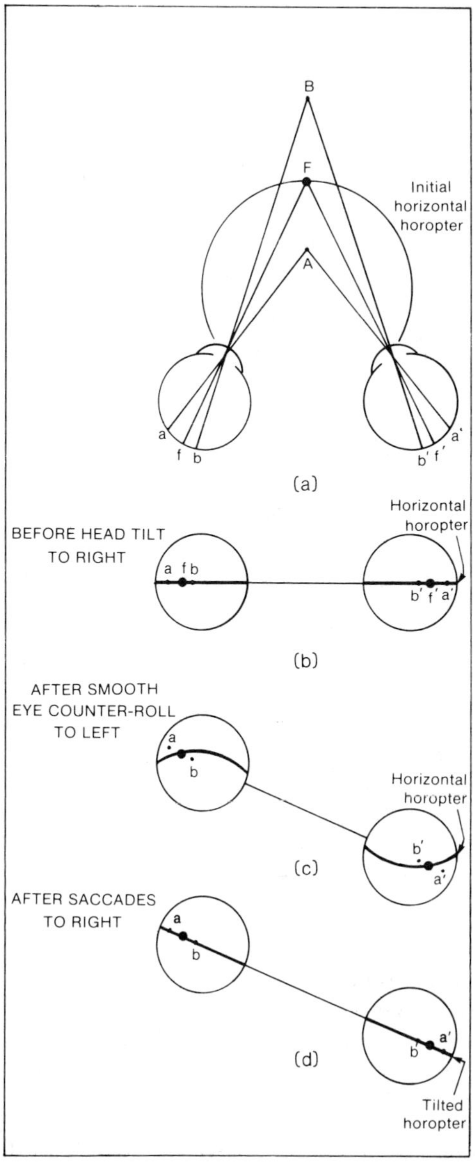

Figure 10.75. Alternating compensations of retinal image slip and binocular disparity during head rolling. (a) Horizontal plane of regard showing left and right eyes converged on the middle of three collinear points AFB. The Vieth-Müller horopter is also shown. (b–d) Eyes viewed from behind. (b) Retinal image positions of the three collinear points before roll of head about axis AFB. (c) Retinal image positions after head roll and equal slow counterrolling of eyes, so as to reduce retinal image slip. This stabilizes the horizontal retinal meridian in space, shown curved in this perspective, but produces vertical disparity because the binocular images *a* and *a′* of *A* and images *b* and *b′* of *B* are no longer on the horizontal retinal meridian. (d) Saccadic rolling eliminates vertical disparity; the new Vieth-Müller horopter is now tilted out of the horizontal plane.

by having the subject set a line to match a linear afterimage imprinted on the originally horizontal retinal meridian. The middle curve in Figure 10.79 (page 10-76) shows net counterrolling as a function of head tilt, when the subject faces a large, static, textured annular display. Parallel measurements show no perceptual errors in assessing the horizontal over this range. The other curves show that rolling the display at $20° \cdot sec^{-1}$ biases the net roll of the eyes by about 4°, as well as altering perception of the horizontal (Merker & Held, 1981). These data support the dissociation of the central processes subserving reflexive eye control and cognitive judgments. However, it should not be forgotten that the dynamic aspects of eye rolling are more behaviorally significant than static measures, such as net counterroll (as was discussed in connection with Figs. 10.75 and 10.76).

3.5.1.3. ***Tilted Stimulus, Erect Head.*** A sufficiently large, static, visual stimulus against a dark background induces generally less than 1° of "optostatic" rolling in the direction of tilt (e.g., a centrally fixated 25° subtense striped display, or the 28°-square standard rod and frame stimulus of psychological testing, but not a 15° long line; see Crone, 1975; Goodenough, Sigman, Oltman, Rosso, & Mertz, 1979; Howard & Templeton, 1964). Subjects are not aware of so small a movement, but the underlying visual mechanism may supplement the otolith drive when the head is held at a tilt in a textured environment.

3.5.1.4. ***Disparately Tilted Stimuli.*** If the two eyes are separately stimulated in a stereoscope, the stimulus to the left eye being given a clockwise tilt, and a similar stimulus to the right eye being given a counterclockwise tilt, then appropriate intorsions of the two eyes leave similar stimulus details at corresponding retinal points and allow binocular single vision (e.g., Crone & Everhard-Halm, 1975). Such disjunctive roll movements (cyclovergence) have been observed with search-coil methods in response to disparate tilts of 50° subtense, photopic grating-patterns, composed of randomly segmented lines (Sullivan & Kertesz, 1978). Cyclovergence is slow relative to ordinary horizontal or vertical vergence movements. Intorsion to a 5.8° symmetrical disparity takes about 12 sec, while extorsion is even slower and less smooth, velocities being in the region of $0.1–0.6° \cdot sec^{-1}$. The responses compensate for 42–75% of the initial retinal disparity. If only the stimulus to one eye is tilted (asymmetric disparity) both eyes equally reduce disparity. Figure 10.80 (page 10-77) illustrates the case where the tilt imposed at time A in the left eye is switched at time B to the right eye, and altered in direction, so as to preserve intorsional disparity. There is no change in the cyclovergence of the eyes, which must clearly be disparity driven, even though the retinal images and the fused percept switch their directions. Responses tend to be slightly larger, the larger the inducing field (Kertesz & Sullivan, 1978).

The retinal periphery plays an important role in vergence movements (e.g., Burian & von Noorden, 1974). Movements such as those of Figure 10.80 can be produced by only the outer annular part of the visual stimulus. If the annulus is large enough, its disparity may be compensated by cyclovergence, while a different disparity in the center is neglected (Sullivan & Kertesz, 1979). Although center and periphery have not yet been compared for equal area stimuli, it is likely that the drive from the central retina is the more powerful, as is true for most visual functions. Cyclovergence is presumably sensitive to training.

Although these disjunctive rolling movements are small, they must play an important role in eliminating small vertical disparities that would otherwise interfere with binocular single vision and stereopsis. Extorsion by about 2°, when accommodating and converging on a near object, changes the vertical horopter (the intersection of the projected planes of the originally vertical retinal meridians) from an infinitely distant vertical line to a slanting line in the median plane through the point of fixation (Helmholtz, 1910/1926). Such extorsion is adaptive for reading a book tilted to catch light from above, because points on the vertical horopter have zero vertical disparity. It may be worth looking for small cyclovergences in more athletic

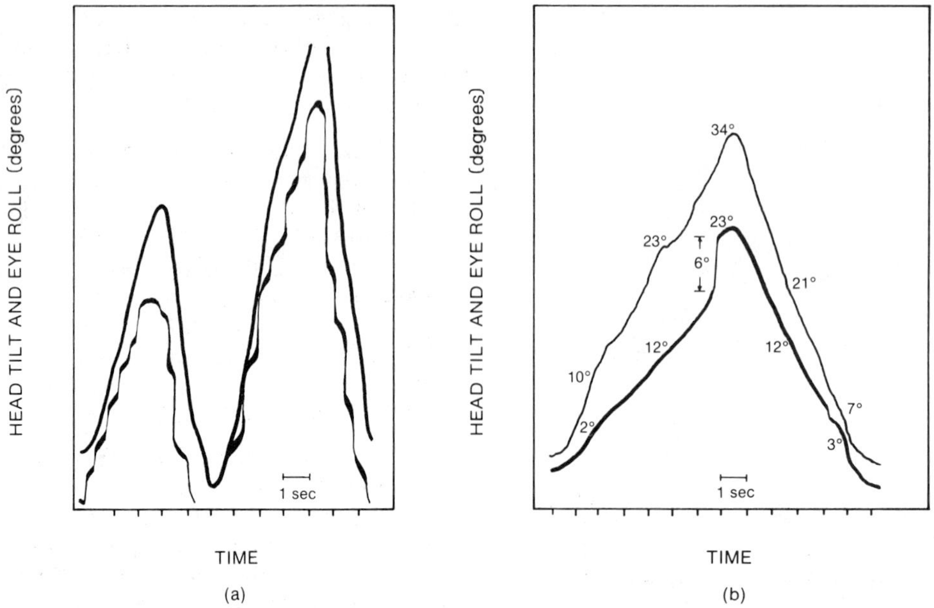

Figure 10.76. Smooth and saccadic rolling eye movements during head tilt about the roll axis. Ordinates are head tilt or eye roll in space in degrees. Abscissas are time in seconds. Top traces are head movement, and bottom traces are eye position in space, registered by a contact lens method, and confirmed by flash photos. Perfect counterrolling would have a slope of 0 in these traces. (a) Head movement, under normal lighting, of up to 25 and 50° in about 3 sec while the subject fixates a small point target. Smooth counterrolling in orbit slows eye roll in space whereas abrupt saccades increase roll, so net result at peak tilt is that eye rolls only about 14° less than head (= "residual torsion"). (b) Similar but dark room with a dim fixation point. Smooth counterrolling in orbit is now less effective than in (a) and saccades are few. Net result is a similar residual torsion to that in (a). The numbers on the traces are calibrated angles. (From A. P. Petrov & G. M. Zenkin, Torsional eye movements and constancy of the visual field, *Vision Research*, *13*. Copyright 1973 by Pergamon Press, Ltd. Reprinted with permission.)

situations. For example, the slanting vertical horopter for a 1° binocular extorsion would run from one's feet to the current point of fixation, which might facilitate trapping a hard-driven but slowly falling ball.

3.5.2. Instruction: Track the Rolling Stimulus with Torsion Movements. Subjects can be trained, given visual feedback as to eye movement, to make substantial voluntary rolling pursuit, saccadic, and fixation movements (Balliet & Nakayama, 1978). Three subjects viewed an 11° initially vertical linear afterimage as a source of feedback, while fixating the center of a dim line stimulus with their right eyes. They were instructed to keep the line and afterimage parallel, and were able to track the line as they rotated it manually in 20-min arc steps clockwise or counterclockwise. Training lasted 1 hr · day^{-1}. Voluntary

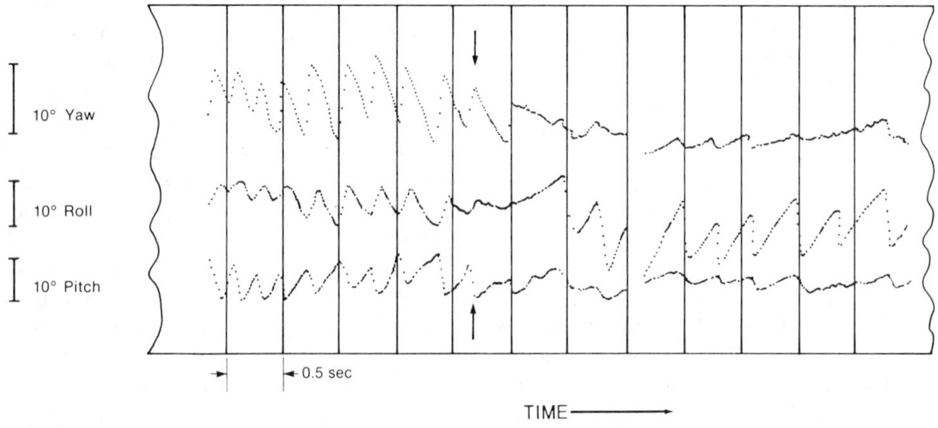

Figure 10.77. Vestibulo-ocular nystagmus during aircraft spin. Records show yaw, roll, and pitch of eyes relative to head, measured photographically. Record at left relates to spinning aircraft which recovers at the time of the arrow. At this moment the mechanical inertia of the semicircular canals stimulates a reverse nystagmus, which is striking in the roll record. The expected vestibular afternystagmus in the pitch and yaw dimensions is probably nulled by opposite optokinetic afternystagmus. (From G. Melvill Jones, Vestibulo-ocular disorganization in the aerodynamic spin, *Aerospace Medicine*, 1965, *36*. Reprinted with permission.)

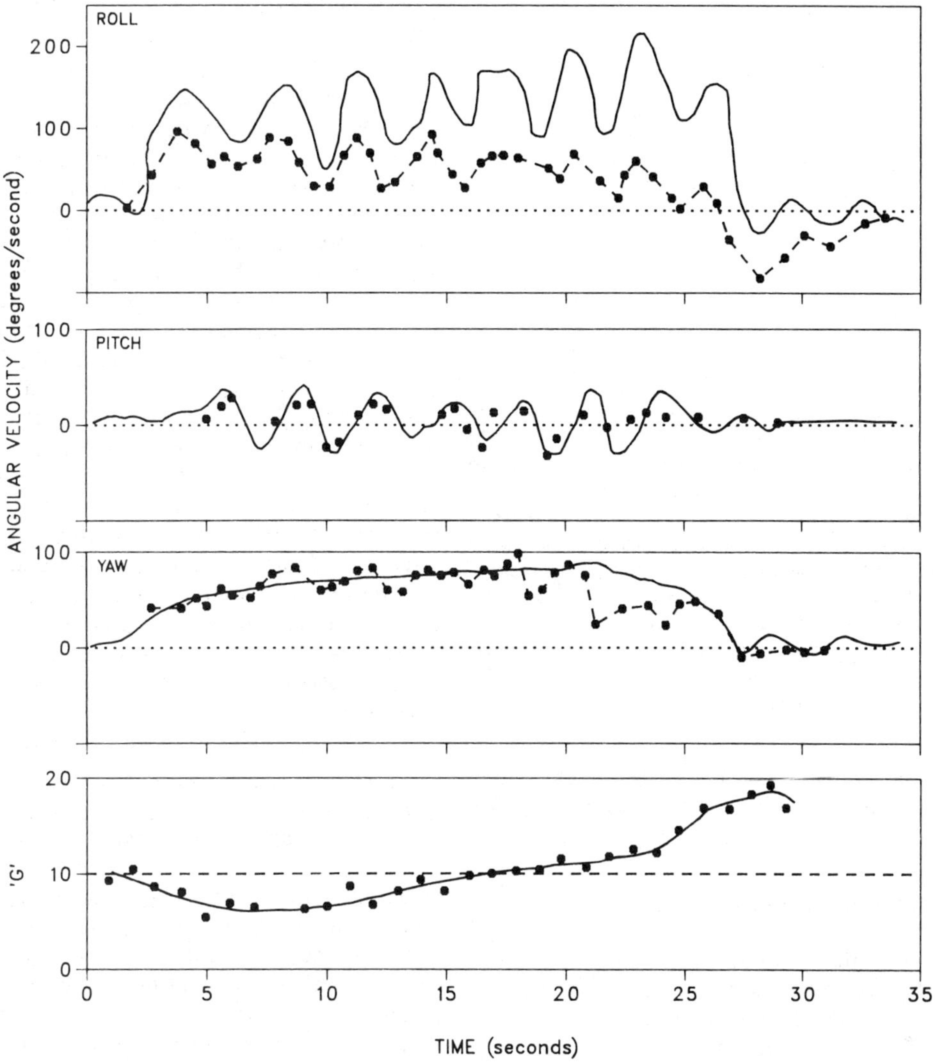

Figure 10.78. Vestibulo-ocular eye movements in aerodynamic spin. Pilot looking through windscreen during eight-turn spin. Aircraft recovers at 27 sec. Plot shows slow-phase eye velocity from photographic measurements of roll, pitch, and yaw components referred to skull. Continuous lines show smooth eye angular velocity required to counteract aircraft angular rotation; points are observed compensatory eye movements. *Yaw*: Intermediate level of stress (about $70° \cdot sec^{-1}$) is well compensated until about 20 sec, at which point vestibular signal wanes owing to mechanical properties of canal (elastic restoration of cupula). Post-rotary nystagmus due to these dynamics is not seen after aircraft recovery, presumably because of compensatory optokinetic afternystagmus. *Pitch*: Mild stress and good compensation along pitch axis in this example. *Roll*: Severe stress of $100–150° \cdot sec^{-1}$ along roll axis with compensation deteriorating with time. *'G'*: Normal acceleration or "g-force" on skull also fluctuates but is of no special oculomotor significance here. (From G. Melvill Jones, Vestibulo-ocular disorganization in the aerodynamic spin, *Aerospace Medicine*, 1965, *36*. Reprinted with permission.)

conjugate torsion developed in both eyes at a rate of about $0.8° \cdot hr^{-1}$ of practice, so that subjects could eventually hold torsions of 20° or more. Voluntary torsion was initially accompanied by sensations of bodily rolling, and even occasional nausea and fatigue during early training, but the movements subsequently became effortless. Once the skill is learned it is probably not forgotten, and special visual feedback is no longer necessary. Figure 10.81 (page 10-78) shows visual pursuit of a smoothly rolling line, in the presence of afterimage feedback. Pursuit velocity is severely limited in range ($1–2° \cdot sec^{-1}$), and faster tracking uses torsional saccades. Subjects had more difficulty pursuing when they were asked to imagine the rotating line and were presented with a black fixation dot and a linear afterimage. Tracking becomes mainly saccadic, as expected, when the subjects are given only a fixation dot and are thus denied perception of movement. Stimulus steps are tracked with a sequence of single or sometimes nearly overlapping saccades which typically undershoot. Dynamic overshoot and glissade can be present, and the amplitude-peak-velocity relations are identical to those already established for horizontal and vertical saccades (e.g., Bahill et al., 1975c). These findings suggest that voluntary torsional movements are generated by the usual brainstem circuits, and are subject to the usual variety of high- and low-level multiple drives. One of the subjects of Balliet and Nakayama had an appreciable horizontal exotropia of about 30°, but his rotary movements were equal; this suggests that

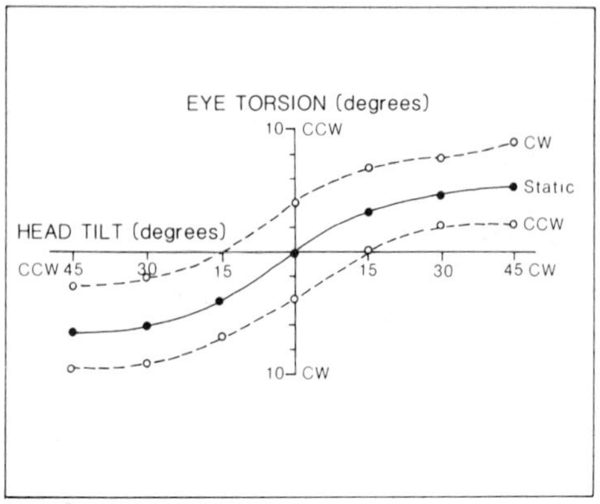

Figure 10.79. Head tilt and eye roll. *Ordinates*: Net eye roll relative to head, measured with an afterimage method for counterclockwise (CCW) and clockwise (CW) directions. *Abscissas*: Static head tilt in counterclockwise or clockwise directions. *Static*: Eye roll for various static head tilts while viewing a static 130° wide annular display (32° center), composed of white flecks on a dark background. *Outer traces*: Biasing of eye roll by clockwise (CW) or counterclockwise (CCW) rolling of the display at $20° \cdot sec^{-1}$. Average data for six subjects. Cycloversional movements such as these are probably very satisfactory in compensating for small head tilts or slow head rolling. (From B. H. Merker & R. Held, Eye torsion and the apparent horizon under head tilt and visual field rotation, *Vision Research, 21*. Copyright 1981 by Pergamon Press, Ltd. Reprinted with permission.)

torsion commands may roll the eyes about the current line of sight—which would seem to be biologically adaptive—rather than about fixed axes in the orbit.

3.6. Eye Movements to Flashing Targets

Repetitively flashing stimuli are used in vision research to assess visual persistence, to freeze the image and eliminate retinal-image slip, or to provide an impression of motion. Under some conditions flashing stimuli generate smooth movement.

3.6.1. Instruction: Fixate the Stationary Target

3.6.1.1. Head Fixed. When subjects fixate a flickering point in darkness, there is a tendency for the flicker to entrain the microsaccadic eye movements, presumably via a high-level mechanism, because most saccades are believed to be voluntary (West & Boyce, 1968). When subjects suppress microsaccades during fixation (<0.2 microsaccades $\cdot sec^{-1}$), which is easy to do (Section 3.1.1.2), and fixate a black point in a flickering field (17° subtense, 540 nm), flicker introduces a matching oscillatory wobble into the vertical or into both horizontal and vertical components of visually controlled drift. See Figure 10.82 (page 10-79). The latency of the oscillation is 130 msec (SD 48). In addition, there is progressive uncompensated drift. The temporal wave form of flickering background is not very material (e.g., sine, square, or triangle), nor is brightness (0.06–6.3 $cd \cdot m^{-2}$), shape, or size (e.g., a central 4° disk, or an annulus with inner and outer diameters of 7 and 17°). Uncompensated drift is reduced when the black fixation point is changed to a clearly visible steady light, but the flickering field still induces oscillation if the modulation depth is above 10–28% (Haddad & Winterson, 1975). Artifacts due to the lids, iris, and ciliary muscle have been excluded, and there does not seem to be any explanation in terms of recognized mechanisms or effects.

A related phenomenon occurs when the entire field of one eye is uniformly strobed, the other eye being occluded. In 24 of 60 subjects, nystagmus occurred with the fast phase toward the stimulated eye (Van Dalen, 1977). The vestibular nucleus may be involved, as it is active in optokinetic nystagmus.

3.6.1.2. Head Moves. When subjects are bodily oscillated about a vertical axis in the dark (at about 0.15 Hz and 10–$60° \cdot sec^{-1}$ peak-to-peak velocity), the eyes counterrotate at a somewhat slower speed. In normal lighting, and for large rotations at least, the speed of these compensatory movements reduces retinal-image slip well below $1° \cdot sec^{-1}$. If the subject puts on reversing goggles, the world rotates in the same direction as the head, but the vestibular system continues to drive what are now inappropriate eye movements, so that useful vision is frustrated by retinal-image slip. This manipulation has quite a different effect if retinal slip is eliminated by stroboscopic lighting, for instance, 3 μsec flashes at 4 Hz (Mandl & Melvill Jones, 1979). Gain (= slow-phase velocity/head velocity, ignoring sign) for ordinary rotation without goggles remains at the normal value of 0.99–1.00. But, in the case of reversing goggles, the smooth movement switches on delivery of the second flash to be in the direction of head rotation, as is appropriate for unfrustrated vision. The authors suggest that reversed smooth eye movement should be self-perpetuating once it is initiated. Such initiation might arise from unstable fixation due to flicker (Haddad & Winterson, 1975), aided by voluntary suppression of the vestibulo-ocular reflex (e.g., Barr et al., 1976). See also Section 3.6.2.3.

3.6.2. Instruction: Pursue the Moving Stimulus

3.6.2.1. Independently Moving Targets. When a row of lights at about 0.5° spacing is flashed *in sequence* at an appropriate interflash interval, with a flash duration of 0.2 msec, the subject perceives and smoothly tracks the apparently smoothly moving target (Morgan & Turnbull, 1978). Tracking became increasingly saccadic at interflash intervals greater than 150 msec (equivalent to an average target velocity of $3° \cdot sec^{-1}$), as shown by the increased standard deviation of the moment-to-moment tracking error. If inadequate visual persistence is a factor at long interflash intervals, one may wonder if reduced luminance or lowered contrast would further impair smooth tracking.

A large (100°) patterned annulus, rolling at 27 $deg \cdot sec^{-1}$ about an empty center, produces cyclotorsion of 1–4° in both normal and stereoblind subjects, even when stroboscopically lit at 8–20 Hz (Wolfe & Held, 1979). Similarly, a vertically oriented optokinetic drum, turning at $26° \cdot sec^{-1}$, induces horizontal optokinetic nystagmus when stroboscopically lit at 2.5–12 Hz in both normal and stereoblind subjects (Wolfe, Held, & Bauer, 1981). Out-of-phase dichoptic stimulation or a faster strobe rate improved the responses in both types of subject in both studies, probably because these eye movements are better when the illusion of motion is improved. Note that developmental abnormalities of binocular vision impair only some binocular functions.

3.6.2.2. Hand-Driven Targets. An actively moved target (±10° amplitude of motion at 1.5–2 Hz) is as well tracked when stroboscopically lit (for 10 msec duration at 5 Hz) as it is when continuously illuminated (Steinbach, 1969). Smooth tracking is still qualitatively good, though interrupted by saccades, during passive movement of the hand and target. A freely moving target is very poorly tracked at these flash frequencies, and the illusion of smooth motion is then largely absent (Fig. 10.83, page 10-80).

3.6.2.3. Stationary Displays. Flashing, spatially repetitive structures sustain an illusion of movement and smooth pursuit,

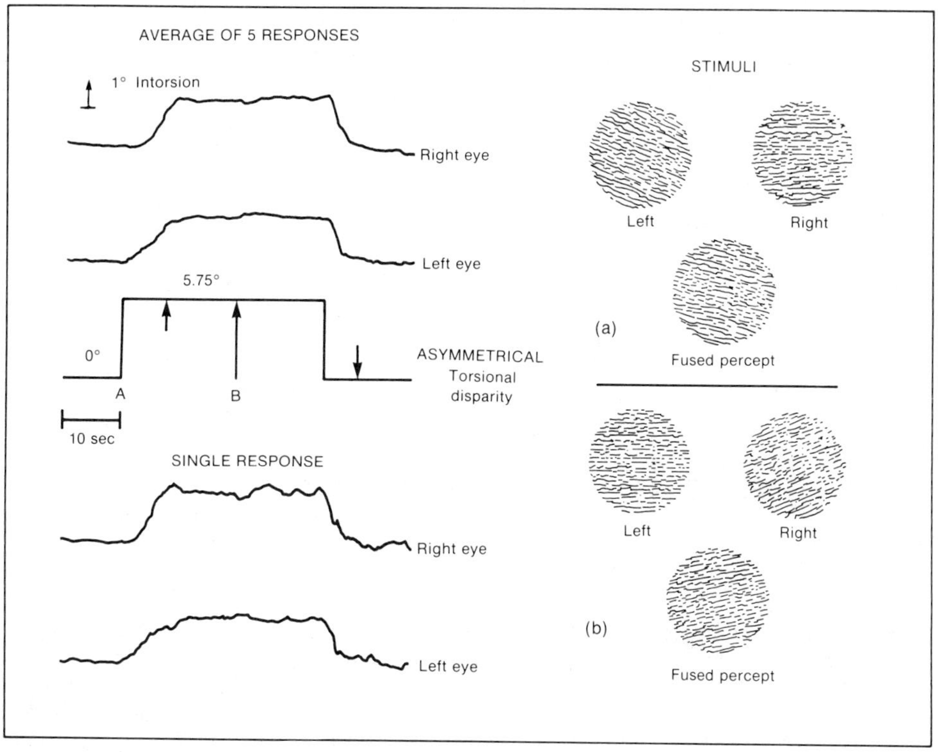

Figure 10.80. Intorsional disjunctive eye movements to asymmetric torsional disparity. *Left*: Subject initially views horizontal segmented grating patterns. At time *A* there is a step roll of the left pattern, which is partly compensated by binocular intorsion (from subject's point of view, left eye rolls clockwise and right eye rolls counterclockwise). The fused percept develops toward the end of the eye movement near the time of the small arrow. Switching the patterns at time *B*, without altering the intorsional disparity, alters the percept but does not affect eye position. Upper contact lens records are averaged to reduce measurement noise. *Right*: The stimuli to the left and right eyes at times *A* and *B*, and the corresponding fused percepts, are shown above and below, respectively. (From M. J. Sullivan & A. E. Kertesz, Binocular co-ordination of torsional eye movements in cyclofusional response, *Vision Research, 18*. Copyright 1978 by Pergamon Press, Ltd. Reprinted with permission.)

once the eyes are set smoothly moving by tracking a finger or some other real or apparently smoothly moving object (e.g., Stoper, 1967, and other references cited by Bridgeman, Mayer, & Glenn, 1976). A particularly striking target is a ring of equally spaced lights, *simultaneously* flashing at frequencies in the region of 0.5 Hz (Behrens & Grusser, 1977), which sustains lengthy circular pursuit, and appears to roll in the direction of pursuit. Clearly, if the eyes move smoothly from one light to another in the interflash interval, the status quo is not disturbed, much as in afterimage tracking. If the eyes move only a half space in an interflash interval, two revolving rings will be seen. Smooth pursuit is also self-perpetuating, once set in motion over stripes of correlated random dots on a background of random-dot noise; the stripes suddenly become visible in front of a snowstorm background. Smooth pursuit, mixed with saccades, can be produced by stroboscopic illumination (at 10 or 25 Hz) of rows of black dots or a continuous black line. The shifting of fixation along the line is subjectively obvious as a more intense black (Heywood, 1973b).

These observations, plus those on afterimage tracking, are consistent with the idea that there is positive feedback of eye velocity signals (Section 2.3.5). Addition of eye velocity and retinal-image velocity gives the spatial velocity of the target. Once the eye is set smoothly moving, a stabilized image, however produced, is seen as a smoothly moving target in space, and movement is sustained.

If a series of static pictures are flashed one after the other, the usual result is cinematographic motion or *apparent motion*, which can provide a stimulus for optokinetic pursuit movements. A recently devised sequence of frames provides moving bright stripes as a stimulus for optokinetic pursuit. The sequence for four frames has alternating equal red and green stripes for the first frame, yellow and dim yellow stripes shifted a half-stripe for the second, red and green stripes shifted a further half-stripe for the third, and yellow and dim yellow stripes shifted another half-stripe for the fourth; the sequence lasts 0.33 sec and repeats at 3 Hz. Apparent motion of bright stripes moving in one direction across the screen can occur only if the red and green stripes differ in luminosity, as well as in color, because only then are the cinematic requirements for motion met. The direction of the moving stripes, and thus the direction of optokinetic nystagmus, is determined by whether red or green is the brighter. This permits objective testing for anomalous color vision (Cavanagh, Anstis, & Mather, 1984).

3.7. Eye Movements to Abrupt Yaw and Pitch Motions of the Target

Abrupt motion of the target generally initiates saccadic tracking if the displacement is large enough, although some target steps in a series of steps may not cause responses. Under certain conditions, appreciable smooth movements may occur if saccades

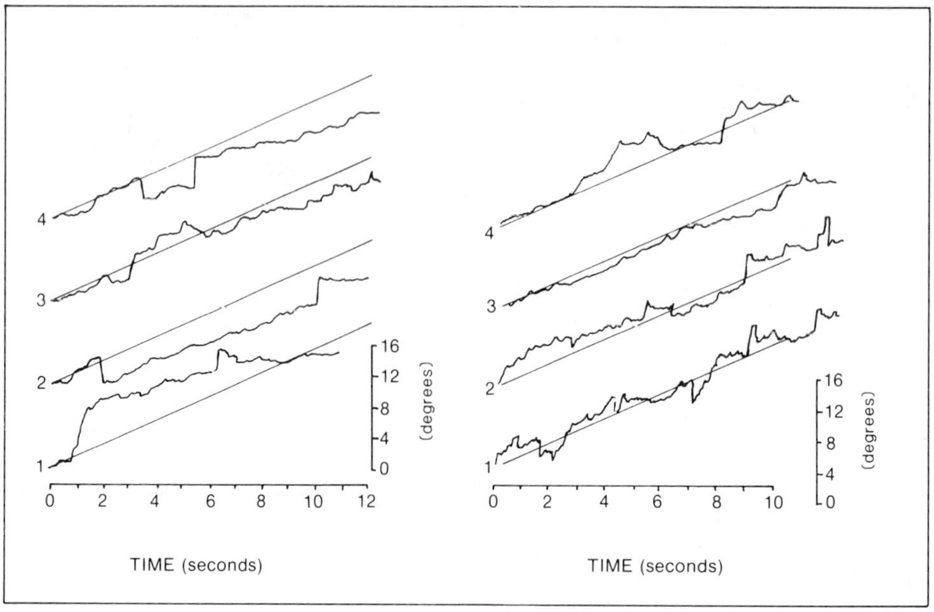

Figure 10.81. Voluntary cycloversional slow pursuit in two different subjects (left and right). Four consecutive trials, from photographic measurements of the right eye, of ocular rolling as the subject tries to make a linear afterimage match a line rolling end over end at 1.6° · sec^{-1}. Ramp shows stimulus rotation. Smooth eye movement is interrupted by occasional saccades. Rolling eye movements are similar to smooth and saccadic movements about the horizontal or vertical axes, though smooth velocities are rather low in degrees per second. (From R. Balliet & K. Nakayama, Training of voluntary torsion, *Investigative Ophthalmology and Visual Space*, 1978, *17*. Reprinted with permission.)

are frustrated. Minor smooth movements have also been demonstrated prior to expected steps.

3.7.1. Instruction: Track the Target When It Steps. The typical response to an unpredictable horizontal or vertical target step is a large primary or main saccade, which may or may not be followed by secondary, tertiary, or smaller saccades, called correction saccades. The adjective "corrective" is best applied to a saccade that can be shown to reduce error. On occasions, subjects will make very small primary saccades, followed by large secondary and tertiary saccades. Such "multiple-step hypometric saccades" are likely pathological in the normal foveating task if the saccades are slowed, or if velocities are normal but frequencies exceed 10–50% (Troost, Weber, & Daroff, 1974).

3.7.1.1. Small Steps. Microsaccades during fixation have a median size of about 4–5 min arc, and are now regarded as an easily suppressed behavioral artifact ("busywork"); see Section 3.1.1.2. Similar minute responses can be voluntarily made to very small target steps, but, in view of the large end-saccade errors (relative to the amplitude of the target step) and the long latencies, it is not clear that these tiny responses are as natural or as highly practiced as larger saccades.

(a) DATA. A contact lens study showed that two subjects would respond, at least part of the time, to a 0.5-Hz, 4–16-min arc horizontal or vertical square-wave motion (Bennet-Clark, 1964). If one disallows saccades at a latency of less than 150 msec from the step as being spontaneous or anticipatory, then horizontal steps of 5–180 min arc in two subjects were tracked with 0.7–1.0 probability, even when head position was rotated 18° left or right between different blocks of trials, altering eye position in the orbit (Timberlake, Wyman, Skavenski, & Steinman, 1972). The saccades were not very accurate by a percentage criterion, for 35–50% of error was left uncorrected. Standard deviation of end-saccadic error increased gradually with size of target step from a SD of 2 min arc for a 5-min step, via a SD of 12 min for a 1° step, to a SD of 21 min for a 3° step. Another experiment used a less-than-2-min arc target stepping in one of four cardinal directions; the two subjects responded to the 1.7-min arc target step on 0.65–0.71 of trials by saccades with a mean size of 2.6–2.8 min arc (Wyman & Steinman, 1973a). Clearly there is no *obligatory* "dead zone" to target steps in the foveation task, which is anatomically or physiologically determined, for some subjects at least (Haddad & Steinman, 1973; Steinman et al., 1973). However, if tracking microsaccades are a form of "busywork," they may not occur for other tasks or instructions, so it is necessary to examine the issue of a *functional* dead zone in the normal foveating task more fully.

In measurements by Young (1981) the stimulus was a thin vertical line, which stepped horizontally in darkness or against a rich visual field. The probability of a saccadic response increased with step size, being maximal for a 0.5° step and half-maximal for a 0.3° step. The model assumes that, as a consequence of previous eye movements, the target is initially at some random position within a vertical retinal strip or dead zone. There is always some probability that even a very small target step will elicit a response, as the initial target position may, by chance, be at the edge of the dead zone. Similar experiments were made by Lightstone (1973) on two subjects in the author's laboratory, but the stimulus was a small blue-green photopic spot (100 × foveal threshold) that stepped horizontally against darkness. The statistical model assumed that the initial target position was randomly and uniformly distributed anywhere within a *circular* dead zone as a consequence of prior motor activity. Despite different experimental and theoretical approaches, both Young and Lightstone agree that the half-width or radius R of this functional dead zone is close to 0.3° (17–30 min arc). Such a zone may approximately match the "foveal bouquet" of Polyak—a retinal area, characterized by densely packed photoreceptors, within which visual functions are assumed to be uniform—but there is a difficulty. Lightstone's model requires that the horizontal SD of initial eye positions within the dead zone be $R/2 = 11–15$ min arc for subject PEH, whereas the measured SD of fixation was 8 (4–12) min arc for 8.26 sec duration fixations, after allowing for apparatus noise. Even 8 min is a high estimate for fixation instability, given contact lens data, a more usual value being nearer 1–5 min arc (Steinman et al., 1973). Thus, unless some other motor activity shifts the point of fixation around the $\pm 0.3°$ zone, there may be a conflict between the well established high stability of fixation and the statistical assumption of random distribution within a large dead zone. One possible mechanism for shifting the point of fixation anywhere within the fovea is the error left by large saccades when the same object point is refixated after a large shift (> 3°) of the eye or target. See Section 3.7.1.5.

(b) Model of Functional Dead Zone for Saccades to Small Steps. Consider a circular dead zone with radius R centered on the fovea. The image of the fixation point is assumed to lie with equal probability at any point in the zone. The probability density for the fixation image being at horizontal position x is the length of the vertical chord at x, relative to the zone area [see Fig. 10.84(a)],

$$f(x) = \frac{2}{\pi R^2}(R^2 - x^2)^{0.5} \qquad \text{for } -R < x < R ,$$

with mean horizontal position 0 and variance $R^2/4$. Consider a horizontal step displacement of the fixation image to the right. There is no threshold size of step; even a small step has a chance of taking the fixation image out of the dead zone, and eliciting a return saccade, if the fixation image is already close to the right edge of the zone. If the step size is W, points within W of the edge will leave the zone. The shaded crescent of width W in Figure 10.84(b) shows the area containing these points. The probability of the fixation image being in the crescent is

$$P(W) = \frac{W}{2\pi R^2}(4R^2 - W^2)^{0.5} + \frac{2}{\pi}\sin^{-1}\frac{W}{2R}$$

$$\text{for } 0 < W < R .$$

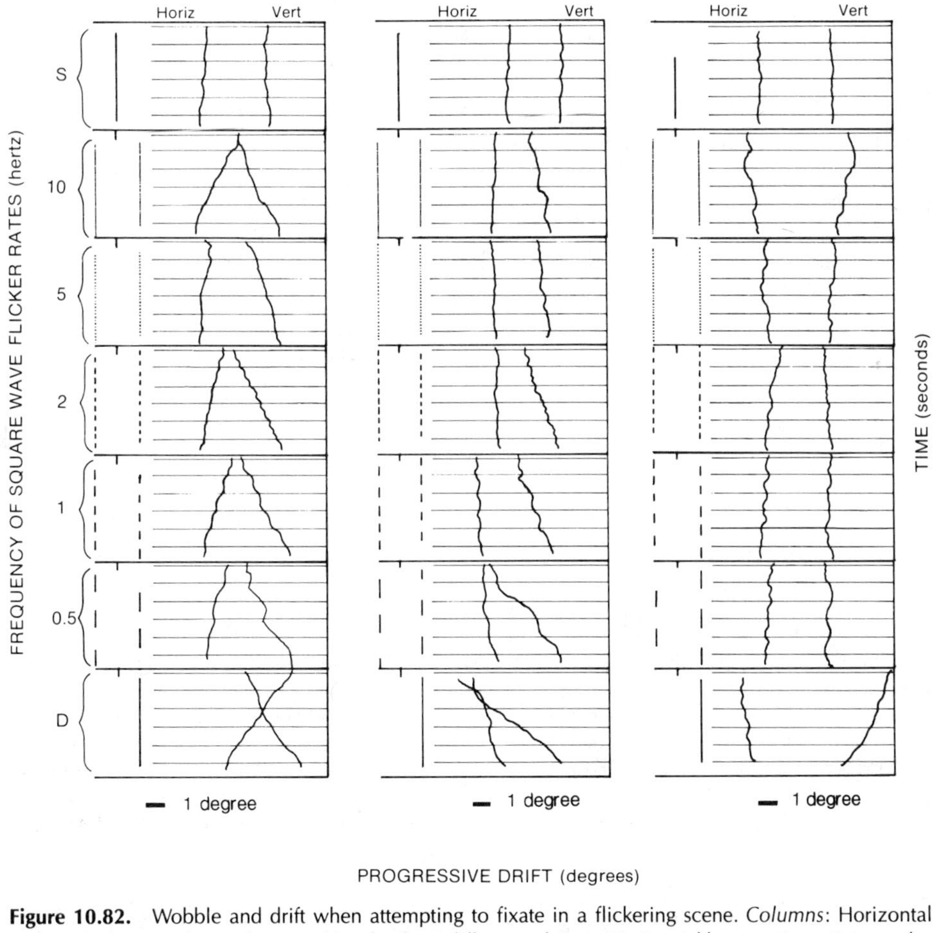

Figure 10.82. Wobble and drift when attempting to fixate in a flickering scene. *Columns*: Horizontal and vertical components of eye position for three different subjects. Horizontal bars are 1-sec time marks, and 1° calibration bars are shown at bottom. From top down. *S*: Small black disk fixated against steady background field. Fixation by slow control without microsaccades. *10, 5, 2, 1, 0.5*: Progressive drift is now apparent in response to 10–0.5 Hz square-wave flicker, plus wobble with an amplitude inversely related to frequency, for example, 6 min arc at 5 Hz and 20 min arc at 0.5 Hz. *D*: Drift in darkness. Note that wobble is not due to invisibility of fixation mark in dark phases, because similar behavior occurs with a continuously visible fixation point. (From G. M. Haddad & B. J. Winterson, Effect of flicker on oculomotor performance, in G. Lennerstrand & P. Bach-y-Rita (Eds.), *Brain mechanisms of ocular motility and their clinical implications*. Copyright 1975 by Pergamon Press, Ltd. Reprinted with permission.)

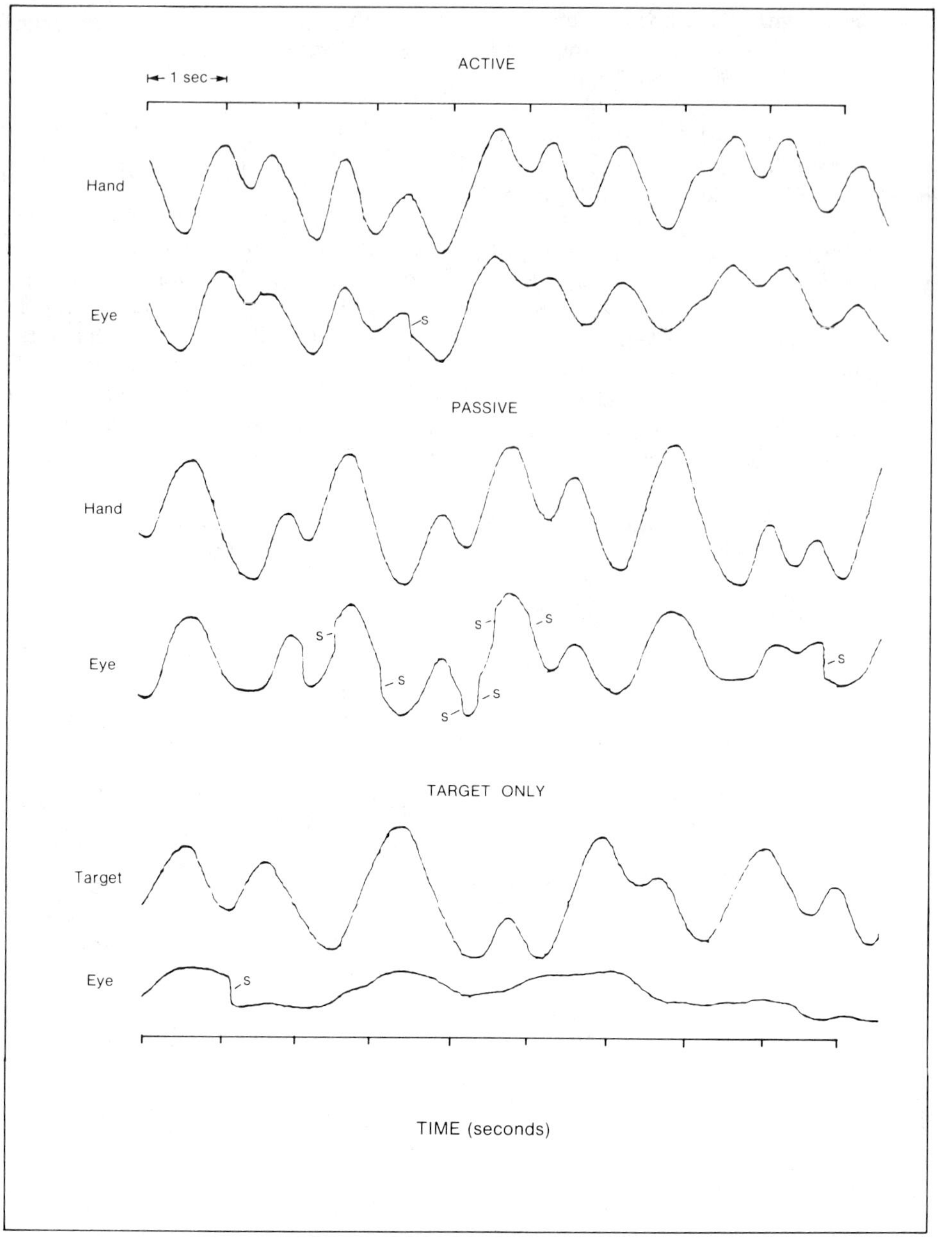

Figure 10.83. Smooth pursuit tracking a moving hand under "strobe" illumination. Actually, the subject was in darkness and did not see his hand; instead he held a lever that controlled a small flickering spot of light optically superposed on the tip of his middle finger. Spot of 10-msec duration and 5-Hz flicker frequency. Five subjects studied, records for one shown here. I have marked obvious saccades with the letter *s*. From top down. *Active*: Subject vigorously moves lever and tracks spot very well. *Passive*: Subject's hand and lever are moved passively by the experimenter. Smooth pursuit is more frequently interrupted by saccades. *Target only*: Subject removes hand from lever and tracking of the vigorous target motion fails. Evidently, it is a matter of the eye and hand being programmed together, rather than the eye "tracking" the hand by means of visual or somatic feedback. (From M. J. Steinbach, Eye tracking of self moved targets: The role of efference, *Journal of Experimental Psychology*, 1969, *82*. Reprinted with permission.)

Thus $P(W)$ is also the probability of the fixation image leaving the dead zone and eliciting a saccade when given a step of size W. It is useful to note that $P(W) = 0.61$ at $W = R$ [Fig. 10.84(c)]. Lightstone's (1973) data supporting this model have already been mentioned and are shown in Figure 10.84(d). The fit of data to the model agrees with the claim of Young (1981) that the functional dead zone for saccades is about $\pm 0.3°$.

Both Young (1981) and Lightstone (1973) explain the functional dead zone in terms of a large dead zone with simple properties. A counter-hypothesis is that the large functional dead zone for saccades to small steps is due to (1) a very small fixation zone of a few minutes of arc width (Fig. 10.36); (2) a high sensory threshold of about 0.3° for saccades to steps, unless subjects are specially instructed (Steinman, 1976); (3) the image being returned to the small fixation zone by visually controlled drift (Section 3.1.1.2) if the step size is less than the sensory threshold for a saccade. More work is needed to decide between the conflicting hypotheses.

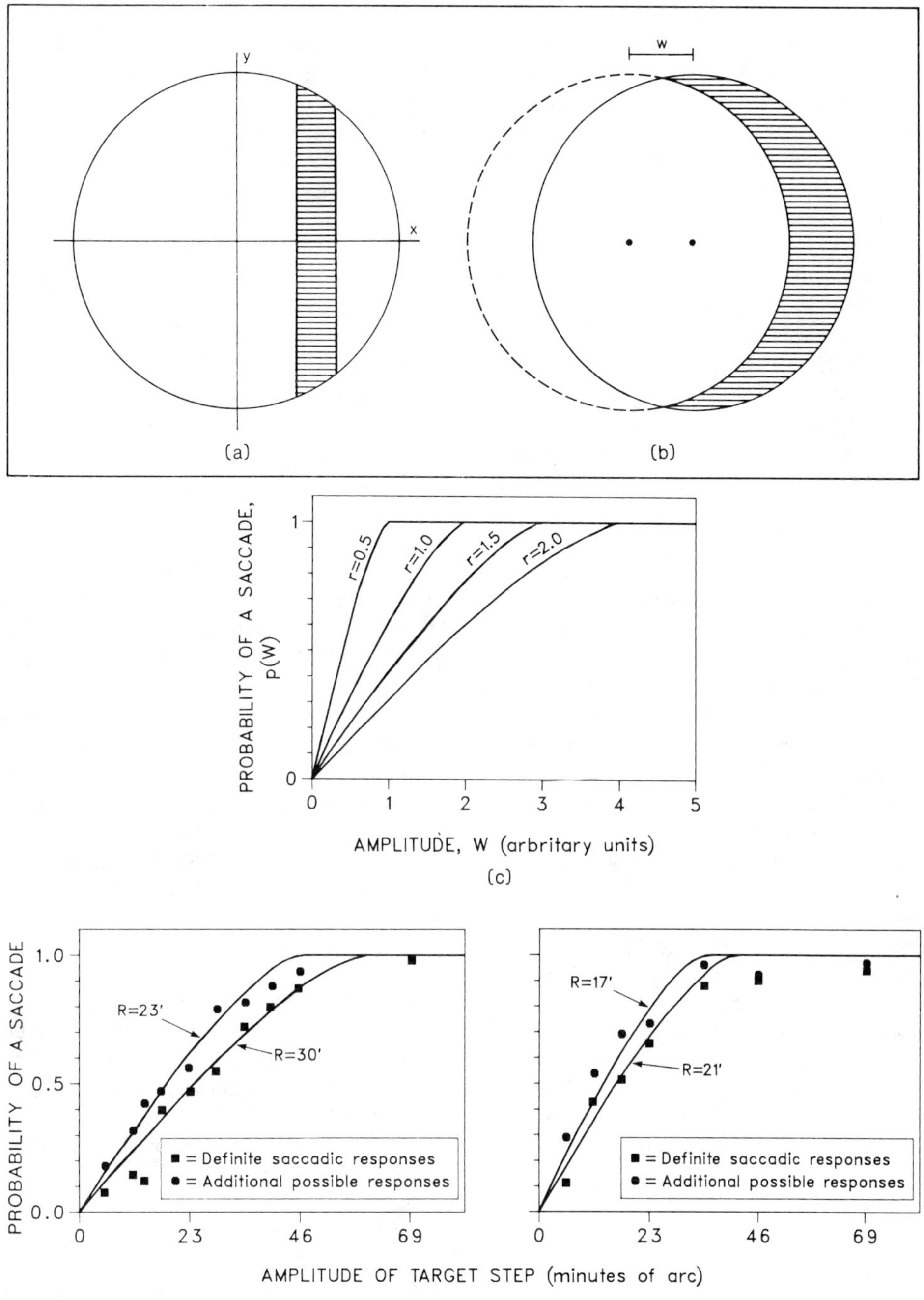

Figure 10.84. Model of the functional dead zone to small target steps. (a) The coordinates represent the retinal surface, and the circle is the dead zone within which the image of the fixation point is randomly distributed. Probability of the fixation point image being at horizontal position *x* is proportional to the area of the narrow vertical chord through *x* relative to the area of the dead zone. (b) The heavy circle is the dead zone; the dashed circle is constructed to evaluate the probability of response. If fixation image lies anywhere within *W* min arc to the left of the right edge of the zone, then a horizontal displacement of the image to the right by *W* will cause the image to leave the dead zone. Actually, the fixation image lies anywhere within the dead zone, so the probability is the area of the shaded crescent of width *W* relative to the area of the dead zone. A tracking saccade occurs if the image leaves the dead zone. (c) Theoretical probabilities of a saccadic response (ordinates) versus horizontal displacement *W* (abscissas) for dead zones of different radii. (d) Observed probabilities of a saccadic response as a function of the amplitude of the target displacement. Data from 1000 and 600 trials by two subjects (left and right plots) for a small bright blue-green target viewed against darkness. Squares are based on definite saccadic responses within 100–500 msec of the step; points include additional possible responses. The dead-zone radii that fit the data are shown against the fitted curves. A functional dead zone of about $\pm 0.3°$ is to be expected if the central fovea is uniform in its visual properties. (Adapted from Lightstone, 1973.)

3.7.1.2. Latency of the Primary Saccade. Although an unpredictable step displacement of the stimulus is frequently used as a control, it is still not completely clear how saccadic latency is influenced by different factors. Two major factors are the subject and the stimulus luminance. Other factors usually amount to only a few milliseconds, and are thus trivial in comparison with the usual mean and standard deviation of latency, but exceptions are frequent. Of course, multiple step displacements involve additional factors.

(a) SUBJECT. Many workers regard mean latencies of 200 or 200–250 msec to randomized targets as being normal values, for example, 213 msec (three subjects of Bartz, 1962) and 250 msec (Heywood & Churcher, 1980). In my laboratory the mean latency has ranged from 163 to 264 msec (median 197 msec) for 13 consecutive subjects and steps of 3.8–15.3° (8–10° on average). Very few or no primary saccadic latencies are less than 140–150 msec, unless the subject anticipates or is visually forewarned (see below). Primary latencies are almost always distributed as a single well-defined peak, which is often skewed toward longer latencies.

(b) LUMINANCE. Most eye movement studies use darkness as a background. The effect of stimulus luminance for a small target stepping 6° left or right can be described by separate linear relations between log latency and log luminance, for scotopic and photopic vision (Wheeless et al., 1967). The scotopic and photopic latency functions intersect at a luminance 0.5 log below the foveal perceptual threshold, which is presumably a reasonable value for the rod/cone transition at 6° retinal eccentricity. These findings have been confirmed in my laboratory (Doma, Note 2), except that we see lesser increases in mean and standard deviation of latency as luminance falls, and would lay more stress on latency approaching an asymptotic minimum at 1.5–2 log above foveal threshold. Obviously, bright stimuli should be used in experiments aimed at dissecting latency mechanisms; otherwise differences in luminance will complicate the comparison of latencies in different studies.

Piéron's law for reaction time versus luminance gives a generally good description of latencies in perceptual and button-pushing tasks, and perhaps for the electroencephalogram also (review and data of Mansfield, 1973). Piéron's law relates reaction time T and stimulus luminance L by

$$T - T_{\infty} = kL^{-\beta}$$

where T_{∞} is the minimal or asymptotic latency for the scotopic or photopic mechanism to very bright stimuli, k is a constant of the scotopic or photopic mechanism, and β varies from 0.33 to 0.5, depending on stimulus size (Mansfield, 1973). My preliminary fits to Doma's data suggest that the deviations from Piéron's law in the photopic range are small for the normal foveating task (e.g., 7 msec).

(c) TARGET DURATION. The primary saccade to a briefly exposed target is normal in latency and amplitude, and probably in velocity profile as well (Barnes & Gresty, 1973; Becker, 1972; Hallett & Lightstone, 1976a, 1976b), though poor performance is also possible (Pernier, Jeannerod, & Gerin, 1969). Normal accuracy and latency are also seen for the saccade toward a small bright target, briefly exposed during a prior saccade against a completely dark background (Hallett & Lightstone, 1976b). It should be realized, however, that the subjects often failed to respond when the target was briefly lit at a position *just ahead* of the prior saccade's eventual termination. A temporal integration period has not been measured. Although normal responses to a target of 1 to 3 msec duration imply a mechanism with transient characteristics, it is possible that a temporal integrating period was missed if the target intensity were sufficient to saturate the response at all target durations.

(d) PREDICTABILITY (INCLUDING REPETITIVE STEPS). Although saccadic eye movements are subject to a large measure of voluntary control, anticipation of the stimulus step or guessing is easily defeated by randomization when measuring latency in the normal foveating task. Reaction time in many behavioral tasks is related to the number of possible alternatives (e.g., the number of bits of information required; Hick, 1952), or to the number of items that must be remembered (e.g., Sternberg, 1969). This is not the case in saccadic tracking. Set size has little or no effect on saccadic latency (Heywood & Churcher, 1980; Saslow, 1967b), perhaps because the well-practiced saccadic response matches the physical dimensions of the stimulus (e.g., spatial direction and amplitude) in a natural fashion (Fitts & Posner, 1967). Indeed, a subject trained on several randomized target positions may continue to track, and not anticipate, when there is only one possibility (Saslow, 1967b), though it would be rash to depend on this. When subjects were told that the target set contained only 8° left- or right-going steps, or only 4 and 8° left-going steps, and so on, the four subjects were able to reduce latency by 12 msec (7–17) when *direction* was known, but not when amplitude was known (Newman, 1972). Knowledge of both amplitude and direction gave a more modest advantage (5 msec) in these particular measurements. These data are interesting because other experiments show a dichotomy in the processing of direction and amplitude (See Section 3.7.2).

When direction is known, *highly* trained monkeys can track with latencies that are very narrowly distributed around 70 ± 4 msec, provided the target displacement is the learned one. There is also suggestive evidence of other potential modes at 140 and 200 msec (Fischer & Boch, 1983).

When a stimulus steps repetitively between two known positions at 0.4–1 Hz, the subject appears to develop a rhythmic internal model of the motion, and may respond with near-zero latency (Stark et al., 1962). This is probably biologically adaptive, because the subject gains more time for perceptual analysis by synchronizing the perceptual disturbances due to the stimulus and saccadic transients. In one study, anticipatory saccades occurred before the step, and visually elicited saccades after it. Saccades were absent in the 0–100-msec region (Horrocks & Stark, 1964). Anticipatory saccades are also seen when the stimulus motion is more random, for example, if the stimulus steps repetitively from center to left or right at random, and then back to center, and so on, with a step every 350–650 msec (i.e., at 1 Hz on average; Findlay, 1981b). A scarcity of saccades in the 100–120-msec region supports the present notion of retinal cancellation with 100–120 msec delay, and allows a clear-cut distinction between earlier anticipatory and later visually guided tracking responses. The two types of saccade show approximately similar amplitude versus peak velocity relations, though more precise measures are definitely needed. Most anticipatory saccades were made to the center position, and were relatively small (75–90% of normal amplitude), their frequency increasing with time since the last step. The results suggest a two-stage process: the probability of a saccade increases with time, but the saccade is only released if the retina or an internal model can supply a goal.

Findlay's data (1981b) also show a reduction in the latency of the visual tracking saccades by about 15 msec as the time from the *previous* step increases from 350 to 650 msec. The broad term "visual warning" is used here to denote latency reductions or increases due to another visual stimulus, the warning stimulus.

(e) VISUAL WARNING. In susceptible subjects, latency may be reduced by an earlier stimulus step, or a stimulus onset, change, or offset, occurring about one normal reaction time before the triggering stimulus. Of these the most potent is stimulus offset (L. Ross & S. Ross, 1980), so the simplest procedure is to blank a single stimulus for a period before it is stepped and relit at a new position (the "gap" condition of Saslow, 1967a). In several studies the latency reduction is reported as large (46–80 msec) and so the forewarned mean latency is only 106–126 msec if the normal single-step latency is short (154–186 msec) in the given subjects (e.g., Becker, 1972; Feinstein, 1970; Henson, 1977; Saslow, 1967a). Forewarned latency is longer (194–208 msec) if the control latency is longer (240–288 msec), for example, Newman (1972) and L. Ross and S. Ross (1980). The above reports do not stress intersubject variation, but Feinstein's (1970) data are intriguing: a small vertical stimulus step of 0.5° or less acted as a potent though inconsistent forewarning stimulus, shortening latency to a subsequent 6° horizontal step for one subject but *not at all* for another! Data for the gap task (11.5° step) in this laboratory show only modest latency reductions for three subjects (ca. 20 msec), once anticipatory responses are identified and removed (Kalesnykas & Hallett, 1983; Kalesnykas, Note 5, for conditions otherwise as Hallett & Adams, 1980). The optimal gap value for latency reduction was around 150 (100–250) msec. Another subject showed a latency *increase*, most marked at the optimal gap value, so it is hard to believe that visual forewarning is a low-level innate mechanism for speeding saccadic tracking.

One can discount a role of microsaccades in forewarning. First, it is highly unlikely that sporadic microsaccades inflate primary latency in the control single-step task (e.g., by introducing additional refractoriness between the stimulus step and the primary saccade), because microsaccades are never seen, even though commonly used recording methods would be sensitive enough to reveal about 30–50% of microsaccades. Second, forewarning occurs with both a dark gap, which should eliminate microsaccades, and with a luminous stimulus which should not (L. Ross & S. Ross, 1980).

Latency is prolonged if the warning stimulus occurs after the triggering stimulus step, an onset being rather more effective than an offset (L. Ross & S. Ross, 1980; S. Ross & L. Ross, 1981). Offset is an easier condition to study, and can be realized by leaving the initial fixation point lit for a period after the presentation of an eccentric stimulus (the "overlap" condition of Saslow, 1967a). Intriguingly, latency appears to be maximally inflated in the overlap task by about the same amount saved in the gap task (Hallett & Adams, 1980; Newman, 1972; Saslow, 1967a).

A variant of the warning paradigm, more relevant to aircraft displays, is where the warning stimulus identifies the subject's task as being one of two possibilities, just in advance of the step of the target. A pilot study on an experienced subject showed that the foveal warning cue should precede the random horizontal target step (3.8–15.3°) by several reaction times, the inflation in latency being particularly marked when the warning was less than one normal reaction time in advance of the target. See Figure 10.85(a). There are probably several factors involved, for a similar though less marked inflation of latency occurred when the subject knew that only one task was possible. Perhaps the visual cue provided an "overlap" condition by remaining at the fixation point after the step of the target. See also Hallett (1978, Figs. 9 and 11).

One would think that a very effective warning would be provided if the target displacement were triggered by the subject rather than by a random clock pulse (Findlay, 1983). However, Hallett and Lightstone (1976a, 1976b) studied a variety of two-step conditions, in which the first step displacement was triggered randomly and the second was triggered by the beginning of the saccade to the first step. Saccadic latencies to the random and saccade-triggered steps were equal. This finding reduces the plausibility of the notion that the primary saccade shortens the latency of the secondary saccade by forewarning (Becker, 1972; Deubel, Wolf, & Hauske, 1982).

(f) STEP SIZE. Latency is not systematically related to step size for a considerable range of amplitudes, but is increased for very small steps of less than 1° or for very large steps of 40° or so. For two subjects mean latency was high (350–400 msec) for a 3.5-min arc step but fell toward more usual values (220–260 msec) for the larger steps (Wyman & Steinman, 1973a). No effect for similar small steps was reported for two subjects by Bennet-Clark (1964), but the predictability of the 0.5-Hz target may have been a factor. No systematic effect of step size is reported for medium amplitude steps (Hallett, 1978; Hallett & Adams, 1980; Heywood & Churcher, 1980; Saslow, 1967b), or large steps (Becker, 1972), though a slow increase of latency with step size is claimed by Bartz (1962); Michard, Tetard, and Levy-Schoen (1974); and White, Eason, and Bartlett (1962). Pirozzolo and Rayner (1980) and Findlay (1983) have similarly commented on the literature. Findlay (1983) has plotted literature values. Systematic studies are badly needed. A longer latency for small steps could reflect more extensive cortical processing of foveal inputs. Of course, if the stimulus is not bright, then any alteration of retinal illumination with eccentricity will complicate responses to large steps. For a comparison with manual reaction times, see Payne (1966).

(g) DIRECTION OF STEP. Because of technical problems, most studies employ only horizontal left/right steps. One recent study pooled data for several different directions (Hou & Fender, 1979), so any direction factor was presumably small. However, direction was the second most important factor in the study of Heywood and Churcher (1980), latencies for upward-going saccades being about 31 msec shorter than for downward saccades, which echoes two older studies (Hackman, 1940; W. R. Miles, 1936). It would seem that direction is *sometimes* a factor.

(h) HANDEDNESS. For small steps to the right, eight right-handers showed slightly shorter latencies than for steps to the left (Pirozzolo & Rayner, 1980). This could reflect a cerebral hemisphere asymmetry in right-handers, given more heavily cerebral processing for targets near the fovea.

(i) BINOCULARITY. Although experimenters are unlikely to mistake abnormal individuals for normal when selecting subjects, it is disturbing that visual acuity can be restored to the normal value of 20/20 (Snellen chart score) by successful orthoptics treatment, and yet the mean latency of primary saccades may remain high for stimuli presented monocularly to the treated eye (ca. 310 msec for 0.3–10° steps). Binocular latency, or latencies for the normal eye, were more normal (ca. 210 msec), as were latencies for secondary saccades (Ciuffreda, Kenyon, & Stark, 1978a, 1978b, 1979). For the probabilistic advantage of using two eyes in a reaction-time experiment, see Blake, Martens, and DiGianfilippo (1980).

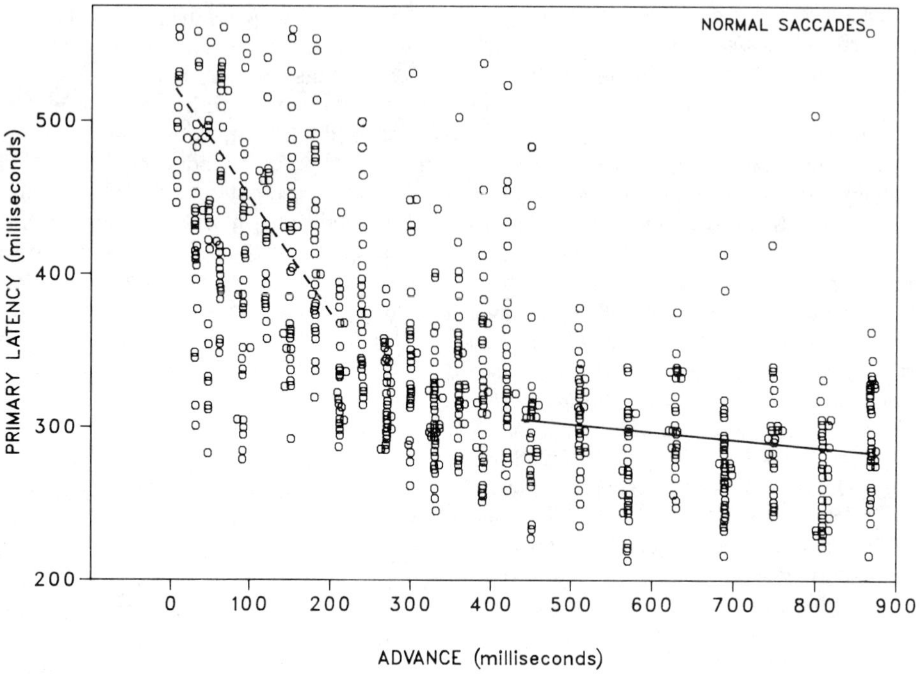

(a)

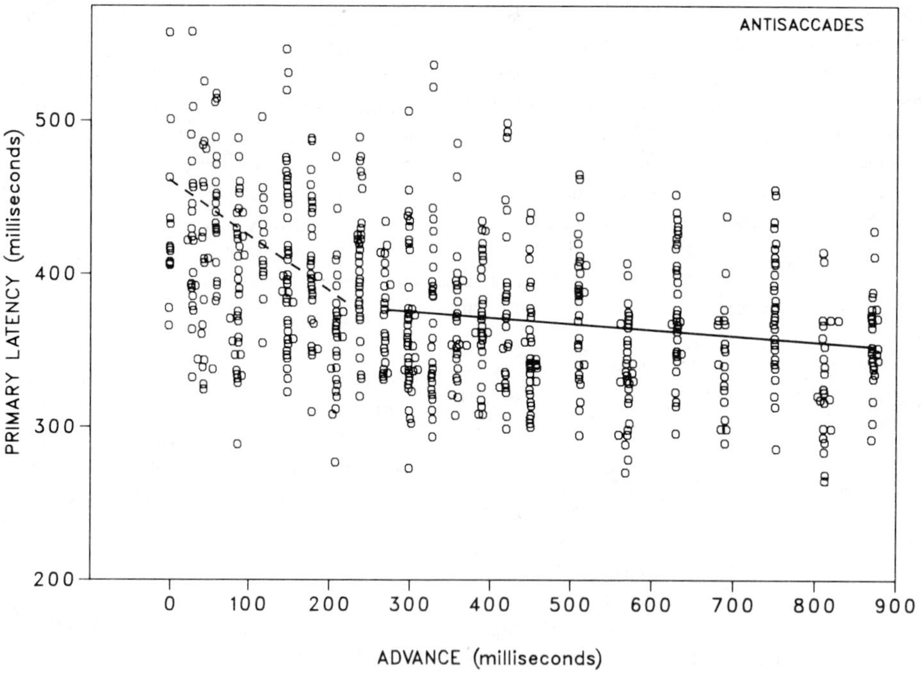

(b)

Figure 10.85. *(Legend opposite).*

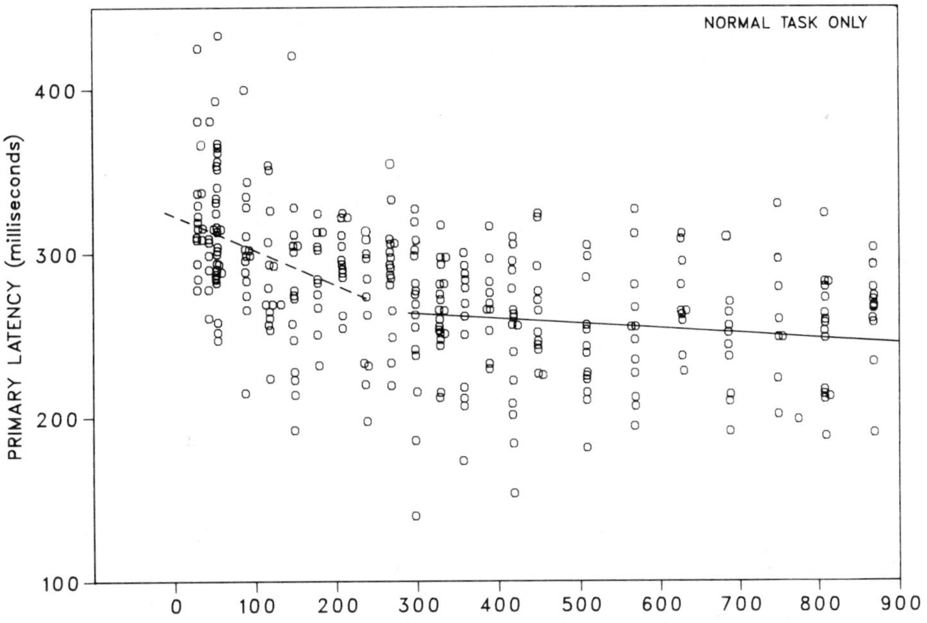

(c)

Figure 10.85. Effect of warning the subject as to the task a short time before the step displacement of the target. Ordinates are latency of the primary saccade. Abscissas are the times at which the cue is delivered in advance of the target step; subject otherwise has no knowledge as to whether the normal foveating task or the "anti" task will be requested. Points show individual trials. Normal task is warned by 0.7° radius foveal C-shape with the gap at the top; "anti" task by the inverted C-shape plus an acoustic tone. Both tasks are randomly mixed in the same session. (a) Data for 700 trials in which the normal task is requested. Latency is longer than the control value (253 msec in this subject), even with 900-msec advance of the cue. Inflation is particularly marked when the advance is less than 250 msec. (b) Data for 700 trials in which the "anti" task is requested (i.e., look away from the target when it steps by an equal and opposite amount). Latency is longer than the control value of 362 msec, even at 900-msec advance, and inflation is increased at advances of less than 250 msec. (c) An additional control experiment. The "warning" cue is as for (a), but the subject knows that every trial will be the normal task. Note change in the range of ordinates. Latencies are normal for advances of more than 500 msec; inflation in latency is particularly marked for advances of less than 250 msec. Small bright target and cues against darkness; pupillary eye monitor. Part of the increase in latency must be due to the cue being lit at the point of fixation just before the target steps, as in (c); part must be due to interpreting what action is requested by the cue. Increase in latency was particularly pronounced when the advance was less than the subject's normal reaction time in all three plots. (Unpublished data of Adams & Hallett, 1980, extending experiments of Hallett, 1978.)

(j) Models of Primary Saccade Latency. A striking feature of the saccadic system is that the latent period between stimulus step and response is so much longer than the duration of the response itself. The system is characterized by considerable delay. According to one model (Carpenter, 1981), neural excitability builds at a constant rate (a "ramp," as it were) and initiates a saccade when a fixed threshold is crossed. If the slope of the ramp is randomly distributed from one trial to the next (Gaussian distribution), the frequency histogram for latencies will not be Gaussian but will be skewed toward longer values, unless transformed and plotted in some appropriate way. Figure 10.86(a) shows cumulative frequency on a probability scale (ordinates) versus the reciprocal of latency (abscissas). This transformation gives a linear result for the normal foveating task, which apparently confirms Carpenter (1981). However, in another task (the "anti" task, Section 3.7.3), where the subject looks away from the stimulus step, the transformation gives a curvilinear result because the original latency histograms were more symmetrically distributed. Also, Figure 10.87 shows that the transformation gives a linear result for a completely different model (the delayed gamma distribution) in which the latent period is modeled as the sum of a constant delay a plus the variable delay associated with passing through a fixed number of stages b of neural stages at c stages per second on average (Poisson process). It would seem, then, that the Carpenter linearization does not succeed for all saccadic tasks and is not restricted to a particular model.

The delayed gamma model has been examined in this laboratory by Doma (Note 2) in two different tasks, using linear fits to plots of mean versus standard deviation of latency. The stimulus stepped to 10° left or right. The normal task and "anti" task data for 12 consecutive subjects imply a constant delay a (latency intercept at zero SD) that is roughly the same in the two tasks (perhaps 138 ± 8 or 142 ± 12 msec, respectively). The "anti" task seems to involve more stages of delay than the normal task (b = squared slopes of mean/SD = 13 ± 2 or 6 ± 2, respectively). Parameter c varied from 4 to 12 msec per stage in the different subjects. However, the latency histograms ac-

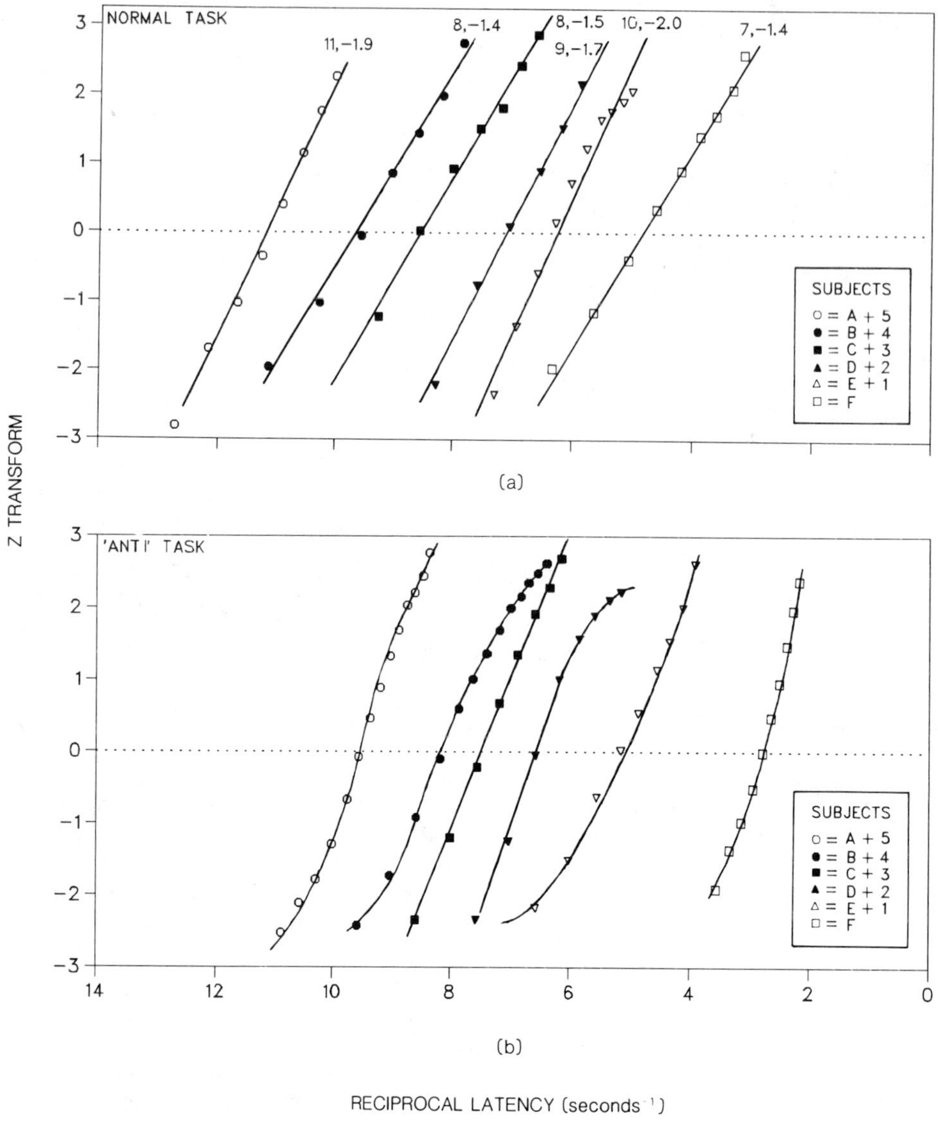

Figure 10.86. Carpenter (1981) transformation of saccadic latencies. Ordinate is a "probability scale" where the z transform of the probability $P(\mathbf{L} < l)$ that latency on a given trial is less than a specific value l is given by

$$P(\mathbf{L} < l) = \frac{1}{\sqrt{2\pi}} \int_{-\infty}^{z} \exp^{-x^2/2} \, dx \; .$$

Abscissas are the reciprocal of latency l. (a) Normal-task latency histograms are skewed to long latencies but are normalized by taking reciprocals and z transforms. The Carpenter transformation for latencies $\overline{N}$ in the normal foveating task is shown for five subjects. For clarity the data have been displaced horizontally by the amounts shown for each subject. Intercepts on $\underline{z}$ and slopes are also given at the upper ends of the curves. (b) Data from the same sessions for latencies $\overline{A}''$ in successful attempts at the "anti" task (which requires that the subject look away from the step stimulus by an equal and opposite amount). Anti-task latency histograms are typically symmetrical. Consequently, the Carpenter transformation does not give a linear result. Small photopic stimulus steps in darkness, left or right by 10°, at an unpredictable time. Experimental conditions otherwise as in Hallett and Adams (1980). (Replotted from data of Doma, Note 2.)

curately matched the delayed gamma distribution in only half the cases. Larger samples are needed. The experiments deserve repeating with more extensive spatial randomization of the stimulus so as to thwart latency-reducing strategies in the "anti" task.

The effects of a warning stimulus have been tentatively formulated by Hallett and Adams (1980) in terms of a model like that in Figure 10.32 (Section 2.3), in which the latent period between a stimulus and its saccade is split into afferent, central, and efferent delays. Thus latency in the normal single-step task is formulated as the sequence of delays ACE. It is suggested that latency in the overlap task of Saslow (1967b) increases toward the sum of the sequence $AC''CE$, as if one variable central decision (**C**) is needed to cancel fixation on the initial stimulus,

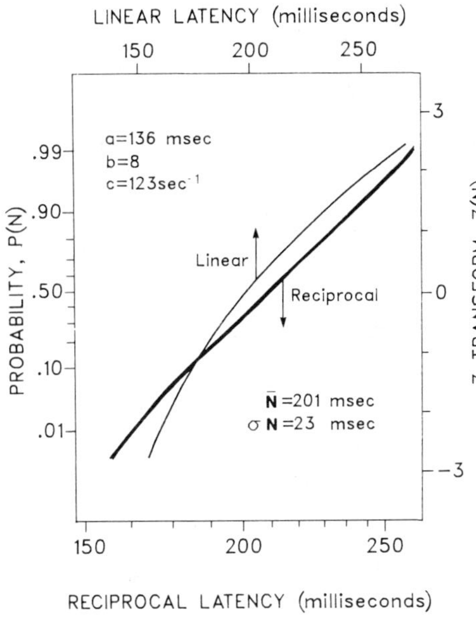

Figure 10.87. Carpenter transformation for the delayed gamma distribution. In this model saccadic latency is due to a constant delay *a*, plus the variable delay due to progressing through *b* stages, at *c* stages per second on average. Top and left scales: Left ordinate is cumulative probability *P*(**N**), on a "Probability scale," that latency is less than the abscissal value. Top abscissa is linear latency and refers to the plot in a thin line, which is curvilinear. Bottom and right scales: Right ordinate is the standard statistical z transform of *P*(**N**). Bottom abscissa is latency on a reciprocal scale and refers to the plot in heavy line. The reciprocal scale effectively linearizes the model data. Thus the gamma model with b = eight stages of delay is similarly skewed to normal-task latencies. The model parameters *a, b, c* were chosen for normal-task latencies with the mean and standard deviation shown. The delayed gamma model simulates anti-task data if *b* is increased by a factor of 2–3.

and another to choose a new goal. In the gap task, latency supposedly shrinks *toward* the sequence of delays *AE*, as if most of the variable **C** decision elapses with the forewarning stimulus. Better data are needed. (Note that $A + E = a$ and $\bar{\mathbf{C}} = b/c$ in the gamma model above.)

3.7.1.3. ***Amplitude, Duration, and Velocity of Primary Saccades.*** It is customary to use plots of amplitude versus peak velocity, and amplitude versus duration, to test whether an eye movement is a normal saccade. Peak velocity reflects the pulse force that overcomes viscous drag, saccadic duration the duration of the pulse, and saccadic amplitude the step force that holds the eye against elastic restoring forces (e.g., Bahill, 1981; Robinson, 1964, 1981). On linear scales, with negative and positive values representing left- and right-going saccades, the plot is a slightly asymmetric sigmoid (like a dose-response curve) with peak velocity saturating around $\pm 700° \cdot \text{sec}^{-1}$ above $\pm 20°$ amplitude (Eizenman et al., 1984). Each half of the plot may be fitted with a saturating exponential function, for example,

$$\dot{\theta}_{\max} = 684\ [1 - \exp(-0.1\ \Delta\theta)]$$

where $\dot{\theta}$ max is peak saccadic velocity and $\Delta\theta$ is saccadic amplitude (Bahill et al., 1981). A plot of log amplitude versus log peak velocity or linear duration, with no regard for direction, is dubbed "the main sequence" by some authors and better emphasizes the smaller saccades (Bahill et al., 1975c; Baloh et al., 1975). See Figures 10.88 and 10.89. The main sequence shifts somewhat with the initial position of the eye. When the eye is strongly abducted or adducted ($\pm 40°$), the velocity of centering saccades is then high, perhaps because of the elastic restoring forces (Abel, Dell'Osso, Daroff, & Parker, 1979).

General aspects of the main sequence that have been studied include variability in the population (Bahill et al., 1981; Baloh et al., 1975), the effect of age (Abel, Troost, & Dell'Osso, 1983), the effect of strabismus (Ishihawa & Terohado, 1973), whether the main sequence is modified for closely successive saccades (Bahill, Bahill, Clark, & Stark, 1975), whether fast phases are saccadic in the "end-point" nystagmus that is seen for extreme deviations of the eyes (Abel, Parker, Daroff, & Dell'Osso, 1978), and whether abrupt head movements can be dubbed "head saccades" (Stark, Zangemeiser, Edwards, Grinberg, Jones, Lehman, Lubock, Narayan, & Nystrom, 1980). Head velocities are, of course, very much lower than eye velocities because of inertia.

A saccadic eye movement frequently ends with a brief duration, monocular, velocity reversal, which has the amplitude-peak-velocity characteristics of a saccade (Bahill et al., 1975a), see Figures 10.25 and 10.26 (Section 2.2), and Figures 10.88 and 10.89. This "dynamic overshoot" is said to be capricious in its occurrence, to be largest (up to 1°) for large (>30°) saccades, and to be most conspicuous for microsaccades, in which the overshoot may equal the steady-state change in eye position. Dynamic overshoot can affect both horizontal and vertical components of oblique saccades, and is responsible for the hook-shaped saccades noted by earlier workers (Llewellyn Thomas & O'Beirne, 1966; compare with Viviani, Berthoz, & Tracey, 1977). In a recent model, the *relatively* large overshoot of microsaccades is attributed to a minimum duration for activating the brainstem pulse generator, whereas dynamic overshoot for larger saccades is due to an inevitable short delay in the local eye-position feedback that quenches the burst neurons. In either case, there is an overshooting error that directly activates the contralateral burst neurons, and thus the antagonist muscles, without the intervention of higher levels (Zee & Robinson, 1979).

Voluntary nystagmus is comparable with dynamic overshoot. Subjects who have the knack can evoke bursts of horizontal pendular oscillations of various amplitudes (0.4–30°) and frequencies (3–42 Hz, i.e., up to 80 saccades per second) while making a forced convergence or, occasionally, when completing a refixation saccade (Sharpe et al., 1975; Stark, Hoyt, Ciuffreda, Kenyon, & Hsu, 1981). At the higher frequencies the velocities of voluntary nystagmus are too high, relative to amplitude, to fit the main sequence. This is plausibly a consequence of overlapping the declining velocity phase of one saccade with the increasing velocity phase of the next (oppositely directed) saccade, so as to achieve resonance.

Glissades, in contrast to saccades, are long-duration movements usually attributed to a monocular mismatch between the underlying pulse and step forces (Bahill et al., 1975b; Easter, 1973). Typical dimensions are about 1.1° (0.2–5) in amplitude, $8° \cdot \text{sec}^{-1}$ (0.5–15) in velocity, and about 280 msec in duration. The quasi-exponential settling characteristics imposed by the viscoelastic restoring forces have already been diagramed (Fig. 10.30), and velocities are comparable to those of vergence movements. Back-drifting glissades are roughly twice as common as forward-drifting glissades (13 versus 7%), but "fatigue" (or inattention?) changes the ratio in favor of forward drifts. The mismatch hypothesis is not accepted by all (Dell'Osso, Daroff, & Troost, 1973).

Fatigue is said to be an important variable affecting saccades (Bahill & Stark, 1975; Schmidt, Abel, Dell'Osso, & Daroff, 1979), although the nature of the fatigue has not been defined. "Fatigue"

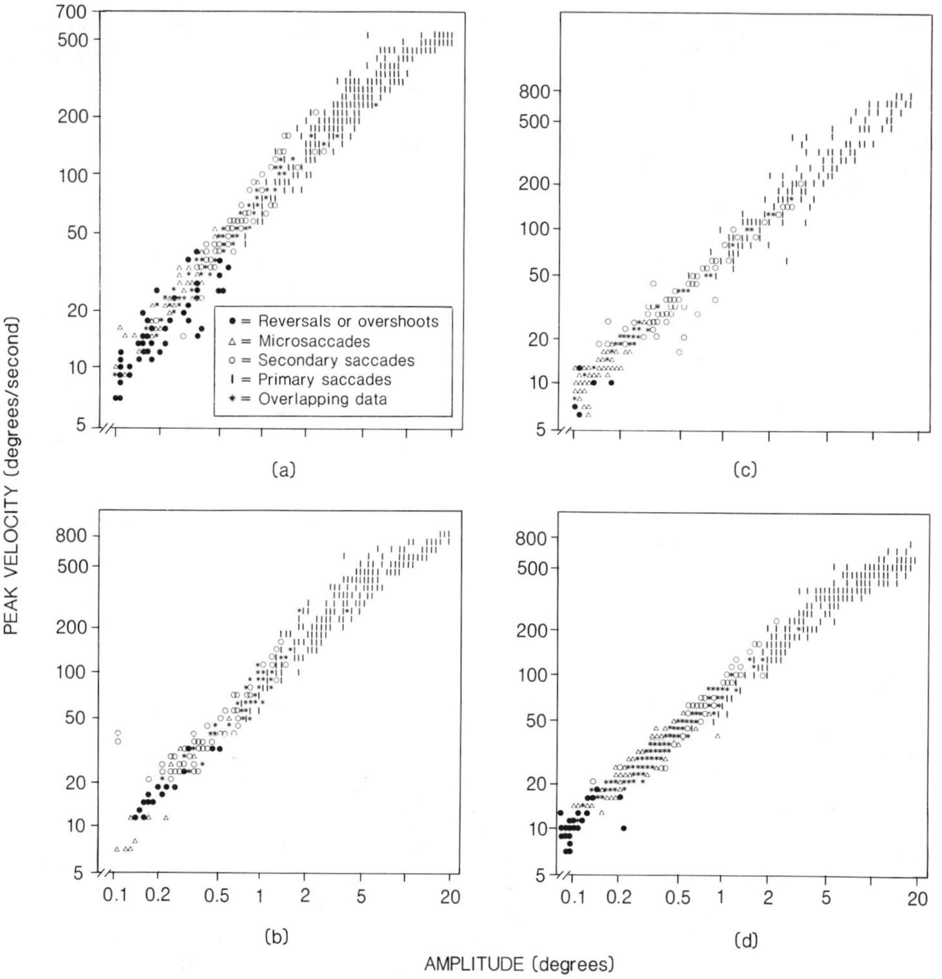

Figure 10.88. Peak velocities versus amplitude plots for four types of saccade. Log coordinates; only nasally directed saccades shown for clarity; data for four subjects (a–d). Symbols are ● for the reversals or overshoots of microsaccades and △ for microsaccades, from the task of fixating a bright target; and ○ for secondary saccades and | for primary saccades, from the task of tracking random horizontal step displacements of the target in the range ±16° (steps every 0.8–1.3 sec). Overlapping symbols are indicated where possible by asterisks, but a number of points along the line of mean trend are omitted for clarity. Precision corneal reflex monitor of Eizenman, Frecker, and Hallett (1984). The continuity of the four types of saccade along a common curve is consistent with all saccades having a single neuromechanical basis. This basis is the powerful pulse of force that accelerates the eye, and the lesser step of force that holds the eye at its new position. (After Eizenman, Frecker, & Hallett 1984.)

suggests some long-lasting impairment (e.g., at the level of the motoneurons or muscles), but simple encouragement restores performance, so it is more likely that lack of attention or arousal is the factor (Fuchs & Binder, 1983). Fatigue favors forward-drifting glissades, overlapping saccades (characterized by double velocity peaks separated by a dip), and long-duration, low-velocity saccades that fall below the main sequence when plotted (Bahill & Stark, 1975). Similarly, some primary saccades in some subjects are qualitatively anomalous in profile when the subject makes an "anti" saccade away from the stimulus, suggesting low peak velocities and multiple-pulse saccades (Hallett, 1978). This is not attributable to fatigue because it occurs early in the session, and is more plausibly attributed to the indirect use of visual information in this task (e.g., Hallett & Adams, 1980). In a similar manner, the fast phases of nystagmus are generally reckoned to be saccadic in their amplitude-velocity characteristics (e.g., Ron et al., 1972), and lessened vision (i.e., darkness) attenuates the velocities of both fast phases and saccades (Sharpe, Troost, Dell'Osso, & Daroff, 1975).

As an alternative to the main sequence approach, one may examine the power spectrum of the temporal frequencies that compose a saccade (Zuber, Semmlow, & Stark, 1968). Other aspects of the mechanics of the eye and its muscles were presented in Sections 1.3.1–1.3.3.

3.7.1.4. End-Primary Error. Several authors have claimed that the mean amplitude of the primary saccade is about 90% of the step (e.g., Becker, 1972; Hallett, 1978; Henson, 1979; Prablanc, Massé, & Echallier, 1978), so if their conclusions are pooled it would seem that undershooting error is the tendency for 4–54° nonpredictable steps. Whether this is an artifact of the customary dental impression, eliminating a small contribution of head turning to gaze, is not known. Frequency distributions of the error at the end of the primary saccade for pooled 4–15° target steps are shown in Figure 10.90(a) which also shows how errors are reduced by corrective saccades and drift in the 650 msec following the primary saccade. The situation for very small steps is variable, one study showing consistent undershooting of 5–180-min arc steps, the end-primary error being 35–50% undershot on average (Timberlake et al., 1972), and another study showing overshooting of 1.7-min steps (Wyman & Steinman, 1973b). The increasing preponderance of undershoots for larger stimulus steps was regarded by Bartz (1967) as being consistent with eye-hand performance in general, though it is not clear to what extent manual errors in eye-hand tasks arise from saccadic errors. Robinson (1973) and Henson (1977, 1979) view systematic undershooting as a mechanism ensuring only occasional (<5%) overshoots of more than 0.5°, thus keeping the retinal image within the visual field of the initially responding hemisphere; but better data are required, and it is not clear why switching *both* sensory and motor processing to a different hemisphere should require extra time.

Amplitude is sometimes different from control values when the target is extinguished at the start of the saccade, but this has not been demonstrated in all subjects and sessions (Deubel et al., 1982; Adams & Kalesnykas, Note 7).

3.7.1.5. End-Primary Error and Secondary Saccades

(a) ROLE OF VOLITION. End-primary error is an important determinant of secondary saccade amplitude (Becker, 1972). It should cause no surprise that a subject can exert considerable freedom in the choice of the goal for a saccade, and can deliberately undershoot the stimulus step by half, or overshoot by a roughly fixed amount, or even look away from the stimulus step by a roughly equal and opposite amount (Hallett, 1978). It is nevertheless very difficult to be accurate on command, and the systematic error is more often undershoot than overshoot, though there are certainly exceptions. Two subjects were asked to take their time and completely suppress secondary saccades, by making very accurate primary saccades to 4–12° left/right step-displacements of a small, bright point target in darkness. End-primary errors were not reduced, being if anything increased, despite constant verbal feedback from the experimenter,

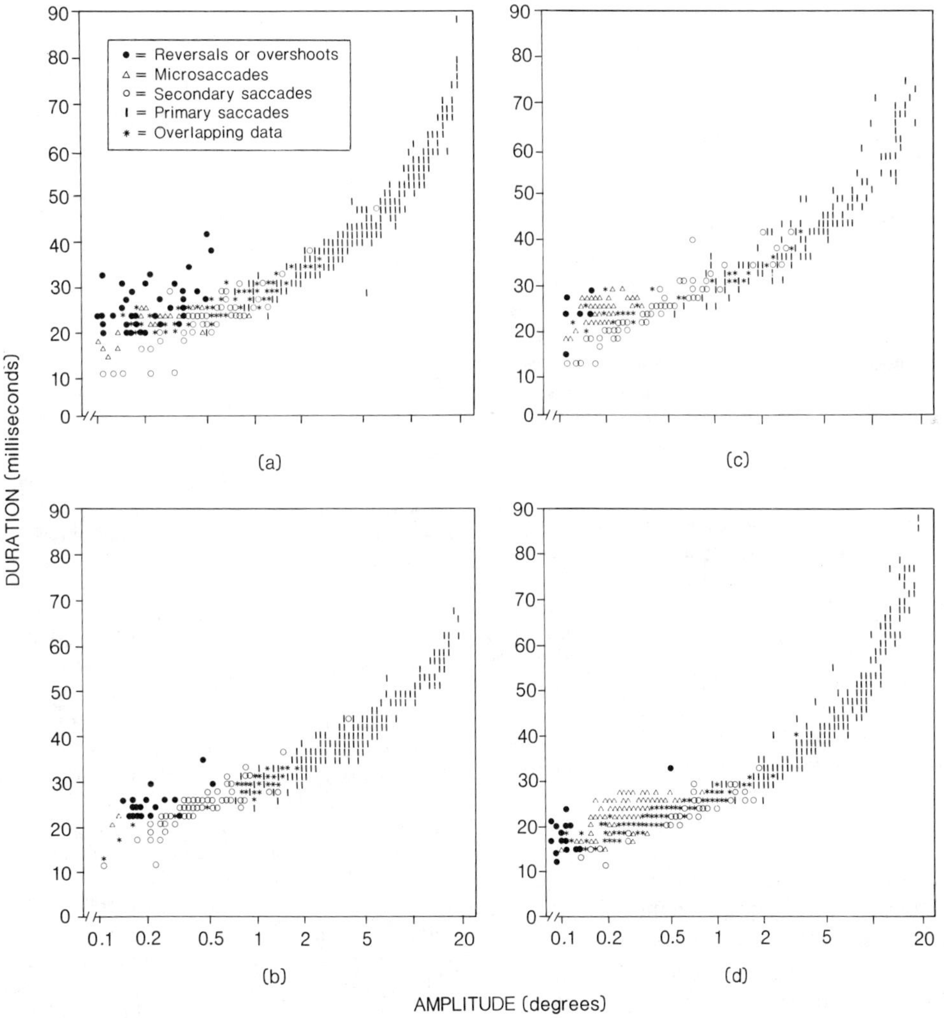

Figure 10.89. Duration versus amplitude plots for four types of saccade. Semilog coordinates; only nasally directed saccades shown for clarity; data for four subjects (a–d). Symbols are ● for the reversals or overshoots of microsaccades and △ for microsaccades, from the task of fixating a point target; and ○ for secondary saccades and | for primary saccades, from the task of tracking a horizontally stepping target. Overlapping symbols are shown by asterisks. Precision corneal reflex monitor of Eizenman, Frecker, and Hallett (1984). The continuity of the four types of saccades is consistent with all saccades having a common neuromechanical basis. (After Eizenman, Frecker, & Hallett, 1984.)

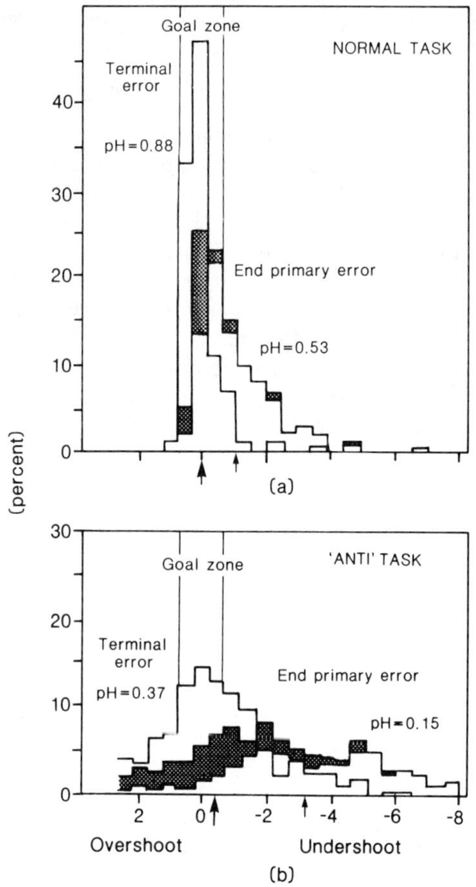

Figure 10.90. Distribution of end-primary and terminal errors for saccadic eye movements in two different tasks. In the normal task the subject is attempting to foveate the stimulus when it steps, whereas in the "anti" task the subject attempts to look away from the stimulus by an equal and opposite amount. *Heavy-line histograms*: Distribution of "terminal error," 650 msec after the end of the primary saccade, is centered near 0 error in both tasks, as shown by the heavy-line histograms and the heavy arrows that mark the means. *Thin-line histograms*: Error at the end of the primary saccade is more dispersed and generally undershooting, and the means are shown by the light arrows. The hatched areas in the thin-line histograms show those generally small end-primary errors that are not corrected by a secondary saccade in less than 350 msec. The remaining areas of the thin-line histograms (unhatched) are the generally large errors that are rapidly corrected by secondary saccades. Relative to the normal task, errors in the "anti" task are relatively large, secondary saccades are relatively fewer, but still corrective, and secondary latency is usually shorter. Probability of a "hit," pH (i.e., an end-primary error within the $+0.7°$ goal zone), is less than normal in the "anti" task. Pupillary eye movement monitor. (From P. E. Hallett, Primary and secondary saccades to goals defined by instructions, *Vision Research, 18*. Copyright 1978 by Pergamon Press, Ltd. Reprinted with permission.)

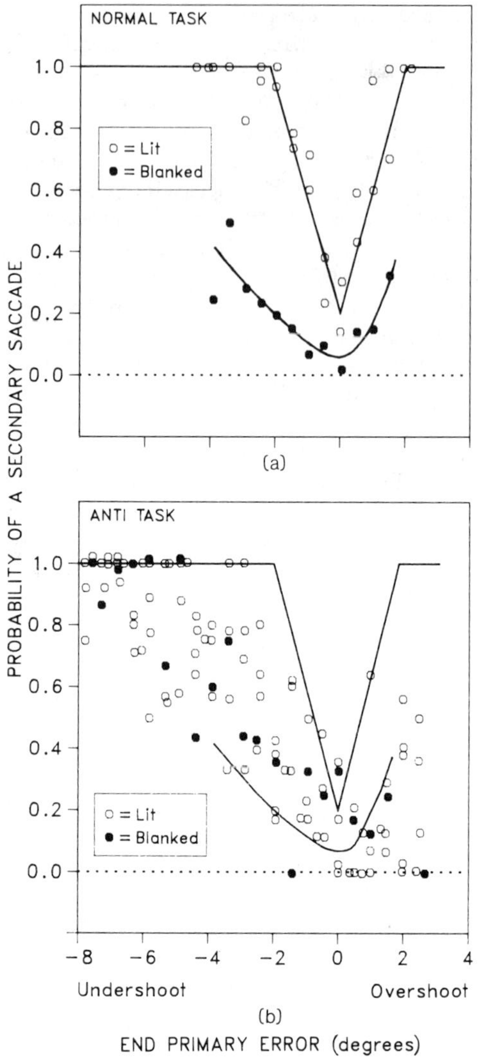

Figure 10.91. Dead zones for secondary saccades to target steps. Ordinate shows probability of a secondary saccade of more than $20° \cdot sec^{-1}$ peak velocity within 350 msec of the end of the primary saccade. Abscissas are the angular extent in degrees of the undershooting or overshooting error left at the end of the primary saccade. (a) Data for the "normal task" in which subject EC attempts to foveate the target. Curves illustrative. When the target remains lit (open symbols) the half-width of the dead zone at 0.61 probability is about 1° in this particular subject. When the target is blanked (dark symbols) at the beginning of the primary saccade (at $20° \cdot sec^{-1}$ velocity), the extrapolated half-width is over 3°. (b) Data for the "anti" task in which the subject attempted to look away from the stimulus step by an equal and opposite amount. Data are more scattered, but the dead zone is clearly large. Blanking the stimulus at the beginning of the primary saccade had no effect. Both blanked and unblanked points fall reasonably close to the curve for blanked saccades from (a). Data for another subject were similar except for absence of overshooting errors. Pupillary eye monitor; small bright photopic stimulus against darkness. The normal task dead zone is appreciably large in this particular subject even when the target is lit; foveation is improved by smooth drifting movements or by eventual saccades. The very large dead zone in the blanked normal task, or in the lit or blanked "anti" task, points to the value of visual feedback and the limited accuracy of eye position signals. (Original data of Hallett, 1978, replotted by E. Conway.)

70–100-msec increases in mean latency, and two- to fourfold increases in standard deviation of latency (Adams, Note 1). The frequency of secondaries was only partly reduced.

(b) Dead Zone for Secondary Saccades. The probabilistic relation between end-primary error and secondary saccades is illustrated in Figure 10.91(a) (open circles). End-primary errors of more than 2° were always corrected by secondary saccades within 350 msec in this subject. Errors smaller than 1° were often left uncorrected by secondaries, though some were reduced by drift or occasional long-latency saccades. Residual (or "terminal") errors 650 msec after the end of the primary saccade are nevertheless appreciable [Fig. 10.90(a)], so one may wonder if large end-primary errors help to shift the fixation image around the fovea, as is required by large dead-zone theories (Section 3.7.1.1). When visual feedback is denied by blanking the target at the beginning of the primary saccade, the dead zone for secondaries is deepened and widened, as expected, given the relatively low accuracy of eye-position feedback for saccadic planning [Fig. 10.91(a), filled circles]. See Section 2.1.11 for comments on the accuracy of eye position signals for saccadic planning; see Section 3.7.1.1 for a model; also see Figure 10.92.

3.7.1.6. *Secondary Saccade Latency and Dependency on Visual Feedback*

(a) LATENCY. How to measure latency is not obvious. The latency of a secondary saccade is conventionally measured from the *end* of the primary saccade as origin, which is reasonable, given evidence for visual feedback at the end of the primary saccade in several subjects (e.g., Becker & Fuchs, 1969; Prablanc et al., 1978). There is also evidence in two subjects for visual input *early* in the primary saccade (Fig. 7 of Hallett & Lightstone, 1976a). In addition, the untested possibility that occasional secondaries are prepared in parallel to the primary saccade, and simply come too late, might justify the use of the stimulus *step* as the time of origin. If secondaries are heterogeneous it is possible that there is no single correct origin.

A common view is that secondary saccades occur less than a normal reaction time from the end of the primary saccade, with a typical end-primary mean latency of about 125 msec (e.g., Weber & Daroff, 1972). However, our consistent experience is that secondary latencies are actually wide-ranging relative to primary latencies (Hallett, 1978; Adams, Note 1; Doma, Note 2). In this laboratory, latency peaks in the normal foveating task (11 subjects) range from about 100 msec to about one anti-task latency (e.g., $\bar{\mathbf{A}}''$ = 270 msec) after the end of the primary saccade, depending on the subject. Whether the longer latencies were learned as a result of practice at the "anti" task (Section

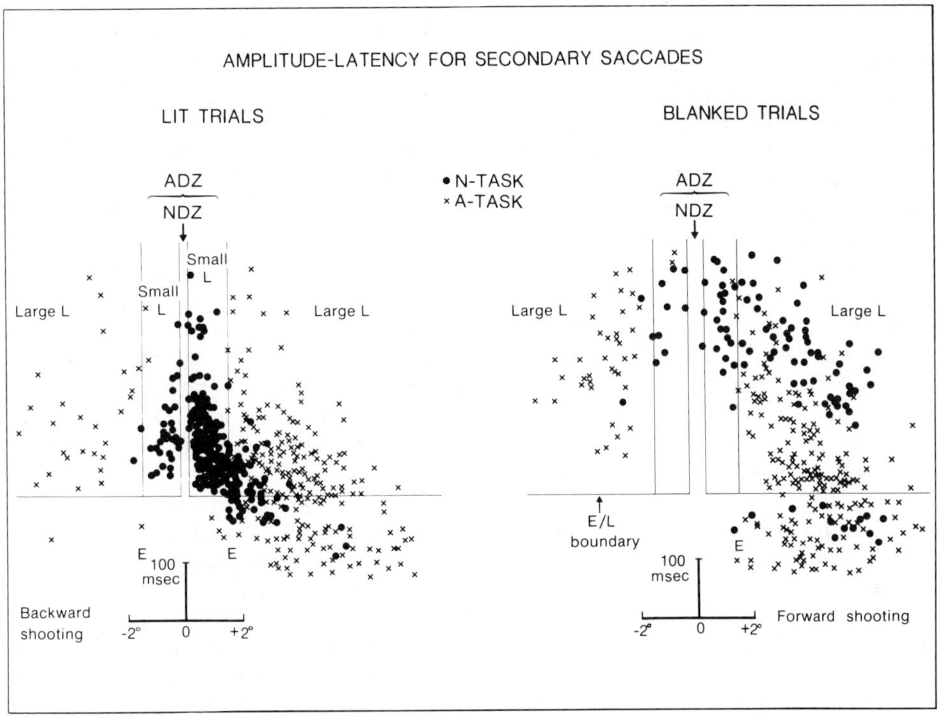

Figure 10.92. Saccadic amplitude versus latency for secondary saccades to step displacements of the stimulus. Two tasks and lighting conditions are shown: "lit trials" on the left, where the stimulus remains lit throughout the trial, and "blanked trials" on the right, in which the stimulus is blanked at the beginning of the primary saccade at a velocity of 20° · sec^{-1}. Data for two different saccadic tasks are shown by separate symbols. In these scatter plots the zero origin is at the center of the axes as shown, but the latency ordinates and the amplitude abscissas have been truncated for simplicity. Latency is measured from the *start* of the primary saccade. Positive abscissas denote forward-shooting secondaries, negative denote backward-shooting. Because the data for individual subjects are variable in range and symmetry, the data for three subjects have been combined, so as to better illustrate the general trends. The thin horizontal lines at 220 msec after the start of the primary correspond to divisions between early (*E*) and late (*L*) secondaries, estimated from dips between peaks in latency histograms. The thin vertical lines at 0.3 and 1.4° approximate the sizes of secondary saccade dead zones and also provide a rough division between smaller and larger secondaries. *Left, filled symbols*: In the normal foveating task, when the target makes a single randomized step and is continually lit, few or no secondaries are smaller than ±0.3°, labeled "normal-task dead zone" (NDZ) here. Most secondaries are small (<1.4°) and of variable, but generally later, latency. The few secondaries larger than 1.4° are usually early. *Right, filled symbols*: When the stimulus is blanked at the start of the primary saccade in the normal task, so as to deny visual feedback, the few early and large secondaries are spared (filled symbols at the bottom of right scatter plot), whereas the numerous small late secondaries are replaced by a few very late, often inappropriately large secondary saccades (filled symbols at top of right scatter plot). *Left, crosses*: In the "anti" task the subject attempts to look away from the stimulus by an equal and opposite amount when it steps. No anti-task secondaries are small and so the anti-task dead zone (ADZ) is quite large (±1.4°). Anti-task secondaries are all large and variable in amplitude and latency. *Right, crosses*: Blanking the stimulus at the start of the primary saccade makes no difference to frequency, amplitude, or latency of anti-task secondaries, except that the later ones may be retarded in some subjects. The small photopic stimulus made 3.8–11.5° horizontal steps in darkness. (Adapted from Adams, Note 1; conditions of Hallett & Adams 1980.)

3.7.3) has not been examined. Clearly, secondary latency must be determined by several factors, including the subject and the step size (which acts by altering the distribution of end-primary error). It is not easy to identify these factors, because the secondary latency distribution for a particular target displacement (e.g., a 10° left or right step) occasionally changes when the same step size is included among a different set of displacements in a new experiment.

(b) Varieties of Secondary Saccade. The issues of separability and classification are not yet settled. Becker (1976) postulated varieties of secondary saccade to reconcile two conflicting sets of data. In one study, small amplitude (<2°), relatively normal-latency secondaries to medium-sized stimulus steps (10°), were dependent on optical feedback as to the effect of the primary saccade (Prablanc & Jeannerod, 1975). These secondaries disappeared if the target was blanked after it was stepped. In the other study, larger, short-latency (120–140 msec) "mixed-mode" secondaries to large stimulus steps (20–60°) did not *depend* on optical feedback, but could still correct error (though after some delay) if the stimulus were blanked before the primary saccade (Becker, 1972). A similar idea comes from Shebilske (1976). He obtained evidence for short-latency nonvisual secondaries, insensitive to blanking the target, and long-latency visual secondaries which were sensitive to blanking. The generality of his claim is weakened by each form being largely restricted to one of his two very different subjects. There is also the possibility that limited randomization may have contributed some artifact, for the stimulus step was of relatively fixed amplitude (21.4 ± 2°, right-going). Hallett (1978, Figs. 8 and 10) observed in two subjects a very few short-latency nonvisual secondaries among longer-latency visual responses in the normal foveating task (4–15° left- or right-going steps); these few responses were apparently unaltered in latency, amplitude, or frequency, when the stimulus was blanked. It is impressive that asking subjects to look away from the stimulus step gives only frequent, large, nonvisual secondaries (Section 3.7.3).

There is a need to examine the possibility of making a useful division of secondaries in the normal foveating task (4–15° steps) into "earlier" or "later" secondaries by a latency cut at about 150 (130–190) msec from the end of the primary saccade. In about one-half of 11 subjects in this laboratory (experimental conditions of Hallett & Adams, 1980), the transition between earlier and later is marked by a dip between two peaks in the histogram of secondary latencies. Because this dip is not present in all subjects, and is slightly variable in position, the existence of separate early and late populations is statistically unproven until tested in many subjects with large numbers of trials. Early secondaries are often larger, and may include a very small component of nonvisual secondaries that appear to survive blanking without change in latency. Late secondaries are purely visual, are widely ranging in peak latency (being at shorter than primary latencies in some subjects and at longer latencies in others), and are often small in amplitude. See Figure 10.23 (Section 2.1). These two groups are consistent with the consequences of encouraging subjects to suppress all secondaries. Although two subjects labored to eliminate all secondaries by attempting accurate primary saccades they were unable to do so, but they were able to reduce the frequency of the small late secondaries, relative to the larger early secondaries, by ignoring the smaller end-primary errors (Adams, Note 1).

(c) Amplitude-Latency Scatter Plots. The two-dimensional relation between the amplitude (abscissa) and latency (ordinate) of secondary saccades in the normal foveating task is shown by scatter plots (Becker, 1972; Henson, 1978; and especially Adams, Note 1), as in Figure 10.92(a), filled circles. The form is an obscure rectangular-hyperbolic, L-shaped, or triangular area. One section (small amplitude and generally any latency, but more usually late) corresponds to "small late" visual secondaries. The other section (short latency and generally any size, but more usually large) corresponds to "large early" secondaries; the latter may include a few nonvisual secondaries in some subjects. Perhaps the correlation between amplitude and latency would be better if the viewing conditions and data analysis were binocular.

Some authors (e.g., Bartz, 1967; M. E. Cohen & Ross, 1978; Henson, 1978) report substantial differences between the mean latencies of forward-shooting corrections of undershot errors and backshooting corrections of overshot errors, namely, forward-shooting/backshooting secondary latencies of 103/57, 217/305, and 148 msec/175 msec for the three studies, respectively. But mean latencies provide a poor summary because the amplitude-latency scatter plots are typically asymmetric in the forward and backshooting directions.

Preliminary data suggest that visual forewarning by blanking the target before the step does not affect mean secondary latency (M. E. Cohen & Ross, 1978).

(d) Denial of Visual Feedback. It will be obvious from the foregoing that denying visual feedback as to the angular error left by the primary saccade, by blanking the stimulus soon after the step or at the beginning of the primary saccade, will have variable results, depending on the types of secondary saccade already present for the given subject and the particular set of stimulus steps (Becker, 1972; Hallett & Lightstone 1976a; Prablanc & Jeannerod, 1975; Prablanc et al., 1978; Shebilske, 1976). The experimenter's criterion is also a factor. If the step size is small, the end-primary errors are generally small; errors will be corrected by small late visual secondaries which will be reckoned to disappear largely or completely on blanking, if one allows only 350 msec to count secondaries (Hallett, 1978; Prablanc & Jeannerod, 1975). But the visual secondaries will be judged to be altered to, or partly replaced by, large amplitude (3°) often erroneous responses if the experimenter allows 650 msec for counting (Adams, Note 1); see Figure 10.92 (right, filled circles). If the stimulus step is large, end-primary errors are generally large; if the subject corrects error with large early nonvisual secondaries, these will be relatively or completely unaffected by blanking (e.g., Becker, 1972).

Denial of visual feedback can have unusual consequences, and should be used with due caution. Following several experiments with a stimulus that stepped twice, one subject was presented with trials in which the single ± 3.8° step was blanked for 370 msec immediately at the beginning of the primary saccade, after which the stimulus was relit at a randomly chosen position (Fig. 8 of Hallett & Lightstone, 1976b). In the majority of trials there was no secondary, which is as expected for a small step, but in 17/66 trials there was a large second saccade during the blanked period, as if the primary saccade was being repeated. There were no afterimages in any of these experiments. The proferred explanation for this strange "secondary saccade" was that blanking eliminated intrasaccadic retinal-image motion, and thus allowed an invisible retinal icon of the target to persist unmasked; consequently, the uncanceled memory trace indicated that the target had jumped with the eye, which elicited a second saccade, as in open-loop tracking. However, a simpler counterexplanation is that the subject may have acquired the *habit* from earlier experiments of making a second large saccade.

In brief, secondary saccades are heterogeneous in latency, amplitude, use of visual feedback, and in the extent to which they can be graded as reflex or voluntary, but classification remains uncertain.

(e) MODELING SECONDARY SACCADES. The *ACE* hypothesis, introduced in Section 2.3.3 and Figure 10.32, provides various routes for the planning of the two saccades to a single step. Time flows from left to right in the timing diagrams of Figure 10.93. The long rectangles are the latent periods between a triggering visual input and its saccade, and the smaller blocks are delays that make up the latent periods (the hatched blocks are of variable duration, the open ones are more constant; disregard the single- and double-headed empty arrows for now). Then diagram (a) in Figure 10.93 can be read as illustrating the possibility that occasional primary and secondary saccades are prepared in parallel. The two latent periods overlap extensively, a normal sequence of delays *ACE* leading to the primary saccade, and a protracted sequence (labeled *AC′CE*) to the secondary. The secondary saccade is automatically smaller, because the primary saccade corrects most of the error and the system is spatially coded. The remainder of Figure 10.93 shows the more important situations where parallel planning fails (if it ever began) and the observed planning is successive. In diagram (b), the central and efferent delays (*CE*) are deferred until triggered by an internal signal at the beginning of the primary saccade (descending black arrow). Secondary latency is short. Thus diagrams (a) and (b) show short-latency or nonvisual modes that do not depend on retinal feedback of end-primary angular error. In diagrams (c) and (e) secondary latency is longer. In the one case a normal sequence of afferent, central, and efferent delays *ACE* is triggered by retinal-image motion early in the primary saccade of duration *s*, and in the other case by retinal input at the end. If one allows that protracted sequences *AC″CE* are also possible, as mentioned in connection with the overlap task above (Section 3.7.1.2) and the "anti" task below (Section 3.7.3.2), then protracted secondary latencies, triggered at the start or end of the primary saccade, are also possible, as in diagrams (d) and (f). This gives four modes of later or visual secondaries dependent on the altered visual feedback created by the primary saccade.

The scheme successfully predicts short-latency nonvisual secondaries, and longer, variable-latency visual secondaries. For example, the latency from the start of the primary saccade to the few nonvisual secondaries seen in the normal foveating task (3.8–15.3° steps) is about 35 msec less than the normal-task reaction time $\bar{N}$ for the 4/11 subjects in this laboratory who show these responses (Hallett, 1978; Adams, Note 1; Doma, Note 2). This latency matches delays *CE* in Figure 10.93(b), if afferent delays $A \simeq 35$ msec, which is not unreasonable (Becker & Jürgens, 1979). As another example, *peak* latency for visual secondaries from the start of the primary saccade ranges from as short as a normal-task latency ($\bar{N}$) in 4/11 subjects, to as long as a primary saccade duration (*s*) plus an anti-task latency in 5/11 subjects [these latencies match delays *ACE* in Fig. 10.93(c) and delays *sAC″CE* in Fig. 10.93(f)]. It would, of course, require many data and many subjects to critically evaluate the plausibility of the six hypothetical modes in Figure 10.93, if a given subject shows evidence of only one or two latency peaks.

The interesting feature of the *ACE* scheme is that numerous possibilities follow from a few simple postulates. For example, if one takes the concept of parallel planning seriously, all the modes of Figure 10.93 could be active simultaneously at the latent level, the observed secondary being the earliest corrective saccade to escape the cross-fire of the cancellation discharges of the other latent secondaries. The observed secondary is thus the sort of "committee decision" that is fully appropriate if several different brain areas are activated by a single target. The timing diagrams in Figure 10.93 allow evaluation of the temporal factors that favor the survival of a particular mode. The double-headed arrows are the times at which cancellation

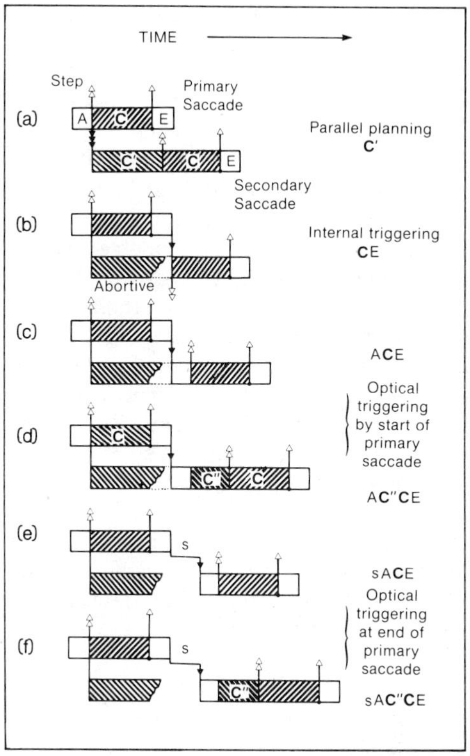

Figure 10.93. Timing diagrams for hypothetical modes of secondary saccades in the normal foveating task. Time flows from left to right. Not to scale. *Upper part of each diagram*: Target step is followed by the primary saccade after delays *A* (= afferent and retinal), **C** (= variable central delay), and *E* (= efferent delay allowing amplitude modification). *Lower part of each diagram*: The sequence of delays leading to a secondary saccade is variable. The saccadic intervals can be expressed as sequences of **ACE** delays, thus providing names for the modes. (a) Parallel planning or mode **C′**. The secondary is triggered by the step after the sequence of delays *AC′CE*, where **C′** is a longer than average value of the variable delay **C**. Saccadic interval between starts of primary and secondary saccades would thus be **C′**. (b–f) Successive planning is more usual, parallel planning being abortive in these cases. (b) Mode **C***E*. The secondary is triggered internally (descending black arrow), giving a saccadic interval of **C***E* between primary and secondary saccades. (c, e) Modes *A***C***E* and *sA***C***E*. The secondary is the normal sequence of delays *A***C***E*, triggered by retinal input at the beginning or end of the primary saccade of duration *s*. Saccadic intervals are *A***C***E* and *sA***C***E*, respectively. (d, f) Modes *A***C″C***E* and *sA***C″C***E*. Triggering retinal input occurs at the beginning or end of the primary saccade, respectively, but the sequence of delays leading to the secondary saccade is extended by a shorter than average value **C″** of the **C** extra delay. *Open-headed arrows*: Cancellation discharges (double-headed arrows) occur at the ends of *A* and **C** delays; their targets are **C** delays. Thus in (a) the occurrence of a latent sequence as the primary saccade is favored by a longer than average delay **C′**, which terminates too late to cancel the decision **C** as to primary goal. Also, in (d) and (f), the shorter than average delay **C″** tends to cancel any alternative secondary saccade and thus favors the sequence being a secondary rather than a tertiary saccade. Amplitude-modifying discharges (single-headed arrows) occur at the end of the **C** delay and are included here only for completeness; their targets are *E* delays. Such discharges are useful for modeling responses to more than one target displacement.

discharges begin and the **C** delays are their targets. A cancellation discharge may be triggered by retinal-image motion after an afferent delay A, or voluntarily after an additional variable delay **C** (which may take long or short values of **C**′ or **C**″ probabilistically). Theoretically, the shorter-latency nonvisual secondaries [timing diagrams (a) and (b) in Fig. 10.93] are favored by primary saccades of long duration s (i.e., large amplitude primaries) and by long delays A [because increase in s and A postpones the cancellation discharges—double-headed arrows—of the longer latency modes (c)–(f)]. Obviously, the shorter-latency secondaries are always favored if their **C** delays, which are the targets for the cancellation discharges, are short (**C**″). The survival of the longer-latency modes [(c)–(f) in Fig. 10.93] is favored by short durations of the cancellation discharges from the shorter-latency modes, by a long primary-saccade duration s, and by a long afferent delay A, all of which curtail the ability of the shorter latency modes a and b to cancel the later ones. Note that increases in both s and A favor the joint survival of both short- and long-latency modes, that is, survival of the shorter-latency modes as secondaries and of the longer ones as tertiaries. Of course, important nontemporal factors (e.g., end-primary error and cognitive factors) should be included in a final scheme.

In summary, several modes of secondary saccade can follow from a few simple postulates (three types of delay; retinal and internal triggering, cancellation, and amplitude-modifying discharges). Such a situation makes correct experimental analysis of the heterogeneity of secondary saccades all the more urgent.

3.7.1.7. ***Smooth Pursuit.*** Although the normal response to a target step is a saccade, there may be a very limited amount of smooth movement, in the form of a glissade (Section 3.7.1.3), or anticipatory visually controlled drift (Section 3.1.1.2). Smooth movement can be substantial in some circumstances.

If a target steps horizontally to and fro through ±2° at 2 Hz, it reverses direction too frequently to be tracked by saccades, but smooth oscillations of about ±1° and 2 Hz are revealed by monocular recording (Stark et al., 1962).

If the beginning of a saccade predictably triggers the return of the target to its origin, then after a few trials the saccade is followed, without any apparent latency, by a smooth return of the eye toward the origin, at 7.7° · sec^{-1} (2–8) in the majority of trials for two subjects [Fig. 10.94(a)]. The eventual return saccade allows for the preceding smooth movement (Lightstone, 1973). If the experimental arrangements are now changed, unknown to the subjects, so that the first saccade does not trigger the stimulus return to origin on 50% of trials (catch trials), then the anticipatory smooth movement occurs with unabated frequency [Fig. 10.94(b)]. In about half of the catch trials, smooth movement builds up sufficient position error to elicit a correction saccade, or even a nystagmus pattern [Fig. 10.94(c) and (d)]. If the apparatus is adjusted again, so that the first saccade now triggers a step to one of eight unpredictable positions, before a final return to origin, then the initial smooth movement is on average abolished [1° · sec^{-1} in Fig. 10.94(e)]. There is now no reasonable expectation on which a movement can be based. However, smooth movement may still occur after the second saccade in anticipation of the final target return to center. Smooth movement has not occurred in other step-stimulus studies in this laboratory, because it is easily defeated by appropriate randomization. "Anticipatory smooth movement" would seem to be the appropriate description, but that term has already been applied to much slower movements (<0.5° · sec^{-1}) that are not defeated by randomization of spatial goals (Section 3.1.1.2).

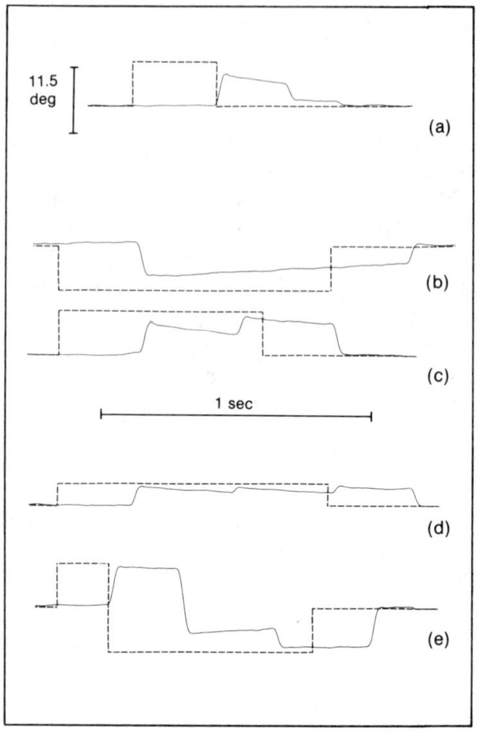

Figure 10.94. Smooth movement compensating for predictable aspects of stimulus motion. Pupil eye movement monitor. Eye and target shown as continuous and dotted lines, respectively. (a) Target steps horizontally by 1.9, 3.8, 7.7, or 11.5° left or right and is triggered to return predictably to origin as soon as primary saccade exceeds a velocity of 37° · sec^{-1}. (b–d) In a second experiment, triggered return to origin occurs only with probability 0.5. In the "catch trials" illustrated, the target returns to origin after a random time, but the smooth movement still occurs, and substantial corrective saccades may yield a nystagmus pattern. (e) In the third experiment the first saccade triggers a step of unpredictable amplitude. Smooth movement after the triggering saccade is now abolished, although it may occur after subsequent saccades in anticipation of the predictable return to origin, as in this example. (After Lightstone, 1973.)

The above smooth movements occurred in circumstances where saccadic response was impractical because of saccadic latency. As an alternative, one can try to penalize saccadic pursuit by stabilizing the retinal image during saccades, that is, by stepping the target in the direction of the saccade during the saccade (Wyatt & Pola, 1981). This procedure does not eliminate saccadic tracking of a step stimulus, although amplitude of saccades may be reduced somewhat, but it does encourage smooth movement toward the target, the movement being graded with a proportionality of 1.4° · sec^{-1} (0.5–3) per degree of step, for 0.5–6° steps.

If the retinal stimulus is stabilized on the retina, and is offset from the fovea, then pursuit may occur (Section 3.1.1.2). If the target is now *stepped* to and fro on the retina as a square wave of ±0.25–3° and 0.5–1 Hz, then the smooth movement also oscillates. Velocity increases with a sensitivity of 14.5° · sec^{-1} (12.6–17) per degree of offset within this range (Pola & Wyatt, 1980). It is possible that sensitivity to small step displacements of less than 0.25° is considerably greater, as one might guess, given the effectiveness of the residual smooth movements of fixation, because extrapolation suggests 10–20° · sec^{-1} velocities for near-zero displacements.

All the above observations support the idea that position error between fovea and target is a major input to the smooth pursuit system, in addition to velocity error and cognitive inputs.

3.7.1.8. Acoustic and Visual Targets Compared. Studies on four to six subjects show that the latency of visual tracking saccades increases with stimulus eccentricity from the fovea, when a red diode is lit at 10 or 20° to the left or right of the initial diode fixation point. In these experiments the head is fixed and the initial fixation point may be straight-ahead or to the left or right of center. The same subjects give similar results when the peripheral stimulus is an acoustic tone burst from a concealed loudspeaker, except that the general trend is for auditory latency to *decline* with increasing eccentricity relative to the *foveal* line of sight. Shorter auditory latency with increasing angular distance from the *midline* of the skull might have been expected, given the better auditory localization, but shorter auditory latency with increasing distance from the fovea must indicate some effect ("visual capture") of an internal auditory coordinate system by a visual one, perhaps at the collicular level (Zahn, Abel, & Dell'Osso, 1978; Zahn, Abel, Dell'Osso, & Daroff, 1979). Auditory latencies are somewhat longer than visual latencies, and auditory saccades are slightly less accurate and somewhat slower in peak velocity than visual saccades. Durations are longer and peak velocities lower than for saccades in the light (Zambarbieri et al., 1981). It may be worthwhile to compare auditory saccades with saccades in the "anti" task, where the subject looks away from the target, as both tasks are less visual than normal (Section 3.7.3).

3.7.1.9. Complex Visual Targets. Most tracking studies have used a small point target that steps to the left or right in darkness. However, there have been a few studies with more complex stimuli; for example, the fixation point may be extinguished and replaced by a pair of horizontally separated spots or squares to one side of the field of view (e.g., Coren & Hoenig, 1972; Findlay, 1982). Subjects show some preference for the nearer parts of the target, so that they slightly undershoot the target's center of gravity. This is not unexpected, given results for tracking a single target that steps twice in rapid succession (e.g., the "staircase" (SC) and the "pulse-under" (PU) target motions of Becker & Jürgens, 1979), and might be consistent with a postulated role for large receptive fields in triggering primary saccades (Findlay, 1982; Hallett, 1978). The data do not depend strongly on whether the task requires detection of a small gap in the side of one of the squares, or requires comparison of global features of the targets in two successive trials. Anticipatory saccades were a serious problem (5–40%) when the stimuli were presented as a continuous sequence (Findlay, 1982).

If the fixation point is relaced by two targets that are diametrically opposite one another (e.g., to left and right), the latency of the first saccade is inflated by about 30–40 msec relative to a single target stepping (Findlay, 1982; Levy-Schoen & Blanc Garin, 1974). Some time-consuming internal conflict is to be expected in this situation, given two-step data (e.g., the pulse-over or PO target motion of Becker & Jürgens, 1979). If the diametrically opposite targets are dissimilar, it is often possible to adjust the parameters of the less attractive target so that the saccadic response is now equally likely to be toward either target. For example, a target at 16° retinal eccentricity may need an area 100 times larger to have the same "visual salience" as a small target at 8° eccentricity (Findlay, 1980). In this way it has been shown that the visual salience of a small target (0.8–0.9°) is determined primarily by its proximity to the fovea, rather weakly by internal motion within the target ($5-40° \cdot sec^{-1}$), and scarcely at all by static internal structure (4 cycles per degree square wave) (Findlay, 1980). These experiments were complicated by the necessity of correcting for innate directional preferences (e.g., toward the upper right visual field).

The variation of photopic perceptual performance with eccentricity is explained by increasingly eccentric perceptual stimuli activating smaller numbers of cortical neurons; that is, the magnification from retina to visual cortex is less in the periphery (e.g., Virsu & Rovamo, 1979). Findlay (1983) suggests that the magnification factors are similar for the visual cortex and the superior colliculus. The decline of "visual salience" with eccentricity is, however, much faster than the decline in the magnification factors.

3.7.1.10. Target Steps During Head Rotation. If the target steps horizontally, from side to side, relative to an earth-fixed reference, then tracking saccades would be accurate if the gain of the vestibulo-ocular reflex were −1 and if slow-phase velocity and saccadic velocity summed completely. In fact, accuracy is normal during sinusoidal rotation en bloc about the yaw axis at 1 Hz ($120° \cdot sec^{-1}$ peak velocity), although the physiology is more complicated. As previously noted in connection with Figure 10.52 (Section 3.2.1.3), summation of slow phase and saccadic velocity is only 70% complete, so uncompensated head movement could potentially affect saccadic accuracy. But the saccadic system is spatially coded and accuracy is maintained by increased saccade duration when the saccade and slow phase are in the same direction, and by reduced saccade duration when the movements are opposite (Jürgens et al., 1981). If the target rotates with the subject, vestibulo-ocular gain is about 0.3 and saccadic accuracy is also normal.

3.7.2. Instruction: Track the Target When It Steps Twice. In two-step tracking tasks the subject fixates the small target, which steps twice in rapid succession *before the subject can respond* (Wheeless, Boynton, & Cohen, 1966). Type-I trials occur when the subject responds to both steps, so that saccade 1 is to step 1 and saccade 2 is to step 2. In type-II trials the first or single saccade is to step 2 (Carlow, Dell'Osso, Troost, Daroff, & Birkett, 1975). See Figure 10.95.

The displacement of the target has been adequately randomized in space and time in most studies, so anticipatory responses are not an obvious problem.

Experimenters implicitly view performance as low level or automatic, the untested assumption being that deliberate voluntary tracking of both steps, or of the second step only, will be reported by the subject or will be obvious from inflated latencies. Actually, the latencies to single steps are inflated by 40 msec when these are randomly introduced as controls (Becker & Jürgens, 1979), so subjects consciously or unconsciously delay saccade 1 to step 1, which increases the time available for canceling or modifying saccade 1. There is also the problem as to what extent the two steps interact at sensory levels by spatial and temporal summation (e.g., Deubel et al., 1982; Deubel, Note 8), visual masking (e.g., Levy-Schoen & Blanc-Garin, 1974), or visual warning effects (L. Ross & Ross, 1980; S. Ross & Ross, 1981). Recently, intermediate responses have been recognized in which saccade 1 of the type-I response is modified in amplitude. Thus it seems that there are two different operations whereby step 2 or saccade 2 can influence saccade 1: all-or-none cancellation of saccade 1, allowing a new saccade (after a reaction

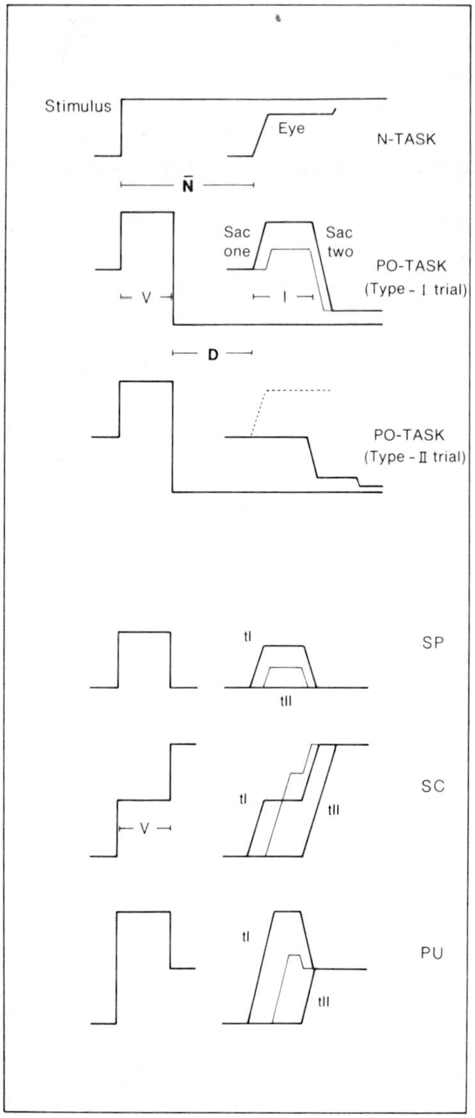

Figure 10.95. Type-I and type-II trials in some two-step tracking tasks. Horizontal target motions. *N-task*: Normal single-step task, which controls for latency. *PO-task* (*type-I trial*): In the "pulse-over" task the stimulus steps to one side, and then to the other, before the eye can react. In type-I trials there is a saccade to each step; in "intermediate" type-I trials at this task (faint line) saccade 1 is attenuated in amplitude. Note definitions of interstep interval *V*, lead **D**, and saccadic interval **I**. *PO-task* (*type-II trial*): The saccade to step 1 is canceled, leaving the saccade to step 2. *SP*: In the "step-pulse" task the target returns to origin. Type-I and type-II trials are shown in heavy line (*tI*, *tII*), and an intermediate type-I trial in faint line. *SC*: "Staircase" task *PU*: "Pulse-under" task. Note that in the "uncrossed" tasks (SP, SC, and PU) a type-II trial can arise either by canceling saccade 1, and responding only to step 2, or by modifying the amplitude of saccade 1 to match step 2. A type-II trial can arise only by cancellation in "crossed" tasks (e.g., PO) because a switch in motor nuclei and muscle action is required.

time), as when a change in *direction* is required, and graded amplitude, modification of saccade 1, which needs little or no extra time (Becker & Jürgens, 1979; Hou & Fender, 1979). Conceivably, cancellation may also be required for an amplitude change if modification is difficult for some reason (e.g., when a change in stimulus position requires that a latent saccade be lengthened; Nam, Park, & Choi, 1975). Graded changes in direction may be possible if the target moves in small steps in two dimensions (Findlay & Harris, Note 9). Following an earlier example (Taümer, Mie, & Kommerell, 1972), later workers have recognized the lead **D** of step 2 on saccade 1 as an important variable that expresses the opportunity for step 2 to cancel or modify saccade 1 (see Fig. 10.95).

3.7.2.1. Type-I Trials (Cancellation). Cancellation of saccade 1 is infrequent, giving a high percentage of type-I trials, when lead **D** of step 2 is small (or interstep interval *V* is long). The percentage of type-I trials decreases in a sigmoid fashion as **D** increases (or *V* shortens). Such a "cancellation function" is shown schematically in the inset to Figure 10.96. (The *ACE*

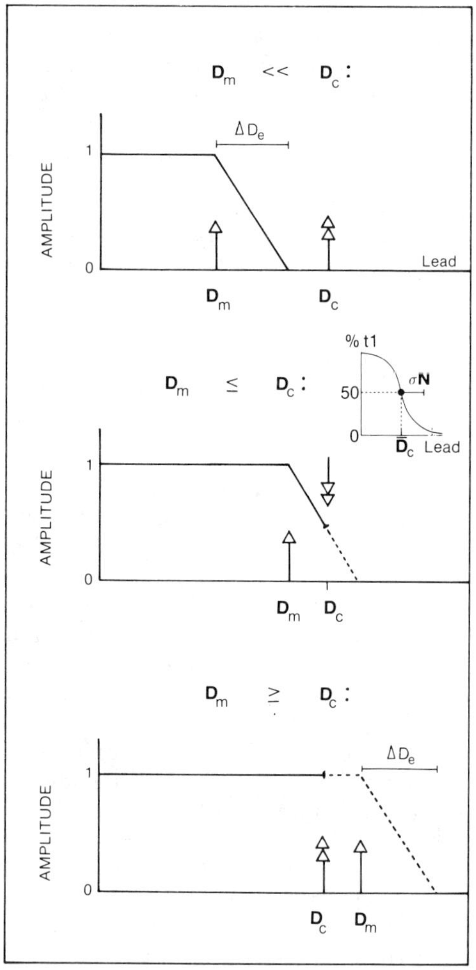

Figure 10.96. Hypothetical amplitude-transition functions for the pulse-over spatial pattern of two-step tracking task, for the parallel-planning mode of the *ACE* model. Three forms of function are possible for type-I trials, depending on the relative magnitudes of the "modification time" $\mathbf{D}_m$ (= sum of delays *AC* in the model) and the "cancellation threshold" $\mathbf{D}_c$ (= sum of delays *AE*). When the lead time **D** of step 2 on saccade 1 is short (lead $<\mathbf{D}_m$), saccade 1 is of normal amplitude. Saccade 1 is attenuated at longer leads (lead $>\mathbf{D}_m$) as shown by the sloping "transition region" of extreme length Δ $\mathbf{D}_e$. Attenuated responses become increasingly rare at long leads (lead $>\mathbf{D}_c$), because saccade 1 is canceled with increasing probability. The insert shows a "cancellation function," which relates the probability of a type-I trial to the lead **D**. The spreads of such sigmoid functions are believed to equal the standard deviation $\sigma\mathbf{N}$ of latencies to a single step (Becker & Jürgens, 1975). The extent of the transition region may thus allow inference about the relative values of $\mathbf{D}_m/\mathbf{D}_c$, or of delays $\overline{C}/E$, for that particular task and subject. Amplitude-transition functions have different shapes for different spatial patterns of the stimulus steps, because some tasks require that saccade 1 be lengthened to match step 2.

model is discussed below.) Plotting percentage type-I trials against lead **D** better normalizes the cancellation functions of different subjects than does a plot against interstep interval *V* (Lisberger et al., 1975). I have made estimates from the literature of the lead $\mathbf{D}_c$ ("cancellation threshold") at which 50% of trials are type-I. (The literature is that cited later in the caption to Fig. 10.97, plus Hou & Fender, 1979.) The overall estimate is about one-half of normal latency, that is, 116 ± 6 msec (range 85–174 msec, about 30 subjects), in good agreement with a more narrowly ranging estimate of 119 ± 3 msec for four different spatial patterns (from Komoda, Festinger, Phillips, Duckman, & Young, 1973), so step pattern is not likely to be a

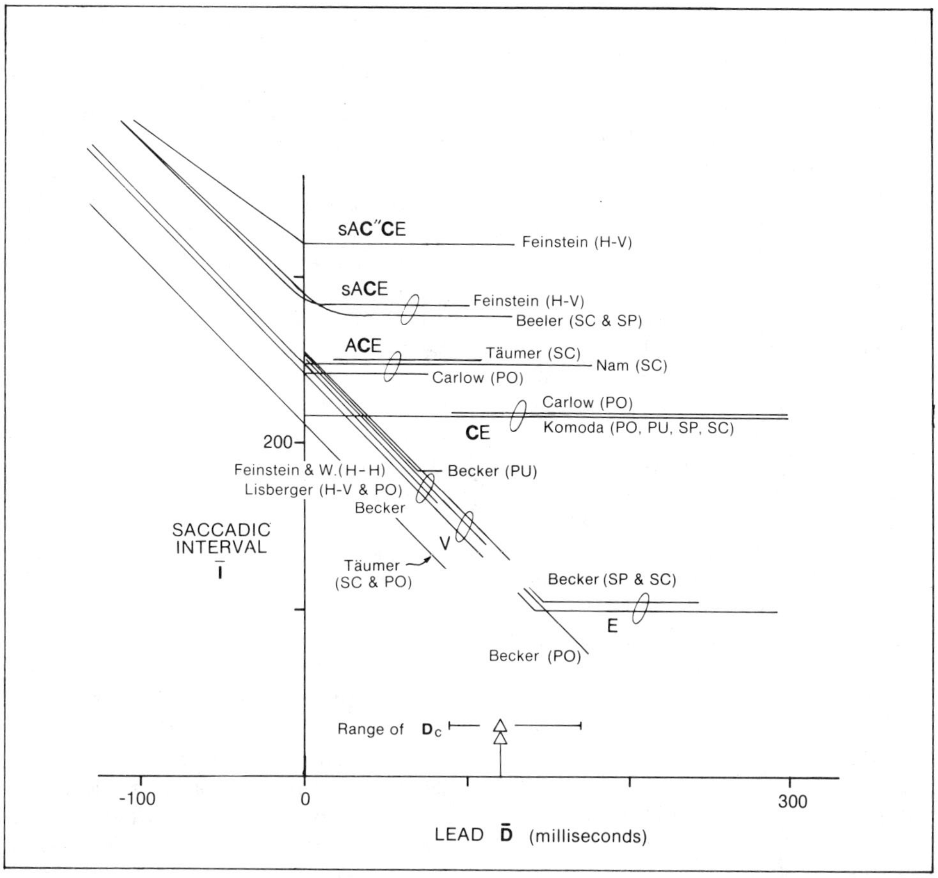

Figure 10.97. Data for two-step tracking tasks in the literature replotted. The original data were mean latencies for type-1 trials at various interstep intervals *V*. The data were replotted as lead **D** of step 2 on saccade 1, versus saccadic interval **I** between the beginnings of saccades 1 and 2; then diagonal and horizontal lines were fitted. The replotted data from the different laboratories have been normalized by displacement upward or downward, according to the extent that the control single-step latency ***N*** was less or greater than 250 msec. Only names of first authors are given, and the different spatial patterns of the two-step stimulus are indicated, for example, PO, PU, SP, SC, H-H, H-V. (In the first five patterns the two steps are both horizontal; in the last pattern one is horizontal and the other vertical.) The data clearly support parallel planning (mode *V*) and a wide range of successive planning. Because the original data are often scattered, it is not certain that there are separable successive planning modes, though some modes are indicated by two studies. If the successive planning data are attributed to particular modes of the *ACE* model, as labeled, then the normalized data (other than Feinstein, 1970) are fitted by $A = 35$ msec, $\bar{\mathbf{C}} = 115$ msec, and $E = 100$ msec, estimating values for saccade duration *s* from mean amplitudes (Hallett, 1978). The predicted and observed values of the cancellation threshold $\mathbf{D}_C$ (= *AE*) are 135 and 120 msec, respectively. The values used for *s* were 25 msec (Beeler, 1965) and 35 msec (Feinstein, 1970; Feinstein & Williams, 1972a). If the data are not normalized, saccadic interval ranges from about 130 msec (Becker & Jürgens, 1979) to much longer than the single-step latency ***N*** (subject JM of Feinstein, 1970). (The saccadic interval can be indirectly estimated in the latter case to be equal to the duration of saccade 1 plus an anti-task latency $\bar{\mathbf{A}}''$.) If the *ACE* model is correct, the different modes should not all be normalized in the same way, as is done here for convenience. For example, mode *E* should not be normalized because it contains no variable delay **C**, whereas mode *sAC″CE* contains two **C** delays and should be displaced by about *twice* the extent that control single-step latency was less or greater than 250 msec. When so normalized, mode *sAC″CE* is also consistent with the fitted values given above if **C″** is 5 msec shorter than **C**. In summary, the data are consistent with the *ACE* model. (Adapted from data of Becker & Jürgens, 1979; Beeler 1965; Carlow, Dell'Osso, Troost, Daroff, & Birkett, 1975; Feinstein, 1970; Feinstein & Williams, 1972a; Komoda, Festinger, Phillips, Duckman, & Young, 1973; Lisberger, Fuchs, King, & Evinger, 1975; Nam, Park, & Choi, 1975; Täumer, 1975; Täumer, Mie, & Kommerell, 1972).

factor here. A related situation is that subjects track predictable repetitive steps without any latencies in the 120-msec region, as if an anticipatory response is cancelled if a stimulus step has occurred about 120 msec earlier (Findlay, 1981b; Horrocks & Stark, 1964). Similarly, the fast phase of optokinetic nystagmus, due to a $40° \cdot sec^{-1}$ optokinetic drum, is cancelled about 150 msec after a fixation point is lit (Judge, 1973). Cancellation is not obligatory, however. For example, cancellation was not seen when subjects tracked a horizontal-vertical step sequence (Feinstein & Williams, 1972a), though other subjects used cancellation when tracking such stimuli (Lisberger et al., 1975). Also, cancellation was seen for only one of four spatial patterns of step (Becker & Jürgens, 1979), although it was present for all four step patterns in another laboratory (Fig. 1 of Komoda et al., 1973).

3.7.2.2. Type-I Trials (Amplitude Modification). In "intermediate" type-I trials the amplitude of saccade 1 is modified (Fig. 10.95). The amplitude of saccade 1 may be plotted against the lead **D** of step 2 to yield scatter plots called the "amplitude transition function" (Becker & Jürgens, 1979). Figure 10.96 shows schematic plots for the *ACE* model that qualitatively imitate two-step data (the model is explained later). In the "pulse-over" or PO pattern, the stimulus might step on a given trial briefly to 25° left and then to 25° right. At short leads **D** the amplitude of saccade 1 is normal; amplitude is progressively reduced as step 2 leads saccade 1 by a lead in excess of $\mathbf{D}_m$ ("modification time"), as in Figure 10.96. $\mathbf{D}_m$ appears to vary with task and subject (e.g., 80–200 msec), which is to be expected if $\mathbf{D}_m$ includes a variable high-level or central delay. The range of leads over which amplitude varies (the sloping "transition region" in Fig. 10.96) is also variable with subject in the Becker-Jürgens data. This is to be expected on general grounds if the cancellation threshold $\mathbf{D}_c$ and the modification time $\mathbf{D}_m$ are separate variables, because amplitude modification cannot be observed if saccade 1 is canceled (i.e., if $\mathbf{D}_c < \mathbf{D}_m$). The extreme extent of the transition region is perhaps more constant ($\Delta\mathbf{D}_e$, Fig. 10.96).

3.7.2.3. Type-I Trials (Saccadic Interval). Lead **D** of step 2 on saccade 1 is a useful parameter against which to plot saccadic interval **I**, and I have done this in Figure 10.97, fitting diagonal and horizontal lines to normalized data from the literature. Becker and Jürgens (1979) caution against using mean latencies in this way, and favor scatter plots of **D** and **I** from individual type-I trials instead. Nevertheless, Figure 10.97 agrees quite well with published scatter plots (Becker & Jürgens, 1975; Täumer, 1975; Täumer et al., 1972). Adding the lead **D** to saccadic interval **I** gives the latency of saccade 2 to step 2. This should be constant and equal to the normal single-step latency **N**, if there is full temporal independence in parallel planning, that is, $\bar{\mathbf{D}} + \bar{\mathbf{I}} = \text{const} \simeq \bar{\mathbf{N}}$. Figure 10.97 shows that the diagonal line of parallel planning has been frequently observed in the literature, both at negative **D** (when step 2 follows saccade 1) and in the more important case when **D** is positive and step 2 precedes saccade 1.

Figure 10.97 also shows a number of horizontal limbs that cover a wide range of saccadic intervals (±100 msec), the data of Becker and Jürgens (1979) being at one extreme. This wide range is in general agreement with the *ACE* scheme of Section 2.3.3 which predicts both parallel planning, with saccadic interval I reciprocally related to lead **D**, and various modes of successive planning for which $\mathbf{I} \simeq$ const. Although the grouping of studies in Figure 10.97 is consistent with separable successive-planning modes, the original data are scattered, and it would be premature to exclude a single broad continuum. Specially collected data are needed, and it will be hard to prove a multiplicity of modes if a given subject shows only one or two modes.

A possible difference between parallel and successive planning is that amplitude modification is observed only in parallel planning (e.g., Becker & Jürgens, 1979; Hou & Fender, 1979), but more data are needed.

3.7.2.4. Type-II Trials (Latency). In type-II trials, the first observed saccade is matched to step 2 (Fig. 10.95). The problem is whether the matching is due to cancellation or to amplitude modification. The simple expectation is that the first or only saccade in type-II trials should occur at normal latency ($\bar{\mathbf{N}}$) after step 2, if the saccade was originally the saccade to step 2, saccade 1 having been cancelled, or at less than normal latency after step 2 (e.g., $\bar{\mathbf{N}}$-V) if the saccade is really saccade 1 modified in amplitude to match step 2. In the case of the well-studied pulse-over (PO) pattern of steps, several authors have simplistically associated extra delay ("cancellation time") with cancellation. Actually, latency in cancelled type-II trials ranges from nearly normal (e.g., +5% for Komoda et al., 1973) to much longer than normal (e.g., +40% for Hou & Fender, 1979), being a function of interstep interval *V* in another study (Carlow, Dell'Osso, Troost, Daroff, & Birkett, 1975). To judge from their Figure 1, Komoda et al. (1973) saw cancellation for all four of their step patterns but type-II latencies were less than normal in three of the patterns, which implies *negative* cancellation time (the PU, SP, and SC patterns of Fig. 10.95)! It has been suggested that cancellation and increased type-II latencies are associated with step patterns that take the image of the stimulus across the fovea into the contralateral hemiretina and half-brain ("crossed patterns," e.g., the PO pattern) (Becker & Jürgens, 1979; Komoda et al., 1973). Lack of cancellation or shorter than normal type-II latencies have been associated with uncrossed patterns which keep the stimulus within one hemiretina and half-brain. However, cancellation and (positive) cancellation time have been reported for an uncrossed pattern which required that a saccade be lengthened to reach a more remote goal (SC pattern, Nam et al., 1975), so it seems that cancellation is possible for *any* target pattern.

In summary, there are basically two possible outcomes in two-step tracking, types I and II, although various degrees of modification of saccade 1 provide intermediate type-I trials. Type-II trials are the more biologically adaptive and can in principle arise by amplitude modification alone if no change in direction is required; otherwise cancellation is necessary. Obviously type-II responses are favored by subjects delaying their responses to step 1, for this allows more time for modification or cancellation, and subjects actually do so (e.g., Becker & Jürgens, 1979). Of the two modes of planning, parallel planning [Fig. 10.98(a)] offers speedy tracking of step 2, with the possibility of cancelling saccade 1 or trimming its size; the eye movements "recapitulate" the direction and *timing* of the steps. In successive planning in type-I trials a normally accurate saccade 1 is followed by a deferred saccade 2, so that the saccades accurately recapitulate the target's changes in *position*. Whether parallel and successive planning offer different perceptual opportunities is not known, but the two modes can be present in the same subject (Täumer, 1975). Amplitude modification is not inevitably associated with parallel planning, because an additional condition is that the cancellation threshold $\mathbf{D}_c$ should be larger than the modification time $\mathbf{D}_m$; otherwise cancellation will occur

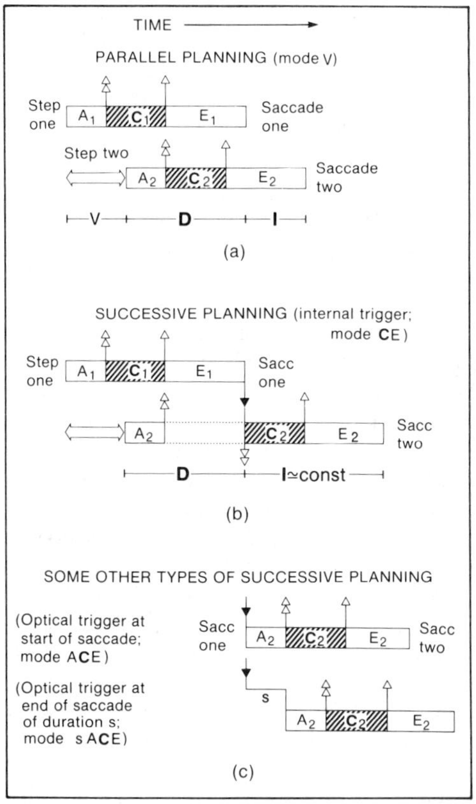

Figure 10.98. Timing diagrams to explain the temporal planning of saccades when the stimulus steps twice in rapid succession (*ACE* model). The long rectangles are the latent period that elapses between a stimulus and its saccade. *V* = interstep interval; **D** = lead of step 2 on saccade 1; **I** = saccadic interval between beginnings of saccades 1 and 2. The smaller blocks are afferent, central, and efferent delays that make up the latent period: *A* = afferent and retinal delay; **C** = variable delay for decision as to goal, during which time cancellation is possible; *E* = efferent delay during which only amplitude modification is possible. (a) Parallel planning. The processing of step 2 and its saccade is unimpeded by saccade 1 in parallel planning, so that the saccadic interval ideally approximates the interstep interval *V*. The open-headed arrows are the times of neural discharges that may cancel (double-headed arrow) or modify (single-headed arrow) a latent saccade if the timing is right; their targets are the **C** and *E* delays, respectively. Timing is determined by the interstep interval and variable delays. (b, c) Successive planning. In these modes the processing of step 2 and its saccade are held up in various ways. Cancellation of saccade 1 is possible if the interstep interval is appropriate, but not amplitude modification because that discharge occurs after saccade 1. The various modes are named according to the delay or sequence of delays that form the characteristic interval between saccades 1 and 2. In mode **C***E*, delays **C** and *E* are held up until triggered internally at the time of the descending black arrow. In mode *A***C***E*, all three delays are deferred until triggered by retinal image motion at the start of saccade 1. In mode *sA***C***E*, the trigger is optical feedback from the end of saccade 1, which has duration *s*. Other modes (not shown) are possible if one allows the possibility of extended sequences due to internal cancellation (e.g., modes *A***C**″*E* and *sA***C**″*E*, where **C**″ is the time needed to cancel an internal decision).

so frequently that there will be few type-I trials in which to observe any amplitude modification. See also Figure 10.96.

3.7.2.5. Modeling the Two-Step Tracking Task. Becker and Jürgens (1979) have used a servomechanistic model to explain their two-step tracking data. The initial step displacement of the target into one hemiretina leads, after an afferent delay, to a variable-duration decision as to left or right direction. This is cancelled if the second step takes the target into the other hemiretina an afferent delay or more before the end of the decision period. Once direction is chosen, the amplitude of the saccade is determined by averaging the error between estimated target position and estimated future eye position. My comment is that the model can be related to the frequently postulated dichotomy between "transient" and "sustained" sensory processing, because the transient of the step displacement initiates the direction decision, while sampling some 30–70 msec later establishes saccade amplitude. Also, if the model is very literally and narrowly interpreted, it is too rigid to account for successive planning, or for the normal accuracy and latency of saccades to very brief flashes (Section 3.7.1.2), or for saccades to goals defined by instructions (Section 3.7.3). The following model shares some of the features of the Becker-Jürgens model but takes all its information from the initial part of each target step.

As noted earlier (Section 2.3.3 and Fig. 10.32) a useful method of discovering models of the saccadic mechanism is to consider the sequence of operations between stimulus and response. In Figure 10.98, time flows from the left to right, the long rectangles are latent periods between target and saccade, and the smaller blocks ($A\mathbf{C}E$) are afferent, central, and efferent components of delay.

In *parallel planning* (upper pair of long rectangles in Fig. 10.98) each of the two steps independently evokes its own sequence of delays $A\mathbf{C}E$, where the time interval between the steps is V, the *lead* of the step 2 on saccade 1 is **D**, and the saccadic interval is **I**. The two $A\mathbf{C}E$ sequences are temporally independent in parallel planning, so there is a reciprocal relation between lead **D** and saccadic interval **I**, as the interstep interval V is altered by the experimenter. Indeed, **I** should equal V if step 2 evokes delays with normal values [Fig. 10.98(a)].

In *successive planning*, some or all of the operations for step 2 and its saccade are held up until after the start of saccade 1; here saccadic interval **I** is constant as lead **D** (or interstep interval V) varies, the actual value of **I** depending on what processes are held up. Successive planning is particularly variable. In one hypothetical mode of successive planning (internal triggering mode), the step-2 delays $\mathbf{C}_2E_2$ are deferred until the **C** delay is initiated by an internal trigger (descending solid arrow) at the beginning of saccade 1 [see Fig. 10.98(b)]. In other modes, the entire step-2 sequence $A_2\mathbf{C}_2E_2$ is deferred until triggered by retinal feedback from the beginning or end of saccade 1. Two such modes are shown in Figure 10.98(c). A plot of lead **D** against saccadic interval **I** for a series of type-I outcomes yields model plots similar to the data of Figure 10.97. In that figure the descending diagonal line represents parallel planning, with **D** reciprocally related to **I**, and the various horizontal limbs match the successive planning modes of Figure 10.98 and 10.93(f).

So far we have considered only type-I outcomes, where each step of a pair produces its own saccade. In type-II outcomes the first observed saccade is appropriate to step 2. This can come about through either cancellation or amplitude modification. In Figure 10.98(a), the double-headed arrow represents the time of onset of a "cancellation discharge." This can cancel another ongoing **C** decision as to goal *if* the discharge occurs before the **C** delay is complete. The cancellation discharge due to step 1 is of no importance (because the oculomotor system should be quiescent at this point in the two-step paradigm), but the cancellation discharge due to step 2 occurs with various delays as the experimenter modifies the interstep interval V. Figure 10.98(a) shows the intermediate situation where V is such that the step-2 cancellation discharge occurs at the time when the $\mathbf{C}_1$ delay typically ends; so, because of statistical variation in $\mathbf{C}_1$, a shorter-than-average latency saccade 1 will escape cancellation, while a longer-than-average latency saccade 1 will not. Cancellation by step 2 can also occur in successive planning, as in Figure 10.98(b), which again shows the intermediate situation. About 50% of outcomes will be type-I (illustrated), and about 50% will be type-II (not illustrated) because the $\mathbf{C}_1$ delay ends too late. In type-II outcomes there is no saccade 1 to hold up the processing of step 2, and so the latency of saccade 2 from step 2 is reduced from the long values typical of successive planning to the sequence $A_2\mathbf{C}_2E_2$, which allows a useful latency saving if the component delays are not inflated. Clearly, the probability of cancellation increases with increase in lead **D**, and so in Figure 10.96 (inset) type-I outcomes become less frequent at large **D**. The lead corresponding to about 50% type-I outcomes may be called the threshold lead for cancellation D_c (the simpler term "cancellation time" is already in use), and is theoretically equal to the sum of the delays A_2E_1 as consideration of Figure 10.98(a) or (b) shows.

If the cancellation discharge is too late or is missing, it remains possible for new events to alter the amplitude of saccade 1, particularly if reduction is appropriate. In parallel planning, step 2 initiates a modifying discharge at the time of the single-headed arrow [Fig. 10.98(a)]. This discharge distinguishes the present scheme from that of Becker and Jürgens (1979) and is postulated because internal events can alter saccade amplitude, as in the "anti" task (Section 3.7.3). If the modifying discharge occurs before the averaging period E_1 is complete, the amplitude of saccade 1 is altered, the more so the earlier the discharge. No amplitude modification should be possible in successive planning, according to Figure 10.98, because the step-2 modifying discharge occurs after saccade 1 has started. The minimum lead or modification time ($\mathbf{D}_m$) for detectable modification is, from Figure 10.98(a), the sum of the delays $A_2\mathbf{C}_2$. Because $\mathbf{D}_m$ varies markedly with task and subject in the literature, it does seem plausible that $\mathbf{D}_m$ includes highly variable terms (e.g., $\mathbf{C}_2$). Amplitude modification occurs over a range of leads: at one extreme, saccade 1 is scarcely modified, so it is still adapted to step 1, whereas at the other extreme saccade 1 matches step 2 (Fig. 10.96). This extreme range of leads $\Delta\mathbf{D}_e$ may be related to the duration (E_1) of the "target" of the modifying discharge. Delay E is constant relative to $\bar{\mathbf{C}}$, and $\Delta\mathbf{D}_e$ does seem to be more constant than $\mathbf{D}_m$ experimentally (Becker & Jürgens, 1979).

3.7.3. Instruction: Look Away from Stimulus When It Steps

3.7.3.1. Results. Most studies of saccadic eye movements are concerned with foveation, although peripheral vision is important for the detection of dim objects at night. Also, the ability of subjects to look away from a conspicuous object is an important aspect of voluntary behavior and one component of visual search. A pilot study showed that a subject was able to look halfway toward a small lit object when it stepped in the dark, or a fixed distance beyond it, or by an equal amount in the opposite direction, when instructed to do so, despite lack of any feedback as to performance (Hallett, 1978). Looking away from the stimulus step was selected for further study, because mistakes are easily recognized as being responses in the direction of the stimulus. Acoustic and visual feedback of performance were introduced as means of keeping the subject alert.

Eight consecutive subjects were able to perform the "anti" task, usually in the first few attempts, although one (EC) began with several tens of mistakes (Hallett, 1978; Hallett & Adams, 1980). The stimulus step was randomized in timing, direction, and amplitude in these studies; that is, there were six (or eight) goals at 3.8, 7.7, and 11.5° (and 15.3°), left or right. The only signs of learning have been a rapid reduction in the mistake rate in the first few tens of trials, usually to the 5–10% level. Two subjects did, however, improve the aim of their primary saccades after several hundreds of trials. These two subjects (EC and CW) were unusual in initially producing primaries of a single roughly constant mean amplitude to all goals, the aim at individual goals being mainly due to the secondary at that stage in their training. Despite rich feedback as to performance, mean latency is always larger than for the normal foveating task, even when the two tasks are mixed in the same session. Occasional primary saccades in some subjects are anomalous in velocity profile, sometimes showing evidence of multiple saccadic pulses. End-primary angular error relative to the instructed goal is more widely scattered than normal, and mean error may be more undershot than normal for some goal positions and overshot for others. Errors of $\pm 1.5°$ are tolerated without correction but, because many primaries are in greater error than this, a good proportion of large early corrective secondaries are seen (e.g., on 30–50% of trials). The frequency and amplitude of these secondaries never depend on visual feedback as to the effect of the primary saccade, although a proportion of the secondaries may be delayed 100 msec or so in some subjects [Fig. 10.92(a), (b); crosses]. Two subjects made frequent "triplet" responses, that is, small primary saccades closely followed by large secondary and tertiary saccades, which are not unlike the multiple-step hypometric saccades of the clinical literature (Teräväinen & Calne, 1980a, 1980b). Subjects do, however, have a good concept of the six to eight goal positions used in these studies, because terminal angular error 650 msec after the end of the primary saccade, though much more scattered than normal, is only a few minutes of arc in mean.

The above features imply a task that is novel and that makes much less use of visual feedback than is normal. On the other hand, the stability of the data over several hundred trials, and other features, suggest that the subjects are exploiting normal mechanisms. In eight consecutive subjects, using well-randomized targets, the latency $\bar{\mathbf{A}}''$ of the primary saccade in successful attempts at the "anti" task is related to primary latency $\bar{\mathbf{N}}$ in the normal foveating task by

$$\bar{\mathbf{A}}'' = 2\bar{\mathbf{N}} - 144(\pm 8) \text{ msec},$$

the SD of latency in the "anti" task being larger than normal by about $\sqrt{2}$. These are surprising relations, unless the normal and "anti" tasks have some latency components in common (Hallett & Adams, 1980). It is also difficult, apart from occasional anomalies in velocity profile, to distinguish records in the "anti" task from those for parallel planning in the equivalent two-step tracking task, the PO task described above (Fig. 10.95). Successful attempts at the "anti" task resemble type-II PO trials in that the only saccade is away from step 1. Mistakes at the "anti" task resemble type-I PO trials in that the direction error saccade (= saccade 1) is toward the step, is of roughly normal latency, and is reduced in amplitude if the large corrective "anti" saccade (= saccade 2) follows after a very short saccadic interval. Because parallel planning in two-step tasks clearly involves competition between the responses to the first and second steps, it is likely that mistakes and successes at the "anti" task similarly involve a competition between foveation and the "look away" instruction. There is good neurosurgical evidence in this paradigm that foveation does not require the frontal lobes in humans, whereas suppressing foveation and looking away do (Guitton et al., 1982). This finding has practical importance, because frontal lobe lesions are often silent. It also suggests that saccades are prepared in parallel at different sites in the brain in certain experimental situations at least (e.g., the frontal lobe cortex and the superior colliculus of the brain stem). This may also be true, for example, of anticipatory saccades (Bronstein & Kennard, Note 10).

Data from the "anti" task are contrasted with normal foveating saccades in a number of figures in earlier sections. Figure 10.23 (A-task, successes) illustrates amplitudes and latencies of correction saccades. Figure 10.85(b) shows the effect of identifying the task just before the stimulus. Figure 10.86(c) shows the effect of the Carpenter normalization on primary latencies. Figure 10.90(b) shows the distribution of end-primary angular errors, and Figure 10.91(b) the dead zone for anti-task secondaries. Figure 10.92 (crosses) shows the amplitude-latency scatter plot for anti-task secondaries. Figure 10.93(a) is also the hypothetical timing diagram for mistakes at the "anti" task, such as are illustrated in Figure 10.23 (A-task, mistakes).

Figure 10.99 contrasts saccadic amplitudes and velocity profiles in the normal and "anti" tasks, when the two tasks are randomly mixed in the same session. It is possible to find triplets of consecutive trials, for comparison purposes, in which one trial is the normal foveating task (N), another is a successful attempt at the "anti" task (A), and the other a direction mistake at the "anti" task. The normal-task responses (N) are highly stereotyped in velocity wave form. In four of the successful anti-task responses illustrated (asterisks), it can be seen that peak-velocity is subnormal for the amplitude, and in two of these the velocity profile is ragged, suggesting multiple saccadic pulses. In a suitable subject pulses can be seen quite clearly (e.g., Fig. 3 of Hallett & Adams, 1980). In every mistake trial in Figure 10.99 the first foveating saccade is the usual foveating stereotype, but each of the large corrective "anti" saccades is of low peak velocity for its size and ragged.

3.7.3.2. ***Models.*** Hallett and Adams (1980) have treated the "anti" task in a simple manner, as a double decision task, and have justified the 144-msec constant in the above equation as being a little longer than the sum of the delays AE in the ACE model. The sum of delays AE was also equated above with the cancellation threshold $\mathbf{D}_c$ for two-step tasks in the literature (116 msec, range 85–171 msec). The inflated SD of latency is due to two variable delays. To be consistent with the above treatment of the overlap task, correction saccades, and two-step tasks, one can formulate the "anti" sequence of delays as $AC''CE$ in parallel to the normal foveating sequence ACE. The first shorter value of the variable delay ($\mathbf{C}''$) is needed to cancel foveation and the second normal value ($\mathbf{C}$) is needed to choose the new goal. For an alternative but compatible approach to modeling (the delayed gamma model), see Section 3.7.1.2.

3.7.4. Instruction: Keep the Eye Marker on the Target When It Steps. While the subject is fixating a target spot on an oscilloscope, another spot (the "eye marker") can be lit and approximately stabilized on an *eccentric* retinal position, the subject's task being to bring the two spots together by eccentrically fixating the target (Zeevi, Peli, & Stark, 1979). Naive subjects usually do this by a damped to-and-fro oscillating pattern of

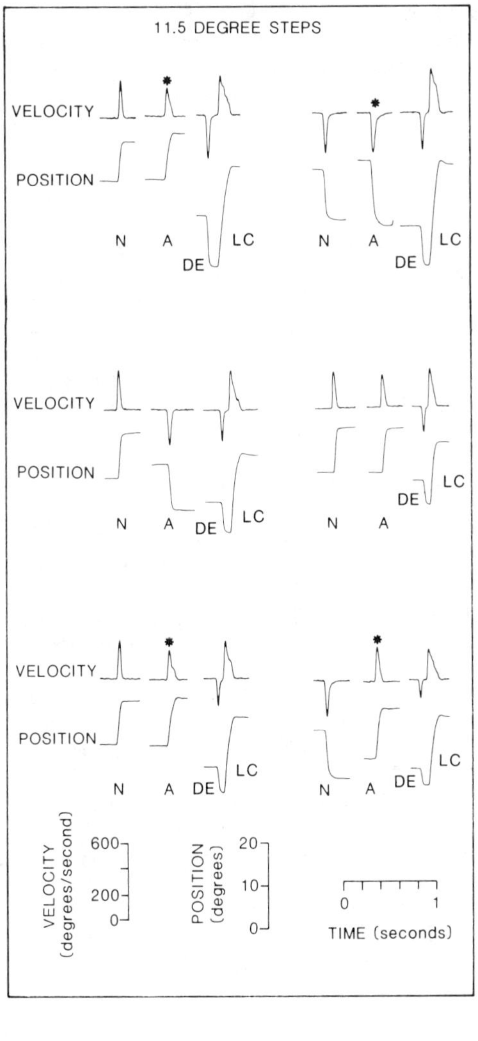

Figure 10.99. Montage of saccadic profiles in the normal and "anti" tasks. When the two tasks are mixed in the same session it is possible to find triplets of consecutive records that allow convenient comparisons. Stimulus not shown. In each triplet the upper trace is eye velocity and the lower is eye position. Scales for these dimensions are given, as well as for time. (N) In the normal foveating task the amplitude and velocity profiles are highly stereotyped. (A) This is not always the case in successful attempts at the "anti" task, in which the subject is required to look away from the stimulus displacement by an equal and opposite amount. In the profiles identified by asterisks, peak velocity is reduced, although the amplitude is larger than for the normal-task saccade in the same triplet of records. Duration is lengthened. The velocity profile may also be ragged; indeed, multiple pulses are seen in occasional subjects. (DE, LC) In direction errors at the "anti" task, the first or foveating saccade is quite normal in appearance, though it may be unusually small, as in the bottom two records, especially if the time interval to the next saccade is short. The large corrective "anti" saccade is of low velocity relative to its peak and is ragged in every case in this particular subject (EC). From an experiment in which the stimulus stepped at random to one of eight horizontal positions in the range ±3.8 to ±15.3°. Pupillary eye monitor. Guitton, Buchtel, and Douglas (1982) have shown in humans that suppressing the foveating saccade and making an "anti" saccade requires frontal cortex; a foveating saccade does not require frontal cortex. It seems likely that the "anti" task involves competition between simultaneously active brain areas (parallel planning). Also in some subjects at least, the frontal cortex does not activate the brainstem saccade generator in the usual manner. (Adapted from original data of Hallett, 1978, by E. Conway.)

saccades, whereas experienced subjects may converge rapidly on the target by consecutive saccades, or by a long slow drift. The stable fixation pattern is a sawtooth nystagmus of about 1° amplitude, which increases with eccentricity of fixation, possibly in the same manner as visual acuity decreases. If the target is now stepped, a long latency, about twice normal, elapses; the subject then foveates the target before looking away and bringing the marker onto the target. Practice reduces the latency of the involuntary foveation to normal (Zeevi & Peli, 1979).

The eccentric fixation task shows much greater practice effects than the related "anti" task, which may be partly due to confusion between the target and the marker. The involuntary foveation, when the target steps, is consistent with the heavy weighting of oculomotor function in favor of foveation. The initially long latency of involuntary foveation may be attributed either to the fixation nystagmus or to the subject attempting to "clamp" the eye to hold the eccentric fixation (perhaps by trying to hold eye velocity low?) and taking extra time to "unclamp."

3.7.5. Instruction: Track Step-Ramp Combinations. Newman (1972) was perhaps the first to describe amplitude modification in two-step tracking tasks. He also pointed out the similar modification of saccadic amplitude that occurs with a *step-wait-ramp* (SWR) stimulus pattern, when the ramp starts at least 110 msec before the saccade to the step. Thus $\mathbf{D}_m \simeq$ 110 msec in this case. See also Barmack (1970). There is a "carry-over" effect from one trial to the next, in which the saccade in a single-step trial is modified if the subject failed to respond to the ramp in the immediately previous SWR trial. This indicates that memories and expectations play a role in the selection of saccadic goals.

The qualitative response to a *step-ramp* stimulus is usually interpreted as showing that the saccadic system predicts smooth pursuit and target motion during the saccadic latent period. Measurements do not, however, reveal any particularly new principles beyond those already culled from studying two-step stimuli. If the stimulus steps rightward to a predictable position (1.8 or 4.4°), and then continues to move smoothly to the right at a randomly chosen speed (3.4–23.9° · sec^{-1}), the saccade is increased in size (Heywood & Churcher, 1981). This may be analogous to the staircase pattern of steps (SC in Fig. 10.95). The amount of error in all three subjects depended on the target velocity. If the target motion is similar, except that the initial step is oppositely directed to the ramp (equivalent to the pulse-over pattern of steps, PO in Fig. 10.95), then there are three patterns of response. (1) At low velocities the first saccade is toward the step after about normal latency (= type-I response). (2) At low to middling velocities, depending on the subject, there is no saccade to the step (= type-II response); this is often so if the stimulus recrosses its initial position in about a normal latency. (3) At high velocities there is no saccade to the step (= type-II response) and inadequate pursuit is supplemented by a large catch-up saccade, which is thus oppositely directed to the step. Analysis suggests that the best correlate of saccadic amplitude is the error that existed prior to the saccade (e.g., about 100 msec earlier = $\mathbf{D}_m$). In addition, it is possible that informed subjects will sometimes look to the expected positions that the target might reach, given its customary range of speeds (Heywood & Churcher, 1981). There is thus no need to postulate elaborate real-time "prediction" by the saccadic system of target movement and smooth pursuit during the saccadic latent period. Amplitude modification by sensory input roughly 100 msec before the saccade is probably sufficient; also, the experienced subject can always guess if randomization is not extensive.

For the eye movements to a stimulus with vertical ramp and horizontal step components, see Feinstein and Williams (1972b).

REFERENCE NOTES

1. Adams, B. D. *Timing parameters of the saccadic oculomotor system.* Master's dissertation, University of Toronto Library, 1978.
2. Doma, H. *An investigation of the effects of different stimuli brightnesses on the human saccadic oculomotor system.* Master's dissertation, University of Toronto Library, 1980.
3. Bahill, A. T., Brendel, G. F., Maskarinec, G. J., Digioia, T., McDonald, J. D., & Friedman, M. B. *Does a baseball player "keep his eye on the ball?"* Paper presented at the 12th Annual Modelling and Simulation Conference, Pittsburgh, Pa., 1981.
4. White, D. B. *The horizontal vestibulo-ocular reflex and its regulation in Parkinson's disease.* Master's dissertation, University of Toronto Library, 1983.
5. Kalesnykas, R. P. *Human saccadic eye movement responses to several varieties of oculomotor tasks.* Master's dissertation, University of Toronto Library, 1982.
6. Tomlinson, R. D. Personal communication, October, 1983.
7. Adams, B. D., & Kalesnykas, R. P. Personal communication, June, 1980.
8. Deubel, H. Personal communication, April, 1982.
9. Findlay, J. M., & Harris, L. R. *Amplitude transition functions for small saccades.* Paper presented at the 2nd European Conference on Eye Movements, Nottingham, U.K., 1983.
10. Bronstein, A. M., & Kennard, C. *Predictive eye movements in normal subjects and in Parkinson's disease.* Paper presented at the 2nd European Conference on Eye Movements, Nottingham, U.K., 1983.

REFERENCES

Abadi, R. V., & King-Smith, P. E. Congenital nystagmus modified orientation detection. *Vision Research*, 1979, *19*, 1409–1411.

Abel, L. A., Dell'Osso, L. F., & Daroff, R. B. Analog model for gaze evoked nystagmus. *IEEE Transactions on Biomedical Engineering*, 1978, *BME-25*, 71–75.

Abel, L. A., Dell'Osso, L. F., Daroff, R. B., & Parker, L. Saccades in extremes of lateral gaze. *Investigative Ophthalmology and Visual Science*, 1979, *18*, 324–327.

Abel, L. A., Parker, L., Daroff, R. B., & Dell'Osso, L. F. End-point nystagmus. *Investigative Ophthalmology and Visual Science*, 1978, *17*, 539–544.

Abel, L. A., Troost, B. T., & Dell'Osso, L. F. The effect of age on normal saccadic characteristics and their variability. *Vision Research*, 1983, *23*, 33–38.

Allen, M. J., & Carter, J. H. The torsional component of the near reflex. *American Journal of Optometry and Archives of the American Academy of Optometry*, 1967, *44*, 343–349.

Alpern, M. Types of movement. In H. Davson (Ed.), *The eye. 3* (2nd ed.). New York: Academic Press, 1969.

Arend, L. E., Jr., & Skavenski, A. A. Free scanning of gratings produces patterned retinal exposure. *Vision Research*, 1979, *19*, 1413–1420.

Bach-y-Rita, P., Collins, C. C., & Hyde, J. E. (Eds.). *The control of eye movements.* New York: Academic Press, 1971.

Bahill, A. T. Development validation and sensitivity analysis of human eye movement models. *CRC Critical Reviews in Bioengineering.* Boca Raton, Fla.: CRC Press, 1981.

Bahill, A. T., Adler, D., & Stark, L. Most naturally occurring human saccades have magnitudes of 15 deg or less. *Investigative Ophthalmology*, 1975, *14*, 468.

Bahill, A. T., Bahill, K. A., Clark, M. R., & Stark, L. Closely spaced saccades. *Investigative Ophthalmology*, 1975, *14*, 317.

Bahill, A. T., Brockenbrough, A., & Troost, B. T. Variability and development of a normative data base for saccadic eye movements. *Investigative Ophthalmology and Visual Science*, 1981, *21*, 116–125.

Bahill, A. T., Clark, M. R., & Stark, L. Dynamic overshoot in saccadic eye movements is caused by neurological control signal reversals. *Experimental Neurology*, 1975, *48*, 107–122. (a)

Bahill, A. T., Clark, M. R., & Stark, L. Glissades—eye movements generated by mismatched components of the saccadic motorneuronal control signal. *Mathematical Biosciences*, 1975, *26*, 303–318. (b)

Bahill, A. T., Clark, M. R., & Stark, L. The main sequence, a tool for studying human eye movements. *Mathematical Biosciences*, 1975, *24*, 191. (c)

Bahill, A. T., Iandolo, M. J., & Troost, B. T. Smooth pursuit eye movements in response to unpredictable waveforms. *Vision Research*, 1980, *20*, 923–931.

Bahill, A. T., & Stark, L. Overlapping saccade and glissades are produced by fatigue in the saccadic eye movement system. *Experimental Neurology*, 1975, *48*, 95–106.

Balliet, R., & Nakayama, K. Training of voluntary torsion. *Investigative Ophthalmology and Visual Science*, 1978, *17*, 303–314.

Baloh, R. W., Sills, A. W., & Honrubia, V. Impulsive and sinusoidal rotatory testing: A comparison with the results of caloric testing. *Laryngoscope*, 1979, *89*, 646.

Baloh, R. W., Sills, A. W., Kumley, W. E., & Honrubia, V. Quantitative analysis of saccadic amplification, duration and velocity. *Neurology*, 1975, *25*, 1065.

Barlow, H. B. Eye movements during fixation. *Journal of Physiology*, 1952, *116*, 290–306.

Barmack, N. H. Modification of eye movements by instantaneous changes in the velocity of visual targets. *Vision Research*, 1970, *10*, 1431–1441.

Barnes, G. R. Vestibulo-ocular function during co-ordinated head and eye movements to acquire visual targets. *Journal of Physiology*, 1979, *287*, 127–147.

Barnes, G. R., Benson, A. J., & Prior, A. R. J. Visual-vestibular interaction in the control of eye movement. *Aviation Space and Environmental Medicine*, 1978, *49*, 557.

Barnes, G. R., & Gresty, M. A. Characteristics of eye movements to targets of short duration. *Aerospace Medicine*, 1973, *44*, 1236–1240.

Barr, C. C., Schultheis, L. W., & Robinson, D. A. Voluntary non-visual control of the human vestibulo-ocular reflex. *Acta Otolaryngologica*, 1976, *81*, 365–375.

Bartz, A. E. Eye movement latency, duration and response time as a function of angular displacement. *Journal of Experimental Psychology*, 1962, *64*, 318–324.

Bartz, A. E. Fixation errors in eye movements to peripheral stimuli. *Journal of Experimental Psychology*, 1967, *75*, 444–446.

Bechai, N. R. L., & Hallett, P. E. Measurement of the rotation of a disk from its elliptical projection, with an application to eye movements. *Journal of the Optical Society of America*, 1977, *67*, 1336–1339.

Becker, W. The control of eye movements in the saccadic system. *Bibliotheca Ophthalmologica*, 1972, *82*, 233–243.

Becker, W. Do correction saccades depend exclusively on retinal feedback? A note on the possible role of nonretinal feedback. *Vision Research*, 1976, *16*, 425–427.

Becker, W. & Fuchs, A. F. Further properties of the human saccadic system: Eye movements and correction saccades with and without fixation points. *Vision Research*, 1969, *9*, 1247–1258.

Becker, W., & Jürgens, R. Saccadic reactions to double step stimuli: Evidence for model feedback and continuous information uptake. In G. Lennerstrand & P. Bach-y-Rita (Eds.), *Basic mechanisms of ocular motility and their clinical implications*. Oxford: Pergamon, 1975.

Becker, W., & Jürgens, R. An analysis of the saccadic system by means of double step stimuli. *Vision Research*, 1979, *19*, 967–983.

Becker, W., & Klein, H. M. Accuracy of saccadic eye movements and maintenance of eccentric eye positions in the dark. *Vision Research*, 1973, *13*, 1021–1034.

Beeler, G. W. Stochastic processes in the human eye movement control system (Doctoral dissertation, California Institute of Technology, 1965). *Dissertation Abstracts International*, 1965, *26*, 2331–2332. (University Microfilms No. 65-11,065)

Beeler, G. W. Visual threshold changes resulting from spontaneous saccadic eye movements. *Vision Research*, 1967, *7*, 769–775.

Behrens, F., & Grusser, O. J. Movement perception and eye movements elicited by stationary visual patterns illuminated by intermittent flashes. In G. Kommerell (Ed.), *Disorders of ocular motility*. Munich: Bergmann, 1977.

Belcher, S. J. Ocular torsion. *British Journal of Physiological Optics*, 1964, *21*, 1–20.

Bengi, H., & Thomas, J. G. Fixation tremor in relation to eyeball-muscle mechanism. *Nature*, 1968, *217*, 773–774.

Bennet-Clark, H. C. The oculomotor response to small target displacements. *Optica Acta*, 1964, *11*, 301–304.

Benson, A. J. Interactions between semicircular canals and gravity receptors. In D. E. Busby (Ed.), *Recent advances in aerospace medicine*. Dordrecht: Reidel, 1970.

Benson, A. J., & Barnes, G. R. Vision during angular oscillation: The dynamic interaction of visual and vestibular mechanisms. *Aviation Space and Environmental Medicine*, 1978, *46*, 340.

Bizzi, E. The co-ordination of eye-head movements. *Scientific American*, 1974, *231*(4), 100–106.

Bizzi, E., Kalil, R. E., & Morasso, P. Two modes of active eye-head coordination in monkeys. *Brain Research*, 1972, *40*, 45.

Blake, R., Martens, W., & Di Gianfilippo, A. Reaction time as a measure of binocular interaction in human vision. *Investigative Ophthalmology and Visual Science*, 1980, *19*, 930–941.

Boeder, P. An analysis of the general type of uniocular rotations. *American Medical Association Archives of Ophthalmology*, 1957, *57*, 200–206.

Boeder, P. The co-operation of extraocular muscles. *American Journal of Ophthalmology*, 1961, *51*, 469–481.

Boghen, D., Troost, B. T., Dell'Osso, L. F., & Birkett, J. E. Velocity characteristics of normal human saccades. *Investigative Ophthalmology*, 1974, *13*, 619.

Boltz, R. L., Smith, E. L., III, Bennett, M. J., & Harwerth, R. S. Vertical fusional vergence ranges of the rhesus monkey. *Vision Research*, 1980, *20*, 83–85.

Boyce, P. R. The effect of change of target field luminance and colour on fixation eye movements. *Optica Acta*, 1967, *14*, 213–217. (a)

Boyce, P. R. Monocular fixation in human eye movement. *Proceedings of the Royal Society, B*, 1967, *167*, 293–315. (b)

Boyce, P. R., & West, D. C. A perceptual effect on the control of fixation. *Optica Acta*, 1967, *14*, 119–126.

Boynton, R. M., & Bush, W. R. Recognition of forms against a complex background. *Journal of the Optical Society of America*, 1956, *46*, 758.

Bozkov, V., Bohdanecky, Z., Radil-Weiss, T., Mitrani, L., & Yakimoff, N. Scanning open and closed polygons. *Vision Research*, 1982, *22*, 721–726.

Brandt, T., & Buchelle, W. Arthrokinetic nystagmus by passive arm or leg rotation. In G. Kommerell (Ed.), *Disorders of ocular motility*. Munich: Bergmann, 1977.

Bridgeman, B., Mayer, M., & Glenn, L. Figural distortion accompanying smooth pursuit eye movements. *Vision Research*, 1976, *16*, 431–433.

Bridgeman, B., & Palca, J. The role of microsaccades in high acuity observational tasks. *Vision Research*, 1980, *20*, 813–817.

Brindley, G. S. *Physiology of the retina and visual pathway* (2nd ed.). Physiological Society Monographs, London: Edward Arnold, 1970.

Brooks, B. A., & Bajandas, F. J. (Eds.). *Eye movements*. New York: Plenum, 1977.

Brooks, B. A., & Fuchs, A. Influence of stimulus parameters on visual sensitivity during saccadic eye movement. *Vision Research*, 1975,

15, 1389–1398.

Brooks, B. A., Impelman, D. M., & Lum, J. T. Influence of background luminance on visual sensitivity during saccadic eye movements. *Experimental Brain Research*, 1980, *40*, 322–329.

Brown, B., & Monk, T. H. The effect of local target surround and whole background constraint on visual search times. *Human Factors*, 1975, *17*, 81–88.

Burian, H. M., & von Noorden, G. K. *Binocular vision and ocular motility*. St. Louis: Mosby, 1974.

Campbell, F. W. Accommodation reflex. *British Orthoptics Journal*, 1954, *11*, 13–17.

Campbell, F. W. The depth of field of the human eye. *Optica Acta*, 1957, *4*, 157–164.

Campbell, F. W., Robson, J. G., & Westheimer, G. Fluctuations of accommodation under steady viewing conditions. *Journal of Physiology*, 1959, *145*, 579–594.

Campbell, F. W., & Westheimer, G. Factors influencing accommodation responses of the human eye. *Journal of the Optical Society of America*, 1959, *49*, 568–571.

Campbell, F. W., & Westheimer, G. Dynamics of accommodation responses of the human eye. *Journal of Physiology*, 1960, *151*, 285–295.

Carlow, T., Dell'Osso, L. F., Troost, B. T., Daroff, R. B., & Birkett, J. E. Saccadic eye movement latencies to multimodal stimuli. *Vision Research*, 1975, *15*, 1257–1262.

Carpenter, R. H. S. *Movements of the eyes*. London: Pion, 1977.

Carpenter, R. H. S. Oculomotor procrastination. In D. F. Fisher, R. A. Monty, & J. W. Senders (Eds.), *Eye movements: Cognition and visual perception*, Hillsdale, N.J.: Lawrence Erlbaum, 1981.

Cavanagh, P., Anstis, S., & Mather, G. Screening for color blindness using optokinetic nystagmus. *Investigative Ophthalmology and Visual Science*, 1984, *25*, 463–466.

Cheng, M., & Outerbridge, J. S. Inter-saccadic interval analysis of optokinetic nystagmus. *Vision Research*, 1974, *14*, 1053–1058.

Ciuffreda, K. J., Kenyon, R. V., & Stark, L. Increased saccadic latencies in amblyopic eyes. *Investigative Ophthalmology and Visual Science*, 1978, *17*, 697–702. (a)

Ciuffreda, K. J., Kenyon, R. V., & Stark, L. Processing delays in amblyopic eyes: Evidence from saccadic latencies. *American Journal of Optometry and Physiological Optics*, 1978, *55*, 187–196. (b)

Ciuffreda, K. J., Kenyon, R. V., & Stark, L. Different rates of functional recovery of eye movements during orthoptics treatment in an adult amblyope. *Investigative Ophthalmology and Visual Science*, 1979, *18*, 213–219.

Clarke, F. J. J., & Belcher, S. J. On the localization of Troxler's effect in the visual pathway. *Vision Research*, 1962, *2*, 53–68.

Coakley, D. (Ed.). *Minute eye movement and brain stem function*. Boca Raton, Fla.: CRC Press, 1983.

Cohen, B. (Ed.). Vestibular and oculomotor physiology (Barany Society). *Annals. New York Academy of Science*, 1981, *374*.

Cohen, M. E., & Ross, L. E. Latency and accuracy characteristics of saccades and corrective saccades in adults and children. *Journal of Experimental Child Psychology*, 1978, *26*, 517–527.

Collewijn, H. The optokinetic system. In B. L. Zuber (Ed.), *Models of oculomotor behavior and control*. Boca Raton, Fla.: CRC Press, 1981.

Collewijn, H., & van der Mark, F. Ocular stability in variable visual feedback conditions in the rabbit. *Brain Research*, 1972, *36*, 47–57.

Collewijn, H., Martins, A. J., & Steinman, R. M. Natural retinal image motion: Origin and change. *Annals. New York Academy of Science*, 1981, *374*, 312–329.

Collins, C. C., Carlson, M. R., Scott, A. B., & Jampolski, A. Extraocular muscle forces in normal human subjects. *Investigative Ophthalmology and Visual Science*, 1981, *20*, 652.

Coren, S., & Hoenig, P. Effect of non-target stimuli upon length of voluntary saccades. *Perceptual and Motor Skills*, 1972, *34*, 499–508.

Cornsweet, T. N. Determination of the stimuli for involuntary drifts and saccadic eye movements. *Journal of the Optical Society of America*, 1956, *146*, 987–993.

Cornsweet, T. N., & Crane, H. D. An accurate eye tracker using first and fourth Purkinje image. *Journal of the Optical Society of America*, 1973, *63*, 921–928.

Crassini, B., & Broerse, J. Monocular rivalry occurs without eye movements. *Vision Research*, 1982, *22*, 203–204.

Crone, R. A. Optically induced eye torsion II. Optostatic and optokinetic cycloversion. *Albrecht von Graefes Archiv fur klinische und experimentelle Ophthalmologie*, 1975, *196*, 1–7.

Crone, R. A., & Everhard-Halm, Y. Optically induced eye torsion. *Albrecht von Graefes Archiv fur klinische und experimentelle Ophthalmologie*, 1975, *195*, 231–239.

Crone, R. A., & Verduyn Lunel, H. F. E. Autokinesis and the perception of movement: The physiology of eccentric fixation. *Vision Research*, 1969, *9*, 89–101.

Dallos, P. J., & Jones, R. W. Learning behaviour of the eye fixation control system. *IEEE Transactions on Automatic Control*, 1963, *AC-8*, 218–227.

Daroff, R. B., Troost, B. T., & Dell'Osso, L. F. Nystagmus and related ocular oscillations. In J. S. Glaser (Ed.), *Neuro-ophthalmology*. New York: Harper & Row, 1978.

Deckert, G. H. Pursuit eye movements in the absence of a moving visual stimulus. *Science*, 1964, *143*, 1192–1193.

Dell'Osso, L. F., Abel, L. A., & Daroff, R. B. "Inverse latent" macro square jerks and macrosaccadic oscillations. *Annals of Neurology*, 1977, *2*, 57–60.

Dell'Osso, L. F., & Daroff, R. B. Clinical disorders of eye movement. In B. L. Zuber (Ed.), *Models of oculomotor behavior and control*. Boca Raton, Fla.: CRC Press, 1981.

Dell'Osso, L. F., Daroff, R. B., & Troost, B. T. Reply to a comment on the glissade. *Vision Research*, 1973, *13*, 883–884.

Dell'Osso, L. F., Gauthier, G., Liberman, G., & Stark, L. Eye movement recordings as a diagnostic tool in a case of congenital nystagmus. *American Journal of Optometry and Archives of the American Academy of Optometry*, 1972, *49*, 3.

Deubel, H., Wolf, W., & Hauske, G. Corrective saccades: Effect of shifting the saccade goal. *Vision Research*, 1982, *22*, 353–364.

Dichgans, J. Optokinetic nystagmus as dependent on the retinal periphery via the vestibular nucleus. In R. Baker & A. Berlioz (Eds.), *Control of gaze by brain stem neurones*. Amsterdam: Elsevier/North-Holland, 1977.

Dichgans, J., & Bizzi, E. (Eds.). *Cerebral control of eye movements and motor perception*. Basel, Switzerland: Karger, 1972.

Dimitrov, G., Yakimoff, N., Mateef, S., Mitrani, L., Radil-Weiss, T., & Bozkov, V. Saccadic eye movements on Bela Julesz' figure. *Vision Research*, 1976, *16*, 411–414.

Ditchburn, R. W. *Eye movements and visual perception*. Oxford: Clarendon, 1973.

Ditchburn, R. W. The function of small saccades. *Vision Research*, 1980, *20*, 271–272.

Ditchburn, R. W., & Drysdale, A. E. The effect of retinal image movements on vision: I. Step-movements and pulse-movements. *Proceedings of the Royal Society*, 1977, *197*B, 131–144.

Ditchburn, R. W., & Foley-Fisher, J. A. Assembled data on eye movements. *Optica Acta*, 1967, *14*, 113–118.

Ditchburn, R. W., & Ginsberg, B. L. Involuntary eye movements during fixation. *Journal of Physiology*, 1953, *119*, 1–17.

ten Doesschate, J. A new form of physiological nystagmus. *Ophthalmologica*, 1954, *127*, 65–73.

Dubois, M. F. W., & Collewijn, H. Optokinetic reactions in man elicited by localized retinal motion stimuli. *Vision Research*, 1979, *19*, 1105–1115.

Duwaer, A. L. Assessment of retinal image displacement during head movement using an afterimage method. *Vision Research*, 1982, *22*, 1379–1388.

Duwaer, A. L., & van den Brink, G. Diplopia thresholds and the initiation of vergence eye-movements. *Vision Research*, 1981, *21*, 1727–1737.

Easter, S. S., Jr. A comment on the "glissade." *Vision Research*, 1973,

13, 881–882.
Ebenholtz, S. M., & Shebilske, W. L. The doll reflex counterrolling with head-body tilt in the median plane. *Vision Research*, 1975, *15*, 713–717.
Eizenman, M., Frecker, R. C., & Hallett, P. E. Precise noncontacting measurement using the corneal reflex. *Vision Research*, 1984, *24*, 167–174.
Eizenman, M., Frecker, R. C., Joy, M. L. G., & Hallett, P. E. A new mathematical approach to the high resolution of eye movements. *Digest of the 8th Canadian Medical and Biological Engineering Confference*, Hamilton, 1980. (Available from the Institute of Biomedical Engineering, University of Toronto.)
Engel, F. L. Visual conspicuity, visual search and fixation tendencies of the eye. *Vision Research*, 1977, *17*, 95–108.
Enoksson, P. Binocular rivalry and monocular dominance studies with optokinetic nystagmus. *Acta Ophthalmology*, 1963, *41*, 544–563.
Enright, J. T. Ocular translation and cyclotorsion due to changes in fixation distance. *Vision Research*, 1980, *20*, 595–602.
Feinstein, R. Interactions of the horizontal and vertical eye movement systems (Doctoral dissertation, University of Michigan, 1970). *Dissertation Abstracts International*, 1970, *31*, 2640 B. (University Microfilms No. 70–21, 651)
Feinstein, R., & Williams, W. J. Interactions of the horizontal and vertical human oculomotor systems: The saccade systems. *Vision Research*, 1972, *12*, 33–44. (a)
Feinstein, R., & Williams, W. J. Interactions of the horizontal and vertical human oculomotor systems: The vertical smooth pursuit and horizontal saccadic systems. *Vision Research*, 1972, *12*, 45–52. (b)
Feldon, S. E., Hoyt, W. F., & Stark, L. Disordered inhibition in internuclear ophthalmoplegia, analysis of eye movement recordings with computer simulations. *Brain*, 1980, *103*, 113.
Feldon, S. E., & Laneston, J. W. Square-wave jerks: A disorder of microsaccades? *Neurology*, 1977, *27*, 278–281.
Fender, D. H. Torsional movements of the eye ball. *British Journal of Ophthalmology*, 1955, *39*, 65–72.
Fender, D. H. Contact lens stability. *Biomedical Sciences Instrumentation*, 1964, *2*, 43–52. (a)
Fender, D. H. Techniques of systems-analysis applied to feedback pathways in the control of eye movements. *Symposia of the Society for Experimental Biology*, 1964, *18*, 401–419. (b)
Fender, D. H., & Nye, P. W. An investigation of the mechanisms of eye movement control. *Kybernetik*, 1961, *1*, 81–88.
Festinger, L. Eye movements and perception. In P. Bach-y-Rita, C. C. Collins, & J. E. Hyde (Eds.), *The control of eye movements*. New York: Academic Press, 1971.
Findlay, J. M. Frequency analysis of human involuntary eye-movements. *Kybernetics*, 1971, *8*, 207–214.
Findlay, J. M. The visual stimulus for saccadic eye movements in human observers. *Perception*, 1980, *9*, 7–21.
Findlay, J. M. Local and global influences on saccadic eye-movements. In D. F. Fisher, R. A. Monty, & J. W. Senders (Eds.), *Eye movements: Cognition and visual perception*. Hillsdale, N.J.: Lawrence Erlbaum, 1981. (a)
Findlay, J. M. Spatial and temporal factors in the predictive generation of saccadic eye movements. *Vision Research*, 1981, *21*, 347–354. (b)
Findlay, J. M. Global visual processing for saccadic eye movements. *Vision Research*, 1982, *22*, 1033–1046.
Findlay, J. M. Visual information for saccadic eye movements. In A. Hein & M. Jeannerod (Eds.), *Spatially oriented behavior*. New York: Springer-Verlag, 1983.
Fischer, B., & Boch, R. Saccadic eye movements after extremely short reaction times in the monkey. *Brain Research*, 1983, *260*, 21–26.
Fisher, D. F., Monty, R. A., & Senders, J. W. (Eds.). *Eye movements: Cognition and visual perception*. Hillsdale, N.J.: Lawrence Erlbaum, 1981.
Fitts, P. M., & Posner, M. I. *Human performance*. Belmont, Calif.: Brooks/Cole, 1967.
Fleming, D. G., Vossius, G. W., Bowman, G., & Johnson, E. L. Adaptive properties of the eye-tracking system as revealed by moving-head and open-loop studies. *Annals. New York Academy of Science*, 1969, *156*, 825–850.
Fox, R., Lehmkuhle, S., & Leguire, L. E. Stereoscopic contours induce optokinetic nystagmus. *Vision Research*, 1978, *18*, 1189–1192.
Fox, R., Todd, S., & Bettinger, L. A. Optokinetic nystagmus as an objective indicator of binocular rivalry. *Vision Research*, 1975, *15*, 849–853.
Frisby, J., & Mayhew, J. The role of spatial frequency tuned channels in vergence control. *Vision Research*, 1980, *20*, 727–732.
Fry, G. A. Nomograms for torsion and direction of regard. *American Journal of Optometry and Archives of the Academy of Optometry*, 1968, *45*, 631–641.
Fuchs, A. F. The saccadic system. In P. Bach-y-Rita, C. C. Collins, & J. E. Hyde (Eds.), *The control of eye movements*. New York: Academic Press, 1971.
Fuchs, A. F., & Becker, W. (Eds.). *Progress in oculomotor research*. Amsterdam: Elsevier/North-Holland, 1981.
Fuchs, A. F., & Binder, M. D. Fatigue resistance of human extraocular muscles. *Journal of Neurophysiology*, 1983, *49*, 28–34.
Fuchs, A. F., & Kaneko, C. R. S. A brain stem generator for saccadic eye movements. *Trends in Neuroscience*, 1981, *(Nov.)*, 283–286.
Gaarder, K. Mechanisms in fixation saccadic eye movements. *British Journal of Physiological Optics*, 1967, *24*, 28–44.
Gauthier, G. M., & Robinson, D. A. Adaptation of the human vestibulo-ocular reflex to magnifying lenses. *Brain Research*, 1975, *92*, 331–335.
Gellert, W. [et al.] (Eds.). *VNR Concise Encyclopedia of Mathematics*. New York: Van Nostrand Reinhold, 1975.
Gibbs, C. B., & Logan, O. Tests of the functions of proprioception and interaction of senses. *Perceptual and Motor Skills*, 1965, *20*, 433–442.
van Gisbergen, J. A. M., Robinson, D. A., & Gielen, S. A quantitative analysis of generation of saccadic eye movements by burst neurons. *Journal of Neurophysiology*, 1981, *45*, 417–442.
Gonshor, A., & Melvill Jones, G. Extreme vestibulo-ocular adaptation induced by prolonged optical reversal of vision. *Journal of Physiology* (London) 1976, *256*, 381–414. (a)
Gonshor, A., & Melvill Jones, G. Short term adaptive changes in the human vestibulo-ocular reflex arc. *Journal of Physiology* (London) 1976, *256*, 361–379. (b)
Goodenough, D. R., Sigman, E., Oltman, P. K., Rosso, J., & Mertz, H. Eye torsion in response to a tilted stimulus. *Vision Research*, 1979, *19*, 1177–1180.
Goodwin, A. W. The effect of colour on time delays in the human oculomotor system. *Vision Research*, 1973, *13*, 1395–1398.
Goodwin, A. W., & Fender, D. H. The interaction between horizontal and vertical eye-rotations in tracking tasks. *Vision Research*, 1973, *13*, 1701–1712.
Green, B. F., & Anderson, L. K. Colour coding in a visual search task. *Journal of Experimental Psychology*, 1956, *51*, 19.
Greenwood, R. E. Some effects of involuntary eye movements. *Journal of the Optical Society of America*, 1972, *62*, 101–103.
Gresty, M. A. Coordination of head and eye movements to fixate continuous and intermittent targets. *Vision Research*, 1974, *14*, 395–404.
Gresty, M., & Leech, J. The assessment of position of stationary targets perceived during saccadic eye movements. *Pflüger's Archiv fuer die Gesante Physiology*, 1976, *366*, 83–88.
Groner, R., Menz, C., Fisher, D. F., & Monty, R. A. (Eds.). *Eye movements and psychological functions*. Hillsdale, N.J.: Lawrence Erlbaum, 1983.
Guitton, D., Buchtel, H. A., & Douglas, R. M. Disturbances of voluntary saccadic eye movement mechanisms following discrete unilateral frontal lobe removals. In G. Lennerstrand et al. (Eds.), *Functional basis of ocular motility disorders*. Oxford: Pergamon Press, 1982.
Hackman, R. An experimental study of variability in ocular latency. *Journal of Experimental Psychology*, 1940, *4*, 11–26.
Haddad, G. M., & Steinman, R. M. The smallest voluntary saccade:

Implications for fixation. *Vision Research*, 1973, *13*, 1075–1086.

Haddad, G. M., & Winterson, B. J. Effect of flicker on oculomotor performance. In G. Lennerstrand & P. Bach-y-Rita (Eds.), *Brain mechanisms of ocular motility and their clinical implications*. Oxford: Pergamon, 1975.

Haegerstrom-Portnoy, G., & Brown, B. Contrast effects on smooth-pursuit eye movement velocity. *Vision Research*, 1979, *19*, 169–174.

Hallett, P. E. Quantum efficiency and false positive rate. *Journal of Physiology*, 1969, *202*, 421–436.

Hallett, P. E. Physiology of vision. In A. Sorsby (Ed.), *Modern ophthalmology 1*. London: Butterworths, 1971.

Hallett, P. E.. Saccades to flashes. In R. A. Monty & J. W. Senders (Eds.), *Eye movements and psychological processes*. Hillsdale, N.J.: Lawrence Erlbaum, 1976.

Hallett, P. E. Primary and secondary saccades to goals defined by instructions. *Vision Research*, 1978, *18*, 1279–1296.

Hallett, P. E., & Adams, B. D. The predictability of saccadic latency in a novel voluntary oculomotor task. *Vision Research*, 1980, *20*, 329–339.

Hallett, P. E., & Lightstone, A. D. Saccadic eye movements to flashed targets. *Vision Research*, 1976, *16*, 107–114. (a)

Hallett, P. E., & Lightstone, A. D. Saccadic eye movements towards stimuli triggered by prior saccades. *Vision Research*, 1976, *16*, 99–106. (b)

Hamann, K.-V. Opposed short latency pairs. In G. Kommerell (Ed.), *Disorders of ocular motility*. Munich: Bergmann, 1977.

Hannen, R. A., Kabrisky, H., Replogle, C. R., Hartzler, V. L., & Roccaforte, P. A. The experimental determination of a portion of the human vestibular system response through measurement of eyeball counterroll. *IEEE Transactions on Biomedical Engineering*, 1966, *BME-13*, 65–70.

Hansen, R. M., & Skavenski, A. A. Accuracy of eye position information for motor control. *Vision Research*, 1977, *17*, 919–926.

Hatamian, M., & Anderson, D. J. Design considerations for a real-time ocular counterroll instrument. *IEEE Transactions on Biomedical Engineering*, 1983, *BME-30*, 278–288.

Hay, J. C. Visual adaptation to an altered correlation between eye movement and head movement. *Science*, 1968, *160*, 429–430.

Hecht, S., Shlaer, S., & Pirenne, M. H. Energy, quanta and vision. *Journal of General Physiology*, 1941, *25*, 819–840.

Heckenmueller, E. G. Stabilization of the retinal image. *Psychological Bulletin*, 1965, *63*, 157–169.

Hedlun, J., & White, C. Nystagmus induced by visual feedback. *Journal of the Optical Society of America*, 1959, *49*, 729–730.

Helmholtz, H. [*Physiological optics*] (J. P. C. Southall, Ed. and trans.). New York: Dover, 1926. (Originally published, 1910.)

Henn, V., Cohen, B., & Young, L. R. Visual-vestibular interaction in motion perception and the generation of nystagmus. *Neurosciences Research Program Bulletin*, 1980, *18*, 459–652.

Henson, D. B. Investigation into corrective saccadic eye movements (Doctoral dissertation, Indiana University, 1977). *Dissertation Abstracts International*, 1977, *38*, 1589 B. (University Microfilms No. 77–22, 657)

Henson, D. B. Corrective saccades: Effects of altering visual feedback. *Vision Research*, 1978, *18*, 63–67.

Henson, D. B. Investigation into corrective saccadic eye movements for refixation amplitudes of 10 degrees and below. *Vision Research*, 1979, *19*, 55–42.

Hering, E. [*The theory of binocular vision*] (B. Bridgeman, Ed. and trans.; with commentaries by B. Bridgeman and L. Stark). New York: Plenum, 1977. (Originally published, 1868.)

Herishanu, Y. O., & Sharpe, J. A. Normal square wave jerks. *Investigative Ophthalmology and Visual Science*, 1981, *20*, 268–272.

Heywood, S. Voluntary control of smooth eye movements and their velocity. *Nature*, 1972, *238*, 408–410.

Heywood, S. Asymmetries related to cerebral dominance in returning the eyes to specified target positions in the dark. *Vision Research*, 1973, *13*, 81–94. (a)

Heywood, S. Pursuing stationary dots: Smooth eye movements and apparent movement. *Perception*, 1973, *2*, 181–195. (b)

Heywood, S., & Churcher, J. Eye movements and the after-image—I. Tracking the after-image. *Vision Research*, 1971, *11*, 1163–1168.

Heywood, S., & Churcher, J. Eye Movements and the after-image—II. The effect of foveal and non-foveal after-images on saccadic behaviour. *Vision Research*, 1972, *12*, 1033–1043.

Heywood, S., & Churcher, J. Structure of the visual array and saccadic latency: Implications for oculomotor control. *Quarterly Journal of Experimental Psychology*, 1980, *32*, 335–341.

Heywood, S., & Churcher, J. Saccades to step-ramp stimuli. *Vision Research*, 1981, *21*, 479–490.

Hick, W. E. On the rate of gain of information. *Quarterly Journal of Experimental Psychology*, 1952, *4*, 11–26.

Holtzman, J. D., Sedgwick, H. A., & Festinger, L. Interaction of perceptually monitored and unmonitored efferent commands for smooth pursuit eye movements. *Vision Research*, 1978, *18*, 1545–1555.

Honrubia, V., Downey, W. L., Mitchell, D. P., & Ward, P. H. Experimental studies on optokinetic nystagmus. II. Normal humans. *Acta Otolaryngologica*, 1968, *65*, 441–448.

Hood, J. D. Electro-nystagmography. *Journal of Laryngology and Otology*, 1968, *82*, 167.

Hood, J. D. Observations upon the role of the peripheral retina in the execution of eye movements. *Journal of Otorhino-laryngology, Borderlands*, 1975, *37*, 65–73.

Horrocks, A., & Stark, L. Experiments on error as a function of response time in horizontal eye movements. *M.I.T. Research Laboratory in Electronics Quarterly Research Report*, 1964, *72*, 267–269.

Hou, R. L., & Fender, D. H. Processing of direction and magnitude by the saccadic eye-movement system. *Vision Research*, 1979, *19*, 1421–1426.

Howard, I. P. *Human visual orientation*. Toronto: Wiley, 1981.

Howard, I. P., & Templeton, W. B. Visually induced eye-torsion and tilt adaptation. *Vision Research*, 1964, *4*, 433–437.

Hughes, A. The topography of vision in animals of contrasting life style: Comparative optics and retinal organization. In F. Crescitelli (Ed.), *The visual system in vertebrates. Handbook of Sensory Physiology 7/5*. Berlin: Springer-Verlag, 1977.

Hyden, D., Istl, Y. E., & Schwarz, D. W. F. Human visuovestibular interaction as a basis for quantitative clinical diagnostics. *Acta Otolaryngologica*, 1982, *94*, 53–60.

Ishihawa, S., & Terohado, R. Maximum velocity of saccadic eye movement in normal and strabismic subjects. *Japan Journal of Ophthalmology*, 1973, *17*, 11.

Jenkins, S. E., & Cole, B. L. The effect of the density of background elements on the conspicuity of objects. *Vision Research*, 1982, *22*, 1241–1252.

Jones, R. Anomalies of disparity detection in the human visual system. *Journal of Physiology (London)*, 1977, *264*, 621–640.

Jones, R., & Kerr, K. E. Vergence eye movements to pairs of disparity stimuli with shape selection cues. *Vision Research*, 1972, *12*, 1425–1430.

Jordan, S. Ocular pursuit movement as a function of visual and proprioceptive stimulation. *Vision Research*, 1970, *10*, 775–780.

Judge, S. J. Temporal interaction between human voluntary saccades and rapid phases of optokinetic nystagmus. *Experimental Brain Research*, 1973, *18*, 114–118.

Jürgens, R., Becker, W., & Kornhuber, H. H. Natural and drug-induced variations of velocity and duration of human saccadic eye-movements: Evidence for a control of the neural pulse generator by local feedback. *Biological Cybernetics*, 1981, *39*, 87–96.

Jürgens, R., Becker, W., & Rieger, P. Different effects involved in the interaction of saccades and the vestibulo-ocular reflex. *Annals. New York Academy of Science*, 1981, *374*, 744–754.

Kalesnykas, R. P., & Hallett, P. E. Anticipatory saccadic eye-movement responses to asynchronous off-on components of step-displacement stimuli. *Supplement to Investigative Ophthalmology and Visual Science*, 1983, *24*(3), 24.

Kaufman, L., & Richards, W. Spontaneous fixation tendencies for visual forms. *Perception and Psychophysics*, 1969, *5*, 85–88.

Keller, E. L. Gain of the vestibulo-ocular reflex in monkey at high rotational frequencies. *Vision Research*, 1978, *18*, 311–316.

Kelly, D. H., & Crane, H. D. *Research study of a fundus tracker for experiments in stabilized vision*. National Aeronautics and Space Administration (CR-1121), 1968.

Kenyon, R. V., Ciuffreda, K. J., & Stark, L. Binocular eye movements during accommodative vergence. *Vision Research*, 1978, *18*, 545–565.

Kenyon, R. V., Ciuffreda, K. J., & Stark, L. Unequal saccades during vergence. *American Journal of Optometry and Physiological Optics*, 1980, *57*, 20–37.

Kenyon, R. V., Ciuffreda, K. J., & Stark, L. Dynamic vergence eye movements in strabismus and amblyopia: Asymmetric vergence. *British Journal of Ophthalmology*, 1981, *65*, 167–176.

Kertesz, A. E., & Hampton, D. R. Fusional response to extrafoveal stimulation. *Investigative Ophthalmology and Visual Science*, 1981, *21*, 600–605.

Kertesz, A. E., & Sullivan, M. J. The effects of stimuli size on human cyclofusional response. *Vision Research*, 1978, *18*, 567–571.

King-Smith, P. E., & Riggs, L. A. Visual sensitivity to the controlled motion of a line or edge. *Vision Research*, 1978, *18*, 1509–1520.

Kishto, B. N., & Saunders, R. Variation of the visual threshold with retinal location. *Vision Research*, 1970, *10*, 745–767.

Kolers, P. Buswell's discoveries. In R. A. Monty & J. W. Senders (Eds.), *Eye movements and psychological processes*. Hillsdale, N.J.: Lawrence Erlbaum, 1976.

Kommerell, G. (Ed.). *Disorders of oculomotor motility*. Munich: Bergmann, 1978.

Kommerell, G., & Klein, V. Über die Visuelle Regelung der Okulomotorik: Die optomotorische Wirking exzentrischer Nachbilder. *Vision Research*, 1971, *11*, 905–920.

Komoda, M. K., Festinger, L., Phillips, L. J., Duckman, R. H., & Young, R. A. Some observations concerning eye movements. *Vision Research*, 1973, *13*, 1009–1020.

Komoda, M. K., Festinger, L., & Sherry, J. The accuracy of two-dimensional saccades in the absence of continuing retinal stimulation. *Vision Research*, 1977, *17*, 1231–1232.

Kowler, E., & Facchiano, D. M. Kid's poor tracking means habits are lacking. *Supplement to Investigative Ophthamology and Visual Science*, 1982, *22*, 103.

Kowler, E., Murphy, B. J., & Steinman, R. M. Velocity matching during smooth pursuit of different targets on different backgrounds. *Vision Research*, 1978, *18*, 603–606.

Kowler, E., & Steinman, R. M. The effect of expectations on slow oculomotor control—I. Periodic target steps. *Vision Research*, 1979, *19*, 619–632. (a)

Kowler, E., & Steinman, R. M. The effect of expectations on slow oculomotor control—II. Single target displacements. *Vision Research*, 1979, *19*, 633–646. (b)

Kowler, E., & Steinman, R. M. Miniature saccades: Eye movements that do not count. *Vision Research*, 1979, *19*, 105–108. (c)

Kowler, E., & Steinman, R. M. Small saccades serve no useful purpose: Reply to a letter by R. W. Ditchburn. *Vision Research*, 1980, *20*, 273–276.

Kowler, E., & Steinman, R. M. The effect of expectations on slow oculomotor control—III. Guessing unpredictable target displacements. *Vision Research*, 1981, *21*, 191–204.

Krauskopf, J., Cornsweet, T., & Riggs, L. An analysis of eye movements during monocular and binocular fixation. *Journal of the Optical Society of America*, 1960, *50*, 572–578.

Kurtzberg, D., & Vaughan, H. G. Differential topography of human eye movement potentials preceding visually triggered and self-initiated saccades. *Brain Research*, 1980, *44*, 203–208.

Lambert, R. H., Monty, R. A., & Hall, R. T. High speed data processing and unobtrusive monitoring of eye movements. *Behavioral Research Methods and Instrumentation*, 1974, *6*, 525–530.

Lancaster, W. B. Fifty years experience in ocular motility. *American Journal of Ophthalmology*, 1941, *24*, 485–496.

Land, M. F. Optics and vision in invertebrates. In H. Autrum (Ed.), *Handbook of Sensory Physiology* VII/6B. New York: Springer, 1981.

Lanman, J. M., Bizzi, E., & Allum, J. The coordination of eye and head movement during smooth pursuit. *Brain Research*, 1978, *153*, 39–53.

Le Grand, Y. *Light, colour and vision*. London: Chapman and Hall, 1957.

Leigh, J. R., Newman, S. A., Zee, D. S., & Miller, N. R. Visual following during stimulation of an immobile eye (the open loop condition). *Vision Research*, 1982, *22*, 1193–1197.

Leigh, R. J., & Zee, D. S. Eye movements of the blind. *Investigative Ophthalmology and Visual Science*, 1980, *19*, 328–331.

Lennerstrand, G., & Bach-y-Rita, P. (Eds.). *Basic mechanisms of ocular motility and their clinical implications*. Oxford: Pergamon, 1975.

Leushina, L. I. On estimation of position of photostimulus and eye movements. *Biofizika*, 1965, *10*, 130–136.

Levy-Schoen, A. Le champ d'activité du regard: Données expérimentales. *L'Année Psychologique*, 1974, *74*, 43–66.

Levy-Schoen, A. Flexible and/or rigid control of oculomotor scanning behavior. In D. F. Fisher, R. A. Monty, & J. W. Senders (Eds.), *Eye movements: Cognition and visual perception*. Hillsdale, N.J.: Lawrence Erlbaum, 1981.

Levy-Schoen, A., & Blanc-Garin, J. On oculomotor programming and perception. *Brain Research*, 1974, *17*, 443–450.

Lightstone, A. D. Visual stimuli for saccadic and smooth pursuit eye movements. (Doctoral dissertation, University of Toronto, 1973. National Library of Canada, Ottawa.)

Lisberger, S. E., Evinger, C., Johanson, G. W., & Fuchs, A. F. Relationship between eye acceleration and retinal image velocity during foveal smooth pursuit in man and monkey. *Journal of Neurophysiology*, 1981, *46*, 229–249.

Lisberger, S. G., Fuchs, A. F., King, W. M., & Evinger, L. C. Effect of mean reaction time on saccadic responses to two step stimuli with horizontal and vertical components. *Vision Research*, 1975, *15*, 1021–1025.

Llewellyn Thomas, E. Movements of the eye. *Scientific American*, 1968, *81*, 288–292.

Llewellyn Thomas, E., & O'Beirne, H. Curvature in saccadic movement. *Archives of Ophthalmology*, 1966, *77*, 105–109.

Locket, N. A. Adaptations to the deep sea environment. In F. Crescitelli (Ed.), *The visual system in vertebrates. Handbook of sensory physiology*. Berlin: Springer-Verlag, 1980.

Luria, S. M., & Strauss, M. S. Eye movements during search for coded and uncoded targets. *Perception and Psychophysics*, 1973, *17*, 303–308.

Mack, A., Fendrich, R., & Pleune, J. Adaptation to an altered relation between retinal displacements and saccadic eye movements. *Vision Research*, 1978, *18*, 1321–1328.

Mack, A., Fendrich, R., & Pleune, J. Smooth pursuit eye movements: Is perceived motion necessary? *Science*, 1979, *203*, 1361–1363.

Mack, A., Fendrich, R., & Wong, E. Is perceived motion a stimulus for smooth pursuit? *Vision Research*, 1982, *22*, 77–88.

Mackworth, N. H., & Llewellyn Thomas, E. Head-mounted eye-marker camera. *Journal of the Optical Society of America*, 1962, *52*, 713–716.

Mandl, G., & Melvill Jones, G. Rapid visual-vestibular interaction during visual tracking in strobe light. *Brain Research*, 1979, *165*, 133–138.

Mansfield, R. J. W. Latency functions in human vision. *Vision Research*, 1973, *13*, 2219–2234.

Matin, L. Measurement of eye movements by contact lens techniques: Analysis of measuring systems and some new methodology for three dimensional recordings. *Journal of the Optical Society of America*, 1964, *54*, 1008–1018.

Matin, L. Saccades and the extraretinal signal for visual direction. In R. Monty & J. Senders (Eds.), *Eye movements and psychological processes*. Hillsdale, N.J.: Lawrence Erlbaum, 1976.

Matin, L. Visual localization and eye movements. In W. A. Wagenaar, A. H. Wertheim, & H. W. Leibowitz (Eds.), *Symposium on the study of motion perception*. New York: Plenum, 1981.

Matin, L., & MacKinnon, G. E. Autokinetic movement: Selective manipulation of directional components by image stabilization. *Science*, 1964, *143*, 145–148.

Matin, L., Matin, E., & Pearce, D. G. Eye movements in the dark during the attempt to maintain a prior fixation position. *Vision Research*, 1970, *10*, 837–857.

Matin, L., & Pearce, D. G. Three dimensional recording of rotational eye movements by a new contact-lens technique. *Biomedical Sciences Instrumentation*, 1964, *2*, 79–95.

Mays, L., & Sparks, D. L. Saccades are spatially not retinocentrically coded. *Science*, 1980, *208*, 1163–1165.

Mays, L., & Sparks, D. L. The localization of saccade targets using a combination of retinal and eye position information. In A. F. Fuchs & W. Becker (Eds.), *Progress in oculomotor research*. Amsterdam: Elsevier/North-Holland, 1981.

McConkie, G. W., & Rayner, K. The span of the effective stimulus during a fixation in reading. *Perception and Psychophysics*, 1975, *17*, 578–586.

McLaughlin, S. C. Parametric adjustment of saccades. *Perception and Psychophysics*, 1967, *2*, 359–362.

Melvill Jones, G. Vestibulo-ocular disorganization in the aerodynamic spin. *Aerospace Medicine*, 1965, *36*, 976–983.

Melvill Jones, G., & Gonshor, A. Oculomotor adaptation to rapid head oscillation after prolonged adaptation to visual reversal. *Experimental Brain Research*, 1982, *45*, 45–58.

Melvill Jones, G., & Mandl, G. Effects of strobe light on adaptation of vestibular-ocular reflex (VOR) to vision reversal. *Brain Research*, 1979, *164*, 300–303.

Melvill Jones, G., & Milsum, J. H. Spatial and dynamic aspects of visual fixation. *IEEE Transactions on Biomedical Engineering*, 1965, *BME-12*, 54.

Merchant, J., Morisette, R., & Porterfield, J. L. Remote measurement of eye direction allowing subject motion over one cubic foot. *IEEE Transactions on Biomedical Engineering*, 1974, *BME-21*, 309–317.

Merker, B. H., & Held, R. Eye torsion and the apparent horizon under head tilt and visual field rotation. *Vision Research*, 1981, *21*, 543–547.

Merton, P. A. The accuracy of directing eyes and the hand in the dark. *Journal of Physiology*, 1961, *156*, 555–577.

Michael, J. A., & Melvill Jones, G. Dependence of visual tracking capability upon stimulus predictability. *Vision Research*, 1966, *6*, 707–716.

Michard, A., Tetard, C., & Levy-Schoen, A. Attente du signal et temps de réaction oculomoteur. *L'Année Psychologique*, 1974, *74*, 387–402.

Miles, F. A., & Eighmy, B. B. Long-term adaptive changes in the primate vestibulo-ocular reflex. 1. Behavioral observations. *Journal of Neurophysiology*, 1980, *43*, 1406–1425.

Miles, F. A., & Fuller, J. H. Adaptive plasticity in the vestibulo-ocular responses of the rhesus monkey. *Brain Research*, 1974, *80*, 512.

Miles, F. A., & Lisberger, S. G. Plasticity in the vestibulo-ocular reflex: A new hypothesis. *Annual Review of Neuroscience*, 1981, *4*, 273.

Miles, W. R. The reaction time of the eye. *Psychological Monograph*, 1936, *47*, 268–293.

Miller, J. E. Electromyographic pattern of saccadic eye movements. *American Journal of Ophthalmology*, 1958, *46*, 183–186.

Miller, J. M. Information used by the perceptual and oculomotor systems regarding the amplitude of saccadic and pursuit eye movements. *Vision Research*, 1980, *20*, 59–68.

Miller, J. M., Ono, H., & Steinbach, M. J. Additivity of fusional vergence and pursuit eye movements. *Vision Research*, 1980, *20*, 43–48.

Mitchell, D. E. Properties of stimuli eliciting vergence eye movements and stereopsis. *Vision Research*, 1970, *10*, 145–162.

Mitrani, L., & Dimitrov, G. Pursuit eye movements of a disappearing moving target. *Vision Research*, 1978, *18*, 537–540.

Mitrani, L., Dimitrov, G., Yakimoff, N., & Mateef, S. Oculomotor and perceptual localization during smooth eye movements. *Vision Research*, 1979, *19*, 609–612.

Monk, T. H., & Brown, B. The effect of target surround density on visual search performance. *Human Factors*, 1975, *17*, 356.

Monty, R. A., & Senders, J. W. (Eds.). *Eye movements and psychological processes*. Hillsdale, N.J.: Lawrence Erlbaum, 1976.

Morasso, P., Bizzi, E., & Dichgans, J. Adjustment of saccade characteristics during head movements. *Experimental Brain Research*, 1973, *16*, 492–500.

Morgan, M. The clinical aspects of accommodation and vergence. *American Journal of Optometry and Physiological Optics*, 1944, *21*, 301–313.

Morgan, M. Accommodation and vergence. *American Journal of Ophthalmology*, 1968, *45*, 417–454.

Morgan, M. J., & Turnbull, D. F. Smooth eye tracking and the perception of motion in the absence of real movement. *Vision Research*, 1978, *18*, 1053–1059.

Muratore, R., & Zee, D. S. Pursuit after-nystagmus. *Vision Research*, 1979, *19*, 1057–1060.

Murphy, B. J. Pattern thresholds for moving and stationary gratings during smooth eye movement. *Vision Research*, 1978, *18*, 521–530.

Murphy, B. J., Haddad, G. M., & Steinman, R. M. Simple forms and fluctuations from the line of sight. *Perception and Psychophysics*, 1974, *16*, 557–563.

Murphy, B. J., Kowler, E., & Steinman, R. M. Slow oculomotor control in the presence of moving backgrounds. *Vision Research*, 1975, *15*, 1263–1268.

Nachmias, J. Two-dimensional motion of the retinal image during monocular fixation. *Journal of the Optical Society of America*, 1959, *49*, 901–908.

Nachmias, J. Meridional variations in visual acuity and eye movements during fixation. *Journal of the Optical Society of America*, 1960, *50*, 569–571.

Nachmias, J. Determiners of the drift of the eye during monocular fixation. *Journal of the Optical Society of America*, 1961, *51*, 761–766.

Nagle, M., Bridgeman, B., & Stark, L. Voluntary nystagmus, saccadic suppression, and stabilization of the visual world. *Vision Research*, 1980, *20*, 717–722.

Nakayama, K. Co-ordination of extraocular muscles. In G. Lennerstrand & P. Bach-y-Rita (Eds.), *Basic mechanisms of ocular motility and their clinical implications*. Wenner-Gren Symposium; Oxford: Pergamon, 1975.

Nakayama, K., & Balliet, R. Listing's law, eye position sense and perception of the vertical. *Vision Research*, 1977, *17*, 453–458.

Nam, N. H., Park, S. H., & Choi, O. Saccadic eye movement characteristics to the double step stimuli. *Yonsei Medical Journal*, 1975, *16*, 65–71.

Newman, C. W. An investigation of the human saccadic visual tracking system (Doctoral dissertation, University of Rochester, 1971) *Dissertation Abstracts International*, 1972, *32*, 3318 B. (University Microfilms No. 72-750)

Ogle, K. N. *Researches in binocular vision*. New York: Hafer, 1964.

O'Neill, W. D., & Stark, L. Triple-function ocular monitor. *Journal of the Optical Society of America*, 1968, *58*, 570–573.

Ono, H. Hering's law of equal innervation and vergence eye movements. *American Journal of Optometry and Physiological Optics*, 1980, *57*, 578–585.

Ono, H. The combination of version and vergence. In C. Schor & K. J. Ciuffreda (Eds.), *Basic clinical aspects of binocular vergence eye movements*. Boston: Butterworths, 1983.

Ono, H., & Nakamizo, S. Saccadic eye movements during changes of fixation to stimuli at different distances. *Vision Research*, 1977, *17*, 233–238.

Ono, H., & Nakamizo, S. Changing fixation in the transverse plane at eye level and Hering's law of equal innervation. *Vision Research*, 1978, *18*, 511–519.

Ono, H., Nakamizo, S., & Steinbach, M. J. Non-additivity of vergence and saccadic eye movement. *Vision Research*, 1978, *18*, 735–739.

Ono, H., & Tam, W. J. Asymmetrical vergence and multiple saccades. *Vision Research*, 1981, *21*, 739–743.

Optican, L. Saccadic dysmetria. In G. Lennerstrand et al. (Eds.), *Functional basis of ocular motility disorders.* Oxford: Pergamon Press, 1982.

O'Regan, K. Saccadic size control in reading: Evidence for linguistic control hypothesis. *Perception and Psychophysics*, 1979, *25*, 501–509.

Paige, G. D. Vestibulo-ocular reflex and its interaction with visual following mechanism in the squirrel monkey. I. Response characteristics in normal animals. *Journal of Neurophysiology*, 1983, *49*, 134–151.

Payne, W. H. Reaction time as a function of retinal location. *Vision Research*, 1966, *6*, 729.

Peck, C. K., Shlag-Rey, M., & Schlag, J. Visuo-oculomotor properties of cells in the superior colliculus of the alert cat. *Journal of Comparative Neurology*, 1980, *194*, 97–116.

Perlmutter, A. L., & Kertesz, A. E. Measurement of human vertical fusional response. *Vision Research*, 1978, *18*, 219–223.

Pernier, J., Jeannerod, M., & Gerin, P. Elaboration et décision de saccades: Adaptation à la trace du stimulus. *Vision Research*, 1969, *9*, 1149–1165.

Petrov, A. P., & Zenkin, G. M. Torsional eye movements and constancy of the visual field. *Vision Research*, 1973, *13*, 2465–2477.

Pirenne, M. H. *Vision and the eye.* London: Chapman and Hall/Science Paperbacks, 1967. (Originally published, 1946.)

Pirozzolo, F. J., & Rayner, K. Handedness, hemispheric specialization and saccadic eye movement latencies. *Neuropsychologica*, 1980, *18*, 225–229.

Pola, J., & Wyatt, H. J. Target position and velocity: The stimuli for smooth pursuit eye movements. *Vision Research*, 1980, *20*, 523–534.

Post, R. B., & Leibowitz, H. W. The effect of convergence on the vestibulo-ocular reflex and implications for perceived movement. *Vision Research*, 1982, *22*, 461–466.

Prablanc, C., & Jeannerod, M. Corrective saccades: Dependence on retinal reafferent signals. *Vision Research*, 1975, *15*, 465–469.

Prablanc, C., Massé, D., & Echallier, J. F. Error-correcting mechanisms in large saccades. *Vision Research*, 1978, *18*, 551–560.

Pritchard, R. Stabilized images on the retina. *Scientific American*, 1961, *204*(6), 72–78.

Puckett, J. W., & Steinman, R. M. Tracking eye movements with and without saccadic corrections. *Vision Research*, 1969, *9*, 695–703.

Pulaski, P. D., Zee, D. S., & Robinson, D. A. The behavior of the vestibulo-ocular reflex at high velocities of head rotation. *Brain Research*, 1981, *222*, 159–165.

Quereau, J. V. D. Rolling of the eye around its visual axis during normal ocular movements. *American Medical Association Archives of Ophthalmology*, 1955, *53*, 807–810.

Rashbass, C. The relationship between saccadic and smooth tracking eye movements. *Journal of Physiology*, 1961, *159*, 326–338.

Rashbass, C. Reflections on the control of vergence. In B. L. Zuber (Ed.), *Models of oculomotor behavior and control.* Boca Raton, Fla.: CRC Press, 1981.

Rashbass, C., & Westheimer, G. Disjunctive eye movements. *Journal of Physiology*, 1961, *159*, 339–360. (a)

Rashbass, C., & Westheimer, G. Independence of conjugate and disjunctive eye movements. *Journal of Physiology*, 1961, *159*, 361–364. (b)

Ratliff, F., & Riggs, L. A. Involuntary motions of the eye during monocular fixation. *Journal of Experimental Psychology*, 1950, *40*, 687–701.

Rattle, J. D. Effect of target size on monocular fixation. *Optica Acta*, 1969, *16*, 183–192.

Rattle, J. D., & Foley-Fisher, J. A. A relationship between vernier acuity and intersaccadic interval. *Optica Acta*, 1968, *15*, 617–620.

Rayner, K. Eye guidance in reading: Fixation locations within words. *Perception*, 1979, *8*, 21–30.

Regan, D., & Beverly, K. I. Looming detectors in the human visual pathway. *Vision Research*, 1978, *18*, 415–421.

Reulen, J. P. H., & Bakker, L. The measurement of eye movements using double magnetic induction. *IEEE Transactions Biomedical Engineering*, 1982, *BME-29*, 500–510.

Richards, W. Anomalous stereopsis and depth perception. *Journal of the Optical Society of America*, 1971, *61*, 410–414.

Richards, W., & Kaufman L. "Centre-of-gravity" tendencies for fixations and flow patterns. *Perception and Psychophysics*, 1969, *5*, 81–84.

Riggs, L. A., & Niehl, E. W. Eye movements recorded during convergence and divergence. *Journal of the Optical Society of America*, 1960, *50*, 913–920.

Robinson, D. A. A method of measuring eye movement using a scleral search coil in a magnetic field. *IEEE Transactions on Biomedical Electronics*, 1963, *BME-10*, 137–145.

Robinson, D. A. The mechanics of human saccadic eye movement. *Journal of Physiology*, 1964, *174*, 245–264.

Robinson, D. A. The mechanics of human smooth pursuit eye movement. *Journal of Physiology*, 1965, *180*, 569–591.

Robinson, D. A. Eye movement control in primates. *Science*, 1968, *161*, 1219–1224.

Robinson, D. A. Models of the saccadic eye control system. *Kybernetik*, 1973, *14*, 71–83.

Robinson, D. A. Oculomotor control signals. In G. Lennerstrand & P. J. Bach-y-Rita (Eds.), *Basic mechanisms of ocular motility and their clinical implications.* Oxford: Pergamon Press, 1975. (a)

Robinson, D. A. A quantitative analysis of extraocular muscle cooperation and squint. *Investigative Ophthalmology and Visual Science*, 1975, *14*, 801–825. (b)

Robinson, D. A. The physiology of pursuit eye movements. In R. A. Monty & J. W. Senders (Eds.), *Eye movements and psychological processes.* Hillsdale, N.J.: Lawrence Erlbaum, 1976.

Robinson, D. A. Models of the mechanics of eye movements. In B. L. Zuber (Ed.), *Models of oculomotor behavior and control.* Boca Raton, Fla.: CRC Press, 1981.

Rogers, B. J., Steinbach, M. J., & Ono, H. Eye movements and the Pulfrich phenomenon. *Vision Research*, 1974, *14*, 181–185.

Ron, S., Robinson, D. A., & Skavenski, A. A. Saccades and the quick phase of nystagmus. *Vision Research*, 1972, *12*, 2015–2022.

Ross, L., & Ross, S. Saccade latency and warning signals: Stimulus onset, offset and change as warning events. *Perception and Psychophysics*, 1980, *27*, 251–257.

Ross, S., & Ross., L. Saccade latency and warning signals: Effect of auditory and visual stimulus onset and offset. *Perception and Psychophysics*, 1981, *29*, 429–437.

Saring, W., & von Cramon, D. Is there an interaction between cognitive activity and lateral eye movements? *Neuropsychologica*, 1980, *18*, 591–596.

Saslow, M. G. Effects of components of displacement step stimuli upon latency for saccadic eye movement. *Journal of the Optical Society of America*, 1967, *57*, 1024–1029. (a)

Saslow, M. G. Latency for saccadic eye movement. *Journal of the Optical Society of America*, 1967, *57*, 1030–1033. (b)

Schiller, P. H., & Sandell, J. H. Interactions between visually and electrically elicited saccades before and after superior colliculus and frontal eye field ablations in the rhesus monkey. *Experimental Brain Research*, 1983, *49*, 381–392.

Schmidt, D., Abel, L. A., Dell'Osso, L. F., & Daroff, R. B. Saccadic velocity characteristics: Intrinsic variability and fatigue. *Aviation Space and Environmental Medicine*, 1979, *50*, 393–395.

Schor, C., & Narayan, V. The influence of field size upon the spatial frequency response of optokinetic nystagmus. *Vision Research*, 1981, *21*, 985–994.

Schor, C. M. The relationship between fusional vergence eye movements and fixation disparity. *Vision Research*, 1979, *19*, 1359–1367.

Schor, C. M., & Levi, D. M. Disturbances of small-field horizontal and vertical optokinetic nystagmus in amblyopia. *Investigative Ophthalmology and Visual Science*, 1980, *19*, 668–683.

Schwarz, D. W. F., & Tomlinson, R. D. Diagnostic precision in a new rotatory vestibular test. *Journal of Otolaryngology*, 1979, *8*, 544.

Semmlow, J. L. Oculomotor responses to near stimuli: The near triad. In B. L. Zuber (Ed.), *Models of oculomotor behavior and control.* Boca Raton, Fla.: CRC Press, 1981.

Semmlow, J., & Tinor, T. Accommodative vergence response to off-foveal retinal images. *Journal of the Optical Society of America*, 1978, *68*, 1497–1501.

Semmlow, J., & Venkiteswaran, N. Dynamic accommodative vergence components in binocular vision. *Vision Research*, 1976, *16*, 403–410.

Senders, J. W., Fisher, D. F., & Monty, R. A. (Eds.). *Eye movements and the higher psychological processes*. Hillsdale, N.J.: Lawrence Erlbaum, 1978.

Shackel, B. Eye movement recording by electro-oculography. *Manual of psycho-physiological methods*. New York: North-Holland, 1967.

Sharpe, J. A. Central eye movement disorders (neuropathology course). *American Academy of Neurology*, 1981, *14*, 77.

Sharpe, J. A., Hoyt, W. F., & Rosenberg, M. A. Convergence-evoked nystagmus. *Archives of Neurology*, 1975, *32*, 191–194.

Sharpe, J. A., & Sylvester, T. O. Effect of aging on horizontal smooth pursuit. *Investigative Ophthalmology and Visual Science*, 1978, *17*, 465–468.

Sharpe, J. A., Troost, B. T., Dell'Osso, L. F., & Daroff, R. B. Comparative velocities of different types of fast eye movements in man. *Investigative Ophthalmology*, 1975, *14*, 689–692.

Shebilske, W. L. Extraretinal information in corrective saccades and inflow *vs* outflow theories of visual direction constancy. *Vision Research*, 1976, *16*, 621–628.

Sheena, D. Pattern-recognition techniques for extraction of features of the eye from a conventional television scan. In Monty R. A. & Senders J. W. (Eds.), *Eye movements and psychological processes*. Hillsdale, N.J.: Lawrence Erlbaum, 1976.

Sherrington, C. *The integrative action of the nervous system*. New York: Cambridge University Press, 1947. (Originally published, 1906.)

Sherrington, C. Postural activity of nerve and muscle. *Brain*, 1915, *38*, 191–234.

Shults, W. T., Stark, L., Hoyt, W. F., & Ochs, A. L. Normal saccadic structure of voluntary nystagmus. *Archives of Ophthalmology*, 1977, *95*, 1399.

Simpson, J. I., & Graf, W. Eye-muscle geometry and compensatory eye movements in lateral-eyed and frontal-eyed animals. *Annals. New York Academy of Science*, 1981, *374*, 20–30.

Skavenski, A. A. Extraretinal correction and memory for target position. *Vision Research*, 1971, *11*, 743–746.

Skavenski, A. A. Inflow as a source of extra-retinal eye-position information. *Vision Research*, 1972, *12*, 221–229.

Skavenski, A. A. The nature and role of extra-retinal eye position information in visual localization. In R. A. Monty & J. W. Senders (Eds.), *Eye movements and psychological processes*. Hillsdale, N.J.: Lawrence Erlbaum, 1976.

Skavenski, A. A., Hansen, R. A., Steinman, R. M., & Winterson, B. J. Quality of retinal image stabilization during small natural and artificial body rotations in man. *Vision Research*, 1979, *19*, 675–684.

Skavenski, A. A., & Steinman, R. M. Control of eye position in the dark. *Vision Research*, 1970, *10*, 193–203.

Smith, K. U., Putz, V., & Molitor, K. Eye movement—retina delayed feedback. *Science*, 1969, *166*, 1542–1544.

Smith, W. M. Control of eye fixation by auditory feedback. *Psychonomic Science*, 1964, *1*, 233–234.

Southall, J. P. C. *Introduction to physiological optics*. New York: Dover, 1961. (Originally published, 1937.)

Sparks, D. L., & Mays, L. E. Spatial localization of saccade targets. I. Compensation for stimulation-induced perturbations in eye position. *Journal of Neurophysiology*, 1983, *49*, 45–63.

Sparks, D. L., & Porter, J. D. Spatial localization of saccade targets. II. Activity of superior collicular neurons preceding compensatory saccades. *Journal of Neurophysiology*, 1983, *49*, 64–74.

Stark, L., & Ellis, S. R. Scanpaths revisited: Cognitive models direct active looking. In D. F. Fisher, R. A. Monty, & J. W. Senders (Eds.), *Eye movements: Cognition and visual perception*. Hillsdale, N.J.: Lawrence Erlbaum, 1981.

Stark, L., Hoyt, W. F., Ciuffreda, K. J., Kenyon, R. V., & Hsu, F. Time optimal saccadic trajectory model and voluntary nystagmus. In B. L. Zuber (Ed.), *Models of oculomotor behavior and control*. Boca Raton, Fla.: CRC Press, 1981.

Stark, L., Vossius, G., & Young, L. Predictive control of eye tracking movements. *IEEE Transactions on Human Factors in Electronics*, 1962, *HFE-3*, 52–57.

Stark, L., Zangemeiser, W. H., Edwards, J., Grinberg, J., Jones, A., Lehman, S., Lubock, P., Narayan, V., & Nystrom, M. Head rotation trajectories compared with eye saccades by main sequence relationships. *Investigative Ophthalmology and Visual Science*, 1980, *19*, 986–988.

St. Cyr, G. J., & Fender, D. H. The interplay of drifts and flicks in binocular fixation. *Vision Research*, 1969, *9*, 245–265. (a)

St. Cyr, G. J., & Fender D. H. Non-linearity of the human oculomotor system: Gain. *Vision Research*, 1969, *9*, 1235–1246. (b)

St. Cyr, G. J., & Fender, D. H. Non-linearities of the human oculomotor system: Time delays. *Vision Research*, 1969, *9*, 1491–1503. (c)

Steinbach, M. J. Eye tracking of self-moved targets: The role of efference. *Journal of Experimental Psychology*, 1969, *82*, 366–376.

Steinbach, M. J. Aligning the eye to the actively or passively positioned head. *Perception and Psychophysics*, 1970, *8*, 287–288.

Steinbach, M. J. Pursuing the perceptual rather than the visual stimulus. *Vision Research*, 1976, *16*, 1371–1376.

Steinbach, M. J. Alternating exotropia: Temporal course of the switch in suppression. *Investigative Ophthalmology and Visual Science*, 1981, *20*, 129–133.

Steinbach, M. J., & Held, R. Eye tracking of observer generated target movements. *Science*, 1968, *161*, 187–188.

Steinbach, M. J., & Pearce, D. G. Release of pursuit eye movements using after-images. *Vision Research*, 1972, *12*, 1307–1311.

Steinman, R. M. Effect of target size, luminance and colour on monocular fixation. *Journal of the Optical Society of America*, 1965, *55*, 1158–1165.

Steinman, R. M. Role of eye movements in maintaining a phenomenally clear and stable world. In R. A. Monty & J. W. Senders (Eds.), *Eye movements and psychological processes*. Hillsdale, N.J.: Lawrence Erlbaum, 1976.

Steinman, R. M., & Collewijn, H. Binocular image motion during active head rotation. *Vision Research*, 1980, *20*, 414–430.

Steinman, R. M., & Cunitz, R. J. Fixation of targets near the absolute foveal threshold. *Vision Research*, 1968, *8*, 277–286.

Steinman, R. M., Haddad, G. M., Skavenski, A. A., & Wyman, D. Miniature eye movement. *Science*, 1973, *181*, 810–819.

Steinman, R. M., Skavenski, A. A., & Sansbury, R. V. Voluntary control of smooth pursuit velocity. *Vision Research*, 1969, *9*, 1167–1171.

Sternberg, S. Memory-scanning: Mental processes revealed by reaction time experiments. *American Scientist*, 1969, *57*, 421–457.

Stevens, J. K., Emerson, R. C., Gerstein, G. L., Kallos, T., Neufeld, G. R., Nichols, C. W., & Rosenquist, A. C. Paralysis of the awake human: Visual perceptions. *Vision Research*, 1976, *16*, 93–98.

Stoper, A. Vision during pursuit movement: The role of oculomotor information (Doctoral dissertation, Brandeis University, 1967). *Dissertation Abstracts International*, 1967, *28*, 2647 B. (University Microfilms No. 67-16, 579)

Sullivan, M. J., & Kertesz, A. E. Binocular co-ordination of torsional eye movements in cyclofusional response. *Vision Research*, 1978, *18*, 943–949.

Sullivan, M. J., & Kertesz, A. E. Peripheral stimulation and human cyclofusional response. *Investigative Ophthalmology and Visual Science*, 1979, *18*, 1287–1291.

Täumer, R. Three reaction mechanisms of the saccadic system in response to a double jump. In G. Lennerstrand & P. Bachy-y-Rita (Eds.), *Basic mechanisms of ocular motility and their clinical implications*. Oxford: Pergamon Press, 1975.

Täumer, R., Mie, K., & Kommerell, G. Three kinds of reaction mechanisms of the human saccadic system. *Biokybernetik*, 1972, *4*, 236–242.

Teräväinen, H., & Calne, D. B. Studies of Parkinsonian movement. I. Programming and execution of eye movements. *Acta Neurologica*

Scandinavica, 1980, *62*, 137–146. (a)

Teräväinen, H., & Calne, D. B. Studies of Parkinsonian movement. II. Initiation of fast voluntary eye movement during postural disturbance. *Acta Neurologica Scandinavica*, 1980, *62*, 149–157. (b)

Ter Braak, J. W. G. Optokinetic control of eye movements, in particular optokinetic nystagmus. *Proceedings of the 22nd International Physiological Congress*, 502–505, 1962.

Thomas, J. G. The dynamics of small saccadic eye movements. *Journal of Physiology*, 1969, *200*, 109–127.

Thomason, T. C., Arbuckle, T., & Cady, D. Test of the eye-movement hypothesis of neurolinguistic programming. *Perception and Motor Skills*, 1980, *51*, 230.

Timberlake, G. T., Wyman, D., Skavenski, A. A., & Steinman, R. M. The oculomotor error signal in the fovea. *Vision Research*, 1972, *12*, 1059–1064.

Tomer, R., & Mintz, M. Hemisphere laterality and smooth pursuit in normal individuals. *Perception and Motor Skills*, 1980, *51*, 31–35.

Tomlinson, R. D., & Robinson, D. A. Is the vestibulo-ocular reflex cancelled by smooth pursuit? In A. F. Fuchs & W. Becker (Eds.), *Progress in oculomotor research*. New York: Elsevier, 1981.

Tomlinson, R. D., Saunders, G. E., & Schwarz, D. W. F. Analysis of the human vestibulo-ocular reflex during active head movements. *Acta Oto-laryngologica*, 1980, *90*, 184.

Trevarthen, C. B. Two mechanisms of vision in primates. *Psychologische Forschung*, 1968, *31*, 299.

Troost, B. T., Daroff, R. B., Weber, R. B., & Dell'Osso, L. F. Hemispheric control of eye movements. II. Quantitative analysis of smooth pursuit in a hemispherectomy patient. *Archives of Neurology*, 1972, *27*, 449–452.

Troost, B. T., Weber, R. B., & Daroff, R. B. Hypometric saccades. *American Journal of Ophthalmology*, 1974, *74*, 1002–1005.

Tulunay-Keesey, U. The role of eye movements in the maintenance of vision. In R. A. Monty & J. W. Senders (Eds.), *Eye movements and psychological processes*. Hillsdale, N.J.: Lawrence Erlbaum, 1976.

Tulunay-Keesey, U., & Riggs, L. Visibility of Mach bands with imposed motions of the retinal image. *Journal of the Optical Society of America*, 1962, *52*, 719–720.

Udo de Haes, H. A. Stability of the apparent vertical and ocular countertorsion as a function of lateral tilt. *Perception and Psychophysics*, 1970, *8*, 137–142.

Van Dalen, J. T. W. Nystagmus induced by stationary stroboscopy. In G. Kommerell (Ed.), *Disorders of ocular motility*. Munich: Bergmann, 1977.

Van Hof-Van Duin, J. Early and permanent effects of monocular deprivation on pattern discrimination and visuomotor behavior in cats. *Brain Research*, 1975, *111*, 261.

Van Vliet, A. G. M. On the central mechanism of latent nystagmus. *Acta Ophthalmologica*, 1973, *51*, 772.

Virsu, V., & Rovamo, J. Visual resolution, contrast sensitivity, and the cortical magnification factor. *Experimental Brain Research*, 1979, *37*, 1–16.

Viviani, P., Berthoz, A., & Tracey, D. The curvature of oblique saccades. *Vision Research*, 1977, *17*, 661–664.

Vossius, G. Adaptive control of saccadic eye movement. *Bibliotheca Ophthalmologica*, 1972, *82*, 244–250.

Waespe, W., Henn, V., & Miles, T. S. Activity in the vestibular nuclei of the alert monkey during spontaneous eye movements and vestibular or optokinetic stimulation. In R. Baker & A. Berthoz (Eds.), *Control of gaze by brainstem neurons*. Amsterdam: Elsevier/North-Holland Biomedical, 1977.

Weber, R. B., & Daroff, R. B. The metrics of horizontal saccadic eye movements in normal humans. *Vision Research*, 1971, *11*, 921–928.

Weber, R. B., & Daroff, R. B. Corrective movements following refixation saccades: Type and control system analysis. *Vision Research*, 1972, *12*, 467–475.

West, D. C., & Boyce, P. R. The effect of flicker on eye movements. *Vision Research*, 1968, *8*, 171–191.

Westheimer, G. Eye movement responses to a horizontally moving visual stimulus. *American Medical Association Archives of Ophthalmology*, 1954, *52*, 932–941.

Westheimer, G. Kinematics of the eye. *Journal of the Optical Society of America*, 1957, *47*, 967–974.

Westheimer, G. Discussion of the control of eye movements. In P. Bach-y-Rita, C. C. Collins, & J. Hyde (Eds.), *The control of eye movements*. New York: Academic Press, 1971.

Westheimer, G. Saccadic eye movements. In V. Zikmund (Ed.), *The oculomotor system and brain function*. Bratislava: Czechoslovakia Publishing House of the Slovak Academy of Science, 1973.

Westheimer, G. Donder's, Listing's, and Hering's laws and their implications. In B. L. Zuber (Ed.), *Models of oculomotor behavior and control*. Boca Raton, Fla.: CRC Press, 1981.

Westheimer, G., & Conover, D. W. Smooth eye movements in the absence of a visual stimulus. *Journal of Experimental Psychology*, 1954, *47*, 283–284.

Westheimer, G., & McKee, S. P. Failure of Donder's law during smooth pursuit eye movements. *Vision Research*, 1973, *13*, 2145–2153.

Westheimer, G., & McKee, S. P. Visual acuity in the presence of retinal image motion. *Journal of the Optical Society of America*, 1975, *65*, 847–850.

Westheimer, G., & Mitchell, A. M. Eye movement responses to convergence stimuli. *American Medical Association Archives of Ophthalmology*, 1956, *55*, 848–856.

Westheimer, G., & Mitchell, D. E. The sensory stimulus for disjunctive eye movements. *Vision Research*, 1969, *9*, 749–755.

Wheeless, L. The effect of intensity on the eye movement control system. (Doctoral dissertation, University of Rochester, 1965). *Dissertation Abstracts International*, 1965, *26*, 3211. (University Microfilms No. 65-12, 30)

Wheeless, L. L., Boynton, R. M., & Cohen, G. H. Eye movement responses to step and pulse-step stimuli. *Journal of the Optical Society of America*, 1966, *56*, 956–990.

Wheeless, L. L., Jr., Cohen, G. H., & Boynton, R. M. Luminance as a parameter of the eye-movement control system. *Journal of the Optical Society of America*, 1967, *57*, 394–400.

White, C. T., Eason, R. G., & Bartlett, N. R. Latency and duration of eye movements in the horizontal plane. *Journal of the Optical Society of America*, 1962, *52*, 210–213.

Whittaker, S. G., & Eaholtz, G. Learning patterns of eye motion for foveal pursuit. *Investigative Ophthalmology and Visual Science*, 1982, *23*, 393–397.

Williams, R. A., & Fender, D. H. The synchrony of binocular saccadic eye movements. *Vision Research*, 1977, *17*, 303–306.

Williams, R. A., & Fender, D. H. Velocity precision in smooth pursuit eye movements. *Vision Research*, 1979, *19*, 343–348.

Wilson, D. A centre for accommodative vergence motor control. *Vision Research*, 1973, *13*, 2491–2503. (a)

Wilson, D. Noise coupling between accommodation and accommodative vergence. *Vision Research*, 1973, *13*, 2505–2513. (b)

Wilson, V. J., & Melvill Jones, G. *Mammalian vestibular physiology*. New York: Plenum Press, 1979.

Winterson, B. J., & Collewijn, H. Microsaccades during finely guided visuomotor tasks. *Vision Research*, 1976, *16*, 1387–1390.

Winterson, B. J., & Steinman, R. M. The effect of luminance on human smooth pursuit of perifoveal and foveal targets. *Vision Research*, 1978, *18*, 1165–1172.

Winterson, B. J., & Steinman, R. M. Proprioception neither improves fixation stability nor reduces autokinesis. *Vision Research*, 1979, *19*, 1289–1291.

Wolfe, J. M., & Held, R. Eye torsion and visual tilt are mediated by different binocular processes. *Vision Research*, 1979, *19*, 917–920.

Wolfe, J. M., Held, R., & Bauer, J. A., Jr. A binocular contribution to the production of optokinetic nystagmus in normal and stereoblind subjects. *Vision Research*, 1981, *21*, 587–590.

Wurtz, R. H., & Albano, J. E. Visual-motor function of the primate superior colliculus. *Annual Review of Neuroscience*, 1980, *180*, 189–226.

Wyatt, H. J., & Pola, J. The role of perceived motion in smooth pursuit

eye movements. *Vision Research*, 1979, *19*, 613–618.
Wyatt, H. J., & Pola, J. Slow eye movements to eccentric targets. *Investigative Ophthalmology and Visual Science*, 1981, *21*, 477–483.
Wyatt, H. J., & Pola, J. Smooth pursuit eye movements under open-loop and closed-loop conditions. *Vision Research*, 1983, *23*, 1121–1131.
Wyman, D., & Steinman, R. M. Latency characteristics of small saccades. *Vision Research*, 1973, *13*, 2173–2175. (a)
Wyman, D., & Steinman, R. M. Small step tracking: Implications for the oculomotor "dead zone." *Vision Research*, 1973, *13*, 2165–2172. (b)
Wyszecki, G., & Stiles, W. S. *Color science*. New York: Wiley, 1967.
Yarbus, A. L. [*Eye movements and vision*] (B. Haigh, trans. and L. A. Riggs, Ed.) New York: Plenum, 1967.
Yasui, S., & Young, L. R. Eye movements during after-image tracking under sinusoidal and random vestibular stimulation. In R. A. Monty & J. W. Senders (Eds.), *Eye movements and psychological processes*. Hillsdale, N.J.: Lawrence Erlbaum, 1976.
Yee, R. D., Baloh, R. W., & Honrubia, V. Eye movement abnormalities in rod monochromacy. *Ophthalmology*, 1981, *88*, 1010–1018.
Yee, R. D., Daniels, S. A., Jones, O. W., Baloh, R. W., & Honrubia, V. Effect of an optokinetic background on pursuit eye movements. *Investigative Ophthalmology and Visual Science*, 1983, *24*, 1115–1122.
Yee, R. D., Goldberg, R. A., Jones, O. W., Baloh, R. W., & Honrubia, V. Effect of eccentric gaze on pursuit. *Investigative Ophthalmology and Visual Science*, 1983, *24*, 1108–1114.
Yoshida, T., & Watanabe, A. Analysis of interaction between accommodation and vergence feedback control systems of human eyes. *Bulletin NHK Broadcasting Science Research Laboratory*, 1963, *3*, 72–80.
Young, L. R. Pursuit eye tracking movements. In P. Bach-y-Rita, C. C. Collins, & J. Hyde (Eds.), *The control of eye movements*. New York: Academic Press, 1971.
Young, L. R. The sampled data model and the foveal dead zone for saccades. In B. L. Zuber (Ed.), *Models of oculomotor behavior and control*. Boca Raton, Fla.: CRC Press, 1981.
Young, L. R., & Sheena, D. Eye movement measurement techniques. *American Psychologist*, 1975, *30*, 315–330.
Young, L. R., & Stark, L. Variable feedback experiments testing a sampled data model for eye tracking movements. *IEEE Transactions on Human Factors in Electronics*, 1963, *HFE-4*, 28–51.
Zahn, J. P., Abel, L. A., & Dell'Osso, L. F. Audio-ocular response characteristics. *Sensory Processes*, 1978, *2*, 32–37.
Zahn, J. R., Abel, L. A., Dell'Osso, L. F., & Daroff, R. B. The audio-ocular response: Intersensory delay. *Sensory Processes*, 1979, *3*, 60–65.
Zambarbieri, D., Schmid, R., Prablanc, C., & Magenes, G. Characteristics of eye movements evoked by the presentation of acoustic targets. In A. F. Fuchs & W. Becker (Eds.), *Progress in oculomotor research*. Amsterdam: Elsevier/North-Holland, 1981.
Zee, D. S., & Robinson, D. A. A hypothetical explanation of saccadic oscillations. *Annals of Neurology*, 1979, *5*, 405–414.
Zeevi, Y. Y., & Ish-Shalom, J. Measurement of eye movement with a ferromagnetic contact ring. *IEEE Transactions Biomedical Engineering*, 1982, *BME-29*, 511–523.
Zeevi, Y. Y., & Peli, E. Latency of peripheral saccades. *Journal of the Optical Society of America*, 1979, *69*, 1274–1279.
Zeevi, Y. Y., Peli, E., & Stark, L. Study of eccentric fixation with secondary visual feedback. *Journal of the Optical Society of America*, 1979, *69*, 669–674.
Zuber, B. L. Control of vergence movements. In P. Bach-y-Rita, C. C. Collins, & J. Hyde (Eds.), *The control of eye movements*. New York: Academic Press, 1971.
Zuber, B. L. (Ed.). *Models of oculomotor behaviour and control*. Boca Raton, Fla.: CRC Press, 1981.
Zuber, B. L., Semmlow, J. L., & Stark, L. Frequency characteristics of the saccadic eye movement. *Biophysical Journal*, 1968, *8*, 1288–1298.
Zuber, B. L., & Stark, L. Dynamical characteristics of the fusional vergence eye-movement system. *IEEE Transactions on Systems, Science and Cybernetics*, 1968, *SSC-4*, 72–79.
Zuber, B. L., Stark, L., & Cook, G. Microsaccades and the velocity-amplitude relationship for saccadic eye movements. *Science*, 1965, *150*, 1459.

SECTION III

BASIC SENSORY PROCESSES II

CARL E. SHERRICK and ROGER W. CHOLEWIAK

Department of Psychology, Princeton University, Princeton, New Jersey

OVERVIEW

CARL E. SHERRICK and ROGER W. CHOLEWIAK

Department of Psychology, Princeton University, Princeton, New Jersey

If it were the intention of this overview to interpret for the reader the major ideas of the authors whose chapters follow, it would correctly be regarded as impertinence. The purpose is more like that of the playbill writer in discussing the play, or of the travel writer in describing a foreign land, that is, to point out some interesting features and in the process prepare the reader for the experience.

The set of chapters that constitute this section of the *Handbook* is greatly varied, including as it does the entire set of senses classified by Aristotle as "touch" and later divided by Weber into *Tastsinn* (sense of touch) and *Gemeingefühl* (general bodily sense; see Boring, 1942, pp. 463ff.). These do not exhaust the list, however. To the cutaneous exteroceptors and the vestibular and kinesthetic proprioceptors is added the teleceptor, hearing, a distant relative of the others in the evolutionary family tree by virtue of its embryological origins as well as of its arousal by mechanical means. This is not the only similarity among the senses, but there is no lack of differences either, as will be seen.

Our purpose is to give a brief description of the senses that are covered, and to note what may be called their major commonalities under the heading of anatomical, physiological, or psychophysical aspects. To the degree that a rigorous account of their interrelation in perception can be given, we attempt to provide it. The expectation is that the readers may thus be prepared to understand the analyses made by chapter authors because there is at hand the outline of a comparative account to assist them.

1. THE SENSES COVERED IN THIS SECTION

1.1. Hearing

Two chapters are devoted to describing the structure, function, and qualitative and quantitative phenomena associated with one of our most fundamental and sophisticated sensory systems, the hearing sense. It is one of the two systems of the group that can be considered to possess an "organized" receptor array, in that the system is confined to a specific geometric space, the design of which enhances its sensitivity and discriminative capacities. The receptor space is reached by an acoustico-mechanical transduction system designed to give airborne sound the most efficient energy transfer, but an effective alternative pathway exists in the bones of the skull.

The quality of the hearing experience is sufficiently different from that of the other senses that it is only rarely confused with them. Most commonly the auditory sensation is referred to objects outside the skin, and separate from the body, unlike touch and the proprioceptive senses. On those rare occasions when auditory sensations that occur actually are generated internally by some upset in the economy of the body, the search is normally conducted for a source outside the head (see McFadden & Wightman, 1983). Patients suffering from tinnitus, as this condition is called, quickly learn to recognize it upon recurrence. This is owing to the superb ability of the auditory system to analyze sounds as temporal patterns, and to store large numbers of them in permanent memory. With this capability we are able to process efficiently the complex structures of speech and music; without it we find ourselves at a serious disadvantage.

1.2. The Vestibular System

This is the other of the systems that can be called organized. Anatomically, the vestibular structures are so closely apposed to the auditory apparatus that they were once (mistakenly) thought to take part in the hearing process. From a phenomenal point of view the appreciation of the vestibular senses is altogether cryptic. The sense of hearing has a set of qualities that, combined with visual patterns, relate to the location and motion of objects, at least in the simple cases of early experience. Touch is aroused by the simple act of placing the hand on an object. At the very same time, one feels the movement of the limb and the force of its placement against the object through kinesthesis. The arousal of the vestibular sense, however, requires a modification of the position of the head, or the head and body, in relation to the gravitational system, and this change is reported as a sensation of position, or of linear acceleration. Such sensations are not the plain and homely variety originating in the skin, which are so clear to introspection that the very word "tangible" is used metaphorically for the most apparent of events and objects. Indeed, when one is first exposed to a pure rotatory stimulus, initial attempts to describe the sensation are fumbling and unsatisfactory. Similarly, trying to describe one's static position in space with only vestibular cues available will give the subject some feeling for the predicament of the aphasic patient. To be sure, it is possible to specify one's spatial position, and to report the very first appearance of the sensation of rotation. It is simply not easy to describe the experiential basis for the decision.

1.3. Kinesthesia

If hearing and the vestibular senses align themselves by virtue of their organized receptor arrays as well as by their close proximity and sharing of a single cranial nerve, the kinesthetic and cutaneous senses may be said to be comparable for the opposite reasons. These are the distributed senses, so to speak. Their receptors are far-flung missionaries from the central nervous system, finding themselves in muscular, tendinous, bony, and cutaneous tissues throughout the body. Here they sit in relative isolation, ready at a millisecond's notice to inform the sensorium of the movement of skin or sinew. The very general term "tissue distortion" describes roughly what it is that arouses them, but it hardly does justice to the discriminative capacities of the various receptors that serve the kinesthetic system. Owing to their responsiveness to varieties of strain and pressure, as well as their disposition within the tissues, the sense organs of the muscles, tendons, and joint capsules apprise the central nervous system of the movement of limbs and body with exquisite precision.

1.4. The Cutaneous Senses

If the functions of the proprioceptive senses are to tell the body where it is and where it is going, the skin senses exist in part to provide proximal information, to tell the body *that* it is and *what* it is. It is no author's invention that shows people pinching themselves or asking others to do so to verify their state of consciousness, and "getting hold of oneself" is more than just an admonition to behave normally.

Besides serving as a fair sea anchor in stabilizing the concept of self, the senses of the skin do occasional duty as supplement to the kinesthetic senses, as well as providing the owner with some appreciation of the texture of surfaces that he or she sits on or handles. Roughness, temperature, and softness are a few of the primary attributes that come to mind. In this function the inseparability of motor and sensory activities in all environmental transactions could not be more clearly exposed; let it be noted that without the kinesthetic component such transactions would be of limited value.

2. COMMONALITIES AMONG THE SENSES

2.1. Anatomical Commonalities

2.1.1. Hearing and the Vestibular System. In addition to the organization of their population of sense organs, these two systems share a common set of features in the appearance of the individual receptors. In both the hearing and vestibular systems the sensory cells are histologically similar, and are usually described as "hair cells" because they commonly have ciliary processes emerging from the ends opposite the point of juncture with the neuron. The clear apposition of the sensory cell body with the neuron is a characteristic of these two systems. In the visual system the bipolar cell intervenes between the sensory cell and the optic nerve, and in the cutaneous and kinesthetic senses the neuron is either free or entwined or encapsulated with a recognizable end organ, but not so clearly synapsed with the cell as in the auditory and vestibular systems (but see Andres & von Düring, 1973). A further commonality is seen in the spatial arrangement of the cells; in both systems the sensory receptors are disposed in single-layered rows upon the receptor surface, with the hairs linking the cells with the tissues that bound the region. Connection of the cells with only one or at most a few neurons is the rule for both systems.

2.1.2. The Kinesthetic and Cutaneous Senses. As we have already described, in these sensory systems the joining of neuron to receptor cell is less formal. If the hair cell systems "shake hands" with the neurons, so to speak, the musculo-tendino-cutaneous systems would appear to do everything from jostling to engaging in the intimacy that vines have with trees. In some of these arrangements is found what may appear to be the precursor of the more advanced hair cell (Sherrick & Cholewiak, Fig. 12.5). Not only are the receptor types and their connections to neurons much more highly varied in these systems, but also their connections to the central nervous system are made through several channels rather than just one major nerve as in the acoustic and vestibular modalities. Thus to collect the messages from the remote outposts of the cutaneous and kinesthetic systems requires the use of 7 cranial and 31 spinal nerves. Such a multiplicity of input lines is required by the functional character of these senses, which serve to locate and qualify a limited set of mechanical (and, on the skin, thermal) activities on the torso, head, or appendages.

At the level of the individual receptor, the connection of neurons to sensory cells is one-to-one only for the Pacinian corpuscle in the skin and joint capsules. This very large mechanoreceptor enjoys a private line to the central nervous system for reasons not yet obvious. Nearly all other receptors either share or are shared by more than one neuron, or both simultaneously.

2.2. Physiological Commonalities

2.2.1. Sensory Thresholds. Without question the most striking functional difference between the organized and diffuse systems is their sensitivity: for hearing and the vestibular senses the power needed to excite a response is about 10E-22 W, whereas for the skin and kinesthetic senses it is about 10E-8 W (Khanna & Sherrick, 1981). Close examination of the response of the various sensory cells demonstrates that a true receptor potential, one that excites the afferent neuron to fire, appears only in the "hair cell" receptors. In the others, that is, those of the skin-and-sinew group, there is produced a "generator potential" whose temporal properties are not perceived as correlated with the nervous discharge so directly. It can be said of almost all the sensory systems that whereas many of the links from physical event to nervous discharge are known and understood, exact step-by-step descriptions of the sequences of events are as yet unavailable.

2.2.2. Adaptation and Inhibition. Physiologists have defined adaptation as the reduction in rate of nervous discharge in a sensory system when the physical stimulus remains at a constant level. Clear evidence of this behavior is present in the cutaneous senses where at least two varieties of slowly adapting and two of rapidly adapting receptors exist (see Section 4.2.2 of Chapter 12, Sherrick & Cholewiak). Such behavior is also apparent in the kinesthetic system (Section 3.3 of Chapter 13, Clark & Horch), as well as in the vestibular systems (Section 2.3.3 of Chapter 11, Howard). Physiological evidence for adaptation in the hearing sense is not so clearly available, because for the most part there appears to be an almost undiminished output of nervous activity with constant physical input. This is true for the first-order neuron; at higher levels of the nervous system, continuous discharge may or may not occur, depending on the type of neuron being excited (Godfrey, Kiang, & Norris, 1975; Kiang, 1965, p. 73).

Inhibition is taken to mean the reduction in rate of nervous discharge when a second stimulus is brought into the field of activity of the sensory system, and nearly all of the senses exhibit the phenomenon in one or more of its several manifestations. In the case of either adaptation or inhibition the argument can be made that information is added to the system by its presence. For adaptation, the information concerns the duration of a constant input, and for inhibition, it concerns the presence of another input. On the other hand, as Thomas (Note 1) points out, because both these processes substitute a series of new functional relations between stimulus and response where only one existed previously, they are adding uncertainty to the situation. The result is that, from this point of view, information is reduced. Howard (Chapter 11, Section 2.3.3) points out that adaptation seems designed to make irregularly responding neural units into phasic detectors, thus enhancing their responsiveness to transient stimuli. The point may also be made that there are very probably dimensions other than rate of discharge to be examined for evidence of change resulting from lasting stimulation or the presence of an additional stimulus. Latency of succeeding responses is one, and changes in absolute or differential threshold are others.

2.2.3. Neural Discharge Rate and Stimulus Magnitude. As a general rule, the rate of nervous discharge for first-order afferents grows with stimulus magnitude over only a very short range of input intensity. For the auditory system, the range is seldom more than 20–50 dB (Kiang, 1965, p. 79) and for the vestibular system, about 10–15 dB (see Sections 1.3 and 2.3 of Chapter 11, Howard). In kinesthesia the range of linear response is quite small for, as Clark and Horch point out (Section 3.6.2.1, Chapter 13), most muscles change less than 20% from their maximum to their minimum lengths. In the cutaneous system the range is similarly short. The dynamic range of response may be as much as 14 dB for the temperature-sensitive neuron (Konietzny & Hensel, 1979, p. 245), and as little as 1–2 dB for the Pacinian corpuscle (see Merzenich & Harrington, 1969, p. 247).

The restricted range of neural activity is surprising to anyone who is familiar with the range of stimulus intensities encompassed by any of these sensory systems in psychophysical studies. There the range of appreciable energies may amount to over 100 dB for the auditory system, as much as 60 dB for touch, and like values for kinesthetic and vestibular stimuli. The common explanation for the discrepancy is that the full range of psychophysical magnitude is represented at the physiological level by rate changes in individual neurons combined with a process that adds more neurons of the same type and level. In this manner, increasing intensity of stimulus is represented by more and more neurons firing at ever-increasing rates. Thus far, however, a wholly satisfactory physiological model of intensity representation is not available.

2.2.4. Higher-Order Neural Activities. Students of the various sensory systems share ignorance of the precise workings of the central nervous system. In almost no case (the auditory and vestibular systems may be the exceptions) is there more than an elementary understanding of the patterns of excitation and inhibition at levels above the first-order neuron. Scharf and Buus discuss in Section 2.4.1 of Chapter 14 the activity of neurons in the cochlear nucleus, and Howard provides similar information for the vestibular system in Sections 1.4 and 2.4 of Chapter 11. Clark and Horch and Sherrick and Cholewiak provide much less in the way of information about central processing mechanisms, presumably because the available material is sparse, or contradictory, or is not readily related to the existing behavioral facts (see Section 3.3 of Chapter 13, Clark & Horch; Section 1.4 of Chapter 12, Sherrick & Cholewiak).

Unique among the sensory systems is the differential input arrangement of the vestibular organs (see Section 2.3.2 of Chapter 11, Howard). The result of the action of the differential input is for higher neural rates from organs on one side of the body to be complemented by lower rates from those of the opposite side. As Howard points out, the linearity and gain of the system are thus significantly improved, and the signal-to-noise ratio should be raised. Whether the latter effect occurs has not been determined, according to this author. Such symmetry of input is not seen in other systems, with the possible exception of the auditory, in which auditory localization and the binaural unmasking effect are thought to depend on a differential mechanism (see Section 3.2.1 of Chapter 14, Scharf & Buus; Section 3.10.2 of Chapter 15, Scharf & Houtsma).

It would be expected that as the apex of neural processing, the cortex, is approached, the currency on which intersensory commerce is based would be the same for all channels. The coding for auditory, vestibular, kinesthetic, and cutaneous events would presumably be comparable so that the needed interactions among the modalities be rapidly and thoroughly accomplished. How this is done, and whether it is done effectively is not well understood, but it is certainly true that neural messages reflecting interaction of modalities have been recorded (see, e.g., Thompson, Smith, & Bliss, 1963). Accounts at the physiological level of such events are also readily found in electroencephalograph (EEG) and auditory evoked response (AER) research (Mysliveĉek, 1983; Papakostopoulos, Crow, & Newton, 1980).

2.3. Psychophysical Commonalities

2.3.1. Thresholds, Magnitude Growth, Adaptation, and Masking. The physiological functions already described are direct correlates of the functions acquired by psychophysical methods in many cases, but certainly not in all. A part of the psychophysical threshold for mechanical vibration as a function of frequency is readily seen in the frequency response of the Pacinian corpuscle (Mountcastle, Talbot, Darian-Smith, & Kornhuber, 1967; Verrillo, 1966). The response curve of single units of the auditory nerve is, however, not congruent with the overall human audiogram (see Section 2.4.2 of Chapter 14, Scharf & Buus). It has already been pointed out that the growth of sensory magnitude occurs over a range far exceeding that found in peripheral neural units, owing presumably to the fact that the mechanism for range expansion requires the organization of higher-order neurons (see Section 2.2.3, Chapter 14, Scharf & Buus).

Adaptation is readily observed in the cutaneous, kinesthetic, and vestibular senses, but with some difficulty in the hearing sense (see Section 2.4.2.5 of Chapter 13; Section 2.3.3 of Chapter 11; Section 1.2.4.2 of Chapter 15; Sections 4.3.3, 4.3.4, 5.3.3, and 6.3.4 of Chapter 12). This statement is true if "adaptation" means that a steady stimulus is applied to the sensory system and a threshold or sensory magnitude measure is then made. There are circumstances under which the auditory system appears to show adaptation, but these have to do with the definition of the adequate stimulus, or with its temporal patterning (see Section 1.2.4.2 of Chapter 15). Although adaptation is often regarded as a failure of transmission of information (see Section 2.2.2, Chapter 15), it has been pointed out by von Békésy (1967, p. 11) that the process is a form of inhibition, and a means of bringing information inflow to a manageable value.

In connection with adaptation a word must be said about the term "habituation," which is occasionally confused with adaptation. Habituation describes the change of conditions in the central nervous system resulting from repeated stimulus occurrences over a prolonged period, and has been suggested as the basis of the "ticking clock" effect. Nearly all our readers can recall occasions on which they realized that a repeated sound, like that of a ticking clock, had not been heard by them for the past few minutes, despite the fact that, as common sense tells them, the sound has continually been present. The chapters in this section do not take up the issue of habituation, but the interested reader can find more about it in Peeke and Petrinovich (1984).

In many of the forms in which it appears, masking may be regarded as the failure of selectivity of the neural coding schemes of the peripheral or central nervous system. When the wanted signal is present and an unwanted signal (or noise) occurs within the same apperceptive sphere, the threshold for the wanted signal is raised or the magnitude of the pattern generated by the signal is reduced, or the recognizability of the pattern is diminished or abolished. This interference is commonly called masking. It was studied early in a systematic way in the hearing sense (Wegel & Lane, 1924), although the phenomenon was well known at a much earlier date (Boring, 1942, p. 394). Masking has been used to great effect in the study of hearing to examine the mechanisms of excitation by the application of masking signals designed to inhibit certain features of the response while allowing others to be revealed (see Sections 3.2, 4.1.7, and 4.2.5 of Chapter 14). Similar applications have been made in the cutaneous system, particularly in the study of the touch sense (see Section 4.3.5 of Chapter 12), and use was made of masking in the vestibular sense to control for irrelevant cues in threshold measurements (see Section 1.5.1 of Chapter 11).

2.3.2. Interrelations of the Mechanoreceptive Senses. It is all very well to draw interesting parallels among the senses, and to show that they are related more or less distantly in function as well as structure. The question that the practical student of the sensory systems will ask is, What of their integrated action in the normal alert organism? It is this question to which J. J. Gibson addressed himself with such unswerving dedication (see Gibson, 1950; 1962; 1966; 1979). To make way in the reader's thinking for the radical notions of information pickup and ecological perception, Gibson adopted the role of iconoclast (literally and figuratively!) to overthrow the notion that the sensory modalities commonly acted separately in the natural behavior of the organism. In the process of promulgating his thesis, Gibson suggested that the study of sensory systems for themselves was a rather one-sided exercise that dealt in the main with passive perceiving, and was usually an overspecialized view of only one or two senses (Gibson, 1966, pp. 1–6). We regard this as an extreme view of the matter. The musician applies with care the pitch pipe or the tuning fork to get his instrument on key, but he does not try to play a tune with it. Similarly, the sensory psychologist or physiologist does not view the behavior of the whole organism through a single modality, nor regard the integrated working of the system as a simple summation of the activities of each sense.

To the degree that independent physical events may affect each sensory modality so as to produce entirely uncorrelated nervous activities, the senses may act separately, at least at the peripheral level. At the level of the second or third neuron, however, integration of the nervous action begins as structural convergence demands it must. In the meantime, whatever motor activity is occurring adds to the influx by way of kinesthetic, proprioceptive, or cutaneous channels, as well as through systems variously named efference copy, corollary discharge, or feedforward neural circuits. Out of this sensory-motor committee meeting there emerges (usually) a report of some unitary event, undoubtedly a chimera generated by the concerted action of the several modalities.

When only one or two modalities are involved, the complexity of the relationship can be enormous. Interactions within the cutaneous senses are known, but not completely understood (see Section 7 of Chapter 12). Similarly, there exist kinesthetic-visual interactions such as Charpentier's illusion, in which the subject lifts separately two vessels of equal weight but very different volume. The illusion occurs when the subject judges the larger volume to be of lighter weight (Anthony, Holding, Lion, & Sluckin, 1962). The interaction of the auditory and vestibular modalities has been shown by Arnoult (1950) to produce a robust effect as well; observers show shifts in auditory localization of 10–20° after being rotated. There are many situations that can be arranged to demonstrate mutual sensory induction effects, and the majority of them involve a degradation of performance. For example, Novak (1965) was able to show that the limen for twoness in vision is significantly raised if a transient electrocutaneous stimulus precedes it by 25 msec. Thus far, no simple mechanism of masking or distraction suffices to explain this effect. Auditory-tactile interactions can be illustrated by experiments by Gescheider and Niblette (1967), who were able to show small but reliable masking effects of vibratory and auditory stimuli on one another, and by the results of research by Sherrick (1976), who could show a disruption of judgments of temporal order in the auditory sense by contravening events in the tactile system. It is not surprising that more interest accrues to this aspect of interaction, because the avoidance of degraded performance is often of greater importance than the discovery of means for improving it, especially in situations involving multiple inputs of information and critical decisions for action (see Sherrick, 1979). There was a series of studies, conducted in Russia, that purported to demonstrate the facilitatory effect of one sense modality on another, but these have not found support in the literature (see, e.g., London, 1954).

One principle that we may be certain will be affirmed in the analysis of cooperative sensory action is redundancy. It appears throughout the structure of the body, including various levels of the nervous system. So too it appears across sensory systems, often when one sense is lost or diminished. For the blind person, the four senses discussed in this section are all that are available besides the chemical senses of smell and taste. Yet the blind person can get around his or her home and business, often commute to work with little aid, read, and appreciate nearly all the esthetic pleasures but the purely visual ones. For such persons the kinesthetic and proprioceptive senses are advanced in station because they bear new responsibilities for maintaining posture and gait, and for monitoring the inflow of information from cane and, perhaps, guide dog. The sense of hearing commands more attention because it analyzes echoes of the walker's footsteps, and of ambient sounds, to tell where the person is and whether sound-reflecting obstacles are ahead. The sense of touch aids the kinesthetic in the handling of the cane, but more important in reading braille text, or in palpating objects to identify tools, foods, and other items most of us classify at a glance (see Chapter 31, Loomis & Lederman).

Even when both sight and hearing are unavailable, a number of people have demonstrated remarkable ability to live, to work, and to enjoy life. In doing so, they teach the rest of us that with the senses as with many abstract talents, it is not what you have so much as how you work with it. Deaf-blind persons avail themselves of the aids that blind persons do, and in some cases replace the hearing sense with the tactile (and almost certainly the kinesthetic) sense to understand speech (Reed, Durlach, & Braida, 1982). The little that is presently known about the potential for the senses to amalgamate the events of the world for processing by the central nervous system could be augmented greatly by studying the behavior of the deaf-blind person (see Walk & Pick, 1981; esp. Millar, 1981). So it is that we may learn most from what at first appear to be flawed constructions of nature, when we should regard them as novae of the behavioral sphere.

REFERENCE NOTE

1. Thomas, J. Personal communication. June 8, 1984.

REFERENCES

Andres, K. H., & Düring, M. von. Morphology of cutaneous receptors. In A. Iggo (Ed.), *Handbook of sensory physiology, Vol. II. Somatosensory system*. Berlin: Springer-Verlag, 1973.

Anthony, W. S., Holding, D. H., Lion, J. S., & Sluckin, W. Size-weight interactions in judgments of compound stimuli. *Quarterly Journal of Experimental Psychology*, 1962, *14*, 77–88.

Arnoult, M. D. Post-rotatory localization of sound. *American Journal of Psychology*, 1950, *63*, 229–236.

Békésy, G. von. *Sensory inhibition*. Princeton, N.J.: Princeton University Press, 1967.

Boring, E. G. *Sensation and perception in the history of experimental psychology*. New York: Appleton-Century-Crofts, 1942.

Gescheider, G., & Niblette, R. K. Cross-modality masking for touch and hearing. *Journal of Experimental Psychology*, 1967, *74*, 313–320.

Gibson, J. J. *The perception of the visual world*. Boston: Houghton Mifflin, 1950.

Gibson, J. J. Observations on active touch. *Psychological Review*, 1962, *69*, 447–491.

Gibson, J. J. *The senses considered as perceptual systems*. Boston: Houghton Mifflin, 1966.

Gibson, J. J. *The ecological approach to visual perception*. Boston: Houghton Mifflin, 1979.

Godfrey, D. A., Kiang, N. Y.-S., & Norris, B. E. Single unit activity in the posteroventral cochlear nucleus of the cat. *Journal of Comparative Neurology*, 1975, *162*, 247–269.

Khanna, S. M., & Sherrick, C. E. The comparative sensitivity of selected receptor systems. In T. Gualtierotti (Ed.), *Symposium on vestibular function and morphology*. Berlin: Springer-Verlag, 1981.

Kiang, N. Y.-S. *Discharge patterns of single fibers in the cat's auditory nerve*. Cambridge, Mass.: MIT Press, 1965.

Konietzny, F., & Hensel, H. The neural basis of the sensory quality of warmth. In D. R. Kenshalo (Ed.), *Sensory functions of the skin of humans*. New York: Plenum Press, 1979.

London, I. D. Research on sensory interaction in the Soviet Union. *Psychological Bulletin*, 1954, *51*, 531–568.

McFadden, D., & Wightman, F. L. Audition: Some relations between normal and pathological hearing. *Annual Review of Psychology*, 1983, *34*, 94–128.

Merzenich, M. M., & Harrington, T. The sense of flutter-vibration evoked by stimulation of the hairy skin of primates: Comparison of human sensory capacity with the responses of mechanoreceptive afferents innervating the hairy skin of monkeys. *Experimental Brain Research*, 1969, *8*, 236–260.

Millar, S. Crossmodal and intersensory perception and the blind. In R. D. Walk, & H. L. Pick, Jr. (Eds.), *Intersensory perception and sensory integration*. New York: Plenum Press, 1981.

Mountcastle, V. B., Talbot, W. H., Darian-Smith, I., & Kornhuber, H. H. Neural basis of the sense of flutter-vibration. *Science*, 1967, *155*, 597–600.

Myslivеček, J. Development of the auditory evoked response in the auditory cortex in mammals. In R. Romand (Ed.), *Development of auditory and vestibular systems*. New York: Academic, 1983.

Novak, S. The effect of electrocutaneous digital stimulation on the detection of single and double flashes of light. *Psychological Monographs*, 1965, *79* (Whole No. 608).

Papakostopoulos, D., Crow, H. J., & Newton, P. Spatiotemporal characteristics of intrinsic evoked and event related potentials in the human cortex. In G. Pfurtscheller, G. Buser, F. Lopes da Silva, & H. Petsche (Eds.), *Rhythmic EEG activities and cortical functioning*. New York: Elsevier, 1980.

Peeke, H. V. S., & Petrinovich, L. (Eds.). *Habituation, sensitization, and behavior*. New York: Academic Press, 1984.

Reed, C. M., Durlach, N. I., & Braida, L. D. Research on tactile communication of speech: A review. *American Speech and Hearing Association Monographs*, 1982, No. 20.

Sherrick, C. E. The antagonisms of hearing and touch. In S. K. Hirsh, D. H. Eldredge, I. J. Hirsh, & S. R. Silverman (Eds.), *Hearing and Davis: Essays honoring Hallowell Davis*. St. Louis: Washington University Press, 1976.

Sherrick, C. E. Combinative sensory processing and modality interactions. *Sensory World*, 1979, Spring, 10–16.

Thompson, R. F., Smith, H. E., & Bliss, D. Auditory, somatic sensory, and visual response interactions and interrelations in association and primary cortical fields of the cat. *Journal of Neurophysiology*, 1963, *26*, 365–378.

Verrillo, R. T. Vibrotactile sensitivity and the frequency response of the Pacinian corpuscle. *Psychonomic Science*, 1966, *4*, 135–136.

Walk, R. D., & Pick, H. L., Jr. (Eds.). *Intersensory perception and sensory integration*. New York: Plenum Press, 1981.

Wegel, R. L., & Lane, C. E. The auditory masking of one pure tone by another and its probable relation to the dynamics of the inner ear. *Physical Review*, 1924, *23*, 226–285.

CHAPTER 11

THE VESTIBULAR SYSTEM

IAN P. HOWARD
York University, Toronto, Ontario

CONTENTS

The sense organs embedded in the temporal bone on each side of the head are known collectively as the labyrinthine organs or simply as the *labyrinths*. They include the organ of hearing, or cochlea, the three semicircular canals, and the otolith organs, or utricle and saccule. The nonauditory labyrinthine organs are known as the *vestibular system*. This chapter is devoted to a review of the structure, physiology, and psychophysics of the vestibular system. The relationships between the vestibular system and other sensory systems are reviewed in Chapter 18 by Howard on "The Perception of Posture, Self Motion, and the Visual Vertical."

Vestibular organs are present in all vertebrate phyla, including the cyclostomes, which is the most primitive extant group of vertebrates, and includes the hagfish and lampreys (Lowenstein, Osborne, & Thornhill, 1968). Analogous organs, in a great variety of forms, also occur in invertebrates (Markl, 1974, pp. 17–74). In vertebrates, vestibular organs evolved from simple fluid-filled pits in the skin. These pits contained hair cells sensitive to vibrations arising from external sources or to vibrations arising from movements of the animal. At a later stage, arrays of interconnected pits evolved into the lateral-line organs of fish and into the vestibular-cochlea organs of the higher vertebrates, including the mammals. There are three subdivisions of the vestibular-cochlea complex on each side of the head: (1) the spiral cochlea, sensitive to acoustic vibrations,

(2) the sack-shaped utricle and saccule, sensitive to gravity and to linear acceleration of the head, and (3) the three canals, sensitive to rotations of the head (see Fig. 11.1). Ducts join the utricle-canal complex to the saccule, and the saccule to the cochlea. Another duct runs from the utricle to a lymphatic reservoir, the endolymphatic sac. The whole system is filled with a fluid, the *endolymph*. The cavities containing the sensory epithelia and endolymph are lined with a membrane that is separated from the bony walls of the labyrinth by a fine network of connective tissue bathed in perilymph fluid.

The sensory end organs of the vestibular system may be stimulated artificially by disturbances of the thermal, chemical, or electrical balance of the endolymph. However, the organs are normally maintained in a dark environment that is thermally and chemically constant so that they usually respond only to mechanical stimulation caused by an appropriate movement of the head. The nature, frequency, direction, and amplitude of the effective movement are determined largely by the mechanical properties of the organ in which the sensory cells lie and the arrangement of sensitive hairs, or cilia, on the surface of each cell.

The vestibular system is concerned with the detection of signals arising from movements of the head; it does not inform us about the state of the external world. Furthermore, the responses induced by vestibular stimulation typically occur automatically, without any need of conscious control. Thus we become aware of the effects of the functioning of the vestibular system only when its mechanism is disturbed. Even then, because the vestibular organs are hidden from view, casual observation does not lead us to an awareness of a distinct sensory modality, as it does in the case of vision and hearing.

It is no wonder, therefore, that the vestibular system was the most recent of the sensory systems of humans to be discovered. Electric sense organs have been discovered more recently, but those organs occur only in certain species of fish. The initial discovery of the true function of the vestibular system was made by Flourens in 1824. He sectioned the vestibular canals of pigeons and rabbits and observed the consequent disturbances of movements of the head and eyes. He revealed a relationship between the damaged canal and the direction in which the head and eyes of the animal turned simultaneously. These discoveries were ignored until 1874. In that and the following year, Breuer in Vienna, Mach in Prague, and Crum Brown in Edinburgh independently proposed the hydrodynamic theory of vestibular function, a theory that stressed the importance of movements of the endolymph induced by accelerative motions of the head. They also proposed that the vestibular canals serve for the detection of rotary acceleration, whereas the utricle and saccule serve for the detection of head position relative to the direction of gravity.

This division between organs sensitive to rotary acceleration and organs sensitive to linear acceleration is very primitive. But the significance of the division has often been misunderstood. Many writers have distinguished between static or head-position receptors (the utricles) and dynamic or head-movement receptors (the canals). This is a false distinction, as Jongkees and Groen (1946) pointed out. Einstein's theory of gravitation tells us that gravity, linear accelerative movement, and centrifugal force are indistinguishable as stimuli. The utricle is sensitive to the magnitude of linear acceleration, however it is produced. This organ is therefore as much a dynamic receptor as the canals, which are sensitive to the magnitude of rotary acceleration. Both receptors also have a static aspect: the utricles are responsive to the direction of linear acceleration, as well as to its amount, and similarly the canals, as a triplet, are sensitive to the direction of rotary acceleration about any head axis as well as to its amount. The two organs are therefore both dynamic and static receptors.

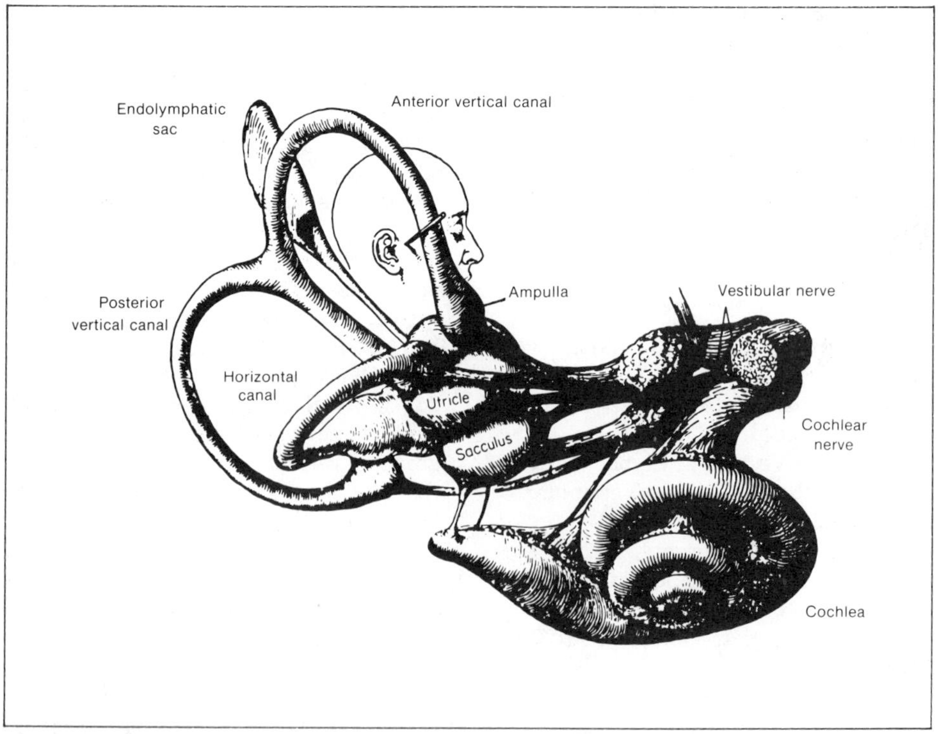

Figure 11.1. Diagram of the inner ear, showing the semicircular canals, utricle, saccule, and cochlea, together with the nerves innervating them. (From Hardy, 1934.)

The development of an adequate theory of the functioning of the vestibular canals was hampered because the crucial working parts of those structures are transparent and thus not visible. These crucial parts are the endolymphatic fluid that fills the canals and a gelatinous structure known as the cupula (see Section 2.1). In 1931, Steinhausen was able to observe the deflection of the cupula in a living fish by injecting pigment into the endolymphatic fluid which fills the canal cavity. In this way it was established that the essential event in the response of the canals to head rotation was a flow of the endolymph round the cavity of the canal and a subsequent deflection of the cupula. It also became obvious from these observations that the cupula forms a seal across the canal, so that the earlier view that the endolymph flows past the cupula was abandoned in favor of the view that the cupula swings back and forth in response to endolymphatic flow. As we shall see below, it has recently become apparent that, although the cupula deflects under the influence of large accelerative forces, ordinary rotations of the head are sufficient only to deform it without displacing its outer margin.

Steinhausen described the behavior of the cupula by the well-known differential equation for the torsion pendulum, which is presented in Section 2.2. Van Egmond, Groen, and Jongkees (1949), using behavioral indices, confirmed that within limits this formula adequately describes the function of the vestibular canals. We shall see below that recent work has led to an elaboration of that basic formula. The quantitative analysis of the dynamics of the otolith organs was carried out by von Holst (1950).

Electrophysiological recordings of the activity of vestibular afferents were first made by Lowenstein and Sand (1940) and Adrian (1943) and, as we shall see below, our knowledge of neural events in the vestibular system has advanced rapidly in recent years through the work of Precht, Llinás, Fernández, Goldberg, and others.

The importance of the vestibular organs is indicated by the fact that their complete ablation leads to persistent behavioral deficits. For instance, after labyrinthectomy, cats cannot land on all fours when dropped (Watt, 1976) and monkeys can no longer run along a moving bar (Igarashi, Watanabe, & Maxian, 1970). People with bilateral loss of vestibular function easily lose their static balance when their eyes are closed and perform poorly when walking along a narrow beam, even with eyes open (Fregly, 1974. pp. 321–360). They are also deficient in their ability to pursue an erratically moving object with their eyes (Cogan, 1958).

Movements of the human head and body are described in terms of the axes and planes shown in Figure 11.2. A fuller kinematic nomenclature for the vestibular system is provided in Hixson, Niven, and Correia (1966). A commonly used standard of force used in vestibular work is that produced by the normal acceleration due to gravity (9.8 m·sec^{-2}), acting on unit mass. Whenever referring to this standard I shall use the symbol g_n to distinguish it from g, the symbol for gram.

1. THE OTOLITH ORGANS

1.1. Structure of the Otolith Organs

The utricle and saccule are small sack-shaped organs situated bilaterally within the head. The utricle on each side is at the junction of the three semicircular canals and its cavity is continuous with the canal cavities. The saccule is just below the utricle. Each organ is filled with endolymph and contains a sensory epithelium, the *macula*, which responds to the magnitude and direction of linear acceleration, including the magnitude and direction of gravity. Organs sensitive to orientation with respect to gravity occurred early in the evolutionary scale. They are represented in every animal phylum and their general mode of functioning is remarkably constant.

The utricular macula lies on the floor of the utricle and is approximately in the same plane as the horizontal canal, although it turns upward at its anterior end. The saccular macula lies on the medial wall of the saccule and is tilted inwards from the vertical by at least 20°. The detailed anatomy of the maculae is given in Lindeman (1973) and Smith (1956). Only a general description is provided here. The surface of each macula is slightly concave (see Fig. 11.3) and is covered with an epithelium of ciliated cells and structural cells, very similar to those found in the cristae of the canals (see Fig. 11.4). The cilia protrude into a plate of material known as the *statoconial membrane*. This consists of a gelatinous substance containing calcite crystals—the *otoliths*, or *statoconia*. The membrane has an area of about 1.5–2 mm^2 and is kept in place by elastic filaments attached to the walls of the utricle or saccule. The specific gravity of the otoliths is 2.74, that is, about three times that of the surrounding endolymph (Carlström & Engström, 1955). Such sense organs have evolved to respond to displacements of the heavy otoliths induced by changes in the extent or direction of the linear acceleration of the head, brought about by changes in the magnitude or direction of the linear velocity of the head or by a tilt of the head with respect to gravity. Note that a person restrained from falling in a gravitational field of strength X m·sec^{-2} is subjected to a constant linear accelerative force of X m·sec^{-2}. Only a nonaccelerating person in the weightless conditions of orbital flight is free of all linear accelerative forces.

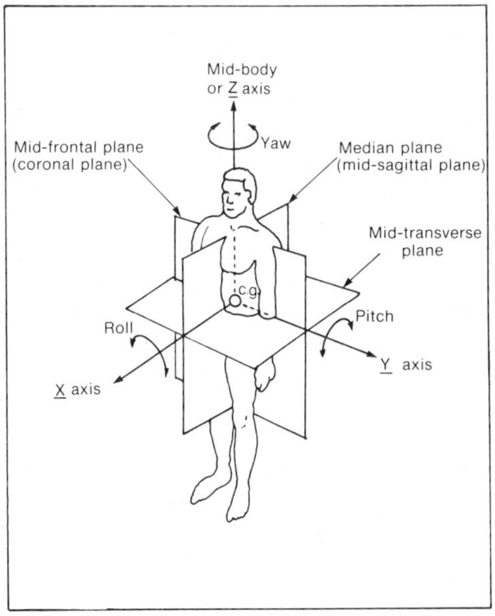

Figure 11.2. Axes and planes of reference for the human body. The three principal axes intersect at the center of gravity of the body. The arrowhead on each axis points in the positive direction along that axis. Other axes, such as the visual axes or the axis joining the centers of the two eyes, are also used.

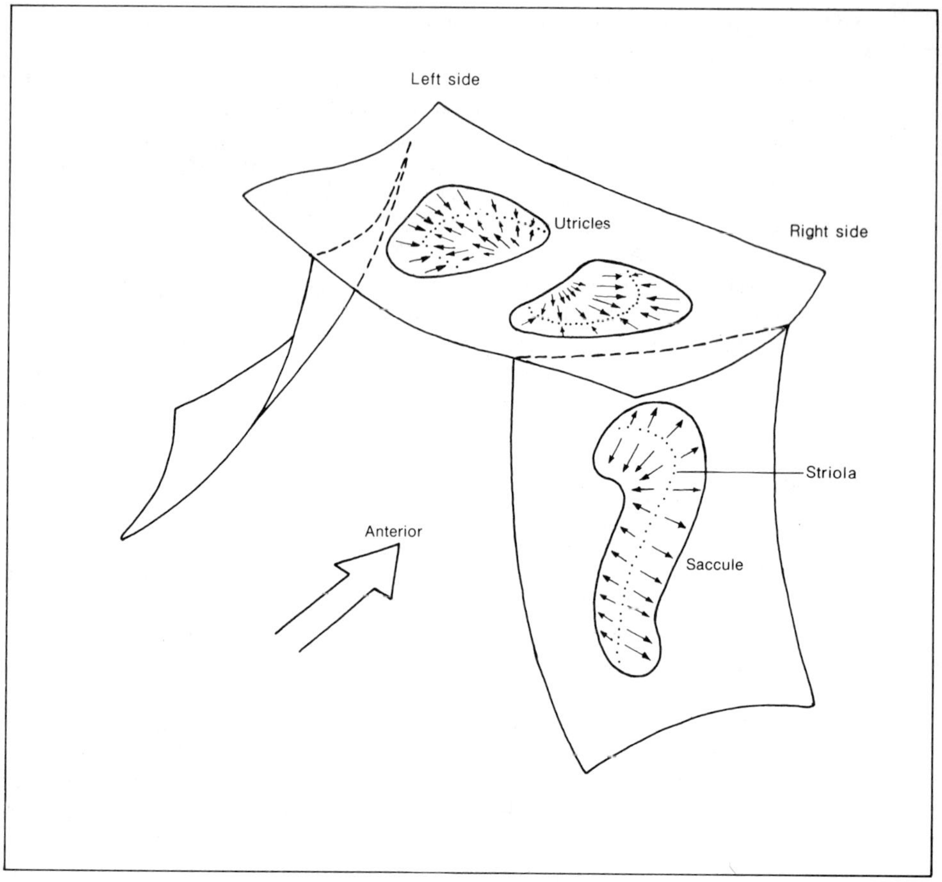

Figure 11.3. Dispositions of the sensory epithelia, or maculae, in the otolith organs on the two sides of the head. The arrows represent the polarization maps of the sensory hair cells lying within the macular surfaces. The arrows point in that direction of shear that produces depolarization of the hair cells in each region. A shear force applied in the opposite direction in each region produces hyperpolarization. The striola is the boundary between regions of opposite polarity. These polarization maps are described in Section 1.3. (From R. Malcolm & G. Melvill Jones, A quantitative study of vestibular adaptation in humans, *Acta Otolaryngologica*, 1970, *70*. Reprinted with permission.)

1.2. Dynamics of the Otolith Organs

By recording the changes in potential in the macula of the guinea pig, Trincker (1962) showed that only shearing forces produced by tangential displacements of the statoconial membrane relative to the macular surface are effective in stimulating the afferent nerve. Pressure or tension applied at right angles to the macular epithelium has no effect. Shearing forces should produce a response proportional to the sine of the angle of tilt of the macular surface from the horizontal, whereas pressure forces should produce a response that is a cosine function of the angle of tilt. Trincker demonstrated a sine function by recording from the macula as the animal was tilted.

The excess mass of the statoconial membrane, β, is its mass m, minus the mass of the same volume of endolymph, which, if the density of the endolymph is assumed to be 1, is given by

$$\beta = \frac{m(\rho - 1)}{\rho}$$

where ρ is the density of the statoconial membrane. The shearing force acting on an otolith organ is equal to the product of the excess mass of the statoconial membrane and the linear acceleration acting in the plane of the macula (α). This is opposed by elastic, or position-dependent resistance k; viscous, or velocity-dependent resistance r; and mass, or acceleration-dependent resistance m. Thus

$$\beta \cdot \alpha = kx + r\frac{dx}{dt} + m\frac{d^2x}{dt^2}$$

where m is the effective mass of the statoconial membrane, that is, the total mass of tissue and fluid that is accelerated, and x is the linear displacement of the otoliths. This is the same well-known equation of motion used to describe the mechanics of the cupula. De Vries (1950) obtained direct measurements of these constants in a fish and found that the statoconial membrane of the saccule was displaced about 33 μm by a tangential force induced on a mass by 1 g_n (9.8 m·sec^{-2}). Assuming a similar value in man, and given that the human threshold for saccular stimulation is about 0.005g_n (Melvill Jones & Young, 1978), the threshold displacement of the saccule turns out to be about 0.15 μm. This distance is within molecular dimensions and suggests that the crucial event is a deformation of organic molecules.

On the basis of measurements of the displacement of the statoconial membrane during oscillatory stimulation, de Vries deduced that the structure is critically damped and is fully

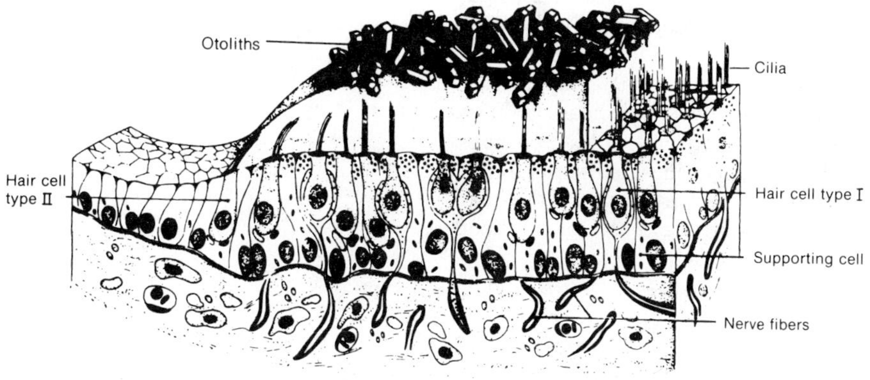

Figure 11.4. Diagramatic representation of the detailed structure of the macular epithelium. Calcite crystals are embedded in a gelatinous substance into which protrude the sensitive hair cells of the macula. A shearing force produced by tilting the macula or by accelerating it within its own plane deflects the otoliths and bends the cilia. If the cilia are deflected toward the kinocilium, the cell membrane is depolarized and the cell's rate of firing increased. A deflection of cilia away from the kinocilium hyperpolarizes the cell membrane and reduces the cell's rate of firing below its resting level. Figure 11.14 shows the structure of the sensory cells in greater detail. (From S. Iurato, Light microscope features, in S. Iurato (Ed.), *Submicroscopic structure of the inner ear*. Copyright 1967 by Pergamon Press, Ltd. Reprinted with permission.)

displaced within 5 msec of the application of a constant tangential force. The membrane apparently restores to its normal position very rapidly after a stimulus has been removed. At least nobody has reported a long recovery time such as is found in the recovery of the vestibular canals. In mammals, the time constants of the statoconial membrane have been inferred from behavioral measurements, but this procedure is open to the objection that behavioral responses reflect properties of neural elements as well as those of the peripheral organ (Young & Meiry, 1968).

There is a fundamental ambiguity in the signals from the otolith organs. For instance, the effect of a horizontal linear acceleration, a, acting in the plane of the utricles is indistinguishable from the effect of tilting the head through the angle whose sine is a. One well-known consequence of this ambiguity is the experience pilots have when there is a change in the speed of the aircraft. If the aircraft gains speed, the otolith organs are stimulated in the same way that they would be by an appropriate upward pitch of the aircraft. If the aircraft is in a cloud, the pilot may correct for this apparent upward pitch by bringing the nose of the aircraft down, and he may then fly the aircraft into the ground (Kirkham, Collins, Grape, Simpson, & Wallace, 1978; Wolfe & Cramer, 1970). The fact that the ambiguous input from the otolith organs is interpreted as a tilt of the body rather than a linear acceleration suggests that the primary function of these organs is the detection of head tilt. However, inputs from the semicircular canals may help to clarify the otolith inputs, as is seen in Chapter 18, "Perception of Posture, Self Motion, and the Visual Vertical."

1.3. The Afferent Signal from Otolith Organs

The microstructure of the maculae of the utricle and saccule is very similar to that of the cristae of the vestibular canals. There are about 33,000 hair cells in the human utricle and about 19,000 in the saccule of the adult human. The number of sensory cells is reduced in the aged (Johnsson & Hawkins, 1972). Some of these cells are known as *type I cells*. Cells of this type are enclosed in a nerve chalice and innervated by large-diameter fibers. Other cells are known as *type II cells*. Cells of this type are cylindrical, do not have a nerve chalice, and are innervated by small-diameter fibers. Cells of both types have about 70 *stereocilia* and one *kinocilium*, with the stereocilia graded in length toward the kinocilium. The resting potential across the cell membrane has been found to be between 60 and 80 mV in amphibians (Bracho, Budelli, & Galey, 1981, pp. 144–159). A general idea of these structures can be gained by inspection of Figure 11.4 and a more detailed idea of the nerve chalice and cilia by inspection of Figure 11.14 in Section 2.3.1.

The membrane of each cell is depolarized when a force shears the stereocilia in the direction of the kinocilium, and hyperpolarized when a force acts in the opposite direction. Depolarization increases the discharge of the afferent neuron above its resting value, and hyperpolarization depresses the discharge rate below its resting value. The directions of most effective hyperpolarization and dipolarization of a hair cell constitute its *polarization axis*. Histological and electrophysiological procedures have been used to map out the polarization axes of cells on the surface of the utricular and saccular maculae (Flock, 1964; Rosenhall, 1972). In each macula, oppositely polarized regions are separated by a central "parting" known as the *striola* (see Fig. 11.3).

Synergistic and inhibitory relationships between different regions of the macula have been worked out (Fluur, 1970). In particular, oppositely directed regions inhibit each other, and this may explain why otolith organs have been found to be unaffected by even intense angular acceleration (Goldberg &

Fernández, 1975). When a person rotates about the z-body axis with the utricular maculae in the plane of rotation, the rotary component of the motion induces a torque in the rigid statoconial membrane and thus stimulates equal numbers of cells with opposite polarization axes in each utricle, producing a zero output. At the same time, the linear, or centrifugal, component of the rotation acting outward from the center of the head produces equal and opposite stimulation of the utricles on the two sides of the head, the effects of which probably cancel in the vestibular nuclei of the brainstem. In a similar way, a rotation of the head about any other axis passing through the center of the head produces rotary effects that cancel in each utricle and saccule, and centrifugal effects that cancel within the vestibular nuclei. When a person is rotated about an off-center axis, the centrifugal linear forces on the two sides will not cancel, because they will be either opposite and unequal or in the same direction.

When the macular surface is at right angles to the accelerative force, the average discharge rate of afferents has been reported as about 60 spikes per second, with a standard deviation of about 27 spikes per second. This represents the resting discharge rate. It has been found that each otolith nerve fiber in the vestibular nerve of the monkey responds most frequently when the head of the animal is tilted at a given angle in a particular plane and least when the head is tilted at 180° in the opposite direction in the same plane (Fernández & Goldberg, 1976a, 1976b, 1976c). This axis of maximum and minimum response of a given nerve fiber defines its polarization axis, which presumably corresponds to the polarization axis of the hair cells that it innervates. The linear polarization of afferent neurons strongly suggests that all the hair cells that any one of them innervates have polarization axes that lie in the same direction, although it remains possible that they are not all of the same sign (they may occur on opposite sides of the striola). Units in the superior region of the nerve have polarization axes in the plane of the utricular macula, and those in the inferior region have axes in the plane of the saccular macula. The rate of discharge of an afferent neuron is a sine function of the angle of tilt of the head (Fernández, Goldberg, & Abend, 1972; Loe, Tomko, & Werner, 1973). This confirms that the effective stimulus is a force acting tangentially on the statoconial membrane. Movement of the head within the plane of the macula, at right angles to the polarization axis of an afferent neuron, has very little effect on its discharge rate, and neither does changing the magnitude of the force acting perpendicularly to the macular surface.

The discharge rates of single fibers have been plotted over a wide range of forces produced by rotating a monkey in a centrifuge. S-shaped force-response curves like that shown in Figure 11.5 have been derived. The function for this particular neuron is linear within the range 0–3 g_n units, and the response levels off at about 5 g_n units. Fernández and Goldberg identified three response parameters to account for differences in the force-response characteristics of different units: the *resting discharge rate*, *sensitivity*, or change in discharge rate produced by a shear force of 1 g_n unit, and an *asymmetry coefficient*, defined as the value of the resting rate with respect to the curve's inflection point.

Most afferent neurons from otolith organs have a regular resting discharge and are designated *regular units*. Those cells in which the resting discharge rate is more variable than a certain arbitrary criterion are designated *irregular units*. Fernández and Goldberg (1976a, 1976b, 1976c) found the sensitivity of most cells to be between 30 and 40 spikes per second per g_n

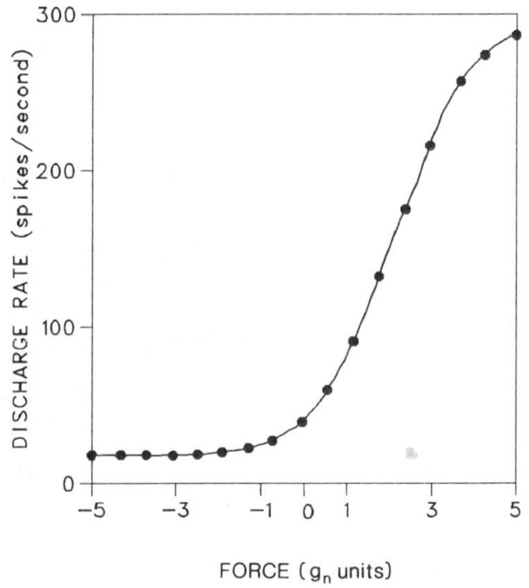

Figure 11.5. A force-response curve for an otolith neuron of the squirrel monkey. The abscissa indicates the shearing force acting on the utricle. The lower asymptote indicates the cell's resting discharge rate, the curve's steepness indicates the cell's sensitivity, and the upper asymptote indicates the cell's saturation discharge. Other units produced curves of the same form but that varied in resting discharge rate, sensitivity, and the positions of the inflection point and saturation level. (From C. Fernández & J. M. Goldberg, Physiology of peripheral neurons innervating otolith organs of the squirrel monkey. II. Directional selectivity and force-response relations. *Journal of Neurophysiology*, 1976, *39*. Reprinted with permission.)

and to be somewhat higher for irregular than for regular cells. They also found that the sensitivity of regular cells is proportional to their resting discharge rate, but that this is not true for irregular cells. Afferent neurons from the utricle were found to have a higher resting discharge rate and higher sensitivity than afferents from the saccule (Fernández et al., 1972; Tomko, Peterka, & Schor, 1981).

During a period of constant stimulation, the discharge rate tends to return toward the resting level, and this *adaptation* is particularly prominent in irregular cells. Adapting cells differentiate the input and are therefore most sensitive to high-frequency changes in head position [see Fig. 11.6(a)]. For this reason irregular cells are designated *phasic cells* to distinguish them from the regular, slowly adapting cells known as *tonic cells*. Adaptation in phasic cells causes their response to become phase advanced as the frequency of head oscillation is increased. By comparison, the response of tonic cells shows an increasing phase lag with increasing frequency of head oscillation [see Fig. 11.6(b)].

1.4. The Central Projections of Otolith Afferents

The primary afferents from the otolith organs project to the ipsilateral vestibular nuclei in the brainstem, particularly to the lateral (Deiter's) and medial nuclei (Gacek, 1975, pp. 21–30). There is evidence that, at least in the cat, a few primary fibers go directly to the abducens nucleus, which is one of the oculomotor nuclei in the brainstem (Lang & Kubik, 1979).

Adrian (1943), working on the cat, was the first to record from cells in the vestibular nuclei and show that some of them change their firing rate as the animal is tilted. Subsequent investigations have revealed that cells of this type that respond to labyrinthine shocks with monosynaptic latencies (second-order cells) fall into two classes: those in which firing rate in-

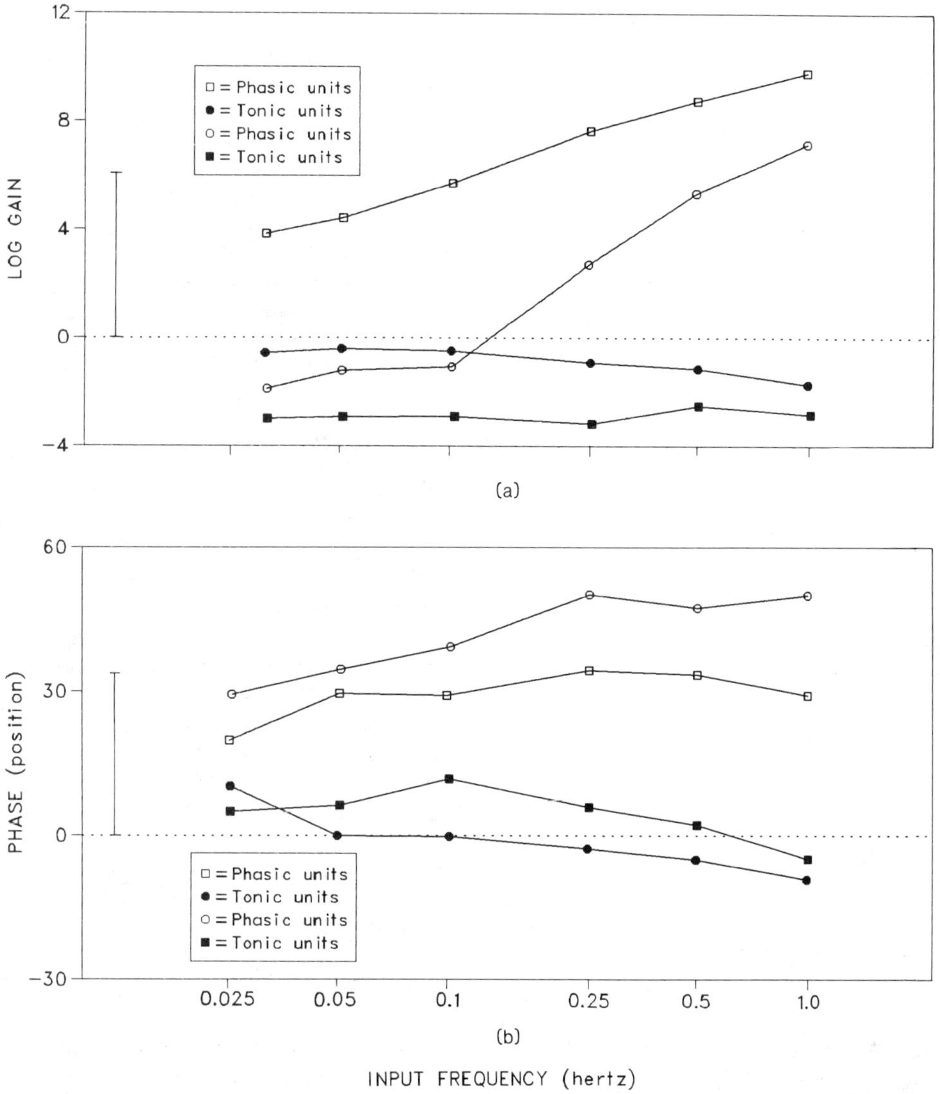

Figure 11.6. Gain of afferent fibers from the utricle of the cat as the animal is tilted sinusodially over a range of frequencies. (a) Gain is defined as impulses per unit of shearing force. (One unit is the force produced on unit mass by an acceleration of 9.8 m·sec^{-2}). In plotting these curves the gains were normalized. (b) Phase is defined as the difference, in degrees, between the position of maximum body tilt and the position of maximum frequency of a cell's response. The open symbols show data from two phasic units and the closed symbols show data from two tonic units. Note how the phase lead and gain of phasic units increase with increasing frequency of body tilt. The vertical bar gives an idea of ±1 SD for both sets of data. (From J. H. Anderson, R. H. I. Blanks, & W. Precht, Response characteristics of semicircular canal and otolith systems in cats. I. Dynamic responses of primary vestibular fibers, *Experimental Brain Research*, 1978, *32*. Reprinted with permission.)

creases to ipsilateral tilt and decreases to contralateral tilt (type I), and those in which firing rate decreases to ipsilateral and increases to contralateral tilt (type II). Both types of cell receive inputs from opposite sides of the striola along the polarization axis that lies in the plane of body tilt. Each otolith organ sends signals to only the ipsilateral vestibular nuclei. Other cells have been found that show a decrease or an increase in firing rate to tilts in either direction, but these cells are not driven directly by vestibular afferents (Matsuoka, Fukuda, Takaori, & Morimoto, 1971; Peterson, 1970). Schor (1974) studied the dynamic responses of second-order neurons of the vestibular nuclei in cats exposed to sinusoidal roll tilts of the body of between 0.01 and 1.0 Hz. The vestibular canals were plugged to ensure that the responses were due to stimulation of only the otolith organs. Cells were found to fall into two classes: a phasic type showing enhanced gain (impulses per degree of head tilt) at higher frequencies of head tilt, and a tonic type showing constant gain over a range of frequencies (see Fig. 11.7).

Although there are no direct inputs from the otolith organs to the contralateral vestibular nuclei, commissural fibers connect the two sides. Excitation of primary afferents from otolith organs on one side facilitates the response produced in the contralateral vestibular nuclei (Shimazu & Smith, 1971; Wilson, Gacek, Uchino, & Susswein, 1978). It will be shown in Section 2.4 that excitatory inputs from semicircular canals on the two sides of the head mutually *inhibit* each other. This difference between the two types of organ makes sense in terms of their differing geometries. Each canal is a *bidirectional* detector in which afferent fibers either all increase or all decrease their firing rates

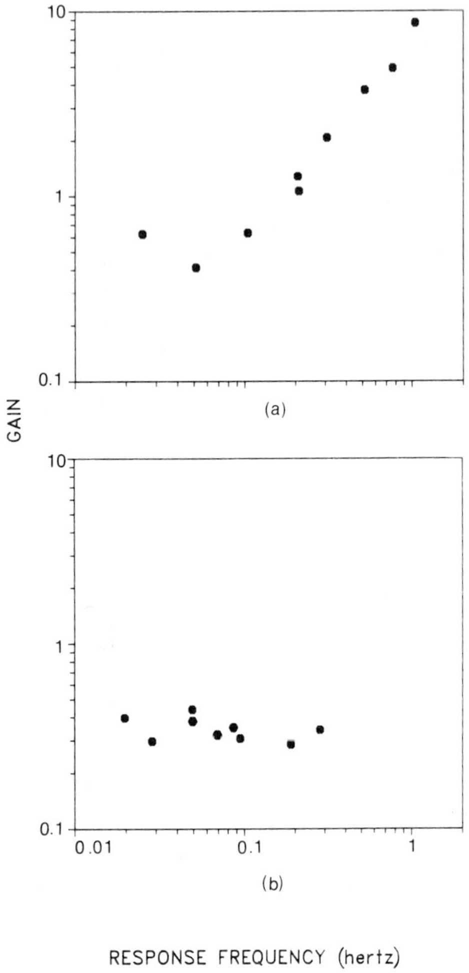

Figure 11.7. Gain of second-order neurons in the vestibular nuclei of the cat as the animal is tilted sinusoidally over a range of frequencies. The vestibular canals were plugged to ensure that only afferents from the otolith organs were stimulated. Gain is defined as impulses per second per degree of body tilt. Data plotted in (a) are from phasic units, that is, units that respond as a function of tilt frequency. These units showed greater modulation of their firing rates as the frequency of body tilt increased. Data plotted in (b) are from static units, that is, units that respond as a function of degree of head tilt and for which the gain as a function of tilt frequency is constant. (From R. H. Schor, Responses of cat vestibular neurons to sinusoidal roll tilt, *Experimental Brain Research*, 1974, *20*. Reprinted with permission.)

according to the direction and magnitude of the rotary force acting in the plane of the canal. Furthermore, a rotation of the head in one direction has opposed effects on synergistic canals on opposite sides of the head. Thus it is the difference, not the sum of the synergistic inputs, that varies with the stimulus. The three canals acting together form a multidirectional detector. Each otolith organ is a multidirectional detector and is therefore analogous to the set of three canals; cells lying along each polarization axis of a macula are analogous to the receptors in a synergistic pair of canals. For a given tilt of the head, the firing rate of receptors along a given polarization axis on one side of the striola increases and that of those on the other side decreases. There are thus two simultaneous and opposed afferent discharges from a macula compared to the single type of discharge from a single canal. Furthermore, a tilt of the head in a given direction has the same effect on equivalently polarized regions of the maculae on the two sides of the head so that, in the case of the otolith organs, it is the summed output from regions with the same polarization axis on the two sides that is the signal for linear acceleration. There are inhibitory relationships within each otolith organ, between detectors with opposite polarization axes (Fluur, 1970), and these may serve to cancel the effects of rotary motions of the macula. There could be similar inhibitory relationships in the vestibular nuclei, between opposed inputs from the two sides of the head, but I have not seen them described. In any case, the resting discharges of opposed inputs cannot be fully canceled. If they were, it would abolish the sustained activity required for the maintenance of postural tone whatever the posture of the body. Loss of vestibular inputs is known to produce prolonged muscular flaccidity (Lowenstein, 1975, pp. 99–108).

There is a natural zero value of rotary acceleration because we are not always turning our heads, and when we are not, the difference signal generated by the resting discharges of synergistic canals is zero. There is no natural zero value of linear acceleration. For one thing, all animals are subjected to a constant force of 1 g_n per unit mass, but even for maculae normal to the direction of this force, resting discharges from the otolith organs are not canceled.

Second-order and higher-order neurons arising from the vestibular nuclei convey information of macular origin to the cerebellum (Marini, Provini, & Rosina, 1976), the reticular formation (Kubin, Magherini, Manzoni, & Pompeiano, 1980; Spyer, Ghelarducci, & Pompeiano, 1974), and the motoneurons of the neck (Wilson, Gacek, Maeda, & Uchino, 1977). These connections mediate postural reflexes. In addition, second-order neurons send fibers to the oculomotor nuclei where they mediate eye-movement reflexes associated with head tilt and linear acceleration (Baker, Precht, & Berthoz, 1973; Schwindt, Richter, & Precht, 1973).

1.5. Psychophysics of Linear Acceleration

1.5.1. Procedures. People are constantly exposed to a linear accelerative force of 1 g_n (9.8 m·sec^{-2}), except for brief periods when they fall or are accelerated in a vehicle. Any determination of the threshold for linear acceleration on earth must therefore be made with respect to a force of at least 1 g_n. Only in the weightless conditions of orbital flight can these thresholds be determined with respect to a zero baseline. Furthermore, any linear accelerative stimulus, whether produced by tilting or by accelerating a subject, does not stimulate only the otolith organs. The somesthetic receptors for touch and pressure and perhaps kinesthetic receptors in muscles and joints are also stimulated. Thus a threshold for linear acceleration is not necessarily an otolith threshold. The device used to accelerate the subject will almost certainly vibrate perceptibly when it begins to move, and the subject may detect these vibrations or the sounds they make before detecting the motion as such. One way to avoid this problem is to vibrate the device at all times, even when it is not moving.

There are two stimulus situations used in the determination of thresholds of linear acceleration. In one, subjects are exposed to an oscillating accelerative force produced by moving them to and fro over a fixed linear path. In the other, they are exposed to a constant linear accelerative force that differs in direction or magnitude, or both, with respect to a baseline condition. The baseline condition is usually the natural force of gravity acting through a specified axis of the body. There are three procedures for achieving maintained alterations in the linear accelerative force acting on the body.

1. The first method is to tilt the subject in a specified plane through a specified angle. If the "upright" posture is one in which the utricular maculae are horizontal, the direction of body tilt specifies the direction of the linear-acceleration vector acting on the statoconial membrane, and the sine of the angle of tilt specifies the magnitude of the shear force.

2. The second method is to rotate the subject in a centrifuge at angular velocity ω, at distance r from the center of rotation, to produce a centrifugal accelerative vector of magnitude $\omega^2 r$. The resultant of the orthogonal centrifugal and gravitational forces is a linear vector of magnitude $\{(\omega^2 r)^2 + g_n{}^2\}^{1/2}$ acting at an angle of arc tan $(\omega^2 r/g_n)$ to the vertical.

For small values of $\omega^2 r$, the increase in vector magnitude is small, and the main factor is its change in direction. If the subject's body remains in line with gravity, then as far as the otolith organs are concerned, the effects of low-magnitude centrifugation are very similar to those produced by tilting the stationary body through arc tan $(\omega^2 r/g_n)$. The associated response of the semicircular canals is different in the two situations. When a person is tilted, the canals that lie in the plane of tilt respond during the tilting motion, and should provide an extra cue to tilt, which may contaminate the linear-threshold determination. In the centrifuge there are no accelerative forces acting in the plane of force displacement. However, the subject's body rotates about a vertical axis every time the centrifuge rotates, and, although the plane of this rotation is orthogonal to the displacement of the linear vector, the turning sensations may distract the subject. Furthermore, if the head is allowed to move, the subject experiences disturbing Coriolis effects (see Section 2.2) owing to the vectorial cross-coupling between the imposed rotation and the self-induced rotation. If one is interested in studying the effects of varying only the direction of a linear vector, it is a cheaper and better procedure to tilt subjects rather than to centrifuge them.

For large values of $\omega^2 r$, the increase in the resultant force becomes the dominant stimulus factor, and the centrifuge provides a unique method for subjecting a person to forces in excess of 1 g_n for long periods of time. Furthermore, the subject's body axis may be inclined at any desired angle with respect to the resultant force. Note that the potentially distracting effects of rotation and Coriolis forces are still present, and if the otolith organs on the two sides of the body lie at different distances from the center of rotation, they are stimulated unequally. Furthermore, a subject moving toward the center of rotation is exposed to a linear Coriolis force acting tangentially in the direction of rotation. A subject moving away from the center of rotation is exposed to a Coriolis force acting in the opposite direction (see Fig. 18.36 in Chapter 18, "The Perception of Posture, Self Motion, and the Visual Vertical").

After the rotation of a centrifuge has started, it takes several seconds before sensations of body tilt are felt, whereas tilt sensations induced by an equivalent tilt of the body are felt immediately. The reason for this is that the absence of appropriate rotary stimuli during the initial period of rotation in the centrifuge informs subjects that they are not actually being tilted. I shall discuss this point more fully in Chapter 18.

3. The third method for producing a sustained linear accelerative stimulus is to accelerate the subject along a linear track in a defined direction with respect to gravity and with respect to the subject's body axis. Long, smooth, linear tracks are expensive and difficult to construct. If a subject is accelerated at a m·sec^{-2} along a horizontal track, the direction of the resultant linear vector is displaced from vertical in the direction of motion through arc tan (a/g_n). Because the component vectors are orthogonal, the magnitude of the resultant vector is increased to $\{a^2 + g_n{}^2\}^{1/2}$. For acceleration along a vertical track the magnitude of the force is changed to $g_n + a$ or $g_n - a$, depending on whether the motion is upward or downward. The direction of the resultant vector is unchanged in this case, although the direction in which it acts on the otolith organs may be controlled by adjusting the orientation of the subject's head. There are no rotary stimuli accompanying horizontal or vertical linear acceleration, and if the track is smooth and the acceleration is free from detectable transients, linear acceleration, especially in a vertical direction, is the least contaminated procedure for measuring thresholds for linear acceleration. The main drawback is that a constant stimulus can be maintained for only a short period of time.

The other type of stimulus used to measure thresholds for linear acceleration is an oscillating acceleration back and forth over a fixed linear path. The velocity profile is usually sinusoidal, but other profiles are possible. With any sinusoidal oscillation, velocity is 90° out of phase with displacement and acceleration. The *parallel swing* is a convenient apparatus for producing sinusoidal linear oscillations without rotary stimulation (see Fig. 11.8). The peak acceleration, which occurs momentarily twice during each cycle, is given by $f^2\theta$, where f is the frequency (in radians per second) and θ the amplitude of oscillation. For moderate accelerations, the periodic variation in the magnitude of the resultant linear vector is small compared with the variation in its direction.

The type of judgment that subjects are asked to make depends on the stimulus. When tilted or rotated in a centrifuge, subjects are usually asked to report when the body first feels that it is tilted relative to its position before stimulation was applied. When accelerated along a track or oscillated back and forth, they are usually asked to report the first sensations of motion or indicate the direction in which they are moving. Note that the threshold for the first sensation of motion is lower than that for reporting the correct direction of motion, which in turn is usually lower than that for the first feelings of being tilted (Jongkees & Groen, 1946).

1.5.2. Thresholds for Linear Acceleration. Perhaps the most satisfactory procedure for measuring thresholds for linear acceleration is to accelerate a subject along a linear track and determine how long each of several accelerations must be maintained before the subject reports the correct direction of motion on a given percentage of occasions. The absolute threshold is that acceleration for which the response latency becomes very long. Figure 11.9 shows the response latency as a function of linear vertical acceleration for subjects in an erect seated posture (Melvill Jones & Young, 1978). It can be seen that the latency becomes long at an acceleration of less than 0.01 g_n. It was inferred from the function relating acceleration to latency that a particular linear *velocity* has to be achieved before a sensation of movement is reported. The mean value of this velocity was reported as 2.16 m·sec^{-1}. Melvill Jones and Young compared their results for acceleration of a seated subject along a vertical path with previous determinations for subjects moved along a horizontal path (Young & Meiry, 1968) and found that they were similar. This suggests that the utricles have about the same sensitivity as the saccules, a conclusion at variance with the results of electrophysiological studies which, as we saw in Section 1.3, show that the receptors in the utricles are more sensitive than those in the saccules. For some unknown

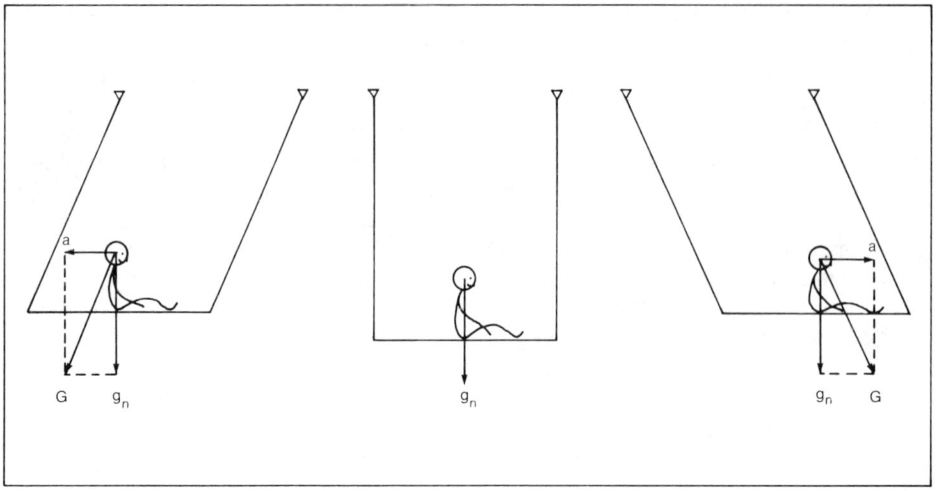

Figure 11.8. The parallel swing used to stimulate the otolith organs sinusoidally. *G* is the resultant of the force due to the applied acceleration, *a*, and that due to gravity g_n. (From L. B. W. Jongkees, On the physiology and examination of the vestibular labyrinths, in R. F. Nauton (Ed.), *The vestibular system*, Academic Press, Inc., 1975. Reprinted with permission.)

reason, subjects are more likely to be confused about the direction of a vertical motion than about that of a horizontal one (Malcolm & Melvill Jones, 1974), even though the direction of the reflex oculomotor response is unambiguously related to the direction of vertical linear acceleration (Melvill Jones, Rolph, & Downing, 1980).

Thresholds for oscillating linear motion, as indicated by the first reported sensation of motion, have been obtained for motion along horizontal and along vertical tracks, with the subject's x, y, or z body axis parallel to the direction of motion. Some of these determinations are shown in Table 11.1. A threshold value of 10 cm·sec^{-2} is equivalent to a utricular shear force of about 0.01 g_n per unit mass. It is not easy to compare these different determinations because the direction and period of the oscillatory motion varied from study to study.

Young and Meiry (1968) developed a servomodel of the otolith system, based on threshold data from experiments in which human subjects were required to report the direction of constant linear acceleration. The model successfully matched several aspects of the subjects' responses, including the variation in response latency as a function of linear acceleration and the continuing sensations of tilt or motion induced by step changes in acceleration. Such models must not be thought of as models of the dynamics of the sensory end organ, because all behaviorally

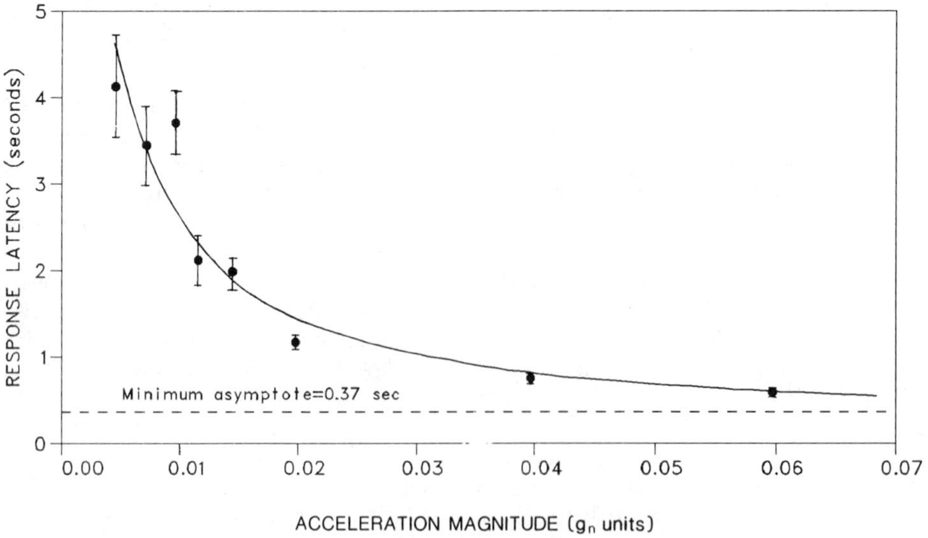

Figure 11.9. Latency of detection of vertical acceleration as a function of rate of acceleration. Based on means of eight subjects (bars give standard errors). The solid line is the regression line fitted to the average latencies according to the relation $T = B/A + T_{min}$ (where T = latency; A = acceleration; T_{min} = latency asymptote; B = slope of regression line when plotting T against $1/A$). B has the dimensions of linear velocity and these results support the conclusion that a constant velocity of 0.022 g_n·sec (i.e., 0.216 m·sec^{-1}) has to be achieved before a sensation is reported. (From G. Melvill Jones & L. R. Young, Subjective detection of vertical acceleration: A velocity-dependent response, *Acta Otolaryngologica*, 1978, *85*. Reprinted with permission.)

Table 11.1. Human Thresholds for the Detection of Linear Acceleration

Investigator	Posture of Subjects	Axis of Oscillation	Period of Oscillation (sec)	Number of Subjects	Maximum Acceleration at Threshold[a] ($cm \cdot sec^{-2}$)
Mach (1875)	Upright	Vertical	7	1	10–12
Travis & Dodge (1928)	Firmly seated facing movement	Horizontal	2–8	2	20–25
	Standing facing movement	Horizontal	2–8	2	8
	Standing sideways to movement	Horizontal	2–8	2	5
Walsh (1962)	Supine	Horizontal	3	13	8.2 (5.9)
	Prone	Horizontal	3	13	7.0 (6.8)
Walsh (1964)	Supine	Vertical	4	7	6.3 (2.7)
	Prone	Vertical	4	7	5.5 (1.9)
Parker, Gulledge, Tubbs, & Littlefield (1978)	Prone	Horizontal	2.6	6	6–12

[a] The threshold represents the peak acceleration of linear sinusoidal motion of the whole body at which subjects reliably detected the motion. The numbers represent the range of threshold values or mean values. Numbers in parentheses indicate standard deviations across subjects.

Travis and Dodge obtained unusually high thresholds for subjects firmly strapped in a seated posture. However, subjects seated without restraint showed thresholds like those reported for freely standing subjects. It can be seen that in most other studies thresholds were about 6 $cm \cdot sec^{-2}$ and did not vary to any great extent with the axis of motion or the posture of the body.

determined thresholds involve a verbal report of a consciously perceived sensation and are therefore thresholds, not only of the sensory end organ, but also of the peripheral and central neural processes involved in generating whichever response is evoked. These neural processes are subject to adaptation and are influenced by events in other sensory systems as well as by factors such as attention and criterion shifts. It is therefore not possible to infer the dynamic properties of the otolith organs from these threshold values. In particular, the long latencies of reports of motion that occur for low rates of acceleration do not imply that the maculae are sluggish in responding to the stimulus. Available data suggest that the maculae are quick to respond, so that delays in report must be due to neural factors, such as the restraining influence of other sensory inputs that conflict with the otolith inputs, for example, those from the semicircular canals. It has been reported that the threshold for linear acceleration temporarily increased following a period of sustained oscillating linear acceleration (Parker, Gulledge, Tubbs, & Littlefield, 1978). It is not clear what caused this change in threshold; it was apparently not due to adaptation of tonic receptors, because there was no change in the threshold after 10 min of maintained unidirectional linear acceleration in a centrifuge.

Magnitude-estimation methods reveal how sensations vary with stimulus magnitude, and thus indicate how the system responds at suprathreshold as well as threshold levels. The subject is asked to rate the magnitude of the stimulus, and the logarithm of the estimates (ordinate) is plotted against the logarithm of the stimulus magnitude. The slope of the resulting function gives an estimate of the exponent in the function $R = kS^n$, where R is the response magnitude indicating the strength of the sensation and S the stimulus magnitude, which in the case of rotary acceleration is equal to the product of head acceleration and the duration over which it is applied (see Stevens & Galanter, 1957). A large value of n (steep slope of the function) indicates that small changes in stimulus magnitude produce large differences in sensation. In one recent study, magnitude estimates of the amplitude of sinusoidal linear oscillation of the body were plotted against the physical displacement of the parallel swing. Mean exponents of the power function varied between 1.45 and 2.2. By comparison, exponents of between 1.3 and 1.5 have generally been found for sensations of rotary acceleration (see Section 2.5.1.2). The exponent was found to be smaller when the subject's head was vertical than when it was tilted, and the exponent was found to increase after a prolonged period of oscillation (Parker, Wood, Gulledge, & Goodrich, 1979).

The results of studies involving tilting or centrifuging subjects are presented in Chapter 18.

2. THE VESTIBULAR CANALS

2.1. The Structure of the Vestibular Canals

Within the temporal bone on each side of the head there are three vestibular canals, roughly at right angles to each other. There are a horizontal canal and two vertical canals. The vertical canals are sometimes referred to as the posterior and anterior canals and sometimes as the inferior and superior canals, respectively. The canals are usually called *semicircular canals*, but the prefix "semi" is misleading because, although they share a common cavity in the utricle, each canal functions as a complete and independent fluid circuit (see Fig. 11.10). The cavity, or *lumen*, of each canal is elliptical in cross section with a mean diameter of about 0.3 mm. The horizontal and posterior canals of humans have a radius of curvature of between 1.6 and 1.9 mm. The anterior canal is larger, with a radius of curvature of about 2.2 mm (Curthoys, Blanks, & Markham, 1977a).

When a person holds the head in a natural erect posture, the fore-aft diameter of each horizontal canal is almost horizontal and inclined about 25° forward with respect to the Horsley-Clark stereotaxic plane (the plane through the lower margins of the orbits of the eyes and the auditory canals). The side-to-side diameter of each canal is tipped down laterally about 9°. The posterior (inferior) vertical canal lies in an almost vertical plane which forms an angle of 45° to the frontal plane of the head, and the anterior (superior) canal lies in a plane inclined

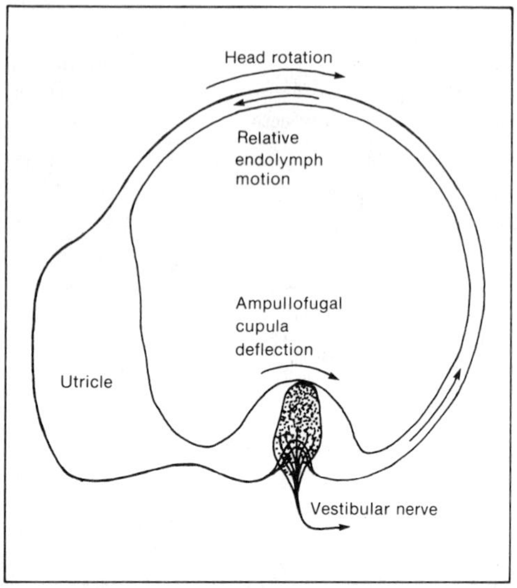

Figure 11.10. Diagram of a vestibular canal showing the complete fluid circuit. The arrows depict the consequences of a clockwise rotation of the head in the plane of the canal. At ordinary levels of threshold the cupula does not deflect as shown in the diagram, but acts like a diaphragm, with the apex not moving. (From J. H. Milsum & G. Melvill Jones, Dynamic asymmetry in neural components of the vestibular system, *Annals of the New York Academy of Sciences*, 1969, *156*. Reprinted with permission.)

at an angle of about 15° to the vertical and which also forms an angle of 45° to the frontal plane (Curthoys et al., 1977b). Each canal has a partner on the other side of the head with which it is most nearly parallel, and which is known as its *synergist*. The three synergistic pairs are the two horizontal canals, the left anterior and right posterior canals, and the left posterior and right anterior canals (see Fig. 11.11). The canals on one side are not exactly at right angles and synergists are not precisely parallel, so that there is no plane of head rotation that stimulates only one pair of synergists (see Blanks, Curthoys, & Markham, 1975).

At one point of each canal, near its junction with the utricle, the *lumen* of the canal swells to form the *ampulla*, which contains the sensory epithelium, or *crista ampullaris*. A crista is a ridge of epithelium protruding into the lumen of the ampulla, carrying many multiciliated sensory cells interspersed with structural cells. The cilia on all the cells project into a common gelatinous fibrillar structure, or *cupula*. The cupula reaches to the far side of the ampulla, which is arched at this point (see Fig. 11.10 and 11.12). When the head is turned in the plane of a canal the endolymph lags behind the walls of the canal and thus flows relative to the walls in a direction opposite to that in which the head is turning. Displacements of the endolymph caused by normal rotations of the head are not sufficient to displace the apex of the cupula; instead they cause the cupula to bulge like a diaphragm (Hillman & McLaren, 1979; McLaren & Hillman, 1979).

2.2. Dynamics of the Vestibular Canals

Consider what happens when a person rotates the head with an angular acceleration of α in the plane of a particular vestibular canal. If H is the moment of inertia of the endolymph and cupula, then the force acting on the cupula is αH. This force displaces the endolymph and cupula through a certain angle, θ', around the canal. To a first approximation the force is related to the displacement by the well-known differential equation for the torsion pendulum,

$$\alpha H = k\theta + r\frac{d\theta}{dt} + H\frac{d^2\theta}{dt^2}$$

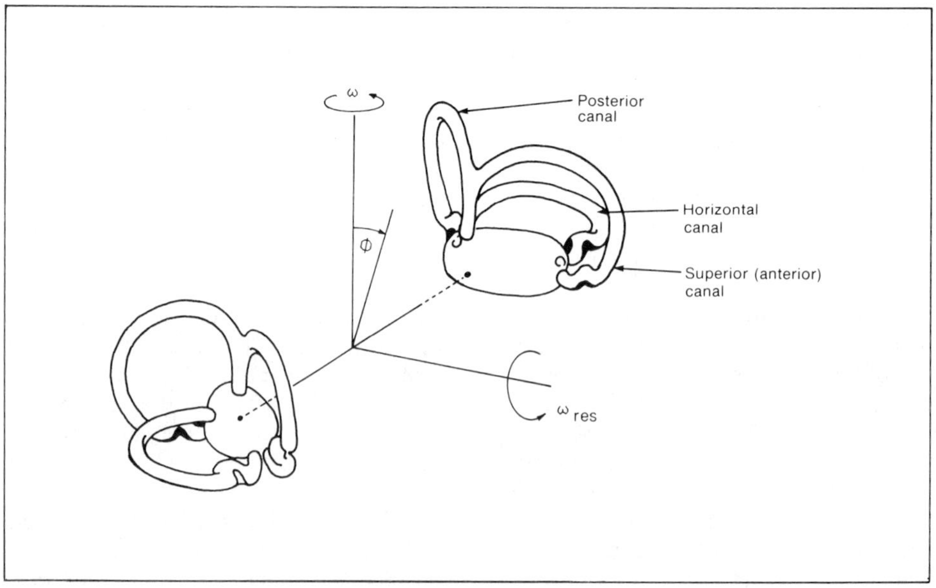

Figure 11.11. Demonstrating cross-coupling between head tilt and body rotation. The head is rotating around a vertical axis at an angular velocity of ω, and the head is suddenly inclined forward through an angle ϕ. A resultant momentum drives the endolymph clockwise and produces a sensation that the head is being tilted to the left through an angle equivalent to a stimulus intensity of $\omega_{res} = \omega\{(1 - \cos\phi)^2 + 2\sin^2\phi\}^{1/2}$. (Adapted from J. J. Groen, The problems of the spinning top applied to semi-circular canals, *Confinia Neurologica*, 1961, *21*. Reprinted with permission.)

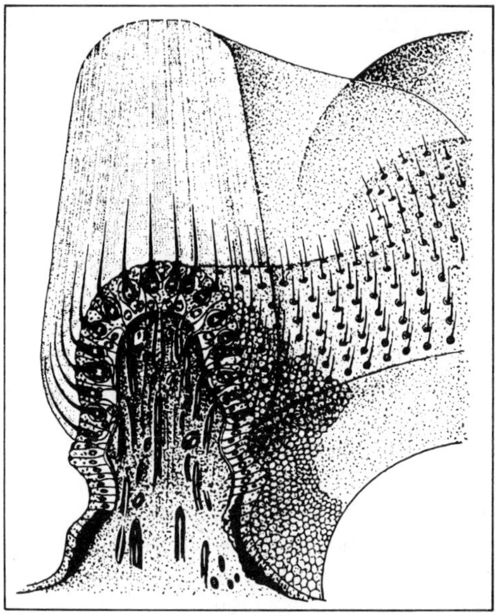

Figure 11.12. Schematic drawing of one-half of a crista ampullaris, showing innervation of its epithelium. Thick nerve fibers form nerve calyxes around type I hair cells at the summit of the crista; medium-caliber fibers innervate type I hair cells on the slopes of the crista; medium-caliber and fine nerve fibers form a nerve plexus innervating hair cells of type II. The sensory hairs pass from the hair cells into fine canals in the cupula, which is separated from the epithelium by a narrow subcupular space. (From J. Wersäll, Studies on the structure and innervation of the sensory epithelium of the cristae ampullaris in the guinea pig, *Acta Otolaryngologica*, 1956, *126* (Suppl). Reprinted with permission.)

in which k is the coefficient of elastic, or position-dependent, resistance, r is the coefficient of viscous, or velocity-dependent, resistance, and H the moment of inertia, or coefficient of mass-dependent resistance, of the cupula and endolymph (Mayne, 1950). A more precise equation that takes the presence of the utricular bulge and the elliptical section of the canal duct into account has been proposed by Oman (1981, pp. 251–274). An approximate value for the moment of inertia of the cupula and endolymph may be calculated from the volume and specific gravity of the endolymph and the mean radius of the canal torus. One estimate is 2.4×10^{-4}g·cm^{-2} (Oman & Young, 1972). The coefficient of viscous resistance may be calculated from Poiseuille's law, and is given by

$$r = 16\, V^2 R^3$$

where V is the viscosity of the endolymph and R is the radius of the canal torus. One estimate yields 0.043 dyne·cm^{-1}·sec^{-1} (Steer, Li, Young, & Meiry, 1967). It has not been possible to calculate the coefficient of elasticity of the cupula because its displacement is at most only about 10 μm and is therefore difficult to observe. However, estimates of this constant have been derived from behavioral measures or from the characteristics of the discharge from primary vestibular afferents. In spite of this lack of precise information, certain general conclusions about the response of the cupula are possible.

Because the lumen of a human vestibular canal is only about 0.3 mm in mean diameter, the viscous resistance is high even for moderate velocities and the mass of the endolymph is small. Furthermore, the elasticity of the cupula is small compared with the viscous resistance. Thus the first and last terms of the torsion-pendulum equation become vanishingly small compared with the second term, and we may write

$$\alpha H = r\frac{d\theta}{dt}.$$

Because H and r are constants, it may be concluded that $d\theta/dt$ is proportional to α or the angular velocity of the cupula is proportional to head acceleration. By integration of both sides of this relationship with respect to time, it follows that the angular displacement of the cupula is proportional to the angular velocity of the head. In other words, the vestibular canals are integrating accelerometers, that is, angular speedometers. Thus at the velocities and durations of normal head rotations, the canals are detectors of angular velocity. When the head rotates very slowly, the viscous resistance becomes smaller than the inertial resistance, so that the third term of the basic differential equation becomes the dominant factor and the response of the system becomes proportional to the acceleration of the head (Melvill Jones, 1976, pp. 3–18). When the head rotates for a period of less than about 3 sec the velocity signals are integrated in the central nervous system to yield a reasonably accurate estimate of the angle through which the head has turned.

The small bore and high viscous resistance of the canal have several advantages. They keep the flow of endolymph smooth, or nonturbulent. They provide viscous damping, which prevents the system from oscillating. They reduce the flow of endolymph and keep the deflection of the cupula within a small range, where its characteristics are most linear and best suited to the process of deforming organic molecules, which is presumably the crucial event. Calculations show that the cupula deflection lies in the range 0.9–5 μm for normal movements of the head (Oman & Young, 1972). The small bore of the canals also reduces the latency of the cupula deflection and helps to keep the deflection in phase with changes in head rotation.

From a behavioral point of view, the important parameters of the physical response of the vestibular canals are their *latency*, *recovery time*, *phase lag*, and *gain*. I shall describe briefly each of these parameters.

2.2.1. Latency. The *latency* of the deflection of the cupula may be defined as the time taken for the defection to reach $1/e$ of its maximum value after a sudden change in the angular velocity of the head, where e is the base of the natural logarithm. This time is given by the *inertial time constant* of the cupula, which is the ratio H/r. This is also known as the *short time constant*. Calculations based on physical measurements in humans (van Egmond, Groen, & Jongkees, 1949) and recordings of the latency of response in the primary sensory neurons of monkeys (Fernández & Goldberg, 1971) have produced values of the short time constant in the range 3–5 msec.

2.2.2. Recovery Time. The time taken for the cupula to regain its normal resting position after cessation of a stimulus is governed by the *elastic time constant*, r/k, also known as the *long time constant*. It is difficult to measure directly, but is estimated by recording the rate of decline of the discharge from primary sensory nerve fibers after the accelerative stimulus has ceased. For the nonadapting, or tonic, receptors of the monkey, this procedure gives a value of the long time constant of 3.8 sec (Goldberg & Fernández, 1971a). Estimates of the long-time constant in man have been based on the persistence of oculomotor responses to vestibular stimulation. But these estimates are at least three times as long as the one just mentioned, which suggests that the persisting oculomotor response does not reflect the restoration time of the cupula, but rather the time taken for central neural events to subside. This suggestion is supported by evidence that will be cited in Section 2.5.1.1.

There is some evidence that with repeated exposure to rotation the long time constant of post-rotatory nystagmus declines to an asymptotic value of about 7 sec, which is close to the value of the long time constant of the cupula. It looks as though repetitive stimulation reduces the neural component of the long time constant to zero (Blair & Gavin, 1979).

2.2.3. Phase Lag. The vestibular canal is essentially a control system in which an input signal (head rotation) is transduced into an output (cupula deflection). The analysis of any control system is simplified if we assume it to be a linear system, which may be defined in terms of its response to sinusoidal inputs. Any time-varying signal, however complex, may be synthesized by superposing a set of simple sinusoids with the correct frequencies, amplitudes, and relative phases. The sinusoidal components of a complex signal are known as its *Fourier components*, and their mathematical derivation from the signal is known as *Fourier analysis*. A *linear system* is one in which the relative frequencies of the Fourier components of an input signal emerge unchanged in the output. If the response of a linear system to a range of sine-wave inputs is known, its response to complex signals can be computed. That is why sinusoidal inputs are useful for analyzing the behavior of linear control systems (see Chapter 6 by Watson).

To describe the properties of a linear control system, we must decide which time function of the input and the output are of interest. In the case of the cupula system it is usual to describe the input signal as a function relating head *velocity* and time. Stimuli used in testing the dynamic properties of the system usually consist of to-and-fro rotations of the head with a fixed amplitude and sinusoidal velocity profile. The output is described as the *displacement* of the cupula as a function of time. With such measures, the *phase shift* of the system is defined as the phase angle between the input function for a defined frequency and the output function when the two functions are superimposed on the same time abscissa. In other words, phase shift defines the extent to which cupula displacement leads or lags behind head velocity. The phase shift varies as a function of the input frequency, and a plot of this function is known as a phase *Bode plot* [see Fig. 11.13(b)].

2.2.4. Gain. The *gain* of the cupula system is defined as the ratio of cupula displacement to head velocity. The gain of a system indicates its *sensitivity*. Where input and output measures differ, some arbitrary ratio may be selected as representing a gain of 1; other values then express *relative gain*. A plot of log gain as a function of input frequency is a *Bode plot of gain* [see Fig. 11.13(a)]. The *transfer function* of a linear control system is a function that describes the phase shift and gain of the system over a range of input frequencies. The transfer function of the cupula is embodied in the torsion-pendulum equation although it is usually expressed in a computationally simpler form known as the *Laplace transform* of the function, denoted by the symbol s.

$$\frac{\theta}{\alpha}(s) = \frac{1}{(T_1 s + 1)(T_2 s + 1)}$$

where θ is the gain of the system, that is, displacement of the cupula per unit of head acceleration, T_1 is the short-time constant, and T_2 is the long-time constant. Numerical solutions are readily available for Laplace transforms, and it is easy to combine transfer functions from different parts of a control system when these functions are expressed in this form. (See Toates, 1975, and Chapter 39 by Wickens for an introduction to these methods. Barnes, 1980, pp. 3–40, and Wilson and Melvill Jones, 1979, show how they are applied in detail to the vestibular system.)

I have already remarked that the range of frequencies of head rotation for which cupula displacement is a function of head velocity is approximately 0.1–5.0 Hz. It can be seen from Figure 11.13(b) that the phase of cupula displacement relative to head velocity is constant over this same range. This means that cupula displacement keeps in step with changes in head velocity over this range. Below this range of frequencies, cupula displacement *leads* head velocity. At very low frequencies the phase lead reaches a limiting value of 90° and it is at this point that cupula displacement becomes proportional to head acceleration. Above the frequency range of natural head movements the cupula displacement *lags* behind head velocity up to a limiting value of 90°, at which point cupula displacement is proportional to head displacement.

It is estimated that the gain of the cupula system is at a maximum and constant over the same range of natural head movements that the phase lag is zero. Above and below this range gain falls off; in other words, the system becomes less sensitive to changes in head velocity.

When a person is rotated at a constant angular velocity for some time, the friction between the endolymph and the canal walls, coupled with the elasticity of the cupula, causes the cupula to become restored to its resting position. After this has happened, the rotation is no longer sensed by the vestibular system. If the person is now decelerated and brought to rest, the inertia of the endolymph displaces the cupula in a direction opposite to that in which it was displaced during the initial acceleration of the body. It can take up to several minutes before the behavioral effects of this deceleratory deflection are dissipated, although the cupula itself regains its central position in a shorter time than this. During about the initial 30 sec of the recovery period, people behave as if they were rotating; they fall to one side, the eyes move nystagmically, they experience turning sensations in the opposite direction to the motion, and perhaps they experience nausea. There follow one or more phases in which the direction of nystagmus and sensations of turning are reversed. If an acceleration is followed immediately by a deceleration, as is usually the case when a person turns voluntarily, the two opposed deflections of the cupulae and the two opposed neural events tend to cancel, leaving little residual deflection or aftereffects (see Chapter 18 for more details about these aftereffects).

If, while a person is being turned steadily, the head rotates out of the plane of primary rotation, the two superposed angular momenta resolve into one at an angle to both components. Anyone who has tried to turn the axis of a spinning wheel or top at right angles to itself will have noticed that the axis tends to rotate at right angles both to itself and to the manually applied torque. This resultant motion is known as precession and the forces that produce it are called *Coriolis forces* (see also Section 1.5.1). The two rotations are said to be cross-coupled. Consider the events on one side of the head when a person is rotated to the left at a steady angular velocity, in the plane of the horizontal canal. If the head is quickly inclined forward through an angle ϕ, the two vertical canals project themselves as narrow ellipses

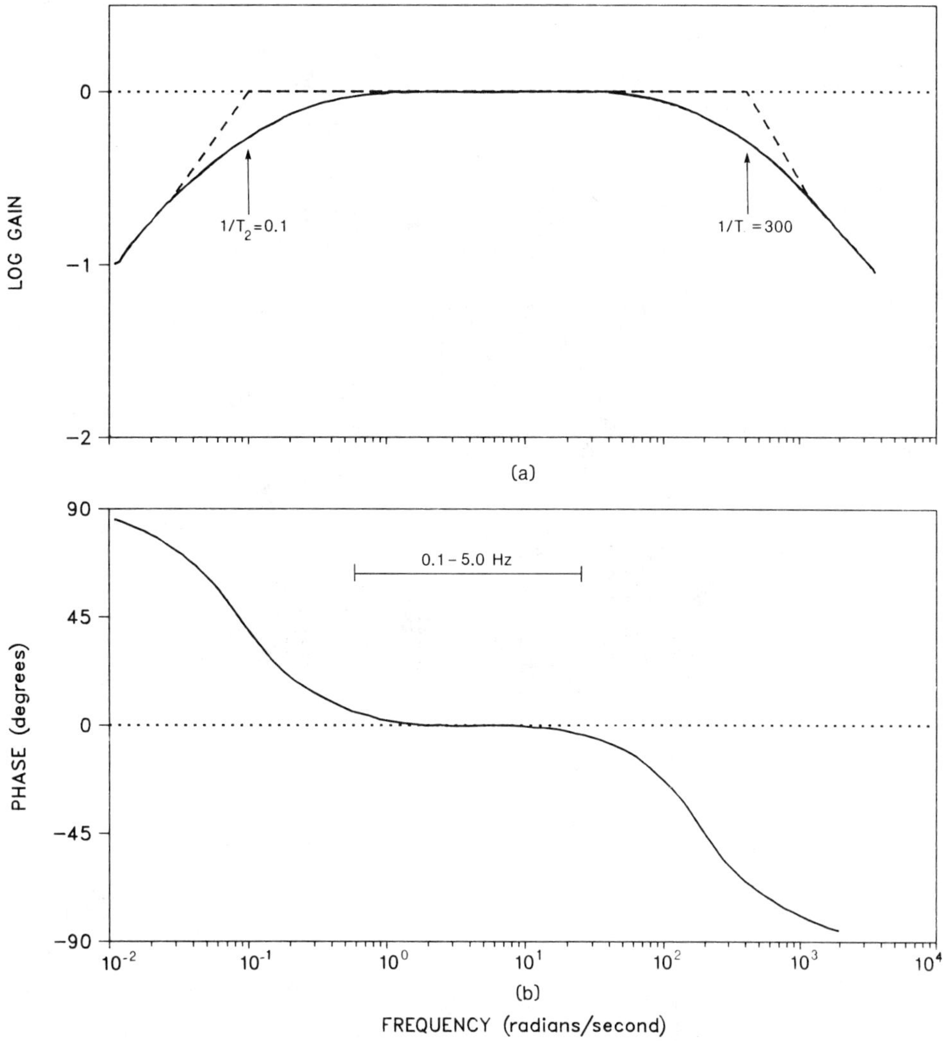

Figure 11.13. Gain (a) and phase (b) Bode plots derived theoretically from the simple torsion-pendulum equation of cupula dynamics. The gain is the degree of cupular deflection per unit of head velocity and the phase is the phase angle between the point of maximum cupula deflection and the point of maximum head velocity. (From G. Melvill Jones & J. H. Milsum, Spatial and dynamic aspects of visual fixation, *IEEE Transactions in Biomedical Engineering, BME-12*. Copyright 1965 by the IEEE. Reprinted with permission.)

in the plane of the original rotation and each becomes subject to a momentum component of that rotation of $\omega \sin \phi$. The horizontal canal moves slightly out of the plane of rotation and loses a fraction of its original momentum, resulting in a change of $\omega\ (1 - \cos \phi)$ (see Fig. 11.11). These three changes in momentum add like vectors to produce a resultant momentum proportional to

$$\omega\{(1 - \cos \phi)^2 + 2 \sin^2 \phi\}^{1/2} .$$

The resultant momentum acts in the plane of head tilt in a direction toward the right shoulder and hence produces a sensation that the head is being tilted to the left. Illusory sensations of this kind are very disturbing and result in illusory movements of the visual surroundings, nausea, and extreme discomfort (Collins, 1968; Melvill Jones, 1970; Reason & Graybiel, 1971). Coriolis inputs from the canals should not in themselves induce nausea, because they resemble the inputs from a true rotation of the head in an equivalent direction. The nausea must result from the conflict between the canal inputs, which produce a nonveridical signal of head tilt, and the otolith, visual, and kinesthetic inputs that signal the veridical direction of head inclination. If movements of the head are confined to the plane of the rotation of the body, these effects are avoided.

2.3. The Afferent Signal from Vestibular Canals

2.3.1. The Basic Response. The microstructure of the sensory epithelium of a crista ampullaris is shown diagramatically in Figure 11.14. The epithelium, like that of the maculae of the otolith organs, consists of sensory hair cells interspersed with structural cells. Here, as in the macula, there are two types of hair cell. *Type I cells* are flask-shaped and almost totally enclosed, singly or several together, in a goblet-shaped nerve chalice. Each nerve chalice feeds into a single nerve fiber in the cristal nerve, usually a large-diameter nerve fiber. *Type II hair cells* are cylindrical, and most of them are innervated by sensory cells with small-diameter fibers, each with several knob-shaped nerve endings (Wersäll & Bagger-Sjöbäck, 1974, pp. 123–170). A single type II cell may be innervated by several nerve fibers and a given nerve may innervate several sensory cells, sometimes a mixture of type I and type II cells (see Wilson

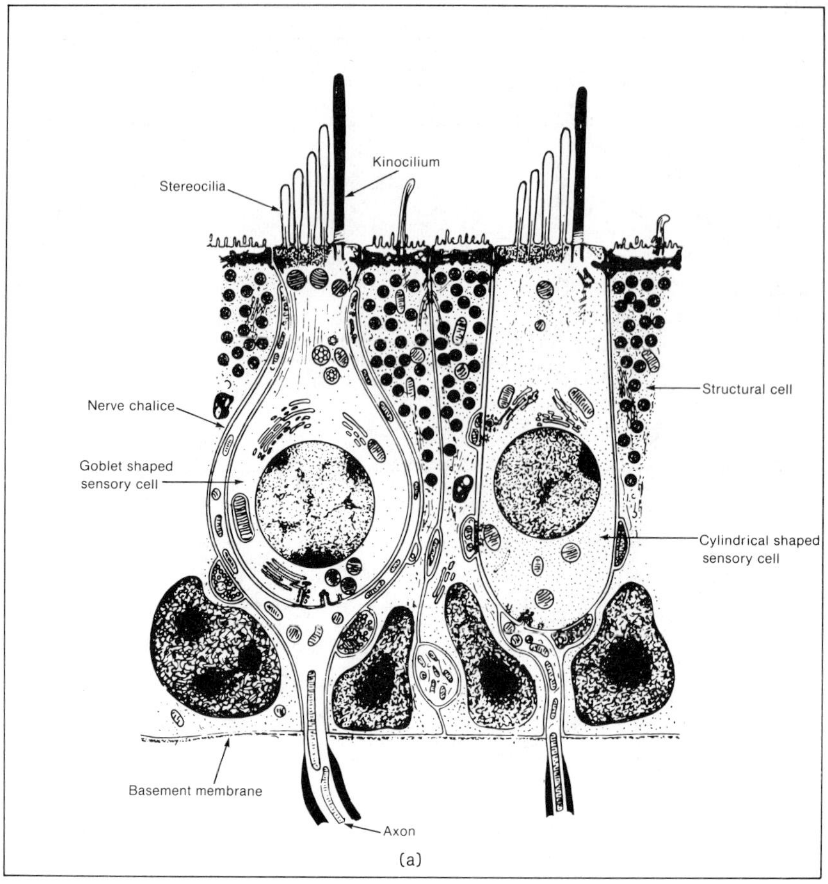

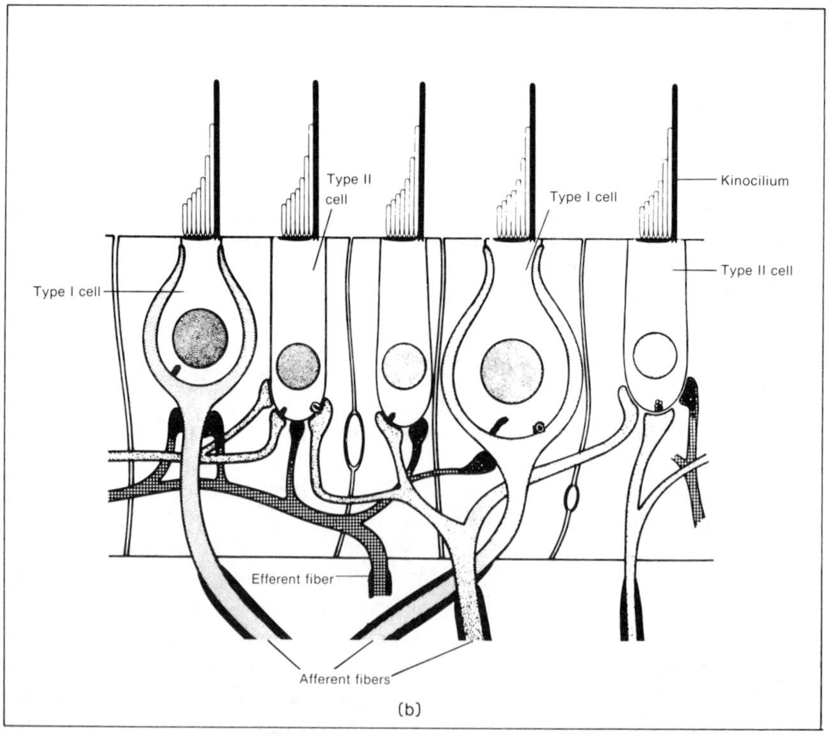

Figure 11.14. (a) Diagramatic representation of the detailed structure of the sensory epithelia of the vestibular system. These figures are based on observations made on the utricle of the squirrel monkey, but the cells of the maculae and cristae have a very similar structure. (b) Schematic representation of afferent and efferent nerve fibers in the end organs of the vestibular system. The flask-shaped type I cells are enclosed in a nerve chalice formed from a large-diameter afferent nerve fiber. Cylindrical type II cells usually feed into a small-diameter nerve fiber. (From H. Engström, B. Bergström, & H. W. Ades, Macula utriculi and maculi sacculi in the squirrel monkey, *Acta Otolaryngologica*, 1972, *301* (Suppl.). Reprinted with permission.)

& Melvill Jones, 1979, p. 35). Type II cells and the nerve chalice of type I cells are also innervated by efferent neurons, that is, neurons that carry impulses from the central nervous system to the peripheral organ. The functional significance of the efferent neurons remains obscure. It has been claimed that they originate in the olivary and vestibular nuclei and are capable of inhibiting the response of sensory cells, but others have suggested that vestibular efferents are parasympathetic fibers of the facial nerve with merely trophic functions (see Klinke & Galley, 1974, and Ross, 1981, pp. 160–183, for a discussion of these issues).

Each sensory cell projects about 70 fine cilia into the cupula mass; these *stereocilia* are distinguishable from a single, larger *kinocilium* in each cell. The stereocilia on each cell are packed into a tight bundle within which they are graded in length toward the kinocilium, which occurs on one side of the bundle, as shown in Figure 11.14. The membrane that covers each cilium is continuous with the membrane that covers the rest of the cell. In the guinea pig a *resting potential* of about 160 mV exists across the cell membrane; the cell interior is negative with respect to the contents of the cupula. This is a higher value than that reported for the cell membrane of the otolith organs (see Section 1.3). This potential is due partly to a polarization of the cell membrane and partly to a concentration of positive ions in the endolymph. Microelectrode studies have revealed that a defection of the cupula in one direction is accompanied by a *depolarization*, or decrease, of the resting potential, and that a defection in the other direction is accompanied by a *hyperpolarization*, or increase, in the resting potential (Trincker, 1962, pp. 289–316). Depolarization of the cell membrane increases the frequency of nerve impulses in the primary afferent nerve above its resting level, and hyperpolarization decreases impulse frequency below the resting level (see Table 11.2). It is thought to be the shearing movement of the cilia, produced by the deflection of the cupula in a given plane, that alters the resting potential; if the cilia are deflected at right angles to their normal plane of action or stretched, the resting potential is not affected (Flock, 1965). Lowenstein and Wersäll (1959) found that the kinocilium of cells of the cristae, like that of cells of the maculae, is always situated on that side of the stereocilia that points in the direction of depolarizing (excitatory) cupula deflection. In any one cupula each kinocilium lies on the same side of its group of stereocilia and each set of stereocilia increases in length in this direction. Some aspect of this structural symmetry must surely be responsible for the bidirectional response of the cupula within a defined plane of rotation. Malcolm (1974) has proposed a model of how this system may work. In the horizontal canals the kinocilia are all on the ampulla side of the stereocilia bundles, so that an *ampullopetal displacement* of the cupula depolarizes the cell membranes and increases each cell's rate of firing. In the vertical canals the kinocilia are on the side away from the ampulla, so that an *ampullofugal displacement* causes the rate of firing to increase in these canals.

Table 11.2. Sensory Events in a Horizontal Semicircular Canal on Rotating a Person to the Right in the Plane of the Canal

Right Canal (Ipsilateral)	Left Canal (Contralateral)
Ampullopetal deflection of cupula	Ampullofugal deflection of cupula
Hair cell membrane depolarized	Hair cell membrane hyperpolarized
Frequency of afferent firing increased above resting level	Frequency of afferent firing decreased below resting level

By recording from single afferent fibers arising from the hair cells of the vestibular system of the squirrel monkey, Goldberg, Fernández, and their collaborators have revealed the way in which cupula deflection is coded into a neural response (Fernández & Goldberg, 1971; Goldberg & Fernández, 1971a, 1971b). Vestibular afferents have a dynamic range of about 0–400 spikes per second, and within this range their sensitivities defined with respect to head acceleration have been found to vary between 0.82 and 3.57 spikes per second per unit of angular acceleration. It is of some interest to note that the sensitivity of the anterior canal in man has been found to be higher than that of the horizontal and posterior canals by an amount proportional to the larger radius of curvature of the anterior canal. There is some evidence that the relative sizes of the three canals are adjusted in different species according to the plane of head rotation to which members of each species are most sensitive (Curthoys et al., 1977a).

Most, if not all, vestibular afferents discharge even when the cupula is not deflected. In the monkey, this *resting discharge* has been found to average about 110 spikes per second, and to vary from cell to cell over a range of 18–160 spikes per second (Keller, 1976). As in the otolith organs, the resting discharge is very regular from moment to moment in some cells, which are therefore called *regular cells*, and variable in others, which are called *irregular cells*. The large-diameter fibers from type I (chalice) hair cells tend to fire irregularly and the thin fibers from type II (cylindrical) hair cells tend to fire regularly. The more stable firing rate of thin fibers may be due to their innervating more hair cells than do thick fibers (Curthoys, 1981; Goldberg & Fernández, 1977). The firing rate of regular cells is closely related to the amount of deflection of the cupula, whereas the firing rate of irregular cells is related to the velocity of cupula displacement as well as to the magnitude of its deflection. This difference reflects the fact that the firing rate of the irregular units adapts to steady displacement of the cupula, which is equivalent to a differentiation of cupular displacement. These differences between the two types of cell may be summed up by saying that the regular units are static, or *tonic receptors*, and the irregular units are dynamic, or *phasic receptors*. Regular tonic afferents have longer elastic time constants and lower sensitivities than do irregular phasic afferents (Goldberg & Fernández, 1971b; Malcolm & Melvill Jones, 1970; Tomko, Peterka, Schor, & O'Leary, 1981). The irregular units seem to be more primitive than the regular units; at least irregular units are present in large numbers in the neonate mammal, whereas most regular units develop later (Romand & Dauzat, 1982).

The function relating frequency of firing of primary afferents to cupula deflection is approximately linear over the middle of the range of deflections to which the cell is sensitive (Goldberg & Fernández, 1971a). At the lower end, firing rate cannot fall below zero and at the higher end it saturates at about 400 spikes per second. The resting discharge rate varies from cell to cell, and in different cells the linear portion of the curve occurs at different positions along the cupula deflection axis, so that there is a continuum of cell types that differ in the value of a "bias," analogous to the bias on an electronic vacuum tube. The net result is that the frequency of discharge of the whole set of primary afferents is a more or less linear function of cupula deflection (head velocity) over a wide range of deflection amplitudes.

The gain, or sensitivity, of the discharge of primary vestibular afferents defined with respect to head velocity is constant over the range of frequencies of normal head movements [see Fig. 11.15(a)]. It can be seen from the figure that at higher frequencies of head oscillation the velocity sensitivity of irregular units is higher than that of regular units. From Figure 11.15(b) it can be seen that the discharge of vestibular afferents keeps in phase with head velocity over approximately the same range of frequencies for which the gain is constant. The solid lines represent the functions to be expected if the afferent discharge were determined by a transfer function derived from the differential equation used to describe the dynamics of the cupula. In Laplace terminology this would be

$$\frac{AR(s)}{V(s)} = \frac{sT_c}{(sT_c + 1)}$$

where AR/V is the gain of the system, that is, the change in rate of neural discharge per unit of head velocity, and T_c is the short-time constant of the system. According to this equation the gain is unity in the higher-frequency range, with a phase lag of zero. At low frequencies of head oscillation, gain is proportional to head acceleration, with a phase lead that approaches 90°. The departure of the neural function for irregular units from the cupula function at low frequencies of head oscillation is due to neural adaptation, which is discussed more fully in Section 2.3.3. The high-frequency gain enhancement and phase advance evident in both neural functions relative to the cupula functions is not fully understood. Fernández and Goldberg (1971) suggest that these high-frequency effects serve to compensate for the increasing importance of the inertia of the endolymph and cupula at high frequencies and also for phase lags and high-frequency gain attenuation that occur in neural pathways into which vestibular afferents feed.

Fernández and Goldberg (1971) added two extra terms to the basic equation, as follows:

$$\frac{AR(s)}{V(s)} = \frac{sT_c}{sT_c + 1}\,\frac{sT_a}{sT_a + 1}\,(sT_z + 1)\ .$$

The first new term describes the adaptation of irregular units with a time constant of T_a, which they set at 80 sec. The second new term describes the high-frequency gain and phase enhancement with a time constant of T_z, which was set at 0.049 sec.

The fact that most canal afferents have a resting discharge enables the system to work bidirectionally; that is, it helps to produce signals which are different for opposed directions of rotation. This point is elaborated upon in Section 2.3.2.

2.3.2. The Difference Signal. The bidirectionality of the canal output means that when the head rotates in the plane of a canal there is an increased rate of firing from the canal in the direction of rotation and a decreased rate of firing from the synergist on the other side of the head. We shall see below that primary vestibular afferents on each side feed into the ipsilateral vestibular nuclei in the brainstem where they synapse with secondary neurons. Commissures connect the vestibular nuclei on the two sides of the head. The net result is that excitatory inputs to the vestibular nuclei on one side inhibit the corresponding contralateral inputs. Thus the inputs combine reciprocally in the vestibular nuclei to form a differential, or *push-pull* system. The push-pull arrangement has several advantages. In the first place, any nonlinearities in one-half of the system are canceled by nonlinearities in the other half so that the "difference signal" produced between them is linear. Second, the gain of a push-pull signal is twice that of each component signal. Third, noise, or an aberrant input, which is uncorrelated between the two sides, produces a difference signal only half as strong as a true stimulus of the same intensity occurring on both sides. In other words, the push-pull arrangement improves

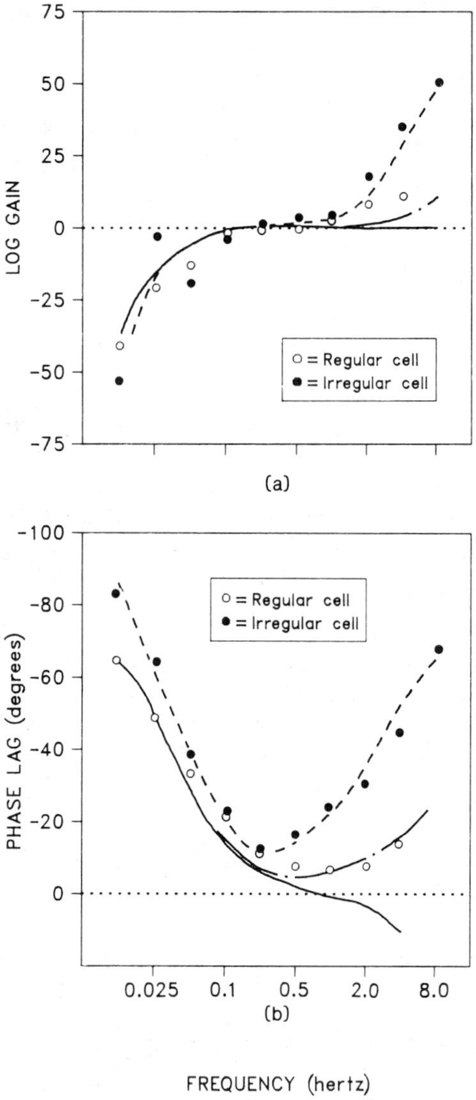

Figure 11.15. Responses of two afferent neurons from the semicircular canals of the squirrel monkey as the animal is rotated sinusoidally about its vertical mid-body axis. In (a) gain is defined as neural spikes per second per unit of head angular velocity. In (b) phase is defined as the angular separation between the position of maximum head velocity and the position of maximum discharge of the cell. The points are experimental values, the solid lines are the functions predicted from the torsion-pendulum equation of the cupula, and the dotted lines are functions predicted by Fernández and Goldberg from a modified equation that takes account of sensory adaptation and high-frequency gain. Note that at high frequencies of head oscillation one of the cells shows markedly increased gain (sensitivity) and phase advance. This is referred to as an irregular or phasic receptor. The other cell is a regular or tonic receptor, which shows a more constant gain and less phase advance as frequency of stimulation is increased. (From C. Fernández & J. M. Goldberg, Physiology of peripheral neurons innervating otolith organs of the squirrel monkey. II. Directional selectivity and force-response relations. *Journal of Neurophysiology*, 1976, *39*. Reprinted with permission.)

the signal/noise ratio of a system. The linearity and gain of the canal system are improved by the push-pull arrangement (Markham, Yagi, & Curthoys, 1976). It has yet to be experimentally determined whether the system's signal/noise ratio is improved.

Any disturbance of the neutral balance point of the vestibular push-pull system, such as is caused by removal of one labyrinth, creates an impression of head rotation when the head is not moving. The fact that animals slowly adapt to such disturbances suggests that they possess a mechanism for automatically adjusting the balance of the system.

In summary of the main points, consider the sequence of events in the right horizontal canal when the head is rotated to the right in the plane of the canal. Inertia causes the endolymph to lag behind the canal walls, which deflects the cupula ampullopetally. This depolarizes the hair cells and increases their frequency of firing. At the same time an ampullofugal deflection of the left-hand cupula hyperpolarizes the hair cells on that side and decreases the frequency of their afferent discharge (see Table 11.2). This decreased discharge reduces the crossed inhibitory influence that left-hand inputs exercised over right-hand inputs and therefore adds to the excitatory response of cells in the vestibular nuclei on the right. The effect on each side is reversed for a head rotation to the left. Remember that in the vertical canals depolarization, and hence increased afferent discharge, is produced by ampullofugal deflection.

Thus behavior associated with vestibular stimulation, such as postural balance and compensatory eye movements, is not related directly to cupula displacement, but rather to the *difference signal* produced in the vestibular nuclei. Consider the consequences of destroying the vestibular organs on the left side of the head. When the head is stationary, the resting discharge from, for example, the intact horizontal canal remains uncanceled because of the absence of inhibitory commissural inputs from the damaged side. This is equivalent to an extreme ampullofugal cupula deflection on the damaged side, which would normally be produced by a rotation of the head to the right. It therefore induces reflex responses, such as compensatory pursuit movements of the eyes to the left, which would normally be induced by such a rotation of the head. If both synergistic canals are destroyed or if both are artificially excited in the same way, no such imbalance of the central difference signal results and reflex responses are not induced (Fluur & Mellström, 1971). That is why, initially, bilateral loss of vestibular organs is not as disturbing as unilateral loss. After several weeks there occurs some compensation for imbalance due to unilateral loss (see Chapter 18).

2.3.3. Adaptation of the Vestibular Signal. The neural discharge from afferent neurons diminishes, or adapts, under conditions of constant cupula deflection produced by a prolonged period of steady angular acceleration (Blanks, Estes, & Markham, 1975; Goldberg & Fernández, 1971a). The rate of adaptation is particularly rapid for normally silent units and for units with irregular rates of resting discharge and greater sensitivity. Adaptation in vestibular afferents is observed after the vestibular nerve is cut, which shows that it does not depend on inhibitory impulses from the central nervous system transmitted along efferent fibers (Lowenstein, 1975, pp. 99–108). Adaptation has been observed at the level of the generator potential in the sensory cells of the crista ampullaris (Taglietti, Rossi, & Casella, 1977) where it is probably due to slow migration of ions across the cell membrane. However, this may not be the only site of the adaptation process.

As we have seen in Section 2.3.1, Fernández and Goldberg (1971) added extra terms to the basic transfer function of the system, one containing a time constant describing the adaptation of neural elements at low frequencies of head oscillation, and one containing a time constant describing the gain enhancement and phase advance at high frequencies. Young and Oman (1970) have also suggested modifications to the basic formula, which they use with success to predict behavioral consequences of vestibular adaptation.

Adaptation seems designed to make irregular afferents into phasic detectors, that is, detectors that respond best to changes in stimulation. As stimulus frequency increases, the sensitivity of phasic receptors increases and their latency (phase lag) decreases (Louie & Kimm, 1976).

2.3.4. Effects of Other Stimuli on Vestibular Afferents. Responses in afferent neurons from vestibular canals may be detected when the head is tilted or subjected to other linear accelerative stimuli. Even a small difference in density between cupula and endolymph would be sufficient to cause such responses, and Goldberg and Fernández (1975) have shown that such density differences may arise from thermal gradients and other disturbances introduced by the surgical exposure necessary to make recordings. By plugging the canals they were able to abolish these thermal effects and, at the same time, abolish the response of the canals to *angular* acceleration. However, the blocked canals still responded to *linear* acceleration. Tilting the head of an animal may disturb the recording electrode mechanically and produce a spurious recording. Estes, Blanks, and Markham (1975) argued that this could not be the main source of tilt-induced responses in canal afferents because the responses differed consistently from cell to cell. It is conceivable that linear accelerative stimuli affect the canals because displacements of the utricular maculae are transmitted to the cristae ampullaris. The behavioral implications of cross talk between linear and rotary accelerations are discussed in Chapter 18.

Alcohol intoxication induces nystagmus when the head is tilted, and it is thought that this form of positional nystagmus is due to a disturbance of the specific gravity of the cupula caused by the differential absorption of alcohol into different parts of the canal system. If alcohol is mixed with heavy water (deuterium oxide) the density of the mixture can be made equal to that of water. A person intoxicated on "heavy" alcohol does not suffer from positional nystagmus and its attendant dizziness (Money, Johnson, & Corlett, 1965; Money & Myles, 1974).

The response of vestibular afferents in the monkey has been found not to be affected by anesthesia of the central nervous system (Keller, 1976). This suggests that if efferent fibers carry impulses from the central nervous system, as many investigators believe, they have nothing to do with the normal maintenance of the system's response. Keller may not have tested over a wide enough range of frequencies or his anesthesia may not have affected the sympathetic system, which is thought by some investigators to be the source of efferent fibers. Goldberg and Fernández (1980) found that electrical stimulation of efferent fibers slightly increased the gain of irregularly discharging primary afferents, and they speculated that efference may serve to extend the dynamic range of the phasic units.

The response of afferent nerve fibers from the canals is not modified by visual stimulation, not even by a movement of the whole visual scene, even though visual movement induces illusory sensations of head rotation. Nor is the response of canal afferents modified by movements of the eyes (Keller, 1976).

2.4. Central Projections of Canal Afferents

2.4.1. Inputs to the Vestibular Nuclei. The vestibular nuclei are the brainstem nuclei for the vestibular system, although some afferent fibers from the vestibular system also go directly to the cerebellum and to the reticular formation (Blanks, Volkind, Precht, & Baker, 1977; Shinoda & Yoshida, 1975). On each side of the brainstem there are four principal vestibular nuclei: the lateral (Deiters'), medial, superior, and inferior nuclei. Together, they form a structure that sits astride the cerebellar peduncle on the floor of the fourth ventricle (Brodal, 1974, pp. 239–352; Gacek, 1974, pp. 213–220). The canals send fibers mainly to the superior and medial nuclei, the utricles mainly to the lateral and inferior nuclei, and the saccules mainly to the inferior nucleus, all on the ipsilateral side. However, these projections are not clear-cut. The cells into which the primary, or afferent, neurons feed are known as second-order vestibular neurons. Each second-order neuron receives excitatory inputs from only one ipsilateral canal. In other words, there is no convergence of inputs from orthogonal canals at this level. However, there is evidence of convergence of canal inputs and of inputs from canals and otolith organs into polysynaptically driven cells of the vestibular nuclei (Abend, 1978; Curthoys & Markham, 1971; Searles & Barnes, 1977).

Although there are no direct inputs from the vestibular organs on one side of the head to the contralateral vestibular nuclei, commissural fibers provide indirect connections between the vestibular nuclei on the two sides. Electrophysiological recordings from second-order vestibular neurons that respond to canal stimulation have revealed two types of cell, which have been called *type I* and *type II* (Duensing & Schaefer, 1958). The side of the head toward which a rotation of the head is occurring is the ipsilateral side; the other is the contralateral side. When the head rotates, the appropriate ipsilateral type I cells increase their rates of firing above their resting values and ipsilateral type II cells decrease their rates of firing below their resting values. At the same time, on the contralateral side, type I cells decrease their rates of firing and type II cells increase their rates of firing (Waespe, Henn, & Miles, 1977, pp. 269–278). There are about equal numbers of each type of cell in the monkey (Fuchs & Kimm, 1975). The input to all type I cells from canals on the side to which the head is turning is direct and exclusively excitatory. Therefore, the decreased response of type II cells to an ipsilateral head rotation cannot be due to inputs arriving from the ipsilateral canals (Keller, 1976). Type II cells must receive their inputs from commissural fibers arising in type I cells in the vestibular nuclei on the other side of the head (Abend, 1977; Kasahara & Uchino, 1974). It has been shown electrophysiologically that the activity of type II cells inhibits that of type I cells, and direct crossed inhibitory links from primary vestibular neurons have also been found (Precht, 1981, pp. 227–250; Shimazu & Precht, 1966) (see Fig. 11.16).

Consider, for example, what happens when the head is turned to the left. The activity of type I cells on the same side is increased by direct inputs from ipsilateral afferents, all of which increase their rates of firing. The activity of type I cells on the right-hand side is reduced because the firing rates of their direct afferents are reduced when the head turns to the left. Commissural fibers convey this reduced activity to type II cells on the left, in turn reducing the inhibitory influence that type II cells were exerting on type I cells while the head was stationary. This should mean that the sensitivity of type I cells to head rotation is enhanced by inputs received from the contralateral side. In line with this prediction, it has been shown that the gain of type I cells is reduced when the contralateral vestibular nerve is sectioned (Markham et al., 1976) or when the contralateral canals are plugged (Abend, 1978).

This arrangement of reciprocal connections provides the basis for the push-pull mechanism by which the behavioral responses of vestibular stimulation are controlled. It also seems to have something to do with the fact that the reflex oculomotor response induced by vestibular stimulation persists for much longer than the long-time constant of the cupula mechanism. The last statement is based on the finding that the two time constants are of similar short duration in monkeys with lesions which sever the commissural fibers. Furthermore, these time constants are again made different in such monkeys by application of a drug which mimics the inhibitory influence of commissural fibers on type I cells of the vestibular nuclei (Blair & Gavin, 1981).

Duensing and Schaefer (1958) also described less common types of cell in the vestibular nuclei, which they designated type III and type IV cells. It was claimed that type III cells are excited by both ipsilateral and contralateral head rotation and type IV cells are inhibited by both directions of rotation. Other evidence suggests that the response features of these cells result from convergence of inputs from orthogonal canals (Abend, 1978). In any case, the functional significance of these cells remains obscure.

The gain and phase characteristics of second-order (monosynaptic) vestibular neurons are very similar to those of primary neurons (Shinoda & Yoshida, 1974), except that second-order neurons have a higher sensitivity (gain), probably because of the enhancing action of the inhibitory commissural input. It is safe to conclude that for normal movements of the head, second-order vestibular nuerons follow closely in the mechanical response of the cupula. Some nonlinearity in the response of vestibular neurons at higher levels of head acceleration probably results from the nonlinearity of the crossed-inhibitory inputs (Abend, 1978). Other cells in the vestibular nuclei are higher than second order, that is, they are driven by vestibular inputs through one or more intervening neurons. The response of polysynaptically driven cells shows a large phase lag and long time constant compared with the response of monosynaptically driven cells (Fuchs & Kimm, 1975; Keller & Kamath, 1975).

2.4.2. Outputs from the Vestibular Nuclei. Efferent pathways from the superior and medial vestibular nuclei provide the largest single source of fibers to the oculomotor nuclei. Each pair of synergistic canals is approximately parallel to the plane of action of a pair of extraocular muscles and each pair of canals projects predominantly to those oculomotor nuclei that control the movements of only one pair of eye muscles (Cohen, Suzuki, Shanzer, & Bender, 1964, Chapter 6; Szentágothai, 1950). This fact is related to the requirement that eye movements that compensate for rotations of the head should be in the same plane as the head rotation. Electrophysiological stimulation of the vestibular nerve on one side has revealed the following pattern of excitatory connections in the rabbit: from the anterior canal to the ipsilateral superior rectus and contralateral inferior oblique, from the horizontal canal to the ipsilateral medial rectus and contralateral lateral rectus, and from the posterior canal to the ipsilateral superior oblique and contralateral inferior rectus. There are also patterns of inhibitory control between specific canals and specific extraocular muscles (see Baker et al., 1973; Highstein, 1972; Ito, Nisimaru, & Yamamoto, 1976a, 1976b). One would expect sensory inputs from a pair of syn-

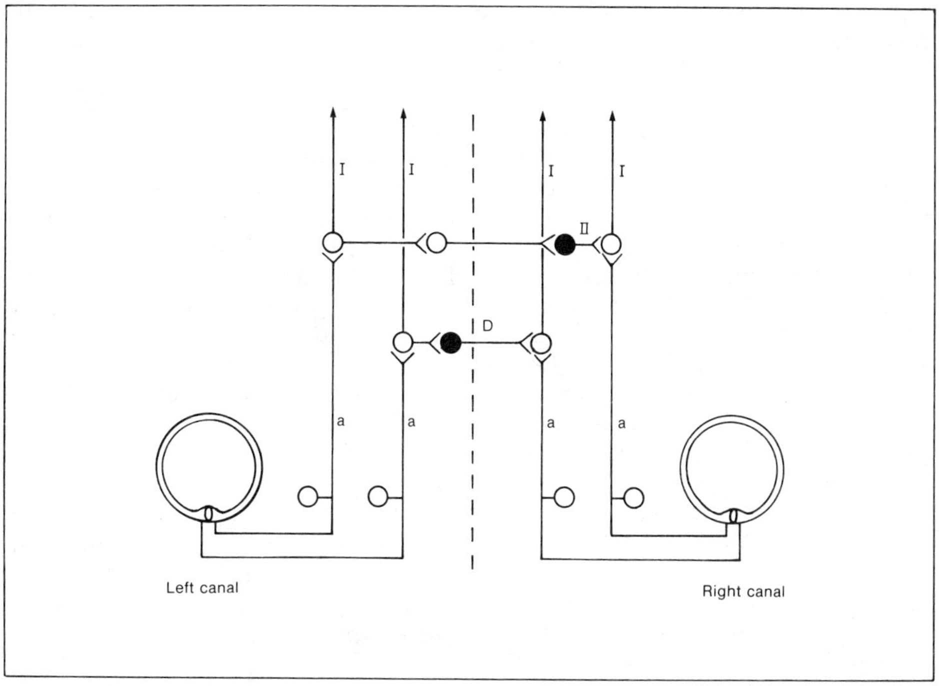

Figure 11.16. Diagramatic representation of the direct and commissural pathways from a pair of synergistic vestibular canals through the vestibular nuclei. Open circles depict excitatory and closed circles inhibitory neurons. Neurons marked a are primary afferent neurons. When the head rotates in a given direction all afferent neurons from the canals on that side increase their rate of firing relative to the resting rate. These inputs are exclusively excitatory on type I secondary neurons in the vestibular nuclei. Type II cells of the vestibular nuclei receive excitatory inputs from the contralateral side through commissural interneurons and are inhibitory on type I cells (which may be second-order cells as depicted here or higher-order cells). In addition, direct commissural inhibitory links occur between type I cells on one side and type I cells on the other side. One such link is denoted by the letter D. The outputs of type I cells pass either to other centers, such as the oculomotor nuclei, or to higher-order cells in the vestibular nuclei. (Adapted from Precht, 1981, Fig. 13-1).

ergistic canals to have a corresponding reciprocal effect on the antagonistic pairs of extraocular muscles which lie in the same plane. In line with this expectation, it has been found that the excitatory and inhibitory inputs that superior rectus motoneurons derive from the anterior and posterior vestibular canals are reciprocally related to the inputs that inferior rectus motoneurons derive from the same canals (Uchino, Suzuki, & Watanabe, 1980).

The pathways along which these excitatory and inhibitory impulses travel form the three-neuron vestibulo-ocular reflex arcs discussed in Chapter 18. Experiments involving acute lesions have revealed that the projections from the horizontal vestibular canals to the lateral and medial recti pass through the ipsilateral *medial longitudinal fasciculus* (Tarlov, 1975, pp. 55–70) and that, at least in the rabbit, the projections from the anterior canals pass through the *brachium conjunctivum* and those from the posterior canals pass through the contralateral longitudinal fasciculus (Ito, Nisimaru, & Yamamoto, 1976c). Other less direct, although no less important, pathways run from the vestibular nuclei to the oculomotor nuclei through the pontine and mesencephalic reticular formations and the tract of Deiters (Reisine & Highstein, 1979; Reisine, Strassman, & Highstein, 1981).

Electrophysiological recordings from single cells in the vestibular nuclei of alert monkeys have revealed the presence of units that fire just before or during eye movements of any kind, not only eye movements evoked by vestibular stimulation. There are also cells that respond to purely visual movement. The vestibular nuclei must therefore be part of the general eye-movement control system and not merely a part of the vestibulo-ocular system (Waespe & Henn, 1979). For instance, Miles (1974) found some cells that fired tonically in relation to the position of the eyes in the orbit; others that fired with a burst of activity just before or during saccades, with a duration which corresponded to the amplitude of the saccade; and others that showed tonic and burst activity in relation to saccades. Some of the burst units responded only when the eyes moved in a certain direction; others were not directionally specific. Some of these neurons responded only in relation to eye movements, but others responded both when the eyes moved and during vestibular stimulation. Other investigators have confirmed the presence of eye-movement related cells in the vestibular nucleus, although there is not full agreement about the types of cell (Fuchs & Kimm, 1975; Keller & Kamath, 1975). The visual-movement and eye-movement related cells of the vestibular nuclei have intimate connections with the cerebellum. Furthermore, the vestibular nuclei, in addition to being important for the control of eye movements, are also important centers for the control of postular reflexes of the head, body, and limbs. See Chapter 18 for further discussion of these issues.

Although doubted for a long time, it is now established that the vestibular apparatus projects to the cerebral cortex (Fredrickson & Schwarz, 1977, pp. 204–210). These inputs, like all other sensory inputs to the cortex, are routed through the thalamus (Deecke, Schwarz, & Fredrickson, 1977). In the monkey, the cells from which short-latency responses to vestibular stimulation may be recorded are situated in area 2v at the lower end of the intraparietal sulcus and in area 3a. Inputs arrive at these sites from both the ipsilateral and contralateral vestibular nuclei after passing through the ventroposterior nucleus of the thalamus (Büttner, Henn, & Oswald, 1977; Magnin & Fuchs, 1977). The use of tracer substances has revealed that there is only a sparse projection of vestibular inputs to the cortex compared with the much heavier projection to the oculomotor nuclei or with the cortical projections of other sensory systems. The thalamic and cortical vestibular neurons of the monkey may, like cells in the vestibular nucleus, be classified as type I and type II cells. The responses of these cells show the same phase and gain relationships to the frequency of stimulation as do their counterparts in the vestibular nucleus (Büttner & Lang, 1979, pp. 581–588). It has been claimed that the thalamic and cortical cells that respond to vestibular stimulation also respond to movements of the visual field (Büttner & Buettner, 1978), although there is some dispute on this point (Magnin & Fuchs, 1977). There is general agreement that most of the thalamic and cortical cells that respond to vestibular stimulation also respond to stimuli arising from proprioceptors in joints and muscles of the limbs and vertebral column, especially from receptors associated with the cervical joints. Furthermore, for some of these cells, the pattern of vestibulo-proprioceptive convergence conforms to patterns of sensory excitation that occur during normal locomotion (Deecke et al., 1977; see Clark & Horch, Chapter 13). In all probability the convergence of inputs from different sense organs occurs initially onto the cells of the vestibular nuclei which then feed to thalamic and cortical levels (Schwarz & Fredrickson, 1971).

The fact that cortical cells respond to vestibular inputs in the same way that they respond to visual and kinesthetic inputs suggests that sensations of body motion may be induced not only by vestibular stimuli, but also by stimuli in these other sense organs. We shall see in Chapter 18 that this is indeed the case.

2.5. The Psychophysics of Rotary Acceleration

2.5.1. Procedures. Methods for the determination of thresholds for rotary acceleration may be classified into *postrotatory procedures*, in which the responses of subjects are recorded when they have been brought to rest after a period of rotation, and *perrotatory procedures*, in which responses are recorded while subjects are rotating.

2.5.1.1. Postrotatory Procedures. In the Bárány procedure the seated subject is rotated in a chair at a steady velocity long enough for perrotatory responses to subside. The subject is then decelerated suddenly and brought to rest. During the immediate postrotatory period the responses to the decelerative impulse are recorded. The duration of postrotatory nystagmus is a commonly used measure. The Bárány test is used for the clinical diagnosis of vestibular disorders, and the decelerative impulse is too massive for the determination of thresholds. A refined version of the test, known as *cupulometry*, was developed by van Egmond et al. (1949) and standardized for clinical and research purposes (Cawthorne, Dix, Hallpike, & Hood, 1956; Groen, 1957). In this procedure the magnitude of the decelerative impulse is controlled by varying the velocity of steady rotation. The duration of one or other of the postrotatory responses is plotted as a function of impulse magnitude, and the resulting function is known as a *cupulogram*. Ideally, the cupulogram is a linear function; its intercept on the impulse magnitude axis is a measure of the subject's threshold for rotary acceleration, and its slope is a measure of the long time constant of the vestibular response. The slope of a cupulogram has been found to vary with practice and the slope obtained by plotting the duration of one postrotatory response, such as eye nystagmus, may not be the same as that obtained from another response, such as the oculogyral illusion (Groen, 1960). It looks as though behavioral measures reflect the time constant of neural processes rather than that of cupula restoration. This is indicated by the fact that the long time constant of discharge of primary vestibular afferents in the monkey, which probably indicates the time constant of the cupula, has been found to be only 6 sec, which is shorter than the time constant of decay of vestibular nystagmus in the monkey (Goldberg & Fernández, 1971a).

The advantages of methods in which the responses are recorded in the postrotatory period are that observations are easier to make when the subject is not rotating, and there are no vibrations or noises present when the subject is still.

2.5.1.2. Perrotatory Procedures. In perrotatory procedures some response which the subject makes when subjected to a rotary acceleration is recorded while the subject is rotating. The response may be one that can be recorded objectively, such as the reflex nystagmic response of the eyes, or it may be some judgment that the subject makes about the movement. The ideal device is one in which a subject may be rotated over a wide range of steady accelerations or oscillated over a wide range of frequencies. In some devices, such as that shown in Figure 11.17, it is possible to set the rotation axis to any angle with respect to the vertical and with respect to the subject's body axis. For routine clinical testing a rotating chair or the *torsion swing*, as shown in Figure 11.18, is used.

The most commonly used stimulus profiles are shown in Figure 11.19. The step-velocity profile provides an impulsive acceleration-deceleration. The Fourier components of an impulse consist of a set of equal-amplitude sine waves covering the whole frequency spectrum. The *frequency-modulation transfer function* of a system is a function that indicates how it responds

Figure 11.17. A rotational device at the Defence and Civil Institute of Environmental Medicine, Toronto, which is capable of rotating a human subject about any axis with reference to the body or gravity.

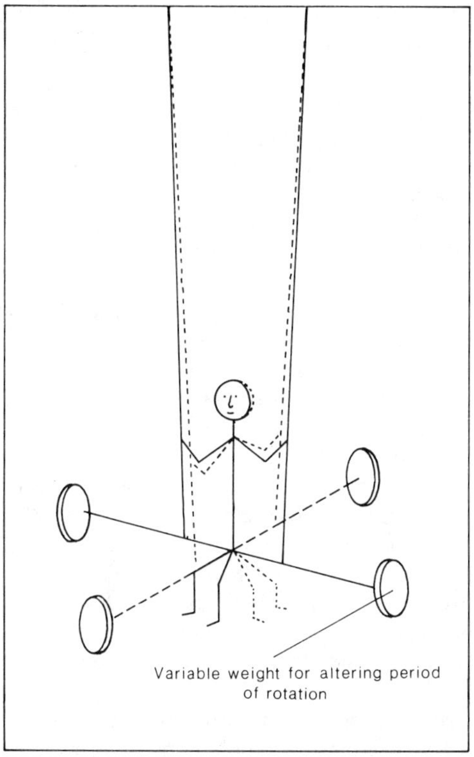

Figure 11.18. The torsion swing, used to vary the period and amplitude of sinusoidal rotation of the body. (From L. B. W. Jongkees, On the physiology and examination of the vestibular labyrinths, in R. F. Nauton (Ed.), *The vestibular system*, Academic Press, Inc., 1975. Reprinted with permission.)

to each of a series of equal-amplitude sine-wave inputs over a defined range of frequencies, and is a convenient summary of the properties of a linear mechanism. Insofar as an impulse contains all frequencies, it should be possible to infer the modulation transfer function of the vestibular system from the way it responds to an impulsive accelerative stimulus, although in practice this approach does not seem to have been very successful. A stimulus that has been designed to serve the same purpose is a pseudorandom sequence of rotational accelerations. The magnitude of the spectral components of this stimulus, like that of the impulse, is constant over a large bandwidth. It is analogous to "white" noise in acoustics (see O'Leary & Honrubia, 1975, for details). The trapezoidal profile allows for the fine control of the accelerative and decelerative impulses and keeps their effects separate by the interposition of a period of constant velocity. The triangular velocity profile has been recommended because it resembles the stimulus profile of ordinary head movements (Guedry, Stockwell, Norman, & Owens, 1971). The sinusoidal velocity profile also resembles natural stimulation and is a standard stimulus for investigating the dynamics of any control system, because any complex stimulus may be analyzed into sine-wave components. One convenient method for varying the period and amplitude of the sinusoid is to adjust weights on a torsion swing, as illustrated in Figure 11.18.

The vestibular canals may also be stimulated by inadequate (unusual) stimuli. (See Sherrick & Cholewiak, Chapter 12.) If the outer ear is irrigated with water at above blood temperature, heat is conducted into the vestibular apparatus, reaching the most lateral part of the horizontal canal first and then the lateral parts of the other canals. If a particular canal is not in a horizontal plane, the thermally induced gradient of specific gravity induces convection currents in the endolymph, which cause a cupula displacement. If cold water is used, a temperature and specific-gravity gradient is induced in the opposite direction and, for a given posture of the head, this deflects a given cupula the other way. Nystagmus induced in this way is known as *caloric* nystagmus, and this theory of the action of thermal gradients has been confirmed by the increase of caloric nystagmus in subjects exposed in a centrifuge to higher than normal g_n forces (Bergstedt, 1961) and by its absence in the weightless conditions of parabolic flight (Kellogg & Graybiel, 1967; Oosterveld & van der Laarse, 1969). With the caloric procedure it is possible to stimulate the vestibular system on either side of the head, and any one canal in either direction. The procedure of caloric stimulation has been standardized for clinical and research use (Baloh, Solingen, Sills, & Honrubia, 1977; Fitzgerald & Hallpike, 1942).

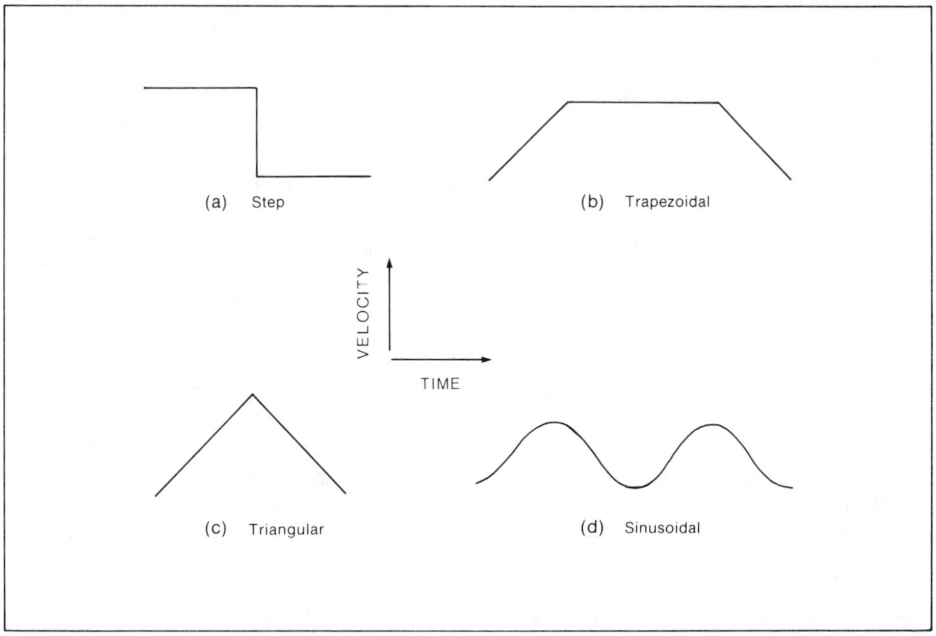

Figure 11.19. Rotary velocity profiles used in the study of vestibular functions.

An electric current, either ac or dc, may be passed through the skull or to inserted electrodes. Faradic (ac) stimulation produces a single-phase nystagmic response. Galvanic (dc) stimulation produces nystagmus with the slow phase directed toward the anode and a sensation of turning toward the cathode. The magnitude of the sensation is roughly proportional to current intensity, with a threshold current of about 600 μA. Reversing the direction of the current reverses the direction of the nystagmus (Spiegel & Scala, 1943; Weiss & Tole, 1973). In animals, the canals may be stimulated directly by inserting a small piston or pneumatic hammer into the lumen of the canals. All these unusual modes of stimulation have the advantage that they allow the various canals to be stimulated separately.

There is a large clinical literature on the use of these procedures for the diagnosis of diseases of the peripheral and central mechanisms of the vestibular system (Hood, 1978; Kornhuber, 1974a, pp. 193–231, 1974b, pp. 581–620; Naunton, 1975).

Three manifestations of vestibular-canal activity have been used to determine threshold values: (1) reports of feelings of rotation, (2) nystagmus, and (3) the oculogyral effect (the apparent movement of a point of light in the dark, induced by vestibular stimulation). It is misleading to regard these thresholds as measures of a single underlying end-organ threshold; they each reflect threshold functions at various levels of partially distinct neural systems.

A variety of psychophysical methods have been used to determine thresholds for angular acceleration. Section 2.5.2 describes these briefly along with typical results.

2.5.2. Thresholds for Angular Acceleration. Several thresholds for angular acceleration have been determined by the *method of limits*, in which angular acceleration is increased either gradually or in discrete steps until the subject shows a response or reports a sensation. Tumarkin (1937) gradually increased acceleration and obtained a sensation-of-rotation threshold of $0.2°\cdot sec^{-2}$. Hilding (1953) increased acceleration in discrete steps and obtained sensation-of-rotation thresholds between 0.25 and $3.0°\cdot sec^{-2}$. It takes several seconds for the cupula to be fully displaced by a near-threshold stimulus, so that unless each acceleration is maintained at a constant level for at least this long, it may fail to evoke a response. On the other hand, the vestibular system adapts to constant acceleration, so that if acceleration is increased gradually, it may never reach threshold. Another problem is that subjects who know that stimuli are increasing in value may give an anticipatory response before the stimulus has reached threshold.

The *method of constant* stimuli overcomes some of these problems. In this method the different stimulus magnitudes are presented several times each, in random order, and the presence or absence of a correct response is noted on each occasion. The threshold is the point in the resulting psychometric function for which correct responses occur either 50 or 75% of the time. This method was used by Hallpike and Hood (1953) and gave thresholds for the oculogyral illusion of between 0.2 and $0.7°\cdot sec^{-2}$.

The method of constant stimuli is time-consuming and a more efficient version is known as the *double staircase method.* Stimuli above threshold alternate at random with stimuli below threshold. Before each trial the stimulus is moved toward or away from the estimated value of the threshold according to how the subject responded on the two previous occasions. After some time the stimuli converge on the threshold. For a description of this method and its elaborations see Taylor and Creelman (1967), and Falmagne, Chapter 1. Clark and Stewart (1968b) obtained thresholds of between 0.05 and $2.2°\cdot sec^{-2}$ by this method.

Signal detection procedures are now used extensively in visual and auditory psychophysics but do not seem to have been used to determine vestibular thresholds. At low magnitudes, any signal becomes indistinguishable from background noise. A person attempting to detect a weak signal may respond to noise as if it were a signal (false alarm) or mistake a signal for noise (miss). The rate of correct detection (hit rate) may be increased if the subject adopts a very lenient *criterion* of what constitutes a signal, but this results in an increased false-alarm rate. On the other hand, a subject may adopt a stringent criterion, in which case the hit rate declines along with the false-alarm rate. A person with higher *sensitivity* will be able to achieve a high hit rate while maintaining a low rate of false alarms. The function relating the hit rate to the false-alarm rate is known as the *receiver operating characteristic curve*, or ROC curve, and can be used to gain independent measures of a person's sensitivity (d') and criterion level (β). These methods are described in detail in Green and Swets (1966). (See also Falmagne, Chapter 1, and Sperling and Dosher, Chapter 2.)

Even when a constant suprathreshold stimulus is applied, it takes time before a detectable response occurs, and the minimum duration of stimulation is an inverse function of stimulus magnitude. The original statement of this relationship was that the product of acceleration and stimulus duration for threshold stimuli is constant. This constant is referred to as *Mulder's constant*, and the relationship is analogous to Bloch's law in vision. More recent studies have confirmed the inverse relationship between acceleration and duration, but the product has been found to be not constant but a linearly increasing function of stimulus duration (Doty, 1969). By extrapolating from the function relating response latency to stimulus magnitude it is possible to determine that magnitude for which latency approaches infinity. This asymptotic value of acceleration is often used as a measure of the threshold. Response latencies obtained by Meiry (1965) are shown in Figure 11.20. The asymptotic acceleration is about $0.3°\cdot sec^{-2}$. The curve was derived by Guedry (1974, pp. 3–154) from the torsion-pendulum equation of the cupula, in which values of the short- and long-time constants were obtained from other experiments and the threshold value of cupula deflection was adjusted to give a best fit to the data points.

In cupulometry, the threshold is derived from the angular velocity that just fails to produce postrotatory responses. These velocities range between about 2.5 and $4.5°\cdot sec^{-1}$ (Aschan, Nylén, Stahle, & Wersäll, 1952). Calculations based upon the basic formula of cupula dynamics show that, for a long time constant of 10 sec, this is equivalent to threshold accelerations of between 0.25 and $0.45°\cdot sec^{-2}$ (Guedry, 1974, pp. 3–154).

Thresholds based upon responses to sinusoidal rotation of the subject are more difficult to determine because maximum acceleration occurs only briefly during each cycle. For a detailed discussion of this issue, see Guedry (1974, pp. 3–154).

Some of the many perrotatory determinations of thresholds for angular acceleration are presented in Table 11.3. It can be seen that they vary between 0.02 and $2°\cdot sec^{-2}$. The lowest thresholds are obtained when the rotating subject is asked to report the apparent motion (oculogyral effect) of a stationary visual target (Clark, 1967; Clark & Stewart, 1968a, 1972b; Huang & Young, 1981; Miller & Graybiel, 1975; Oosterveld, 1970).

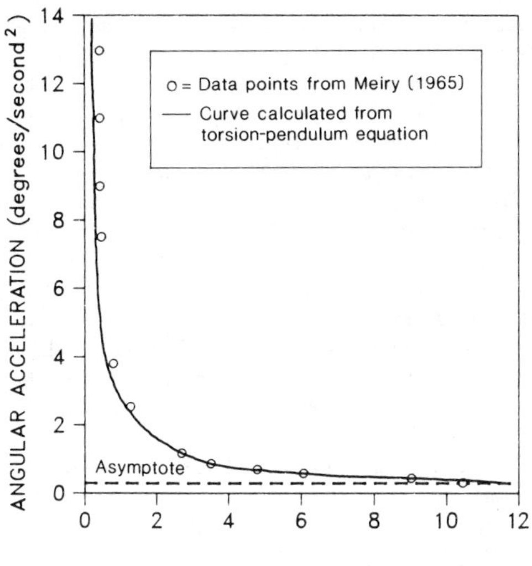

Figure 11.20. Latency of detection of rotation as a function of rotary acceleration. Data points from Meiry (1965). Curve calculated by Guedry from the torsion-pendulum equation of the cupula, in which the time constants were obtained from other experiments, and the threshold cupula deflection was adjusted to give a best fit to the data points. The asymptotic value of acceleration at which latency approaches infinity provides a measure of the threshold for acceleration. For these data the threshold determined in this way is about $0.3°\cdot sec^{-2}$. (From F. E. Guedry, Psychophysics of vestibular sensation, in In H. H. Kornhuber (Ed.), *Handbook of sensory physiology, 6(2)*. Springer-Verlag, Inc., 1974. Reprinted with permission.)

It is not surprising that there is so much variation between the different determinations of the threshold of rotary acceleration, even when the same indicator is used. It is not easy to accelerate a human subject smoothly, avoiding all extraneous sources of stimulation, and experimenters have differed in the extent to which they were successful. The threshold here, as in other modalities, is a function of the signal/noise ratio: reduce the "noise" and the threshold is reduced. In any case, many other factors modify the results. One of these is the psychophysical method used. For instance, a perrotatory double staircase method yields lower thresholds than cupulometry (Clark & Stewart, 1968b; Dockstader, 1971).

There seem to be no published reports of a direct comparison between acceleration thresholds in different planes of rotation. Clark (1967) reviewed an unpublished experiment by Meiry in which it was shown that the threshold for rotation about the z-axis (head erect, axis of rotation vertical) was between 0.1 and $0.2°\cdot sec^{-2}$ and the threshold for rotation about the x-axis (head supine, axis of rotation vertical) was $0.5°\cdot sec^{-2}$. Gundry (1978) compared the threshold for rotation of an erect person about the x-axis (roll) with those for rotation of a prone person about the same body axis. The threshold and time for detection were lower for the erect person, and this was probably because with this posture the canals and the utricles would be stimulated, whereas in the prone posture only the canals would be stimulated (see also Guedry, 1965).

Several investigators have used magnitude-estimation procedures to derive functions relating the perceived velocity of rotation to various parameters of the stimulus (Brown, 1966, 1968; Clark & Stewart, 1968c, 1972a; Elsner, 1971; Guedry, Stockwell, & Gilson, 1971). Values of the exponent relating sensation magnitude to stimulus magnitude (the product of acceleration and stimulus duration) have generally been found to lie between 1.3 and 1.5. The vestibular system adapts to maintained acceleration. Therefore, the value of this exponent must fall as the sensitivity of the system declines during adaptation.

This completes this review of the vestibular system. The full behavioral significance of this system cannot be appreciated until its relationships with the motor system and with other senses, especially vision and kinesthesis, have been considered. These relationships are described in Chapter 18.

Table 11.3. Human Thresholds for the Detection of Rotary Acceleration

Response	Stimulus	Subjects	Threshold Acceleration ($°\cdot sec^{-2}$)	Study[a]
First reports of rotation	Rotating chair	30	Range 0.23–2.0 Mean 0.8	Groen & Jongkees (1948)
	Rotating chair	92	Range 0.05–3.18 Mean 0.44	Clark & Stewart (1972b)
Oculogyral illusion	Human centrifuge	5	Mean 0.12	Graybiel, Kerr, & Bartley (1948)
	Rotating chair	92	Range 0.03–0.59 Mean 0.11	Clark & Stewart (1972b)
	Rotating chair	300	Range 0.02–0.95 Median 0.1	Miller & Graybiel (1975)

[a] In the study by Groen and Jongkees subjects were rotated continuously in a chair about the z-body axis and the threshold was indicated by the minimum acceleration that produced a sensation of rotation after about 30 sec of exposure. In the study by Clark and Stewart, subjects were accelerated about the z-body axis for 10 sec and thresholds were determined by a forced-choice staircase procedure. Graybiel, Kerr, and Bartley rotated subjects in a centrifuge about the z-body axis and asked them to report the direction of apparent motion of a light (the oculogyral illusion) every 20 sec over an acceleration time of 80 sec.

In the Miller and Graybiel study, subjects were rotated about the z-body axis and asked by a forced-choice staircase procedure to report the oculogyral illusion between 5 and 20 sec after acceleration commenced. It can be seen that mean thresholds for the first reports of rotation lie between 0.44 and $0.8°\cdot sec^{-2}$ and are higher than the mean thresholds for reports of the oculogyral illusion, which lie between 0.1 and $0.12°\cdot sec^{-2}$.

3. KEY REFERENCES

Wilson and Melvill Jones (1979), in their book *Mammalian Vestibular Physiology* have provided the most recent review of this subject. Part 1 of the *Handbook of Sensory Physiology* edited by Kornhuber (1974c) contains authoritative reviews of vestibular physiology by a number of authors, and so does a recent volume edited by Gualtierotti (1981). Earlier, but still useful, reviews of vestibular physiology are contained in books edited by Brodal and Pompeiano (1972), Hood (1978), Naunton (1975), and Stahle (1970). Barnes (1980) provides a useful review of vestibular dynamics. The whole subject of vestibular psychophysics has been very thoroughly reviewed by Guedry (1974, pp. 3–154).

REFERENCES

*References preceded by an asterisk are "key references."

Abend, W. K. Functional organization of the superior vestibular nucleus of the squirrel monkey. *Brain Research*, 1977, *132*, 65–84.

Abend, W. K. Response to constant angular accelerations of neurons in the monkey superior vestibular nucleus. *Experimental Brain Research*, 1978, *31*, 459–473.

Adrian, E. D. Discharge from vestibular receptors in the cat. *Journal of Physiology*, 1943, *101*, 389–407.

Anderson, J. H., Blanks, R. H. I., & Precht, W. Response characteristics of semicircular canal and otolith systems in cat. I. Dynamic responses of primary vestibular fibers. *Experimental Brain Research*, 1978, *32*, 491–508.

Aschan, G., Nylén, C. O., Stahle, J., & Wersäll, R. The rotation test. Cupulometric data from 320 normals. *Acta Otolaryngologica*, 1952, *42*, 451–459.

Baker, R., Precht, W., & Berthoz, A. Synaptic connections to trochlear motoneurons determined by individual vestibular nerve branch stimulation in the cat. *Brain Research*, 1973, *64*, 402–406.

Baloh, R. W., Solingen, L., Sills, A. W., & Honrubia, V. Caloric testing. *Annals of Otology, Rhinology, & Laryngology*, 1977, *86*, Suppl. 43.

*Barnes, G. R. Vestibular control of oculomotor and postural mechanisms. *Clinical Physics and Physiological Measurement*, 1980, *1*, 3–40.

Bergstedt, M. The effect of gravitational force on the vestibular caloric test. *Acta Otolaryngologica*, 1961, *53*, 551–562.

Blair, S., & Gavin, M. Response of the vestibulo-ocular reflex to differing programs of acceleration. *Investigative Ophthalmology*, 1979, *18*, 1086–1090.

Blair, S. M., & Gavin, M. Brainstem commissures and control of time constant of vestibular nystagmus. *Acta Otolaryngologica*, 1981, *91*, 1–8.

Blanks, R. H. I., Curthoys, I. S., & Markham, C. H. Planar relationships of semicircular canals in man. *Acta Otolaryngologica*, 1975, *80*, 185–196.

Blanks, R. H. I., Estes, M. S., & Markham, C. H. Physiologic characteristics of vestibular first-order canal neurons in the cat. II. Response to constant angular acceleration. *Journal of Neurophysiology*, 1975, *38*, 1250–1268.

Blanks, R. H. I., Volkind, R., Precht, W., & Baker, R. Responses of cat prepositus hypoglossi neurons to horizontal angular acceleration. *Neuroscience*, 1977, *2*, 391–403.

Bracho, H., Budelli, R., & Galey, F. Ionic mechanisms in the vestibular apparatus: The resting state. In T. Gualtierotti (Ed.), *The vestibular system*. New York: Springer, 1981.

Breuer, J. Über die Function der Bogengänge des Ohrlaberynthes. *Wien Medizinisches Jahrbuch*, 1874, *4*, 72–124.

*Brodal, A. Anatomy of the vestibular nuclei and their connections. In H. H. Kornhuber (Ed.), *Handbook of sensory physiology* (Vol. 6/1). New York: Springer, 1974.

*Brodal, A., & Pompeiano, O. *Basic aspects of central vestibular mechanisms*. New York: Elsevier, 1972.

Brown, J. H. Magnitude estimation of angular velocity during passive rotation. *Journal of Experimental Psychology*, 1966, *72*, 169–172.

Brown, J. H. Cross-model estimation of angular velocity. *Perception and Psychophysics*, 1968, *3*, 115–117.

Büttner, U., & Buettner, U. W. Parietal cortex (2v) neuronal activity in the alert monkey during natural vestibular and optokinetic stimulation. *Brain Research*, 1978, *153*, 392–397.

Büttner, U., Henn, V., & Oswald, H. P. Vestibular-related neuronal activity in the thalamus of the alert monkey during sinusoidal rotation in the dark. *Experimental Brain Research*, 1977, *30*, 435–444.

Büttner, U., & Lang, W. The vestibulocortical pathway: Neurophysiological and anatomical studies in the monkey. In R. Granit & O. Pompeiano (Eds.), *Reflex control of posture and movement*. New York: Elsevier, 1979.

Carlström, D., & Engström, H. The ultrastructure of statoconia. *Acta Otolaryngologica*, 1955, *45*, 14–18.

Cawthorne, T. E., Dix, M. R., Hallpike, C. S., & Hood, J. D. Vestibular function. *British Medical Bulletin*, 1956, *12*, 131–142.

*Clark, B. Thresholds for the perception of angular acceleration in man. *Aerospace Medicine*, 1967, *38*, 443–450.

Clark, B., & Stewart, J. D. Comparison of sensitivity for the perception of bodily rotation and the oculogyral illusion. *Perception and Psychophysics*, 1968, *3*, 253–256. (a)

Clark, B., & Stewart, J. D. Comparison of three methods to determine thresholds for perception of angular acceleration. *American Journal of Psychology*, 1968, *81*, 207–216. (b)

Clark, B., & Stewart, J. D. Magnitude estimates of rotational velocity during and following prolonged increasing, constant, and zero angular acceleration. *Journal of Experimental Psychology*, 1968, *78*, 329–339. (c)

Clark, B., & Stewart, J. D. Comparison of the sensitivity to rotation of pilots and nonpilots. *Aerospace Medicine*, 1972, *43*, 8–12. (a)

Clark, B., & Stewart, J. D. The power law for the perception of rotation by airline pilots. *Perception and Psychophysics*, 1972, *11*, 433–436. (b)

Cogan, D. G. Some objective and subjective observations on the vestibulo-ocular system. *American Journal of Ophthalmology*, 1958, *45*, 74–78.

Cohen, B., Suzuki, J., Shanzer, S., & Bender, M. B. Semicircular canal control of eye movements. In M. B. Bender (Ed.), *The oculomotor system*. New York: Harper & Row, 1964.

Collins, W. E. Coriolis vestibular stimulation and the influence of different surrounds. *Aerospace Medicine*, 1968, *39*, 125–130.

Crum Brown, A. On the sense of rotation and the anatomy and physiology of the semicircular canals of the inner ear. *Journal of Anatomy*, 1875, *8*, 327–331.

Curthoys, I. S. The response of primary semicircular canal neurons to angular accelerations of varying magnitude. In T. Gualtierotti (Ed.), *The vestibular system*. New York: Springer, 1981.

Curthoys, I. S., Blanks, R. H. I., & Markham, C. H. Semicircular canal functional anatomy in cat, guinea pig, and man. *Acta Otolaryngologica*, 1977, *83*, 258–265. (a)

Curthoys, I. S., Blanks, R. H. I., & Markham, C. H. Semicircular canal radii of curvature (R) in cat, guinea pig, and man. *Journal of Morphology*, 1977, *151*, 1–16. (b)

Curthoys, I. S., & Markham, C. H. Convergence of labyrinthine influences on units in the vestibular nuclei of the cat. I. Natural stimulation. *Brain Research*, 1971, *35*, 469–490.

Deecke, L., Schwarz, D. W. F., & Fredrickson, J. M. Vestibular responses in the rhesus monkey ventroposterior thalamus. II. Vestibulo-proprioceptive convergence at thalmic neurons. *Experimental Brain Research*, 1977, *30*, 219–232.

de Vries, H. The mechanics of the labyrinth otolith. *Acta Otolaryngologica*, 1950, *38*, 262–273.

Dockstader, S. L. Comparison of cupulometric and psychophysical thresholds for perception of rotation and the oculogyral illusion. *Perception and Psychophysics*, 1971, *9*, 299–302.

Doty, R. L. Effect of duration of stimulus presentation on the angular acceleration threshold. *Journal of Experimental Psychology*, 1969, *80*, 317–321.

Duensing, F., & Schaefer, K. P. Die Aktivität einzelner Neurone im Bereich der Vestibulariskerne bei Horizontalbeschleunigungen unter besonderer Bericksichtigung des vestibularen Nystagmus. *Archiv für Psychiatrie und Nervenkrankheiten*, 1958, *198*, 225–252.

Elsner, W. Power laws for the perception of rotation and the oculogyral illusion. *Perception & Psychophysics*, 1971, *9*, 418–420.

Engström, H., Bergström, B., & Ades, H. W. Macula utriculi and maculi sacculi in the squirrel monkey. *Acta Otolaryngologica*, 1972, *Suppl. 301*, 75–126.

Estes, M. S., Blanks, R. H. I., & Markham, C. H. Physiologic characteristics of vestibular first-order canal neurons in the cat. I. Response plane determination and resting discharge characteristics. *Journal of Neurophysiology*, 1975, *38*, 1232–1249.

Fernández, C., & Goldberg, J. M. Physiology of peripheral neurons innervating semicircular canals of the squirrel monkey. II. Response to sinusoidal stimulation and dynamics of peripheral vestibular system. *Journal of Neurophysiology*, 1971, *34*, 661–675.

Fernández, C., & Goldberg, J. M. Physiology of peripheral neurons innervating otolith organs of the squirrel monkey. I. Response to static tilts and to long-duration centrifugal force. *Journal of Neurophysiology*, 1976, *39*, 970–984. (a)

Fernández, C., & Goldberg, J. M. Physiology of peripheral neurons innervating otolith organs of the squirrel monkey. II. Directional selectivity and force-response relations. *Journal of Neurophysiology*, 1976, *39*, 985–995. (b)

Fernández, C., & Goldberg, J. M. Physiology of peripheral neurons innervating otolith organs of the squirrel monkey. III. Response dynamics. *Journal of Neurophysiology*, 1976, *39*, 996–1008. (c)

Fernández, C., Goldberg, J. M., & Abend, W. K. Response to static tilts of peripheral neurons innervating otolith organs of the squirrel monkey. *Journal of Neurophysiology*, 1972, *35*, 978–996.

Fitzgerald, G., & Hallpike, C. S. Studies in human vestibular function: I. Observations on the directional preponderance ("Nystagmus-bereitschaft") of caloric nystagmus resulting from cerebral lesions. *Brain*, 1942, *65*, 115–137.

Flock, Å. Structure of the macula utriculi with special reference to directional interplay of sensory responses as revealed by morphological polarization. *Journal of Cell Biology*, 1964, *22*, 413–431.

Flock, Å. Electron microscopic and electrophysiological studies on the lateral line canal organ. *Acta Otolaryngologica*, 1965, *Suppl. 199*, 1–90.

Flourens, P. *Recherches experimentales sur les propriétés et fonctions du system nerveux dans les animaux vertébrés*. Paris: Crevot, 1824.

Fluur, E. The interaction between the utricle and the saccule. *Acta Otolaryngologica*, 1970, *69*, 17–24.

Fluur, E., & Mellström, A. Vestibular nystagmus—A differential reaction. *Acta Otolaryngologica*, 1971, *71*, 299–302.

Fredrickson, J. M., & Schwarz, D. W. F. Vestibulo-cortical projection. In R. F. Naunton (Ed.), *The vestibular system*. New York: Academic Press, 1977.

Fregly, A. R. Vestibular ataxia and its measurement in man. In H. H. Kornhuber (Ed.), *Handbook of sensory physiology* (Vol. 6/2). New York: Springer, 1974.

Fuchs, A. F., & Kimm, J. Unit activity in vestibular nucleus of the alert monkey during horizontal angular acceleration and eye movement. *Journal of Neurophysiology*, 1975, *38*, 1140–1161.

Gacek, R. R. Morphological aspects of the efferent vestibular system. In H. H. Kornhuber (Ed.), *Handbook of sensory physiology* (Vol. 6/1). New York: Springer, 1974.

Gacek, R. R. The innervation of the vestibular labyrinth. In R. F. Naunton (Ed.), *The vestibular system*. New York: Academic Press, 1975.

Goldberg, J. M., & Fernández, C. Physiology of peripheral neurons innervating semicircular canals of the squirrel monkey. I. Resting discharge and response to constant angular accelerations. *Journal of Neurophysiology*, 1971, *34*, 635–660. (a)

Goldberg, J. M., & Fernández, C. Physiology of peripheral neurons innervating semicircular canals of the squirrel monkey. III. Variations among units in their discharge properties. *Journal of Neurophysiology*, 1971, *34*, 676–684. (b)

*Goldberg, J. M., & Fernández, C. Responses of peripheral vestibular neurons to angular and linear accelerations in the squirrel monkey. *Acta Otolaryngologica*, 1975, *80*, 101–110.

Goldberg, J. M., & Fernández, C. Conduction times and background discharge of vestibular afferents. *Brain Research*, 1977, *122*, 545–550.

Goldberg, J. M., & Fernández, C. Efferent vestibular system in the squirrel monkey: Anatomical location and influence on afferent activity. *Journal of Neurophysiology*, 1980, *43*, 986–1025.

Graybiel, A., Kerr, W. A., & Bartley, S. H. Stimulus thresholds of the semicircular canals as a function of angular acceleration. *American Journal of Psychology*, 1948, *61*, 21–36.

Green, D. M., & Swets, J. A. *Signal detection theory and psychophysics*. New York: Wiley, 1966.

Groen, J. J. Cupulometry. *Laryngoscope*, 1957, *67*, 894–910.

Groen, J. J. Problems of the semicircular canal from a mechanico-physiological point of view. *Acta Otolaryngologica*, 1960, *Suppl. 163*, 59–67.

Groen, J. J. The problems of the spinning top applied to the semicircular canals. *Confinia Neurologica (Basel)*, 1961, *21*, 454–455.

Groen, J. J., & Jongkees, L. B. W. The threshold of angular acceleration perception. *Journal of Physiology*, 1948, *107*, 1–7.

*Gualtierotti, T. *The vestibular system: Function and morphology*. New York: Springer, 1981.

Guedry, F. E. Orientation of the rotation-axis relative to gravity. *Acta Otolaryngologica*, 1965, *60*, 30–48.

*Guedry, F. E. Psychophysics of vestibular sensation. In H. H. Kornhuber (Ed.), *Handbook of sensory physiology* (Vol. 6/2). New York: Springer, 1974.

Guedry, F. E., Stockwell, C. W., & Gilson, R. D. Comparison of subjective responses to semicircular canal stimulation produced by rotation about different axes. *Acta Otolaryngologica*, 1971, *72*, 101–106.

Guedry, F. E., Stockwell, C. W., Norman, J. W., & Owens, G. G. Use of triangular waveforms of angular velocity in the study of vestibular function. *Acta Otolaryngologica*, 1971, *71*, 439–448.

Gundry, A. J. Experiments on the detection of roll motion. *Aviation, Space and Environmental Medicine*, 1978, *49*, 657–664.

Hallpike, C. S., & Hood, J. D. The speed of the slow component of ocular nystagmus induced by angular acceleration of the head. *Proceedings of the Royal Society, B*, 1953, *141*, 216–221.

Hardy, M. Observations on the innervation of the macula saculi in man. *Anatomical Record*, 1934, *59*, 403–478.

Highstein, S. M. Electrophysiological investigation of the organization of the vestibulo-ocular pathways in rabbit. *Bibliotheca Ophthalmologia*, 1972, *82*, 89–98.

Hilding, A. C. Studies on the otic labyrinth III: On the threshold of minimum perceptible angular acceleration. *Annals of Otology, Rhinology and Laryngology*, 1953, *62*, 5–14.

Hillman, D. E., & McLaren, J. W. Displacement configuration of semicircular canal cupulae. *Neuroscience*, 1979, *4*, 1989–2000.

Hixson, W. C., Niven, J. I., & Correia, M. J. Kinematics nomenclature for physiological accelerations. Monograph 14, Navel Aerospace Medical Center, Pensacola, Fla., 1966.

Holst, E. von. Die Arbeitsweise des Statolithenapparates bei Fischen. *Zeitschrift Vergleichender Physiology*, 1950, *32*, 60–120.

*Hood, J. D. (Ed.). *Vestibular mechanisms in health and disease*. New York: Academic Press, 1978.

Huang, J., & Young, L. R. Sensation of rotation about a vertical axis with a fixed visual field in different illuminations in the dark. *Experimental Brain Research*, 1981, *41*, 172–183.

Igarashi, M., Watanabe, T., & Maxian, P. M. Dynamic equilibrium in squirrel monkey after unilateral and bilateral labyrinthectomy.

Acta Otolaryngologica, 1970, *69*, 247–253.

Ito, M., Nisimaru, N., & Yamamoto, M. Inhibitory interaction between the vestibulo-ocular reflexes arising from semicircular canals of rabbits. *Experimental Brain Research*, 1976, *26*, 89–103. (a)

Ito, M., Nisimaru, N., & Yamamoto, M. Pathways for the vestibulo-ocular reflex excitation arising from semicircular canals of rabbits. *Experimental Brain Research*, 1976, *24*, 257–271. (b)

Ito, M., Nisimaru, N., & Yamamoto, K. Postsynaptic inhibition of oculomotor neurons involved in vestibulo-ocular reflexes arising from semicircular canals of rabbits. *Experimental Brain Research*, 1976, *24*, 273–283. (c)

Iurato, S. Light microscope features. In S. Iurato (Ed.), *Submiscroscopic structure of the inner ear*. Oxford: Pergamon, 1967.

Johnsson, L-G., & Hawkins, J. E. Sensory and neural degeneration with aging, as seen in microdissections of the human inner ear. *Annals of Otology, Rhinology, and Laryngology*, 1972, *81*, 179–193.

Jongkees, L. B. W. On the physiology and examination of the vestibular labyrinths. In R. F. Nauton (Ed.), *The vestibular system*. New York: Academic Press, 1975.

Jongkees, L. B. W., & Groen, J. J. The nature of the vestibular stimulus. *Journal of Laryngology*, 1946, *61*, 529–541.

Kasahara, M., & Uchino, Y. Bilateral semicircular canal inputs to neurons in cat vestibular nuclei. *Experimental Brain Research*, 1974, *20*, 285–296.

Keller, E. L. Behavior of horizontal semicircular canal afferents in alert monkey during vestibular and optokinetic stimulation. *Experimental Brain Research*, 1976, *24*, 459–471.

Keller, E. L., & Kamath, B. Y. Characteristics of head rotation and eye movement related neurons in alert monkey vestibular nucleus. *Brain Research*, 1975, *100*, 182–187.

Kellogg, R. S., & Graybiel, A. Lack of response to thermal stimulation of the semicircular canals in the weightless phase of parabolic flight. *Aerospace Medicine*, 1967, *38*, 487–490.

Kirkham, W. R., Collins, W. E., Grape, P. M., Simpson, J. M., & Wallace, T. F. Spatial disorientation in general aviation accidents. *Aviation, Space and Environmental Medicine*, 1978, *49*, 1080–1086.

Klinke, R., & Galley, N. Efferent innervation of vestibular and auditory receptors. *Physiological Review*, 1974, *54*, 316–357.

Kornhuber, H. H. (Ed.). *Handbook of sensory physiology* (Vol. 6). *Vestibular system*. New York: Springer, 1974. (a)

Kornhuber, H. H. Nystagmus and related phenomena in man: An outline of otoneurology. In H. H. Kornhuber (Ed.), *Handbook of sensory physiology* (Vol. 6/2). New York: Springer, 1974. (b)

*Kornhuber, H. H. The vestibular system and the general motor system. In H. H. Kornhuber (Ed.), *Handbook of sensory physiology* (Vol. 6/2). New York: Springer, 1974. (c)

Kubin, L., Magherini, P. C., Manzoni, D., & Pompeiano, O. Responses of lateral reticular neurons to sinusoidal stimulation of labyrinth receptors in decerebrate cats. *Journal of Neurophysiology*, 1980, *44*, 922–936.

Lang, W., & Kubik, S. Primary vestibular afferent projections to the ipsilateral abducens nucleus in cats. *Journal of Neurophysiology*, 1980, *44*, 922–936.

Lang, W., & Kubik, S. Primary vestibular afferent projections to the ipsilateral abducens nucleus in cats. *Experimental Brain Research*, 1979, *37*, 177–181.

Lindeman, H. H. Anatomy of the otolith organs. *Advances in Otology, Rhinology, and Laryngology*, 1973, *20*, 405–433.

Loe, P. R., Tomko, D. L., & Werner, G. The neural signal of angular head position in primary afferent vestibular nerve axons. *Journal of Physiology*, 1973, *230*, 29–50.

Louie, A. W., & Kimm, J. The response of 8th nerve fibers to horizontal sinusoidal oscillation in the alert monkey. *Experimental Brain Research*, 1976, *24*, 447–457.

Lowenstein, O. The peripheral neuron. In R. F. Naunton (Ed.), *The vestibular system*. New York: Academic Press, 1975.

Lowenstein, O., Osborne, M. P., & Thornhill, R. A. The anatomy and ultrastructure of the labyrinth of the lamprey (*Lampetra fluviatilis L.*). *Proceedings of the Royal Society, B*, 1968, *170*, 113–134.

Lowenstein, O., & Sand, A. The individual and integrated activity of the semicircular canals of the elasmobranch labyrinth. *Journal of Physiology*, 1940, *99*, 89–101.

Lowenstein, O., & Wersäll, J. A functional interpretation of the electron-microscopic structure of the sensory hairs in the cristae of the elasmobranch, *Raja clavata*, in terms of directional sensitivity. *Nature*, 1959, *184*, 1807–1808.

Mach, E. *Grundlinien der Lehre von der Bewegungsempfindungen*. Leipzig: Engelman, 1875.

Magnin, M., & Fuchs, A. F. Discharge properties of neurons in the monkey thalamus tested with angular acceleration, eye movement and visual stimuli. *Experimental Brain Research*, 1977, *28*, 293–299.

Malcolm, R. A mechanism by which the hair cells of the inner ear transduce mechanical energy into a modulated train of action potentials. *Journal of General Psychology*, 1974, *63*, 757–772.

Malcolm, R., & Melvill Jones, G. A quantitative study of vestibular adaptation in humans. *Acta Otolaryngologica*, 1970, *70*, 126–135.

Malcolm, R., & Melvill Jones, G. Erroneous perception of vertical motion by humans seated in the upright position. *Acta Otolaryngologica*, 1974, *77*, 274–283.

Marini, G., Provini, L., & Rosina, A. Gravity responses of Purkinje cells in the nodulus. *Experimental Brain Research*, 1976, *24*, 311–323.

Markham, C. H., Yagi, T., & Curthoys, I. S. Influence of the contralateral labyrinth on resting and dynamic activity of cat vestibular nucleus cells. *Neuroscience Abstracts*, 1976, *2*, 1059.

Markl, H. The perception of gravity and of angular acceleration in invertebrates. In H. H. Kornhuber (Ed.), *Handbook of sensory physiology* (Vol. 6/1). New York: Springer, 1974.

Matsuoka, I., Fukuda, N., Takaori, S., & Morimoto, M. Responses of single neurons of the vestibular nuclei to lateral tilt and caloric stimulation in the intact and hemilabyrinthectomized cats. *Acta Otolaryngologica*, 1971, *72*, 182–190.

Mayne, R. The dynamic characteristics of the semicircular canals. *Journal of Comparative and Physiological Psychology*, 1950, *43*, 309–319.

McLaren, J. W., & Hillman, D. E. Displacement of the semicircular canal cupula during sinusoidal rotation. *Neuroscience*, 1979, *4*, 2001–2008.

Meiry, J. L. The vestibular system and human dynamic space orientation. Doctoral thesis, Massachusetts Institute of Technology, 1965 (cited in Guedry, 1974).

Melvill Jones, G. Origin, significance and amelioration of Coriolis illusions from the semicircular canals: A non-mathematical appraisal. *Aerospace Medicine*, 1970, *41*, 483–490.

Melvill Jones, G. The vestibular system for eye movement control. In R. A. Monty & J. W. Senders (Eds.), *Eye movements and psychological processes*. Hillsdale, N.J.: Erlbaum, 1976.

Melvill Jones, G., & Milsum, J. H. Spatial and dynamic aspects of visual fixation. *IEEE Transactions in Biomedical Engineering*, 1965, *BME-12*, 54–62.

Melvill Jones, G., Rolph, R., & Downing, G. H. Comparison of human subjective and oculomotor responses to sinusoidal vertical linear acceleration. *Acta Otolaryngologica*, 1980, *90*, 431–440.

Melvill Jones, G., & Young, L. R. Subjective detection of vertical acceleration: A velocity-dependent response. *Acta Otolaryngologica*, 1978, *85*, 45–53.

Miles, F. A. Single unit firing patterns in the vestibular nuclei related to voluntary eye movements and passive body rotation in conscious monkeys. *Brain Research*, 1974, *71*, 215–224.

Miller, E. F., & Graybiel, A. Thresholds for the perception of angular acceleration as indicated by the oculogyral illusion. *Perception and Psychophysics*, 1975, *17*, 329–332.

Milsum, J. H., & Melvill Jones, G. Dynamic asymmetry in neural components of the vestibular system. *Annals of the New York Academy of Science*, 1969, *156*, 851–871.

Money, K. E., Johnson, W. H., & Corlett, B. M. A. Role of semicircular

canals in positional alcohol nystagmus. *American Journal of Physiology*, 1965, *208*, 1065–1070.
Money, K. E., & Myles, W. S. Heavy water nystagmus and effects of alcohol. *Nature*, 1974, *247*, 404–405.
*Naunton, R. F. (Ed.). *The vestibular system*. New York: Academic Press, 1975.
O'Leary, D. P., & Honrubia, V. On-line identification of sensory systems using pseudorandom binary noise perturbations. *Biophysics Journal*, 1975, *15*, 505–532.
Oman, C. M. The influence of duct and utricular morphology on semicircular canal response. In T. Gualtierotti (Ed.), *The vestibular system*. New York: Springer, 1981.
Oman, C. M., & Young, L. R. The physiological range of pressure difference and cupula deflection in the human semicircular canal. *Acta Otolaryngologica*, 1972, *74*, 324–331.
Oosterveld, W. J. Threshold value for stimulation of the horizontal semicircular canals. *Aerospace medicine*, 1970, *41*, 386–389.
Oosterveld, W. J., & van der Laarse, W. D. Effect of gravity on vestibular nystagmus. *Aerospace Medicine*, 1969, *40*, 382–385.
Parker, D. E., Gulledge, W. L., Tubbs, R. L., & Littlefield, V. M. A temporary threshold shift for self-motion detection following sustained oscillating acceleration. *Perception and Psychophysics*, 1978, *23*, 461–467.
Parker, D. E., Wood, D. L., Gulledge, W. L., & Goodrich, R. L. Self-motion magnitude estimation during linear oscillation: Changes with head orientation and following fatigue. *Aviation, Space and Environmental Medicine*, 1979, *50*, 1112–1121.
Peterson, B. W. Distribution of neural responses to tilting within vestibular nuclei of the cat. *Journal of Neurophysiology*, 1970, *33*, 750–767.
Precht, W. Functional characteristics of central vestibular neurons. In T. Gualtierotti (Ed.), *The vestibular system*. New York: Springer, 1981.
Reason, J. T., & Graybiel, A. The effect of varying the time interval between equal and opposite Coriolis accelerations. *British Journal of Psychology*, 1971, *62*, 165–173.
Reisine, H., & Highstein, S. M. The ascending tract of Deiters' conveys a head velocity signal to medial rectus motoneurons. *Brain Research*, 1979, *170*, 172–176.
Reisine, H., Strassman, A., & Highstein, S. M. Eye position and head velocity signals are conveyed to medial rectus motoneurons in the alert cat by the ascending tract of Deiters'. *Brain Research*, 1981, *211*, 153–157.
Romand, R., & Dauzat, M. Modifications of threshold activity in primary vestibular neurons during development in the cat. *Experimental Brain Research*, 1982, *45*, 265–268.
Rosenhall, U. Vestibular macular mapping in man. *Annals of Otology, Rhinology, and Laryngology*, 1972, *81*, 339–351.
Ross, M. D. Centrally originating efferent terminals on hair cells: Fact or fancy? In T. Gualtierotti (Ed.), *The vestibular system*. New York: Springer, 1981.
Schor, R. H. Responses of cat vestibular neurons to sinusoidal roll tilt. *Experimental Brain Research*, 1974, *20*, 347–362.
Schwarz, D. W. F., & Fredrickson, J. M. Rhesus monkey vestibular cortex: A bimodal primary projection field. *Science*, 1971, *172*, 280–281.
Schwindt, P. C., Richter, A., & Precht, W. Short latency utricular and canal input to ipsilateral abducens motoneurons. *Brain Research*, 1973, *60*, 259–262.
Searles, E. J., & Barnes, C. D. Ipsilateral utricular and semicircular canal interactions from electrical stimulation of individual vestibular nerve branches recorded in the descending medial longitudinal fasciculus. *Brain Research*, 1977, *125*, 23–36.
Shimazu, H., & Precht, W. Inhibition of central vestibular neurons from the contralateral labyrinth and its mediating pathway. *Journal of Neurophysiology*, 1966, *29*, 467–492.
Shimazu, H., & Smith, C. M. Cerebellar and labyrinthine influences on single vestibular neurons identified by natural stimuli. *Journal of Neurophysiology*, 1971, *34*, 493–508.
Shinoda, Y., & Yoshida, K. Dynamic characteristics of responses to horizontal head angular acceleration in vestibuloocular pathway in the cat. *Journal of Neurophysiology*, 1974, *37*, 653–673.
Shinoda, Y., & Yoshida, K. Neural pathways from the vestibular labyrinths to the flocculus in the cat. *Experimental Brain Research*, 1975, *22*, 97–112.
Smith, C. Microscopic structure of the utricle. *Annals of Otology, Rhinology, and Laryngology*, 1956, *65*, 450–469.
Spiegel, E. A., & Scala, N. P. Response of the labyrinthine apparatus to electrical stimulation. *Archives of Otolaryngology*, 1943, *38*, 131–138.
Spyer, K. M., Ghelarducci, B., & Pompeiano, O. Gravity responses of neurons in main reticular formation. *Journal of Neurophysiology*, 1974, *37*, 705–720.
*Stahle, J. (Ed.). *Vestibular function on earth and in space*. New York: Pergamon, 1970.
Steer, R. W., Li, Y. T., Young, L. R., & Meiry, J. L. Physical properties of the labyrinthine fluids and quantification of the phenomenon of caloric stimulation. In third symposium on the role of the vestibular organs in space exploration. (NASA SP-152). Washington, D.C.: National Aeronautics and Space Administration, 1967.
Stevens, S. S., & Galanter, E. H. Ratio scales and category scales for a dozen perceptual continua. *Journal of Experimental Psychology*, 1957, *54*, 377–411.
Steinhausen, W. Über den Nachweis der bewegung der Cupola in der intakten Bogengansampulle des Labyrinths bei der naturlichen rotatorischen und calorischen Reizung. *Pflüger's Archiv fuer die Gesamte Physiologie*, 1931, *228*, 322–328.
Szentágothai, J. The elementary vestibulo-ocular reflex arc. *Journal of Neurophysiology*, 1950, *13*, 395–407.
Taglietti, V., Rossi, M. L., & Casella, C. Adaptive distortions in the generator potential of semicircular canal sensory afferents. *Brain Research*, 1977, *123*, 41–57.
Tarlov, E. Synopsis of current knowledge about ascending projections from the vestibular nuclei. In R. F. Naunton (Ed.), *The vestibular system*. New York: Academic Press, 1975.
Taylor, M. M., & Creelman, C. D. PEST: Efficient estimates of probability function. *Journal of the Acoustical Society of America*, 1967, *41*, 782–787.
Toates, F. M. *Control theory in biology and experimental psychology*. London: Hutchinson, 1975.
Tomko, D. L., Peterka, R. J., & Schor, R. H. Responses to head tilt in cat eighth nerve afferents. *Experimental Brain Research*, 1981, *41*, 216–221.
Tomko, D. L., Peterka, R. J., Schor, R. H., & O'Leary, D. P. Response dynamics of horizontal canal afferents in barbiturate-anesthetized cats. *Journal of Neurophysiology*, 1981, *45*, 376–396.
Travis, R. C., & Dodge, R. Experimental analysis of the sensorimotor consequences of passive oscillation, rotary and rectilinear. *Psychological Monographs*, 1928, *38* (Whole No. 175).
Trincker, D. E. W. The transformation of mechanical stimulus into nervous excitation by the labyrinthine receptors. In Symposium of the Society of Experimental Biology, No. 16, *Biological receptor mechanisms*. Cambridge: Cambridge University Press, 1962.
Tumarkin, I. A. Some observations on the function of the labyrinth. *Proceedings of the Royal Society of Medicine*, 1937, *30*, 599–610.
Uchino, Y., Suzuki, S., & Watanabe, S. Vertical semicircular canal inputs to cat extraocular motoneurons. *Experimental Brain Research*, 1980, *41*, 45–53.
van Egmond, A. A. J., Groen, J. J., & Jongkees, L. B. W. The mechanics of the semicircular canal. *Journal of Physiology*, 1949, *110*, 1–17.
Waespe, W., & Henn, V. The velocity response of vestibular nucleus neurones during vestibular, visual, and combined angular acceleration. *Experimental Brain Research*, 1979, *37*, 337–347.
*Waespe, W., Henn, V., & Miles, T. S. Activity in the vestibular nuclei of the alert monkey during threshold eye movements and vestibular or optokinetic stimulation. In R. Baker and A. Berthoz (Eds.), *Control of gaze by brain stem neurons*. New York: Elsevier, 1977.
Walsh, E. G. The perception of rhythmically repeated linear motion in

the horizontal plane. *British Journal of Psychology*, 1962, *53*, 439–445.

Walsh, E. G. The perception of rhythmically repeated linear motion in the vertical plane. *Quarterly Journal of Experimental Physiology*, 1964, *49*, 58–65.

Watt, D. G. D. Responses of cats to sudden falls: An otolith-originating reflex assisting landing. *Journal of Neurophysiology*, 1976, *39*, 257–265.

Weiss, A. D., & Tole, J. R. Effect of galvanic vestibular stimulation on rotation testing. *Advances in Otology, Rhinology, and Laryngology*, 1973, *19*, 311–317.

Wersäll, J. Studies on the structure and innervation of the sensory epithelium of the cristae ampullaris in the guinea pig. *Acta Oto-laryngologica, Suppl.*, 1956, *126*, 1–85.

Wersäll, J., & Bagger-Sjöbäck, D. Morphology of the vestibular sense organs. In H. H. Kornhuber (Ed.), *Handbook of sensory physiology* (Vol. 6/1). New York: Springer, 1974.

Wilson, V. J., Gacek, R. R., Maeda, N., & Uchino, Y. Saccular and utricular input to cat neck motoneurons. *Journal of Neurophysiology*, 1977, *40*, 63–73.

Wilson, V. J., Gacek, R. R., Uchino, Y., & Susswein, A. J. Properties of central vestibular neurons fired by stimulation of the saccular nerve. *Brain Research*, 1978, *143*, 251–261.

*Wilson, V. J., & Melvill Jones, G. *Mammalian vestibular physiology*. New York: Plenum, 1979.

Wolfe, J. W., & Cramer, R. L. Illusions of pitch induced by centrifugal acceleration. *Aerospace Medicine*, 1970, *41*, 1136–1139.

Young, L. R., & Meiry, J. L. A revised dynamic otolith model. *Aerospace Medicine*, 1968, *39*, 606–608.

Young, L. R., & Oman, C. M. Modeling adaptation in human semicircular canal response to rotation. *Transactions of the New York Academy of Science*, 1970, *32*, 489–494.

CHAPTER 12

CUTANEOUS SENSITIVITY

CARL E. SHERRICK and ROGER W. CHOLEWIAK

Department of Psychology, Princeton University, Princeton, New Jersey

CONTENTS

1. GENERAL CONSIDERATIONS

1.1. History of the Scientific Study of the Skin Senses

The origins of classification of the human senses are commonly traced to Aristotle, who specified the five known presently to the layperson: vision, hearing, taste, smell, and touch. Aristotle himself was unsure of the unitary character of bodily sensations, and E.H. Weber in 1826 confirmed the Greek sage's doubts by observing that touch could be divided into a sense of location, a sense of weight, and a sense of temperature. Pain and other, more diffuse feelings, for example, kinesthetic, vestibular, and visceral sensations, were relegated to *das Gemeingefühl*, or general sensations (see Boring, 1942, p. 463; Weber, 1978).

In the 1830s Johannes Müller published his doctrine of specific nervous energies, which was to influence physiological and psychological thought well into the twentieth century and, in its unrevised form, to confound the thinking of investigators of cutaneous phenomena for nearly a century.

Müller's doctrine, it will be recalled, stated that any given nerve, however excited, will evoke the sensation normally attributable to that nerve. Designed to oppose the theory that eidola or simulacra of scenes or sounds must travel to the brain to be experienced, Müller's doctrine proposed that nervous activity was the only message to the sensorium, that all nervous activity was similar, and that the specificity of experience depended on the peripheral source and the central projection of the nerve tract in question (see Boring, 1942, p. 71).

The demonstration by Weber that location, pressure, warmth, and cold could all be discriminated by humans whose skin was appropriately stimulated suggested that the necessary subdivisions of nervous function must exist in the skin. The exact nature and degree of the specificity became apparent only later in the nineteenth century with the discovery of isolated peaks of sensitivity to touch, warmth, cold, or pain over most of the body surface (Boring, 1942, p. 467). A hunt for histological evidence of specialized nerve endings underlying the spots proved fruitless. Nevertheless, there was proposed a theory that postulated the presence of specialized endings, one for each sensation, and having nerves that projected to specific centers in the brain, in keeping with the doctrine of Müller. The theory, proposed by Max von Frey in 1895, was repeated in the literature of physiology and medicine until the middle of the twentieth century, when Weddell and his coworkers in England (see Sinclair, 1967, p. 16) enlarged upon an alternative theory, originally proposed by Nafe (1934), that emphasized the importance of patterns of nervous activity. The pattern theory asserts that a particular quality of experience is contingent upon the collocation of a number of separate and more elementary nervous events, not all of which need be present in each token of the pattern. A similar theory has been proposed for the sense of taste (Pfaffmann, 1959).

Some views of the English pattern theorists were quite extreme, for example, that specialized nerve endings in the skin were mainly histological artifacts or else the product of local tissue activities unrelated to the job of "tuning" the nerve to specific classes of physical activity. These views, along with earlier ideas of cutaneous neurophysiology, were modified and reconciled by Melzack and Wall (1962) in a paper that should be regarded as a landmark in the theory of cutaneous sensitivity. Evidence generated by more sophisticated electrophysiological and histological techniques since that time has not greatly altered the basic assumptions of their theory, as we shall see later, and it is regarded by most serious investigators as one of the clearest and most empirically oriented set of statements currently available to research workers. In the cutaneous system, as in all other senses, the majority of theorists have puzzled over how the *quality* of sensation is encoded by the nervous system.

1.2. Gross Anatomy

The total area of skin surface of an average-sized adult human is about 1.8 m^2, which is about 1000 times the area of the retinas. It has a density of 1250 kg/m^3 and weighs about 5 kg. The apparently smooth texture of skin is, upon close examination with a low-power lens, a highly variegated surface full of ridges and valleys, pores, hair, and uneven flecks of pigment. Excepting the highly vascular areas, such as the vermilion of the lips, the areolae (nipples), and the genitalia, two major types of skin are described, namely, hairy and glabrous. Glabrous skin is that which covers the palm and sole; nearly all other skin surfaces contain hair follicles and hairs that are more or less visible. Most of the skin surface includes sweat ducts of two types. The commonly distributed eccrine sweat glands serve, in part, the purpose of reducing the body temperature, including that of the skin itself (see Section 5.3.4); the apocrine glands, most densely located in the axillary and genital regions, are active in a more complex manner that need not concern us (see Montagna, 1956, chapter 4).

The skin is a system of layers, the outermost of which is called the *corneum*, and consists of tough, anuclear cells that overlay their source, the *germinative* layer. As the cells of the corneum are lost through friction and natural growth and senescence, the germinative layer below replaces them. Together these compose the *epidermis*, and below them lies the *dermis*, or *corium*, in which are the nerve endings and tiny capillary loops, located in microscopic gulfs formed by the corrugation of the dermis. The *papillae*, as these irregularities are called, are mirrored in the outer layer and produce the characteristic "print" pattern seen most readily on the palms and soles.

Below the corium lies the *reticulated dermis*, a network of connective tissue containing larger blood vessels, small nerve trunks, sweat and sebaceous glands, and hair follicles, in addition to an elastic tissue that secures it to the overlying structures. Beneath this begins the subcutaneous tissue, which contains additional sweat and sebaceous glands, larger nerve trunks, and hair follicles, interspersed with fatty deposits and fibrous structures that extend to the *fascia*, which is the "chain mail" covering for the muscles, bones, and some organs.

1.3. Degree of Dedication of the Central Nervous System to the Skin Senses

It is impossible to characterize the skin with a single set of biophysical values unless the location is specified; thickness, vascularity, density, electrical conductivity, and more derived properties, such as moduli of shear and elasticity, vary over a wide range of values (see Tregear, 1966). The density of innervation is similarly variable, as is the character of nervous end organs. The total number of sensory axons converging on the central nervous system (CNS) is estimated at 1.1×10^6 (Piéron, 1952), which suggests that, considering the territory covered, the sensory pickets are indeed a thin line when compared to their counterparts in the retina (10^6 axons) and the cochlea (6×10^4 axons) (see Brown, 1973). The individual fibers in the skin are moreover a motley collection in comparison to those in the optic and acoustic nerves, in that those in the skin exhibit a wide range of fiber diameters from 0.1–16 μm (see Section 4.2.1). From the fact that the degree of overlap of fiber ends at the periphery is commonly very great, one perceives the sense of Sinclair's statement that "activity in a single fiber is quite unphysiological" (1967, p.73). To put this rather succinct statement another way, it is impossible under normal conditions to stimulate a single fiber alone, just as it is quite impossible to stimulate by itself a single cone or rod in the retina or a single auditory hair cell. Not only does the stimulus energy, in whatever form, propagate widely throughout the skin tissues, but even small areas of skin, when broached, reveal the presence of endings from several different axons.

1.4. Peripheral, Spinal, and Central Receptive Fields

Because this chapter deals primarily with the functional characteristics of the cutaneous system, there is no section devoted to descriptive neuroanatomy. More traditional approaches to the neuroanatomy and neurophysiology of the skin system may be found in Carterette and Friedman (1978), Darian-Smith (1984), Geldard (1972), Iggo (1973, 1982), and Sinclair (1967).

It is nevertheless of some utility to understand what may be characterized as the functional anatomy of the cutaneous nervous system. It has already been noted that the tiny nerves underlying the corium and reticulated dermis exhibit large degrees of overlap. A number of these fibrils ultimately join to form the main nerve fiber, which is one of the first-order afferents. The fibers then collect (in their ascent to the spinal cord) in small bundles, characterized anatomically as cutaneous nerves, usually with the adjective describing their location. In recent years (see, e.g., Vallbo, Hagbarth, Torebjörk, & Wallin, 1979; Vallbo & Johansson, 1978) neurophysiologists have been able to plunge small electrode wires into the arms of conscious (and consenting) humans to contact single afferent units in the cutaneous nerves, to record the activity of the nerve while the skin area it serves is stimulated by pressure, vibration, or other forms of energy. Figure 12.1(a) and (b) shows the arrangement for such an experiment and the results obtained.

When a unit has been contacted, the investigators explore the skin to determine what loci appear to excite the fiber. Following this a systematic exploration of the so-called receptive field is undertaken to characterize the unit according to the area of skin served, the response to various stimuli, and other attributes, such as adaptation and dynamic range. Examples of the receptive fields thus obtained are shown in Figure 12.1(c), along with a brief description of their properties. We should be clear concerning the meaning of this experimental approach and its results. What has been studied is not a "touch nerve" but a neural unit that responds to the kind of physical energy that in the human commonly elicits a report of "touch." The

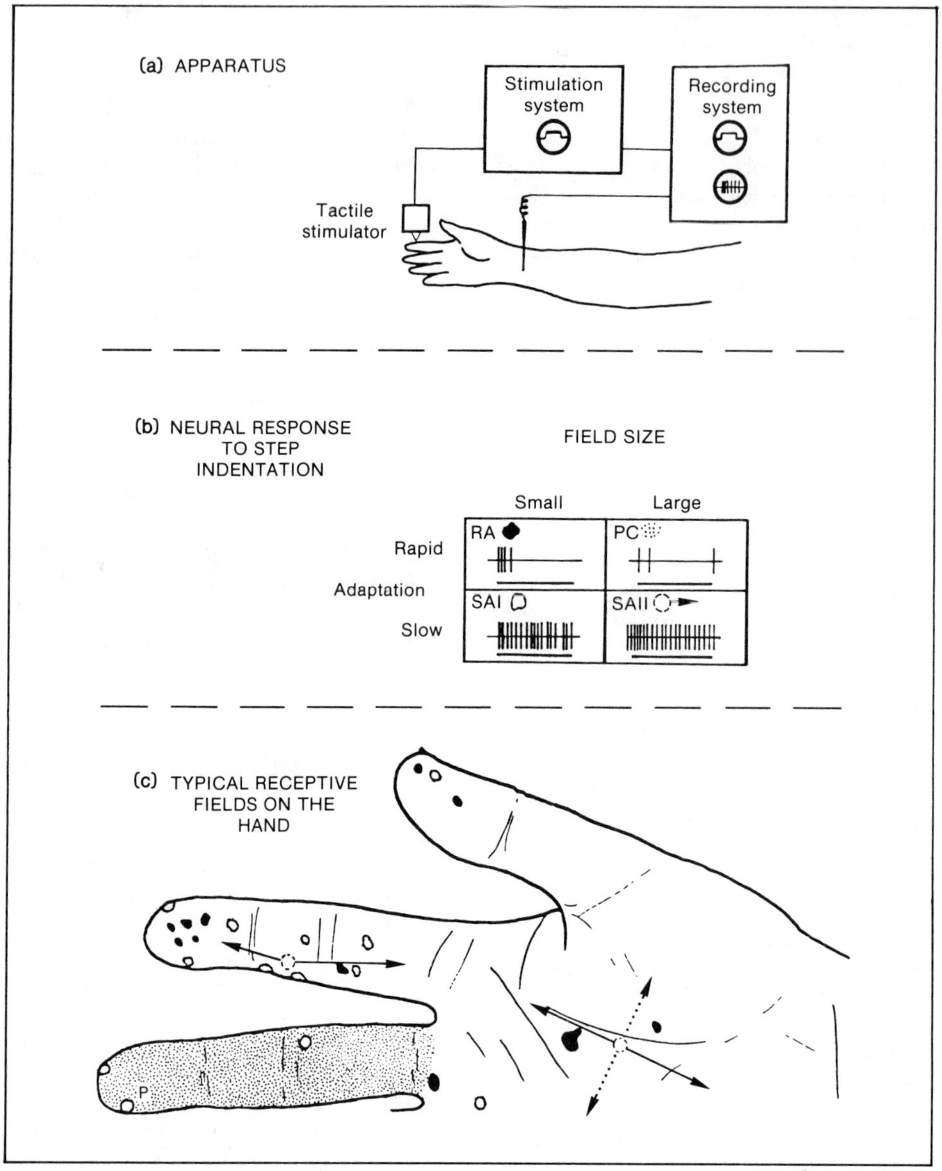

Figure 12.1. Apparatus and results from typical microneurography experiments. (Adapted from Johansson, 1979). (a) The apparatus for such an experiment involves fine tungsten recording microelectrodes that may be inserted into the arm of the awake human at any of several levels, from the wrist to the upper arm. After the nerve has been penetrated, single afferent units are isolated by gentle stroking of the periphery until an area from which activity can be recorded is located. After this receptive field is mapped, providing some information about the underlying receptor classification, an electromechanical stimulator may be applied to the most sensitive point and controlled stimuli presented. Such stimuli have included sinusoidal, as well as step or ramp, functions. (b) Typically, afferent units may be classified into two main groups according to their rate of adaptation to step-indentation stimuli (indicated by the solid bar beneath the neural records). These may be further subdivided on the basis of certain receptive field characteristics, such as size. Within this 2 × 2 matrix fall the four receptor types: rapidly adapting units (RA), Pacinian corpuscles (PC), slowly adapting Type I (SAI), and slowly adapting Type II (SAII). (c) The PC and SAII field sizes can be quite large, encompassing an entire digit on the hand (arrows indicate the stretch-sensitive extent of the representative SAII fields). In contrast, RA and SAI fields are smaller, with punctate foci. Of the four classes, only one, the SAII, demonstrates sensitivity to stretch, as well as to perpendicular, indentation. Ongoing ("spontaneous") activity, typically recorded from these receptors, can be increased by skin stretch in the appropriate direction (indicated by the solid arrows), as well as inhibited by stretch orthogonal to the excitatory direction (dotted arrows). Representative locations and extents of the receptive fields are shown, not their density, which varies over the hand for each type. Although it is tempting to attribute one type of sensation or another to these receptor classes based on the awake subject's response to stimulation, it must be repeated that such experiments are only recording information from one of a number of receptors with extensively overlapping fields. Stimulation of a single point may indeed activate the receptive unit being recorded from, but any number of others are also providing information about the external world to more central processors from the same site in response to the same stimulus (see Vallbo & Johansson, 1979).

unit response may well be one component of the whole required to produce the sensation. We do not know the other necessary components because the experimental method focuses only on the one (Vallbo & Johansson, 1979).

Microneurography, as this method has been labeled, reveals an important set of details, not only about the distribution of sensitivity of single peripheral fibers but also that a few fairly distinct classes of fibers emerge from repeated explorations with different neural units. The majority of those described thus far are responsive to mechanical stimuli (Vallbo & Johansson, 1978), but a number have been reported to respond as thermoreceptors and as *nociceptors* (i.e., units responsive to tissue-damaging levels of these stimuli; see Torebjörk, 1979). A much older technique, capable of exposing the responsive area of a nerve fiber bundle, rather than a single fiber, is *neurotomy*, in which a small cutaneous nerve in the human is severed and the cut ends rejoined to permit regrowth of the nerves. The material distal to the cut disappears, of course, and growth moves from the proximal side of the cut out to the original area served by the nerve bundle. The process takes many months, however, and the area thus denervated may be studied to determine the extent of loss, as well as the quality of sensation induced by different stimuli as growth progresses. A well-known study of this kind was done on himself by Head, the English neurologist (Head, 1920; see also Boring, 1942, p. 471; Munger, 1982). Shortly after the surgery is performed, there is a substantial loss of sensitivity for all types of stimuli, and careful exploration of the region shows an area of primary loss, such as that depicted in Figure 12.2. In addition, an area of somewhat reduced sensitivity borders the primary zone, suggesting that this is an area of overlap with another nerve trunk. Third, exploration with thermal, pressure, and pain-inducing stimuli reveals that (1) the area of loss varies with stimulus type and (2) the quality of experience evoked varies with the region stimulated as well as over the period of regrowth. Finally, the location of the area on the skin served by a given cutaneous nerve varies markedly from one person to another or even bilaterally in the same person (see, e.g., Lanier, 1934).

The nerves of the periphery gather in larger branches as they move downstream to the spinal cord, where they first enter the paired dorsal roots at 1 of 30 segments situated between the sacrum and the cervical area. If one of these roots which contain the cell bodies of the nerves is severed or disabled by spinal trauma or disease, the area of skin that it serves will be differentially responsive to mechanical probing (Keegan & Garrett, 1948). From injury cases and experiments, it has been found that a given dorsal root serves a restricted area of skin, seen most readily on the torso as a band circling the body. These areas are called *dermatomes* (see Figure 12.3). Because there are several ways of damaging the dorsal roots, or otherwise interrupting or enhancing their activities to reveal their outline, a number of different dermatomal maps exist in the literature. Moreover, individual differences among humans undoubtedly are a factor here as in the distribution of cutaneous nerve trunks (see, e.g., Section 6.1.2). Most investigators agree, however, that there is a great amount of overlap across adjacent dermatomes, so that the loss of a single dorsal root does not produce an area of total anesthesia (see Geldard, 1982; Kerr & Wilson, 1978).

The orofacial region, the scalp, the ear canals and drum membrane, the tongue and oral mucosa, the pharynx, and some internal organs are innervated by four cranial nerves: the trigeminal, facial, glossopharyngeal, and vagus nerves. Of these the trigeminal is the most elaborate and far-flung system, as any victim of trigeminal neuralgia will testify. The trigeminal is also the source of complaint in the common toothache, as well as the mediator of the exquisite sensitivity to touch found in the lip region. Functional field maps for the cranial nerves are demonstrable in primates (see Darian-Smith, 1973); for humans, excellent descriptions are given by Anderson and Matthews (1977) and Dubner, Sessle, and Storey (1978).

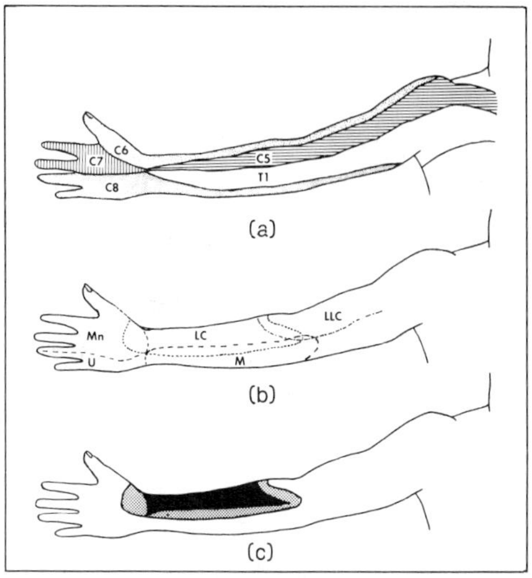

Figure 12.2. Results from section of the lateral cutaneous nerve of the arm, comparing the extent of anesthesia (c) to the distributions of peripheral cutaneous nerves (b) and dermatomes (a). (Adapted from Sinclair, 1967.) The effects of section of nerves at any level of the nervous system must be examined with the realization that at every stage of processing, some degree of spatial redundancy exists. At the first-order afferent level, stimulation of a point excites many types of receptors with overlapping receptive fields. The first-order fibers travel centrally in the peripheral cutaneous nerves, each of which receives information from specific areas of the skin. However, as seen in (b), in which the areas served by the medial (M), ulnar (U), median (Mn), lateral cutaneous (LC), and lower lateral cutaneous nerves (LLC) are defined, a great degree of overlap exists in their peripheral representation. Thus if, for example, LC is severed centrally, only a small area of its receptive field is rendered anesthetic (c, dark stipple). A surrounding area in which overlapping representation exists demonstrates only partial sensory loss (c, light stipple). The extent to which further division of the periphery occurs is seen by comparing (a) and (b). In (a), the dermatomes (areas served by individual spinal roots; see Figure 12.3) further segregate the peripheral representation. This segregation occurs, however, in such a manner as to cut across peripheral neural boundaries because a given nerve may enter the spinal cord through several different dorsal roots. Additional patterns of division and multiple representation may be seen at more central levels of the nervous system, with as many as four or more somatotopic areas known to exist at the cortex (see Figure 12.4).

Understanding of the organization of the spinal cord has advanced greatly in the last decade, with the result that some of the accepted doctrine of the 1960s has been brought into serious question. For example, the division of the spinal transmission system into two major and opposing segments, the dorsal column medial lemniscal system and the lateral spinothalamic system (Sinclair, 1967), is now seen to be an oversimplification. Beginning at the dorsal horn, that is, the grey matter of the cord, there are now discernible four classes of the larger neurons, based on electrophysiologic measures (Iggo, 1982, p. 392). Class 1 neurons are excited only by cutaneous mechanoreceptors. Class 2 neurons are excited by mechanoreceptors and those nociceptors with unmyelinated fibers. Both these classes are

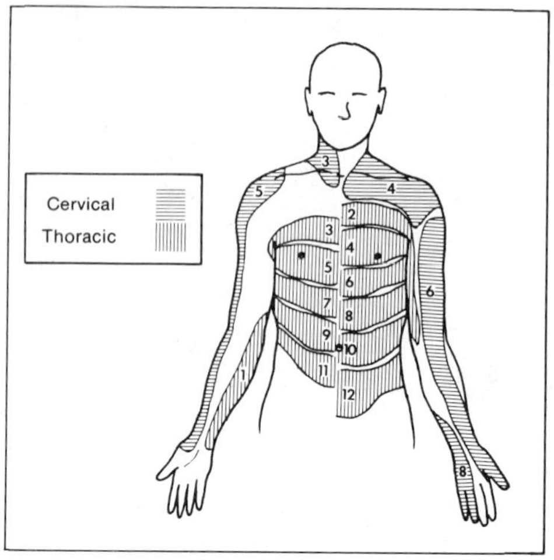

Figure 12.3. The areas of skin known as dermatomes, supplied by the cervical and some of the thoracic posterior spinal nerve roots, taken from the data of Foerster (1933). The cervical dermatomes are indicated by horizontal hatching, while the thoracic roots are shown with vertical hatching. Even-numbered dermatomes are shown on the right side of the figure and the odd-numbered dermatomes on the left. Note that no cervical dermatomes exist above the C3 level. The region along the midline of the body has been purposely left undefined owing to the current uncertainty regarding the precision of lateralization in this region. Also note the considerable degree of overlap of adjacent dermatomes evident in the figure, which, according to some authors, may be conservatively represented here. This particular map was determined by the method of remaining sensibility, resulting from the isolation of one spinal root produced by injury to those above and below the one of interest. This operation leaves a region of sensitivity surrounded by an area of anesthesia. Although many methods have been employed in attempts to define the dermatomes, the general feature common to all such maps is the striated appearance of the dermatomes on the trunk of the body, reflecting the orderly progression of the individual spinal roots. This segregation is rapidly lost at higher neural centers, in which somatotopic organization is typically based on whole digits or limbs, for example, with a single area of the CNS receiving input from regions that cut across dermatomal boundaries (see Werner & Whitsel, 1973).

found in the same restricted layers, or laminae, of the dorsal horn, to wit, laminae IV and V.

The class 3 dorsal horn neurons are smaller than class 1 and 2 types and are responsive to nociceptor stimulation. Finally, class 4 neurons respond to thermoreceptor stimulation, mainly "cold" units. The last two classes are found in the outermost layer of the dorsal horn, that is, lamina I. When receptive fields for these neurons are examined, they tend to be clearly delimited and are smaller on the distal portions of limbs than they are on the trunk.

Packed between the lamina I cells of classes 3 and 4 and the lamina IV and V cells of classes 1 and 2 are cells of lamina II, called the *substantia gelatinosa*. The interesting characteristic of these cells, to be discussed in greater detail later (see Section 9.3), is that they respond to stimuli that affect classes 1, 2, and 3 dorsal horn neurons, except that they are inhibited instead of being excited (Iggo, 1982, p. 393).

The inhibitory effect of the activity of one class of neuron upon another has also been demonstrated. Thus, for example, the nociceptive stimulus will excite the class 3 neurons, but if class 1 and 2 receptors are simultaneously excited, the class 3 neuronal activity is reduced. This effect is called *segmental inhibition* by Iggo (1982, p. 394).

The spinal cord is commonly regarded by the layperson as a transmission system, and the presence of many second-order neurons is not surprising. The axons of one important group of first-order neurons, however, ascend in the posterior funiculus of the cord to terminate in two nuclei in the medulla oblongata. These are the *cuneate* and *gracile fasciculi*, ending in nuclei of the same name. The neurons that synapse with cells in the cuneate nuclei arise mainly in the upper limbs and torso, whereas those synapsing in the gracile nuclei arise in the lower limbs and trunk. When cell bodies of the second-order neurons of these nuclei are examined electrophysiologically (mainly in cats but also in monkeys), they respond to either exteroceptive or interoceptive mechanical stimulation, that is, cutaneous receptors or receptors in muscles, tendons, or joints. The exteroceptive cell types can be shown to have peripheral receptive fields, located on the same side of the body as the nucleus, that are usually small and clearly defined. Light mechanical stimuli will excite them, but some are specific to skin displacement, others to hair movement, and still others to claw movement. Some are inhibited but others facilitated by stimuli applied near the receptive field. Careful exploration of groups of these cells has revealed that a somatotopic "map" of the ipsilateral body can be outlined by judicious sampling of adjacent cells. For a discussion of interoceptive systems, see Chapter 13 by Clark and Horch.

The nuclei just described project afferents to the contralateral ventral posterior lateral nucleus of the thalamus as a band of fibers called the *medial lemniscus* (earlier called the *band of Reil* or the *fillet*). Although there are other sources of second-order (and perhaps third-order) fibers contributing to it, one major branch of the cutaneous system containing these fibers is named the *medial lemniscal system,* and its receptive field characteristics, response to mechanical stimuli, and presence of inhibitory zones, typify the behavior described above for the cuneate and gracile nuclei. For thalamic neurons of this system similar behavior is observed, but there are exceptions in both nuclei. It is now known that class 2 (nociceptor) dorsal horn neurons also ascend in the dorsal column–medial lemniscal system (Iggo, 1982).

A tract that is perceived to be much more complex in its sources, organization, and central projections is the spinothalamic tract, which ascends superficially on the anterolateral quadrant of the cord. The tract contains neurons from classes 1, 2, 3, and 4 of the dorsal horn contralateral to it. Thus all classes of stimuli will excite the neurons within the spinothalamic tract.

Within the thalamus the spinothalamic tract is distributed among at least three major somesthetic areas, where interactions may occur among submodalities in its tract, as well as between it and the other major sensory tracts.

Two other tracts should be noted. First, the spinocervical tract, containing class 1 and 2 dorsal horn neurons, has an uncertain role in the sensory process but contributes axons to the medial lemniscal system already described, terminating in the thalamic nucleus to which the system goes. A second is the spinoreticular tract, which contains neurons from deeper laminae of the dorsal horn that are excited by mechanoreceptors and nociceptors. These project to the contralateral reticular formation of the brain stem, but their receptive fields may be bilateral, cover extensive skin areas, and be both excitatory and inhibitory (Iggo, 1982, p. 397). It is presumed that this tract serves in part the function of alerting the organism.

Projections from the thalamus to the cortex culminate in two major areas: SI, the primary, and SII, the secondary somatosensory area. The area SI receives fibers from the contra-

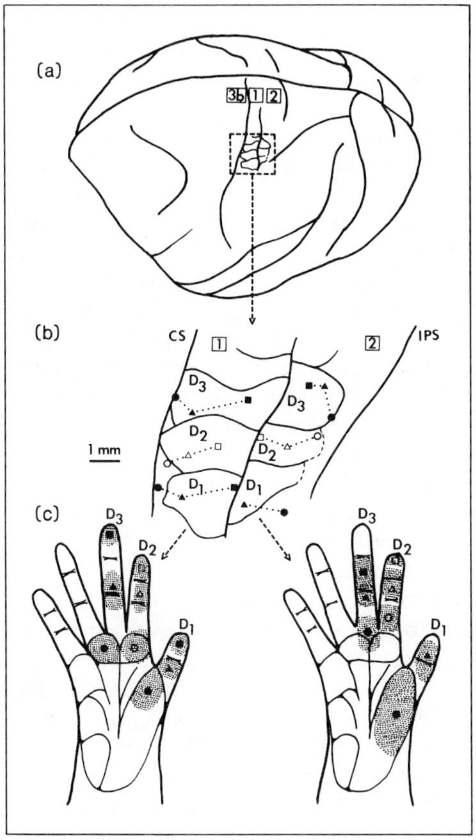

Figure 12.4. Somatotopic representation of the skin's surface at the cortex of the brain of macaque monkeys, as determined by microelectrode mapping techniques (after Kaas, Nelson, Sur, Lin, & Merzenich, 1979). Two regions of the cortex (a) are shown that receive information from the digits of the hand. By microelectrode mapping, in which recording sites are systematically shifted across the surface of the cortex while the peripheral receptive field is established for each, a spatial mapping (albeit distorted) of the body's surface can be described. Such a somatotopic representation for the region of the somatosensory cortex devoted to the fingers is seen in (b). Each of the first three digits (shown in c) is separately represented in the two areas (1 and 2, bounded by the central sulcus, CS, and the interparietal sulcus, IPS). Corresponding symbols in (b) and (c) represent recording sites and their associated receptive fields. The ordering of the receptive fields, shown by the stippled regions in (c), indicates that a mirror-image representation exists on the cortex, such that the regions are joined at the fingertips. These data are representative of similar maps obtained from over 24 animals and almost 8000 recording sites in the primary postcentral parietal somatosensory cortex by these workers. In general, receptive fields show an orderly progression across a particular cortical area correlated with peripheral body regions. As many as four (and possibly more) such representations exist, each of which appears to subserve some unique class of somatic sensations. Other peripheral organizing principles, such as the dermatomes (Figure 12.3) or major nerve trunks (Figure 12.2), appear to be lost at higher levels of the nervous system. Indeed, these authors view the hierarchical model CNS organization as probably incorrect (see also Merzenich & Kaas, 1980).

lateral body, but bilaterally from the face and scalp. Area 3b of this region is the primary projection area for specific skin receptors (see Figure 12.4). On the superior wall of the Sylvian gyrus is found area SII, which is smaller than SI. Its cells suggest from their activity that several different afferent inputs converge upon them. Moreover, the body is bilaterally represented here. Posterior regions of SII are active when nociceptive pathways are excited. So far as interhemispheric connections go, SI receives input from its opposite hemisphere and SII receives input from its opposite, as well as from opposite SI.

One further characterization of these systems should be noted: in addition to a segregation by body region that persists to the cortex, there is simultaneously a segregation by receptor type at some levels (see Werner & Whitsel, 1973, p. 649), including columnar segregation in area SI. Figure 12.4 shows a diagram of the sensory cortex of an anesthetized macaque monkey, showing the location of cortical areas responsive to tactile stimuli. Kaas, Nelson, Sur, Lin, and Merzenich (1979), from whose results the diagram is taken, were able to demonstrate that, in addition to the mirror-image duplication of skin areas shown in the figure, a third cortical area appears responsive to heavier pressures, and a fourth area may also be present (see also Merzenich & Kaas, 1980). In general, the cortex is responsive to the contralateral skin area, but a few ipsilateral units exist. The presence of surround inhibition is common, and responsiveness to mechanical tactile stimuli has most commonly been observed. Recently, responsiveness in area SII to nociceptor activity has been noted (Iggo, 1982, p. 400), and cortical activity resulting from thermal stimulation is also seen in the cat and rat but not yet in primates (Darian-Smith, 1984).

Inhibition has been mentioned and will be again, but it should be noted that neurophysiologists classify three kinds. *Surround inhibition*, as we have noted, occurs when the response of, say, a cortical unit is depressed by stimulation of a skin area adjacent to the receptive field. *Complementary inhibition* occurs when the response is depressed by stimulation of a corresponding contralateral skin area. *Cross-modality inhibition* occurs when the response is depressed by a stimulus of a different class being presented to a nearby or distant skin area. The parallel of these phenomena in psychophysical studies is commonly called *masking* (e.g., see Section 4.3.4).

In addition to the primary, secondary, and tertiary (perhaps also quaternary) cortical somatic areas, there are other regions of the cortex, called *polysensory areas*, in which may be found cells responsive to touch, sound, or visual stimuli (Jabbur & Atweh, 1975). It would be a disservice to leave the reader with the false impression that all the pathways described here are engaged solely in the process of transporting information from the skin to some projection room in the central nervous system (CNS) for the enlightenment of a resident homunculus. Indeed, a recent review (Merzenich & Kaas, 1980) has concluded that the classical view of hierarchically organized processing centers from periphery to association cortex is entirely fallacious. A realistic picture of the activity of the CNS in relation to any single modality is not yet possible. Without correlated research efforts between psychophysics and neurophysiology, it is doubtful that a complete description of CNS function relative to behavior will ever be made.

2. OUTLINE OF THIS CHAPTER

The remainder of this chapter is devoted to a description of the sensory and perceptual phenomena associated with the stimulation of the skin by pressures, vibrations, thermal stimuli of various kinds, noxious stimuli, and percutaneous electrical stimuli. The experimental methods will involve mainly psychophysical manipulations, but electrophysiological studies will be cited where helpful in further describing, explaining, or clarifying theory.

The relatively few studies concerned with interactions among cutaneous modalities are considered, and a final discussion deals with some current and potential applications of the cutaneous channels to problems of information processing.

3. GENERAL REFERENCES IN CUTANEOUS SENSITIVITY

For an excellent historical review of experiment and theory in psychophysics up to 1940, Boring's (1942) book is unparalleled. A more exhaustive account may be found in von Skramlik (1937). A general overview of the skin senses of more recent vintage may be found in Geldard (1972) or Iggo (1982), and a somewhat more extensive but laconic description is given by Sinclair (1967). The chapters by Rose and Mountcastle (1959), Zotterman (1959), and Sweet (1959), are classics in neurophysiology and are updated by the newer handbooks edited by Iggo (1973) and Loewenstein (1971a). Lederman (1977) has compiled a bibliography on touch, amounting to about 4000 titles taken mainly from *Psychological Abstracts* but including references from the National Technical Information Service, as well as selected books and conference proceedings.

Special topics ranging fairly broadly from anatomy to psychophysics are dealt with by the two books edited by Kenshalo (1968, 1979), and one by Gordon (1978). Similar works are those edited by Carterette and Friedman (1978), de Reuck and Knight (1966), Kornhuber (1975), and Zotterman (1976). Morphologic and biophysical properties of the skin are described in Montagna (1956) and Tregear (1966). Finally, the *Annual Review of Psychology*, *Annual Review of Physiology*, and *Annual Review of Neuroscience* have regularly published chapters on cutaneous senses under the heading *somesthesis*, the *somatosensory system*, or specific modalities.

References to more complex perceptual or cognitive functions of the skin will be found in Chapter 31 by Loomis and Lederman.

4. THE SENSE OF TOUCH

Whereas "touch" is the word commonly applied to any skin sense, it is more precisely given to those mechanical contacts with the skin that elicit reports of "touch," "contact," "tap," "pressure," "vibration," and so forth. It is thus necessary to specify both a stimulus event and a response class to limit the possible domain of discussion or inquiry. Without such dual specification it is possible to infer (falsely) that every mechanical impact produces experiences of touch or to infer (falsely) that a report of "touch" or other responses in the class was preceded by a mechanical impact. It is only after a continuing intimate and active association with devices for stimulating the skin that one discovers the wealth of qualitative experiences afforded by the various modes of stimulation, as well as, to one's dismay, the ineffability of many of these experiences. There are, therefore, many borrowed terms in touch: A contact may be "bright" or "ponderous"; a vibration may be "high pitched" or "loud." Far more exotic descriptions may be found in the literature; what determines their acceptability in experimental discourse is their repeatability under controlled conditions.

4.1 Anatomic Correlates

4.1.1. The Skin as a Transmission Medium. The skin extends on the average only 1 or 2 mm below the outer layer, although it is thinner in some regions than others. The facial skin is as thin as 0.5 mm, whereas the skin of the sole may be 4.0 mm or thicker. This semiplastic membrane overlays a viscoelastic substrate that varies greatly in local density, hardness, and other physical properties that affect its ability to propagate mechanical disturbances. Studies of biophysical properties of the skin have shown, in general, that skin tissue overlying muscle will attenuate such disturbances along its surface according to the inverse-square law (see Franke, von Gierke, Oestreicher, & von Wittern, 1951). The manner of propagation is a continually damped traveling wave on the skin surface, generated by a combination of shear and compression waves within the substrate (von Békésy, 1967, p. 119). A theoretical discussion of the problem of propagation is provided by Franke and coworkers (1951). A more elaborate and neurophysiologically oriented model, involving principles of continuum mechanics, is presented by Phillips and Johnson (1981).

When care is taken to explore a grid-marked patch of skin with a so-called von Frey hair (a horse hair or nylon filament, calibrated for force and attached to a handle), it is readily seen that some skin locations are far more sensitive than others to the displacements produced by the hair. A consistent finding with respect to such sensitivity "peaks" has been their location with reference to skin hair; such spots are near the base of the hair and on its "windward" side. Similar spots, obviously without the hirsute landmark, can be found on glabrous skin, such as that near the volar carpal folds. On glabrous palmar skin, sensitivity is uniformly high.

The density of sensitivity peaks varies over the body surface, and at one time it was thought that the spot density was correlated with innervation density. A careful psychophysical study (Guilford & Lovewell, 1936) demonstrated that spot density for a given skin area increases with force of the stimulator as a culmulative normal distribution function. This suggests that, far from being an outcropping of a sensory end organ, the pressure spot is a convenient port of variable admittance through which mechanical energy may be propagated. Our understanding of the exact manner and degree of distribution of energy below the surface of the skin is based mainly on measurements made of mechanical impedance at the driving point (i.e., at the point of stimulator contact) or of propagation distances over the surface (see, e.g., Franke et al., 1951; Geldard, 1975; Kiedel, 1956, 1968; Moore, 1970; Moore & Mundie, 1972; Sherrick, 1953). Further understanding of these processes awaits such measures as the transfer impedance through the layers of skin tissue (cf. Quilliam, 1978, p. 14).

4.1.2. Receptor Types, Location, Density, and Neural Connections. Although there is still some disagreement among histologists concerning the typical locations of cutaneous end organs, how best to expose them to view, or the range of forms a receptor may take and still remain a member of a single class, there is general agreement on a fair-sized group of end organs thought to be skin mechanoreceptors. Their distribution differs in hairy and glabrous skin.

The most common nervous termination of either hairy or glabrous skin is the free nerve ending, perceived microscopically like the mouse's tale of Lewis Carroll, that is, a fine hairlike proliferation that dwindles in size and disappears. The dermal nerve net comprises thousands of such tiny fibers wandering over, around, and through the various skin layers. One class of stimuli that excites them appears to be strong mechanical displacements (Kruger, Perl, & Sedivec, 1979). A more clearly organized set of such endings appears at the follicle of the hair, however. Here the fibers, numbering two or more, surround the follicle cylindrically, as well as running parallel to its axis. Some histologists have described this formation as a "basket ending," from the weaving effect perceived, but others object to the implication that these are encapsulated in some way. The previously mentioned finding of pressure spots near the hair bases has been explained by the action of these nerve endings (von Békésy, 1939; Geldard, 1974b; Merzenich & Harrington, 1969). Other than basket endings, the dermal layers of human hairy skin contain *Merkel discs* near the hairs (Iggo, 1974) and *Ruffini endings*, spindle-shaped capsules 0.5–2 mm in length (Iggo & Andres, 1982).

In glabrous skin, encapsulated receptors are common, and two or three categories are agreed on by the majority of histologists. The dermal nerve net is still a dominant feature, to be sure, but in addition careful excision and staining reveals tiny corpuscles located in greatest quantities in the papillary ridges of the fingertips, as seen in Figure 12.5. These are called *Meissner corpuscles*, and, from their position, high density, and general appearance, are thought to transmit transient electrochemical surges to their nerves in response to ambient pressures. A single Meissner corpuscle may accept up to nine separate nerves, any of which may also branch to supply other nearby Meissner corpuscles. Even at the organized receptor level, therefore, simultaneous convergence and divergence of the neural code is present. Exactly how this arrangement acts in coding neural signals is as yet only dimly perceived.

Another end organ commonly found in glabrous skin is the Merkel receptor complex, or hederiform ending, appearing as expanded tips of nonmyelinated ends of myelinated axons, lying apposed to the Merkel cell. Some authors suspect that they are modified Meissner corpuscles (see, e.g., Sinclair, 1967, p. 46), but others accord them independent status (Iggo, 1974; Iggo & Andres, 1982, pp. 4ff; Quilliam, 1978, p. 7).

The best-described and, physiologically speaking, best-understood end organ is the Pacinian corpuscle, an encapsulated nerve ending that dwarfs all others and is served exclusively by a single dedicated nerve fiber. It is considered by some to be of equivocal value as a *cutaneous* receptor (Sinclair, 1967, p. 57), but others regard its moderate distance from the skin surface (2–3 mm) and its "private line" to the central nervous system (via medium-sized myelinated fibers) to place it high on the list of candidates for tactile receptor (Iggo & Andres, 1982, pp. 15ff). The total number of these corpuscles in strategic locations, such as the palmar side of the hands and fingers, is about 1000 to 1500, with greatest density in the distal joints. They may also be found near blood vessels, in the joint capsules, and near lymph nodes (Sinclair, 1967, p. 43), where their sensory role is less clearly defined by their location.

4.1.3. Central Connections. The initial colligation of the nerves from these various receptor types occurs in the peripheral cutaneous nerve bundles already described, whence they proceed with their neighbors to the dorsal roots of the spinal cord. It is of some interest to note that, for example, the two or more fibers innervating a single hair follicle may proceed to entirely separate dorsal roots, that is, dermatomal segments (Munger, 1982; Sinclair, 1967). Whatever functional advantage may accrue to such a broadcasting structural arrangement has not yet been thoroughly analyzed, but it does guarantee against total loss of sensation in a skin area if a dorsal root is blocked.

As we have already described, the central projections of the receptors for mechanical energy are by no means completely understood, but rapidly evolving techniques in neuroanatomy are changing this picture (see, e.g., E.G. Jones & Hartman, 1978). It is worth repeating that the vast majority of subcortical and cortical responses thus far reported are to mechanical stimulation of the skin (see Darian-Smith, 1982; Kaas et al., 1979; Merzenich & Kaas, 1980). To this should be added the statement that electrical stimulation will also elicit responses, but, as will be seen, no one can be certain about what neural complexes the electrical energy distribution excites at the periphery.

4.2. Physiological Aspects

4.2.1. Classification of Receptor Systems by Function. It is rarely possible for physiologists to devise a preparation that gives them the histologists' view of receptors and at the same time affords them the opportunity to record their activities electrically. Except for the study of the Pacinian corpuscle, the common technique has been that of microneurography, that is, to isolate a single peripheral nerve fiber in a bundle with a microelectrode, then to probe the likely area of skin to find the receptive field for the unit thus obtained. As a result, physiological receptor types are not often described by their structural properties but *instead* by their functional characteristics. Thus receptors may be classified as slowly adapting (meaning that the nerve response continues for a second or more with unabated discharges) or rapidly adapting (i.e., discharge rate falls precipitously in a fraction of a second to a low or zero value). In addition, they may be described as displacement-, velocity-, acceleration-, or jerk-sensitive, depending on frequency response. The character of the receptive field may also be used to typify a receptor, as well as determine whether it responds better to one direction of pull on the skin than to another. Differential sensitivity to various rates of vibration have been used to sort receptor classes, and the presence of the receptive field in hairy, as opposed to glabrous, skin permits some differentiation of classes.

Differentiation of nerve fibers according to their conduction velocities can also be made, and it has been well known since the pioneer work of Erlanger, Gasser, and Bishop (1924) that fiber size, threshold, and conduction velocity are highly correlated quantities. Another dichotomy included within the spectrum of fiber size is that of myelination, that is, the fatty sheath surrounding the fiber or the lack of it. In general, conduction velocities are known to vary (in humans) from 120 m/sec to about 1.0 m/sec in peripheral nerves. When measurements are made in human physiological preparations, the values are frequently used to characterize the size of fiber from which the reading was made, in conjunction with such other data as nerve firing rate, refractory period, spontaneous activity, and threshold.

4.2.2. Microneurography. The use of the technique just described with alert humans has been advanced particularly by Swedish electrophysiologists (Johansson, 1979; Torebjörk, 1979; Vallbo & Johansson, 1978; Vallbo et al., 1979). The third cited reference contains a description of four receptor classes that the authors were able to segregate by their method: two slowly adapting and two rapidly adapting types found in the glabrous skin of the palms and fingers (see Figure 12.1). One of the rapidly adapting types of unit appears to have a fairly extensive receptive field (e.g., a whole digit), with indistinct borders, and a single point of maximal sensitivity, that is, the point at which a reliable increase in neural firing rate is seen for the least energy input to the skin. Because its behavior closely parallels that seen in other physiological preparations that have dissected out the identifiable receptor and the nerve

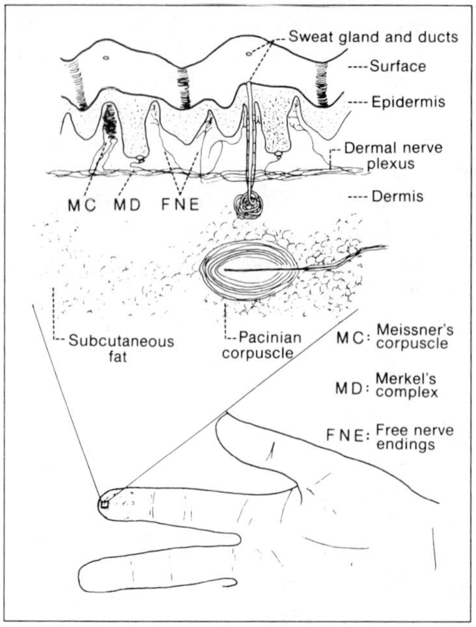

Figure 12.5. The structure of glabrous skin, as illustrated by a section through the finger pad. (Adapted from Vallbo & Johansson, 1978.) The figure illustrates the major organized neural structures found in fingerprint skin and their relationship to its important noneural components. The surface of the skin itself is usually covered by a layer of dead epidermal cells, sloughing off throughout the life of the individual. These cells can increase the resistance to current flow through the skin's surface and often are removed by abrasion or cleansers for electrocutaneous stimulation or recording (see Section 8.1). Below these cells lie the live cells of the epidermis, made up of several layers (totaling to as much as 1.0 mm in thickness in the fingerpad) distinguishable from one another on morphological grounds. The layers are actually intermediate stages in the 20–30-day cycle of cell migration outward to the skin's surface. The epidermal–dermal interface is a highly convoluted surface with pits and plugs, each of which is often concerned with some neural structure. In the skin of the finger pad, the ridges and depressions in this interface mirror those on the surface which make up the fingerprint. Large dense plugs underlie each superficial ridge, and through these pass the ducts of the sweat glands, which actually lie much deeper, at the bottom of the dermal layer. The dermis is a layer of connective tissue ranging in thickness from 0.4 mm in the prepuce to 3 mm or more in the palms of the hands, averaging 1–2 mm over the body's surface. It is this layer that contains the majority of the cutaneous vascular system (blood and lymph), some smooth and striated muscles, and most of the major components of cutaneous innervation, including nerve fibers and both free and encapsulated endings. Below the dermis lies the superficial fascia, separating it from the deeper-lying structures, such as muscle and bone. This layer is often fatty and contains fibers interconnecting the dermis with deeper tissues. The major neural elements of glabrous skin consist of the free nerve endings (FNE), Merkel cell-neurite complexes (MD; once believed to be encapsulated endings known as Merkel's discs), Meissner's corpuscles (MC), and the Pacinian corpuscles. Although each of these components has, at one time or another, been associated by theory with some class of tactile sensitivity, caution must be advised in such attribution (see, e.g., Kenshalo & Nafe, 1962). The axons from the first three of these travel back to the CNS through the dermal nerve plexus. The FNE can enter the epidermis and has been supposed at one time to mediate all forms of stimulation: mechanical, thermal, and noxious stimuli may excite these endings. The MC, which may be 30 × 80 μm in size and sits 0.5 mm below the surface, lies within the upwellings of dermal tissue and may be served by five or more nerve fibers. It appears to be maximally sensitive to mechanical deformation, as do the MD. The MD consists of enlarged ends of nerve fibers apposed to specialized cells lying at the bottom of the dermal plugs. This position could provide a mechanical filter for "tuning" the response of these receptors, which also appear to be maximally sensitive to mechanical stimuli. The largest structure to be found in the skin is the Pacinian corpuscle (as large as 1 × 4 mm), lying 2–3 mm below the skin's surface (as well as in muscles, joints, and mesentery). This mechanoreceptor has its own mechanical filter in the form of its lamellate encapsulation. The characteristics of this receptor have been extensively studied, owing primarily to the ease with which it may be identified and dissected (Loewenstein, 1971b; Sato, 1961). See Quilliam (1978) for a more complete description of the structure of the skin.

together, Vallbo and Johansson infer that the receptor from which they have recorded is the Pacinian corpuscle. By means of somewhat less direct lines of evidence, the second type of rapidly adapting unit is thought to be the Meissner corpuscle, the two slowly adapting units Merkel's receptor complexes and Ruffini endings (Vallbo & Johansson, 1978, p. 38). The Ruffini endings are regarded by some histologists as morphologically too ambiguous to be called encapsulated (Sinclair, 1967, p. 47; but see Iggo & Andres, 1982).

4.2.3. The Pacinian Corpuscle. The largest and most easily identified end organ in the somesthetic system is the Pacinian corpuscle, which can achieve a size of 1 by 4 mm (Sinclair, 1967, p. 43). Besides having the ovoid shape of an onion, the core is surrounded by layer on layer of tissue that gives the corpuscle its lamellate appearance in cross section. A single myelinated nerve fiber of moderately large diameter emanates from the core and proceeds without branching to the CNS: Pacinians have "private lines." Calculation of the power required to stimulate a single Pacinian at its best frequency (sinusoidal mechanical vibrotactile stimulus) yields a value of 2×10^{-8} W which, although a small value, is many orders of magnitude greater than the calculated minimal auditory or visual stimulus intensities of 10^{-22} W (Khanna & Sherrick, 1981).

The proximal stimulus for the excitation of the Pacinian body appears to be a gradient of pressure across its long axis (Loewenstein, 1971b). As was noted, the gradient, if sustained, will produce a high-frequency burst of impulses in the nerve fiber that quickly subsides to a low or zero rate as befits a rapidly adapting receptor. This response to transients is not owing solely to mechanical design; Loewenstein was able to divest the Pacinian of its laminar coats and stimulate the core. Although the generator potential of the corpuscle showed faithful reproduction of the pressure variation, the nerve impulses appeared only with onset or offset of the potential.

Direct recording from other observable end organs in the skin has not been made, so that the pairing of encapsulated receptor types with functional properties is as yet an interesting but speculative exercise (see Iggo & Andres, 1982, pp. 9, 12). Current hypotheses concerning the role of any end organ in the mediation of a particular class of sensory experiences must be tempered with the caveat that even a complete knowledge of the functioning of a single unit in the system tells us no more about concerted nervous activity than the knowledge of behavior of a single railway passenger tells us of the probable response of a group of individuals in the Grand Central Terminal of New York City.

4.3. Psychophysical Aspects

4.3.1. Methods of Stimulation. Three major classes of mechanical stimuli can be described: *step functions*, in which a displacement is effected and held for a significant period, say 1 sec or more; *impulse functions*, in which a transient of some given waveform is produced for a few milliseconds; and *periodic functions*, which displace the skin at constant or variable frequencies for several milliseconds. For the most part, these forms of mechanical energy are currently imparted to the skin by electromechanical transducers, usually modified loudspeakers (Geldard, 1940a) or electrodynamic mechanical shakers employed by engineers for testing electronic systems (Sherrick, 1975). The recent acquisition of piezoceramic elements has permitted the design of compact arrays of mechanical transducers in large numbers (Cholewiak & Sherrick, 1981; Sherrick, 1975). An early source of mechanical stimulation was the air jet (Bellows, 1936), as was the tuning fork and the von Frey hair. The hair produces a fairly clean step function when properly applied, inasmuch as it bends, when pressed briskly on the skin, to exert a constant force at its calibrated value even when small vertical displacements by the experimenter's hand occur (see von Békésy, 1967, p. 119).

To give quantitative expression to the mechanical stimulus, a variety of ingenious solutions have been found. Geldard (1940a, p. 272) described a method employing stroboscopic illumination on the vibrating contactor, with the flash frequency mistuned to allow the viewer to see the slow excursions of the skin and its stimulator. Most recently, small accelerometers or solid-state resistive strain gauges have been recruited to the task of quantifying the movement of the driver element (Cholewiak & Sherrick, 1981; Sherrick, 1975; Verrillo, 1968).

Whereas the von Frey hair is calibrated in units of force, or force per unit radius or per unit area of hair tip, the common physical value measured in most experimental work is displacement. There is some reason to believe that energy is a better measure of stimulus intensity, inasmuch as the skin impedance varies with frequency of the stimulus, but a majority of studies have reported only amplitude or force values (see Moore & Mundie, 1972).

4.3.2. Thresholds for Touch. For step-function inputs produced by von Frey hairs, the most recent survey was performed by Weinstein (1968), who examined a variety of body loci in 47 subjects of both sexes. Threshold values were obtained by the method of limits, that is, increasing the hair force until a report of touch sensation occurred. Mean values of absolute thresholds varied from 5 mg on the faces of the females (nose, cheek, upper lip) to 355 mg on the great toes of the males. Moreover, the expected significant differences among body loci were accompanied by significant differences between sexes, significant interactions between body loci and laterality (right vs. left sides), and between body loci and sex. Figure 12.6 is taken from Weinstein's data and shows threshold values for selected body loci. Note that the face and torso are most sensitive to pressure, followed by the fingers and lower extremities.

A similar survey of vibrotactile thresholds was made by Wilska (1954). Figure 12.6 shows a sample of body loci for which vibrotactile thresholds were measured. Wilska measured threshold sensitivity (as amplitude of vibration) to a 1-cm^2 contactor vibrating at 200 Hz. In view of the fact that poorest vibratory sensitivity is found at the buttocks, it is clear that flying "by the seat of one's pants" may have been even more hazardous than the early aviators thought. It may seem somewhat puzzling to note the discrepancy of pressure and vibrotactile thresholds on some body areas; the lips, which are most sensitive to pressure, rank well below the fingers in vibrotactile sensitivity. A partial explanation for this may come from comparing the measures employed. Weinstein's pressure measurements were made with fine nylon hairs, calibrated for force. Wilska employed a comparatively large contactor (1.1 cm diameter) and measured amplitude of a 200-Hz sinusoidal vibration. Considering local differences in skin impedance, as well as the temporal characteristics of the mechanical energy, it is difficult to say which stimulus carried more energy at a given site.

4.3.2.1. Spatial Summation. The problem of comparison among stimulus classes and body areas is compounded by the integrative action of the receptive system. Spatial summation of energy is believed to take place in the skin under certain

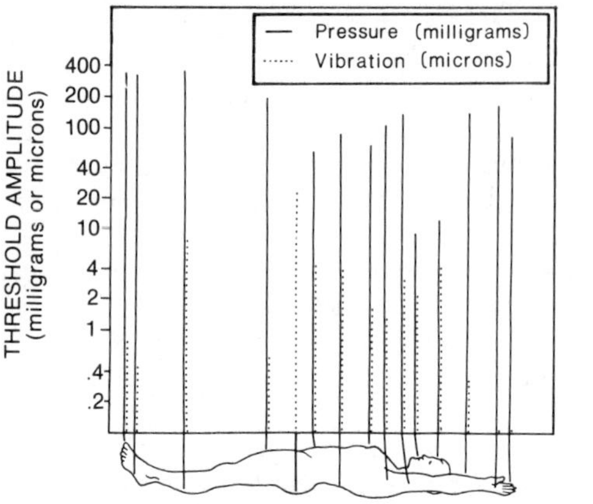

Figure 12.6. Thresholds for pressure (solid bars) and vibration (dots) at several selected body sites. (Adapted from Weinstein, 1968.) Thresholds for pressure were obtained by Weinstein (1968) using von Frey nylon filaments that bend at a calibrated force. These were applied to selected body sites in six alternating series of increasing or decreasing force. The observer's task was to indicate the appearance or disappearance of the sensation, respectively. Threshold was defined as the mean of the six determinations. Although Weinstein tested both sides of the body on males and females, the mean level across sides is presented for only the male observers. In terms of pressure sensitivity, the most sensitive area is the face, followed by the trunk and fingers. Whereas the sensitivity profile across the body was similar for males and females, females were generally more sensitive by approximately 0.4–0.6 log unit. In the case of pressure sensitivity, thresholds did not decrease proximodistally (Vierordt's law) as occurs with point localization and two-point thresholds (see Figure 12.16), as well as with vibrotactile sensitivity (dotted lines). Thresholds for vibration are taken from Wilska's (1954) data, obtained with a 1-cm^2 contactor presenting a 200-Hz sinusoidal signal. Threshold varies at these body sites over a 46-dB (re 1 μm) range. It is notable that there is little correspondence between thresholds for the two types of stimulation. The palm of the hand, for example, has one of the lowest thresholds to vibration and yet one of the highest to pressure. Differences, however, in the stimuli both temporally and spatially may make direct comparisons difficult. Furthermore, different types of skin (e.g., sole of the foot versus lips) have different biophysical and biomechanical characteristics that could easily interact with the mode of stimulation. It does appear, however, that vibratory sensitivity is well correlated with cortical representations of particular body sites. For example, the digits are represented in an area of somatosensory cortex (of the owl monkey) that is some 10 times greater than that for the thigh (Kaas, Nelson, Sur, Lin, & Merzenich, 1979).

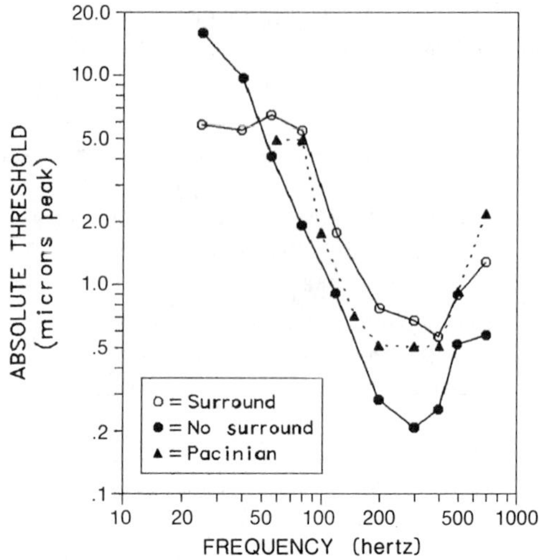

Figure 12.7. Absolute threshold at the thenar eminence as a function of stimulus frequency, with and without a static surround (adapted from Gescheider, Capraro, Frisina, Hamer, & Verrillo, 1978), compared with the physiological response of a single cutaneous receptor. For the human vibrotactile thresholds (filled and solid circles), stimuli were presented with 5-mm-diameter contactors indented 1 mm into the skin of the thenar eminence (fleshy pad on the palmar surface at the base of the thumb). In the surround condition, the contactor touched the skin through a 7-mm hole. In the no-surround condition, stimuli were actually presented through a 60-mm-diameter hole, providing a 27.5-mm gap around the contactor. Stimuli consisted of 1-sec bursts of vibration with 100-msec rise–fall times presented once every two sec. For each of the 10 frequencies of vibration, five adult observers tracked their thresholds using the von Békésky tracking method, raising the intensity of the signal when it disappeared, lowering the intensity when it reappeared. Typically, thresholds for samples of 5–10 young adult males produce a standard error about the mean of 1–3 dB for stimulus frequencies in this range. In both cases, the high-frequency portion of the frequency response curve shows a similar shape. The presence of a surround, however, raises the overall threshold in the high-frequency region by some 6–8 dB. In the low-frequency region, the presence of the surround reduces thresholds. It has been proposed by Gescheider and colleagues that the function obtained with a surround describes the interaction of at least two receptor systems. The presence of a surround allows for the disclosure of a less sensitive, quickly adapting (QA) population of receptors whose threshold is normally about 6 μm. Without a surround, it is proposed that this threshold is raised well above 15 μm. Thus in this condition the thresholds recorded are a function of the response characteristics of a much more sensitive receptor system. It has been hypothesized that the Pacinian corpuscle provides the anatomical basis for this sensitive system. Indeed, the response of a single corpuscle (triangles), recorded by Sato (1961), shows a similarly shaped high-frequency response curve to those recorded psychophysically when the isolated corpuscles from cat mesentery, held at 37° C, were stimulated with comparable frequencies of vibration. The voltage levels from his paper (his Fig. 7) were transformed to microns peak displacement using his calibration plot (his Fig. 1). Talbot, Darian-Smith, Kornhuber, and Mountcastle (1968) later confirmed the shape of this function with single unit recordings from Pacinian corpuscles (PC) in the intact hand of the monkey. For the psychophysical conditions described above, absence of a surround results in thresholds lower than that for a single PC, presumably through the mechanism of spread of energy and spatial summation. No such system, however, has been described to account adequately for the higher-threshold, lower-frequency portion of the function. This fact, as well as several other complicating factors (see Section 4.3.2.1), suggest that the variables underlying the human psychophysical response to vibration are incompletely understood as yet.

conditions (Verrillo, 1968), as is temporal summation (Gescheider, 1976; Verrillo, 1968). It has been the contention of Verrillo that the threshold response of observers to a wide range of vibrotactile frequencies is based on the activities of two mechanoreceptive systems (Verrillo, 1968). The curve for vibrotactile thresholds is shown in Figure 12.7 for two sets of stimulus conditions, one without a static surround and one with a static surround. The first of these was the mode of stimulation chosen by most investigators and reveals what appears to be the action of a broadly tuned bandpass filter. The second curve is the form obtained by Verrillo when he stimulated the thenar eminence of the palm (the fleshy area medial to the base of the thumb) with a contactor of more than 2 mm diameter, through a hole in a heavy plate (on which the palm rested securely). If the hole diameter is 2 mm larger than the contactor, and the contactor indents the skin by 0.5–1.0 mm, the results shown are obtained over the frequency range of 20–700 Hz for sinusoidal vibrations.

The discontinuity in the response curve appears at a frequency of about 40 Hz. The low-frequency limb of the function appears to be a constant value; thus, Verrillo suggests, this part of the curve is generated by receptive systems that are not frequency dependent, hence show no temporal summation. The middle- and upper-frequency portions of the curve are determined by receptive systems that exhibit temporal summation and hence are frequency sensitive. By manipulating the diameter of the vibrating contactor (and the surround as well), Verrillo could show that, below a critical contactor diameter (about 1.0 mm), thresholds over the entire range of frequencies were very nearly constant. The inference drawn has been that these conditions expose the response function of a receptive system that exhibits neither spatial nor temporal integrative capacities. When a large contactor with no surround is employed, the system just described is not revealed because the second system, which has both spatial and temporal integrative properties, possesses the lower threshold.

Studies in electrophysiology support, in part, the duplex hypothesis that Verrillo has proposed. The work of Mountcastle and his colleagues in particular demonstrates the parallel between the response of the Pacinian corpuscle to vibration and the human psychophysical function (see, e.g., Merzenich & Harrington, 1969; Mountcastle, Talbot, Darian-Smith, & Kornhuber, 1967; Talbot, Darian-Smith, Kornhuber, & Mountcastle, 1968). Two aspects of Verrillo's hypothesis are not supported by electrophysiological findings, however. First, no receptive system has been found to respond at a constant amplitude over the entire frequency range, as Verrillo has hypothesized. Second, the Pacinian corpuscle shows not only the same rate of decrease in threshold amplitude as the psychophysical function but also responds more readily as coupling of the vibrotactile energy to the tissue is improved (Merzenich & Harrington, 1969, p. 252). These findings suggest that spatial summation of receptor responses is not necessarily what results if contactor area is increased. Indeed, Craig and Sherrick (1969), Geldard, Sherrick, and Cholewiak (1980, p. 18), and B. G. Green and Craig (1974) have shown that increases of static force of the contactor (which normally must occur when contactor area is increased and indentation held constant) will similarly reduce thresholds to vibration when they alone are manipulated.

Craig (1968), who reviewed the literature on the subject, was able to demonstrate spatial summation on the ventral thigh by presenting two spatially separated 100-Hz vibrotactile stimuli simultaneously. He found that approximately 2.5 dB less amplitude was required when the two stimuli were presented together than when either was presented alone. Probability summation was ruled out when its predicted value was shown to be 0.5 dB. Craig's finding held for three spatial separations (8, 12, and 20 cm), as well as for separate fingers on one hand and even bilateral presentations. When a frequency of 9 Hz was employed, or when two different frequencies (160 and 360 Hz) were used, no significant summation appeared, however. A report by Franzén, Markowitz, and Swets (1970) challenged Craig's conclusions, pointing out that, under the assumption of a single-channel model of attention, spatial summation appears to occur when the observer does not know whether one or both loci will be stimulated but does not occur when the observer knows the loci beforehand. In a later paper, Shiffrin, Craig, and Cohen (1973) demonstrated that the single-channel model of attention is not applicable to vibrotactile processing or, under similar conditions, to visual processing and that the criticism of Franzén and coworkers was not valid.

Does the sense of touch exhibit spatial summation? If we consider only absolute-threshold or weak-signal conditions, we may conclude that the amount of summation is small, that is, about 2 dB for two loci. Moreover, this summation is probably not peripheral, since widely separated sites can be involved (Craig, 1968). The local summation effects that Verrillo has described (1968, p. 142) are not clearly attributable to areal summation because the effects of static force of the contactor are not partialled out. In recent work, Geldard and coworkers (1980, pp. 15–20) were able to show that when number (hence area) of contactors was varied over a factor of 8 and static force was systematically varied to produce several degrees of skin indentation, the simplest relation of physical value to absolute threshold involved static force of the contactor, at least for a 250-Hz sinusoidal vibration.

4.3.2.2. Temporal Summation. It was mentioned earlier that a second hypothesis of the duplex mechanoreceptor theory for vibrotactile sensitivity is that one receptor class (the low-frequency branch) exhibits no temporal summation, which accounts for the flat low-frequency section of Figure 12.7. The other receptor class, however, does exhibit this behavior, and Verrillo (1968, p. 147) and Gescheider (1976) have documented these facts, as well as pointing out that Zwislocki's (1960) theory of auditory temporal summation predicts the empirical results very well. B. G. Green (1976) examined the effects of signal duration on absolute threshold at several frequencies and confirmed, in part, Verrillo's findings, that temporal summation occurs for higher frequencies and larger-sized contactors and that the data fit Zwislocki's theoretical predictions. In addition, Green found that both large and very small contactor areas (i.e., less than 1 mm diameter) produce some temporal summation, albeit less than that for larger contactors, at low frequencies of vibration. It is Green's conclusion that not only is temporal summation a CNS phenomenon but also that contactor area and signal duration determine vibrotactile thresholds in a manner suggesting that these physical variables interact strongly. The exact nature of the interaction is yet unclear, but it is probably not peripheral.

The problem of threshold shifts with area or duration of stimulation is equally refractory for waveforms other than sinusoidal. For example, let us examine Boring's (1942, p. 490) interpolations from the curves of von Frey and Kiesow, who measured the area and force at absolute threshold for a variety of "microscopic" and "macroscopic" hair stimulators (i.e., producing step functions of force on the skin). If one examines the variation of threshold values for microscopic stimuli, with tension (grams per millimeter of radius) as the stimulus dimension, the variation is almost zero. Thus von Frey and Kiesow concluded that tension is the adequate stimulus, since it is constant when other measures vary. As the contactor area grows further, however, the simple relation of tension to threshold disappears, and no equally simple dimension appears to replace it.

When a stimulus of the impulse form is presented to the skin, it can be shown that temporal summation occurs. Hill (1967, p. 240) was able to measure thresholds as a function of duration of a unidirectional mechanical pulse and found a functional relation between duration and threshold (in peak amplitude of displacement) that satisfied the equation

$$A_t = \frac{2}{(1 - \exp - [t \div 1.5])},$$

where A_t is the threshold amplitude in μm; t is the pulse duration in msec. The model for such an equation is an integrator with a time constant of 1.5 msec, and the data fit the curve very well (see Figure 12.8). The data apply only to the fingerpad and probably only for the small area of stimulation employed (0.6-mm-diameter contactor). So far as we know, there are no systematic studies characterizing the temporal integrating properties of the skin for impulsive stimuli as a function of locus and area of stimulation.

Examination of vibrotactile sensitivity on skin areas where separate pressure-sensitive spots can be isolated has been infrequent. Geldard (1940b, p. 286) examined a number of such spots on the volar wrist, where no hairs were observable. He

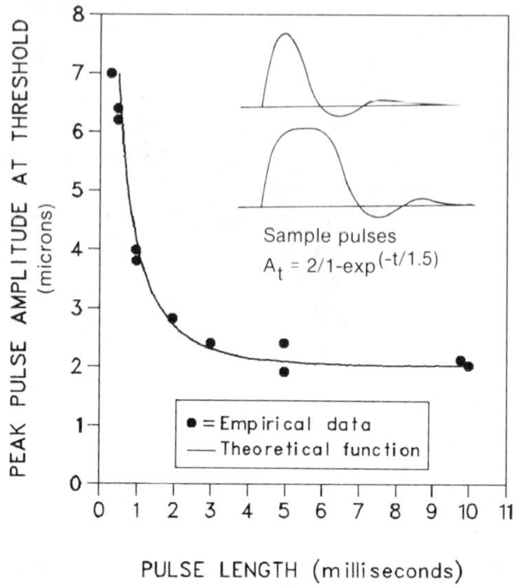

Figure 12.8. Evidence for temporal summation, shown by a plot of amplitude of a rectangular pulse at threshold as a function of its duration. Stimuli were presented to the finger by a stiff, short piezoceramic bender with a 0.64-mm-diameter contactor through a plate with a 2.3-mm hole. Thresholds were obtained by presenting rectangular pulses (as shown in the inset, 1 msec/division) at 2 pulses per second and slowly increasing their amplitude until the observer just felt the taps. The pulse duration was varied, on successive trials, from 0.35–100 msec. Only those data from the first 10 msec are shown since threshold was constant at 2 μm for pulse durations of 10–100 msec. These thresholds were repeatable on the same locus to less than 1 dB on successive trials. The data are well fit by the exponential function shown on the graph, which has a 1.5-msec time constant and may be compared with those obtained with electrocutaneous stimuli in the strength-duration curves shown in Figure 12.33. Although the mode of stimulation was quite different, similarly shaped functions result on the logarithmic coordinates. (From J. W. Hill, *The perception of multiple tactile stimuli*, Tech. Rep. No. 4823-1, Stanford University, 1967. Reprinted with permission.)

found that the frequency response of these spots was, on the average, a flat function, when five values from 64 to 1024 Hz were examined. Von Békésy (1939), however, claimed that pressure- and vibration-sensitive spots near hairs were separate and that the latter showed a U-shaped sensitivity function for frequency with a minimum somewhat below that found for the finger. Thus not only did von Békésy find a possible spatial separation of two functional aspects of tactile sensitivity, but also evidence for temporal summation of the receptive system on hairy skin. Sherrick (1960) attempted to replicate the studies of Geldard and von Békésy and found occasional separation of vibrotactile- and pressure-sensitive spots but only in a random relation. By employing three contactor diameters, Sherrick was able to show that the flat function is most apparent for the smallest contactor, and that the U shape appeared as contactor area increased, implying that temporal summation on pressure spots near hairs will occur only when a large enough area of tissue is disturbed. More recently, Geldard and coworkers (1980, pp. 17–18) have shown that, for a 1-mm-diameter contactor acting through a 3-mm hole in a static surround on the thenar eminence of the hand, a frequency function will be obtained that appears flat if the commonly chosen values of frequency are examined. When smaller frequency separations are tested, however, particularly in the range 150–300 Hz, systematic "dips" in threshold are observed. Moreover, such dips will increase in depth as the static force of the contactor increases. We cannot be certain at this point whether the observed frequency response of the skin is owing to the action of a dual (or more; see Capraro, Verrillo, & Zwislocki, 1979) receptive system, skin mechanics, or a combination of these associated with patterns of integration in the CNS.

4.3.2.3. ***Differential Intensitive Sensitivity for Step, Impulse, and Periodic Pressure Stimuli.*** The determination of the *differential sensitivity* (also called difference limen [DL]; *difference* threshold; or just-noticeable difference) of a sensory system has a history in quantitative psychology that extends beyond Weber at least to Sauveur, who in the early part of the eighteenth century determined the differential threshold for the pitch of musical tones (see Boring, 1942, p. 339). Systematic experimentation on the resolving power of the senses appeared after Weber's studies (Boring, 1942, p. 495) and Fechner's formalization of the psychophysical law. According to Weber, who did not employ any of the now commonly accepted psychophysical methods, the Weber fraction $\Delta I/I$ for pressure on the finger was about 0.05, or 5% over the range 50–800 g. A later study by Biederman and Löwit (Boring, 1942, p. 495), employing more systematic psychophysical methods, suggested that the fraction varies as a U-shaped function over the range 10–500 g, falling from 7% at 10 g to 1.3% at 400 g and rising to 5% at 500 g.

By the end of the nineteenth century it was made clear that very heavy forces were involving more than the cutaneous system, and when care was taken to restrict the forces to values that would displace mainly the superficial layers of skin, the Weber fraction was found to be in the range 14–20% (see Boring, 1942, p. 497).

All the values cited thus far are for step-function stimuli, involving the placing of successive values of weight on the skin or the application of von Frey hairs. When an impulsive stimulus is presented to the skin, the Weber fraction, measured by Craig (1972), shows variation from a value of 35 to 20% over a range of displacement amplitudes of 30 dB (see Figure 12.9). For a periodic stimulus, such as a sinusoidal vibration, Craig found that the Weber fraction exhibits almost no change in its value of 20% over the same range, as Figure 12.9 shows. It must again be pointed out that the step-function stimuli were measured as forces or tensions in grams or grams per millimeter, whereas the impulse and periodic functions of Craig were measured as contactor displacements in micrometers. Moreover, contactor size and the level of static force can affect the mechanical impedance of the skin and hence the manner and amount of energy propagation into the receptor sheet. Ready comparisons of the values obtained by different methods are therefore difficult, and the biophysical data required to reconcile the variations in method of measurement were not provided by the investigators whose values are given.

It has generally been assumed that the DL for intensity is a measure of the discriminative capacity of the system such that the small DL indicates heightened capacity. However, von Békésy has taken some pains to dispute this as a universal truth, by demonstrating that the DL may be larger for areas having lower absolute thresholds and will decrease if the system is obtunded by anesthesia, cooling, or other blocking methods (see, e.g., von Békésy, 1960a, p. 626). It must be noted that von Békésy was careful to state that he was discussing only the DL near the absolute threshold.

4.3.2.4. ***Differential Sensitivity for Rate of Periodic Stimuli.*** Interest in the frequency-resolving powers of the skin has generally centered around the problem of employing cutaneous vibratory stimuli in a sensory aid for the hard of hearing (see,

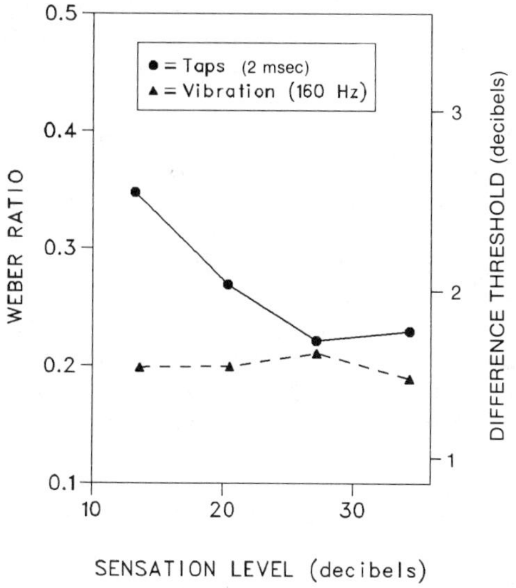

Figure 12.9. The Weber fraction and difference thresholds for vibrotactile stimuli and impulsive taps as a function of stimulus intensity (after Craig, 1972). The difference thresholds for stimuli presented to the right index finger by 6-mm-diameter contactors driven by electromechanical vibrators were determined by a two-interval forced-choice procedure. The two subjects were presented with a pair of stimuli, one of which was stronger than the other. The subject indicated which, the first or second, was the more intense. Depending on the response and its relation to the preceding response, the difference between the stimuli was increased or decreased (block up-and-down two-interval forced-choice procedure; Campbell, 1963). The stimuli were either 200-msec bursts of 160-Hz vibration with 10-msec rise-fall times or taps generated by a 2-msec square wave. After determining threshold for the particular stimulus, it was raised 14, 21, 28, or 35 dB above threshold (dB SL). Approximately 100 trials were required for each determination, and 10 measurements were made for each combination of intensity and mode of presentation. The results are plotted in terms of both the Weber fraction, $\Delta I/I$ and the relative DL, $20 \log (I + \Delta I/I)$, in decibels as a function of intensity for both taps and bursts of vibration. The DL for vibration is relatively constant over the range of intensities, possibly owing to the fact that even the lowest intensity produces quite a strong vibrotactile sensation, at which point DLs tend to reach some constant level. The results for single taps, on the other hand, do show some decrease in DL, eventually reaching the same level as the bursts, about 20%. This level is roughly the same as that obtained for step functions of pressure.

e.g., Kirman, 1973). The possibility of representing the pitch of sounds by direct transposition of the frequency dimension of the acoustic stimulus to vibrotactile frequency values holds appeal, and a number of investigators have examined the difference threshold for rate of vibration in the useful frequency range, that is, 20–500 Hz. The problem is not as easy as it may first appear. In the visual and auditory systems, the size of the DL for hue or pitch is fairly small, and the shift in brightness or loudness with wavelength or frequency is not great in relation to the DL. For sinusoidal vibrotactile stimuli this is not the case; the DL is large, and shifts in sensory magnitude, with change in vibration frequency, may be large. The result is that if one shifts frequency while holding vibration displacement amplitude constant, the observer may be detecting a magnitude, rather than a rate, shift. One is therefore constrained to conduct a preliminary study to ensure that a frequency contour of equal sensation magnitude is generated, such that whatever two frequencies may be presented, they appear the same in sensory magnitude to the observer.

When care is taken to specify pattern sets of this kind, the DL for frequency expressed as a Weber fraction has been found to lie between 20% and 25% in the range of 20–300 Hz, according to Rothenberg, Verrillo, Zahorian, Brachman, and Bolanowski (1977). This means that a just noticeable difference (jnd) of rate is about 4 Hz at 20Hz, but is 60–75 Hz at 300 Hz. An additional complication, documented by von Békésy (1967, p. 167), appears when the intensity of vibration is changed while frequency is constant. At certain levels, a noticeable change in rate occurs as well. It is clear that the acquisition of data for an uncontaminated estimate of the DL for frequency or rate of vibration is an iterative task that Sisyphus could appreciate.

The problems just cited are ameliorated if, instead of sinusoidal vibrations, unidirectional pulses are employed. Rothenberg and coworkers (1977) reviewed several previous studies and examined the DL for the rate when short pulses having rise and fall times of 1 msec were presented in trains. These authors found that the sensory magnitude of such stimuli did not vary so much when rate was varied, which eliminated that source of complication. The Weber fraction for the rate of pulse trains was only 10% for rates of 10–50 pps but rose steadily to values as high as 30% for rates of 200 pps. Compared to auditory frequency Weber fractions of 1%, the vibratory DL is extremely obtuse.

4.3.3. Adaptation. The general definition for adaptation in psychophysical work has been the rise in absolute threshold values from normal for the stimulus, or the reduction from normal of sensory magnitude of the stimulus, following the presentation of some finite suprathreshold value of it. By this definition the differentiation of adaptation from forward masking is possible only if the time course of the masking process is well understood. It is also reasonable to assume that absolute thresholds and sensory magnitude measures are not the sole criteria by which adaptation can be inferred. The DL for intensity, changes in quality (e.g., "brightness" or "pitch" of the stimulus), or shifts in spatial localization may also be manifestations of the adaptation process. In the study of touch and vibration, however, only the absolute-threshold and magnitude shifts have been examined carefully.

Probably the most systematic study of adaptation to static pressure was the series of experiments conducted by Nafe and Wagoner (1941). These authors arranged to allow a set of cylindrical masses having various cross-sectional areas, suitably constructed to eliminate heat conductivity, fall freely into the skin of the thigh just proximal to the patella. The depth of skin indentation was recorded on a kymograph, as was the observer's report of disappearance of pressure sensation. For a wide range of contactor sizes and masses that varied from 9 to 70 g, the report of disappearance of a sensation of pressure coincided with an almost constant value of velocity of indentation. From this and other experiments Nafe and Wagoner concluded that adaptation of the pressure sense resulted not from a physiological process in the neural substrate but from stimulus failure, that is, the slowing of indentation or tissue displacement rate to a just-not-noticeable value. Whereas this study is commonly taken as a classic in the field, and deservedly so, it should be noted that it is not in any sense definitive. First, only the anterior thigh with its hairy skin was examined; the properties of glabrous skin may yield entirely different results. Second, the definition of adaptation as stimulus failure implies that the stimulus is known, but the stimulus, that is, indentation or tissue displacement rate, was defined by the same experiment. Third, neither the course of the adaptation process nor recovery from it were studied; only the final stage, at which the threshold for noticeable sensation occurred, was recorded. The questions whether existing pressure raised the absolute or differential threshold for pressure, or decreased the sensory magnitude of the pressure were not quantitatively answered. Further work on the problem awaits the interest of a skilled and patient experimenter.

4.3.4. Adaptation to Vibrotactile Stimuli. Given the fact that the adaptation to a step function of pressure occurs when the tissue displacement velocity falls below a critical value, one might expect that a periodic displacement wave of sufficient velocity would not show adaptation. That this is untrue was demonstrated clearly by Hahn (1966, 1968a), who was able to show both the course of adaptation and the course of recovery from adaptation by two methods. Hahn arranged to stimulate the distal joint of the index finger with a 6-mm contactor driven by an electrodynamic vibrator excited with a 60-Hz sinusoid. A single moderate level of intensity, 200 μm (about 50 times threshold value), was used to adapt the observer. At various times after the onset of the adapting stimulus, ranging from 10 to 1500 sec, the observer was either required to match the sensation on the adapted finger to that on the corresponding contralateral finger stimulated by means of an identical system or to be tested for absolute threshold at the adapted finger (see Gescheider & Wright, 1968, for an alternative technique). Correction of results was made for the delays produced by the measuring methods. The results are shown in Figure 12.10, where it is seen that the course of adaptation for the two methods is the same, despite the fact that the degrees of shift in threshold

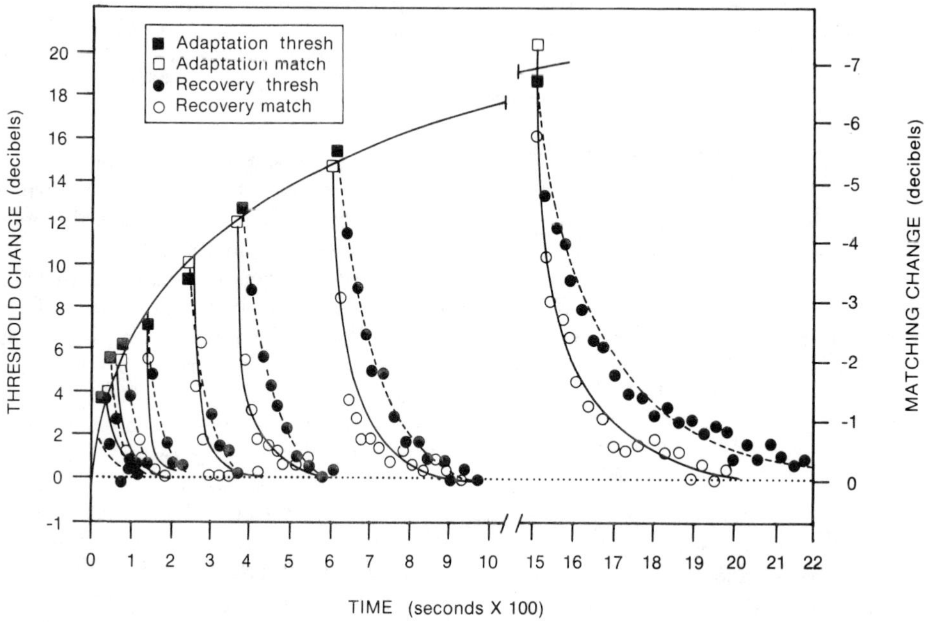

Figure 12.10. Vibrotactile adaptation and recovery as measured by threshold and matching techniques. The change in sensitivity to durative 60-Hz vibration presented at a constant intensity of 200μm (34 dB above threshold for the three observers) to the pad of the index finger was examined by two different methods. In the first, the threshold technique, absolute thresholds were taken with a modified method of limits at regular intervals during and after the end of the adapting period. Here, change is defined as the logarithm of the ratio of postadaptation-to-preadaptation threshold. In the second method, matching, a 1-sec comparison burst was periodically presented to the contralateral index finger, and the observer was required to match its apparent intensity to that at the test site. In this case, change is defined as the logarithm of the ratio of postadaptation-to-preadaptation loudness matches. These procedures were followed during both adaptation to and recovery from vibration presented for eight different stimulus durations ranging from 10 to 1500 sec. Stimuli were presented to the fingerpad by a Goodmans V-47 vibrator, fitted with a 6-mm-diameter contactor and mounted to provide a static force of 20 g. For the matching series, a duplicate system contacted the contralateral index fingerpad. All measurements were made with the left and right index finger pads as the test site for all observers. Seven threshold measurements and 12 matching measurements for each site and observer contributed to each of the points plotted in the figure, while time errors resulting from the measurement techniques were accounted for in the treatment of the data. In the figure, threshold data (filled symbols) are referred to the left ordinate, while matching data (open symbols) are referred to the right ordinate. From the difference in the scales, it is apparent that, for the same temporal course, the relative changes in adaptation were some 2.8 times greater for the threshold measure. In addition, the course of recovery (open and filled circles) differed, with more rapid recovery occurring with the matching series. In both cases, adaptation appears to be continuing after some 25 min, with recovery to baseline levels occurring within a time equal to about 50% of the duration of the adapting stimulus. Hahn suggested that the course of adaptation may mirror the changes in the characteristics of the skin under repeated blows from the stimulus, affecting the viscosity, resistance, and elasticity of the tissue. (From J. F. Hahn, Vibrotactile adaptation and recovery measured by two methods, *Journal of Experimental Psychology, 71*. Copyright 1966 by American Psychological Association. Reprinted with permission.)

and in sensation are unalike. The courses of recovery from adaptation, on the other hand, are different for the two methods, particularly in the early stages.

In a later study, Hahn (1968a) was able to show that threshold changes for 10- and 200-Hz sinusoids are similar in their courses of adaptation and recovery, but there is almost no cross-adaptation between these frequencies. Hahn's conclusion from these findings was that the lack of cross-adaptation implies that two different receptive processes are involved at these frequencies but the similarities in the course and recovery of adaptation suggest similar mechanisms within systems.

Evidence that a significant part of vibrotactile adaptation involves central nervous mechanisms was supplied by von Békésy (1960a, p. 606), who was able to show that two different frequencies harmonically related (e.g., 160 and 480 Hz), when periodically shifted in phase and presented at separate skin loci will produce a sensation of vibration moving from one to the other locus and back again at the rate of the phase shift. If the process continues for a time, the skin adapts more completely to the 480-Hz vibration (cf. Hahn, 1968b), however, and the sensation becomes that of feeling vibration beginning at the 160-Hz site, then moving to the 480-Hz site and disappearing entirely. This shows that the 480-Hz stimulus, although adapted, still acts centrally to inhibit the 160-Hz stimulus. If adaptation were solely a peripheral process, the 480-Hz stimulus would disappear and the 160-Hz vibration would be felt as stationary.

Little beyond these facts is known about adaptation in the perception of pressure and vibration, but Verrillo and Gescheider and their colleagues have taken advantage of the apparent independence of low- and high-frequency adaptation processes to disassociate them for separate study. This "psychophysical surgery," in which one or the other frequency range is adapted and maintained in its obtunded state by continued injections of the adapting stimulus, is believed to permit the application of test stimuli in the other frequency range to examine the "pure" form of the receptor process, uncontaminated by the activity of the now-quiescent system (see, e.g., Gescheider, Frisina, & Verrillo, 1979; Verrillo & Gescheider, 1977).

The problem of adaptation should not be left without some discussion of the meaning of this term. That it means quite different things to physiologists and psychophysicists is apparent from the discussion of Hahn's paper (1968b, pp. 326–330), in Kenshalo's *The Skin Senses*, by physiologists and psychologists. In the same book, Geldard (1968, pp. 593–594) attempted to distinguish the psychophysical from other meanings by suggesting the revival of a term coined by Troland, *minuthesis*, meaning "a reduction." The physiologists' distinction of rapidly or quickly adapting from slowly adapting mechanoreceptors rests entirely on the observation that recordings from the first type show a fast decline in firing rate when a step-function displacement is presented to the former but little or no decline (during a reasonable period) when the latter is presented the same steady stimulus. Here what diminishes is neural firing rate, a dimension that may be related to sensitivity and is commonly taken as the measure of relative responsiveness of a system. It is not, however, necessarily the measure of sensation magnitude or the invariant index of threshold for psychophysical measures.

It has been known for some time (see, e.g., Geldard, 1972, p. 459) that some nerve preparations show little or no decline in neural firing rates to steady-state stimulus conditions but that psychophysical measurements in comparable conditions reveal large reductions in sensory magnitude, sometimes down to absolute threshold, as stimulation continues. Once again we are enjoined to take care that the operational definitions of words common to several fields of study are examined to be certain that the elementary terms (here, "stimulus," "sensitivity," "responsiveness," "sensation magnitude," and "firing rate") are properly matched before we argue the problem of meaning.

In this connection it should be mentioned that processes other than excitatory ones may be affected by continuing stimulation. Thus, von Békésy has noted that lateral inhibition, the process by which excitation of an area is accompanied by simultaneous "silencing" of surrounding areas, may be reduced by prolonged stimulation (von Békésy, 1960a, p. 627). Evidence for such effects is as yet principally phenomenological, but Cholewiak,(1976) was able to demonstrate clear time-dependent changes in cutaneous saltation (see Section 4.4) after an adapting stimulus was presented to a nearby area. The saltation effect is certainly dependent in part on lateral inhibitory mechanisms but is not strongly affected by shifts in stimulus magnitudes. It is admittedly a speculative exercise, however, to advance this idea with no further evidence.

4.3.5. Masking of Pressure and Vibratory Stimuli. A masking stimulus may be said to have an effect if its apposition in space or time to the test signal affects some aspect of the latter in a quantifiable manner. Thus the absolute threshold of the test signal may be raised, its sensory magnitude may be reduced, or its intensitive DL may be shifted. Yet other aspects, such as "pitch," "brightness," or apparent locus of the test signals, may also be shifted, in which case we would submit that a masking effect has occurred. The majority of studies of tactile masking have involved periodic or impulsive stimuli.

It was suggested earlier in the discussion of adaptation that there may be conditions under which it may not be clear whether masking or adaptation is responsible for the shift in the attributes of a test signal (see Section 4.3.3). In general, the differentiation cannot be made in the measurement operations except along the temporal dimension. If we examine the course of adaptation from Hahn's data in Figure 12.10, we see that a relatively short adapting stimulus of moderate intensity (10 sec, 200 μm) produced initially a threshold shift of about 4 dB that falls to zero within 100 sec. If a masking stimulus of this level were presented for 0.5 sec, the increase in the test signal (presented simultaneously and at the same site) required for its detection would be more than 10 times normal (see Sherrick, 1964, p. 49). If the masker is moved ahead of the signal in time (forward masking), the shift in threshold falls continuously to zero within 200 msec. Similarly, if the masker follows the signal in time (backward masking), the same continuous decrease in test signal threshold shift appears, although in this condition somewhat more precipitously (Sherrick, 1964, p. 47). What emerges from this set of facts is that the effects of adaptation manifest themselves after a relatively long period of stimulation and are generally small but will increase with duration. Masking effects, on the other hand, are commonly very large even for short durations when measured by a concurrent test signal but decrease rapidly as the test signal is moved out of synchrony with them. Figure 12.11 shows the time course of masking for impulsive stimuli.

It is possible to separate a masker and test signal in space (remote masking), as well as time, and when this is done, the masking effect is reduced. In general, the greater the spatial separation between the two, the less the masking effect for a given temporal relation (Sherrick, 1964). Even contralaterally

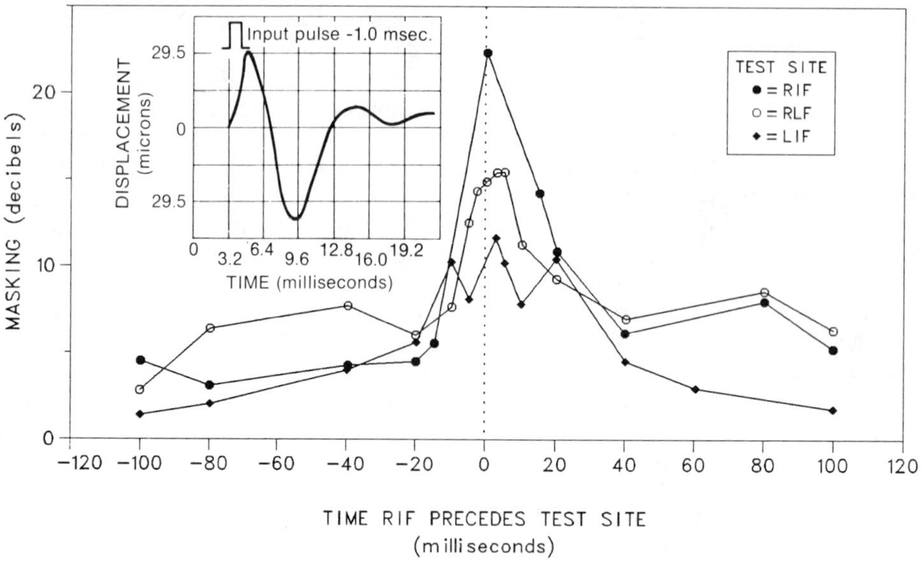

Figure 12.11. Masking of one mechanical pulse by a second pulse as a function of the interstimulus interval and locus of the test pulse. Pairs of 1.0-msec pulses were presented through Goodmans V-47 vibrators to the fingers of three observers to examine the shift in threshold at one site, the test locus, as a function of both the temporal and spatial proximity of the second stimulus. The vibrators touched the fingers with 6.5-mm-diameter plastic contactors. Owing to the impedance relationships between the electronic components, the unipolar pulse was transformed at the skin's surface into the biphasic wave form shown in the inset. In all cases, the masking stimulus was presented to the right index finger, while the test sites included the right index finger (RIF), the right little finger (RLF), and the left index finger (LIF). The masking stimulus at the RIF was set to an intensity of 20 dB above threshold. After threshold was determined for the test site, the observer was presented with pairs of pulses at the rate of one pair per 1.5 sec, at the particular interstimulus interval (ISI) chosen. The ISI ranged from 0 to 100 msec, with the test stimulus either preceding or following the masker. Using a recording attenuator, the observer raised or lowered the intensity of the test signal until it disappeared. Two such determinations were made by each observer for each condition. Standard errors of the mean ranged from 1 to 2 dB across sites and ISIs. The results indicate that a considerable amount of masking can be recorded when stimuli are presented to the same or to different sites, as far apart as the two hands. The farther apart the two stimuli, the less the masking, yet for these conditions the amount never falls to zero. Furthermore, the bilateral masking indicates that the site of the interaction is not solely in the periphery but requires some degree of central involvement. These masking functions are not unlike those recorded with electrocutaneous and auditory stimuli. (From C. E. Sherrick, Effects of double simultaneous stimulation of the skin, *American Journal of Psychology*, *77*. Copyright 1964 by University of Illinois Press. Reprinted with permission.)

placed masker stimuli will show masking effects, however. Gilson (1969) adduced evidence that remote masker effectiveness could be increased if the onset time of masker and test signals were shifted slightly; he suggested that the increase might be owing to the compensation for differences in arrival time of the stimuli in the CNS.

Localization or lateralization phenomena are, of course, subjects in themselves, but, as we saw in the problem of central adaptation, they play a secondary role in the study of many phenomena. When von Békésy (1960a, p. 602) has shown, for example, that two vibrotactile stimuli at different skin sites appear to be a single stimulus commuting between the loci as phase relations between the sinusoids are shifted, he is illustrating masking as well. After all, the energies of periodic stimulation at the loci never change, only the phase relation between them does, yet the location of a single signal is what seems to change, and the physical point of energy transfer is felt during only a fraction of the phase cycle.

It has already been noted that shifts in absolute threshold and of localization are not the only measures of masking effects. Changes in the sensory magnitude of vibrotactile stimuli (see Section 4.3.6) and shifts in the intensive DL have also been quantified. Craig (1974) for example, examined the change in the DL for a 160-Hz sinusoid at the index fingertip when a masking signal of the same frequency was presented to the little finger of the same hand simultaneously. Careful measures of the DL were made when no masker appeared and when three levels of masker intensity were presented, at signal intensities of 1–20 dB SL.

Figure 12.12(a) shows Craig's results when the Weber ratio is plotted against intensity represented as sensation level, decibels above absolute or masked threshold. The progressive vertical separation among the masking levels suggests that the DL is indeed strongly affected by the masking stimulus. Craig reasoned, however, that the presence of the masking stimulus will not only increase the absolute threshold at the test site but will also contribute to the base intensity level against which the jnd must be perceived. Thus the Weber fraction should be calculated from the equation

$$\text{Weber fraction} = \frac{\Delta I}{(I_s + I_m)},$$

where

ΔI is the DL,
I_s is the level of signal intensity,
I_m is the effective level of the masker at the test site.

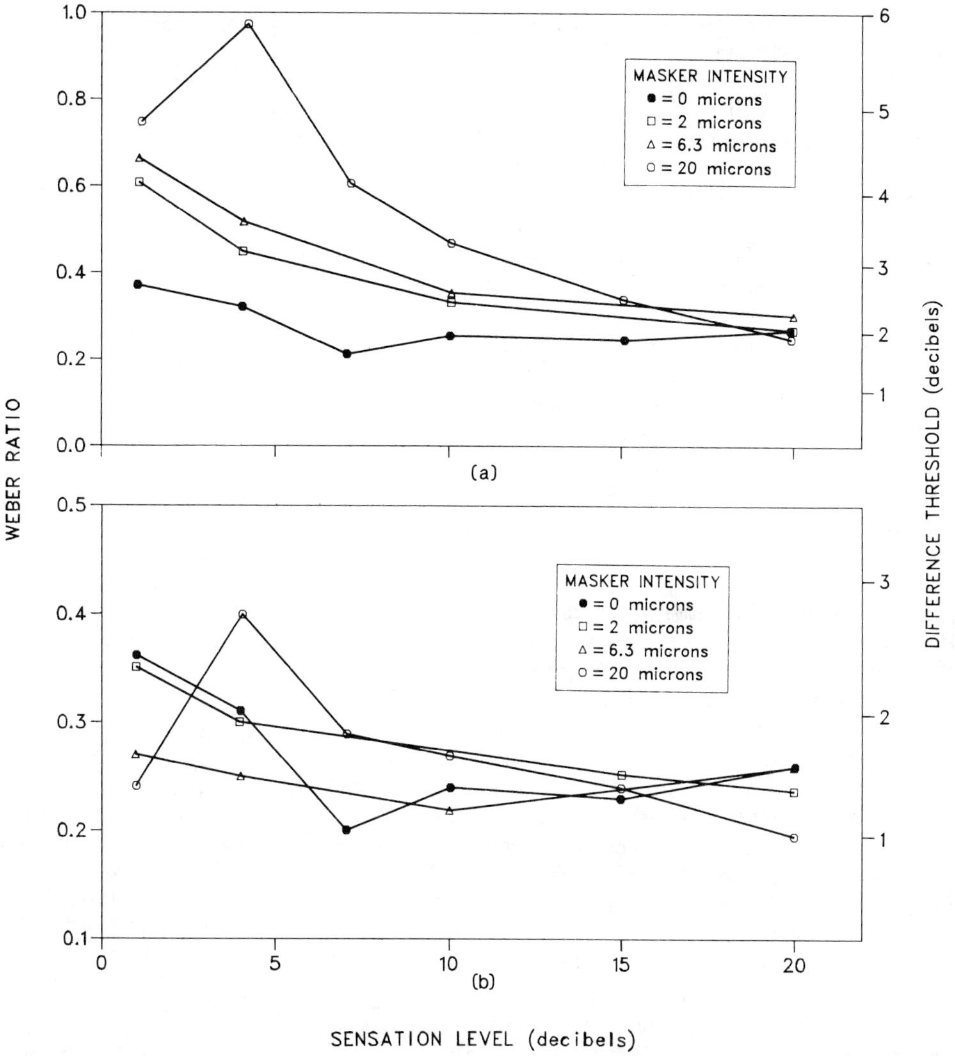

Figure 12.12. The difference threshold, or difference limen, for vibrotactile stimuli as a function of stimulus intensity with the intensity of a masking stimulus as the parameter. In this study, Craig obtained three different vibrotactile threshold measures: the absolute threshold for the test stimulus, its masked threshold in the presence of three different masker intensities, and the difference threshold (DL) for the test stimulus under the same conditions. The test stimuli were presented at six different suprathreshold intensities and in the presence of three levels of masking stimuli. In all cases, the test site was the right index finger, while the right little finger was the site for the masker. The test and masking stimuli consisted of 200-msec bursts of 160-Hz vibration with rise—fall times of 10-msec. These were presented by Goodmans V-47 vibrators fitted with 6-mm contactors touching the fingers through 8-mm-diameter holes with 20 g of static force. Thresholds were determined with the same procedure used in Craig's earlier (1972) study, described in Figure 12.9: the block up-and-down two-alternative forced-choice procedure, which tends to maximize the number of observations in the near-threshold intensity region. For the DL measurements, observers indicated which of two 1-sec observation intervals contained the more intense stimulus. The test stimulus was presented at 1, 4, 7, 10, 15, and 20 dB SL in the unmasked condition (closed symbols) and at the same levels above the masked threshold for three different intensities of masker (open symbols) for masked DLs. Three observers judged each condition with the results of approximately 100 trials contributing to each data point. Standard errors of the mean ranged from 0.1 to 0.4 dB. The results are shown in (a), in which the DLs are plotted for both unmasked and masked stimulus levels. On the left ordinate thresholds are plotted in terms of the Weber ratio $\Delta I/I$, for each condition. On the right ordinate the relative difference limen is given in dB. These data suggest that, in the presence of a masker, the relative change in amplitude that can be discriminated must increase with masker intensity for a given level above threshold. It is possible, however, that the Weber ratio should be calculated as a function of not just the test signal intensity but of that intensity plus some proportion of the masker. When Craig recalculated the Weber ratio taking into account the level of the masker, the functions shown in (b) resulted. These tend to support the idea that a single function can describe the increment in intensity that can just be detected above a given level, regardless of the masking level. (From J. C. Craig, Vibrotactile difference for intensity and the effect of a masking stimulus, *Perception and Psychophysics*, 1974. Reprinted with permission.)

When the DL was recalculated by means of the modified equation, using values for I_m calculated from masking effects, the new plot of the Weber ratio versus intensity appeared as in Figure 12.12(b). The likelihood of fitting all the curves by a single equation is obviously greatly increased. What Craig's finding implies, of course, is that masking does not affect the difference threshold, provided that the effective masking energy is included in the baseline signal. Sherrick (1959) presented a similar argument in discussing the auditory DL in noise. It should be pointed out that when masker and test are at the same site, consist of the same signal (or are additive energies), and are coincident in time, the paradigm could be considered the same as that for the DL. Indeed, Hirsh (1952, p. 197) was able to show that the intensitive DL for hearing obtained by the intensity modulation method was predictable from masking results.

4.3.6. Sensory Magnitude Functions. The method of magnitude estimation so effectively championed by S. S. Stevens (1975) was tested early against vibrotactile stimulation (S. S. Stevens, 1959b). When sinusoidal vibrations at 60 Hz were presented at various suprathreshold intensities to the fingertip, the sensation magnitude grew as a power function with an exponent of 0.95. When Verrillo (1974) examined magnitude growth for the palm, fingers, and the arm by means of the combined magnitude estimation and production techniques, he found curves that were slightly concave, similar to that found by S. S. Stevens on the arm (1959b, p. 214). Figure 12.13 shows the curve for a vibrotactile stimulus at the finger tip. Verrillo found in addition that the exponent for the power function varied somewhat with the locus of stimulation. Later (Verrillo & Capraro, 1975), he determined that frequency of stimulation had little effect on the exponent, contrary to an earlier finding by S. S. Stevens (1968) and a later one by Marks (1979b).

The growth of sensory magnitude with intensity is affected by the duration of the stimulus, at least at higher frequencies (ca. 100 Hz); the intercept, not the exponent, is altered, however (see, e.g., Gescheider, 1976). When different signal frequencies excite the same vibrator, will their (additive) combination produce a sensory magnitude that results from summation of energy, summation of displacement amplitudes, or summation of separate magnitudes? Marks (1979b) was able to show that the result of such two-frequency combinations depends on the degree of separation of the frequencies. For combined 200- and 250-Hz signals, sensory magnitudes increase in proportion to the total energy in the signal. When 20- and 250-Hz signals are combined, sensory magnitudes grow in proportion to the combined values of sensory magnitudes for each signal. When 50- and 600-Hz signals were added, sensory summation occurred as it did for 20 and 250 Hz. Marks was able to show that a model involving summation of displacement amplitudes was inadequate to predict the data (1979b, p. 197). The analogy between these results and those found for auditory stimuli at frequencies within and across critical bands was drawn by Marks (see, e.g., 1979a).

If intensity of vibration is held constant and the number of vibrators (from 1 to 64) is increased, the sensory magnitude grows in direct proportion, that is, a doubling in sensory magnitude with a doubling of number (Cholewiak, 1979). This applies for frequencies of more than 40 Hz. At 20 Hz, the growth rate is halved. The effect of adding numbers of vibrators does not appear to be altered by changing the distance between them, in the range of 1.5–10.5 cm (Cholewiak, 1979, p. 148). Figure 12.14 shows the growth of sensory magnitude with an increasing

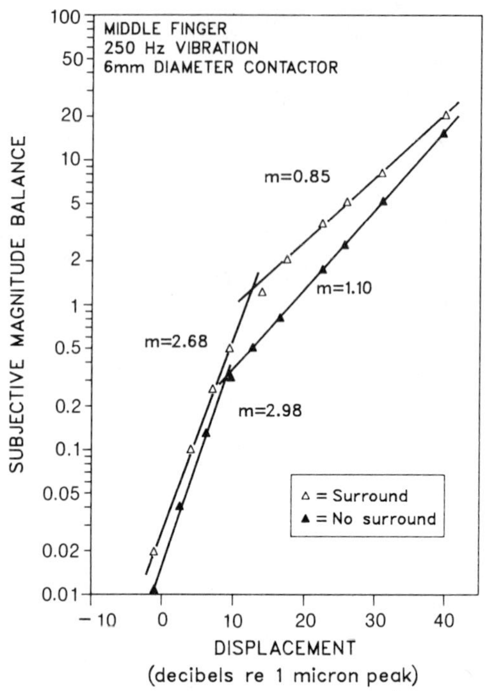

Figure 12.13. The growth of vibrotactile loudness for 250-Hz stimuli on the middle finger as a function of stimulus intensity (after Verrillo, 1974). The rate of growth of sensation for vibrotactile stimuli was examined by Verrillo and Chamberlain (1972) for several different body sites. The results are shown for the middle finger pad as a function of stimulus displacement for two different contactor configurations. In both cases, the 900-msec bursts of 250-Hz vibration were presented to the distal pad of the right middle finger by a Goodmans 360 A vibrator fitted with a 6-mm-diameter contactor indented into the skin 0.5 mm. In the surround condition, the contactor protruded through a plate with an 8-mm hole, providing a 1-mm gap of free skin. In the no-surround condition, no such plate was used. The subjective magnitude balance functions are a combination of two methods of direct judgment of stimulus magnitudes: magnitude estimation and magnitude production. In the first procedure, the nine subjects were required to assign numbers to 10 different stimulus intensities in proportion to their sensation magnitudes, with no reference standard given. In the second method, magnitude production, subjects were required to adjust the intensity of the stimulus to match the magnitude of numbers presented in random order by the experimenter. In both cases, three runs of 10 randomized levels were judged by each subject, and only the geometric mean of the second and third runs were taken as the data points. The results of the two procedures were averaged from the group and plotted. The expected value of the standard deviation for the magnitude estimation procedure can range from 10 dB to 3 dB re the mean as stimulus intensity increases, while that for the magnitude production procedure may vary from 3 to 8 dB over a comparable range (see Verrillo, Fraioli, & Smith, 1969). Although these functions are typically fitted with smooth curves, two intersecting functions, as drawn here, could describe the data well. Only the upper portion of the function is usually considered when such a set of data is discussed, since the steeper arm probably reflects near-threshold properties that might not be representative of the system's operation. Nevertheless, the general finding is that loudness at this site grows less rapidly when a surround is present ($m = 0.85$) than when it is not ($m = 1.10$). This relationship, however, does interact with the site of stimulation, and Verrillo (1974) hypothesized that the ratio reflects the interaction of the spread of energy over space with the density of innervation (neural units) in a particular area.

number of vibrators having the same intensities. It is clear that spatial magnitude summation of the stimulus is occurring for the suprathreshold values.

That adaptation can affect the slope and intercept of the magnitude growth function was shown by Gescheider and Wright (1968). These authors further demonstrated that the correction for threshold, originally suggested by J.C. Stevens and S. S. Stevens (1963) (see also Section 5.3.4), adjusted the lower portions of the functions to linearity in the logarithmic plot (Gescheider & Wright, 1968, p. 312).

Temporal interactions of suprathreshold values of brief stimuli can be shown in a set of paradigms employed by Zwislocki and Ketkar (1972) for audition. Verrillo and Gescheider (1975, 1976) have repeated these methods for vibrotactile stimuli. In one paradigm, two identical suprathreshold values of short bursts are presented, and the observer is asked to match a third (variable-intensity) stimulus to equal the overall magnitude of the pair. Variation in the magnitude of the third stimulus, called summation, occurs as the temporal relation of the pair is shifted,

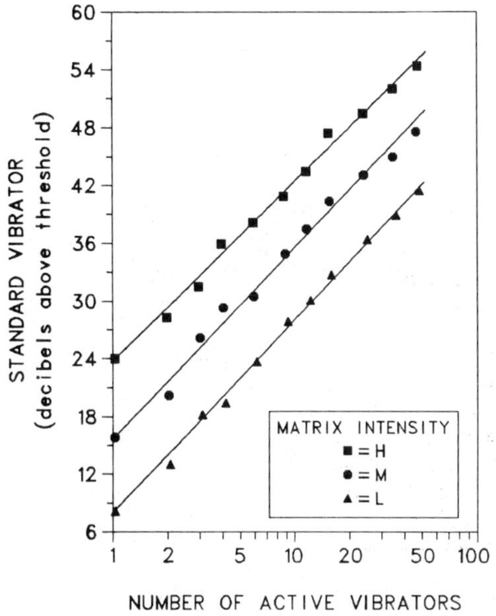

Figure 12.14. The growth of vibrotactile loudness in a multicontactor array as a function of number of contiguous active vibrators. The sensation magnitude of vibrotactile patterns presented by a 64-contactor array was examined as a function of number of active vibrators. The computer-controlled array (see Cholewiak & Sherrick, 1981) consisted of 64 independent piezoceramic benders contacting the skin with 5-mm-diameter hemispherical buttons on 15-mm centers in an 8 × 8 square configuration. The array was fitted to the ventral surface of the observer's left thigh, with an average force of 10 g per contactor. The 11 patterns consisted of 1–49 adjacent elements in as close to a square pattern as possible with the number chosen. Each element was energized for 200-msec at 250 Hz at one of three different intensity levels (L = 92 μm, M = 136 μm, and H = 202 μm). Observers were required to match the sensation produced by each pattern to that produced by adjusting the intensity of a Goodmans V-47 vibrator contacting the middle finger of the left hand. The standard vibrator presented 200-msec bursts at 200 Hz, alternating with the matrix patterns at an interstimulus interval of 500 msec. After the match was achieved, the intensity of the standard was recorded in decibels above threshold, which was determined for each observer at the beginning of the session. The results shown are for four observers who judged each pattern 5 times over a total of 15 sessions. The standard errors of the mean for each intensity for the 16-vibrator matches were less than 2 dB. The data indicate that the growth of loudness owing to addition of increasing numbers of vibrators having the same vibration amplitude progresses in a linear fashion. The slopes of the functions drawn to fit the data range from 0.93 to 1.0 on the log-log coordinates and indicate almost perfect summation of loudness. These results imply that suprathreshold spatial summation, as defined by the addition of active areas on the matrix, progresses at a constant rate regardless of the intensity of the individual element. (From R. Cholewiak, Spatial factors in the perceived intensity of vibrotactile patterns, *Sensory Processes*, 1979, *3*. Reprinted with permission.)

as Figure 12.15(a) shows. When similar frequencies are employed, the maximum value of summation amounts to 3 dB, implying that energy summation occurs. When widely separated frequencies are involved, however, magnitude summation occurs, as though separate channels are interacting (see Verrillo & Gescheider, 1975, p. 132; cf. Marks, 1979b).

In a second paradigm, the observer is asked to match the variable to only the *second* of the pair in magnitude, ignoring as much as possible the first burst. An example of the results of such a study is shown in Figure 12.15(b). The increase in the perceived magnitude of the test burst (measured by the change in intensity setting of the variable burst with and without the conditioning burst) is called enhancement. The effect can be shown to occur when different loci are involved (Verrillo & Gescheider, 1976), but not when widely different frequencies are presented. When different loci are stimulated, the effect of the conditioning burst at near-zero time differences is to inhibit or mask the test burst by reducing its perceived magnitude below the value it has when presented alone (see Verrillo & Gescheider, 1976, p. 130). This was also noted by Sherrick (1960, p. 157), when auditory and vibrotactile sensory magnitudes were estimated in quiet and noisy conditions. Finally, Verrillo and Gescheider (1979) have been able to show that the enhancement paradigm produces its effect when the same site is stimulated and the conditioning stimulus follows the test, that is, backward enhancement. When the test and conditioning stimuli are at different sites, only suppression (masking) occurs in this arrangement.

4.3.7. Temporal Acuity for Touch. The comparative resolving power of the senses has often been discussed with the aim of shedding light on the basis of their capacities for processing information (see, e.g., Geldard, 1970; Miller, 1956). Of the domains in which resolution is measurable, by no means the least important is time. A variety of measures have been applied to the senses, and the sense of touch has not been neglected in the effort to assess channel capacities.

In measures of the perception of successiveness, Gescheider (1974) was able to show that two impulsive stimuli of about 1 msec duration each must be separated by 5.5 msec to be perceived as two stimuli at a single locus on the fingertip. The comparable value for the ear, for two 10-μsec pulses, is 10 μsec (Leshowitz, 1971). The basis for the ear's superiority was shown to be its exquisite discriminative capacity for differences in spectral energy distributions of one- and two-click patterns. In a similar paradigm, Kietzman (1967) was able to determine the two-flash threshold for the eye as about 25 msec. For such methods, therefore, the three senses span three orders of magnitude in time, with touch lying between audition and vision.

Successiveness is not the only measure of temporal acuity, of course. A second means of appraisal is the fusion threshold, the rate of occurrence of bursts of stimuli that is indiscriminable from a steady train. The measure is well known in vision as the critical fusion frequency (cff) and has been measured in the auditory system as well. In the latter system, the controlling variables for fusion rate of noise bursts seem to be the silent period duration and the onset–offset times of the bursts (Harbert, Young, & Wenner, 1968). This is not true of visual cff, which can be shown to depend on a great variety of conditions (Riggs, 1972). Vibrotactile bursts and impulsive pressure stimuli have not been tested for fusion, in part owing to transducer limitations, but the likelihood is that the skin would behave more like the ear than the eye. Although von Békésy (1960a, p. 600) described a kind of tactile fusion, it is not of the type commonly understood

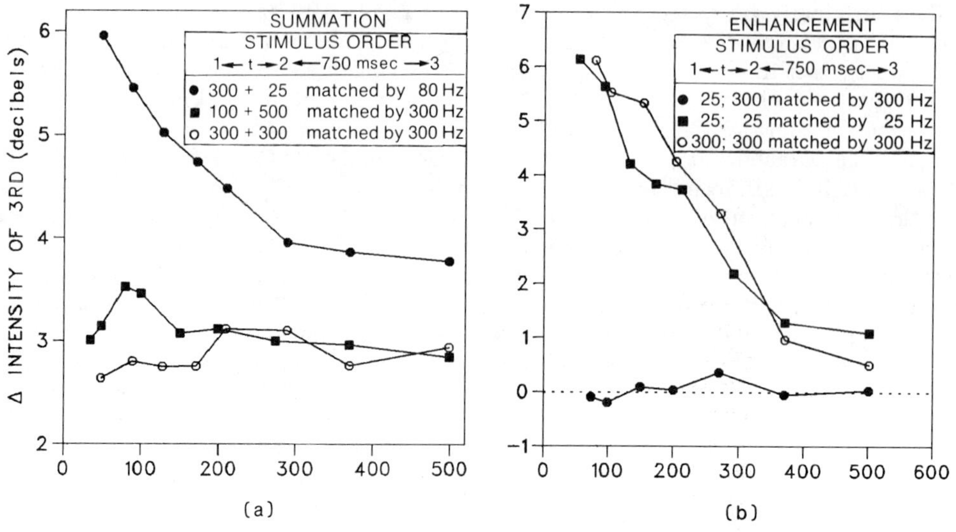

Figure 12.15. Enhancement and summation of vibrotactile bursts as a function of their interburst interval and frequencies. If a vibrotactile stimulus is followed within a brief period of time by a second similar stimulus, at the same or at different sites, two different measures of apparent intensity can be taken. In one case, if certain conditions are met, an increment in the apparent loudness of the second stimulus may occur, owing to the presence of the first stimulus. This is operationally defined as enhancement. In the second case, increases in the overall loudness of the pair can be measured. This has been defined as summation. These phenomena have been found to occur in audition and are described here for vibrotactile sensitivity employing loudness-matching procedures, in which the intensity of a third burst, following the first two, is adjusted until its loudness matches that of either the second burst (enhancement) or the total loudness of the pair (summation). In these experiments, five or six observers judged stimulus sequences presented to the thenar eminence of the hand with a vibrator fitted with a 19-mm-diameter contactor protruding through a 21-mm-diameter hole in the support plate and indented into the skin by 0.5 mm. Stimuli were 20 msec in duration at the half-power points with a 25-msec rise–fall time. In all the experiments reported here, the second stimulus in the pair has a sensation level of 24 dB. The comparison stimulus (3) always occurred 750 msec after the second stimulus in the pair,and its intensity was controlled by the observer. The first stimulus in the sequence preceded the second by 35–500 msec, and its loudness was equated to that of the second burst in the summation experiments. The first stimulus here was set to a level 10 dB greater than the second, although similar but weaker effects are recorded when they are equal in loudness. The means of the matches of the third stimulus to the total loudness of the pair (summation) are shown in (a) and the matches of the third to the second (enhancement) are shown in (b). The standard deviations ranged from 0.09 to 1.88 dB. By varying the frequency relationships among the three stimuli, several underlying principles of summation and enhancement were disclosed. Under the conditions of summation, if the frequencies of the components are either similar (squares) or identical (open circles), summation reaches a maximum of approximately 3 dB and appears to be independent of the interstimulus interval. When the members of the sequence are very dissimilar (filled circles), however, the effect was as much as 6 dB and was time dependent over this range. These relationships are identical to those obtained with auditory stimuli (Zwislocki & Ketkar, 1972) and imply that within a channel passing some band of frequencies, energy summation can occur, resulting in the 3-dB increment in loudness. With very dissimilar frequencies, it becomes difficult for the observer to attend to the total loudness of the pair, and summation judgments become contaminated with enhancement judgments (filled circles). With dissimilar frequencies falling into different channels, equally loud stimuli should result in loudness addition in which the total loudness should be judged to be twice as loud as either alone (resulting in a 6-dB increment). This appears to be the case here. In the enhancement condition (b), the first stimulus was set to a level 10 dB greater in loudness than that of the second. In these cases, the influence of the first stimulus on the second occurs only when the conditioning and test stimuli fall within the same frequency channel. Furthermore, the effect of the first, enhancing the loudness of the second, is a function of their interstimulus interval. With dissimilar frequencies, no such effect is seen. Thus in these two different processes, similar frequencies result in maximal enhancement, whereas dissimilar frequencies are required for maximal summation. Verrillo and Gescheider have interpreted these results to support the hypothesis that two different and independent receptor systems exist in the skin, which are maximally sensitive to different frequency ranges and which provide separate vibrotactile input channels not unlike the critical bands in audition. (From R. T. Verrillo & G. A. Gescheider, Enhancement and summation in two successive vibrotactile stimuli, *Perception and Psychophysics*, 1975, *18*. Reprinted with permission.)

in the auditory or visual literature; rather, it is the transition from a perception of separate pulses on the skin to the perception of a steady pressure underlying the interruptions.

A third measure of temporal acuity is numerousness. The term describes the observer's ability to count accurately a series of events presented within a temporal epoch. Recent investigations by Lechelt (1975) have yielded figures that place touch (impulsive stimuli) between audition (clicks) and vision (flashes) in processing capacity, as was found for perception of successiveness. When more than one skin site was used for the signal input, the capacity improved in a manner that depended on the patterning of the multiple input (Lechelt, 1974). In the simple (single-locus) paradigm, when events are presented at the rate of 5 per sec, the observer will count 9 auditory events when 9 occur, but slightly fewer than 9 tactile events and fewer than 8 visual events, on the average.

The perception of temporal order of events may be considered an acuity measure requiring somewhat higher-level activity, since the observer is required to identify two events for the purpose of saying which came first in time. It is possible to design the task in a number of ways, as Hirsh (1976) has pointed out, and obtain different results. Hirsh and Sherrick (1961) opted to present two successive impulsive stimuli at separate sites on the skin and asked which site was stimulated first. Under these conditions, the limen for order was about 20 msec for 75% detection. For similar tasks in the auditory (dichotic) and visual (dichoptic or binocular) systems, the limen is the same. Moreover, if intersensory events are presented, such as a tap to the skin and an acoustic click or a visual flash, the limen is still the same (Hirsch & Sherrick, 1961, p. 430). It is interesting, however, that when two auditory stimuli (left ear–right ear) are presented and a judgment of order is required, and two tactile stimuli (left hand–right hand) are presented simultaneously, the auditory limen increases by more than 100% if the tactile ordering opposes the auditory, that is, auditory left–right, tactile right–left, and decreases if the tactile order agrees with the auditory (Sherrick, 1976). This interference appears to be mutual between touch and hearing and may occur among all three senses, owing perhaps to the fact that the basis for identification, side of the body stimulated, is the same for all three modalities in this task.

When a number of body sites are stimulated and a report of their ordering is required, observers require increasing amounts of time (Sherrick, 1982). It seems that increasing degrees of spatial separation would improve discrimination in this case, but the difference in acuity between multiple loci on a single finger and those spread across all five fingers is not significant.

4.3.8. Spatial Acuity for Touch. The two classic measures of the spatial resolving power of the skin are the *two-point limen* and the *error of localization*, and the history of early studies of these measures is thoroughly reported by Boring (1942, pp. 475–487). The common method for measuring the two-point limen is to replace the points of a draftsman's compass with somewhat more blunt, thermally indifferent contactors. The device is set to some distance larger than the two-point limen and presented to the observer's skin at the locus of interest. The observer is asked to report "one" or "two." In successive trials, the distance is reduced until a consistent report of "one" is given. Similarly, ascending trials are presented. In an earlier day it was the custom to present a single stimulus (the so-called *Vexierversuch*) to check the observer's criterion. Recently, Johnson and Phillips (1981) have reexamined the two-point limen by means of signal detection analysis and have shown that "one" can always be discriminated from "two" even when the points (0.5 mm diameter) are side by side.

The error of localization can be measured in a variety of ways, depending on whether the observer reports on the sameness or the difference of locus of two successive contacts, or touches his/her skin at the point he or she thinks the experimenter did, and so forth.

It is not unusual to find modern investigators criticizing the classical studies for failing to yield the smallest value of the spatial limen obtainable, for example, by offsetting the stimuli in time or allowing the observer to palpate two points. These critics miss the point of the original studies, whose authors were in fact well aware of the possibilities of reducing, say, the two-point limen by "rocking" the compass points commonly used in testing. The fact is that the original studies sought to determine the spatial, not the spatiotemporal limen, for comparison to the minimum separable acuity measure for vision, which at the time was thought to lack a temporal aspect also.

The classic studies have been repeated by Weinstein (1968), who measured both the two-point limen and the error of localization at several body sites in both males and females. Figure 12.16 illustrates Weinstein's findings for a sample of body sites. It is worth noting that for these measures, as for the measures of pressure sensitivity described earlier, significant effects of body locus and sex were found, as well as first-order interactions of these variables with laterality. The fingers are in general the most sensitive sites for both measures, amounting to about 2.5 mm on the index fingertip for the two-point limen and 1.5 mm for the error of localization. It is readily shown that practice will reduce the two-point limen considerably and that observers can discriminate between different distances, even though they all yield reports of "one" (Boring, 1942, p. 482).

The fact that the error of localization of a single point is less than the distance needed to perceive two points seems paradoxical. Boring (1930) explained the discrepancy on essentially methodological grounds, not physiological, as others have done and von Békésy (1967, p. 44) has suggested that the size of the two-point limen and the change of sensation magnitude of the contacts at the liminal point are evidence of neural "funneling." He believes that lateral inhibitory effects account for the size of the limen and has attempted to quantify the excitatory–inhibitory activities in a model of the funneling process (von Békésy, 1960b).

In recent years, less conventional methods applied to the problem of spatial acuity have revealed considerably smaller liminal values. Vierck and Jones (1969) were able to show that the discrimination of two sizes of cylinder on the skin is much smaller than might be predicted by the two-point limen for the site. Loomis (1979; Loomis & Collins, 1978) has been able to show a considerable improvement in tactile acuity by means of innovative apparatus and methodological developments. Indeed, Loomis applies the term *hyperacuity* to the capability of the skin, borrowing the term from Westheimer's visual studies. Acuity does not seem to be much affected by intensity of the stimulus (Johnson & Phillips, 1981; Pritchard, 1931), but it is affected by the temporal frequency pattern (Bliss, 1974). Whether or how acuity is affected by adaptation, masking, temperature, or anoxia have not thus far been answered. It is figuratively but not literally true to say the surface has barely been scratched.

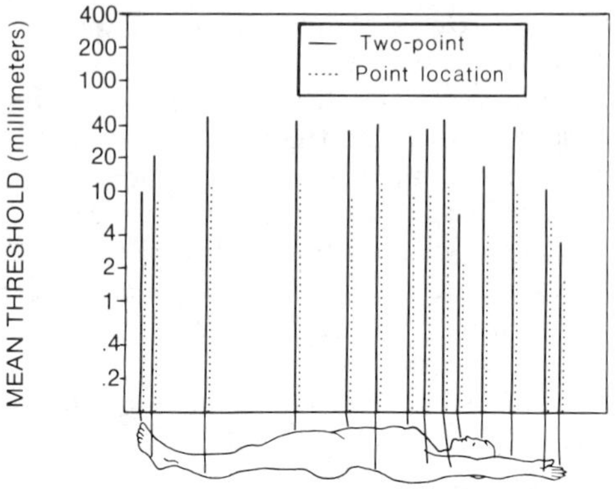

Figure 12.16. Thresholds for tactile point localization and two-point discrimination on several different body sites (after Weinstein, 1968). In this study of intensive and extensive aspects of tactile sensitivity, Weinstein (1968) employed three different measures. The first, pressure sensitivity, was discussed in Figure 12.6. The present figure illustrates his results for the second and third measures: thresholds for two-point discrimination and point localization. Two-point thresholds were measured with a pair of machinist's calipers. An additional single point was used whose surface area (3.2 mm^2) totaled that of the two individual points combined. To determine the threshold at a site, six alternating ascending and descending series were presented in which the subject had to identify correctly two double and two single stimulations randomly presented for each separation. For the point localization series, a Y-shaped grid with arms diverging at 120° angles from one another was stamped on the skin's surface. The single point used in the previous set of measures was then touched first to the center of the grid, then to a point on one of the three rays. The subject was to report whether the second point was coincident with the first. The point most distant that was so identified was taken as the error of localization for that ray. This was repeated on each ray and the mean of the three values is reported as the threshold for that body site. Although both male and female observers were tested, only the results obtained from the 24 males are shown, with the means of the left and right side of the body plotted in the figure for each measure of sensitivity. It is not inappropriate to plot these means since laterality was not a significant primary variable and showed a significant interaction with body part for only two-point discriminations. The data, plotted on a logarithmic scale identical to that in Figure 12.6, indicate a reasonably high correlation between the two measures as a function of body part. The rank-order correlation between the two is .92 and is highly significant. In general, there is a proximodistal gradient of increasing sensitivity for both spatial measures, contrary to the general findings for pressure sensitivity. The mean ratio of the threshold for the two measures shown in this figure is 3.5 : 1, with a standard error of 10%, suggesting a relatively constant difference. The seemingly paradoxical results in which two points are discriminated at longer distances than might be expected by the error of localization were explained by Boring (1942) on the basis of methodological differences and, later, by von Békésy (1967) on the basis of mutual inhibitory and excitatory influences indicative of neural funneling (see Section 4.3.8).

The implications of acuity studies for processing more complex patterns are left for Chapter 31 by Loomis and Lederman.

4.3.9. Deep Pressure Sensations. Somewhat oblique reference has already been made to the fact that the measurement of tactile sensitivity lies within certain limits of force or of displacement of tissues. Beyond certain upper limits we must presume that the set of tissues underlying the integument are involved when very large forces are exerted on the body part. When a force of half a kilogram is exerted on the (supported) dorsal forearm, it is impossible to ignore the fact that a substantial amount of muscular tissue is compressed between the applied force and the radial bone. If the force is prolonged, the expression of blood from capillaries must also occur, with attendant effects of partial anoxia from the pressure block. Receptors in the muscles and tendons must be stimulated along with a considerable area of ambient skin that is stretched by the deformation occurring at the surface. (See also Clark & Horch, Chapter 13.)

The term *deep sensibility* was coined by Head (1920) to describe the various qualities of sensation that were aroused in areas anesthetic to superficial stimuli. Thus when Head exerted forces of more than a few grams with a blunt probe on the portion of his arm made anesthetic by neurotomy, he reported a dull "pressury" sensation. He believed this resulted from stimulation of deep-lying receptors subserved by deep cutaneous nerves. It is entirely possible that Pacinian corpuscles lying within the musculotendinous system were excited, but we should not overlook the possibility that areas of skin unaffected by the neurotomy were called into play at the lateral stretching of the tissues. Such activity as might be aroused by this process would go unnoticed in the presence of the higher level of local activity that would occur in normal skin. Other attempts to dissociate superficial and deep aspects of pressure sensitivity, as, for example, topical anesthetic blocks of small areas of skin (see Boring, 1942, p. 523), can be questioned on the same basis as Head's study. However, so far as we know, there is no reason to dispute Boring's conclusion that the distinction between deep and kinesthetic sensibility "may be only functional, the former having to do with stimuli superficially applied and the latter with movement" (1942, p. 524).

4.4. Similarities of Touch to Hearing and Vision

It is tempting to dwell at considerable length on the metaphoric possibilities of tactile experience, either in relation to spatial vision or in relation to auditory temporal patterning, but such qualitative sallies are not commonly the stuff of which applications are made. Besides, there are a sufficient number of quantitative analogies available among the senses to provide the creative investigator with enough food for constructive thought to span a professor's sabbatical.

Some analogies that we have already considered are methodologically comparable, such as common procedures and instrumentation for measuring temporal and spatial acuity or threshold, masking, and adaptation functions. Other analogies are comparable in both method and phenomenal outcome, for example, the experience of space or of rhythm. Still others exhibit comparability in the first two ways, as well as in the quantitative relations that emerge from variation of stimulus conditions. Some effects are better researched than others, and these deserve elaboration.

Perhaps the most familiar of such analogies is that of lateralization (less precisely, localization), which was described briefly in Section 4.3.5. In hearing, the effect is readily produced by sinusoidal or repetitive impulsive stimuli (von Békésy, 1960a, pp. 571, 605; see Scharf & Houtsma, Chapter 15). For the ear, two identical, equally loud sinusoids (200–1000 Hz) delivered dichotically, but with a slowly changing phase relation, will produce a sensation that appears to move, at the rate of the phase shift, from one ear to the other. When successive clicks are presented dichotically and the click to one ear is delayed relative to the other, the sensation is localized toward the ear that leads in time. When the clicks are equally loud and simultaneous, the sensation seems to be between the ears, although not necessarily on the interaural axis. The perception of location by the skin can be very similar when two vibrators are placed about 10 cm apart (they can be bilaterally placed,

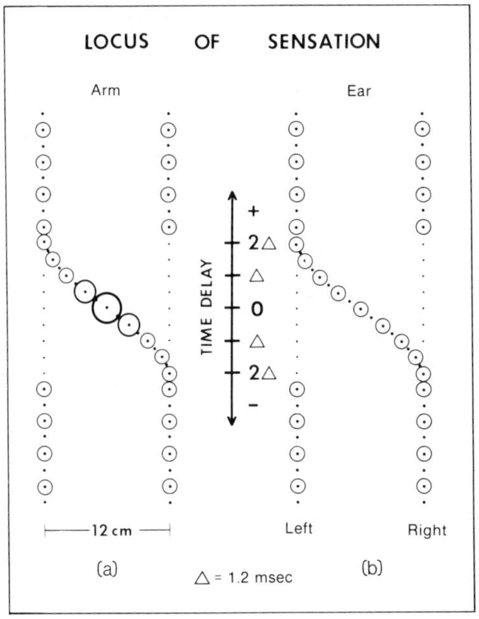

Figure 12.17. The lateralization of two impulsive auditory or tactile stimuli as a function of small temporal shifts in their onset times. The figure illustrates the apparent locus of equally loud stimuli presented either to the volar surface of the arm (a) or dichotically by headphones to the ears (b). As the time delay between the first and the second pulses approached zero, the apparent magnitudes and loci of the two stimuli changed in a striking fashion. The following pulse, on the right in the upper half of (a) and (b), decreased in apparent intensity until it was completely suppressed. This reduction in loudness was complemented by a regular increase in the magnitude of the leading pulse, eventually resulting in a single sensation felt, in these cases, at the site indicated on the left of the drawings. As the interpulse interval continued to decrease toward zero delay, the apparent locus of the loud sensation began to move toward the center of the field, between the two sites of stimulation, finally reaching the center when the onsets of the two pulses were simultaneous. As the delay continued to change, with the previously leading pulse now following, the reverse of the pattern of localization and loudness shifts took place, with the stimuli returning to their original sites and apparent intensities. The time course for these effects is relatively brief: ±2 msec or less around simultaneity. This interval is the same for both senses, as are all of the phenomena described. One significant difference does exist between the two modalities: with tactile stimuli the apparent intensity of the single phantom decreased as it moved toward the center of the field accompanied by an increase in its apparent size. As the sign of the time delay became negative the intensity of the tactile sensation increased again and became smaller. A similar pattern of results can be obtained if only the relative loudnesses of the two taps is changed (see Alles, 1970). Furthermore, identical patterns of spatiointensive changes took place when von Békésy used electrocutaneous stimuli and when he anesthetized the surface of the skin with ethyl chloride spray. Thus the lateralization effect must occur at higher levels of the nervous system, similar to other such phenomena, for example, sensory saltation (see Figure 12.18). The strength of the illusion can be shown by Alles' (1970) use of the location of the phantom in a vibrotactile feedback system to indicate limb angle in an elbow prosthesis. The illusion was rapidly learned and provided some degree of useful information, although that produced by amplitude variation alone appeared to be superior to the sensation produced by the time delay alone. (From G. von Békésy, *Experiments in hearing*, McGraw-Hill, 1960. Reprinted with permission.)

but the effect is less impressive). Under these conditions, the phase-shifted sinusoid (frequencies of 40–500 Hz) produces the same shift in localization from one energy source to the other. When clicks are presented, the production of a single "phantom" occurs, just as in hearing. The time of delay required to move the image from center to one side is about 1.0 msec for hearing and about the same for touch, according to von Békésy (1960a). Figure 12.17 illustrates the lateralization effect. Gescheider (1974, p. 34) was unable to replicate these results for the skin, however, and found temporal differences on the order of 2–4 msec needed for full phantom lateralization. It is possible that the precision of localization of the phantom, and consequently the precision of adjustment of time relations, depends on the temporal properties of the tactile displacement. Gescheider's taps were generated by an electrodynamic vibrator (Goodmans V-47) that has a natural period of about 10 msec. Occasionally von Békésy has mentioned the necessity for "tuning" mechanical transducers to ensure very sharp taps for best results (see, e.g., von Békésy, 1967, pp. 91–92). In both senses, it can be shown that a time delay may be compensated by an intensity adjustment such that an appropriate increase in loudness of the lagging stimulus will bring the phantom back to the center position. For lateralization, therefore, the analogy holds for method, phenomenal report, and quantitative relations, owing, von Békésy claims, to the fact that the processes underlying the phenomena are nearly identical (von Békésy, 1960a).

Within the time domain there dwells another analogy that has withstood both qualitative and quantitative tests in the three senses of touch, audition, and vision. This is the so-called saltation effect (Geldard, 1975, 1982; Geldard & Sherrick, 1972, 1983). In its simplest form, it consists of presenting an impulsive stimulus (tap, click, or flash) at one spatial location and a second stimulus at a second location a short time later. If the time between stimuli is short (say, 20–30 msec), the first (in time) will appear near to or coincident with the second. As the time disparity increases, the first stimulus seems to travel in space back to its veridical locus, arriving there when the lag amounts to 250 msec. The phenomenon can be produced with multiple impulsive stimuli by presenting several taps at one skin locus followed immediately by a single tap at a second locus. The sensation is that of a set of taps more or less equally spaced between the loci. This "hopping" perception led to the more refined term saltation. It is easy to show that observers can fractionate the distance between sites by adjusting the time between single taps (see Figure 12.18).

By a similar means,the distance between two sound sources or two flashes of light can be fractionated (Geldard, 1975, p. 90, p. 96; Figure 12.18). In the case of vision, however, the two veridical sites are always perceived; what is seen additionally is a somewhat dimmer phantom between the sites and nearer to the lagging one. Geldard (1976) has been able to demonstrate a variety of interesting effects in the visual system, including the fact that, as in touch, saltation cannot be induced across the midline. For the skin, this means the anatomical midline, that is to say, the sagittal plane. For the eye, of course, it means the retinal midline; homonymous areas of the two eyes will show saltation. Moreover, the saltatory phantom can be perceived in the blind spot (Lockhead, Johnson & Gold, 1980). For the ear, however, a "midline barrier" has not yet been demonstrated.

Yet a third phenomenon, separable qualitatively and quantitatively from the preceding two, is also a spatiotemporal delegate with portfolio in all three senses. It is synthetic movement, called by some *apparent movement* or (inaccurately) *phi* movement, or (more precisely) *beta* movement (Kenkel, 1913). Most familiar in vision, it is readily produced by flashing two spatially separated light sources on and off in succession. The observer sees a moving light progress from the first to the second source when the time between flashes is within a critical range. For touch, the optimal stimulus is a periodic one, for example,

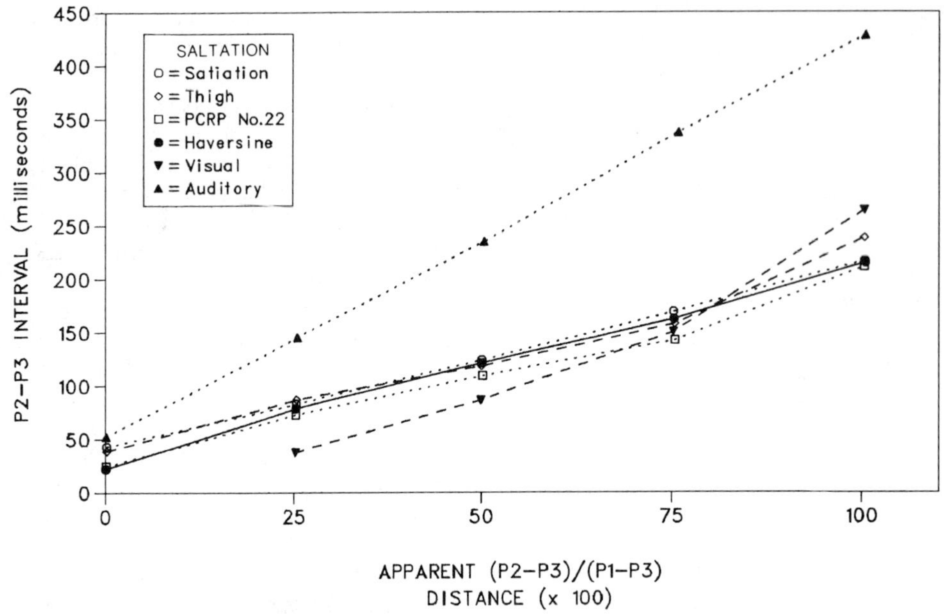

Figure 12.18. Functional relation between the apparent spatial location of a stimulus and its temporal proximity to a succeeding stimulus. (Adapted from Geldard, 1975; Sherrick, 1982.) Sensory saltation involves the systematic change in the apparent locus of one stimulus when it is followed within a brief period of time by a second stimulus at a different location. A typical pattern of pulses delivered to the skin (or flashes to the eye or clicks to the ear) includes 2 taps P_1 and P_2 at one locus L_1, separated temporally by 700–800 msec. Following these at a second locus L_2, is the third tap P_3, which may occur 20–500 msec after P_2. The P_1 pulse is so far removed temporally that it serves only as a locator and does not enter into the P_2–P_3 interaction. In a typical fractionation experiment, after the stimuli have been equated for apparent intensity, the pattern is presented to the observer at the rate of about 10 sequences/min. The observer, by varying the P_2–P_3 time, is able to set the apparent locus of P_2 to several different points representing the proportions of the total apparent P_1–P_3 distance. In some cases the data from as many as 50 series from each of five observers are reported here (PCRP No. 22), although usually fewer series are run. The first four experiments listed in the legend were performed with tactile stimuli typically placed 10–15 cm apart on the forearm or, in the case of the series labeled "Thigh," on the anterior surface of that limb. The contactors rested with 10 g of static force, and the stimuli, brief haversine or unidirectional square pulses, were set to 10–12 dB SL. The four studies were conducted over a period of some 8 years, with different experimenters and over a dozen different observers. The standard errors of the mean of these data were quite consistent and ranged over studies from 1.3 msec at the 0% setting to 34.5 msec at the 100% setting. For further details regarding the procedures for the individual studies, see Geldard (1975) or Sherrick (1982). In the study of visual saltation, three observers judged the amount of saltation produced by brief strobe flashes presented to 0.5° fields separated by 5° of visual angle and viewed with an eccentricity of 35° from the fixation point against a constant 0.03 cd/m^2 surround (Geldard, 1975). For these conditions, it was impossible to achieve complete displacement of the second pulse. The last set of data plotted are from a study of auditory saltation (Geldard, 1975). In this experiment, stimuli were presented by TDH-39 earphones suspended 1.25 m from the observer in a sound-attenuated room draped to reduce reflected energy. The stimuli were 0.1-msec rectangular pulses filtered to pass 2400–3200 Hz and set to 40 dB SL. The sources were 60° apart and to the left of the observer's sagittal plane. Standard errors of the mean ranged from 8.5–45.5 msec with increasing judged distance. The results of these studies are remarkably consistent, although somewhat steeper functions are apparent for both the visual and auditory stimuli. The differences among modalities may be owing to a variety of factors. Even within a modality, such as vision, the form of the function varies somewhat with such variables as the eccentricity of the fixation point and the separation between the stimuli. Larger individual differences were recorded for the auditory series than for the tactile series, but the sample of observers was more heterogeneous, particularly in length of training period.

vibrotactile bursts of 150 Hz, as Sherrick and Rogers (1966) were able to show. They demonstrated further that the interval between stimulus onsets for best beta motion was a nonmonotonic function of the duration of the first stimulus and that the same function held for vision, as Neuhaus (1930) had shown earlier. Figure 12.19 depicts the relation for touch and vision, as well as for electrocutaneous stimuli. More recently Kirman (1974) has replicated the tactile results almost exactly with different methods and at different loci, and Perrott (1974) has succeeded in replicating the movement effects in hearing for a single stimulus duration.

An interesting error common to the three modalities crops up when observers are asked to equate the silent interval between stimuli to the stimulus duration itself. Craig (1973) examined this effect for vibrotactile, auditory, and visual stimuli over a range of stimulus durations of 100–1200 msec and discovered that a constant error of about 600–700 msec occurs when observers are asked to equate the silent, or dark, interval between bursts to the burst duration. When the gap between auditory stimuli (1000-Hz tones) was filled by white noise, however, the error was eliminated. No similar experiment was done for the vibrotactile or visual stimuli. No ready explanation is at hand for this puzzling effect, but it would certainly be of interest to vary the level and quality of the stimulus presented in the silent interval.

A number of other effects that have counterparts in other senses could be described. For example, the autokinetic effect reported in vision will occur in touch (Langford, Hall, & Monty, 1973). But most of them are more or less metaphorical and therefore, arise (possibly) from imagery across modalities. Marks (1978) has written at some length on such relationships.

It is clear that the analogies shared by two or more senses and having similar functional relations between stimulus variables are very probably dependent in the main on common central mechanisms. At present, the most highly developed model that provides an explanatory mechanism for some of the

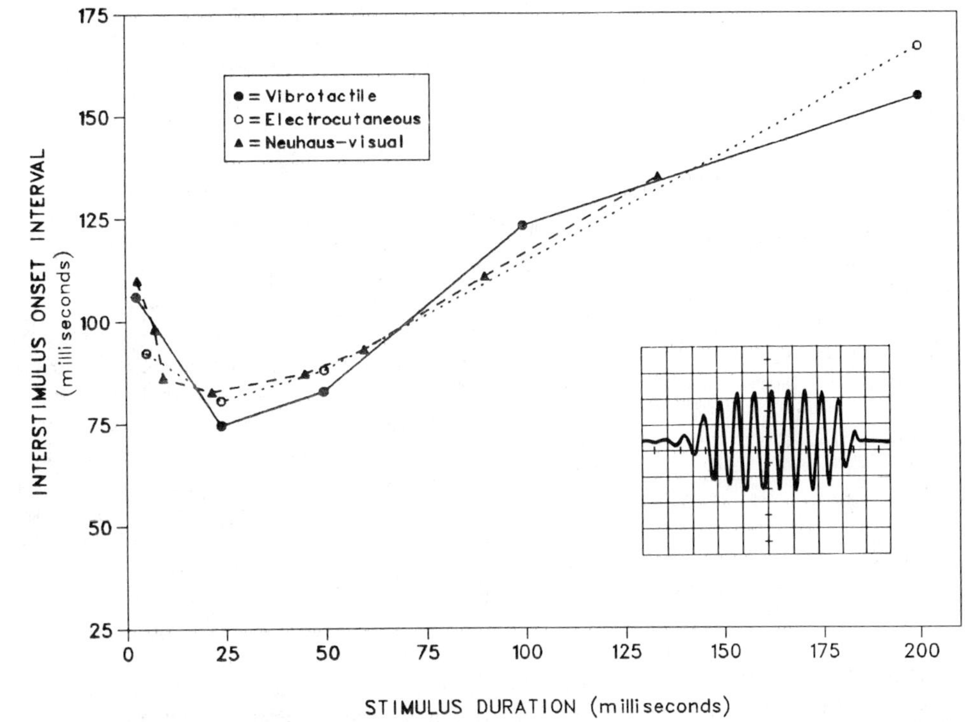

Figure 12.19. The stimulus onset asynchrony between two stimuli for optimal apparent movement for vibrotactile, electrocutaneous, and visual events as a function of stimulus duration. Sherrick and Rogers (1966) presented vibrotactile stimuli consisting of bursts of a 150-Hz sinusoid (see inset for an oscillographic tracing of a 50-msec burst) exciting Goodmans V-47 vibrators fitted with 6-mm contactors touching the skin through 11-mm-diameter holes in fixed 25-mm-diameter Teflon rings. The contactors rested on two sites on the ventral thigh with a static force of 100 g. After adjusting both stimuli to produce a sensation level of about 15 dB, observers manipulated the interburst interval to produce the best movement. This criterion was defined as the longest uninterrupted feeling of movement between the first site and the second. The observer was free to trigger the sequence at a comfortable rate and to adjust the interval as desired. Furthermore, a standard sequence that had previously produced good apparent movement could be switched into the circuit to provide a comparison against which to measure the current settings. A total of four observers served in the experiment, which took place over a period of about 14 months. The means of the interstimulus onset intervals (ISOIs) for good movement are plotted as a function of stimulus duration. Standard errors of the mean ranged from about 3 to 11 msec over the series of durations. At best, the movement was described as being equivalent to that produced by actually moving a vibrating source along the skin's surface, although often movement might only be felt near one source or the other. The ISOI for best movement was not affected by distances of less than 30 cm between sites. For greater distances, the quality of the movement was quickly degraded. Of the variables tested, the only one having any major effect on the ISOI required for high-quality movement was stimulus duration. The results are shown, therefore, for burst durations ranging from 25 to 200 msec (filled circles). To provide for an even shorter duration, a single transient tap was used as the stimulus for the point plotted at 3-msec duration. In addition, the data from a second experiment are plotted in which durations for electrocutaneous stimuli required for good movement were measured by the same technique (open circles). The only significant differences involved replacing the vibrators with wet, concentric electrodes having 0.5-cm^2 center encircled by a 6.8-cm^2 surround, and using 1-kHz bursts at 3 dB SL, a level roughly equivalent to the magnitude of the 15 dB SL vibrotactile stimulus (see Figure 12.34). Finally, the data from Neuhaus (1930) for visual movement are also plotted (as triangles) to allow comparison of ISOIs across the three stimulus modalities. It is striking that the conditions required for good movement not only are comparable for the two tactile modalities but are virtually equivalent to those for good visual movement. (From C. E. Sherrick & R. Rogers, Apparent haptic movement, *Perception and Psychophysics*, 1966 *1*. Reprinted with permission.)

commonalities among sensory processes is the funneling hypothesis of von Békésy (1967). By means of an elaborate series of converging psychophysical experiments, this investigator was able to show that the processes of summation and inhibition arise in space and time in a regular manner, at several levels of the nervous system, to clarify the structure of the stimulus pattern in preparation for interpretative processing at cognitive levels. If either the sensory register or the precategorical store are valid as information-processing constructs, funneling by the nervous system is the signal-conditioning network that precedes them.

5. THE TEMPERATURE SENSES

5.1. Anatomic Correlates

5.1.1. Early Evidence: Hering, Goldscheider, and von Frey. Whereas Weber believed that the sensations of warm and cold were qualitative variants of the touch sense, physiologists by the middle of the nineteenth century were moving to the opinion that touch and temperature were separate modalities. Among these was Ewald Hering, more famous now for his opponent processes theory of color perception. It should surprise few that Hering proposed a similar theory for the perception of cold and warm sensations (see Boring, 1942, p. 466). Hering viewed cold and warm as antagonistic processes whose activation formed the upper and lower bounds of the *Nullpunktstemperatur*, or physiological zero, of the skin (see Section 5.3.2). Unfortunately, no clearly described end organs had been shown to exist in the skin to provide the concrete evidence for Hering's argument, and electrophysiology was an embryonic field at the time.

We have already noted that the discovery of specific sensory spots on the skin in the 1880s was the occasion for certifying the existence of separate modalities. Three independent investigators, Blix in Sweden, Goldscheider in Germany, and Donaldson in America, all found evidence, by varying procedures, of the punctate distribution of pressure, warm, cold, and pain. Both Donaldson and Goldscheider excised the skin areas containing cold and warm spots and found nothing but free nerve endings (Boring, 1942, p. 467). Nevertheless, von Frey repeated the measurements of the first investigators and also examined painstakingly those skin tissues that seemed insensitive to pressure but sensitive to temperature, for example, the glans penis. In these areas he found the Krause end bulb, which he assigned to cold. Because the reaction time for warmth is longer than that for cold, von Frey then assigned Ruffini endings, which lie deeper in the skin tissue, to warmth.

5.1.2. Nafe and the Neurovascular Theory. The troublesome findings (or lack of them) by Donaldson and Goldscheider, relating cold and warm spots only to free nerve endings, were replicated by the early 1930s by several histologists, when J. P. Nafe offered his quantitative theory of temperature sensitivity (see Kenshalo & Nafe, 1962, p. 18). Nafe was able to marshal a considerable body of evidence that the arterioles in the skin, comprising smooth muscle tissue that includes a vestment of sensory nerve fibers, can respond to warmth and cold by dilatation and contraction. In the process of modulation of the caliber of the arteriole, the sensory nerves are excited, and the patterns of local activity thus produced are interpreted in the CNS as warm and cool sensations (see, e.g., Nafe, 1934; Nafe & Kenshalo, 1962). The theory is made to order for Hering's opponent-process hypothesis, but several details, qualitative and quantitative, have failed experimental scrutiny (see, e.g., Geldard, 1972, p. 372). As an early example of pattern theory, however, Nafe's ideas were undoubtedly seminal.

5.1.3. Current Evidence for Receptor Systems. As of the present writing, the majority of authorities on the subject agree that the temperature senses are still in search of a certifiable receptor (Geldard, 1972, p. 362; Kenshalo, 1972, p. 140; Sinclair, 1967, p. 105). As we shall see, there is no dearth of evidence from electrophysiology that first-order neurons are excited by temperature changes on the skin, nor do we lack reports from clinical neurology of dissociation of temperature and other modalities by spinal cord lesions. What is wanted (by some theorists) is a *caloriceptor*, an encapsulated nerve ending that can be shown to shift the neural firing rate as its temperature alone is raised and lowered.

5.1.4. Spinal Tracts and Higher Representation of Temperature Detectors. It has been argued, in the absence of direct anatomical evidence for specificity of peripheral receptor types (see Iggo & Andres, 1982), that there is nonetheless a specificity of nerve fiber types for the cutaneous modalities. This hypothesis results from both experimental observations on the sensations remaining following nerve block by means of pressure, anoxia, cold, or anesthetics and clinical observations following nerve injury at various CNS levels. The dissociation of sensations resulting from selective interference with particular fiber groups, by size, degree of myelination, or position in the nerve bundle, was thought to be strong evidence for a fiber-specificity theory of cutaneous quality. Sinclair (1967, pp. 117–122) has examined the evidence for the hypothesis and concluded that it is seriously flawed by variations in methods of measurement and procedure. Hansen's disease (leprosy), which produces over time a progressive loss of cutaneous sensitivity, has been studied by a number of anatomists, physiologists, and psychologists, with the hope of showing a distinct relation of loss of fiber class to loss of sensations of warmth, cold, pain, or touch as the disease progresses. Findings have been sufficiently contradictory that one cannot say whether a given group of fibers "belongs" to a given sensory modality. It cannot be conclusively stated that the poor relationship results from a real lack of association. It may be that the variation in methods of observation among studies obscures the relation with "noisy" data.

5.2. Physiological Aspects

5.2.1. Animal Studies of Temperature Detection: The Response of Temperature-Sensing Units. A common method for locating warm and cold spots on the human skin involves the use of metallic cylinders tapering to a blunt point. These may be warmed or cooled in a constant-temperature bath and applied to the grid-marked skin area. The human observer can readily differentiate "touch" from "touch plus warm" or "touch plus cold" for the most part. When an animal is prepared for electrophysiological recording of peripheral sensory nerve activity in a region of skin, and the same testing procedure is conducted, two problems are encountered:

1. The simultaneous occurrence of the mechanical action and the temperature change in the skin are not separable by the single nerve fiber being examined. Each pressure-plus-thermal stimulus would require a pressure-alone control for comparison.

2. Even with such a control, it has been found that some mechanoreceptive nerve fibers exhibit a modulation of firing rate with temperature change.

All nerves, of course, show such temperature coefficients under appropriate conditions; therefore, some physiologists are suspicious of preparations that seem to respond to both mechanical and thermal stimuli. Hensel (1962, p. 191) has offered five functional criteria for specification of a temperature receptor:

1. A rise in neural discharge rate when cooled if a "cold" receptor, a fall if a "warm" receptor.
2. If the nerve has a resting discharge, a reduction of rate when warmed if a cold receptor and reduction when cooled if a warm receptor. If the nerve is silent, no response to warming if a cold receptor and none to cooling if a warm receptor.
3. A steady rate of discharge that depends on the temperature.
4. No response or a very high threshold to mechanical stimuli.
5. Sensitivity to thermal levels comparable to that determined psychophysically.

Kenshalo and his colleagues described a stimulating device that avoids the problem of generating transient pressures or other cues concomitant with heating of the skin (Kenshalo, 1963). The *Peltier effect* is the name given to the physical result of passing a dc electric current through the junctions of unlike metals; in a sense it is the reciprocal of the thermoelectric effect. The Peltier thermode, when designed properly, yields heat on one surface and cold on the other with one current polarity and the reverse of this with the opposite current polarity. By means of this device, Kenshalo (1964; Brearly & Kenshalo, 1970; Kenshalo, Decker, & Hamilton, 1967) and his coworkers were able to demonstrate, with avoidance-conditioning techniques, that the cat exhibits over much of its body insensitivity to warm and cold until the temperatures reach aversive (heat- or cold-pain) levels. Over the region of the lips, however, the cat's behavioral threshold function lies close to that of humans (Brearley & Kenshalo, 1970). When electrophysiological measurements of twigs of the cat's infraorbital nerve (part of the trigeminal system subserving the lip area) were made, Kenshalo and Brearley (1970) could show that a 15% increase in activity with cooling or 30% suppression of activity with warming, described the same threshold function as had been determined behaviorally (see Kenshalo, 1972, p. 150).

Electrophysiological studies of nerve activities in humans were pioneered by Hensel and Boman (1960), who severed a superficial branch of the radial nerve in seven human volunteers and recorded responses from the distal cut ends to mechanical and thermal stimuli at the area of skin subserved by the nerve. Out of a total of 34 identified nerve fibers, 21 were described as single fibers, of which 16 responded to touch or pressure, 5 to touch, pressure, and temperature, and 4 to temperature alone. Of the last 4, 1 fiber exhibited responsiveness that approximated psychophysical threshold values, and it behaved like a "cold" fiber, according to Hensel's definition. More recently Konietzny and Hensel (1979) have reported measurements by means of the microneurographic methods. Again, the superficial radial nerve was selected, and tungsten microelectrodes were inserted at a point 2 cm proximal to the wrists of 28 subjects. Recordings were made of responses to mechanical and thermal stimuli in the receptive fields of the units, and about 22 were identified as "warm" units. Other similar studies of this kind have found neural units responsive to cold and warm stimuli and note, in general, their association with the slowly conducting "C" fiber type or with small myelinated fibers of 1–6 μm diameter.

The response of such fibers to temperature is divided into dynamic and static segments. A steady-state response at a constant rate to a constant temperature characterizes the static component; a burst of activity with a step function of temperature change, diminishing in rate over time, characterizes the dynamic component. However, neither of these components proves to be a linear function of temperature or of rate of temperature change, (see, e.g., Konietzny & Hensel, 1979, p. 245). On the other hand, the plot of cumulative number of discharges (dynamic phase) against temperature increment (rate constant) does yield a linear relation, as though temperature shift could be calculated if the peripheral fiber were followed by an integrator network (Konietzny & Hensel, 1979, p. 248).

5.2.2. Responses to Warmth and Cold in Higher Centers. Attempts to record responses in higher-order neurons to temperature changes have been made but with limited success. The work of Landgren (1960) on thalamic recording of responses to cooling of the cat's tongue has been cited by some as evidence of central activity to temperature. Responses to warmth were not present, however. The more recent work by Hellon and colleagues (Dostrovsky & Hellon, 1978; Hellon & Mitchell, 1975) on the rat's scrotum and the cat's muzzle is more promising. The cold- and warm-responsive areas on the cat's lip and nostril areas were stimulated and recordings were made of responses from second-order neurons in the caudal portion of the trigeminal nucleus. The degree to which these findings can be applied to primate forms is not yet well established.

5.3. Psychophysical Aspects

5.3.1. Methods of Stimulation. The two major classes of stimulating device are, of course, those that conduct heat toward or away from the skin surface and those that radiate energy toward the surface. Cooling or warming by air convection has been employed but to a limited degree (see, e.g., Bujas, 1938; Marks & J. C. Stevens, 1972). Of the radiant group, high-intensity lamps, infrared heating lamps, and microwave energy sources are the kinds employed; one of the earliest-used sources, the burning glass, is in this group. Early conductive devices were generally made of metals with high-heat capacity and conductivity, such as copper, copper alloys, or aluminum. These were fabricated as cylinders tapering to blunt points for stimulation of small skin areas and usually with sufficient mass to maintain a relatively constant surface temperature over short time periods. Later developments for conductive devices included the *Dallenbach stimulator* (Geldard, 1972, p. 263), a liquid heat exchanger that permits rapid changes in the temperature of its conductive surface by alteration in the flow of hot or cold water through its outer jacket. A number of variants of this device have been constructed, and all have to some degree the same undesirable feature. The flow of water will produce mechanical motions of the *thermode*, as it is called, thus adding an unwanted stimulus dimension to the thermal changes.

The development of the Peltier electrical thermode was a step toward purification of the stimulus pattern, particularly in the design that Kenshalo (1963) reported. The system Kenshalo described can achieve quite rapid changes in temperature but also, by means of feedback circuitry, attain and hold temperatures over most of the range of usable values for thermal stimulation.

Radiant-heating devices of the type developed by Hardy and his colleagues for thermal pain production (see Geldard, 1972, p. 320) have been adapted for measurement of warmth sensitivity (see, e.g., J. C. Stevens, Okulicz, & Marks, 1973), owing to the fact that provision is made for direct measurement of radiated heat in physical units (g·cal/sec·cm^2). Microwave-heating devices have been used to measure warmth thresholds in the skin (Eijkman & Vendrik, 1961), but these have not seen widespread use, owing in part perhaps to fears of radiation trauma, in part to the differing requirements for calibration, energy measurement, and so forth.

5.3.2. Thresholds for Warmth and Cold: "Physiological Zero." The problem of specification of the stimulus at the skin is no less complicated for thermal modalities than for touch. As Kenshalo has pointed out, measurement of the temperature of the contacting surface of a thermode does not specify the skin temperature, since the specific heats and conductivities of thermode and skin are also involved in its determination (Kenshalo, 1972, p. 141). In addition, comparison of stimulus values between experiments employing radiant heat and those employing conductive devices can be awkward, as Kenshalo has also noted. The ideal solution is to insert small temperature sensors to the average calculated depth of the sensory sheet under the skin. For humans, however, the generally accepted technique has been to place tiny sensors (thermistors or thermocouples) between the thermode and the skin surface (see, e.g., Konietzny & Hensel, 1979).

An additional complication in the study of thermal sensations arises from the fact that the skin has ordinarily a temperature somewhat above the surroundings, about 33° C, but higher or lower depending on the skin site, state of health, person, sex, and time of day, among other variables. Objects at skin temperature that are contacted are judged as neutral or indifferent, that is, neither warm nor cold. This value of tem-

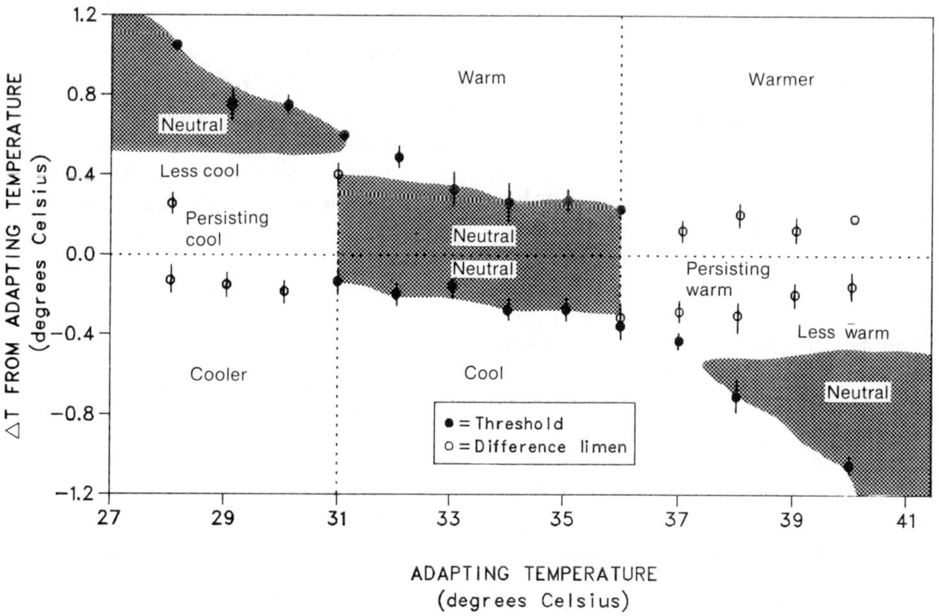

Figure 12.20. Absolute and difference thresholds for warm and cool stimuli as a function of the temperature to which the skin was adapted. Thresholds for warm and cool stimuli vary considerably as a function of area of the stimulator, duration of the temperature change, and, shown here, state of adaptation of the skin. Seven observers were required to report (1) a change in the quality of the sensation and (2) the identity of the sensation, that is, either warm or cool. Stimuli were delivered to the dorsal surface of the forearm, 3 cm distal to the point of the elbow, with a Peltier effect stimulator having a contact area of 14.44 cm^2 and resting on the shaved skin with a pressure of 11.5 g/cm^2. After 20 min of adaptation to the room temperature (ca. 23° C), the stimulator set at the adapting temperature for that session was placed on the arm. Threshold measurements began 45 min later and were taken by the method of limits in which temperature changes occurred at the rate of 0.3° C/sec. The durations of the test steps in the ascending and descending series were 10 sec, after which the temperature of the stimulator was returned to the adapting level. Adapting temperatures ranged from 28° to 40° C in 1° increments. The results are shown in the figure with the filled circles indicating absolute thresholds and open circles indicating the difference thresholds with standard errors of the mean indicated by the vertical lines. Despite the long period of adaptation, only adapting temperatures between 31 and 36° produced thermally neutral sensations during the threshold measurements. Persisting sensations of cool and warmth remained for adapting temperatures below and above this range, respectively. Owing to these persisting sensations, temperature changes in the opposite direction passed through thermally neutral zones (indicated by the stippling) before entering a zone in which the sensation changed sign. Only in the regions of persisting sensation could difference thresholds be differentiated from the absolute threshold; they coincided in the thermally neutral zone of adapting temperatures from 31° to 36°. In this neutral zone they are defined as absolute thresholds because a change occurs in the quality of the sensation when the temperature is raised or lowered. (From D. R. Kenshalo, The cutaneous senses. In J. W. Kling & L. A. Riggs (Eds.), *Woodworth and Schlosberg's experimental psychology: Sensation and perception*, 3rd ed., Vol. 1, Holt, Rinehart & Winston, 1972. Reprinted with permission.)

perature is called *physiological zero*, on either side of which a change of sufficient rate and amount will produce a report of "warm" or "cool." The skin thermal sensory system may be said to be adapted to its local physiological zero, since it is possible (within limits) to warm or cool the skin at a slow rate to a new temperature without eliciting a report of change. The size of this "zone of neutrality" varies with the adapting temperature, the rate of change, and the skin site and amount of area stimulated. An example of the zone for the forearm is shown in Figure 12.20. It should be noted that two kinds of thresholds can be measured to produce the various areas bounded by the curves. The absolute threshold is defined as the change from neutral to warm or to cool. The difference threshold is defined as a change from warm to warmer or less warm or from cool to cooler or less cool. At temperature levels below about 31° C or above 36° C, the sensation of cool or warm persists. Thus the static neutral zone for these conditions has about 5° width, within which a sufficiently rapid dynamic change of about 0.2° C will elicit a report of "warm" or "cool."

It has been mentioned that rate of temperature change determines threshold to some extent. Figure 12.21 is a plot of one function for the human forearm, showing that, for the conditions of the experiment, rates above 0.1° C/sec require about the same increment above physiological zero to be perceived. Below that rate, the functions can be described by the equation for a rectangular hyperbola (see Figure 12.21).

5.3.2.1. Temporal Summation of Temperature Thresholds. A recent study by J. C. Stevens and coworkers (1973) has reviewed some of the earlier work on temporal summation of warmth and examined the process over the range of 0.5–10 sec for two sizes of exposure area on the forehead, for radiated heat. Thresholds to warmth were measured in six observers by presenting controlled pulses of radiant energy until reports of warmth were obtained for the durations studied. The results show nearly perfect temporal summation from 0.5 to 1.0 sec and above 1.0 sec ("critical duration") no further effect to 10 sec. In addition, spatial summation (computed from the two areas employed) shows only an additive relation to temporal summation at all points, implying no complex interactive effects in these ranges. For cold stimuli, there appears to be no equivalent set of functions describing temporal summation later than observations by Bujas (1938), who directed jets of cold air against the forehead for various durations and found the threshold for temperature change to decrease with the square root of duration, with a critical duration of about 1.5 sec. The question of temporal summation will recur in the discussion of adaptation (see Section 5.3.3).

5.3.2.2. Spatial Summation of Temperature Thresholds. The ability of the skin surface to summate the stimulus energy over increasingly larger extents is directly observable. Press the edge, then the flat, of a cooled (or warmed) coin (insulated from the fingers holding it!) on the skin successively, and note the dramatic increase in sensory magnitude of cold (or warmth). The same effects appear for absolute thresholds (see, e.g., Kenshalo et al., 1967). Spatial summation, like temporal summation, is nearly complete; a doubling of exposed area reduces the temperature change required for threshold to one-half the original value. Kenshalo (1972, p. 146) provides the equation for spatial summation of warmth at threshold:

$$I = kA^{-b} + c ,$$

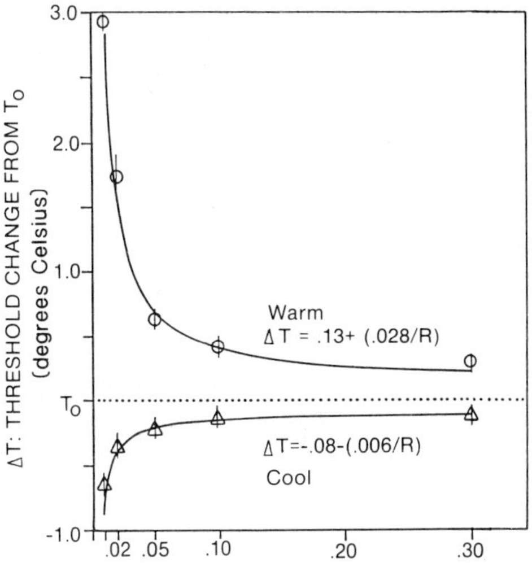

Figure 12.21. Warm and cool thresholds as a function of the rate of change of the thermal stimulus (after Kenshalo, Holmes, & Wood, 1968). In this study of thermal sensitivity as a function of the rate of change of the thermal stimulus, stimuli were presented with a Peltier effect device that produces either a temperature increase or decrease at the contacting surface depending on the polarity of the driving current. The rate of warming or cooling was similarly dependent on the rate and final level of the current change. The stimulator had a surface area of 14.44 cm^2 and rested on the shaved skin of the observer's forearm with a pressure of 10.5 g/cm^2. After setting the device to normal skin temperature (previously measured), thresholds were obtained by the method of limits for rates of change of 0.3, 0.1, 0.05, 0.02, and 0.01° C/sec. Six measurements were made of the warm and cool thresholds for the five rates of change in each of three sessions on three observers. The results, shown in the figure, are the means of 48 threshold determinations, with the standard error of the mean indicated on each point. For these observers, normal skin temperature T_o was approximately 31.5° C, and asymptotic levels of threshold were reached for both warmth and cold at a rate of 0.1° C/sec. Slower rates of change, however, resulted in increases in both thresholds. Both sets of data may be fitted by a rectangular hyperbola of the form $\Delta T = K + L/R$, where ΔT is the temperature change in °C, K is the asymptotic threshold level at very high rates of change (in °C), L is a range-specific constant in $°C^2$/sec, and R is the rate of change in °C/sec. The authors suggest that the difference in the effects of small rates of change on the two thresholds reflect differences in the rates of thermal adaptation (see Figure 12.23). (From D. R. Kenshalo, The cutaneous senses. In J. W. Kling & L. A. Riggs (Eds.), *Woodworth & Schlosberg's experimental psychology: Sensation and perception*, 3rd ed., Vol. 1, Holt, Rinehart & Winston, 1972. Reprinted with permission.)

where

I = radiant intensity in g·cal/sec·cm^2
A = area in cm^2
k = constant depending on the site stimulated
b = constant of approximately 1.0 for these data
c = threshold for very large areas, that is, greater than 2000 cm^2

Figure 12.22 shows the summation functions for three sites, forehead, forearm, and back. Both conducted heat, and radiant heat yield similar functions over the range of areas shown. Of additional interest in this regard is the fact that two separate areas will (partially) summate spatially as well (see Kenshalo, 1972, p. 147), suggesting that the process occurs at both peripheral and central levels of the nervous system. Evidence for

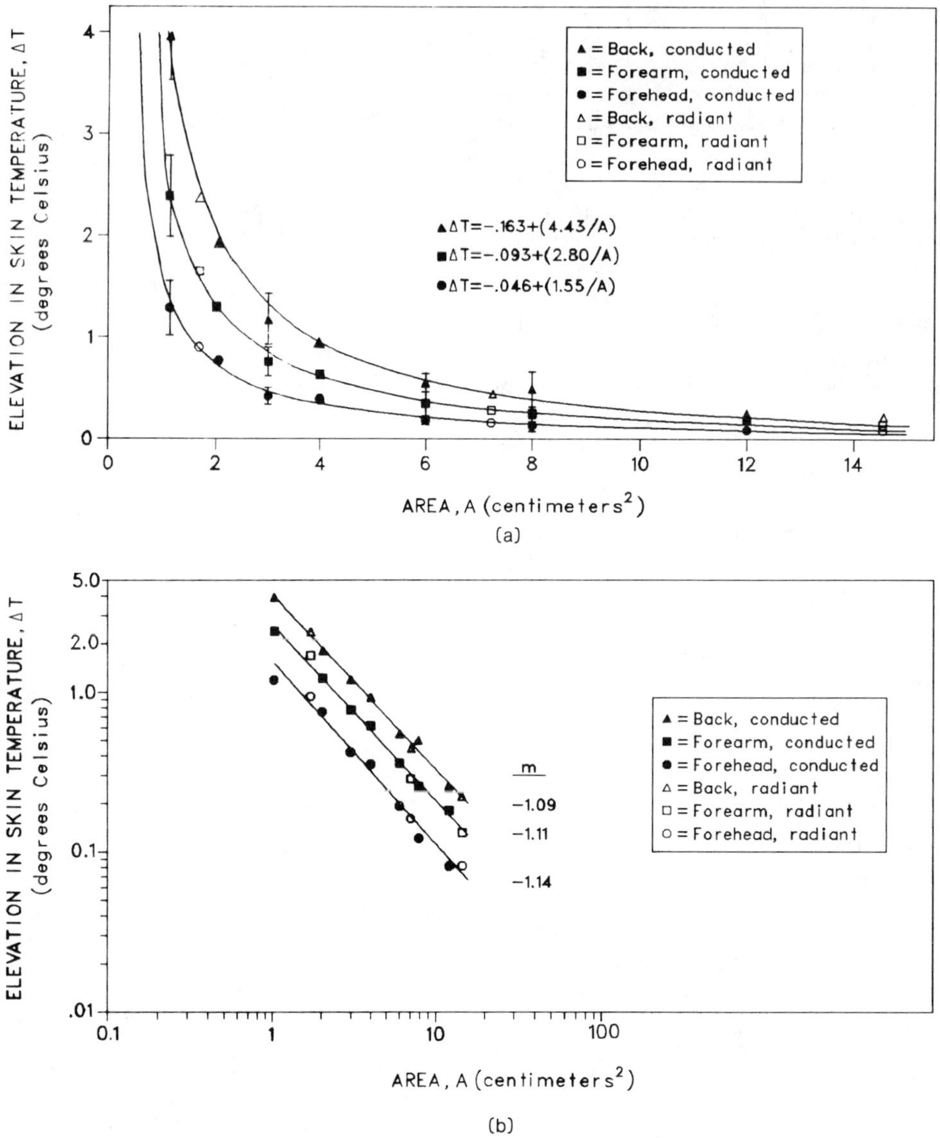

Figure 12.22. Thresholds for warmth as a function of the area of stimulation at three different body sites showing spatial summation for both radiant and conducted heat. Kenshalo and colleagues examined the manner in which thresholds for warmth varied as a function of different areas of conducted heat (1.7, 7.1, and 14.4 cm^2), as well as for seven different areas of radiant heat (ranging from 1 to 12 cm^2). These thresholds were obtained using the method of limits from three observers on the forehead, the volar surface of the forearm, and the back. The level of radiant energy was varied by increasing or decreasing its intensity, while the level of conducted heat was varied by changing its rate of increase over the 3 sec of exposure to equate the temporal characteristics of the two methods. The calculated rise in skin temperature at threshold is plotted for the three body sites as a function of the area of skin stimulated on linear coordinates in (a) and on logarithmic coordinates in (b). The bars in (a) represent the standard errors of the means of eight threshold measurements for each condition. When the data are plotted on linear coordinates, they may be well fit with a rectangular hyperbola of the form $\Delta T = K + L/A$, with the constants shown for each body site. In this equation, ΔT is the threshold for warmth in °C, K is the threshold in °C for very large areas, L is a site-dependent constant expressed in °C·cm^2, and A is the area of stimulation in cm^2. In this form, the functions readily describe the asymptotic behavior of threshold as the area of stimulation grows in size. However, the degree to which these data show spatial summation may be better seen if they are plotted on logarithmic coordinates, for then the slopes of the functions reflect the amount of summation (b). The functions described in (b) are of the form $\Delta T = K + LA^{\beta}$ in which ΔT is the elevation in skin temperature in °C necessary to reach threshold for area A in cm^2, K is the threshold in °C for a very large area, and L is a site-dependent constant in °C·cm^2. The exponent of the function, β, ranging here from -1.09 on the back to -1.14 on the forehead, indicates the degree to which summation is complete. Because the exponents are approximately equal to -1.0, a doubling in area results in a halving of threshold. Thus almost perfect spatial summation does occur for both radiant and conducted heat. Furthermore, any tactile component present with conducted heat does not appear to interact with either threshold or the rate of summation since these data fall along the same lines as do the radiant thresholds. (From D. R. Kenshalo, The cutaneous senses. In J. W. Kling & L. A. Riggs (Eds.), *Woodworth & Schlosberg's experimental psychology: Sensation and perception*, 3rd ed., Vol. 1, Holt, Rinehart & Winston, 1972. Reprinted with permission.)

for spatial summation of cold at threshold has been reported by Hardy and Oppel (1938).

5.3.3. Adaptation to Thermal Stimuli. It has already been mentioned that the physiological zero for a given skin area represents a level of temperature at which the site is completely adapted; that is, no thermal sensation is reported. As Figure 12.20 shows, an approximate 5° C zone of indifference holds for the forearm, but when this range is exceeded, a persisting sensation of warmth or cold exists. The temporal course of adaptation can be shown by a tracking method, as Kenshalo and Scott (1966) did, by having observers increase the temperature of a Peltier thermode from physiological zero (here, about 33° C) until a just noticeable warmth appeared, then wait until the sensation disappeared, increase it again to noticeablity, hold, and so on. Similarly, the course of adaptation to cold was studied. The results for five observers are shown in Figure 12.23. The rate of adaptation is highest for small deviations from normal skin temperature, and individual differences are marked. When very small areas—"temperature spots" of 1 or 2 mm diameter—are stimulated, a much wider range of temperatures will produce complete adaptation, suggesting that areal summation affects both threshold and adaptive processes (see e.g., Geldard, 1972, p. 359).

5.3.4. Sensory Magnitude Functions for Warmth and Cold. An early study of the growth of sensory magnitude of warmth and cold was done by J. C. Stevens and S. S. Stevens (1960), who applied large aluminum cylinders to the volar forearms of 12 observers. The results are shown in Figure 12.24. To obtain a power function for these data, it was necessary to provide an additive constant in the expression for the stimulus intensity, after converting temperature to degrees Kelvin. The expressions are then

$$\text{For Warmth } W = M\,(T_K - 305.7)^{1.6}$$

where

W is the numerical estimate of warmth sensation,
T_K is the temperature of the stimulus in degrees Kelvin,
M is a constant,
305.7 is the additive constant (near physiological zero).

$$\text{For Cold } C = M'\,(304.2 - T_K)^{1.0}$$

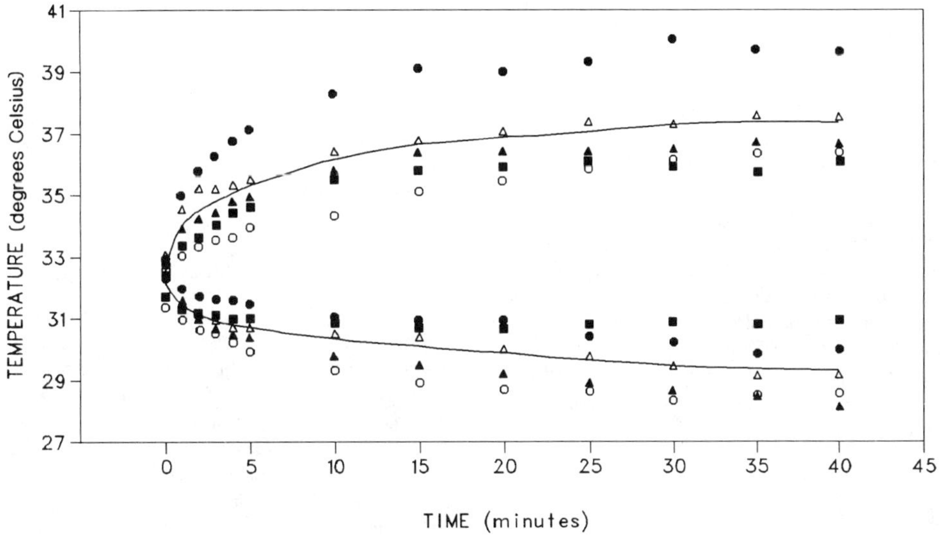

Figure 12.23. The course of adaptation to near-threshold warm and cool stimuli for five observers. Kenshalo and Scott (1966) employed a Peltier effect stimulator (a device whose temperature is dependent on the amount of current applied) in a tracking paradigm. After adapting to room temperature, the device, with a contacting area of 14.4 cm^2, was applied to the forearm 3 cm distal to the point of the elbow and set to the previously measured skin temperature. The five subjects were then required to keep the stimulator at a "just perceptibly warm" or "just perceptibly cool" temperature with a control lever that would raise or lower the stimulator temperature at 0.3°C/sec when moved. Continuous records were kept of the temperature at the contacting surface. At 5-min intervals the temperature of the stimulator was changed by the experimenter towards neutral, forcing the observer to return it to the warm or cool threshold. Four such series were run with each of the five observers for the two temperature ranges. The means of the settings for each observer at 5-min intervals for both the warm and cool functions are shown in the figure. The range of responses across observers increases as adaptation progresses, but observers appear to reach their own final level at their own rate. Criterion differences probably would not account for these variations because the observers all had considerable experience detecting such stimuli. Furthermore, their thresholds at physiological zero did not vary by more than ±0.05°C. Depending on the individual, therefore, adaptation appears to take some 20 to 40 min with this method and reaches asymptote at 36–40°C for warmth and 28–31°C for cool stimuli. These results also indicate that it is possible to shift the neutral point (physiological zero) over the 28–40°C range as long as the stimulus temperature changes slowly enough (less than 0.007°C in this series). Within these boundaries it is possible to achieve complete adaptation. Outside these limits, however, persisting warm or cool sensations will result (see Figure 12.20). (From D. R. Kenshalo, The cutaneous senses. In J. W. Kling & L. A. Riggs (Eds.), *Woodworth & Schlosberg's experimental psychology: Sensation and perception*, 3rd ed., Vol. 1, Holt, Rinehart & Winston, 1972. Reprinted with permission.)

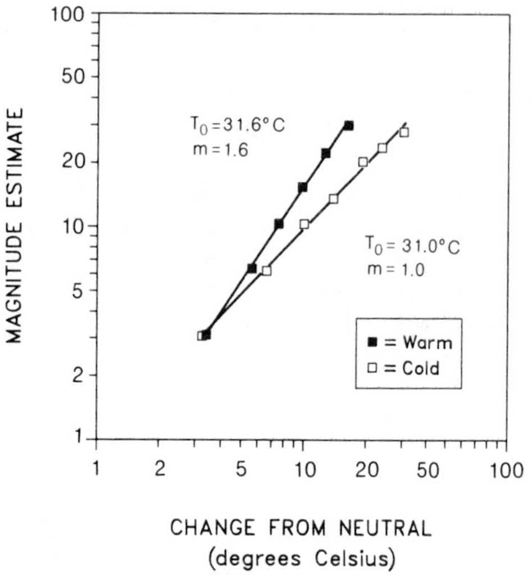

Figure 12.24. The growth of sensation magnitude of warmth and cold as a function of stimulus intensity above or below physiological zero. (Adapted from J. C. Stevens & S. S. Stevens, 1960.) J. C. Stevens and S. S. Stevens (1960) examined the growth of magnitude of warmth and cold on the volar surface of the forearm using large aluminum cylinders with contacting surfaces 20 mm in diameter (3.14-cm^2 area). The cylinders were kept in constant-temperature baths and held at the stimulating temperature to within 0.2°C. Warm stimulus temperatures ranged from 35–47.2°C in six roughly equal log increments, while the cold stimuli ranged from 0.5–27.7°C in seven increments. Twelve observers made 3 magnitude estimates of each of the warm stimuli, while 13 observers made 2 estimates of the cold stimuli. Geometric means of the data were plotted on logarithmic coordinates, but when these data were plotted in terms of absolute temperature (Kelvin), the functions obtained showed significant curvature (concave downward) over their lengths. If, on the other hand, the data are plotted in terms of degrees above or below thermal neutrality for the skin as shown in the figure, the best-fitted functions become linear on the logarithmic coordinates, indicating a power relationship. The resulting slope of the function for warmth is 1.6 referred to a neutral point at 31.6°C while the slope of the magnitude estimation function for cold is 1.0 referred to a neutral point at 31°C. This manipulation only calls for the introduction of a constant into the psychophysical law, subtracting threshold from the actual stimulus level, and points out the importance of considering threshold in the measurement of the relationship between sensation magnitude and stimulus intensity.

where

C is the numerical estimate of cold sensation,
T_K is the temperature of the stimulus in degrees Kelvin,
M' is a constant,
304.2 is the additive constant (near physiological zero).

The slopes resulting are obviously quite different: 1.6 for warmth and 1.0 for cold. Similar values were obtained when the entire hand was immersed in water at various temperatures. A change in physiological zero would seem to affect only the value of the additive constant. Variations in methods of measurement, such as the site tested or the area of skin stimulated, can produce different slopes. (See, e.g., Figure 12.30 and B. G. Green, 1977b.)

Marks and J. C. Stevens and their colleagues have applied the techniques of direct estimation of sensory magnitudes to several fundamental problems of thermal sensitivity (see, e.g., Marks, 1974; Marks & J. C. Stevens, 1973a, 1973b; Marks, J. Stevens, & Tepper, 1976; J. C. Stevens & Marks, 1971; J. C. Stevens, Marks, & Simonson, 1974). Marks and coworkers (1976) were able to show spatiotemporal summation of warmth at absolute threshold, as well as at suprathreshold, levels for radiant energy to the forehead. The investigators examined spatial, temporal, and spatiotemporal summation by exposing restricted areas of the forehead to radiant heat of controlled intensity and duration. For absolute threshold measures, observers were required to report feelings of warmth as the stimulus intensity of a 100-msec pulse of radiation was increased under one of several conditions: 1. one stimulus presented to one or the other area, 2. one stimulus presented to both areas simultaneously, 3. one stimulus presented to one area followed, after a delay of 0.25, 0.5, 0.75, or 1.0 sec, by a second stimulus to the other area, or to the same area. Appropriate counterbalancing of the sides was done.

The results of this experiment are shown in Figure 12.25, where it is clear that the drop in threshold from one stimulus to two simultaneous bilateral stimuli (conditions 1 and 2) shows partial spatial summation (reduction to 80% of single value, or about 1.0 dB). The summation thus demonstrated is probably not peripheral, since isolated areas across the midline of the body were involved. When the same area was stimulated successively at various intervals (condition 3), thresholds for short interstimulus intervals were the same as for the bilateral si-

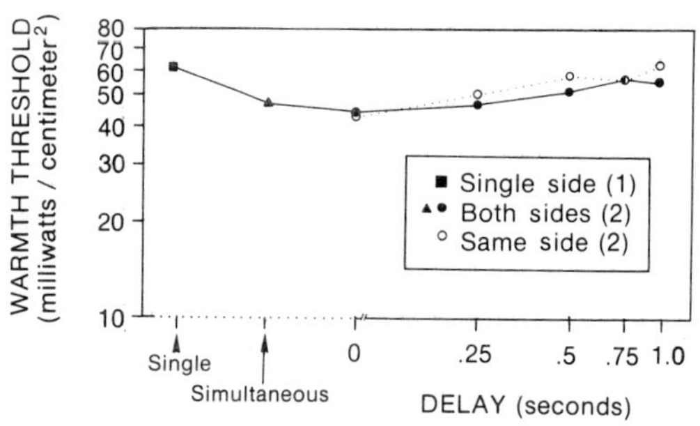

Figure 12.25. Spatiotemporal summation of warmth at absolute threshold for brief pulses of radiant heat (after Marks, J. C. Stevens, & Tepper, 1976). The purpose of this experiment was to determine the degree to which warm stimuli presented to two different body sites will summate and how such summation is dependent on the temporal separation between the stimuli. The sites chosen were two 11-cm^2 rectangles on either side of the midline of the forehead, separated horizontally by 3 cm. The rest of the forehead was shielded by an aluminum plate. The voltages on two 1000-W projection lamps fitted with shutters were controlled by two variable autotransformers, providing different levels of irradiation that were measured in the plane of the subject's forehead with a Hardy radiometer. The shutters in front of the lamps could be opened simultaneously or successively for any duration and in any order. Thresholds were measured in three subjects by the method of limits in ascending order only; the series ended with two affirmative responses to a stimulus level. Seven different stimulus patterns were presented in counterbalanced orders with shutter-open durations of 100 msec: a single pulse to one side only, simultaneous pulses presented to both sides of the forehead, or successive pulses to one or both sides separated by 0, 250, 500, 750, or 1000 msec. Note that the 0-msec delay condition involves back-to-back pulses, not simultaneous ones. Each observer judged the set of stimuli 14 times. The mean thresholds are shown for each condition. Spatial summation is indicated by the fact that thresholds are lower when both sides are stimulated simultaneously (solid triangle) than when a single site is stimulated (solid square). Temporal summation is shown by the lower thresholds for two pulses on the same side versus a single one (open circles versus square, respectively). Finally, spatiotemporal summation is indicated by the difference between the single-site short stimulus (square) and the two-site delayed stimuli (filled circles). The similarity between the one- and the two-site conditions indicates that summation is not a peripheral phenomenon, nor does it matter whether signals originate in the same or different sides of the body: they add in the same manner.

multaneous condition (2) and for longer intervals rose until thresholds were about that for the single unilateral condition (1). Thus stimuli that are temporally separated by intervals of 250 msec or less can be ipsilateral or contralateral and yield the same threshold; that is, stimuli that summate temporally summate as well when processed by separated or common channels. Moreover, the course of decline of temporal summation is the same for the two-channel conditions.

With the same stimulus arrangement, these investigators presented suprathreshold stimuli at 6 intensity levels to 18 observers and asked for numerical estimates of magnitude of warmth. Again, several conditions were examined.

The results are shown in Figure 12.26. A unilateral short pulse is rated as the same as a unilateral long pulse when radiation levels are low but rated as weaker with higher levels. This suggests that temporal summation is dependent on stimulus level, at least for these durations and areas. When the magnitude of a unilateral 4-sec pulse is compared to that of successive bilateral 2-sec pulses, no difference is apparent at any given intensity level, which implies that spatiotemporal summation is complete; dividing the total energy flux between two areas yields the same magnitude of warmth as when the flux impinges on a single area. Finally, simultaneous bilateral stimuli of the same duration and intensity as a unilateral stimulus yield 3–1 dB of spatial summation, as intensity increases. Again, because of the stimulus conditions, the summation effects observed here are central in origin. Marks and colleagues (1976) argue that these data, in particular the spatiotemporal data of the second and fourth conditions, demonstrate that the skin does not act as a passive heat transfer system that integrates energy over time and sends a resulting thermometric message on to the CNS. Instead, it appears to convey an energy-dependent signal that is integrated by the CNS over its spatiotemporal-intensitive frame of reference.

To those who believe that symmetry is beauty in science as in art, it would provide pleasure to report that a similar set of experiments has been carried out for the perception of cold. Alas, such gratification awaits the talents and inclinations of this or another group. In another study, however, Marks and J. C. Stevens (1972) reported the effects of decreasing radiant heat levels over the whole ventral body surface with ambient cold temperatures of 3–4°C, 30% relative humidity, and average wind velocity of 0.3 m/sec. After determining the minimum radiant heat levels required to produce a report of neutral temperature levels, the effects of decreasing intensity for various durations and amounts of decrement were assessed by having the observers estimate the magnitude of cold sensation thus produced. Skin temperatures were measured on a sample of the 14 observers who participated.

The growth of magnitude of cold is shown in Figure 12.27, with stimulus duration as parameter. Figure 12.28(a) shows the growth of magnitude with duration, with intensity as parameter. Clearly, adaptation to cold occurs, but under the conditions of whole-body radiation it is never complete. Figure 12.28(b), which is taken from a similar study of growth of magnitude of warmth (Marks & J. C. Stevens, 1968), shows that warmth sensations adapt except at the higher levels. Marks and J. C. Stevens explain the differing functional relations by appealing to the homeostatic mechanisms involved. For cold, only vasoconstriction can compensate for loss of body heat, and skin temperature levels (which correlate well with perception of cold) fall with almost no autonomic restraint. For heat, in contrast, both vasodilatation and sweating occur to compensate for the rise in skin temperature (which does not correlate well with perception of warmth), and potentially dangerous deviations from ambient levels are mitigated.

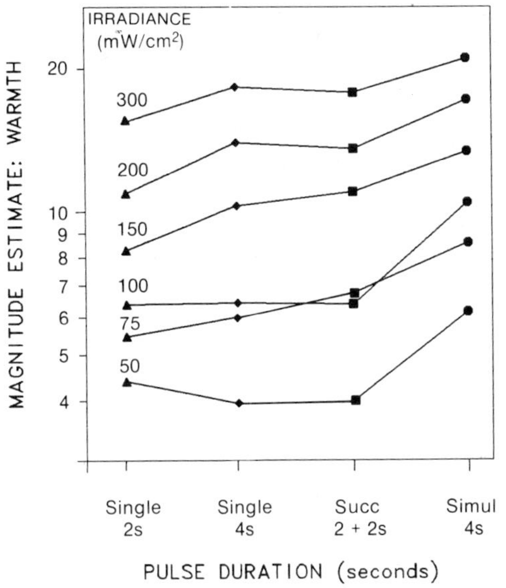

Figure 12.26. Suprathreshold spatiotemporal summation of warmth for durative pulses of radiant heat (after Marks, J. C. Stevens, & Tepper, 1976). The apparatus used to produce the durative pulses of radiant heat to the foreheads of the observers was identical to that described in Figure 12.25, except for the duration of the pulses (increased here to 2 or 4 sec each) and the introduction of white noise to mask the sound of the shutters. The procedure in this case involved magnitude estimation, in which the subjects were required to assign numbers to the stimuli in proportion to the degree of apparent warmth. Neither a standard nor a range was suggested for the numbers. The stimuli consisted of 2-sec or 4-sec pulses of heat presented at six different levels of irradiance. Each of these levels was presented in four different conditions: 2 sec on one side of the forehead, 4 sec to one side, 4 sec to both sides simultaneously, and the successive presentation of 2 sec to one side followed immediately with a 2-sec pulse to the other side. In all conditions the sides and order of patterns were counterbalanced. The results are shown for 18 male observers who judged each of the 24 different stimuli twice. Comparing the geometric means of the magnitude estimates, the following conclusions may be reached. (1) Temporal summation, as indicated by an increase in the estimates to the single 4-sec presentation (diamonds) above those to the single 2-sec stimulus (triangles), takes place only at higher levels of irradiance. The amount of summation, however, is no more than about 2 dB/doubling of duration. (2) Spatial summation, indicated by the increase in estimates between the 4-sec stimulus at one site (diamonds) and the 4-sec stimulus at two sites (circles), occurs as a decreasing function of irradiance. At low stimulus levels, the 6-dB increase in area results in a 3.5-dB increase in perceived warmth, while at higher intensities, the same areal increase results in about a 2-dB increase in sensation magnitude. (3) Spatiotemporal summation was tested by comparing the results of stimulation with two successive 2-sec pulses to two sites (squares) with a single 4-sec pulse to a single site (diamonds). Because the heat in the first case, which was spread out spatially as well as temporally, produced essentially the same perceived warmth as a single pulse at a single site, the conclusion was that spatiotemporal summation occurred. The amounts of spatiotemporal summation described both in this figure and in Figure 12.25 indicate that the summation is the same regardless of whether successive presentations are made to different sites or one longer presentation to a single site. Furthermore, owing to the bilateral nature of the stimuli, it must be assumed that the classes of summation described here are central in origin, much like those described for audition and vibrotactile sensitivity.

5.3.5. Paradoxical Cold and Heat Sensations. Certain phenomena appear in the course of laboratory studies of sensory systems and are duly reported by the discoverers as deviants from the orderly relations sought in psychophysical studies.

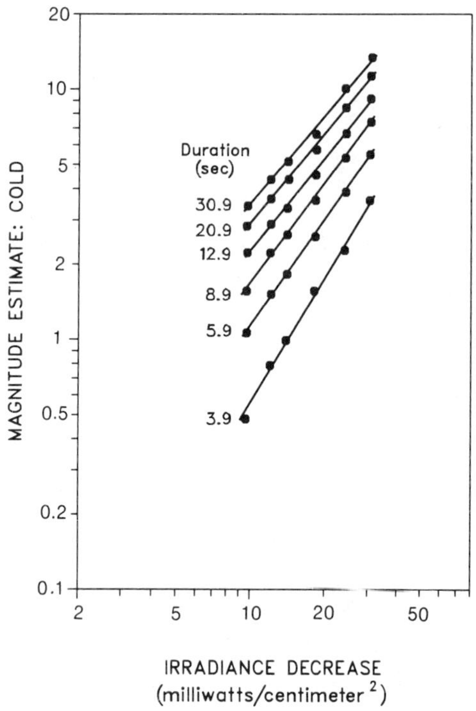

Figure 12.27. The growth of perceived cold as a function of the magnitude of the decrease in irradiance with duration of stimulation as the parameter. This study examined how the sensation of cold grows as a function of both the intensity of cold (here defined by the *de*crease in the magnitude ofheat flux irradiating the subject) and the duration of the cooling stimulus. Fourteen blindfolded subjects lay supine on a bed, clad in briefs, socks, and shoes, 1.65 m below a bank of quartz lamps mounted in a shuttered system. The room was maintained at an air temperature of 3–4°C, but the level of radiation produced by the lamps was adjusted for each subject to produce thermal neutrality in the cold air. Changes in irradiance could be achieved by rapidly switching from one subset of lamps to a second at the desired level using the shutter system. The changes in irradiance were monitored at 30 points on the body surface, and the reported values are averages of these readings, corrected for skin reflection. During the calibration session the level of irradiation necessary to maintain thermal neutrality was determined, along with those required to produce the six levels to be used in the estimation series. During the test sessions these were presented at each of six different effective exposure durations ranging from 3.9 to 30.9 sec. Subjects were required to assign numbers to the 36 stimuli in proportion to the degree of experienced cold, that is, by the method of magnitude estimation. Geometric means of the estimates are plotted in the figure as a function of irradiance decreases, with the best-fitted power functions drawn through the estimates for each duration. For each duration, the data were well fitted by power functions that had exponents ranging from 1.18 for a duration of 30.9 sec to 1.71 for a duration of 3.9 sec. The family of functions has a convergence point of approximately 1000 mW/cm^2. These exponents are somewhat larger than that recorded by J. C. Stevens and S. S. Stevens (1960) for brief contact cold stimulation on the forearm with a smaller area of stimulation (see Figure 12.24). However, either spatial or temporal summation of cold could readily account for the discrepancy (see, e.g., Figure 12.28). (From L. E. Marks & J. C. Stevens, Perceived cold and skin temperature as functions of stimulation level and duration, *American Journal of Psychology, 85*. Copyright 1972 by University of Illinois Press. Reprinted with permission.)

Some of these are remarkably dependable and get repeated and repeatedly cited; others have the quality of the will o' the wisp. Both types are the stepping stones for one theory and the impediments of another. *Paradoxical cold* is of the first kind. If a skin spot, previously identified as yielding a consistent report of "cold" when stimulated by a thermode at less than the physiological zero, is stimulated by a very warm thermode, say 45°C, the report of "cold" is sometimes given. This has been repeated by many students (see Geldard, 1972, p. 359; Kenshalo, 1972, p. 148; Sinclair, 1967, p. 168). The parallel to this phenomenon, *paradoxical warmth* is of the second kind. Stimulating a warm spot with a cold stimulus should occasionally yield a report of "warm.". It almost never does, if 1 report in 13,000 (see Geldard,

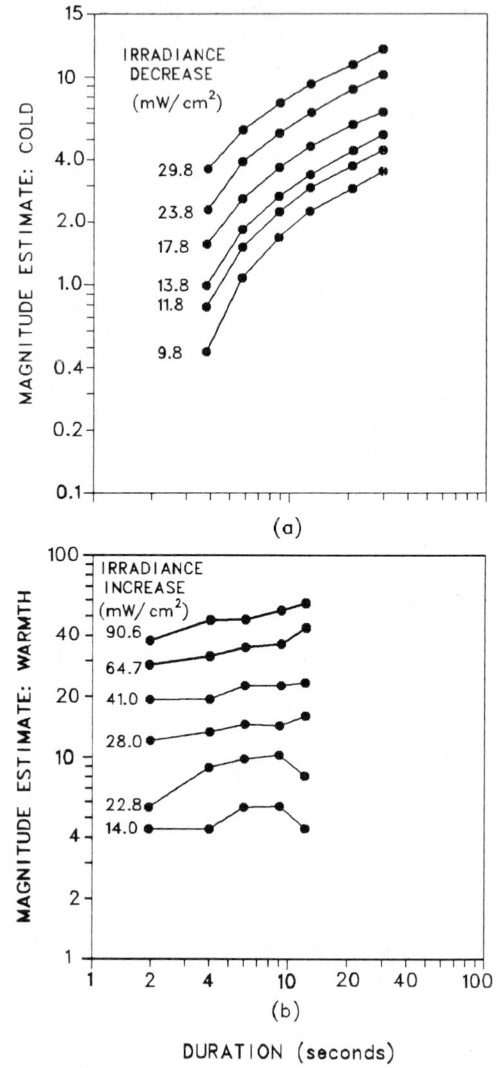

Figure 12.28. Magnitude estimates of cold (a) and warmth (b) as a function of stimulus duration with stimulus intensity as the parameter. The results from Marks and J. C. Stevens' (1972) study of the magnitude of perceived cold, shown in Figure 12.27, were replotted in (a) as a function of duration with the intensity (irradiance *de*crease) as the parameter. For comparison, comparable functions are plotted in (b) for warmth (irradiance increase) from the data of Marks and J. C. Stevens (1968). In this study, room temperature was maintained at 20°C, and 16 male subjects served in the 2 sessions; the apparatus was essentially the same as that used for estimates of cold. Cold grows as a negatively accelerated function of duration, indicating the occurrence of adaptation. Yet, over the 30+-sec period of exposure, estimates are still growing slightly, indicating that complete adaptation has not been achieved for any stimulus level. Furthermore, the relatively parallel functions suggest similar rates of change across levels. In the case of warmth, however, adaptation appears to be close to complete at all levels within the first 2 sec of stimulation, with no significant rise in apparent warmth with increases in duration from 2 to 12 sec. (From L. E. Marks & J. C. Stevens, Perceived cold and skin temperature as functions of stimulation level and duration, *American Journal of Psychology, 85*. Copyright 1972 by University of Illinois Press. Reprinted with permission.)

1972, p. 360) defines "almost never." Other investigators report more frequent occurrences, but still others deny ever finding it (Geldard, 1972, p. 360; Kenshalo, 1972, p. 148; Sinclair, 1967, p. 168). The appearance of paradoxical sensations of both kinds, even with large stimulating surfaces (when no paradoxical sensations are reported by persons with intact peripheral nerves), occurs when nerve blocks have been affected (Sinclair, 1967, p. 169).

The sensation of heat can be aroused paradoxically, so to speak, by presenting the observer with a stimulus pattern of alternating (in space) warm (43°C) and cool (10°C) surfaces. The uninformed observer will often recoil from such a stimulus as though it were hot, that is, in the 50–60°C range. Although moderately reliable, this demonstration, which was once a standard laboratory instructional aid but is now a quaint museum piece, fails with many observers. It happens just often enough, as Geldard (1972, p. 362) points out, to add the unwanted straw to the back of the theorist's camel.

5.3.6. Localization of Temperature Sensations. To examine the spatial acuity of the temperature senses, it is obviously necessary to eliminate cues from the sense of touch. For warmth, the use of radiant heat solves the problem, since no mechanical contact is made with the skin. Taus, J. C. Stevens, and Marks (1975) were able to show that the error of localization for warmth varies with the intensity of the stimulus, and that a 4-cm^2 patch of skin at a low stimulus intensity was correctly localized 75% of the time when 5.5 cm from a touch reference point. A similar patch at 2.5 cm from the reference point was equally well localized only when the intensity was raised by 7 dB (Taus et al., 1975, p. 195). Similar data for cold are not available, but the relative ease with which the location of both warm and cold sensations can be displaced by appropriately timed and located tactile stimuli suggests that the localization of cold is not much better than that for warmth (see B. G. Green, 1979; see Section 7.1).

The temperature senses are not commonly thought of as useful for communicative purposes, owing to their relatively slower response, their poor localizability, and their comparatively prodigious capacity for adaptation and summation. Under appropriate circumstances, however, they could be recruited to serve as alternative background cutaneous stimuli, as color is used in visual displays, or voice pitch in auditory displays, to add optional channels in information transmission. This and related possibilities will be discussed later (see Sections 7 and 10).

6. CUTANEOUS PAIN

6.1. Anatomic Correlates

6.1.1. Early Conclusions: Goldscheider, von Frey, and Head. It has already been noted that pain was consigned by Weber to the rather large category of general bodily feelings. When Blix, Goldscheider, and Donaldson independently reported their findings of spots on the skin seemingly separately responsive to touch, warmth, cold, and pain, it might be thought that pain would, along with the others, be considered an independent modality. After all, the microscopic probe method employed, which is a kind of partial correlational technique, gave status to touch, warmth, and cold as independent modalities. Initially, in fact, this was the case; pain was thought to be a separable modality of the cutaneous system. Goldscheider, however, had second thoughts (following additional experiments). He noted, for example, that pain spots were more dense than all the other qualities combined and that they often coincided with other kinds of spots. He decided, therefore, that pain was more likely the product of summation of stimulations of the pressure sense or thermal senses, just as summation seemed to explain the aversive quality of bright visual stimuli or very loud auditory stimuli (see Boring, 1942, pp. 467, 469).

On the other hand, von Frey took the high density of pain spots to be the behavioral correlate of the high density of free nerve endings in the skin and argued for the existence of cutaneous pain as a distinct modality with the same simplistic application of Müller's doctrine of specific nervous energies as he had made for touch and temperature. The appeal of the idea of pain as a separate entity was no doubt heightened by its inclusion as a separate receptor group (the nociceptors) in Sherrington's classification scheme (Sherrington, 1906). Medical textbooks commonly did not dispute and sometimes encouraged the belief that a specific class of stimuli would excite, among others, a group of nerve endings that carry the message "pain" to the CNS without the need for a plebescite among the neural population. This was done in the absence of good evidence for such a process, which in more recent years is being adduced (Kerr & Wilson, 1978).

Head's (1920) dichotomy of epicritic and protopathic sensations, which resulted in part from experiments on his own skin as the severed radial and external nerves recovered (see Boring, 1942, pp. 472–475), was heavily dependent on the peculiar intrusions of pain sensations into nearly every qualitative analysis that he and his colleagues attempted. Touch, deep pressure, warmth, and cold could arouse unpleasant, burning, itching, or excruciating pain sensations at some location on the affected skin area at some time during the recovery period. These were the products of what Head called the *protopathic division* of the cutaneous sense and were produced, he believed, by the presence of the faster-growing fine nerve twigs coupled with the relative absence of the larger nerve fibers. Such a theory demands the incorporation of the concept of central interaction of patterns of activity from the periphery. As such, it holds appeal for neurophysiologists whose orientation is central. Because of its introspective data base, however, and perhaps owing to the fact that Head fell victim to a neurological disorder himself at a relatively early age (see Munger, 1982), the needed continuing advocacy of Head's theory was lacking. Nevertheless, as Sinclair points out (1967, p. 14) certain aspects of the Head duality theory have found support from electrophysiological evidence.

When the early electronically mediated studies of nerve thresholds and conduction velocities in animals led to the popular but short-lived theory relating fiber types and sensory quality, pain was perceived as the exclusive product of the slower, small, unmyelinated skin nerves that comprise much of the total neural population (see, e.g., Sinclair, 1967, p. 114). The lack of consistent results from nerve block studies on humans (mentioned in Section 5.1.4), which were intended to correlate fiber sizes and quality, played no small part in the disintegration of this theory. Findings by neurophysiologists that there exist a class of nociceptive, myelinated, peripheral neurons with high conduction velocities provide the *coup de grace* for the theory (see Burgess & Perl, 1973; Perl, 1982).

6.1.2. Clinical Evidence. Just as with the evidence for modality separation from nerve blocks, the clinical reports of dissociation of pain, temperature, and touch from peripheral nerve disease is equivocal (see, e.g., Sinclair, 1967, p. 117). Again, it may be owing to inconsistency of method on the part of physicians, the necessary dependence on the patient's report (who, after all, is neither a disinterested nor an expert observer under the conditions), or the fact that modality-specific fiber systems do not exist. The conclusion must be once again the Scotch verdict: not proved (ergo: not disproved!)

It might appear that hope for a clearer outcome is greater for lesions, from disease, injury, or surgical treatment, of the CNS. The most intensely investigated of such lesions has followed the kind of surgery done for relief of intractable pain, of which anterolateral chordotomy is one. In general, the incision in this operation is made at a spinal level well below the cervical group, so that whatever sensory testing is done takes place in the lower limbs or thorax. These are sites much less familiar to the patient as areas for the discrimination of tactile sensations. Thus the probability for a precise and accurate determination of pain or other sensory thresholds is seriously reduced by both the experience and the mood of the observer.

The original intention of the anterolateral chordotomy was to sever the lateral spinothalamic tract, which, it will be recalled, is a major pathway in the lateral spinothalmic system, an entity having the (not wholly deserved) reputation for diffuse, unpleasant, and generally sinister sensory activity. Sinclair has shown (1967, p. 128) how the extent of the operation (in terms of total spinal area cut) has grown, along with the hypothesized size of the tract, over the years of surgical practice. The earlier operations of smaller extent too often produced no or only temporary relief, and the size was enlarged progressively by surgeons over a period of several years until a full quarter of the cord is now incised. Results are nevertheless not consistent, and other incision sites can appear to produce similar results, as Sinclair (1967, p. 130) has pointed out.

More recently, Sweet (see Kerr & Casey, 1978, pp. 148–154) has reviewed the results of a variety of surgical procedures and remarked upon the large range of individual differences in structure and organization of the ascending pathways. About 70% of the 144 specimens in a group of fetal and neonatal spinal sections examined were similarly structured, but even in these the tracts were "patently unequal" in size or location (see Figure 12.29). Such data as these rarely appear in the psychological literature, with the result that the putative structural model of the nervous system for most of us is as unchanging as the position of Polaris.

The search for pain "centers" in the thalamus and cortex has generally proved to be unsatisfactory. Although vascular lesions in the thalamic region produce a characteristic "thalamic syndrome" that has as a prominent symptom spontaneous and very unpleasant pain, tumors of the thalamus seldom produce such effects. The rare cases in which the thalamus has been stimulated or partially ablated in humans have yielded some evidence for partitioning of the sensory quality, but a reliable body of evidence is not yet available. It is not uncommon for recovery of sensory function to follow fairly extensive destruction of the region, but no more than the ad hoc explanation of "plasticity" has been offered for this result.

The cortex lends no comfort to the phrenological inclinations of those who search for a pain center there. To be sure, injuries to the parietal lobes (where somesthesis is mainly represented) can result in loss of pain sensation, and operations in this area have successfully relieved pain. Total hemispherectomy may not, however, abolish pain sensations, as Sinclair has indicated (1967, p. 135). Moreover, the technique of Penfield and Rasmussen (1950) involving direct electrical cortical stimulation in awake humans, as well as the more recent studies of Libet, Alberts, Wright, Lewis, and Feinstein (1975, p. 299), almost never aroused pain sensations.

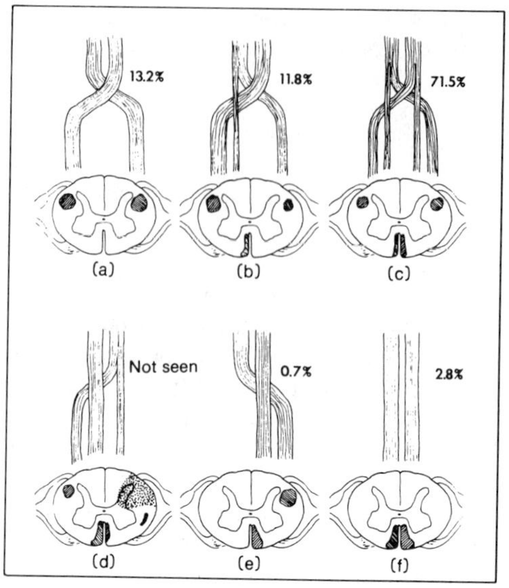

Figure 12.29. The range of variation in the location of pyramidal tracts in the spinal cords of a sample of human fetal or neonatal specimens. Yakovlev and Rakic (1966) examined sections of the spinal cord from 144 human fetal and neonatal specimens and plotted the course of descent of the pyramidal tracts through the medulla and cord. These tracts are the main pathways involved in the voluntary control of movement. The patterns of distribution in the spinal cord fell into five major groups as shown in the figure, with a sixth (d) added for symmetry, although this pattern was never encountered in their sample. The percentage of the sample falling into each category is indicated. The most common pattern appears to be the bilaterally symmetrical configuration shown in (c). Of the 103 specimens in this group, however, 81 were described as clearly asymmetrical. Sweet (in Kerr & Casey, 1978) describes these data as relevant to the problem of the lack of consistent results in the operative treatment of acute pain, which typically consists of anterolateral cordotomy. This procedure severs the spinothalamic tract, the putative pain pathway shown by the solid areas in (d). If it can be assumed that the degree of variability in the course of the pyramidal tract reflects that of the spinothalamic tract, certain predictions might be made regarding the degree of success expected with a particular surgical procedure. For example, in an attempt to divide the pyramidal tract by a lesion in the posterolateral quadrant indicated by the stippled region in (d), some degree of success might be recorded in a small proportion of the patients. In the case of total tissue destruction as extensive as that shown by the stippling, cases (a) and (e) would have a complete section of the descending pathways, presumably resulting in successful contralateral disruption of motor control. Because only 14% of the cases fall into these categories, 86% of the cases might result in partial or no paralysis if this were the only operative target region. Data such as these might explain the surprising success in the relief of pain that occasionally follows lesions placed well outside the anterolateral target zone pathways. Sinclair (1967, pp. 129–132) further supports these notions by describing how the presumed size of the lateral spinothalamic tract has grown as a necessary consequence of the need for larger and deeper incisions to increase the probability of success in abolishing pain. In fact, other pathways and collaterals might just as well be involved either as "pain pathways" or as contributing to the pattern of activity judged as pain, and these are being severed with the larger cuts. (From F. W. L. Kerr & K. L. Casey, Pain, *Neurosciences Research Program Bulletin, 16*. Copyright 1978 by MIT Press. Reprinted with permission.)

It is perhaps not wise to dwell at length on the wraithlike structural character of pain as a distinct modality, but a liberal portion of skepticism in such matters is necessary to the recipe for effective research, whether basic or applied. It never hurts in such cases to doubt the early returns, and much of the research thus far done undoubtedly is just that.

6.2. Physiological Aspects

6.2.1. Animal Studies of Response to Tissue Injury. It has been already noted that the theory relating nerve fiber types to sensory quality has been discredited (see Section 6.1.1). The review by Douglas and Ritchie (1962), however, lends support to the view, arising from experiments with animals, that small unmyelinated nerve fibers play a definite role in pain perception. When mild mechanical or thermal stimuli or noxious extremes of these agents are presented, such fibers respond. Moreover, it has been shown that strong stimuli appear to inhibit the responses of neural elements that have low thresholds to thermal or mechanical stimuli (see Kenshalo, 1972, p. 163). The response of small unmyelinated nerves to several kinds of stimuli has occasioned the designation *polymodal nociceptor* for these fibers, and whereas some physiologists consider them to be exclusively pain receptors, others remain to be convinced (see, e.g., Kenshalo, 1979, p. 409).

A recent microneurographic study in humans (Torebjörk, 1979) has succeeded in disclosing the activities of small single units of unmyelinated ("C") fibers. Insertion of tiny tungsten electrodes into the radial, peroneal, or saphenous nerves permitted recording of activity that proved, from measures of conduction velocity, to be that of the C fiber group. The skin areas served were the dorsum of the hand, forearm, or foot or the side of the calf of the leg. The typical fiber showed responses to firm pressure, to heating at painful levels, and to pricking. If the skin was slightly injured by a superficial burn (50°C for 90 sec over the small area of the receptive field for the fiber—about 6mm^2), the responsiveness of the unit was reduced, and the subject reported a raised threshold for pain. Over the next hour, however, lowered pain thresholds appeared, and responsiveness of the unit increased (hypersensitivity) for some but not all units. Recordings from larger fibers showed some increase in responsiveness on their part as well, however, and Torebjörk concluded that the so-called nociceptors may very well not act alone in signaling pain (1979, p. 319; see also Vallbo et al., 1979, p. 935).

6.2.2. Responses in Higher CNS Centers. The lengthy article on pain edited by Kerr and Casey (1978) contains a number of reports of research by various investigators on the responses of several tracts of the spinal cord, the brainstem, thalamic nuclei, and cortex. At the spinal level, cells of the spinothalamic tract have been shown to respond differentially to stimuli that produce avoidance behavior in awake animals. At the thalamic level, the problem of level of wakefulness intervenes. In lightly anesthetized animals, certain cells respond only to aversive stimulus levels, whereas in fully awake animals, the cells respond to a spectrum of innocuous and noxious stimuli. More recent research (see, e.g., Iggo, 1982) suggests that a number of thalamic nuclei respond to nociceptive stimulation, and limited parts of cortical areas SII are excited by the same input.

Evidence for cortical and subcortical systems controlling pain has been gathered from the protocols of neurosurgeons, but these investigators caution the reader that the personality and mood of the patient are often altered by surgery and that reaction to the noxious signal is perhaps more affected than is the nervous signal itself (see, e.g., Kerr & Casey, 1978, p. 153). To the complexity of the neural structure of the CNS is now added the recent discoveries of endorphins, endogenous opiates in the CNS, that are husbanded and released within restricted brain areas (see Kerr & Casey, 1978, p. 141). The additional cytochemical dimension has been only partially surveyed thus far, but its influence on the magnitude, quality, and duration of pain may be far reaching (see also Fields & Basbaum, 1978).

6.3. Psychophysical Aspects

6.3.1. Methods of Stimulation. The full array of devices and bodily loci employed in the study of pain would bring a smile to the lips of the Marquis de Sade and a shudder of anticipation to the Graf von Sacher-Masoch. Mechanical, thermal (conductive and radiant), chemical, and electrocutaneous stimuli have been applied to or injected into the limbs, torso, genitalia, face, cornea, palate, scalp, and tooth pulp of humans and animals in an unremitting search for either the conditions of stable production of pain or of reliable relief from it (see Beecher, 1959; Geldard, 1972, p. 317, Kerr & Wilson, 1978; Sweet, 1959, p. 461).

In general, psychophysical studies assume that the perceiving organism can be maintained in a semblance of a steady state for at least short time intervals. The steady-state condition does not truly obtain, of course; *dynamic equilibrium*, such as the physicist postulates, is the more appropriate term. Even so, progressive changes like those seen in adaptation and recovery of sensitivity occur but are generally seen to be regular. More to the point, such changes are almost invariably reversible. Noxious stimuli, on the other hand, are by definition those that may produce tissue damage and hence may induce irreversible changes. The resulting modification of physiologic state can be at the site of the damage, or it may be at various stations in the CNS, up to and including a change in the human observer's general attitude to the experiment or the experimenter.

Evidence for such changes is readily marshaled from a number of reviews of behavioral studies of pain (see, e.g., Beecher, 1957, 1959; Nafe & Kenshalo, 1962; Sweet, 1959). A sharp pin attached to a von Frey hair provides a good mechanical stimulus for pain of the pricking variety, but its repeated placement at the same skin site will produce a reddening of the tissue accompanied by aftersensations (Sweet, 1959). Radiant heat focused on a patch of skin repeatedly will produce aftereffects (Geldard, 1972), as will repeated electrocutaneous stimuli, whether in the form of small sparks from noncontacting electrodes (Bishop, 1943) or of currents through contacting electrodes (Gibson, 1968). Chemical stimuli placed on the skin or subcutaneously injected, or passed transcutaneously by iontophoresis, produce varying degrees of flaring or even wheals on the skin surface (Kenshalo, 1968, pp. 458–511). If only qualitative analyses are to be made, a variety of such stimuli will do, but if reliable quantification is needed, involving measures of thresholds or magnitude of pain, or pain tolerance levels, the number of useful modes of stimulation shrinks to a very few alternatives that will yield stable day-to-day and person-to-person values. However, there is almost no method that boasts a lack of critics who find serious fault with its application.

6.3.2. Thresholds for Pain. In addition to the variation in the physiologic state of the organism when painful stimuli are presented, there is, as in all psychophysical work, the added problem of semantics. One may hope that the observer will adopt a criterion that he or she will apply to the series of stimulus events for sorting purposes. The response is the name of the bin into which the event gets placed. Depending on the kind of stimulus employed to produce the pain, we may find that the categories of response range from "something felt," through "something strong but not unpleasant felt," "something strong and unpleasant but not painful felt," "something strong, unpleasant, and mildly painful felt," to "something strong and clearly painful felt." The series is not unlike the progression for the two-point limen: "one," "one with some length," "one with great elongation," "a dumbbell-shaped pattern," and, finally, "two." The difference between the two series is that in the study of the two-point limen, the experimenter knows when "one" or "two" is presented. In pain threshold studies, one may know the stimulus level, but pain does not exist as a fixed a priori stimulus category.

In recent years, there have been published a number of studies on pain reports, analyzed by signal detection methods, and their modulation by analgesics, acupuncture, and hypnotic suggestion, among other things (Chapman, 1977; Kerr & Casey, 1978, pp. 14–27; Rollman, 1977). It has been the claim of some investigators using the techniques of the theory of signal detection (TSD) that the sensory and motivational components of responses to noxious stimuli can be separately analyzed, with the result that, unlike the older psychophysical methods, TSD methods permit the experimenter to distinguish between conditions that modify sensory discriminability and those that affect the observer's criterion. For some time, as we have already mentioned, it has been apparent to investigators that the *threshold for pain* is a highly labile quantity, and other measures have suggested that a part of the difficulty lies in the observer's shifting criterion for reporting pain. The investigators who apply TSD methods believe that they can attribute changes in behavior toward noxious stimulus levels to either sensory discrimination shifts, criterion shifts, or both. If true, the method would seem to permit investigators to separate the sensory and motivational determinants of pain and arrive at more stable measures of the pain experience and, hence, more stable measures of its reduction, by the variety of real and fancied treatments available.

Rollman (1977) has cast a pall over this sunny prospect by suggesting that the measures involved in TSD research on pain do not deal with pain and noxious signals as much as they deal with discriminations of signal levels. Rollman further suggests that d', the measure of discriminability between two levels of signal intensity, may be unchanged by treatment that reduces pain owing to the the fact that, for example, the means of both distributions could be equally shifted on the decision axis (see Rollman, 1977, p. 200; see also Falmagne, Chapter 1). The author goes on to show that TSD cannot guarantee the exact partitioning of sensory and motivational changes resulting from pain production or therapeutic treatment because it is not an appropriate model for pain perception.

In response to this critique, Chapman (1977) has emphasized that the separation of sensory and emotional components of pain is not the goal of TSD pain researchers (Chapman, 1977, p. 303). Clark (see Kerr & Casey, p. 23) has said, however, that the apparent rise in pain thresholds upon placebo administration, as measured by traditional methods, could be shown to result from the shift in criterion C, not from a change in d', implying that the separation of these measures is important. It is therefore not clear that all investigators of pain thresholds are in agreement concerning the power or the analytic value of the TSD methods. Here, as in other testing methods, what may be wanted is not a single index but a battery of tests to provide converging operations on the concepts under analysis. If the multidimensional model for pain experience that Chapman (1977, p. 301) proposes (derived from Melzack & Casey, 1968) is correct, multiple measurements are certainly demanded. Thus far, such an approach has not been undertaken systematically.

6.3.3. Spatial and Temporal Summation of Pain. Kenshalo (1972, p. 160) reported that evidence for spatial summation of pain stimuli (using traditional psychophysics) is weak or altogether lacking. Radiant or conductive heat measures over areas 2.5–70 cm^2 show only a very slight but reliable threshold drop. Mechanical stimuli do not appear to summate at all. Evidence for temporal summation of pain was adduced by Gibson(1968, p. 229). When rectangular, unidirectional, 0.5-msec pulses were delivered through 10-mm-diameter electrodes disposed on either hairy or glabrous skin, a reduction of peak current required for reports of pain occurred as pulse number, at constant frequency, was increased or as repetition rate increased with constant pulse number. Evidence that electrocutaneous pulse width will produce summation of pressure sensations to yield pain was also described qualitatively by Gibson (1968, p. 225).

6.3.4. Adaptation to Pain. Boring (1942, p. 501) was doubtful of studies that employed sharp objects to produce cutaneous pain which adapted completely in a minute or less. Since that time studies of electrocutaneous, mechanical, thermal (both heat and cold), and chemical stimulation of the skin have reported adaptation to some degree if not complete (Geldard, 1972, p. 327; Kenshalo, 1972, p. 158; Sinclair, 1967, p. 204). It should be borne in mind that we are discussing cutaneous pain, not visceral pain, tooth pain, headache, or the pain involving nerve trauma. We assume that the general systemic conditions contributing to such pain experiences extend more profoundly into the vegetative neurohumoral system than would superficial injuries confined to small areas of skin.

The phenomenon of *double pain* (second pain) is often noted by physiologists and was at one time the introspective source of data used to support the fiber-class modality theory. If one immerses the finger in water at 57°C to a depth of 2.5 cm for 1 sec, as Sinclair and Stokes (1964) did, the person will very likely perceive first a pricking or stinging pain almost immediately, followed in about 2 sec by a longer-lasting burning pain. Forty naive subjects were tested by this method, and about 70% felt double pain. The question is not entirely settled, but many physiologists believe that this phenomenon is the result of activity in two groups of nerves that conduct their signals at greatly differing velocities (see Croze & Duclaux, 1979; Geldard, 1972, p. 332; Sinclair, 1967, p. 197).

Referred pain is a phenomenon known almost since the practice of medicine began. It is actually visceral in origin; that is, some trauma, disease process, or vascular problem has occasioned nervous signals from the visceral afferents. Instead of localizing the activity at the site of damage, the central interaction or convergence of the somatosensory and autonomic systems produces a displacement of the pain to superficial sites. Anginal pain in cardiac distress may be reported at the chest wall, in the jaw, or down the left arm. Pain resulting from passing a kidney stone (urethral distention) may be referred to the lower back or loins. In appendicitis, the discomfort may first be thought to reside in a knee. In nearly all cases, the evidence for a convergence of cutaneous and visceral afferents on a central location is strong (see Iggo, 1982, p. 405; Sweet, 1959, p. 500).

7. INTERRELATIONS OF THE CUTANEOUS MODALITIES

When we contact or are contacted by objects in our environment, we learn to identify them in part by their mechanical and thermal properties. Texture, weight, thermal conductivity, and size are common attributes employed in classification. One may wonder whether some tactile stimulus dimensions interact with others when several are simultaneously present. As we shall see, some do interact in interesting ways.

7.1. Touch–Temperature Interactions

7.1.1. Localization Effects. It has already been mentioned (see Section 5.3.6) that the localization for radiant warmth is poor. B. G. Green (1977b, 1978, 1979) was able to show that this capacity is readily confounded by a relatively simple set of conditions. Two pennies are cooled to 0°C, and a third is held in the hand to maintain it at skin temperature (about 35°C). The three are placed side by side, with the warmer penny in the middle. If now the index, middle, and ring fingertips are placed on the pennies simultaneously, the middle (warmer) finger will be perceived as very much cooler than when the outside fingers are lifted from the cold pennies.

B. G. Green quantified these observations (1977b) by having observers place their fingers on three independently controlled Peltier thermodes. In one condition the fingers were placed on the thermodes and the outer stimulators were kept at skin temperature while the center one was varied from 10–45°C, and observers made magnitude estimates of cold or warmth of the center finger. In a second condition, the outer stimulators were varied over the same range, the center one kept at skin temperature, with magnitude estimates of the center finger again being given. The results were that the perceived warmth or cold for the two conditions is quantitatively indistinguishable (see Figure 12.30). In a later study B. G. Green (1979) was able to show that (1) the touch component is necessary to produce the referred sensation, (2) warmth is more readily referred than cold, (3) when the middle finger temperature is raised or lowered, the reported magnitude is modulated by the temperature conditions of the outside stimulators, and (4) experiments with only two or with four fingers, or with sites on the forearm, produce similar effects.

7.1.2. The Weber Illusion. In his original monograph on cutaneous sensations Weber reported an interesting illusion. A silver thaler (a German coin somewhat larger than a U.S. half-dollar) that is cold feels heavier on the forehead of the supine observer than does a warm one (see Boring, 1942, p. 466). Weber took this demonstration to signify that touch and temperature were interdependent. Only one or two quantitative replications of this experiment have been made since 1846, but recently J. C. Stevens (1979a; J. C. Stevens & B. G. Green, 1978) repeated Weber's work. Metal cylinders of various weights and contacting areas were warmed to skin temperature or to 45°C or cooled to 0°C. These were carefully placed, in quasi-random order, on the foreheads of observers who were told to ignore the thermal quality and to estimate the magnitude of the pressure sensation. Just as Weber had found, J. C. Stevens determined that the cold objects felt heavier than the warm ones of equal weight. The warm and neutral objects felt about equally heavy on the forehead, but on the forearm both cold and warm objects felt heavier than the neutral ones. J. C. Stevens conjectured that the lack of warmth facilitation on one area but not the other ruled out a central summation hypothesis. The difference in magnitude of weight was less for heavier weights, and the effect of temperature fell off with smaller area of contact. These two facts led J. C. Stevens to hypothesize that the effect was the result of action of peripheral nerve groups that are excited by both temperature and pressure (see Section 5.2.1). Small areas that are warmed or cooled do not yield reports of strong sensations of temperature, whereas strong pressure sensations can occur, so the synergy of temperature and pressure signals cannot take place. When heavy pressures are present, the addition of the temperature signal is again a minute change that the observer does not detect. For larger areas and moderate pressures (12.6 cm^2 and 10–100 g) the phenomenon is apparent; a weight of 10 g at skin temperature will seem to be one-fifth that of a 10-g weight at 0°C. Whether estimates of warm and cold magnitudes are similarly modulated by pressure variations has not yet been tested.

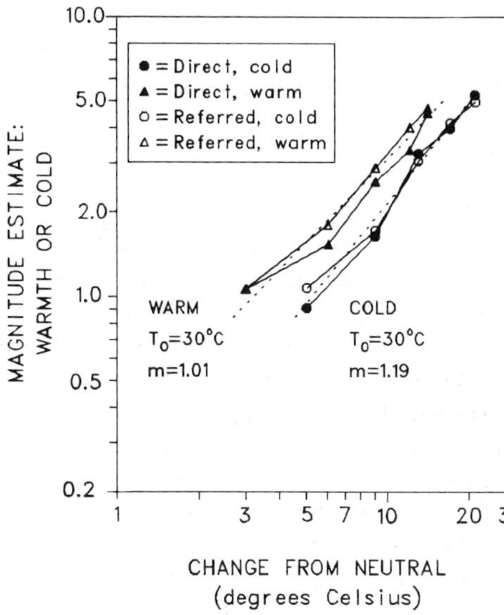

Figure 12.30. Magnitude estimates of warmth and cold as a function of stimulus intensity in degrees above neutral (30°C) for direct and "referred" thermal sensations. (Adapted from B. Green, 1977b.) B. Green tested the power of thermal referral by having observers give estimates of the warmth or cold produced by Peltier effect stimulators contacting the fingers. In the control ("direct") condition, the temperature of the device contacting the middle finger was varied, while the two neighboring fingers were held at thermal neutrality (30°C). The estimates of warmth or cold at the middle finger are shown by the filled symbols on the graph. These results were then compared to those made when the middle finger was held at a neutral temperature and only the temperature of the adjacent fingers was varied. Again, judgments were made of the thermal sensation at only the middle finger. These data, shown by the open symbols for each range of temperatures, were not significantly different from the control estimates. Standard errors of the mean ranged from 2 to 5%. Functions fitted to the two conditions over each temperature range are shown, with the exponents of the power functions ranging from 1.01 for warm to 1.19 for cold. It is obvious that subjects judge referred or induced thermal sensations in the same manner as they judge direct contact sensations. The difference between the slopes of these functions and those shown in Figure 12.24 could be owing to differences in the neutral points defined (which would change the log ranges over which the stimuli were judged, thereby affecting the slope) to the sites stimulated (finger vs. arm), area of the stimulator (ca. 1.5 versus 3.14 cm^2), or other procedural differences.

In a later paper J. C. Stevens (1979b) reported that tests for the Weber, or thermal intensification, effect on (1) males and females, (2) both sides of the body, and (3) six body sites revealed substantial differences in degree of effect as a function of body locus. No sex effect appeared, and laterality effects were present but only for the main variable of perceived weight. Of further interest was his finding that the rank ordering of body sites according to how heavy a given weight was perceived was not correlated with pressure thresholds, as determined by Weinstein, or vibration thresholds, as determined by Wilska (see Figure 12.6). Instead, the order of body part by weight estimation correlated with order for the error of localization ($\rho = 0.94$) and two-point limens ($\rho = 0.98$) determined by Weinstein! No explanation for these results is at hand.

7.1.3. Temperature Effects on Touch Thresholds. The Weber illusion is paradoxical in a superficial sense because it occurs at all; in a more profound sense it is paradoxical because we think of cold as a desensitizer or anesthetic. In fact, cold has been used for just that purpose, and anyone who has been outdoors in zero weather (Celsius or Fahrenheit) knows the feeling of numbness that encroaches with exposure of body parts. Why then should a cold object feel heavier instead of lighter? J. C. Stevens' explanation (1979a, p. 214) is very persuasive, particularly in light of other data that he has reported. When the skin of the fingertip was cooled to 10°C, thresholds to step-function forces (von Frey hairs) rose by 7 dB. In the range of 20–45°C, however, thresholds varied by only ± 3 dB from that at 30°C. Cold does not lower pressure threshold, therefore, so a cold object does not feel heavier because of direct effects of temperature on pressure receptors. In a similar manner, the threshold for high-frequency sinusoidal vibrotactile stimuli (250 Hz) is raised by 15 dB over the range of 34–20°C and by 5 dB over the range 34–43°C (B. G. Green, 1977a; Weitz, 1941). No change in threshold for low-frequency (30 Hz) vibrations is produced, however (B. G. Green, 1977a). Green has suggested (1977a, p. 247) that whereas Verrillo's (1968) dual mechanoreceptor hypothesis explains in part the differential action of temperature on frequency sensitivity, it leaves other findings unclarified. Why the vibrotactile threshold is raised by so much more than the touch threshold, and over a narrower temperature range, is as yet unexplained. Once again, we note that the touch thresholds are force measures (actually, tension in g/mm; J. C. Stevens, 1979a, p. 210), whereas the vibration thresholds are amplitude measures (B. G. Green, 1977a, p. 245). Studies of sensitivity of the fingers in detecting a gap between edges have shown a rise in threshold with cooling of the skin (see Provins & Morton, 1960).

Effects of warming and cooling of the skin on the quality or acuity of the sense of touch has been reported by von Békésy (1960a). In his experiments on fusion of repetitive pulses (see Section 4.3.6.) von Békésy noted that cooling the skin produced the same effect as stimulating a less sensitive site; that is, it raised the frequency required for fusion of pulses (1960a, p. 600). On the other hand, when one of two fingers, both stimulated by the same vibration amplitude, is warmed, the localization of vibration shifts to the normal finger. When amplitude is raised, the warmer finger now seems to be the site for vibration. Consequently, von Békésy assumed that the warming and cooling effects merely obtunded the receptor systems, but it remains for more systematic study to show that the modulation of skin temperature has only a simple influence on excitatory processes, particularly in light of B. G. Green's (1977a) and J. C. Stevens' (1979b) findings just mentioned. The effects could be far more profound, for example, modifying inhibitory mechanisms or adaptation or summating temperature-sensitive and pressure-sensitive systems, as J. C. Stevens suggests, and so on. Indeed, von Békésy himself observed that the speed of nervous conduction could be affected by temperature of the body surface (von Békésy, 1967, p. 158), and this could affect the patterns of sensory inflow to the CNS.

7.2. Touch–Pain Interactions: Masking of Pain by Touch or Vibration

It is part of the lore of folk medicine that pain can be reduced by a variety of counterirritants or even by simply pressing on the affected part. Melzack, Wall, and Weisz (1963) induced pain by electrocutaneous stimulation, then attempted to mask the pain by applying mechanical vibration near the pain site. Low levels of vibration did mask the pain, but higher levels increased it. When Melzack and Schecter (1965) put cowage (the active ingredient of itching powder) on the skin to induce itch, they successfully eliminated this annoying sensation (thought by some to be a low order of pain) with vibration near the site or at the contralateral site, but not at ipsilateral or contralateral distant sites (see also Kerr & Wilson, 1978).

7.3. Temperature–Pain Interactions: Radiant Heat, Warmth, and Pain

The sensations of heat, warmth, and pain (pricking or burning in quality) are seemingly intervals on the continuum of energy delivered by the radiant heat lamps used by researchers. One may conclude then that the summation of energy flux is the simplest model for excitation of a continuum of receptor systems. Moderate warming of a painful injury site, as well as cooling, can reduce the pain; however, the question of the mobilization of circulatory mechanisms and their influence has not been settled in such cases. The interaction of pain and temperature as purely nervous activities is not presently understood.

The effects of painful stimuli on perception of sensations of pressure or temperature may be considerable, as Benjamin (1956) has reported. The degree to which such effects result from sensory interactions, as opposed to "distraction" or attentional factors, remains to be determined by the application of TSD methods of psychophysical analysis. With regard to the kind of interaction produced by the various methods of acupuncture, there is little research available on the subject (see Jenerick, 1973; Kerr & Wilson, 1978).

8. ELECTROCUTANEOUS STIMULATION

Reference has been made to the passage of electrical currents through the skin as an "inadequate" stimulus (Geldard, 1972, p. 267). This is a derivation of the term applied by Sherrington (1906) to the natural or proper stimulus for a particular modality. Thus the adequate stimulus for vision is light of wavelength 400–700 ηm; for touch, it is mechanical energy. Electrical current is inadequate because it has no receptor designed or evolved to detect it in preference to other forms of energy (in humans at least; but see Bullock, 1974). It is well know that electricity can arouse almost any sensory (or motor) channel at nearly every way station from periphery to cortex. Physiologists have for years employed one or another electrical waveform to excite a portion of the nervous system or, selectively, to reveal the presence of weak signals by means of combined adequate and electrical stimuli (see, e.g., Torebjörk, 1979, p. 314). The utility of the electrical stimulus, its relatively simple interface with the tissues, and the very low power consumption entailed in its application have combined to make this form of stimulus energy an attractive alternative to the natural mechanical stimuli for rapid signaling to the skin. As we shall see, like the other blessings people have bestowed upon people, it is mixed.

8.1. Methods of Stimulation: Electrode Characteristics

A very great variety of electrode sizes, shapes, compositions, configurations, and sites of placement has been devised over the years (see, e.g., Gibson, 1968; Girvin, Marks, Antunes, Quest, O'Keefe, Ning, & Dobelle, 1982; Hahn, 1958; Prior, 1972; Rollman, 1974; Saunders, 1974). "Dry" electrode pairs of metallic composition from aluminum to zinc have been employed, with brass, gold, silver, stainless steel (austenitic), and zinc the favorites. The word "dry" is in quotes because the term is entirely relative. The placing of a solid on any normal skin area entails covering a number of sweat ducts, with the result that some bodily fluids having electrolytic characteristics will eventually moisten (and perhaps react chemically at) the electrode–skin junction. Nevertheless, the conductance (or, better, admittance) of the untreated corneum is very low (10^{-6} mhos or less) but labile under dry electrodes, in part owing to the unpredictable vaso- and sudamotor activities of the autonomic nervous system. The result is that large, rapid, and unexpected swings of electrical current may take place in the process of stimulating the skin (see, e.g., Gibson, 1968, p. 254). Such effects may be reduced by prior treatment of the skin, for example, "peeling" the corneum by pressing adhesive tape on the site and removing it, scrubbing the area with alcohol or a wetting agent, or carefully grinding away the corneum itself.

Increasing the skin conductance to a higher level (about 10^{-3}–10^{-4} mhos) guarantees against extreme variations, and wet electrodes have been adapted for this purpose. Such preparation may be especially appropriate when multiple-electrode arrays are designed, since intersite variations in skin conductance can be quite large in the same individual when the skin is untreated. In general, some form of electrode paste or gel (often the brands used for electroencephalogram, or electrocardiogram, electrodes) is applied to the skin, and the metallic electrodes are placed over the treated area. Another form of wet electrode is a variant of the "wick" electrode, a cotton-wool or gauze material soaked in an isotonic salt or Ringer's solution (see Sherrick & Rogers, 1966; Turksy, Watson, & O'Connell, 1965). Such electrodes are generally more stable electrically, but they are messy and can cause trouble if the two poles of the electrode configuration are too close, by short-circuiting across the skin surface. In recent studies the electrocutaneous stimuli have been applied through silver concentric electrodes with no paste (Saunders, 1974), through brass concentric electrodes with paste (Prior, 1972), through dry stainless steel electrodes either concentric or apposed (Gibson, 1968), or through a doublet of silver Grass EEG electrode cups filled with electrode cream (Rollman, 1974). An unusual electrode is one made from silver powder (Silflake) and Du Pont Duco cement and acetone. The slurry resulting can be poured on the skin and impaled with an electrode wire. The plastic clump, of any desired size, will dry in less than 1 min and adhere very well to the skin surface to provide a fair conductive interface (Geldard & Sherrick, 1973, p. 15).

8.1.1. Electrode Shape, Size, and Placement. Gibson (1968) has reported success with what may be called a monopolar configuration, in which a very large metal ("indifferent") electrode is placed under the sole of the foot, and smaller ("active") electrodes (0.5–3 cm^2) placed at the sites where the stimulation is to be localized. This arrangement could, however, produce stray current paths through the body that might give unwanted effects, and most investigators have elected to use either apposed bipolar arrays (Rollman, 1974) or concentric arrays with a larger annular indifferent electrode (0.5–1.25 cm^2) and a smaller (0.3–0.5 cm^2) central active electrode of the unipolar variety (Prior, 1972; Saunders, 1974). The advantage of the concentric electrode is that the inevitable stray currents flowing through the more conductive subdermal tissues are better confined to the area of stimulation than are those flowing between separated bipolar electrodes (see, e.g., von Békésy, 1967, pp. 123, 156). Figure 12.31 shows some examples of electrode configurations. It has been argued that metal-salt electrodes (e.g., Ag-AgCl) are superior in the interest of electrochemical equilibrium, but when large currents are passed, the equilibrium condition is probably violated (see Prior, 1972, pp. 21f.).

If location on the body is an option, most investigators have suggested that glabrous skin has a threshold for touch that lies further below that for pain than does hairy skin, although such a generalization must be tempered with the caution that stimulus waveform interacts with placement and mode of stimulation (i.e., constant-current versus constant-voltage or constant-power systems; see Prior, 1972, p. 146; see Section 8.1.3).

8.1.2. Stimulus Waveform. Although it is theoretically possible to generate as great a variety of waveforms as electrode types, the number actually studied is relatively small. Sinusoids, rectangular, and triangular alternating waveforms and white noise have been tested. Unidirectional rectangular, triangular, and rectified sinusoids have also been examined, along with biphasic forms having equal waveforms of opposite polarities or equal areas but different time courses and of opposite polarities. The latter stimuli are intended to stimulate the cutaneous nerves but to produce an average zero total current flow, thereby preventing the accrual of unwanted electrochemical products in the tissues (see Gibson, 1968, p. 226; Saunders, 1974, p. 25). Figure 12.32 illustrates some of the various waveforms that have been employed.

The majority of electronic systems for delivery of the electrical signal to the skin are designed to present a constant waveform at a given repetition rate and to vary only the voltage or current amplitude to increase the stimulus intensity. One system, described by Saunders (1974, p. 25) and applied to a tactile vocoder aid for the deaf, presents a train of very short (about 5–20 μsec) biphasic pulses at a burst repetition rate of 250/sec and constant peak current. Increasing intensity for this waveform could be achieved by increasing the widths of the individual pulses or increasing the number of biphasic pulses per burst (see Sachs, Miller, & Grant, 1980). Saunders has reported that his system works best on hairy skin and that discomfort or frank pain has almost never been reported.

8.1.3. The Effective Stimulus Dimension. Whereas there has been some debate concerning the appropriate dimension of the electrical signal for characterizing stimulus intensity, or the effective threshold stimulus (see e.g., Girvin et al., 1982; R. T. Green, 1962; Prior, 1972; Saunders, 1974), most investigators have measured stimulus current (e.g., Gibson, 1968; Hahn, 1958; Rollman, 1974; Rosner, 1964; Schmid, 1961; Uttal &

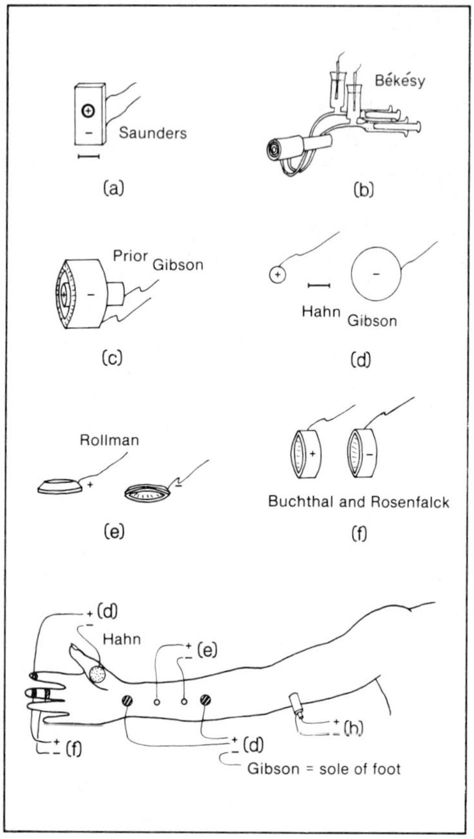

Figure 12.31. Several different electrode configurations and sites used in electrocutaneous stimulation. A representative sample of the types of electrodes used for electrical stimulation of the skin are shown. Of these, the first three (a), (b),and (c) are concentric configurations that tend to limit the spread of current somewhat better than other designs, since the indifferent site completely encircles the active one. The remaining configurations involve bipolar arrays. In these cases, the closer the electrodes are to one another, the less likely it is that stray currents produce undesirable effects. Commonly, these electrodes consist of metal or metal–metal-salt combinations. For example, Saunders (1974) used silver concentric electrodes, Prior (1972) brass, and Gibson (1968) stainless steel for the same configuration. The plates, rings, and cups shown in (d) through (f) may be made of the same materials. To improve contact with the skin, several methods can be used. Rollman's (1974) EEG cups were filled with electrode paste, whereas Hahn (1958) and Prior (1972) used paste between their electrodes and the skin. Saunders (1974) only scrubbed the skin with a saline solution before applying his electrodes. On the other hand, von Békésy (1963) employed a completely different arrangement, using a concentric system in which cotton gauze, soaked with saline, contacts the skin, eliminating the need for electrode paste. In this system, silver–silver chloride electrodes are used to pass current into the saline solution. Some of the sites used in the studies cited in the text are shown in the lower portion of the figure. Hawkes and Warm (1961), for example, used electrodes and sites similar to those shown for Hahn. Gibson (1968) used several different configurations and sites in his studies, including those shown. Prior (1972) examined electrotactile thresholds over the whole surface of the body, and Saunders' electrodes have been used on the arm and abdomen.

Krissoff, 1968). Considering the fact that the excitatory processes are occurring in a volume of tissue containing electrolytes, active electrical cells, and reactive systems capable of changing resistive and capacitative properties of the tissues, it is not surprising that psychophysical measures of response to electrode composition, size, and configuration, or to waveform variations of the signal, have not revealed the "true" dimension for electrocutaneous stimulation. Such manipulations alone have not revealed the true stimulus for touch, vibration, temperature, or pain, either.

It may be better to speak of the "useful" stimulus for electrocutaneous work instead. Clearly the choice is electrical current, with the provision that a constant-current stimulator be inserted in the electrode circuit. In the interest of precision of description and better understanding of the mechanisms of electrocutaneous stimulation, it would be well for the investigator to record the voltage and current and their time course or, for sinusoids, the phase angle between them. The idea of the constant-current device is that no matter what happens in the electrode circuit, the level of current flow set by the controls is held. Thus if the skin impedance doubles, the voltage does also; conversely, if impedance falls to one-half, so does the volt-

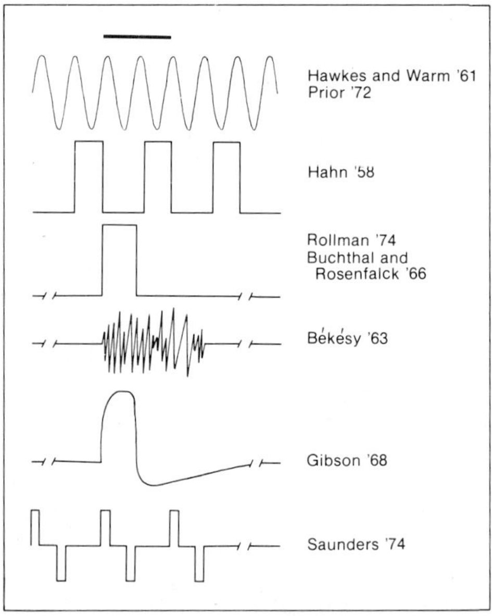

Figure 12.32. Some representative waveforms employed in electrocutaneous stimulation. A large variety of stimulus waveforms have been used in electrocutaneous stimulation. Prior (1972) has reported data on the greatest number of potential waveforms, including sinusoids, triangular, and rectangular waveforms, as well as half-wave rectified versions of these, both positive and negative going. Of this variety, however, unipolar or bipolar square-wave pulses have been used most commonly. For the waveforms in the figure, the time scale shown by the solid bar at the top of the series represents 1 msec, except for Saunders' (1974) waveform in which the bar represents 100 μsec and Hawkes and Warm's (1961) sinusoid in which the bar represents 10 msec. Most of the studies cited varied the frequency or pulse duration, so the examples are only indicative of the type of waveform used. For example, Prior (1972) examined many frequencies of sinusoids, as well as of other waveforms. Hahn (1958) varied pulse durations from 0.1 to 7.0 msec while presenting them at continuous pulse rates in five steps between 60 and 1000 pulses/sec. Rollman (1974) varied pulse duration from 0.02 to 100 msec, a range that encompassed that of Buchthal and Rosenfalck (1966). And von Békésy (1963) was the only investigator to use white noise bursts of either 0.5 or 1.5 msec duration. Biphasic waveforms, such as the lower two shown, are advocated by some investigators since the reversal of polarity produces an average zero net current flow, limiting electrochemical polarization of the skin. Gibson's (1968) 0.5-msec positive-going pulse was followed by a longer-lasting negative-going phase. Saunders (1974) employed a different technique that involved extremely brief (5–20 μsec) constant-amplitude biphasic pulses presented in bursts consisting of 1–40 pulses at an interpulse interval of 100 μsec at a burst frequency of 250 burst/sec. With this method, intensity of stimulation is a function of the number of pulses in each burst, since each pulse is presented at a constant-current amplitude. In every other case, stimulus amplitude is a function of current amplitude, with thresholds ranging from 0.6 to over 6 mA, depending on such other factors as pulse duration or site of stimulation.

age. The simplest kind of constant-current stimulator is a high-voltage source with a series resistor in the electrode circuit. The resistor has a value so large that any change in skin impedance is small by comparison. More sophisticated constant-current stimulators are available; these commonly incorporate active feedback circuitry to hold a set level (see Prior, 1972, pp. 26–27). In addition, such systems often have isolator circuits to prevent the inadvertent connection of the subject to the electric mains. In this more than any other mode of stimulation the considerations of risk and safety are paramount. This is especially applicable to cases in which electrode placements circumscribe the heart (see Dalziel, 1973).

8.2. Psychophysical Aspects

8.2.1. Thresholds: Spatial and Temporal Summation. It should be plain at this juncture that the absolute threshold for electrical stimulation will depend heavily on electrode character and configuration, locus of stimulation, waveform and repetition rate, and on the subject. Hahn (1958) examined thresholds for rectangular unidirectional pulses from a constant-current source. The electrodes were wetted with electrode paste and placed on the hand. The active (positive) electrode, 24 mm diameter, was placed on the thenar eminence. Five repetition rates of 60, 100, 200, 500, 1000 pulses/sec (p/sec) were presented to three observers by the ascending method of limits, with eight observations per condition. The main variable was pulse width, which was set to 0.1, 0.2, 0.4, 0.7, 1.0, 2.0, 4.0, and 7.0 msec. Figure 12.33 shows the variation of threshold in decibels re threshold at 1.0 msec, with pulse width. The repetition rate had no effect on threshold. This may be owing to the fact that the lowest rate employed was 60 p/sec, for when Rollman (1974, p. 42) examined thresholds on the volar forearm of four observers for single pulses of varying width, he obtained the curve shown also in

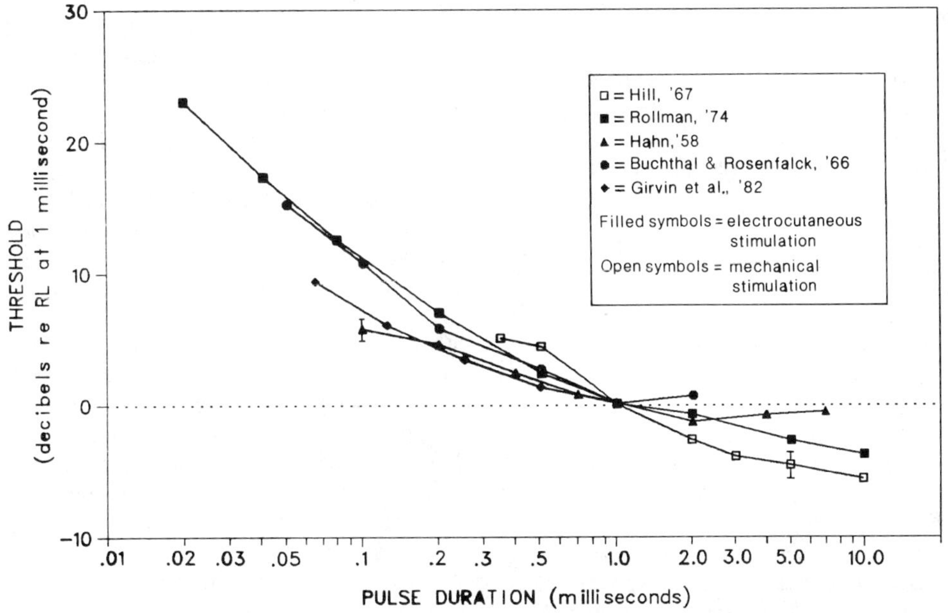

Figure 12.33. Strength-duration functions for electrocutaneous stimulation, compared with a similar function for mechanical stimuli. The filled symbols describe data points derived from four studies of threshold for electrocutaneous stimulation as a function of the duration of the electrical pulse and are compared with a function obtained with mechanical pulses (indicated by the open symbols). The data are normalized to the threshold obtained for pulses of 1-msec duration for comparison and plotted on log-log coordinates. In Hill's (1967) experiment, described in Figure 12.8, brief mechanical pulses were presented to the fingertip of one observer. In this case threshold for a 1-msec pulse averaged 3.9 μm. Rollman (1974) presented unidirectional pulses to the forearms of four male subjects through a pair of Grass silver EEG electrodes spaced 2.5 mm apart over the ulnar nerve on the volar surface of the arm (see Figures 12.31 and 12.32). Twenty-five judgments were made by each observer for each duration over a series of five sessions. Threshold for 1-msec pulses averaged 0.44 mA. Hahn (1958) also presented unidirectional pulses, but in continuous trains at rates of 60, 100, 200, and 500 pulses/sec. Although adaptation might have been taking place, thresholds for one to three subjects for 1-msec pulse durations averaged 0.76 mA. Buchthal and Rosenfalck (1966) examined the strength-duration function for unidirectional pulses presented to the middle finger of one observer at 1 pulse/sec through ring electrodes (anode on the distal part of the distal phalanx, cathode 10–20 mm proximal to it). At a pulse duration of one msec, threshold averaged 1.76 mA. Finally, Girvin and colleagues (1982) derived a similar function from their study of the effects on sensitivity of body site, electrode configuration, stimulus waveform, and pulse duration. Neither body site (forehead vs. abdomen) nor electrode configuration (Saunders' concentric electrodes vs. 1.13-mm-diameter unifocal electrodes with the indifferent on the left leg) produced significant changes in absolute threshold as a function of pulse duration. Similarly, biphasic (+/− or −/+) and monophasic cathodal (−) waveforms collapsed into a single function. Thresholds were somewhat higher for monophasic anodal (+) pulses. The data shown were collapsed over all conditions and three subjects, with each point representing 72 threshold determinations obtained with a modified staircase procedure. Threshold for 1-msec pulses averaged about 1.82 mA. It is notable that these data demonstrate comparable rates of change over the durations examined, showing near-asymptotic levels in the 1–10-msec range. The ranges for two of the points are shown on the figure.

Figure 12.33. Despite the difference in form of stimulation and electrode placement, the values obtained differ by only 4–11 dB re 1.0 mA.

Temporal summation for single pulses is evident in Rollman's data (Figure 12.33). Complete summation occurs for pulse durations less than 0.1 msec, and partial summation for durations between 0.1 and 1.0 msec. Beyond 1.0 msec summation is almost negligible; the current threshold is almost independent of pulse duration (see Rollman, 1974, p. 42). Another way to express the result is that the constant dimension for electrocutaneous thresholds, for pulses below 0.1 msec, is electrical charge in coulombs:

$$I \times t = K,$$

where

I is peak current, mA,
t is pulse duration, msec,
K is a constant .

It is of some interest to note that Rollman's data for single pulses can be fitted to the curve form described by Hill (1967; see also Section 4.3.1) for mechanical unidirectional pulses. The expression for Rollman's data would then be (approximately)

$$I_T = \frac{0.25}{1 - e^{-t/0.5}},$$

where

I_T is threshold current, mA,
t is pulse width, msec.

This is, by analogy to Hill's model, an integrating network with a time constant of 0.5 msec. The data of Hahn (1958), as well as those of Buchthal and Rosenfalck (1966) and Girvin and coworkers (1982), can also be described by this model, with small changes in the two parameters (see Figure 12.33).

When several pulses are presented, there appears to be additional temporal summation. This was shown by Gibson (1968, p. 227), who found between 3- and 6-dB reduction of threshold for touch with a tenfold increase in the number of pulses at a repetition rate of 100 p/sec. The summation found by Rollman amounted to 12 dB for single pulses from 0.02 to 0.2 msec width, and he has suggested (1974, p. 43) that temporal summation over single pulse durations is owing to the properties of the peripheral nerves, whereas the summation over repeated pulses is the result of interactions at higher centers.

Spatial summation of electrocutaneous stimuli has not been directly examined, but certain measurements have some bearing on the evidence for it. Vernon and Wessman (1956) tested for interaction between two 500-Hz sinusoidal stimuli presented through isolated apposed electrode pairs. The stimulus array was wet electrodes placed along the palmar surface of the middle finger, with one pair of electrodes in the center, the other pair flanking these at the end and base of the finger. When a current at a value of 75% of the threshold was presented through the outside pair, the threshold for the inside pair was decreased or increased around normal as a function of the phase relation between the two stimuli. The maximum decrease in threshold was 13 dB, whereas the increase was 2.5 dB. Localization of sensation for the decreased threshold was at the distal inner electrode, for the increased threshold at the distal outer electrode. It is possible that the interaction observed was based on the addition of current fields in the subdermal electrode paths. Evidence from masking studies by Schmid (1961) is not subject to the same criticism as Vernon and Wessman's study, but the effective facilitation in threshold is less than 1 dB. And von Békésy (1959, p. 1242) has shown that electrical stimuli through pairs of concentric electrodes do not seem to interact as do mechanical stimuli, even when they are only 1 or 2 cm apart. Moreover, the Mach band phenomemon, which can be produced by appropriately arranged mechanical stimulation of the skin (von Békésy, 1958, p. 410) did not occur for an analogous electrical array (von Békésy, 1959, p. 1243).

Hawkes and his colleagues have done considerable research on the problems of differential thresholds and information transmission for electrocutaneous stimuli. Hawkes (1961) found the Weber fraction for intensity of electrocutaneous stimulation to be about 3% and constant over the range of 100–1500 Hz for sinusoids. This is about one-sixth the value for mechanical vibration (see Section 4.3.2). The Weber fraction for duration was found by Hawkes and Warm (1961) to be 5–10% for durations ranging from 0.5–1.5 sec. Following studies of absolute identification of intensities and durations of electrical stimulation, Hawkes (1960, 1961) concluded that three levels of intensity and three of duration could be usefully employed in a communications system (see also Sachs et al., 1980, p. 261). The small number of absolute levels of intensity seems to be contradicted by the small Weber fraction; one might assume that high differential sensitivity should permit the absolute identification of a large number of categories of intensity. The explanation may lie in a very small dynamic range for electrical stimulation, amounting to perhaps 10 or 15 dB from threshold for touch to the first reports of discomfort or pain. Compare this to the 60–80-dB dynamic range for vibration or the 100-dB range for audition. The range for radiant heat, on the other hand, appears to be about 15 dB from warmth to pain and another 3 dB to tissue damage (Geldard, 1972, p. 321).

Prior (1972, pp. 88, 108) performed a preliminary study of the Weber fraction for frequency of sinusoids and of 1-msec unidirectional rectangular pulses. He found Weber fractions of 3–16% over the range of 1–20 Hz for the sinusoid, and 3–23% over a 5–50-p/sec range for the pulses. The results are for a single observer, however. Prior noted that discrimination of frequency or pulse rate above 50 Hz was poor if not impossible. Temporal acuity for electrocutaneous pulses is similarly poor. Rosner (1961) determined a threshold for successiveness for two brief pulses to be 15–45 msec, whereas Uttal (1959) estimated the limen at 10 msec. The threshold for temporal order, on the other hand, is similar to that for touch, 20 msec (Sherrick, 1970; but see Marks, Girvin, O'Keefe, Ning, Quest, Antunes, & Dobelle, 1982). Rollman (1974, p. 47) demonstrated that reaction times (RTs) to electrical stimuli are equal to those for mechanical taps when their sensory magnitudes are equated; the range of RTs was 120–200 msec, depending on magnitude. Sparks (1979) has reported somewhat different values for temporal order and movement effects on a multielectrode array (see also Chapter 31 by Loomis and Lederman for more information on multiple-contactor arrays).

8.2.2. Masking Effects. A number of authors have been able to demonstrate masking effects of electrocutaneous stimuli. Uttal (1960) reported the effects of a suprathreshold electrocutaneous stimulus at one finger on the threshold for a simultaneously presented test stimulus at another. Masking effects were dependent in part on the juxtaposition of the fingers; the index masked the middle more than it did the ring finger. Schmid

(1961) examined the temporal relations of test and masker stimulus when they appeared at the index and ring fingers and found that forward masking (i.e., masker precedes test) was much less than backward masking but that the total amount of masking was no more than 4 or 5 dB threshold shift. Rosner (1964) examined forward masking of electrocutaneous stimuli when masker and test were delivered to the same site, and found 6–10 dB when masker preceded test by 30 msec.

Rollman (1974, p. 45) examined the masking of electrocutaneous stimuli by mechanical impulsive stimuli and vice versa, as a function of the time between test and masker. The asymmetric effects of the two modes are illustrated by the fact that the electrical masker produced a 13-dB shift in the mechanical test threshold, whereas the mechanical masker produced only a 3-dB shift in the electrocutaneous threshold.

8.2.3. Sensory Magnitude Scales. S. S. Stevens, Carton, and Shickman (1958) examined the growth of sensory magnitude for a 60-Hz stimulus delivered to the fingers. A pair of glass jars filled with saline solution and containing metal electrodes formed the contacting surface. A total of about 30 observers made estimates of the magnitude of 0.5- or 1-sec shocks varying from 0.25 to 1.1 mA in strength. Figure 12.34 is a plot of the results combined from the three experiments reported. The striking feature of the power function is its steepness; the exponent was calculated as 3.5, the steepest of any sensory magnitude function yet determined. S. S. Stevens (1959a) found a similar exponent when he had observers perform cross-modality matching of shock to auditory loudness and to vibration magnitude. Rollman (1974, pp. 40f) has discussed the fact that a number of investigators could not get the large exponent obtained by S. S. Stevens and suggests that the disagreement may arise from the method of treating the data. When Rollman included threshold values in his calculation of power function intensity levels, the slope dropped from a value of 3.0 to 1.1 (Rollman, 1974, p. 41, Fig. 6). Sachs and coworkers (1980), who used the circuit devised by Saunders (1974) and described in Section 8.1.1, determined the power function for increasing number of pulses per burst with pulse width as parameter. From the data adduced by a cross-modality matching technique, Sachs and coworkers concluded that the exponent was not different from those obtained by varying current levels, that is, between 1.0 and 2.0.

8.2.4. Relation to Touch and Vibration Patterns. The applications of electrocutaneous stimulation in basic research have often been for the purpose of control. Sherrick and Rogers (1966) substituted an electrocutaneous sinusoid for the mechanical vibration in their study of synthetic movement to determine whether wave propagation through tissue affected the results. Similarly, Geldard and Sherrick (see Geldard, 1975, p. 66) substituted rectangular unidirectional electrical pulses for the mechanical taps to ensure that wave propagation through tissue was not producing the saltatory effect. In innumerable cases, von Békésy (1967) has applied the same control for similar purposes. When conditions are right, the electrocutaneous stimulus often cannot be distinguished from its mechanical counterpart as a tap, a buzz, or an asynchronous train. Rollman (1974, p. 43) has suggested that the electrical stimulus bypasses the receptors and stimulates the nerves directly. He cites as supporting evidence the known temporal properties of nerve fiber compared to those adduced for cutaneous electrical stimuli. S. S. Stevens and colleagues (1958) have argued for this hypothesis by comparing the normally shallow power function in

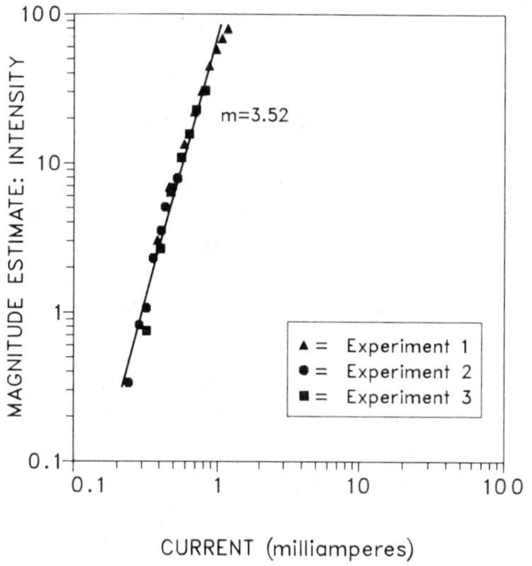

Figure 12.34. The growth of apparent intensity of electric shock as a function of stimulus current. S. S. Stevens, Carton, and Shickman (1958) examined the growth of subjective magnitude of electric shocks. These were presented to the index and ring fingers through electrodes consisting of saline-filled glass jars in which the fingers were immersed up to the first joint. The results of three experiments are indicated by the filled triangles, circles, and squares, respectively. In the first experiment, 60-Hz constant-current bursts lasting about 1 sec were judged by 10 subjects using the method of magnitude estimation. The 0.79-mA stimulus was presented first, and subjects were instructed to call that sensation "10." The remaining eight stimuli were then presented twice each in irregular order and judged by assigning numbers in proportion to the subjective magnitude produced by each. In the second experiment (circles), the shocks lasted 0.5 sec, the standard was set at 0.37 mA, and the stimuli were judged by 15 subjects. Otherwise the procedure was identical to that used in experiment I. Experiment III was similar to Experiment II except that the standard was set at 0.5 mA and 10 subjects served in the study. Interquartile ranges for the estimates obtained from the first experiment ranged from 1.5 to 5.5 dB re the geometric mean, somewhat greater than usually obtained from magnitude estimates of other stimuli, such as the loudness of tones. The slope of the power function fit to these data, 3.52, is remarkable for its steepness. One may compare it with the slopes of 0.85–1.10 for vibrotactile loudness (Figure 12.13) or 1.0–1.6 for thermal stimuli (Figure 12.24). Electric shock is also notable in that it is one of the few stimuli that produce a function demonstrating "expansion" (slope >1.0) as opposed to "compression" (slope <1.0) of the rate of growth of sensation magnitude relative to the change in physical stimulus magnitude. These authors suggest that the compression function normally seen is a result of processing at the end organ. This inference follows because direct electric shock to the auditory nerve bypasses the receptor, and the resulting expansion function may be indicative of the gain produced by the transduction of electrical into neural energy. (From S. S. Stevens, A. S. Carton, & G. M. Shickman, A scale of apparent intensity of electric shock, *Journal of Experimental Psychology*, *56*. Copyright 1958 by American Psychological Association. Reprinted with permission.)

hearing (exponent = 0.6) to the steep value of 3.5 obtained when the acoustic branch of the VIIIth nerve is directly stimulated electrically (S. S. Stevens et al., 1958, pp. 332f.).

8.3. Potential Applicability of Electrocutaneous Stimulation

Two primary considerations in applications will be the convenience of the attachment of the signal system to the human and the low-power requirements of the system. In this respect, the electrocutaneous mode is superior (particularly when size and weight of display are considered), since power dissipation at the electrode–skin junction is approximately 30 μW at threshold and rises at the tolerable limit to no more than 300 mW (see R. T. Green, 1962; Sachs et al., 1980; S. S. Stevens et al., 1958). This range (of 40 dB) is not owing to the large dynamic range of electrocutaneous stimulation; rather, it takes into account a number of variants of electrode arrays and efficiencies. With appropriate treatment, electrodes can be maintained on the skin for periods of at least an hour or two (Sachs et al., 1980, p. 262, note 1; Saunders, 1974), and generally are easy to apply and remove.

From the standpoint of brightness, clarity, attention-demanding value, and resistance to masking, the electrical stimulus is superior. Temporal acuity is poor, and spatial localization is no better than for touch, although the study of the latter property is complicated by the necessary spatial distribution of electrodes (see F. N. Jones, 1956). The major drawback of electrocutaneous stimulation is the problem of pain; on occasion, stinging, burning, or, with deep tissue involvement, aching pain can appear and prove to be sufficiently traumatic that the subject is seriously distracted or avoids further contact with the system. Moreover, if an electrode configuration includes a muscle group in the current path, the involuntary movements induced by higher intensities of stimulation can be very discomforting. The subject's apprehension is not necessarily unfounded; unless great care is taken to ensure that current paths remain entirely superficial to the body, life-threatening shocks may result. This is particularly true when power from electric mains is converted to stimulus values, since electric grounds for such a source (e.g., radiators, pipes, and metal window frames) may be contacted inadvertently (see Dalziel, 1973).

9. THEORIES OF CUTANEOUS SENSITIVITY

Intensive experimental studies of the optics and spectrophotometric properties of the eye have for years been a part of the structure of fact incorporated in theories of vision. For a similar purpose, the mechanical, acoustical, and hydrodynamic properties of the outer, middle, and inner ear have been carefully investigated. The measurement of the mechanical characteristics of the skin has only rarely been undertaken with a view to understanding the manner of propagation and distribution through the skin of mechanical, electrical and thermal energies (see von Békésy, 1939; Franke et al., 1951; Geldard, 1975; Keidel, 1956; Moore, 1970; Moore & Mundie, 1972; Phillips & Johnson, 1981; Sherrick, 1953; Stolwijk & Hardy, 1965; Tregear, 1966). In comparison to the detailed knowledge of the morphology of receptive structures in the skin tissues, the understanding of the dermal layers as propagation media is in a primitive state.

It is not enough to know the response characteristics of, for example, the Pacinian corpuscle as measured in situ in the mesentery of the cat, as Catton (1970, p. 316), Hahn (1974, p. 237), and Quilliam (1978, p. 14) have pointed out. The receptor is a captive of the tissues surrounding it and will have its functional properties augmented or diminished by theirs (Phillips & Johnson, 1981).

A fully integrated theory of cutaneous sensitivity will ultimately require models for the propagation, reflection, and absorption of various energy forms in the pathways from skin surface to receptors. At present, only qualitative statements or rough quantitative approximations can be made. The result is that theories of cutaneous sensitivity do not begin at the skin surface; they begin at the nerve ends. Nevertheless, the theories maintain an orientation to the ultimate psychological problem of quality of experience, that is, how we discriminate (and integrate) the seemingly elemental sensations of touch, warmth, cold, and pain.

9.1. Specificity Theories

It would be difficult to find two more knowledgeable guides than Melzack and Wall (1962) in our attempt to reduce the confusion in the labyrinthine structure of cutaneous theory, in particular the portions erected by von Frey and reinforced by his followers. Melzack and Wall reviewed the specificity theory of von Frey and the fiber-type modality theory that supplemented it, and they arrived at three conclusions. First, the von Frey theory comprises three major assumptions: (1) specific receptors are "tuned" to particular forms and dimensions of environmental energy, (2) the sensory spots on the skin overlie the receptors, and (3) the activitation of the receptor is encoded by the nerve fiber and transmitted to a cerebral station that registers the appropriate sensation. Their second conclusion is that the assumption of specific tuning of receptors (1, above) is a physiological truth so universally accepted that von Frey's theory is supported by those who see this assumption as its major and essential feature. Their third conclusion is that the assumption of psychological specificity (3, above) is regarded as so abhorrent by those who perceive it as the major feature that they reject the whole theory.

Of the three assumptions that von Frey makes, only the first can be said to be supported by direct evidence. The study of the response of specialized receptors to various forms of energy in several sensory modalities provides convincing evidence that the end organ is a filter of ambient energies, with low thresholds to a very few forms and high thresholds to the rest.

The second assumption of von Frey was anatomic. It has almost never been upheld, even from the beginning, as Boring (1942, p. 471) pointed out (see also Kenshalo & Nafe, 1962). In fact, what the spot–receptor coincidence assumption demands is that the skin propagate energy just as it issues sweat, through restricted ducts. The point of interest concerning this feature of von Frey's theory, as Melzack and Wall so clearly express it, is that the coincidence of sensory spots and underlying end organs is not critical to the theory. The anatomic assumption is not only unproven and unrealistic, it is unnecessary, at least at this juncture since, as we have already pointed out, so little is known about the manner of energy propagation.

The third assumption made by von Frey is the critical one, and the evidence against it marshaled by Melzack and Wall (1962) is best given in their words:

1. There is considerable evidence that there is no simple one-to-one relationship between perceptual dimensions and the dimensions of the physical stimulus. . . .
2. . . . The four "modalities" of von Frey seem to represent broad categories of different perceptions lumped together solely on the basis of introspection and labelled in terms of those perceptions that are most easily named. . . .
3. von Frey's theory also assumes that a physical stimulus is differentiated into four "modalities" entirely at the receptor level and that the information concerning each is transmitted directly to the brain. The potentials as generated by skin receptors, however, mark only the beginning of the whole afferent sensory process. The impulses may be inhibited or modified. . . . They may summate with impulses ascending in other fibers. . . . Moreover, if differentiation

were indeed completed in skin receptors, one would expect to find a predominance of "modality-specific cells" in the dorsal horns of the spinal cord; but such cells have never been found. (pp. 336–337).

In recent years (Christensen & Perl, 1970) it has been shown that some dorsal horn cells respond only to nociceptor activity. This is still not evidence for a predominance of modality-specific activity.

After the initial determinations by Erlanger, Gasser, and Bishop (1924) that nerve fiber diameters and myelination determine threshold and conduction velocity, there was an attempt to correlate the cutaneous modalities with particular categories of nerves grouped by fiber diameter. Repeated attempts to dissociate nerve groups by pressure, cold, anesthetic, or ischemic block in humans while testing for the sensory qualities remaining have not yielded univocal results, as we have already reported (see Section 5.1.4). Moreover, it has been pointed out that the various blocking techniques do more than simply silence a particular fiber group. Sinclair (1955) discussed five factors that are altered by various blocks: (1) relative activities among fiber groups, (2) maximum frequency of impulses transmitted, (3) total number of active fibers, (4) levels of spontaneous activity, and (5) transduction properties (owing to altered circulatory conditions) of the receptors. The presently available facts concerning fiber diameter and modality suggest instead that more than one group of fibers is active under almost any set of stimulus conditions that can be specified (Melzack & Wall, 1962, p. 338; Torebjörk, 1979, p. 318; Vallbo et al., 1979).

9.2. Activity Pattern Theories

If the von Frey theory errs on the side of rigid specificity, the pattern theory proposed by Nafe (1934; Nafe & Kenshalo, 1962) and elaborated by Weddell and his associates (see Sinclair, 1967, p. 15; Weddell & Miller, 1962) has proved to be altogether too vague to be of use in generating testable hypotheses about the activity of the cutaneous system. The neurovascular theory of temperature sensitivity proposed by Nafe (1934) was unable to explain certain well-known facts about warmth and cold sensations (see Geldard, 1972, p. 372); its core mechanism of vascular dilatation and contraction as the necessary condition for stimulation was shown by Dawson (1964) to be uncorrelated with warmth and cold perception. Similarly, the pattern theory of Weddell and the English school, which denied the selective action of cutaneous receptors, has been refuted on that issue by physiologic and anatomic research results (Iggo, 1982; Iggo & Andres, 1982; Sinclair, 1967, p. 17).

Nafe's idea that the influx of a variety of nervous signals is organized into a pattern of central activities was anticipated by other authors. Certainly Sherrington (1906) and Head (1920) had postulated such a process, and nothing in current physiological research refutes the idea that a single external event can produce new levels of activity in several areas of the cerebrum. This portion of the pattern theory, therefore, is supportable in the light of both clinical and experimental evidence (see also Merzenich & Kaas, 1980).

9.3. An Eclectic Theory of Cutaneous Sensitivity

The problem for explanation, as Melzack and Wall (1962) see it, has two components:

1. What kind of information is generated at the periphery to impinge on the CNS when a stimulus is presented to the skin?
2. How do the cells of the CNS analyze and integrate this peripheral code to produce the various qualities that compose what we call sensation?

Melzack and Wall have offered eight propositions intended to present what is known and what can reasonably be assumed about the activities of the somesthetic system, in a manner that permits the generation of testable hypotheses concerning the processes involved in transduction, coding, and integration of these activities. The propositions are as follows:

1. There is specialization of receptor activity in response to particular dimensions of the energy impinging on the skin, and this activity results in the production of neural patterns, not modality-specific codes.
2. The terminal endings of peripheral nerves may, at the presynaptic level, filter selectively some features of the neural patterns thus generated.
3. Central nerve cells may also select certain features of the impulses from the terminal endings owing to their special properties of differential sensitivity, temporal summation, and adaptation.
4. These same cells may select features by means of the property of spatial summation of impulses arriving from converging fibers.
5. Central cells have special connections, for example, spatial positioning on their bodies of particular incoming fiber systems, or both excitatory and inhibitory connections, or internuclear connecting systems allowing comparison between, say, dorsal horn cells and the medial lemniscal system.
6. More than one nerve impulse, or more than one fiber carrying a single impulse, is necessary for the detection of a stimulus by the central cells.
7. The somesthetic system is a unitary integrated system comprising specialized component parts.
8. Every discriminably different somesthetic perception is the product of a unique pattern of nerve impulses.

With these eight propositions, Melzack and Wall have been able to provide reasonable explanations for the facts adduced from physiological and psychophysical research, as well as to suggest areas for further needed investigation. One of these is the problem of pain, and in subsequent publications these authors presented a special theory of pain based on the propositions cited (Melzack & Wall, 1965; see also Melzack & Casey, 1968).

The theory of pain is now generally referred to as the *gate control theory*, after its salient feature. A schematic diagram of the major parts of the nervous system involved is shown in Figure 12.35. What Melzack and Wall have proposed is that both large and small fiber activity occur when a noxious stimulus is presented, and the special connections (proposition 5) of these to two spinal systems permit the range of higher-order activities demanded by the facts given clinically and experimentally.

The theory not only has a rational appeal but also conforms to some of the presently known anatomical and physiological facts. In the later paper by Melzack and Casey (1968, p. 427) additional systems were added to account for motivational and central determinants of pain experience. In more recent years,

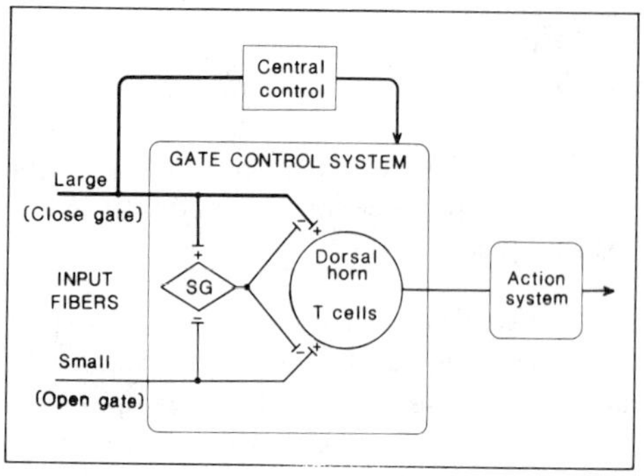

Figure 12.35. The gate control theory of pain, according to Melzack and Wall (1965). Schematically shown are the major anatomical points of interaction in the spinal cord that would account for several of the major characteristics of pain sensation. The sites of interaction are in the dorsal horn areas of the spinal cord, in which lie the "transmission," or T, cells. These provide patterned information to the CNS's "action systems" that could signal the difference between innocuous and noxious stimuli. The activity in these cells is modulated by inputs from both large, myelinated nerve fibers receiving input from mechanoreceptors in the skin and from smaller nonmyelinated fibers, some of which may be activated by noxious thermal, mechanical, or chemical stimuli at the skin's surface. The activity in these fibers, which is excitatory to the T cells, is itself controlled by presynaptic inhibitory influences from cells that lie in a deeper portion of the dorsal horn, in the substantia gelatinosa (SG). These inhibitory influences are, in turn, controlled by collateral branches from both populations of input fibers: excitation from the large fibers but inhibition from the smaller fibers. This pattern of interaction completes the early model of the gate control system. Activity from mechanoreceptors initially excites the T cells, but then, through the SG excitation, T-cell input is reduced by the inhibitory collaterals on the large-fiber synapses. Concurrent activity in smaller fibers, however, releases the inhibitory influences of the SG cells by inhibiting the SG cells themselves (producing "disinhibition"). Thus the output of the T cells is increased by small-fiber influences and may be prolonged beyond that produced solely by large-fiber inputs. Main branches of the large fibers ascend in the dorsal tracts of the spinal cord to the cerebral centers that, in turn, may send modulating signals back down the cord, influencing activity within the gate. The model can account for several characteristics of tactile pain, such as the modulating influence of rubbing an adjacent area (increasing large-fiber activity, closing the gate). The actual sites of and polarities of the activities described are, however, still a matter for investigation. (From R. Melzack & P. D. Wall, Pain mechanisms: A new theory, *Science, 150*. Copyright 1965 by American Association for the Advancement of Science. Reprinted with permission.)

the added knowledge of endogenous opioids (see Section 6.2.2), as well as findings in spinal neurophysiology (see Casey, 1978; Kerr & Wilson, 1978), demands some revision in the theory, but that is beyond the scope of the present chapter. If there is a better theory of pain, we have not been apprised of it.

10. APPLICATIONS OF CUTANEOUS SENSORY CAPACITIES

A later chapter of this handbook will deal in considerably greater detail with complex information processing by the skin (see Chapter 31 by Loomis and Lederman). There are a few applications of the skin sensory system to relatively simple skills involving such tasks as tracking and vigilance that can be described here. In general the applications have been made when it is anticipated that the human operator will be involved in a complex task structure that demands heavy use of the auditory and visual modalities. The cutaneous system is recruited either to provide a third independent input channel or, by adding redundant information, to increase the cueing power of one of the other modalities. When the individual is handicapped by a sensory disability, the cutaneous channel can be employed to augment the reduced inflow of the deficient sense or to replace it entirely for such limited purposes as alerting the handicapped user.

10.1. Vigilance and Cueing Studies

Systematic work on the comparative value of mechanical and electrocutaneous (EC) signals in task situations requiring watchkeeping or monitoring behavior was undertaken by Hawkes and Loeb (1961). In the standard vigilance paradigm, in which subjects are required to report the appearance of a transient stimulus or a change in the stimulus intensity level or other dimension, it was found that weak mechanical vibrotactile signals and EC signals were not detected as efficiently as weak auditory signals. Poorest efficiency, that is, longest reaction latencies, most misses, and most false alarms, occurred for weak EC signals (set to 1.6 dB SL, i.e., 1.2 times threshold). Comparable levels of auditory and vibrotactile stimuli were set by allowing subjects to equate the sensory magnitudes of the latter two to the EC signal. Mechanical vibratory signals were significantly more efficiently processed, but auditory signals were most efficiently monitored. In subsequent studies (Hawkes & Loeb, 1962; Loeb & Hawkes, 1961, 1962) signal strength, signal duration, and signal rise–fall time were examined to compare the efficiency of auditory and EC signals. In general, EC signals at comparable values were less effectively processed, but nevertheless sufficiently well detected to suggest their utility in vigilance tasks of an extended nature. When Hawkes, Meighan, and Alluisi (1964) examined vigilance in the presence of several cognitive subtasks, they found that, when EC signals (at 6 dB SL) were added redundantly to provide both temporal and spatial cues to a visual monitoring task, performance in the visual tasks not only improved but also resisted the decrement commonly produced by other tasks without interfering with their performance.

In an experiment designed to examine the problem of division of attention, Glucksberg (1963) required subjects to perform a standard rotary pursuit task while responding to visual, auditory, or EC signals that appeared during the trial. The response was either simple detection, disjunctive spatially, or disjunctive intensitively (i.e., respond to one spatial position but not another or to one intensity but not another). Glucksberg found that the visual detection and disjunctive tasks reduced the (visual) tracking performance significantly, as would be expected, but the auditory and EC tasks did not, nor did they differ from each other. No discriminable effect of the tracking behavior on response latency for detection was noted.

It appears that the cutaneous system has utility as either an independent or an adjunctive channel in situations demanding a relatively simple level of processing of discrete and clearly discriminable signals. A somewhat more complex task is that of tracking signals that vary in one or more attributes in a continuous but unpredictable manner, and we examine this next.

10.2. Tracking with Cutaneous Signals

10.2.1. Simple Compensatory and Pursuit Tracking. There are two excellent critical reviews of cutaneous tracking studies, by Hill (1970) and by Triggs, Levison and Sanneman (1974).

One of the earlier studies of cutaneous tracking was reported by Howell (1960), who compared a quantized compensatory vibrotactile display with both a quantized and a continuous visual display. Displays with and without quickening were examined when various rates of sinusoidal target motion were imposed. Performance, measured as average error, on the cutaneous and visual displays was comparable up to about 0.1 Hz. At higher frequencies performance for the cutaneous display declined at twice the rate as for the visual displays. With extended training on the cutaneous and visual tasks at the 0.08-Hz tracking rate, it was found that performance improved on the cutaneous display at 4 times that for the visual quantized display.

In a similar task setting that added intensity increase to the error signal, Hahn (1965) compared a two-vibrator quantized display to a continuous visual display (a horizontally moving spot on an oscilloscope face). With 6 hours of practice, the mean error for the cutaneous display was about 2.5 times that for the visual.

Hill (1970) examined a number of different conditions for cutaneous tracking, including vibrator number, stimulus properties (vibration or air jets), locus on the body, and display gain. In addition, this author provided a describing-function analysis of the various tasks and conditions and concluded that error-amplitude information added to directional information is used effectively by the subject. Hill confirmed Hahn's results by showing that the mean-square tracking error is about twice that for the standard visual display. Of particular interest is what Hill called a "ripple" display, which appears more like the continuous visual display, in that a sequence of contacts occurs across the cutaneous sheet. At some rates, apparent (beta) movement is perceived, but the expected conjunction of this phenomemon and improved performance did not occur. Overall, performance with this display did, however, improve to the point that equivalent operator gain was two-thirds that for the visual display and equivalent operator time delay was shorter than for visual tracking (see Figure 12.36).

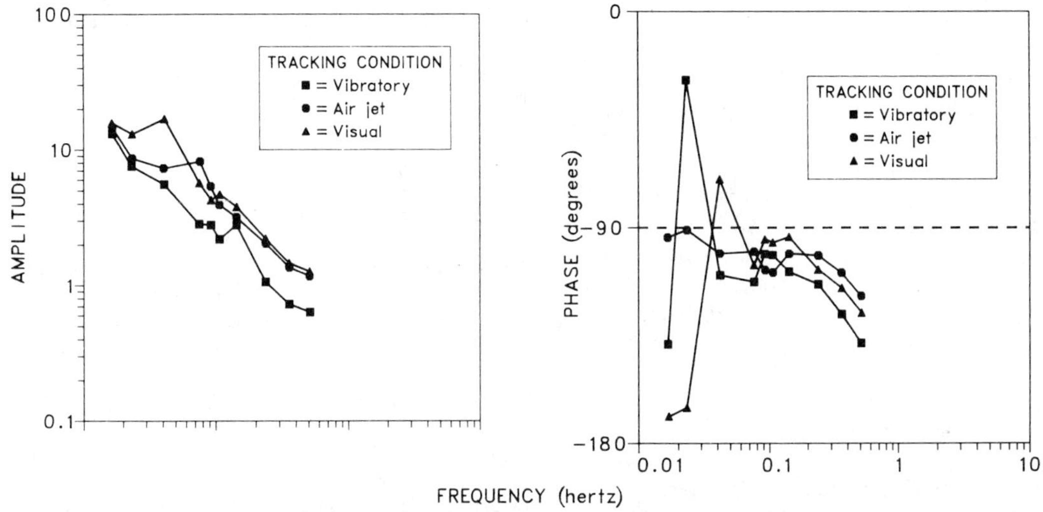

Figure 12.36. A describing function plotting the relative amplitudes of several different frequencies included in a tracking response, and the associated phase lags for those frequencies, for three different feedback conditions. (Adapted from Hill, 1970.) Of the several different good methods available for scoring tracking data, (see, e.g., Poulton, 1974), the describing function is one of the better because it allows for comparisons across many different experimental procedures. The analysis shows the gain and time delay of an operator independent of signal bandwidth, vehicle dynamics, feedback method, or other conditions of the system. The function is obtained by means of a Fourier analysis of the data, in which the coefficients are determined at the command signal frequencies and often others as well. The resulting plot is comparable to the Bode plot of the input–output responses of electronic signal processing equipment. In this study, Hill presented observers with a command signal composed of the sum of 10 different equal-amplitude sinusoids ranging in frequency from 0.0167 to 0.508 Hz. In the three cases shown, compensatory tracking was performed using different conditions of error feedback. Observers tracked the command signal using a lightly loaded joystick for 2 min. In the vibratory condition, two vibrotactile transducers were strapped to the arm. One indicated error in one direction, the other indicated error in the other direction. The air jet display consisted of seven jets in a line on the hand holding the joystick. The stimulus consisted of a serial pulsing from an outside jet toward the center one, to create a rippling sensation on the skin. The amplitude of the error was indicated by the maximum number of jets activated, while direction of the error was indicated by the direction of movement. The visual display showed a horizontal line that moved up or down in proportion to the amplitude and direction of the error. The task for the observer, in all cases, was to minimize the error by attempting to maintain the display in the neutral ("zero") position, that is, no signal on either vibrator, only the center air jet active, or, in the visual display, the horizontal line in the center of the screen. The results shown indicate that the air jet tactile display, when conditions were optimal, was better than the best vibratory display. This was indicated by greater response magnitudes at all command signal frequencies for the air jet feedback. Furthermore, the data show that the air jet and visual displays are equally effective in signaling error conditions, as indicated by nearly equivalent tracking performance. A more rigorous mathematical treatment of the describing function may be found in Graham and McRuer (1961).

In a study that compared mechanical vibrotactile and electrocutaneous display modes, Triggs, Levison, and Sanneman (1974) examined a number of display conditions. In addition, they reported some preliminary findings on judgments of temporal order and number of points stimulated. When the two-dimensional tactile was compared to the equivalent quantized visual display, no difference in performance was noted. The electrocutaneous and mechanical displays were judged to be equally effective, but the latter was reported to be more acceptable. The general conclusion from these studies must be that, under relatively limited conditions of practice, the subjects do not perform as well with cutaneous display information as they do with the usual visual (continuous) displays. Whether increasing the practice time or varying the dimensions of the tactile display will reduce this gap in display effectiveness remains for experiment to determine.

10.2.2. Tracking with a Subsidiary Task. An interesting study by Schori (1970a, 1970b) involved a unidimensional compensatory tracking task having either a visual, an auditory, or an electrocutaneous display of the quantized type. The error was indicated by spatial location of the stimulus, which was a light on the right or left side of a console, noise in the right or left ear, or an electrical stimulus to one of the concentric electrodes attached to the right and left forearms of the subject. To the tracking task was added a subsidiary monitoring task that required the subject to press buttons mounted on a tracking control wheel in response to the appropriate lights mounted on the console display. These were situated well to either side of the visual tracking display lights. Three levels of subsidiary task difficulty could be employed with this display: level 0, in which neither subsidiary display was presented; level 1, in which either the right or left display lights appeared during the tracking trial, and level 2, in which both sides appeared (not simultaneously). The subject's subsidiary task was to respond to the appearance of a light by pressing its corresponding button within the 1.3-sec interval of its appearance.

The level of difficulty of the subsidiary task was varied contingently. Following a trial on which tracking performance was above a critical value, difficulty level was increased, and when performance fell below criterion, difficulty level decreased. This "cross-adaptive" loading technique was intended to control for differences in tracking performance that might be owing to different cognitive strengths among display modes. The results of Schori's experiments were that no difference in tracking performance was found for the three displays but that the performance on the subsidiary task was poorest when the cutaneous display was being tracked.

All the above studies are simulations of actual tasks involving monitoring displays in military or industrial settings or controlling vehicle motions in ground, underwater, or air transport situations. One or two studies of in-flight or automobile control have been made (see, e.g., Fenton, 1966; Gilson & Fenton, 1974). Of further interest was the study by Mann and Reimers (1970) of the improvement in positioning of an artificial arm with an elbow joint. These investigators made use of the phantom sensation produced by near-simultaneous stimulation of two separate skin loci (see Section 4.4; Alles, 1970; von Békésy, 1967, p. 90). By means of sensing and control circuitry, the angle of the elbow joint was detected and sent to vibratory devices that controlled the position of the phantom touch in cutaneous space. Position of the phantom was the correlate of joint angle. A reduction of 50% in errors was achieved over a standard mechanical prosthesis when visual feedback was unavailable, during extended trial periods.

11. CONCLUDING REMARKS

Elsewhere one of us has remarked upon the lack of application of the capacities of the cutaneous senses (Sherrick, 1974, 1975). Beyond the special adaptations of the hand for palpating space-occupying and textured objects or the occasional fortuitous circumstances in which informative encounters of the skin and the environment may occur, very little has been done to enhance the altogether subordinate role of the skin sensory system in communications (Geldard, 1974a, p. 11). In part such neglect was owing to the lack of availability of compact transducers and processing circuitry either for applications or basic research. We are happy that this deficiency has been reduced in recent years, for with it perhaps will recede the very large gaps in our understanding of the working of the cutaneous system. At the same time we may anticipate the appearance of further attempts to integrate processing capacities of this modality into the general pool of information handling now controlled by sight and hearing. It is possible that the insistent and growing demands on the major senses will at long last force workers in research and development to enlarge the channel capacity of the human operator by recruiting and training the cutaneous senses.

REFERENCES

* References preceded by an asterisk are "key references."

Alles, D. S. Information transmission by phantom sensation. *IEEE Transactions on Man–Machine System*, 1970 *MMS-11*, 85–91.

Anderson, D. J., & Matthews, B. M. (Eds.) *Pain in the trigeminal system.* Amsterdam: Elsevier, 1977.

Beecher, H. K. The measurement of pain: Prototype for the quantitative study of subjective responses. *Pharmacological Reviews*, 1957, *9*, 59–209.

*Beecher, H. K. *Measurement of subjective responses.* New York: Oxford University Press, 1959.

Békésy, G. von. Über die Vibrationsempfindung. *Akustische Zeitschrift*, 1939, *4*, 316–334.

Békésy, G. von. Funneling in the nervous system and its role in loudness and sensation intensity in the skin. *Journal of the Acoustical Society of America*, 1958, *30*, 399–412.

Békésy, G. von. Neural funneling along the skin and between the inner and outer hair cells of the cochlea. *Journal of the Acoustical Society of America*, 1959, *31*, 1236–1249.

Békésy, G. von. *Experiments in hearing.* New York: McGraw-Hill, 1960. (a)

Békésy, G. von. Neural inhibitory units of the eye and skin. Quantitative description of contrast phenomena. *Journal of the Optical Society of America*, 1960, *50*, 1060–1070. (b)

Békésy, G von Interaction of paired sensory stimuli and conduction in peripheral nerves. *Journal of Applied Physiology*, 1963, *18*, 1276–1284.

*Békésy, G von. *Sensory inhibition.* Princeton, N.J.: Princeton University Press, 1967.

Bellows, R. M. An experimental isolation of some factors determining response to rhythmic cutaneous stimulation. I. Frequency, pressure, and time. *Journal of Experimental Psychology*, 1936, *19*, 716–731.

Benjamin, F. B. Effect of pain on simultaneous perception of non-painful sensory stimulation. *Journal of Applied Physiology*, 1956, *8*, 630–634.

Bishop, G. H. Responses to electrical stimulation of single sensory units of skin. *Journal of Neurophysiology*, 1943, *6*, 361–382.

Bliss, J. C. Summary of three Optacon-related cutaneous experiments. In F. A. Geldard (Ed.), *Cutaneous communication systems and devices.* Austin, Tex.: The Psychonomic Society, 1974.

Boring, E. G. The two-point limen and the error of localization. *American Journal of Psychology*, 1930, *42*, 446–449.

*Boring, E. G. *Sensation and perception in the history of experimental psychology.* New York: Appleton-Century, 1942.

Brearley, E. A., & Kenshalo, D. R. Behavioral measurements of the sensitivity of cat's upper lip to warm and cool stimuli. *Journal of Comparative and Physiological Psychology*, 1970, *70*, 1-4.

Brown, J. L. Sensory systems. In J. R. Brobeck (Ed.), *Best & Taylor's Physiological basis of medical practice* (9th ed.). Baltimore: Williams & Wilkins, 1973.

Buchthal, F., & Rosenfalck, A. Evoked action potentials and conduction velocity in human sensory nerves. *Brain Research*, 1966, *3*, 1–122.

Bujas, Z. La sensibilité au froid en fonction du temps. *Anneé Psychologique*, 1938, *38*, 140.

Bullock, T. H. An essay on the discovery of sensory receptors and the assignment of their functions together with an introduction to electroreceptors. In A. Fessard (Ed.), *Handbook of sensory physiology: Electroreceptors and other specialized receptors in lower vertebrates* (Vol. 3/3.) New York: Springer-Verlag, 1974.

Burgess, P. R., & Perl, E. R. Cutaneous mechanoreceptors and nociceptors. In A. Iggo (Ed.), *Handbook of sensory physiology: Somatosensory system* (Vol. 2). New York: Springer-Verlag, 1973.

Campbell, R. A. Detection of a noise signal of varying duration. *Journal of the Acoustical Society of America*, 1963, *35*, 1732–1737.

Capraro, A. J., Verrillo, R. T., & Zwislocki, J. J. Psychophysical evidence for a triplex system of mechanoreception. *Sensory Processes*, 1979, *3*, 334–352.

*Carterette, E. C., & Friedman, M. P. *Handbook of perception: Feeling and hurting* (Vol. 4B). New York: Academic Press, 1978.

Casey, K. L. Neural mechanisms of pain. In E. C. Carterette & M. P. Friedman (Eds.), *Handbook of perception: Feeling and hurting* (Vol. 4B) New York: Academic Press, 1978.

Catton, W. T. Mechanoreceptor function. *Physiological Reviews*, 1970, *50*, 297–318.

Chapman, C. R. Sensory decision theory methods in pain research: A reply to Rollman. *Pain*, 1977, *3*, 295–305.

Cholewiak, R. W. Satiation in cutaneous saltation. *Sensory Processes*, 1976, *1*, 163–175.

Cholewiak, R. W. Spatial factors in the perceived intensity of vibrotactile patterns. *Sensory Processes*, 1979, *3*, 141–156.

Cholewiak, R. W. & Sherrick, C. E. A computer-controlled matrix system for presentation to the skin of complex spatiotemporal patterns. *Behavior Research Methods & Instrumentation*, 1981, *13*, 667–673.

Christensen, B. N., & Perl, E. R. Spinal neurons specifically excited by noxious or thermal stimuli: Marginal zone of the dorsal horn. *Journal of Neurophysiology*, 1970, *33*, 293–307.

Craig, J. C. Vibrotactile spatial summation. *Perception & Psychophysics*, 1968, *4*, 351–354.

Craig, J. C. Difference thresholds for intensity of tactile stimuli. *Perception & Psychophysics*, 1972, *11*, 150–152.

Craig, J. C. A constant error in the perception of brief temporal intervals. *Perception & Psychophysics*, 1973, *13*, 99–104.

Craig, J. C. Vibrotactile difference thresholds for intensity and the effect of a masking stimulus. *Perception & Psychophysics*, 1974, *15*, 123–127.

Craig, J. C., & Sherrick, C. E. The role of skin coupling in the determination of vibrotactile spatial summation. *Perception & Psychophysics*, 1969, *6*, 97–101.

Croze, S., & Duclaux, R. Burning and second pain: An alternative interpretation. In D. R. Kenshalo (Ed.), *Sensory functions of the skin of humans*. New York: Plenum, 1979.

Dalziel, C. F. Electric shock. In J. H. U. Brown & J. F. Dickson, III (Eds.), *Advances in biomedical engineering* (Vol. 3). New York: Academic Press, 1973.

Darian-Smith, I. A. The trigeminal system. In A. I. Iggo (Ed.), *Handbook of sensory physiology: Somatosensory system* (Vol. 2). New York: Springer-Verlag, 1973.

Darian-Smith, I. A. Touch in primates. *Annual Review of Psychology* (Vol. 33). Palo Alto, Calif.: Annual Reviews, 1982, pp. 155–194.

*Darian-Smith, I. A. Touch and thermal sensibility. In R. D. Luce, R. J. Herrnstein, R. C. Atkinson, & G. Lindzey (Eds.), *Stevens' Handbook of Experimental Psychology*. New York: Wiley, in press.

Dawson, W. W. Thermal stimulation of experimentally vasoconstricted human skin. *Perceptual & Motor Skills*, 1964, *19*, 775–788.

de Reuck, A. V. S., & Knight, J. *Touch, heat, and pain. A Ciba Foundation Symposium*. London: Churchill, 1966.

Dostrovsky, J. O., & Hellon, R. F. The representation of facial temperature in the caudal trigeminal nucleus of the cat. *Journal of Physiology* (London), 1978, *277*, 29–47.

Douglas, W. W., & Ritchie, J. M. Mammalian non-myelinated nerve fibers. *Physiological Reviews*, 1962, *42*, 297–334.

Dubner, R., Sessle, B. J., & Storey, A. T. *The neural basis of oral and facial function*. New York: Plenum, 1978.

Eijkman, E., & Vendrik, A. J. H. Dynamic behavior of the warmth sense organ. *Journal of Experimental Psychology*, 1961, *62*, 403–408.

Erlanger, J., Gasser, H. S., & Bishop, G. H. Compound nature of the action current of nerve as disclosed by the cathode ray oscillograph. *American Journal of Physiology*, 1924, *70*, 624–666.

Fenton, R. E. An improved man–machine interface for the driver–vehicle system. *IEEE Transactions on Human Factors in Electronics*, 1966, *HFE-7*, 150–157.

Fields, H. L., & Basbaum, A. I. Brainstem control of spinal pain—Transmission neurons. *Annual Review of Physiology* (Vol. 40). Palo Alto, Calif.: Annual Reviews, 1978, pp. 217–248.

Foerster, O. The dermatomes in man. *Brain*, 1933, *56*, 1–39.

Franke, E. K., Gierke, H. E. von., Oestreicher, H. L., & Wittern, W. W. von. *The propagation of surface waves over the human body*. (USAF Technical Report No. 6464.) United States Air Force, Aero Medical Laboratory, Wright-Patterson Air Force Base, June 1951.

Franzén, O., Markowitz, J., & Swets, J. A. Spatially-limited attention to vibrotactile stimulation. *Perception & Psychophysics*, 1970, *7*, 193–196.

Geldard, F. A. The perception of mechanical vibration. II. The response of pressure receptors. *Journal of General Psychology*, 1940, *22*, 271–280. (a)

Geldard, F. A. The perception of mechanical vibration. III. The frequency function. *Journal of General Psychology*, 1940, *22*, 281–289. (b)

Geldard, F. A. A note on "adaptation" and allied terms. In D. R. Kenshalo (Ed.), *The skin senses*. Springfield, Ill.: Thomas, 1968.

*Geldard, F. A. Vision, audition, and beyond. In W. D. Neff (Ed.), *Contributions to sensory physiology* (Vol. 4). New York: Academic Press, 1970.

Geldard, F. A. The human senses (2nd ed.). New York: Wiley, 1972.

*Geldard, F. A. (Ed.) *Cutaneous communication systems and devices*. Austin, Tex.: The Psychonomic Society, 1974. (a)

Geldard, F. A. Vibratory reception in hairy skin. In G. B. Flores d'Arcais (Ed.), *Studies on perception*. Milan, Italy: Martello-Giunti, 1974. (b)

Geldard, F. A. *Sensory saltation: Metastability in the perceptual world*. Hillsdale, N. J.: Erlbaum, 1975.

Geldard, F. A. The saltatory effect in vision. *Sensory Processes*, 1976, *1*, 77–86.

Geldard, F. A. Saltation in somesthesis. *Psychological Bulletin*, 1982, *92*, 136–175.

Geldard, F. A., & Sherrick, C. E. The cutaneous "rabbit": A perceptual illusion. *Science*, 1972, *178*, 178–179.

Geldard, F. A., & Sherrick, C. E. *Princeton Cutaneous Research Project* (Report No. 21), Princeton University, 1973.

Geldard, F. A., & Sherrick, C. E. The cutaneous saltatory area and its presumed neural basis. *Perception & Psychophysics*, 1983, *33*, 299–304.

Geldard, F. A., Sherrick, C. E., & Cholewiak, R. W. *Princeton Cutaneous Research Project* (Report No. 36), Princeton University, 1980.

Gescheider, G. A. Temporal relations in cutaneous stimulation. In F. A. Geldard (Ed.), *Cutaneous communication systems and devices*. Austin, Tex.: The Psychonomic Society, 1974.

Gescheider, G. A. Evidence in support of the duplex theory of mechanoreception. *Sensory Processes*, 1976, *1*, 68–76.

Gescheider, G. A., Capraro, A. J., Frisina, R. D., Hamer, R. D., & Verrillo, R. T. The effects of a surround on vibrotactile thresholds. *Sensory Processes*, 1978, *2*, 99–115.

Gescheider, G. A., Frisina, R. D., & Verrillo, R. T. Selective adaptation of vibrotactile thresholds. *Sensory Processes*, 1979, *3*, 37–48.

Gescheider, G. A., & Wright, J. H. Effects of sensory adaptation on the form of the psychophysical magnitude function for cutaneous vibration. *Journal of Experimental Psychology*, 1968, *77*, 308–313.

Gibson, R. H. Electrical stimulation of pain and touch. In D. R. Kenshalo (Ed.), *The skin senses*. Springfield, Ill.: Thomas, 1968.

Gilson, R. D. Vibrotactile masking: Some spatial and temporal aspects. *Perception & Psychophysics*, 1969, *5*, 176–180.

Gilson, R. D., & Fenton, R. E. Kinesthetic-tactual information presentations—Inflight studies. *IEEE Transactions on Systems, Man, and Cybernetics*, 1974, *SMC-4*, 531–535.

Girvin, J. P., Marks L. E., Antunes, J. L., Quest, D. O., O'Keefe, M. D., Ning, D., & Dobelle, W. H. Electrocutaneous stimulation. I. The effects of stimulus parameters on absolute threshold. *Perception & Psychophysics*, 1982, *32*, 524–528.

Glucksberg, S. Rotary pursuit tracking with divided attention to cutaneous, visual, and auditory signals. *Journal of Engineering Psychology*, 1963, *2*, 119–125.

*Gordon, G. (Ed.) *Active touch. The mechanism of recognition of objects by manipulation: A multi-disciplinary approach.* Oxford: Pergamon, 1978.

Graham, D., & McRuer, D. *Analysis of nonlinear control systems*. New York: Wiley, 1961.

Green, B. G. Vibrotactile temporal summation and the effect of frequency. *Sensory Processes*, 1976, *1*, 138–149.

Green, B. G. The effect of skin temperature on vibrotactile sensitivity. *Perception & Psychophysics*, 1977, *21*, 243–248. (a)

Green, B. G. Localization of thermal sensation: An illusion and synthetic heat. *Perception & Psychophysics*, 1977, *22*, 331–337. (b)

Green, B. G. Referred thermal sensations: Warmth versus cold. *Sensory Processes*, 1978, *2*, 220–230.

Green, B. G. Thermo-tactile interactions: Some influences of temperature on touch. In D. R. Kenshalo (Ed.), *Sensory functions of the skin of humans*. New York: Plenum, 1979.

Green, B. G., & Craig, J. C. The role of vibration amplitude and static force in vibrotactile spatial summation. *Perception & Psychophysics*, 1974, *16*, 503–507.

Green, R. T. The absolute threshold of electric shock. *British Journal of Psychology*, 1962, *53*, 107–115.

Guilford, J. P., & Lovewell, E. M. The touch spots and the intensity of the stimulus. *Journal of General Psychology*, 1936, *15*, 149–159.

Hahn, J. F. Cutaneous vibratory thresholds for square-wave electrical pulses. *Science*, 1958, *127*, 879–880.

Hahn, J. F. Unidimensional compensatory tracking with a vibrotactile display. *Perceptual and Motor Skills*, 1965, *21*, 699–702.

Hahn, J. F. Vibrotactile adaptation and recovery measured by two methods. *Journal of Experimental Psychology*, 1966, *71*, 655–658.

Hahn, J. F. Low-frequency, vibrotactile adaptation. *Journal of Experimental Psychology*, 1968, *78*, 655–659. (a)

Hahn, J. F. Tactile adaptation. In D. R. Kenshalo (Ed.), *The skin senses*. Springfield, Ill.: Thomas, 1968, pp. 322–330. (b)

Hahn, J. F. Somesthesis. *Annual Review of Psychology* (Vol. 25). Palo Alto, Calif.: Annual Reviews, 1974, pp. 233–246.

Harbert, F., Young, I. M., & Wenner, C. H. Auditory flutter fusion and envelope of signal. *Journal of the Acoustical Society of America*, 1968, *44*, 803–806.

Hardy, J. D., & Oppel, T.W. Studies in temperature sensation. IV. The stimulation of cold sensation by radiation. *Journal of Clinical Investigation*, 1938, *17*, 771–778.

Hawkes, G. R. Cutaneous communication: Absolute identification of electrical intensity level. *Journal of Psychology*, 1960, *49*, 203–212.

Hawkes, G. R. Information transmitted via electrical cutaneous stimulus duration. *Journal of Psychology*, 1961, *51*, 293–298.

Hawkes, G. R., & Loeb, M. Vigilance for cutaneous and auditory signals. *Journal of Auditory Research*, 1961, *4*, 272–284.

Hawkes, G. R., & Loeb, M. Vigilance for cutaneous and auditory stimuli as a function of intersignal interval and signal strength. *Journal of Psychology*, 1962, *53*, 211–218.

Hawkes, G. R., Meighan, T. W., & Alluisi, E. A. Vigilance in complex task situations. *Journal of Psychology*, 1964, *58*, 223–236.

Hawkes, G. R., & Warm, J. S. ΔT for electrical cutaneous stimulation. *Journal of Psychology*, 1961, *51*, 263–271.

Head, H. *Studies in neurology*. London: Oxford University Press, 1920.

Hellon, R. F., & Mitchell, D. Convergence in a thermal afferent pathway in the rat. *Journal of Physiology* (London), 1975, *248*, 359–376.

Hensel, H. Electrophysiology of thermosensitive nerve endings. In C.M. Herzfeld (Ed.), *Temperature—Its measurement and control in science and industry* (Vol. 3). New York: Reinhold, 1962.

Hensel, H., & Boman, K. Afferent impulses in cutaneous sensory nerves in human subjects. *Journal of Neurophysiology*, 1960, *23*, 564–578.

Hill, J. W. *The perception of multiple tactile stimuli* (Stanford Electronics Laboratory Technical Report No. 4823-1). Stanford University, 1967.

Hill, J. W. Describing function analysis of tracking performance using two tactile displays. *IEEE Transactions on Man–Machine Systems*, 1970, *MMS–11*, 92–100.

Hirsh, I. J. *The measurement of hearing*. New York: McGraw-Hill, 1952.

Hirsh, I. J. Order of events in three sensory modalities. In S. K. Hirsh, D. H. Eldredge, I. J. Hirsh, & S. R. Silverman (Eds.), *Hearing and Davis: Essays honoring Hallowell Davis*. St. Louis, Mo.: Washington University Press, 1976.

Hirsh, I. J., & Sherrick, C. E. Perceived order in different sense modalities. *Journal of Experimental Psychology*, 1961, *62*, 423–432.

Howell, W. C. On the potential of tactual displays. An interpretation of recent findings. In G. R. Hawkes (Ed.), *Symposium on cutaneous sensitivity*. Fort Knox: U.S. Army Medical Research Laboratory, 1960.

Iggo, A. I. (Ed.) *Handbook of sensory physiology: Somatosensory system* (Vol. 2). New York: Springer-Verlag, 1973.

Iggo, A. I. Cutaneous receptors. In J. I. Hubbard (Ed.), *The peripheral nervous system*. New York: Plenum, 1974.

Iggo, A. I. Cutaneous sensory mechanisms. In H. B. Barlow & J. D. Mollon (Eds.), *The senses*. Cambridge, England: Cambridge University Press, 1982.

*Iggo, A. I., & Andres, K. H. Morphology of cutaneous receptors. *Annual Review of Neuroscience*, 1982, *5*, 1–31.

Jabbur, S. J., & Atweh, S. F. Visual, auditory, and somatic interactions in the cuneate nucleus. In H. H. Kornhuber (Ed.), *The somatosensory system*. Stuttgart: Georg Thieme, 1975.

Jenerick, H. P. *Proceedings NIH acupuncture research conference*. Washington, D.C.: DHEW Publication No. (NIH) 74-165, 1973.

Johansson, R. S. Tactile afferent units with small and well demarcated receptive fields in the glabrous skin area of the human hand. In D. R. Kenshalo (Ed.), *Sensory functions of the skin of humans*. New York: Plenum, 1979.

Johnson, K. O., & Phillips, J. R. Tactile spatial resolution. I. Two-point discrimination, gap detection, grating resolution, and letter recognition. *Journal of Neurophysiology*, 1981, *46*, 1177–1191.

Jones, E. G., & Hartman, B. K. Recent advances in neuroanatomical methodology. *Annual Review of Neuroscience*, 1978, 1, 215–296.

Jones, F. N. Space-time relationships in somesthetic localization. *Science*, 1956, *124*, 484.

Kaas, J. H., Nelson, R. J., Sur, M., Lin, C.-S., & Merzenich, M. M. Multiple representations of the body within the primary somatosensory cortex of primates. *Science*, 1979, *204*, 521–523.

Keegan, J. J., & Garrett, F. D. Segmental distribution of cutaneous nerves in the limbs of man. *Anatomical Record*. 1948, *102*, 409–437.

Keidel, W.-D. Vibrationsreception. Der Erschütterungssinn des Menschen. Erlanger Forschungen, 1956, Reihe B. Band 2.

Keidel, W.-D. Electrophysiology of vibratory perception. In W. D. Neff (Ed.), *Contributions to sensory physiology* (Vol. 3). New York: Academic Press, 1968.

Kenkel, F. Untersuchungen über den Zusammenhang zwischen Erscheinungsgrösse und Erscheinungsbewegung bei einigen sogenannten optischen Täuschungen. *Zeitschrift für Psychologie*, 1913,

67, 358–449.

Kenshalo, D. R. Improved method for the psychological study of the temperature sense. *Review of Scientific Instruments*, 1963, *34*, 883–886.

Kenshalo, D. R. The temperature sensitivity of furred skin of cats. *Journal of Physiology* (London), 1964, *172*, 439–448.

*Kenshalo, D. R. (Ed.) *The skin senses.* Springfield, Ill.: Thomas, 1968.

Kenshalo, D. R. Psychophysical studies of temperature sensitivity. In W. D. Neff (Ed.), *Contributions to sensory physiology*. New York: Academic Press, 1970.

Kenshalo, D. R. The cutaneous senses. In J. W. Kling & L. A. Riggs (Eds.), *Woodworth & Schlosberg's Experimental Psychology* (3rd ed., Vol. 1): *Sensation and perception.* New York: Holt, Rinehart & Winston, 1972.

*Kenshalo, D. R. (Ed.) *Sensory functions of the skin of humans.* New York: Plenum, 1979.

Kenshalo, D. R., & Brearley, E. A. Electrophysiological measurements of the sensitivity of cat's upper lip to warm and cool stimuli. *Journal of Comparative and Physiological Psychology*, 1970, *70*, 5–14.

Kenshalo, D. R., Decker, T., & Hamilton, A. Comparisons of spatial summation on the forehead, forearm, and back produced by radiant and conducted heat. *Journal of Comparative and Physiological Psychology*, 1967, *63*, 510–515.

Kenshalo, D. R., Holmes, C. E., & Wood, P. B. Warm and cool thresholds as a function of rate of stimulus temperature change. *Perception & Psychophysics*, 1968, *3*, 81–84.

Kenshalo, D. R., & Nafe, J. P. A quantitative theory of feeling: 1960. *Psychological Review*, 1962, *69*, 17–33.

Kenshalo, D. R., & Scott, H. H. Temporal course of thermal adaptation. *Science*, 1966, *151*, 1095–1096.

*Kerr, F. W. L., & Casey, K. L. (Eds.) Pain. *Neuroscience Research Program Bulletin*, 1978, *16*, 1–207.

Kerr, F. W. L., & Wilson, P. R. Pain. *Annual Review of Neuroscience*, 1978, *1*, 83–102.

Khanna, S., & Sherrick, C. E. The comparative sensitivity of selected receptor systems. In T. Gualtierotti (Ed.), *Symposium on vestibular function and morphology.* New York: Springer-Verlag, 1981.

Kietzman, M. L. Two-pulse measure of temporal resolution as a function of stimulus energy. *Journal of the Optical Society of America*, 1967, *57*, 809–813.

*Kirman, J. H. Tactile communication of speech: A review and an analysis. *Psychological Bulletin*, 1973, *80*, 54–74.

Kirman, J. H. Tactile apparent movement: The effects of interstimulus onset interval and stimulus duration. *Perception & Psychophysics*, 1974, *15*, 1–6.

Konietzny, R., & Hensel, H. The neural basis of the sensory quality of warmth. In D. R. Kenshalo (Ed.), *Sensory functions of the skin of humans.* New York: Plenum, 1979.

Kornhuber, H. H. *The somatosensory system.* Stuttgart: Georg Thieme, 1975.

Kruger, L., Perl, E. R., & Sedivec, M. J. Electron microscopic identification of cutaneous delta nociceptors of cat. *Neuroscience Letters*, 1979, Supplement 3, p. 5262.

Landgren, S. Thalamic neurons responding to cooling of the cat's tongue. *Acta Physiologica Scandinavica*, 1960, *48*, 255–267.

Langford, N., Hall, R. J., & Monty, R. A. Cutaneous perception of a track produced by a moving point across the skin. *Journal of Experimental Psychology*, 1973, *97*, 59–63.

Lanier, L. H. An experimental study of cutaneous innervation. *Proceedings of the Association for Research in Nervous and Mental Disease*, 1934, *15*, 437–456.

Lechelt, E. C. Pulse number discrimination in tactile spatio-temporal patterns. *Perceptual & Motor Skills*, 1974, *39*, 815–822.

Lechelt, E. C. Temporal numerosity discrimination: Intermodal comparisons revisited. *British Journal of Psychology*, 1975, *66*, 101–108.

*Lederman, S. J. *A bibliography on the sense of touch.* Unpublished manuscript. Queen's University at Kingston, Kingston, Ontario, Canada K7L 3N6, 1977.

Leshowitz, B. Measurement of the two-click threshold. *Journal of the Acoustical Society of America*, 1971, *49*, 462–466.

Libet, B., Alberts, W. W., Wright, E. W., Jr., Lewis, M., & Feinstein, B. Cortical representation of evoked potentials relative to conscious sensory responses, and of somatosensory qualities in man. In H. H. Kornhuber (Ed.), *The somatosensory system.* Stuttgart: Georg Thieme, 1975.

Lockhead, G. R., Johnson, R.C., & Gold, F. M. Saltation through the blind spot. *Perception & Psychophysics*, 1980, *27*, 545–549.

Loeb, M., & Hawkes, G. R. Rise and decay time in vigilance for weak auditory and cutaneous stimuli. *Perceptual and Motor Skills*, 1961, *13*, 235–242.

Loeb, M., & Hawkes, G. R. Detection of differences in duration of acoustic and electrical cutaneous stimuli in a vigilance task. *Journal of Psychology*, 1962, *54*, 101–111.

*Loewenstein, W. R. (Ed.) *Handbook of sensory physiology: Principles of receptor physiology* (Vol. 1). New York: Springer-Verlag, 1971. (a)

Lowenstein, W. R. Mechano-electrical transduction in the Pacinian corpuscle: Initiation of sensory impulses in mechanoreceptors. In W. R. Loewenstein (Ed.), *Handbook of sensory physiology: Principles of receptor physiology* (Vol. 1). New York: Springer-Verlag, 1971. (b)

Loomis, J. M. An investigation of tactile hyperacuity. *Sensory Processes*, 1979, *3*, 289–302.

Loomis, J. M., & Collins, C. C. Sensitivity to shifts of a point stimulus: An instance of tactile hyperacuity. *Perception & Psychophysics*, 1978, *24*, 487–492.

Mann, R. W., & Reimers, S. D. Kinesthetic sensing for the EMG-controlled "Boston arm." *IEEE Transactions on Man–Machine Systems*, 1970, *MMS-11*, 110–114.

Marks, L. E. Spatial summation in the warmth sense. In H. R. Moskowitz, B. Scharf, & J. C. Stevens (Eds.), *Sensation and measurement: Papers in honor of S. S. Stevens.* Dordrecht, Holland: Reidel, 1974.

Marks, L. E. *The unity of the senses.* New York: Academic Press, 1978.

Marks, L. E. A theory of loudness and loudness judgments. *Psychological Review*, 1979, *86*, 256–285. (a)

Marks, L. E. Summation of vibrotactile intensity: An analog to auditory critical bands? *Sensory Processes*, 1979, *3*, 188–203. (b)

Marks, L. E., Girvin, J. P., O'Keefe, M. D., Ning, P., Quest, D. O., Antunes, J. L., & Dobelle, W. H. Electrocutaneous stimulation III. The perception of temporal order. *Perception & Psychophysics*, 1982, *32*, 537–541.

Marks, L. E., & Stevens, J. C. Perceived warmth and skin temperature as functions of the duration and level of thermal stimulation. *Perception & Psychophysics*, 1968, *4*, 220–228.

Marks, L. E., & Stevens, J. C. Perceived cold and skin temperature as functions of stimulation level and duration. *American Journal of Psychology*, 1972, *85*, 407–419.

Marks, L. E., & Stevens, J. C. Spatial summation of warmth: Influence of duration and configuration of the stimulus. *American Journal of Psychology*, 1973, *86*, 251–267. (a)

Marks, L. E., & Stevens, J. C. Temporal summation related to the nature of the proximal stimulus for the warmth sense. *Perception & Psychophysics*, 1973, *14*, 570–576. (b)

Marks, L. E., Stevens, J. C., & Tepper, S. J. Interaction of spatial and temporal summation in the warmth sense. *Sensory Processes*, 1976, *1*, 87–98.

Melzack, R., & Casey, K. L. Sensory, motivational, and central control determinants of pain: A new conceptual model. In D. R. Kenshalo (Ed.), *The skin senses.* Springfield, Ill.: Thomas, 1968.

Melzack, R., & Schecter, B. Itch and vibration. *Science*, 1965, *147*, 1047–1048.

*Melzack, R., & Wall, P. D. On the nature of cutaneous sensory mechanisms. *Brain*, 1962, *85*, 331–356.

Melzack, R., & Wall, P. D. Pain mechanisms: A new theory. *Science*, 1965, *150*, 971–979.

Melzack, R., Wall, P. D. & Weisz, A. K. Masking and metacontrast phenomena in the skin sensory system. *Experimental Neurology*,

1963, *8*, 34–46.

Merzenich, M. M., & Harrington, T. The sense of flutter-vibration evoked by stimulation of the hairy skin of primates: Comparison of human sensory capacity with the response of mechanoreceptive afferents innervating the hairy skin of monkeys. *Experimental Brain Research*, 1969, *9*, 236–260.

*Merzenich, M. M., & Kaas, J. H. Principles of organization of sensory-perceptual systems in mammals. In J. M. Sprague & A. N. Epstein (Eds.), *Progress in Psychobiology and Physiological Psychology* (Vol. 9). New York: Academic Press, 1980.

*Miller, G. A. The magical number seven, plus or minus two: Some limitations on our capacity for processing information. *Psychological Review*, 1956, *63*, 81–97.

Montagna, W. *The structure and function of skin*. New York: Academic Press, 1956.

Moore, T. J. A survey of the mechanical characteristics of skin and tissue in response to vibratory stimulation. *IEEE Transactions on Man–Machine Systems*, 1970, *MMS-11*, 79–84.

Moore, T. J., & Mundie, J. R. Measurement of specific mechanical impedance of the skin: Effects of static force, site of stimulation, area of probe, and presence of a surround. *Journal of the Acoustical Society of America*, 1972, *52*, 577–584.

Mountcastle, V. B., Talbot, W. H., Darian-Smith, I., & Kornhuber, H. H. Neural basis of the sense of flutter-vibration. *Science*, 1967, *155*, 597–600.

Munger, B. L. Multiple afferent innervation of primate facial hairs—Henry Head and Max von Frey revisited. *Brain Research Reviews*, 1982, *4*, 1–43.

*Nafe, J. P. The pressure, pain, and temperature senses. In C. A. Murchison (Ed.), *Handbook of General Experimental Psychology*. Worcester, Mass.: Clark University Press, 1934.

Nafe, J. P., & Kenshalo, D. R. Somesthetic senses. *Annual Review of Psychology* (Vol. 13). Palo Alto, Calif.: Annual Reviews, 1962, pp. 201–224.

Nafe, J. P., & Wagoner, K. S. The nature of pressure adaptation. *Journal of General Psychology*, 1941, *25*, 323–351.

Neuhaus, W. Experimentelle Untersuchung der Scheinbewegung. *Archiv für die Gesamte Psychologie*, 1930, *75*, 315–458.

Penfield, W., & Rasmussen, T. *The cerebral cortex of man*. New York: Macmillan, 1950.

*Perl, E. R. Pain and nociception. In I. Darian-Smith (Ed.), *Handbook of physiology, Section I: Sensory processes* (Vol. 2). Washington, D.C.: American Physiological Society, 1982.

Perrott, D. R. Auditory apparent motion. *Journal of Auditory Research*, 1974, *14*, 163–169.

Pfaffman, C. The afferent code for sensory quality. *American Psychologist*, 1959, *14*, 226–232.

*Phillips, J. R., & Johnson, K. O. Tactile spatial resolution. III. A continuum mechanics model of skin predicting mechanoreceptor responses to bars, edges, and gratings. *Journal of Neurophysiology*, 1981, *48*, 1204–1225.

Piéron, H. *The sensations: Their functions, processes and mechanisms*. London: Frederick Muller, 1952.

Poulton, E. C. *Tracking skills and manual control*. New York: Academic Press, 1974.

Prior, R. E. *Study of electrocutaneous parameters relevant to dynamic tactual communication systems*. Unpublished doctoral dissertation, University of California, Los Angeles, 1972.

Pritchard, E. A. B. Cutaneous tactile localization. *Brain*, 1931, *54*, 350–371.

Provins, K. A., & Morton, R. Tactile discrimination and skin temperature. *Journal of Applied Physiology*, 1960, *15*, 155–160.

Quilliam, T. A. The structure of finger print skin. In G. Gordon (Ed.), *Active touch. The mechanism of recognition of objects by manipulation: A multi-disciplinary approach*. Oxford: Pergamon, 1978.

Riggs, L. A. Vision. In J. W. Kling & L. A. Riggs (Eds.), *Woodworth & Schlosberg's experimental psychology* (3rd ed.), Vol. 1: *Sensation and perception*. New York: Holt, Rinehart & Winston, 1972.

Rollman, G. B. Electrocutaneous stimulation. In F.A. Geldard (Ed.), *Cutaneous communication systems and devices*. Austin, Tex.: The Psychonomic Society, 1974.

Rollman, G. B. Signal detection theory measurement of pain: A review and critique. *Pain*, 1977, *3*, 187–211.

Rose, J. E., & Mountcastle, V. B. Touch and kinesthesis. In J. Field, H. W. Magoun, & V. E. Hall (Eds.), *Handbook of physiology, Neurophysiology I*. Washington, D.C.: American Physiological Society, 1959.

Rosner, B. S. Neural factors limiting cutaneous spatiotemporal discriminations. In W. A. Rosenblith (Ed.), *Sensory communication*. New York: Wiley, 1961.

Rosner, B. S. Temporal interaction between electrocutaneous stimuli. *Journal of Experimental Psychology*, 1964, *67*, 191–192.

*Rothenberg, M., Verrillo, R. T., Zahorian, S. A., Brachman, M. L., & Bolanowski, S. J., Jr. Vibrotactile frequency for encoding a speech parameter. *Journal of the Acoustical Society of America*, 1977, *62*, 1003–1012.

Sachs, R. M., Miller, J. D., & Grant, K. W. Perceived magnitude of multiple electrocutaneous pulses. *Perception & Psychophysics*, 1980, *28*, 255–262.

Sato, M. Response of Pacinian corpuscles to sinusoidal vibration. *Journal of Physiology* (London), 1961, *159*, 391–409.

Saunders, F. A. Electrocutaneous displays. In F. A. Geldard (Ed.), *Cutaneous communication systems and devices*. Austin, Tex.: The Psychonomic Society, 1974.

Schmid, E. Temporal aspects of cutaneous interaction with two-point electrical stimulation. *Journal of Experimental Psychology*, 1961, *61*, 400–409.

Schori, T. R. A comparison of visual, auditory, and cutaneous tracking displays when divided attention is required to a cross-adaptive loading task. Unpublished doctoral dissertation, University of South Dakota, 1970.

Schori, T. R. Tracking performance as a function of precision of electrocutaneous feedback information. *Human Factors*, 1970, *12*, 447–452. (b)

Sherrick, C. E. Variables affecting sensitivity of the human skin to mechanical vibration. *Journal of Experimental Psychology*, 1953, *45*, 273–282.

Sherrick, C. E. Effect of background noise on the auditory intensive difference limen. *Journal of the Acoustical Society of America*, 1959, *31*, 239–242.

Sherrick, C. E. Observations relating to some common psychophysical functions as applied to the skin. In G. R. Hawkes (Ed.), *Symposium on cutaneous sensitivity*. Fort Knox: U. S. Army Medical Research Laboratory, 1960.

Sherrick, C. E. Effects of double simultaneous stimulation of the skin. *The American Journal of Psychology*, 1964, *77*, 42–53.

Sherrick, C. E. Temporal ordering of events in haptic space. *IEEE Transactions on Man–Machine Systems*, 1970, *MMS-11*, 25–28.

Sherrick, C. E. Current prospects for cutaneous communication. In F. A. Geldard (Ed.), *Cutaneous communication systems and devices*. Austin, Tex.: The Psychonomic Society, 1974.

Sherrick, C. E. The art of tactile communication. *American Psychologist*, 1975, *30*, 353–360.

Sherrick, C. E. The antagonisms of hearing and touch. In S. K. Hirsh, D. H. Eldredge, I. J. Hirsh, & S. R. Silverman (Eds.), *Hearing and Davis: Essays honoring Hallowell Davis*. St. Louis, Mo.: Washington University Press, 1976.

Sherrick, C. E. Cutaneous communication. In W. D. Neff (Ed.), *Contributions to sensory physiology* (Vol. 6). New York: Academic Press, 1982.

Sherrick, C. E., & Rogers, R. Apparent haptic movement. *Perception & Psychophysics*, 1966, *1*, 175–180.

Sherrington, C. S. *The integrative action of the nervous system*. London: Constable, 1906.

Shiffrin, R. H., Craig, J. C., & Cohen, E. On the degree of attention and capacity limitation in tactile processing. *Perception & Psy-*

chophysics, 1973, *13*, 328–336.

Sinclair, D. C. Cutaneous sensation and the doctrine of specific energy. *Brain*, 1955, *78*, 584–614.

*Sinclair, D. C. *Cutaneous sensation*. London: Oxford University Press, 1967.

Sinclair, D. C., & Stokes, B. A. R. The production and characteristics of "second pain." *Brain*, 1964, *87*, 609–618.

*Skramlik, E. von. Psychophysiologie der Tastsinne. *Archiv für die Gesamte Psychologie*, 1937, Ergänzungsband *4*.

Sparks, D. W. The identification of the direction of electrocutaneous stimulation along lineal multistimulator arrays. *Perception & Psychophysics*, 1979, *25*, 80–87.

Stevens, J. C. Thermo-tactile interactions: Some influences of temperature on touch. In D. R. Kenshalo (Ed.), *Sensory function of the skin of humans*. New York: Plenum, 1979. (a)

Stevens, J. C. Thermal intensification of touch sensation: Further extensions of the Weber phenomenon. *Sensory Processes*, 1979, *3*, 240–248. (b)

Stevens, J. C., & Green, B. G. Temperature–touch interaction: Weber's phenomenon revisited. *Sensory Processes*, 1978, *2*, 206–219.

Stevens, J. C., & Marks, L. E. Spatial summation and the dynamics of warmth sensation. *Perception & Psychophysics*, 1971, *9*, 391–398.

Stevens, J. C., Marks, L. E., & Simonson, D. Regional sensitivity and spatial summation in the warmth sense. *Physiology & Behavior*, 1974, *13*, 825–836.

Stevens, J. C., Okulicz, W. C., & Marks, L. E. Temporal summation at the warmth threshold. *Perception & Psychophysics*, 1973, *14*, 307–312.

Stevens, J. C., & Stevens, S. S. Warmth and cold: Dynamics of sensory intensity. *Journal of Experimental Psychology*, 1960, *60*, 183–192.

Stevens, J. C., & Stevens, S. S. Brightness function: Effects of adaptation. *Journal of the Optical Society of America*, 1963, *53*, 375–385.

Stevens, S. S., Cross-modality validation of subjective scales of loudness, vibration, and electric shock. *Journal of Experimental Psychology*, 1959, *57*, 201–209. (a)

Stevens, S. S. Tactile vibration: Dynamics of sensory intensity. *Journal of Experimental Psychology*, 1959, *57*, 210–218. (b)

Stevens, S. S. Tactile vibration: Change of exponent with frequency. *Perception & Psychophysics*, 1968, *3*, 223–228.

*Stevens, S. S. *Psychophysics: Introduction to its perceptual, neural, and social prospects*. New York: Wiley, 1975.

Stevens, S. S., Carton, A. S., & Shickman, G. M. A scale of apparent intensity of electric shock. *Journal of Experimental Psychology*, 1958, *56*, 328–338.

Stolwijk, J. A. J., & Hardy, J. D. Skin and subcutaneous temperature changes during exposure to intense thermal radiation. *Journal of Applied Physiology*, 1965, *20*, 1006–1013.

*Sweet, W. H. Pain. In J. Field, H. W. Magoun, & V. E. Hall (Eds.), *Handbook of physiology, Neurophysiology I*. Washington, D.C.: American Physiological Society, 1959.

*Talbot, W. H., Darian-Smith, I., Kornhuber, H. H., & Mountcastle, V. B. The sense of flutter-vibration: Comparison of the human capacity with response patterns of mechanoreceptive afferents from the monkey hand. *Journal of Neurophysiology*, 1968, *31*, 301–334.

Taus, R. F., Stevens, J. C., & Marks, L. E. Spatial localization of warmth. *Perception & Psychophysics*, 1975, *17*, 194–196.

Torebjörk, H. E. Activity in C nociceptors and sensation. In D. R. Kenshalo (Ed.), *Sensory functions of the skin of humans*. New York: Plenum, 1979.

*Tregear, R. T. *Physical functions of the skin*. New York: Academic Press, 1966.

Triggs, T. J., Levison, W. H., & Sanneman, R. Some experience with flight-related electrocutaneous and vibrotactile displays. In F. A. Geldard (Ed.), *Cutaneous communication systems and devices*. Austin, Tex.: The Psychonomic Society, 1974.

Tursky, B., Watson, P. D., & O'Connell, D. N. A concentric shock electrode for pain stimulation. *Psychophysiology*, 1965, *1*, 296–298.

Uttal, W. R. A comparison of neural and psychophysical responses in the somesthetic system. *Journal of Comparative and Physiological Psychology*, 1959, *52*, 485–490.

Uttal, W. R. Inhibitory interaction of responses to electrical stimuli in the fingers. *Journal of Comparative and Physiological Psychology*, 1960, *56*, 47–51.

Uttal, W. R., & Krissoff, M. Response of the somesthetic system to patterned trains of electrical stimuli. In D. R. Kenshalo (Ed.), *The skin senses*. Springfield, Ill.: Thomas 1968.

Vallbo, Å. B., Hagbarth, K. E., Torebjörk, H. E., & Wallin, B. G. Somatosensory, proprioceptive, and sympathetic activity in human peripheral nerves. *Physiological Reviews*, 1979, *59*, 919–957.

Vallbo, Å. B., & Johansson, R. S. The tactile sensory innervation of the glabrous skin of the human hand. In G. Gordon (Ed.), *Active touch. The mechanism of recognition of objects by manipulation: A multidisciplinary approach*. Oxford: Pergamon, 1978.

Vallbo, Å. B., & Johansson, R. S. Coincidence and cause: A discussion on correlations between activity in primary afferents and perceptive experience in cutaneous sensibility. In D. R. Kenshalo (Ed.), *Sensory functions of the skin of humans*. New York: Plenum, 1979.

Vernon, J. A., & Wessman, A. The effect of phase manipulation upon electrocutaneous stimulation. *Journal of Comparative and Physiological Psychology*, 1956, *49*, 293–296.

*Verrillo, R. T. A duplex mechanism of mechanoreception. In D. R. Kenshalo (Ed.), *The skin senses*. Springfield, Ill.: Thomas, 1968.

Verrillo, R. T. Vibrotactile intensity scaling at several body sites. In F. A. Geldard (Ed.), *Cutaneous communication systems and devices*. Austin, Tex.: The Psychonomic Society, 1974.

Verrillo, R. T. & Capraro, A. J. Effect of extrinsic noise on vibrotactile information processing channels. *Perception & Psychophysics*, 1975, *18*, 88–94.

Verrillo, R. T., & Chamberlain, S. C. The effect of neural density and contactor surround on vibrotactile sensation magnitude. *Perception & Psychophysics*, 1972, *11*, 117–120.

Verrillo, R. T., Fraioli, A. J., & Smith, R. L. Sensation magnitude of vibrotactile stimuli. *Perception & Psychophysics*, 1969, *6*, 366–372.

Verrillo, R. T., & Gescheider, G. A. Enhancement and summation in the perception of two successive vibrotactile stimuli. *Perception & Psychophysics*, 1975, *18*, 128–136.

Verrillo, R. T., & Gescheider, G. A. Effect of double ipsilateral stimulation on vibrotactile sensation magnitude. *Sensory Processes*, 1976, *1*, 127–137.

Verrillo, R. T., & Gescheider, G. A. Effect of prior stimulation on vibrotactile thresholds. *Sensory Processes*, 1977, *1*, 292–300.

Verrillo, R. T., & Gescheider, G. A. Backward enhancement and suppression of vibrotactile sensation. *Sensory Processes*, 1979, *3*, 249–260.

Vierck, C. J., & Jones, M. B. Size discrimination on the skin. *Science*, 1969, *63*, 488–489.

*Weber, E. H. The sense of touch. (*De Tactu*. H. E. Ross, trans., & *Der Tastsinn*, D. J. Murray, trans. Originally published in 1826.) New York: Academic Press, 1978.

Weddell, G., & Miller, S. Cutaneous sensibility. *Annual Review of Physiology* (Vol. 24). Palo Alto, Calif.: Annual Reviews, 1962, pp. 199–222.

*Weinstein, S. Intensive and extensive aspects of tactile sensitivity as a function of body part, sex, and laterality. In D. R. Kenshalo (Ed.), *The skin senses*. Springfield, Ill.: Thomas, 1968.

Weitz, J. Vibratory sensitivity as a function of skin temperature. *Journal of Experimental Psychology*, 1941, *28*, 21–36.

Werner, G., & Whitsel, B. L. Functional organization of somatosensory cortex. In A. I. Iggo (Ed.), *Handbook of sensory physiology: Somatosensory system* (Vol 2). New York: Springer-Verlag, 1973.

Wilska, A. On the vibrational sensitivity in different regions of the body surface. *Acta Physiologica Scandinavica*, 1954, *31*, 285–289.

Yakovlev, P. I., & Rakic, P. Patterns of decussation of bulbar pyramids and distribution of pyramidal tracts on two sides of the spinal cord. *Transactions of the American Neurological Assocation*, 1966, *91*,

337–370.

Zotterman, Y. Thermal sensations. In J. Field, H. W. Magoun, & V. E. Hall (Eds.), *Handbook of physiology, Neurophysiology I*. Washington, D.C.: American Physiological Society, 1959.

*Zotterman, Y. (Ed.) *Sensory function of the skin in primates, with special reference to man*. Oxford: Pergamon Press, 1976.

*Zwislocki, J. J. Theory of temporal auditory summation. *Journal of the Acoustical Society of America*, 1960, *32*, 1046–1060.

Zwislocki, J. J., & Ketkar, I. Loudness enhancement and summation in pairs of short sound bursts. *Journal of the Acoustical Society of America*, 1972, *51*, 140(A).

CHAPTER 13

KINESTHESIA

FRANCIS J. CLARK

Department of Physiology & Biophysics, University of Nebraska College of Medicine, Omaha, Nebraska

KENNETH W. HORCH

Department of Physiology, University of Utah School of Medicine, Salt Lake City, Utah

CONTENTS

Kinesthesia (or kinesthesis) taken literally means a sense of movement, though current usage of the term often includes a sense of static limb position as well. In this chapter, we use the term kinesthesia in the broadest sense to include the awareness of the positions and movements of the limbs and other body parts whether self-generated or externally imposed. We include, as well, sensations arising from the contractions of the muscles but exclude sensations arising from the visual and vestibular systems. We will use another term, *proprioception*, interchangeably with kinesthesia. Proprioception originally referred to sensations produced by action of the body itself, as distinct from exteroceptive sensations arising from the action of the external environment on the body. Now the term proprioceptive lacks a precise definition, but it usually connotes sensations of movement, position, and muscle tension arising from muscles and associated structures, such as tendons and joints, largely replacing the term *muscle sense*, which originally meant sensations believed associated with muscle contraction.

Our kinesthetic sense arises from activity in specialized sensory receptors that provide information about the angles of the joints, the lengths of the muscles and the tensions they produce, and the rates at which these values change. This chapter explores the nature of these kinesthetic sensations and describes the possible sources of the sensory input that elicit them.

1. HISTORICAL PERSPECTIVES

Our current understanding of the mechanisms underlying the kinesthetic sense differs remarkably little from views that prevailed at the turn of the century, although the intervening years saw these early ideas systematically challenged, discarded, reexplored, and finally reinstated.

The emphasis and controversy over these many years involved mainly the nature and the source of the sensory inflows that provide our kinesthetic awareness whether from skin, muscle, or joint, and the role played by an internal "sense of innervation," meaning a sensory experience resulting from some internal monitoring of the impulses originating in the brain and destined for the muscles.

During the nineteenth century, the concept of a sense of innervation prevailed, and some people believed that kinesthetic awareness arose entirely from such internally derived signals, with little contribution from sensory receptors (see Jones, 1972, for a discussion of the early development of these ideas). Helmholtz's experiments with eye movements provided a compelling argument favoring the sense of innervation hypothesis. Helmholtz (1867/1925) noted that when we voluntarily move our eyes, our visual surroundings seem to remain stationary; we merely shift our gaze. However, when we impose a comparable movement on the eye by pushing it with our finger, the visual world seems to jump about. Although the eyeball and the image on the retina might move the same way in each case, only the externally imposed movements cause any apparent shift in our surroundings. With movements we produce by our voluntary effort, our surroundings remain appropriately stationary. Similarly, if we attempt to shift the gaze voluntarily but now prevent any movement of the eye (e.g., by grasping the anesthetized sclera with a fine forceps), the visual world appears to shift even though the eye remains stationary and the subject remains largely unaware of the restraint. It seems that whether the visual world jumps about depends not upon the actual displacement of the eyeball or the retinal image but on whether the image shifts in the way we expect from our attempt to move the eyes voluntarily (see Brindley & Merton, 1960). From these and related experiments, Helmholtz concluded that our perception of eye movement and of the direction of gaze came not from sensory receptors that monitor the position of the eyeballs or the contractions of the muscles but from the effort of willing the eyes to move (a sense of "innervation"). The brain in some way compares shifts in the visual image to the internally generated command signals to move the eyes as outlined in Figure 13.1. Sperry (1950) later coined the term *corollary discharge* to specify that part of the command signals for muscle contraction fed back into the perceptual regions of the brain. Helmholtz's observations still stand as a convincing demonstration of a sense of innervation.

Another argument put forth in favor of a sense of innervation came from illusions of limb movement associated with the phantom-limb phenomenon. After an amputation, many persons have powerful illusions that the amputated limb, or portions of it, still exists, and they feel they can move the missing limb (see Henderson & Smyth, 1948, for descriptions of the phantom-limb phenomenon they observed while in a World War II prisoner-of-war camp). These illusions may come from abnormal activity arising from the *neuroma*, or tumor, that forms on the stump of a severed nerve as the fibers attempt to regrow, but more likely, the phantom arises from some internal *body schema* the brain has. Any kinesthetic sensations associated with attempts to flex or extend a phantom joint voluntarily would clearly need to arise internally because no sensory receptors remain to provide a sensation. However, as Goodwin, McCloskey, and Matthews (1972b) point out, when speaking of movement

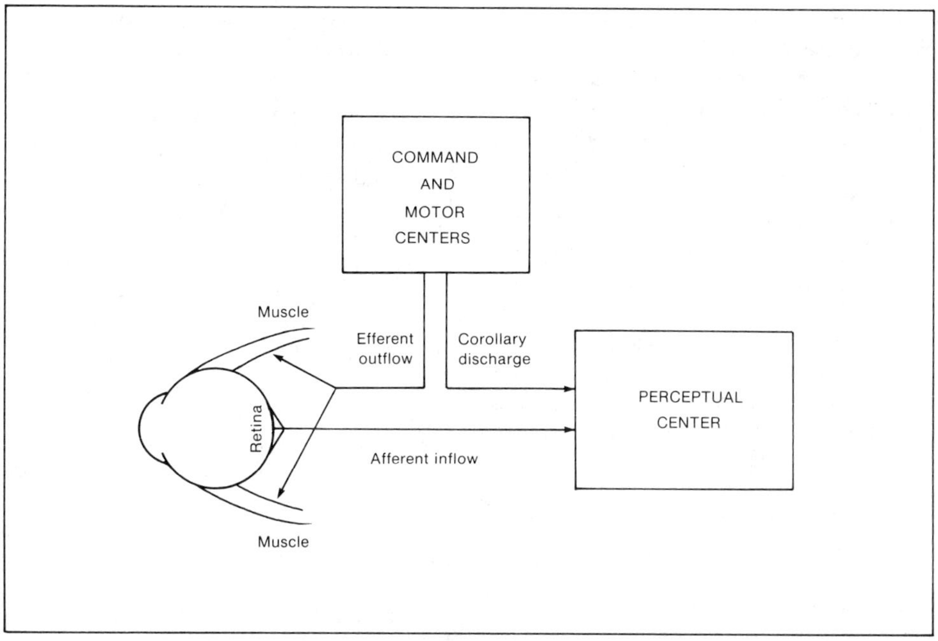

Figure 13.1. Corollary discharge. Sperry noted that rotating the eyes of a fish 180° around the visual axis caused the fish to swim in circles. He hypothesized that this resulted from an illusory spinning of the visual field. An image will move across the retina if either the object moves or the eye moves. In the latter case, self-movement does not cause an illusion that the environment moves because a corollary discharge is introduced into the visual centers to compensate for the retinal displacement. When the eye is rotated, this compensation fails (see Sperry, 1950). The figure shows a block diagram of the sources of perceptual input suggested by this hypothesis.

of a phantom limb, one must distinguish between a movement of the phantom as a whole, because the remaining stump moved, and a "bending" of a nonexistent joint within the phantom. Only the latter situation would involve the generation of new signals related to the phantom. Henderson and Smyth (1948) observed that amputees feel that they can bend a nonexistent joint only when some portion of the muscles that once moved the joint remains in the stump. Eliminate these bits of muscle and the sensory receptors they contain, and the person loses this feeling of movement. Therefore, the feeling that one can voluntarily bend a phantom joint does not demonstrate the existence of a sense of innervation.

The sense of innervation hypothesis began losing favor at the end of the nineteenth century, largely as a result of discoveries that revealed how importantly motor control depends on sensory information. The further discovery that muscles themselves contain sensory receptors provided another major blow to the hypothesis. The skin, muscles, and joints appeared to contain an abundance of sensory receptors to signal events happening in the limbs. Although at the time people knew almost nothing about the nature of the signals these receptors provided, one no longer needed to invoke a sense of innervation to explain kinesthetic sensation.

Sherrington, a physiologist of considerable authority, vigorously opposed the concept of a sense of innervation and favored sensory receptors in muscles as the main source of kinesthetic sensation. In a textbook of physiology published in 1900, he maintained that the sensation of innervation remained unproven, and he argued in favor of a muscle sense "based on a specific set of sensations obtained by accessory organs of movement" (Sherrington, 1900, p. 1006). He thought that our kinesthetic sense resulted largely from this muscle sense with some contributions from receptors in joints. The skin, he said, "does not much assist muscular sense," although "that it has some influence is undeniable" (p. 1011). Sherrington's views prevailed for about the next 50 years, but by the 1950s the view that receptors in muscles contributed to kinesthesia began to erode. New evidence emerged to argue, first, that signals from muscle receptors do not reach conscious levels and therefore cannot contribute to perception and, second, that kinesthesia depends vitally on joint receptors. (We now believe that muscle receptors do contribute to kinesthesia, whereas joint receptors seem hardly involved at all.)

Provins (1958), using finger joints, and Browne, Lee, and Ring (1954), using the joint of the big toe, found that deadening the joint and skin around the joint abolished a person's ability to detect passive (externally imposed) rotations of the joint. The muscles that move these joints lie in the forearm or the leg, so they would remain unaffected by the anesthetic. Therefore, eliminating skin and joint receptors, leaving only the muscle receptors, sufficed to abolish kinesthetic sensations. Their subjects could still voluntarily move the joint, but they could not detect whether an intended movement, restrained by the experimenter, had actually occurred; they appeared to lack a conscious muscle sense. Gelfan and Carter (1967) took a more direct approach to the question of a muscle sense by pulling on tendons exposed in the wrists of patients in surgery under a local anesthetic for the carpal tunnel syndrome. When they stretched the muscle by pulling on the tendon, taking care not to move the finger, their patients reported no kinesthetic sensations. However, if pulling the tendon moved a finger, the patient felt unmistakable movement of the correct finger. Merton (1964) summarized these results and the earlier arguments of Helmholtz to argue strongly against the possibility of any conscious muscle sense, favoring now a "joint" sense along with a sense of innervation.

Meanwhile, laboratory experiments in animals appeared to corroborate the lack of a conscious muscle sense observed in people and also to provide some neurological basis for its absence. Attempts failed to condition behavior in normal, awake cats or to elicit signs of arousal in their electroencephalogram (EEG) by electrical stimulation of nerve fibers from muscle receptors (Swett & Bourassa, 1967). However, similar stimulation of skin nerves proved quite effective for both conditioning behavior and producing arousal (Bourassa & Swett, 1967). Other studies at the time offered an explanation for why animals did not respond to stimulation of muscle nerves. It seemed that impulses from muscle receptors never reached those parts of the cerebral cortex believed dedicated to sensation. Early attempts failed to find electrical activity in the sensory cortex elicited by impulses in muscle receptor nerve fibers, yet one could elicit clear cortical responses from stimulation of cutaneous nerves (see Rose & Mountcastle, 1959, for a discussion and references). Obviously, the important task of regulating the contraction of muscles, served by the muscle receptors, remained best left to the subconscious portions of our nervous system.

Leksell (1945) unintentionally provided a finishing touch to the case against a muscle sense when he showed that the small-diameter nerve fibers innervating the muscle length receptors (the muscle spindles) served a motor function. The central nervous system could regulate the response of the spindle itself via *gamma-efferent* nerve fibers. Merton (1964) and others (see Rose & Mountcastle, 1959) argued that although muscle spindles respond to changes in muscle length, they also respond to activity in the gamma-efferent fibers, making them unsuitable to serve as absolute length detectors. Merton felt that "not only are signals from muscle receptors unsuited to subserve conscious position sense, but the information they do give if it reached consciousness, could only confuse" (p. 397).

Meanwhile, animal experiments presented evidence that the ligaments and capsules of joints contained many receptors that appeared ideally suited to encode joint angle and, therefore, to signal limb position. The regular and sustained discharge of these articular receptors correlated well with joint angle (Boyd & Roberts, 1953), and their location in the joint made them relatively insensitive to changes in muscle tension, at least compared with muscle receptors. Joint receptors thus seemed the ideal position sensors. Skoglund's (1956) study with the cat knee presented an especially appealing model of how joint receptors signal angle. He described a population of spatially tuned receptors in which the individual receptors responded over only a portion of the range of joint angles but as a group they covered the entire range (see Figure 13.32 (a)). Skoglund's model gained quick acceptance and found its way into many contemporary textbooks.

At about the same time, Mountcastle and his colleagues (Mountcastle & Powell, 1959) found cells in the sensory portions of the cerebral cortex of animals that showed sustained activity with discharge rates well correlated to joint angle and presumably driven by impulses from the joint receptors. Mountcastle apparently accepted Skoglund's model of spatially tuned receptors, although his own work revealed monotonically increasing or decreasing responses as a function of joint angle, quite unlike the presumed sharply tuned behavior of the joint receptors. Rose and Mountcastle in the 1959 *Handbook of Physiology* stated:

> It is now apparent that the sense of position or of movements of the joints depends solely on the appropriate receptors in the joints themselves. There is no need to involve a mysterious muscle sense to explain kinesthetic sensations and to do so runs contrary to all the known facts concerning the muscle stretch receptors. (p. 426)

Ten years later Burgess and Clark (1969) published their study of joint receptor responses from the cat knee, the same joint used for most of the previous work on articular receptors. They suspected that the previous work had employed highly biased methods of sampling the receptor population. When they examined the receptor responses over the whole range of joint angles, taking care to minimize sampling bias, a different picture emerged. The vast majority of receptors responded only near the extremes of flexion or extension of the joint, and those few units that did respond in the midrange of positions appeared incapable of encoding joint angle. They found no evidence for a population of spatially tuned receptors as proposed by Skoglund. Others have since found a similar absence of spatial tuning and a lack of activity over a wide range of intermediate joint angles in the cat wrist, elbow, and hip and the monkey knee. Joint receptors faced a major challenge in their role as the primary kinesthetic detectors.

Orthopedic surgeons apparently never favored the idea of a joint sense over a muscle sense, so when technology allowed, they began to replace various diseased joints (and their associated receptors) with metal and plastic. They saw no loss in a patient's kinesthetic sense. Laboratory tests on humans confirmed the preservation of kinesthesia with artificial hip or finger joints, or with anesthetized knee joints, where a subject's ability to sense joint rotations of only a few degrees remained essentially normal. Removal of the joint failed to cause the profound loss of position sense one might expect if joint receptors provided the main source of information about limb position.

For a while it seemed that perhaps no particular group of receptors made a clear contribution to kinesthesia. However, new and careful studies of sensations elicited from muscle receptors soon proved otherwise. Brown, Engberg, and Matthews (1967) demonstrated that vibration of only a few microns amplitude applied to the muscle tendon powerfully excites muscle spindle receptors. The vibration appeared rather selective for exciting the spindle primary endings, leaving the spindle secondary endings and the Golgi tendon organs much less influenced (see Figure 13.2 and Section 3.6). This same kind of vibration applied over a muscle tendon in humans produces striking illusions of movement of a limb that actually remains stationary (Goodwin, McCloskey, & Matthews, 1972b). If subjects ignore the movement sensations and pay attention to the position of the vibrated limb, they reveal that the limb feels somewhat more flexed or extended than its true position, depending on whether an extensor or a flexor muscle gets vibrated. Sometimes the limb might even feel in an impossible position clearly beyond its normal range (Craske, 1977). It would appear from such tests that not only can impulses from muscle receptors reach conscious levels but they can elicit clear and striking kinesthetic sensations. We should keep in mind that vibration constitutes an abnormal stimulus, and it may not reveal how the nervous system normally goes about sensing limb position and movement. Nonetheless, such tests demonstrate that we do possess a conscious muscle sense.

Most of the older experiments that searched unsuccessfully for a conscious muscle sense, when carefully repeated, yielded different results. Matthews and Simmonds (1974) pulled on finger muscle tendons exposed in the wrist during surgery, but in contrast to Gelfan and Carter's (1967) results, they discovered that patients could sense the stretch of a muscle. Moreover,

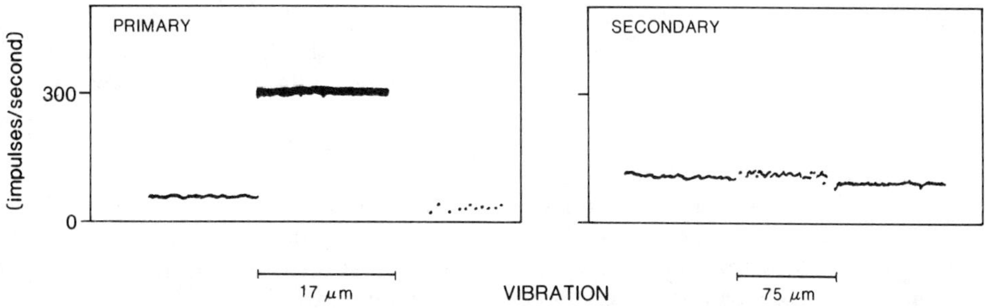

Figure 13.2. Effects of tendon vibration on muscle spindles. Shown are the firing rates of a primary and secondary muscle spindle ending in response to a logitudinal vibration at 300 Hz applied to the muscle, with a peak-to-peak amplitude as indicated. See Section 3.6 for a description of the differences between these two types of muscle spindle receptors. Note the vigorous response of the primary muscle spindle ending and the virtual absence of a response from the secondary ending. The soleus muscle was deefferented to eliminate any reflex contraction. (From M. C. Brown, I. E. Engberg, & P. B. C. Matthews. The relative sensitivity to vibration of muscle receptors of the cat, *Journal of Physiology*, 1967, *192*. Reprinted with permission.)

they had sensations of movement of the appropriate finger. These different results may have arisen because of the way the experimenters instructed their subjects. Gelfan and Carter (1967) had asked about sensations "referable to muscles," whereas Matthews and Simmonds concentrated on sensations at the fingers. More recently, McCloskey, Cross, Honner, and Potter (1983) repeated the experiment of pulling on exposed tendons and concluded, like Matthews and Simmonds, that stretch of a muscle does elicit kinesthetic sensations. McCloskey even had a tendon in his own foot severed to experience the sensation himself. It seems odd that the question of whether humans can sense stretch of a muscle would remain unresolved for so long, but recently Moberg (1983), in the very same journal as McCloskey and colleagues (1983), reported a similar experiment involving pulling on tendons but with the opposite results. Moberg, agreeing with the earlier findings of Gelfan and Carter, concluded that subjects could not sense stretch of their muscles. The reasons for these differences remain obscure, but for such differences to still exist underscores the difficulty in getting answers to seemingly simple, straightforward questions about kinesthesia.

Goodwin, McCloskey, and Matthews (1972b, 1972c) retested position sense in the fingers with the hand anesthetized, a condition that previous reports had claimed abolished kinesthetic sense in the fingers (Browne, Lee, & Ring, 1954; Provins, 1958). Goodwin and coworkers (1972a, 1972b) found that the sense of finger movement, although blunted by the anesthesia, remained. It seems that previous experimenters had moved the fingers too slowly; subjects would probably have easily detected more rapid movements. Again, contrary to previous results, their subjects could sense when the experimenter unexpectedly restrained an intended voluntary movement of the finger. The long muscles in the forearm, unaffected by anesthesia of the hand, apparently on their own can elicit sensations of finger movement. That anesthesia of the hand substantially blunts kinesthetic sensation did emerge as one finding all such studies with the fingers have in common.

Several laboratories have since demonstrated convincingly that impulses from muscle receptors reach both the sensory and the motor areas of the cerebral cortex, providing us with at least some neurological basis for the perception of their activity (Landgren & Silfvenius, 1969; McIntyre, 1962; Oscarsson & Rosén, 1963).

The new findings as a whole have again placed muscle receptors in the forefront as candidates for the kinesthetic detectors (Matthews, 1982). Most researchers would probably still include as candidates the receptors in joints, although we think they contribute relatively little to kinesthesia. The role of cutaneous receptors remains less clear. We think that skin receptors can signal joint movement but not joint position. This "new" understanding of kinesthesia appears remarkably similar to the views that existed at the turn of the century. However, the new view goes even further toward reconfirming the existence of a sensation of innervation. Sherrington seemed to consider the sense of innervation as counter to the view that peripheral sense organs mediate sensation, and so he discarded sense of innervation because it did not explain such effects as our ability to sense passive (externally imposed) movements. However, Helmholtz's observations with the eye endure as powerful arguments favoring a sense of innervation, one that coexists with a sensory system that depends on information from peripheral receptors.

This chapter reviews several of the experiments that have led to our current understanding of kinesthesia. Though we may have altered the conclusions drawn originally from the older studies in light of subsequent evidence, the data can still provide us with useful information about human kinesthetic ability.

2. PSYCHOPHYSICS OF KINESTHESIA

Our knowledge of kinesthesia comes mainly from psychophysical studies with humans, studies that probe the dimensions and the nature of the kinesthetic experience, seek to reveal what kinds of information the nervous system requires for kinesthesia, and to locate the sources of this information.

Kinesthesia encompasses several different aspects of our awareness of the movements and relative positions of the various parts of our bodies, and the consequences of contracting our muscles. We possess an awareness of both the rate and the direction of movement of our limbs, whether voluntarily produced or externally imposed, and of the static position when movement has stopped. We can gauge the amount of weight supported by a limb or the force produced by contraction of our muscles. And we have a sense of the "effort" necessary to contract our muscles. This section considers each of these dimensions in turn.

2.1. Perception of Passive Movements

2.1.1. Methods. Most tests of limb-movement sense involve passively flexing or extending a joint and asking for a signal when the subject feels the movement or can identify its direction. Subjects generally can perceive that a movement has occurred before they can sense its direction (Laidlaw & Hamilton, 1937), and McCloskey (1978) argues that any true test of proprioception requires identification of direction. Typically, the joint, out of view of the subject, gets rotated at a uniform rate using a motor-driven apparatus that provides a smooth, steady movement with a minimum of vibration. The limb or digit rests in a carrier or a clamp lightly but firmly grips the part with care to minimize tactile cues. Rotation begins after a warning signal, and the subjects give an indication as soon as they feel the movement with confidence. Generally, the subject has instructions not to guess but to wait for a sufficiently clear sensation. To score a subject's performance, one notes the displacement required for reliable detection at each velocity tested. Smaller displacements would indicate a higher movement acuity.

Having the subject make a response while the movement progresses can introduce errors because of reaction time, especially with fast movements. To eliminate reaction time errors, the experimenter can present runs of fixed-amplitude excursions and allow the subject a few seconds after movement has stopped to make a judgment. To score a subject's performance, the experimenter records, for each velocity, the amplitude where the subject could correctly identify the movement or its direction a certain percentage of the trials (e.g., 70%).

The experimenter might include dummy (no movement) trials and/or a variable time delay between the warning signal and the onset of movement to discourage guessing. The subject tries for the highest score possible while maintaining false-alarm rate (mistaking dummy trials for movements) as low as possible. The experimenter might set the maximum permissible false-alarm rate at some small value like 5%. Unless instructed to minimize false alarms, subjects will use their own strategies, some with a conservative approach to avoid mistakes, while others might opt for a high score with less concern for errors. One must clearly establish the criterion for the task and take into account any subject bias in order to compare results from one subject to the next or even from one time to the next with the same subject. Signal detection theory (see Chapter 1 by Falmagne) offers a powerful method of accounting for subject bias. Note that these comments about establishing a criterion and accounting for subject bias apply to most of the tests we discuss in this section.

Another type of test uses a fixed displacement (method of constant stimulus) presented at some variable delay after a warning signal. The subject then has a brief period of time to indicate whether a movement ocurred and/or to tell its direction. This method has the advantage of eliminating errors introduced by a subject's reaction time. The subject receives instructions to try for a high score but not to guess. One scores the subject's performance by computing the percentage of correct choices at each of several different rates of rotation. Variations on this method include moving in only one direction or having the subject tense the muscles or support a load during the movement.

2.1.2. Results from Tests of Movement Perception. The various methods used to evaluate perception of passive joint rotation have yielded reasonably comparable results, although one sees variations in the minimum detectable displacement with the same subject on different occasions and from one subject to the next. These variations often become obscured by the presentation of the data as mean values (Cleghorn & Darcus, 1952).

Proximal joints (those closer to the torso) appear to have a smaller minimum detectable angle with passive movements than do distal joints (see Sherrington, 1900). This seems an intuitively reasonable finding if one associates minimum detectable angle with the accuracy of our awareness of limb position, as most authors have done. For example, a small error in setting the angle of a proximal joint like the shoulder with its long radius arm would affect positioning of the finger tip much more than a comparable angular error in a distal finger joint.

Laidlaw and Hamilton (1937), using a rate of rotation of 10° /min, compared various joints on the right and left sides of the body in subjects classified as younger or older than 40 years, for the purpose of establishing reference values useful in clinical testing of movement sense in patients. They established threshold values (the smallest excursion required for detection) by averaging the results from five trials (three with older subjects) for each joint in each direction. Table 13.1 summarizes their findings. They found no right–left (R–L) differences, so the values in the table represent the combined R–L data. They noted a slight tendency for smaller minimum detectable angles with the proximal joints that with the distal joints. Laidlaw and Hamilton emphasized that the hip had the greatest sensitivity, but their data show the minimum detectable angle for the hip differs from several other joints by only 0.1° .

Laidlaw and Hamilton's values for the smallest detectable angle differed from the values reported earlier by Goldscheider

Table 13.1. The Smallest Rotation of the Joint Subjects Can Detect: A Comparison of Several Joints and Subjects in Two Age Groups

	Threshold Displacement in Degrees			
	Under 40 yrs of Age		Over 50 yrs of Age	
Joint	Up	Down	Up	Down
Shoulder	0.4	0.3	0.5	0.5
Elbow	0.4	0.4	0.5	0.7
Wrist	0.3	0.5	0.5	0.5
First MCP	0.5	0.6	0.5	0.5
Second MCP	0.5	0.5	0.5	0.5
Third MCP	0.4	0.4	0.6	0.5
Fourth MCP	0.4	0.5	0.6	0.6
Fifth MCP	0.5	0.7	0.5	0.5
Hip	0.2	0.2	0.4	0.5
Knee	0.3	0.3	0.5	0.6
Ankle	0.3	0.3	0.5	0.6
First MTP	0.7	0.7	not done	not done

The table lists the smallest externally imposed (passive) excursion at a velocity of 10°/min that younger (<40 years) and older subjects could detect with different joints. The examiner moved the joint at a constant rate by turning a crank in synchrony with a metronome. The subjects responded when they sensed the direction of movement, whereupon the examiner stopped cranking and noted the angular displacement. The table lists modal (not mean) values of this minimum displacement needed for detection for 20 subjects in each of the two age groups (right and left sides combined). The authors note that subjects showed considerable variability, so one should consider as abnormal only values more than twice those listed. MCP = metacarpophalangeal, MTP = metatorsophalangeal. (From Laidlaw & Hamilton, 1937.)

Table 13.2 The Smallest Angular Excursions of the Elbow Joint Subjects Can Detect: A Comparison of the Results from Different Investigators

Investigator	Number of Subjects	Range of Speeds (Degree/sec)	Range of Thresholds (Degrees)
Goldscheider (1889)	1	0.7–1.4	0.40–0.76 ^1
Pillsbury (1901)	3	0.33	0.43–0.85 ^2
Winter (1912)	7	0.08–0.56	0.20–2.80 ^2
Laidlaw & Hamilton (1937)	60	0.16	0.30–2.50 ^2
Cleghorn & Darcus (1952)	4	0.10–0.25	0.80–1.80 ^3

All the tests listed used passive (externally imposed) movement of the joint, with ^1 = threshold defined as the value "just perceived" on half or more of the trials, ^2 = average value of displacement where subjects perceived movement, and ^3 = direction of movement identified correctly on 80% of the trials. (From Cleghorn & Darcus, 1952.)

(1889; also in Sherrington, 1900). However, one cannot always compare results from different studies in a meaningful way because of differences in procedure, in the definition of "threshold," and in the rates of rotation used. Cleghorn and Darcus (1952), addressing this problem, compared the threshold sensitivity of the elbow obtained from four different studies, plus their own. They found a range of 0.2–2.80° (Table 13.2), with their own values falling within this range. Nonetheless, despite differences in actual angular values, Laidlaw and Hamilton (1937) drew the same conclusions as Goldscheider: proximal joints have a greater sensitivity to movement (i.e., a smaller minimum discriminable angle) than distal joints. Sherrington (1900) had explained this observation by noting that proximal joints such as the shoulder or hip move more slowly than the distal joints because of the longer length of their lever. Therefore, it stands to reason they ought to show a greater sensitivity to movement. Hall and McCloskey (1983) reconfirmed with the finger, elbow, and shoulder that the more proximal joints do move the more slowly when subjects do a pointing task in their own time. They also discovered that the velocities subjects use spontaneously fall in a range where the joints show a high sensitivity to passive movement (see Figure 13.3 and a further discussion of the Hall and McCloskey work below). Other values for the minimum excursions needed to perceive movement with various joints appear in Table 13.3.

A major problem when attempting to establish thresholds for detection of movements and displacements of different joints stems from an interaction between rate and displacement (Figure 13.3). Joint rotation so slow that it goes unnoticed with a small excursion may become apparent with a larger excursion. Similarly, a displacement too small for perception at one rate may become apparent at a faster rate.

Hall and McCloskey (1983) reexamined proprioception in proximal versus distal joints and tested how the minimum detectable excursion varied with rate of movement. They tested the shoulder, the elbow, and the terminal joint of the middle finger. At each of several angular velocities, they varied the excursion until they found an amplitude where the subject could correctly identify the direction of the movement 70% of the time. Figure 13.3(a) shows how the 70% detection levels varied versus angular velocity for the three joints tested. With all three joints, the slower the velocity, the larger the excursion needed by subjects to detect the movement, and this velocity–excursion interaction showed most prominantly with the finger.

As one might have expected, the finger showed the poorest acuity; subjects required considerably larger excursions at all velocities to sense finger movements than they needed to detect elbow or shoulder movements. However, when Hall and McCloskey recomputed their data to express rotation of all three joints in terms of linear velocity of the finger tip (instead of angular velocity of each joint itself), an opposite ordering resulted. The distal joint (finger) emerged as superior to the proximal joint (shoulder) with the elbow falling in between (Figure 13.3[b]). To position our fingers accurately, these three joints (and others) must act together, and findings such as these underscore the close matching between the various joints to perform this common task. No joint shows better performance than any other, but each does what it does quite adequately. The authors went a step further and converted angular velocity of the joint into rate of stretch of the muscles that move the joint (Figure 13.3 [c]). When compared according to velocity of muscle stretch, all three joints appeared similar. This similarity supports the idea that the central nervous system pays close attention to activity in muscle stretch receptors for proprioception.

Most likely some complex interaction exists between rate and displacement in the detection of movement, but some of the apparent interaction may stem from flaws in the experiments. Subjects may use different mental processes to make position and movement discriminations (see Burgess, Horch, & Tuckett, 1983) and become confused if they must attend to both variables. We found in our own experiments that subjects given no instruction tended to pay more attention to movement sensations than to position sensations. Subjects experienced in making movement discriminations might tend to miss subtle positional sensations. Thus an experiment intended to measure both position and movement senses may turn out, in fact, to measure only movement sense.

Tensing the muscles that move the fingers can enhance the perception of movements imposed on the finger joints. This becomes quite evident with anesthesia of either the whole hand or just a finger joint including the surrounding skin, which substantially reduces perception of movement at the joint. Tensing the muscles that move the joint seems to restore much though not all of the sensitivity to movement (see Goodwin, McCloskey, & Matthews, 1972b, 1972c, for a discussion of the effects of finger anesthesia). Patients who have a spastic weakness of the fingers (a sustained involuntary contraction of the muscles superimposed upon a partial loss of voluntary control) experience much less loss of movement sense in fingers experimentally rendered anesthetic than do normal subjects (Chambers & Gilliatt, 1954). The tensing of their muscles, even though involuntary, preserves movement sense to a large degree. Patients with a flaccid paralysis (relaxed muscles with a loss of voluntary control) experience the usual, substantial loss of movement perception in anesthetized fingers. We do not know how tensing muscles improves movement sense, but tensing likely enhances the responses of receptors in the muscles.

2.2. Perception of Position

2.2.1. Methods. Position sense tests usually require a subject to judge the orientation of a limb or a digit and to provide some measurable indication of the perception of its position.

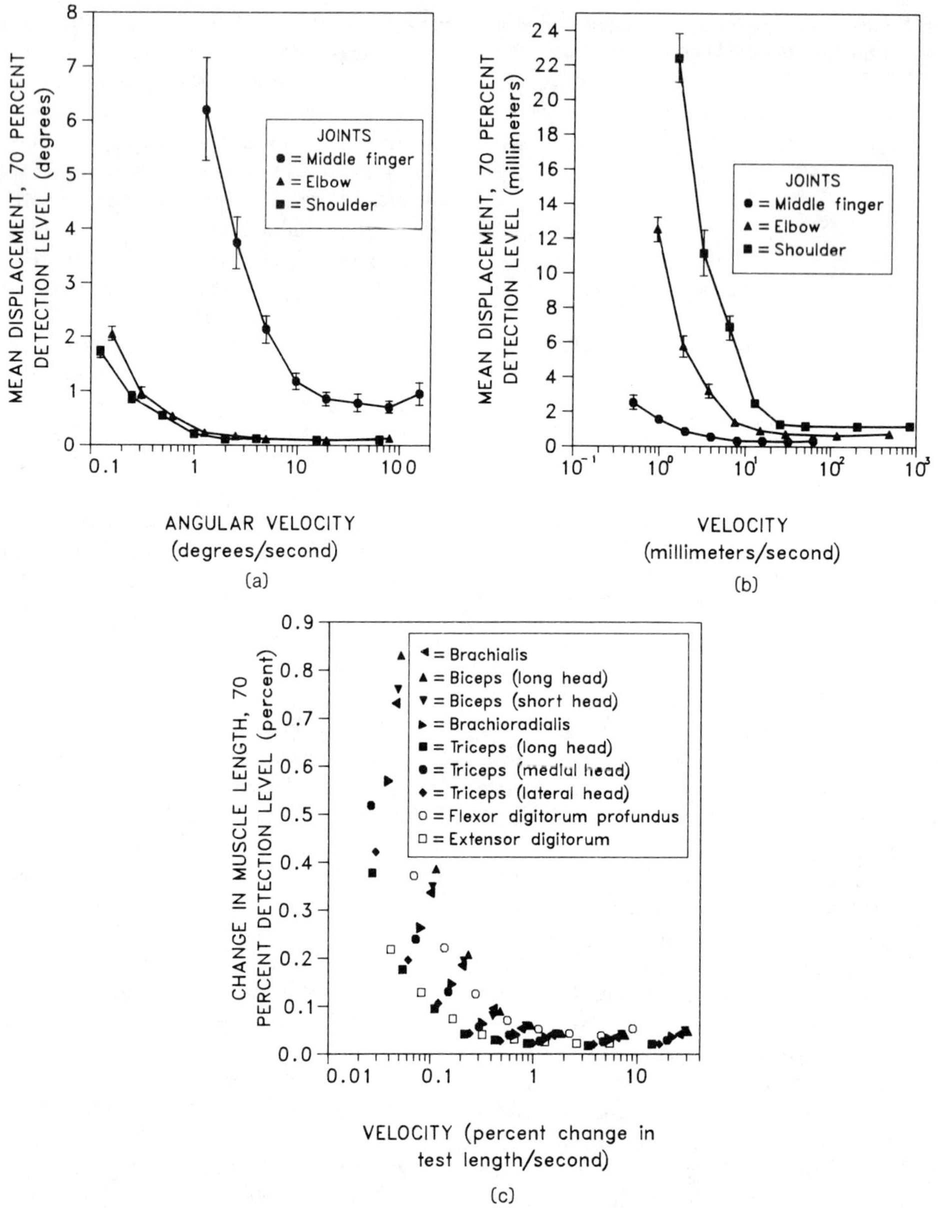

Figure 13.3. Detection thresholds for movements of different forelimb joints. The arm was comfortably positioned in an apparatus that passively moved the joint to be tested and shielded it from the view of the subject. A movement of a given amplitude and velocity was made, and the subject was asked to identify the direction of movement upon its completion. The data shown are from ten subjects. The graphs illustrate the mean (± standard error of the mean) in (a) displacement necessary for 70% correct nomination of direction of movement of randomly mixed flexions and extensions imposed at various velocities (on a log scale). Data from the terminal middle finger joint are given as circles, for the elbow joint as triangles, and for the shoulder joint as squares. (a) The data expressed in terms of angular velocity and displacement of the joint. At all angular velocities tested, larger angular displacements were required for 70% detection for the finger joint than for the more proximal joints. (b) The data expressed in terms of linear velocity and displacement. Assessed in these terms proprioceptive performance is superior at more distal joints. (c) The data expressed in terms of percentage change in muscle length for different muscles. Muscles operating the elbow joint are shown as filled symbols, and muscles operating at the distal joint of the middle finger are shown as open symbols. Assessed in these terms, proprioceptive performance is similar at the elbow and finger joint, particularly over the range of optimal performance. (From L. A. Hall & D. I. McCloskey, Detections of movements imposed on finger, elbow, and shoulder joints, *Journal of Physiology*, 1983, *335*. Reprinted with permission.)

Table 13.3. The Smallest Angular Excursions of the Joints Subjects Can Detect: A Comparison of Several Joints and Values Obtained from Different Investigators.

Joint (Investigator)	Number of Subjects	Velocity (Degree/sec)	Average Threshold (Degree)
Hip (Grigg, Finerman, & Riley, 1973)	2	0.15	0.22 ˆ1
	7	0.6	0.66 ˆ2
Second MCP (Provins, 1958)	12	0.63	6.10 ˆ2,3 5.47 ˆ2,4 4.20 ˆ2,5
Second and fifth MCP and first MTP (Kokmen, Bossemeyer, & Williams, 1977)	14	0.5 ˆ6 5.0	0.8–1.0 0.4–0.6
First MTP (Browne, Lee, & Ring, 1954)	82	1 & 2	4.4 ˆ2

All the tests used passive (externally imposed) movements of the joints. Note that MCP = metacarpophalangeal (finger joint); MTP = metatarsophalangeal (toe joint); ˆ1 = method of constant stimuli (constant amplitude displacement); ˆ2 = the joint moved passively at a constant rate, and the subjects indicated when they had a definite sensation of movement; ˆ3 = finger relaxed; ˆ4 = with voluntary flexion (25–50-g force); ˆ5 = with voluntary extension (25–50-g force); and ˆ6 = sinusoidal rotation of the joint with a slowly increasing amplitude until the subject perceived the movement, whereupon the amplitude decreased until the sensation disappeared: threshold defined as amplitude halfway between these two values. Movement at 0.5 Hz gives a maximum velocity of 1.26–1.57°/sec for the amplitudes used, and 5.0 Hz corresponds to peak velocities in the range 6.28–9.42°/sec.

Performance of this task involves two separate steps: presentation of the target position by the experimenter and indication of the perceived location by the subject. The experimenter must take care to eliminate visual and other nonkinesthetic cues in at least one of these steps. Almost all these tests use some sort of screen or other means to prevent the subject from viewing the limb under test.

The usual test involves position sense with a single joint, such as the hip, knee, shoulder, elbow, ankle, wrist, or a finger joint. Here, joint angle provides the most convenient measure of position. Some tests involve the combined movement of several joints, for example, where a subject must point to some location in three-dimensional space with no restriction on arm movement. In this kind of test, the linear distance between the target and the indicated positions often provides the most convenient measure of joint position. Sections 2.2.1.1 to 2.2.1.3 outline the commonly used methods of testing position sense in the limbs and digits.

2.2.1.1. Methods of Presenting the Target Position

2.2.1.1(a) Passive Placement. The experimenter moves the subject's relaxed limb to the target position, usually after having made several large excursions to try to confound movement cues. In many tests an apparatus supports the limb to provide smooth rotation at a constant speed and allow accurate setting of angular position.

2.2.1.1(b) Active Positioning. The subject moves his or her own limb as directed by the experimenter. The subject may move the limb through large excursions until told to stop or may move the limb until it strikes a mechanical stop. Some tests have the subject move the limb or digit at a prescribed speed, whereas others make no restrictions in speed.

2.2.1.1(c) Visual Presentation. The subject briefly views a target in space, specified by its location along some line or arc or in a plane. In some tests the subject can see the entire target area with the desired position marked by a pointer or a tab. Features in the background must not provide the subject with an opportunity to develop a strategy that might bias the tests. In other tests, a spot of light on a screen in a darkened room serves as the target.

2.2.1.1(d) Verbal Presentation. The experimenter specifies target location, usually along some scale familiar to the subject. For example, the subject might imagine a protractorlike scale in a horizontal plane with the 0° position straight ahead and the 90° position to the right or left. To ensure familiarity, the subject could practice locating points expressed in degrees along the scale. The distance from some established reference point or the coordinates on some imaginary grid might also serve as measures of position.

2.2.1.2. Methods of Indicating Perceived Target Position. These methods involve variations of those used for presenting target position but with some differences in procedure.

2.2.1.2(a) Passive Positioning. A carrier of some type supports the limb or digit so the subject can keep the part relaxed. To indicate the position of the target, the subject either verbally instructs the experimenter how to move the limb or perhaps manipulates a control that moves the carrier.

2.2.1.2(b) Active Positioning. The subject simply moves the limb or digit to the perceived target location by contracting the muscles in the normal way. The movements usually have some restrictions imposed; for example, in an experiment with the shoulder, the subject might receive instructions to hold the arm outstretched in front of his or her body and to make only vertical movements.

2.2.1.2(c) Active Pointing. The subject points with the index finger to the perceived location of some part of the body, usually the opposite limb. This method differs from the preceding two in that it typically involves movement of several joints. Frequently, a screen hides one or both limbs from view and the subject must point to some part of the target limb, such as the finger tip, a knuckle, or the wrist. The subject does not actually touch the target part but makes a mark on an overlying screen to serve as a pointer for measuring the distance between the actual and the indicated positions. By using a transparent screen, one can photograph the limb in place under the marked screen and measure positional errors from an enlargement of this permanent record. Pointing has an additional advantage of familiarity to the subject.

2.2.1.2(d) Visual Indication. The subject indicates position by reading aloud a number or a letter from a scale or the coordinates from a grid. Altering the scale in some unpredictable way between trials helps discourage guessing or the adoption of undesired strategies. Alternatively, the subject may receive a visual presentation that includes one correct choice among several alternatives or may manipulate a control to position a spot or a line on a screen.

2.2.1.2(e) Verbal Indication. The subject verbally states the perceived location on some imaginary scale or perhaps the perceived distance between two points expressed in some familiar or comfortable units.

2.2.1.3. Limitations of the Methods. The number of factors that can complicate position sense tests, plus the variety of methods used, makes it difficult to compare data between experiments. The usual pitfalls that plague psychophysical ex-

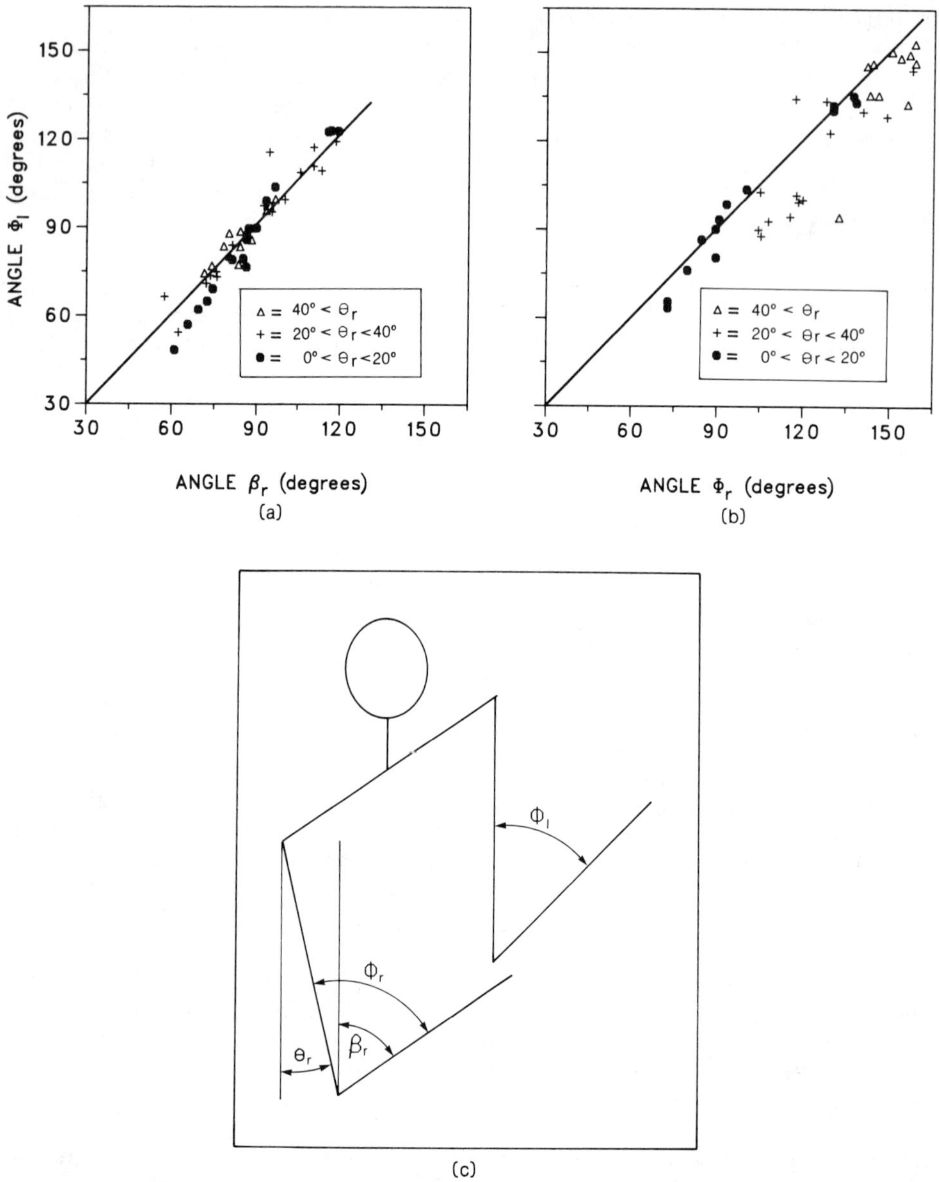

Figure 13.4. Comparison of the sense of limb orientation and sense of joint angle. Angles are defined in (c). The angle between the vertical and the upper arm is denoted by θ_r for the right arm and θ_e for the left arm. The left arm was kept vertical so $\theta = 0$. The angle of the elbow is denoted by ϕ. For the left arm, the angle of the elbow was the same as the angle between the vertical and the forearm. For the right arm, this angle is denoted by β. The data shown are from one subject, and each point represents one trial. (a) The results from experiment where the subject attempted to match the orienation of forearms (i.e., to equalize ϕ_l and β_r). Plotted is the angle between the left arm and the vertical as a function of the angle between the right arm and the vertical. (b) The results from attempts to reproduce the same amount of extension of the elbow (i.e., to equalize ϕ_l and ϕ_r). Plotted is the angle of the left elbow as a function of the angle of the right elbow. The subjects did significantly better at matching orientation in space than in matching joint angle. For all six subjects tested, the standard deviation of the error was 9.6° when matching elbow angles. This was statistically significantly ($p < .005$) greater than the 6.7° standard deviation observed when matching limb orientation. (From J. F. Soechting, Does position sense at the elbow reflect a sense of elbow joint angle or one of limb orientation? *Brain Research*, 1982, *248*. Reprinted with permission.)

periments in general exist here. These include the introduction of experimenter bias; the presence of unintentional or unknown extraneous cues that may influence the subject; the availability to the subject of certain strategies he or she may use, however unwittingly, to circumvent the intended purpose of the experiment; and the effects of fatigue, boredom, and the different reinforcement schedules used in various tests (e.g., see Sebeok & Rosenthal, 1981).

To this we must add secondary variables an experimenter might easily overlook. For instance, in a task where a free-standing subject points to a fixed target, body sway can introduce an unknown error in the position measurement. Tasks that seem simple and straightforward may, in fact, require subjects to make unfamiliar judgments that give the impression of poor accuracy. Granit (1978) discusses how an experimenter can get misleading information from tests that may have relevance to the experimenter but not necessarily to the subjects. Though he cites animal experiments, his comments apply as well to humans. As an example, matching the angles of the elbows certainly would seem a reasonable test of our basic position sense ability, but Soechting (1982) has recently shown that subjects can match orientations of the arms in space more accurately than they can match elbow joint angles (Figure 13.4). Adequate training with a task might minimize errors introduced by a novel situation, but training may introduce its own biases. Subjects may unwittingly develop strategies to circumvent the purpose of the test or learn to use the subtlest cues from the apparatus, the procedure, or the experimenter (Sebeok & Rosenthal, 1981).

Another major problem with devising a test for position or movement sense involves separating these two parameters. One cannot have a movement without a change in position and vice versa, and a subject might confuse movement cues and positional cues. For studies that seek to determine the underlying sensory mechanisms, a distinction between movement and position becomes important. Finally, it remains unclear whether mean error or variable error (standard deviation) better assesses the accuracy of a positional match. Mean error, the more commonly used measure, ignores the possibility of a precise sense of position but with the addition of a consistent offset or bias. In this case a significant "error" results even though the subject may reliably match to this offset position with little variability. In the opposite case, a subject may have almost no idea of the true position of the target but might match around some intermediate position close to the target angle resulting in a large variability but only a small mean error.

With these caveats in mind, we survey the results from several representative studies that deal with perception of the static positions of the joints.

2.2.2. Results from Tests of Position Perception. Most position sense studies with the limbs or digits have dealt with the sensory mechanisms that underlie this perception. We therefore have information about our position sense performance only under a few limited and specialized conditions. Nonetheless, the data can provide us with a reasonable estimate of "what we can do." Sections 2.2.2.1 to 2.2.2.8 examine the accuracy of our sense of position, including some factors that seem to affect this position sense.

2.2.2.1. Accuracy of Position Sense. The accuracy of matching or reproducing target positions can vary over time and between subjects (Figures 13.5 and 13.6). McCloskey (1980) tested the accuracy of matching elbow position in a population of 50 normal, sighted individuals and seven normal but congenitally blind subjects. His subjects sat with the tips of their elbows resting on a table before them and with their forearms free to move in a vertical plane. A clear plastic screen marked out in degrees and placed between the arms served to measure elbow angle. The subject moved one forearm as directed by the experimenter and placed the tip of the index finger on the scale at some angle between 10 and 110° of full extension. Ten sec after establishing this target angle, the subject moved the opposite forearm and attempted to touch the tips of his or her index fingers together (the plastic screen prevented the fingers from actually touching). Subjects made five estimates at each of five different target angles (10, 20, 50, 70, and 80°). Figure 13.7 illustrates the distribution of matching error for each of the 57 subjects. Note that each subject had a particular bias in the perception of the target position (as indicated by the mean values of the angle errors), but all the subjects matched to this perceived angle with about the same precision (as indicated by the similar values of the standard deviation).

In another, similar test of elbow position sense, McCloskey (1973) used the same target angle for all trials (50° from full extension). Table 13.9 (the column labeled "Control") illustrates the different bias or offset (mean error) from one subject to the

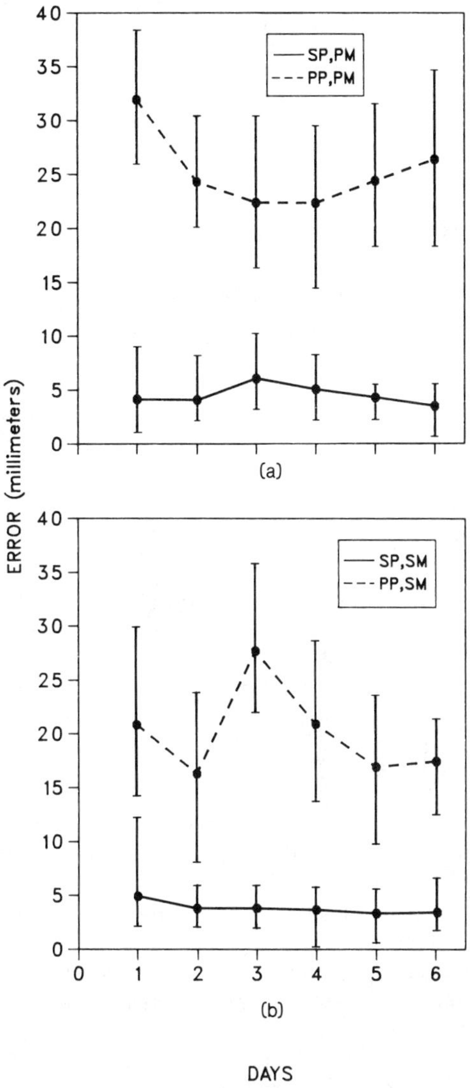

Figure 13.5. Variability in judging joint position. Shown are mean errors and interquartile ranges in judging the final position of one hand with the other hand. The subject's left hand was positioned along a vertical track, either actively or passively, and maintained there, either actively or passively. The position of the left hand was then matched, 0–12 sec later, with the right hand moving along a parallel vertical track. Each data point is based on 40 trials. Graph (a) shows passively maintained, and graph (b) shows actively (self-) maintained trials. Note; SP = self-positioned; PP = passively positioned; SM = self-maintained; and PM = passively maintained. Although there was no training effect, there was daily variability in the accuracy of the matches. (From J. Paillard & M. Brouchon, A proprioceptive contribution to the spatial encoding of position cues for ballistic movements, *Brain Research*, 1968, *71*. Reprinted with permission.)

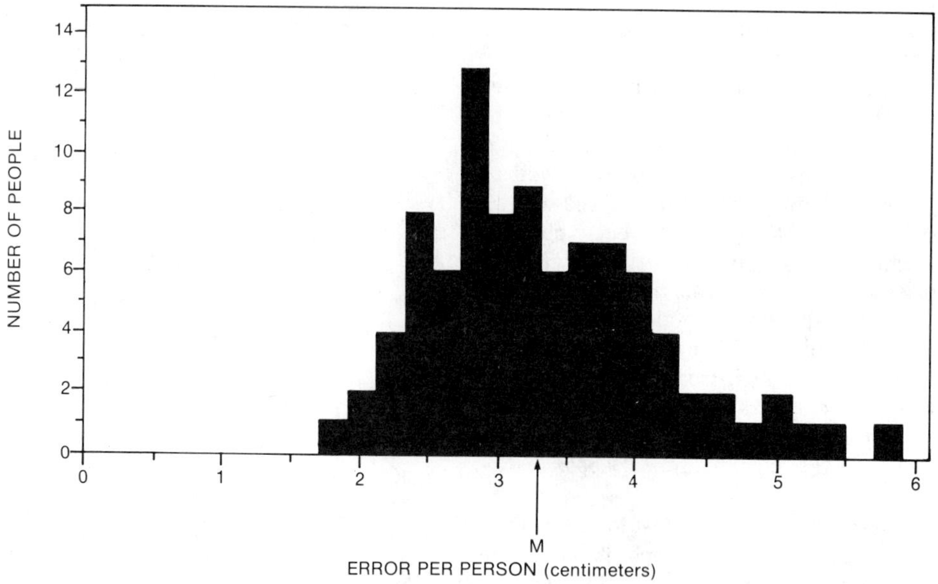

Figure 13.6. Distribution of overall shoulder position sense accuracy in 91 young adults. The subject used the arm to point to a visually presented reference point. After closing the eyes, the subject lowered the arm and then again pointed to the target 2–8 sec later. Data are based on one trial pointing to each of 48 reference points. Note the large variation in accuracy among the subject population. (From L. A. Cohen, Analysis of position sense in human shoulder, *Journal of Neurophysiology*, 1958, *21*. Reprinted with permission.)

next, although each subject matched the offset position with a similar precision as indicated in this case by the standard error. One sees a similar variability in accuracy with constancy in precision between subjects with the knee (see Figure 13.15 in Section 2.2.2.4).

In the studies mentioned, McCloskey either combined and averaged matching error values from tests that spanned a 70° range of target angles or else used a single target angle. Caution is needed when using such data to estimate matching performance. Matching accuracy appears to vary with target angle in a systematic manner, so combining data or using a single target angle can give a misleading estimate of accuracy. Figure 13.8 illustrates how matching error varies versus target position for the elbow from six subjects. In this study, subjects had to duplicate the position of one arm using the other arm (no further details given about methods). If we interpret mean error as a measure of matching accuracy, subjects tended to match most accurately near some midposition close to 90° and tended to undershoot the mark in a direction toward the midposition, more so as the target position approached either extreme. However, the variability or precision in matching, as indicated by the standard deviation, behaved in the opposite manner. Variability decreased near the extremes. It seems that near the extreme positions the subjects showed the least accuracy in their matching ability but they had the greatest precision! Monster, Herman, and Altland (1973) noted a similar behavior in the ankle, and we, too, have observed characteristics very similar to those in Figure 13.8 for the shoulder, knee, and ankle. The midposition for the shoulder lies close to the horizontal position, and for both the knee and the ankle it lies at joint angle of about 90°.

2.2.2.2. ***Active Versus Passive Positioning.*** These experiments ask whether we perceive position more accurately in a limb placed actively (by the voluntary contraction of the muscles) than in one passively placed (by an apparatus, with muscles relaxed). Apparently, we do.

Paillard and Brouchon (1968) studied position sense in the shoulder with active and passive placement of the reference arm to find out whether the improvement seen with active positioning resulted from the act of moving the arm into position or whether actively holding the arm in place after reaching the target position had importance. They compared four combinations of self (active) versus passive placing and maintaining the reference arm in position:

1. Self-positioned and self-maintained (SP–SM).
2. Self-positioned and passively maintained (SP–PM).
3. Passively positioned and self-maintained (PP–SM).
4. Passively positioned and passively maintained (PP– PM).

In this experiment they restricted the range of motion to vertical displacements of the shoulder joint. The subject sat in an apparatus and held both arms outstretched and straight ahead. Each index finger moved a slider on a vertical track placed in front of the subject. The left index finger in its slider provided the target position, and the subject indicated the perceived target position by attempting to align the right hand slider with the left. For passive conditions, the subject's left arm rested in a cradle moved by the experimenter. The subject actively matched position with the right shoulder. Figure 13.9 illustrates the results from 7 subjects with 20 trials under each of the 4 conditions. Active positioning of the arm produced clear improvement in both accuracy and precision, showing a reduction in the median value of the error and in the dispersion. Active versus passive maintenance of the final position had little influence on the error.

Lloyd and Caldwell (1965) and Lloyd (1968) compared the accuracy of active versus passive positioning of the knee joint. In their experiments, the subject placed each leg in a separate carrier, counterbalanced to provide equal ease of flexing and extending the knee. Displacements covered the range from 10 (near maximum extension) to 100° flexion, in 10° steps to provide 10 goal angles. For passive positioning the experimenter moved the leg through several complete swings before stopping at some goal angle. The subject indicated an estimate of position verbally by selecting one of 12 possible goal angles (including 0 and 110°). For the active condition, the subject moved his or her own leg at about the same rate and extent as with the passive movements until the experimenter called out the goal angle, whereupon the subject immediately stopped the movement and went to the target position. The authors computed matching error from the difference between the actual leg position measured on a protractor scale and the stated goal angle.

Figure 13.10 shows Lloyd and Caldwell's overall results. They found no difference between the right and left legs, so for the illustrations they combined the data for the two sides. They compared errors under the active versus passive conditions in two ways: an arithmetic mean (mean constant error), which emphasizes the bias in the subjects' perception of position, and the mean of the absolute values of the error (average error), which gives an estimate of the subjects' overall accuracy. Active positioning showed only a slightly smaller average error, except near the end position. However, the subjects' bias as revealed by the arithmetic-mean error appeared quite different for the two conditions, as a function of both direction and position.

Lloyd (1968) measured the electrical activity (EMG) in one of the knee extensor muscles (rectus femoris) during some of the passive positioning tests outlined above. He monitored activity in both the relaxed, passively moved leg and in the opposite relaxed leg. (With most attempts to relax, the muscles will show some background activity; complete relaxation of the muscles requires training.) He found no significant correlation between muscle activity (EMG) in either leg and positioning accuracy. However, he did see a general low-level background activity in both legs that increased in one leg when the opposite (contralateral) leg moved passively but not when it moved actively. This increase appeared more pronounced with passive movements of the nondominant limb. Lloyd's results illustrate the complex interaction between various muscle groups even under seemingly simple and well-controlled laboratory conditions. Also, one cannot assume the "passive" conditions mean complete absence of muscle activity.

We will see in Section 2.2.2.3 that contracting the muscles during position discriminations, as a subject must do to support the limb for active positioning, can influence matching accuracy. Whether muscle contraction to support the limb alone or to carry additional weights (muscle loading) degrades or improves matching accuracy may depend more on the particular conditions of the experiment than on any fundamental differences between the active and passive conditions.

2.2.2.3. Effects of Muscle Loading and Force Production. Cohen (1958a, 1958b) tested how distorted sensory cues from the skin and from the muscles affected position sense with the shoulder. To distort skin cues during repositioning, Cohen applied a net made from strips of adhesive tape to the subject's shoulder, and to alter cues from the muscles, the subject held a 1-kg weight in the hand. To establish the target position, the subject stood with the arm held straight with the finger pointing to a specified location on a screen (the subject could see the screen). The subject then closed the eyes and returned the arm to the side. To indicate target position, the subject, keeping the eyes closed, attempted to reposition the finger on the target point. Cohen applied the weight and/or the net only during the repositioning (indicating) portion of the trial, never while establishing target position. He computed matching error as the distance in centimeters between the target and the match, corrected to a standard arm length of 70 cm, and compared the effect of adding the tape and/or the weight with the normal, unencumbered accuracy. Either loading the arm or taping the shoulder caused a small but statistically significant increase (about 20%) in matching error compared to the control trials.

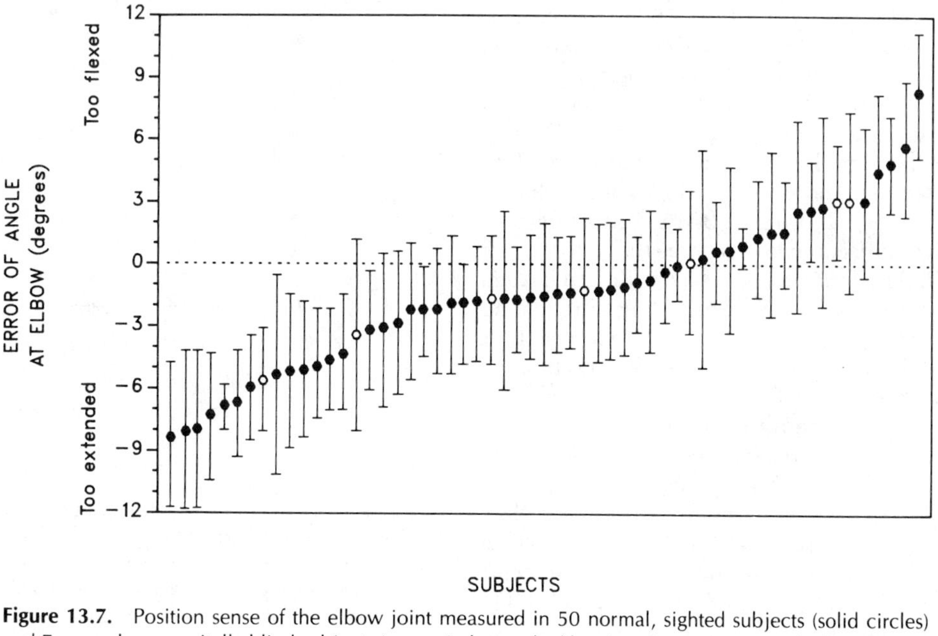

Figure 13.7. Position sense of the elbow joint measured in 50 normal, sighted subjects (solid circles) and 7 normal, congenitally blind subjects (open circles) ranked by size of mean error. Each subject made five attempts at each of 10, 20, 50, 70, and 80° from full extension to touch the index fingers together. A Perspex board prevented the fingers actually touching. Given are the mean error of alignment ± standard deviation for 25 trials in each subject. There is no correlation between mean and variable error, the latter being similar for nearly all the subjects. (From D. I. McCloskey, Kinaesthetic sensations and motor commands in man, *Progress in Clinical Neurophysiology*, 1980, *8*. Reprinted with permission.)

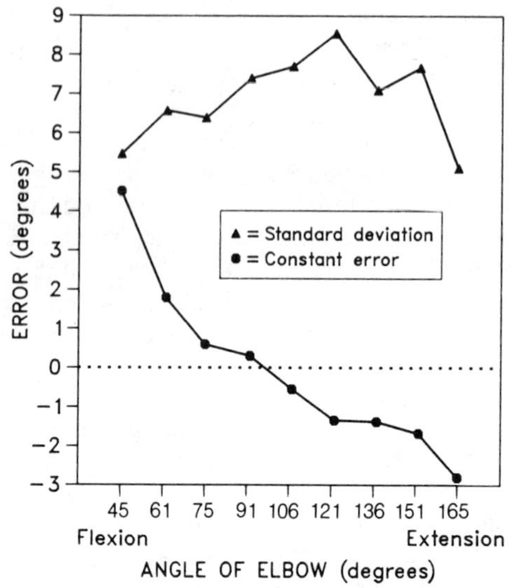

Figure 13.8. Accuracy of positioning the elbow. The six subjects were asked to duplicate the position of one arm using the other arm. The average position taken is given as the constant error from the correct position. Although this error is greatest at the extreme positions, the reliability (as indexed by the standard deviation) is greatest toward extreme flexion and extension. That is, subjects were more precise in returning to a given position with the matching arm at the extremes. (From R. P. Erickson, Parrallel "population" neural coding in feature extraction, in F. O. Schmitt & F. G. Worden (Eds.), *The neurosciences. Third study program*, MIT Press, Inc., 1974. Reprinted with permission.)

The loading and the tape net applied together produced a larger error, close to the sum of the individual errors from loading or taping alone.

Cohen measured absolute error, the distance between the rematch point and the target point, so we have no idea whether his subject's perception of limb position shifted on the average in the direction of the applied force or in the opposite direction. Apparently either can happen. McCloskey (1973) showed that when a force on the wrist tended to extend the elbow joint from a fixed position of 50°, the subject felt the forearm as more extended than its true position. Table 13.9 (compare the columns labeled "Control" and "Load Alone") illustrates this effect for a 12-or 15-lb force applied to the wrist with a rope and pulling the elbow toward extension. The force caused an average change in perceived position of +4.2° (range 1.2–8.8° in 15 subjects). A second group of five subjects opposed a force that tried to flex the elbow. Loading in this direction caused errors toward flexion, opposite to the errors produced by a force that tried to extend the arm. However, Soechting (1982) recently reported that loading one arm with a 2.5-kg weight had no effect on subjects' ability to match the orientation of the forearms in space.

We can use McCloskey's data to point out a caution one must exercise when designing an experiment to measure how a force (loading) might affect matching accuracy. In the control test (no force), most subjects erred toward flexion; that is, they indicated the arm as less extended than its true position, whereas a loading force that tried to extend the arm produced an error toward extension. Presumably, one could have found a level of force that would have made the matching error approach zero and perhaps concluded that muscle loading improves the accuracy of position sense.

Monster, Herman, and Altland (1973) studied how loading affected position sense with the ankle joint. They compared errors in matching the position of one ankle to the other under two different loading conditions, isotonic and isometric, and also with no load. In the isotonic condition, force exerted by the reference foot remained constant though position could vary. In the isometric case, position remained constant, set by the apparatus, and the subject exerted some predetermined force. The subject actively positioned both the reference (target) foot and the indicator foot. In the isotonic case (comparable to McCloskey's elbow experiment), Monster and colleagues found an offset in perceived position produced by the forces, but surprisingly, the direction of the force made no difference. Forces in either direction produced the same offset. A load torque of 1.4 kg-m in either direction on the reference foot produced a 4° difference in error compared to the no-load case, with the reference foot feeling more plantar/flexed. In the isometric case, when the subject exerted a force with the reference foot, the foot felt displaced in the direction of the exerted force (although the actual position of the foot did not change). Figure 13.11 illustrates the effect of isometric loading. The figure also includes the effect of tapping the Achilles tendon to elicit the tendon tap reflex (a "knee-jerk" kind of reflex in muscles acting across the ankle that generates a short-lasting force toward plantar flexion). The reflex contraction affects matching error in the same direction as the voluntary contraction.

Rymer and D'Almeida (1980) also found a difference in perceived position between isotonic and isometric loading. Their experiments used the interphalangeal joint (second joint) of the index finger, with the right finger usually serving as the reference and the left finger as the indicator. An electromagnetic servo device configured to maintain either a position or a force

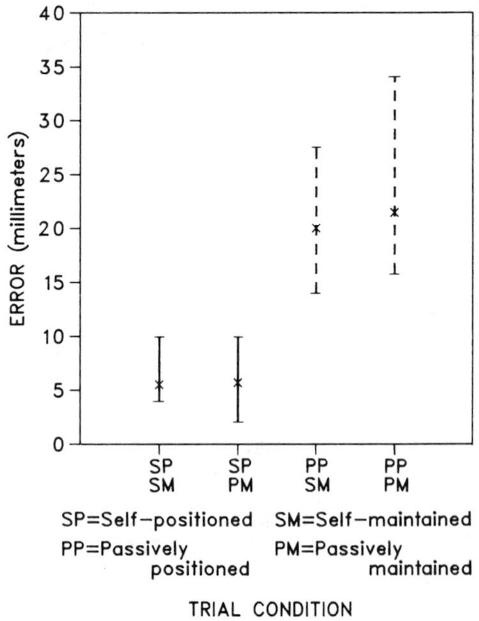

Figure 13.9. Median error and interquartile range of errors in locating with one hand a target held in the other hand. The hands were positioned by moving the extended arm vertically at the shoulder. The left index finger provided the target position which was then actively matched by the right index finger. Each of 7 subjects made 20 trials under each condition. Active positioning of the target hand, whether actively or passively maintained, was superior to passive positioning of the target arm. (From J. Paillard & M. Brouchon, Active and passive movements in the calibration of position sense, in S. J. Freedman, Ed., *The neuropsychology of spatially oriented behavior*. Copyright 1968 by Dorsey Press. Reprinted with permission.)

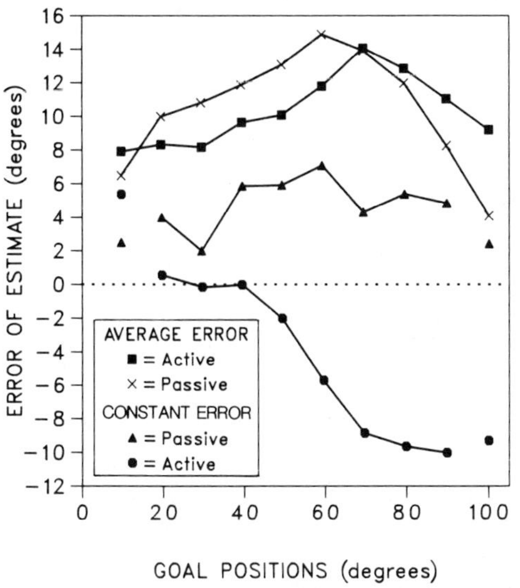

Figure 13.10. Accuracy of estimating knee joint angle with active versus passive positioning of the leg. Subjects were asked to identify the position of a passively positioned leg by verbally indicating knee joint angle or to actively match to a verbally presented goal angle. The constant error (lower curves, not connected to end points) is the arithmetic mean of the errors from a true match, and average error (upper curves, connected to end points) is the mean of the absolute values of the errors. Mean constant and average errors at each of the goal positions are based on 48 trials in each of 40 subjects. Positive error indicates an overestimation in the direction of flexion. (From A. Lloyd & L. S. Caldwell, Accuracy of active and passive positioning of the leg on the basis of kinesthetic cues, *Journal of Comparative and Physiological Psychology*, 60. Copyright 1965 by the American Psychological Association. Reprinted with permission.)

held the reference (right) finger. The subject had a visual display of position or force, depending on the test, to help establish the initial position of the reference finger or to maintain a particular force. An apparatus attached to the indicator finger monitored its position.

As one might expect, the subjects could track and duplicate imposed displacements of a finger quite accurately. Figure 13.12 shows an example of the accuracy in a simple matching experiment in which the right finger moved passively and the subject matched the displacement with the left finger.

However, loading the reference finger had two quite different effects on its perceived position, depending on how the finger moved. With the finger free to move in response to the force (isotonic case), loading had little influence on perceived finger position. With this test the apparatus operated as a force servo. The subject established the desired initial position by pressing against the servo using the visual display of actual versus desired positions as a guide. After blanking the display, the force increased or decreased, causing the finger to achieve a new position. The subject then matched the displacement with the other finger. Figure 13.13 illustrates tracking accuracy under no-load and the isotonic low and high-force conditions. Applying different forces to the tracking (indicator) finger to oppose or assist its movements likewise had little effect on matching accuracy.

When subjects exerted different forces with the finger, but with a fixed constraint on displacement ("isometric" loading), they confused force and displacement. In these tests, the apparatus operated as a position servo. The apparatus displaced the finger while the subject exerted a force with the reference finger to achieve the target force presented on a visual display. Once the force and position had stabilized, the subject reproduced the perceived position of the reference finger using the indicator finger. Unknown to the subject, every trial used an identical 4° displacement. As Figure 13.14 shows, the displacements of the indicator finger correlated with the force exerted by the reference finger and not its displacement. Thus if a finger exerts a force while its movement is constrained, the finger feels displaced in the direction of the force by an amount proportional to the force.

This finding resembles that of Monster and colleagues (1973) with the ankle (see Figure 13.11), though the illusion appears more pronounced in the finger. However, this illusion of increased displacement with increased force in the fingers has the opposite direction from what McCloskey found in the elbow (see Table

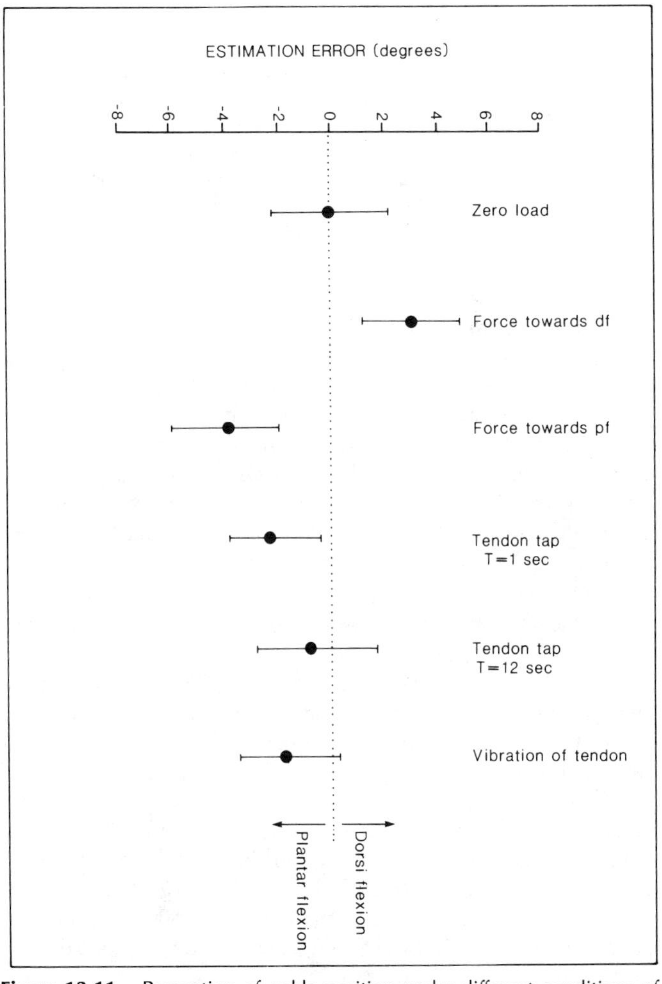

Figure 13.11. Perception of ankle position under different conditions of muscle contraction in the reference foot. Both feet were initially relaxed and aligned. The subject then tried to move the reference ankle with a predetermined force of muscle contraction, or a reflex contraction was initiated either by a tendon tap or by vibration of the tendon. After a stable situation was achieved, the subject then estimated the position of the reference foot by actively positioning the other foot. Maintained voluntary force toward dorsiflexion or toward plantar flexion led to an estimation error in the same direction. A phasic stretch reflex induced a reflex response also leading to a dynamic error in the direction of plantar flexion. Vibration induced a tonic vibration reflex of the ankle extensors and led to an estimation error toward plantar flexion. The authors provided no other details of how the data are plotted. (From A. W. Monster, R. Herman, & N. R. Altland, Effect of the peripheral and central "sensory" component in the calibration of position, in J. E. Desmedt, Ed., *New developments in electromyography and clinical neurophysiology*, Karger, 1973. Reprinted with permission.)

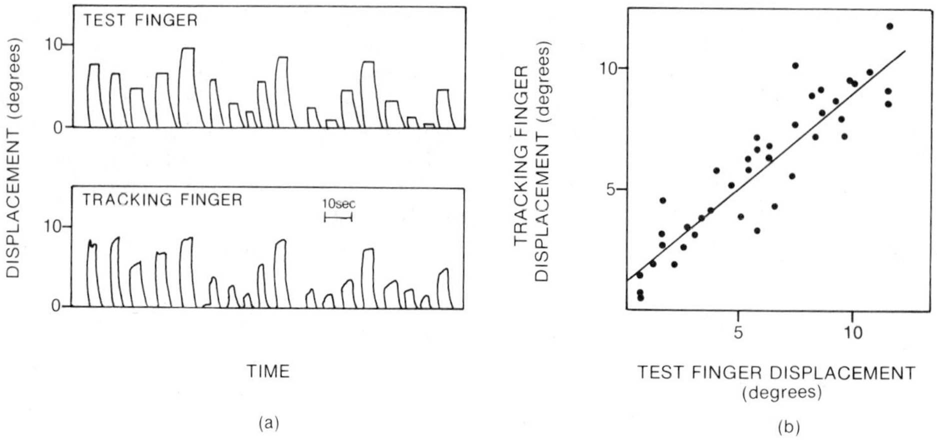

Figure 13.12. Perception of passive displacements of the right index finger. The subject indicated perceived displacement with the left index finger. In (a) a sequence of trials is depicted in which the motion of the proximal interphalangeal joint of the right index (test) finger is illustrated above and perceived motion, as reflected in movements of the proximal interphalangeal joint of the left index (tracking) finger, is shown below. In (b) tracking finger movement is plotted on the ordinate and test finger movement is plotted on the abscissa for a sequence of 40 trials collected from the same subject at one sitting. The subject could accurately track the displaced finger. The least-squares line has a slope of 0.76 (which was significant at $p < .01$) and an intercept of 1.13. (From W. Z. Rymer & A. D'Almeida, Joint position sense: The effects of muscle contraction, *Brain, 103*. Copyright 1980 by Oxford University Press. Reprinted with permission.)

13.9). The cause of these differences remains unclear though they may result from differences in procedure or perhaps confusion on the part of the subject due to inadequate or inappropriate training. Rymer and D'Almeida did several control tests to check whether their illusion with isometric loading might stem from some artifact in their procedure and concluded that although they could not explain the effect, it appeared genuine. Such differences in findings underscore the difficulty in interpreting results even from experiments that seem relatively straightforward.

2.2.2.4. Speed, Direction, and Extent of the Positioning Movement. Clark, Horch, Bach, and Larson (1979) tested how accurately subjects could realign their legs after one knee had slowly rotated through a few degrees, starting from a position where the subject perceived the legs as aligned. Their method came from the observation that while movement of the knee at a rate less than about 1°/min went undetected by the subject, after a few degrees displacement subjects could nonetheless detect a misalignment, even though they could not always tell which leg had moved (Horch, Clark, & Burgess, 1975). The authors thought this procedure provided an appropriate measure of our awareness of static position, unconfused by signals derived during movement of the limb.

In these experiments, the subject sat in an apparatus with the legs in stirrups driven by hydraulic motors that provided smooth, quiet rotation of the joint. The left leg remained fixed at some angle between 115 and 125° (180° = maximum extension), and the experimenter moved the right leg as verbally directed to achieve what felt to the subject like the closest alignment of the legs. The experimenter then either rotated the right leg very slowly (less than 1°/min) through an angle of 5° flexion or extension or did nothing for an equivalent period of time. The subjects then indicated verbally whether their right leg felt higher than, lower than, or in the same position as their left leg. Subjects could reliably detect 80–90% of these excursions. The majority of errors occurred in mistaking control trials for displacements, probably due to the various illusions of movement experienced by the subjects. These illusions appeared unrelated to true movement. If the subjects reported that a displacement had occurred (i.e., the right leg felt either higher or lower than the left), they could realign the legs by instructing the experimenter how to move the right leg to again achieve "the best match." For rematching, the experimenter moved the stirrups by hand. Figure 13.15 illustrates the rematching error (left–right) for five subjects over two blocks of

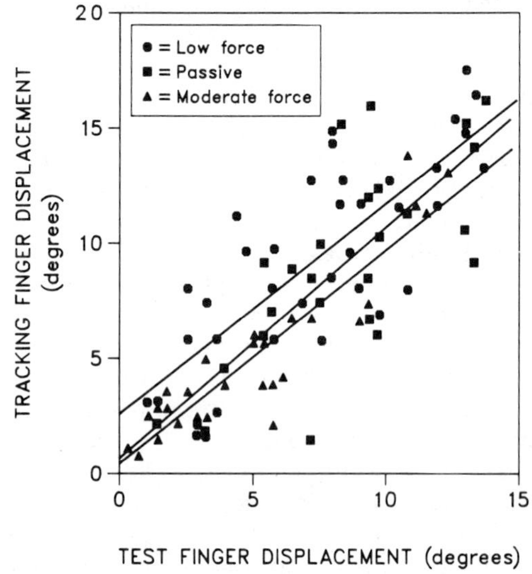

Figure 13.13. Perception of joint position in a finger supporting a load. The magnitude of perceived movement (indicated by tracking the displacement with the opposite finger) was tested under three different operating conditions in one subject. These conditions are passive movement (solid square), low initial force (solid circle), and moderate initial force (triangle). Test finger movements were imposed by loading the finger with a constant, initial force and then introducing ramp and hold decreases in load. This induced a change in finger position that was tracked by the opposite finger (see Figure 13.12). The regression slopes all have values near 1.0 and do not differ significantly from each other. (From W. Z. Rymer & A. D'Almeida, Joint position sense: The effects of muscle contraction, *Brain, 13*. Copyright 1980 by Oxford University Press. Reprinted with permission.)

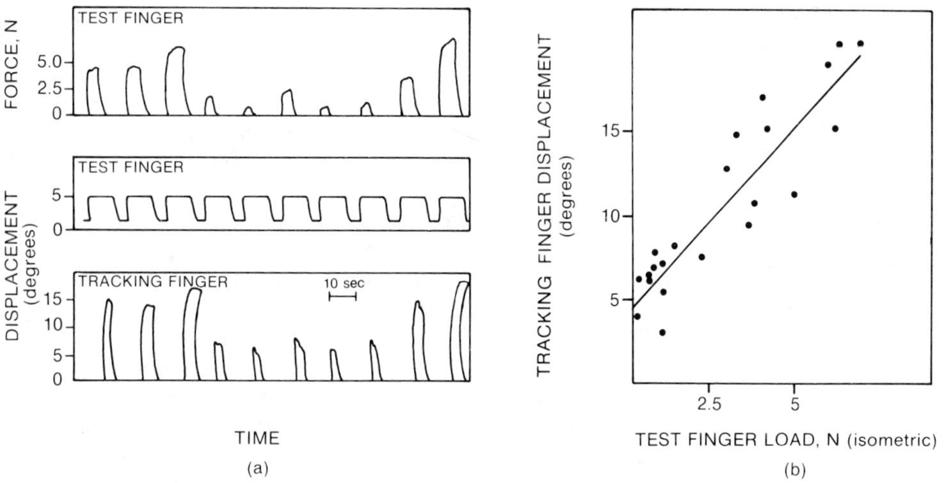

Figure 13.14. Sense of finger position with muscle contraction showing how production of isometric force interferes with the estimation of joint position. In (a), the test finger (right index) was periodically flexed while the subjects tried to match a visually displayed target force by increasing flexion force. The resultant force is shown in the top panel. Unknown to the subjects, all displacements were 4° in magnitude. The final position of the right index was estimated during the "hold," or isometric phase, of the movement, using matched movements of the left index (bottom panel; see also Figure 13.12). In (b), the magnitude of perceived displacement is plotted as a function of isometric force. The slope of the regression line, a measure of error magnitude, is 2.25°/N, with an intercept of 4.55° (compared to the actual 4° movement). Increasing isometric load on the finger produced an increasing overestimate of the displacement of the finger. (From W. Z. Rymer & A. D'Almeida, Joint position sense: The effects of muscle contraction, *Brain, 13*. Copyright 1980 by Oxford University Press. Reprinted with permission.)

test. It appeared that each subject had a different "bias" in the perception of the target angle (the mean values), but all the subjects matched to this perceived angle with about the same precision (standard deviation) (also see Section 2.2.2.1, and Figure 13.7).

The subjects perceived the movements during rematching, made at rates well over 100 times faster than the slow rotations, as having a dramatically larger extent than they really had. Even with tiny displacements subjects often made comments that the excursion had far overshot the mark. However, after sitting motionless for a few moments, the subjects commonly requested a further displacement in the same direction. A subject might request several such adjustments in the same direction. Subjects tended to underestimate the correction needed to rematch to the starting position; the size of the correction for the best perceived rematch fell a degree or two short of the original 5° displacement.

Paillard and Brouchon (1974) examined how the speed of moving the reference limb to the target position influenced the perceived position of the hand in a task that combined the action of several joints over a wide range of angles. The task involved holding a target plate in the left hand with the tip of the index finger at the center. The subject then attempted to touch the center of the target (lying over the left index fingertip) with a stylus held in the right hand. A series of concentric metal rings on the target, each connected to a separate channel of an event recorder, provided a direct readout of targeting error. The left hand changed location either passively (moved by the experimenter) or actively (by the subject's own movement). Figure 13.16 illustrates the error in locating the target center for three speeds of repositioning the target hand either actively or passively. Active positioning produced a smaller error under all three speed conditions, and increasing the speed decreased the error with both the active and passive positioning in a parallel fashion. The medium speed of 5 m/sec approximates

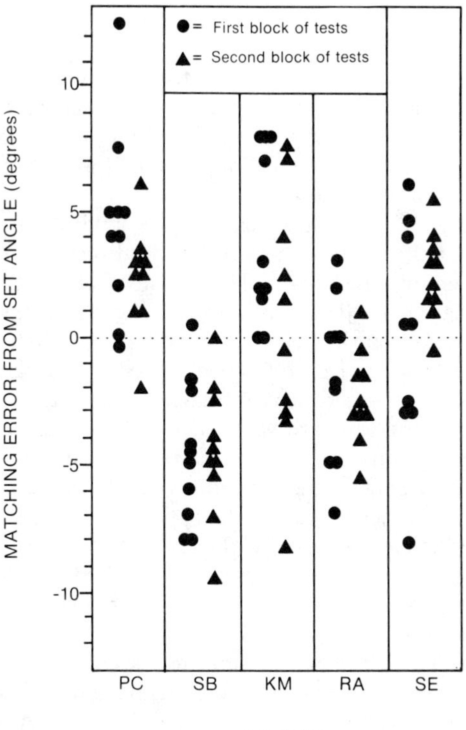

Figure 13.15. Accuracy of matching knee joint angles. Data are from 5 subjects each with two serial blocks of tests, with each block having four extension, four flexion, and two control (no movement) trials. The left knee was fixed in position, and all movements were done with the right leg. Angle plus error indicates the right knee was more extended than the left after matching. Note that each subject had a different bias angle, around which his or her matches fell, but comparable scatter around the bias angle. (From F. J. Clark, K. W. Horch, S. M. Bach, & G. F. Larson, Contribution of cutaneous and joint receptors to static knee-position sense in man, *Journal of Neurophysiology*, 1979, *42*. Reprinted with permission.)

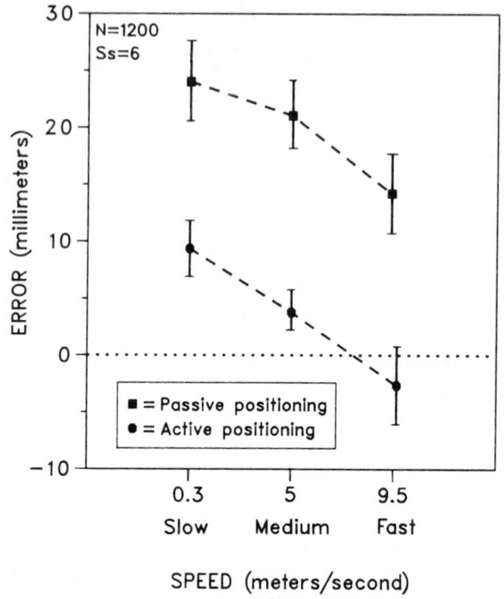

Figure 13.16. Effect of changing the speed of moving the target hand to the reference position on the accuracy of locating the target with the opposite hand. Three ranges of speed were used. The subject held a lightweight target in the left hand, with the index finger at the center. In the right hand, the subject had a stylus aligned with the index finger. The subject tried to touch the center of the target with the stylus, thus aligning the index fingertips. Each point represents the mean constant errors ± probable error of 1200 measures from 6 subjects. (From J. Paillard & M. Brouchon, A proprioceptive contribution to the spatial encoding of position cues for ballistic movements, *Brain Research*, 1974, *71*. Reprinted with permission.)

the speed used spontaneously by most subjects when instructed to reposition the target without mentioning speed. While increasing speed reduced the mean error in locating the target, the reliability of the match as indicated by the scatter did not change noticeably.

Brown, Knauft, and Rosenbaum (1948) studied the accuracy of positioning the hand as a function of the direction and extent of the positioning movement. The test apparatus consisted of a movable tab on a slider set in a featureless background except for two position markers along the slider. The first marker remained at the zero or reference position, and the second marker, set by the experimenter, established the target position. The subject sat in the dark with the hands resting in the lap. For target presentation, a light went on for 2.5 sec for the subject to view the markers. When the light went off, the subject used the hand to try to position the slider opposite the target marker, hold it there for two seconds, and then return it to zero. Matching error consisted of the distance between the target position and the estimate, with positive values indicating the subject moved beyond the target. Tests involved combinations of slider orientations and excursions; the slider moved in a horizontal (H) or vertical (V) plane and movements included near to far (NF) and the reverse, center to the right (CR) and the reverse, and bottom to top (BT) and the reverse. Errors from six combinations of these movements as a function of distance moved appear in Figure 13.17(a). The figure shows the mean error values, the variability (standard deviation), and the mean error expressed as a percentage of the distance moved. The general findings from this study suggested a tendency to overestimate the shorter distances and underestimate the longer extents, with the exception of the top-to-bottom movement. Variability in positioning, Figure 13.17(b), increased with distance. The accuracy of movements away from the body proved slightly greater than those toward the body, Figure 13.17(c).

In a related experiment with the shoulder, Caldwell (1956) likewise found that both the direction of movement and its end point (locus) influenced the accuracy of estimating 10° displacements in the horizontal plane. Caldwell's subjects had their right arm outstretched and resting in a sling that allowed free rotation of the shoulder in the horizontal plane. The 0° position on the scale pointed straight ahead, with the 90° position set to the right. Trials started from one of 10 positions spaced at 10° intervals along the scale. The subject knew the starting position of the arm and had to move 10° to the right or the left (the goal position). For example, the experimenter would tell each subject that the arm rested at 40° and that on cue the subject should move it to 50° and say "50°" when satisfied with the setting. After each trial, the experimenter told the subjects how close they came to the target point. The participants had access to each other's test scores in order to foster competition among the members of the group.

Figure 13.18 shows the mean and variable (standard deviation) errors as a function of goal position from a combined sample of 12 subjects. From these data Caldwell, like Brown and colleagues (1948), concluded that, overall, subjects located angular positions more accurately when the arm moved toward the side than when it moved toward the front. This difference became even more pronounced near the extreme (90°) position. Although Caldwell says his results measure subjects' ability to locate angular positions, it seems to us he measured instead how their ability to reproduce a 10° displacement varied with location.

2.2.2.5. Nonkinesthetic Sensory Cues. Position sense tests involve two steps: (1) establishing the target position and (2) indicating the perception of the target position. One can specify the position of a limb, digit, or joint in a variety of ways apart from using kinesthetic cues. For example, some studies have used "tactile" cues, such as having subjects feel two points and then attempt to reproduce their separation by moving a slider (Cheng, 1968). However, only two nonkinesthetic methods have had much use: (1) verbally stating an angle or position or (2) visually observing a point along some scale or in space. A nonkinesthetic method used at one of the two steps introduces its own type of error into the final measurement. (See Boring, 1942, for a discussion of a related problem, localizing points of stimulation on the skin, and the possible interactions between tactile, visual, and kinesthetic methods of presenting and localizing the target point.)

Verbal presentation requires that the subject have an internal calibration of position or angle, and this may vary considerably with a subject's background and experience. For example, one might expect a person with a high degree of mechanical aptitude to have a more accurate internal calibration of angle than someone less mechanically inclined. A few studies have attempted to control for such variations in their subject population: some employed laboratory personnel (Caldwell, 1956), while some used graduate and undergraduate students (Brown et al., 1948).

Visual presentation of a target position, or visual methods used to indicate perceived position, can introduce factors that affect matching accuracy in complex ways. For example, when Connolly and Jones (1970) used the same modality, whether vision or kinesthesis, for both the target presentation and the indication of perceived location (intramodal matching), they found greater accuracy than with cross-modal matching

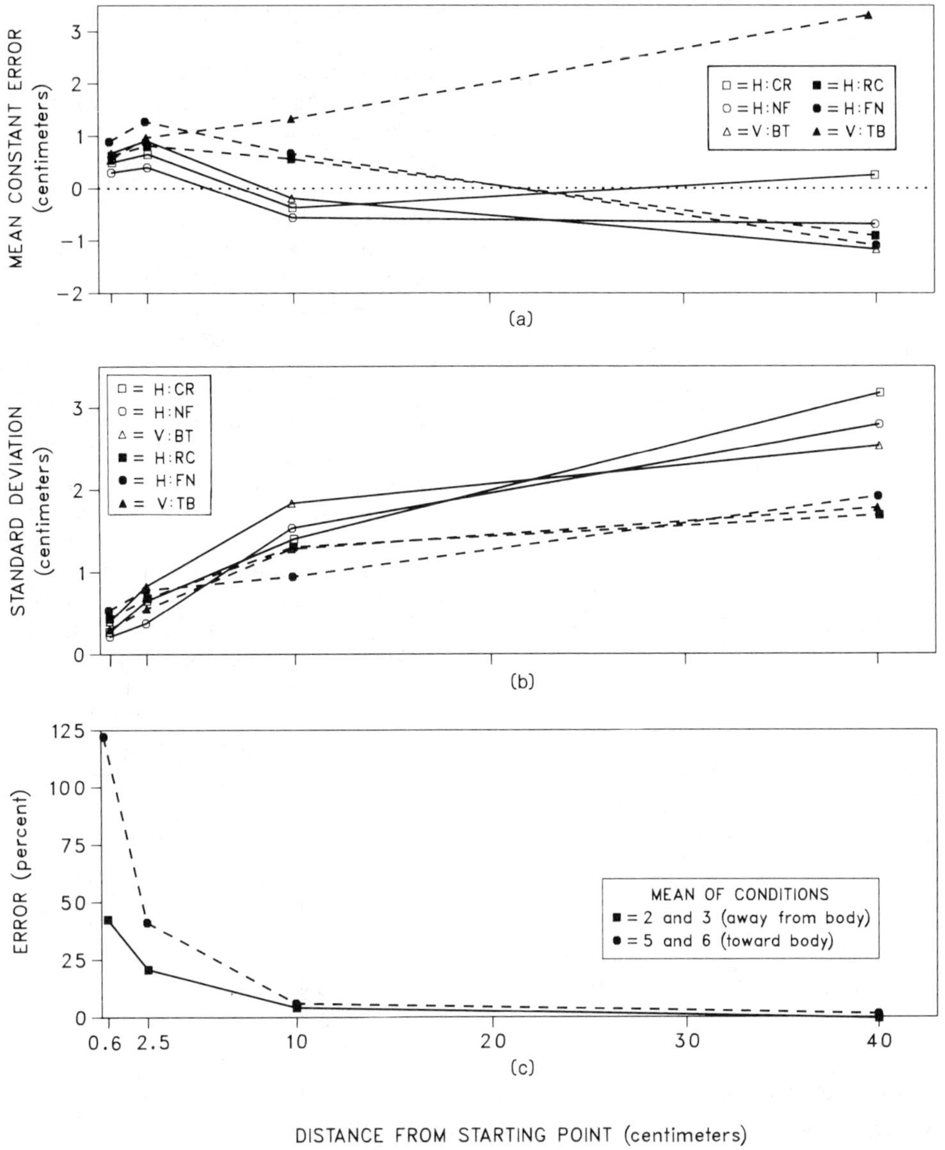

Figure 13.17. Accuracy of positioning a slider on a track as a function of distance from the starting point for various directions of movement. A target marker was briefly illuminated for subjects in a darkened room. After the light went off, the subjects moved a slider to the perceived location of the target. The track was placed either horizontally (H) or vertically (V), and movements went from near to far (NF) or vice versa, top to bottom (TB) or vice versa, and center to right (CR) or vice versa. Plotted are (a) mean constant error, (b) variability (standard deviation), and (c) percentage error (the magnitude of the error relative to the displacement). Movement occurred mainly at the shoulder and elbow. Data are from 24 subjects making 10 consecutive estimations at each target position. In general, subjects tended to overestimate short distances and to underestimate long distances. (From J. S. Brown, E. B. Knauft, & G. Rosenbaum, The accuracy of positioning reactions as a function of their direction and extent, *American Journal of Psychology, 61*. Copyright 1948 by University of Illinois Press. Reprinted with permission.)

(using different modalities for matching and indicating). In a later study, Salmoni and Sullivan (1976) likewise found a greater accuracy with intramodal matching when subjects used location (position) cues for the different matching tasks. However, when subjects matched extents (distances), rather than locations, a different trend emerged. Cross-modal matches proved no less accurate than the intramodal kinesthetic matches. Figure 13.19 shows an example of the influence of modality on accuracy when using distance versus location cues for matching. The authors observed that the visual–visual condition in their tests showed a consistently greater accuracy than any of the other conditions.

Cross-modal matching using vision and kinesthesis may show an asymmetry. Millar (1972) found that kinesthetic matching to a visually presented target proved more accurate than the reverse condition. Jones (1973) found a further interaction when he compared vision to active and to passive positioning in tests that involved matching distances. For visual presentations and indications, the experimenter moved a small spot of light either for a distance to establish the standard or until told to stop by the subject for a visual reproduction of the standard. For passive kinesthetic presentations the experimenter moved the subject's relaxed arm. With active positioning, the subject simply moved a slider. Jones found little asymmetry

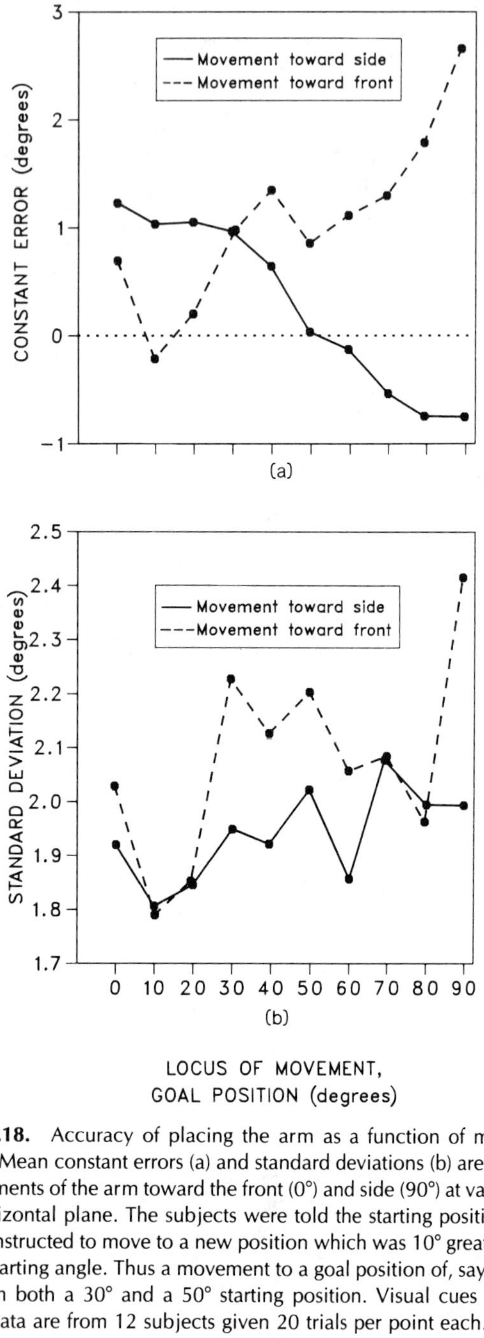

Figure 13.18. Accuracy of placing the arm as a function of movement direction. Mean constant errors (a) and standard deviations (b) are given for 10° movements of the arm toward the front (0°) and side (90°) at various loci in the horizontal plane. The subjects were told the starting position of the arm and instructed to move to a new position which was 10° greater or less than the starting angle. Thus a movement to a goal position of, say, 40° was made from both a 30° and a 50° starting position. Visual cues were not present. Data are from 12 subjects given 20 trials per point each. In terms of constant error, movements toward the side were more accurate, especially at lateral starting positions.

between vision and kinesthesis with passive movement but a clear asymmetry with active movement. Visual presentation paired with active movement showed a greater absolute error and a greater overshoot. Table 13.4 summarizes these results.

Another aspect of visual–kinesthetic interaction comes from a dominance which vision appears to have over kinesthesis. If the two senses conflict, visual localization of a target will usually dominate (Harris, 1965; Rock & Harris, 1967). This effect becomes apparent if one views the limbs through prism spectacles that displace the visual world by 20–30°. After some period of acclimation, vision and kinesthesis match, and the arms feel positioned exactly as they appear through the prisms. This effect persists with the eyes closed and lingers for some time after removing the prism spectacles (readapting to normal requires another time period). Position sense, rather than visual perception, appears to recalibrate. Acclimation to shifted visual fields can take place in a surprisingly short time; sometimes only a few minutes and a few tens of trials suffice. The less the distortion produced by the prisms, the shorter the time required. Watching the limb move greatly helps acclimation, with active movements proving considerably more effective than passive movements (Lackner, 1977). To acclimate, the subject must experience a discordance between vision and kinesthesis (Mather & Lackner, 1975), though the subject need not consciously perceive the discordance (Lackner, 1977). Apparently, the acclimation affects only the body part involved in the discordance and only the joints that move and does not transfer to other joints. Putterman, Robert, and Bregman (1969) demonstrated the lack of transfer to noninvolved joints by having the subject point to various target positions by moving the wrist. During the adaptation with prisms that displaced the visual field 23°, only the wrist could move and both the head and forearm remained fixed in place. After the adaptation period and removal of the prisms, the subject could again freely move the arm, though it remained out of view. The subject then received instructions to straighten the wrist and point to targets with the whole arm using the elbow as a pivot. Figure 13.20 illustrates the results. The forearm accurately pointed to the target, but the subject held the wrist bent despite repeated instructions during the test to hold it straight. The wrist had acclimated to the prisms, but this acclimation did not transfer to the forearm.

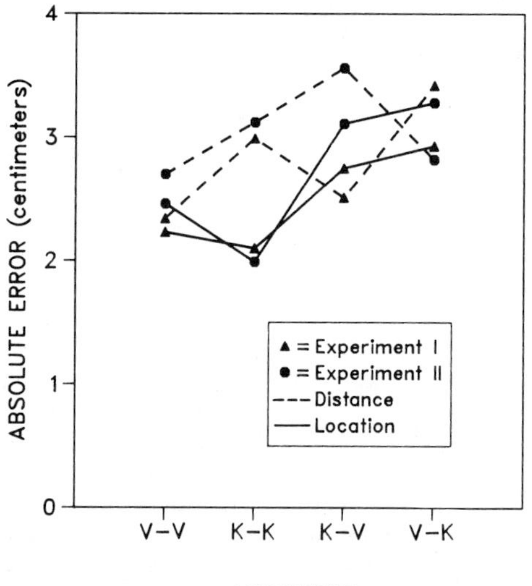

Figure 13.19. Error in matching distance or location as a function of the modalities used. For visual (V) presentations, the subject watched while the experimenter moved a pointer along a rod from a start position to some target position and back again after a 2-sec pause. For visual matches, the experimenter moved the pointer until told to stop by the subject. For kinesthetic (K) presentations, a mechanical stop was placed at the target position, and the subject moved the pointer from the start position to the stop and back again. For kinesthetic matching, the subject moved the pointer to match his or her perception of the target position. Two different starting positions and three different target distances were used. Data from experiment I are based on 10 subjects per group, while experiment II used a total of 72 subjects divided among 8 groups. Intramodal matches were superior to cross-modal matches for location but not for distance. (From A. W. Salmoni & S. J. Sullivan, The intersensory integration of vision and kinesthesis for distance location cues, *Journal of Human Movement Studies*, Teviot Scientific Publishers, 1976.)

Table 13.4. Cross Modal Matching: The Accuracy of Reproducing and Estimating Distances with the Standard Presented in One Mode (Visual or Kinesthetic) and the Reproduction or Estimate Made in the Other Mode.

Length of standard (cm)		Errors in cm Condition V–P	P–V	V–A
2	(abs)	1.12 ± 0.05	1.32 ± 0.25	2.29 ± 0.84
	(alg)	−0.76 ± 4.34	−1.30 ± 1.02	−0.13 ± 2.16
4	(abs)	1.88 ± 0.89	2.06 ± 1.02	3.30 ± 1.42
	(alg)	−1.30 ± 1.60	−1.98 ± 1.78	+0.36 ± 3.58
6	(abs)	1.68 ± 0.71	1.73 ± 1.02	2.92 ± 1.37
	(alg)	−1.27 ± 1.30	−1.30 ± 1.27	+1.40 ± 2.90
8	(abs)	3.12 ± 1.27	2.08 ± 0.97	4.70 ± 1.50
	(alg)	−2.24 ± 2.49	−1.52 ± 1.70	+0.94 ± 4.85
10	(abs)	2.57 ± 1.14	2.57 ± 1.17	3.94 ± 1.75
	(alg)	−1.91 ± 1.91	−2.01 ± 1.14	+0.10 ± 4.11

These tests compared vision (V) and two kinesthetic modes: imposed (passive) movement (P) and voluntary (active) movement (A). The subject sat before an apparatus with the index finger in a thimble that slid along a rail. The subject could also see a small light that moved behind a long slot. To present the standard, the experimenter either moved the thimble to a stop and back to the starting point (P) or moved the light through a preset distance along the slot and back again (V). The subject then tried to reproduce the standard either by voluntarily moving the thimble (A), by reporting when the experimenter had moved the thimble (and the subject's finger) the correct distance (P), or by indicating when the light had traversed an equivalent distance (V). The table shows mean absolute errors (abs) and mean algebraic errors (alg) (both ± standard deviation) in estimating each of five standard lengths as a function of mode. (From Jones, 1973.)

(See Chapter 25 by Welch and Warren for a further discussion on sensory interaction.)

The mechanism of this apparent lability in position sense remains unclear. The bulk of the evidence suggests that the change occurs in the perception of the position of the limb and not from any visual effect. Perhaps this phenomenon reflects our amazing ability to modify our body image to incorporate objects held in our hands, such as tools, as extensions of our bodies.

Bairstow and Laszlo (1978) investigated interactions between vision and kinesthesis using a test somewhat different from those in the usual matching experiments. They used a pattern recognition task, with a polygonal pattern presented in one of four ways: (1) by active kinesthesis, where the subject traced the outline of the pattern with a stylus in a groove; (2) by passive kinesthesis, similar to the active kinesthesis except the subject, after training to relax, had the arm moved around the pattern by the experimenter; (3) visually, where a spot of light traced the pattern on a screen; and (4) visually, with the pattern itself presented for five sec. The subject then had to select the correct pattern from a visual array of four alternatives that differed slightly. Figure 13.21(a) shows two sample pattern arrays. Figure 13.21(b) shows the frequency of selection of the different choices in the pattern array for the four experimental conditions. As one might expect, visual presentation of the pattern gave the highest percentage of correct choices, but little difference emerged among the other three experimental conditions.

2.2.2.6. Influence of Time on Position Sense Accuracy. The length of time elapsed between establishing a target position and making an indication of the perceived position can markedly influence matching accuracy. These alterations in accuracy with time may involve one or another different mechanisms, depending on the nature of the task. With information about target position continuously available, for example, by maintaining one limb at the reference position while matching with the other limb, the sensation of limb position may change with time due to adaptation of the sensory receptors in the reference limb or perhaps to other higher-order central nervous system effects. Where a subject must rely on a remembered target position when making an indication, the memory may fade or otherwise alter in some way. Finally, prior joint positions and movements can influence one's perception of the current position of a limb, digit, or joint (aftereffects).

Paillard and Brouchon (1968) examined variations in matching error over a 12-sec interval, using arm matching tests that involved vertical movement of the shoulder joint. The right arm (held straight) moved to some target position and remained there for a specified time before the subject actively matched its position with the left arm. Figure 13.22 shows how matching error varied with time for either active or passive positioning of the right (reference) arm. Both active and passive positioning of the reference arm revealed a steady drift in error with time toward an underestimation of target position.

Monster and colleagues (1973) found that the error in matching one ankle joint position to the other varied with time much like that reported for the shoulder. However, they also discovered that imposing a torque on the reference foot produced a dramatically different behavior in how the error changed with time. Figure 13.23 shows matching error versus time interval for the load and no-load conditions. Note in particular

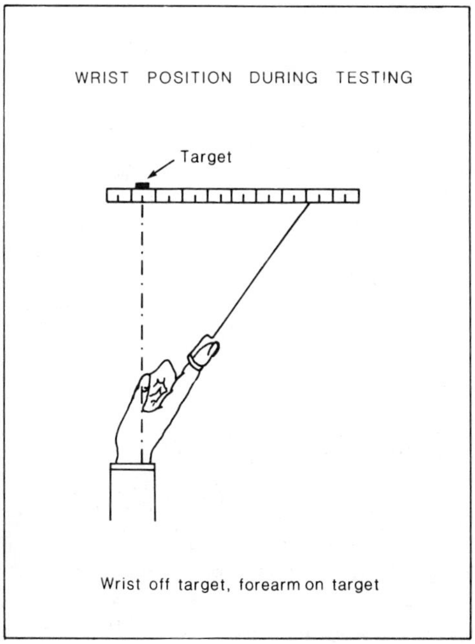

Figure 13.20. Drawing of the wrist position assumed by subjects pointing to a target after acclimation to a displaced visual field produced by prism glasses. During acclimation, the forearm and pointer were hidden from view, and only the wrist was free to move. The subject was asked to point to the target and then allowed to view the position of the pointer. After the acclimation period, the prisms were removed and the subject was instructed to straighten his or her arm and point to a target but was not shown the position of the pointer at this time. The forearm accurately pointed to the target, but the wrist was held bent. (From S. H. Putterman, A. L. Robert, & A. S. Bregman, Adaptation of the wrist to displacing prisms, *Psychonomic Science*, 1969, 69. Reprinted with permission.)

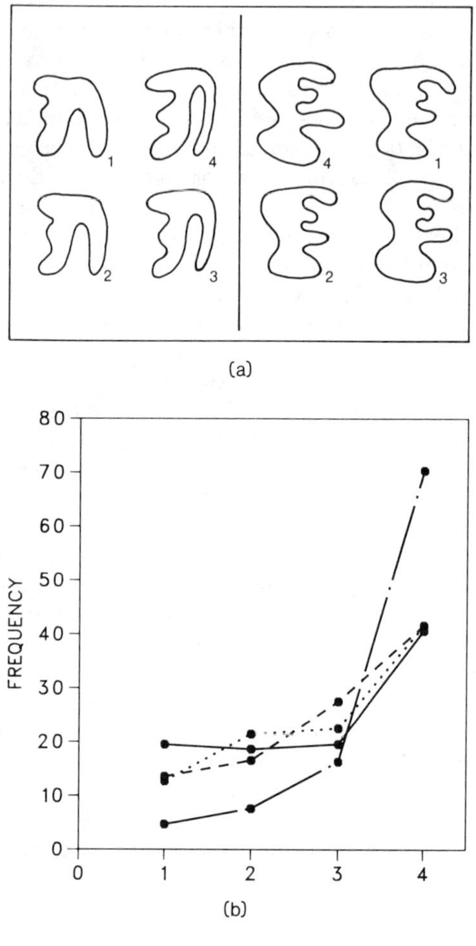

Figure 13.21. Pattern recognition with vision and kinesthesis. (a) Examples of the patterns used for the recognition tests. Pattern 4 is the standard, 1 the least similar. The subjects either traced the outline of the standard, had the hand moved around the outline by the experimenter, saw the outline traced by a light, or saw the whole pattern illuminated for 5 sec. (b) The frequency of patterns chosen from the visual arrays over 10 trials. Solid line, active kinesthesis; dashes, passive kinesthesis; dotted line, vision with moving light; chain-dashed line, vision with illuminated pattern. The last condition produced the best matches. (From P. J. Bairstow & J. I. Laszlo, Perception of movement patterns. Recognition from visual arrays of distorted patterns, *Quarterly Journal of Experimental Psychology*, 1978, *30*. Reprinted with permission.)

that the direction of the torque applied to the reference foot had no effect on the direction of the error.

One might feel tempted to relate changes in position estimates with time to adaptation in the sensory receptors that signal limb position because most sensory receptors do show some degree of adaptation (a decline in response during a maintained, constant stimulus; see Chapter 12 by Sherrick and Cholewiak). Some adaptation might occur also within the central nervous system. In support of adaptation as a possible cause of the change in matching error with time, Monster and colleagues (1973) observed a striking similarity in the time course of ankle position matching errors in their experiments and the firing rate of an individual sensory unit recorded from the thalamus of a monkey by Mountcastle, Poggio, and Werner (1963). This neuron increased its discharge upon rotation of the monkey's wrist, but this increase in activity adapted with the time course shown in Figure 13.24. Because the thalamus serves as the major sensory relay to the brain, this parallel in the behavior of a central neuron and a limb matching task seemed reasonable and appropriate. However, our lack of understanding of the mechanisms involved in position sense, especially concerning central mechanisms and memory for limb position, dictates that we exercise a great deal of caution in interpreting the results of such experiments.

While some type of alteration over time in those sensory inputs that signal limb position might parallel the shift in perceived position, the true explanation for the shifts may involve altogether different mechanisms. We seem to possess some internal image or schema of our bodies that can exist independently of sensory input. Sensory inputs may enhance the clarity or vividness of this image or alter the orientation of its various parts, but sensory inputs per se apparently do not produce this image. Persons who have lost a limb usually retain some vestige of the missing part in their body image—the phantom-limb phenomenon (see Henderson & Smyth, 1948). Phantom-limb sensations can also result after spinal cord injury (Conomy, 1973) and from anesthesia of a limb, produced by blocking a major nerve trunk with a local anesthetic (Melzack & Bromage, 1973).

Gross and Melzack (1978) studied how perceived position of the arm changes over time as the arm slowly becomes anesthetized. To anesthetize the arm, they used a blood pressure cuff on the upper arm inflated to 180 mm Hg, a pressure high enough to occlude the blood flow (the reader should not use this procedure without expert counsel). Anesthesia progresses slowly and becomes complete in about 20 min. The subject sat with the arm resting semiflexed on a table and hidden from view, as illustrated in Figure 13.25(a). The subject indicated the perceived positions of several landmarks on the hand, wrist, and arm by pointing with the opposite index finger. Markings made on a sheet of clear plastic placed over the reference arm served to record the various position estimates. Photographs of the reference arm taken afterward through the clear plastic sheet with the markings provided a means of measuring positioning errors.

Gross and Melzack found that the perceived position of the arm systematically approached the waistline and felt closer to the body with increasing duration of ischemia (no blood flow). Also, the greater the distance between the arm and the body, the larger the discrepancy between the perceived and the real arm location. Having the subject lie supine with the arm supported above the chest and parallel to the body produced similar shifts in perceived position, as shown in Figure 13.25(b). The striking dissociation in orientation between the real and perceived arms resembles the phantom limb reported by patients with lesions (damage) or anesthetic block of the brachial plexus (nerves to the arm).

Apparently the arm need not lack sensation in order to experience shifts in position. Gross, Webb, and Melzack (1974) observed simply keeping the normal arm in place for several minutes can produce positional shifts similar in direction, though smaller in magnitude (see Figure 13.26(a)). Additional sensory input to the arm unrelated to position (in the form of a vibration) had no effect on the spatial localization of the arm. In another test, the subject made small circular movements of the concealed arm every 60 sec, moving as many joints as possible for 30 sec. It is interesting that with these small active movements, localization of the arm actually worsened (see Figure 13.26(b)). This finding appears to conflict with the usual observation of improved positioning accuracy with active positioning. One

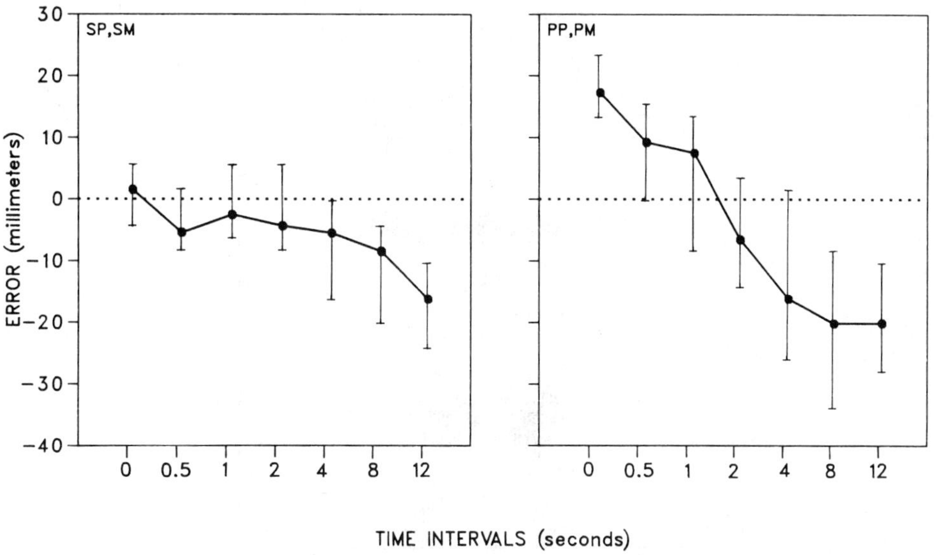

Figure 13.22. Accuracy of matching the position of one arm to that of the opposite arm over a period of time. The arms were held straight, and movement occurred at the shoulders. Median and interquartile range of errors in the judgment of the final position of the hand are shown as a function of the time interval between positioning and judging. The subjects either actively positioned the reference arm and actively matched it with the other arm after the indicated time (SP, SM) or both the positioning and matching were done passively (PP, PM). Both methods showed a similar drift with time toward underestimation. Points are based on means from 5 subjects, each of whom made 24 trials at each time interval. (From J. Paillard & M. Brouchon, Active and passive movements in the calibration of position sense, in S. J. Freedman, Ed., *The neuropsychology of spatially oriented behavior*. Copyright 1968 by Dorsey Press. Reprinted with permission.)

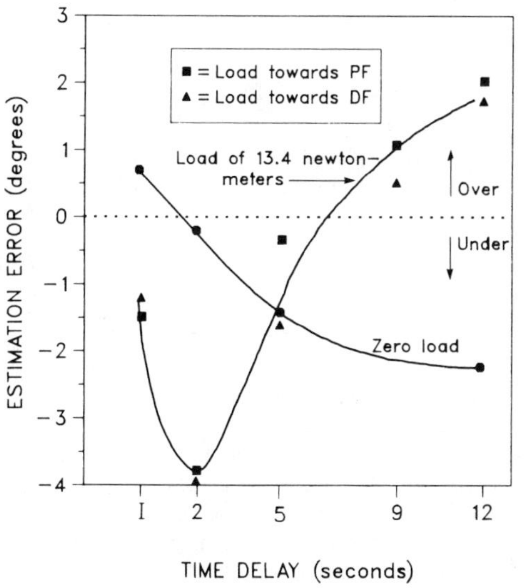

Figure 13.23. Estimation of ankle position as a function of time with and without a load applied to the reference foot. Initially, both feet were lined up. The reference foot was then actively moved to the reference position and maintained in that position against a load applied toward plantarflexion (PF) or dorsiflexion (DF). The position of the reference foot was then estimated by matching it with the other foot. A negative error implies excessive plantarflexion of the matching foot. Lines are drawn to connect the points smoothly. The direction of the load did not affect the error induced by loading the ankle. (From A. W. Monster, R. Herman, and N. R. Altland, Effect of the peripheral and central "sensory" component in the calibration of position, in J. E. Desmedt, Ed., *New developments in electromyography and clinical neurophysiology*, Karger, 1973, Reprinted with permission.)

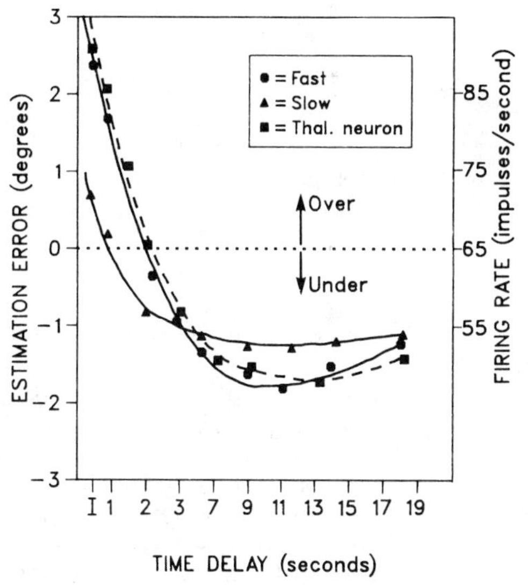

Figure 13.24. Change in the perception of ankle position over time for two rates of positioning the reference ankle. Plotted on the same time scale with the psychophysical data is the rate of decay of discharge of a neuron in the ventrobasal thalamus of a macaque monkey during a maintained position of the animal's wrist (from Mountcastle, Poggio, & Werner, 1963). The symbol I indicates immediate matching. Lines are the authors' smooth curves through the points. Note the similarity in the curves for the neuronal adaptation and the decay of sensation after rapid joint movement. (From A. W. Monster, R. Herman, & N. R. Altland, Effect of the peripheral and central "sensory" component in the calibration of position, in J. E. Desmedt, Ed., *New developments in electromyography and clinical neurophysiology*, Karger, 1973, Reprinted with permission.)

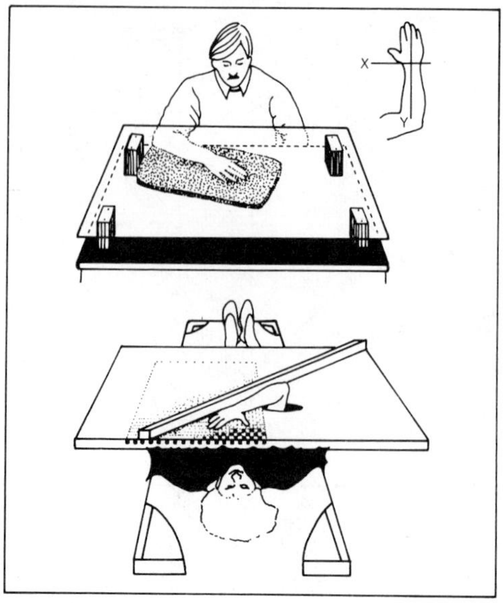

(a)

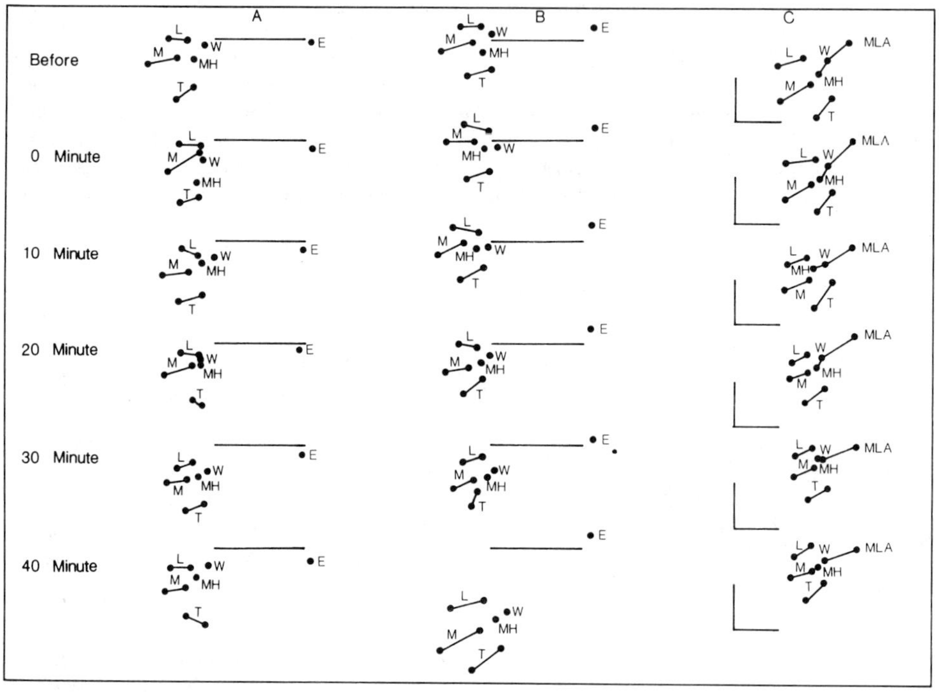

(b)

Figure 13.25. Shifts over time in the apparent positions of limbs during ischemia. (a) Drawings of the experimental setup. During testing, the Plexiglas table was covered with a black cloth, and a pressure cuff was applied to the subject's upper arm. In the lower drawing, the subject is lying on a cot, with the arm above and parallel to the body. The right arm was positioned on the surface, and the subject's task was to point to a specified part of the unseen arm with the left index finger (upper drawing) or with a needle held in the left hand (lower drawing). (b) The perceived location of the nine tested points of the right forearm and fingers before and at various times after inflation of the pressure cuff to a level known to produce ischemia and sensory loss, with E = elbow, MLA = middle of the lower arm, W = wrist, MH = middle of the hand, T = thumb, M = middle finger, and L = little finger. The horizontal solid line is the midline of the real lower-arm position between elbow and wrist. The real elbow position was about 100° for the left column and near 150° in the middle column. The third column shows the results from the experiment in which the subject was lying on the cot. The coordinate axes correspond to the axes shown in the upper-right drawing. The apparent position of the hand shifts toward the waist with time in all three cases. (From Y. Gross & R. Melzack, Body image: Dissociation of real and perceived limbs by pressure-cuff ischemia, *Experimental Neurology*, 1978, *61*. Reprinted with permission.)

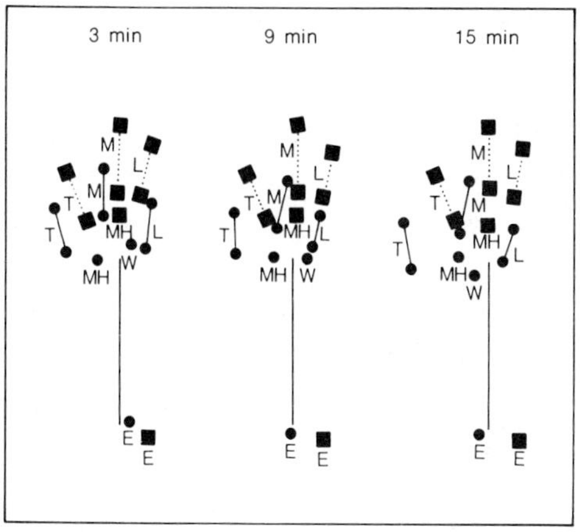

(a)

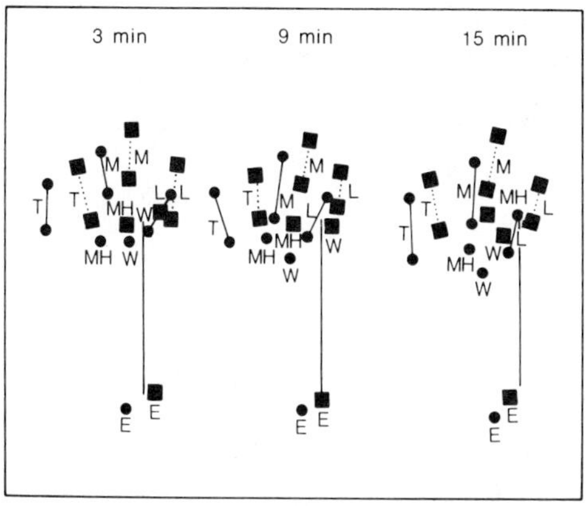

(b)

Figure 13.26. Shifts over time in the apparent positions of the forelimb. Real and perceived locations of nine tested points of the resting forearm and hand at different times after beginning the experiment without (a) and with (b) intervening small random movements of the hand, with E = elbow, W = wrist, MH = middle of hand, T = thumb, M = middle finger, and L = little finger. The vertical solid line is the midline of the forearm. Squares show actual locations; circles represent perceived points. The changes in perceived position with time are similar to, but smaller than, those seen with ischemia and were not influenced by active movement of the hand. See Figure 13.25 for more detail. (From Y. Gross, R. Webb, & R. Melzack, Central and peripheral contributions to localization of body parts: Evidence for a central body schema, *Experimental Neurology*, 1974, *44*. Reprinted with permission.)

might wonder if this apparent shift over time could arise from some peculiarity in the way the subject indicated position. However, the same shifts appeared when the subject verbally indicated perceived location of the target part by specifying a position on a checkerboard placed over the arm.

2.2.2.7. Memory for Limb Position. Many tests of limb position sense require that the subject remember the target position during the interval between the presentation of the target and the indication of its perceived position. Humans apparently exhibit a remarkable ability to remember positions of their limbs quite accurately and for a long period of time. Horch, Clark, and Burgess (1975) found no difference in the accuracies of matching leg positions with a direct-comparison match (one leg matched to the other) versus a memory match (one leg matched to the remembered position of the other, Table 13.5). For the memory match, the reference leg moved passively, remained at the target position for 15 sec, and returned to the neutral position (knee at 90°). Then 45 sec later, the subject actively matched the remembered target position. For the direct-comparison match, the reference leg moved passively and remained at the target position for one min before the subject matched.

Our memory for limb position seems to endure far beyond the few minutes needed to perform most positioning tasks. Clark and Burgess found little decrement in the accuracy of memory matching of the shoulder even after a 24-hour interval (Figure 13.27). In these tests the subject had the arm supported outstretched in a carrier and moved passively to one of 12 target positions, held there for five sec, and then returned to the side. Twenty-four hours later, the subject returned to the apparatus and reproduced the most recent target position from memory. Clark and Burgess found a small decrease with time in the slope of the regression line relating target position and the subject's estimate from memory and an increase in the variability of the match. Nonetheless, subjects could rematch the remembered positions remarkably well.

The existence of this memory for limb position, whatever its mechanism, seriously complicates interpretation of experiments that attempt to determine what sensory inputs provide position sense. For example, simple limb matching experiments cannot distinguish between a system that derives position from signals available only during movement, storing the result in a memory, and a mechanism that relies upon continuously available position signals. Horch, Clark, and Burgess (1975) sought to get around this dilemma and test whether our awareness of static knee position depends on signals from movement detectors. They reasoned that if every sensory receptor has some threshold below which it fails to respond to the stimulus, there should exist some rate of joint rotation slow enough that movement receptors will not respond. They tested this idea and found that if they rotated the subject's knee at a rate less than 1°/min, the subject failed to detect the movement. However, when starting from a position where the subject felt the legs aligned, only a few degrees of rotation sufficed for a subject to detect the misalignment, though the subject could not tell which leg

Table 13.5. The Accuracy of Matching Knee Joint Angle to Remembered Target Positions

Subject	Set Angle	Direct Comparison	Memory Match
JF	81	79.8 ± 1.89	79.3 ± 2.15
LF	85	87.5 ± 2.66	89.3 ± 4.46
ML	74.5	79.4 ± 2.25	78.4 ± 2.48
BM	79	83.0 ± 5.48	79.3 ± 4.16
NJ	131	133.2 ± 7.16	135.0 ± 6.92
MAL	131.5	127.7 ± 4.89	130.6 ± 8.36
MM	134	131.1 ± 3.67	127.6 ± 9.41
MR	126	120.5 ± 5.50	122.3 ± 9.76

Subjects matched knee joint position in two different ways: matching one leg directly to the other and matching one leg to the remembered position of the other. For a direct-comparison match, the experimenter passively moved the reference leg to the target angle and held it. After one min, the subject moved the other leg to match the reference leg. For the memory match, the reference leg got moved to the target, held for 15 sec, and then replaced to a "neutral" position. Then 45 sec later, the subject moved the other leg to the remembered target angle. The table shows the mean matching error (± standard deviation) in degrees, with 180° equivalent to full extension. Matching from memory showed no significant difference from direct matches except for an increase in variance with one subject (MM). (From Horch, Clark & Burgess, 1975.)

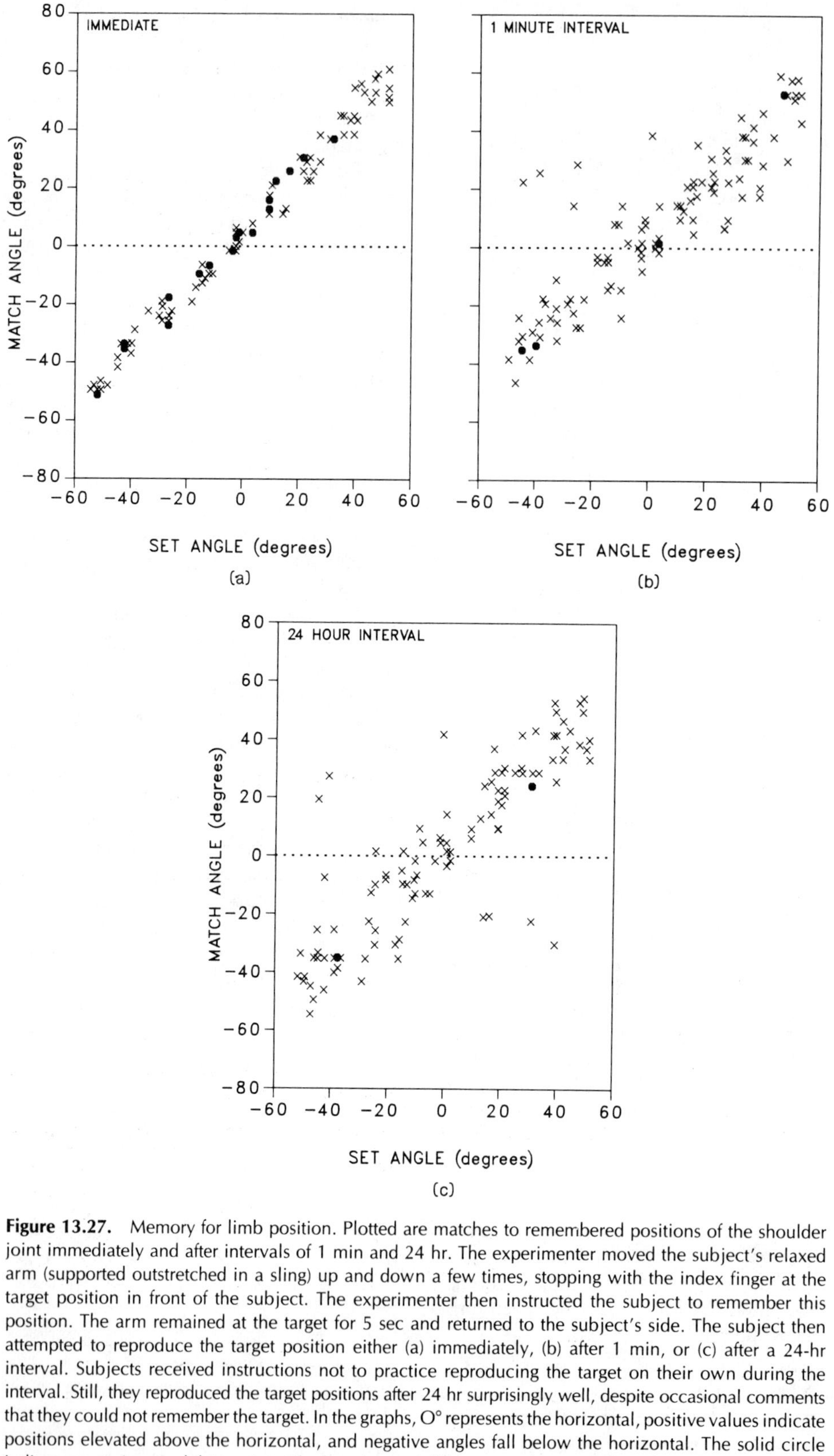

Figure 13.27. Memory for limb position. Plotted are matches to remembered positions of the shoulder joint immediately and after intervals of 1 min and 24 hr. The experimenter moved the subject's relaxed arm (supported outstretched in a sling) up and down a few times, stopping with the index finger at the target position in front of the subject. The experimenter then instructed the subject to remember this position. The arm remained at the target for 5 sec and returned to the subject's side. The subject then attempted to reproduce the target position either (a) immediately, (b) after 1 min, or (c) after a 24-hr interval. Subjects received instructions not to practice reproducing the target on their own during the interval. Still, they reproduced the target positions after 24 hr surprisingly well, despite occasional comments that they could not remember the target. In the graphs, O° represents the horizontal, positive values indicate positions elevated above the horizontal, and negative angles fall below the horizontal. The solid circle indicates superimposed data points. The long interval did increase the variability of the reproduction and reduce the slope of the regression line. Least-squares regression analysis of the data produced slopes of 1.01 for the immediate matches, 0.790 for the 1-min matches, and 0.809 for the 24-hr matches, respectively, and gave correlation coefficients .99, .89, and .85, respectively. In other words, subjects showed a reduced precision in reproduction with time, and they tended to err in a direction toward the horizontal position of the shoulder. Data from five subjects. (From Clark & Burgess, Note 1.)

had actually moved. This sensation of misalignment did not fade with time. While most subjects experienced illusions of movement that sometimes confused their judgment of position, these illusions appeared unrelated to any actual movement; they occurred even when the leg remained stationary. (These illusions remind one of the shifts over time in perceived position of a stationary limb studied by Gross & Melzack, 1978, and discussed in Section 2.2.2.6). Horch and colleagues (1975) concluded that subjects could not have relied on movement signals and, therefore, they must have access to some form of continuously available position information. These experiments also suggest that we can sense the relative position of the two limbs more accurately than absolute position of a single limb. However, this idea needs verification.

2.2.2.8. Aftereffects and Postural Persistence. Prior movements or postures of a limb can influence our perception of its position. This aftereffect, or "postural persistence" (a term used in the earlier literature), produces an offset in perceived position directed away from the previously held position. One sees sensory aftereffects with a variety of different tasks, such as estimating the thickness of a block using the thumb and finger (Cameron & Wertheimer, 1965), gauging slopes (Cratty & Duffy, 1969; Day & Singer, 1964) or the tilt of a bar or the taper of a rod (Gibson, 1933; Koehler & Dinnerstein, 1947), or with estimating shapes (Gibson, 1933) or weights (de Mendoza, 1979).

Craske and Crawshaw (1974) found an offset in perceived arm position produced by maintaining the arm motionless and relaxed in a "treatment" position. The location of the treatment position and the exposure time affected the magnitude of this offset. The test used horizontal movements of the right arm. The subject first moved the arm to one of two treatment positions (25 or 40° right of straight ahead). After a 3 or 30 sec exposure time, with the arm relaxed, the subject moved the arm to the left until signaled to stop. One sec after stopping at this test position, the subject indicated perceived arm position by reading a value from a scale placed over the hand, using the right index finger as a landmark. The subject could not see the hand and kept the eyes closed during the test except for brief intervals to read the scale. Craske and Crawshaw found greater amounts of offset with longer exposure times and with larger distances between the treatment position and the test position (Table 13.6). Offsets appeared directed away from the treatment position.

Table 13.6. The Effect of Previously Held Positions of the Arm on the Perception of Subsequent Arm Position

	Mean Localization Error (Degrees)		
	Exposure Time		
Treatment position	3 sec	30 sec	Mean
25°	0.15	0.82	0.48
40°	1.33	1.23	1.28
Mean	0.75	1.02	0.88

The table shows mean error (in degrees) of estimating the location of a limb previously held in one or the other treatment positions (25 or 40° to the right) for either 3 or 30 sec. The subject moved the right arm (supported on a cradle) until told to stop at the selected treatment position. After the 3- or 30-sec interval, the subject moved the arm to the left until told to stop at one of 10 judgment positions 1° apart, centered about the "straight ahead." The subject then indicated perceived position by reading a value from a scale placed over the hidden hand to indicate the apparent location of the index finger. In all cases the subjects overestimated the distance moved from the treatment position to the test position. (From Craske & Crawshaw, 1974).

One can easily demonstrate for oneself a postural aftereffect as follows (Jackson, 1954). Hold both arms outstretched horizontally in front of yourself. Take a brief glimpse of your arms to verify their alignment; then close your eyes. Next, raise your right arm about 45° above the horizontal, hold it there about 15 sec, and return it to the horizontal. Now, look at your arms. You probably will find the right arm positioned above the horizontal by 4 or 5° (about 5 or 6 cm measured at the fingertips). Holding the arm below the horizontal for 15 sec will produce the appropriately opposite offset; the arm then feels higher than its true position, so you position it a bit lower to achieve what feels like a match.

Table 13.7 from Howard and Anstis (1974) provides another example of a kinesthetic aftereffect, demonstrating in this case an offset in perceived head position produced by turning and holding the head at 24° to the right for 10 min. Howard and Anstis also tested whether the resulting offset in perceived position depended on the treatment position of the head, on the contraction of the neck muscles during the adaptation period, or simply as a result of holding the head motionless for 10 min irrespective of its position. To test the influence of muscle contraction, the subject maintained the head for 10 min in the straight-ahead (0°) position while opposing a torque of about 0.035 kg·m that tried to rotate the head to the left. For the control condition, the subject simply held the head relaxed in the straight-ahead position. They measured aftereffects in two ways: (1) by having subjects align their heads to the perceived straight-ahead position starting from a variety of initial positions and (2) by having the subjects slide a metal tab along a curved track, using both hands, until they judged the tab to lie directly in front of their nose. The experiment took place in a darkened room.

Howard and Anstis found that previous position emerged as the important variable in their test. Neither muscle contraction nor the control condition produced an offset. Heide and Molbech (1973) likewise found that an isometric contraction of muscles in the arms at 50% of the maximum strength had little effect on subjects' accuracy in pointing to a target, though some increase in uncertainty (a decrease in precision) became apparent. The authors concluded that "an isometric muscle contraction thus can be assumed to have little influence on a subsequent selection of buttons and handles without using the eyes" (p. 795).

2.3. Sense of Effort and Muscle Force

We have the ability to gauge the forces produced by the contractions of our muscles. This ability appears to arise via two separate and quite different mechanisms. The first uses sensory inputs presumably from tension receptors in the muscles (the Golgi tendon organs) to provide us with a subtle awareness of muscle tension. The second mechanism appears to monitor the command signals generated in the brain and destined for the muscles to provide us with a vivid sense of "effort." We briefly review here some of the sensations arising from these kinesthetic mechanisms and explore the relationships between them.

2.3.1. Estimating Weight. We use the terms *heaviness* and *lightness* to describe our perception of the weight of an object. The perceived heaviness or weight of an object depends not only on its actual weight but also on the condition of the muscles that support the weight (Stevens, Note 2). Recall the common experience of a parcel feeling heavier and heavier as the arm that carries it becomes progressively fatigued. One can objec-

Table 13.7. The Effect of Previous Positions of the Head on the Perception of Subsequent Head Position

	Tests			
		Fingers to Head At		
Treatment Condition	Head to Straight Ahead	+24°	0°	−24°
Head at 24° to the right	+5.9 ± 1.3[a]	−6.2 ± 1.6[a]	−6.8 ± 1.6[a]	−3.4 ± 1.0[a]
Head at 0° strained to the left	+0.9 ± 2.1	−0.4 ± 1.2	−1.0 ± 1.5	−0.3 ± 1.7
Head at 0°, relaxed	−0.01 ± 1.1	+0.8 ± 0.8	+0.4 ± 1.1	−0.5 ± 1.8

The table shows the error in judging the position of the head caused by three treatment conditions. The test, done before and after each treatment, consisted of having subjects: (1) position the head forward, starting from one of six randomly selected positions, (2) position the head at each of three angles (−24, 0, and +24°), and (3) position a tab held between the two index fingers until it felt straight ahead of the nose. For the treatment, subjects held their heads as indicated for 10 min, with 2-min "top-up" periods interspersed through the testing phase. The values represent differences in the means (±95% confidence limits) for the pre- and posttreatment tests. Positive values indicate shifts to the right. (From Howard & Anstis, 1974).

[a] Significant at $p < .001$.

tively demonstrate this effect of muscle fatigue on the perception of weight or heaviness by having a subject continuously support a weight in one hand, thus allowing the arm muscles to fatigue, and periodically match this weight using the opposite, nonfatigued arm (McCloskey, Ebeling, & Goodwin, 1974). As the one arm fatigues, subjects select larger and larger weights with the nonfatigued arm to match the reference weights (Figure 13.28).

Fatigue weakens a muscle by reducing the amount of force it can produce for a given level of excitation or neural "drive." This weakness apparently accounts for the increase in perceived heaviness. Muscle weakness produced by disease, injury, or drugs, like curare, that block transmission of nerve impulses to the muscle fibers likewise causes an increase in apparent heaviness of weights lifted with the affected limb (Gandevia & McCloskey, 1977). Neurological disorders within the central

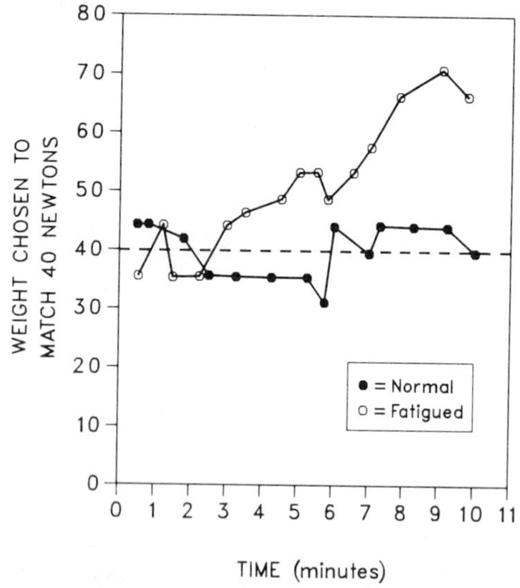

Figure 13.28. Weight matching and the sense of heaviness in fatigued muscles. The subject was given a 9-lb (4.09-kg) weight to support by contraction of the biceps brachialis of one arm and, in a series of trials, was to choose apparently equal weights supported in the same way by other arm. When the reference arm was rested between trials (closed circles), the subject chose weights close to the reference weight in attempts to match it. When the reference arm supported the weight continuously (open circles), it became fatigued, and weights heavier than the reference weight were chosen to match it. (From D. I. McCloskey, P. Ebeling, & G. M. Goodwin, Estimation of weights and tensions and apparent involvement of a "sense of effort," *Experimental Neurology*, 1974, *42*. Reprinted with permission.)

nervous system, such as stroke, may also cause an apparent muscle weakness (paresis) that produces the same altered sense of weight discrimination found with muscle fatigue (Gandevia, 1982). Weights feel heavier when lifted with a limb on the affected side compared to the normal side. The weakness need not come about because of any alterations in the muscle itself or the peripheral nerve supplying the muscle in order to affect perceived heaviness.

Recent studies suggest that our perception of heaviness arises mainly from signals derived entirely within the central nervous system (CNS) (see Section 4.4). A portion of the command signals generated during willed or voluntary movements and destined for the muscles apparently get routed as well to the perceptual portions of the brain where they can alter or perhaps even produce sensations. We usually call the signals that get fed back to the perceptual areas *corollary discharges*, a term first used by Sperry (1950). The concept is schematized in Figure 13.1. In short, the CNS internally monitors its own efforts to produce muscle contractions, and our perception of heaviness derives from this internal sense of effort (Gandevia & McCloskey, 1977). To support an object with muscles weakened by fatigue, drugs, or disease, or with a partial blockage in the motor pathways, would require a greater than normal level of command signals, and the CNS would interpret this increased level of command signals as an increased heaviness of the object. (For an excellent review of corollary discharges and perception, see McCloskey, 1981.)

Involuntary muscle contractions may occur without an accompanying sense of effort. Patients suffering from CNS disorders that produce involuntary movements rarely feel any effort associated with the movement. However, involuntary or reflex contractions can indirectly alter perceived effort by reducing or increasing the amount of command signals needed to accomplish a task. A reflex contraction that assists a voluntary contraction will reduce the apparent effort, and conversely, one that opposes the voluntary contraction will increase the feeling of effort (Hagbarth & Eklund, 1966). For example, if one vibrates the biceps tendon in the arm while supporting a weight in the hand, the weight feels lighter. Biceps tendon vibration elicits a reflex contraction (the tonic vibration reflex) that assists lifting of the weight, so that a smaller level of voluntary command suffices to support the load. Conversely, vibrating the antagonist muscles to oppose the lifting causes the weight to feel heavier (McCloskey, Ebeling, & Goodwin, 1974). Recently, Cafarelli and Kostka (1981) reported exactly the opposite results. Vibration applied to the patellar tendon to elicit a reflex that assists voluntary extension of the knee caused weights lifted with the foot to feel heavier, rather than lighter. They could not explain why their results differed from McCloskey's or Hagbarth's.

Contracting the lifting muscles prior to estimating a test weight can alter the estimate, an aftereffect called the *weight expectancy illusion*. See de Mendoza (1979) for further details. Lifting a heavy weight several times in seccession before lifting a lighter weight causes underestimation of the lighter weight, and, likewise, lifting a lighter weight prior to estimating a heavier weight causes an overestimation. Another example of a postcontraction effect that influences our sense of heaviness comes from an old parlor game where one's arms seem to rise almost effortlessly following a brief but forceful attempt to raise them against a restraint (Kohnstamm effect, see Cratty & Duffy, 1969; Forbes, Baird, & Hopkins, 1926). To demonstrate this effect stand in a doorway with your arms at your side. Keeping your arms straight, push the backs of your hands very firmly against the doorjambs for about 10–20 sec. Step out of the doorway and with little effort your arms will rise, seemingly almost by themselves. The mechanism of these illusions remains unresolved.

Sensory inputs from the skin can also influence perceived effort or heaviness. To demonstrate the complexity of the interaction between perception of heaviness and cutaneous sensation in the hand, Gandevia and McCloskey (1977) had subjects lift a reference weight, either by flexing or extending the terminal joint of the thumb or by flexing the middle (interphalangeal) joint of the index finger, and then select a matching weight identically presented to the opposite thumb or finger. Figure 13.29 illustrates their procedure and summarizes the results.

In general, anesthetizing the thumb caused weights lifted by flexing the thumb to feel heavier than normal, and weights lifted by extending the thumb to feel lighter than normal (see Figure 13.29(b)). They found a close interaction between the thumb and the index finger: anesthesia of the index finger caused weights lifted by thumb flexion to feel heavier, and electrical stimulation of the unanesthetized index finger caused weights lifted by thumb flexion to feel lighter (Figure 13.29(c)). Perceived heaviness with the index finger behaved much like the thumb. Weights lifted by finger flexion felt lighter with stimulation of the thumb and heavier with anesthesia of the thumb (Figure 13.29(d)).

This interaction between thumb and index finger apparently did not extend to all the fingers. Neither anesthesia nor electrical stimulation of the fifth (little) finger had much influence on perceived heaviness when lifting weights with thumb flexion. In addition, thumb anesthesia did not cause an increase in perceived heaviness if muscles in the arm and shoulder did the lifting and the thumb muscles served only to stabilize the wrist and thumb.

Whether the effects of anesthesia and stimulation of the skin alter the sense of effort directly by influencing the central command signals or indirectly by altering some reflex contraction of the thumb or finger muscles remains unclear. Marsden, Rothwell, and Traub (1979) proposed that anesthesia or stimulation of the digits influences the sense of effort via an effect on muscle reflexes, primarily by altering the contraction of the antagonist (opposing) muscle. A reflex-cocontraction of the antagonist muscles would necessitate a greater level of command signals to the lifting muscles to produce the same net external force. However, Gandevia, McCloskey, and Potter (1980) subsequently demonstrated that blocking the nerve to the antagonistic muscles, thus preventing their contraction, did not systematically alter the increase in perceived heaviness due to anesthesia. Therefore changes in contraction of the antagonist muscles probably do not explain why perceived heaviness increases with thumb anesthesia. This does not rule out other reflex effects that might, for example, act within the spinal cord. Cutaneous sensory inputs affect the spinal component of the stretch reflex of the thumb flexor muscle much as they affect perception of heaviness. Anesthesia of either the thumb or the index finger can abolish the reflex (see Marsden, Merton, & Morton, 1977), and electrical stimulation of the unanesthetized digit can restore the reflex (Dyhre-Poulsen & Djørup, 1976). Like alterations in perceived heaviness, the effect of stimulating or anesthetizing the skin appears confined to the muscles that actually move the joints; thumb anesthesia has no effect on the stretch reflex of the arm and shoulder muscles. We note with interest that unlike the finger, peripheral anesthesia of the great toe does not affect the stretch reflex in muscles that move the toe (Marsden et al., 1977).

One observation about the sense of effort with weakened muscles remains puzzling. As muscles become progressively weaker, the feeling of heaviness or effort increases (see Figures 13.28 and 13.30). One might expect that with total paralysis the feeling of heaviness would reach some maximal level. However, with certain lesions (damage) in the brain, sense of effort and heaviness can disappear entirely (Gandevia, 1982; McCloskey, 1981). The account by the physicist Ernst Mach (here quoted from Gandevia, 1982, p. 152) concerning his own motor stroke describes this phenomenon well:

> I was in a railway train, when I suddenly observed, with no consciousness of anything else being wrong, that my right arm and leg were paralyzed; the paralysis was intermittent, so that from time to time I was able to move again in an apparently normal way. After some hours it became continuous and permanent, there also set in an affection of the right facial muscle, which prevented me from speaking except in a low tone and with some difficulty. I can only describe my condition during the period of complete paralysis by saying that when I formed the intention of moving my limbs I felt no effort, but that it was absolutely impossible for me to bring my will to the point of executing the movement. On the other hand, during the phases of imperfect paralysis, and during the period of convalescence, my arm and leg seemed to me enormous burdens which I could only lift with the greatest effort. . . . The paralyzed limbs retained their sensibility completely . . . and thus I was enabled to be aware of their position and of their passive movement.

One does not see this absence of a sense of effort with complete paralysis produced by relaxant drugs or nerve blocks that exert their effect outside the CNS, or by disorders of the motor neurons in the spinal cord (Gandevia, 1982). Subjects have a clear perception of their attempts to contract their muscles and also of their inability to move. Even if the experimenter tries to fool the subject by eliciting cutaneous sensations consistent with a successful voluntary movement with paralyzed muscles, a subject still reports that no movement occurred (McCloskey & Torda, 1975).

2.3.2. Estimating Muscle Tension. Humans normally rely on their sense of effort to judge the force of muscle contractions, but they also possess a subtle awareness of the actual tension produced by their muscles. Effort and tension normally go hand in hand, so one must disturb the usual relationship between them to demonstrate independent senses of tension and effort. This dissociation becomes apparent with muscles weakened by

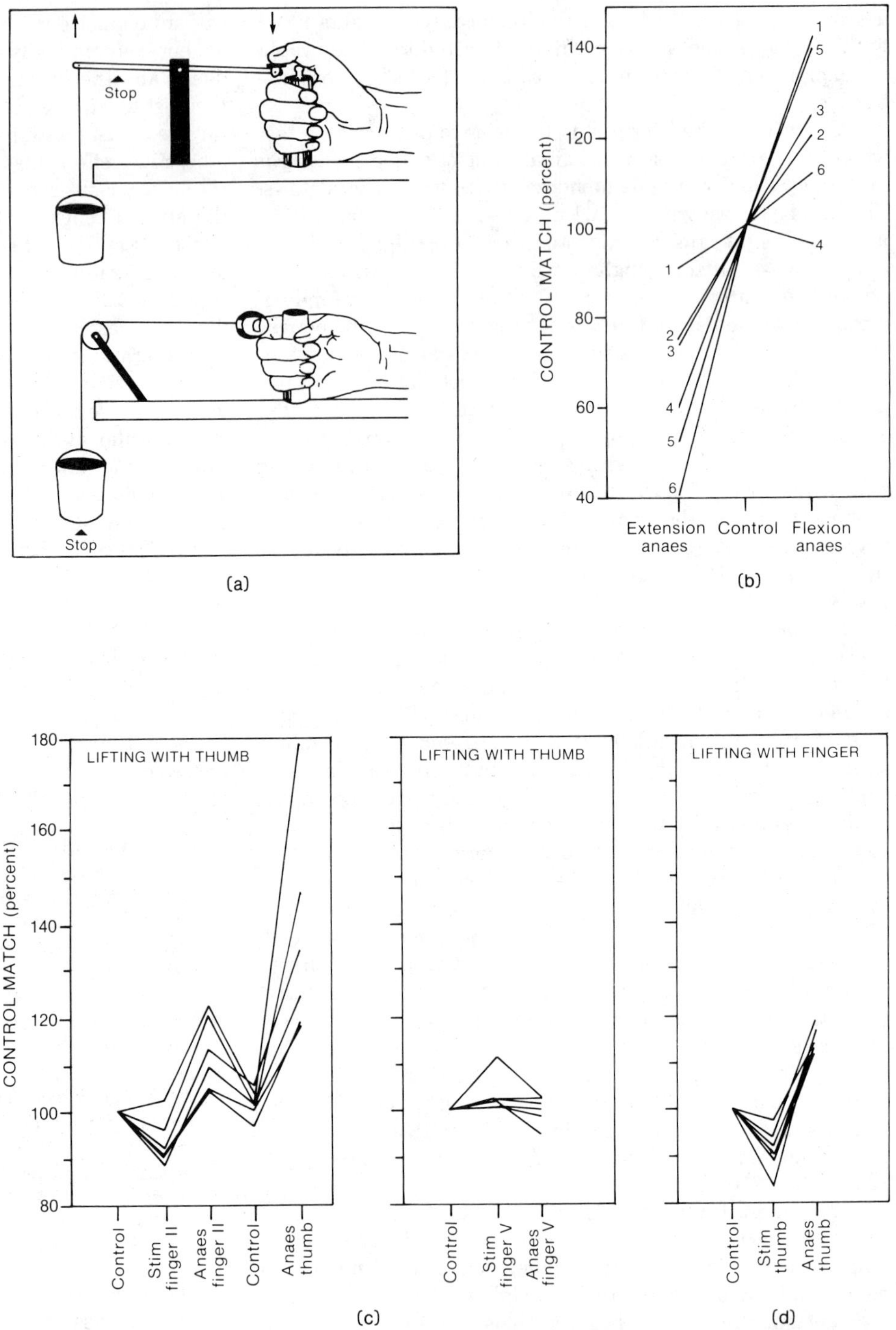

Figure 13.29. Altering sensory inputs from parts not related to lifting of weights can alter the sense of heaviness. (a) The position of the right hand and apparatus used when weights were lifted by flexing the distal joint of the thumb. The fingers were placed around a cylindrical upright, and the pulp of the thumb rested on a flat circular rocker. Flexing the thumb depressed one end of the "seesaw" and lifted the weight contained in a bucket hung on the other end. The apparatus could be arranged for lifting with extension of the thumb. Below: this shows the position of the right hand and the pulley used when weights were lifted by flexing the index finger predominantly at the proximal interphalangeal joint. The adjacent fingers were placed around a cylindrical upright. A wire ran from a thick piece of rubber tubing around the distal interphalangeal joint over a pulley to support the bucket containing the weights. For all modes of lifting, the left hand used a similar apparatus to that used by the right hand, and each apparatus had an adjustable stop mechanism so that the weights were "engaged" when the positions of the lifting digits were similar. (b) The results from six subjects when estimating the weight of 1 kg lifted by thumb flexion and 0.5 kg lifted by thumb extension. Results obtained with an anesthetized thumb are shown on the left for extension and the right for flexion and are expressed as percentages of control matches. Results from individual subjects are indicated by numerals at the left and right edges of the figure. For the group, removal of the sensory input from the thumb caused an increase in the perceived heaviness of the reference when it was

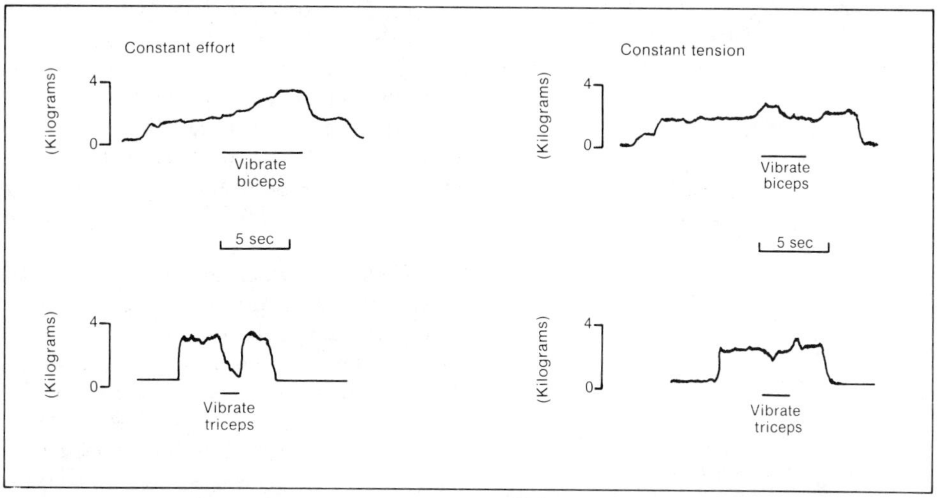

Figure 13.30. Estimation of weights and sense of heaviness. A subject exerted a force against a strain gauge by contracting his biceps brachialis muscles. The wrist through which he exerted the force and the tip of his supporting elbow were anesthetized, and vision was excluded. He was asked to keep either his effort (traces at left) or the tension he exerted (traces at right) constant. Vibration at 100 Hz of the contracting muscle or of its antagonist (triceps) was applied where shown. The records of tension achieved show that vibration led to considerable changes when the subject was asked to keep his effort constant. When he was asked to keep tension constant, he was able to adjust his effort so as to do so. (From D. I. McCloskey, P. Ebeling, & G. M. Goodwin, Estimation of weights and tensions and apparent involvement of a "sense of effort," *Experimental Neurology*, 1974, *42*. Reprinted with permission.)

fatigue or muscle relaxants like curare or by eliciting a tonic vibration reflex either to assist or to oppose a voluntary contraction.

McCloskey, Ebeling, and Goodwin (1974) tested subjects' ability to maintain either a constant effort or a constant tension in the biceps (arm flexor) muscle during vibration of either the biceps muscle, which reflexly assisted the contraction, or the triceps (arm extensor) muscle, which reflexly opposed the contraction. The subjects sat at a table with their arms held to the front in a slightly flexed position and the elbows resting on a pad. Three of 12 subjects had the skin around the elbows anesthetized as a check that pressure cues from skin on the elbow did not cause the observed results. A blindfolded subject pulled against a strain gauge (attached to the wrist with a cable) by flexing the arm to produce some target force, whereupon the experimenter vibrated either the biceps or the triceps tendons. With a simple instruction to "keep the effort constant" or "do not change effort," the subjects exerted a greater or lesser force depending on whether the tonic vibration reflex assisted or opposed the contraction. However, with instructions to "keep the tension in the cable constant," force remained fairly constant during vibration of either muscle (see Figure 13.30). The 12 subjects could hold tension constant with an accuracy of 20% or better.

Roland and Ladegaard-Pedersen (1977) demonstrated a similar ability to distinguish between tension and effort in the fingers with the muscles weakened by curare injected into the arm through a vein. An inflated blood pressure cuff around the upper arm occluded the circulation to the arm and prevented the curare from entering the general circulation. Subjects slowly

lifted by flexion and a reduction in the perceived heaviness when lifted by extension. (c) The results from six subjects when estimating the weight of 1 kg lifted by flexing the thumb. Results are expressed as a percentage of control estimates. On the left are results obtained when the sensory input from the index finger (finger II) was increased by electrical stimulation and removed by anesthesia and later when the thumb was anesthetized (paralyzing its joint and cutaneous afferents but not its muscle afferents). On the right are results obtained from the same subjects when lifting by flexing the thumb while the sensory inputs from the little finger (finger V) were enhanced by stimulation and then when they were removed by anesthesia. For the group, stimulation of the index finger reduced the perceived heaviness of the reference weight, and anesthesia increased it. Anesthesia of the thumb produced a large increase in the perceived heaviness of the reference weight. For the group, modification of the sensory input from the little finger did not significantly alter the heaviness of the reference weight. (d) The results from six subjects when estimating the weight of 2 kg lifted by flexing the index finger at the proximal interphalangeal joint. The sensory input from the thumb was increased by electrical stimulation or removed by digital anesthesia. For the group, stimulation of the thumb reduced and anesthesia of the thumb increased the perceived heaviness of the reference weight lifted by flexing the finger. (From S. C. Gandevia & D. I. McCloskey, Changes in motor commands, as shown by changes in perceived heaviness during partial curarization and peripheral anaesthesia in man, *Journal of Physiology*, 1977, *272*. Reprinted with permission.)

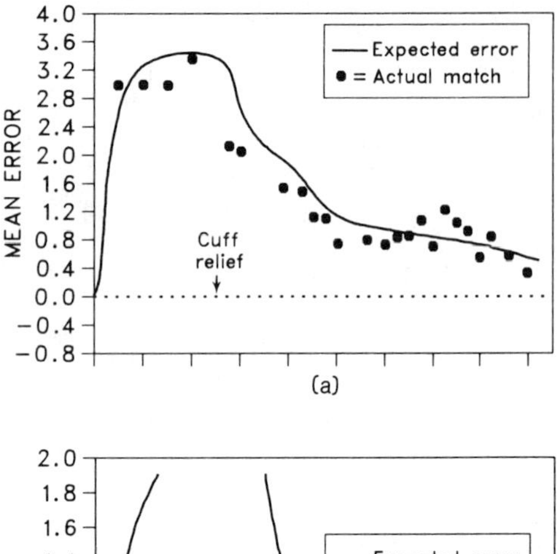

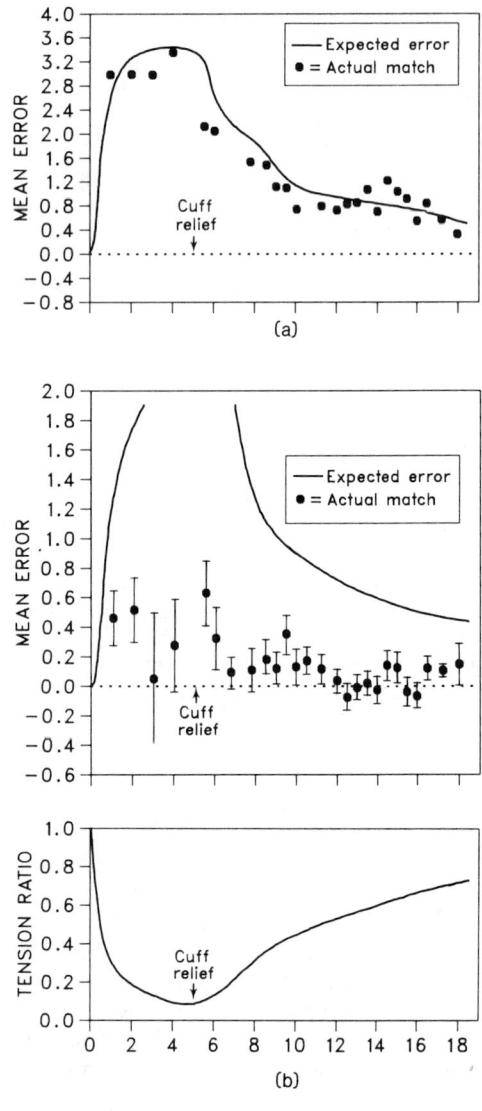

Figure 13.31. The effect of weakening the muscles on the sense of effort and the ability to estimate muscle tension. A pressure cuff was placed around one arm which was then injected with curare. The subject squeezed a strain gauge with the weakened hand to some level of force set by the experimenter (P_{set}), then matched the apparent force or effort with the other hand, producing a matching force (P_{obt}). The error in matching is expressed as the logarithm of the ratio of these two values. The expected error was estimated by measuring the maximal tension the subject could produce prior to curarization and at different times after paralysis. (a) Matching of effort during gallamine blockade, 1 subject. The points refer to the actual match. The curve is the error expected if the subject had a perfect match of effort by virtue of matching outgoing motor discharges (estimated as the ratio of maximal, uncurarized tension to maximal tension at times after injection of curare). Shown is the mean error (average of ln $[P_{obt}/P_{set}]$) as a function of time. (b) Matching of force isometrically during gallamine blockade, 11 subjects. The skin and joints were anesthetized. Mean error and standard error of the mean for the matches are shown. The upper line shows the matching error expected if matching were based on corollary discharges. Note the discrepancy between expected and actual errors. The time course of paralysis is shown in the lower part of figure as the fraction of normal maximal force of compression that could be exerted with thumb and index finger. Paralysis-induced weakness produced a significant error in force when matching effort but not when matching force. (From P. E. Roland & H. Ladegaard-Pederson, A quantitative analysis of sensations of tension and of kinaesthesia in man: Evidence for a peripherally originating muscular sense and for a sense of effort, *Brain, 100*. Copyright 1977 by Oxford University Press. Reprinted with permission.)

squeezed an isometric strain gauge between the thumb and the index finger, first with the weakened hand until told to stop by the experimenter (this established the "set force,"P_{set}) and then with the nonweakened hand to match either the force or the effort (this established the "obtained matching force," P_{obt}). They computed matching error from the logarithm of the ratio of these two force values. Paralysis produced a significant error when matching effort but not when matching force (Figure 13.31).

These experimenters also measured the force of a maximal voluntary contraction in the test hand before (P_{max},o) and at intervals during the muscle paralysis (P_{max},t). This measure provided an estimate of the degree of paralysis and allowed the calculation of error expected if the subject relied on the sense of effort to make judgments (lower curves in Figure 13.31(b)). The difference between the expected and actual errors in matching force indicates that the sense of muscle tension in this case did not derive from the sense of effort.

2.4. Summary

2.4.1. Perception of Passive Movement. The majority of tests of limb-movement sense involve passively rotating a joint to determine the smallest excursion the subject can detect. The clarity or vividness of the sensation depends on the rate of movement. Excursions that go unnoticed at one speed may become readily detected at a faster speed. Amplitude plays a part as well; increasing the amplitude of an excursion may improve its detectability.

Humans can detect joint rotations of a fraction of a degree. Reported values range from 0.20 to 6.10° , depending on the joint tested and the rate of rotation used. Authors tend to agree that proximal joints like the hip show a greater sensitivity to movement than distal joints like those in the fingers. For example, Laidlaw and Hamilton (1937) list the joints in order of decreasing sensitivity as follows: hip, shoulder, knee, ankle, elbow, the first three metacarpophalangeal joints (knuckles), wrist, the last two metacarpophalangeal joints, and the metatarsophalangeal joint (toe).

2.4.2. Perception of Limb Position. Humans possess independent senses of joint movement and position, but our awareness of movement has a more vivid character than our sense of position. Subjects instructed or trained, perhaps inadvertently, to attend to movement may not notice small changes in position. Some studies claiming to have studied position sense have actually tested movement sense.

The most straightforward test of limb-position sense requires a subject to match the position of one limb to that of the other. The experimenter sets the target position of the reference limb either by moving the subject's relaxed limb (passive positioning) or by asking the subject to move the limb voluntarily to the target as instructed (active positioning). The subject indicates perception of the target position by aligning the opposite limb with the reference limb. Many variants of this paradigm exist, but this example illustrates the main aspects of the procedure.

2.4.2.1. Bias. Subjects match to a target position with an offset or bias (revealed by the mean value of the matching error) that varies from subject to subject (see Figures 13.7 and 13.15) and also depends on the target angle (see Figure 13.8). Some subjects may show large offsets representing as much as 10% of the full range of joint excursion. One might conclude from such large and varied offsets that we possess a rather inaccurate sense of joint position. However, subjects all seem to match positions around this offset position with about the same precision or variability, as reflected in the standard deviation about the mean of the errors. For some situations precision may provide a better measure of performance than accuracy. Figure 13.8 reveals that subjects match elbow position with a slightly greater precision (smaller standard deviation) near the extreme positions where they show the least accuracy (largest mean error). The figure also shows that subjects match most accurately near the middle of the angle range. At either extreme, they tend to err in a direction toward this middle position. We have found a similar behavior with the knee, ankle, and shoulder.

2.4.2.2. ***Active versus Passive Positioning of the Reference Arm.*** Paillard and Brouchon (1968) found that subjects could match their outstretched arm (shoulder joint) more accurately when they themselves placed the reference arm by voluntary contraction of the muscles (active positioning) than when the experimenter moved the relaxed arm into place (passive positioning). Self-positioning proved the more accurate whether the subject continued to support the arm at the target angle or rested it relaxed in a cradle. The act of self-placement seems the important factor.

2.4.2.3. ***Effect of Muscle Loading on Position Sense Accuracy.*** We do not yet have a clear picture of how muscle loading affects our perception of the position of a limb. Some studies indicate that we should experience an offset in perceived position in the direction of the force; others say the opposite. McCloskey (1973) found an offset in the direction of the applied force with the elbow when pulling against a weight. This seems an intuitively reasonable finding. However, Monster and colleagues (1973) found an offset in the perceived position of the ankle toward a plantar flexion when pulling or pushing against a torque, but the direction of the torque did not affect the direction of the offset. Altering the experimental conditions slightly produced yet another effect. Having the subject flex the ankle isometrically to produce a force without actual rotation of the joint caused an offset in perceived position in a direction opposite to the exerted force. In other words, the subjects exerted a force toward dorsiflexion and perceived an offset toward dorsiflexion, an effect opposite that seen by McCloskey.

2.4.2.4. ***Effect of Speed of Movement on Positioning Accuracy.*** Subjects accustomed to discriminating passive displacements executed at very slow rates may subsequently overestimate the magnitudes of rapid excursions. When subjects attempt to locate a target position by self-movement (e.g., by pointing with the finger), the speed, direction, and magnitude of movement, as well as the locus of the target, can all affect accuracy. The speeds they choose without prompting by the experimenter tend to correspond to speeds that give the best accuracy in tests of accuracy versus speed. Unfortunately, we lack a coherent picture of how these variables influence perception of position.

2.4.2.5. ***Influence of Time on the Perception of Position.*** The length of time elapsed between establishing the target position and making an indication can substantially influence matching accuracy in some cases. The perceived position of a limb maintained in place changes with time, presumably due to adaptation in the receptors that signal position and perhaps to some internal, CNS mechanism as well. We do possess an internal, mental image of our body in space that does not of itself depend on sensory inflow as evidenced by the phantom-limb phenomenon. Sensory inputs may alter the clarity of this image and the relative positions of its various components, but the image can exist without sensory inflow. People who lose a limb usually feel that the limb, or at least portions of it, still exists. Blocking nerves to anesthetize a limb also produces a phantom.

2.4.2.6. ***Memory.*** Humans seem to have a remarkable memory for limb position. Subjects can match the remembered position of a limb, even after many hours, about as accurately as they match one limb directly to another. Subjects can also tell that a limb has changed its position by only a few degrees even when the change has occurred slowly over a period of 15 min or so, and they can do so without using the opposite limb as a reference. The mechanisms for this remarkable memory remain obscure.

2.4.2.7. ***Aftereffects.*** Previous positions of a limb can influence perceived position. It appears that previous position, rather than muscle contraction involved in achieving or maintaining the position, serves as the important factor. Previous muscle contractions can, however, affect our sense of heaviness. A test weight lifted after several liftings of a heavier weight will feel lighter and vice versa.

2.4.3. Sense of Heaviness, Effort, and Muscle Tension. Humans have independent senses of the actual tension developed by their muscles and the "effort" required to contract the muscles. One can observe the difference in these two senses with muscles experimentally weakened by fatigue or drugs. Weights lifted by weakened muscles feel heavier; it requires more effort to lift them. Subjects will select a heavier weight with a normal arm to match a test weight supported by the weakened arm. However, with proper instruction, subjects with weakened muscles can match muscle tensions as well. Our sense of effort has a much more vivid character than our sense of tension, and normally subjects will rely on this sense of effort to discriminate weights. Our sense of muscle tension derives from sensory receptors in the muscles, presumably the Golgi tendon organs. Sense of effort derives from an internal monitoring of the command signals leaving the brain destined for the muscles. A portion of these command signals, the *corollary discharges*, get routed to the sensory regions of the brain to influence perception.

3. PHYSIOLOGY OF KINESTHETIC MECHANORECEPTORS

The CNS potentially has two ways of obtaining information about the positions and movements of the limbs. The CNS could monitor its own commands to the muscles, with the expectation that a given command produces the desired action, or it could use information from sensory receptors. In fact, it uses both methods. Monitoring its own commands or issuing a set of "prerecorded" commands, or *engrams*, from a bank of well-rehearsed alternatives has the advantage of speed; waiting for feedback from sensory receptors would actually limit the speed of our movements (van der Gon & Wienke, 1968). However, this method provides the CNS with no information about passive movements or whether a limb has successfully executed a desired action. Such information needs to come from sensors located in the periphery. Of course, the CNS can use information from a variety of sources to determine limb position and movement. We might look at our limbs, touch an object that has a known location, or perhaps even hear a sound when the limb makes contact with a familiar object. However, we shall limit our discussion to those receptors located in the limbs themselves that might signal limb position and movement or supply information about the contractions of our muscles. These receptors provide the bulk of our kinesthetic sensations from the limbs.

Receptors responding to mechanical events associated with joint rotation can potentially signal information about active and passive changes in limb position, as well as about muscle contraction. Such mechanoreceptors include articular receptors, cutaneous touch receptors, muscle spindles, and tendon organs. In this section we examine the kinds of signals available from sensory mechanoreceptors in the skin, joints, and muscle that might suitably serve as kinesthetic detectors.

3.1. Classification of Mechanoreceptors

We find two broad classes of input from mechanoreceptors: position or displacement signals and movement or transient signals. The former refers to information about joint angle continuously available during a maintained position of a limb or digit, and the latter refers to signals available only during the actual movement of a limb or digit. Movement signals could include information about the rate (velocity) at which a limb or digit changes its position and about acceleration or higher-order derivatives.

We can associate these position and movement signals with two broad classes of mechanoreceptors, the slowly adapting and the quickly or rapidly adapting types, respectively. Adaptation refers to the decline in the response of a sensory receptor to a maintained, static stimulus. Applying these definitions to kinesthetic receptors, if one rotates a joint from one position to another and maintains the new position, the rapidly adapting receptors would respond during the movement, and their response would decline to zero (adapt) within the first several seconds after reaching the new position. The response of the slowly adapting receptors would not diminish or would diminish only slightly over this period. Classifying receptors on the basis of their adaptation provides only a rough guide to the type of signals they carry, but the scheme has gained wide usage (see Burgess & Perl, 1973). According to this scheme, true position signals (meaning continuously available position signals) can come only from slowly adapting receptors. This does not rule out the possibility of deriving position information from signals produced by rapidly adapting receptors and available only during movement.

A rough correlation exists between a receptor species and the conduction velocity of its nerve fiber. A similar correlation exists for motor nerve fibers that innervate muscle. In addition, an approximately linear relationship exists between the conduction velocity of a nerve fiber and its diameter. See Mann (1981, p. 196) for further details about the different classification schemes. These relationships form the basis for much of the terminology found in the literature about kinesthetic receptors. Our discussion will mainly refer to A-alpha fibers (conducting impulses at 70–120 m/sec) that innervate skeletal (voluntary) muscle cells and signal them to contract and A-gamma fibers (15–40 m/sec) that carry control signals to the muscle spindle receptors. In discussing sensory innervation of muscle receptors, we will refer mainly to groups Ia, Ib, and II, the sensory fibers that innervate the muscle spindle primary endings, the Golgi tendon organ receptors, and the muscle spindle secondary endings, respectively. The reader might note that most of our data on conduction velocity comes from cats; human nerve fibers conduct impulses about 20% slower.

3.2. Methods

Most studies of mechanoreceptor responses involve recording electrical activity from individual afferent fibers while applying suitable stimuli to the structure containing the receptor. For limb position and movement ("kinesthetic") receptors, suitable stimuli consist of rotating and positioning the joint in various ways and perhaps probing around the joint and muscles to pinpoint the location of the receptor or receptors. To record activity from an individual nerve fiber (single-unit recordings), one either teases a thin bundle containing only a few fibers away from the nerve and places the filaments on wire hook electrodes or uses sharpened wire or glass microelectrodes.

To study the responses of kinesthetic receptors properly, one must manipulate joints. Unfortunately, the usual methods of recording unit responses from nerves will not accommodate much movement, and many of the earlier studies restricted joint rotation. Restricted movement in conjunction with a bias of unknown proportions in sampling the activity from the population of nerve fibers can yield a highly inaccurate picture of how the population as a whole responds to position or movement. This problem occurred in most of the early studies of joint receptors and it led to incorrect conclusions about the role of articular receptors in position sense.

3.3. Coding of Position and Movement

Sensory receptors show a selectiveness in the type of stimulus energy to which they respond. Each type or class of receptors has its own preferred stimulus, the so-called adequate stimulus, to which it responds most sensitively. Our ability to distinguish one kind of stimulus from another depends to a large extent on this differential sensitivity of the various receptor types. This high degree of specificity in the receptors themselves, combined with particular neural channels to carry the information, forms a *dedicated channel*, or *labeled line*, system of sensory coding. Within somesthesis ("body sense") the CNS uses the labeled line approach to encode location of a stimulus on the surface of the body and also to encode the various subdivisions or submodalities of the body sense, such as touch, temperature, and kinesthesia. Differences in the activity between the various receptor types (pattern codes) within a particular submodality provide the many shades or qualities of our sensory experience. For example, our ability to recognize the great many subtle variations in our sense of touch, including discriminating differences in textures, size of the contact, sharpness, and numerous other features, relies on pattern codes.

Kinesthetic receptors probably use both dedicated channels and pattern codes to provide information about the positions and movements of the limbs and digits. We know surprisingly little about how these stimulus features get encoded by the various receptors, but we can make some educated guesses. Humans can detect the occurrence of a movement without necessarily sensing its direction or speed, and they can independently judge the direction and the speed of a movement and the position of a limb. It seems reasonable, therefore, to expect that these features get encoded independently by the receptor population and that they may utilize different neural circuits (see Burgess, Horch, & Tuckett, 1983). For the case of movement signals, we find an ample supply of suitable receptor types, especially in skin and muscles, that can provide the requisite information, though we do not know which receptors actually do the job.

The signaling of limb position seems a bit easier to understand, at least in principle. After first establishing (or, more precisely, assuming) that our awareness of static limb position depends on continuously available information from the periphery, we would look to the slowly adapting receptors in the skin, muscle, or joint as the most probable source of the signals. One generally finds this assumption made, and most studies have concentrated on seeking slowly adapting receptors, especially in joints, that appear capable of encoding joint angle. We possess far fewer slowly adapting receptors than the rapidly adapting type, and thus slowly adapting responses prove easier to isolate for study. In addition, static joint angle provides a simple, well-defined stimulus feature, so we stand a reasonable chance of identifying how the neural discharge encodes angle. Most studies have sought to demonstrate that the rate of discharge (number of impulses per second) of individual receptors varies with joint angle in some unambiguous way capable of encoding the angle.

However, a continuously available signal does not necessarily require an ongoing signal, as one would get from slowly adapting receptors. Conceivably, true position signals could derive from rapidly adapting receptors that respond transiently to brief subtle contractions of the muscles, contractions too small to produce a noticeable movement. Transiently available signals coupled with a good memory for position might serve well to provide static position sense. We discuss this idea further in Section 4.

While many schemes for encoding static position appear possible, two in particular have received the most attention. The first uses spatially tuned receptors, where each receptor responds only over a limited range of joint angles but the group as a whole covers the entire range. Skoglund (1956) claimed that receptors in the joints encode angle in this manner as shown in Figure 13.32(a). This scheme resembles the coding of sound frequency along the cochlea of the inner ear. Other workers have not found spatially tuned responses in joints (Clark, 1975; Clark & Burgess, 1975; Millar, 1975; Rossi & Grigg, 1982; Tracey, 1979), so we have little corroboration for a population of spatially tuned receptors of the type proposed by Skoglund. Still, we cannot entirely rule out some form of spatial tuning as contributing to position sense. For example, most slowly adapting receptors in joints respond only near the extreme positions of the joint. Whether impulses from these receptors produce conscious sensations or whether they initiate muscle reflexes to protect the joint remains unknown.

An opponent system provides an attractive alternative to the spatially tuned receptor model. In the opponent scheme, we find two groups of receptors anatomically arranged so that one group increases its discharge as the joint moves toward one extreme position and the other increases its discharge as the joint moves toward the other extreme, as shown in Figure 13.32(b). This resembles the way the retina encodes the wavelength of light (color) (Erickson, 1974; Richards, 1979). Neither of the two opponent populations needs to respond over the entire range of angles; as long as the two response profiles overlap, the CNS can uniquely derive position from the combined response. The receptors in muscles that signal muscle stretch would seem prime candidates for this kind of a signaling system. Almost all of our muscles work in opposing groups: agonist (aiding) and antagonist (opposing). For virtually every movement we make, some muscles shorten and other muscles lengthen.

In most opponent systems, total neural activity would vary over the range, with maximums at the extremes and a minimum near the midrange. Erickson (1974) attempted to correlate matching accuracy in the elbow with hypothetical opponent systems having differently shaped neural response functions (the curve relating receptor response to joint angle; see Figure 13.33). He observed that the best reliability of matching, as indicated by the smallest standard deviation (dispersion) of the matching errors, occurred near the end positions which had the greatest total neural activity. Note that the smallest mean or constant error occurred near the midposition, a common finding (see Section 2).

An opponent system has an advantage if the receptors respond to rate of movement in addition to position, as most do. A velocity response will reduce or even silence the output of a receptor as the position changes in the direction of decreasing response (see Figure 13.34). In an opponent system, this decrease in one-half the population gets compensated by the increased vigor of response from the other half of the population.

For sensations with an intensitive dimension, stimulus magnitude gets encoded by the total amount of neural activity reaching the CNS from all the receptors affected by the stimulus. When stimulus strength increases, the impulse rate goes up in those receptors already discharging, and additional sensory units reach threshold and begin discharging (see Chapter 12 by Sherrick and Cholewiak). This model matches our common experience for such sensations as the brightness of a light, the loudness of a sound, or the heaviness of a weight. However, position sense lacks a corresponding sense of intensity. We can easily gauge the amplitudes of joint displacements, but larger amplitudes do not feel "stronger" than smaller amplitudes. Likewise, changing the position of a limb does not result in any change in sensation that one would describe as stronger or weaker. We simply feel the limb in a different place. It seems unlikely that the total neural activity representing position remains constant over all positions (especially if the CNS uses an opponent system to measure position). Therefore, for the sense of limb or joint position, the CNS probably interprets changing levels of neural activity as a change in location, instead of a change in "amount" (Burgess, Wei, Clark, & Simon, 1982).

Keeping these concepts in mind, we now consider each of the three possible sources of kinesthetic sensory information: mechanoreceptors in skin, joints, and muscle.

3.4. Mechanoreceptors in Skin

Since virtually any movement we make will stretch and bend some regions of skin and relax others, cutaneous mechanoreceptors could play a significant role in kinesthesia.

We find in the skin about a dozen different mechanoreceptor types, identified on the basis of their responses to mechanical deformation of the skin (Burgess & Perl, 1973; Horch, Tuckett, & Burgess, 1977; see Chapter 12 by Sherrick and Cholewiak). Most of these receptor types now have a clear association with specific receptor structures in the skin (see reviews by Chouchkov, 1978; Iggo, 1976; Iggo & Andres, 1982), and the majority show rapidly adapting responses and signal the velocity or the acceleration of skin or hair displacement. Two receptor species, called type I (T1) and type II (T2) receptors and associated with Merkel cell complexes and Ruffini endings, respectively, show slowly adapting responses. They continue to discharge with a maintained deformation of the skin and receive innervation from axons conducting at velocities in the middle of the A-alpha range.

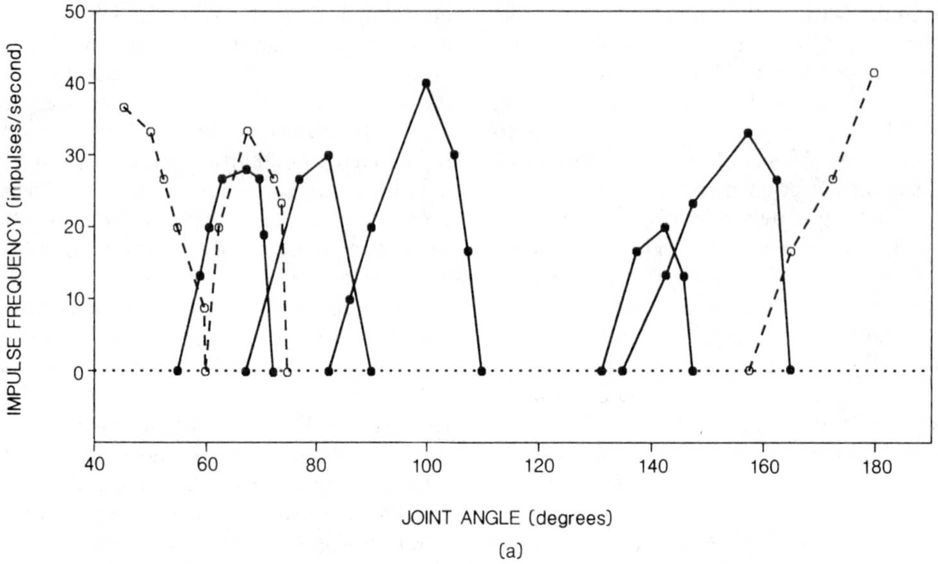

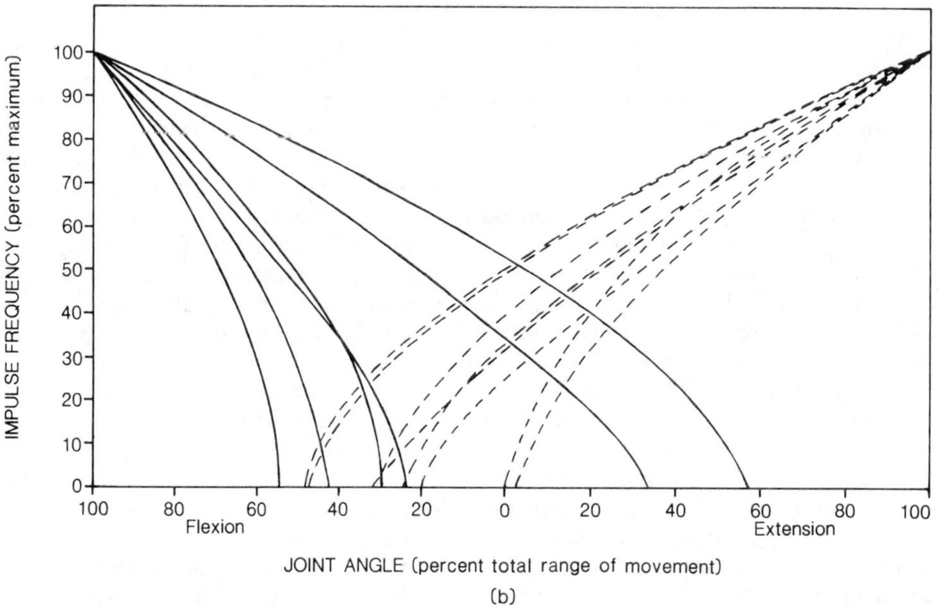

Figure 13.32. Two possible schemes for encoding joint angle. (a) A spatially tuned system in which each receptor responds over a very limited portion of the range. One would know joint angle by knowing which members of the population are active. In the extreme case, the bell-shaped curves could be replaced by idealized "on–off" pulse functions as it is not necessary to know the actual level of activity in the individual members of the population. (From S. Skoglund, Anatomical and physiological studies of knee joint innervation in the cat, *Acta Physiologica Scandinavica*, 1956, *36*. Reprinted with permission.) (b) An opponent system in which two populations of receptors produce a graded discharge with angle over more than half the total range. The populations are biased toward opposite extremes, so the ratio of activity between the two populations gives a measure of joint angle. Overall changes in level of activity or sensitivity of the populations would not degrade the coding of joint position. (From V. B. Mountcastle, G. F. Poggio, & G. Werner, The relation of thalamic cell response to peripheral stimuli varied over an intensive continuum, *Journal of Neurophysiology*, 1963, *26*. Reprinted with permission.)

Several candidates might seem to exist among the cutaneous mechanoreceptor types for signaling kinesthetic information; however, few of these receptors respond much to skin stretch, a prerequisite for signaling the bending of a joint. Only the T2 receptor type (a slowly adapting candidate for sensing position) responds well to skin stretch and alters its discharge in response to changes in joint position (see Figure 13.35), though a recent report indicates that some rapidly adapting hair follicle receptors can fire in a predictable manner during movement of the jaw (Appenteng, Lund, & Seguin, 1982). An arrangement of T2 receptors either in a "spatially tuned" array or as opponent populations could, in principle, allow signaling of joint angle while compensating for activation due to objects contacting the skin. However, the T2 receptors make up only a small proportion of the total receptor population in the skin. Therefore, one wonders if they exist in sufficient numbers to encode angle except very crudely, though they may suffice to signal joint movement.

With recently available techniques in microneurography (see Chapter 12 by Sherrick and Cholewiak), one can activate single nerve fibers from the various cutaneous receptors to reveal

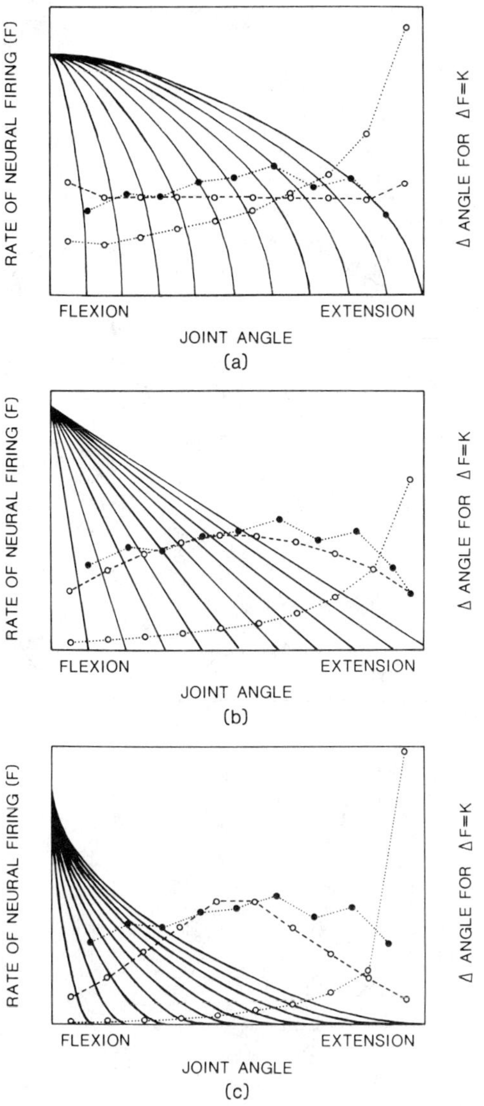

Figure 13.33. Coding of position by an "opponent" system. Three possible forms of neural response functions, (a), (b), and (c), of individual kinesthetic neurons (solid lines). Only those peaking in activity at flexion are shown; for clarity, extensor neurons are not shown. Dotted line with open circles are just noticeable difference curves based on equal changes in the neural response functions ($\Delta F = K$). The curves peaking at extension are derived from the flexion functions shown. Dashed lines with open circles are curves derived from the population of both extensor and flexor neural response functions. In (b) and (c), better discrimination is predicted toward the end of the continuum. Dotted lines with closed circles are the experimentally determined reliability of localization of elbow joint in humans (see Figure 13.8). Note correspondence with derived curves based on both flexors and extensors. (From R. P. Erickson, Parallel "population" neural coding in feature extraction, in F. O. Schmitt & F. G. Worden, Eds., *The neurosciences. Third study program*, MIT Press, Inc., 1974. Reprinted with permission.)

the kind of sensations they elicit. To our knowledge, no one has ever reported kinesthetic sensations arising from the stimulation of cutaneous receptors, and the T2 receptors (the prime candidates) do not appear to elicit any sensation at all when activated in isolation (Vallbo, Olsson, Westberg, & Clark, 1984). One should keep in mind that studies of this type have just begun. Though we think skin plays at most only a minor role in kinesthesia, new discoveries might alter our opinions. Perhaps cutaneous receptors that in isolation elicit sensations associated with the skin (touch, pressure, etc.) or no sensations at all (like the T2 receptors) might elicit kinesthetic sensations if the appropriate pattern of activity arose in the appropriate receptor population. As an example, muscle spindle receptors can elicit clear kinesthetic sensations when excited by vibration but apparently not when excited by squeezing the muscle.

In the fingers, skin receptors serve a facilitatory or supportive role; they enhance kinesthetic sensations elicited from other sources. This apparently holds true even for those classic rapidly adapting receptors, the Pacinian corpuscles, found on deeper bone and joint tissues, as well as in the dermis of the hands and feet. Pacinian receptors exhibit an exquisite sensitivity to acceleration and probably provide our ability to detect low-amplitude, high-frequency (60–400 Hz) vibrations (LaMotte & Mountcastle, 1975; Mountcastle, LaMotte, & Carli, 1972).

These reservations notwithstanding, skin may play an important role in kinesthesia in the hands, feet, and face, regions of skin that have an especially high innervation density compared to other skin areas. Anesthesia of the skin covering the tongue or the lips makes speech difficult, and people tend to bite their tongue if they cannot feel it. Anesthesia of the skin on the hands can produce a striking inability to use the fingers even with visual guidance, whereas anesthesia of a wide band of skin around the knee joint goes barely noticed. Cutaneous mechanoreceptors in the hand probably do not provide suitable information about the position of the fingers though they might signal movement, thus providing kinesthetic information to supplement position and movement signals from other sources (notably, muscle receptors). In addition, cutaneous receptors in the hand, particularly the thumb and the index finger, provide a facilitative input that the CNS needs in order to process kinesthetic information from other receptors. We discuss these ideas further in Section 4.

3.5. Mechanoreceptors in Joints

The ligaments and capsules of joints contain numerous slowly adapting mechanoreceptors that respond to stretching the ligament and stretching or bending the capsule (Freeman & Wyke, 1967; Skoglund, 1973; Wyke, 1967). In the ligaments, slowly adapting responses arise mainly from Golgi type endings formed by a profuse branching of the nerve terminals. The parent fiber may branch to several clusters of endings. Golgi receptors receive innervation from large-diameter, rapidly conducting axons (O'Connor & Gonzales, 1979).

When tested in the isolated ligament, the Golgi receptors show a vigorous and almost nonadapting response to stretch, though tension appears a more relevant variable than stretch because of the very low compliance of ligaments (Andrew, 1954). Andrew tested receptor responses in ligaments either removed from the knee (leaving the nerve supply intact) or left in place and stretched by means of a string looped under one end. He concluded that because the ligaments stretch when the knee moves, these receptors would provide ideal kinesthetic signals. However, when one tests the responses of these receptors with the knee intact and using natural stimulation (joint movement), they respond only at the very extreme positions of the joint (Clark, 1975). Moreover, many of the receptors respond only upon forceful hyperextension of the joint. Grigg (1975, 1976) found the receptor responses correlated best with torque applied to the joint, rather than joint position, and concluded that they served a protective function. Thus ligament receptors seem incapable of encoding position or movement of the joints, except perhaps to signal the extremes of flexion and extension.

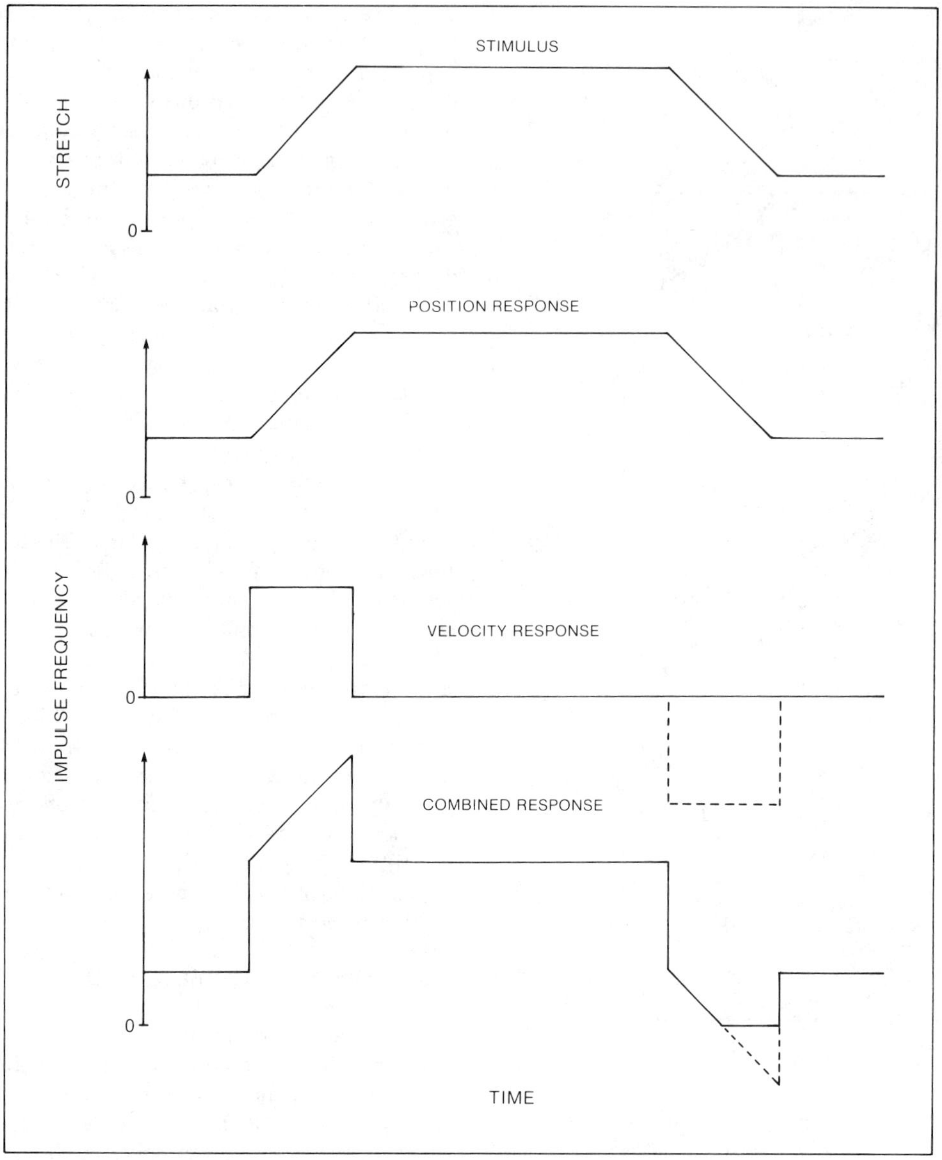

Figure 13.34. Idealized response profiles of receptors responding to a ramp displacement in joint angle. Shown are the displacement, the response from a receptor responding only to displacement, the response from a receptor responding to stimulus velocity, and the response from a receptor responding to both displacement and velocity. The last profile characterizes most "tonic" mechanoreceptors. Discharge frequencies below 0 are not possible, so the responses during the return ramp are truncated.

In the joint capsule, slowly adapting responses arise mainly from Ruffini type endings (Boyd, 1954; Skoglund, 1956). Ruffini endings appear very similar to the Golgi receptors, though a bit smaller, and they respond to stretch of the capsule. Ruffini endings in the joint resemble those in the skin that provide the slowly adapting T2 responses to skin stretch. Grigg, Hoffman, and Fogarty (1982) also found Golgi type receptors in the joint capsule. However, because the arrangement of the Golgi type differed from that of the Ruffini type, the Golgi receptors responded to compression of the capsule but not to stretch.

Several studies beginning around the 1950s reported the presence in the cat knee of mechanoreceptors that appeared ideally suited to encode joint angle (see Skoglund, 1973, for a discussion and references). Contraction of the muscles crossing the joint can influence the response of joint receptors, perhaps making them less suitable for accurately coding joint angle (Grigg, 1976; Grigg & Greenspan, 1977; Millar, 1973). However, joint receptors seemed far less subject to such external forces than skin or muscle receptors. Therefore, these early studies became generally accepted, and for a while the question of the origin of limb position signals appeared resolved.

Some years later, Burgess and Clark (1969) reexamined how knee joint mechanoreceptors respond to joint rotation. They came to a quite different conclusion: joint receptors could not encode joint position, except perhaps at extreme positions of the joint. Burgess and Clark, like others, noted that recordings from the whole knee joint nerve showed a great deal of activity at extreme positions of the joint and considerably less activity over the midranges of position (see Figure 13.36). However, the previous studies had focused on these responses in the midrange but did not attempt to determine how well this sample might represent the response of the population as a whole. When Bur-

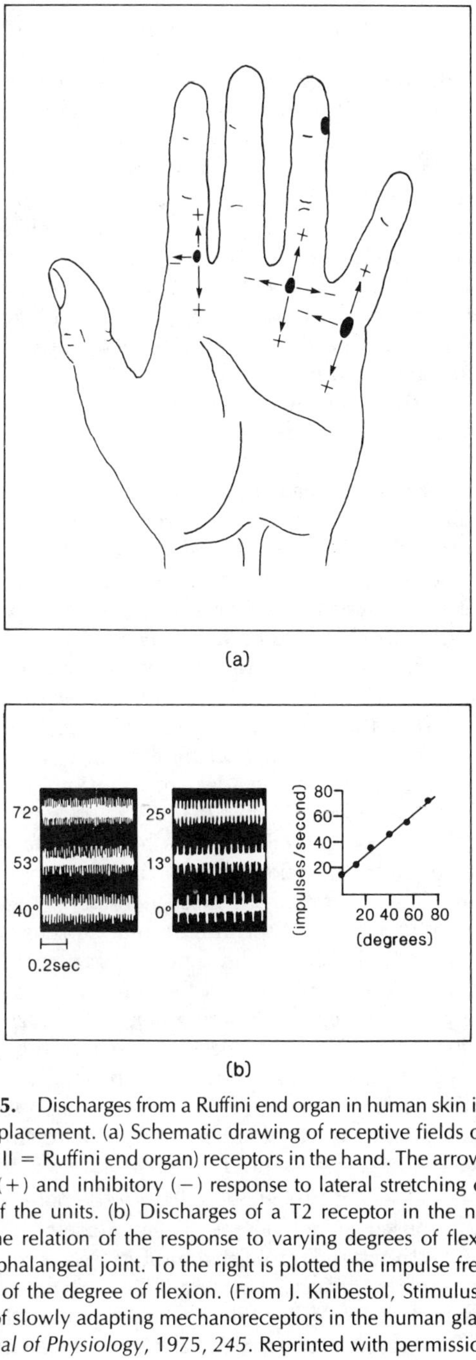

Figure 13.35. Discharges from a Ruffini end organ in human skin in response to joint displacement. (a) Schematic drawing of receptive fields of sampled T2 (= type II = Ruffini end organ) receptors in the hand. The arrows indicate excitatory (+) and inhibitory (−) response to lateral stretching of the skin for three of the units. (b) Discharges of a T2 receptor in the nail region, showing the relation of the response to varying degrees of flexion at the distal interphalangeal joint. To the right is plotted the impulse frequency as a function of the degree of flexion. (From J. Knibestol, Stimulus–response functions of slowly adapting mechanoreceptors in the human glabrous skin area, *Journal of Physiology*, 1975, *245*. Reprinted with permission.)

gess and Clark (1969) surveyed the entire population, they found that only a very small proportion of receptors responded in midrange positions.

Those receptors that did respond in midpositions of the joint appeared incapable of encoding flexion and extension of the joint (Clark & Burgess, 1975). Furthermore, at least some of the midrange responding receptors resided in the muscle behind the joint and not in the joint tissue itself. McIntyre, Proske, and Tracey (1978) have since confirmed the presence of muscle spindle receptor responses in the knee joint nerve. O'Connor and Seipel (1983) have provided anatomical evidence of muscle receptor afferents in the knee joint nerve, a nerve that most of us believed innervated only the joint. They found considerable variability in the origin and the courses of the posterior articular nerve of the cat knee, with as many as 14 out of 20 nerves containing nonarticular fibers, mostly from muscles around the knee.

Grigg (1975, 1976) corroborated this paucity of activity in the joint nerve over a wide range of midpositions in the knee, and others have observed a similar pattern in the wrist (Tracey, 1979) and the elbow (Millar, 1975). Thus receptors in these joints appear poorly suited to encode static angle in the midrange. Relatively few receptors respond, and one can often find positions with only one or two units active that show little change in response with alterations in position. In many cases, the nerve shows no activity at all. This lack of activity over a wide range of angles provides a powerful argument against joint receptors serving as the crucial source of position signals. Had there existed any appreciable activity, even though apparently uncorrelated to joint angle, we could not say for sure what infor-

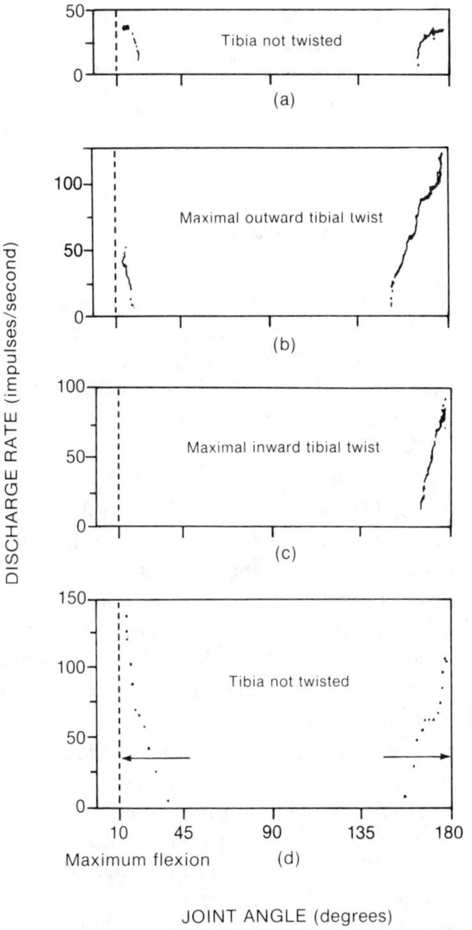

Figure 13.36. Flexion–extension receptor responses from cat knee joint. Impulse activity was recorded from a slowly adapting afferent fiber in the posterior articular nerve while the knee joint was held at different angles. "Instantaneous" discharge rate was calculated from time intervals between pairs of impulses and marked by a dot placed along the horizontal axis at the angle of occurrence. The angle between the tibia and femur was 10° at maximum flexion, 180° at maximum extension. Shown is steady-state response versus joint angle for tibia: (a) not twisted, (b) maximum outward twist, (c) maximum inward twist, (d) joint rotated at 150°/sec, with arrows indicating direction of movement (tibia not twisted). Note the similarity to an "opponent" type response pattern (Figure 13.33). (From P. R. Burgess & F. J. Clark, Characteristics of knee joint receptors in the cat. *Journal of Physiology*, 1969, *203*. Reprinted with permission.)

mation it provided. However, it seems reasonably safe to presume that one cannot build much of a code on silence.

If receptors in the knee, ankle, and wrist do encode angle at all, they would do so near the end positions, but inputs from other sources would be needed to handle the midrange, where psychophysical testing for position or movement sense usually takes place. Joint receptors might play an entirely protective role, providing a fast mechanism to prevent hyperextending the knee during a vigorous movement (such as trying to kick a football and missing it).

Some controversy yet remains over the role of joint receptors in position sense. Ferrell (1980) found midrange responses from receptors in the cat knee joint that he claims can encode angle over the whole range. Though few in number, they may suffice. Carli, Farabollini, Fontani, and Meucci (1979) concluded that receptors in the hip joint can encode angle, and Godwin-Austen (1969) found mechanoreceptors that could encode angle in the costovertebral joints (rib joints) of the cat. Though the final chapter in this story about joint receptors remains unwritten, we believe that they play their major role in protective reflexes and not in position sense.

Having argued that cutaneous and joint receptors make at most a limited contribution to signaling joint position, we now turn our attention to the possible role of muscle receptors in kinesthesia.

3.6. Mechanoreceptors in Muscles

Muscles contain two types of slowly adapting mechanoreceptors: the Golgi tendon organs and the muscle spindles. Golgi tendon organs lie in series with the main muscle fibers, well situated to measure tension in the muscle. Muscle spindles lie in parallel with the main muscle fibers, well situated to measure muscle length and rate of change of length. Figure 13.37 diagrams the arrangement of these two receptor types in muscle.

3.6.1. Golgi Tendon Organs. The Golgi tendon organ consists of a thinly encapsulated bundle of small tendon fascicles with a fusiform (spindlelike) shape, innervated by a single large-diameter group Ib nerve fiber. These receptor endings respond to stretch of the tendon fascicles, but due to the very low compliance of tendon, tension seems the more appropriate variable. The tendon organ monitors the tension produced in its muscle and feeds the information back to the CNS.

A skeletal muscle consists of a bundle of long, slender fibers arranged in parallel (often called *extrafusal* fibers, referring to their location outside of the muscle spindle). Upon command from the CNS, these muscle fibers will produce a force to make them contract. Whether they actually shorten, lengthen, or remain the same length depends on the external forces (loading) on the muscle. Muscles produce only shortening forces by active contraction: they only pull; they cannot push. The CNS triggers contraction by sending impulses down the efferent nerve fibers (A-alpha motor axons) that innervate the muscle fibers. A single nerve impulse will elicit only a single, brief twitch in the muscle fiber, but a train of impulses (imp) at a sufficiently high rate (20–100 imp/sec, depending on the "speed" of contraction of the muscle) will cause the twitches to fuse into a smooth sustained contraction (a tetany). The CNS grades (i.e., smoothly regulates) force of contraction of the whole muscle by altering both the number of muscle fibers activated (recruitment) and the rate of firing of the recruited fibers. The CNS rarely controls individual muscle fibers; rather, it controls the fibers in groups or units.

An individual muscle fiber receives innervation from only one A-alpha nerve fiber. However, a single A-alpha motor axon innervates several muscle fibers to comprise a motor unit (a motor neuron, its axon, and all the muscle fibers it innervates). Motor units vary in "size." In large postual muscles, a single motor neuron may innervate 2000–3000 muscle fibers, whereas in the small muscles found in the eye or the hand, a single axon may contact 10 or every fewer muscle fibers. The muscle fibers of an individual motor unit do not lie clustered together; they lie scattered over the muscle cross section, thus distributing the tension they produce. This tension gets transmitted to the skeleton via thin tendonous filaments that eventually join together to form the main tendon.

The Golgi tendon organs lie at the musculotendonous junction, where tendonous filaments from 10 to 20 individual muscle fibers, mostly associated with different motor units, join on their way to adding to the main muscle tendon. The Golgi tendon organ therefore lies in series with a small group of muscle fibers, ideally situated to monitor the tension developed by them (Binder, 1981; Binder, Kroin, Moore, & Stuart, 1977). The individual muscle fibers monitored by a single Golgi tendon organ come from several different motor units so that with the 50 or so tendon organs found in a "typical" muscle, the CNS can obtain an excellent sampling of the tension developed in the muscle, a sampling that includes contributions from most if not all the motor units.

Signals from Golgi tendon organs no doubt inform the CNS about tension in the muscle useful for the regulation of muscle contraction. They stand as the most attractive candidates for providing our ability to discriminate muscle tension or force (see Section 2.3). Though Golgi tendon organ receptors seem unlikely candidates for limb position sensors, showing no response to position, per se, they might nonetheless contribute to position sense. If the true position sensors lie within the muscles (e.g., the spindles), they measure length within the muscle. Tension information could provide a signal to correct for the compliance of the tendons and attachments that lie outside of the region measured by such length detectors. We have no evidence one way or the other on this point.

3.6.2. Muscle Spindle Organs. The muscle spindle measures muscle stretch and rate of change of stretch. A sophisticated sensory organelle, surpassed in complexity among mammalian sensory structures only by the eye and the ear, the spindle consists of a long, slender bundle of 2–12 modified muscle fibers (intrafusal fibers) encased in a fluid-filled capsule (Figure 13.38). A key feature of the muscle spindle resides in the two types of innervation it receives: sensory and motor. Each spindle receives innervation by one large, primary sensory fiber (Group Ia) and by 0–5 intermediate-sized, secondary sensory fibers (Group II). In addition, the spindle receives 6–12 small-diameter motor fibers in the gamma range, the gamma efferents. Activity in the motor nerve fibers can substantially alter the activity in the sensory fibers. In essence, the CNS can regulate the characteristics of the muscle spindle receptors, presumably to optimize their response over a wide variety of muscle lengths and loading conditions. The CNS devotes a substantial portion of its motor outflow to the regulation of muscle spindles (about 48% in the cat hindlimb muscle nerves: Boyd & Davey, 1968), attesting to the importance of spindles in the systems that control muscle contraction.

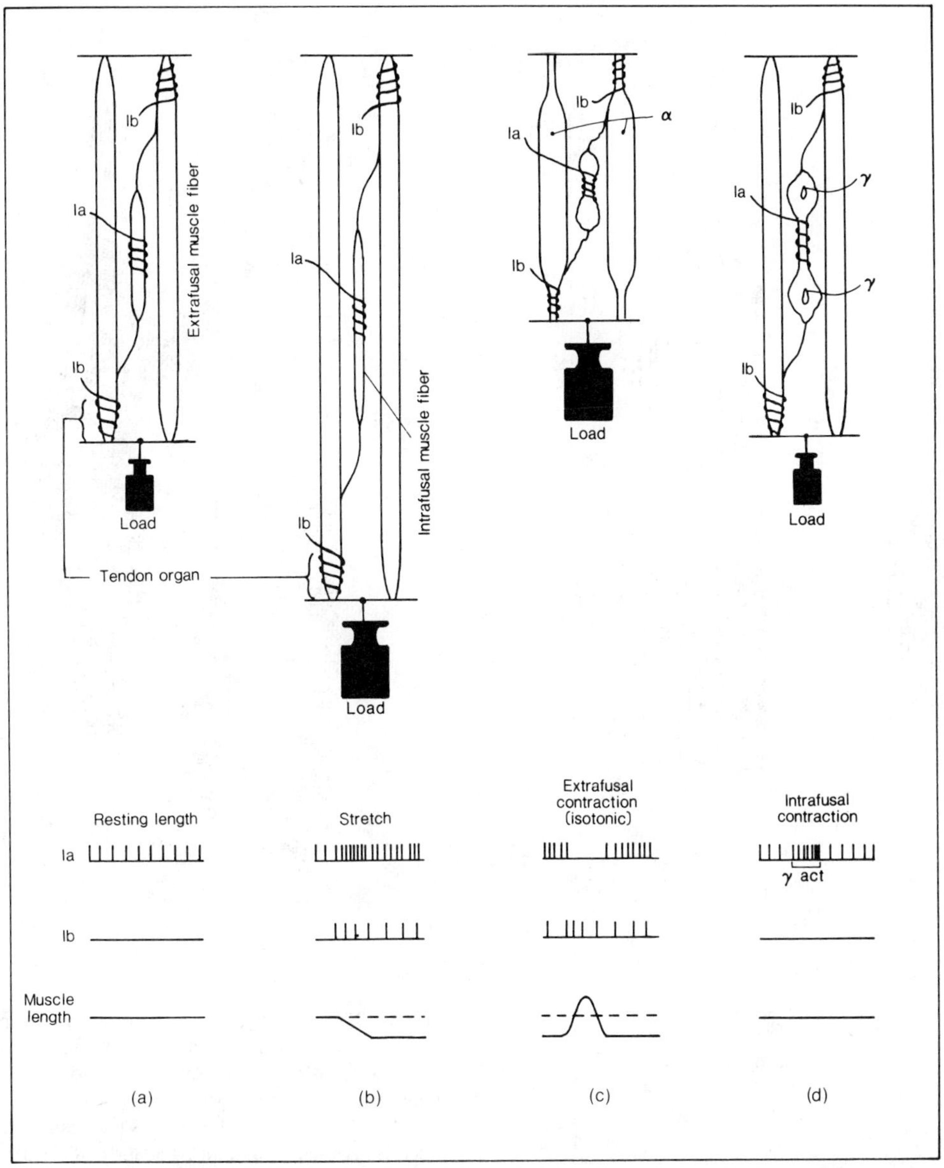

Figure 13.37. Schematic drawing of the arrangement of sensory elements in a muscle and their discharge patterns as a function of muscle length. Shown are the positions and shapes of the muscle spindles (1a) and Golgi tendon organs (1b) with the muscle at rest (a) and passively stretched (b), during isotonic contraction of the extrafusal fibers (c), and during contraction of the intrafusal fibers alone (d). The muscle spindles lie in parallel and measure length and rate of stretch of the spindle receptor region (note the 1a discharge pattern). The Golgi tendon organs lie in series with the extrafusal contractile fibers and measure tension (1b discharge pattern). (From R. F. Schmidt & G. Thews, Eds., *Human physiology*, Springer-Verlag, Inc., 1983. Reprinted with permission.)

Almost every mammalian skeletal muscle contains spindles (Barker, 1974). The various muscles contain different numbers of spindles, ranging from only a few in small muscles to well over 500 in the largest muscles. (Barker, 1974, pp. 88 and 89, and Matthews, 1972, p. 48 and 50, list the spindle counts in several different muscles from the cat and the human.) The spindle receptors lie in parallel with the main muscle fibers. Smaller muscles have fewer spindles than larger muscles, but if we compare muscles not by the total number of spindles but by the spindle density (spindles per gram of muscle), the smallest muscles have the highest density. One cannot say which variable has the greater relevance for kinesthesia, total count or density, though it seems reasonable that the more spindles available to encode angle, the better the accuracy. However, such logic can prove misleading, so we must wait for experimental evidence before committing ourselves.

The discussion that follows emphasizes features of muscle spindle function likely to relate to kinesthesia. We have either simplified or simply omitted much detail. We urge the interested reader to consult the many excellent reviews on muscle receptors for further information (e.g., Barker, 1974; Binder, Houk, Nichols, Rymer, & Stuart, 1982; Hulliger, 1984; Hunt, 1974; Matthews, 1972, 1974, 1981; McCloskey, 1978; McIntyre, 1974).

Inside the muscle spindle, we find two different types of intrafusal fibers, the nuclear bag and the nuclear chain. Recent evidence supports a further subdivision of the bag fibers (bag

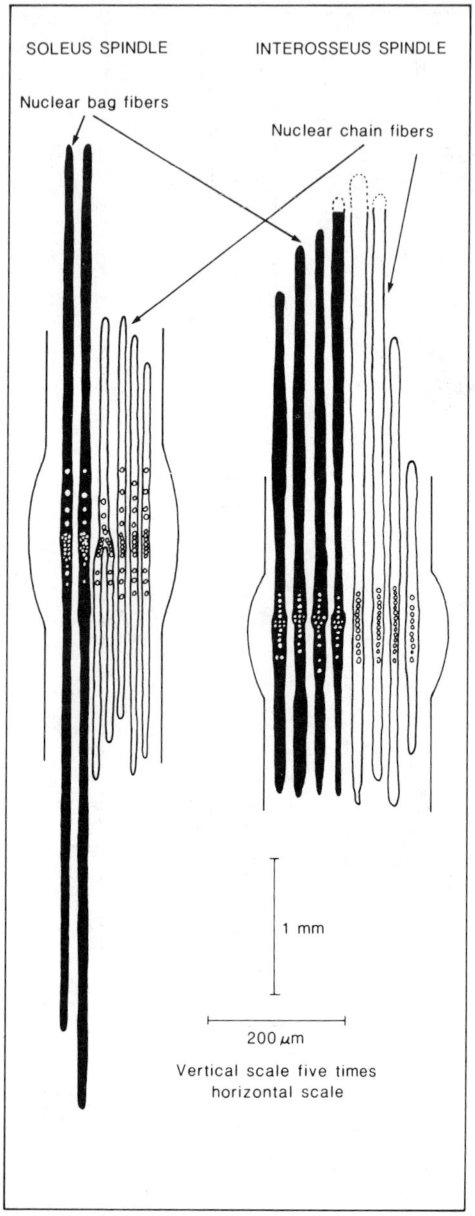

(a)

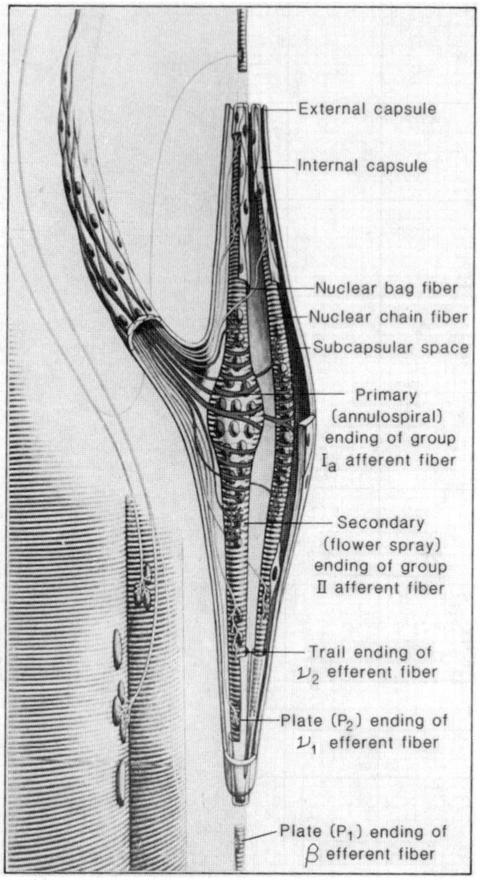

(c)

Figure 13.38. Muscle spindles. (a) The arrangement of intrafusal fibers in typical spindles from two different cat muscles. The drawings are to scale and are based on serial transverse sections. The nuclear bag and nuclear chain regions are indicated diagrammatically. Bag fibers, black; chain fibers, stippled. The outermost line shows the position of the spindle capsule. The interosseus spindle was from the adductor digiti longus V muscle. (b) Illustration of the parts of a cat muscle spindle drawn to relative scale to emphasize its great length. Only the afferent nerve endings are shown. (From P. B. C. Matthews, *Mammalian muscle receptors and their central actions*, Williams & Wilkins, 1972. Reprinted with permission.) (c) Detailed drawing of the central region of a muscle spindle. (From R. Warwick & P. L. Williams, Eds., *Gray's anatomy*, Saunders, 1973. Reprinted with permission.)

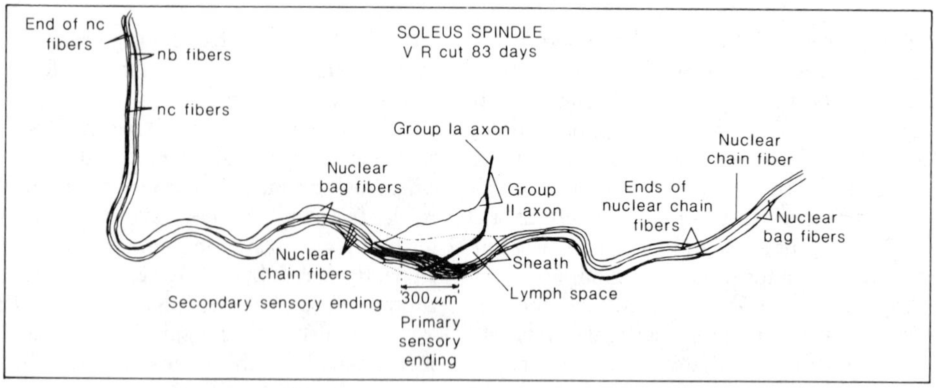

(b)

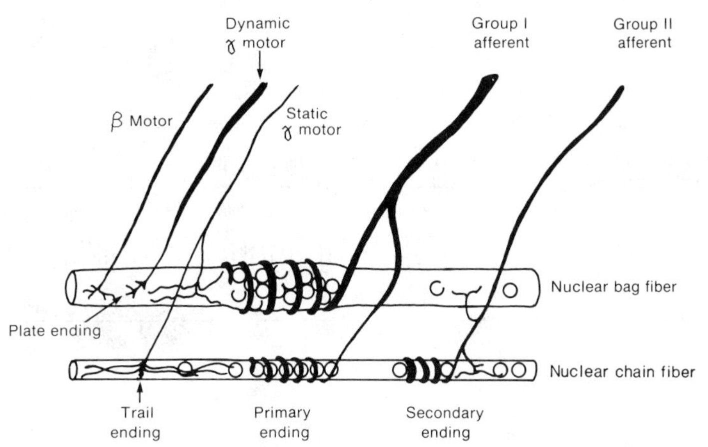

Figure 13.39 Simplified diagram of the central region of the muscle spindle to show the relation of the two kinds of afferent endings to the two kinds of intrafusal fibers. For purposes of illustration, the fibers are truncated at the ends of the central region, and relative size relationships are not maintained. (From P. B. C. Matthews, *Mammalian muscle receptors and their central actions*, Williams & Wilkins, 1972. Reprinted with permission.)

1 and bag 2), based largely on the speed of contraction of the fibers (see Matthews, 1981). The terms *bag* and *chain* come from the arrangement of the cellular nuclei in the fibers (see Figure 13.39). A spindle may contain from 2 to 12 intrafusal fibers, with an average between 7 and 8. Chain fibers outnumber bag fibers by about 2 to 1. These numbers vary somewhat for spindles from different muscles. Each intrafusal fiber consists of a single muscle fiber resembling the extrafusal (main) muscle fibers, though much shorter in length and somewhat thinner. Like extrafusal muscle fibers, each single-celled intrafusal fiber forms during its development by the fusion of many smaller cells, each contributing a nucleus. In the intrafusal fibers these nuclei aggregate near the middle of the fiber either in a cluster (nuclear bag) or in a line (nuclear chain). This middle (or equitorial) region forms the sensory portion of the intrafusal fiber. The Groups Ia and II sensory nerve fibers have their receptor endings in the middle region (see Figure 13.39), and stretch of the nuclear region generates action potentials in the receptor endings.

The end portions (polar regions) of the intrafusal fibers look much like skeletal muscle, and like skeletal muscle, these end regions can contract and shorten. Contraction of the few hundred or so intrafusal fibers in a muscle adds almost nothing to the tension developed by the muscle. This intrafusal contraction functions to alter the response properties of the sensory portions of the fiber. Also like the extrafusal fibers, the intrafusal fibers contract only on command from the nervous system (via action potentials in the gamma efferent fibers). However, the intrafusal fibers have different pattern of innervation and different mechanical properties than do the main muscle (extrafusal) fibers.

An intrafusal fiber usually receives motor innervation from several different A-gamma motor nerve fibers, thereby receiving control signals over several different channels, which provides a flexible and precise control of the response of the sensory portion of the spindle. In contrast, each extrafusal muscle fiber in skeletal muscle receives innervation from only a single nerve fiber (the A-alpha motor neurons), although a few exceptions to this single innervation rule do exist (e.g., the extraocular muscles). The multiple-motor innervation of the individual intrafusal fibers and the clustering of the nerve–muscle contacts suggest that individual segments of an intrafusal fiber might contract under command of the CNS. This could provide a fine control of mechanical properties of specific portions of the fiber. In contrast, extrafusal muscle fibers carry action potentials (much like nerves) that quickly travel along the muscle to trigger near-simultaneous contraction of all parts of the fiber (an all-or-none contraction of the entire fiber).

*3.6.2.1. **Afferent Component***. We recognize two main types of muscle spindle sensory endings, the primary found at the middle of the intrafusal fibers and the secondary found just off the middle. Older literature refers to the primary ending as *annulospiral*, and the secondary ending as *flower spray*, because of their appearance under the microscope. The primary ending receives innervation by Group Ia nerve fibers and the secondary endings by Group II fibers. Many workers use the terms *Group Ia afferents* and *Group II afferents* in reference to the primary and secondary endings, respectively. Similarly, *Group Ib afferents* refer to Golgi tendon organ receptors.

Signals from muscle spindles provide the CNS with information about the length of a muscle and its rate of change of length. Both the length and the rate responses stand out clearly in the discharge of the sensory fibers, with the secondary endings showing mainly a length response and the primary endings showing a pronounced rate response, as well as a length response (see Figure 13.40(a) and (b)). Note that muscle spindles can signal increases in length much better than decreases. During rapid shortening of a muscle, a pronounced velocity response can cause the spindles to go silent with a loss of information. This may happen with many movements initiated by the CNS despite coactivation of the gamma system that would tend to

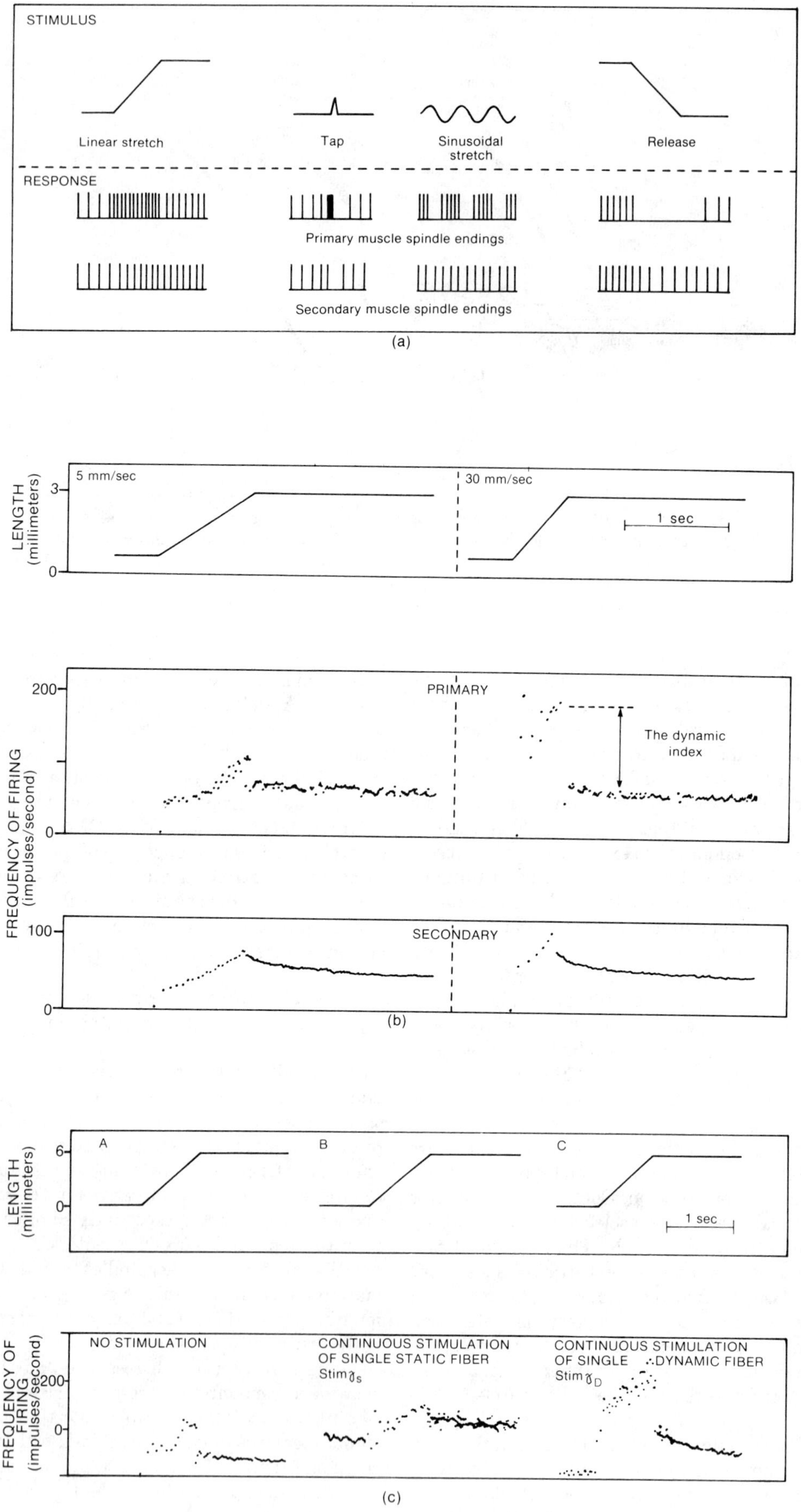

Figure 13.40. *(Legend opposite.)*

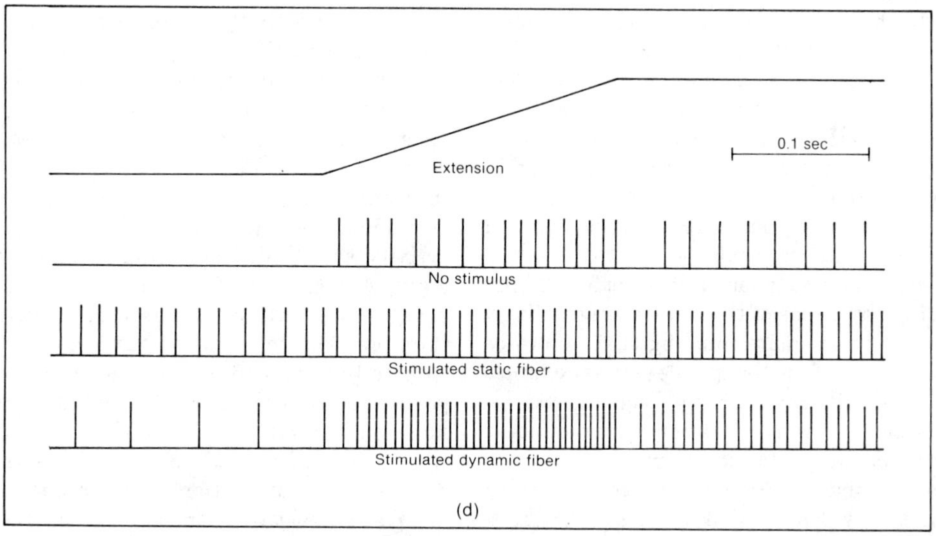

Figure 13.40. Discharge patterns of muscle spindles. (a) Schematic diagram of the responses of primary and secondary muscle spindle endings to four kinds of stimuli as a function of time. Each vertical line on the lower two traces represents a single action potential in the afferent nerve fiber. (From P. B. C. Matthews, Muscle spindles and their motor control, *Physiological Reviews,* 1964, *44.* Reprinted with permission.) (b) Comparison of the responses of deefferented primary and secondary muscle spindle endings to a ramp stretch. Shown is the "instantaneous" frequency of firing: each spot represents an action potential and its vertical displacement is proportional to the reciprocal of the time interval since the immediately preceding action potential. The "dynamic index" is the difference in frequency between the discharge near the termination of the dynamic phase of stretching and that occurring when the muscle has been maintained at the final length for 0.5 sec. The stretch of 3 mm was applied to the tibialis posterior muscle at either 5 mm/sec (left) or 30 mm/sec (right). The 1-sec time marker applies only while the muscle is at a constant length; during the phase of dynamic stretching the time scale is somewhat expanded. (From M. C. Brown, A. Crowe, & P. B. C. Matthews, Observations on the fusimotor fibres of the tibialis posterior muscle of the cat, *Journal of Physiology*, 1965, *177*. Reprinted with permission.) (c) The contrasting effects of the two kinds of A-gamma efferent fiber on the response of a primary muscle spindle ending to stretching. The soleus muscle was stretched 6 mm at 30 mm/sec, (A) in the absence of fusimotor stimulation, (B) during continuous stimulation of a single static fiber at 70 impulses/sec, and (C) during continuous stimulation of a single dynamic fiber at 70 impulses/sec. The time scale is expanded during the dynamic phase of stretching, and the time bar applies only when the length is constant. (From P. B. C. Matthews, *Mammalian muscle receptors and their central actions*, Williams & Wilkins, 1972. Reprinted with permission.) (d) Schematic diagram of the different effects of stimulation of static and dynamic fusimotor fibers. The response of a primary ending to stretch is shown as action potentials on a linear time scale. Based on data shown in (c). (From A. Crowe & P. B. C. Matthews, Further studies of static and dynamic fusimotor fibres, *Journal of Physiology*, 1964, *174*. Reprinted with permission.)

maintain the spindle discharge (Prochazka, 1980; Prochazka, Westerman, & Ziccone, 1976). However, in some cases gamma coactivation may actually cause spindle discharge to increase during muscle shortening (Critchlow & von Euler, 1963). Rapid and unexpected shortening imposed on a muscle frequently causes the spindles to go silent, but the CNS appears well equipped to manage this loss of information from the shortening muscle; it simply monitors the activity of lengthening antagonist muscles. With few exceptions, for every muscle that shortens, another muscle lengthens.

Small-signal (sinusoidal) linear analysis of the steady-state spindle response as a function of length has revealed similar transfer functions for the primary and secondary endings over a range of frequencies from 0.1to about 2 Hz (Matthews & Stein, 1969; Poppele & Bowman, 1970). However, analysis has also demonstrated important differences between the two endings. The secondary response to sinusoidal stretching depends on its spontaneous discharge rate (its carrier rate), whereas the primary ending shows no such carrier dependence. The primary, but not the secondary, endings show a pronounced temperature dependence. This suggests that the two endings have different decoder mechanisms.

Linear analysis can serve to characterize spindle behavior for natural movements but only for very small displacements. Using the cat soleus muscle (about 3 or 4 cm in length), Matthews and Stein (1969) found that sinusoidal frequencies up to 3 Hz, with an amplitude of 50 μm for the primary endings and 500 μm for the secondary endings, kept the endings in their linear range. At higher frequencies of 100–300 Hz the appropriate amplitude fell to 1 μm for the primary and 10 μm for the secondary endings. Larger displacements revealed the existence of substantial nonlinearities, some different for the two endings and some common to both (Hasan & Houk, 1975; Poppele, 1981). In an attempt to relate linear analysis of spindle responses to our normal, natural activity, we might note that most muscles in the body undergo less than a 20% change in length from their maximum to their minimum lengths, and many movements, especially skilled movements, probably use only a small fraction of this range. Also, few voluntary movements exceed rates of a few hertz (though some involuntary tremors have frequency components in excess of 10 or 15 Hz).

The spindle primary endings respond especially strongly to the velocity of stretching, even with extremely small displacements. A sharp tap of a tendon produces a small but rapid stretch of the muscle that synchronously activates primary endings in many spindles, as shown in Figure 13.40(a). This volley of activity in the Ia fibers has a potent excitatory effect on the alpha motor neurons that innervate the extrafusal fibers of the muscle that contains the spindle, causing the muscle to contract (e.g., the knee-jerk reflex). This stretch reflex, seen in its simplest form with a tendon tap, forms a neural control system that can help compensate for unexpected changes in muscle length (Houk, 1980; Merton, 1953).

Vibration applied to a muscle tendon can powerfully excite primary spindle endings by virtue of their velocity sensitivity (see Figure 13.2), and with adequate coupling of the vibrator to the tendon, the Ia discharges from the spindle primary endings will lock in phase with the vibration (Brown, Engberg, & Matthews, 1967). The Ia activation by vibration may produce a reflex muscle contraction (the tonic vibration reflex), largely via the same mechanism that produces the tendon-tap reflex but with greater complexity (Hagbarth & Eklung, 1966; Matthews, 1966), because excitation of the spindles by vibration continues much longer than activation by a simple tendon tap, so other more complex neural circuits come into play. In addition, vibration can sometimes excite spindle secondaries and Golgi tendon organs and always activates some cutaneous receptors. However, the primary endings probably provide the major sensory input for the tonic vibration reflex.

3.6.2.2. ***Efferent Component.*** Gamma motor activity appears capable of independently altering both the length and the rate responses of primary and secondary spindle afferents (Brown & Matthews, 1966). Electrical stimulation of one type of gamma fiber (gamma static) in isolation can enhance the length response, whereas involvement of another type (gamma dynamic) can enhance the rate response (see Figure 13.40(c) and (d).

Differences in the contractile properties and the sensory innervation of the bag and chain intrafusal fibers can account for at least some of the observed response patterns. Note first that the Ia nerve fiber forms a primary ending on every intrafusal fiber (see Figure 13.39), thus both chain and bag fibers contribute to the primary response. In contrast, the secondary endings lie largely on the chain fibers.

We can visualize an intrafusal fiber as divided lengthwise into three portions, two contractile portions, one at each end, and the middle (sensory) region. We can model each of these three regions as a compliance in parallel with a viscous element (see Matthews, 1964). To model the whole fiber, we then place these three parallel combinations in series. In this simple model for the chain fibers, the ratio of viscosity to compliance has the same value for each of the parallel combinations, so a stretch of the whole fiber will distribute among the three regions in direct proportion to their compliances. This apportionment occurs independently of rate of stretch. For the bag fibers, the ratios of viscosity to compliance in the end regions exceeds the ratio for the middle region, and apportionment of the total stretch no longer remains independent of rate of stretch (see Figure 13.41). The viscosity of a region may relate to the speed at which it can contract; bag fibers contract more slowly than do chain fibers (Boyd, Gladden, McWilliam, & Ward, 1977).

The model in Figure 13.41 also suggests a possible strategy for adjustment of the length sensitivity of an intrafusal fiber, namely by altering the compliance of the elastic element in the contractile end sections. The stiffer or less compliant the ends become relative to the middle, the more the middle will stretch for any given overall increase in length.

Gamma activity exerts its effect on the spindle response via the contractile mechanism in the intrafusal fiber, and as our simple model implies, this might affect the compliance or viscosity of the fiber. Gamma activity can also cause the contractile ends to shorten and thereby stretch the middle sensory region (Bessou & Pages, 1972). This would produce an increase in spindle discharge even though the overall length of the spindle remained constant. In fact, with a sufficiently strong gamma activity, spindle discharge might even increase despite a shortening of the muscle (Critchlow & von Euler, 1963). The shortening of the contractile ends of the intrafusal fiber could more than compensate for the shortening of the muscle in which the spindle lies and cause a net elongation of the middle sensory portion. A coactivation of the gamma system occurs with most muscle contractions. We call this alpha–gamma coactivation, where the *alpha* refers to the main (extrafusal) muscles that receive their innervation from A-alpha motor neurons.

Gamma activity can serve to "bias" the spindle, meaning to adjust its operating point so the spindle can respond optimally over the full range of possible muscle lengths (see Matthews, 1972). For instance, an ending that discharges at a long muscle length may go silent if the muscle shortens. However, an increase in gamma activity at the shorter length could return the sensory region to a portion of its operating range where it can once again signal small changes in length. However, in common usage the term *gamma bias* often lacks a precise definition; it does not necessarily mean bias as defined here, but simply refers to any activity in the gamma motor fibers.

Merton (1953) proposed that the CNS might accomplish voluntary movements via a servomechanism that involved gamma activition of the spindles and the stretch reflex. It would function as follows. Command signals to the spinal reflex circuits establish a "set point" for the desired muscle length, and the spinal reflexes function as a length servo to maintain this desired length. Muscle spindles serve as the length sensors. An unexpected change in muscle length, for example, from a sudden increase in the weight of a load, would stretch the spindles, causing an increase in their discharge, which in turn would cause an increase in the excitation of the motor neurons supplying the muscles containing the spindles. The muscles would therefore contract a little more forcefully to carry the added load and restore the muscle to near its original length. (The system would behave as a proportional-length servo, so some error would remain. The magnitude of the error would depend on the "gain" of the reflex servo loop.) Merton suggested that the CNS could adjust muscle length by altering the gamma outflow, which in turn would change the spindle activity. Muscle length would then adjust automatically via the stretch reflex to a new equilibrium condition corresponding to the new level of gamma activity. In other words, the CNS would change the length set point by altering gamma activity. He suggested that many normal, voluntary movements occur via this follow-up servomechanism, though many movements could also come about via a more direct activation of the alpha motor neurons. The neural circuits to support such a mechanism clearly exist, and Merton's hypothesis became rather popular. However, subsequent evidence has not favored such a role for the gamma system (see Matthews, 1981, for further discussion).

One could argue that gamma control of the spindle discharge precludes the spindles from providing information about absolute muscle length and therefore limb position (Merton, 1964; Rose & Mountcastle, 1959). The spindle responds not only to changes in length but also to changes in gamma activity, and the nervous system presumably could not extract true length information

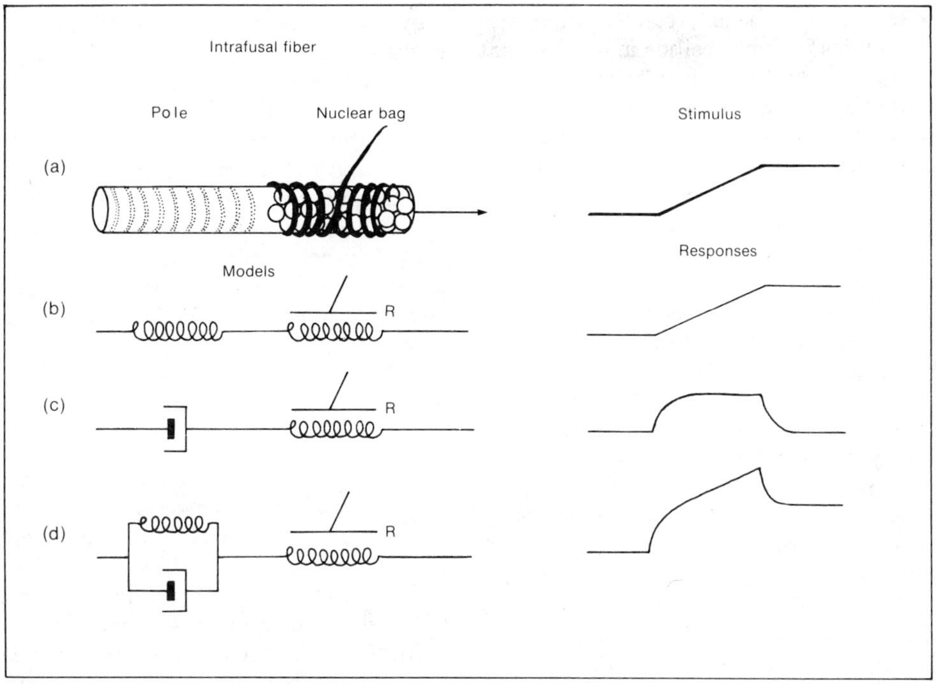

Figure 13.41. Viscoelastic model of a muscle spindle. In (a) a simplified intrafusal nuclear bag fiber is stretched linearly in time as shown to the right. In (b) to (d) models of the intrafusal fiber and resulting response of the receptor to stretching are shown as a function of time. The models consist of elastic elements (springs) and simple viscous elements (dashpots). The receptor region (R) is assumed to lie in a region dominated by elastic elements, so the viscous component is omitted, and the response is assumed to be directly proportional to the deformation of this region. The model in (d) most closely mimics the observed responses of muscle spindles to ramp stretches. The time constant of such a model is the product of the elastic compliance and viscosity, where compliance = displacement/force and viscosity = force/velocity. Similar responses are seen in a model with a parallel viscous element in the receptor region, provided that the viscosity of the receptor region is much less than that of the polar regions. For simplicity, only one polar region is illustrated. (From P. B. C. Matthews, Muscle spindles and their motor control, *Physiological Reviews*, 1964, *44*. Reprinted with permission.)

from the spindle discharge. Such a view greatly underestimates the CNS by implying that it does not have access to its own output or that it cannot accurately predict what effect gamma activity might have on the spindles. Of all the candidates for position detectors, muscle spindle receptors, especially the secondary or Group II afferents, seem the best suited. Amazingly, this has provided difficult to demonstrate, and even the general role of secondary spindles remains somewhat of a mystery. We discuss this problem further in Section 4.

3.7. Summary

We have examined sensory receptors in the skin, joints, and muscles and evaluated their potential for signaling the positions and movements of the limbs and the state of contraction of the muscles. We have looked at how these various receptors respond to mechanical stimuli, such as bending a joint, for evidence that the receptor response might encode the movement or the position of the joint. We must acknowledge that by looking at a receptor's response we can only infer what it signals and speculate on how the CNS uses the information. However, evidence that a receptor population can or cannot encode particular stimulus features, such as movement or position, provides us with a basis for further experimentation to discover the source of kinesthetic signals. We summarize the findings about the various receptors below.

3.7.1. Articular Receptors. Mechanoreceptors in joints seem poorly suited to signal joint position, except perhaps at the extremes of flexion and extension. In several joints, including the knee, ankle, and wrist, the receptor population shows little response over a wide range of angles. However, a few joints, like the hip and the costovertebral (rib) joints, do show position coding. Nonetheless, if joints did serve as the major source of position information, we might reasonably expect to find evidence of coding in all or at least most joints.

Joint receptors might provide information about the rate and direction of movement of the joint, but based on the responses of the majority of joint mechanoreceptors, they appear best suited to signal tension in the capsule and ligaments as the joint approaches one or the other limits of its range. This would suggest some sort of protective role for the receptors, probably to elicit fast-acting spinal reflexes to prevent damage to the joint. Forceful hyperextensions of a joint elicit sensations that feel "pressury" and perhaps threatening, at first, and painful if continued.

3.7.2. Cutaneous Receptors. The bending of any joint will stretch some region of skin around the joint and relax another. Thus mechanoreceptors in skin might serve to signal joint position and movement. One type of cutaneous mechanoreceptor, the slowly adapting, type II (T2) responds sensitively to skin stretch with a slowly adapting discharge. Though a population of these receptors might encode static joint position, they appear too few in number to provide much accuracy. However, we cannot rule out the possibility that they play a role. The skin also contains an abundance of rapidly adapting mechanoreceptors that certainly could signal joint movement.

3.7.3. Muscular Receptors. Mechanoreceptors in muscle emerge as the best candidates for limb position and movement detectors (the muscle spindles) and for signaling the tension produced by a muscle (the Golgi tendon organs). Muscle spindles lie in parallel with the contractile elements of the muscle, well situated to encode muscle length, and a have a slowly adapting discharge that increases with stretch of the muscle. Thus muscle spindles can encode the static length of a muscle and also signal rate of length increase and higher-order time derivatives. The presence of the fusimotor (gamma) control of spindles complicates the encoding of length and movement; gamma activity can alter spindle discharge in the absence of any length change. However, the CNS presumably can compensate for the effects of its own output.

Muscle spindles signal increases in length much better than decreases, and the rate-sensitive component of their response may cause the spindle to go silent with rapid shortening of the muscle, resulting in a loss of information from the shortening spindles. However, in almost all situations muscles work in opposing groups, so for every muscle that shortens, another lengthens. Thus spindles in antagonistic muscle pairs can keep the CNS informed of movement under any conditions.

The Golgi tendon organs lie in series with the tension-producing elements of the muscles and display an exquisite sensitivity to the tension produced by contraction of the motor units within the muscles. As a group, the tendon organs provide a good sample of the overall tension developed in the muscle. The tendon organs appear well suited for providing our awareness of muscle tension. It seems unlikely that tendon organs would contribute much to limb position sense, but we cannot say this with certainly.

4. MECHANISMS OF KINESTHESIA

Human subjects can utilize information from a variety of sources to make kinesthetic judgments, often using information we would not regard as "kinesthetic." For example, a subject might simply look at his or her limbs to discover their positions. People also have an uncanny ability to use subtle, seemingly irrelevant cues and to employ clever strategies to perform a kinesthetic task in ways that can bypass the intent of an experiment. One should keep this in mind when interpreting the psychophysical literature. In addition, humans might "know" the position of a limb even without using kinesthetic information because a reliable and accurate motor control system set the limb into place. We have ample evidence that the motor control system can accurately place the limbs without the benefit of any feedback whatever (Bossom, 1974; Rothwell, Traub, Day, Obeso, Thomas, & Marsden, 1982; Taub & Berman, 1963). Probably many of the rapid, skilled movements we make every day require little sensory information. The movements occur too rapidly for feedback during the movement to have much effect on the trajectory or the end position.

Nonetheless, we apparently do rely heavily upon kinesthetic information from the periphery. Animals with limbs rendered insentient by cutting sensory nerve fibers in the dorsal roots of the spinal cord can move and position their limbs with remarkable accuracy (Taub & Berman, 1963), but these animals cannot detect passive movements of the affected limb, nor can they tell if a voluntary movement occurred as intended. Without visual guidance, they cannot compensate for unexpected changes in loading of a limb. Humans who have lost sensation in their hands have great difficulty with all but the simplest tasks of grasping and holding, even under visual guidance (Moberg, 1972; Rothwell et al., 1982)

We review here those psychophysical studies that have contributed most to our understanding of the neural mechanisms underlying kinesthesia and the roles played by sensory receptors in skin, muscle, and joint. As we mentioned, humans can use a variety of cues to make kinesthetic judgments, but we believe that they possess fundamental kinesthetic mechanisms that depend on position, movement, and tension signals from sensory receptors in the periphery. We concentrate on these basic mechanisms.

4.1. Methods

In the previous section we discussed the responses of sensory receptors and concluded that muscle receptors emerged as the best candidates for sensing limb position and movement; skin and joint receptors seemed less well suited. However, acceptance or rejection of a receptor population as kinesthetic detectors on the basis of their response properties alone requires caution. Evidence that receptors can encode a particular stimulus feature may indicate that the information exists, but rejecting a population of receptors because their discharge seems to the experimenter unrelated to the stimulus may not have validity. We do not know for certain what information the CNS requires. Consider the commonly held assumption that limb position sense must derive from ongoing signals from slowly adapting receptors. With a memory for position, the CNS might well rely on signals available only during movements and stored in memory.

Measurements of the response characteristics of sensory receptors can suggest a role for the receptors in kinesthesia, but to establish their participation in kinesthetic sensation, one must use experiments with awake and functioning animal or human subjects (psychophysical experiments). These experiments usually attempt to establish some baseline performance in a kinesthetic task, and measure the effect of selectively eliminating or distorting particular sensory inputs. Some tests attempt to distort the sensory inputs under investigation, using, for example, tape on the skin or weights to alter muscle loading or vibrating the tendons of a muscle. Other tests rely on a particular strategy to alter the contribution from a particular group of receptors, such as rotating a joint slowly enough not to excite movement receptors or, with the fingers, positioning certain joints to slacken the associated muscle tendons, thereby decoupling the muscles from the joint.

4.2. Cutaneous Receptors

Movement of a joint involves stretching or bending the skin around the joint, so we might reasonably expect that cutaneous stretch receptors could provide kinesthetic information. Skin receptors might signal joint movement but apparently not the static position of the joint.

Most receptors in skin, whether on the hands or elsewhere, have rapidly adapting responses not suited to signal static position or slow displacements of the skin (or a joint), but these receptors can respond to rapid movements. In this sense, they act as high-pass filters having a low-frequency time constant on the order of seconds or milliseconds.

The slowly adapting cutaneous mechanoreceptors that potentially might signal static skin position appear not to support a sense of static position (see Section 3.4). Horch, Clark, and Burgess (1975) demonstrated that subjects failed to detect slowly produced indentations of the skin on the forearm (1.6–1.9 mm, at rates 0.05 mm/sec or less). In addition, the sensation from a skin indentation rapidly produced and then maintained faded over a period of a few minutes in marked contrast to sensations of misalignment of the limbs that do not fade with time. In regard to kinesthesia, Clark, Horch, Bach and Larson (1979) report that anesthesia of the skin around the knee joint produced no deficits in knee position sense (see Figure 13.42) and in fact went almost unnoticed by the subjects. Indeed, skin anesthesia may actually have improved their subjects' matching precision slightly, as indicated by a smaller standard deviation of the matching errors with skin block.

While skin sensation may play only a minor role, if any, in position sense of the knee, a quite different situation exists with the fingers. Loss of sensation in the skin of the hand produces a severe deficit in the ability to use the hand or to detect passive movements of the fingers even though the muscles and their associated sensory receptors remain unaffected. Subjects can still move their fingers, but they have a severely disabled hand (Moberg, 1972; Rothwell et al., 1982).

The finger skin has a very high density of innervation and a large representation in the cerebral cortex, both of which support a high degree of tactile resolution. Considering how extensively we use our hands with their well-developed sense of touch for manipulating objects and exploring our surroundings (Gibson, 1962), it seems reasonable that the skin of the fingers might play a special role in kinesthesia. Furthermore, the receptors in the fingers muscles acting on their own may not have the capability of signaling finger position. Though we possess a remarkable dexterity with our hands, we cannot independently move or position individual finger joints the way we can position most other joints. If the muscles cannot independently position a joint, the receptors in those muscles probably cannot unambiguously encode the angle of that joint. The CNS then could not rely on muscle receptors alone to establish finger position but would require supplementary information perhaps from the rich sensory input afforded by cutaneous receptors. Still, one wonders whether cutaneous receptors could supply information about static position of the fingers.

Clark, Burgess, and Chapin (1983) reinvestigated the nature of kinesthesia in the hands and found that humans lack a sense of static position in some of the finger joints. They compared position sense in the fingers and the ankle, using as their test a subject's ability to detect 3.5 or 5° angular displacements made at various rates. They reasoned that if a person had an awareness of the static position of a joint, then rate of displacement should have little effect on ability to sense the change. However, if the subject relied on movement signals, the slow displacements would go undetected. With the ankle, subjects could reliably detect 3.5° displacements produced as slowly as 0.5°/min, but with the finger, the subject's ability to detect 5° displacements began to deteriorate at 120°/min and approached zero at 1.5°/min. These tests involve a memory for limb position; a subject had to tell whether a final position differed from an initial position that existed as much as 7 or 8 min previously. They seemed able to do this with little difficulty.

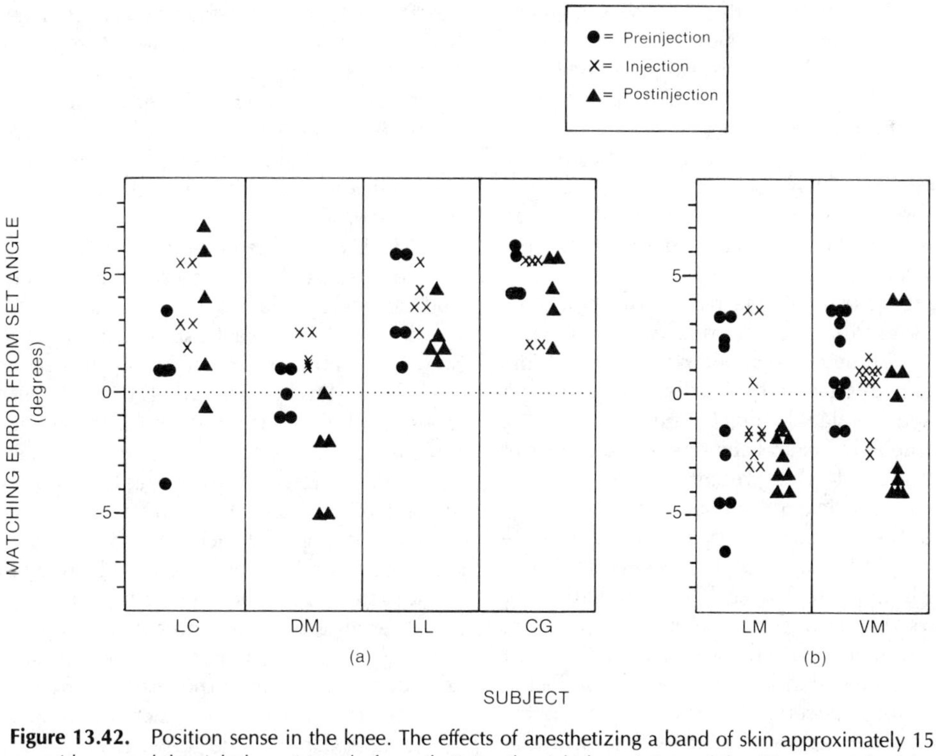

Figure 13.42. Position sense in the knee. The effects of anesthetizing a band of skin approximately 15 cm wide around the right knee (a) and of anesthetizing the right knee joint and the skin around the joint (b) on individual subjects' accuracy of matching knee joint angles are shown by the distributions of errors before, during, and after anesthesia. The left leg was fixed in position and all movements were of the right leg. A + error indicates the right knee was more extended and a − error indicates it was more flexed than the left. Neither procedure produced a deterioration in the performance of the subjects. (From F. J. Clark, K. W. Horch, S. M. Bach, & G. F. Larson, Contribution of cutaneous and joint receptors to static knee-position sense in man, *Journal of Neurophysiology*, 1979, *42*. Reprinted with permission.)

In addition to providing movement signals, cutaneous receptors in the fingers supply some sort of supportive or facilitatory input that the CNS needs to interpret kinesthetic information from other sources. Clark and colleagues (1983) found that anesthetizing the fingertip, but not the skin around the moving joint, substantially impaired subjects' ability to sense slow rotations. Anesthetizing the thumb also diminished subjects' ability to detect slow displacements of the index finger. Anesthesia injected into the joint produced no noticeable impairment. The facilitatory effect of cutaneous inputs makes it difficult to ascertain how cutaneous receptors signal movement by using tests that involve anesthetic block of the skin. Any deficit from anesthesia would involve both mechanisms, a reduction in facilitatory inputs and in the movement signals.

Gandevia and McCloskey (1976) took advantage of an anatomical oddity in the fingers to separate the contributions of skin and joint receptors from those of muscle without using anesthesia. They positioned the fingers in a way that slackens the muscle tendons to the terminal joint of the middle finger. If one holds the middle finger flexed while keeping the remaining fingers fully extended, as shown in Figure 13.43, the terminal joint of the middle finger becomes impossible to move. This maneuver disengages the muscles crossing the joint leaving only skin and joint mechanisms intact. Gandevia and McCloskey found that with only skin and joint to signal movement, the ability of subjects to detect a 10° rotation fell as rate of rotation decreased. Below 1°/sec the excursions went almost undetected by the subjects (see Figure 13.43).

When Gandevia and McCloskey positioned the fingers to reengage the muscles, subjects could readily detect the slower rotations (Figure 13.43). With the muscles engaged, they did not observe a decrement in subjects' ability to detect displacements at the slower rates. However, the slowest rate they used exceeded by more than 60 times the slowest rate used by Clark and colleagues (1983). A later study by Gandevia, Hall, McCloskey, and Potter (1983) confirmed the earlier findings with this finger joint and did employ slower rates but still nowhere near as slow as those used by Clark and colleagues. Had Gandevia and colleagues tried slower rates of rotation, they may have seen the same decrement in performance with rate reported by Clark and colleagues.

Clark and colleagues (1983, 1985) tested the contributions of skin and joint receptors to kinesthesia with the ankle joint by paralyzing the nerves to the ankle dorsiflexor muscles. This nerve block paralyzes the muscles that raise the foot, producing "foot-drop," and interrupts the signals from the muscle receptors. Only about a third of the skin around the ankle and a part of the joint gets anesthetized with this procedure. With the foot positioned downward (plantarflexed) to slacken the unaffected plantar/flexor muscles, thereby partly decoupling the muscle from the joint, subjects' ability to sense displacements decremented with rate much as in the finger. Thus left with only skin and joint receptors they lacked a sense of static position, but they could sense movement. With the foot set in an upward (dorsiflexed) position to tense and thus reengage the unaffected plantar/flexor muscles, subjects could detect most of the slow displacements. Clark and colleagues concluded that skin and joint mechanisms may contribute to movement sense but an awareness of static position requires sensory inputs from muscle.

Before we can summarize how cutaneous receptors might contribute to kinesthesia, we must examine further the contribution of joint receptors. Many of the tests cited so far have studied skin and joint mechanisms in combination, because one cannot easily decouple the skin from the joint to study skin in isolation.

4.3. Articular Receptors

At first glance, articular receptors would seem ideally suited for kinesthetic tasks. Given the rigid nature of our skeleton, the angles of the joints uniquely determine the location of any appendage relative to the test of the body. What could better serve to measure joint angle than receptors in the joints themselves? Actually, little of our kinesthetic awareness apparently derives from receptors in the ligaments and capsules of joints. Laboratory data show that while some joint receptors do respond during movement, and many respond with the joint held in extreme flexion or extension, all but a few receptors go silent in midrange positions. The receptors appear incapable of encoding position over a substantial portion of angular range. However, mindful of our caveat in regard to jumping to conclusions about function from receptor data alone, let us look at other evidence regarding the role of articular receptors in kinesthesia.

4.3.1. Role of Articular Receptors in Kinesthesia. The psychophysical data suggest an absence of a "joint sense." Grigg, Finerman, and Riley (1973) tested movement sense in the hip with patients who had one of their hip joints entirely replaced with a prosthesis but whose other hip appeared normal. They found only a slight difference between the normal and the operated sides in the patient's ability to detect small lateral excursions of the hip at 0.6°/sec (Table 13.8) and in estimating the magnitude of an excursion made at 2°/sec (see Figure 13.44).

Cross and McCloskey(1973) tested movement sense in the fingers with patients who had all the finger joints replaced on both hands with silicone rubber implants. (While they said they tested position sense, we believe they actually tested movement sense.) They found normal joint sense in all the joints tested. Such findings would come as no surprise to surgeons who have long known that replacing entire joints with prostheses results in apparently normal function with no obvious deficiency in kinesthesia.

Clark and colleagues (1983) found that local anesthetic injected into the middle interphalangeal joint of the index finger had no observable effect on subjects' ability to detect joint movement. In contrast, anesthesia of the skin on the finger produced a marked deficit in movement sense with the finger.

Clark, Horch, Bach, and Larson (1979) examined the effect of anesthetizing the knee joints on subjects' ability to match the position of the two legs and subsequently detect 5° misalignments in knee position created by slow (less than 1°/min) rotation of the knee. This slow rotation produced no sensation of movement, nor did such slow speeds activate rapidly adapting receptors when tested in animals. They said the method allowed a test of static position sense unconfused by movement signals. Anesthetizing the knee joint had no apparent effect on either the subjects' ability to detect the excursions correctly or on the accuracy of rematching the position afterward (Figure 13.45(a)). The authors gauged the effectiveness of the anesthetic block by using a comparable amount of the drug (scaled by body weight) in animals. In all cases the anesthetic completely or almost completely silenced activity in the joint nerves, as shown in Figure 13.45(b), and the effect lasted several hours.

In that same experiment, Clark and colleagues tested the effect of anesthetizing a 15–20-cm band of skin around the joint, both alone and in combination with the joint anesthesia.

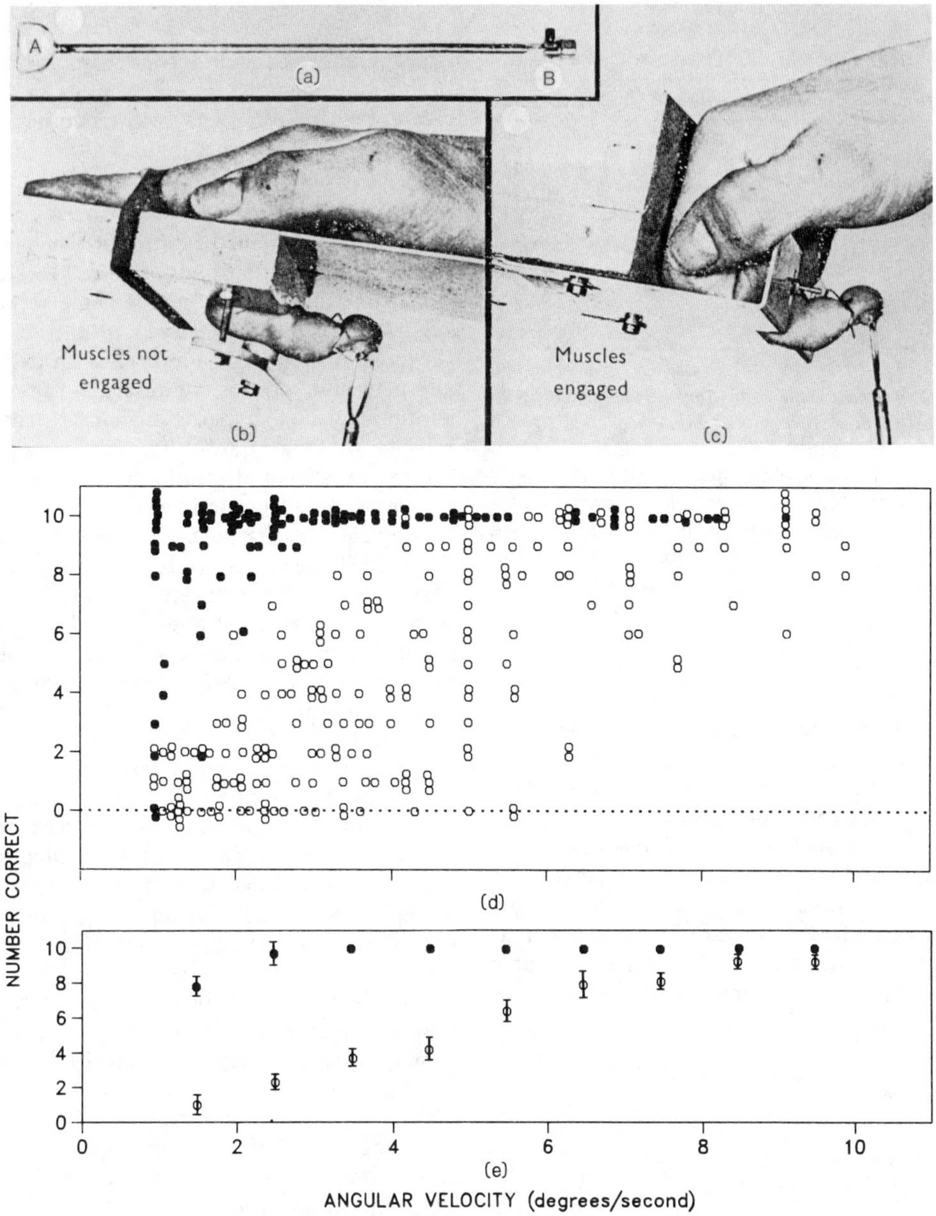

Figure 13.43. Ability to sense displacements of the terminal joint of the middle finger at different speeds relying only on receptors in the skin and joint. The photographs show the apparatus used to connect the terminal phalanx of the middle finger to the finger displacer and to position the hand so that muscle could be engaged or not engaged at the distal interphalangeal joint. (a) The brass rod which has a forked end (A), over which a section of hypodermic needle, glued to the subject's fingernail, was fitted, completing a stirrup arrangement. Torsional forces on the fingernail were minimized by having two mechanical joints (a and b) with axes in the same plane as the axis of movement of the joint. (b) The position of the hand when the muscles were unable to move the joint and were effectively disengaged from it. The middle finger passed through a hole in a board and was clamped fully flexed, while the remaining fingers were fully extended. In this position only joint and cutaneous mechanisms contribute to position sense. (c) The position of the hand when the muscles were engaged and able to flex the terminal phalanx of the middle finger. This finger was fully flexed at the proximal interphalangeal joint and slightly flexed at the distal interphalangeal joint, while the remaining fingers were fully flexed at both distal and proximal interphalangeal joints. In this position, joint, cutaneous, and muscular mechanisms could contribute to position sense. In both positions of the hand a paper clip was placed across the nail, thus depressing it and reducing pressure sensations. The results are from 12 subjects with displacements of 10° at various angular velocities, when the muscles were not engaged (open circles) and when the muscles were engaged (filled circles). No distinction is made between movements into flexion and into extension. (d) The data from the subjects are plotted together. (e) The data have been grouped into velocity ranges (1.0–1.9°/sec, 2.0–2.9°/sec, etc.), averaged for all subjects, and plotted as mean number of correct judgments (± standard error) in 10 trials at each point. Acuity of position sense was enhanced by engagement of muscles at the joint. For both cases, detection improved as the angular velocity increased, although the angular displacement remained constant. (From S. C. Gandevia & D. I. McCloskey, Joint sense, muscle sense, and their combination of position sense, measured at the distal interphalangeal joint of the middle finger, *Journal of Physiology*, 1976, *260*. Reprinted with permission.)

Table 13.8. Movement Sense in the Hip after Total Joint Replacement

Patient	Normal Joint	Operated Joint	Difference
JS	0.34	1.06	0.72[a]
RH	0.60	0.61	0.01
HM	0.54	2.78	2.24[a]
SS	1.32	2.48	1.16[a]
BW	0.53	0.62	0.09
WM	0.45	1.80	1.35
MS	0.84	0.62	−0.22
Mean	0.66	1.42	

The table lists the smallest hip joint excursion (in degrees) patients could reliably detect after total joint replacement, comparing the operated hip with the opposite, normal hip. The hip passively moved outward (abduction) at 0.6°/sec until the patient could just detect the excursion. Values shown represent the means of these just detectable excursions from 10 trials. Three of the seven patients showed a statistically significant difference between the normal and operated sides, but the differences amounted to a few degrees at most. (From Grigg, Finerman, & Riley, 1973.) Note that Grigg and colleagues claimed to have tested position sense, but we think they actually tested movement sense.

[a] $p < 0.01$.

In neither case did they find any impairment in the task performance (Figure 13.42). These results suggest that neither skin nor joint receptors provide an important sensory input for the awareness of the static position of the knee.

We can summarize these findings regarding a kinesthetic role for receptors in skin and joint as follows: neither articular receptors nor cutaneous receptors alone or in combination provide an essential input for awareness of the static position of a proximal joint. These receptors can signal joint movement at rates higher than about 1°/sec (Figure 13.43), but the evidence suggests

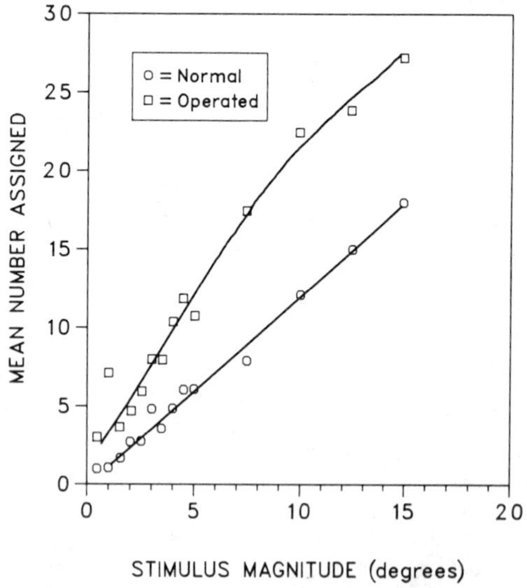

Figure 13.44. Ability to sense displacements of the hip after replacement of the joint. Results are from subjective magnitude estimation of hip abduction by one subject with a unilateral, total hip replacement. The leg was moved at 2°/sec. Shown are the magnitude estimates for abduction of the normal hip joint and the replaced joint. For the four subjects tested, there was no difference in correlation between leg position and magnitude estimate for normal and operated hips. (From P. Grigg, G. A. Finerman, & L. H. Riley, Joint-position sense after total hip replacement, *Journal of Bone and Joint Surgery*, 1973, *55A*. Reprinted with permission.)

a far greater role for cutaneous receptors than for joint receptors in this movement sense. Additionally in the fingers, cutaneous receptors even in regions away from the moving joint supply a supportive or facilitatory input that the CNS needs for detecting joint movement. Joint receptors seem not to serve a similar supportive or facilitatory role.

4.3.2. Functions of Articular Receptors. Since articular receptors play little, if any, role in kinesthesia, we might ask what function they do serve. Their response characteristics suggest that they may serve a protective function. One might expect that as a joint approaches an extreme position, rapid and powerful reflexes would brake the movement to prevent joint injury due to hyperextension. Searches for such protective reflexes in experimental animals have given mixed results. The reflex effects of stimulating nerve fibers from joint mechanoreceptors show only weak and sometimes quite inappropriate reactions for such a protective function (Andersson & Stener, 1959; Ekholm, Eklund, & Skoglund, 1960; Petersen & Stener, 1959; Ramacharan & Wyke, 1972). However, most of these tests have used anesthetized animals under quite unnatural conditions. Perhaps under normal and natural conditions, especially with vigorous movements, such reflexes would become clearer.

Barron and Coote (1973) found that gentle manipulation of the knee produced an increase in heart rate, blood pressure, and respiration rate in anesthetized animals. By electrically stimulating the joint nerve at different strengths, they determined that activity in the slower conducting nerve fibers (less than 30 m/sec) caused this effect. Most studies of joint mechanoreceptors concentrate on afferents conducting somewhat faster, so one cannot easily say what receptors produce these autonomic reflexes.

Little data about the sensations elicited by selective stimulation of mechanoreceptors in the joints exist in the literature. In one heroic experiment, Samuel (1949) dissected his own knee and pulled on the joint capsule to investigate the sensations evoked. He reported feeling pressure in and around the knee with gentle manipulation of the capsule and pain when he pulled harder. Samuel never experienced sensations of movement or altered position. One of us (FJC) injected saline into his own knee joint to expand the capsule and activate articular mechanoreceptors. Like Samuel, he experienced only sensations of pressure deep in the joint.

Injecting a local anesthetic into a normal knee joint produces an effect people find difficult to describe. For the most part, the effect goes unnoticed after the first few moments. However, with a forced extension or flexion of the joint, one sometimes has a subtle but noticeable feeling some subjects describe as "sort of swollen." (One gets a "swollen" feeling with saline as well, but it lasts only a short time. The feeling with the local anesthetic sometimes lasted for hours.) Injecting a local anesthetic into the metacarpophalangeal joint (first knuckle) of the index finger produces an initial feeling of pressure that subsides after a while. When we tried this with ourselves (FJC &KWH), we experimented with forcibly hyperextending the joint to test the sensation. We compared the injected finger with the opposite normal finger and noticed no particular difference—until the following day. The injected joint hurt. We believe this happened because we tolerated greater force in the injected joint than in the normal joint and caused some minor injury. This supports the view that articular receptors may serve a protective function by signaling noxious forces applied to the joint. The majority

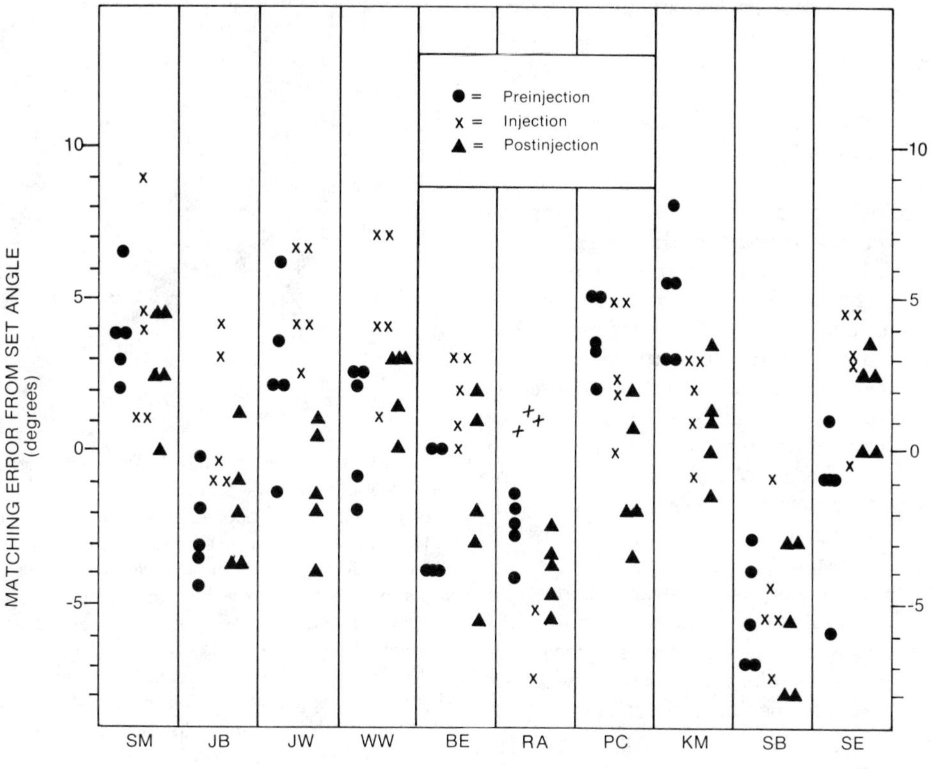

(a)

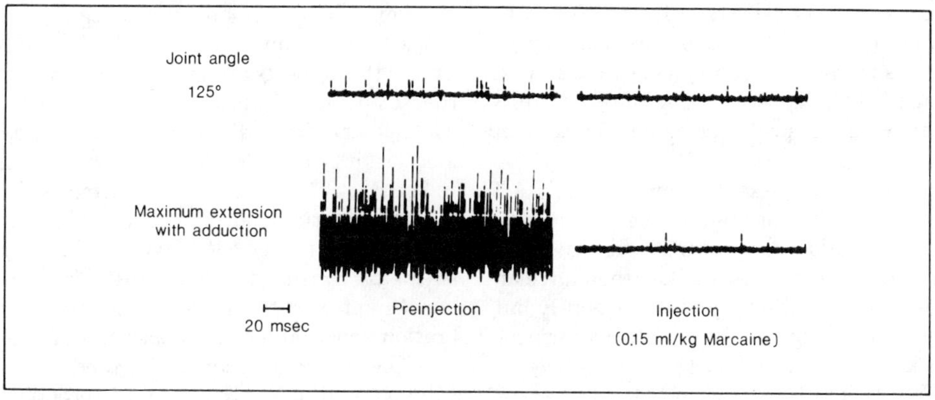

(b)

Figure 13.45. Position sense in anesthetized knee joints. (a) Effect of injecting a local anesthetic into both knee joints on individual subjects' accuracy of rematching knee joint angles after slowly applied misalignments. See Figure 13.42 for format. (b) Effect of a local anesthetic injected into the knee joint of a monkey on tonic activity in the posterior articular nerve. Activity is shown at two positions, 125° and maximum extension with abduction of the tibia. Note the almost complete absence of any myelinated fiber activity after the injection. Marcaine is a long-acting anesthetic, so this block persisted for several hours. (From F. J. Clark, K. W. Horch, S. M. Bach, & G. F. Larson, Contribution of cutaneous and joint receptors to static knee-position sense in man, *Journal of Neurophysiology*, 1979, *42*. Reprinted with permission.)

of the receptors in articular tissue have maximal discharges under such conditions, responses well suited for a protective role.

4.4. Muscle Spindle Receptors

Just as knowledge of joint angle allows one to determine the orientation of an appendage, knowledge of the lengths of the muscles around these joints also allows determination of limb position and movement. The muscle spindle receptors appear quite capable of encoding muscle length. The argument that gamma control, which can alter spindle activity indepedently of muscle stretch, precludes encoding of absolute length seems without merit. Such arguments assume that the CNS cannot take into account the effects of its own output to derive true length from the spindle discharge. Muscles act in opponent (antagonistic) groups, so that CNS has access to receptors operating in a "push–pull" arrangement that likely enhances the quality and reliability of the signals from the muscles.

If we acknowledge that humans have an awareness of static limb position, and neither skin nor joint receptors contribute to this position sense, then it would seem that muscle receptors alone remain as contenders for the role. Let us examine whether our logic holds up in the face of experimental evidence.

4.4.1. Kinesthetic Sensations from Muscle Spindles. A major argument against a role for muscle receptors in kinesthesia centered around the belief that impulses from muscle receptors do not reach conscious levels and therefore cannot contribute to kinesthesia. One of the most striking demonstrations, that impulses from muscle receptors not only do reach consciousness but elicit kinesthetic sensations as well, comes from the illusions of limb movement and altered limb position produced by vibrating a muscle. Gentle vibration at a frequency in the range of about 20–200 Hz applied to a muscle tendon can powerfully excite the spindle receptors in the muscle and produce kinesthetic illusions.

One can easily demonstrate these illusions for one's self using the arms. Sit before a table of comfortable height with both elbows resting on the table, as shown in Figure 13.46. Tense the biceps of one arm to locate the tendon; then have an assistant hold an ordinary physiotherapy vibrator gently but firmly on the tendon as shown in the figure. With your eyes closed, hold the vibrated arm fairly relaxed with the elbow at about a 110° angle. Use the opposite forearm to track the perceived movement and position of the vibrated arm. The vibration will usually cause a mild reflex contraction of the biceps, so have your assistant gently support your forearm so it does not move. When the vibration begins, you should feel your forearm extending outward. You can heighten this movement illusion by having your assistant very slowly extend the vibrated forearm, and you can diminish the illusion by tensing your muscles. You can ignore the sensation of movement and focus instead on matching the position of your two forearms. You will find that though your forearms feel perfectly matched, they will actually have a misalignment similar to that shown in Figure 13.46: the vibrated arm feels more extended than its true position.

Subjects become aware of several different sensations during the tendon vibration. First, one feels the contact of the vibrator on the skin and vibration of the arm, feelings that localize to the arm and which we do not regard as kinesthetic. Next, one has an often striking feeling that the forearm continually moves outward into extension. Finally, one has an impression of arm position. The movement illusion catches the attention of most subjects, so the altered sense of limb position may go unnoticed unless the subjects attempt to align the arms and then observe the resulting mismatch or unless the limb feels situated in some clearly impossible position (Craske, 1977). Subjects can also visually track the apparent movement of a vibrated arm in the dark (Lackner, 1975). Normally, one can make smooth pursuit (tracking) movements with the eyes only when following some visual target. Otherwise, voluntary eye movements to shift gaze consist of rapid, ballistic movements called *saccades* (see Chapter 10 by Hallett). The movement illusions from vibration apparently can engage the visual tracking mechanisms.

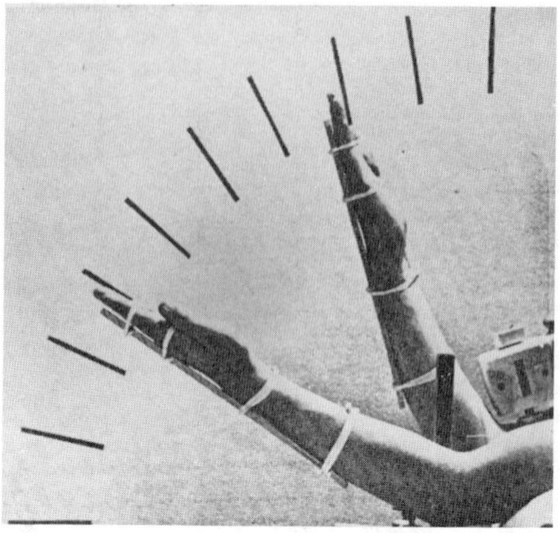

Figure 13.46. Kinesthetic illusion produced by tendon vibration. The biceps tendon of one arm was stimulated, with a vibrator, while being held in a fixed position, and its apparent position was tracked by the subject with the other arm. Shown is a posed photograph to illustrate the magnitude of the difference in position of the vibrated and the tracking arm that can occur while the subject believes he is managing to keep them aligned. The scale is marked in tens of degrees. The more extended arm represents the apparent position of the more flexed, vibrated arm. (From G. M. Goodwin, D. I. McCloskey, & P. B. C. Matthews, The contribution of muscle afferents to kinaesthesia shown by vibration-induced illusions of movement and by the effects of paralysing joint afferents, *Brain*, 95. Copyright 1972 by Oxford University Press. Reprinted with permission.)

The illusions produced by tendon vibration arise mainly from activation of the spindle receptors. Tendon vibration strongly excites spindle primary endings because of their high sensitivity to rate of stretch (velocity). The CNS interprets the increased discharge from the spindles as a lengthening of the muscle, and one feels the limb moving in a direction that corresponds to a lengthening of the muscle. When tracking the perceived movement with the opposite limb, a subject soon becomes aware of a conflict between the sense of continuing movement and the perceived position of the arm, which seems to remain fixed. The vibration activates spindles in only one or a few muscles, so other nonvibrated muscles still contribute signals that conflict with those from the vibration. However, the vividness of the illusions underscores the powerful contribution possible from the spindle primary endings.

In laboratory experiments one can connect a vibrator directly to the muscle tendon to produce a longitudinal vibration that can selectively activate the primary endings (group Ia fibers). The discharge of the primary ending will lock in phase with the vibration (Matthews, 1972). Transverse vibration of a muscle belly in the cat will excite both secondary and primary endings (Bianconi & van der Meulen, 1963), but transverse vibration of the tendon at sufficiently high frequencies appears to excite mainly the primary endings. In humans, tendon vibration applied transversely can excite some spindle secondary endings and Golgi tendon organs, as well as the primary endings (Burke, Hagbarth, Wallin, & Löfstedt, 1980). Nonetheless, it appears safe to regard tendon vibration as a nearly selective activator of spindle primary endings (Roll & Vedel, 1982). Comparing the effects of vibrating the muscle tendon versus the belly of the muscle provides a way to separate the contributions of the spindle primary and secondary endings. In this respect, McCloskey (1973) found he could selectively alter the movement and positional components of the illusion by vibrating the tendon or the muscle belly. We discuss his experiment further in Section 4.4.2.

Vibration provides a way of making the primary spindle response independent of muscle stretch, a technique that has proven useful for analyzing the role of the various components of the spindle discharge. With the discharge locked in phase with the vibration, the primary ending no longer responds to changes in muscle length. Using vibration to excite spindles can introduce its own complications. Sinusoidal vibration can sometimes produce "double driving" of the spindle with two impulses per cycle of vibration. In addition, resonances in the vibrator and the coupling to the tendon can cause substantial changes in amplitude as frequency varies. McGrath and Matthews (1973) found that using a bell-shaped pulse, instead of a sinusoid, eliminated many of the problems of double driving and resonances.

4.4.2. Independence of Movement and Position Sensations. Experimental manipulations reveal an independence in the sensations of position and movement. People can attend to either sensation. Position and movement have an interrelationship, as one cannot move without changing position and vice versa, but under most circumstances movement and position vary in a consistent manner, so one would not notice any separation of the sensations. However, one can experimentally dissociate position and movement sensations. Horch and colleagues (1975) found that subjects cannot sense very slow joint rotations (less than 1°/min), but they can sense the resulting small misalignments. Perhaps the nervous system might use different signals or different central-processing mechanisms to sense position and movement (see Burgess, Horch, & Tuckett, 1983), much like a piece of electronic equipment might use different circuits to separate dc and low-frequency signals from high-frequency signals.

McCloskey (1973) found he could differentially alter the illusion of movement and the positional errors produced by vibrating a muscle either by loading the muscle or by changing the amplitude and frequency of vibration. Loading a muscle during vibration by having the subject support a weight made the movement illusion feel slower (see Figure 13.47), but it increased the position error (Table 13.9).

McCloskey (1973) also found that vibration frequency and the method of application affect the displacement and movement illusions differently. He used two kinds of vibrators: a physiotherapy type operating at 100Hz with a one-mm displacement applied to the tendon, and a variable-speed jigsaw, with a padded plunger applied to the belly of the muscle. The jigsaw produced a series of taps of about 0.5-cm displacement at a frequency of 2–48 Hz. The positional errors obtained with the low-frequency jigsaw vibrator exceeded those from the physiotherapy vibrator, and the low-frequency vibrator could produce a positional error without a movement illusion.

McCloskey supported the idea of separate lines of information from muscle to signal position and movement and argued that position sense does not result from integrating rate information. He pointed out first that the movement illusions appear too great to produce the relatively smaller positional errors by simple integration. Second, the positional error does not change with time during the vibration (although this might just reflect a "leaky" or sliding integration). Third, loading the muscle slows the movement illusion but increases positional errors. And, finally, low-frequency vibration can produce a positional error in the absence of a movement illusion. An especially attractive hypothesis arising from these findings would assign movement signals to the primary endings and positional signals to the secondary endings. This hypothesis awaits confirmation.

4.5. Sense of Muscle Tension

We have little data about our awareness of muscle tension except to note that humans can make judgments of muscle tension independent of any sense of effort (McCloskey et al., 1974; Roland & Ladegaard-Pedersen, 1977). Tendon organs, by nature of their response properties, appear the most likely candidates to signal the forces (tension developed by muscles. Binder, Kroin, Moore, and Stuart (1977) have shown that activity in single motor units can powerfully excite tendon organs and have suggested that these receptors serve to regulate contraction in the motor units linked to them. However, the 40 or 50 Golgi tendon organs in the "average" large muscle, on the whole, provide an accurate measure of the total tension produced by the muscle (Crago, Houk, & Rymer, 1982) and could serve as the source of our subtle sense of muscle tension.

4.6. Corollary Discharge and Efference Copy

If muscle spindles contribute to kinesthesia, the nervous system must somehow compensate for the effect of fusimotor (A-gamma efferent) activity on muscle spindle responsiveness. We have no idea how the CNS does this, but it could monitor its own outflow to the muscle spindles and use this information to adjust the incoming spindle signals. We do have evidence that such monitoring occurs, particularly in the case of our "sense of effort."

Recent studies have marshaled compelling evidence that our perception of heaviness arises mainly from signals derived entirely within the CNS. Command signals generated during willed or voluntary movements and destined for the muscles get routed, as well, to the perceptual portions of the brain, where they can alter or perhaps even produce sensations. In short, the CNS internally monitors its own efforts to produce muscle contractions, and out perception of heaviness comes from this internal sense of effort (Gandevia & McCloskey, 1977).

We apply the term *corollary discharge* to that component of the internally generated command signal that radiates to the perceptual portion of the brain to affect sensations. The term *efference copy* often gets used interchangeably with the term corollary discharge, although these terms originally referred to quite different hypotheses (see Figure 13.48). In using these terms, we will follow the suggestion of McCloskey (1981) and reserve the term corollary discharge "for those internal consequences of motor commands that affect sensations, either by central modification of the processing of sensory signals gen-

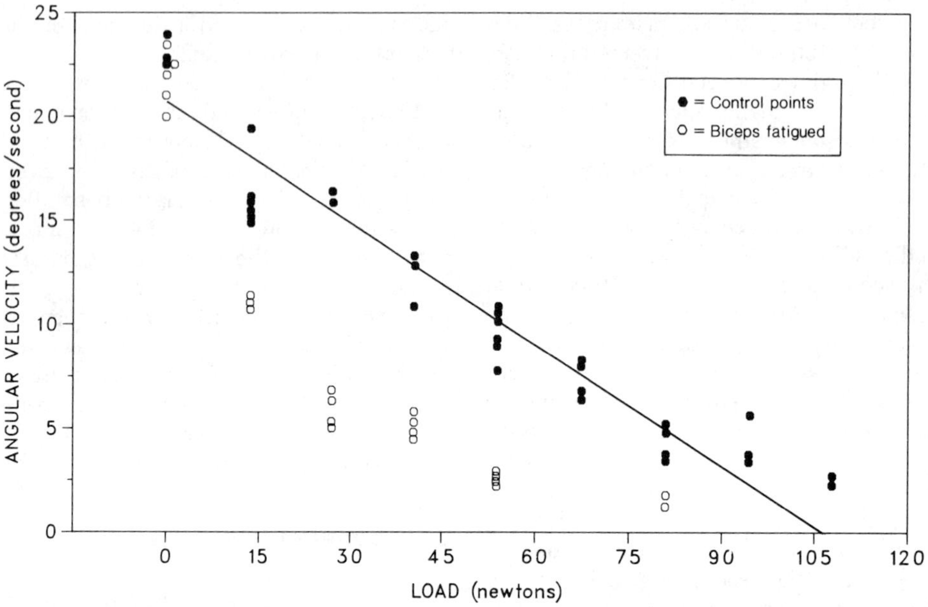

Figure 13.47. Contracting a muscle alters the movement illusion induced by tendon vibration. The angular velocity of the illusory movement of the elbow joint into extension, induced by vibration of biceps brachii at 100 Hz, is plotted against the load at the wrist borne by tensing the biceps. The closed circles show the control points, and the line drawn is the line of best fit drawn by the least-squares method. The open circles are points obtained when biceps were fatigued through a prolonged period of weight bearing. The speed of movement was indicated by having the subject track the illusion with the opposite arm (see Figure 13.46). (From D. I. McCloskey, Differences between the senses of movement and position shown by the effects of loading and vibration of muscles in man, *Brain Research*, 1973, *63*. Reprinted with permission.)

Table 13.9. Positions Sense at the Elbow: Errors in Matching Positions of the Elbows during Vibration and Loading of the Elbow Flexor (Biceps) Muscle

Subject	Control (Degrees)	Load Alone (Degrees)	Vibration Alone (Degrees)	Vibration Plus Load (Degrees)	Movement Illusion (Degree/sec)
CG	−0.8 ± 0.95	+1.6 ± 1.77[a]	+6.0 ± 3.23[a]	+ 4.9 ± 3.70	2.5
PE	−4.5 ± 1.58	+0.9 ± 1.90[a]	+0.9 ± 1.17[a]	+ 7.7 ± 2.75[b]	1.5
IN	−0.1 ± 1.90	+6.6 ± 3.64[a]	+8.8 ± 2.81[a]	+12.9 ± 1.71[b]	6.5
PC	−0.4 ± 1.61	+4.3 ± 0.44[a]	+3.1 ± 4.11[a]	+10.9 ± 2.88[b]	3.0
MS	−3.3 ± 1.39	+1.6 ± 1.58[a]	−1.0 ± 1.45[a]	+ 3.6 ± 1.17[b]	8.5
JC	−7.5 ± 2.12	+0.3 ± 2.12[a]	+6.4 ± 2.15[a]	+11.9 ± 1.08[b]	12.5
EM	−3.8 ± 2.12	+5.0 ± 3.86[a]	+5.2 ± 4.46[a]	+ 7.8 ± 3.98	10.0
RM	+0.7 ± 1.45	+1.9 ± 2.28	+3.3 ± 2.85[a]	+ 6.6 ± 1.77[b]	4.0
AL	−5.4 ± 1.99	+0.6 ± 1.26[a]	+4.3 ± 1.61[a]	+ 4.7 ± 3.26	22.5
JM	−2.7 ± 1.49	+0.5 ± 0.70[a]	+4.8 ± 2.47[a]	+ 3.7 ± 2.06	35.0
IC	−2.7 ± 2.02	+0.7 ± 1.64	+0.2 ± 1.74	+ 7.0 ± 1.52[b]	1.0
RH	−2.3 ± 2.28	+5.3 ± 1.01[a]	+ 2.1 ± 1.42	+ 5.8 ± 1.17[b]	
MP	−1.9 ± 2.28	+3.4 ± 2.81	+4.0 ± 2.47[a]	+ 7.9 ± 1.30[b]	
RB	0.0 ± 2.02	+1.4 ± 2.91	+3.2 ± 1.01[a]	+ 5.8 ± 0.76[b]	
MJ	−1.2 ± 2.02	+3.4 ± 3.10			
Mean	−1.7	+2.5	+3.7	+ 7.2	

Blindfolded subjects attempted to match the position of one elbow to the opposite, reference elbow by aligning the index fingers of both hands. Unknown to the subjects, all trials used the same target position, 50° from full extension. The table lists the matching errors as mean values ± standard deviation for 10 trials, with positive values indicating an error in extension (matching arm more extended than the reference arm). Negative values indicate error in flexion. The column labeled "Movement Illusion" gives an estimate of the angular velocity of the movement illusion induced with vibration at 100 Hz with no loading (mean of five trials.) (From McCloskey, 1973.)

[a] Deviated significantly from control (no-load) values by the *t*-test ($p < .01$ or more).
[b] Deviated significantly from vibration alone values by the *t*-test ($p < .01$ or more).

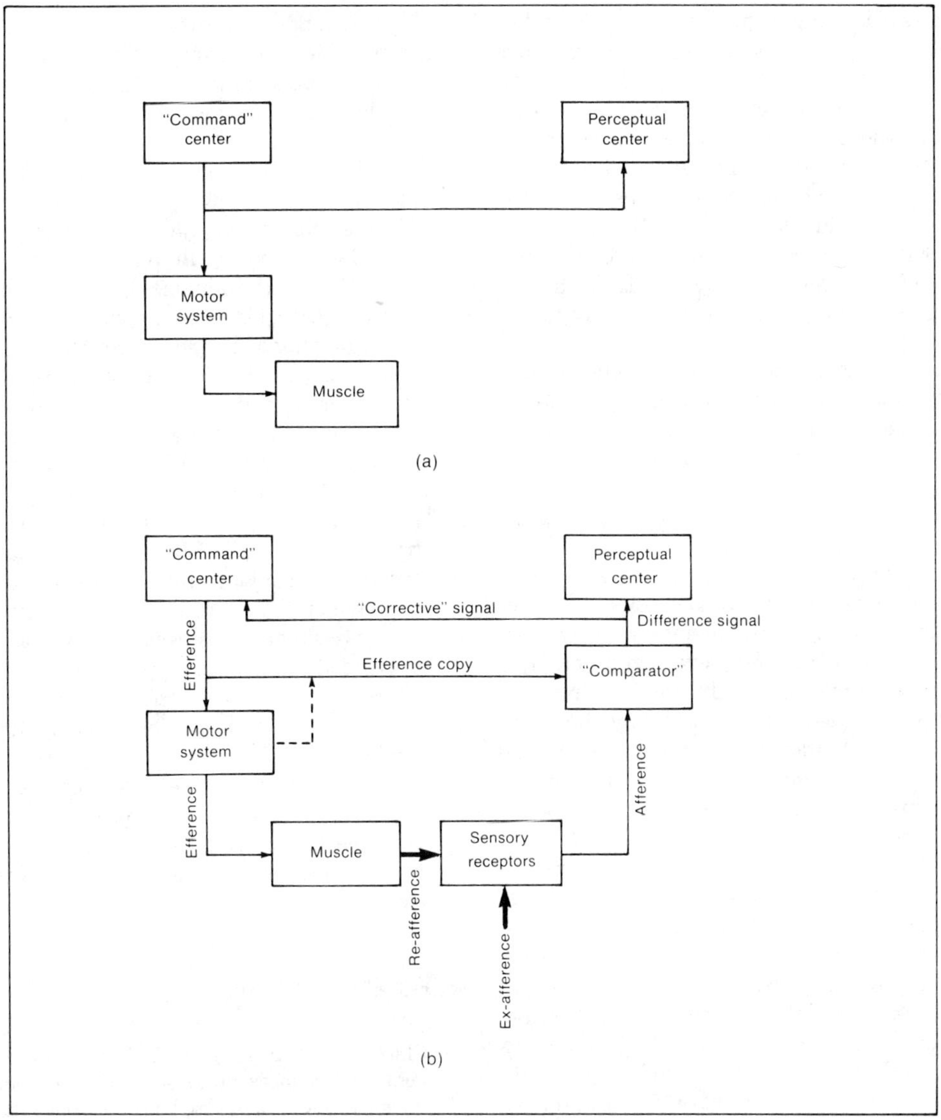

Figure 13.48. Corollary discharge versus efference copy. Corollary discharge (a) hypothesizes a copy of the efferent command signal to the motor systems being also directed to perceptual centers, where it has a direct influence on perception. See Figure 13.1 for a historical perspective on this concept. Efference copy (b) also involves a copy of the efferent command signal being directed elsewhere. In contrast to the corollary discharge model, however, the signal is not sent directly to perceptual centers. Rather, it is directed to a lower, "comparator" system, which then provides a difference signal between this input and the input from sensory receptors responding to the result of the motor activity. This difference signal can be used either to influence perception or to modulate the motor commands. If the sensory input matches the efference copy signal, the desired motor act is being performed properly and no corrective signal is produced. The sensory signal originating from skin, muscle, and joint mechanoreceptors has two components: re-afference, stimulation produced by the muscle activity created by the efferent signal, and ex-afference, stimulation produced by external factors. The function of the comparison of the sensory input with an efferent copy is to distinguish between the two sources of sensory input. Ideally, the output of the comparator is an image of ex-afference. (Based on Sperry, 1950; von Holst, 1954; von Holst & Mittelstaedt, 1973.)

erated peripherally, or by their own independent actions" (p. 1420).

Just where corollary discharges arise in the CNS remains unclear, though tests on patients suffering a partial block in a motor pathway do provide some clues. For example, to support a weight in the hand requires a particular muscle force that in turn requires a particular neural signal to the muscles. With a partial block in the pathway, the CNS must generate a greater amount of neural activity upstream of the block to provide the required level below the block. If such a block causes an increase in the sense of effort (e.g., people complain of weakness) or if weights feel heavier on the side with a block, we conclude that the corollary discharge originates above the block. Lesions of the motor cortex can cause weakness and a sense of heaviness of the limbs, suggesting perhaps that the corollary discharges arise at a fairly high level in the CNS. However, as McCloskey (1981) warns, many lesions (injuries) involve sensory mechanisms, as well as motor systems, and the contribution of each becomes unclear. Furthermore, Gandevia (1978) suggested that corollaries arise not at the highest levels but further down along the motor pathway. He studied patients who had undergone brain surgery to control epilepsy. The surgical procedure involved separating the two hemispheres of the brain ("split brain") by cutting their interconnecting nerve bundles (the commissures). He found these patients could accurately match weights held in the hands. This presumably requires an exchange of information between the two hemispheres of the brain, but with the brain commissures cut, the first opportunity for any crossover would occur in the brainstem. However, one cannot rule out the possibility of a corollary pathway arising at a higher level and following a descending path before crossing to the opposite side.

Corollary discharges seem associated mainly (and perhaps exclusively) with willed or voluntary movements, suggesting that the corollary discharges arise close to the origin of the voluntary command signals, though we know almost nothing about the location and the nature of any "voluntary command center." Various nonwilled or involuntary movements, for example, those produced by neurological disorders in the cerebrum (especially those involving the basal ganglia), occur without feelings of effort by patients, as though some external force produced the movement. Some of these involuntary movements, particularly of the face and mouth, may even go unfelt by a patient, his or her first awareness of any disorder coming from comments by a friend or relative. It seems likely that both voluntary commands and involuntary commands produce muscle contractions through a common motor machinery, but the involuntary commands may enter the system at a level below where the corollary discharges arise.

Note that a lack of feelings of effort with involuntary muscle contractions does not rule out the existence of some sort of efference copy (see Figure 13.48) associated with the contractions: it implies only that the copy does not reach levels of perception, so we would not call it a corollary discharge.

The corollary discharge model provides a very attractive hypothesis to explain our sense of effort and how the CNS derives true muscle length and velocity signals from spindle discharges. However, the evidence does not yet rule out other mechanisms not involving corollary discharges. We may yet find that all sensation comes entirely from incoming signals and that the CNS analyzes the patterns of discharge from all the different receptor types affected by a stimulus to produce an appropriate sensation. Scientists tend to look for particular stimulus features encoded in receptor discharges in a recognizable way and, finding none, conclude that the receptor plays no role in sensing the stimulus. However, the CNS might encode data in ways not yet apparent to us. Our sense of effort might derive from the overall pattern of discharge from muscle spindles and tendon organs, as well as other receptor types, and not require or even involve corollary discharges. Muscle weakness caused by strokes, drugs, or fatigue might alter the balance of activity among these receptors and thereby alter our sense of heaviness. The discharge of the ensemble of receptors might encode the effects of the gamma motor activity, as well as the various features of the stimulus. Though we personally favor the corollary discharge hypothesis as conceptually the simplest and most direct, we suggest caution in accepting it uncritically.

4.7. Summary

1. Though humans may use a variety of nonkinesthetic cues to ascertain the positions and movements of their limbs, we possess an important, fundamental kinesthetic system that depends on position, movement, and tension signals from sensory receptors in the periphery. These inputs arise from receptors in joints, skin, and muscle.
2. We have independent senses of joint movement and joint position.
3. Muscle spindle receptors provide our awareness of the static positions of the limbs.
4. Muscle spindle receptors and probably cutaneous receptors provide our sense of limb movement.
5. Kinesthetic mechanisms for the fingers differ from those in most other joints. We apparently lack a true sense of the static positions of some of the finger joints (the interphalangeal joints). Presumably our sense of finger position derives from a variety of cues, including movement signals that come from muscle and skin receptors and other cues we might ordinarily call nonkinesthetic. Additionally, cutaneous receptors in the fingers supply some sort of facilitatory input the CNS requires to interpret movement signals from other sources. Elimination of regions of skin not associated with a joint can impair subjects' ability to perceive movement of the joint.
6. We possess an awareness, however subtle, of the tension developed by our muscles, and an independent "sense of effort."
7. Our sense of muscle tension probably derives from the Golgi tendon organs, the tension receptors found in muscles.
8. Our sense of effort likely derives from signals generated entirely within the CNS. A portion of the command signals destined for the muscles gets fed as corollary discharges into the perceptual regions of the brain to influence sensation.

REFERENCE NOTES

1. Clark, F. J., & Burgess, R. C. *Longterm memory for position.* Unpublished manuscript, 1984. (Available from F. J. Clark, Dept. of Physiology & Biophysics, University of Nebraska College of Medicine, Omaha, NE 68105).
2. Stevens, J. C. *Psychophysical invariances in proprioception.* Paper presented at the Conference on Cutaneous Communication Systems and Devices, Monterey, California, April 1973.

REFERENCES

*References marked by an asterisk are "key references."

Andersson, S., & Stener, B. Experimental evaluation of the hypothesis of ligamentomuscular protective reflexes. II. A study in cat using the medial collateral ligament of the knee joint. *Acta Physiologica Scandinavica*, 1959, *48* (Suppl. 166), 27–49.

Andrew, B. L. The sensory innervation of the medial ligament of the knee joint. *Journal of Physiology*, 1954, *123*, 241–250.

Appenteng, K., Lund, J. P., & Seguin, J. J. Behavior of cutaneous mechanoreceptors recorded in mandibular division of Gasserian ganglion of the rabbit during movements of lower jaw. *Journal of Neurophysiology*, 1982, *47*, 151–166.

Bairstow, P. J., & Laszlo, J. I. Perception of movement patterns. Recognition from visual arrays of distorted patterns. *Quarterly Journal of Experimental Psychology*, 1978, *30*, 311–317.

*Barker, D. The morphology of muscle receptors. In C. C. Hunt (Ed.), *Handbook of sensory physiology, (Vol. III/2): Muscle receptors.* New York: Springer-Verlag, 1974.

Barron, W., & Coote, J. H. The contribution of articular receptors to cardiovascular reflexes elicited by passive limb movement. *Journal of Physiology*, 1973, *235*, 423–436.

Bessou, P., & Pages, B. Intracellular potentials from intrafusal muscle fibres evoked by stimulation of static and dynamic fusimotor axons in the cat. *Journal of Physiology*, 1972, *227*, 709–728.

Bianconi, R., & van der Meulen, J. P. The response to vibration of the end organs of mammalian muscle spindles. *Journal of Neurophysiology*, 1963, *26*, 177–198.

Binder, M. D. Further evidence that the Golgi tendon organ monitors the activity of a discrete set of motor units within a muscle. *Experimental Brain Research*, 1981, *43*, 186–192.

*Binder, M. D., Houk, J. C., Nichols, T. R., Rymer, W. Z., & Stuart, D. G. Properties and segmental actions of mammalian muscle receptors: An update. *Federation Proceedings*, 1982, *41*, 2907–2918.

Binder, M. D., Kroin, J. S., Moore, G. P., & Stuart, D. G. The response of Golgi tendon organs to single motor unit contractions. *Journal of Physiology*, 1977, *271*, 337–349.

Boring, E. G. *Sensation and perception in the history of experimental psychology*. New York: Appleton-Century-Crofts, 1942.

Bossom, J. Movement without proprioception. *Brain Research*, 1974, *71*, 285–296.

Bourassa, C. M., & Swett, J. E. Sensory discrimination thresholds with cutaneous nerve volleys in the cat. *Journal of Neurophysiology*, 1967, *30*, 515–529.

Boyd, I. A. The histological structure of the receptors in the knee joint of the cat correlated with their physiological response. *Journal of Physiology*, 1954, *124*, 476–488.

Boyd, I. A., & Davey, M. R. *Composition of peripheral nerves*. Edinburgh, Scotland: Livingstone, 1968.

Boyd, I. A., Gladden, M. H., McWilliam, P. M., & Ward, J. Control of dynamic and static nuclear bag fibres and nuclear chain fibres by gamma and beta axons in isolated cat mucles spindles. *Journal of Physiology*, 1977, *265*, 133–162.

Boyd, I. A., & Roberts, T. D. M. Proprioceptive discharges from stretch-receptors in the knee joint of the cat. *Journal of Physiology*, 1953, *122*, 38–58.

Brindley, G. S., & Merton, P. A. The absence of position sense in the human eye. *Journal of Physiology*, 1960, *153*, 127–130.

Brown, M. C., Crowe, A., & Matthews, P. B. C. Observations on the fusimotor fibres of the tibialis posterior muscle of the cat. *Journal of Physiology*, 1965, *177*, 140–159.

Brown, M. C., Engberg, I. E., & Matthews, P. B. C. The relative sensitivity to vibration of muscle receptors of the cat. *Journal of Physiology*, 1967, *192*, 773–800.

Brown, J. S., Knauft, E. B., & Rosenbaum, G. The accuracy of positioning reactions as a function of their direction and extent. *American Journal of Psychology*, 1948, *61*, 167–182.

Brown, M. C., & Matthews, P. B. C. In B. L. Anderson (Ed.), *Control and innervation of skeletal muscle*. Dundee, Scotland: Thomson, 1966.

Browne, K., Lee, J., & Ring, P. A. The sensation of passive movement at the metatarso-phalangeal joint of the great toe in man. *Journal of Physiology*, 1954, *126*, 448–458.

Burgess, P. R., & Clark, F. J. Characteristics of knee joint receptors in the cat. *Journal of Physiology*, 1969, *203*, 317–335.

Burgess, P. R., Horch, K. W., & Tuckett, R. P. Boring's forumulation: A scheme for identifying functional neuron groups in a sensory system. *Federation Proceedings*, 1983, *42*, 2521–2527.

Burgess, P. R., & Perl, E. R. Cutaneous mechanorecetors and nociceptors. In A. Iggo (Ed.), *Handbook of sensory physiology, (Vol. II): Somatosensory system*. New York: Springer-Verlag, 1973.

Burgess, P. R., Wei, J. Y., Clark, F. J., & Simon, J. Signaling of kinesthetic information by peripheral sensory receptors. *Annual Review of Neuroscience*, 1982, *5*, 171–187.

Burke, D., Hagbarth, K. E., Wallin, B. G., & Löfstedt, L. Muscle spindle activity induced by vibration in man: Implications for the tonic stretch reflex. *Progress in Clinical Neurophysiology*, 1980, *8*, 243–253.

Cafarelli, E., & Kostka, C. E. Effect of vibration on static force sensation in man. *Experimental Neurology*, 1981, *74*, 331–340

Caldwell, L. S. *The accuracy of constant angular displacement of the arm in the horizontal plane as influenced by the direction and locus of the primary adjustive movement* (Report No. 233). Fort Knox, KY: Army Medical Research Laboratory, 1956.

Cameron, P., & Wertheimer, M. Kinesthetic after-effects are in the hands, not in the phenomenal space. *Perceptual and Motor Skills*, 1965, *20*, 1131–1132.

Carli, G., Farabollini, F., Fontani, G., & Meucci, M. Slowly adapting receptors in cat hip joint. *Journal of Neurophysiology*, 1979, *42*, 767–778.

Chambers, R. A., & Gilliatt, R. W. The clinical assessment of postural sensation in the fingers. *Journal of Physiology*, 1954, *123*, 42 P.

Cheng, M. Tactile–kinesthetic perception of length. *American Journal of Psychology*, 1968, *81*, 74–82.

Chouchkov, C. Cutaneous receptors. *Advances in Anatomy, Embryology and Cell Biology*, 1978, *54*, 1–61.

Clark, F. J. Information signaled by sensory fibers in medial articular nerve. *Journal of Neurophysiology*, 1975, *38*, 1464–1472.

Clark, F. J., & Burgess, P. R. Slowly adapting receptors in cat knee joint: Can they signal joint angle? *Journal of Neurophysiology*, 1975, *38*, 1448–1463.

Clark, F. J., Burgess, R. C., & Chapin, J. W. Humans lack of sense of static-position of the fingers. *Society for Neuroscience Abstracts*, 1983, *9*, 1033.

*Clark, F. J., Burgess, R. C., Chapin, J. W., & Lipscomb, W. T. The role of intramuscular receptors in the awareness of limb position. *Journal of Neurophysiology*, 1985, *54*, 1529–1540.

Clark, F. J., Horch, K. W., Bach, S. M., & Larson, G. F. Contribution of cutaneous and joint receptors to static knee-position sense in man. *Journal of Neurophysiology*, 1979, *42*, 877–888.

Cleghorn, T. E, & Darcus, H. D. The sensibility to passive movement of the human elbow joint. *Quarterly Journal of Experimental Psychology*, 1952, *4*, 66–77.

Cohen, L. A. Analysis of position sense in human shoulder. *Journal of Neurophysiology*, 1958, *21*, 550–562. (a)

Cohen, L. A. Contributions of tactile, musculo-tendinous and joint mechanisms to position sense in human shoulder. *Journal of Neurophysiology*, 1958, *21*, 563–568. (b)

Connolly, K., & Jones, B. A developmental study of afferent-reafferent integration. *British Journal of Psychology*, 1970, *61*, 259–266.

Conomy, J. P. Disorders of body image after spinal cord injury. *Neurology*, 1973, *23*, 842–850.

Crago, P. E., Houk, J. C., & Rymer, W. Z. Sampling of total muscle force by tendon organs. *Journal of Neurophysiology*, 1982, *47*, 1069–1083.

Craske, B. Perception of impossible limb positions induced by tendon vibration. *Science*, 1977, *196*, 71–73.

Craske, B., & Crawshaw, M. Differential errors of kinesthesis produced by previous limb positions. *Journal of Motor Behavior*, 1974, *6*, 273–278.

Cratty, B. J., & Duffy, K. E. Studies of movement aftereffects. *Perceptual and Motor Skills*, 1969, *29*, 843–860.

Critchlow, V., & von Euler, C. Intercostal muscle spindle activity and its gamma motor control. *Journal of Physiology*, 1963, *168*, 820–847.

*Cross, M. J., & McCloskey, D. I. Position sense following surgical removal of joints in man. *Brain Research*, 1973, *55*, 443–445.

Crowe, A., & Matthews, P. B. C. Further studies of static and dynamic fusimotor fibres. *Journal of Physiology*, 1964, *174*, 109–131.

Day, R. H., & Singer, G. The relationship between the kinesthetic spatial aftereffect and variations in muscular involvement during stimulation. *Australian Journal of Psychology*, 1964, *16*, 200–208.

de Mendoza, J.-L. J. Demonstration of an aftereffect occurring in the tactile–kinesthetic domain: The gravimetric aftereffect. *Psychological Research*, 1979, *40*, 415–422.

Dyhre-Poulsen, P., & Djørup, A. The effect of sensory input on reflex load compensation. *Acta Physiologica Scandinavica*, 1976, *98* (Suppl. 440), 58.

Ekholm, J., Eklund, G., & Skoglund, S. On the reflex effects from the knee joint of the cat. *Acta Physiologica Scandinavica*, 1960, *50*, 167–174.

Erickson, R. P. Parallel "population" neural coding in feature extraction. In F. O. Schmitt & F. G. Worden (Eds.), *The neurosciences. Third study program.* Cambridge, Mass.: MIT Press, 1974.

Ferrell, W. R. The adequacy of stretch receptors in the cat knee joint for signalling joint angle throughout a full range of movement. *Journal of Physiology*, 1980, *299*, 85–99.

Forbes, A., Baird P. C., & Hopkins, A. M. The involuntary contraction following isometric contraction of skeletal muscle in man. *American Journal of Physiology*, 1926, *78*, 81–103.

Freeman, M. A. R., & Wyke, B. The innervation of the knee joint: An anatomical and histological study in the cat. *Journal of Anatomy*, 1967, *101*, 505–532.

Gandevia, S. C. The sensation of heaviness after surgical disconnection of the cerebral hemispheres in man. *Brain*, 1978, *101*, 295–305.

Gandevia, S. C. The perception of motor commands or effort during muscular paralysis. *Brain*, 1982, *105*, 151–159.

Gandevia, S. C., Hall, L. A., McCloskey, D. I., & Potter, E. K. Proprioceptive sensation at the terminal joint of the middle finger. *Journal of Physiology*, 1983, *335*, 507–517.

Gandevia, S. C., & McCloskey, D. I. Joint sense, muscle sense, and their combination as position sense, measured at the distal interphalangeal joint of the middle finger. *Journal of Physiology*, 1976, *260*, 387–407.

Gandevia, S. C., & McCloskey, D. I. Changes in motor commands, as shown by changes in perceived heaviness, during partial curarization and peripheral anaesthesia in man. *Journal of Physiology*, 1977, *272*, 673–689.

Gandevia, S. C., McCloskey, D. I., & Potter, E. K. Alterations in perceived heaviness during digital anaesthesia. *Journal of Physiology*, 1980, *306*, 365–375.

Gelfan, S., & Carter, S. Muscle sense in man. *Experimental Neurology*, 1967, *18*, 469–473.

Gibson, J. J. Adaptation, aftereffect and contrast in the perception of curved lines. *Journal of Experimental Psychology*, 1933, *16*, 1–33.

Gibson, J. J. Observations on active touch. *Psychological Review*, 1962, *69*, 477–491.

Godwin-Austen, R. B. The mechanoreceptors of the costo-vertebral joints. *Journal of Physiology*, 1969, *202*, 737–753.

Goldsheider, A. Untersuchungen über den Muskelsinn. *Archiv für Anatomie und Physiologie*, 1889, *3*, 369–502.

Goodwin, G. M., McCloskey, D. I., & Matthews, P. B. C. Proprioceptive illusions induced by muscle vibration: Contribution to perception by muscle spindles? *Science*, 1972, *175*, 1382–1384. (a)

*Goodwin, G. M., McCloskey, D. I., & Matthews, P. B. C. The contribution of muscles afferents to kinesthesia shown by vibration induced illusions of movement and by the effects of paralysing joint afferents. *Brain*, 1972, *95*, 705–748. (b)

Goodwin, G. M., McCloskey, D. I., & Matthews, P. B. C. The persistence of appreciable kinesthesia after paralysing joint afferents but preserving muscle afferents. *Brain Research*, 1972, *37*, 326–329. (c)

Granit, R. The case for relevance in sensorimotor physiology. *Trends in Neuroscience*, 1978, *1*, 17–18.

Grigg, P. Mechanical factors influencing response of joint afferent neurons from cat knee. *Journal of Neurophysiology*, 1975, *38*, 1473–1484.

Grigg, P. Response of joint afferent neurons in cat medial articular nerve to active and passive movements of the knee. *Brain Research*, 1976, *118*, 482–485.

Grigg, P., Finerman, G. A., & Riley, L. H. Joint-position sense after total hip replacement. *Journal of Bone and Joint Surgery*, 1973, *55A*, 1016–1025.

Grigg, P., & Greenspan, B. J. Response of primate joint afferent neurons to mechanical stimulation of knee joint. *Journal of Neurophysiology*, 1977, *40*, 1–8.

Grigg, P., Hoffman, A. H., & Fogarty, K. E. Properties of Golgi-Mazzoni afferents in cat knee joint capsule, as revealed by mechanical studies of isolated joint capsule. *Journal of Neurophysiology*, 1982, *47*, 31–40.

Gross, Y., & Melzack, R. Body image: Dissociation of real and perceived limbs by pressure-cuff ischemia. *Experimental Neurology*, 1978, *61*, 680–688.

Gross, Y., Webb, R., & Melzack, R. Central and peripheral contributions to localisation of body parts: Evidence for a central body schema. *Experimental Neurology*, 1974, *44*, 346–362.

Hagbarth, K.-E., & Eklund, G. Tonic vibration reflexes (TVR) in spasticity. *Brain Research*, 1966, *2*, 201–203.

Hall, L. A., & McCloskey, D. I. Detections of movements imposed on finger, elbow, and shoulder joints. *Journal of Physiology*, 1983, *335*, 519–533.

Harris, C. S. Perceptual adaptation to inverted, reversed, and displaced vision. *Psychological Review*, 1965, *72*, 419–444.

Hasan, Z., & Houk, J. C. Transistion in sensitivity of spindle receptors that occurs when muscle is stretched more than a fraction of a millimeter. *Journal of Neurophysiology*, 1975, *38*, 673–689.

Heide, J., & Molbech, S. Influence of after-movement on muscle memory following isometric muscle contraction. *Ergonomics*, 1973, *16*, 787–796.

Helmholtz, H. [*Helmholtz's treatise on physiological optics* (3rd ed.)] (J. P. C. Southall, Ed. and trans.) Menasha, Wisc.: Optical Society of America, 1925. (Originally published, 1867.)

*Henderson, W. R., & Smyth, G. E. Phantom limbs. *Journal of Neurology, Neurosurgery and Psychiatry*, 1948, *11*, 88–112.

Horch, K. W., Clark, F. J., & Burgess, P. R. Awareness of knee joint angle under static conditions. *Journal of Neurophysiology*, 1975, *38*, 1436–1447.

Horch, K. W., Tuckett, R. P., & Burgess, P. R. A key to the classification of cutaneous mechanoreceptors. *Journal of Investigative Dermatology*, 1977, *69*, 75–82.

Houk, J. C. Homeostasis and control principles. In V. B. Mountcastle (Ed.), *Medical physiology* (14th ed.). St. Louis: Mosby, 1980.

Howard, I. P., & Anstis, T. Muscular and joint-receptor components in postural persistence. *Journal of Experimental Psychology*, 1974, *103*, 167–170.

*Hulliger, M. The mammalian muscle spindle and its central control. *Reviews of Physiology, Biochemistry and Pharmacology*, 1984, *101*, 1–10.

*Hunt, C. C. The physiology of muscle receptors. In C. C. Hunt (Ed.), *Handbook of sensory physiology* (Vol. III/2): *Muscle receptors.* New York: Springer-Verlag, 1974.

Iggo, A. Is the physiology of cutaneous receptors determined by morphology? In A. Iggo & O. B. Ilyinsky (Eds.), *Somatosensory and visceral receptor mechanisms. Progress in brain research* (Vol. 43). New York: Elsevier, 1976.

Iggo, A., & Andres, K. H. Morphology of cutaneous receptors. *Annual Review of Neuroscience*, 1982, *5*, 1–31.

Jackson, C. V. The influence of previous movement and posture on subsequent posture. *Quarterly Journal of Experimental Psychology*, 1954, *6*, 72–78.

Jones, B. When are vision and kinaesthesis comparable? *British Journal of Psychology*, 1973, *64*, 587–591.

*Jones, E. G. The development of the "muscular sense" concept during the nineteenth century and the work of H. Charlton Bastian. *Journal of the History of Medicine*, 1972, *25*, 298–311.

Knibestol, J. Stimulus–response functions of slowly adapting mechanoreceptors in the human glabrous skin area. *Journal of Physiology*, 1975, *245*, 63–80.

Koehler, W., & Dinnerstein, D. Figural after-effects in kinesthesis. In Universitas Catholica Lovaniensis, *Miscellanea psychologica Albert Michotte.* Paris: Joseph Vrin, 1947.

Kokmen, E., Bossemeyer, R. W., Jr., & Williams, W. J. Quantitation of motion perception in the digits: A psychophysical study in normal human subjects. *Annals of Neurology*, 1977, *2*, 279–284.

Lackner, J. R. Pursuit eye movements elicited by muscle afferent information. *Neuroscience Letters*, 1975, *1*, 25–28.

Lackner, J. R. Adaptation to visual and proprioceptive rearrangement: Origin of the differential effect of active and passive movements. *Perception and Psychophysics*, 1977, *21*, 55–59.

Laidlaw, R. W., & Hamilton, M. A. A study of thresholds in apperception of passive movement among normal control subjects. *Bulletin of the Neurological Institute of New York*, 1937, *6*, 268–273.

LaMotte, R. H., & Mountcastle, V. B. Capacities of humans and monkeys to discriminate between vibratory stimuli of different frequency and amplitude: A correlation between neural events and psychophysical measurements. *Journal of Neurophysiology*, 1975, *38*, 539–559.

Landgren, S., & Silfvenius, H. Projection to cerebral cortex of group I muscle afferents from the cat's hind limb. *Journal of Physiology*, 1969, *200*, 353–372.

Leksell, L. The action potential and excitatory effects of the small ventral root fibres to skeletal muscle. *Acta Physiologica Scandinavica*, 1945, *10* (Suppl. 31), 1–84.

Lloyd, A. J. Muscle activity and kinesthetic position responses. *Journal of Applied Physiology*, 1968, *25*, 659–663.

Lloyd, A. J., & Caldwell, L. S. Accuracy of active and passive positioning of the leg on the basis of kinesthetic cues. *Journal of Comparative and Physiological Psychology*, 1965, *60*, 102–106.

Mann, M. D. *The nervous system and behavior*. Philadelphia: Harper & Row, 1981.

Marsden, C. D., Merton, P. A., & Morton, H. B. The sensory mechanism of servo action in human muscle. *Journal of Physiology*, 1977, *265*, 521–535.

Marsden, C. D., Rothwell, J. C., & Traub, M. M. Effect of thumb anaesthesia on weight perception, muscle activity and the stretch reflex in man. *Journal of Physiology*, 1979, *294*, 303–315.

Mather, J., & Lackner, J. R. Adaptation to visual rearrangement elicited by tonic vibration reflexes. *Experimental Brain Research*, 1975, *24*, 103–105.

Matthews, P. B. C. Muscle spindles and their motor control. *Physiological Reviews*, 1964, *44*, 219–288.

Matthews, P. B. C. The reflex excitation of the soleus muscle of the decerebrate cat caused by vibration applied to its tendon. *Journal of Physiology*, 1966, *184*, 450–472.

*Matthews, P. B. C. *Mammalian muscle receptors and their central actions*. Baltimore: Williams & Wilkins, 1972.

Matthews, P. B. C. Receptors in muscles and joints. In J.I. Hubbard (Ed.), *The peripheral nervous system*. New York: Plenum, 1974.

*Matthews, P. B. C. Muscle spindles: Their messages and their fusimotor supply. In V. B. Brooks (Ed.), *Handbook of physiology. Section 1: The Nervous System* (Vol. 2). Bethesda, Md.: American Physiological Society, 1981.

*Matthews, P. B. C. Where does Sherrington's "muscular sense" originate? Muscles, joints, or corollary discharges? *Annual Review of Neuroscience*, 1982, *5*, 189–218.

Matthews, P. B. C., & Simmons, A. Sensations of finger movement elicited by pulling upon flexor tendons in man. *Journal of Physiology*, 1974, *239*, 27–28P.

Matthews, P. B. C., & Stein, R. B. The sensitivity of muscle spindle afferents to small sinusoidal changes in length. *Journal of Physiology*, 1969, *200*, 723–743.

McCloskey, D. I. Differences between the sense of movement and position shown by the effects of loading and vibration of muscles in man. *Brain Research*, 1973, *63*, 119–131.

*McCloskey, D. I. Kinesthetic sensibility. *Physiological Reviews*, 1978, *58*, 763–820.

McCloskey, D. I. Kinaesthetic sensations and motor commands in man. *Progress in Clinical Neurophysiology*, 1980, *8*, 203–214.

*McCloskey, D. I. Corollary discharges: Motor commands and perception. In V. B. Brooks (Ed.), *Handbook of physiology. Section 1: The nervous system* (Vol. 2). Bethesda, Md.: American Physiological Society, 1981.

McCloskey, D. I., Cross, M. J., Honner, R., & Potter, E. K. Sensory effects of pulling or vibrating exposed tendons in man. *Brain*, 1983, *106*, 21–37.

McCloskey, D. I., Ebeling, P., & Goodwin, G. M. Estimation of weights and tensions and apparent involvement of a "sense of effort." *Experimental Neurology*, 1974, *42*, 220–232.

McCloskey, D. I., & Torda, T. A. G. Corollary motor discharges and kinaesthesia. *Brain Research*, 1975, *100*, 467–470.

McGrath, G. J., & Matthews, P. B. C. The use of repetitively applied sharply rising mechanical pulses to excite spindle primary endings and thus minimize the double driving occasionally produced by high frequency sinusoidal stretching. *Journal of Physiology*, 1973, *230*, 60–61P.

McIntyre, A. K. Central projection of impulses from receptors activated by muscle stretch. In D. Barker (Ed.), *Symposium on muscle receptors*. Hong Kong: Hong Kong University Press, 1962.

McIntyre, A. K. Central actions of impulses in muscle afferent fibres. In C. C. Hunt (Ed.), *Handbook of sensory physiology (Vol. III/2); Muscle receptors*. New York: Springer-Verlag, 1974.

McIntyre, A. K., Proske, U., & Tracey, D. J. Afferent fibres from muscle receptors in the posterior nerve of the cat's knee joint. *Experimental Brain Research*, 1978, *33*, 415–424.

Melzack, R., & Bromage, P. R. Experimental phantom limbs. *Experimental Neurology*, 1973, *39*, 261–269.

Merton, P. A. Speculations on the servo-control of movement. In G. E. W. Wolstenholme (Ed.), *The spinal cord*. London: Churchill, 1953.

Merton, P. A. Human position sense and sense of effort. *Symposia of the Society for Experimental Biology*, 1964, *18*, 387–400.

Millar, J. Joint afferent fibres responding to muscle stretch, vibration and contraction. *Brain Research*, 1973, *63*, 380–383.

Millar, J. Flexion–extension sensitivity of elbow joint afferents in cat. *Experimental Brain Research*, 1975, *24*, 209–214.

Millar, S. The development of visual and kinaesthetic judgements of distance. *British Journal of Psychology*, 1972, *63*, 271–282.

Moberg, E. Fingers were made before forks. *The Hand*, 1972, *4*, 201–206.

Moberg, E. The role of cutaneous afferents in position sense, kinaesthesia, and motor function of the hand. *Brain*, 1983, *106*, 1–19.

Monster, A. W., Herman, R., & Altland, N. R. Effect of the peripheral and central "sensory" component in the calibration of position. In J. E. Desmedt (Ed.), *New developments in electromyography and clinical neurophysiology* (Vol. 3). Basel, Switzerland: Karger, 1973.

Mountcastle, V. B., Lamotte, R. H., & Carli, G. Detection thresholds for stimuli in humans and monkeys: Comparison with threshold events in mechanoreceptive afferent nerve fibers innervating the monkey hand. *Journal of Neurophysiology*, 1972, *35*, 122–136.

Mountcastle, V. B., Poggio, G. F, & Werner, G. The relation of thalamic cell response to peripheral stimuli varied over an intensive continuum. *Journal of Neurophysiology*, 1963, *26*, 807–834.

Mountcastle, V. B., & Powell, T. P. S. Central nervous mechanisms subserving position sense and kinesthesis. *Bulletin of the Johns Hopkins Hospital*, 1959, *105*, 173–200.

O'Connor, B. L., & Gonzales, J. Mechanoreceptors of the medical collateral ligament of the cat knee joint. *Journal of Anatomy*, 1979, *129*, 719–729.

O'Connor, B. L., & Seipel, J. Anatomical variations of the posterior articular nerve to the cat knee joint. *Journal of Anatomy*, 1983, *136*, 27–34.

Oscarsson, O., & Rosén, I. Projection to cerebral cortex of large muscle-spindle afferents in forelimb nerves of the cat. *Journal of Physiology*, 1963, *169*, 924–945.

Paillard, J., & Brouchon, M. Active and passive movements in the calibration of position sense. In S. J. Freedman (Ed.), *The neuropsychology of spatially oriented behavior*. Homewood, Ill.: Dorsey, 1968.

Paillard, J., & Brouchon, M. A proprioceptive contribution to the spatial encoding of position cues for ballistic movements. *Brain Research*, 1974, *71*, 273–284.

Petersen, I., & Stener, B. Experimental evaluation of the hypothesis of ligamento-muscular protective reflexes. *Acta Physiologica Scandinavica*, 1959, *48* (Suppl. 166), 51–61.

Pillsbury, W. B. Does the sensation of movement originate in the muscle? *American Journal of Psychology*, 1901 *12*, 346–353.

Poppele, R. E. An analysis of muscle spindle behavior using randomly applied stretches. *Neuroscience*, 1981, *6*, 1157–1165.

Poppele, R. E., & Bowman, R. J. Quantitative description of linear behavior of mammalian muscle spindles. *Journal of Neurophysiology*, 1970, *33*, 59–72.

Prochazka, A. Muscle spindle activity during walking and during free fall. *Progress in Clinical Neurophysiology*, 1980, *8*, 282–293.

Prochazka, A., Westerman, R. A., & Ziccone, S. P. Discharges of single hindlimb afferents in the freely moving cat. *Journal of Neurophysiology*, 1976, *39*, 1090–1105.

Provins, K. A. The effect of peripheral nerve block on the appreciation and execution of finger movements. *Journal of Physiology*, 1958, *143*, 55–67.

Putterman, A. H., Robert, A. L., & Bregman, A. S. Adaptation of the wrist to displacing prisms. *Psychonomic Science*, 1969, *16*, 79–80.

Ramcharan, J. E., & Wyke, B. D. Articular reflexes at the knee joint: An electromyographic study. *American Journal of Physiology*, 1972, *223*, 1276–1280.

Richards, W. Quantifying sensory channels: Generalizing colorimetry to orientation and texture, touch, and tones. *Sensory Processes*, 1979, *3*, 207–229.

Rock, I., & Harris, C. S. Vision and touch. *Scientific American*, 1967, *216*(5), 96—104.

Roland, P. E., & Ladegaard-Pedersen, H. A quantitative analysis of sensations of tension and of kinaesthesia in man: Evidence for a peripherally originating muscular sense and for a sense of effort. *Brain*, 1977, *100*, 671–692.

Roll, J. P., & Vedel, J. P. Kinaesthetic role of muscle afferents in man, studied by tendon vibration and microneurography. *Experimental Brain Research*, 1982, *47*, 177–190.

Rose, J. E., & Mountcastle, V. B. Touch and kinesthesis. In J. Field & H. W. Magoun (Eds.), *Handbook of physiology. Section 1: Neurophysiology* (Vol. 1). Washington, D.C.: American Physiological Society, 1959.

Rossi, A., & Grigg, P. Characteristics of hip joint mechanoreceptors in the cat. *Journal of Neurophysiology*, 1982, *47*, 1029–1042.

Rothwell, J. C., Traub, M. M., Day, B. L., Obeso, J. A., Thomas, P. K., & Marsden, C. D. Manual motor performance in a deafferented man. *Brain*, 1982, *105*, 515–542.

Rymer, W. Z., & D'Almeida, A. Joint position sense: The effects of muscle contraction. *Brain*, 1980, *103*, 1–22.

Salmoni, A. W., & Sullivan, S. J. The intersensory integration of vision and kinesthesis for distance and location cues. *Journal of Human Movement Studies*, 1976, *2*, 225–232.

Samuel, E. P. *The innervation and sensitivity of the articular capsule of the human and feline knee joint.* Unpublished doctoral dissertation, Victoria University, England, 1949.

Schmidt, R. F., & Thews, G. (Eds.) *Human physiology.* New York: Springer-Verlag, 1983.

Sebeok, T. A., & Rosenthal, R. (Eds.) The Clever Hans phenomenon: Communication with horses, whales, apes, and people. *Annals of the New York Academy of Science*, 1981 *364*, 1–311.

Sherrington, C. S. The muscular sense. In E. A. Schaefer (Ed.), *Textbook of physiology.* New York: Macmillan, 1900.

Skoglund, S. Anatomical and physiological studies of knee joint innervation in the cat. *Acta Physiologica Scandinavica*, 1956, *36* (Suppl. 124), 1–101.

Sloglund, S. Joint receptors and kinaesthesis. In A. Iggo (Ed.), *Handbook of sensory physiology (Vol. II); Somatosensory system.* New York: Springer-Verlag, 1973.

Soechting, J. F. Does position sense at the elbow reflect a sense of elbow joint angle or one of limb orientation? *Brain Research*, 1982, *248*, 392–395.

Sperry, R. W. Neural basis of the spontaneous optokinetic response produced by visual neural inversion. *Journal of Comparative and Physiological Psychology*, 1950, *43*, 482–489.

Swett, J. E., & Bourassa, C. M. Comparison of sensory discrimination thresholds with muscle and cutaneous nerve volleys in the cat. *Journal of Neurophysiology*, 1967, *30*, 530–545.

Taub, E., & Berman, A. J. Avoidance conditioning the absence of relevant proprioceptive and exteroceptive feedback. *Journal of Comparative and Physiological Psychology*, 1963, *56*, 1012–1016.

Tracey, D. J. Characteristics of wrist joint receptors in the cat. *Experimental Brain Research*, 1979, *34*, 165–176.

Vallbo, Å. B., Olsson, K. Å., Westberg, K.-G., & Clark, F. J. Microstimulation of single tactile afferents from the human hand: Sensory attributes related to unit types and properties of receptive fields. *Brain*, 1984, *107*, 727–749.

van der Gon, J. J. D., & Wienke, G. H. The concept of feedback in motorics against that of preprogramming. In L. D. Proctor (Ed.), *Biocybernetics of the central nervous system.* Boston: Little, Brown, 1968.

von Holst, E. Relations between the central nervous system and the peripheral organs. *British Journal of Animal Behavior*, 1954, *2*, 89–94.

von Holst, E., & Mittelstaedt, H. [The reafference principle. Interaction between the central nervous system and the periphery.] In R. Martin (Ed. and trans.), *Selected papers of Eric von Holst: The behavioural physiology of animals and man* (Vol. 1). London: Methuen, 1973.

Warwick, R., & Williams, P. L. (Eds.). *Gray's anatomy* (35th British ed.). Philadelphia: Saunders, 1973.

Winter, J. E. The sensation of movement. *Psychological Review*, 1912, *19*, 374–385.

Wyke, B. The neurology of joints. *Annals of the Royal College of Surgery*, 1967, *41*, 25–50.

CHAPTER 14

AUDITION I

Stimulus, Physiology, Thresholds

BERTRAM SCHARF

Auditory Perception Laboratory, Northeastern University, Boston, Massachusetts
and
Laboratoire de Mécanique et d'Acoustique, Centre National de la Recherche Scientifique, Marseilles, France

SØREN BUUS

Auditory Perception Laboratory, Northeastern University, Boston, Massachusetts
and
Laboratory of Psychophysics, Harvard University, Cambridge, Massachusetts

CONTENTS

In this *Handbook*, audition is treated in two chapters that cover acoustics, physiological acoustics, and psychoacoustics. The emphasis is largely on psychoacoustics, on the relations between stimulus and auditory response. Accordingly, this chapter, Audition I, is about acoustics and physiological acoustics and also contains sections on detection and discrimination. Chapter 15 by Scharf and Houtsma, "Audition II," is about loudness, pitch and timbre, localization, and aural distortion. More complex auditory behavior, such as that involved in auditory speech processing, speech perception, or auditory pattern recognition, is treated in Chapter 26 by Hawkins and Presson, Chapter 27 by Jusczyk, and Chapter 32 by Deutsch. For a fairly recent review of all aspects of hearing, see the *Handbook of Perception, Volume 4, Hearing* (Carterette & Friedman, 1978).

The history of audition was, until relatively recently, the history of acoustics and of physiological acoustics. A century ago, Helmholtz's *On The Sensations of Tone* (1885/1954) provided detailed information about the physics of sound and the anatomy of the peripheral auditory system but only introspective observations about auditory behavior. Stimulated by Helmholtz's work and by Fechner's (1860/1966) development of the psychophysical procedures needed for the experimental investigation of sensory behavior, research on hearing (as well as on the other senses) made great progress during the next 40 years, especially on the perception of pitch, sound localization, and detection.

The modern era in auditory research began in the 1920s when it became possible to produce, control, and measure sound by electronic means. By 1938 Stevens and Davis could write a book on hearing that is still relevant and that summarized the status of the field up to that time. Their book contained precise physiological and psychological data. Since the 1930s the major developments have been in the broadening of theories of pitch perception to encompass both place and temporal coding in the auditory system, the discovery and investigation of large interaural interactions in masking, the measurement of loudness by direct scaling, and the advent of signal-detection theory with its refinement of the measurement and understanding of detection and discrimination. In physiology, the transmission characteristics of the middle and inner ear have been described in some detail, and the responses of single fibers of the auditory nerve related to stimulus characteristics and to auditory behavior. The increased use of the computer to synthesize sounds and to run experiments continues to affect all aspects of auditory research and is basic to the vast increase in knowledge of neural function and of the refinement of many psychoacoustic measurements. For recent, brief reviews of the history of hearing research see Carterette (1978) and Schubert (1978).

In this chapter, Section 1 is a review of the measurement and representation of the acoustic stimulus. The various ways of expressing the intensity of a sound are defined. Because the production of the stimulus as well as its control and measurement are so important in the study of audition, calibration and instrumentation are reviewed with attention to problems of noise and distortion. Several published reviews cover those areas in more detail. A general, mathematically oriented introduction to physical acoustics and measurement is provided by Beranek (1954). Leshowitz (1978) provides a careful treatise on sound as it relates to psychoacoustics. Richards (1976) gives a simple introduction to terminology, instrumentation, and calibration in psychoacoustics. Shaw (1966b) discusses the calibration and use of headphones.

Section 2 is about sound transmission from the sound field through the outer and middle ears to the inner ear. The anatomy and physiology of all parts of the auditory system are reviewed and their relevance to hearing emphasized. Much attention is paid to the mechanics of the inner ear where sound energy is transduced into neural energy in the form of potentials in the fibers of the auditory nerve. The basic findings from neurophysiology are also discussed. Mention is made of the cochlear implant, which converts sound to electrical pulses that stimulate the auditory nerve directly, thus bypassing a defective transducer mechanism in an impaired auditory system. Many general reviews of auditory physiology are available. A clear introduction is provided by Gelfand (1981). The classic papers of Békésy are gathered and translated in *Experiments in Hearing* (1960). Recent reviews of various aspects of the auditory system include Dallos (1973a) on the auditory periphery, Keidel and Neff (1975) on all aspects of the system, and Woolsey (1982) on the auditory cortex. The rapidly evolving area of cochlear prostheses is reviewed in a volume edited by Parkins and Anderson (1983).

Section 3 is about the detection of sound, with emphasis on the minimum sound pressure required to detect pure tones of different frequencies. Results are divided into two main categories, those obtained in the quiet and those obtained in the presence of another sound, usually noise. The dependence of threshold on frequency has been measured both in a free field and through earphone listening. Differences between these results are explained, and the general shape of the threshold curve is related to the transmission characteristics of the peripheral auditory system. Threshold also depends on stimulus duration and bandwidth (for complex sounds), on whether one ear or two ears are stimulated, and on the listener's age and sex. The effects of all these variables are treated in detail. Threshold in the quiet often increases following exposure to a noise. The amount of this so-called temporary threshold shift (TTS) depends on duration of the exposure (from seconds to many hours) and characteristics of the noise (intensity, frequency, bandwidth, etc.). Much attention has been devoted to TTS because it may be related to noise-induced permanent hearing loss, which is also discussed together with other types of auditory pathology. Noise raises the threshold for signals presented simultaneously or nearly so, and this masking of one sound by another has been extensively studied. Findings are reviewed both for simultaneous presentation of the masker and the signal and for nonsimultaneous presentation, with the signal preceding or following the masker within a few hundred milliseconds. Zwislocki (1978) and R. D. Patterson and Green (1978) review auditory masking in detail. The books *Effects of Noise on Hearing* (Henderson, Hamernik, Dosanjh, & Mills, 1976) and *New Perspectives on Noise-induced Hearing Loss* (Hamernik, Henderson, & Salvi, 1982) cover both the temporary and permanent effects of noise, as does a recent review paper by Kryter (1983).

Section 4 deals with the discrimination of small differences in the properties of sound arriving at one or both ears. (Differences between sound at one ear and at the other ear are treated in Chapter 15, Audition II, under localization.) Intensity, frequency, and temporal discrimination are treated separately for sounds presented in the quiet and in noise. The effects of experimental paradigm, signal level, and signal duration are described and often related to predictions from models of discrimination. The effect of auditory impairment is also described. No comprehensive reviews of auditory discrimination are available in the recent literature, but Durlach and Braida (1969) and Harris (1963) provide earlier reviews of the issues in intensity discrimination. More recently, Florentine and Buus (1981) reviewed the effect of stimulus variables such as level, frequency, and masking on intensity discrimination.

1. SOUND

To understand psychoacoustic experiments it is important to understand the physical properties of sound and to avoid confusing these properties with the sensation a sound produces. For example, a listener usually reports that a 1,000-Hz tone has a higher pitch than a 200-Hz tone, but under special circumstances may report that they have the same pitch (Houtgast, 1976). Whereas the difference between the two stimuli is invariant in terms of their physical frequencies, the sensations of pitch they evoke vary.

These first sections describe the physical properties of sound. After a discussion of sound as a wave of pressure changes in an elastic medium, the fundamental acoustic measures are presented, as well as resonance and standing waves. Next the different ways of describing stimuli in psychoacoustic experiments are explained and the associated units of measurement are presented. Then acoustical measuring instruments are discussed. The final subsection discusses possible stimulus artifacts such as distortion and extraneous noise from the equipment that generates the stimuli.

1.1. Sound Waves

Sound is a physical disturbance in an elastic medium and cannot exist in the absence of a medium, that is, in a vacuum. The disturbance can be described in terms of pressure changes, particle velocity, or particle displacement. These three measures are not independent but depend on one another according to the laws of physics for elastic media. Particle displacement and particle velocity oscillate around a value of zero. In contrast, sound pressure is a change in pressure that takes place around some reference or static pressure, usually normal atmospheric pressure.

Many acoustical measurements are conveniently made in a standardized condition such as a free field. A free field is the sound field in free space far away from any objects that could reflect or otherwise disturb it. Good approximations to a free field exist over a snow-covered field and in specially designed rooms, anechoic chambers, in which reflections are minimized by covering all surfaces with large wedges of sound-absorbing material.

Sound originates from vibrating bodies. For example, when a tuning fork is struck, its prongs vibrate. Moving in one direction, the prongs push the air particles before them to create a small increase in pressure. When the prongs reach the end of their displacement, as shown in Figure 14.1, the pressure is maximal. Then they move the opposite way, bringing the pressure through its static value to a minimum that occurs at the

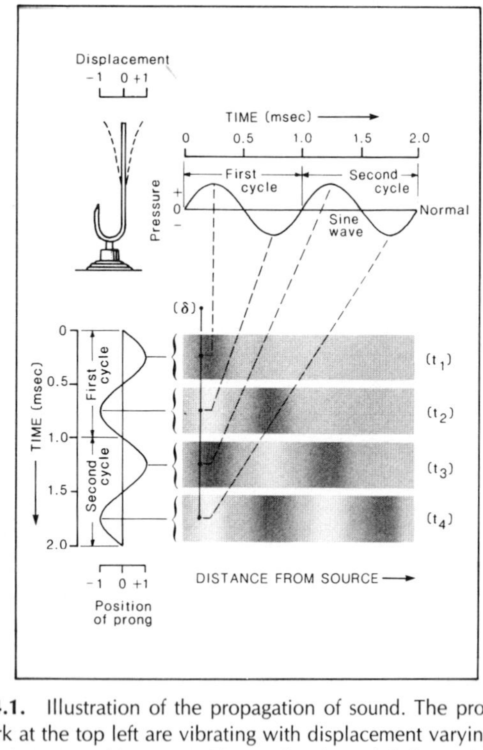

Figure 14.1. Illustration of the propagation of sound. The prongs of the tuning fork at the top left are vibrating with displacement varying between plus and minus one arbitrary unit. The graph at lower left shows displacement as a function of time and the four gray areas illustrate the instantaneous sound pressure at various places in front of the tuning fork at 0.25, 0.75, 1.25, and 1.75 msec relative to a positive-going zero crossing of the prong's displacement. The pressure is indicated by the darkness of the gray area, with static pressure being medium gray. Dark gray areas indicate positive sound pressures (pressures greater than the static pressure) and light gray areas indicate negative sound pressures (pressures less than the static pressure). The four bars show propagation of the disturbance generated by vibration of the tuning fork. The graph at top right shows sound pressure, measured at a fixed place, as a function of time and illustrates sinusoidal sound pressure variation generated by the tuning fork's vibration. (From W. L. Gulick, *Hearing, physiology, and psychophysics*, Oxford University Press, 1971. Reprinted with permission.)

other end of their displacement. The particles set in motion by the tuning fork set neighboring particles in motion. These particles then set their neighboring particles in motion, and so on. Thus the pressure changes (i.e., the sound) propagate through the air as a traveling wave. Sound cannot propagate through a vacuum, because there are no particles to transfer the motion.

The propagation of sound through a medium takes time; how much time depends on the medium. In air, the *speed of sound* is approximately 343 $m \cdot sec^{-1}$ measured in dry air at 20°C. The speed of sound, c, in any gas can be calculated as

$$c = \sqrt{\frac{\gamma R T}{M}} \tag{1}$$

where γ ($\approx$ 1.401 in dry air at 20°C) is the ratio of the specific heat at constant pressure to that at constant volume, R (= 8,314.3 $g \cdot m^2 \cdot sec^{-2} \cdot K^{-1} mol^{-1}$) is the gas constant, T is the absolute temperature (in degrees Kelvin), and M ($\approx$ 28.98 $g \cdot mol^{-1}$ for dry air) is the molecular weight of the gas. Thus the speed of sound in air is approximately proportional to $\sqrt{T}$ and independent of the static pressure. Because the molecular weight of air decreases as the humidity increases, the speed of sound is faster in humid air than in dry air, although the effect is relatively small. For example, the speed of sound is about 0.4% faster in air with 100% relative humidity than in dry air at 20°C. In liquids and solids, on the other hand, speed of sound is considerably faster. In water, for example, it is about 1,500 $m \cdot sec^{-1}$. Generally, the lighter and the stiffer the medium, the faster the sound travels. The speed of sound is proportional to $(K/\rho)^{0.5}$, where K is the *bulk modulus* and ρ is the density of the medium. (The bulk modulus is a measure of the stiffness of a liquid or solid. It is the inverse of the relative change in volume of the medium per unit of pressure. For example, if a cube of steel is subjected to a uniform pressure of 1 $N \cdot m^{-2}$, its volume shrinks 6.25×10^{-10}%. Thus the bulk modulus for steel is 16×10^{10} $N \cdot m^{-2}$ [= 1 $N \cdot m^{-2}/(6.25 \times 10^{-10}/100)$].) Extensive tables for the speed of sound and its temperature dependence in various media can be found in Kaye and Laby (1966).

1.2. Fundamental Measures of Sounds

1.2.1. Sound Pressure. Many physical phenomena in acoustics are more readily understood when sound is considered in terms of particle velocity or displacement. In psychoacoustics, however, it is usually most convenient to consider sound as a change in pressure. Sound pressure can be expressed in many different units, but the presently preferred unit for sound pressure is the micropascal ($\mu Pa = 10^{-6}\ N \cdot m^{-2} = 10^{-6}\ kg \cdot m^{-1} \cdot sec^{-2}$), which is useful for expressing the very small pressure changes encountered in acoustics. Other units are dynes per square centimeter and microbars. Both 1 $dyne \cdot cm^{-2}$ and 1 μbar are equal to 10^5 μPa.

Sound pressure is usually measured as the *root-mean-square* (RMS) value of the pressure deviation from the static pressure. The RMS value is the square root of the mean (over some time interval) of the squared instantaneous deviations. Peak sound pressure and peak-to-peak sound pressure are also useful to describe some aspects of sound. The *peak sound pressure* is the highest sound pressure encountered during the measurement interval. The *peak-to-peak sound pressure* is the difference between the highest and the lowest (most negative) sound pressure encountered during the measurement interval. For a sine wave, the peak sound pressure is $\sqrt{2}$ times higher than the RMS sound pressure and the peak-to-peak sound pressure is twice the peak pressure. The *crest factor* of a sound is the ratio of the peak sound pressure to the RMS sound pressure.

1.2.2. Intensity. When combining sounds of different frequencies, the total sound power equals the sum of the powers of each individual sound. For this reason, it is often practical to measure the strength of a sound in terms of power. To limit the measurement to a specific place (e.g., at the center of a listener's head), the sound is not measured by its total power, but rather in terms of *intensity*, which is a measure of power flow per unit area. The *unit* for intensity is watts per square meter ($W \cdot m^{-2}$). The *RMS sound pressure* and the *intensity* of a sound are closely related; for a plane sound wave

$$I = \frac{p^2}{\rho c} \tag{2}$$

where I is the intensity, p is the RMS sound pressure, ρ is the density of the medium, and c is the speed of sound (for air at atmospheric pressure and standard temperature of 20°C, $\rho c \approx 410\ N \cdot sec \cdot m^{-3}$). A *plane sound wave* can be assumed when the distance to the sound source exceeds a few wavelengths and reflections are absent.

1.2.3. The Inverse Square Law. The area over which the intensity of a sound is measured can be regarded as a small part of the surface of a sphere whose center is at the sound source. If the distance to the sound source is doubled, the power flowing through the measurement area will be spread out over an area four times as large. Consequently, the intensity of the sound will be one-fourth. In general, the intensity is inversely proportional to the square of the distance. This law is the *inverse square law.* In a plane sound field the intensity is proportional to the square of the sound pressure; hence sound pressure is inversely proportional to the distance.

1.2.4. Frequency, Period, and Wavelength. The *wave form* of a sound is the instantaneous sound pressure plotted as a function of time. The *frequency* of a sinusoidal wave form is defined as the number of repetitions in one second. The contemporary unit for frequency is hertz (Hz), after the German physicist H. R. Hertz (1857–1894), but the older literature often used cycles per second (cps). The *period*, T, is the duration of one complete cycle and is the inverse of the frequency, f:

$$T = \frac{1}{f}\,. \tag{3}$$

The distance in space between repetitions of a sinusoidal sound (or between two adjacent, simultaneous pressure peaks) is the *wavelength* of the sound. The wavelength, λ, can be calculated as

$$\lambda = \frac{c}{f} \tag{4}$$

where c is the speed of sound and f is its frequency.

1.2.5. Fundamental Frequency, Harmonics, and Overtones. Most sounds are not simple sinusoids and therefore are called *complex.* Wave forms that repeat themselves are called *periodic.* The *fundamental frequency*, f_0, of a complex, periodic wave form is defined as the inverse of the period, T_0:

$$f_0 = \frac{1}{T_0}\,. \tag{5}$$

A complex, periodic wave form can be broken down into a series of sinusoids whose frequencies are multiples of f_0. Frequencies that are integral ($n \geqq 2$) multiples of a fundamental frequency are called *harmonics* or *overtones* of that fundamental. The *harmonic number* of a frequency equals the ratio of that frequency to the fundamental. The *number of an overtone* is its harmonic number minus 1. For example, 800 Hz is the fourth harmonic, but the third overtone of 200 Hz.

1.2.6. Frequency and Musical Notes. Most musical instruments produce complex, periodic wave forms. Figure 14.2 shows the relation between frequency and the range of notes that can be produced by different voices and instruments. The range of fundamental frequencies is well within the range of human hearing. Even the highest fundamental frequency produced by the piccolo is three to four times lower than the highest audible frequency (see Section 3.1.2). Thus a couple of overtones may be audible, even for a piccolo. (For further discussion of the perception of music, see Deutsch, Chapter 32.)

1.3. Resonance

Many objects, such as a tuning fork or a crystal glass, vibrate at a specific frequency when struck. This *natural* or *resonant frequency* of vibration is determined by the mass and stiffness of the object. A sound source with the same frequency as the natural frequency of an object can easily set it into vibration. This phenomenon is called *resonance.* A special example of a resonating object is the *Helmholtz resonator* (1885/1954) which is shaped like a bottle or vase, as shown in Figure 14.3(a). The air in the neck of the bottle provides the mass, and the compressibility of the air enclosed in its body provides the stiffness of the resonating system.

Resonance can also occur when some dimension of an object such as the length of a pipe or a room matches the wavelength of the sound. What constitutes a match depends in part on the shape of the resonating enclosure, as shown in Figure 14.3. When the resonator is closed, as for the room (b), the instantaneous particle velocity at both ends must always be zero. This condition is fulfilled whenever an integral multiple of half the wavelength equals the length of the room. When a room is excited by a sound at such a resonant frequency, the maxima and minima in RMS particle velocity and RMS sound pressure are at fixed places in the room. Thus a *standing wave* is produced. As indicated by the deviation of the thin line from the midline, the RMS particle velocity is zero at both end walls and reaches a maximum in the middle of the room. On the other hand, the RMS sound pressure is maximal at the ends of the room and minimal in the middle of the room.

The open pipe shown in Figure 14.3(c) has the same resonant frequencies as the room. Because the pipe is open at both ends, however, the RMS particle velocity is maximal at the ends as shown by the thin lines. This condition is also fulfilled whenever the integral multiple of half the wavelength equals the length of the pipe. The RMS sound pressure, on the other hand, is maximal in the middle of the pipe where the particle velocity is zero.

A pipe closed at one end requires a different wavelength for resonance as shown in Figure 14.3(d). It resonates when an odd multiple of one-fourth the wavelength equals the length of the pipe. As shown by the thin lines, the particle velocity is

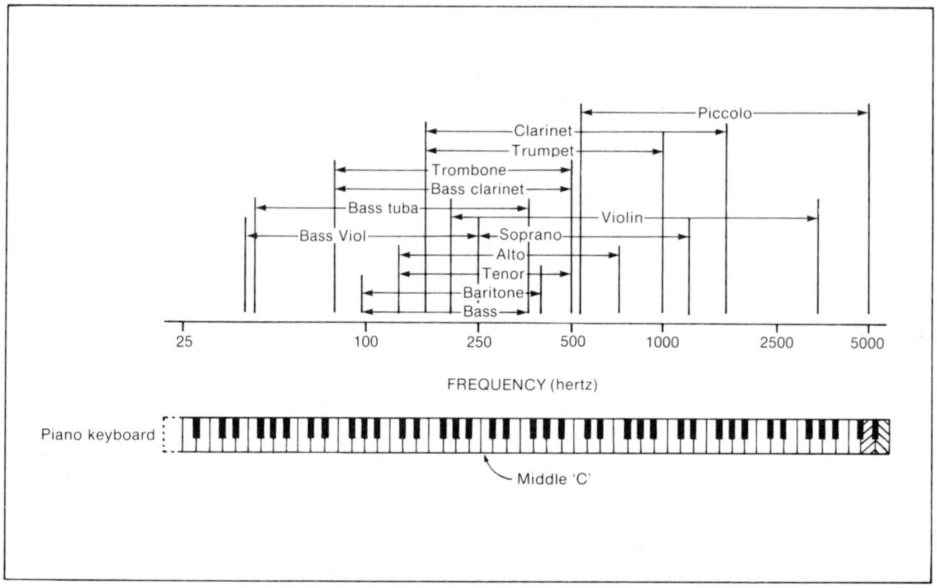

Figure 14.2. Range of fundamental frequencies that can be produced by various singing voices and musical instruments. The ranges of fundamental frequencies in hertz are shown by the frequency scale in the middle, and the piano keyboard at the bottom shows corresponding musical notes ranging from more than 3 octaves below to more than 4 octaves above middle C. (From V. O. Knudsen & C. M. Harris, *Acoustical designing in architecture*, Acoustical Society of America, 1980. Reprinted with permission.)

zero at the closed end and maximal at the open end. The RMS sound pressure in a closed pipe is maximal at the closed end and minimal at the open end.

1.4. Measurement of Psychoacoustic Stimuli

1.4.1. Level: The Decibel Scale. The range of sound pressures that can be heard exceeds 1:10^6 and the range of intensities exceeds 1:10^{12}. It is therefore convenient to express sound pressure and intensity as *level* on a logarithmic scale. A special scale, the *decibel* (dB) scale, is used almost universally in acoustics. The *intensity level*, L, of a sound is defined as follows:

$$L = 10 \log\left(\frac{I}{I_0}\right) \text{ dB} \tag{6}$$

where I is the intensity of the sound and I_0 is an arbitrarily chosen reference intensity. If the intensity of sound A is chosen as reference (I_0), and the intensity of sound B is I, the equation yields the level difference in decibels between A and B. For example, if I equals 10^{-4} W·m^{-2} and I_0 equals 10^{-6} W·m^{-2},

$$L = 10 \log\left(\frac{10^{-4}\text{ W·m}^{-2}}{10^{-6}\text{ W·m}^{-2}}\right) \text{ dB} = 20 \text{ dB} , \tag{7}$$

showing that B is 20 dB (100 times) more intense than A. It is often desirable to express the intensity of a sound relative to a *standard reference intensity* of 10^{-12} W·m^{-2}. This standard intensity is close to the threshold of audibility for a 1,000-Hz tone.

The *sound pressure level* can be derived from Equations (2) and (6):

$$L = 10 \log\left(\frac{I}{I_0}\right) \text{ dB}$$

$$L = 10 \log\left(\frac{p^2/\rho c}{p_0^2/\rho c}\right) \text{ dB}$$

$$L = 20 \log\left(\frac{p}{p_0}\right) \text{ dB} , \tag{8}$$

where L is the level of the sound, p is its RMS sound pressure (with the corresponding intensity I), p_0 is the reference sound pressure corresponding to I_0, ρ is the density of the medium, and c is the speed of sound [see Equation (2)]. In air, the *standard reference sound pressure* corresponding to $I_0 = 10^{-12}$ W·m^{-2} is $p_0 = 20$ μPa. When the level of a sound is expressed relative to 20 μPa (= 0.0002 dyne·cm^{-2}) it is referred to as *sound pressure level* (SPL) which is always expressed in decibels. Thus

$$L = 20 \log\left(\frac{p}{20\ \mu\text{Pa}}\right) \text{ dB SPL} . \tag{9}$$

In air, the SPL of a sound is equal to the intensity level of the sound, provided the reference intensity equals 10^{-12} W·m^{-2}.

Figure 14.4 shows the relation between intensity, sound pressure, and SPL and indicates where some familiar sounds would fall on the scale. The levels that are usually considered in psychoacoustics range from a little below 0 dB SPL to somewhat above 100 dB SPL.

The distinction between intensity level and sound pressure level is often blurred, although it is important when calculating the total level of a combination of sounds. Consider two sounds at 60 dB SPL, which means that their sound pressure is 2 × 10^4 μPa and their intensity is 10^{-6} W·m^{-2}. If their frequencies are different, the total intensity is the sum of their intensities. Thus their total level is

$$L = 10 \log\left(\frac{2 \times 10^{-6}\ \mathrm{W{\cdot}m^{-2}}}{10^{-12}\ \mathrm{W{\cdot}m^{-2}}}\right) \text{ dB SPL}$$

$$= 63 \text{ dB SPL} \qquad (10)$$

or 3 dB higher than each of the sounds. However, if the two sounds are identical (same frequency and phase) their sound pressures add to yield the total sound pressure. Then their total level is

$$L = 20 \log\left(\frac{2.4 \times 10^4\ \mu\mathrm{Pa}}{20\ \mu\mathrm{Pa}}\right) \text{ dB SPL} = 66 \text{ dB SPL} \qquad (11)$$

or 6 dB higher than each of the sounds.

According to the inverse square law, the level of a sound decreases 6 dB every time the distance from the sound source doubles because

$$L = 10 \log\left(\frac{1/4\, I}{I}\right) \text{ dB} = -6 \text{ dB} . \qquad (12)$$

The 6-dB decrease also follows from the rule that the sound pressure is inversely proportional to the distance.

1.4.2. Sensation Level, Hearing Level, and Hearing Threshold Level. The level is always a relative measure, that is, the ratio between the sound in question and some reference sound. The level is meaningful only when the reference is stated. The level in dB SPL is always relative to 20 μPa, but this is not the only reference that may be used. In many psychoacoustic experiments, the level is expressed relative to the listener's threshold for the sound. The level in decibels above a listener's threshold is the *sensation level* (dB SL). The listener's threshold for the sound—the sound pressure, p_{TH}, at which he can just hear the sound (see Section 3)—is first measured, and the level of sound is calculated with p_{TH} as the reference sound pressure:

$$L = 20 \log\left(\frac{p}{p_{TH}}\right) \text{ dB SL} . \qquad (13)$$

From this formula it follows that the sensation level, L_{SL}, can also be calculated as the difference between the SPL corresponding to L, and the SPL corresponding to p_{TH}, L_{TH}:

$$L_{SL} = L - L_{TH} \text{ dB SL} . \qquad (14)$$

Another commonly used reference is the average threshold of normal listeners as codified in national and international standards (American National Standards Institute, 1969; International Standards Organization, 1975). The level relative to such a standard threshold is the *hearing level* (HL) or *hearing threshold level* (HTL). The intensity of a sound at a given SL depends on the frequency, the sound source, and the listener. The intensity of a sound at a given HTL depends only on the frequency and the sound source. (Section 3.1.1 and Table 14.1

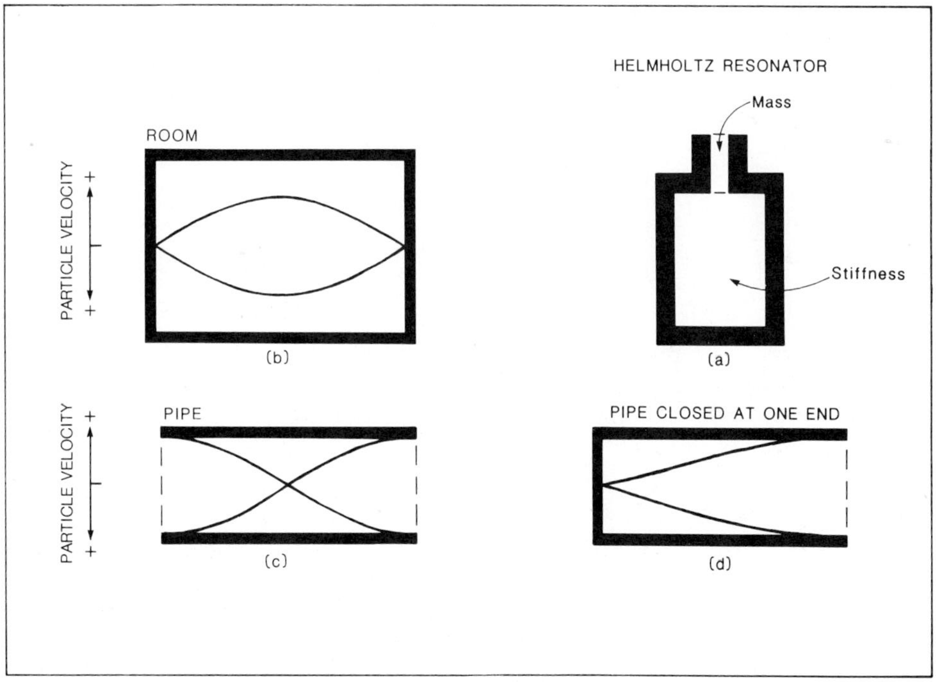

Figure 14.3. Resonating enclosures. (a) A Helmholtz resonator, which can be viewed as a mass coupled to a spring. The mass is the air in the neck of the enclosure and the spring is the stiffness of the volume of air enclosed in the body of the enclosure. (b) A principal resonance in a closed enclosure such as a box or a room. Resonance occurs when an integral multiple of half wavelengths is equal to the length of the enclosure. The thin lines illustrate how the particle velocity in the standing wave varies along the length of the enclosure. (c) Resonance in a pipe that is open at both ends. Resonance occurs when an integral multiple of half wavelengths is equal to the length of the pipe. (d) Resonance in a pipe that is closed at one end and open at the other. Resonance occurs when an odd multiple of quarter wavelengths is equal to the length of the pipe.

SOUND INTENSITY (W/m^2)	SOUND PRESSURE ($dynes/cm^2$)	SOUND PRESSURE (μ Pa)	SOUND PRESSURE LEVEL (dB SPL)	
10^{10}	2×10^{7}	20×10^{11}	220	12" cannon, 4 m in front and below muzzle
			210	
10^{8}	2×10^{6}	20×10^{10}	200	
			190	(Equivalent normal atmospheric pressure)
10^{6}	2×10^{5}	20×10^{9}	180	
			170	
10^{4}	2×10^{4}	20×10^{8}	160	
			150	
100	2000	20×10^{7}	140	
10	630	63×10^{6}	130	
1	200	20×10^{6}	120	Threshold of pain Rock band or loud discoteque
10^{-1}	63	63×10^{5}	110	Hammering on steel, 1 m
10^{-2}	20	20×10^{5}	100	Subway station, express passing
10^{-3}	6.3	63×10^{4}	90	Electric power station Average factory
10^{-4}	2	20×10^{4}	80	Very loud radio in home
10^{-5}	0.63	63×10^{3}	70	Ordinary conversation, 1 m
10^{-6}	0.2	20×10^{3}	60	Department store, noisy office
10^{-7}	0.063	63×10^{2}	50	Quiet residential street
10^{-8}	0.02	20×10^{2}	40	Average residence
10^{-9}	0.0063	630	30	
10^{-10}	0.002	200	20	Quiet whisper, 1.5 m
10^{-11}	0.00063	63	10	Out of door minimum
10^{-12}	0.0002	20	0	Threshold of audibility

Figure 14.4. Sound pressure, intensity, and sound pressure level (dB re 20 μPa) compared for some familiar sounds, which are indicated at appropriate points on these scales.

in Section 3 give standard threshold values; Fig. 14.42 in Section 3 gives examples of audiograms on which hearing level is plotted as a function of frequency.)

1.4.3. Temporal Parameters. Level and frequency of a sound are the two most important variables used to specify a sound, but temporal characteristics such as those shown in Figure 14.5 are also important. Figure 14.5 shows the wave form of two modulated sinusoids. The sinusoid on top is switched on and off with slow onset and offset to form a tone burst. The wave form on the bottom is cut from a continuous sinusoid whose amplitude varies over time.

When the *envelope* of a wave form can be defined, it often serves to describe temporal characteristics of a sound. It can be formally defined as a slowly changing function $A(t)$ of time when the equation of the wave form is

$$f(t) = A(t) \sin(2\pi ft + \Theta) \qquad (15)$$

where $\sin(2\pi ft + \Theta)$ is a sine wave with frequency f and phase θ. However, this definition becomes meaningless if $A(t)$ changes too fast. The *envelope* may be described more loosely as the curve connecting successive peaks in the wave form. So defined, it represents, for example, the modulating wave form of an amplitude-modulated tone. For the amplitude-modulated tone shown at the bottom of Figure 14.5,

$$A(t) = K \cdot (1 + m \cdot \sin(2\pi f_m t + \Theta_m)) \qquad (16)$$

and

$$f(t) = K[1 + m \cdot \sin(2\pi f_m t + \Theta_m)]\sin(2\pi ft + \Theta) \qquad (17)$$

where K is the average amplitude, m is the modulation depth or modulation index ($0 \leqq m \leqq 1$), f_m is the modulation frequency, and Θ_m is the phase of the modulating wave form.

The *duration* of a sound is usually defined as the time from the beginning of the onset to the beginning of the offset. Although arbitrary, this definition is convenient because it relates directly to the timing of events in the experimental apparatus. Moreover, when the onset and offset have the same shape and are symmetrical around the half-amplitude points, the energy of the stimulus is nearly proportional to the duration so defined. The *rise time* is the duration of the envelope's increase from 10 to 90% of its maximal value. The *fall time* is defined as the duration of the envelope's decrease from 90 to 10% of the maximal value. (See Fig. 14.5.)

Phase is also an important temporal parameter of sounds. *Phase* is a relative measure of the temporal relationship between individual sinusoids in a complex wave form or of the temporal relationship between a sinusoid and some fixed event such as the onset of the sound. The *phase*, Θ, is measured in degrees or radians, and is expressed by the following equation:

$$\Theta = 2\pi f \Delta t \text{ rad} = 360° \cdot f \Delta t \qquad (18)$$

where f is the frequency and Δt is the time between the reference event and the positive-going zero crossing of the sinusoid in question. When phase is measured between two sinusoids, the reference event is a positive-going zero crossing of the reference sinusoid. The wave form of a complex sound composed of several sinusoids can vary greatly depending on the phase relations among the component sinusoids.

1.5. Spectra and Spectrograms

1.5.1. Amplitude and Phase Spectra. Describing sounds in terms of their wave forms is complicated and generally not very useful in psychoacoustics. Although the wave form gives a complete physical description, it cannot readily be related to the perception of the sound. Sounds whose wave forms are very dissimilar may be perceived as very similar and vice versa. On the other hand, sounds composed of the same set of frequencies, with each frequency at some fixed level, are heard as very similar. Therefore, it is useful to describe a sound in terms of its *amplitude spectrum*, which shows intensity or sound pressure as a function of frequency. The amplitude spectrum is customarily shown in terms of spectrum level as a function of frequency. The *spectrum level* is the intensity level within a band 1 Hz wide. The intensity corresponding to the spectrum level is often referred to as N_0.

Figure 14.6 shows amplitude spectra of different sounds. Two types of spectra are shown, line spectra and continuous spectra. Sounds with *line spectra* consist of sinusoids at specific frequencies. All periodic sounds of long duration have line spectra. Sounds with *continuous spectra* have their energy distributed

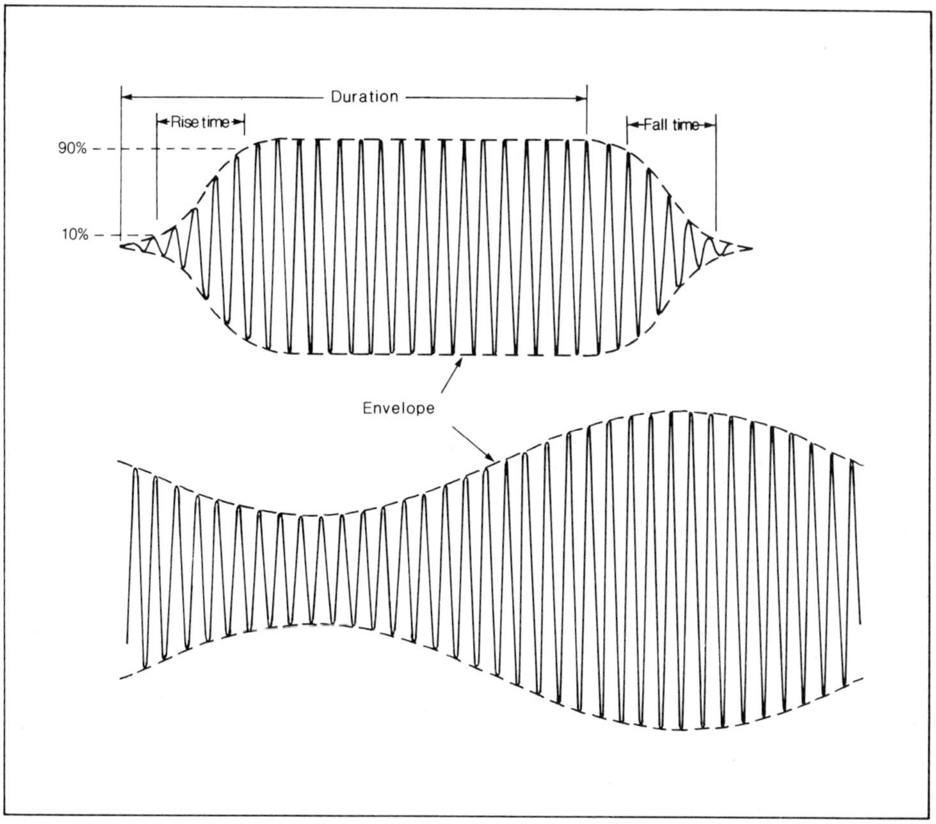

Figure 14.5. Wave form and temporal parameters of sounds. The wave form (solid lines) and envelope (broken lines) are shown for a tone burst (top) and an amplitude-modulated tone (bottom). At the top, some temporal parameters for the tone burst are indicated by dotted lines. The duration is the time from the beginning of the onset of the burst to the beginning of the offset. The rise time is the duration of the envelope's increase from 10 to 90% of its maximal value and the fall time is the duration of the envelope's decrease from 90 to 10% of its maximal value.

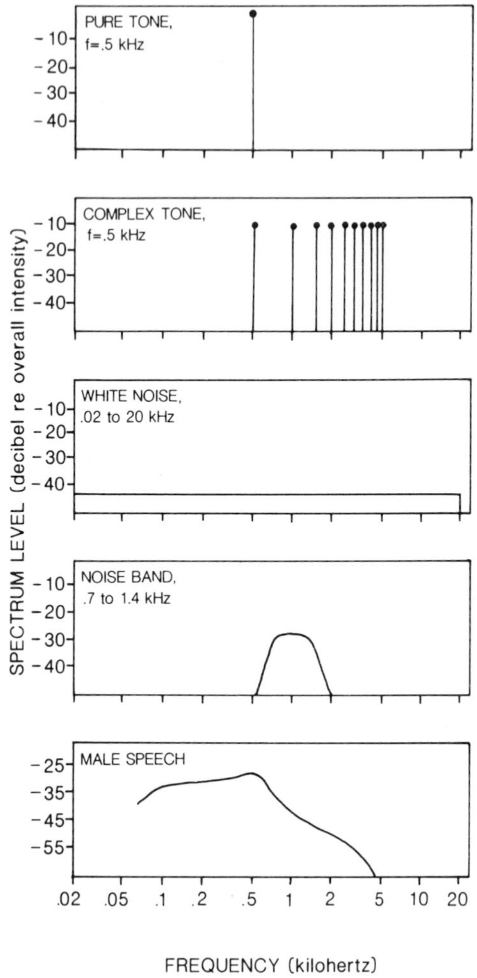

Figure 14.6. Amplitude spectra of various sounds. The spectrum level in decibels relative to the overall level of the sound is plotted as a function of frequency for a 500-Hz pure tone (top), a 500-Hz complex tone, band-limited white noise, an octave band of noise centered at 1,000 Hz, and male speech (long-term average) (bottom). The spectrum for the pure tone is one line at 500 Hz whose height is equal to the level of the tone (0 dB re its overall level). The complex tone has a fundamental of 500 Hz and consists of the first ten harmonics of 500 Hz. The harmonics' levels are equal and so the spectrum has ten lines 500 Hz apart whose height is 10 dB less than the overall level of the complex tone. The white noise has a continuous spectrum with a constant spectrum level throughout the range of audible frequencies. The spectrum level of this 20,000-Hz-wide noise is 43 dB below its overall level. The octave band of noise is centered at 1,000 Hz and has cutoff frequencies of 700 and 1,400 Hz. Its continuous spectrum has a spectrum level 28 dB below the overall level in the passband and 3 dB lower at the cutoff frequencies. The long-term average spectrum of male speech also has a continuous spectrum. The spectrum level is maximal, about 28 dB less than the overall level, around 500 Hz and drops slowly toward the lower frequencies down to about 70 Hz, below which it drops sharply. Above 500 Hz, the spectrum level decreases approximately 12 dB·octave^{-1} (Dunn & White, 1940).

across a range of frequencies. Random wave forms such as a white noise and wave forms of short duration have continuous spectra.

The phase plotted as a function of frequency is the *phase spectrum* of a sound. Together the amplitude and phase spectra form a complete description of a sound.

1.5.2. Fourier Transformation. A one-to-one correspondence between spectrum (amplitude plus phase) and wave form can be shown. A mathematical transform, the *Fourier transformation*, converts a wave form into its spectrum. The *inverse Fourier transformation* converts a spectrum into its wave form. It follows from the theory of Fourier transformation that the spectrum of a periodic sound whose period is T consists of lines (some of which may have zero amplitude) with a frequency spacing equal to $1/T$. For example, a complex tone whose period is 2 msec (f_0 = 500 Hz, second from top of Fig. 14.6) has a line spectrum with lines 500 Hz apart.

1.5.3. Long-Term and Short-Term Spectra. In mathematical Fourier transformation, the spectrum of a nonperiodic signal is defined through integration over an infinite time interval. Thus the true spectrum of nonperiodic physical events can never be arrived at in practice, but may be approximated by measuring over a long period of time. Such spectra are often referred to as *long-term spectra*.

The ear, however, integrates sound only over a relatively short period of time (no more than 500 msec). Therefore, *short-term spectra* measured over less than 500 msec provide important information. Spectral resolution becomes poorer as integration time is shortened: Whereas the long-term spectrum of a continuous pure tone is a line whose width is essentially zero, the short-term spectrum of the tone encompasses a range of frequencies. The *bandwidth*, Δf, which is the frequency region containing most of the sound energy, and the integration time, t, fulfill thc following relation:

$$\Delta f \cdot t \geqq k \approx 1 \tag{19}$$

where k is a constant close to 1. The exact value of k depends on the shape of the weighting function used to limit the integration time and on how large a percentage of the energy is required to lie within the frequency region Δf.

1.5.4. Energy Splatter. Because integration beyond the duration of a signal does not alter the shape of its spectrum, the relation shown in Equation (19) also applies to signals of different durations. Thus signals with short durations (such as tone pips or clicks) have their energy distributed over a wider frequency range than do signals with long durations. This "*energy splatter*" is also present in the short-term spectra during the onset and offset of a sound, whereas the short-term spectrum is close to the long-term spectrum during the steady-state part of a sound. The shorter and more abrupt the onset and offset, the greater the energy splatter. In general, the more abruptly a wave form changes, the wider its bandwidth.

1.6. Calibration and Instrumentation

Direct calibration of an auditory stimulus requires the measurement of the acoustic spectrum in some well-specified location. However, direct acoustic measurements are somewhat difficult and time consuming. Therefore, calibration usually is done on the electric wave form that drives the electroacoustic transducer (loudspeaker or headphone). This electrical calibration is less rigorous than acoustic calibration because it assumes that the acoustic output of the transducer is specified exactly for a given electrical input and remains stable over time. Whether the calibration measurements are made on the acoustical or the electrical wave form, at some point they involve electrical wave forms, because the acoustic wave forms almost always are converted into electrical wave forms by means of a microphone. Therefore, after a brief discussion of calibration microphones, most of this section considers measurements on an electrical wave form.

1.6.1. Calibration Microphones. To be useful for calibration, the electrical output voltage of the microphone must be specified exactly for any given acoustical input. Although the conversion of acoustical wave forms into electrical wave forms can be achieved in many different ways, calibration measurements are made almost exclusively with condenser microphones. The condenser microphone is preferred because its conversion characteristics are relatively stable. Moreover, its frequency response, which is its electrical output as a function of frequency when the SPL is kept constant, is flatter than that of most other types of microphones. Often the condenser microphone gives a constant electrical output with an acoustical input of constant SPL, regardless of the frequency up to some limiting frequency. Such a flat frequency response makes measurements particularly simple.

To make measurements where the microphone itself does not fit, such as in the ear canal, or is so large that it disturbs the sound field, a probe microphone is often used. This is a microphone with a thin metal or plastic tube (the probe) attached to it. The resonances of the tube alter radically the frequency characteristic of the microphone. The resonant peaks and valleys can be made smaller and broader by damping the probe with sound-absorbing material such as thread, steel wool, or cotton.

Whether the probe is damped or not, the probe and microphone must be calibrated together as a unit to yield useful measurements. Calibration is typically done by measuring the output of the probe microphone in response to a constant sound pressure generated in a small enclosure such as an acoustic coupler (see Section 1.6.6). However, it has been shown that the acoustical characteristics of the coupler can change the measured frequency response of the probe microphone by as much as 15 dB in some frequency ranges (Studebaker & Zachmann, 1970). Therefore, calibration should preferably be made in an acoustical environment that is similar to the environment in which the measurements are to be made. These problems must be kept in mind when evaluating measurements by probe microphone.

To circumvent the problems of interaction between the probe microphone and the acoustical environment, the entire acoustical system including the probe microphone may be modeled mathematically (Egolf, 1977). If the model predicts the measurements, the response of the probe microphone can be evaluated by eliminating the probe microphone from the model. However, this approach requires that the acoustical properties of the system be known and may not be practical for complex systems like the ear.

1.6.2. Voltmeters and Sound Level Meters. The level of a sound is usually measured with a *voltmeter*. Most voltmeters measure the RMS voltage of the wave form, but may also measure peak or peak-to-peak voltage. The precision of voltmeters is quite good; often their accuracy is within $\pm 2\%$ corresponding to ± 0.2 dB. From the frequency response of the measuring microphone, the voltage is easily translated into SPL. In fact, the voltmeter may be calibrated for use with a specific microphone and the SPL read directly from the instrument. The combination of a microphone and a voltmeter calibrated in SPL is called a *sound level meter* (see Fig. 14.7). The accuracy of sound level meters is usually less than that of voltmeters, owing to the characteristics of the microphone, but can be within ± 0.5 dB at a specified frequency and within ± 1 dB over most of the audible frequency range.

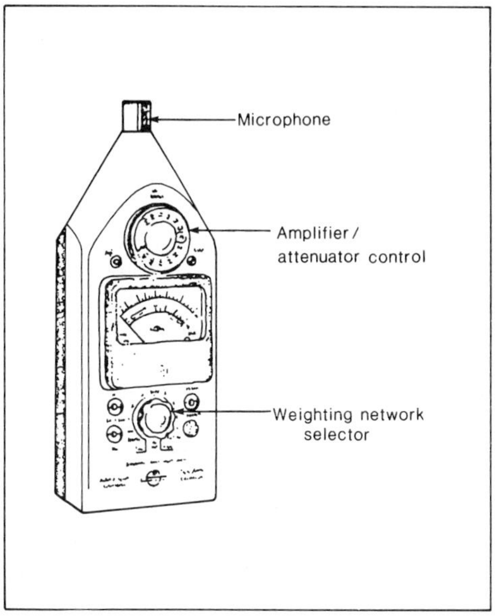

Figure 14.7. Sound level meter. The sound level meter consists of a microphone (top), an amplifier and attenuator (below microphone), weighting networks selected by the knob at the bottom, and a meter calibrated in decibels SPL (middle). (From Brüel & Kjaer Instruments, Inc., *Instrumentation and applications: Precision sound level meter type 2203/1613* (Instruction Manual), Author, 1970. Reprinted with permission.)

Many sound level meters have weighting networks that emphasize some frequencies and attenuate others. These weighting networks (designated A, B, and C) provide objective, weighted measurements of noise levels that are meant to correspond more closely to its subjective effects than unweighted measurements. Normally, the SPL specified in psychoacoustics is the unweighted SPL. The weighted sound pressure level is often called *sound level* and is stated with the weighting network indicated in parentheses after the measured sound level, such as 65 dB (A). The weighting networks are standard filters whose frequency responses approximate the pure-tone equal-loudness contours with loudness levels between 30 and 60 phons for the A weighting, between 60 and 90 phons for the B weighting, and above 90 phons for the C weighting. (The loudness level in *phons* is the SPL of a 1-kHz tone that is judged equally loud to the test sound.) In principle, these weighting networks should yield values that correspond to the loudness level of a single pure tone at any frequency; they are not expected to yield values that correspond to the loudness level of complex sounds due to the increased loudness of wide-band sounds. (See Scharf & Houtsma, Chapter 15, for further discussion of loudness and loudness level.) However, even for tones the weighted level only approximates the loudness level, because the weighting curves were chosen with as much attention to the ease by which they could be implemented electronically as to their agreement with equal-loudness measurements.

1.6.3. Calibration in Free Field. The method used to calibrate the level of a sound depends on the sound source and the listening environment. If the sound source is a loudspeaker, level is customarily measured at the location corresponding to the center of the listener's head. Thus the level is measured without disturbance of the sound field by the presence of the listener. If necessary the disturbance caused by the microphone or sound level meter should be taken into account. Special free-field microphones, whose frequency response is corrected to compensate for their disturbance of the sound field, are available.

1.6.4. Calibration of Headphones. Calibration of the acoustical wave form produced by a headphone is usually performed by means of an *acoustic coupler* such as that shown in Figure 14.8. The coupler provides a standard connection between headphone and microphone. The microphone should have a pressure response that changes little as a function of frequency up to 15–20 kHz. The acoustic coupler is sometimes called an *artificial ear*, because it is designed to provide an acoustical environment like that of the average human ear. This resemblance, however, is at best restricted to a very narrow frequency range and then only for some commonly used audiometric headphones (Shaw, 1966b). Moreover, the geometry of standardized acoustic couplers is different from that of an ear so that corresponding sites of measurement in the coupler and a real ear cannot be specified. Therefore, the SPL produced by a headphone in a coupler cannot be simply related to that in a real ear, nor can it be simply related to SPL in a free field (see Fig. 14.9). It does, however, provide a reproducible, standardized calibration that permits comparison of results from different laboratories.

1.6.5. Spectrum Analyzers. The instruments just discussed permit calibration of the overall SPL and, if it is periodic, the frequency of a sound. However, they do not provide information about spectrum. The amplitude spectrum of a wave form may be measured with a spectrum analyzer or wave analyzer. Most *spectrum analyzers* measure amplitude of a narrow band of frequencies by passing the signal through a sharply tuned filter. The center frequency of this filter may be swept across the audible frequency range to measure spectrum level at different frequencies, which in turn may be displayed graphically. Recently, analyzers performing a Fourier transformation on the wave form have become available. These *FFT-analyzers* (fast Fourier transformation) use computer technology to specify quickly and conveniently the precise amplitude spectrum of wave forms.

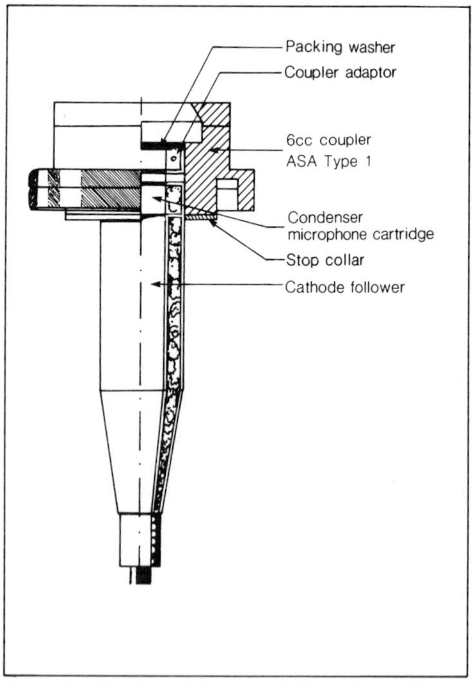

Figure 14.8. Coupler for earphone calibration. The ASA Type 1 (NBS-9A) coupler, mounted on a condenser microphone and cathode follower, is shown in cross section. By means of the 6-cm^3 volume, the coupler provides a rough approximation to the acoustic impedance of an average human ear. (From Brüel & Kjaer Instruments, Inc., *Instruction and applications: Artificial ear type 4151* (Instruction Manual), Author, 1961. Reprinted with permission.)

1.7. Stimulus Artifacts

A careful spectral analysis of a sound provides detailed information not only about the intended components, but also about those arising from imperfect behavior of electroacoustic equipment. These additional spectral components arise from two sources, distortion and noise in the equipment.

1.7.1. Distortion. Distortion is caused by nonlinearities in the equipment. If the input is a sine wave, the nonlinearity produces spectral components at harmonic frequencies of the sine wave. This is *harmonic distortion*. If the input is complex, intermodulation distortion is produced in addition to harmonic distortion. *Intermodulation distortion* produces spectral components at frequencies that are the sum of or the difference between the input frequencies and their harmonics.

The *amount of distortion* is conveniently specified by the level difference (measured at the output) between the input frequencies and the distortion components. The distortion, D, may also be specified in percent:

$$D = \sqrt{\frac{A^2(\text{overall}) - A^2(\text{input frequencies})}{A^2(\text{overall})}} \cdot 100 \qquad (20)$$

where A(overall) is the RMS value (measured in volts or micropascals) of the total signal at the output, and A(input frequencies) is the RMS value of the input frequencies at the output. In other words, D is specified as the percentage of the squared RMS value of the unintentional part of the signal (which is the distortion) relative to the squared RMS value of the total signal (intentional plus distortion). If the input signal is a pure tone, D is equal to the total harmonic distortion plus noise (THD + N), which is a commonly stated specification for audio equipment. To measure D in practice, it is necessary to eliminate the input frequency from the output signal to get a direct measurement of the unintentional part of the output. Otherwise, when D is less than about 10%, the difference between the total output and the intentional part tends to be swamped by variability of the voltage measurements.

The measurement of very low values of D requires almost complete elimination of the intentional part of the signal, which is difficult to achieve. Therefore, when the distortion is low it is often measured by means of a spectral analysis of the output in response to a sinusoidal input. THD is calculated in percent on the basis of the amplitudes of each of the harmonics:

$$\text{THD} = \sqrt{\frac{\sum_{n=2}^{N} A_n^2}{\sum_{n=1}^{N} A_n^2}} \cdot 100 \qquad (21)$$

where A_n is the amplitude of the nth harmonic. In other words, THD is specified as the percentage of the squared RMS value of all harmonics except the fundamental (which is the desired output) relative to the squared RMS value of the fundamental plus the distortion. In most instances only the first three to

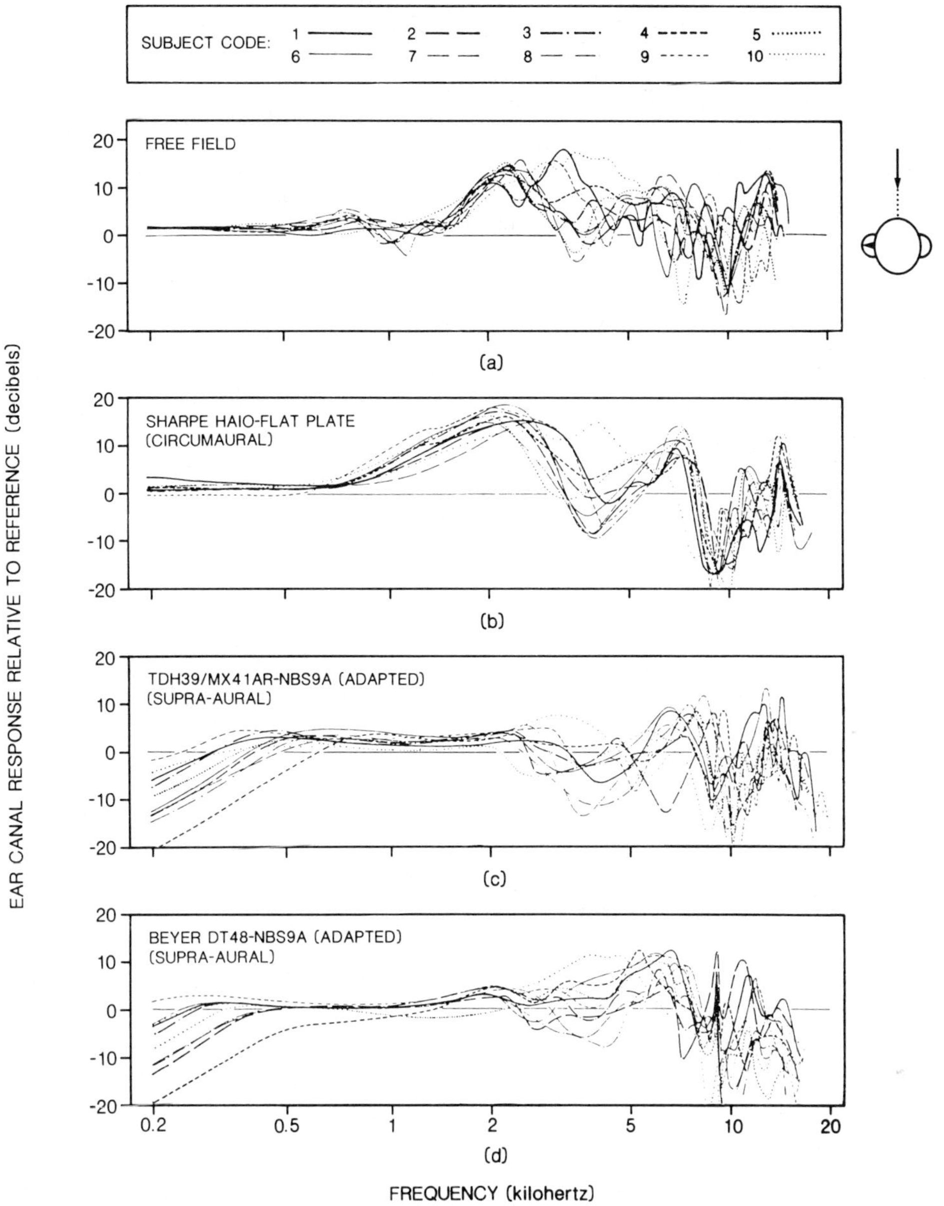

Figure 14.9. Difference between the SPL measured in a free field or in a coupler and the SPL measured at the entrance to the ear canal. The level measured by a probe microphone at the entrance to the ear canal relative to that measured in frontally incident free field (a) or in a coupler with various headphones (b–d) is plotted as a function of frequency. The relative levels in decibels are plotted individually for ten listeners. Transfer functions from free field show that the SPL at the entrance to the ear canal is about equal in all listeners up to approximately 2,000 Hz, but above 2,000 Hz the SPL at the entrance to the ear canal varies widely among listeners. Note that above 3,000 Hz individual differences of 20 dB are common and that above 1,000 Hz the average SPL at the entrance to the ear canal differs from the free-field SPL. The SPL at the entrance to the ear canal tends to be higher than the free-field SPL between 1,500 and 8,000 Hz and lower around 10,000 Hz. The circumaural headphone (b) also shows large variation among listeners at high frequencies. Also note the difference between the free-field and the headphone transfer functions for frequencies above 700 Hz. The surpra-aural (audiometric) headphones (c) and (d) show large variation among listeners at both low and high frequencies. The variation at low frequencies is due to differences in leakage between the headphones cushion and the listener's ear. (The low-frequency response decreases with increasing leakage.) The circumaural headphone is not prone to such leakage because its cushion surrounds the pinna and rests against the listener's head; the supra-aural headphones have cushions that rest directly on the listener's pinnae. Generally, the SPL at the entrance to the ear canal is about the same for all listeners and close to the SPL measured in a coupler only in the frequency range from 700 to 2,000 Hz. Outside this range variations of 20 dB among listeners are common and even the average SPL may deviate 5–10 dB from tht measured in a coupler. Finally, the transfer functions from free field and from audiometric headphones are generally dissimilar. Thus free-field SPLs are not directly comparable to SPLs generated in a coupler by a headphone. [(a) From E. A. G. Shaw, Ear canal pressure generated by a free sound field, *Journal of the Acoustical Society of America*, 1966, *39*. Reprinted with permission. (b), (c), and (d) From E. A. G. Shaw, Ear canal pressure generated by circumaural and supra-aural earphones, *Journal of the Acoustical Society of America*, 1966, *39*. Reprinted with permission.]

seven harmonics are taken into consideration because they are usually the dominant part of the distortion. If higher harmonics contribute substantially to the THD calculation they should be included as long as their frequencies are within the audible range. Moreover, if the high harmonics are relatively strong they may be more audible than the lower harmonics owing to the limited spread of masking. [When the desired (fundamental) frequency is far below the frequency of the distortion, it is much less effective in masking the distortion; for more information on masking, see Section 3.]

1.7.2. Equipment Noise. Equipment noise is caused by the random flow of electrons in electronic equipment. As contrasted with distortion, the noise is unrelated to the stimulus and has a continuous spectrum. The noise on the output of most kinds of electroacoustic equipment remains at a fixed voltage level regardless of the signal level. The noise produced by electroacoustic equipment is often computed as a *signal-to-noise* ratio in decibels as follows:

$$N = 20 \log\left(\frac{V_S}{V_N}\right) \text{ dB} \qquad (22)$$

where V_S is the maximal or the nominal signal voltage at the output and V_N is the noise voltage at the output.

Noise and distortion are always present as stimulus artifacts in any experiment. The extent to which they influence the results depends on their level and on the experimental task. Often they can be ignored even if they are clearly audible together with the intentional part of the stimulus, but in some tasks (e.g., intensity discrimination; see Section 4) they may influence the results even if only barely audible.

2. AUDITORY SYSTEM

The auditory system has three basic functions: (1) sound transmission through the outer, middle, and inner ears, (2) sensory transduction by the hair cells of the inner ear, and (3) neural processing within and transmission through the eighth nerve and four or five neural levels to the auditory cortex. Figure 14.10 gives an overview of the whole auditory system. So much is known about sound transmission and neural responses in the eighth nerve that many psychoacoustic data can be understood in terms of transduced neural signals at this level. The relation of sensation to neural events at more central levels of the auditory system remains obscure. This section presents basic information about the auditory transmission system and about subsequent neural processing; some of this information will serve to clarify psychoacoustic data.

2.1. Outer Ear

The outer ear comprises the pinna and the ear canal (also called external meatus). Upon reaching the outer ear, sound continues on through air in the ear canal, but the configuration of the pinna and canal imposes frequency-dependent changes on the sound vibrations that reach the middle ear.

2.1.1. Pinna. The pinna (or auricle) concentrates sound, and thereby increases sound amplitude at the entrance of the ear canal. Owing to its complex configuration, the pinna also reflects sound. As a result, sound is amplified or attenuated—depending on its direction and frequency—on the way to the ear canal by as much as 10 dB. Effects are greatest at frequencies above 2,000 Hz (Shaw & Teranishi, 1968). Thus the spectrum of a complex sound containing many high frequencies varies at the entrance to the ear canal in a manner that depends on the direction from which a sound comes. These pinna effects provide cues to location of a sound source; they also seem necessary to give an impression that a sound source is external to the listener. Section 3.1.2 discusses the role of the pinna in detection, and Section 3 of Chapter 15 discusses its role in localization. Figure 14.11 shows how the level of a sound at the entrance to the ear canal differs from that measured at the same place in a free sound field with no listener present. Each curve is for a sound source coming from a different angle. These measurements were made by first recording the response of a microphone located where the middle of a listener's head would be and then again with a probe microphone placed at the entrance to the ear canal. Such measurements thus include effects of the head and body on the sound field.

Because sound pressure levels are usually measured with the listener absent, effects of the presence of the listener on the sound field must be taken into account if precise knowledge of sound pressure at the ear canal is required. Shaw (1966a) has shown that the effects of the pinna and body on the sound field differ from one individual to another, by as much as 25 dB at particular frequencies (see Fig. 14.9).

When headpones are worn, sound arrives directly at the ear canal bypassing the pinna and body so that most of their effects disappear. Despite the wide range encompassing individuals with normal pinnae, a few persons with missing or deformed pinnae fall outside that range. Gross abnormalities of the pinna are usually accompanied by other auditory defects caused by congenital malformation in other parts of the auditory system.

2.1.2. Ear Canal. The ear canal isolates the sensitive structures of the middle and inner ears from the external world, thereby reducing the chance of mechanical injury and disease. Hairs and wax formation within the canal keep insects, small objects, and dirt away from the eardrum. The mean dimensions of the canal are approximately 0.7 cm in diameter and 2.5–3 cm in length. With these dimensions, the ear canal acts as a resonant pipe that amplifies frequencies near 4000 Hz by as much as 10 dB. (See Section 1.3.) Figure 14.12 (page 14-17) gives the change in SPL from the input of the ear canal to the eardrum as a function of frequency. This change accounts, in part, for the way in which detection depends on sound frequency, as shown in Section 3.1.

Sound transmission through the ear canal may be altered by the accumulation of wax (cerumen). A large accumulation can reduce the amplitude of sound reaching the eardrum. According to Saltzman (1949), impacted wax may raise the threshold by as much as 40 dB. On the other hand, D. W. Robinson, Shipton, and Hinchcliffe (1981) found no threshold elevation in 18 ears whose eardrums were partially or totally covered by wax. The effect of wax depends on how much wax accumulates and how impacted it is. The shape of the ear canal must also affect sound transmission and a person's detection of sound. Although no information seems to be available on this point, the shape of the canal probably contributes to variability of thresholds among persons with normal hearing.

2.2. Middle Ear

Figure 14.13 (page 14-18) is a schematic drawing of the human ear, showing relations between outer, middle, and inner ears.

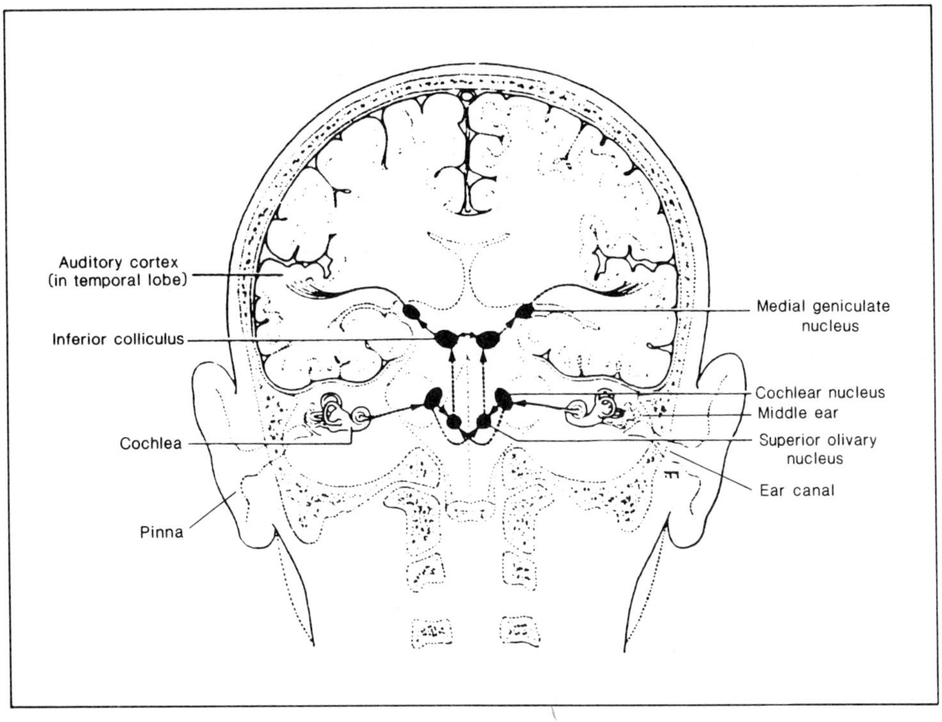

Figure 14.10. Overview of the human auditory system, from the outer ear to the auditory cortex. Shown are the pinna, ear canal, and middle ear. The cochlea and vestibular canals (the latter are not involved in hearing) are also shown. Beyond lies the complex neural network with synapses at the cochlear nucleus, superior olivary nucleus, inferior colliculus, and medial geniculate. Many nerve fibers cross from one side of the head to the other. Only afferent fibers, which send signals to the brain, are shown; a small number of efferent fibers also send signals toward the cochlea. (Adapted from Wever, 1949, in E. B. Goldstein (Ed.), *Sensation and perception* (2nd Ed.), Wadsworth Publishing Co., 1984. Reprinted with permission.)

The middle ear is a complex mechanical system designed to match, in effect, impedance of air in the outer ear to that of fluid in the inner ear. The impedance of the cochlear fluid is greater than that of air, which means that it takes more force to move the fluid than to move air. If sound waves went directly to the oval window of the cochlea, much of the sound energy would be reflected back. The impedance matching of the middle ear prevents this loss and permits most of the sound energy to reach the inner ear. The middle ear comprises the eardrum (called also tympanic membrane), the three ossicles (malleus, incus, and stapes), middle-ear muscles, oval window, round window, and entrance to the Eustachian tube. The ossicles transmit sound waves to the oval window from the eardrum.

2.2.1. Eardrum. The eardrum is a fibrous membrane with a diameter of approximately 0.9 cm. Shaped somewhat like a filter cone, or a loudspeaker diaphragm, it concentrates sound on the malleus, the first of the three ossicles of the middle ear. For a constant input, it transmits impinging sound energy approximately uniformly up to about 1,500 Hz; at higher frequencies displacement amplitude decreases (Tonndorf & Khanna, 1968).

Movement of the eardrum is quite small, only 0.3 μm in response to a 3,000-Hz tone at 100 dB SPL (Tonndorf & Khanna, 1968). Because the amplitude of eardrum movement is a linear function of sound pressure, the eardrum must move over a distance of only 3×10^{-6}μm when extrapolation is made down to threshold near 0 dB SPL (Green, 1976).

If the middle ear were airtight, the enclosed air would be gradually absorbed by the linings of the cavity, and a pressure differential between the two sides of the eardrum would result. However, air is able to enter the middle ear through the Eustachian tube, which connects the middle-ear cavity with the nasopharynx. Thus the air in the cavity is replenished, and pressure in the cavity is kept the same as the environmental pressure of the ear canal. The Eustachian tube normally opens only for a short time during swallowing. When it cannot open, owing to congestion caused by disease or to an allergic reaction or other pathology, then changes in atmospheric pressure are not compensated for. The resulting pressure difference on the eardrum is felt as a tightening in the ears and may cause threshold to increase as much as 20 dB at 1,000 Hz in extreme cases. As shown in Figure 14.14 (page 14-18) the threshold loss decreases at lower and higher frequencies, but is still over 10 dB at 100 Hz.

Perforation of the eardrum also results in threshold elevations, especially at low and middle frequencies (Anthony & Harrison, 1972). However, the size of these hearing losses cannot be reliably measured audiometrically through earphone listening. Such measurements exaggerate the hearing loss because perforation of the eardrum reduces middle-ear impedance (Kruger & Tonndorf, 1978). As a consequence, the sound pressure generated in the ear canal under an earphone is also reduced. The size of the hearing loss in sound-field listening and its frequency dependence are unknown for humans. In the cat, a small perforation of the eardrum results in a loss that decreases—at a rate of 12 dB·octave^{-1}—from about 30 dB at 300 Hz to near 0 dB at 1,200 Hz (Kruger & Tonndorf, 1978).

2.2.2. Ossicular Chain. The three ossicles of the middle ear—malleus (hammer), incus (anvil), and stapes (stirrup)—have a total length of approximately 18 mm and weigh ap-

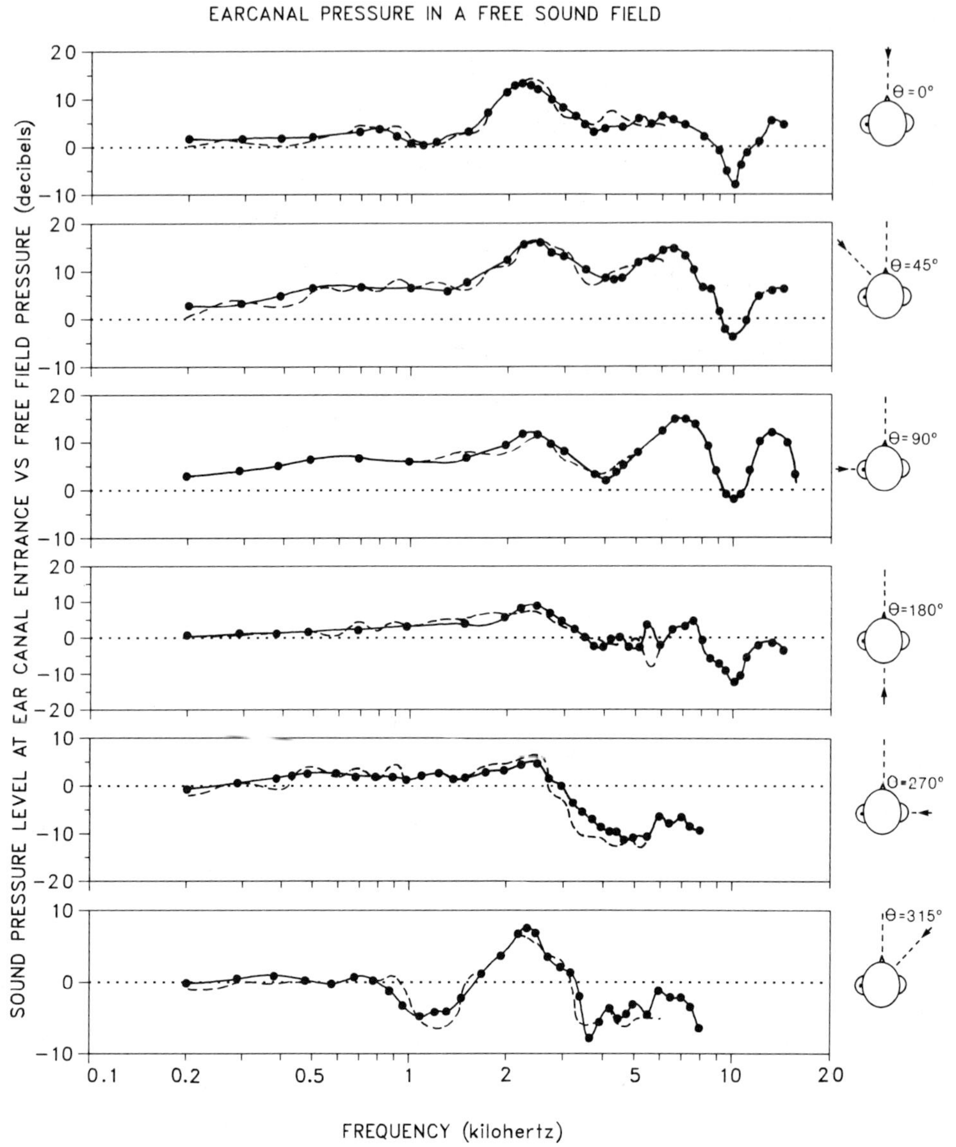

Figure 14.11. Sound pressure level at the entrance to the ear canal. Measurements of sound pressure level in an empty anechoic chamber were subtracted from measurements via a microphone recording from a probe tube whose orifice was located at the entrance of a subject's ear canal. The difference is plotted as a function of sound frequency. Results are shown for the sound source located at six different azimuths. Each point is the mean for nine subjects. Repeated measurements on three of the subjects showed good reliability with deviations mostly less than 3 dB; the differences were probably due to inaccurate positioning of the head. Differences among subjects were greater than within subjects. The smooth curves through the data do not reflect the sharper contours of the individual curves. Dashed lines are taken from a previous study by Wiener (1947). For the most part, SPL is greater at the ear-canal entrance than in the empty free field. Diffraction by torso, head, and pinna give rise to maxima at 2,400 and 13,000 Hz and to minima around 4,000 and at 10,000 Hz. The relative positions of the curves do not change dramatically with azimuth. (From E. A. G. Shaw, Ear canal pressure generated by a free sound field, *Journal of the Acoustical Society of America*, 1966, *39*. Reprinted with permission.)

proximately 60 mg. The malleus is attached at its manubrium (or handle) to the eardrum. The malleus and incus are connected by a joint with limited movement and act nearly as a unit, whereas the joint between incus and stapes is of the ball-and-socket type and is very flexible. These tiny bones serve to match the impedance in air to the higher impedance of the cochlear fluid behind the oval window, essentially by concentrating the pressure from the eardrum onto the oval window. The small pressures needed to move air particles are thus built up to the larger pressures needed to send vibrations through the cochlear fluid. The surface area of the eardrum ranges from 50 to 90 mm, whereas that of the stapedial footplate which abuts the oval window is about 3 mm. The reduction of nearly 25-fold in the area against which the force of a sound wave is exerted increases the pressure on the oval window by almost 28 dB. In addition to concentrating force, the ossicles provide a leverage action that further amplifies the pressure about 1.3-fold or 2 dB. However, transmission through the middle ear is frequency dependent. Figure 14.15 shows the relation between volume displacement at the eardrum and volume displacement at the oval window as a function of frequency. The relation is given in terms of volume displacement of the stapes. Transmission is about equally efficient at all frequencies up to approximately 1,000 Hz, above which it decreases at roughly 15 dB·octave^{-1}. [However, according to Dallos (1973a) measurements in the cat, as opposed to humans, indicate that transmission becomes less efficient as frequency decreases below 1,000 Hz.]

The middle ear not only matches acoustic impedances; to a limited extent it also protects the inner ear from intense external sound, primarily by the acoustic reflex. Attached to the malleus and to the stapes are two small muscles, the tensor tympani and the stapedius muscle, which contract in response to sounds above about 85 dB SPL. In humans, only the stapedius muscle seems to be involved in the acoustic reflex (Møller, 1972). When the stapedius muscle contracts, the whole ossicular chain and the eardrum become difficult to move. Consequently, the threshold for sounds below 500 Hz increases by as much as 20 dB. The muscle does not contract directly in response to an intense sound. First, the sound is transduced. Activation of the reflex is via the trigeminal and facial nerves. As a result, the muscles do not contract until at least 10 msec after onset of an intense sound. During those 10 msec a very intense sound could damage the auditory system. To avoid such damage from an anticipated intense sound, it has been suggested that a less intense sound be introduced 15–20 msec prior to the potentially damaging sound. The preceding sound would cause the stapedius muscle to contract, and so reduce the impact of the later and more intense sound (Fletcher & Riopelle, 1960; Ward, Selters, & Glorig, 1961). For example, rifles could be equipped with a device that would make a noise just before the actual shot.

The level necessary to activate the acoustic reflex depends on the characteristics of the eliciting stimulus. A wide-band noise elicits the reflex at levels 6–10 dB lower than does a high-frequency pure tone (Flottorp, Djupesland, & Winther, 1971); an ipsilateral sound (to the same ear on which the reflex is measured) elicits the reflex at a level 2–14 dB lower than a contralateral sound; a bilateral (binaural) sound elicits it at a level 3 dB lower than an ipsilateral, monaural sound (Møller, 1962a); a 500-msec sound elicits it at a level a few decibels lower than a 25-msec sound (Møller, 1962b).

The middle ear also attenuates intense sounds by a change in rotation of the footplate of the stapes (Békésy, 1960, pp. 112–115). Instead of rotating on a "vertical axis," the footplate rotates on a horizontal axis, reducing the pressure on the oval window.

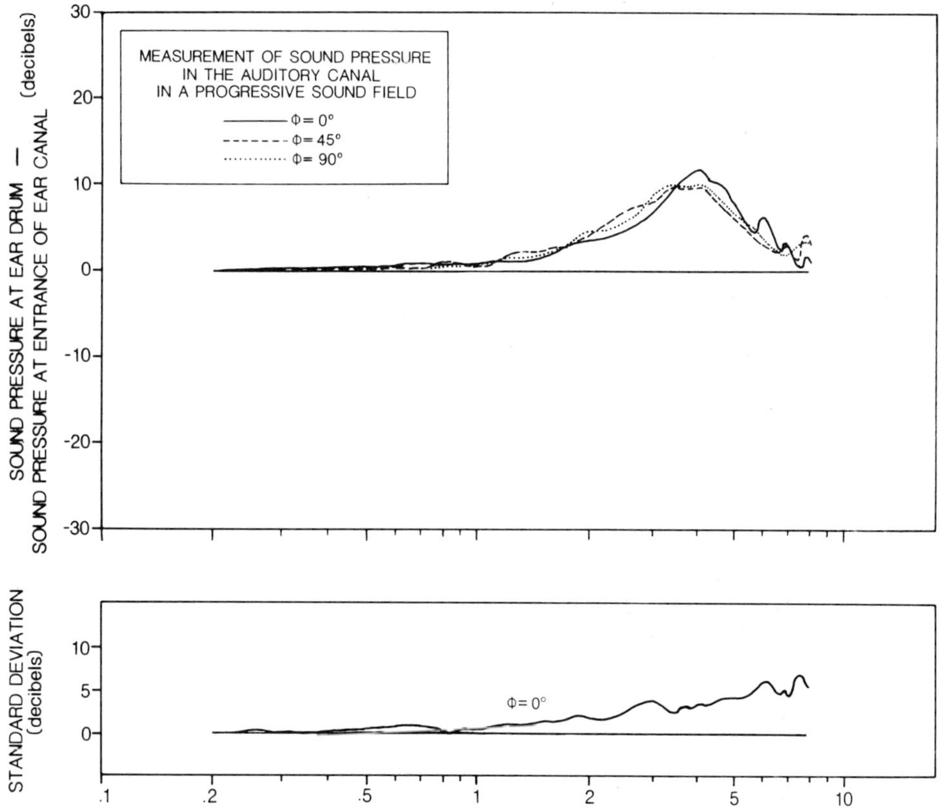

Figure 14.12. Sound pressure level at the eardrum. The SPL at the eardrum minus the SPL at the entrance to the ear canal is plotted as a function of sound frequency. Measurements were made with a probe microphone whose orifice was located at the ear canal entrance or at the eardrum. The subject sat in an anechoic chamber with his head fixed. Curves shown are the means from 6–12 male ears. Measurements were made with sound source at the three azimuths depicted in the inset. Standard deviations are plotted at the bottom of the graph. Resonance of the ear canal results in a peak of approximately 10 dB near 4,000 Hz. The curves change little as the sound source moves from directly in front at 0° azimuth to the side at 90°. (From F. M. Wiener & D. Ross, The pressure distribution in the auditory canal in a progressive sound field, *Journal of the Acoustical Society of America*, 1946, *18*. Reprinted with permission.)

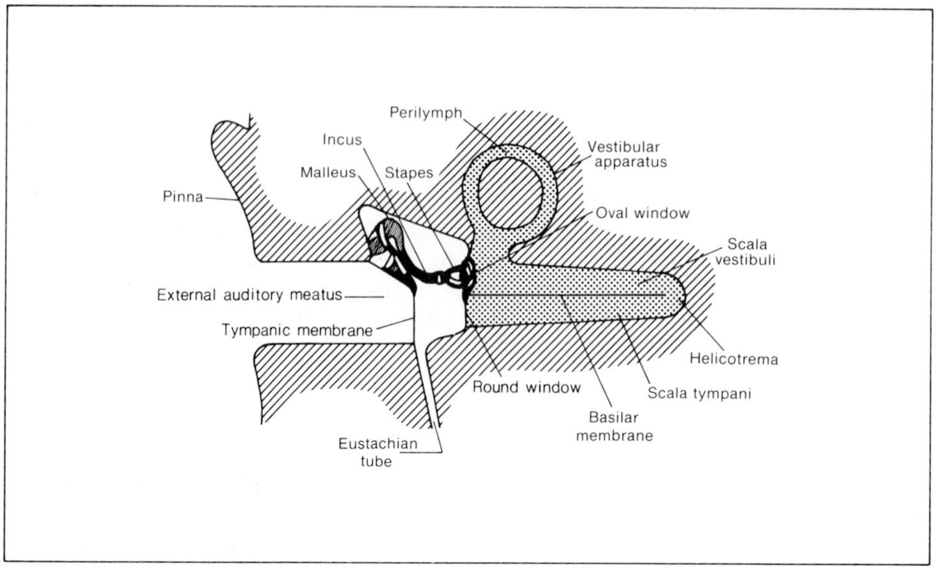

Figure 14.13. Schematic drawing of the human ear. The outer ear comprises the pinna and external auditory meatus or ear canal. The middle ear comprises the tympanic membrane or eardrum and the ossicles (malleus, incus, and stapes), as well as the air cavity around the ossicles, which opens to the Eustachian tube. The inner ear comprises the cochlea, which is depicted unrolled, and the vestibular canal, which is not involved in hearing. The separation of the inner ear from the external sound field provides protection from disease and injury and permits impedance matching between air and the perilymph of the inner ear. (From G. von Békésy, Über die akustische Reizung des Vestibularapparates, *Pflügers Archiv, European Journal of Physiology*, 1935, *236*. Reprinted with permission.)

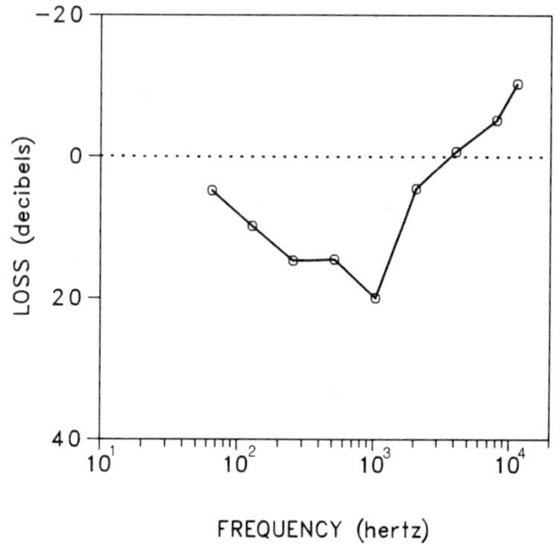

Figure 14.14. Effect on threshold of increasing air pressure in the middle ear. Static air pressure was increased to 102 cm H_2O (approximately 5,000 Pa), and the threshold of a normally hearing young adult measured audiometrically at most octave frequencies from 64 to 8,200 Hz and at 11,600 Hz. Threshold is elevated as indicated by the positive hearing loss on the ordinate, except at the highest frequencies. (Hearing loss is the increase in threshold relative to that of a group of normally hearing young adults.) The unequal air pressure on the two sides of the eardrum causes the greatest hearing loss, of 20 dB, at 1,000 Hz. The loss decreases toward both lower and higher frequencies. (From H. Rasmussen, Studies on the effect on the air conduction and bone conduction from changes in the meatal pressure in normal subjects and otosclerotic patients, *Acta Oto-Laryngologica*, 1948, *74* (Supplement). Reprinted with permission.)

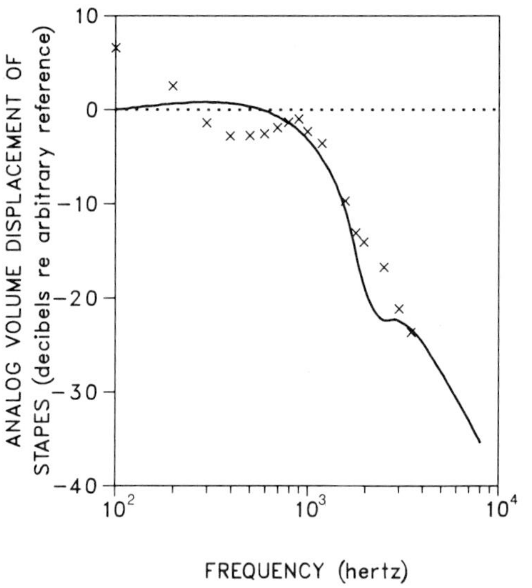

Figure 14.15. Transmission characteristic of the middle ear. The volume displacement of the stapes produced by a constant sound pressure at the eardrum is plotted as a function of frequency. Crosses are data from human ear preparations. The curve is an electrical network analog of the ear. Transmission through the middle ear is independent of stimulus frequency up to approximately 1,000 Hz, but falls off at more than 10 dB·octave^{-1} at higher frequencies. (From J. J. Zwislocki, Analysis of some auditory characteristics, in R. D. Luce, R. R. Bush, & E. Galanter (Eds.), *Handbook of mathematical psychology*, Vol. 3. Copyright 1965, R. Duncan Luce. Reprinted with permission of John Wiley & Sons, Inc.)

Even though restricted to frequencies below 100 Hz, this mechanism can protect the inner ear from injury by intense natural sounds, such as thunder and windstorms, which contain mostly low frequencies.

The middle ear connects with the inner ear at the oval window, an ellipsoidal opening about 4 mm long in the bony wall of the cochlea. This opening is filled by the footplate of the stapes, which is held in place by an annular ligament; it is here that pressure waves are set in motion in the cochlear fluid. The round window is a second membrane-covered opening in the cochlea. It faces into the middle-ear cavity which is filled with air. Pressure exerted by the stapes on the cochlear fluid is relieved by outward movement of the round window. Sounds arriving at the middle ear from within the body, including vocalization, have little effect in the cochlea, owing partly to the orientation and mass of the ossicles (Békésy, 1949). Furthermore, such internal sounds exert pressure on the oval and round windows at the same time, and so tend to be cancelled within the cochlear fluid, which is nearly incompressible (Békésy, 1960, pp. 429–438).

2.2.3. Disorders of the Middle Ear. The middle ear is subject to a number of disorders that are viral, bacterial, or allergic in origin. Regardless of the cause, the effect is similar: Fluid that collects in the middle ear loads the eardrum unnaturally. Pure-tone thresholds may rise as much as 40 dB between 250 and 8,000 Hz. Unless the disorder is prolonged, the threshold usually returns to normal once the middle ear clears.

More serious problems are tympanosclerosis and otosclerosis. In these disorders, parts of the ossicular chain are immobilized by the buildup of bony or fibrous deposits. Tympanosclerosis refers to fixation of the junction between the eardrum and malleus; otosclerosis refers to fixation at the coupling between the footplate of the stapes and the oval window. The sclerotic disorders occur mainly among young people between adolescence and the 30th year (Davis & Silverman, 1970).

These middle-ear disorders are generally signaled by elevated thresholds at all frequencies when sound arrives via air conduction (the usual path), but by normal thresholds when sound arrives by bone conduction. A middle-ear disorder can also be diagnosed by measurement of the impedance at the eardrum. A disorder is indicated by abnormal changes in impedance as a function of changes in air pressure in the external ear canal and as a function of contralateral stimuli that elicit the acoustic reflex. Although surgical intervention such as stapes mobilization can often correct these disorders, some otologists may recommend the use of hearing aids (bone-conduction aids), which are especially helpful in conductive hearing impairment.

2.3. Inner Ear

The terms "inner ear" and "cochlea" describe the same anatomical entity, except that the three vestibular canals, vital to equilibrium and the sensation of bodily rotation (see Chapter 18 by Howard), are usually considered part of the inner ear. The snail-shaped cochlea contains the hair cells that transduce into neural energy the mechanical waves set up in the cochlear fluid by a sound. The crucial questions are just how does transduction take place, how is stimulus information coded in the neural signal, and what aspects of the neural code are relevant to sensation.

2.3.1. Anatomy of the Cochlea. In humans, the cochlea is about 5 mm high from base to apex and about 9 mm broad at the base. Figure 14.16 shows a cross section of the cochlear duct of the guinea pig. The cochlear duct forms a rough triangle with the basilar membrane on one side, the wall of the cochlea on the second side, and Reissner's membrane on the third side. The basilar membrane is a fibrous elastic structure which in humans makes 2¾ turns as it winds approximately 35 mm around the cochlea's central bony core, the modiolus. The modiolus contains fibers of the eighth nerve and blood capillaries. On the basilar membrane lie the receptor cells. The space between the basilar membrane and Reissner's membrane forms the scala media, which is filled with endolymph at a high potassium ion concentration. On the basilar membrane lies the organ of Corti covered by the tectorial membrane. The whole duct coils around the modiolus almost to the apex of the cochlea. The helicotrema, the small opening between the end of the duct and the apex, connects the perilymph of the scala vestibuli with that of the scala tympani; the perilymph's ionic content is high in sodium and low in potassium, just the opposite of the endolymph in the scala media. [Davis (1957) incorporates this difference in his electric model of cochlear excitation.]

The hair cells line up in four or five rows along the length of the basilar membrane. The 3500 inner hair cells lie in a single row on the modulus side of the triangle formed by the rods of Corti, a stiff supporting structure, shown in Figure 14.16. They are slightly larger than the outer hair cells, with a mean diameter of 12 μm, have fewer stereocilia per cell (40–60), and are less numerous. Some 25,000 outer hair cells lie in three or four rows on the other side of the rods of Corti toward the outer wall of the cochlea. The outer hair cells, with a diameter of 6–7 μm, are smaller than the inner hair cells and have a different shape and internal structure. They are also more easily damaged by ototoxic drugs and intense sounds. The tips of their longest cilia are apparently embedded in the overlying tectorial membrane.

2.3.2. Displacement Patterns and Frequency Analysis. The complex and delicate structures of the cochlea are designed to transduce sound into neural events while performing a frequency analysis by responding differentially to sounds of different frequencies. Frequency analysis is achieved by a translation of stimulus frequency into place of maximum excitation on the basilar membrane. As explained below, this so-called tonotopic organization is achieved by the nature of the sound transmission within the cochlea.

Set in motion by an incident sound, the vibrating footplate of the stapes swings in and out against the perilymph of the scala vestibuli, setting up a pressure wave that travels along to the helicotrema. When the stapes presses in, the round window moves out. The pressure wave travels from the oval window to the helicotrema at the speed of sound in fluid. As a result, a pressure difference arises almost instantaneously between the scala vestibuli and scala tympani with the cochlear partition in between. This pressure difference displaces the basilar membrane from its resting position, but because the membrane is about 100 times stiffer near the oval window than near the helicotrema, not all parts of the membrane are displaced by the same amount and at the same time. This nonhomogeneity may be seen as a displacement wave that travels up the basilar membrane and has the form shown in Figure 14.17. The traveling wave is shown at two successive moments, the solid line preceding the heavy, dashed line. The light, dashed curve depicts the envelope of the wave and shows the largest displacement attained at each point along the basilar membrane. Note that

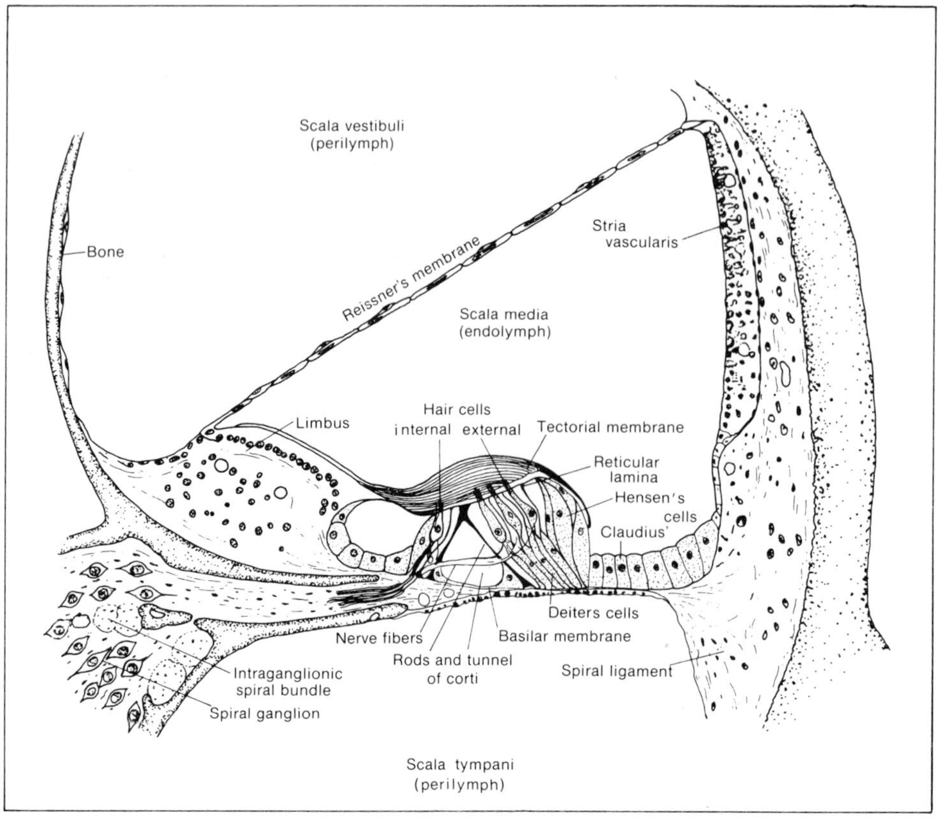

Figure 14.16. Cross section of the second turn of the cochlea of the guinea pig. The three cochlear canals—scala vestibuli, scala media, and scala tympani—are shown with the dividing membranes, Reissner's and the basilar membrane. The organ of Corti lies on the basilar membrane and contains the hair cells, tectorial membrane, and associated structures. Sensory transduction takes place in the hair cells upon the bending of the cilia embedded in the tectorial membrane. (From H. Davis, Advances in the neurophysiology and neuroanatomy of the cochlea, *Journal of the Acoustical Society of America*, 1962, *34*. Reprinted with permission.)

the displacement decreases much more slowly toward the stapes than away from the stapes. The traveling wave moves much less rapidly than the pressure wave and takes about 5 msec to go from the stapes to the helicotrema (Zerlin, 1969).

Frequency analysis occurs in the cochlea because the traveling wave has its maximum displacement at different places along the basilar membrane. The locus of maximum displacement depends upon the frequency of the stimulating sound: High frequencies cause maximum displacement near the oval window, low frequencies near the helicotrema. The distance of peak displacement from the stapes is approximately a logarithmic function of the frequency. The size of the peak displacement is not the same along the basilar membrane, but decreases with distance from the stapes, which means that it increases as a function of frequency as shown in Figure 14.18.

Our understanding of cochlear mechanics is based primarily upon the visual observations of Békésy (1942, 1943, 1960). Nonvisual observations have permitted an extension of measurements to higher frequencies and lower levels (Johnstone & Boyle, 1967; Rhode, 1971; Wilson & Johnstone, 1972). These new data raise questions about the linearity in the vibration of the basilar membrane. It is not clear whether displacement of the membrane increases linearly as a function of sound pressure from threshold to the very high levels at which the experimental observations have been made. The recent data also raise questions about the sharpness of tuning on the basilar membrane, that is, about how rapidly the displacement amplitude decreases on either side of the place of maximum displacement. We return to this point in the discussion of neural tuning curves in Section 2.4.2.

Békésy's observations confirm Helmholtz's (1885/1954) earlier hypothesis that stimulus frequency is mapped out tonotopically on the basilar membrane. At the same time they invalidate Helmholtz's assumption that the basilar membrane acts like a series of finely tuned resonators. Although wrong about the hypothesized mechanism, Helmholtz was right about the fundamental translation of frequency into place on the basilar membrane.

2.3.3. Sensory Transduction. Displacement of the basilar membrane results in a bending of the cilia of the hair cells. The cilia are thought to be bent by a shearing motion between the tectorial membrane and the reticular membrane (see Fig. 14.16); they project through the reticular membrane and some are embedded in the tectorial membrane (cf. Wever, 1971). A shearing motion comes about because the tectorial membrane and the basilar membrane (on which the hair cells and the reticular membrane sit) are attached at different points of the cochlear wall, so that they rotate around different center points when displaced. A sliding action between the tectorial membrane and the basilar membrane, including the reticular membrane, bends those cilia that are firmly anchored in the reticular membrane and in the tectorial membrane. Cilia not anchored in the tectorial membrane are bent either via lateral attachments to

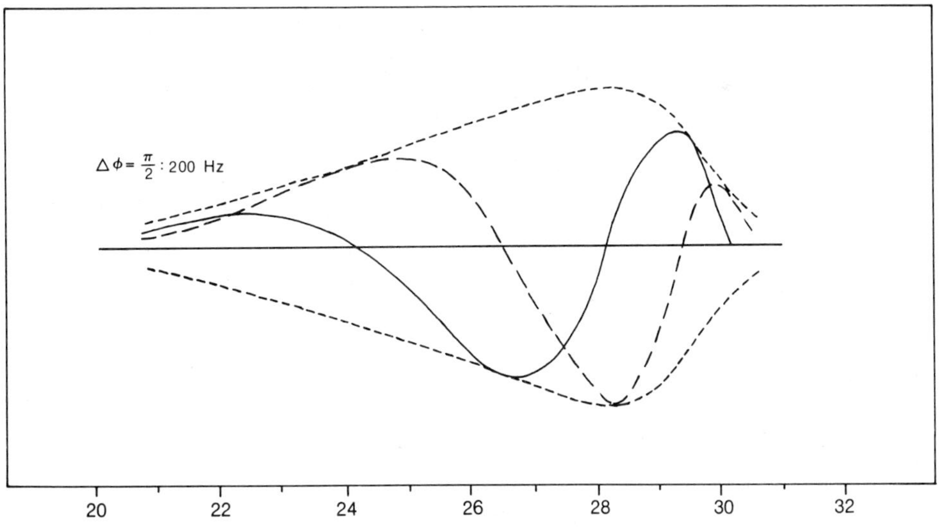

Figure 14.17. Vibration of the cochlear partition. Amplitude of the vibration produced by a 200-Hz tone is plotted as a function of distance from the stapes. The solid curve shows the pattern at one moment and the dark inner dashed curve 1.25 msec later (corresponding to 90° later in a cycle of the tone). The enclosing, light, dashed curve represents the maximum amplitude at each point calculated over several cycles. (From G. von Békésy, The variation of phase along the basilar membrane with sinusoidal vibration, *Journal of the Acoustical Society of America*, 1947, *19*. Reprinted with permission.)

anchored cilia or by fluid movement between the two sliding surfaces. (The latter scheme would apply mainly to inner hair cells, none of whose cilia are embedded in the tectorial membrane.)

The bending of the cilia is generally thought to stimulate the hair cells that in turn excite the sensory neurons of the eighth nerve with which they synapse (Dallos, 1978). Thus the hair cells transduce sound energy, by the bending of their cilia, into neural energy in the form of the all-or-none spikes of the eighth nerve. Dallos (1973a, 1973b) believes that the deformation of the cilia produces a receptor potential near the stereocilia that travels to the other end of the hair cell where it mediates the release of chemical transmitters from the presynaptic region. Measurements made from within hair cells of the receptor cells

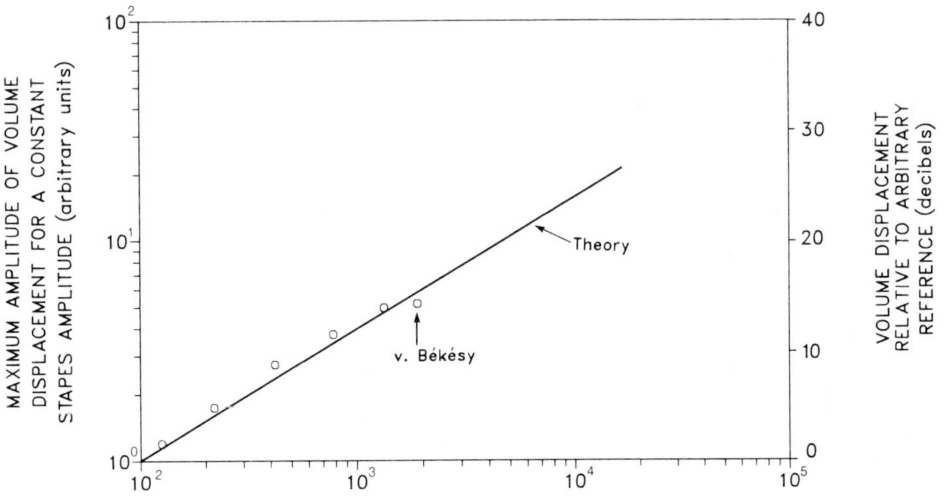

Figure 14.18. Amplitude of vibration of the cochlear partition. The maximum amplitude of volume displacement relative to a constant amplitude of stapes displacement is plotted as a function of sound frequency. Circles are measurements of cochlear partition displacement that Békésy (1960) made by visual observation under stroboscopic illumination at six positions along the basilar membrane. According to the theoretical line, amplitude increases as the 0.6 power of frequency. (From J. J. Zwislocki, Analysis of some auditory characteristics, in R. D. Luce, R. R. Bush, & E. Galanter (Eds.), *Handbook of mathematical psychology*, Vol. 3. Copyright 1965, R. Duncan Luce. Reprinted with permission of John Wiley & Sons, Inc.)

do not yet permit firm conclusions about the functioning of the hair cells (Russell & Sellick, 1977).

During transduction, a cochlear microphonic potential and several types of summating potentials can be recorded from the cochlea (Dallos, 1978). According to Dallos, these electrical signals result from receptor potentials of many hair cells. The cochlear microphonic is generated in response to "instantaneous variations in the deformation of the receptive region of the hair cell," whereas the summating potential is related to the envelope of these variations (Dallos, 1978, p. 153). The cochlear microphonic has been the subject of many studies since its discovery by Wever and Bray (1930). It has been called the cochlear microphonic because its wave form looks so much like the acoustical input. Its amplitude increases with the amplitude of the signal up to about 90 dB SPL. For a given level, the amplitude of the microphonic is greatest when measured in that part of the basilar membrane that is maximally displaced by the input frequency. Like the cochlear microphonic, the summating potentials vary with stimulus level and frequency, but their interpretation is more complex.

2.3.4. Echoes and Acoustic Emissions from the Inner Ear. The ear not only receives sounds but also emits them, either for some tens of milliseconds after impulsive stimulation by a pressure pulse (Kemp, 1978; Wilson, 1980) or spontaneously (Zurek, 1981). Stimulated acoustic emissions generally have an SPL of less than 20 dB SPL as measured by a probe microphone in the closed ear canal. Increasing the stimulus level causes the emission level to increase nonlinearly, so that in one subject, when the stimulus went from 20 to 60 dB SPL, the emission went from around 0 to 20 dB. The increase in emission level also depended strongly on stimulus frequency. A likely source of these "echoes" is in the cochlea itself, possibly in the cochlear partition (Kemp, 1980). They may be related to peaks and dips in auditory threshold curves that reflect marked and rapid changes in sensitivity as stimulus frequency is changed (see Section 3.1.2).

Spontaneous narrow-band signals are also emitted from human ears. They seem to occur mostly between 1,000 and 2,000 Hz and seldom exceed 20 dB SPL as measured in the occluded ear canal. Zurek (1981) detected them in 22 ears out of a total of 32 ears tested on 16 persons. Suppression of these emissions by an external tone depends in the same way on the frequency of the tone as masking of a low-level tonal signal. This similarity suggests that the source of the emission is in the cochlea and that it may be related to the source of stimulated emissions. Zurek speculates on a possible role for them in the sharpening of cochlear frequency analysis.

2.3.5. Cochlear Disorders. A cochlear disorder seems nearly always to mean that hair cells are abnormal. The source of the disorder may be heredity, presbycusis (old-age deafness), noise exposure, ototoxic drugs, general infections such as mumps or rubella, or cochlear disease such as Ménière's. Whatever the cause, the anatomical outcome is clear: Hair cells are deformed or missing. The behavioral consequences are elevated thresholds, especially at frequencies above 2,000 Hz; above the elevated thresholds there is an abnormal growth of loudness known as loudness recruitment (see Scharf and Houtsma, Chapter 15, Section 1.5.3.1). These effects are described in detail in some of the following sections. Recent evidence from measurements of masking and loudness summation suggests that cochlear disorder results in impaired frequency analysis (Scharf & Florentine, 1982). Owing to loudness recruitment and impaired frequency analysis, hearing aids often are of limited use to the listener with a cochlear disorder, especially in noise.

When hearing is so profoundly impaired that the patient hears almost nothing, stimulating the auditory nerve directly may be the only way to restore hearing. Much research on *cochlear implants* is underway. The implant comprises one or more electrodes inserted into the cochlea. The electrodes are energized from processing circuitry located in the ear canal or implanted under the skin. Electrical stimulation yields an auditory sensation, but the patient is rarely able to understand speech. (See Parkins & Anderson, 1983.)

2.4. Neural Transmission

Innervation of the cochlea is complex and the ascending neural pathways to the auditory cortex are even more sophisticated; they involve four to five synapses with crossovers between the left and right sides of the head. Much has been learned about the neural responses of the auditory nerve fibers, and this section emphasizes that information.

2.4.1. Anatomy of the Auditory Nervous System. Figure 14.19 is a schematic view of the ascending neural pathway from the cochlea to the auditory cortex. Within the cochlea of the cat, 95% of the more than 50,000 afferent fibers originating from the cochlear nucleus innervate the 2,500–3,000 inner hair cells, so that there are about 20 afferents innervating each inner hair cell (Spoendlin, 1974). About 5% of the fibers make their way through a tortuous route to the 25,000 outer hair cells, which means that more than ten outer hair cells are served by a single fiber. All auditory nerve fibers have myelin sheaths and diameters of 3–10 μm. Their cell bodies lie within the bony center of the cochlea, where they form the spiral ganglion.

From the spiral ganglion, the bipolar auditory nerve fibers send axons to the cochlear nucleus, a complex structure with two main divisions that probably have interconnections (Gacek, 1972). As Figure 14.19 shows, fibers from the cochlear nucleus go to a number of different places in the auditory nervous system, on both sides of the brain. The important neural stations on the way to the cortex include the superior olive, the inferior colliculus, and the medial geniculate. Within the cortex, the temporal lobes contain the auditory areas.

The auditory nervous system includes about 500 efferent fibers to each cochlea. Originating in the superior olive of the brainstem, about 400 go to the contralateral cochlea and 100 to the ipsilateral cochlea. They make connections with the afferent dendrites innervating the inner hair cells, and directly with the cell bodies of the outer hair cells (Dallos, 1978). The results of experiments involving electrical stimulation of the nerves of the olivocochlear bundle suggest that their main function is to reduce activity in the auditory nerve fibers (Gifford & Guinan, 1983; Wiederhold & Kiang, 1970).

Throughout the auditory system, from basilar membrane to auditory cortex, the rule is tonotopic organization, an orderly representation of stimulus frequency according to the place of maximum excitation (for a review see Gelfand, 1981, pp. 162–171). Within the auditory nerve, the fibers are organized approximately in accordance with the part of the cochlea they innervate. Fibers from the basal end of the cochlea, where high frequencies are mediated, are found near the peripheral margins of the nerve (Gacek, 1972). Fibers from the apical end, where low frequencies are mediated, are found in the central portions of the nerve. The cochlear nucleus of the cat has three distinct

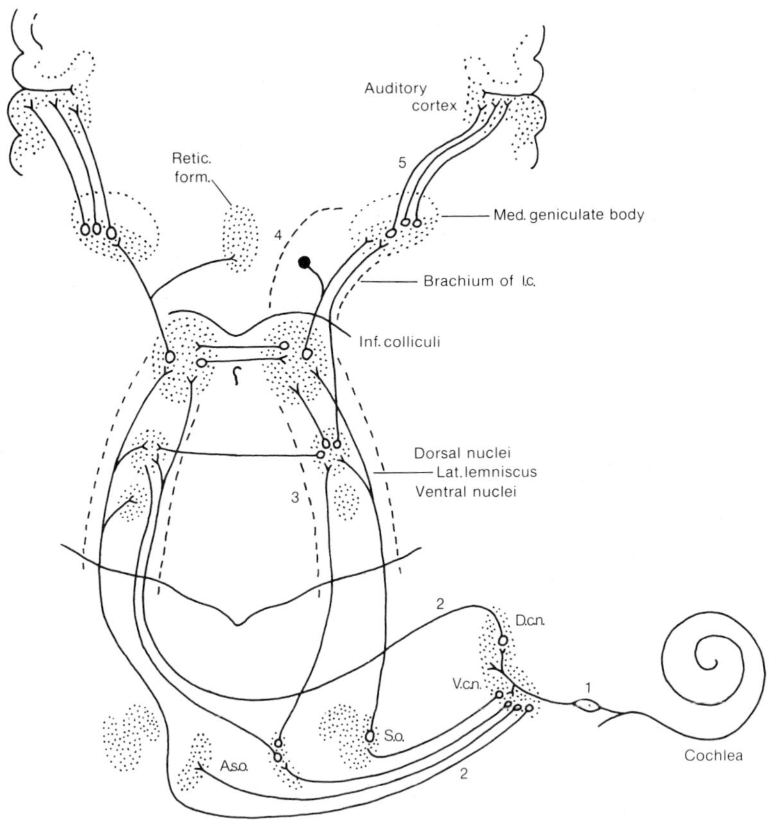

Figure 14.19. Ascending neural pathway of the auditory system. The first neural elements are the bipolar cochlear neurons going from the cochlea to the dorsal and ventral cochlear nuclei (D.c.n. and V.c.n.). Fibers from the cochlear nucleus terminate at the superior olivary complex (S.o.), the associate superior olivary complex (A.s.o.), and the inferior colliculi. The neural pathway continues on via the medial geniculate body to the auditory cortex. (From R. R. Gacek, Neuroanatomy of the auditory system, in J. V. Tobias (Ed.), *Foundations of modern auditory theory*, Vol. 2, Academic Press, Inc., 1972. Reprinted with permission.)

frequency mappings, with low frequencies evoking the largest neural responses ventrally and high frequencies dorsally (Rose, 1960). The next level, the superior olivary complex, also shows clear tonotopic organization (Tsuchitani & Boudreau, 1966). Within the cat's lateral lemniscus, neurons sensitive to higher frequencies are found in ventral portions of the nuclei whereas neurons sensitive to low frequencies are located in dorsal portions (Aitkin, Anderson, & Brugge, 1970). A consistent tonotopic organization has been demonstrated in the cat at the next level as well, in the inferior colliculus (Rose, Greenwood, Goldberg, & Hind, 1963). Tonotopic organization also exists in the auditory cortex of the monkey (Merzenich & Brugge, 1973), but the division of the auditory cortex into several distinct areas complicates matters. Woolsey (1960) measured three distinct areas in the cat's auditory cortex, each with its neurons arranged tonotopically.

2.4.2. Single-Fiber Responses in the Auditory Nerve. Much effort has been devoted to determining how the responses of auditory nerve fibers depend on stimulus frequency and level. A common procedure is to measure over a wide range of frequencies the stimulus levels at which a neuron first reaches a criterion response (a given number of action potentials per second). Results are mapped as a threshold curve with the criterion level plotted as a function of frequency. The resulting curve is called a tuning curve because each eighth-nerve fiber responds best to a particular frequency. The frequency to which a fiber is most sensitive (has thc lowest threshold) is the characteristic or best frequency of that fiber. Overall, the way in which responses in auditory nerve fibers depend on frequency and level can be understood in terms of the displacement patterns measured by Békésy (1960) on the basilar membrane.

Figure 14.20 presents tuning curves from 18 auditory fibers in the cat. On the logarithmic frequency scale, most of the curves show a more gradual rise in threshold toward lower frequencies than toward higher frequencies. This asymmetric pattern corresponds to the form of the traveling-wave envelope in Figure 14.17. The reasoning goes as follows. Presumably the characteristic frequency indicates that the fiber innervates the place on the basilar membrane where displacement is maximum

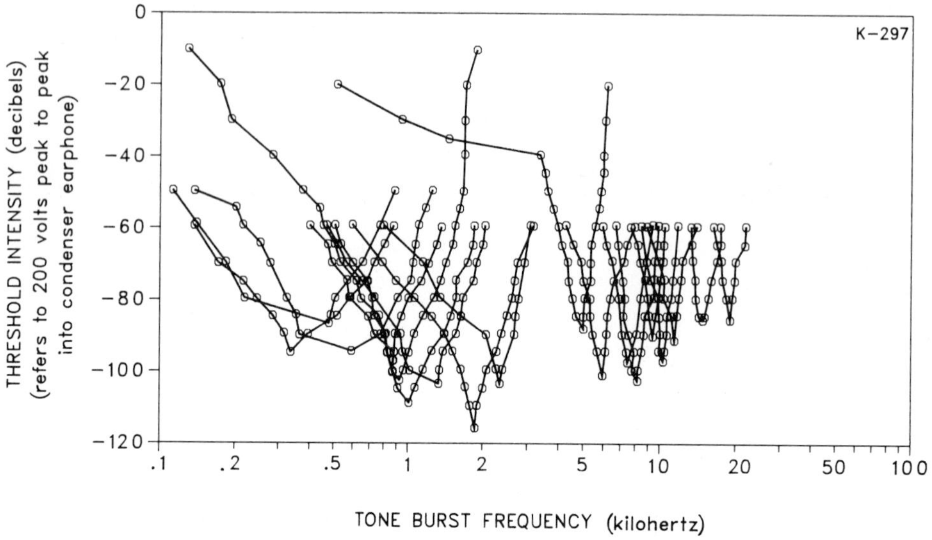

Figure 14.20. Tuning curves of auditory nerve fibers. Curves for 18 fibers from a single cat are shown. Relative threshold is plotted as a function of frequency of the tone bursts. Criterion threshold was a 10–20% increase in discharge rate over a neuron's spontaneous rate. A tone burst (duration of 50 msec, rise-fall time of 2.5 msec) was set to a constant level and varied in frequency to determine the range of frequencies over which the neuron gave a threshold response. The limits of these ranges are the pairs of points on a horizontal line through a tuning curve. All points for a given neuron are connected from the lowest to the highest frequency. Plotted on a logarithmic frequency scale, these tuning curves appear to be very sharp at high frequencies. At lower frequencies, for a given unit the threshold increases more rapidly toward the high than toward the low frequencies. (From N. Y.-S. Kiang, Discharge of single fibers in the cat's auditory nerve, *Research Monograph*, No. 35, 1965. Reprinted with permission of MIT Press.)

for that frequency. (For example, according to Fig. 14.17, a 200-Hz tone would be the characteristic frequency of a fiber innervating the basilar membrane at a distance of about 28 mm from the stapes.) Decreasing the stimulus frequency would move the whole pattern toward the right. Given the long tail of the pattern, displacement at the place innervated by the fiber being measured would be only slightly reduced. Thus to keep the fiber firing, the stimulus level would need to be raised only a little. In contrast, increasing the stimulus frequency moves the pattern to the left and, owing to the strong asymmetry in the pattern, displacement at the fiber's location would be reduced much more. To keep the fiber firing, the stimulus level would then have to be raised much more. The thresholds increase more rapidly on either side of the characteristic frequency than would be predicted from Békésy's measurements, but current studies indicate better agreement between mechanical and neural tuning. If all injury to the cochlea can be avoided and measurements are made down to low sound pressure levels, then "tuning" on the basilar membrane itself is about as sharp as in the eighth nerve (Khanna & Leonard, 1981; Sellick, Russell, Patuzzi, & Johnstone, 1981). Even so, Evans and Wilson (1973) have argued that the filtering is still not sharp enough to account for the eighth-nerve results. They postulate a "second filter" located somewhere between the basilar membrane and the dendrites of auditory nerve fibers. This second filter would provide the sharpening necessary to account for the neural measurements, but its identity remains unspecified.

By adding a second tone to a tone set at a fiber's characteristic frequency, Sachs and Kiang (1968) caused a reduction in the discharge rate of single fibers provided the added tone was at frequencies slightly above and slightly below the characteristic frequency. The level of the added tone had to be in the vicinity of the excitation threshold at those frequencies. Sachs and Kiang called this phenomenon two-tone inhibition, which implies a neural basis for the reduction in discharge rate. Others call it suppression (Hind, 1970). Legouix, Remond, and Greenbaum (1973) ascribe the suppression to mechanical events on the cochlear partition.

Tuning curves like those of the auditory nerve fibers have been measured in the cochlear nucleus (Galambos & Davis, 1943; Møller, 1969) and in the superior olive (Tsuchitani & Boudreau, 1967). In the cat, however, the tuning curves are sharper in the primary auditory nerve fibers than in the cochlear nucleus and in the superior olive (Møller, 1972).

2.4.3. Temporal Coding. Single fibers of the eighth nerve retain much of the temporal information in sinusoidal stimuli. Neural discharges are time-locked to individual cycles of a pure tone whose frequency does not exceed about 4,000 Hz (Kiang, 1965; Rose, Brugge, Anderson, & Hind, 1967). Almost all the action potentials elicited by a low-frequency pure tone occur during half of each cycle of the wave, which means that the neuron fires only when the stapes is either moving in or moving out. Kiang (1965) interprets his data as suggesting that it is the outward movement that elicits neural activity. During the half cycle of response, the number of neural spikes is far from uniform but increases to a peak that is in phase with the peak of the sine wave. Figure 14.21 is an example of the time locking of neural spikes measured in the squirrel monkey over one or two periods of single tones at 907 and 1,814 Hz (top left). When the stimulus is a complex sound such as a two-tone complex, the number of spikes varies over time as a function of the amplitude of the complex waveform (Brugge, Anderson, Hind, & Rose, 1969; Evans, 1978). Figure 14.21 gives examples of how the wave pattern changes as a function of the phase shift of one tone relative to the other and of how the number of spikes per unit time changes accordingly.

Some units of the cochlear nucleus of various species also show time locking. In the rat, Møller (1970) has recorded from units that show a precise relationship between nerve discharges and clicks, with one discharge per click up to repetition rates from 200 to 800 pulses per second depending on the unit. Unlike eighth-nerve fibers, these particular units of the cochlear nucleus have almost no temporal jitter, which suggests that they summate from a large number of primary fibers to achieve a spatial averaging (Møller, 1970). Such temporal precision is needed to account for sound localization based on interaural time differences in the microsecond range (see Scharf & Houtsma, Chapter 15, Section 3.2.12).

The superior olive also has units that show phase locking to a sinusoidal stimulus (Moushegian, Rupert, & Whitcomb, 1972). Temporal coding in units at more central stations of the auditory nervous system has not been reported to date.

2.4.4. Measured Neuroelectric Responses in Humans. Measures of single-unit responses in the human auditory nervous system have not been possible, but recent advances have facilitated measures of overall activity. Evoked potentials are measured at the scalp and can be analyzed to indicate the overall response at various levels in the auditory system down to the eighth nerve. Electrical responses in the cochlea are measured at the ear canal on one side or the other of the eardrum. Both types of measure are used in clinics to ascertain degree of hearing loss in patients such as infants and retardates for whom behavioral measures are difficult and unreliable. (See Hoke, Kauffmann, & Bappert, 1980.)

2.4.5. Neural Disorders. Disorders of the eighth nerve are due mainly to tumors. Disorders of more central neural structures have a variety of causes including tumors, hemorrhage, cerebral embolisms or thrombosis, multiple sclerosis, arteriosclerosis, birth injuries, wounds, skull fractures, and so forth (Dirks, 1978).

Auditory symptoms of eighth-nerve tumors vary greatly depending upon the site and size of the tumor. Usually thresholds for pure tones are close to normal, whereas intensity discrimination for continuous tones may be poor (Buus, Florentine, & Redden, 1982a). The latter effect may be related to the rapid and sizable tone decay often found in patients with an eighth-nerve tumor. The tone decay shows up as an inability to hear a soft, continuous tone for more than a few seconds without an increase in its level. Threshold for a continuous tone may increase as much as 60–70 dB within a few minutes, whereas for the same tone presented intermittently, threshold may be normal and remain so over sustained periods of listening. Speech discrimination is often poor, but loudness recruitment is absent. If done soon enough, surgical removal of the tumor, which is the usual treatment, may terminate the auditory deficits.

Disorders of the central auditory nervous system seldom lead to either elevated pure-tone thresholds or reduced speech discrimination, unless the speech is distorted by masking, fre-

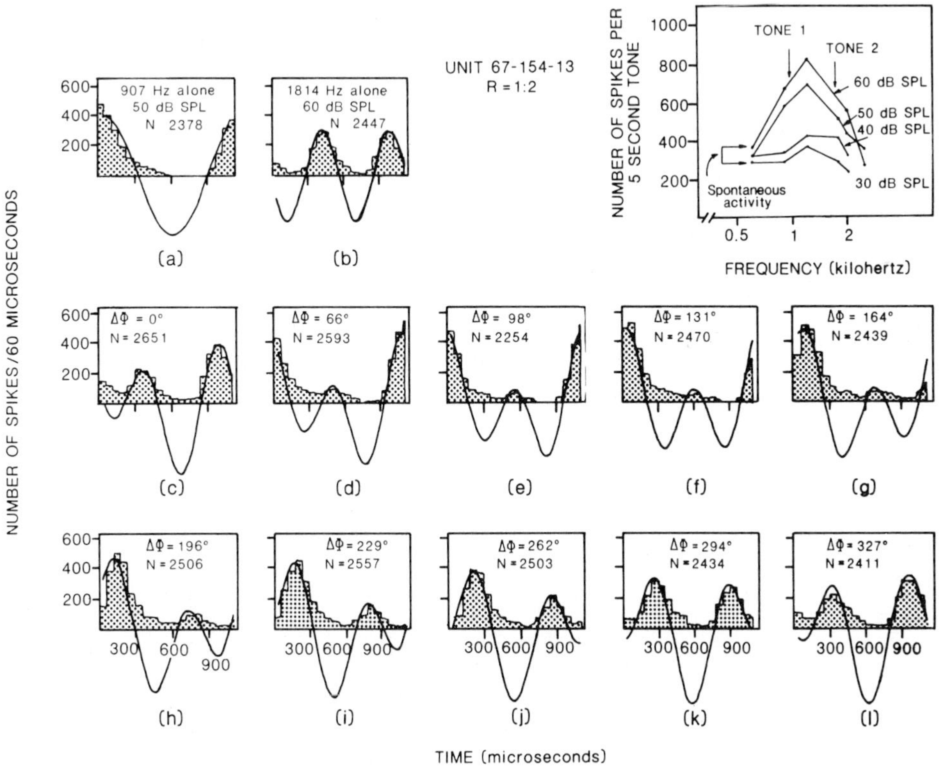

Figure 14.21. Temporal coding in the auditory nerve. Responses of a single fiber in the auditory nerve of a squirrel monkey were measured for a 907-Hz tone at 50 dB SPL, an 1,814-Hz tone at 60 dB SPL, and the two together with various phase relations. The number of neural spikes per unit time is plotted as a function of time. The wave forms of the single tones are shown with the responses in the top two panels. The wave forms of the two-tone complexes are shown in the rest of the panels. Both simple and complex tones give rise to discharge patterns that are closely tied to the temporal course of the signal. Thus, information about the temporal properties of a sound is often available in single units of the auditory nerve. (From J. F. Brugge, D. J. Anderson, J. E. Hind, & J. E. Rose, Time structure of discharges in single auditory nerve fibers of the squirrel monkey in response to complex periodic sounds, *Journal of Neurophysiology*, 1969, *32*. Reprinted with permission.)

quency changes, time compression, acceleration, or interruption (cf. Korsan-Bengtsen, 1973). In almost all cases, discrimination is poorer for speech presented to the ear contralateral to the lesion than to the ipsilateral ear, where discrimination may be entirely normal.

3. DETECTION

3.1. Thresholds in Quiet

3.1.1. Measurement Procedures. In this section, we describe briefly those psychophysical methods most often used to assess auditory threshold. Many different ways to present stimuli and gather judgments are available. In the two-interval, forced-choice procedure, the signal is presented in one of two successive time intervals, and the subject indicates which interval contained the signal. This method is commonly used in conjunction with *adaptive* procedures, which keep the signal near threshold by adjusting the level in accordance with the subject's previous responses. One example of an adaptive rule is that the signal level increases if the subject indicates the incorrect interval on a single trial and decreases if the subject designates the correct interval on two trials in a row. The threshold derived from this rule corresponds to the signal level at which the subject responded correctly nearly 71% of the time. [The value is 71% because the sequences of signals converge on the level at which the probability of the signal being decreased equals the probability of its being increased. Thus the probability of two correct responses in a row, which is the square of the probability of a single correct response, must be .5. It follows that the probability of being correct at "threshold" is $\sqrt{.5}$ or .707 (see Levitt, 1971, 1978.)] The value of 71% is close to the signal level for 75% correct responses calculated by interpolation in nonadaptive procedures using two intervals.

Auditory thresholds are also measured by the method of constant stimuli, in which the subject is presented a signal at varying levels in a single interval and reports whether it was heard. This yes-no procedure yields reliable data with highly trained listeners who have developed approximately the same consistent criterion.

Another procedure is the Békésy tracking method, which is popular both in the laboratory and in the clinic. The subject presses a switch to decrease signal level as long as the signal is heard and releases it to increase the level as soon as the signal is no longer heard. Continued over a few minutes, the procedure yields a zigzag pattern of increasing and decreasing signal levels. Figure 14.22 is an example of the results of tracking by a normally hearing young adult and by a patient with a hearing impairment. In this example, the frequency of the pure-tone signal increased gradually as the subject tracked the threshold. Threshold is usually taken as the average of the median values between successive valleys and peaks. This procedure is much quicker than the forced-choice procedures but has the disadvantage of depending upon the subject's criterion as to when the signal is heard and when it is not, which results in less reliable measurement.

The Békésy tracking procedure is often used in clinical assessments of hearing loss. With signal frequency increasing (or decreasing) while threshold is tracked by the patient the procedure can provide a threshold curve from 125 to 8,000 Hz in about 15 min, depending on the speed at which the frequency changes. Not only does it show the amount of hearing loss (threshold increase in decibels), but it also provides diagnostic information. For example, patients with a cochlear disorder often have excursions on the order of 1–2 dB at frequencies

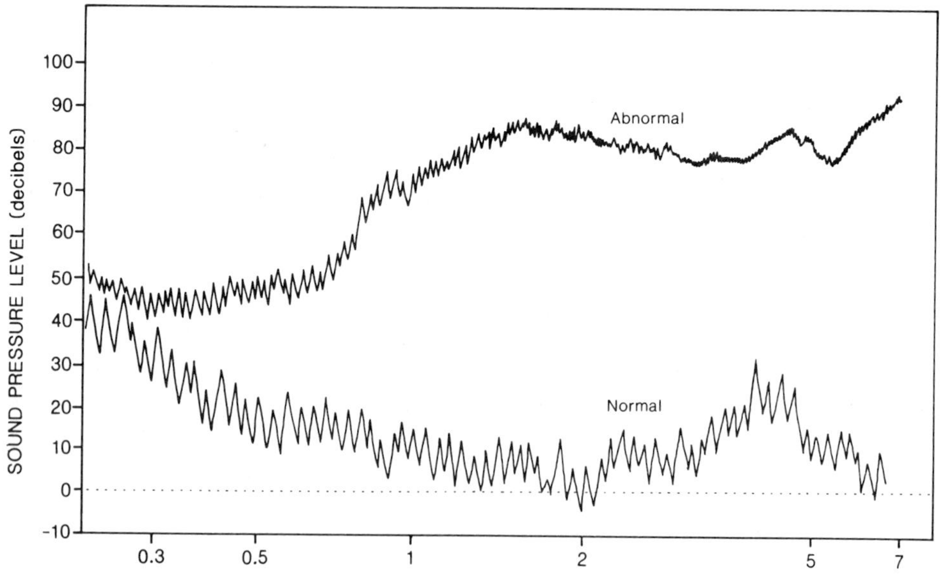

Figure 14.22. Two examples of monaural threshold curves obtained by the Békésy tracking method. The curves were generated by a normally hearing young adult and by a patient with a cochlear hearing impairment. As the frequency of the tone gradually increased, the subject alternately pressed a switch to increase the level until the tone was heard and then released the switch to decrease the level until the tone was not heard. Frequency increased about one octave every 2 min.; level changed at the rate of 2 dB·sec.$^{-1}$ The tracking procedure permits the rapid measurement of threshold over much of the audible frequency range. It also reveals the narrower excursions characteristic of cochlear disorders at higher frequencies. (From B. Scharf, Audition, in B. Scharf (Ed.), *Experimental sensory psychology*. Scott, Foresman & Co., 1975. Reprinted with permission.)

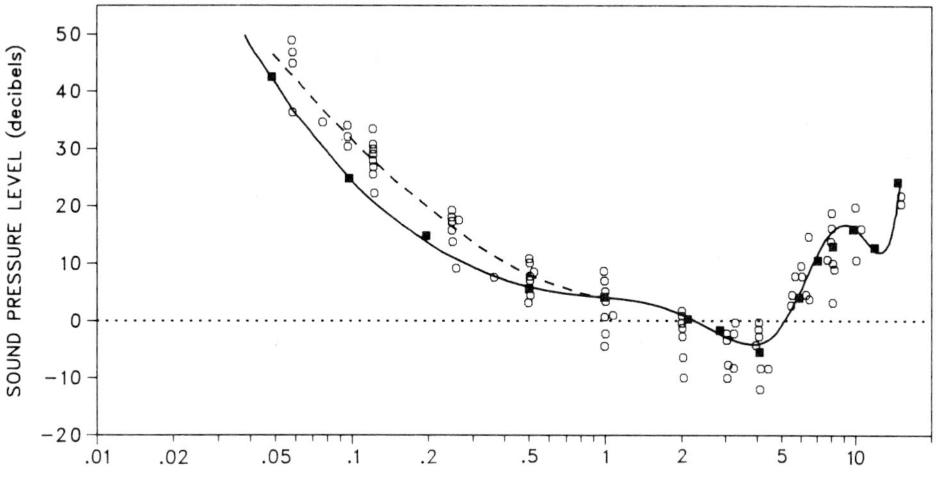

Figure 14.23. Threshold for pure tones in the free field. The SPL at threshold is plotted as a function of frequency. See Table 14.1 for tabulated values. Solid curve is the international standard (ISO, 1961) and was based largely on measurements on 51 people between 18 and 25 years old made by Robinson and Dadson (1956, filled squares). It is less regular at high than at low frequencies, owing to diffraction effects from the subject's body above 1,000 Hz. Data points are averages from nine studies, involving nearly 200 subjects, as compiled by Berger (1981). Dashed curve is the second-order polynomial,

$$\text{SPL} = 17.18 (\log_{10} f)^2 - 144.65 (\log_{10} f + 192.02)$$

where f is frequency in hertz. This curve fits the ensemble of data below 1,000 Hz better than does the ISO curve. Above 1,000 Hz, where it was visually adjusted to meet the ISO curve, the dashed curve is identical to the ISO curve. Despite some disagreements among studies, it is clear that the hearing of young adults is most sensitive between about 400 and 7,000 Hz, where the average does not exceed 10 dB SPL. (From E. H. Berger, Re-examination of the low-frequency (50-1,000 Hz) normal threshold of hearing in free and diffuse sound fields, *Journal of the Acoustical Society of America*, 1981, *70*. Reprinted with permission.)

above 2,000 Hz, compared to excursions of 5–10 dB for normal listeners. Figure 14.22 gives a typical example of a tracking curve in cochlear impairment.

Nonbehavioral methods are seldom used in the laboratory to measure threshold. In the clinic, however, measurements of evoked potentials from the scalp and from the cochlea (the cochleogram) have become increasingly frequent. Neither method is as easy or reliable as a behavioral measure with most patients, but when the patient is too young, too retarded, or too disturbed to understand instructions, such a nonbehavioral procedure is the only recourse. On the whole, neuroelectric thresholds are about 10 dB higher than behavioral thresholds (Pratt & Sohmer, 1978). Limiting the sensitivity of the neuroelectric measurements is the large amount of background electrical activity ("noise") in the nervous system.

3.1.2. Threshold Curves as a Function of Frequency. Auditory thresholds most often refer to the detection of sound, but thresholds for pain and for loudness discomfort caused by intense stimuli have also been measured. Section 1 of Chapter 15 by Scharf and Houtsma covers these topics.

Auditory threshold curves usually show the minimum SPL required to detect a pure tone in the quiet as a function of the tone's frequency. Measurements are made either in a free field (see Section 1.1) or under earphones. Because a free field is not usually available, most threshold measurements are made via earphones, which require only a sufficiently quiet environment (ANSI, 1977). Earphones are perfectly suited to comparisons among subjects as in audiometric testing. However, free-field tests are more natural because the ears are unrestricted and the sound is externally localized.

The solid curve in Figure 14.23 is the international standard (ISO, 1961) for absolute thresholds measured in the free field. The SPL at threshold is plotted as a function of frequency. The data on which the ISO curve is based are represented by the filled squares and were obtained by D. W. Robinson and Dadson (1956). Table 14.1 tabulates the ISO values in the column marked minimum audible field (MAF), with standard deviations reported by Robinson and Dadson. Robinson and Dadson made their measurements in an anechoic room with the subject facing the loudspeaker. The ISO MAF values are the means for 51 subjects aged from 18 to 25 years. A method of limits was used with repetition at a level in the neighborhood of the minimum audible level. The other data points in Figure 14.23 are from Berger's (1981) analysis of nine different studies. The dashed line represents a second-order polynomial fitted to the data and set to meet the ISO curve at 1,000 Hz. Berger concludes from all the data that the dashed curve [which is close to that proposed by Killion (1978)] represents the free-field threshold better than does the ISO standard. Indeed, except for the data of Robinson and Dadson (1956) most of the low-frequency data fall fairly close to the dashed curve. Later measurements in the same anechoic room by Robinson and his colleagues (Whittle, Collins, & Robinson, 1972) yielded a threshold value at 50 Hz close to the dashed curve. Comparing their data to those of Robinson and Dadson, Whittle et al. ascribe their higher thresholds at 50 Hz to the use of a Békésy tracking procedure in place of the method of limits and to less practice by the subjects. At frequencies above 500 Hz, the ISO standard seems to provide a reasonable fit to all of the data. The variability among the studies is due to procedural, calibration, and subject differences.

Table 14.1. Threshold Values in Free Field (MAF) and under Earphone Listening (MAP)

Frequency (Hz)	Sound Pressure Level (dB)			
	ISO Minimum Audible Field (Standard Deviation)[a]	Modified MAF[b]	ISO (W.E. 705-A) Minimum Audible Pressure (Standard Deviation)[c]	ISO (TDH-39)[d]
50	41.7 (6.0)	43.5	— —	—
120/125	21.4 (5.0)	28.5	45.5 (5.6)	45.0
250	11.2 (4.5)	17.5	24.5 (5.0)	25.5
500	6.0 (4.5)	8.0	11.0 (5.4)	11.5
1,000	4.2 (4.5)	4.2	6.5 (5.4)	7.0
2,000	1.0 (5.0)	1.0	8.5 (5.9)	9.0
4,000	−3.9 (8.0)	−3.9	9.0 (7.6)	9.5
6,000	4.6 (8.5)	4.6	8.0 (7.4)	15.5
8,000	15.3 (8.5)	15.3	9.5 (9.9)	13.0
10,000	16.4 —	16.4	— —	—
12,000	12.0 —	12.0	— —	—
15,000	24.1 —	24.1	— —	—

[a] From the international standard (ISO, 1961), based primarily on threshold data of Robinson and Dadson (1956), whose Tables 1 and 2 provided the standard deviations.
[b] From Berger's (1981) fitted curve as shown in Figure 14.23.
[c] From the international standard (ISO, 1975), also in the USA standard (ANSI, 1969); these values are for the Western Electric 705-A earphone mounted in a MX-41/AR cushion and calibrated on a National Bureau of Standards 9-A coupler. The standard deviations, from Weissler's (1968) Table VIII, are associated with the original threshold determinations.
[d] MAP values for the Telephonics TDH-39 earphone mounted in the MX-41/AR cushion. (On the basis of new measurements and a review of the literature, Robinson et al., 1981, suggest that the MAP values for the TDH-39 phone are 2.0–2.5 dB too high at 500 and 4000 Hz.)

Within the individual studies, differences among listeners is the primary source of variability.

Although thresholds are most often measured under earphone listening, few extensive and systematic studies are available. Figure 14.24 presents the international standard (ISO, 1975) threshold values for the minimum audible pressure (MAP), which are also given in Table 14.1. The precise threshold values depend upon the type of earphone used in the measurements and on the artificial ear used to calibrate the earphone. Figure 14.24 gives threshold values for the Western Electric 705-A earphone calibrated on a National Bureau of Standards type 9-A coupler. Table 14.1 gives these same threshold values as well as those for the TDH-39 earphone. Other earphones give slightly different values, especially at higher frequencies.

The dashed curve, marked MAF, is Berger's (1981) proposed curve for the minimum audible field as shown in Figure 14.23. The free-field curve lies below the earphone curve for several reasons. First, free-field listening is binaural whereas earphone listening is monaural, and the binaural threshold is about 3 dB lower than the monaural (Section 3.1.6). Second, at many frequencies, diffraction by the body, head, and pinnae augments the SPL at the ear-canal entrance as compared to the SPL measured with the listener absent; it is the latter SPL that is given as the minimum audible pressure (see Section 2.1.1). Third, low-frequency noise under the earphone may raise the threshold at frequencies below 500 Hz by about 6 dB (Anderson & Whittle, 1971; Killion, 1978).

Values for the MAP in Table 14.1 extend only to 8,000 Hz because earphone calibration at higher frequencies is uncertain. Recent attempts to overcome this problem show that for teenagers and young adults, threshold at first slowly rises, by 6–8 dB, as frequency goes from 8,000 to 14,000 Hz and then jumps another 12–14 dB between 14,000 and 16,000 Hz (Stelmachowicz, Gorga, & Cullen, 1982; see also Fausti, Frey, Erickson, Rappaport, Cleary, & Brummett, 1979).

All the data in Figures 14.23 and 14.24 are based on measurements at frequencies fairly far apart, often an octave apart. Measurements at intervals of 10–20 Hz reveal surprisingly large threshold changes over small frequency intervals. For example, one subject's threshold went down 15 dB when signal frequency was increased from 1,450 to 1,490 Hz (Cohen, 1982). Other data, gathered at frequencies where a subject was expected to have low and high thresholds on the basis of low-level loudness judgments, are shown in Figure 14.25. Measurements on two subjects over a period of two weeks show both how large and how stable are the threshold shifts between frequencies. The cause of these shifts is unknown.

Detection of pure tones has also been measured under water, notably by Brandt and Hollien (1967). On the same subjects, thresholds were measured for tones presented under water from a specially built loudspeaker and in air via earphones. Table 14.2 presents the mean thresholds at seven frequencies for eight subjects in water at a depth of 10.5 m and in air. Low-frequency fan noise in the room where the air tests were made raised low-frequency thresholds, so that the differences between air and water thresholds in Table 14.2 probably should be 10–15 dB larger at frequencies of 1,000 Hz and below.

On the basis of various findings, Hollien and Feinstein (1975) concluded that underwater thresholds depend predominantly on bone-conducted sound. For example, Hollien and Brandt (1969) showed that thresholds under water were the same whether the ear canal was filled with water or had an air bubble trapped against the tympanic membrane.

Sounds are harder to hear under water than in air for one or all of the following reasons: (1) energy transfer across the eardrum is poorer under water owing to the impedance mismatch

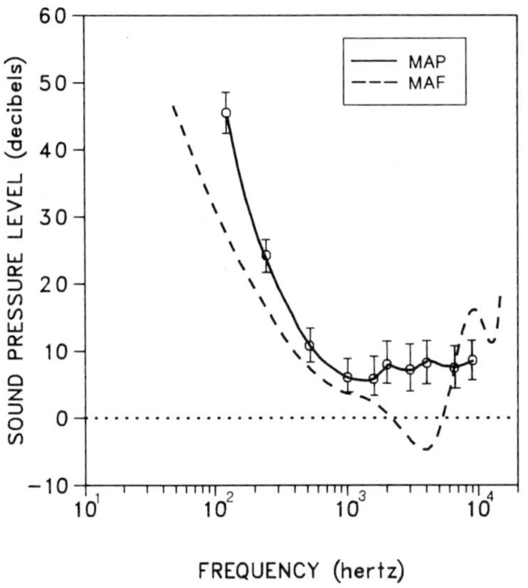

Figure 14.24. Thresholds for earphone listening (MAP). The SPL at threshold for monaural listening through an earphone is plotted as a function of frequency. The solid line is from the international standard (ISO R389, 1975) for the United States earphone-coupler combination (WE 705A earphone type and NBS 9-A coupler) as reported by Weissler (1968). Vertical lines are plus and minus one standard deviation which is the average of the standard deviations of four studies as summarized by Weissler (1968, column 4 of Table VIII). The dashed line is from Figure 14.23 and is the modified threshold curve measured in the free field. Although higher than the MAF, the MAP is approximately the same function of frequency, with the greatest differences at higher frequencies where diffraction effects are important. At most frequencies the MAP is higher than the MAF because only one ear was stimulated instead of two, because of noise under the earphone at lower frequencies, and because of diffraction in the free field by the subject's torso, head, and pinnae at higher frequencies. (Adapted from Berger, 1981.)

at the eardrum; (2) hearing under water is mainly by bone conduction, which is much less efficient than by air conduction; and (3) mass loading of the eardrum and middle ear by the water reduces energy transfer to the cochlea.

3.1.3. Physiological Basis of the Threshold Curve. The average thresholds shown in Figure 14.23 would be some 30 dB lower if only noise due to the Brownian motion of the air molecules set the lower limit to our hearing (Green, 1976). A tone must be about 20 dB above the spectrum level of a noise to be detected, but by Green's calculations, our lowest threshold (in the vicinity of 3,000 Hz) is 50 dB above the spectrum level of Brownian motion. Accordingly, factors other than the Brownian motion of air particles must limit our sensitivity. One factor is internal noise generated by blood flow in the vicinity of the cochlea.

Although the limiting factors cannot be clearly identified, the way in which threshold depends on frequency can be closely tied to physiological events, mainly in the transmission path of the ear. Section 2 includes several curves showing how the stimulus amplitude changes as a function of frequency as a sound wave progresses through the peripheral auditory system. Figure 14.11 shows how the SPL, initially measured in the free field with the listener absent, changes when the listener is introduced into the sound field and the level is measured at the entrance to the ear canal. This curve accounts for part of the difference between free-field (MAF) and earphone (MAP) thresholds at high frequencies, as seen in Figure 14.24. Figure 14.12 shows how the resonances of the ear canal further change the SPL measured at the eardrum. Figure 14.15 shows the frequency-dependent changes imposed by the ossicular chain. Finally, Figure 14.18 shows how the maximum amplitude of the traveling wave on the basilar membrane increases with the frequency of a pure-tone stimulus. Zwislocki (1965) took all these effects into account to predict the *form* of the free-field threshold curve. His predicted curve and the curve of Figure 14.23 are shown in Figure 14.26, where they are arbitrarily assigned the same value at 1,000 Hz. Threshold improves somewhat more with increasing frequency than predicted. Zwislocki suggests that this difference can largely be accounted for by assuming that there is temporal integration and that neural activity follows the individual cycles of a sine wave, giving an advantage to higher frequencies. Every time frequency is doubled, the effective intensity is doubled or increased by 3 dB. Indeed, the discrepancy

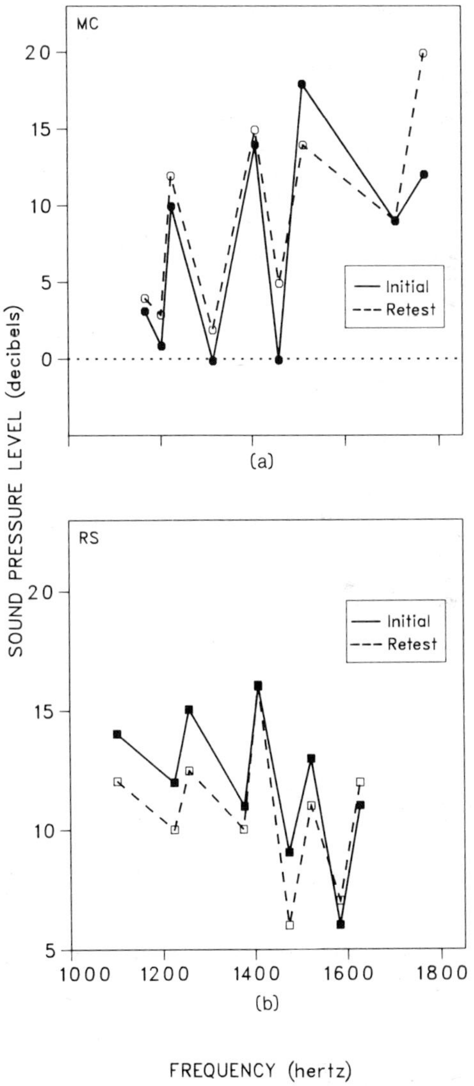

Figure 14.25. Fine structure of the threshold curve. The SPL at threshold is plotted as a function of frequency for subject MC at the top and for subject RS at the bottom. Thresholds were measured monaurally by an adaptive two-interval forced-choice procedure. Each point is based on 240 trials. Signals were 250-msec tone bursts separated by 400-msec silent intervals; linear rise-fall times were 25 msec. Retests indicated by dashed lines were conducted 2 weeks after the initial measurements, which are indicated by solid lines. Data show that large shifts in the absolute threshold may occur over frequency ranges as small as 50 Hz, and that these shifts are stable over at least a 2-week period. (Adapted from Cohen, 1982.)

Table 14.2. Mean SPL at Threshold under Water and in Air

Frequency (Hz)	Pure-Tone Threshold[a] (dB) Under Water[b]	In Air[b]	Difference (Water Minus Air)[c]
125	70 (4.4)	52 (3.1)	18
250	64 (6.9)	44 (4.2)	20
500	58 (3.0)	30 (5.6)	28
1,000	60 (6.5)	27 (5.1)	33
2,000	66 (8.5)	17 (6.1)	49
4,000	67 (9.8)	31 (11.2)	36
8,000	74 (4.1)	18 (8.2)	56

[a] The mean SPL is given for frequencies spaced an octave apart. Measurements were made first via a pair of earphones in a quiet room above water, and then under water with the diver wearing a wet suit and scuba equipment. A Békésy tracking procedure was used. Tones were 500 msec with a rise-fall time of 2.5 msec and were repeated every second. Eight subjects served, five men and three women, ranging in age from 25 to 40 years with a mean of 29.2 years. Underwater thresholds shown were measured 10.5 m below the surface of the water; thresholds were the same at 3.6 m.
[b] Standard deviations are in parentheses.
[c] Differences between air and underwater thresholds at low frequencies should be larger than shown because the air thresholds at low frequencies were artifactually elevated by fan noise in the room. Adding 10–15 dB to the listed difference at 1,000 Hz and below would reduce the dependence on frequency of the air-water difference. The higher underwater thresholds are ascribed to poor energy transfer across the middle ear with the result that most of the acoustic energy is transmitted through the bones of the head. (J. F. Brandt and H. Hollien, Underwater hearing thresholds in man, *Journal of the Acoustical Society of America*, 1967, *42*. Reprinted with permission.)

in Figure 14.26 is roughly 3 dB·octave^{-1}. So by assuming temporal integration, Zwislocki was able to bring the two curves into close alignment.

This analysis points out the critical role of the mechanical properties of the ear's sound transmission system in determining the form of the threshold curve. Such a conclusion is fully in accord with the observation that hair cells appear to be uniform in anatomy, orientation, and density along most of the basilar membrane. Thus hair cells serving middle frequencies, to which we are most sensitive, are probably no better able to respond to stimulation than are hair cells serving other frequencies. Sensitivity depends not on which hair cells are excited but on how much they are excited, which is directly related to the amplitude of displacement of the basilar membrane. At a given SPL, a sound at a middle frequency results in greatest displacement of the basilar membrane because those frequencies are transmitted more efficiently through the peripheral auditory system than are lower and higher frequencies.

3.1.4. Temporal Summation. The duration of the signals used in the measurements shown in Figures 14.23 and 14.24 was of the order of 1 sec. Signals much shorter in duration must be set to higher levels to be detected. The general rule is that as duration decreases from approximately 200 msec, the threshold increases. At durations longer than 200 msec, threshold remains constant. Figure 14.27 shows data from several studies in which threshold for a 1,000-Hz tone was measured as a function of duration. At durations shorter than about 200 msec, signal intensity must be doubled every time duration is halved so that energy remains constant at threshold. However, this finding cannot be interpreted as showing energy summation in the auditory system which has no mechanism for storing acoustic energy. Rather, as Zwislocki (1960) has argued, temporal summation must take place in the auditory nervous system, probably at some level beyond the cochlea.

Temporal summation also extends over silent intervals so that two tone bursts separated by up to 100 msec are easier to detect than either burst alone. The advantage is about 3 dB, which means that at threshold each of the two bursts is half as intense as it would be if presented alone or if the two were separated by long intervals (Zwislocki, 1960). Although they are generally similar, the functions relating threshold intensity to stimulus duration may vary somewhat with such stimulus variables as frequency, bandwidth, and background noise level.

Stimulus duration affects detection at long time intervals as well. A tone that remains on beyond 10 or 20 sec at a level a few dB above threshold usually becomes inaudible after 30 sec or so (Scharf, 1983). However, it is unclear whether this inaudibility is the same as nondetectability. When the tone is turned off, the listener often reports hearing a change. If the sound is turned off and then on again, the subject easily hears the tone come on even though it had seemed inaudible at the same level a moment before. Whether or not threshold increases with duration, the subjective quality of a continuous sound at or near threshold does change over time, and the sound often seems to become inaudible (see Section 1.2.4.2 of Chapter 15).

3.1.5. Bandwidth. Two tones separated in frequency are easier to detect than either one alone, provided their separation is not too large. The implication is that the auditory system summates signals close in frequency but not those far apart in frequency. Just what is close and what is far? The answer is somewhat unclear with respect to two-tone thresholds, because the data from several studies are equivocal (e.g., Green, 1958;

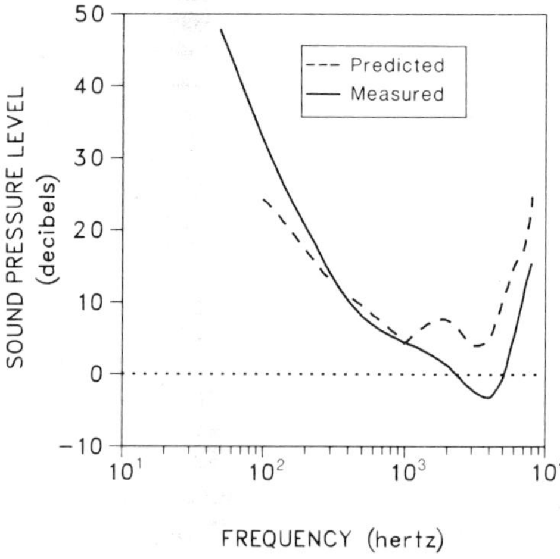

Figure 14.26. Predicted versus measured free-field threshold curves. The measured curve is the modified ISO curve shown in Figure 14.23. The predicted curve is based on measured and calculated transformations in the sound pressure of sounds from the free field through the outer and middle ear to the basilar membrane. The predicted curve is arbitrarily equated to the measured curve at 1,000 Hz. The obtained threshold decreases more rapidly as a function of frequency than predicted but otherwise the two curves have the same general form. Differences can be largely accounted for by temporal summation in the auditory nervous system. (From J. J. Zwislocki, Analysis of some auditory characteristics, in R. D. Luce, R. R. Bush, & E. Galanter (Eds.), *Handbook of mathematical psychology*, Vol. 3. Copyright 1965, R. Duncan Luce. Reprinted with permission of John Wiley & Sons, Inc.)

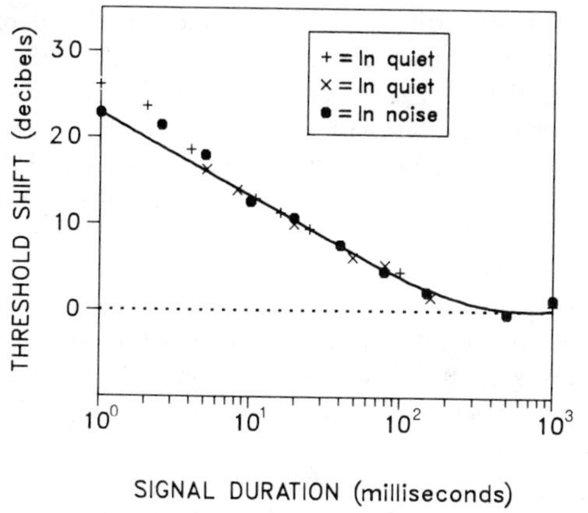

Figure 14.27. Threshold as a function of signal duration. The threshold for 1,000-Hz tone bursts set at the durations given on the abscissa was measured in the quiet in two studies (pluses from Garner, 1947, and crosses from unpublished data of Zwislocki & Pirodda as reported by Zwislocki, 1965) and against a background of white noise in one study (circles from Feldtkeller & Oetinger, 1956). The shift in threshold from its value at long durations is plotted as a function of the tone's duration. The data from the three studies fall close to the solid line, which assumes that the following equation relates threshold shift to duration:

$$10 \log \frac{I}{I_0} = 10 \log \frac{1}{1 - e^{-st}}$$

where I_0 is the asymptotic threshold at long signal durations, t (in seconds). Departure from the calculated line at durations shorter than 10 msec may be caused by the spread of signal energy outside a single critical band. Once outside the critical band, the energy contributes little to detection. As a result, intensity would have to be increased to compensate not only for the briefer duration but also for the greater spread of energy over frequency. The data and calculations show that threshold intensity decreases with increasing duration, following an exponential function such that threshold energy is nearly constant at durations shorter than about 100 msec. Beyond 200 msec there is little further decrease in threshold with duration. (From J. J. Zwislocki, Analysis of some auditory characteristics, in R. D. Luce, R. R. Bush, & E. Galanter (Eds.), *Handbook of mathematical psychology*, Vol. 3. Copyright 1965, R. Duncan Luce. Reprinted with permission of John Wiley & Sons, Inc.)

Marill, 1956; van den Brink, 1964.) One reason for this lack of clarity is that the threshold advantage of two tones over one is, at most, 3 dB. However, when many tones or bands of noise of varying bandwidth were examined by Gässler (1954), the result was clear.

Gässler measured the threshold for a multitone complex as a function of the number of components. Because each component tone was 10 or 20 Hz from its neighbor, the number of components and the overall spacing varied together. As the number of tones increased from 1 to 40, the overall SPL remained constant at threshold until the overall spacing exceeded a particular value, the critical band. Results were the same for thresholds both in the quiet and against a background noise. Typical results, at a center frequency of 1,000 Hz, are shown in Figure 14.28. To keep the overall level constant as tones were added, the level of each tone was decreased. Gässler was careful to use subjects who had flat threshold curves in the frequency range tested with no large changes in the fine structure. In any case, in a background noise, such irregularities would have little influence on the masked threshold. Gässler reported similar results at various center frequencies and for bands of white noise. The results show that the total energy necessary for a sound to be heard remains constant as long as the energy is confined to a single critical band. The total energy must be increased if spread over more than one critical band. (Section 3.2.1.2 reviews the critical band in more detail.)

3.1.6. Binaural Summation. Binaural thresholds are about 3 dB lower than monaural thresholds; Chocholle (1954) showed convincingly that this advantage cannot be interpreted as purely statistical. The advantage does not come about because a listener has a greater chance of detecting a sound to two ears if each ear acts independently of the other. He measured the psychometric function for both monaural and binaural inputs. As Figure 14.29 shows, the entire binaural psychometric function is shifted by 3 dB; if statistical summation was the reason for the threshold shift (measured at the 50% point), then the listener could not have reached 100% detection until at least one ear was at 100%. Instead, the listener was at 100% for the binaural input at a

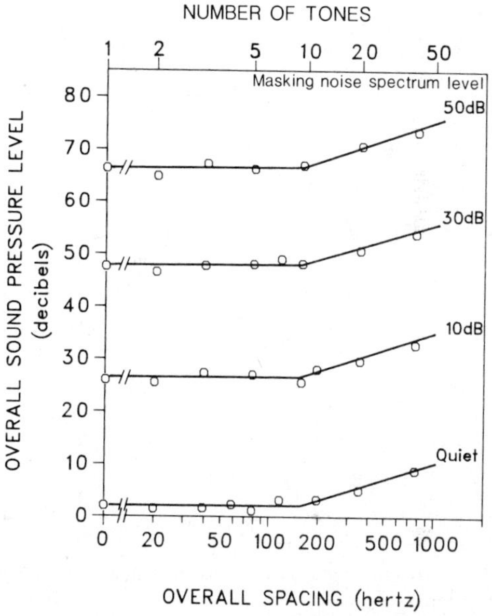

Figure 14.28. Dependence of the threshold for a multitone complex on the overall bandwidth (or frequency spacing). The SPL at threshold of the complex is plotted as a function of the frequency separation between the lowest and the highest component tones. Overall spacing was varied by adding single tones which were 20 Hz apart and at equal intensity to the complex; phase relations were random. A Békésy tracking procedure lasting about 1 min was used for each threshold measurement. Each point is based on one or two measurements, all on the same subject who listened monaurally. The single tone was originally set at 1,100 Hz and other tones were added at lower frequencies. Measurements were made in the quiet and also against a uniform masking noise whose spectrum level is the parameter on the curves. (A uniform masking noise is a white noise whose level decreases 3 dB·octave^{-1} above 1,000 Hz, raising the threshold for all audible frequencies to the same level.) Horizontal lines are drawn through the data points at the level of the single tone (overall frequency spacing = 0 Hz) and diagonal lines are drawn through data points beyond the critical band with a slope of 3 dB·octave$_{-1}$. These lines give an excellent account of the data both in the quiet and under masking and show that the threshold for a multitone complex is constant so long as all energy is within a single critical band. Energy outside the critical band does not contribute to threshold. Accordingly, threshold depends on the overall level of those components within the same critical band. To keep that level at its threshold value, the level of the whole complex must be increased once tones outside the critical band are added to the complex. (From B. Scharf, Critical bands, in J. V. Tobias (Ed.), *Foundations of modern auditory theory*, Academic Press, Inc., 1970. Reprinted with permission.)

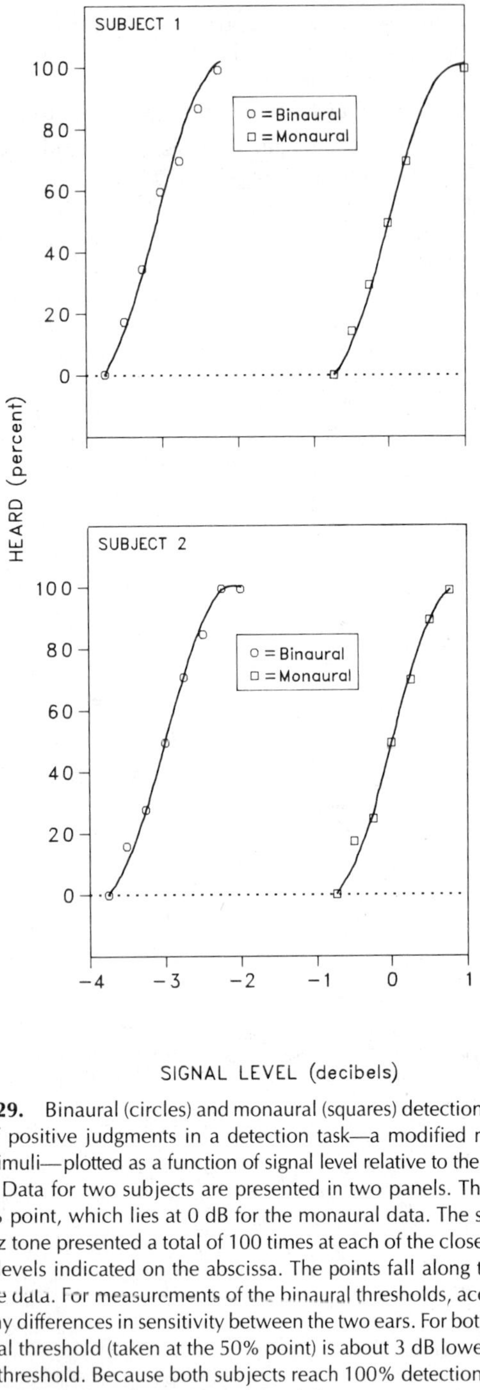

Figure 14.29. Binaural (circles) and monaural (squares) detection. The percentage of positive judgments in a detection task—a modified method of constant stimuli—plotted as a function of signal level relative to the monaural threshold. Data for two subjects are presented in two panels. Threshold is at the 50% point, which lies at 0 dB for the monaural data. The signal was a 1,000-Hz tone presented a total of 100 times at each of the closely spaced (0.25 dB) levels indicated on the abscissa. The points fall along the ogives fitted to the data. For measurements of the binaural thresholds, account was taken of any differences in sensitivity between the two ears. For both subjects the binaural threshold (taken at the 50% point) is about 3 dB lower than the monaural threshold. Because both subjects reach 100% detection at a level more than 1 dB below that monaural level that was never detected, the binaural threshold must depend on summation between the ears and not on statistically dependent summation. (From R. Chocholle, Etude statistique des seuils auditifs monauraux et binauraux; interprétation des résultats, *Acustica*, 1954, *4*. Reprinted with permission.)

level that yielded only 0% detection for the monaural input. Thus we may conclude that the binaural advantage results from true sensory summation. This conclusion is buttressed by the finding of binaural loudness summation, as discussed in Chapter 15.

3.1.7. Dependence of Threshold on Age and Sex. Hearing deteriorates with age, less so for women than for men. Many investigations have shown this to be true for large numbers of people. D. W. Robinson and Sutton (1979) review and summarize eight of those studies. (See also Møller, 1983.) Typical of the kind of data obtained are those of Hinchcliffe (1959), who randomly sampled 400 persons from a rural population of 9,000. After rejecting ears for which any sort of otological abnormality was suspected, the investigator tested a total of 645 clinically normal ears on men and women between 18 and 74 years old. Table 14.3 gives the medians (boldface type) and the 25th and 75th percentiles of the hearing levels relative to the thresholds of the youngest age group at the corresponding frequency. Single scores in a column mean that the men and women did not differ significantly at that frequency and age. Where they did differ, the women's scores are given first and the men's second. The median curves are shown in Figure 14.30. Hearing loss in decibels is plotted as a function of age in years with frequency in hertz as the parameter. At all frequencies, threshold increases (hearing loss increases) continuously as a function of age from young adulthood, but the loss is greatest at frequencies above 2,000 Hz, and is particularly striking at 12,000 Hz.

With respect to sex, Table 14.3 shows that at frequencies from 3,000 to 6,000 Hz, women of all ages had lower thresholds than men. Other studies (e.g., Corso, 1963) suggest that women have better thresholds at all ages and frequencies, and that their advantage increases with both age and frequency.

Increasing exposure to noise with age is considered one of the reasons for the deterioration of hearing. This factor accounts for part of the sex difference because men traditionally had been more likely to be exposed to noise than women. The relative role of other age-associated environmental factors such as diet and stress is unknown. Nevertheless, the reduced hearing sensitivity with advancing age is called *presbycusis*, a term that suggests that it is a normal part of the aging process. Kryter (1983) supports that view and suggests that the term *sociocusis* be used to refer to hearing loss induced by the noise of everyday living. *Nosocusis* would then refer to hearing losses caused by pathogenic conditions including high-level workplace noise.

Whatever the cause, thresholds increase steadily from about age 20, whereas they do not deteriorate during early years. In fact, children generally have higher thresholds than adults. Yoneshige and Elliott (1981) showed that adults are more sensitive even when such factors as middle-ear disorders, differences in ear-canal sound pressure, and possible procedural difficulties are taken into account.

3.2. Thresholds in Noise

One sound, usually referred to as a masker, may raise the threshold for another sound, the signal. The elevated threshold is called the *masked threshold*. The amount of *masking* is the difference between the masked threshold and the threshold in quiet. The amount of masking depends upon the masker's level, bandwidth, and frequency content relative to the signal. The temporal relations between masker and signal also play a role. Masking is simultaneous when noise and signal occur at the same time and is nonsimultaneous when they occur at different times.

3.2.1. Simultaneous Masking

3.2.1.1. ***Broad-Band Noise.*** The ability to detect a pure tone in a wide-band noise such as white noise tells us much about the analytical properties of the auditory system. Possibly the most comprehensive study of pure-tone masking by white noise was carried out by Hawkins and Stevens (1950). They measured the monaural thresholds of four male subjects at 15

Table 14.3. Threshold as a Function of Subject's Age and Stimulus Frequency

	Threshold (dB) re Youngest Age Group					
Frequency (Hz)	Age 8–24 (176)	Age 25–34 (104)	Age 35–44 (93)	Age 45–54 (104)	Age 55–64 (74)	Age 65–74 (94)
	4.3	5.5	6.1	9.5	13.1	17.1
125	**0.0**	**1.7**	**2.6**	**4.8**	**8.7**	**10.1**
	−3.9	−2.1	−1.1	1.8	4.6	6.0
	2.9	5.3	5.6	7.6	11.6	16.4
250	**0.0**	**1.0**	**1.7**	**3.2**	**6.5**	**9.6**
	−3.4	−2.8	−1.5	0.1	2.3	4.5
	4.0	4.1	5.7	8.7	12.8	20.8
500	**0.0**	**0.7**	**1.7**	**3.9**	**7.0**	**9.7**
	−2.7	−2.4	−2.0	0.4	2.4	4.8
	3.7	4.1	6.4	9.5	10.0	24.7
1000	**0.0**	**1.0**	**1.7**	**4.7**	**5.6**	**12.8**
	−3.6	−2.4	−2.1	0.8	1.3	5.2
	4.6	4.8	6.9	10.9	14.9 17.9	26.6 41.1
2000	**0.0**	**0.4**	**2.5**	**5.5**	**8.7 12.1**	**14.6 25.1**
	−4.2	−3.5	−0.5	1.2	4.6 5.7	9.4 15.6
	4.6 8.0	6.9 11.1	10.3 16.5	18.2 29.4	20.2 45.3	40.6 53.1
3000	**0.0 2.1**	**1.5 5.8**	**5.5 8.6**	**9.9 18.2**	**14.8 31.5**	**19.8 40.9**
	−4.0 −0.9	−2.8 1.1	0.4 3.7	4.8 6.3	8.8 18.7	10.1 30.7
	4.3 10.2	8.5 12.9	10.0 19.8	18.9 45.3	26.3 59.6	45.6 59.6
4000	**0.0 3.5**	**3.8 7.5**	**5.3 12.6**	**13.2 22.2**	**19.4 37.8**	**22.2 45.5**
	−4.3 −1.6	−0.2 2.4	1.7 5.4	6.6 12.4	8.7 30.7	12.1 29.9
	5.8 9.6	8.8 12.9	13.6 20.9	22.4 36.7	28.7 59.7	47.2 66.5
6000	**0.0 2.5**	**3.6 5.3**	**6.2 12.4**	**11.2 23.1**	**22.3 49.5**	**33.9 50.9**
	−6.6 −2.6	0.5 −1.2	0.6 5.9	3.5 14.0	11.3 30.6	17.4 34.9
	5.6	9.6	15.7	28.4 45.1	39.7 67.8	52.2 68.5
8000	**0.0**	**3.3**	**7.2**	**8.2 20.7**	**24.7 53.5**	**42.2 57.2**
	−6.3	−5.4	−2.3	2.6 10.7	11.0 30.1	32.2 48.7
	9.2	17.6	28.5	58.0	70.0	70.0
12000	**0.0**	**5.2**	**14.4**	**41.7**	**64.2**	**70.0**
	−6.6	−4.0	3.9	19.0	54.2	63.1

Note: Relative threshold for different age groups at frequencies from 125 to 12,000 Hz. The boldface value in each triplet is the median value; the bottom value is the 25th percentile and the top value is the 75th percentile. Thresholds were measured by a method of limits on a total of 645 ears, 326 male and 319 female. The number of ears within each age group is given in parentheses. From a rural population of 9,000, 400 persons were chosen at random. Only clinically normal ears were included in the survey. Monaural thresholds are given relative to the threshold of the youngest age group at a given frequency. Accordingly, the median is always 0 dB in the first column. Where two sets of triplets appear together, the set on the left is for women and that on the right for men. In all these cases the men had significantly higher thresholds than the women. Where only one set is given, male and female thresholds did not differ significantly and were combined. Threshold increases with age, more so at high frequencies than at low, and more rapidly after 45–54 years. Above 1,000 Hz, males usually have higher thresholds than women in most age groups. These trends are more clearly seen in Figure 14.30. (From R. Hinchcliffe, The threshold of hearing as a function of age, *Acustica*, 1959, *9*. Reprinted with permission.)

different frequencies against eight levels of noise (see Fig. 14.31). The SPL at threshold is plotted as a function of the frequency of the pure-tone signal. The parameter on the curves is the spectrum level (SPL per cycle) of the masking noise. Owing to the response characteristics of the PDR-10 earphone used, the bandwidth of the white noise did not go much beyond 9,000 Hz. The subject heard the sounds through a single earphone mounted in a sponge neoprene cushion; he adjusted the level of the continuous tone so that it "could just be recognized as having a definite pitch" (p. 6). The subject was able to interrupt the tone as desired by means of a mercury switch. The bottom curve is for thresholds measured in the quiet.

Smooth lines drawn through the data represent them well except at the high frequencies. The plotted SPLs were measured in a 6-cm^3 coupler, and those values differ from the levels generated in the ear canal at frequencies above 6,000 Hz, as Hawkins and Stevens (1950) showed. Thus the aberrant points would fall close to the smooth curves if the pressure in the ear canal were plotted. The most striking feature of these curves is that they are parallel to each other and equidistant except near the threshold in quiet. Accordingly, at all the measured frequencies, increasing the level of a wide-band masking noise raises the threshold for a pure tone by the same number of decibels across all frequencies. For example, when the spectrum level goes up 10 dB, a tone's threshold goes up 10 dB. While parallel, these curves are not entirely flat but increase slowly with frequency from about 400 Hz; between 100 and 400 Hz the curves decrease somewhat. The conclusion to be drawn is that, except below

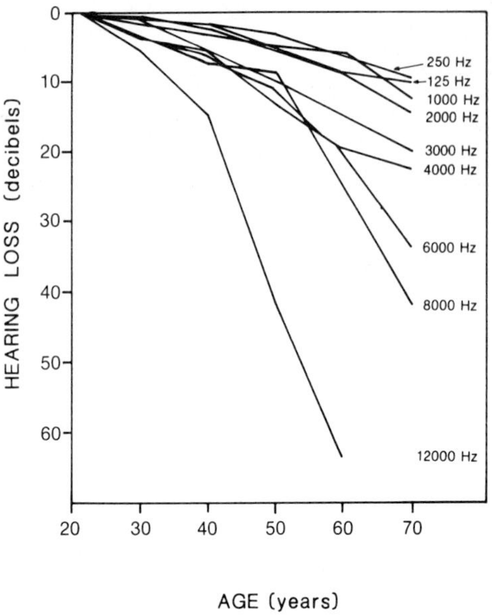

Figure 14.30. Hearing loss as a function of age. Hearing losses are given relative to the median threshold in the youngest age group, 18–24. The median values in Table 14.3 for women and men or women alone (where women have significantly lower thresholds) are plotted as a function of age. At all frequencies, hearing loss increases with age, but in this rural population of nearly 400 persons, the average loss is not greater than 20 dB until frequency is at least 4,000 Hz. At the higher frequencies the increase in hearing loss, that is, in threshold, is especially rapid after 40–50 years of age. (From R. Hinchcliffe, The threshold of hearing as a function of age, *Acustica*, 1959, 9. Reprinted with permission.)

400 Hz, tones become harder to detect in noise as their frequency increases. Had their noise been perfectly flat, Hawkins and Stevens calculated that the threshold would have increased between 10 and 11 dB from 500 to 9,000 Hz. The basis for the relation between the masked threshold and frequency is discussed in the next section.

3.2.1.2. ***Critical Band.*** The concept of a critical band originated with H. Fletcher (1940), who hypothesized that the masking of a tone by a broad-band noise is mainly determined by those frequencies close to the frequency of the tone. Only a narrow part of the noise actually serves to mask any given tone. Fletcher called this band the *critical band.* He guessed that at the masked threshold, the level of the tone and that of the surrounding critical band would be the same. To test this hypothesis it was necessary to measure the threshold for the tone against bands of noise of various widths. According to the critical-band hypothesis, if the spectrum level of the noise were kept constant, the threshold for a pure tone located at the center frequency of the band of noise would remain unchanged as the bandwidth of the noise narrowed from very wide to the critical band. Making the noise narrower than the critical band would cause the threshold to decrease because some of the frequencies contributing to masking would be discarded. Preliminary measurements of this kind by Fletcher confirmed his basic hypothesis that only a small part of the noise contributes to masking. Furthermore, those results seemed to support his secondary hypothesis that at the critical bandwidth the level of the noise and of the tone are equal.

On the basis of Fletcher's secondary hypothesis, it is easy to calculate what part of the white noise in Hawkins and Stevens's (1950) experiments falls within the critical band. Because this calculated critical band is derived from the ratio of the intensity of the tone (at threshold) to the spectral density per cycle of the noise, it is now called the *critical ratio.* The formula, in decibels, for a critical ratio is

$$\text{CR in dB} = T - L_0 \tag{23}$$

where T is the threshold in decibels for the pure tone, and L_0 is the spectrum level of the wide-band noise. To calculate the critical ratio as a bandwidth in hertz, the following formula is used:

$$\text{CR in Hz} = \text{antilog}\,(10^{-1} \times \text{CR in dB})\ . \tag{24}$$

It has become clear that the critical ratio underestimates the size of the critical band. Measurements by Greenwood (1961), Hamilton (1957), and Zwicker (1958) show that at critical bandwidth the noise must be more intense than a pure tone at its center frequency to just mask it. The measured signal-to-noise ratios vary from −3 to −8 dB. By assuming that the correct ratio is −4 dB or that the critical band is 2.5 times wider than the critical ratio in hertz, we calculate critical-band values that correspond closely to those measured in other types of experiments. Critical bandwidths thus estimated correspond closely to those measured by Gässler (1954) in the detection of multitone complexes and bands of noise (Section 3.1.5), by Zwicker (1954) in two-tone masking, and by a number of other authors in a variety of psychoacoustic tasks discussed in Chapter 15. All these experiments show that the critical band depends on frequency in the manner shown in Figure 14.32. Table 14.4

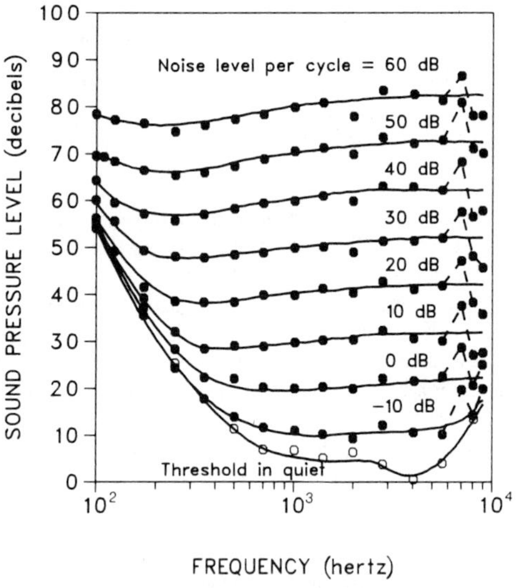

Figure 14.31. Detection of pure tones in white noise. The SPL at the monaural threshold is plotted as a function of signal frequency. Parameter on the curves is the spectrum level (level per cycle) of the noise; adding 40 dB to the spectrum level gives the approximate overall level of the noise. The lowest points were measured in the quiet. Four experienced subjects adjusted the level of a continuous tone until it had a recognizable pitch. Data are the means of two to six threshold measurements on each of the subjects. Smooth curves are drawn through the points up to 5,000 Hz. At the higher frequencies calibration of the earphone renders the plotted data unreliable, and the smooth curves represent better the true thresholds. At all frequencies the masked threshold increases in nearly direct proportion to the level of noise so the curves are approximately parallel. Threshold also increases with frequency above about 400 Hz. (From J. E. Hawkins & S. S. Stevens, The masking of pure tones and of speech by white noise, *Journal of the Acoustical Society of America*, 1950, *22*. Reprinted with permission.)

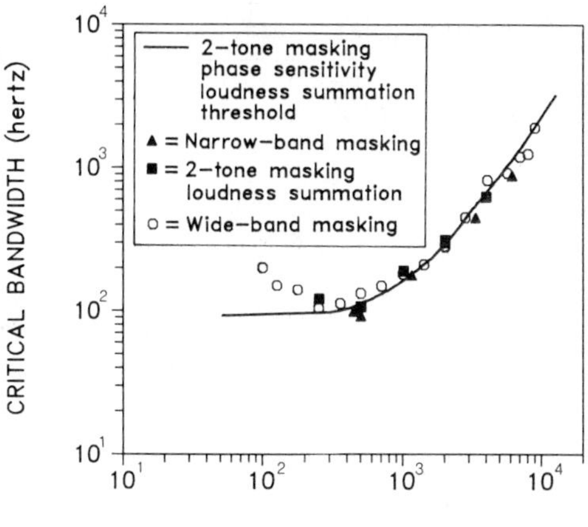

Figure 14.32. Critical bandwidth as a function of center frequency. The solid line represents the average critical bandwidth estimated from measurements of two-tone masking, phase sensitivity, loudness summation over bandwidth, and the threshold for multitone complexes. Data points are from measurements of masking by bands of noise of varying width (triangles), of two-tone masking and loudness summation of a two-tone complex (squares), and of wide-band masking (circles). (See text for the calculation of the values for the circles.) The critical band has a nearly constant value of 100 Hz up to a center frequency of about 500 Hz. Thereafter it is equal to 10–15% of the center frequency. (From B. Scharf, Critical bands, in J. V. Tobias (Ed.), *Foundations of modern auditory theory*, Academic Press, Inc., 1970. Reprinted with permission.)

gives the critical-band values for selected center frequencies together with the cutoff frequencies. Table 14.4 also gives values for the critical ratio. The open circles in Figure 14.32 are from Hawkins and Stevens (1950) and were computed from the following formula:

$$\text{CB in Hz} = 2.5 \text{ antilog } [10^{-1}(T - L_0)] \qquad (25)$$

where T and L_0 have the same meaning as in Equation (23) for the critical ratio in decibels. The curve is based on Gässler's threshold data, Zwicker's two-tone masking data, and two other critical-band measures that do not involve masking. The triangles are for the masking of pure tones by bands of noise. The squares are for two-tone masking and loudness summation. Except below 200 Hz, all the data agree closely. The higher values of the wide-band masking data of Hawkins and Stevens at low frequencies may reflect a change in the signal-to-noise ratio there. If a 100-Hz wide noise can be less than 4 dB above the level of the low-frequency tone it just masks, the critical bandwidth would be overestimated. A study of masking at low frequencies by Fidell, Horonjeff, Teffeteller, and Green (1983) does suggest that listeners are less efficient at detecting low-frequency than higher-frequency signals in noise. Indeed, their analysis of the data led them to suggest that the effective masking band decreases with decreasing frequency down to at least 124 Hz.

According to Figure 14.32, up to about 500 Hz, the critical band is constant at approximately 100 Hz. Above 500 Hz it begins to increase, and above 1,000 Hz it is 15–20% of the center frequency, with the percentage increasing with center frequency. A more precise approximation to the critical bandwidth is given by the equation

$$\text{CB in Hz} = 25 + 75(1 + 1.4f^2)^{0.69} \qquad (26)$$

where f is center frequency in kilohertz. According to Zwicker and Terhardt (1980), their formula yields values within 10% of those in Table 14.4.

Moore and Glasberg (1983b) have offered another formula for critical bandwidth (expressed as the equivalent rectangular bandwidth [ERB] of the assumed auditory filter), based on data obtained by measuring the threshold for a tone as a function of the width of a spectral notch in a noise masker. The formula is

$$\text{ERB} = 6.23f^2 + 93.39f + 28.52 \qquad (27)$$

where f is center frequency measured in kilohertz. Above about 800 Hz the obtained values are about 20% smaller than the critical bandwidths in Table 14.4. Below 800 Hz the two estimations diverge further and further as frequency decreases.

Experimental and clinical practice often call for bands of noise one critical band wide. They are readily obtained, although only approximately, by passing a white noise through a commercially available third-octave band filter. The third-octave bands are 20–30% wider than the critical bandwidths in Table 14.4 at center frequencies above 500 Hz and are narrower at lower frequencies.

Two important properties of the critical band supposedly are that it varies little with stimulus level and is independent of duration. Some controversy exists on both these points, however. Scharf and Meiselman (1977) concluded from a review of the available data that the critical band is independent of level up to 80–90 dB SPL. Forming an important basis for this conclusion are the data from Hawkins and Stevens (1950), shown in Figure 14.31. Their masking noise went from about 30 to near 100 dB in *overall* SPL (the level shown as parameter on the graph is the spectrum level in decibels per hertz). Over that range, there is no consistent trend for the masked threshold to increase with level, which it would do if the critical band widened as level increased from threshold. However, Scharf and Meiselman (1977) suggested that above about 90 dB, the critical band may begin to widen, perhaps doubling at levels above 110 dB.

One basis for assuming a wider critical band at higher levels is the so-called two-tone masking experiment. Zwicker (1954) measured the threshold for a narrow-band noise located between two tones. Increasing the difference in frequency, ΔF, between the two tones leaves the masked threshold unchanged until ΔF equals the critical bandwidth. Beyond that ΔF, the threshold falls sharply and continues to fall as ΔF increases. The drop is sharp enough to provide a clear measure of the critical band, provided the level of the tones is below 70–80 dB SPL. At 77 dB SPL, Green (1965) obtained two-tone masking functions that showed no sharp break and that suggested much wider critical bands than Zwicker measured. However, in this masking paradigm, unlike the wide-band noise paradigm, combination and difference tones play a role and are at the root of the apparent widening of the critical band (D. A. Nelson, 1979).

The effect of duration on the critical band is more complex, but a consensus has been reached that the critical band remains constant even at very brief durations (Scharf, 1970b; Zwicker & Fastl, 1972). The complications with respect to duration arise because of temporal dependencies in simultaneous masking (see Section 3.2.1.7).

The physiological basis for the critical band is obscure. Evans and Wilson (1973) have related it to the Q-value (center frequency divided by bandwidth at the 10-dB value) of the tuning

Table 14.4. Examples of Critical Bandwidth and Critical Ratio

Critical-Band Rate (barks)	Center Frequency (Hz)	Critical Band (Hz)	Lower Cutoff Frequency (Hz)	Upper Cutoff Frequency (Hz)	Critical Ratio (dB)
1	50	—	—	100	—
2	150	100	100	200	17.75
3	250	100	200	300	17.00
4	350	100	300	400	16.75
5	450	110	400	510	16.75
6	570	120	510	630	17.00
7	700	140	630	770	17.25
8	840	150	770	920	17.50
9	1,000	160	920	1,080	18.00
10	1,170	190	1,080	1,270	18.50
11	1,370	210	1,270	1,480	18.75
12	1,600	240	1,480	1,720	19.50
13	1,850	280	1,720	2,000	20.00
14	2,150	320	2,000	2,320	20.50
15	2,500	380	2,320	2,700	21.00
16	2,900	450	2,700	3,150	21.75
17	3,40	550	3,150	3,700	22.25
18	4,000	700	3,700	4,400	23.25
19	4,800	900	4,400	5,300	24.00
20	5,800	1,100	5,300	6,400	25.50
21	7,000	1,300	6,400	7,700	26.75
22	8,500	1,800	7,700	9,500	28.25
23	10,500	2,500	9,500	12,000	—
24	13,500	3,500	12,000	15,500	—

Note: The critical band is given in hertz in the third column for each of the center frequencies listed in the second column. The first column gives the critical-band value in barks, a unit proposed by Zwicker (1958). One bark corresponds to the width of one critical band. The fourth and fifth columns give the lower and upper cutoff frequencies of the corresponding critical band. The critical-band values are plotted as the solid line in Figure 14.32. The last column gives critical ratios for center (i.e., signal) frequencies from 150 to 8,500 Hz. They are the ratios of the power of a pure-tone signal at threshold relative to the power per cycle of a wide-band masking noise. The tabled values are from a smooth curve published by French and Steinberg (1947). The curve summarizes threshold measurements from Bell Telephone Laboratories and fits very well the data of Hawkins and Stevens (1950) shown in Figure 14.31. Ratios published by Reed and Bilger (1973), who used an adaptive forced-choice procedure, are 2.5–5 dB smaller but are the same function of signal frequency. Green, McKey, and Licklider (1959) also measured a very similar function for 100-msec tone bursts. (From B. Scharf, Critical bands, in J. V. Tobias (Ed.), *Foundations of modern auditory theory*, Vol. 1, Academic Press, Inc., 1970. Reprinted with permission.)

curves of individual eighth-nerve fibers in the cat. One problem with this interpretation is that the tuning of most fibers broadens as stimulus level increases, whereas the critical band remains invariant up to at least 80 dB SPL. Nevertheless, most of the critical-band measurements can be interpreted as evidence for a cochlear origin for the critical band. The usual analogy is a bank of band-pass filters, and the bank is located prior to the eighth nerve. Nevertheless, the possibility of a more central origin cannot be excluded. The filter analogy facilitates calculations of the *shape* of the postulated filter in terms of the steepness of the filter skirts (e.g., R. D. Patterson, 1976). Leaving aside the filter model (which is extremely useful) and the question of the physiological site, we note that the critical band defines the frequency limits within which simultaneous signals are integrated for purposes of detection and, as shown in Chapter 15, of loudness summation. Signals that are more than a critical band apart are treated more readily by the auditory system as separate inputs.

3.2.1.3. Narrow-Band Maskers. From the description of the critical band, one might expect that a narrow-band masker, such as a pure tone or a narrow band of white noise, would raise threshold a great deal more when masker and signal fall within the same critical band than when they are in different critical bands. But narrow-band masking shows no discontinuity near the critical band. Masking decreases continuously as the signal moves away from the masker. Figure 14.33 presents an idealized set of masking curves for a narrow-band masker centered on 1,200 Hz and set at the indicated levels. Masking is greatest when the signal is within the frequency limits of the masker and then declines gradually as the signal increases in frequency and more rapidly as the signal decreases in frequency. This asymmetry in masking leads to the rule that low frequencies mask higher frequencies more effectively than the other way around. The rule applies, however, only at masker levels above about 40 dB SPL; the higher the level, the greater the asymmetry. Below 40 dB, masking tends to become somewhat greater toward the *lower* frequencies than toward the higher frequencies (Zwicker, 1980; Zwicker & Jaroszewski, 1982).

Pure-tone maskers give rise to similar curves. However, an important difference is seen when masker and signal are within about 20 Hz of each so that beats make the signal easily detected, as is evident in Figure 14.34. Beating occurs also at harmonic frequencies. Consequently, narrow-band noise maskers give a better picture of masking patterns than do pure tones. Zwicker and Feldtkeller (1967) and Zwicker and Scharf (1965) provide sets of masking curves at various center frequencies. Dips in the masking patterns of pure-tone and of narrow-band-noise maskers also occur at frequencies about 1.5 times the masker frequency (Ehmer, 1959; Greenwood, 1971; Small, 1959). Greenwood (1971) has shown that those dips reflect the presence of cubic difference tones, which arise at frequencies below the masker owing to aural distortion (see Chapter 15). The listener detects the difference tone, and masked threshold goes down.

Why is the critical band not reflected in narrow-band masking patterns? R. D. Patterson and Green (1978) suggest that because the masker and the tonal signal give rise to excitation at frequencies far removed from the masker, the listener can take advantage of a more favorable signal-to-noise ratio at these remote frequencies by "off-frequency" listening. In this case "the width of the critical band is not nearly so important as the detailed shape of the filter, especially the skirt of the filter, because this determines the signal-to-noise ratio at remote frequencies" (R. D. Patterson & Green, 1978, p. 334). This hypothesis is reasonable and emphasizes the limited resolving power of the auditory system as well as the fact that interaction within a critical band and segregation outside it are far from perfect.

One last point about narrow-band masking should be made. Recent years have seen a spate of measurements of the so-called *psychoacoustic tuning curve*. Zwicker (1974) pointed out the similarity between physiological tuning curves (see Fig. 14.20) and masking patterns. This is evident when masking is measured in the following manner: The signal is a tone set 5 or 10 dB above its threshold in the quiet, and the masker is a narrow-band noise or pure tone whose frequency is varied. The level of the masker is set to where the signal is just masked. This arrangement is the opposite of the usual masking paradigm in which the masker is fixed in frequency and level and the signal is varied. Two examples of the resulting masking patterns are shown in Figure 14.35. The left pattern is for a 500-Hz signal, and the right for a 4,000-Hz signal. Masker level required to just mask the signal is plotted as a function of the masker's frequency. The resulting plot is qualitatively similar to tuning curves measured on single eighth-nerve fibers. This similarity is ascribed to the fact that the signal is weak and so excites only a restricted group of fibers, all close to a particular characteristic frequency. To mask the signal, it is assumed that the masker must excite the same restricted group of fibers to prevent them from responding to the signal. This analysis follows the "line-busy" notion of masking, that is, that masking takes place when the neural elements that normally respond to a stimulus are kept busy by the masking sound.

Even at the low levels used for the signal, however, there is evidence that fibers other than those primarily responsive to the signal affect the shape of the psychoacoustic tuning curve. Johnson-Davies and Patterson (1979) found that they needed lower levels of a narrow-band masker at frequencies below the signal frequency when they added a high-pass broad-band masker to the stimuli. Conversely, a low-pass masker permitted lower masker levels for narrow-band maskers above the signal frequency. They ascribe the overall broadening of the tuning curve

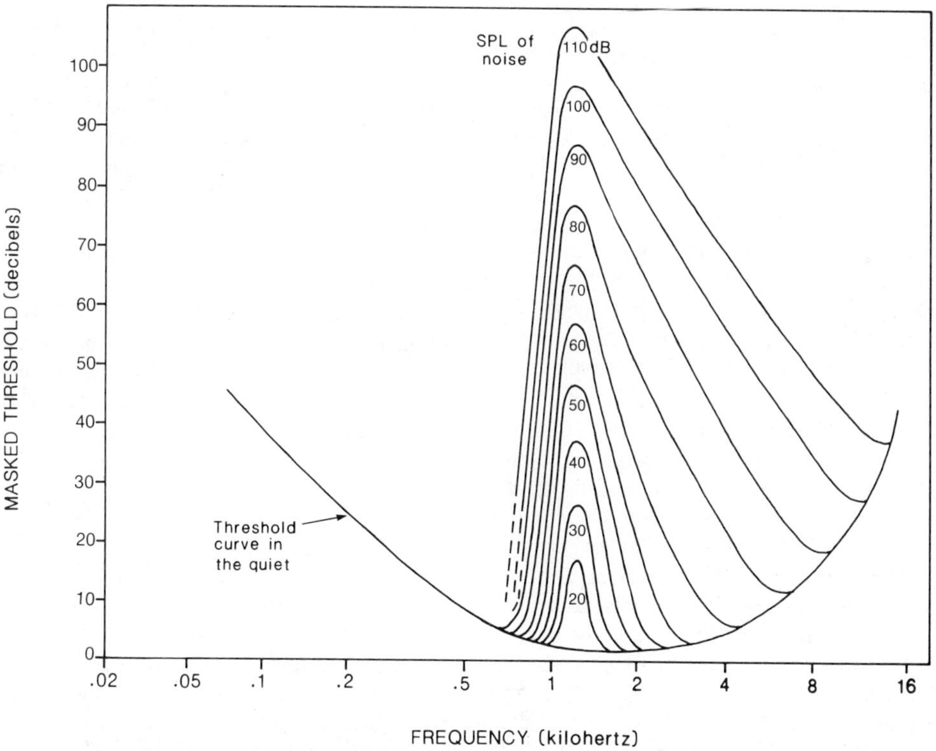

Figure 14.33. Masking patterns produced by a narrow-band masker. Smoothed curves are based on threshold measurements on eight observers who heard tone bursts against a narrow-band noise centered on 1,200 Hz and with cuttoff frequencies at 1,100 and 1,300 Hz. The skirts of the band-pass filter were very steep in order to reveal the steep psychoacoustic curves of the masking patterns on the low-frequency side. Parameter on the curves is the SPL of the noise. The bottom curve is the threshold curve in the quiet. At the center frequency of the band of noise, the threshold increases in direct proportion to the level of noise. Up to about 40 dB of noise the masking patterns are roughly symmetrical; at higher levels masking spreads more and more to the higher frequencies and spreads hardly at all to the lower frequencies. These patterns show that at all but the lowest masking levels, a sound masks higher-frequency sounds better than lower-frequency sounds. (From E. Zwicker & B. Scharf, A model of loudness summation, *Psychological Review*, 1965, *72*. Copyright 1965 by American Psychological Association. Reprinted with permission.)

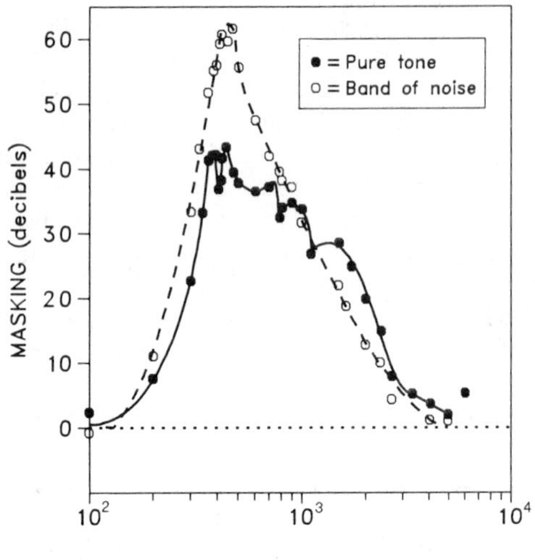

Figure 14.34. Masking by a pure tone and by a narrow band of noise. Masking is plotted as a function of signal frequency. (Masking is the SPL at threshold for a signal in noise minus the SPL of the threshold for the same signal in the quiet.) The masker was either a pure tone (filled circles) at 400 Hz or a 90-Hz-wide band of noise (open circles) centered on 410 Hz. Both maskers were at 80 dB SPL. Masking by the noise is much more regular than by the tone, and is like the somewhat idealized curves of Figure 14.33. The level of masking by the tone decreases when beating occurs between the masking tone and the masked tone because of their simple harmonic relation (when the masker is at 400 and 800 Hz, for example) or because of the presence of a harmonically related distortion product such as the cubic difference tone at 1,200 Hz. Despite the irregularities and reduced masking by the tone, the greater degree of masking toward the higher frequencies is evident in both patterns. (From J. P. Egan & H. W. Hake, On the masking pattern of a simple auditory stimulus, *Journal of the Acoustical Society of America*, 1950, *22*. Reprinted with permission.)

to the masking in those portions of the auditory system where off-frequency listening is possible. Without off-frequency listening, the patterns resemble tuning curves less closely. That resemblance is turning out to be less important than the usefulness of the psychoacoustic tuning curve as a measure of interactions within the auditory system.

3.2.1.4. Masking and Auditory Physiology. The line-busy hypothesis—the notion that the relevant neurons are too busy responding to the masker to respond adequately to the signal—receives some support from consideration of displacement patterns on the basilar membrane. Recall that the place where the amplitude of displacement is maximum almost certainly determines the characteristic frequency of the eighth-nerve fibers innervating that portion of the basilar membrane. The pattern gradually decreases in amplitude toward the stapes, that is, toward those parts of the basilar membrane serving *higher* frequencies; the decrease in amplitude is much steeper in the other direction (see Fig. 14.17). This asymmetry in the displacement pattern corresponds to the asymmetry of narrow-band masking patterns. Low frequencies mask high frequencies better than the reverse. This occurs because the low frequencies set up displacement patterns with long tails. Excitation from these tails keeps busy the fibers whose characteristic frequency is that of the higher-frequency signal.

Although in qualitative agreement with cochlear mechanics and simple physiological tuning curves, the line-busy hypothesis does have problems with some fundamental neural data. First there is the general problem that most auditory fibers respond over a stimulus range of only 30–40 dB. Yet a signal at 70 dB can be masked by introducing a 100-dB masker. A possible explanation is that the signal is already causing the fibers to respond in synchrony with the stimulus input. Thus introducing a masker at a different frequency or with an aperiodic structure (i.e., noise) would decrease the synchrony and thereby mask the tone. The line-busy hypothesis may stand up better if extended to mean that the masker not only keeps neurons busy but keeps them busy according to its own temporal pattern.

3.2.1.5. Binaural Effects. In the quiet, the threshold for a binaural tone is about 3 dB lower than for a monaural tone, but in noise it may be as much as 9 dB higher. The threshold for a binaural low-frequency tone (< 500 Hz) is approximately 9 dB higher when both tone and noise are out of phase at the two ears or both are in phase. On the other hand, when tone and noise have different interaural phase relationships, the threshold for the binaural tone is lower than for a monaural tone heard against the same binaural noise. For example, keeping the binaural tone out of phase while putting the noise to the two ears in phase reduces the threshold 15 dB. These phenomena, called the *masking level difference* (MLD) or *binaural unmasking*, have been extensively studied and conceptualized in several sophisticated theories. (See Colburn & Durlach, 1978, and Durlach & Colburn, 1978, for comprehensive reviews of the data and theories.) Table 14.5, adapted from Green (1976), shows how much lower the threshold is under various binaural configurations than under monaural listening with both tone and noise going to only one and the same ear. No improvement is obtained when the tone and noise have the same interaural phase or when the noise is uncorrelated and the tone is monaural. The greatest improvement is with the noise in phase and the tone out of phase. According to Green, these values are correct to within ±0.5 dB. They apply to low-frequency tones heard in noise at levels above about 50 dB SPL, as suggested in the next two figures.

Binaural unmasking is a complex phenomenon that not only depends on the relation between the interaural phase of the signal and noise, but also depends strongly on the frequency of the tone and the level of the noise. Figure 14.36 from Durlach and Colburn (1978) plots the threshold improvement as a function of the frequency of the tonal signal. The improvement was measured as the decrease in the threshold for an out-of-phase tone relative to that for an in-phase tone, each heard against in-phase noise. Data are from a number of studies. The dependence on frequency is evident in the first study by Hirsh (1948, upright triangles), who discovered binaural unmasking. It is unclear whether the masking-level difference decreases at 100 Hz. Otherwise the difference is roughly constant up to about 500 Hz, then declines to 3 dB in the vicinity of 1,500 Hz and thereafter remains constant with increasing frequency. The asymptote at 1,500 Hz corresponds to the frequency beyond which the human auditory system is insensitive to interaural phase information (cf. Scharf & Houtsma, Chapter 15, Section 3). Durlach (1964) suggests that the 3-dB masking-level difference above 1,500 Hz results from larger interaural power differences when the tone is out of phase and the noise in phase than when both are in phase.

Figure 14.37, also from Durlach and Colburn (1978), shows how the masking-level difference for low-frequency tones depends on the spectrum level of a broad-band masking noise. In these experiments, the signal was 180° out of phase and the noise was in phase. The plotted MLD is relative to a monaural tone and noise. These data show that the difference increases over

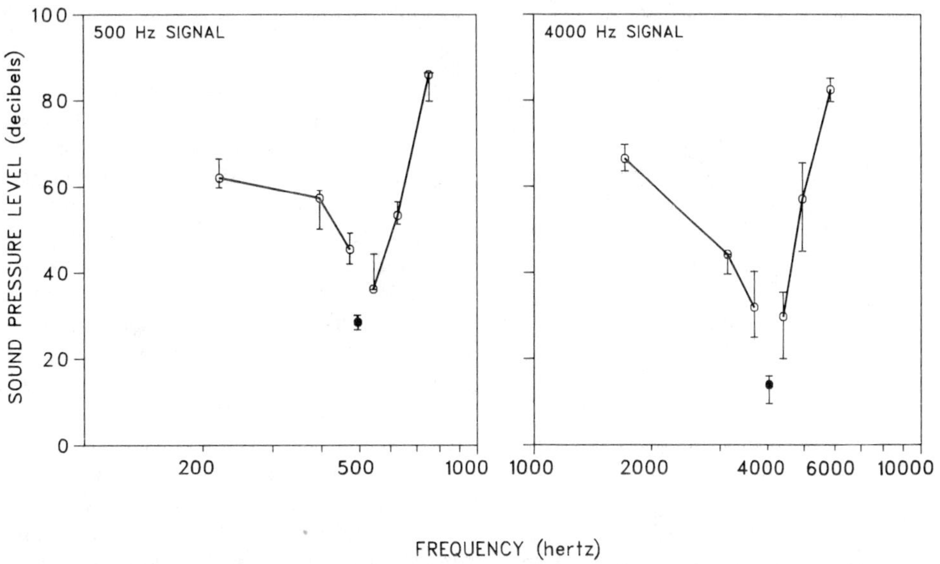

Figure 14.35. Psychoacoustic tuning curves. The SPL at which a pure-tone masker just masks a 500-Hz or 4,000-Hz signal is plotted as a function of the masker's frequency. The signal was presented every 1,200 msec for 600 msec at 10 dB above its threshold in the quiet; the masker was on continuously and the level required to just mask the signal was tracked by the Békésy procedure. Each point is the median of data from ten normally hearing subjects. Vertical bars are the interquartile ranges. The lowest point gives the median SPL at which the signal was at 10 dB SL. At both signal frequencies the level of the masking tone must be raised much more rapidly when its frequency increases than when it decreases. This asymmetry in the psychoacoustic tuning curve resembles that of single-neuron physiological tuning curves (see, e.g., Fig. 14.20). Both types of function are believed to reflect the pattern of mechanical excitation on the basilar membrane. (From M. Florentine, S. Buus, B. Scharf, & E. Zwicker, Frequency selectivity in normally hearing and hearing-impaired observers, *Journal of Speech and Hearing Research*, 1980, *23*. Reprinted with permission.)

about a 40-dB range. Above about 50 dB spectrum level, the MLD remains constant. According to Colburn and Durlach (1978), this is the predominant finding in the literature. The literature also tends to confirm the finding that the MLD increases more rapidly at very low frequencies than at around 500 Hz. Figure 14.37 also shows a binaural threshold in the quiet ($-\infty$) that is 4.5 dB lower than a monaural threshold. This is 1.5 dB more than the usual 3-dB binaural advantage for an in-phase signal. Diercks and Jeffress (1962) had measured a similar difference at 250 Hz. They ascribed the advantage for

Table 14.5. Binaural Unmasking

Interaural Condition	Decrease in Threshold (dB)
S and N monaural in same ear	0
S and N both in phase	0
S and N both out of phase	0
N uncorrelated, S monaural	0
N uncorrelated, S out of phase	3
N uncorrelated, S in phase	4
N out of phase, S monaural	6
N in phase, S monaural	9
N out of phase, S in phase	13
N in phase, S out of phase	15

Note: Estimated decreases in threshold under the defined stimulus conditions are relative to the threshold measured when a monaural noise and tone go to the same ear. S means tonal signal, and N means masking noise. Except where indicated, S and N were presented to both ears. Out of phase means 180° out of phase at the two ears. The tabled values apply to signals below 1,000 Hz and to noises with a spectrum level of at least 20 dB. (From D. M. Green, *An introduction to hearing*, Lawrence Erlbaum Associates, 1976. Reprinted with permission.)

the binaural out-of-phase tone to the presence of correlated internal noise which masks an in-phase or monaural signal better.

A number of other stimulus variables have been manipulated, including the noise's interaural phase, amplitude ratio, time delay, correlation, and bandwidth. All these variables influence the MLD, and often interact with the frequency of the signal. When the background noise is in phase, varying the interaural phase of the signal from 0° (in phase) to 180° (out of phase) yields a continuous increase in the MLD (Jeffress, Blodgett, & Deatherage, 1952).

The enormous detail available in results of numerous experiments on MLD presents a severe challenge to any modeling or theorizing. In addition, the binaural system performs a number of other tasks, notably localization, that a theory of MLD cannot easily ignore. Probably the most successful and best known of the many theories offered is the equalization-cancellation model of Durlach (1963). In their excellent review of the various MLD models, Colburn and Durlach (1978) write the following:

> The basic idea of the equalization-cancellation model is to adjust the received signals so that the masking components are equal in the two channels (equalize) and then to subtract (cancel). If these operations are performed perfectly, and the interaural relations of the target signal are different from those of the masking signal, then the resultant output will contain a component due to the target signal but not the masking signal. (p. 481)

Noise in the form of random effects in the amplitude and delay parameters brings predicted performance in line with observed performance. In general, neither this model nor any other binaural model has yet proved capable of explaining such phe-

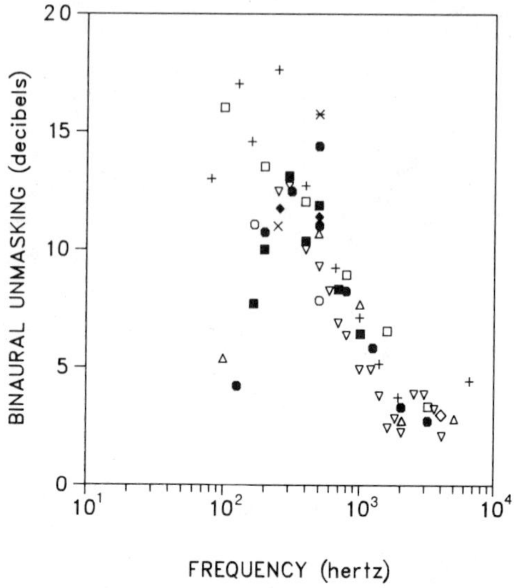

Figure 14.36. Dependence of binaural unmasking on signal frequency. The ordinate shows the decrease in masking by a noise that is in phase at the two ears as a function of the signal's frequency. Masking decreases when the signal is a tone that is out of phase in the two ears in place of a tone that is in phase. Data points are from 16 different studies in which noise was relatively broad band and had a spectrum level of 45 dB or higher, and where the signal lasted at least 100 msec. Above about 150 Hz, unmasking first increases with frequency to a maximum of about 15 dB around 250 Hz. Unmasking then decreases with increasing frequency until it reaches a minimum of about 3 dB near 1,500 Hz. Below 150 Hz, results depend on the exact noise level and on training of the subject. It is apparent that only at low frequencies does the interaction between the signal's and the noise's interaural phase relations substantially affect masking. (From N. I. Durlach & H. S. Colburn, Binaural phenomena, in E. C. Carterette & M. P. Friedman (Eds.), *Handbook of perception Vol. 4: Hearing*, Academic Press, Inc., 1978. Reprinted with permission.)

nomena as the ability to pick a desired signal out of multiple sound sources (the cocktail party effect), the precedence effect, or the reduced localization ability in some forms of peripheral hearing impairment. Models such as Durlach's do clarify the kinds of signal processing that are likely to occur. Colburn (1983) continues his development of a binaural model that includes explicit neural networks based on available neurological data. The existence of masking-level differences shows that auditory masking is not determined entirely in the cochlea but is strongly influenced by more central neural processing.

3.2.1.6. ***Interaural Masking.*** A sound to one ear may mask a weak sound to the other ear. Unless precautions are taken to prevent the masking sound from reaching the test ear via bone conduction, the measured masking may be monaural masking. A sound presented to one ear via the typical earphone will be attenuated approximately 50 dB upon arrival at the other ear (Zwislocki, 1953). Insert earphones—tiny phones inserted in the auditory meatus—increase the attenuation to 80 dB and permit measurement of true interaural masking, which takes place entirely within the auditory nervous system. Zwislocki, Damianopoulos, Buining, and Glantz (1967) prefer to call such interaural masking "central" masking to emphasize the almost certain site of the interference within the auditory system. Figure 14.38 shows the threshold shift for a 10-msec test tone masked by a 60-dB, 1,000-Hz tone that lasted 250 msec in the contralateral ear. Signal frequency was varied. The signal started 20 msec after the masker. The delay is a crucial parameter, because masking decays rapidly, with a time constant of 50–60 msec, as a function of onset delay of the signal. Moreover, the masking pattern—threshold plotted as a function of signal frequency—becomes considerably flatter.

At a delay of 20 msec, the pattern is much sharper than in monaural masking. Indeed, as marked on the two panels of Figure 14.38, the critical band seems to determine the limits of masking. The signal is so weak that it produces no usable excitation at remote frequencies that can serve off-frequency listening. Furthermore, because the tones are in separate ears, there is no chance for combination tones to play a role. These results would seem to lend some support to the explanation proffered by R. D. Patterson and Green (1978) for the failure of the critical band to show up in monaural pure-tone masking. A number of other theoretically interesting aspects of interaural masking are reviewed by Zwislocki (1978).

3.2.1.7. ***Temporal Effects.*** As noted in Section 3.1.4, the detectability of a sound in the quiet increases with duration up to about 200 msec. The same rule holds in noise. However, detectability of a short-duration signal depends also on its onset relative to the onset of the masker. Threshold is highest when the masker and signal come on together and then decreases as the signal is delayed up to about 100 msec. Figure 14.39 shows the masked threshold for a 2-msec, 4,800-Hz tone burst as a function of its onset delay. (The threshold in the quiet for the same tone burst is approximately 30 dB SPL.) The parameter on the curves is the bandwidth of the masking noise in critical bands. The widest noise of 24 critical bands covers the whole audible frequency range.

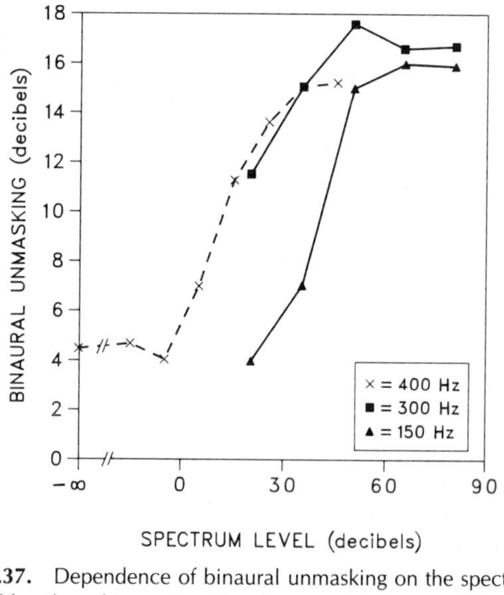

Figure 14.37. Dependence of binaural unmasking on the spectrum level of a broad-band masking noise. Signal was a pure tone at 150 or 300 Hz (from Dolan, 1968) or at 400 Hz (from McFadden, 1968). The ordinate gives the decrease in threshold for an out-of-phase tone in the presence of an in-phase noise as compared to the threshold for a monaural tone and noise. The unmasking increases from about 4 dB at low noise levels to over 15 dB at levels of 50 dB and greater. Having a higher absolute threshold, the 150-Hz tone does not begin to increase until masked by a higher-level noise. The "unmasking" in the quiet reflects the advantage of binaural over monaural listening and of the out-of-phase signal presentation. Binaural unmasking increases from threshold as the noise level increases up to a spectrum level of about 50 dB. (From N. I. Durlach & H. S. Colburn, Binaural phenomena, in E. C. Carterette & M. P. Friedman (Eds.), *Handbook of perception Vol. 4: Hearing*, Academic Press, Inc., 1978. Reprinted with permission.)

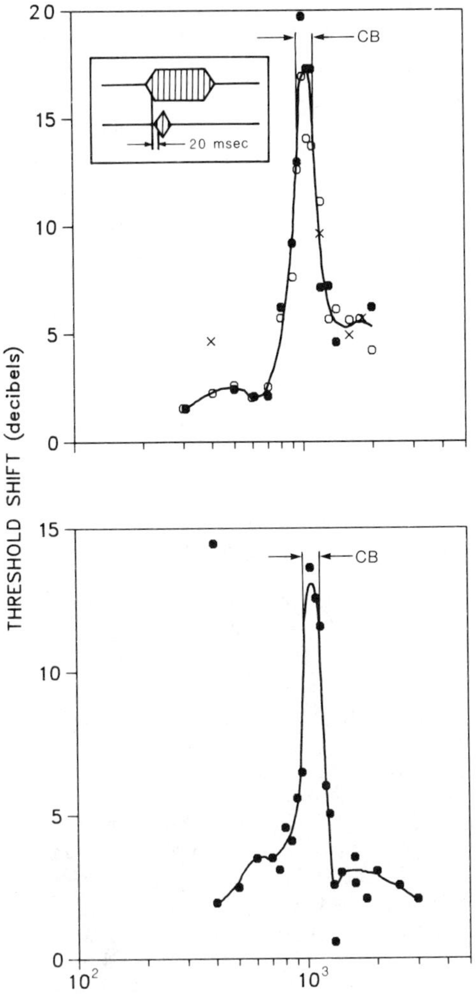

Figure 14.38. Interaural masking. The increase in threshold from its value *in the quiet* is plotted as a function of the signal frequency. The masker—presented to one ear—was a 250-msec, 1,000-Hz tone set 60 dB above threshold. The signal—presented to the other ear—was a 10-msec tone burst that came on 20 msec after masker onset, as shown in the figure. A Békésy tracking procedure was used. Each point is the median of threshold crossings in a single run by one of the two subjects in which tracking reversed direction 20 times. The top panel is for subject JZ and the bottom panel is for subject JG. Insert earphones were used to ensure interaural attenuation of at least 75 dB at 1,000 Hz. Interaural masking reaches a maximum of about 15 dB when the signal lies within half a critical band (CB) on either side of the contralateral masking tone. The asymmetry so characteristic of more intense monaural masking is not seen in interaural masking. (From J. J. Zwislocki, E. N. Damianopoulos, E. Buining, & J. Glantz, Central masking: Some steady-state and transient effects, *Perception and Psychophysics*, 1967, *2*. Reprinted with permission.)

All maskers have the same spectrum level of 25 dB, so they should all be equally effective maskers because they are at least one critical band wide. This equality is true only when the signal is delayed more than 100 msec. At shorter delays the threshold is as much as 10 dB higher in the wide-band noise than in the narrow-band noise. Similar measurements at 1,000 Hz showed a 5-dB difference between wide- and narrow-band noise. The cause of this elevation is unclear, but it cannot be the widening of the critical band at short durations. Zwicker (1965) showed that a tone outside the frequency limits of a narrow-band masker does not have a higher threshold near masker onset than later. If the critical band were wider under such circumstances, an increased spread of masking should take place. Earlier, Elliott (1965) had measured such an effect, but her masker onsets were abrupt, scattering energy well outside the frequency limits of a narrow-band noise, which meant that the masker was physically broader at onset.

3.2.2. Nonsimultaneous Masking. A masker can raise the threshold for a second sound presented either after the masker is turned off (forward masking) or before the masker is turned on (backward masking). Nonsimultaneous masking provides information about temporal integration and resolution in the auditory system.

3.2.2.1. ***Forward Masking.*** The two stimulus parameters that largely determine the amount of simultaneous masking, namely, masker level and the frequency relation between masker and signal, are also important in forward masking. The most important new parameter is the delay of the signal after termination of the masker, often measured as the time between the offset of the masker and the offset of the signal. The duration of the signal and masker must also be considered; usually the masker is at least 200 msec long and the signal is less than 50 msec long.

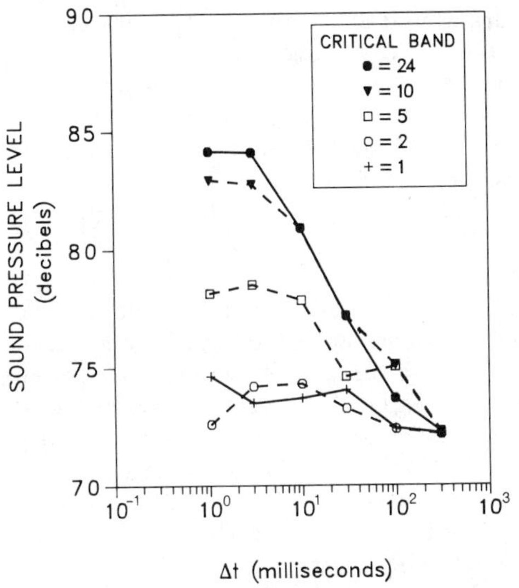

Figure 14.39. Effect on the masked threshold of the temporal relation between masker and signal. Threshold for a 4,800-Hz, 2-msec tone burst is plotted as a function of the delay of its onset relative to that of the masker. The bandwidth, in critical bands, of the masking noise is the parameter on the curves. The narrowest noise, one critical band wide, had cutoffs at 4,300 and 5,100 Hz. The masker came on every 1,200 msec for 600 msec, and the signal came on in the noise every other time. Tone and noise passed through the same filter so as to keep energy in the signal from spreading beyond the frequency limits of the noise. Each listener's monaural threshold was tracked by the Békésy procedure. Each data point is the median from four listeners. (Threshold in the quiet for the tone burst is about 30 dB SPL.) Against a wide-band noise, the masked threshold decreases over 10 dB as its onset is delayed relative to the onset of the noise. Against narrow-band noise, threshold does not change with onset delay. Beyond 100 msec, threshold is the same against all five bandwidths because the spectrum level (and hence the level within a single critical band) is constant. The basis for this "overshoot" at the beginning of wide-band noise is unknown. (From E. Zwicker, Temporal effects in simultaneous masking and loudness, *Journal of the Acoustical Society of America*, 1965, *38*. Reprinted with permission.)

Several general rules emerge from the many papers on forward masking. Forward masking is less effective than simultaneous masking, and the amount of masking decreases with signal delay up to about 200 msec. Beyond 200 msec the threshold is generally the same as in the quiet. The amount of masking increases with masker level (Jesteadt, Bacon, & Lehman, 1982; Moore & Glasberg, 1983a; Widin & Viemeister, 1979; Zwislocki, 1978). The shorter the delay between masker and signal, the more rapid the increase with level; the increase is always less rapid than in simultaneous masking, which means that for a given increase in masker level, the forward masking increases by a lesser amount (Widin & Viemeister, 1979). The effect of frequency differences between masker and signal is qualitatively the same in forward as in simultaneous masking. Masking is greatest when the frequencies are the same or very close and decreases as the signal moves away in frequency, more rapidly toward lower than toward higher frequencies (Fastl, 1976/77; Munson & Gardner, 1950; Widin & Viemeister, 1979). However, the decrease in masking is greater in forward than in simultaneous masking. Consequently, in forward masking, the patterns of masking extend over a narrower frequency range (Fastl, 1976/77) and psychoacoustic tuning curves (see Section 3.2.1.3) are sharper (Moore, 1978). As in simultaneous masking, the effect of the frequency difference between signal and masker interacts with the masker level: Forward masking increases more rapidly with level when the signal frequency lies above the masker frequency than when it lies below. In fact, masking grows more rapidly for a higher-frequency signal than for a signal at the masking frequency.

Figure 14.40 shows how the threshold for a 1-msec tone burst changes as a function of the time delay between the end of the critical-band masker centered on 8,500 Hz and the signal offset. The masker's level was 70 dB SPL and its duration was 500 msec. Each curve is for a different signal frequency, as shown by the inset. Arrows indicate thresholds in the quiet. Masking declines at different rates for the three frequencies. These different rates compensate for large initial differences in the amount of masking, so that the forward masking continues for about the same duration, 200 msec, at all three frequencies. These data are based on a tracking procedure by one subject. Very high frequencies were used to allow a signal duration as short as 1 msec. Above 8,000 Hz, the critical band is so wide that the energy splatter associated with a 1-msec duration remains confined to a single critical band and so would have little effect on the threshold. Data by other authors are similar, despite much variability among subjects in forward masking.

Jesteadt et al. (1982) and also Moore and Glasberg (1983a) have proposed to summarize forward masking with a formula of the form

$$M = a(b - \log \Delta t)(L_0 - c) \qquad (28)$$

where M is the amount of masking in decibels, Δt is the signal delay, L_0 is the masker spectrum level, and the constants a, b, and c are chosen to provide the best fit to the data from individual listeners.

Part of the variability in forward masking is caused by the qualitative cues available for detecting the signal. These cues depend upon the type of signal and masker (whether tone or noise), their durations, the signal delay, and so forth. Mainly they concern the qualitative similarity between masker and signal. For example, Weber and Moore (1981) showed that when a 2,000-Hz signal has a duration of 5 msec, it is more effectively

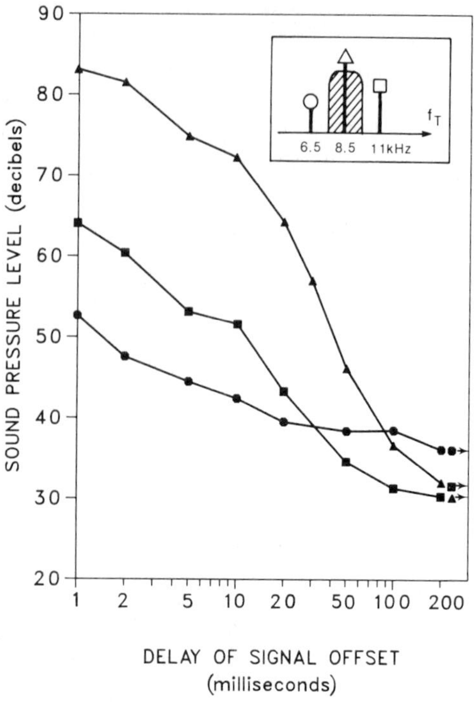

Figure 14.40. Forward masking by narrow-band noise. A noise one critical-band wide with a center frequency of 8,500 Hz and an SPL of 70 dB masked a 1-msec tone pulse. The pulse came on with a Gaussian rise time of 0.5 msec and terminated from 1 to 200 msec after the noise terminated. The noise came on every 1,100 msec for 500 msec; the tone pulse came on every other time. The subject's monaural threshold was tracked by the Békésy procedure. The different symbols correspond to the frequency of the tone pulse as shown in the inset. Arrows indicate thresholds *in the quiet*. At all three frequencies, the masked threshold decreases monotonically as a function of signal delay up to between 100 and 200 msec. The decrease is most rapid where threshold began highest, namely, at the signal frequency located in the middle of the noise band. Masking of the higher frequency is, as usual, greater than masking of the lower frequency at short delays but it decreases more rapidly so that at all three frequencies, the threshold 200 msec after termination of the noise is the same as *in the quiet*. (From H. Fastl, Temporal masking effects: II. Critical band noise masker, *Acustica*, 1976–77, *36*. Reprinted with permission.)

masked by a preceding narrow-band noise than by a preceding 2,000-Hz tone. (Masker level was 82 dB SPL, and duration was 400 msec.) However, when the duration of the signal is increased from 5 to 35 msec, it is masked more by the tone than by the noise. The proposed explanation for this finding goes as follows: The 35-msec tone has a clear tonal quality that resembles that of the masking tone much more than that of the masking noise and so is easier to detect after the noise than after the tone. On the other hand, the 5-msec tone burst sounds more like the narrow-band noise and so is easier to distinguish from the preceding tone than from the noise. Reasoning along such lines, Moore (1980) has been able to explain why various kinds of experimental manipulations lead to changes in forward masking. Other things being equal, the more qualitatively alike the masker and the signal, the greater the forward masking.

Forward masking seems also to reflect *suppression* in the auditory system. Suppression refers to the presumed reduction in neural activity evoked by one sound when a second sound is introduced (Houtgast, 1972). Thus adding a second sound to a masking sound may suppress neural activity evoked by the masker in the neural channel subsequently to be activated by the signal. If the suppression decays rapidly enough so that its effects are gone by the time the signal arrives, then forward masking would be lessened. Suppression is not evident in simultaneous masking because the suppressing sound reduces activity evoked by both masker and signal, leaving undiminished the signal-to-noise ratio within the signal channel.

The relative importance of qualitative cues and suppression in forward masking depends on the temporal and spectral relations of signal and masker. For example, Moore (1980) showed that adding a tone at a lower or higher frequency to a narrow-band noise masker reduced the forward masking of a 45-msec tonal signal by as much as 16 dB but had no effect on the masking of a 5-msec signal. Because suppression is assumed to take place while the suppressing tone and noise are on, the duration of the signal ought not to matter. That it does matter may mean that in this particular paradigm, the added tone makes it easier for the subject to detect the change from masker to signal because the added tone reduces the fluctuations inherent in the narrow-band masker.

3.2.2.2. Backward Masking. One sound can raise the threshold for a preceding sound that is turned off before the masker is turned on. The time interval for this backward effect is generally well under 100 msec, the value depending upon the type of stimuli. One click masks a preceding click over a 10-msec interval (Raab, 1961). A broad-band noise masks a preceding click over intervals as long as 25 msec at 80 dB SPL and over less than 10 msec at 40 or 55 dB (C. E. Robinson & Pollack, 1971). When the click precedes the noise by 4 msec or less, the amount of masking is of the order of 20–30 dB. Because a click has a broad spectrum, these data cannot tell us about frequency resolution. Measuring backward masking of narrow-band stimuli such as tones is difficult because of the brief durations involved, and of the energy splatter that occurs when a tone is very brief or turned on and off quickly.

Wright (1964) attempted to overcome this handicap by varying the duration of a relatively long tonal signal that always terminated 100 msec before the end of a 600-msec narrow-band masker. Figure 14.41 gives the threshold for a 1,000-Hz tone as a function of its duration. At all three masker levels the threshold begins to increase in the vicinity of 700 msec. Part of this increase comes about because the noise shortens the tone's effective duration to less than 200 msec. The noise onset acts to terminate temporal summation in the quiet as well as to exert a backward masking effect. To determine the threshold shift due to masking alone, Wright first calculated the expected shift due to interference with temporal summation. As thus determined, backward masking appears to be extremely effective over a 30-msec interval prior to masker onset; during those 30 msec, the tone's threshold rose to within 10 dB of the masker's level. At 50 msec masking is decaying rapidly and by 100 msec there is almost no masking. One difficulty with these calculations is that they assume uniform temporal summation throughout the pre-noise interval. It may be that the last 30 msec of a signal are more important than the first 30 msec for detection so that the interference by the noise with temporal summation is greater than calculated. This would mean that the interval over which backward masking occurs is shorter than shown by Wright.

Fastl's (1976/77) data do suggest, indeed, that backward masking does not extend back more than 30–40 msec prior to masker onset. Fastl made his measurements around 8,000 Hz where energy splatter, even for a signal as brief as 1 msec, is confined to a single critical band. Within 4 msec prior to masker onset, masking of an 8,500-Hz signal by an 1,800-Hz wide band of noise centered on 8,500 Hz was more than 40 dB; when the signal came on 15 msec before the noise, backward masking had decreased to less than 10 dB.

3.3. Noise-Induced Threshold Shift

Measurements of noise-induced threshold shift are a kind of extension of forward masking in that a noise precedes a signal whose threshold is measured as a function of various parameters of the noise. However, the durations of both the noise and the interval separating the noise from the signal are much longer than in forward masking. We distinguish two types of induced threshold shifts: those that are permanent (threshold never returns to its preexposure level) and those that are temporary (threshold does return to normal, usually within a few days). Permanent threshold shift (PTS) usually comes about from years of exposure to noise, often in the work environment. Temporary threshold shift (TTS) occurs in many environments, and may be induced in the laboratory. A primary motivation for the study of TTS has been its possible elucidation of PTS. Many of the numerous studies of noise-induced threshold shift are referred to in the books by Henderson et al. (1976) and by Hamernik et al. (1982).

3.3.1. Temporary Threshold Shift. Generalizations about the effects of various stimulus parameters are not simple, owing to interactions among the parameters and to large individual differences (e.g., Mills, Gilbert, & Adkins, 1979). The amount of TTS depends on the level, frequency content, duration, bandwidth, and temporal characteristics of the inducing sound, which may be a noise or a tone. It depends also on the frequency content of the signal. Because recovery begins once the noise is turned off, the TTS also depends on how long after noise offset it is measured.

In general TTS does not begin until the A-weighted sound level (see Section 1.6.2) exceeds 60–80 dB even for exposures lasting as long as a day (J. D. Miller, 1974). Once induced, the amount of TTS increases monotonically with the intensity of the noise. For example, an octave band of noise produces no TTS until it reaches a level of 80 dB. At 95 dB it produces 15 dB of TTS after a 50-min exposure, and at 105 dB it produces 30 dB of TTS. In this example, TTS increases at about 1.5 dB per decibel increase in noise level above 95 dB. However, the rate of increase in TTS depends on duration and other parameters as well as level.

The frequencies that seem to produce the greatest TTS, for a constant noise level, are between about 2,000 and 6,000 Hz. However, Botte (Note 1) found that the maximum TTS is the same when induced by pure tones from 250 to 6,000 Hz all set to the same sensation level (level above absolute threshold before any TTS). Moreover, the TTS extends over a wider range of signal frequencies when induced by low-frequency tones than when induced by high-frequency tones. A striking characteristic of TTS is that the maximum shift is generally not at the frequency location of the fatiguing sound but, depending somewhat on level, at a frequency about half an octave higher (e.g., Mills et al., 1979; Ward, 1962). For example, a fatiguing tone at 1,000 Hz causes a larger threshold shift at 1,500 Hz than at 1,000 Hz. In contrast, simultaneous and even forward masking are almost always maximum at the center frequency of the masker and decrease at higher frequencies. The reason for this difference between TTS and masking is unclear. McFadden and Plattsmier (1983) suggest that the half-octave shift in TTS is associated with changes in the displacement patterns on the basilar mem-

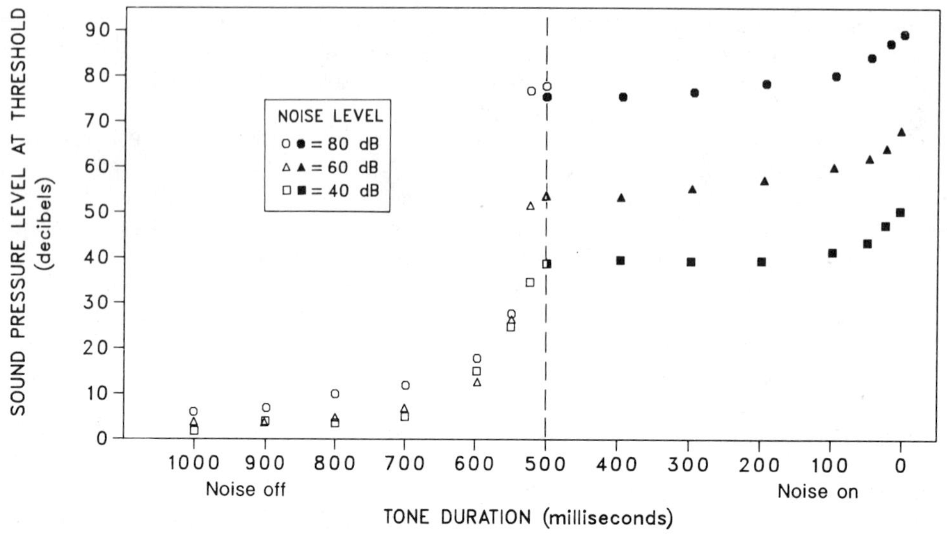

Figure 14.41. Backward masking by narrow-band noise. Threshold for a 1,000-Hz tone burst is plotted as a function of the tone's duration. The tone always terminated 100 msec before the end of the 600-msec masking noise. Rise-fall time for both signal and noise was 10 msec. Parameter on the curves is the SPL of the masking noise, which had a bandwidth of 160 Hz centered on 1,000 Hz. Monaural thresholds were measured by a bracketing procedure in which the experimenter varied the signal in 2-dB steps to find the level at which the subject reported hearing the signal 50% of the time. Mean thresholds of three subjects are plotted as unfilled symbols for backward masking where the tone began prior to noise onset and as filled symbols for simultaneous masking where the tone began after noise onset. As tone onset approaches noise onset, threshold begins to increase substantially starting at about 200 msec prior to noise onset (700 msec on the abscissa). By 10 msec (510 msec on the abscissa), the threshold is almost as high as during simultaneous masking. Results are similar at all three masking levels. After taking into account the role of temporal summation at threshold, these findings suggest that backward masking extends at most to 50–100 msec prior to masker onset. (From H. H. Wright, Temporal summation and backward masking, *Journal of the Acoustical Society of America*, 1964, *36*. Reprinted with permission.)

brane. Not only does the frequency locus of the fatiguing sound affect TTS, but so also does the bandwidth. Pure tones and narrow-band noise produce more TTS than does wide-band noise.

The TTS increases as the logarithm of the duration of the noise (Ward, Glorig, & Sklar, 1959), but only up to an exposure duration of 8–16 hr. With further exposure, the amount of TTS remains at a plateau (Melnick, 1976; Mills et al., 1979). This plateau is referred to as the *asymptotic threshold shift* (ATS). In an extensive study of ATS, Mills et al. (1979) exposed 60 normally hearing young men and women for as long as 24 hr to various levels of octave-band noise. Results showed that ATS is less than about 5 dB until the noise exceeds a critical level. The critical level depended on the center frequency of the noise, decreasing from 82 dB SPL at 500 Hz to 74 dB at 4,000 Hz. This means that a weaker high-frequency noise causes as much TTS as a stronger low-frequency noise (see also Ward, 1963). For wide-band noise the critical level was 78 dB (Mills, Adkins, & Gilbert, 1981). The rate of increase above the critical level was 1.7 dB per decibel increase in the exposure level, regardless of the center frequency of the noise.

Much attention has been given to recovery from TTS. At intervals of 2 min and longer after termination of the fatiguing sound, TTS declines as the logarithm of the recovery time (Ward et al., 1959). At intervals less than 2 min, the relation between recovery and duration is less clear. Accordingly, TTS is usually measured after 2 min or longer of recovery.

3.3.2. Permanent Threshold Shift. Although TTS and PTS must be related, extrapolation from TTS to noise-induced permanent threshold shift (NIPTS) is not possible. Information on NIPTS is based primarily on industrial surveys. Passchier-Vermeer summarized the literature in 1968, and Ward (1984) has brought that summary up to date. Generalizations are based on threshold measurements of workers after exposure in the workplace during at least 10 years to continuous noise for 8 hr·day^{-1}. On the average, no PTS appears until the A-weighted SPL (see Section 1.4) has exceeded 80 dB. An exposure of 85 dB leads to a median loss at 4,000 Hz of about 10 dB. With further increases in exposure level, PTS increases approximately 10 dB for every 5-dB increase in exposure level. Hearing loss is greatest around 4,000 Hz and is 20–30 dB less below 2,000 Hz and at 8,000 Hz [see Fig. 14.42(c)]. Evidence is not available concerning the degree to which hearing loss depends on the frequency content of the noise.

The role of temporal factors is also unclear. A rule often used is that NIPTS depends on the overall energy to which the ears have been exposed. Such a rule implies that hearing loss is the same whether or not rest periods occur between noise exposures. However, Ward (1984) argues that periods of quiet permit recovery by the auditory system from preceding noise exposure. Thus, for example, daily 4-hr exposures may be less damaging than 8-hr exposures to a noise at a level 3 dB lower (which means half the intensity). These controversies are not readily resolved because the effects of workplace noise on hearing are usually confounded by the effects of aging, exposure to noise outside the workplace, and nonacoustic sources of hearing damage. Nonetheless, it is clear that long-term daily exposure for 8 hr to noise levels of 80–90 dB (A) leads to significant PTS (20 dB or more) in many people.

3.4. Effects of Auditory Disorders on Detection

As made so evident in PTS, the hallmark of a hearing disorder is an increase in absolute threshold at some or all frequencies. Threshold measurements are by far the most important tool in the audiologist's hands. Audiologists measure thresholds in terms of *hearing level* rather than SPL. They are interested primarily in hearing loss, defined as the amount of elevation from the normal threshold (which is one reason for the importance of the standardized curves in Fig. 14.24). The hearing level is the difference in decibels between the SPL at which the patient detects a given frequency and the SPL at which the standard, normally hearing listener detects it (see Section 1.4.2). A positive hearing level means threshold is higher than normal, and a negative hearing level means that it is lower.

Figure 14.42 gives the *audiograms*, hearing level plotted as a function of frequency, for four types of hearing disorder. Audiograms are usually obtained by having the patient report whether or not he hears a tone presented at various levels and frequencies. A method of limits with steps of 5 dB is typical; sometimes the Békésy tracking procedure is used. Tones are presented at frequencies spaced at octave intervals from 125 or 250 Hz to 8,000 Hz. Results are nearly always given in terms of hearing level, relative to the standard threshold curve (ANSI, 1969; and see Table 14.1).

Measurements of detection under masking by hearing-impaired listeners have been carried out almost exclusively in the laboratory. In conductive impairment, masking seems to be the same as in normal hearing with respect to its magnitude, its spread to other frequencies, and so forth, provided measurements are made at the same sensation level, that is, the same level above threshold. The pathological transmission loss acts like an attenuation that reduces the input to the cochlea. Sound amplification can overcome the pathological attenuation so that hearing is nearly normal.

In cochlear disorders, the input to the cochlea is normal, but changes within the cochlea itself result in abnormal sensory transduction. Not only is detection poor and thresholds elevated, but masking, loudness, and other suprathreshold auditory functions are also abnormal. Masking by wide-band noise is greater than in normal ears, which means that critical ratios are larger and that critical bands are probably wider (e.g., Tyler, in press). Masking by narrow-band noise extends to higher frequencies where the threshold shift is greater than normal (Florentine, Buus, Scharf, & Zwicker, 1980). Determining just how much masking increases in cochlear disorders is difficult because in normal ears, the spread of masking to higher signal frequencies becomes greater with increasing masker level, as shown in Figure 14.33. Yet even in terms of sound pressure level, the upward spread of masking in cochlear disorders may be greater than in normal hearing. It is unclear to what extent the greater spread of masking is due to abnormal mechanical events within the inner ear and to what extent to pathological processing in the impaired hair cells. Physiological tuning curves are presumably flattened. Evidence for this comes mainly from psychoacoustic tuning curves that are considerably less sharp in patients with cochlear disorders than in normals, even when compared for signals at the same sound pressure levels (Florentine et al., 1980). Moreover, Evans (1975) has shown that hypoxia and ototoxic drugs cause the tuning curves measured in the eighth nerve of animals to become flat, with almost no sharp tuning near the characteristic frequency.

Aging, which probably involves cochlear deterioration, appears also to result in a greater spread of masking than in normally hearing young adults. R. D. Patterson, Nimmo-Smith, Weber, and Milroy (1982) ascribe this change both to a slow increase in the width of the critical band after age 20 and to a reduction in its dynamic range, meaning that frequencies well outside a given critical band are "attenuated" less. (In terms of the auditory-filter model, the tails of the filter are elevated.) Consequently, there is more masking of the signals at frequencies remote from the masker frequencies.

4. MONAURAL DISCRIMINATION

This section describes the ability of the auditory system to detect small differences between monaural sounds that vary along a single stimulus continuum, such as intensity or frequency. Measurements of this ability provide much information about the way in which the auditory system processes sounds and permit setting design criteria for allowable deviations from some ideal stimulus specification such as the frequency of a tonal signal. Following a brief discussion of measurements of discrimination in general, intensity discrimination is discussed in Section 4.1, frequency discrimination in Section 4.2, and temporal resolution and discrimination of duration in Section 4.3.

Most measurements of discrimination have focused on the smallest difference between two sounds that a listener can detect. This difference is usually called the just noticeable difference (JND) or, less commonly, the difference limen (DL), and is measured in stimulus units. The JND for a given continuum varies with the stimulus condition and with factors unrelated to the basic resolving power of the auditory system. Some of these factors are the criterion of percentage correct responses required to call the difference just noticeable, the psychophysical method, and the method by which the stimulus difference is introduced (e.g., by modulating a continuous sound or by presenting separate, slightly different sounds).

The effect of these extra-auditory factors can often be specified approximately by means of signal-detection theory (for a discussion of signal-detection theory, see Falmagne, Chapter 1). Because the magnitude of their effect on the JND depends on the stimulus, however, these variables are discussed separately for each stimulus dimension.

For many stimulus dimensions, the JND, $\Delta\phi$, is approximately proportional to the stimulus magnitude, ϕ, that is,

$$\Delta\phi = k\phi \quad (29)$$

where k is a constant known as the Weber fraction. This relationship is Weber's law (after the German physicist Ernst H. Weber, 1795–1878), which states that the just noticeable difference between stimuli is proportional to the stimulus magnitude (see also Falmagne, Chapter 1). For example, the JND for duration is about 5 msec for a 50-msec stimulus and about 50 msec for a 500-msec stimulus, and the Weber fraction, $\Delta\phi/\phi$, is 0.1. Weber's law provides a good first approximation of much of the data for discrimination of intensity, frequency, and duration. Even when it fails, the data are often described in terms of the deviation from Weber's law.

4.1. Intensity Discrimination

One of the most studied properties of the auditory system is its ability to discriminate among sounds differing only in intensity

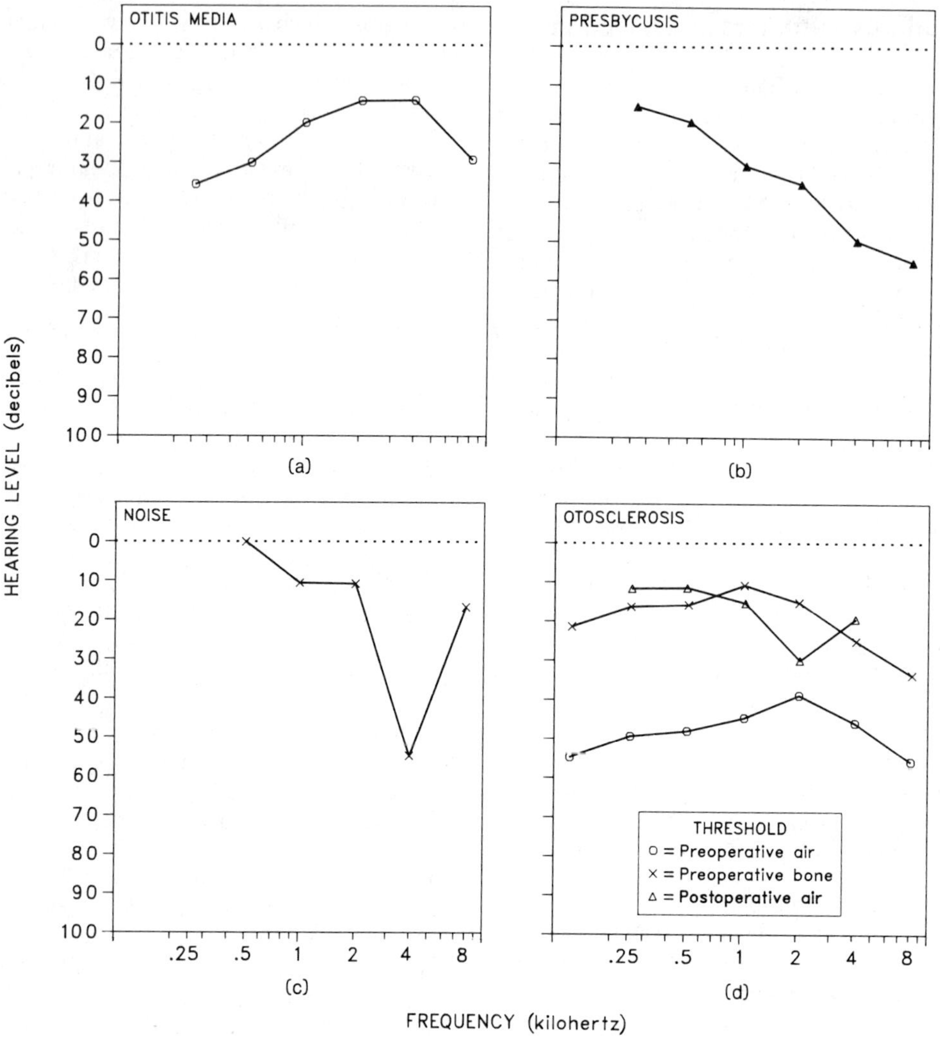

Figure 14.42. Effect of auditory pathology on thresholds. Hearing loss is plotted as a function of frequency for four individuals with different types of hearing impairment. Hearing losses are calculated by subtracting the average normal threshold (minimum audible pressure) at a given frequency (see Table 14.1 and Fig. 14.23) from the individual's threshold at that same frequency. Audiogram (a) is for the right ear of a 5-year-old child with serous otitis media (fluid in the middle ear). Audiogram (b) is for the left ear of a 70-year-old man with presbycusis. Audiogram (c) is for the left ear of a 34-year-old person with noise-induced hearing loss after 20 years of employment in a weaving factory. Unlike otitis media and presbycusis, which result in patterns of hearing loss that vary greatly from one patient to another, noise-induced hearing loss is usually characterized by normal thresholds at lower frequencies and a sharp increase in threshold above 3,000 Hz, often with some recovery above 4,000 Hz. Audiogram (d) shows the preoperative air thresholds (circles) of a 40-year-old patient with otosclerosis resulting in fixation of the stapes. This flat curve at 50 dB is the maximum loss observed in pure middle-ear losses. Preoperative bone-conduction thresholds (measured by placing a vibrator in back of the pinna) are normal. After surgery to mobilize the stapes, air-conduction thresholds (triangles) are normal for a person of the patient's age. Although air-conduction thresholds provide an indication of the severity and possible nature of a hearing loss, they must be supplemented by other hearing tests in order to assess the impact on speech perception and to pinpoint the site and nature of the impairment. [(a), (b), (d) From D. D. Dirks, Effects of hearing impairment on the auditory system, in E. C. Carterette & M. P. Friedman (Eds.), *Handbook of perception Vol. 4: Hearing*, Academic Press, Inc., 1978. Reprinted witth permission. (c) From T. S. Littler, Noise measurement, analysis, and evaluation of harmful effects, *Annals of Occupational Hygiene, 1*. Copyright 1958 by Pergamon Press, Inc. Reprinted with permission.]

(or equivalently, in SPL). The JND for intensity can be expressed several different ways and unfortunately all have been used in the literature. In this section, the JND for SPL is stated in terms of ΔL, which is the level difference, in decibels, between two sounds that are just noticeably different. To clarify the conversion of the original data from various studies to the form used in this section, the relations among the various measures of intensity JNDs are discussed below. For a further discussion and tables of the relationship among the various measures of intensity discrimination, see Grantham and Yost (1982).

4.1.1. Measures of Intensity Discrimination. The ΔI is the just noticeable intensity difference between a standard (reference) sound and a comparison sound. We will call the intensity of the standard I and of the comparison I'. Then

$$\Delta I = I' - I \tag{30}$$

or

$$I' = I + \Delta I \tag{31}$$

and to convert to level difference (ΔL) in decibels,

$$\Delta L = 10 \log \frac{I'}{I} = 10 \log \frac{I + \Delta I}{I} \ . \tag{32}$$

Note that Weber's law suggests that ΔL should be constant, or stated in terms of the Weber fraction,

$$k = \frac{\Delta I}{I} \tag{33}$$

which can also be expressed in decibels as

$$K = 10 \log \frac{\Delta I}{I} \ . \tag{34}$$

Many studies have viewed intensity discrimination as a special case of masking, in which masker and signal are identical (e.g., Green, Nachmias, Kearney, & Jeffress, 1979; Hirsh, 1951). Accordingly, they present their data as the "signal" level, 10 $\log[\Delta I/(10^{-12}\text{W}\cdot\text{m}^{-2})]$, necessary for detection in presence of the masker with level 10 $\log(I/10^{-12}\text{W}\cdot\text{m}^{-2})$. ($10^{-12}\text{W}\cdot\text{m}^{-2}$ is the reference intensity corresponding to 0 dB SPL in air; see Section 1.4.1.) Presenting the data in this manner implicitly assumes that the "signal" and the masker are 90° out of phase, so that their intensities (I) add linearly. When "masker" and "signal" are identical and in phase, the intensity of the masker plus signal is greater than the sum of their intensities, because their sound pressures (p) add linearly. In this case, the "signal" level may be presented as 20 $\log(\Delta p/20\ \mu\text{Pa})$ and the "masker" level as 20 $\log(p/20\ \mu\text{Pa})$, and the level difference is

$$\Delta L = 20 \log \frac{p + \Delta p}{p} \ . \tag{35}$$

Some authors have presented their results in terms of ΔI even if they added the "masker" and the "signal" in phase. The ΔIs reported are not the "signal" intensities, but are calculated as the ΔIs that would yield the same ΔL as the Δps actually used in the experiment. It can be shown that

$$\Delta I = \frac{\Delta p^2}{\rho c} + \frac{2p \cdot \Delta p}{\rho c} \tag{36}$$

and

$$\frac{\Delta I}{I} = \frac{\Delta p^2}{p} + \frac{2\Delta p}{p} \tag{37}$$

where ρ is the density of the medium (air) and c is the speed of sound (see also Section 1.2.2). In these various types of "masking" curves, Weber's law is indicated by a line with a slope of 1.0.

Finally, some experimenters (e.g., Zwicker & Feldtkeller, 1967) have measured intensity discrimination in terms of detection of amplitude modulation and presented their results in terms of the modulation index, m (see Section 1.4.3). For a modulated wave form the maximum RMS sound pressure is $(1 + m)p$ and the minimum is $(1 - m)p$, where p is the unmodulated RMS sound pressure. Thus

$$\Delta p = (1 + m)p - (1 - m)p = 2mp \tag{38}$$

and

$$\Delta L = 20 \log\left(\frac{p + 2mp}{p}\right) = 20 \log(2m + 1) \ . \tag{39}$$

4.1.2. The Effect of Paradigm. Besides being presented in different forms, data for intensity discrimination may also vary among different studies owing to differences in the experimental paradigm. Two major sources of variability are the way in which the level difference is presented and the memory load. The memory load is determined by the psychophysical method and the stimulus timing.

The level difference can be presented either as amplitude modulation of a continuous sound or as separate bursts differing only in intensity. Amplitude modulation was used in several classic experiments (e.g., Riesz, 1928) whereas the method of burst comparison has been the preferred method in modern experiments (e.g., Jesteadt, Wier, & Green, 1977, and references cited therein). Although the results for amplitude modulation and burst comparison have much in common, they differ sufficiently that some authors have concluded that a single mechanism is unlikely to explain both sets of results (Green et al., 1979). For example, outside the mid-frequency range, there are marked differences in the frequency dependence of the amplitude-modulation ΔLs measured by Riesz (1928) and burst-comparison ΔLs measured in modern experiments (e.g., Jesteadt et al., 1977).

In theory, amplitude modulation may be adequately detected by onset-detectors responding to the onset of the intensity increase (Evans & Whitfield, 1965; P. Nelson, Erulkar, & Bryan, 1966). Amplitude modulation may also be detected on the basis of the activity or excitation pattern evoked by the stimulus, which can be expected to vary with the modulation. Burst comparison, on the other hand, can be based only on the excitation pattern evoked by the separate bursts, because both reference and comparison bursts have onsets. Therefore, ΔLs for amplitude modulation and burst comparison should differ to the extent that the onset detectors play an important role.

For a 1,000-Hz tone, the ΔI versus I functions for amplitude modulation and burst comparison have similar slopes above 30 dB SPL. However, the psychometric functions are steeper, and shortening the signal duration from 100 to 10 msec increases the JND more for modulation than for comparison (Green et al., 1979). Also, the JNDs for the 100-msec signals are smaller for amplitude modulation than for burst comparison above 30 dB SPL. These results indicate that at the difference threshold, the onset response probably plays a minor role in the detection of amplitude modulation, but its contribution increases with the amount of modulation. This conclusion is supported by Harris's (1963) finding that increasing the steady-state duration of an intensity increment in a continuous 1,000-Hz tone decreased the JND much more than shortening the rise time of the increment.

The other major variable that can affect the JNDs for intensity is the memory requirements of the experimental task. Memory load is primarily a problem in burst-comparison experiments because amplitude modulation permits a nearly immediate comparison of the lower and higher intensities. Burst comparison requires the temporal separation between successive bursts, and the larger the separation, the poorer discrimination becomes.

To account for this and related effects, Durlach and Braida (1969) developed their "preliminary theory of intensity resolution." This model accounts for a variety of phenomena in intensity discrimination, and may also account for similar phenomena in discrimination along other continua. The model consists of three parts: a stimulus-transformation stage, a short-term (trace) memory, and a long-term (context) memory. Stimulus intensity is first transformed into a "sensation magnitude" according to an empirically defined transfer function. This transformation is imperfect and has associated variability, represented by a "sensation noise" that limits discrimination even if memory were perfect.

The trace memory presumably enables the listener to recall the sensation of the preceding stimulus, but accuracy decreases over time. How fast the trace fades depends on the amount of interference. As the interstimulus interval increases, the trace-memory noise increases and quickly renders the trace ineffective. Then the model predicts that discrimination will be performed via context memory, unless context memory is compromised by other manipulations, as described next.

The model assumes that context memory permits long-term storage of a label that represents the sensation and that can be recalled perfectly regardless of interstimulus interval. Variability is associated with the labeling process, and depends on the range of stimuli used in a given experiment. Thus the model states that aside from fundamental resolving power, which is determined by the sensation noise, intensity discrimination depends on the interstimulus interval and the total range of stimuli presented. When the range of stimuli is small, changing interstimulus interval has a relatively small effect on the JNDs because the variability associated with context memory is small. When the interstimulus interval is short, changing the overall range has a relatively small effect on the JNDs because the variability associated with trace memory is small (Berliner, Durlach, & Braida, 1977). On the other hand, when the interstimulus interval is large, changing the range has a substantial effect on the JND and vice versa. At the limit of interstimulus intervals, that is, in identification experiments in which only one stimulus is presented at a time, the model predicts that the JND is nearly proportional to the total range of levels encompassed by the stimuli to be identified. Thus the model explains why the number of stimuli that can be identified correctly is relatively constant at about 7 ± 2 (G. A. Miller, 1956) regardless of the range. The model also predicts that in a given experiment the sensitivity, d', is proportional to the level difference, ΔL, between the two stimuli. This prediction is well supported by data in the literature (Pynn, Braida, & Durlach, 1971; Rabinowitz, 1970; Rabinowitz, Lim, Braida, & Durlach, 1976).

4.1.3. The Effect of the Stimulus: The Multiband Excitation-Pattern Model. The model of Durlach and Braida (1969) limits itself to the role of memory load in discrimination. Other models seek to explain the effects of stimulus variables such as level, frequency, and bandwidth on intensity discrimination. Some of these models adhere more or less closely to physiological data (Siebert, 1965, 1968; Teich & Lachs, 1979), whereas others are based almost entirely on psychoacoustic data (Florentine & Buus, 1981; Maiwald, 1967a, 1967b; Viemeister, 1972; Zwicker, 1956, 1970). One other class of models takes a rather abstract view of the stimulus transformations in the auditory system and applies almost exclusively to pure tones (Luce & Green, 1974; McGill & Goldberg, 1968a, 1968b).

The physiological and psychoacoustic models differ in many respects, but share the critical assumption that intensity discrimination is based upon changes in a pattern of activity. The notion is that as a tone increases in intensity, it produces activity that spreads to more and more frequency-selective channels which are tuned to frequencies further and further from the test frequency. Because intensity discrimination is based on the change in activity within each channel, even channels remote from the test frequency can contribute substantially to intensity discrimination of intense tones. The importance of this concept is clearly illustrated by the multiband excitation-pattern model (Florentine & Buus, 1981).

The model is based on Zwicker's (1956, 1970) excitation-pattern model, which derives a pattern of activity (excitation pattern) for a stimulus from the masking pattern for that stimulus. The multiband excitation-pattern model assumes that intensity discrimination is the outcome of an optimum decision based on the difference in each of the 24 critical bands between the levels of excitation caused by the standard and the comparison. According to standard excitation patterns (see Zwicker & Feldtkeller, 1967), excitation level increases with stimulus level with a slope between 1 and 1.6 in every critical band that is excited above threshold. Moreover, the sensitivity to a given change in excitation level is the same in all critical bands. Therefore, the model predicts that the width of the excitation pattern is the most important determinant of intensity discrimination. To a first approximation the model predicts that ΔL is inversely proportional to the square root of the number of critical bands excited by the stimulus. For example, ΔL for a 1,000-Hz tone ought to decrease by a factor of about 6 as the level increases from near threshold to 90 dB SPL. (The predicted increase is somewhat larger than the square root of the increase in number of critical bands excited, because the excitation level in some bands above the test frequency grows with a slope greater than 1, which increases their sensitivity to a given change in stimulus level.) Because the model uses information along the entire excitation pattern, it also predicts that masking any part of the excitation pattern ought to result in poorer JNDs. As described in the following sections, these and other predictions by the model are generally well supported by the data.

4.1.4. Intensity Discrimination of Pure Tones. Figure 14.43 shows how the JND varies as a function of level for a 1,000-Hz tone. Rabinowitz et al. (1976) summarized the results from 15 studies; they normalized the data from each study by dividing the ΔL at each level by the ΔL at 40 dB SL. The ΔLs at 40 dB SL varied from 0.83 to about 1.5 dB for studies using stimulus durations of 100 msec or longer. (For short stimulus durations, the ΔLs can become very large, as shown in Fig. 14.49.) The normalized data are in good agreement with the average data for the three highly practiced listeners of Jesteadt et al. (1977). The function derived from the excitation-pattern model is in good agreement with the data except, perhaps, at the lowest levels. According to both theory and data, the JND decreases from about 2 to about 0.4 dB as the level increases from threshold to 90 dB SL. This deviation from Weber's law, which predicts a constant JND, is called the "near miss" to Weber's law.

Whether the near miss to Weber's law also obtains at high frequencies is a matter of some controversy (see also Falmagne, Chapter 1). Most studies do not permit firm conclusions because

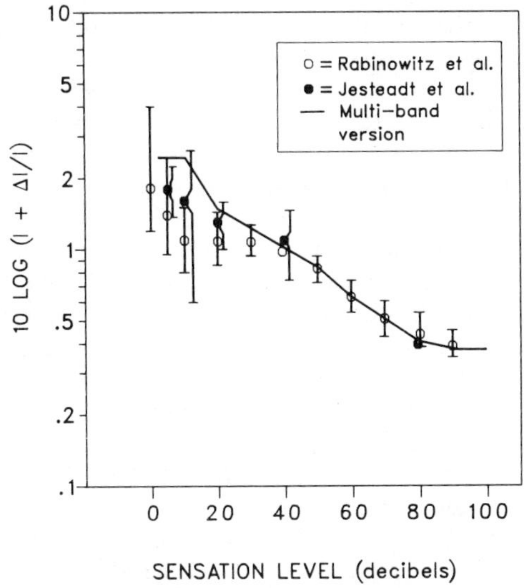

Figure 14.43. JNDs for level, ΔL, [$=10\log(I+\Delta I/I)$] of a 1,000-Hz tone as a function of sensation level. The JNDs were measured in burst comparison experiments, in which the listener is presented with two tone bursts differing only in intensity. The listener's task is to judge which burst was the more intense. Rabinowitz, Lim, Braida, and Durlach's (1976) data (open circles) are the averages of data from 15 studies, normalized by dividing each ΔL with the ΔL at 40 dB SL. The bars show plus and minus one standard deviation, calculated on a linear scale of $\delta' = 10/\Delta L$. Jesteadt, Wier, and Green's (1977) data (filled circles) are the means for three well-trained listeners who were presented 500-msec tone bursts 500 msec apart. The ΔLs were determined by an adaptive one-up, two-down procedure (Levitt, 1971). The bars show plus and minus three standard errors of the means, calculated on a linear scale of ΔL on the basis of the standard deviations of five measurements in each individual listener. The solid line shows the ΔLs predicted by the excitation-pattern model for intensity discrimination (Florentine & Buus, 1981). The prediction is based on Zwicker's standard excitation patterns (see Zwicker & Feldtkeller, 1967) and the free parameter k was set to $0.406\cdot dB^{-1}$ to fit the data at 40 dB SL. The data show that the ΔL for a 1,000-Hz tone decreases by a factor of 4–5—from about 2 to about 0.4 dB—as the sensation level is increased from threshold to about 90 dB SL. The model prediction is in good agreement with the data except, perhaps, below 20 dB SL. (From M. Florentine & S. Buus, An excitation-pattern model for intensity discrimination, *Journal of the Acoustical Society of America*, 1981, *70*. Reprinted with permission.)

the JNDs at high frequencies were measured over too restricted a range of levels. In a recent study, however, Florentine (1983) measured intensity JNDs at 1,000 and 14,000 Hz at levels encompassing almost the entire dynamic range. Her results are shown in Figure 14.44; the ΔLs at 1,000 Hz are about as large as those at 14,000 Hz at low levels but smaller at high levels. According to the excitation-pattern model the ΔLs at 14,000 Hz more closely follow Weber's law owing to the severely limited upward spread of excitation. The limited availability of critical bands above 14,000 Hz prevents the ΔLs from decreasing with increasing level. At low levels, on the other hand, the spread of excitation is not very large at any frequency and can be accommodated at high as well as at low frequencies. Thus the model predicts that the JND is independent of frequency at low levels.

In the following discussion, the frequency dependence of the ΔLs is examined further by comparing data for burst comparison and amplitude modulation. Using a burst comparison paradigm, Jesteadt et al. (1977) measured intensity JNDs at frequencies between 200 and 8,000 Hz (see also Fig. 14.43). The results for three listeners are shown in Figure 14.45. An analysis of variance showed that sensation level had the only significant effect. The excitation-pattern model predicts an interaction between frequency and level. Among the conditions used by Jesteadt et al. (1977), however, the effect on ΔL should be measurable only at 8,000 Hz and 80 dB SL. In fact, the ΔL at this point tends to be higher than at the ΔLs at the same level and lower frequencies, but the variability in the data and the many measurements at relatively low frequencies rendered the interaction insignificant. Thus the frequency independence of the ΔLs obtained by Jesteadt et al. (1977) agrees roughly with the model.

To permit approximation of the JND at a given sensation level (SL), Jesteadt et al. gave the following formula:

$$\Delta L = 1.644\ \text{dB} - 0.0141 \times \text{SL} \qquad (40)$$

which accounted for 50% of the variance in their data. Their formula for the Weber fraction in decibels is

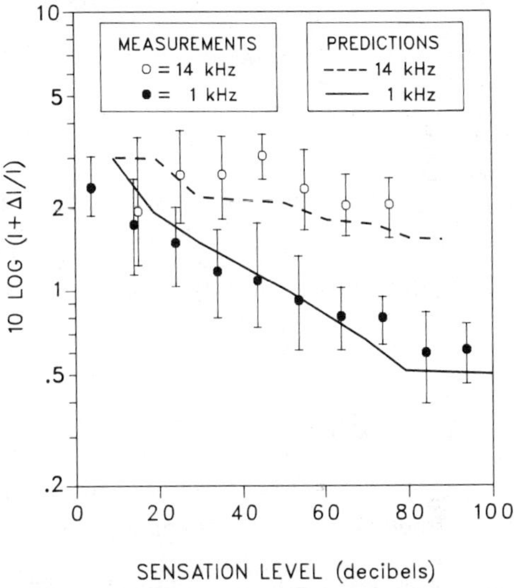

Figure 14.44. JNDs for level, ΔL, [$= 10\log(I+\Delta I/I)$] for tones at 1,000 and 14,000 Hz as a function of sensation level. The ΔLs were measured in a burst comparison paradigm using the method of constant stimuli. On each trial, two 500-msec monaural tone bursts 250 msec apart were presented and the listeners judged which burst was more intense. For each listener and condition, the ΔL was calculated as the geometric mean of the ΔLs obtained in two to seven blocks of 100 trials. The ΔL for one block of trials was calculated as the level increment used for that block of trials divided by the sensitivity, d', obtained in the block of trials. This calculation yields the ΔL corresponding to $d' = 1$. The data are geometric means for five listeners. The bars show plus and minus one standard deviation. The lines show the predictions by the excitation-pattern model for intensity discrimination. The predictions are based on Zwicker's standard excitation patterns (Zwicker & Feldtkeller, 1967) and the free parameter in the model, k, was set to $0.333\cdot dB^{-1}$. Note that the ΔLs for 14,000 Hz are equal to those at 1,000 Hz at low levels, but about three times larger at high levels. The 1,000-Hz data show the usual four- to fivefold decrease of the ΔLs as the level increases from near threshold to 90 dB. In contrast, the 14,000-Hz data closely follow Weber's law and show almost no decrease in the ΔLs with increasing level. According to the excitation-pattern model, the decrease of the ΔLs at 1,000 Hz results primarily from upward spread of excitation. At 14,000 Hz, no critical bands are available for upward spread of excitation, and thus one would not expect the ΔLs to decrease with increasing level. (The slight decrease in the predicted ΔLs at 14,000 Hz is the result of the small downward spread of excitation.) (From M. Florentine, Intensity discrimination as a function of level and frequency and its relation to high-frequency hearing, *Journal of the Acoustical Society of America*, 1983, *74*. Reprinted with permission.)

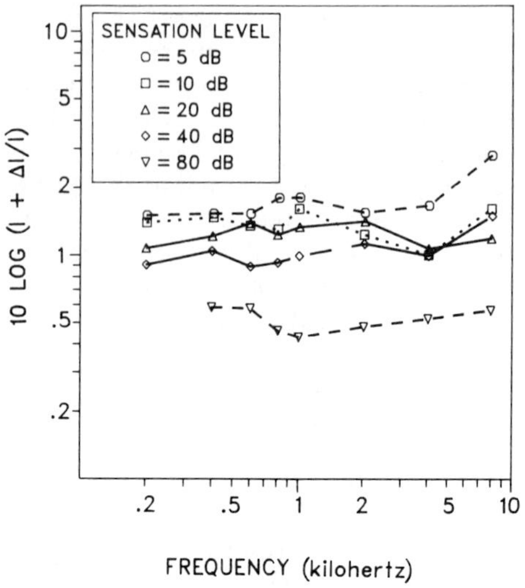

Figure 14.45. JNDs for level, ΔL, [$= 10\log(I + \Delta I/I)$] measured in a burst comparison paradigm as a function of frequency (data from Jesteadt, Wier, & Green, 1977). The average ΔLs for three well-trained listeners, measured with an adaptive one-up, two-down procedure (Levitt, 1971), are plotted as a function of frequency with sensation level as the parameter. Five adaptive runs, 100 trials each, were obtained for each listener and condition. On each trial the listeners were presented two 500-msec tone bursts differing only in level. Their task was to judge which burst was more intense. Note that the ΔLs appear relatively independent of frequency at all levels, contrary to Florentine's (1983) data (see Fig. 14.44). However, the excitation-pattern model predicts that even for the highest frequency used by Jesteadt et al. (8,000 Hz), any effect of frequency should occur only above 40 dB SL. Thus it is hardly surprising that Jesteadt et al. found no significant effect of frequency.

$$K = -3.344\text{ dB} - 0.072 \times \text{SL} \quad (41)$$

which accounted for 71% of the variance. These formulas are independent of frequency, because the data showed no effect of frequency.

Whereas the effect of frequency on intensity JNDs for burst comparison is small, Riesz (1928) in his classic study found a considerable effect for amplitude modulation. Figure 14.46 shows his average data for 12 listeners tested at frequencies from 35 to 10,000 Hz. The ΔL for a given level is smallest at 4,000 Hz and increases at lower and higher frequencies. The effect of frequency is probably highly significant, because Riesz's (1928) observations in terms of ΔL were within ±10% for small ΔLs and within ±5% for the highest ΔLs, indicating remarkably small variability. (In burst-comparison experiments the standard deviation across listeners typically is about 40% of ΔL.) Furthermore, the effect of level is more pronounced in Riesz's (1928) data than in those of Jesteadt et al. (1977). This is consistent with other data that show equal JNDs at low sensation levels but smaller JNDs for amplitude modulation than for burst comparison at high sensation levels (Green et al., 1979; Viemeister 1983).

4.1.5. The Effect of Stimulus Duration on Intensity Discrimination. Riesz (1928) also found that the ΔL increased by about a factor of 3 as the modulation rate was lowered from 3 to about 0.2 Hz or raised to about 30 Hz. The increase of ΔL at modulation rates lower than 3 Hz probably results from decay of memory during the slow transition from minimum to maximum levels. The increase of the ΔLs toward modulation rates higher than 3 Hz probably results from the auditory system's temporal integration which, in effect, diminishes the intensity differences at high rates. (See also Section 4.3.)

For burst comparison, temporal integration ought not to diminish the intensity difference provided the bursts are separated by an interstimulus interval longer than the integration time. However, auditory integration may still result in smaller JNDs for long than for short stimulus durations. Consider a general model in which the sensitivity, d', is determined by the ratio of the difference in activity evoked by the two stimuli to the standard deviation of some random process (e.g., Siebert, 1968). Owing to temporal integration, the standard deviation of the activity will be inversely proportional to the square root of stimulus duration up to the maximum integration time. Thus ΔL ought to be inversely proportional to the square root of the stimulus duration for durations less than the maximum integration time and constant for longer durations. Indeed, Henning's (1970) data, shown in Figure 14.47, are consistent with this prediction. Note that on the average the critical duration above which the ΔLs are constant decreases from about 70 msec at 250 Hz to about 12 msec at 4,000 Hz, indicating that the integration time in the model may depend on test frequency. However, some recent, more comprehensive data by Florentine (in press) make this simple model less tenable. Whereas her ΔLs for three listeners agree reasonably well with Henning's, the overall trend is quite different. Florentine's data show a steady decrease of ΔL as duration increases up to about 750 msec at 250 Hz and up to 2,000 msec at 1,000 and 8,000 Hz. Moreover, the decrease of ΔL has an average slope of only about -0.3, not the -0.5 predicted by the model. Some data for amplitude modulation agree with the predictions of the model and indicate that the integration time also may vary with level. Harris's (1963) data for detection of a brief level increment in a continuous tone indicate that the critical duration for a 1,000-Hz tone decreases from about 300 msec at 5 dB SL to 60 msec at 80 dB. Garner and Miller's (1944) data for a 500-Hz tone are in the same direction. However, Chocholle and Krutel's (1968) data for tones are not well matched by the predictions of the model and indicate an integration time of about 130 msec independent of frequency.

The implications of the studies using amplitude modulation are unclear, because the auditory integration impairs discrimination by reducing the effective size of a rapid level change whereas detection of the onset of the increment could aid discrimination. At the limit, the onset alone may be detectable, in which case one would predict that ΔL should be independent of duration, as is evident in Garner and Miller's data for durations less than about 50 msec. Thus the interpretation of the amplitude-modulation data must necessarily be cautious.

4.1.6. Intensity Discrimination of Complex Sounds. The intensity discrimination of complex sounds lends itself to analysis by the multiband excitation-pattern model (Florentine & Buus, 1981). For a broad-band stimulus such as an unfiltered click or a white noise, the model predicts that Weber's law holds at levels well above threshold because all available critical bands are excited. At absolute threshold, on the other hand, only one band is excited, as in the case of a pure tone. Thus the model predicts that near threshold, ΔL is the same for a broad-band noise as for a pure tone. As the level increases, ΔL for the noise ought to decrease more rapidly than for a pure tone, because the noise even at low levels excites many critical bands in the mid-frequency range, where the threshold curve is relatively flat. Above 70 dB SPL, however, the ΔL should be lower for a pure tone than for the noise owing to the faster-than-linear

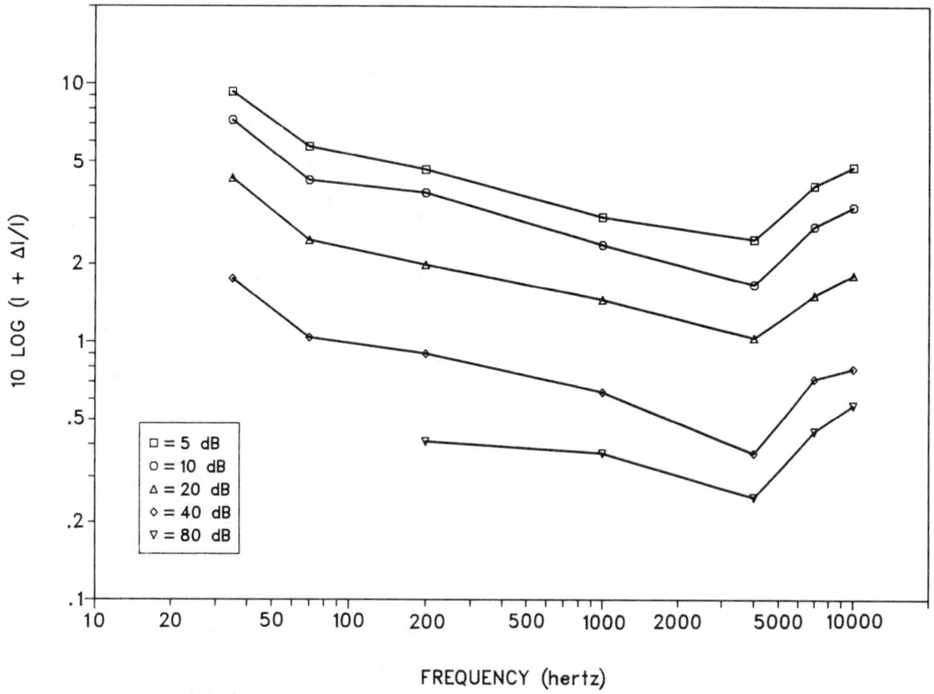

Figure 14.46. JNDs for level, ΔL, [$= 10 \log(I + \Delta I/I)$] measured in a modulation paradigm as a function of frequency (data from Riesz, 1928). The average ΔLs for 12 listeners are plotted as a function of frequency, f, with sensation level as the parameter. The listeners were presented two continuous tones with frequencies f and $(f + 3)$ Hz. Their task was to adjust the level of the $(f + 3)$-Hz tone so the resulting 3-Hz amplitude modulation was just audible. The data in the figure are the ΔLs calculated from the average Weber fractions, $\Delta I/I$, presented by Riesz. Note that at all frequencies, the ΔLs decrease about a factor of 10 as the level of the test tone increases from 5 to 80 dB SL. Moreover, the data show a pronounced effect of frequency in contrast to the data for burst comparison ΔLs of Jesteadt et al. (1977) (see Fig. 14.45). Although the ΔLs for burst comparison and amplitude modulation are quite similar in magnitude, they obviously differ in respect to the effect of frequency and, to some extent, the effect of level.

growth of excitation in critical bands far above the frequency of the tone. As shown in Figure 14.48, Houtsma, Durlach, and Braida's (1980) measurements of ΔLs for a 1,000-Hz tone and for white noise are consistent with these predictions. The slight bump in the data for the white noise between 60 and 90 dB is probably not significant. Other data for white noise closely follow Weber's law above 20 dB SL (Harris, 1963; G. A. Miller, 1947; Zwicker & Feldtkeller, 1967), as do those of Penner and Viemeister (1973) for 100-μsec broad-band clicks and Buus and Florentine (1981) for broad-band 18-tone complexes.

The different shapes of the ΔL functions for a 1,000-Hz tone and for a white noise clearly illustrate the strong dependence of ΔL on the width of the excitation pattern. Further support for this notion comes from studies on intensity discrimination of two-tone complexes and filtered clicks. The ΔLs for two-tone complexes tend to be lower when the tones are separated by about two critical bands than when they are separated by less than one critical band (Chaves, 1965; Morton & Carpenter, 1963). The ΔLs for high-pass clicks (cutoff frequency, $f_c = 2{,}000$ Hz) closely follow Weber's law and tend to be higher than those for broad-band clicks (about 1.8 vs. 1.4 dB) (Penner & Viemeister, 1973). (The excitation pattern is about 12 critical bands wide for the high-pass clicks and about 23 critical bands wide for the broad-band clicks at all but the lowest levels.) On the other hand, the ΔLs for low-pass filtered clicks ($f_c = 780$ Hz) are nearly the same as for high-pass clicks at low levels but decrease to about 0.8 dB at the high levels (Penner & Viemeister, 1973). Presumably, the low ΔLs at high levels result from the broad upward spread of excitation and the faster-than-linear growth of excitation in bands tuned to frequencies far above the cutoff frequency.

Intensity discrimination of narrow-band noises differs from that of other complex stimuli because the level of separate bursts of the same noise fluctuates from burst to burst. This randomness may hamper intensity discrimination. For example, with a signal duration of 100 msec, ΔL ought not to be less than 0.73 dB when the bandwidth is 300 Hz and 1.2 dB when the bandwidth is 100 Hz. These values for ΔL result from considering only the fluctuations in the stimulus and assuming no randomness in the detection process, so they are the smallest possible. The literature on intensity discrimination of narrow-band noise is rather inconsistent, but the improvement of ΔL with increasing noise bandwidth is usually less than expected (for review see Schacknow & Raab, 1976). The reason for this probably is that the ΔLs for most noise bands approach those for tonal stimuli with similar spectral characteristics. For example, using a burst comparison procedure Schacknow and Raab found ΔLs of 0.97 dB at a 100-Hz bandwidth, 0.85 dB at a 300-Hz bandwidth, and 0.6 dB at a 10,000-Hz bandwidth for 100-msec noise bursts with a spectrum level of 45 dB SPL. [The ΔL for the 100-Hz wide noise is lower than the theoretical limit stated above, because the effective statistical bandwidth is wider (186 Hz) than the half-power bandwidth of 100 Hz, owing to the relatively shallow cutoff of the filter skirts.]

According to the excitation-pattern model, ΔL for these stimuli ought to be about 0.6 dB, if random level variations of

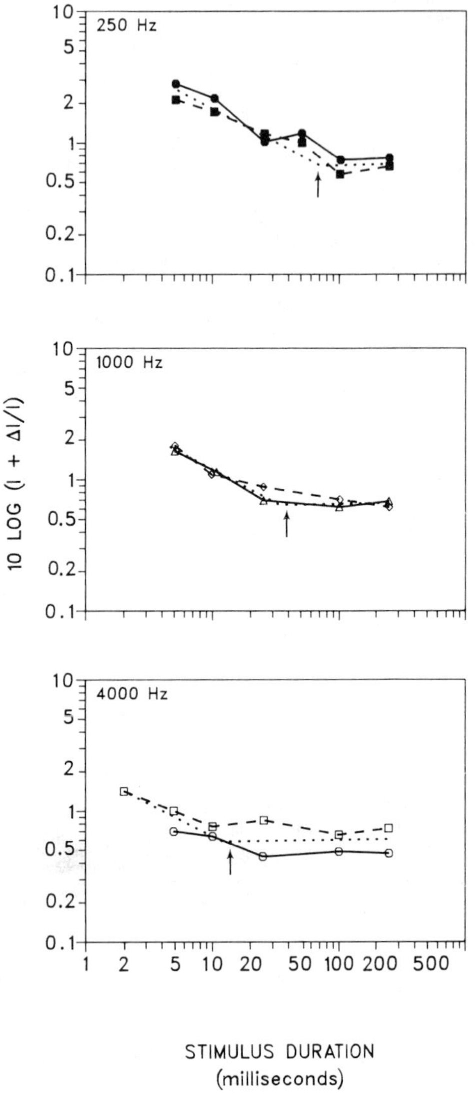

Figure 14.47. JNDs for level, ΔL, [= 10 log(I + $\Delta I/I$)] as a function of stimulus duration (data from Henning, 1970). The data points are the ΔLs calculated for each of Henning's two listeners. (Points are connected by solid lines for listener 1 and by dashed lines for listener 2.) The JNDs were measured in a burst comparison paradigm using the method of constant stimuli. The dotted lines show predictions of a general model in which the integration time (indicated by the arrows) is a free parameter. The model predicts that the ΔLs should be inversely proportional to the square root of the stimulus duration for durations shorter than the integration time and constant for longer durations. This prediction is represented by two line segments, one with a slope of −0.5 for durations shorter than the integration time and a horizontal one for longer durations. The line segments were fitted to the data by eye and the integration time is at their intersection. The predictions are in good agreement with the data and indicate that the integration time decreases with increasing stimulus frequency.

the noise bursts are ignored. Thus it appears that the random level variation of the stimulus contributes about as much as the randomness of the auditory system to the ΔLs for the 300-Hz wide noise band, but more for the 100-Hz wide noise band.

4.1.7. The Effect of Partial Masking on Intensity Discrimination. The excitation-pattern model predicts that masking any part of the excitation pattern can increase the ΔLs. As shown in Figure 14.49, this prediction is supported by data for several different conditions of masking. Masking frequencies below the test tone has relatively little effect (bottom left; Viemeister, 1972), owing to the limited downward spread of excitation. Masking frequencies above the test tone has a considerable effect (top, left and right; Moore & Raab, 1974; Viemeister, 1972), owing to the large upward spread of excitation. Masking frequencies both above and below the test tone has the greatest effect (middle right; Moore & Raab, 1974). Of course, the magnitude of the effect depends on how much of the excitation pattern is masked. A weak white noise that masks only the tails of the excitation pattern has relatively minor effect (bottom right; Moore & Raab, 1974). Results from other experiments (Hellman, 1978; Zwicker & Feldtkeller, 1967) are also consistent with predictions by the excitation-pattern model.

4.1.8. Intensity Discrimination in Impaired Listeners. The data on partial masking make it evident that excitation above the test frequency is very important for intensity discrimination at high SPLs. Thus the ΔLs for listeners with sensorineural hearing loss ought to depend, at least in part, on the amount of loss at high frequencies. Figure 14.50 shows that, indeed, impaired listeners with low-frequency losses have ΔLs similar to those for normal listeners; listeners with more or less flat losses have slightly larger ΔLs; listeners with high-frequency (sloping) losses have the largest ΔLs (Florentine, Reed, Durlach, & Braida, Note 2; see also Scharf & Florentine, 1982). However, at the same sensation level, all groups of impaired listeners have lower ΔLs than normal listeners, owing to the difference

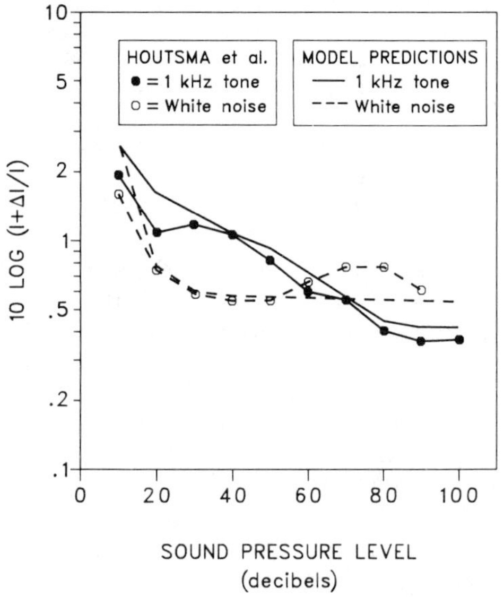

Figure 14.48. JNDs for level, ΔL, [= 10 log(I + $\Delta I/I$)] for a 1,000-Hz tone and white noise as a function of sound pressure level (data from Houtsma, Durlach, & Braida, 1980). The ΔLs were measured in a burst comparison paradigm using the method of constant stimuli. On each trial, two 500-msec bursts were presented 250 msec apart and the listeners judged which burst had the higher level. The data are the geometric means of three listeners' ΔLs for the 1,000-Hz tone (filled circles) and the white noise (open circles). The thick lines show predictions by the excitation-pattern model for intensity discrimination (Florentine & Buus, 1981). Note that the ΔLs for white noise decrease very rapidly with increasing level at low levels but closely follow Weber's law above 20–30 dB SPL. According to the model, the rapid decrease in the ΔLs resulted from the rapid increase in the number of critical bands excited by the white noise as the level increases from threshold to about 30 dB SPL. Above 30 dB SPL almost all critical bands are excited by the white noise and the model predicts Weber's law, because the number of excited bands is approximately constant. (From M. Florentine & S. Buus. An excitation-pattern model for intensity discrimination, *Journal of the Acoustical Society of America*, 1981, *70*. Reprinted with permission.)

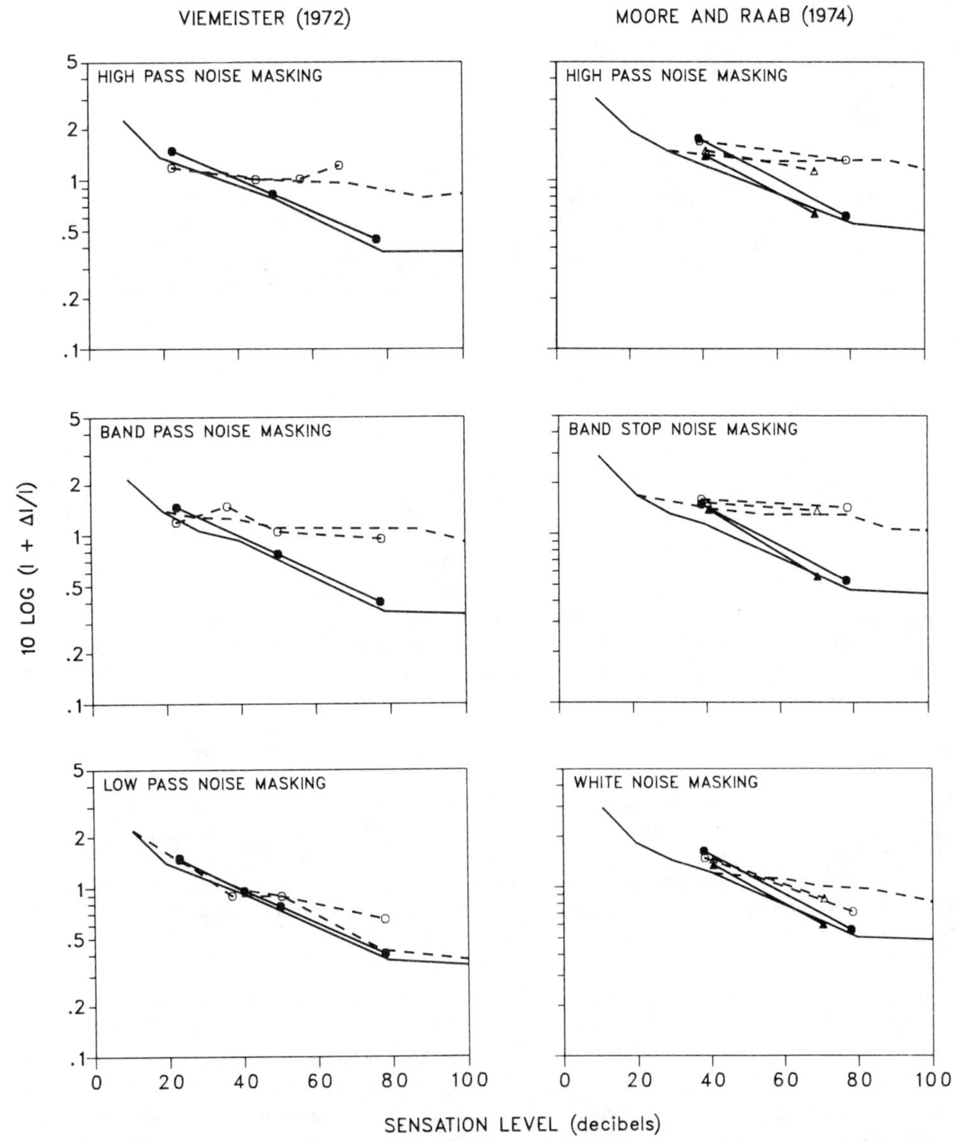

Figure 14.49. JNDs for level, ΔL, [= 10 log(I + $\Delta I/I$)] under various conditions of partial masking (data from Viemeister, 1972, and Moore & Raab, 1974). The ΔLs, measured in burst comparison paradigms, are plotted as a function of sensation level of the test tone. Viemeister's data are the averages for two listeners tested with a 950-Hz tone in the quiet (filled circles) or in the presence of the maskers indicated on the figures (open circles). Moore and Raab's data are for two individual listeners tested with a 1,000-Hz tone in the presence of a masker 50 dB below the level of the test tone (filled circles and triangles) or in the presence of the various maskers indicated (open circles and triangles). The lines without data points (dashed for tones in noise, solid for tones in quiet), show predictions by the excitation-pattern model for intensity discrimination (Florentine & Buus, 1981). In both studies the level of each masker was kept constant relative to the level of the test tone. In Viemeister's study, the high-pass masker had a cutoff frequency of 1,900 Hz and a spectrum level of −25 dB relative to the test tone's level, the band-pass masker had a center frequency of 1,900 Hz and a spectrum level of −15 dB, and the low-pass masker had a cutoff frequency of 800 Hz and a spectrum level of −25 dB. In Moore and Raab's study the high-pass masker had a cutoff frequency of 2,000 Hz. Note that the data closely follow Weber's law for maskers above the test tone and that Moore and Raab's (1974) band-stop masker has a larger effect than their high-pass masker despite its 5-dB lower spectrum level. These results indicate that frequencies above the test tone are the most important for intensity discrimination, and that masking any part of the excitation-pattern can result in increased ΔLs. (From M. Florentine & S. Buus, An excitation-pattern model for intensity discrimination, *Journal of the Acoustical Society of America*, 1981, *70*. Reprinted with permission.)

in SPL. At a given SL, the tone is set to a higher SPL for the impaired listeners than for the normal listeners. Consequently, the excitation patterns are wider for the impaired listeners. Moreover, many impaired listeners tend to have abnormally broad masking patterns at a given SPL (cf. Section 3 on masking). The finding that ΔL at a low SL is smaller in listeners with sensorineural impairments is the basis for the short increment sensitivity index (SISI) test that is used by audiologists in the differential diagnosis of hearing impairment (for review, see Buus, Florentine, & Redden, 1982a, 1982b).

4.1.9. Intensity Discrimination Summary. Intensity discrimination has been investigated for a wide variety of stimuli

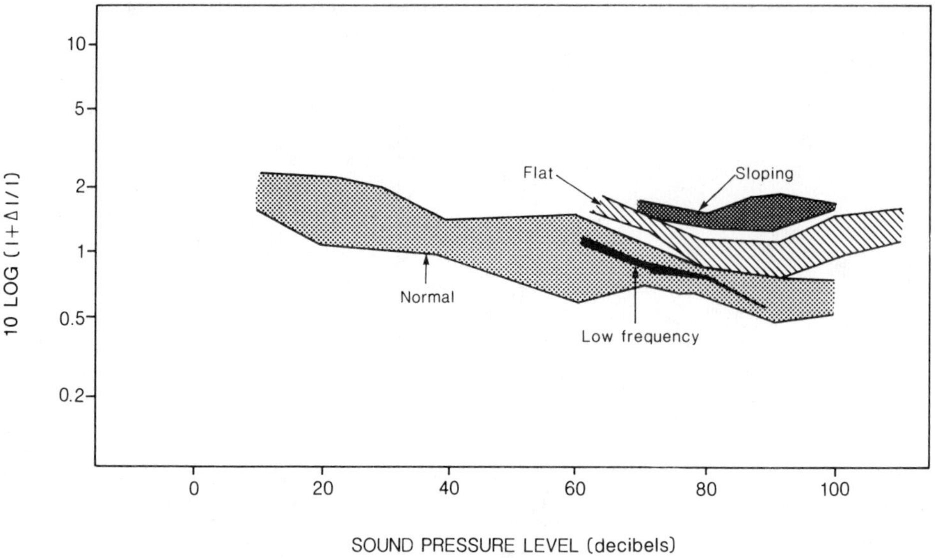

Figure 14.50. JNDs for level, ΔL, [$= 10 \log(I + \Delta I/I)$], for three groups of listeners with impairments of primarily cochlear origin (data from Florentine et al., Note 2; see also Scharf & Florentine, 1982). The medians of ΔLs for two listeners with bowl-shaped audiograms (primarily low-frequency hearing losses), and interquartile ranges for four listeners with relatively flat hearing losses and four listeners with sloping (primarily high-frequency) hearing losses are plotted as a function of SPL. Also shown are the interquartile ranges for a group of ten normal listeners. The interquartile ranges are for data that have been pooled across various test frequencies. The ΔLs were measured in a burst comparison paradigm using the method of constant stimuli. On each trial, the listeners were presented with two 500-msec tone bursts 250 msec apart. Their task was to judge which burst was more intense. For each listener and condition, ΔLs were determined on the basis of two to seven blocks of 100 trials. Note that for levels well above threshold listeners with low-frequency losses have ΔLs equal to those of normal listeners, listeners with flat losses have slightly larger ΔLs, and listeners with high-frequency losses have the largest ΔLs. This shows the importance of high-frequency hearing for intensity discrimination of mid-frequency tones.

and paradigms. With the exception of identification experiments using stimuli encompassing a wide range of levels and experiments using stimuli of very short durations, the ΔLs are about 2 dB near threshold and decrease to between 0.6 and 0.3 dB at levels above about 60 dB SPL. At high levels, somewhat increased ΔLs may result from masking, random level variations in narrow-band noise, and high-frequency hearing loss. Most of the data on intensity discrimination can be understood by Durlach and Braida's (1969) memory model and the multiband excitation-pattern model for intensity discrimination (Florentine & Buus, 1981).

4.2. Frequency Discrimination

The auditory system's ability to discriminate frequency is typically measured as the smallest change, ΔF, in frequency that is just detectable. Experimenters report the results directly in terms of the JND in hertz, ΔF, or as the Weber fraction, $\Delta F/F$.

4.2.1. The Effect of Method on Frequency Discrimination. Like intensity discrimination, frequency discrimination depends on two major variables: the mode of stimulus presentation and the memory load.

The frequency difference can be presented either as frequency modulation, that is, as a continuous tone whose frequency varies over time, or as separate bursts differing only in frequency. Frequency modulation was used in several classic studies (e.g., Shower & Biddulph, 1931, and references cited therein), whereas burst comparison has been the preferred method in modern experiments (e.g., Wier, Jesteadt, & Green, 1977, and references cited therein). These two methods yield radically different results at low and high frequencies; ΔFs are larger for frequency modulation than for burst comparison at frequencies below 2,000 Hz, but smaller above 2,000 Hz (Wier et al., 1977, Figs. 14.51 and 14.52 in Section 4.2.3; see also Jesteadt & Sims, 1975; Verschuure & van Meeteren, 1975). Moreover, there is no correlation ($r < 0.06$) between ΔFs for frequency modulation and ΔFs for burst comparison measured in the same listeners (Moore, 1976). The differences and total lack of correlation between frequency modulation and burst comparison is surprising, for one would expect the two tasks to depend on the same basic mechanisms.

The other major source of difference among studies of frequency discrimination is the psychophysical procedure. Modern studies have used at least three different procedures: a symmetrical two-interval, two-alternative forced-choice (2I, 2AFC) procedure, a same-different procedure, and an adjustment procedure. For example, Wier et al.'s (1977) listeners indicated which of two stimulus intervals contained the higher-frequency tone; Buus's (1980, 1983) listeners judged whether two successive tone bursts were the same or different; Nordmark's (1968) listeners adjusted the frequency of a variable tone to match that of the alternately presented standard. Direct comparisons show that the ΔFs are about 1.88 times larger for the same-different than for the 2I, 2AFC procedure (Jesteadt & Sims, 1975). Signal-detection theory predicts a smaller ratio, amounting to 1.41 ($= \sqrt{2}$) (Sorkin, 1962), but memory effects similar to those suggested by Durlach and Braida's (1969) model for intensity discrimination probably inflate the same-different ΔFs. The adjustment procedure yields ΔFs about $2\sqrt{2}$ times smaller than those obtained with the 2I, 2AFC procedure (Wier, Jesteadt, & Green, 1976). The basis for this difference is unclear.

4.2.2. Models of Frequency Discrimination. The mechanisms for frequency discrimination are not well understood. Current models do not satisfactorily explain the dependence of ΔF on frequency and intensity of a pure tone. Moreover, there is no quantitative model for frequency discrimination of complex tones. Nonetheless, the existing models do help us to understand qualitatively the many experiments on frequency discrimination.

Historically, attempts to explain frequency discrimination have been based either on a temporal theory or on a place theory. The temporal theory, originally proposed by Seebeck (1841), maintains that frequency is encoded in the timing of the neural activity. Indeed, many physiological experiments have shown that the spikes in the eighth nerve are synchronized to the frequency of a pure tone at frequencies below 4,000 to 5,000 Hz (e.g., Rose, Brugge, Anderson, & Hind, 1968; see also Section 2). Interspike intervals could be the source of information about the frequency, for example, by an autocorrelation process (Licklider, 1951; Siebert, 1970). From a model of auditory- nerve activity, Siebert (1970) estimated that if the listener could make optimal use of neural timing information, the ΔF ought be about 0.01 Hz at 1,000 Hz, which is about two orders of magnitude smaller than the observed ΔFs. Although rejecting the temporal theory, he pointed out that mechanisms could be envisioned that degrade the temporal information, thereby leading to less than optimal discrimination.

The other general theory, the place theory, was originally implied by Ohm (1843) and later explicitly developed by Helmholtz (1885/1954). Its physiological basis is that tones of different frequencies excite different parts of the basilar membrane and consequently different fibers in the auditory nerve. As the frequency of a tone increases, the place of maximum activity moves along the basilar membrane from the apex toward the oval window (Békésy, 1960; see also Section 2). The place of maximum activity is not sharply defined, but other features of the activity pattern may serve for the detection of a change in frequency. Zwicker (1956, 1970) suggested that two tones are just discriminable when their excitation patterns (see Section 4.1.3) differ by 1 dB in any critical band. This suggestion implies that ΔF is determined by the steepest slope on the masking pattern, which at high levels is below the signal frequency (see Section 3). Zwicker (1970) calculated that ΔF ought to be about 1/27 of the critical bandwidth. Although compelling in its simplicity, the model's current formulation and the standard excitation patterns (Zwicker & Feldtkeller, 1967) imply that ΔF should be invariant with level, which it is not, as shown in Section 4.2.3. However, Zwicker and Jaroszewski (1982) have shown that the slopes on the low-frequency side of masking patterns become shallower with decreasing level, which might account for the increase in ΔF with decreasing level. More elaborate versions of an excitation-pattern model may account for many of the empirical phenomena observed in frequency discrimination.

A different quantitative version of a place model has been investigated by Siebert (1970). He again based his calculations on a model of the activity in the auditory nerve, but disregarded timing information and considered only the total number of spikes in a given fiber. Siebert concluded that place information alone could account for the observed ΔFs, but he did not attempt to account for the effect of level. Moreover, his model incorrectly suggested that the Weber fraction $\Delta F/F$ is constant. The difference between Siebert's and Zwicker's predictions stems from the assumed activity patterns. For a given frequency difference, Zwicker (1970) assumes parallel translation of the patterns along the critical-band scale, which leads to the prediction of proportionality between ΔF and the critical bandwidth, whereas Siebert assumes parallel translation along a logarithmic frequency scale, which leads to the prediction of proportionality between ΔF and F.

Empirical support is weak for current theories of frequency discrimination, whether temporal or place. It is often suggested that temporal coding operates at low frequencies and place coding at high frequencies (e.g., Moore, 1982). The boundary between low and high may be near 5,000 Hz, where many phenomena associated with frequency coding show a more or less abrupt change (Moore, 1982).

4.2.3. Frequency Discrimination of Pure Tones: The Effect of Frequency and Level. Because the data obtained with frequency modulation and with burst comparison differ in many respects, we consider them separately. The most comprehensive study of frequency discrimination was performed by Shower and Biddulph (1931), who measured the just detectable amount of frequency modulation in ten ears of five listeners for ten frequencies at 6–11 levels. Figure 14.51 gives their monaural results. Several features are evident. The ΔF is nearly constant up to about 1,000–2,000 Hz, but thereafter increases faster than proportionally with the frequency; the ΔF decreases rapidly with increasing level up to about 20 dB SL, but only slightly

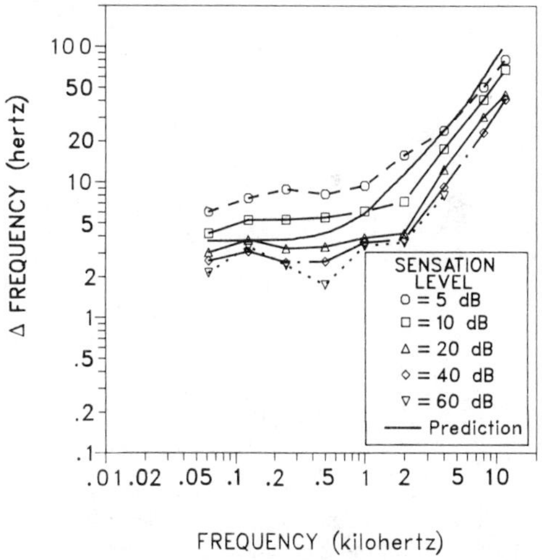

Figure 14.51. JNDs for frequency, ΔF, for frequency-modulated tones (data from Shower & Biddulph, 1931). The ΔFs for ten ears of five listeners are plotted as a function of frequency with sensation level as the parameter. The solid line shows the prediction of Zwicker's (1956) excitation pattern model that ΔF should be equal to 1/27 of the critical bandwidth. The ΔFs were measured with an ascending method of limits. The listeners' task was to indicate when they just detected a frequency modulation. The modulation frequency was 2 Hz and the modulation wave form consisted of two plateaus at the minimum and maximum frequencies with a smooth 125-msec sinusoidal transition between the two plateaus. Note that ΔF is relatively constant up to 1,000 or 2,000 Hz and increases faster than proportionally with frequency above 2,000 Hz. Also note that the effect of level changes with frequency. Generally, ΔF decreases more with increasing level at low than at high frequencies. A comparison with Figure 14.52, which shows ΔFs for burst comparison, reveals considerable difference between the two methods for measuring ΔF.

at higher levels. The function $\Delta F = 1/27 \times$ critical bandwidth, which is the prediction from Zwicker's (1956, 1970) excitation-pattern model, roughly describes the data at 10 dB SL. Shower and Biddulph (1931) also measured binaural ΔFs and found they that were 1.5 times lower than the monaural ΔFs. This factor is close to the value of 1.41 ($=\sqrt{2}$) that signal-detection theory predicts for independent detection of frequency modulation by each ear.

Data on discrimination between two successively presented tone bursts are given in Figure 14.52. Only the data of Wier et al. (1977) are given because they are the most comprehensive and because, after adjustment for procedural differences, they are in good agreement with other burst-comparison data in the literature (J. D. Harris, 1952; Henning, 1970; Moore, 1973a; Nordmark, 1968; Rosenblith & Stevens, 1953). The ΔF is roughly constant up to about 500 Hz, increases slowly up to about 1,000 Hz, and increases faster than proportionally to F above 1,000 Hz. [This description ignores the sharp peak around 800 Hz, which appears to be significant at the low levels but not at the high. This peak may be related to the fine structure in individual threshold curves (cf. Section 3); the average threshold at 800 Hz was about 2 dB lower than the thresholds at 0.6 and 1,000 Hz.] The ΔFs decrease rapidly with increasing level up to about 40 dB SPL, but only slightly thereafter.

Recently, D. A. Nelson, Stanton, and Freyman (1983) showed that Wier et al.'s, J. D. Harris's (1952), and their own data are well described by equations of the form

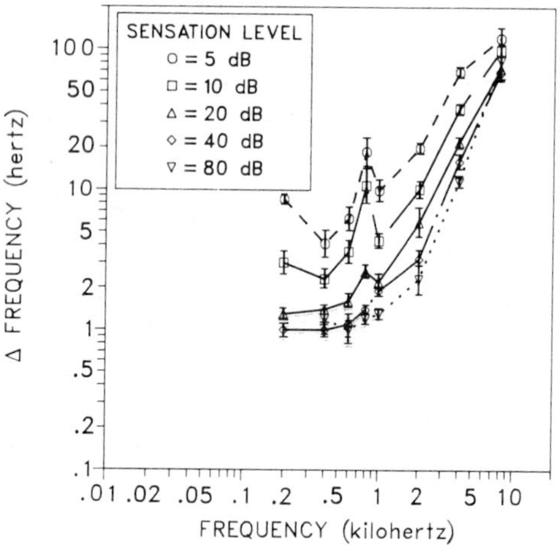

Figure 14.52. JNDs for frequency, ΔF, for tone bursts (data from Wier et al., 1977). The ΔFs for four highly trained, selected listeners are plotted as a function of frequency with sensation level as the parameter. The bars show the range of plus and minus one standard error of the mean. Listeners who could not produce a ΔF less than 3 Hz at 1,000 Hz and 70 dB SPL within the first 400 trials were excluded from the study. The ΔFs were measured with an adaptive one-up, two-down procedure (Levitt, 1971), and are based on four or five runs of 100 trials for each listener and condition. On each trial, two 500-msec tone bursts differing only in frequency were presented 500 msec apart. The listeners' task was to judge which burst was higher in frequency. The ΔFs are relatively constant up to a frequency of 600 Hz and increase rapidly above 2,000 Hz. Between 600 and 2,000 Hz ΔF either grows slowly (at high levels) or is nonmonotonic (at levels of 20 dB SL or less). The effect of level is largest for frequencies below 2,000 Hz; the ΔFs decrease about a factor of 8 as the level increases from 5 to 80 dB SL. At 8,000 Hz the decrease is less than a factor of 2. At all frequencies, most of the decrease occurs between 5 and 20 dB SL. A comparison with Figure 14.51, which shows ΔFs for frequency-modulated tones, reveals considerable difference between the two methods of measuring ΔF.

$$\log \Delta F = a\sqrt{F} + k + \left(\frac{m}{\mathrm{SL}}\right) \tag{42}$$

where a, k, and m are constants, F is the frequency of the tone, and SL is the sensation level. For Wier et al.'s data, the constants obtained by a least-squares fit were $a = 0.0238$, $k = -0.24$, and $m = 4.295$; for D. A. Nelson et al.'s data they were $a = 0.0214$, $k = -0.15$, and $m = 5.056$. (These values are for ΔF in a four-alternative forced-choice paradigm; to obtain ΔFs for the standard two-interval, two-alternative forced-choice paradigm divide the ΔFs by 1.91, or subtract 0.28 from the k values given above.)

A comparison of Figures 14.51 and 14.52 makes obvious that the ΔFs are different for frequency modulation and for burst comparison. The ΔFs for burst comparison increase sooner and more sharply with increasing frequency and decrease faster and longer with increasing level than those for frequency modulation. A common feature is the decreasing slope of the ΔF curves at low levels and at frequencies above 4,000 Hz. It probably results from the listeners' detection of a change in stimulus level at the eardrum that accompanies a small change in frequency. These changes are the consequence of resonances and antiresonances in the ear canal at frequencies around 6,000 Hz and above (cf. Section 1). The level in the ear canal changes rapidly with frequency, as made evident in Figure 14.10. The change in signal level may well be more audible than the change in frequency. Support for this analysis comes from an experiment by Henning (1966), who eliminated the level cues by randomly varying the levels of the two comparison tone bursts in a trial over a range of 12 dB. Henning (1966) reported ΔFs of about 150 Hz at 8,000 Hz and about 400 Hz at 12,000 Hz for tones presented near 63 dB SPL. Stucker (1908) also found extremely large ΔFs at high frequencies. His stimulus levels must have been more or less random because the level of the stimuli produced by his Galton whistle could not be controlled precisely. However, the extent to which the data of Stucker and Henning accurately represent frequency resolution is uncertain, because random variation of level could interfere with memory and decision processes. Moreover, if frequency discrimination is mediated by a place mechanism, as is most plausible at frequencies above 5,000 Hz, then variation would tend to obscure the changes in activity needed to signal the change in frequency. Indeed, Henning's ΔFs are in good agreement with other data below 5,000 Hz, but considerably higher at frequencies above 5,000 Hz. It is likely that the ΔFs obtained with random level variations of the test tone are inflated at high frequencies, whereas the ΔFs obtained without level variation probably are too small. Thus it is unclear which data best represent the frequency resolution.

4.2.4. The Effect of Duration on Frequency Discrimination. As the duration of a stimulus becomes very brief, frequency discrimination, like intensity discrimination, should deteriorate. Furthermore, if frequency discrimination is mediated by a "place" mechanism, ΔF should behave like ΔL (see Section 4.1.5) and be inversely proportional to the square root of the duration, T, up to some maximum integration time, T_{max}, beyond which ΔF should be constant. If frequency discrimination is mediated by a temporal mechanism, on the other hand, a different relationship between ΔF and T is predicted. The exact prediction depends on the statistics of the temporal information. For example, Siebert's (1970) model of auditory-nerve activity predicts that ΔF is inversely proportional to $T^{1.5}$ for durations less than T_{max}. J. L. Goldstein and Srulovicz (1977), on the other hand, arrived at a different, considerably more complicated prediction by using different assumptions about the distribution of time intervals in the neural activity.

These predictions ignore the possible effects of the broadening of the spectra of tones at short durations, often referred to as energy splatter (see Section 1.5.4). Moore (1973a) argued that energy splatter ought to interfere with frequency discrimination based on a place mechanism. However, he measured smaller ΔFs at low frequencies than would be expected on the basis of energy splatter. Moreover, Ronken (1971) found that ΔFs for 1,000-Hz tone bursts with different envelopes did not depend on energy splatter, but rather on the duration for which the stimulus had "an acceptable signal-to-noise ratio," that is, the duration for which it was clearly above threshold. Thus energy splatter may not be a critical factor in frequency discrimination of brief, low-frequency tones. This supports the notion that frequency discrimination at low frequencies is based on a temporal mechanism that is less likely to be disturbed by energy splatter.

If discrimination is based on a temporal mechanism at low frequencies and on a place mechanism at high frequencies, then the function relating ΔF to duration should be steeper at low frequencies ($\Delta F \approx kT^{-1.5}$) than at high ($\Delta F \approx kT^{-0.5}$). Moore's (1973a) data for ΔF measured over wide ranges of frequencies and durations in one listener are in general agreement with this prediction (see Fig. 14.53). (Two other listeners yielded similar data.) At 2,000 Hz and above, the slopes of the functions are near -0.5, as predicted by the place model. Below 2,000 Hz, the slopes are steeper, about -1.0, but not as steep as the slope of -1.5, predicted by Siebert's temporal model. The low-frequency functions closely follow the predictions by J. L. Goldstein and Srulovicz (1977). Similar data have been obtained by Henning (1970) and others.

The foregoing data were obtained in a burst-comparison paradigm. Data obtained by frequency modulation are different. Shower and Biddulph (1931) measured a three- to fourfold increase in ΔF for a 1,000-Hz tone as the modulation frequency was doubled from 2.8 to 5.6 Hz (i.e., $\Delta F \approx kT^{-2}$). On the other hand, the results of Zwicker and Feldtkeller (1967, p. 169) closely follow the place-model prediction of $\Delta F \approx kT^{-0.5}$ for tones between 1,000 and 8,000 Hz modulated with rates between 5 Hz and half the critical bandwidth. The reason for the discrepancy between Zwicker and Feldtkeller's data and Shower and Biddulph's data is not clear. In general, the effect of T on ΔF is poorly understood, and the differences among studies are generally greater than among the studies of the effect of T on ΔL (cf. Section 4.1.5).

4.2.5. The Effect of Masking on Frequency Discrimination. Harris (1966) and Henning (1967) showed that ΔF increases markedly as the level of a white-noise masker is increased so that thc test tone approaches its masked threshold. However, at 20 dB or more above the masked threshold, frequency discrimination is about the same as in the quiet. Buus (1980) also found the 20-dB rule adequate to account for the frequency discrimination of tones partially masked by narrow-band noise. Thus it appears that frequency discrimination is far less susceptible to masking than is intensity discrimination (cf. Section 4.1.7).

4.2.6. Frequency Discrimination of Complex Sounds. Like pure tones, the frequency of a complex sound can be discriminated in at least two ways. One, spectral-shape discrimination, calls

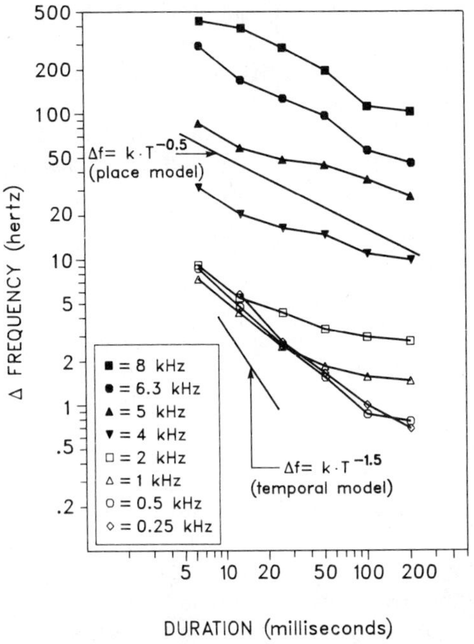

Figure 14.53. JNDs for frequency, ΔF, as a function of stimulus duration (data from Moore, 1973a). The ΔFs for one listener (TC) are plotted as a function of the stimulus duration with frequency as the parameter. Two other listeners showed similar results. The ΔFs were measured in a burst comparison paradigm using the adaptive PEST procedure (Taylor & Creelman, 1967) for TC and the method of constant stimuli for the two other listeners. The stimuli were presented via electrostatic headphones with a relatively smooth high-frequency response to minimize variations in level with changes in frequency and the loudness level of all stimuli kept constant at 60 phons. On each trial, two tone bursts differing only in frequency were presented and the listeners judged which burst had the higher frequency. The ΔFs plotted in the figure are averages for several runs. Moore stated that the standard deviation of repeated measurements in the same listener is 15–20%. Also plotted are two line segments representing predictions of Siebert's (1970) place model (upper line, slope = -0.5) and temporal model (lower line, slope = -1.5). Note that the decrease in ΔFs is considerably steeper at low than at high frequencies. In fact, for frequencies of 1,000 Hz and below, the slopes of the measured functions are close to that predicted by the temporal model and for frequencies above 4,000 Hz the slopes of the measured functions are close to that predicted by the place model. These results lend support to the notion that frequency discrimination is mediated by a temporal mechanism at low frequencies and by a place mechanism at high frequencies.

for a place mechanism for the detection of a frequency difference, such as that introduced by changing the center frequency of a filter. (A temporal mechanism can be excluded either by presenting a complex tone whose fundamental frequency is kept constant or by using a narrow-band noise whose temporal structure is too variable to provide a usable cue.) The other type of frequency discrimination, envelope-frequency discrimination, requires a temporal mechanism for detection of the frequency difference, such as that introduced by varying the fundamental frequency of a complex tone. (A place mechanism can be excluded by keeping the overall spectrum nearly independent of the fundamental frequency, for example, by filtering.) Some stimuli can be discriminated on the basis of both spectral shape and envelope frequency (e.g., Ritsma, 1963), but the available data can be interpreted in terms of only one of these two mechanisms.

4.2.6.1. Spectral-Shape Discrimination. Spectral-shape discrimination can be thought of as discrimination of timbre (see Scharf & Houtsma, Chapter 15). Although many experiments have investigated the perception of timbre, none seems to have measured directly JNDs in the frequency domain except for some measurements of the JND for filtering frequency of a noise band (Gabrielsson, Johansson, Lindblad, Persson, Pettersson, & Rosenquist, 1975; Maiwald, 1967a; Michaels, 1957; Moore, 1973b; Zwicker & Feldtkeller, 1967).

Zwicker and Feldtkeller (1967) studied the discrimination of the cutoff frequency, F_c, of high- and low-pass noises. According to Zwicker's (1970) excitation-pattern model, the JND for cutoff frequency, ΔF_c, of high-pass noise should be approximately like that of pure tones; both are thought to depend on the detection of a change in excitation level on the steep low-frequency side of the excitation pattern. The ΔF_cs for noise may be expected to be larger than the ΔFs for tones due to the variability inherent in the noise. Zwicker and Feldtkeller (1967) did find that the ΔF_c for a high-pass noise is about eight times larger ($\approx$12 Hz) than the ΔF for pure tones at low frequencies and about four times larger (e.g., about 160 Hz for F_c = 10,000 Hz) at high frequencies. Predictions for low-pass noise depend on level, because discrimination is thought to depend on the detection of a change in the excitation pattern along the high-frequency slope, which becomes shallower with increasing level. Thus ΔF_c of a low-pass noise ought to increase with increasing level, but at a given level, it ought to be proportional to the pure-tone ΔF. Here too, the data of Zwicker and Feldtkeller (1967) closely follow the predictions. At 1,000 Hz, ΔF_c for a low-pass noise increases from about 18 Hz (equal to the ΔF_c for a high-pass noise) near 30 dB SL to about 75 Hz at 90 dB.

Zwicker (1956) and Maiwald's (1967a) data for noises that are one critical band wide are also in good agreement with predictions of the excitation-pattern model. The ΔF_cs increase from about 12 Hz at low center frequencies, to 20 Hz at 1,000 Hz, and to 40 Hz at 4,000 Hz. Standard deviations across six listeners were about 25% (Maiwald, 1967a). Gabrielsson et al.'s (1975) data for relatively wide bands of noise also seem consistent with the excitation-pattern model. In general, discrimination of center or cutoff frequency of noises of critical bandwidth or wider appears to be mediated by a place mechanism, as exemplified by the excitation-pattern model.

In contrast, the data for very narrow bands of noise do not follow the excitation-pattern model very well, at least below 5,000 Hz. A probable explanation is that a temporal mechanism may provide useful information about the center frequency of such a noise (Moore, 1973b). Owing to variation in the short-term level and instantaneous frequency, the information from a temporal mechanism is more precise for a very narrow band of noise than for a wide band of noise. For noises with a duration of 100 msec, Moore (1973b) predicted that ΔF_cs for very narrow bands of noise ought to be relatively small and should reach a minimum for bandwidths of about 8 Hz if a temporal mechanism mediated the discrimination of center frequency. For center frequencies of 2,000 and 4,000 Hz he found minima in the ΔF_cs for a bandwidth of 8 Hz. Moreover, the ΔF_cs were only slightly larger than pure-tone ΔFs, and considerably lower than the ΔF_cs for relatively wide bands of noise. At 6,000 Hz, ΔF_cs were like those for a pure tone and were considerably lower than those for wider bands of noise, but increased monotonically with bandwidth. Moore (1973b) interpreted these findings as consistent with a temporal mechanism below about 5,000 Hz.

4.2.6.2. Envelope-Frequency Discrimination. Lacking a model of envelope-frequency discrimination, we present the results in two groups with quite different patterns of results. One large group of studies finds that the JND for envelope frequency closely follows Weber's law. Another, smaller group finds that the JND is constant across a limited range of envelope frequencies, but depends on center frequency.

In these experiments, the listener detects a small change in the envelope frequency of a complex sound, which can be an amplitude-modulated noise (e.g., Ahroon & Fay, 1977; Harris, 1963; G. A. Miller & Taylor, 1948; Mowbray, Gebhard, & Byham, 1956; R. D. Patterson, Johnson-Davies, & Milroy, 1978; Pollack, 1952), an amplitude-modulated tone (Ritsma, 1963; Small, 1955), a filtered pulse train (Hoekstra, 1979; Long & Cullen, 1983), or a two-tone complex (Buus, 1983; Schodder & David, 1960). The discrimination is almost certainly mediated by a temporal mechanism, except when the components of a complex tone can be resolved and discriminated individually.

The limit at which envelope discrimination becomes pure-tone discrimination of individual components varies with the center frequency and with the change in individual component frequencies relative to the change in envelope frequency. For example, Hoekstra's (1979) filtered pulse trains appear to be discriminated on the basis of individual components for envelope frequencies higher than about 1/25 of the center frequency, at which point the individual components are separated by about one-fourth of a critical band. In contrast, Buus (1983) suggested that his two-tone complexes were discriminated on the basis of the individual components for envelope frequencies higher than about one-third the center frequency, at which point the components were separated by about two critical bands. While disagreeing in absolute values, both studies show that the envelope frequency, above which discrimination was performed on the basis of individual components, is an approximately constant proportion of the critical bandwidth.

Studies of envelope-frequency discrimination with broadband noise stimuli indicate that the just noticeable difference in modulation frequency, ΔF_m, is nearly proportional to modulation frequency, F_m, from 2.5 Hz (Pollack, 1952) to 200 Hz (Ahroon & Fay, 1977; Miller & Taylor, 1948; Mowbray et al., 1956) or even up to 750 Hz (Harris, 1963). Hoekstra (1979) reported that ΔF_m was about 2% of F_m for ⅓-octave wide filtered pulse trains at center frequencies between 1,000 and 10,000 Hz and for pulsed white noise, provided F_m was less than about 1/25 of the center frequency.

In contrast to the studies just discussed, a few experiments indicate that Weber's law does not hold for envelope-frequency discrimination. The most comprehensive of these studies measured discrimination of two-tone complexes (Buus, 1983). The equally intense two sinusoids in the complex differed in frequency by an amount equal to the envelope frequency, F_m, and they were geometrically centered. Thus when the envelope frequency was increased, the lower frequency decreased slightly and the higher frequency increased slightly. These two-tone complexes minimize the influence of the discrimination of individual components and thus permit the measurement of ΔF_m over a wide range of F_ms. As shown in Figure 14.54, ΔF_m (which is the same as the just noticeable increase in the frequency separation between the components) is nearly independent of F_m up to some critical F_m; except at the 1,000-Hz center frequency, the critical F_m is equal to the standard critical bandwidth. For a given subcritical F_m, the value of ΔF_m depends on the center frequency, increasing from about 2.5 Hz at 500 Hz, to about 3.1 Hz at 1,000 Hz, to about 4.6 Hz at 2,000 Hz, and to 10.9 Hz

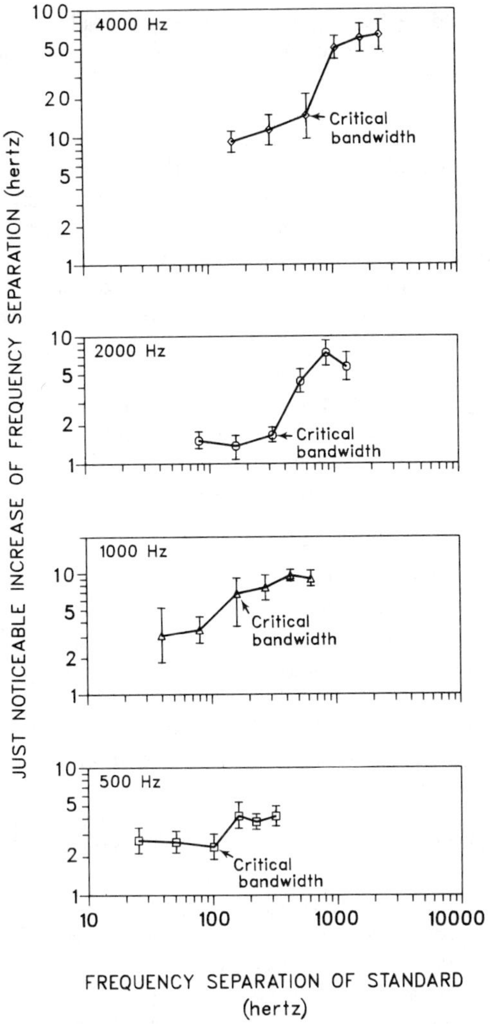

Figure 14.54. JNDs for envelope frequency, Δf_m, as a function of envelope frequency, f_m. The Δf_ms were measured as the just noticeable increase in bandwidth (Δf_m) of two-tone complexes as a function of bandwidth (f_m). The points are the geometric means of Δf_ms for six listeners tested at a center frequency of 500 Hz, three listeners at 1,000 Hz, nine listeners at 2,000 Hz, and five listeners at 4,000 Hz. The Δf_ms were measured in a same-different paradigm using an adaptive procedure. On each trial, the listeners were presented two 600-msec two-tone complexes 600 msec apart. Either the standard was followed by the variable, which had a bandwidth wider than that of the standard, or the standard was presented twice. The listeners' task was to judge whether the two-tone complexes were the same or different. The results show that Δf_m is nearly constant for f_m less than the standard critical bandwidth (see Zwicker & Feldtkeller, 1967; and Scharf, 1970a), except perhaps at the 1,000-Hz center frequency. For f_m less than the critical bandwidth, Δf_m increases with increasing center frequency. Beyond the critical bandwidth, Δf_m increases rapidly until it reaches a maximum for a f_m between two and three critical bandwidths, probably owing to the deterioration of the envelope cue and partial resolution of the two tones that result from the action of the auditory filter. (From S. Buus, Discrimination of envelope frequency, *Journal of the Acoustical Society of America*, 1983, *74*. Reprinted with permission.)

at 4,000 Hz. For supercritical F_ms, ΔF_m increases rapidly until F_m is about 40% of the center frequency; beyond that, the two tones appear to be discriminated individually (Buus, 1983). Presumably, the increase in ΔF_m for supercritical F_ms reflects the deterioration of the envelope as the two tones gradually become separated by the auditory filter.

Buus's (1983) finding of constant ΔF_ms for the subcritical F_ms is in opposition to the studies finding Weber's law (i.e., constant $\Delta F_m/F_m$), but it is supported by some other studies. Long and Cullen (1983) also reported ΔF_ms that were independent of F_m between 50 and 400 Hz for high-pass filtered pulse trains. R. D. Patterson et al. (1978) found that the modulation-depth required to detect a 20% change in F_m for a partially masked, white-noise carrier decreased as F_m increased up to about 80 Hz, which means that Weber's law does not hold in this range. Finally, Fay and Passow (1982) reported that discrimination of envelope frequency by goldfish is based on temporal cues and that ΔF_m is independent of F_m.

The reason for the discrepancy between the studies reporting constant Weber fractions for discrimination of envelope frequency and those reporting constant ΔF_m is not clear. Buus (1983) speculated that different envelope properties of the stimuli used in the various studies might account for the discrepancy, but until an appropriate model for envelope discrimination is available, predictions of ΔF_ms for arbitrary stimuli cannot be made. Unless the stimuli are very similar to those used in one of the various studies discussed above, it is uncertain which set of data would apply.

4.2.7. Frequency Discrimination in Impaired Listeners. Several studies have measured pure-tone frequency discrimination in impaired listeners, both in burst comparison and modulation paradigms (e.g., DiCarlo, 1962; Filling, 1956; Gengel, 1973; Hoekstra, 1979; Zurek & Formby, 1981). Generally, adult listeners with impairments of primarily cochlear origin have ΔFs that are two to three times larger than those for normal listeners. However, in many studies this difference was not significant owing to large variability among individuals, both normal and impaired. This variability also tends to obscure any correlation between ΔF and amount of hearing loss. For example, Ross, Huntington, Newby, and Dixon (1965) and Gengel (1969) obtained significant correlations at 500 Hz, but not at other frequencies. Hoekstra (1979), summarizing data from four studies, showed that despite considerable variability among listeners and studies ΔF increased by about a factor of 10 as thresholds increased from normal (0 dB HL) to 100 dB HL. Some of Hoekstra's (1979) data suggested that the deterioration of frequency discrimination might not be a smoothly increasing function, but occurs rather suddenly when the hearing loss exceeds 35 dB.

4.3. Temporal Discrimination

The auditory system's ability to detect and discriminate temporal properties (other than frequency) of sound has been studied in several different ways. This section includes discussions of (a) temporal resolution as measured by the just-detectable depth of amplitude modulation, (b) detection of a brief pause (gap) in an otherwise continuous sound, (c) the perception of temporal order, (d) the JND for duration of auditory events, and (e) temporal discrimination by hearing-impaired listeners.

4.3.1. Detection of Amplitude Modulation as a Function of Modulation Rate. Many experiments have shown that the auditory system tends to smooth rapid variations in the amplitude of sounds. For example, the perceived roughness of an amplitude-modulated tone decreases with increasing modulation frequency (Terhardt, 1974). Similarly, the difference between the minimum and maximum masked thresholds for a brief probe such as a click presented at various phases of an amplitude-modulated masker decreases with increasing modulation frequency (e.g., Fastl, 1977; Viemeister, 1973, cited by Green, 1973; Zwicker, 1976). Also, the modulation depth necessary to detect amplitude modulation increases with increasing modulation frequency (e.g., Riesz, 1928; Viemeister, 1977, 1979; Zwicker, 1952; cf. Section 4.1.4). (For a review of these phenomena, see Viemeister, 1979.)

A common interpretation of all these experiments is that the amplitude fluctuation of an auditory signal is smoothed by a leaky integrator or, equivalently, by a low-pass filter acting on the envelope of the signal. Many experimenters have concluded that the transfer function of this filter, the temporal modulation transfer function (TMTF), is similar to that of a simple low-pass filter. Estimates of the cutoff frequency vary from about 24 Hz by Dubrovsky and Tumarkina (1967) to about 85 Hz by Buunen (1975). The corresponding integration times are 6.7 and 1.9 msec, which are much shorter than those observed in measurements of temporal integration for detection (see Section 3) and loudness (Scharf & Houtsma, Chapter 15). One explanation of this discrepancy is that the nonlinearity of the auditory system distorts the measurements of integration time. Divenyi and Shannon (1983) showed that a compressive power function followed by an integrator with a time constant of about 3 msec can account for the long time constants observed in measurements of loudness and threshold, as well as the short ones measured as the TMTF. Another explanation is that the auditory system adapts its integration time to a given task. A long integration time is inefficient for the detection of brief events but efficient for the detection of long-duration tones. Finally, it is possible that some mechanism other than the TMTF is responsible for the improvement in detection threshold and increase in loudness that results from increasing stimulus duration. In the following, we consider only the TMTF.

A comprehensive set of measurements of the TMTF has been presented by Viemeister (1979). He measured the just-detectable depth of amplitude modulation as a function of modulation frequency, and found no effect of level on the TMTF for white-noise carriers with spectrum levels between 0 and 50 dB. The modulation thresholds (20 log m, where m is the modulation depth necessary for detection of the modulation) were nearly equal for spectrum levels between 20 and 50 dB, but about 3 dB higher at 0 dB. Viemeister did find that the TMTF for band-pass noises changed somewhat with center frequency. The cutoff frequency of the TMTF, defined as the 3-dB-down point, increased from 27 Hz at a center frequency of 200 Hz to 31 Hz at 1,000 Hz and to 45 Hz at 10,000 Hz. As the center frequency of the noise increased, the modulation thresholds decreased, and at 10,000 Hz the results were almost identical to those for white noise. This indicates that the high-frequency channels bear the primary responsibility for detecting the modulation in white noise.

An assumption underlying the derivation of the TMTF is that auditory processing is linear, at least locally. Linearity cannot be assumed generally because nonlinearity is often evident as in masking (cf. Section 3) and aural distortion (see Scharf & Houtsma, Chapter 15). However, the amplitude variations at modulation threshold are usually small compared to the overall amplitude of the carrier, and thus linearity may be assumed within the range of amplitudes encompassed by the modulated carrier even if the overall processing is nonlinear.

To the extent that the local linearity assumption is tenable, the TMTF ought to predict modulation thresholds for different modulating wave forms. Viemeister (1979) found that modulation thresholds for sine-wave, square-wave, and pulse modulation could be accounted for by a single TMTF. As shown in Figure 14.55, Viemeister (1979) found that modulation thresholds are about 2 dB lower for square-wave modulation than for sine-wave modulation for F less than 1,000 Hz. This difference corresponds to the 2.1-dB difference between the amplitudes of the fundamental frequency for sine and square waves with equal peak amplitude (corresponding to equal m). This indicates that the modulation depth corresponding to the fundamental component of the square wave accounts for the detection of modulation. The fundamental component ought to dominate because the higher components of the square-wave have lower initial amplitude and are attenuated more by the TMTF than is the fundamental. At high modulation frequencies the difference between sine-wave and square-wave modulation increases to about 3 dB. Viemeister (1979) showed that this difference was due to the observer's detection of the overall increase in power that results from square-wave modulation. Thresholds for pulse modulation can be accounted for by a more elaborate version of the TMTF model (Viemeister, 1979). In general, the TMTF can provide a useful description of many aspects of temporal resolution in the auditory system.

4.3.2. Temporal Resolution in Gap Detection. A more direct measure of temporal resolution is afforded by measurements of the just-detectable duration, ΔT, of a pause (gap) in an otherwise continuous sound or of a pause between two bursts of sound. Plomp (1964) measured the just-detectable gap between two bursts of white noise. The level of the second burst was equal to or lower than that of the first. He suggested that the gap is detectable whenever the auditory activity at the end of the gap has decayed to a value below some fixed fraction of that caused by the sound following the gap. Thus measurements of ΔT as a function of the level difference between the sounds before and after the gap ought to show directly the rate of decay of auditory activity. Plomp (1964) found that the logarithm of ΔT decreased linearly with increasing level of the second white-noise burst. The slope of these decay functions increased with the level of the initial burst. In fact, the lines obtained for three different initial-burst levels appeared to intersect at a second-burst level equal to threshold, with ΔT equal to about 250 msec. This finding indicates that, regardless of stimulus level, after turning off a stimulus it requires about 250 msec before the auditory activity decays to a value corresponding to no stimulation. Similar results have been obtained in forward-masking experiments (see Section 3). Because the decay functions change slope and are linear when decibels are plotted against log time scales, the decay of auditory activity defies a straightforward description. (In simple exponential decay, the decay measured in decibels is a linear function of time.) Nonetheless, models that incorporate an exponential integration window (consistent with the TMTF concept discussed in the previous section and indicating a simple exponential decay of activity) provide a reasonable account of a relatively large body of gap-detection data.

In these models, auditory temporal resolution is limited by two factors: temporal integration (the TMTF) and the peripheral auditory filter. Duifhuis (1972, 1973) pointed out that auditory frequency selectivity ought to limit temporal resolution, especially at low frequencies where the auditory filters are relatively narrow. This suggestion follows from the fact that the output of a physical filter decays with a time constant that is inversely proportional to its bandwidth. On the basis of a model of auditory nerve activity that incorporated a peripheral filter and a short-term exponential integrator, he suggested that the

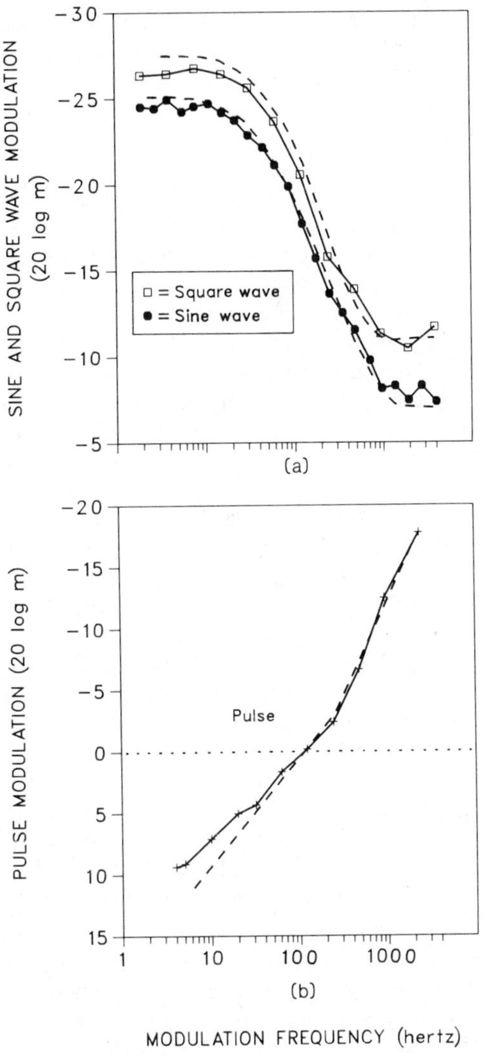

Figure 14.55. Detection thresholds for amplitude modulation as a function of modulation frequency and modulation wave form. The modulation thresholds are plotted in terms of 20 log *m*, where *m* is the modulation depth that was just detectable, as a function of modulation frequency. Note that the y-axes are inverted to reflect the low-pass filter characteristic of the temporal modulation transfer function, TMTF. The data are the averages for two listeners and the dashed lines are the result of simulations on an electrical model consisting of a band-pass filter followed by a half-wave rectifier, a leaky integrator (which is a low-pass filter simulating the TMTF), and an RMS voltmeter. The modulation thresholds were measured in a two-interval, two-alternative forced-choice paradigm using an adaptive one-up, two-down procedure (Levitt, 1971). The listeners were presented a continuous white noise with a spectrum level of 40 dB. On each trial, amplitude modulation was introduced during one of the two 500-msec observation intervals. The listeners' task was to judge which interval contained the amplitude modulation. The curves for sine- and square-wave modulation shown in the upper panel are almost parallel and increase with increasing modulation frequency above 30 Hz, indicating that the magnitude of the fundamental frequency of the modulating frequency after filtering by the TMTF can account for the modulation thresholds. In contrast, the data for pulse modulation shown in the lower panel decrease with increasing modulation frequency. For modulation frequencies above 250 Hz, the slope of the pulse function is nearly 6 dB·octave^{-1} and the modulation thresholds correspond to a ΔL of about 0.4 dB, which is close to the JND for level of amplitude-modulated white noise reported by G. A. Miller (1947). Thus discrimination of the overall amplitude difference between the modulated and unmodulated noise probably accounts for detection of pulse modulation for modulation frequencies above 250 Hz. (This critical frequency can be expected to vary with pulse duration because the overall RMS amplitude of the pulse-modulated noise is proportional to pulse duration. The pulse duration in Viemeister's experiment was 200 μsec.) (From N. F. Viemeister, Temporal modulation transfer functions based upon modulation thresholds, *Journal of the Acoustical Society of America*, 1979, 66. Reprinted with permission.)

peripheral filter bears the primary responsibility for the short-term decay of auditory activity as measured in nonsimultaneous masking.

If the auditory filter is the primary determinant of short-term temporal resolution, gap detection ought to improve with increasing stimulus frequency because the bandwidth of the auditory filter increases with center frequency. This prediction is supported by several experiments (Buus & Florentine, 1982; Fitzgibbons, 1979, 1983; Fitzgibbons & Wightman, 1982; Florentine & Buus, 1983b; Shailer & Moore, 1983). The most comprehensive set of data, published by Florentine and Buus (1983b), gives ΔTs for octave bands of noise of varying center frequency and a wide-band noise. As shown in Figure 14.56, the ΔT decreases as overall level increases up to about 60 dB; at still higher levels, ΔT tends to increase. The effect of frequency is readily apparent: ΔT decreases by a factor of 10 as the frequency of the octave bands of noise increases from 250 to 8,000 Hz. These data are similar both in form and magnitude to other data for wide-band noise (Irwin, Hinchcliff, & Kemp, 1981; Irwin & Purdy, 1982; Penner, 1977; Plomp, 1964) and similar in form to Shailer and Moore's (1983) and Fitzgibbons's (1983) data for bands of noise slightly narrower than one octave. All these data can be accounted for by a simple model that is essentially an energy detector preceded by a critical-band filter (Buus & Florentine, 1982). It appears that most of the improvement of temporal resolution with increasing frequency results from the widening of the auditory filters with increasing center frequency.

4.3.3. Separation and Discrimination of Successive Stimuli. The experiments discussed above provide a measurement of the auditory system's ability to detect rapid changes in amplitude. A somewhat different aspect of temporal resolution is the discrimination of two successive auditory events.

In one type of experiment, the listener is presented with two sounds, typically clicks, in rapid succession, and judges whether one or two clicks are perceived. In a variation of this procedure, Leshowitz (1971) asked listeners to discriminate one 20-μsec click from two 10-μsec clicks presented in rapid succession and found a discrimination threshold of about 10 μsec. He ascribed this extremely low threshold to the difference in the spectrum between the 20-μsec click and the two 10-μsec clicks. When such a spectral difference is not present, a separation of about 2 msec is necessary to perceive two clicks as separate (Exner, 1875; Gescheider, 1966; Hirsh, 1959; Wallach, Newman, & Rosenzweig, 1949). This value is close to the just-detectable gap duration for broad-band noise, which at moderate levels is 2–3 msec. Although the discrimination of successive clicks may appear to depend on the decay of auditory excitation invoked to explain gap detection, this explanation is suitable only when the two clicks go to the same auditory channels. Presenting clicks alternately to the left and right ears (Exner, 1875; Gescheider, 1966; Wallach et al., 1949) or in different frequency regions (Hirsh, 1959) yields minimum temporal separations almost identical to those obtained in the monaural, single-frequency experiments. Also, experiments on discrimination of Huffman sequences yield estimates of about 2 msec as the limit

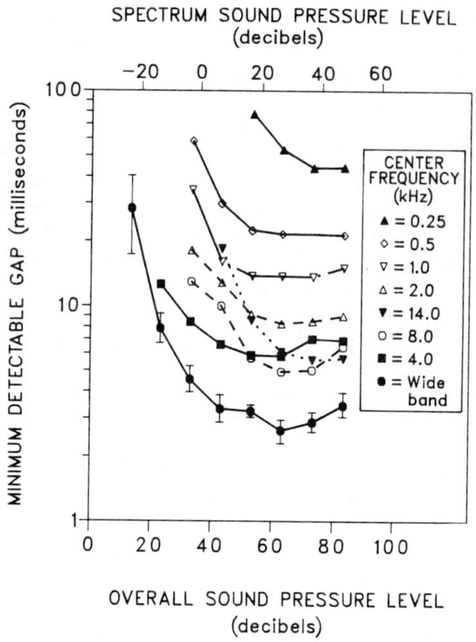

Figure 14.56. Gap detection thresholds as a function of level and frequency. The just-detectable duration, ΔT, of a brief pause (a gap) in an otherwise continuous noise is plotted as a function of overall sound pressure level of the noise. The spectrum level is shown on the top axis. Center frequency of the signal is the parameter. Data for a wide-band noise (low-pass noise, F_c = 7,000 Hz) are also shown. Except for the wide-band noise, the signals were octave-bands of noise. To eliminate detection of energy splatter from the rapid offset and onset of the noise (fall and rise times were 1 msec), the octave-bands of noise were presented with their complementary band-stop maskers. The spectrum level of the masker was always equal to that of the signal. The points are the geometric means for three listeners and vertical bars indicate the standard deviations. The ΔTs were measured in a two-interval, two-alternative forced choice paradigm using a modified BUDTIF procedure (Campbell, 1963). On each trial, the two observation intervals (500 msec in duration and separated by 500 msec) were marked by lights and the gap was introduced in one of the intervals by briefly turning off and on the otherwise continuous signal. The listeners' task was to judge which interval contained the gap. Note that ΔT decreases rapidly with increasing level up to 50–60 dB SPL, after which it is relatively constant, and that it decreases by about a factor of 10 as the center frequency increases from 250 to 14,000 Hz. This pattern of results is consistent with the notion that the auditory filters bear the primary responsibility for the auditory system's limited temporal resolution. (From M. Florentine & S. Buus, Temporal acuity as a function of level and frequency, *Proceedings of the 17th International Congress on Acoustics*, Paris, 1983. Reprinted with permission.)

of temporal resolution for stimuli presented to different auditory channels (Green, 1971, 1973). In essence, a Huffman sequence is the response of an all-pass filter to a pair of clicks. The first click excites the filter, and the excitation is terminated after a given duration by the second click. The effect of the all-pass filter is to delay the onset of energy in a specific frequency region (for a more detailed description of Huffman sequences, see Green, 1971, 1972; J. H. Patterson & Green, 1970). Thus the discrimination of Huffman sequences, which have equal durations and the same long-term spectra, seems to depend on the discrimination of the time between the onsets in the delayed frequency region and the surrounding undelayed frequency regions. That this task is unrelated to the decay of auditory activity as measured in gap detection is illustrated by the finding that the just-discriminable difference in delay of Huffman sequences is almost independent of frequency (Green, 1973).

These results are most easily understood by assuming that two different mechanisms govern the perceptual separation of successive events in the auditory system. One is the decay of auditory activity, which appears necessary to separate two events stimulating the same auditory channels. The other may be related to the precision by which the time of onset in different auditory channels can be judged. For high-frequency or broadband stimuli, resolution by the two mechanisms is about the same—2–3 msec—but for low-frequency stimuli it is not. At low frequencies, the decay of auditory sensation is slowed considerably by the action of the auditory filters, whereas the precision of onset-time judgments across different channels appears to be independent of frequency.

The experiments just discussed required the listener to perceive only a difference in the time of auditory events. Many authors have assumed that if events were perceived to occur at different times, the order of events could also be perceived (e.g., Piéron, 1952; for review, see Hirsh & Sherrick, 1961), but Hirsh (1959) showed this assumption to be wrong. For his listeners to tell which of two qualitatively different stimuli, such as a noise and a tone, occurred first, the onsets of the stimuli had to be separated by about 20 msec. This value was nearly independent of how the stimuli differed, whether clicks of different frequencies, tones and clicks, clicks and noise, and so on. Later Hirsh and Sherrick (1961) showed that the 20-msec threshold for judgment of temporal order holds in the auditory, visual, and tactile modalities whether the successive stimuli are presented in different modalities or to different (left vs. right) organs in the same modality (see also Sherrick & Cholewiak, Chapter 12). These results suggest that the judgment of temporal order depends on central mechanisms.

4.3.4. Discrimination of Duration. We now consider the discrimination of a change in duration, either of a brief interval separating two sounds or of a single, brief sound. Four studies have measured the JND for duration of tone bursts and various noise bursts (Abel, 1972a; Fleet & Shelton, 1983; Shelton, 1982; Small & Campbell, 1962) and one study has measured the JND for duration of a silent interval (gap) bounded by bursts of white noise (Abel, 1972b).

The JND for duration of a burst of sound follows a simple pattern as shown in Figure 14.57. It is largely independent of the bandwidth and is the same at 65 and 85 dB SPL (Abel, 1972a). For durations less than about 50 msec the JND is approximately proportional to the square root of the duration; for durations greater than 50 msec the JND is approximately 10% of the duration. The JND's independence of level and bandwidth and its dependence on the square root of duration are consistent with central theories of duration discrimination (Allan, Kristofferson, & Wiens 1971; Creelman, 1962). However, peripheral theories of energy discrimination may also account for the square-root dependence. Moreover, the JND for duration is almost exactly that predicted from Henning's (1970) data for intensity discrimination. The intensity JNDs can be converted to JNDs for duration by assuming that increases in duration and in intensity are equivalent whenever they provide the same overall increase in energy. The breakpoint at 50 msec is in reasonable agreement with the 35-msec integration time found by Henning (1970). For stimulus durations longer than the integration time the peripheral energy discrimination model is not valid, because the peak output of the integrator then becomes independent of the stimulus duration. At that point, it seems plausible that a central timing mechanism takes over.

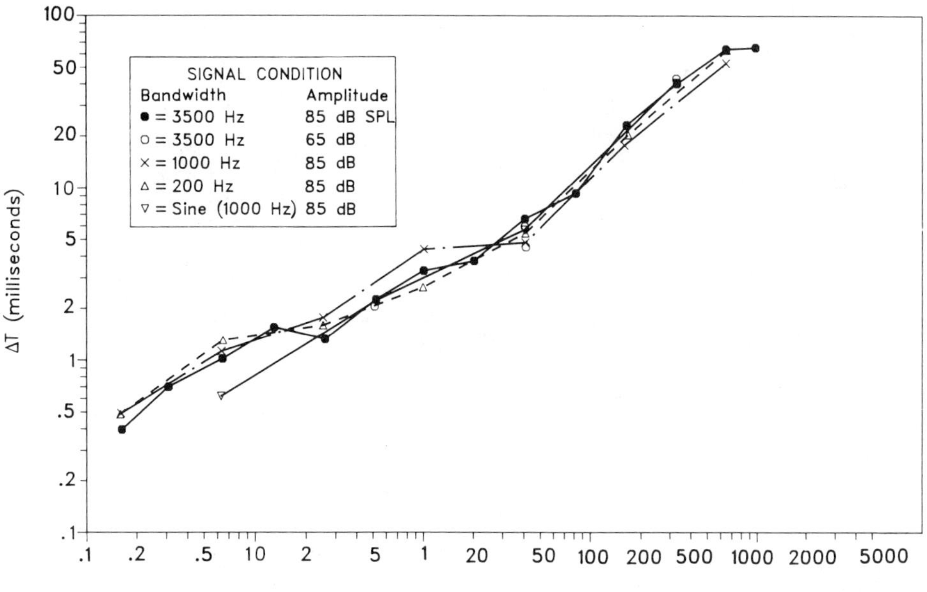

Figure 14.57. JNDs for duration of a burst of sound as a function of stimulus duration. The averages of the just-detectable increase in stimulus duration, ΔT, for two listeners are plotted as a function of the stimulus duration, T, of a 1,000-Hz tone, low-pass noises with F_c = 3,500 Hz and 1,000 Hz, and a band-pass noise with a bandwidth of 200 Hz centered at 1,000 Hz. The ΔTs were measured in a two-interval, two-alternative forced-choice paradigm using the method of constant stimuli. On each trial, the listeners were presented with two sounds differing only in duration separated by a 500-msec interstimulus interval. Their task was to judge which burst had the longer duration. The ΔTs are well described by a line with a slope of 0.5 for durations less than 50 msec and a line with a slope of 1 for durations greater than 50 msec. The data for durations less than 50 msec are consistent with Henning's (1970) data on intensity discrimination, indicating that duration discrimination for short durations probably depends on discrimination of the difference of energy in the two bursts. (From S. M. Abel, Discrimination of temporal gaps, *Journal of the Acoustical Society of America*, 1972, *51*. Reprinted with permission.)

The data indicate that this central timing mechanism obeys Weber's law. The breakpoint of 50 msec may depend on the interstimulus intervals (ISI). Shelton (1982) found that the JND was 8% of the duration, at least down to 25 msec when the interstimulus interval was 1600 msec. For shorter ISIs, the JND increased at short durations. Fleet and Shelton (1983) suggested that this increase is due to peripheral interaction between the two bursts to be discriminated because presenting the two bursts to different ears improved discrimination at short ISIs.

The data for discrimination of duration of a silent interval are more complicated, as shown in Figure 14.58 (Abel, 1972b). At durations greater than about 200 msec the JNDs for duration are reasonably described by Weber's law. The Weber fraction is about 20% and nearly independent of the duration (10 or 300 msec) and level (70 or 85 dB SPL) of the markers. For gap durations less than 200 msec the Weber fraction increases as duration decreases to about 10 msec. For durations less than 5 msec the JND is nearly constant at about 2 msec.

At long durations the results appear reasonably consistent with a central timing mechanism that follows Weber's law. For durations between 10 and 200 msec, the results are roughly consistent with a central Weber's-law mechanism that measures the interval between two markers with a constant timing uncertainty. This timing uncertainty could arise from the slow decay of the auditory activity following the offset of a sound. Finally, the JND of about 2 msec at the shortest durations is to be expected if the listeners discriminated the gap duration by detecting the longer comparison gap. For standard gap durations of 2.5 msec or less, the brief gap was probably not audible, and thus the task became one of gap detection.

To the extent that they reflect the properties of a common timing mechanism, the data for discrimination of burst and gap duration ought to be comparable. The larger JNDs for gap duration may be due to differences in procedure and training. Moreover, the discrimination of burst duration probably benefits from the energy difference between bursts, a cue that is unavailable in discriminating gap duration. Thus it may be that discrimination of gap duration better reflects the properties of the central timing mechanism.

4.3.5. Temporal Resolution in Impaired Listeners. Temporal resolution in impaired listeners has been assessed primarily by nonsimultaneous masking (e.g., Elliott, 1971; see Section 3) and gap detection (e.g., Fitzgibbons, 1979; Florentine & Buus, 1982, 1983a, 1984; Irwin, Hinchcliff, & Kemp, 1981; Irwin & Purdy, 1982). These studies indicate that some, but not all, listeners have impaired temporal resolution as shown by higher thresholds in nonsimultaneous masking and longer gap detection thresholds, for broad-band noise. However, Florentine and Buus (1982, 1983a, 1984) pointed out that, at least for gap detection, part of the poorer JNDs can be accounted for by these listeners' inability to hear high frequencies where temporal resolution is best. Thus such listeners ought to have larger ΔTs for broad-band noise even if their temporal resolution is normal. Nevertheless, some listeners with impairments of primarily cochlear origin do have impaired temporal resolution, even after the

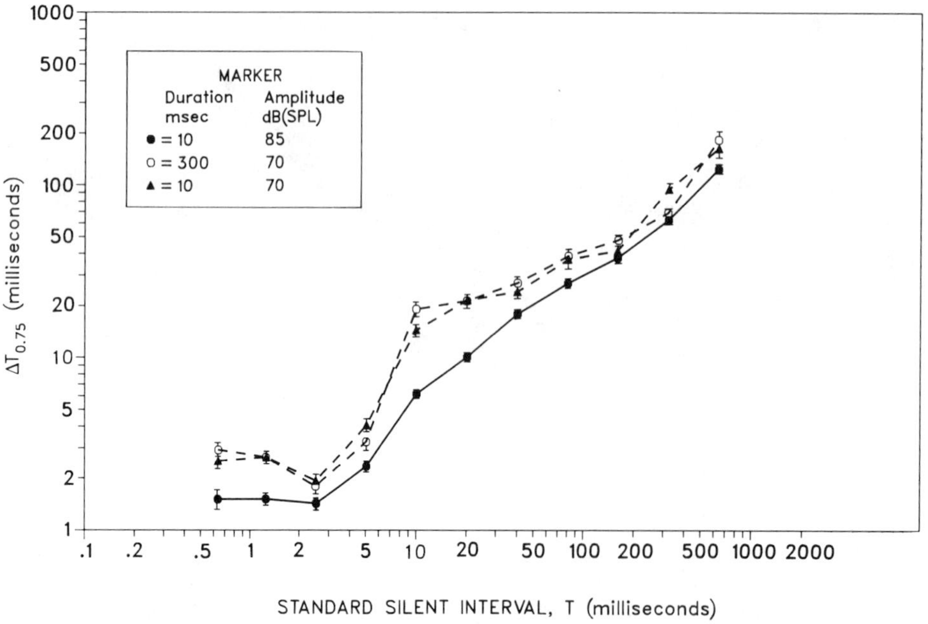

Figure 14.58. JNDs for duration of a silent interval as a function of duration. The averages of the just-detectable increase in duration, ΔT, of a silent interval (a gap) for three listeners (two for the 10-msec, 70 dB SPL markers) are plotted as a function of duration of the standard silent interval, T. The bars show the standard errors of the means. Each silent interval was bounded by two acoustic markers (bursts of white noise) with the levels and durations indicated in the figure. Note that the overall energy is the same for the 10-msec, 85 dB SPL marker and the 300-msec, 70 dB SPL marker. The ΔTs were measured in a two-interval, two-alternative forced-choice paradigm in which seven different comparison gap durations were presented in seven consecutive trials while the standard gap duration was kept fixed during a block of trials. Psychometric functions were derived from 25 observations for each of the seven comparisons obtained in a block of 175 trials. On each trial, the listeners were presented four noise bursts, the first two marking the duration of the first silent interval, the last two marking the duration of the second silent interval. The time between the noise burst marking the end of the first interval and the noise burst marking the beginning of the second interval was fixed at about 500 msec. The listeners' task was to judge which silent interval had the longer duration. Note that ΔT is approximately constant (about 2 msec) for Ts less than 5 msec. Below 5 msec, duration discrimination probably was based on detection of the comparison gap with the longer duration, because the standard gap probably was inaudible (cf. Fig. 14.56). The rapid increase in ΔT for Ts between 5 and 10 msec probably results from a change in discrimination process. (From S. M. Abel, Duration discrimination of noise and tone bursts, *Journal of the Acoustical Society of America*, 1972, *52*. Reprinted with permission.)

inaudibility of the high frequencies are taken into account (Florentine & Buus, 1983a, 1984).

5. SUMMARY

This chapter has (1) covered the basic physics of sound, (2) reviewed fundamental knowledge of the auditory system, and (3) summarized the data and issues in detection and discrimination. Once defined and explained, sound was then followed through the outer, middle, and inner ears to the hair cells where transduction from acoustic to neural energy takes place. It is largely the mode of sound transmission that determines the way in which the detection of pure tones depends on frequency. On the other hand, interactions between sounds, such as the masking of one sound by another, are understandable on the basis of the displacement patterns on the basilar membrane and the responses of the auditory nerve fibers. Excitation patterns derived from psychoacoustical masking data help explain the discrimination of small changes in sound intensity and frequency.

Our review reveals the great sensitivity of the human auditory system in terms both of the minimum detectable sound pressure and the smallest detectable change in the intensity or frequency of a sound. Many of the data on thresholds are embodied in several international and national standards, and are listed in the references under ISO and under ANSI. Revisions and new standards can be obtained from ANSI (1413 Broadway, New York, NY 10018). Current research and modeling in auditory physiology are concentrated on the cochlea, and especially on the microscopic details of cochlear mechanics. More peripherally, increasingly refined measures of the middle ear are becoming available. More centrally, the internal anatomy and physiology of the hair cells are now being studied so that a clear understanding of sensory transduction may not be so far in the future. The source and role of induced and spontaneous acoustic emissions from the inner ear are also being investigated. At the same time attempts continue to unravel the neural codes in the auditory nerve and at more central neural levels. Impetus for this work comes not only from its theoretical importance, but also from its relevance to cochlear implants. For the most part, current research on detection and discrimination involves a refining process, with much of the excitement having to do with the formulation of successful models of the underlying mechanisms. New endeavors are in the area of the discrimination of complex sounds. The next chapter, "Audition II" by Scharf and Houtsma, covers the remaining areas of psychoacoustics—loudness, pitch, localization, and distortion.

REFERENCE NOTES

1. Botte, M.-C. Personal communication, 1984.
2. Florentine, M., Reed, C., Durlach, N., & Braida, L. Intensity perception XII. Intensity resolution and loudness in sensorineural hearing loss. In preparation.

REFERENCES

*References preceded by an asterisk are "key references."

Abel, S. M. Discrimination of temporal gaps. *Journal of the Acoustical Society of America*, 1972, *52*, 519–524. (a)

Abel, S. M. Duration discrimination of noise and tone bursts. *Journal of the Acoustical Society of America*, 1972, *51*, 1219–1223. (b)

Ahroon, W. A., & Fay, R. R. Temporal modulation discrimination function. *Journal of the Acoustical Society of America* (Suppl. 1), 1977, *61*, S88.

Aitken, L. M., Anderson, D. J., & Brugge, J. F. Tonotopic organization and discharge characteristics of single neurons in nuclei of the lateral lemniscus of the cat. *Journal of Neurophysiology*, 1970, *33*, 521–449.

Allan, L. G., Kristofferson, A. B., & Wiens, E. W. Duration discrimination of brief light flashes. *Perception and Psychophysics*, 1971, *9*, 327–334.

American National Standards Institute. *American national standard specifications for audiometers S3.6*. New York: ANSI, 1969.

American National Standards Institute. *American national standard criteria for permissible ambient noise during audiometric testing S3.1*. New York: ANSI, 1977.

Anderson, C. M. B., & Whittle, L. S. Physiological noise and the missing 6 dB. *Acustica*, 1971, *24*, 261–272.

Anthony, W. P., & Harrison, C. W. Tympanic membrane perforations: Effect on audiograms. *Archives of Otolaryngology*, 1972, *95*, 506–510.

Békésy, G. von. Über die akustische Reizung des Vestibular-apparates. *Pflügers Archiv, European Journal of Physiology*, 1935, *236*, 59–76.

Békésy, G. von. Über die Schwingungen der Schneckentrennwand beim Präparat und Ohrenmodel. *Akustische Zeitschrift*, 1942, *7*, 173–186.

*Békésy, G. von. Über die Resonanzkurve und die Abklingzeit der verschiedenen Stellen der Schneckentrennwand. *Akustische Zeitschrift*, 1943, *8*, 66–76.

*Békésy, G. von. The variation of phase along the basilar membrane with sinusoidal vibration. *Journal of the Acoustical Society of America*, 1947, *19*, 452–460.

Békésy, G. von. The structure of the middle ear and the hearing of one's own voice by bone conduction. *Journal of the Acoustical Society of America*, 1949, *21*, 217–232.

*Békésy, G. von. *Experiments in hearing*. New York: McGraw-Hill, 1960.

Békésy, G. von, & Rosenblith, W. A. The mechanical properties of the ear. In S. S. Stevens (Ed.), *Handbook of experimental psychology*. New York: Wiley, 1951.

*Beranek, L. L. *Acoustics*. New York: McGraw-Hill, 1954.

Berger, E. H. Re-examination of the low-frequency (50–1000 Hz) normal threshold of hearing in free and diffuse sound fields. *Journal of the Acoustical Society of America*, 1981, *70*, 1635–1645.

Berliner, J. E., Durlach, N. I., & Braida, L. D. Intensity perception VII. Further data on roving-level discrimination and the resolution and bias edge effects. *Journal of the Acoustical Society of America*, 1977, *61*, 1577–1585.

Brandt, J. F., & Hollien, H. Underwater hearing thresholds in man. *Journal of the Acoustical Society of America*, 1967, *42*, 966.

Brüel & Kjaer Instruments. *Instructions and applications: Artificial ear type 4151 (Instruction Manual)*. Naerum, Denmark: Brüel & Kjaer Instruments, 1961.

Brüel & Kjaer Instruments. *Instructions and applications: Precision sound level meter type 2203/1613 (Instruction Manual)*. Naerum, Denmark: Brüel & Kjaer Instruments, 1970.

Brugge, J. F., Anderson, D. J., Hind, J. E., & Rose, J. E. Time structure of discharges in single auditory nerve fibers of the squirrel monkey in response to complex periodic sounds. *Journal of Neurophysiology*, 1969, *32*, 386–401.

Buunen, T. J. F. Two hypotheses on monaural phase effects. *Acustica*, 1975, *34*, 78–105.

Buus, S. *The role of the critical band in discrimination of complex sounds*. Unpublished doctoral dissertation, Northeastern University, 1980.

Buus, S. Discrimination of envelope frequency. *Journal of the Acoustical Society of America*, 1983, *74*, 1709–1715.

Buus, S., & Florentine, M. Intensity discrimination of simple and complex sounds. *Journal of the Acoustical Society of America* (Suppl. 1), 1981, *70*, S87–S88.

Buus, S., & Florentine, M. Detection of a temporal gap as a function of level and frequency. *Journal of the Acoustical Society of America* (Suppl. 1), 1982, *72*, S94.

*Buus, S., Florentine, M., & Redden, R. B. The SISI test: A review. I. *Audiology*, 1982, *21*, 273–293. (a)

*Buus, S., Florentine, M., & Redden, R. B. The SISI test: A review. II. *Audiology*, 1982, *21*, 365–385. (b)

Campbell, R. A. Detection of a noise signal of varying duration. *Journal of the Acoustical Society of America*, 1963, *35*, 1732–1737.

Carterette, E. C. Some historical notes on research in hearing. In E. C. Carterette & M. P. Friedman (Eds.), *Handbook of perception Vol. 4: Hearing*. New York: Academic Press, 1978.

Carterette, E. C., & Friedman, M. P. (Eds.). *Handbook of perception Vol. 4: Hearing*. New York: Academic Press, 1978.

Chaves, J. F. *Critical bands and the discrimination of intensity relations in two-tone complexes*. Unpublished master's thesis, Northeastern University, 1965.

Chocholle, R. Etude statistique des seuils auditifs monauraux et binauraux; interprétation des résultats. *Acustica*, 1954, *4*, 341–350.

Chocholle, R., & Krutel, J. Les seuils auditifs différentiels d'intensité en fonction de la durée des stimuli. *Comptes rendus de la Société de Biologie*, 1968, *162*, 848–851.

Cohen, M. Detection threshold microstructure and its effect on temporal integration data. *Journal of the Acoustical Society of America*, 1982, *71*, 405–409.

Colburn, H. S. Recent developments in binaural modeling. In R. Klinke & R. Hartmann (Eds.), *Hearing—Physiological bases and psychophysics*. Berlin: Springer, 1983.

*Colburn, H. S., & Durlach, N. I. Models of binaural interaction. In E. C. Carterette & M. P. Friedman (Eds.), *Handbook of perception Vol. 4: Hearing*. New York: Academic Press, 1978.

Corso, J. F. Age and sex differences in pure tone thresholds. *Archives of Otolaryngology*, 1963, *77*, 385–405.

Creelman, C. D. Human discrimination of auditory duration. *Journal of the Acoustical Society of America*, 1962, *34*, 582–593.

*Dallos, P. *The auditory periphery: Biophysics and physiology*. New York: Academic Press, 1973. (a)

Dallos, P. Cochlear potentials and cochlear mechanics. In A. Møller (Ed.), *Basic mechanisms of hearing*. New York: Academic Press, 1973. (b)

Dallos, P. Biophysics of the cochlea. In E. C. Carterette & M. P. Friedman (Eds.), *Handbook of perception Vol. 4: Hearing*. New York: Academic Press, 1978.

Davis, H. Initiation of nerve impulses in the cochlea and other mechanoreceptors. In T. H. Bullock (Ed.), *Physiological triggers and discontinuous rate processes*. Washington, D.C.: American Physiological Society, 1957.

Davis, H. Advances in the neurophysiology and neuroanatomy of the cochlea. *Journal of the Acoustical Society of America*, 1962, *34*, 1377–1385.

Davis, H., & Silverman, S. R. (Eds.). *Hearing and deafness* (3rd ed.). New York: Holt, Rinehart & Winston, 1970.

DiCarlo, L. M. Some relationships between frequency discrimination by hearing impaired listeners. *Journal of Auditory Research*, 1962, *2*, 37–49.

Diercks, K. J., & Jeffress, L. A. Interaural phase and the absolute threshold for tone. *Journal of the Acoustical Society of America*, 1962, *34*, 981–984.

*Dirks, D. D. Effects of hearing impairment on the auditory system. In E. C. Carterette & M. P. Friedman (Eds.), *Handbook of perception Vol. 4: Hearing*. New York: Academic Press, 1978.

Divenyi, P., & Shannon, R. V. Auditory time constants unified. *Journal of the Acoustical Society of America* (Suppl. 1), 1983, *74*, S10.

Dolan, T. R. Effect of masker spectrum level on masking-level difference at low signal frequencies. *Journal of the Acoustical Society of America*, 1968, *44*, 1507–1512.

Dubrovsky, N. A., & Tumarkina, L. N. Investigation of the human perception of amplitude-modulated noise. *Soviet Physical Acoustics*, 1967, *13*, 41–47.

Duifhuis, H. *Perceptual analysis of sound*. Unpublished doctoral dissertation, Technische Hogeschool, Eindhoven, Holland, 1972.

Duifhuis, H. Consequences of peripheral frequency selectivity for nonsimultaneous masking. *Journal of the Acoustical Society of America*, 1973, *54*, 1471–1488.

Dunn, H. K., & White, S. D. Statistical measurements on conversational speech. *Journal of the Acoustical Society of America*, 1940, *11*, 278–288.

*Durlach, N. I. Equalization and cancellation theory of binaural masking-level differences. *Journal of the Acoustical Society of America*, 1963, *35*, 1206–1218.

Durlach, N. I. Note on binaural masking-level differences at high frequencies. *Journal of the Acoustical Society of America*, 1964, *36*, 576–581.

*Durlach, N. I., & Braida, L. D. Intensity perception. I. Preliminary theory of intensity resolution. *Journal of the Acoustical Society of America*, 1969, *46*, 372–383.

*Durlach, N. I., & Colburn, H. S. Binaural phenomena. In E. C. Carterette & M. P. Friedman (Eds.), *Handbook of perception Vol. 4: Hearing*. New York: Academic Press, 1978.

Egan, J. P., & Hake, H. W. On the masking pattern of a simple auditory stimulus. *Journal of the Acoustical Society of America*, 1950, *22*, 622–630.

Egolf, D. P. Mathematical modeling of a probe tube microphone. *Journal of the Acoustical Society of America*, 1977, *61*, 200–205.

Ehmer, R. H. Masking patterns of tone. *Journal of the Acoustical Society of America*, 1959, *31*, 1115–1120.

Elliott, L. L. Changes in the simultaneous masked threshold of brief tones. *Journal of the Acoustical Society of America*, 1965, *38*, 738–746.

Elliott, L. L. Backward and forward masking. *Audiology*, 1971, *10*, 65–76.

Evans, E. F. The sharpening of cochlear frequency selectivity in the normal and abnormal cochlea. *Audiology*, 1975, *14*, 419–442.

Evans, E. F. Place and time coding of frequency in the peripheral auditory system: Some physiological pros and cons. *Audiology*, 1978, *17*, 369–420.

Evans, E. F., & Whitfield, I. Classification of unit responses in the auditory cortex of the unanesthesized and unrestrained cat. *Journal of Physiology*, 1965, *171*, 476–493.

Evans, E. F., & Wilson, J. P. The frequency selectivity of the cochlea. In A. Møller (Ed.), *Basic mechanisms of hearing*. New York: Academic Press, 1973.

Exner, S. Experimentelle Untersuchung der einfachsten psychischen Process. *Pflügers Archiv für gesamter Physiologie*, 1875, *11*, 403–432.

Fastl, H. Temporal masking effects: II. Critical band noise masker. *Acustica*, 1976/77, *36*, 317–331.

Fastl, H. Subjective duration and temporal masking patterns of broadband noise impulses. *Journal of the Acoustical Society of America*, 1977, *61*, 162–168.

Fausti, S. A., Frey, R. H., Erickson, D. A., Rappaport, B. Z., Cleary, E. J., & Brummett, R. E. A system for evaluating auditory function from 8000 to 20000 Hz. *Journal of the Acoustical Society of America*, 1979, *66*, 1713–1718.

Fay, R. R., & Passow, B. Temporal discrimination in the goldfish. *Journal of the Acoustical Society of America*, 1982, *72*, 753–760.

Fechner, G. T. *Elemente der Psychophysik*. Leipzig: Breitkopf und Härtel, 1860. [Translated by H. Adler, New York: Holt, Rinehart & Winston, 1966.]

Feldtkeller, R., & Oetinger, R. Die Hörbarkeitsgrenzen von Impulsen verschiedener Dauer. *Acustica*, 1956, *6*, 489–493.

Fidell, S., Horonjeff, R. T., Teffeteller, S., & Green, D. M. Effective masking bandwidths at low frequencies. *Journal of the Acoustical Society of America*, 1983, *73*, 628–638.

Filling, S. *Audiometrical measurement of difference limen for frequency in pathological ears*. La Puenta, Calif.: Allison Laboratories, 1956.

Fitzgibbons, P. *Temporal resolution in normal and hearing-impaired listeners*. Unpublished doctoral dissertation, Northwestern University, 1979.

Fitzgibbons, P. J. Temporal gap detection in noise as a function of frequency, bandwidth, and level. *Journal of the Acoustical Society of America*, 1983, *74*, 67–72.

Fitzgibbons, P. J., & Wightman, F. L. Gap detection in normal and hearing-impaired listeners. *Journal of the Acoustical Society of America*, 1982, *72*, 761–765.

Fleet, G. J., & Shelton, B. R. A demonstration of peripheral constraint on an auditory duration discrimination task. *Journal of the Acoustical Society of America*, 1983, *74*, S10.

*Fletcher, H. Auditory patterns. *Review of Modern Physics*, 1940, *12*, 47–65.

Fletcher, J. L., & Riopelle, A. J. Protective effect of the acoustic reflex for impulsive noises. *Journal of the Acoustical Society of America*, 1960, *32*, 401–404.

Florentine, M. Intensity discrimination as a function of level and frequency and its relation to high-frequency hearing. *Journal of the Acoustical Society of America*, 1983, *74*, 1375–1379.

Florentine, M. Level discrimination as a function of duration. *Journal of the Acoustical Society of America*, in press.

*Florentine, M., & Buus, S. An excitation-pattern model for intensity discrimination. *Journal of the Acoustical Society of America*, 1981, *70*, 1646–1654.

Florentine, M., & Buus, S. Is the detection of a temporal gap frequency dependent? *Journal of the Acoustical Society of America*, 1982, *71*, S48.

Florentine, M., & Buus, S. Gap detection in sensori-neural and simulated impairments. *Journal of the Acoustical Society of America*, 1983, *74*, S110. (a)

Florentine, M., & Buus, S. Temporal acuity as a function of level and frequency. *Proceedings of the 11th International Congress on Acoustics*, Paris, 1983, 103–106. (b)

Florentine, M. & Buus, S. Temporal gap detection in sensori-neural and simulated impairments. *Journal of Speech and Hearing Research*, 1984, *27*, 449–455.

*Florentine, M., Buus, S., Scharf, B., & Zwicker, E. Frequency selectivity in normally-hearing and hearing-impaired observers. *Journal of Speech and Hearing Research*, 1980, *23*, 646–669.

Flottorp, G., Djupesland, G., & Winther, F. The acoustic stapedius reflex in relation to critical bandwidth. *Journal of the Acoustical Society of America*, 1971, *49*, 457–461.

French, N. R., & Steinberg, J. C. Factors governing the intelligibility of speech sounds. *Journal of the Acoustical Society of America*, 1947, *19*, 90–119.

Gabrielsson, A., Johansson, B., Lindblad, A.-C., Persson, L., Pettersson, A., & Rosenquist, B. Frequency discrimination for bands of noise. *Audiology*, 1975, *14*, 1–20.

*Gacek, R. R. Neuroanatomy of the auditory system. In J. V. Tobias

(Ed.), *Foundations of modern auditory theory* (Vol. 2). New York: Academic Press, 1972.

*Galambos, R., & Davis, H. The response of single auditory nerve fibers to acoustic stimulation. *Journal of Neurophysiology*, 1943, *6*, 39–57.

Garner, W. R. The effect of frequency spectrum on temporal integration of energy in the ear. *Journal of the Acoustical Society of America*, 1947, *19*, 808–815.

Garner, W. R., & Miller, G. A. Differential sensitivity to intensity as a function of the comparison tone. *Journal of Experimental Psychology*, 1944, *34*, 450–463.

Gässler, G. Ueber die Hörschwelle für Schallereignisse mit verschieden breitem Frequenzspektrum. *Acustica*, 1954, *4*, 408–414.

*Gelfand, S. A. *Hearing*. New York: Dekker, 1981.

Gengel, R. W. Practice effects in frequency discrimination by hearing-impaired children. *Journal of Speech and Hearing Research*, 1969, *12*, 847–856.

Gengel, R. W. Temporary effects in frequency discrimination by hearing-impaired listeners. *Journal of the Acoustical Society of America*, 1973, *54*, 11–15.

Gescheider, G. Resolving of successive clicks by the ears and skin. *Journal of Experimental Psychology*, 1966, *39*, 378–381.

Gifford, M. L., & Guinan, J. J., Jr. Effects of crossed-olivocochlear-bundle stimulation on cat auditory nerve fiber responses to tones. *Journal of the Acoustical Society of America*, 1983, *74*, 115–123.

Goldstein, E. B. *Sensation and perception* (2nd ed.). Belmont, Calif.: Wadsworth, 1984.

Goldstein, J. L., & Srulovicz, P. Auditory-nerve spike intervals as an adequate basis for aural frequency measurement. In E. F. Evans & J. P. Wilson (Eds.), *Psychophysics and physiology of hearing*. New York: Academic Press, 1977.

Grantham, D. W., & Yost, W. A. Measures of intensity discrimination. *Journal of the Acoustical Society of America*, 1982, *72*, 406–410.

Green, D. M. Detection of multiple component signals in noise. *Journal of the Acoustical Society of America*, 1958, *30*, 904–911.

Green, D. M. Masking with two tones. *Journal of the Acoustical Society of America*, 1965, *37*, 802.

Green, D. M. Temporal auditory acuity. *Psychological Review*, 1971, *78*, 540–551.

Green, D. M. Minimum integration time. In A. R. Møller (Ed.), *Basic mechanisms in hearing*. New York: Academic Press, 1972.

Green, D. M. Temporal acuity as a function of frequency. *Journal of the Acoustical Society of America*, 1973, *54*, 373–379.

Green, D. M. *An introduction to hearing*. New York: Wiley, 1976.

Green, D. M., McKey, M. J., & Licklider, J. C. R. Detection of a pulsed sinusoid in noise as a function of frequency. *Journal of the Acoustical Society of America*, 1959, *31*, 1446–1452.

Green, D. M., Nachmias, J., Kearney, J. K., & Jeffress, L. A. Intensity discrimination with gated and continuous sinusoids. *Journal of the Acoustical Society of America*, 1979, *66*, 1051–1056.

Greenwood, D. D. Auditory masking and the critical band. *Journal of the Acoustical Society of America*, 1961, *33*, 484–502.

Greenwood, D. D. Aural combination tones and auditory masking. *Journal of the Acoustical Society of America*, 1971, *50*, 502–543.

Gulick, W. L. *Hearing, physiology and psychophysics*. New York: Oxford University Press, 1971.

*Hamernik, R. P., Henderson, D., & Salvi, R. (Eds.). *New perspectives on noise-induced hearing loss*. New York: Raven, 1982.

Hamilton, P. M. Noise masked thresholds as a function of tonal duration and masking noise bandwidth. *Journal of the Acoustical Society of America*, 1957, *29*, 506–511.

Harris, J. D. Pitch discrimination. *Journal of the Acoustical Society of America*, 1952, *24*, 750–755.

*Harris, J. D. Loudness discrimination. *Journal of Speech and Hearing Disorders*, 1963, *11*, 1–63. (Monograph Supplement)

Harris, J. D. Masked DL for pitch memory. *Journal of the Acoustical Society of America*, 1966, *40*, 43–46.

*Hawkins, J. E., & Stevens, S. S. The masking of pure tones and of speech by white noise. *Journal of the Acoustical Society of America*, 1950, *22*, 6–13.

Hellman, R. P. Dependence of loudness growth on skirts of excitation patterns. *Journal of the Acoustical Society of America*, 1978, *63*, 1114–1119.

*Helmholtz, H. *On the sensations of tone*. New York: Dover, 1954. (Originally published, 1885.)

*Henderson, D., Hamernik, R. P., Dosanjh, D. S., & Mills, J. H. (Eds.). *Effects of noise on hearing*. New York: Raven, 1976.

Henning, G. B. Frequency discrimination of random-amplitude tones. *Journal of the Acoustical Society of America*, 1966, *39*, 336–339.

Henning, G. B. Frequency discrimination in noise. *Journal of the Acoustical Society of America*, 1967, *41*, 774–777.

Henning, G. B. A comparison of the effects of signal duration on frequency and amplitude discrimination. In R. Plomp & G. F. Smoorenburg (Eds.), *Frequency analysis and periodicity detection in hearing*. Leiden, Netherlands: Sijthoff, 1970.

*Hinchcliffe, R. The threshold of hearing as a function of age. *Acustica*, 1959, *9*, 303–308.

Hind, J. E. Two-tone masking effects in squirrel monkey auditory nerve fibers. In R. Plomp & G. F. Smoorenburg (Eds.). *Frequency analysis and periodicity detection in hearing*. Leiden, Netherlands: Sijthoff, 1970.

*Hirsh, I. J. The influence of interaural phase on interaural summation and inhibition. *Journal of the Acoustical Society of America*, 1948, *20*, 536–544.

Hirsh, I. J. *The measurement of hearing*. New York: McGraw-Hill, 1951.

Hirsh, I. J. Auditory perception of temporal order. *Journal of the Acoustical Society of America*, 1959, *31*, 759–767.

Hirsh, I. J., & Sherrick, C. E., Jr. Perceived order in different sense modalities. *Journal of Experimental Psychology*, 1961, *62*, 423–432.

Hoekstra, A. *Frequency discrimination and frequency analysis in hearing*. Unpublished doctoral dissertation, Rijksuniversitet te Groningen, Holland, 1979.

Hoke, M., Kauffmann, G., & Bappert, E. Cochlear and brainstem evoked response audiometry and electrical stimulation of the VIIIth nerve. *Scandinavian Audiology Supplement 2*, 1980.

Hollien, H., & Brandt, J. F. Effect of air bubbles in the external auditory meatus on underwater hearing thresholds. *Journal of the Acoustical Society of America*, 1969, *46*, 384–387.

Hollien, H., & Feinstein, S. Contribution of the external meatus to auditory sensitivity underwater. *Journal of the Acoustical Society of America*, 1975, *57*, 1488–1492.

Houtgast, T. Psychophysical evidence for lateral suppression in hearing. *Journal of the Acoustical Society of America*, 1972, *51*, 1885–1894.

Houtgast, T. Subharmonic pitches of a pure tone at low S/N ratio. *Journal of the Acoustical Society of America*, 1976, *60*, 405–409.

Houtsma, A. J., Durlach, N. I., & Braida, L. D. Intensity perception XI. Experimental results on the relation of intensity resolution to loudness matching. *Journal of the Acoustical Society of America*, 1980, *68*, 807–813.

International Standards Organization. *Normal equal-loudness contours for pure tones and normal threshold of hearing under free field listening conditions R226*. New York: ISO, 1961.

International Standards Organization. *Standard reference zero for the calibration of pure-tone audiometers 389*. New York: ISO, 1975.

Irwin, R. J., Hinchcliff, L. K., & Kemp, S. Temporal acuity in normal and hearing-impaired listeners. *Audiology*, 1981, *20*, 234–243.

Irwin, R. J., & Purdy, S. C. The minimum detectable duration of auditory signals for normal and hearing-impaired listeners. *Journal of the Acoustical Society of America*, 1982, *71*, 967–974.

Jeffress, L. A., Blodgett, H. C., & Deatherage, B. H. Masking and interaural phase. II. 167 cycles. *Journal of the Acoustical Society of America*, 1952, *34*, 1124–1126.

Jesteadt, W., Bacon, S. P., & Lehman, J. R. Forward masking as a function of frequency, masker level, and signal delay. *Journal of the Acoustical Society of America*, 1982, *71*, 950–962.

Jesteadt, W., & Sims, S. L. Decision processes in frequency discrimination. *Journal of the Acoustical Society of America*, 1975, *57*,

1161–1168.

*Jesteadt, W., Wier, C. C., & Green, D. M. Intensity discrimination as a function of frequency and sensation level. *Journal of the Acoustical Society of America*, 1977, *61*, 169–177.

Johnson-Davies, D., & Patterson, R. D. Psychophysical tuning curves: Restricting the listening band to the signal region. *Journal of the Acoustical Society of America*, 1979, *65*, 765–770.

Johnstone, B. M., & Boyle, A. J. F. Basilar membrane vibration examined with the Mossbauer technique. *Science*, 1967, *158*, 389–390.

Kaye, G. W. C., & Laby, T. H. *Tables for physical and chemical constants and some mathematical functions* (13th ed.). London: Longmans, Green, 1966.

*Keidel, W. D., & Neff, W. D. (Eds.). *Handbook of sensory physiology Vol. 5: Auditory system*. New York: Springer-Verlag, 1975.

*Kemp, D. T. Stimulated acoustic emissions from within the human auditory system. *Journal of the Acoustical Society of America*, 1978, *64*, 1386–1391.

Kemp, D. T. Towards a model for the origin of cochlear echoes. *Hearing Research*, 1980, *2*, 533–548.

Khanna, S. M., & Leonard, D. G. B. Laser interferometric measurements of basilar membrane vibrations in cats using a round window approach. *Journal of the Acoustical Society of America*, 1981, *69*, S51.

*Kiang, N. Y.-S. Discharge of single fibers in the cat's auditory nerve. *Research Monograph* No. 35. Cambridge, Mass.: MIT Press, 1965.

Killion, M. C. Revised estimate of minimum audible pressure: Where is the "missing 6 dB?" *Journal of the Acoustical Society of America*, 1978, *63*, 1501–1508.

Knudsen, V. O., & Harris, C. M. *Acoustical designing in architecture*, New York: Acoustical Society of America, 1980. (Originally published, 1950.)

Korsan-Bengtsen, M. Distorted speech audiometry. *Acta Oto-Laryngologica* (Suppl. 310), 1973.

Kruger, B., & Tonndorf, J. Tympanic membrane perforations in cats: Configurations of losses with and without ear canal extensions. *Journal of the Acoustical Society of America*, 1978, *63*, 436–441.

*Kryter, K. D. Presbycusis, sociocusis and nosocusis. *Journal of the Acoustical Society of America*, 1983, *73*, 1897–1917.

Legouix, J. P., Remond, M. C., & Greenbaum, B. Interference and two-tone inhibition. *Journal of the Acoustical Society of America*, 1973, *53*, 409–419.

Leshowitz, B. Measurement of the two-click threshold. *Journal of the Acoustical Society of America*, 1971, *49*, 462–466.

*Leshowitz, B. Measurement of the auditory stimulus. In E. C. Carterette & M. P. Friedman (Eds.), *Handbook of perception Vol. 4: Hearing*. New York: Academic Press, 1978.

*Levitt, H. Transformed up-down methods in psychoacoustics. *Journal of the Acoustical Society of America*, 1971, *49*, 467–477.

Levitt, H. Adaptive testing in audiology. In C. Ludvigsen & J. Barfod (Eds.), Sensorineural hearing impairment and hearing aids. *Scandinavian Audiology Supplement 6*, 1978, 241–291.

*Licklider, J. C. R. A duplex theory of pitch perception. *Experientia*, 1951, *7*, 128–134.

Littler, T. S. Noise measurement, analysis and evaluation of harmful effects. *Annals of Occupational Hygiene*, 1958, *1*, 11.

Long, G. L., & Cullen, J. K., Jr. Some aspects of signal processing in individuals with residual high-frequency hearing. In R. Klinke & R. Hartman (Eds.), *Hearing—Physiological bases and psychophysics*. Berlin: Springer-Verlag, 1983.

Luce, R. D., & Green, D. M. Neural coding and psychophysical discrimination data. *Journal of the Acoustical Society of America*, 1974, *56*, 1554–1564.

Maiwald, D. Berechnung von Modulationsschwellen mit Hilfe eines Funktionsschemas. *Acustica*, 1967, *18*, 193–207. (a)

Maiwald, D. Beziehungen zwischen Schallspektrum, Mithörschwelle und Erregung des Gehörs. *Acustica*, 1967, *18*, 69–80. (b)

Marill, T. M. *Detection theory and psychophysics*. (Tech. Rep. 319). Cambridge, Mass.: Massachusetts Institute of Technology, Research Laboratories of Electronics, 1956.

McFadden, D. Masking-level differences determined with and without interaural disparities in masker intensity. *Journal of the Acoustical Society of America*, 1968, *44*, 212–223.

McFadden, D., & Plattsmier, H. S. Frequency patterns of TTS for different exposure intensities. *Journal of the Acoustical Society of America*, 1983, *74*, 1178–1184.

McGill, W. J., & Goldberg, J. P. Pure-tone intensity discrimination and energy detection. *Journal of the Acoustical Society of America*, 1968, *44*, 576–581. (a)

McGill, W. J., & Goldberg, J. P. A study of the near-miss involving Weber's law and pure-tone intensity discrimination. *Perception and Psychophysics*, 1968, *4*, 105–109. (b)

Melnick, W. Human asymtotic threshold shift. In D. Henderson, R. P. Hamernik, D. S. Dosanjh, & J. H. Mills (Eds.), *Effects of noise on hearing*. New York: Raven Press, 1976.

Merzenich, M. M., & Brugge, J. F. Representation of the cochlear partition on the superior temporal plane of the macaque monkey. *Brain Research*, 1973, *50*, 275–296.

Michaels, R. M. Frequency DLs for narrow bands of noise. *Journal of the Acoustical Society of America*, 1957, *29*, 520–522.

Miller, G. A. Sensitivity to changes in the intensity of white noise and its relation to masking and loudness. *Journal of the Acoustical Society of America*, 1947, *19*, 609–619.

Miller, G. A. The magical number seven, plus or minus two: Some limits on our capacity for processing information. *Psychological Review*, 1956, *63*, 81–97.

Miller, G. A., & Taylor, W. G. The perception of repeated bursts of noise. *Journal of the Acoustical Society of America*, 1948, *20*, 171–180.

*Miller, J. D. Effects of noise on people. *Journal of the Acoustical Society of America*, 1974, *56*, 729–764.

Mills, J. H., Adkins, W. Y., & Gilbert, R. M. Temporary threshold shifts produced by wideband noise. *Journal of the Acoustical Society of America*, 1981, *70*, 390–396.

Mills, J. H., Gilbert, R. M., & Adkins, W. Y. Temporary threshold shifts in humans exposed to octave bands of noise for 16 to 24 hours. *Journal of the Acoustical Society of America*, 1979, *65*, 1238–1248.

*Møller, A. R. Acoustic reflex in man. *Journal of the Acoustical Society of America*, 1962, *34*, 1524–1534. (a)

Møller, A. R. The sensitivity of contraction of the tympanic muscles in man. *Annals of Otology, Rhinology, and Laryngology*, 1962, *71*, 86–95. (b)

Møller, A. R. Unit responses in the rat cochlear nucleus to repetitive, transient sounds. *Acta Physiologica Scandinavica*, 1969, *75*, 542–551.

Møller, A. R. Two different types of frequency selective neurons of the rat. In R. Plomp & G. F. Smoorenburg (Eds.), *Frequency analysis and periodicity detection in hearing*. Leiden, Netherlands: Sijthoff, 1970.

Møller, A. R. Coding of sounds in lower levels of the auditory system. *Quarterly Reviews of Biophysics*, 1972, *5*, 59–155.

Møller, M. B. Changes in hearing measures with increasing age. In R. Hinchcliffe (Ed.), *Hearing and balance in the elderly*. Edinburgh: Churchill-Livingstone, 1983.

Moore, B. C. J. Frequency discrimination for short-duration tones. *Journal of the Acoustical Society of America*, 1973, *54*, 610–619. (a)

Moore, B. C. J. Frequency discrimination limens for narrow bands of noise. *Journal of the Acoustical Society of America*, 1973, *54*, 888–896. (b)

Moore, B. C. J. Comparison of frequency DLs for pulsed tones and modulated tones. *British Journal of Audiology*, 1976, *10*, 17–20.

Moore, B. C. J. Psychophysical tuning curves measured in simultaneous and forward masking. *Journal of the Acoustical Society of America*, 1978, *63*, 524–532.

Moore, B. C. J. Detection cues in forward masking. In G. van den Brink & F. A. Bilsen (Eds.), *Psychological, physiological, and behavioural studies in hearing*. Netherlands: Delft University Press, 1980.

*Moore, B. C. J. *Psychology of hearing*. New York: Academic Press, 1982.

Moore, B. C. J., & Glasberg, B. R. Growth of forward masking for sinusoidal and noise maskers as a function of signal delay; implications for suppression in noise. *Journal of the Acoustical Society of America*, 1983, *73*, 1249–1259. (a)

Moore, B. C. J., & Glasberg, B. R. Suggested formulae for calculating auditory-filter bandwidths and excitation patterns. *Journal of the Acoustical Society of America*, 1983, *73*, 750–753. (b)

Moore, B. C. J., & Raab, D. H. Pure-tone intensity discrimination: Some experiments relating to the "near-miss" to Weber's law. *Journal of the Acoustical Society of America*, 1974, *55*, 1049–1054.

Morton, J., & Carpenter, A. Experiments relating to the perception of formants. *Journal of the Acoustical Society of America*, 1963, *35*, 475–480.

Moushegian, G., Rupert, A., & Whitcomb, M. A. Processing of auditory information by medial superior-olivary neurons. In J. V. Tobias (Ed.), *Foundations of modern auditory theory* (Vol. 2). New York: Academic Press, 1972.

Mowbray, G. H., Gebhard, J. W., & Byham, C. L. Sensitivity changes in the interruption rate of white noise. *Journal of the Acoustical Society of America*, 1956, *63*, 1904–1911.

Munson, W. A., & Gardner, M. B. Loudness patterns—a new approach. *Journal of the Acoustical Society of America*, 1950, *22*, 177–190.

Nelson, D. A. Two-tone masking and auditory critical bandwidths. *Audiology*, 1979, *18*, 279–306.

Nelson, D. A., Stanton, M. E., & Freyman, R. L. A general equation describing frequency discrimination as a function of frequency and sensation level. *Journal of the Acoustical Society of America*, 1983, *73*, 2117–2123.

Nelson, P., Erulkar, S., & Bryan, J. Responses of units of the inferior colliculus to time-varying acoustic stimuli. *Journal of Neurophysiology*, 1966, *29*, 834–860.

Nordmark, J. O. Mechanisms of frequency discrimination. *Journal of the Acoustical Society of America*, 1968, *44*, 1533–1540.

Ohm, G. S. Über die Definition des Tones nebst daran geknupfter Theorie der Sirene und ähnlicher tonbildender Vorrichtungen. *Annalen der Physikalische Chemie*, 1843, *59*, 513–565.

*Parkins, C. W., & Anderson, S. W. (Eds.). *Cochlear prostheses: An international symposium*. Annals of the New York Academy of Sciences, *Volume 405*, 1983.

Passchier-Vermeer, W. *Hearing loss due to exposure to steady-state broadband noise* (IG-TNO Report 35). Delft, Netherlands, 1968.

Patterson, J. H., & Green, D. M. Discrimination of transient signals having identical energy spectra. *Journal of the Acoustical Society of America*, 1970, *48*, 894–905.

Patterson, R. D. Auditory filter shapes derived with noise stimuli. *Journal of the Acoustical Society of America*, 1976, *59*, 640–654.

*Patterson, R. D., & Green, D. M. Auditory masking. In E. C. Carterette & M. P. Friedman (Eds.), *Handbook of perception Vol. 4: Hearing*. New York: Academic Press, 1978.

Patterson, R. D., Johnson-Davies, D., & Milroy, R. Amplitude-modulated noise: The detection of modulation versus the detection of modulation rate. *Journal of the Acoustical Society of America*, 1978, *63*, 1904–1911.

Patterson, R. D., Nimmo-Smith, I., Weber, D. L., & Milroy, R. The deterioration of hearing with age: Frequency selectivity, the critical ratio, the audiogram, and speech threshold. *Journal of the Acoustical Society of America*, 1982, *72*, 1788–1803.

Penner, M. J. Detection of temporal gaps in noise as a measure of the decay of auditory sensation. *Journal of the Acoustical Society of America*, 1977, *61*, 552–557.

Penner, M. J., & Viemeister, N. F. Intensity discrimination of clicks: The effects of click bandwidth and background noise. *Journal of the Acoustical Society of America*, 1973, *54*, 1184–1188.

Piéron, H. The phenomenon of toneless hearing in light sleep. *L'Année Psychologique*, 1952, *52*, 393–395.

Plomp, R. Rate of decay of auditory sensation. *Journal of the Acoustical Society of America*, 1964, *36*, 277–282.

Pollack, I. Auditory flutter. *American Journal of Psychology*, 1952, *65*, 544–554.

Pratt, H., & Sohmer, H. Comparison of hearing threshold determined by auditory pathway electric responses and by behavioural responses. *Audiology*, 1978, *17*, 285–292.

Pynn, C. T., Braida, L. D., & Durlach, N. I. Intensity perception. III. Resolution in small-range identification. *Journal of the Acoustical Society of America*, 1971, *51*, 559–566.

Raab, D. H. Forward and backward masking between acoustic clicks. *Journal of the Acoustical Society of America*, 1961, *33*, 137–139.

Rabinowitz, W. M. *Frequency intensity resolution in audition*. Unpublished master's thesis, Massachusetts Institute of Technology, 1970.

Rabinowitz, W. M., Lim, J. S., Braida, L. D., & Durlach, N. I. Intensity perception. VI. Summary of recent data on deviations from Weber's law for 1000-Hz tone pulses. *Journal of the Acoustical Society of America*, 1976, *59*, 1506–1509.

Rasmussen, H. Studies on the effect upon hearing through air conduction brought about by variations of the pressure in the auditory meatus. *Acta Oto-Laryngologica*, 1946, *34*, 415–424.

Rasmussen, H. Studies on the effect on the air conduction and bone conduction from changes in the meatal pressure in normal subjects and otosclerotic patients. *Acta Oto-Laryngologica, Supplement*, 1948, *74*, 54–64.

Reed, C. M., & Bilger, R. C. A comparative study of S/N and E/N. *Journal of the Acoustical Society of America*, 1973, *53*, 1039–1044.

Rhode, W. S. Observations of the vibration of the basilar membrane in squirrel monkeys using the Mossbauer technique. *Journal of the Acoustical Society of America*, 1971, *49*, 1218–1231.

Richards, A. M. *Basic experimentation in psychoacoustics*. Baltimore: University Park Press, 1976.

Riesz, R. R. Differential intensity sensitivity of the ear. *Physics Review*, 1928, *31*, 867–875.

Ritsma, R. J. Existence region of the tonal residue. II. *Journal of the Acoustical Society of America*,1963, *35*, 1241–1245.

Robinson, C. E., & Pollack, I. Forward and backward masking: Testing a discrete perceptual-moment hypothesis in audition. *Journal of the Acoustical Society of America*, 1971, *50*, 1512–1519.

Robinson, D. W., & Dadson, R. S. A re-determination of equal-loudness relations for pure tones. *British Journal of Applied Physics*, 1956, *7*, 166–181.

Robinson, D. W., Shipton, M. S., & Hinchcliffe, R. Audiometric zero for air conduction. *Audiology*, 1981, *20*, 409–431.

Robinson, D. W., & Sutton, G. J. Age effect in hearing—A comparative analysis of published threshold data. *Audiology*, 1979, *18*, 320–324.

Ronken, D. A. Some effects of bandwidth duration constraints on frequency discrimination. *Journal of the Acoustical Society of America*, 1971, *49*, 1232–1242.

Rose, J. E. Organization of frequency sensitive neurons in the cochlear nuclear complex of the cat. In G. L. Rasmussen & W. F. Windle (Eds.), *Neural mechanisms of the auditory and vestibular systems*. Springfield, Ill.: Thomas, 1960.

Rose, J. E., Brugge, J. F., Anderson, D. J., & Hind, J. E. Phase-locked response to low-frequency tones in single auditory nerve fibers of the squirrel monkey. *Journal of Neurophysiology*, 1967, *30*, 769–793.

Rose, J. E., Brugge, J. F., Anderson, D. J., & Hind, J. E. Patterns of activity in single auditory nerve fibers of the squirrel monkey. In A. V. S. de Reuck & J. Knight (Eds.), *Hearing mechanisms in vertebrates*. London: Churchill, 1968.

Rose, J. E., Greenwood, D. D., Goldberg, J. M., & Hind, J. E. Some discharge characteristics of single neurons in the inferior colliculus of the cat. I. Tonotopical organization, relation of spike-counts to tone intensity, and firing patterns of single elements. *Journal of Neurophysiology*, 1963, *26*, 294–320.

Rosenblith, W. A., & Stevens, K. N. On the DL for frequency. *Journal of the Acoustical Society of America*, 1953, *25*, 980–985.

Ross, M., Huntington, D. A., Newby, H. A., & Dixon, R. F. Speech discrimination of hearing-impaired individuals in noise. *Journal of Auditory Research*, 1965, *5*, 47–72.

*Russell, I. J., & Sellick, P. M. The tuning properties of cochlear hair cells., In E. F. Evans & J. P. Wilson (Eds.), *Psychophysics and* *physiology of hearing*. London: Academic Press, 1977.

*Sachs, M. B., & Kiang, N. Y.-S. Two-tone inhibition in auditory nerve fibers. *Journal of the Acoustical Society of America*, 1968, *43*, 1120–1128.

Saltzman, M. *Clinical audiology*. New York: Grune & Stratton, 1949.

Schacknow, P. N., & Raab, D. H. Noise-intensity discrimination: Effects of bandwidth conditions and mode of masker presentation. *Journal of the Acoustical Society of America*, 1976, *60*, 893–905.

*Scharf, B. Critical bands. In J. V. Tobias (Ed.), *Foundations of modern auditory theory*, Vol. 1. York: Academic Press, 1970. (a)

Scharf, B. Loudness and frequency selectivity at short durations. In R. Plomp & G. F. Smoorenburg (Eds.), *Frequency analysis and periodicity detection in hearing*. Leiden, Netherlands: Sijthoff, 1970. (b)

Scharf, B. Audition. In B. Scharf (Ed.), *Experimental sensory psychology*. Glenview, Ill.: Scott, Foresman & Company, 1975.

Scharf, B. Loudness Adaptation. In J. V. Tobias & E. D. Schubert (Eds.), *Hearing research and theory*. New York: Academic Press, 1983.

Scharf, B., & Florentine, M. Psychoacoustics of elementary sound perception. In G. A. Studebaker & F. H. Bess (Eds.). *The Vanderbilt hearing-aid report*. Monographs in Contemporary Audiology, 1982.

Scharf, B., & Meiselman, C. H. Critical bandwidth at high intensities. In E. V. Evans & J. P. Wilson (Eds.), *Psychophysics and physiology of hearing*. London: Academic Press, 1977.

Schodder, G. R., & David, E. E., Jr. Pitch discrimination of two-frequency complexes. *Journal of the Acoustical Society of America*, 1960, *32*, 1426–1435.

Schubert, E. D. History of research on hearing. In E. C. Carterette & M. P. Friedman (Eds.), *Handbook of perception Vol. 4: Hearing*. New York: Academic Press, 1978.

Seebeck, A. Beobachtungen über einige Bedingungen der Entstehung von Tönen. *Annalen der Physikalische Chemie*, 1841, *53*, 417–436.

Sellick, P. M., Russell, I. J., Patuzzi, R., & Johnstone, B. M. Generation of hair cell receptor potentials and basilar membrane tuning. *Journal of the Acoustical Society of America*, 1981, *70*, S51.

Shailer, M. J., & Moore, B. C. J. Gap detection as a function of frequency, bandwidth, and level. *Journal of the Acoustical Society of America*, 1983, *74*, 467–473.

*Shaw, E. A. G. Earcanal pressure generated by a free sound field. *Journal of the Acoustical Society of America*, 1966, *39*, 465–470. (a)

Shaw, E. A. G. Earcanal pressure generated by circumaural and supraaural earphones. *Journal of the Acoustical Society of America*, 1966, *39*, 471–479. (b)

Shaw, E. A. G., & Teranishi, R. Sound pressure generated in an external-ear replica and real human ears by a nearby point source. *Journal of the Acoustical Society of America*, 1968, *44*, 240–249.

Shelton, B. R. Duration discrimination of noise bursts presented at a rapid rate. *Journal of the Acoustical Society of America*, 1982, *72*, S89.

Shower, E. G., & Biddulph, R. Differential pitch sensitivity of the ear. *Journal of the Acoustical Society of America*, 1931, *3*, 275–287.

Siebert, W. M. Some implications of the stochastic behavior of primary auditory neurons. *Kybernetik*, 1965, *2*, 206–215.

Siebert, W. M. Stimulus transformations in the peripheral auditory system. In P. A. Kolers & M. Eden (Eds.). *Recognizing patterns*. Cambridge, Mass.: MIT Press, 1968.

Siebert, W. M. Frequency discrimination in the auditory system: Place or periodicity mechanisms. *Proceedings of the IEEE*, 1970, *58*, 723–730.

Small, A. M., Jr. Some parameters influencing the pitch of amplitude modulated signals. *Journal of the Acoustical Society of America*, 1955, *27*, 751–760.

Small, A. M., Jr. Pure-tone masking. *Journal of the Acoustical Society of America*, 1959, *31*, 1619–1625.

Small, A. M., & Campbell, R. A. Temporal differential sensitivity for auditory stimuli. *American Journal of Psychology*, 1962, *75*, 401–410.

Sorkin, R. D. Extension of the theory of signal detectability to matching procedures in psychophysics. *Journal of the Acoustical Society of America*, 1962, *34*, 1745–1751.

*Spoendlin, H. Neuroanatomy of the cochlea. In E. Zwicker & E. Terhardt (Eds.), *Facts and models in hearing*. New York: Springer-Verlag, 1974.

Stelmachowicz, P. G., Gorga, M. P., & Cullen, J. K. A calibration procedure for the assessment of thresholds above 8000 Hz. *Journal of Speech and Hearing Research*, 1982, *25*, 618–623.

*Stevens, S. S., & Davis, H. *Hearing: Its psychology and physiology*. New York: Wiley, 1938.

Stucker, H. Über die Unterschiedsempfindlichkeit für Tonhöhen. *Zeitschrift für Sinnesphysiologie*, 1908, *42*, 392–408.

Studebaker, G., & Zachmann, T. A. Investigation of the acoustics of earmold vents. *Journal of the Acoustical Society of America*, 1970, *47*, 1107–1115.

Taylor, M. M., & Creelman, C. D. PEST: Efficient estimates on probability functions. *Journal of the Acoustical Society of America*, 1967, *41*, 782–787.

Teich, M. C., & Lachs, G. A neural-counting model incorporating refractoriness and spread of excitation. I. Application to intensity discrimination. *Journal of the Acoustical Society of America*, 1979, *66*, 1738–1749.

Terhardt, E. On the perception of periodic sound fluctuations (roughness). *Acustica*, 1974, *30*, 201–213.

Tonndorf, J., & Khanna, S. H. Submicroscopic displacement of the tympanic membrane (cat) measured by a laser interferometer. *Journal of the Acoustical Society of America*, 1968, *44*, 1546–1569.

Tsuchitani, C., & Boudreau, J. C. Single unit analysis of cat superior olive S segment with tonal stimuli. *Journal of Neurophysiology*, 1966, *29*, 684–697.

Tsuchitani, C., & Boudreau, J. C. Encoding of stimulus frequency and intensity by cat superior olive S-segment cells. *Journal of the Acoustical Society of America*, 1967, *42*, 794–805.

Tyler, R. S. Frequency resolution in hearing-impaired listeners. In B. C. J. Moore (Ed.), *Frequency resolution in hearing*. London: Academic Press, in press.

van den Brink, G. Experiment on cochlear summation. *Journal of the Acoustical Society of America*, 1964, *36*, 1213–1214.

Verschuure, J., & van Meeteren, A. A. The effect of intensity on pitch. *Acustica*, 1975, *32*, 33–44.

Viemeister, N. F. Intensity discrimination of pulsed sinusoids: The effects of filtered noise. *Journal of the Acoustical Society of America*, 1972, *51*, 1265–1269.

Viemeister, N. F. Temporal modulation transfer functions for audition. *Journal of the Acoustical Society of America*, 1973, *47*, 119.

Viemeister, N. F. Temporal factors in audition: A system analysis approach. In E. F. Evans & J. P. Wilson (Eds.), *Psychophysics and physiology of hearing*. New York: Academic Press, 1977.

Viemeister, N. F. Temporal modulation transfer functions based upon modulation thresholds. *Journal of the Acoustical Society of America*, 1979, *66*, 1364–1380.

Viemeister, N. F. On the form of the masking function for intensity discrimination of pure tones. *Journal of the Acoustical Society of America* (Suppl. 1), 1983, *74*, S34.

Wallach, H., Newman, E. B., & Rosenzweig, M. R. Precedence effect in sound localization. *American Journal of Psychology*, 1949, *62*, 315–336.

Ward, W. D. Damage-risk criteria for line spectra. *Journal of the Acoustical Society of America*, 1962, *34*, 1610–1619.

Ward, W. D. Auditory fatigue and masking. In J. Jerger (Ed.), *Modern developments in audiology*. New York, London: Academic Press, 1963.

*Ward, W. D. Noise-induced hearing loss. In D. M. Jones & A. J. Chapman (Eds.), *Noise and society*. London: Wiley, 1984.

Ward, W. D., Glorig, A., & Sklar, D. L. Relation between recovery from temporary threshold shift and duration of exposure. *Journal of the Acoustical Society of America*, 1959, *31*, 600–602.

Ward, W. D., Selters, W., & Glorig, A. Exploratory studies on temporary threshold shift from impulses. *Journal of the Acoustical Society of*

America, 1961, *33*, 781–793.

Weber, D. L., & Moore, B. C. J. Forward masking by sinusoidal and noise maskers. *Journal of the Acoustical Society of America*, 1981, *69*, 1402–1409.

Weissler, P. B. International Standard reference zero for audiometers. *Journal of the Acoustical Society of America*, 1968, *44*, 264–275.

Wever, E. G. *Theory of hearing*. New York: Wiley, 1949.

Wever, E. G. The mechanics of hair cell stimulation. *Annals of Otology, Rhinology, and Laryngology*, 1971, *80*, 786–805.

Wever, E. G., & Bray, C. Action currents in the auditory nerve in response to acoustic stimulation. *Proceedings of the National Academy of Science*, 1930, *16*, 344–350.

Whittle, L. S., Collins, S. J., & Robinson, D. W. The audibility of low-frequency sounds. *Journal of Sound and Vibration*, 1972, *21*, 431–448.

Widin, G. P., & Viemeister, N. F. Intensive and temporal effects in pure-tone masking. *Journal of the Acoustical Society of America*, 1979, *66*, 388–395.

Wiederhold, M. L., & Kiang, N. Y.-S. Effects of electric stimulation of the crossed olivocochlear bundle on single auditory-nerve fibers in the cat. *Journal of the Acoustical Society of America*, 1970, *48*, 950–965.

Wiener, F. M. On the diffraction of a progressive sound wave by the human head. *Journal of the Acoustical Society of America*, 1947, *19*, 143–146.

*Wiener, F. M., & Ross, D. The pressure distribution in the auditory canal in a progressive sound field. *Journal of the Acoustical Society of America*, 1946, *18*, 401–408.

Wier, C. C., Jesteadt, W., & Green, D. M. A comparison of method-of-adjustment and forced-choice procedures in frequency discrimination. *Perception and Psychophysics*, 1976, *19*, 75–79.

*Wier, C. C., Jesteadt, W., & Green, D. M. Frequency discrimination as a function of frequency and sensation levels. *Journal of the Acoustical Society of America*, 1977, *61*, 178–184.

Wilson, J. P. Evidence for a cochlear origin for acoustic re-emissions, threshold fine structure, and tonal tinnitus. *Hearing Research*, 1980, *2*, 527–532.

Wilson, J. P., & Johnstone, J. R. Capacitive probe measures of basilar membrane vibrations. In *Hearing theory*. Eindhoven, Netherlands: Institut voor Perceptie Onderzoek, 1972.

Woolsey, C. N. (Ed.), Organization of cortical auditory system: A review and a synthesis. In G. L. Rasmussen & W. F. Windle (Eds.). *Neural mechanisms of the auditory vestibular systems*. Springfield, Ill.: Thomas, 1960.

*Woolsey, C. N. *Cortical sensory organization. Vol. 3. Multiple auditory areas*. Clifton, N.J.: Humana Press, 1982.

Wright, H. N. Temporal summation and backward masking. *Journal of the Acoustical Society of America*, 1964, *36*, 927–932.

Yoneshige, Y., & Elliott, L. L. Pure-tone sensitivity and ear canal pressure at threshold in children and adults. *Journal of the Acoustical Society of America*, 1981, *70*, 1272–1276.

Zerlin, S. Traveling-wave velocity in the human cochlea. *Journal of the Acoustical Society of America*, 1969, *46*, 1011–1015.

*Zurek, P. M. Spontaneous narrowband acoustic signals emitted by human ears. *Journal of the Acoustical Society of America*, 1981, *69*, 514–523.

Zurek, P. M., & Formby, C. Frequency-discrimination ability of hearing-impaired listeners. *Journal of Speech and Hearing Research*, 1981, *24*, 108–112.

Zwicker, E. Die Grenzen der Hörbarkeit der Amplitudenmodulation und der Frequenzmodulation eines Tones. *Acustica*, 1952, *2*, 125–133.

Zwicker, E. Die Verdeckung von Schmalbandgeräuschen durch Sinustöne. *Acustica* (Akustische Beiheft), 1954, *4*, 415–420.

Zwicker, E. Die elementaren Grundlagen zur Bestimmung der Informationskapazität des Gehörs. *Acustica*, 1956, *6*, 365–381.

Zwicker, E. Über psychologische und methodische Grundlagen der Lautheit. *Acustica*, 1958, *8*, 237–258.

Zwicker, E. Temporal effects in simultaneous masking and loudness. *Journal of the Acoustical Society of America*, 1965, *38*, 132–141.

Zwicker, E. Masking and psychological excitation as consequences of the ear's frequency analysis. In R. Plomp & G. F. Smoorenburg (Eds.), *Frequency analysis and periodicity detection in hearing*. Leiden, Netherlands: Sijthoff, 1970.

*Zwicker, E. On a psychoacoustical equivalent of tuning curves. In E. Zwicker & E. Terhardt (Eds.), *Facts and models in hearing*. Berlin: Springer, 1974.

Zwicker, E. Masking period patterns of harmonic complex tones. *Journal of the Acoustical Society of America*, 1976, *60*, 429–439.

Zwicker, E. Reversed behavior of masking at low levels. *Audiology*, 1980, *19*, 330–334.

Zwicker, E., & Fastl, H. On the development of the critical band. *Journal of the Acoustical Society of America*, 1972, *52*, 699–702.

*Zwicker, E., & Feldtkeller, R. *Das Ohr als Nachrichtenempfänger*. Stuttgart, West Germany: Hirzel Verlag, 1967.

Zwicker, E., & Jaroszewski, A. Inverse frequency dependence of simultaneous tone-on-tone masking patterns at low levels. *Journal of the Acoustical Society of America*, 1982, *71*, 1508–1512.

Zwicker, E., & Scharf, B. A model of loudness summation. *Psychological Review*, 1965, *72*, 3–26.

Zwicker, E., & Terhardt, E. Analytical expressions for critical-band rate and critical bandwidth as a function of frequency. *Journal of the Acoustical Society of America*, 1980, *68*, 1523–1525.

Zwislocki, J. J. Acoustic attenuation between the ears. *Journal of the Acoustical Society of America*, 1953, *25*, 752–759.

*Zwislocki, J. J. Theory of temporal auditory summation. *Journal of the Acoustical Society of America*, 1960, *32*, 1046–1060.

*Zwislocki, J. J. Analysis of some auditory characteristics. In R. D. Luce, R. R. Bush, & E. Galanter (Eds.), *Handbook of mathematical psychology Vol. 3*. New York: Wiley, 1965.

*Zwislocki, J. J. Masking: Experimental and theoretical aspects of simultaneous, forward, backward, and central masking. In E. C. Carterette & M. P. Friedman (Eds.), *Handbook of perception Vol. 4: Hearing*. New York: Academic Press, 1978.

Zwislocki, J. J., Damianopoulos, E. N., Buining, E., & Glantz, J. Central masking: Some steady-state and transient effects. *Perception and Psychophysics*, 1967, *2*, 59–64.

CHAPTER 15

AUDITION II

Loudness, Pitch, Localization, Aural Distortion, Pathology

BERTRAM SCHARF

Auditory Perception Laboratory, Northeastern University, Boston, Massachusetts

and

Laboratoire de Mécanique et d'Acoustique, Centre National de la Recherche Scientifique, Marseilles, France

ADRIANUS J. M. HOUTSMA

Instituut voor Perceptie Onderzoek (IPO), Eindhoven, The Netherlands

CONTENTS

The preceding chapter, Audition I (Scharf & Buus, Chapter 14), presents information about the physics of sound and the physiology of the auditory system, information needed to understand the large body of data and theory on auditory perception and performance. That chapter covers signal detection in free field and under earphones, in the quiet and in noise, in monaural and binaural listening, and so forth; it also covers discrimination of intensity, frequency, and duration. This chapter turns to the suprathreshold attributes of sound, loudness, and pitch, to the localization of sound with respect to direction and distance, and to auditory distortion.

Much is known about the loudness of pure tones and complex sounds. Much of this knowledge concerns the dependence of loudness on stimulus variables such as intensity, frequency, duration, bandwidth, background noise, as well as on observer variables such as auditory fatigue and mode of listening. Whenever possible in this chapter, the effects of these diverse variables are anchored to the basic loudness function that relates the loudness of a 1,000-Hz tone to sound pressure level. Pitch, too, depends on a number of stimulus and observer variables, but for pure tones the fundamental variable is frequency; intensity, other sounds, stimulus envelope, and right-ear versus left-ear presentation play relatively minor roles. The pitch of multitone sounds depends on the frequency content and the relations among the component frequencies. These effects are complex, and a number of different theories have been offered to clarify and explain them. Pitch sensations are also reported when nontonal stimuli are subjected to temporal or spectral manipulations. In contrast to loudness and pitch, sound localization concerns not a subjective attribute of a sound but the ability of listeners to identify correctly a physical property, namely, locus in space. This ability depends mainly on fine differences in the intensity and timing of a sound at the two ears. Additional information comes from head movements and pinna effects. The last section of this chapter deals with distortion within the auditory system, mainly in the inner ear. The frequency, level, and even phase of various combination tones have been measured and these data provide grist for theories of their likely source in the auditory system. Their effects in various auditory tasks, especially detection in noise, are discussed.

1. LOUDNESS

Loudness is the perceived intensity of a sound. It varies most closely with the physical intensity or sound pressure of the stimulus but also depends on frequency, frequency content (especially bandwidth), duration, presence of other sounds, and on a number of observer variables such as previous exposure to sound, one-ear versus two-ear listening, and so forth. This section deals with these stimulus and observer variables as well as the probable relation between loudness and physiological variables. It concludes with a presentation of objective methods for estimating the loudness of complex sounds, which are the only kind that occur naturally.

1.1. Background

In modern psychophysics, loudness has served as the preferred sensation around which theories and methods of scaling have been built and tested. Ever since Fechner (1860), the general consensus among sensory psychologists has been that sensation can be quantitatively studied and sensation magnitude expressed as a mathematical function of stimulus intensity. Controversy has raged over the way to measure sensation—whether it can be measured directly or indirectly—and about the validity of such procedures (see Chapter 1 by Falmagne). Within this controversy, loudness has been a favorite target of theoretical analyses and theoretically inspired experimental studies. Furthermore, loudness is crucial in our interaction with the environment. The sensation of loudness serves both to provide information about the environment and to help protect the auditory system from acoustic overload. Loudness tells us about the identity of sound sources and their distance; in communication, loudness changes are one source of meaning. Loudness, as the major component of sound aversiveness, serves also to keep the organism away from aversively loud sounds; very loud sounds lasting a short time or moderately loud sounds lasting a long time can cause permanent damage to the hair cells of the inner ear and thereby produce a hearing loss (Henderson, Hamernik, Dosanjh, & Mills, 1976). A third area in which loudness plays an important role is in audiology—the study and diagnosis of auditory pathology. Reduction of loudness is usually the first cue to patients that something is wrong with their hearing; the particular form of loudness reduction is an important diagnostic clue to the type of pathology. The convergence of theoretical and practical interests has led to studies of all aspects of loudness that permit a thorough empirical description. Nevertheless, the physiological basis for loudness—the neural code of sound intensity—remains obscure.

1.2. Stimulus Variables

Loudness is most closely related to stimulus magnitude but it also depends on frequency, bandwidth, duration, temporal properties, and masking. Each of these is discussed in turn.

1.2.1. Intensity. A variety of procedures have been used to determine how loudness, in particular how the loudness of a 1,000-Hz tone, depends on stimulus intensity or level. These procedures are mostly "direct" in that the listener estimates numerically the loudness of each presentation as the level is varied. An especially popular procedure has been magnitude estimation, which requires the listener to match number magnitude to loudness magnitude (S. S. Stevens, 1956). The subject listens to a tone at a number of different levels, such as from 40 to 100 dB in 10-dB steps. In one version, the experimenter assigns the number 10 to the initial sound which serves as a standard. The subject then assigns numbers to the rest of the sounds relative to 10. Alternatively, the experimenter leaves the subject entirely free to choose any number without providing a "modulus" or standard. Somewhat surprisingly, greater freedom yields more consistent data (S. S. Stevens, 1975).

Figure 15.1 summarizes a large number of these direct measurements as the straight line taken from the standard of the International Standards Organization (ISO R532-1966). Loudness in sones is plotted as a function of sound pressure level in decibels. The straight line (solid and dashed sections) represents the equation

$$L = kP^{0.6} \tag{1}$$

where L is loudness in sones, $k = 0.01$, and P is sound pressure in micropascals. The sone is a unit of loudness such that a 1,000-Hz tone heard binaurally at 40 dB SPL has a loudness of 1 sone. On the graph, loudness and pressure are expressed logarithmically, because a power function is a straight line in log-log coordinates. Sones are scaled logarithmically, and pressure is transformed logarithmically to decibels or phons (as described in Scharf & Buus, Chapter 14), by the following equation:

$$\text{number of dB} = 20 \log \frac{P}{20}\ \mu\text{Pa}\ . \tag{2}$$

In the present case the decibels are called phons and sound pressure level (SPL) becomes the loudness level, which is the level at which a 1,000-Hz tone is judged equal in loudness to a given sound. Here the stimulus is a 1,000-Hz tone so SPL and loudness level are identical, because a 1,000-Hz tone is as loud as itself. Table 15.1 gives the sone values and sound pressure levels corresponding to the solid line in Figure 15.1. (The basis of the values for white noise is discussed in the caption to Table 15.1.)

The circles in Figure 15.1 are from a recent experiment carried out in an anechoic chamber. The tone came from a loudspeaker 3 m from the subjects, who were 70 in number and who were run in groups of 4–11. Each subject wrote down the estimate on a sheet of paper; no standard was given. The stimulus presentation conformed to the conditions of measurement of loudness level, whereby the 1,000-Hz tone is to be presented frontally in a free field. The figure shows that above 30 dB the mean estimates follow closely the standard loudness function with its slope of 0.6. As determined by least-squares fits, individual exponents varied from less than 0.2 to over 1.4; their distribution is given in the inset. Of the 70 subjects, about two-thirds (or 67%) have exponents between 0.3 and 0.7.

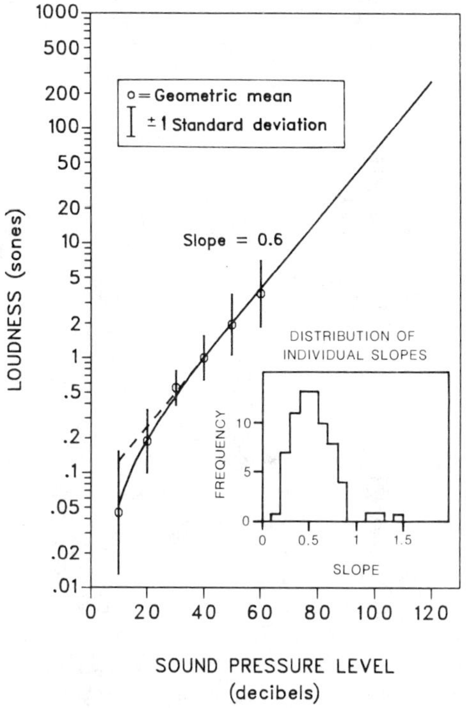

Figure 15.1. Loudness function for a binaural, 1,000-Hz tone. Loudness in sones is plotted as a function of the sound pressure level in decibels measured at the center of the locus of the listener's head with the listener absent. The straight portion of the solid line is from the international standard for a 1,000-Hz tone (ISO, 1966) and has a slope of 0.6. The curved portion was taken from Scharf (1978) and is based on a number of studies near threshold. The loudness of a 1,000-Hz tone increases with an exponent of 0.6 according to the power law, $L = 0.01\ (P - P_0)^{0.6}$, where L is loudness in sones, P is sound pressure in micropascals, and P_0 has the value of 45 μPa, which is the effective threshold at which loudness begins to increase with sound pressure; the subtractive constant is included to reflect the curvature of the loudness function at low levels. The slope of the straight line drawn in log-log coordinates is the exponent of the power function. An exponent of 0.6 means that loudness doubles whenever sound pressure level increases by 10 dB. The data in the figure are from Canévet, Hellman, Marchioni, and Scharf (1983) and are the geometric means of magnitude estimates by 70 naive listeners who were run in groups of 4–11 in an anechoic room with the loudspeaker at a distance of about 3 m. Curves fitted to individual data by the method of least squares yielded the 70 slopes plotted in the inset. The mean of these individual slopes is 0.6, and the slope of the best fitting curve through the geometric means is 0.55.

Table 15.1. Some Values for a Binaural 1,000-Hz Tone and for a Binaural White Noise Listed as a Function of Sound Pressure Level

SPL (dB)	Tone	Noise	SPL (dB)	Tone	Noise	SPL (dB)	Tone	Noise
10	0.052	—	50	2.00	3.85	90	32.0	46.0
12	0.072	—	52	2.30	4.45	92	36.8	50.5
14	0.095	—	54	2.64	5.20	94	42.2	57.5
15	0.110	—	55	2.83	5.60	95	45.3	61.0
16	0.125	—	56	3.03	6.00	96	48.5	65.0
18	0.155	—	58	3.48	7.00	98	55.7	72.0
20	0.190	—	60	4.00	7.85	100	64.0	80
22	0.230	—	62	4.59	8.9	102	73.5	91
24	0.280	—	64	5.28	10.2	104	84.4	102
25	0.305	—	65	5.66	10.9	105	90.5	108
26	0.330	—	66	6.06	11.5	106	97.0	114
28	0.395	.450	68	6.96	13.0	108	111	128
30	0.460	.580	70	8.00	14.7	110	128	—
32	0.550	.720	72	9.19	16.4	112	147	—
34	0.640	.900	74	10.6	18.5	114	169	—
35	0.700	1.00	75	11.3	19.5	115	181	—
36	0.750	1.10	76	12.1	20.6	116	194	—
38	0.860	1.36	78	13.9	23.2	118	223	—
40	1.00	1.65	80	16.0	26.0	120	256	—
42	1.15	2.00	82	18.4	29.0			
44	1.32	2.40	84	21.1	32.5			
45	1.41	2.60	85	22.6	34.8			
46	1.52	2.80	86	24.3	36.5			
48	1.74	3.28	88	27.9	41.0			

A value of 1 sone is assigned to the loudness of a binaural 1,000-Hz tone at 40 dB SPL. Above 1 sone, the values listed for the tone are from the international standard (ISO R532-1966). Below 1 sone, the values are based on the curve in Figure 15.1, which summarizes a number of studies of loudness at low intensities. The sone values for a white noise are based on measurements of the loudness of white noise (see Fig. 15.8). (From B. Scharf, Loudness, in E. C. Carterette & M. P. Friedman (Eds.), Handbook of perception Vol. 4: Hearing, *Academic Press, Inc., 1978. Reprinted with permission.)*

Because loudness measured in sones is a ratio scale, a sound of 2 sones is four times louder than a sound of 0.5 sones, and a sound of 1 sone is one-tenth as loud as a sound of 10 sones. Given that the exponent is smaller than 1.0, loudness grows less rapidly than sound pressure. For every 10-dB increase in SPL, loudness doubles, but a 10-dB increase corresponds to a pressure increase of $\sqrt{10}$ or 3.2. Over a 100-dB range, which is less than the intensity range of 140 dB or so encompassed by the human ear, loudness increases a little more than 1,000-fold whereas sound pressure increases 100,000-fold.

Where the power relation holds, equal stimulus ratios yield equal sensation ratios. That a 10-dB increase in pressure means a doubling of loudness is but one example of this general rule. In the perception of loudness, as in the perception of most sensory magnitudes, ratios are more important than differences.

Although the function in Figure 15.1 is defined for presentation from a loudspeaker in a free field, the function applies equally well to presentation via a pair of earphones. For monaural presentation via a single earphone, the function must be shifted to the right, to compensate in part for the higher monaural threshold (see Scharf & Buus, Chapter 14) and in part for the difference between binaural and monaural loudness (see Section 1.5.1).

The simple power function Equation (1) is valid only above 30 phons. At lower levels, loudness decreases more and more rapidly as threshold is approached, as shown by the curve in Figure 15.1 (cf. Hellman & Zwislocki, 1961; Robinson, 1957; Scharf & Stevens, 1961; Zwicker, 1958). To represent this curvature, the power law must be modified. One modification is

$$L = k(P - P_0)^{0.6} \quad (3)$$

where P_0 is the "effective" threshold at which the sound first begins to have a sensory effect in the experimental context. A value of 45 μPa for P_0, which corresponds to a loudness level of 8 phons, is a few phons higher than the expected detection threshold. The value of k remains 0.01. The important point here is that loudness changes more rapidly, as a function of level, up to about 30 phons than at higher levels. This steepening of the power function near threshold also occurs when the auditory threshold is elevated by such conditions as noise or pathology.

1.2.2. Frequency. Figure 15.2 gives the equal-loudness contours obtained by Fletcher and Munson (1933) for binaural, earphone listening. Sound pressure level is plotted as a function of frequency, with loudness level as the parameter. All points on a contour represent equally loud tones. Thus on the 13-phon contour, a 100-Hz tone at 40 dB, a 1,000-Hz tone at 13 dB, and a 10,000-Hz tone at 33 dB are all equally loud.

Fletcher and Munson not only measured equal loudness but also measured thresholds which are given as the curve marked "threshold." The threshold curve is at 3 phons because their subjects' average binaural threshold for a 1,000-Hz tone was approximately 3 dB. It is noteworthy that despite the marked difference in procedure between equating loudness and determining thresholds, the 3-phon threshold curve is nearly parallel to the 13-phon equal-loudness curve. Although the procedure employed by Fletcher and Munson to measure threshold depended on the subject's deciding whether the signal was heard,

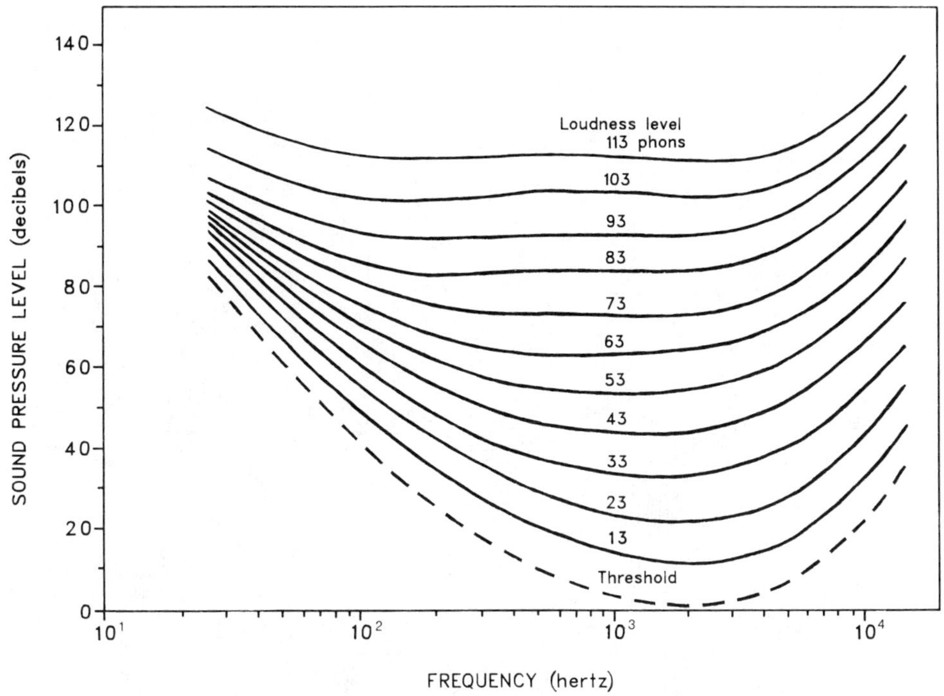

Figure 15.2. Equal-loudness contours for pure tones presented through a pair of earphones. The ordinate gives the sound pressure level at which a tone at the frequency given on the abscissa sounded equal in loudness to a 1,000-Hz reference tone. The level of the 1,000-Hz tone is the loudness level shown as the parameter on the curves. A method of constant stimuli was used in which the variable frequency was presented for 1 sec followed 0.5 sec later by the 1,000-Hz tone for 1 sec. Rise-fall times were 100 msec. After two such presentations the subject responded whether the reference tone was louder or softer than the variable-frequency tone. Eleven experienced subjects each made 27 judgments at each loudness level for a total of 297 judgments, the median of which served in the construction of the curves in the figure. These curves were drawn through the median points and smoothed. The standard error of the combined results was between 1 and 2 dB, with the variability somewhat larger when the variable frequency was far from 1,000 Hz than when it was close. A given contour gives the combinations of frequency and sound pressure level that yield the loudness level indicated on that contour. The bottom curve is different from the others; it is based on threshold measurements by a method of limits. It appears that for these 11 subjects the binaural threshold under earphone listening was about 3 dB rather than the 8 dB presented in the version of Fletcher and Munson's (1933) equal-loudness contours presented by Stevens and Davis (1938) and often reproduced (e.g., Scharf, 1978). [Stevens and Davis used a summary threshold curve from Sivian and White (1933) for monaural listening as the threshold curve. It is more appropriate to position the curve according to the binaural threshold measured by Fletcher and Munson (1933) at 1,000 Hz. That value of 3 dB is in accord with the international standard, which is 6.5 dB for the *monaural* threshold at 1,000 Hz (see Table 14.1 in Scharf & Buus, Chapter 14).] The loudness levels are labeled accordingly from 3 phons for the "threshold curve" to 113 phons for the topmost contour.

modern criterion-free detection procedures such as the two-interval, forced-choice procedure reveal essentially the same relation between threshold and frequency. The concordance between loudness matching near threshold and detection measures attests to the validity of the matching procedures. (As shown in Section 3.1.3 of Scharf & Buus, Chapter 14, threshold, and therefore loudness, varies with frequency primarily because of the way in which sound is transmitted through the peripheral auditory system.)

Figure 15.3 gives the equal-loudness contours measured by Robinson and Dadson (1956) in a free field; these serve as the international standard (ISO/R 522-1962). Robinson and Dadson used the method of constant stimuli to determine the point of subjective equality. About 30 subjects served in these experiments. The free-field contours resemble the earphone contours at frequencies below 1,000 Hz where both sets are bunched together and show a rapid increase in level as frequency decreases. The bunching together of the contours means that as the lower-frequency tones become more intense, their loudness grows faster than that of tones at middle and higher frequencies.

Above 1,000 Hz, the free-field contours are lowest near 4,000 Hz and peak near 8,000 Hz. Otherwise the two sets of contours—for free field and for earphones—show the same general increase in level with frequency above about 4,000 Hz and the same constant distance between curves. At the higher frequencies the irregular shape of the threshold curve (dashed line) and of the equal-loudness contours is caused by diffraction around the head. The presence of the listener alters the sound field so that the sound pressure in the ear canal is greater around 4,000 Hz and smaller around 8,000 Hz than in earphone listening. Because the free-field SPL is measured with the listener absent, and threshold and loudness with the listener present, the SPL at the ear canal varies as a function of frequency in accordance with diffraction by the head and pinnae. Plotting

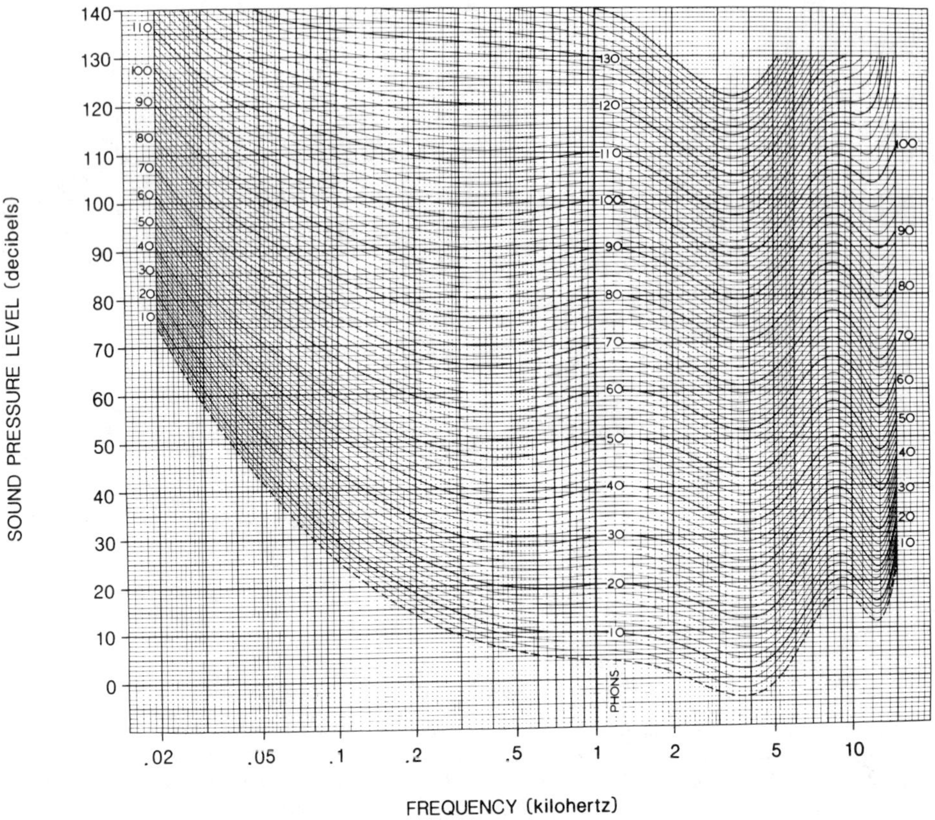

Figure 15.3. Equal-loudness contours for pure tones presented in a free field. The meaning of the ordinate, abscissa, and parameter is the same as in Figure 15.2. Data were collected by the method of constant stimuli in a fashion similar to that used by Fletcher and Munson (1933) and described in Figure 15.2. The results from a group of about 30 men and women aged 18–25 years were used to construct these contours, which constitute the international standard. Variability for the entire original group depended upon the difference in frequency between the variable tone and the reference 1,000-Hz tone and also on level. For moderate frequency separations the standard deviation was about 5 phons, increasing to 10 phons for wide separations and also at high levels. The free-field contours differ from the earphone contours primarily at the high frequencies where the head, torso, and pinnae render the sound pressure generated at the ear-canal entrance different from that measured in the sound field with the listener absent. Differences at low frequency are related more to leakage under the ear cushion and to greater influence of internal noise. (From D. W. Robinson & R. S. Dadson, A re-determination of the equal-loudness relations for pure tones, *British Journal of Applied Physics*, *7*. Copyright 1956, by The Institute of Physics. Reprinted with permission.)

the level at the ear canal instead of the free-field SPL would yield contours in Figure 15.3 with the same regular form as those in Figure 15.2, at frequencies above 1,000 Hz. (The low-frequency differences between earphone and free-field listening are discussed in Section 3 of Scharf & Buus, Chapter 14.) Going further and plotting on the ordinate the level of mechanical energy at the hair cells instead of the SPL at the ear canal would yield nearly flat contours in Figure 15.3.

Because the equal-loudness contours are reasonably parallel above 1,000 Hz, the loudness function shown in Figure 15.1 for a 1,000-Hz tone is valid at higher frequencies as well. However, the bunching together of the low-frequency contours means that the loudness functions become progressively steeper as frequency decreases below 1,000 Hz. At the same time, threshold is rising. We have here, at the low frequencies, an example of a general relationship between threshold and the steepness of the loudness function: the higher the threshold, the steeper the loudness function.

On the basis of the equal-loudness contours and the loudness function at 1,000 Hz, it is a straightforward matter to construct a loudness function at any desired frequency. The loudness level (parameter) at a given frequency can be related to a corresponding SPL on the ordinate, and these levels can in turn be translated to loudness in sones from Table 15.1. Figure 15.4 plots loudness in sones as a function of SPL with frequency, the parameter on the curves, varying from 100 to 8,000 Hz. These functions are from the earphone curves in Figure 15.2. Free-field loudness functions would have the same form at corresponding frequencies, but the SPLs would be different owing to the diffraction effects already discussed.

The functions at 100 and 250 Hz begin at higher levels than at 1,000 Hz because thresholds are elevated at the lower frequencies. Once audible, the loudness rises more rapidly; the loudness of the lower-frequency tones eventually catches up to the loudness of the 1,000-Hz tone, and the curves coincide at the higher levels. This coincidence follows from the flatness of the equal-loudness contours at higher levels. Also when measured directly (Hellman & Zwislocki, 1968; Marks, 1979b; Schneider, Wright, Edelheit, Hock, & Humphrey, 1972), the loudness functions are steeper at low frequencies than at 1,000

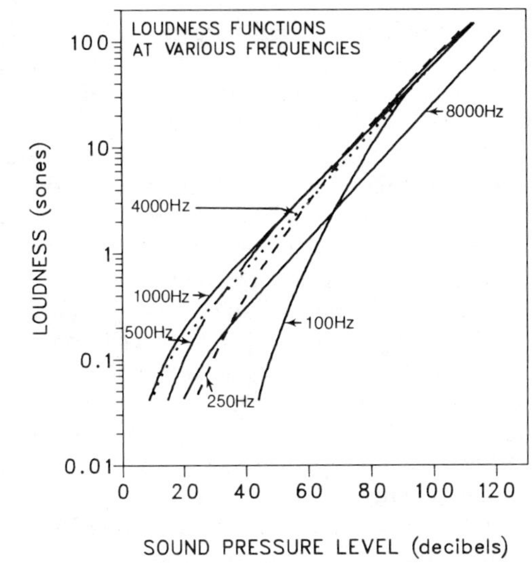

Figure 15.4. Loudness functions for tones at frequencies from 100 to 8,000 Hz. Loudness in sones is plotted as a function of the sound pressure level of the tone in decibels. The functions are derived from the earphone equal-loudness contours of Figure 15.2 and the loudness function for a 1,000-Hz tone of Figure 15.1, which is reproduced here. By finding the loudness level for a given frequency at a particular sound pressure level, the value in sones can be obtained either from Figure 15.1 or from Table 15.1. Functions are steepest at the lower frequencies where internal noise partially masks the tone. At 1,000 Hz and higher, functions are parallel. (From B. Scharf, Loudness, in E. C. Carterette & M. P. Friedman (Eds.), *Handbook of perception Vol. 4: Hearing*, Academic Press, Inc., 1978. Reprinted with permission.)

Hz, thereby showing agreement between direct estimation and loudness matching.

The steep functions exemplify "loudness recruitment," the more rapid rise in loudness as a function of level by comparison with a 1,000-Hz tone in the quiet. Loudness recruitment has been most often associated with cochlear pathology and with sounds heard in noise. At 4,000 and 8,000 Hz, where the equal-loudness contours are parallel to one another, there is no loudness recruitment. However, the 8,000-Hz curve is shifted to the right by over 10 dB, which is the difference in threshold between 1,000 and 8,000 Hz.

The equal-loudness contours of Figure 15.3 reach to 140 phons, which corresponds to an extremely loud sound, of the order of 1,000 sones. At such high levels most listeners would find the sound exceedingly aversive, and indeed if they were exposed for too long a period, hearing might be permanently damaged. Well below the threshold of pain and damaging intensities, listeners find sounds unpleasant or uncomfortable. Given its potential usefulness in revealing loudness recruitment in cochlear pathology (see Section 1.5.3.1), investigators have attempted to define the normal loudness-discomfort or uncomfortable loudness levels. Using an ascending method of limits, Hood and Poole (1966) measured the SPL at which 200 listeners first reported "a feeling of loudness discomfort." Mean levels were near 98 dB for monaural tones at 500, 1,000, and 2,000 Hz; it was 95 dB at 4,000 Hz. Using a tracking procedure, Stephens and Anderson (1971) measured an uncomfortable loudness level of about 108 dB SPL for a pulsed 1,000-Hz tone presented monaurally and 102 dB for the tone presented binaurally. Standard deviations for the 22 naive subjects were about 8 dB. Morgan, Wilson, and Dirks (1974) reported a more extensive study on nine young adults at octave frequencies from 125 to 4,000 Hz. Their method of constant stimuli yielded the mean loudness discomfort levels and standard deviations shown in Figure 15.5. Except for the values at 125 and 250 Hz, the contour in Figure 15.5 is essentially the same as those measured at 120 phons for loudness by Fletcher and Munson (1933, our Fig. 15.2) and by Robinson and Dadson (1956, our Fig. 15.3). Morgan et al. ascribe the discrepancy at the low frequencies to the overestimation of the sound pressure in the ear canal. The reported sound pressure levels were based on earphone calibration in an artificial ear, which often gives a higher value at low frequencies than is developed in the ear canal. They also measured the discomfort levels for a narrow-band and a wide-band noise. The results in Figure 15.5 show a 4-dB lower level for the wide-band noise, which is about what would be expected for equal loudness at this high level (see next section). Accordingly, the authors conclude that judgments of discomfort reflect primarily the effect of loudness.

1.2.3. Bandwidth. Pure tones are convenient, readily specified stimuli that excite limited portions of the auditory nervous system, especially at low levels of stimulation. However, natural sounds contain many frequencies and usually have a continuous spectrum, and so they—in addition to pure tones—have been studied in detail. It is also theoretically important to know how the auditory system puts together inputs at many

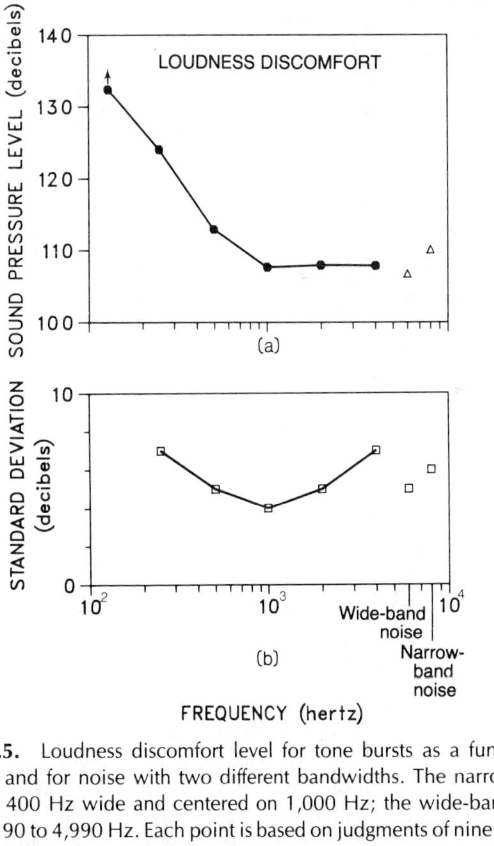

Figure 15.5. Loudness discomfort level for tone bursts as a function of frequency and for noise with two different bandwidths. The narrow-band noise was 400 Hz wide and centered on 1,000 Hz; the wide-band noise went from 90 to 4,990 Hz. Each point is based on judgments of nine subjects in three sessions, with each stimulus presented 120 times per session to each subject over a 10-dB range. Standard deviations are shown at the bottom of the graph. The apparent increase in the discomfort level at low frequencies is caused by a calibration discrepancy; in fact discomfort level is fairly flat over the range of frequencies and noises used and corresponds closely to the equal-loudness contour. (From D. E. Morgan, R. H. Wilson, & D. D. Dirks, Loudness discomfort level: Selected methods and stimuli, *Journal of the Acoustical Society of America*, 1974, *56*. Reprinted with permission.)

frequencies to produce a unitary sensation of loudness. Studies of the loudness of complex sounds have examined stimulus characteristics such as bandwidth, number of components, and internal frequency spacing.

Complex sounds are generally either line spectra or continuous spectra. Line spectra are produced by combining two or more tones. The major independent variable has been the frequency difference, ΔF, between the components of lowest and highest frequency. Continuous spectra are usually produced by filtering white noise and varying the bandwidth (defined as the frequency difference between the half-power points, where the power has dropped by half) which we likewise designate as ΔF. The listener's task is to match the loudness of complex sounds of varying ΔF to a comparison sound, which may be a pure tone or a complex sound of unchanging ΔF. Matches are usually made by the method of adjustment or of constant stimuli.

Figure 15.6 shows the results of a series of measurements of the loudness of a complex sound composed of two tones whose geometric mean was 2,000 Hz and whose frequency separation is given on the abscissa. The two-tone complex was matched in loudness to another two-tone, comparison complex, whose ΔF was fixed at 220 Hz. Individual results are shown for six subjects; the last panel gives the medians. The symbol "C" means the comparison was adjusted in level to match in loudness the experimental complex, and "[" means the experimental complex was adjusted. It is necessary to have each sound serve as the standard because, as these results and many others show, subjects tend to set whichever sound they are adjusting higher than would be expected from the adjustment made when the roles of the standard and variable are reversed. Thus the "Cs" fall mostly above the "[s." The median results show clearly how the loudness of a complex sound depends on ΔF. Up to a ΔF of about 300 Hz the difference between comparison and experimental is approximately 0 dB, which means that the loudness of the two-tone complex remains constant up to a ΔF of 300 Hz. Beyond 300 Hz, the comparison must be set higher relative to the experimental complex as the latter's ΔF increases; thus beyond 300 Hz, loudness increases with ΔF. The 300-Hz ΔF is the critical bandwidth at a center frequency of 2,000 Hz (see Scharf & Buus, Chapter 14).

The finding that loudness does not change with bandwidth up to the critical band, but then increases beyond it, is the

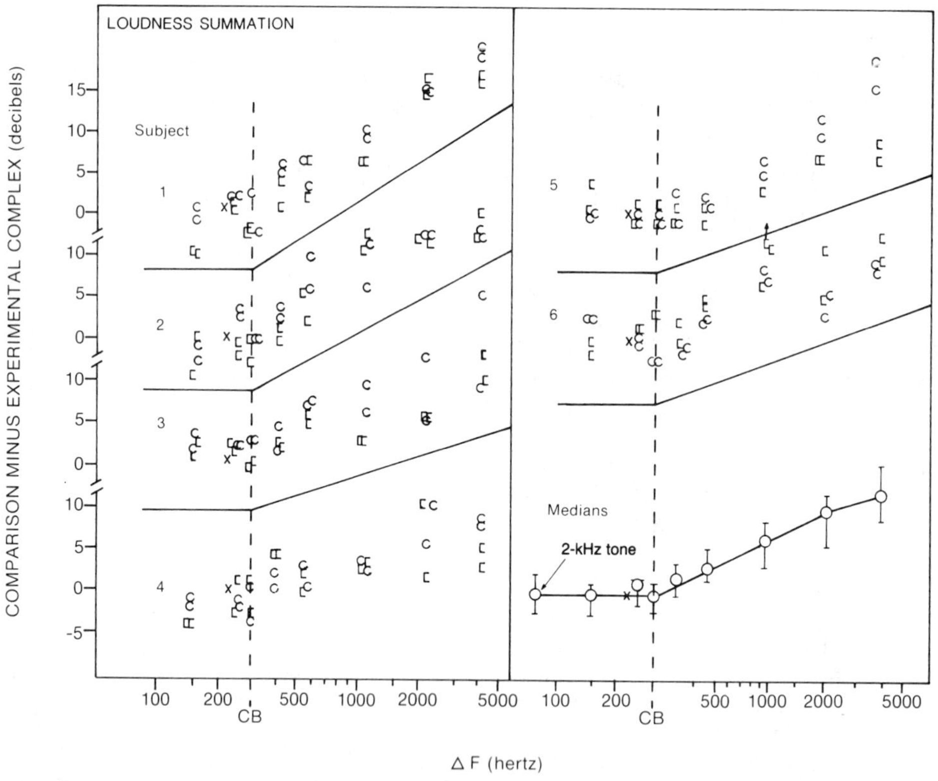

Figure 15.6. Loudness summation for a 53-dB, two-tone complex centered on 2,000 Hz as a function of the frequency separation between the two components. Individual data are shown for six subjects; median results with interquartile ranges are given in the lower right corner. The symbol "C" means the comparison complex whose frequency separation was 220 Hz was adjusted in level to match the loudness of the experimental complex. The symbol "[" means the experimental complex was adjusted. Each subject made two judgments of each type at each frequency separation. The symbol "X" marks the ΔF of the comparison complex. The average results show that the loudness of the complex remains constant as the frequency separation increases from 0 Hz (a single 2,000-Hz tone) to the critical bandwidth, which is 300 Hz at this center frequency. Beyond the critical band, loudness increases with frequency separation, that is, the level of the comparison has to be set higher and higher for it to remain as loud as the experimental complex. These findings illustrate the way in which the loudness of multitone complexes depend on frequency separation at most levels. (From B. Scharf, Critical bands, in J. V. Tobias (Ed.), *Foundations of modern auditory theory* (Vol. 1). Academic Press, 1970. Reprinted with permission.)

general rule of loudness summation. But it does not hold for narrow-band noise at high frequencies and moderate levels where rapid amplitude fluctuations appear to enhance the loudness of subcritical bands of noise (cf. Zwicker, 1977). Otherwise, the rule applies generally to line spectra, regardless of the number of components, as well as to continuous spectra (which may be considered line spectra with an infinite number of components). The role of the critical band is of special importance. As described in Section 3.2.1.2 of Scharf & Buus, Chapter 14, the width of the critical band varies with center frequency going from about 100 Hz below a center frequency of 600 Hz to 4,000 Hz at a center frequency of 15,000 Hz. It is noteworthy that four of the six individuals in Figure 15.6 show critical bands of approximately 300 Hz; the other two seem to have broader critical bands. The amount of loudness increase beyond the critical band is more variable, going from a maximum at the widest ΔF (4,000 Hz) of about 5 dB for one listener to nearly 20 dB for another.

The amount of loudness summation depends on level, being maximum between 40 and 60 dB and becoming less at higher and lower levels. In Figure 15.6 the average maximum amount of loudness summation is approximately 12 dB, for two-tone complexes with an overall level of 53 dB. Figure 15.7 shows the amount of loudness summation at levels from 20 to 80 dB for bands of filtered white noise. Loudness level is plotted as a function of ΔF, with the SPL of the bands of noise given as the parameter on the curves. As the bandwidth of these continuous spectra was changed, the overall level was kept constant at the indicated values. Accordingly, the spectrum level (SPL per hertz) decreased with increasing ΔF. Clearly, it is the overall level and not the spectrum level that is important for the loudness level of a band of noise.

At 20 dB SPL, the loudness of the band of noise tends to decrease beyond the critical band, which is around 160 Hz at the center frequency, 1,000 Hz, of these noises. In a subsequent study of loudness summation near threshold, Scharf (1959a) showed that this decrease is not caused simply by extending energy to frequencies to which the ear is less sensitive. With all the components of a four-tone complex set equally loud at all ΔF, loudness still decreased with ΔF beyond the critical band at 5 dB above threshold and remained constant at 10 dB. These results at low levels as well as those at higher levels can be understood in terms of the loudness function for a 1,000-Hz tone (Fig. 15.1) and the nature of loudness summation as described in Section 1.3.

Figure 15.7 shows the increase in the loudness of bands of noise out to a bandwidth of nearly 2,000 Hz. Although loudness appears not to have reached a plateau at all levels, in fact the widest possible band, a white noise, has a loudness level generally between 10 and 15 phons greater than its SPL. In other words, a white noise at a moderate level is as loud as a 1,000-Hz tone 10–15 dB more intense, and one would expect the curves in Figure 15.7 to reach a plateau at a level 10–15 phons above the corresponding SPL of the noise. This relation is the inverse of that which holds at threshold and at low levels. The threshold for a white noise is about 10 dB *higher* than that for a 1,000-Hz tone (e.g., Gässler, 1954; Hellman, 1976). At about 25 dB SPL, noise and tone are equally loud. At moderate levels, the difference in loudness is maximum; at still higher levels, the difference decreases but the advantage remains with the wideband noise. Given the nonlinear relation between a 1,000-Hz tone and white noise, a relation that is evident in Figure 15.7, it follows that the loudness function of a white noise must be

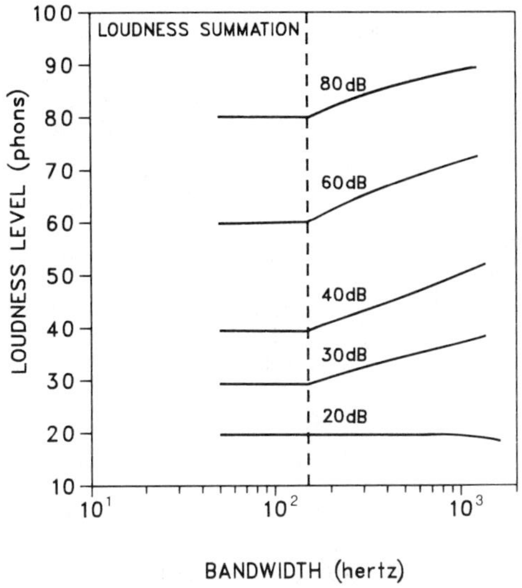

Figure 15.7. Loudness level of a band of continuous noise centered on 1,000 Hz as a function of its bandwidth. The overall level of the band of noise was held constant at the value shown as the parameter on the curves. The data upon which these curves are based were obtained by a tracking procedure in which the subject increased the level of a 1,000-Hz comparison tone until it was louder than the noise and then decreased it until it sounded softer. The tone and noise alternated in time, each lasting about 600 msec. Because the overall level of the noise was constant for a given curve, these results show that the loudness of a band of noise remains constant up to the critical band (indicated by the dashed line at 160 Hz), beyond which the loudness increases with bandwidth except at a low level. The dependence of loudness level on bandwidth was found to be similar at a number of different center frequencies, and for multitone complexes as well as for bands of noise. Although Zwicker and Feldtkeller (1955) did not report the number of subjects they tested and did not give any measure of variability, later measurements by Zwicker, Flottorp, and Stevens (1957) yielded essentially the same results. Zwicker et al. used a method of adjustment with 12 subjects. Interquartile ranges varied from 1–2 dB to about 8 dB depending primarily on how alike the variable and comparison sounds seemed. Like Zwicker and Feldtkeller, they found similar relations at a number of center frequencies, both for multitone complexes and bands of noise. (From E. Zwicker & R. Feldtkeller, Über die Lautstarke von gleichformigen Gerauschen, *Acustica*, 1955, *5*. Reprinted with permission.)

different from that of a 1,000-Hz tone and that it cannot be a simple power function even above 30 dB. Direct magnitude estimation and magnitude production of a white noise presented at a number of different levels reveal the expected relation between the loudness of a white noise and its SPL. Figure 15.8 presents the standard tone function (from Fig. 15.1) together with the white-noise function. The bulge in the noise function follows from the dependence of loudness summation on level. Accordingly, at low levels the loudness of white noise increases more rapidly than that of a 1,000-Hz tone, and at high levels it increases somewhat more slowly. At all levels above about 25 dB, a white noise is louder than an equally intense 1,000-Hz tone. Table 15.1 presents the values for white noise corresponding to the noise curve in Figure 15.8. For complex sounds with ΔF between the critical bandwidth and that of white noise, the loudness functions can be expected to lie between the two functions shown in Figure 15.8.

In going from a two-tone complex to bands of noise and to white noise, the number of components goes from the smallest possible, two, to an infinitely large number. Yet the basic rules of loudness summation are the same at these two extremes.

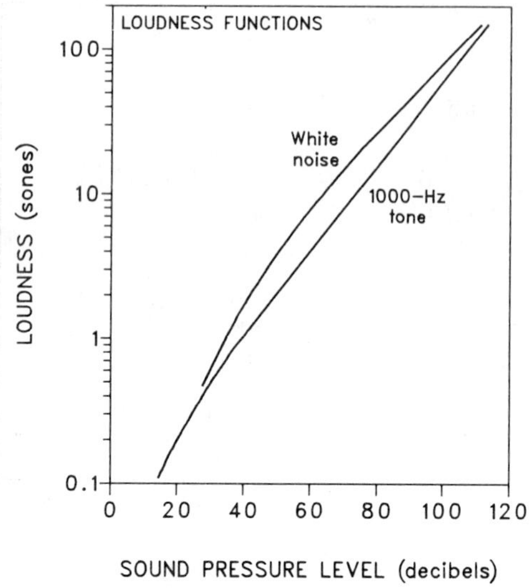

Figure 15.8. Loudness function for white noise compared to that for a 1,000-Hz tone. Loudness in sones is plotted as a function of the level of the tone or noise. The tone function is taken from Figure 15.1. The noise function is based on magnitude estimations and magnitude productions (in which the subject adjusted the loudness of the noise to match the magnitude of a number given by the experimenter). Fifteen subjects judged the noise presented binaurally through a pair of TDH-39 earphones. In magnitude estimation the noise was presented at levels from 40 to 110 dB. In magnitude production the numbers presented went from 1 to 160. Because the subjects were given no standard for the magnitude estimation, their numbers were reduced to a common modulus before combining across subjects. Interquartile ranges were about 50% of the geometric mean at a given level for the magnitude estimates and 10 dB for the productions. The curves fitted to the estimation and production data were reduced to the single curve in Figure 15.8 by taking their geometric means. In contrast to the tone curve, which is a power function above about 30 dB, the noise curve is bowed on these log-log coordinates. Near its threshold, the noise grows more rapidly than a 1,000-Hz tone, and above about 60 dB, it grows more slowly. (From B.Scharf & D. Fishken, Binaural summation of loudness: Reconsidered, *Journal of Experimental Psychology, 86*. Copyright 1970 by the American Psychological Association. Reprinted with permission.)

The question arises as to whether the degree of loudness summation is greater when there are more components than when there are fewer. Scharf (1959b) found at three center frequencies and four levels that loudness summation does not change as the number of components goes from two to the infinite number contained in a continuous spectrum. A similar conclusion is reached when one compares loudness summation for four-tone complexes and for bands of noise in the paper by Zwicker, Flottorp, and Stevens (1957)—again no significant differences between the four-tone complexes and the noise. Nevertheless, Florentine, Buus, and Bonding (1978) found as much as a 10-phon difference between the loudness levels of a two-tone complex and a band of noise that were equally intense and had the same bandwidth. The reason for the discrepant results may be procedural, but remains to be clarified.

A number of other details of loudness summation have been worked out. Loudness summation is greatest when the components in a multitone complex are evenly spaced in terms of critical bands (Zwicker et al., 1957). As many as 4 phons are lost if, for example, three of four tones are bunched together instead of being evenly distributed across critical bands within a four-tone complex with a wide ΔF. Closely related is the finding that loudness is greatest when the components are all equally loud, instead of some components being louder and some softer (Scharf, 1962a). On the other hand, the physical distribution of sound sources in space is unimportant. The complex sound can be presented via one or two earphones or from a loudspeaker or even broken up so that low-frequency components come from one loudspeaker and high-frequency components from a second speaker at a different location (Niese, 1960, 1961; Scharf, 1974b).

1.2.4. Duration. Loudness varies with duration in complex ways that have not been entirely clarified. The effect of duration falls into two distinct categories: durations shorter than about 1 sec and durations longer than about 1 sec. At brief durations, loudness increases with duration whereas at long durations, it remains constant or—under certain conditions—decreases as duration lengthens. The increase is called temporal summation of loudness; the decrease is called loudness adaptation, but adaptation is the exception rather than the rule. (See Section 1.2.4.2.)

1.2.4.1. Temporal Summation. Although there is no doubt that loudness increases as sound duration goes from a few msec to hundreds of msec, the rapidity and limits of the increase remain uncertain. Experimental results are many and varied. For the most part they are based on matching the loudness of sounds of various durations to a comparison sound of constant duration. A convenient way of presenting the data is illustrated by Figure 15.9. The sounds were narrow bands of noise centered on 2,500 Hz. Set to a duration whose value is given on the abscissa, the experimental noise was matched in loudness to a comparison noise of long duration (1,200 msec). The level at which the short-duration noise sounded as loud as the long-duration noise is given on the ordinate. First the short-duration noise was adjusted in level (filled circles) to match in loudness the long-duration comparison noise set at 60 dB; in later measurements the long-duration noise was adjusted (open circles). Because all the loudness matches were made—in effect—to the

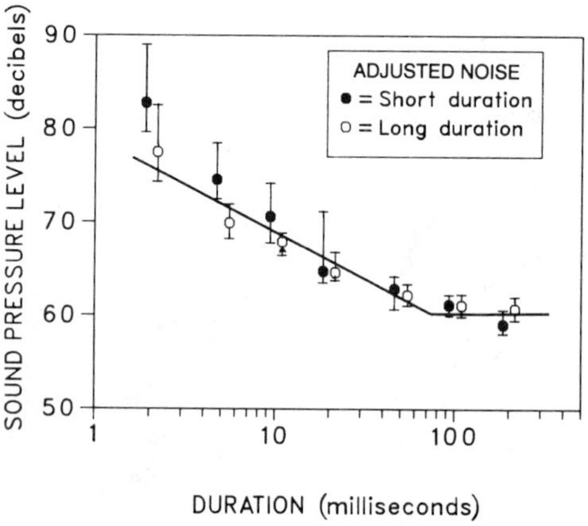

Figure 15.9. Loudness as a function of duration. The sound pressure level at which a narrow-band noise of variable duration (shown on the abscissa) sounds as loud as a noise of constant duration (1,200 msec). Sounds were presented from a loudspeaker in an anechoic room. Eight subjects adjusted the level of either the short-duration noise (filled circles) or the long-duration noise (open circles) by a tracking method. Medians and interquartile ranges are given in the graph. The straight line drawn through the data represents constant sound energy up to a duration of 70 msec, beyond which level is constant. The implication is that up to 70 msec loudness depends on the integrated sound energy and beyond 70 msec it depends only on the sound pressure level. (From E. Port, Über die Lautstarke einzelner kurzer Schallimpulse, *Acustica*, 1963, *13*. Reprinted with permission.)

same comparison, the data map out an equal-loudness contour, which is approximated by the straight lines. According to the straight lines, loudness remains constant so long as intensity (or sound pressure) decreases in direct proportion as duration increases, up to a critical duration of 70 msec. This complete inverse proportionality means that constant sound energy (energy = intensity × time) yields constant loudness up to 70 msec. Beyond 70 msec, intensity (and sound pressure) must remain constant to achieve constant loudness. A somewhat better fit to the data would be obtained by an exponential function of the following form:

$$I(t) = \frac{I_\infty}{1 - e^{-t/\tau}} \quad (4)$$

where $I(t)$ is the sound intensity required to maintain constant loudness, I_∞ is the asymptotic intensity at long durations, t is stimulus duration, and τ is the time constant (see also Section 4.3.2.2 of Sherrick & Cholewiak, Chapter 12). Such a function accounts better for the departure of the points from the straight line at 2 msec and for the gradual change between 50 and 200 msec.

Besides Port (1963a), some of whose results are shown in Figure 15.9, a number of other investigators have measured the loudness of brief sounds. Table 15.2 gives the results of 16 studies. Despite many disparities in the results, the time constants—other than those measured by Niese (1956, 1959; Reichardt & Niese, 1970)—hover around 100 msec. The critical durations are often difficult to define and so it is not surprising that they are more variable than the time constants; critical durations go from 15 msec to over 500 msec. The trading relation between intensity and time is also variable, with nine cases in which constant energy is required for equal loudness, five cases

Table 15.2. Dependence of the Loudness of Brief Tones and Noises on Duration[a]

Study	Number of Subjects	Stimulus	Rise-Fall Time (msec)	Trading Relation[b]	Critical Duration[c] (msec)	Time Constant[d] (msec)	Effect of Level
Miller, 1948	3	White noise	Abrupt	Energy increases	60–140	—	Critical duration decreases as level increases
Pollack, 1958	7–10	White noise	Abrupt	Energy constant	100	—	—
Small, Brandt, & Cox, 1962	12	White noise	—	Energy decreases	15–50	—	Critical duration decreases as level increases
Stevens & Hall, 1966	12	White noise	—	Energy decreases	150	—	None
	83	White noise	Abrupt	Energy constant	200–400	100	—
Zwicker, 1966	74	1,000 Hz	1–2	Energy constant	200–400	100	—
Békésy, 1929	—	800 Hz	Abrupt	Energy increases	120–180	—	Critical duration shorter at higher level
Boone, 1973	14–20	500, 1,000, 4,000 Hz	5	Energy constant	150	120	—
Ekman, Berglund, & Berglund, 1966	10	1,000 Hz	10	Energy increases	Over 500	—	Steeper trading relation at high levels
Garner, 1949	6	1,000 Hz	Abrupt	Energy increases	500	—	Steeper trading relation at higher level
Munson, 1947	—	125, 1,000, 5,650 Hz	3	Energy decreases	200	—	Steeper trading relation at higher level
Niese, 1956	12	500, 1,000, 3,000 Hz	Abrupt	Energy constant	65	23	—
Niese, 1959	10	1,000 Hz	1–2	Energy increases	100	23	None
Pedersen, Lyregaard, & Poulsen, 1977	381	1,000 Hz	1–2	Energy constant or decreases	160–320	80	Steeper trading relation at lower levels
Reichardt & Niese, 1970	50	1,000 Hz	3	Energy constant	100	30	—
		250 Hz			100		
		1,000			90		
Stephens, 1974	10	4,000	Abrupt	Energy constant	10	—	—
Port, 1963a	8	Narrow-band noise at 350, 2,000, 10,000 Hz	1–2	Energy constant	70	70	None

A dash means the information either was not relevant to the study or was not provided.

[a] Despite much heterogeneity in the results, the overall picture is that loudness increases with duration up to about 100 msec. At durations shorter than 100 msec, energy (intensity times duration) is approximately constant for constant loudness. (From B. Scharf, Loudness, in E. C. Carterette & M. P. Friedman (Eds.), *Handbook of perception Vol. 4: Hearing*, Academic Press, Inc., 1978. Reprinted with permission.)

[b] Trading relation refers to the relation between intensity and time. As stimulus duration increases up to the critical duration, to keep loudness constant, total sound energy ($l \times t$) has been found to remain constant, decrease, or increase.

[c] For constant loudness, intensity must be reduced as duration is increased up to the critical duration.

[d] The time constant was calculated from an exponential function of the form $I(t) = I_\infty/(1 - e^{-t/\tau})$, where I_∞ is the asymptotic intensity at long duration, t is the stimulus duration, and τ is the time constant.

in which the energy must be increased (meaning that intensity decreases more slowly than time increases), and four cases in which the energy must be decreased. Among the 16 studies, that by Pedersen, Lyregaard, and Poulsen (1977) which involved 381 subjects, far exceeds the others in size. Their report summarizes an international study undertaken in 20 laboratories, using the same stimuli and procedures. Despite a heroic attempt to achieve uniform conditions, results showed considerable scatter across laboratories. After detailed statistical analyses and careful consideration of the data, the authors concluded that the time constant over the range of levels investigated—from 55 to 95 phons—is close to 80 msec and that the trading relation is nearly constant. These results are for a 1,000-Hz tone. As can be seen in Table 15.2, the time constant may be different at other frequencies but no consistent effect of frequency can be discerned. Nor is there a consistent difference between pure tones and white noise.

The variability in the data is due, no doubt, mainly to differences in the criteria that listeners adopt in comparing the loudness of long- and short-duration sounds (cf. Reichardt, 1965; Stephens, 1974). To the extent that this interpretation is true, the wisest policy is to average data across as many subjects and laboratories as possible. The report by Pedersen et al. (1977) does just that, and then comes up with a summary that is encouragingly close to results obtained in the majority of the other studies in Table 15.2. Thus the description by Pedersen et al. (1977), of how the loudness of brief sounds depends on duration, is the best available. According to them, an exponential function with a time constant of 80 msec gives the relation between loudness and duration for brief sounds. This means that loudness level comes to within 1 phon of its asymptotic value when duration reaches 180 msec.

1.2.4.2. Loudness Adaptation. Studies of the temporal summation of loudness agree in showing that beyond a few hundred msec, the loudness of a constant-intensity sound remains the same as duration increases. However, these measures do not extend beyond a few sec. An entirely different set of experiments has been concerned with the course of loudness at durations from a few sec to many minutes and even hours. These experiments have attempted to determine whether loudness, like most other sensation magnitudes, decreases with prolonged stimulation. Such a decrease is usually referred to as *adaptation*. We distinguish adaptation operationally from fatigue and habituation, terms with which adaptation is often confused. By adaptation, we mean the decrease in sensation magnitude (loudness) or detectability of a continuous stimulus *during* stimulation. By fatigue, we mean the measured decrease in sensation magnitude or detectability of a stimulus that comes on *after* termination of a preceding stimulus. By habituation, we mean changes in the *response* to a stimulus either during or after stimulation. Fatigue and habituation are referred to in later sections. On the whole, results leave no doubt that loudness does not adapt under most listening conditions. Nevertheless, the exceptions to the general rule are important to note and eventually must be taken into account in any theory of loudness coding. These exceptional conditions are (1) a steady sound within about 30 dB of threshold, (2) a steady sound accompanied by an intermittent increment, (3) the presence of a retrocochlear lesion (usually an acoustic neuroma). This section discusses the first two conditions only.

Figure 15.10 gives an overview of loudness adaptation under earphone and free-field listening. Ten listeners assigned numbers

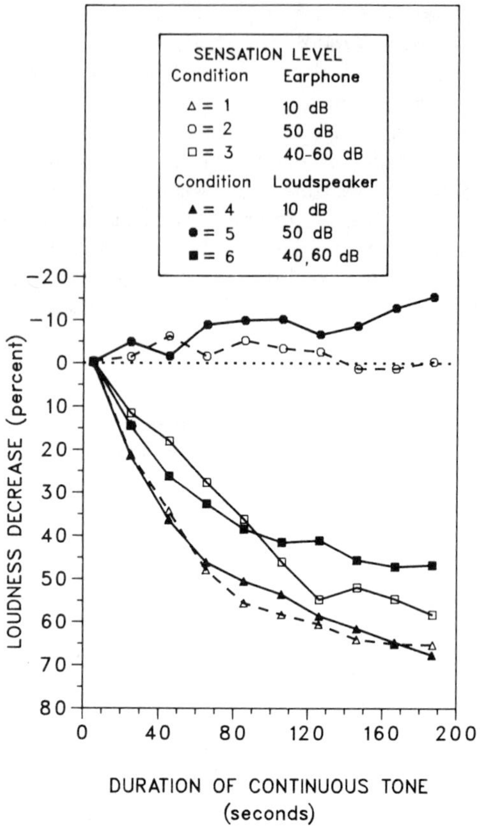

Figure 15.10. Loudness adaptation under various listening conditions. The percentage decrease in the loudness of a 1,000-Hz tone is plotted as a function of its duration. The tone was presented either via an earphone or from a loudspeaker in an anechoic room. Its sensation level is the parameter on the curves. In conditions 1 and 4 (triangles), the tone was presented alone at 10 dB above threshold. In conditions 2 and 5 (circles), it was presented at 50 dB above threshold. In condition 3 (unfilled squares), a 40-dB tone was on continuously in the right ear, and a 60-dB, 1,000-Hz turned on every 20 sec for 15 sec in the left ear. Loudness was judged during the 5-sec intervals that the tone was on in the right ear only. In condition 6 (filled squares) the tone was increased from 40 dB SL to 60 dB every 20 sec for 15 sec. Loudness was judged during each of the 5-sec intervals that the tone was at 40 dB. Ten subjects judged loudness by the method of successive magnitude estimations, assigning a number to represent the loudness at the moment a computer terminal signaled them to do so. They then entered their numerical judgment into the terminal. Each data point is the mean of ten such judgments. Standard deviations were approximately 30%. The results show that the loudness of a 1,000-Hz tone does not change at 50 dB SL over a duration of at least 3 min, whether heard via an earphone or in a sound field. When presented at 10 dB SL, loudness decreased by about 65% within 3 min. A more intense tone can also be made to decrease in loudness (i.e., to adapt) by increasing its level intermittently (filled squares) or by introducing an intermittent tone (the inducing tone) in the contralateral ear (open squares). (This figure also appears in Canévet, Scharf, & Botte, in press.)

to represent the loudness of a steady 1,000-Hz tone every 20 sec for 3 min. In conditions 2 and 5, the tone was at a sensation level of 50 dB and was presented alone. (Sensation level, SL, is the number of decibels above threshold; it is equal to the SPL of the sound minus its SPL at the subject's threshold.) Under monaural earphone listening (open circles) loudness remains constant, on the average, with the percentage change varying among listeners from −33% (meaning an increase in loudness) to 30%, standard deviation = 19%. Under free-field listening (filled circles) in a large anechoic room, with the loudspeaker 1.6 m from the subject, loudness increases 14% (range from −80 to 20%, standard deviation = 28%), a statistically insignificant change. In conditions 1 and 4, the tone was set at 10 dB SL. Under both earphone (open triangles) and free-field (filled triangles) listening, loudness decreases nearly 70% within 3 min (range from 0–99%, standard deviations = 30 and 26%). In condition 3 (open squares), a steady tone at 40 dB SL in the right ear was accompanied by an intermittent tone (15 sec on, 5 sec off) at 60 dB in the left ear. In condition 6 (filled squares), the steady tone was presented at 40 dB SL from a loudspeaker; it was increased to 60 dB for 15 sec every 20 sec, the same duty cycle as condition 3. The loudness of the 40-dB tone decreases by 40–50% (range 10–96%, standard deviations = 19 and 29%). These last two conditions are examples of *induced* loudness adaptation because a 40-dB tone presented alone does not decrease in loudness over 3 min (Scharf, 1983).

Although we can make these statements about loudness adaptation with confidence, the literature contains many reports of large amounts of adaptation ascribed solely to prolonged stimulation (e.g., Békésy, 1929; de Maré, 1939; Egan, 1955; Hood, 1950; Kärjä, 1968). Most of these reports were based on interaural loudness matching, which involved the presentation of a steady sound to one ear and an intermittent sound to the other. The intermittent sound was usually adjusted in level to be as loud as the steady sound. As many investigators have shown, it is the interaction between the intermittent comparison sound and the steady sound that induces the drop in loudness of the latter (for a complete list of references see Scharf, 1983). Procedures that avoid interaural interaction or the introduction of any kind of intermittent increment reveal no loudness adaptation in normally hearing persons, except at low stimulus levels. These procedures include tracking (Harris & Pikler, 1960; Mirabella, Taug, & Teichner, 1967; Wiley, 1972), cross-modality matching (Gruber & Braune, 1974), successive magnitude estimation (Canévet, Germain, Marchioni, & Scharf, 1981; Scharf, 1983), and delayed interaural loudness matching (e.g., Fraser, Petty, & Elliott, 1970; Margolis & Wiley, 1976; Stokinger, Cooper, Meissner, & Jones, 1972). Before discussing adaptation induced by an intermittent sound, we review the results on loudness adaptation at low levels.

A tone 10 dB above threshold decreases in loudness on the average 60–70% within 2–3 min; the particular results in Figure 15.10 are typical of many experiments (cf. Canévet et al., 1981; Scharf, 1983). Closer to threshold the decrease in loudness is greater. At 5 dB SL, a 4,000-Hz tone disappears altogether for most listeners. At 20 dB SL, monaural loudness decreases by 50%. By 30 dB SL, monaural adaptation is 20%, which is not significantly different from 0%.

Adaptation also depends on frequency. Adaptation of a tone at 10 dB SL increases from about 30% at 250 Hz to over 60% at 4,000 Hz (Scharf, 1983, Fig. 8). At still higher frequencies, up to at least 12,000 Hz, the percentage decrease remains approximately constant (Canévet et al., 1981).

For maximum adaptation, the sound must be steady. A beating tone, an intermittent tone, and a tone sinusoidally modulated in amplitude all show less adaptation than a steady tone (Scharf, 1983). Noise also adapts less than a pure tone, and that is true for narrow-band as well as for wide-band noise (Scharf, 1983).

Although average results are reliably reproduced for groups of ten or more subjects, individuals show large differences in the degree of adaptation, as could be inferred from the ranges for the data in Figure 15.10. So far, no basis for these individual differences has been uncovered. Neither absolute threshold nor sex correlates with the degree of adaptation. Children under about 16 years of age show slower and weaker adaptation than adults but there is no correlation with age among adults (Canévet et al., 1981; Scharf, 1983). To what extent interindividual differences reflect differences in the auditory system or judgmental differences is unknown. Although differing from each other, people are consistent in the degree of adaptation they undergo. Moreover, the large variability is not simply a result of number matching. Variability was just as large when a delayed tone in the contralateral ear was matched in loudness to the last part of a steady tone in the ipsilateral ear by a method of constant stimuli (Scharf, 1983).

People also differ widely in the degree of adaptation induced by an intermittent sound or increment. Incidental evidence suggests that people who adapt strongly at low levels adapt strongly in the presence of intermittent stimulation, but no careful study of this possible relation has yet been undertaken. On the other hand, much has been learned about how adaptation depends on the characteristics of the inducing sound in dichotic listening. For the most part contralaterally induced loudness adaptation is independent of the level and frequency of the inducing sound relative to the adapting sound; adaptation is about the same (approximately 50%) whether the contralateral sound is 20 dB more intense, as in condition 3 of Figure 15.10, or 20 dB less intense (Botte, Canévet, & Scharf, 1982). The frequency can be four or five critical bands lower or higher than that of the adapting sound. Moreover, the rate of intermittency matters little and can be as rapid as 200 msec on, 200 msec off or as slow as 10 sec on, 10 sec off. Though much is known about the inducing sound, little is known about how the characteristics of the adapting sound affect the degree of adaptation. Some preliminary data suggest that a wide-band noise cannot be induced to adapt nearly as much as a pure tone. It also turns out that adaptation is greater when the steady tone is in the right ear and the intermittent tone in the left ear than the contrary (Botte & Scharf, 1983).

As seen in Figure 15.10 (condition 6), adaptation can also be induced by periodically increasing the level of a steady tone. The duration of the increment need not be so long or so frequent as in Figure 15.10 to induce adaptation; a 20-dB increment every 30 sec for only 5 sec suffices (Botte & Scharf, 1983). However, the longer and more frequent the increment, the greater the adaptation. The size of the increment must be between 0 and 5 dB for adaptation to be measurable; the degree of adaptation increases as the increment goes from 5 to 20 dB (Canévet, Scharf, & Botte, 1983). Adaptation also tends to increase as the level of the steady, weaker portion goes down. Of particular practical importance is the finding that the amount of adaptation is about the same when the steady sound comes from one loudspeaker and the increment comes from another loudspeaker in a different location (Scharf, Botte, & Canévet, 1983a). That means that induced loudness adaptation probably takes place whenever a more or less steady sound is accompanied by a stronger intermittent sound from a different source. It remains to be determined whether such induced adaptation holds for noises as well as for pure tones.

Despite the many data gathered on low-level and on induced loudness adaptation, the fact remains that loudness adaptation is the exception rather than the rule. Because adaptation in other sensory modalities is strong and increases with stimulus intensity (Marks, 1974), the most interesting theoretical question is what keeps loudness from adapting under most listening conditions. A major clue to a possible mechanism is the finding that adaptation for fluctuating sounds such as a beating tone or noise is less than for a nonfluctuating pure tone. It may be that fluctuations within the neural system prevent adaptation at all but low levels. Induced adaptation by an intermittent sound may then reflect an overriding of the normal fluctuations by those in the inducing sound.

A difficulty for any theory of loudness adaptation is the discovery that dichotically induced loudness adaptation is highly resistant to recovery (Scharf, Botte, & Canévet, 1983b). After 3 min of simultaneous presentation of an intermittent tone and a steady tone, adaptation reaches 50–60%; turning off the intermittent tone does not return loudness to its preadaptation value. The loudness of the steady tone rises only slightly to 40–50% of its original value. To reattain full loudness, first the steady tone as well as the intermittent tone must be turned off. After at least 30 sec of silence the steady tone is turned on again and has its full preadaptation loudness; however, its loudness begins to decrease again, as if the intermittent tone were back on, over the next 3 or more min. We have yet to determine the stimulus conditions necessary to return loudness to its original value without "readaptation." Full and permanent recovery does take place when the subject leaves the experimental room. Perhaps recovery requires intermittent stimulation of the adapted ear, such as occurs in the natural acoustic environment.

1.2.4.3. Rise-Fall Time. The most important temporal characteristic of a sound is its duration, but duration implies a beginning and an end. Does the speed with which a sound comes on and goes off affect loudness? If the sound is a "pure" tone or narrow-band noise of brief duration (under 25 msec or so), then a very rapid onset and offset produce a spread of spectral energy that enhances loudness. This increased loudness is only indirectly a temporal effect; it is more directly a bandwidth effect, reflecting the loudness summation across frequency at bandwidths greater than the critical band, as noted. If the sound is longer in duration, the fast rise-fall time gives rise to audible clicks at the beginning and end of the stimulus; the subject may ignore these clicks in judging loudness or may integrate them in his overall loudness judgment. Once rise-fall time is lengthened beyond a few msec so that the spread of energy does not exceed the critical band, it has a negligible effect on loudness (Gjaevenes & Rimstad, 1972).

1.2.5. Intermittency. Many sounds are intermittent in nature, alternating with intervals of silence. We consider first the simplest case of a single repetition, that is, two pulses, and then the more complex case of many repetitions, in other words, a pulse train.

1.2.5.1. Double Pulses. As in the studies of the effect of duration on loudness, the literature on the loudness of double pulses is discordant with respect to the maximum time interval over which the loudness of two tone bursts summates. Agreement is general, however, that the loudness level of two equally loud tone bursts (each one generally 10 msec or less in duration) is 3 phons greater than the level of either burst alone, provided the interval separating the two bursts is only 1 or 2 msec. As the interval lengthens, the loudness level decreases until the two bursts are no louder than either one alone. The limit over which temporal summation takes place is 25 msec according to Niese (1956), 50 msec according to Schwarze (1963), 150–200 msec according to Irwin and Zwislocki (1971), Scharf (1970b) and, for dichotic clicks, Botte (1974). Such discrepancies in the measured limit of temporal summation are inevitable when one tries to measure changes in loudness level of the order of 3 phons, as did Neise and Schwarze. By using two tone bursts very different in frequency, Scharf (1970b) and Irwin and Zwislocki (1971) obtained a 10-phon advantage for two tone bursts separated by 1 or 2 msec, as did Botte (1974) by putting two clicks in different ears. These investigators could then trace reliably the decrease in level as a function of the temporal separation. It is these results that show that loudness summates over a silent interval as long as 200 msec. This interval is about twice the duration for temporal summation of a brief, continuous sound. During the silent interval, inhibitory off-effects may dissipate, thereby allowing greater summation (Zwislocki, 1969).

In the experiments described in the preceding paragraph, subjects judged the overall loudness of the two bursts. Subjects can also judge one of the bursts apart from the other. When they do so, the loudness level of the second burst is strongly elevated by a preceding, more intense burst (Elmasian & Galambos, 1975). This *loudness enhancement* is absent when the two tones are equally intense or separated by more than about 500 msec. Enhancement becomes decrement if the first burst is less intense than the second burst. The basis for these effects remains obscure (see also Section 4.3.6 of Sherrick & Cholewiak, Chapter 12).

1.2.5.2. Repeated Pulses. Brief sounds repeated over and over are called pulse trains. For the pulse train to have the same loudness as a continuous sound of the same overall duration, the individual pulses must be set to a higher intensity. However, if one computes the overall energy (intensity times time) of the pulse train over both on and off periods, then the pulse train contains less energy than an equally loud continuous sound. Accordingly, a pulse train is louder than a continuous sound of equal overall energy, but softer than a continuous sound of equal intensity. This rule applies to pulse rates exceeding 2 pulses per sec. At slower rates the pulses are nearly 500 msec apart, too far for temporal summation to take place. (For a report and references, see Port, 1963b.)

1.2.6. Loudness Reduction Under Masking. Sounds are seldom heard in the quiet. The presence of other sounds usually raises the threshold for a given sound and reduces its loudness. Threshold elevation or complete masking is discussed in Section 3.2 of Scharf & Buus, Chapter 14. Loudness reduction or *partial masking* is the subject of the current section. First we give the results for partial masking by a wide-band noise, which permits a careful study of the effect of noise level on loudness. Then we give results for partial masking by a narrow-band noise, which permits a study of both the effects of level and the frequency relation between masker and signal.

1.2.6.1 Wide-Band Noise. Most studies of partial masking, beginning with the classic paper by Steinberg and Gardner (1937), have concentrated on pure tones, usually at 1,000 Hz, in white noise. The most extensive set of data has been gathered by S. S. Stevens and Guirao (1967). Figure 15.11 presents a summary of these data in the form of loudness functions. Loudness in sones is plotted as a function of the sound pressure level of the tone in noise. The parameter on the curves is the level of the masking noise. Data are based on loudness matching by two to nine subjects who heard the tone in noise and tone in quiet presented alternately through a pair of earphones. S. S. Stevens and Guirao (1967) published the SPL of the tone in the quiet as a function of its level in the noise. Because the SPLs

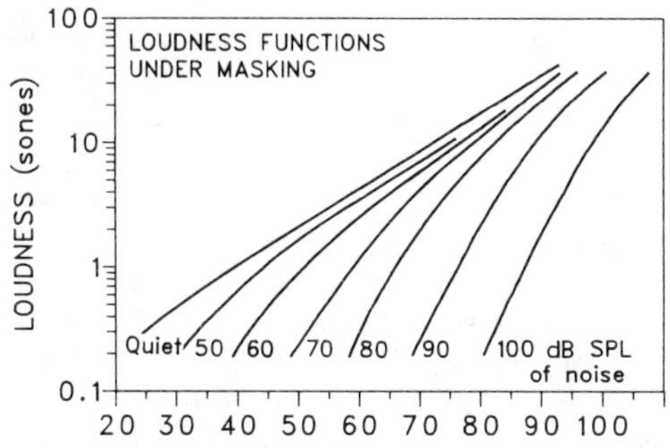

Figure 15.11. Loudness functions under masking by a white noise. Loudness of a partially masked, binaural 1,000-Hz tone is plotted as a function of its level. The parameter on the curves is the level of the masking noise. Curves are based on loudness matches between a 1,000-Hz tone in the quiet and in noise except for the function labeled "quiet," which is taken from Figure 15.1. From two to nine subjects adjusted the level of the tone in the quiet so that it sounded as loud as the tone in the noise. They later adjusted the tone in the noise. The noise lasted 2.8 sec and the tones nearly 2 sec. Matches were made by some subjects with the tone set at many different levels—separated by only a few decibels—in a given noise. These matches yielded average levels at which the unmasked and the partially masked tones were equal in loudness. Because these levels in the quiet are the same as loudness levels, they could be converted to loudness in sones by means of Table 15.1. The resulting sets of points were fitted by the smooth curves in the figure. As the level of the masking noise increases, the loudness function steepens, which also means that the higher the masked threshold, the more rapidly loudness grows. Against noises less than about 80 dB, the tone is just as loud in the noise as in the quiet once it is 20–30 dB above its masked threshold. Against more intense noise, loudness does not appear to reach its full, unmasked value. (From B. Scharf, Loudness, in E. C. Carterette & M. P. Friedman (Eds.), *Handbook of perception Vol. 4: Hearing*, Academic Press, Inc., 1978. Reprinted with permission.)

in the quiet are for a 1,000-Hz tone, they could be converted directly into loudness in sones from Table 15.1. It is these converted values that are shown in Figure 15.11.

Compared to the standard function in quiet, the loudness functions in white noise are steeper, the more so the more intense the noise. Rising from its elevated threshold, the tone in noise eventually comes close to full unmasked loudness when the noise level is less than 80 dB. In noise more intense than 80 dB, loudness does not reach its full unmasked value although, at high signal levels, the function under masking is parallel to the function in the quiet. As a general rule, the loudness functions in wide-band noise are no steeper than in the quiet once the signal is about 30 dB above the masked threshold. Above 30 dB SL, the loudness functions in Figure 15.12 have the usual slope of 0.6. Unfortunately, the modified power function in Equation (3) (see Section 1.2),

$$L = k(P - P_0)^{0.6}$$

does not provide a good fit to these functions. Other, more complicated modifications have been proposed (S. S. Stevens, 1966; Zwicker, 1963; Zwislocki, 1965).

The steepening of the loudness function by noise was observed originally by Steinberg and Gardner (1937), who also pointed out the similarity between loudness recruitment in noise and the recruitment observed in cochlear pathology. As noted in Section 1.2.2, loudness recruitment also occurs at low frequencies, but the term generally refers to the abnormally steep growth of loudness found in the presence of noise and in cochlear pathology. Pathological recruitment is discussed in Section 1.5.3.

1.2.6.2. Narrow-Band Noise. By filtering a white noise, one can study the effect on loudness of the frequency relations between masker and signal. Figure 15.12 presents data for four subjects obtained in a similar manner to those shown in Figure 15.11, by the method of adjustment. The noise was a 70-dB, 160-Hz wide band of sharply filtered noise centered on 1,000 Hz. Loudness functions were obtained by transforming loudness level into loudness in sones by means of Table 15.1. Parameter on the curves is the frequency of the signal. As noted in Section 3.2.1.3 of Scharf and Buus, Chapter 14, complete masking is greatest when the tone is located within the frequency confines of the noise. Once above the masked threshold, the loudness of a 1,000-Hz tone increases extremely fast, reaching full loudness at 20 dB SL. Gleiss and Zwicker (1964) found full loudness within 15 dB of threshold, with narrow-band maskers at 40 and 60 dB.

At frequencies below and above the limits of the noise, complete masking is less than at 1,000 Hz. Nevertheless, tones slightly above the noise in frequency had very steep loudness functions, so steep that, for example, the loudness of a 1,170-Hz tone overtook that of a 840-Hz tone although the latter's

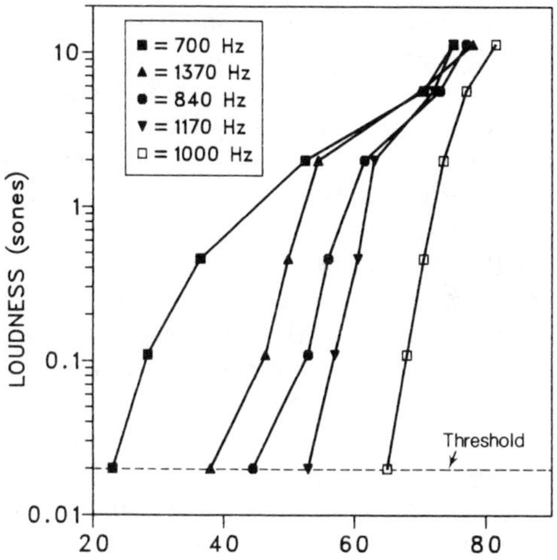

Figure 15.12. Loudness functions under masking by a narrow-band noise. Loudness in sones at five frequencies is plotted as a function of the sound pressure level of the tone in noise. Noise was 160 Hz wide, centered on 1,000 Hz, and set to 70 dB SPL. Four subjects adjusted the tone in noise to match in loudness the tone in quiet, which was set at a known loudness level (on the basis of individual equal-loudness contours). Later they adjusted the tone in quiet. Loudness levels went from 15 to 75 phons. Masked thresholds were also measured by a method of adjustment; the median levels are shown. Tones had a duration of 700 msec and came on in the middle of the noise, which lasted 1,500 msec. The four subjects made a total of 16 judgments at each frequency. Medians were converted to loudness from Table 15.1 and plotted in the figure. Loudness functions steepen with increasing threshold. Thus although tones at frequencies above those of the masking noise have higher thresholds than tones equally far below the noise, they increase in loudness so rapidly as to reach or even overtake their lower-frequency counterparts. (From B. Scharf, Patterns of partial masking, *Proceedings of the 7th International Congress of Acoustics*, 1971, 3. Reprinted with permission.)

masked threshold was 8 dB lower. In general, for a given degree of complete masking, tones lying above a narrow-band noise have steeper loudness functions than do tones lying below. These findings are readily accounted for in terms of the spread of excitation within the auditory system (see Section 1.3). Results along similar lines have been reported by Scharf (1964), for narrow-band noise whose center frequency was varied, and by Chocholle and Greenbaum (1966), who measured the partial masking of one pure tone by another. When, however, a pure tone is used to mask a narrow-band noise, the amount of partial masking (and of complete masking) is some 20 dB less than when the noise is the masker (Hellman, 1972).

1.3. Acoustical, Physiological, and Psychoacoustic Determinants of Loudness

The dependence of loudness on stimulus variables is well documented. Without attempting to account for individual differences or for such observer variables as attention and habituation, we can understand reasonably well why loudness varies with frequency, intensity, bandwidth, and background as it does.

1.3.1. Transmission Characteristics of the Ear. The form of the equal-loudness contours, which define the way in which loudness varies with frequency, is determined primarily in the transmission of sound from the sound source to the hair cells. For a sound in a free field, as discussed above, diffraction by the torso, head, and pinnae accounts for the irregular form of the threshold curve and the equal-loudness contours at high frequencies. Beginning with the ear canal, frequency-dependent transmission through the eardrum, middle ear, and endolymph of the cochlea accounts for the general form of the threshold curve and, in part, of the equal-loudness contours at all frequencies (see Scharf & Buus, Chapter 14). Because the equal-loudness contours above 1,000 Hz are parallel to one another and to the threshold curve, the dependence of loudness on frequency must have the same origin as does the dependence of absolute threshold. However, at low frequencies the equal-loudness contours do not stay parallel to the threshold curve but become flatter with increasing level. Therefore, loudness increases more rapidly as a function of level at low frequencies than at 1,000 Hz and above (Fig. 15.4). Both the dependence of loudness on frequency below about 500 Hz and the steeper loudness functions are thought to result from (1) physiological noise (heartbeat, breathing, blood flow, etc.), which is strongest at the low frequencies where, accordingly, masking would be greatest, and (2) the rapid extension of the long tail of the excitation pattern produced by a low-frequency tone as its intensity increases. The broadening of the tail takes place because a low-frequency tone produces maximum displacement on the basilar membrane toward the apex, leaving plenty of room for the tail to spread out as level increases (see Scharf & Buus, Chapter 14). At high levels, these two effects are negligible but by then the low frequencies have caught up to the higher frequencies in loudness. This analysis assumes essential equality in the response of the hair cells and auditory nerve fibers regardless of their locus. Indeed, anatomically and physiologically these neural structures do not appear to vary along the length of the basilar membrane.

1.3.2. Model of Loudness. The transmission characteristics from sound source to hair cells explain only the dependence of loudness on frequency. The dependence of loudness on intensity and, concomitantly, on bandwidth and acoustical background can be understood not in acoustical and physiological terms but in psychoacoustic terms that can only indirectly be interpreted physiologically. A direct physiological interpretation is not feasible because the neural code for intensity is unknown. Nevertheless, it is often assumed that the neural correlate of loudness is the number of nerve impulses per sec (cf. Davis, 1959); the assumption often works well, as in the detailed neural-counting model of Lachs and Teich (1981). This plausible notion, however, remains to be confirmed experimentally. Moreover, many physiological data from the auditory system suggest that the mechanism is not simple, and some psychoacoustic data speak against it (e.g. Hellman, 1978; Viemeister, 1983). Nevertheless, we shall make a similar assumption, namely, that loudness increases with level because neural fibers fire more frequently and because more fibers are excited with increasing stimulus level. Both these changes occur in the activity of auditory nerve fibers and are reflected in the masking of a pure tone by other pure tones or by narrow-band noise.

Figure 15.13 provides examples of idealized excitation patterns produced by tones at a fixed level and by a narrow-band noise at three different levels. (The interactions between patterns are discussed shortly.) These excitation patterns differ little from masking patterns that are based on psychoacoustic measurements of the masking of pure tones by narrow-band noise. As described in Chapter 14 (Section 3.2.1.3), the measurements consist of determining the thresholds for tones at many frequencies in the presence of a masker whose level and frequency location are held constant. Masking is greatest within the frequency limits of the noise, declining rapidly when the signal's frequency descends below the lower limit of the masker and declining more slowly when the signal goes above the masker. As the level of the masker increases, both the amount of masking (expressed as excitation level on the ordinate of Figure 15.13) and the spread of masking toward higher frequencies increase. Masking patterns, drawn from responses of the whole organism rather than of single neurons, provide a basis for understanding and calculating the effects of level, bandwidth, and background noise on loudness. This approach to modeling loudness was first taken by Fletcher and Munson (1937) and reappears in the models of Howes (1950), Munson and Gardner (1950), and C. M. Harris (1959). Its most comprehensive expression is to be found in Zwicker's model (Zwicker, 1958, 1963; Zwicker & Scharf, 1965). [Other kinds of loudness models have used, for example, intensity resolution as a point of departure (Lim, Rabinowitz, Braida, & Durlach, 1977) or an inferred hierarchy of stages of information processing (Marks, 1979b).]

Two fundamental assumptions underlie Zwicker's model: (1) a sound's masking pattern reflects the spread and amplitude of the excitation evoked by the masker in the auditory system and (2) the amount of excitation directly determines loudness. Thus by measuring the masking of one sound by another, we can estimate the excitation and its frequency distribution in the auditory system. Zwicker's model permits the conversion of masking patterns to excitation patterns and then to loudness patterns. Adding 3 or 6 dB, depending on frequency, to the threshold for a tone masked by a given sound yields the excitation level for that sound. Excitation level is then plotted as a function of frequency, as in Figure 15.13, to yield an excitation pattern, which is nearly the same as the original masking pattern raised a few decibels. An excitation pattern is then converted to a loudness pattern essentially by raising to the fourth power the excitation within each critical band encompassed by the pattern. (For a detailed description of the model, see Zwicker & Scharf,

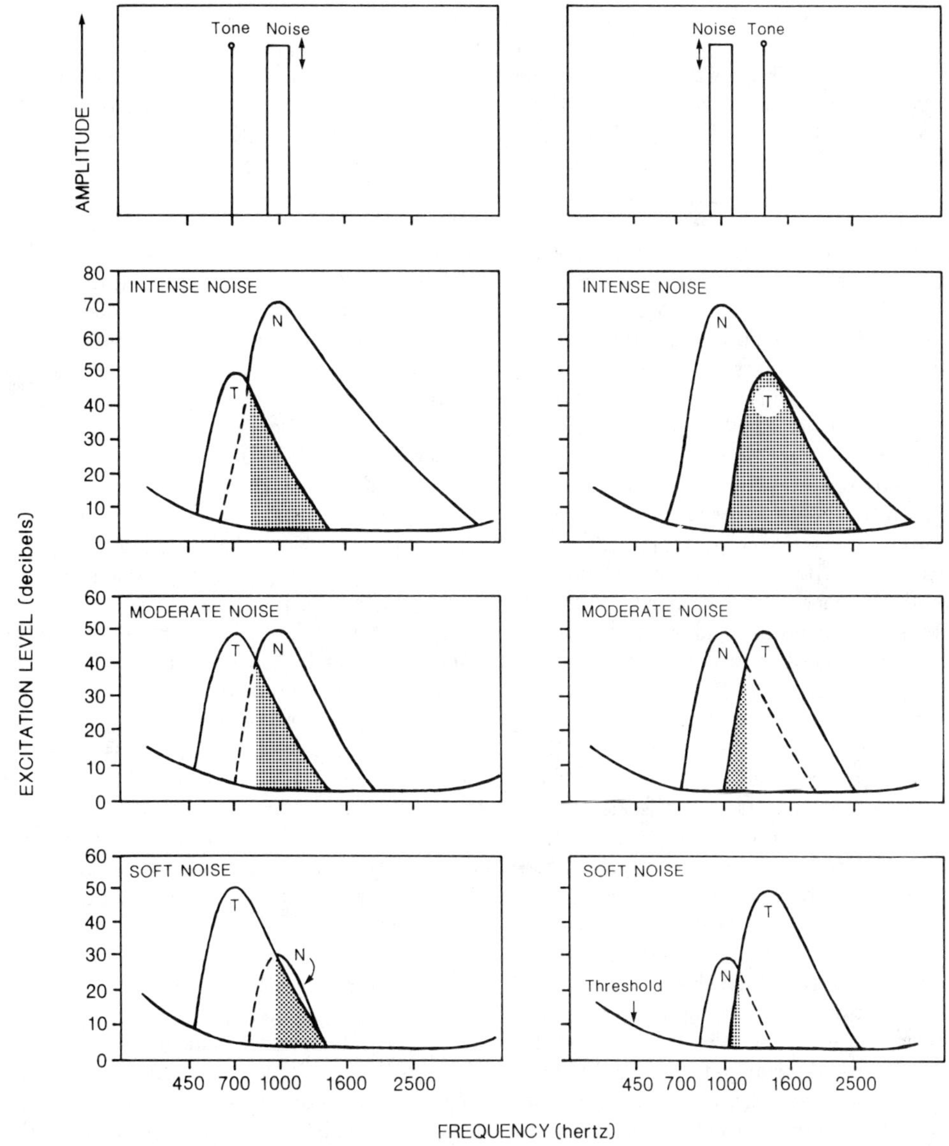

Figure 15.13. Interactions between excitation patterns as the basis for partial masking. The top panels give idealized spectra of two pairs of signal and noise. The bottom three panels plot excitation level as a function of frequency. In the left panels the tonal signal lies below the frequencies of the narrow-band noise, whose level goes from intense to soft. In the right panels the tone lies above the noise. The excitation patterns for the tone and noise are nearly the same as their masking patterns, which are generated by using a given tone or noise to mask pure tones at many frequencies. The masking pattern is a plot of the masked threshold for the signal as a function of its frequency. The derived excitation patterns are assumed to reflect the spread of excitation evoked in the auditory system. The loudness of the tone is proportional to the integral of the excitation pattern. Hence the more the noise interferes with that pattern, the softer the tone becomes. At an intense level, the noise completely engulfs the pattern of the higher-frequency tone, making it inaudible. The same noise pattern only partially covers the lower-frequency tone's pattern, leaving it faint but audible. The assumption is that the noise pattern must have a higher level in order to eliminate corresponding parts of the tone's pattern; these subtracted areas are darkened in the figure. When the noise becomes weaker, only a small part of its pattern remains above that of the higher-frequency tone, whereas much of it remains above that of the lower-frequency tone. Consequently, the loudness of the higher-frequency tone is reduced little by the soft and moderately intense noises, but the loudness of the lower-frequency tone is reduced significantly. The asymmetry of excitation within the auditory system can explain why complete masking (making a signal inaudible) is more effective toward higher than toward lower frequencies whereas partial masking (reducing a signal's loudness) is greater toward lower frequencies. It also explains why a tone at a frequency above the masker's frequency range grows more rapidly in loudness than a tone at a lower frequency. (From B. Scharf, Partial masking, *Acustica*, 1964, *14*. Reprinted with permission.)

1965.) The model permits accurate calculation of loudness as a function of bandwidth both in the quiet and in noise, and in persons with a hearing impairment. Whereas the model's ability to predict increasing loudness with increasing bandwidth is built in, its ability to predict the differential effects of low- and high-frequency partial maskers on loudness is less evident.

The spread of complete masking toward the high frequencies can be understood on the basis of the asymmetry of the displacement patterns on the basilar membrane (see preceding section). In similar fashion, patterns of partial masking—the reduction in the loudness of a signal caused by a masker—can be understood on the basis of the asymmetry of excitation patterns. Indeed, the model predicts that whereas complete masking by a moderate or intense masker is greater toward higher than toward lower frequencies, partial masking has just the opposite effect and is greater toward lower frequencies. The cause of this striking reversal is illustrated in Figure 15.13. The reasoning behind it goes as follows. Masking patterns indicate that a narrow-band sound generally evokes more excitation toward higher than toward lower frequencies. Because loudness is assumed to be a monotonic function of excitation, events at higher frequencies are more important for loudness than events at lower frequencies. Accordingly, a tone is usually reduced more in loudness by a noise lying above it at higher frequencies than by a noise at lower frequencies. This outcome is schematized in the lower two panels of Figure 15.13, where the reduction in the loudness of the tone, represented by the pattern marked "T," is proportional to the dark area. The dark area is the section of the tone's pattern where the intersecting noise pattern, "N," has a higher level. That section presumably is swamped by the noise and contributes nothing to the tone's loudness. As the figure shows, the tone loses more loudness when its frequency (shown at the top) lies below the noise than when it lies above, provided the noise is not too intense. When the noise becomes very intense (top excitation patterns), it then completely masks the higher-frequency tone but not the lower one. The same effects of the asymmetry of the excitation patterns hold when, as is more usual, the masker's level is held constant and the signal's level is increased. Consequently, the loudness of tones higher in frequency than the masker increases more rapidly with signal level than the loudness of tones lower in frequency, as already seen in Figure 15.12.

No serious attempt appears to have been made to model the dependence of loudness on temporal factors except for a physiological model by Zwislocki (1969), who puts much emphasis on short-term inhibition and adaptation that follow the onset and offset of stimuli.

1.4. Objective Calculation of Loudness

Owing largely to the importance of loudness as the primary factor in sound annoyance, a number of procedures have been developed for calculating loudness on the basis of the acoustic spectrum without recourse to additional subjective tests. Zwicker's model, described in the preceding section, is one such procedure that permits a precise calculation of the loudness of any steady sound lasting more than a couple of hundred milliseconds. It does so by providing a set of excitation patterns for tones separated by one critical band over a wide range of levels. As indicated in the preceding section, excitation patterns are derived from masking. The model uses a set of standard patterns based on measurements of the masking of pure tones by narrow-band noise set at many center frequencies and levels. By analysis of the spectrum of any sound into its component critical bands, the excitation and thereby the loudness patterns for any sound can be constructed by interpolation. Originally requiring a somewhat complicated graphical procedure to calculate loudness level and loudness (ISO R532-1966), Zwicker's system is now available as a computer program in Fortran (Paulus & Zwicker, 1972) which greatly facilitates its use. Another system for calculating loudness directly from the objective spectrum was originally developed by S. S. Stevens (1961; ANSI S3.4-1980; ISO R532-1966) and later revised (S. S. Stevens, 1972). This procedure makes no attempt to model the way the auditory system works and therefore is simpler than Zwicker's. For wideband natural sounds, the two procedures yield similar results except that Zwicker's procedure usually gives a loudness level about 6 phons higher than Stevens's, and Stevens's outcome is generally closer to subjective estimations of loudness (Scharf, Hellman, & Bauer, 1977).

None of these procedures takes temporal factors into account. Only Niese (1965; see also Reichardt, 1970) includes a time constant, 25 msec, in his calculation procedure to permit the evaluation of the loudness of brief sounds. Recently, Zwicker (1977) has described an apparatus that incorporates temporal effects such as temporal summation at durations under 200 msec, loudness enhancement under modulation (see Section 1.2.3), and masking. The loudness meter, a complex series of high-pass, band-pass, and low-pass filters, nonlinear devices, time constants, and so forth, provides a measure of the loudness of sounds of brief duration, such as impulse noise, and also of time-varying sounds, such as speech. Limited data presented by Zwicker (1977) suggest a close correspondence (within 1–2 dB) between subjectively measured loudness and readings on the meter.

1.5. Observer Variables

Loudness is almost always measured with the listener instructed to pay full attention to the sound. No data are available on the effects of such observer variables as attention and habituation; a limited set exists on personality factors in the direct estimation of loudness (de Barbenza, Bryan, & Tempest, 1970; Stephens, 1970). Except for auditory pathology, it is usually impossible to evaluate the extent to which individual differences in loudness judgments are caused by differences in the auditory system and by judgmental or cognitive differences. One exception is a study by Ross (1968), who showed that variations in the impedance of the middle ear could account for the equal-loudness contours of two of four listeners. On the other hand, the slopes of 11 individual loudness functions measured by J. C. Stevens and Guirao (1964) went from 0.4 to 1.1 and seem to reflect mainly extra-auditory factors. The same subjects did not give very reliable exponents; when the magnitude estimations and productions were repeated 1–6 months later, exponents had changed. The correlation between the exponents in the first and second series was 0.53, which accounts for only about one-fourth of the variance. Other investigators (Hellman, 1981; Logue, 1976; Teghtsoonian & Teghtsoonian, 1983) have measured larger correlations, ranging from 0.6 to 0.8. However, Teghtsoonian and Teghtsoonian (1983) have shown that the correlation is small when the experimenter assigns *different* numbers to a standard sound in each session instead of leaving the subject free to choose his own modulus. That experimental manipulation apparently prevents the subjects from using the same numbers in the repeated magnitude estimations, and leads to zero correlation even when one session follows the other immediately. Support for this interpretation comes from Hellman's (1981) finding that the correlation between exponents went from 0.95 to insignificance when the intersession delay was increased from about 1 to 6 months. These results strongly suggest that individual differences in the slope of the loudness function do not usually reflect true, permanent differences in auditory functioning.

Furthermore, if differences in the slope of the loudness function of the order of 3:1 represented differences in the way the auditory system works, they would imply unrealistically extreme divergence in people's perception of the environment. For example, a person with a slope of 1.1 would hear speech at conversational levels (60–70 dB) more than 100 times louder than a person with a slope of 0.4, and a jet passing overhead (some 100 dB) would be over 3,000 times louder! Such enormous divergence surely reflects differences in the way subjects evaluate their sensory experience and use numbers rather than in what they hear.

In the rest of this section, we consider several carefully documented observer variables that affect loudness: binaural versus monaural listening, auditory fatigue, and auditory pathology.

1.5.1. Monaural versus Binaural Loudness. All the functional relations between loudness and stimulus variables such as intensity, frequency, bandwidth, duration, and so forth are essentially the same whether the sound is presented to one ear via a single earphone or to two ears. Nevertheless, binaural loudness and monaural loudness are not the same. A sound to two ears is nearly twice as loud as the same sound presented to one ear. For pure tones, estimates in the literature range from a ratio of 1.7 (Caussé & Chavasse, 1942; Hellman & Zwislocki, 1963; Porsolt & Irwin, 1967; Scharf & Fishken, 1970) to 2.0 (Fletcher & Munson, 1933; Marks, 1979b). Reynolds and Stevens (1960) measured approximately a 2:1 ratio for a band of noise. Whatever ratio one accepts, the corresponding number of decibels varies with level and the nature of the sound, whether pure tone—and which frequency—or wide-band noise. At threshold, detection is 3 dB better for a binaural sound than for a monaural sound (Section 3.1.6, Scharf & Buus, Chapter 14). Right near threshold, where the loudness function is steep, a doubling of loudness also corresponds to 3 dB. As level increases, the number of decibels required for double loudness increases so that by about 30 dB SL, above which the loudness of a 1,000-Hz tone changes as a power function of pressure with an exponent of 0.6, 10 dB is required to double loudness. Thus the loudness function in Figure 15.1 is defined for binaural loudness (a frontally incident sound in a free field); the loudness function for a monaural sound would have to be shifted to the right about 3 phons near threshold and 8–10 phons at loudness levels above 30 phons.

If one takes 1.7 as the binaural-to-monaural ratio for a 1,000-Hz tone and 3 dB as the threshold difference, then from the revised binaural loudness function Equation (3), the following monaural function can be derived:

$$L = \frac{0.01}{1.7}(P - 1.4P_0)^{0.6} \qquad (5)$$

where, as before, L is in sones, P is in micropascals, and P is the effective threshold with a value of 45 μPa. If one takes 2.0 as the ratio, then the denominator is 2.0 instead of 1.7.

Binaural loudness has also been measured with tones of different frequency to the two ears (Scharf, 1969). Even when tones differ greatly in frequency, the overall loudness is 1.7–2.0 times greater than the loudness of either tone alone. However, owing to the difficulty of the judgment, especially for those listeners who readily hear two separate images, the intersubject variability is large.

1.5.2. Auditory Fatigue. Exposure to one sound often results in a reduced response to another sound. The reduction is called masking when the first sound or masker is on at the same time as the second sound or signal; it is usually called fatigue when the first sound is turned off before the second sound comes on. However, this distinction is less clear in forward masking where the masker is also turned off before the signal comes on. The basis for the distinction then depends on the duration of the masker and, especially, on the interval separating masker and signal: In forward masking the masker usually lasts less than 1 sec and the silent interval less than 0.5 sec. In fatigue the fatiguing sound usually lasts many minutes or even hours and the silent or recovery interval is usually at least several seconds long and may be as long as many hours or days. (For the distinction between adaptation and fatigue, see Section 1.2.4.2.)

Scharf and Buus (Section 3.3.1 of Chapter 14) review the many experiments on temporary threshold shift (TTS), the temporary increase in threshold after exposure to a fatiguing sound. Few studies have measured the reduction in loudness caused by a fatiguing sound. The effect was already noted in psychoacoustic studies during the early 1940s and reported by Davis, Morgan, Hawkins, Galambos, and Smith in 1950. They showed that temporary loudness shift (TLS), like TTS, is greatest at a frequency a half octave higher than that of the fatiguing sound. Using the method of magnitude estimation, Riach, Elliott, and Reed (1962) measured the loudness function for a 2,800-Hz tone 4 min after the ear had been fatigued by a 2,000-Hz tone. The level of the fatiguing tone was between 100 and 110 dB and was on long enough to produce a TTS of 10, 20, or 30 dB. Owing to the elevated threshold, loudness was reduced at low sound pressure levels but, as under masking, the loudness functions under fatigue were steeper than normal; by 60 dB above the *un*fatigued threshold, loudness was back to its usual value, and the loudness function had its usual slope. The greater the TTS, the greater the loudness recruitment, with the slope going from 0.62 to 1.06 as TTS increased from 10 to 30 dB. Similar results have been reported for a 1,500-Hz tone after 45 min of fatigue by a 1,000-Hz tone at 97 dB SPL (Botte & Scharf, 1980). According to Botte (Botte, Beagley, & Chocholle, 1979; Botte & Scharf, 1980), recovery of loudness is slower than recovery of threshold; both take about as long to recover completely because threshold shift is always greater than loudness shift.

Loudness recruitment is found under both masking and fatigue. Recruitment is greater, that is, loudness increases more rapidly from the elevated threshold, under masking by a pure tone than after fatigue (Botte & Scharf, 1980). Recruitment is complete at about 15 dB above the masked threshold but not until about 30 dB above the threshold elevated by fatigue. Thus fatiguing by a low-frequency tone resembles masking by a wide-band noise, at least with respect to the slope of the loudness function.

Under natural conditions, after exposure to a fatiguing sound, the listener hears a signal accompanied by other masking sounds. Some limited measurements in the laboratory show that after fatigue, both complete and partial masking are greater than would be expected by a simple combination of TTS or TLS caused by fatigue and that caused by masking (Botte & Scharf, 1980; Parker, Tubbs, Johnston, & Johnston, 1976). Interaction between fatigue and masking suggests that masking is more detrimental to the fatigued ear than to the rested ear.

One last point concerns the relation between fatigue and adaptation. Because exposure to a fatiguing sound results in a loss of loudness, why does loudness not decrease under prolonged exposure to a moderate- or high-intensity sound? The answer is that fatigue results in loudness loss only of sounds at levels well below that of the fatiguing sound. The results of Riach et al. (1962) and of Botte and Scharf (1980) show that only the loudness of a tone at least 40–50 dB weaker than the fatiguing sound is reduced. In measurements of adaptation, the sound remains at the same level throughout the listening period. Accordingly, if the adapting sound were turned off, TLS would be measurable for much weaker sounds but not for a sound at the same level as the adapting sound itself. Because by definition adaptation is measured for a sound at a constant level, there is no contradiction between the effects of fatigue on loudness and the failure of loudness adaptation at levels above 30 dB.

1.5.3. Auditory Pathology. After threshold, loudness provides the most important psychoacoustic cue to the type and extent of auditory pathology. Experimental and clinical information is available on the loudness function, loudness summation, and loudness adaptation in each of the three broad categories of auditory impairment: conductive, cochlear, and retrocochlear.

1.5.3.1. Loudness Function. In cochlear pathology, loudness often increases more rapidly than normal. This phenomenon is commonly called "recruitment" in clinical audiology. The greater the hearing loss, the steeper the loudness function (e.g., Miskolczy-Fodor, 1960). Although the resemblance between recruitment under masking and in cochlear pathology has long been noted (e.g., Steinberg & Gardner, 1937), it remains uncertain whether the underlying mechanism is the same or even similar. Recruitment is particularly clear in Ménière's disease (Hallpike & Hood, 1959) and in noise-induced hearing loss (Ward, Fleer, & Glorig, 1961); indeed, patients with such pathology often complain that sounds at 80–90 dB SPL are disturbingly loud. Thus one indirect measure of recruitment has been the loudness discomfort level, on the assumption that a patient with recruitment finds sounds uncomfortably loud at a level at or below the normal discomfort threshold. In contrast, a patient with the same elevated threshold but with a discomfort threshold that is much higher than normal does not have recruitment. Hood and Poole (1966) showed that the mean discomfort level of 100 persons with monaural Ménière's disease (which is almost always accompanied by loudness recruitment) was only a couple of decibels higher than that of 200 normally hearing persons, and that the distribution over individuals was very similar. Of course, such a finding is to be expected from the clinical reports that even moderately loud sounds disturb such patients.

Loudness recruitment is seldom seen in conductive or retrocochlear neural pathology (Hallpike, 1967). In conductive pathology, the threshold is raised because acoustic energy reaching the cochlea is attenuated by poor conduction, usually in the middle ear. As long as the cochlea and associated neural structures are intact, sensory transduction and neural transmission are normal. Accordingly, the loudness function has the normal form but is shifted to higher sound pressure levels. Were loudness measured as a function of, for example, amplitude of displacement of the basilar membrane, then the function would be entirely normal. The effect of a retrocochlear lesion on the loudness function is less well known and understood, but recruitment is not characteristic of such pathology.

1.5.3.2. Loudness Summation. Summation of loudness over frequency is absent or greatly reduced in cochlear pathology (Florentine, Buus, Scharf, & Zwicker, 1980; Martin, 1974; Scharf & Hellman, 1966) but is normal in conductive pathology (Scharf, 1962b). Thus the difference between the loudness of a broadband sound, such as white noise, and that of a pure tone is much less in cochlear pathology than in normal hearing or in conductive hearing loss. In more severe hearing losses, loudness does not increase at all with ΔF, suggesting a wider critical band. This interpretation is in accord with a number of other measures of frequency selectivity in cochlear impairment (e.g., Florentine et al., 1980; Scharf & Florentine, 1982). However, some of the reduced summation can be ascribed to loudness recruitment (Martin, 1974). Loudness summation is not easily measured in the clinic and care must be taken that pathological equal-loudness contours do not obscure the reduction in loudness summation (see Bonding, 1979 and Scharf & Florentine, 1982).

1.5.3.3. Loudness Adaptation. Few measurements have been published on the adaptation of loudness in auditory pathology. The large amounts of adaptation at threshold that are a hallmark of retrocochlear neural pathology (Scharf & Buus, Chapter 14) suggest that loudness does adapt in such patients, but the literature provides no confirmation. With respect to both conductive and cochlear pathology, there is no evidence of abnormal adaptation.

2. PITCH AND TIMBRE

The American National Standards Institute (1973) defines pitch as ". . . that attribute of auditory sensation in terms of which sounds may be ordered on a scale extending from high to low." Timbre is defined as ". . . that attribute of auditory sensation in terms of which a listener can judge that two sounds similarly presented and having the same loudness and pitch are dissimilar." (See also Deutsch, Chapter 32.) These definitions raise several questions. How can pitch, a subjective attribute, be ordered on a physical scale? Are there other possible pitch scales besides musical scales? Is a negative definition of timbre as everything that is not loudness or pitch very useful? Adequate definitions for pitch, loudness, and timbre are hard to come by because they are subjective sensations of unknown dimensionality and each is a complex function of more than one physical sound attribute. For example, although timbre may depend primarily on the sound spectrum, it also varies with sound pressure level and wave form envelope. It is therefore unclear whether timbre represents a single subjective attribute that depends on several physical dimensions or whether it represents different attributes that are referred to by the same name.

Definitions of subjective attributes such as pitch and timbre are very important in psychoacoustic research, because they often determine the experimental strategy to be followed. If, for instance, one defines pitch operationally as the subjective correlate of the frequency of a sinusoidal matching tone, one is likely to perform pure-tone pitch matching experiments. If, on the other hand, one defines pitch as that subjective attribute of sound that allows a listener to judge one sound as higher or lower than another sound, one may end up doing mostly pitch discrimination experiments. Pitch is an attribute that should not be arbitrarily defined because in music the expression is specific and meaningful. Terms such as "a major third above" or "an octave apart" are meaningful musical expressions that indicate that the subjective pitch dimension has ratio properties. Recognition of these ratio properties tends to lead to experiments that involve musical paradigms such as recognition of melodic or harmonic intervals, or musical dictation. Studies of this kind are more difficult to perform than discrimination or matching studies, but offer greater assurance that the phenomenon under study is the same as musical pitch.

This section covers pure-tone pitch, complex-tone pitch, and the pitch of noisy sounds with continuous spectra. Special attention is given to absolute pitch, the apparent ability of some people to identify tonal sounds by their musical name without the aid of any reference. Some modern studies on the multidimensionality of musical timbre are reviewed, and finally some pathologies affecting pitch perception are discussed.

2.1. Pure-Tone Pitch

Pure-tone pitch scales with ratio properties can be obtained directly through scaling experiments. Magnitude estimation and halving and doubling have been among the procedures used. In the first type of experiment subjects assign numbers proportional to pitches of sequential sinusoidal tones, whereas in the second type they adjust the frequency of a test tone until it sounds "half as high" or "twice as high" as the pitch of a reference tone. The classical result is the mel scale (S. S. Stevens & Volkmann, 1940; S. S. Stevens, Volkmann, & Newman, 1937) shown in Figure 15.14. The original mel scale was derived from determinations of pitch half-values (solid curve). The revised scale was obtained by having listeners divide certain frequency intervals into four subjectively equal pitch intervals (dashed curve). For both scales, a 1,000-Hz tone has been assigned a value of 1,000 pitch units (mels from melody). Several features of these results should be noted. First, the mel scale depends on the method of measurement. This dependence has been investigated in detail by Beck and Shaw (1962, 1963). Secondly, the frequency ratios of traditional musical intervals such as octaves and fifths are not preserved in the mel scale; if they were, the mel function would have a simple exponential shape on the coordinates of Figure 15.14. Finally, certain musical intervals, such as the octave, are subjectively unequal in different frequency regions, a fact that a musician finds difficult to accept. The discrepancy between mel pitch and musical pitch as it is commonly understood by musicians is probably the principal reason why the mel scale never became as popular as the sone scale for loudness (see Section 1.2.1).

The pitch of a pure tone depends not only on frequency, but also on intensity. Sometimes the pitch of a tone increases with intensity, but it may also decrease or remain unchanged. An early study on this subject is by S. S. Stevens (1935), but there are many others, for example, by Snow (1936), Morgan, Garner, and Galambos (1951), Terhardt (1974b), and Verschuure and van Meeteren (1975). Stevens had subjects listen to two alternating tones of slightly different frequency, one tone having a fixed intensity, the other an intensity controlled by the listener. Subjects adjusted the intensity of the second tone until both tones had equal pitch. Continuous pitch-intensity functions were constructed from all of the matched pairs; three such functions are shown in Figure 15.15. The ordinate represents percentage

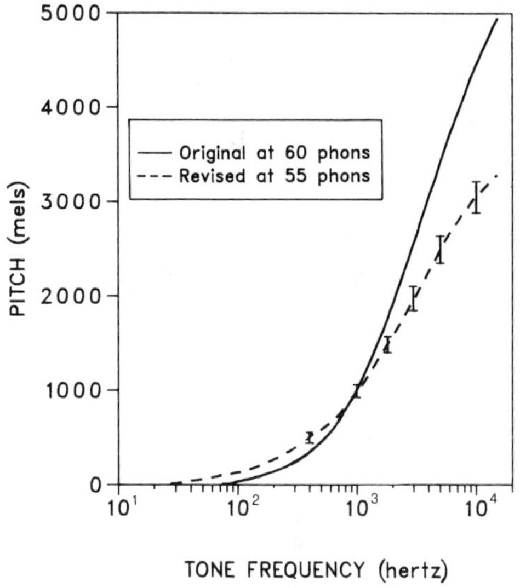

Figure 15.14. Pitch in mels as a function of frequency of a pure tone. The original mel function was obtained by having subjects adjust the frequency of a tone until its subjective pitch was half as high as that of a reference tone (from S. S. Stevens, Volkmann, & Newman; 1937). The revised mel function (S. S. Stevens and Volkmann, 1940) was obtained by division of a musical interval into four subjectively equal parts. Intra-observer average deviations for the latter experiment are shown by vertical bars (from S. S. Stevens & Volkmann, 1940). The pitch of a 1,000-Hz tone at 40 dB SPL is arbitrarily assigned a value of 1,000 mels. The relation between pitch and frequency is not linear, and a factor of two on either mel scale does not necessarily correspond to a physical octave on the frequency scale. (From S. S. Stevens, J. Volkmann, & E. B. Newman, A scale for the measurement of the psychological magnitude pitch, *Journal of the Acoustical Society of America*, 1937, *8*. Reprinted with permission.)

pitch change with arbitrarily chosen origin. The dashed lines represent the 25th and 75th percentiles of the distribution averages of results for 18 observers studied by Morgan et al. (1951) under similar signal conditions. With increasing intensity, high-frequency tones increase in pitch, low-frequency tones decrease, and middle-range tones (1,000–2,000 Hz) remain unchanged. Terhardt's more recent study (1974b) confirms this basic trend, although his 15 subjects showed larger intersubject variability than the interquartile range of Morgan et al. suggests.

Another factor that influences the pitch of a pure tone is the presence of other interfering sounds. Figure 15.16 shows pitch shifts of a test tone of frequency f_T and intensity L_T, induced by an interfering tone of frequency f_I and intensity L_I. The interfering tone is always an octave below (top of figure) or an octave above the test tone (bottom of figure). The ordinate shows percentage induced pitch shift, measured through a monaural pure-tone pitch match, as a function of intensity of the interfering tone. The general rule is that if the masking tone frequency is below that of the test tone, an upward pitch shift of the test tone is observed for all frequencies. If the frequency of the interfering tone is above that of the test tone, a downward pitch shift of the test tone is seen only at low frequencies. Figure 15.17 shows data on pure-tone pitch shifts induced by band-pass noise. The data points represent means, averaged over two matches, four subjects, and two masker bandwidths. Results are similar to those for tonal maskers. Masking noise below the test-tone frequency causes a general upward pitch shift, whereas masking noise above the test-tone

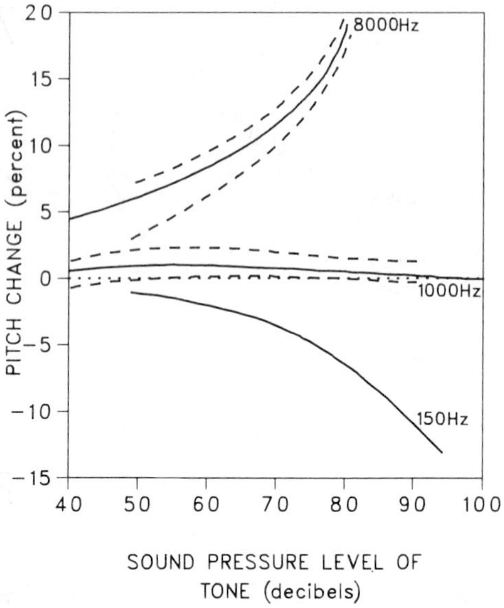

Figure 15.15. Pitch change of a pure tone as a function of its intensity. Results were obtained by measuring the intensity difference between two free-field tones of slightly different frequency needed to obtain equal pitch sensation. Summation of the resulting pairs of intensity and frequency differences over tone intensity provides the curves shown. Curve parameters are the tone frequencies (from S. S. Stevens, 1935). Dashed curves indicate 25th (lower) and 75th (upper) percentile of the distribution of average pitch changes in 18 ears measured in a similar experiment, in which both tone intensities were kep at a fixed difference and subjects adjusted the frequency of one tone for equal pitch. (From S. S. Stevens, The relation of pitch to intensity, *Journal of the Acoustical Society of America*, 1935, 6; C. T. Morgan, W. R. Garner, & R. Galambos, Pitch and intensity, *Journal of the Acoustical Society of America*, 1951, *23*. Reprinted with permission.)

frequency causes a shift whose direction depends on the frequency region of the tone. These findings are largely consistent with older studies on noise-induced pitch shift (see Terhardt, 1974a).

Pitch can also be altered by previous exposure to a tone of similar frequency. Pitch shifts following exposure to a tone have been studied by Békésy (1929), Christman and Williams (1963), Hall and Soderquist (1978), and Larkin (1978); they are often referred to as tone adaptation, but we avoid that term. The general finding is that a prior tone presented for a minute or longer can change the perceived pitch of a subsequent test tone in a direction *away* from the prior frequency, provided the test-tone frequency is within about 5% of the prior frequency. The shift is *upward* if the test tone frequency is higher than the prior tone frequency, and *downward* if it is lower. The maximum shift is about 1% so that, from a musical standpoint, this effect is rather small (one minor second or semitone is a 6% frequency step). Pitch shifts caused by prior exposure are also strongly time dependent and, according to some investigators (Hall & Soderquist, 1978), typically last only about 30 sec. Pitch matches measured by Larkin (1978), which took more than 30 sec to perform, must therefore represent some kind of average taken over the entire decay period of the effect. Other post-stimulatory pure-tone pitch shifts, such as those reported by Hartmann and Blumenstock (1976) and Rakowski and Hirsh (1978), show similar trends.

Stimulus envelope can also affect the pitch of a pure tone. Figure 15.18 shows the frequency difference required to match in pitch two pure tones that differed in envelope, one having an exponentially decaying envelope (120 dB over 120 msec), and the other a 20-msec rectangular envelope. The tones had equal energy, appeared roughly equal in loudness and subjective duration, and were adjusted in frequency to have equal pitch. The criterion for equal pitch was the 50% point of the psychometric function obtained from a two-alternative forced choice pitch discrimination test between the two tones. The data points, representing averages of three subjects, show by what percentage the frequencies of the exponentially decaying tone (f_E) differed from those of the tone with the rectangular envelope (f_R).

Finally, a pure tone of a certain frequency may not have exactly the same pitch when presented to the left or right ear. When a subject adjusts the frequency of a pure tone in one ear to match the pitch of a tone in the other ear, small interaural frequency differences are typically found. This effect, known as binaural diplacusis, is found in every listener. Figure 15.19 shows four diplacusis patterns measured over a period of several years on one subject by van den Brink (1970). These data dem-

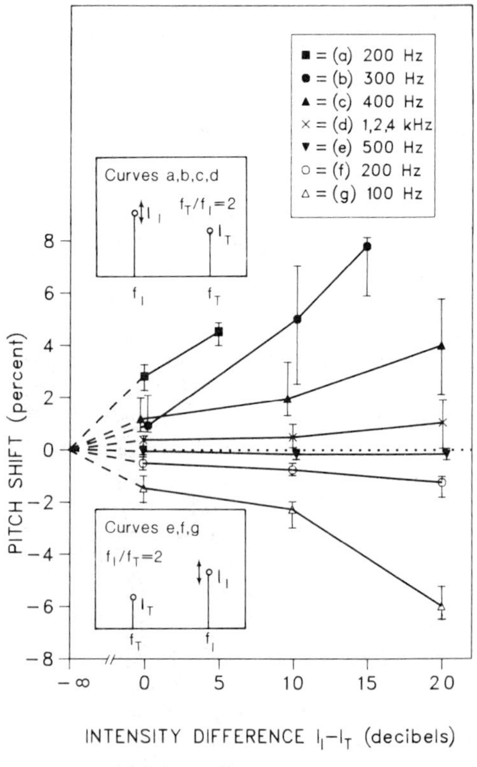

Figure 15.16. Pitch shift of one sinusoidal test tone induced by another sinusoidal tone. Subjects adjusted the frequency f_V of a comparison tone to match the pitch of a test tone of frequency f_T and intensity I_T in the presence of an interfering tone of frequency f_I and intensity I_I. The phase relation between test tone and interfering tone was always such that positive maxima coincided. Test tone and comparison tone levels, I_T and I_V, were kept at 50 phons. Matches were monaural, and subjects could select the combination of test and interfering tone or the comparison tone by means of a switch. The interfering frequency was 1 octave below (curves a–d) or 1 octave above (curves e–g) the test-tone frequency. Parameter is the test tone frequency. Percentage pitch shift, 100 $(f_V - f_T)/f_T$, is plotted as a function of level difference (in dB) between interfering tone and test tone. Data points are medians of eight matches and bars indicate the range of the six middle values. The pitch of a pure tone is always increased by an interfering tone of lower frequency. (From E. Terhardt & H. Fastl, Zum einfluss von störtönen und störgeräuschen auf die tonhöhe von sinustönen, *Acustica*, 1971, *25*. Reprinted with permission.)

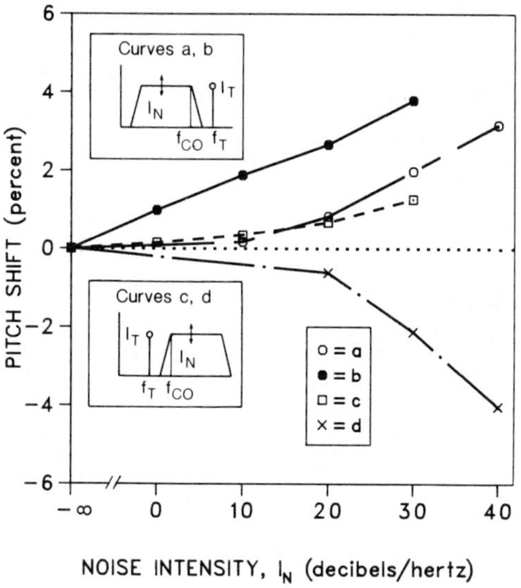

Figure 15.17. Pitch shift of a sinusoidal test tone induced by band-pass noise spectrally located just below (curves a and b) or just above (curves c and d) the test-tone frequency. The experiment was performed in a manner similar to the one shown in Figure 15.16. Levels of the test tone (I_T) and comparison tone (I_V) were 50 dB SPL. Percent pitch shift, $100 (f_V - f_T)/f_T$, is plotted against the spectral density of the noise band I_N (dB/Hz). Test tone, f_T, and nearest noise-edge frequencies, f_c, were $f_T = 300$ Hz, $f_c = 250$ Hz (curve a); $f_T = 3{,}800$ Hz, $f_c = 2{,}800$ Hz (curve b); $f_T = 3{,}400$ Hz, $f_c = 3{,}600$ Hz (curve c); $f_T = 100$ Hz, $f_c = 125$ Hz (curve d). The far noise-edge frequencies are not significant. Data points are means of six matches. The pitch of a pure tone always increases in the presence of interfering noise of lower frequency. (From E. Terhardt & H. Fastl, Zum einfluss von störtönen und störgeräuschen auf die tonhöhe von sinustönen, *Acustica*, 1971, *25*. Reprinted with permission.)

onstrate that pitch shifts vary greatly with frequency and that details of the interaural shift pattern can change with time, but that the main features of the pattern remain rather stable.

Although little is known about the causes or exact mechanisms of pure-tone pitch shift, it is generally agreed that they represent "place" effects. It is easy to imagine how excitation patterns may systematically change under adaptation or interference from other stimuli (S. S. Stevens, 1935). On the other hand, there is no physiological evidence so far that temporal synchrony to stimulus frequency, found in auditory nerve fibers as well as in higher nerve centers, changes systematically into synchrony to other (e.g., higher) frequencies when interfering sounds such as noise or tones are added.

Ratio properties of pitch sensations have manifested themselves probably for as long as music has existed. Musicians can generally recognize specific musical intervals or frequency ratios not only when they see them written, but also when they hear them played. Anyone who can carry a tune produces distinct and systematic frequency ratios. Active exposure to music at an early age may be very important in acquiring this ability, and ear training or "solfege," that is, to "sol-fa" or to "run the scales," is a regular component of elementary school education in many cultures.

Ward (1954) investigated the ability of trained musicians to tune the frequency of one tone to the octave of another fixed tone. He found that subjective octaves are tuned consistently sharp compared to the physical octave ratio of two. Some of his results are shown in Figure 15.20, where the difference between the subjective and physical octave is expressed in cents (one-hundredth of an equally tempered semitone) for several reference frequencies. This work shows that pitch has ratio properties slightly but systematically different from the physical musical scale. In a recent study, Burns and Ward (1978) showed that pure-tone frequency ratios are perceived in a categorical manner, similar to speech sounds (Liberman, Harris, Hoffman, & Griffith, 1957). This means that if a subject is presented a frequency interval anywhere in the continuum between, say, a major third (frequency ratio 5:4) and a minor third (ratio 6:5), such an interval is perceived as either a major or a minor third. Burns and Ward presented experienced listeners with melodic intervals (sequential pure-tone frequency ratios) which could assume 20 different values in the range from 2.5 to 5 semitones, and asked them to identify these intervals in five categories ranging from a major second to an augmented fourth in one-semitone steps. The same subjects also performed a discrimination task on pairs of melodic intervals in this range. The results showed that melodic intervals are perceived in categories and that discrimination performance is best at category boundaries.

Pitch is not necessarily a simple unidimensional attribute, but may contain two distinct components. One is often referred to as "pitch chroma," which represents circular properties of pitch, the fact that notes 1 octave apart have something in common. The other, referred to as "tone height," represents the fact that a continuously increasing frequency causes a continuously rising pitch sensation. These two components of pitch can be represented by a helix (Revesz, 1913; Shepard, 1982; Ward & Burns, 1982) where chroma is given by angular position

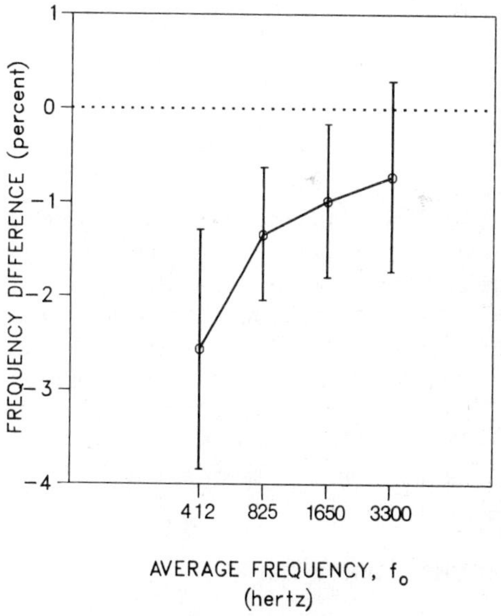

Figure 15.18. Percent frequency difference between tones of the same pitch that have either exponential or rectangular envelopes. Exponential and rectangular envelopes were set so that tone bursts had the same energy, and the tone with the rectangular envelope was at 89 dB SPL. The criterion for equal pitch was chance performance in a forced choice discrimination test. The abscissa shows f_0, which is the average of the frequencies f_E of the exponentially shaped tone and f_R of the rectangularly shaped tone. Data points are averages of three subjects; bars indicate plus or minus one standard deviation for a typical subject. The negative values on the ordinate mean that a tone with exponentially decaying envelope sounds higher in pitch than a tone of the same frequency with a rectangular envelope. (From W. M. Hartmann, The effect of amplitude envelope on the pitch of sinewave tones, *Journal of the Acoustical Society of America*, 1978, *63*. Reprinted with permission.)

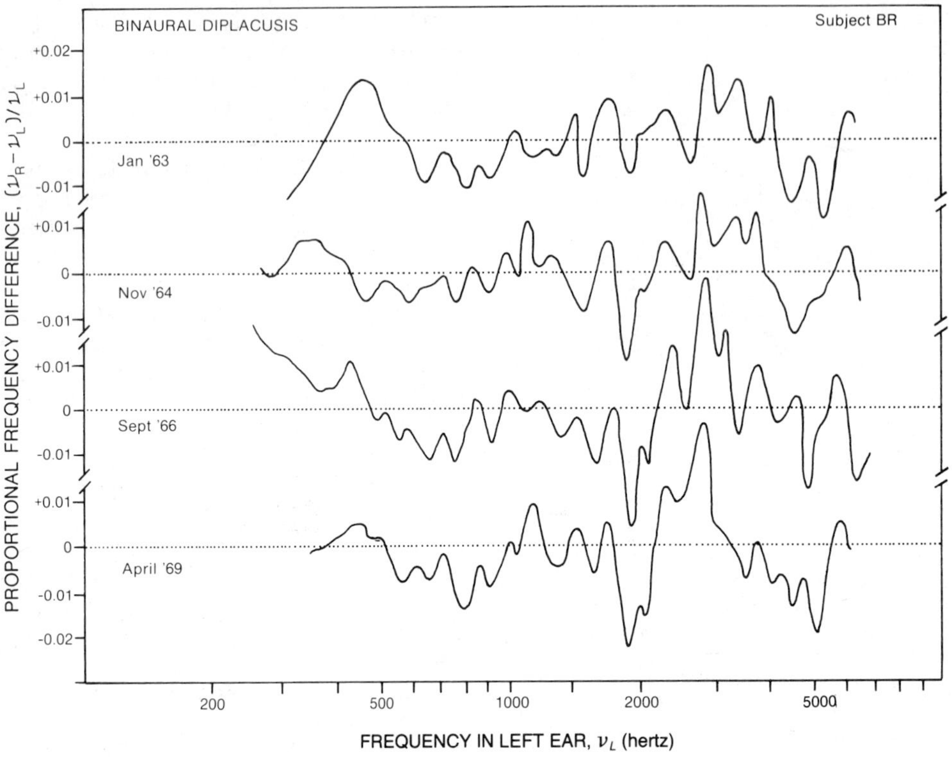

Figure 15.19. Binaural diplacusis patterns of one subject measured at intervals of several years. Patterns represent interaural pitch matches in which the subject adjusted the frequency of a tone in one ear until it matched the pitch of a tone in the other ear. The graphs show the fractional difference between the frequencies of sinusoidal tones in the left (ν_L) and right (ν_R) ears as a function of the frequency in the left ear. Patterns do not depend much on intensity as long as there are no interaural intensity differences. Differences between the two ears follow an irregular but highly stable pattern. (From G. van den Brink, Experiments on binaural displacusis and tone perception, in R. Plomp & G. F. Smoorenburg (Eds.), *Frequency analysis and periodicity detection in hearing*, Sijthoff & Noordhoff International Publishers, 1970. Reprinted with permission.)

on a turn, and tone height by axial position. Such a model is supported by the observation that musicians with absolute pitch (see Section 2.4) usually can quickly identify a note as a G or an A, for example, but make mistakes about a note's proper octave. Shepard (1964) provided the first direct demonstration of circular properties in pitch judgments using complex tones with octave partials. By continuously increasing the frequencies of all octave partials, and passing the signal through a filter with a smooth and constant spectral envelope, he created a continuously rising pitch sensation.

2.2. Complex-Tone Pitch

Complex tones are composites of two or more sinusoidal components whose frequencies may or may not be harmonically related. A harmonic tone complex represents in the time domain a periodic wave form whose period equals the period of the fundamental frequency. Most "natural" periodic sounds have a fundamental component and harmonics whose frequencies are multiples of the fundamental frequency. When the fundamental frequency is absent, the periodicity of the wave form still equals that of the (missing) fundamental. A number of theories have been offered to explain the pitch of complex tones; these are discussed in the following sections.

2.2.1. Early Theories. An interesting feature of complex-tone pitch perception is that a musical message, such as a melody, can be perceived from a sequence of periodic sounds, more or less without regard to spectral details. Ohm (1843) proposed a theory known as "Ohm's acoustic law" that the ear performs a real-time spectral analysis of complex sounds and maps the frequency of the lowest spectral component into pitch. Seebeck (1841), on the other hand, had demonstrated that a sound with only a very weak fundamental component still evoked a relatively strong fundamental pitch sensation, much stronger than the actual spectral energy at the fundamental seemed to justify. He argued that the higher harmonics also contributed to the sensation of fundamental pitch. Ohm's and Seebeck's argument eventually led to what is now known as the place and periodicity theories of pitch. Place theorists (Békésy, 1944: Fletcher, 1924; Helmholtz, 1885/1954) found physiological support for Ohm's law in the tonotopic organization of the cochlea and tried to account for Seebeck's observations by assuming that, if the fundamental frequency of a harmonic stimulus was absent from the original stimulus, nonlinear distortion in the middle-ear could resupply that fundamental as a (quadratic) difference tone. Other theorists (Wever & Bray, 1930; Wundt, 1880) argued that it is not which nerve units are active, but synchrony between nerve impulses and the stimulus frequency that gives rise to the sensation of pitch.

2.2.2. Residue Theory. Schouten (1940) devised an ingenious version of periodicity theory that combined peripheral frequency analysis and central periodicity detection. According

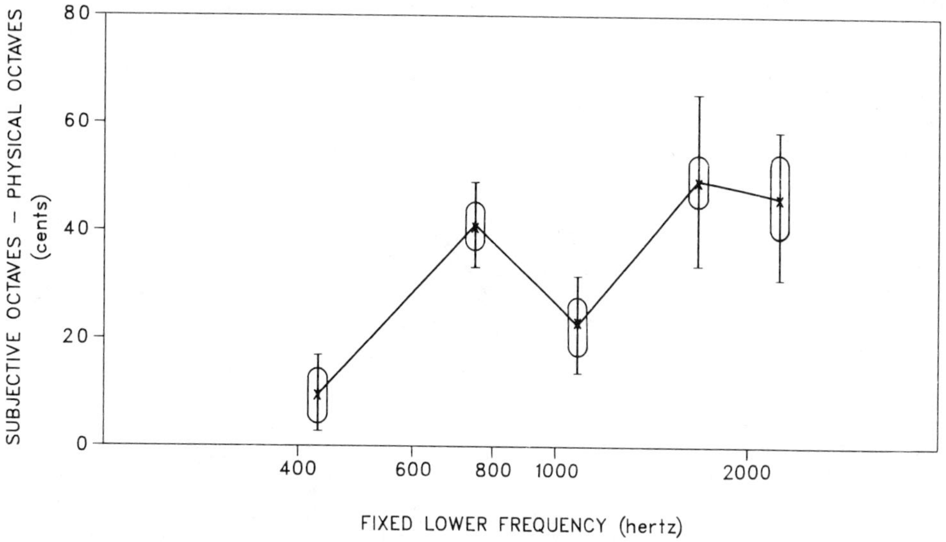

Figure 15.20. Melodic octave judgments for trained musicians. Subjects adjusted the frequency of one of two alternating pure tones until it sounded an octave above the pitch of the other tone. Tones were at 50 dB SPL. The difference between the obtained frequency (SO) and twice the lower frequency (PO), expressed in cents, is plotted against the lower frequency. One cent equals one-hundredth of an equally tempered semitone. Crosses are the means from nine observers (18 ears). Vertical bars show plus or minus one standard error of the mean for all observers, and length of ovals show the same for a typical observer. According to these results, the subjective octave is consistently larger than the physical octave. (From W. D. Ward, Subjective musical pitch, *Journal of the Acoustical Society of America*, 1954, *26*. Reprinted with permission.)

to this theory, the lower components of a harmonic complex are spectrally resolved in the cochlea and each component maps into its own pitch. The higher components, which are not resolved in the cochlea, create a periodic interference pattern that reflects the periodicity of the wave form. This periodicity is detected by the nervous system and maps into a sensation of (fundamental) pitch. Missing fundamental pitch became known as "residue pitch" because, according to Schouten, it results from the residue of spectral components that the cochlea fails to resolve. (See de Boer, 1976, for an excellent review of the "residue.")

Subsequent studies showed that "residue" pitch is not related to a simple difference tone or other distortion product. It can be masked by a band of noise at the component frequencies, but not at the perceived (fundamental) pitch frequency. Experiments on inharmonic frequency shift (de Boer, 1956; Schouten, Ritsma, & Cardozo, 1962; Smoorenburg, 1970), in which the difference between component frequencies was kept constant, showed convincingly that residue pitch is not related to difference frequency. If one starts with a harmonic complex of tones at 800, 1,000, and 1,200 Hz and increases each frequency by 20 Hz to obtain a complex of tones of 820, 1,020, and 1,220 Hz, pitch changes from 200 to about 204 Hz. If one keeps shifting the three frequencies upward, however, the pitch cannot increase indefinitely because for a shift of 200 Hz a new harmonic position is reached for the three components (1,000, 1,200, and 1,400 Hz), that should evoke a pitch sensation of 200 Hz again. Figure 15.21 shows pitch matching data from Smoorenburg's study in which the higher tone of a two-tone complex was always kept 200 Hz above the lower tone frequency, which is plotted on the abscissa. The ordinate shows the fundamental of a two-tone harmonic matching signal whose components were in the same spectral region as the test signal and whose fundamental could be controlled by the subject. The apparent pitch rises with increasing frequency shift of the test tones in a sawtooth-like pattern. There is much pitch ambiguity when the frequency shift is halfway between two harmonic positions. For example, a complex of 900 and 1,100 Hz evokes an ambiguous pitch sensation of 227 and 176 Hz. Later experiments (Gerson & Goldstein, 1978; Houtsma, 1979) have shown that such a stimulus of successive odd harmonics can, when the subject's attention is properly drawn to it, also evoke a pitch sensation at the true fundamental of 100 Hz. All these types of pitch data on inharmonically shifted tone complexes are reasonably well described by the law:

$$dP = \frac{dF}{n_e}, \tag{6}$$

where dP is the pitch shift away from the original fundamental, dF the frequency shift away from the nearest harmonic condition, and n the effective (weighted average) harmonic number of the stimulus. For example, an inharmonic complex tone with frequencies 810, 1,010, and 1,210 Hz is obtained from the harmonic complexes of frequencies 800, 1,000, and 1,200 Hz by a positive frequency shift of 10 Hz. If all three harmonics carry equal weight, the effective average harmonic number, n_e, equals 5. The expected pitch shift dP equals 10/5, or 2, so that the inharmonic complex tone has a pitch of 202 Hz. Bounds imposed by this relation are shown in Figure 15.21 by the solid lines, where n_e is taken as the lower harmonic number for one line of each pair and as the higher number for the other line at each harmonic position of the test stimulus. Systematic differences between measured slopes and predicted bounds, especially at high harmonic numbers, suggest that the effective harmonic number can be lower than the lowest harmonic in the stimulus. This is possible because the effective stimulus may contain aural combination tones, which are discussed in Section 4.

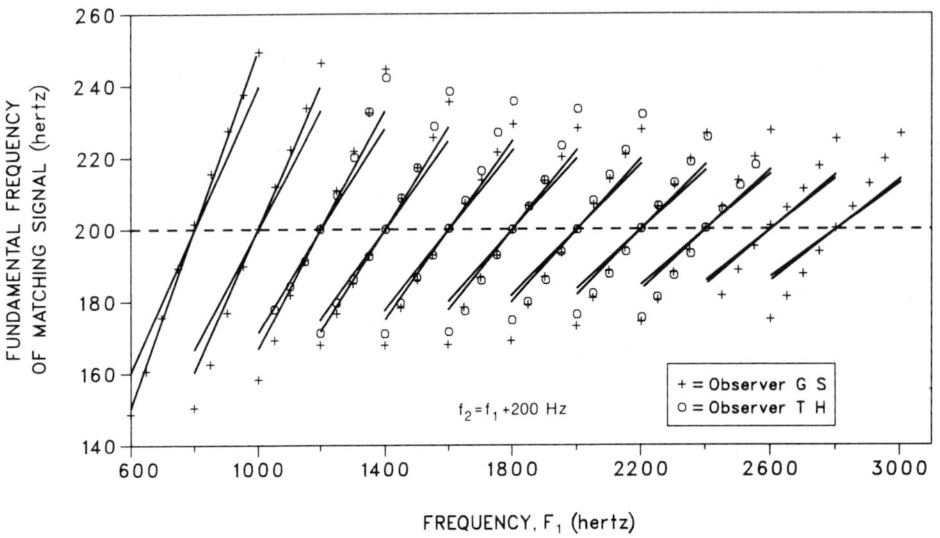

Figure 15.21. Pitch matches by two observers between a (generally inharmonic) two-tone test stimulus with a fixed frequency difference (200 Hz) and a harmonic two-tone comparison stimulus of known pitch. Tones were presented monaurally at 40 dB SL. Subjects could select the test stimulus, the comparison stimulus, or silence by means of a switch. They adjusted the (missing) fundamental of the comparison stimulus for equal pitch. The abscissa shows the lower frequency of the test stimulus, the ordinate shows the (missing) fundamental of the matching stimulus. Solid lines represent pitch bounds of a simple descriptive formula, $dP = dF/n_e$, where dP is the pitch shift away from the original fundamental, dF is the frequency shift away from the nearest harmonic condition, and n_e is the effective (weighted average) harmonic number of the stimulus. (From G. F. Smoorenburg, Pitch perception of two-frequency stimuli, *Journal of the Acoustical Society of America*, 1970, *48*. Reprinted with permission.)

"Residue" pitch can be perceived only when fundamental frequency and harmonic numbers are within certain limits. Ritsma (1962) measured the existence region of what he called the "tonal residue" by asking subjects whether a harmonic test complex sounded equal in pitch to a harmonic reference complex of the same (missing) fundamental frequency whose tonal character had earlier been established by other means. If the answer was positive it was concluded that the test complex evoked a tonal residue pitch, whereas if the answer was negative an atonal residue sensation was assumed. Some of his results are shown in Figure 15.22 as the solid contour, which represents the boundary between tonal (left) and atonal (right) residue. The other contours (dashed curves) were derived from a study by Houtsma and Goldstein (1971), in which the tonality of complex tones was investigated by having subjects identify melodic intervals played with three-tone and two-tone harmonic tone complexes. The contours represent conditions for a three-tone complex under which levels of 100, 60, and 20% correct identification were reached. All contours are plotted in terms of equivalent carrier (frequency of the middle tone) and modulation frequency (missing fundamental). The results show how different experimental criteria for tonality of a sound, one being the impression of similar versus dissimilar, the other the correct identification of a musical interval, can lead to very different results.

Ritsma's existence region data provided the first early clues that there was something wrong with the residue theory. The theory implies a lower bound on harmonic number, not an upper bound. Harmonics below a certain order (approximately the tenth) are resolved in the cochlea and cannot, according to the residue theory, contribute to a low pitch sensation. Ritsma (1967) provided further evidence that the dominant spectral region through which "residue" pitch is conveyed is typically between the third and fifth harmonics, which are known to be resolved in the cochlea. It is therefore not surprising that eventually the residue theory was challenged.

2.2.3. Modern Pitch Theories. Terhardt (1970) proposed on the basis of a study of periodicity pitch and roughness perception that the "residue" may be a product of resolved rather than of unresolved components. Much more direct evidence for the central rather than peripheral origin of "residue" pitch was provided in a study by Houtsma and Goldstein (1971, 1972). Musically trained subjects were asked to identify melodic intervals (e.g., major second, minor third) for stimuli of two sequential complex tones, where each complex consisted of two successive harmonics in random order. The two harmonics were either monotic (both to one ear) or dichotic (one to each ear). Identification performance deteriorated monotonically with increasing harmonic order, contrary to the predictions of the residue theory, but performance contours remained also unchanged when the two stimulus harmonics were presented dichotically (one to each ear) compared to monotically (both to one ear). Some results from this experiment are shown in Figure 15.23 for three subjects. They firmly established the notion that complex-tone pitch must be accounted for with a central mechanism that operates on neural signals, derived from those stimulus partials that are peripherally resolved. The term "residue," which has been used to designate complex-tone pitch, therefore seems no longer appropriate because it implies the wrong mechanism.

Figure 15.24 shows a schematic representation of one of the modern pitch theories that have been proposed during the past decade. The optimum processor theory (Gerson & Goldstein, 1978; Goldstein, 1973) assumes that the frequencies f_i of spectrally resolved stimulus components are transformed into random variables X_i; each X_i has a Gaussian distribution with mean equal to f_i and a variance that is a function of f only. A

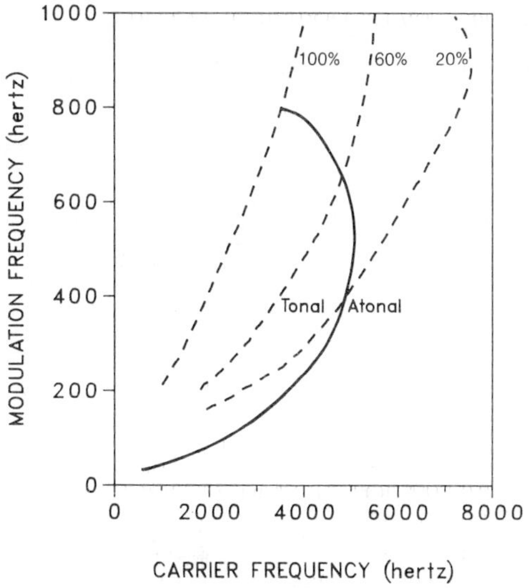

Figure 15.22. Existence region of "tonal residue" pitch for three-tone harmonic stimuli, expressed as modulation frequency (missing fundamental) as a function of carrier frequency (center tone frequency). Solid curve is the boundary of subjects' ability to tell whether or not a three-component test tone had the same pitch as a complex comparison tone of the same fundamental frequency. Tones were at 35 dB SL (from Ritsma, 1962). Dashed curves are equal percent-correct performance contours from a melodic interval identification experiment in which notes were represented by three-tone harmonic complexes at 20 dB SL (from Houtsma & Goldstein, 1971). Differences between the existence region of the tonal residue, measured by Ritsma, and musical performance contours, measured by Houtsma and Goldstein, are assumed to reflect differences in the criteria for what makes a stimulus tonal. (From R. J. Ritsma, Existence region of the tonal residue I, *Journal of the Acoustical Society of America*, 1962, *34*. Reprinted with permission.)

central processor, which has only the set of random variables X_i to look at and assumes that they are noisy representations of harmonic frequencies, estimates the unknown harmonic numbers and fundamental frequency in an optimal way. Important features of this theory are that its formulation is stochastic, that it utilizes only frequency information, ignoring component amplitude and phase, and that its only free parameter is a frequency-dependent variance function.

The pattern transformation theory (Wightman, 1973) is a deterministic signal processing scheme in which the stimulus spectrum is first smeared to represent crudely the peripheral excitation patterns in the cochlea and eighth nerve, and next is Fourier-transformed. Pitch corresponds to the first major maximum of the transformed pattern away from the origin. The resolution power of the coarse spectral analyzer is the model's only free parameter. The virtual pitch theory (Terhardt, 1974a, 1979) assumes that spectral frequencies are transformed at the periphery into spectral pitch cues according to certain empirical rules. More centrally, virtual pitch is derived from these spectral cues by finding the best-fitting common subharmonics. The model is similar to the optimum processor model in that both are template matching models. Important differences are that the virtual pitch theory is deterministic, recognizes the effects of learning and exposure on virtual pitch images, and implies that all pure-tone pitch shift effects described in the preceding section should also be found to the same degree in complex-tone pitch.

Recent attempts to evaluate predictions of these theories in a quantitative manner on the basis of new data (Hall & Soderquist, 1982; Houtsma, 1979, 1981a, 1981b) have shown that the pattern transformation theory cannot account for some of these data and that some pure-tone pitch and complex-tone pitch phenomena are rather independent, which is inconsistent with predictions of the virtual pitch theory. A practical application of the optimum processor theory for determining pitch of running signals such as speech has recently been developed by Duifhuis, Willems, and Sluyter (1982). Such an application is important if prosodic properties are to be preserved in speech transmitted via a vocoder, a device for sending speech in a coded form.

2.3. Nontonal Pitch

The clearest pitch sensations are evoked by sounds that are periodic or, equivalently, sounds that have line spectra of harmonically related frequencies. Most string and wind instruments produce near-periodic sounds and are therefore very efficient in conveying melodic information. Other instruments, such as bells or chimes, produce line spectra with inharmonically related frequencies that evoke the ambiguous pitch sensations characteristic of these instruments. Still other instruments, such as the snare drum or cymbals, produce sounds with continuous spectra that evoke a sensation of noise without any pitch. Accordingly, these are instruments used for rhythmic rather than for melodic or harmonic purposes.

2.3.1. Repetition Pitch. Some noise-like sounds, however, do evoke pitch sensations. One example is repetition pitch or echo pitch, first described by Huygens in the 17th century (1693/1905). He noticed that the noise of a water fountain, reflected by some marble stairs, produced a distinct musical pitch equal to that of an organ pipe whose length matched the depth of the stairs. He essentially discovered that when one or more systematically delayed images of a sound interfere with the original sound wave form, one hears a pitch that corresponds to the inverse of the time delay. The original sound wave form can be noise, music, speech, or just about any other sound. Because the frequency response characteristic of such a time-delay system has a periodic comblike structure, this process is often referred to as comb filtering. The effect is audible for time delays ranging from 1 to 10 msec and is commonly used as a special effect in recorded or synthesized music. It sometimes shows up as an accidental and undesirable effect. If a concert hall or auditorium has a strong sound reflection that arrives at the listener's ear between 1 and 10 msec after the direct wave front, the listener hears a constant pitch or tone coloration superimposed on the sound.

Figure 15.25 shows results of a study in which white noise $n(t)$ plus its delay $n(t - \tau)$ were presented monotically (Bilsen, 1968) and dichotically (Bilsen & Goldstein, 1974) to subjects who adjusted the reference signal for equal pitch. The reference signal in the monotic study was a pure tone, and in the dichotic study a monotic, repeated noise signal. The solid lines represent pitch matching results when the delayed noise is added in phase, and the dashed lines when it is added out of phase. In the first case, the perceived pitch corresponds to the inverse of the delay, but in the second case two pitches are heard, one slightly above and the other slightly below the inverse of the delay. The results can be summarized by the following empirical formulas:

$$RP_0 = \frac{1}{\tau}\ ;\ RP_{180} = \frac{8}{7\tau} \text{ or } RP_{180} = \frac{6}{7\tau} \qquad (7)$$

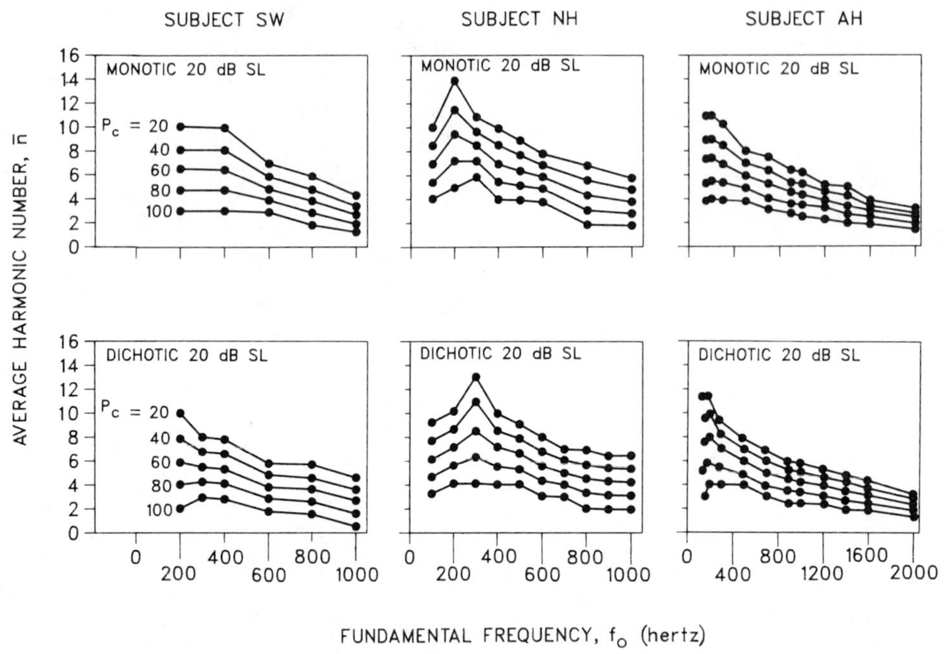

Figure 15.23. Equal percent-correct performance contours for melodic interval identification with notes of harmonic two-tone stimuli of random harmonic order, presented monotically (both tones to one ear) and dichotically (one tone to each ear). There were eight possible melodic intervals, with (missing) fundamental frequency ratios 5/4, 6/5, 9/8, 16/15, 15/16, 8/9, 5/6, and 4/5. Harmonic numbers were random for each note, within a range of three. The abscissa gives (missing) fundamental frequency f_0; the ordinate gives the average harmonic number. Similarity of monotic and dichotic performance contours underscores the role of central processing in the formation of a missing fundamental percept. (From A. J. M. Houtsma & J. L. Goldstein, The central origin of the pitch of complex tones: Evidence from musical interval recognition, *Journal of the Acoustical Society of America*, 1972, *51*. Reprinted with permission.)

where RP_0 is the repetition pitch of noise with its delay added in-phase, RP_{180} is the pitch(es) of noise with its delay added out-of-phase, and τ is the time delay. The ambiguous behavior in the antiphasic case may be interpreted the same way as behavior observed with inharmonically shifted tone complexes. The power spectrum of $n(t) + n(t - \tau)$ shows periodic peaks and valleys, with peaks at $t = 0, 1/\tau, 2/\tau, 3/\tau$, etc. The spectrum of $n(t) - n(t - \tau)$ has maxima at $t = 1/2\tau, 3/2\tau, 5/2\tau$, and so forth, which can be considered as derived from the in-phase spectrum by a frequency shift of $1/2\tau$. From the observed pitch shifts and the empirical inharmonic shift law we find that the effective harmonic number n_e, representing the rank order of the peak in this wide-band spectrum, equals 3.5, which is similar to Ritsma's finding for the spectrally dominant region in complex-

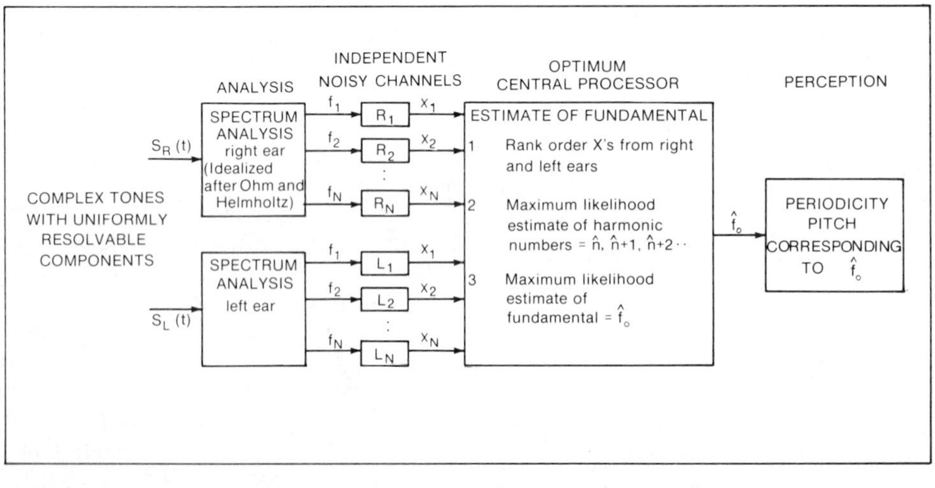

Figure 15.24. Optimum processor theory for pitch of complex tones. Spectral analyzers supply independent noisy channels with separate frequency representations, f_i, of resolved spectral components. Amplitude and phase information is ignored. Frequency information, X_i, is conveyed stochastically to the central processor, which estimates the most likely harmonic numbers and fundamental frequency. (From J. L. Goldstein, An optimum processor theory for the central formation of the pitch of complex tones, *Journal of the Acoustical Society of America*, 1973, *54*. Reprinted with permission.)

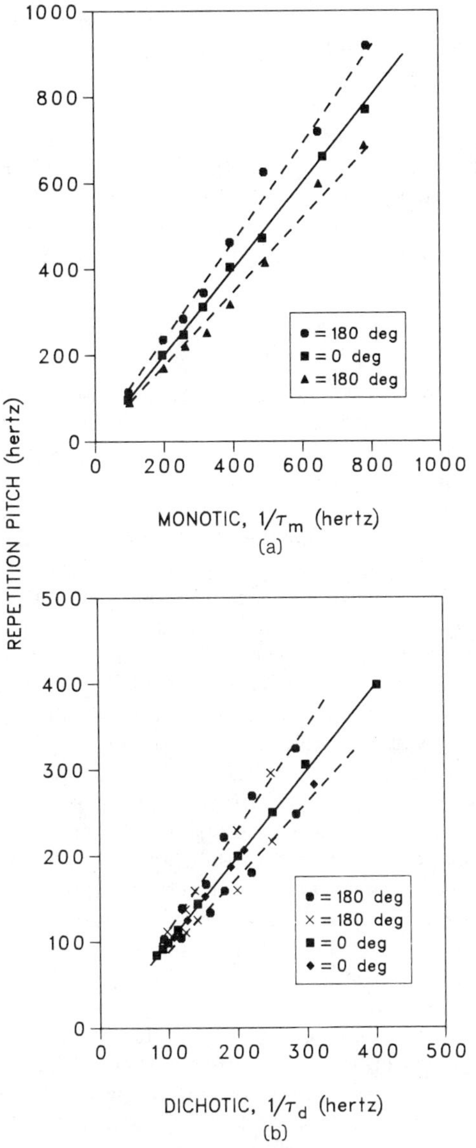

Figure 15.25. Monotic and dichotic repetition pitch evoked by adding broadband noise $n(t)$ to its own delay $n(t - \tau)$. (a) Frequency of a pure tone judged equal in pitch to the noise, plotted as a function of the reciprocal of the delay. Stimuli were presented to one ear. (b) Results when $n(t)$ and $n(t - \tau)$ were presented to different ears, and a monotic repetition pitch signal was the comparison stimulus. Monotic results were obtained in a free field at 40 dB SL, dichotic results with earphones at 25 dB SL. Function parameters indicate in-phase and out-of-phase relations between noise source $n(t)$ and delayed source $n(t - \tau)$. Symbols designate different subjects. Although monotic and dichotic results appear similar, dichotic repetition pitch is much weaker than monotic repetition pitch. (From F. A. Bilsen & J. L. Goldstein, Pitch of dichotically delayed noise and its possible spectral basis, *Journal of the Acoustical Society of America*, 1974, *55*; F. A. Bilsen, *On the interaction of a sound and its repetitions*, Unpublished doctoral dissertation, 1968. Delft University of Technology, Netherlands. Reprinted with permission.)

tone pitch processing. The dichotic results suggest the existence of a central spectral representation of the total dichotic signal.

2.3.2. Edge Pitch. The idea of a central spectrum has gained additional momentum with recent experiments on monaural and binaural edge pitch. Monaural edge pitch refers to a pitch sensation evoked by low-pass or high-pass noise with a sufficiently sharp spectral edge. Such stimuli can be matched to pure tones with frequencies slightly in (toward the noise band) from the spectral edge (Fastl, 1971; Klein & Hartmann, 1981). Binaural edge pitch is evoked when white noise is presented to both ears with an interaural phase shift of 0° below a certain frequency f_0, and 180° above f_0. Under those conditions, two pitches are observed, one slightly above f_0, the other slightly below f_0. Klein and Hartmann measured these pitches. They had their subjects adust the frequency of a partially masked tone so that its pitch matched that of a broadband noise with such an interaural phase transition. Results are shown in Figure 15.26, where the ratio of matching tone frequency to phase-transition frequency, f_m/f_0, is plotted as a function of f_0. These data can be interpreted as resulting from central addition and subtraction, which yield central low-pass and high-pass filtered signals, respectively. The results are then equivalent to those obtained in monaural experiments, and support the notion of central spectral signal representation.

Binaural edge pitch also bears some resemblance to "Huggins' pitch" (Cramer & Huggins, 1958). Huggins' pitch is heard when the phase of a binaural noise is shifted interaurally 360° over a narrow frequency range around f_0. In this case, central subtraction yields a central narrow-band signal around f_0.

2.3.3. Adaptation Pitch. Another noise-pitch phenomenon was discovered by Zwicker (1964). If the ear is exposed to wideband noise with a spectral notch of about ½ octave, a weak tonal afterimage is heard when the noise is suddenly turned off. The pitch of the afterimage matches the center frequency of the notch. Its duration depends on the duration of noise ex-

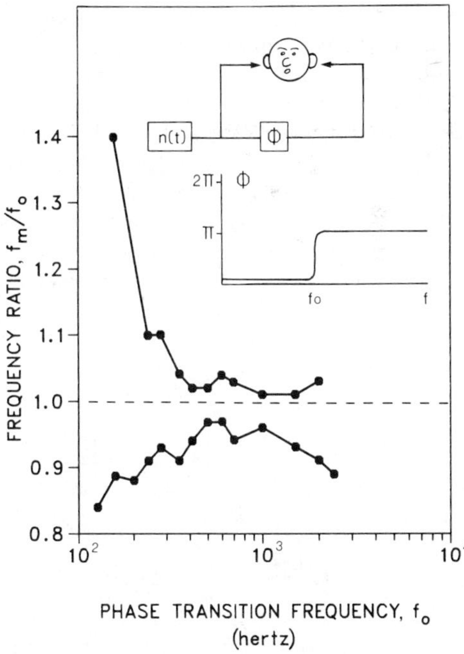

Figure 15.26. Binaural edge pitch evoked by binaurally presented broadband noise with a sudden interaural phase transition from 0 to 180° around a frequency f_0. Subjects compared the pitch of such a signal to that of a comparison sinusoid, partially masked by noise, and adjusted the sinusoid's frequency for equal pitch. Stimuli were at 60 dB SPL. Two pitches were heard, one slightly above f_0, the other slightly below. Graph shows ratio of pure-tone matching frequency to phase-transition frequency, f_m/f_0, as a function of the phase-transition frequency f_0. Data are average pitch matches from four subjects. Bimodal pitch distribution suggests central addition and/or subtraction of the signals in the two ears. (From M. A. Klein & W. M. Hartmann, Binaural edge pitch, *Journal of the Acoustical Society of America*, 1981, *70*. Reprinted with permission.)

posure, but never lasts more than a few seconds. The effect is evidence for place encoding of pure-tone pitch and can be explained as a result of adaptation or fatigue and lateral suppression. The noise fatigues or causes adaptation of all sensory units except those tuned to the spectral notch where there is no adaptation stimulus. When the noise is turned off, adapted units are less active and therefore less effective in suppressing spontaneous activity in sensory units tuned to the notch frequency. The physiological effect is increased activity of a small, clustered group of units, which is what happens under stimulation with a weak sinusoidal tone.

2.3.4. Pitch of Amplitude-Modulated Noise. Periodically amplitude-modulated noise is cited as a classic example of temporally based pitch. Miller and Taylor (1948) reported that listeners could match the pitch of periodically gated white noise to that of a square wave or pure tone with roughly the same accuracy as they could match the pure tone to the square wave, at least for rates below 100 Hz. They also measured sensitivity to changes in noise-interruption rate, which is shown in Figure 15.27, along with just noticeable differences in pure-tone pitch measured by Shower and Biddulph (1931). Sensitivities are roughly comparable below 100 Hz, but diverge rapidly beyond that point. This "noise-pitch" phenomenon was considered significant because the signal has a flat power spectrum and therefore contains no spectral pitch clues. Any sensation of pitch was therefore thought to be derived from temporal characteristics of the wave form. Modern empirical and theoretical studies, however, cast doubt on this simple explanation. First, spectra of such signals are flat only over very long time intervals. Short-term spectra, as would be measured by any set of filters with limited resolution power, contain all kinds of clues to noise interruption or modulation rate (Pierce, Lipes, & Cheetham, 1977). Comparing some of those short-term spectral clues with temporal clues, Houtsma, Wicke, and Ordubadi (1980) found that temporal processing gives a better account of the data than does short-term spectral processing. Another unresolved problem is whether the sensation of periodically amplitude-modulated noise is a pitch sensation. Investigators have come to different conclusions, based on the outcome of their experiments and

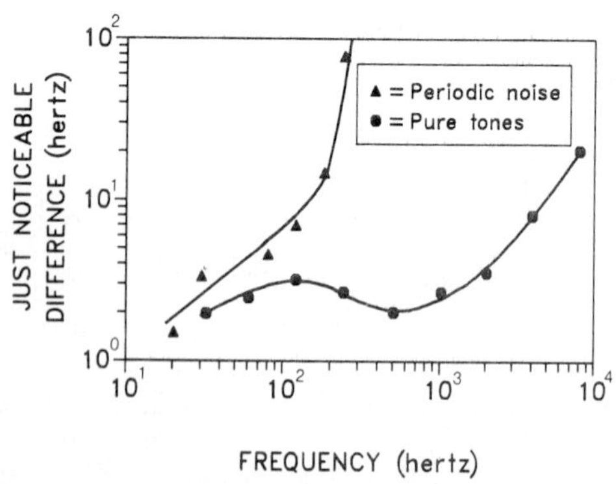

Figure 15.27. Just noticeable differences in periodic noise interruption rates. Triangles represent average thresholds of six listeners at which they were able to detect changes in interruption rate half of the time (Miller & Taylor, 1948). Stimulus level was 100 dB. Pure tone JNDs are shown as circles for comparison. Convergence of the two functions below 100 Hz suggests that at low frequencies a similar, temporally based mechanism is operative. (From G. A. Miller & W. G. Taylor, The perception of repeated bursts of noise, *Journal of the Acoustical Society of America*, 1948, *20*. Reprinted with permission.)

their criteria for what constitutes a pitch sensation (Burns & Viemeister, 1976, 1981; Miller & Taylor, 1948; Mowbray, Gebhard, & Byham, 1956; Pollack, 1969). Impeding the solution of this debate is the difficulty of determining why recognizing melodic intervals or performing musical dictation is so difficult with such sounds. It is unclear whether the limitations are due to severely reduced sensitivity (see Fig. 15.27) or to the fact that the sensation has only ordinal and not ratio properties, which would disqualify it as a true musical pitch effect.

2.4. Absolute Pitch

Absolute pitch, sometimes also referred to as "perfect pitch," is the relatively rare ability to identify isolated tonal sounds by their proper note name, or to name the key of a tonal piece of music, without an apparent reference. This ability, sometimes considered a coveted sign of true musicianship but often a mixed blessing, has been studied by many investigators for well over a century. Unfortunately our understanding of the phenomenon is still minimal, owing in part to the difficulty of performing reliable experiments on absolute pitch.

Some of the more comprehensive among the older studies were done by Bachem (1937, 1940, 1954). He examined a large number of people who claimed to possess absolute pitch. Experimenting with different kinds of sounds and employing a variety of techniques, he established three categories of people: (1) those with genuine absolute pitch, (2) those with acquired absolute pitch, and (3) those with imagined absolute pitch. People in the first category can make absolute pitch judgments quickly (within 2 sec) and accurately, with octave errors the prevailing type of mistake. Those in the second category are slower in their judgments and seem to use some learned reference such as a concert "A" (orchestra players) or vocal chord position (singers). Those in the third category show average errors of five to nine semitones, which is close to chance performance after compensation for octave errors. Figure 15.28 shows some time-error functions for pure-tone pitch discrimination for four subjects, two without (top) and two with absolute pitch (bottom). The first group shows a steadily growing error with time, whereas the second shows a constant error of about 2% (a semitone is near 6%), independent of time, except for frequencies above 4,000 Hz.

The question whether absolute pitch can be acquired by training has been studied by several investigators. Prolonged training to recognize a certain tone proved not only to help subsequent recognition of that tone when presented in a larger context, but improved pitch identification across the board (Cuddy, 1968). However, people so trained still seem to have great difficulty in recognizing the key of a passage of tonal music, which is a trivial task for musicians with genuine absolute pitch (Brady, 1970).

Absolute pitch may not be exceptional, but rather may represent an extreme on a scale of musical ability. Perfect relative pitch, which is the ability to recognize frequency ratios or musical intervals without the aid of a reference, is much more common among musicians, and can be learned. Tone-deaf people or "tin ears" are on the other end of this scale. It is not known whether all these phenomenological differences represent differences in physiology, although there is some indication (Bachem, 1937) that absolute pitch requires an innate ability combined with the proper exposure and training during a critical development period at an early age.

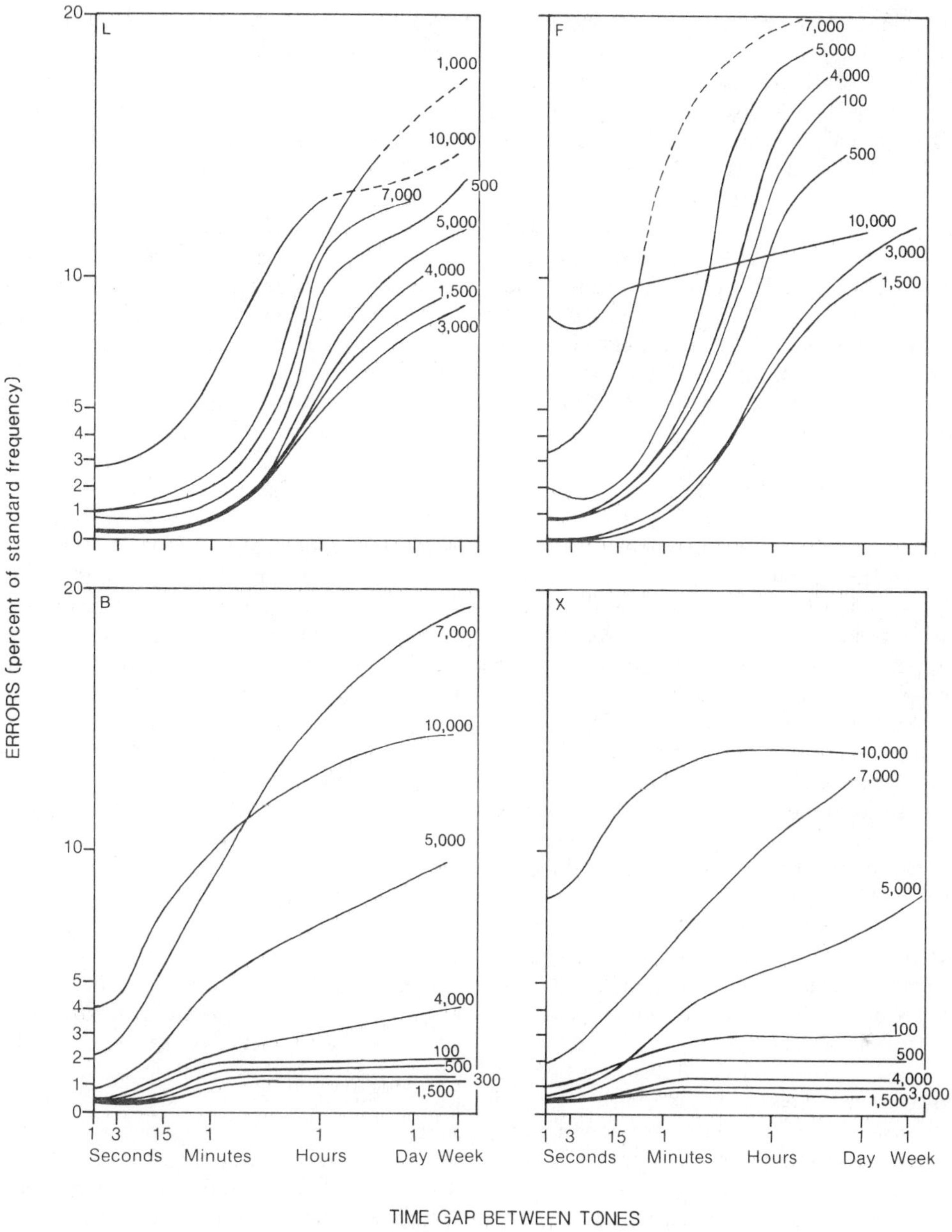

Figure 15.28. Time-error curves for pure-tone pitch from four subjects. The just noticeable frequency difference, Δf, between two pure tones was measured as a function of frequency and the time gap between the tones. Tones lasted 2 sec and were presented at a comfortable listening level in a free field. Ordinate represents pitch discrimination errors, expressed in percentages ($100\Delta f/f$). The time scale along the abscissa is logarithmic. Subjects B and X claim absolute pitch, subjects L and F do not. Tone frequencies are shown as curve parameters. With small time gaps results are virtually identical for all subjects. With large time gaps and at frequencies below 5,000 Hz, JNDs are smaller and more stable for the subjects with absolute pitch. (From A. Bachem, Time factors in relative and absolute pitch discrimination, *Journal of the Acoustical Society of America*, 1954, *26*. Reprinted with permission.)

2.5. Timbre

Timbre is probably not a specific attribute of auditory sensation, but may represent many attributes. The advance of electronic musical instruments and computer music has increased the need to understand timbre, but the lack of basic knowledge and the absence of clear theoretical concepts have hindered progress considerably. Hardly more than a handful of studies on timbre exists. Older experiments on the perceptual distinctions among musical instruments revealed that not only spectral features but also temporal features such as attack and decay characteristics play a role in determining timbre (Clark, Luce, Abrams, Schlossberg, & Rome, 1964). These studies provided significant empirical details, but failed to develop a model or to define a formal approach to the study of timbre.

Plomp (1970) developed a spectral vector model in which the sound pressure levels in n frequency bands are interpreted as an n-dimensional vector. Triadic comparison of speech vowels, musical instrument tones, and organ tones enabled him to examine this vector space, but he was unable to determine whether a vector space with Euclidean metrics or a space with city block metrics provided the best fit.

Von Bismarck (1974) asked subjects to rate sounds that differed in spectral envelope on 30 verbal scales (e.g., bright-dull, broad-narrow). Factor analysis showed that four orthogonal factors account for 90% of the variance. These factors correspond to the verbal scales dull-sharp (44%), compact-scattered (26%), colorful-colorless (12%), and full-empty (9%). In a study of similarity judgments for timbres of computer-synthesized musical instrument tones, Grey (1977) found that a three-dimensional spatial solution was sufficient to account for perceptual relationships. One subjective dimension is related to spectral energy distribution, another to presence of high-frequency energy in the attack segment, and the third to synchronicity in high-harmonic transients.

2.6. Pathologies in Pitch Perception

Some hearing pathologies directly affect pitch perception. Tinnitus is a condition in which the patient reports that a tone or noise is continuously heard in the absence of an external stimulus. Tinnitus often follows cochlear damage caused by mechanical injury or ototoxic drugs. One possible explanation for the effect is the absence of lateral inhibition by damaged cells of intact neighboring cells that are consequently more spontaneously active. Sometimes tinnitus is accompanied by oto-acoustic emissions, in which a physical tone or narrow-band signal is actually emitted from the ear. Oto-acoustic emissions by themselves are not necessarily pathological, for they can be found in about half the population (McFadden & Wightman, 1983; Wilson & Sutton, 1983; Zurek, 1981).

Monaural diplacusis is said to exist when a monaural tone evokes a multiple pitch image. This image may be a noise sensation (atonal monaural diplacusis) or a complex tone (tonal monaural diplacusis). Ward (1955) found in two subjects exhibiting tonal monaural diplacusis that the additional pitch components resembled aural combination tones (see Section 4.4) generated by the stimulus frequency and another tone of unknown origin. Monaural diplacusis is often accompanied by transient tinnitus when the stimulus tone is turned off. Such an aftertone is referred to as an "idiotone."

Binaural diplacusis is to a small degree found in every listener, but can sometimes become pathological. The few pathological cases that have been systematically studied suggest that pathological interaural pitch shifts can be as large as an octave and are often associated with significant permanent threshold shifts (de Maré, 1948; Shambaugh, 1940). A problem in studying pathological binaural diplacusis is that it is often accompanied by monaural diplacusis, so that it is difficult to establish whether interaural pitch shifts reflect monaural or binaural diplacusis.

3. LOCALIZATION

3.1. Background

The ability to localize sound in space is fundamental to an organism's ability to cope with environmental dangers and opportunities. Humans have a fine sense of localization based primarily on differences between the sounds reaching the two ears, differences that vary with the direction and distance of the sound source relative to the listener. These interaural cues are complemented by monaural cues from the pinna and from head movements. Research on sound localization goes back to at least the end of the 18th century (cf. Gulick, 1971). By the beginning of the 20th century, investigators had identified intensity, phase, and onset time differences as the major cues for sound localization, although their relative importance and their dependence on frequency were undetermined. Earlier investigators used external sounds produced mechanically (by musical instruments, sirens, tuning forks, etc.) at some distance from the listener. The use of small tubes as wave guides to lead the sound to the listener's two ears permitted the separation of time cues from intensity cues. With the advent of electrical amplifiers, it became possible in the 1920s to produce signals sufficiently intense to use loudspeakers and earphones as the sound sources. Earphones are used (in place of tubes) to control precisely the interaural differences and to manipulate them independently of each other. However, certain complementary monaural cues are missing and the sounds are heard inside the head instead of being externalized. Despite these differences between localization of actual sound sources in space and lateralization, as it is called, through earphones, comparison of data on localization and on lateralization have led to a detailed understanding of how we localize sounds. Much of this understanding concerns localization in the horizontal plane, that is, with respect to displacement to the left and right of the listener at the level of the ears. Less is known about localization in the median plane and about front-back discrimination. Furthermore, horizontal and vertical angles define the locus of a sound in only two dimensions. Distance defines the third dimension. The ability to judge the distance of a sound source is poorly understood, despite a number of careful studies.

Although localization is also affected by noise and competing sounds, and depends strongly on temporal relations among multiple inputs, few data concerning these problems are available. On the other hand, much attention has been paid to the effect on localization of repeating a sound, which occurs when the original sound is reflected by surrounding surfaces on its way to the listener's ears; because the original or leading sound source generally determines perceived locus, the effect is called the *precedence effect* or the Haas effect (see Section 3.6). With respect to *moving* sound sources, whether in quiet or in noise, few systematic data on localization have been collected.

Besides the distinction between localization and lateralization, studies differ as to whether they measure accuracy or precision. By accuracy we mean the margin within which a listener can identify the absolute direction of an external sound source or locus of a sound image inside the head. By precision, we mean the error with which a listener judges a change in direction of a sound source or of the intracranial locus. Most studies of localization have been concerned with accuracy—with notable exceptions (e.g. Mills, 1958)—whereas most studies of lateralization have been concerned with precision, but some have measured sidedness or lateral position (e.g. Blauert, 1983, Fig. 3.20; Sayers & Cherry, 1957; Yost, 1981). Both approaches are discussed in this section.

The available experimental results concern mainly discrimination between left and right in the horizontal plane. (The horizontal plane is an imaginary surface that cuts through the head from left to right at ear level.) Data are also presented on discrimination between front and back and between up and down in the median plane. [The median (or sagittal) plane is an imaginary two-dimensional surface that splits the head from front to back.] The other sections deal with discrimination of distance, and the effects on localization of noise, reflections, movement, and auditory pathology.

3.2. Localization in the Horizontal Plane

Most studies of localization have examined the accuracy of localizing a sound in the horizontal plane, toward the left and toward the right in front of the listener. Studies of lateralization have measured the discrimination of left from right, where "left" usually means a sound that arrives earlier or at a greater intensity in the left ear than in the right, and "right" means the opposite. The primary bases for discrimination in the horizontal plane are *binaural cues.* In lateralization those are the only available cues, but in localization, *monaural cues* are available as well. We discuss first binaural cues.

3.2.1. Binaural Cues. The location of the ears on each side of the head means that a sound not coming from a source in the median plane reaches the two ears at different times and with different intensities. Given the speed of sound in air and the maximum acoustical distance between the ears, the ear closer to the sound source receives the sound as much as 700 μsec sooner than the ear farther away. Successive sound waves continue to arrive sooner to the nearer ear. Given the size of the head relative to the wavelength of most audible sounds, the sound in the farther ear may be attenuated at certain frequencies as much as 40 dB relative to the nearer ear (Blauert, 1983).

These interaural time and intensity differences provide the primary cues for sound localization, but their utility depends strongly on the spectral content of the sound. The interaural differences also depend upon the distance of the sound source from the listener. Beyond a distance of 1 m, however, the effect of distance becomes negligible (Blauert, 1974). Accordingly, we limit our discussion mainly to sources in the "far field," that is, locations more than 1 m from the head.

A complicating factor in the study of localization is that sound is reflected from most surfaces, so that a single sound source gives rise to multiple acoustic inputs at the two ears. To avoid this complication, Stevens and Newman (1936) sat their subject on a tall chair on top of a four-story building. The only reflecting surface was the roof 4 m below the listener. A loudspeaker at the end of a boom emitted tone bursts with smooth envelopes (thus avoiding audible clicks). The loudspeaker was rotated in the horizontal plane around the listener, at ear level. The listener indicated the direction of the sound to the nearest 15°. Figure 15.29 shows the mean localization error as a function of frequency. (Front-back reversals were not scored as incorrect; they occurred about one-third of the time at frequencies below 2,500 Hz.) The most important point to be drawn from this curve is that errors are greatest between about 2,000 and 4,000 Hz. Here was the first clear, quantitative evidence in support of the duality theory of localization which by the 1930s was generally accepted largely on logical grounds. According to this theory, localization below about 2,000 Hz is based mainly on interaural time differences (ITD) and above 4,000 Hz mainly on interaural intensity differences (IID). The finding that localization was poorest at the middle frequencies suggests that neither binaural cue works well in the transition region. Indeed, Stevens and Newman pointed out that interaural phase differences are unambiguous only up to about 1,500 Hz and that interaural intensity differences begin to be substantial starting at about 3,000 or 4,000 Hz.

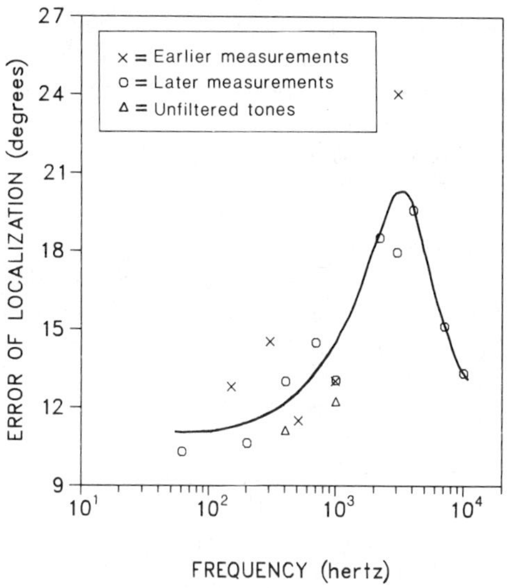

Figure 15.29. Localization in the horizontal plane. The difference in degrees between the reported and actual azimuth of a pure-tone source is plotted as a function of the tone's frequency. Clickless tones were presented from a small, 10-cm speaker located 3.6 m from the subject on the end of a boom. The subject was seated on a high chair on top of a roof so as to reduce reflections. Tones between 400 and 4,000 Hz were at 50–60 phons; lower and higher frequencies were at about 30 phons. Distant traffic noise was intense enough to raise thresholds nearly 30 dB, which suggests that the level of the noise at the experimental site was about 50 dB. The two experimenters served also as the only subjects. They judged the locus of the speaker set in steps of 15° at 13 positions to the subject's right from 0 to 180°. Differences between the named position and the actual position were averaged across all azimuths and the two subjects. Front-back confusions were not counted as errors. Crosses and circles are for earlier and later series of measurements, separated by about 1 year. Triangles are for unfiltered tones. The smooth line drawn through the data highlights the finding that localization is poorest in the middle-frequency range and better at below 2,000 and above 5,000 Hz. (Stevens & Newman, 1936.)

The errors in Figure 15.29 are rather large because they are for pure tones. Localization is better with broad-band spectra, which provide multiple cues. For example, in Figure 15.29 errors were smaller for unfiltered tones (triangles) with their broader spectra than for filtered tones; for a click (not shown) the error was 8°, for a hiss only 5.6°. To determine how localization depends on frequency, however, pure tones or narrow-band noises are required.

Other studies have used other procedures for measuring the accuracy of localization; these include pointing to the source or indicating its locus according to numerals on a clock (Teas, 1962), adjusting an air puff on the forehead (Békésy, 1960), and adjusting the locus of a broad-band noise that served as an auditory pointer (Moushegian & Jeffress, 1959). The outcomes of these various procedures are in good agreement.

Mills (1958) used a different procedure to measure the *precision* of localization. He determined the minimum audible angle (MAA), the smallest angle of displacement of a sound source needed by a listener to tell whether the source had moved to the left or to the right. The listener was seated in an anechoic room with the sound source, a small speaker, mounted on the end of a movable boom. A tone burst was presented first from one position, and then the speaker was moved either to the left or to the right according to a random schedule, and the tone was presented again. The angle at which the listener correctly reported the direction of change 75% of the time was taken as the MAA. Figure 15.30 gives the MAA as a function of frequency with azimuth as the parameter. (In the horizontal plane, azimuth is the angle between two lines, one from a given sound source to the center of a listener's head, the other from a point directly in front of the listener.) The dependence of the MAA on frequency varies with the azimuth. At 0° azimuth, the MAA is smaller than 4° at all frequencies, whereas at 75°, discrimination could not be measured between about 1,000 and 3,000 Hz or at high frequencies. At those frequencies where discrimination is nearly impossible when the azimuth is 75°, it is also generally poorest when the azimuth is 0°. Compared to the accuracy judgments of Stevens and Newman (1936), the precision judgments of Mills (1958) suggest that the region of poorest localization lies at lower frequencies, between 1,500 and 2,200 Hz. The lower values are in better agreement with the physical measures of IID as shown below.

Mills (1972, pp. 301–348) has suggested that the maximum error in accuracy judgments is at a higher frequency because of a bias in those judgments that is excluded from precision judgments; subjects underestimate the deviation from the median plane more at frequencies between 1,500 and 5,000 Hz than at other frequencies.

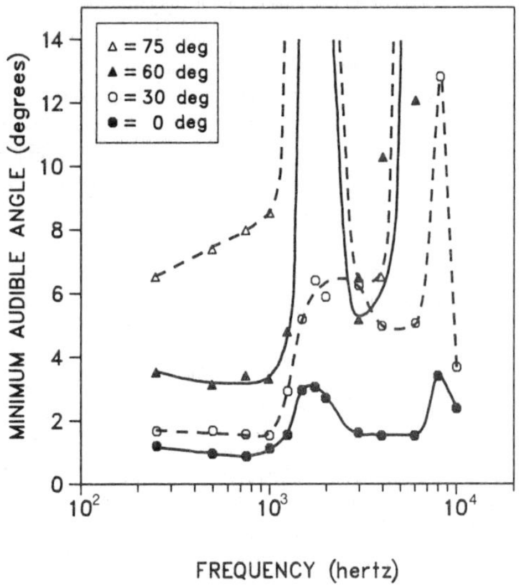

Figure 15.30. Accuracy of localization of pure tones. Minimum audible angle for pure tones is plotted as a function of frequency at four azimuths. The sound source was located 50 cm from the center of the listener's head on the end of a movable boom. On each trial a 1-sec tone burst, with a rise-fall time of 70 msec, was presented first from a reference azimuth; the sound source was then moved either to the left or right, and the tone presented again after a 1-sec interval. The subject judged whether the source had moved to the left or right. A method of constant stimuli was used to determine the change of azimuth required for correct judgments on approximately 75% of the trials. The reference azimuth of 0° was established by having the subject judge when he heard the sound as coming from the median plane. The other references, at 30, 45, 60, 75, and 90° were set relative to 0°. Tones were presented at approximately 50 dB SL. All measurements were carried out in an anechoic room. Three subjects served in the experiments. Their average data at four of the six reference azimuths studied are given in the figure. Localization is best at 0° at all frequencies. At all azimuths, localization is poorest between 1,500 and 2,200 Hz, and becomes poor again above about 5,000 Hz. (From A. W. Mills, Auditory perception of spatial relations, *Proceedings of the International Congress on Technology and Blindness*, 1963, 2. Material from *Proceedings of the International Congress on Technology and Blindness* is copyrighted by the American Foundation for the Blind, Inc., and is reproduced by kind permission of the American Foundation for the Blind, 15 West 16th Street, New York, N.Y. 10011.)

These results can be related roughly to physical measures of IID. But they are even better understood in terms of lateralization data. The next sections consider first IID and then ITD.

3.2.1.1. ***Interaural Intensity Differences.*** For pure tones coming from different directions, Figure 15.31 gives the IID in decibels as a function of azimuth in degrees for frequencies from 200 to 6,000 Hz. Three features are especially noteworthy: (1) the intensity difference is largest at azimuths between about 60 and 120°, that is, when the sound source is to one side; (2) at a given azimuth, the difference generally increases with frequency; (3) at a given frequency, the difference changes most rapidly as a function of azimuth near 0° and very slowly near 90°.

The dependence of the physical IID on frequency helps explain some of the results shown in Figure 15.30. The IID is unlikely to serve as a cue to direction until above about 2,500 Hz, where it begins to change more rapidly with azimuth. The interactive dependence of localization on both azimuth and frequency is also understandable in terms of Figure 15.31. At 0° the IID changes rapidly as a function of azimuth at frequencies above about 1,800 Hz. At 30° the IID changes more slowly than at 0°; this difference can probably account for the larger MAAs when the source moves away from the midline. At 75°, the IID changes so little with azimuth that discrimination may well be based on cues other than IID. However, the neat contours in Figure 15.31 oversimplify the relations depicted, especially at higher frequencies. Interaural differences change irregularly and sharply as a function of frequency above about 6,000 Hz (Blauert, 1983). Moreover, the difference exceeds 40 dB at particular frequencies and azimuths.

The extent to which listeners use the available IIDs as cues in localization has been demonstrated by Mills (1960) as follows. He presented 1-sec tone bursts via carefully calibrated earphones and measured the smallest intensity difference that was discernible 75% of the time as a function of the tone's frequency. The black circles in Figure 15.32 are the median just noticeable differences (JNDs) for five subjects. The same figure gives the physical IIDs that were available when the subjects were just able to detect a displacement of the loudspeaker from the median plane, that is, the MAA at 0° azimuth as measured by Mills (1958, open circles). Similar estimates of the required IID were obtained from data of Sandel, Teas, Feddersen, and Jeffress (1955). Between 1,500 and 6,000 Hz the just detectable difference in intensity between the two ears is close to the IID that was available at the ears when the loudspeaker positions differed by one MAA. This correspondence suggests that IID was the primary, possibly the sole, cue used in that frequency range. At 8,000 Hz and 10,000 Hz, the physical IID corresponding to one MAA was above the range of JNDs, suggesting that cues other than IID were used at the higher frequencies or that the IIDs were rendered erratic by irregularities of the head, and so had to be larger than those measured with earphones. Below 1,500 Hz, the available IID was much smaller than the JND, and could not have served as the localization cue. Hence at low frequencies, temporal cues take over.

3.2.1.2. ***Interaural Temporal Differences.*** For a periodic sound, two temporal cues are possible. One cue is related to the time of arrival of the sound or, more generally, to the sound's envelope. The other cue is related to phase or fine structure, which refers to cycle-by-cycle changes. The sound reaches the ear nearer the sound source before it reaches the other ear farther away. It also leads in phase in the nearer ear. When

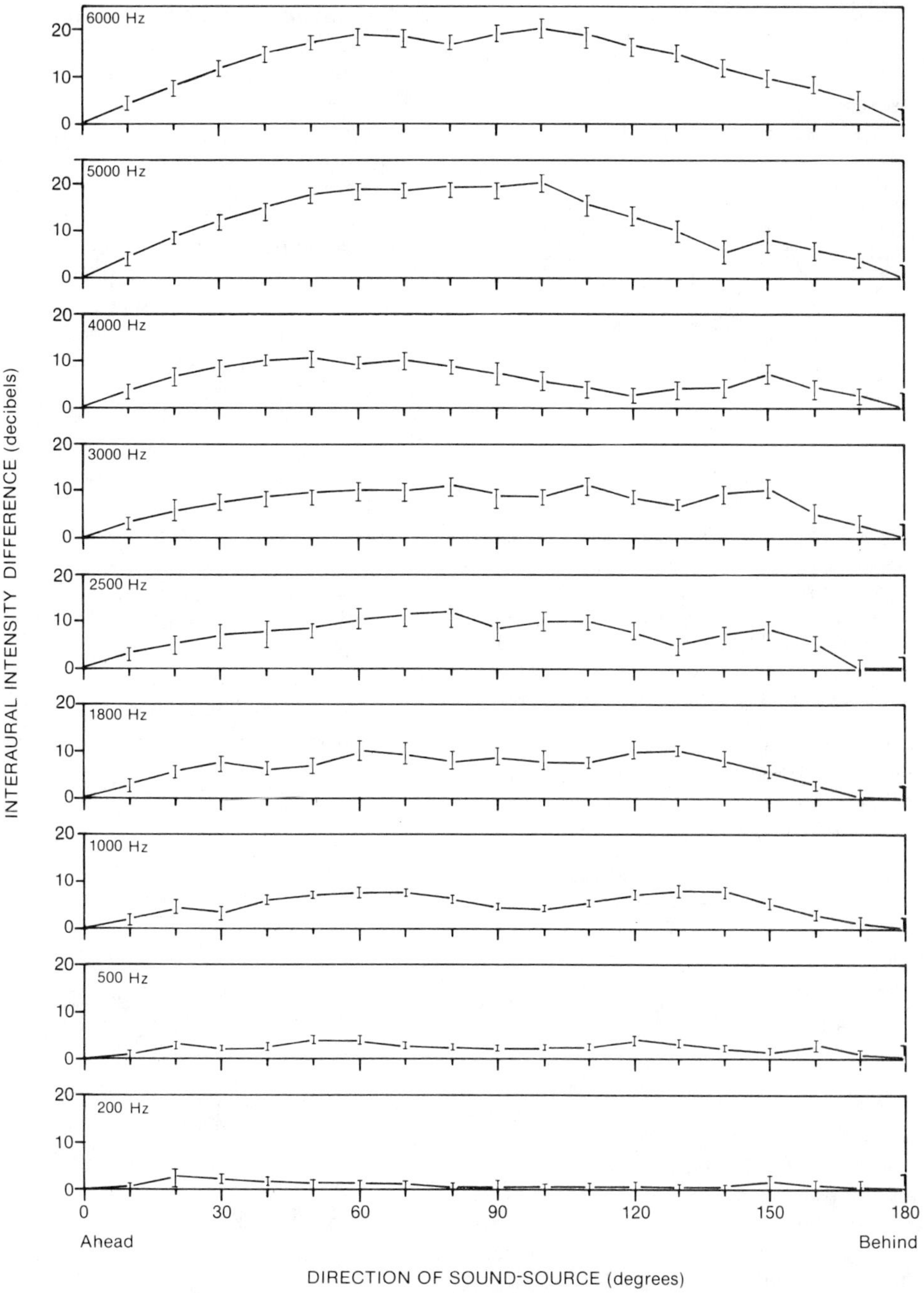

Figure 15.31. Interaural intensity differences measured as a function of sound-source azimuth at nine frequencies. Measurements were made on five persons with a probe microphone introduced a small distance into one ear. The sound source mounted on a boom 2 m long slowly rotated around the subject while the level from the microphone was continuously recorded. Similar measurements were made in the subject's other ear, and the differences between corresponding measures were averaged across the same azimuths to the left and right. Measurements were made twice in each ear to yield a total of four measures for each subject for each data point. Thus each point in the figure is the mean of 20 measurements; each vertical line is plus and minus two standard errors of the mean. Lines connecting the points show that the interaural intensity difference increases with frequency, and that it is generally maximum between 60 and 120° azimuth. (From W. E. Fedderson, T. T. Sandel, D. C. Teas, & L. A. Jeffress, Localization of high-frequency tones, *Journal of the Acoustical Society of America*, 1957, *29*. Reprinted with permission.)

the sound is a pure tone, as in the experiments of Stevens and Newman (1936) and of Mills (1958), the interaural phase difference is constant and persists as long as the tone continues. However, phase cues appear to be useful only when successive cycles of a tone are sufficiently far apart for the auditory nervous system to keep track of them separately. Experimental evidence shows that this limit lies between 1,000 and 2,000 Hz, close to 1,600 Hz. Phase cues are also limited by the effective aerial distance between the two ears. The maximum acoustical path between the two ears, for a sound source at 90° azimuth, is about 23 cm, which exceeds the half wavelength of frequencies above 750 Hz. That means that after the first cycle of the sound wave, it is unclear to the listener which ear leads in phase; the first cycle in the lagging ear begins prior to the second cycle in

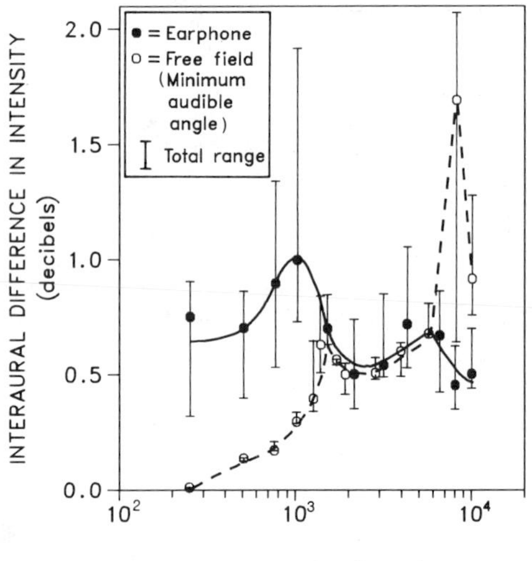

Figure 15.32. Just noticeable interaural intensity difference as determined from earphone listening (filled circles) and from listening in a free field (open circles). The filled circles are the medians for five subjects who judged whether a dichotic tone burst was to the left or right of a preceding burst. Tone bursts were 1 sec long with a rise-fall time of 20 msec. A method of constant stimuli was used to arrive at the 75% point for each subject. The dichotic tone burst was first centered for the subject by introducing a constant interaural intensity difference. Subsequently this difference was increased or decreased in a series of trials during which the subject judged to which side the tone had moved. The open circles are based on the MAA (minimum audible angle) data at 0° in Figure 15.30 and estimates of the physical intensity difference between the ears culled from measurements by Sivian and White (1933). The close fit between the earphone and free-field measurements at frequencies from 1,500 to 6,000 Hz suggests that localization at those frequencies is based on interaural intensity differences. At lower frequencies the JND is too large for the small IIDs to serve as cues; at higher frequencies the available IIDs are larger than the JND but they may be too erratic to serve as reliable cues. (Adapted from A. W. Mills, Lateralization of high-frequency tones, *Journal of the Acoustical Society of America*, 1960, *32*. Reprinted with permission.)

the leading ear, which it precedes by less than half a period. When the sound source moves toward the midline, that is, 0° azimuth, the binaural time difference decreases so that this ambiguity begins at a higher frequency. For a sound source directly in front of the listener at 0° azimuth, and for displacements smaller than about 3°, the problem of ambiguous phase cues does not present itself within the audible frequency range. But the successive cycles are so close in time at higher frequencies that the auditory system cannot keep track of them and so cannot use the available phase cues to discriminate direction.

Cues based on time of arrival do not suffer from this ambiguity. Figure 15.33 plots the interaural time delay as a function of azimuth, θ. The solid curves come from measurements in an anechoic environment with pure tones and clicks (Shaw, 1974a). The lower dashed curve is from the formula $t = (r/s)(\theta + \sin \theta)$, and the upper curve from the formula $t = (r/s)(3 \sin \theta)$, where $r = 0.0875$ m, head radius, and $s = 344 \text{ m}\cdot\text{sec}^{-1}$, speed of sound in air. In this model the head is treated as a hard sphere with the ears replaced by two holes on opposite ends of the diameter. (A better approximation would put the holes 10° in back of the diameter.) The same curve adequately represents all frequencies at 2,000 Hz and above as well as clicks. The time delay increases at lower frequencies, as shown.

To explain most of the results of Mills's measurements shown in Figure 15.30, interaural phase and intensity cues must suffice; rise times of his stimuli were too slow for interaural differences in onset time to play a significant role. First we consider the data at 0° azimuth (filled circles). Up to about 1,500 Hz, discrimination is based on phase differences. Above 800 Hz this cue begins to become less effective because of the brief time between successive cycles of the sound wave. (It is sometimes stated that discrimination becomes poorer above 800 Hz because of phase ambiguity, but that ambiguity at 800 Hz is true only near 90° azimuth; as noted above, it begins at higher and higher frequencies as the sound moves toward the center.) The difficulty arises for the auditory nervous system because it simply cannot follow such rapid changes. Discrimination then depends on IID. Thus the duality theory serves the data based on these precision measurements as well as those based on accuracy measurements from S. S. Stevens and Newman (1936).

Just as Figure 15.32 shows the relation between the MAA and the JND for IID, so Figure 15.34 shows the relation between the MAA and the JND for ITD. The solid curve is based on measurements by Zwislocki and Feldman (1956) of the JND for interaural phase difference at 50 dB above detection threshold. Beyond 1,300 Hz the five subjects could not discriminate phase differences. The dashed curve shows the phase difference between the ears when the sound source moves one MAA away

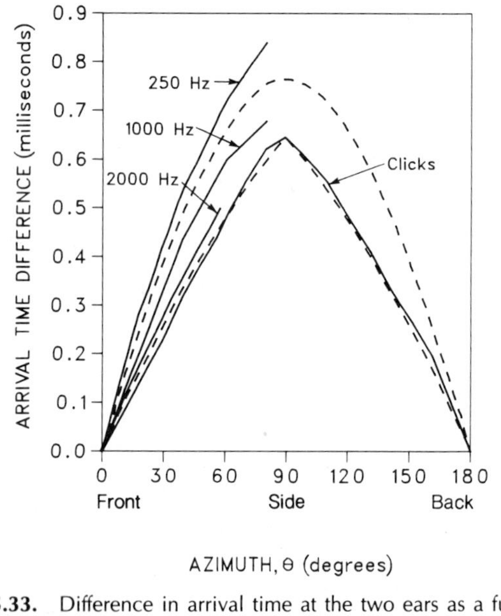

Figure 15.33. Difference in arrival time at the two ears as a function of azimuth. Parameter on the curves is the frequency of the tonal signal, except for the curve marked "clicks." Dashed curves are derived from a formula that assumes a hard sphere with two holes for the head without diffraction (lower dashed curve) and with diffraction (upper dashed curve). Measurements were made on the heads of a number of subjects in various experiments. For example, the click data are from Feddersen, Sandel, Teas, and Jeffress (1957), who placed a probe microphone in each ear of a subject and measured the time difference between the arrival of the click in each ear. The tonal data are based on several studies summarized by Shaw (1974a). Although measured time differences decrease somewhat with decreasing frequency below 2,000 Hz, they are reasonably close to the theoretical curves and have their maximum at 90° as expected. (From N. I Durlach & H. S. Colburn, Binaural phenomena, in E. C. Carterette & M. P. Friedman (Eds.), *Handbook of perception Vol. 4: Hearing*, Academic Press, Inc., 1978. Reprinted with permission.)

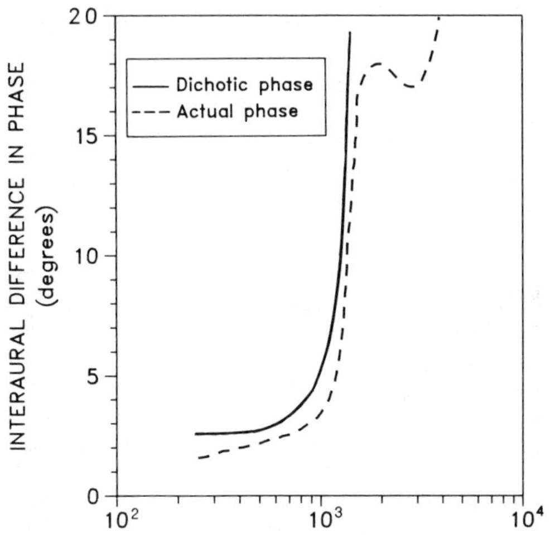

Figure 15.34. Interaural temporal discrimination for pure tones. Just noticeable interaural difference in phase is plotted as a function of frequency. The dark line is based on dichotic earphone listening (see Sec. 4.2.1.2) and shows the difference in phase of a dichotic pure tone that listeners could just detect. The dashed line gives the phase change that takes place when a sound source is moved out of the median plane (0°) by one MAA. The MAA values used in the calculation are those shown at 0° in Figure 15.30. Up to about 1,300 Hz, the two curves lie close together, suggesting that phase differences determine the MAA at low frequencies. (Adapted from A. W. Mills, Lateralization of high-frequency tones, *Journal of the Acoustical Society of America*, 1960, *32*. Reprinted with permission.)

from 0° azimuth. Up to 1,300 Hz the curves lie close together, which means that phase serves as the cue for localization at low frequencies. Above 1,300 Hz, the actual phase differences, although very large, are not discriminable and so are useless. But that is where the intensity cue becomes useful, as Figure 15.32 shows. Because the transition from intensity to phase is not perfect, the MAA is higher between 1,300 and 2,000 Hz than elsewhere (see Fig. 15.30).

Because the dichotic phase difference in earphone listening is wholly unaffected by the acoustic distance between the ears, we can safely conclude that the inability to discriminate interaural phase differences at frequencies above 1,500 Hz is due to failure of the nervous system, most likely due to its inability to follow successive cycles in the *same ear*, where a separation of less than 0.7 msec (700 μsec) between successive periods of a 1,500-Hz tone is too short. This monotic failure contrasts with the dichotic ability to detect interaural time differences under 10 μsec. For the binaural system to detect such small differences, the successive periods in each ear must give rise to distinct neural events, but that becomes impossible when periods are less than about 700 μsec.

3.2.1.3. Envelope Delay (Transient Disparity). In the experiments described above, onset time differences were not considered because either they were greatly attenuated by slow rise times or they were wholly absent as in the dichotic phase measurements under earphone listening. (In the dichotic measurements, tones started and ended simultaneously in the two ears.) Natural sounds usually have more abrupt onsets, and may have additional abrupt changes later on in their envelopes; such onset and ongoing envelope delays may give rise to interaural time differences that serve as cues in localization. To separate envelope delay (also called transient disparity) from interaural intensity differences, it is necessary to present the sounds via earphones; to distinguish them from ongoing differences in the fine structure, it is necessary to use very brief stimuli such as clicks (e.g., Hall, 1964), to pit ongoing fine-structure differences against onset differences (Tobias & Schubert, 1959), or to use sounds with different frequency content at the two ears (Scharf, Florentine, & Meiselman, 1976). Dichotic earphone measurements have shown that listeners can detect onset time differences of 100–200 μsec for tone bursts at frequencies above 1,500 Hz where fine-structure cues are not usable (Scharf et al., 1976).

A click lasts no longer than about 1 msec, often much less, and its energy is spread over a wide range of frequencies. Thus there is no ongoing information, only the transient temporal disparities at onset and offset (given earphone presentation with equal intensity at the two ears). The auditory image is usually clearly defined within the head. Figure 15.35 shows how the image moves from the left ear to the right ear through the middle of the head as the ITD goes from −1,000 μsec (left ear leading) (see Section 4.4 of Sherrick and Cholewiak, Chapter 12) through 0 μsec (no time difference) to +1,000 μsec (right ear leading). The relation is clear and monotonic. With respect to the just noticeable time difference for clicks, Hall (1964) measured values between 20 and 50 μsec at 80 phons and Klumpp and Eady (1956) 28 μsec at 60–80 dB SPL. Yost, Wightman, and Green (1971) passed clicks through a high-pass

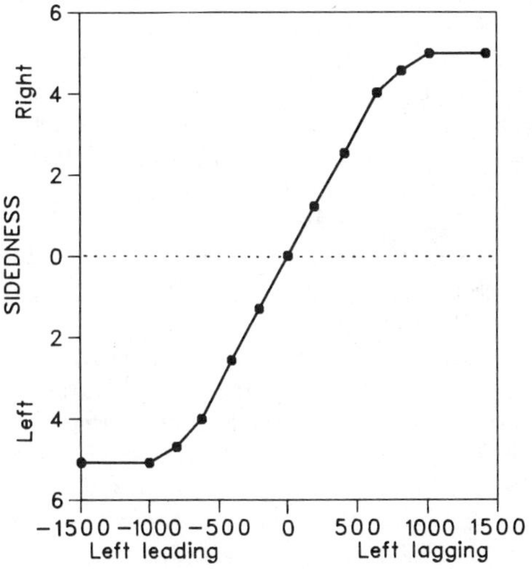

Figure 15.35. Lateralized position of a dichotic click. Judged sidedness is plotted as a function of the interaural onset time difference in microseconds. The stimulus was a 100-μsec click repeated every 6 msec until the listener reported the position of the image according to a visual scale on which, for example, 5 meant the image was at the ear (left or right depending on direction) and 0 meant it was in the middle of the head. Clicks were in phase and at equal intensity in the two ears. Their sensation level was between 40 and 50 dB. The data shown are, apparently, the averages of at least ten judgments per point by a single subject who judged the "dominant impulsive image." Similar data were reported for three to five other subjects. The average judgments follow a linear course for delays between about −630 and +630 μsec. At longer delays the image is located at the ear. Similar results were found for noise and speech (data from Toole & Sayers, 1965, Figure 1, as plotted by Blauert, 1974). (From J. Blauert, *Spatial hearing, The psychophysics of human sound localization*, MIT Press, 1983. Reprinted with permission.)

filter and found that against a low-level background noise the JND remained constant at 50 μsec for cutoff frequencies lower than 800 Hz, above which it began to increase, reaching about 150 μsec when the cutoff frequency was 5,000 Hz. Hafter and de Maio (1975) also measured smaller JNDs for low-frequency than for high-frequency clicks.

The JND for clicks lies within the range measured for interaural phase discrimination for pure tones, as shown in Figure 15.34. Translated into ITD, these phase differences correspond to time differences of 10–30 μsec depending on frequency. Zwislocki and Feldman (1956) measured the JND in dichotic phase for 1-sec tone bursts with rise-fall times of 50 msec. Frequency of the burst was 250, 500, 1,000, or 1,250 Hz. The first tone burst was set to appear centered in the median plane, and the phase of the second burst was varied randomly so that on half the trials the left ear led in phase. Measured in degrees, the means for three to six subjects were converted to ITDs from the formula $\Delta T = \Delta\varphi/360f$, where $\Delta\varphi$ is the JND in degrees, f is the frequency, and ΔT is the ITD. At each of six levels tested, the JND was smallest at 1,000 Hz; at 65 dB SPL it was down to 11 μsec. The order of variability is indicated by standard deviations at 500 Hz, which were 50–75% of the mean value at most levels.

As noted, time differences are not limited to the initial or first wave front, if we consider changes in the *envelope* of the sound instead of in its *fine structure*. The envelope connects all the peaks on both sides of a wave form. (Fig. 14.5 in Scharf & Buus, Chapter 14, gives examples of several wave forms.) The fine structure refers to changes in instantaneous value within the envelope. When the sound is a pure tone, the envelope is flat, and usable interaural differences must be in the initial onset time, in ongoing phase, or in ongoing amplitude. Natural sounds usually have envelope variations that can provide temporal information as well. In the laboratory, Henning (1974) and others (Young & Carhart, 1974) have shown that an amplitude-modulated high-frequency tone can be lateralized just as well—with the same minimum interaural time difference—as a tone with the same frequency as the modulation rate.

Henning (1974) measured the smallest interaural time delay required to lateralize a high-frequency tone burst toward the leading ear, as well as a low-frequency tone burst, and a modulated high-frequency tone burst. Signals were presented at 50 dB SPL for 250 msec with rise-fall times of 50 msec. On each trial, the sounds were presented twice, once with the left ear leading and once with the right ear leading. A psychometric curve was based on 200 trials at each of a number of interaural delays. When the signal was a high-frequency (3,600 Hz) tone burst, none of three subjects was able to lateralize correctly on more than about 50% of the trials, even with delays as long as 180 μsec. As Figure 15.36 shows, when the signal was a 300-Hz tone burst (crosses), one subject could lateralize correctly on 75% of the trials with ΔT set close to 50 μsec. A second subject needed about 70 μsec. Results were similar when a 3,900-Hz tone was sinusoidally amplitude modulated at a rate of 300 Hz (triangles). It did not matter whether only the envelope was delayed (open triangles) or the whole wave form, that is, both envelope and fine structure, was delayed (filled triangles). Delaying the whole wave form means that there is phase information available within the fine structure of the signal as well as in the envelope. But the auditory system cannot use such information in the fine structure above about 1,600 Hz, so delaying only the envelope or both envelope and fine structure is equivalent for the listener.

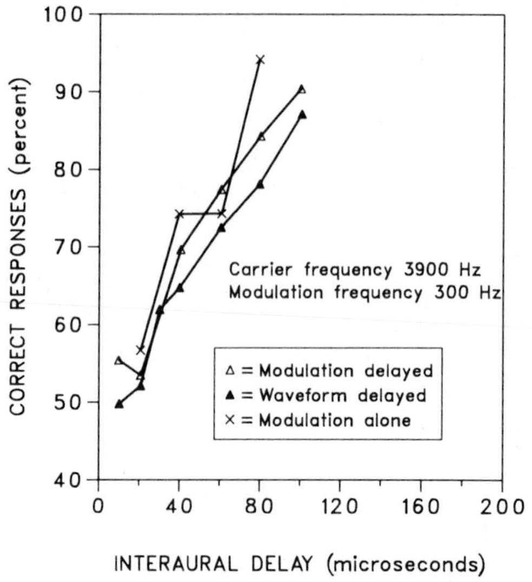

Figure 15.36. Accuracy of lateralizing a modulated tone. Percentage of correct judgments of the image toward the leading ear is plotted as a function of the interaural delay in microseconds. Procedure was two-interval forced choice in which the interaural delay was to one ear in the first interval and to the other ear in the second interval. The subject reported which interval contained the sound that was more to the left. Each point is based on 200 judgments by a single subject, who was also the experimenter. A second subject gave similar functions. Lateralization accuracy was essentially the same under three different conditions: when only a 300-Hz tone burst was presented (crosses), when a 3,900-Hz burst sinusoidally modulated by 300 Hz was presented and the whole wave form delayed (that is, both modulation frequency and carrier frequency were delayed), and when the same modulated 3,900-Hz burst was presented but only the modulation frequency was delayed and not the carrier frequency. Signals were 250 msec in duration with a rise-fall time of 50 msec and were set at 50 dB SPL. The data suggest that with a high carrier frequency, delaying only the low-frequency modulation suffices as a cue to lateralization with no help from the interaural time delay of the carrier frequency. (From G. B. Henning, Detectability of interaural delay in high-frequency complex waveforms, *Journal of the Acoustical Society of America*, 1974, *55*. Reprinted with permission.)

Presenting the modulated tone burst against a low-pass noise (600-Hz cutoff) did not degrade performance even though the masking noise presumably rendered low-frequency auditory channels incapable of transmitting information. Thus ongoing interaural time differences can be used by the auditory system even when they occur in high-frequency channels, provided they are based on monaural temporal events that are not too rapid. At 300 Hz, the envelope of the modulated high-frequency tone changes slowly enough that the nervous system can keep track of the changes and small interaural differences become usable. Henning also tested performance with a number of other modulation frequencies, and found that lateralization was best between 50 and 300 Hz. At 600 Hz subjects could not lateralize much above chance even with interaural delays of 500 μsec. For two of the three subjects, performance was best when the carrier frequency was 3,900 Hz, and became poorer at lower and higher frequencies. Results for the individual subjects were similar under most conditions, except that one of the three could lateralize on the basis of much smaller interaural delays than the other two.

3.2.1.4. Effect of Rise-Fall Time. The duration of the onset and offset disparities between the two ears depends on how fast the sound comes on and goes off, and is generally referred to as the rise-fall time. In lateralization, the role of rise time has received much attention; offset or fall time is relatively unimportant. In localization, only one paper appears to have investigated systematically the role of rise time. Perrott (1969) measured the minimum audible angle for 2-sec tone bursts with frequencies of 500, 2,000, and 5,000 Hz. At 500 and 5,000 Hz the MAA remained the same for his four subjects as the rise time was varied from 1 to 500 msec. At 2,000 Hz, the MAA increased with rise time. Perrott interpreted these results as showing that listeners do not use onset time cues in localization. However, an alternative explanation is that listeners do not need the onset disparity when other interaural differences are available. At 500 Hz ongoing fine-structure differences (phase) are available and at 5,000 Hz intensity differences are large. At 2,000 Hz the interaural time delay in the fine structure is too short to be used by the auditory system, and the intensity differences are small. Accordingly, the onset time difference is important, but with increasing rise time, it becomes less useful and the MAA increases.

Results from lateralization measurements lead to a similar interpretation. For example, Hafter, Dye, and Gilkey (1979) tested the importance of onset and offset disparities by presenting the signal against a masking noise that was turned off after signal onset and turned on again before signal offset. They measured lateralization of a 500-Hz tone burst with a constant rise-fall time of 10 msec. For three of four subjects, the interaural time difference required for lateralization was the same whether the onset and offset transients were masked or not, provided the signal duration exceeded 100–200 msec. Thus if the signal is long enough so that sufficient information is available, onset and offset cues are unimportant, and rise-fall time irrelevant. A direct test of changes in rise-fall time was made by Kunov and Abel (1981) who varied both the rise-fall time and phase of a 1,000-Hz tone whose duration was about 200 msec. Rise and fall were linear. As long as the phase delay was less than 180° the lateralization JND did not depend on the rise-fall time, which varied from 5 to 500 msec. But when the phase was greater than 180° so that it became an ambiguous cue, lateralization varied with onset time difference as long as rise time did not exceed 50–100 msec. For one of the two subjects, the envelope completely determined the lateralization when rise time was 5 msec, and for the other when rise time was 0 msec. These results suggest that for brief signals, rise times faster than about 100 msec do provide usable cues, and these cues become determinant when rise time is very rapid. Scharf and Florentine (1975) found for a group of six listeners that the lateralization JND declined from nearly 90 μsec with a rise time of 10 msec, to 50 μsec with a rise time of 1 msec. Their signals were 30-msec, 2,000-Hz tone bursts with exponential rises. These results at 2,000 Hz together with others at 4,000 and 6,000 Hz (Scharf et al., 1976) show unequivocally that high-frequency tone bursts can be lateralized on the basis of onset-time differences, albeit not as well as low-frequency bursts. In one other study that varied rise-fall time, Elfner and Tomsic (1968) measured interaural time differences needed to lateralize 600- and 6,000-Hz tone bursts at 20 dB SL. Owing in part to the low level the JNDs were very large, from 2 to 40 msec; the rise times varied from 10 to 250 msec. Subjects apparently used interaural intensity cues during the slow onset of the tone.

3.2.1.5. Effect of Duration. Studies of the effect of rise time have already made apparent the importance of signal duration in lateralization. The longer the signal lasts, the less important is the information at the onset, and the more that ongoing time and intensity disparities between the two ears contribute to lateralization. A number of studies have shown that the lateralization threshold decreases as duration increases (Hafter & Dye, 1983; Houtgast & Plomp, 1968; McFadden & Moffitt, 1977; Nuetzel & Hafter, 1976; Ricard & Hafter, 1973; Tobias & Zerlin, 1959). Although lateralization threshold does decrease with signal duration, it decreases less rapidly than would be predicted if the listeners had made optimal use of the available information in the signal. Figure 15.37 presents data from three studies, all of which show slopes less than −0.5, the slope that would be expected if variability were being reduced maximally, that is, as the square root of duration. Hafter, Dye, and Wenzel (1983) have shown that lateralization based on interaural intensity differences depends in a similar fashion on duration. It appears that onset does have a special place in lateralization and localization, and that later-arriving parts of the signal provide relatively less information (see precedence effect below). Nevertheless, if the onset information is missing (as by masking) or is degraded (long onsets) then the ongoing information can become determinant. Thus temporal integration applies to localization just as it does to detection and loudness. The results in Figure 15.37 suggest that integration occurs over durations at least as long as 500 msec.

Among these studies, those by Hafter and Dye (1983) and by Hafter et al. (1983) involved not a continuous stimulus but

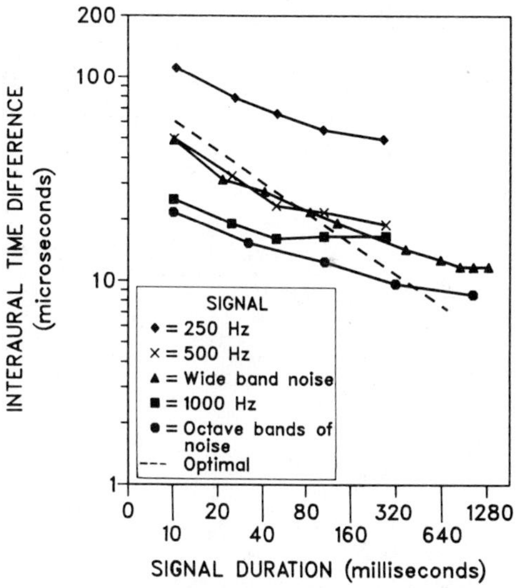

Figure 15.37. Dependence of lateralization on signal duration. The interaural time difference required to lateralize a signal toward the leading ear is plotted as a function of the signal duration. Results are from three studies that used different sounds. Data for pure tones at 50 dB SPL at three frequencies are from Ricard and Hafter (1973). Data for octave bands of noise centered on 500 Hz and set to a level equivalent to 50 dB SL at long durations are from Houtgast and Plomp (1968), who ran two subjects. Data for wide-band noise, which was 5,000-Hz low-pass filtered white noise at 68 dB SPL, are from Tobias and Zerlin (1959), who ran five subjects. Data are based on two-interval, forced-choice judgments which required the listener to judge the position of the second of a pair of signals relative to the first. Although the interaural time difference decreases with increasing duration for all the sounds represented, the decrease is less than optimal. The dashed line is the decrease expected if the auditory system used the information throughout the stimulus interval in optimal fashion. One interpretation of these findings is that listeners use onset cues—when available—as well as ongoing cues in lateralization. (From E. R. Hafter, R. H. Dye, & R. H. Gilkey, Lateralization of tonal signals which have neither onsets nor offsets, *Journal of the Acoustical Society of America*, 1979, *65*. Reprinted with permission.)

a succession of 4,000-Hz pulses. Duration was varied by changing the number of pulses and the interpulse interval. With an interval of 10 msec, the interaural time JND decreased in direct proportion to the square root of the number of pulses. With shorter intervals, the decrease was shallower. The auditory system appears to accumulate information over repetitions of high-frequency pulses, and this accumulation can continue for over 1 sec (Yost et al., 1971). In contrast, no accumulation takes place at low frequencies where a single pulse suffices to yield the minimum time JND. Yost et al. (1971) measured a JND of about 20 μsec for a low-pass pulse and nearly 200 μsec for a high-pass pulse; the high-pass pulse had to be repeated 64 times before the JND came close to 20 μsec. It does not seem that temporal integration differs at low and high frequencies, but that onset time differences are much more effective at low frequencies where a single sample suffices; at high frequencies many samples are needed.

3.2.1.6. Effect of Level. The dependence of localization and lateralization on signal level has received scant attention, probably because the dependence appears to be rather weak. No one seems to have measured localization systematically as a function of stimulus level, and only a few investigators have measured lateralization as a function of level. The results of four studies are presented in Table 15.3. (Note that levels are given as the number of decibels above detection threshold; this measure is called sensation level or SL.) One study (Rowland & Tobias, 1967) measured only ΔI as a function of level, another (Zwislocki & Feldman, 1956) only ΔT, and two others (Hall, 1964; Hershkowitz & Durlach, 1969) both ΔI and ΔT. All the investigators used tone bursts as the stimuli, except Hall, who used a broad-band click. The results of these four studies make evident that these lateralization JNDs, like monaural intensity and frequency JNDs (see Section 4 of Scharf & Buus, Chapter 14), do not become much larger at low levels. Intensity JNDs continue to decrease slowly as level increases up to 60 dB SL, according to the data of Hershkowitz and Durlach. Apparently, only one study (Scharf & Meiselman, 1977) measured the lateralization JND based solely on onset disparity as a function of signal level. They measured the onset time difference required to lateralize a 2,000-Hz tone burst at levels from 25 to 110 dB SPL. The mean threshold decreased markedly with increasing level, from 4,000 μsec at 25 dB to about 125 μsec at 80 dB. Similar results were found at 4,000 and 6,000 Hz. Because in this study the rise time was always 10 msec, and the envelope exponential in shape, we cannot be sure that the effect of level will not be different with other rise times or other envelope shapes.

Table 15.3. Discrimination of Interaural Time and Intensity Differences

ΔI (dB)

SL (dB)	Frequency (Hz) 250[1]	500[2]	2000[1]	6000[1]	BBN[3]
5	—	—	—	—	2.2
10	—	1.9	—	—	—
20	1.5	1.5	1.0	1.1	1.5
30	.9	—	.8	.9	—
50	.6	1.0	.5	.6	1.6
70	—	.8	—	—	2.8

ΔT (μsec)

SL (dB)	Frequency (Hz) 250[4]	500[4]	500[2]	1000[4]	1250[4]	BBN[3]
10	44	49	60	37	—	53
30	26	26	15	20	38	29
50	28	14	11	16	26	—
70	22	18	11	11	17	37
90	28	14	—	12	20	—
110	—	22	—	15	26	—

The JND for intensity (ΔI) and the JND for time (ΔT) are listed for tones of different frequencies and broad-band noise (BBN) at sensation levels from 5 to 110 dB. Data are from four studies, indicated by the superscripts. Study 1 is Rowland and Tobias (1967); study 2 is Hershkowitz and Durlach (1969); study 3 is Hall (1964); study 4 is Zwislocki and Feldman (1956). Each study measured the minimum time or intensity difference required to discriminate a sound leading or stronger in one ear from the same sound leading or stronger in the other ear.

On the whole, scant as they are, these data suggest that once a sound is audible, it can be localized reasonably well and improves only marginally as level increases. Data on localization in noise support this conclusion. (This rule may not apply to low-frequency clicks, which must be localized primarily on the basis of onset time disparity and so may be difficult to localize at low levels.)

3.2.1.7. Time versus Intensity (Trading Relation). In localization, interaural intensity and time differences are perfectly correlated; the ear receiving the more intense sound also receives it first. In lateralization, time and intensity cues can be manipulated independently of one another. By pitting one cue against the other, many experiments have sought to determine their relative importance. The typical approach has been to determine the combinations of ΔI and ΔT that yield an auditory image in the middle of the head. Figure 15.38 shows how the trading relation for a broad-band click depends on signal level. The ordinate gives the interaural time difference required to overcome the intensity difference shown on the abscissa in order to center the image. The relative importance of ΔT increases with sensation level; at 10 dB SL a ΔT of about 0.5 msec compensates a 1-dB interaural difference, whereas at 70 dB less than 0.1 msec overcomes 1 dB. These results are for a single subject.

Although a number of measurements have been made using the trading paradigm, the results must be viewed with great caution because such artificial stimuli generally give rise to multiple images or to a spatially broad image. The outcome inevitably depends on which of the available images the listener bases the judgment.

Rotuolo, Stern, and Colburn (1979) sought to overcome the criterion problem by having subjects distinguish a 500-Hz tone burst that had ΔT and ΔI opposed in one direction ($+\Delta T$ and $-\Delta I$) from a 500-Hz burst with ΔT and ΔI opposed in the opposite way ($-\Delta T$ and $+\Delta I$). With a constant ΔT of 15 μsec, three listeners could not distinguish between the two stimuli more than by chance when ΔI was 0.6 dB. For smaller and larger values of ΔI discrimination improved. One could conclude that a ΔT of 15 μsec is equivalent to a ΔI of 0.6 dB except that for two other listeners no value of ΔI reduced their discrimination to chance levels. These two experienced subjects reported that they heard more than one auditory image and that they could base their judgment on one of them and ignore the other. Thus training and the ability to use subtle cues become very important in such measurements.

Although trading functions might have been expected to yield useful information about the relative importance of time and intensity cues in lateralization and localization, in practice

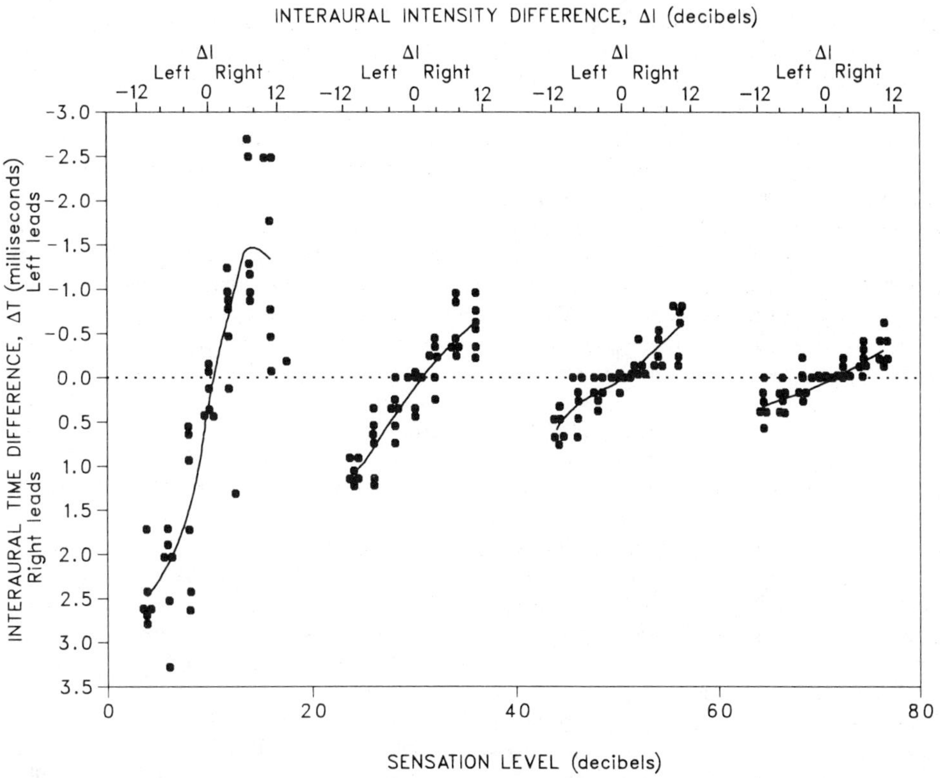

Figure 15.38. Trading of interaural intensity (ΔI) and time differences (ΔT) to center an auditory image. The ΔT required to center a stimulus is plotted as a function of the ΔI. The parameter on the curves, which is given on the long abscissa, is the sensation level. Signals were a 100-μsec noise pulse, which was sent through a high-pass filter (cutoff at 2,000 Hz) and presented with correlated phase at the two ears and a noise click, which was uncorrelated at the two ears. Both stimuli were presented at a rate of 20 pulses per second. The signal was presented with an ΔI of between −12 and +12 dB, symmetrically distributed between the two ears. The listener adjusted the ΔT until she heard the sound image in the center of her head. Data are for one of six teen-age female subjects. Each point is the mean of two trials. Three points are for the uncorrelated click and three for the noise pulse; the two signals gave comparable results. Results indicate that with increasing intensity, a smaller interaural time delay is required to offset a given interaural intensity difference to center a click or noise pulse. (From E. E. David, N. Guttman, & W. A. von Bergeijk, Binaural interaction of high-frequency complex stimuli, *Journal of the Acoustical Society of America*, 1959, *31*. Reprinted with permission.)

they are beset with many problems that render the data uncertain. We agree with Blauert (1983) that "results of trading experiments must be regarded with great skepticism."

3.2.1.8. Head Movements. Head movements serve to enhance binaural cues as well as to provide monaural cues. Rotating the head in the horizontal plane gives rise to a rate of change of the ITD that specifies the azimuth of a stationary sound source. Such movement can also specify the elevation of the source. Wallach (1939, 1940) showed that listeners make use of these cues in the judgment of both the azimuth and elevation of a stationary sound source.

Attention must be paid to the possible role of head movements in measurements of localization. However, for head movements to be effective, the sound's duration must exceed 250–300 msec (Blauert, 1974, p. 79). At shorter durations the cues change too little to be perceptible. Even with sounds lasting 1 sec, subjects can keep their heads sufficiently still when so instructed. Blauert (1969, 1974, pp. 79–80) found a mean amplitude of movement of 0.22° for ten subjects with nearly 90% of the amplitudes under 0.4°. The probability of movements greater than 1° was less than 5%. Because the MAA is at best 1°, measurements of localization can be carried out without special precautions to fixate the head other than instructions and the use of signals shorter than 1 sec.

3.2.1.9. Pinna Differences. Searle, Braida, Cuddy, and Davis (1975) have shown that differences between the left and right pinnae are large enough in a given individual to give rise to usable spectral differences that depend on the elevation angle of the sound source. Differences also depend on the azimuth in the horizontal plane. However, these subtle spectral differences may well be swamped by the more powerful IIDs and ITDs so that interaural pinna differences seem unlikely to play a significant role in localization in the horizontal plane. Some authors have argued that monaural pinna cues play an important role in localization; this point is discussed in the next section.

3.2.2. Monaural Cues. Although interaural differences provide the major cues to the localization of sounds in the horizontal plane, monaural cues are also available and are particularly useful to persons with unilateral deafness (e.g., Gatehouse, 1976) and to normally hearing listeners for resolving front-back ambiguities (see Section 3.3.1). The pinnae, head shadow, and head movements are the primary sources of monaural cues.

3.2.2.1. ***Pinna Effects and Head Shadow.*** Together with the effect of head shadow and shoulder bounce, the folds of the pinna and the ear canal modify the spectrum of a sound as it travels to the eardrum. These modifications depend on the sound's frequency content and azimuth. Of special relevance is the anatomy of the pinna, which is shown in Figure 15.39. Averaged and smoothed over many subjects, the curves in Figure 15.40 show how the sound pressure differs between the free field and eardrum as a function of frequency. Parameter on the curves is the azimuth of the sound source. The effect of azimuth is especially large at frequencies above 2,000 Hz. Thus the timbre of a complex sound changes as its locus changes. Presumably a person with only one good ear can make use of these cues, although no direct test has been made of this assumption. Studying normal listeners, Batteau and Plante (1962) found that azimuth errors increased from ±4° to around ±30° when one ear was occluded, even though head movements were permitted. On the other hand, listeners were able to judge fairly accurately the azimuth of sounds heard via earphones when the sounds had been picked up and recorded via microphones placed into casts of actual pinnae (Batteau, 1967). In addition, although presented via earphones, the sounds were externalized, heard as coming from outside the head. Thus the pinnae provide usable cues to azimuth and play a major role in the externalization of sound. It remains unclear how much they contribute to localization under normal binaural listening. In monaural listening with the pinna occluded, localization is reduced to a restricted region in the horizontal plane (Butler, 1975). Within that region, apparent locus depends more on the high-frequency content of the signal than on its azimuth (Musicant, 1983).

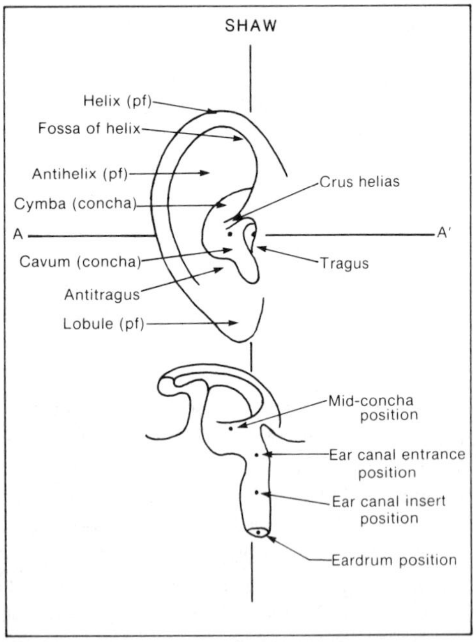

Figure 15.39. Schematic diagram of the external ear and horizontal cross section from A to A′. The ear canal opens into a wide shallow cavity called the concha, which is partially divided into the cavum and the cymba by the crus helias. Structures surrounding the concha are grouped under the name of pinna flange or pinna extension. Dots in the cross section of the ear canal indicate various loci where insert microphones are placed for sound measurements. (From A. E. G. Shaw, The external ear, in W. D. Keidel & W. D. Neff (Eds.), *Handbook of sensory physiology, Vol. 5/1*, Springer-Verlag, Inc., 1974. Reprinted with permission.)

3.2.2.2. ***Head Movements.*** Movement of the head or of the sound source may render monaural cues as effective as binaural cues. For three subjects who listened with one ear plugged, muffed, and masked by noise, the monaural MAA was as small for white noise coming from a moving source as the binaural MAA (Harris & Sargeant, 1971). For tonal signals the monaural MAA was twice as large as the binaural. From Figure 15.40 we surmise that the predominant cue must be loudness changes, for a displacement of 15° results in a 2- to 3-dB change in level at the eardrum at nearly all audible frequencies. For a sound coming from the side, spectral changes that cause changes in timbre can also play a role because at frequencies below 2,000 Hz the level is independent of azimuth, whereas at higher frequencies the level changes noticeably with frequency.

3.3. Localization in the Median Plane

Although most previous research has concentrated on discrimination in the horizontal plane in front of the listener, that is, to the left and right, more and more attention is being given to discrimination in the median plane. Such research tells us much about the mechanism of localization as well as being germane to discrimination of the elevation of a sound source and of front from back. Given the placement of the ears, interaural time and intensity differences are absent (except for those caused by head asymmetry and by differences between the left and right pinnae) when a sound source is located directly in front or in back of the listener. A change in the height of the sound source leaves these interaural differences equal to zero, except for asymmetries in the head and pinnae. Outside the median plane, discrimination of elevation and of front from back is complicated by the so-called cones of confusion. The basis for the cone of confusion can be understood by first considering a sound source that moves along a hyperbola at the level of the two ears as in part (a) of Figure 15.41. The difference between the time of arrival at the left ear and at the right ear remains constant all along the hyperbola so that ITD cannot distinguish back from front (nor the distance of the sound source). If now the hyperbola is rotated, the surface of the resulting cone [part (b) of Fig. 15.41] defines a family of points all of which give rise to the same ITDs. Thus up-down as well as front-back discrimination cannot be based reliably on ITD. However, the pinnae and head impose changes in the spectrum that differ for sounds coming from the front and back. Elevation of the sound also results in spectral changes. We discuss first front-back discrimination.

3.3.1. Front-Back Discrimination. Despite the lack of interaural differences in the median plane, we are able to distinguish front from back for most sound sources, either by moving the head or through familiarity with the sound. Moving the head puts the sound source outside the median plane, and interaural differences become available. Familiar sounds can be distinguished owing to the differential effects of the pinna; the sound pressure transformation in Figure 15.40 for a sound source at 0° is 3–5 dB greater than for a source at 180° at frequencies above 2,000 Hz. Accordingly, a wide-band signal will be softer and different in timbre when in back than in front. (The loudness cue would have to be accompanied by cues to the distance of the sound source.) The role of frequency was evident in the results of Stevens and Newman (1936). Front-back reversals of tone pulses hovered around 35% for frequencies up to about 2,500 Hz; above 3,000 Hz reversals were down to 10%. These

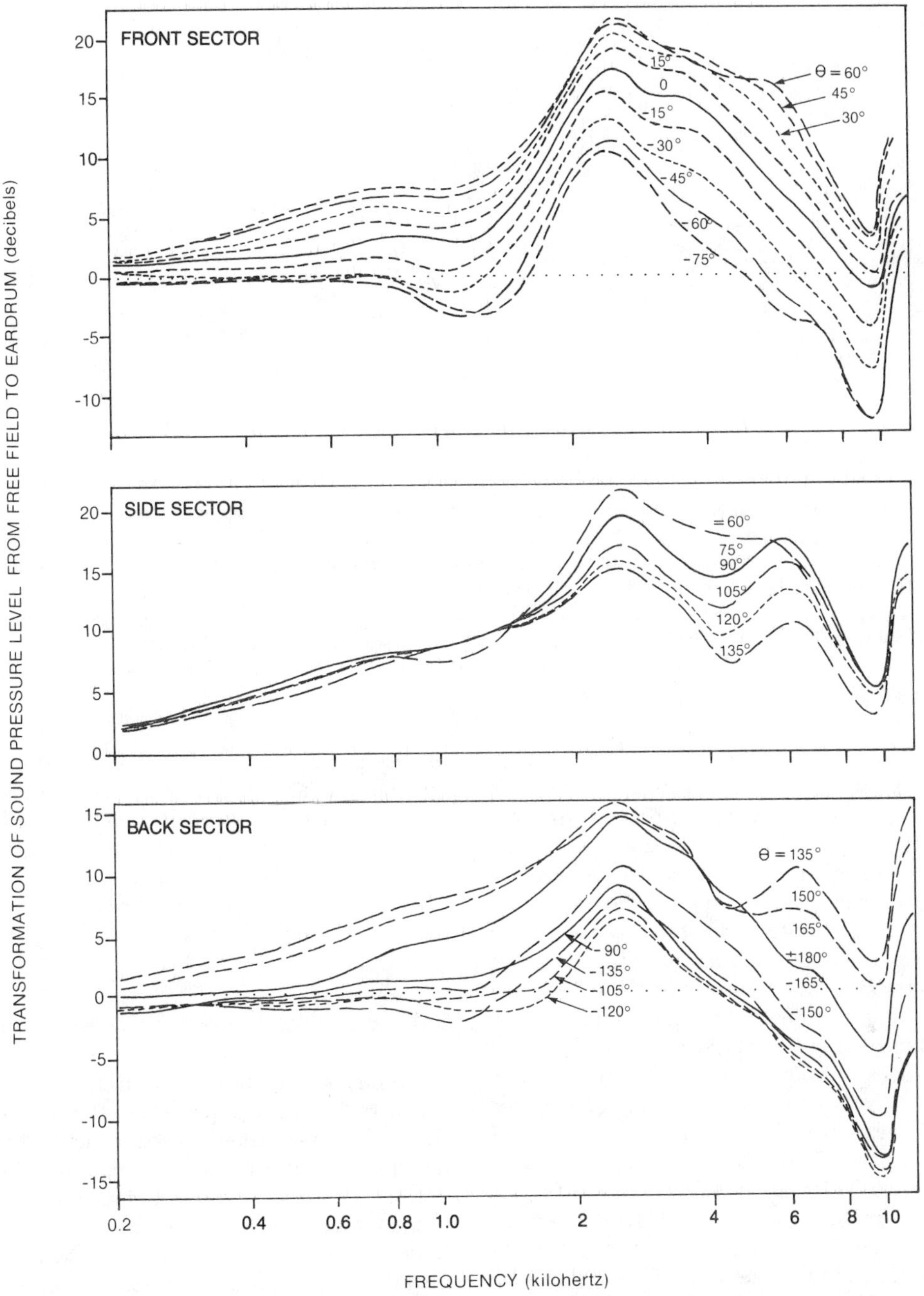

Figure 15.40. Difference in sound pressure level when measured in a free field with the subject absent and when measured at the eardrum. The change in level is plotted as a function of signal frequency with the azimuth, θ, of the sound source given as the parameter. For convenience, the curves are separated into the front, side, and back sectors. Curves are based on direct (probe microphone at the eardrum) and indirect (probe at an outer-ear position) measurements from 12 laboratories. Signals were tones or narrow-band noises. Number of subjects varied from 3 to 20 per study. The fitted curves show strong sound amplification owing to the subject's presence at around 2,500 Hz and strong attenuation at high frequencies. The amount of transformation in sound pressure depends on azimuth, more so at frequencies above 1,000 Hz than below and more so in the front and back sectors than at the side. (From A. E. G. Shaw, Transformation of sound pressure level from the free field to the eardrum in the horizontal plane, *Journal of the Acoustical Society of America*, 1974, *56*. Reprinted with permission.)

reversals were for sources in the horizontal plane at various azimuths. According to Mills (1972, p. 332), "When the intensity is varied from trial to trial, the percentage of errors increases to nearly that expected by chance." Varying the intensity prevents the listener from using the intensity cues provided by the torso, head, and pinnae at high frequencies. Not varying intensity allows even pure tones to become familiar sounds in an experimental context.

When subjects are deprived of relevant information to help discriminate front from back, they tend to bias their judgments toward one or the other (and, less so, toward above) according to the frequency of the sound (Blauert, 1969/70; Hebrank &

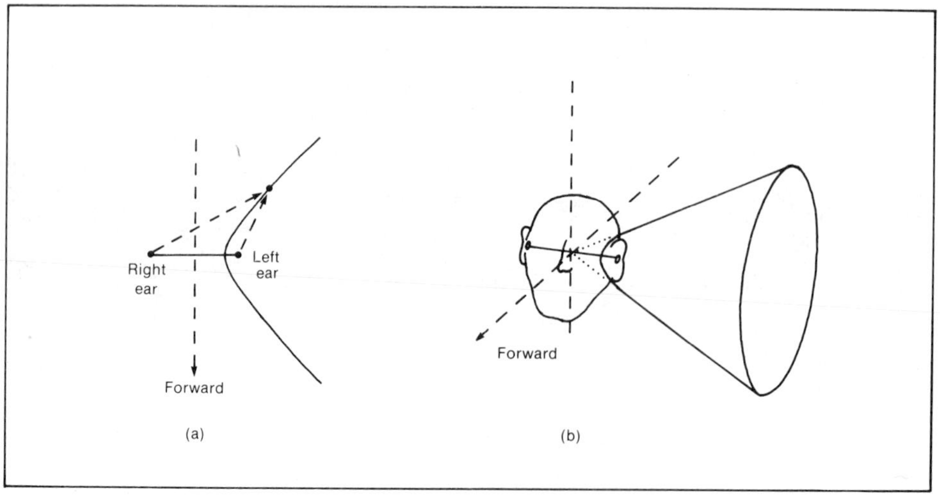

Figure 15.41. Positions of a sound source in space that yield the same interaural time differences (ITD). Panel (a) shows the hyperbola along which all sounds in the same plane give identical ITDs. On the basis of ITD alone a listener could not distinguish sound sources in front from those in back when they lie along the same hyperbola. Panel (b) is the same hyperbola rotated to yield a cone of confusion, so-called because all sounds on the cone's surface produce the same ITDs, which means that sound sources could be mislocated with respect to elevation as well as to front and back. (Adapted from J. Blauert, *Spatial hearing, The psychophysics of human sound localization*, MIT Press, 1983. Reprinted with permission.)

Wright, 1974). Figure 15.42 shows in three panels the percentage of behind (a), above (b), and front (c) judgments made by 20 subjects who judged ⅓-octave bands of noise presented randomly at four different levels (30–60 dB SPL) from the front or from the back. Level had no effect on localization. The dependence of the responses on center frequency is a psychoacoustic effect that may reflect the transformations imposed by the pinnae and other structures on the amplitude reaching the ear canal. Blauert (1969/70) has named "directional bands" the frequency ranges over which particular directions predominate. These bands, illustrated at the top of the figure, correspond roughly to the relative amplitudes of front-to-back transformation. That is, between 250 and 500 Hz the front source is slightly stronger (about 1 dB) than the back source; between about 800 and 1,800 Hz, the back source is about 2 dB stronger; around 4,000 Hz the back source is about 5 dB weaker (see Fig. 15.40). At higher frequencies, the bases for the directional bands are less clear. [Butler and Flannery (1980) have reported a dependence on frequency also in the horizontal plane when listening monaurally.]

3.3.2. Up-Down Discrimination. Humans can distinguish the vertical position of a sound source. The basis for this discrimination appears to lie in physical differences imposed on the sound reaching the ears by the head and pinnae. That humans can use these differences was shown by Roffler and Butler (1968) who measured the ability of six listeners to localize a 10-msec sound burst from a louspeaker located between $-13°$ and $+20°$ in the median plane. Pure tones of any frequency and complex sounds with no energy above 7,000 Hz could not be localized in the median plane, that is, sounds coming from $-13°$ were judged, on the average, to have the same locus as sounds coming from $+20°$. But to make use of these high-frequency cues in complex sounds the subjects had to have unoccluded pinnae. Covering their pinnae with a plastic sheet destroyed their ability to localize in the median plane. The authors concluded that localization in the median plane requires complex sounds with energy above 7,000 Hz and with the pinnae unobstructed. Gardner (1973) has substantiated these findings but has also shown that some useful information is provided in the frequency range from 500 to 4,000 Hz.

Wettschureck (1973) has measured the precision of localizing white noise in the median plane. He found that the MAA was smallest, 4°, in the forward direction (as compared to as little as 1° in the horizontal plane) and was largest, 10°, directly overhead.

3.4. Localization and Lateralization

Much has been learned about localization by studying the lateralization of sounds presented through a pair of earphones. Generally, the listener's task is to discriminate between sounds internalized toward the left and right. The question arises as to whether the same binaural processing takes place when the sound image is located inside the head as when located outside. Lateralization is the usual task when sounds are presented through earphones and localization when they are presented from the original sound source or from loudspeakers. However, it is possible to arrange loudspeakers symmetrically around the listener so as to give rise to a sound image inside the head, at least initially. It is also possible to present sounds via earphones that give rise to externalized images. This externalization is achieved by presenting sounds that had been recorded via microphones inserted in real or artificial pinnae (e.g., Plenge, 1974). Corroborating the subjective reports is the finding by Molino (1974) that three listeners gave the same psychometric functions to pure tones at 500, 1,000, and 8,000 Hz whether they were presented via a pair of earphones or from a loudspeaker located 9 m from the center of the listener's head. Earlier, Jeffress and Taylor (1961) had found that four subjects could discriminate the position of wide-band noise presented via earphones just as well as the subjects of Stevens and Newman (1936), who judged the locus of actual sources of sound in a sound field. Moreover, the subjects of Jeffress and Taylor made their judgments by reference to a set of lights set 1.8 m away in a semicircle. Even

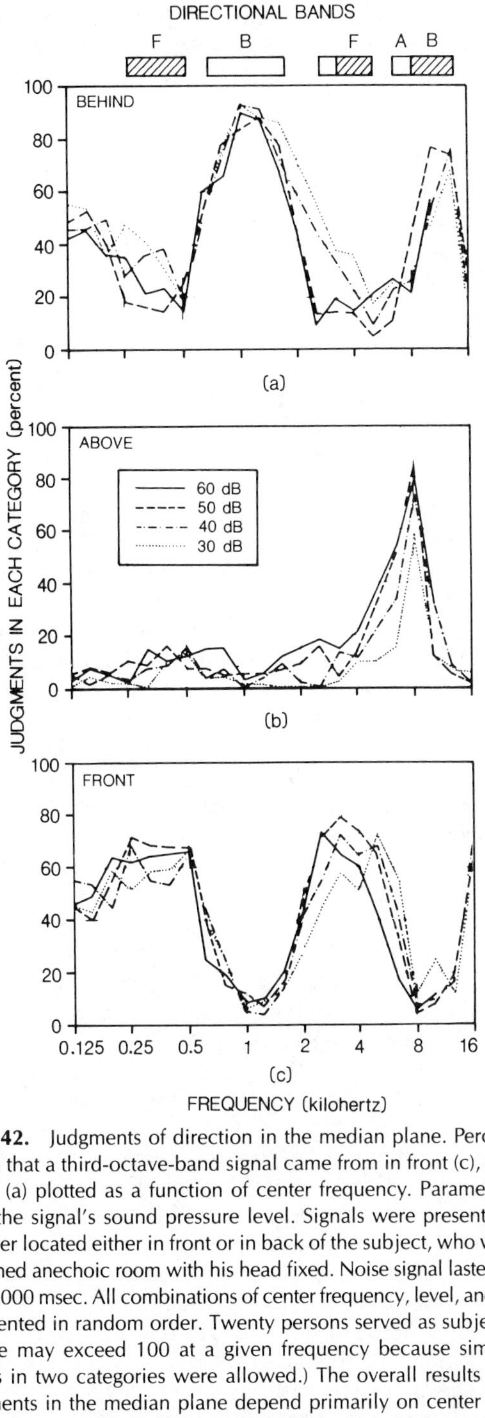

Figure 15.42. Judgments of direction in the median plane. Percentage of judgments that a third-octave-band signal came from in front (c), above (b), or behind (a) plotted as a function of center frequency. Parameter on the curves is the signal's sound pressure level. Signals were presented from a loudspeaker located either in front or in back of the subject, who was seated in a darkened anechoic room with his head fixed. Noise signal lasted between 100 and 1,000 msec. All combinations of center frequency, level, and direction were presented in random order. Twenty persons served as subjects. (Total percentage may exceed 100 at a given frequency because simultaneous judgments in two categories were allowed.) The overall results show that the judgments in the median plane depend primarily on center frequency and not at all on level. The bars at the top indicate the frequency ranges where each of the three categories of judgment predominates. Although the noises were presented half the time from the front speaker and half the time from the back, accuracy of judgments is not indicated. (Adapted from J. Blauert, *Spatial hearing, The psychophysics of human sound localization*, MIT Press, 1983. Reprinted with permission.)

after many trials the sound image remained almost always located inside the head but its lateral position could be correlated with the external lamps.

3.5. Distance

The primary cue to distance is sound intensity, which decreases as the square of the distance of the sound source. However, for this cue to be usable the listener must be familiar with the sound. Coleman (1962) showed that after some familiarity with a broad-band noise presented at various distances, listeners could make reasonably accurate judgments of actual distance although they underestimated it by about 25%. At first, judgments were essentially unrelated to physical distance but with practice accuracy improved significantly. Because these measurements were carried out with louspeakers placed at various distances, other cues could have served as well as intensity changes. However, a number of other studies reviewed by Blauert (1974, 1983) have shown that intensity alone may serve as a cue to distance. (See also Coleman, 1963.) For example, Gardner (1969) had five subjects judge the distance of speech coming from a speaker at a distance of either 3 or 9 m. As the sound pressure level at the ears increased, the judged distance decreased in the same way whether the sound came from 3 or from 9 m. The perceived change in distance was much smaller than expected from the rule that doubling the distance decreases the sound pressure level by 6 dB. To double the perceived distance, the level had to be decreased 20 dB.

Other cues to distance come from changes in the timbre of a broad-band sound. Timbre changes for two reasons, one physical, the other psychophysical. Beyond some 15 m the differential attenuation by air of low and high audible frequencies becomes noticeable with the higher frequencies more strongly attenuated than the low so that the timbre becomes deeper. At the same time the intensity decreases and the contribution of low frequencies diminishes because the loudness of low frequencies decreases more rapidly with decreasing level than does that of high frequencies (see Section 1.2.1). Just how the physical and psychophysical effects interact must depend upon the absolute levels and the spectra of the sounds.

The experiments described above were carried out in anechoic spaces that have no or little reverberation. Under most listening conditions, reverberation does occur, and it serves as an indication of the distance of the sound source, as Mershon & King (1975) demonstrated with 80 listeners. Like intensity and spectral cues, reverberation requires some familiarity with the environment. It appears that listeners obtain sufficient familiarity very rapidly, often in a matter of minutes or even seconds.

3.6. Precedence Effect

As noted, reverberation is the rule rather than the exception. Hearing usually occurs in environments with hard surfaces that reflect sounds, producing the multiple reflections that constitute reverberation. We hear these reflections only when they reach the ear at least 50 msec after the direct sound. The suppression of the reflected sound is referred to as the precedence effect (Wallach, Newman, & Rosenzweig, 1949) or Haas effect (Haas, 1951). In the laboratory, the direct and reflected sounds can be simulated by a leading sound from one loudspeaker and by a lagging sound from a second speaker. For delays between 1 and 50 msec a single sound image, such as that produced by continuous speech, is heard at the leading speaker. (The boundary value of 50 msec varies somewhat with the type and duration of the signal, being usually shorter for noncontinuous sounds.) For delays less than 1 msec, the image is located between the speakers, moving toward a midway position as the delay decreases further. With no delay, the image is generally centered between the two speakers. These rules apply (for somewhat different delays) not only when the lagging sound is equal in intensity to the leading sound, but also when it is as much as 10 dB stronger. If the two sounds are simultaneous, a level difference will cause the image to move toward the stronger speaker; a difference of 10 dB or greater yields a single-locus image at the stronger source.

Delays greater than 50 msec result in the perception of an echo, although the precise time delay required depends on the type of sound and on the listener. Generally, with delays between about 30 and 50 msec, listeners report that speech quality is reduced even though a single-locus sound is heard (Haas, 1951). The early findings of Haas, which have been influential in concert-hall design and amplification schemes, demonstrated that although the lagging sound might not contribute to the perceived locus of the direct or leading sound, it did affect its quality. Later studies have demonstrated that the lagging sound contributes fully to the overall loudness of the sound, so that the combined sound may be twice as loud as either one alone (Scharf, 1974b). Moreover, if the two sounds differ spectrally, both contribute to the overall pitch and timbre of the single-locus sound; thus if the leading sound is a tone of one frequency and the lagging sound is of another frequency, the single-locus sound will have a chord-like quality (Scharf, 1974a).

The precedence effect is a powerful phenomenon that is poorly understood in terms of physiological mechanisms, the time delays involved being much longer than those usually observed in neurological measurements. Clearly, it is not simply inhibitory because the lagging sound contributes fully to the loudness and quality of the total sound. In this respect, it resembles the funneling described by Békésy (1958).

3.7. Localization in Noise

Although localization of one sound usually takes place in the presence of other sounds that may be considered interfering or masking sounds, few studies exist on localization under masking. Jacobsen (1976) measured the localization of 500-Hz and 3,000-Hz tone bursts as a function of sensation level. His principal finding was that at 10–15 dB above the masked threshold localization was as good in the presence of the wide-band masking noise as in the quiet. In these studies the noise was on continuously, and the signals were gated on for 1 sec. Later studies by Scharf and Canévet (1980) and by Canévet, Germain, and Scharf (1980) have shown that spectral and temporal relations between the signal and noise have a considerable influence on localization. Thus when the signal and noise share the same critical band, localization is reduced more than when they do not. If noise onset precedes signal onset by about 20 msec, and if signal and noise are close in frequency, then localization is not as good as in the quiet until the sensation level is about 15 dB. As the frequency separation between signal and noise becomes greater, the detection threshold decreases more rapidly than the localization threshold so that a signal well below or above the frequency of a narrow-band masking noise must be some 30 dB above the masked threshold to be localized (Scharf, Canévet, Buus, & Marchioni, 1982). These interactions probably reflect the influence of the precedence effect, for the lagging signal's locus would be dominated by that of the preceding noise.

3.8. Perception of Moving Sounds

The preceding sections dealt with discrimination of stationary sound sources by listeners who were usually also stationary. Also discussed was the effect of head movements. Under natural conditions, often the sound source is moving while the listener is stationary, or both may be moving. In a recent review, Perrott (1982) reports a number of experiments, mainly by his own group, on apparent movement of stationary sources and of the perception of moving sources; he could find no experimental reports of measurements where both source and listener were moving. Perrott also reported measurements of perceived motion under dichotic stimulation, where two brief sounds appear to move through the head when one is presented 20–70 msec after the other; the optimal onset time difference increases with the duration of the signals.

Measurements of the perception of the motion of actual sound sources have been concerned with detection of motion and the estimation of the velocity of motion. Detection turns out to be rather crude. For listeners to distinguish a moving sound source from a stationary source, the source (a loudspeaker emitting a 500-Hz tone burst) must move through 8–21° depending on the velocity. Because the lowest velocity Perrott used was $90°\cdot sec^{-1}$, which is fairly fast, we may assume that if the velocity was slow enough, the MAA for motion would reduce to the 1° or so found for two successive sources (Mills, 1958). On the other hand, once velocity is detected, changes can be discriminated quite well, with the Weber fraction equal to about 0.05; that is, subjects could distinguish a 5% change in velocity. Moreover, perceived velocity increases in direct proportion to physical velocity; under some conditions listeners can even estimate fairly closely the absolute velocity (in miles per hour).

Perrott (1982) also summarizes a number of experiments on auditory autokinesis, in which a stationary source is heard as moving, and on induced motion, in which a stationary source is induced to seem to move owing to other actually moving sources. Many of these effects resemble visual phenomena. Perrott interprets these similarities as indicating a central processor for the perception of motion that is common to seeing and hearing (the commonality may extend to touch: see Section 4.4 of Sherrick & Cholewiak, Chapter 12).

3.9. Effects of Auditory Pathology on Localization

Most types of bilateral hearing loss seem to cause some degradation in sound localization (Durlach, Thompson, & Colburn, 1981). The amount of degradation varies greatly from patient to patient and is not readily predicted from the audiogram. Generally, middle-ear lesions and acoustic neuromas lead to more severe disturbance of localization than do cochlear lesions (Abel, Birt, & McLean, 1982; Durlach et al., 1981). However, once the sound is 10 dB above threshold, disturbances are often minimal. Even persons with unilateral or highly asymmetric losses can learn to localize sufficiently well for most ordinary situations. The monaural cues discussed above are used by these patients. Similarly, patients with intact high-frequency hearing in at least one ear can localize well in the median plane, but the need for high-frequency input prevents patients with bilateral high-frequency loss from scoring much above chance (Butler, 1970). Despite the high correlation between age and hearing loss after 30 years, the ability to discriminate sources separated by 7.5° shows no change with age until past 70 years (Röser, 1965).

3.10. Models of Auditory Localization

Models of localization constitute one of two categories of models of binaural interaction, the other category being concerned with detection of signal in noise and masking level differences (see

Section 3.2.1.5 of Scharf & Buus, Chapter 14). A detailed review of many models of binaural interaction of both types is contained in the chapter by Colburn and Durlach (1978). Blauert (1983) presents a more general review of models of localization including his own model (see also Blauert, 1974). Most models of localization are either cross-correlation models or count-comparison models, to use the terms of Colburn and Durlach (1978).

3.10.1. Cross-Correlation Models. Jeffress (1948) laid the foundation for the cross-correlation approach when he proposed that the auditory system effects a comparison between neural inputs from the left and right ears. To explain the lateralization of the auditory image toward the leading ear, Jeffress hypothesized that neural excitation is greatest where simultaneous input is received in corresponding fibers in the left and right auditory tracts. Simultaneous input would be in the left tract when the left ear leads, and in the right tract when the right ear leads. Thus interaural time differences are translated into a place code in the auditory system, the place of maximum excitation depending on the precise time difference between the left and right inputs. To handle interaural intensity differences, Jeffress invoked the so-called latency hypothesis according to which the weaker signals lead to later firings in the nerve fibers. Thus intensity differences are equivalent to time differences and both are ultimately translated into place differences. Later modifications permitted the application of this model to problems of detection as well as lateralization. As originally formulated, the model had many inadequacies that are reviewed by Colburn and Durlach (1978), but later modifications have led to improvements, and the idea of a coincidence detector as the basis for lateralization and, presumably, for localization remains very much alive.

A more explicitly quantitative use of the coincidence model was made by Sayers and Cherry (1957), who described lateralization in terms of interaural correlation, calculated in the statistical sense. The degree of correlation between the inputs from the two ears will depend, in part, on their time difference, such that the greater the difference the smaller the correlation. The degree of lateralization (and of fusion) corresponds to the degree of correlation. Interaural intensity differences are included as a weighting function. This basic approach has also inspired many papers, most of which have been concerned with detection rather than localization. Many of the later developments and refinements of the cross-correlation approach are contained in the model of Blauert (1974, 1982, 1983; see also Lindemann, 1982). Figure 15.43 presents an overview of this model, which includes transformations imposed on the signal by the external and middle ears as well as the filtering in the auditory periphery (critical bands). Interaural comparisons are assumed to be made only in corresponding critical bands (see Scharf et al., 1976). Interaural time differences are handled by a binaural coincidence processor; level differences are handled separately by difference weighting. The resulting neural place-time pattern accounts for such binaural phenomena as fusion and spaciousness as well as lateral position. This model is not incompatible with the explicitly physiological model developed by Colburn (see Colburn & Durlach, 1978) to account for de-

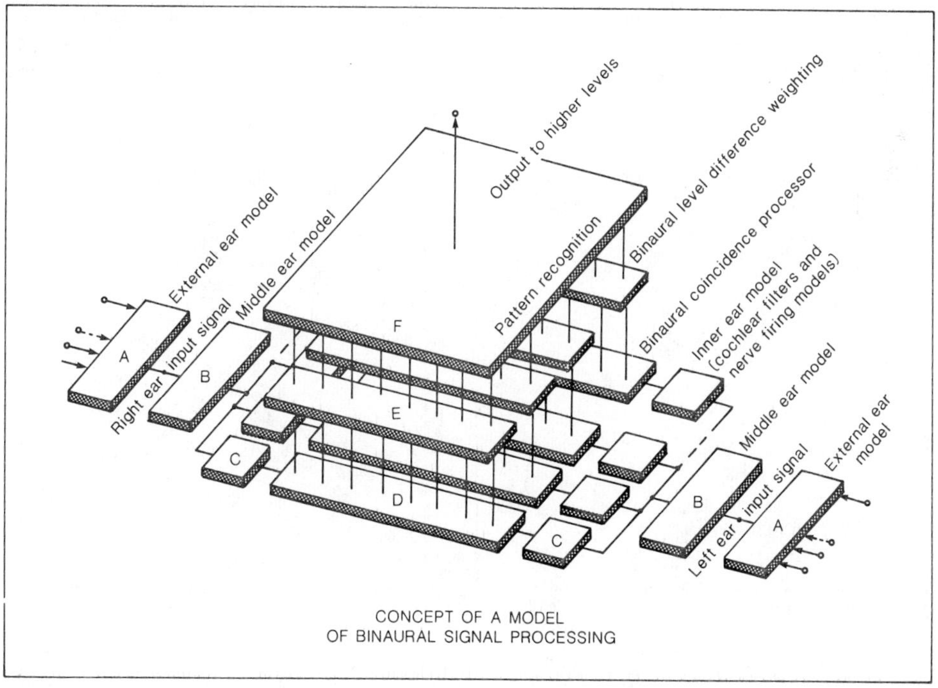

Figure 15.43. Conceptual model of binaural processing, designed especially to account for localization, lateralization, and subjective impressions of spaciousness and fusion. The model includes six functional elements: A and B simulate the transfer functions of external and middle ear; C simulates the frequency selectivity (critical bands) of the cochlea and the sensory transduction of stimulus energy to neural impulses; D evaluates interaural time differences and interaural correlation; E evaluates interaural intensity differences; F integrates information from D and E and "decides" about the locus, size, and presence of signals; that is, F localizes and detects. By means of these functional elements, the model schematizes the sequences and the kinds of physiological processing that may take place in the auditory nervous system. (From J. Blauert, *Spatial hearing, The psychophysics of human sound localization*, MIT Press, 1983. Reprinted with permission.)

tection by the binaural system. Combining these two models would represent a distinct advance and could lead to a clearer understanding of both binaural detection and localization.

3.10.2. Count-Comparison Models. These models assume that lateralization is based on a comparison of the amount of activity in two neural populations. The greater the activity in one set of neurons, the more to one side the sound is perceived. Békésy (1930, 1960) offered this model originally, and it has since been extended by van Bergeijk (1962) and given explicit physiological support by data and modeling of Hall (1964). The count-comparison model has received little attention in recent years, but as Colburn and Durlach (1978) suggest, it remains a viable alternative to the correlation models.

4. AURAL DISTORTION

Although often treated for convenience as a linear system, the ear is by no means linear. One sign of nonlinearity is the existence of spectral distortion products or "aural combination tones," which are tones that can be heard but are not present in the original sound stimulus. An early report of such tones came from the Italian violinist and composer Tartini (1754), and so they are sometimes called "Tartini tones." Tartini observed that when he played on the violin a harmonic interval of two notes with a frequency ratio of, for example, 5:6 he heard a lower note corresponding to the next lower number (4 in this case). Early explanations can be grouped as (1) spectral theories that invoked a distortion mechanism (Helmholtz, 1885/1954), and (2) temporal theories that invoked a "beat tone" heard when two sinusoids are slightly mistuned (Hermann, 1891). Helmholtz ascribed the origin of aural combination tones primarily to the quadratic component of a general overloading-type distortion in the middle ear. If S is an arbitrary signal to the ear, the effective signal after overload distortion can be described by a Taylor series expansion,

$$F(S) = \alpha_0 + \alpha_1 S + \alpha_2 S^2 + \alpha_3 S^3 + \cdots + \alpha_n S^n \quad (8)$$

where the coefficients α_i are constants. For a signal S containing two frequencies f_1 and f_2, the expected quadratic distortion frequencies resulting from the term $\alpha_2 S^2$ are $2f_1$, $2f_2$, $f_1 + f_2$, and $f_2 - f_1$. For nearly a century Helmholtz's view prevailed, and aural combination tones were thought to be aural harmonics, summation tones, and difference tones. Few investigators were bothered by the failure of Helmholtz's theory to account for Tartini tones. Later studies have shown that the middle ear does introduce quadratic distortion, but that much more complex distortion takes place in the cochlea.

4.1. Modern Experiments on Aural Combination Tones

Plomp (1965) presented two pure tones, one at 1,000 Hz and the other at a higher and variable frequency. Subjects tuned the frequency of a third tone to match any "other" component they could hear. Figure 15.44 shows the results at two intensity levels, 50 and 80 dB SPL. The abscissa gives the frequency ratio, f_2/f_1, of the primary tones; the ordinate gives the ratio of the perceived combination tone to the lower primary tone. Results for each of four subjects are represented by different lines. The distortion components $2f_1 - f_2$ and $3f_1 - 2f_2$ were heard by all four observers at both levels, but over a reduced frequency range at the lower level. The quadratic difference tone, $f_2 - f_1$, was more difficult to hear at the lower primary level, where only two of the four subjects heard it.

Zwicker (1955) used a cancellation procedure to measure the intensity of combination tones. He fixed the primary tone

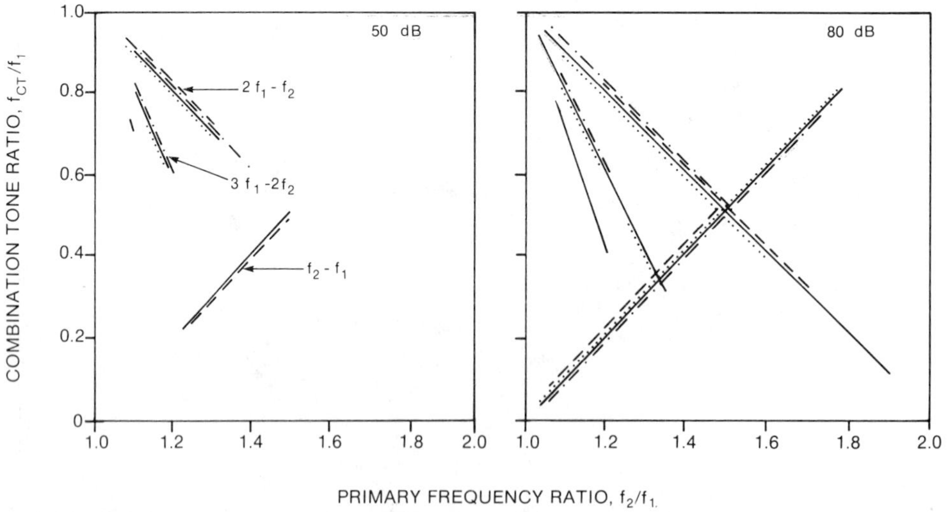

Figure 15.44. Aural combintion-tone (CT) frequencies heard by four subjects, with two-tone stimuli at frequencies f_1 and f_2 presented at two different sound pressure levels. The tone f_1 was kept at 1,000 Hz, and f_2 was varied between 1,000 and 2,000 Hz. Subjects listened alternately to the two-tone combination and to a single comparison tone, which they tuned to the frequency of any combination tone they could distinguish. The ratio of the observed CT frequency to 1,000 Hz (primary frequency, f_1) is plotted as a function of the primary frequency ratio f_2/f_1. Each subject's results are represented by a different line. The range of observed CTs increases with intensity of the primary tone. No summation tones ($f_1 + f_2$) were heard. (Adapted from R. Plomp, Detectability threshold for combination tones, *Journal of the Acoustical Society of America*, 1965, *37*. Reprinted with permission.)

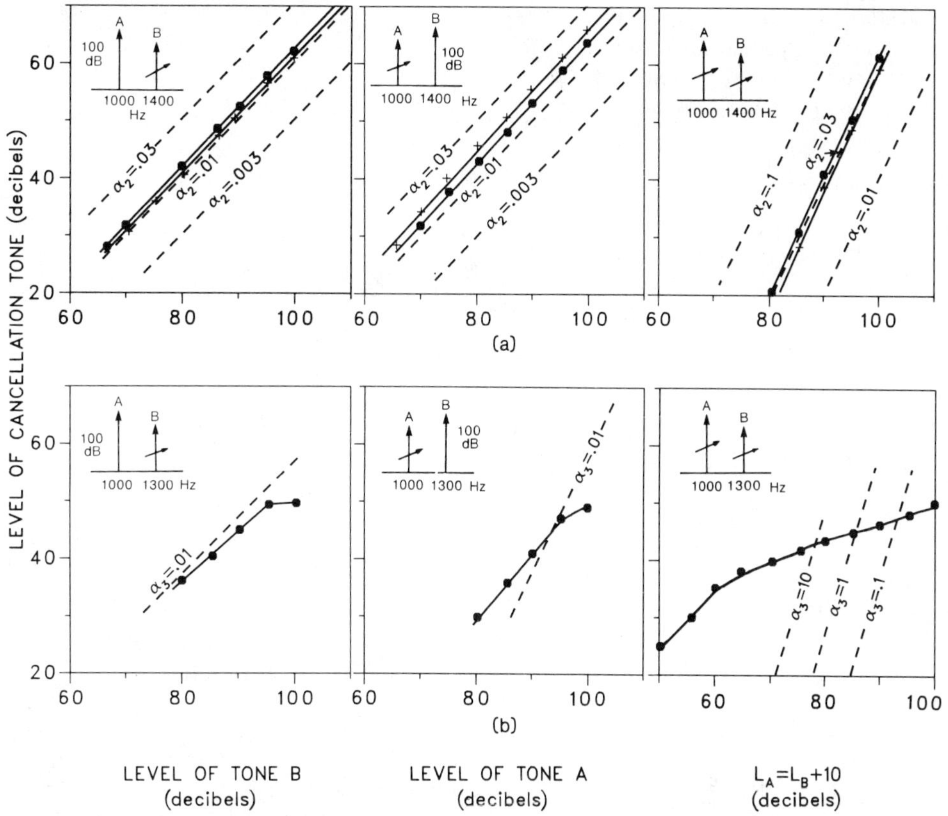

Figure 15.45. Cancellation-tone intensities for aural combination tones $f_B - f_A$ (top) and $2f_A - f_B$ (bottom) plotted as a function of primary-tone intensities. In addition to the primary frequencies f_A and f_B, a phase-locked cancellation tone at the expected combination-tone frequency was presented. The subject adjusted its amplitude and phase until the cancellation tone could no longer be heard. Primary-tone intensities are indicated on the abscissa and on the inserts. Dashed lines are theoretical predictions from a Taylor series expansion with various values of the quadratic coefficient α_2 (top) and the cubic coefficient α_3 (bottom). The $f_B - f_A$ combination tone is well described as a quadratic distortion product, but the $2f_A - f_B$ combination tone clearly does not behave as a cubic distortion product. (From E. Zwicker, Der ungewöhnliche Amplitudengang der nichtlinearen Verzerrungen des Ohres, *Acustica*, 1955, *5*. Reprinted with permission.)

frequencies at f_A and f_B. The levels of the lower tone, the higher tone, or both were varied. Subjects adjusted the amplitude and phase of a third "cancellation" tone, which was set at the combination-tone frequency, until that tone could not be heard. Figure 15.45 shows the results for the quadratic difference tone $(f_B - f_A)$ at the top, and for the cubic difference tone $(2f_A - f_B)$ at the bottom. The quadratic difference tone behaves like a simple quadratic distortion product. When only one primary intensity is varied, the difference-tone intensity varies linearly with primary-tone intensity, but when the intensities of both primary tones were varied, difference-tone intensity varies as the square of primary tone intensity. The Taylor expansion coefficient α_2 of the quadratic term is between 1 and 3% of the linear term coefficient α_1. If the cubic difference tone were a component of the third-order term of the Taylor power expansion, $\alpha_3 S^3$, it would grow linearly with the intensity of f_B, quadratically with the intensity of f_A, and as the third power of primary intensity when both tones are simultaneously varied. The bottom panels of Figure 15.45 show that these relations do not hold. Goldstein (1967) found with a similar cancellation procedure that the cubic difference tone is nearly a linear function of primary-tone intensity when both primaries are varied.

Another reason why combination tones of the set $f(n) = f_1 - n(f_2 - f_1)$ cannot be explained as odd-order terms of a distortion power-series expansion is their dependence on the frequency ratio between the primary tones. Figure 15.46 shows how combination-tone strength depends on this ratio (Goldstein, 1967). The ordinate gives the difference between the levels of the primary tone and the cancellation tone as a function of the ratio, f_2/f_1, between the primary tones for three different odd-order combination tones ($n = 1, n = 2, n = 3$). The quadratic difference tone, $(f_2 - f_1)$, whose cancellation-tone level is shown at the bottom of the figure, varies little with f_2/f_1, whereas the odd-order combination tones depend strongly on f_2/f_1. Cancellation tone amplitudes for combination tones, $f(n)$, can be approximated by the empirical relation sketched in Figure 15.46:

$$L - L_c(n) = 125\left(1 - \frac{f(n)}{f_1}\right) \text{ dB} \tag{9}$$

where L is the sound pressure level of the equally intense primary tones and $L_c(n)$ is the level of the cancellation tone, which is presumably equal to the level of the combination tone. More general descriptive formulas for calculation levels of combination tones have been developed and tested by Zwicker (1981). They include low- and high-frequency effects in the quadratic difference tone, and dependence on individual primary-tone levels. The quadratic difference tone, for primary frequencies greater than 200 Hz, is given by

$$L(f_2 - f_1) = L_1 + L_2 - 126 + 10 \log[1 + (0.25f_1)^2] + 10 \log\left[1 + \left(\frac{0.5}{f_1}\right)^2\right] \quad (10)$$

where L_1, L_2, and $L(f_2 - f_1)$ are expressed in decibels, f_1 is in kilohertz, and logarithms are decimal. The level of the first odd-order combination tone, $f(1) = 2f_1 - f_2$, is for primary frequencies between 600 Hz and 7 kHz and is given by the relation

$$\begin{aligned} L(2f_1 - f_2) = 1.1L_1 - 10\{&\log(1 + 10^{0.2(L_1 - L_2) + 0.6(0.1L_2 - \Delta z^2 - 7)}) \\ &+ \log(1 + 10^{0.05(L_2 - L_1)(1 - 0.35\Delta z)}) \\ &+ \log(1 + 10^{0.04(L_2 - 40)}) \\ &+ \log[1 + (0.25f_1)^2] \\ &+ \log\left[1 + \left(\frac{0.5}{f_1}\right)^2\right] \\ &+ 1.2(\Delta z)^2[1 - 0.01(L_2 - 50)]\}^{-2} \end{aligned} \quad (11)$$

where L_1, L_2, and $L(2f_1 - f_2)$ are the levels of the primary tones and combination tone in decibels, f_1 is the frequency of the lower primary tone in kilohertz, and Δz is the critical-band rate difference $z_2 - z_1$ in barks (1 bark corresponds to one critical band; see Scharf & Buus, Chapter 14, Section 3.3.1.2). Critical-band rates, which approximately translate frequency into place along the basilar membrane, can be computed with the aid of the simple linear relation

$$z_n = 8.7 + 14.2 \log f_n \quad (12)$$

with z_n expressed in barks and f_n in kilohertz. Approximate levels of higher odd-order combination tones are

$$L(3f_1 - 2f_2) = L(2f_1 - f_2) - \Delta z - 18 \quad (13)$$

$$L(4f_1 - 3f_2) = L(2f_1 - f_2) - 2\Delta z - 30 \quad (14)$$

again with all levels L in decibels and $\Delta z = z_2 - z_1$ in barks. The principal conclusion from Zwicker's and Goldstein's findings is that the difference tone $f_2 - f_1$ behaves largely as a simple quadratic distortion component and does not involve a filtering process. Its origin is therefore probably in the middle ear where tuning is very broad. The other odd-order combination tones represent a different kind of nonlinearity. Because they are frequency dependent, their origin involves a filtering process and must therefore be located beyond the middle ear.

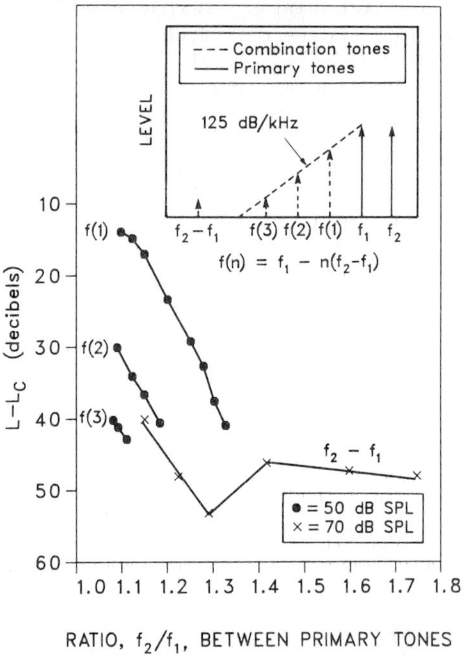

Figure 15.46. Relative cancellation-tone intensities, L_c, of three odd-order combination tones, CTs, ($2f_1 - f_2$, $3f_1 - 2f_2$, and $4f_1 - 3f_2$) and of the quadratic combination tone, $f_2 - f_1$, plotted as a function of primary frequency ratio f_2/f_1. The frequency of f_1 was always 1,000 Hz. Measurements were made by a cancellation procedure similar to that described in Figure 15.45. The level, L, of the primary tones was 50 dB SPL for the odd-order CTs and 70 dB SPL for the quadratic CT. As shown by the three lines to the left, all three odd-order CTs decrease in level as the f_2/f_1 ratio increases. In contrast, the quadratic CT does not vary monotonically with the f_2/f_1 ratio, and this lack of dependence is true when the primaries are decreased to 50 dB. The dependence of CT intensity on primary-tone frequency ratio shows that odd-order CTs can not be regarded as products of middle-ear distortion, but must originate in the filter process of the cochlea. (From J. L. Goldstein, Aural combination tones, in R. Plomp & G. F. Smoorenberg (Eds.), *Frequency analysis and periodicity detection in hearing*, Sijthoff and Noordhoff, 1970. Reprinted with permission.)

Physiological experiments have revealed direct neural correlates of combination tones in units of the eighth (auditory) nerve and the anteroventral cochlear nucleus of the cat. Goldstein and Kiang (1968) showed that units in the cat's eighth nerve with a characteristic (most sensitive) frequency, CF, would not respond readily to pure tones at frequencies f_1 or f_2, but would respond to both tones together when the frequency $2f_1 - f_2$ was close to CF. Interspike interval histograms measured by Smoorenburg, Gibson, Kitzes, Rose, and Hind (1976) in a unit of the cat's antroventral cochlear nucleus with a characteristic frequency of 160 Hz showed similar behavior. When the primary frequencies f_1 and f_2 are such that the combination frequency $2f_1 - f_2$ is close to the unit's characteristic frequency, there are many interspike intervals equal to the inverse of the combination-tone frequency, whereas when $2f_1 - f_2$ is away from the fiber's best frequency, the firing rate is lower and the distribution of interspike intervals is more random. In addition, cancellation experiments similar to the psychophysical ones have been carried out physiologically on the cat's ear. By adding to the primary tones f_1 and f_2 a cancellation tone, with a frequency of $2f_1 - f_2$ with proper phase and amplitude, the response of single units that initially responded to the combination of f_1 and f_2 is reduced to spontaneous activity. A salient feature of the data of Goldstein and Kiang (Goldstein, 1970) is that the combination-tone response is canceled in several units for the same amplitude and phase conditions of the cancellation tone. These findings have been confirmed in a recent study of a large number of fibers (Kim, Molnar, & Matthews, 1980).

Helmholtz (1885/1954) predicted audible distortion products above as well as below the stimulus frequencies. Modern attempts to find such tones directly with cancellation methods have failed, but their presence has been indirectly demonstrated. Clack (1967), who measured a listener's threshold for an interrupted 2,000-Hz tone in the presence of a phase-locked 1,000-Hz masker, found that detection threshold depended on the phase relation between the two tones. He explained this by vectorial summation of the 2,000-Hz test tone and a subthreshold 2,000-Hz aural harmonic of the masker. Clack measured variations of as much as 6 dB above or below the quiet threshold of the 2,000-Hz tone. Zurek and Sachs (1979) presented monaural two-tone stimuli at frequencies f_1 and f_2 to one ear, and a single contralateral tone at frequencies $2f_1 - f_2$, $2f_2 - f_1$, $f_1 + f_2$, $2f_1 + f_2$, or $2f_2 + f_1$ to the other ear. Only the first of these frequencies is below the primaries; the others are above. The subject adjusted the amplitude and phase of the contralateral tone until its image was intracranially centered. The fact that this task could be done repeatedly shows that, at least for relatively low primary frequencies, combination tones above the primary frequencies exist at anywhere from 20 to 40 dB below the level of the primary tones. They are not audible, however, because they are masked by the lower-frequency primary tones (see Section 3.2.1.3 of Scharf & Buus, Chapter 14).

Aural distortion products arise also when the primary stimulus components are narrow bands of noise. Greenwood (1971, 1972), measured the masking pattern of a 1,000-Hz tone plus a narrow noise band centered at 1,250 Hz. He found distinct elevations in the masking pattern at frequencies of 750 and 500 Hz. These elevations, located at the odd-order combination-tone frequencies, indicate the presence of combination bands of noise added to the tone-plus-noise masking pattern. Moreover, the level of these combination bands depends on the primary component frequency ratio in a manner similar to combination tones.

The demonstration that odd-order combination tones show tuning behavior and that neural correlates exist in the eighth nerve firmly established the cochlea as the place where they originate. It is unclear, however, whether they are generated mechanically or electrophysiologically. Do aural combination tones result from nonlinearities in basilar membrane motion and propagate as components of a mechanical wave along the membrane, or do they result from transducer nonlinearity in the hair cells? Support for a mechanical coherent wave theory comes from the simultaneous cancellation of the response to the cubic difference tone in different eighth-nerve units. If the cancellation tone eliminates a particular mechanical wave distortion component, all nerve units tuned to that component should simultaneously fail to respond. Another phenomenon that supports the wave theory is the so-called "Kemp-echo" (Kemp, 1978), an acoustic reflection from the cochlea that can be measured in the ear canal. Quadratic and cubic distortion products have been found in this "echo" in animals (Kim et al., 1980) and in humans (Wilson, 1980). It is difficult to account for such nonlinear emissions on the basis of transducer nonlinearity alone. The chief argument against the coherent wave theory was an initial failure of physiologists to find correlates of traveling distortion components in electrical potentials across the cochlear partition (Dallos, 1969; Rhode, 1977). This failure encouraged speculation that the hair cells might be where the distortion originates. Duifhuis (1976) proposed a two-stage filter model with compressive nonlinearity in the second filter, thus making the hair-cell transducers responsible for combination tone-generation. Recently, however, physiologists found cochlear microphonic evidence for mechanical propagation of combination tones along the basilar membrane (Gibian, 1980). This success is attributed to improved physiological techniques, requiring less invasive surgery of the cochlea. It makes it more likely that aural combination tones originate in mechanical filtering on the basilar membrane, and propagate as components of a traveling wave along the membrane.

4.2. Combination-Tone Models

Representation of basilar-membrane motion by transmission-line or wave models has a lengthy history (e.g., Schroeder, 1973; Siebert, 1974; Zwislocki, 1948). All these models employ linear elements or sets of linear equations, and therefore cannot account for combination tones. Hall (1974) proposed a transmission-line model with nonlinear elements. This model, which incorporates ideas of Kim (1972) and Hubbard and Geisler (1972), is illustrated in panel (a) of Figure 15.47. The initial, intermediate, and final stages are shown. Panel (b) of Figure 15.47 shows results simulated by this model, with appropriately chosen parameter values, for an input of two tones at f_1 and f_2; the displacement component at $2f_1 - f_2$ is measured across the various capacitors C_i. The solid curve shows the spatial distribution of the $2f_1 - f_2$ component, the dashed curve shows the distribution of the same component when an appropriately chosen cancellation tone of frequency $2f_1 - f_2$ is added to the input. Salient features of this model are (1) that the $2f_1 - f_2$ component is found everywhere basal to the characteristic place of $2f_1 - f_2$, that is, the place of maximal response to a single frequency of $2f_1 - f_2$, but nowhere apical to this place, and (2) that upon cancellation the $2f_1 - f_2$ component is suppressed only in the apical and not in the basal direction. The model also explains why only distortion components below the primary frequencies are heard. Distortion components above the primary frequencies, for example, $2f_2 - f_1$, appear in the model's output only at the place of the primary frequencies where they are masked by these primaries. The lower distortion components, however, appear both basal and apical to the characteristic place of the primary frequencies. Apically, the response is not masked by other frequency components.

Hall's wave model does not account for the psychophysical observation that the phase at which cancellation tone nulls the sensation of the $2f_1 - f_2$ combination tone depends strongly on the intensity of the primary tones (Goldstein, 1967). A 40-dB increase in level requires that the phase angle between primary tones and cancellation tone be decreased as much as 100–150°. Cancellation measurements in single auditory neurons do not show this dependence. Although the difference between psychophysical and physiological behavior is not yet well understood, psychophysical phase behavior can be accounted for by modifying Hall's wave model (Furst & Goldstein, 1980).

4.3. Effects of Combination Tones

Psychophysical experiments that employ monaural complex sounds must be performed with careful attention to possibly

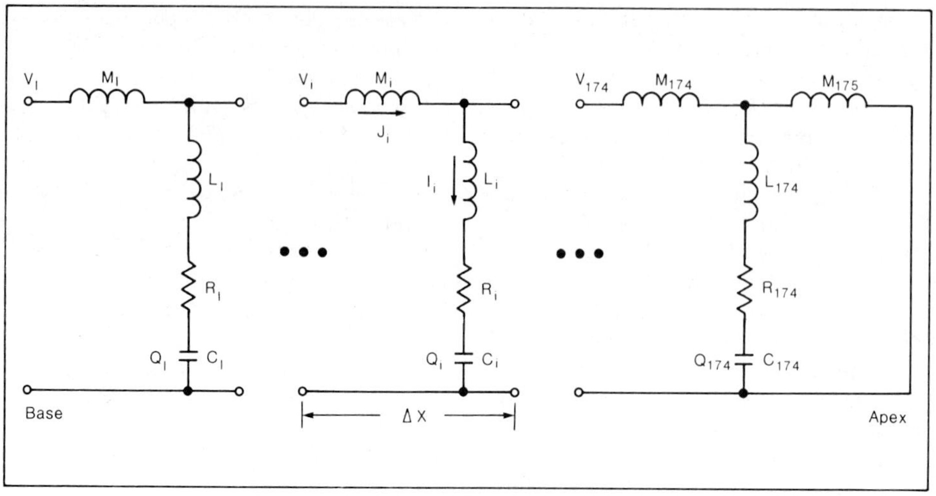

(a)

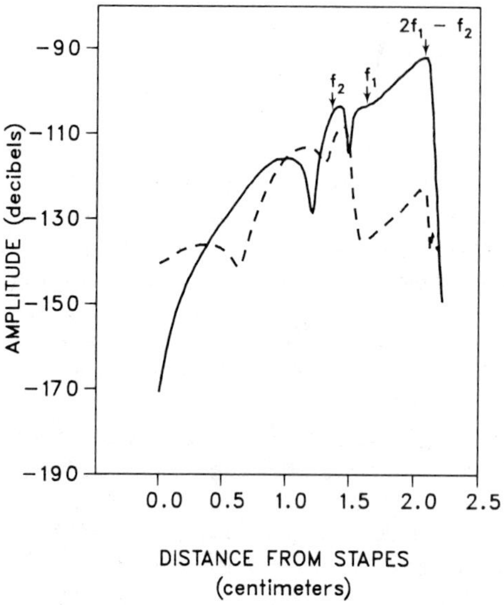

(b)

Figure 15.47. Nonlinear basilar-membrane model comprising 175 sections, where section 1 is near the stapes and section 175 is near the apex. The voltage *V* represents pressure differences across the basilar membrane, the current *J* represents fluid velocity in the periotic space, the current *I* the velocity on the basilar membrane, and the charge *Q* on capacitor *C* the displacement of the basilar membrane. The inductance *M* represents the fluid mass, the inductance *L* the basilar-membrane mass (and laterally moving fluid), and the capacitance *C* the compliance of the basilar membrane. The nonlinear resistances R_i represent loss associated with membrane motion, and are a function of the current passing through them. With a linear current term, quadratic distortion can be accounted for, whereas cubic-order distortion requires a quadratic current term in the resistance function. (b) Model response, that is, voltages across capacitors C_i, as a function of section number or length along the cochlea. Input is a two-tone stimulus of 1,000 and 1,450 Hz and third-order nonlinearity is introduced by taking $R_i = R_0(1 + 0.1I_i)^2$. The solid line is the response at frequency $2f_1 - f_2$; the dashed line is the same when a (third) cancellation tone is added at 550 Hz and 30 dB below the primary tone level at optimum cancellation phase. Vertical arrows indicate places of maximum model response for the frequencies specified. Notice that nonlinear activity spreads only to places associated with frequencies below the primary tones. (From J. L. Hall, Two-tone distortion products in a nonlinear model of the basilar membrane, *Journal of the Acoustical Society of America*, 1974, *56*. Reprinted with permission.)

confounding effects of aural combination tones. Because combination tones are generated in the cochlea and are to the brain indistinguishable from other spectral stimulus components, they may often provide misleading clues. In the investigation of complex-tone pitch, for instance, it was long thought that the phase relation between complex-tone components was critical in creating a "residue pitch" sensation (de Boer, 1956). It is now known that fundamental pitch perception of complex tones is essentially phase-insensitive (Houtsma & Goldstein, 1971; Wightman, 1973), but that monaural phase effects can be accounted for by the strongly phase-dependent combination tones (Goldstein, 1970), which enhance the complex-tone stimulus.

Aural combination tones can have a particularly confounding effect in masking experiments (see Section 3.2 of Scharf & Buus, Chapter 14). A test tone may interact with a masking tone to generate combination tones that are outside the masking region of the masker. Therefore the combination tones may be detected, whereas the test tone is completely masked. Smoorenburg (1972) has shown that the masked threshold for a test tone can be raised as much as 10 dB when the cubic difference tone resulting from interaction between the test and masking tones is covered with appropriate masking noise.

A useful audiometric application of aural combination tones is the determination of the effect of the acoustic middle-ear reflex by measuring the phase of the cubic difference tone. The middle-ear reflex effectively attenuates sound conduction through the middle ear by stiffening the middle-ear muscles, and is elicited in both ears simultaneously by exposure to relatively loud sounds. Effective attenuation can be measured as follows. For a given subject, a calibration curve is established by measuring the cubic difference tone's cancellation phase as a function of the intensity of two primary tones f_1 and f_2 (Goldstein, 1967). Cancellation phase measurements are then made for a fixed two-tone test stimulus both before and after the middle-ear reflex has been activated by contralateral noise. The observed cancellation phase difference can then be translated into a measure of effective middle-ear attenuation by means of the calibration curve (Rabinowitz & Goldstein, 1973).

5. SUMMARY

This chapter, Audition II, and its companion, Audition I, provide most of the basic information gathered largely during the past 50 years on how humans discriminate and perceive sounds. The sounds of concern have been tones, clicks, and noises; auditory patterns and sounds that carry symbolic information are considered in chapters by Deutsch, by Hawkins and Presson, and by Jusczyk. Audition I outlined basic concepts of the physics of sound, reviewed the complex anatomy and physiology of the auditory system, and gave detailed information on the detection of sounds in the quiet and in noise and also on the discrimination of spectral and temporal changes. Audition II has been about the perception of suprathreshold sounds—about loudness, pitch and timbre, localization, and aural distortion. Each section deals with the effects of stimulus and observer variables on these auditory phenomena. Among the important stimulus variables are intensity, frequency, bandwidth, duration, and the presence of other sounds (partial masking). Among the relevant observer variables are mode of sound presentation (to one ear or two ears or from a sound field), experience, and auditory pathology. Not being able to present or catalog all the psychoacoustic facts, we have attempted to present the most important and salient; we have provided an extensive bibliography to help the reader locate additional information. We also discuss models and theories that provide conceptual homes for the myriad facts.

Many of the data and models serve to solve problems in noise pollution, music, audiology, architectural acoustics, communication (especially speech), and so forth. We discuss some of these practical applications; others appear in other chapters. Primarily, we have sought to provide the data base and the conceptual groundwork to the reader who wishes to use the vast knowledge that constitutes psychoacoustics.

ACKNOWLEDGMENTS

We appreciate the many wise comments of Professor Jens Blauert about the section on sound localization. Sharon Quigley, with the aid of Barbara Passarelli and Anna-Liisa Scharf, handled most efficiently and effectively the complex word processing of these large chapters.

REFERENCES

*References preceded by an asterisk are "key references."

Abel, S. M., Birt, B. D., & McLean, J. A. Sound localization in hearing-impaired listeners. In R. W. Gatehouse (Ed.), *Localization of sound: Theory and applications*. Groton, Conn.: Amphora Press, 1982.

American National Standards Institute. *American national psychoacoustical terminology*. S3.20. New York: Anonymous, 1973.

American National Standards Institute. *American national standard procedure for the computation of loudness of noise*. S3.4. New York: Anonymous, 1980.

Bachem, A. Various types of absolute pitch. *Journal of the Acoustical Society of America*, 1937, *9*, 146–151.

Bachem, A. The genesis of absolute pitch. *Journal of the Acoustical Society of America*, 1940, *11*, 434–439.

Bachem, A. Time factors in relative and absolute pitch determination. *Journal of the Acoustical Society of America*, 1954, *26*, 751–753.

Batteau, D. W. The role of the pinna in human localization. *Proceedings of the Royal Society of London, Series B*, 1967, *168*, 158–180.

Batteau, D. W., & Plante, R. L. *Localization of sound: Part 2. The mechanism of human localization of sound with application in remote environments* (Report TP 3109). China Lake, Calif.: U.S. Naval Ordnance Testing Station, 1962.

Beck, J., & Shaw, W. A. Magnitude estimations of pitch. *Journal of the Acoustical Society of America*, 1962, *34*, 92–98.

Beck, J., & Shaw, W. A. Single estimates of pitch magnitude. *Journal of the Acoustical Society of America*, 1963, *35*, 1722–1724.

Békésy, G. von. Zur Theorie des Hörens: Über die Bestimmung des einem reinen tonempfindend entsprechenden Erregungsgebietes der Basilarmembran vermittelst Ermüdungserscheinungen. *Physikalische Zeitschrift*, 1929, *30*, 115–125.

Békésy, G. von. Zur Theorie des Hörens: Über das Richtungshören bei einer Zeitdifferenz oder Lautstärkeungleichheit der beidseitigen Schalleinwirkungen. *Physikalische Zeitschrift*, 1930, *31*, 824–838; 857–868.

Békésy, G. von. Über die Frequenzauflösung in der menschlichen Schnecke. *Acta Oto-Laryngologica*, 1944, *32*, 60–84.

Békésy, G. von. Funneling in the nervous system and its role in loudness and sensation intensity on the skin. *Journal of the Acoustical Society of America*, 1958, *30*, 399–412.

*Békésy, G. von. *Experiments in hearing*. New York: McGraw-Hill, 1960.

Bilsen, F. A. *On the interaction of a sound with its repetitions*. Unpublished doctoral dissertation, Delft University, The Netherlands, 1968.

Bilsen, F. A., & Goldstein, J. L. Pitch of dichotically delayed noise and its possible spectral basis. *Journal of the Acoustical Society of America*, 1974, *55*, 292–296.

Bismarck, G. von. Timbre of steady sounds: A factorial investigation of its verbal attributes. *Acustica*, 1974, *30*, 146–159.

Blauert, J. *Untersuchungen zum Richtungshören in der Medianebene bei fixiertem Kopf.* Unpublished doctoral dissertation, Technische Hochschule Aachen, West Germany, 1969.

Blauert, J. Sound localization in the median plane. *Acustica*, 1969/70, *22*, 205–213.

*Blauert, J. *Räumliches Hören.* Stuttgart, West Germany: S. Hirzel, 1974. (English translation with addendum: see Blauert, 1983.)

Blauert, J. Binaural localization. In O. J. Pedersen and T. Poulsen (Eds.), *Binaural effects in normal and impaired hearing. Scandinavian Audiology Supplement*, 1982.

*Blauert, J. *Spatial hearing.* Cambridge, Mass.: MIT Press, 1983.

Bonding, P. Critical bandwidth in Ménière's disease. *Audiology*, 1979, *18*, 197–211.

Boone, M. M. Loudness measurements on pure tone and broad band impulsive sounds. *Acustica*, 1973, *29*, 198–204.

Botte, M. -C. Effet du delai interaural pour des clics binauraux sur la sonie et sur les réponses évoquées. *Acustica*, 1974, *31*, 256–265.

Botte, M. -C., Beagley, H. -A., & Chocholle, R. Temporary threshold shift, loudness, and auditory evoked potentials. *Clinical Otolaryngology*, 1979, *4*, 49–56.

Botte, M. -C., Canévet, G., & Scharf, B. Loudness adaptation induced by an intermittent tone. *Journal of the Acoustical Society of America*, 1982, *72*, 727–739.

Botte, M. -C., & Scharf, B. La sonie—Effets simultanés de fatigue et de masque. *Acustica*, 1980, *46*, 100–106.

Botte, M. -C., & Scharf, B. La sonie. Interactions entre flux sonores simultanés. *Proceedings of 11th International Congress on Acoustics*, 1983, 83–86.

Brady, P. T. Fixed-scale mechanism of absolute pitch. *Journal of the Acoustical Society of America*, 1970, *48*, 883–887.

Brink, G. van den. Experiments on binaural diplacusis and tone perception. In R. Plomp & G. F. Smoorenburg (Eds.), *Frequency analysis and periodicity detection in hearing.* Leiden, The Netherlands: Sijthoff, 1970.

Burns, E. M., & Viemeister, N. F. Nonspectral pitch. *Journal of the Acoustical Society of America*, 1976, *60*, 863–869.

Burns, E. M., & Viemeister, N. F. Played-again SAM: Further observations on the pitch of amplitude-modulated noise. *Journal of the Acoustical Society of America*, 1981, *70*, 1655–1660.

Burns, E. M., & Ward, W. D. Categorical perception—Phenomenon or epiphenomenon: Evidence from experiments in the perception of melodic musical intervals. *Journal of the Acoustical Society of America*, 1978, *63*, 456–468.

Butler, R. The effect of hearing impairment on locating sound in the vertical plane. *International Audiology*, 1970, *1*, 117–126.

*Butler, R. A. The influence of the external and middle ear on auditory discriminations. In W. D. Keidel & W. D. Neff (Eds.), *Handbook of sensory physiology Vol. 5: Auditory system.* Berlin: Springer-Verlag, 1975.

Butler, R. A., & Flannery, R. The spatial attributes of stimulus frequency and their role in monaural localization of sound in the horizontal plane. *Perception and Psychophysics*, 1980, *28*, 449–457.

Canévet, G., Germain, R., Marchioni, A., & Scharf, B. Adaptation de sonie. *Acustica*, 1981, *49*, 239–244.

Canévet, G., Germain, R., & Scharf, B. Localisation d'une information sonore en presence de bruit masquant. *Acustica*, 1980, *46*, 90–95.

Canévet, G., Hellman, R. P., Marchioni, A., & Scharf, B. Estimations de sonie en champ libre et semi-réverbérant. *Proceedings of 11th International Congress on Acoustics*, 1983, 87–90.

Canévet, G., Scharf, B., & Botte, M.-C. Loudness adaptation, when induced, is real. *British Journal of Audiology*, 1983, *17*, 49–57.

Canévet, G., Scharf, B., & Botte, M.-C. Simple and induced loudness adaptation. *Audiology*, in press.

Caussé, R., & Chavasse, P. Différence entre l'écoute binauriculaire et monauriculaire pour la perception des intensités supraliminaire. *Comptes Rendus des Séances de la Société de Biologie*, 1942, *136*, 405–406.

Chocholle, R., & Greenbaum, H. B. La sonie de sons purs partiellement masqués. *Journal de Psychologie*, 1966, *4*, 385–414.

Christman, R. J., & Williams, W. E. Influence of the time interval on experimentally induced shifts of pitch. *Journal of the Acoustical Society of America*, 1963, *35*, 1030–1033.

Clack, T. D. Aural harmonics: The masking of a 2000-Hz tone by a sufficient 1000-Hz fundamental. *Journal of the Acoustical Society of America*, 1967, *42*, 751–758.

Clark, M., Luce, D., Abrams, R., Schlossberg, H., & Rome, J. Preliminary experiments on the aural significance of parts of tones of orchestral instruments and on choral tones. *Journal of the Audio Engineering Society*, 1964, *12*, 28–31.

*Colburn, H. S., & Durlach, N. I. Models of binaural interaction. In E. C. Carterette & M. P. Friedman (Eds.), *Handbook of perception Vol. 4: Hearing.* New York: Academic Press, 1978.

Coleman, P. D. Failure to localize the source distance of an unfamiliar sound. *Journal of the Acoustical Society of America*, 1962, *34*, 345–346.

*Coleman, P. D. An analysis of cues to auditory depth perception in free space. *Psychological Bulletin*, 1963, *60*, 302–315.

Cramer, E. M., & Huggins, W. H. Creation of pitch through binaural interaction. *Journal of the Acoustical Society of America*, 1958, *30*, 413–417.

Cuddy, L. L. Practice effects in the absolute judgment of pitch. *Journal of the Acoustical Society of America*, 1968, *43*, 1069–1076.

Dallos, P. Combination tone $2f_1 - f_2$ in microphonic potentials. *Journal of the Acoustical Society of America*, 1969, *46*, 1437–1444.

David, E. E., Guttman, N., & van Bergeijk, W. A. Binaural interaction of high-frequency complex stimuli. *Journal of the Acoustical Society of America*, 1959, *31*, 774–782.

Davis, H. Excitation of auditory receptors. In J. Field, H. W. Magou, & V. E. Hall (Eds.), *Handbook of physiology Vol. 1: Neurophysiology.* Baltimore: Waverly Press, 1959.

Davis, H., Morgan, C. T., Hawkins J. E., Galambos, R., & Smith, F. W. Temporary deafness following exposure to loud tones and noise. *Acta Oto-Laryngologica Supplement*, 1950, *88*, 1–87.

de Barbenza, C. M., Bryan, M. E., & Tempest, W. Individual loudness functions. *Journal of Sound and Vibration*, 1970, *11*, 399–410.

de Boer, E. *On the "residue" in hearing.* Unpublished doctoral dissertation, University of Amsterdam, The Netherlands, 1956.

de Boer, E. On the "residue" and auditory pitch perception. In W. D. Keidel & W. D. Neff (Eds.), *Handbook of sensory physiology Vol. 5: Auditory system, Part 3: Clinical and special topics.* New York: Springer-Verlag, 1976.

de Maré, G. Audiometrische Untersuchungen. Über das Verhalten des normalen und schwerhörigen Ohres bei funktioneller Belastung nebst Bemerkungen zur Theorie des Gehörs. *Acta Oto-Laryngologica*, 1939, *Supplement 31.*

de Maré, G. Investigations into the functions of the auditory apparatus in perception deafness. *Acta Oto-Laryngologica*, 1948, *Supplement 74.*

Duifhuis, H. Cochlear nonlinearity and second filter: Possible mechanism and implications. *Journal of the Acoustical Society of America*, 1976, *59*, 408–423.

Duifhuis, H., Willems, L. F., & Sluyter, R. J. Measurement of pitch in speech: An implementation of Goldstein's theory of pitch perception. *Journal of the Acoustical Society of America*, 1982, *71*, 1568–1580.

Durlach, N. I., & Colburn, H. S. Binaural phenomena. In E. C. Carterette & M. P. Friedman (Eds.), *Handbook of perception Vol. 4: Hearing.* New York: Academic Press, 1978.

Durlach, N. I., Thompson, C. L., & Colburn, H. S. Binaural interaction in impaired listeners. *Audiology*, 1981, *20*, 181–211.

Egan, J. P. Perstimulatory fatigue as measured by heterophonic loudness balances. *Journal of the Acoustical Society of America*, 1955, *27*, 111–120.

Ekman, G., Berglund, B., & Berglund, U. Loudness as a function of the duration of auditory stimulation. *Scandinavian Journal of*

Psychology, 1966, *7*, 201–208.

Elfner, L. F., & Tomsic, R. T. Temporal and intensive factors in binaural lateralization of auditory transients. *Journal of the Acoustical Society of America*, 1968, *43*, 746–751.

Elmasian, R., & Galambos, R. Loudness enhancement: Monaural, binaural and dichotic. *Journal of the Acoustical Society of America*, 1975, *58*, 229–234.

Fastl, H. Über Tonhöhenmpfindungen bei Rauschen. *Acustica*, 1971, *25*, 350–354.

Fechner, G. T. *Elemente der Psychophysik*. Leipzig: Breitkopf & Harterl, 1860.

Fedderson, W. E., Sandel, T. T., Teas, D. C., & Jeffress, L. A. Localization of high-frequency tones. *Journal of the Acoustical Society of America*, 1957, *29*, 988–991.

Fletcher, H. The physical criterion for determining the pitch of musical tone. *Physical Review*, 1924, *23*, 427–437.

Fletcher, H. F., & Munson, W. A. Loudness, its definition, measurement and calculation. *Journal of the Acoustical Society of America*, 1933, *5*, 82–108.

Fletcher, H., & Munson, W. A. Relation between loudness and masking. *Journal of the Acoustical Society of America*, 1937, *9*, 1–10.

Florentine, M., Buus, S., & Bonding, P. Loudness of complex sounds as a function of the standard stimulus and the number of components. *Journal of the Acoustical Society of America*, 1978, *64*, 1036–1040.

*Florentine, M., Buus, S., Scharf, B., & Zwicker, E. Frequency selectivity in normally-hearing and hearing-impaired observers. *Journal of Speech and Hearing Research*, 1980, *23*, 646–669.

Fraser, W. D., Petty, J. W., & Elliott, D. N. Adaptation: Central or peripheral? *Journal of the Acoustical Society of America*, 1970, *47*, 1016–1021.

Furst, M., & Goldstein, J. L. Differences of CT ($2f_1 - f_2$) phase in psychophysical and physiological experiments. *Hearing Research*, 1980, *2*, 379–386.

Gardner, M. B. Distance estimation of 0° or apparent 0°-oriented speech in anechoic space. *Journal of the Acoustical Society of America*, 1969, *45*, 47–53.

Gardner, M. B. Some monaural and binaural facets of median plane localization. *Journal of the Acoustical Society of America*, 1973, *54*, 1489–1495.

Garner, W. R. The loudness and loudness matching of short tones. *Journal of the Acoustical Society of America*, 1949, *21*, 398–401.

Gässler, G. Über die Hörschwelle für Schallereignisse mit verschieden breitem Frequenzspektrum. *Acustica*, 1954, *4*, 408–414.

Gatehouse, R. W. Further research in localization of sound by completely monaural subjects. *Journal of Auditory Research*, 1976, *16*, 265–273.

Gerson, A., & Goldstein, J. L. Evidence for a general template in central optimal processing for pitch of complex tones. *Journal of the Acoustical Society of America*, 1978, *63*, 498–510.

Gibian, G. L. *Cochlear microphonic evidence for mechanical propagation of distortion products* ($f_2 - f_1$) *and* ($2f_1 - f_2$). Unpublished doctoral dissertation, Washington University, St. Louis, 1980.

Gjaevenes, K., & Rimstad, E. R. The influence of rise time on loudness. *Journal of the Acoustical Society of America*, 1972, *51*, 1233–1239.

Gleiss, N., & Zwicker, E. Loudness function in the presence of masking noise. *Journal of the Acoustical Society of America*, 1964, *36*, 393–394.

*Goldstein, J. L. Auditory nonlinearity. *Journal of the Acoustical Society of America*, 1967, *41*, 676–689.

Goldstein, J. L. Aural combination tones. In R. Plomp and G. F. Smoorenburg (Eds.), *Frequency analysis and periodicity detection in hearing*. Leiden, The Netherlands: Sijthoff, 1970.

Goldstein, J. L. An optimum processor theory for the central formation of the pitch of complex tones. *Journal of the Acoustical Society of America*, 1973, *54*, 1496–1516.

Goldstein, J. L., & Kiang, N. Y.-S. Neural correlates of the aural combination tone $2f_1 - f_2$. *Proceedings of the IEEE*, 1968, *56*, 981–992.

Greenwood, D. D. Aural combination tones and auditory masking. *Journal of the Acoustical Society of America*, 1971, *50*, 502–543.

Greenwood, D. D. Masking by combination bands: Estimation of the levels of the combination bands $(n+1)f_1 - nf_2$. *Journal of the Acoustical Society of America*, 1972, *52*, 1144–1154.

Grey, J. M. Multidimensional perceptual scaling of musical timbres. *Journal of the Acoustical Society of America*, 1977, *61*, 1270–1277.

Gruber, J., & Braune, H. Auditory adaptation measured by cross-modality matching. *Eighth international congress on acoustics*. Trowbridge, England: Goldcrest Press, 1974.

Gulick, W. L. *Hearing: Physiology and psychophysics*. New York: Oxford University Press, 1971.

Haas, H. Über den Einfluss eines Einfachechos auf die Hörsamkeit von Sprache. *Acustica*, 1951, *1*, 49–58.

Hafter, E. R., & De Maio, J. Difference threshold for interaural delay. *Journal of the Acoustical Society of America*, 1975, *57*, 181–187.

Hafter, E. R., & Dye, R. H., Jr. Detection of interaural differences of time in trains of high-frequency clicks as a function of interclick interval and number. *Journal of the Acoustical Society of America*, 1983, *73*, 644–651.

Hafter, E. R., Dye, R. H., Jr., & Gilkey, R. H. Lateralization of tonal signals which have neither onsets nor offsets. *Journal of the Acoustical Society of America*, 1979, *65*, 471–477.

Hafter, E. R., Dye, R. H., Jr., & Wenzel, E. S. Detection of interaural differences of intensity in trains of high-frequency clicks as a function of interclick interval and number. *Journal of the Acoustical Society of America*, 1983, *73*, 1708–1713.

Hall, J. L. Minimum detectable change in interaural time or intensity difference for brief impulsive stimuli. *Journal of the Acoustical Society of America*, 1964, *36*, 2411–2413.

Hall, J. L. Two-tone distortion products in a nonlinear model of the basilar membrane. *Journal of the Acoustical Society of America*, 1974, *56*, 1818–1828.

Hall, J. W. III, & Soderquist, D. R. Adaptation of residue pitch. *Journal of the Acoustical Society of America*, 1978, *63*, 883–893.

Hall, J. W., & Soderquist, D. R. Transient complex and pure tone pitch changes by adaptation. *Journal of the Acoustical Society of America*, 1982, *71*, 665–670.

Hallpike, C. S. The loudness recruitment phenomenon: A clinical contribution to the neurology of hearing. In A. B. Graham (Ed.), *Sensorineural hearing processes and disorders*. Boston: Little, Brown, 1967.

Hallpike, C. S., & Hood, J. P. Observations upon the neurological mechanism of the loudness recruitment phenomenon. *Acta Oto-Laryngologica*, 1959, *50*, 472–486.

Harris, C. M. Residual masking at low frequencies. *Journal of the Acoustical Society of America*, 1959, *31*, 1110–1115.

Harris, J. D., & Pikler, A. G. The stability of a standard loudness as measured by compensatory tracking. *American Journal of Psychology*, 1960, *73*, 573–580.

Harris, J. D., & Sargeant, R. L. Monaural/binaural minimum audible angle for a moving sound source. *Journal of Speech and Hearing Research*, 1971, *14*, 618–629.

Hartmann, W. M. The effect of amplitude envelope on the pitch of sinewave tones. *Journal of the Acoustical Society of America*, 1978, *63*, 1105–1113.

Hartmann, W. M., & Blumenstock, B. J. Time dependence of pitch perception-pitch step experiment. *Journal of the Acoustical Society of America*, 1976, *60*, S40.

Hebrank, J., & Wright, D. Spectral cues used in the localization of sound sources on the median plane. *Journal of the Acoustical Society of America*, 1974, *56*, 1829–1834.

Hellman, R. P. Asymmetry of masking between noise and tone. *Perception and Psychophysics*, 1972, *11*, 241–246.

Hellman, R. P. Growth of loudness at 1000 and 3000 Hz. *Journal of the Acoustical Society of America*, 1976, *60*, 672–679.

Hellman, R. P. Dependence of loudness growth on skirts of excitation patterns. *Journal of the Acoustical Society of America*, 1978, *63*, 1114–1119.

Hellman, R. P. Stability of individual loudness functions obtained by magnitude estimation and production. *Perception and Psychophysics*, 1981, *29*, 63–70.

Hellman, R. P., & Zwislocki, J. J. Some factors affecting the estimation of loudness. *Journal of the Acoustical Society of America*, 1961, *33*, 687–694.

Hellman, R. P., & Zwislocki, J. J. Monaural loudness function at 1000 cps and interaural summation. *Journal of the Acoustical Society of America*, 1963, *35*, 856–865.

Hellman, R. P., & Zwislocki, J. J. Loudness determination at low sound frequencies. *Journal of the Acoustical Society of America*, 1968, *43*, 60–64.

Helmholtz, H. *On the sensations of tone*. New York: Dover, 1954. (Originally published, 1885.)

Henderson, D., Hamernik, R. P., Dosanjh, D. S., & Mills, J. H. (Eds.), *Effects of noise on hearing*. New York: Raven, 1976.

Henning, G. B. Detectability of interaural delay in high-frequency complex waveforms. *Journal of the Acoustical Society of America*, 1974, *55*, 84–90.

Hermann, L. Zur Theorie der Combinationstöne. *Archiv für gesamte Physiologie*, 1891, *49*, 499–518.

Hershkowitz, R. M., & Durlach, N. I. Interaural time and amplitude JND's for a 500-Hz tone. *Journal of the Acoustical Society of America*, 1969, *46*, 1464–1467.

Hood, J. D. Studies in auditory fatigue and adaptation. *Acta Oto-Laryngologica*, 1950, *S92*, 1–57.

Hood, J. D., & Poole, J. P. Tolerable limit of loudness: Its clinical and physiological significance. *Journal of the Acoustical Society of America*, 1966, *40*, 47–53.

Houtgast, T., & Plomp, R. Lateralization threshold of a signal in noise. *Journal of the Acoustical Society of America*, 1968, *44*, 807–812.

Houtsma, A. J. M. Musical pitch of two-tone complexes and predictions by modern pitch theories. *Journal of the Acoustical Society of America*, 1979, *66*, 87–99.

Houtsma, A. J. M. Noise-induced shifts in the pitch of pure and complex tones. *Journal of the Acoustical Society of America*, 1981, *70*, 1661–1668. (a)

Houtsma, A. J. M. Pitch of unequal-amplitude dichotic two-tone harmonic complexes. *Journal of the Acoustical Society of America*, 1981, *69*, 1778–1785. (b)

Houtsma, A. J. M., & Goldstein, J. L. *Perception of musical intervals: Evidence for the central origin of the pitch of complex tones* (Tech. Rep. 484). Cambridge, Mass.: Research Laboratory of Electronics, 1971.

*Houtsma, A. J. M., & Goldstein, J. L. The central origin of the pitch of complex tones: Evidence from musical interval recognition. *Journal of the Acoustical Society of America*, 1972, *51*, 520–529.

Houtsma, A. J. M., Wicke, R. W., & Ordubadi, A. Pitch of amplitude-modulated low-pass noise and predictions by temporal and spectral theories. *Journal of the Acoustical Society of America*, 1980, *67*, 1312–1322.

Howes, D. H. The loudness of multicomponent tones. *American Journal of Psychology*, 1950, *63*, 1–30.

Hubbard, A. E., & Geisler, C. D. A hybrid-computer model of the cochlear partition. *Journal of the Acoustical Society of America*, 1972, *51*, 1895–1903.

Huygens, C. *Oeuvres complètes (Vol. 10)*. Haarlem, The Netherlands: Société Hollandaise des Sciences, 1905. (Originally published, 1693.)

International Organization for Standardization. *Normal equal-loudness contours for pure tones and normal threshold of hearing under free field listening conditions*. R226. New York: Anonymous, 1962.

International Organization for Standardization. *Method for calculating loudness level*. R532. New York: Anonymous, 1966.

Irwin, R. J., & Zwislocki, J. J. Loudness effects in pairs of tone bursts. *Perception and Psychophysics*, 1971, *10*, 189–192.

Jacobsen, T. *Localization in noise* (Tech. Rep. 10). Lyngby, Denmark: Technical University of Denmark, Acoustics Laboratory, 1976.

Jeffress, L. A. A place theory of sound localization. *Journal of Contemporary Physiology and Psychology*, 1948, *61*, 468–486.

Jeffress, L. A., & Taylor, R. W. Lateralization versus localization. *Journal of the Acoustical Society of America*, 1961, *33*, 482–483.

Kärjä, J. Perstimulatory suptrathreshold adaptation. I. Basic studies on normal-hearing persons. *Acta Oto-Laryngologica*, 1968, Supplement 241.

Kemp, D. T. Stimulated acoustic emissions from within the human auditory system. *Journal of the Acoustical Society of America*, 1978, *64*, 1386–1391.

Kim, D. O. *A nonlinear model for basilar membrane motion and related phenomena of single cochlear nerve fibers*. Unpublished doctoral dissertation, Washington University, St. Louis, 1972.

Kim, D. O., Molnar, C. E., & Matthews, J. W. Cochlear mechanics: Nonlinear behavior in two-tone responses as reflected in cochlear nerve fiber responses and in ear canal sound pressure. *Journal of the Acoustical Society of America*, 1980, *67*, 1704–1721.

Klein, M. A., & Hartmann, W. M. Binaural edge pitch. *Journal of the Acoustical Society of America*, 1981, *70*, 51–61.

Klumpp, R. G., & Eady, H. R. Some measurements of interaural time difference thresholds. *Journal of the Acoustical Society of America*, 1956, *28*, 859–860.

Kunov, H., & Abel, S. M. Effect of rise/decay time on the lateralization of interaurally delayed 1-kHz tones. *Journal of the Acoustical Society of America*, 1981, *69*, 769–773.

Lachs, G., & Teich, M. C. A neural-counting model incorporating refractoriness and spread of excitation. II. Application to loudness estimation. *Journal of the Acoustical Society of America*, 1981, *69*, 774–782.

Larkin, W. D. Pitch shifts following tone adaptation. *Acustica*, 1978, *41*, 110–116.

Liberman, A. M., Harris, K. S., Hoffman, H. S., & Griffith, B. S. The discrimination of speech sounds within and across phoneme boundaries. *Journal of Experimental Psychology*, 1957, *54*, 358–368.

Lim, J. S., Rabinowitz, W. M., Braida, L. D., & Durlach, N. I. Intensity perception VIII. Loudness comparisons between different types of stimuli. *Journal of the Acoustical Society of America*, 1977, *62*, 1256–1267.

Lindenmann, W. Evaluation of internal signal differences. In O. J. Pedersen & T. Paulson (Eds.), *Binaural effects in normal and impaired hearing. Scandinavian Audiology Supplement*, 1982.

Logue, A. W. Individual differences in magnitude estimation of loudness. *Perception and Psychophysics*, 1976, *19*, 279–280.

Margolis, R. H., & Wiley, T. L. Monaural loudness adaptation at low sensation levels in normal and impaired ears. *Journal of the Acoustical Society of America*, 1976, *59*, 222–224.

Marks, L. E. *Sensory processes*. New York: Academic Press, 1974.

Marks, L. E. Sensory and cognitive factors in judgments of loudness. *Journal of Experimental Psychology: Human Perception and Performance*, 1979, *5*, 426–443. (a)

Marks, L. E. A theory of loudness and loudness judgments. *Psychological Review*, 1979, *86*, 256–285. (b)

Martin, M. C. Critical bands in sensori-neural hearing loss. *Scandinavian Audiology*, 1974, *3*, 133–140.

McFadden, D., & Moffitt, C. M. Acoustic integration for lateralization at high frequencies. *Journal of the Acoustical Society of America*, 1977, *61*, 1604–1608.

McFadden, D., & Wightman, F. L. Audition: Some relations between normal and pathological hearing. *Annual Review of Psychology*, 1983, *34*, 95–128.

Mershon, D. H., & King, L. E. Intensity and reverberation as factors in the auditory perception of egocentric distance. *Perception and Psychophysics*, 1975, *18*, 409–415.

Miller, G. A. The perception of short bursts of noise. *Journal of the Acoustical Society of America*, 1948, *20*, 160–170.

Miller, G. A., & Taylor, W. G. The perception of repeated bursts of noise. *Journal of the Acoustical Society of America*, 1948, *20*, 171–182.

*Mills, A. W. On the minimum audible angle. *Journal of the Acoustical Society of America*, 1958, *30*, 237–246.

Mills, A. W. Lateralization of high-frequency tones. *Journal of the Acoustical Society of America*, 1960, *32*, 132–134.

*Mills, A. W. Auditory localization. In J. V. Tobias (Ed.), *Foundations of modern auditory theory* (Vol. 2). New York: Academic Press, 1972.
Mirabella, A., Taug, H., & Teichner, W. H. Adaptation of loudness to monaural stimulation. *Journal of General Psychology*, 1967, *76*, 251–273.
Miskolczy-Fodor, F. Relation between loudness and duration of tonal pulses. III. Responses in cases of abnormal loudness function. *Journal of the Acoustical Society of America*, 1960, *32*, 486–492.
Molino, J. A. Psychophysical verification of predicted interaural differences in localizing distant sound sources. *Journal of the Acoustical Society of America*, 1974, *55*, 139–147.
Morgan, C. T., Garner, W. R., & Galambos, R. Pitch and intensity. *Journal of the Acoustical Society of America*, 1951, *23*, 658–663.
Morgan, D. E., Wilson, R. H., & Dirks, D. D. Loudness discomfort level: Selected methods and stimuli. *Journal of the Acoustical Society of America*, 1974, *56*, 577–581.
Moushegian, G., & Jeffress, L. A. Role of interaural time and intensity differences in the lateralization of low-frequency tones. *Journal of the Acoustical Society of America*, 1959, *31*, 1441–1445.
Mowbray, G. H., Gebhard, J. W., & Byham, C. L. Sensitivity to changes in the interruption rate of white noise. *Journal of the Acoustical Society of America*, 1956, *28*, 106–110.
Munson, W. A. The growth of auditory sensation. *Journal of the Acoustical Society of America*, 1947, *19*, 584–591.
Munson, W. A., & Gardner, M. B. Loudness patterns—A new approach. *Journal of the Acoustical Society of America*, 1950, *22*, 177–190.
Musicant, A. D. Behavioral evidence for central coding of azimuth as a function of stimulus frequency. *Journal of the Acoustical Society of America*, 1983, *74*, S9.
Niese, H. Vorschlag für die Definition und Messung der Deutlichkeit nach subjectiven Grundlagen. *Hochfrequenztechnik und Elektroakustik*, 1956, *65*, 4–15.
Niese, H. Die Trägheit der Lautstärkebildung in Abhängigkeit vom Schallpegel. *Hochfrequenztechnik und Elektroakustik*, 1959, *68*, 143–152.
Niese, H. Subjektive Messungen der Lautstärke von Bandpassrauschen. *Hochfrequenztechnik und Elektroakustik*, 1960, *68*, 202–217.
Niese, H. Die Lautstärkebildung bei binauralem Hören komplexer Geräusche. *Hochfrequenztechnik und Elektroakustik*, 1961, *70*, 132–141.
Niese, H. Eine Methode zur Bestimmung der Lautstärke beliebiger Geräusche. *Acustica*, 1965, *15*, 117.
Nuetzel, J. M., & Hafter, E. R. Lateralization of complex waveforms: Effects of fine structure, amplitude, and duration. *Journal of the Acoustical Society of America*, 1976, *60*, 1339–1346.
Ohm, G. W. Über die Definition des Tones, nebst daran geknupfter Theorie der Sirene und ähnlicher tonbildender Vorrichtungen. *Annalen für Physik und Chemie*, 1843, *59*, 513–565.
Parker, D. E., Tubbs, R. L., Johnston, P. A., & Johnston, L. S. Influence of auditory fatigue on masked pure tone thresholds. *Journal of the Acoustical Society of America*, 1976, *60*, 881–885.
Paulus, E., & Zwicker, E. Program zur automatischen Bestimmung der Lautheit aus Terzpegeln oder Frequenzgruppenpegeln. *Acustica*, 1972, *27*, 253–266.
*Pedersen, O. J., Lyregaard, P. E., & Poulsen, T. E. *The round robin test on evaluation of loudness level of impulsive noise* (Report No. 22). Copenhagen: Technical University of Denmark, Acoustics Laboratory, September 1977.
*Perrott, D. R. Role of signal onset in sound localization. *Journal of the Acoustical Society of America*, 1969, *45*, 436–445.
Perrott, D. R. Studies in the perception of auditory motion. In R. W. Gatehouse (Ed.), *Localization of sound: Theory and applications*. Groton, Conn.: Amphora Press, 1982.
Pierce, J. R., Lipes, R., & Cheetham, C. Uncertainty concerning the direct use of time information in hearing: Place clues in white-spectra stimuli. *Journal of the Acoustical Society of America*, 1977, *61*, 1609–1621.
Plenge, G. On the difference between localization and lateralization. *Journal of the Acoustical Society of America*, 1974, *56*, 944–951.
*Plomp, R. Detectability threshold for combination tones. *Journal of the Acoustical Society of America*, 1965, *37*, 1110–1123.
Plomp, R. Timbre as a multidimensional attribute of complex tones. In R. Plomp & G. F. Smoorenburg (Eds.), *Frequency analysis and periodicity detection in hearing*. Leiden, The Netherlands: Sijthoff, 1970.
Pollack, I. Loudness of periodically interrupted white noise. *Journal of the Acoustical Society of America*, 1958, *30*, 181–185.
Pollack, I. Periodicity pitch for interrupted white noise—Fact or artifact. *Journal of the Acoustical Society of America*, 1969, *45*, 237–238.
Porsolt, R. D., & Irwin, R. J. Binaural summation in loudness of two tones as a function of their bandwidth. *American Journal of Psychology*, 1967, *80*, 384–390.
Port, E. Über die Lautstärke einzelner kurzer Schallimpulse. *Acustica*, 1963, *13*, 212–223. (a)
Port, E. Zur Lautstärkeempfindung und Lautstärkemessung von pulsierenden Geräuschen. *Acustica*, 1963, *13*, 224–233. (b)
Rabinowitz, W. M., & Goldstein, J. L. Middle-ear transmission change as measured by aural combination tone phase behavior. *Journal of the Acoustical Society of America*, 1973, *54*, 293.
Rakowski, A., & Hirsh, I. Post-stimulatory pitch shift and its dependence on signal parameters. *Journal of the Acoustical Society of America*, 1978, *63*, S50.
Reichardt, W. Zur Trägheit der Lautstärkebildung. *Acustica*, 1965, *15*, 345–354.
Reichardt, W. Subjective and objective measurement of the loudness level of single and repeated impulses. *Journal of the Acoustical Society of America*, 1970, *47*, 1557–1562.
Reichardt, W., & Niese, H. Choice of sound duration and silent intervals for test and comparison signals in the subjective measurement of loudness level. *Journal of the Acoustical Society of America*, 1970, *47*, 1083–1090.
Revesz, G. *Zur Grundlagung der Tonpsychologie*. Leipzig: Veit, 1913.
Reynolds, G. S., & Stevens, S. S. Binaural summation of loudness. *Journal of the Acoustical Society of America*, 1960, *32*, 1337–1344.
Rhode, W. S. Some observations of two-tone interactions measured using the Mossbauer effect. In E. F. Evans & J. P. Wilson (Eds.), *Psychophysics and physiology of hearing*. New York: Academic Press, 1977.
Riach, W., Elliot, D. N., & Reed, J. C. Growth of loudness and its relationship to intensity discrimination under various levels of auditory fatigue. *Journal of the Acoustical Society of America*, 1962, *34*, 1764–1767.
Ricard, G. L., & Hafter, E. R. Detection of interaural time differences in short-duration low-frequency tones. *Journal of the Acoustical Society of America*, 1973, *53*, 335.
Ritsma, R. J. Existence region of the tonal residue I. *Journal of the Acoustical Society of America*, 1962, *34*, 1224–1229.
Ritsma, R. J. Frequencies dominant in the perception of the pitch of complex sounds. *Journal of the Acoustical Society of America*, 1967, *42*, 191–198.
Robinson, D. W. The subjective loudness scale. *Acustica*, 1957, *7*, 217–233.
Robinson, D. W., & Dadson, R. S. A re-determination of the equal-loudness relations for pure tones. *British Journal of Applied Physics*, 1956, *7*, 166–181.
Roffler, S. K., & Butler, R. A. Factors that influence the localization of sound in the vertical plane. *Journal of the Acoustical Society of America*, 1968, *43*, 1255–1259.
Röser, D. *Schallrichtungsbestimmung bei krankhaft verändertem Gehör* (The determination of the direction of sound with defective hearing). Unpublished doctoral dissertation, Technische Hochschule, Aachen, West Germany, 1965.
Ross, S. On the relation between the acoustic reflex and loudness. *Journal of the Acoustical Society of America*, 1968, *43*, 768–779.
Rotuolo, B. R., Stern, R. M., & Colburn, H. S. Discrimination of symmetric time-intensity traded binaural stimuli. *Journal of the Acoustical Society of America*, 1979, *66*, 1733–1737.
Rowland, R. C., & Tobias, J. F. Interaural intensity difference limen.

Journal of Speech and Hearing Research, 1967, *10*, 745–756.

Sandel, T. T., Teas, D. C., Feddersen, W. E., & Jeffress, L. A. Localization of sound from single and paired sources. *Journal of the Acoustical Society of America*, 1955, *27*, 842–852.

Sayers, B. A., & Cherry, E. C. Mechanism of binaural fusion in the hearing of speech. *Journal of the Acoustical Society of America*, 1957, *29*, 973–987.

Scharf, B. Critical bands and the loudness of complex sounds near threshold. *Journal of the Acoustical Society of America*, 1959, *31*, 365–370. (a)

Scharf, B. Loudness of complex sounds as a function of the number of components. *Journal of the Acoustical Society of America*, 1959, *31*, 783–785. (b)

Scharf, B. Loudness summation and spectrum shape. *Journal of the Acoustical Society of America*, 1962, *34*, 228–233. (a)

Scharf, B. Loudness summation in conductive deafness. *Proceedings of the 4th International Congress on Acoustics*, 1962, *1*, H53. (b)

Scharf, B. Partial masking. *Acustica*, 1964, *14*, 16–23.

Scharf, B. Dichotic summation of loudness. *Journal of the Acoustical Society of America*, 1969, *45*, 1193–1205.

Scharf, B. Critical bands. In J. V. Tobias (Ed.), *Foundations of modern auditory theory* (Vol. 1). New York: Academic Press, 1970. (a)

Scharf, B. Loudness and frequency selectivity at short durations. In R. I. Plomp & G. F. Smoorenburg (Eds.), *Frequency analysis and periodicity detection in hearing*. Leiden, The Netherlands: A. W. Sijthoff, 1970, 455–461. (b)

Scharf, B. Patterns of partial masking. *Proceedings of the 7th International Congress on Acoustics*, 1971, *3*, 461–464.

Scharf, B. Localization of unlike tones from two loudspeakers. In H. R. Moskowitz, B. Scharf, & J. C. Stevens (Eds.), *Sensation and measurement—Papers in honor of S. S. Stevens*. Dordrecht, Holland: Reidel Press, 1974. (a)

Scharf, B. Loudness summation between two tones from two loudspeakers. *Journal of the Acoustical Society of America*, 1974, *56*, 589–593. (b)

*Scharf, B. Loudness. In E. C. Carterette & M. P. Friedman (Eds.), *Handbook of perception Vol. 4: Hearing*. New York: Academic Press, 1978.

*Scharf, B. Loudness adaptation. In J. V. Tobias & E. D. Schubert (Eds.), *Hearing research and theory*. New York: Academic Press, 1983.

Scharf, B., Botte, M.-C., & Canévet, G. Loudness adaptation induced interaurally and monaurally. In R. Klinke & R. Hartmann (Eds.), *Hearing—Physiological bases and psychophysics*. New York: Springer-Verlag, 1983. (a)

Scharf, B., Botte, M.-C., & Canévet, G. Récuperation après adaptation induite de sonie. *L'Année Psychologique*, 1983, *83*, 9–24. (b)

Scharf, B., & Canévet, G. Role of frequency selectivity in localization and lateralization. In G. van den Brink & F. A. Bilsen (Eds.), *Psychophysical, physiological, and behavioral studies in hearing*. Delft, Holland: Delft University Press, 1980.

Scharf, B., Canévet, G., Buus, S., & Marchioni, A. *Localization in noise by hearing impaired listeners*. International Congress of Audiology, Helsinki, Finland, May, 1982, C27 (A).

Scharf, B., & Fishken, D. Binaural summation of loudness: Reconsidered. *Journal of Experimental Psychology*, 1970, *86*, 374–379.

Scharf, B., & Florentine, M. Critical bandwidth in lateralization. *Journal of the Acoustical Society of America*, 1975, *57*, S25 (A).

Scharf, B., & Florentine, M. Psychoacoustics of elementary sound perception. In G. A. Studebaker & F. H. Bess (Eds.), *The Vanderbilt hearing-aid report, Monographs in contemporary audiology*, 1982, 3–15.

Scharf, B., Florentine, M., & Meiselman, C. H. Critical band in auditory lateralization. *Sensory Processes*, 1976, *1*, 109–126.

Scharf, B., & Hellman, R. P. Model of loudness summation applied to impaired ears. *Journal of the Acoustical Society of America*, 1966, *40*, 71–78.

Scharf, B., Hellman, R., & Bauer, J. Comparison of various methods for predicting the loudness and acceptability of noise. *Report to Environmental Protection Agency*, August, 1977.

Scharf, B., & Meiselman, C. Critical bandwidth at high intensities. In E. V. Evans & J. P. Wilson (Eds.), *Psychophysics and physiology of hearing*. New York: Academic Press, 1977.

Scharf, B., & Stevens, J. C. The form of the loudness function near threshold. *Procedings of the third congress of acoustics* (Vol. 1). Amsterdam: Elsevier, 1961.

Schneider, B., Wright, A. A., Edelheit, W., Hock, P., & Humphrey, C. Equal loudness contours derived from sensory magnitude judgments. *Journal of the Acoustical Society of America*, 1972, *51*, 1951–1959.

*Schouten, J. F. The residue and the mechanism of hearing. *Proceedings of the Koninklijke Nederlandse Akademie van Wetenschappen*, 1940, *43*, 991–999.

Schouten, J. F., Ritsma, R. J., & Cardozo, B. L. Pitch of the residue. *Journal of the Acoustical Society of America*, 1962, *34*, 1418–1424.

Schroeder, M. R. An integrable model for the basilar membrane. *Journal of the Acoustical Society of America*, 1973, *53*, 429–434.

Schwarze, D. *Die Lautstärke von Gausstönen*. Unpublished doctoral dissertation, Technische Universität, Berlin, 1963.

Searle, C. L., Braida, L. D., Cuddy, D. R., & Davis, M. F. Binaural pinna disparity: Another auditory localization cue. *Journal of the Acoustical Society of America*, 1975, *57*, 448–455.

Seebeck, A. Beobachtungen über einige Bedingungen der Entstehung von Tönen. *Annalen für Physik und Chemie*, 1841, *53*, 417–436.

Shambaugh, G. C. Diplacusis: A localizing symptom of disease of the organ of Corti. *Archives of Otolaryngology*, 1940, *31*, 160.

*Shaw, E. A. G. The external ear. In W. D. Keidel & W. D. Neff (Eds.), *Handbook of sensory physiology* (Vol. 5). New York: Springer-Verlag, 1974. (a)

*Shaw, E. A. G. Transformation of sound pressure level from the free field to the eardrum in the horizontal plane. *Journal of the Acoustical Society of America*, 1974, *56*, 1848–1861. (b)

Shepard, R. N. Circularity in judgments of relative pitch. *Journal of the Acoustical Society of America*, 1964, *36*, 2346–2353.

Shepard, R. N. Geometrical approximations to the structure of musical pitch. *Psychological Review*, 1982, *89*, 305–333.

Shower, E. G., & Biddulph, R. Differential pitch sensitivity of the ear. *Journal of the Acoustical Society of America*, 1931, *3*, 275–287.

Siebert, W. M. Ranke revisited—A simple short-wave model. *Journal of the Acoustical Society of America*, 1974, *56*, 594–600.

Sivian, L. J., & White, S. D. On minimum audible sound fields. *Journal of the Acoustical Society of America*, 1933, *5*, 228–321.

Small, A. M., Jr., Brandt, J. F., & Cox, P. G. Loudness as a function of signal duration. *Journal of the Acoustical Society of America*, 1962, *34*, 513–514.

Smoorenburg, G. F. Pitch perception of two-frequency stimuli. *Journal of the Acoustical Society of America*, 1970, *48*, 924–942.

Smoorenburg, G. F. Audibility region of combination tones. *Journal of the Acoustical Society of America*, 1972, *52*, 603–614.

Smoorenburg, G. F., Gibson, M. M., Kitzes, L. M., Rose, J. E., & Hind, J. E. Correlates of combination tones observed in the response of neurons in the anteroventral cochlear nucleus of the cat. *Journal of the Acoustical Society of America*, 1976, *59*, 945–962.

Snow, W. B. Change of pitch with loudness at low frequencies. *Journal of the Acoustical Society of America*, 1936, *8*, 14–19.

*Steinberg, J. C., & Gardner, M. B. The dependence of hearing impairment on sound intensity. *Journal of the Acoustical Society of America*, 1937, *9*, 11–23.

Stephens, S. D. G. Personality and the slope of loudness function. *Quarterly Journal of Experimental Psychology*, 1970, *22*, 9–13.

Stephens, S. D. G. Methodological factors influencing loudness of short duration sounds. *Journal of Sound and Vibration*, 1974, *37*, 235–246.

Stephens, S. D. G., & Anderson, C. M. B. Experimental studies on the uncomfortable loudness level. *Journal of Speech and Hearing Research*, 1971, *14*, 262–270.

Stevens, J. C., & Guirao, M. Individual loudness functions. *Journal of the Acoustical Society of America*, 1964, *36*, 2210–2213.

Stevens, J. C., & Hall, J. W. Brightness and loudness as functions of stimulus duration. *Perception and Psychophysics*, 1966, *1*, 319–327.

*Stevens, S. S. The relation of pitch to intensity. *Journal of the Acoustical Society of America*, 1935, *6*, 150–154.

*Stevens, S. S. The direct estimation of sensory magnitudes—Loudness. *American Journal of Psychology*, 1956, *69*, 1–25.

*Stevens, S. S. Perceived level of noise by Mark VII and decibels (E). *Journal of the Acoustical Society of America*, 1972, *51*, 575–601.

Stevens, S. S. Procedure for calculating loudness, Mark VI. *Journal of the Acoustical Society of America*, 1961, *33*, 1577–1585.

Stevens, S. S. Power-group transformations under glare, masking, and recruitment. *Journal of the Acoustical Society of America*, 1966, *39*, 725–735.

Stevens, S. S. *Psychophysics*. New York: Wiley, 1975.

Stevens, S. S., & Davis, H. *Hearing: Its psychology and physiology*. New York: Wiley, 1938.

Stevens, S. S., & Guirao, M. Loudness functions under inhibition. *Perception and Psychophysics*, 1967, *2*, 459–465.

*Stevens, S. S., & Newman, E. B. The localization of actual sources of sound. *American Journal of Psychology*, 1936, *48*, 297–306.

Stevens, S. S., & Volkmann, J. The relation of pitch to frequency: A revised scale. *American Journal of Psychology*, 1940, *53*, 329–353.

Stevens, S. S., Volkmann, J., & Newman, E. B. A scale for the measurement of the psychological magnitude pitch. *Journal of the Acoustical Society of America*, 1937, *8*, 185–190.

Stokinger, T. E., Cooper, W. A., Jr., Meissner, W. A., & Jones, K. O. Intensity, frequency, and duration effects in the measurement of monaural perstimulatory loudness adaptation. *Journal of the Acoustical Society of America*, 1972, *51*, 608–616.

Tartini, G. *Trattato di musica secondo la vera scienza dell' armonia*. Padua, Italy: 1754.

Teas, D. C. Lateralization of acoustic transients. *Journal of the Acoustical Society of America*, 1962, *34*, 1460–1465.

Teghtsoonian, M., & Teghtsoonian, R. Consistency of individual exponents in cross-modal matching. *Perception and Psychophysics*, 1983, *33*, 203–214.

Terhardt, E. Frequency analysis and periodicity detection in the sensations of roughness and periodicity pitch. In R. Plomp & G. F. Smoorenburg (Eds.), *Frequency analysis and periodicity detection in hearing*. Leiden, The Netherlands: Sijthoff, 1970.

Terhardt, E. Pitch, consonance and harmony. *Journal of the Acoustical Society of America*, 1974, *55*, 1061–1069. (a)

Terhardt, E. Pitch of pure tones: Its relation to intensity. In E. Zwicker & E. Terhardt (Eds.), *Facts and models in hearing*. Stuttgart, West Germany: Springer-Verlag, 1974. (b)

Terhardt, E. Calculating virtual pitch. *Hearing Research*, 1979, *1*, 155–182.

Terhardt, E., & Fastl, H. Zum Einfluss von Störtönen und Störgeräuschen auf die Tonhöhe von Sinustönen. *Acustica*, 1971, *25*, 53–61.

Tobias, J. V., & Schubert, E. D. Effective onset duration of auditory stimuli. *Journal of the Acoustical Society of America*, 1959, *31*, 1595–1605.

Tobias, J. V., & Zerlin, S. Lateralization threshold as a function of stimulus duration. *Journal of the Acoustical Society of America*, 1959, *31*, 1591–1594.

Toole, F. E., & Sayers, B. M. Lateralization judgments and the nature of binaural acoustic images. *Journal of the Acoustical Society of America*, 1965, *37*, 319–324.

van Bergeijk, W. A. Variation on a theme of Békésy: A model of binaural interaction. *Journal of the Acoustical Society of America*, 1962, *34*, 1431–1437.

Verschuure, J., & van Meeteren, A. A. The effect of intensity on pitch. *Acustica*, 1975, *32*, 33–44.

Viemeister, N. F. Auditory intensity discrimination at high frequencies in the presence of noise. *Science*, 1983, *221*, 1206–1208.

Wallach, H. On sound localization. *Journal of the Acoustical Society of America*, 1939, *10*, 270–274.

*Wallach, H. The role of head movements and vestibular and visual cues in sound localization. *Journal of Experimental Psychology*, 1940, *27*, 339–368.

*Wallach, H., Newman, E. B., & Rosenzweig, M. R. The precedence effect in sound localization. *American Journal of Psychology*, 1949, *57*, 315–336.

Ward, W. D. Subjective musical pitch. *Journal of the Acoustical Society of America*, 1954, *26*, 369–380.

Ward, W. D. Tonal monaural diplacusis. *Journal of the Acoustical Society of America*, 1955, *27*, 365–372.

Ward, W. D., & Burns, E. M. Absolute pitch. In D. Deutsch (Ed.), *The psychology of music*. New York: Academic Press, 1982.

Ward, W. D., Fleer, R. E., & Glorig, A. Characteristics of hearing losses produced by gunfire and by steady noise. *Journal of Auditory Research*, 1961, *1*, 325–356.

Wettschureck, R. Die absoluten Unterschiedswellen der Richtungswahrnehmung in der Medianebene beim naturlichen Hören, sowie beim Hören über ein Kunstkopf-Übertragungssystem (The absolute difference threshold of directional perception in the median plane in natural hearing and in hearing over a dummy-head reproducing system). *Acustica*, 1973, *28*, 197–208.

Wever, E. G., & Bray, C. W. Present possibilities for auditory theory. *Psychological Review*, 1930, *37*, 365–380.

Wightman, F. L. The pattern-transformation model of pitch. *Journal of the Acoustical Society of America*, 1973, *54*, 407–416.

Wiley, T. *Monaural loudness adaptation*. Unpublished doctoral dissertation, University of Iowa, 1972.

Wilson, J. P. The combination tone $2f_1 - f_2$, in psychophysics and ear canal recording. In G. v. d. Brink & F. A. Bilsen (Eds.), *Psychophysical, physiological and behavioral studies in hearing*. Delft, Holland: Delft University Press, 1980.

Wilson, J. P., & Sutton, G. J. A family with high-tonal objective tinnitus—An update. In R. Klinke and R. Hartmann (Eds.), *Hearing—Physiological bases and psychophysics*. Berlin: Springer-Verlag, 1983.

Wundt, W. *Grundzüge der physiologischen Psychologie* (Vol. I). Leipzig: Engelmann Verlag, 1880.

Yost, W. A. Lateral position of sinusoids presented with interaural intensive and temporal differences. *Journal of the Acoustical Society of America*, 1981, *70*, 396–409.

Yost, W. A., Wightman, F. L., & Green, D. M. Lateralization of filtered clicks. *Journal of the Acoustical Society of America*, 1971, *50*, 1526–1531.

Young, L. L. Jr., & Carhart, R. Time-intensity trading functions for pure tones and a high-frequency AM signal. *Journal of the Acoustical Society of America*, 1974, *56*, 605–609.

Zurek, P. M. Spontaneous narrowband acoustic signals emitted by human ears. *Journal of the Acoustical Society of America*, 1981, *69*, 514–523.

Zurek, P. M., & Sachs, R. M. Combination tones at frequencies greater than the primary tones. *Science*, 1979, *205*, 600–602.

Zwicker, E. Der ungewöhnliche Amplitudengang der nichtlinearen Verzerrungen des Ohres. *Acustica*, 1955, *5*, 67–74.

*Zwicker, E. Über psychologische und methodische Grundlagen der Lautheit. *Acustica*, 1958, *8* (Beiheft 1), 237–258.

Zwicker, E. Über die Lautheit von ungedrosselten und gedrosselten Schallen. *Acustica*, 1963, *13* (Beiheft 1), 194–211.

Zwicker, E. Negative afterimage in hearing. *Journal of the Acoustical Society of America*, 1964, *36*, 2413–2415.

Zwicker, E. Ein Beitrag zur Lautstärkemessung impulshaltiger Schalle. *Acustica*, 1966, *17*, 11–22.

Zwicker, E. Procedure for calculating loudness of temporally variable sounds. *Journal of the Acoustical Society of America*, 1977, *62*, 675–682.

Zwicker, E. Formulae for calculating the psychoacoustical excitation level of aural difference tones measured by the cancellation method. *Journal of the Acoustical Society of America*, 1981, *69*, 1410–1414.

Zwicker, E., & Feldtkeller, R. Über die Lautstärke von gleichformigen Geräuschen. *Acustica*, 1955, *5*, 303–316.

*Zwicker, E., Flottorp, G., & Stevens, S. S. Critical bandwidth in loudness summation. *Journal of the Acoustical Society of America*, 1957, *29*, 548–557.

*Zwicker, E., & Scharf, B. A model of loudness summation. *Psychological Review*, 1965, *72*, 3–26.

Zwislocki, J. J. Theorie der Scheckenmechanik. *Acta Oto-Laryngologica*, 1948, S72.

Zwislocki, J. J. Analysis of some auditory characteristics. In R. D. Luce, R. R. Bush, & E. H. Galanter (Eds.), *Handbook of mathematical psychology* (Vol. 3). New York: Wiley, 1965.

*Zwislocki, J. J. Temporal summation of loudness: An analysis. *Journal of the Acoustical Society of America*, 1969, *46*, 431–441.

Zwislocki, J. J., & Feldman, R. S. Just noticeable differences in dichotic phase. *Journal of the Acoustical Society of America*, 1956, *28*, 860–864.

SECTION IV

SPACE AND MOTION PERCEPTION

H. A. SEDGWICK

S.U.N.Y. College of Optometry, New York, New York

OVERVIEW

H. A. SEDGWICK

S.U.N.Y. College of Optometry, New York, New York

The topic of this section is the perception of space and motion by human observers. People live and act in an extended, three-dimensional environment. They find their way about in this environment and interact with various objects in it, some of which may also be moving around. All these actions are guided by, and depend on, perception.

To interact successfully with a moving object, whether it is to catch hold of it or to avoid being run down by it, requires that its motion be accurately perceived. Some motions are simple; the motion of a car traveling down Fifth Avenue may be adequately characterized by its velocity. Other motions are complex; a person riding a unicycle up Fifth Avenue while juggling five oranges is not just motion; it is an event—there is a complex hierarchy of relative motions here that needs to be correctly untangled.

Motion of the self also may be simple or complex, but in either case successful behavior can depend on perceiving one's own motion accurately. If one is moving rapidly in the direction of a brick wall, whether it is a collision course or a "near-miss" course is an important piece of information, as is the remaining time until collision or near-miss will occur. Understanding the limits of perception is also important. If one's aircraft is executing a nauseating combination of turning, banking, and acceleration, how accurately will one's motion be perceived? If systematic distortions of perception are going to occur in such situations, it is important to know about and plan for them in advance.

These problems of motion perception take up a large portion of this section, being a primary concern of the next four chapters and a central topic in one other chapter as well. Much of the rest of the section is taken up with various aspects of the problem of perceiving where things are, both in relation to oneself and in relation to the framework of the environment.

There is an emphasis in this section on visual perception, as befits the importance of vision in space and motion perception. Vestibular and somatosensory inputs do play an essential role in the perception of one's own posture and motion, however, and the functions of these systems are considered in detail in one chapter. Also, the last two chapters of the section are concerned with the interactions of the other sense modalities with vision. The remainder of this overview briefly introduces the issues dealt with by each of the chapters in this section.

"Motion Perception in the Frontal Plane: Sensory Aspects," by Stuart Anstis, explores some of the basic properties of the mechanisms by which motion is registered by the visual system. As indicated in this chapter, some of the most telling phenomena concerning the inner workings of motion perception are those in which motion is perceived where or when no real motion is present in the environment. The phenomenon of *motion contrast*, in which a stationary patch of texture appears to drift in the opposite direction to the motion of the textured background that surrounds it, is a clear example of this. The phenomenon of motion contrast is taken to imply the existence of lateral inhibition between neural motion detectors. Detailed examination of the properties of motion contrast helps to reveal the properties of this inhibitory network. Moreover, direct electrophysiological recording has begun to confirm these inferred characteristics.

A second example of motion perception in the absence of real motion dealt with by Anstis arises from the *aftereffects* of *motion adaptation*, in which the prolonged viewing of a steadily moving field causes a subsequently viewed stationary test field to appear to be moving in the opposite direction. Other "distortions" of motion perception occur in this situation as well; for example, the adapting field itself appears to slow down with continued viewing, and a subsequently viewed test field that is moving in the same direction also appears to have its velocity reduced. All these results can again be interpreted at a neural level, as selectively producing adaptation and subsequent insensitivity of neural motion analyzers. Extensive experimentation in this area has led to a wealth of suggestions about the properties of these motion analyzers—their location in the visual system, directional sensitivity, spatial sensitivity, temporal characteristics, interactions, and so on—all of which are discussed by Anstis.

The third, and perhaps most familiar, example of perceived motion in the absence of real motion that Anstis discusses is that of *apparent motion*, in which a succession of stationary objects presented with the appropriate temporal and spatial displacements gives rise to the perception of a single smoothly moving object. This phenomenon, which has great practical importance because it is the basis of "moving pictures," both in cinema and in video, is also an important key to the understanding of how real motion is perceived. Recent work on apparent motion discussed by Anstis suggests the existence of two processes in motion perception—a short-range process mediated by motion-analyzing neurons that work over a limited range of spatial and temporal parameters and a long-range process that is mediated by more cognitive processes and operates over a wider range of spatial and temporal parameters.

The promise held out by all this research is that a coherent model can eventually be found that will explain the neural mechanisms underlying the perception of motion. In the final section of his chapter, Anstis examines several candidates for such a model, including contributions recently made from the area of computer sciences.

To study motion perception at the level of neural analyzers, certain simplifying conditions are helpful. Typically, the observer is required to maintain steady fixation so that whatever motion or events are present in the visual field are mapped directly into motions or events on the retina; also, displays are constructed to stimulate fairly narrowly localized patches of the retina. These restrictions are consistent with the known anatomy of the visual system, in which, at the early stages of processing, each neuron receives its inputs, either directly or indirectly, from only a small area of the retina.

When these restrictions are relaxed, either by allowing the observer's head or eyes to move or by presenting more complicated, global visual displays, then a wide range of motion phenomena arise that can no longer be accounted for solely by the properties of local motion-analyzing neurons. Instead, higher-order perceptual processes, such as those encountered in long-range apparent motion, must be postulated. These motion phenomena are discussed by Arian Mack in her chapter "Perceptual Aspects of Motion in the Frontal Plane."

Mack structures her discussion around the distinction between *subject-* and *object-relative* determinants of motion perception. When an isolated object is viewed in total darkness, its motion must be defined relative to the observer. The determinants of such subject-relative motion are complicated, however, because parts of the observer can move relative to each other. Thus, for example, a smoothly moving object may be tracked by eye movements, by head movements, or by some combination of the two, so that its image has little if any motion on the retina. Nevertheless, motion is perceived. Some information about eye and head movements must be made available to the visual system. Mack examines the thresholds for subject relative motion, the perceived stability of the visual world when saccadic or smooth pursuit movements occur, and the characteristics of motion perception during smooth pursuit eye movements. She also discusses some striking motion illusions that occur under subject-relative conditions and that help clarify limitations in the perceptual system's use of information about eye movements.

In a normal, richly structured, and illuminated environment, the motion of an object generally takes place against, or relative to, the stationary background of the environment. This object-relative motion thus provides another basis for determining perceived motion. In normal circumstances, subject- and object-relative determinants of motion are consistent with each other and both tend to produce the same perceptions of motion. An important key to understanding the workings of motion perception, however, comes from putting these two sets of determinants into conflict with each other. When this is done, the visual system is revealed as being heavily weighted toward the use of object-relative determinants. The outcome of this conflict is clearly seen in the phenomenon of *induced motion*, in which a small stationary object appears to move in the opposite direction to the motion of a larger surrounding frame. The varieties of induced motion and their implications for the properties of the motion perception system are carefully examined by Mack.

Real motions in the environment are often arranged in complex hierarchies. A leaf flutters on a branch that sways in the wind, or a person waves from a moving train. The visual system's ability to deal with these complexities of object-relative motion is examined by Mack under the heading of *configurational event perception*. Here she examines some powerful laboratory demonstrations of such motion analysis and discusses the models that have been offered to explain how the visual system performs this analysis.

In a final section, Mack discusses the subject- and object-relative determinants of velocity and examines an object-relative explanation of *velocity constancy*, the phenomenon that the velocities of objects at different distances from the observer tend to be seen more in terms of their relative physical velocities than in terms of their relative image velocities at the retina.

A further complication in our understanding of motion and space perception occurs when we take into consideration the posture and motion of the observer within the environment. Self motion adds yet another transformation to the image motions occurring at the retina. In addition, the perception of the observer's own posture and motion is complicated by the input of several contributing perceptual subsystems. Visual, vestibular, and proprioceptive factors are all closely interwoven. The properties of these systems and their interactions are examined in "The Perception of Posture, Self Motion, and the Visual Vertical," by Ian Howard.

Howard begins with a discussion of the *control of posture* in vertebrates, with special attention given to the control of vertical stance in humans. The contributions of postural reflexes, of passive stiffness in joints and muscles, and of somatosensory, vestibular, and visual factors are all considered. The somatosensory, vestibular, and visual systems are seen to complement each other by resolving ambiguities and by covering different frequency ranges of sway in postural stabilization.

A critical aspect of postural stabilization for visual perception is the stabilization of the eye relative to the environment when the observer's head moves. The *vestibulo-ocular reflexes* that subserve this function are discussed in detail by Howard. *Vestibular nystagmus* is based on vestibular signals arising from head rotation and causes the eyes to rotate in the opposite direction. *Optokinetic nystagmus* serves a similar function but is based instead on the rotation of the visual field, which leads the eyes to rotate in the same direction. Howard compares the properties (gain, latency, and phase lag) of these two systems and shows how they complement each other.

The differing temporal properties of the vestibular and visual systems contribute to an illusion of self motion that arises when, somewhat unnaturally, the visual environment rotates continuously around the observer. The visual system attributes the relative motion between observer and environment to the observer, rather than to the environment; the vestibular system, which is attuned to fairly rapid changes in rotational velocity, does not effectively oppose this perception, so that a compelling illusion of self rotation results. This and other illusions arising from visual–vestibular interactions are examined by Howard for the information that they can provide about the properties and interactions of these two systems.

A second and perhaps even more striking effect that occurs when the vestibular and visual systems are placed into conflict with each other is that the vestibular system eventually adapts. Thus placing in front of the eyes prisms that reverse the direction of visual flow on the retina when the head turns will lead to a reduction in gain and eventual reversal of direction in vestibular nystagmus. This vestibular recaliberation, which has profound implications for our understanding of how the oculomotor system can adapt to changing conditions of visual perception, is also discussed by Howard.

Echoes of the distinction made in Mack's chapter between subject-relative and object-relative factors can be seen in the interactions between the vestibular and visual systems. The vestibular system provides information that is of necessity purely subject-relative, while the visual system provides both subject- and object-relative information. The tendency toward stability of the visually perceived framework of the environment enters into vestibular recalibration and illusory self rotation just as it did into the perception of induced motion.

The interactions of vestibular and visual factors and of subject- and object-relative factors both enter into the observer's perception of the visual vertical. Howard explores the intricacies of this area in detail, including questions of how the visual vertical is perceived in unusual but important environments, such as those encountered under water, under weightless conditions, and during centrifugal rotation.

The chapters by Anstis and Mack deal primarily with motion that is in the frontal plane and that is either of constant or sinusoidally varying velocity. The motion considered by Howard is primarily rotational. Two additional important aspects of motion perception are considered by David Regan, Lloyd Kaufman, and Janet Lincoln in their chapter "Motion in Depth and Visual Acceleration."

The first portion of this chapter is concerned with observers' sensitivity to *visual acceleration* of objects, primarily in the frontal plane. Given the considerable evidence, discussed by Anstis, that the visual system contains neurons directly sensitive to velocity, it is natural to ask whether the visual system might also contain neurons directly sensitive to change in velocity, that is, acceleration. After a careful review of the characteristics of acceleration perception, Regan and colleagues conclude that acceleration is probably not directly sensed by the perceiver but is inferred from a difference in the velocity that is perceived at two successive times. This tentative conclusion is important because it helps delimit the classes of neuronal mechanisms involved in motion perception.

An important set of results that work in the opposite direction—that is, that expand the suggested range of neuronal specificities—is discussed in the second section of this chapter. Here evidence is reviewed concerning an observer's visual sensitivity to two somewhat complementary types of visually perceived events, the movement in depth of an object toward the observer, called *visual looming*, and the *self motion in depth* of the observer toward an object or extended surface. The authors suggest for both of these events that observers possess neural mechanisms specifically sensitive to them. The ability to produce adaptation and aftereffects specific to these types of events plays a key role in these conclusions, as it does in the conclusions concerning neural mechanisms of motion discussed by Anstis. These results are of particular interest because they point to neural mechanisms that are specifically sensitive to some types of more complicated, or "higher-order," stimulation that are of functional significance to the organism.

"Visual Localization and Eye Movements," by Leonard Matin, is not primarily concerned with motion perception, but both the fundamental problem addressed in this chapter and one of the central problems of motion perception addressed by Mack stem from the same underlying issue. This underlying issue concerns the integration of retinal information with extraretinal information about the position of the eye. In motion perception, particularly during smooth pursuit, the perception of an object's motion can depend on the combination of retinal information about the object's motion with extraretinal information about the pursuit movements of the eye. In visual localization, the perception of where an object is—its direction from the observer—likewise can depend on combining information about image location on the retina with extraretinal information about the position of the eye in its orbit.

While the availability to perception of at least some information about eye position has long been recognized, the origin of this extraretinal information remains a subject of research and discussion. Matin carefully explains the different models suggested and examines the still inconclusive evidence concerning them, including a series of dramatic studies in which observers voluntarily underwent nearly total muscular paralysis to test the perceptual effects of attempting to make eye movements when little or no eye movement could actually occur.

After a discussion of the concepts of local signs and reference directions, Matin reviews the evidence concerning visual localization under three different eye movement conditions: steady gaze, voluntary saccades, and pursuit. In each of these areas an important distinction arises between localization of isolated targets viewed in darkness and localization of targets viewed against the background of an illuminated environment. In the former case, the observer is forced to rely on subject-relative information about the position of the eye in the orbit and of the image on the retina. In the latter case, the observer has the alternative of using object-relative information about the location of the object in relation to the rest of the visible environment. Just as Mack observes concerning motion perception, Matin concludes that in visual localization this object-relative information tends to dominate perception when it is available, with subject-relative information being used only when object-relative information is not available.

In the chapter "Space Perception," I discuss how and how well the spatial layout of the environment is perceived. At issue here is the visual perception of the sizes and distances, the shapes and slants, of the surfaces that make up the environment. Central to this chapter is the question of how the two-dimensional array of light reaching the eyes can provide the basis for the perception of a three-dimensional environment. The answer lies in the constraints that characterize the normal environment; to function effectively, perception does not have to deal with any conceivable environment but only with the environments that nature and people have provided. Within these constraints, the two-dimensional optical structure in the light reaching the eyes often uniquely specifies a three-dimensional structure in the environment. The nature of this specificity and the human observer's ability to make use of it are discussed in detail in this chapter.

The following chapter, "Representation of Motion and Space in Video and Cinematic Displays," by Julian Hochberg, takes up a different perspective on the perception of motion and space and in doing so offers a unique overview of the subject of this section. The problem considered by Hochberg is how the characteristics of visual perception make it possible to successfully represent motion-filled events occurring in three-dimensional environments using media (video and cinema) that can present only a succession of two-dimensional displays containing no real motion. The solution to this problem, in addition to being of considerable practical importance, requires a deep understanding of the processes by which motion and space are normally perceived; the search for the solution has added very significantly to our understanding of visual perception in normal environments.

In approaching this problem of representation, Hochberg carefully examines the technical workings of video and cinema and discusses how the characteristics of these media interact with the characteristics of the visual system. The parameters of apparent motion, for example, place constraints on the rate at which successive frames can be presented and also on the types of motion that can successfully be represented as occurring between frames.

In normal perception, an image of the environment is projected onto the retina; the task of the perceptual system is then to find the inverse of this transformation—to work backward from the structure of light available at the eye to the structure of the environment. In video and cinema, the sequence of transformations is much more complicated; an image of the environment is projected onto a light-sensitive surface within the camera; this image is then conveyed in some way to a viewing surface from which it is projected onto the retina. In addition, the camera itself, as well as the objects in the environment, may be in motion, or the camera may be continuously transforming its projection characteristics through the use of a zoom lens. All these transformations can introduce distortions and ambiguities that would not be present in normal perception. Hochberg's systematic exploration of these possibilities and of the perceptual system's responses to them reveals both some of the limits of cinematic representation and some of the flexibility of the perceptual system.

An even more radical departure from the conditions of normal perception occurs in the cinematic technique, essential for the representation of complex, extended events, of cutting abruptly from one scene to another. The varied characteristics of these cuts and the visual system's successes and failures in dealing with such rapid, discontinuous shifts in place and time are discussed in detail by Hochberg. The exploration of this area is making a substantial contribution to our still meager understanding of how the visual system normally integrates the flow of information that it receives as the observer moves through the environment and as the eyes scan around in it.

Another type of information integration must occur between the inputs received by the visual system from the two eyes. The perceptual characteristics of this process are reviewed in the chapter, "Binocular Vision," by Aries Arditi.

Although certain functions, most notably stereopsis, are clearly possible only with binocular vision, it is also true that some functions that can be performed in monocular vision are nevertheless done better with two eyes than with one. What has received most attention here is the comparison of monocular with binocular sensitivities to patches of light. Arditi gives a detailed discussion of the different models and supporting evidence that have been offered to describe the ways in which such input from the two eyes is combined.

Because the two eyes are separated from each other by several centimeters, they have two slightly different views of the world. Thus the image present on the retina of one eye usually differs somewhat from that on the other eye. Such differences between the two eyes can lead to *suppression*, in which some portion of one eye's input is perceptually suppressed in favor of the other's, and to *rivalry*, in which there is an alternation between the eyes. Arditi reviews the methods of studying suppression and rivalry and discusses the circumstances under which they occur.

The other important consequence of the two eyes having disparate views of the world is of course *stereopsis*, the vivid perception of depth that arises from binocular disparity, and it is to this feature of binocular vision that much of Arditi's chapter is devoted. Arditi carefully lays out the geometrical analysis of stereoscopic space and describes in detail the various empirical attempts made to characterize the perceived space that arises from stereopsis. In addition, he describes the principal methods by which stereoscopic displays are generated for research purposes and discusses such functional parameters of stereopsis as *stereoacuity* and the limits of the range of image disparities over which stereopsis operates. In a final section dealing with what is often considered to be the central theoretical problem of stereopsis, Arditi reviews the various models offered to account for the visual system's ability to match up corresponding parts of the images reaching the two eyes, considering both the "classical" theories and more recent models that have their origins in computer science.

Several of the chapters already mentioned touch on the human organism's ability to adapt to alterations in the relation between the perceiver and the environment. In Howard's chapter, he discusses the adaptation of vestibular nystagmus that occurs when the relation between head rotation and image motion at the retina is optically altered. Howard also describes the shift, or "normalization," in the perceived vertical that is produced by prolonged viewing of tilted lines. Matin describes the adjustments that occur in the saccadic system when the normal relation between size of eye movement and amount of image shift on the retina is artificially altered. The ability to adapt is pervasive, however, in an observer's perceptually guided interactions with the surrounding environment, and it is in "Adaptation of Space Perception," by Robert Welch, that this ability is systematically surveyed.

The adaptation paradigm most extensively investigated is that of *prismatic displacement*, in which the visual world is shifted somewhat to the right or left by placing a prism in front of the eye. This of course introduces systematic errors into visually guided motor behaviors, such as manual pointing. Adaptation to this situation is rapid, and removal of the prism after adaptation produces a characteristic *aftereffect*, in which pointing errors now occur in the opposite direction. The research described by Welch has shown that it is unnecessary to postulate changes within the visual system to account for this adaptation. Instead, it can be accounted for by proprioceptive changes that occur in the felt positions of the arm, of the head, or of the eye within the orbit, depending on the specific nature of the adaptation situation. Such changes can be both rapid and extensive.

Many of the other types of adaptation discussed by Welch can also be accounted for by proprioceptive or motoric changes. Left–right reversing prisms, for instance, lead to the adaptation of the vestibular system described by Howard, and distortions in depth produced by magnifying lenses appear to lead to adaptation in the ocular convergence system.

Nevertheless, it is clear that some flexibility does exist within the visual system itself. A clear example of this occurs with adaptation to prismatically induced curvature, in which all the straight lines in the visual field appear to be systematically curved in one direction. After prolonged exposure to this situation, these lines appear less curved, and when the prism is removed, there is an aftereffect of perceived curvature in the opposite direction. The amount of such change that can occur, however, appears to be strictly limited. Even after prolonged exposure to prismatically induced curvature, adaptation only reaches about 30% of its theoretical maximum, and at least some of the changes that occur must be attributed to normalization processes within the visual system, rather than to true adaptation.

The organism's overall adaptation is thus a composite of changes occurring at many levels, within and between different sensory systems and sometimes at the cognitive level of "conscious correction" as well. Welch carefully explores the intricacies of this process, both at an empirical and at a theoretical level, for a wide variety of adaptation situations, including adaptation to auditory rearrangement and adaptation to underwater optical distortions.

The theme of the relations between the senses is taken up again in the last chapter of this section—"Intersensory Interactions," by Robert Welch and David Warren. Whereas adaptation requires the detection through repeated experience that some error or mismatch exists between the spatial information being received by two different sensory modalities, the focus of this chapter is on the immediate effects that activity in one sense modality may have on activity in another sense modality. These effects can range from the nonspecific to the highly specific. An example of a nonspecific intersensory interaction is the reported effect of illumination on increasing auditory sensitivity. An example of a specific effect is the shift in the heard location of an event toward its seen location, a phenomenon referred to as *visual capture*.

The existence of visual capture suggests that vision is the dominant modality, but as Welch and Warren point out, the situation is more complicated. Visual spatial localization can also be somewhat influenced by audition and proprioception. Vision tends to be dominant for spatial localization, but audition tends to be dominant for temporal events. A rich and complicated pattern of intersensory interactions is systematically laid out by Welch and Warren, and the various theoretical approaches that have been made to this area are discussed.

In addition to the chapters in this section, a number of other chapters in this Handbook have an important bearing on the perception of space and motion. Chapter 3 by Freeman in Section I, "Theory and Methods," gives an introduction to methods and algorithms for simulating space and motion with graphic displays. In Section II, "Basic Sensory Processes I," Hallett's Chapter 10, which outlines the basic characteristics of the oculomotor system, provides a helpful background to this section's descriptions of oculomotor functioning in motion perception, spatial localization, and binocular vision. Howard's Chapter 11 in Section III, "Basic Sensory Processes II," describes the vestibular system, whose essential contribution to the perception of self motion is considered in Howard's other chapter, in this section. Chapter 38, by Barrow and Tenenbaum in Section VI, "Perceptual Organization and Cognition," examines significant recent work in computer vision relevant to problems both of space and of motion perception. In the same section, Chapter 33 by Rock and Chapter 36 by Pomerantz and Kubovy deal with some problems of perceptual organization in motion perception and thus complement the chapter by Mack in this section.

CHAPTER 16

MOTION PERCEPTION IN THE FRONTAL PLANE

Sensory Aspects

STUART ANSTIS

Department of Psychology, York University, Downsview, Ontario

CONTENTS

There are two ways in which we can see movement. Suppose you are sitting on a beach gazing at a rock. A seagull flies into view, and its image moves across your retina. This provokes a fixation reflex which makes your eyes jump over to look at the bird. Your eyes then follow it, holding its image virtually stationary on the retina. Gregory (1966) has dubbed these the *image-retina* and the *eye-head systems*. One might expect some kind of jarring visual thump as one switches from one system to the other, but in fact the changeover is effortless and generally unnoticed.

This section reviews some phenomena of visual motion. Table 16.1 shows whether these effects are related to eye movements or to motion of the retinal image. The table may not command universal assent—few topics in motion perception do—but it may be helpful.

For further reading, review chapters on motion perception are available by Neff (1936), Graham (1965), Sekuler and Levinson (1974), Sekuler, Pantle, and Levinson (1978), and Anstis (1978, 1980). Chapter 19 by Regan, Kaufman, and Lincoln reviews the perception of motion in depth. Grusser and Grusser-Cornehls (1973) and Berkley (1982) have reviewed the physiology of neural motion detectors. Self-review articles, in which authors describe their own work on motion perception, include Wallach (1959), Kolers (1963), and Anstis (1983). Textbooks by Robinson (1972), Kaufman (1974), Rock (1975), and Caelli (1981) contain useful chapters on motion perception. Spigel (1965) edited a book of readings motion perception. Japanese-speaking readers might enjoy Mori's (1982) profusely illustrated survey. The January 1984 issue of the journal *Vision Research*, edited by Guy Orban, is devoted to the proceedings of a conference on motion perception, and a forthcoming issue of *Perception*, edited by V. S. Ramachandran, is also devoted to motion perception. Three recent books, each compiled from conference proceedings, contain plenty of good material on motion perception: Leibowitz, Osaka, and Oyama (1978), Longuet-Higgins and Sutherland (1980), and Wertheim, Wagenaar, and Leibowitz (1982). Kolers' book (1972) reviews motion perception well, especially apparent or stroboscopic motion, and includes many experiments by Kolers himself. Ullman (1979) published a seminal book which forces us to change the way we think about motion perception. His book has been critically reviewed by Runeson and Lind (1981). Ullman's student Hildreth has also published a valuable book (1984). Marr's posthumous book on vision (1982), which is already exerting a huge influence, contains many ideas on motion perception (pp. 159–215). Both books, which draw heavily on ideas from computation and artificial intelligence, are recommended to the reader, since it is impossible to do them justice here.

1. MOTION CONTRAST

Motion contrast is a form of induced movement. Induced movement is an illusion in which real movement is attributed to the wrong part of the stimulus array. For instance, when clouds drift slowly to the left across the moon, the moon appears to sail to the right. High buildings viewed from below against a sky with moving clouds appear to be falling. Sometimes the movement is falsely attributed to the observer's own body. The train in which we sit appears to be moving forward when in fact it is the train on the next line which is moving backward. This phenomenon, known as *self vection*, has been reviewed by Dichgans and Brandt (1978), Berthoz and Droulet (1982), and Leibowitz, Post, Brandt, and Dichgans (1982), and it is not discussed here.

There are two schools of research on induced movement. One school, founded by Duncker (1929/1938), kept the inducing and test objects spatially far apart. Typical stimuli were large frames made of straight luminous lines, surrounding a dot seen in the dark. Experiments concentrate on eye movements, and explanations are often cognitive, based on frames of reference. The other school, including Tynan and Sekuler (1975) and Sekuler, Pantle, and Levinson (1978), kept the inducing and test objects adjacent. Typical stimuli were adjacent fields of random-dot texture moving past each other with a shearing motion. Experiments concentrate on local apparent shearing seen at the borders, and explanations are often physiological, based on lateral inhibition between neural motion detectors. These contrasting research styles may reflect two separate perceptual processes. The first process, which operates over a long spatial range and can be called *induced motion*, is reviewed in Mack, Chapter 17. The second process, which operates over a short spatial range and can be called *motion contrast*, is reviewed now.

Motion contrast is an analogy of brightness contrast (Loomis & Nakayama, 1973). A gray test patch looks darker against a white surround than it does against a black surround, probably because receptors that respond to the white surround will laterally inhibit receptors that respond to the gray test patch (Ratliff, 1965). In a similar way, a test patch of stationary texture will appear to drift upward if it is centered in a surround of downward-drifting texture, presumably because of lateral inhibition between motion detectors. Walker and Powell (1974) exposed two adjacent fields of dots, meeting at a horizontal border and both drifting to the right at different speeds. The upper region moved at 0.3°/sec, the lower region at 0.6°/sec. As a result, near the border rapidly moving dots seemed to move even faster and slowly moving dots seemed to move even more slowly. This was true only within about 20 min arc of the border; dots further away from the border were unaffected. No motion contrast was found in dichoptic conditions, when each field was seen by a different eye; however, Over and Lovegrove (1973) have reported dichoptic motion contrast.

Tynan and Sekuler (1975) exposed a 1.23° square test patch of random-dot texture, centered in a moving textured surround and found that the velocity of the surround dots affected the perceived speed of the center dots. When the center dots were stationary, the rightward-moving surround dots made the center dots appear to move to the left, whatever the speed of the surround. When the center dots were moving in the same direction as the surround, the apparent speed of the center was diminished, and as the surround speed increased toward the center's speed and then grew to exceed it, the perceived speed of the center first decreased and then increased again in a U-shaped function. The perceived center speed reached a minimum at about the point where surround and center were moving at the same speed. When the center and surround moved in opposite direc-

Table 16.1

	Image-Retina	Eye-Head
Real movement	Yes	Yes
Apparent movement	Yes	(Occasionally)
Motion aftereffect	Yes	No
Motion contrast	Yes	No

tions, the perceived speed of the center was enhanced and grew systematically over the entire range of surround speeds used. Tynan and Sekuler also noted that the center region appeared to lie in a depth plane in front of or behind the surround, owing to depth cues of occlusion and motion parallax.

Nakayama and Tyler (1978) used a display consisting of four horizontal lines, as shown in Figure 16.1. The two inner test lines were stationary. Counterphase oscillation of the two outer lines induced the sensation of counterphase motion in the two inner lines, in a direction opposite to the nearest outer lines. First, they measured the threshold for seeing the real motion of the outer lines, for different frequencies of oscillation, as shown in Figure 16.1(b). Sensitivity was best for an oscillation rate of 2 cycles/sec. Below 2 cycles/sec there was an inverse

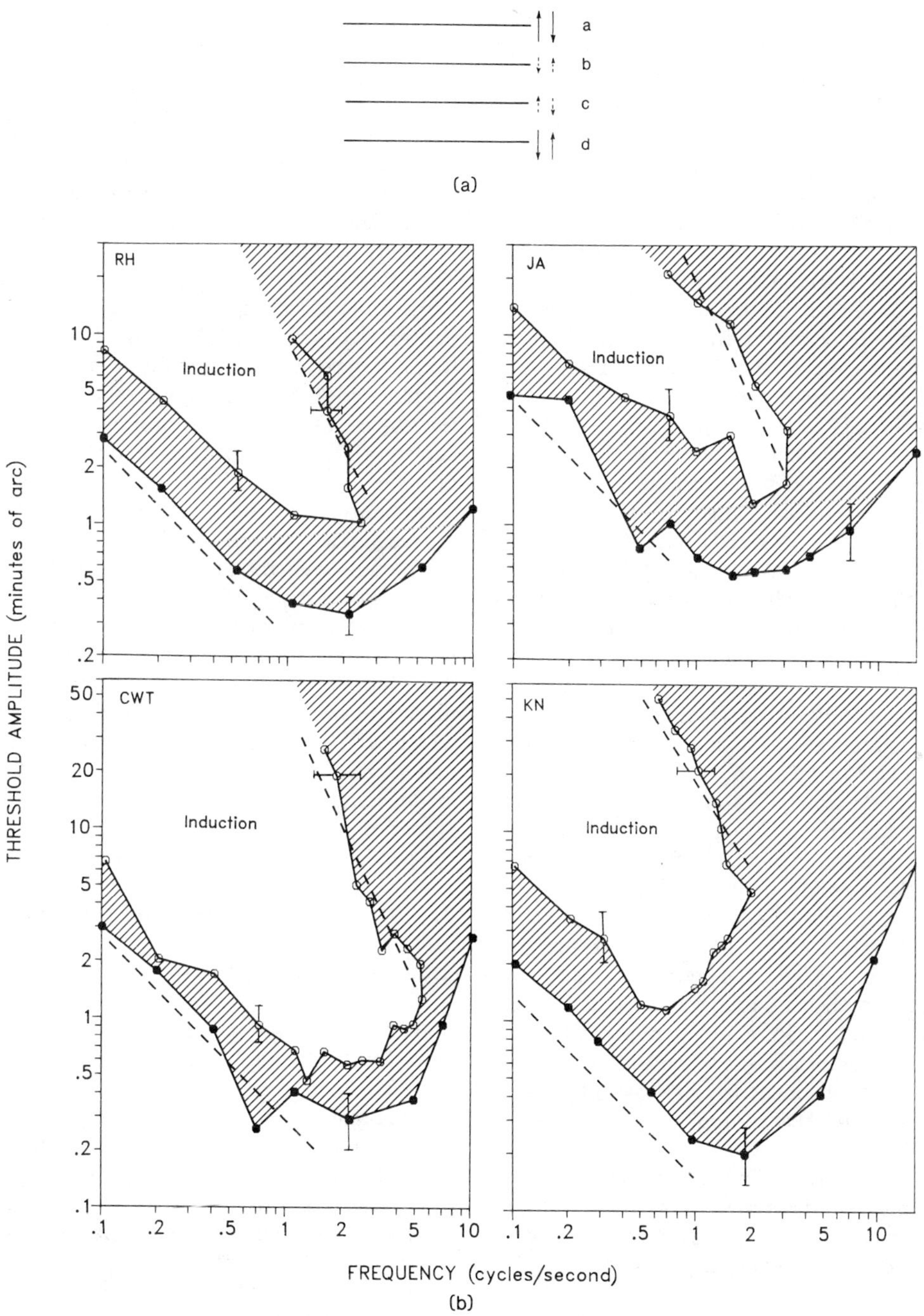

Figure 16.1. (a) Motion is induced into the stationary lines *b* and *c*. When line *a* moves up and line *d* moves down, they induce aparent motion upward into line *b* and downward into line *c*. (b) Frequency characteristics of real and induced motion for four observers. Filled circles (lower curve) show peak-to-peak threshold amplitude to see real movement in the outer lines. Open circles show the upper and lower threshold limits for induced motion. Lower dashed line represents a slope of −1; upper dashed line represents a slope of −2. Shadow area represents conditions where real motion is seen, but induced motion is not. Induced motion is restricted to the tongue-shaped area of the graph labeled "induction." (From K. Nakayama & C. W. Tyler, Relative motion induced between stationary lines, *Vision Research 18*. Copyright 1978 by Pergamon Press, Ltd. Reprinted with permission.)

relationship between frequency and threshold, with a slope of −1 (dashed line in Figure 16.1(b)). This suggests that the threshold was set exclusively by the maximum velocity in the stimulus, not merely by amplitude of displacement. Next, they measured the lower limit for induced motion (IM)—the smallest amplitude of the outer lines for which IM could be seen on the inner lines. A marked loss of sensitivity was found at high frequencies: whereas real motion could be seen above 10 cycles/sec, IM was not seen above 2 – 5 cycles/sec. This agrees with Duncker (1929/1938) and Over and Lovegrove (1973), who found that slow real movement (RM) was more effective as an inducer than fast real movement. (But Tynan and Sekuler, 1975, disagree.) However, at low frequencies the IM and RM threshold curves ran parallel with a slope of −1. The minimum velocity to see real motion (at frequencies below 2 cycles/sec) was constant at about 25–50 arc sec/sec, which is consistent with earlier reports (Leibowitz 1955). The minimum velocity for IM was 2 or 3 times as high, at about 60–120 arc sec/sec. Note that real movement could be seen anywhere in the shaded region of Figure 16.1 (b), but IM could be seen only in the tongue-shaped region labeled "induction." The upper edge of the tongue is the maximum amplitude of real movement that could give rise to IM.

The results of all these experiments can be attributed to lateral inhibitory interactions between motion detectors. Many visual neurons are selective for velocity and direction (reviewed by Grusser & Grusser-Cornehls, 1973), and some of these neurons have inhibitory surrounds that are also velocity sensitive (Bridgeman, 1972; Collett, 1972; Frost & Wong, 1977; Sterling & Wickelgren, 1969). Frost and Nakayama (1983) found cells in the optic tectum of the pigeon which responded best when a textured background pattern moved in the opposite direction to a test spot but did not respond at all when spot and background moved in the same direction. The response was invariant with absolute direction, being equally strong whether the spot moved down and the background moved up, or the spot moved left and the background moved right, and so on.

The U-shaped function which Tynan and Sekuler (1975) found when the center and surround motion were in the same direction could result from inhibition exerted by mechanisms sensitive to motion in the surround upon mechanisms sensitive to motion in the center. This inhibition, with resulting reduction in apparent speed, was greatest when the center and surround moved at the same speed, so when the center and surround moved in the same direction, their inhibitory interaction showed velocity tuning; the apparent speed reduction depended on the center–surround speed differential. But when center and surround moved in opposite directions, their interaction was not inhibitory, nor did it show velocity tuning; instead the center velocity was increased, suggesting a release from inhibition. Nakayama and Tyler (1981) attribute induced motion to neurons having a center-surround organization with respect to velocity and suggest that units with small receptive fields are sensitive to a slower range of velocities than are units with larger receptive fields.

Further support comes from the fact that motion aftereffects can be produced by motion which is not real but induced (Anstis & Reinhardt-Rutland 1976). A stationary patch of texture was centered in a rightward-moving surround and appeared to be moving to the left. Subsequently a rightward motion aftereffect could be seen in the test patch. The motion-sensitive neurons in the test patch must presumably have been active during the adapting period, owing to lateral inhibition from the surround, in order to adapt and give a motion aftereffect.

To these examples of *velocity repulsion* in motion contrast we can add *directional repulsion*. Marshak and Sekuler (1979) and Mather and Moulden (1980) superimposed two intermingled fields of sparse random dots, presented simultaneously and moving in slightly different directions, say toward 12 and 1 o'clock. They found that the perceived directions of movement appeared shifted away from each other, toward 11 and 2 o'clock, respectively. As the angular separation between the two motion paths was increased, the amount of mutual repulsion between them increased rapidly, peaked for a separation of 22.5°, and gradually declined thereafter, reaching zero when the two paths were about at right angles. The maximum directional repulsion was 15–20° for each set of dots. Effects were the same whether the observer tracked the moving dots or fixated, so eye movements did not play a significant role. Dichoptic viewing, in which the two sets of dots were presented to different eyes, halved the repulsion effect but did not destroy it, so there is probably a component central to the point of binocular fusion. The effect is much bigger than the simultaneous orientation shift or apparent expansion of acute angles (Blakemore, Carpenter, & Georgeson, 1970), which rarely exceeds 3 or 4°, and it can be produced by motion paths which differ by up to 90°, whereas angle expansion occurs only for acute angles. Thus it may be caused by lateral inhibition, not between orientation detectors but between motion detectors that are tuned to different directions (and velocities). The directional tuning of each unit is probably broad, up to ± 45°. Many such directional tuning curves plotted on polar graph paper are conceivable, each with a different preferred direction, like the petals of a rose. Motion in any given direction will adapt an overlapping set of these units, and some measure of central tendency in the response of the population of stimulated units will signal the perceived direction. Now if these units tend to inhibit each other, stimulation in two directions at once will produce mutual inhibition, which will shift the two distributions away from each other and give a perceived mutual repulsion of direction. The same model can fit much of the data from adaptation and aftereffects of motion, which we now discuss.

2. ADAPTATION AND AFTEREFFECT

2.1. The Phenomena

If an observer inspects a field of steadily moving contours, four perceptual effects can occur:

1. The inspection motion itself gradually appears to slow down as the observer adapts to it. A subsequently viewed test field can show the following three different aftereffects.
2. A stationary test field will appear to move back in the opposite direction. This is the negative aftereffect of motion, or *motion aftereffect* (MAE).
3. A low-contrast test field which moves in the same direction will be harder to see, whereas if it moves in the opposite direction, its visibility will be relatively unaffected. This is called *direction-specific adaptation* (DSA) (Sekuler & Ganz 1963).
4. A test pattern that moves in the same direction will have its apparent velocity reduced (or occasionally increased), whereas if it moves in the opposite direction, its apparent speed will be relatively unaffected. This has been called the *velocity aftereffect* (Thompson, 1982).

2.1.1. Early Studies. The MAE was first reported by Aristotle in his treatise on dreams. He noted that after one gazes at a flowing river, the stationary river bank appears to move. However, he mistakenly claimed that the aftereffect was positive, in the same direction as the adapting motion (Gregory, 1982). Wohlgemuth (1911) reviewed nineteenth-century work on the MAE, and Holland (1965) reviewed work up to the 1960s. We shall concentrate on more modern studies, which have been inspired by the physiological models of Sutherland (1961), Barlow and Hill (1963), and Sekuler and Pantle (1967).

2.1.2. Modern Studies: A Model from Physiology. Hubel and Wiesel (1962) described neurons in the mammalian visual system that respond most vigorously to a contour moving through the visual field in a particular direction. (Motion-sensitive neurons have since been extensively reviewed by Grusser & Grusser-Cornehls, 1973, and by Berkley, 1982. See also Chapter 5 by Hood & Finkelstein.) This led Sutherland (1961) to suggest that "the direction in which something is seen to move might depend upon the ratios of firing in cells sensitive to movement in different directions, and after prolonged movement in one direction a stationary image would produce less firing in the cells which had just been stimulated than normally, hence apparent movement in the opposite direction would be seen to occur" (p. 222). Barlow and Hill (1963) found such adaptation of a motion-sensitive ganglion cell in the rabbit retina. When the retina was exposed to a moving surface, the ganglion cell's firing rate was initially brisk but gradually reduced over the first 15–20 sec. During the next 40 sec it fell only slightly further as the cell adapted. When the motion was stopped, the firing rate fell below its baseline rate, recovering gradually over 30 sec. This depression in firing rate is thought to correspond to the MAE. Incidentally, these ganglion cells showed only maintained baseline activity when tested with motion in the opposite, nonpreferred direction. Srinivasan and Dvorak (1980) found similar adaptation and aftereffect (AE) in the firing of a neuron in the blowfly lobulus, accompanied by corresponding behavioral changes; the tethered blowfly attempted to follow the adapting motion by making walking movements that turned a Ping-Pong ball held in its feet, and during the stationary test phase it turned the Ping-Pong ball back in the opposite direction for a few seconds.

Sekuler and Pantle (1967), following Sutherland (1961), attributed MAE and DSA to the supposed adaptation of motion analyzers, tuned to different velocities, which would gradually reduce their activity when exposed to prolonged motion and fall below their baseline level of activity when exposed to a static test field thereafter, recovering at a rate that was proportional to the amount of adaptation. The duration of the MAE would reflect this recovery time. This model is supported by measurements of three types of aftereffects—DSA, MAE, and velocity aftereffects—as a function of the contrast and velocity of the adapting and test stimuli.

2.2. Direction-Specific Adaptation

Sekuler and Ganz (1963) found that after an observer inspected bars moving in one direction, the observer's luminance threshold for bars moving in that same direction was raised in comparison to the threshold for bars moving in the opposite direction. They attributed this to adaptation in directionally selective neural elements. The amount of DSA depended on the contrast of the moving adapting grating: DSA increased linearly with the logarithm of the adapting contrast in the low-contrast region but reached an asymptote and became independent of adapting contrast once this contrast exceeded threshold by more than a factor of 5 or 6 (Pantle, Lehmkuhte & Caudill, 1978; Pantle & Sekuler, 1969). A similar relationship was found for the MAE (Keck, Palella, & Pantle, 1976).

2.3. Motion Aftereffect

The MAE, like piano music, is easy to record badly but hard to record well. Its duration can be measured with a stopwatch, but this method has its problems because it is hard to be sure when the MAE has finally stopped: it is apt to stop and then start up again. If one thinks of an exponentially decaying MAE sinking into a bed of neural noise (Reason, Note 1; Leguire, 1982), its slope will be very shallow when it disappears, so its perceived duration will be very sensitive to small changes in the noise level or in the criterion adopted. Also, the apparent velocity of the MAE can be nulled by moving the test pattern slowly in the direction opposite to the MAE until it appears stationary (Johnston & Wright, 1983; Thompson, 1981). One problem here is that the MAE involves apparent motion without change in position—it makes a pattern appear to move without getting anywhere, so visible landmarks in a test pattern will appear to move even at the null point. One solution is to use a very brief test period of a second or so (Johansson, 1950). The nulling motion itself may produce adaptation and affect the MAE. Mayhew (1973) attacked these problems by nulling the MAE with an extremely low-contrast, almost spatially uniform test field made of white tracing paper. Some authors have used magnitude estimation to measure the velocity of the MAE, which will do as a method of last resort.

2.3.1. Animal Studies. In a technical tour de force, Scott and Powell (1963) showed that a rhesus monkey sees an MAE. The animal was trained to press a key when it saw an expanding circle. Following adaptation to a contracting spiral, it was shown a static circle and pressed the key, as though it saw the circle apparently expanding. Srinivasan and Dvorak (1980) demonstrated an MAE in the blowfly (see Section 2.1.2).

2.3.2. Effects of Adapting and Test Contrast. Keck, Palella, and Pantle (1976) measured the MAE resulting from adaptation to moving vertical gratings as a function of grating contrast from threshold up to 10.5%. They measured both the duration of the MAE and its estimated magnitude, obtaining similar results from both measures. They varied the adapting and test gratings independently and found that when the test grating was held constant, the MAE magnitude increased rapidly with the contrast of the adapting grating up to about 3% (about 6 times threshold) but much more slowly above 3%. When the adapting grating contrast was held constant, the MAE was strongest for the lowest test contrasts and became weaker as the test contrast was increased. Thus MAE was greatest for high adapting contrast and low test contrast. This shows that an adapted neural substrate does not always give a visible MAE; any aftereffect may remain latent if the test contrast is too high or if the situation is unfavorable for other reasons, for instance, if there is no surround (Anstis, 1961; Day & Strelow, 1974) or if the room is totally darkened (Spigel, 1965).

Green, Chilcoat, and Stromeyer (1983) reported a brief but strong MAE when the test field was spatially uniform and sinusoidally flickered. This flicker MAE has distinct properties: the adapting grating must be of low spatial frequency; the MAE was promoted by high contrast and high temporal frequency of both the adapting and test fields; and it did not transfer interocularly. This flicker MAE seemed to tap a class of transient mechanisms that were selective both for flicker and for rapidly moving stimuli of low spatial frequency.

2.3.3. Effects of Adapting Velocity. Motion-sensitive neurons in mammals are selective for direction of motion, and they are tuned to a range of preferred velocities, so that a given neuron responds maximally to a particular rate of motion (Barlow, Hill, & Levick, 1964; Berkley, 1982; Grusser & Grusser-Cornehls, 1973; Hubel & Wiesel, 1965; Reichardt, 1961). There are two plausible ways in which the human visual system could code velocity. On an "intensity" model, velocity would be coded rather as luminance is: the neurons would be selective for direction but not for velocity, so that an increase in velocity would simply increase the firing rate of all the neurons. On a "tuning-curve" model, velocity would be coded rather like color or orientation: each neuron could be tuned to a limited range of velocities, and different neurons would have different but overlapping tuning curves, like color cones or orientation detectors (Anstis, 1975; Coltheart, 1971). Slow velocities would maximally excite "slow" neurons and fast velocities would maximally excite "fast" neurons. Two predictions follow from the tuning-curve but not from the intensity model: (1) after adaptation to a particular velocity, DSA should be greatest for the adapting velocity and should be less severe for slower or faster test velocities and (2) adaptation to a medium velocity would selectively adapt a subset of tuned neurons, and the resulting skewed response of the adapted neural population would make slow test velocities look slower, and fast velocities look faster, than they really were. In other words, test fields that moved at about the adapting velocity would be depressed or repulsed. Neither of the models predicts much change in the appearance of test fields that move in the opposite direction.

Experimental tests of these prediction give some support for the tuning-curve model. Pantle and Sekuler (1968) measured the luminance threshold elevation (DSA) for contours moving at 2, 5, or 9°/sec, after adaptation periods in which contours moving at each of several velocities were viewed. The range of adapting velocities included 1/2–45°/sec. Threshold elevations were direction specific; that is, they were greatest when test and adapting motions were in the same direction. Moreover, they were greatest when the velocities were about the same and were less if the adapting and test velocities were mismatched. In practice, the greatest DSA occurred when the adapting bars moved slightly faster than the test bars, not when they moved at exactly the same speed. For test velocities of 2, 5, and 9°/sec, the most effective adapting velocities were 7, 9, and 22°/sec, respectively. This might reflect an asymmetry in the underlying tuning curves. The DSA effect was very broadly tuned for velocity, with a half-amplitude half-bandwidth of over 2 octaves, so that to halve the threshold elevation, the test and adapting velocities had to differ by a factor of 5 or 6.

2.3.4. Neural Site of the Motion Aftereffect. There have been various psychophysical attempts to jump over the peripheral visual system and locate effects in more central parts. The simplest experiment of this kind involves interocular transfer (IOT): if only one eye is adapted, the MAE can be elicited from the other eye, although its duration is roughly halved (Anstis, 1961; Favreau, 1976; Wohlgemuth, 1911). Interocular transfer is a form of cross-adaptation experiment. The argument is that since the adapting stimulus alters the appearance of the test stimulus, the two stimuli must share a binocular visual channel that receives inputs from both eyes. The logic is like a tuning-curve experiment, in which an apparent change in one test spatial frequency brought about by adaptation to another spatial frequency is taken as evidence for a single channel sensitive to both. Unfortunately, it happens that interocular transfer does not really demonstrate a central origin for the MAE, because it is always possible that the adapted eye may be sending up the message of an MAE, which the brain combines with the stationary test field viewed by the unadapted eye. Craik (1940) devised an ingenious though risky solution, which he used to study the neural site of afterimages. If the eyeball is pressed firmly against the bony orbit, the optic artery can be compressed until the retinal blood supply is cut off. This makes the retina functionally blind until the pressure is released. Barlow and Brindley (1963) adapted one eye to motion, then pressure blinded it, and opened the unadapted eye to view a stationary test field. Subjects reported an MAE, which could not have resided in the retinal ganglion cells.

Other studies confirm that the MAE is probably central, not retinal, and can involve both monocular and binocular pathways in the brain. Movshon, Chambers, and Blakemore (1972), Mitchell and Ware (1974), and Mitchell, Reardon, and Muir (1975) found conventional interocular transfer of the MAE in normal subjects, predominantly from the dominant to the nondominant eye. However, they found no interocular transfer in subjects who lacked stereopsis. This suggests that interocular transfer is mediated by binocular cells in the cortex that receive inputs from both eyes. Wade (1976) extended these findings, using 24 normally binocular subjects and 18 who lacked stereopsis as a result of childhood strabismus. His normal subjects showed an interocular transfer slightly but not significantly greater from the dominant to the nondominant eye. The strabismic subjects seemed to fall into two groups. One group, including 7 out of the 18 subjects, showed the same pattern of interocular transfer as the normals, whereas the others showed no interocular transfer in either direction. Wade concluded that "neither stereoblindness alone, nor its combination with a history of childhood strabismus is a sufficient condition for the failure of interocular transfer: for this to occur stereoblindness in combination with eye deviation (continuing into adulthood) is required, but eye deviation together with stereopsis will yield transfer" (p. 117).

Wohlgemuth (1911) alternately exposed one eye to an expanding spiral and the other to a contracting spiral and was able to elicit opposite MAEs from each eye separately, although no MAE was visible when both eyes were open. These MAEs presumably lie in monocular channels. Anstis and Duncan (1983) used a variation of this technique that was devised by Vidyasagar (1976). In their adapting period, the left eye viewed a disc rotating clockwise, and the right eye viewed the same disc still rotating clockwise, and both eyes together viewed the same disc now rotating counterclockwise. When a stationary test field was presented, the left eye alone saw a counterclockwise MAE, and so did the right eye, but when both eyes were open together, a clockwise MAE was seen. Thus the MAE in each eye condition was opposite in direction to the adapting motion. Each eye saw equal and opposite overall motion, so in a linear system any MAEs would have canceled out. Therefore the visual system was behaving in a nonlinear fashion. The "monocular" MAE is thought to reside in visual channels excited by one eye and inhibited by the other. Such neurons have been found in the cat (Bishop, Henry, & Smith 1971). The "binocular" MAE is thought to reside in visual channels that give only a weak response to stimulation from either eye alone, but a very much stronger response to simultaneous stimulation from the two eyes. Such neurons have been found by Pettigrew, Nikara, and Bishop (1968).

Moulden (1980) measured the duration of MAE produced by adapting one or both eyes and then testing either the same eye, the other eye, or both eyes. He concluded that MAEs resulted from the adaptation of a subset of monocular or binocular neurons and that the strength of the MAE depended on how much overlap there was between the adapted and the tested subsets of neurons.

Papert (1964) demonstrated MAEs central to the point of binocular fusion. He used dynamic random-dot stereograms (Julesz, 1971), in which either eye on its own saw an incoherent snowstorm of twinkling dots but moving stereoscopic bars could be seen when the two eyes fused the disparate sets of random dots. Inspection of these cyclopean bars gave rise to a short-lived MAE, which must have been central. Anstis and Moulden (1970) also shared out the motion information between the two eyes with an interleaved stroboscopic display designed so that the left eye on its own saw clockwise apparent motion and so did the right eye but the two eyes together saw counterclockwise apparent motion. Subsequently, the two eyes together saw a brief clockwise MAE, which must have been central to the point of binocular fusion. On the other hand, Lehmkuhle and Fox (1975) viewed an adapting motion stimulus with one eye while the other eye viewed a rival stimulus that masked the adapting stimulus, leaving it subjectively visible for only about half the time. This did not, however, reduce the subsequent MAE, which must therefore be peripheral to the point of binocular rivalry. O'Shea and Crassini (1981) confirmed that binocular rivalry during adaptation did not reduce the intraocular MAE (adapt and test the same eye), nor did it reduce the interocular MAE (adapt one eye and test the other). Incidentally, the McCollough effect (McCollough, 1965; White, Petry, Riggs, & Miller, 1978) and the tilt aftereffect (Wade & Wenderoth, 1978) are also independent of binocular rivalry. However, it is most unlikely that the MAE can be both peripheral to the rivalry point and central to the fusion point, since the fusion point itself probably lies central to the rivalry point. We suggest that MAEs can probably occur at various different sites within the visual system.

Bonnet, Le Gall, and Lorenceau (1982) find that MAEs contain a long-lasting residual component contingent upon the properties of the stationary test pattern. They attribute this component to an associative conditioning process, which would presumably be central.

2.3.5. Motion Adaptation in Two Dimensions. Adaptation to motion can alter not only the visibility and apparent velocity but also the apparent direction of a moving test target. Levinson and Sekuler (1976) and Mather and Moulden (1980) have shown that following prolonged inspection of a sparse random-dot field drifting toward 4 o'clock, a test field drifting toward 3 o'clock appeared to be moving toward 2 o'clock. The maximum apparent shift in direction was about 10° and occurred when the adapting and test directions differed by 30°, falling off steadily as this angle increased. The shift was always away from the adapting direction. Adaptation to motion toward 10 o'clock, that is, at 180° to the best direction, produced no apparent shift in a test field drifting toward 3 o'clock, so it was the direction of motion and not merely its axis (horizontal or vertical) that mattered.

Unlike, say, the tilt aftereffect, this alteration in motion depended on the direction of the adapting motion (left or right), not simply on its axis (horizontal), so an adapting field which drifted toward 10 o'clock, instead of 4 o'clock, produced no shift in a test field which drifted toward 3 o'clock. Moreover, a pair of superimposed adapting fields, drifting toward 4 and 10 o'clock, respectively, did shift the test field's motion toward 2 o'clock. Any MAEs from these two opposed adapting fields would have canceled out, so the direction shift cannot simply be a form of MAE.

The fact that the directional shift peaked when the adapting and test field directions differed by as much as 30° suggests that the underlying motion channels are tuned rather broadly for direction of motion. This is confirmed by measurements of the directional tuning of the DSA made by Levinson and Sekuler (1980). They showed that adaptation to an isotropic pattern of sparse random dots, moving uniformly in one direction, elevated the luminance detection threshold for patterns of dots moving in various directions. Threshold elevation, or DSA, was maximal when the adapting and test directions were the same and fell to zero for opposite directions. They found rather broad tuning curves for directional selectivity, with some threshold elevation being present even when the adapting and test directions differed by 45 °, as seen in Figure 16.2. Mather (1980) and Mather and Moulden (1980) base a model of the perception of direction on these findings. Sutherland (1961) suggested that motion is seen, say upward, by taking the ratio of responses in visual channels selective for "upward" to the response of channels selective for "downward." However, Mather and Moulden suggest that channels tuned to directions all around the clock face play a part. Adaptation to motion upward toward 12 o'clock would fatigue the stimulated channels but leave relatively unaffected the channels tuned to directions all round the clock face from 1 to 11 o'clock. A stationary test field would excite all these channels somewhat, giving a net signal of "minus 12 o'clock," that is, motion downward.

For a review of MAE in depth, see Chapter 19 by Regan, Kaufman, and Lincoln.

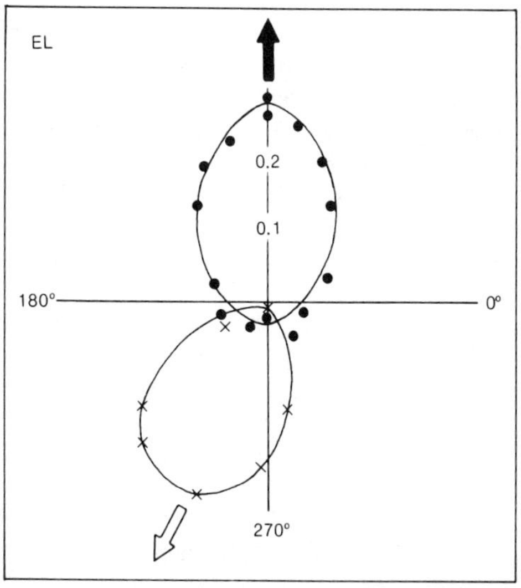

Figure 16.2. Directional tuning of motion-sensitive visual channels as revealed psychophysically by direction-specific adaptation: Log threshold elevation for moving dot patterns as a function of direction of drift (in polar coordinates) produced by adaptation to a sheet of random dots drifting upward (filled circles, filled arrow) or toward 7 o'clock (crosses, open arrow). (From E. Levinson & R. Sekuler, A two-dimensional analysis of direction specific adaptation, *Vision Research, 20*. Copyright 1980 by Pergamon Press, Ltd. Reprinted with permission.)

2.3.6. Velocity Aftereffects. In an MAE one adapts to some velocity and tests on a stationary field. It is also possible to measure the apparent velocity of moving test patterns after adaptation to movement. In the special case when the adapting and test velocities are the same, Wohlgemuth (1911), Gibson (1937), and A.G. Goldstein (1957) found adaptation to motion, in which the perceived velocity of a constant-velocity test stimulus decreased during prolonged inspection. Carlson (1962) examined the effects of adaptation to one velocity upon a range of test velocities in the same and in the opposite direction. He found an apparent reduction in the speed of test velocities that were slower than, but in the same direction as, the adapting velocity, and this was confirmed by Rapoport (1964), Clymer (1973), and Thompson (1981). Rapoport (1964), using rotary movement, found that velocities equal to or slower than the adpating velocity appeared slower and, furthermore, test velocities in the same direction as the adapting velocity, but faster, appeared faster after adaptation. Clymer (1973) found that patterns moving in the same direction as the adapting motion generally appeared to be slower but with slow adapting velocities fast test velocities appeared faster after adaptation. However, Thompson (1981) has suggested that this apparent speeding up of rapid test velocities may be artificial. He measured the effect of adaptation to movement on various test velocities, using a matching method. He found that low test velocities were reduced in apparent speed by a wide range of velocities, from 1 to 8°/sec. In fact, a fast velocity was more effective than a slow one in reducing the apparent velocity of a slow test speed, and a fast adapting velocity would reduce the apparent speed of all slower test velocities. This is consistent with Pantle and Sekuler's (1968) threshold elevation data. However, a test velocity was not slowed down if it was faster than the adapting velocity. Thompson found no evidence for apparent speeding up of test velocities. It is known that adaptation to a high-contrast grating will reduce the apparent contrast of a medium-contrast test grating (Blakemore, Muncey, & Ridley, 1973). Thompson (1976) found that perceived speed of a moving grating depended on its contrast, with a reduction in contrast at high velocities leading to an overestimation of velocity. So previous reports of velocity overestimation may merely reflect the results of the adapting pattern's reducing the apparent contrast of the test grating.

Thompson (1981) also investigated whether motion was coded by velocity in degrees per second or by temporal frequency in Hertz, that is, by the number of spatial periods that crosses a fixed retinal point per unit time. He varied the spatiotemporal frequency of his adapting and test gratings and found that his different curves gave the best superimposition when he plotted them in terms of velocity, not of temporal frequency. Thus the aftereffect following adaptation to an 8 Hz, 8 cycles/degree (1°/sec) grating resembled the adaptation produced by a 2 Hz, 2 cycles/degree (1°/sec) grating, as predicted by velocity coding, and was not at all like the adaptation produced by an 8 Hz, 2 cycles/degree (4°/sec) grating, as would have been predicted by temporal frequency coding. This is at variance with Pantle's (1974) report that magnitude of MAE depended on the temporal frequency, not on the velocity of the adapting grating. This discrepancy is still unresolved.

However, there is little evidence for a population of velocity-detecting channels with tuning curves each tuned to a different preferred velocity. Instead, the data are compatible to a simple model of some channels that peak at relatively low velocities but also respond to stationary fields. In the MAE the appearance of a stationary test field is altered by prior adaptation to upward motion, so presumably the same channels are involved in seeing both the upward-adapting motion and the stationary test field. The data are compatible to a model in which some channels have tuning curves ranging from zero to medium velocities, peaking at slow velocities, while other channels have tuning curves that completely cover these, peaking at high velocities. The tuning curves of the former would be a subset of the latter.

3. ILLUSIONS OF MOTION

3.1. Motion Perception in Peripheral Vision

It is sometimes mistakenly claimed that the peripheral retina is "more sensitive" to motion than the fovea. In fact, the threshold for motion rises steadily with eccentricity (Johnson & Leibowitz, 1976; McKee & Nakayama, 1984; Tyler & Torres, 1972; Tynan & Sekuler, 1982). However, the threshold of resolution for static detail rises even more rapidly, so the periphery is relatively better at seeing motion than seeing form. A wiggling finger in the extreme visual periphery is perceived as something moving, but one cannot see what that something is. Motion in the peripheral visual field is important in sensing the motion of one's whole body through space, and an observer sitting in a slowly rotating drum will start to feel after about 30 sec that the drum is stationary and that the observer is moving. This "vection" phenomenon occurs if the parafoveal region is masked off and the peripheral field is visible. The parafoveal region on its own does not produce vection (Dichgans & Brandt, 1978). Peripheral vision is important in judging one's speed when driving, so goggles which cut-off peripheral vision are a bad idea.

Tynan and Sekuler (1982) found that the lower threshold for movement increased steeply with eccentricity, being about 0.03°/sec at the fovea, rising to 0.22°/sec at an eccentricity of 22.5° and to 0.45°/sec at 30° eccentricity. Johnston and Wright (1983), using drifting gratings of various spatial frequencies, also found that the lower velocity threshold for movement increased with eccentricity (although it was independent of spatial frequency). However, when they scaled their results by the human magnification factor (Cowey & Rolls, 1974; Rovamo & Virsu, 1979), they found that the lower velocity threshold, expressed in terms of cortical velocity, was constant for all retinal eccentricities. Its value was 0.16 mm/sec for one observer and 0.15 mm/sec for the other, where mm refers to millimeters across the cortical surface.

Lichtenstein (1963) noticed that slow velocities look even slower in peripheral vision. Campbell and Maffei (1979, 1981) measured this peripheral slowdown. A striped or spotted disc, viewed foveally and rotating at 1 rpm, was compared with a similar disc at different eccentricities, whose rotation the subject adjusted to match the foveal disc. The greater the eccentricity, the higher the frequency of rotation required to match the foveal standard of 1 rpm. At 10° eccentricity it was 2 rpm, and at 25° it was 5 rpm. This apparent slowing in eccentric velocity closely matched the increase in motion threshold with eccentricity. Sometimes an eccentric rotation looked actually stopped. Similarly, Hunzelman and Spillman (1983) found that a slowly rotating sectored disc viewed peripherally appeared to slow down and come to a standstill within 5–20 sec. The time required for this full adaptation decreased with (1) increasing retinal eccentricity (30–70°), (2) increasing number of sectors (10–20), and (3) decreasing speed of rotation (1–0.2 revolution/sec). At high speeds sectors tended to disappear, instead of becoming stationary. These results could not be obtained with aperiodic discs. Movement presented to the temporal retina adapted about twice as fast as movement presented to the nasal side.

Tynan and Sekuler (1982) investigated the role of velocity in peripheral slowdown. They found that the more slowly they moved their peripheral stimulus—a field of sparse drifting dots—the greater the percentage slowdown. At an eccentricity of 30° random dots moving at 16°/sec still appeared to have 90% of their true velocity, but dots moving at 4°/sec were apparently slowed to 70%, dots moving at 1°/sec to 40%, and dots moving at 0.25°/sec to 0% (so that they looked stationary).

On the other hand, Mather and Anstis (in press) found that a spot oscillating at 6–8 Hz on an oscilloscope screen in a darkened room appeared to speed up by 25% when viewed in the near periphery (2–10° eccentricity). The apparent path length of the motion was not increased, and a stationary flickering spot showed almost the same speedup, so the effect was probably temporal rather than spatial. The peripheral retina may be relatively more sensitive to transient than to steady-state events.

Mackay (1980) found that slow motion was seen more readily than fast motion in the periphery. A spot on an oscilloscope screen in a normally lit room was driven by a modified ramp waveform, so that it deflected instantaneously through 1 or 2° upward and then moved steadily downward. This was seen veridically in foveal vision, but viewed 3 or 4° off the fovea, the ramps were seen but the temporal spikes were not: the spot appeared to move continuously downward. Oddly enough, although the sharp rise times were not perceived, they were seen quite clearly when the spot was made to jump up and down, driven by a square wave. Here the spikes were the same but the ramps were missing. Perhaps the ramps inhibit the perception of the spikes.

Richards and Lieberman (1982) discovered a parafoveal "shear blindness." Two adjacent random-dot fields moved parallel to their common boundary, in the same direction but at different speeds, creating a shearing motion. Of the population 20% were unable to use this differential motion to locate the boundary when it was presented to the parafovea, although they could all perform the task when the fields sheared in opposite directions or when they moved differentially at right angles to the common boundary (occluding motion). Richards and Leiberman concluded that different mechanisms process shearing and occluding motion.

McKee and Nakayama (1984) measured the peripheral differential motion threshold, which expresses the ability to detect relative motion or shear between adjacent visual stimuli. This threshold increased linearly with eccentricity, but it was smaller than the minimum angle of resolution at all retinal loci tested (as in the fine-grain motion illusion described in the next paragraph). They concluded that the spatial determinants of velocity discrimination followed the magnification factor, that is, the progressive loss of resolution and coarsening of the spatial grain with eccentricity, but that temporal sensitivity must be almost as good in the periphery as in the fovea. However, van Doorn and Koenderink (1982) and Nakayama and Silverman (1984) argue that the coding of high velocities by peripherally placed receptive fields is probably handled by two complementary approaches: increasing the receptive field size and decreasing the processing time. The role of spatial and temporal factors in peripheral motion perception merits more research.

Thorson, Lange, and Biederman-Thorson (1969), Biederman-Thorson, Thorson, and Lange (1971), and Foster, Thorson, McIlwain, and Biederman-Thorson (1981) reported an apparent expansion of small peripheral displacements. They called this the *fine-grain movement illusion*. When two spots were flashed in sequence to peripheral vision, a strong sensation of movement was produced even though the separation of the two spots was well below the static acuity threshold. The apparent jump size increased from 2 to 6° as the retinal eccentricity was increased from 10 to 24°. However, when mapped on to the visual cortex by means of the human cortical magnification factor, the illusion spanned a patch of cortex about 3 mm in diameter, regardless of eccentricity. This corresponds to the locus of cortical cells that "see" a given retinal point.

This may look at first like evidence that motion and position occupy separate visual channels, but a simpler explanation can be found by comparing position perception with color perception (Anstis, 1983). Location in the retinal periphery is probably signaled by the large, overlapping receptive fields of ganglion cells. Analogously, color is signaled by cones with overlapping spectral sensitivity curves. A patch alternating in hue between red and green will be seen veridically, since it stimulates red and green cones in succession. If the patch contains a mixture of monochromatic red and green, the visual system cannot resolve the two colors but takes an average and sees metameric yellow. (Color vision, unlike hearing, cannot resolve two frequencies or wavelengths presented simultaneously.) Now imagine two receptive fields viewing two adjacent, overlapping retinal regions in the retinal periphery. These two units respond to position, instead of wavelength. A spot jumping between two positions will stimulate the two units in succession, and motion will be correctly seen. If two nearby spots are exposed simultaneously instead of successively, the pair of overlapping receptive fields cannot resolve the two positions but takes an average and sees the spot in an intermediate, "metameric" position (Anstis, 1983).

3.2. Phantom Gratings

Tynan and Sekuler (1975) occluded the central portion of a vertical sinusoidal or square-wave grating with an opaque horizontal strip. When the grating was made to drift across the screen, or simply flicker on and off (Genter & Weisstein, 1981), the grating appeared to continue, dimly but unmistakably, across the occluded region of the screen. The *phantom grating* could be produced dichoptically in a display of which the top half was seen only by the right eye, the bottom half only by the left eye. Adaptation to a (monoptic) drifting phantom grating could lead to an MAE (Weisstein & Harris, 1980). An adapting grating drifted to the left, and a phantom grating filled the occluded gap in the middle. Then the grating was stopped; the top and bottom appeared to drift to the right, and the gap was filled by a phantom grating that also appeared to drift to the right.

3.3. Motion and Flicker

When a large homogeneous field is flickered at rates between 2 and 50 Hz, observers report seeing patterns called *stroboscopic patterns* that under suitable conditions are composed of hexagons, squares, grids, and other geometric elements (Smythies, 1959a, 1959b; Young, Cole, Gamble, & Rayner 1975). These do not directly involve motion. Staebler (1975) found an apparent motion phenomenon when each eye saw a separate flickering Ganzfeld. Each field flickered sinusoidally with a 90° temporal phase delay between the eyes. If the temporal phase between the eyes was suddenly changed, a low-contrast pattern of stripes was seen that moved either to the left or right. Suppose the left eye's field had a 90° phase lead but was switched to a 90° phase lag (by suddenly inverting the phase seen by one eye). The subjective stripes now appeared to move to the left. The effect diminished over several seconds. When the initial conditions were restored, the stripes appeared to move to the right. Motions were observed at flicker rates of 10– 30 Hz, and the patterns became larger and moved more slowly at lower frequencies.

Flicker perception and motion perception are clearly related. Levinson and Sekuler (1975b) found that the detection threshold for a counterphase flickering grating was twice that for a moving grating, suggesting that the visual system may analyze a counterphase grating as the sum of two half-contrast gratings that moved in opposite directions. Tolhurst (1973), King-Smith and Kulikowski (1975), and Gorea (1979) have suggested that flicker and motion are detected separately; but Green (1981) found that adaptation to drifting gratings raised the detection threshold for a uniform flickering field, and conversely adaptation to flicker impaired sensitivity to drifting gratings. These data pointed to broadly tuned temporal channels that responded to both flicker and motion.

3.4. Apparent Distortions of Moving Stimuli

Some patterns appear to contract or distort when they move. Ansbacher (1944) noted that an arc of 30° drawn on a rotating disc appeared to shrink when the disc was rotated at speeds rather below the flicker fusion rate. Most shrinkage occurred at 1.3 revolutions/sec. Stanley (1970) measured this phenomenon. An object in linear motion also appears to shrink, and as it moves faster, it must be made larger in order to reach threshold (Bhatia & Verghese, 1963). Caelli (1981) has compared this to the Fitzgerald-Lorentz contraction.

Mace (1971) and Harris, Schwartz, Patashnik, and Lappin (Note 2) noticed that when two identical dots, moving at the same constant speed in opposite directions, meet and pass through each other, they seem to pause momentarily. The spots must coincide or at least touch: near misses do not suffice. If the two spots are separated in apparent depth via the Pulfrich technique, pausing still occurs. Goldberg and Pomerantz (1982) concluded that the observer takes the vector average of the velocity of the two spots.

Matin, Boff, and Pola (1976) and Boff and Matin (1977) found that a rotating vernier target, or two radii forming a broken diameter on a disc, showed an apparent vernier offset of about 4 min arc when the disc was rotated at 0.7 revolution/sec. The direction of the vernier offset was reversed when the direction of rotation was reversed. See Figure 16.3. They suggest that the radius at one position in time induces a figural or tilt aftereffect into the same radius when it reaches a fresh position an instant later.

The artists Fred Duncan and Marcel Duchamp have produced rotating patterns of eccentric circles that appear as three-dimensional cones coming off the surface of the disc in a "stereokinetic depth illusion" (Braunstein, 1976). Some of these are exhibited at the Exploratorium in San Francisco. Several of these patterns are reproduced as illustrations in Wade's (1982) book, and others can be found in Fineman's textbook (1981), conveniently printed large enough to cut out and glue on a disc to rotate. For a recent review see Wilson, Robinson, and Piggins (1983).

Mori (1981) was able to reduce the Poggendorff illusion by moving the oblique lines. This probably reduced the interaction between the test and inducing lines. Wade and Swanston (1984) placed a short line inclined at 45° on a large grating of fine vertical lines. Expansion or contraction of the display, produced by head movements or by a television link with a zoom lens, made the 45° line appear to rotate through as much as 6°. Foster and Gravano (1982) exposed a curved horizontal line, convex upward, followed by a straight horizontal line below it. During apparent motion the straight line appeared to be slightly concave upward.

A detuned television set shows a snowstorm of randomly twinkling points known as dynamic visual noise. If this is viewed with both eyes open, with a neutral density filter over the left eye, it seems to separate out into two or more depth planes, with a streaming motion which is leftward in front of the point of fixation and rightward behind it. The direction of movement reverses with the filter over the right eye. The effect is probably related to Pulfrich's (1922) pendulum, which actually swings in the frontoparallel plane but appears to swing in depth in an ellipse. Pulfrich's effect occurs because the filter introduces a physiological delay of up to 100 msec (Rogers & Anstis, 1972),

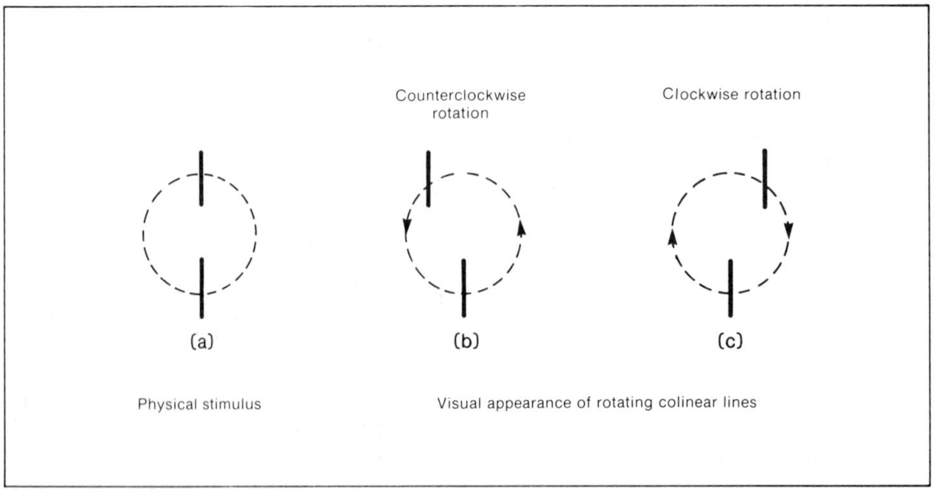

Figure 16.3. Two radii rotating about their central point appear to be offset like a vernier target. (From L. Matin, K. Boff, & J. Pola, Vernier offset produced by rotary target motion, *Perception and Psychophysics*, 1976, 20. Reprinted with permission.)

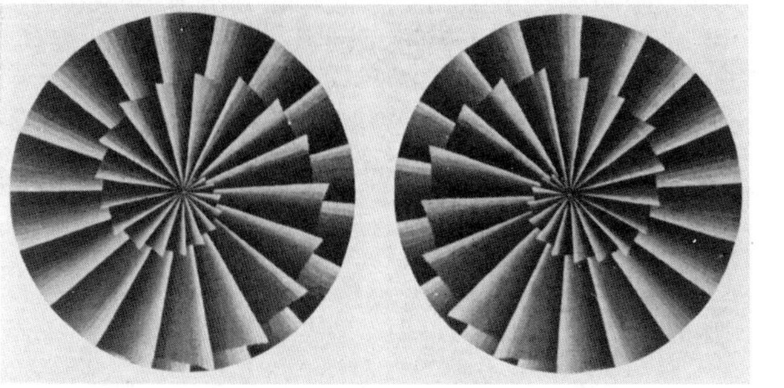

Figure 16.4. The escalator illusion. On fixating between the two shaded disks, most observers will see them in slow apparent rotation in peripheral vision. (From A. Fraser & K. J. Wilcox, Perception of illusory movement, *Nature, 281*. Copyright 1979 by Macmillan Journals, Ltd. Reprinted with permission.)

so the filtered eye sees the bob in the past and the effective binocular disparity is interpreted as depth. Some fine papers have been written on stereopsis in dynamic visual noise by Burr and Ross (1979), Morgan (1979), Neill (1982), Ross (1974), and Tyler (1974, 1977), among others, but to this reviewer such literature is still a noisy stimulus from which no clear picture emerges.

Fraser and Wilcox (1979) report an "escalator" illusion, in which stationary spatially shaded stripes seen in peripheral vision appear to move (Figure 16.4). The explanation is unknown.

4. APPARENT MOVEMENT

Walls (1942) wrote, "If asked what aspect of vision means the most to them, a watchmaker may answer 'acuity,' a night flier, 'sensitivity,' and an artist 'color.' But to the animals which invented the vertebrate eye, and hold the patents on most of the features of the human model, the visual registration of movement was of the greatest importance" (p. 342). Motion perception, "the most ancient and primitive form of vision" (p. 342), evolved early probably because motion is the unmistakable mark of living things, and the first thing an animal needs to know about is smaller living things that it can eat or larger ones that might eat it. Color vision may help a vegetarian to find red fruit among green leaves, but then the fruit "wants" to be found and eaten to spread its seeds abroad, so it uses color to advertise. Tasty animals do not want to be eaten so they have evolved camouflage that makes color vision useless to a predator, but they have to move, if only to run away, so a predator that can see motion is at an advantage. Seeing motion is, of course, equally valuable to the prey.

An object in *real motion* (RM) changes its position continuously over time, but if the displacement of the object is intermittent or discontinous and we still see motion, we speak of *apparent motion* (AM) or stroboscopic motion (Kaufman, Cyrulnik, Kaplowitz, Malnick, & Stoff, 1971). This ability of the visual system to see discontinuous jumps as if they were smooth continuous trajectories has been beneficial to technology. We are surrounded by AM technology, from flashing neon signs to television, movies, and computer graphics, which could barely exist without this physiological oddity of the visual system. It is beneficial because it allows vision engineers to simulate real motion with signals of limited bandwidth. Does this fact merely reflect the limited bandwidth of the visual system itself? After all, the three-color television system that is indistinguishable from a full-spectrum device is itself a simulation using limited bandwidth for hues matching the visual system's own limited bandwidth in color resolution, otherwise known an metamerism. Existing TV and movie systems have reached their present reasonably efficient level by evolving under market pressures, drawing hardly at all on psychophysical data but relying instead on engineers' folklore and intuition. But by looking at them we can form a rough impression of the visual system's limited ability to resolve motion and flicker.

4.1. Space and Time

The intervals of space and time giving the best AM have been much studied. If two adjacent spots are flashed in alternation, a rate that is "too slow" yields the impression of two spots appearing in succession, a rate that is "just right" gives good AM, and a rate that is "too fast" gives the impression of two spots flickering in place simultaneously. How fast is "just right"? It depends on the spatial properties of the stimuli.

Koffka's student Korte (1915) formulated three "laws" of AM. (Perhaps rules of thumb would be a better description.)

1. For a fixed interstimulus interval (ISI), the spatial separation S and the intensity I of the stimulus are directly related: $S \simeq I$ and $I \simeq S$.
2. For a fixed spatial separation, ISI and intensity are inversely related: $I \simeq 1/\text{ISI}$ and $\text{ISI} \simeq 1/I$.
3. For a fixed intensity, ISI and spatial separation are directly related: $\text{ISI} \simeq S$ and $S \simeq \text{ISI}$.

These laws have a fine scientific ring to them, like Ohm's laws for electrical circuits. In practice, however, the visual system tolerates wide departures from these functions. Neuhaus (1930) reported good AM between spots separated by 0.5° for ISIs of 50–250 msec. At larger separations the range of permissible ISIs was narrower: for spots separated by 4°, the ISI had to lie between about 100 and 160 msec. The likelihood of seeing AM can be predicted better from stimulus onset asynchrony (SOA), or onset-to-onset time, than it can from the ISI. (SOA = stimulus duration + ISI.) Kolers (1972, chap. 2) has replotted Neuhaus's data and provides a good summary of the early literature.

Zeeman and Roelofs (1953) obtained AM over a range of spatial separations of 2–18° separations, and Smith (1948) even reported dichoptic AM across 100° or more when one light was presented to the temporal margin of each eye, stimulating monocular regions in each eye.

The spatial pattern affects the best timing. Braddick (1973, 1974) found that overlapping random-dot patterns, separated by 15 min arc or less, gave good AM only for SOAs under 100 msec, whereas longer jumps between isolated single spots, as used by Wertheimer (1912/1961), Korte (1915), and Neuhaus (1930), could give AM for SOAs of up to several hundred msec. He dubbed these, respectively, the "short-range" process, which has a short time constant, and the "long-range" process, which has a longer time constant. The short-range, but not the long-range, process is disrupted by a uniform, bright ISI interposed between the two stimuli.

Petersik (1980) exposed his subjects to discontinuous, that is, stroboscopic, computer simulations of a transparent sphere partially filled with randomly positioned luminous dots and rotating about the y axis in depth. These simulations gave sensations of continuous rotation and internal volume of the sphere for SOAs which ranged from about 50 to 200 msec. In an important paper, Burt and Sperling (1981) exposed in succession a series of horizontal rows of small shapes and asked subjects to report whether the diagonal AM they saw was diagonally down to the left or diagonally down to the right. They found short optimal SOAs for these multiitem patterns, in the order of 20 msec. This is about the duration of a movie frame. Thus, as Korte (1915) realized, finely patterned displays with short jumps require shorter SOAs than large isolated spots jumping through large distances. Farrell and Shepard (1981) exposed a spiky polygon, alternating with the same polygon at a different orientation. At rapid alternation rates the shape appeared to change, but at slower alternation rates a rotating, rigid polygon was seen. The minimum SOA that gave rigid rotation increased linearly with the amount of angular rotation and was also influenced by the symmetry of the polygon.

Tyler and Torres (1972) measured the amplitude threshold for sinusoidal (real) oscillation of a bright line in the dark as a function of temporal frequency and found that sensitivity was greatest at 1–2 Hz. The authors interpreted the slope of their frequency response plots as evidence for both position- and velocity-sensitive mechanisms in the movement detection system. Nakayama and Tyler (1981) found a way to dissociate position cues from motion cues. Normally these are inseparable, since any moving object visibly changes its position. When an object moves really slowly, such as the minute hand of a clock, it is not clear whether one sees motion at all or merely infers it from the change in position. They measured threshold sensitivity, as a function of temporal frequency, for an oscillating "kinetic grating" of moving random dots, which was rather like a set of many speckled fingers drumming on a table top. They were able to measure pure sensitivity to motion without contamination from position sensitivity, for two reasons: (1) a snapshot of their stimulus at any instant would give merely a static field of random dots, with virtually no positional cues, and (2) they found that sensitivity depended on peak velocity (which varies with temporal frequency), not on displacement. Subjects could detect motions as small as 5 or 6 sec arc, which is comparable to vernier acuity, when the spatial frequency of the grating was between 0.1 cycle/degree, the lowest frequency tested, and 1 cycle/degree. Note that the kinetic grating was defined purely by differential motion, not by luminance profile as in a conventional grating.

Tyler (1973) exposed two lines in alternation on an oscilloscope, driven by a square wave so that one saw a single line jumping back and forth between two positions. As the alternation frequency was increased from 1 to 7 Hz, the duration of AM decreased rapidly. It was replaced mainly by the impression of omega movement (Zeeman and Roelofs, 1953), in which a dark smudge or shadow appeared to move in antiphase with the line position, as though a dark occluder were jumping back and forth, covering and uncovering two stationary lines. Omega movement peaked at 3–5 Hz. By 7 Hz very little motion was reported; subjects just saw two lines flickering in place. Sigman and Rock (1974) have also studied this occlusion effect, which they take as a sign of "perceptual intelligence" in interpreting a potentially ambiguous AM stimulus.

Shepard and Zare (1983) have recently reported a striking effect. Two alternately flashing black dots give AM along an imaginary straight line joining them, but when a curved gray path was briefly flashed between them, a compelling illusion was seen of a single dot moving back and forth over that path. Suppose the dots lay at 7 and 5 o'clock on an imaginary clock face and the curved path comprised an almost complete circle running from 7 through 12 o'clock to 5 o'clock. If the 7 o'clock dot was flashed, then the curved path, then the 5 o'clock dot, the AM ran clockwise around the long circular path. Furthermore, the minimum time interval yielding this AM increased not with the direct distance between the dots but, linearly, with the length of the curved path.

4.2. Smoothing, Interpolation, and Fourier Synthesis

The tip of a swinging pendulum moves in real, sinusoidal motion. A spot jumping back and forth in AM can be said to describe a spatiotemporal square wave. As is well known, a square wave can be thought of as the sum of a set of odd harmonics, that is, sine waves of frequencies 1, 3, 5, 7 . . . and relative amplitudes 1, 1/3, 1/5, 1/7 . . .; thus its seems a reasonable speculation to intepret the visual system's response to square-wave AM in terms of its spatiotemporal frequency response. Kelly (1979) measured the human spatiotemporal frequency response to real movement of a drifting grating. He plotted his results in the form of a three-dimensional surface whose axes were the spatial frequency of the grating x, its temporal frequency, or number of cycles that pass a fixed point per second of time y, and threshold sensitivity z. This argument can be extended to sensitivity for AM. Thus a grating jumping back and forth between two positions is undergoing a square-wave motion, which can be thought of as the sum of a set of sinusoidal oscillations.

Adelson (1982) has studied visual responses to the spatial components of AM, and Caelli (1981), Burr (1979), Morgan (1980a,b), Watson, Ahumada, and Farrell (1983) and Watson (Chapter 6) have studied visual responses to temporal and spatiotemporal components.

What is it that appears to move in AM? More specifically, what are the spatial features, displayed at successive times, between which the visual system establishes correspondences? Ternus (1926/1938) called this the problem of *phenomenal identity*. Ullman (1979) called it the correspondence problem and believes that the correspondence tokens are low-level features, such as blobs and ends of lines. Adelson (1982), on the other hand, believes that correspondences are established between Fourier components. He considered a grating with a square-wave luminance profile that jumped successively through one-quarter of a spatial period (half a bar width) to the right. This is equivalent to a set of harmonic gratings of relative frequencies 3, 5, 7 . . . jumping through 3/4, 5/4, 7/4 . . . spatial periods to the right. Note that the third harmonic's jump of 3/4 spatial period to the right is identical to a jump of 1/4 period to the left. Higher harmonics will jump every which way, but their amplitudes are too low to have much perceptual effect. Adelson then presented a square-wave grating minus its fundamental and made it jump successively through 1/4 cycle to the right. Observers saw it as apparently jumping to the left. This result would not be predicted if the visual system extracted edges or other pattern features, which do jump to the right. However, a system acting as a Fourier analyzer would give the result he obtained. It may sound intuitively unlikely that the visual system would break a jumping pattern down into its harmonics, figure out the phase shift of each harmonic, and put them together again to give a pure spatial (minimum phase) jump, but that is what his results suggest.

Anstis (1970) and Rogers and Anstis (1975) described *reversed apparent motion*, in which a picture was replaced by its own photographic negative, shifted a few minutes of arc to the right. Strong AM was seen to the left, in a direction opposite the physical displacement. This would also be expected from a Fourier analyzer that broke a picture down into its harmonic components, since inverting the contrast of a component grating is equivalent to phase-shifting it by 180 °, so shifting a negative through 1 ° of phase angle to the right is equivalent to shifting a positive through 179 ° to the left. Gregory and Heard (1982) have made careful measurements of these and related phenomena.

An object moving in discrete spatial jumps is difficult to distinguish from a continuously moving object, provided that the time between jumps is not too great. Morgan (1979, 1980) has depicted the changes in spatial position over time of an object in real motion as a ramp and of an object in AM as a staircase. A staircase can by synthesized from a continuous motion ramp plus a higher frequency modulation of spatial position that takes the form of a sawtooth. See Figure 16.5 (a)–(c). The sawtooth gives rise to the discreteness of motion. If this motion signal has its higher frequencies progressively removed by physical filtering, it is perceived as increasingly continuous. The fact that such filtering is not necessary for perceived continuity when the discrete jumps occur at rates greater than about 30 Hz suggests that frequencies greater than this limit are removed by the visual system itself. So a commercial movie is indistinguishable from real motion because both provide the same effective stimulus to the visual system. They differ only in higher frequencies, to which the visual system is blind.

A cricketer can predict the momentary position of a flying cricket ball accurately enough to catch it. But how is this achieved? We know from experiments on flicker fusion thresholds that the visual system is relatively sluggish in its response to temporal change. Morgan relates this sluggishness to the apparent continuity of apparent motion, and to the problem of localizing a moving target in space, by examining a curious illusion of spatial interpolation, discovered independently by Morgan (1979) and by Burr (1979). Consider a vertical vernier target moving steadily to the right, with the upper line slightly leading. The target will be seen veridically and with surprisingly little loss of vernier acuity (Westheimer & McKee, 1975, 1978). But Morgan and Burr, arranged to illuminate it intermittently, so that the targets made discrete spatial jumps separated by periods of rest (or of invisibility), with the upper and lower targets occupying identical spatial locations but occupying these positions at slightly different times. It turned out that this temporal phase lag appeared to the subject as a spatial offset between the stimuli, even though the spatial positions were actually aligned. A subject, if asked to make a spatial adjustment to align the stimuli, would advance the spatial position of the temporally lagging stimulus in the direction of motion. The stimuli were produced electronically under computer control, but in theory they could be produced by moving a vernier target behind a row of spatial separated vertical slits, as in Figure 16.6. (At first this might sound reminiscent of the apparent compression and spatial distortions in a figure seen moving behind a stationary slit, Parks, 1965, in which eye movement may be painting a distorted image on the retina, Anstis & Atkinson, 1967, but control experiments have ruled out eye movements in this vernier task). Morgan showed that this apparent spatial offset is an interpolation effect caused by the visual system's sluggish temporal response or visual persistence, which forces an averaging of visual direction over time and thus a confusion between a temporal and a spatial effect. The visual persistence has a time constant in the order of 30 msec and is longer in the dark adapted eye (Rogers & Anstis, 1972).

This may not be the whole story, since an oscilloscope display with a slow phosphor also has a sluggish temporal response but would not confuse space with time. In fact, this spatial interpolation effect has inspired much theorizing on visual coding of position and motion and on reconstruction of the retinal image in space and time (Anstis, 1983; Barlow, 1979; Fahle & Poggio, 1980).

Whereas Morgan (1979, 1980) compared AM and RM in the spatiotemporal domain, Watson, Ahumada, and Farrell (1983) compared them in the Fourier domain (Figure 16.5 (d) to (g)). They compared the Fourier spectrum of AM, which contains many high-frequency components, with the low-pass "visibility window" of the visual system in the Fourier domain and concluded that after AM has undergone low-pass filtering by the visual system, it is barely distinguishable from RM. They derived the spatiotemporal frequency spectra of some simple moving images and showed how these spectra are altered by sampling in the time domain. They constructed a simple model of the human observer which predicted the critical sampling rate required to render continuous (RM) and sampled (AM) images indistinguishable; this rate depended on the spatial and temporal acuity of the observer and on the velocity and spatial frequency content of the image. For a fuller treatment see Chapter 6 by Watson. Caelli (1981) has also pointed out that the trajectory of a spot jumping back and forth in AM between two positions is a spatiotemporal square wave, containing high frequencies that are filtered out physiologically, plus a sinusoidal fundamental that is retained to give the impression of motion.

Visual low-pass filtering, which makes AM effectively equivalent to RM, is restricted to short-range AM and does not apply to long-range AM. The vernier interpolation effect disappears when the ISI exceeds about 50 msec; at an ISI of 200 msec the vernier targets appear aligned when they actually are spatially aligned. However, they are still seen as moving, presumably via the long-range AM mechanism.

4.3. Braddick's Two-Process Theory

Korte's third law states that the optimal timing increases with spatial separation. Braddick (1973, 1974) has taken this dictum to an extreme, finding a difference in kind, not merely in degree, produced by spatial separation between two stimuli. Anstis (1970), Julesz (1971), Braddick (1973, 1974), Ramachandran and Anstis (1983), and Nakayama and Silverman (1984) have examined AM between a pair of random-dot patterns, which Julesz (1971) has called random-dot *kinematograms* (by analogy from the stereograms which they closely resemble). A region of the dots is identical in the two patterns of the pair, except for a uniform displacement; when the two patterns are presented alternately at an appropriate rate, this region appears to oscillate to and fro. The oscillating region is visible as a shape segrated from the surround by clear boundaries. No such shape is visible in either pattern taken alone, since each is a homogenous random array; the shape is defined only by the relationship between the two patterns. To see the shape, the visual system must compare the successive patterns, probably by some kind of correlation process (Lappin & Bell, 1972). The perception of motion must precede and define the perception of this cyclopean shape, and its visibility can be used as an index of the motion-detecting process (Braddick, 1973). Thus random-dot kinematograms can isolate early motion processing from other visual mechanisms.

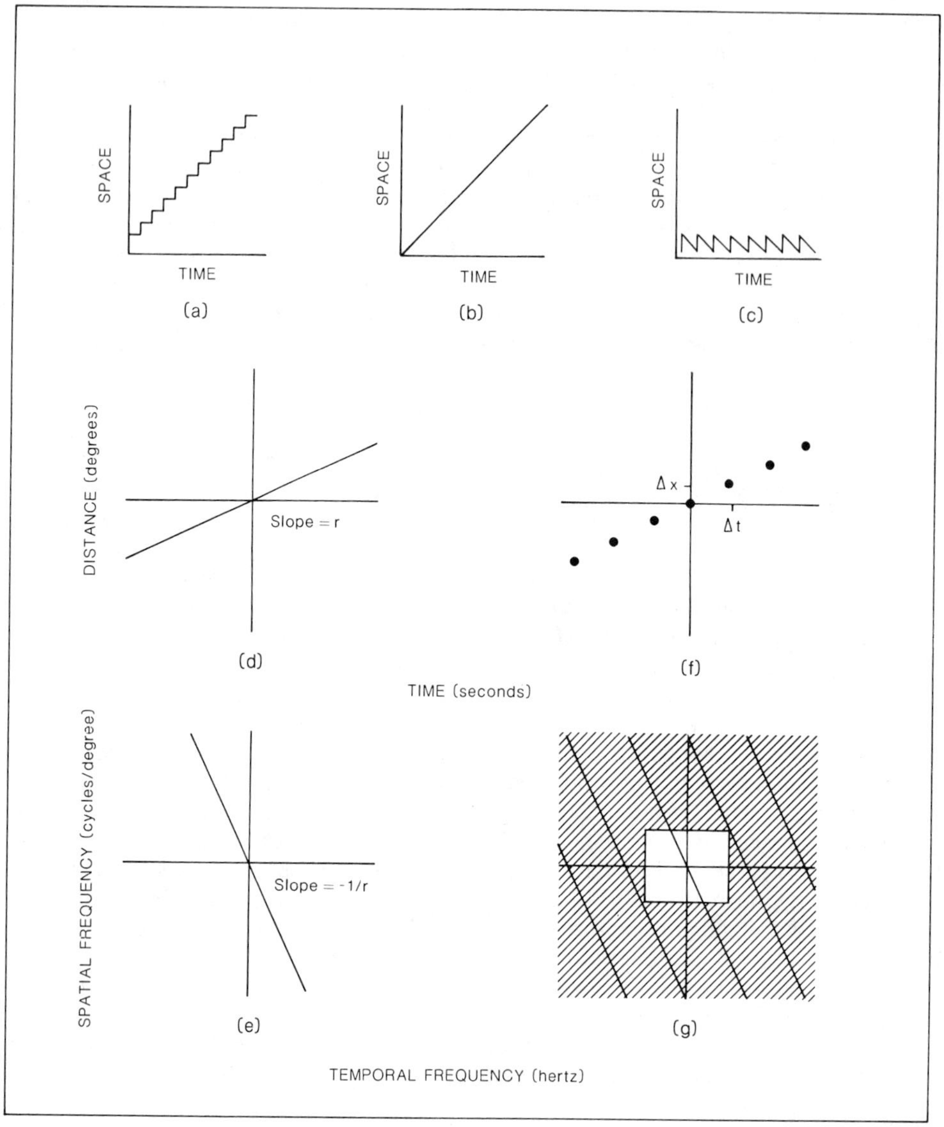

Figure 16.5. (a) Apparent motion can be depicted as a spatiotemporal staircase. (b) This can be thought of as a real motion or spatiotemporal ramp with (c) a superimposed sawtooth. If the sawtooth is rapid, compared with the visual integrating time, it will be progressively filtered out, so that AM will look indistinguishable from real movement (Morgan 1980). (d) Real motion on a space-time axis has (e) a Fourier spectrum consisting of a straight line on axes of spatial and temporal frequency. (f) A stroboscopically lit apparent motion has (g) a Fourier spectrum consisting of straight parallel lines. Superimposed is the "window of visibility" of the visual system. The shaded region contains combinations of spatial and temporal frequency that are invisible to the human eye, so here AM and RM cannot be told apart (Watson, Ahumada, & Farrell 1983). ((a), (b), and (c) from M. J. Morgan, Analogue models of motion perception, *Philosophical Transactions of the Royal Society of London*, 1980, *290*. Reprinted with permission.)

Braddick found that motion between random-dot patterns cold be seen only for spatial separations of about 1/4 ° or less, regardless of the size of the picture elements (pixels). At larger separations each dot jumped to its nearest neighbor of the same brightness, giving an overall chaotic incoherent motion in all directions. The maximum distance over which the observer can see coherent motion is generally known as D_{max}, or the *Braddick limit.* Beyond this limit the visual system cannot solve the correspondence problem (Ullman, 1979). Braddick also found that AM was destroyed by an SOA longer than about 100 msec, by a bright ISI interposed between the two pictures, or by dichoptic presentation in which one eye saw the first picture and the other eye saw the second picture. However, AM between single isolated spots was immune to all these. It could still be seen over tens of degrees, for SOAs up to 500 msec or longer, in spite of bright ISIs and in both monocular and dichoptic presentations. Braddick concluded that there may be two separate AM processes in the visual system. The short-range process has a short space constant (jumps of 15 min arc or less) and a short time constant (SOAs below 100 msec). This process mediates perceptual segregation in random-dot kinematograms. Its breakdown in dichoptic conditions suggests that it operates early in the visual system, and it is probably mediated by the neural motion detectors studied by Barlow and Levick (1965),

Michael (1968), and many others. These detectors respond well to discontinuous stimulation. (Neural motion detectors have been reviewed by Grusser & Grusser-Cornehls, 1973, and by Berkley, 1982.) The long-range process, which is more central, has large space and time constants, accepting jumps of tens of degrees and time intervals of 500 msec or more. It probably underlies the classical AM of isolated spots jumping over large distances.

In Section 4.4 we discuss the different spatial and temporal ranges of the two processes and their different solutions to the correspondence problem (Ullman, 1979)—how they decide which feature in the first picture is to be paired off with which feature in the next picture.

4.4. Evidence for Two Processes

We review the evidence that two AM processes exist, which differ in (1) their spatiotemporal range, (2) their ability to produce an MAE, and (3) the correspondence between pictures to which they are sensitive.

4.4.1. Spatiotemporal Range of the Short-Range System. How short is the spatial range or Braddick limit (D_{max}) of the short-range process? There is some controversy whether it is to be expressed as a visual angle or as a number of pixel diameters, but it is agreed that it varies with the size and shape of the moving area and with retinal locus (Baker & Braddick, 1982a, 1982b; Chang & Julesz, 1983a, 1983b; Nakayama & Silverman, 1984).

Braddick (1974) used random-dot kinematograms containing dense arrays of dots and used perceptual segregation of a central rectangle as his criterion for AM. He reported AM only when the jump size was less than about 15 min arc. This differs from classical studies in which two isolated dots, illuminated in succession, gave AM for separations that range 2–18° (Zeeman & Roelofs, 1953). Braddick varied independently both the jump size and the pixel size. He found that the curves showing his subjects' responses lay far apart on his graphs when displacement was plotted in numbers of pixels or pattern elements but were neatly superimposed when displacement was expressed as a visual angle. He found that perceptual segregation began to deteriorate at a displacement of about 5 min arc, and this deterioration was complete for displacements of about 20 min arc. Inserting an ISI of 10–80 msec greatly degraded the short-range AM, and dichoptic presentation of the two random-dot stimuli destroyed it altogether.

Lappin and Bell (1976) measured their subjects' ability to discriminate the direction of AM in a similar random-dot display and found that performance fell off as the ISI was increased in steps from 0 to 100 msec and as displacement was increased in steps from one to four pattern elements. These results agree with those obtained by Braddick. However, they concluded from a second experiment that the spatial range over which coherent motion could be detected was not a fixed visual angle of about 15 min arc but a fixed number of pattern elements. This makes sense intuitively because a fixed number of pixels implies a fixed number of possible false matches that the visual system must reject. They pointed out that when Braddick increased his dot size, he held the total pattern size constant, reducing the total number of pixels and hence the size of the statistical sample of dots. On Lappin and Bell's cross-correlation model of motion detection, this might be expected to halve the signal–noise ratio available to the visual system. In this model the visual system slid the first picture around over the second picture, so to speak, until it found the best match. Bell and Lappin (1979) found very similar results when one random-dot field was rotated, instead of translated, relative to the other. Baker and Braddick (1982a) riposted with further evidence that the spatial range was independent of dot size. However, they did find that the spatial range increased as the area of moving dots increased, as Lappin and Bell would predict. Baker and Braddick pointed out that this increase in stimulus area artifactually spread the stimulus on to more peripheral regions of the retina, where the spatial range may be larger owing to the coarser grain of the retina; but this may not be the whole story. It is still not settled whether D_{max} is a function of visual angle or of pixel diameter.

Chang and Julesz (1983a) and Nakayama and Silverman (1984) both measured D_{max}, whilst van Doorn and Koenderink (1984) measured the threshold signal–noise ratio in AM, as a function of size and shape of the target area. In the latter paper a spatially and temporally random snowstorm of dynamic visual noise was electronically added to a random-dot kinematogram. All three groups of authors found that the perception of AM improved (D_{max} and threshold signal–noise ratio were larger) as the square root of the target was increased and, if the target area was a long, thin strip, when its long axis was parallel to, rather than perpendicular to, the direction of motion. The fact that motion perception was best for long, thin strips suggests simple pooling of motion-sensing units, perhaps of the type proposed by Reichardt (1961), as width was increased but recruitment of new units as length was increased (van Doorn & Koenderink, 1982).

Chang and Julesz (1983b) presented spatially filtered random-dot kinematograms using a low-, medium-, or high-pass filter. And D_{max} was greatest (5 dots, or 18 min arc) for the "blobby" low-pass and least (1.4 dots, or 5 min arc) for the "edgy" high-pass filtered images, suggesting that the motion detection mechanism is inefficient at coding high spatial frequency information. They then filtered the dots in the horizontal direction only, turning each dot into a horizontally elongated blob, and found that D_{max} was increased for horizontal but not vertical motion. This implies that detectors for horizontal and vertical motion are independent, and probably contain spatially tuned channels.

Nakayama and Silverman (1984) ingeniously measured the time it takes the visual system to encode a displacement. Suppose a random-dot display jumps through a distance D_{max}, pauses 5 sec, and makes a further jump in the same direction. Clearly both motions will be seen, and the upper displacement limit will increase from one Braddick limit to two. They measured the minimum pause needed between jumps to encode a second D_{max} and found it was surprisingly short: about 40 msec for a small area and 10 msec for a large area. Thus the mechanisms mediating directional selectivity can be very fast, especially if they have large receptive fields. Large fields that made a series of jumps revealed enhanced motion perception or *sequential recruitment*. Perhaps this can be traded off against the spatial recruitment found by van Doorn and Koenderink (1984), since these authors reported a trade-off between target area and presentation time such that a 5° square target could be seen in coherent motion in three successive frames but ten times as many frames had to be presented for a 10 min square target. The advantage conferred by "many looks" at a moving target reveals an important difference between motion perception and stereo. These two tasks seem alike since AM involves two (or more) successive looks at a displaced field, while stereo involves two simultaneous looks by the two eyes (Anstis, 1970). However, while stereo may involve sophisticated pattern matching of just two images (Marr & Poggio, 1979), motion may rely on much cruder spatial correlations between many more successive images (Nakayama & Silverman, 1984).

Kolers (1972, p. 37) displayed a line in a succession of positions. When only two positions were used, good AM occurred with separations as large as 7.5°. However, with more than two positions, smooth continuous motion was only perceived if the interline separation was as small as 14 min arc, a figure close to Braddick's limit. Perhaps the long-range "interpretative" process cannot couple a series of displacements into a continuous perception of uniform motion, whereas the lower-level short-range process can.

4.4.2. Motion Aftereffects and the Short-Range Process. The short-range process may be mediated by directionally selective neurons in the visual pathways, which in other species are known to respond to discontinuous stimulation (Barlow & Levick, 1965). The long-range process may involve more cognitive processes in interpreting AM (Rock, 1975). It is likely that the well-known MAE is mediated by adaptation of neural motion detectors (Barlow & Hill, 1963; Sutherland, 1961), so we would expect an MAE from short-range AM but not from long-range AM. Banks and Kane (1972) measured the MAE from AM, using a pattern of jumping thin lines and found that it became vanishingly small when the spatial discontinuity of the stimulus reached 12.5 min arc. However, Pantle has pointed out (Note 3) that it would be worth repeating this experiment with sinusoidal gratings to rule out contamination from the rich high harmonics present in thin lines, which might be jumping the wrong way and artifactually reducing the MAE.

4.5. The Correspondence Problem in Apparent Motion

If two pictures are presented in rapid succession to the same retinal area, AM will be seen between corresponding features of the two pictures. The question is, How does the visual system know, or decide, which features are to be placed in correspondence? Ullman (1979) has called this the *correspondence problem*. More simply, we can ask how similar successive pictures need to be for AM to be seen between them.

Wertheimer (1912/1961) and Korte (1915) used single, isolated spots in each picture. Their work revealed the best spacing and timing for AM, but this problem reduces to one of spatiotemporal geometry. Their artificially simple stimuli oversimplified the problem, barely allowing the correspondence problem to arise. Few decisions are required of the visual system, because it is obvious which spots are to be paired together—if there is only one spot in each picture, then there is no choice. More complex stimuli, such as successive frames of a movie, do pose visual decision problems. For instance, the limbs of a racing athlete in a movie constantly change their configuration, but the observer correctly identifies the body in each frame as "the same." If the camera cuts from a sprint event to the pole vault, the observer correctly identifies the new athlete as a "different" body, and no false AM is seen from sprinter to jumper. Where does the perceptual boundary lie for identifying two stimuli as the same or different? A special-effects film editor can deliberately cross this boundary by juxtaposing two different people in such close succession that a "jump cut," or false AM, is seen between them or by doing a slow trick dissolve from a toad to a prince. In real life this rarely happens, and the visual system nearly always gets things right.

So false AM looks like a nosocomial problem, unknown in real life and seen, like hospital cross-infections, only in the artificial stimuli of a perception laboratory. In real movement, an object moves continuously by infinitesimal steps; since there are no stroboscopes in nature, there is no problem in establishing correspondence. The "correct" solution gives a thousand times better fit than any potential imposter. But once experimenters pry two successive pictures apart, inserting gaps in time and space, there is room for impostors to creep in, and the brain is like an examiner faced with a myriad false candidates whose credentials may not be much worse than those of the true heir. Imagine Prince Charming's dilemma if he found that the ugly sisters could slip their feet into the glass slipper as well as Cinderella could. Who would adjudicate, and how?

In random-dot kinematograms the correspondence problem arises not so much because the rival candidates are so well qualified as because they are so numerous. Such patterns contain 50% black and 50% white dots, so any given dot will have a partner of the same color in the other pattern, but there is a probability of 0.5 that any nearby position in the other pattern will be occupied by a dot of the same color. Why and how does the perceived motion correspond to the relationship between partners, rather than between any other pairs of identical nearby dots? And the more dots each picture contains, the worse the problem becomes. The number of false matches goes up factorially with the number of points in the picture. If there are two points in each picture, there are two possible pairings. Three points give 3! = six possible pairings, and four points give 4! = twenty-four. If the two pictures consist of 8 × 8 random-dot kinematograms, the number of possible or phantom matchings is equal to 64!, which is about 10^{89}, or far more than the number of particles in the universe. Clearly the visual system cannot consider and reject even a tiny fraction of these possible pairings; it would take it centuries to respond. Any plausible model of motion perception must explain not only how the correspondence problem is solved but also how it is solved so quickly, in a fraction of a second. We can exclude any model based upon an exhaustive search of all the possible correspondences between the two pictures. There must be some ruthless early culling that rejects many unpromising candidates out of hand. Generally there is only one correct match, and all the others must be ignored or discarded. The visual system might save processing time by restricting its search to a small neighborhood, comparing each dot in the first picture with only those dots in the second picture that lie within, say, a few min arc. This would work for densely packed random-dot pictures but would fail for the case of two isolated dots, one in each picture, which were several degrees apart. We know that the visual system sees AM between such isolated dots with ease. Perhaps it considers only near neighbors, comparing each dot with, say, the ten (or N) dots that lie nearest it. This solution would limit the search to a few min arc if the dots were densely packed but would efficiently extend the search to a few degrees if the pictures contained only a few isolated dots. Thus a search confined to a limited number of pixels sounds better than a search restricted to a fixed visual angle. Nevertheless, as we have seen, Baker and Braddick (1982a, 1982b) found evidence that the search area is defined in terms of visual angle, not in terms of number of pixels.

The simple experiment of looking at a random-dot kinematogram and seeing AM within a fraction of a second is powerful, perhaps analogous to asking whether a subject has ever seen a particular word before, such as "carinel." The correct answer ("no") springs to one's lips immediately. Clearly one had no time to search through every location in one's memory of English words to see if it was there or not. Human memory must have a highly efficient cross-indexing and interrogation system. Motion perception must have its own efficient algorithms too. The human observer is obviously not scanning all possible phantom matches but is taking some shortcuts somewhere.

The short-range process is thought to select only strict correspondences between points and edges of the same luminance polarity (light on dark or dark on light). However, the long-range process is thought to be much more flexible, and if zones can be perceptually segregated within pictures on any basis, these zones can be set in correspondence and can give a signal of long-range AM. Ramachandran, Rao, and Vidyasagar (1973) exposed in succession two fields of uncorrelated random dots, which gave incoherent local motions, like television snow. One picture contained a central, textured square composed of vertical black and white random dashes, while the other picture contained a similar central square, shifted to the right, but with a texture composed of horizontal, not vertical, dashes. Thus there was no local correspondence between the dashes in the two central zones. Nevertheless, subjects readily saw a central square jumping back and forth in long-range AM. Pantle (1973) likewise obtained AM between two fields of sparse, uncorrelated green dots, containing central zones of sparse, uncorrelated red dots. The central zone was shifted between pictures, and when the pictures were exposed in alternation, with one picture turning off sharply as the other turned on, the central square was seen jumping back and forth in long-range motion. If one picture was faded down as the other was faded up, in a dissolve instead of a cut, the percept was radically altered. Observers now saw each dot gliding into its nearest neighbor in the following picture, regardless of its color. The percept was an incoherent set of random, local short-range motions in all directions. A small change in timing switched the percept from long- to short-range AM.

The problem of false correspondences arises with equal force in stereopsis (Julesz, 1971). See Arditi, Chapter 23.

Pantle and Picciano (1976) used a simpler display containing only three dots. Following Ternus (1926/1938), they presented three spots in positions a, b, c at time 1, which were replaced by three spots in positions b', c', d' at time 2. If these were presented sequentially with no ISI, subjects reported "element motion" of a single spot jumping from a to d while the spots at b and c remained stationary. However, if a blank ISI was introduced between the two stimuli, "group motion" was reported, with all three spots jumping together to the right as a trio. (See Figure 16.6.) Group motion also occurred if the two pictures were presented one to each eye or if the two central spots shifted very slightly, that is, when the spots at b' and c' in the second picture were not precisely aligned with those at b and c in the first picture. These maneuvers weakened the perceptual links between the two pictures.

Braddick and Adlard (1978), noting that element motion occurred if there was no ISI, applied an ISI selectively to the outer spot at a, but not to the inner spots at b and c, and found this made no difference; they still got element motion. When they applied the ISI selectively to the inner spots at b and c, and not to the outer spot at ISI, they did get group motion. This surprising result showed that an ISI, or a tiny displacement, applied to the inner spots and perturbing their positions, gave an AM signal showing that they had moved, allowing all three spots to move as a group. When there was no ISI on the inner spots, the short-range process signaled not motion but stationariness of the inner spots, which locked them in position, leaving the outer spot to undergo element motion.

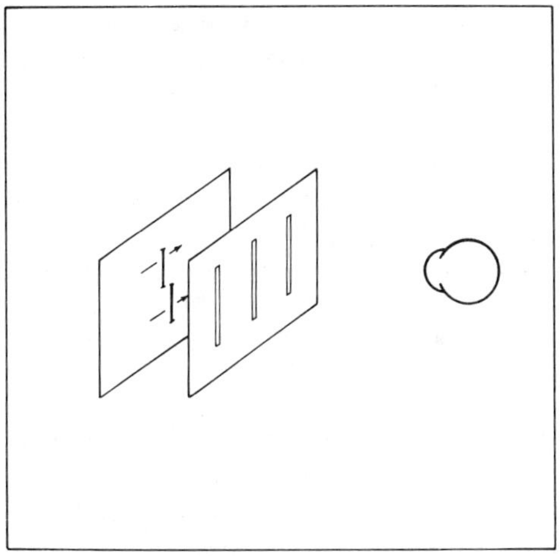

Figure 16.6. Simulation of the moving vernier targets used by Burr (1979) and by Morgan (1979). Two vertical lines placed end to end jumped along and were flashed with a brief relative delay but with no spatial offset. To an observer the line which flashed later appeared to lag spatially behind the earlier line. (From D. C. Burr, Acuity for apparent vernier offset, *Vision Research*, *19*. Copyright 1979 by Pergamon Press, Ltd. Reprinted with permission.)

4.6. Apparent Motion and Real Motion—Same or Different?

To ask whether AM is "equivalent" to RM is to ask whether both stimulate the same or different channels in the visual system. Dependable methods have been developed over the past decade to find out whether two stimuli are processed by the same visual (or auditory) channels. If two stimuli are perceived independently, they are assumed to stimulate different channels, but if they summate or interact, they are thought to stimulate the same channel or channels. These methods have been used to establish *critical bands* of auditory frequencies (Scharf, 1970) and, correspondingly, to estimate the width of tuning curves for hypothetical spatial-frequency detectors used in seeing gratings (Campbell, 1976). These methods are:

1. *Discrimination.* Ohm's auditory law states that the ear can distinguish the different notes or frequencies in a musical chord, presumably by means of fairly narrowly tuned frequency-selective auditory channels. However, the visual system cannot distinguish red and green wavelengths (frequencies) in a color mixture but takes an average and sees yellow. This is because the wavelength analyzers—the red, green, and blue cones—are very broadly tuned for wavelength.
2. *Adaptation.* Adaptation to one auditory frequency raises the threshold for a range, or critical band, of nearby auditory frequencies. This frequency range probably corresponds to the frequency tuning curve of the auditory detectors.
3. *Masking.* One auditory frequency can mask a second nearby frequency presented simultaneously and raise its detection threshold.
4. *Subthreshold Summation.* Two frequencies, both just below threshold, can summate and become audible if they lie within

a critical band, so that they presumably stimulate the same auditory detector. If they differ too much in frequency, both remain inaudible.

To establish whether AM and RM have common underlying channels, one could measure human ability to discriminate AM from RM when both were presented simultaneously; adapt to AM and test the threshold elevation produced on RM, and vice versa; see whether AM could mask RM, and vice versa; or look for subthreshold summation between RM and AM. I have found no experiments on discrimination but one good experiment on subthreshold summation. There are various experiments on adaptation and masking, but they do not follow the conventional methods just described, so they are hard to interpret.

Banks and Kane (1972) found that adaptation to collapsing circles, which jumped in AM, did give MAEs just as RM does. The MAE was progressively less as the size of the jumps increased and disappeared for jumps greater than about 15 min arc. This is evidence that AM is seen by a short-range process (Braddick, 1974) that also responds to RM. It would be interesting to look for direction-specific adaptation to AM, to see if it raised contrast thresholds for RM in the same direction.

Banks and Kane's experiment demonstrated cross-adaptation from AM to RM. Kolers (1964) looked at self-adaptation within AM and within RM. He noted that AM and RM look subjectively different after prolonged fixation. A spot moving sinusoidally in RM is seen as moving to and fro for as long as one cares to view it. But a spot which jumps to and fro in AM, driven by a spatial square wave, shows rapid adaptation when fixated, and the AM gives way to a percept of two spots flickering in place. Anstis, Giaschi, and Cogan (1985) found that this adaptation increased linearly with log alternation rate and with log spatial separation: thus AM was strongest at low alternation rates and small jump sizes. Moreover, preexposure to two spots flickering in phase produced very little adaptation, whereas preexposure to two spots flickering in antiphase (AM) did give marked adaptation. This shows that the adaptation affected visual channels specific to movement, not merely to flicker.

Kolers (1964) took this subjective difference as evidence for the nonidentity of RM and AM. But Frisby (1973) and Clatworthy and Frisby (1973) suggested that RM detectors may underlie both phenomena but become fatigued (Barlow & Hill, 1963), so that the AM stimulation, which is only marginally strong enough to give an impression of movement, gradually becomes inadequate to keep the RM detectors responding strongly, whereas the RM stimulus remains adequate. The differences may reflect not two different mechanisms but simply the unusual operation of the AM-RM mechanism when exposed to AM stimuli close to its limits of tolerance, like a lock with a badly fitting key. Anstis, Giaschi, and Cogan (1985) found strong cross-adaptation from RM to AM, suggesting a common visual channel.

Kolers (1963) also questioned the identity of RM and AM on the grounds that they have different effects in masking a stationary stimulus. He presented a vertical bar that moved along a path, either in RM or in AM, by being flashed first at one endpoint and then at the other. He flashed a dim test bar somewhere along the motion path and measured its detection threshold. During RM its threshold was raised most when it was exposed just as the moving line passed over it, but during AM the threshold of the test bar was not affected. He concluded that since AM and RM have different masking effects, they must have different underlying mechanisms. But this is not proven. The timing of AM cannot be mapped on to RM, since the direction and velocity of the AM are indeterminate until after the second flash. Attneave and Block (1974) realized this and used a wider range of onset times for their test target. They also found no masking from AM. However, this tells us that AM and RM are physically different stimuli differing in some of their effects, in this case, their masking effects. It does not prove that AM and RM involve different visual channels.

Green (1983) combined RM and AM by displaying a window containing a grating. The window jumped from left to right in apparent motion. The grating within the window was either stationary, drifting to the left, or drifting to the right. Reports of apparent motion of the window were greatly increased (reduced) when the real motion of the drifting grating was in the same (opposite) direction as the window's jump. This is evidence for a common mechanism for RM and AM.

Barbur (1981) convincingly demonstrated the identity of RM and AM by discovering subthreshold summation between them. A dim test spot moved at 23°/sec in RM along a horizontal path 2.5 ° long. Simultaneously, a dim, subthreshold spot jumped in AM between the end points of this path, at either the same or different effective velocities and in the same or the opposite direction. In another experiment the AM path was set overlapping the horizontal RM path but at an angle to it, say toward 2 instead of 3 o'clock. Subjects adjusted the luminance of the RM test spot until it was at threshold. Barbur found that the subthreshold AM spot summated with the RM spot, making the RM easier to see, but only if the AM spot had an effective velocity within ± 8°/sec of the RM spot and if the direction of its path lay within 25° of the horizontal RM path. These results suggest that AM and RM were seen by common visual channels specific to motion, which were tuned to velocities of 23 ± 8°/sec and were tuned to directions of motion within ± 25°. These estimates of the directional and velocity tuning of human motion channels are consistent with those which Sekuler and Levinson (1974) obtained from threshold measurements, following adaptation to continuously moving random-dot stimuli. Barbur found no subthreshold summation when the AM and RM spots moved in opposite directions. This fits with Levinson and Sekuler's (1975b) finding that motion-detecting mechanisms, selectively sensitive to opposite directions of movement, act independently at threshold level (although Moulden & Mather, 1978, have disputed this independence at threshold).

Note that Barbur's jump size of 2.5° was a "long-range" jump (Braddick, 1974), as described in Section 4.3. Kaufman, Cyrulnick, Kaplowitz, Melnick, and Stoff (1971), using a comparable jump size of 2.34°, reached conclusions that differed sharply from Barbur's. They presented three stimulus conditions: (1) AM, in which a spot jumped back and forth between two positions, (2) RM, in which a spot ran smoothly from one position to the other and back again, and (3) RM + AM, in which the spot was stationary at one end of the path, then ran continuously along the path, stopped at the other end, and ran back. Upper- and lower-velocity thresholds for seeing movement were collected. In the RM + AM condition a clearly moving object was reported up to a mean angular velocity of 10.6°/sec, at which point the image became blurred or streaked. This blurred motion was seen up to a velocity of 27.9°/sec, at which speed an undifferentiated or fused blinking stimulus was seen. In the RM condition the blur threshold was reached at 7.9 °/sec, the fusion threshold at 17.9°/sec. In the AM condition the lower threshold at which subjects reported seeing a dot moving back and forth was equivalent to 8.6°/sec. This is in the region of the blur threshold for RM, so AM did not occur until the object in RM became blurred. The upper (fusion) threshold for AM was at 21°/sec, about the same as for RM and about the same as Barbur's (1981) stimulus velocity. Kaufman concludes (Note 4) that such a speed produces a blurred streak but that if the spot has a definite onset and offset, as in the RM + AM condition, its appearance and disappearance would lead to two stimuli that allow for AM, which is simply superimposed on the streak, thus increasing the "dynamic range" of motion perception. Thus at high RM velocities where the spot starts to blur, AM takes over, so (although there is no essential difference between AM and RM) AM in one velocity range is independent of RM in another range.

In summary, the evidence suggests that AM and RM are detected by the same, or by overlapping, visual channels.

4.7. Luminance and Color in the Short-Range Process

Correspondence can depend on similarity. Many studies have manipulated size, shape, and position of corresponding elements, but only a few have consistently manipulated luminance and color.

Anstis and Mather (in press) exposed a pair of parallel, separated bars of different luminances on a gray background that suddenly changed places. The background stayed the same. Frame 1 contained a light bar above a dark bar, frame 2 a dark bar above a light bar. Subjects were asked whether they saw a light bar jumping down or a dark bar jumping up. As a result, the bar with the higher contrast, that is, which differed more from the background, was seen as moving. This is consistent with opponent channels for seeing motion, which accept the stronger (higher contrast) of two countermanding motion signals that lie along the same path. Results were the same whether the spatial separation between the bars was a few min arc or several degrees so no differences could be found here between the short- and long-range processes.

Color seems to have virtually no input into motion perception. Anstis (1970) and Ramachandran and Gregory (1978) exposed in alternation a pair of random-dot kinematograms with a shifted central region and asked subjects to detect the presence of the jumping central square. The AM and the central square, which it defined, were easy to see if the random dots were black and white but disappeared if the dots were made equiluminous red and green. Cavanagh (Note 5) has extended these results and found that AM can occur for certain spatiotemporal conditions at equiluminance but is always very weak. Cavanagh and Favreau (Note 6) have found dramatic evidence that color plays little or no part in real motion. A drifting grating of low spatial frequency ($<$ 0.5 cycle/degree) and composed of equiluminous red and green bars appears to move extremely slowly or even look stationary. Anstis and Cavanagh (1983) devised a minimum-motion technique for judging the equiluminance of colors. A square-wave grating of red and green stripes was exposed, followed by an overlapping grating of black and white stripes shifted by half a bar width. If the red stripes looked lighter than the green, they were seen as jumping to the left, into the white bars. If the red stripes looked darker than the green, they were seen as jumping to the right, into the black bars. A continuous sequence of red-green bars alternating with black-white bars gave a grating that appeared to drift to the left or right according to the red–green brightness ratio or to remain stationary at equiluminance. Results were consistent with minimum-border and minimum-flicker methods. This technique has been used to measure color blindness (Cavanagh, Anstis, & Mather, 1984).

5. MODELS OF MOTION PERCEPTION

5.1. Motion Perception and the Brain

Evidence that movement is perceived directly and not merely inferred from perceived time and distance comes from occasional reports of specific impairment of movement perception following brain damage. Early reports (Bender & Teuber, 1949; Goldstein & Gelb, 1918; Potzl & Redlich, 1911) have been supplemented by a fascinating recent case study by Zihl, von Cramon, and Mai (1983). Their patient, who suffered from bilateral lesions to the lateral temporo-occipital cortex, enjoyed normal color vision and acuity but had lost movement vision in all three dimensions. She had difficulty in pouring a cup of tea because the liquid appeared frozen like a glacier, and she could not stop pouring at the right time because she was unable to perceive the movement in the cup when the fluid rose. Clinical tests showed a complete inability to see motion in depth. The ability to see a target moving along the vertical or horizontal axes was reduced within 15° of the fovea and was almost completely lost at greater eccentricities.

An important brain area subserving motion perception has been identified in the monkey as area V5 in the prestriate cortex (Zeki, 1974). Normal development of neural directional selectivity seems to require exposure to visual motion, since strobe-reared cats show abnormal directional properties in their cortical neurons, together with severe psychophysical losses in spatial contrast sensitivity and in motion detection (Pasternak, Merigan, & Movshon, 1981). Exposure of these cats to RM to the right improved both the neural and the psychophysical deficit—but only for motion to the right, not for vertical or leftward motion (Pasternak, Movshon, & Merigan, 1981).

5.2. Motion Perception as a Computational Problem

Ullman's excellent book (1979) proposes possible algorithms for seeing AM. The main task is to solve the correspondence problem, namely: Which item at time *t*1 corresponds to which item at time *t*2? Thus what are the items, or "tokens," on which the matching is done? Ullman gives evidence that they are at a higher level than the luminances or gray-scale values of individual points but lower than complete shapes, such as squares or triangles. He identifies the correspondence tokens as edges and blobs.

How are items matched up between frames? It is clear on statistical grounds that the closer and more similar two items are in successive frames, the more likely it is that they correspond. Ullman believes that the human visual system incorporates a permanent, or "hard-wired," table of similarities, which he calls *affinity measures*. However, these do not by themselves determine the correspondence process. A vertical line in one frame might be followed by two lines with the same affinity, for instance, a line of the same length but tilted 45° and a vertical line that is 50% longer. Here split motion will be seen. When more elements are present, more pairings are possible. In Ternus's (1926) display, three dots at positions A, B, C are replaced in the next frame by three dots at positions B′, C′, D′.

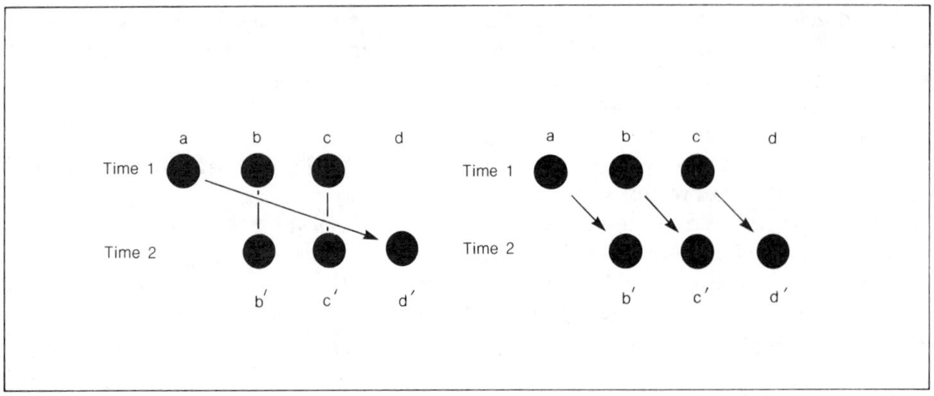

Figure 16.7. Three spots *a, b,* and *c* were flashed up at time t_1, followed at time t_2 by three spots b', c', and d'. Spots were superimposed, not vertically displaced, as shown in this illustration. Perceptual organization depended on timing: when presented with no interstimulus interval (ISI), the two middle spots appeared stationary (probably the short-range AM process signaled this), while the end element jumped to and fro (element motion). With an ISI, or with dichoptic presentation, the three spots jumped back and forth as a trio in group motion.

Depending on the timing, one perceives either *element motion* ($A \rightarrow D'$) or *group motion* ($A \rightarrow B'$, $B \rightarrow C'$, $C \rightarrow D'$) (Pantle & Picciano, 1976). See Figure 16.7.

The pairing actually established is the one that maximizes overall similarity between frames according to a cost function, related to the total path length, which Ullman (1979, chap. 3) calls *minimum mapping.* The Gestalt theorists wrongly thought that global operations were necessary to bind elements (dots) into groups, but Ullman shows that purely local competitive interactions between affinities can establish the *correspondence strengths,* which, in turn, determine what motion is seen.

For an antidote to Ullman's book read the highly critical review written by Runeson and Lind (1981) from a Gibsonian standpoint.

Burt and Sperling (1981) also measured correspondence strengths by setting up competitive interactions between rival possible motions. They found linear trade-offs between distance and time in AM paths. They briefly flashed a horizontal row of dots and then flashed another row of dots, displaced both vertically and horizontally, *t* msec later (Figure 16.8). This sequence continued. When the interflash interval *t* was long, subjects saw AM only along path *P*1 to the succeeding dot that was nearest in time. For shorter *t*, they saw AM along path *P*2 that was closer in space though further away in time, and for even shorter *t*, along path *P*3 that was even closer in space but even further away in time. Although each motion path presented on its own gave clear AM, they competed and suppressed each other when presented together and only one path was seen. Stable transition times were found at which the percept changed from *P*3 to *P*2 and from *P*2 to *P*1. At transition times between two paths, where both path percepts were equiprobable, the time *t* and distance *d* between successive points along the paths was described by a log linear relationship, that is, $t = A - \log (d1/d2)$. Path selections were unaffected by the viewing distance, and this so-called scale invariance showed that the motion selection mechanism was primarily sensitive to relative, not absolute, distances between dots along competing paths; from this the authors concluded that the contributions of time and distance to stimulus motion strength were independent. Their model deduced the precise trade-off function between *d* and *t* and suggested a neural array of Reichardt units that were scaled replicas of each other, all having the same geometry and time delays and differing only in size and orientation.

Ambiguities inherent in the information supplied by a moving image are discussed by Ullman and Hildreth (1983) and by Hildreth (1983). These include the *aperture problem,* known to older psychologists as the "barber pole illusion," and related ambiguities, such as a translating sine wave that could be either translating or undergoing plastic deformation or could be the shadow of a rotating corkscrew. Algorithms to disambiguate these rely on local constraints and assumptions about the physical world, for example, the assumption that most physical surfaces are smooth.

5.3. Computer Simulations of Motion Perception

Computer simulations have been developed for various subareas of motion perception. The IEEE published a special issue of their *Transactions of Pattern Analysis and Machine Intelligence* in November 1980. In this issue, Jacobus, Chien, and Selander (1980) discuss the matching of successive pictures by means of

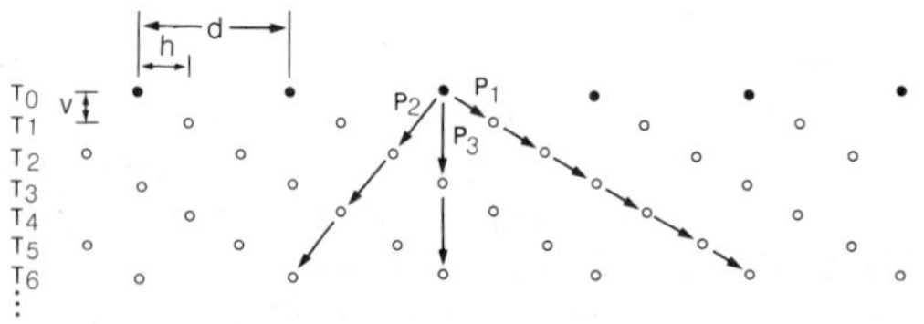

Figure 16.8. Ambiguous motion stimulus. A multiple-motion path stimulus is generated by repeatedly flashing a horizontally oriented row of dots on a CRT screen. Dot spacing within row is *d.* With each new presentation the row is displaced downward a distance *v* and to the right a distance *h.* Solid circles show position of dots at time $T'0$; open circles show dot positions at subsequent time $T'1$, where $T'1 = T'0 + t$. Arrows show some possible paths for AM of a dot presented at time $T'0$. Path $P'1$ represents AM to the position of the nearest dot at time $T'1$. Generally, all dots of the row appear to move together along the same path. Path dominance is determined by the particular values of *t, d, v,* and *h.* (From P. Burt & G. Sperling, Time, distance, and feature trade-offs in visual apparent motion, *Psychological Review, 88.* Copyright 1981 by the American Psychological Association. Reprinted with permission.)

a new primitive, the half-chunk, and derive depth information from a moving image where the camera is moving through a real-world scene, based on error measures derived by interimage comparisons of point values.

Tsuji, Osada, and Yachida (1980) present a dynamic scene analyzer that separates moving objects from the background and analyzes their motion patterns in dynamic line images, such as cartoon films. Since the objects move and rotate in a three-dimensional world and since occlusion often occurs, the shapes, sizes, and structures of the images of moving objects change from frame to frame. The task of the analyzer is to segment the scene into meaningful constituents and to obtain a structural description of each object containing properties, spatial relations, and motion patterns. The correspondence problem is attacked by a flexible template method in which the analyzer tracks moving regions and their segments in the dynamic images and merges segments of each moving object into groups having similar motion patterns, in order to obtain a meaningful partition corresponding to its components such as hands or legs. Yachida, Ikeda, and Tsuji (1980) implemented a system which analyzed the low-quality, noisy pictures produced by cineangiograms, which are X-ray motion pictures of a beating heart in which X-ray opaque dye is injected through a catheter. Tsotsos, Mylopoulos, Covvey, and Zucker (1980) also devised algorithms for the computer abstraction of motion concepts from sequences of images and applied them to an automated cineangiogram analyzer.

Roach and Aggarwal (1980) set out to determine the three-dimensional motion of an object from a sequence of two-dimensional images. Ullman (1979) has called this the *structure from motion* problem. Roach and Aggarwal found that a minimum of two views of six points or three views of four points were necessary to solve the problem. Rashid (1980) worked on the related problem of segmenting the points of a moving light display of a wire-frame person into body parts. This was inspired by Johansson's discovery (1977) that 12 moving lights, attached to the joints of a person walking in the dark, can evoke the immediate perception of the walker.

Further interesting papers are contained in the Proceedings of the SIGGRAPH Conference on Motion: Representation and Perception, held in Toronto in 1983. These are edited by J. Tsotsos.

All this work by computer engineers is of great interest to students of perception, and the lists of references in these articles show that their authors are familiar with the psychophysical literature.

5.4. Correlation Models and Gradient Models of Directional Selectivity

Longuett-Higgins and Prazdny (1980) presented a mathematical account of the information available in a moving retinal image. This tells modelers what needs to be modeled.

There are two kinds of model for directional selectivity: correlation models devised by physiologists (Figure 16.9(a) and (b)) and gradient models devised by computer people who have read what the physiologists write (Figure 16.9(c)).

Barlow and Levick (1965) measured the directional response to moving stimuli in the ganglion cells of the rabbit retina. They suggested that receptors *A* and *B* sample adjacent retinal regions, and *B*'s output is delayed and subtracted from *A*'s output. If a stimulus spot moves in the null direction from *B* to *A*, then *B* inhibits *A* and the cell does not respond. But if a spot moves in the preferred direction from *A* to *B*, then *B*'s output arrives too late to inhibit *A*, and the cell responds. Barlow and Levick also considered a rival model that summed, instead of subtracted, the outputs of *A* and *B*, but they concluded that their evidence supported the subtractive model. Reichardt (1961) proposed a model of motion detection in the insect eye, in which B's delayed output B' is multiplied by A's output (Figure 16.9(b)). Multiplication measures the correlation between the patterns seen by *A* and *B*, and the product AB' reaches a maximum when the patterns seen by *A* and *B* are identical but separated in time by a delay equal to *B*'s internal delay.

These models all compare the luminance distributions seen at position *A* and time *t*1 to that seen at position *B* and time *t*2. In this respect they resemble the short-range process, which responds to luminance points, but not the long-range process, which responds to subtle correlations of cyclopean edges and the like, to which these models would be blind. In fact, Lappin and Bell (1972, 1976) have invoked correlation models to explain their psychophysical results for short-range motion. These models are easy enough to simulate on a computer, or with simple special-purpose hardware. I have described an electronic version of Reichardt's model, made from two photocells, a shift-register delay, and an electronic multiplier (Anstis, 1980). The device responded readily to moving patterns. Moreover, changing the internal time delay altered the preferred velocity to which the device gave the maximum response.

Marr and Ullman (1981) proposed a different kind of model (Figure 16.9(c)), in which the second spatial derivative (SSD) of a stimulus edge is taken by convolving it with a Mexican hat operator. The position of the edge is represented by the zero crossing, namely, the point at which the SSD changes in sign from positive to negative. The temporal derivative of this SSD is always positive at the zero-crossing point when the SSD is moving to the right and negative when it is moving to the left and thus signals the direction of motion. In other words, their model has two components: a spatial component that detects the polarity of the edge and a temporal component that detects net dimming or brightening at the edge. Thus a light–dark edge produces net brightening when it moves to the right because the light region moves to cover a previously dark region. Moulden (Note 7) adapted the temporal component by exposing his subjects to a spatially uniform, gradually brightening field (Anstis, 1967) and found that it raised their threshold for detecting a light–dark edge that moved to the right. Adaptation to a dimming field raised the detection threshold for the same edge moving to the left. These cross-adaptation results support Marr and Ullman's model.

This scheme has several advantages over Barlow and Levick's scheme: it requires only local measurements, no time delay is involved beyond that required to compute the temporal derivative, and it is extremely reliable and will respond to a very wide range of speeds.

Marr and Ullman suggested that the lateral geniculate *X* cells could carry the positive and negative parts of the SSD via on- and off-center cells, respectively. The zero crossing could be found simply by connecting the on- and off-center *X* cells via a logical AND gate, and the temporal derivative is computed by a *Y* (transient) cell. Psychophysical tests of this model will doubtless begin to appear in the literature soon.

Adelson and Bergen (1985) have proposed a spatiotemporal energy model of motion perception. The idea is this: a bar that stimulates a cortical unit could be plotted as a line on an *xy* graph and, analogously, a moving spot that stimulated a motion

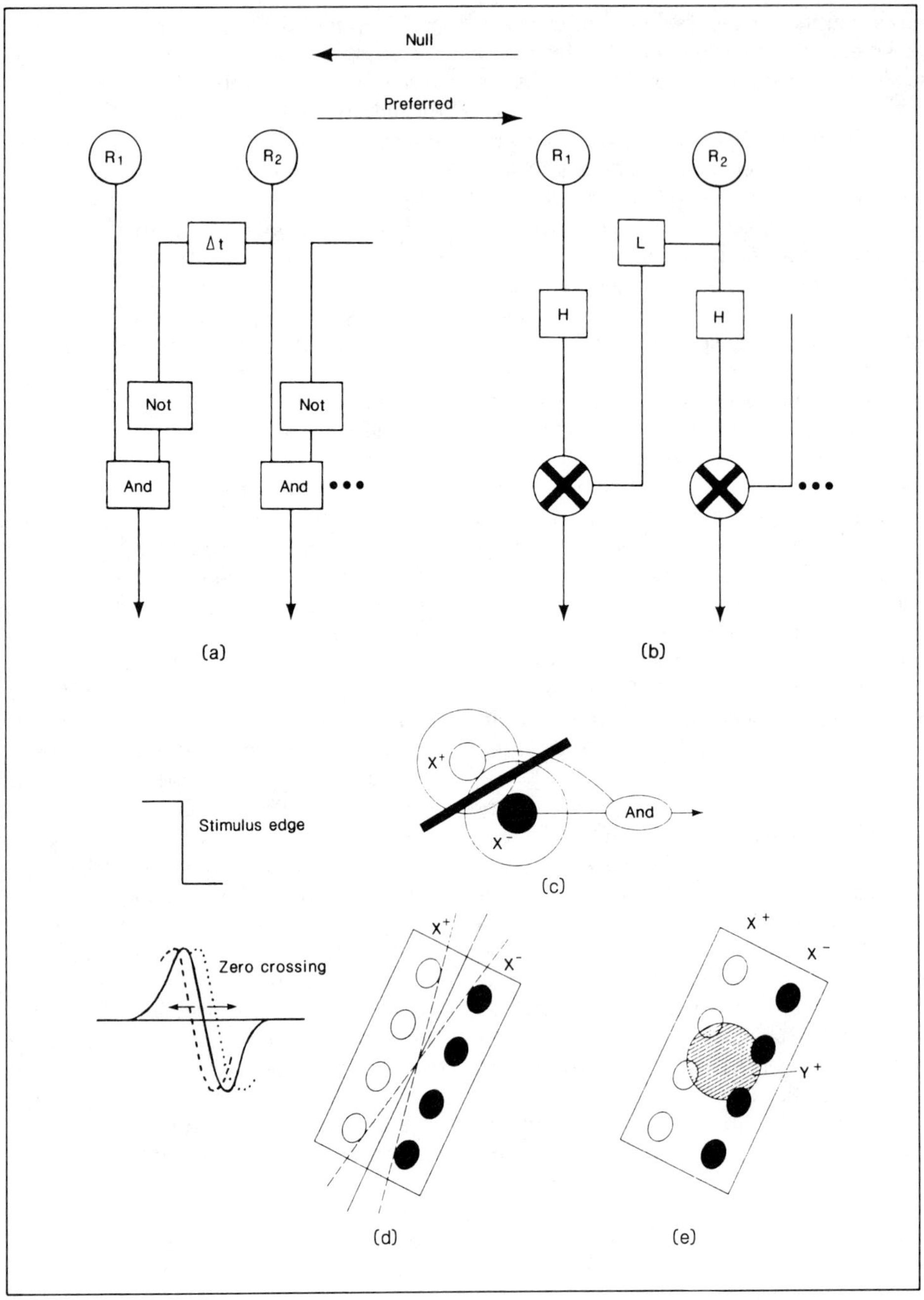

Figure 16.9. (a) Barlow and Levick's (1965) model for directional selectivity connects two detectors to an AND-NOT gate, one via a delay. This detector responds to motion to the right (its preferred direction), not to the left (its null direction). (From H. B. Barlow & W. R. Levick, The mechanism of direction selective units in rabbit's retina, *Journal of Physiology*, 1965, *178*. Reprinted with permission.) (b) Reichardt's (1961) model, here simplified, is similar except that the delay is replaced by a temporal low-pass filter *L* and the subtractive inhibition is replaced by correlation or multiplication. The high-pass filter is *H*. (From W. Reichardt, Autocorrelation, a principle for the evaluation of sensory information by the central nervous system, in W. Rosenblith (Ed.), *Sensory Communication*, MIT Press, 1961. Reprinted with permission.) (c) Marr and Ullman's (1981) gradient model detects motion of a zero-crossing. On-center ($X+$) and off-center ($X-$) subunits, connected by a logical AND gate, signal the presence of a zero-crossing of a particular sign running between the two subunits. (From D. Marr, *Vision*. Copyright 1982 by W. H. Freeman and Company. Reprinted with permission.) (d) A row of these units connected through a logical AND would detect the presence of a zero-crossing within the orientation bounds given by the dotted lines. (e) A *Y* unit is added to the detector in (d). If the unit is $Y+$, it would respond when the zero-crossing segment is moving from the $X+$ to the $X-$. If the unit is $Y-$, it would respond to motion in the opposite direction.

detector could be plotted as the same line, simply by changing the ordinate from y to t (time). On this xt plot the spot velocity determines the slope of the line, and AM of a jumping spot would give a staircase (Figure 16.5(a)). The receptive field of the motion detector would have excitatory and inhibitory regions on the xt plot and would comprise linear filters oriented in space and time and tuned for spatial frequency. Such a motion detector is phase sensitive, responding differently to a moving black spot than to a moving white spot. To get rid of phase sensitivity, the output of quadrature pairs of such filters would be taken and then squared and summed to give a measure of motion energy. These responses are then fed into an opponent stage. Burr and Ross (in press) have proposed a similar model.

An elaboration of Reichardt's (1961) model has been proposed by van Santen and Sperling (1984), in which a local correlation or multiplication is performed across space and time, with filters tuned for spatial frequency serving as the inputs to the correlator stages. Their model, like those of Adelson and Bergen and of Burr and Ross, can make correct predictions about a wide range of motion displays, and its turns out that under appropriate conditions the three models, although developed from different philosophies, are formally identical. The appearance of such sophisticated models may mean that the study of motion perception is at last emerging from obscurity into maturity.

REFERENCE NOTES

1. Reason, J. Personal communication, 1983.
2. Harris, C. S., Schwartz, B. J., Patashnik, O., & Lappin, J. S. *Illusory pausing of moving dots.* Paper presented at the nineteenth annual meeting of the Psychonomic Society, San Antonio, Texas, November 1978.
3. Pantle, A. Personal communication, 1983.
4. Kaufman, L. Personal communication, 1985.
5. Cavanagh, P. C. Personal communication, 1985.
6. Cavanagh, P. C., & Favreau, O. E. Unpublished observations, 1984.
7. Moulden, B. P. Paper presented at the European Congress of Visual Perception, Cambridge, England 1984.

REFERENCES

Adelson, E. H. *Investigative Ophthalmology and Visual Science*, 1982, *34* (Suppl.).

Adelson, E. H., & Bergen, J. K. Spatio-temporal energy models for the perception of motion. *Journal of the Optical Society of America*, 1985, *2*, 284–299.

Ansbacher, H. L. Distortion in the perception of real movement. *Journal of Experimental Psychology*, 1944, *34*, 1–23.

Anstis, S. M. *Aftereffects of seen movement and brightness.* Doctoral dissertation, University of Cambridge, 1961.

Anstis, S. M. Visual adaptation to gradual change of intensity. *Science*, 1967, *155*, 710–712.

Anstis, S. M. Phi movement as a subtraction process. *Vision Research*, 1970, *10*, 1411–1430.

Anstis, S. M. What does visual perception tell us about visual coding? In M. Gazzaniga & C. Blakemore (Eds.), *Handbook of psychobiology.* New York: Academic Press, 1975.

Anstis, S. M. Apparent movement. In R. H. Held & H. W. Leibowitz (Eds.), *Handbook of sensory physiology* (Vol. 8): *Perception.* New York: Springer-Verlag, 1978.

Anstis, S. M. The perception of apparent movement. *Philosophical Transactions of the Royal Society of London.* (Series B), 1980, *290*, 153–168. (Reprinted in *The psychology of vision.* London: The Royal Society, 1980.)

Anstis, S. M. Visual coding of position and motion. In D. L. Braddick & A. Sleigh (Eds.), *Biological and physical processing of images.* New York: Springer-Verlag, 1983.

Anstis, S. M., & Atkinson, J. Distortions in moving figures viewed through a stationary slit. *American Journal of Psychology*, 1967, *80*, 572–585.

Anstis, S. M., & Cavanagh, P. A minimum-motion technique for judging equiluminance. In J. Mollon & E. Sharpe (Eds.), *Colour vision: Physiology and psychophysics.* London: Academic Press, 1983.

Anstis, S. M., & Duncan, K. Separate motion aftereffects from each eye and from both eyes. *Vision Research*, 1983, *13*, 161–169.

Anstis, S. M., Giaschi, D., & Cogan, A. Adaptation to apparent motion. *Vision Research*, 1985, *25*, 1051–1062.

Anstis, S. M., & Mather, G. Effects of luminance and contrast in apparent motion. *Perception*, in press.

Anstis, S. M., & Moulden, B. P. Aftereffect of seen movement: Evidence for peripheral and central components. *Quarterly Journal of Experimental Psychology*, 1970, *22*, 222–229.

Anstis, S. M., & Reinhardt-Rutland, A. H. Interactions between motion aftereffects and induced movement. *Vision Research*, 1976, *16*, 1391–1394.

Anstis, S. M., & Rogers, B. J. Illusory reversal of depth and movement during changes of contrast. *Vision Research*, 1975, *15*, 957–961.

Attneave, F., & Block, G. Apparent movement in tridimensional space. *Perception and Psychophysics*, 1974, *13*, 301–307.

Baker, C. L., & Braddick, O. L. The basis of area and dot number effects in random dot motion perception. *Vision Research*, 1982, *22*, 1253–1260.

Baker, C. L., & Braddick, O. L. Does segregation of differently moving areas depend on relative or absolute displacement? *Vision Research*, 1982, *22*, 851–856. (b)

Banks, W. P., & Kane, D. A. Discontinuity of seen motion reduces the motion aftereffect. *Perception and Psychophysics*, 1972, *12*, 69–72.

Barbur, J. L. Subthreshold addition of real and apparent motion. *Vision Research*, 1981, *21*, 557–564.

Barlow, H. B. Reconstructing the retinal image in space and time. *Nature*, 1979, *279*, 189–190.

Barlow, H. B., & Brindley, G. S. Inter-ocular transfer of movement after-effects during pressure-blinding of the stimulated eye. *Nature*, 1963, *200*, 1347.

Barlow, H. B., & Hill, R. M. Evidence for a physiological explanation of the waterfall illusion and figural aftereffects. *Nature*, 1963, *200*, 1434–1435.

Barlow, H. B., Hill, R. M., & Levick, W. R. Retinal ganglion cells responding selectively to direction and speed of image motion in the rabbit. *Journal of Physiology*, 1964, *173*, 377–407.

Barlow, H. B., & Levick, W. R. The mechanism of direction selective units in rabbit's retina. *Journal of Physiology*, 1965, *178*, 477–504.

Bell, H. H., & Lappin, J. S. The detection of rotation in random-dot patterns. *Perception and Psychophysics*, 1979, *26*, 415–417.

Bender, M. B., & Teuber, H.-L. Disturbances in visual perception following cerebral lesions. *Journal of Psychology*, 1949, *28*, 223–233.

Berkley, M. Neural substrates of the visual perception of motion. In A. H. Wertheim, W. A. Wagenaar, & H. W. Leibowitz (Eds.), *Tutorials on motion perception.* New York and London: Plenum Press, 1982.

Berthoz, A., & Droulet, J. Linear self motion perception. In A. H. Wertheim, W. A. Wagenaar, & H. W. Leibowitz (Eds.), *Tutorials on motion perception.* New York and London: Plenum Press, 1982.

Bhatia, B., & Verghese, C. A. Constancy of the visibility of a moving object viewed from different distances with the eyes fixed. *Journal of the Optical Society of America*, 1963, *53*, 283–286.

Biederman-Thorson, M., Thorson, J., & Lange, G. D. Apparent motion due to closely spaced sequentially flashed dots in the human peripheral field of vision. *Vision Research*, 1971, *11*, 889–903.

Bishop, P. O., Henry, G. H., & Smith, C. S. Binocular interaction fields of single units in the cat striate cortex. *Journal of Physiology*, 1971, *216*, 39–68.

Blakemore, C. B., Carpenter, R. H. S., & Georgeson, M. A. Lateral inhibition between orientation detectors in the human visual system. *Nature*, 1970, *228*, 37–39.

Blakemore, C. B., Muncey, J. P., & Ridley, R. M. Stimulus specificity in the human visual system. *Vision Research*, 1973, *13*, 1915–1931.

Boff, K., & Matin, L. The velocity response of vernier offset with rotary motion. *Investigative Ophthalmology*, 1977.

Bonnet, C., Le Gall, M., & Lorenceau, J. Visual motion aftereffects: Adaptation and conditioned processes. In L. Spillmann & B. R. Wooten (Eds.), *Sensory experience, adaptation, and perception: Festschrift for Ivo Kohler*. Hillsdale, N.J.: Lawrence Erlbaum Associates, 1982.

Braddick, O. The masking of apparent motion in random-dot patterns. *Vision Research*, 1973, *13*, 355–369.

Braddick, O. A short-range process in apparent motion. *Vision Research*, 1974, *14*, 519–527.

Braddick, O., & Adlard, A. J. Apparent motion and the motion detector. In J. Armington, J. Krauskopf, & B. R. Wooten (Eds.), *Visual psychophysics: Its physiological basis*. New York: Academic Press, 1978.

Braunstein, M. L. *Depth perception through motion*. New York: Academic Press, 1976.

Bridgeman, B. Visual receptive fields sensitive to absolute and relative motion during tracking. *Science*, 1972, *178*, 1106–1108.

Burr, D. C. Acuity for apparent vernier offset. *Vision Research*, 1979, *19*, 835–838.

Burr, D. C., & Ross, J. How does binocular delay give information about depth? *Vision Research*, 1979, *19*, 523–532.

Burr, D. C., & Ross, J. Seeing objects in motion. *Nature*, in press.

Burt, P., & Sperling, G. Time, distance, and feature trade-offs in visual apparent motion. *Psychological Review*, 1981, *88*, 171–195.

Caelli, T. On the spatio-temporal determinants of some motion effects. *Acta Psychologica*, 1981, *48*, 175–185.

Campbell, F. W. The transmission of spatial information through the human visual system. In F. O. Schmitt (Ed.), *The neurosciences: Third study series*. Cambridge, Mass.: MIT Press, 1976.

Campbell, F. W., & Maffei, L. Stopped visual motion. *Nature*, 1979, *278*, 192–193.

Campbell, F. W., & Maffei, L. The influence of spatial frequency and contrast on the perception of moving patterns. *Vision Research*, 1981, *21*, 713–721.

Carlson, V. R. Adaptation in the perception of visual velocity. *Journal of Experimental Psychology*, 1962, *64*, 192–197.

Cavanagh, P., Anstis, S. M., & Mather, G. Screening for color blindness using optokinetic nystagmus. *Investigative Ophthalmology*, 1984, *25*, 463–466.

Chang, J. J., & Julesz, B. Displacement limits, directional anisotropy and direction versus form discrimination in random-dot cinematograms. *Vision Research*, 1983, *23*, 639–646. (a)

Chang, J. J., & Julesz, B. Displacement limits for spatial frequency random-dot cinematograms in apparent motion. *Vision Research*, 1983, *23*, 1379–1386. (b)

Clatworthy, J. L., & Frisby, J. P. Real and apparent visual movement: Evidence for a unitary mechanism. *Perception*, 1973, *2*, 161–164.

Clymer, A. B. *The effect of seen motion on the apparent speed of subsequent test velocities: Speed tuning of movement aftereffects*. Doctoral dissertation, Columbia University, N.Y., 1973.

Collett, T. Visual neurons in the anterior optic tract of the privet hawk moth. *Journal of Comparative Physiology*, 1972, *78*, 396–433.

Coltheart, M. Visual feature-analysers and after-effects of tilt and curvature. *Psychological Review*, 1971, *78*, 114–121.

Cowey, A., & Rolls, E. T. Human cortical magnification factor and its relation to visual acuity. *Experimental Brain Research*, 1974, *21*, 447–454.

Craik, K. Origin of visual afterimages. *Nature*, 1940, *145*, 512.

Day, R. H., & Strelow, E. S. Reduction or disappearance of visual aftereffect of movement in the absence of a patterned surround. *Nature*, 1974, *230*, 5–56.

Dichgans, J., & Brandt, T. Visual vestibular interactions: Effects on self-motion perception and in postural control. In R. H. Held, H. W. Leibowitz, & H.-L. Teuber (Eds.), *Handbook of sensory physiology* (Vol. 8): *Perception*. Berlin: Springer-Verlag, 1978.

Duncker, K. Ueber induzierte Bewegung (ein Beitrag zur Theorie optisch (Wahrgenommenor). *Psychologische Forschung*, 1929, *12*, 180–259. (Excerpts translated and reprinted in W. D. Ellis (Ed.), *A source book of Gestalt psychology*. London: Routledge & Kegan Paul, 1938.)

Fahle, M., & Poggio, T. Visual hyperacuity: Spatiotemporal interpolation in human vision. *Proceedings of the Royal Society of London* (Series B), 1980, *213*, 451–477.

Farrell, J. E., & Shepard, R. N. Shape, orientation, and apparent rotational motion. *Journal of Experimental Psychology*, 1981, 7, 477–486.

Favreau, O. E. Motion aftereffects: Evidence for parallel processing in motion perception. *Vision Research*, 1976, *16*, 181–186.

Fineman, M. *The inquisitive eye*. Oxford University Press, 1981.

Foster, D. H., & Gravano, S. Overshoot of curvature in visual apparent motion. *Perception and Psychophysics*, 1982, *31*, 411–420.

Foster, D. H., Thorson, J., McIlwain, J. T., & Biederman-Thorson, M. The fine-grain motion illusion: A perceptual probe of neuronal connectivity in the human visual system. *Vision Research*, 1981, *21*, 1123–1128.

Fraser, A., & Wilcox, K. J. Perception of illusory movement. *Nature*, 1979, *281*, 565–566.

Frisby, J. Aftereffects: A further investigation. *Perception*, 1973, *2*, 113–115.

Frost, B. J., & Nakayama, K. Single visual neurons code opposing motion independent of direction. *Science*, 1983, *220*, 744–745.

Frost, B. J., & Wong, S. C. P. The effect of relative motion on directionally specific pigeon tectal units. *Society of Neurosciences* (Abstract), 1977, *3*, 560.

Genter, C. R., & Weisstein, N. Flickering phantoms: A motion illusion without motion. *Vision Research*, 1981, *21*, 963–966.

Gibson, J. J. Adaptation with negative after-effect. *Psychological Review*, 1937, *44*, 22–244.

Goldberg, D. M., & Pomerantz, J. R. Models of illusory pausing and sticking. *Journal of Experimental Psychology*, 1982, *8*, 547–561.

Goldstein, A. G. Judgments of visual velocity as a function of length of observation time. *Journal of Experimental Psychology*, 1957, *54*, 457–461.

Goldstein, K., & Gelb, A. Psychologische Analysen hirnpathologischer Falle auf Grund von Untersuchungen Hirnverletzter. I. Abhandlung. Zur Psychologie des optischen Wahrnehmungs- und Erkennungsvorganges. *Zeitschrift fur die gesamte Neurologie und Psychiatrie*, 1918, *41*, 1–142.

Gorea, A. Directional and non-directional coding of a spatio-temporal modulated stimulus. *Vision Research*, 1979, *19*, 545–551.

Graham, C. H. Perception of movement. In Graham, C. H. (Ed.), *Vision and visual perception*. New York: Wiley, 1965.

Green, M. Psychophysical relationships among mechanisms sensitive to pattern flicker and motion. *Vision Research*, 1981, *21*, 971–984.

Green, M. Inhibition and facilitation of apparent motion by real motion. *Vision Research*, 1983, *23*, 861–865.

Green, M., Chilcoat, M., & Stromeyer, C. F. Rapid motion aftereffect seen within uniform flickering fields. *Nature*, 1983, *304*, 61–62.

Gregory, R. L. *Eye and brain: The psychology of seeing*. New York: McGraw-Hill, 1966.

Gregory, R. L. *Mind in science: A history of explanations in psychology and physics*. Cambridge University Press, 1981.

Gregory, R. L., & Heard, P. Dissociation between depth, motion and stereopsis: A phenomenal phenomenon. *Quarterly Journal of Experimental Psychology*, 1983, *35A*, 217–237.

Grusser, O-J., & Grusser-Cornehls, U. Neuronal mechanisms of visual movement perception and some psychophysical and behavioral correlations. In R. Jung (Ed.), *Handbook of sensory physiology* (Vol. 7/3): *Central processing of visual information*. New York: Springer-Verlag, 1973.

Harris, C. S., Schwartz, B. J., Patashnik, O., & Lappin, J. S. *Illusory pausing of moving dots*. Paper presented at the nineteenth annual

meeting of the Psychonomic Society, San Antonio, November 1978.
Hildreth, E. Computing the velocity field along contours. In J. Tsotsos (Ed.), *Motion: Representation and perception. Proceedings of the SIGGRAPH/SIGART conference*, Toronto. New York: Association for Computing Machinery, 1983.
Hildreth, E. C. *The measurement of visual motion*. Cambridge, Mass.: MIT Press, 1984.
Holland, H. C. The spiral aftereffect. *International monographs in experimental psychology*. London: Pergamon Press, 1965.
Hubel, D. H., & Wiesel, T. N. Receptive fields, binocular interaction, and functional architecture in the cat's visual cortex. *Journal of Physiology*, 1962, *10*, 106–154.
Hubel, D. H., & Wiesel, T. N. Receptive fields and functional architecture in two nonstriate areas (18 and 19) of the cat. *Journal of Neurophysiology*, 1965, *28*, 229–289.
Hunzelman, J., & Spillmann, L. Adaptation to movement in the peripheral retina. *Investigative Ophthalmology* (Suppl.), 1983, *24*, 92.
Jacobus, C. J., Chien, R. T., & Selander, J. M. Motion detection and analysis of matching graphs of intermediate-level primitives. *IEEE Transactions: Pattern Analysis and Machine Intelligence*, 1980, PAMI-2, 495–510.
Johansson, G. *Configurations in event perception*. Uppsala: Almquist & Wiksell, 1950.
Johansson, G. Studies on visual perception of locomotion. *Perception*, 1977, *6*, 365–376.
Johnson, C. A., & Leibowitz, H. W. Velocity-time reciprocity in the perception of motion: foveal and peripheral determinants. *Vision Research*, 1976, *16*, 177–180.
Johnston, A., & Wright, M. J. Visual motion and cortical velocity. *Nature*, 1983, *304*, 436–437.
Julesz, B. *Foundations of cyclopean perception*. Chicago: University of Chicago Press, 1971.
Kaufman, L. *Sight and mind*. New York: Oxford University Press, 1974.
Kaufman, L., Cyrulnik, I., Kaplowitz, J., Melnick, G., & Stoff, D. The complementarity of apparent and real motion. *Psychologische Forschung*, 1971, *34*, 343–348.
Keck, M. J., Palella, T. D., & Pantle, A. J. Motion aftereffect as a function of the contrast of sinusoidal gratings. *Vision Research*, 1976, *16*, 187–191.
Kelly, D. H. Motion and vision. II. Stabilized spatio-temporal threshold surface. *Journal of the Optical Society of America*, 1979, *69*, 1340–1349.
King-Smith, P. E., & Kulikowski, J. J. Pattern and flicker detection analyzed by subthreshold summation. *Journal of Physiology, 1975, 249*, 519–548.
Kolers, P. A. Some differences between real and apparent visual movement. *Vision Research*, 1963, *3*, 191–206.
Kolers, P. A. The illusion of movement. *Scientific American*, 1964, *211*, 98–106.
Kolers, P. A. *Aspects of motion perception*. New York: Pergamon Press, 1972.
Korte, A. Kinematoskopische Untersuchungen. *Zeitschrift für Psychologie*, 1915, *72*, 193–296.
Lappin, J. S., & Bell, H. H. Perceptual differentiation of sequential visual patterns. *Perception and Psychophysics*, 1972, *12*, 129–134.
Lappin, J. S., & Bell, H. H. The detection of coherence in moving random-dot patterns. *Vision Research*, 1976, *16*, 161–168.
Leguire, L. *Investigative Ophthalmology*, (Suppl.), 1982.
Lehmkuhle, S. W., & Fox, R. Effect of binocular rivalry suppression on the motion aftereffect. *Vision Research*, 1975, *15*, 855–859.
Leibowitz, H. W. The relation between the rate threshold for the perception of movement and luminance for various durations of exposure. *Journal of Experimental Psychology*, 1955, *49*, 209–214.
Leibowitz, H. W., Osaka, R., & Oyama, T. (Eds.) *Perception of space and motion: An international symposium*. Kyoto University, Japan, Psychologia Society, 1978.
Leibowitz, H. W., Post, R. B., Brandt, T., & Dichgans, J. Implications of recent developments in dynamic spatial orientation and visual resolution for vehicle guidance. In M. Wertheim, W. A. Wagenaar, & H. W. Leibowitz (Eds.), *Tutorials on motion perception*. New York and London: Plenum Press, 1982.
Levinson, E., & Sekuler, R. Inhibition and disinhibition of direction-specific mechanisms in human vision. *Nature*, 1975, *254*, 692–693. (a)
Levinson, E., & Sekuler, R. The independence of channels in human vision selective for direction of movement. *Journal of Physiology*, 1975, *250*, 247–266. (b)
Levinson, E., & Sekuler, R. Adaptation alters the perceived direction of motion. *Vision Research*, 1976, *16*, 779–781.
Levinson, E., & Sekuler, R. A two-dimensional analysis of direction-specific adaptation. *Vision Research*, 1980, *20*, 103–107.
Lichtenstein, M. Spatio-temporal factors in cessation of smooth apparent motion. *Journal of the Optical Society of America*, 1963, *53*, 302–306.
Longuett-Higgins, H. C., & Prazdny, K. The interpretation of a moving retinal image. *Proceedings of the Royal Society of London* (Series B), 1980, *208*, 385–397.
Longuett-Higgins, H. C., & Sutherland, N. (Eds.). *The psychology of vision*. London: The Royal Society, 1980.
Loomis, J. M., & Nakayama, K. A velocity analogue of brightness contrast. *Perception*, 1973, *2*, 425–428.
Mace, W. M. *An investigation of spatial and kinetic information for separation in depth using computer generated dot patterns*. Doctoral dissertation, University of Minnesota, 1971. (Dissertation Abstracts International, 1972, 32, 6687B. University Microfilms No. 72-14, 333.)
Mackay, D. M. Illusory reversal of extrafoveally perceived displacement. *Nature*, 1980, *284*, 257.
Marr, D. *Vision*. Cambridge, Mass.: MIT Press, 1982.
Marr, D., & Ullman, S. Directional selectivity and its use in early visual processing. *Proceedings of the Royal Society of London* (Series B), 1981, *211*, 151–180.
Marr, D., & Poggio, T. A computational theory of human stereo vision. *Proceedings of the Royal Society of London* (Series B), 1979, *204*, 301–328.
Marshak, W., & Sekuler, R. Mutual repulsion between moving targets. *Science*, 1979, *205*, 1399–1401.
Mather, G. The movement aftereffect and a distribution-shift model for coding the direction of visual movement. *Perception*, 1980, *9*, 379–392.
Mather, G., & Anstis, S. M. Motion and flicker look faster in peripheral vision. *Vision Research*, in press.
Mather, G., & Moulden, B. P. A simultaneous shift in apparent direction: Further evidence of a "distribution-shift" model of direction coding. *Quarterly Journal of Experimental Psychology*, 1980, *32*, 325–333.
Matin, L., Boff, K., & Pola, J. Vernier offset produced by rotary target motion. *Perception and Psychophysics*, 1976, *20*, 138–142.
Mayhew, J. E. W. Aftereffects of motion contingent on direction of gaze. *Vision Research*, 1973, *13*, 877–880.
McCollough, C. Color adaptation of edge-detectors in the human visual system. *Science*, 1965, *149*, 1115–1116.
McKee, S., & Nakayama, K. The detection of motion in the peripheral visual field. *Vision Research*, 1984, *24*, 25–32.
Michael, C. R. Receptive fields of single optic nerve fibers in a mammal with an all-cone retina: II. Directionally selective units. *Journal of Neurophysiology*, 1968, *31*, 268–281.
Mitchell, D. E., Reardon, J., & Muir, D. Inter-ocular transfer of motion aftereffect in normal and stereoblind observers. *Experimental Brain Research*, 1975, *22*, 163–173.
Mitchell, D. E., & Ware, C. Inter-ocular transfer of a visual aftereffect in normal and stereoblind humans. *Journal of Physiology*, 1974, 263, 707–721.
Morgan, M. J. Spatio-temporal filtering and the interpolation effect in apparent motion. *Perception*, 1980, *9*, 161–174. (a)
Morgan, M. J. Analogue models of motion perception. *Philosophical Transactions of the Royal Society of London* (Series B), 1980, *290*, 117–135. (b)

Mori, T. Reduction of the Poggendorff effect by the motion of oblique lines. *Perception and Psychophysics*, 1981, *29*, 15–20.

Mori, T. *Visual motion perception.* (Circulars of the Electrotechnical Laboratory #207.) Electrotechnical Laboratory, 1-1-4 Umezono, Sakura, Niihara, Japan, 1982.

Moulden, B. P. After-effects and the integration of patterns of neural activity within a channel. *Philosophical Transactions of the Royal Society of London* (Series B), 1980, *290*, 39–56.

Moulden, B. P., & Mather, G. In defence of a ratio model for movement detection at threshold. *Quarterly Journal of Experimental Psychology*, 1978, *30*, 505–520.

Movshon, J., Chambers, B., & Blakemore, C. Interocular transfer in normal humans, and those who lack stereopsis. *Perception*, 1972, *1*, 483–490.

Nakayama, K., & Silverman, G. Temporal and spatial characteristics of the upper displacement limit for motion in random dots. *Vision Research*, 1984, *24*, 293–300.

Nakayama, K., & Tyler, C. W. Relative motion induced between stationary lines. *Vision Research*, 1978, *18*, 1663–1668.

Nakayama, K., & Tyler, C. W. Psychophysical isolation of movement sensitivity by removal of familia position cues. *Vision Research*, 1981, *21*, 427–433.

Neff, W. S. A critical investigation of the visual apprehension of movement. *American Journal of Psychology*, 1936, *48*, 1–42.

Neill, R. A. Spatio-temporal averaging and the dynamic visual noise stereophenomenon. *Vision Research*, 1981, *21*, 673–682.

Neuhaus, W. Experimentelle Untersuchung der Scheinbewegung. *Archiv für Gesanite Psychologie*, 1930, *75*, 315–458.

Orban, G. A. (Ed.). Symposium on movement perception: 5th European conference on visual perception. *Vision Research*, 1984, *24*.

O'Shea, R. P., & Crassini, B. Interocular transfer of the motion aftereffect is not reduced by binocular rivalry. *Vision Research*, 1981, *21*, 801–804.

Over, R., & Lovegrove, W. Color-selectivity in simultaneous motion contrast. *Perception and Psychophysics*, 1973, *14*, 445–448.

Pantle, A. J. Stroboscopic movement based upon global information in successively presented visual patterns. *Journal of the Optical Society of America*, 1973, *63*, 1280A.

Pantle, A. J. Motion aftereffect magnitude as a measure of the spatio-temporal properties of direction sensitive analyzers. *Vision Research*, 1974, *14*, 1229–1236.

Pantle, A. J., Lehmkuhle, S., & Caudill, M. On the capacity of directionally selective mechanisms to encode different dimensions of moving stimuli. *Perception*, 1978, *7*, 261–268.

Pantle, A. J., & Picciano, L. A multistable movement display: Evidence for two separate motion systems in human vision. *Science*, 1976, *193*, 500–502.

Pantle, A. J., & Sekuler, R. Velocity-sensitive elements in human vision: Initial psychophysical evidence. *Vision Research*, 1968, *8*, 445–450.

Pantle, A. J., & Sekuler, R. Contrast response of human visual mechanisms sensitive to orientation and direction of motion. *Vision Research*, 1969, *9*, 397–406.

Papert, S. *Regularities in the time courses of some visual processes.* (Quarterly Progress Report no. 73.) Research Lab in Electronics, MIT, 1964, 244–247.

Parks, T. Post-retinal visual storage. *American Journal of Psychology*, 1965, 145–147.

Pasternak, T., Merigan, W. H., & Movshon, J. A. Motion mechanisms in strobe-reared cats: Psychophysical and electrophysiological measures. *Acta Psychologica*, 1981, *48*, 321–332.

Pasternak, T., Movshon, J. A., & Merigan, W. H. Creation of direction selectivity in adult strobe-reared cats. *Nature*, 1981, *292*, 834–836.

Petersik, J. T. The effects of spatial and temporal factors on the perception of stroboscopic rotation simulations. *Perception*, 1980, *9*, 271–283.

Pettigrew, J. D., Nikara, T., & Bishop, P. O. Responses to moving slits by single units in cat striate cortex. *Experimental Brain Research*, 1968, *6*, 373–390.

Potzl, O., & Redlich, E. Demonstration eines Falles von bilateraler Affektion beider Occipitallappen. *Wiener Klinische Wochenschrift,* 1911, *24*, 517–518.

Pulfrich, C. Die Stereoscopie im Dienste der isochromen und heterochromen Photometrie. *Naturwissen*, 1922, *10*, 553–564.

Ramachandran, V. S. (Ed.). Special issue on motion perception. *Perception*, 1984.

Ramachandran, V. S., & Anstis, S. M. Displacement thresholds for coherent apparent motion in random dot-patterns. *Vision Research*, 1983, *23*, 1719–1724.

Ramachandran, V. S., Rao, V. M., & Vidyasagar, T. R. Apparent movement with subjective contours. *Vision Research*, 1973, *13*, 1399–1401.

Ramachandran, V. S., & Gregory, R. L. Does colour provide an input to motion perception? *Nature*, 1978, *275*, 55–57.

Rapoport, J. Adaptation in the perception of rotary motion. *Journal of Experimental Psychology*, 1964, *67*, 263–267.

Rashid, R. F. Towards a system for the interpretation of moving light displays. *Transactions of the IEEE*, Vol. PAMI-2, 1980, *6*, 574–581.

Ratliff, F. *Mach bands. Quantitative studies on neural networks in the retina.* San Francisco: Holden-Day, 1965.

Reichardt, W. Autocorrelation, a principle for the evaluation of sensory information by the central nervous system. In W. Rosenblith (Ed.), *Sensory communication*, Cambridge: MIT Press, 1961.

Richards, W., & Lieberman, H. Velocity blindness during shearing motion. *Vision Research*, 1982, *22*, 97–100.

Roach, J. W., & Aggarwal, J. K. Determining the movement of objects from a sequence of images. *Transaction of the IEEE*, Vol. PAMI-2, 1980, *6*, 554–562.

Robinson, J. *The psychology of visual illusion.* London: Hutchinson University Library, 1972.

Rock, I. *Introduction to perception.* New York: Macmillan, 1975.

Rogers, B. J., & Anstis, S. M. Intensity versus adaptation and the Pulfrich stereophenomenon. *Vision Research*, 1972, *12*, 909–928.

Rogers, B. J., & Anstis, S. M. Reversed depth from positive and negative stereograms. *Perception*, 1975, *4*, 193–201.

Ross, J. Stereopsis by binocular delay. *Nature*, 1974, *248*, 363–364.

Rovamo, J., & Virsu, V. An estimation and application of human magnification factor. *Experimental Brain Research*, 1979, *37*, 495–510.

Runeson, S., & Lind, M. S. Ullman's "The interpretation of visual motion": A critical review. *Journal of Mathematical Psychology*, 1981, *23*, 273–284.

Scharf, B. Critical bands. In J. V. Tobias (Ed.), *Foundations of modern auditory theory.* New York: Academic Press, 1970.

Scott, T. R., & Powell, D. A. Measurement of a visual motion aftereffect in the rhesus monkey. *Science*, 1963, *140*, 57–59.

Sekuler, R., & Ganz, L. A new aftereffect of seen motion with a stabilized retinal image. *Science*, 1963, *139*, 419–420.

Sekuler, R., & Levinson, E. Mechanisms of motion perception. *Psychologia*, 1974, *17*, 38–49.

Sekuler, R., & Pantle, A. A model for the aftereffects of seen movement. *Vision Research*, 1967, *7*, 427–439.

Sekuler, R., Pantle, A., & Levinson, E. Physiological basis of motion perception. In H.-L. Teuber, R. H. Held, & H. W. Leibowitz, (Eds.), *Handbook of sensory physiology* (Vol. 8). New York: Springer-Verlag, 1978.

Shepard, R. N., & Zare, S. L. Path-guided apparent motion. *Science*, 1983, *220*, 632–634.

Sigman, E., & Rock, I. Stroboscopic movement based on perceptual intelligence. *Perception*, 1974, *3*, 9–28.

Smith, K. R. Visual apparent movement in the absence of neural interaction. *American Journal of Psychology*, 1948, *61*, 73–78.

Smythies, J. R. The stroboscopic patterns: I. The dark phase. *British Journal of Psychology*, 1959, *50*, 106–116. (a)

Smythies, J. R. The stroboscopic patterns: II. The phenomenology of the bright phase and after-images. *British Journal of Psychology*, 1959, *50*, 305–324. (b)

Spigel, I. (Ed.). *Readings in the perception of movement.* New York:

Harper & Row, 1965.

Srinivasan, M. V., & Dvorak, D. Spatial processing of visual information in the movement-detecting pathway of the fly. *Journal of Comparative Physiology*, 1980, *140*, 1–23.

Staebler, D. L. Binocularly induced motion of flicker patterns. *Journal of the Optical Society of America*, 1975, *66*, 156–157.

Stanley, G. Static visual noise and the Ansbacher effect. *Quarterly Journal of Experimental Psychology*, 1970, *22*, 43–48.

Sterling, P., & Wickelgren, B. Visual receptive fields in the superior colliculus of the cat. *Journal of Neurophysiology*, 1969, *32*, 1–15.

Sutherland, N. S. Figural aftereffects and apparent size. *Quarterly Journal of Experimental Psychology*, 1961, *13*, 222–228.

Ternus, J. Experimentelle Untersuchung ueber phaenomenale Identitaet. *Psychologische Forschung*, 1926, *7*, 81–136. (Excerpts translated in W. D. Ellis (Ed.), *A source book of Gestalt psychology*. London: Routledge Kegan Paul, 1938.)

Thompson, P. G. *Velocity after-effects and the perception of movement*. Doctoral dissertation, University of Cambridge, 1976.

Thompson, P. G. Velocity after-effects: The effects of adaptation to moving stimuli on the perception of subsequently seen moving stimuli. *Vision Research*, 1981, *21*, 337–345.

Thompson, P. G. Perceived rate of movement depends on contrast. *Vision Research*, 1982, *22*, 377–380.

Thorson, J., Lange, G. D., & Biederman-Thorson, M. Objective measure of the dynamics of a visual movement illusion. *Science*, 1969, *164*, 1087–1088.

Tolhurst, D. J. Separate channels for the analysis of shape and the movement of a moving stimulus. *Journal of Physiology*, 1973, *231*, 385–402.

Tsotsos, J. K. (Ed.) *Motion: Representation and perception. Proceedings of the SIGGRAPH/SIGART Conference*, Toronto. New York: Association for Computing Machinery, 1983.

Tsotsos, J. K., Mylopoulos, J., Covvey, H. D., & Zucker, S. A framework for visual motion understanding. *Transactions of the IEEE*, Vol. *PAMI-2*, 1980, 563–573.

Tsuji, S., Osada, M., & Yachida, M. Tracking and segmentation of moving objects in dynamic line images. *Transactions of the IEEE*, Vol. *PAMI-2*, 1980, 516–522.

Tyler, C. W. Temporal characteristics in apparent movement: Omega movement vs. phi movement. *Quarterly Journal of Experimental Psychology*, 1973, *25*, 182–192.

Tyler, C. W. Stereopsis in dynamic visual noise. *Nature*, 1974, *250*, 781–782.

Tyler, C. W. Stereomovement from interocular delay in dynamic visual noise: A random spatial disparity hypothesis. *American Journal of Optometry*, 1977, *54*, 374–386.

Tyler, C. W., & Torres, J. Frequency response characteristics for sinusoidal movement in the fovea and periphery. *Perception and Psychophysics*, 1972, *12*, 232–236.

Tynan, P., & Sekuler, R. Simultaneous motion contrast: Velocity, sensitivity, and depth response. *Vision Research*, 1975, 15, 1231–1238.

Tynan, P., & Sekuler, R. Motion processing in peripheral vision: Reaction time and perceived velocity. *Vision Research*, 1982, *22*, 61–68.

Ullman, S. *The interpretation of visual motion*. Cambridge, Mass.: MIT Press, 1979.

Ullman, S., & Hildreth, E. C. The measurement of visual motion. In O. L. Braddick & A. C. Sleigh (Eds.), *Physical and biological processing of images*. New York: Springer-Verlag, 1983.

van Doorn, A. J., & Koenderink, J. J. Spatial properties of the visual detectability of moving spatial white noise. *Experimental Brain Research*, 1982, *45*, 189–195.

van Doorn, A. J., & Koenderink, J. J. Spatiotemporal integration in the detection of coherent motion. *Vision Research*, 1984, *24*, 47–54.

van Santen, J. P. H., & Sperling, G. Temporal covariance model of human motion perception. *Journal of the Optical Society of America*, 1984, *1*, 451–473.

Vidyasagar, T. R. Orientation specific colour adaptation at a binocular site. *Nature*, 1976, *261*, 39–40.

Wade, N. J. On interocular transfer of the movement aftereffect in individuals with and without normal binocular vision. *Perception*, 1976, *5*, 113–118.

Wade, N. J. *The art and science of visual illusions*. London: Routledge and Kegan Paul, 1982.

Wade, N. J., & Swanston, M. T. Illusory line rotation in expanding and contracting displays. In L. Spillmann & B. R. Wooten (Eds.), *Sensory experience, adaptation, and perception: Festschrift for Ivo Kohler*. Hillsdale, N.J.: Lawrence Erlbaum, 1984.

Wade, N. J., & Wenderoth, P. The influence of colour and contour rivalry on the magnitude of the tilt aftereffect. *Vision Research*, 1978, *18*, 827–835.

Walker, P., & Powell, D. J. Lateral interaction between neural channels sensitive to velocity in human visual system. *Nature*, 1974, *252*, 732–733.

Wallach, H. The perception of motion. *Scientific American*, 1959, *201*, 56–60.

Walls, G. *The vertebrate eye and its adaptive radiations*. Bloomfield Mills, Mich.: Cranbrook Institution of Science Bulletin, 1942.

Watson, A. B. *Models, modules, and visual representations*. Paper delivered at the Symposium on Mechanisms of Spatial Vision, University of Rochester, 1984.

Watson, A. B., Ahumada, A., & Farrell, J. *The window of visibility: A psychophysical theory of fidelity in time-sampled visual motion displays*. (NASA Technical Paper 2211) 1983.

Weisstein, N., & Harris, C. S. In Harris, C. S. (Ed.), *Sensory coding and adaptation*. Hillsdale, N.J.: Lawrence Erlbaum, 1980.

Wertheim, M., Wagenaar, W. A., & Leibowitz, H. W. (Eds.). *Tutorials on motion perception*. New York and London: Plenum Press, 1982.

Wertheimer, M. Experimentelle Studien ueber das Sehen von Bewegung. In T. Shipley (Ed. & Trans.), *Classics in Psychology*. New York: Philosophical Library, 1961. (Originally published in *Zeitschrift für Psychologie*, *61*, 161–265.)

Westheimer, G., & McKee, S. Visual acuity in the presence of retinal-image motion. *Journal of the Optical Society of America*, 1975, *65*, 847–850.

Westheimer, G., & McKee, S. Stereoscopic acuity for moving retinal images. *Journal of the Optical Society of America*, 1978, *68*, 450–455.

White, K. D., Petry, H. M., Riggs, L. A., & Miller, J. Binocular interaction during the establishment of McCollough effects. *Vision Research*, 1978, *18*, 1201–1215.

Wilson, J. A., Robinson, J. O., & Piggins, D. J. Wobble cones and wobble holes: The stereokinetic effect revisited. *Perception*, 1983, *12*, 187–194.

Wohlgemuth, A. On the aftereffect of seen movement. *British Journal of Psychology Monographs* (Suppl. No. 1), 1911.

Yachida, M., Ikeda, M., & Tsuji, S. A plan-guided analysis of cineangiograms for measurement of dynamic behavior of heart wall. *Transactions of the IEEE*, Vol. *PAMI-2*, 1980, 537–543.

Young, R. S. L., & Cole, R. E., Gamble, M., & Rayner, M. D. Subjective patterns elicited by light flicker. *Vision Research*, 1975, *15*, 1291–1293.

Zeeman, W., & Roelofs, C. Some aspects of apparent motion. *Acta Psychologica*, 1953, *9*, 158–181.

Zeki, S. M. Functional specialisation of a visual area in the posterior bank of the superior temporal sulcus of the rhesus monkey. *Journal of Physiology* (London), 1974, *236*, 549–573.

Zihl, J., von Cramon, D., & Mai, N. Selective disturbance of movement vision after bilateral brain damage. *Brain*, 1983, *106*, 313–340.

CHAPTER 17

PERCEPTUAL ASPECTS OF MOTION IN THE FRONTAL PLANE

ARIEN MACK

New School for Social Research, New York, New York

CONTENTS

1. DETERMINANTS OF PERCEIVED OBJECT MOTION

1.1. Primary Sources of Information

The perception that an object is moving in the world is not a simple event and does not arise solely or even primarily from the motion of its image on the retina. There is, in fact, no necessary connection between image motion and seeing an object move. We may track a moving object with our eyes so that its image remains fixed and nevertheless see it move. Conversely, the image of a stationary object will move as our eyes move, and the object will appear stationary.

There are two major sets of determinants of perceived object motion, each of which belongs to a distinct and different perceptual category. One involves *subject-relative* sensory information, while the other is based on *object-relative* information. Subject-relative information is distinguished from object-relative information by the coordinate system. Subject-relative information is based on an egocentric coordinate system in which retina, head, or torso serves as the frame of reference. Object-relative information is based on an external reference system in which one or more objects in the visual field serve as the frame of reference for another.

1.2. Subject-Relative Determinants

Subject-relative information, as defined here, specifies the relation between an aspect of the visual world and the head, for example, orientation with respect to the head or motion with respect to the head. Perceptions based on this information are referred to as *absolute, egocentric, headcentric*, or *scalar* (Gogel, 1977b; Howard, 1982; Mack, 1978; Rock, 1975; Wallach, 1976). These labels are all equally apt as each refers to a distinctive characteristic. For example, these percepts are egocentric, since the object is perceived in relation to the self. They are scalar or absolute because they permit judgments of how far, how fast, how much, and so on.

The sensory source of subject-relative information is twofold. It entails retinal (afferent) information about some absolute feature of the proximal stimulus, for example, visual angle, retinal orientation, retinal location or retinal displacement, and sensory information about the relationship between the relevant aspect of the imaged object and the observer. This latter information is frequently but not necessarily nonvisual and extraretinal; in the case of perceived object motion it is invariably nonvisual and extraretinal.

The subject-relative determinants of object motion are retinal image motion and extraretinal information about head and eye movements. (For the most part information about eye movement is thought to be derived from the efferent signals that control the extraocular muscles.) Image motion alone does not signal object motion, but the relationship between image and eye and head movement information does. When the image motion signal matches, cancels, or is accounted for by the extraretinal eye and/or head motion signal, the object is generally perceived as stationary. A match between these two kinds of information defines the perceptual phenomenon known as *position constancy*.

1.3. Position Constancy

Position constancy refers to the perception that an object is stationary despite the displacement of its image over the retina caused by eye movements or displacements of the object relative to the head caused by head movements. When the retinal and extraretinal motion signals do not match, object motion is generally perceived. The hypothetical mechanism that relates afferent motion signals to extraretinal eye motion information is referred to as a *motion comparator*, a term associated most frequently with von Holst (1954), although a version of this general hypothesis has a longer history (see Teuber, 1960). (For a discussion of the roles of the vestibular system and of neck receptors in providing extraretinal signals, see Howard, Chapter 18.) The motion comparator receives a copy of the efferent signal to the extraocular muscles, frequently referred to as a corollary discharge (von Holst, 1954), and afferent signal from the retina. It calculates the difference between them, and its output is the result of this calculation. Thus when object motion is a function of subject-relative information, it is based on the output from this hypothetical mechanism. Considerable research has been done on the precision with which this position constancy mechanism operates, given different kinds of extraretinal eye movement signals, that is, saccadic and pursuit. The questions asked are either, How good are we at detecting object motion during eye movements? or To what extent do stationary objects appear stationary during eye movements? A similar issue arises in connection with head movements. To what extent do stationary objects appear stationary despite the displacement of the visual field produced by head movements? This question must be phrased in terms of visual field, rather than retinal image displacements, since head turns are frequently accompanied by compensatory eye movements known as vestibulo-ocular reflexes, which serve to stabilize the images of stationary objects on the retina. This research is reviewed in the following sections.

1.4. Object-Relative Determinants

Percepts based on object-relative information are not determined by information that relates some aspect of an object to the observer, but by information that relates one object in the visual field to another. Unlike percepts based on subject-relative information, they depend entirely on visual or retinal information and entail no extraretinal input. While motion percepts determined by information about displacements with respect to the self are derived from image and observer motion signals, motion percepts determined by object-relative information are derived from the displacement of one object relative to another. Percepts based on this information are also referred to as *metric, exocentric* (Gogel, 1977a) relative (Harvey & Michon, 1974; Kinchla, 1971) or configurational perceptions (Wallach, Bacon, & Schulman, 1978). These labels are descriptive and point to the distinctive features of these percepts. Object-relative information permits only metric judgments, for example, faster than, more than, in a different direction from. They are exocentric or relative because one object is perceived in relation to another object, not the self. They are configurational because they are based on information that is formlike, and in the case of motion they are based on formlike changes in the visual array. Gogel's *principle of adjacency* (1977a) states, "The effectiveness of relative cues decreases as the perceived distance between objects producing the relative cues increases" (p. 162). This suggests a decrease in the probability that relative displacement between objects in the field will be the basis of perceived motion as the separation between objects increases.

Unlike subject-relative–based motion perception, object-relative–based motion perception cannot be studied in isolation. In every case where the conditions for object-relative motion perceptions exist, the conditions for motion perception based on subject-relative information are also present. The reverse is not the case. In any situation in which there is a solitary object moving through an otherwise unstructured field, only subject-relative motion information is potentially present. If a second object is introduced into the field, providing object-relative motion information, this information necessarily coexists with the available subject-relative information.

A characteristic aspect of object-relative motion information is that it provides no information about which object is moving, that is, which object is responsible for the relative displacement. Logically, a displacement between two objects might be the result of the motion of either or both objects. Since perceived motion based on object-relative information is frequently ambiguous, information specifying which object is moving must come from some other source. This other source is either subject-relative motion information or (when this information is not available because the object producing the relative displacement is moving too slowly and its motion is therefore below the subject-relative motion threshold) the specification appears to rest on principles of motion organization (see Sections 4.2 and 4.3).

1.5. Gibson's Analysis

Gibson (1968) has argued for a radically different account. For Gibson there is perceived self motion and perceived object motion. The distinction between object motion based on subject-relative input and object motion based on object-relative displacement is simply not recognized. He rejects the view that position constancy is to be accounted for by a calculating process comparing retinal image motion to extraretinal eye and/or head motion signals, and this rejection entails an implicit rejection of the subject- and object-relative motion distinction.

Gibson proposes the notion of "sensationless proprioception" (p. 341) or "visual kinesthesis" (p. 341) to account for position constancy:

> It is important to realize that motion perspective caused by locomotion entails a change in the *whole* of the textured ambient array whereas the alteration of perspective caused by an objective motion entails only a change in *part* of the array, the remainder being frozen. If this part–whole distinction can be picked up by a visual system, the difference between motion in the world and locomotion of the self would be specified by the input of the system, and an explanation in terms of special brain processes to correct the retinal sensation would not be necessary. (p. 341)

The motion of the entire retinal array specifies observer movement and accounts for position constancy. Relative motion within the ambient array specifies object motion. Thus for Gibson *all* perceived object motion is a function of retinal displacement information and the distinction between subject- and object-relative determinants of perceived object motion has no validity.

Gibson's approach, briefly sketched here, is recommended by its simplicity. Unfortunately, it has serious difficulty in accounting for a variety of motion phenomena easily accounted for by the view that there is subject-relative information about object motion derived from observer and image motion signals. When we press gently against the eyeball, the visual scene appears to displace despite the fact that the retinal image motion produced by the manual manipulation of the eye mimics that produced by a normal eye motion that causes the *whole* ambient array to displace. According to Gibson, motion of the entire array specifies self motion and therefore no scene motion should be perceived. If an observer tries to move a paralyzed or immobilized eye, scene motion may again be reported, and this presents another problem for Gibson's analysis. Why should object motion be perceived if there is no image displacement at all? These observations are easily accounted for by the alternative view which posits that a mismatch between eye and image movement signals leads to perceived object motion. In the first instance, there is image motion and no eye motion signal since the eye movement signal is a corollary of the efferent command to the extraocular muscles. In the second instance, there is an eye motion signal produced by the effort to move the immobilized eye, but there is no image motion.

Gibson's view cannot account for other common observations. Why does an afterimage, a retinally stabilized visual array, or a single point moving in the dark and tracked by the eye, appear to move? In each of these instances, there is no image motion at all. The alternative view once again attributes the perceived object motion in each of these situations to the mismatch between eye and image motion produced by the absence of image displacement and the presence of an eye motion signal. Gibson dismisses these observations and others that might have been described as atypical laboratory phenomena, but the sheer number of them suggests a different account. Although this evidence weighs against Gibson's analysis, his analysis does focus on characteristic differences between image motions generated by objects and those generated by self movements. For example, his analysis easily accounts for the perceptual dominance of object-relative motion and the induced motion phenomena that follow from this. Furthermore, in a normal, richly patterned visual environment, which for Gibson is the only environment appropriate for the study of visual perception, relative retinal displacement is an invariant feature of object motion, while homogeneous retinal displacement is an invariant of self motion. Empirical support for Gibson's analysis is provided by an experiment (Rock, 1968) in which observers were slowly and smoothly moved along a wall of a dark room. When the visual stimuli consisted of a series of small, widely spaced luminous discs, separated from each other by interposed shields so that only one disc was visible at a time as observers were moved along, the observers reported that the discs appeared to move. They did not perceive themselves as moving. However, when the wall was covered with a luminous, textured pattern, the observers no longer perceived the pattern as moving but experienced themselves as moving.

1.6. Subject- and Object-Relative Motion Thresholds

The subject-relative motion threshold refers to the limit of our sensitivity or ability to detect the motion of a single luminous object in an otherwise dark field. The object-relative threshold refers to the capacity to detect object motion when at least one other object is present in the field. Bonnet (1975, 1982) distinguishes between three kinds of motion display presentations which have differential effects on motion thresholds. These are continuous, discrete and stop-go-stop presentations. (Kaufman et al., 1971, also report threshold differences for discrete and continuous motion.) In a continuous presentation the stimulus comes into view and disappears from view while moving and is never viewed in a stationary position. In a discrete presentation a stimulus is presented in two different positions in space separated by a temporal interval (phi motion). In a stop-go-stop presentation the motion stimulus is viewed in a stationary position prior to and following the motion interval.

Shaffer and Wallach (1966) measured the *extent of motion threshold*, how far a stimulus had to move for its motion to be reliably reported 50% of the time, under both subject- and object-relative viewing conditions using stop-go-stop presentations. Velocity was held constant and three velocities were tested: 41, 82, and 164 min arc/sec. When stimulus motion was purely subject-relative and the moving stimulus, which was a luminous outline square, was all that was visible, the extent of motion threshold varied inversely with velocity. At the highest velocity, 164 min arc/sec, the median threshold was 1.1 min arc; at the medium velocity, it was 2.4 min arc; and at the lowest velocity, it was 4.4 min arc. When stimulus motion was object-relative, a stationary luminous disc was centered within the outline square. The median extent of motion threshold ranged from 1.0 to 1.1 min arc and was unaffected by stimulus velocity. Shaffer and Wallach report that at all velocities tested and for every subject, larger extents were needed to detect subject- than object-relative motion and this difference decreased as velocity increased.

The finding that the threshold for the detection of object-relative motion is lower than that for subject-relative motion is supported by the results of other investigators, for example, Kinchla (1971), J. F. Brown (1931b), Aubert (1886), Harvey and Michon (1974). However, Leibowitz (1955), Hanes (1965), Mates (1969), and Bonnet (1975) report that there are conditions in which there is no difference between subject- and object-relative motion thresholds. Bonnet (1975) who, like Wallach, measured extent of motion thresholds but, unlike Wallach, used a continuous motion display, reports that stationary reference lines do not lower threshold when the motion interval is short (less than 180 msec) or when velocity is high. See Figure 17.1 (Bonnet, 1975), which presents extent of motion threshold data as a function of exposure time for four display conditions.

Leibowitz reports similar findings from an experiment in which he measured velocity thresholds, rather than extent of motion, as a function of luminance, stationary referents, and motion duration using a continuous motion display. He reports that with his short motion interval (250 msec), the presence of stationary referents in the visual display did not alter the threshold, which ranged from 62.72 to 8.80 min arc/sec, depending on the luminance of the motion stimulus and amount of prior practice. With a motion interval of 16 sec (the longest motion interval), Leibowitz found that stationary referents lowered the threshold by about 48%. (See Figure 17.2.)

The fact that high-velocity, short-duration motions are not affected by stationary referents, whereas slower motions over longer intervals are, has led some investigators to postulate a dual basis for motion perception (Bonnet, 1975; R. H. Brown, 1955; Exner, 1875; Leibowitz, 1955). According to one statement of this view, movingness that is distinguished from displacement detection results from a "single sensory event; such an event can be conceived of basically as a critical neural event (rate of firing or number of firings) which make the movingness detectors fire at a rate discriminable from their maintained rate of discharge" (Bonnet, 1975, pp. 36–37). The perceived motion of slower-moving stimuli viewed for a longer period, however, is thought to be based on the detection of position change, and this depends on the processing of position information. If this

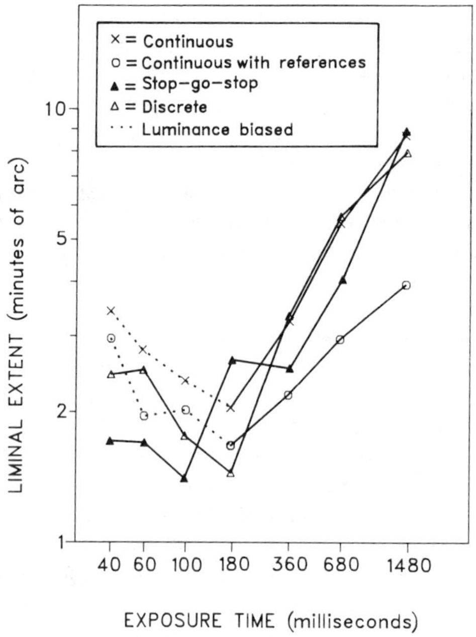

Figure 17.1. Extent of motion thresholds as a function of exposure time. Liminal extent (*S* lim) as a function of exposure time *T* on log scales for different modes of presentation: continuous, continuous with references, stop-go-stop, discrete (motion to succession instructions), and data known as luminance biased (CRT device). The graphed results are from one observer who monocularly viewed a 2.4. min arc spot on a CRT (P 31). In continuous motion displays the extent of motion thresholds are not lowered by stationary reference lines when the motion interval is short (less than 180 msec). (From C. Bonnet, A tentative model for visual motion detection, *Psychologia*, 1975, *18*. Reprinted with permission.)

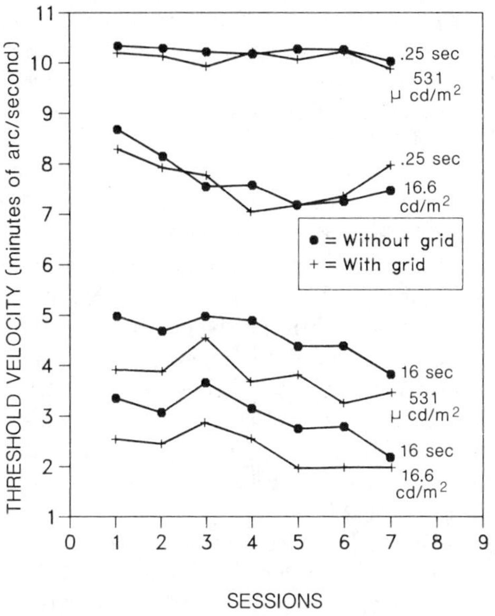

Figure 17.2. Velocity detection thresholds as a function of duration luminance, and presence or absence of stationary grid. An increase in duration (0.25–16 sec) or luminance (0.016–500 cd) lowers the velocity threshold. The effect of luminance is more pronounced for shorter than for longer exposure. The grid lines lower the threshold velocity at the longer duration but have no consistent effect for the shorter duration. The data represent the means for eight subjects run over seven experimental sessions. (From H. W. Leibowitz, Effects of reference lines on the discrimination of movement, *Journal of the Optical Society of America*, 1955, *45*. Reprinted with permission.)

were a correct description, it would follow that stationary referents would facilitate the latter and have no affect on the former.

Since many factors influence our sensitivity to motion, for example, size of the motion stimulus, size of the motion field, amount of practice, luminance of the motion stimulus, and location of the retina stimulated, no precise general statements about either subject- or object-relative motion sensitivity are possible. However, it is possible to conclude from the available data that except when motion intervals are exceedingly brief or velocities are high, the presence of object-relative displacement information increases sensitivity.

1.7. A Developmental Hypothesis about the Relation between Subject- and Object-Relative Motion

Wallach (1965) has argued that absolute image displacement is the ontogenetically primary stimulus for perceived object motion. Perceived object motion based on the relative displacement between objects in the field or based on the pursuit of a moving stimulus is seen as derivative, the result of an associative learning process in which one stimulus comes to stand for another. Since every instance of object-relative displacement is conjoined with a subject-relative displacement and ocular pursuit is normally elicited by image displacement, if neither pursuit nor relative displacement initially signal motion, they might come to do so as a result of their consistent and repetitive association with absolute image displacement. The same argument, of course, could be phrased in adaptive, evolutionary terms that would entail no assumptions about learning. The hypothesis that perceived motion based on object-relative displacement is the result of a learned association with absolute displacement provides a ready explanation for the fact that when the information about which object is moving is ambiguous, for example, when motion is below the absolute threshold, it is always the smaller, enclosed object that appears to move while the larger surrounding object or objects appear stationary. In most situations a moving object is viewed against a stationary background scene, so not only might relative displacement come to signify motion but the rule that the smaller object is moving and the larger object is stationary also might be simultaneously encoded.

The validity of Wallach's learning hypothesis is clearly an empirical matter, although apart from relevant data, there are grounds for skepticism. First, it is not clear whether absolute image displacement unallied with observer movement information is in and of itself ever a condition for motion perception, except perhaps for high-velocity, brief-interval displacements. Second, recent reports of cells uniquely responsive to relative, rather than absolute, retinal image motion (Bridgeman, 1972; Burns, Gassanov, & Webb, 1972; Frost & Wong, 1977; Sterling & Wickelgren, 1977) do not suggest a learning hypothesis although these data do not eliminate it. Third, the characteristic dominance of object- over subject-relative motion is not obviously compatible with the hypothesis that subject-relative motion is the primitive motion stimulus, although this evidence is also not conclusive.

Wallach reports the only relevant empirical data (Wallach, Bacon, & Schulman, 1978). The experiment involved prolonged exposure to a subject- and object-relative motion conflict and demonstrated a subsequent decrease in the extent of the perceived object-relative component of motion. This is viewed by the authors as a perceptual adaptation in which the salience of relative displacement, referred to as configurational change, is diminished as a cue to motion because of its prolonged pairing with absolute, angular displacement.

The investigators concluded that object-relative displacement had become a less effective basis for perceiving object motion, and this result is at least compatible with, although not proof of, the claim that object-relative displacement is a learned source of motion information.

1.8. Perceptual Dominance of Object-Relative Displacement

It is a general rule of perception that when object- and subject-relative motion information conflict, object-relative input will determine the perception if it derives from adjacent objects in the field. This is so despite the fact that only the subject-relative information provides a basis for veridical perception. Every instance of induced motion, the effect of size of the motion field on perceived object velocity, and the perception of the motion of Lissajous-like motion combinations (see Section 5.2 for discussion of this phenomenon) provide evidence of the weight assigned to relative displacement by the perceptual system. This is further exemplified by the effects of eliminating all visual referents from the field when viewing either a moving or a stationary object. If the object is moving, its motion will be far more difficult to detect, and if it is stationary, it will most likely appear to move after a brief period of fixation, a phenomenon referred to as the *autokinetic effect*. (See Section 3.4.7.)

While there is overwhelming evidence of the importance of relative displacement in the perception of object motion, the role of this information in the control of orienting responses to visual targets is far less clear.

2. ORIENTING RESPONSES: MOTION AND POSITION INFORMATION

Eye movement and pointing responses have been examined under conditions in which the perceived position or motion of a target stimulus, specified by object-relative determinants, is discrepant with its actual position, specified by retinal and eye motion information.

2.1. Perceived Motion and Pursuit Eye Movements

When the appearance of motion is induced in a stationary target by the motion of a surrounding visual frame, its perceived motion instantiates the salience of relative displacement information for perception. (The reader is referred to Section 5.1.) If an observer is required to fixate a stationary target undergoing induced motion, the perceived motion fails to elicit pursuit eye movements despite the fact that observers believe that they are, in fact, tracking. Since pursuit of such a stationary target would cause the image of the target to slip away from the fovea, it is perhaps not surprising that perceived induced motion fails to engage the oculomotor system (Mack, Fendrich, & Pleune, 1979). Pursuit eye movements might well be constrained by the potential retinal error information. However, even if this information is eliminated, perceived induced motion fails to act as a stimulus for smooth pursuit. This was demonstrated in an experiment in which the retinal error information normally produced by pursuit of an apparently moving, but actually stationary, target was eliminated by retinal stabilization of the entire induced motion display (Mack, Fendrich, & Wong, 1982). Under these conditions, pursuit of an apparently moving, actually stationary, target does not generate constraining retinal error information, so that if perceived object motion based on relative displacement information can be a stimulus for pursuit, this situation should reveal it. Despite consistent reports that the stabilized, stationary induction target appeared to be moving, there was no evidence of pursuit eye movements. Other experiments in this series confirmed these results. Pursuit eye movements were always governed by subject-relative motion information when perceived motion was a function of the object-relative displacement. (It might be noted that if the perception of induced motion were accompanied by the visual capture of oculomotor information, a possibility suggested by at least two groups of investigators—McConkie & Farber, 1979; Rock, Auster, Schiffman, & Wheeler, 1980—no actual pursuit movement should be elicited by the perceived induced motion. See Section 5 for a discussion of this issue.)

The sensitivity of the oculomotor system to subject-relative motion information is further illustrated by the finding that a single stimulus moving too slowly for its motion to be perceived is nevertheless reliably tracked by smooth pursuit eye movements. This is illustrated in Figure 17.3, which summarizes the results of an experiment in which eye motions were monitored while observers watched a slowly moving stimulus. There were no noticeable differences between the tracking of above- and below-threshold motions.

The only evidence that perceived motion per se governs or acts as a stimulus for smooth pursuit comes from situations in which the pursuit target has no conflicting retinal counterpart, for example, when the path of motion is remembered (Holtzman,

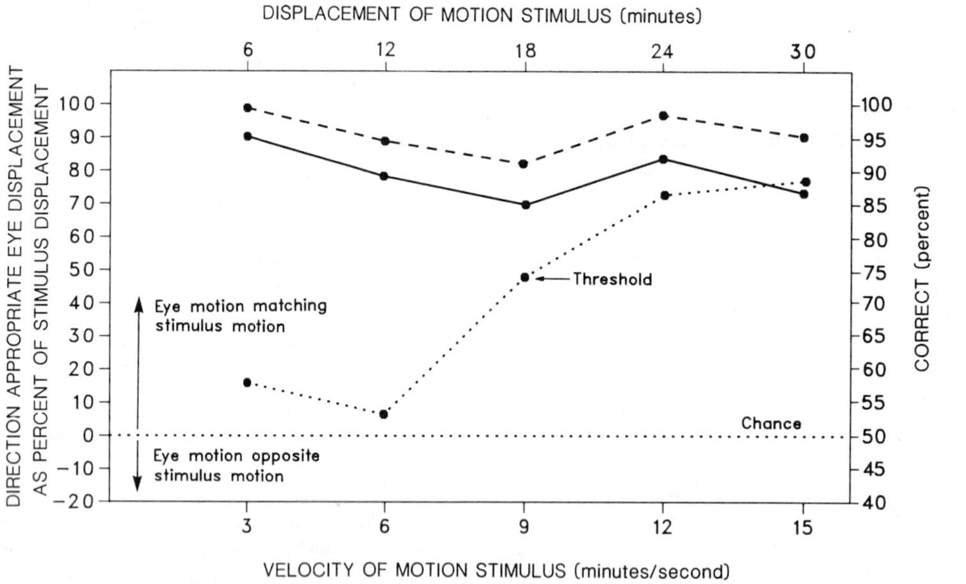

Figure 17.3. Eye motion and psychophysical report as a function of stimulus velocity. Dashed line represents total change in eye position; solid line, pursuit component in eye position change; dotted line, percentage correct in psychological report of direction. Eye motions are plotted against the left ordinate as a percentage of total stimulus displacement. Psychological reports are plotted against the right ordinate. Subjects viewed a single point of light on a fast phosphor CRT (P 15). The point was present for 2 sec and moved left or right at velocities of 3–15 min arc/sec. Eye movements were recorded by a SRI Double Purkinje Image Eye Tracker. A forced-choice procedure was used in which observers responded "left" or "right" to indicate the direction of motion at the end of each trial. Tracking of below-threshold motion did not differ from tracking of above-threshold motion. This suggests that pursuit eye movements do not depend on perceived motion. (From A. Mack, R. Fendrich, & J. Pleune, Smooth pursuit eye movements: Is perceived motion necessary? *Science, 203*. Copyright 1979 by the American Association for the Advancement of Science. Reprinted by permission.)

Sedgwick, & Festinger, 1978) or when the perceived target is presented anorthoscopically (Steinbach, 1976). *Anorthoscopic perception* occurs when a form or figure is moved behind a narrow vertical slit. Under the appropriate conditions, the observer perceives the figure passing behind the slit despite the fact that all that is visible at any instant is some small fraction of the figure's contours moving vertically within the slit. Evidence that observers can track an anorthoscopic stimulus (Mack, Fendrich, & Wong, 1982; Steinbach, 1976) is consistent with the evidence indicating that perceived motion governs pursuit only when the target has no conflicting retinal counterpart and is thus consistent with the view that subject-relative information, image and eye movement information, is the principle determinant of smooth pursuit eye movements.

2.2. Perceived Displacements and Saccadic Eye Movements

Similar results have been obtained with saccadic eye movements. In one investigation of the effect of perceived displacement on saccades (Wong, 1981; Wong & Mack, 1981), a visual frame was discretely stepped relative to an enclosed target point. Observers were required to fixate the target point which was initially centered within a rectangular frame. Target and frame were blanked for a brief interval and then reappeared, the target for 100 msec, the frame for 500 msec. The reappearance of target and frame was the signal for the observer to refixate the briefly presented target. (The refixation saccade, of course, generated no retinal error signal, since the target vanished well before the saccade was executed.) Observers reported whether and by how much the target appeared to jump.

In every instance the saccade was directed to the actual, rather than perceived, position of the target, which was consistently a function of its position relative to the framing rectangle. Since actual position is signaled by subject-relative information, that is, by eye position and retinal position information, it is clear that, as in the case of pursuit, it is this information that is critical to the oculomotor orienting system.

Evidence from the work of other investigators confirms this. Hallett and Lightstone (1976a, 1976b) report that saccades are accurately directed to a target flashed during the time course of a saccade even though the position of the target is misperceived (Matin, 1972). Ono and Nakamizo (1977) also reported that in a situation in which perceived and actual location differ, observers saccade to the actual, rather than the perceived, location. The question this study addressed was whether a saccade made during a change in fixation to a stimulus at a different distance is directed toward the actual or perceived location of that stimulus.

> The stimulus situation used was that of Panum's limiting case where the farther of two stimuli is occluded from one eye by a near stimulus, thus there is no diplopia for the far target. In this stimulus arrangement, when a subject is fixating on the near stimulus, the far stimulus is perceived in an illusory location. (Ono & Nakamizo, 1977, p. 234)

(See Figure 17.4 for a schematic representation of the stimulus arrangement.)

Recent work also indicates, however, that if a saccade is made to the remembered position of a target, the saccade tends to be directed to perceived, rather than actual, target position (Mack, Fendrich, & Chambers, 1982). When the signal to saccade occurs more than 500 msec after the onset of the flashed, apparently stepped target, the saccade is likely to be directed to perceived target position. This result, too, is consistent with the evidence concerning perceived motion and pursuit, in particular the evidence reported by Holtzman, Sedgwick, and Festinger (1978).

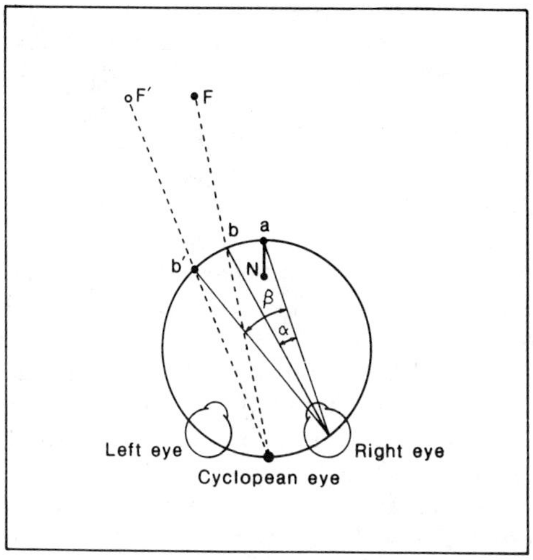

Figure 17.4. Scheme of display in which actual and perceived location of an eye movement target are discrepant. Illustrations of the experimental stimuli and of the difference in predictions based on the actual and perceived locations *F* and *F′*, respectively. The angular magnitude defined by *a* and *b* from the right eye is the prediction based on the direction of the actual location, and that by *a* and *b′* is the prediction based on the visual direction of the perceived location. (From H. Ono & S. Nakamizo, Saccadic eye movements during change in fixation to stimuli at different distances, *Vision Research, 17*. Copyright 1977 by Pergamon Press, Ltd. Reprinted with permission.)

2.3. Perception of Motion and Position and Other Orienting Responses

There is some evidence that subject-relative motion and position information are the principal determinants of pointing and other related orienting responses. In an experiment examining the ability to point to the position of a target displaced near the time of a saccade, the investigators found pointing was as accurate when the observer failed to report the displacement as when it was correctly reported (Bridgeman, Lewis, Heit, & Nagle, 1979).

In another experiment (Hansen, 1979) a ballistic-orienting act (striking a target with a hammer) was accurately performed even under conditions that led to significant misperception of target position, for example, when the target was presented during an interval in which a moving stimulus was being tracked. In this experiment the observer tracked a small projected spot in the dark. During a period of accurate tracking, a second spot was flashed. The observer's task was to hit this second spot with a hammer. The speed of the tracking stimulus ranged from 15 to 1800 min arc/sec.

Bridgeman, Kirch, and Sperling (1981) report that observers point accurately to a target that either appears to step when it is in fact stationary or appears stationary when in fact it has displaced. An induced displacement display, similar to the one used by Wong and Mack (1981), described in Section 2.2, served to produce the conflict between perceived and actual position. The Bridgeman and coworkers findings are, however, discrepant with results reported by Sugarman and Cohen (1968), Farber (1979), and Bacon, Gordon, and Schulman (1982). These studies indicate that observers' pointing or manually tracking is significantly influenced by perceived induced motion; that is, observers respond to apparent, rather than actual, target position or motion. The reason for this discrepancy is not clear although it is possible, as Bridgeman and coworkers suggest, that the observers in the Farber study, the Sugarman and Cohen studies, and the Bacon study might have been confronted with a conflict, the resolution of which might well have led to manual tracking or pointing to induced motion. Perhaps if observers are asked to report perceived induced motion at the same time they are required to point to or manually track the induction target, they will point to or track in a way that is consistent with the perceptual report. Not to do so would be to appear self-contradictory. In the Bridgeman study pointing immediately followed target presentation and was the only response required of the subject. Psychophysical measures of perceived induced motion or displacement were obtained prior to trials in which pointing responses were made. This was not the case in the Farber study or Bacon study. It ought to be noted, however, that Bridgeman and coworkers failed to obtain robust induced motions. The induced target motion ranged from 14 to 21% of complete induction. It is therefore possible that the Bridgeman and coworkers findings simply reflect the weakness of the induction. Further work is required to explain these differences in results.

3. PERCEIVED MOTION AND OBSERVER MOVEMENT: SUBJECT-RELATIVE PHENOMENA

Since information about eye and head motion and position is the principle factor in the subject-relative determination of perceived object motion and stability, our ability to perceive motion and stability accurately during intervals in which our eyes and/or head is moving must depend both on the accuracy of the extraretinal eye and head motion information and on the precision with which it is matched against image position and motion signals. Inaccuracies in extraretinal information or imprecision in this match must lead to misperceptions of object motion, in situations in which perception is based on this information. How good are we at perceiving whether something is moving or stationary when we are moving our eyes and our heads?

3.1. Head Movement: Perceived Motion and Position

Head movements, like eye movements, cause relative displacement between the environment and the eyes or head. These movements are indistinguishable from those caused by actual motion of objects in the world. (As noted previously, head rotations do not necessarily cause image motions since head rotations generally release the vestibulo-ocular reflex.) Fortunately, these frequently indistinguishable events have quite different perceptual consequences. Field motions caused by our own movement, what von Holst (1954) termed *reafferent stimulation*, are generally appropriately attributed to our own movements while field motions caused by the motion of some object, what von Holst termed *exafferent stimulation*, are generally perceived as such. The basis for this discrimination seems to be the relationship between extraretinal, observer movement information and retinal information. A match between them signifies stability; a mismatch signifies motion. (If, rather than comparing the two inputs, the system simply discounted all field motion that was contemporaneous with head or eye motion, it would be impossible to distinguish between a moving and stable object during head or eye motions. This is clearly not the case.)

Studies of the perceptual modifiability of position or direction constancy provide the only data pertinent to the human capacity to detect object motion during head movements. This research investigates whether the normal correlation between head and field motion that signifies constancy can be modified by visual experience with an altered correlation. Normally a turning of the head, for example, to the right by 10°, causes a turning of the visual field to the left by 10° relative to the head. A compensation or matching process causes this subject-relative displacement to be discounted so that position constancy prevails. The question of interest concerns the accuracy with which this process operates. For example, will a relative displacement of 9 or 11° also lead to position constancy? Investigation of this question indicates that the answer is "no" (Wallach & Kravitz, 1965a). Only displacements between 9.7 and 10.3° will generate position constancy. Clearly the tolerance for an inexact mismatch is very small.

A study by Wallach and Kravitz (1965a), which is representative of others in this area, determined the range of the *displacement ratio* (DR), the ratio between the angular extent of head rotation and angular extent of field rotation which defined the range of perceived object stability. This provided the baseline against which perceptual adaptation was later assessed. The investigators found that the match between head and field displacement associated with perceived object stability was quite precise. The point of subjective stability was defined by a DR of 1.5%, and the range of uncertainty had a mean DR of 6.6%. In other related experiments these investigators found uncertainty ranges with mean widths of 5.2 (Wallach & Kravitz, 1965b) and 3.8% (Wallach & Kravitz, 1968). In this latter experiment the midpoint of the uncertainty range, that is, the point of subjective stability, was as low as 0.58% DR. These findings indicate that only the smallest motions of the display in the direction of head rotation go unreported, and all displacements in the opposite direction and larger displacements in the same direction are correctly reported. Thus it would appear that we are able to detect stimulus motion during head rotations with a high degree of reliability when the only relevant, available information concerns head rotation, eye movement, and field motion, that is, when the only information is subject relative.

3.2. Saccadic Eye Movements: Perceived Motion and Stability

Our ability to detect object motion during a saccade, while less good than during head rotation, is nevertheless considerable, and the relevant data make clear that there is by no means a simple and complete suppression of image displacement during saccades. (Data reported by Wallach & Lewis, 1966, might be interpreted as indicating complete suppression, but these data are not representative and have not been replicated.) Like work on position constancy during head rotation, this research also requires that displacements of the visual stimulus be contingent upon observer movement, in this case upon a saccade, and that the visual stimulus be all that is visible.

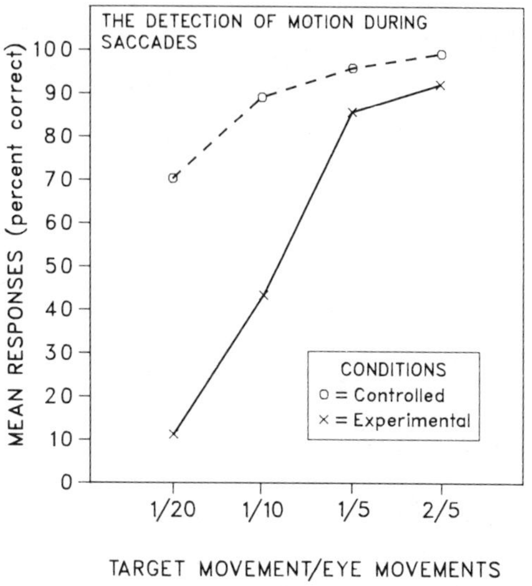

Figure 17.5. The detection of motion during saccades. To assess the degree of position constancy during saccades, a single luminous point displayed on an oscilloscope screen was displaced during a saccade. Saccades were horizontal with a mean amplitude of 13°. The point displaced up or down, left or right, a fraction of the distance through which the eye moved. Four target motion to eye movement ratios (TM:EM) were tested: 1:20, 1:10, 1:5, 2:5. Control observations were of identical stimulus displacements that, however, were not contingent on an eye movement. Each of 14 subjects served in both the control and experimental conditions. Stimulus displacements 1/5 of the saccadic displacements were almost always reported, whereas displacements only 1/20 of the saccadic displacements rarely were. (From A. Mack, An investigation of the relationship between eye and retinal image movement in the perception of movement, *Perception and Psychophysics*, 1970, *8*. Reprinted with permission.)

In one experiment (Mack, 1970) the displacement of a visual stimulus, a light point on a cathode-ray tube (CRT), was made contingent upon a saccade (results are reported in Figure 17.5). The visual stimulus was displaced with, against, or at right angles to the direction of the saccade. Saccades were either leftward or rightward, and their average amplitude was 10°. The eye movement–target movement displacement (EM:TM) ratios examined were 1, 1:2, 2:5, 1:5, 1:10, 1:20, and 0. The results were that all displacements greater than 20% of the saccadic displacement were reported, whereas displacements of 5% or less were rarely reported. Target displacements that were 10% of the eye displacement were reported about 43% of the time. It is perhaps surprising that the direction of target displacement did not significantly affect reports of target movement, a finding corroborated by at least one other group of investigators (Stark, Kong, Schwartz, Hendry, & Bridgeman, 1976).

Stark and colleagues (1976) examined motion detection during saccades, with the relationship between onset of target motion and onset of saccade as one of the experimental variables. They found maximum suppression of target displacement in the 60–70-msec interval that began 20 msec prior to saccade execution. There were again no differences between collinear and orthogonal target displacements. During steady fixation (no saccade) observers were able to detect a 2–3 min arc target displacement 50% of the time. During a saccade, target displacements of 6 min arc were rarely detected if they occurred during the interval of maximum suppression. The probability of detection increased rapidly as the time between the interval of maximum suppression and displacement increased. As the amplitude of target displacement increased, so did the probability of its being reported. The results of this experiment appear in Figure 17.6.

In another study (Bridgeman, Hendry, & Stark, 1975) the investigators failed to find any effect of direction of target displacement relative to direction of saccade, which is consistent with Mack (1970). What they did find was that the absolute size of the error between saccade and retinal displacement was more important than the sign of the error in accounting for detection. A major factor in determining whether target motion was detected was the size of the displacement relative to the size of the saccade. In general, target displacements less than one-third of the saccade amplitude were not reliably detected. This means, of course, that a small displacement is more likely to be detected during a small saccade than during a large one. The investigators again found maximum suppression of target displacements around the time of saccade onset. Figure 17.7 presents these results.

Whipple and Wallach (1978) report the only data indicating that the motion detection threshold during saccades is affected by the *direction* of stimulus displacement. These data are presented in Figure 17.8. The investigators report that threshold was lower when saccade and stimulus displacement occur along the same axis if the saccade is either horizontal or vertical. When a horizontal saccade was accompanied by horizontal stimulus displacement, the 80% threshold occurred when the target displacement was 8.2% of the saccade displacement. In the case of vertical saccades and congruent target displacement, the 80% threshold occurred when target displacement was 9.3% of saccade amplitude. These thresholds are substantially lower than those reported by Mack (1970) and Bridgeman, Hendry, and Stark (1975). When the axis of stimulus and saccade displacement differed, thresholds increased to between 19.7 and 25.3%. With oblique saccades and congruent image displacement an even more dramatic threshold elevation was obtained. The reason for the discrepancy between these results and those obtained by others is not clear.

These data indicate that while our capacity to detect object motion during saccades is less than during head rotation or during fixation, it is nevertheless considerable. Since the only information that permits the visual system to distinguish between a moving and a stationary object in these experiments is image and eye movement information, the fact that we are able to distinguish between the two is evidence that the match between eye and image motion constitutes a source of perceived motion and stability.

Bridgeman and colleagues (1975) have pointed out that the evidence indicating that the match signifying stability is imprecise may reveal nothing about the quality of the extraretinal eye position information. It may only reflect the degraded quality of image displacement information during a saccade caused by saccadic suppression. With degraded image displacement information, the match between eye and image motion could not be precise so that some target motion necessarily might be undetected. This speculation remains to be investigated.

3.3. Pursuit Eye Movements: Perceived Motion and Stability

While the raised threshold for the detection of object motion during saccades could possibly be attributed to degraded retinal information, differences in the perception of motion and stability during pursuit have generally been attributed to the degraded

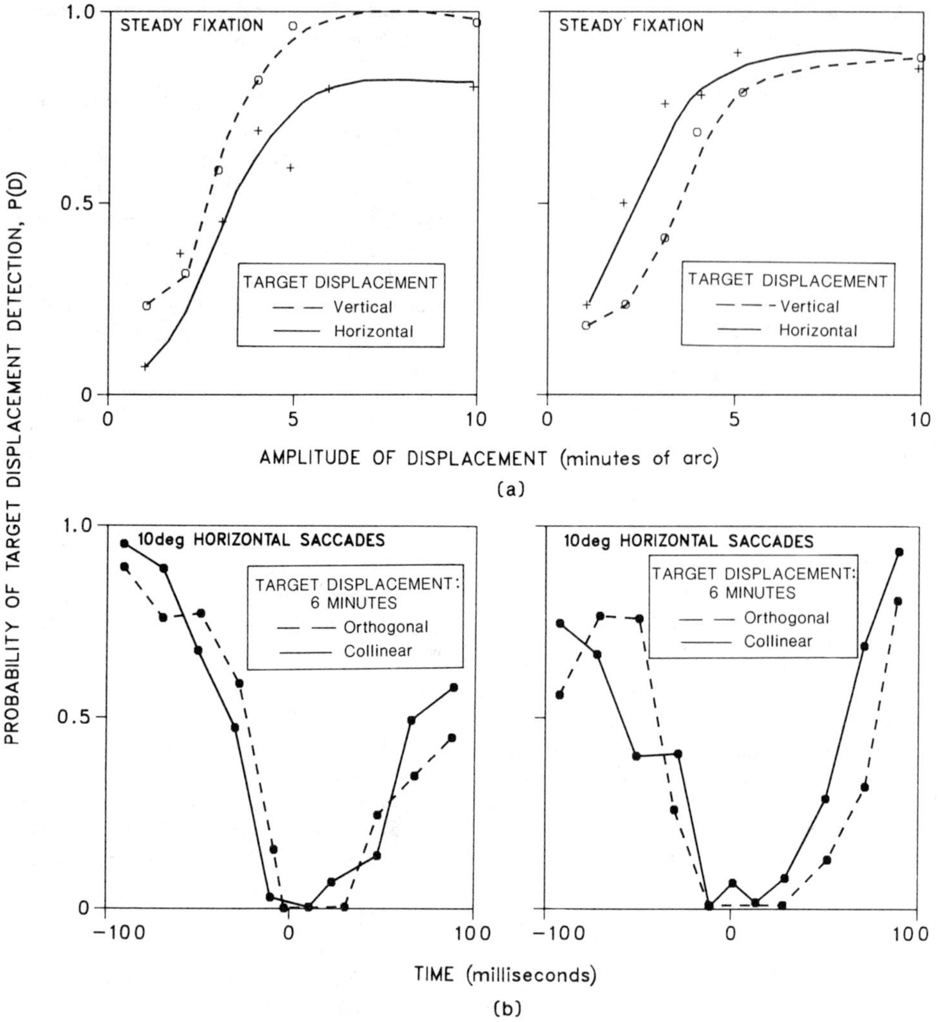

Figure 17.6. Detection of target displacements during fixation and during a saccade. (a) Vertical and horizontal target displacement detection sensitivity for subjects BK (left column) and SS (right column) during steady fixation. Dashed lines represent vertical target displacement; solid lines, horizontal displacement. Probability of target displacement detection *P(D)* is plotted on the ordinate, and amplitude of displacement is represented on the abscissa in minutes of arc. (b) Detection of collinear and orthogonal target displacements of 6 min arc with 10° horizontal saccades. Dashed lines represent orthogonal displacement; solid lines, collinear displacement. Probability of target displacement detection is plotted on the ordinate, and time, in milliseconds, with respect ot the initiation of eye movement, on the abscissa. Negative time refers to time before the eye movement begins. Target displacements of 2–3 min arc were detected 50% of the time during steady fixation. Target displacements of 6 min arc were rarely detected if they occurred during the interval of maximum suppression of a saccade. (From L. Stark, R. Kong, S. Schwartz, D. Hendry, & B. Bridgeman, Saccadic suppression of image displacement, *Vision Research, 16*. Copyright 1976 by Pergamon Press, Ltd. Reprinted with permission.)

quality of the eye motion information. An extreme and early version of this view was stated by Dodge (1904) who argued that the perceptual system receives *no* information at all about the pursuit movements of the eye and consequently a moving stimulus, accurately tracked, will never appear to be moving. Dodge attempted to validate this conclusion with the report that an intermittently luminous point, fixated while the observer rotates his or her head slowly from side to side, does not appear to move. Dodge purposely chose a compensatory pursuit eye movement, rather than pursuit elicited by a slowly moving target, to eliminate the retinal velocity signal that normally precedes the initiation of "voluntary" pursuit, which he believed to be the sole source of motion information during pursuit.

The stimulus conditions were, however, ill chosen. Dodge managed to create a situation in which, given the appropriate head and eye movement information, position constancy ought to prevail. The fact that his observers reported that the fixated stimulus was stationary then could either reflect what Dodge thought it reflected, the absence of any pursuit eye movement information or, more likely, the operation of a position constancy process involving eye and head motion information. In fact, we know from Wallach's work on the constancy of visual direction that there is a high degree of constancy during head rotation. Furthermore, a study, which examined perceived stability during intervals in which an observer rotated his or her head from side to side while fixating a stationary stimulus, yielded results

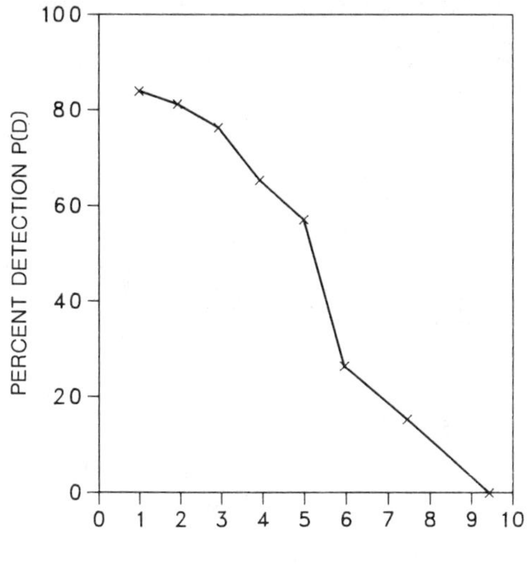

Figure 17.7. Percentage detection versus size of saccade for a 2° target displacement. Decrease in *P*(*D*) as eye movements increase in size. Data are plotted for two target displacements occurring between 10 msec before and 40 msec after the start of a saccade. As saccade size increases, the probability that target displacement is detected decreases. Target displacements less than a third of the amplitude of the saccade are usually not detected. (From B. Bridgeman, D. Hendry, & L. Stark, Failure to detect displacement of the visual world during saccadic eye movements, *Vision Research, 15*. Copyright 1975 by Pergamon Press, Ltd. Reprinted with permission.)

demonstrating that only at the point at which compensatory eye movements are no longer possible, because of the extremeness of the head turn, does a stationary target suddenly appear to lurch into motion with the head (Mack, Fendrich, & Fisher, 1974). It would appear therefore that Dodge's demonstration not only fails to support his claim but supports an opposite one.

There are a number of both early and recent studies relevant to the issue of perceived motion and stability during pursuit. Filehne (1922) reported that stationary objects whose images are caused to displace over the retina, when the eye tracks a moving object, appear to move. This apparent failure of position constancy is now known as the *Filehne illusion* (Stoper, 1967). Filehne reported not only that stationary background objects appeared to move but that the apparent velocity of the pursued stimulus was half of its objective velocity. This underrestimation of target velocity during pursuit was first reported by Fleischl (1882) and is known as the *Aubert-Fleischl paradox*. Filehne believed that both the loss of position constancy for background objects and the underestimation of pursuit target velocity resulted from the fact that the objective motion of the target was shared equally between background and target; that is, the target appeared to move at one-half its objective velocity while the background moved at the same velocity in the opposite direction. Both the Filehne illusion and the Aubert-Fleischl paradox point to disturbances in the perception of motion and rest during pursuit.

The Filehne illusion has been attributed to the fact that the perceptual system fails to evaluate image displacements of the nontracked objects in terms of pursuit eye movement information, although this information is assumed to add to or account for motion of the tracked, retinally stable stimulus (Stoper, 1967, 1973). This is a modified version of the Dodge hypothesis. The Filehne illusion has also been attributed to an underregistration of pursuit eye movement velocity and to the salience of the relative displacement between tracked and background objects when they are adjacent (Mack & Herman, 1973, 1978).

Stoper (1967, 1973) reports that the perception of stroboscopic motion during pursuit depends on the stimulation of two separate retinal loci, which distinguishes stroboscopic motion during pursuit from stroboscopic motion during saccades. Stroboscopic motion during saccades has been found to depend on stimulation from two apparently different locations in space (Rock & Ebenholtz, 1962). In both the Rock and Ebenholtz and the Stoper studies actual spatial location was isolated from retinal location. In Stoper's study, modeled on Rock and Ebenholtz, two points were successively flashed while the observer pursued a moving target. If the flashes emanated from two different places in space but fell on the same retinal position, no stroboscopic motion was reported. If the flashes emanated from the same or nearly the same place in space but stimulated different retinal positions, stroboscopic motion was likely to be reported. These data were the primary grounds for Stoper's conclusion that the extraretinal signal is not used in evaluating image displacements.

In another study (Stoper, 1967) that examined perceived position during pursuit, the data revealed increasing position constancy with increasing separation between judged target and tracking stimulus, or, with what amounted to the same thing, increasing time between the presentation of the two stimuli whose positions were being reported. During tracking, observers judged whether a second flashed stimulus appeared to the left or right of one presented earlier. With an interstimulus interval of 306 msec, the mean loss of constancy was 76%, whereas it was only 36.2% when the interstimulus interval was 1734 msec.

Two other experiments examining the Filehne illusion support a different account of perceived position and motion during pursuit (Mack & Herman, 1973, 1978; see also Festinger, Sedgwick, & Holtzman, 1976). In both these studies the point of subjective stability (PSS) for background stimuli was determined during intervals in which the observer tracked a moving stimulus. Observers reported whether the background stimulus appeared to move and the direction of the motion. A nulling procedure was used. The background stimulus moved at some fraction of the speed of the tracked target until the PSS was located. In the earlier study (1973) the background stimulus consisted of a large patterned array, which filled the observer's visual field. In the later study (1978) the background was reduced to a single point to determine the extent to which the apparent movement of the background might have been reduced in the earlier study, by the tendency of the large surrounding stimulus to appear stationary (Duncker, 1929; see also Section 4).

The results of the study with the large background array (1973) revealed a small position constancy loss during pursuit, amounting to about 19%. Tracking target speed was either 3 or 10.5°/sec. In either case the background motion in the direction of target motion was correctly reported when its velocity fell between 3/8 and 1/2°/sec. Background motion in the opposite direction was consistently reported even at the slowest speeds. The later experiment (1978) in which the background was reduced to a single point yielded somewhat different results. If the background stimulus, presented when the tracking target reached the midpoint of its path, remained visible for the remainder of the tracking (1.2 sec), the loss of position constancy was less than if the background stimulus presentation was very brief (0.2 sec). Tracking target velocity was 5°/sec, and again a

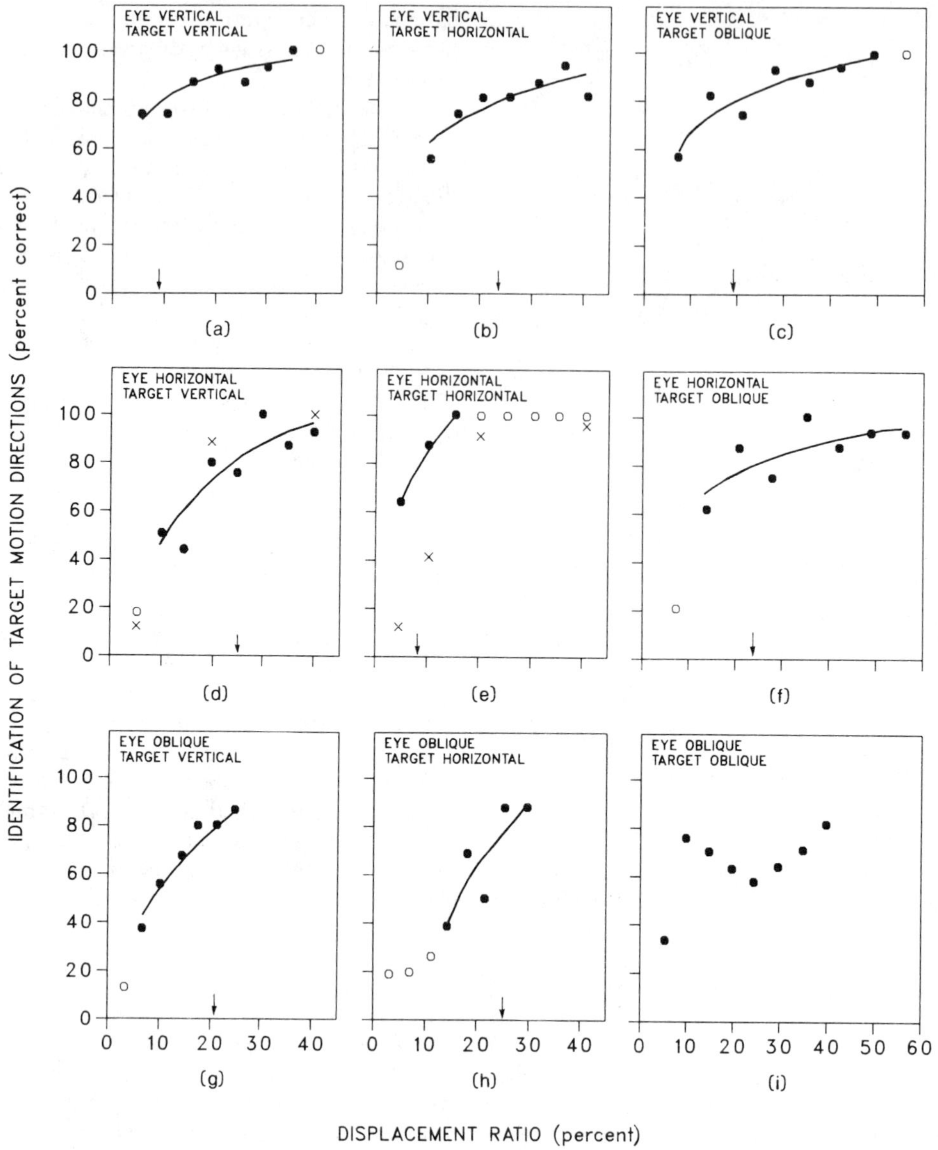

Figure 17.8. Direction-specific motion thresholds for abnormal image shifts during a saccade. Percentage correct identification of target motion directions as a function of displacement ratio (*DR*) for nine conditions of eye movement and target movement directions. Crosses represent data from Mack's (1970) experiment; arrows, the 80% thresholds. A ring 7° in diameter displayed on a CRT screen was moved during a saccadic eye movement. Thresholds were low when both the eye and target moved horizontally or vertically. Thresholds increased by a factor of 2 or more when the axis of target motion differed from that of the eye movement. (From W. Whipple & H. Wallach, Direction-specific motion thresholds for abnormal image shifts during saccadic eye movements, *Perception and Psychophysics*, 1978, *24*. Reprinted with permission.)

nulling procedure was used. The longer background presentation yielded a position constancy loss of 19%. Brief exposure of the background, however, yielded a 67% loss of constancy, which was comparable to the large loss reported by Stoper. These results are summarized in Figure 17.9.

The difference between these two conditions was attributed to the difference in the perceptual salience of the relative displacement between background and target in the two conditions. In both conditions the background stimulus first appeared aligned with the tracking target and, in the brief presentation condition, was visible only while adjacent to the tracking target. With longer presentations there was increasing separation between background and target, reducing the salience of the relative displacement, with the result that perceived position increasingly became a function of the relationship between eye and image motion information. When the relative displacement between tracking target and background stimulus was salient, it led to perceived background motion.

This explanation received strong support from data showing only a small position constancy loss during an interval in which the observer tracked an "invisible" target, as compared to the loss when the tracking target was visible. In both cases the background stimulus was present for only the *brief* interval, but when the tracking target was invisible, there, of course, could be no displacement between it and the background stimulus.

These results suggested a two-factor explanation of the disruption of perceived motion and position during pursuit. One

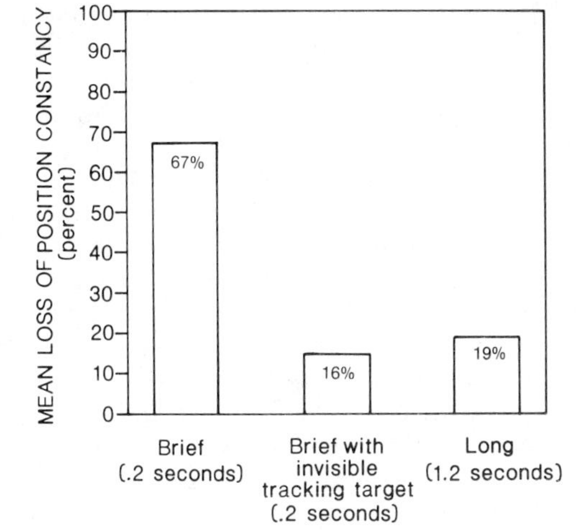

Figure 17.9. Position constancy loss for single background stimulus during pursuit of a moving target. Data are based on the mean of six observers. A 0.5° vertical line presented on a CRT screen (P 15) moved from left to right at 5°/sec over a 15° path. This was the pursuit target. When this target reached the middle of its path, a background stimulus appeared and was aligned with the pursuit target. The background stimulus was visible for either 0.2 sec (brief interval) or 1.2 sec (long interval) and moved either left or right at a velocity ranging 0–5°/sec. Eye movements were monitored by an SRI Double Purkinje Image Eye Tracker. Observers reported whether the background stimulus moved left, right, or was stationary. On trials in which the background was stationary, it appeared to be moving opposite the pursuit target on 61% of the trials with long exposure and on 58% of the trials with brief exposure. The mean background velocity judged stationary in the long-interval condition was 0.96°/sec in the same direction as the pursuit target, while in the brief condition it was 3.35°/sec. In a follow-up experiment (brief exposure with invisible tracking target) the background stimulus was presented during a 0.2-sec interval, during which the observer tracked in the absence of a visible target. Under these conditions the stationary background appeared to move on 67% of the trials and had to move 0.79°/sec in the direction of the pursuit eye movement to appear stationary. (From A. Mack & E. Herman, The loss of position constancy during pursuit eye movements, *Vision Research, 18*. Copyright 1978 by Pergamon Press, Ltd. Reprinted with permission.)

factor, which accounts for the modest loss of position constancy, is the underregistration of pursuit velocity. This underregistration is the basis for, and evidenced by, the Aubert-Fleischl paradox, the apparent slowing of a tracked target. If pursuit velocity is underregistered, stationary objects viewed during pursuit should appear to move against the direction of pursuit by about as much as the velocity is underregistered, assuming, of course, that the match between image and eye motion information is the basis of perceived motion or stability. The second factor, which seems to be responsible for the larger loss of position constancy, is the salience of the relative displacement between target and background when the two are adjacent.

Evidence for an underregistration of pursuit velocity comes from several sources. Mack and Herman (1973) found a high degree of correlation between the magnitude of the position constancy loss for background stimuli and the magnitude of the apparent slowing (Aubert-Fleischl paradox) of a tracked target, which was about 12%. Dichgans, Koener, and Voigt (1969) report that the perceived speed of a smoothly tracked target is 63% of its perceived speed when the eye is stationary. J. F. Brown (1931a) reports a ratio of 1.43 between perceived tracked and untracked target speed. Under somewhat different conditions Festinger, Sedgwick, and Holtzman (1976) found a far greater underestimation of velocity. Their data led them to conclude that the perceptual system has only poor information about pursuit. It has information that the eye is moving and its direction of motion. The system then inputs some low value for the speed of movement. In another careful study Miller (1980) reports that repetitive pursuit, pursuit of a target oscillating sinusoidally at 0.33 Hz, produces a 33% underregistration of pursuit amplitude, whereas nonrepetitive pursuit, pursuit of a target moving sinusoidally through only one-half a cycle, causes an 11% underestimation. The difference between the results of various investigations may be accounted for by Miller's findings about the difference between repetitive and nonrepetitive pursuit.

There is reason to conclude from the evidence reviewed that the perception of motion and position during pursuit is determined by both object- and subject-relative factors, and characteristically when the object-relative information is salient, it appears to mask or inhibit the subject-relative information if they conflict.

3.4. Motion Illusions and Pursuit Eye Movements

Correlative with the effects of eye movements on the detection of object motion and rest are a set of illusory motion phenomena associated with pursuit. The fact that these illusions are associated with pursuit, rather than with saccades, may reflect the difference in the source of the disruption of motion perception during these two kinds of eye motions. Two of these illusions have been discussed in Section 3.3, namely, the Filehne and the Aubert-Fleischl illusions.

3.4.1. Motion of the Afterimage. An afterimage or stabilized retinal image viewed in an otherwise dark field will appear to move if the observer engages in smooth pursuit eye movements during its observation (Heywood & Churcher, 1971; Kömmerell & Taumer, 1972; Mack & Bachant, 1969; Yasui & Young, 1975). Apart from the question of what stimulates pursuit in this situation, the phenomenon itself attests to the participation of pursuit eye movement information. It seems likely that the only reason a stabilized image appears to move when we move our eyes is that there is eye movement information that is not canceled by the appropriate retinal displacement information. This mismatch signals object motion. Furthermore, there is evidence that the perceived movement of the afterimage parallels the eye movement (Mack & Bachant, 1969). Saccades occurring during observation of an afterimage similarly generate perceived displacement, which is most likely stroboscopic in character because of the speed of the eye movement.

3.4.2. Perceived Motion of Random Dynamic Noise and Pursuit. Ward and Morgan (1978) report that if observers engage in smooth pursuit while viewing a dynamic random noise pattern, they will perceive a "vaguely defined area of the noise field . . . , perceptually detach itself from the background and move back and forth across the display with the eyes" (p. 158). As soon as the observer ceases to track, the target disappears. The investigators aptly attribute this phenomenon to the same factors responsible for the perceived motion of an accurately tracked moving stimulus or an afterimage. "The movement of the eye fails to induce movement of the contours on the retina, thereby producing the same feedback as that obtained when the eye tracks a real moving target" (p. 159). Again the absence of retinal displacement information in the presence of pursuit eye movement generates an illusory perception of motion that, in this instance, serves to organize a segment of the pattern into a distinct and coherent unit. An obvious critical aspect of this display is that no dot or set of dots in the display is distinguishable from any other.

3.4.3. Stroboscopically Lit Displays and Pursuit. There is at least one other illusory motion phenomenon associated with the *apparent* absence of retinal displacement during pursuit:

> If a row of dots or of other simple stimuli is observed in stroboscopic illumination, and a small continuous light source or finger is tracked beneath the row of dots, then the whole row jumps into apparent smooth movement in the same direction as the moving stimulus, despite the opposite direction of retinal image displacement—the retinal image of a stationary row of dots displaces in a direction opposite to and equal to that of the eye movement as does the image of any stationary object in the world. (Heywood, 1973, pp. 181–182)

This same phenomenon has been reported by at least two other investigators (LaMontagne, 1973; Stoper, 1967). The illusion occurs most easily when the motion of the tracking target is synchronized with the flashed presentation of the pattern. It depends both on tracking and on the phenomenal identity of the elements in the pattern. (The interflash and interdot intervals are also important.) If, every time the array is flashed, an element in it is aligned with the tracking target and no element is distinguishable from another, no retinal displacement signal is produced by the eye movement, which could cancel or match the eye movement signal, and so object motion is perceived. Figure 17.10 provides a schematic representation of the display used by LaMontagne.

3.4.4. Amplitude of Perceived Motion during Pursuit. The perceived *extent* of motion is reduced during tracking (Mack & Herman, 1972). These investigators found a 10–20% reduction in perceived extent of target motion (dependent on target velocity) when a target was tracked, compared to when it moved across the retina. Miller (1980) reports an 11% reduction for nonrepetitive pursuit and a 33% reduction for repetitive pursuit.

It is reasonable to assume that the factors responsible for the underestimation of velocity during pursuit are also responsible for the underestimation of amplitude of motion, since it is difficult to imagine an independent source of motion amplitude

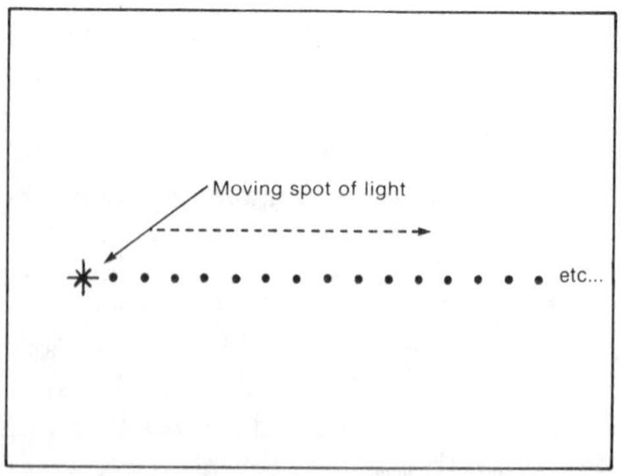

Figure 17.10. Schematic drawings of the basic stimulus setup for perceived motion during pursuit of a stroboscopically lit array. The observer tracked a small moving spot across a row of 250 static black dots that were stroboscopically illuminated. If flash rate was similar to the rate at which the pursuing eye passed across the dots, the static dot array appeared to move with the eye. (From C. Lamontagne, A new experimental paradigm for the investigation of the secondary system of human visual motion perception, *Perception*, 1973, *2*. Reprinted with permission.)

information when the tracking stimulus is all that is visible, as is the case in these studies. Data showing that the underestimation of extent is highly correlated with the underestimation of velocity support this speculation (Mack & Herman, 1972). If, as seems likely, the extraretinal signal associated with pursuit encodes rate and direction of motion, rather than position, then when a single moving point is tracked in an otherwise homogeneous field, information about tracked distance must be derived from velocity information and, if it is underestimated, amplitude must be correlatively underestimated.

3.4.5. Shape of Motion Path and Pursuit. Hayashi (1971) reports that the diameter of the perceived path of a tracked spot describing a circle is underestimated and the shape of the motion path is distorted into an ellipse or shrinking spiral. Rotational speeds between 0.2 and 1 Hz were tested. The rate of apparent underestimation decreased as velocity increased, and the diameter of the apparent path decreased as the number of rotations of the spot increased. Judgments following observation of one rotation decreased apparent diameter by about 50%, while judgments following observations of ten rotations reduced apparent diameter by 75%. Eye movements were not monitored, so it is difficult to determine to what extent these path distortions were a function of pursuit eye movements.

Another investigation of the perceived distortions associated with tracking a circularly moving spot, which included electrooculographic monitoring of eye movements, yielded somewhat different results (Coren, Bradley, Hoenig, & Girgus, 1975). The rotational velocities tested ranged between 0.18 and 5.2 Hz. The diameter of the actual path of motion was 20°. The investigators report virtually no underestimation of diameter at the slowest rotational velocity and maximum underestimation, which was about 40%, at rotational velocities of 1.13 and 1.73 Hz. With faster rotational velocities, apparent diameter increased toward veridicality, and at the fastest velocities, no distortions were reported. Thus at the fastest and slowest velocities, no distortions occurred. The eye movement records revealed accurate tracking at the slowest velocities. As velocity increased, smooth pursuit was increasingly interrupted by saccades, until at the fastest velocity, tracking was accomplished by saccadic eye movements only. At the rotational velocities which produced maximum shrinkage, smooth pursuit accounted for less than 60% of the eye motion (the remainder involved saccades). The data also revealed that the diameter of the tracked path decreased as velocity increased, so that at a rotational velocity of 1.73 Hz, the diameter of the tracked path was only 40% of the diameter of the actual path. The investigators conclude that it is only "the path the eye smoothly tracks which is utilized in the perceptual computation of path diameter" (p. 53). This conclusion is based on the assumption that the principal function of smooth pursuit is to match target velocity, so that the system is relatively insensitive to retinal error information below some threshold value.

This reasoning is at odds with the view that pursuit velocity is consistently underregistered, and the data showing no underestimation of perceived path diameter at the slowest rotational velocities are discrepant with reports of the underestimation of the velocity and extent of motion reported by other investigators (Aubert, 1886; Dichgans et al., 1969; Mack & Herman, 1972; Miller, 1980). The reasons for this discrepancy are not obvious.

There are other reports of distortions of motion path during pursuit. Fujii (1943) described a set of experiments in which the path of a point moving about the perimeter of a square, a circle, or a triangle is misperceived. Festinger and Easton (1974) refer to this as the Fujii illusion in a paper reporting the results of an investigation of these phenomena. Festinger and Easton examined the Fujii illusion while simultaneously recording eye motions. The observed target traveled along a square path at uniform speeds of 3 and 18°/sec. Analysis of eye records revealed that the eye never accurately tracks the spot as it turns the corners of the square. Although the spot changes direction abruptly, the eye does so only gradually, continuing to move for a period in the direction of the previous motion. The investigators point out that during these intervals, the motion path of the spot on the retina would be "an indentation from the corner, similar to what is reported perceptually" (p. 52). If the assumption is made that information about pursuit is based solely on the efferent signal to the eye muscles and that the efferent command to the eyes differs from the actual path of the eyes in the neighborhood of the corners, then eye movement information will fail to match the retinal image motion, and the perceived distortion occurs. Figure 17.11 pictures the typical distortion obtained by these investigators when the tracked point described a square.

The same argument was proposed earlier to account for a different but related illusion associated with pursuit (Mack, Fendrich, & Sirigatti, 1973). If a target moving at a constant velocity is tracked by the eyes and comes to an abrupt stop, it will appear to rebound sharply backward. Investigation of this *rebound illusion* revealed that the eye continues to track, that is, overshoots the target, at the point at which the target stops abruptly. If we again assume that the information about eye movement is derived solely from the efferent command signal to the extraocular muscles and that the efferent system signals the eye to stop at the moment the target stops, then there would be no extraretinal information about the overshoot of the eye muscle system. Because the eye continues to move after the target has stopped, its image displaces on the retina, and in the absence of the appropriate eye movement information, this

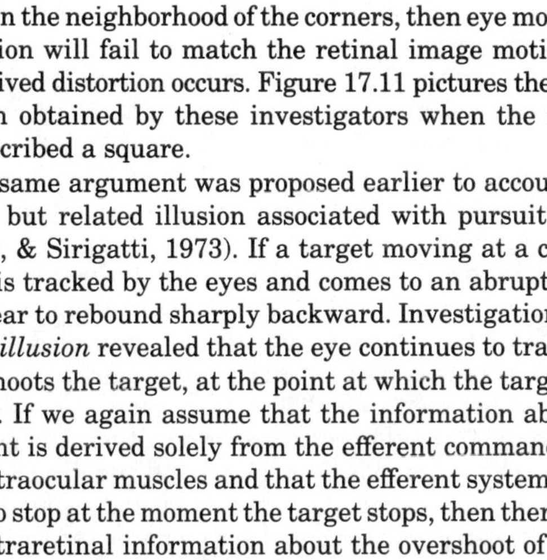

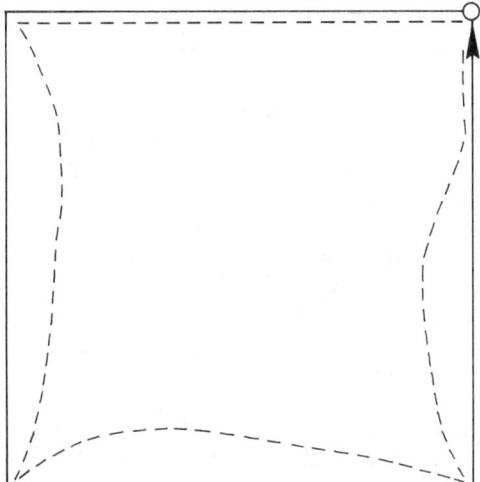

Figure 17.11. Perception of the path of a tracked target moving in a square path. A single spot displayed on an oscilloscope moved in a square path at frequencies between 0.5 and 0.6 Hz and was tracked by the eye. Distortions of the perceived shape occurred at the corners and presumably are the result of faulty eye movement information. (From L. Festinger & A. M. Easton, Inferences about the efferent system based on a perceptual illusion produced by eye movements, *Psychological Review, 81*. Copyright 1974 by the American Psychological Association. Reprinted with permission.)

image displacement results in the perceived rebound of the target. Experimental support for this reasoning was provided by data showing that the overshoot of the eye was commensurate with the magnitude of perceived target rebound.

Finally, there is a set of experiments showing no distortion in the perceived path of a tracked point (Rock & Halper, 1969). An opaque black screen with a narrow vertical aperture was moved over a luminous curved line, revealing the contour as it moved. Observers either tracked the luminous element within the slit or fixated a stationary luminous point; next they matched the shape of the figure, revealed through the slit, to a figure present among a group of similar shapes. Correct identification was frequent in both conditions, and there were no differences between fixation and pursuit. It is possible that this failure to find any path distortion associated with pursuit in this study may have been due to the testing technique, which may have been insensitive to relatively subtle path distortions.

3.4.6. The Pendular-Whiplash Illusion. If one of two luminous points at opposite ends and equidistant from the center of a counterbalanced, swinging pendulum is tracked, it appears to move at a slower velocity and through a smaller angle than the untracked point. Furthermore, at the extreme positions, the tracked point may appear to stop while the untracked one continues to move (whiplash). This perception occurs despite the fact that points equidistant from the center of rotation of a pendulum move through equal arcs at equal velocities. The phenomenon was first reported by Dodge (1904) and subsequently labeled the *pendular-whiplash illusion* by Carr (1907), in a paper reporting the outcome of an investigation of the illusion. At about the same time it was also the subject of another study (Ford, 1910). More recent studies have not been published.

Dodge (1904, 1910) took the illusion as evidence for "the utter inability of the pursuit movement either to subserve the perception of motion of the fixated point or to correct the exaggerated data from the displacement of the retinal image of the non fixated point" (p. 14). Carr (1907) offered a different explanation, having to do with the afterimages generated by the tracked and untracked points, which is sufficiently untenable to be ignored.

Ford (1910) reported that the nontracked target appears to move about twice as far as the tracked target and faster, but no velocity data were reported. He attributed the illusion to attentional factors, an explanation not well supported by his findings. The illusion is another instance of a motion distortion associated with pursuit, and as such was the subject of an unpublished series of experiments in our laboratory. In most of these experiments, pendulum motion was simulated on a fast phosphor oscilloscope. Two vertically separated points of light swept sinusoidally from left to right out of phase at 0.5 Hz. Eye movements were monitored. The tracked stimulus moved through an angle of 2°, while the untracked stimulus could be moved through a variable angular distance ranging from 0 to 2° in steps of 0.167°. The point of subjective equality (PSE) for the extent of motion of the tracked and untracked points was established by varying the distance through which the untracked point moved. In another experiment the observers also reported the apparent distance one or the other of the points moved by adjusting the distance between two horizontally separated points presented at the end of each trial (see Figure 17.12).

In the first experiment, the two points appeared to be moving through equal distances, when the untracked point traveled through 46% of the distance actually traveled by the tracked point. The illusion obtained in the second experiment was even

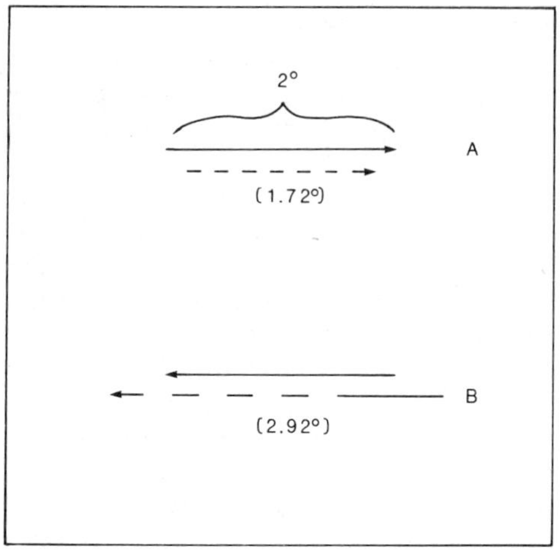

Figure 17.12. Points *A* and *B* move sinusoidally in opposite directions. Solid lines indicate actual motion; dashed arrows, perceived motion when point *A* is tracked. The tracked point appears to move through a smaller extent (1.72°) than the actual motion extent (2°). The untracked point may continue to be seen as moving when the tracked point stops and is seen moving through a larger extent (2.92°) than the actual extent (2°).

larger. The two points appeared to move through equal distance when the untracked point moved through only 33% of the distance of the tracked point. (Two of the four observers in the second experiment were highly practiced in pursuit, which may have accounted for the increment in the illusion.) The mean underestimation of the distance through which the tracked point moved was relatively small, less than 12%, which was also true in other experiments in this series, in which perceived extent of motion was measured. The mean overestimation of the distance through which the untracked point moved, however, was quite large, more than 46%, which again was true in other experiments. Clearly there was no parity between perceived overestimation and underestimation of path length. Overestimation was greatest when the untracked point was actually stationary.

These data suggest that this illusion cannot be accounted for only by an underregistration of pursuit eye movement velocity, for if this were the case, either the underestimation would have had to be greater or the overestimation smaller. Since the conditions in which the illusion occurs are closely related to those which produce the Filehne illusion (in both there is a tracked and untracked stimulus, and in both perceived motion is added to the untracked stimulus), it seems reasonable to propose that the two illusions have similar causes. If so, the underestimation of the perceived extent and velocity of the tracked point's motion would be a function of the underregistration of pursuit velocity, while the perceived overestimation of the extent and velocity of the untracked stimulus would be primarily a function of the salience of its displacement relative to the tracked stimulus. The finding that the illusory overestimation of movement path is greatest when the untracked stimulus is stationary supports this analysis, since it remains most adjacent to the tracked point in this location. Although nothing in the data is inconsistent with this explanation, further work is necessary to validate it.

3.4.7. Autokinetic Motion. Autokinetic motion (AKM) is by far the most widely studied and best-known motion illusion, attributed by some investigators to the eye movement system. Its origin dates back to observations of early astronomers who noticed that the same star appeared to be moving in different directions during the same period of time. When it became apparent that this *sternschwanken* was a frequent phenomenon with no apparent physical basis, it became the subject of laboratory investigation. The phenomenon was labeled *autokinetic motion* by Aubert (1886). If a dimly luminous stationary point is fixated in an otherwise dark field, after a brief period (ranging from several seconds to several minutes) it will appear to move. Autokinetic motion has been the subject of countless studies and several extensive reviews (Adams, 1912; Carr, 1907; Crone & Verduyn Lunel, 1969; Levy, 1972; Reinwald, 1952; Royce, Carran, Aftanas, Lehman, & Blumenthal, 1966). Despite the large number of investigations, there is no single accepted explanation of the phenomenon.

Reports of the speed, amplitude, and character of AKM vary considerably, partly as a function of the method of measurement of the illusion (Levy, 1972). Motions as large as 30° have been reported (Charpentier, 1886), while other investigators report a maximum of 16° of motion with an average between 3 and 4° (Graybiel & Clark, 1945). Reports of the speed of AKM vary even more widely. Pearce and Matin (1966), using a nulling technique, estimate the speed of AKM at 20 min arc/sec for primary fixation and 40 min arc/sec for fixation at an extreme angle of regard. Carr (1907) reports motion of 15°/sec, and Gregory and Zangwill (1963) report an angular velocity between 2 and 3°/sec. Graybiel and Clark (1945), using a measurement technique that involved a comparison between AKM and real motion, report that perceived speed averaged 12 min arc/sec and ranged between 10 and 50 min arc/sec.

Autokinetic motion is paradoxical motion. The light stimulus may appear to move considerably while displacing little or not at all (Carr, 1907; Gilbert, 1967), and there appears to be no relationship between speed and amplitude of motion. There are large individual differences in the magnitude, direction, and susceptibility to AKM. Graybiel and Clark (1945) report that 50% of a group of naive observers failed to report the illusion spontaneously. Alerting the observer to the illusion in advance is reported to sharply increase the likelihood that AKM will be reported. The initial motion perceived is likely to have a jerky quality, following which the motion appears quite smooth and continuous. The stimulus appears to glide around in the dark.

Fatigue and prolonged fixation increase the illusion, while the presence of other objects in the visual field decreases it. Suggestion or set can influence the direction of movement. Fatigue of neck and eye muscles also predictably influences the direction of AKM (Gregory & Zangwill, 1963). The position of the stimulus influences the illusion. A stimulus in the median plane is likely to require a longer period of initial fixation before the movement begins, and the direction of movement is not predictable. A stimulus placed at an extreme gaze angle will generally appear to move almost at once and in the same direction as the ocular deviation (Carr, 1907).

Explanations of the illusion fall into several distinct categories, two of which implicate eye movements. Investigations of the role of eye movements in the illusion have been extremely numerous (Adams, 1912; Barlow, 1952; Bourdon, 1902; Carr, 1907; Charpentier, 1886; DeSisto & McLaughlin, 1968; Exner, 1896; Guilford & Dallenbach, 1928; Hoppe, 1879; Jordan, 1968; Lehman, 1965; Matin & MacKinnon, 1964; Piggens, 1965; Skolnick, 1940; Vaegan, 1976). A review of the earlier work is presented in Skolnick (1940). Autokinetic motion has been attributed to uncompensated retinal displacements produced by involuntary drifts of the eye that occur during fixation, fixation nystagmus (Hoppe, 1879; Matin & MacKinnon, 1964; Vaegan, 1976). The principal support for this view is the finding that retinal stabilization of the autokinetic stimulus along the horizontal axis decreases reports of horizontal AKM (Matin & MacKinnon, 1964); that is, eliminating horizontal image displacement produced by horizontal eye drift is reported to decrease horizontal AKM sharply.

This explanation of the illusion faces some difficulties, however. It has difficulty explaining how very small fixational drifts, which are interrupted by corrective saccades, produce the appearance of smooth and continuous motion. Furthermore, since these drifts tend to be small, less than 50 sec arc (Nachmias, 1961), particularly when the target is in the median plane, it is necessary to assume not only that the slow phase of the nystagmus is unregistered but also that these small image displacements, less than 50 sec arc, engendered by these slow drifts mediate the perception of motion over quite large extents (between 2 and 30°). The report that a foveal afterimage and autokinetic target will appear to move together (Gregory & Zangwill, 1963; Levy, 1972) simply cannot be explained at all by this hypothesis. (Recent data collected in our own laboratory involving stabilization of an autokinetic target in either the horizontal or vertical axis so far fail to confirm the data reported by Matin & MacKinnon, 1964. On the contrary, as of 1983 we are finding an increase in reports of movement along the stabilized axis, which is consistent with the view that any eye motion in that direction should generate perceived motion because of the absence of image displacement, which, in turn, should elicit further eye movement in that direction, and so on. Since this work is still in progress and the methods of stabilization and AKM reports are different from those used by previous investigators, more work is needed to resolve the discrepancy in the findings. They are mentioned here only because this is, to our knowledge, the first attempt to replicate these important results.)

Another general account of AKM, which implicates eye movements, attributes the illusion to the corollary discharge (eye movement) signal associated with the control of the extraocular muscles. While the previous explanation rests on retinal afference (image motion) caused by actual involuntary drifts of the eye, this explanation rests on the efferent command signal necessary to maintain stable fixation, which is generally not associated with any actual eye motion. Thus both views share the Helmholtzian or von Holstian assumption that object motion is perceived when there is a mismatch between image and eye motion signals. They differ only in their assumptions about the source of the mismatch. Matin & MacKinnon attribute it to the absence of an efferent signal; Gregory and Zangwill to the absence of an afferent, image motion signal. A clear statement of this account of the illusion first proposed by Carr (1907) can be found in Gregory and Zangwill (1963). Any differential fatigue or imbalance of the eye muscles necessitates alterations in the command signals to maintain fixation. Since these signals serve to keep the eye still, they are unaccompanied by image displacements and, therefore, lead to illusory target motion. Following a period of extreme fixation, Gregory and Zangwill found that observation of a centrally located target light leads to AKM in the same meridian but opposite the direction of the ocular deviation. This supports their view.

A third account of AKM does not relate it to the eye motion system at all but attributes it to apparent shifts in egocentric position that are assumed to occur spontaneously when an observer is placed in a dark environment. If, for whatever reason, the observer experiences such a shift in position while viewing a stationary light point, the light must appear to move (Brosgole, 1967; Jordan, 1968). According to Brosgole, the observers perceive the target light moving opposite the direction of their own perceived shift in spatial position. This explanation is dubious for several reasons, not the least of which is the fact that there is no evidence that observers experience self movement. If perceived body shift were the cause of the illusion, then AKM ought to be in the same direction as the perceived egocentric shift, since if the target does not actually displace on the retina when the observer moves, this mismatch should signal motion in the direction of observer movement. Brosgole reports that a stationary point made to appear displaced to the left or right because of its relative displacement to a larger surrounding rectangular frame will appear to drift back to center after the frame is removed from the field. He takes this as support for his account of AKM. He reasons that the induced shift of the stationary target is the result of an apparent shift in median plane caused by the displacement of the frame (see Section 4.1.4). The apparent drift of the point back toward the objective median plane when the frame is extinguished is caused by the correlative shift in apparent egocentric position. There is little other evidence that explicitly supports this explanation of the illusion, and in its absence the explanation does not appear compelling. It seems possible that the phenomenon reported by Brosgole and described previously is not normal AKM. Furthermore, there is no reason to assume that brief periods of observation in the dark typically produce shifts in experienced egocentric position. Finally, this account would appear to have difficulty explaining the sharp reduction in AKM when a second point is introduced into the field. Does merely introducing a second point into the field eliminate shifts in egocentric position? It does not seem likely.

Autokinetic motion remains something of a puzzle. However, it seems safe to describe it as a subject- rather than object-relative motion illusion. This would seem to be established by the fact that the presence of a second visible stimulus either entirely eliminates or sharply reduces AKM. This must be because the presence of the additional stimulus provides object-relative information. The question remains whether it is the eye position information or image displacement that is the central source of the illusion.

4. OBJECT-RELATIVE MOTION PERCEPTION

Induced motion is the principal exemplar of perceived motion based on object-relative motion information. It depends for its occurrence on the presence of at least two objects or points in the visual field, one of which moves. The displacement of one object relative to the other is the source of the motion percept. It is more likely to be perceived when the elements in the display are viewed in an otherwise homogeneous field.

4.1. Two-Point Induced Motion

When the field contains only two points of light, one of which is at rest and the other moving, either or both points may appear to move. Duncker's (1929) classic paper on induced motion not only contains this observation but is a rich source of information about the phenomenon. This is the simplest case of induced motion. If the motion of the displacing stimulus is below the absolute motion threshold, then either or both stimuli may appear to move, and the direction of the perceived motion will be a function of the relative displacement between them. Duncker believed that when the motion of the moving point in this situation was below the subject-relative (absolute) motion threshold, the point fixated would most likely carry the perceived motion. A recent examination of two-point induced motion (Mack, Fendrich, & Fisher, 1975), however, failed to confirm this. The fixated and nonfixated and the moving and stationary stimuli were equally likely to appear moving. This was true when stimulus motion was below threshold as well as when stimulus motion was liminal. In all cases observers correctly reported the direction of relative displacement between stimuli. Thus if the point on the left moved right and motion was attributed to the right point, it appeared to move left. If the point on the left moved left, the point on the right appeared to move right.

4.2. Center-Surround Induced Motion

If instead of two points, one of the two stimuli in the field is larger and encloses the other, then regardless of which stimulus actually moves, only the enclosed stimulus will appear to move if stimulus motion is near or below threshold. Figure 17.13 pictures a typical center-surround induced motion display. If stimulus motion is clearly above threshold and it is the surrounding stimulus that moves, both center and surround may appear to move. The tendency to perceive the larger, surrounding stimulus as stationary and the enclosed, smaller stimulus as moving, when there is relative displacement between them, is generally considered an organizing principle that governs perception. The enclosing stimulus acts as the frame of reference for the enclosed, smaller stimulus. "That which is displaced relative to its phenomenal reference system, appears phenomenally moved" (Duncker, 1929, chap. 2, p. 204. All quotations have been translated by F. Heuer and D. Seaman).

4.3. Frame of Reference

There is considerable ambiguity concerning the appropriate definition of the term *frame of reference*. There is some evidence

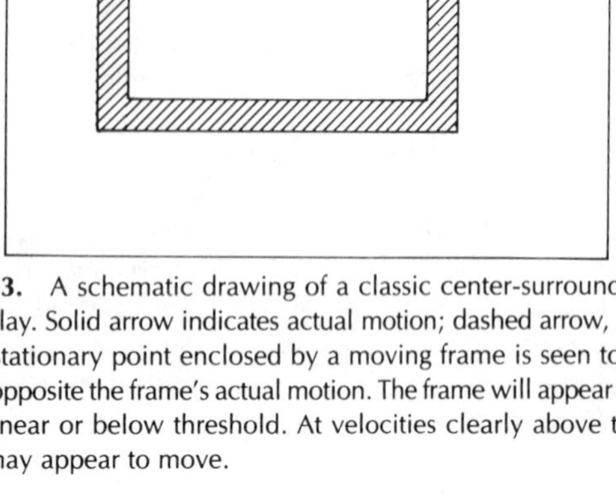

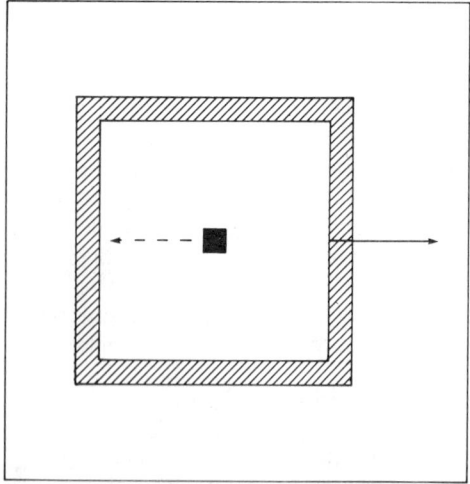

Figure 17.13. A schematic drawing of a classic center-surround induced motion display. Solid arrow indicates actual motion; dashed arrow, perceived motion. A stationary point enclosed by a moving frame is seen to move in a direction opposite the frame's actual motion. The frame will appear stationary if it moves near or below threshold. At velocities clearly above threshold, the frame may appear to move.

(Day, Millar, & Dickinson, 1979) that the background stimulus need not actually surround or enclose the figural stimulus. These investigators found that the frequency with which perceived induced motion of a point was reported was not affected by whether the point was inside or alongside a rectangular frame. On the other hand, Duncker observed that simply making one stimulus larger than another was not sufficient to turn it into a phenomenal frame of reference, that is, into the stimulus which would invariably be seen as stationary when its motion was below or marginally above threshold. This observation led him to conclude that the frame of reference must be a surrounding stimulus.

Despite a lack of clarity about the precise attributes of a frame of reference, the concept plays a central role in all accounts of induced motion, and although it appears that surroundedness is not a necessary attribute, it may well be a sufficient one.

4.4. Separation of Systems

The concept of frame of reference is invoked by Duncker to account for the perception of induced motion that occurs when the surrounding stimulus moves at suprathreshold speeds. He reported that when this is the case, *both* frame and enclosed stimulus may appear to move in opposite directions. He proposed that the motion of the frame was based on subject-relative information, with the observer as the frame of reference, at least when the display is observed in a dark field. The induced motion of the enclosed stimulus is based soley on its displacement relative to the enclosing surround. Duncker described this as a *separation of systems*. The enclosed stimulus and its surround comprise one motion system, the frame and the observer (or other more remote background objects) another. The systems are independent so that both the enclosed stimulus and the frame may appear to move despite the fact that the motion of either may be sufficient to account for the total displacement between them. Duncker (1929) saw this outcome as apparently paradoxical and referred to it as the *distance paradox*:

> If the observer perceives the veridical motion of the surround and simultaneously perceives induced motion of the enclosed stimulus, it follows directly that the sum of the opposed phenomenal movement excursions of the enclosed stimulus and the frame is greater than the phenomenal distance change between them, under certain circumstances, almost twice as great. This fact poses a "distance paradox." Through closer examination, however, this state of affairs is clarified. Namely, it must not be overlooked that under the experimental conditions like ours, the distance change between enclosed stimulus and frame is not the only relevant change that generally occurs. There occurs, in addition, still another distance change between the frame and the surround of the room and the frame and the egocentric system. Although the induction stimulus undergoes its phenomenal movement solely as a result of its distance change with respect to the frame, the frame, on the other hand, receives its phenomenal movement relative to the surround of the room and to the egocentric system. This can only mean that the frame owes its phenomenal movement directly to these systems which are of no significance to the phenomenal movement of the induction stimulus, and, on the contrary, are even obtrusive. (chap. 1, pp. 196–197)

The distance paradox is thus resolved by the notion of separation of systems. If the frame and enclosed stimulus are luminous and viewed in an otherwise dark environment, as is the case in most induced motion studies, then the separation of systems is between subject- and object-relative frames of reference. Since these motions are mediated by different kinds of information, it is no longer paradoxical to perceive both the induced motion and the actual motion of the frame even though this means perceiving more motion than is present in the display.

Data have recently been presented that argue against the occurrence of the distance paradox (Rock, Auster, Schiffman, & Wheeler, 1980). These investigators report that if the motion of the surrounding stimulus (a luminous rectangle) is perceived at the same time induced motion of the enclosed stimulus (a luminous point) is perceived, then the motion of the frame generally will be perceived as much less than if no induced motion were perceived. Furthermore, they report that at frame speeds ranging from 0.44 to 1.33°/sec, the calculated combined perceived displacement of both point and rectangle, when both were perceived to move, was not significantly greater than the perceived displacement when only the frame appeared to move or only the point appeared to move. (On control trials the point moved and the frame was stationary.) On many induction trials, particularly at the slower velocities, the frame was not perceived to move at all even though its motion was suprathreshold.

These findings led Rock and his collaborators (1980) to reject the notion of separation of systems and to propose an *apportionment hypothesis*, which states:

> The relative displacement is apportioned phenomenally to either the induced object, the inducing object or both. The objective motion of the inducing object is thus, in whole or in part, transferred to the induced object. Thus excess phenomenal motion does not occur. (p. 391)

Data reported by others are at odds with those reported by Rock and colleagues (1980). Gogel and Koslow (1971) examined the effects of a depth separation between inducing and induction stimuli and report results that support Duncker's original observations. As in the Rock study, the induction stimulus was a luminous rectangle enclosing a luminous point. On control trials only the point moved, while on the induction trials only the frame moved. In either case the speed of movement was 1.27°/sec, which is quite close to one of the speeds used in the Rock study. At the end of each trial, the observer reported the distance through which the frame and point had appeared to move. On induction trials the frame moved an average of 16.51 cm. The median perceived movement of frame and point was 15.24 and 17.78 cm, respectively. Thus a total of 33.02 cm of displacement was reported although the actual displacement was 16.51 cm. In the corresponding control trials in which the point moved through 16.51 cm and the frame was stationary, the median perceived displacement was 19.30 cm.

There are a number of differences in procedure which conceivably might account for the sharp differences in outcomes. Rock and colleagues speculate that the differences might be a function of the difference in the duration of a single trial. In the Gogel and Koslow study a trial lasted 30 sec, during which time the moving stimulus oscillated back and forth repeatedly. In the Rock and coworkers study a trial lasted only 9 sec and the moving stimulus traveled in one direction only. The speculation is that, during the longer repetitive oscillation, attention might have shifted from frame to point and there may have been moments when only frame or only point appeared to move. This may then have led the observers to assume that both stimuli moved throughout a trial. This speculation is itself based on the assumption that shifts in attention have predictable effects on perceived induced motion, an assumption for which no evidence is cited. Another difference in procedure, which Rock and coworkers consider important, is the difference in the question asked the observer at the end of each trial. In the Rock study, observers were asked to report the motion of either the frame or the point and were not aware at the start of a trial which stimulus would be reported on. In the Gogel and Koslow study, observers reported on each stimulus at the end of every trial. However, a later experiment by Gogel (1979) confirms his own earlier finding even though in the more recent study, the observer reported on the motion of only the frame or only the point on any single trial. This would therefore seem to rule out this difference as the critical one.

Using a somewhat different display, Wallach and colleagues (1978) also report that observers perceive full induced motion while perceiving the motion of the induced stimulus. There is therefore some reason to question the Rock and colleagues rejection of the concept of separation of systems and to question the conclusion that induced motion is simply motion subtracted from the induction stimulus.

4.5. Velocity of the Induction Stimulus

Duncker (1929) observed that increases in the velocity of the induction stimulus are associated with decreases in the magnitude and robustness of induced motion, particularly if the stationary stimulus is fixated. Results reported by Rock and colleagues (1980) confirm this observation. There were 65% fewer reports of induced motion at the fastest speed tested (1.33°/sec) than at the slowest speed (0.44°/sec). Gogel (1979), however, reports no decrease in the perceived magnitude of induced motion with frame speeds of 2.85°/sec as compared to frame speeds of 0.17°/sec. In this experiment the *extent* of motion of the frame was held constant. Duncker reports that the breakdown in induced motion occurs with frame speeds between 4 and 11°/sec. He reports strong induced motion with a frame speed of 1°/sec. Thus again there are discrepancies in reported data, although there appears to be general agreement that there are frame speeds too high to induce motion. Duncker attributes the breakdown of induced motion with high frame velocities to a breaking of the connection between frame and enclosed stimulus such that the frame no longer serves as the reference for the enclosed stimulus. When this occurs, the behavior of the enclosed stimulus is determined by its relation to the observer, that is, by the subject-relative information, and is perceived as stationary.

Although high velocities of frame motion inhibit induced motion, stroboscopic motion of the frame does not, despite the fact that the velocities of stroboscopic motion are extremely high. Duncker devotes an entire chapter of his monograph to a description of experiments on induced motion generated by stroboscopically displaced frames. Because the velocity of stroboscopic displacement is high, frame motion is always perceived in these displays, If a frame is displaced stroboscopically to the left, and enclosed stationary point appears displaced to the right. This observation has been repeated many times (see, e.g., Wong & Mack, 1981). Why fast motion of a continuously displacing frame inhibits induced motion, whereas the much faster displacements associated with stroboscopic displacements do not, remains an unanswered question. It is difficult to imagine, however, that stroboscopically induced motion is motion subtracted from the frame's motion.

4.6. Separation between Induction Target and Frame

The amount of separation between target and frame has a significant influence on induced motion; the greater the separation, the weaker the induced motion. Gogel has demonstrated this adjacency effect in several experiments (Gogel & Koslow, 1971, 1972; Gogel & MacCracken, 1979; Gogel & Tietz, 1976). Introducing a depth separation between target and frame decreases the induced motion of the target (Gogel & Koslow, 1972). In a display in which two frames are present, located at different depths and moving counterphase, the depth separation between a particular frame and target decreased its contribution to the induced motion of the stationary target.

4.7. Perceived or Retinal Adjacency between Target and Frame

Is it retinal or perceived adjacency between target and frame that is critical for induced motion? The question is important because it is relevant to the more general issue of the level of processing responsible for induced motion. Do prior perceptions play a role in induced motion? The outcomes of several experiments by Gogel and his collaborators suggest that perceived, not retinal, adjacency is the important factor. In one experiment (Gogel & Koslow, 1972) in which two frames located at different depths from the induction target moved in opposite directions, one of the frames was larger than the other. The smaller of the two frames was always retinally adjacent to the target. If retinal adjacency were critical, the smaller of the frames should consistently control induced motion regardless of the perceived depth separation between target and frame. The induction target was placed either midway between the frames or in the same plane as one of the frames. The effect of the large frame increased significantly when the target was positioned at the same distance. (The visual angle subtended by the larger frame was always greater than that of the smaller frame, regardless of its depth location.)

If perceived, rather than retinal, adjacency plays a role in determining which of several simultaneously present surrounds at different depths governs the induced motion of an enclosed stimulus, it is possible that perceived, rather than retinal, adjacency between enclosed stimulus and surround influences the induced motion. A demonstration described by Wallach (1959, 1965) addresses this issue.

4.8. Wallach's Demonstration of Separation of Systems

The demonstration by Wallach led to an elaboration of Duncker's notion of separation of systems. Wallach's display consisted of three elements (see Figure 17.14). A stationary point was surrounded by a horizontally moving rectangle that, in turn, was surrounded by a vertically moving circle. The motion of the two concentric frames was below threshold, above threshold, or stroboscopic. If motion was above threshold or stroboscopic, the vertical motion of the circle was correctly perceived. The rectangle appeared to move obliquely, as a result of its objective horizontal motion and the vertical motion induced by the circle. The point appeared to move horizontally opposite the actual motion of the rectangle.

Given this outcome, the induced motion of the stationary point must be entirely a function of its *retinal* displacement relative to the adjacent square, rather than of its displacement relative to the square's perceived motion, which is oblique, the actual motion of the circle, or the motion of both surrounds. On the basis of this demonstration, Wallach concluded that the induced motion of the point is an instance of separation of systems

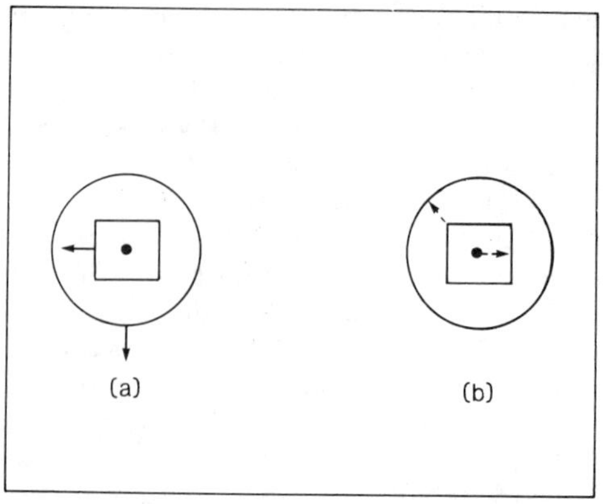

Figure 17.14. A schematic drawing of Wallach's separation of systems. (a) The actual motion. The circle moves down as the rectangle moves left. The dot is stationary. (b) The perceived motions when actual motions are slow. The circle appears stationary. The rectangle appears to move obliquely up, and the dot appears to move to the right. The perceived motion of the stationary point is a function of its displacement relative to the adjacent square and is not a function of the displacement relative to the perceived motion of the surround. (From H. Wallach, *On perception*, Quadrangle Press, 1976. Copyright Random House. Reprinted with permission.)

where the retinally adjacent surround alone governs the point's induced motion. It also stands as evidence against the hypothesis that induced motion is a function of the displacement of the induction target relative to the *perceived* motion of the surround. If the induced motion of the point were a function of the perceived motion of the square, its perceived path of motion would have to be oblique opposite the perceived oblique motion of the square. This never occurs.

Repeated observation of Wallach's three-element display in our own laboratory by many subjects, however, indicates that the observations Wallach reported may not be typical. Subjects more frequently report that the point appears to move vertically opposite the motion of the circle or obliquely opposite the motions of both surrounds.

The fact that Wallach's observations are not easily duplicated is supported by another study (Bassili & Farber, 1977). These investigators report that observations of a display similar to that described by Wallach yielded different results. Observers tended to report that the stationary point moved vertically, opposite the motion of the outermost circular frame. Brosgole (1968) using a somewhat different display consisting of two concentric rectangles, one larger than the other, which moved in opposite directions, found that the larger or outermost rectangle controlled the induced motion of the enclosed induction target. Thus the evidence as it now stands would seem to suggest that separation of systems as defined by Wallach is difficult to obtain. In addition, these failures to duplicate Wallach's observations do not support Gogel's conclusion that perceived adjacency is an important factor in determining whether the motion of a surround will induce motion. The circle is both perceptually and retinally more remote than the rectangle. Nevertheless, it frequently governs the perceived motion of the point. More research is needed to isolate what attributes define the frame of reference for induced motion, particularly when there are multiple frames.

4.9. Individual Differences in Induced Motion

A consistent finding in every study of induced motion is the marked difference in reports given by subjects, which seems to result from the very nature of the phenomenon. A principal characteristic of induced motion which may, at least in part, account for these differences and the differences between the reports of various investigators is that it is based on what Wallach (1968) describes as a *cue conflict*. Induced motion entails a conflict between the subject- and object-relative determinants of motion of the induction target. It may be that the solution of this conflict is influenced by a variety of factors, including subtle differences in displays.

4.10. Rotary Induced Motion

Induced motion need not involve a distance change between visual stimuli. Duncker (1929) observed and studied the induced rotary motion of a patterned stationary disc produced by the rotation of a surrounding concentric-patterned annulus. An example of a rotary induced motion display is pictured in Figure 17.15. Both annulus and disc contained a series of regularly spaced radial lines. When the annulus was rotated at an angular velocity of 4°/sec around the stationary disc, the disc and surrounding annulus appeared to move in opposite directions. The rotary motion of the annulus causes no change in distance between annulus and disc but produces a directional change between the radial lines of the inner and outer stimuli. The orientation of the radial lines of the annulus displaces relative to the radial lines of the disc, and this purely configurational change appears to be the basis of the perceived induced motion.

To assess the magnitude of the induced motion, Duncker used a compensation method. The inner disc was rotated with increasing speed in the same direction as the rotating annulus until the point of subjective stability (PSS), or what Duncker describes as the *zone of indifference*, was determined. The zone of indifference consists of the disc velocities at which the observer perceives only slight tiltings of the inner disc to the left and right. With an annulus velocity of 8.44°/sec, the PSS for the disc was found to lie at 5.36°/sec (standard deviation: 34 min arc). If, instead of an inner disc, the annulus surrounded a single shaft that had the same length as the radius of the inner disc, a higher velocity was required for compensation. The PSS was found to lie at 7.53°/sec.

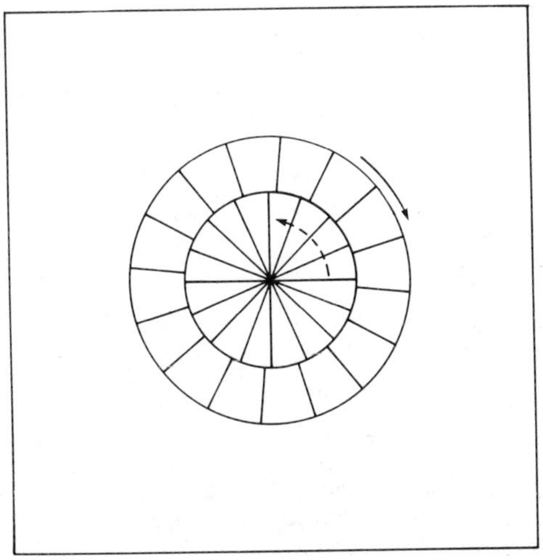

Figure 17.15. Rotary induced motion display. The inner disc is stationary; the surrounding annulus rotates. This induces an apparent opposite motion in the disc. Continuous line indicates real motion; dashed line, perceived motion. (From K. Duncker, Uber induzierte Bewegung, *Psychologische Forschung*, 1929, *22*. Reprinted with permission.)

As the speed of the rotary motion of the surround increased, Duncker again found predictable effects on the perception of the induced motion. With annulus velocity between 2 and 6°/sec, the motion of the annulus and disc appeared about equal. With rotational velocities greater than 6°/sec, the induced motion was increasingly inhibited until, at speeds of 36°/sec, the induced motion disappeared entirely. Of course, at this speed, the radial lines of the rotating annulus became completely blurred. Duncker (1929) also reports that increasing observation time beyond 3 sec also decreased perceived induced motion. He attributes both the effect of frame speed and observation time to the increased influence of subject-relative motion information:

> With constant exposure time and increasing inducing velocity . . . as well as with constant inducing velocity and increasing exposure time, the position change (the angle of rotation) which the induction object (more precisely the radii extending to the induction object), should have undergone in relation to the egocentric system (i.e., subject relatively) increases. In other words its position and direction liabilities increase proportionally with exposure time and inducing velocity. (p. 10)

Duncker continues:

> Also one must imagine that with the use of rotary movement, the egocentric system of the induction object must become "cheated" out of, not merely as otherwise, a change in position, but a change in direction as well. The egocentric system appears to be more sensitive to differences in direction than to differences in position. . . . (chap. 3, p. 216)

Duncker examined whether the rotation of the inner disc could induce motion in the surrounding stationary annulus even though he had already noted that the motion of a point within a frame failed to induce motion in the frame. If the surrounding annulus was placed forward of the inner disc, which was now located behind the annulus and served as its ground, and the disc was rotated, induced motion of the annulus was perceived. However, Duncker reports that this induced rotation is less strong than when the inducing stimulus surrounds the induction stimulus. For Duncker these observations illustrated the importance of the phenomenal frame of reference in induced motion. The ground or phenomenal frame of reference resists motion, while the figure, which is localized with reference to the ground, accrues motion.

There are two other recent reports of rotary induced motion (Anstis & Reinhardt-Rutland, 1976; Day, 1981). (The Anstis and Reinhardt-Rutland study is described in Chapter 16 by Anstis.) Day's results, for the most part, confirm Duncker's original observations. But unlike Duncker, he found *no* decrease in the frequency of induced motion reports with rotary induction velocities ranging between 4 and 15°/sec. Like Duncker, Day used a compensation technique to locate the PSS for the enclosed disc. With an annulus velocity of 8.7°/sec, he found a PSS of 2.41°/sec. He, too, reports weak induction if the disc is rotated and the annulus is stationary.

4.11. Induced Motion in Depth

Induced motion in depth is not a well-investigated phenomenon, but it has been studied by at least one investigator (Farne, 1972). Farne reports that two lines drawn on a stationary transparent sheet of glass appeared to move in depth opposite the motion in depth of a patterned surface that lay behind the glass. Greater induced motion in depth was perceived as observation time increased from 1 to 3 min and as frame velocity increased from 4 to 32 min arc/sec. Perceived induced motion in depth was also produced stroboscopically. The brief presentation of a circular outer contour 13.5 cm in diameter and an inner circular contour 6 cm in diameter was alternated with an outer circle of 10.5 cm and an inner circle, again, of 6 cm. All circles were concentric. With the appropriate temporal presentation rate, the outer circle was perceived to loom and recede in depth and to induce an opposite motion in depth in the inner circle. It should be noted that neither relative retinal displacement nor a configurational change can be the basis for this induced motion. It would seem that the apparent looming of the outer circle is the immediate cause of the induced counterlooming of the inner circle. If so, this is an instance in which a prior "perceptual" process, namely, that which leads to the apparent looming of the surround, is the basis for the induced motion, which therefore derives from a perceived, rather than a retinal, displacement between surround and target.

4.12. The Locus of Induced Motion

The finding that an apparently looming stimulus can induce motion in depth and the finding that perceived, rather than retinal, adjacency may govern induced motion (Gogel & Koslow, 1972) strongly suggest that induced motion is based on more central, rather than on peripheral, processing. This is supported by data reported by Bassili and Farber (1977) and corroborated by Day and Dickinson (1977), indicating that induced motion occurs with dichoptically presented stimuli. Bassili and Farber presented their observers with a dichoptic version of the Wallach three-element display. One eye viewed the outer circle and inner stationary point while the other viewed the inner rectangle and point. The outer circle displaced vertically. The inner rectangle displaced laterally in phase with the circle. As Wallach had reported earlier, the rectangle appeared to move obliquely, demonstrating a dichoptic induced motion. These results suggest induced motion derives from a stage of processing that follows the binocular combination of retinal inputs.

The Bassili and Farber results appear to conflict with results reported by another group of investigators (Over & Lovegrove, 1973). However, there are grounds for asserting that these investigators were studying a phenomenon that, while superficially similar to induced motion, is not the same. The rationale for the Over and Lovegrove study, which also involved dichoptic presentation of a moving surround and stationary inner-target pattern, grew out of earlier work on motion aftereffects (MAEs). Previous work on MAEs had shown that if the stationary test pattern has the same spectral characteristics as the moving induction pattern, the MAE is stronger. This was only true, however, when induction and test pattern were presented to the same eye. No color specificity was evidenced when the test pattern was presented to one eye and the moving pattern to the other. Motion aftereffects involve successive presentations of induction and test patterns. Over and Lovegrove wished to determine whether similar effects would also be obtained with simultaneous presentation of induction and test patterns, a condition which produces *simultaneous motion contrast* (SMC) or conceivably induced motion. They therefore used both monoptic and dichoptic viewing conditions.

The display consisted of a pair of concentric circular patterns (see Figure 17.16). The outer surrounding pattern was 3° 20′ arc in diameter, the inner circle 1°. Both test and induction stimuli contained a vertical square-wave grating pattern that was either the same or different colors. The pattern within the boundaries of the inducing stimulus moved at 0.5°/sec. The inner induction pattern was stationary. The investigators report that the apparent motion of the stationary pattern was greatest

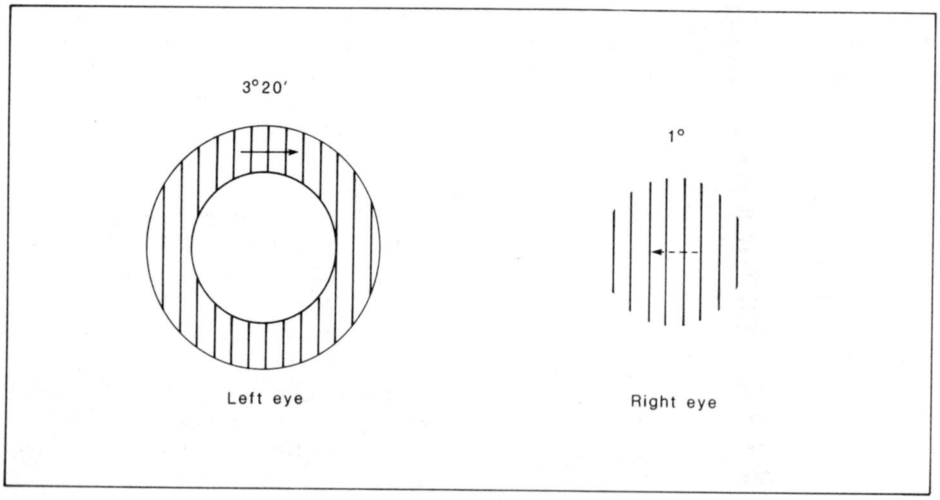

Figure 17.16. A schematic drawing of a dichoptic simultaneous motion contrast display. Left eye: Vertical bars in the 3° 20′ arc diameter surround drift rightward (solid arrow) in the annular window at 0.5°/sec. Right eye: Vertical bars are stationary within a 1° circular test field. The patterns were square-wave gratings formed on separate oscilloscopes and were presented to 32 subjects. Four color combinations of inducing and test gratings were used: red-green, green-red, green-green, red-green. The patterns were presented either monoptically or dichoptically by the use of polarizing filters to enable the left eye to see the inducing pattern, the right eye the test grating. When the test field was the same color as the inducing pattern, the simultaneous motion contrast under monoptic conditions was maximal and reduced when they differed in color. Color has no significant effect under the dichoptic presentation. The vertical bars in the test stimuli appear to drift left (dotted arrow) if the display is presented monoptically. The apparent movement is severely reduced by dichoptic presentation. (Data from Over & Lovegrove, 1973.)

when the vertical bars were the same color in the monoptic condition, but no differences were found in the dichoptic condition in which the stationary pattern was viewed by one eye and the induction pattern was viewed by the other. However, and more relevant to the issue under consideration, they also report that the motion induced in the test pattern in the dichoptic condition was so slight as to be almost nonexistent (see Chapter 16 by Anstis for additional discussion of this experiment).

The apparent conflict between these results and those reported by Bassili and Farber are resolved by an experiment by Day and Dickinson (1977). These investigators demonstrated that the Over and Lovegrove finding of minimum induction is specific to the situation in which the moving induction pattern is *contained* or *surrounded* by a *stationary contour* or aperture. They report that when the inducing stimulus is a moving contour surrounding a stationary target (a moving rectangle and stationary point) or is a moving grating surrounding a stationary grating, the induced motion of the stationary target is not affected either by color differences or by dichoptic presentations. Furthermore, Day and Dickinson report a significant reduction in the velocity of the perceived motion of the stationary target when the moving induction pattern has a stationary boundary compared to the perceived induced motion when the entire inducing stimulus (bars and surrounding contour) moved. When this was the only difference between conditions, there was an 83% reduction in the velocity of the perceived motion of the stationary stimulus.

Day and Dickinson (1977) conclude that the effect studied by Over and Lovegrove is not induced motion.

> The stationary boundary serves as a reference which prevents the smooth, continuous, gliding effect commonly associated with Duncker-type induced movement. It seems likely that the marked reduction in the effect with target and field bars of a different color is simply due to the greater distinguishability of the two. When the target bars are more distinguishable, they can be more easily related perceptually to the stationary contour which serves as a reference. In consequence, they seem hardly to move. (p. 319)

This study provides persuasive grounds for the authors' conclusion that the phenomenon studied by Over and Lovegrove is not classic induced motion and thus removes the apparent conflict between the outcomes of the Over and Lovegrove and the Bassili and Farber studies. Over and Lovegrove studied *simultaneous motion contrast*, which is likely to be the result of processes operating at a much lower level in the visual system than those responsible for induced motion. This evidence is reviewed in Section 4.13.

4.13. Comparison of Induced Motion with Simultaneous Motion Contrast

The principle stimulus difference between SMC and the superficially similar phenomenon of induced motion appears to be the one singled out by Day and Dickinson (1977), namely, the presence or absence of a stationary contour that surrounds the moving induction pattern. This enclosing stationary contour in SMC displays is a source of conflicting object-relative information about the induction target. While the target displaces relative to the moving inducing pattern, it is stationary with respect to this contour. Since this object-relative information is consistent with the available subject-relative information about target position, it is unlikely that SMC engenders any misperception of position and, instead, only affects the perception of velocity. If this is so, this phenomenon is more properly grouped with MAEs (see Chapter 16 by Anstis) which engenders the perception of paradoxical motion, rather than with induced motion, which seems to involve both the perception of motion and position change.

A number of motion phenomena reported in the literature, sometimes referred to as induced motion, seem to be instances of SMC. These include studies by Loomis and Nakayama (1973), whose display consisted of two horizontally separated dots moving with equal angular velocity against a background of moving dots with a shallow velocity gradient; Tynan and Sekular (1975), whose display consisted of a field of horizontally drifting dots surrounding a central square array of dots whose direction and velocity of motion could be varied independently; and Nakayama and Tyler (1978), whose display consisted of two stationary horizontal lines separated by 1° and flanked by two horizontal lines moving counterphase toward and away from the stationary lines (for a detailed discussion of these studies, see Section 1, Chapter 16 by Anstis).

Although induced motion and SMC appear to be different phenomena, both may be present in any given display. The distinguishing feature of induced motion is the relative displacement or directional shift between objects in the visual field where, except in the case of two-point induced motion, one object acts as the phenomenal background or frame of reference for another. Perceived induced motion produces a shift in perceived position. Simultaneous motion contrast, which seems to be based on local velocity differences between patterned stimuli, probably involves no shift in position and therefore may entail the perception of paradoxical motion.

4.14. Theories of Induced Motion

There are two general kinds of explanations of induced motion that correspond to the major categories of motion information (subject and object-relative). Duncker (1929) proposed the original object-relative account, in which perceived induced motion occurs as the result of the relative displacement between objects in the visual field. If one object has a framelike character, for example, if it surrounds another object, it will serve as the background against which movement of the figural object is perceived. Its motion will induce motion in the enclosed object. The fact that the background will appear stationary, when its motion is below or near threshold, is attributed to the general tendency to perceive backgrounds as stable. Perceived motion of the background implies a separation of systems. The motion of the background is subject relative; the induced motion is object relative.

Brosgole (1968) has proposed a subject-relative account of induced motion. On this analysis, a stationary point within a moving surround appears to move because the movement of the surround shifts the observer's apparent median plane, which tends to be located toward the center of a visual framework (Roelofs, 1935). The shift in apparent median plane is the immediate source of induced motion. As the median plane shifts in the direction of frame displacement, it induces an apparent shift in the opposite direction in an enclosed stationary object, and this displacement is subject relative. (See Section 3.4.7 for a discussion of Brosgole's analysis of AKM, which parallels his explanation of induced motion.)

Several investigators have proposed lateral inhibition accounts of induced motion (Anstis & Reinhardt-Rutland, 1976; Over & Lovegrove, 1973; Tynan & Sekular, 1975), but it is argued here that this explanation is more appropriately restricted to SMC.

A patently untenable account of induced motion attributes it to involuntary eye movements elicited by motion of the surround which causes the image of the stationary target to displace on the retina. Since these eye movements are assumed to be involuntary, they are unaccompanied by an extraretinal signal; consequently, the image displacement is unmatched by an eye movement signal, and object motion is perceived (Kaufman, 1974). Kaufman has recognized that this version of a subject-relative account of induced motion faces a variety of difficulties, and there is ample evidence that induced motion is not a function of eye movements. Induced motion occurs in retinally stabilized displays (Mack, Fendrich, & Wong, 1982). It can occur simultaneously in the opposite direction in different parts of the visual field (Gogel, 1977a). In a direct test of the eye movement hypothesis, eye movement–caused image displacement was pitted against object-relative displacement. The outcome was that induced motion was governed by the object-relative displacement (Schulman, 1979). Two horizontal lines separated vertically by 3.6° moved back and forth in opposite directions. A stationary point, the induction target, was placed immediately below the upper line, immediately above the lower line, or midway between the two (see Figure 17.17). In one condition of the experiment, the observers were required to track one of the moving lines when the stationary point was adjacent to the other line. The stationary point was perceived to move opposite the motion of the adjacent line despite the fact that displacement of the image of the stationary point produced by the tracking was in the opposite direction. Finally two investigations in which eye movements were directly monitored produced no evidence that tracking of the surround motion was the cause of induced motion (Brosgole, Cristal, & Carpenter, 1968; Mack, Fendrich, & Pleune, 1979).

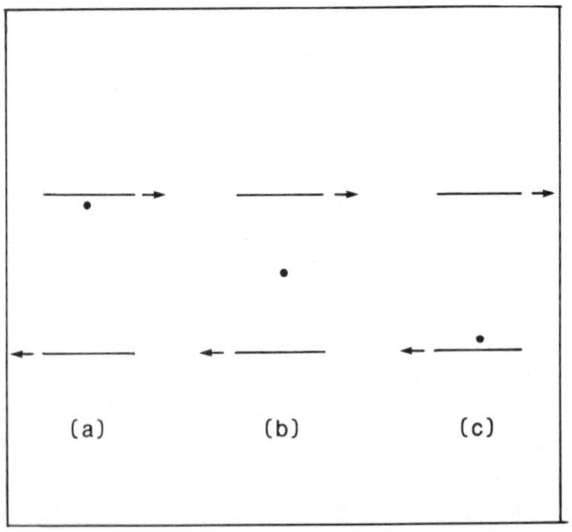

Figure 17.17. Eye movements do not cause induced motion. The stationary target (a) was 0.24° below the upper line, (b) midway between the lines, and (c) 0.24° above the lower line. In the fixation condition, subjects fixated the stationary target. In the tracking condition, an additional spot was placed in the middle of one of the lines and moved with it. The horizontal lines, which were separated by 3.6° moved in counterphase motion through two full cycles at a rate of 0.48°/sec. If the lower line is tracked in (a), the induction target adjacent to the upper line appears to move left. If the induced motion is caused by the eye movement, it should appear to move right. Adjacency determined the direction of induced motion in the fixation and tracking conditions for the 13 subjects. This suggests that eye movements do not cause induced motion. (From P. Schulman, eye movements do not cause induced motion, *Perception and Psychophysics*, 1979, *26*. Reprinted with permission.)

A subtler version of the egocentric eye movement hypothesis has been proposed. Both McConkie and Farber (1979) and Rock and colleagues (1980) have proposed that induced motion is mediated by visual capture of oculomotor information. By this account oculomotor visual capture is the result of induced motion. The tendency to perceive backgrounds or surrounds as stationary leads to the assignment of motion to the enclosed object when there is relative displacement between the two. If the enclosed object is fixated, visual capture would result in a registered pursuit eye movement opposite the motion of the surround. The retinal displacement of the surround, which is a function of its real motion, is attributed to the eye's tracking motion, and the absence of retinal displacement of the fixated induction object is consistent with the perception of its induced motion. A parallel argument can be made if the observer fixates and tracks the moving surround.

4.15. Evaluation of Evidence

Perhaps not surprisingly, there is evidence that both supports and fails to support the several subject- and object-relative accounts of induced motion. In support of the subject-relative account, Brosgole (1968) found that the *larger* of two concentric rectangles, moving counterphase and surrounding a small sphere, governed induced motion. Since the larger frame should have greater influence over apparent median plane (its frame character for the observer is greater), the fact that it, rather than the more adjacent, smaller rectangle, controls the induced motion is taken as support for the subject-relative theory. Brosgole's finding is at odds with Wallach's three-element display demonstrating separation of systems but is not necessarily at odds with Duncker's account in which the principal separation is between object- and subject-relative systems. The central issue is what constitutes the frame of reference. Is it the subject or some visual object? For Brosgole, it is the subject, and by this view, the larger frame controls induced motion by inducing a displacement in the observer's apparent median plane. This is not the only way of accounting for the fact that the larger frame controls the induction. Its displacement might act directly rather than indirectly. If the larger surround had a more "framelike appearance," the enclosed point would be seen in relation to it, rather than the smaller surround.

Brosgole (1968) found no induced motion when two rectangular frames were placed one above the other (see Figure 17.18). A stationary sphere was enclosed within each rectangle, and the two rectangles displaced from left to right, counterphase. This failure to find induced motion is taken as further evidence that induced motion is caused by a shift in apparent median plane produced by a displaced frame. The presence of two equal-sized frames moving in opposite directions prevents either frame from influencing apparent median plane and thus makes induced motion impossible. This, however, may not be the reason why no induced motion is perceived. It may be that the absence of relative displacement between the two vertically aligned, stationary targets, which are surrounded by oppositely moving rectangles, successfully counteracts the induction effects of the frames and destroys any possibility of induced motion. A related study by Gogel (1977a) provides evidence for this speculation. The principal difference between the Gogel and the Brosgole studies is that in the Gogel study the two oppositely moving rectangles were separated horizontally, thus sharply reducing

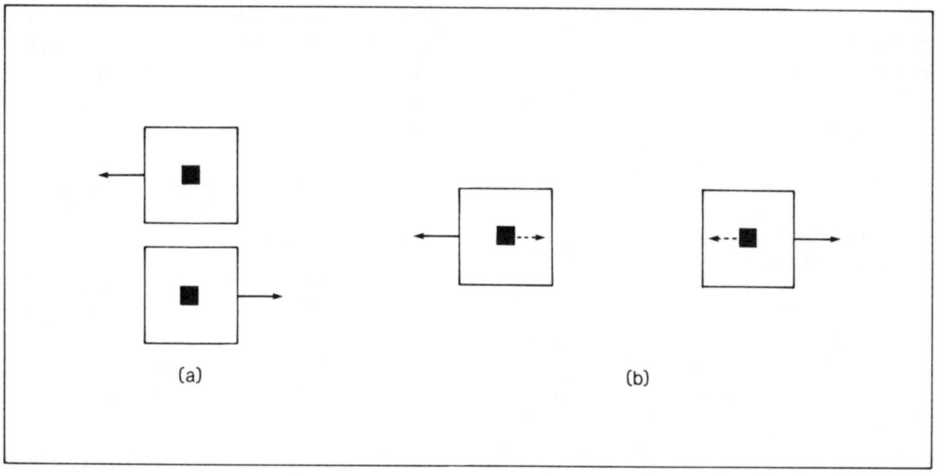

Figure 17.18. Schematic drawing of Brosgole and Gogel double induced motion displays. Dashed lines indicate perceived motion; Solid lines, actual motion. (a) Two frames, consisting of a 1.91-cm luminous band attached to a 101.6- × 27.9-cm posterboard, were placed one above the other. Each frame had a 2.54-cm-diameter luminous sphere at its center. The spheres were in the subject's objective median plane. Subjects fixated a point midway between an imaginary vertical line connecting the two spheres. The frames moved 2.54 cm/sec in counterphase motion. Brosgole reported that induced motion was not elicited when the frames were in counterphase motion. (b) Electroluminescent strips were used to create two frames, 1.3 × 8.9 cm at 91.4 cm (near) from the observers or 2.6 × 17.8 cm at 182.8 cm (far) from the observers. Within each frame was a disc, 27 cm (near) or 54 cm (far) in diameter. The discs were separated horizontally 18.2 cm (near), 36.4 cm (far). The frames moved at 1.34 cm/sec, in counterphase motion. At both distances, induced motion was elicited in the discs by the frames presented simultaneously in counterphase motion. Thirty-one subjects viewed the display. (Data from Brosgole, 1968; Gogel, 1977a.)

the salience of the relationship of the targets to each other (see Figure 17.18). This one change dramatically affected the outcome. Gogel reports that observers perceive the two stationary targets moving in opposite directions. This result not only suggests an alternative explanation of Brosgole's results but must also be considered evidence against Brosgole's general account of induced motion. It is hardly likely that apparent median plane can simultaneously shift in opposite directions.

Brosgole's subject-relative theory cannot explain the Schulman (1979) data, described in Section 4.14, in which induction occurred in the presence of oppositely moving induction stimuli (horizontal lines), for the same reasons that it cannot account for Gogel's results. Two-point induced motion also is not easily accounted for by Brosgole's subject-relative view of induced motion.

The view that induced motion produces visual capture of oculomotor information is an alternative subject-relative account that entails no assumptions about apparent shifts in the median plane. Since subject-relative position or motion information is based on eye position information, if induced motion causes a misregistration of this information, it would necessarily be an instance of egocentric motion. This view is neither confirmed nor unconfirmed by available data. While the fact that observers may report that their eyes are moving when they fixate a stationary stimulus undergoing induced motion is consistent with the occurrence of visual capture, these reports do not permit us to conclude that visual capture has occurred. These reports may merely reflect the observers' wish to appear consistent. The only relevant, less ambiguous evidence comes from a study reported by Wong and Mack (1981) in which observers were required to saccade to the initial position of a no-longer-visible stimulus after it had undergone induced motion. If the induction target was actually stationary and appeared to move to the right, observers saccaded to the left, to the position the target would have occupied if it had actually displaced. Unfortunately these results are also vulnerable to an interpretation in terms of the observers' wish to behave consistently and cannot be taken as conclusive evidence of visual capture. Experiments currently underway in our laboratory are designed as a more rigorous test of this hypothesis. In one of these experiments, observers are required to saccade to an invisible auditory target after fixating a stationary stimulus that undergoes induced motion. If the auditory target is actually to the left of the induction stimulus but induced motion causes this stimulus to appear to move to the left, then oculomotor visual capture should result in a saccade in the wrong direction.

If perceived induced motion is mediated by oculomotor visual capture, other orienting responses should reflect this. Undistorted eye position information is the only basis for accurate guidance of (nonvisually) guided orienting responses, like pointing, when induced motion is perceived. If that information suffers visual capture, then the single source of veridical position information is eliminated, and an orienting response ought then to reflect the induced motion. This evidence that induced motion causes oculomotor visual capture would be consistent with data indicating that induced motion is manually tracked and inconsistent with the report that pointing to an induction target is accurate (Bridgeman et al., 1981).

4.16. Induced Motion of the Self

The phenomenon of induced motion of the self was first described by Duncker (1929). It is described in detail in Chapter 18 by Howard, and therefore is only briefly discussed here. Like induced object motion, induced motion of the self, also called *vection*, is a phenomenon that occurs in ordinary experience. When a train across the platform or a car stops alongside us then pulls away, we experience the train or car in which we are seated, which is actually stationary, to be moving in the opposite direction.

Duncker (1929) described the conditions for induced motion of the self in terms similar to those necessary for inducing object motion.

> The same object structure of the visual field that determines object-relative movement and rest values of the object, also determines the object-relative movement and rest values of the subject. For example, the strongest impetus to movement that can be given for an object, namely, a change in distance relative to its entire environment, is at the same time the strongest impetus to movement for the perceiving subject. Or: whether the subject finds himself at phenomenal rest, depends—exactly as it is with the phenomenal rest of an object—in the highest degree on whether there is something in the environment onto which it can anchor itself. (chap. 2, p. 207)

In other words, induced motion of the self is likely to occur when the entire field surrounding the observer moves. The observer then becomes the enclosed object, and the motion of the surround leads to perceived motion of the self.

In the laboratory the phenomenon is usually demonstrated by placing the observer within a vertically oriented, cylindrical, patterned field, which is then set into rotary motion around the observer. After a brief period in which the observer may perceive the field as rotating, the observer comes to experience self movement and the field as stationary. When this occurs, a stationary target located between the observer and the patterned surround will also be perceived as moving with the observer. The relative displacement between surround and observer is attributed to motion of the observer in accordance with the principle, "that which is displaced relative to a phenomenal reference system appears phenomenally moved" (Duncker, 1929, chap. 2, p. 13).

Induced motion of the self is a prototypical example of the power of object-relative information to override available subject-relative information, which in this situation is sensory information that the observer is stationary.

Recent evidence indicates that vection depends on stimulation of the retinal periphery by the moving pattern (Brandt, Dichgans, & Koenig, 1973) and does not require a moving pattern that fills the observer's visual field. Thus it would seem that the primary feature of the background or frame motion that induces vection is that it extends to the sides of the observer and therefore literally surrounds her or him. This finding suggests that the stimulus difference, which distinguished vection from induced object motion, may depend on where in the visual field the moving pattern is located. If it lies in the periphery, it may engender vection. If it is located more centrally, it may engender induced object motion. There is now also evidence that the visual stimulation, which produces vection, is associated with a pattern of vestibular responses comparable to those which occur with actual observer motion (Henn, Young, & Finley, 1974). This finding is completely consistent with the view that the perception of induced self motion causes visual capture of vestibular signals. Therefore, if induced object motion is, in fact, comparable to the phenomenon of induced self motion and what distinguishes them is simply that the motion of the surround in one instance is attributed to an enclosed visual stimulus, whereas in the other it is attributed to the self, we ought to expect visual capture of oculomotor signals when there is induced object motion. Failure to find evidence of visual capture of oculomotor information with induced object motion would therefore suggest an important difference between these phenomena. In any case, evidence concerning the presence or absence of visual capture with induced object motion should elucidate their relationship.

4.17. The Relation between Induced and Real Motion

There has been some discussion in the literature about whether induced and real motion are distinguishable. Existing relevant data are not consistent. The fact that a compensation technique can be used to assess the magnitude of induction (Bridgeman et al., 1981; Duncker, 1929) suggests that real and induced motion are not perceptually distinct, since real motion of a target is capable of nulling perceived induced motion. This is supported by the finding that, at least under certain conditions, observers are unable to distinguish between the real and induced motion (Bassili & Farber, 1977).

Gogel and Koslow (1971) compared the extent of perceived induced motion when observers fixated a stationary point surrounded by a moving frame with the perceived extent of motion when the point, rather than the frame moved. In both cases, stimulus motion was 1.27°/sec. In general, they found that the perceived extent of point motion was greater when the point moved than when its motion was induced. This difference is interpreted by the investigators as evidence that observers can discriminate between real and induced motion. However, the fact that the perceived extent of point motion was less when motion was induced may be attributed to the fact that induced motion involves a conflict between subject- and object-relative motion information and does not indicate that the motions are necessarily discriminable. In fact, a frame motion of greater than 1°/sec is probably too fast to induce optimal motion, which could account for the discriminability of the two types of motion.

5. CONFIGURATIONAL EVENT PERCEPTION

5.1. The Rolling Wheel

Duncker (1929; see also Rubin, 1927) describes the perceived motion of a luminous point on the rim of a rolling wheel viewed in a dark room, a phenomenon which has been the subject of much recent investigation and discussion (Johansson, 1950; Proffitt & Cutting, 1979, 1980a, 1980b; Proffitt, Cutting, & Steir, 1979; Restle, 1979). If only one point is visible, it will be seen to move along a series of arches or a wavelike path, which, in fact, is its subject-relative motion path (see Figure 17.19). If a second point is added to the rim opposite the first or is attached to the hub, there is a dramatic shift in the perceived motion path of the point on the rim. If the two points are both on the rim of the wheel, they will both appear to rotate around the unseen center of the wheel as they travel together along a horizontal path. If the second point is added to the hub, the point on the perimeter will appear to rotate around the hub point, while both points together move along a horizontal path. In other words, the addition of the second point in both cases results in the perception of wheellike motion, that is, rotation and translation. In the case of the single point, its actual path of motion is perceived, and this is given by purely subject-relative motion information. The addition of the second point adds object-relative information, which has a profound effect

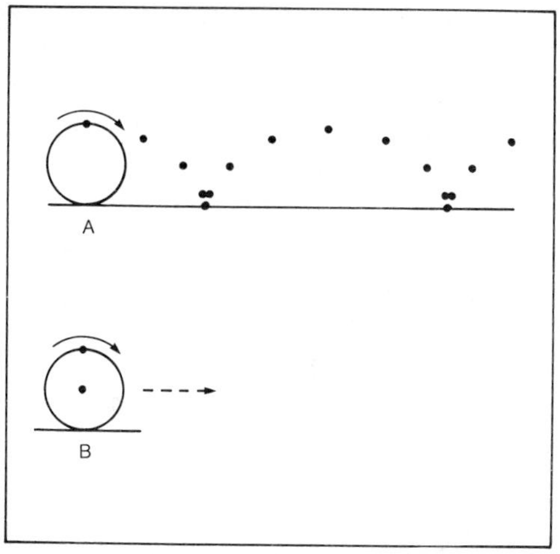

Figure 17.19. The rolling wheel. In *A*, a single light on the rim of a rolling wheel viewed in darkness appears to move along a wavelike path. In *B*, with a second light attached to hub, the rim light appears to rotate around the center light, and both lights appear to translate to the right, yielding apparent wheellike motion. (From H. Wallach, *On perception*, Quadrangle Press, 1976. Copyright Random House. Reprinted with permission.)

on the perceived outcome. "The rotary fate of the point on the perimeter with respect to the hub is separated from its translatory fate with respect to the surround and the observer" (Duncker, 1929, chap. 5, p. 1). In other words, there is a separation of systems, but the separation is between the rotary component of motion, which is object relative, and the translatory fate with respect to the surround and the observer. Note that the object-relative component is based on a change of direction between the two points, not on a change of distance between them.

There is an important difference between the separation of systems that occurs in the case of the rolling wheel and the separation that occurs in classic center-surround induced motion. In the induced motion case, one element encloses another, and this is the basis upon which motion is assigned to the elements that displace relative to each other. The enclosing stimulus is the phenomenal frame of reference for the enclosed stimulus carrying the relative motion. The separation of systems that occurs between subject- and object-relative motions corresponds to the organization of elements in the field into a figure and a background. The motion of the background, when it is fast enough to be seen, is given by subject-relative information. The motion of the enclosed element carries the object-relative motion. In the case of two-point induced motion where there is no basis for figure-ground segregation, either or both elements may carry the relative motion, and therefore observers will perceive this array idiosyncratically.

The separation that occurs in the case of the rolling wheel is not such that one element carries the object-relative motion while the other carries the subject-relative motion. The separation is between the subject- and object-relative *components* of motion that the elements simultaneously undergo. In other words, there is a simultaneous dissociation. In classical induced motion, induction occurs to the extent that the actual subject-relative behavior of the induction target is not perceived (if the induction target has a real motion, its perceived motion is a function of the induced motion and the real motion). In the case of the rolling wheel, both the subject- and object-relative motion components of the rim elements are perceived; that is, each element carries both components of motion which are, however, perceptually segregated. Together, these components yield the perception that the outer point or points are rotating and simultaneously translating through space. The frame of reference for the object-relative rotary motion is the center of the wheel, while the subject and or visual background is the reference for the translatory motion component. Similar to classical induced motion, the object-relative motion is generally perceptually salient; consequently, at low angular velocities it may be the only motion that is perceived (Wallach, 1965, 1982).

In a series of studies of the perceived path of motion of light points attached to invisible rolling wheels, investigators found that the perceived motion can be best described in terms of rotation about the centroid of the geometric figure defined by the light points (Proffitt & Cutting, 1979, 1980a, 1980b; Proffitt, Cutting, Steir, 1979). "The relative motion of the points to each other is best described as perceived rotation about the mathematically defined center of the moving array. The subject relative motion of the entire system of points is perceived as motion of the system's centroid" (Proffit & Cutting, 1979, p. 390). To the extent that the centroid of a system of points coincides with the actual center of the wheel, the motion of the entire system is perceived as linear and wheellike. The more the centroid departs from the actual center of the wheel on which the lights are placed, the more the entire system of points will be perceived to hop along a cycloidal path.

5.2. Lissajous Combinations

The perceived motion of points attached to a rolling wheel is an instance of what Johansson (1950) has called a *configuration in event perception*. (This discussion of Johansson patterns is limited to two-dimensional configurations. The reader is referred to Chapter 19 for a discussion of three-dimensional motion configurations.) The perception of displays, like the rolling wheel, all involve a dissociation or separation of subject- and object-relative motion components and therefore of the multiple frames of reference. Johansson has referred to these motion configurations as *Lissajous combinations*. A Lissajous figure results when a single point simultaneously undergoes two simple harmonic motions that are at right angles to each other. The shape of the resultant motion path is a function of the frequency and phase relation of the two motions. Figure 17.20 depicts the motion paths that result from different combinations of frequencies and phase relations. Johansson tells us (pp. 87–88) that the term Lissajous pattern derives from the French physicist Lissajous (1822–1880), who first produced these patterns using two tuning forks placed at right angles to each other. Small mirrors were attached to a tine of each fork. A light beam was reflected from one mirror to the other and then onto a screen. Variations in the frequency and phase relations between the forks predictably altered the motion path of the light beam. The configurations studied by Johansson were generated on a CRT screen and are called Lissajous combinations, rather than Lissajous figures, because "these give, in the same perceptual field, a single harmonic vertical motion and also a horizontal such motion. As opposed to Lissajous figures, we have one carrier for each motion and thus two objects in motion" (p. 88).

The first example of a Lissajous pattern is the most frequently described (see Figure 17.21). Two moving elements (e.g., light points presented on a CRT) travel at right angles to each other along the legs of an invisible "L." Both elements travel at the same sinusoidal velocity, and their phase relation is such that they arrive at their common point simultaneously.

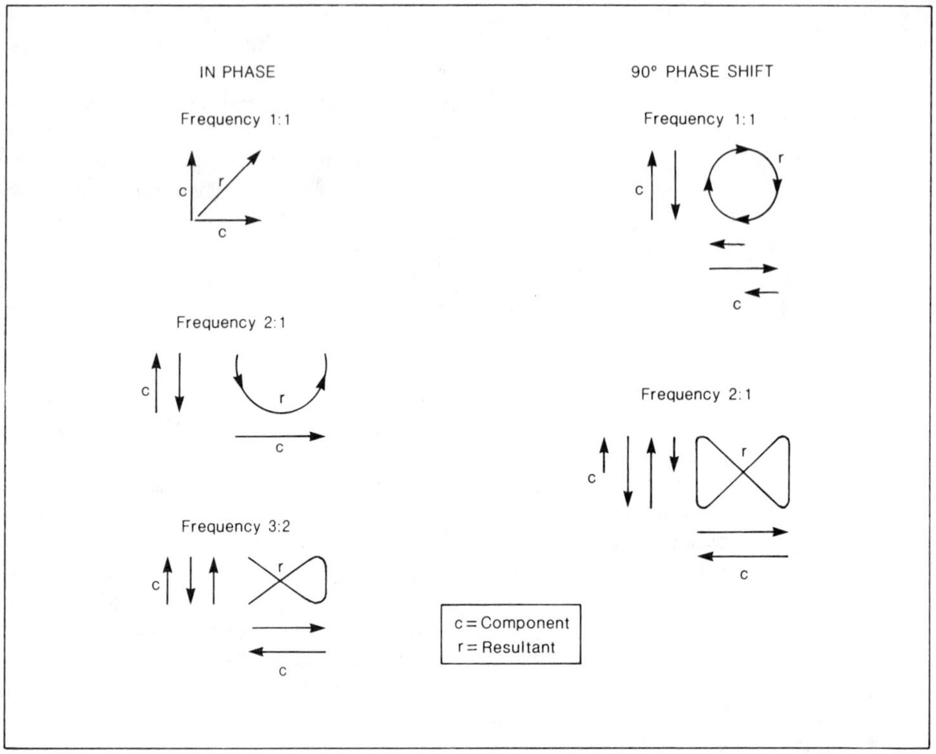

Figure 17.20 Simple Lissajous combinations. Different motion paths result when two simple harmonic motions, oriented at right angles to each other, are combined in various ways. The shape of the resultant motion path is a function of the frequency and phase relation of the two motions.

When this display is viewed, the observer does not see the actual motion of the two points but the two points appear to move toward and away from each other along an oblique path, and the entire configuration may appear to move obliquely up and down along a path at right angles to the object-relative motion path. The motions appear to be separated into their object- and subject-relative components, with perception dominated by the object-relative component. The dominant oblique perceived motion of the elements toward and away from each other is the actual motion of the elements, with respect to each other; it is their object-relative motion. The remaining oblique motion at right angles to this motion path is the subject-relative component of the motion, that is, the motion of the elements with respect to the observer.

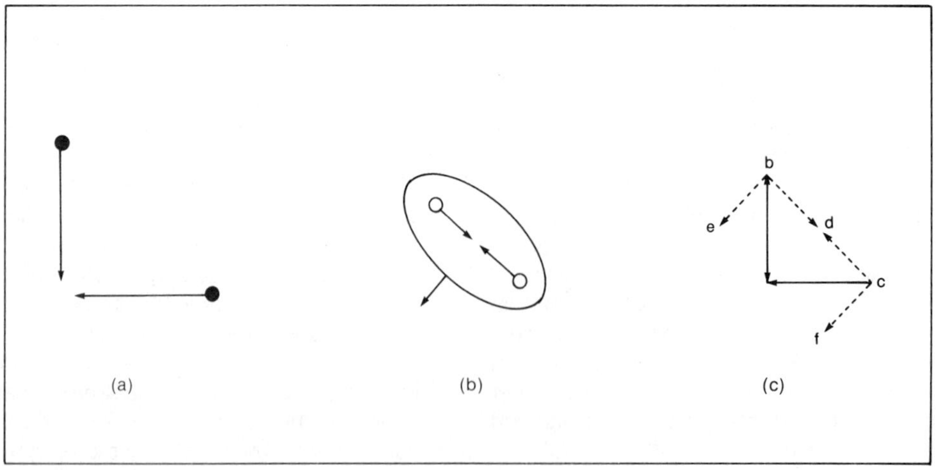

Figure 17.21. Johansson Lissajous combinations. (a) Actual Motion: Two points move in phase at the same sinusoidal velocity. (b) Perceived motion: The two points are seen moving toward and away from each other along an oblique path. The entire configuration may also appear to move along its common motion path. (c) Vector analysis: Vectors ***bd*** and ***cd*** are divergent verctors; vectors ***cf*** and ***be***, common vectors. Divergent vectors dominate the perception. (From G. Johansson, *Configurations in event perception*, Almquist & Wicksell International, 1950. Reprinted with permission.)

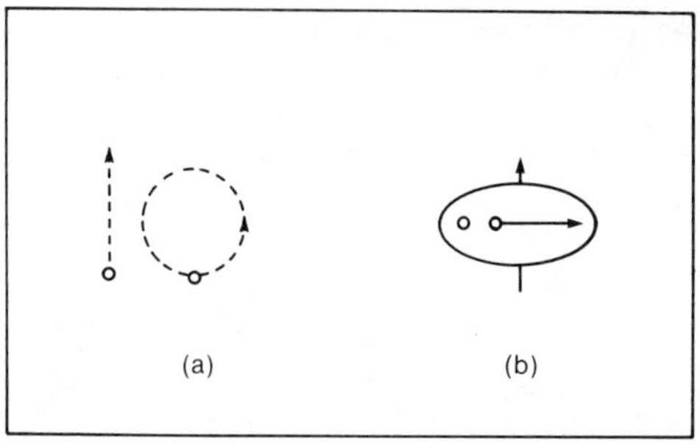

Figure 17.22. Johansson Lissajous combination. (a) Real motion: One point moves up and down in a vertical path, and one point describes a circle. The points move in a phase. (b) Perceived motion: The point moving in a circular path is seen moving horizontally toward and away from the point moving vertically. Both points may appear to move conjointly up and down as a unit. (From G. Johansson, *Configuration in event perception*, Almquist & Wicksell International, 1950. Reprinted with permission.)

Another example of Lissajous combination described by Johansson again consists of two elements. One of the elements oscillates up and down along a vertical path, while the second element describes a circle (see Figure 17.22). The motion of the elements is in phase, so that they arrive at their uppermost and lowermost positions at the same time. If either element is presented alone, its actual path of motion is perceived. Presented together, the point moving in a circular orbit is perceived to move horizontally toward and away from the point moving vertically. Simultaneously both points may appear to move conjointly up and down as a unit. Again the subject- and object-relative components of the motion are dissociated. The perceived horizontal motion of the point describing a circle is its actual motion relative to the point moving vertically; that is, it is its relative motion. Its perceived vertical motion is its motion relative to the observer or the background it has in common with the other element. Again two distinct reference systems provide the basis for the perceived dissociation of motion paths. The grouping of the common subject-relative motion is in accord with the Gestalt grouping principle of *common fate*. (See Chapter 33 by Rock.)

5.3. Vector Analysis

Johansson (1950) accounts for the perception of these two arrays and for others belonging to the same class in terms of his theory of *vector analysis*. He proposes that the visual system engages in an analysis of the motion vectors present in a moving visual array. This analysis leads to the segregation of common and divergent vectors of motion, such that the common vector provides the frame of reference or background for the divergent and perceptually dominant or figural vector. The frame of reference for the common motion is either the static environment, the observer, or both.

In the case of the two elements moving along the legs of the L, vector analysis leads to the abstraction of the common motion vector (labeled **be** and **cf** in Figure 17.21) and the divergent vector (labeled **bd** and **cd**). In the case in which one element moves up and down while the other travels in a circular path, vector analysis leads to the abstraction of the common vertical vector, which the circularly moving element shares with the vertically moving element, and the residual or divergent horizontal vector, which is the perceptually dominant motion. The two vectors added together account for the motion that is present. (The perception of the motion of Lissajous patterns does not seem to involve what Duncker described as distance paradox. See Section 4.4. Since here the separation of systems does not entail seeing surplus motion, this may be one of the distinguishing differences between induced and Lissajous pattern perception.)

If one of the two points in the L display is tracked, the perceived paths of motion are significantly altered. The tracked point is perceived to move along its actual path, while the other point appears to move along an oblique path toward and away from it. It is as if the tracked point becomes the frame of reference for the relative motion between elements. There is, however, another way of describing the effects of tracking. If, as Dodge (1904) or Stoper (1967, 1973) have argued, there is no compensation for the displacement of images of tracked stimuli during pursuit of a moving target, then one would expect the perceived path of motion of the tracked element to be determined solely by its retinal path of motion, which in the case of L is oblique. However, since there are reasons to believe that there is compensation for image displacements during pursuit (see Section 3.3), this description is unlikely to be correct.

A somewhat different account has been offered by Festinger, Sedgwick, and Holtzman (1976), which derives from an experiment examining the perceived extent of motion of a tracked stimulus and the perceived orientation of the motion path of a stimulus moving at an angle between 60 and 75° or between 105 and 120° to the horizontally moving, tracked stimulus. These displays resembled the L display although a 90° phase angle was not examined. The results indicated that the perceived orientation of the untracked element was much closer to its retinal than its actual motion path. The investigators concluded, "The perceptual system has access to information about direction of tracking and assumes a relatively low speed, almost irrespective of the actual speed of the eye" (p. 1377). If these investigators are correct, the perceived motion path of the untracked element in the L display may be a function of the only minimal compensation for retinal image displacements engendered by pursuit, rather than of a process of vector analysis.

According to Johansson, pursuit of either of the moving elements in the configuration depicted in Figure 17.22 does not alter its appearance. If this is actually so, this argues against the Festinger and colleagues (1976) explanation. If the observer tracks the vertically moving element, the path the circularly moving element traces on the retina will be horizontal. If there were no compensation for image displacement during pursuit, this would account for the perception that the circle element is moving horizontally. On the other hand, if the circle element is tracked, the image of the vertically moving element will displace horizontally on the retina. If there were only minimal compensation for pursuit, then this point should appear to move more or less horizontally. If Johansson's statement, "Fixation of a specific object does not lead to any appreciable alterations in the motion pattern" (1950, p. 10), is correct, then the fact that the element actually describing a circle continues to appear to move horizontally when it is tracked cannot be accounted for by retinal painting. Verification of this report is desirable and would have important theoretical consequences.

5.4. Principle of Lowest Velocity

Johansson (1950) states a principle of motion organization to account for the fact that pursuit affects some Lissajous arrays but not others. This is the *principle of lowest velocity*. "The lower velocity becomes the frame of reference for the divergent higher velocity" (Johansson, 1950, p. 136). The evidence that leads Johansson to this principle is derived from other motion configurations not described here, but it may be applicable to the two configurations described in this section. In the case of the L configuration where the elements are moving at equal velocities, the "slowing" of the velocity of the tracked element may be sufficient to cause it to become the frame of reference for the untracked point, consistent with the principle of lowest velocity. In the case in which one of the elements moves vertically while the other moves in a circle, the velocity of the circle point is almost three times greater than the velocity of the vertically moving element. Tracking of the circle element might therefore not cause sufficient slowing to register its motion as less than that of the untracked point, so, by the principle of lowest velocity, tracking could not cause the motion of the circle element to become the frame of reference for the other element.

5.5. Difficulties with Vector Analysis

The finding that the adjacency between elements in a Lissajous motion configuration affects the perceived motion paths of the elements suggests restrictions on the generality of the vector analysis account (Gogel, 1974). Gogel examined the effects of element adjacency in a variation of the Johansson L. Three elements moving at right angles to each other were presented (see Figure 17.23). The points moved along paths of equal length at the same constant velocity. If the motion of the three points

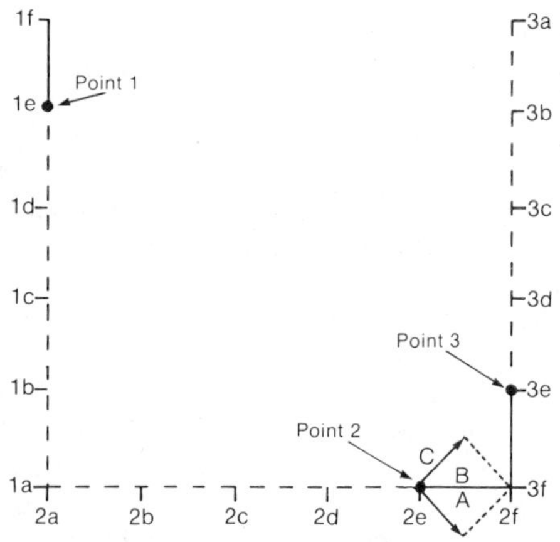

Figure 17.23. Adjacency and Lissajous combinations. Physical paths of motion of three points of light (1, 2, and 3) moving from positions e toward *f* and the analysis of the motion of point 2 in terms of the absolute vector ***B*** and the relative vectors ***A*** and ***C***. The relative motion vector of point 2 is ***C*** with respect to point 3 and ***A*** with respect to point 1. The common motion vector of point 2 is ***A*** with respect to point 3 and ***C*** with respect to point 1. Twenty-four subjects monocularly viewed the three points of light projected by three oscilloscopes onto a rear projection screen. For ease of identification, points 1 and 3 were blue, point 2 red. Points 1 and 3 moved vertically 180° out of phase, point 2 horizontally. All points moved at 17.5 cm/min. Subjects indicated the perceived orientation of the path of movement of point 2 by means of an adjustable 21-cm rod located in the subjects frontoparallel plane. The path of point 2 was influenced by the adjacent stimulus at the beginning and end of its excursion and essentially by neither at its midpoint. The relative motion cue between more adjacent points, rather than more separated points, influenced the perceived path of motion. (From W. C. Gogel, Relative motion and the adjacency principle, *Quarterly Journal of Experimental Psychology, 26*. Copyright 1974 by the Experimental Psychology Society. Reprinted with permission.)

is analyzed into vectors at right angles to each other, then point 2 shares one vector with point 1 and another with point 3; that is, it has one common vector with point 1 and another with point 3. According to Johansson, the perceived motion path of point 2 should be determined conjointly by these two different vectors of divergent motion. Observers were asked to report the slope of the motion path traveled by point 2 at the beginning, middle, and end of its excursion when both or only one of the vertically moving points was present (points 1 and/or 3). The report of this experiment fails to indicate whether observers were required to fixate point 2, although it seems likely that they did, since they were required to report its path of motion.

When only two points were present, observers perceived point 2 traveling along an increasingly less inclined path as the distance between the points increased. A strict interpretation of Johansson leads to the unconfirmed prediction that point 2 should appear to move along a path whose slope is 45°. Gogel reports that the perceived slope varied from 25°, when the points were closest, to 14°, when they were most separated. When all three points were present in the display, the path of point 2 was influenced by the adjacent stimulus at the beginning and end of its excursion and essentially by neither at its midpoint.

These results suggest that the salience of object-relative displacement or divergent motion may be a function of the proximity of the moving elements. Then if common and divergent motion vectors are dissociated as Johansson suggests, this dissociation must operate only over locally adjacent stimuli. When the stimuli are separated by some undefined threshold distance, the relative change between them may no longer be a decisive determinant of the motion percept, which then becomes a function of subject-relative motion information.

This conclusion is supported by a finding that divergent and common motions continue to be segregated even when the motion configuration is observed while fixating a stationary element placed off to one side of the motion pattern (Hochberg & Fallon, 1976). The authors point out that in the presence of a stationary element, there is no common vector greater than zero. The fact that the motion of the elements is segregated, nevertheless, again suggests that vector analysis, if it occurs, may operate only locally over adjacent elements.

5.6. Motion Configurations and Induced Motion

There are a number of similarities and differences between the perceived motion of Lissajous configurations and the perception of classic induced motion. Both illustrate the potency of object-relative displacement for perception of motion, and both may involve a separation of systems, such that object- and subject-relative motion operate independently of each other, although this point has been disputed (Rock et al., 1980). The primary difference between them may be the one alluded to earlier (see Section 5.3), namely, the difference in the nature of the separation of systems. In induced motion (typically a center-surround display), one element carries the subject-relative motion, while the other carries the object-relative motion. In the Lissajous combinations one element carries both motions simultaneously, so that its motion in one direction is its object-relative motion and its motion in another direction is its subject-relative motion.

The perceptual effects associated with the motion configurations appear to be more robust than those involving classic induced motion. For example, Johansson effects may *not* be inhibited by viewing them in lit environments or with neighboring stationary elements, while induced motion normally is.

The special characteristics associated with these Lissajous motion configurations need to be better understood. Duncker and subsequent investigators have observed that if the enclosed point in a center-surround display is given a vertical motion while the enclosing frame moves horizontally, the induced motion is more potent. Induced motion displays in which there is an enclosed stimulus and a frame of reference, and in which the enclosed point moves at an angle to the motion of the surround, would seem to combine the features of induced motion and event perception, which might account for the special potency of this kind of display. Another difference between perception of Lissajous combinations and induced motion is that the former appears to involve grouping by common fate, while the latter does not. In event perception the common or subject-relative motion is the vector of motion shared by two or more of the elements in the display and consequently grouped as a unit of motion. The various differences and similarities between induced motion, event perception, and SMC need to be better understood.

5.7. Coding Theory and Motion Event Perception

Restle (1979) offers an alternative explanation of Johansson's two-dimensional motion patterns derived from Leeuwenberg (1978). (The reader is referred to Chapter 36 by Pomerantz and Kubovy for a fuller account of this theory.) According to this theory, a *code* is an abstract representation of a display, which is complete enough to specify the display. Any given motion array can give rise to a large number of interpretations and consequently can be coded in many different ways. Each code has a specific information load determined by the number of parameters used to specify a particular interpretation. The information load may be reduced if the number of parameters can be reduced without loss of translatability. Restle isolated five parameters to describe the Johansson configurations involving simple harmonic and circular motion, like those described in Section 5.2. They are amplitude, phase, frequency, orientation, and tilt. The first three in particular play an explicit role in Johansson's own analysis.

The theory as formulated by Restle (1979) states that the observer will perceive the *simplest* interpretation, that is, the interpretation with the minimum information load. "If two or more interpretations have equal information loads, then the display will be ambiguous and either or both interpretations may be seen" (p. 2). One of the configurations Restle discusses is the Johansson L (see Figure 17.21). He demonstrates that according to his analysis there are four quite possible interpretations of this configuration, three of which have equal information load and therefore ought to be seen with equal probability. This is depicted in Figure 17.24.

One of the possible interpretations is the one consistent with the actual motion paths of the two elements. This is designated (a) in Figure 17.24. This has the highest informational load of the interpretations considered and thus ought not to be perceived and is not. The other three interpretations have equal information loads and therefore should be seen equally often. While we already know that each of these possible motion patterns may be seen, we know from Johansson that whether (c_1) or (c_2) is seen depends on whether one of the elements is tracked, and if so, which one it is. Johansson's principle of lowest velocity can account for this outcome. Restle's formulation in its present form does not. According to coding theory interpretations (b), (c_1), and (c_2) are equally economical and therefore should be equally stable and equally likely to be seen. "At present there

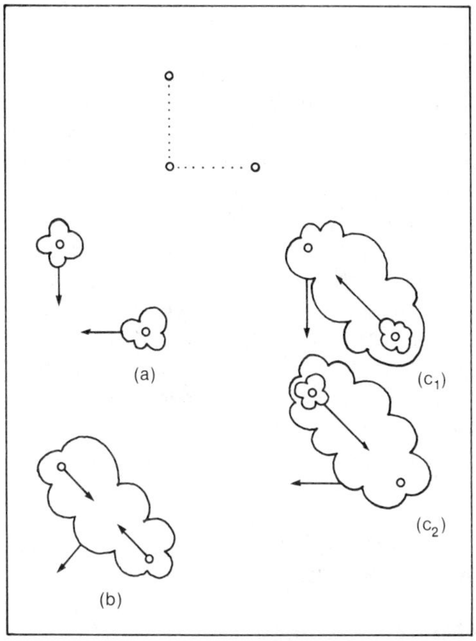

Figure 17.24. Schematic drawing of four possible analyses of the Johansson L. A given motion array can give rise to different interpretations and be coded in different ways. A code has a specific information load determined by the number of parameters used to specify a particular interpretation. The interpretation with the most economical information load will be perceived. Interpretation *a*, is consistent with the actual motion of the two elements, interpretation *b* has two sloping components, and interpretation *c* has one sloping and one vertical or horizontal component. Interpretation a is not perceived because its information load is higher than interpretations *b*, c_1 and c_2. The coding model states that interpretations *b*, c_1 and c_2 have equal information loads and should be seen with equal probability. (From F. Restle, Coding theory of the perception of motion configurations, *Psychological Review, 86*. Copyright 1979 by the American Psychological Association. Reprinted with permission.)

is no clear reason why fixating one point tends to produce a particular interpretation" (Restle, 1979, p. 10).

Restle also considers the other Johansson configuration (discussed in Section 5.2) in which one point moves circularly while another moves vertically up and down (see Figure 17.22). Coding theory appears to account for this perception as adequately as the competing account. "Again grouping of common motion reduces information load from 20 to 10. Thus the model selects the interpretation identified by Johansson's vector analysis" (p. 10).

The major assumption of coding theory, which it shares with a number of other perceptual theories, is that perception is governed by a simplicity or minimum principle. Coding theory may be seen as an attempt to calibrate simplicity in terms of minimum information load. Its major assumption is that one perceives what is easiest to remember. Thus coding theory, as an instance of this general class of perceptual theories, shares the difficulties faced by all such theories. If the perceptual system opts for the simplest outcome, simplicity must be definable. In informational terms, the simplest description is the one with lowest informational load or the fewest elements. How are these elements, the so-called atomic units, selected?

The reader is referred to Hochberg (1968) for a critical discussion of simplicity principles and to Peterson and Hochberg (1983) in particular for a critical discussion of coding theory and the difficulties it faces in accounting for the perception of static forms. Peterson and Hochberg report data indicating that both the locus of fixation and set predictably influence the perception of reversible figures, and they argue, "Coding theories of figure perception and the direct theory of object and event perception must be redesigned to consider the limits of the information present within each glance and the viewer's perceptual intention or set" (p. 192). Evidence that fixation of one of the elements affects the perceptual organization of many of the Johansson configurations may bear the same relationship to a coding theory account of event perception as the data that locus of fixation affects static form perception bears to a coding theory account of static form perception. If, for whatever reason, fixation and pursuit affect the perception of these dynamic arrays, then it simply cannot be the case that their perception is strictly a function of informational load, at least if this is defined in terms of the visual array alone, since there is no obvious reason why fixation should alter informational load.

6. VELOCITY PERCEPTION: SUBJECT- AND OBJECT-RELATIVE DETERMINANTS

6.1. Velocity Constancy

Retinal image velocity, like retinal image extent, is inversely proportional to the distance of the imaged object from the observer. The perceived constancy of an object's velocity despite changes in its distance from the observer is another aspect of motion perception that has been explained in terms of object- and subject-relative motion information.

6.2. Subject-Relative Determinants of Velocity

Since velocity is defined as the extent of motion traversed in a given unit of time, the relation between extent and velocity is obvious. Both the angular extent of the distance traversed by a moving object and its angular velocity decrease directly as distance from the observer increases. If perceived extent were to remain constant with changes in viewing distance, in other words, if size constancy prevailed, perceived constancy of velocity might reasonably be considered a derivative. On this account both perceived extent and velocity constancy would be based on sensory information about an object's distance from the observer. Evidence that both perceived extent and velocity are a function of subject-relative information about absolute, egocentric distance must therefore demonstrate commensurate perceptions of extent and velocity under conditions in which access to distance information is carefully controlled and other possible determinants of perceived velocity are eliminated. J. F. Brown (1931a) found that the perceptions of extent and velocity were incommensurate and concluded that perceived velocity was not a derivative of perceived size or extent of the motion path.

More recently, evidence supporting a subject-relative account of perceived velocity has been reported (Rock, Hill, & Fineman, 1968). These investigators set out to show that perceived velocity constancy, in fact, may be a function of size constancy. The observers were required to compare the speeds of two vertically moving, luminous circles, which were viewed in an otherwise dark field. One of the circles was to the right of the observer at a distance of 45.7 cm, while the other was to the observer's left at four times the distance (182.8 cm). Observers were also required to compare the size of two luminous triangles placed at the same distances and in the same positions as the moving stimuli. This permitted a comparison between perceived velocity and perceived extent. Observations were made with both binocular and monocular viewing. When viewing was monocular, vision was restricted by an artificial pupil that effectively eliminated all sensory information about distance. With binocular observation, perceived size and velocity departed only slightly from constancy. Brunswick ratios indicated that mean perceived velocity was 86% and mean perceived size 93% of complete constancy. With monocular observation, Brunswick ratios were effectively zero. These results thus support a subject-relative account of perceived velocity. Under conditions in which a single object moved through an otherwise unstructured field, perceived velocity was a function of retinal velocity and information about the distance of the object from the observer.

6.3. Object-Relative Determinants of Velocity

J. F. Brown (1931a) found that perceived velocity was a function of the proportion of the field traversed in a given unit of time. If the velocity of an object moving through one field was compared to the velocity of an object moving through a field that was, for example, four times as large and if the moving object was also four times as large, then the velocity of the larger object in the larger field had to be about four times as fast, to appear equal to the velocity of the smaller object in the smaller field. This relationship between perceived velocity and relative displacement held over a wide range. If the movement field was transposed in its linear dimensions by a factor of 10, velocity had to be transposed by a factor of about 8 to be perceived as equal. Brown called this the *principle of the transposition of velocity*. If a movement field is transposed in its linear dimensions, the stimulus velocities must be transposed in an approximately like amount for perceived velocity to appear equal (see Figure 17.25).

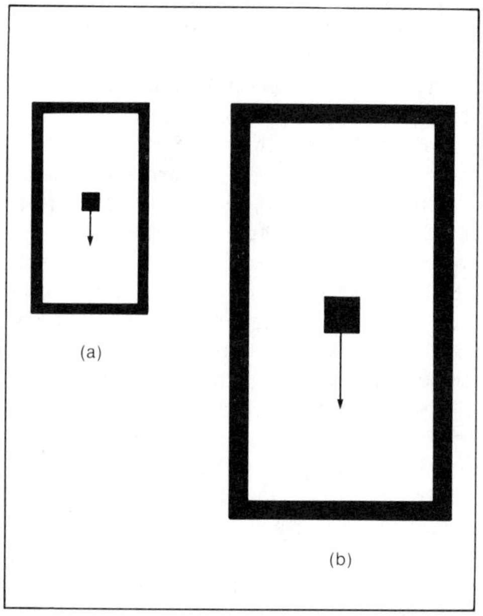

Figure 17.25. Velocity transposition display. Motion field *a* is half the size of motion field *b*. Moving square in field *a* must move about 50% of the velocity of moving square in field *b* to appear to move at equal velocity. If a movement field is transposed in its linear dimensions, the stimulus velocities must be transposed in an approximately like amount for perceived velocity to appear equal. (From J. F. Brown, The visual perception of velocity, *Psychologische Forschung*, 1931, *14*. Reprinted with permission.)

The influence of the size of the field on perceived velocity holds despite information about the distance of the object from the observer and thus despite subject-relative velocity information. In many of Brown's experiments, the observer viewed the movement stimuli, dark circles enclosed in rectangular lit fields, placed at the *same* distance but in different directions from the observer. The size of one movement field and the moving stimuli within it were transposed in linear dimensions relative to the other. One array was designated the standard, the other the comparison. The observer's task was to adjust the velocity of the comparison stimuli to match the velocity of the standard. When the observer adjusted the velocity of the comparison stimulus so that rate of displacement relative to size of field was matched, actual velocities were of course widely divergent, and if those same stimuli were presented in isolation, the Rock and colleagues study indicates their absolute velocities would be matched.

Evidence that the threshold for the change of position of a point within a visual frame reflects the same dependence on size of the frame as perceived velocity (Cartwright, 1938) suggested to Wallach (1939) that there probably was a close relationship between perceived speed and the threshold for change of position. Wallach speculated that both may be understood in terms of Weber's law:

> Actually, several phenomena in the field of visual speed can be explained, if we realize that our sensitivity for changes of position depends on a great many factors. Here it seems relevant that this sensitivity follows Weber's law within certain limits. Strict validity of Weber's law for spatial changes would mean that the threshold for changes of position is proportional to the size of the openings in which the threshold is measured. From this point of view one might expect the transposition principle of velocities to be fully realized. Actually, Weber's law does not strictly hold in this field. This follows clearly from Cartwright's experiments. But the departure from Weber's law seems to be of about the same magnitude as the departure from ideal transposition of velocity. Thus the departure from ideal transposition of velocity may be attributed to the fact that Weber's law does not strictly hold in the case of spatial changes. (p. 159)

It has been suggested (Smith & Sherlock, 1957) that a "counting" artifact might explain the velocity transposition effect. If the standard and comparison displays consisted of a series of spots moving on continuous belts through the apertures and one display was magnified or minified in all respects in relation to the other, then in any given time interval more spots would pass through the small aperture than through the large one, and the ratio between the number of spots passing through the two apertures would be identical to the ratio between the sizes of the two displays. Only if the velocity of the spots in the large display were increased by as much as the size of the display had been magnified, would the frequency of the spots passing through the apertures be equal. Thus velocity matches based on the frequency with which elements pass in or out of the aperture could account for the transposition effect. Smith and Sherlock report results of an experiment that indicate that velocity matches between a standard and comparison stimulus, obtained when observers were instructed to judge frequency, were indistinguishable from those obtained when observers were instructed to match velocity. However, since Brown found the transposition effect even when the spacing between the moving spots in the standard and comparison displays differed, which, of course affects the number of spots which traverse the aperture during a given interval, it is unlikely that frequency is the primary explanation of this phenomenon. Rock (1975) correctly points out, "One method for avoiding this possible artifact is to present only one moving element within each aperture and to restrict observation to one half cycle" (p. 227).

6.4. Velocity Constancy: An Object-Relative Explanation

The principle of transposition of velocity has provided the basis for Wallach's object-relative explanation of perceived velocity constancy (Wallach, 1939). If perceived velocity is a function of the *proportion* of the field traversed per unit of time, then since this proportion remains constant despite changes in the object's distance from the observer, the transposition of velocity can account for perceived velocity constancy without reference to distance information. Consider the fact that a moving stimulus four times as large as another in a field four times as large must move four times as fast to appear to move at an equal speed when both are at the same distance from the observer. The retinal dimensions of these two configurations are identical to those that would be produced by two arrays of equal size, one of which was four times as far away as the other. If perceived velocity is a function of the proportion of the field traversed per unit of time, then despite the fact that the retinal angular velocity of the distant stimulus is one-fourth that of the near stimulus, perceived velocity should be equal since the retinal extent of the field through which it moves is also reduced by a factor of 4.

Epstein (1978) recently has reported evidence confirming Wallach's account of velocity constancy. In one experiment observers compared the velocity of one stimulus, a 0.5° point of light, with another equal-sized stimulus designated the standard. Both stimuli were enclosed by equal-sized apertures, the boundaries of which were clearly marked. The stimuli designated as standard was placed at the same distance as the comparison or at two, three, four, or five times that distance. The comparison stimulus was always 1 m from the observer. The observers viewed the arrays binocularly or monocularly through a small aperture. Constancy of velocity was found to be nearly perfect for both viewing conditions; that is, *relative* angular velocity accounted for perceived velocity whether or not egocentric distance information was available. [See Figure 17.26(b)]

If perceived velocity were a function of perceived extent of movement, that is, of subject-relative distance information, this outcome could not have been obtained since monocular viewing deprived the observer of all distance information. Monocular viewing should therefore have produced retinal velocity matches. These results were confirmed by the results of another experiment which showed that, under similar conditions of viewing, perceived *size* and *distance were*, as expected, predictably affected by mode of viewing, whether monocular or binocular. [See Figure 17.26(a)]

Additional evidence was provided by an experiment in which the standard array was again placed at different distances, but now its dimensions varied in direction proportion to its distance, so that its retinal size was always constant. As distance of the standard increased, its angular velocity decreased (since its physical velocity remained constant), but the angular size of the frame remained constant. This differs from the previous experiment in which angular velocity and angular size of the standard both varied concomitantly with distance, so that physical size and velocity remained constant. If perceived velocity is a function of *relative* angular velocity, then the velocity of

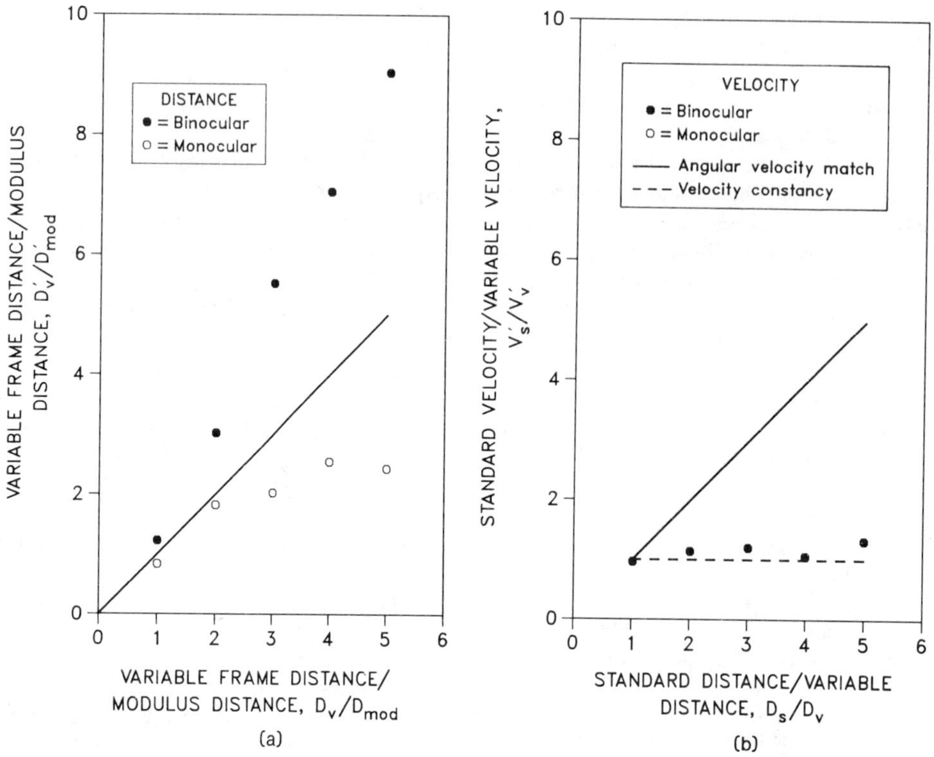

Figure 17.26. Velocity transposition data. (a) The modulus was a 7.5 × 2.5-cm frame at 1 m from the observer. The variable frame consisted of nine size-distance combinations (ranging from 7.5 × 2.5 at 1 m from the observer to 37.5 × 12.5 cm at 5 m). The variable frames were presented individually. The variable and modulus were successively presented. No moving points were included in either frame. Twelve subjects (six binocular and six monocular viewing) assigned to a whole number estimate of the perceived distance of the variable frame relative to the distance of the modulus (D'_v/D'_{mod}). The actual ratio of the variable frame's distance to the modulus distance is D_v/D_{mod}. When the two displays subtended the same visual angle, the relative objective distances were discriminated with binocular viewing but were not discriminated monocularly. There was a tendency to overestimation in binocular viewing. Monocular viewing reduces distance information available in binocular input. (b) The variable and standard frames were both 37.5 × 12.5 cm, viewed successively, and separated by 90°. Both enclosed a projected spot traversing the frames 2.4 or 7.5 cm/sec. The standard was presented, individually, at distances of 1, 2, 3, 4, and 5 m from the subject. The variable was presented at 1 m from the subject. Subjects used a potentiometer to adjust the velocity of the dot in the variable to match that of the standard. The ratio of standard distance to variable distance is D_s/D_v. The ratio of perceived velocity of dot in standard to variable is V'_s/V'_v. Constancy of velocity was obtained with both monocular and binocular viewing. The effect of the frame on the perceived velocity is unaffected by the reduction of distance cues in monocular viewing. (From W. Epstein, Two factors in the perception of velocity at a distance, *Perception and Psychophysics*, 1978, *24*. Reprinted with permission.)

the comparison stimulus, which is at a constant distance, must be decreased as the distance of the standard is increased if the two are to appear equal. Results consistent with this prediction were obtained. When the standard was five times the distance of the comparison, the ratio of standard to comparison velocity judged equal was 4.75. If perceived velocity were determined by absolute angular velocity and distance information, the velocity of the standard should have been perceived as constant over the various distances, since viewing was binocular and angular velocity decreased proportional to distance. The fact that perceived velocity decreased as distance increased reflects the influence of angular size of the field, which remained constant and led to a decrease in relative angular velocity.

A more recent study (Epstein & Cody, 1980) provides evidence that the transposition effect occurs even in the absence of a visible frame. When two light spots moved through a dark field containing no visible static contours and one spot moved three times the distance of the other, the velocity of the spot traversing the greater distance had to be increased for the velocities to appear equal. This increase was not statistically different from the increase in the control condition in which rectangular frames defined the motion paths. This result, as well as the results of other experiments, allowed the investigators to conclude, "The perceived relative velocities of two objects are significantly affected by the proportions of the retinal projections of the respective movement fields traversed by the two objects in the same unit of time, even when the motion fields consist only of the objects' motion paths" (Epstein & Cody, 1980, p. 47). It should be noted that both J. F. Brown and Epstein failed to find complete transposition of velocity, and the results reported by Epstein (1978) fall short of those reported by J. F. Brown (1931a). (See Table 17.1, which presents both the Epstein and the Brown results.)

In conclusion, the available evidence indicates that perceived velocity may be determined by the subject-relative input, which involves registered distance information, or by object-relative

Table 17.1. Ratio of Velocities (Standard/Variable) for Perceived Equality of Velocity in Conventional Arrangement

Ratio of Projective Sizes of Frames (Standard/Variable)	Transposition Ratio	Linear Velocity Ratio	Obtained Ratio of Velocities		Brown's Results
			Mean	Standard Deviation	
1	1	1	1.007	0.106	
2	2	1	1.447	0.246	1.91
3	3	1	1.818	0.389	2.61
4	4	1	2.139	0.675	3.09
5	5	1	2.531	0.461	3.48

The variable display was a 7.5 × 2.5-cm rectangle at 1 m from the subject. The standard display consisted of five rectangular frames presented individually, ranging from 7.5 × 2.5 to 37.5 × 12.5 cm at 1 m from the subject. Both standard and variable displays enclosed an oscilloscope spot of light traversing the entire frame at a linear velocity of 2.5 or 7.5 cm/sec. The variable display was separated by 90° from the standard. The displays were viewed successively. The six subjects adjusted the perceived velocity of the point of light moving across the variable frame to match that of the perceived velocity of the dot moving across the standard. Transposition of the linear dimensions of the standard display had systematic effects on relative perceived velocity. The effects fell short of Brown's (1931a) results but were in the same direction predicted by the transposition of velocity principle. In the right-hand column are results reported by J. F. Brown (1931a).

Source: J. F. Brown, The visual perception of velocity. *Psychologische Forschung*, 1931, vol. 14. Reprinted with permission of Springer-Verlag, publishers.

information, namely, the proportion of the field traversed per unit of time. Consistent with other evidence indicating the potency of object-relative determinants of motion perception, Epstein's results clearly demonstrate the salience of the object-relative determinants of perceived velocity when these conflict with available subject-relative input. It might be noted, however, that despite the importance of relative retinal displacement for the perception of velocity, this information signifies nothing about the absolute velocity of an object. It signifies only that an object in one field is moving faster or slower than an object in another field. This is, of course, a characteristic of all object-relative input. Despite its potency in the motion perception process, it provides no information about how fast, how far, or which object is moving.

REFERENCES

Adams, H. F. Autokinetic sensations. *Psychological Monographs*, 1912, *14*, 1–45.

Anstis, S., & Reinhardt-Rutland, A. Interaction between motion aftereffects and induced movement. *Vision Research*, 1976, *16*, 1391–1394.

Aubert, H. Die Bewegungsempfindungen. *Pfluger's Archiv fur Die Gesamte Physiologie Des Menschen und Der Tiere*, 1886, *39*, 347–370.

Bacon, J., Gordon, A., & Schulman, P. The effect of two types of induced motion displays on perceived location of the induced target. *Perception and Psychophysics*, 1982, *32*, 353–359.

Barlow, H. B. Eye movements during fixation. *Journal of Physiology*, 1952, *116*, 290–306.

Bassili, J. N., & Farber, J. M. Experiments on the locus of induced motion. *Perception and Psychophysics*, 1977, *21*, 157–161.

Bonnet, C. A tentative model for visual motion direction. *Psychologia*, 1975, *18*, 35–50.

Bonnet, C. Thresholds of motion perception. In A. H. Wertheim, W. A. Wagenaar, & H. W. Leibowitz (Eds.), *Tutorials on motion perception.* New York: Plenum Press, 1982.

Bourdon, B. *La perception visuelle de l'espace*. Paris: Schleicher Freres, 1902.

Brandt, T., Dichgans, J., & Koenig, E. Differential effects of central versus peripheral vision on egocentric and exocentric motion perception. *Experimental Brain Research*, 1973, *16*, 476–491.

Bridgeman, B. Visual receptive fields sensitive to absolute and relative motion during tracking. *Science*, 1972, *178*, 1106–1108.

Bridgeman, B., Hendry, D., & Stark, L. Failure to detect displacement of the visual world during saccadic eye movements. *Vision Research*, 1975, *15*, 719–722.

Bridgeman, B., Kirch, M., & Sperling, A. Segregation of cognitive and motor aspects of visual function using induced motion. *Perception and Psychophysics*, 1981, *29*, 336–342.

Bridgeman, B., Lewis, S., Heit, G., & Nagle, M. Relation between cognitive and motor-oriented systems of visual position perception. *Journal of Experimental Psychology*, 1979, *5*, 692–700.

Brosgole, L. Induced autokinesis. *Perception and Psychophysics*, 1967, *2*, 69–73.

Brosgole, L. Analysis of induced motion. *Acta Psychologia*, 1968, *28*, 1–44.

Brosgole, L., Cristal, R., & Carpenter, O. The role of eye movements in the perception of visually induced motion. *Perception and Psychophysics*, 1968, *3*, 166–168.

Brown, J. F. The visual perception of velocity. *Psychologische Forschung*, 1931, *14*, 249–268. (a)

Brown, J. F. The thresholds for visual movement. *Psychologische Forschung*, 1931, *14*, 189–192. (b)

Brown, R. H. Velocity discrimination and the intensity time relation. *Journal of the Optical Society of America*, 1955, *45*, 189–192.

Burns, B. Delisle, Gassanov, U., & Webb, A. C. Responses of neurons in the cat's visual cerebral cortex to relative movement of patterns. *Journal of Physiology*, 1972, *226*, 113–151.

Carr, H. A. Studies from the Psychological Laboratory of the University of Chicago. *Psychological Review*, 1907, *17*, 42–75.

Cartwright, D. On visual speed. *Psychologische Forschung*, 1938, *22*, 320–342.

Charpentier, A. Sur une illusion visuelle. *Academie des Sciences, Paris, Comptes Rendus*, 1886, *102*, 1155–1157.

Coren, S., Bradley, D. R., Hoenig, P., & Girgus, J. The effect of smooth tracking and saccadic eye movements on the perception of size: The shrinking circle illusion. *Vision Research*, 1975, *15*, 49–55.

Crone, R. A., & Verduyn Lunel, H. F. E. Autokinesis and the perception of movement: The physiology of eccentric fixation. *Vision Research*, 1969, *9*, 89–101.

Day, R. H. Induced rotation with concentric patterns. *Perception and Psychophysics*, 1981, *29*, 493–499.

Day, R. H., & Dickinson, R. G. Absence of color selectivity in Duncker-type induced visual movement. *Perception and Psychophysics*, 1977, *22*, 313–320.

Day, R. H., Millar, J. H., & Dickinson, R. G. Induced movement as nonveridical resolution of displacement ambiguity: Effect of enclosure and number of field elements. *Perception and Psychophysics*, 1979, *25*, 23–28.

DeSisto, M. J., & McLaughlin, S. C. Change in judgement of direction of gaze after autokinetic perception. *Psychonomic Science*, 1968, *10*, 221–222.

Dichgans, J., Koener, F., & Voigt, K. Verleichende Skalierung des afferenten und efferenten Bewegungssehen beim Menschen: Lineare Funktionen mit Verschiedener Ansteigssteilheit. *Psychologische Forschung*, 1969, *32*, 277–295.

Dodge, R. The participation of the eye movements in the visual perception of motion. *Psychological Review*, 1904, *11*, 1–14.

Dodge, R. The pendular whiplash illusion. *Psychological Bulletin*, 1910, *7*, 390–393.

Duncker, K. Uber induzierte Bewegung. *Psychologische Forschung*, 1929, *22*, 180–259.

Epstein, W. Two factors in the perception of velocity at a distance. *Perception and Psychophysics*, 1978, *24*, 105–114.

Epstein, W., & Cody, W. J. Perception of relative velocity: A revision of the hypothesis of relational determination. *Perception*, 1980, *9*, 47–60.

Exner, S. Uber das sehen von Bewegungen und die theorie des zusammengesetzen Auges. *Sitzungsberichts Akademie Wissenschaft Wein*, 1875, *72*, 156–190.

Exner, S. Uber autokinestische Empfindungen. *Zeitschrift fur Psychologie und Physiologie der Sinnesorgane*, 1896, *12*, 313–330.

Farber, J. Manual tracking of induced motion. *Investigative Opthalmology*, 1979, *18*, 3.

Farne, M. Studies on induced motion in the third dimension. *Perception*, 1972, *1*, 351–357.

Festinger, L., & Easton, A. M. Inferences about the efferent system based on a perceptual illusion produced by eye movements. *Psychological Review*, 1974, *81*, 44–58.

Festinger, L., Sedgwick, H. A., & Holtzman, J. D. Visual perception during smooth pursuit eye movements. *Vision Research*, 1976, *16*, 1377–1386.

Filehne, W. Ueber das optische Wahenehmen von Bewegungen. *Zeitschrift fur Sinnesphysiologie*, 1922, *53*, 134–145.

Fleischl, E. von Physiologischoptische notizen. *Sitzungsberichte der Akademie der Wissenschaften*, 1882, *86*, 17–25.

Ford, A. The pendular whiplash illusion. *Psychological Review*, 1910, *17*, 192–204.

Frost, B. J., & Wong, S. The effect of relative motion on directionally specific pigeon tectal units. *Society for Neuroscience Abstracts*, 1977, *3*, 560.

Fujii, E. Forming a figure by movements of a luminous point. *Japanese Journal of Psychology*, 1943, *18*, 196–232.

Gibson, J. J. What gives rise to the perception of motion. *Psychological Review*, 1968, *75*, 335–364.

Gilbert, D. A factor analytic study of autokinetic responses. *Journal of Experimental Psychology*, 1967, *73*, 354–357.

Gogel, W. C. Relative motion and the adjacency principle. *Quarterly Journal of Experimental Psychology*, 1974, *26*, 425–437.

Gogel, W. C. Independence of motion induction in separated portions of the visual field. *Psychonomic Science*, 1977, *10*, 408–415. (a)

Gogel, W. C. The metric of visual space. In W. Epstein (Ed.), *Stability and constancy in visual perception*. New York: Wiley, 1977. (b)

Gogel, W. C. Induced motion as a function of the speed of the inducing object, measured by means of two methods. *Perception*, 1979, *8*, 255–262.

Gogel, W. C., & Koslow, M. A. The effect of perceived distance on induced movement. *Perception and Psychophysics*, 1971, *10*, 142–146.

Gogel, W. C., & Koslow, M. A. The adjacency principle and induced movement. *Psychonomic Science*, 1972, *11*, 309–314.

Gogel, W. C., & MacCracken, P. J. Depth adjacency and induced motion. *Perceptual and Motor Skills,* 1979, *48*, 313–350.

Gogel, W. C., & Tietz, J. D. Adjacency and attention as determiners of perceived motion. *Vision Research*, 1976, *16*, 839–845.

Graybiel, A., & Clark, B. The autokinetic illusion and its significance in night flying. *Journal of Aviation Medicine*, 1945, *16*, 111–151.

Gregory, R. L., & Zangwill, O. L. The origin of the autokinetic effect. *Quarterly Journal of Experimental Psychology*, 1963, *15*, 252–261.

Guilford, J. P., & Dallenbach, K. M. A study of the autokinetic sensation. *American Journal of Psychology*, 1928, *40*, 83–91.

Hallett, P. E., & Lightstone, A. D. Saccadic eye movements towards stimuli triggered by prior saccades. *Vision Research*, 1976, *16*, 99–106. (a)

Hallett, P. E., & Lightstone, A. D. Saccadic eye movements to flashed targets. *Vision Research*, 1976, *16*, 107–114. (b)

Hanes, L. F. Discrimination of direction of movement at short exposure durations. *Dissertation Abstracts International*, 1965, *25*.

Hansen, R. Spatial localization during pursuit eye movements. *Vision Research*, 1979, *19*, 1213–1221.

Harvey, L., & Michon, J. Detectability of relative motion as a function of exposure duration, angular separation, and background. *Journal of Experimental Psychology*, 1974, *103*, 317–325.

Hayashi, K. *The apparent path of a circular moving spot* (Report No. 5). Hiyoshi, Japan: Keio University, Psychological Laboratory, 1971.

Henn, V., Young, L. R., & Finley, C. Vestibular nucleus units in alert monkeys are also influenced by moving visual fields. *Brain Research*, 1974, *71*, 144–149.

Heywood, S. Pursuing stationary dots: Smooth eye movements in apparent movement. *Perception*, 1973, *2*, 181–195.

Heywood, S., & Churcher, J. Eye movements and the afterimage—I. Tracking the afterimage. *Vision Research*, 1971, *11*, 1163–1168.

Hochberg, J. In the mind's eye. In R. N. Haber (Ed.), *Contemporary theory and research in visual perception*. New York: Holt, Rinehardt & Winston, 1968.

Hochberg, J., & Fallon, P. Perceptual analysis of moving patterns. *Science*, 1976, *194*, 1081–1083.

Holtzman, J., Sedgwick, H., & Festinger, L. Interaction of peripherally monitored and unmonitored efferent commands for smooth pursuit eye movements. *Vision Research*, 1978, *18*, 1545–1555.

Hoppe, J. I. *Die Schein-Bewegung*. Wurzberg: A. Stuber, 1879.

Hoppe, J. I. Studie zur Erklarung gewisser Scheinbewgungen. *Zeitschrift fur Psychologie und Physiologie der Sinnesorgane*, 1894, *7*, 29–37.

Howard, I. *Human visual orientation*. New York: Wiley, 1982.

Johansson, G. *Configurations in event perception*. Uppsala, Sweden: Almquist & Wilksell, 1950.

Jordan, S. Autokinesis and felt eye position. *American Journal of Psychology*, 1968, *81*, 497–512.

Kaufman, L. *Sight and Mind*. New York: Oxford University Press, 1974.

Kaufman, L., Cyralnick, I., Kaplowitz, J., Melnick, G., & Stoff, D. The complementarity of apparent and real motion. *Psychologische Forschung*, 1971, *34*, 343–348.

Kinchla, R. A. Visual movement perception: A comparison of absolute and relative movement discrimination. *Perception and Psychophysics*, 1971, *9*, 165–171.

Kömmerell, G., & Taumer, R. Investigations of the eye tracking system through stabilized retinal images. *Bibliotheca Ophthalmologica*, 1972, *82*, 288–297.

LaMontagne, C. A new experimental paradigm for the investigation of the secondary system of human visual motion perception. *Perception*, 1973, *2*, 167–180.

Leeuwenberg, E. L. J. Quantification of certain visual pattern properties: Salience, transparency, similarity. In E. L. J. Leeuwenberg & H. F. J. Buffart (Eds.), *Formal theories of visual perception*. New York: Wiley, 1978.

Lehman, R. Eye movements and the autokinetic illusion. *American Journal of Psychology*, 1965, *78*, 490–492.

Leibowitz, H. W. Effects of reference lines on the discrimination of movement. *Journal of the Optical Society of America*, 1955, *45*, 829–830.

Levy, J. Autokinetic illusion: A systematic review of theories, measures and independent variables. *Psychological Review*, 1972, *78*, 457–474.

Loomis, J., & Nakayama, K. A velocity analogue to brightness contrast. *Vision Research*, 1973, *18*, 425–428.

Mack, A. An investigation of the relationship between eye and retinal image movement in the perception of movement. *Perception and*

Psychophysics, 1970, *8*, 291–298.

Mack, A. Three modes of visual perception. In H. L. Pick & E. Saltzman (Eds.), *Modes of processing information*. Hillsdale, N.J.: Lawrence Erlbaum, 1978.

Mack, A., & Bachant, J. Perceived movement of the afterimage during eye movements. *Perception and Psychophysics*, 1969 *6*, 379–384.

Mack, A., Fendrich, R., & Chambers, D. Retinal and perceptual location in saccadic control. *Supplement to Investigative Opthalmology and Visual Science*, 1982, *22*, 104.

Mack, A., Fendrich, R., & Fisher, C. B. A new illusion of movement dependent on eye movement during head rotation. *Perception*, 1974, *3*, 53–62.

Mack, A., Fendrich, R., & Fisher, C. B. A re-examination of two-point induced movement. *Perception and Psychophysics*, 1975, *17*, 273–276.

Mack, A., Fendirch, R., & Pleune, J. Smooth pursuit eye movements: Is perceived motion necessary? *Science*, 1979, 2, 1361–1363.

Mack, A., Fendrich, R., & Sirigatti, S. A rebound illusion in visual tracking. *American Journal of Psychology*, 1973, *86*, 425–433.

Mack, A., Fendrich, R., & Wong, E. Is perceived motion a stimulus for smooth pursuit? *Vision Research*, 1982, *22*, 77–88.

Mack, A., & Herman, E. A new illusion: The underestimation of distance during pursuit eye movements. *Perception and Psychophysics*, 1972, *12*, 471–473.

Mack, A., & Herman, E. Position constancy during eye pursuit movement: An investigation of the Filehne illusion. *Quarterly Journal of Experimental Psychology*, 1973, *25*, 7–84.

Mack, A., & Herman, E. The loss of position constancy during pursuit eye movements. *Vision Research*, 1978, *18*, 55–62.

Mates, B. Effect of reference marks and luminance on discrimination of movement. *Journal of Psychology*, 1969, *73*, 209–221.

Matin, L. Eye movements and perceived visual direction. In H. Autrum, R. Jung, W. R. Loewenstein, D. M. McKay, & H. L. Teuber (Eds.), *Handbook of sensory physiology* (Vol. VII). Berlin: Springer-Verlag, 1972.

Matin, L., & MacKinnon, G. E. Autokinetic movement: Selective manipulation of directional components by image stabilization. *Science*, 1964, *143*, 147–148.

McConkie, A., & Farber, J. Relation between perceived depth and perceived motion in uniform flow-fields. *Journal of Experimental Psychology: Human Perception and Performance*, 1979, *5*, 501–508.

Miller, J. Information used by the perceptual and oculomotor systems regarding the amplitude of saccadic and pursuit eye movements. *Vision Research*, 1980, *20*, 59–68.

Nachmias, J. Determiners of the drift of the eye during monocular fixation. *Journal of the Optical Society of America*, 1961, *51*, 761–766.

Nakayama, K., & Tyler, W. C. Relative motion induced between stationary lines. *Vision Research*, 1978, *18*, 1663–1668.

Ono, H., & Nakamizo, S. Saccadic eye movements during changes in fixation to stimuli at different distances. *Vision Research*, 1977, 233–238.

Over, R., & Lovegrove, W. Color selectivity in simultaneous motion contrast. *Perception and Psychophysics*, 1973, *14*, 445–448.

Pearce, D. G., & Matin, L. The measurement of autokinetic speed. *Canadian Journal of Psychology*, 1966, *20*, 160–172.

Peterson, M. A., & Hochberg, J. Opposed set procedure: Measure of the role of local cues and intention in form perception. *Journal of Experimental Psychology: Human Perception and Performance*, 1983, *9*, 183–194.

Piggens, D. R. Autokinesis with an afterimage. *Journal of Physiology*, 1965, *78*, 509–510.

Proffitt, D. R., & Cutting, J. E. Perceiving the centroid of configurations on a rolling wheel. *Perception and Psychophysics*, 1979, *25*, 389–398.

Proffitt, D. R., & Cutting, J. E. An invariant for wheel-generated motions and the logic of its determination. *Perception*, 1980, *9*, 435–449. (a)

Proffitt, D. R., & Cutting, J. E. Perceiving the centroid of curvilinearly bounded rolling shapes. *Perception and Psychophysics*, 1980, *28*, 484–487. (b)

Proffitt, D. R., Cutting, J. E., & Steir, D. M. Perception of wheel generated motions. *Journal of Experimental Psychology: Human Perception and Performance*, 1979, *5*, 289–302.

Reinwald, F. L. *An experimental investigation of conditions affecting autokinetic sensations*. Unpublished doctoral dissertation, University of Texas, 1952.

Restle, F. Coding theory of the perception of motion configurations. *Psychological Review*, 1979, *86*, 1–24.

Rock, I. The basis of position constancy during passive movement of the observer. *American Journal of Psychology*, 1968, *81*, 262–265.

Rock, I. *An introduction to perception*. New York: Macmillan, 1975.

Rock, I., Auster, M., Schiffman, H., & Wheeler, D. Induced movement based on the subtraction of motion from the inducing object. *Journal of Experimental Psychology: Human Perception and Performance*, 1980, *6*, 391–403.

Rock, I., & Ebenholtz, S. Stroboscopic movement based on change of phenomenal rather than retinal location. *American Journal of Psychology*, 1962, *75*, 193–207.

Rock, I., & Halper, F. Form perception without a retinal image. *American Journal of Psychology*, 1969, *82*, 425–440.

Rock, I., Hill, L., & Fineman, M. Speed constancy as a function of size constancy. *Perception and Psychophysics*, 1968, *4*, 37–40.

Roelofs, C. O. Optische Localisation. *Archiv fur Augenheilkunde*, 1935, *109*, 395–415.

Royce, J. R., Carran, A. B., Aftanas, M., Lehman, R. S., & Blumenthal, A. The autokinetic phenomenon: A critical review. Psychological Bulletin, 1966, *65*, 243–260.

Rubin, E. Visuell Wahrgenommene Wirkliche Bewegungen. *Zeitschrift fur Psychologie*, 1927, *103*, 382–392.

Schulman, P. Eye movements do not cause induced motion. *Perception and Psychophysics*, 1979, *26*, 381–383.

Shaffer, O., & Wallach, H. Extent-of-motion thresholds under subject-relative and object-relative conditions. *Perception and Psychophysics*, 1966, *1*, 447–451.

Skolnick, A. The role of eye movements in the autokinetic phenomenon. *Journal of Experimental Psychology*, 1940, *26*, 373–393.

Smith, O. W., & Sherlock, C. A new explanation of the velocity transposition phenomenon. *American Journal of Psychology*, 1957, *70*, 102–105.

Stark, L., Kong, R., Schwartz, S., Hendry, D., & Bridgeman, B. Saccadic suppression of image displacement. *Vision Research*, 1976, *16*, 1185–1187.

Steinbach, M. Pursuing the perceptual rather than the retinal stimulus. *Vision Research*, 1976, *16*, 1371–1376.

Sterling, P., & Wickelgren, B. Visual receptive fields in the superior colliculus in the cat. *Neurophysiology*, 1977, *3*, 560.

Stoper, A. *Vision during pursuit eye movements: The role of oculomotor information*. Unpublished doctoral dissertation, Brandeis University, 1967.

Stoper, A. Apparent motion of stimuli presented stroboscopically during pursuit eye movements. *Perception and Psychophysics*, 1973, *13*, 301–311.

Sugarman, R. C., & Cohen, W. Perceived target displacement as a function of field movement and asymmetry. *Perception and Psychophysics*, 1968, *3*, 169–173.

Teuber, H. L. Perception. In H. W. Magoun & V. E. Hall (Eds.), *Handbook of physiology* (Vol. 3): *Neurophysiology*. Washington, D.C.: American Physiological Society, 1960.

Tynan, P., & Sekular, R. Simultaneous motion contrast: Velocity sensitivity and depth responses. *Vision Research*, 1975, *15*, 1231–1238.

Vaegan, **X**. The position of random autokinetic movement and the physiological position of rest are frequently stable and identical. *Perception and Psychophysics*, 1976, *19*, 240–245.

von Holst, E. Relations between the central nervous system and the peripheral organs. *British Journal of Animal Behavior*, 1954, *2*, 89–94.

Wallach, H. On constancy of visual speed. *Psychological Review*, 1939, *46*, 541–552.

Wallach, H. The perception of motion. *Scientific American, 1959, 201*, 56–60.

Wallach, H. Visual perception of motion. In G. Kepes (Ed.), *The nature of art and motion*. New York: George Braziller, 1965.

Wallach, H. Informational discrepancy as the basis for perceptual adaptation. In S. J. Freedman (Ed.), *The neuropsychology of spatially oriented behavior*. Homewood, Ill.: Dorsey Press, 1968.

Wallach, H. *On perception*. New York: Quadrangle, 1976.

Wallach, H. Eye movement and motion perception. In A. H. Wertheim, W. A. Wagenaar, & H. W. Leibowitz (Eds.), *Tutorials on motion perception*. New York: Plenum Press, 1982.

Wallach, H., Bacon, J., & Schulman, P. Alteration of induced motion. *Perception and Psychophysics*, 1978, *24*, 509–514.

Wallach, H., & Kravitz, J. The measurement of the constancy of visual direction and its adaptation. *Psychonomic Science*, 1965, *2*, 217–218. (a)

Wallach, H., & Kravitz, J. Rapid adaptation in the constancy of visual direction with active and passive rotation. *Psychonomic Science*, 1965, *3*, 165–166. (b)

Wallach, H., & Kravitz, J. Adaptation in the constancy of visual direction tested by measuring the constancy of auditory direction. *Perception and Psychophysics*, 1968, *4*, 299–303.

Wallach, H., & Lewis, C. The effect of abnormal displacement of the retinal image during eye movements. *Perception and Psychophysics*, 1966, *1*, 25–29.

Ward, R., & Morgan, M. J. Perceptual effects of pursuit eye movements in the absence of a target. *Nature*, 1978, *274*, 158–159.

Whipple, W., & Wallach, H. Direction-specific motion thresholds for abnormal image shifts during saccadic eye movements. *Perception and Psychophysics*, 1978, *24*, 509–514.

Wong, E. *Information used by the oculomotor system in saccadic programming and the relationship of perceptual and saccadic responses*. Unpublished doctoral dissertation, New School for Social Research, 1981.

Wong, E., & Mack, A. Saccadic programming and perceived location. *Acta Psychologia*, 1981, *48*, 123–131.

Yasui, S., & Young, L. R. Perceived visual motion as effective stimulus to pursuit eye movements. *Science*, 1975, *190*, 906–908.

Ziehen, T. L. Einige BemerKungen Uber das sog. Punktschwanken. *Zeitschrift fur Sinnesphysiologie*, 1927, *58*, 59–72.

CHAPTER 18

THE PERCEPTION OF POSTURE, SELF MOTION, AND THE VISUAL VERTICAL

IAN P. HOWARD

York University, Toronto, Ontario, Canada

CONTENTS

Portions of this chapter are adapted from *Human spatial orientation*, I. P. Howard and W. B. Templeton, Wiley, 1966.

1. THE CONTROL OF POSTURE

1.1. Postural Reflexes

1.1.1. Background. Postural reflexes are subcortically controlled patterns of behavior concerned with maintaining and restoring an animal's upright posture both while the animal is standing still and while it is moving about. The eyes, the vestibular system, and receptors in skin, muscles, tendons, and joints all contribute afferent signals that initiate component reflexes in the total pattern of postural-reflex behavior. Responses involve movements of the limbs, trunk, and neck, with associated movements of the eyes. Stimuli are conveyed to, and responses are organized in, nerve centers at several levels of the central nervous system, including the spinal cord, upper brain stem nuclei, basal ganglia, cerebellum, and diencephalon. The cerebral cortex may coordinate or override the subcortical reflex patterns of behavior. Reflexes operating in an animal in which the spinal cord has been severed from the brain stem are known as *spinal reflexes*. Spinal reflexes for which the sense organs and effectors are in the same body segment are known as *segmental reflexes*. One segmental reflex to be discussed is the *myotatic reflex*, which is a reflex contraction of a muscle evoked when it is stretched passively. In this reflex, afferent signals from sensory muscle spindles in the muscle are conveyed to the spinal cord along sensory fibers, which enter the dorsal root and make direct connections with motoneurons, which emerge in the ventral root to reach the contractile elements of the stretched muscle. Spinal reflexes involving stimuli and responses in more than one body segment are known as *intersegmental reflexes*. Those that depend on subcortical structures of the upper brain stem are known as *suprasegmental reflexes*.

In higher mammals, and particularly in humans, postural reflexes are subservient to cortical control. This dominance has developed because intelligently guided behavior often requires movements that run counter to the demands of reflex control. Furthermore, reflex actions are too slow for many learned skills. Learned skills are preprogrammed according to contingencies that the animal anticipates before stimuli have had time to evoke basic reflex mechanisms. For instance, an animal running over rough ground plans its movements with respect to obstacles it can see at some distance (Lee & Lishman, 1977). If the environment is familiar, the animal may be able to ignore sensory inputs by executing a sequence of preplanned actions. Nevertheless, even well-executed performances, such as those of gymnasts and athletes, still show the postural attitudes and movement sequences typical of subcortical reflex patterns (Fukuda, 1961). Furthermore, drawings and statues of animals and humans look most natural and aesthetically pleasing when the postures resemble those evoked by basic reflexes. This similarity between well-executed voluntary movements and subcortically controlled movements may be due to the fact that voluntary control can involve the evocation of basic reflex patterns. Another reason why well-learned motor skills conform to these patterns is that they are the most efficient ways of moving, whichever centers control them.

The cerebral cortex of a neonate human is unmyelinated and, therefore, nonfunctional. For this reason subcortical postural reflexes are evident at this age (see Peiper, 1963, for a review of this topic). Later in life they become much less evident, although they may show in pathological states. They are certainly evident in decerebrate animals, as we shall see in what follows. This section ends with a brief description of the pathways and centers involved in postural reflexes, illustrated in Figure 18.1. The vestibular nuclei of the upper brain stem, working in conjunction with the cerebellum, constitute the hub of the postural reflex system. Other important centers include the colliculi, basal ganglia, and diencephalon.

Each lateral vestibular nucleus conveys signals originating in the utricle and saccule to the *lateral vestibulospinal tract,* which descends ipsilaterally to exert mainly excitatory influences on extensor and flexor motoneurons at all levels of the spinal cord (Nyberg-Hansen, 1975, pp. 71–96). Many of these pathways are polysynaptic, especially those reaching motoneurons of the limbs (Maeda, Maunz, & Wilson, 1975). Some axons in the vestibulospinal tract branch to supply motoneurons at more than one level and thus control distinct muscle groups simultaneously (Abzug, Maeda, Peterson, & Wilson, 1974).

On each side of the head the lateral, medial, and inferior vestibular nuclei convey signals from the otolith organs and semicircular canals to the *medial vestibulospinal tract* which descends bilaterally to exert excitatory and inhibitory influences on motoneurons in the upper spinal cord. Fibers in this tract also branch to supply motoneurons at more than one level (Rapoport, Susswein, Uchino, & Wilson, 1977). Many of the axons in the two vestibulospinal tracts, which reach motoneurons in the neck, do so directly, rather than through multisynaptic networks, and are involved in easily identified reflex movements of the head. Direct fibers in the lateral tract are excitatory and reach ipsilateral neck motoneurons; those in the medial tract are both excitatory and inhibitory and reach motoneurons on both sides (Akaike, Fanardjian, Ito, & Ohno, 1973; Wilson & Maeda, 1974). The predominant effects of utricular stimulation on neck motoneurons is ipsilateral inhibition and contralateral excitation. The effects of saccular stimulation are opposite to those produced by utricular stimulation (Wilson, Gacek, Maeda, & Uchino, 1977). There are also very extensive two-way connections between the vestibular nuclei and the reticular formation from which originate the *reticular spinal tracts* (Brodal, 1974, pp. 239–398). These tracts convey signals, some of vestibular origin, to all levels of the spinal cord and, like the lateral vestibulospinal tract, mediate spinal reflexes and exercise reciprocal control over flexor and extensor motoneurons of the back, neck, and limbs through both monosynaptic and polysynaptic connections (Gernandt, 1974, pp. 541–564; Pompeiano, 1975, pp. 147–184). Other nerve fibers involved in the control of reflex activity in the muscles of the neck arise in the superior colliculus and descend in the *tectospinal* and *tectoreticulospinal* pathways to contralateral neck motoneurons (M. E. Anderson, Yoshida, & Wilson, 1972). Still other fibers arise in the diencephalon and descend to the spinal cord in the *rubrospinal* and *central tegmental tracts*. These diencephalic centers receive inputs from the vestibular nuclei, cerebellum, and spinothalamic tracts (Hess, 1957).

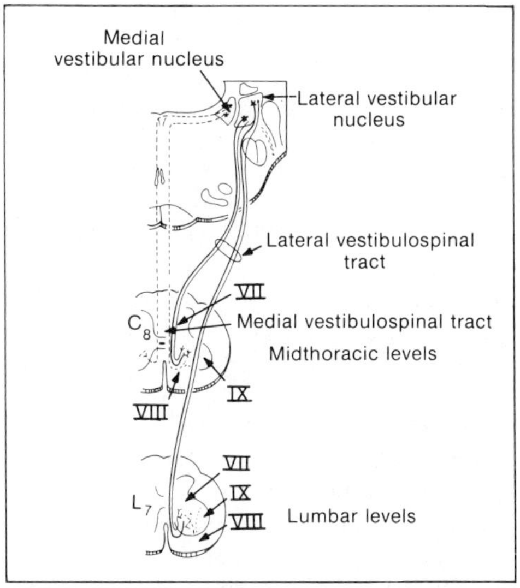

Figure 18.1. Diagrammatic representation of the lateral and medial vestibulospinal tracts. The lateral tract originates in the lateral vestibular nucleus and descends ipsilaterally to all levels of the spinal cord. The smaller medial tract originates mainly in the medial vestibular nucleus and descends to ipsilateral and contralateral midthoracic levels. Both pathways terminate mainly on interneurones in laminae VII—VIII of the spinal cord. (From R. Nyberg-Hansen, Anatomical aspects of the functional organization of the vestibulo-spinal pathways, *The vestibular system*. Academic Press, Inc., 1975. Reprinted with permission.)

Inputs from the vestibular sense organs reach the vestibular nuclei along the vestibular branch of the eighth cranial nerve. Inputs from receptors in the skin, joints, and muscles reach the vestibular nuclei along tracts that ascend in the spinal cord. These somesthetic and kinesthetic inputs, acting back through the vestibulospinal tracts, exert an excitatory influence on spinal motoneurons. The *cerebellum* also receives inputs from somesthetic and kinesthetic receptors (Kolb & Rubia, 1980; Rubia & Tandler, 1981; Thach, 1978). In addition, signals of vestibular origin reach the fastigial and vermal cortex of the cerebellum, either directly or through the ipsilateral vestibular nuclei (Pompeiano, 1974, pp. 417–476; Stanojević, Erway, Ghelarducci, Pompeiano, & Willis, 1980).

Pathways from the cerebellum project to the vestibular nuclei where they modulate the excitatory activity generated by somesthetic, kinesthetic, and vestibular inputs (Akaike, Fanardjian, Ito, & Nakajima, 1973; Bloedel, 1975; Higgins & Glaser, 1964; Orlovsky, 1972; Walberg, 1975, pp. 31–54). The cerebellum also controls muscle tonus by adjusting the gain of the gamma muscle-spindle system (see Chapter 11, "The Vestibular System," by Howard). More will be said about the cerebellum in Section 4.3.

Signals arising from proprioceptors in the neck play a crucial role in postural and eye-movement reflexes. Inputs initiating neck-postural reflexes ascend to the cerebellum and to the vestibular nuclei, often impinging on cells that also receive vestibular inputs (Abrahams & Rose, 1975; Anastasopoulos & Mergner, 1982; Boyle & Pompeiano, 1980a, 1980b; Kasper & Thoden, 1981; Stanojević, 1981). Inputs from neck proprioceptors that initiate eye-movement reflexes project to the cerebellum, superior colliculi, nucleus prepositus hyperglossi, and the frontal eye field (Dubrovsky & Barbas, 1977; Gresty & Baker, 1976; Wilson, Maeda, & Franck, 1975).

Excitation of stretch receptors in the extraocular muscles of the cat gives rise to discharges in those brain stem motor nuclei that control movements of the head and forelimbs (Easton, 1972). Cells discharging to the same stimulus have been found in the cerebellum of the monkey (Hepp, Henn, & Jaeger, 1982). These connections presumably serve to initiate reflex postural adjustments in response to movement of the eyes.

In this chapter the longitudinal axis of the human body will be referred to as the z axis; the axis in the median plane, at right angles to the z axis, will be referred to as the x axis; and the axis in the midfrontal plane will be referred to as the y axis. It is assumed that all these axes pass through the center of gravity of the body.

1.1.2. Tonic Reflexes of the Decerebrate Animal. When the brain stem is sectioned just above the vestibular nuclei, the antigravity extensor muscles of the body go into a continuous spasm, resulting in a rigid extension of the limbs, known as *decerebrate rigidity.* If the head of a decerebrate animal is placed in different positions, the distribution of tonus in the whole body is changed in characteristic ways. Two groups of reflexes are involved in these responses: the *tonic-neck reflexes*, resulting from stimulation of proprioceptors in the neck, and *the tonic-labyrinthine reflexes*, resulting from stimulation of the utricles.

Tonic-neck reflexes are studied in the decerebrate animal in which the labyrinths have been removed. When this is done, rotation of the head about the z axis causes extension of the forelimbs and hindlimbs on the side toward which the jaw is rotated and relaxation of the limbs on the side toward which the back of the head is rotated. Inclination of the head toward one shoulder causes extension of the limbs on that side of the body and relaxation of the limbs on the opposite side. Elevation of the head causes an extension of the forelimbs and relaxation of the hindlimbs. Lowering of the head causes flexion of the forelimbs and extension of the hindlimbs (Magnus, 1924, 1926).

Tonic-neck reflexes occur in many newborn or premature human infants. Figure 18.2 shows a typical reflex pattern induced by a sideways deflection of the head in a newborn infant, a pattern known as the "fencing position." Such reflexes are less obvious beyond the first half-year of life, when the cerebral cortex gains control over the lower reflex centers (Riesen & Kinder, 1952).

The tonic-neck reflexes are abolished after the dorsal (sensory) roots of the first three cervical segments have been severed. These nerves originate in receptors associated with the joints of the neck, especially the atlantoaxial and atlanto-occipital joints (McCouch, Deering, & Ling, 1951). Intravertebral joint receptors have not been found in the neck, and it has been suggested that the crucial sense organs for the tonic-neck reflexes are the small muscle spindles and Golgi tendon organs that abound in the small intravertebral and perivertebral muscles of mammals, including humans (Abrahams, 1977).

Monosynaptic, or myotatic, reflexes have not been demonstrated in the dorsal muscles of the neck (Abrahams, Richmond, & Rose, 1975). Any reflex responses of these muscles must therefore involve polysynaptic pathways in the spinal cord or higher levels of the central nervous system. The most important pathway for tonic-neck reflexes seems to be one involving those regions of the vestibular nuclei from which originate the vestibulospinal pathways (Abrahams, 1977). The fact that cerebellectomy has been found to weaken but not abolish tonic-neck reflexes in the cat suggests that pathways carrying neck-proprioceptive signals to the cerebellum have only a secondary role in controlling these reflexes (Wenzel, Thoden, & Frank, 1978).

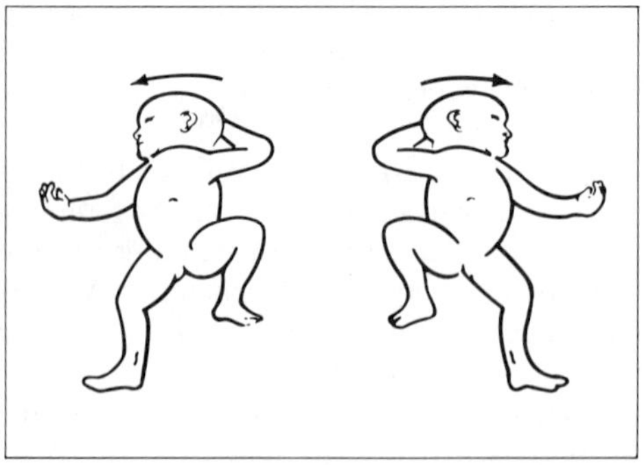

Figure 18.2. The tonic-neck reflex (fencing position) in a 2-month-old infant, induced by a sideways deflection of the head. Note the extension of the ipsilateral limbs and the flexion of the contralateral limbs (from Peiper, 1963, fig. 24).

Anesthetic blockage of the first three cervical dorsal roots in monkeys has been found to cause severe defects in balance, orientation, and motor coordination of the entire body (L. A. Cohen, 1961). The musculature of cervically deafferented animals becomes hypotonic, and the gain of vestibular reflexes is reduced (Ezure, Sasaki, Uchino, & Wilson, 1976, pp. 461–489). Humans with cervical rheumatism or spondylosis suffer from a condition known as *cervical vertigo.* There are sensations of spinning, falling, and nausea whenever an attempt is made to move the head. If such symptoms persist when the patient wears a collar that prevents movement of the head relative to the body, they are due to a vestibular disorder, such as Ménière's disease, rather than to cervical vertigo (Cope & Ryan, 1959).

The tonic-neck reflexes are clearly very important in the control of posture and movement, and it has been claimed that poor postural habits associated with the way the head is carried on the trunk are responsible for inefficient movements and general tension. Procedures for reeducating poor postural habits have been proposed (Jones, 1963, 1965).

Tonic-labyrinthine reflexes are investigated in the decerebrate animal after the first three dorsal cervical roots have been severed. In this way vestibular reflexes are not confused with tonic-neck reflexes. Sideways tilting of the head produces ipsilateral extension and contralateral flexion of the limbs. Nose-down tilting produces bilateral forelimb extension and hindlimb flexion. Nose-up tilting produces bilateral hindlimb extension and forelimb flexion (Roberts, 1971a). These tonic-labyrinthine responses serve to stabilize the position of the skull relative to the ground. It looks as though each vestibular organ controls the contralateral limbs, because when the cat is hemilabyrinthectomized, the response in ipsilateral limbs remains unchanged (Lindsay, & Rosenberg, 1978b).

The tonic-labyrinthine reflexes are partly under the control of the cerebellum. When this organ is removed in the cat, a side-down tilting of the head in either direction results in a flexion of both forelimbs (Lindsay & Rosenberg, 1978a). It may have been this response that led Magnus (1924) to conclude falsely that the tonic-labyrinthine reflexes act on all four limbs in the same way.

The tonic-labyrinthine responses persist when the head is held in a tilted position, which demonstrates that, under these circumstances, they are controlled by nonadapting inputs from the otolith organs.

One would expect the contribution of inputs from the canals to be evident only while the animal is being tilted. One way to dissociate the contributions of otolith and canal inputs to the vestibular-tonic reflex is to compare the responses in intact cats with those in cats with plugged vestibular canals. This procedure has revealed that the canal contribution becomes evident only when the cat is tilted at frequencies above 0.1 Hz; below this frequency the response is controlled by otolith inputs (Schor & Miller, 1981).

The effects produced on the limbs by the tonic-neck reflexes are opposite to those produced by the tonic-labyrinthine reflexes. Thus when an intact animal moves its head, the effects of the two groups of the reflexes cancel. This allows the animal to place and hold its head in any posture without interference from those reflexes (Lindsay, Roberts, & Rosenberg, 1976). The tonic-neck reflexes act alone when the body of an animal is tilted and its head is erect, as shown in Figure 18.3(a). This situation develops when an animal stands on a slanted surface, and responses result in a posture that holds the animal upright (Figure 18.3(d)). The tonic-labyrinthine reflexes act alone when the head and body of an animal are tilted together, as in Figure 18.3(b). The responses help to restore the animal to the upright posture. When the head is tilted alone, the two reflexes tend to cancel, thus allowing the animal to hold its head in a desired posture (Figure 18.3(c)).

Unilateral destruction of the cervical spinal roots in the cat produces hypertonicity of the ipsilateral limbs and hypotonicity of the contralateral limbs. This posture asymmetry is opposite in sign to that produced by destruction of the vestibular apparatus on the same side (Manzoni, Pompeiano, & Stampacchia, 1979).

A physiological basis for this reciprocal interaction between the tonic-labyrinthine and tonic-neck reflexes has been revealed by Boyle and Pompeiano (1981). They recorded from single cells in the lateral vestibular nucleus of the cat and found that about half the cells encountered responded to either sinusoidal tilt of the whole body or to rotation of the neck. Most of the cells upon which vestibular and neck inputs converged were excited by ipsilateral tilt of the whole body and inhibited by ipsilateral tilt of the head, and it is these cells which are presumably responsible for the reciprocal control of tonic-labyrinthine and tonic-neck reflexes. This view gains further support from the fact that cells in the vestibular nucleus of the cat that respond to stimulation of cervical and vestibular nerves are cells that project into the vestibulospinal tracts (Brink, Hirai, & Wilson, 1980). Cells that respond reciprocally to stimulation of neck and macular receptors have also been found in the spinal cord (Ehrhardt & Wagner, 1970), lateral reticular nucleus (Kubin, Manzoni, & Pompeiano, 1981), and cerebellum (Boyle & Pompeiano, 1980a; Stanojević, 1981).

1.1.3. Righting Reflexes of the Thalamic Animal. The reflexes discussed so far can be elicited in a decerebrate animal where the section is made just rostral to the vestibular nuclei. If the section is even more rostral, leaving the midbrain and thalamus intact, the animal is known as a thalamic, or decorticate, preparation. Such an animal no longer manifests decerebrate rigidity and is able to restore itself to an upright posture when disturbed.

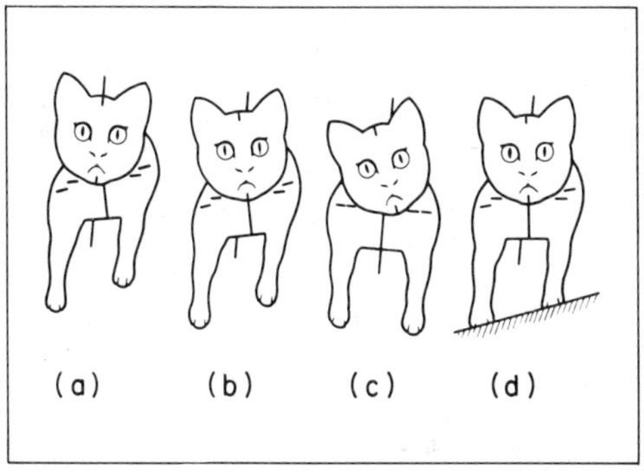

Figure 18.3. Schematic illustration of interactions between tonic-neck and tonic-labyrinthine reflexes. (a) Neck reflex acting alone—body tilted, head erect. (b) Labyrinthine reflex acting alone—body and head tilted together. (c) Head tilted alone—reflexes cancel. (d) Effect of standing on a slanting surface—vector sum of neck and labyrinthine reflexes induces compensatory posture, with head at any desired angle. (From T. D. M. Roberts, Reflex balance, *Nature, 244*. Copyright 1973 by Macmillan Journals Limited. Reprinted with permission.)

Magnus (1924) identified four groups of reflexes that cooperate in righting responses. To demonstrate any one of these components, the animal must first be placed in such a state that none of them is active. This so-called zero condition is fulfilled when a thalamic animal, after bilateral labyrinthectomy, is freely suspended out of contact with any surface.

1.1.3.1. Labyrinthine-Righting Reflexes. If a decorticate animal is held by the pelvis and its body rotated into various positions, its head remains upright as far as is physically possible. This pattern of reflexes is controlled by stimuli arising in the otolith organs. In the human neonate, labyrinthine-righting reflexes are only faintly demonstrable, but they develop during the first year of life and enable the growing infant to lift the head and later to sit up and to stand.

1.1.3.2. Neck-Righting Reflexes. This pattern of reflexes serves to bring the torso into alignment with the head. If the body is tilted, the head regains the upright position by the action of the labrinthine-righting reflexes. The resulting twisting of the neck evokes a neck-righting reflex, which in turn causes the thorax and then the lower parts of the body to be brought back into line with the upright head.

1.1.3.3. Body-Righting Reflexes. These reflexes may be demonstrated by holding a decorticate labyrinthectomized animal freely as if lying on its side. If the animal is now placed upon a surface, it immediately rotates its head until it is at right angles to the surface. This reflex is evoked by the asymmetrical stimulation of the touch receptors in the skin. If a board is pushed against the animal so that the tactile stimulation on each side of the body is symmetrical, the head will return to the lateral position. If an animal is held in the air in a lateral position and again lowered onto a board, but this time with its head held firm, its torso will right itself. The asymmetrical stimulation of the skin induces this reflex also, in spite of a tendency for the torso to remain in line with the laterally placed head in response to the tonic-neck reflex.

1.1.3.4. Optic-Righting Reflexes. In intact higher mammals, such as cats, dogs, and primates, the orientation of the head is controlled largely by vision. If such an animal, with labyrinths removed, is freely suspended in the air, its head remains disoriented until the eyes are opened and the animal fixates on something in the environment.

1.1.4. Righting Responses of the Falling Animal. Many animals, such as the rabbit and the cat, are adept at landing on all fours after being suddenly dropped in an unusual posture. To bring the body into a prone posture suitable for landing, the animal must rotate while falling. Any freely falling object, animate or inanimate, is unable to gain angular momentum unless it rejects mass. However, by applying a sequence of relative movements of body parts, it is possible for a falling animal to alter its attitude without any net change in angular momentum. For instance, by executing the following four maneuvers, a weightless person is able to change attitudes in space. See Figure 18.4.

1. Initially the body is straight, arms down, and legs spread to the sides, giving the lower part of the body, a high moment of inertia and the upper part a low moment of inertia.
2. The torso is twisted about the z axis as far as possible; the upper part of the body rotates further than the lower because of its lower moment of inertia.

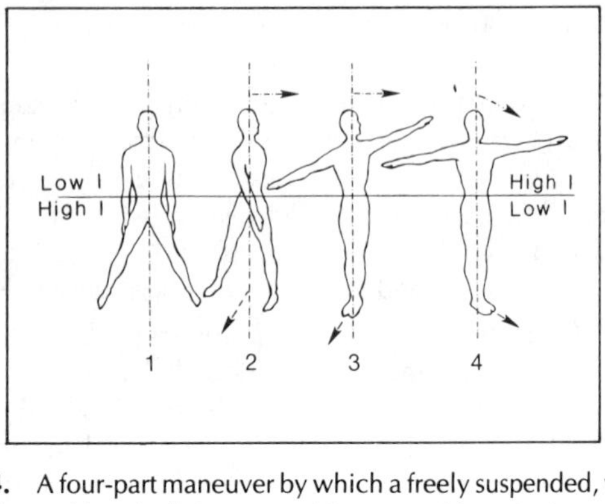

Figure 18.4. A four-part maneuver by which a freely suspended, weightless man may change his attitude in space without acquiring angular momentum. (From I. P. Howard & W. B. Templeton, *Human spatial orientation*. Copyright 1966 by John Wiley & Sons, Inc. Reprinted with permission.)

3. The moment of inertia of the upper part of the body is increased by spreading the arms out to the sides, and the moment of inertia of the lower part of the body is decreased by bringing the legs in.
4. The torso is now straightened. During this process the lower part of the body rotates further than the upper part, because it now has the lower moment of inertia.

Many animals execute such maneuvers when falling. For instance, the cat arches its back to increase the moment of inertia of its hindquarters, then rotates its head to an upright posture, as signaled by the otoliths, reduces the moment of inertia of its hindquarters by straightening its back, and, finally, turns its body into alignment with the head through the mediation of the tonic-neck reflex. At the same time, stimuli from the vestibular system and neck proprioceptors cause the limbs to extend into a posture suitable for landing.

When a cat is dropped, the early component of the reflex response can be detected electromyographically 10–50 msec after release. This early component is present in animals with plugged semicircular canals but not in animals with complete loss of vestibular organs. It must therefore be controlled by the otolith organs. The second component of the cat's righting maneuver begins 70–100 msec after release and occurs if the vestibular organs are absent, which shows that it is instigated by either proprioceptive or visual stimuli (Watt, 1976). When an upright human subject is dropped suddenly, the first muscular response in the gastrocnemius muscle of the lower leg occurs with a mean latency of 74 msec (Melvill Jones & Watt, 1971a). This is presumably the vestibular response. After the vestibular organs have been destroyed in monkeys, the motion of the retinal image becomes more effective in instigating motor responses to a sudden release of the body (Lacour & Xerri, 1980).

During free-fall an animal is in a weightless condition, and the otolith organs no longer signal the direction of gravity. Therefore, if the otolith organs are to help in righting a falling animal, they can do so only on the basis of signals received just before the animal was released. This point has been nicely demonstrated by Brindley (1965). He exposed a rabbit for several seconds to a centrifugal force that displaced the direction of the gravitoinertial force through about 15° from the vertical. He then released the animal and found that during the fall its head became aligned with the direction of the "false" gravity to which it had been exposed.

1.1.5. The Diencephalon and Postural Reflexes. Hess (1957) and his coworkers in Zurich have contributed to the understanding of the way in which postural motor patterns are organized by the central nervous system. Fine electrodes were embedded in the diencephalic region in an otherwise intact cat. For any one site and type of stimulation, the cat executed reproducible attitudinal responses of the head or head and body. Figure 18.5(a) shows the head-lowering–legs-flexing response to stimulation of the posterior commissure. Figure 18.5(b) shows the opposite response to stimulation in a medial, narrow zone over the posterior hypothalamus. Figure 18.5(c) shows a head-rotation response to stimulation of the thalamus or subthalamus; the direction of turning depends on the exact site of stimulation. The turning movement shown in Figure 18.5(d) is in response to stimulation of the thalamus lateral to the tract of Meynert. Hess noted that the exact counterparts of the various head responses produced by diencephalic stimulation are the vestibular-reflex head movements induced by the different vestibular canals. He concluded that the normal mode of stimulation of these diencephalic centers was from the vestibular canals, via the cerebellum and brachium conjunctivum. He also traced routes from spinothalamic tracts and trigeminal tracts, which carry information regarding the relative position of body parts to these diencephalic centers.

A further set of diencephalic responses was observed, which involved lifting of the forelimbs and perhaps a whole side of the body. That these were not related to nociceptive (pain) reflexes was evident from the calm demeanor of the animal. Hess concluded that they are related to postural reflexes under the control of proprioception. Hess has thus shown how postural reflexes are organized by central nuclei and do not represent merely the interplay of separate, peripherally determined reflexes. The hierarchical organization of postural and locomotor responses in humans has been demonstrated by Nashner, Woollacott, and Tuma (1979).

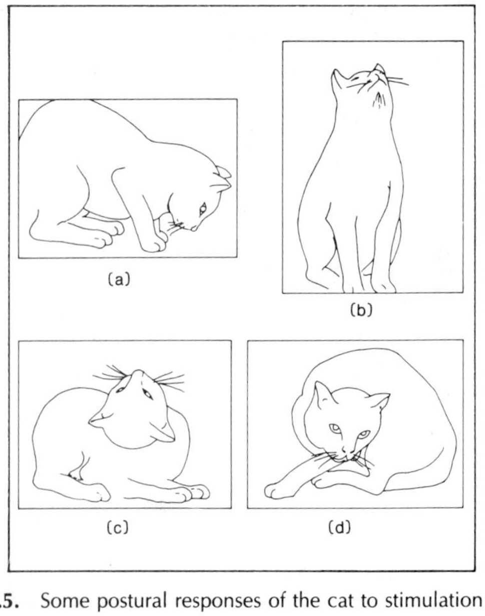

Figure 18.5. Some postural responses of the cat to stimulation of various parts of the diencephalon. (a) Lowering of the head and foretrunk. (b) Raising of the head and foretrunk. (c) Rotation of the head in the frontal plane. (d) Turning of the body in the horizontal plane. (From W. R. Hess, *The functional organization of the diencephalon*, Grune & Stratton, 1957. Reprinted with permission.)

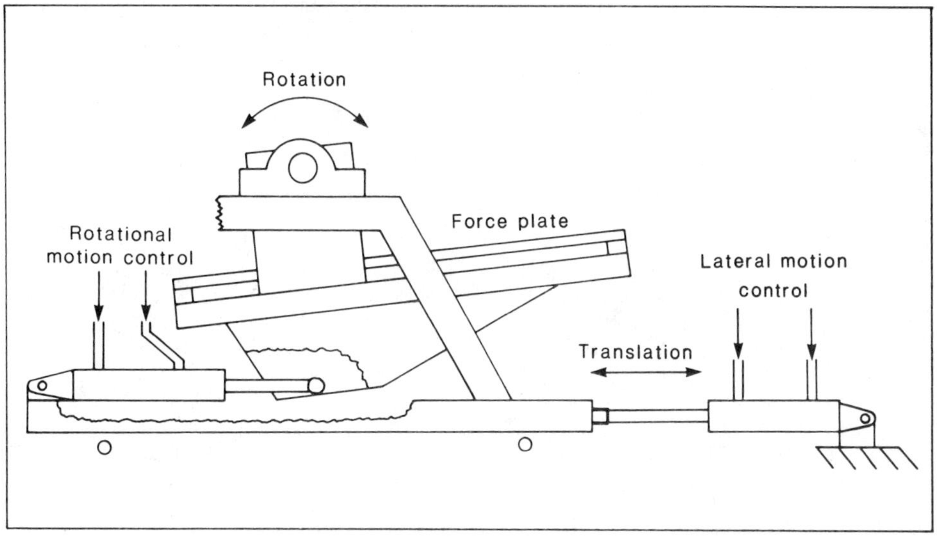

Figure 18.6. A stabilometer with control for rotating and translating the platform. The subject stands on the force plate while the lateral motor control imposes a sway in the fore-aft direction. By coupling outputs from transducers in force plate to the rotational control, the angle between the foot and leg of the swaying subject may be held constant. (From L. M. Nashner, A model describing vestibular detection of body sway motion, *Acta Otolaryngologica*, 1971, *72*. Reprinted with permission.)

1.2. The Control of Vertical Stance

1.2.1. Background. Humans are the only mammals to have adopted a predominantly bipedal posture. A person can maintain a vertical posture with very little expenditure of effort. Furthermore, the anatomical arrangement of bones, ligaments, and muscles is such that a given change in muscular tension produces the same turning moment at the knee, whatever the angle of the knee joint (Roberts, 1971b).

Postural stability is adversely affected by a variety of clinical conditions, including Ménière's disease, which affects the vestibular system, and tabes dorsalis, which damages the dorsal columns that carry proprioceptive inputs from the lower body. Blindfolded patients with such diseases sway or fall when attempting to stand erect or walk, a condition known as *postural ataxia*. Many diagnostic tests of postural ataxia have been devised, the best known being the *Romberg test* in which the blindfolded patient's degree of body sway is measured as the patient stands with feet together. This test is not sensitive enough for the diagnosis of vestibular damage, and other, more discriminating tests have been devised that require the patient to stand or walk in more demanding conditions. For instance, Fregly and Graybiel (1970) have devised a battery of tests in which the subject stands or walks on a narrow beam, with or without a blindfold (see Fregly, 1974, pp. 321–360, for a review of this topic).

The measurement of static postural stability is known as *posturography*. For research purposes, postural stability is measured either by the *sway test*, which is similar to the Romberg test, or by the use of a *stabilometer* (Edwards, 1942; Travis, 1944). The stabilometer consists of a platform mounted either on a spring at each corner or on a central square steel shaft. Strain gauges mounted at the corners, or on each side of the steel shaft, record the pressure changes caused by the swaying of a subject standing in the center of the platform. The platform support is stiff so that its motion is not apparent to the subject. The signals from the strain gauges are usually displayed as two traces on an oscilloscope or pen recorder, one indicating sway in the fore–aft direction and the other in the side-to-side direction. Such traces are known as *stabilograms*. The recorder may also be used to compute changes in the projection of the subject's center of gravity onto the base plate (see Santschi, Dubois, & Omoto, 1963, for data on moments of inertia and centers of gravity of the human body and its parts). For studying the effects of imposed rotation or translation of the platform, rotary and linear motion controls may be added, as shown in Figure 18.6. The motions of other parts of the body may be recorded at the same time by photographing lights attached to knee, hip, shoulder, or head.

Computer simulations of human postural responses have been devised in which the feedback gains of the model are adjusted until its response is close to human performance. In this way the sensory feedback gains used by the human subject may be estimated (Camana, Hemami, & Stockwell, 1977).

Human postural stability is conveniently represented by its *power spectral density* plotted as a function of frequency. Such a function indicates the degree of sway at each frequency. It turns out that the highest amplitudes of sway are between 0 and 0.4 Hz and that the cut-off frequency is about 1.0 Hz (see Figure 18.7). There is a small peak of sway activity in the 8–12 Hz band, which probably represents the effects of high-frequency synchronous muscular tremor due to oscilations in the myotatic reflex (Lippold, 1970; Mori, 1973). This high-frequency tremor probably plays no specific role in the maintenance of vertical stance and will be ignored in what follows. The mean power density of sway at all frequencies increases as a steady posture is maintained (see Figure 18.7). There are also large individual differences in the mean spectral density (Bensel & Dzendolet, 1968).

It is often assumed that the standing human body behaves like a simple inverted pendulum, with all its motion occurring about the ankle joint. However, it has been shown that some motion also occurs about the hip joint (Roberts & Stenhouse, 1976).

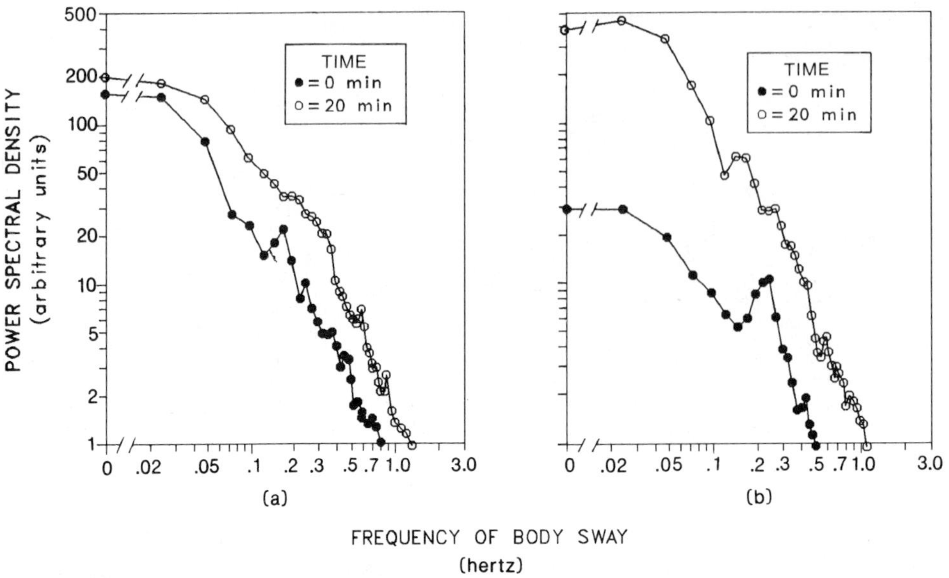

Figure 18.7. (a) The amount of anteroposterior sway at each of several frequencies in the standing adult. The bottom curve (time 0 min) was obtained from observations made on six adult males during the first minute of standing, and the top curve (time 20 min), from observations made during the twentieth minute of standing. The amount of sway is indicated by the power spectral density. An autocorrelation function was first computed with a variable time lag of between 0 and 20 sec, and a Fourier transform of this function yielded the power spectral density. It can be seen that the curve of time 20 min shows an increase in the amount of sway and a suppression of the peaks shown at time 0 min. (b) Similar curves based on results from three male subjects, to illustrate how these functions vary across subjects. (From C. K. Bensel & E. Dzendolet, Power spectral density analysis of the standing sway of males, *Perception and Psychophysics*, 1968, *4*. Reprinted with permission.)

Factors found to affect the magnitude of sway include muscle tension, fatigue, alcohol, and nitrogen narcosis (Adolfson, Bjerver, Fluur, & Goldberg, 1974; Edwards, 1943; Fearing, 1925). The amplitude of body sway with eyes closed is affected by suggestions to subjects that they are falling. Hull (1933) first used the amplitude of postural sway as a test of suggestibility and hypnotizability. Subsequently, Eysenck (1947) and Furneaux (1946) have shown high correlations between the extent to which the suggestion "you are falling forward" affects body sway and susceptibility to trance-inducing suggestions. The effect of suggestion on sway has also been found to relate to neuroticism and extroversion (Furneaux, 1961) although, even without suggestion, neurotics have been found to sway more than normal subjects (Ingham, 1954).

Static postural stability depends on four factors: (1) the passive stiffness of joints and muscles, (2) responses induced by stretching of muscles in the leg, (3) responses induced by stimulation of the vestibular organs, particularly the semicircular canals, and (4) visually instigated responses. Each of these factors will be discussed in more detail.

1.2.2. Passive Stiffness of Joints and Muscles. Gurfinkel, Lipshits, and Popov (1974) stood human subjects on a stabilometer platform that was rocked in a heel-to-toe direction, with an amplitude between 0.1 and 0.2° and a velocity of 0.6°/sec. The angular movement of the ankle joint was measured, and the ratio of the change in the moment of forces acting on the ankle to the change in joint angle was used to calculate the coefficient to stiffness of the ankle joint. Electromyographic records from the tricep muscles revealed that no active contractions of the leg muscles were evoked by the rotation of the platform, so that the stiffness of the joint was due entirely to its inherent stiffness plus whatever tonic muscular contraction was present.

The coefficient of stiffness varied between 1.3 and 1.7 kg·m/degree and was greater for taller or heavier subjects and for subjects carrying a load. The elastic torque generated by this degree of stiffness is sufficient to compensate for small deviations of the body of the erect person.

1.2.3. Proprioceptive Factors in Postural Stability. The fact that Gurfinkel and colleagues (1974) did not find any evidence of an active muscular response when the ankle of the standing person was rotated suggests that the myotatic response is not evoked in the standing posture. The latency of the normal myotatic response of the human biceps to sudden stretch is 15 msec or less (Dufresne, Soechting, & Terzuolo, 1980; Hammond, Merton, & Sutton, 1956; Pierrot-Deseilligny, Morin, Bergego, & Tankov, 1981). The earliest detectable contraction of the leg muscles in response to an imposed sway of the standing body occurs with a latency of about 120 msec. A response of this latency must be a supraspinal reflex, rather than a segmental one. This view is confirmed by the absence of this long-latency reflex in patients with spinal transections or postcentral lesions (Chan, Melvill Jones, & Watt, 1979; Marsden, Merton, Morton, & Adam, 1978, pp. 334–342). Furthermore, the response is not limited to the muscles that are stretched, which it would be if it were a myotatic response (Burke & Eklund, 1977; Nashner, 1977). This supraspinal reflex response to stretching of the leg muscles has been called the *functional stretch reflex* (Melvill Jones & Watt, 1971b). That muscle-spindle activity is involved in this reflex is indicated by the fact that blockage of gamma innervation to muscle spindles of the ankle muscles has been found to increase postural sway (Shambes, 1969).

Gurfinkel and colleagues (1974) did not find any evidence of the long-latency stretch reflex when they rotated the ankles of the standing subject, but they did observe it when the subject's body was induced to sway. This makes sense because normally the ankles of a standing person are rotated in the absence of body sway when a person stands on uneven ground, and under these conditions a response to muscle stretch would destabilize the person's posture. On the other hand, the reflex stabilizes posture when it occurs in response to a turning of the ankles induced by body sway. In other words, the functional stretch reflex is evoked only when other sensory information informs the system that the body is swaying. See Figure 18.8.

Nashner (1976) took a closer look at the conditions under which the functional stretch reflex is evoked. Subjects were placed on a platform controlled by a servo-activated tilt mechanism that responded to the pressure changes caused by the sway of the subject's body. In this way the angle of the subject's ankle was kept constant as the subject's body swayed, and the stretch reflex was put out of action. This abolished those sway-induced muscular responses that have a latency of 120 msec, the latency of the functional stretch reflex. The first responses occurred with a latency of 200–300 msec. As we shall see later, these responses were of vestibular origin.

Nashner revealed the adaptive properties of the stretch reflex in the following way. Subjects were exposed to several trials in which the stabilometer platform was moved backward, causing them to sway and manifest a compensatory stretch reflex. Then, without warning, the platform was rotated, rather than translated. For the first trial or two after the change, subjects continued to produce an inappropriate stretch reflex, but then the response disappeared. Thus the "set" of subjects is a factor governing whether the stretch reflex is evoked by ankle torque. It looks as though the cerebellum is involved in the inhibitory control of the stretch reflex, because patients with cerebellar defects show an enhanced gain of this reflex and are unable to adapt their response to ankle rotation to changing circumstances (Mauritz, Schmitt, & Dichgans, 1981; Nashner & Grimm, 1978).

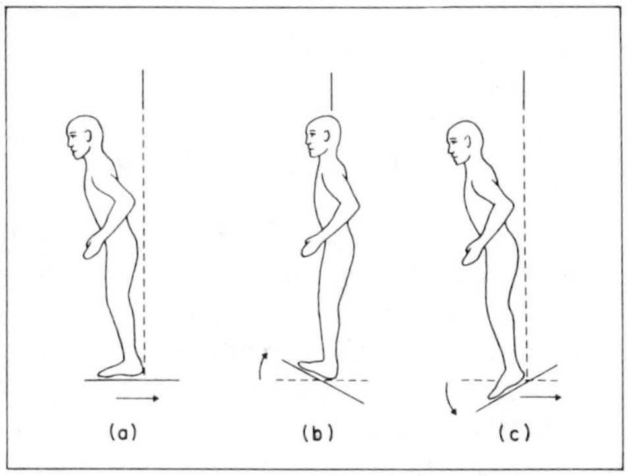

Figure 18.8. Illustration of interactions between ankle proprioception and vestibular inputs in postural control. (a) A backward motion of the stabilometer platform rotates the ankle and accelarates the head. Resulting proprioceptive and vestibular stimuli induce compensatory postural responses. (b) Rotation of the platform rotates the ankle, but the resulting proprioceptive stimuli do not induce postural responses because the vestibular system is not stimulated. (c) A motion of the platform combined with servo-controlled tilt of the platform induces vestibular stimuli without rotating the ankle. Under these circumstances compensatory responses in the dark are due only to vestibular stimulation. (From L. M. Nashner, Adapting reflexes controlling the human posture, *Experimental Brain Research*, 1976, *25*. Reprinted with permission.)

The simplest way to explain these findings is that the stretch reflex is inhibited by vestibular inputs. But it is not necessary to assume a central gating mechanism; at least part of the interaction could arise at a peripheral level in the following fashion. The threshold of the stretch reflex to passive flexion of the relaxed soleus muscle is much higher than the threshold to passive flexion when the muscle is in a state of voluntary contraction (Gottlieb, Agarwal, & Jaeger, 1981). When the muscle is actively contracted, concomitant innervation of contractile fibers in muscle spindles potentiates the feedback from sensory receptors in muscle spindles. For instance, when a person exerts a flexing force against an imposed sinusoidal rotation of the foot around the ankle joint, the stretch reflex in the calf muscles is enhanced (Evans, Fellows, Rack, Ross, & Walters, 1983). Therefore, when a person sways, the contraction of leg muscles induced by vestibular stimulation automatically augments the stretch reflex. The lack of response to ankle rotation in the absence of body sway would be due to the high threshold of the stretch reflex when leg muscles are relatively relaxed. The fact that subjects may initially show a stretch reflex when their ankles are rotated may be due to the fact that they have not learned to relax.

Gurfinkel and colleagues (1974) and Nashner (1977) used rather low rates of ankle turning. With more intense stimulation of ankle proprioceptors, the functional stretch reflex might occur whether or not there is an accompanying sway of the body. For instance, Melville Jones and Watt (1971b) obtained a response on every occasion following a sharply applied, and maintained, dorsiflexion of the foot. This is probably because intense stimulation exceeds the threshold of stretch receptors, even when there is no appreciable voluntary contraction of the muscles.

The functional stretch reflex may also be induced by an externally applied vibration of the Achilles tendon. This causes subjects to fall backward. If prevented from falling, subjects feel that they are falling forward, and if a small light in dark surroundings is visible, it appears to move with the body (Eklund, 1972; Lackner & Levine, 1979). Vibration applied to the leg muscles induces a sustained displacement of the body from the vertical posture, through an angle that is proportional to the enhancement of electromyographic activity in leg muscles, which the vibration induces (Hayashi, Miyake, Jijiwa, & Watanabe, 1981). Externally applied stimulation of the muscles of one leg induces a simultaneous stretch reflex in both legs if both legs are supporting the body. If only the stimulated leg supports the body, only that leg shows the functional stretch reflex (Dietz & Berger, 1982). The responses of the two legs are thus coupled when the situation requires it.

When a person transfers weight from one leg to the other, as in walking, running, or hopping, the muscular tension in the leg required to give support builds up before the foot touches the ground. Therefore, under these circumstances, the response must be preplanned, rather than triggered by externally applied stretching of the muscles. The stretch reflex may well play a role in initiating the muscular contraction that launches each stepping motion in running or hopping, and its latency is probably a factor determining the frequency of the preferred rate of repetitive hopping (Melvill Jones, & Watt, 1971b). For data on the proprioceptive control of patterns of postural activity, see Gahéry and Legallet (1981), Marsden, Merton, and Morton (1981), and Thach (1978).

1.2.4. Vestibular Factors in Postural Stability. To study the contribution of vestibular inputs to postural stability, one must eliminate the influence of visual and proprioceptive stimuli.

Visual stimuli are easy to eliminate. Proprioceptive stimuli, at least those from the ankle, may be nulled by standing the subject on a servo-controlled platform that rotates so as to keep the angle between the foot and leg constant. Nashner (1971) exposed subjects to these conditions and measured the compensatory responses of muscles in the lower leg to body sway induced by controlled translatory motion of the platform. A computer simulation based on the parameters of subjects' performance was compared with the known properties of the vestibular organs. This analysis indicated that movements of the head that are sufficient to induce responses in the legs were well below the threshold of the utricles but somewhere near the threshold of the semicircular canals. He concluded that only the canals contribute to static postural stability in humans.

By ignoring movements of the hip joint, Nashner may have used an exaggerated measure of how far the head moves in static sway. Perhaps neither vestibular organ is stimulated above threshold in the static standing posture. People with bilateral labyrinthine loss maintain a steady posture when standing with eyes closed. Their balance is not noticeably worse than that of a normal person unless the task is made demanding, for instance, by perturbation of the platform or by requiring them to lift one leg (Birren, 1945; Rademaker, 1935).

As seen in Section 1.1.4, the otolith organs (utricles and saccules) are involved in righting reflexes, and there is no reason to doubt that they are also involved in restoring upright posture when a standing animal is pushed to one side with a force sufficient to accelerate the body above the utricular threshold. However, there is a problem here because utricular stimuli, like those arising from ankle rotation, are ambiguous with respect to corrective postural adjustments. This ambiguity arises in at least three ways.

The first source of ambiguity may be illustrated by the following example. If an animal's body is pushed to the left, the appropriate response is to extend the limbs on the left. However, if the platform upon which the animal stands is accelerated to the left, the utricles are deflected in the same way as before, but now the appropriate response is to extend the limbs on the right. The proprioceptive stimuli from the two legs and tactile stimuli from the feet are opposite in the two cases and so are the inputs from the vestibular canals if the animal sways in response to the applied force. See Figure 18.9(a) and (b). The sign of any utricular reflexes induced in these two cases would therefore have to be suitably adjusted by proprioceptive or canal inputs (Barnes, 1980).

As an illustration of the second source of ambiguity in vestibular stimuli, consider the following. When the body of an animal is pushed to the left, the appropriate response is an extension of limbs on the left. When the body is tilted to the right, the utricle is stimulated as before, and yet the appropriate response is now an extension of limbs on the right. So here again the utricular responses must be reversed under the influence of stimuli from the semicircular canals or from proprioceptors. See Figure 18.9(a) and (c).

A third source of ambiguity in the postural significance of vestibular stimulation becomes apparent when changes in head posture are considered. When a person stands with the head facing over the left shoulder, a forward sway of the body stimulates the vestibular system in a right-ear–down fashion. However, when the head is facing over the right shoulder, the same body sway stimulates the vestibular system in a left-ear—down fashion. In other words, a given corrective postural response would be triggered by opposite vestibular inputs in the two cases. It has been known for some time that spinal motoneuron activity induced by vestibular stimulation is modified by simultaneous inputs from neck proprioceptors (Kim & Partridge, 1969). More recently, Nashner and Wolfson (1974) have demonstrated that the sign of electromyographically recorded postural responses of human leg muscles to electrical stimulation of the vestibular system is reversed when the head is turned from left to right.

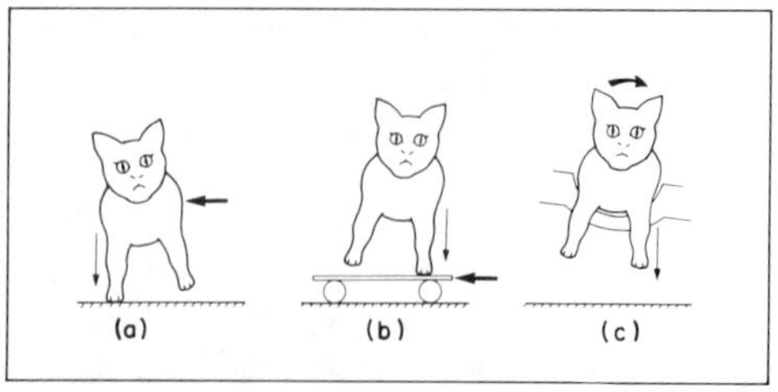

Figure 18.9. Illustrating the appropriate responses of leg muscles to (a) a force pushing an animal to the left, (b) a force pushing the platform, upon which the animal is standing, to the left, and (c) rotating the animal to the right. The large arrows indicate the direction of the disturbing force, the small arrows the direction of the force that the animal must exert to restrain its body. Note that in each case the utricles are stimulated in the same way, so that for the animal's responses to be adaptive, the effects of the utricular inputs on the leg musculature must be modified by stimuli arising in the vestibular canals, proprioceptors, or pressure receptors in the feet. (From G. R. Barnes, Vestibular control of oculomotor and positional mechanisms, *Clinical Physics* and *Physiological Measurement*, 1980, *1*. Reprinted with permission.)

1.2.5. The Visual Control of Posture. When enclosed in a large illuminated box whose walls and ceiling are swaying back and forth, a person begins to sway in synchrony with the box (Lishman & Lee, 1973). Young children who have just learned to sit upright or to walk fall over in the direction of any motion of the visual scene (Butterworth & Hicks, 1977; Lee & Aronson, 1974). After a child reaches the age of 5, the effects of visual motion on postural stability slowly decrease; the normal adult shows only moderate body sway in the direction of visual motion (Brandt, Wenzel, & Dichgans, 1976). The ability of subjects to stand steadily has been compared under four conditions: (1) room lights on, (2) room lights off, leaving in view only a cube with one side horizontal, (3) nothing in view, and (4) an unstable rocking cube in view. Steadiness decreased progressively from conditions 1 to 4 (Wapner & Witkin, 1950; Witkin & Wapner, 1950).

Direct recording from the extensor and flexor motoneurons of the cat has revealed that their pattern of response to large visual stimuli rotating about the animal's line of sight in a given direction is similar to that produced by tilting the animal in the opposite direction (Thoden, Dichgans, & Savidis, 1977). Therefore, under normal circumstances, an animal may use both vestibular and visual reflex responses to restore itself to an upright position. Motion of the retinal image resulting from movements of the eyes does not induce postural instability, but similar image motion caused by movements of the visual surroundings does (White, Post, & Leibowitz, 1980). This is to be expected because the first type of image motion does not signify that the body is moving, whereas the second type of movement usually does.

Postural sway is not improved by vision when the visual surroundings are illuminated stroboscopically (Amblard & Cremiéux, 1976). This is probably because intermittent illumination removes visual motion signals that provide the visual information that the body is swaying.

Visual sway detected by the visual periphery has been found to be more effective in stabilizing posture than that detected by the fovea (Amblard & Carblanc, 1980). This fact is in line with findings reported at various places in this chapter, which show that peripheral vision is particularly significant for spatial orientation.

Although vestibular, somatosensory, and visual signals cooperate in the control of posture, there is little redundancy of stimulation because, as we have seen, their interaction helps to resolve ambiguities and because the different types of signal are effective over different ranges of frequency. Signals from the vestibular canals and somatosensory system stabilize posture most effectively at higher frequencies of body sway, while visual and otolith-organ signals are most effective in stabilizing postural sway at lower frequencies.

One way to determine the frequency range of body sway for which visual inputs are effective is to compare the power spectrum of body sway when the eyes are open with that obtained when the eyes are closed. This procedure has revealed that the increase in the amplitude of body sway that occurs when a person closes the eyes is mainly confined to frequencies below about 0.3 Hz (Dichgans & Brandt, 1978, pp. 755–804).

Another procedure is to measure the Fourier spectrum of postural sway when subjects' eyes are closed and again while they observe a moving visual scene. The results of this procedure reveal that the destabilizing effects of anomalous visual inputs show a peak effect at about 0.1 Hz (Dichgans, Mauritz, Allum, & Brandt, 1976; Lestienne, Soechting, & Berthoz, 1977). However, the effects of anomalous visual inputs have no direct bearing on the normal role of visual inputs because normal visual inputs confirm, rather than contradict, vestibular and somatosensory inputs.

In a third procedure for determining the frequencies of body sway most affected by vision, subjects stand on a platform that is tilted sinusoidally at various frequencies, and their postural responses are recorded with and without vision. With this procedure the stabilizing effects of vision have been found to be maximal at an imposed body sway of 0.3 Hz. The destabilizing effects of imposed body sway below 0.01 Hz and above 1 Hz were the same with as they were without vision. At frequencies below 0.01 Hz the visual motion signals generated by the imposed body sway were probably below the threshold of the visual-motion detection system (Diener, Dichgans, Bruzek, & Selinka, 1982).

For patients with *postural ataxia*, such as arises in tabes dorsalis, in whom the nonvisual mechanisms of postural stability are defective, the destabilizing effects of sinusoidal visual motion extend to higher frequencies of body sway than in normal subjects. This suggests that such patients use vision to compensate for postural sway to a greater extent than do normal subjects (Dichgans, Mauritz, Allum, & Brandt, 1976).

The sensations of illusory self motion induced by visual tilt require a threshold displacement of over 2° and have a latency of several seconds, whereas visually induced corrections of posture occur for sways of less than 2° to either side of the vertical and have a reaction time of only 100–140 msec (Dichgans et al., 1976; Nashner & Berthoz, 1978). The higher threshold for illusory self motion could, like its longer latency, be due to the absence of vestibular and proprioceptive inputs, which normally accompany body sway (see Section 3.3 for further discussion on this point).

Postural stability is severely disturbed by optical devices that reverse the direction of headcentric scene motion induced by motion of the head. Subjects wearing reversing prisms continuously gradually learn to regain their postural stability over a period of days (Gonshor & Melvill Jones, 1980). This improvement is probably related to the reversal of vestibular nystagmus, which is known to occur under such circumstances (see Section 4.3).

When a person walks or runs over a natural terrain, the visual scene is perceived as an optical flow pattern. The convergence and curvature in the flow pattern indicates changes in the observer's direction of movement, and the rate and symmetry of the frontal looming of the pattern indicate the observer's heading and time to impact with obstacles (Harrington, Harrington, Wilkins, & Koh, 1980; Lee & Lishman, 1977). This topic is discussed at greater length in Chapter 11, "The Vestibular System," by Howard.

1.3. Key References

The standard sources on spinal reflexes are Sherrington (1947), Lloyd (1960, pp. 929–949), and Denny-Brown (1966). The classic studies of postural reflexes carried out by Rudolph Magnus at the University of Utrecht are reviewed in *The Cameron Prize Lectures* for 1926 (see Magnus, 1926). The best single review of the neurophysiology of postural mechanisms is provided in the book by Roberts (1978). Useful collections of papers on the whole subject of posture and motor control are contained in books edited by Granit and Pompeiano (1979), Stein, Pearson, Smith, and Redford (1973), and Talbot and Humphrey (1979). Fregly (1974) has reviewed vestibular ataxia in the *Handbook of Sensory Physiology*. Peiper (1963) has provided a thorough review of the development of reflexes and cerebral control of motion. The most complete review of muscle receptors and their central actions is provided in Matthews (1972). Grillner (1975) has reviewed the subject of locomotion in vertebrates.

2. VESTIBULO-OCULAR REFLEXES

2.1. Background

If the gaze moves smoothly over a stationary scene, the retinal image is blurred and objects become difficult to recognize. This fact may easily be verified by observing the appearance of the stationary background as one allows the gaze to follow a finger moving smoothly from side to side. For effective vision, the eyes must be held reasonably steady with respect to the object of regard for at least as long as it takes to recognize it. Two kinds of eye-stabilizing reflex are therefore required, one to compensate for movements of the head and the other to compensate for movements of the visual object. All animals with mobile eyes possess these two basic reflexes, and in lower animals, eye movements probably serve no other purpose (Walls, 1962).

The eye movements that compensate for head movements are driven by stimuli arising in the otolith organs, vestibular canals, and the joints of the neck, trunk, and legs. Those driven by vestibular stimuli are known as *vestibulo-ocular reflexes*, and those driven by receptors in the neck are known as *cervico-ocular reflexes*. There are no agreed terms to describe eye movements induced by movements of the trunk and legs. I shall refer to them as *arthro-ocular responses*. The cervico-ocular reflex is a form of arthro-ocular response. Stationary sound sources may also provide a stimulus generating compensatory eye movements. This may be called the *audiokinetic response* (Hennebert, 1960).

As a person is rotated to the left about a vertical axis, stimuli arise in the horizontal vestibular canals that cause a simultaneous rotation of the two eyes to the right, that is, in a direction that stabilizes the retinal image. This is known as the pursuit (slow) phase of the response. After the eyes have rotated a certain distance, they quickly return to begin another compensatory movement. The return movement, known as the *quick phase* of the response, is in the anticompensatory direction and thus smears the image across the retina and impairs vision. The sooner this movement is complete, the better, and that is why the quick phase is rapid, or *saccadic*; it can reach velocities up to 800°/sec.

Any rhythmic involuntary motion of the eyes is known as *nystagmus*; that induced by vestibular stimulation is known as *vestibular nystagmus*. Vestibular nystagmus occurs around an axis parallel to that about which the head rotates. Thus rotation of the head about the z axis induces *horizontal nystagmus*, rotation of the head about the y axis (in the median plane) induces *vertical nystagmus*, and rotation of the head about the x axis (in the frontal plane) induces nystagmus about the visual axis—a response known as *torsional nystagmus*. Quick phases usually alternate with slow phases, but *pendular nystagmus* consists only of alternating slow phases. A nystagmic movement of the eyes tends to occur about a constant mean position of gaze. This mean position will be referred to as the *deviation component* of the nystagmus. If the mean position of gaze is the primary position of the eyes, the deviation component is zero. But this is not usually the case. As we shall see later, the mean deviation of the eyes often undergoes a slow oscillation during nystagmus. Rapid nystagmic oscillations are thus superimposed on a slower oscillation of the eyes.

Steady excitation of the otolith organs produces a more or less constant deviation of the eyes. For instance, a sideways tilt of the head induces a persisting torsional deviation of the eyes around the visual axis up to about 8°. This is known as *countertorsion*. Reflex elevation and depression of gaze are induced by inclining the head forward and backward (U. Brandt & Fluur, 1967b; Ebenholtz & Shebilske, 1975). These responses are known as the *doll's eye reflex*. Rhythmic stimulation of the otolith organs, such as is produced by rotating a prone person about an earth horizontal axis, induces alternating deviations of the eyes. In some people, tilting the head to one side induces an involuntary nystagmus, which is known as *positional nystagmus*. If this response is large in amplitude and persistent, it is a sign of pathology or alcohol intoxication (Barber & Wright, 1973).

Cervico-ocular reflexes are evoked experimentally by rotating a person's torso relative to the stationary head, although the response evoked in this way is prominent only in very young infants and in adults with some pathology. In normal adults, the response is small and occurs with only very slow movements of the head. Horizontal eye movements are induced by rotating the vertical torso about the midbody axis and vertical eye movements by inclining the torso forward or backward. However, eye torsion is apparently not induced when a supine subject tilts the head toward the shoulder, indicating that stimulation of neck receptors in the absence of stimulation of the otolith organs does not induce this response (Scott, 1967).

Arthro-ocular responses are induced by twisting the trunk of an otherwise stationary subject or by having the subject walk around a rotating platform, so that there is no rotation of the body (see Section 2.8).

Some people show nystagmic movements of the head when they are rotated in the dark. This is known as the *vestibulocollic reflex*. This reflex is very pronounced in animals, like the owl, which do not move their eyes far (Outerbridge & Melvill Jones, 1971; Steinbach & Money, 1973; Wilson, Peterson, Fukushima, Hirai, & Uchino, 1979). Such animals rely on movements of the head to maintain a stable retinal image as the body moves about. The to-and-fro head movements of birds, like the hen, also serve to stabilize vision as the animal moves forward. The eye movements induced by movements of the body are summarized in Table 18.1.

2.2. Vestibular Nystagmus

2.2.1. General Features. Vestibular nystagmus occurs in all vertebrates with mobile eyes and is controlled by mechanisms in the brain stem although, as we shall see later, the response may be modified to some extent by higher centers. It occurs in human neonates, often with greater amplitude than in an adult (Ornitz, Atwell, Walter, Hartmann, & Kaplan, 1979; Tibbling, 1969). The response is weakened by prolonged visual deprivation in early life (Harris & Cynader, 1981a). It is also weakened in states of relaxed attention (W. E. Collins, 1974a, pp. 361–368; Sokolovski, 1966) and is replaced by maintained ocular deviation in the compensatory direction during light sleep. It is entirely absent during deep sleep (Melvill Jones & Sugie, 1972).

If a person rotates at a steady *velocity* for longer than about 20 sec, the absence of an accelerative stimulus causes the cupula to become restored to its central position and the discharge from the hair cells resembles that present when the head is stationary. If a person is decelerated after a period of rotation at constant angular velocity, the acquired momentum of the endolymph in the canals lying in the plane of the rotation causes a deflection of the cupulae in the same direction as the previous rotation. This initiates *postrotary nystagmus*, which is opposite in direction to the preceding perrotary nystagmus. This response lasts for up to 30 sec in the dark, which is longer than it takes for the cupulae to become restored to their resting positions or for primary afferents to cease firing (Büttner & Waespe, 1981). The duration of postrotary nystamus depends on the strength of the stimulus, attention, practice, and the axis of rotation (Melvill Jones, Barry, & Kowalsky, 1964). It tends to be inhibited when stationary objects are in view (see Section 2.3.3).

During a period of constant rotary *acceleration* the firing rate of phasic vestibular afferents tends to return toward the resting level in spite of the fact that the cupula remains deflected (see Chapter 11, "The Vestibular System," by Howard). This is true sensory adaptation, analogous to light adaptation in vision. It should not be confused with the restoration of the cupula and concomitant restoration of afferent firing rate to the resting level that occurs during a period of constant angular velocity. Adaptation to constant acceleration is never complete and reveals itself as a decrement in the velocity of the slow phase of vestibular nystagmus and a decrease in the perceived velocity of body rotation (Brown & Wolfe, 1969; Luster, 1972). If the body is brought to rest after adaptation to constant acceleration has occurred, it takes time for the system to adapt back to its normal state, and during this time there is a continuation of nystagmus in phase with the perrotary response. This is known as *secondary nystagmus*. During the initial postrotary period, in-phase secondary nystagmus is overshadowed by the antiphase postrotary

Table 18.1. Types of Eye Movement Induced by Movements of the Head and Body

Origin of Signals	Response of Eyes	Characteristics
Vestibular Canals		
Rotary acceleration	Nystagmic slow phase	A short-latency, high-gain, compensatory pursuit movement of the eyes in phase with head position
Rotary acceleration	Nystagmic deviation	A deviation of the eyes in phase with head velocity
Unknown	Nystagmic quick phase	A saccadic return of gaze, following slow phase of nystagmus
Deceleration	Postrotary nystagmus	Phase-reversed nystagmus persisting for about 20 sec after rotation ceases
Recovery from vestibular adaptation	Secondary nystagmus	A second phase-reversed nystagmus following postrotary nystagmus
Ferris-wheel rotation of the body	Nystagmus	Possibly due to of "roller pump" action working on the canals
Vision		
Visual motion	Optokinetic pursuit of stationary scene	A long-latency pursuit of the visual scene supplementing vestibular nystagmus at low or constant velocities of body rotation
Visual integrator	Optokinetic afternystagmus	A continuation of optokinetic nystagmus after cessation of stimulation
	Secondary optokinetic nystagmus	A phased-reversed nystagmus following optokinetic afternystagmus
Audition	Audiokinetic nystagmus	Nystagmus in pursuit of a sound source, stationary with respect to the rotating body
Utricles and Saccules		
Linear acceleration	Deviation	Steady eye deviation opposite to linear body acceleration
Head tilt	Countertorsion	Tendency of eyes to remain upright when head is tilted
Head inclination	Doll's eye reflex	Tendency of eyes to remain level
Head inclination	Nystagmus induced or increased	Pathological
Rotating linear vector (barbecue rotation of body)	Alternating deviation	Induced by alternating stimulation of the utricles
Proprioceptors		
Neck rotation	Cervico-ocular nystagmus	A low-gain nystagmus induced by neck proprioceptors
Neck rotation	Cervico-ocular deviation	A deviation of eyes induced by neck proprioceptors
Twisting of trunk or walking round	Artho-ocular nystagmus	Eye movements induced by walking, etc.
Centrally Programmed	Anticipatory saccades	Saccades just preceding a head movement
	Coordinate compensatory pursuit	Pursuit eye movements with zero latency made in conjunction with a head movement

nystagmus induced by the deceleration of the body. However, the time constant for recovery from adaptation is about 80 sec and that for postrotary nystagmus is only about 20–30 sec, so that secondary nystagmus reveals itself as an in-phase response after the antiphase postrotary effect was worn off (Malcolm & Melvill Jones, 1970). This sequence of events is depicted in Figure 18.10. Mathematical models of these processes have been developed (Stockwell, Gilson, & Guedry, 1973; Young & Oman, 1969).

If the head of a person is rotated rapidly to one side, the eyes make a brief compensatory slow-phase movement followed by a large saccade in the direction of head turn, before finally settling down into the primary position of gaze. Under ordinary circumstances, rapid head movements are executed to bring the gaze toward an object situated off to one side, so that the large saccade can be understood as part of the strategy of fixating such an object (see Section 2.4).

The pathways that convey signals from the vestibular nuclei to the oculomotor nuclei are described briefly in Chapter 11, "The Vestibular System," by Howard and more fully in B. Cohen (1974, pp. 477–540) and Wilson and Melvill Jones (1979).

2.2.2. The Gain of Vestibular Nystagmus. The *gain* of vestibular nystagmus induced by unidirectional rotation of the head is the ratio of the angular velocity of the eyes during the slow phase to the angular velocity of the head. Gain must be measured while the subject is in the dark, so as to avoid the intrusion of optokinetic nystagmus, that is, nystagmus induced by sight of the countermoving scene. If the gain is 1, the slow phase compensates perfectly for the head rotation and stabilizes the retinal image of a distant stationary scene. If the gain is less than 1, the eyes fail to keep up with the moving image of a stationary scene.

A point easily overlooked is that the velocity of eye movements necessary to stabilize the retinal image of an object when the head rotates varies with the distance of the object. This is because a rotation of the head causes the eyes to be translated as well as rotated. For a head rotation of θ, the compensatory rotation of an eye required to stabilize the image of a stationary object at distance D is

$$\theta + \arctan\frac{d \sin\theta}{D},$$

where d is the distance from the axis of head rotation to the nodal point of the eye. For a distant object the second term of this equation, which represents the effects of head translation, is negligible, but for near objects the translatory term approaches the value of θ, so that the velocity of eye movements required

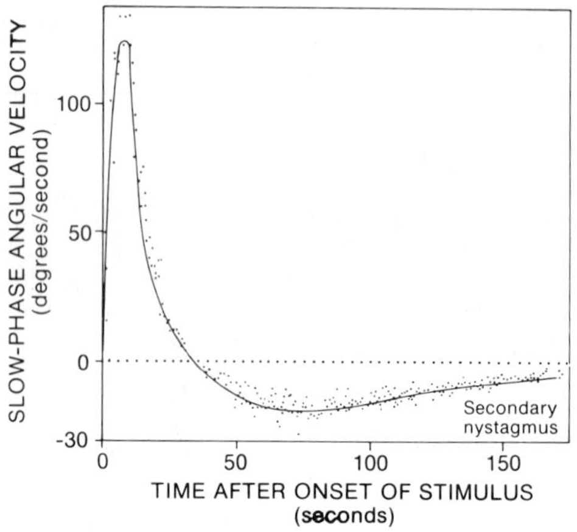

Figure 18.10. The angular velocity of the slow phase of vestibular nystagmus plotted beat by beat after onset of a 10-sec period of deceleration of the body from a rotary velocity of 270°/sec to zero. Note that the direction of the postrotary response reverses in direction after about 30 sec. (From R. Malcolm & G. Melvill Jones, A quantitative study of vestibular adaptation in humans, *Acta Otolaryngologica*, 1970, *70*. Reprinted with permission.)

to stabilize the retinal image becomes about double the velocity required for distant objects. In other words, the gain of the slow phase of vestibular nystagmus required for image stabilization increases from 1 for distant objects to 2 for near objects.

Under normal conditions of viewing, the visual system presumably serves to adjust the gain of compensatory eye movements for different distances. However, Biguer and Prablanc (1981) have shown that once the distance of a visual object is known, compensatory eye movements appropriate to its distance are still made during an interval in which the visual target is not visible. It is conceivable that the accommodative and vergence state of the eyes would automatically adjust the gain of vestibulo-ocular responses. There are cells in the flocculus of the cerebellum which respond to changes in the convergence of the eyes, and the flocculus is known to exert control over cells in the vestibular nucleus (Miles, Fuller, Braitman, & Dow, 1980). Hay and Sawyer (1969) have shown that a change in the convergence of the eyes alters the velocity at which a visual scene must be moved to appear stationary when the head rotates. Similar findings have been reported by Post and Leibowitz (1982). However, there is still a lack of direct evidence that vestibulo-ocular gain is directly controlled by accommodative vergence.

When a person is rotated back and forth sinusoidally about a given axis, the gain of vestibular nystagmus is indicated by the peak velocity of nystagmus relative to that of the head. For a person rotated sinusoidally in the dark, nystagmic gain varies with the frequency of the oscillation of the body. See Figure 18.11. It is only about 0.6 when a subject is oscillated at 0.1 Hz, rises to 1 at about 2 Hz, and to above 1 at higher frequencies in humans (Benson, 1970, pp. 249–261; Meiry, 1971, pp. 483–906) and in monkeys (Keller, 1978). It is significant that, where the gain is 1 at a frequency of 2 Hz, the acceleration of the head is about the same as it is in natural head movements. The gain remains at 1 at frequencies higher than 2 Hz when a stationary background is in view (Koenig, Allum, & Dichgans, 1978). For instance, the nystagmic gain of the monkey is 1 up to a frequency of 6 Hz, when there are objects in view (Keller, 1978). Part of this improvement in gain may be due to the fact that animals are more alert when not in the dark. More alert animals are known to have a higher gain of the vestibulo-ocular reflex (Furman, O'Leary, & Wolfe, 1981). Another cause of the improvement of gain when things are in view is the recruitment of optokinetic nystagmus, although gain is improved when a stationary target is merely imagined (see Section 2.3).

The gain is also 1 up to higher frequencies when the head is oscillated in the dark by the voluntary efforts of the subject rather than by the experimenter (Tomlinson, Saunders, & Schwarz, 1980). The reason for this improvement over passive oscillation is not known; it could be due to increased alertness, to the contribution of efference, or to the recruitment of the cervico-ocular and arthro-ocular responses (see Sections 2.7 and 2.8). The gain of nystagmus with slow phase downward is less than that of nystagmus with slow phase upward (Darlot, Lopezbarneo, & Tracey, 1981). Both upward and downward nystagmus have a lower gain than horizontal nystagmus (Böhmer & Henn, 1983).

The only systematic data on the gain of the vestibulo-ocular reflex as a function of head velocity have been provided by Pulaski, Zee, and Robinson (1981). The gain was found to be approximately unity for voluntary or passive rotations of the head up to about 350°/sec, both when the subjects could see a fixed visual target and when they imagined a fixed target. See Figure 18.12.

2.2.3. The Latency and Phase Lag of Vestibular Nystagmus. When people rotate their own heads voluntarily at mod-

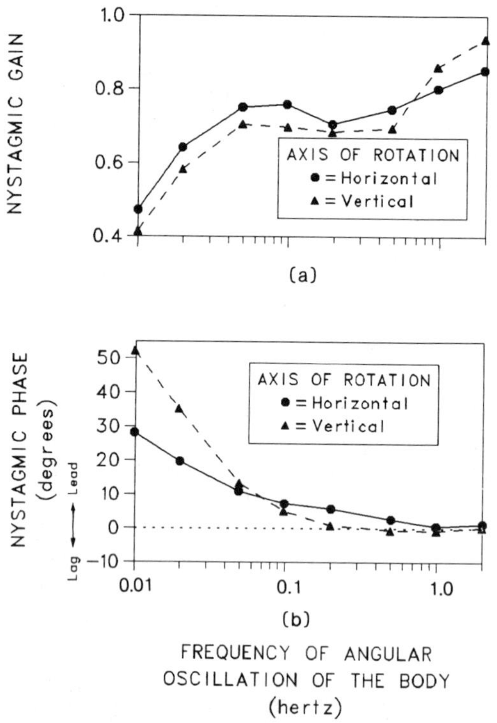

Figure 18.11. Gain and phase plots of nystagmus evoked by oscillation of the human body about the z axis, with this axis vertical (dotted curves) and horizontal (solid curves). Peak angular velocity of body rotation was ± 30°/sec at all frequencies. Mean values were for nine subjects. Gain (sensitivity) is defined as the ratio of the velocity of the slow phase of nystagmus to the velocity of body rotation. Phase is defined as the phase angle between the instant of peak head velocity and the instant of peak eye velocity. Note the characteristic reduction in phase lead and increase in gain of the compensatory eye movements as the frequency of body rotation is increased 0.01–0.5 Hz. (From A. J. Benson, Interactions between semicircular canals and graviceptors, in D. E. Busby (Ed.), Recent *advances in aerospace medicine*, D. Reidel Publishing Company, 1970. Reprinted with permission.)

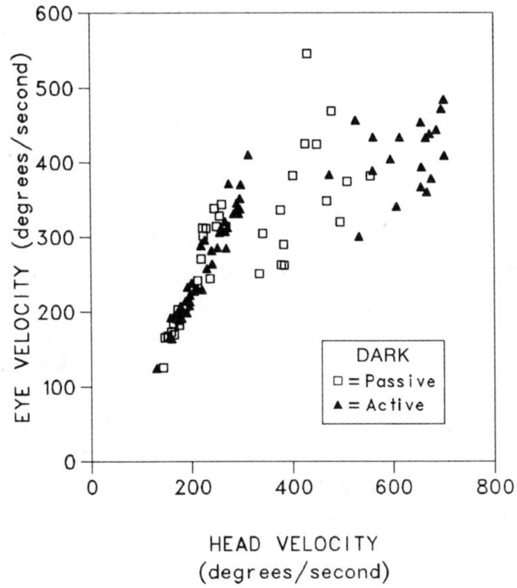

Figure 18.12. Peak slow-phase velocity as a function of peak head velocity during active and passive rotation of the head of a human subject in the dark. The subject was asked to imagine a stationary visual target. Note that the vestibulo-ocular response was compensatory for a head velocity of up to about 350°, after which it became saturated and variable. (From P. D. Pulaski, D. S. Zee, & D. A. Robinson, The behavior of the vestibulo-ocular reflex at high velocities of head rotation, *Brain Research*, 1981, *222*. Reprinted with permission.)

erate velocities the compensatory movement of the eyes may begin at the same time as the head movement. Under these circumstances the latency of the ocular response is zero because the head and eye movements are preprogrammed as one. These eye movements have been called *coordinate compensatory eye movements*. The latency of vestibular nystagmus, defined as the first sign of eye movements, is not easy to measure for slow accelerations of the body. It is not easy to tell when the compensatory movement of the eyes begins. Fluur and Mendel (1966) measured the time to the completion of the first nystagmic beat and found that it varied with the magnitude of the acceleration of the body. With a rotary acceleration of 1.0°/sec the latency defined in this way was found to be several seconds, and with an acceleration of 8°/sec it was 0.5 sec or less. The latency was found to be less variable with higher rates of acceleration. Once the response was initiated and the subject was accelerated at a steady rate, it was found to take several seconds for the response to reach its maximum frequency. This so-called crescendo time was found to be shorter with higher rates of acceleration (Fluur & Mendel, 1970). A more useful measure of nystagmic latency than the first signs of response to constant acceleration is the phase lag of the response when subjects are exposed to sinusoidal to-and-fro rotation of the body. In a linear system the slope of the function relating phase lag to input frequency defines the latency of the system.

When a person is rotated back and forth sinusoidally, the nystagmic response is said to be in phase with head movement when the slow phases are in the compensatory direction and the peak velocities of the slow phases coincide with the peak velocities of head rotation. The nystagmus is 180° out of phase when the slow phases are in the anticompensatory direction and when opposite peak velocities coincide. Other phase angles indicate the extent and relative direction of the mismatch between the two peak velocities. In practice, nystagmus shows a phase lead at low frequencies and no lead or a lag at higher frequencies of head oscillation.

The question of the phase lag of vestibular nystagmus is complicated by the fact that if a person in the dark is oscillated about a vertical axis, slowly and sinusoidally, a slow change in the mean position of the eyes relative to the skull is superimposed on the nystagmic response (see Figure 18.13). This drift in mean eye position has the same frequency as the oscillatory motion of the body but is phase-advanced 90° with respect to changes in head position (Mishkin & Melvill Jones, 1966). This puts the drift in phase with the angular velocity of the head, which suggests that it is driven by cupula deflection, because cupula deflection is also in phase with head velocity (see Chapter 11, "The Vestibular System," by Howard).

Figure 18.11(b) shows the phase of human vestibular nystagmus for angular oscillations of the body up to 2 Hz. For the monkey, in the dark, it has been found that the eyes are approximately in phase with the head over the frequency range 0.04–3.5 Hz, after which there is an increasing phase lag (Keller, 1978; Skavenski & Robinson, 1973). The input from the canals over this range of frequencies is proportional to head velocity, not to head acceleration or to head position (see Chapter 11 by Howard). The signals from the oculomotor nucleus, which drive the eyes, are coded in terms of both eye position and velocity, rather than in terms of eye velocity alone. The position component is required because the eyes move against an elastic load that increases linearly with increasing eccentricity of the eyes. In any sinusoidal motion, velocity and displacement are 90° out of phase. Thus if the velocity signal from the vestibular canals is to drive the position-coded component of the eye-movement system, a 90° phase lag is required in the control channel that links them. The vestibular velocity signal can drive the velocity component of the eye-movement system directly, except that there will have to be compensation for phase lags that tend to occur in any control channel. The absence of a significant phase lag in vestibular nystagmus at moderate frequencies of head oscillation led Robinson (1971, pp. 519–538) to postulate the presence of a neural integrator between the vestibular nuclei and the oculomotor nuclei. The operation of integrating a velocity signal is equivalent to converting it into a position signal, which, in turn, is equivalent to the required

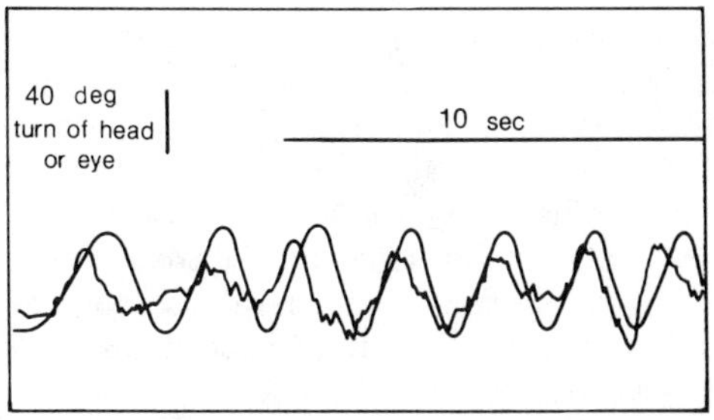

Figure 18.13. The jagged curve represents movements of the eye of a human subjected to oscillatory rotation of the head about a vertical axis at 0.5 Hz in the dark. The smooth curve represents the movements of the head. Upward displacement indicates displacement to the right. It can be seen that nystagmic beats are superimposed on a slower displacement of eye position, which is phase-advanced about 90° with respect to head position. This suggests that the slow deviation is driven by a velocity signal arising in the vestibular system. (From S. Mishkin & G. Melvill Jones, Predominant direction of gaze during slow head rotation, *Aerospace Medicine, 37*. Copyright 1966 by Aerospace Medical Association. Reprinted with permission.)

90° phase shift in the signal controlling eye position. Deactivation of the cerebellum has been found to increase the phase lag of vestibular nystagmus but not by the full 90° that one would expect if this organ were solely responsible for the required phase shift (Carpenter, 1972; Robinson, 1974). Furthermore, cells in the cerebellum, which fire in relation to the slow phase of nystagmus, show a phase lag intermediate between that of canal afferents and cells in the oculomotor nucleus (Gardner & Fuchs, 1975). Electrophysiological recordings in an alert monkey have revealed that the required 90° phase shift is evident in the activity of polysynaptically driven cells in the vestibular nuclei (Buettner, Büttner, & Henn, 1978; Keller & Kamath, 1975). The results of recording from, and stimulating, cells in the pontine reticular formation suggest that the required integration may be achieved by recurrent interactions between this center and the vestibular nuclei (B. Cohen & Komatsuzaki, 1972; Luschei & Fuchs, 1972).

2.2.4. Control of the Quick Phase of Vestibular Nystagmus. The quick phases and slow phases of vestibular nystagmus are affected in different ways by drugs and brain lesions, which suggests that they are controlled by distinct mechanisms (Ford & Walsh, 1936; Haciska, 1973). The rhythmic discharge of motoneurons in the oculomotor nerves can be detected after the eye and its muscles have been removed (McIntyre, 1939). This demonstrates that the quick phase is not mediated by stretching of the extraocular muscles. Furthermore, nystagmus occurs in the dark, so that the motion of the retinal image cannot be responsible for initiating the quick phase. Electrophysiological evidence suggests that the signals for the quick phase of both vestibular and optokinetic nystagmus originate in, or at least pass through, the pontine reticular formation (Berthoz, Baker, & Goldberg, 1974; Hikosaka & Kawakami, 1977). Neural activity associated with the quick phase of nystagmus has also been recorded in neurons of the vestibular nuclei. Furthermore, these cells were found to inhibit cells receiving vestibular inputs, that is, cells responsible for generating the slow-phase signal (Nakao, Sasaki, Schor, & Shimazu, 1982). Perhaps one signal from the reticular formation goes to inhibit the slow phase in the vestibular nucleus, while a second signal triggers the quick phase in the oculomotor nuclei. The quick phase tends to occur at regular intervals, although this regularity may not be apparent because of interaction between this inherent periodicity and the periodicity of the rotational stimulus (Cheng & Outerbridge, 1974).

A model of a mechanism for generating the quick phase of vestibular nystagmus has been proposed by Chun and Robinson (1978). In this model it is assumed that there is a primitive coupling between head rotation and the generation of a saccadic eye movement. The eye movement carries the gaze in the direction in which the head is moving and enables the animal to see where it is going. This saccade is directed toward a "center of interest" in headcentric space, the position of which is determined by vestibular signals induced by head turning. The subsequent slow phase of nystagmus carries the eyes away from this point until the discrepancy between present eye position, as indicated by an internal efferent copy, and the center of interest exceeds a threshold value. At this point a new quick phase is initiated. It is not clear how this model can explain the variability in amplitude of human quick phases. Perhaps the variability is due to fluidity in setting the center of interest or in setting the threshold value of discrepancy between the present and the desired position of the eyes.

2.3. The Interaction between Vestibular Nystagmus and Visual Pursuit

2.3.1. Background. When a person's head rotates under normal circumstances, the vestibular canals are stimulated and the visual scene moves relative to the head. There are thus two stimuli, both of which evoke nystagmus; the vestibular stimulus evokes vestibular nystagmus and the visual stimulus evokes *optokinetic nystagmus*. In its simplest form the slow phase of optokinetic nystagmus is controlled by the so-called retinal-slip velocity. The velocity of the eye movements is adjusted to reduce the retinal slip of the image to zero. In animals with foveate eyes this mechanism is supplemented by a visual pursuit system that seeks to keep a given feature of the visual scene on the fovea (see Hallett, Chapter 10). The vestibular and visual responses cooperate to achieve optimal stability of the retinal image both during and just after a period of body rotation. This section is devoted to a description of how this cooperation is achieved. The general problem of how visual stability is affected by eye movements is discussed by Anstis, Chapter 16, and Mack, Chapter 17.

2.3.2. Visual Enhancement of Vestibular Nystagmus. It has been mentioned already that if stationary objects are in view, the gain of the slow phase of nystagmus is unity at higher frequencies of head oscillation than is the case in the dark. This suggests that visually induced pursuit eye movements supplement the vestibular response. This supplementary input is required because the vestibular system does not respond at low frequencies of head oscillation. In particular, during a period of steady rotation of the body the absence of an accelerative stimulus causes the cupula to become restored to its resting position and the vestibular signal to decline to zero over a period of about 20 sec. The optokinetic system, on the other hand, is sensitive to low-frequency motion of the retinal image but relatively insensitive to high-frequency motion. When a person rotates the head in illuminated surroundings, the vestibular and optokinetic systems thus cooperate to produce adequate compensatory eye movements over a wider range of frequencies of head oscillation than either system could produce alone.

One indication of the efficiency of combined vestibular and visual inputs in achieving image stability during head movements is the fact that a person can read a stationary display of digits while being oscillated about a vertical axis up to frequencies of about 9 Hz. When only visual signals operate, as when a display of digits is oscillated from side to side in front of a stationary observer, the ability to read the display is impaired even at a frequency of 0.5 Hz, and at 2 Hz, reading speed is only about 10% of normal (Benson & Barnes, 1978).

Some improvement in the gain of vestibular nystagmus has been reported in subjects oscillated, either passively or actively, at 0.3 Hz in the dark when they were merely asked to imagine that they were fixating on a stationary scene (Barr, Schultheis, & Robinson, 1976; Takahashi, Uemura, & Fujishiro, 1980). Perhaps the angle of convergence of the eyes increased when subjects imagined a visual scene, and this may have caused the change in gain (see Section 2.2.2).

In a recent study Steinman and Collewijn (1980) found that the gain of the vestibulo-ocular response was considerably less than one in some of their subjects when they made voluntary head movements in lighted surroundings. In spite of the imperfect image stabilization, subjects reported that the scene appeared stable. This evidence suggests that even large imperfections in image stability do not impair visual performance. However, Duwaer (1982) repeated these measurements using an afterimage method for recording the adequacy of fixation, which he claims is more reliable than the search-coil method used by Steinman and Collewijn. He found that the gain of visual fixation remained close to unity with a frequency of voluntary head oscillation of 0.66 Hz at an amplitude of 20°, which were the values used in the Steinman and Collewijn study. Further measurements are needed to resolve this issue.

The way in which inputs from the vestibular system complement visual signals arising from a stationary scene can be seen in the activity of type I second-order neurons in the vestibular nuclei of the monkey (Waespe & Henn, 1979, pp. 683–693). The rate of discharge per unit of stimulus rotation (gain) of these cells in response to body rotation in the dark is low for low rates of acceleration but high for high rates of acceleration, as shown in Figure 18.14(a). Their gain in response to visual motion is high for low rates of acceleration and low for high rates of acceleration, as shown in Figure 18.14(b). When the animal is rotated in the presence of a stationary scene, gain becomes a function of velocity of rotation and more or less independent of acceleration, as shown in Figure 18.14(c).

Several models of these interactive processes have been devised, one of which is shown in simplified form in Figure 18.15. For a detailed treatment of models of the eye-movement system see Henn, Cohen, and Young (1980) and Robinson (1981).

2.3.3. Visual Inhibition of Vestibular Nystagmus. Vestibular nystagmus is inhibited when a person's gaze is fixed on an object that rotates with the head. Nystagmus is more or less completely inhibited during sinusoidal head oscillations up to about 0.5 Hz. Above this frequency the eyes show increasing evidence of nystagmus until, at a frequency of about 2 Hz, its amplitude is about as great as with eyes closed, even though the subject tries to maintain steady fixation (Benson & Barnes, 1978). Accompanying this increase in nystagmic amplitude is a progressive deterioration in the subject's ability to read a display of digits, which is rotated with the head (Barnes, Benson, & Prior, 1978). Vestibular nystagmus induced by a forward inclination of the head is less adequately suppressed by vision than is nystagmus induced by a backward inclination or sideways rotation of the head (Benson & Guedry, 1971; Darlot, Lopez-barneo, & Tracey, 1981). When a person attempts to fixate on an object that rotates with the head, vestibular nystagmus is in conflict with the needs of visual fixation. The most effective stabilization of the retinal image is achieved when vestibular nystagmus and visual pursuit are in harmony. The two responses are in harmony when the accelerating or oscillating subject visually fixates a stationary object (Guedry, Lentz, & Jell, 1979).

Pilots in vibrating aircraft are required to read displays that move with the vibrating body. This is especially the case when a pilot is required to read a display mounted on the helmet. Visual stabilization is poor under these circumstances because, as we have just seen, visual-vestibular reflexes are best suited to stabilizing scenes which do not move with the head (Guedry, Benson, & Moore, 1982). The visual effects of the whole body vibration are reviewed in A. M. Collins (1973) and in Griffin and Lewis (1978). For a person, moving or rotating at a steady velocity, in whom the vestibular signals have subsided, the visual and vestibular responses will be most harmonious when the person fixates a point moving with the head. For this reason subjects are, in these circumstances, best able to read a display that moves at the same velocity as the head. Visual suppression

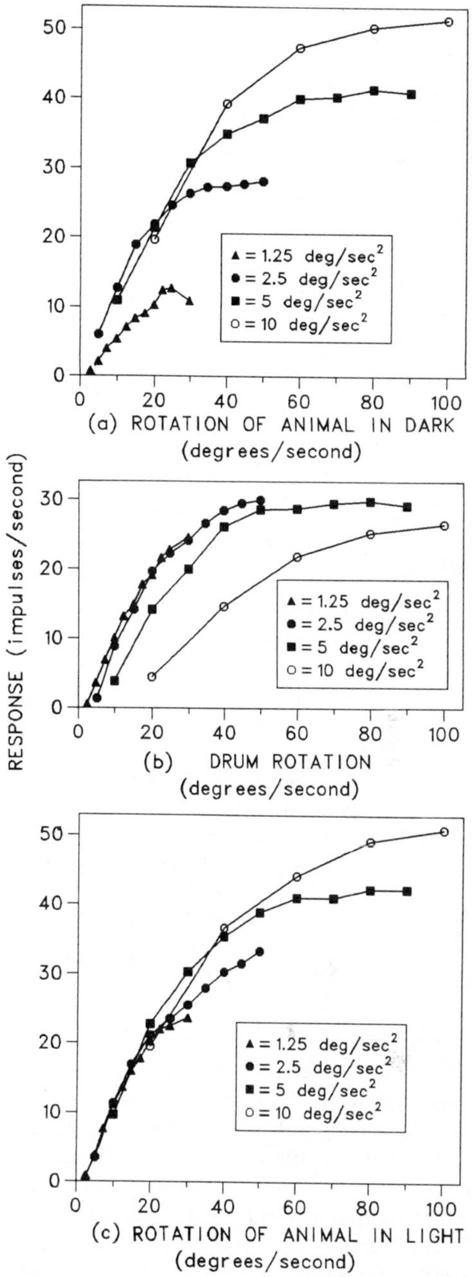

Figure 18.14. Mean activity of four type I neurons in the vestibular nucleus of an alert monkey as a function of stimulus velocity for various stimulus accelerations during (a) rotation of the animal around its vertical z axis in the dark, (b) rotation of a cylinder covered with black and white vertical stripes around the stationary animal, and (c) rotation of the animal in the presence of a stationary striped scene. The ordinate represents discharge frequency above the resting level. During combined visual-vestibular stimulation, discharge frequency is a function of stimulus velocity, independent of acceleration. (From W. Waespe & V. Henn, Motion information in the vestibular nuclei of alert monkeys: Visual and vestibular input vs. optomotor input, in R. Granit & O. Pompeiano (Eds.), *Reflex control of posture and movement*, Elsevier Biomedical Press, 1979. Reprinted with permission.)

of vestibular nystagmus is less effective when visual velocity information is degraded either by presenting the visual target in the periphery or by having it illuminated intermittently (Barnes, 1982; Barnes & Edge, 1983).

The duration of postrotary nystagmus is shortened from about 30 sec to about 5 sec when the subject is asked to fixate

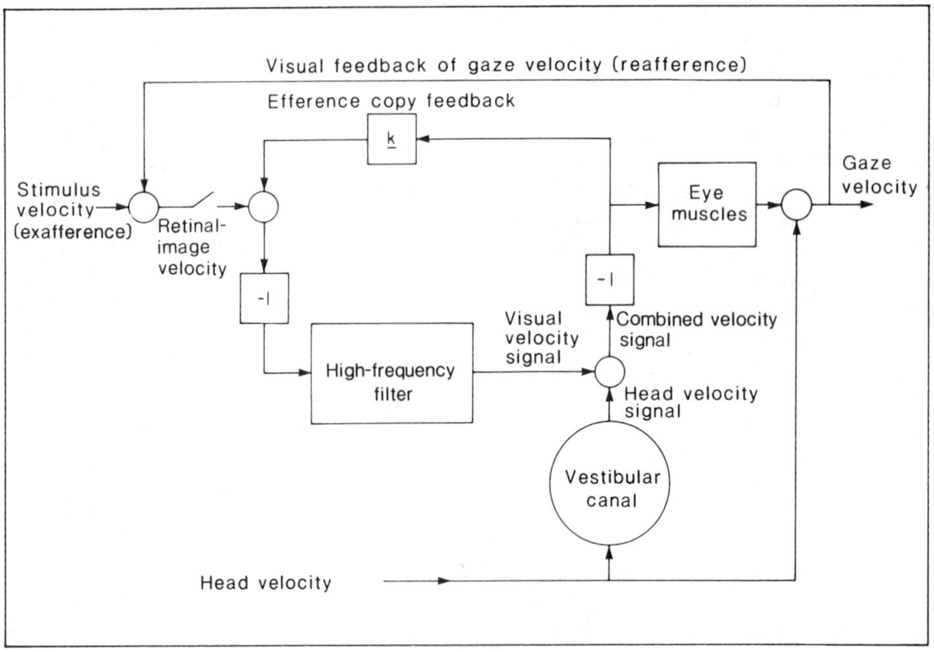

Figure 18.15. A simplified version of the model proposed by Robinson to account for how visual and vestibular signals cooperate in producing eye movements that stabilize the retinal images. In this model the retinal image moves across the retina at a velocity that depends on the velocity of the stimulus and the adequacy of combined pursuit eye movements and head movements. The resulting retinal-slip velocity constitutes an error signal assessed in terms of feedback from the efferent signals to the eye muscles. Image motion due to eye movements is thus discounted, and an estimate of the headcentric velocity of the visual signal is derived. This is equal to head velocity when the visual scene is stationary. A filter rejects high-frequency visual signals, and the resulting visual velocity signal is combined with a head-velocity signal from the vestibular system. The combined velocity signal, after suitable phase adjustment, drives the oculomotor system in such a way as to stabilize the retinal image in relation to perturbations introduced by movements of the stimulus and head. (From D. A. Robinson, Linear addition of optokinetic and vestibular signals in the vestibular nucleus, *Experimental Brain Research*, 1977, *30*. Reprinted with permission.)

a feature of a visual scene (Ornitz, Brown, Mason, & Putnam, 1974). It looks as though the duration of postrotary nystagmus with visual fixation is governed by the long time constant of the primary vestibular inputs, which is of the order of 5 sec.

In spite of the inhibitory relationships between visual and vestibular inputs, visual pursuit and vestibular nystagmus may occur at the same time. For instance, Holm-Jensen (1982) found that a high-frequency vestibular nystagmus induced by caloric stimulation of the ear could be superimposed on a low-frequency visual pursuit induced by slow movements of the visual surroundings (see Figure 18.16). When the two responses were in opposite directions, the amplitude of the visually driven response was found to be less than when they were in the same direction. It seems that visual inputs inhibit vestibular responses most effectively when the visual and vestibular stimuli are of similar strength and frequency, as they are when rotating subjects view a scene that moves with them.

The site of the mechanism responsible for visual suppression of nystagmus is not known, but the activity of second-order neurons in the vestibular nuclei of an alert monkey is attenuated and their time constants are shortened when nystagmus is inhibited (Figure 18.17). There are indications that the cerebellum is involved in this inhibitory process (see Section 4.3). People with lesions in the cerebellum, brain stem, or cerebral hemispheres do not suppress inappropriate nystagmus effectively (Dichgans, Reutern, & Römmelt, 1978). The effectiveness of this suppression improves with age in young people, but whether this is due to a learning process or a maturational process is not known (Herman, Maulucci, & Stuyck, 1982).

The fact that vestibular nystagmus may be superimposed on low-frequency visual pursuit suggests that interactions between the two systems when they are of similar frequency is due to competition between two initially distinct systems for entry into the final common path through the oculomotor nuclei.

2.3.4. Temporal Cooperation between Vestibular and Optokinetic Nystagmus. The temporal features of vestibular nystagmus were described in Section 2.2.3. The slow phase of optokinetic nystagmus takes 20–60 sec to reach its full velocity after a visual scene has started to move. This is known as the *recruitment time* of the response. Several lines of evidence suggest that response recruitment is due to the presence of a mechanism that accumulates, or integrates, the velocity signal driving the slow phase of optokinetic nystagmus (Raphan, Cohen, & Matsuo, 1977, pp. 37–48). Optokinetic nystagmus persists as an *after-nystagmus* for a period of 20–60 sec after visual stimulation has ceased, and this is probably caused by the slow discharge of the velocity integrator (Collewijn, Winterson, & van der Steen, 1980). We may now consider how these features of optokinetic nystagmus mesh with temporal features of vestibular nystagmus when a person is rotated for some time and then brought to rest.

If a person is rotated for some time at a steady angular velocity, the cupulae become restored to their central positions and the stimulus for vestibular nystagmus ceases. If the subject's

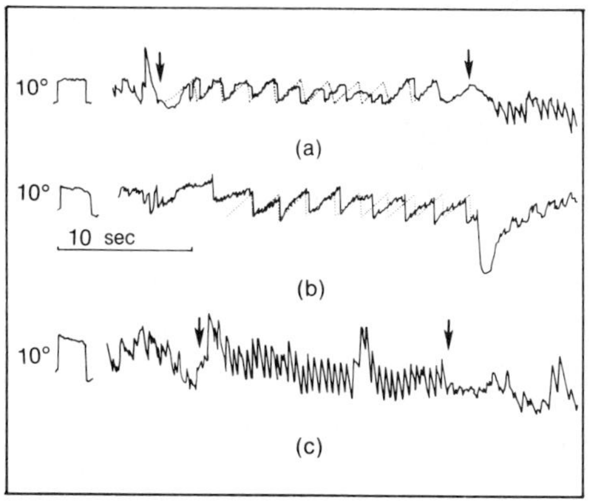

Figure 18.16. Simultaneous vestibular (caloric) and optokinetic nystagmus. In (a) right-beating caloric nystagmus is superimposed on a slow, visually driven nystagmus in the opposite direction (velocity: 5°/sec). In (b) the two responses are in the same direction. The dotted lines represent the visual response expected when there is no vestibular stimulus. It can be seen that the visual response is reduced or enhanced relative to this baseline, according to whether it is in the same or opposite direction to the slow phase of the vestibular response. The trace in (c) shows how a right-beating caloric nystagmus is suppressed by ipsilateral optokinetic stimulation when the two responses have a similar frequency. Arrows indicate onset and offset of visual stimulation. (From S. Holm-Jensen, Interference between synchronous optokinetic nystagmus and vestibular nystagmus. *Acta Otolaryngologica*, 1982, *93*. Reprinted with permission.)

eyes are open, nystagmus is nevertheless maintained by optokinetic stimuli arising from the motion of the retinal image. Vestibular nystagmus has a short latency, whereas it takes some time for the optokinetic response to be recruited to full strength. It is probably no accident that this recruitment time is about the same as the time taken for the vestibular response to decline after the start of a period of steady rotation. Thus when a person rotates at a steady velocity, the vestibular system ceases to respond, but by this time the optokinetic system will have taken over to generate adequate pursuit movements of the eyes. When the head comes to rest, the inertia of the endolymph causes a deflection of the cupula in a direction opposite to that in which it was deflected during head acceleration. This, together with neural aftereffects of vestibular stimulation, induces postrotary vestibular nystagmus, which, if unchecked, would destablize the retinal image. If the eyes remain open in the postrotary period, fixation on the stationary scene will inhibit the vestibular response. But even if the eyes are closed when turning ceases, the stored "charge" in the integrator of the optokinetic system induces optokinetic afternystagmus. The slow phases of postrotary nystagmus and of optokinetic afternystagmus are in opposite directions and therefore cancel each other. Recent evidence shows that the two aftereffects decay at the same rate (Collewijn et al., 1980; Raphan & Cohen, 1981; Raphan, Matsuo, & Cohen, 1979). They thus continue to cancel until the two aftereffects have decayed to zero. The fact that these two functions have similar time constants suggests that they both depend on the same neural integrator. However, it has been found that the decay rates of postrotary nystagmus and optokinetic afternystagmus can be made different by selective habituation (Skavenski, Blair, & Westheimer, 1981). Demer and Robinson (1983) account for this finding by suggesting that the two aftereffects share one integrator but that postrotary nystagmus has a second integrator not shared by the optokinetic system.

After optokinetic stimulation, a second phase of afternystagmus is often observed, opposite in sign to the first phase (Brandt, Dichgans, & Büchele, 1974; Waespe & Henn, 1978b; Waespe, Huber, & Henn, 1978). This secondary optokinetic afternystagmus coincides with the secondary phase of postrotary nystagmus, which was described in Section 2.2.1. These two secondary aftereffects are in opposite directions, so that they, too, cancel. These relationships between visual and vestibular responses are illustrated in Figure 18.18.

All this suggests that visual and vestibular inputs converge at some point in the nervous system. Electrophysiological recordings of the activity of cells in the vestibular nuclei in a monkey have shown that certain cells discharge at a rate correlated with the velocity of the slow phase of optokinetic afternystagmus and cease firing when the afternystagmus is inhibited by the sight of stationary stimuli. Furthermore, these same units respond transiently when the animal's head is rotated (Waespe & Henn, 1977a, 1977b). Rabbits, monkeys, and humans with bilateral loss of the vestibular system lack optokinetic afternystagmus and have a measurable defect in the ability to visually pursue stripes moving at high velocities (B. Cohen, Uemura, & Takemori, 1973; Collewijn, 1976; Zee, Yee, & Robinson, 1976).

Other aspects of visual-vestibular interaction will be discussed in Sections 3 and 4.

2.4. The Coordination of Active Head and Eye Movements

It is not comfortable to hold the eyes in an eccentric position of gaze. The natural reaction when a person looks at an object some distance off to the side is to move both the eyes and the head to face the object so that the eyes can return to their primary position in the head. When a person executes a combined movement of head and eyes, the motor commands to the neck muscles are usually initiated before those to the eye muscles, but because of their low inertia, the eyes start to move about 20 msec before the head and reach the target before the head has accelerated to its peak velocity. While the head continues to move toward the target, the eyes make a compensatory return movement that stabilizes the retinal image (Bizzi, Kalil, & Tagliasco, 1971; Uemura, Arai, & Shimazaki, 1980). The amplitude of a saccade made in conjunction with a head movement is reduced to take account of the fact that the head is also moving (Morasso, Bizzi, & Dichgans, 1973). This sequence of movements is depicted in Figure 18.19. The evidence reviewed next suggests that this coordinated sequence of eye and head movements is partly preprogrammed and partly under vestibular control, although visual, kinesthetic, and attentional factors may modify it.

When a person's head is moved by the experimenter, a saccadic eye movement occurs in the same direction, and the saccade is initiated after the head has started to move, not before, as in voluntary movements of the head (Melvill Jones, 1964). This delayed saccadic response is not evoked visually, since it occurs in the dark. The saccadic response may also be delayed if the head is moved voluntarily in the dark or even in illuminated surroundings if the subject makes no effort to fixate a visual object (Barnes 1979; Henriksson, Novotny, & Tjernström, 1974). The fact that under these circumstances the saccade occurs *after* the onset of the head movement suggests that it is a response to vestibular stimulation, namely, the quick phase of vestibular nystagmus. When a person's gaze is actively di-

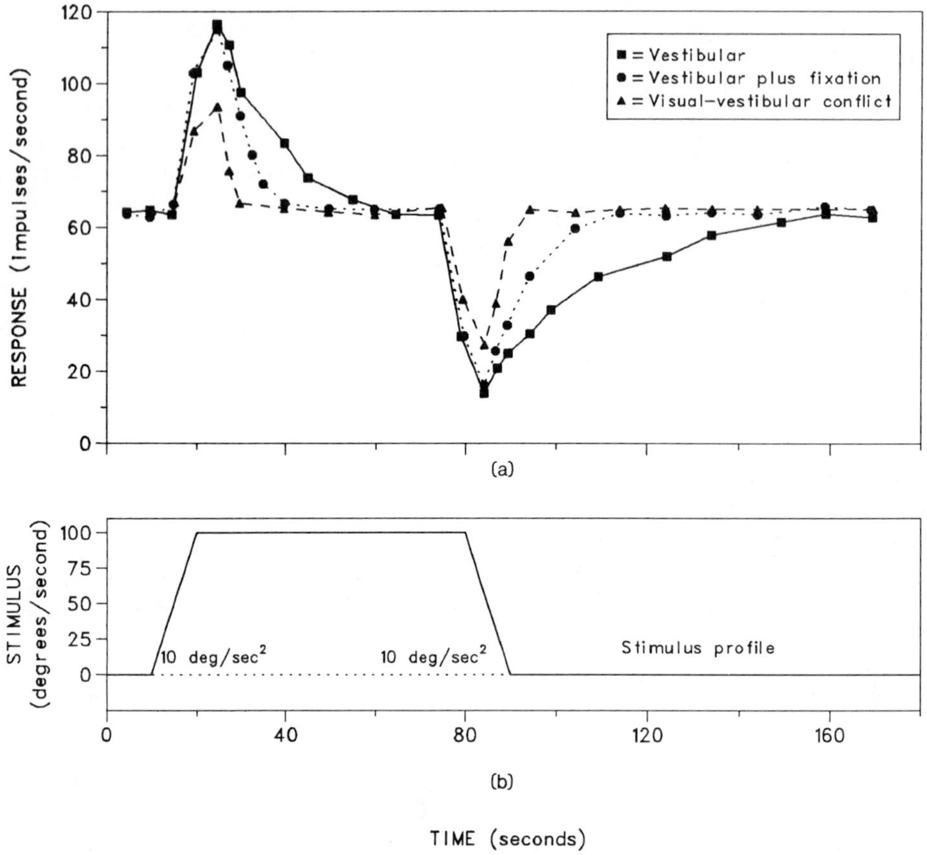

Figure 18.17. (a) Responses of a type I neuron in the vestibular nucleus of an alert monkey during and after rotary acceleration and deceleration of the animal. The stimulus profile is shown in (b). The solid curve was obtained when the animal was rotated in the dark, the dotted curve when the rotating animal fixated a stationary visual target, and the dashed curve when the rotated animal fixated a visual target which remained in the median plane of its head. Note that visual fixation reduces the postrotatory response. Fixation on a target rotating with the animal reduces the gain of the perrotary response. Although the gain of the cell was not reduced to zero, the animal showed no sign of nystagmus under these circumstances. (From U. W. Buettner & U. Büttner, Vestibular nuclei activity in the alert monkey during suppression of vestibular and optokinetic nystagmus, *Experimental Brain Research*, 1979, *37*. Reprinted with permission.)

rected toward an eccentrically placed object, the saccade occurs *before* the head movement and must therefore be preprogrammed along with the head movement.

Even when the head movement is voluntary, the compensatory return motion of the eyes is apparently not preprogrammed but is triggered by vestibular inputs. If the head movement is arrested by a brake when a person attempts to direct the gaze to an eccentric target, the initial saccade occurs but the compensatory return movement does not (Bizzi et al., 1971). The brake should not interfere with a preprogrammed slow eye movement, but it does forestall vestibular stimulation. Furthermore, if a person's head is rotated in the dark voluntarily or by an external agent, the slow return motion of the eyes occurs, showing that vestibular and perhaps also proprioceptive inputs from the neck are sufficient to induce it (Barnes, 1979). Nevertheless, if objects are in view, the gain of the return movement is improved by the recruitment of the optokinetic pursuit system, and visually evoked saccades may correct for large errors (Gresty, 1974; Lanman, Bizzi, & Allum, 1978).

If subjects know when and where a visual target is going to appear, they may move their heads before the target is presented and apply corrective saccades when the target appears, followed by secondary head movements and compensatory eye movements if these are required (Bizzi, Kalil, & Morasso, 1972).

When subjects pursue a visual target, moving with either a high-velocity regular motion or randomly, along a horizontal track, they do so with their eyes alone, not with the eyes and head. This is because the low inertia of the eyes allows for accurate tracking of the target. When the target moves regularly to and fro with a frequency below 1 Hz, subjects often pursue it with a more or less adequate combination of head and eye movements, interrupted when necessary by corrective saccades (Gresty & Leech, 1977).

2.5. Eye Movements in Response to Combined Rotary and Linear Acceleration

The most easily observed response of the eyes to a linear acceleration of the body is a steady deviation in the opposite direction. This is the normal response of the eyes to stimulation of the otolith organs. The residual eye torsion, which is evident when a person tilts the head to one side, is an example of an eye deviation induced by stimulation of the otolith organs.

Each receptor cell in the maculae of the utricles and saccules responds best to an accelerative stimulus acting in a certain direction. This most effective direction defines the *polarization axis* of the receptor cell. Electrical stimulation of an afferent fiber from a utricle or saccule of the cat has been found to induce

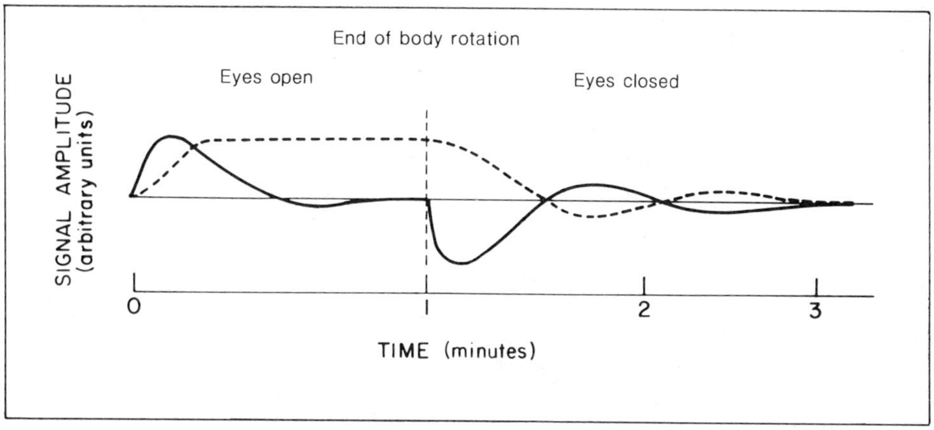

Figure 18.18. A diagrammatic and hypothetical representation of relationships between vestibular (solid line) and optokinetic signals (dotted lines) that generate nystagmus during and after a period of body rotation. It is assumed that the eyes are open during the 1-min rotation period and closed after rotation has stopped. In the initial period of rotation the vestibular signal drives nystagmus. As this signal decays, the optokinetic signal is recruited and stabilizes the retinal image. After rotation, the postrotatory vestibular signal and the optokinetic-afternystagmus signal tend to cancel. Signals also cancel in subsequent reversed phases of these two response systems.

a steady deviation of gaze in a direction corresponding to the polarization axis of the receptors that the stimulated afferent fiber innervates (Fluur & Mellström, 1970a, 1970b, 1971; Janeke, Jongkees, & Oosteveld, 1970; Suzuki, Tokumasu, & Goto, 1969).

Some uncoordinated deviations and torsional movements of the eyes may also occur with this type of stimulation. Occasional nystagmic responses are probably due to incidental stimulation of the canals, since they are not found in cats with sectioned ampullar nerves but intact afferents from utricle and saccule (Fluur & Siegborn, 1973a) and they are not evoked by direct stimulation of utricle afferents in rabbits (Janeke et al., 1970). See Howard, Section 2.3, Chapter 11, "The Vestibular System."

Human subjects exposed to a linear acceleration of the body along the interaural axis have been found to exhibit nystagmus with an amplitude of a few degrees. The accelerative stimulus required to produce this response is well in excess of that required for the perception of acceleration, and it is not clear whether the response is due to stimulation of the otolith organs or to some indirect effect of linear acceleration on the semicircular canals (Buizza, Léger, Droulez, Berthoz, & Schmid, 1980; Niven, Hixson, & Correia, 1966).

A human subject exposed to sinusoidal linear motion in the dark executes involuntary oscillations of the eyes, the frequency of which varies systematically with the frequency of the stimulus (Melvill Jones, Downing, & Rolf, 1973). This response is probably due to the alternate stimulation of oppositely polarized receptors in the utricular or saccular maculae.

If human subjects with head erect are rotated in a centrifuge in the dark, in such a way that the body always faces the same direction relative to the stationary surroundings, they are subjected to a *rotating linear acceleration* in a horizontal plane, without any angular movement of their body. This type of stimulation, which may be called *ferris-wheel rotation*, induces a horizontal nystagmus. The most obvious conclusion is that ferris-wheel nystagmus represents the sequential eye deviations induced by the rotating linear vector acting on the utricles (Benson, 1968; Benson & Barnes, 1973, pp. 221–236). In line with this view is the fact that the response persists when the six vestibular canals are blocked (B. Cohen, Suzuki, & Raphan, 1983; Correia & Money, 1970). However, other evidence reviewed now suggests that the canals also contribute to ferris-wheel nystagmus.

It has been found that cells in the vestibular nucleus of the cat that normally respond when the head is rotated also respond

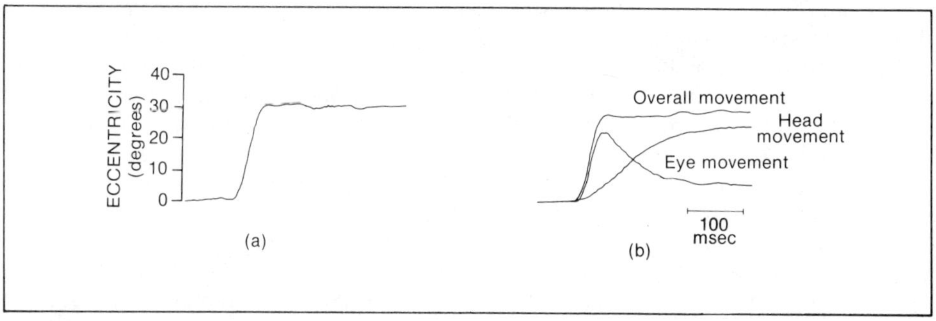

Figure 18.19. Records of eye and head movements during a change of gaze from straight ahead toward a visual target appearing at an eccentricity of 30°. In (a) this is done by a saccadic eye movement, with the head held stationary. In (b) a similar overall change in gaze is produced by a combined movement of the head and eyes. (From P. Morasso, E. Bizzi, & J. Dichgans, Adjustment of saccade characteristics during head movements, *Experimental Brain Research*, 1973, *16*. Reprinted with permission.)

to ferris-wheel stimulation (Benson, Guedry, & Melvill Jones, 1970). Canal afferents in the monkey have been found to respond to linear acceleration even when the canals are plugged so that they cannot respond to rotary acceleration (Goldberg & Fernández, 1975). If this response were due to a direct effect of linear acceleration on the cupula, there would have to be some difference in specific gravity between the cupula and endolymph. But no such difference has been found (Money, Bonen, Beatty, Kuehn, Sokoloff, & Weaver, 1971). There is a difference in density between the endolymph and perilymph, and it has been suggested that a rotating linear vector causes a cyclic motion of the membranous duct of the canal within its bony cavity, in the manner of a roller pump. This would cause a cyclic pressure change in the endolymph and deflect the cupula, even in a plugged canal (Benson & Bodin, 1966a).

Even though the otolith organs are primarily responsible for ferris-wheel nystagmus, the response has been found to be abolished by section of the semicircular canal nerves (B. Cohen et al., 1983). It was suggested that the resting discharge from canal nerves is necessary for integrating the velocity signal from the otolith organs.

A recumbent person rotated about an earth-horizontal z axis is subjected to a rotary acceleration in the plane of the horizontal canals and a rotating linear-acceleration vector in the plane of the utricles. This type of stimulation is known as *barbecue rotation*. While it lasts, nystagmus persists, even when the velocity of rotation is constant and the subject is in the dark (Benson & Bodin, 1966b; Guedry, 1965b). Any canal-induced response should cease during constant angular velocity, as it does when the head is rotated about a vertical z axis, so that the persisting nystagmus must be due to the changing direction of gravity acting on the otolith organs. This conclusion is confirmed by the fact that barbecue nystagmus ceases in rabbits in which the otolith organs have been removed, leaving the canals intact (Janeke et al., 1970), and by the fact that it is present in human patients with loss of canal functioning but with intact otolith organs (Graybiel, Stockwell, & Guedry, 1972).

It can be seen from Figure 18.20 that postrotary nystagmus decays more rapidly after barbecue rotation than after rotation about the vertical z axis (Benson & Bodin, 1966a). Presumably, after barbecue rotation, inputs from the utricles, which inform subjects that they are not rotating, inhibit the postrotary effects of canal stimulation.

Stimuli arising in the otolith organs may modify nystagmus induced by rotary acceleration. These influences have been studied in some detail in the cat (Fluur & Siegborn, 1973a, 1973b, 1974). After unilateral labyrinthectomy monkeys show a spontaneous lateral nystagmus when held in a fixed posture in the dark. This symptom soon disappears, leaving a permanent loss of gain in the slow phase of nystagmus induced by rotation of the body toward the operated side. After bilabyrinthectomy, there is a reduction of nystagmic gain in both directions (Igarashi, Takahashi, Reschke, & Wright, 1977). When human patients with unilateral vestibular damage tilt the head toward the affected side, the frequency of spontaneous nystagmus increases, and when they tilt it the other way, it decreases. This is probably the reason why such patients sleep on their sound ear (Fluur, 1973, 1974). Nystagmus induced or increased by head tilt is referred to as *positional nystagmus* and is thought to be due either to defects in the cervico-ocular system or to the defective interplay between inputs from otolith organs and semicircular canals (Bergstedt, 1961; Biemond & de Jong, 1969). Positional nystagmus due to alcohol ingestion probably results from a

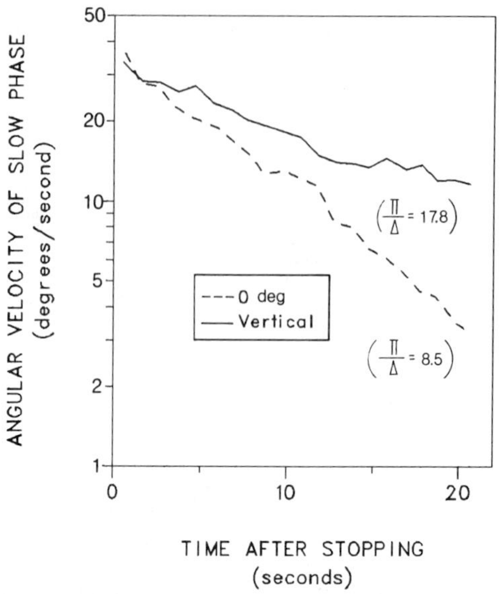

Figure 18.20. The decay of the angular velocity of postrotary nystagmus (mean of 11 subjects) when the body was brought to rest after being rotated about the vertical z axis (top curve) and after being brought to rest in a supine posture after being rotated about the horizontal z axis (bottom curve). The numbers in parentheses represent the time constants in seconds in the two cases. It can be seen that nystagmus declines more rapidly after rotation about a horizontal axis than after rotation about a vertical axis. In the former case, utricular inputs inform subjects that they are not rotating and probably inhibit the postrotary canal effects. (From A. J. Benson & M. A. Bodin, Effects of orientation to the gravitational vertical on nystagmus following rotation about a horizontal axis, *Acta Otolaryngologica*, 1966, *61*. Reprinted with permission.)

disturbance of the specific gravity of the endolymph (Money & Myles, 1974). In clinical practice a distinction is made between postional nystagmus that occurs just after a tilting motion of the head, referred to as *positioning nystagmus*, and that which occurs for as long as a tilted posture is maintained, referred to as *postural nystagmus*.

These interactions between otolith and semicircular canal stimulation suggest that inputs from the two types of sense organs converge. Cells have been found in the fastigial nuclei of the cerebellum of the cat that respond to both linear and rotary acceleration. Most of the cells were found to respond only to one or the other type of stimulation, which suggests that the activity of the dual-purpose cells is due to convergence of afferents rather than to interactions at the level of the sense organs (Favilla, Ghelarducci, Hill, & Spyer, 1980). Convergence of inputs from the utricles and semicircular canals has also been recorded in second-order neurons in the vestibular nuclei of the cat. By recording from these cells after selective sectioning of brain stem pathways, patterns of facilitations and inhibition have been worked out that may explain some of the pathological symptoms described above (Searles & Barnes, 1977).

It may thus be stated that constant stimulation of the otolith organs induces a corresponding deviation of the eyes but not nystagmus. Nystagmus may be induced by an alternating or rotating linear vector. A rotating linear vector may also excite the canals in the manner of a roller pump. If the balance of the vestibular system is disturbed by unilateral damage, the resulting spontaneous nystagmus is modified by otolith stimulation, and this interaction probably depends on the presence of cells in the brain stem that respond to inputs from the otolith organs and the canals.

2.6. Countertorsion

In many animals, including humans, the eyes tend to remain upright relative to gravity when the head is rotated about an axis parallel to a visual axis. This response is known as *countertorsion.* In animals, like the rabbit, countertorsion is sufficient to keep the same retinal meridian upright, but in humans countertorsion is only about 10% of the angle of head tilt. It is of greater amplitude when the resultant force acting on the body is increased beyond the normal value of 980 cm/sec^2—a fact that demonstrates the role of the otolith organs (Schöne, 1962). In the dark, the response is fairly smooth, with an occasional nystagmic beat that probably arises from stimulation of the vestibular canals. More prominent nystagmic beats, evident in illuminated surroundings (see Figure 18.21), are probably due to optikinetic stimulation from the moving retinal image (Petrov & Zenkin, 1973).

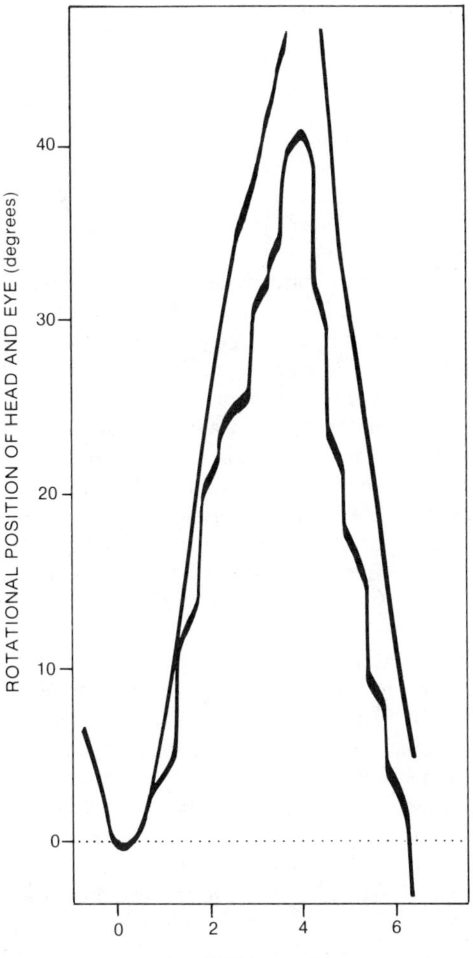

Figure 18.21. The smooth curve is a record of the head tilting toward the left shoulder through 50° and back in illuminated surroundings. The rippled curve is a record of rotation of the eye around the visual axis during the head movement. The basic response is probably due to utricular stimuli, with the nystagmic ripples due to stimulation of the vestibular canals plus an optokinetic response. Note that the magnitude of eye torsion is indicated by the extent to which the eyes lag behind the head rotation. (From A. P. Petrov & G. M. Zenkin, Torsional eye movements and constancy of the visual field, *Vision Research, 13*. Copyright 1973 by Pergamon Press, Ltd. Reprinted with permission.)

The amplitude of countertorsion is a function of the sine of the angle of head tilt, which suggests that it is induced by the shearing force acting on the utricular maculae (Miller & Graybiel, 1971; Schöne, 1962). The amplitude of the response is not reduced if the head is held in a tilted position for several hours, which suggests that it is driven by nonadapting utricular receptors (Miller & Graybiel, 1974). The response is absent when the head is tilted toward the shoulder with the body in a supine posture. The utricles do not respond to this type of head movement, and the absence of countertorsion demonstrates that there is no cervico-ocular reflex under these circumstances (Scott, 1967).

With sinusoidal oscillation of the head, countertorsion is in phase with head displacement over the frequency range 0.025–0.25 Hz. At higher frequencies the response shows some phase lag, which must be neural in origin, because the output from the utricles shows a phase lead at these frequencies of head oscillation (J. H. Anderson & Precht, 1979).

Utricular involvement in countertorsion is confirmed by the fact that after unilateral labyrinthine loss, the response is absent when the head tilts toward the defective side. The labyrinthine control of motoneurons serving the superior and inferior oblique muscles of the eye has been investigated by direct recording from these motoneurons in the cat (Berthoz, Baker, & Precht, 1973; Blanks, Anderson, & Precht, 1978).

After bilateral vestibular loss, countertorsion is reduced in both directions (Krejčová, Highstein, & B. Cohen, 1971; Nelson & Cope, 1971). The cause of the residual response after bilateral vestibular loss is not known, but it occurs in the dark, so that it is not visually instigated, and it occurs with whole-body rotation, so that it is not a cervico-ocular response (Smiles, Hite, Hyams, & Junker, 1975).

2.7. The Cervico-ocular Response

If the head of a seated person is held in a fixed position while the torso is rotated about a vertical axis, the eyes execute a small-amplitude horizontal nystagmus and become deviated in a direction opposite to the movement of the torso. A forward or backward inclination of the torso, with respect to the stationary head, induces nystagmus and deviation in a vertical plane, but a sideways tilt of the torso does not induce eye torsion (Scott, 1967). The horizontal and vertical eye movements are induced by stimulation of joint receptors in the neck and are referred to as *cervico-ocular reflexes* and sometimes as *spino-ocular reflexes* (Meiry, 1971; Takemori & Suzaki, 1971). These responses are more evident in infants, in certain animals, and in adults with pathologies than they are in normal human adults (Jongkees, 1969).

Any discussion of the cervico-ocular reflex is complicated by the fact that there is no agreement about which aspect of the response indicates its gain and phase. Figure 18.22 shows a typical record of the response. It can be seen that body rotation induces small nystagmic movements superimposed on an overall to-and-fro drift of eye position that is approximately 120° out of phase with body position. One could take the mean velocity of the response divided by stimulus velocity at any one part of the stimulus cycle as a measure of response gain, and this would be analogous to the gain of vestibular nystagmus. But this is not what is always done. Instead, gain and phase are sometimes derived from the fundamental Fourier component of the response. In other words, the response is defined as the overall to-and-fro deviation of the eyes. This is analogous to the to-and-fro

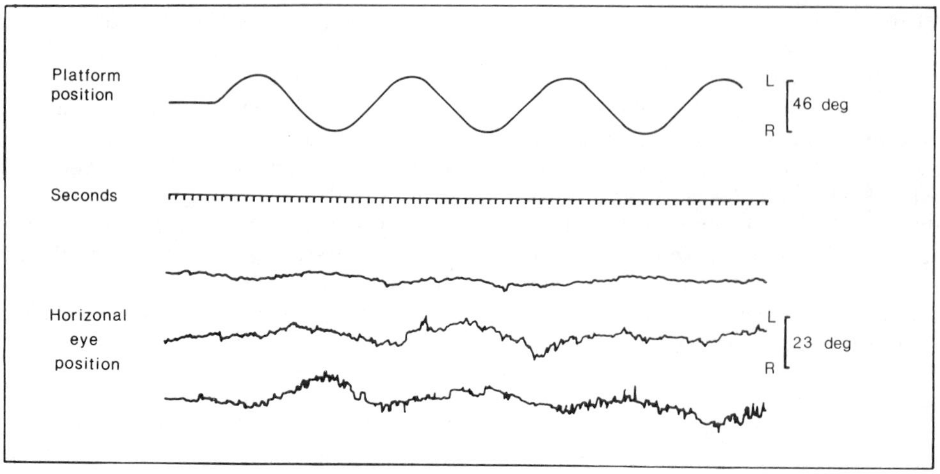

Figure 18.22. The cervico-ocular response. A subject was exposed to sinusoidal side-to-side rotation of the body with head held stationary (top curve). The middle curve is a record of eye movements before body rotation, the bottom two curves, records of eye movements during rotation. Body rotation induces a rapid nystagmic motion of the eyes superimposed on a slow drift that lags the body motion by about 120°. (From D. Barlow & W. Freedman, Cervico-ocular reflex in the normal adult, *Acta Otolaryngologica*, 1980, *89*. Reprinted with permission.)

deviation found in records of the vestibulo-ocular response that was shown in Figure 18.13. Measures derived from this component give a misleading indication of the relationship between the cervico-ocular response and vestibulo-ocular nystagmus. It is therefore not surprising that there is no agreement about how the two responses are related.

One measurement of the gain of the normal human cervico-ocular response in the dark put it at 0.05 when the torso was oscillated passively within the range 0.2–2.3 Hz (Barnes & Forbat, 1979). This measure was based on the small nystagmic responses. A more recent study has revealed a similar small gain over the same frequency range (amplitude 23°), but a rise in gain to 0.2 as the frequency of body oscillation was reduced to 0.025 Hz (Barlow & Freedman, 1980). In this case, gain was derived from the overall deviation of the eyes. High-gain, compensatory cervico-ocular responses have been found in the rabbit but only for frequencies of body oscillation below 0.08 Hz (Barmack, Nastos, & Pettorossi, 1981). In this case, the response was a smooth to-and-fro deviation with no small nystagmic steps. It looks as though the cervico-ocular response is designed to operate only at low frequencies of head movement where the vestibular signal is probably an ineffective indicator of the velocity of head rotation. Even at these low frequencies the gain of the human response, however it is measured, is no more than 0.2. Furthermore, in several mammalian species, the gain and even the direction of the response have been found to vary from animal to animal and from trial to trial in the same animal (Fuller, 1980). Confusion over measures may be partly responsible for some of these reported differences.

Before it is concluded that the human cervico-ocular response is largely ineffective, it must be realized that the above determinations involved passive rotation of the subject's torso by the experimenter, rather than active rotation by the subject. Perhaps the gain of the response is higher when it is evoked by active movements of the torso. In many animals the unrestrained head stays in a stationary attitude, with respect to the ground, when the body is oscillated about any of its three orthogonal axes. In the owl, for instance, the head remains stubbornly in a fixed position even when a body is oscillated rapidly from side to side through 360°. The cervico-ocular reflex is absent under these circumstances because its presence would destabilize the retinal image. Perhaps it is inhibited by the vestibulocollic reflex, that is, the reflex which stabilizes the head. Let us consider what happens when an animal's torso is passively rotated with respect to a restrained head. If the vestibulocollic reflex is evoked, the cervico-ocular reflex will be inhibited, which would explain why it has such a low gain under these circumstances. If the animal relaxes and allows its head to be stabilized passively by the mechanical restraint, these hypothetical inhibitory influences would be removed from the cervico-ocular reflex and its gain should improve. If the animal is sometimes alert and sometimes relaxed, this would account for the variability of gain found by Fuller. The cervico-ocular reflex should be evoked consistently only when an animal moves its head actively with respect to a stationary body, because this is when eye movements are needed to stabilize the retinal image. But under these circumstances it is difficult to distinguish from the vestibulo-ocular response. One way to dissociate the two reflexes is to ask subjects to rotate the torso actively, with respect to the restrained head. Barlow and Freedman (1980) applied such a test but found that the gain of the response was no greater than when the torso was rotated by the experimenter. The absence of vestibular signals in both the active and passive conditions may have indicated to subjects that the head was stationary and therefore that a cervico-ocular response was inappropriate. A better way to dissociate the cervico-ocular response from vestibular responses is to test animals lacking a vestibular system. Labyrinthine-defective monkeys and humans exhibit effective compensatory eye movements for low-frequency head oscillations, and presumably these movements are controlled by the cervico-ocular reflex (Dichgans, Bizzi, Morasso, & Tagliasco, 1974; Kasai & Zee, 1978). Furthermore, in normal humans, the gain of vestibular nystagmus in the dark is one over a wider range of head velocities when the head is moved actively compared with when it is moved passively (Tomlinson et al., 1980). This could be due either to the contribution of efference or to the recruitment of the cervico-ocular reflex.

Afferent fibers arising in properioceptors in the muscles and ligaments of the neck project directly or indirectly to several subcortical and cortical centers concerned with the organization of eye movements, including the superior colliculus, the nucleus prepositus hyperglossi, the reticular formation, the vestibular nuclei, and the frontal eye fields (Abrahams & Rose, 1975; Dubrovsky & Barbas, 1977; Gresty & Baker, 1976; Hikosaka & Maeda, 1973). The vestibular nuclei are the most probable sites of processes that control the interactions between the vestibulo- and cervico-ocular reflexes, and certain cells in the vestibular nuclei of the cat have been found that respond in a similar way to sideways tilt of the whole animal and sideways neck rotation (Boyle & Pompeiano, 1981).

2.8. Arthro-Ocular Responses

Warabi (1978) demonstrated a trunk-ocular response by twisting the lower trunk of seated human subjects while the head and shoulders were firmly clamped. When the trunk was rotated sinusoidally through about 20° at a frequency of 0.25 Hz in the dark, the eyes deviated out of phase with a gain of about 0.5. Smaller nystagmic ripples were sometimes superimposed on the to-and-fro deviation.

Bles and Kapteyn (1977) recorded nystagmic eye movements in subjects who walked round a small rotating platform at such a rate that the subjects did not actually move. The direction of the nystagmus was such that it would have helped to stabilize the visual surroundings had subjects been actually moving. When the walking stopped, the nystagmic eye movements persisted for about half a minute with direction unchanges. This means that the aftereffect of this kind of stimulation is opposite in direction to postrotatory nystagmus of vestibular origin.

Nystagmus induced by active rotation of the body should be of higher gain relative to that produced by passive rotation because in the active case the vestibular response is augmented by one induced by trunk and leg movements. Furthermore, postrotary vestibular nystagmus should be reduced after active rotation because it and trunk nystagmus are opposite in phase. The results of a study by Guedry, Mortenson, Nelson, and Correia (1978) confirm these predictions.

It is reasonable to conclude that the twisting action in the legs and trunk induces these eye movements. They are not induced by walking in a straight path (Bles, 1981). Another possibility is that nystagmic eye movements are induced by anything convincing a person that he or she is rotating. On this view eye movements induced by twisting motions of the neck, trunk, and limbs would not be distinct reflexes but aspects of a more general mechanism in which all such inputs make a contribution to a central process that "decides" whether or not the person is rotating. This is not to imply that the decision process is conscious although, as we shall see in Section 3.3, sensations of self rotation are induced by active movements of the trunk and legs. The types of eye movements induced by movements of the head and body were summarized in Table 18.1.

2.9. Key References

The most thorough and recent review of vestibulo-ocular reflexes has been provided by Henn, B. Cohen, and Young (1980). An earlier review is contained in the chapter by B. Cohen (1974, pp. 477–540) in the *Handbook of Sensory Physiology.* Kornhuber's chapter in the same handbook (1974, pp. 193–232) reviews the clinical aspects of vestibulo-ocular responses. Useful review chapters are contained in Wilson and Melvill Jones (1979) and in edited volumes of papers on eye movements by Brooks and Bajandas (1977), Lennerstrand and Bach-y-Rita (1975), and Monty and Senders (1976).

3. ILLUSIONS DUE TO VISUAL-VESTIBULAR INTERACTIONS

3.1. Background

When we perceive the motion of a visual object, it may be because we are detecting the motion of the image of the object over the retina. But we still experience visual motion when we pursue the moving object with the eyes or the head, that is, when the image is stationary on the retina. The experience of visual motion may therefore depend on a purely visual mechanism but also on signals that inform us about the movements of the eyes and head. The relationship between perceived motion and eye movements is discussed in Antis, Chapter 16, and Mack, Chapter 17. The relationship between motion perception and movements of the head and body will be considered in this section. There are two cases to be considered: the effect of self motion on visual sensations of motion and the effect of scene motion on sensations of self motion.

When we walk or turn, with respect to a stationary scene, the image of the scene moves relative to the retina and excites visual motion detectors. We nevertheless perceive the scene as stationary and ascribe the motion signals to self motion. When we are moved passively, rather than by our own effort, our ability to judge whether an external object is stationary is impaired and we are subject to illusory impressions of object motion known as *oculogyral illusions.* These illusions and their causes are discussed in Section 3.2.

Sometimes, stationary people exposed to an actually moving scene mistakenly perceive that they are moving and not the scene. This illusion is often experienced by people when they watch a neighboring train pull out of the station, and it is known as *illusory self motion.* This effect is discussed in Section 3.3.

The vestibular system is designed for the detection of linear and rotary motion of the head and is known to be intimately associated with the visual mechanism for the detection of retinal motion. Excitation of either of these sensory systems can produce the same illusory impressions of visual motion or of self motion. Recent physiological evidence, which is reviewed in Section 3.3.3, indicates that the vestibular nuclei in the brain stem are the site of the interactions between visual and vestibular signals that are responsible for the oculogyral illusion and illusory self motion.

3.2. Visual Effects of Self Motion—The Oculogyral Illusion

It is a common experience that the world appears to spin when one has come to rest after a period of body rotation. An illusion of visual movement experienced during or just after rotation of the body is known as an oculogyral illusion (Graybiel & Hupp, 1946). I shall describe several illusory phenomena that come under this heading, some of which are less interesting than others.

That the stationary visual scene should in some sense appear to move when the body is rotated is not remarkable. After all, the retinal image of the scene is being alternately fixated and swept across the retina as the eyes execute nystagmic movements. The visual motion-detection system is excited, even during the pursuit phases of nystagmus, because visual pursuit is usually not perfect, especially during the recruitment time of the response. Sensations of visual movement therefore arise, although they are usually not interpreted as being due to an actual movement of the visual scene. In the immediate postrotary period, the eyes continue to execute nystagmic movements and thus generate strong visual motion signals which create an impelling impression that the scene is moving.

More interesting oculogyral illusions arise when rotating subjects, in dark surroundings, fix their gaze on a luminous object that rotates with them and maintains a constant headcentric direction. At moderate angular velocities subjects are able to suppress nystagmus under these circumstances. If subjects are asked to report their impressions of the movement of the fixated object, they should say it is moving in the same direction and at the same velocity as themselves, because that is what it is doing. This impression of movement is not an illusion but is the baseline with respect to which any illusory movement of the fixated object should be measured. If, for any reason, subjects misperceive the angular rotation of their body, they should experience a corresponding change in the apparent velocity of the fixated object, with respect to the unseen stationary surroundings. For instance, if they feel that their body is no longer rotating, then they should report that the visual object is no longer moving, because to say otherwise would imply a contradiction. This would be a mistaken judgment, and in that sense an illusion, but it is a trivial phenomenon. Remember, the object is rotating with them so that there is no oculocentric motion to report. A more interesting phenomenon—perhaps the only one worthy of the name oculogyral illusion is an experience that the fixated object moves with respect to the head. This is an illusion because the object remains in the median plane of the head. This illusion has important theoretical implications. To prove that subjects are experiencing an illusion of headcentric motion, rather than a trivial illusion of objective (exocentric) movement, one must be sure that they obey instructions to report impressions only of headcentric motion. Not all experimenters have taken this precaution, but there is little doubt that headcentric motion is misperceived under the conditions I have described.

The oculogyral illusion can produce disturbing effects in a pilot's perception of the instrument panel in an aircraft. For instance, pilots sometimes report an apparent visual bending of the artificial horizon that is designed to indicate the true position of the horizon. This illusion occurs when pilots are subjected to strong vestibular inputs during rolling maneuvers (Lentz & Guedry, 1982).

Parsons (1970) rotated seated subjects about the midbody axis and asked them to use a rating scale to estimate the headcentric velocity of a visual object, fixed with respect to the head. Subjects were accelerated at 2, 3, 6, and 9°/sec^2 for periods of 1, 3, 6, and 9 sec, after which they were rotated constantly at whatever terminal velocity they had reached. Estimates of the motion of the visual object were made every 5 sec. A sample of results for an acceleration of 9°/sec^2 is shown in Figure 18.23. It can be seen that the illusory visual movement in the direction of body rotation increased during a period of acceleration, although acceleration was not continued long enough for an accurate determination of the *crescendo time* of the illusion. After steady velocity was reached, the illusory movement declined to 0 in about 40 sec, which is about the same duration as postrotary nystagmus. After 9 sec of acceleration the illusion passed into a reversed phase, which lasted for about 2 minutes. This phase corresponds to the period during which the vestibular system recovers from the effects of neural adaptation to the preceding acceleration (see Howard, Section 2.3.3, Chapter 11, "The Vestibular System"). As one would expect, this reversed phase did not occur after brief periods of acceleration. It was also found not to occur when acceleration was only 2°/sec^2, whatever its duration.

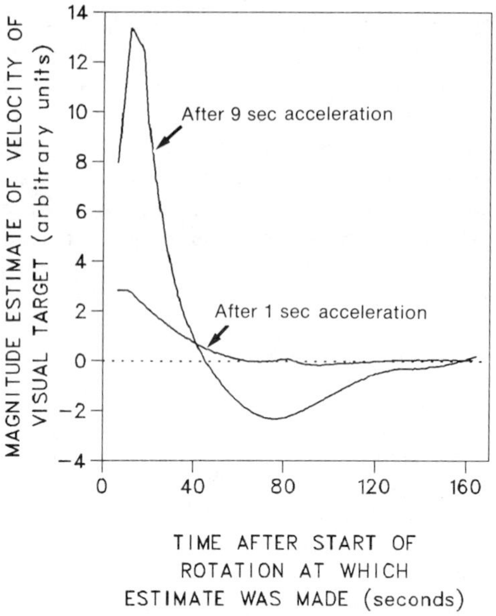

Figure 18.23. Mean magnitude estimates of the oculogyral illusion for ten subjects rotating at constant velocity after being subjected to an acceleration of 9°/sec^2 for periods of 1 and 9 sec. Positive apparent movement is in the direction of body rotation. The illusion increases during the period of acceleration and declines asymptotically during steady rotation. After a longer period of acceleration the positive phase of the illusion is followed by a negative phase. (From R. D. Parsons, Magnitude estimates of the oculogyral illusion during and following angular acceleration, *Journal of Experimental Psychology, 84*. Copyright 1970 by American Psychological Association. Reprinted with permission.)

The oculogyral illusion under these conditions cannot be due to movements of the retinal image, because the gaze is fixed on the visual target, and the illusion occurs when the target is an afterimage (Göthlin, 1946). It could be due to the effects of the visually inhibited oculmotor signals, but this is unlikely to be the only cause of the illusion, because it occurs during accelerations that are too weak to induce nystagmus and lasts longer than nystagmus (Guedry, Collins, & Sheffey, 1961). On logical grounds, the oculogyral illusion cannot be due to any misjudgment of the velocity of body rotation. It looks as though the illusion is due to a direct effect of vestibular stimulation on the visual centers concerned with the assessment of headcentric visual motion (Clark & Stewart, 1969). Interaction between vestibular and visual inputs is a two-way process, as we shall see.

3.3. Illusions of Self Motion

When one is sitting in a stationary train watching the neighboring train pull out of the station, it often feels as if one's own train is moving in the opposite direction. This is not only a visual illusion; there are also illusory sensations of body acceleration. The illusion is particularly pronounced when the neighboring train is viewed out of the corner of the eye. Similar compelling illusions are often experienced in the wide-screen cinema; the whole cinema seems to be a vehicle moving through space. Such illusions are referred to as *illusions of self motion.* Illusions of self motion are also experienced when sound sources or felt objects are moved relative to a stationary observer in the dark (T. Brandt, Büchele, Arnold, Fallert, & Wassermeyer, 1977; Dichgans & T. Brandt, 1978; Hannebert, 1960; Lackner, 1977).

Illusions of self motion were first investigated by Mach (1875) who induced them by placing the subject at the center of a rotating cylinder painted with vertical stripes. Illusory self rotation induced by rotating scenes is known as *circularvection*, and illusory self translation induced by scenes moving in a flat plane is known as *linearvection* (Fisher & Kornmüller, 1930). Early investigators concluded that illusory self motion is due to the effects of optokinetic nystagmus induced by the moving scene. However, this cannot be the main cause of the illusion, because the effect produced by a large moving display remains the same when the direction of optokinetic nystagmus is reversed by reversing the motion of a small display at the center of the larger one (T. Brandt, Dichgans, & Koenig, 1973).

The similarity between the effects of illusory and real motion of the body is vividly illustrated by the fact that if subjects incline the head forward while experiencing illusory rotation about the z axis, they have the same sensations or Coriolis vertigo that are induced when the head is tilted during a real rotation., Coriolis sensations experienced during illusory self motion are known as *pseudo-Coriolis sensations* (Dichgans & T. Brandt, 1973).

During prolonged rotation of the body the vestibular inputs cease, and the most effective cue that the body is still moving is the sight of the countermoving scene. It is not often that a whole visual scene rotates around a stationary observer, so that if it is seen to rotate, this is convincing evidence that it is the self that is rotating, not the scene. Similarly, when people move along a straight path, the optical array they experience is transformed; there is a parallactic gradient of motion over horizontal surfaces on either side, translation of vertical surfaces on either side, and expansion outward from the front. This optical flow pattern contains normally reliable information regarding the observer's velocity, heading, and distance from surfaces (Gibson, 1966, 1968; Nakayama & Loomis, 1974; Warren 1976). It is therefore not surprising that a large moving visual display induces an illusion of self translation—it is the natural cue for such motion. See Regan, Kaufman, and Lincoln, Chapter 19.

A moving observer assesses the headcentric motion of a visual scene by summing the motion of the retinal image of the scene and the motion of pursuit eye movements. For a given type and velocity of body motion, the more there is of one, the less there is of the other. Illusory self motion is induced by the perceived headcentric motion of the scene and not merely by the motion of the retinal image; it occurs whether or not the eyes move in pursuit of the moving scene.

Illusory self rotation is also produced in a person who is actively walking in the dark around a rotating platform at such a rate that the body does not actually rotate. These sensations are presumably induced either by proprioceptors in the trunk and limbs or by the muscular activity associated with walking.

3.3.1. Temporal Features of Illusory Self Motion. When subjects are first exposed to a rotating visual array, they perceive the scene as rotating and themselves as stationary. This impression lasts for several seconds; then gradually the observer begins to experience illusory self motion until, after 30 sec or more, only self rotation is experienced and the scene looks stationary (Brandt et al., 1973). This sequence of experiences is depicted in the curves shown in Figure 18.24, which were obtained from magnitude estimations of self motion and scene motion at different times after exposure to a rotating scene as velocities between 20 and 40°/sec (Wong & Frost, 1978). If an initially stationary scene is accelerated at below about 5°/sec^2, the latency for onset of illusory self motion is less than at lower or higher accelerations of the stimulus. Furthermore, at accelerations of less than about 5°/sec^2, illusory self motion is not preceded by a period of perceived visual motion, as it is at higher rates of acceleration (Melcher & Henn, 1981).

Consider what happens when a person is actually accelerated and then rotated at constant angular velocity. During the period of acceleration, eye movements and sensations of rotation are largely under the control of vestibular inputs. During the period of constant rotation, the vestibular inputs weaken as the cupula returns to its central position and associated neural activity ceases. At the same time, visual inputs become more dominant as the optokinetic system is recruited into activity until, finally, sensations of body rotation are governed wholly by visual inputs. A stationary person who observes a rotating scene will know, initially, that it is the scene that is moving and not the self, because the vestibular inputs that a natural acceleration of the body would produce are absent. Gradually, the restraint imposed

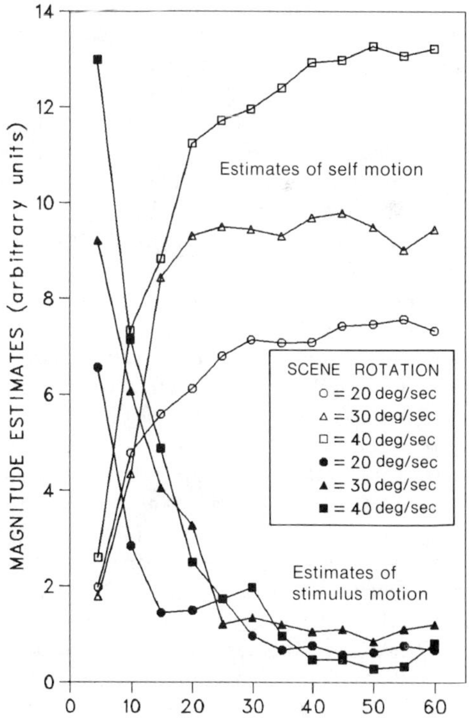

Figure 18.24. Mean magnitude estimates of velocity of stimulus motion (bottom curve) and self motion (top curves) of four subjects at different times after a striped drum is set in motion around them at each of three velocities. Note that as the sensation of self motion increases, the estimate of motion of the scene decreases. (From S. C. P. Wong & B. J. Frost, Subjective motion and acceleration induced by the movement of the observer's entire visual field, *Perception and Psychophysics*, 1978, *24*. Reprinted with permission.)

by the absence of vestibular inputs lessens, finally leaving the visual motion of the scene to be interpreted wholly as self rotation. This exactly describes the sequence of experiences depicted in Figure 18.24 and accounts for why, at low accelerations of the stimulus, illusory self motion is not preceded by apparent visual motion; vestibular stimuli would be ineffective at low accelerations.

The latency of illusory self motion is shortened by an impulsive rotation of the body in the direction of the illusory motion (T. Brandt et al., 1974). This is because any actual vestibular stimulation counter to the scene motion will encourage the observer to interpret scene motion as due to body motion. An actual rotation of the body in the other direction promptly destroys any illusory self motion (Young, Dichgans, Murphy, & T. Brandt, 1973).

Patients with Ménière's disease show reduced vestibular sensitivity to one direction of turning and have been found to have a shorter latency of induced self motion in that direction (Wong & Frost, 1981). These findings confirm the view that the latency of induced self motion is due to conflicting visual-vestibular inputs in the early period of exposure to scene motion.

The orienting responses triggered by peripheral vision are important at all times for general coordination and balance. It is therefore not surprising that illusory self motion has been found not to be influenced by a reduction in luminance to scotopic levels or by defocusing the image (Leibowitz, Rodemer, & Dichgans, 1979).

The apparent velocity of illusory self rotation is proportional to stimulus velocity up to about 90°/sec, although this relationship is complicated by the fact that the apparent velocity of a display of stripes depends on the spatial frequency of the pattern, as well as on its actual velocity. Furthermore, for any one angular velocity of stimulus motion, illusory self motion depends on how far away the scene is from the observer (Wist, Diener, Dichgans, & T. Brandt, 1975). At stimulus velocities above 90°/sec there are interludes when self motion is not experienced. Such high velocities of continued real self motion are rarely met with, so it is not surprising that people are undecided as to how to interpret such signals.

If the lights are put out after a moving scene has been observed for some time, the illusory self rotation continues as a *positive aftereffect* followed by a *negative aftereffect* in the opposite direction. The positive aftereffect must be due at least in part to the fact that there are no vestibular or other cues to inform subjects that they have stopped rotating. But there is another factor that explains both aftereffects. The time course of the positive and negative aftereffects of appearent self rotation as a function of stimulus duration is similar to the time course of positive and negative optokinetic afternystagmus (see Section 2.3). The two positive aftereffects increase in duration to about 36 sec, as stimulus exposure increases up to 60 sec, and both decrease in duration with longer stimulus exposures. The two negative aftereffects increase with increasing stimulus duration, at least up to 15 min, the longest duration tested (T. Brandt et al., 1974). Thus the initiation of illusory self motion follows the time course of recruitment of optokinetic nystagmus, and its aftereffects follow the time course of the positive and negative phases of optokinetic afternystagamus. Furthermore, optokinetic and self-motion aftereffects both occur whether the subject pursues the moving scene or fixates on a headcentrically stable object when exposed to the inducing stimuli. This is not to say that illusory self motion is caused by optokinetic nystagmus, only that both effects seem to depend on the recruitment of the same underlying process. Optokinetic nystagmus is known to be associated with neural impulses in the vestibular nuclei, so perhaps these same circuits are related to sensations of body rotation.

In all these studies, subjects gave magnitude estimations of the sensations of self rotation. Zacharias and Young (1981) asked subjects to control their own body rotation so as to null their sensations of self motion. Due allowance was first made for the dynamic characteristics of the nulling task. Subjects were then exposed to various combinations of sideways scene motion and oscillation of the body about the vertical midbody axis. Visual motion was found to dominate sensations of body rotation at low frequencies of body oscillation, and vestibular stimuli arising from body rotation were dominant at higher frequencies. However, their data did not fit the assumption that sensations of rotation represent a linear summation of visual and vestibular inputs. They propose what they call a *cue-conflict model*. Vestibular inputs, which signal rotation or absence of expected rotation, outweigh highly conflicting visual signals. This occurs when subjects are rotated with an acceleration that generates appreciable vestibular signals or when conditions lead subjects to expect such signals, as when a visual scene is first set in motion. When there is less conflict between the two cues, the inputs are averaged. This occurs during that period when illusory self rotation increases at the expense of sensations of scene motion. When visual motion cues are present with confirming vestibular inputs, sensations of body motion are governed by the visual inputs. Confirming vestibular inputs do not add to sensations induced by visual motion. In this way the two cues are selectively weighted to give a best estimate of self motion.

3.3.2. The Effects of Stimulus Position and Direction on Illusory Self Motion. A moving display that stimulates the retinal periphery is a much more effective stimulus for illusory self motion than one confined to the center of the visual field, even when the two displays have the same area. Furthermore, if a peripheral display moves one way and a central display of equal area moves in the opposite direction, the illusion of self motion is determined by the motion of the peripheral display even though the eyes may pursue the central display (Brandt, et al., 1973). When there are moving displays at different distances, the one farther away from the subject is more effective in inducing illusory self motion (T. Brandt, Wist, & Dichgans, 1975).

When subjects inspect a scene rotating in the frontal plane, they experience an illusory rotation and tilt of the body in the opposite direction. These *illusory sensations of tilt* are paradoxical in that the body seems to be rotating continuously and yet seems to be tilted only to a limited extent. The sensation of limited tilt is due to restraining influences from the otolith organs, which inform subjects that they are not actually being tilted. When subjects lying on the back view a display rotating in the frontal plane, the sensation is simply one of continuous rotation, because signals from the otolith organs are irrelevant in this situation and, therefore, do not inform observers that they are not rotating. Illusory sensations of tilt for the upright observer start soon after the stimulus is applied and reach a steady state after about 18 sec. As before, peripheral stimuli are more effective than stimuli in the center of the visual field. The extent of the apparent body tilt increases with increasing velocity of the stimulus and reaches a mean value of about 15° (Held, Dichgans, & Bauer, 1975). Accompanying the sensation of body tilt is an apparent tilt of a vertical line in the same direction. This effect is discussed in more detail in Section 5.6.5.

The sensation of self tilt induced by a scene rotating about the visual axis is increased if the head is inclined 90° or inverted, compared with when the utricular maculae are horizontal (Young, Oman, & Dichgans, 1975). The utricles are known to be less sensitive when tilted or inverted, and therefore, in these positions they provide less effective information about the true orientation of the head (see Howard, Chapter 11, "The Vestibular System").

A scene that rotates about a person so as to produce an upward or downward movement of the frontal visual scene induces *illusory sensations of self inclination.* A sensation of continuous body rotation is accompanied by a paradoxical sensation of constant body inclination (pitch) against the direction of stimulus motion. For a given velocity of stimulus motion the illusion of pitch backward is larger than that of pitch forward (Young et al., 1975). It will be recalled from Section 2.2.2 that there are similar asymmetries in vertical vestibular nystagmus. Inspection of a stationary tilted scene induces illusory sensations of body tilt in the opposite direction (see Section 5.6.4).

Translatory motions of the visual scene induce *illusory sensations of linear motion*, which are often referred to as linearvection. These illusions have been known for a long time. For instance, in the nineteenth century there was a fairground device, known as the "haunted swing." People entered a boat-shaped chamber, and artificial scenery was slowly swung backward and forward outside the windows. This gave a compelling illusion that the chamber was rocking, and the people felt all the body sensations of real motion, including loss of postural stability and vertigo (Wood, 1895). An apparatus resembling the haunted swing has recently been used to investigate illusory self motion. The subject is enclosed within a large illuminated box that swings back and forth along a path parallel to the subject's median plane. At the same time, the subject may stand on a trolley and be moved passively back and forth, either in phase or out of phase with the box, or may walk actively forward while the box moves in the opposite direction. The sensations of self motion are determined by the direction of motion of the visual scene relative to the observer. Even if observers are actually moved one way, they experience a motion of the body the other way if that is what the relative motion of the scene indicates. When a person walks in one direction and the scene induces a sensation of self motion in the opposite direction by moving at a faster rate than the subject, the subject has the feeling of walking on a moving treadmill. Subjects sway in synchrony with the scene as they attempt to counter the sensation of body sway that the moving scene induces. For some time after the movement has stopped, they sway in the opposite direction (Reason, Wagner, & Dewhurst, 1981). Young children who have just learned to walk fall over as soon as the scene begins to move (Lishman & Lee, 1973). The topic of vision and postural stability is discussed in Section 1.2.5.

Illusory linear motion has a latency and saturation velocity similar to those for illusory rotary motion and, like other forms of illusory self motion, is more readily induced by motion in the visual periphery than by motion in the center of the visual field (Berthoz, Pavard, & Young, 1975; Johansson, 1977; Rock, 1968).

3.3.3. Nonvisual Induction of Illusory Self Motion. Illusory sensations of rotation are produced in a person who is actively turning in the dark, and it seems that vestibular stimulation is not required under these circumstances. Bles (1981) had subjects walk around the rim of a rotating platform at such a speed that they did not actually rotate. This action of "apparent stepping around" induced a sensation of self rotation in the direction of intended motion. Pseudo-Coriolis effects were also produced when subjects tilted their heads to one side.

Postrotary sensations of self rotation, which occur after passive rotation of the body, are in the opposite direction to the motion that induced them and are thought to be due to the persisting mechanical and neural effects of deceleration. Guedry, Mortenson, Nelson, and Correia (1978) found that after active rotation of the body subjects experience sensations of self rotation that are much reduced or even reversed, with respect to those produced by passive rotation. It is reasonable to suppose that the action of actively stepping around produces its own aftereffect that partly or completely cancels that produced by vestibular stimulation.

It is not possible to say as yet whether these effects of active rotation are induced by proprioceptors in the trunk and legs or by the efference associated with the muscular activity. Perhaps the effects are nonspecific, being induced by any input that "persuades" subjects that they are rotating.

Illusions of self rotation presumably occur because the visual or proprioceptive inputs trigger some mechanism that in other circumstances is triggered by the vestibular system. What this mechanism might be is considered in Section 3.3.4.

3.3.4. The Neurology of Illusory Self Motion. The illusions of self motion suggest that movements of large peripheral visual displays, relative to a stationary observer, produce some of the same physiological effects as stimulation of the vestibular system. The two types of input must converge somewhere in the central nervous system, and the results of electrophysiological investigations suggest that this convergence occurs in the vestibular nuclei. Cells have been found in the vestibular nuclei of a variety of species, including goldfish, rabbits, cats, and monkeys, which respond to both vestibular stimulation and visual motion (Dichgans & T. Brandt, 1978). For instance, cells in the vestibular nuclei of a monkey, which are excited when the head turns to the left in the dark, are also excited when the head is stationary and the visual scene moves to the right. At higher angular velocities of the stimulus the response of these cells to purely visual motion is less vigorous than their response to body rotation in the dark. At lower angular velocities and accelerations the response to visual motion is more vigorous than the response to body rotation. When the body is rotated in illuminated surroundings, the responses to the two types of input complement each other to produce a vigorous response over a wide range of stimulus velocities (see Figure 18.14).

Other cells in the vestibular nuclei that respond to a linear motion of the body also respond to a translatory motion of the scene. In other words, each cell responds to that head motion and that scene motion that normally occur together when the animal moves. The behavior of these cells accords with many of the behavioral features of illusory motion that have just been described. After a scene has stopped moving, activity in dual-purpose cells persists, just like the positive aftereffect of illusory self motion. The response of the cells to scene motion is enhanced or inhibited by body rotation in the opposite or same direction, respectively, in just the same way that illusory self motion is enhanced or inhibited by body rotation (Daunton & Thomsen, 1979; Henn, Young, & Finley, 1974; Waespe & Henn, 1977a, 1977b).

There is some uncertainty about how visual inputs reach the vestibular nuclei. These nuclei do not receive direct visual inputs from the optic tract or superior colliculus. Visual inputs reach the flocculus of the cerebellum by a route that passes through the nucleus of the optic tract (NOT) and the nucleus reticularis tegmenti pontis (Maekawa & Kimura, 1981), and the flocculus has direct connections with the vestibular nuclei. For instance, lesions of the flocculus impair the visual suppression of vestibular nystagmus (see Section 4.3). However, a route through the cerebellum cannot be the only one by which visual signals reach the vestibular nuclei, because cells in these nuclei respond to visual motion after the cerebellum has been removed (Keller & Precht, 1979b). The superior colliculus does not seem to be implicated, because it does not have cells with the required sensitivities to visual motion. Cells in the nucleus of the optic tract have the required sensitivities, and cells have been found in the nucleus reticularis tegmenti pontis that respond to both head movement and visual movement in much the same way as the dual-purpose cells in the vestibular nuclei (Cazin, Precht, & Lannou, 1980; Collewijn, 1975). It looks as though the crucial visual input reaches the vestibular nuclei by a route involving the nucleus of the optic tract and the nucleus reticularis tegmenti pontis but not necessarily the cerebellum.

There is some recent evidence that the interaction between visual and vestibular inputs may also occur in the visual cortex. Vanni-Mercier and Magnin (1982) recorded the activity of cells in the visual cortex of the cat and found that about 40% of them responded to both visual and vestibular inputs.

Interactions between vestibular and proprioceptive stimuli could be mediated by the cells in the vestibular nuclei, which receive both types of input (see Section 1.1.1). But the cerebral cortex may also be involved. The posterior parietal lobes are richly endowed with cells that receive inputs from several senses, including the proprioceptive and vestibular senses (see Hyvärinen, 1982, for a review of this topic).

The last few sections of this chapter have described several illusions associated with movements of the head or body. These illusions are listed in Tables 18.2 and 18.3 (see Section 5.7.6), together with an indication of the conditions that induce them.

3.4. Key References

Henn, B. Cohen, and Young (1980) have produced a comprehensive review of visual-vestibular interactions. The volume edited by Monty and Senders (1976) contains several review papers on this topic. The chapter by Dichgans and T. Brandt (1978) in the *Handbook of Sensory Physiology* provides a thorough review of illusions of self motion.

4. THE ADAPTABILITY OF THE VESTIBULAR SYSTEM

4.1. Background

When people are exposed for some time to atypical combinations of vestibular and visual stimulation, their responses to these stimuli undergo long-lasting modifications. These modifications may involve directly observable responses, such as postural stability and the gain or direction of vestibular nystagmus; they may also involve subjective responses, such as sensations of rotation, the oculogyral illusion, and nausea. Long-term changes in vestibular responses take time to develop, last for hours and even days, and have characteristics related to the specific stimuli that induce them. Short-term changes, such as those caused by adaptation and inattention, are induced rapidly, last only seconds or minutes, and are usually nonspecific (see W. E. Collins, 1974a, for a review of the effects of arousal on vestibular responses).

There are two ways to think about long-term changes in responses to vestibular stimulation. In the first place they may be put under the heading of *habituation*, or the gradual dropping out of inappropriate responses. In the second place, they may be put under the heading of *recalibration*. The vestibulo-ocular system is adjusted to cope with the normal relationships between head movements and headcentric movements of the visual scene. When unusual pairings of these two movements occur repeatedly, the system shows evidence of adapting its internal calibration. Although habituation and recalibration may be related specifically to the conditions that induce them, habituation implies a mere dropping out of unwanted responses, whereas recalibration implies that new response patterns are set up, which are more suited to the anomalous stimulus conditions to which the subject has been exposed. I shall now review some of the evidence for these two types of process, but it should be borne in mind that they may both be manifestations of one underlying process.

4.2. Vestibular Habituation

The term *habituation* was originally used to signify a type of simple learning in which a response to a stimulus associated with a threatening event gradually weakens if the stimulus is repeated in benign circumstances. For instance, a snail rapidly withdraws into its shell when lightly touched, but if it is touched repeatedly, the withdrawal response gradually declines. The signal regains its previous potency if accompanied by a noxious event. Atypical visual-vestibular stimulation is threatening, because it signifies that the animal is in an unusual situation with which it may not be able to deal. Furthermore, several poisons upset the specific gravity of the cupula, and the earliest symptom of their presence is a feeling of body motion that conflicts with visual inputs. This is probably why anomalous vestibular inputs have evolved to trigger nausea, vomiting, and depression (Treisman, 1977). Dogs in which the vestibular organs have been removed do not vomit after ingesting certain poisons (Money & Cheung, 1983).

Motion sickness also induces anxiety and depression, which perhaps serve to keep the animal still so that the circulation of poisons is reduced. Repeated attacks of vertigo can lead to severe anxiety neurosis (Pratt & McKenzie, 1958), and patients with anxiety neurosis show exaggerated responses to caloric vestibular stimulation (Hallpike, Harrison, & Slater, 1951; Lader, 1969, pp. 53–56). Furthermore, people with loss of vestibular function are less susceptible to anxiety neurosis than are normal people (Altshuler, 1971; Winokur, Cadoret, Dorzab, & Baker, 1971). Recovery from motion sickness during a long sea voyage can be understood as habituation of vertigo-induced nausea under conditions in which the potentially noxious visual-vestibular conflict is repeated without undesirable consequences.

On this theory of vestibular habituation one would not expect responses to normal vestibular stimulation to habituate. After all, these responses serve a useful purpose, and ordinary living involves the continual stimulation of the vestibular system, so that whatever habituation may occur will already have done so. Rabbits oscillated continuously in the dark for 2 days at a frequency of 0.17 Hz showed no evidence of response decrement (Kleinschmidt & Collewijn, 1975). Nor did men who were rotated sinusoidally for 1 hour each day for 3 days (Gonshor & Melvill Jones, 1973). Note that during this type of stimulation there is no conflict between vestibular and visual inputs, and because the motion is oscillatory, there are no postrotary effects in which such conflicts could arise.

There has been a long and heated debate about whether postrotary nystagmus decreases in duration, velocity, or amplitude after repeated rotation of the body in one direction (see W. E. Collins, 1974b, pp. 369–388). One might expect postrotary responses to habituate because they are not induced by normal movements of the body and they involve conflicting vestibular and visual inputs. In most studies claiming to demonstrate vestibular habituation under these circumstances, subjects were repeatedly exposed to 10–20 periods of rotation or caloric irrigation of the ear over several hours or days. Each period of rotation lasted a few minutes; in some studies all the periods involved rotation in the same direction, and in others, periods of left rotation alternated with periods of right rotations. In earlier studies there was lack of control over the subject's level of arousal, and a lack of consistency in the measure of nystagmus (duration, frequency, velocity, or amplitude) and in whether the eyes were open during and after rotation. These deficiencies in stimulus control led to unwarranted conclusions. For instance, if a subject is not kept alert, nystagmus elicited in the dark may gradually decline, but this is not true habituation because the response retains its full vigor and may even increase in amplitude if subjects are kept alert (Johnson & Torok, 1970). Furthermore, if subjects have the eyes open when being tested in the postrotary period, they may inhibit nystagmus visually, and this, too, is not true habituation. Figure skaters and ballet dancers are particularly adept at inhibiting postrotary symptoms by visual fixation. When they are not allowed to see in the postrotary period, they lose their balance like anybody else (W. E. Collins, 1966, 1968; Dix & Hood, 1969; Schroeder, 1971).

Nevertheless, when all these precautions have been allowed for, there is abundant evidence that postrotary nystagmus, subjective reactions, and the oculogyral illusion all show a response decrement after repeated rotation of the body (see W. E. Collins, 1974b, for a review of this evidence). That this response reduction is due to central factors rather than fatigue or sensory adaptation is shown by the fact that (1) the rate of habituation may be higher for some responses than for others (Guedry & W. E. Collins, 1968), (2) the effects may persist for several months (W. E. Collins, 1964), and (3) habituation is specific to the direction and complexity of the rotary stimulus that induced it (Graybiel & Knepton, 1972; Guedry, 1965a; Guedry, W. E. Collins, & Graybiel, 1964).

In a recent well-designed study, a long-lasting reduction in the time constant and gain of vestibular nystagmus was obtained in cats exposed to periods of unidirectional rotation over a span of 5 days (Clément, Courjon, Jeannerod, & Schmid, 1981). The response changes were produced only for rotation in the practiced direction, which suggests that they were not due merely to loss of attention or to visual suppression. In spite of the resulting asymmetry in gain, the animals showed no spontaneous nystagmus, which suggested to Clément and colleagues that the habituation was confined to receptors having no resting discharge. Such receptors are known to respond only to steady or low-frequency oscillatory movement, and this might explain why habituation has been found not to occur when animals are oscillated at relatively high frequencies. Recently, evidence of habituation of vestibular nystagmus has been obtained after animals were rotated sinusoidally in the dark at frequencies below 0.1 Hz (Jäger & Henn, 1981). Perhaps continued oscillation of the head at low frequencies induces habituation because continued excitation of the tonic vestibular receptors is an unusual stimulus, exposure to which widens the range of head movements the system accepts as indicating that the head is not moving.

Coriolis stimulation is one of the most atypical and nausea-inducing modes of vestibular stimulation. A rotation of the head is imposed on an existing rotation in another plane and, as was explained in Chapter 11, "The Vestibular System," by Howard, this produces a resultant vector in a third plane, which conflicts with visual, utricular, and other inputs.The way people adjust to long periods of exposure to Coriolis stimulation has been studied in the slow rotating room at the Aerospace Medical Institute in Pensacola. Subjects lived for days in the rotating room, and every time they tilted or inclined their heads, they were subjected to Coriolis effects and experienced nystagmus, dizziness, and nausea. When head tilting was practiced in a given direction, the symptoms gradually subsided but only for the practiced direction (Guedry, 1964). When the speed of the room was increased very gradually and many head movements made at each velocity step, subjects adapted to the Coriolis effects produced by an eventual rotation of 10 rpm without showing signs of disequilibrium or nausea (Graybiel, Deane, & Colehour, 1969). After leaving the rotating room, subjects experienced an oppositely directed nystagmus when the head was tilted in the practiced direction (Dowd & Cramer, 1967). This suggests that their adaptation to Coriolis stimulation was not due merely to a decrease in disturbing responses but to an active recalibration of the system. The active nature of the process is suggested by the fact that subjects deprived of sleep have been found not to adapt to Coriolis stimulation as readily as well-rested subjects (Dowd, 1974). Perhaps all so-called vestibular habituation may be more profitably considered to represent a recalibration of the vestibular system to anomalous inputs.

4.3. Vestibular Recalibration

Compensatory eye movements triggered by vestibular stimulation in the dark operate in a feed-forward mode, which means that there are no error signals indicating to what extent the eye movements match head velocity. In illuminated surroundings, the stationary visual scene provides visual signals that trim the gain of compensatory movements on a moment-to-moment basis. But if the vestibular control system adjusts to changes occurring during the growth of an animal, vision must also provide the necessary feedback for these long-term, or parametric, adjustments. These visually driven parametric adjustments of the gain of the vestibulo-ocular system have been studied by artificially disturbing the visual feedback accompanying head rotation.

The most severe disturbance of feedback is created by optical devices that reverse visual scene motion. If people wear spectacles that reverse the visual scene from left to right, a sideways motion of the head causes the image of the stationary scene to move across the retina in a direction opposite to that in which it would normally move. If subjects pursue the image motion with the eyes, its retinal motion is annulled, but now there is a reversal of the sign of the nystagmus that normally accompanies a rotation of the head. Whether they pursue the moving image or not, the scene is experienced as moving with the head at twice the angular velocity of the head. Stratton (1897a, 1897b) observed this phenomenon in his classic study of the effects of wearing spectacles that reversed and inverted the visual scene.

After 6 days of wearing these devices, he reported that the sensation of anomalous motion of the visual scene had disappeared. Stratton made no attempt to record his eye movements, but at least part of his adaptation was probably due to his learning to reverse the direction of his vestibular nystagmus and thus restabilize the image of the scene on the retina. More recent studies have demonstrated that the gain and direction of the vestibulo-ocular reflex may be changed. For instance, Hay and Goldsmith (1973) found that subjects soon learn to pursue visually a light that moves up and down while the head moves from side to side (see also Wallach & Frey, 1969; Wallach, Frey, & Romney, 1969). See Welch, Chapter 24, for a fuller treatment of how people adapt to anomalous visual inputs.

Gonshor and Melvill Jones (1976a) exposed human subjects to optical reversal of the visual scene for periods of between 2 and 27 days. Periodically, the gain of the slow phase of nystagmus induced by rotation of the body in the dark was measured and was found to decrease steadily until, by the end of 1 week, it was almost zero. During the second week, a nystagmus of reversed phase began to appear, the gain of which gradually improved. It took about 2 hours for nystagmus to return to its usual state after normal vision had been restored. Exposure to only 16 min of reversed vision on each of 3 consecutive days produced a 25% reduction in the gain of nystagmus induced by rotation of the body in the dark (Gonshor & Melvill Jones, 1976b). The experience of illlusory self motion has also been found to be reduced after subjects walked about for several hours wearing left–right reversing prisms. Indeed, illusory self motion was found to reverse in sign before there was any evidence of a change in the vestibulo-ocular reflex (Oman, Bock, & Huang, 1980).

A less severe form of visual disturbance is created by optical magnification. For instance, when people first wear spectacles that magnify the visual scene, they experience visual instability when they move the head. These sensations eventually subside, which suggests that the gain of vestibular nystagmus has increased to match the increased headcentric motion of the scene. Gauthier and Robinson (1975) found that subjects, wearing lenses that magnified by a factor of 2, regained visual stability after 4 days and showed an associated 70% increase in the gain of nystagmus. Similar adaptive changes in the gain of vestibular nystagmus have been reported in cats (Melvill Jones & Davies, 1976) and in monkeys (Miles & Eighmy, 1980; Miles & Fuller, 1974).

Even these disturbances are large compared with those likely to be induced by natural growth. Collewijn, Martins, and Steinman (1983) had subjects actively oscillate the head while exposed to an optical magnification requiring a 36% change in the gain of compensatory eye movements. Adaptation of the gain of vestibular nystagmus in the dark was largely complete after only between 4 and 20 min of this experience. When the two eyes were exposed to unequal magnification, the movements of the two eyes adapted equally to a level intermediate between that required of each.

A movement of the whole visual scene unaccompanied by a head movement is, in effect, an anomalous conjunction of visual and vestibular stimuli. It is therefore not surprising that repeated exposure of stationary subjects to a moving array of vertical stripes has been found to lead to a reduction in the gain of vestibular nystagmus induced by rotation in the dark (Pfaltz & Ohtsuka, 1975; Young & Henn, 1974).

Adaptive changes in nystagmic gain are specific to the plane within which visual feedback was distorted. For instance, exposure to left–right reversed vision has no effect on nystagmus induced by head oscillations in the sagittal plane (Melvill Jones & Gonshor, 1982). A subject who wore dove prisms for 19 days was found to show a reduction in the gain of torsional nystagmus induced by sinusiodal rotation of the backward-tilted head about an earth-vertical axis (Berthoz, Melvill Jones, & Bégué, 1981). These dove prisms did not reverse images in the vertical plane, and therefore the gain of vertical nystagmus was not affected by this experience. Nevertheless, stimuli from the same four vertical canals produce both torsional and vertical nystagmus, so that this adaptation of one type of response demonstrates that adaptation occurs after central neural mechanisms have coded the various patterns of inputs into "egocentric planes." Callan and Ebenholtz (1982) exposed subjects for 30 min to a scene observed through dove prisms that tilted the image through 30°. Vestibular nystagmus produced by oscillation of the head about the vertical z axis in the dark was found to be displaced in the direction of the optical tilt.

There is electrophysiological evidence that cells in the vestibular nuclei that control the vestibulo-ocular response also fire during optokinetic nystagmus, that is, nystagmus induced by visual movement with the head stationary (Waespe & Henn, 1977a). Because of this shared component, one might expect that adaptive changes in the gain of the vestibulo-ocular response would also be manifest in the gain of the optokinetic response. Lisberger, Miles, Optican, and Eighmy (1981) adapted the gain of the vestibulo-ocular response of monkeys and tested their optokinetic response to a constantly rotating striped drum. Eye velocity during the first 100 msec was not affected, but the maximum velocity of the steady-state response was sensitive to changes in the gain of the vestibulo-ocular response. These results have been confirmed in cats (Demer, 1981). It looks as though the two nystagmic systems share a component with a long time constant but the optokinetic system has a component with a short time constant not shared with the vestibular mechanism. Melvill Jones and Gonshor (1982) found that the gain of the optokinetic response of humans was not affected by up to 49 days of reversed vision. However, they tested visual tracking with an oscillating visual display, a procedure that would not reveal changes in the steady-state response. I now review the physiological evidence bearing on the question of the site of these adaptive changes.

There is little or no change in the response characteristics of vestibular afferents when the vestibulo-ocular system is adapted to anomalous inputs, so that we must look in the central nervous system for the mechanism responsible (Lisberger & Miles, 1980; Miles & Braitman, 1980). A part of the cerebellum, referred to as the *vestibulocerebellum*, is known to be involved because the adaptive plasticity of the vestibulo-ocular system is absent when this part of the cerebellum is lost (Robinson, 1976). The cerebellar vermis does not seem to be involved because its ablation in monkeys has been found not to affect the animal's capacity to adapt the vestibulo-ocular reflex to unusual visual inputs, although its ablation has been found to abolish the animal's capacity to habituate to repeated rotation (Blair & Gavin, 1979).

The vestibulocerebellum is the most ancient part of the cerebellum and includes the uvula, nodulus, and flocculus. It receives inputs from the vestibular organs, both directly and through the vestibular nuclei, from the retina through the accessory optic tract and inferior olivary nucleus, and from the pontine reticular formation, a center associated with eye movements (Baker, Gibson, Glickstein, & Stein, 1976; Hepp, Henn,

& Jaeger, 1982; Nakao, Curthoys, & Markham, 1980; Simpson, Precht, & Llinás, 1974; Walberg, 1975). It apparently also receives inputs from eye muscle afferents that indicate passive movements of the eyes (Kimura & Maekawa, 1981) and from proprioceptors in the neck (Wilson, Maeda, & Franck, 1975). Outputs from the vestibulocerebellum travel along Purkinje cells and impinge on cells in the vestibular nuclei, where they exert inhibitory control over signals passing from the vestibular organs to the oculomotor nuclei. The vestibulocerebellum thus receives information about head motion, retinal-image motion, and eye movements (both passive and active), in other words, all the information required to assess the adequacy of image stabilization produced by the combined movements of head and eyes. Furthermore, because of its inhibitory control of oculomotor signals, the vestibulocerebellum is able to adjust the gain of the vestibulo-ocular response. A diagrammatic representation of these structures and pathways is provided in Figure 18.25.

The output from Purkinje cells in the flocculus is related to the algebraic sum of head and eye velocities. It is apparently part of a system for reciprocally adjusting head and eye velocities when an object is pursued by various combinations of head movement and eye movement (Lisberger & Fuchs, 1978). The output of Purkinje cells in the vermal region of the vestibulocerebellum is related to the algebraic sum of the velocity of pursuit eye movements and the velocity of retinal-image motion (Kase, Noda, Suzuki, & Miller, 1979). This part of the system seems to be a mechanism for assessing the velocity of target motion relative to the head.

It has been suggested that over a period of time the cerebellar system becomes calibrated to the recurring features of head, eye, and image motion in such a way that it performs as a feedforward (anticipatory) system that improves the gain and phase of the oculomotor response. If the normal relationships between head, eye, and image motions are disturbed, synaptic connections in the cerebellum become modified so as to repair the calibration of the system. This shifted balance of activity in the cerebellum plays upon the vestibular inputs to the vestibular nuclei and modifies the gain of the vestibulo-ocular reflex to suit the new

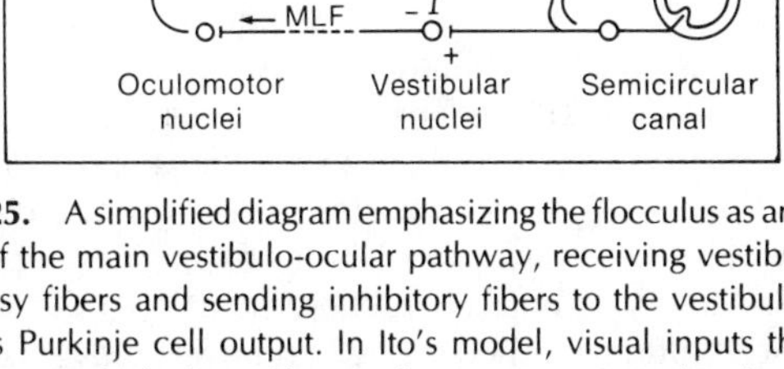

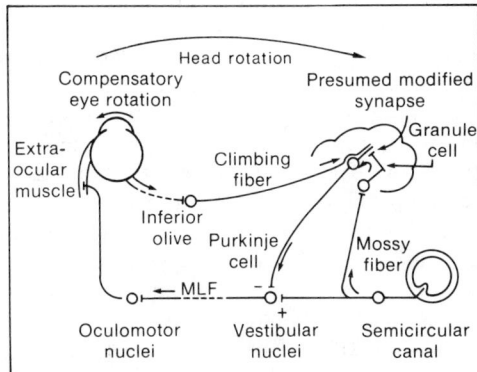

Figure 18.25. A simplified diagram emphasizing the flocculus as an inhibitory sideloop of the main vestibulo-ocular pathway, receiving vestibular inputs along mossy fibers and sending inhibitory fibers to the vestibular nucleus through its Purkinje cell output. In Ito's model, visual inputs through the inferior olive and climbing fibers indicate an error in the slow phase of nystagmus and cause a gradual change in the inhibitory control of the vestibular nucleus, which, in turn, adjusts the gain of the slow phase of vestibular nystagmus until it is again adequate. (From F. A. Miles, The primate flocculus and eye–head coordination, in B. A. Brooks & F. J. Bajandas (Eds.), *Eye movements*, Plenum Publishing, 1977. Reprinted with permission.)

stimulus conditions (Ito, 1972, 1976, pp. 1–21). Davies and Melvill Jones (1976) have proposed a dynamic model of the adaptive mechanism.

This scheme is supported by the fact that the cat's adaptive control of vestibulo-ocular responses is lost when either the vestibulocerebellum or the superior olive is ablated (Haddad, Demer, & Robinson, 1980; Robinson, 1976). It is also lost in cats reared in darkness, which shows that visual experience is required for the growth of the adaptive mechanism (Harris & Cynader, 1981b). Furthermore, changes in the response characteristics of single cells in the flocculus of the rabbit's vestibulocerebellum have been found to be related to behavioral changes induced by exposing the animal to anomalous visual-vestibular inputs (Duffossé, Ito, Jastreboff, & Miyashita, 1978). Similar changes have been recorded in the response characteristics of cells in the flocculus of the monkey (Miles, Braitman, & Dow, 1980). Sometimes, behavioral responses showed evidence of having been modified by anomalous inputs before corresponding changes were observed in the cells of the vestibulocerebellum. Miles and Lisberger (1981) concluded that the vestibulocerebellum generates the signals that indicate the vestibulo-ocular response is in need of recalibration but is not the site of the synaptic changes ultimately responsible for the recalibration. They suggested that these changes occur somewhere in the brainstem, at a site which also has some effect on the slow phase of optokinetic nystagmus (see Lisberger, Miles, Optican, & Eighmy, 1981, for details). Changes in the gain and phase relationships between head velocity and the firing rates of cells in the vestibular nuclei have also been found to accompany adaptive changes in the vestibulo-ocular reflex of cats (Keller & Precht, 1979a: Waespe & Henn 1978a). However, these modifications of response characteristics showed only in certain cells, particularly in cells that normally have a high gain, and were not large enough to account for the behavioral changes. Keller and Precht also suggested that the floccular mechanism proposed to account for vestibulo-ocular recalibration may have to be modified or supplemented by adaptive changes outside the cerebellum. This suggestion gains support from the fact that recalibration of the vestibulo-ocular system is lost while the climbing-fiber inputs to the flocculus are temporarily silenced by the local application of a drug (Demer & Robinson, 1982). This procedure would not be expected to affect modified synapses within the flocculus immediately but it would cut it off from inputs from modified synapses in other structures. In a recent review of the subject Ito (1982) suggests that the relevant adaptive changes occur in only one local region of the flocculus and that recordings have not yet been made in the correct location. Ito sees the flocculus as a sideloop of several reflexes having to do with visual stability, such as the optokinetic reflex, the cervico-ocular reflex, as well as the vestibulo-ocular reflex. According to Ito, this sideloop is called into action whenever sensory feedback systems of control are absent or inadequate to stabilize the visual input.

4.4. Compensation for Vestibular Loss

Destruction of the vestibular system on one side of the head results in a spontaneous nystagmus with the quick phase toward the normal side, postural instability, a tendency to hold the head tilted toward the intact side, and nausea. There may also be an apparent tilt of the visual scene one way or the other, depending on the type and extent of the unilateral damage (Friedmann 1971). With unilateral vestibular loss, the resting discharge from each canal of the intact labyrinth is not canceled in the vestibular nuclei by synergistic inputs from the damaged side of the head. Thus when the head is stationary, difference signals are produced in the vestibular nuclei. In the case of the horizontal canals, the anomalous difference signal is equivalent to rotation of the head about a vertical axis toward the intact labyrinth. This imbalanced input induces spontaneous nystagmus with fast phase toward the intact side. The resulting conflict between visual and vestibular stimulation induces nausea. For the vertical canals, the imbalanced input is equivalent to that produced by tilting the head toward the intact side. This induces postural instability and torsional nystagmus. The apparent tilt of vertical lines is presumably due to the loss of otolith organs on one side. Otolith imbalance also induces a deviation of the eyes to the affected side, which enhances the spontaneous canal-driven nystagmus when the head is tilted toward the defective side and reduces it when the head is tilted the other way (see Section 2.5). That is one reason why patients tilt the head toward and sleep on their sound side (Fluur, 1973), but another reason is that a sideways tilt of the head is induced by the otolith imbalance (Hallpike, 1975). After between 1 and 4 weeks the spontaneous nystagmus subsides; aged patients compensate more slowly than younger patients. Symptoms engendered by movements of the head take longer to subside, and careful testing reveals asymmetry of postrotary nystagmus months, or even years, after the injury (Precht, Shimazu, & Markham, 1966; Schaefer & Meyer, 1974, pp. 463–490). It seems that recovery is due to a reappearance of spontaneous activity in neurons of the vestibular nuclei that are normally driven by the damaged canals (Precht et al., 1966). There are several possible sources of this spontaneous activity.

One possibility is that there is a change in the effects caused by signals conveyed to the damaged side over commissural fibers originating on the intact side. It was explained in Howard, Chapter 11, "The Vestibular System," that the cells in the vestibular nuclei that receive ipsilateral excitatory inputs (type I cells) are inhibited by cells (type II cells) that receive excitatory inputs from reciprocally active type I cells on the contralateral side. After hemilabyrinthectomy the type II cells on the damaged side still receive their normal input. During compensation for vestibular loss, some restoration of balance in the activity of the two sides would be achieved if the inhibitory influences conveyed to the damaged side were decreased. The evidence on this point is equivocal (see Precht, 1974, pp. 451–462), although it has been reported recently that compensation for spontaneous nystagmus does not occur if the commissural connections are cut (Bienhold & Flohr, 1978). In any case, decreased inhibition cannot be the sole cause of restoration of spontaneous activity on the damaged side because this activity recovers on both sides in bilabyrinthectomized animals (Ryu & McCabe, 1976).

Another possibility is that the restoration of vestibular balance is due to adaptive changes in the vestibulocerebellum. One way to investigate this matter is to see whether recovery occurs in animals in which the cerebellum has been removed. Care must be taken to remove the cerebellum some weeks before performing labyrinthectomy; otherwise, the trauma of the first operation will interfere with recovery from the second. The evidence indicates that cerebellectomy delays but does not prevent recovery from hemilabyrinthectomy (Haddad, Friendlich, & Robinson, 1977; Llinás, Walton, Hillman, & Soleto, 1975; Schaefer & Meyer, 1973, pp. 203–232). Removal of the cerebellum some time after cats had recovered from hemilabyrinthectomy produced only a transient regression in their recovery (Courjon, Flandrin, Jeannerod, & Schmid, 1982). Evidence of another sort suggests that the cerebellum ameliorates the symptoms in the immediate postoperative period, even through it may not be essential to the recovery process. McCabe and Ryu (1969) recorded from the vestibular nuclei of cats after hemilabyrinthectomy and found an almost complete absence of spontaneous activity in the medial nuclei on both the damaged and intact sides, which returned to normal levels in both nuclei as the animal recovered from the effects of the hemilabyrinthectomy. In animals lacking a cerebellum, there was resting activity in the previously silent neurons in the medial nucleus of the intact side. It looks as though the cerebellum suppresses the resting discharge in the intact vestibular nucleus and helps maintain the balance of the system until activity on the damaged side has had time to recover. Spontaneous nystagmus and other forms of asymmetry of functioning found after hemilabyrinthectomy must be due either to incomplete cerebellar suppression or to vestibular inputs that bypass the vestibular nuclei.

The final possibility is that restoration of vestibular balance is due to a potentiation of effects of inputs from other motor or sensory systems on cells of the vestibular nuclei. Recovery from unilateral vestibular loss is known to depend on the integrity of other sensorimotor systems. For instance, recovery is delayed in immobilized baboons and has been found to be reversed by spinal transection in guinea pigs (Azzena, 1969; Lacour, Roll, & Appaix, 1976). It is also delayed in animals prevented from making contact with the ground in the recovery period (Schaefer & Meyer, 1973). Furthermore, cats do not recover from hemilabyrinthectomy if kept in the dark (Courjon, Jeannerod, Ossuzio, & Schmid, 1977; Putkonen, Courjon, & Jeannerod, 1977). Blindfolding a hemilabyrinthectomized animal, after it has recovered, causes its symptoms to reappear (Schaefer & Meyer, 1974). The inferior olive is perhaps the major route of visual inputs to the vestibular nuclei, so that it is not surprising that compensation for unilateral vestibular loss is absent in animals in which the inferior olive has been destroyed (Llińas et al., 1975). MacKay and Murphy (1979) have suggested that the inferior olive may achieve restoration of vestibular balance by producing a reduction in the inhibitory influence normally exerted by the vestibulocerebellum on the vestibular nucleus. Removal of the vestibulocerebellum should have the same effect, and this is perhaps why recovery was found not to be much hindered by removal of that organ.

When both labyrinths are removed, there is an absence of the resting discharge from both sides, so that there is no anomalous difference signal in the resting state. There is therefore no spontaneous nystagmus or other sign of imbalance after bilabyrinthectomy. There is also no nausea, and patients with bilateral vestibular loss do not suffer from motion sickness. The loss of vestibular inputs leads to a loss of muscular tone throughout the body, and there is a predictable decrease in postural stability, especially when the eyes are closed or when the patient attempts to walk along a narrow rail (Fregly 1974; Fregly & Graybiel, 1970). There is a gross deficiency in the compensatory movements of the eyes during head movement (D. G. Cogan, 1958). Over a period of months the disturbing symptoms of bilateral loss of vestibular functions partially subside, but recovery is not so complete as after unilateral loss. For instance, a bilabyrinthectomized cat never recovers its ability to land smoothly when dropped, and a monkey never recovers its ability to run along a rotating bar (Igarashi, Watanabe, & Maxian, 1970; Watt, 1976.)

The gain of the slow phase of nystagmus induced by head turning in monkeys has been found to regain about 30% of its normal value in about two months after a bilateral labyrinthectomy (Dichgans, Bizzi, Morasso, & Tagliasco, 1973). This recovery is probably due in part to a potentiation of the cervico-ocular reflex and in part to increased voluntary control over pursuit eye movements (Bizzi, Kalil, Morasso, & Tagliasco, 1972, pp. 220–232).

4.5. Key References

The subject of vestibular habituation has been reviewed by W. E. Collins (1974a, 1974b). Reason and Brand (1975) have thoroughly reviewed the subject of motion sickness. The recalibration of vestibular responses is reviewed in Wilson and Melvill Jones (1979) and Miles and Lisberger (1981). MacKay and Murphy (1979) and Ito (1982) have reviewed the literature on the cerebellar modulation of vestibular responses in general. Compensation for vestibular loss has been reviewed by Schaefer and Meyer (1974, pp. 463–490) and more recently by Henn, B. Cohen, and Young (1980).

5. JUDGING THE VISUAL VERTICAL

5.1. Background

When people judge the position of one part of the body with respect to some other part, they are making *proprioceptive judgments*. When people make judgments about the position of an external object with respect to some feature of the body, they are making *egocentric judgments*. There are three types of egocentric judgment; *oculocentric*, *headcentric*, and *bodycentric* (torsocentric). Oculocentric judgments are involved when people fixate an object (align it with the visual axis) or set a line parallel to the normally vertical meridian or the retina. People make headcentric judgments when they face an object (align it with the frontal parallel plane of the head), and they make bodycentric judgments when they set an object parallel to the *z* axis of the body.

When people make a judgment about the position of one object with respect to another object or with respect to an external system of coordinates, such as geographical directions or the direction of gravity, they are making *exocentric judgments*. Setting a line of light to the vertical is an exocentric judgment. Exocentric judgments may involve proprioceptive and egocentric components, as we shall see.

Let us look more closely at the task of setting a line to the vertical. Assume that the line of light is the only thing in view. In the first place, the subject must register the orientation of the image of the line on the retina. This is the oculocentric component of the task, and it requires for its execution the presence of a mechanism in the visual system that can detect the orientation of images. The pioneering work of Hubel and Wiesel has revealed that the mammalian visual cortex contains cells selectively responsive to the retinal orientation of stimuli (see Olzak and Thomas, Chapter 7). Oculocentric judgments of the orientation of a line are disturbed by long inspection of a tilted line, an effect known as *tilt normalization*. They are also disturbed by other lines in different orientations, an effect known as *tilt contrast*. These two effects are discussed in Sections 5.3 and 5.4, respectively.

The task of setting an isolated line of light to the vertical requires the subject to also register the torsional position of the eyes in the head. This is a purely proprioceptive component of the task. Evidence suggests that we register the position of the eyes in terms of the motor commands (efference) involved in holding them in position, although a contribution from proprioceptors in the extraocular muscles has not been finally ruled out (see Howard, 1982, for details on this issue). The torsional position of the eyes changes when people assume an eccentric position of gaze or tilt the head, and the effects of such changes on judgments of the vertical are discussed in Sections 5.5 and 5.7.2.

Finally, the task of setting an isolated line of light to the vertical requires the subject to register the angular position of the head with respect to gravity. This is the headcentric component of the task, and it depends on signals from the otolith organs (see Howard, Chapter 11). When people tilt the head, otolith organs become less sensitive, and judgments of head tilt are subject to constant errors. Furthermore, the otolith organs may be defective, or they may be affected by changes in the gravitational vector produced by weightlessness or by centrifuging the subject. These effects are discussed in Section 5.7. Note that when the two egocentric components and the proprioceptive component are combined, the final product is an exocentric judgment about the orientation of the line with respect to gravity.

Up to now it was assumed that subjects were making judgments about a line of light in otherwise dark surroundings. If the judgment is made in the presence of familiar visual surroundings, such as the inside of a room, subjects can succeed simply by aligning the line with those features of their surroundings, such as the walls of the room, which they know to be vertical. Spatial features of a scene surrounding a given object may constitute a spatial *frame of reference*. If people use such things as the walls of a room as their frame of reference for making judgments of the vertical, they need not register the position of the eyes or of the head; the task reduces to that of aligning one visual stimulus with respect to another. If the frame of reference is not vertical and subjects assume that it is, they will misjudge the visual vertical. Such effects are discussed in Section 5.6.

5.2. The Precision of Judgments of the Vertical

Accuracy in judging the visual vertical is indicated by the mean signed error with which a person is able to set a line to the vertical. Accuracy is indicated by the *constant error*, or bias. The *point of subjective equality* (PSE) in this task is the mean position of the line that the subject judges to be vertical and may be referred to as the *apparent vertical*. A person's *precision*, or sensitivity, in judging the vertical is indicated by the reciprocal of the mean unsigned error of a series of judgments, with respect to the PSE. The reciprocal of error variance or its standard deviation is an alternative measure of precision. Note that the mean unsigned error with respect to the true vertical confounds accuracy and precision and should be avoided. Accuracy and precision, properly defined, are independent parameters of human performance.

A person is able to set a luminous line in dark surroundings to the vertical or horizontal with a precision of 1° or less (Mann, Berthelot-Berry, & Dauterive, 1949; Witkin & Asch, 1948). Westheimer, Shimamura, and McKee (1976) found that on 75% of trials subjects could detect when a line, subtending 0.5° at the eye, was about 0.5° from vertical. The precision of judgments of orientations other than vertical and horizontal are much worse than 1° (Gibson & Radner, 1937; Muller, Sidorsky, Slivinske, Alluisi, & Fitts, 1955; Volkmann & Pufall, 1972). We have natural subjective standards, or norms, for the vertical and horizontal, whereas other orientations must be estimated with respect to a learned scale (Kaufman, Reese, Volkmann, & Rogers, 1953). A secondary region of higher precision tends to occur at orientations of 45°, with respect to the vertical, although the variation of precision within each quadrant of orientation depends on the categories with which the subject is asked to operate (Keene, 1963).

The precision of judgments of the visual vertical is highest when the body is in its normal upright position and decreases with increasing tilt of the body (Miller, Fregly, van den Brink, & Graybiel, 1965). This decrease in precision is related to the decrease in the sensitivity of the utricles with increasing tilt of the body; it is particularly evident when the somesthetic inputs are eliminated by immersing the subject in water (Lechner-Steinleitner & Schöne, 1980).

Performance on a number of visual tasks shows higher sensitivity for displays aligned with the normally vertical and horizontal meridans than for displays aligned with oblique meridians. For instance, grating acuity, contrast sensitivity, and luminance sensitivity are all higher for vertical and horizontal lines than for oblique lines. This type of visual anisotropy is known as *meridional astigmatism* and is reviewed by Howard (1982). In the present context it is relevant to note that the variability in setting a line parallel or perpendicular to another line is less for lines that fall on vertical or horizontal axes than for those that fall on oblique axes (Andrews, 1967a, 1967b; Bouma & Andriessen, 1968), and the variability in matching the orientations of successively presented lines is also less for lines that fall on main retinal axes (Matin & Drivas, 1979). Vernier acuity is essentially the ability to detect a change in the slope of the imaginary line joining the ends of two offset target lines, so that it is not surprising that vernier acuity has also been shown to be better for vertical or horizontal lines (Ludvigh & McKinnon, 1967; McKee & Westheimer, 1978).

Meridional astigmation has been shown not to be due to optical factors (Campbell, Kulikowski, & Levinson, 1966) although optical astigmation of long standing may cause a neural anisotropy to develop (Freeman & Thibos, 1973). Neural anisotropy is most likely due to a preponderance of cortical cells preferentially tuned to vertical and horizontal stimuli.

5.3. Tilt Normalization

The vertical and horizontal are natural *norms* in the dimension of visual tilt. There are norms in other visual spatial dimensions; for instance, eye level is a norm in the dimension of elevation and the median plane is a norm in the dimension of azimuth. Generally speaking, a stimulus in a given sensory scale that is displaced with respect to a norm comes increasingly to resemble the norm as the stimulus is inspected. Thus after a period of inspection, a curved line appears to get straighter (Gibson, 1933), a moving array appears to slow down, and two objects at different distances from the observer appear to become more equidistant (Howard & Templeton, 1964a). Any such apparent displacement of a stimulus attribute toward a norm is known as *normalization.*

In *tilt normalization*, a line near a principal visual meridian appears to rotate toward that meridian as the line is inspected. Inspection of a vertical or horizontal line will obviously not produce normalization, and if it is assumed that the vertical and horizontal norms are equally strong, one would expect a line at 45° to be also immune to the effects of normalization, because its tendency to normalize to the vertical would cancel its tendency to normalize to the horizontal. We shall see that in fact the two tendencies cancel at an angle of about 60° to the vertical.

A vertical line, seen after an inspection line tilted a few degrees with respect to the vertical, appears to be tilted in the opposite direction for several seconds. This phenomenon is known as the *tilt aftereffect*. The tilted line that induces such an aftereffect is called the *inspection line*, and the vertical line seen subsequently is known as the *test line*. It is not easy to measure the tilt normalization of a single line directly, because it is not easy to judge the orientation of a tilted line. The tilt aftereffect is measured by asking the subject to set the test line to the apparent vertical, and that is an easy judgment to make. That is why Gibson and Radner (1937) and others attempted to measure tilt normalization indirectly, by measuring the tilt aftereffect. However, the tilt aftereffect operates between two lines irrespective of their relation to the principal meridians. For instance, it has been found that inspection of a vertical line affects the apparent orientation of a test line tilted 10° from the vertical (Templeton, Howard, & Easting, 1965). This effect cannot be due to normalization of the inspection line, since vertical lines do not normalize. The tilt aftereffect is probably due to at least two processes working in the same direction, and one can at least be sure that if there is no tilt aftereffect, there is no tilt normalization.

A second procedure used to measure tilt normalization involves asking the subject to select which of several briefly exposed test lines appears to be parallel to a continuously exposed inspection line. It is assumed that the test lines are exposed too briefly for them to normalize and that they are sufficiently far from the inspection line to not be affected by it. One problem with this method is that the subject may rely on the cues of equality of distances between parts of the lines, rather than on their orientation. By the use of the parallel-matching procedure, lines have been found to normalize up to a maximum extent of about 2° (Prentice & Beardslee, 1950).

Tilt normalization may also be measured by asking the subject to align a dot with the perceived extension of a tilted inspection line. This method works only to the extent that the imaginary extension of the line does not also normalize. Bouma and Andriessen (1968) used this procedure and obtained maximum mean normalization effects of about 4° for lines tilted about 15° to the nearest principal meridian. With lines shorter than about 1° of visual angle, normalization effects of up to 10° were found. Smaller effects were obtained with inspection lines longer than this.

Tilt normalization has also been measured by asking subjects to set a rod they can feel, but not see, to match the orientation of a line, first, when the line is exposed only briefly and, second, after it has been inspected for some time. Templeton (1972) used this method and reported a normalization effect of about 2° for an inspection tilt of 20°. This procedure depends on the unsubstantiated assumption that there are no constant errors in the felt position of the comparison rod.

A tilted visual framework, such as a tilted room, may appear to be displaced toward the vertical through very large angles. This is the *visual frame effect*, which is discussed in Section 5.6.1. The visual frame effect formally resembles tilt normalization but may be distinguished from it on the following grounds.

1. The apparent shifts in orientation induced by a tilted frame may be 20° or more, whereas tilt normalization has a maximum value of only about 4° for all but very short lines.
2. The visual frame effect is more in evidence with frames that fall on the periphery of the retina than with frames

presented in the central region of the visual field. The tilt aftereffect is only a little larger in the periphery than in the center of the visual field (Muir & Over, 1970), and insofar as the tilt aftereffect indicates the upper limit of tilt normalization, it may be concluded that normalization is also similar in the two regions of the visual field.

3. A tilted visual frame affects all objects seen in the context of the frame, whereas the tilt aftereffect is confined to within a few degrees of visual angle of the inspection line (Muir & Over, 1970; Rieser & Banks 1981).
4. When a person views a tilted realistic scene that fills the entire field of view, the apparent vertical is displaced in the same direction, even for frame tilts of up to 75°, the largest angle tested. On the other hand, tilt normalization reaches a maximum when the inspection line is between 10 and 20° from the vertical and reverses in sign when the inspection line is tilted at an angle of somewhere between 45 and 60°.
5. The visual frame effect has been reported to be influenced by cognitive variables, such as the degree of realism in the tilted scene and the instructions given to the subject. There are no reports that tilt normalization is affected by these variables.

I suspect that tilt normalization, like tilt contrast and the tilt aftereffect discussed in the Section 5.4, is an oculocentric shift arising at an early stage in visual processing, probably in the primary visual cortex. The visual frame effect is probably not an oculocentric shift but most likely depends on a higher level of processing involving the assessment of the orientation of objects relative to internal standards of vertical and horizontal. Gibson and Radner (1937) explained normalization in terms of adaptation processes in *oppositional* sensory dimensions, that is, dimensions in which there is a neutral point in the scale. So-called intensitive sensory dimensions do not contain a neutral or symmetrical stimulus value; examples are weight and loudness. The point or axis of symmetry in an oppositional dimension is the norm; it is the point or axis from which the scale values increase in either direction. It is also the most frequent stimulus value to be experienced, and in many cases it is the stimulus value about which discrimination is most acute. Gibson and Radner suggested that inspection of an off-norm stimulus produces an alteration over the whole scale of correspondence between the physical values and the perceived values of the sensory dimension, although this shift in correspondence may be maximal in the region of the inspected value. The precise nature of the physiological process responsible for this type of adaptation is not known.

5.4. Tilt Contrast

The apparent orientation of a line is affected by a neighboring line in a different orientation. For instance, the central discs of vertical lines in Figure 18.26 are apparently tilted because of the presence of the tilted surrounding lines. Effects such as these are known as *tilt contrast*. Many well-known geometrical illusions, such as the Hering illusion and the Zöllner illusion, depend, at least partly, on tilt contrast. The simplest stimulus array in which such an effect is produced consists of two lines meeting at an angle. One line is normally designated the *induction line* (line I), the other the *test line* (line T). The angle between them is the intersect angle. Two lines mutually repel each other when they form an acute angle of between 5 and 60°. In other words, acute angles appear to be larger than they would be if there were no tilt contrast. It is generaly agreed that tilt contrast is at a maximum when the angle between the induction and test lines is between 10 and 20°; the exact position of the maximum varies with the orientation of the angle in the frontal plane. Several investigators have reported that angles of less than 5° are underestimated, an effect known as *small angle assimilation*. Angles between 60 and 90° are also found to be underestimated, an effect known as the *indirect effect*.

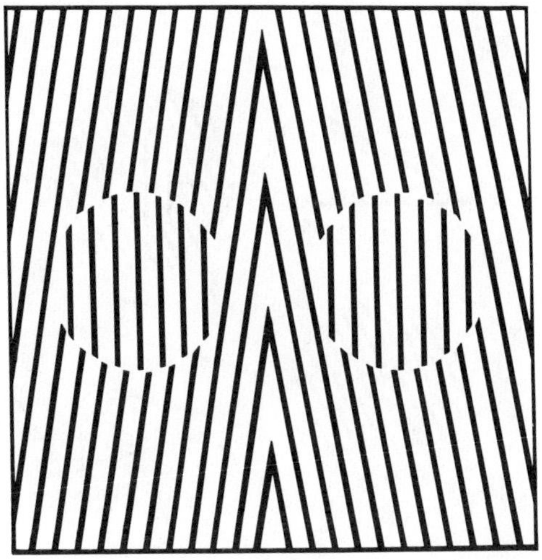

Figure 18.26. Tilt contrast. The lines in the two central discs are vertical but appear tilted, because of the contrasting tilt of the background lines.

Tilt contrast persists for a while after the induction figure has been removed. This is referred to as *successive tilt contrast*, or the *tilt aftereffect* (see Figure 18.27). Most of the evidence suggests that the simultaneous and successive effects are manifestations of the same physiological processes (Magnussen & Kurtenbach, 1980; Ware & Mitchell, 1974).

The types of display used to measure tilt contrast are shown in Figure 18.28. Perphas the most useful procedure for measuring tilt contrast is one in which the subject is asked to set a comparison line to appear parallel with the test line when the test

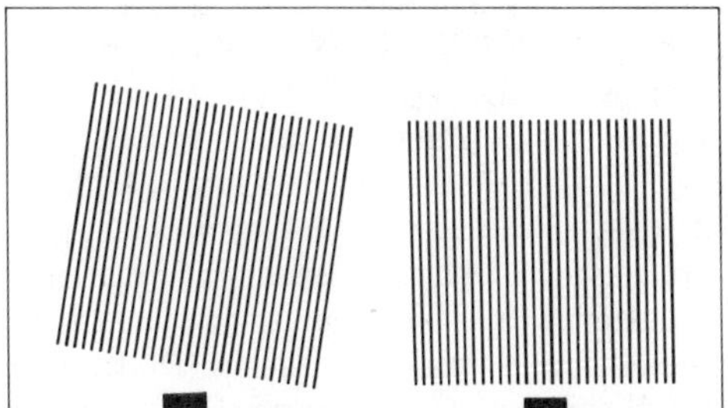

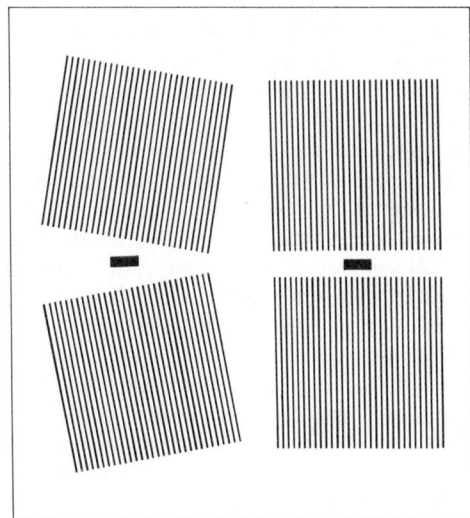

Figure 18.27. Successive tilt contrast. Inspect the small black rectangle on the left for about half a minute, and then transfer the gaze to the rectangle on the right. Each test grating should appear to tilt in the opposite direction, with respect to its corresponding inspection grating.

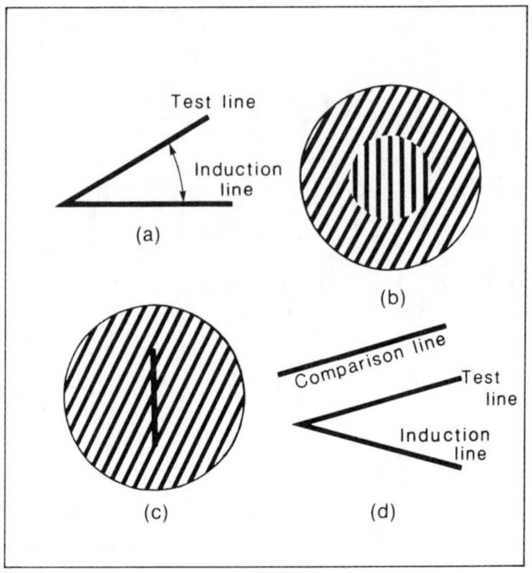

Figure 18.28. Stimulus displays for measuring tilt contrast. (a) Intersecting induction and test lines. (b) Disc of test lines with an annulus of induction lines. (c) Test line superimposed on induction lines. (d) Subject sets the comparison line to appear parallel to the test line in the presence of an induction line.

line is presented with an induction line, as shown in Figure 18.28(d). It is essential that the induction line affects the test line but not the comparison line. This will probably be the case as long as the induction and test lines touch or overlap and the comparison line is at least 1° of visual angle away from the two other lines. This assumption is justified because evidence suggests that contrast effects, at least those in the central visual field, are confined to a region around the induction line subtending less than 1° (Campbell & Maffei, 1971; Tolhurst & Thompson, 1975). Care must be taken to make control readings in the absence of the induction line because, as Carpenter and Blakemore (1973) found, subjects may show systematic errors in setting two lines parallel.

There is no completely satisfactory explanation of tilt contrast. One factor may be that optical blur in an acute angle makes it appear more obtuse than it otherwise would (Chiang, 1968). But this cannot be the only factor, because the illusion persists when the region of intersection between the two lines is omitted (Oyama, 1975; Weale, 1978). Furthermore, the effect is still present when the test line is presented to one eye and the induction line to the other (Campbell & Maffei, 1971; Virsu & Taskinen, 1975). Tyler (1975) obtained a tilt aftereffect of normal size when the induction grating and test grating were stereoscopically synthesized as cyclopean images from monocular random-dot patterns. In a cyclopean image formed in this way, there are no monocular images of lines, so that the presence of the cyclopean illusion provides a very powerful argument against a purely optical theory of the tilt aftereffect, in addition to strengthening the notion that the tilt aftereffect and, probably also, successive tilt contrast depend largely, if not entirely, on neurons in the visual cortex. It is generally believed that tilt contrast is due to adaptation of or inhibition between cortical cells selectively responsive to particular orientations of the stimulus. This question has been reviewed by Howard (1982). One type of process that may be involved has been proposed by Carpenter and Blakemore (1973). In Figure 18.29 each curve represents the hypothetical pattern of activity across a population of cortical orientation detectors, resulting from the combined effects of both excitation and inhibition. Each detector in the population responds maximally to a line in one orientation, as indicated on the abscissa, and is inhibited by lines in neighboring orientations. The two top curves represent the distribution of activity set up by each of two lines when presented in isolation, one tilted 6° to the left and one tilted 6° to the right. In each case a set of orientation detectors with preferred orientations similar to the stimulus is excited, and sets of orientation detectors with preferred orientations more remote from that of the stimulus are inhibited. The bottom curve represents the distribution of activity which results when the two lines are superimposed to form an acute angle. An inhibitory flank of each distribution overlaps one side of the excitatory region of the other distribution, resulting in a skewing of the two modes away from each other on the tilt axis. If we assume that the mode of any such distribution of activity across orientation detectors determines perceived tilt, then this process will result in an apparent enlargement of the angle between the two lines, from 12 to 16° in this hypothetical case.

5.5. The Effects of Eccentric Gaze on the Visual Vertical

The normally vertical meridian of the eye is that meridian which passes through the fovea and is vertical when the head is upright and the eye is in its primary position of gaze. When the head is upright, the image of a vertical line remains parallel to the vertical meridian of the eye as long as the eye is in a

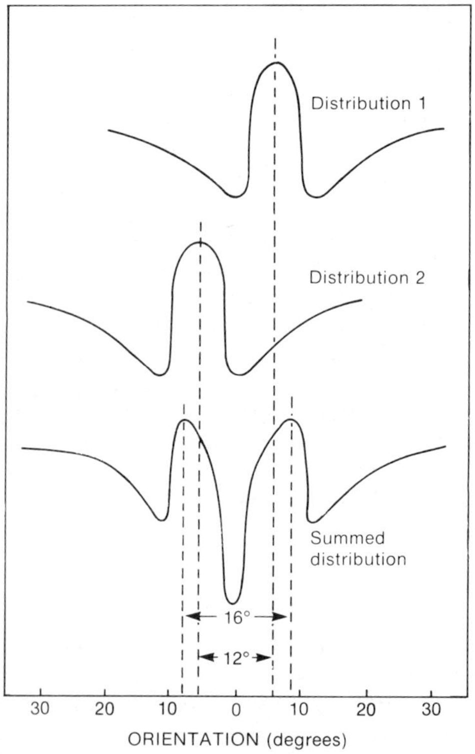

Figure 18.29. An illustration of the processes suggested by Carpenter and Blakemore (1973, fig. 1), as an explanation of tilt contrast. The curves represent hypothetical distributions of excitation across the population of cortical orientation detectors in response to a line at 6° (distribution 1), − 6° (distribution 2), and two lines intersecting at an angle of 12° (summed distribution). If the mode of such distributions determines perceived tilt, then this interactive process will cause acute angles to appear enlarged. (From R. H. S. Carpenter & C. Blakemore, Interactions between orientations in human vision, *Experimental Brain Research*, 1973, *18*. Reprinted with permission.)

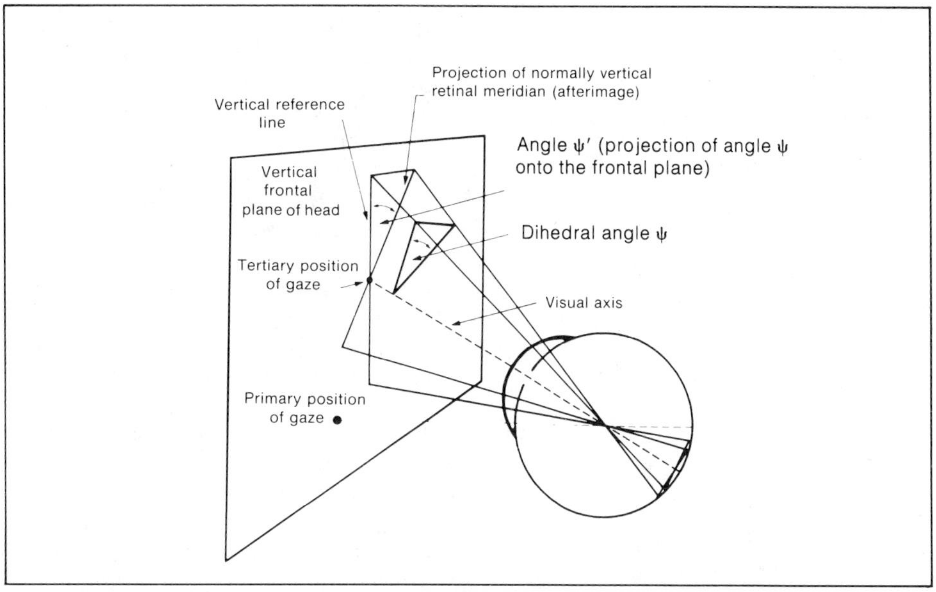

Figure 18.30. Showing how an afterimage imposed on the normally vertical meridian of the eye is projected at an angle ψ to the objective vertical when the eye is in a tertiary position of gaze. The angle ψ′ is the projection of the dihedral angle ψ, contained in the frontal plane of the eye, onto the frontal plane of the head. (From I. P. Howard, *Human visual orientation*. Copyright 1982 by John Wiley & Sons, Inc. Reprinted with permission.)

primary or secondary position of gaze. A secondary position of gaze is any position that can be reached by elevating or depressing the eye from the primary position along a vertical meridian or by abducting or abducting it from the primary position along a horizontal meridian of the eye's orbit. A position of gaze reached by moving along any other meridian of the orbit is a tertiary, or oblique, position of gaze. The image of a vertical line is no longer parallel to the normally vertical meridian of the eye when the eye is in an oblique position of gaze. This deviation is due to the fact that the eyes move as if they rotate about axes within Listing's plane (see Chapter 10 by Hallett). If the position of an eye is defined with respect to its elevation θ and its azimuth ϕ, then according to Listing's law the orientation of the normally vertical meridian of the eye with respect to the vertical is given by

$$\Psi = \arcsin \frac{\sin\theta \sin\phi}{(1 + \cos\theta \cos\phi)} \quad \text{(Robinson, 1963).}$$

It can be seen from Figure 18.30 that angle Ψ is the dihedral angle between a vertical plane through the nodal point of the eye and a plane through the nodal point and the normally vertical meridian of the eye. In other words, angle Ψ lies in the frontal plane of the eye. A person may impress an afterimage of a line on the normally vertical meridian of an eye and then, while holding the eye in an oblique position, rotate a line within the frontal plane of the head until it is aligned with the projection of the afterimage. The deviation of the test line from the vertical defines angle Ψ', which, according to Listing's law, should be the projection of angle Ψ into the frontal plane of the head. Actual measurements of angle Ψ' have confirmed that eyes rotate according to Listing's law (Nakayama & Balliet, 1977; Quereau, 1954).

The question now arises as to how a line in the frontal plane of the head must be oriented to appear vertical when the eyes are in a position of oblique gaze. One possibility is that the image of the line must fall on the normally vertical meridian of the eye, in which case the line will be inclined at an angle of Ψ' to the vertical. Another possibility is that the image must fall on the meridian of the eye that is actually vertical, in which case the line will also be vertical and the subject will exhibit orientation constancy. *Orientation constancy* refers to the ability of a person to judge the true vertical when, for any reason, the normally vertical meridian of the eye is not vertical.

Nakayama and Balliet (1977) sought an answer to this question by asking subjects to set a luminous line seen monocularly in dark surroundings to appear vertical for each of several positions of gaze. The mean settings are indicated by dashed lines in Figure 18.31. The bold lines represent the projections of the normally vertical meridian of the eye onto the frontal plane of the head. It can be seen that for oblique angles of gaze the apparent vertical is a compromise between a veridical setting and the projection of the eye's normally vertical meridian. Thus orientation constancy breaks down when only a single line in dark surroundings is in view. However, judgments of the vertical for oblique gaze were found to be veridical when the room lights were left on so that, under normal viewing conditions, orientation constancy is maintained by the simple process of referring objects to the visual frame of reference.

With binocular viewing, the situation is more complex because for any line not lying in the horizontal or vertical horopter, its orientation with respect to a particular retinal meridian of one eye will differ from its orientation with respect to the corresponding meridian of the other eye. Any disparity in the orientations of binocular images is known as *cyclodisparity*. This may explain reports that the apparent vertical is displaced to the right when the right eye is used and to the left when the left eye is used (Schneider, 1966; Wade, 1969a). The eyes may rotate about the visual axes so as to nullify a cyclodisparity, and this complicates matters even more.

Up to now we have considered judgments of the vertical with respect to tilt within the frontal plane of the head. People

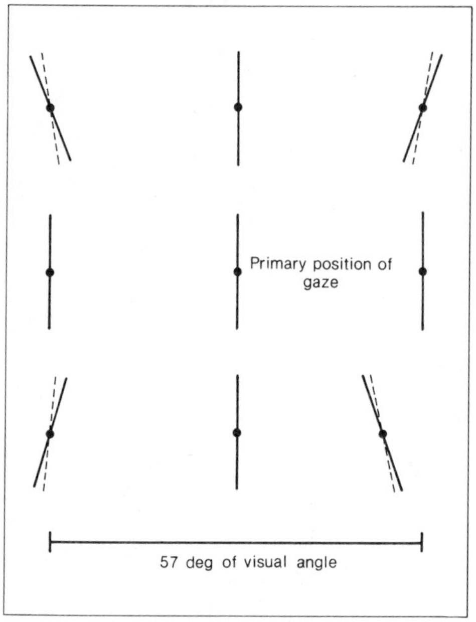

Figure 18.31. An afterimage of a vertical line is impressed on the eye while the eye is in its primary position of gaze. Each solid line shows the orientation of this afterimage on a frontal plane of the head for that position of gaze. The apparent vertical corresponds to the direction of the normally vertical meridian, except for teriary (oblique) positions of gaze. At these positions the apparent vertical is represented by dashed lines and is a compromise between the normally vertical meridian and the true vertical. (From K. Nakayama & R. Balliet, Listing's law, eye position sense, and perception of the vertical, *Vision Research, 17*. Copyright 1977 by Pergamon Press, Ltd. Reprinted with permission.)

may also make judgments about the *inclination* of lines within the median plane of the head. This question is complicated by the fact that the normally vertical meridians of the eyes are not binocularly corresponding meridians. In other words, images that fall along normally vertical meridians excite noncorresponding points and are said to have a cyclodisparity. Such lines do not fuse into an impression of a single line or, at least, are not at the midpoint of Panum's fusional area. For a line in the median plane of the head to stimulate corresponding meridians, it must be inclined away from the observer. Such a line is said to fall on the *vertical horopter* (Helmholtz, 1866/1962). This means that corresponding retinal meridians in the vertical direction are extorted about 2° with respect to the vertical meridians (see Figure 18.32). It is a fact of geometry that for a fixed amount of extortion of corresponding meridians, the inclination of the vertical horopter increases with increasing viewing distance until, at infinity, it is parallel to the ground. The relation between the inclination of the vertical horopter i and the angle between corresponding meridia θ is given by

$$\tan\,\theta = \frac{a\,\tan\,i}{b},$$

where a is the interpupillary distance and b is the viewing distance (Ogle, 1964). The slant of the vertical horopter is probably due to the tuning of patterns of binocular correspondence by the frequent exposure of people to surfaces that slant away from them (Krekling & Blika, 1983).

In spite of this inclination of the vertical horopter, it has been found that, on average, people correctly estimate the vertical position of a line within the median plane (A. I. Cogan, 1979; Ebenholtz & Paap, 1973).

5.6. The Visual Vertical and the Visual Frame of Reference

5.6.1. The Effects of Tilted Frames. Most objects and surfaces maintain a more or less constant orientation with respect to gravity. A scene comprised of such objects and surfaces constitutes a *frame of reference*, which serves as a basis for judgments about the orientation of particular objects. A frame of reference may be defined in general as an attribute of certain objects that does not normally vary and in terms of which variations of the same attribute in other objects are judged. If the visual scene is tilted with respect to gravity, it may still be accepted as vertical and cause the observer to experience illusions of visual tilt. For instance, a person in an airplane perceives the inside of the plane as vertical even when it is tilted through a large angle; a pilot flying in a cloud may not be aware that the plane is upside-down. A water surface or plumb line seen in the cabin of a listing boat seems to be slanted at a large angle (Dixon & Dixon, 1966). Wertheimer (1912) noticed that a room seen in a tilted mirror soon came to appear upright, and it has been reported that people living in buildings tilted 8° by an earthquake perceived the rooms as vertical (Kitahara & Uno, 1967).

The tilt contrast and normalization effects discussed in Sections 5.3 and 5.4 rarely exceed 2°, are limited to the retinal location of the inducing figure, and depend on the relative ocu-

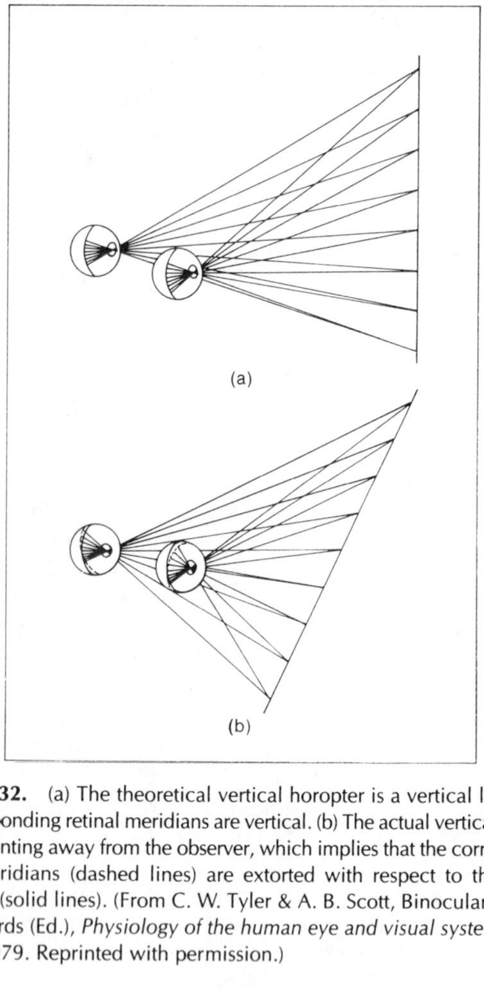

Figure 18.32. (a) The theoretical vertical horopter is a vertical line only if the corresponding retinal meridians are vertical. (b) The actual vertical horopter is a line slanting away from the observer, which implies that the corresponding retinal meridians (dashed lines) are extorted with respect to the vertical meridians (solid lines). (From C. W. Tyler & A. B. Scott, Binocular vision, in R. E. Records (Ed.), *Physiology of the human eye and visual system*, Harper & Row, 1979. Reprinted with permission.)

locentric orientations of inducing and test figures. The effects of a tilted visual scene may be much larger than 2°, are not limited to one location in the visual field, and are not tied to retinal coordinates. Tilt adaptation effects outlast the presence of the inducing figure for several seconds. There are conflicting reports about whether frame-of-reference effects outlast the presence of the frame (Morant & Aronoff, 1966; Wallace, Singer, Mottram, & Purcell, 1975).

Asch and Witkin (1948) measured the effect of a tilted visual frame on the apparent vertical by asking subjects to face a model room tilted 22° and set a rod contained within it to appear vertical with respect to gravity. When subjects could see nothing but the tilted room, the apparent vertical position of the rod was displaced on average 15° in the direction of the tilt of the room. Similar effects were produced when the test rod was seen within a large luminous square in completely dark surroundings (Witkin & Asch, 1948). Subjects differ in the extent to which their judgments of verticality are disturbed by a tilted frame. Some people place the rod nearly parallel to the sides of the frame even though carefully instructed to set it to the gravitational vertical. Such people are called *frame dependent*. Those who set it closer to the true vertical are called *frame independent*. Witkin developed a standardized *rod-and-frame test* for measuring frame dependency and found this measure to be correlated with performance on a variety of perceptual and personality tests (see Witkin, Oltman, Cox, Ehrichman, Hamm, & Ringler, 1973, for a bibliography on this topic). Men are less frame dependent than women, although this difference does not show before the age of about 15 years (Nyborg, 1980). It is unfortunate that in many applications of the rod-and-frame test, crucial variables have not been controlled, including the stability of the head (Lester, 1968), the starting position of the rod (Nyborg, 1974), the speed of rotation of the rod (Corah, 1965), and the exposure time (Hayes & Venables, 1972). Furthermore, the test is often scored in terms of the unsigned deviation from the true vertical, a measure confounding the item of prime interest, namely, the constant error, with variability (Fine & Danforth, 1975).

The apparent vertical is displaced more by a frame that subtends a large angle at the eye than by one which subtends a small angle. For instance, a frame that subtended less than 10° at the eye, irrrespective of its distance, was found to displace the apparent vertical by only 2°, whereas a frame that subtended 40° produced an effect of 8° (Ebenholtz, 1977). However, it is not clear whether the greater effect of larger frames is due to their larger size or to the fact that they stimulate more peripheral regions of the retina. The central–peripheral factor is probably the crucial one, because other evidence reviewed in this chapter suggests that peripherally viewed stimuli are particularly potent cues to stimulus orientation. The effectiveness of a tilted frame is reduced when it is surrounded by a luminous circle, whereas inscribing a circle inside the frame has no effect (Ebenholtz & Utrie, 1982). Thus the most peripheral components of a visual display is the dominant frame of reference for verticality. A frame has less effect on a rod the more the two stimuli are separated in depth (Gogel & Newton, 1975).

A square frame has no natural top or bottom and when tilted at 45° may be regarded as an erect diamond. It therefore comes as no surprise to learn that a square frame has no effect on an enclosed rod when the frame is tilted at multiples of 45° (Beh & Wenderoth, 1972; Beh, Wenderoth, & Purcell, 1971).

Natural scenes, such as a room, have an intrinsic top and bottom and appear upright in only one orientation. One would therefore expect the apparent vertical position of the rod to be displaced in the direction of tilt of a room for all angles of tilt up to 180°, that is, until the room is upside-down. I refer to features that determine the intrinsic top and bottom of an object or scene as *polar features*. The direction linking the top and bottom of a scene is its *polar axis*. The addition of polar features to an otherwise bare box tilted at 45° has been found to displace the apparent vertical position of a rod 17° in the direction of the polar axis, although the addition of polar features did not have much effect for larger angles of tilt of the box (Singer, Purcell, & Austin, 1970). With a tilted projected image of an outdoor scene, the apparent vertical was displaced in the direction of the polar axis of the scene when the scene was tilted up to 75°, at which angle the tilt illusion was zero. In these experiments the visual frame was a box or a projected scene, which may not be very compelling frames of reference. One might expect effects at even larger degrees of tilt when a person views a tilted natural scene that fills the entire field of view. Morant and Beller (1965) had subjects judge the vertical while viewing the world through prisms. Even at an angle of 75° the test rod was still displaced in the direction of the tilted frame. It is a pity that larger angles of tilt were not used. In some instances, an inverted scene may be accepted as upright. For instance, pilots in an inverted aircraft may not realize they are inverted, although of course, in this case, the pilot is also upside-down.

5.6.2. Causal Factors in the Frame Effect. If all cues to the vertical other than that provided by the visual frame were removed, subjects would have no option but to set a rod parallel to the polar axis of the frame, when asked to set it vertical. This would be the situation inside a spacecraft orbiting the earth. On earth, utricular, kinesthetic, and tactile stimuli inform the subject about the true direction of gravity. The extent to which a rod is displaced toward the polar axis of a tilted frame depends on the strength of the visual cues in relation to the strength of other cues to the vertical. There are two main factors determining the strength of visual cues. The first is the impellingness of the visual frame, which depends, as we have just seen, on its size and the richness of the polar features that define its polar axis. The second is the extent of tilt contrast between the test rod and the sides of the frame. Tilt contrast is of minor importance because, as we saw in Section 5.4, it rarely exceeds 2° in magnitude and operates only when the rod is near the sides of the tilted frame. We shall see in later sections of this chapter that there are several factors which determine the strength of nonvisual cues to the vertical. Within the context of the tilted frame effect, as observed by an upright seated observer, there are two nonvisual factors that almost certainly contribute to the illusion. The first factor is that a tilted frame induces torsion of the eyes in the direction of tilt, so that the normally vertical meridian is deflected toward the polar axis of the frame. The second factor is that a tilted frame induces an apparent tilt of the body in the same direction. I shall now comment on each of these factors.

5.6.3. Optostatic Eye Torsion and the Visual Frame Effect. Inspection of a tilted line or grating induces the eyes to tort about their visual axes in the direction of visual tilt. This movement of the eyes may be called *optostatic torsion*. For instance, a disc-shaped grating subtending 25° to the eye has been found to induce a maximum optostatic torsion of about 1° when the lines of the grating were 15° from the vertical (Crone, 1975). It can be seen from Figure 18.33 that the effect is also

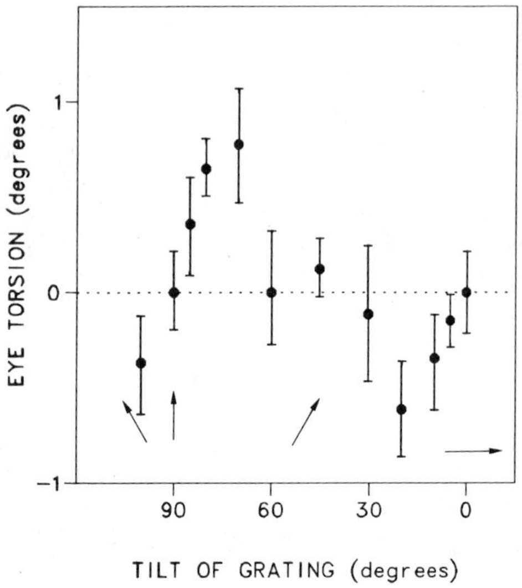

Figure 18.33. Optostatic eye torsion induced in one subject by inspection of a grating tilted at various angles and subtending 25° in the frontal plane. The arrows represent the orientation of the stimulus. Bars are standard deviations. Note that eye torsion of up to 1° is induced by a field of lines tilted with respect to the horizontal or vertical. (From R. A. Crone, Optokinetically induced eye torsion, *von Graefe's Archiven von Ophthalmologie*, 1975, *196*. Reprinted with permission.)

induced by off-horizontal lines and is absent for lines at 45°. A tilted visual framework subtending 28° has also been found to induce up to about 1° of eye torsion (Goodenough, Sigman, Oltman, Rosso, & Mertz, 1979). The response was not found for a single line that subtended only 10° at the eye (Howard & Templeton, 1964b). It looks as though large displays are needed, although it is not known whether the crucial factor is the size of the display or the part of the retina it stimulates.

The eyes respond with oppositely directed torsion when presented with stereotargets having a cyclodisparity. This *cyclofusional response* of the eyes serves to keep corresponding parts of disparate images on corresponding retinal meridians (Kertesz & Jones, 1970). This response is also smaller when the angular size of the stimulus is reduced (Kertesz & Sullivan, 1978).

Eye torsion is not normally under voluntary control. However, it has been claimed that human subjects may learn to make voluntary torsional movements of the eyes of up to a total amplitude of 30° (Balliet & Nakayama, 1978b). Furthermore, a vertical luminous line was found to be apparently displaced in the opposite direction to the voluntarily induced torsion (Balliet & Nakayama, 1978a). Under ordinary circumstances eye torsion can be only a minor factor in illusions of tilt induced by tilting frames.

5.6.4. Apparent Body Tilt and the Visual Frame Effect. Several investigators have reported that inspection of a tilted frame induces an apparent tilt of the body in the opposite direction. For instance, Sigman, Goodenough, and Flannagan (1979) found that the apparent vertical position of a rod was displaced, on average, 7° in the direction of a 28° tilted frame and that the apparent vertical position of the body was displaced 2.5° in the same direction. There was a high correlation between the two settings. This suggests that part, but not all, of the effect of a tilted frame on the apparent orientation of a rod is due to a change in the apparent orientation of the body (see also Ebenholtz & Benzschawel, 1977).

Subjects lying in a supine position inspecting a horizontal visual frame tilted with respect to the body axis have been found to experience a sensation of body rotation in a horizontal plane relative to the unseen walls of the room (Goodenough, Nowak, Oltman, Cox, & Sigman, 1982). These effects are the static counterpart of the sensations of the body tilt and motion induced by visual displays rotating about the visual axis (see Section 3.3.2).

If the instructions require subjects to set the rod parallel to the body axis, rather than to the direction of gravity, any effect due to an apparent tilt of the body should be eliminated. Sigman and colleagues (1979) found that bodycentric instructions reduced the mean effect of the tilted frame by 2.4°, which is, as one would expect, about the same as the apparent tilt of the body that the tilted frame has been found to induce.

Tilt adaptation, eye torsion, and apparent body tilt all contribute something to the visual frame effect, but even if all these effects are added together, they do not equal the apparent displacements of the visual vertical induced by large realistic tilted scenes. The main cause of the visual frame effect must be the tendency of subjects to use the polar axis of the visual scene as their standard of reference for judgments of the vertical.

5.6.5. Rotating Backgrounds and the Visual Vertical. A large visual display rotating in a given direcion in the frontal plane of an observer's head induces sensations of body tilt and body rotation in the opposite direction. These effects were discussed in Section 3.3.2. It was mentioned there that a rotating display of this kind also induces an apparent angular displacement of a vertical line in a direction opposite that of scene rotation. This effect was first reported by Brecher (1934). The most satisfactory type of display for studying this effect is one consisting of a random array of dots. Lines are best avoided because tilted lines induce tilt illusions, which may contaminate any effects due to the motion of the scene.

The main stimulus parameters determining the magnitude of the effect are the oculocentric location of the stimulus, its angular velocity, and, if the stimulus is oscillated, its amplitude of oscillation.

An annulus-shaped display of a given area rotating in the frontal plane about the fixation point displaces the apparent vertical more when it stimulates peripheral regions of the visual field than when it stimulates regions closer to the fovea (Held, Dichgans, & Bauer, 1975). This confirms what has been observed repeatedly in this chapter, that the sense of orientation of observers, with respect to their visual surroundings, depends more on stimuli falling on the retinal periphery than on centrally placed stimuli. The central regions of the retina seem to have more to do with perceiving oculocentric features (pattern features) of the visual stimulus.

The illusory tilt of a test line increases as the angular velocity of the display increases. One determination of this relationship is shown in Figure 18.34. The mean size of the effect was found to increase to an asymptotic value of 15° when the angular velocity of the 130° background reached 30°/sec. At each velocity the apparent tilt of the test line reached its steady level after about 18 sec and returned to its normal position in about the same time after the background stopped rotating (Dichgans, Held, Young, & T. Brandt, 1972). The reasons for these latency effects were discussed in Section 3.3.1. A rotating background subtending only 19° of visual angle has been found to produce an asymptotic effect of only 3° when velocity reaches about 30°/sec (Hughes, Brecher, & Fishkin, 1972). Presumably, the smaller display produces less effect because it stimulates more central regions of the retina.

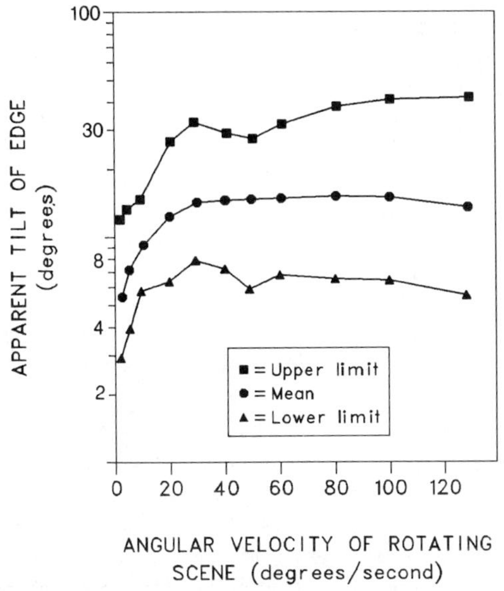

Figure 18.34. Apparent tilt of a stationary vertical edge as a function of the angular velocity of a surrounding 130° field of random dots. The middle curve represents the mean results of seven subjects, the other curves the largest and smallest apparent tilt of the edge, respectively. Note that the mean size of the effect increases to a limiting value of about 15° as the angular velocity of the scene increases. (From J. Dichgans, R. Held, L. R. Young, & T. Brandt, Moving visual scenes influence the apparent direction of gravity, *Science*, 1972. Copyright 1972 by Association for the Advancement of Science. Reprinted with permission.)

Visual scenes rarely rotate or sway, so that when people observe such a thing, they interpret it as due to motion of the body. In other words, the headcentric rotation of a scene is a natural signal that the body is swaying or rotating. The importance of visual motion as a cue to postural stability is illustrated by the fact that infants fall over as soon as the visual scene is moved (Section 1.2.3) and by the fact that the stabilizing effect of a visual scene is reduced if it is flashed on and off at rates below 6 Hz, that is, at rates where visual motion signals become ineffective (Amblard & Cremieux, 1976). The body normally sways with an amplitude of less than 2°, so that one would expect visually induced tilt to occur for background rotations of this amplitude. However, it has been found that backgrounds oscillating sinusoidally around the midpoint of the frontal plane do not induce tilt illusions unless the amplitude of the movement is more than about 5° (Maurtiz, Dichgans, & Hufschmidt, 1977). Probably the threshold is high because of the absence of vestibular stimulation that normally accompanies body sway. Its absence informs subjects that they are not swaying. This interpretation is supported by the fact that the apparent displacement of the visual vertical has been found to be larger when the head is tilted into a position where the utricles are known to be less sensitive (Dichgans, Diener, & T. Brandt, 1974).

Part of the illusion of tilt induced by scene rotation must be due to the illusion of body tilt that such rotation induces. One way to partition out this effect from a purely visual effect would be to ask subjects to set the test rod parallel with the midbody axis, rather than to set it to the apparent vertical. This experiment does not seem to have been done, but if it were, any residual illusion would reflect an apparent headcentric tilt of the test rod. A residual headcentric effect of several degrees might arise because a rotating scene induces a torsional displacement of the eyes of up to about 6° in the same direction (Brecher, 1934; Crone, 1975; Howard & Templeton, 1964b). If the subject failed to take some or all of this so-called optokinetic torsion into account when estimating the orientation of the test rod, the rod would appear displaced in a direction opposite that of the motion of the scene.

Although the amplitude of optokinetic nystagmus, like the illusion of tilt, increases with increasing angular velocity of the rotating background (Kertesz & Jones, 1969), the magnitude of illusory tilt has been found not to correlate with the amplitude of optokinetic torsion (Finke & Held, 1978). The relationship between the two effects remains enigmatic.

5.7. The Visual Vertical and Nonvisual Stimuli

5.7.1. The Aubert and Müller Effects. A luminous vertical line seen in completely dark surroundings appears to tilt when the head is tilted toward the shoulder. For large angles of head tilt a vertical or horizontal line typically appears to be tilted in the opposite direction up to a maximum angle of about 10°. Put another way, the position a line occupies to appear vertical (the apparent vertical) is displaced in the same direction as the body tilt. This effect is known as the *Aubert effect* after the man who first reported it in 1861. For small angles of head tilt a vertical or horizontal line usually appears to be tilted in the same direction—an effect known as the *Müller effect* (Bauermeister, 1964; Müller, 1916; Wade 1969c). It can be seen from the data plotted in Figure 18.35 that the two effects cancel each other when the head is tilted about 60° (Miller, Fregly, van den Brink, & Graybiel, 1965).

There are wide individual differences in the Aubert and Müller effects, although results from experiments also differ because of variations in stimuli and procedures. Particular care must be taken to dissociate tilt effects that occur in the period during and just after the movement of the head from those that arise after the head has been held in one position for some time. In the initial period there are stimuli from the semicircular

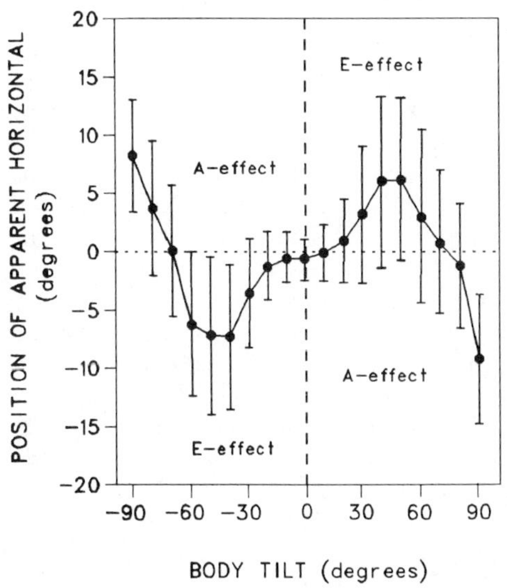

Figure 18.35. The position of the apparent horizontal as a function of body tilt. Means of three subjects. Bars are ± one standard deviation. For small angles of body tilt, the apparent horizontal is displaced in the same direction as the body tilt (E-effect). In other words, a horizontal line appears displaced in the opposite direction to the body. For larger angles of body tilt, the illusion is typically the reverse of that at small angles (A-effect). (Based on Miller, Fregly, Van den Brink, & Graybiel, 1965, fig. 1.)

canals in addition to those from the utricles and receptors in the neck. After the canal inputs have subsided there are stimuli only from the utricles and neck. When the body has been rotating about its x axis for some time and is then suddenly stopped, there is an apparent displacement of a vertical line in the direction opposite to that of the rotation of the body. This effect decays over a period of a minute or two and is replaced by the typical Müller or Aubert effect. Presumably the transitory effect is due to the postrotary deflection of the cupula. The magnitude and duration of the transitory illusion are least if the head is brought to rest in a vertical position, where the otolith organs most effectively restrain the canal influences from exerting their effects, and greatest when the head is brought to rest at an angle of 150°, where the otolith organs are least effective (Udo de Haes & Schöne, 1970). Similar factors probably account for the fact that the Aubert effect is more prominent when the head is tilted rapidly, rather than slowly (Stockwell & Guedry, 1970). The vestibular canal inputs would of course be stronger when the head rotates more rapidly, and the transitory illusion of tilt would enhance the Aubert illusion, because the two are in the same direction.

Care must also be taken to ensure that subjects understand that they must set the test line to the apparent vertical and not parallel to the midbody axis (Wade, 1970b). Effects are greater with some psychophysical procedures than with others (Wade, 1970a).

Similar apparent inclinations of a vertical line occur in the median plane of the head as the head is inclined backward (Ebenholtz, 1970), and there is evidence that illusory tilts produced by a sideways rotation of the head are independent of illusory inclinations produced by a backward rotation of the head (Wade, 1972)

The *variability* of estimates of the vertical also increases with increasing tilt of the whole body (Miller et al., 1965). This increase in variability is presumably related to the decrease in the sensitivity of the utricles with increasing tilt of the head, and it probably accounts for the fluctuations observed in the apparent orientation of a luminous line when the head is held in a tilted position (Aubert, 1861; Miller & Graybiel, 1963).

It was suggested in Section 3.3.2 that visual stimuli in the peripheral visual field are more potent cues to headcentric orientation than are stimuli confined to the center of the visual field. One would therefore expect head tilt to affect peripherally placed lines less than it affects centrally placed lines. Nobody has made this direct comparison, keeping the length of the line constant, but it has been reported that a line subtending 40° of visual angle produces a smaller Müller effect than one subtending only 7° (Wade, 1969b). Other evidence in support of this view comes from an experiment by Wallach and Bacon (1976). They found that a radial pattern of lines confined to the peripheral visual field had to be rotated in excess of 5% of the angle of head tilt for its motion in the same direction to be noticed, whereas a pattern confined to the central few degrees of the visual field had to rotate in excess of 18% of the angle of head tilt before its motion was noticed. Both these ratios of undetected motion are equivalent in direction to the Müller effect and support the notion that this effect is smaller with stimuli confined to the visual periphery.

The fact that the function relating the magnitude of the two effects to the degree of body tilt resembles a sine function prompted Schöne (1962) to suggest that the illusions are related to the shearing force acting on the utricular surface, which is also a sine function of body tilt. However, utricular shear cannot be the only factor because, as we shall see in Section 5.7.5, Aubert and Müller illusions are present in people with loss of vestibular function.

Several factors may contribute to these illusions, including (1) countertorsion of the eyes, (2) changes in vestibular inputs, particularly those from the otolith organs, (3) changes in somesthetic inputs arising from contact between the body and surfaces that support it, and (4) changes in kinesthetic inputs from the joints and musculature of the legs, back, and neck. Experiments have been done to disentangle the contributions of these various factors to the visual perception of the vertical and are reviewed briefly in the following sections.

5.7.2. Eye Torsion and the Visual Vertical. When the head is in a tilted position, the eyes are counterrotated with respect to the head, so that the normally vertical meridians of the eyes do not tilt as far as the head. This counterrotation is about 10% of the angle of head tilt (see Section 2.6). If the system failed to take this countertorsion into account, the resulting error would be in the same direction as the Müller effect. However, Udo de Haes (1970) could find no relationship between the variability of judgments of the vertical and the intensity and duration of postrotary torsional nystagmus. Merker and Held (1981) used a line that subtended 2° of visual angle and found no consistent relationship between static eye torsion and the amount or the variability of the apparent angular displacement of the line as the head tilted. U. Brandt and Fluur (1967a) found no consistent relationship between the apparent tilt of a line and the direction of the resultant gravitionertial force. Furthermore, the Müller effect has been found in people whose eyes do not undergo a torsion because of vestibular malfunction (Miller, Fregly, Graybiel, 1968). The fact that countertorsion has no consistent effect on the apparent vertical suggests that it is normally allowed for. Balliet and Nakayama (1978b) found that voluntarily induced eye torsion was accompanied by a corresponding shift in the apparent vertical, so that not all types of torsion are allowed for.

5.7.3. The Visual Vertical under Water. All cues to the vertical, other than those provided by the otoliths, may be eliminated by suspending a person in water in a state of neutral buoyancy. Care must be taken to exclude extraneous cues to the vertical, such as visual cues, thermal gradients, and air bubbles. Comparison of submerged subjects' ability to set a luminous line to the vertical, with their ability when seated in a chair in air, should indicate the contribution that tactile cues make to the perception of the visual vertical. Early experiments of this type were unsatisfactory because subjects were tested just after they had been rotated several times and before rotational aftereffects had subsided (J. L. Brown, 1961). Recent investigations have shown that the precision and accuracy of setting a line to the vertical under water are much the same as in air for body tilts of up to 90°. Beyond 90° the variability of settings becomes relatively larger, reaching a maximum value when subjects are in the upside-down position (Ross, Crickmar, Sills, & Owen, 1969; Schöne, 1964; Wade, 1973).

The general conclusion from experiments on immersion is that the somesthetic senses contribute little to the accuracy or precision of judgments of the visual vertical for small angles of body tilt but supplement the otolith organs at larger angles of tilt, where the sensitivity of the otolith organs is diminished.

5.7.4. The Visual Vertical under Weightless Conditions. A person falling freely within a gravitational field, as, for instance, in a spacecraft orbiting the earth, is said to be weightless. In such conditions changes in the attitude of the body produce no persisting changes in any sense organ. One is aware only of changes in the relative positions of body parts. The otolith organs still respond if the person is accelerated along a straight path, and the vestibular canals respond to rotary acceleration. In weightless conditions the notion of gravitational vertical is meaningless, although if the inside of the spacecraft is in view, the occupants usually regard the surface nearest to their feet as "down," and this impression is reinforced if familiar, normally erect objects are appropriately oriented with respect to the "floor." If the astronaut is strapped into a seat, contact cues will provide a frame of reference for "vertical," even in the dark (Lackner & Graybiel, 1983).

Subjects exposed to weightlessness for 8 days in the Gemini space flights were asked to set a line of light in dark surroundings to be parallel to a remembered feature of a control panel in front of them. This task was performed just as precisely and accurately under weightless conditions as it was under normal gravity conditions, and it was concluded that lifting the gravitational load from the otolith organs did not result in a disturbance of the perceived direction of space (Graybiel, Miller, Billingham, Waite, Berry, & Deitlein, 1967). But the subjects remained in the same position while being tested, so that they could succeed simply by setting the visible line parallel to the z axis of the body, a task that does not depend on the otolith organs or on tactile cues. A more informative procedure would be one in which weightless subjects are asked to set a line to a remembered external reference when the direction of application of contact cues is varied. For instance, a subject could be secured with cushioned straps against a hard board so that tactile cues are localized along one surface of the body. In one condition subjects could be positioned at each of several angles with respect to the board and in each case asked to orient a visual line with respect to the board. This would test their ability to orient a visual object with respect to the direction of application of tactile stimuli. In another condition the subjects and board could be rotated together, and the subjects asked to set the visual line to its original position in space. This would test subjects' ability to judge the extent and direction of their movement on the basis of inputs from the vestibular canals, with somesthetic inputs held constant.

Under normal conditions of gravity, supporting a person with cushions that weaken tactile cues has been found not to affect the precision of judgments of the visual vertical. However, for subjects tilted 28° the provision of localized tactile contact with a hard surface has been found to improve the precision of judgments (Nysborg, 1971). Lechner-Steinleitner (1978) found that for subjects strapped to a bed, the orientation of the bed became the factor determining the precision of judgments of the visual vertical only when the bed was tilted 90° or more. It was concluded that performance was limited by inputs from the otolith organs for smaller angles of body tilt but that as the reliability of these inputs declined at higher tilt angles, the performance became limited by somesthetic inputs (see also Schöne & Udo de Haes, 1968).

Soviet cosmonauts and American astronauts had a sensation of being upside-down when they closed their eyes while exposed to the weightlessness conditions of orbital flight. The Soviets reported that the illusion was dispelled if they pushed themselves against the surface of their chairs. This phenomenon has been called the *inversion illusion*, although, in weightless conditions, it is no more an illusion to believe that you are upside-down than it is to believe that you are right-side up. Labyrinthine-defective subjects do not experience this illusion when exposed to conditions similar to those that give rise to it in normal subjects (Graybiel & Kellogg, 1967). In the upside-down position on earth the discharge from the utricles is at a minimum, and it is probably the association between this position and reduced utricular activity that causes subjects to interpret an absence of utricular inputs as signifying that they are upside-down.

5.7.5. Vestibular Loss and the Visual Vertical. The only way to eliminate the contribution of the vestibular organs to the perception of the visual vertical is to use subjects with bilateral loss of vestibular function. One must be alert to the possible presence of residual function, and patients with recent vestibular loss should not be used, because they will be subject to transitory disturbances during the period of recovery. At the same time, subjects with a long-standing loss will probably have learned to use their other senses in a way that is not typical of normal subjects.

As we saw in Section 1.2.4 people with loss of vestibular function have no difficulty balancing or orienting themselves when they can see their surroundings. Their constant and variable errors in setting a luminous line to the horizontal have been found to be similar to those of normal people when the body is maintained in an active standing posture, either erect or with the head, or head and trunk, tilted up to 20° (Clark & Graybiel, 1967). The kinesthetic and motor activity associated with actively maintained posture and the differential pressure on the feet allow both groups of subjects to judge the visual vertical accurately and precisely.

Both normal and labyrinthine-defective subjects have been found to show a Müller effect for up to about 60° of body tilt and an Aubert effect at larger angles of tilt, when passively tilted in a chair. However, the defective subjects showed larger illusory effects, and the variability of their settings increased with increasing body tilt at a faster rate than that of normal subjects (Miller, Fregly, & Graybiel, 1968).

5.7.6. The Visual Vertical in the Human Centrifuge—The Oculogravic Illusion. A human centrifuge is a device that rotates at various speeds about a vertical axis and carries a small cabin within which a person can be strapped in various postures. The cabin, which is usually between 5 and 10 m from the center of rotation, may be held in a fixed orientation or allowed to swing out so as to remain in line with the resultant force as the centrifuge speeds up. The centrifugal force per unit mass acting on a subject at distance r from the center of rotation of a centrifuge, rotating at an angular velocity ω, is given by $\omega^2 r$. This force and the force of gravity g_n form a resultant gravitoinertial force per unit mass of $[(\omega^2 r)^2 + g_n^2]^{1/2}$, which acts at an angle with respect to the vertical, where $\theta = \arctan \omega^2 r/g_n$.

Spinning a human being in a centrifuge has seven main effects on the sense organs.

1. It displaces the direction of the force acting on the body, unless the cabin is hinged so that it is free to align itself and the subject with the direction of the resultant force.
2. It increases the magnitude of the force acting on the body.
3. As the centrifuge changes its angular velocity, the otolith organs and somesthetic senses are stimulated as if the body were being tilted, but the vestibular canals do not register a rotation of the head in the same plane as the apparent tilt, as they would if the body were really being tilted.
4. The centrifuge rotates the subject about a body axis parallel to the axis of rotation of the centrifuge.

5. It produces a gradient in the direction and magnitude of the force acting on the body. Thus if a subject faces in the direction of motion, the utricles are stimulated unequally.
6. A subject moving with velocity v, with respect to the rotating surface of the centrifuge, is subjected to a Coriolis force that varies in magnitude and direction according to the angle θ between the rotation vector of the centrifuge ω and the v vector. The magnitude of this force acting on each point of an object moving with respect to a centrifuge is given by

$$F_c = 2\omega v \sin\theta$$

and its direction is given by the rule for vector cross products. Figure 18.36 illustrates the directions of the Coriolis forces to which a "small" person would be exposed when moving within a "large" rotating cylinder. These effects are critical factors in the design of artificial gravitational fields in rotating spacecraft.
7. If a person rotates the head about any axis other than one parallel to the axis of rotation of the centrifuge, each point of the head is subjected to a Coriolis force of magnitude $2\omega v \sin\theta$. If these forces are integrated, the net effect is that the head is subjected to a rotary force at right angles to the two applied rotations. This effect is known as *precession*, or *rotational cross coupling*. It is also referred to as the Coriolis effect because ultimately that is what it depends on.

The most convenient and least contaminated procedure for studying the effects of changing the direction of the force acting on the body is simply to tilt a person (Howard & Templeton, 1963). Effects in item 4 are equivalent to those produced by simply rotating a person, and these have been discussed. Effects

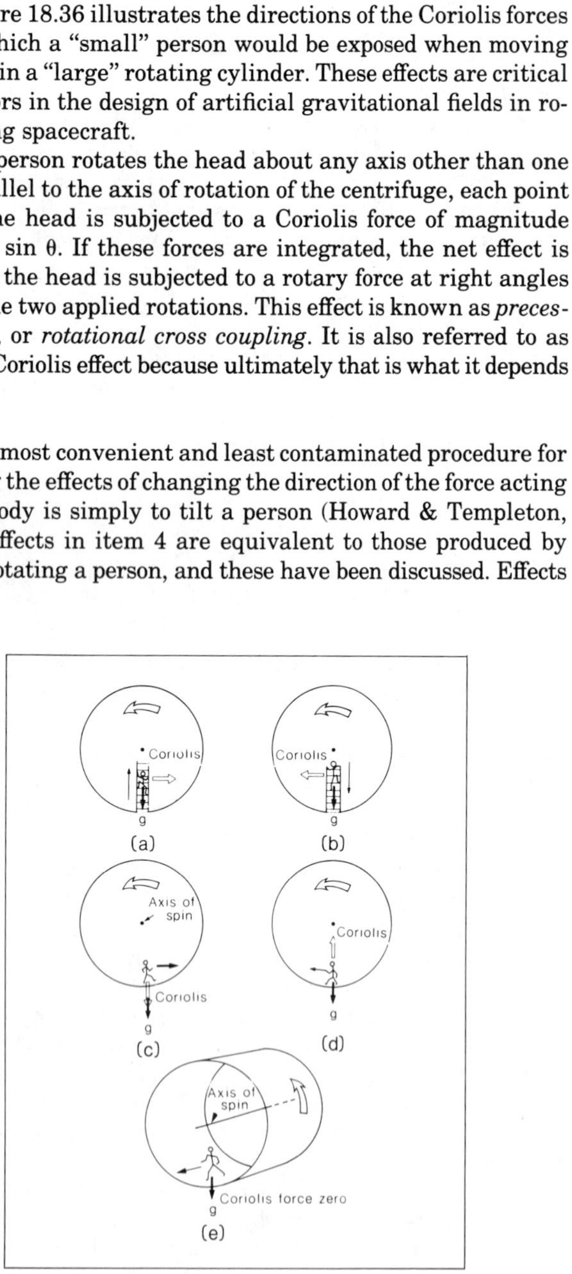

Figure 18.36. Diagrammatic representation of the direction of the Coriolis force acting on a person moving in various directions with respect to the axis of rotation of a cylinder. Moving (a) toward the axis of rotation of the cylinder, (b) away from the axis, (c) with the spin of the cylinder, (d) against the spin of the cylinder, and (e) parallel to the axis of rotation. (Adapted from Loret, 1961, fig. 6.)

in items 5, 6, and 7 have been studied in subjects living in the slow rotating room and were mentioned briefly in Section 4.3. I now discuss effects listed in items 1, 2, and 3.

5.7.6.1. **Displacing the Direction of Gravitoinertial Force.** It is a cornerstone of Einstein's theory of relativity that inertial and gravitational forces are indistinguishable. It follows from this that when subjects are rotated in a centrifuge at a steady velocity in the dark, they have no option but to regard the direction of the resultant gravitoinertial force as vertical. If we disregard the fact that the resultant force is larger than g and consider only the static situation, a gravitoinertial force that is displaced $\theta°$ relative to a person's upright body has the same effect on the sense organs as a normal gravitational force acting on the body when it is tilted through the same angle. Mach first formulated this proposition in 1875, and it has come to be known as *Mach's hypothesis*. An upright subject facing toward the center of a centrifuge, which has been rotating at a steady velocity for some time, experiences a backward inclination of the body, produced by the change in the shearing force acting on the utricles, and an equivalent apparent elevation of a point of light at eye level (M. M. Cohen, 1973; Schöne, 1964). A subject facing in the direction of rotation of the centrifuge experiences a tilt of the body and an equivalent apparent tilt of a vertical or horizontal luminous line positioned in the frontal plane (Clark & Graybiel, 1951; Schöne, 1964). Illusions of visual movement, displacement or tilt, experienced as a result of a change in the direction and magnitude of the gravitoinertial force produced by a linear acceleration of the body are called *oculogravic illusions* (Graybiel, 1952). The oculogravic illusions just described are not illusions when considered from the subject's point of view. The point *is* elevated and the line *is* tilted relative to the subject's gravitoinertial frame, and that is the judgment that the subject is asked to make. I shall refer to this form of the oculogyral illusion as the trivial form of the illusion. An oculogravic illusion would be nontrivial only if the apparent vertical position of the line were *not* reported to be parallel to the resultant direction of the gravitoinertial force. One would expect a person tilted with respect to a resultant force to be subject to Aubert and Müller illusions, as are subjects tilted to a normal gravitational field. A nontrivial oculogravic illusion is one uniquely determined by linear acceleration of the body, and that does not occur when the body is tilted. I shall now look at the evidence that such illusions exist.

5.7.6.2. **Increasing the Magnitude of the Resultant Gravitoinertial Force.** Assume that the centrifugal force is $1g_n$, so that the resultant force of $\sqrt{2}g_n$ acts at an angle of 45° to the utricular maculae of a subject facing in the direction of rotation. Bearing in mind that the shearing force on the utricles is proportional to $\sin\theta$, where θ is the angle between the force and the normal to the macula, then a force of $\sqrt{2}g_n$ acting at an angle of 45° to the macular surface is equivalent to a shearing force of $1g_n$ acting at an angle whose sine is $\sqrt{2}\sin 45°$. This angle is 90°. Similar calculations show that when the resultant force is displaced to 20 or 30°, the shearing forces are equivalent to those produced by tilting the body 21.3 and 35° deg, respectively. Thus it is not until the resultant force is displaced more than about 30° that the deviation from Mach's hypothesis on account of the magnitude factor can be expected to be significant. If the subject's utricular maculae are kept normal to the direction of the resultant force, then increasing the force should have no effect on the utricles and hence no effect on the apparent tilt of the body. The increased force will affect the saccular macula under these circumstances, but this should induce a sensation of being in a rising elevator, rather than a sensation of tilt. Under these circumstances subjects experience an apparent elevation of a visual object, an effect known as the *elevator illusion* (Whiteside, 1961). When the utricular maculae are not normal to the resultant force, increasing the magnitude of the resultant force should increase the shearing force and induce an impression of increasing body tilt. The results of studies by Miller and Graybiel (1966) and Wade and Schöne (1971) are in approximate agreement with this analysis. In these studies, the resultant force, although well over $1g_n$, was not large enough to produce a shearing of the maculae beyond the normal limit of $1g_n$ acting at 90° to the macula surface. In other studies, in which supernormal shearing of the maculae was induced, it was found that increases beyond the normal limit did not produce impressions of increased body tilt or visual tilt (Schöne, Parker, & Mortag, 1967; Schöne & Wade, 1971). It looks as though a force of $1g_n$ acting at 90° to the macula is the saturation point for impressions of body tilt. This is not surprising, because body tilts of more than 90° produce *less* deflection of the maculae than a 90° tilt, so that deflections in excess of those produced by $1g_n$ acting at 90° should not be interpreted as due to a tilt of the body of more than 90°. Correia, Hixson, and Niven (1968) plotted the apparent tilt of a visual line as a function of the tangent of the resultant force and got a better fit for normal and supernormal stimulus strengths than by plotting apparent tilt against its sine. Compression forces are related to the tangent of the resultant force, so that this finding suggests that compression forces come into play with higher *g* forces, although a precise mechanism was not presented.

With the body at a given angle to the resultant force, an increase in the force does not alter its direction of application on the surface of the body. The tactile and kinesthetic sensations should therefore not induce a change in the apparent tilt of the body. However, tactile and kinesthetic inputs should be enhanced, and this should perhaps lead to a more veridical appreciation of the angle at which the resultant force is acting on the body. On the other hand, the muscular effort required to maintain the body in its posture will increase with increasing magnitude of the resultant force, and this should give rise to the impression of increased body tilt. There seem to be no experimental data bearing on these points.

5.7.6.3. Conflicting Cues of Rotation and Tilt. In the centrifuge, "tilt" information from the utricles is contradicted by the absence of the canal inputs that normally accompany a real head tilt. The impression of tilt should therefore be less in the centrifuge than when a person is being tilted in a chair. Furthermore, the cupulae do not return to their central position until several seconds after the head has been tilted, so that the absence of cupula displacement in the centrifuge should delay the impression of body tilt for some time after the machine has reached a steady velocity. The lower curve in Figure 18.37 shows the gradual shift in the apparent visual vertical that occurs when a centrifuge is accelerated so as to displace the gravitoinertial force through 30° (Clark & Graybiel, 1966a). It can be seen that it takes between 60 and 80 sec before the apparent vertical comes to lie close to the direction of the displaced force. The upper curve in Figure 18.37 shows that when subjects were actually tilted through 30° in a padded chair, the apparent vertical was almost immediately close to the gravitational vertical. The delay in the centrifuge case is due to signals from the vestibular canals that inform subjects that they are not tilting. This restraining influence decays after the new steady state is reached, with a time course that matches the decay of

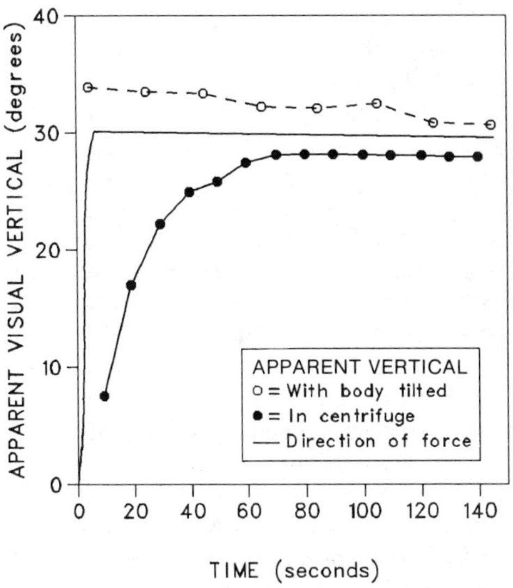

Figure 18.37. The mean position of the apparent visual vertical, with respect to the body axis for various angles of sideways body tilt (top curve) and for various directions of gravitoinertial force imposed in a centrifuge (lower curve). The middle curve shows the actual direction of the force acting on the body in both cases. The change in the apparent vertical is more gradual in the centrifuge than when the body is tilted, which is probably due to the absence of signals from the vestibular canals in the centrifuge. This absence of signals informs subjects that they are not actually tilting. (From C. W. Stockwell & F. E. Guedry, The effect of semicircular canal stimulation during tilting on the subsequent perception of the visual vertical, *Acta Ololaryngologica*, 1970, *70*. Reprinted with permission.)

postrotary vestibular responses (Stockwell & Guedry, 1970).

When a person is oscillated back and forth along a linear path, the illusory changes in body tilt and in the visual vertical are much less than when the same otolith shear is produced by actually tilting the person (Niven, Hixson, & Correia, 1966; Schöne & Mortag, 1968). In this case, also, otolith stimulation is not accompanied by changes in canal stimulation that accompany body tilt, so that the subject should be predisposed to experience linear motion, rather than body tilt. With continued linear acceleration in one direction, the signals from the otolith organs become ambiguous. It has often been reported that when an aircraft is accelerated in clouds, the pilot may interpret signals from the otolith organs as being due to an upward pitch of the aircraft and may turn the nose of the plane down in an effort to correct its altitude, only to drive the plane into the ground.

Subjects sitting sideways in an aircraft accelerated so that the gravitoinertial force was displaced 28° were found to experience a displacement of the visual vertical of only about 16° (Graybiel, Johnson, Money, Malcolm, & Jennings, 1979). If the aircraft accelerated for longer than 25 sec, the visual vertical would presumably have been displaced to a greater extent. Graybiel and colleagues (1979) reported that the subjects in this experiment experienced an apparent *headcentric* rotation of the vertical line as they were accelerated, although the only data they provide refer to the apparent orientation of the line relative to the *subjective vertical*. Furthermore, we are not told to what extent subjects experienced an apparent tilt of the body, so that we cannot tell from these data whether the apparent vertical orientation of body and line remained congruent. To establish quantitatively that linear acceleration produces an apparent headcentric shift in the orientation of a line, over and above any effect that might occur when a subject is tilted, would require an experiment in which subjects are asked to set a luminous line parallel to the *z* body axis under each of these two conditions. However, the subjects in the study by Graybiel and colleagues (1979) may have been making headcentric judgments, because they unequivocally reported a headcentric motion of the vertical line in the centrifuge but not when tilted.

The only forms of the oculogravic illusion for which we have quantitative evidence are (1) the trivial form of the illusion produced both by accelerating people and tilting them through an equivalent angle, (2) effects due to increasing the magnitude of the gravitoinertial force, and (3) the delay in shifts of the apparent vertical position of a line or the apparent elevation of a point, which occurs in the centrifuge and which seems to be due to the absence of relevant rotary stimulation. In all these effects the apparent orientation of the body and the visual line should be the same. In other words, these illusions do not imply any shift in the apparent headcentric orientation of the visual line. The headcentric shifts that the subjects in the study by Graybiel and colleagues (1979) reported would be analogous to the purely visual form of the oculogyral illusion induced by rotary acceleration. In Sections 3.2 and 3.3.3 this and similar effects were explained in terms of a direct effect of vestibular inputs on cells in the vestibular nuclei, which also receive visual inputs.

At various places in this chapter and in Chapter 10, "The Vestibular System," I have described illusions associated with stimulation of the otolith organs and vestibular canals. The effects are listed in Tables 18.2 and 18.3, in which the numbers in brackets indicate the sections of this chapter where each effect is described.

Table 18.2. Illusory Sensations Associated with Stimulation of the Otolith Organs[a]

Name or Description	Inducing Conditions
Illusory tilt	Linear acceleration is interpreted as tilt of the body. Affects pilots in accelerating aircraft. (2.2)
Unperceived tilt	A pilot in a banked turn fails to feel the tilt of the aircraft because his or her body is aligned with the resultant gravitoinertial force. (2.5.1)
Oculogravic illusion	Changes in the direction and magnitude of gravitoinertial force produce apparent displacement of visual objects. (5.7.6)
Elevator illusion	Changes in the magnitude of gravitoinertial force produce apparent elevation or depression of visual objects. (5.7.6)
Inversion illusion	Subjects in zero-gravity conditions or in a prone posture may experience sensation of being upside-down. (5.7.4)
Coriolis effects of linear motion in rotating field	Subjects moving toward or away from center of rotating vehicle experience tangential displacement of gravitoinertial force. (2.5)
Aubert effect	Apparent tilt of a line in opposite direction to body tilt. (5.7.1)
Müller effect	Apparent tilt of a line in same direction as body tilt. (5.7.1)

[a]Numbers in parentheses refer to the section of this chapter where each illusion is discussed.

Table 18.3. Illusory Sensations Associated with Stimulation of the Vestibular Canals[a]

Name or Description	Characteristics
Unperceived constant velocity	Rotation of constant velocity is undetected by the vestibular system. (3.2)
Postrotary sensations	Deceleration produces sensations of turning. (2.3.3)
Negative	An initial sensation in the opposite direction to the inducing rotation. Due to persisting mechanical and neural effects of deceleration and lasting about 30 sec.
Postitive	A subsequent sensation in the same direction as the inducing rotation, due to recovery from vestibular adaptation.
Adaptation to constant acceleration	Decrease in effective strength of stimulation during period of maintained acceleration. (3.2)
Coriolis, or cross-coupling effects	Sensations of turning at right angles to two superimposed rotations of the head. (3.2)
Oculogyral illusion	Illusions of headcentric visual motion and displacement induced by rotation. (3.2)

[a]Numbers in parentheses refer to the section of this chapter where each illusion is discussed.

5.8. Key References

The earlier literature on the visual vertical was reviewed in Howard and Templeton (1966). More recent reviews are contained in chapters by Bischof (1974, pp. 155–190) and Lackner (1978, pp. 805–846) in the *Handbook of Sensory Physiology*. Several chapters of a recent book by Howard (1982) are devoted to the topics covered in this section.

6. VISUAL DIRECTION AND POSTURAL ASYMMETRY

6.1. Background

It is well known that the sense of position of a part of the body is affected when the part is held in an eccentric posture. Furthermore, the disturbed sense of position persists for some time after the body part has been restored to its normal posture. I shall discuss only those effects due to an eccentric posture of the head or eyes. An effect experienced while the eccentric posture is maintained is a *perdeviation effect*, and one experienced after the organ has been restored to a central position is a postdeviation effect, or *postural aftereffect*. Typically, the eccentrically positioned organ is experienced as being less eccentrically placed than it is, so that when it is returned to a central position, it feels as though it is displaced in the opposite direction, until the effect has worn off. In the absence of other factors it is to be predicted that in the case of the head and eyes, these postural effects will be accompanied by an equivalent apparent visual displacement. For instance, if the head feels elevated $x°$ when it is actually level, a light on the horizon should also appear to be elevated $x°$ above the horizon. Similarly, an apparent sideways rotation of the head about the z axis should be accompanied by an apparent displacement of a straight-ahead visual object in the same direction, and an apparent tilt of the head should be accompanied by an apparent tilt of a vertical line in the same direction. Note that whenever a vertical line appears tilted to the left, the position into which a line must be placed to appear vertical (the apparent vertical) is displaced to the right.

6.2. Posturally Induced Displacements of the Visual Horizon and Straight Ahead

MacDougall (1903) asked subjects to strain the eyes upward for a few seconds and then return them to a normal position and set a light, seen in dark surroundings, to eye level. It was found that the apparent eye level was displaced upward, which is the direction one would expect from a postural aftereffect. Straining the eyes downward had the opposite effect.

Several investigators have reported that when the head is inclined backward, the apparent eye level is higher than it is when the head is erect (MacDougall, 1903; Schubert & Brecher, 1934; Tschermak-Seysenegg, 1952, p. 214). This effect is what one would expect from adaptation of neck proprioceptors or of the utricles. MacDougall also found that a backward inclination of the whole body caused a 3° elevation of apparent eye level (see also U. Brandt & Fluur, 1967b). This effect could be due to adaptation of the utricles or of touch and pressure receptors in the skin.

The apparent visual straight ahead has been found to be shifted while the eyes are held in an eccentric position of lateral gaze. As one would predict from perdeviation postural adaptation, a light in dark surroundings, which is objectively straight ahead, appears displaced in the direction opposite to an eccentric position of gaze (Goldstein & Riese, 1923; Werner, Wapner, & Bruell, 1953). Figure 18.38 shows the magnitude of the displacement of the apparent straight-ahead position of a visual target while the eyes are fixated on a stimulus at various angles of eccentricity. It can be seen that the shift in the apparent straight ahead is a more or less linear function of the eccentricity of gaze, reaching a maximum of 6° at a deviation of gaze of 42° (Morgan, 1978). It has been established that this effect is due to the eccentric posture of the eyes, rather than to the eccentric position of the visual target (Hill, 1972). The effects of an eccentric posture of the eyes persist for some time after the eyes have been returned to the straight-ahead position (Craske, Crawshaw, & Heron, 1975; Park, 1969). The displacement of the apparent visual straight ahead, experienced just after the eyes have been restored from an eccentric position of gaze, increases as a function of the previous eccentricity of the eyes and of the period of time during which the eccentric position was maintained (see Figure 18.39). Furthermore, the visual aftereffect decays more rapidly after shorter periods of eccentric gaze (see Figure 18.40). The data displayed in Figure 18.40 also show that the initial visual aftereffect is followed by a second aftereffect of opposite sign. The secondary aftereffect did not show for the 8-min induction period but might have done so if testing had been continued beyond 4 min.

An eccentric posture of the head about the vertical axis leads to perdeviation and postdeviation effects analogous to those produced by a deviation of the eyes (Ebenholtz, 1976; Howard & Anstis, 1974; Shebilske & Fogelgren, 1977; Shebilske & Karmiohl, 1979). Holding the head straight against a moderate load has been found not to disturb the visual straight ahead, so that the aftereffects of head posture must be due to adaptation of proprioceptors, rather than to asymmetrical muscular tension (Howard & Anstis, 1974).

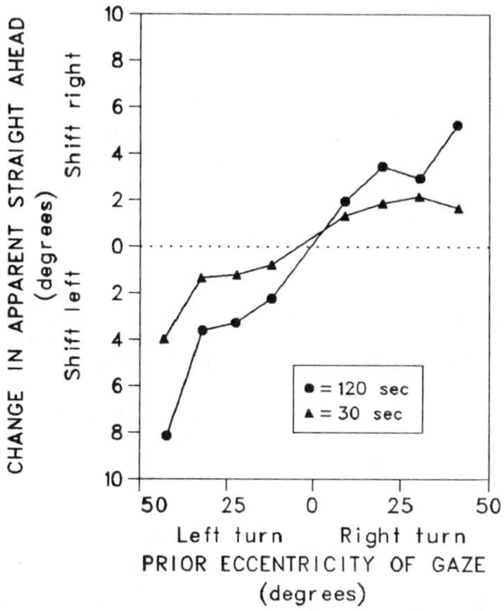

Figure 18.39. Changes in the apparent visual straight-ahead after holding the eyes at various angles of eccentricity for 30 and 120 sec. The change in the apparent straight ahead increases as a function of the magnitude and duration of the previous eccentricity of the eyes. (From K. R. Paap & S. M. Ebenholtz, Perceptual consequences of potentiation in the extraocular muscles: An alternative explanation for adaptation to wedge prisms, *Journal of Experimental Psychology: Human Perception and Performance, 2*. Copyright 1976 by American Psychological Association. Reprinted with permission.)

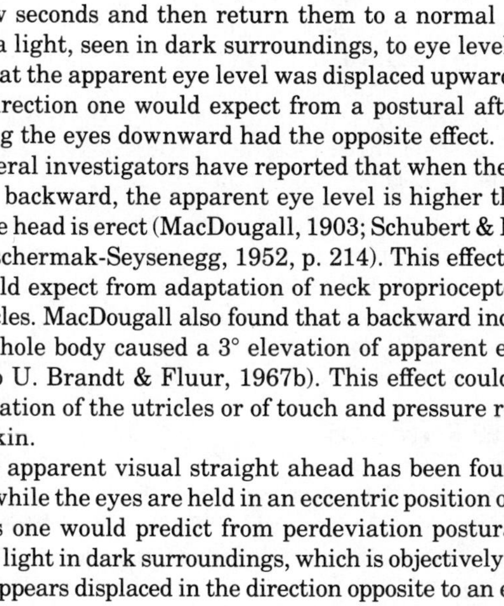

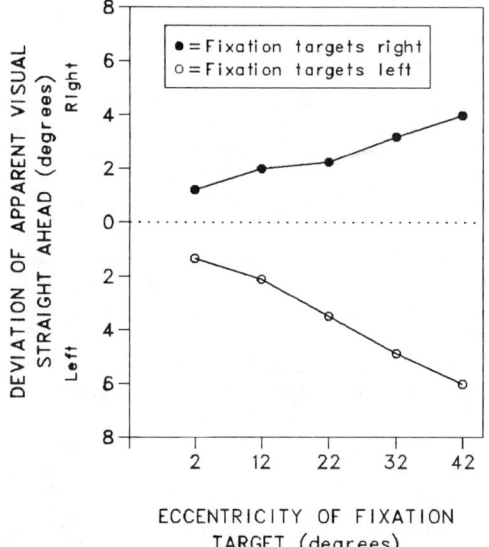

Figure 18.38. Deviation of the apparent visual straight ahead as a function of eccentricity of gaze. Data based on means of six subjects. The shift in the apparent straight ahead is approximately a linear function of the eccentricity of gaze. (From C. L. Morgan, Constancy of egocentric visual direction, *Perception and Psychophysics*, 1978, *23*. Reprinted with permission.)

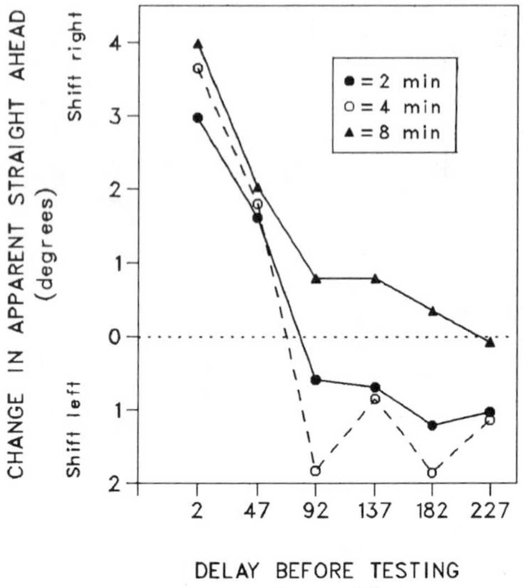

Figure 18.40. Progressive changes in the apparent straight ahead after holding the eys at an eccentricity of 32° right for various periods of time. The aftereffect declines more rapidly after shorter periods of eccentric gaze. A negative phase is evident for the shorter exposure periods. (From K. R. Paap & S. M. Ebenholtz, Perceptual consequences of potentiation in the extraocular muscles: An alternative explanation for adaptation to wedge prisms, *Journal of Experimental Psychology: Human Perception and Performance, 2*. Copyright 1976 by American Psychological Association. Reprinted with permission.)

6.3. Posturally Induced Displacements of the Visual Vertical

The perdeviation effects of a maintained sideways tilt of the head on the apparent vertical were discussed in Section 5.7.1. These effects are more complex than would be predicted on the basis of adaptation of sensory inputs that signal head position. One complicating factor is the presence of countertorsion of the eyes, although nobody has found a consistent relationship between countertorsion and apparent visual tilt (Fischer, 1930; Merker & Held, 1981; Miller, Fregly, & Graybiel, 1968; Udo de Haes, 1970).

The only information on the effects of a maintained torsion of the eyes on the apparent vertical comes from a study by Balliet and Nakayama (1978b), in which they found that voluntarily induced eye torsion was accompanied by a corresponding shift in the apparent vertical, an effect presumably due to the torsion not being allowed for in the visual judgment. But the effects of voluntary eye torsion may not be the same as those produced by involuntary torsion.

When the head has been returned to a vertical posture after being tilted for some time, the apparent vertical positions of the head and of a luminous line are displaced up to 6° in the direction of head tilt (Day & Wade, 1966). The size of the postural effect has been found to be about the same as the size of the visual effect for head tilts up to about 20°, but the size of the visual effect was found to exceed that of the postural effect for larger head tilts (Wade & Day, 1968a). The size of both effects depends on how long the head is held in the tilted position, and both decay exponentially after the head has been returned to its normal posture (Wade & Day, 1968b).

When subjects were asked to set a luminous line in dark surroundings to be parallel to the *z* body axis, the aftereffect of head tilt was much the same when the head was tilted, with the body erect, as it was when the head was inclined toward the shoulder, with the body in a supine posture. This suggests that the aftereffects are due to adaptation of proprioceptors in the neck, rather than to adaptation of the otolith organs. This cannot be their only cause because similar visual and postural aftereffects are also produced after the whole body has been held in a tilted posture (Clark & Graybiel, 1963; Schöne & Lechner-Steinleitner, 1978). These whole-body aftereffects are presumably due to adaptation of somesthetic receptors. That these receptors, rather than the otolith organs, are involved is supported by the following evidence:

1. Subjects with defective labyrinths show larger aftereffects than do normal subjects (Clark & Graybiel, 1966b).
2. The effects are least when the whole body is vertical, that is, in the posture where otolith organs are most sensitive, and greatest at angles of tilt of 90° or more, where the otolith organs are least sensitive.
3. With the posture of the head held constant, the effects are larger when the trunk is erect and the somesthetic receptors are more heavily stimulated than when the trunk is prone and the somesthetic receptors are less heavily stimulated (Schöne & Lechner-Steinleitner, 1978).

It may be concluded that the visual vertical is affected by adaptation of proprioceptors in the neck and by adaptation of somesthetic receptors. Golgi tendon organs and ligament receptors are known to adapt when subjected to steady tension (Ferrell, 1980; Houk, 1967), and there is no shortage of physiological evidence that somesthetic receptors adapt.

6.4. Key References

The literature of the topics covered in the last section of this chapter is reviewed in Howard (1982). The physiological background to proprioception is reviewed in Granit (1966), Matthews (1972), Yahr and Purpura (1967), and in Howard, Chapter 11, "The Vestibular System."

REFERENCES

* References preceded by an asterisk are "key references."

Abrahams, V. C. The physiology of neck muscles; Their role in head movement and maintenance of posture. *Canadian Journal of Physiology & Pharmacology*, 1977, *55*, 332–338.

Abrahams, V. C., Richmond, F., & Rose, P. K. Absence of monosynaptic reflex in dorsal neck muscles of the cat. *Brain Research*, 1975, *92*, 130–131.

Abrahams, V. C., & Rose, P. K. Projections of extraocular, neck muscle, and retinal afferents to superior colliculus in the cat: Their connection to cells of origin of tectospinal track. *Journal of Neurophysiology*, 1975, *38*, 10–18.

Abzug, C., Maeda, M., Peterson, B. W., & Wilson, V. J. Cervical branching of lumbar vestibulospinal axons. *Journal of Physiology*, 1974, *243*, 499–522.

Adolfson, J., Bjerver, K., Fluur, E., & Goldberg, L. Balance disturbance in man at 10 ATA ambient air pressure. *Försvarsmedicin*, 1974, *10*, 148–156.

Akaike, T., Fanardjian, V. V., Ito, M., & Nakajima, H. Cerebellar control of the vestibulospinal tract cells in rabbit. *Experimental Brain Research*, 1973, *18*, 446–463.

Akaike, T., Fanardjian, V. V., Ito, M., & Ohno, T. Electrophysiological analysis of the vestibulospinal reflex pathway of rabbit. II. Synaptic actions upon spinal neurones. *Experimental Brain Research*, 1973, *17*, 497–515.

Altshuler, K. Z. Studies of the deaf: Relevance to psychiatric theory. *American Journal of Psychiatry*, 1971, *127*, 1521–1526.

Amblard, B., & Carblanc, A. Role of foveal and peripheral visual information in maintenance of postural equilibrium in man. *Perceptual & Motor Skills*, 1980, *51*, 903–912.

Amblard, B., & Cremieux, J. Rôle de l'information visuelle du mouvement dans le maintien de l' équilibre. *Aggressologie*, 1976, *17c*, 25–37.

Anastasopoulos, D., & Mergner, T. Canal-neck interaction in vestibular nucleus of the cat. *Experimental Brain Research*, 1982, *46*, 269–280.

Anderson, J. H., & Precht, W. Otolith responses of extraocular muscles during sinusoidal roll rotations. *Brain Research*, 1979, *160*, 150–154.

Anderson, M. E., Yoshida, M., & Wilson, V. J. Tectal and tegmental influences on cat forelimb and hindlimb motoneurons. *Journal of Neurophysiology*, 1972, *35*, 463–470.

Andrews, D. P. Perception of contour orientation in the central fovea. Part I: Short lines. *Vision Research*, 1967, *7*, 975–997. (a)

Andrews, D. P. Perception of contour orientation in the central fovea. Part II. Spatial integration. *Vision Research*, 1967, *7*, 999–1013. (b)

Asch, S. E., & Witkin, H. A. Studies in space orientation: II. Perception of the upright with displaced visual fields and with body tilted. *Journal of Experimental Psychology*, 1948, *38*, 455–477.

Aubert, H. Eine scheinbare bedeutende Drehung von Objekten bei Neigung des Kopfes nach rechts oder links. *Virchows Archives*, 1861, *20*, 381–393.

Azzena, G. B. Role of the spinal cord in compensating the effects of hemilabyrinthectomy. *Archives of Italian Biology*, 1969, *107*, 43–53.

Baker, J., Gibson, A., Glickstein, M., & Stein, J. Visual cells in the pontine nuclei of the cat. *Journal of Physiology*, 1976, *255*, 415–433.

Balliet, R., & Nakayama, K. Egocentric orientation is influenced by trained voluntary cyclorotory movements. *Nature, New Biology*, 1978, *275*, 214–216. (a)

Balliet, R. & Nakayama, K. Training of voluntary torsion. *Investigative Opthalmology*, 1978, *17*, 303–314. (b)

Barber, H. O., & Wright, G. Positional nystagmus in normals. *Advances in Oto-Rhino-Laryngology*, 1973, *19*, 276–285.

Barlow, D., & Freedman, W. Cervico-ocular reflex in the normal adult. *Acta Otolaryngologica*, 1980, *89*, 487–496.

Barmack, N. H., Nastos, M. A., & Petterossi, V. E. The horizontal and vertical cervico-ocular reflexes of the rabbit. *Brain Research*, 1981, *224*, 261–278.

Barnes, G. R. Vestibulo-ocular function during coordinated head and eye movements to acquire visual targets. *Journal of Physiology*, 1979, *287*, 127–147.

*Barnes, G. R. Vestibular control of oculomotor and postural mechanisms. *Clinical Physics and Physiological Measurement*, 1980, *1*, 3–40.

Barnes, G. R. The effects of retinal location and strobe rate of head-fixed visual targets on suppression of vestibular nystagmus. In A. Roucoux (Ed.), *Physiological and pathological aspects of eye movements*. The Hague: W. S. Junk, 1982.

Barnes, G. R., Benson, A. J., & Prior, A. R. J. Visual vestibular interaction in the control of eye movement. *Aviation, Space & Environmental Medicine*, 1978, *49*, 557–564.

Barnes, G. R., & Edge, A. The effects of strobe rate of head-fixed visual targets on suppression of vestibular nystagmus. *Experimental Brain Research*, 1983, *50*, 228–236.

Barnes, G. R., & Forbat, L. N. Cervical and vestibular afferent control of oculomotor responses in man. *Acta Otolaryngologica*, 1979, *88*, 79–87.

Barr, C. C., Schultheis, L. W., & Robinson, D. A. Voluntary non-visual control of the human vestibulo-ocular reflex. *Acta Otolaryngologica*, 1976, *81*, 365–375.

Bauermeister, M. Effect of body tilt on apparent verticality, apparent body position, and their relation. *Journal of Experimental Psychology*, 1964, *67*, 142–147.

Beh, H. C., & Wenderoth, P. M. The effect of variation of frame shape on the angular function of the rod-and-frame illusion. *Perception and Psychophysics*, 1972, *11*, 35–38.

Beh, H., Wenderoth, P. M., & Purcell, A. T. The angular function of a rod-and-frame illusion. *Perception and Psychophysics*, 1971, *9*, 353–355.

Bensel, C. K., & Dzendolet, E. Power spectral density analysis of the standing sway of males. *Perception and Psychophysics*, 1968, *4*, 285–288.

Benson, A. J. Lateral eye movements produced by a rotating linear acceleration vector. *Journal of Physiology*, 1968, *197*, 85–86P.

Benson, A. J. Interactions between semicircular canals and gravireceptors. In D. E. Busby (Ed.), *Recent advances in aerospace medicine*. Dordrecht, Holland: Reidel, 1970.

Benson, A. J., & Barnes, G. R. Responses to linear acceleration vectors considered in relation to a model of the otolith organs. In *5th Symposium on the Role of the Vestibular Organs in Space Exploration*. Washington, D.C.: NASA SP-314, 1973.

Benson, A. J., & Barnes, G. R. Vision during angular oscillation: The dynamic interaction of visual and vestibular mechanisms. *Aviation, Space & Environmental Medicine*, 1978, *49*, 340–345.

Benson, A. J., & Bodin, M. A. Effect of orientation to the gravitational vertical on nystagmus following rotation about a horizontal axis. *Acta Otolaryngologica*, 1966, *61*, 515–526. (a)

Benson, A. J., & Bodin, M. A. Interaction of linear and angular acceleration on vestibular receptors in man. *Aerospace Medicine*, 1966, *37*, 144–154. (b)

Benson, A. J., & Guedry, F. E. Comparison of tracking-task performance and nystagmus during sinusoidal oscillation in yaw and pitch. *Aerospace Medicine*, 1971, *42*, 593–601.

Benson, A. J., Guedry, F. E., & Melvill Jones, G. Responses of semicircular canal dependent units in vestibular nuclei to rotation of a linear acceleration vector without angular acceleration. *Journal of Physiology*, 1970, *210*, 475–494.

Bergstedt, M. Studies of positional nystagmus in the human centrifuge. *Acta Otolaryngologica*, 1961, *Suppl. 165*, 1–144.

Berthoz, A., Baker, R., & Goldberg, A. Neuronal activity underlying vestibular nystagmus in the oblique oculomotor system of the cat. *Brain Research*, 1974, *71*, 233–238.

Berthoz, A., Baker, R., & Precht, W. Labyrinthine control of inferior oblique motoneurons. *Experimental Brain Research*, 1973, *18*, 225–241.

Berthoz, A., Melvill Jones, G., & Bégué, A. E. Differential visual adaptation of vertical canal-dependent vestibulo-ocular reflexes. *Experimental Brain Research*, 1981, *44*, 19–26.

Berthoz, A., Pavard, B., & Young, L. R. Perception of linear horizontal self-motion induced by peripheral vision (linear vection): Basic characteristics and visual-vestibular interactions. *Experimental Brain Research*, 1975, *23*, 471–489.

Biemond, A., & de Jong, J. M. B. V. On cervical nystagmus and related disorders. *Brain*, 1969, *92*, 437–458.

Bienhold, H., & Flohr, H. Role of commissural connexions between vestibular nuclei in compensation following unilateral labyrinthectomy. *Journal of Physiology*, 1978, *284*, 178P.

Biguer, B., & Prablanc, C. Modulation of the vestibulo-ocular reflex in eye-head orientation as a function of target distance in man. In A. F. Fuchs & W. Becker (Eds.), *Progress in oculomotor research*. New York: Elsevier, 1981.

Birren, J. E. Static equilibrium and vestibular function. *Journal of Experimental Psychology*, 1945, *35*, 127–133.

*Bischof, N. Optic vestibular orientation to the vertical. In H. H. Kornhuber (Ed.), *Handbood of sensory physiology* (Vol. VI/2). New York: Springer-Verlag, 1974).

Bizzi, E., Kalil, R. E., & Morasso, P. Two modes of active eye–head coordination. *Brain Research*, 1972, *40*, 45–48.

Bizzi, E., Kalil, R. E. Morasso, P., & Tagliasco, V. Central programming and peripheral feedback during eye–head coordination in monkeys. In J. Dichgans & E. Bizzi (Eds.), *Cerebral control of eye movements and motion perception.* Basel: Karger, 1972.

Bizzi, E., Kalil, R. E., & Tagliasco, V. Eye–head coordination in monkeys: Evidence for centrally patterned organization. *Science*, 1971, *173*, 452–454.

Blair, S., & Gavin, M. Modification of the macaque's vestibulo-ocular reflex after ablation of the cerebellar vermis. *Acta Otolaryngologica*, 1979, *88*, 235–243.

Blanks, R. H. I., Anderson, J. H., & Precht W. Response characteristics of semicircular canal and otolith systems in cat. II. Responses of trochlear motoneurons. *Experimental Brain Research*, 1978, *32*, 509–528.

Bles, W. Stepping around: Circular vection and Coriolis effects. In J. Long & A. Baddeley (Eds.), *Attention and performance* (Vol. IX). Hillsdale, N.J.: Lawrence Erlbaum, 1981.

Bles, W., & Kapteyn, T. S. Circular vection and human posture. I. Does the proprioceptive system play a role? *Aggressologie*, 1977, *18*, 325–328.

*Bloedel, J. R. Cerebellar afferent systems: A review. *Progress in Neurobiology*, 1975, *2*, 1–68.

Böhmer, A., & Henn, V. Horizontal and vertical vestibulo-ocular and cervico-ocular reflexes in the monkey during high frequency rotation. *Brain Research*, 1983, *277*, 241–248.

Bouma, H., & Andriessen, J. J. Perceived orientation of isolated line segments. *Vision Research*, 1968, *8*, 493–507.

Boyle, R., & Pompeiano, O. Response characteristics of cerebellar, interpositus and intermediate cortex neurons to sinusoidal stimulation of neck and labyrinthine receptors. *Neuroscience*, 1980, *5*, 357–372. (a)

Boyle, R., & Pompeiano, O. Responses of vestibulospinal neurones to sinusoidal rotation of the neck. *Journal of Neurophysiology*, 1980, *44*, 633–64. (b)

Boyle, R., & Pompeiano, O. Convergence and interaction of neck and macular vestibular inputs in vestibulospinal neurons. *Journal of Neurophysiology*, 1981, *45*, 852–868.

Brandt, T., Büchele, W., Arnold, F., Fallert, M., & Wassermeyer, B. Arthrokinetic nystagmus and ego-motion sensation. *Experimental Brain Research*, 1977, *30*, 331–338.

Brandt, T., Dichgans, J., & Büchele, W. Motion habituation: Inverted self-motion perception and optokinetic after-nystagmus. *Experimental Brain Research*, 1974, *21*, 337–352.

Brandt, T., Dichgans, J., & Koenig, E. Differential affects of central versus peripheral vision on egocentric and exocentric motion perception. *Experimental Brain Research*, 1973, *16*, 476–491.

Brandt, T., Wenzel, D., & Dichgans, J. Die Entwicklung der visuellen Stabilisation des aufrechten Standes beim Kind: Ein Reifezeichen in der Kinderneurologie. *Archiven von Psychiatrie und Nervenkranken*, 1976, *223*, 1–13.

Brandt, T., Wist, E. R., & Dichgans, J. Foreground and background in dynamic spatial orientation. *Perception and Psychophysics*, 1975, *17*, 497–503.

Brandt, U., & Fluur, E. Postural perceptions and eye displacements during the variation of a force field acting in the mid-frontal plane. *Acta Otolaryngologica*, 1967, *63*, 49–64. (a)

Brandt, U., & Fluur, E. Postural perceptions and eye displacements produced by a resultant vector acting in the median sagittal plane of the head. II: Continuous responses along the *Y* axis with the subject in a vertical position heading centripetally and centrifugally. *Acta Otolaryngologica*, 1967, *63*, 564–578. (b)

Brecher, G. A. Die optokinetische Auslösung von Augenrollung und rotatorischem Nystagmus. *Pflüger's Archiven Gesamt Physiologie*, 1934, *234*, 13–28.

Brindley, G. S. How does an animal that is dropped in a non-upright posture know the angle through which it must turn in the air so that its feet point to the ground? *Journal of Physiology*, 1965, *180*, 20–21.

Brink, E. E., Hirai, N., & Wilson, V. J. Influence of neck afferents on vestibulospinal neurons. *Experimental Brain Research*, 1980, *38*, 285–292.

*Brodal A. Anatomy of the vestibular nuclei and their connections. In H. H. Kornhuber (Ed.), *Handbook of sensory physiology* (Vol. VI/I). New York: Springer-Verlag, 1974.

*Brooks, B. A., & Bajandas, F. J. *Eye movements.* New York: Plenum, 1977.

Brown, J. H., & Wolfe, J. W. Adaptation to prolonged constant angular acceleration. *Acta Otolaryngologica*, 1969, *67*, 389–398.

Brown, J. L. Orientation to the vertical during water immersion. *Aerospace Medicine*, 1961, *32*, 209–217.

Buettner, U. W., & Büttner, U. Vestibular nuclei activity in the alert monkey during suppression of vestibular and optokinetic nystagmus. *Experimental Brain Research*, 1979, *37*, 581–593.

Buettner, U. W., Büttner, U., & Henn, V. Transfer characteristics of neurons in vestibular nuclei in the alert monkey. *Journal of Neurophysiology*, 1978, *41*, 1614–1628.

Buizza, A., Léger, A., Droulez, J., Berthoz, A., & Schmid, R. Influence of otolithic stimulation by horizontal linear acceleration on optokinetic nystagmus and visual motion perception. *Experimental Brain Research*, 1980, *39*, 165–176.

Burke, D., & Eklund, G. Muscle spindle activity in man during standing. *Acta Physiologica Scandinavica*, 1977, *100*, 187–199.

Butterworth, G., & Hicks, L. Visual proprioception and postural stability in infancy. A developmental study. *Perception*, 1977, *6*, 255–262.

Büttner, U., & Waespe, W. Vestibular nerve activity in the alert monkey during vestibular and optokinetic nystagmus. *Experimental Brain Research*, 1981, *41*, 310–315.

Callan, J. W., & Ebenholtz, S. M. Directional changes in the vestibular ocular response as a result of adaptation to optical tilt. *Vision Research*, 1982, *22*, 37–42.

Camana, P. C., Hemami, H., & Stockwell, C. W. Determination of feedback for human posture control without physical intervention. *Journal of Cybernetics*, 1977, *7*, 199–225.

Campbell, F. W., Kulikowski, J. J., & Levinson, J. The effect of orientation on the visual resolution of gratings. *Journal of Physiology*, 1966, *187*, 427–436.

Campbell, F. W., & Maffei, L. "The tilt after-effect": A fresh look. *Vision Research*, 1971, *11*, 833–840.

Carpenter, R. H. S. Cerebellectomy and the transfer function of the vestibulo-ocular reflex in the decerebrate cat. *Proceedings of the Royal Society* (B). 1972, *181*, 353–374.

Carpenter, R. H. S., & Blakemore, C. Interactions between orientations in human vision. *Experimental Brain Research*, 1973, *18*, 287–303.

Cazin, L., Precht, W., & Lannou, J. Firing characteristics of neurons mediating optokinetic responses to rat's vestibular neurons. *Pflüger's Archiv European Journal of Physiology*, 1980, *386*, 221–230.

Chan, C. W. Y., Melvill Jones, G., & Watt, D. G. D. The "late" electronmyographic response to limb displacement in man. I. Evidence for supraspinal contribution. *Electroencephalography & Clinical Neurophysiology*, 1979, *46*, 173–181.

Cheng, M., & Outerbridge, J. S. Inter-saccadic interval analysis of vestibular nystagmus. *Acta Otolaryngologica*, 1974, *77*, 348–353.

Chiang, C. A new theory to explain geometrical illusions produced by crossing lines. *Perception and Psychophysics*, 1968, *3*, 174–176.

Chun, K. S., & Robinson, D. A. A model of quick phase generation in the vestibuloocular reflex. *Biological Cybernetics*, 1978, *28*, 209–221.

Clark, B., & Graybiel, A. Visual perception of the horizontal following exposure to radial acceleration on a centrifuge. *Journal of Comparative & Physiological Psychology*, 1951, *44*, 525–534.

Clark, B., & Graybiel, A. Perception of the postural vertical in normals and subjects with labyrinthine defects. *Journal of Experimental Psychology*, 1963, *63*, 490–494.

Clark, B., & Graybiel, A. Factors contributing to the delay in the perception of the oculogravic illusion. *American Journal of Psychology*, 1966, *79*, 377–388. (a)

Clark, B., & Graybiel, A. Perception of the visual horizontal in normal and labyrinthine defective observers during prolonged rotation. *American Journal of Psychology*, 1966, *79*, 608–612. (b)

Clark, B., & Graybiel, A. Egocentric localization of the visual horizontal in normal and labyrinthine-defective observers as a function of head and body tilt. *Perception and Psychophysics*, 1967, *2*, 609–611.

Clark, B., & Stewart, J. D. Effects of angular acceleration on man: Thresholds for the perception of rotation and the oculogyral illusion. *Aerospace Medicine*, 1969, *40*, 952–956.

Clément, G., Courjon, J. H., Jeannerod, M., & Schmid, R. Unidirectional habituation of vestibulo-ocular responses by repeated rotational or optokinetic stimulations in the cat. *Experimental Brain Research*, 1981, *42*, 34–42.

Cogan, A. I. The relationship between the apparent vertical and the vertical horopter. *Vision Research*, 1979, *19*, 655–665.

Cogan, D. G. Some objective and subjective observations on the vestibulo-ocular system. *American Journal of Ophthalmology*, 1958, *45*, 74–78.

*Cohen, B. the vestibulo-ocular reflex arc. In H. H. Kornhuber (Ed.), *Handbook of sensory physiology* (Vol. VI/1). New York: Springer-Verlag, 1974.

Cohen, B., & Komatsuzaki, A. Eye movements induced by stimulation of the pontine reticular formation: Evidence for integration in oculomotor pathways. *Experimental Neurology*, 1972, *36*, 101–117.

Cohen, B., & Suzuki, J., & Raphan, T. Role of the otolith organs in generation of horizontal nystagmus: Effects of selective labyrinthine lesions. *Brain Research*, 1983, *276*, 159–164.

Cohen, B., Uemura, T., & Takemori, S. Effects of labyrinthectomy on optokinetic nystagmus (OKN) and optokinetic after-nystagmus (OKAN). *Equilibrium Research*, 1973, *3*, 80–93.

Cohen, L. A. Role of eye and neck proprioceptive mechanisms in body orientation and motor coordination. *Journal of Neurophysiology*, 1961, *24*, 1–11.

Cohen, M. M. Elevator illusion: Influences of otolith organ activity and neck proprioception. *Perception and Psychophysics*, 1973, *14*, 401–406.

Collewijn, H. Direction-selective units in the rabbit's nucleus of the optic tract. *Brain Research*, 1975, *100*, 489–508.

Collewijn, H. Impairment of optokinetic (after-) nystagmus by labyrinthectomy in the rabbit. *Experimental Neurology*, 1976, *52*, 146–156.

Collewijn, H., Martins, A. J., & Steinman, R. M. Compensatory eye movements during active and passive head movements: Fast adaptation to changes in visual magnification. *Journal of Physiology*, 1983, *340*, 259–286.

Collewijn, H., Winterson, B. J., & van der Steen, J. Post-rotatory nystagmus and optokinetic after-nystagmus in the rabbit; Linear rather than exponential decay. *Experimental Brain Research*, 1980, *40*, 330–345.

Collins, A. M. Decrements in tracking and visual performance during vibration. *Human Factors*, 1973, *15*, 379–393.

Collins, W. E. Task-control of arousal and the effects of repeated unidirectional angular acceleration of human vestibular responses. *Acta Otolaryngologica*, 1964, *Suppl. 190*, 1–34.

Collins, W. E. Vestibular responses from figure skaters. *Aerospace Medicine*, 1966, *37*, 1098–1104.

Collins, W. E. Special effects of brief periods of visual fixation on nystagmus and sensations of turning. *Aerospace Medicine*, 1968, *39*, 257–266.

*Collins, W. E. Arousal and vestibular habituation. In H. H. Kornhuber (Ed.), *Handbook of sensory physiology* (Vol. VI/2). New York: Springer-Verlag, 1974. (a)

*Collins, W. E. Habituation of vestibular responses with and without visual stimulation. In H. H. Kornhuber (Ed.), *Handbook of sensory physiology* (Vol. VI/2). New York: Springer-Verlag, 1974. (b)

Cope, S., & Ryan, G. M. S. Cervical and otolith vertigo. *Journal of Laryngology*, 1959, *73*, 113–120.

Corah, N. L. Effects of the visual field upon perception of change in spatial orientation. *Journal of Experimental Psychology*, 1965, *70*, 598–601.

Correia, M. J., Hixson, W. C., & Niven, J. I. On predictive equations for subjective judgments of vertical and horizon in a force field. *Acta Otolaryngologica*, 1968, *Suppl. 230*, 3–20.

Correia, M. J., & Money, K. E. The effect of blockage of all six semicircular canal ducts on nystagmus produced by dynamic linear acceleration in the cat. *Acta Otolaryngologica*, 1970, *69*, 7–16.

Courjon, J. H., Flandrin, J. M., Jeannerod, M., & Schmid, R. The role of the flocculus in vestibular compensation after hemilabyrinthectomy. *Brain Research*, 1982, *239*, 251–257.

Courjon, J. H., Jeannerod, M., Ossuzio, I., & Schmid, R. The role of vision in compensation of vestibulo-ocular reflex after hemilabyrinthectomy in the cat. *Experimental Brain Research*, 1977, *28*, 235–248.

Craske, B., Crawshaw, M., & Heron, P. Disturbance of the oculomotor system due to lateral fixation. *Quarterly Journal of Experimental Psychology*, 1975, *27*, 459–465.

Crone, R. A. Optokinetically induced eye torsion. *von Graefe's Archiven von Ophthalmologie*, 1975, *196*, 1–7.

Darlot, C., Lopezbarneo, J., & Tracey, D. Asymmetries of vertical vestibular nystagmus in the cat. *Experimental Brain Research*, 1981, *41*, 420–426.

Daunton, N., & Thomsen, D. Visual modulation of otolith-dependent units in cat vestibular nuclei. *Experimental Brain Research*, 1979, *37*, 173–176.

Davies, P., & Melvill Jones, G. An adaptive neural model compatible with plastic changes induced in the human vestibulo-ocular reflex by prolonged optical reversal of vision. *Brain Research*, 1976, *103*, 546–550.

Day, R. H., & Wade, N. J. Visual spatial aftereffect from prolonged head tilt. *Science*, 1966, *154*, 1201–1202.

Demer, J. L. The variable gain element of the vestibulo-ocular reflex is common to the optokinetic system of the cat. *Brain Research*, 1981, *229*, 1–13.

Demer, J. L., & Robinson, D. A. Effects of reversible lesions and stimulation of olivocerebellar system on vestibuloocular reflex plasticity. *Journal of Neurophysiology*, 1982, *47*, 1084–1107.

Demer, J. L., & Robinson, D. A. Different time constants for optokinetic and vestibular nystagmus with a single velocity-storage element. *Brain Research*, 1983, *276*, 173–177.

*Denny-Brown, D. *The cerebral control of movement.* Liverpool: Liverpool University Press, 1966.

Dichgans, J., Bizzi, E., Morasso, P., & Tagliasco, V. Mechanisms underlying recovery of eye–head coordination following bilateral labyrinthectomy in monkeys. *Experimental Brain Research*, 1973, *18*, 548–562.

Dichgans, J., Bizzi, E., Morasso, P., & Tagliasco, V. The role of vestibular and neck afferents during eye–head coordination in the monkey. *Brain Research*, 1974, *71*, 225–232.

Dichgans, J., & Brandt, T. Optokinetic motion sickness and pseudo-Coriolis effects induced by moving visual stimuli. *Acta Otolaryngologica*, 1973, *76*, 339–348.

*Dichgans, J., & Brandt, T. Visual-vestibular interaction: Effects on self-motion perception and postural control. In R. Held & W. Leibowitz (Eds.), *Handbook of sensory physiology* (Vol. VIII). New York: Springer-Verlag, 1978.

Dichgans, J., Diener, H. C., & Brandt, T. Optokinetic-graviceptive interaction in different head positions. *Acta Otolaryngologica*, 1974, *78*, 391–398.

Dichgans, J., Held, R., Young, L. R., & Brandt, T. Moving visual scenes influence the apparent direction of gravity. *Science*, 1972, *178*, 1217–1219.

Dichgans, J., Mauritz, K. H., Allum, J. H. J., & Brandt, T. Postural sway in normals and atactic patients: Analysis of the stabilizing and destabilizing effects of vision. *Aggressologie*, 1976, *17c*, 15–24.

Dichgans, J., Reutern, G. M., & Römmelt, U. Impaired suppression of vestibular nystagmus by fixation in cerebellar and noncerebellar patients. *Archiven Psychiatrie und Nervenkranken*, 1978, *226*, 183–199.

Diener, H. C., Dichgans, J., Bruzek, W., & Selinka, H. Stabilization of human posture during induced oscillations of the body. *Experimental Brain Research*, 1982, *45*, 126–132.

Dietz, V., & Berger, W. Spinal coordination of bilateral leg muscle activity during balancing. *Experimental Brain Research*, 1982, *47*, 172–176.

Dix, M. R., & Hood, J. D. Observations upon the nervous mechanism of vestibular habituation. *Acta Otolaryngologica*, 1969, *67*, 310–318.

Dixon, N. F., & Dixon, P. M. "Sloping water" and related framework illusions: Some informal observations. *Quarterly Journal of Experimental Psychology*, 1966, *18*, 369–370.

Dowd, P. J. Sleep deprivation effects on the vestibular habituation process. *Journal of Applied Psychology*, 1974, *59*, 748–752.

Dowd, P. J., & Cramer, R. L. Habituation transference in Coriolis acceleration. *Aerospace Medicine*, 1967, *38*, 1103–1107.

Dubrovsky, B. O., & Barbas, H. Frontal projections to dorsal neck and extraocular muscles. *Experimental Neurology*, 1977, *55*, 680–693.

Dufossé, M., Ito, M., Jastreboff, P. J., & Miyashita, Y. A neuronal correlate in rabbit's cerebellum to adaptive modification of the vestibulo-ocular reflex. *Brain Research*, 1978, *150*, 611–616.

Dufresne, J. R., Soechting, J. F., & Terzuolo, C. A. Modulation of the myotatic reflex gain in man during intentional movements. *Brain Research*, 1980, *193*, 67–84.

Duwaer, A. L. Assessment of retinal image displacement during head movement using an afterimage method. *Vision Research*, 1982, *22*, 1379–1388.

Easton, T. A. Patterned inhibition from single eye muscle stretch in the cat. *Experimental Neurology*, 1972, *34*, 497–510.

Ebenholtz, S. M. Perception of the vertical with body tilt in the median plane. *Journal of Experimental Psychology*, 1970, *83*, 1–6.

Ebenholtz, S. M. Additivity of Aftereffects of maintained head and eye rotations: An alternative to recalibration. *Perception and Psychophysics*, 1976, *19*, 113–116.

Ebenholtz, S. M. Determinants of the rod and frame effect: The role of retinal size. *Perception and Psychophysics*, 1977, *22*, 531–538.

Ebenholtz, S. M., & Benzschawel, T. L. The rod and frame effect and induced head tilt as a function of observation distance. *Perception and Psychophysics*, 1977, *22*, 491–496.

Ebenholtz, S. M., & Paap, K. R. The constancy of object orientation: Compensation for ocular rotation. *Perception and Psychophysics*, 1973, *14*, 458–470.

Ebenholtz, S. M., & Shebilske, W. The doll reflex: Ocular counterrolling with head–body tilt in the median plane. *Vision Research*, 1975, *15*, 713–717.

Ebenholtz, S. M., & Utrie, J. W. Inhibition of the rod-and-frame effect by circular contours. *Perception and Psychophysics*, 1982, *32*, 199–200.

Edwards, A. S. The measurement of static ataxia. *American Journal of Psychology*, 1942, *55*, 171–188.

Edwards, A. S. Factors tending to decrease the steadiness of the body at rest. *American Journal of Psychology*, 1943, *56*, 599–602.

Ehrhardt, K. J., & Wagner, A. Labyrinthine and neck reflexes recorded from spinal single motoneurons in the cat. *Brain Research*, 1970, *19*, 87–104.

Eklund, G. General features of vibration-induced effects on balance. *Upsala Journal of Medical Science*, 1972, *77*, 112–124.

Evans, C. M., Fellows, S. J., Rack, P. M. H., Ross, R. F., & Walters, D. K. W. Response of the normal human ankle joint to imposed sinusoidal movement. *Journal of Physiology*, 1983, *344*, 483–502.

Eysenck, H. J. *Dimensions of personality*. London: Routledge & Kegan Paul, 1947.

Ezure, K., Sasaki, S., Uchino, Y., & Wilson, V. J. A role of upper cervical afferents on vestibular control of neck motor activity. In S. Homma (Ed.), *Progress in brain research* (Vol. 44): *Understanding the stretch reflex*. New York: Elsevier, 1976.

Favilla, M., Ghelarducci, B., Hill, C. D., & Spyer, K. M. Vestibular inputs to the fastigial nucleus: Evidence of convergence of macular and ampular inputs. *Pflüger's Archiv European Journal of Physiology*, 1980, *384*, 193–206.

Fearing, F. S. Factors influencing static equilibrium: An experimental study of the effect of controlled and uncontrolled attention upon sway. *Journal of Comparative Psychology*, 1925, *5*, 1–24.

Ferrell, W. R. The adequacy of stretch receptors in the cat knee joint for signalling joint angle throughout a full range of movement. *Journal of Physiology*, 1980, *299*, 85–100.

Fine, B. J., & Danforth, A. V. Field-dependence, extraversion, and perception of the vertical: Empirical and theoretical perspectives of the rod-and-frame test. *Perceptual & Motor Skills*, 1975, *40*, 683–693.

Finke, R. A., & Held, R. State reversals of optically induced tilt and torsional eye movements. *Perception and Psychophysics*, 1978, *23*, 337–340.

Fischer, M. H. Messende Untersuchungen über die Gegenrollung der Augen und die Lokalisation der scheinbaren Vertikalen bei seitlicher Neigung des Gesamtkörpers bis zu 360°: II. Mitteilung. Untersuchungen an Normalen. *von Graefe's Archiven von Ophthalmologie*, 1930, *123*, 476–508.

Fischer, M. H., & Kornmüller, A. E. Optokinetisch ausgelöste Bewengungswahrnehmung und optokinetischer Nystagmus. *Journal von Psychologie und Neurologie* (Leipzig), 1930, *41*, 273–308.

Fluur, E. Interaction between the utricles and the horizontal semicircular canals. IV. Tilting of human patients with acute unilateral vestibular neuritis. *Acta Otolaryngologica*, 1973, *76*, 349–352.

Fluur, E. Positional and positioning nystagmus as a result of utriculocupular integration. *Acta Otolaryngologica*, 1974, *78*, 19–27.

Fluur, E., & Mellström, A. Saccular stimulation and oculomotor reactions. *Laryngoscope*, 1970, *80*, 1713–1721. (a)

Fluur, E., & Mellström, A. Utricular stimulation and oculomotor reactions. *Layngoscope*, 1970, *80*, 1701–1712. (b)

Fluur, E., & Mellström, A. The otolith organs and their influence on oculomotor movements. *Experimental Neurology*, 1971, *30*, 139–147.

Fluur, E., & Mendel, L. Relation between strength of stimulus and duration of latency time in vestibular rotatory nystagmus. *Acta Otolaryngologica*, 1966, *61*, 463–474.

Fluur, E., & Mendel, L. Crescendo time for per-rotatorily elicited nystagmus. *Acta Otolaryngologica*, 1970, *69*, 239–246.

Fluur, E., & Siegborn, J. Interaction between the utricles and the horizontal semicircular canals. I. Unilateral selective sectioning of the horizontal ampuller nerve followed by tilting around the longitudinal axis. *Acta Otolaryngologica*, 1973, *75*, 17–20. (a)

Fluur, E., & Siegborn, J. The otolith organs and the nystagmus problem. *Acta Otolaryngologica*, 1973, *76*, 438–442. (b)

Fluur, E,, & Siegborn, J. Interaction between the utricles and the vertical semicircular canals. VI. Unilateral selective sectioning of the horizontal and vertical ampullar nerves, followed by tilting around the horizontal axis. *Acta Otolaryngologica*, 1974, *77*, 167–170.

Ford, F. R., & Walsh, F. B. Clinical observations on the importance of the vestibular reflexes in ocular movements: The effects of section of one or both vestibular nerves. *Bulletin of the Johns Hopkins Hospital*, 1936, *58*, 80–83.

Freeman, R. D., & Thibos, L. N. Electrophysiological evidence that abnormal early visual experience can modify the human brain. *Science*, 1973, *80*, 876–878.

*Fregly, A. R. Vestibular ataxia and its measurement in man. In H. H. Kornhuber (Ed.), *Handbook of sensory physiology* (Vol. VI/2). New York: Springer-Verlag, 1974.

Fregly, A. R., & Graybiel, A. Labyrinthine defects as shown by ataxia and caloric tests. *Acta Otolaryngologica*, 1970, *69*, 216–222.

Friedmann, G. The influence of unilateral labyrinthectomy on orientation in space. *Acta Otolaryngologica*, 1971, *71*, 289–298.

Fukuda, T. Studies on human dynamic postures from the viewpoint of postural reflexes. *Acta Otolaryngologica*, 1961, *Suppl. 161*, 1–52.

Fuller, J. H. The dynamic neck–eye reflex in mammals. *Experimental Brain Research*, 1980, *41*, 29–35.

Furman, J. M., O'Leary, D. P., & Wolfe, J. W. Changes in the horizontal vestibulo-ocular reflex of the rhesus monkey with behavioral and pharmacological alerting. *Brain Research*, 1981, *206*, 490–494.

Furneaux, W. D. The prediction of susceptibility to hypnosis. *Journal of Personality*, 1946, *14*, 281–294.

Furneaux, W. D. Neuroticism, extroversion, drive, and suggestibility. *International Journal of Clinical and Experimental Hypnosis*, 1961, *9*, 195–214.

Gahéry, Y., & Legallet, E. Influence of initial posture on posturo-kinetic co-ordination in the cat. *Experimental Brain Research*, 1981, *44*, 177–186.

Gardner, E. P., & Fuchs, A. F. Single-unit responses to natural vestibular stimuli and eye movements in deep cerebellar nuclei of the alert monkey. *Journal of Neurophysiology*, 1975, *38*, 627–649.

Gauthier, G. M., & Robinson, D. A. Adaptation of the human vestibular-ocular reflex to magnifying lenses. *Brain Research*, 1975, *92*, 331–335.

Gernandt, B. E. Vestibulo-spinal mechanisms. In H. H. Kornhuber (Ed.), *Handbook of sensory physiology* (Vol. VI/1). New York: Springer-Verlag, 1974.

Gibson, J. J. Adaptation, after-effect and contrast in the perception of curved lines. *Journal of Experimental Psychology*, 1933, *16*, 1–31.

Gibson, J. J. *The senses considered as perceptual systems.* Boston: Houghton Mifflin, 1966.

Gibson, J. J. What gives rise to the perception of motion? *Psychological Review*, 1968, *75*, 335–364.

Gibson, J. J., & Radner, M. Adaptation, after-effect, and contrast in the perception of tilted lines. I. Quantitative studies. *Journal of Experimental Psychology*, 1937, *20*, 453–467.

Gogel, W. C., & Newton, R. E. Depth adjacency and the rod-and-frame illusion. *Perception and Psychophysics*, 1975, *18*, 163–171.

Goldberg, J. M., & Fernández, C. Responses of peripheral vestibular neurons to angular and linear accelerations in the squirrel monkey. *Acta Otolaryngologica*, 1975, *80*, 101–110.

Goldstein, K., & Riese W. Über induzierte Veränderungen des Tonus (Halsreflexe, Labyrinthreflexe und ähnliche Erscheinungen): III. Blickrichtung und Zeigeversuch. *Klinishe Wirkshrift*, 1923, *2*, 2338–2340.

Gonshor, A., & Melvill Jones, G. Changes of human vestibulo-ocular response induced by vision-reversal during head rotation. *Journal of Physiology*, 1973, *234*, 102–103.

*Gonshor, A., & Melvill Jones, G. Extreme vestibulo-ocular adaptation induced by prolonged optical reversal of vision. *Journal of Physiology*, 1976, *256*, 381–414. (a)

Gonshor, A., & Melvill Jones, G. Short-term adaptive changes in the human vestibulo-ocular reflex. *Journal of Physiology*, 1976, *256*, 361–379. (b)

Gonshor, A., & Melvill Jones, G. Postural adaptation to prolonged optical reversal of vision in man. *Brain Research*, 1980, *192*, 239–248.

Goodenough, D. R., Nowak, A., Oltman, P. K., Cox, P. W., & Sigman, E. A visually induced illusion of body tilt in a horizontal plane. *Perception and Psychophysics*, 1982, *31*, 268–272.

Goodenough, D. R., Sigman, E., Oltman, P., Rosso, J., & Mertz, H. Eye torsion in response to a tilted visual stimulus. *Vision Research*, 1979, *19*, 1177–1180.

Göthlin, G. F. Entopic analysis of vestibular nystagmus. *Acta Otolaryngologica*, 1946, *34*, 230–245.

Gottlieb, G. L., Agarwal, G. C., & Jaeger, R. J. Response to sudden torques about ankle in man. IV. A functional role of α–γ linkage. *Journal of Neurophysiology*, 1981, *46*, 179–190.

Granit, R. (Ed.). *Muscular afferents and motor control.* Stockholm: Almquist and Wiksell, 1966.

*Granit, R., & Pompeiano, O. (Eds.) *Reflex control of posture and movement.* New York: Elsevier, 1979.

Graybiel, A. The oculogravic illusion. *Archives of Opthalmology*, 1952, *48*, 605–615.

Graybiel, A., Deane, F. R., & Colehour, J. K. Prevention of overt motion sickness by incremental exposure to otherwise highly stressful Coriolis accelerations. *Aerospace Medicine*, 1969, *40*, 142–148.

Graybiel, A., & Hupp, D. I. The oculo-gyral illusion: A form of apparent motion which may be observed following stimulation of the semicircular canals. *Journal of Aviation Medicine*, 1946, *17*, 3–27.

Graybiel, A., Johnson, W. H., Money, K. E., Malcolm, R. E., & Jennings, G. L. Oculogravic illusion in response to straight-ahead acceleration of a CF-104 aircraft. *Aviation, Space & Environmental Medicine*, 1979, *50*, 383–386.

Graybiel, A., & Kellogg, R. S. The inversion illusion in parabolic flight: Its probable dependence on otolith function. *Aerospace Medicine*, 1967, *38*, 1099–1102.

Graybiel, A., & Knepton, J. Direction-specific adaptation effects acquired in a slow rotation room. *Aerospace Medicine*, 1972, *45*, 1179–1189.

Graybiel, A., Miller, E. F., Billingham, J., Waite, R., Berry, C. A., & Deitlein, L. F. Vestibular experiments in Gemini flights V and VII. *Aerospace Medicine*, 1967, *38*, 360–370.

Graybiel, A., Stockwell, C. W., & Guedry, F. E. Evidence for a test of dynamic otolith function considered in relation to responses from a patient with idiopathic progressive vestibular degeneration. *Acta Otolaryngologica*, 1972, *73*, 1–3.

Gresty, M. A. Coordinations of head and eye movements to fixate continuous and intermittent targets. *Vision Research*, 1974, *14*, 395–403.

Gresty, M. A., & Baker, R. Neurons with visual receptive field, eye movement and neck displacement sensitivity within and around the nucleus prepositus hypoglossi in the alert cat. *Experimental Brain Research*, 1976, *24*, 429–433.

Gresty, M. A., & Leech, J. Coordination of the head and eyes in pursuit of predictable and random target motion. *Aviation, Space & Environmental Medicine*, 1977, *48*, 741–744.

Griffin, M. J., & Lewis, C. H. A review of the effects of vibration on visual acuity and continuous manual control. Part I: Visual acuity. *Journal of Sound & Vibration*, 1978, *56*, 383–413.

Grillner, S. Locomotion in vertebrates: Central mechanisms and reflex interaction. *Physiological Review*, 1975, *55*, 247–306.

Guedry, F. E. Visual control of habituation to complex vestibular stimulation in man. *Acta Otolaryngologica*, 1964, *58*, 377–389.

Guedry, F. E. Habituation to complex vestibular stimulation in man: Transfer and retention of effects from twelve days of rotation at 10 rpm. *Perceptual & Motor Skills*, 1965, *21*, 459–481. (a)

Guedry, F. E. Orientation of the rotation-axis relative to gravity: Its influence on nystagmus and sensations of rotation. *Acta Otolaryngologica*, 1965, *60*, 30–48. (b)

Guedry, F. E., Benson, A. J., & Moore, H. J. Influence of a visual display and frequency of whole-body angular oscillation on incidence of motion sickness. *Aviation, Space & Environmental Medicine*, 1982, *53*, 564–569.

Guedry, F. E., & Collins, W. E. Duration of angular acceleration and ocular nystagmus from cat and man: II. Responses from the lateral canals to varied stimulus durations. *Acta Otolaryngologica*, 1968, *65*, 257–269.

Guedry, F. E., Collins, W. E., & Graybiel, A. Vestibular habituation during repetitive complex stimulation: A study of transfer effects. *Journal of Applied Physiology*, 1964, *19*, 1005–1015.

Guedry, F. E., Collins, W. E., & Sheffey, P. L. Perceptual and oculomotor reactions to interacting visual and vestibular stimulation. *Perceptual & Motor Skills*, 1961, *12*, 307–324.

Guedry, F. E., Lentz, J. M., & Jell, R. M. Visual-vestibular interactions: I. Influence of peripheral vision on suppression of the vestibulo-ocular reflex and visual acuity. *Aviation, Space & Environmental Medicine*, 1979, *50*, 205–211.

Guedry, F. E., Mortensen, C. E., Nelson, J. B., & Correia, M. J. A comparison of nystagmus and turning sensations generated by active and passive turning. In J. D. Hood (Ed.), *Vestibular mechanisms in health and disease.* New York: Academic Press, 1978.

Gurfinkel, V. S., Lipshits, M. I., & Popov, K. Y. Is the stretch reflex the main mechanism in the system of regulation of the vertical posture in man? *Biofizika*, 1974, *19*, 761–766.

Haciska, D. T. The influence of drugs on caloric-induced nystagmus. *Acta Otolaryngologica*, 1973, *75*, 477–484.

Haddad, G. M., Demer, J. L., & Robinson, D. A. The effect of lesions of the dorsal cap of the inferior olive on the vestibulo-ocular and optokinetic systems of the cat. *Brain Research*, 1980, *185*, 265–275.

Haddad, G. M., Friendlich, A. R., & Robinson, D. A. Compensation of nystagmus after VIIIth nerve lesions in vestbulo-cerebellectomized cats. *Brain Research*, 1977, *135*, 192–196.

Hallpike, C. S. Directional preponderance 1942–1974: A review. *Acta Otolaryngologica*, 1975, *79*, 409–418.

Hallpike, C. S., Harrison, M. S., & Slater, E. Abnormalities of the caloric test, results in certain varieties of mental disorder. *Acta Otolaryngologica*, 1951, *30*, 1–36.

Hammond, P. H., Merton, P. A., & Sutton, G. C. Nervous gradation of muscular control. *British Medical Bulletin*, 1956, *12*, 214–219.

Harrington, T. L., Harrington, M. K., Wilkins, C. A., & Koh, Y. O. Visual orientation by motion-produced blur patterns: Detection of divergence. *Perception and Psychophysics*, 1980, *28*, 293–305.

Harris, L. R., & Cynader, M. The eye movements of the dark-reared cat. *Experimental Brain Research*, 1981, *44*, 41–56. (a)

Harris, L. R., & Cynader, M. Modification of the balance and gain of the vestibulo-ocular reflex in the cat. *Experimental Brain Research*, 1981, *44*, 57–70. (b)

Hay, J. C., & Goldsmith, W. M. Space-time adaptation of visual position constancy. *Journal of Experimental Psychology*, 1973, *99*, 1–9.

Hay, J. C., & Sawyer, S. Position constancy and binocular convergence. *Perception and Psychophysics*, 1969, *5*, 310–312.

Hayashi, R., Miyake, A., Jijiwa, H., & Watanabe, S. Postural readjustment to body sway induced by vibration in man. *Experimental Brain Research*, 1981, *43*, 217–225.

Hayes, R. W., & Venables, P. H. An exposure time effect on the Witkin rod-and-frame test. *Psychonomic Science*, 1972, *28*, 243–244.

Held, R., Dichgans, J., & Bauer, J. Characteristics of moving visual areas influencing spatial orientation. *Vision Research*, 1975, *15*, 357–365.

Helmholtz, H. von. *Treatise on physiological optics*. New York: Dover, 1962. (Originally published, 1866.)

Henn, V., Cohen, B., & Young, L. R. Visual-vestibular interaction in motion perception and the generation of nystagmus. *Neurosciences Research Progress Bulletin*, 1980, *18*, 459–651.

Henn, V., Young, L. R., & Finley, C. Vestibular nucleus units in alert monkeys are also influenced by moving visual fields. *Brain Research*, 1974, *71*, 144–149.

Hennebert, P. E. Nystagmus audiocinétique. *Journal of Auditory Research*, 1960, *1*, 84–87.

Henriksson, N. G., Novotny, M., & Tjernström, Ö. Eye movements as a function of active head turnings. *Acta Otolaryngologica*, 1974, *77*, 86–91.

Hepp, K., Henn, V., & Jaeger, J. Eye movement neurons in the cerebellar nuclei of the alert monkey. *Experimental Brain Research*, 1982, *45*, 253–264.

Herman, R., Maulucci, R., & Stuyck, J. Development and plasticity of visual and vestibular generated eye movements. *Experimental Brain Research*, 1982, *47*, 69–78.

Hess, W. R. *The functional organization of the diencephalon*. New York: Grune & Stratton, 1957.

Higgins, D. C., & Glaser, G. H. Stretch responses during chronic cerebellar ablation. A study of reflex instability. *Journal of Neurophysiology*, 1964, *27*, 49–62.

Hikosaka, O., & Kawakami, T. Inhibitory reticular neurons related to the quick phase of vestibular nystagmus—Their location and projection. *Experimental Brain Research*, 1977, *27*, 377–396.

Hikosaka, O., & Maeda, M. Cervical effects on abducens motoneurons and their interaction with vestibulo-ocular reflex. *Experimental Brain Research*, 1973, *18*, 512–530.

Hill, A. L. Direction constancy. *Perception and Psychophysics*, 1972, *11* 175–178.

Holm-Jensen, S. Interference between synchronous optokinetic nystagmus and vestibular nystagmus. *Acta Otolaryngologica*, 1982, *93*, 375–385.

Houk, J. A viscoelastic interaction which produces one component of adaptation in responses of Golgi tendon organs. *Journal of Neurophysiology*, 1967, *30*, 1482–1493.

*Howard, I. P. *Human visual orientation*. London: Wiley, 1982.

Howard, I. P., & Anstis, T. Muscular and joint-receptor components in postural persistence. *Journal of Experimental Psychology*, 1974, *103*, 167–170.

Howard, I. P., & Templeton, W. B. A critical note on the use of the human centrifuge. *American Journal of Psychology*, 1963, *76*, 150–152.

Howard, I. P., & Templeton, W. B. The effect of steady fixation on the judgement of relative depth. *Quarterly Journal of Experimental Psychology*, 1964, *16*, 193–203. (a)

Howard, I. P., & Templeton, W. B. Visually-induced eye torsion and tilt adaptation. *Vision Research*, 1964, *4*, 433–437. (b)

*Howard, I. P., & Templeton, W. B. *Human spatial orientation*. London: Wiley, 1966.

Hughes, P. C., Brecher, G. A., & Fishkin, S. M. Effects of rotating backgrounds upon the perception of verticality. *Perception and Psychophysics*, 1972, *11*, 135–138.

Hull, C. L. *Hypnosis and suggestibility*. New York: Appleton-Century-Crofts, 1933.

Hyvärinen, J. Posterior parietal lobe of the primate brain. *Physiological Reviews*, 1982, *62*, 1060–1129.

Igarashi, M., Takahashi, M., Reschke, M. F., & Wright, W. K. Effect of otolith end organ ablation on pendular rotation nystagmus in squirrel monkey. *Archives of Oto-Rhino-Laryngology*, 1977, *217*, 183–188.

Igarashi, M., Watanabe, T., & Maxian, P. M. Dynamic equilibrium in squirrel monkeys after unilateral and bilateral labyrinthectomy. *Acta Otolaryngologica*, 1970, *69*, 247–253.

Ingham, J. G. Body sway and suggestibility. *Journal of Mental Science*, 1954, *100*, 432–441.

Ito, M. Neural design of the cerebellar motor control system. *Brain Research*, 1972, *40*, 81–84.

Ito, M. Cerebellar learning control of vestibulo-ocular mechanisms. In T. Desiraju (Ed.), *Mechanisms in transmission of signals for conscious behavior*. Amsterdam: Elsevier, 1976.

*Ito, M. Cerebellar control of the vestibulo-ocular reflex around the flocculus hypothesis. *Annual Review of Neuroscience*, 1982, *5*, 275–296.

Jäger, J., & Henn, V. Habituation of the vestibulo-ocular reflex (VOR) in the monkey during sinusoidal rotation in the dark. *Experimental Brain Research*, 1981, *41*, 108–114.

Janeke, J. B., Jongkees, L. B. W., & Oosteveld, W. J. Relationship between otoliths and nystagmus. *Acta Otolaryngologica*, 1970, *69*, 1–6.

Johansson, G. Studies on visual perception of locomotion. *Perception*, 1977, *6*, 365–376.

Johnson, D. D., & Torok, N. Habituation of nystagmus and sensations of motion after rotation. *Acta Otolaryngologica*, 1970, *69*, 206–221.

Jones, F. P. The influence of postural set on pattern of movement in man. *International Journal of Neurology*, 1963, *4*, 60–71.

Jones, F. P. Method for changing stereotyped response patterns by the inhibition of certain postural sets. *Psychological Review*, 1965, *72*, 196–214.

Jongkees, L. B. W. Cervical vertigo. *Laryngoscope*, 1969, *79*, 1473–1483.

Kasai, T., & Zee, D. S. Eye–head coordination in labyrinthine-defective human beings. *Brain Research*, 1978, *144*, 123–142.

Kase, M., Noda, H., Suzuki, D. A., & Miller, D. C. Target velocity signals of visual tracking in vermal Purkinje cells of the monkey. *Science*, 1979, *205*, 717–720.

Kasper, J., & Thoden, U. Effects of natural neck afferent stimulation on vestibulo-spinal neurons in the decerebrate cat. *Experimental Brain Research*, 1981, *44*, 401–408.

Kaufman, E. L., Reese, E. P., Volkmann, J., & Rogers, S. In E. P. Reese, (Ed.), *Psychophysical research*. (Report No. 5DC. 131-1-5.) Psychophysical Research Unit, Mount Holyoke College, 1953.

Keene. G. C. The effect of response codes on the accuracy of making absolute judgments of linear inclination. *Journal of General Psychology*, 1963, *69*, 37–50.

Keller, E. L. Gain of the vestibulo-ocular reflex in monkey at high rotational frequencies. *Vision Research*, 1978, *18*, 311–315.

Keller, E. L., & Kamath, B. Y. Characteristics of head rotation and eye movement related neurons in alert monkey vestibular nucleus. *Brain Research*, 1975, *100*, 182–187.

Keller, E. L., & Precht, W. Adaptive modification of central vestibular neurons in response to visual stimulation through reversing prisms. *Journal of Neurophysiology*, 1979, *42*, 896–911. (a)

Keller, E. L., & Precht, W. Visual-vestibular responses in vestibular nuclear neurons in the intact and cerebellectomized alert cat. *Neuroscience*, 1979, *4*, 1599–1613. (b)

Kertesz, A. E., & Jones, R. W. The effect of angular velocity of stimulus on human torsional eye movements. *Vision Research*, 1969, *9*, 995–998.

Kertesz, A. E., & Jones, R. W. Human cyclofusional response. *Vision Research*, 1970, *10*, 891–896.

Kertesz, A. E., & Sullivan, M. J. The effect of stimulus size on human cyclofusional response. *Vision Research*, 1978, *18*, 567–571.

Kim, J. H., & Partridge, L. D. Observations on types of response to combinations of neck, vestibular and muscle stretch signals. *Journal of Neurophysiology*, 1969, *32*, 239–250.

Kimura, M., & Maekawa, K. Activity of flocculus Purkinje cells during passive eye movements. *Journal of Neurophysiology*, 1981, *46*, 1004–1017.

Kitahara, M., & Uno, R. Equilibrium and vertigo in a tilting environment. *Annals of Otology*, 1967, *76*, 166–178.

Kleinschmidt, H. J., & Collewijn, H. A search for habituation of vestibulo-ocular reactions to rotatory and linear sinusoidal accelerations in the rabbit. *Experimental Neurology*, 1975, *47*, 257–267.

Koenig, E., Allum, J. H. J., & Dichgans, J. Visual-vestibular interaction upon nystagmus slow phase velocity in man. *Acta Otolaryngologica*, 1978, *85*, 397–410.

Kolb, F. P., & Rubia, F. J. Information about peripheral events conveyed to the cerebellum via the climbing fiber system in the decerebrate cat. *Experimental Brain Research*, 1980, *38*, 363–374.

*Kornhuber, H. H. Nystagmus and related phenomena in man: An outline of otoneurology. In H. H. Kornhuber (Ed.), *Handbook of sensory physiology* (Vol. VI/2). New York: Springer-Verlag, 1974.

Krejčová, H., Highstein, S., & Cohen, B. Labyrinthine and extralabyrinthine effects on ocular counterrolling. *Acta Otolaryngologica*, 1971, *72*, 165–171.

Krekling, S., & Blika, S. Development of the tilted vertical horopter. *Perception and Psychophysics*, 1983, *34*, 491–493.

Kubin, L. Manzoni, D., & Pompeiano, O. Responses of lateral reticular neurons to convergent neck and macular vestibular inputs. *Journal of Neurophysiology*, 1981, *46*, 48–64.

Lackner, J. R. Induction of illusory self motion and nystagmus by a rotating sound field. *Aviation, Space & Environmental Medicine*, 1977, *44*, 129–131.

*Lackner, J. R. Some mechanisms underlying sensory and postural stability in man. In R. Held & W. Leibowitz (Eds.), *Handbook of sensory physiology* (Vol. VIII). New York: Springer-Verlag, 1978.

Lackner, J. R., & Graybiel, A. Perceived orientation in free-fall depends on visual, postural, and architectural factors. *Aviation, Space & Environmental Medicine*, 1983, *54*, 47–51.

Lackner, J. R., & Levine, M. S. Changes in apparent body orientation and sensory localization induced by vibration of postural muscles: Vibratory myesthetic illusions. *Aviation, Space & Environmental Medicine*, 1979, *50*, 346–354.

Lacour, M., Roll, J. P., & Appaix, M. Modifications and development of spinal reflexes in the alert baboon (*Papio papio*) following a unilateral neurotomy. *Brain Reserch*, 1976, *113*, 255–269.

Lacour, M., & Xerri, C. Compensation of postural reactions to free-fall in the vestibular neurectomized monkey. *Experimental Brain Research*, 1980, *40*, 103–110.

Lader, M. H. *Studies of anxiety*. New York: Headley Brothers, 1969.

Lanman, J., Bizzi, E., & Allum, J. The coordination of eye and head movements during smooth pursuit. *Brain Research*, 1978, *153*, 39–54.

Lechner-Steinleitner, S. Interaction of labyrinthine and somatoreceptor inputs as determinants of the subjective vertical. *Psychological Research*, 1978, *40*, 65–76.

Lechner-Steinleitner, S., & Schöne, H. The subjective vertical under "dry" and "wet" conditions at clockwise and counterclockwise changed positions and the effect of a parallel background field. *Psychological Research*, 1980, *41*, 305–318.

Lee, D. N., & Aronson, E. Visual proprioceptive control of standing in human infants. *Perception and Psychophysics*, 1974, *15*, 529–532.

Lee, D. N., & Lishman, R. Visual control of locomotion. *Scandinavian Journal of Psychology*, 1977, *18*, 224–230.

Leibowitz, H. W., Rodemer, C. S., & Dichgans, J. The independence of dynamic spatial orientation from luminance and refractive error. *Perception and Psychophysics*, 1979, *25*, 75–79.

Lennerstrand, G., & Bach-y-Rita, P. (Eds.). *Basic mechanisms of ocular motility and their clinical implications*. New York: Pergamon, 1975.

Lentz, J. M., & Guedry, F. E. Apparent instrument horizon deflection during and immediately following rolling maneuvers. *Aviation, Space & Environmental Medicine*, 1982, *53*, 549–553.

Lester, G. The rod-and-frame test: Some comments on methodology. *Perceptual & Motor Skills*, 1968, *26*, 1307–1314.

Lestienne, F., Soechting, J., & Berthoz, A. Postural readjustments induced by linear motion of visual scenes. *Experimental Brain Research*, 1977, *28*, 363–384.

Lindsay, K. W., Roberts, T. D. M., & Rosenberg, J. R. Asymmetric tonic labyrinth reflexes and their interaction with neck reflexes in the decerebrate cat. *Journal of Physiology*, 1976, *261*, 583–601.

Lindsay, K. W., & Rosenberg, J. R. The effect of cerebellectomy on tonic labyrinth reflexes in the forelimb of the decerebrate cat. *Journal of Physiology*, 1978, *273*, 76–77. (a)

Lindsay, K. W., & Rosenberg, J. R. Tonic labyrinth reflexes in the forelimb of the acute and chronic hemilabyrinthectomized cat. *Journal of Physiology*, 1978, *275*, 43–44. (b)

Lippold, O. C. G. Oscillation in the stretch reflex arc and the origins of the rhythmic 8–12 c/s component of physiological tremor. *Journal of Physiology*, 1970, *206*, 359–382.

Lisberger, S. G., & Fuchs, A. F. Role of primate flocculus during rapid behavioral modification of vestibuloocular reflex. I. Purkinje cell activity during visually guided horizontal smooth-pursuit eye movements and passive head rotation. *Journal of Neurophysiology*, 1978, *41*, 733–763.

Lisberger, S. G., & Miles, F. A. Role of primate medial vestibular nucleus in long-term adaptive plasticity or vestibuloocular reflex. *Journal of Neurophysiology*, 1980, *43*, 1725–1745.

Lisberger, S. G., Miles, F. A., Optican, L. M., & Eighmy, B. B. Optokinetic response in monkey: Underlying mechanisms and their sensitivity to long-term adaptive changes in vestibuloocular reflex. *Journal of Neurophysiology*, 1981, *45*, 869–889.

Lishman, J. R., & Lee, D. N. The autonomy of visual kinaesthesis. *Perception*, 1973, *2*, 287–294.

Llinás, R., Walton, K., Hillman, D. E., & Soleto, C. Inferior olive: Its role in motor learning. *Science*, 1975, *190*, 1230–1231.

*Lloyd, D. P. C. Spinal mechanisms involved in somatic activities. In J. Field (Ed.), *Handbook of physiology* (Sec. 1, Vol. II). Washington, D.C.: American Physiological Society, 1960.

Loret, B. J. *Optimization of manned orbital satellite vehicle design with respect to artificial gravity*. ASD Technical Report 61-688. Wright-Patterson Air Force Base, Ohio, 1961.

Ludvigh, E., & McKinnon, P. The effect of orientation on the three-dot alignment test. *American Journal of Ophthalmology*, 1967, *64*, 261–265.

Luschei, E. S., & Fuchs, A. F. Activity of brain stem neurons during eye movements of alert monkeys. *Journal of Neurophysiology*, 1972, *35*, 445–461.

Luster, T. Vestibular adaptation in man: Effects of increased acceleration during different phases of adaptation. *Journal of Experimental Psychology*, 1972, *96*, 263–272.

MacDougall, R. The subjective horizon. *Psychological Review Monograph*, 1903, *Suppl 4*.

Mach, E. *Grundlinien der Lehre von der Bewegungsempfindungen.* Leipzig: Engelmann, 1875.

*MacKay, W. A., & Murphy, J. T. Cerebellar modulation of reflex gain. *Progress in Neurobiology*, 1979, *13*, 361–417.

Maeda, M., Maunz, R. A., & Wilson, V. J. Labyrinthine influence on cat forelimb motoneurons. *Experimental Brain Research*, 1975, *22*, 69–86.

Maekawa. K., & Kimura, M. Electrophysiological study of the nucleus of the optic tract that transfers optic signals to the nucleus reticularis tegmenti pontis—The visual mossy fiber pathway to the cerebellar flocculus. *Brain Research*, 1981, *211*, 456–462.

*Magnus, R. *Körperstellung.* Berlin: Springer, 1924.

Magnus, R. Some results of studies in the physiology of posture. The Cameron Prize Lectures. *Lancet*, 1926, *2*, 531–536; 583–588.

Magnussen, S., & Kurtenbach, W. Linear summation of tilt illusion and tilt aftereffect. *Vision Research*, 1980, *20*, 39–42.

Malcolm, R., & Melvill Jones, G. A quantitative study of vestibular adaptation in humans. *Acta Otolaryngologica*, 1970, *70*, 126–135.

Mann, C. W., Berthelot-Berry, N. H., & Dauterive, H. J. The perception of the vertical: I. Visual and non-labyrinthine cues. *Journal of Experimental Psychology*, 1949, *39*, 538–547.

Manzoni, D., Pompeiano, O., & Stampacchia, G. Cervical control of posture and movements. *Brain Research*, 1979, *169*, 615–619.

Marsden, C. D., Merton, P. A., & Morton, H. B. Human postural responses. *Brain*, 1981, *104*, 513–534.

Marsden, C. D., Merton, P. A., Morton, H. B., & Adam, J. The effect of lesions of the central nervous system in long-latency stretch reflexes in the human thumb. In J. E. Desmedt (Ed.), *Cerebral motor control in man: Long loop mechanisms. Progress in clinical neurophysiology.* Basel: Karger, 1978.

Matin, E., & Drivas, A. Acuity for orientation measured with a sequential recognition task and signal detection methods. *Perception and Psychophysics*, 1979, *25*, 161–168.

*Matthews, P. B. C. *Mammalian muscle receptors and their central action.* London: Arnold, 1972.

Mauritz, K. H., Dichgans, J., & Hufschmidt, A. The angle of visual roll motion determines displacement of subjective visual vertical. *Perception and Psychophysics*, 1977, *22*, 557–562.

Mauritz, K. H., Schmitt, C., & Dichgans, J. Delayed and enhanced long latency reflexes as the possible cause of postural termor in late cerebellar atrophy. *Brain*, 1981, *104*, 97–116.

McCabe, B. F., & Ryu, J. H. Experiments on vestibular compensation. *Laryngoscope*, 1969, *79*, 1728–1736.

McCouch, G. P., Deering, I. D., & Ling, T. H. Location of receptors for tonic neck reflexes. *Journal of Neurophysiology*, 1951, *14*, 191–195.

McIntyre, A. K. The quick component of nystagmus. *Journal of Physiology*, 1939, *97*, 8–16.

McKee, S. P., & Westheimer, G. Improvement in vernier acuity with practice. *Perception and Psychophysics*, 1978, *24*, 258–262,

Meiry, J. L. Vestibular and proprioceptive stabilization of eye movements. In P. Bach-y-Rita, C. C. Collins, & J. E. Hyde (Eds.), *The control of eye movements.* New York: Academic Press, 1971.

Melcher, G. A., & Henn, V. The latency of circular vection during different accelerations of the optokinetic stimulus. *Perception and Psychophysics*, 1981, *30*, 552–556.

Melvill Jones, G. Predominance of anti-compensatory oculomotor response during rapid head rotation. *Aerospace Medicine*, 1964, *35*, 965–968.

Melvill Jones, G., Barry, W., & Kowalsky, N. Dynamics of the semicircular canals compared in yaw, pitch and roll. *Aerospace Medicine*, 1964, *35*, 984–989.

Melvill Jones, G., & Davies, P. Adaptation of cat vestibulo-ocular reflex to 200 days of optically reversed vision. *Brain Research*, 1976, *103*, 551–554.

Melvill Jones, G., Downing, D., & Rolf, R. *Human subjective and reflex responses to sinusoidal vertical acceleration.* Ames Progress Report, NASA, 1973. (Cited in Melvill Jones, G. The vestibular system for eye movement control. In R. A. Monty & J. W. Senders (Eds.), *Eye movements and psychological processes.* Hillsdale, N.J.: Lawrence Erlbaum, 1976.)

Melvill Jones, G., & Gonshor, A. Oculomotor response to rapid head oscillation (0.5–50 Hz) after prolonged adaptation to vision reversal. *Experimental Brain Research*, 1982, *45*, 45–58.

Melvill Jones, G., & Sugie, N. Vestibulo-ocular responses in man during sleep. *Electroencephalography and Clinical Neurophysiology*, 1972, *32*, 43–53.

Melvill Jones, G., & Watt, D. G. D. Muscular control of landing from unexpected falls in man. *Journal of Physiology*, 1971, *219*, 729–737. (a)

Melvill Jones, G., & Watt, D. G. D. Observations on the control of stepping and hopping movements in man. *Journal of Physiology*, 1971, *219*, 709–727. (b)

Merker, B. H., & Held, R. Eye torsion and the apparent horizontal under head tilt and visual field rotation. *Vision Research*, 1981, *21*, 543–547.

Miles, F. A. The primate flocculus and eye–head coordination. In B. A. Brooks, & F. J. Bajandas (Eds.), *Eye movements.* New York: Plenum, 1977.

Miles, F. A., & Braitman, D. J. Long-term adaptive changes in primate vestibulo-ocular reflex. II. Electrophysiological observations on semicircular canal primary afferents. *Journal of Neurophysiology*, 1980, *43*, 1426–1436.

Miles, F. A., Braitman, D. J., & Dow, B. M. Long-term adaptive changes in primate vestibuloocular reflex. IV. Electrophysiological observations in flocculus of adapted monkeys. *Journal of Neurophysiology*, 1980, *43*, 1477–1493.

Miles, F. A., & Eighmy, B. B. Long-term adaptive changes in primate vestibuloocular reflex. I. Behavioral observations. *Journal of Neurophysiology*, 1980, *43*, 1406–1425.

Miles, F. A., & Fuller, J. H. Adaptive plasticity in the vestibuloocular responses of the rhesus monkey. *Brain Research*, 1974, *80*, 512–516.

Miles, F. A., Fuller, J. H., Braitman, D. J., & Dow, B. M. Long-term adaptive changes in primate vestibuloocular ocular reflex. III. Electrophysiological observations in flocculus of normal monkey. *Journal of Neurophysiology*, 1980, *43*, 1437–1476.

*Miles, F. A., & Lisberger, S. G. Plasticity in the vestibuloocular reflex: A new hypothesis. *Annual Review of Neuroscience*, 1981, *4*, 273–299.

Miller, E. F., Fregly, A. R., & Graybiel, A. Visual horizontal-perception in relation to otolith-function. *American Journal of Psychology*, 1968, *81*, 488–496.

Miller, E. F., Fregly, A. R., van den Brink, G., & Graybiel, A. *Visual localization of the horizontal as a function of body tilt up to* $\pm 90°$ *from gravitational vertical.* (NSAM-942. NASA Order No. R-47.) Naval School of Aviation Medicine, Pensacola, Fl., 1965.

Miller, E. F., & Graybiel, A. *Rotary autokinesis and displacement of the visual horizontal associated with head (body) position.* (MROOS.13-6001, Subtask 1, Report No. 77.) Naval School of Aviation Medicine, Pensacola, Fl., 1963.

Miller, E. F., & Graybiel, A. Magnitude of gravitoinertial force; An independent variable in egocentric visual localization of the horizontal. *Journal of Experimental Psychology*, 1966, *71*, 452–460.

Miller, E. F., & Graybiel, A. Effect of gravitoinertial force on ocular counterrolling. *Journal of Applied Psychology*, 1971, *31*, 697–700.

Miller, E. F., & Graybiel, A. Human ocular counterrolling measured during eight hours of sustained body tilt. *Minerva Otorinolaringologica*, 1974, *24*, 247–252.

Mishkin, S., & Melvill Jones, G. Predominant direction of gaze during slow head rotation. *Aerospace Medicine*, 1966, *37*, 897–900.

Money, K. E., Bonen, L., Beatty, J. D., Kuehn, L. A., Sokoloff, M., & Weaver, R. S. Physical properties of fluids and structures of vestibular apparatus of the pigeon. *American Journal of Physiology*, 1971, *220*, 140–147.

Money, K. E., & Cheung, B. S. Another function of the inner ear: Facilitation of the emetic response to poisons. *Aviation, Space & Environmental Medicine*, 1983, *54*, 208–211.

Money, K. E., & Myles, W. S. Heavy water nystagmus and the effects of alcohol. *Nature*, 1974, *247*, 404–405.

*Monty, R. A. & Senders, J. W. *Eye movements and psychological processes*. Hillsdale, N.J.: Lawrence Erlbaum, 1976.

Morant, R. B., & Aronoff, J. Starting position, adaptation, and visual framework as influencing the perception of verticality. *Journal of Experimental Psychology*, 1966, *71*, 684–686.

Morant, R. B., & Beller, H. K. Adaptation to prismatically rotated visual fields. *Science*, 1965, *148*, 530–531.

Morasso, P., Bizzi, E., & Dichgans, J. Adjustment of saccade characteristics during head movements. *Experimental Brain Research*, 1973, *16*, 492–500.

Morgan, C. L. Constancy of egocentric visual direction. *Perception and Psychophysics*, 1978, *23*, 61–68.

Mori, S. Discharge patterns of soleus motor units with associated changes in force exerted by foot during quiet stance in man. *Journal of Neurophysiology*, 1973, *36*, 458–471.

Muir, D. W., & Over, R. Tilt aftereffects in central and peripheral vision. *Journal of Experimental Psychology*, 1970, *85*, 165–170.

Müller, G. E. Uber das Aubertsche Phänomenon. *Zeitschrift fur Psychologie und Physiologie der Sinnesorganen*, 1916, *49*, 109–246.

Muller, P. E., Sidorsky, R. C., Slivinske, A. J., Alluisi, E. A., & Fitts, P. M. *The symbolic coding of information on cathoderay tubes and similar displays*. (U.S.A.F. WADC Technical Report No. 55-375.) 1955.

Nakao, S., Curthoys, I. S., & Markham, C. H. Eye movement related neurones in the cat pontine reticular formation Projection to the flocculus. *Brain Research*, 1980, *183*, 291–300.

Nakao, S., Sasaki, S., Schor, R. H., & Shimazu, H. Functional organization of premotor neurons in the cat medial vestibular nucleus related to slow and fast phases of nystagmus. *Experimental Brain Research*, 1982, *45*, 371–384.

Nakayama, K., & Balliet, R. Listing's law, eye position sense, and perception of the vertical. *Vision Research*, 1977, *17*, 453–457.

Nakayama, K., & Loomis, J. M. Optical velocity patterns, velocity-sensitive neurons, and space perception: A hypothesis. *Perception*, 1974, *3*, 63–80.

Nashner, L. M. A model describing vestibular detection of body sway motion. *Acta Otolaryngologica*, 1971, *72*, 429–436.

Nashner, L. M. Adapting reflexes controlling the human posture. *Experimental Brain Research*, 1976, *25*, 59–72.

Nashner, L. M. Fixed patterns of rapid postural responses among leg muscles during stance. *Experimental Brain Research*, 1977, *30*, 13–24.

Nashner, L., & Berthoz, A. Visual contribution to rapid responses during postural control. *Brain Research*, 1978, *150*, 403–407.

Nashner, L. M., & Grimm, R. J. Analysis of multiloop dyscontrols in standing cerebellar patients. *Progress in Clinical Neurophysiology*, 1978, *4*, 300–309.

Nashner, L. M., & Wolfson, P. Influence of head position and proprioceptive cues on short latency postural reflexes evoked by galvanic stimulations of the human labyrinth. *Brain Research*, 1974, *67*, 255–268.

Nashner, L. M., Woollacott, M., & Tuma, G. Organization of rapid responses to postural and locomotor-like perturbations of standing man. *Experimental Brain Research*, 1979, *36*, 463–476.

Nelson, J. R., & Cope, D. The otoliths and the ocular countertorsion reflex. *Archives of Otolaryngology*, 1971, *94*, 40–50.

Niven, J. I., Hixson, W. C., & Correia, M. J. Elicitation of horizontal nystagmus by periodic linear acceleration. *Acta Otolaryngologica*, 1966, *62*, 429–441.

Nyberg-Hansen, R. Anatomical aspects of the functional organization of the vestibulo-spinal pathways. In R. F. Naunton (Ed.), *The vestibular system*. New York: Academic Press, 1975.

Nyborg, H. Tactile stimulation and perception of the vertical. I. Effects of diffuse vs. specific tactile stimulation. *Scandinavian Journal of Psychology*, 1971, *12*, 1–13.

Nyborg, H. A method for analysing performance in the rod-and-frame test. I. *Scandinavian Journal of Psychology*, 1974, *15*, 119–123.

Nyborg, H. Psychological differentiation in school children. Maturation, cognition, and personality development. *Psychological Reports Aarhus*, vol. 5, no. 2. Denmark: University of Aarhus, 1980.

Ogle, K. N. *Researches in binocular vision*. New York: Hafner, 1964.

Oman, C. M., Bock, O. L., & Huang, J. K. Visually induced self-motion sensation adapts rapidly to left–right visual reversal. *Science*, 1980, *209*, 706–708.

Orlovsky, G. N. Activity of vestibulospinal neurons during locomotion. *Brain Research*, 1972, *46*, 85–98.

Ornitz, E. M., Atwell, C. W., Walter, D. O., Hartmann, E. E., & Kaplan, A. R. The maturation of vestibular nystagmus in infancy and childhood. *Acta Otolaryngologica*, 1979, *88*, 244–256.

Ornitz, E. M., Brown, M. B., Mason, A., & Putnam, N. H. The effect of visual input on post-rotatory nystagmus in normal children. *Acta Otolaryngologica*, 1974, *77*, 418–425.

Outerbridge, J. S., & Melvill Jones, G. Reflex vestibular control of head movement in man. *Aerospace Medicine*, 1971, *42*, 935–940.

Oyama, T. Determinants of the Zöllner illusion. *Psychological Research*, 1975, *37*, 261–280.

Paap, K. R., & Ebenholtz, S. M. Perceptual consequences of potentiation in the extraocular muscles: An alternative explanation for adaptation to wedge prisms. *Journal of Experimental Psychology: Human Perception & Performance*, 1976, *2*, 457–468.

Park, J. N. Displacement of apparent straight ahead as an after effect of deviation of the eyes from normal position. *Perceptual & Motor Skills*, 1969, *28*, 591–597.

Parsons, R. D. Magnitude estimates of the oculogyral illusion during and following angular acceleration. *Journal of Experimental Psychology*, 1970, *84*, 230–238.

*Peiper, A. *Cerebral function in infancy and childhood*. London: Pitman, 1963.

Petrov, A. P., & Zenkin, G. M. Torsional eye movements and constancy of the visual field. *Vision Research*, 1973, *13*, 2465–2477.

Pfaltz, C. R., & Ohtsuka, Y. The influence of optokinetic training upon vestibular habituation. *Acta Otolaryngologica*, 1975, *79*, 253–258.

Pierrot-Deseilligny, E., Morin, C., Bergego, C., & Tankov, N. Pattern of group I fibre projections from ankle flexor and extensor muscles in man. *Experimental Brain Research*, 1981, *42*, 337–350.

Pompeiano, O. Cerebello-vestibular interrelations. In H. H. Kornhuber (Ed.), *Handbook of sensory physiology* (Vol. VI/1). New York: Springer-Verlag, 1974.

Pompeiano, O. Vestibulo-spinal relationships. In R. F. Nauton (Ed.), *The vestibular system*. New York: Academic Press, 1975.

Post, R. B., & Leibowitz, H. W. The effect of convergence on the vestibulo-ocular reflex and implications for perceived movement. *Vision Research*, 1982, *22*, 461–465.

Pratt, R. T. C., & McKenzie, W. Anxiety following vestibular disorders. *Lancet*, 1958, *2*, 347–349.

Precht, W. Characteristics of vestibular neurons after acute and chronic labyrinthine destruction. In H. H. Kornhuber (Ed.), *Handbook of Sensory Physiology* (Vol. VI/2). New York: Springer-Verlag, 1974.

Precht, W., Shimazu, H., & Markham, C. H. A mechanism of central compensation of vestibular function following hemilabyrinthectomy. *Journal of Neurophysiology*, 1966, *29*, 996–1010.

Prentice, W. C. H., & Beardslee, D. C. Visual "normalization" near the vertical and horizontal. *Journal of Experimental Psychology*, 1950, *40*, 355–364.

Pulaski, P. D., Zee, D. S., & Robinson, D. A. The behavior of the vestibulo-ocular reflex at high velocities of head rotation. *Brain Research*, 1981, *222*, 159–165.

Putkonen, P. T. S., Courjon, J. H., & Jeannerod, M. Compensation of postural effects of hemilabyrinthectomy in the cat. A sensory substitution process? *Experimental Brain Research*, 1977, *28*, 249–257.

Quereau, J. Some aspects of torsion. *Archives of Ophthalmology*, 1954, *51*, 783–788.

Rademaker, G. G. J. *Reactions Labyrinthiques et Equilibre: L'Ataxie Labyrinthique*. Paris: Masson, 1935.

Raphan, T., & Cohen, B. The role of integration in oculomotor control.

In B. L. Zuber (Ed.), *Models of oculomotor behavior and control.* Boca Raton, Fl.: CRC Press, 1981.

Raphan, T., Cohen, B., & Matsuo, V. A velocity-storage mechanism responsible for optokinetic nystagmus (OKN), optokinetic after-nystagmus (OKAN) and vestibular nystagmus. In R. Baker & A. Berthoz, (Eds.), *Control of gaze by brain stem neurons.* New York: Elsevier, 1977.

Raphan, T., Matsuo, V., & Cohen, B. Velocity storage in the vestibulo-ocular reflex arc (VOR). *Experimental Brain Research,* 1979, *35,* 229–248.

Rapoport, S., Susswein, A., Uchino, Y., & Wilson, V. J. Synaptic actions of individual vestibular neurones on cat neck motoneurones. *Journal of Physiology,* 1977, *272,* 367–382.

*Reason, J. T., & Brand, J. J. *Motion sickness.* New York: Academic Press, 1975.

Reason, J., Wagner, H., & Dewhurst, D. A visually-driven postural after-effect. *Acta Psychologica,* 1981, *48,* 241–251.

Riesen, A. H., & Kinder, E. F. *Postural development in infant chimpanzees.* New Haven: Yale University Press, 1952.

Rieser, J. J., & Banks, M. S. The perception of verticality and the frame of reference of the visual tilt aftereffect. *Perception and Psychophysics,* 1981, *29,* 113–120.

Roberts, T. D. M. Changes in stretch reflexes in limb extensor muscles during position reflexes from the labyrinth in the cat. *Journal of Physiology,* 1971, *211,* 5–6. (a)

Roberts, T. D. M. Standing with a bent knee. *Nature,* 1971, *230,* 499–501. (b)

Roberts, T. D. M. Reflex balance. *Nature,* 1973, *244,* 156–158.

*Roberts, T. D. M. *Neurophysiology of postural mechanisms* (2nd ed.). London: Butterworth, 1978.

Roberts, T. D. M., & Stenhouse, G. The nature of postural sway. *Aggressologie,* 1976, *17,* 11–14.

Robinson, D. A. A method of measuring eye movement using a scleral search coil in a magnetic field. *IEEE Transactions in Biomedical Electronics,* 1963, *10,* 137–145.

Robinson, D. A. Models of oculomotor neural organization. In P. Bach-y-Rita, C. C. Collins, & J. E. Hyde (Eds.), *The Control of eye movements.* New York: Academic Press, 1971.

Robinson, D. A. The effect of cerebellectomy on the cat's vestibuloocular integrator. *Brain Research,* 1974, *71,* 195–207.

Robinson, D. A. Adaptive gain control of vestibuloocular reflex by the cerebellum. *Journal of Neurophysiology,* 1976, *39,* 954–969.

Robinson, D. A. Linear addition of optokinetic and vestibular signals in the vestibular nucleus. *Experimental Brain Research,* 1977, *30,* 447–450.

*Robinson, D. A. The use of control systems analysis in the neurophysiology of eye movements. *Annual Review of Neuroscience,* 1981, *4,* 463–503.

Rock, I. The basis of position-constancy during passive movement. *American Journal of Psychology,* 1968, *81,* 262–265.

Ross, H. E., Crickmar, S. D., Sills, N. V., & Owen, E. P. Orientation to the vertical in free divers. *Aerospace Medicine,* 1969, *40,* 728–732.

Rubia, F. J., & Tandler, R. Spatial distribution of afferent information to the anterior lobe of the cat's cerebellum. *Experimental Brain Research,* 1981, *42,* 249–259.

Ryu, J. H., & McCabe, B. F. Central vestibular compensation. *Archives of Otolaryngology,* 1976, *102,* 71–76.

Santschi, W. R., DuBois, J., & Omoto, C. *Moments of inertia and centers of gravity of the living human body.* (Aerospace Medical Research Laboratories, Report No. AMRL-TDR-63-36.) Wright-Patterson Air Force Base, Ohio, 1963.

Schaefer, K.-P., & Meyer, D. L. Compensatory mechanisms following labyrinthine lesions in the guinea-pig: A simple model of learning. In H. P. Zippel (Ed.), *Memory and transfer of information.* New York: Plenum, 1973.

*Schaefer, K.-P., & Meyer, D. L. Compensation of vestibular lesions. In H. H. Kornhuber (Ed.), *Handbook of sensory physiology* (Vol. VI/1). Berlin: Springer-Verlag, 1974.

Schneider, C. W. Monocular and binocular perception of verticality and the relationship of ocular dominance. *American Journal of Psychology,* 1966, *79,* 632–636.

Schöne, H. Über den Einfluss der Schwerkraft auf die Augenrollung und auf die Wahrnehmung der Lage im Raum. *Zeitschrift für Vergleichende Physiologie,* 1962, *46,* 57–87.

Schöne, H. On the role of gravity in human spatial orientation. *Aerospace Medicine,* 1964, *35,* 764–772.

Schöne, H., & Lechner-Steinleitner, S. The effect of preceding tilt on the perceived vertical. *Acta Otolaryngologica,* 1978, *85,* 68–73.

Schöne, H., & Mortag, H. G. Variation of the subjective vertical on the parallel swing at different body positions. *Psychologische Forschung,* 1968, *32,* 124–134.

Schöne, H., Parker, D. E., & Mortag, H. G. Subjective vertical as a function of body position and gravity magnitude. *Naturwissenschaften,* 1967, *54,* 288.

Schöne, H., & Udo de Haes, H. Perception of gravity—Vertical as a function of head and trunk position. *Zeitschrift fur Vergleichende Physiologie,* 1968, *60,* 440–444.

Schöne, H., & Wade, N. J. The influence of force magnitude on the perception of body position: II. Effect of body posture. *British Journal of Psychology,* 1971, *62,* 347–352.

Schor, R. H., & Miller, A. D. Vestibular reflexes in neck and forelimb muscles evoked by roll tilt. *Journal of neurophysiology,* 1981, *46,* 167–178.

Schroeder, D. J. Influence of alcohol in vestibular responses to angular accelerations. *Aerospace Medicine,* 1971, *42,* 959–970.

Schubert, G., & Brecher, G. A. Uber optische Lokalisation und Augenstellung bei Vor-Rückwärtsneigung oder excentrischer Rotation des Körpers. *Zeitschrift für Sinnesphysiologie,* 1934, *65,* 1–26.

Scott, A. B. Extraocular muscles and head tilting. *Archives of Ophthalmology,* 1967, *78,* 397–399.

Searles, E. J., & Barnes, C. D. Ipsilateral utricular and semicircular canal interactions from electrical stimulation of individual vestibular nerve branches recorded in the descending medial fasciculus. *Brain Research,* 1977, *125,* 23–36.

Shambes, G. M. Influence of the fusimotor system on stance in volitional movements in normal man. *American Journal of Physical Medicine,* 1969, *48,* 225–236.

Shebilske, W. L., & Fogelgren, L. Eye-position aftereffects of backward head tilt manifested by illusory visual direction. *Perception and Psychophysics,* 1977, *21,* 77–82.

Shebilske, W. L., & Karmiohl, C. M. Illusory visual direction during and after backward head tilts. *Perception and Psychophysics,* 1979, *24,* 543–545.

*Sherrington, C. *Integrative action of the nervous system.* Cambridge: Cambridge University Press, 1947.

Sigman, E., Goodenough, D. R., & Flannagan, M. Instructions, illusory self-tilt and the rod-and-frame test. *Quarterly Journal of Experimental Psychology,* 1979, *31,* 155–165.

Simpson, J. I., Precht, W., & Llinás, R. Sensory separation in climbing and mossy fiber inputs to cat vestibulocerebellum. *Pflüger's Archiv European Journal of Physiology,* 1974, *351,* 183–195.

Singer, G., Purcell, A. T., & Austin, M. The effect of structure and degree of tilt on the tilted room illusion. *Perception and Psychophysics,* 1970, *7,* 250–252.

Skavenski, A. A., Blair, S. M., & Westheimer, G. 1981. The effects of habituating vestibular and optokinetic nystagmus on each other. *Journal of Neuroscience,* 1981, *1,* 351–357.

Skavenski, A. A., & Robinson, D. A. Role of abducens neurons in the vestibulo-ocular reflex. *Journal of Neurophysiology,* 1973, *36,* 724–738.

Smiles, K. A., Hite, D., Hyams, V. J., & Junker, A. M. Effect of labyrinthectomy on the dynamic vestibulo-ocular counterroll reflex in the rhesus monkey. *Aviation, Space & Environmental Medicine,* 1975, *46,* 1017–1022.

Sokolovski, A. The influence of mental activity and visual fixation upon calorie-induced nystagmus in normal subjects. *Acta Otolaryngologica,* 1966, *61,* 209–220.

Stanojević, M. Responses of cerebellar fastigial neurons to neck and macular vestibular inputs. *Pflüger's Archiv European Journal of Physiology*, 1981, *391*, 267–272.

Stanojević, M., Erway, L., Ghelarducci, B., Pompeiano, O., & Willis, W. D. A comparison of the response characteristics of cerebellar fastigial and vermal cortex neurons to sinusoidal stimulation of macular vestibular receptors. *Pflüger's Archiv European Journal of Physiology*, 1980, *385*, 95–104.

*Stein, R. B., Pearson, K. G., Smith, R. S., & Redford, J. B. (Eds.), *Control of posture and locomotion*. New York: Plenum, 1973.

Steinbach, M. J., & Money, K. E. Eye movements of the owl. *Vision Research*, 1973, *13*, 889–891.

Steinman, R. M. & Collewijn, H. Binocular retinal image motion during active head rotation. *Vision Research*, 1980, *20*, 415–430.

Stockwell, C. W., Gilson, R. D., & Guedry, F. E. Adaptation of horizontal semicircular canal responses. *Acta Otolaryngologica*, 1973, *75*, 471–476.

Stockwell, C. W., & Guedry, F. E. The effect of semicircular canal stimulation during tilting on the subsequent perception of the visual vertical. *Acta Otolaryngologica*, 1970, *70*, 170–175.

Stratton, G. M. Upright vision and the retinal image. *Psychological Review*, 1897, *4*, 182–187. (a)

Stratton, G. M. Vision without inversion of the retinal image. *Psychological Review*, 1897, *4*, 341–360. (b)

Suzuki, J. I., Tokumasu, K., & Goto, K. Eye movements from single utricular nerve stimulation in the cat. *Acta Otolaryngologica*, 1969, *68*, 350–362.

Takahashi, M., Uemura, T., & Fujishiro, T. Studies of the vestibulo-ocular reflex and visual-vestibular interactions during active head movements. *Acta Otolaryngologica*, 1980, *90*, 115–124.

Takemori, S., & Suzuki, J. I. Eye deviations from neck torsion in humans. *Annals of Otology, Rhinology, & Laryngology*, 1971, *80*, 439–444.

*Talbot, R. E., & Humphrey, D. R. (Eds.). *Posture and movement*. New York: Raven Press, 1979.

Templeton, W. B. Visual tilt normalization: The method of kinaesthetic matching. *Perception and Psychophysics*, 1972, *12*, 422–424.

Templeton, W. B., Howard, I. P., & Easting, G. Satiation and the tilt after-effect. *American Journal of Psychology*, 1965, *78*, 656–659.

Thach, W. T. Correlation of neural discharge with pattern and force of muscular activity, joint position, and direction of intended next movement in motor cortex and cerebellum. *Journal of Neurophysiology*, 1978, *41*, 654–676.

Thoden, U., Dichgans, J., & Savidis, Th. Direction-specific optokinetic modulation of monosynaptic limb reflexes in cats. *Experimental Brain Research*, 1977, *30*, 155–160.

Tibbling, L. The rotatory nystagmus response in children. *Acta Otolaryngologica*, 1969, *68*, 459–467.

Tolhurst, D. J., & Thompson, P. G. Orientation illusions and aftereffects: Inhibition between channels. *Vision Research*, 1975, *15*, 967–972.

Tomlinson, R. D., Saunders, G. E., & Schwarz, D. W. F. Analysis of human vestibulo-ocular reflex during active head movements. *Acta Otolaryngologica*, 1980, *90*, 184–190.

Travis, R. C. A new stabilometer for measuring dynamic equilibrium in the standing position. *Journal of Experimental Psychology*, 1944, *34*, 418–424.

Treisman, M. Motion sickness: An evolutionary hypothesis. *Science*, 1977, *197*, 493–495.

Tschermak-Seysenegg, A. von. *Introduction to physiological optics*. Springfield, Ill.: Thomas, 1952.

'Tyler, C. W. Stereoscopic tilt and size aftereffects. *Perception*, 1975, *4*, 187–192.

Tyler, C. W., & Scott, A. B Binocular vision. In R. E. Records (Ed.), *Physiology of the human eye and Visual system*. New York: Harper & Row, 1979.

Udo de Haes, H. A. Stability of apparent vertical and ocular countertorsion as a function of lateral tilt. *Perception and Psychophysics*, 1970, *8*, 137–142.

Udo de Haes, H. A., & Schöne, H. Interaction between statolith organs and semicircular canals on apparent vertical and nystagmus. Investigations on the effectiveness of the statolith organs. *Acta Otolaryngologica*, 1970, *69*, 25–31.

Uemura, T., Arai, Y., & Shimazaki, C. Eye–head coordination during lateral gaze in normal subjects. *Acta Otolaryngologica*, 1980, *90*, 191–198.

Vanni-Mercier, G., & Magnin, M. single neuron activity related to natural vestibular stimulation in the cat's visual cortex. *Experimental Brain Research*, 1982, *45*, 451–455.

Virsu, V., & Taskinen, H. Central inhibition interactions in human beings. *Experimental Brain Research*, 1975, *23*, 65–74.

Volkmann, F. C., & Pufall, P. B. Adjustment of visual tilt as a function of age. *Perception and Psychophysics*, 1972, *11*, 187–192.

Wade, N. J. The effect of monocular and binocular observation on visual orientation during head tilt. *American Journal of Psychology*, 1969, *82*, 384–388. (a)

Wade, N. J. The effect of stimulus line variations on visual orientation with head upright and tilted. *Australian Journal of Psychology*, 1969, *21*, 177–185. (b)

Wade, N. J. Visual orientation as a function of head tilt. *Perceptual and Motor Skills*, 1969, *29*, 573–574. (c)

Wade, N. J. The effect of different psychophysical methods on visual orientation during tilt. *Psychonomic Science*, 1970, *19*, 201–203. (a)

Wade, N. J. Effect of instructions on visual orientation. *Journal of Experimental Psychology*, 1970, *83*, 331–332. (b)

Wade, N. J. Effect of forward head inclination on visual orientation during lateral body tilt. *Journal of Experimental Psychology*, 1972, *96*, 203–205.

Wade, N. J. The effect of water immersion on perception of the visual vertical. *British Journal of Psychology*, 1973, *64*, 351–361.

Wade, N. J., & Day, R. H. Apparent head position as a basis for a visual aftereffect of prolonged head tilt. *Perception and Psychophysics*, 1968, *3*, 324–326. (a)

Wade, N. J., & Day, R. H. Development and dissipation of a visual spatial aftereffect from prolonged head tilt. *Journal of Experimental Psychology*, 1968, *76*, 439–443. (b)

Wade, N. J., & Schöne, H. The influence of force magnitude on the perception of body position: I. Effect of head posture. *British Journal of Psychology*, 1971, *62*, 157–163.

Waespe, W., & Henn, V. Neuronal activity in the vestibular nuclei of the alert monkey during vestibular and optokinetic stimulation. *Experimental Brain Research*, 1977, *27*, 523–538. (a)

Waespe, W., & Henn, V. Vestibular nuclei activity during optokinetic after-nystagmus (OKAN) in the alert monkey. *Experimental Brain Research*, 1977, *30*, 323–330. (b)

Waespe, W., & Henn, V. Conflicting visual-vestibular stimulation and vestibular nucleus activity in alert monkeys. *Experimental Brain Research*, 1978, *33*, 203–212. (a)

Waespe, W., & Henn, V. Reciprocal changes in primary and secondary optokinetic after-nystagmus (OKAN) produced by repetitive optokinetic stimulation in the monkey. *Archiv für Psychiatrie und Nervenkrankheiten*, 1978, *225*, 23–30. (b)

*Waespe, W., & Henn, V. Motion information in the vestibular nuclei of alert monkeys: Visual and vestibular input vs. optomotor input. In R. Granit & O. Pompeiano (Eds.), *Reflex Control of posture and movement*. New York: Elsevier, 1979.

Waespe, W., Huber, T., & Henn, V. Dynamic changes of optokinetic after-nystagmus (OKAN) caused by brief visual fixation periods in monkey and in man. *Archiv für Psychiatrie und Nervenkrankeiten*, 1978, *226*, 1–19.

Walberg, F. The vestibular nuclei and their connections with the eighth nerve and the cerebellum. In R. F. Naunton (Ed.), *The vestibular system*. New York: Academic Press, 1975.

Wallace, M., Singer, G., Mottram, J., & Purcell, T. Effects of exposure to a tilted room on kinesthetic postexposure responses. *Perception*, 1975, *4*, 447–451.

Wallach, H., & Bacon, J. The constancy of the orientation of the visual field. *Perception and Psychophysics*, 1976, *19*, 492–498.

Wallach, H., & Frey, K. J. Adaptation in the constancy of visual direction measured by a one-trial method. *Perception and Psychophysics*, 1969, *5*, 249–256.

Wallach, H., Frey, K. J., & Romney, G. Adaptation to field displacement during head movement unrelated to the constancy of visual direction. *Perception and Psychophysics*, 1969, *5*, 253–256.

Walls, G. L. The evolutionary history of eye movements. *Vision Research*, 1962, *2*, 69–80.

Wapner, S., & Witkin, H. A. The role of visual factors in the maintenance of body-balance. *American Journal of Psychology*, 1950, *63*, 385–408.

Warabi, T. Trunk-ocular reflex in man. *Neuroscience Letters*, 1978, *9*, 267–270.

Ware, C., & Mitchell, D. E. The spatial selectivity of the tilt aftereffect. *Vision Research*, 1974, *14*, 735–737.

Warren, R. The perception of egomotion. *Journal of Experimental Psychology: Human Perception & Performance*, 1976, *2*, 448–456.

Watt, D. G. D. Responses of cats to sudden falls: An otolith-originating reflex assisting landing. *Journal of Neurophysiology*, 1976, *39*, 257–265.

Weale, R. A. Experiments on the Zöllner and related optical illusions. *Vision Research*, 1978, *18*, 203–208.

Wenzel, D., Thoden, U., & Frank, A. Forelimb reflexes modulated by tonic neck positions in the cat. *Pflüger's Archiv European Journal of Physiology*, 1978, *374*, 107–113.

Werner, H., Wapner, S., & Bruell, J. H. Experiments on sensory-tonic field theory of perception: VI. Effect of position of head, eyes, and of object on position of the apparent median plane. *Journal of Experimental Psychology*, 1953, *46*, 293–299.

Wertheimer, M. Experimentelle Studien über das Sehen von Bewegung. *Zeitschrift für Psychologie und Physiologie der Sennesorganen*, 1912, *61*, 161–265.

Westheimer, G., Shimamura, K., & McKee, S. P. Interference with line-orientation sensitivity. *Journal of the Optical Society of America*, 1976, *66*, 332–338.

White, K. D., Post, R. B., & Leibowitz, H. W. Saccadic eye movements and body sway. *Science*, 1980, *208*, 621–623.

Whiteside, T. C. D. Hand–eye co-ordination in weightlessness. *Aerospace Medicine*, 1961, *32*, 719–725.

Wilson, V. J., Gacek, R. R., Maeda, M., & Uchino, Y. Saccular and utricular input to cat neck motoneurons. *Journal of Neurophysiology*, 1977, *40*, 63–73.

Wilson, V. J., & Maeda, M. Connections between semicircular canals and neck motoneurons in the cat. *Journal of Neurophysiology*, 1974, *37*, 346–357.

Wilson, V. J., Maeda, M., & Franck, J. I. Input from neck afferents to the cat flocculus. *Brain Research*, 1975, *89*, 133–138.

*Wilson, V. J., & Melvill Jones, G. *Mammalian vestibular physiology*. New York: Plenum, 1979.

Wilson, V. J., Peterson, B. W., Fukushima, K., Hirai, N., & Uchino, Y. Analysis of vestibulocollic reflexes by sinusoidal polarization of vestibular afferent fibers. *Journal of Neurophysiology*, 1979, *42*, 331–346.

Winokur, G., Cadoret, R., Dorzab, J., & Baker, M. Depressive disease. A genetic study. *Archives of General Psychiatry*, 1971, *24*, 135–144.

Wist, E. R., Diener, H. C., Dichgans, J., & Brandt, T. Perceived distance and the perceived speed of self-motion: Linear vs. angular velocity? *Perception and Psychophysics*, 1975, *17*, 549–554.

Witkin, H. A., & Asch, S. E. Studies in space orientation: IV. Further experiments on perception of the upright with displaced visual fields. *Journal of Experimental Psychology*, 1948, *38*, 762–782.

Witkin, H. A., Oltman, P. K., Cox, P. W., Ehrichman, E., Hamm, R. M., & Ringler, R. W. Field-dependence and psychological differentiation: A bibliography through 1972 with index. Princeton, N.J.: *Educational Testing Service Research Bulletin*, 1973, 73–62.

Witkin, H. A., & Wapner, S. Visual factors in the maintenance of upright posture. *American Journal of Psychology*, 1950, *63*, 31–50.

Wong, S. C. P., & Frost, B. J. Subjective motion and acceleration induced by the movement of the observer's entire visual field. *Perception and Psychophysics*, 1978, *24*, 115–120.

Wong, S. C. P., & Frost, B. J. The effect of visual-vestibular conflict on the latency of steady-state visually induced subjective rotation. *Perception and Psychophysics*, 1981, *30*, 228–236.

Wood, R. W. The "haunted-swing" illusion. *Psychological Review*, 1895, *2*, 277–278.

*Yahr, M. D., & Purpura, D. P. *Neurophysiological basis of normal and abnormal motor activities*. Hewlett, N.Y.: Raven Press, 1967.

Young, L. R., Dichgans, J., Murphy, R., & Brandt, T. Interaction of optokinetic and vestibular stimuli in motion perception. *Acta Otolaryngologica*, 1973, *76*, 24–31.

Young, L. R., & Henn, V. S. Selective habituation of vestibular nystagmus by visual stimulation. *Acta Otolaryngologica*, 1974, *77*, 159–166.

Young, L. R., & Oman, C. M. Model for vestibular adaptation to horizontal rotation. *Aerospace Medicine*, 1969, *40*, 1076–1080.

Young, L. R., Oman, C. M., & Dichgans, J. M. Influence of head orientation on visually induced pitch and roll sensation. *Aviation, Space & Environmental Medicine*, 1975, *46*, 264–269.

Zacharias, G. L., & Young, L. R. Influence of combined visual and vestibular cues on human perception and control of horizontal rotation. *Experimental Brain Research*, 1981, *41*, 159–171.

Zee, D. S., Yee, R. D., & Robinson, D. A. Optokinetic responses in labyrinthine-defective human beings. *Brain Research*, 1976, *113*, 423–428.

CHAPTER 19

MOTION IN DEPTH AND VISUAL ACCELERATION

DAVID MARTIN REGAN

Department of Biomedical Engineering, Rutgers University, New Brunswick, New Jersey

LLOYD KAUFMAN

Department of Psychology and Department of Physiology and Biophysics, New York University, New York, New York

JANET LINCOLN

Department of Psychology, New York University, New York, New York

CONTENTS

Motion perception is one of the central topics of this *Handbook*. Apparent motion, aftereffects of exposure to motion, induced motion, and the visually induced sense of self-motion (vection) are discussed by Howard, Chapter 11, Mack, Chapter 17, and Rock, Chapter 33. Thresholds for seeing motion are considered in Chapter 16 by Anstis. This chapter goes further in discussing motion that is nonuniform in time or in space. For example, the velocity of a ball thrown through the air is not uniform in time, but changes from instant to instant. The velocity at any point on a river's surface may remain constant from moment to moment, but the velocity is different at different locations on the water's surface. Section 1 discusses motion that is nonuniform in time and is especially concerned with sensitivity to the acceleration of targets moving in the frontal plane; Sections 2 and 3 discuss motion that is nonuniform in space. Section 2 discusses empirical results of studies of perceived motion in depth due to changing size and to changing disparity, which produces effects that differ from the classic static disparity discussed by Arditi in Chapter 23. Section 3 deals with the direction of self-motion in depth and with optic flow patterns, for the two subjects are strongly related to each other.

A pervasive concept in vision research is that the visual system has multiple specific sensitivities; the visual system responds to some specific abstract feature of the retinal image, rather independently of other stimulus parameters, and there are a limited number of these specific sensitivities. (See Chapter 6 by Watson, Chapter 34 by Ginsburg, and Chapter 35 by Treisman in this *Handbook* for discussions of related concepts.) It has been suggested that the effect of these multiple sensitivities is to make an initial analysis of the retinal image by reducing the available information to a limited number of dimensions, without recourse at this stage of perception to any conscious or unconscious inferential processes. A component mechanism underlying such specific sensitivity is exemplified by a hypothetical "motion detector" in the visual system that is selectively sensitive to movement of the image across the retina. As we shall see in Section 1.1, such a component is insufficient to account for detection of nonuniformity in the motion of the image over time and other processes must be postulated at a later stage which, in this case, could include an inferential process.

Without denying the likelihood that higher-order processes may follow the analysis of the proximal stimulus by the visual system, a central theme in this chapter is to use the "multiple specific sensitivity" idea to explain visual responses to motion that is nonuniform in space. Section 3 discusses experimental evidence that the human visual system is specifically sensitive to certain relationships between the velocities at different locations in the retinal image, and that there are several such specific sensitivities to spatial relationships. One example of specific sensitivity is the visual response to looming or changing size; the visual system responds accurately to the algebraic difference between the simultaneous velocity at two locations that can be a degree or so apart in the visual field. Because this is a sensitivity to a relationship between two velocities, it cannot be explained in terms of classic sensitivity to velocity, for example, in terms of the action of simple "motion detectors." However, unlike sensitivity to nonuniform motion in time (which also cannot be explained solely in terms of simple motion detectors), evidence exists to support the applicability of the concept of "specific sensitivities" as an explanatory device.

Section 3.1 discusses visual responses to optic flow patterns produced by self-motion in terms of specific sensitivities to relationships between velocities at different locations. The approach is to identify by experiment those specific sensitivities that exist in the visual system, as well as those that are absent. Flow pattern parameters to which the visual system specifically responds seem more likely to be behaviorally significant than cues to which the visual system does not respond in any specific manner.

The spatial distribution of velocities in an optic flow pattern can be described in the notation of vector analysis (vector calculus). In this formalism, the spatial properties of the flow pattern are described in terms of the mathematically independent quantities grad **V**, div **V**, and curl **V**, where **V** is the local velocity at any given instant. The Appendix provides definitions of the terms "div," "grad," and "curl," but for those unfamiliar with vector calculus the book by Schey (1973) contains an excellent introduction. Section 3 summarizes experimental evidence that the human visual pathway is selectively sensitive to attributes of the optic flow pattern caused by self-motion that roughly approximate div **V** and also may be sensitive to a rough approximation of curl **V**.

Section 4 discusses specific multiple sensitivities in the context of channel theories of motion in depth. This example illustrates how such theoretical notions may lead to useful practical results. This point is elaborated in Section 5, which discusses applied research in which the "multiple specific sensitivity" idea informed the study of flying performance in simulator and real aircraft.

1. VISUAL ACCELERATION

1.1. Background

As the eye moves to scan a scene, the images of stationary objects in that scene move across the retina. However, in normal circumstances the objects are not perceived as moving. Also, a stationary target within a moving frame may be perceived as moving opposite to the direction of motion of the frame (induced motion). The general conclusion from such observations is that a single mechanism cannot be the basis for sensing motion.

Chapter 17 by Mack, Chapter 22 by Hochberg, and Chapter 21 by Sedgwick distinguish between *object-relative motion* and *subject-relative motion*. Although this distinction (and the similar distinction between *exocentric* and *egocentric* motion) is of considerable theoretical interest, we do not dwell on it here. Instead we deal with processes that are presumed to underlie both kinds of motion, namely those related to information associated with image translation across the retina and eye-head motion involved in tracking objects.

Although several mechanisms must be postulated in models designed to explain the perception of motion, we do have knowledge of one type of mechanism that can account for the detection of motion in the frontal plane. Cells in the visual system of the cat (Hubel & Wiesel, 1962), rabbit (Barlow & Hill, 1963), and monkey (Hubel & Wiesel, 1968) respond when bars or edges are moved across their receptive fields. In fact, the majority of motion-sensitive neurons in the medial temporal cortex of macaque respond to movement in one direction only (van Essen, 1979; Zeki, 1974). Also, some neurons in primary visual cortex respond to unidirectional motion in depth (Cynader & Regan, 1978; Poggio & Talbot, 1981).

The existence of such cells in the cortex suggests that velocity is directly encoded at a relatively early stage of visual processing in parallel with the detection of successive positions of a target over time. One model of a system capable of detecting motion relative to the retina in a single direction is schematized in Figure 19.1.

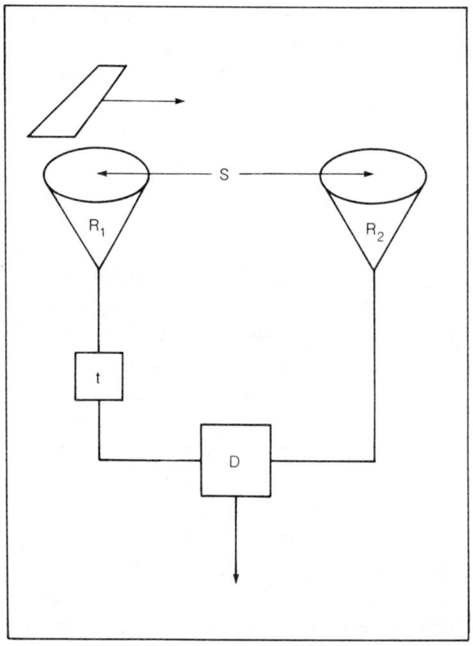

Figure 19.1. Schematic version of a model of a polarized velocity detector. When the image of the bar stimulates receptor R_1, the unit t delays the output of R_1 before transmitting it to the movement detector D. If the bar arrives at R_2 concurrently with the arrival of the output of t at D, the movement detector responds to the coincidence of the signals originating at R_1 and R_2. This movement detector cannot respond when the bar moves from R_2 toward R_1. (From L. Kaufman. *Sight and Mind*, Oxford University Press, 1974. Reprinted with permission.)

There are several possible variations of the scheme depicted in Figure 19.1. For example, if unit t should respond in a sustained manner some time after stimulation of R_1, then the movement detector would respond regardless of the speed of the stimulus as long as it exceeded some minimum value. In this case the circuit would detect movement over a wide range of speeds, provided they were not too great, and the narrowness of its velocity tuning would thus be reduced. An alternative scheme is to have the detector perform an analog operation, such as multiplication. Such directionally selective movement detectors have been proposed by Barlow, Hill, and Levick (1964), Foster (1971), Poggio, Reichardt, and Hausen (1983), Reichardt (1961), and Reichardt and Poggio (1979).

Anstis and Rogers (1975) suggested that motion detectors could be incorporated in a network analogous to the projection field employed in some models of stereopsis (see Chapter 23 by Arditi). In this application each point in one eye may interact with many other points in the same eye. The resulting network effectively multiplies events occurring at one point with events occurring at other points. This multiplication is similar to the cross-correlation presumed to be involved in the detection of disparity in a projection field (Kaufman, 1974).

As pointed out by Arditi, to obtain stereopsis the perceptual system must match corresponding stimuli of the two eyes to avoid the problem of "ghosts," that is, the fusion of unrelated points imaged in the two eyes. The same is true in motion perception, where the problem is referred to as that of phenomenal identity (Ternus, 1938) or, alternatively, as the problem of correspondence (Ullman, 1979). In motion perception, an image formed at different places and times on the retina must be identified as belonging to the same object. A cross-correlating network could make it possible to solve the problem of identity by comparing the retinal image at one time with the image at other times. In fact, virtually all theories of the perception of motion based on translation of the images of objects across the retina incorporate the operation of cross-correlation.

All versions of the basic cross-correlation model described above fail to distinguish between targets that move with the same average speed but whose speed changes as they traverse a portion of the retina. Consider the simple model shown in Figure 19.1. If a target moves rapidly across R_1 and then slows down before reaching R_2, the motion detector would still respond. Now, if the perceptual system is capable of sensing acceleration directly, as it presumably senses velocity, either a second-order correlation process must occur—for example, the comparison of three representations of the retinal image occurring at three different times—or a comparison of velocities must occur at some higher level. In this chapter we consider the evidence concerning the sensitivity of the perceptual system to change of speed per se.

Thus far we have restricted discussion to the so-called *image-retina* system (Gregory, 1966). This is the hypothetical system that uses information about the translation of an image across the retina to compute the motion of the image. Motion may also be perceived when the eye and head are rotated to track a moving target. Theoretically, this need not involve the image-retina system for, in such cases, the retinal velocity of the image may be zero. The eye-head system (Gregory, 1966) is presumed to be capable of detecting motion even when there is little or no slip of the image on the retina. This actually occurs when an afterimage is seen to move during voluntary eye movements, and it makes it possible for the observer to fixate a moving target (to prevent its becoming blurred due to high retinal velocity) and still detect the motion. To a first approximation, the velocity given by the image-retina system is added to the velocity given by the eye-head system to obtain the net velocity of the target. Of course, the two systems are not equally sensitive; that is, a target moving across the visual field while the eye is stationary appears to move more rapidly than it does when it is tracked by the eye (see Mack, Chapter 17), and therefore are not given equal weight in the perception of speed. Even so, as Gregory (1966) proposed, there can be little doubt that they work in tandem.

It appears that the eye-head system is capable of responding to the nonuniformity of motion. Although there is little evidence that proprioceptive feedback enables observers to consciously monitor eye position during smooth pursuit eye movements (Festinger, Sedgwick, & Holtzman, 1976), observers can still move their eyes with great precision in tracking a target moving with a nonuniform velocity. Moreover, Purkinje cells in the cerebellar flocculus fire in step with the eyes as they move in smooth pursuit of a sinusoidally moving target (Noda, 1981). There is substantial evidence that the control of eye movements in visual tracking tasks is mediated by the cerebellum (Lisberger & Fuchs, 1978; Miles & Fuller, 1974; Miles, Fuller, Braitman, & Dow, 1980; Noda & Suzuki, 1979). It seems likely that the cerebellum is effectively "programmed" to accomplish fine motor control, as in oculomotor tracking, and that it is capable of extracting higher derivatives of motion to make such tracking possible (Pellionisz & Llinas, 1979). Even if true, it does not necessarily follow that the nonuniformity of motion is consciously perceived.

As we shall see below, much of the evidence to date suggests that acceleration is not directly sensed by the perceiver, although the question is still open. In fact, most theorists assume that the observer infers the presence of a change in speed from the fact that velocity at one time differs from velocity sensed at some other time. Hence the critical data in this area are those pertaining to difference thresholds for velocity. These thresholds were measured by Hick (1950) and by Notterman and his colleagues (Mandriota, Mintz, & Notterman, 1962; Notterman, Cicala, & Page, 1960) among others. In general, these investigators found that the discrimination of differences in velocity does not follow Weber's law; that is, the just detectable increment in the velocity of a moving target is not a constant percentage of the velocity of the target. Rather, the difference threshold is at a minimum when the target moves with a velocity of between 1 and $2°\cdot sec^{-1}$, and is higher at both lower and higher velocities. This minimum varies from as little as 3–4% of the $1–2°\cdot sec^{-1}$ to as much as 15%, depending upon experimental circumstances. Of course, such results are valid only for comparisons of the velocities of small spots moving across a display at two different times, and it is difficult to generalize from them to other more complicated targets and backgrounds. Even so, a Weber ratio of about 12% provides a very rough index of sensitivity to differences in velocity, and it is of some interest that this difference threshold has not been used in testing the notion that the detection of acceleration is essentially a matter of comparison of velocity at two different times.

So one of the central concerns of researchers in this area is determining the degree to which the perceiver is sensitive to change of velocity (acceleration) per se. Section 1.3 reviews the experimental results obtained in this area.

1.2. Basic Concepts

So that the discussion in the following sections will be clear, let us define the basic terms used:

1. Uniform motion: the linear motion of an object or point at a single speed in a constant direction.
2. Velocity: a vector quantity (having magnitude and direction) indicating the speed of an object or point in a particular direction at a given moment in time (i.e., instantaneous velocity).
3. Speed: a scalar quantity indicating the magnitude of the velocity of a target regardless of its direction.
4. Acceleration: the rate of change of velocity.
5. Jerk: the rate of change of acceleration.
6. Circular motion: the motion of an object or point along a circular path.

The speed, velocity, or acceleration of a moving object (distal stimulus) need not be the same as the speed, velocity, or acceleration of the image of that object on the retina (proximal stimulus). All the foregoing definitions may be applied to the retinal stimulus as well as to the distal stimulus. Where needed, this distinction is made clear in the text.

1.3. Observations and Experimental Results

1.3.1. Natural Observations. Science often begins with observations of natural occurrences that require explanation. This may lead to the reproduction of the observed phenomena in the laboratory, where hypotheses as to their causes may be tested under controlled experimental conditions. Although this is not necessarily the course of events leading to experimentation, it certainly is a major factor in influencing work in perception, where phenomena such as naturally occurring illusions may lead to scientific investigations.

Some observations of naturally occurring events are so common that they are often simply overlooked. For example, an object moving along a circular path is continually changing the direction of its motion. Hence by definition it is accelerating, and the acceleration (change in velocity) is perceived. Also, the increase in the rate of change of the area of a surface increases more rapidly as one gets closer to the surface. This too is a fairly common observation, and this acceleration in change of size is probably used as a cue in estimating stopping distance when braking one's automobile. However, it is not so obvious that one is sensitive to the change in speed of an object as it moves along a linear path. For if humans were highly sensitive to such a phenomenon, it would not have required the insight of Galileo to establish that falling objects move faster as they approach the center of the earth.

As already indicated, natural observations are often brought into the laboratory for further study. One example is the work of Michotte (1946), who wondered about the kinds of patterns of motion that lead to the impression that one of two moving objects may seem to cause the other object to move. He found that some kinds of nonuniform motion lead to such a perception, whereas other kinds of motion do not. "Causation" is perceived when one object moves toward the other and continues moving for a short period of time while the other object begins to move in the same direction (see Figure 19.2). It appears as though the motion of the first object is carried on by the second. Similarly, if an object moves toward a stationary object and, after reaching it, abruptly reverses its direction, the moving object has the appearance of having bounced off the stationary object. Although Michotte focused on the question of why one interprets some events as caused by others, he failed to consider the role of the higher derivatives of motion in producing these effects. In the case of perceived rebound, for example, there is a very rapid reversal of direction of motion. Such an event can be described as an abrupt change in velocity, which implies the presence of large second and third derivatives of motion. These higher derivatives affect the phenomenal quality of the motion.

Despite this apparent effect of nonuniformity on the perception of motion, doubt has been raised about the sensitivity of observers to acceleration. Levelt (Michotte, 1963), for example, noted that when a target moves from side to side in a simple harmonic manner, it is difficult to see any change in its speed except at the very ends of its transit. However, this "insensitivity" may well be due to the fact that the changes in speed are insufficiently strong.

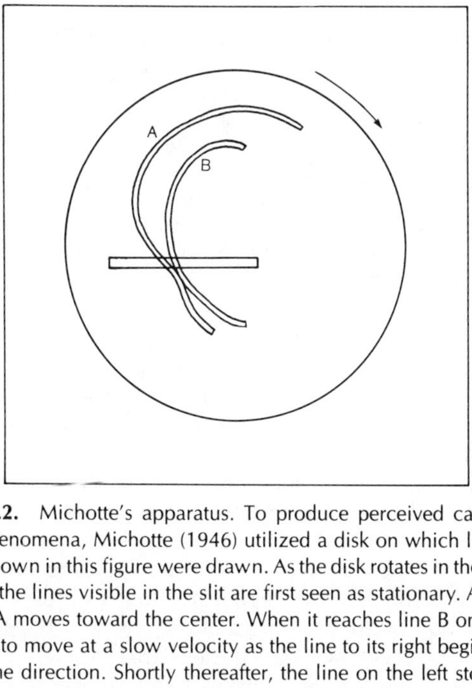

Figure 19.2. Michotte's apparatus. To produce perceived causality and related phenomena, Michotte (1946) utilized a disk on which lines similar to those shown in this figure were drawn. As the disk rotates in the clockwise direction, the lines visible in the slit are first seen as stationary. After a short time line A moves toward the center. When it reaches line B on its right, it continues to move at a slow velocity as the line to its right begins to move in the same direction. Shortly thereafter, the line on the left stops moving while the line on the right continues to move at a higher velocity. This produces the impression of "caused motion." If the line on the left had stopped moving before the onset of motion of the line to its right, then the two events would have been perceived as independent of each other.

The reader may perform a little experiment to test the validity of this point. If a sinusoidal signal of about 1 Hz is applied to one x-axis of a dual-beam oscilloscope, and a triangular function of the same fundamental frequency is applied to the other x-axis, two spots can be made to move from side to side on the face of the cathode-ray tube at the same fundamental frequency. It is immediately obvious that the spot moving as a triangular function of time seems to bounce back and forth from one end of its transit to the other, whereas the spot executing simple harmonic motion lacks the "bounce" and seems to slow up gradually at the ends of its transit. This difference in the perceived motion of the two spots could be due to the detection of the difference in the magnitudes of the higher derivatives of motion of the two spots. Alternatively, it could be mediated by an overshoot error that must occur when the eye tracks the target moving as a triangular function of time (see Mack, Chapter 17). Even so, there is a great need to obtain quantitative data to establish the degree to which individuals are sensitive to changing velocity.

Two-dimensional shadows of rotating three-dimensional wire objects may exhibit nonuniform motion, depending upon the shapes of the objects. In some cases these two-dimensional projections are perceived as rigid objects rotating in depth (Gibson & Gibson, 1957; Wallach & O'Connell, 1953). To explain these results, some experimenters focused on the transformations in the shape of the projections of three-dimensional objects onto the frontal plane; however, Ullman (1979) called attention to the important role of the change in speed of elements of the projection of a rotating three-dimensional object. These changes in speed do seem to play a significant role in perceiving the projected image as rigid and three-dimensional. More details are given by Sedgwick, Chapter 21.

The work of Johansson (1950, 1958, 1974) on the perceived organization of patterns of moving dots in the frontal plane and in depth includes several demonstrations in which nonuniform motion plays a role. This is amply treated by Mack, by Anstis, and by Pomerantz and Kubovy in Chapters 17, 16, and 36, respectively.

As already indicated, objects that move along circular paths must also be considered as exhibiting nonuniform motion, for the velocity of an object undergoing circular motion in the frontal plane is continually changing because its direction of motion is changing. In fact, an object moving at a constant speed v in a circle of radius r can be regarded as having an acceleration v^2/r directed toward the center of the circle. Some very interesting phenomena are associated with circular motion. Forms painted on a rotating disk, as shown in Figure 19.3, give rise to some surprising illusions (Musatti, 1924; Tauber & Kaufman, 1977; Wallach, Weisz, & Adams, 1956).

There is a tendency for position constancy to be lost for objects undergoing circular motion. This is in contrast with the perception of linear motion of objects in a normal illuminated environment, where the relative motions of the objects are perceived veridically, that is, in accord with the distal stimulus. However, with circular motion the perception tends to be in accord with the retinal motion of the objects. This is especially true of objects that are largely circular in shape (Wallach et al., 1956). Configurational factors strongly influence the resulting perception. The planetary motion experienced when an observer fixates one of the two circles on a rotating disk may disappear when this fixation is not maintained. As we shall see below, illusions that occur during circular motion can produce some interesting effects of motion in depth. Also, Matin, Boff,

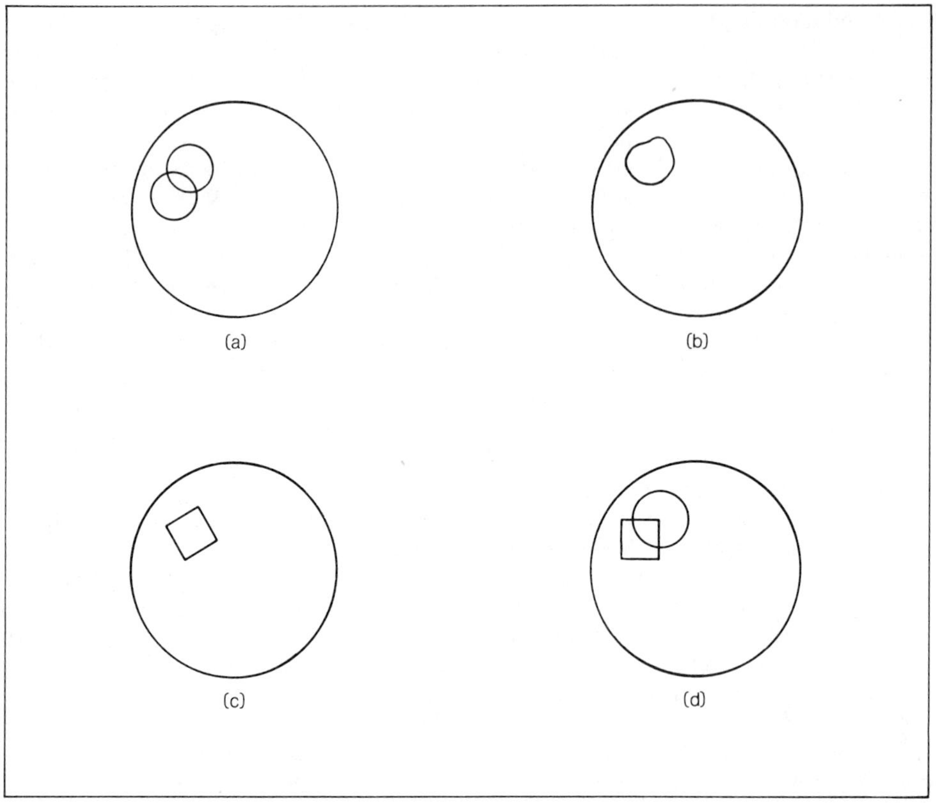

Figure 19.3. Some rotating figures. The eccentric intertwined circles in (a) rotate about the center of the disk, with one circle leading the other. However, when the disk rotates no faster than about 8 rpm, the observer generally reports that the two circles actually seem to execute a planetary motion, with one of the circles as the "sun" and the other the "planet" (Wallach, Weisz, & Adams, 1956). This effect has been found to occur when the eye of the observer moves to track one of the circles (Tauber & Kaufman, 1977), with the tracked circle seen as the sun and the other circle as the planet. A single circle containing a slight distortion (b) gives rise to the perception of a circle that remains "upright" during rotation of the disk, whereas the distorted portion independently "wobbles" around the circle (Wallach et al., 1956). The reason given for this is that circles have an inherently ambiguous orientation, that is, as a circle rotates about its center it undergoes no change at all. Because of this tendency to remain upright during rotation, the largely circular portion provides a frame of reference for the distorted segment, which moves around the "underlying" circle. A square, such as the one in (c), is unlike a circle because it has a determinate spatial orientation, and therefore it is seen as rotating as the disk turns. Tauber and Kaufman (1977) demonstrated that fixating one corner of a square on a rotating disk results in the perception of the square as turning about the fixated corner. This corresponds to the actual motion of the image of the square on the retina, just as the planetary motion of the intertwined circles is consistent with the motion of their images on the retina. Finally, when a square and a circle are intertwined, as in (d), fixation of the circle results in seeing the square rotate smoothly in planetary fashion about the circle. However, when fixation is switched to the square, the circle cannot be seen as rotating about the square, presumably because the unambiguous orientation of a square prevents the appearance of planetary motion.

and Pola (1976) and Boff (1978) observed that when a pair of collinear lines are rotated about their center, the upper line continuously appears offset from the lower line in the direction of rotation. This vernier offset is not fully understood (see further discussion in Chapter 16 by Anstis). Unfortunately, not enough is known about circular motion, because it has not been a popular research topic.

1.3.2. Experimental Results

1.3.2.1. Visually Guided Tracking of Accelerating Targets. We now turn to more formal experiments designed to elicit a clearer picture of the degree to which a person is sensitive to nonuniformity of motion. We begin with a visually guided manual tracking task, for it is reasonable to assume that the tracker must perceive the motion of the target if it is to be tracked accurately.

During a typical pursuit tracking task a target is made to move on a visual display, and the subject must use a joystick to keep a cursor aligned with the moving target. The difficulty of pursuit tracking is related to a number of factors, for example, vehicular dynamics (which is reflected in lag in response of the cursor relative to the tracking motion, etc.) and the speed and complexity of target motion. All these are reviewed in Chapter 39 by Wickens. For present purposes we consider only the complexity and speed of target motion and how these may affect accuracy of tracking.

The complexity and speed of target motion are commonly described in terms of its Fourier transform. It is relatively easy to track a target moving in a simple harmonic manner at a single low frequency. If the frequency is increased so that the target moves back and forth too fast for it to be followed, then performance obviously declines. When the target's motion includes several frequency components, or even when its motion can be described as a continuous spectrum of band-limited noise, tracking also becomes difficult, even at low frequencies.

This approach to tracking behavior implies the applicability of linear systems analysis to predict the performance of the human operator. Under the assumption that the operator can be described as a linear or quasilinear system, it is possible to determine the human's transfer function by having the operator track targets that move with different frequencies. The phase lag and attenuation of the tracking motion relative to the phase and amplitude of the target motion at each frequency fully characterize the operator's transfer function. Under the assumption of linearity (i.e., that the principle of superposition holds), it is possible to predict from the transfer function the accuracy of the operator's tracking behavior when confronted with target motions of any degree of complexity.

The foregoing approach is oversimplified because the operator rarely behaves as a linear system. Rather ingenious methods have been employed to predict operator tracking behavior despite evident nonlinearities (see Wickens, Chapter 39). For our purposes, it suffices to use this example to illustrate the way in which tracking performance, as measured in terms of its Fourier amplitude spectrum and its phase spectrum, can be evaluated in the frequency domain. This approach to motor performance is conceptually the same as current approaches to the study of sensitivity to spatial patterns and time varying stimuli (see Olzak and Thomas, Chapter 7, Ginsburg, Chapter 34, and Watson, Chapter 6).

To successfully track a target moving in a simple harmonic manner, the operator must be able to predict its future velocity. In fact, the velocity of such a target changes continuously over time. To keep pace with the target, the velocity of the cursor must be matched to that of the target. If the target is moving in a sinusoidal manner, its position at time t is $s = a \sin \omega t$, where a is the amplitude of the sine wave, ω is 2π times the frequency of the target in hertz, and ωt is the phase of the motion at t. Because phase can be measured from any arbitrary point in time, it is usually represented as $y = \omega t + p$. Now the velocity and acceleration are given by differentiation. Thus

$$s = a \sin(\omega t + p) \tag{1}$$

$$\frac{ds}{dt} = a\omega \cos(\omega t + p) \tag{2}$$

$$\frac{d^2s}{dt^2} = a\omega^2 \sin(\omega t + p) \tag{3}$$

As can be seen from Eq. (2), the velocity of the target is proportional to the product of its amplitude and frequency, whereas by Eq. (3) its acceleration is proportional to the product of the amplitude and the square of its frequency. Moreover, the phase of the acceleration lags that of the velocity by 90°.

To track a target moving in a sinusoidal manner, the operator must match a velocity that changes as a function of time. The amount of this change in velocity (the acceleration) increases rapidly with frequency. Therefore, one limiting factor governing tracking behavior may well be the rate at which the perceptual-motor system can sample and compare velocities.

It should now be obvious that the accuracy of visually guided tracking behavior depends on the way in which the operator processes the visual information, as well as the precision with which his or her motor system can respond to this information. According to one theory, the observer samples velocity in one interval of time and again in some other interval of time. If the two sampled velocities differ, then the operator infers that the target is accelerating. Alternatively, to account for the high accuracy with which operators learn to track simple harmonic motion, we may postulate an ability to extrapolate the rate of change in velocity integrated over short periods of time to allow the predictive behavior associated with successful tracking. Still another possibility is that operators simply generate a motor output at a particular frequency and adjust its phase and amplitude until the cursor being controlled matches the motion of the target; that is, operators minimize positional error, with no need to directly sense velocity or acceleration.

The foregoing discussion lays the groundwork for interpreting the results to be described in this section. Unfortunately, these results are somewhat meager, although they are highly suggestive.

Gottsdanker (1952) had a target move along the length of a horizontal slit at two different nonuniform speeds: positively accelerated with the velocity $v = 0.4t^2$ and negatively accelerated with $v = 16(5t)^{1/2}$. The uniformly moving and positively accelerating targets were visible for 10 sec whereas the negatively accelerating target was visible for 5 sec. In all cases the terminal velocity was 8 mm·sec^{-1}.

The subject tracked the moving target with a pencil held in the slit and was asked to continue marking the projected path of the target even after it had disappeared. The continuous belt apparatus used to generate these stimuli is illustrated in Figure 19.4. Sample stimuli and tracks are shown in Figure 19.5.

The tracks made by these subjects suggest that they tended to follow the tangent to the target's motion at or near the time of its disappearance. They were clearly unable to project the acceleration of the target into its future, but they could predict the position of the target if it maintained the same velocity it had at the time of its disappearance. For negatively accelerated targets they were able to maintain the projected velocity with an accuracy of about 11% on the average. However, they departed from the target's actual path by tracking about 30% too fast. By contrast, the error in tracking the uniform target was no more than about 1%.

Averaging over subjects, the uniformly moving target was tracked at a rate of 7.92 mm·sec^{-1} (SD = 0.85). At the point of its disappearance the positively accelerating target had a physical velocity of 10.4 mm·sec^{-1}. It was tracked after disappearance at a mean velocity of 6.97 mm·sec^{-1} (SD = 1.17). There was no significant difference between tracking velocity during the first second after disappearance and tracking velocity during the sixth second; that is, the target was tracked at a constant velocity. Gottsdanker concluded that tracking was based either on the velocity of the target at some time prior to its disappearance or on velocity integrated over a period of time prior to its disappearance. The subjects were unable to store and use information about the rate of change of the target's velocity prior to its disappearance.

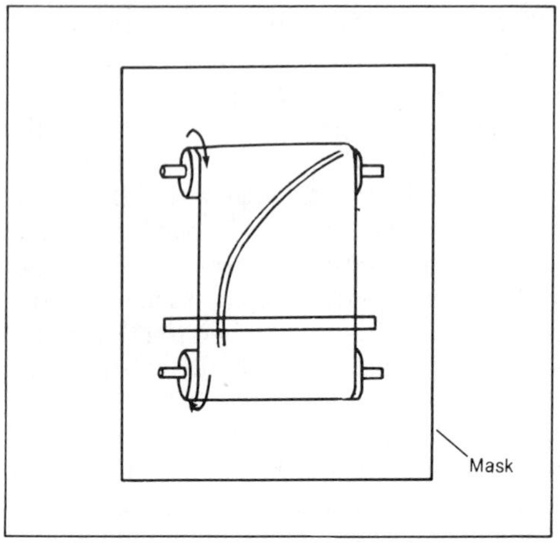

Figure 19.4. Schematic representation of apparatus used in motion tracking task (Gottsdanker, 1952). A printed target of parallel black lines 5 mm apart was moved downward behind a narrow slit (6.35 × 30.48 mm). The small visible segments of the lines (the target) were seen as moving horizontally across the length of the aperture in the mask. The speed of this motion was determined by the shapes of the lines. Line shapes generating positively accelerated, constant rate, and negatively accelerated motion were used. The velocity of the uniform motion and the terminal velocity of the nonuniform motion was 8 mm·sec^{-1}. (Unfortunately, Gottsdanker did not provide the stimulus dimensions in angular terms. If we assume a viewing distance of 50 cm, then the aperture was about 0.7° high by about 34° wide, and the terminal velocity was about 0.9°·sec^{-1}.) Subjects tracked the targets as they moved across the slit with a pencil held between the lines. In some trials the target disappeared before reaching the end of its transit, and subjects had to continue tracking the target at an appropriate speed.

Although this conclusion is valid for Gottsdanker's untrained subjects, it must be accepted with some circumspection. It is well known that the ability of a subject to track targets moving in a complicated manner improves significantly with training. For example, the visual-motor skills involved in shooting at moving targets improve considerably with practice. The skills developed by today's youngsters who play video games also testify to this conclusion. This kind of performance becomes quite automatic, suggesting that the higher derivatives are not responded to effectively when the performance is under cortical control. The question remains, however, as to whether acceleration is sensed or handled in some other way even when complex motion is successfully tracked.

1.3.2.2. Effect of Acceleration on Estimated Time to Collision. The phenomenological observations and the tracking study discussed above are complemented by a number of investigations based on more traditional psychophysical methods. These methods provide a more direct indication of the human's ability to detect changing velocity.

One useful technique in the study of motion perception is to have a subject estimate the future position of a target some time after it disappears. Estimation methods avoid dependence on motor skill, as in the tracking paradigm, and thus minimize the problem of effects of practice on performance.

In an experiment by Runeson (1975), one target (the standard) moved vertically along a 48° path. A "comparison" target moved horizontally across the display, beginning its transit 18° to the left of the vertical path and intercepting the path at its center. The edges of the display were blurred and several "landmarks" provided visual structure (see Fig. 19.6).

The velocity of the standard was always 9.6°·sec^{-1}. It should be noted that this is almost too fast to be seen clearly without eye movements (Kaufman, Cyrulnick, Kaplowitz, Melnick, & Stoff, 1971). The comparison target moved either with a uniform velocity or with a velocity described by the power function

$$s = kt^n \tag{4}$$

where s is the speed of the target, k is a scale factor chosen so that the average velocity is 9.6·sec^{-1}, and the exponent n defines the magnitude of acceleration at any time t. With $n = 1$ the motion is uniform. With $n < 1$ the target decelerates and with $n > 1$ the target accelerates. For example, when $n = 2$ the target exhibits a uniform acceleration and when $n = 1.6$ it exhibits a decreasing acceleration.

The onset of motion of the two targets differed from trial to trial so that the targets reached the point of intersection at different times. In addition, the target paths were partially occluded so that they disappeared before they crossed each other. The size of the mask was adjusted from trial to trial so that it occluded more or less of both target paths. The task of the subject was to judge whether the comparison target would reach the point of intersection before or after the standard ("same" judgments were not allowed).

Data were averaged to determine the point of subjective equality (PSE), or the point where the comparison target was judged equally often to be "ahead of" or "behind" the standard.

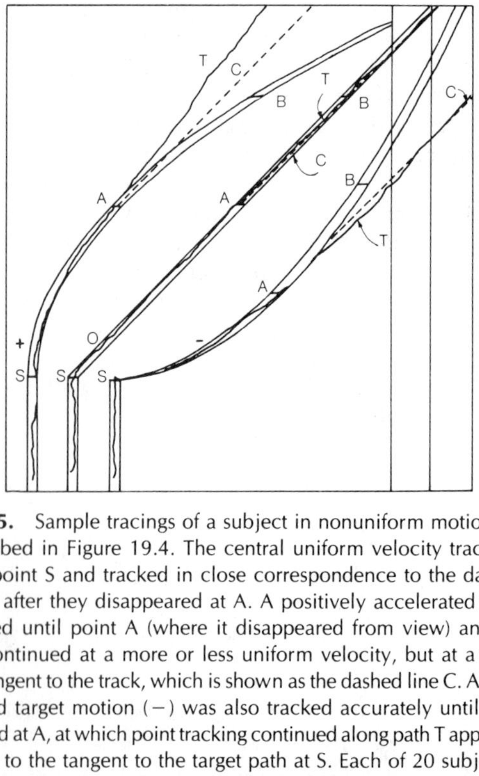

Figure 19.5. Sample tracings of a subject in nonuniform motion tracking task described in Figure 19.4. The central uniform velocity track (O) was begun at point S and tracked in close correspondence to the dark double lines even after they disappeared at A. A positively accelerated target (+) was tracked until point A (where it disappeared from view) and tracking along T continued at a more or less uniform velocity, but at a faster rate than the tangent to the track, which is shown as the dashed line C. A negatively accelerated target motion (−) was also tracked accurately until the target disappeared at A, at which point tracking continued along path T approximately equivalent to the tangent to the target path at S. Each of 20 subjects had 8 tracking runs with each of the three types of moving target. The third through eighth runs were evaluated by measuring the departure of the target at intervals of 1 sec for 6 sec after the target disappeared. (Point B on all tracks represents the end of the 6-sec measurement period.) As illustrated by these tracings, subjects were unable accurately to predict accelerated or decelerated motion and instead tended to follow the tangent to the target's motion at or near the time of its disappearance. (From Gottsdanker, 1952.)

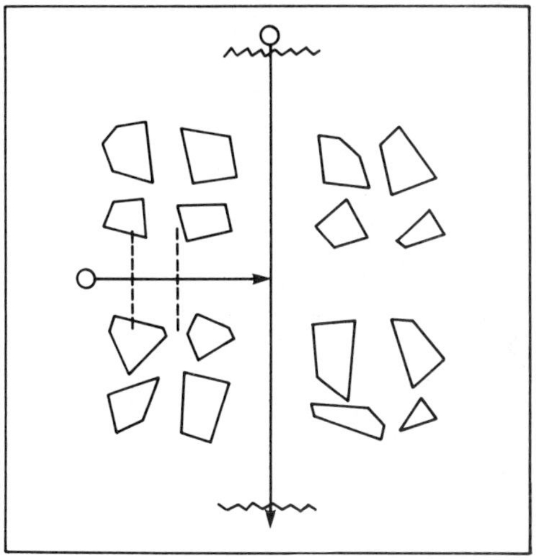

Figure 19.6. Schematic view of the display used by Runeson (1975) to study effects of different types of motion on estimated time to collision. Targets were bright blue rings 1.5° in diameter moving in a horizontal direction. A comparison stimulus moved from the top to the bottom of the display, as indicated by the vertical arrow, at a constant speed of 9.6°·sec^{-1}. The ends of its 48° path were occluded by diffuse invisible screens (wavy lines). The target moved horizontally along an 18° path with an average velocity of 15°·sec^{-1}. It was occluded by a sharp invisible edge after traversing one-fourth or one-half of its path (vertical dotted lines). Irregular shapes were placed on the surface of the screen to provide a frame of reference for the movement. The field outside the screen was dark. Subjects had to judge whether the target stimulus would arrive at the point of intersection before or after the comparison stimulus. (From S. Runeson, Visual prediction of collision with natural and nonnatural motion functions, *Perception and Psychophysics*, 1975, *18*. Reprinted with permission.)

Psychometric functions showing how the PSE varied with the kind of motion are shown in Figure 19.7.

When the comparison target moved at a uniform velocity of 15°·sec^{-1} and was occluded for all but one-fourth of its transit, the PSE departed from zero by −190 msec; that is, the targets were judged to arrive simultaneously when the comparison target arrived 190 msec after the standard. With late occlusion (one-half the track), the PSE was −43 msec, and did not differ significantly from zero. However, the PSE for the target with decreasing acceleration (n = 1.6) did not differ significantly from zero with either early or late occlusion. Large errors were observed for both the deceleration (n = 0.7) and uniformly accelerating (n = 2) comparison targets. Subjects showed a significant tendency to judge that a decelerating target collided with the standard when it actually lagged the standard. Conversely, the uniformly accelerating target was judged to lag the standard even though the two targets were actually on a collision course.

If subjects can sense or otherwise use the higher derivatives of these smoothly changing velocities, such errors should not occur. However, even in the case of uniform acceleration, where no higher terms (e.g., jerk) are needed for accurate prediction, there was considerable variability in performance. More important, variability was also high when both targets moved with uniform velocity; that is, there were no higher derivatives and there was no need to sense them to make predictions. Thus the targets may have been moving so fast that subjects used both the image-retina and eye-head systems to track one of them, thus producing highly nonuniform retinal motion. The better performance with the target moving with decreasing acceleration could be attributed partly to the fact that, during the latter portion of its transit, it had a velocity of about 4–5°·sec^{-1}. This velocity is well within the range where the target is clearly perceptible as its image moves across the retina.

Although they are conjectural, the foregoing reservations illustrate a potentially important problem with studies such as this one by Runeson (1975). That is, the dynamic range of the velocity-sensing system based on motion across the retina is quite narrow. When velocities are higher than, say, 5–6°·sec^{-1} it may be impossible to "keep track" of the target (e.g., because of blur) as its image travels across a relatively small distance on the retina. At very slow uniform velocities (< 5–6°·sec^{-1}), on the other hand, prediction may become extremely accurate. Similarly, nonuniform motion may be evaluated to predict future position provided that the velocity of the target does not exceed some critical value. In short, it appears that many workers in this field may have used targets that moved too fast. This remains to be evaluated in future research.

One experiment whose outcome is consistent with this point of view is that of Rosenbaum (1975). In his study subjects judged when an occluded target would reach a fixed point in space. Subjective velocity was tacitly defined as the judged speed of the hidden target, the index of which was the time when the invisible target was assumed to intersect a visible stationary marker. Rosenbaum found that the distance over which the moving target was visible had no effect on accuracy. This led him to conclude that velocity per se was employed in making the judgment. Also, objective target velocity was highly correlated with subjective velocity; that is, it accounted for over 90% of the variance in subjective velocity. However, no other details were published so it is difficult to fully evaluate this report.

Rosenbaum provides more information on a second experiment which used moving targets accelerating at 7.97°·sec^{-2}, 13.6°·sec^{-2}, and 15.1°·sec^{-2}. The six subjects had to judge how long after these accelerating targets disappeared they would reach a fixed visible marker.

Performance was best for the smallest of the three accelerations; in this condition the objective acceleration accounted for 85% of the variance in judged time to intersection. For the highest of the three accelerations, objective acceleration accounted for only 5% of the variance. Here performance was more nearly like that reported by Gottsdanker (1952). It is worth noting that subjects trained in physics did no better in this task than did "naive" subjects. Although the data are incomplete, they certainly force us to remain circumspect regarding any claims about the ability or inability of observers to sense acceleration.

1.3.2.3. Initial versus Terminal Velocity. One crude measure of sensitivity to acceleration is an observer's ability to judge correctly whether the velocity of a target at one point in time is the same or different from its velocity at another point in time. The ratio of velocity at time C_2 to velocity at time C_1 would be unity for a target moving with a uniform velocity, greater than 1 for a target increasing in speed, and less than 1 for a decelerating target.

Schmerler (1976) showed subjects a film of a target that emerged from a "tunnel" at one speed and then, after traversing a distance of 11.2°, entered another "tunnel" at the same or at a different speed. Target acceleration was 0, 2.3, 6.9, or 11.3°·sec^{-2}. Running the films backward provided comparable values of deceleration. The lowest initial velocity was 1.4°·sec^{-1} and the highest 12.4°·sec^{-1}.

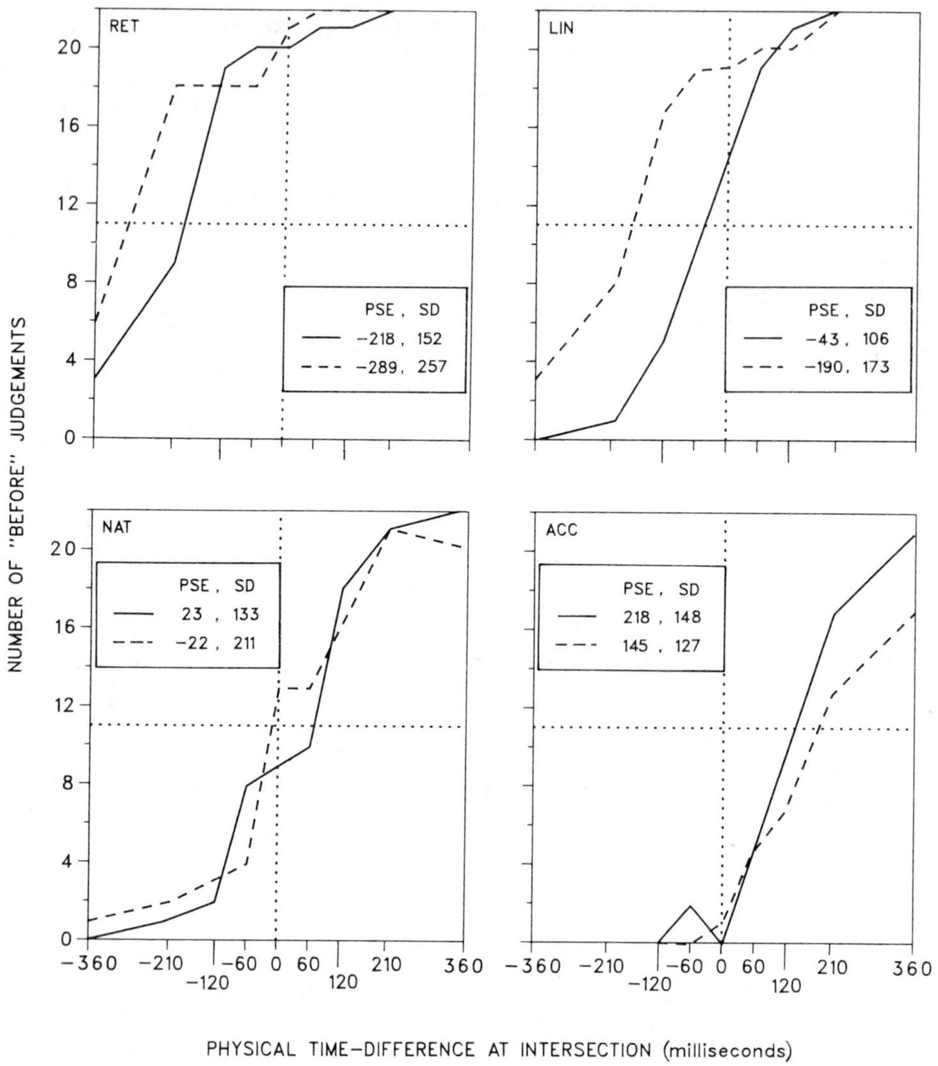

Figure 19.7. Effect of type of target motion on predictions of collision of targets traveling along partially occluded paths. Eleven subjects viewed the display shown in Figure 19.6 and judged whether a target moving with various degrees of acceleration would arrive at the point of intersection with a comparison (standard) stimulus before or after the standard. The number of trials on which the target was judged as arriving before the standard is plotted as a function of the physical time difference in their arrival at the intersection. Four kinds of target motion were used: RET—constant deceleration; LIN—constant velocity; NAT—"natural motion" (acceleration followed by a leveling to a constant velocity); ACC—constant acceleration. Broken and solid lines show results of early and late occlusion (see Figure 19.6). PSE (point of subjective equality) corresponds to the time difference at which the target and standard are estimated to have arrived simultaneously at the point of intersection. This PSE differed significantly from zero—that is, was either too early or too late relative to the objective time of intersection—for all but the motion with diminishing acceleration (NAT). Runeson concluded that the visual system does not utilize acceleration or deceleration in predicting motion but instead applies the stereotype of a "natural motion function." (From S. Runeson, Visual prediction of collision with natural and nonnatural motion functions, *Perception and Psychophysics*, 1975, *18*. Reprinted with permission.)

Only group thresholds were reported. In the case of acceleration, the threshold is defined as the terminal-to-initial velocity ratio at which the target was judged to be speeding up 50% of the time. The threshold for deceleration was determined in analogous fashion. Each of 60 subjects was given 12 trials for acceleration and 12 for deceleration.

Unfortunately, the results of this experiment are inconclusive because the threshold terminal-to-initial velocity ratios did not differ significantly across conditions even though the actual ratios presented varied by almost a factor of five. If all the subjects did not use the same criterion in making their judgments, the resulting grouped data were bound to be quite variable, and any changes in sensitivity to differences between initial and terminal velocity could have been masked when data were combined across subjects.

It may be of some interest to note that when the velocity near the end of an 11° traverse was approximately 2.7 times that near the beginning of the run, observers were likely to judge that the target had speeded up. Thus sensitivity to acceleration was unaffected by an increase in average velocity, although the data are too noisy to state this as a firm conclusion.

Discrimination between terminal and initial velocity improved when the target passed through a third tunnel placed midway between the two end tunnels, thus interrupting the appearance of the target. This result is consistent with the view that the subject senses velocity at one time and compares it with velocity sensed at another time. This is supported by experiments in which other criteria are employed, as described in the following section.

1.3.2.4. Direct Comparisons. Runeson (1974) investigated the question of how well subjects can judge the difference between uniform and nonuniform motion. In this experiment a target moved horizontally along a track subtending 48° at the observer's eye. The motion had either a uniform velocity or one of three nonuniform velocities described by the power function given in Eq. (4). In this case, however, the scale factor k was chosen so that the average velocity was $48°\cdot sec^{-1}$.

In this particular experiment subjects viewed a target that moved across the screen twice. Their task was to judge on which of the two presentations the target moved with uniform velocity. In fact, the target that moved with a constant velocity appeared to subjects to be moving with a nonuniform speed. The target they judged to be moving with uniform velocity actually moved with decreasing acceleration (i.e., with $n = 1.3$ or 1.6). To appear as constant, a target must begin its motion with a certain amount of acceleration which later falls off to a nearly constant velocity. Runeson called this "natural motion," because it is typical of naturally occurring horizontal motions of objects influenced by the drag of a medium that causes them to slow down.

This explanation is not entirely convincing, despite its apparent "ecological" validity. For one thing, it is well known that sensitivity to motion is greater when a moving target is close to an edge than when the target is far from edges and in an empty visual field. Therefore, the motion of the target used by Runeson is not strictly accounted for by its physical velocity and acceleration, simply because the perception of its speed at any instant may well be affected by its position in the display. In fact, none of the studies described here has incorporated factors such as proximity to the edges of a display in their treatment of perception of acceleration. Also, the average velocity of $48°\cdot sec^{-1}$ used in this experiment by Runeson is extremely high. It is unlikely that a target moving so fast can be seen clearly unless the eye moves to track it (Kaufman et al., 1971). Second, Runeson's results illustrate a subtle point about the reported appearance of motion. That is, if we accept Runeson's results at face value, they actually imply that observers can discriminate between uniform and nonuniform motion, except that they misname the two kinds of motion. Thus the observers can discriminate between objects moving with decreasing acceleration and those moving at a constant velocity. If these observers had been given feedback, they might well have come to label the different kinds of motion correctly. Once again, we must conclude that when higher derivatives of motion are present, they often have an effect on the appearance of the stimulus as described by the subject. This still leaves open the question of whether acceleration is perceived directly or is inferred from the sampling of velocities at different times.

Gottsdanker, Frick, and Lockard (1961) performed an experiment similar to Runeson's, in which they reached the conclusion that acceleration is not sensed directly. In their study, 160 college students were given 100 trials each in which they viewed consecutive runs of a moving target. Each trial contained two runs. The target moved with a constant velocity on one run and with an accelerating or decelerating motion on the other. The subject had to tell on which run the motion was constant. Because this method is much less criterion-sensitive, some of the problems associated with Schmerler's (1976) study are avoided.

The velocity of the target ranged from 0.96 to $15.4°\cdot sec^{-1}$, and acceleration ranged from 0.26 to $67.6°\cdot sec^{-2}$. Presentation time varied from 0.45 to 3.6 sec. Because the stimuli were presented via motion pictures, playing the film backward gave decelerating stimuli. Unlike Schmerler (1976), Gottsdanker et al. (1961) found that sensitivity to acceleration decreased as mean velocity was increased. They also found sensitivity to be adversely affected by decreasing presentation time. Finally, the ability to discriminate acceleration from uniform velocity is affected more by the total change in velocity than by the duration of the stimulus. This supports the view that subjects compare early and late velocities. The minimum detectable accelerations are associated with stimuli whose initial and terminal velocities differ by as little as 26% and as much as 157%, depending upon the stimulus conditions. These values are quite a bit larger than any reported by Notterman and his colleagues, as described in Section 1.1, and much smaller than those observed by Schmerler. Of course, subjects may have been making their judgments on the basis of changes in velocity that were actually smaller than these terminal values.

1.3.3. Summary. It is obvious that none of the studies discussed thus far in this chapter allows a definitive statement concerning human sensitivity to acceleration, differences in velocity, or the mechanisms that may make it possible to detect either differences in velocity or any of the higher derivatives of motion. For one thing, the parameters of the various experiments may not have been appropriate; for example, the velocities employed were frequently too fast (e.g., Kaufman et al., 1971). Often there was no consideration of or adequate control for the abrupt onsets and offsets of motion, the effect of the presence of a framework (Brown, 1931), target size, luminance contrast, and other factors (e.g., Kaufman & Williamson, in press). Effects of differences in criteria were not considered either. Even so, all of this prior work is instructive in the sense that it makes it possible to conduct experiments in which the range of velocities is appropriate, and it helps to define the methods and stimuli that would lead to more general conclusions. All these considerations led to one recent parametric study.

1.4. Parametric Study

Kaufman and Williamson (in press) reported an experiment designed to overcome some of the problems described above. Rather than the moving spots used by previous investigators, stimuli were computer-generated gratings produced by sinusoidally modulating the luminance of a raster on the screen of an oscilloscope. These gratings had one of three different spatial frequencies, 0.5, 2.0, or 4.5 cycles per degree. The average luminance was the same for all gratings and was set at $40\ cd\cdot m^{-2}$. The luminance contrast of each grating had one of two values, 0.2 or 0.5 (see Ginsburg, Chapter 34). The gratings drifted across the display at one of three different average velocities—0.5, 2.0, or $5.0°\cdot sec^{-1}$—and thus they were in the range of the velocity-sensing capabilities of the image-retina system. The direction of motion was either to the left or to the right, and was varied at random from trial to trial to prevent adaptation to a given direction. To introduce acceleration, the speed of the grating was sinusoidally modulated at a frequency of 1, 2, 4, or 6 Hz. Sensitivity to this acceleration was measured by determining a threshold for the amount of modulation of speed needed for its detection as a function of all the foregoing parameters (luminance contrast, spatial frequency, average speed, frequency of modulation of speed, and direction of motion).

The thresholds (75%) were determined by means of a modified staircase method (see Falmagne, Chapter 1), in which the subject had to decide which of two presentations of the same spatial frequency or average velocity, for example, included a modulation of speed. This two-interval forced-choice procedure is criterion-free.

It is instructive to evaluate the data of this experiment in two different ways. First, by analogy with the Michelson contrast used to describe the luminance contrasts of grating stimuli, the thresholds can be expressed as the difference between the maximum and minimum velocities at threshold, divided by their sum. This is essentially the same as a Weber ratio. The main findings were that sensitivity to the acceleration was significantly related to the average velocity of the grating. On the average, the threshold for detecting the modulation was at a minimum (12%) when the average velocity was $2°\cdot sec^{-1}$, and was significantly greater at lower and higher average velocities. At velocities above $5°\cdot sec^{-1}$, the higher spatial frequency patterns could not be resolved by a subject fixating a point in the center of the screen, so changes in speed of gratings moving at or above this average speed could not be detected at all. For lower average velocities, the lowest threshold is in the vicinity of $1–3°\cdot sec^{-1}$. The other main effect was that of modulation frequency. Here too there was evidence for "tuning" in the sense that the threshold was lowest (17%) when the modulation frequency was 2 Hz, and greater at lower and higher modulation frequencies. Finally, the threshold was significantly lower for the higher spatial frequencies than it was for the lowest spatial frequency, varying from 24 to about 18%. There were no main effects of direction of motion or of luminance contrast.

Although thresholds for detecting changing speed are not a constant percentage of average velocity, there is evidence of a shift in magnitude of the threshold level in the direction predicted by Weber's law. Thus the threshold expressed as the absolute amplitude of the change in velocity is nearly proportional to average velocity for each modulation frequency. It is of some interest to note that the detectable increment in velocity varies from about 7.5 min $arc\cdot sec^{-1}$ for the lower average velocity to as much as $1.8°\cdot sec^{-1}$ for the highest. Thus the lowest threshold (expressed as a difference in velocity) is only about twice the magnitude of the absolute threshold for motion, which, in a structured visual field, is on the order of 3 min $arc\cdot sec^{-1}$.

There are other ways in which to express the results of this study. For example, it is possible to describe a stimulus like a moving grating in terms of the temporal frequency with which a point on the retina is stimulated by alternating levels of luminance. In fact, the temporal frequency of stimulation is the product of the average velocity and the spatial frequency of the stimulus. If this were a higher-order variable to which the subject responded, then it could be claimed that the results are not due to some sensitivity to velocity and to velocity change but rather to a change in temporal frequency—a kind of frequency modulation of a pattern. However, Kaufman and Williamson (in press) analyzed their data in terms of temporal frequency and found a highly nonuniform relationship between temporal frequency and threshold. The analysis suggested that the main effect was of average velocity, and this contributed 56% of the variance in the data. Clearly, more data are needed to fully explore the parameters that affect sensitivity to changing velocity.

1.5. Conclusions

The various experiments described in this chapter thus far are not necessarily inconsistent with each other. For example, Gottsdanker's (1952) early finding that subjects track at or near the terminal velocity of a target after it disappears from view might have been because subjects were tracking at high velocities and therefore had too little time to observe the target and could not respond to the change in velocity per se. The demonstration by Kaufman and Williamson (in press) of sensitivity to changing velocity may have been due to the fact that subjects had ample time to view the pattern as it moved, and the fact that the motion did not have a definable onset or offset. Also, the conditions under which such sensitivity could be demonstrated were confined to a rather narrow range of temporal and spatial parameters. These parameters simply were not sampled in the experiments by Runeson (1975) or any of the others discussed here.

In a way, the fact that one is sensitive to acceleration only over a narrow range of velocities, temporal frequencies, and spatial frequencies does make adaptive sense. If the visual system were capable of sensing acceleration, regardless of velocity or other parameters, the amount of neural circuitry involved would be enormous. By narrowing the range of conditions under which detection of changes in velocity is possible, the requirements placed on the organism are similarly narrowed. Also, if the image-retina system detects acceleration, it should do so only when it is capable of resolving moving objects. If the object is moving very fast, then it can be tracked with the moving eye, and if the eye should start to lag or lead the tracked target, the resulting change in the velocity of its image should also be detected if the error in tracking is to be corrected. Hence the visual system should be better suited for detecting changes in the velocity of objects whose images move relatively slowly on the retina. At the same time, the visual system may well tolerate slight changes in the speed of images that move very slowly on the retina, because such images correspond to targets that are already being tracked fairly well. The fact that the visual system is somewhat less sensitive to changing velocity of very low spatial frequencies is also an interesting finding, because it is consistent with the notion that such sensitivity is an attribute of central vision rather than of the peripheral retina. However, this and other issues remain for future investigation.

1.6. Key References

An excellent review of the older literature on acceleration is given by Gottsdanker (1956), who begins with the complication experiment of Bessel and its application by Wundt to the study of the perception of acceleration of the pendulum bob (Boring, 1950). He goes on to discuss the problem of measuring thresholds for sudden changes in velocity, his own impressive contributions to this literature, and the relevant work of Metzger (1953) and Johansson (1950).

The most recent key publication is by Schmerler (1976); his article goes over some of the ground already covered by Gottsdanker and brings us up to date. Apparently Schmerler did not have access to the paper by Rosenbaum, which appeared in 1975. The latter author comes to conclusions opposed to those of Gottsdanker and Schmerler.

2. MOTION IN DEPTH

2.1. Background

Animals and humans, including infants, tend to avoid objects that approach them rapidly. Rapid changes in angular size ("looming") and changes in textural density of surfaces lead to avoidance reactions or some other behavior indicating that the object is perceived as drawing near (Ball & Tronick, 1971; Bower, Broughton, & Moore, 1970; Fishman & Tallarico, 1961; Hayes & Saiff, 1967; Regan & Beverley, 1978a, 1978b; Schiff, 1965; Schiff, Caviness, & Gibson, 1962; Schiff & Detwiler, 1979; Tronick, 1967; Wheatstone, 1852). Similar changes in angular size and in texture of physically stationary surfaces may aid the locomoting observer toward an object or point on a surface (Gibson, 1950, 1957, 1958; Gibson, Olum, & Rosenblatt, 1955; Lee, 1974; Regan & Beverley, 1979b, 1982).

This section emphasizes the changing of size and of textural density as objects approach observers and as observers approach objects and surfaces. Because so little information exists concerning how extravisual information interacts with visual information, it is not dwelt on here.

Information other than changing size and texture is available to an observer moving relative to objects and surfaces. For example, the amount of visible texture occluded by an object at right angles to a textured surface changes in proportion to the square of the distance to the object (Gillam, 1981). Also, objects that are relatively nearby form disparate images on the two retinas when a distant point is fixated. The amount of this disparity changes as the object approaches or recedes. Thus binocular disparity may also play a role in perceiving changes in depth. Similarly, both accommodation and convergence may covary with slow changes in distance to a fixated object.

There are two kinds of changes in depth. One is the change in distance between an observer and an object. The other is the change in distance between two objects along the observer's line of sight. This corresponds to the distinction between "egocentric" and "exocentric" described in Chapter 16 by Anstis and Chapter 17 by Mack. We consider both kinds of motion here, but our main focus is on egocentric changes in depth.

It is important to recognize that an object may be perceived as moving in depth even though it is undergoing no physical motion in depth. As long ago as 1852, Wheatstone reported that, when the magnification of an object's retinal image changes, observers have the impression that the object is moving in depth. Thus changing size alone can be sufficient to produce an impression of motion in depth. The kinetic depth effect (KDE) in a shadowgraph is a second example (Wallach & O'Connell, 1953). As illustrated in Chapter 22 by Hochberg, this fact is exploited in film and television. Also, an observer may move through an environment so that objects in that environment are displaced toward him or away from him. Yet the observer may perceive himself as moving and the objects as stationary. Thus "motion in depth" is a phrase that covers object motion, illusory object motion, real self-motion, and illusory self-motion. The usage of the term "motion in depth" will be made explicit in the context in which the phrase is used.

2.2. Experimental Results

2.2.1. Phenomenological Data. Section 1.3.1 described the planetary motion often perceived when two circles painted on a flat disk are rotated (see Rock, Chapter 33). As illustrated in Figure 19.3, planetary motion is perceived when the eye fixates one of the circles as it rotates about the center of the disk. This is not the only perceptual consequence of viewing such stimuli, however. When a small circle is drawn inside a larger circle, as illustrated in Figure 19.8, the resulting perception may take several forms. One is a depth effect in which the observer perceives a solid truncated cone with either its apex or its base nearer the observer. The cone has a nutating motion; that is, its nearer portion appears to wobble as the entire cone moves along its circular path. Wallach et al. (1956) attribute this phenomenon to the classic kinetic depth effect (KDE), because the relative motions of the retinal images of the two circles satisfy the conditions for perceiving a moving two-dimensional image as a rigid object in depth. The KDE and other depth effects related to motion parallax are described in Chapter 21 by Sedgwick and Chapter 22 by Hochberg.

The depth effect described above illustrates that changing image size is not a necessary condition for the perception of motion in depth. Even when objects do not move, there is a tendency to see the larger of two otherwise identical objects as nearer (Epstein, 1963; Gogel, Hartman, & Harker, 1957; Hochberg & Hochberg, 1952; Ittelson, 1951). The question addressed next is the degree to which changing size provides a reliable basis for accurately judging the motion of objects in depth in both simple and complicated visual settings.

2.2.2. "Looming" or Changing Size

2.2.2.1. Visual Sensitivity to Changing Size. As an object draws nearer to an observer, its boundaries expand away from each other. Regan and Beverley (1978a) investigated whether the visual system is specifically sensitive to changing size or whether sensitivity to changing size can be reduced to sensitivity to motion per se. In brief, they demonstrated a specific sensitivity to looming.

In their experiments subjects viewed bright squares on a dimmer background. The edges of the squares moved in one of two different ways. In the inphase condition the opposite edges of the square moved in phase with each other so that the whole

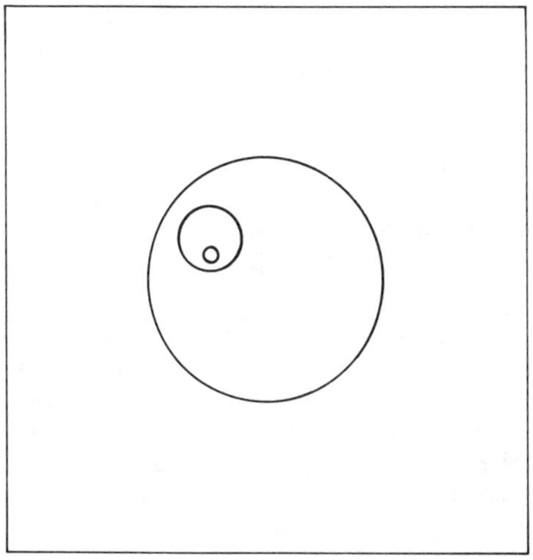

Figure 19.8. The stereokinetic effect. A large circle painted on a disk and containing a smaller eccentrically located circle may appear as a solid cone executing a nutating motion as the disk rotates about its center. The smaller circle appears to wobble about the inner circumference of the larger circle when fixation is on a point on the rim of the larger circle. The appearance of the pattern as a depthful truncated cone is attributed by Wallach et al. (1956) to the classic kinetic depth effect.

square moved along a diagonal path without changing size. In the antiphase condition the edges moved in opposite directions and the square's size oscillated. The reason for selecting these two stimuli was that motion stimulation was identical in the two cases: local motion detectors would merely "see" any given edge moving from side to side. The difference between the two stimuli was that, at any given instant, opposite edges moved either in the same direction (inphase) or in opposite directions (antiphase). This is illustrated in Figure 19.9(a).

The smallest detectable oscillation amplitude was measured for inphase test oscillation and for antiphase oscillation using the method of adjustment. The subjects then inspected a strong antiphase oscillation for 25 min and the two thresholds were measured again. Figure 19.9(b) shows that this resulted in an appreciable loss of visual sensitivity to oscillating size. However, sensitivity to the inphase oscillation was only slightly affected. Because motion stimulation was the same for inphase and antiphase test stimuli, the difference must have been due to some other factor, and it was proposed that the visual pathway is specifically sensitive to the *difference* between the retinal velocities at two retinal locations. When the experiment was repeated by having the subject inspect an inphase oscillation, visual sensitivity was hardly affected at all either for the inphase or the antiphase test oscillations. In the latter case, adaptation could only have been due to motion per se and not to changing size. The relative weakness of this adaptation can be attributed to the fact that the motion was oscillatory and that few contours were present. The stronger aftereffects of motion, such as the waterfall illusion, occur only with exposure to unidirectional motion which, in addition, involves stimulation by many moving contours. The fact that threshold elevation for looming was larger (up to 500%) in the antiphase adaptation condition than in the inphase condition suggests that in this case subjects were adapting to looming and not to motion of the edges of the square, and that looming adaptation can be induced by much weaker stimuli than is required to induce classical motion adaptation.

Changing luminance could not account for the aftereffect described above because flickering a stationary square produced no appreciable adaptation. Furthermore, similar looming adaptation was obtained when the adapting stimulus was a bright square on a dark background and the test stimulus a dark square on a bright background (Regan & Beverley, 1978a). In point of fact, stimulus contrast has little influence on looming adaptation, provided that the stimulus is clearly visible (Petersik, Beverley, & Regan, 1981).

The experiments just described were limited to only two directions of motion: motion parallel to the frontal plane (inphase oscillation) and motion along the line of sight (antiphase oscillation, or looming). However, both kinds of motion may be superimposed on each other, as when an object moves along a slanted path toward the observer. Such motion has an inphase component as well as an antiphase component. Regan and Beverley (1980b) used a wide range of object trajectories to discover if the hypothesized looming system (Regan & Beverley, 1978b) is independent of the moving object's trajectory. The rationale is illustrated in Figure 19.10(a)–(c).

If looming adaptation were unaffected by added frontal plane motion (inphase oscillation), then all adaptation trajectories should have produced the same antiphase threshold elevation. Figure 19.10(d) shows that this prediction was verified within an accuracy of $\pm 5\%$ over a wide range of trajectories.

These findings are consistent with the view that the visual system contains functional subunits or "channels" for looming that operate as illustrated in Figure 19.11. As shown in the figure, motion-sensitive filters supply velocity signals (x and y) to a hypothetical changing size filter whose output is proportional to the algebraic difference between x and y (the velocities of widely separated edges). It is a striking finding that the visual system computes this difference to a high precision that is almost independent of the absolute values of x and y [Figure 19.10(d)].

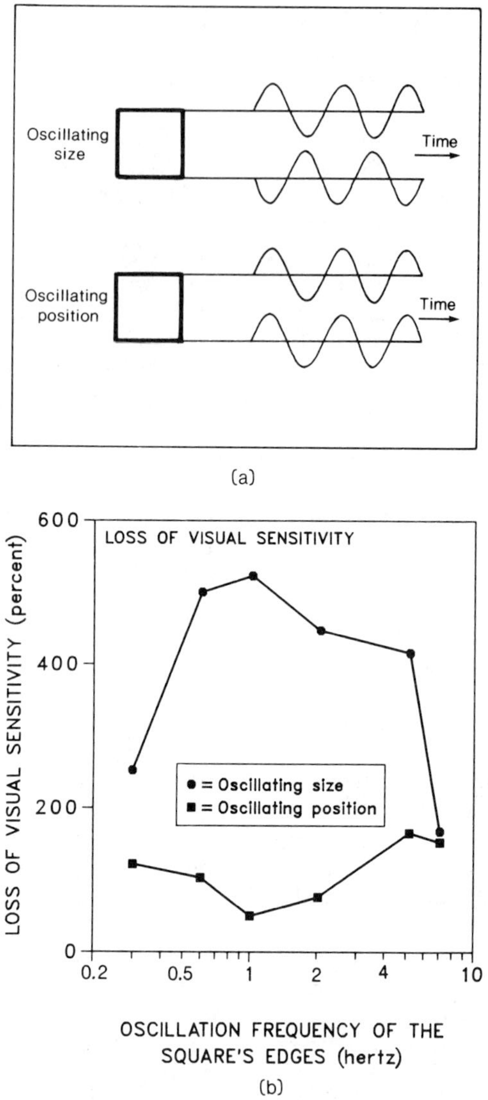

Figure 19.9. Specific threshold elevation due to adaptation to changing size. Stimulus conditions used are illustrated in (a). Solid squares (mean side length = 0.5°) were shown in two modes of motion. In one (oscillating size), parallel edges of the square moved toward and away from each other in a periodic manner. This oscillatory antiphase motion of the edges is shown for two sides only, but the square was actually increasing and decreasing in size. In the other mode, opposite edges oscillated in phase with each other (oscillating position) so that the square's position shifted. This changing position occurred along a diagonal path, because all four edges of the square were moving. As shown in (b), after 25 min of adaptation to a strong (6 min of arc peak to peak) 2 Hz oscillation in size, visual threshold for changing size was elevated about 500%, whereas threshold for inphase oscillation showed little change. Adaptation to a 6 min arc inphase oscillation and adaptation to a flickering stationary square had little effect on sensitivity to changing size. This effect was also independent of the amount or direction of contrast of the adapting square, which could be different from that of the test square. (From D. Regan & K. I. Beverley, Looming detectors in the human visual pathway, *Vision Research*, 1978, *18*. Reprinted with permission.)

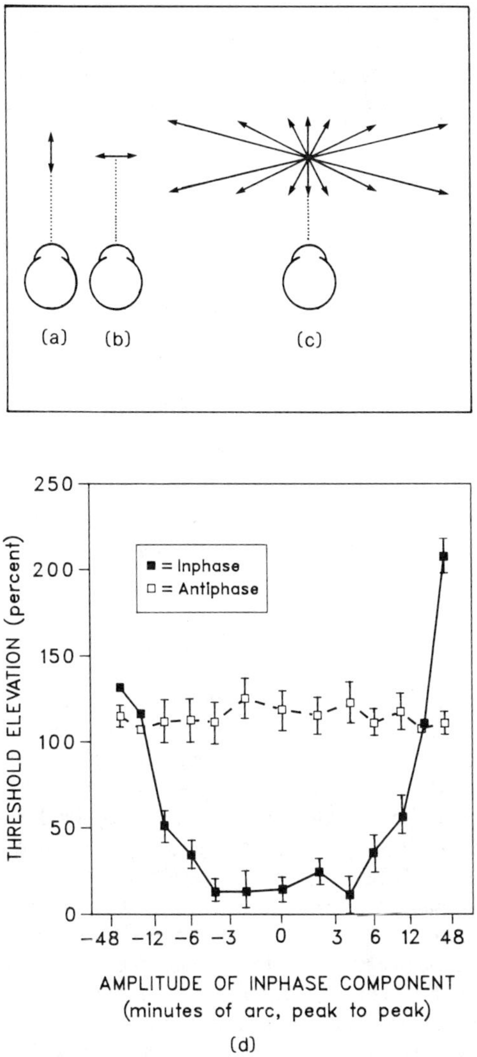

Figure 19.10. Independence of adaptation to changing size and adaptation to changing position. A target moving directly toward and away from the eye is shown in (a), and a target moving left and right in the frontal plane is shown in (b). A target moving as in (a) would change in size, whereas one moving as in (b) would change in position. Both kinds of motion may be combined, as in (c), to produce several trajectories. Regan and Beverley (1980b) used targets with 11 different trajectories to determine if adaptation to changing size is independent of adaptation to changing lateral position. Stimuli were bright squares 0.5° on a side. Targets at all trajectories had the same antiphase (changing size) component; that is, the component of motion toward and away from the observer was the same, but the component in the frontal plane (the inphase component) differed, depending on the trajectory. The graph in (d) shows how the thresholds for pure inphase motion and pure antiphase motion were affected after adaptation to stimuli at each trajectory. Elevation of antiphase thresholds was independent of the amount of inphase motion, whereas inphase threshold elevation progressively increased with the amplitude of the inphase component. (From D. Regan & K. I. Beverley, Visual responses to changing size and to sideways motion for different directions of motion in depth: Linearization of visual responses, *Journal of the Optical Society of America*, 1980, *70*. Reprinted with permission.)

These findings imply that the visual system directly responds to the line of sight component of an object's velocity independently of its velocity in the frontal plane. Regan and Beverley's experiments were restricted to the case of an object moving in relation to a stationary observer. The possible roles of head and eye movements have yet to be formally studied in situations such as those described above.

There are interesting hints about the possible effects of eye and head movements, however. For the case of motion in depth along a line through the eye, the absolute amount of looming adaptation was about the same when the retinal image was stabilized and when it was unstabilized as in the experiment shown in Figure 19.9 (Regan & Beverley, 1978b). However, the situation seems to be very different when trajectory is varied as shown in Figure 19.10(d). The data in Figure 19.10(d) were obtained when the stimulus was slightly "jittered," mimicking the amount of retinal image jitter associated with free head movements. Without this jitter the looming channels seem to be much less independent of trajectory. Thus it seems that the motion "noise" introduced by free head and eye movements is essential for independent operation of the looming channels (Regan & Beverley, 1980a).

2.2.2.2. Temporal Tuning of Changing-Size Channels. At first sight, Figure 19.9 suggests that the hypothetical looming channels are most sensitive over a frequency range of about 0.6–4.0 Hz. However, in this experiment, the adaptation frequency had a single value of 2.0 Hz. To resolve this point, the experiment was repeated with adaptation oscillation frequencies ranging from 0.25 to 24 Hz. The peak of threshold elevation was found to vary with adaptation frequency. This result is consistent with a multiplicity of looming channels tuned to different temporal frequencies of oscillation (Regan & Beverley, 1980b).

Searching for a physiological basis for specific sensitivity to looming, Regan and Cynader (1979) studied 108 neurons in area 18 of the cat's visual cortex. Almost all responded to changes in stimulus size. Control experiments, however, showed that most of these neurons were sensitive to the changes in total light flux that accompanied size changes. Only two units were shown to respond specifically to changing size. The response was similar whether the bar was brighter or darker than its surroundings and also when the bar was placed in widely separated portions of the visual field. However, an appreciable proportion of the neural population responded more strongly to expansion or contraction of width than was predicted by the responses to motion of a single edge. Thus whereas very few units are sharply tuned to changing size per se, the statistical

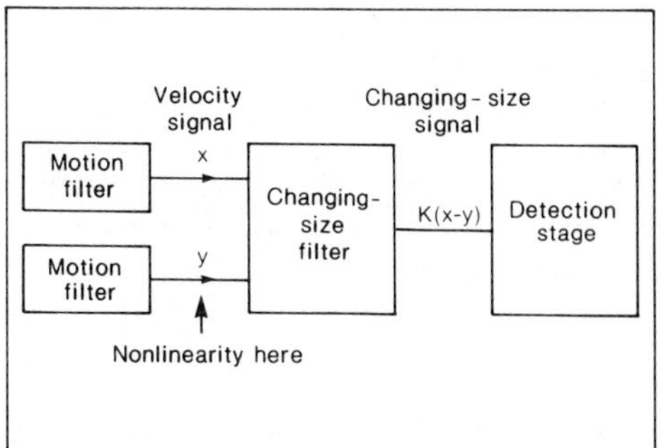

Figure 19.11. Model of changing-size channels. This model, based on psychophysical evidence (Regan & Beverley, 1980b, 1981), includes three stages. The first is a set of motion-sensitive elements ("motion filters") that supply velocity signals (labeled x and y) to a hypothetical changing-size filter whose output is proportional to the difference between x and y (the velocities of widely separated edges). The output of the changing-size filter is fed to a threshold detection stage. (From D. Regan & K. I. Beverley, Motion sensitivity measured by a psychophysical linearizing technique, *Journal of the Optical Society of America*, 1981, *71. Reprinted with permission.)*

distribution of the activity across a large population of neurons may be involved in the organism's sensitivity to changing size.

2.2.2.3. Nonlinear Aspects of Looming Sensitivity. As mentioned above, when head and eye movements are small, so that the jitter of the retinal image is correspondingly low, this nonlinearity causes the output of the changing-size channel to be erroneously low for objects with trajectories that just graze the eye (Regan & Beverley, 1980a). Under such conditions, a subject would underestimate the motion in depth (i.e., would underestimate the component of the velocity vector along the line of sight). However, in daily life free head motion produces appreciable image jitter, which has the effect of "linearizing" the system. In a nonlinear system whose output frequency in response to a sinusoidal input is twice that of the input, the addition of substantial high-frequency jitter to the input results in an output at the fundamental frequency of the input. The reasons for this are described by Spekreijse and Reits (1982), and at an elementary level by Kaufman (1974). Thus adding jitter to antiphase oscillation of the square linearizes the system, and this effect can be used in analyzing the dynamic properties of the changing-size channel in Figure 19.11 as described below.

Threshold elevations were produced by adaptation to changing-size oscillation of a given temporal frequency. The effects of head motion were mimicked by adding auxiliary "jitter" oscillations of different frequencies to the changing-size oscillation. The frequency and amplitude of the auxiliary oscillation were adjusted to produce a constant linearizing effect (Regan & Beverley, 1981). In this way it was shown that (1) the first stage of the changing-size channel behaves linearly, and nonlinearity is introduced after the first stage; and (2) the high-frequency attenuation in the first stage roughly accounts for the high-frequency attenuation for the whole channel.

2.2.2.4. Time to Collision. Astrophysicist Fred Hoyle, in his science fiction novel *The Black Cloud* (1957), seems to have been the first to point out that the time to collision with an approaching object is given by $(\theta/\dot{\theta})$, where $\dot{\theta}$ is the object's angular size and θ is its rate of increase of angular size at any given instant. This relation can be understood as follows. Suppose that an object's absolute width is S and its distance is d at time t, and that its distance has decreased to $(d - \Delta d)$ at time $(t + \Delta t)$. The change in its angular size is given by $\Delta\theta = S/(d - \Delta d) - (S/d) = (S\Delta d/d^2)$ approximately. Dividing both sides by Δt, we have $\dot{\theta} = \Delta\theta/\Delta t = S/d^2 \times \Delta d/\Delta t$. If the velocity toward the eye remains constant and the object does not rotate, then the time to collision is given by $d/(\Delta d/\Delta t) = \theta/\dot{\theta}$, because $\theta = S/d$. In words, time to collision = (angular size at any given instant)/(instantaneous rate of change of angular size). This formula is given added physiological interest by the finding that the human visual system is specifically sensitive to the rate of change of size $(\dot{\theta})$, and may contain a neural mechanism sensitive to $\dot{\theta}$.

Although in Hoyle's novel the calculation was of the time to collision with a black cloud approaching the earth from outside the solar system, the formula applies equally well to earthbound events, and is involved in a model of anticipatory braking by automobile drivers in traffic. Lee (1976, 1980) points out that drivers do not normally initiate full power braking as soon as they see an obstacle—if only to avoid being hit from behind. On the other hand, if they brake too lightly at first, they will run out of braking power so that they are in a "crash state" well before the actual collision. How do drivers use visual cues to adjust their braking? Lee suggests that this could be done on the basis of rate of change of time to collision. Suppose that at time t the driver is at distance d from the obstacle, the vehicle's instantaneous velocity is v, and the driver is braking with deceleration a. Clearly, the deceleration is adequate if the distance that it will take the vehicle to stop is less than distance d, that is,

$$\frac{v^2}{2a} < d \ .$$

Therefore

$$\frac{da}{v^2} > 0.5 \ . \tag{5}$$

Now the instantaneous time to collision is given by

$$T = \frac{d}{v} \ . \tag{6}$$

Differentiating Eq. (6) with respect to time,

$$\frac{da}{v^2} = 1 + \frac{dT}{dt} \ . \tag{7}$$

Hence from Eqs. (5) and (7) the driver's braking is adequate if $dT/dt > -0.5$. In words, the driver's braking is adequate if the rate of change of time to collision is greater than -0.5.

A second problem discussed by Lee (1980) is how long jumpers adjust their stride length as they approach the takeoff board. Movie films showed that jumpers do not use a standard run-up. Instead, they adjust their stride length during the approach. Lee suggested that the relevant cue was time to reach the board, and that the task of zeroing in on the board can be conceived of as programming the durations of the forthcoming strides to just fill the time remaining to reach the board. Thus Lee proposed a temporal conception of this visual-motor coordination task rather than a spatial conception such as, for example, programming stride lengths.

Schiff and Detwiler (1979) studied the information used in judging impending collision. They had 36 subjects view motion pictures of plain black disks that appeared to move toward them along a simulated "terrain" separated from a "sky" by a horizontal line. In some conditions a rectangular grid added texture to the terrain, the sky, or both. The simulated approaching velocities and distances of motion are summarized in Table 19.1.

The experimenters found that judgments of time to collision increased monotonically with the actual time to collision, as shown in Figure 19.12. However, there was a consistent tendency to underestimate time to collision as its actual value increased. In addition, variance in the judgment of time to collision also increased, nearly in proportion to the actual time to collision. As illustrated in Figure 19.12(b), there was a similar relationship between object velocity and judged time to collision.

The study suggested that the primary information used by the subject was the changing size of the target. The stimuli were all motion pictures, so no stereoscopic three-dimensional information was available. Also, there were no significant differences in performance that could be attributed to the presence or absence of texture (the grids). Finally, the judgments were essentially invariant over several object sizes, object velocities, and viewing distances. One major limitation in this experiment is that the moving target was never permitted to get closer than a simulated distance of about 300 m. Because in normal

Table 19.1. Stimulus Conditions for the Experiment in Judging Time to Collision, T_C (see Figure 19.12)

T_C	Simulated Distance (*m*) Start	Final	Velocity km·hr^{-1}	cm·sec^{-1}
10	660	300	18	11
10	720	600	36	22
8	375	300	22.5	14
8	750	600	45	28
6	399	300	30	19
6	798	600	60	38
4	450	300	45	28
4	900	600	90	56
2	600	300	90	56

Subjects viewed films of a black disk approaching along one of several stylized backgrounds. In one condition, only a "horizon" line was present to differentiate sky and terrain; in other conditions, the "terrain," the "sky," or both were covered by a grid pattern. Stimuli were produced by filming black forms using animated tabletop photography. The camera was aimed slightly downward to approximate the direction of gaze of an erect pedestrian watching an approaching automobile. Actual distances and velocities were rescaled to provide the corresponding real-world equivalents shown in the table on the assumption that the 3-cm disk corresponded to an object that was actually 150 cm in diameter (the approximate width of an automobile). (From W. Schiff & M. L. Detwiler, Information used in judging impending collisions, *Perception*, 1979, *8*. Reprinted with permission.)

life estimates of time to collision can be highly accurate when the distance is short—as, for example, in avoiding a cricket ball (Regan, Beverley, & Cynader, 1979), these data have limited applicability. Even so, the predominant role of changing size and the weak effect of background texture are highly significant. A similar failure of background texture to aid performance was found in judgments of the impact point on the surface of an aircraft carrier during a simulated landing (Kaufman, 1964).

2.2.2.5. Looming and Texture Changes. The studies by Schiff and Detwiler (1979) and Kaufman (1964) cited above suggest that background texture has little effect on the perception of changing size and motion in depth. The situation is quite different, however, with regard to object texture, which exerts a strong effect on the perception of motion in depth. In a study of visual responses to changes in depth, Regan and Beverley (1983b) attempted to compare the contributions of texture and looming by pitting one against the other. Figure 19.13 illustrates some of the electronically generated stimuli they used.

As described in Section 2.2.3.2, after inspection of an adapting square whose size increases, a subsequently viewed test square of constant size appears to be moving away in depth, provided that the adapting and test squares are about the same size. This motion-in-depth aftereffect was used to quantify the effectiveness of the displays in Figure 19.13 as stimuli for motion in depth. This indirect procedure was used because (1) the motion-in-depth aftereffect is supposed to be due to a specific motion-in-depth mechanism in the visual pathway (Regan & Beverley, 1978a); (2) the aftereffect was usually an unequivocal sensation of motion in depth, unaccompanied by any confounding sensations such as size change or texture change.

In this experiment, texture change either assisted looming or opposed it. A motion-in-depth aftereffect was produced by inspecting a textured square that contracted in overall size at 24%·sec^{-1}. The magnification of the texture of the adapting square increased or decreased at different rates. The motion-in-depth aftereffect was roughly constant when texture contracted as for a real-world solid object (24%·sec^{-1}) or faster. However, when texture was static or opposed looming, the motion-in-depth aftereffect was virtually destroyed (see Figure 19.14). A similar but reversed effect was observed for an expanding square.

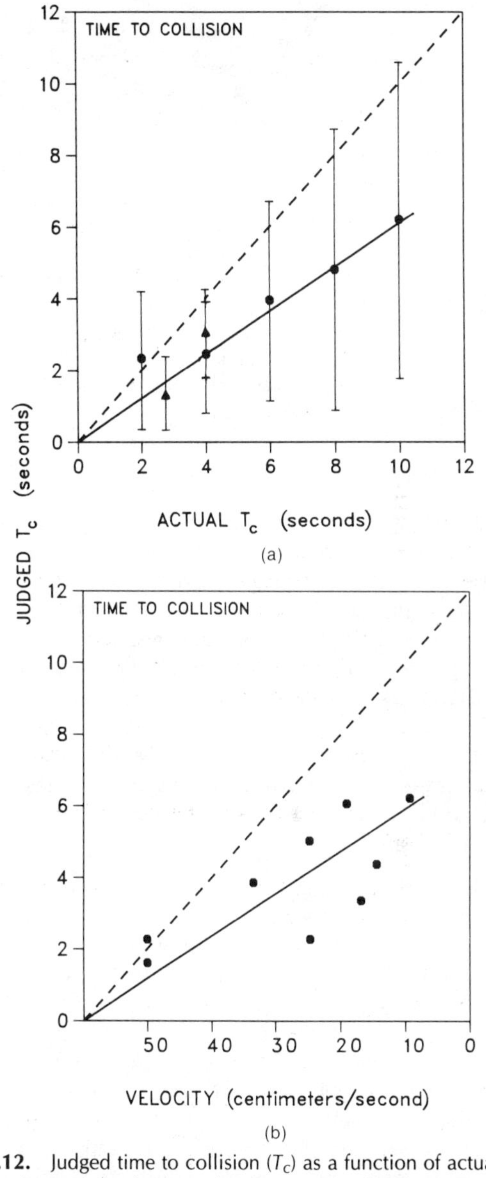

Figure 19.12. Judged time to collision (T_C) as a function of actual time to collision and stimulus velocity. Subjects viewed a film sequence in which a black disk approached at various speeds along a stylized terrain and estimated the time at which the disk would reach them. (See Table 19.1 for a listing of the stimulus conditions.) Panel (a) shows an approximately linear relationship between estimated time to collision (ordinate) and actual time to collision (abscissa) with the disk (round symbols). Data points for 4–10 sec are averages of 144 responses by each of 36 subjects; the data point for 2 sec is based on 36 judgments by 18 subjects. Triangles are averages of 36 similar time-to-collision judgments by each of 36 subjects in response to films of automobiles approaching head-on at about 64 km·hr^{-1}. There is an approximately proportional increase in variability of judgments with time to collision (vertical bars show standard deviations). The slope of the function is < 1.0, indicating a tendency to underestimate time to collision. Panel (b) shows that judged time to collision was also underestimated relative to actual object velocity, especially for real velocities less than about 40 cm·sec^{-1}. (From W. Schiff & M. L. Detwiler, Information used in judging impending collisions, *Perception*, 1979, *8*. Reprinted with permission.)

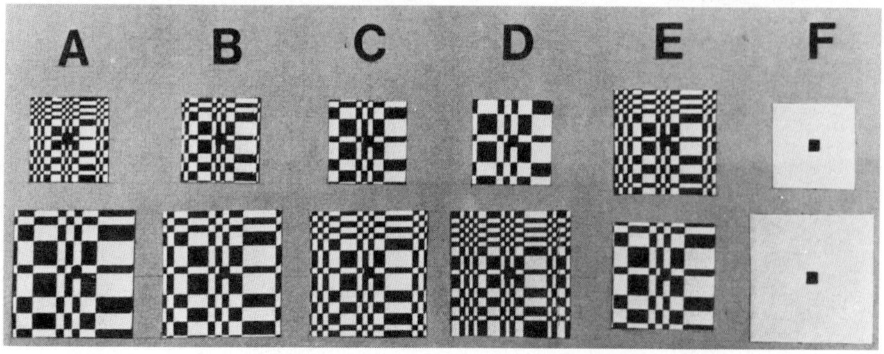

Figure 19.13. Independent manipulation of size and texture grain. A–F show some of the different adapting stimuli used to compare the effectiveness of size and texture changes in producing the sensation of motion in depth. Stimulus B corresponds to a solid real-world object whose magnification is changing. In A texture elements contract faster than square size and in C texture grain is constant. Changes in texture and size are antagonistic in D. In E size is constant whereas texture contracts. F is an untextured square. Mean square side length was 1.2°, square size contracted or expanded at 17 min arc·sec^{-1}, and presentation duration was 1.7 sec. These are photographs of the CRT displays used. (From K. I. Beverley & D. Regan, Texture changes versus size changes as stimuli for motion in depth, *Vision Research*, 1983, *23*. Reprinted with permission.)

Even with the fastest rates of texture change, an untextured square was usually a better motion-in-depth stimulus than a textured square. These findings suggest that, although texture may well be important in representing such static features as curvature, in terms of the monocular simulation of motion in depth the presence of object texture adds little at best, and if texture dynamics and looming dynamics are not accurately matched, texture detracts from motion in depth. This experiment draws attention to the importance of dynamic features of visual flight simulation, in contrast to the emphasis on static picture quality that has traditionally been the chief criterion of quality in simulator displays.

2.2.3. Stereopsis and Changing Size. Stereoscopic depth perception has been a research topic since Wheatstone (1838) demonstrated that binocular disparity alone produces a compelling impression of solidity and depth. In recent years the topic has been given a fresh impetus by Julesz's (1971) development of random dot and dynamic random dot stimuli. The classical stereoscopic system in the human visual pathway mediates the perception of position in depth, and in particular the perception of depth relative to the point of ocular convergence. This section discusses the hypothesis that there is a second stereoscopic system that is substantially independent of the classical stereoscopic depth system. This second system is sensitive to the direction of motion in depth. It operates in parallel with the classical system rather than sequentially, and is not merely derived from the rate of change of disparity. The stimulus for this second system is the ratio of the retinal image velocities in the left and right eyes. There is evidence that different neurons mediate the classical depth system and the motion-in-depth system.

A compelling sensation of motion in depth can be produced either by stereoscopic stimulation or by looming stimulation. The following section also discusses the relative effectiveness of these two stimuli in generating a sensation of motion in depth.

2.2.3.1. Two Stereoscopic Systems: One for Motion, One for Position. Beverley and Regan (1973a, 1973b) pointed out that the relative velocities of the left and right retinal images provide a precise stereoscopic cue to the direction of motion in depth (Figure 19.15). In psychophysical experiments they found that the threshold for detection of motion in depth along a straight line was elevated after inspection of a stimulus that oscillated in depth. This effect occurred only over a limited range of directions of motion in depth. As shown in Figure 19.16, inspection of an object that moved along a line inclined to the left of the nose elevated the threshold for stereoscopic motion in depth for all test trajectories inclined to the left of the nose, but had little effect for test trajectories inclined to the right of the nose. Similarly, inspecting an object oscillating in depth along a line inclined to the right of the nose elevated threshold for stereoscopic motion in depth for all test directions inclined to the right of the nose, but had little effect for test trajectories inclined to the left of the nose. Beverley and Regan proposed that the data shown in Figure 19.16 demonstrate a specific visual sensitivity to the direction of motion in depth. They postulated four pairs of stereoscopic motion-in-depth channels, tuned to different ratios of left/right image velocity and hence to four different directions of motion in depth. Figure 19.17(b) shows the directional tuning of these channels as derived from the data of Figure 19.16.

The dynamic properties of the system mediating perception of motion in depth are quite different from the dynamic properties of vision for frontal plane motion. In one experiment (Regan & Beverley, 1973) subjects viewed a bar or dot pattern that oscillated from side to side at a slightly different frequency in each eye. The target appeared to change its position in depth at the difference frequency of the oscillations in each eye, although neither eye alone had access to this frequency. With this technique, it is possible to measure monocular sensitivity to motion in the frontal plane while simultaneously measuring stereoscopic sensitivity to motion in depth. Visual sensitivity to frontal plane oscillations was found to reach a maximum at 1–4 Hz. Such motion was visible at frequencies as high as 25 Hz. In contrast, sensitivity to stereoscopic motion in depth was greatest at the lowest frequency measured (difference frequency of 0.75 Hz). Stereoscopic visual sensitivity breaks down so that

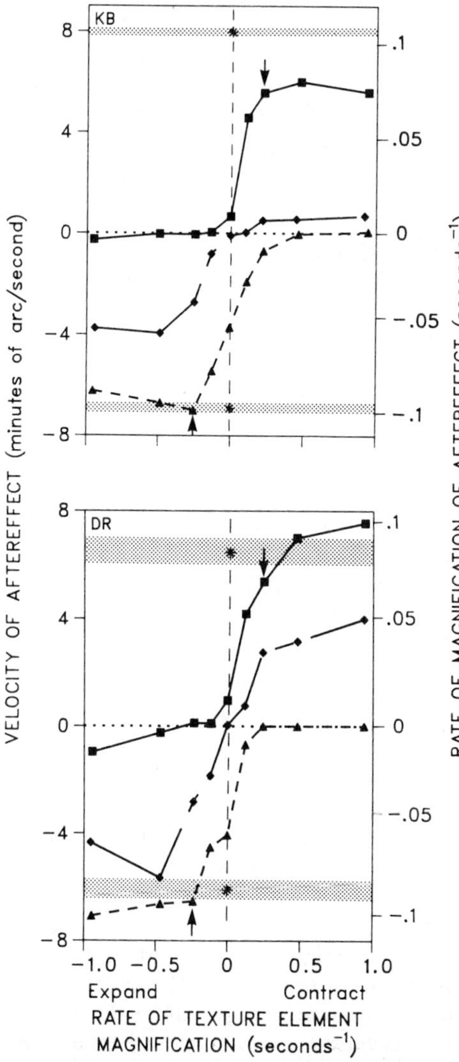

Figure 19.14. Size and texture compared as stimuli for motion in depth. Subjects viewed textured squares similar to those in Figure 19.13 that changed in overall size and in magnification of texture elements. After 10 min of adaptation to one of these stimuli, subjects viewed an untextured test square that changed in size and adjusted the rate of size change just to cancel the motion-in-depth aftereffect produced by the adapting stimulus. Ordinates plot the strength of motion-in-depth aftereffects caused by adapting to textured squares that contracted at a fixed rate (upper curves, squares), expanded at the same fixed rate (lower curves, triangles), or remained constant in size (middle curves, diamonds). Magnification of the texture elements of the adapting square decreased or increased independently of the square's overall size change at the rates shown on the abscissas. Arrows mark the points at which rate of change in the magnification of texture elements matched rate of change in overall size of the stimulus square ($24\% \cdot sec^{-1}$). The asterisks at zero on the abscissas plot the aftereffect caused by an untextured adapting square. The vertical extent of the shaded areas shows ± 1 SE. Otherwise, SEs were smaller than the symbols. Data are shown for two subjects. For rates of texture magnification equal to or greater than the rate of overall size change, the motion-in-depth aftereffect remained relatively constant; however, the aftereffect was virtually absent when texture was static or texture element magnification was in a direction opposite to overall size change. (From K. I. Beverley & D. Regan. Texture changes versus size changes as stimuli for motion in depth, *Vision Research*, 1983, *23*. Reprinted with permission.)

no oscillation in depth can be seen at all at frequencies higher than about 4–5 Hz. These data are illustrated in Figure 19.18.

This sluggishness of the stereoscopic system may be connected with the slow convergence response to an abruptly introduced disparity (Rashbass & Westheimer, 1961; Westheimer & Mitchell, 1956). The reaction time for convergence is about 160 msec, and convergence to a new position may take as long as 800 msec—a substantial time as compared with conjugate saccadic or pursuit eye movements.

The ability to discriminate between different directions of stereoscopic motion in depth is remarkably acute. A difference of as little as 0.1–0.2° in direction may be detectable (Beverley & Regan, 1975).

Figure 19.17(a) summarizes about 10,000 observations in which subjects had to discriminate between different directions of motion in depth. The retinal velocity ratios of the images in the two eyes (V_L/V_R) were adjusted to simulate objects that hit or just missed the head as they approached the observer.

The high acuity of 0.1–0.2° shown in Figure 19.17(a) cannot be entirely explained by assuming that the most active of the four directionally selective channels of Figure 19.17(b) signals direction. This model would predict an acuity of only about 1–2°. To account for this higher acuity, Beverley and Regan (1975) proposed that discrimination among different directions of motion in depth is determined by the relative outputs of the four channels of Figure 19.17(b), a proposal similar to the ideas that our acute wavelength discrimination is determined by the balance of activity of three rather broadly tuned color mechanisms, that spatial frequency discrimination is determined by the relative activities of spatial frequency channels (Campbell, Nachmias, & Jukes, 1970; Regan & Beverley, 1983b) and that orientation discrimination is determined by the relative activity of orientation-tuned mechanisms (Regan, 1982; Regan & Beverley, 1984c; Westheimer, Shimamura, & McKee, 1976).

2.2.3.2. Aftereffects of Motion in Depth and of Changing Size. Prolonged inspection of an object whose size is changing causes a subsequently viewed object of constant size to appear to be either changing in size or changing in depth. Regan and Beverley (1978a) had subjects view a bright square that increased in size for 1.0 sec. After steadily fixating the square over repeated expansion cycles, subjects looked at a static test square which then appeared to be moving away in depth. An aftereffect was also observed when the adapting square shrank horizontally but remained constant in size vertically (Beverley & Regan, 1979). At first the test square did not appear to move forward in depth, but it did appear to expand in width. However, this initial aftereffect was replaced (often abruptly) by a motion-in-depth aftereffect in which the square appeared to be moving forward rather than expanding.

These aftereffects were measured by having subjects adjust rate of size change in a test square that shrank horizontally so as to null either its apparent motion in depth or its apparent changing size. Figure 19.19 shows that both aftereffects decay exponentially, but the aftereffect of changing size has a much shorter time constant than does the aftereffect of motion in depth. For four subjects, the mean time constants for changing size ranged from 7.9 to 9.9 sec, whereas the time constants for motion in depth ranged from 21 to 47 sec. It may be significant that the decay time constant for the elevation of stereoscopic motion-in-depth threshold following exposure to changing binocular disparity (Beverley & Regan, 1973a) is roughly equivalent to the 21–47 sec decay time constants for motion in depth aftereffects due to a stimulus that is changing in size, as described above.

Regan and Beverley (1978b) tested the hypothesis that the motion-in-depth aftereffect is truly an aftereffect of velocity. When only one test ramp duration is used (where the slope of the test ramp represents the rate of size change), the rate of expansion of the test square whose changing size is being ad-

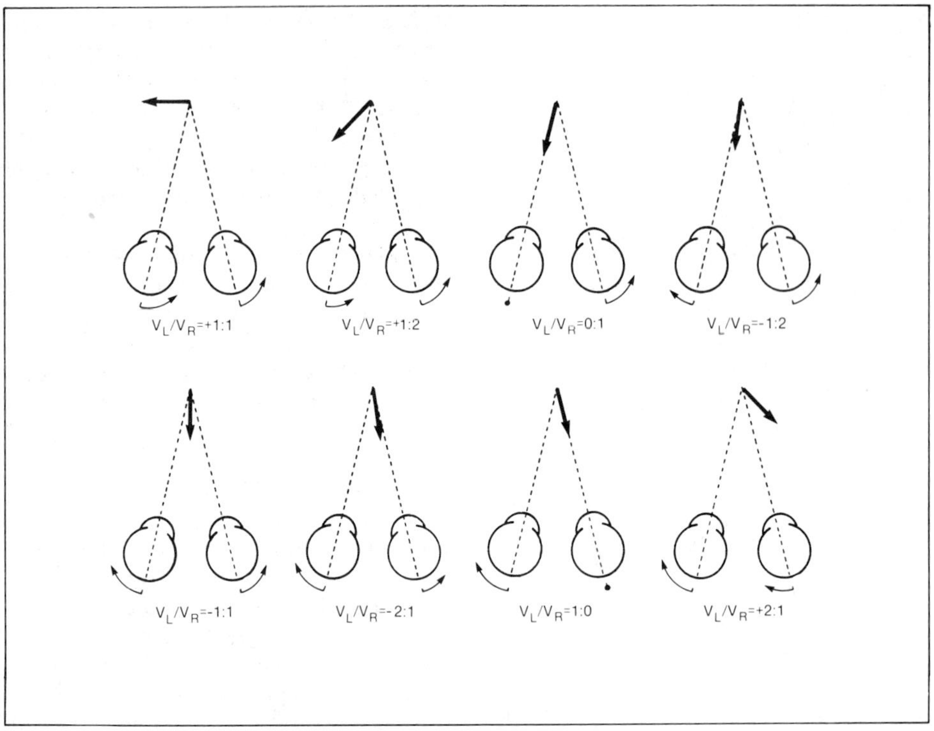

Figure 19.15. Relative velocities of left and right retinal images for different target trajectories. When the target moves along a line passing between the eyes, its retinal images move in opposite directions in the two eyes; when the target moves along a line passing wide of the head, the retinal images move in the same direction, but with different speeds. The ratio (V_L/V_R) of left- and right-eye image velocities provides an unequivocal indication of the direction of motion in depth. (Modified from Beverley & Regan, 1973a.)

justed by the subject is confounded with the absolute increase in size of the test square. To unconfound these two parameters, the experiment described above was repeated using two different test ramp durations—3.3 and 1.0 sec. When canceling velocity is plotted against time, the data points superimpose for both test durations. However, when the amplitude of the canceling stimulus (final side length minus initial side length) is plotted against time, the data points for the two durations do not coincide. This finding indicates that the effective feature of the canceling stimulus is the rate of change of size.

The growth of the motion-in-depth aftereffect follows a function that differs from the one describing its decay. Buildup continues for at least 10 min and is not exponential. The canceling rate of change of size is proportional to the square root of the time of exposure, so growth follows a power law. For decay, the canceling rate of change in size falls exponentially, and at time t in seconds is

$$V_t = K \exp\left(\frac{-t}{\tau}\right)$$

where τ is the time constant and V_t is the canceling rate of change of size (Regan & Beverley, 1978b).

2.2.4. Kinetic Aftereffects and Motion in Depth. As we have seen, an increase in an object's retinal image size can mean either that it is expanding or that it is moving in depth. As described previously, other kinds of transformations in the picture plane also produce impressions of motion in depth. The kinetic depth effect (KDE) of Wallach and O'Connell (1953) is one example. In their view, the perception of a rigid object rotating in depth depends on change in both the lengths and directions of its contours over time. Objects with contours that do not change along one of these dimensions are ambiguous stimuli in that they may be seen as moving in depth at some times, or undergoing rubbery transformations at other times. Fieandt and Gibson (1959) also noted that rigid objects seen from a succession of different vantage points constitute one kind of stimulus to vision, whereas "rubbery transformations" constitute another. Beverley and Regan (1979) suggested that a "safest guess" strategy may operate in that the visual system is biased to signal that a looming predator is approaching rather than the predator is growing in size. Their suggestion was based on the finding that a changing-size aftereffect is *not* produced by adaptation to a target whose size changes uniformly as though viewed through a zoom lens: a motion-in-depth aftereffect alone is seen. Only when the object's shape is distorted while its size changes is a changing-size aftereffect produced, suggesting that the visual system is biased toward motion-in-depth rather than changing-size responses.

Ullman (1979) made a similar suggestion and in one experiment created a stimulus composed of dots distributed at random on the surfaces of two concentric and transparent cylinders. The cylinders were invisible and the dots were projected onto a screen where they looked like a flat array of random dots. When the cylinders were made to rotate stroboscopically in opposite directions, the subject saw two rigid cylinders rotating in depth about their vertical axes. This perception was but one of several alternatives. Because the dots were moving stroboscopically, they might just as well have been perceived as executing a random snowlike motion. However, the resulting KDE was clearly the preferred alternative for the perceptual system.

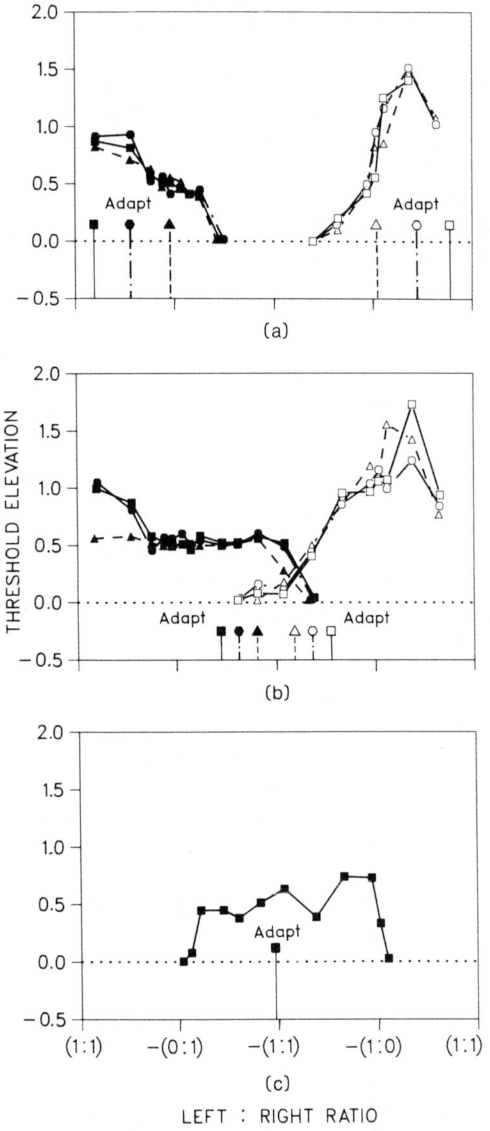

Figure 19.16. Elevation of threshold for detecting stereoscopic motion in depth after adaptation to different left/right image velocity ratios. Stimuli were stereoscopic dot patterns whose central portions appeared to oscillate in depth. In separate sessions subjects were adapted to 1 of 13 different directions of motion in depth (see Figure 19.15). Threshold elevations were measured for up to 13 different test trajectories after a 10-min exposure to each of the adapting trajectories. Panel (a) shows that all three adapting trajectories directed to the left of the head produced the same threshold elevations, as did all three different adapting trajectories to the right of the head. In panel (b), similar results are seen for the three adapting trajectories directed between the nose and the left eye and between the nose and the right eye. As shown in panel (c), motion directly toward the nose produced symmetrical elevations. The pattern of threshold elevations produced by the 13 different trajectories can be parsimoniously explained in terms of four mechanisms tuned to different values of V_L/V_R, as shown in Figure 19.17(b). (From K. I. Beverley & D. Regan, Evidence for the existence of neural mechanisms selectively sensitive to the direction of movement in space, *Journal of Physiology*, 1973, 235. Reprinted with permission.)

As noted earlier, inspecting a rectangle that changes in size in one dimension only produces first an aftereffect in which a static test rectangle appears to change size (and thus shape) without moving in depth; then this aftereffect abruptly changes into one in which the test rectangle appears to move in depth without changing size. This suggests that the perceptions of changing size and of motion in depth are mediated by at least partially different neural mechanisms, and that there is some antagonism between these two mechanisms (Beverley & Regan, 1979).

2.2.4.1. Interaction of Kinetic Aftereffects with Disparity. Although partially independent mechanisms may mediate alternative modes of perception, there is strong evidence that kinetic cues to depth affect the depth perception related to static binocular disparity. Wallach and Karsh (1963) had subjects

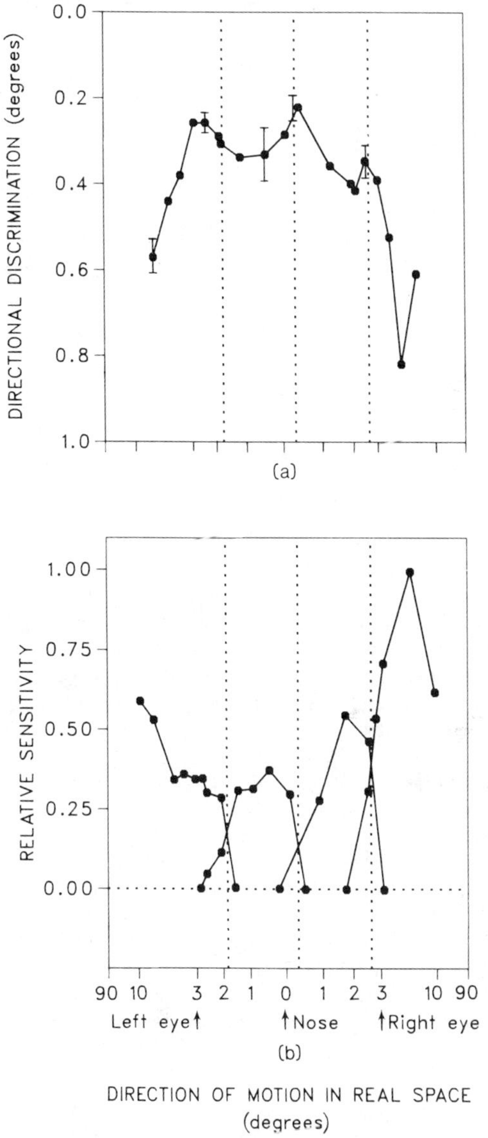

Figure 19.17. Stereoscopic discrimination of the direction of motion in depth. Panel (a) shows how angular discrimination of direction (ordinate) is related to the actual direction of a target's trajectory (abscissa). This figure, based on about 10,000 observations, demonstrates a very accurate discrimination of roughly 0.2° among trajectories hitting or just missing the head. Standard deviations are represented by the vertical bars. Panel (b) is derived from the data of Figure 19.16. The results of Figure 19.16 can be explained in terms of four pairs of channels tuned to different values of V_L/V_R (left/right image velocity ratios). These hypothetical channels underlie the operation of a stereoscopic subsystem that responds to motion in depth, as opposed to the classic stereoscopic subsystem that responds to static disparity (relative static position in depth). (From K. I. Beverley & D. Regan, The relation between discrimination and sensitivity in the perception of motion in depth, *Journal of Physiology*, 1975, 249. Reprinted with permission.)

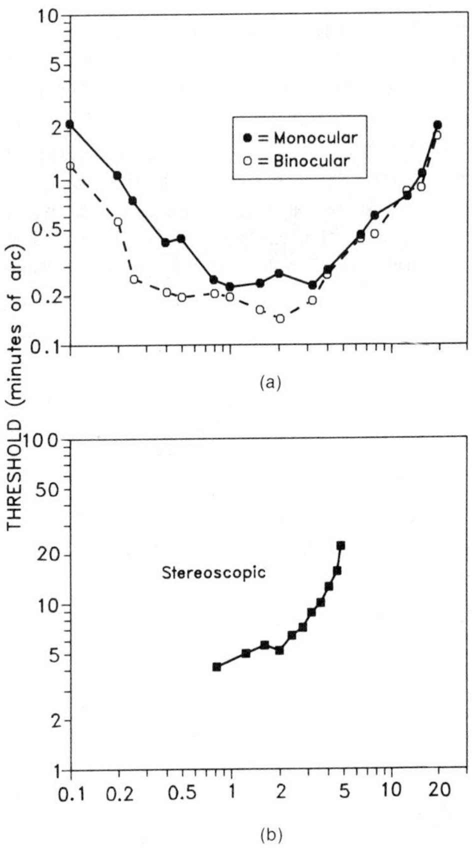

Figure 19.18. Comparison of visual sensitivity to positional oscillations in the frontal plane and to stereoscopic oscillations in depth. The subject's left eye viewed a bar or dot pattern that oscillated from side to side at a frequency *F* Hz while the right eye viewed a similar pattern oscillating at ($F + \Delta F$) Hz. At the difference frequency of ΔF, oscillations in depth waxed and waned, but monocular signals were at either *F* or ($F + \Delta F$) and had no component at frequency ΔF. Thus the technique provides a subjective distinction between stereoscopic and monocular processing by giving them quite different frequency "signatures." Panel (a): sensitivity to oscillation in the frontal plane is maximal at 1–4 Hz, with somewhat greater sensitivity at low frequencies under binocular viewing conditons with ΔF at zero (dashed curve). Frontal plane oscillations are still visible at 25 Hz, although sensitivity is much reduced. Panel (b): sensitivity for stereoscopic oscillation in depth falls off with increasing frequency from the lowest frequency measured (0.75 Hz). Oscillation in depth could not be seen at or above 3 Hz for one subject, and 5 Hz for another. (From D. Regan & K. I. Beverley, The dissociation of sideways movements from movements in depth: Psychophysics, *Vision Research*, 1973, *13*. Reprinted with permission.)

view a slanted wire pyramid through a telestereoscope that increased the disparity of its half images (see Figure 19.20). The enhanced disparity caused subjects to judge the distance between the nearer apex of the pyramid and its more distant base as being much greater than when the pyramid was seen without the telestereoscope. Then the pyramid was rotated so that each eye obtained the same kinetic information as to depth (the KDE was the same for both eyes), except that it was in opposite phases in the two eyes. At first the pyramid exhibited a rubbery distortion, but after a while it was perceived as rigid and rotating in depth.

After viewing the rotating pyramid through the telestereoscope for several minutes, subjects judged the depth between the apex and base of the static pyramid once again while looking at it directly. It was found that the amount of depth given by the static disparity was substantially altered as a result of adaptation to the kinetic cues. This rapid modification of the stereoscopic depth effect suggests that the amount of depth associated with different disparities can be rescaled by exposure to (monocular) kinetic cues.

Wallach and Frey (1972) placed changing size in conflict with the cues of accommodation, convergence, and disparity. This was done by moving a luminous diamond-shaped object toward and away from an observer, but expanding and diminishing its size as it moved. The actual path length was 55 cm, with the nearer point 25 cm from the subject and the farther point 80 cm away. Although the path was only 55 cm long, the size of the diamond was varied while it moved to simulate a path length of 367 cm. Thus the change in image size was greater than the changes induced in absolute disparity and accommodation.

As pointed out in Chapter 23 by Arditi, the amount of depth perceived between two objects is a function of both the distance to the objects and the relative binocular disparity. For a constant relative disparity, the amount of perceived depth between two objects increases as the square of the average distance to them. Hence a change in perceived distance should result in a marked change in perceived depth based on relative disparity. If the changing size utilized by Wallach and Frey resulted in an increase in perceived distance, then a stereoscopic depth effect should be enhanced.

It is also well known that the perceived frontal size of an object of constant linear size is proportional to its perceived distance (Emmert's law). Hence an increase in perceived distance due to exposure to the changing-size stimulus should also result in an increase in judged frontal size.

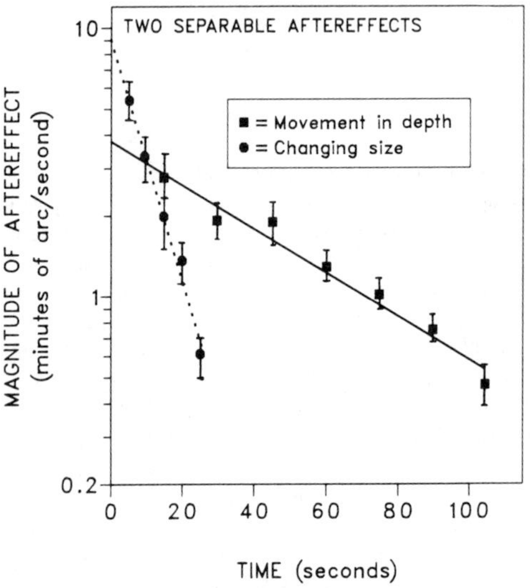

Figure 19.19. Decay curves for motion-in-depth and changing-size aftereffects. The adapting stimulus was a bright solid square of mean size 1° on a side. During adaptation, the vertical edges moved toward each other at a rate of $0.25°\cdot sec^{-1}$ for 1 sec; horizontal edges remained stationary. The square then disappeared for 0.25 sec and the cycle was repeated. After 20 min of exposure to the adapting stimulus, a static test square appeared either to expand in size or to move forward in depth. In one experiment, subjects canceled the changing-size aftereffect by adjusting the rate of size change in a 1° test square whose vertical edges moved toward each other (dotted line). In another experiment, subjects canceled apparent movement in depth in the same manner (continuous line). (Modified from Beverley & Regan, 1979.)

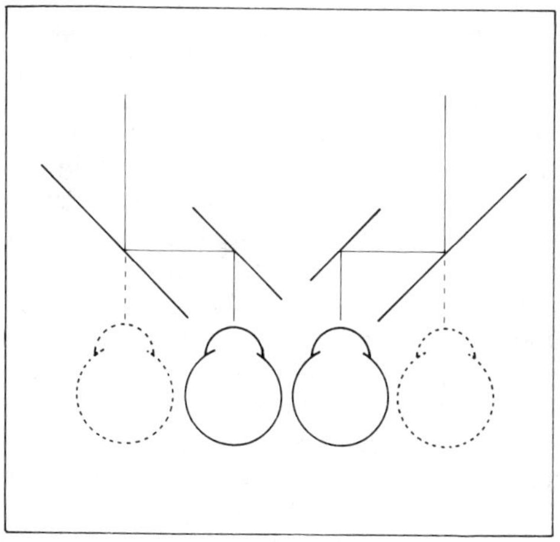

Figure 19.20. The principle of the telestereoscope. The images of the world reflected by the mirrors to the two eyes are "seen" from station points that are set farther apart than the eyes themselves. This has the effect of enlarging the interpupillary distance. It also enhances the magnitude of depth between points at different distances, because the disparity of these points is increased. (From L. Kaufman, *Sight and mind*, Oxford University Press, 1974. Reprinted with permission.)

To test for these effects Wallach and Frey had observers estimate the size of the base of a luminous wire pyramid facing them, and also the depth between the base and the more distant apex of the pyramid. This was done for pyramids at two different distances both before and after adaptation to the changing-size diamond. The estimates of size and depth were made by having subjects adjust the length of a rod held in their hands but not seen. In general, the rod was made longer after adaptation than before. The base of the near pyramid was judged to be about 10% larger after adaptation than before; the base of the more distant pyramid, about 16% larger. The judgments of depth were even more markedly affected. Although the disparity of both the near and more distant pyramids was the same before and after adaptation, the perceived depth increased by 19% for the near pyramid and 28% for the far pyramid. This finding indicates that the distance information given by absolute disparity and accommodation was altered by observation of nonveridical changing size.

2.2.4.2. Comparison of Changing Size and Changing Disparity as Stimuli for Motion in Depth Perception. As shown in Figure 19.21, when an object moves directly toward the head, the two retinal images move away from each other (their disparity increases), and the images also grow larger. As discussed above, either of these two consequences of object motion is capable of producing a sensation of motion in depth. In the real visual world the situation is almost always as shown in Figure 19.21, but Regan and Beverley (1979a) placed changing size and changing disparity in opposition to each other in order to measure their relative efficacy as stimuli for motion in depth. In their experiment, when decreasing disparity indicated that a square was coming closer, the sizes of its retinal images grew smaller rather than larger.

The task of the subject was to null the motion in depth of a square produced by changing size by adjusting the rate of change in the disparity of its two retinal images. Figure 19.22 shows the relationship between the rate of change in disparity and the rate of change in size that was nulled by this rate of change in disparity. The fact that nulling is possible at all indicates that the perception of motion in depth is the same thing, whether produced by looming stimulation or by changing disparity stimulation; presumably, signals generated by these two stimuli converge before reaching the neural mechanism whose activity corresponds to the sensation of motion in depth. The plots are roughly linear on log-log axes, indicating a power function relationship. The relative effectiveness of the two stimuli is also affected by the duration of the inspection period. Furthermore, in a sample of five subjects, an 80:1 intersubject difference was seen in the relative effectiveness of changing size and changing disparity as stimuli for perception of motion in depth.

Now we turn to the question of what effect viewing distance has on the relative effectiveness of changing disparity and changing size as stimuli for motion in depth perception. It can be shown that, on geometric grounds, viewing distance has no effect on the ratio between change in stimulus size and change in stimulus disparity.

As shown in Figure 19.23, when an object of linear width S moves from a viewing distance D to distance $(D - \Delta D)$, the size of its retinal images increases from θ_S to θ'_S radians, and the binocular disparity changes from θ_D to θ'_D radians. Approximately, $\theta_D = I/D$, $\theta'_D = I/(D - \Delta D)$, $\theta_S = S/D$ and $\theta'_S = S/(D - \Delta D)$. Hence $(\theta'_D - \theta_D) = \Delta\theta_D = (I\Delta D)/D^2$ and $(\theta'_S - \theta_S) = \Delta\theta_S = (S\Delta D)/D^2$. Thus $\Delta\theta_S/\Delta\theta_D = S/I$. Hence $\dot{\theta}_S/\dot{\theta}_D = S/I$. This means that the ratio between the rate of change in binocular disparity ($\dot{\theta}_D$) and the rate of change in size ($\dot{\theta}_S$) does not depend on viewing distance, but does depend on the absolute width of the object and on the observer's interpupillary distance. A more detailed proof is given in the Appendix. The independence of viewing distance may seem counterintuitive since classical binocular depth perception is almost ineffective at ranges greater than about 100 m. However, it is the ratio $\dot{\theta}_D/\dot{\theta}_S$ that is important here, whereas classical depth perception depends on absolute disparity rather than a ratio.

The effect of viewing distance is not necessarily only a geometrical issue, however, for binocular convergence is different for different viewing distances, and the angle of convergence

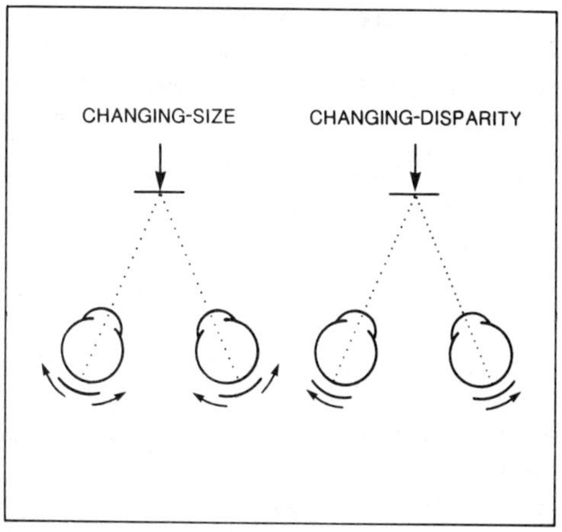

Figure 19.21. Effect on retinal images of changing size and changing disparity. When a solid and nonrotating object moves toward the head, its half-images change in size, as shown on the left. Also, the left and right half-images move away from each other (change in absolute disparity), as shown on the right. Both kinds of change, that of image size and that of absolute disparity, occur simultaneously when an object moves toward the head in real space. (From D. Regan & K. I. Beverley. Binocular and monocular stimuli for motion-in-depth: Changing-disparity and changing-size inputs feed the same motion-in-depth stage, *Vision Research*, 1979, *19*. Reprinted with permission.)

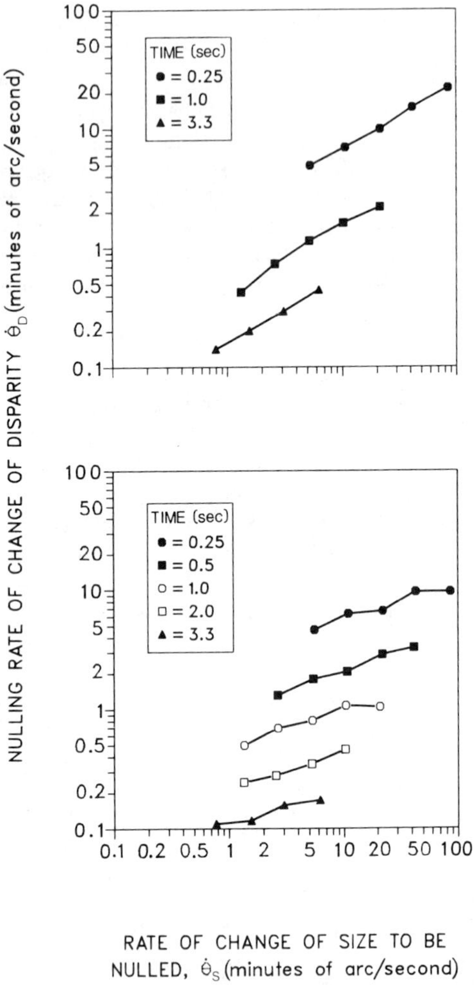

Figure 19.22. Relative effectiveness of binocular and monocular cues for motion in depth. Subjects viewed a square of mean size 1° that expanded at a uniform speed for 0.25, 1.0, or 3.3 sec. The disparity of the square could be altered simultaneously by the subject so as to cancel the impression of motion in depth produced by the changing size. Repeated observations were made at each inspection time until a satisfactory null was achieved. Ordinates plot the rate of change of binocular disparity required to cancel the sensation of motion in depth produced by different rates of size change (abscissas). Data are shown for two subjects. The relative effectiveness of changing size and changing disparity as stimuli for motion in depth depends on rate of size change and inspection time. (From D. Regan & K. I. Beverley, Binocular and monocular stimuli for motion-in-depth: Changing-disparity and changing-size inputs feed the same motion-in-depth stage, *Vision Research*, 1979, *19*. Reprinted with permission.)

is known to affect perceived size. Control experiments in which the angle of convergence was varied by means of prisms upheld the conclusion that viewing distance does not substantially alter the relative effectiveness of changing size and changing disparity as cues to motion in depth (Regan & Beverley, 1979a).

It is clear from Figure 19.21 that changing-size stimulation is available either binocularly or monocularly. However, changing disparity is only available binocularly. A question that has attracted considerable interest is whether the absence of binocular vision affects pilot performance. Three flight studies revealed that landing performance of pilots in daylight was not degraded by the occlusion of one eye (Grosslight, Fletcher, Masterton, & Hagen, 1978; Lewis, Blakeley, Swaroop, Masters, & McMurty, 1973; Pfaffman, 1948), and one study reported that landing performance could even be improved by loss of binocular vision (Lewis & Kriers, 1969). This latter finding was challenged by other researchers who, nevertheless, found that monocular performance was no worse than binocular performance (Grosslight et al., 1978). The suspicion that pilots might try harder when one eye is occluded was addressed by performing an experiment with relatively inexperienced ("low-time") pilots rather than experienced military pilots. Even though the low-time pilots were presumably stressed when landing normally with full binocular vision, monocular occlusion produced no reduction in landing performance (Lewis & Kriers, 1969).

The results of these flight tests are consistent with the notion that, when other depth cues are available, static binocular depth perception is unimportant at ranges in excess of about 90 m. (Of course, there may well be other advantages to binocular vision in piloting aircraft because, for example, it provides a wider field of view than does vision with one eye occluded.)

There is evidence, however, that stereoscopic sensitivity to motion in depth is a different matter from classical stereoscopic sensitivity to position in depth. As discussed above, the ratio between sensitivity to binocular motion cue and to the looming cues is little affected by viewing distance over a large range of distances. Laboratory experiments (Regan & Beverley, 1979a) suggest that the flight tests discussed above may have confounded several factors, so that their results may be applicable to only a narrow range of visual situations. To make this clear, consider the consequences of loss of binocular vision for sensitivity to motion in depth of objects on the ground during landing. This sensitivity would depend on the following four factors (Regan & Beverley, 1979a):

1. *Inspection Duration.* A loss of binocular vision would be less important for short periods of inspection.
2. *The Target's Velocity in Depth.* Visual sensitivity to low velocities would be less affected by losing binocular vision.
3. *The Absolute Width of the Object.* Visual sensitivity to motion in depth of wider objects would be less affected by loss of binocular vision than would sensitivity to motion in depth of narrower objects (except at very short distances; see Regan and Beverley, 1979a).
4. *Individual Differences.* There are very large individual differences in relative sensitivity to changing size and to changing disparity; for example, as noted earlier, individuals differ in sensitivity to changing disparity by as much as 80 to 1.

Calculations have been published (Regan & Beverley, 1979a) to illustrate how the relative effectiveness of monocular and binocular stimuli to motion in depth can be computed for individual observers in real visual situations, including aircraft landings.

The following calculation illustrates how targets of narrow width (in centimeters rather than angular subtense) favor the stereoscopic (binocular) stimulus for motion in depth over the changing size stimulus. Suppose that an object 15.24 cm in diameter is 90 m from an aircraft and approaching it at a closing line-of-sight velocity of 260 km·hr^{-1}. From geometric considerations the ratio of the rate of change in disparity to the rate of change in angular size is equal to I/S, where I is the interpupillary distance and S the angular size of the object. At 90 m the object's angular size is about 10 min of arc and its rate of change in size is about 3.6 min arc·sec^{-1}. Now consider the psychophysical data for one subject shown in Figure 19.22 (lower panel). If the inspection time is 1.0 sec, then, before

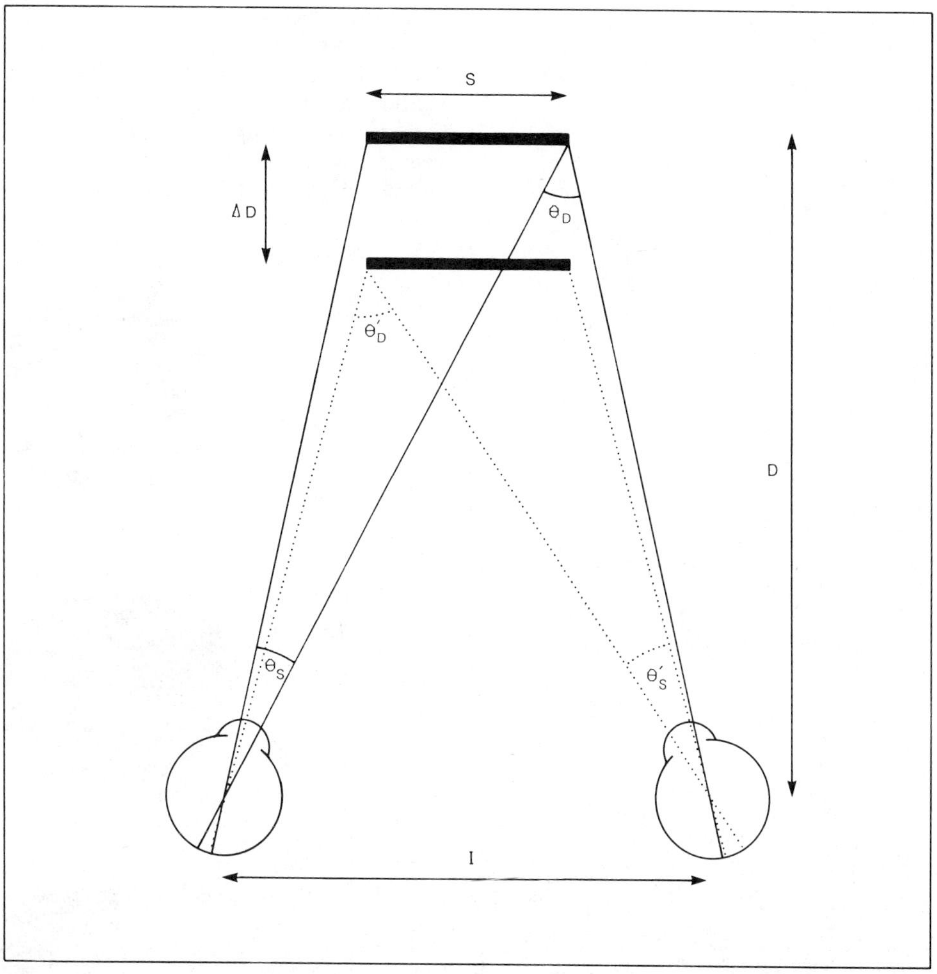

Figure 19.23. Geometric relation between rate of change of size and rate of change of disparity. When an object of linear width S moves from viewing distance D to distance $(D - \Delta D)$, retinal image size increases from θ_S to θ'_S rad, and binocular disparity changes from θ_D to θ'_D. See text for proof that the ratio between the rate of change of binocular disparity and the rate of change of size does not depend on viewing distance, but does depend on the linear width of the object and the observer's interpupillary distance. (From D. Regan & K. I. Beverley. Binocular and monocular stimuli for motion-in-depth: Changing-disparity and changing-size inputs feed the same motion-in-depth stage, *Vision Research*, 1979, *19*. Reprinted with permission.)

allowance for geometric factors, the ratio of the effectiveness of stereoscopic and changing size stimulation is about 0.28 for this subject; after allowance for geometry, the binocular stimulus of changing disparity would be about 1.5 times more effective than changing size as a stimulus for motion in depth of this narrow object. Of course, this applies only to one particular subject, and relative effectiveness would have to be computed for other subjects on an individual basis.

Figure 19.22 compares the effectiveness of brief unidirectional changes of size and disparity in producing the sensation of motion in depth. As noted earlier, oscillations in the size of a bright square can give rise to two different sensations: motion in depth and changing size. Figure 19.24 compares the effectiveness of changing size in producing each of these sensations as a function of frequency of size oscillation. Changing size is ineffective as a stimulus for motion in depth at frequencies above about 3 Hz. However, at frequencies of 3–5 Hz the subject can detect a change in size without experiencing a change in depth.

2.2.4.3. Motion in Depth and Motion in the Frontal Plane. The effects of oscillation frequency on the perception of motion in depth and motion in the frontal plane were compared in Figure 19.18(a) and (b). Both the left eye's target and the right eye's target oscillated from side to side. The only difference between the binocular stimulus in (a) and the stereoscopic stimulus in (b) is that the left and right eyes' oscillations were inphase in (a) and in antiphase in (b). It is clear that sensitivity to motion in depth due to oscillating disparity falls off at a lower frequency of oscillation than does sensitivity to motion in the frontal plane caused by oscillating position [binocular in (a)]. A similar difference was also found for motion in depth due to changing size (see Figure 19.24). To summarize, motion in depth caused by change in disparity and motion in depth caused by change in size both collapse at frequencies in excess of about 3 Hz, but the subject continues to perceive motion in the frontal plane at much higher frequencies.

2.2.4.4. Comparison of Static Disparity and Changing Disparity. Regan and Beverley (1973) suggested that responses

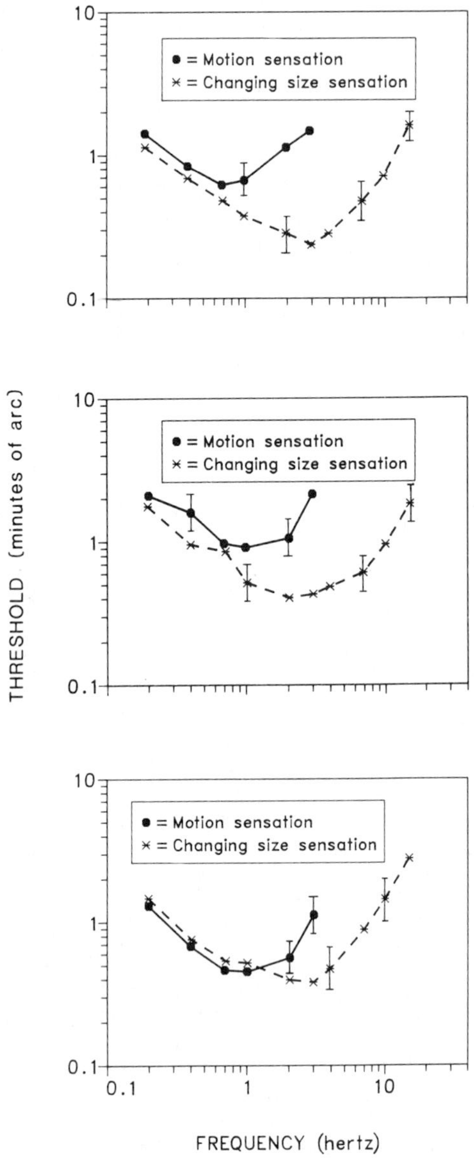

Figure 19.24. Effect of frequency of size oscillation on perception of motion in depth and changing size. The stimulus was a solid bright square (mean size 0.5° on a side) that alternately expanded and contracted in size at different oscillation rates. Subjects were instructed to set the amplitude of the size change to make the motion in depth barely visible on some trials and to make changing size just visible on other trials. Solid curves show the minimum oscillation amplitude (in minutes of arc) that produced a sensation of motion in depth; dashed curves, the minimum oscillation amplitude that produced a sensation of changing size. Data are from three different subjects who viewed the stimuli binocularly. Vertical lines indicate ±1 SD. Motion in depth sensation fails above about 3 Hz, but the sensation of changing size persists to above 10 Hz. (From D. Regan & K. I. Beverley, Binocular and monocular stimuli for motion-in-depth: Changing-disparity and changing-size inputs feed the same motion-in-depth stage. *Vision Research*, 1979, *19*. Reprinted with permission.)

to changing disparity are fundamentally different from responses to static binocular disparity. One reason for this is that stereoscopic sensitivity to motion in depth cannot be predicted from acuity for static relative disparity.

As pointed out earlier, the direction of stereoscopic motion in depth is indicated by the stimulus velocity ratio V_L/V_R (Figure 19.15). However, classic stereoscopic depth perception is related to the positional disparities of the half-images on the two retinas. The two are not equivalent because a given rate of change of disparity corresponds to an indefinite number of values of V_L/V_R. Furthermore, the binocular disparity of any given object is different for different angles of ocular convergence, because disparity is measured relative to the frontal plane passing through the point of binocular convergence and thus relates not to absolute depth but rather to depth relative to this plane.

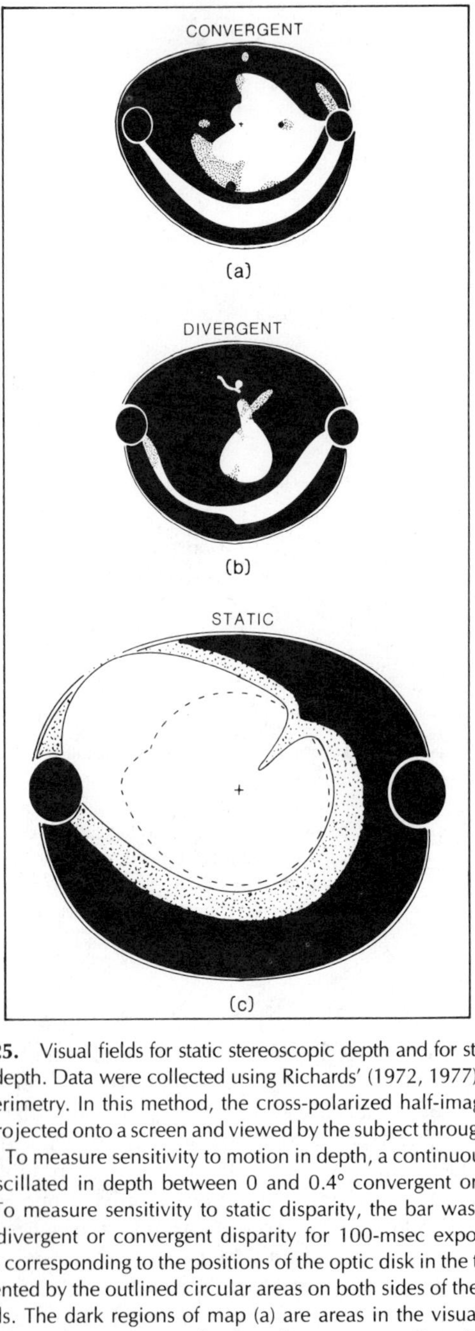

Figure 19.25. Visual fields for static stereoscopic depth and for stereoscopic motion in depth. Data were collected using Richards' (1972, 1977) technique of stereoperimetry. In this method, the cross-polarized half-images of a 1° bar were projected onto a screen and viewed by the subject through Polaroid spectacles. To measure sensitivity to motion in depth, a continuously visible bar was oscillated in depth between 0 and 0.4° convergent or divergent disparity. To measure sensitivity to static disparity, the bar was presented with 0.4° divergent or convergent disparity for 100-msec exposures. The blind spots corresponding to the positions of the optic disk in the two retinas are represented by the outlined circular areas on both sides of the portrayed visual fields. The dark regions of map (a) are areas in the visual field that were "blind" to the motion in depth with convergent disparity. Stippled areas show where unstable depth sensations could sometimes be elicited. Panel (b) shows a similar map for motion in depth in a divergent direction. Both maps differ substantially from map (c), where the solid curve encloses the region in which the subject could correctly estimate the position in depth of a stationary bar. Comparison of (b) and (c) shows that some areas of the visual field are "blind" to motion in depth but still are sensitive to static disparity, and vice versa. (From W. Richards & D. Regan, A stereo field map with implications for disparity processing, *Investigative Ophthalmology*, 1973, *12*. Reprinted with permission.)

In contrast, the value of V_L/V_R is approximately the same for different angles of ocular convergence. The origin of the coordinates of disparity-based geometry varies with the point of convergence, whereas the coordinates of V_L/V_R geometry are fixed in the head.

Evidence that physiological responses to disparity and to V_L/V_R are different comes from the finding that the visual fields of many observers contain regions that are "blind" to stereo motion in depth but not to the classic static disparity and vice versa (Richards & Regan, 1973). Figure 19.25 shows a visual field of this type. The subject had normal visual acuity and perimetric examination revealed no scotomas. The white areas in Figure 19.25(a) and (b) show where the subject could see the motion in depth of a bar that oscillated back and forth in depth. Outside these areas the subject was essentially blind to motion in depth. Figure 19.25(c) shows the regions where the subject could accurately judge the position in depth of a stationary bar. Areas that were blind to motion in depth differ in location from areas that were blind to static disparity. Apparently, it is fairly common for stereo fields to contain areas blind to motion in depth, even in normally sighted individuals. However, the locations of these "motion blind" areas seem to be peculiar to the individual. In any event, the conclusion is that the neural mechanisms subserving sensitivity to static disparity and to kinetic disparity are sufficiently separate that one can be impaired and the other spared.

Richards' and Regan's findings suggest that subjects who have extensive areas of the visual field that are "blind" to stereoscopic motion in depth might misjudge the trajectories of objects in the affected areas of the visual field. However, because changing size is an additional stimulus for motion in depth, it could offset the effects of "blindness" to changing disparity. Confirming this suggestion, Regan and Beverley (1983a) found that sensitivity to changing size was normal in regions of the visual field of a subject that were blind to changing disparity.

Cynader and Regan (1978, 1982) found neurons in area 18 and in the 17/18 border of the cat that were selectively sensitive to the ratio between left and right retinal image velocities. In other words, these neurons were tuned to the direction of motion in depth. Some of the most sharply tuned neurons fired most briskly when the retinal images moved in opposite directions, corresponding to a range of directions spanning no more than 1–2°. Some of these neurons maintained their directional tuning over a fourfold range of speeds [Regan & Cynader, 1982; Figure 19.26 (a)]. A second class of neuron fired best for trajectories that missed the head. These were tuned to a broader range of directions than the "hitting the head" class of neurons.

Cynader and Regan (1978) found that the well-known "binocular depth" class of neurons is also very selectively sensitive to the direction of motion in depth. These neurons show strong interocular facilitation (up to 100-fold) when motion is accurately parallel to the frontal parallel plane [Figure 19.26(b)]. However,

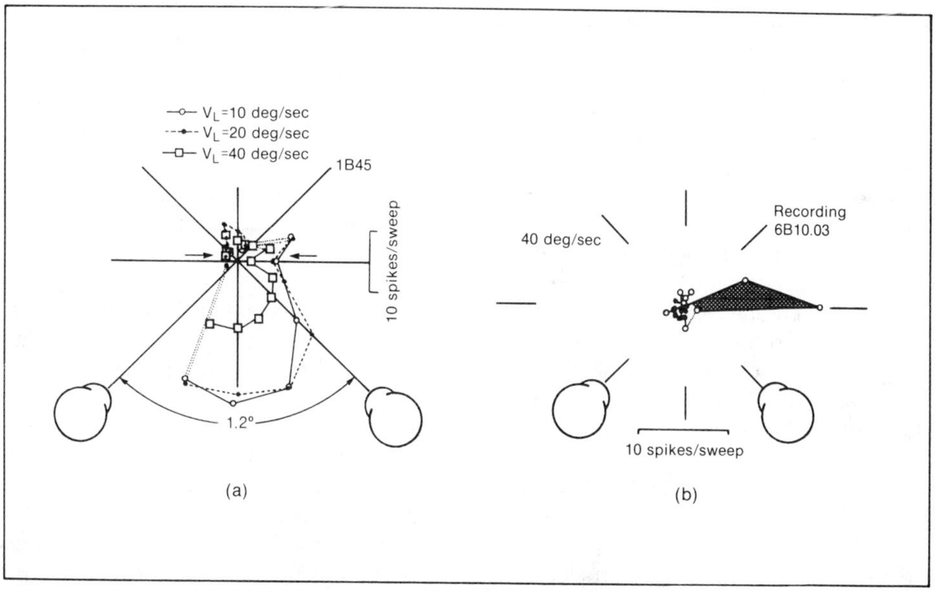

Figure 19.26. Selective sensitivity of neurons in the visual cortex of the cat to direction of motion in depth. Number of spikes per unit time is plotted radially as a function of the direction of motion in depth. The ratio of retinal image velocities (V_L/V_R) is plotted as azimuthal angle. This scale exaggerates the cone of angles subtended by the eyes. Panel (a) shows the response properties of a "hitting the head" neuron. This cell fired strongly to binocular stimulation only when the test bar moved along a path of collision with the right side of the head. Strong firing was restricted to a cone of directions about 1.0° wide. The cell maintained its sharp selectivity even when stimulus speeds were doubled and redoubled. This unit's selectivity was achieved by interocular inhibition, as indicated by the arrows. Panel (b) shows a unit that fired at an appreciable rate only when (1) the target's disparity was near zero; (2) its direction of motion was closely parallel to the frontal plane in a left-right direction; and (3) vision was binocular. Closed circles show firing when the two eyes were stimulated separately, and open circles show firing with binocular vision. The black area marks the very strong interocular facilitation observed with binocular vision. (From D. Regan & M. Cynader, Neurons in cat visual cortex tuned to the direction of motion in depth: Effects of stimulus speed, *Investigative Ophthalmology and Visual Science*, 1982, *22*. Reprinted with permission.)

the chief property of this type of neuron is its comparatively sharp tuning to disparity, that is, to relative position in depth. It was suggested that the first two classes of neuron are involved in the perception of stereoscopic *motion* in depth (Cynader & Regan, 1978); the third class, it has been suggested, is involved in the perception of relative *position* in depth (Barlow, Blakemore, & Pettigrew, 1967). Extrapolating to human vision, these "motion-in-depth" and "position-in-depth" neurons provide a possible physiological basis for findings such as selective "blindness" for motion in depth while visual sensitivity to position in depth is preserved and vice versa (Figure 19.25).

Some of the first two classes of "motion-in-depth" neurons maintain their tuning to the direction of motion in depth over a range of disparities as wide as 12° (Cynader & Regan, 1982). Other neurons of the first two classes systematically change their tuning as a function of disparity, for example, by favoring motion towards the plane at which the eyes are converged (the plane of fixation) for objects that lie either nearer or farther than the plane of fixation.

3. THE DIRECTION OF SELF-MOTION IN DEPTH AND OPTIC FLOW PATTERNS

Studies on visual cues to self-motion encompass several different problems. Some investigators are concerned with the sensation of self-motion that can be produced by visual stimulation. For example, when sitting in a stationary train parked next to a moving train, one may perceive the outside world as stationary and oneself as in motion (Dichgans & Brandt, 1978). Peripheral retinal stimulation is particularly effective in generating this illusion, and even a small area of peripheral stimulation can be effective (Brandt, Dichgans, & Koening, 1978; Johansson, 1974). The discussion here does not treat the sensation of locomotion caused by visual stimulation, but is restricted to a different problem: what visual cues are used for accurate visual guidance of locomotion.

Changing size and changing disparity are potentially of help in guiding a person's locomotion, and it has been empirically shown that the use of visual cues to motion in depth is particularly important in landing an aircraft. Other sources of information that may be employed by a pilot include flow gradients of the terrain, perspective, and the angular distance between the horizon and an aim point on the ground.

3.1. Analysis of Visual Flow Patterns by the Human Visual System

As an observer moves through the external world, the location from which the world is viewed continually changes and, because the world is three-dimensional, what the observer sees is different from one instant to the next. This continuous change of viewpoint makes available information about the outside world that is not available in a view from a static position. An analogy with that famous medical instrument, the CAT scanner, might be useful here. Comparing many X-ray photographs of the brain taken from different angles provides information not available in one single photograph, and this comparison is performed rapidly and automatically by a computer using special-purpose algorithms. Turning back to self-motion, the brain might, in principle, parallel the CAT computer's ability to extract information by comparing views from different locations. Rather than operating on an ordered sequence of single "snapshots," however, the brain has available a continuous ordered flow of different views so that information about the outside world could, in principle, be extracted by means of specific visual sensitivities to different aspects of motion. Indeed, there is experimental evidence that the visual pathway does have several different motion sensitivities that would allow the extraction of visual information unavailable to a stationary observer. For example, depth perception can be generated by motion parallax (Graham & Rogers, 1982; Rogers & Graham, 1982). Camouflaged objects that are invisible in the absence of relative motion can be rendered visible by motion parallax alone (Anstis, 1970; Braddick, 1974; Foster, 1971; Poggio et al., 1983; Regan & Spekreijse, 1970; Reichardt & Poggio, 1979) by means of visual processing that is quite different from the processing involved in detecting noncamouflaged objects (Regan & Beverley, 1984b). Further to this point, evidence is discussed below that the visual pathway is sensitive to mathematical elements of the optic flow field such as divergence and curl.

Anticipating such recent empirical studies, in his seminal writings Gibson (1950) pointed out that the extra information potentially made available to an observer by self-motion includes visibility of three-dimensional camouflaged objects, and the three-dimensional relationships between external objects as well as the observer's direction of self-motion. Gibson's theoretical approach to this topic was via the concept of the "optic array." The optic array contains visual information that is potentially available to the observer. This information includes motion perspective and the focus of expansion in the flow of optical texture. Chapter 21 by Sedgwick describes the Gibsonian concept of the optic array, and the concept is also briefly discussed by Hochberg in Chapter 22. For present purposes, it suffices to follow Gibson (1979), who defined the ambient optic array at a point of observation as a "nested set of adjacent solid angles . . . [where each solid angle corresponds to] one of the large facets or small facets of the environment. The solid angles are separated by contours or contrasts" (Gibson, 1979, p. 310). Thus the optic array is the set of all possible retinal images of a scene projected onto the picture plane.

Recent theoretical work on visual flow patterns has included attempts to represent the flow pattern as a velocity field that is completely described by assigning a magnitude (i.e., speed) and direction to every point in the field. Several authors have sought to describe this vector field in terms of the vector calculus notation conventionally used to describe vector fields such as electrical fields and the field of local velocity in flowing water (Gordon, 1965; Koenderink & van Doorn, 1976, 1981; Longuet-Higgins & Prazdny, 1980; Prazdny, 1980). In these terms the flow pattern can be analyzed into mathematically independent elements that include the divergence, curl, and gradient of velocity at each point in the field (i.e., div **V**, curl **V** and grad **V** respectively; see Appendix). At an intuitive level, these mathematical quantities can be understood in terms of the flow pattern in an emptying bath. The divergence of surface velocity (i.e., div **V**) is large near the drain hole where div **V** expresses the loss of water. The curl of surface velocity (i.e., curl **V**) is large where there are vortices in the water. Longuet-Higgins and Prazdny (1980) conjectured that the visual pathway might have evolved neural mechanisms that were specifically sensitive to these mathematically independent quantities. They pointed out that the "looming detectors" of Regan and Beverley (1978b) can be regarded as roughly approximating detectors for div **V**.

Further support for their conjecture is provided by a recent suggestion that the visual system is specifically sensitive to a rough approximation of vorticity or curl **V** (Regan & Beverley, 1984a). The problem addressed by this study was whether visual responses to rotary motion can be explained in terms of the known sensitivity to linear motion. The rationale of the experiment is illustrated in Figure 19.27.

Subjects were adapted to one of two circular areas of moving dots, divided into quadrants. The dots in each quadrant oscillated back and forth linearly. In one stimulus pattern, the dots in all quadrants moved "clockwise" or "counterclockwise" together, providing a strong rotary component of motion about the center, although no individual dots actually moved along a curve [Figure 19.27(a)]. In the other pattern, dots in two opposite quadrants moved "clockwise" whereas those in the other two quadrants moved "counterclockwise," so that no rotary motion component was present [Figure 19.27(b)]. After adapting to these patterns, subjects viewed a test circle of random dots that rotated about its center [Figure 19.27(c)]. It was envisaged that a curl (i.e., vorticity) mechanism might be adapted by Figure 19.27(a) but would not be adapted by Figure 19.27(b). On the other hand, (a) and (b) would have identical effects on linear motion mechanisms, for the dot motion within any quadrant was identical in the two stimuli.

After viewing one of the adapting patterns for 5 min, subjects set the test pattern to the smallest rotary oscillation that could just be seen. Base-line thresholds were established after adapting to a stationary dot pattern. The main finding was that stimulus (a) produced threshold elevations up to 600% greater than stimulus (b). This difference was greatest when oscillatory frequency was about 4–6 Hz. Arguing that this difference could not be explained in terms of visual sensitivity to linear motion, Regan and Beverley (1984a) concluded that the visual system is specifically sensitive to rotary motion. They went on to suggest that the visual system contains detectors sensitive to some rough approximation to curl **V**.

3.2. The Direction of Self-Motion in Depth

Gibson (1950, 1979) pointed out that, when an observer moves forward, the optic array (see above) contains a radially expanding flow pattern, and the focus of expansion coincides with the moving observer's destination in the outside world. The focus of expansion in the optic array is potentially available as a guide to self-locomotion. Going further, Gibson (1958) suggested that humans and animals can, in practice, use the focus of expansion in the optic array to guide self-locomotion. This prediction is, of course, open to experimental test.

First, it should be noted that the flow pattern in the optic array is not necessarily the same as the flow pattern in the retinal image. This happens, for example, when moving observers do not look at their destination or gaze at a fixed angle to their destination, but rather look at some nearby feature in the world. In this important case, their eyes rotate continuously and add to the radial expansion pattern a translational velocity of the whole retinal image. This changes the flow pattern, and the focus of expansion may be displaced so that it no longer coincides with the destination. In other cases the focus may be abolished altogether (Koenderink & van Doorn, 1976; Regan & Beverley, 1982; Richards, 1975). A specific example in which the focus of expansion does not coincide with the destination is illustrated in Figure 19.28. Figure 19.28(a) represents the focus of expansion in the optic array. This differs from the flow pattern on the retina [Figure 19.28(b)] when the eye moves to track a point (B) on a vertical surface toward which the observer is moving. It is clear that in this special instance there is a flow outward from the impact point A in Figure 19.28(a). Figure 19.28(c)–(e) illustrate this with photographic multiple exposures. In (c) the camera is moving toward the nose and pointing at the nose; this illustrates the flow pattern in the optic array. In (d) the camera is moving toward the nose, but pointing at the arrowed dot. Can a subject separate the translational flow introduced by the eye movements from the radial flow in the optic array and respond to the latter? Although the expanding component and the translational component due to eye rotation "are, in principle, separable" (Lee, 1976, p. 140), it is an empirical question whether or not the visual system can separate them in practice. Experimental evidence on this point includes Regan and Beverley's (1982) demonstration that in at least one situation observers are not able to separate the effects of one-dimensional

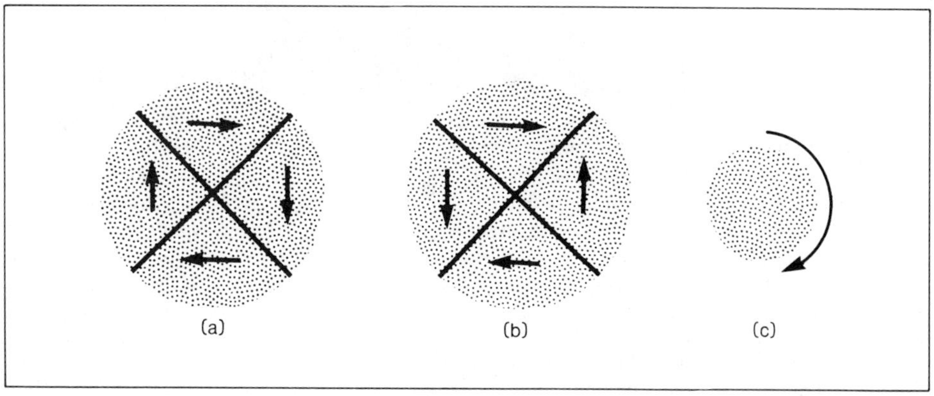

Figure 19.27. Adaptation to rotary motion. (a) and (b) were adapting patterns consisting of a 2° diameter area of random dots divided into four quadrants. Dots in any given quadrant oscillated sinusoidally along a straight line at the same frequency and with the same peak-to-peak amplitude of 1°, but the directions of oscillation were different for the four quadrants. Adapting stimuli (a) and (b) differed only in the relative phasing of the quadrants, as shown by the arrows. In (a) all dots moved clockwise or counterclockwise together, so the circular disk had a strong rotary component of motion about the center. In (b) the relative phasing of the quadrants gave the disk a zero net rotary component of motion about the center. Test stimulus (c) was a 1° diameter area of random dots that rotated sinusoidally to and fro about the center with an amplitude adjustable by the subject. Adaptation to (a) had a much greater effect on sensitivity to the rotary motion of the test stimulus than did adaptation to (b) (Regan & Beverley, 1984a).

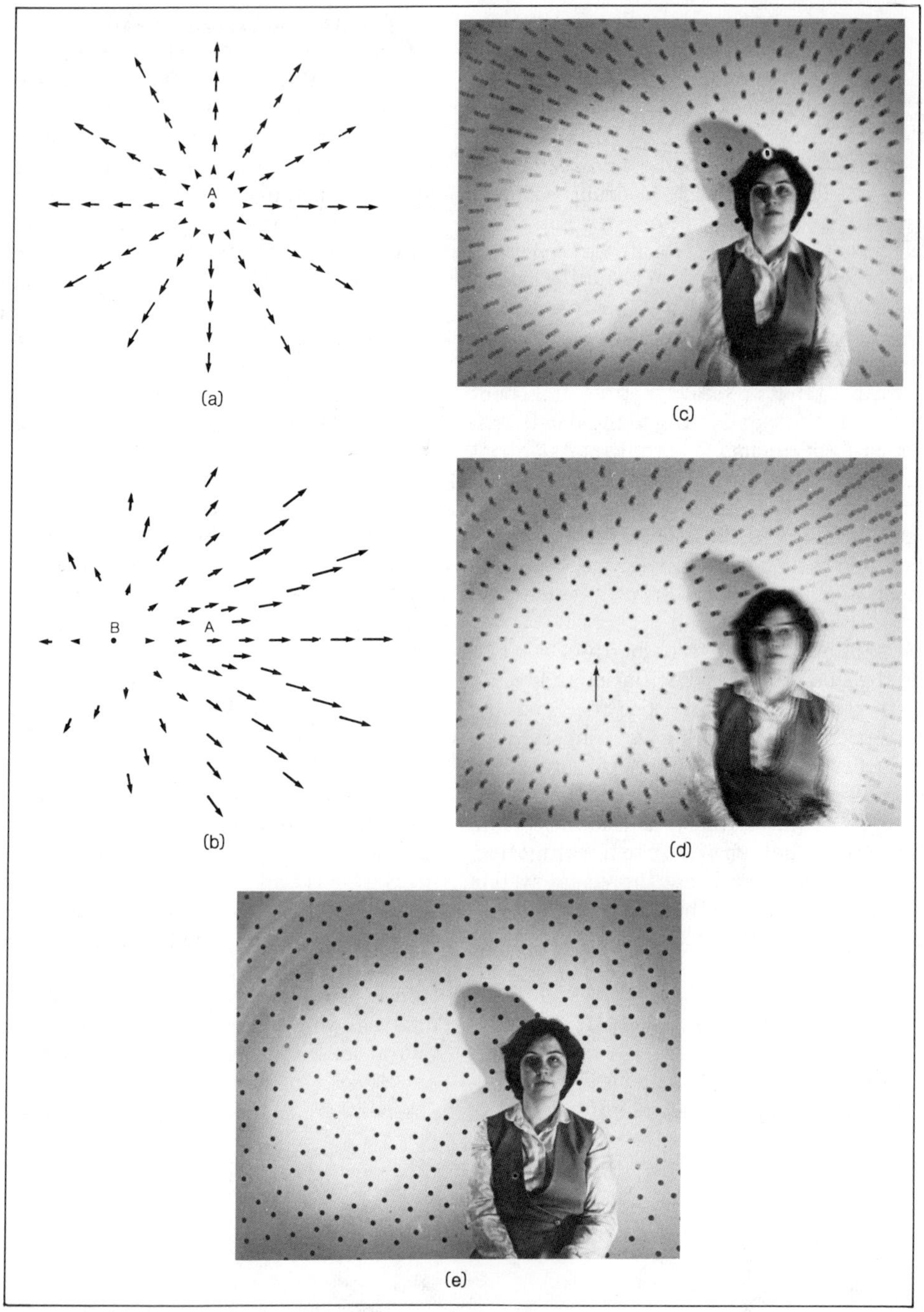

Figure 19.28. Expanding flow patterns with direction of gaze at focus of expansion and with direction of gaze off to one side. In pattern (a) the observer's gaze is fixed at the focus of expansion at A, and all elements of texture in the image of the surface expand away from this focus. This symmetrical expansion pattern occurs in the optic array and also in the retinal image when the direction of gaze remains fixed at the point of impact with the surface. The surface in (b) is identical to the surface in (a) except that the observer fixates on point B rather than on the actual impact point A. This introduces a sideways component of motion in the image at point A. In both patterns, for simplicity, the rate of change of magnification is the same for all points in the field of view. Photograph (c) is a multiple exposure taken with the camera moving toward the head and always pointing at the head. The center of expansion of flow coincides with the point toward which the camera is both moving and "gazing." Photograph (d) is a multiple exposure of the same scene, but the camera is pointing at the arrowed dot while moving toward the head. This corresponds to the situation depicted in (b). Photograph (e) is a single exposure of the scene in (c) and (d). (From Regan & Beverley, 1982.)

translational flow from expansion in order to locate the focus of expansion. This and other experimental evidence are discussed below.

First, let us consider situations in which observers can use the center of expansion in the optic array to guide locomotion. As an observer moves along a straight-line path in space the texture of the terrain projected onto the frontal plane undergoes a time-varying transformation. As shown schematically in Figure 19.29, if the observer is the pilot of an airplane that is descending toward the ground on a straight flight path, a single point (the projected impact point) remains stationary in the optic array. However, this is true for the retinal image only if the observer gazes at the impact point or if the gaze is maintained at a fixed angle to a distant point. Provided one of these conditions is met, all other points in the retinal image move away from the impact point. Thus the terrain becomes magnified in such a way that all points retreat radially from the focus of expansion. The rates are higher for points in the lower part of the visual field than for those near the impact point. Rate also increases (accelerates) with distance upward of the impact point on the projection plane, but then the rate becomes smaller with further distance upward until it diminishes to zero at the horizon (see Figure 19.29). Thus the aim point (focus of expansion) in the optic array is a precise indicator of the momentary place of impact. Moreover, changes in the position of the focus of expansion correlate perfectly with changes in the flight path.

As implied above, although the foregoing account is correct geometrically, there is no direct evidence that observers can use the focus of expansion with the same precision under all possible stimulus conditions. At the very least, there must be some zone of confusion in detecting the precise position of the aiming point. Furthermore, as illustrated in Figure 19.28, translational flow may be introduced in the retinal image by eye movements toward one side of the impact point, and this may interfere with the detection of the center of expansion.

In any case, many factors require additional study. One is the role of inhomogeneities of texture in the visual field. Another is the amount of texture that is visible to the observer. The magnitude of the flight path angle, the distance between the observer and the impact point, "visual noise" or jitter introduced by turbulence, and the crab angle of the aircraft due to wind may also affect the detection of the focus of expansion by an aircraft pilot. So, for practical reasons, it is not sufficient simply to point to the invariant relationship between properties of the optic array and the motion in depth of the observer. Unfortunately, too little experimental work has been done on this problem.

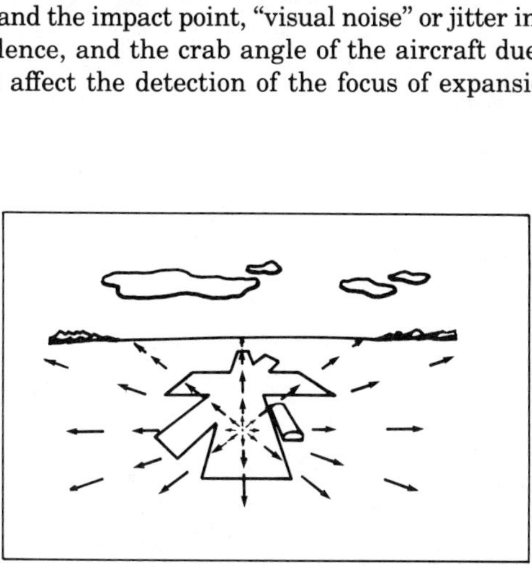

Figure 19.29. Expanding flow pattern in the optic array during final approach of an aircraft landing at an airfield. The focus of expansion in the optic array is the impact point of the aircraft provided it continues along the same path, though as shown in Figure 19.28, this is not necessarily the case for the retinal-image flow pattern. (From James J. Gibson, *The perception of the visual world*, Copyright 1950, renewed 1977 by Houghton Mifflin Company. Reprinted with permission.)

3.3. Experimental Studies of the Focus of Expansion

3.3.1. Simulated Aircraft Carrier Landings. Kaufman (1964) utilized a shadowgraph technique to study the sensitivity of observers in detecting the aim point in simulated landing of an aircraft on an aircraft carrier. In one experiment, subjects viewed a scene in which the aircraft approached a carrier deck at a simulated speed of 118 knots. The glide slope was held constant at 5°. Five glide paths were used: one intercepted the deck at the "correct" aim point (in the middle of the arresting cables), and the others at different distances either fore or aft of the correct aim point. All approaches began from an equivalent distance of approximately 1983 m from the desired aim point on the deck and closed to one of four ranges from 915 to 92 m away from the aim point. Viewing was restricted to the time the image was in motion.

Subjects were given a training period in which descents to the deck were simulated with subjects in control of their flight path. Subjects then observed each simulated approach segment and were instructed to judge the projected point of impact with the deck. The choices given the subject were "on," to indicate an aim point at the desired position on the deck; "short," to indicate landing too low in the projection plane; and "high," to indicate an overshoot of the desired aim point. Judgments were also made under static conditions in which the carrier deck was viewed from equivalent distances.

Data are shown in Figure 19.30. Static sensitivity is equal to or higher than dynamic sensitivity for all but the 458 m range. The biases are small—8 m or less—and variable, for all ranges.

When static and dynamic data are combined (Figure 19.31), it is evident that sensitivity increases with decreasing range. Thus at the shortest range of 92 m, subjects are able to judge the position of the aim point with an accuracy of about $+17$ m, whether they see an expanding pattern or not. Clearly, cues other than the focus of expansion were being used by subjects in this experiment. Nevertheless, these results do not prove that subjects cannot use the focus of expansion to determine the impact point when no other cues are present. Several follow-up experiments were performed to determine more precisely what cues the subject was able to use. In one the aircraft carrier was replaced by a pattern of random dots toward which the subject made simulated approaches from 1983 m along straight-line glide paths ranging from 224 to 1464 m in length. In half the trials a horizon was present, but it was absent in the other half of the trials. The subject viewed the scene through an artificial pupil, as in the previously described experiment. The presence or absence of a horizon made no difference to accuracy of performance. The angular size of the vertical error in detecting the aim point was 1.5°, which corresponds to a very large linear error at all of the distances at which the judgments were made, for example, about 24 m at a range of 92 m, and proportionately larger at longer distances. In fact, an error of such magnitude would be intolerable in an actual flight situation.

In still another experiment, the aircraft carrier was present, but the textured background was eliminated so that the subject saw the deck from a distance in a uniform dark gray "sea."

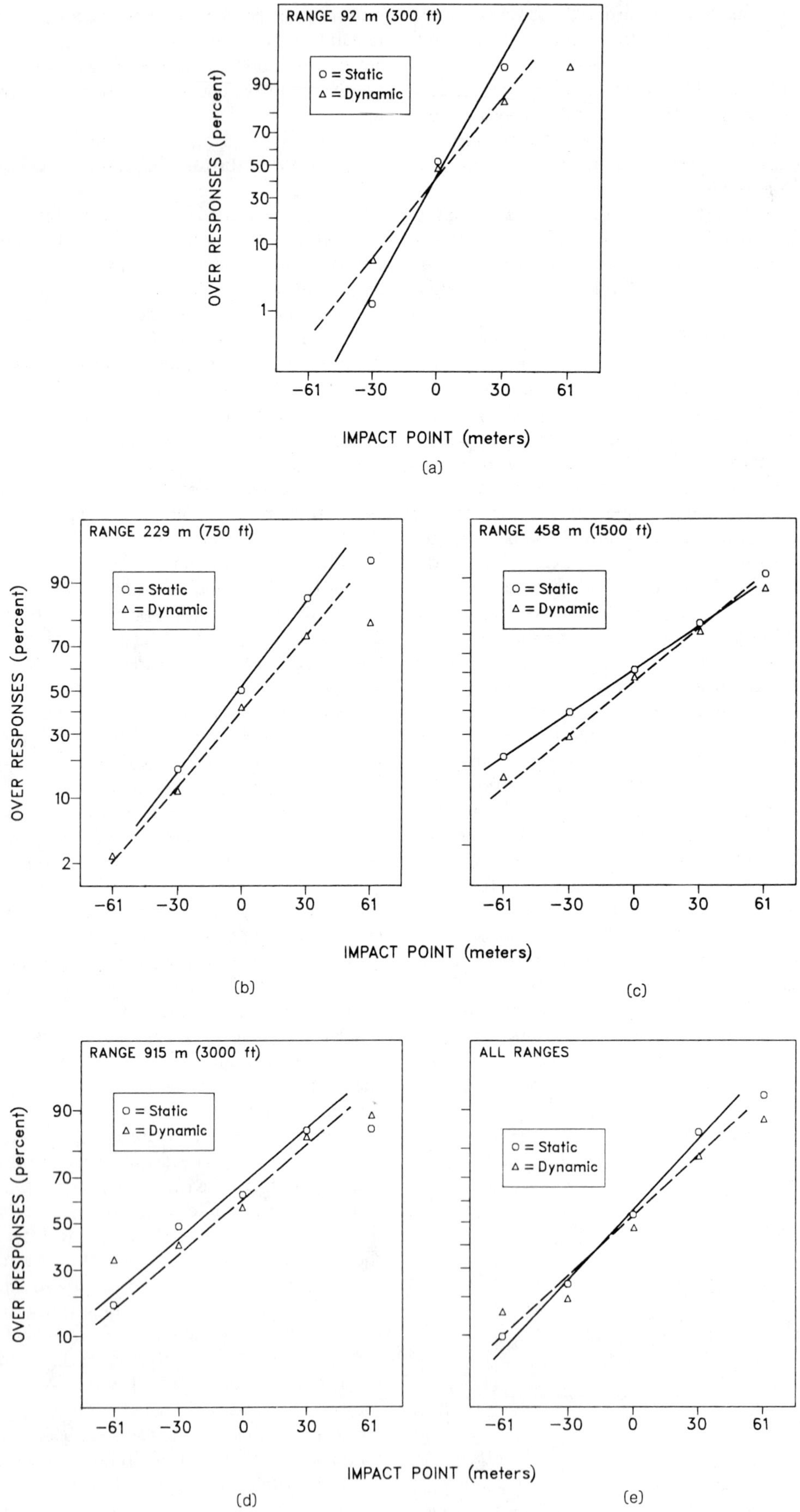
RANGE 92 m (300 ft)
o = Static
Δ = Dynamic
OVER RESPONSES (percent)
1
10
30
50
70
90
−61
−30
0
30
61
IMPACT POINT (meters)
(a)
RANGE 229 m (750 ft)
o = Static
Δ = Dynamic
OVER RESPONSES (percent)
2
10
30
50
70
90
RANGE 458 m (1500 ft)
o = Static
Δ = Dynamic
−61
−30
0
30
61
IMPACT POINT (meters)
(b)
(c)
RANGE 915 m (3000 ft)
o = Static
Δ = Dynamic
OVER RESPONSES (percent)
10
30
50
70
90
ALL RANGES
o = Static
Δ = Dynamic
−61
−30
0
30
61
IMPACT POINT (meters)
(d)
(e)

Performance was no different under these conditions than in the first experiment.

It is clear from these experiments that time-varying changes in texture were not used by subjects in detecting the impact point. Static perspective information given by the texture was not used by subjects either. In fact, when it was available, subjects used configurational information inherent in the scene. In this particular situation it was apparent that subjects could judge the aim point solely on the basis of the ratio of the vertical angles subtended by the stern and the deck of the aircraft carrier (see Kennedy, Collyer, May, & Dunlap, 1982; and Kruk & Regan, 1983, for a similar discussion regarding recognition of aircraft shapes). When the constant flight path is such that the impact point is too low, the stern is large relative to the deck. The reverse is true when the impact point is too high. Subjects seem to detect this without specific training or instructions. This cue does not exist except in situations similar to that investigated in these experiments, but it should alert us to the fact that even when the eye is fixed and the scene is viewed through an artificial pupil, the focus of expansion can be detected only with limited accuracy and that other information, when available, may be used. Llewellyn (1971) reached a similar conclusion using a quite different stimulus pattern.

3.3.2. Effects of Translational Motion of the Retinal Image on Use of Focus of Expansion. The flow pattern in the optic array may differ considerably from one situation to another, depending on the nature and locations of surfaces in the environment. Several discussions that bear on this point are available (Gordon, 1965; Koenderink & van Doorn, 1976, 1981; Lee, 1976; Lee & Lishman, 1977; Nakayama & Loomis, 1974). In addition, eye movements may cause the flow patterns in the retinal image and the optic array to be different, as noted earlier. For example, when an observer gazes at an object to one side of the impact point, the eye rotates and a uniform translational velocity of the whole retinal image is superimposed on the expanding flow pattern, as illustrated in Figure 19.28(a) and (b).

Regan and Beverley (1982) compared subjects' ability to locate the focus of expansion of a flow pattern when a translational velocity was impressed on the whole pattern, and when there was no translational velocity. To isolate the expanding flow pattern from other stimulus variables (such as div **V**) they chose a flow pattern similar to that produced by a zooming lens; that is, the rate of increase of magnification was the same at every point in the pattern. In Regan and Beverley's (1982) three experiments the target was a grating of vertical bars whose magnification continuously increased so that it expanded horizontally (Figure 19.32). Total stimulus field size was constant. In Experiment 1, translational velocity was always zero. A black reference bar was located at the center of the pattern. In successive trials the center of expansion was located at different distances to the left or right of the reference bar, and the subject's task was to judge left or right. Subjects found the laboratory task easy, and could locate the center of expansion to better than 1°. In this condition, with no translational velocity, any given trial was equivalent to the real-world situation of a subject's gazing at a fixed angle relative to the impact point as, for example, when a car driver gazes at a fixed angle relative to the car body while the car travels the way it is pointing.

The finding is consistent with Gibson's (1950) estimate of about $\pm 1°$ for the accuracy with which subjects could judge the impact point when viewing movie films taken from a fixed camera on an aircraft during landing. (If we regard the movie camera as an eye aligned at a fixed angle relative to the aircraft and assume that the aircraft maintained a fixed orientation relative to its trajectory, then the two stimulus situations are geometrically similar.) Such measurements may have some practical interest in that they estimate how accurately subjects use the focus of the expanding flow pattern to estimate the direction of self-motion in the special case where the eye is pointing at the impact point or maintains a fixed angle relative to the impact point. But this experiment does not address the question of how accurately subjects can use the focus of the expanding flow pattern in the general case of arbitrary direction of gaze.

Regan and Beverley (1982) attempted to address this question in their second experiment. Experiment 2 resembled Experiment 1 except that horizontal translational velocities were added to the stimulus pattern so as to mimic the effect of slow pursuit eye movements. As illustrated in Figure 19.28(b) and (d), the effect of gazing at an object to one side of the impact point is to impress a uniform translational velocity on the whole

Figure 19.30. (*Opposite*) Perception of point of impact for simulated aircraft carrier landings. Subjects saw expanding scenes of a carrier deck that simulated the viewpoint of an aircraft approaching the carrier at a speed of 118 knots along one of five glide paths intercepting the deck at different impact points. Glide slope was constant at 5°. All approaches began from a distance of 1983 m and closed to a range of 915, 458, 229, or 92 m. Subjects judged whether the aircraft would undershoot, overshoot, or land right on the correct aim point in the middle of the arresting cables. The five panels are psychometric functions plotted on probit paper which give the probability of judging that the aircraft would overshoot the desired aim point as a function of the actual miss distance (negative values represent undershoot; positive values, overshoot). (For analysis, "on" judgments were distributed equally among undershoot and overshoot categories.) In each panel, the stimulus condition corresponding to 50% probability of an "over" response represents the response bias. The slope of each line is a direct measure of variability and represents the standard deviation. In panels (a)–(d), the dynamic condition (solid line) is data obtained after viewing the simulated scene throughout the entire descent of the aircraft from the starting distance to the range given at the top of each panel. The static condition (dotted line) represents the same function obtained when the subject viewed only a static scene of the carrier deck from the range given. Data are based on 190 trials per subject, averaged across four male subjects with normal vision who viewed the scenes through an artificial pupil. Panel (e) shows data combined over all ranges. Performance did not differ significantly for the static and dynamic conditions. Thus it appears that subjects did not use the information provided by the expanding texture in the display, but employed configural information that was inherent in the static scene. (From Kaufman, 1964.)

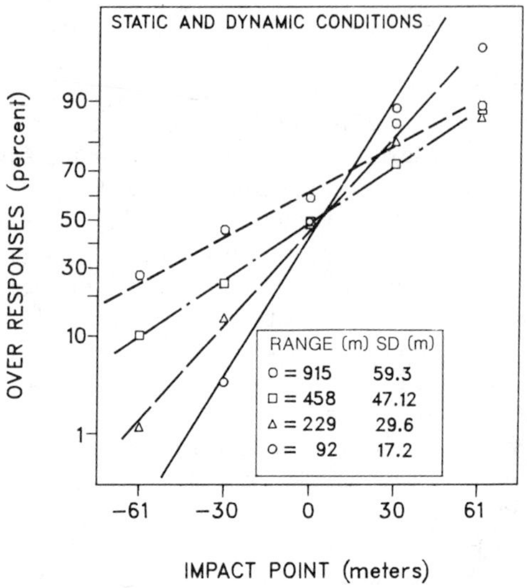

Figure 19.31. Effect of range on judgment of impact point for simulated aircraft carrier landings. Data for the static and dynamic conditions of the carrier landing task portrayed in panels (a)–(d) of Figure 19.30 were combined, and the resulting psychometric functions are superimposed here. The increase in the slopes of the psychometric functions as the range at which judgments are made decreases provides graphic evidence that the sensitivity of subjects to deviations from the actual aim point increases monotonically in linear distance as range is shortened; this is to be expected for a constant angular error of about 1.5°. (From Kaufman, 1964.)

retinal image. Regan and Beverley found that adding translational velocity severely reduced subjects' ability to locate the focus of expansion: accuracy fell from better than 1° to a level where subjects' responses were essentially random and accuracy could not be reliably estimated, but was considerably worse than 10°. Extrapolating to real-world conditions, Regan and Beverley suggested that in the general situation where the eye is not maintained at a fixed angle relative to the impact point so that overall translational motion is added to the expansion pattern, subjects cannot accurately locate the focus of expansion. It should be noted that rough estimates of the direction of self-motion are a different matter. Richards (1975) calculated that gazing to one side of the impact point creates an asymmetry in the flow pattern that is particularly evident when a very wide field of view is provided, and points out that this asymmetry might be used to estimate roughly the impact point to an accuracy of 10–20°. This accuracy would seem far inferior to that required for precise self-location.

A different kind of flow pattern was used in Regan and Beverley's (1982) third experiment. This flow pattern had a center of expansion as in Experiment 2, but also had a local region where div **V** was larger than elsewhere on the pattern. In other words, the rate of increase of magnification was not uniform over the whole pattern, being larger in a local region than elsewhere. The point of this experiment was that eye movements can disturb the expansion pattern and shift its focus, but do not affect the location of the point where div **V** is maximal. (A uniform translational velocity does not affect the magnification at any point in the pattern.) Experiment 2 was repeated using several different expansion patterns. In some the rate of increase of magnification was very different at different points in the pattern; in others the rate of increase of magnification was almost uniform over the pattern. Figure 19.33(a) formally describes three of these different patterns. Instantaneous velocity of any point in the pattern was a power function of distance across the screen for all expansion patterns. Different patterns had different exponents. Figure 19.32 shows the flow pattern when translational velocity was set to zero. The maximum rate of increase of magnification was the same for all patterns. A real-world equivalent is the maximum rate of expansion seen from an automobile traveling at 55 km·hr^{-1} directly at a wall 81 m away. The straight line with exponent $n = 1.0$ in Figure 19.33(a) represents the pattern used in Experiment 2 where velocity linearly increased across the screen so that the rate of magnification was uniform (i.e., div **V** was the same at all points on the pattern). For the pattern with exponent 0.3 in Figure 19.33(a), there was a very clear region in the pattern where div **V** was greater than elsewhere (see Appendix). Results for two subjects are shown in Figure 19.33(b) and (c), which plot subjects' accuracy in judging the location of the point where magnification increased fastest for several exponents n of the pattern. As noted in Experiment 2, accuracy was too poor to be measured when $n = 1.0$, and with $n = 0.9$ was still only 10° or so. However, for exponents less than about 0.8, subjects performed the task easily with an accuracy better than 1°, even when substantial translational velocities were imposed on the flow pattern.

Regan and Beverley's (1982) conclusion can be stated as follows. Subjects can accurately locate a local maximum of div **V** in a flow pattern, even in the presence of translational motion that virtually abolishes the ability to locate the focus of expansion in the same pattern.

This finding raises the question of whether the visual system's specific sensitivity to looming (Section 2.2.2 above) might be implicated in behavioral responses to flow patterns in the optic array. The basis for this supposition is, first, that specific sensitivity to looming can be regarded as a specific sensitivity to div **V** and, second, that the receptive fields involved in looming sensitivity seem to be smaller than about 1.5° diameter so that they are potentially capable of mediating accurate localization.

Regan and Beverley's (1979b) laboratory study is relevant to this point. In this experiment, subjects adapted to radial flow patterns, and the effect of this adaptation on sensitivity to changing size was measured. Subjects were instructed to aim their gaze at a fixed angle relative to the focus of expansion of a flow pattern [either 2.0° to the left of the focus, as illustrated in Figure 19.34(b) or, in different experiments, directly at the focus]. The test stimulus and the adapting stimulus are illustrated in Figure 19.34(a) and (b). The adapting stimulus was a pattern of short line segments that alternately moved radially away from a focal point and back toward it at constant radial speed. The individual line segments were lengthened and shortened in proportion to their distance from the focus, and the direction of flow was reversed at 5-sec intervals. As shown in Figure 19.34(c), adaptation to this flow pattern results in a loss of sensitivity to the changing size of a test square located near the focus.

The flow pattern used in this experiment has the property that div **V** is low except immediately near the focus, where it rises to a sharp maximum [see the Appendix and Figure 19.35(d)]. This line of argument leads to the prediction that findings would have been different if the velocity across the radially expanding pattern had not varied with an abrupt transition at the focus as shown by the continuous line in Figure 19.35(c), but instead had varied linearly across the screen as shown by the broken line. Such a pattern would have the same value of div **V** at every point on the pattern [broken line, Figure

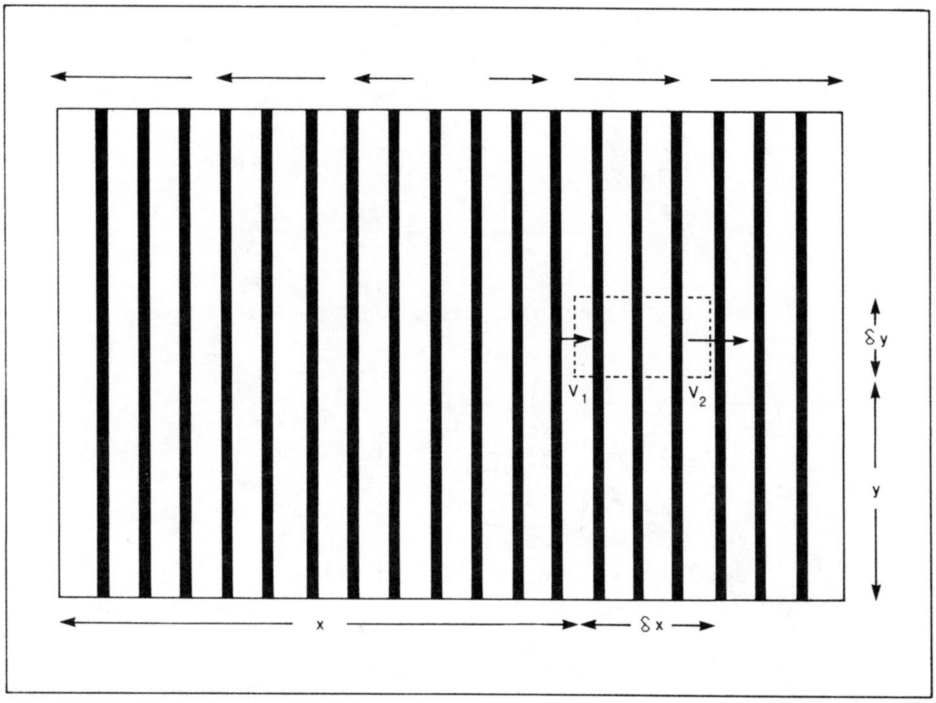

Figure 19.32. Expanding grating pattern used to study sensitivity to various cues to the direction of self-motion. The focus of expansion of the retinal flow pattern during self-motion depends on the direction of gaze and does not coincide with the direction of motion unless the observer is looking at the destination point (see Figure 19.28). However, in some (but not all) situations the point of maximum rate of change in magnification of the retinal image does coincide with the direction of self-motion and is independent of the direction of gaze. The grating shown here illustrates the type of stimulus used to study sensitivity to this local maximum in the rate of expansion in the flow pattern. The vertical grating expanded horizontally (thus changing in spatial frequency) as indicated by the arrows at the top of the figure. In addition, an overall translational motion was imposed on the pattern so that some predetermined point on the pattern simulated the point of gaze by becoming stationary. An arbitrarily small area of the grating (bounded by the rectangle and designated as dxdy) could be created whose vertical boundaries had velocities V_1 and V_2 that differed from the horizontal velocities of other points on the grating. Location of this area of maximum change in magnification rate was varied with respect to the focus of expansion of the grating to simulate the flow patterns that would arise during self-motion when center of gaze is shifted different distances away from the destination point. The subject's task was to locate the point of maximum rate of change in magnification. Figure 19.33 presents data showing that subjects were generally able to make this determination given appropriate rates of change in magnification at a local maximum.

19.35(d)]. This prediction is that changing-size threshold would be much less elevated than in the experiment of Figure 19.34(c), and that there would be no maximum at the focus. To date this prediction does not seem to have been tested.

Regan and Beverley's (1979b) conclusion was that visual mechanisms for looming would be strongly stimulated only near the focus of the flow pattern of Figure 19.34(b), that is, where div **V** is largest, and that these activated looming detectors would "mark" the location of the focus. Presumably, looming detectors would also "mark" the location where div **V** is largest in the Figure 19.33(a) patterns with exponents $n = 0.5$ and $n = 0.3$. Because visual sensitivity to changing size is not much affected by translational motion (Section 2.2.2.1), it seems possible that looming detectors could continue to "mark" the focus of the pattern in Figure 19.34(b) even if the pattern were moving across the retina while expanding. This could explain the finding [Figure 19.33(b) and (c)] that subjects could accurately locate the point on the expanding grating pattern where div **V** was largest, even when the pattern was in translational motion.

The foregoing hypothesis has not yet been subjected to definitive testing. However, sufficient experimental evidence has already been described to make such a conjecture seem more than merely plausible—for example, subjects can pick up the simulated impact point with considerable accuracy in cases where it is associated with nonuniformity in rate of change of magnification. On the other hand, the impact point does not necessarily coincide with the point at which div **V** is greatest: the two can be quite different (Regan & Beverley, 1982). Thus it is certainly not the case that the ability to visually locate the point of maximum div **V** can completely explain visually guided self-motion. The recent studies described above have suggested that the center of expansion is of limited value in guiding self-motion, but have not provided other than a limited alternative explanation.

Given that information for visually guided locomotion is computed from the optic flow pattern and eye movement data, the problem becomes to propose specific ways in which this might be achieved and to test these various hypotheses exper-

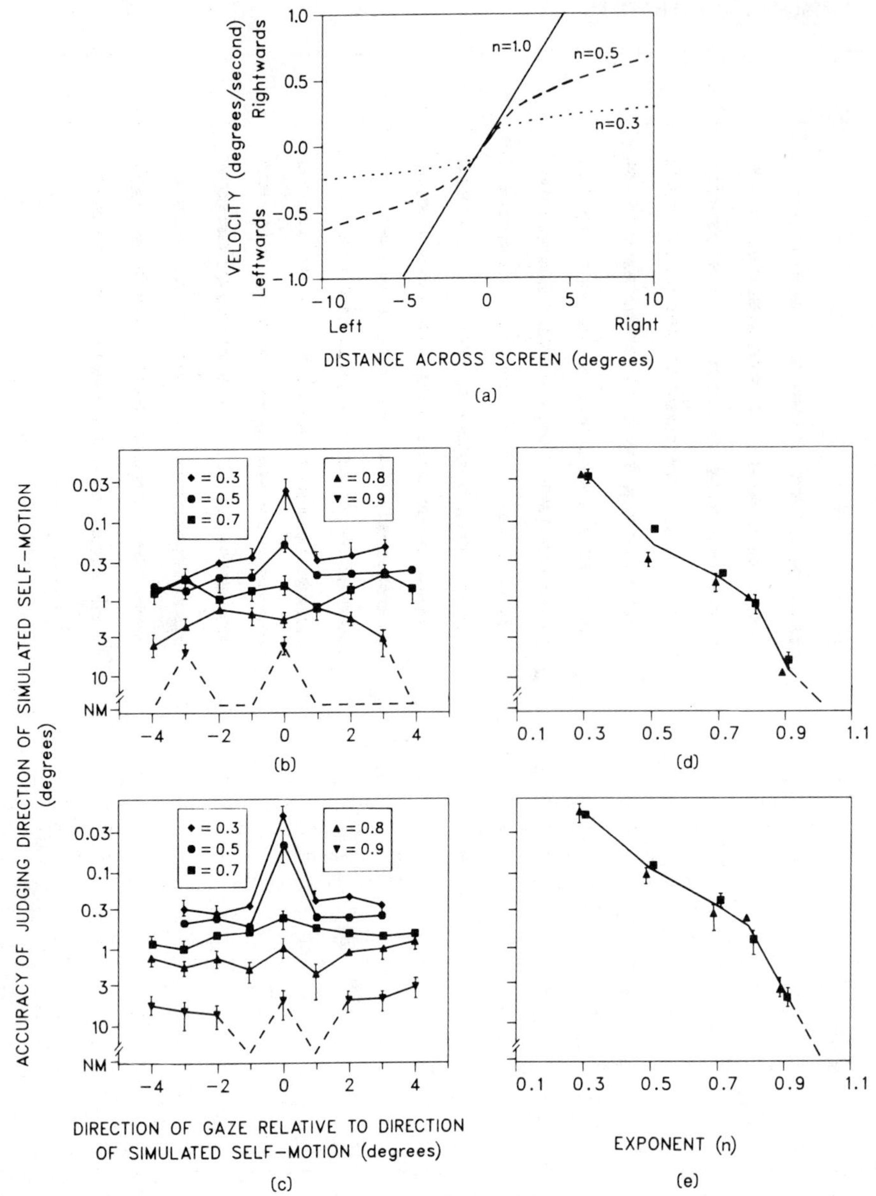

Figure 19.33. Relative usefulness of rate of change in magnification and center of expansion in judging the direction of simulated self-motion. Subjects viewed expanding grating patterns such as that shown in Figure 19.32. Panel (a) gives a formal description of the horizontal expansion of the gratings for three of the patterns used. The instantaneous velocity of any point in the pattern was first made a power function of distance across the pattern. Then a uniform translational speed was added that defined the point of gaze. The solid line in the graph represents the pattern in which the rate of change of magnification was uniform across the pattern ($n = 1.0$). The dashed line ($n = 0.5$) describes a pattern in which the rate of change in magnification was slightly greater at one point than elsewhere. This local maximum could be made more pronounced by adjusting the value of n, as in the dotted curve where $n = 0.3$. The rate of expansion in all cases was equivalent to impact with the target 5 sec after onset of stimulation. Initial spatial frequency was 5 cycles per degree; field size was 20° vertically and 12° horizontally. Each pattern presentation lasted 2 sec. For patterns with $n = 1.0$ (uniform expansion rate), the subject's task was to judge the position of the center of expansion, and for patterns with $n < 1.0$, subjects judged the position of the maximum rate of change in magnification. As shown in panels (b)–(e), when rate of change in magnification was uniform or nearly uniform over the pattern ($n = 1.0$ and $n = 0.9$) subjects could not perform the task at all. However, when the rate of change of magnification was appreciably greater at one point in the pattern than elsewhere, subjects were able to identify the local maximum almost independently of the direction of gaze ($n = 0.8$, $n = 0.7$). For $n = 0.5$ or $n = 0.3$, subjects were somewhat more accurate when the direction of gaze coincided with the direction of simulated self-motion. Panels (d) and (e) show how accuracy of judging direction of self-motion varied with the value of the exponent n when subjects were looking approximately along the direction of motion. The results suggest that the focus of expansion is not a generally useful cue to the direction of self-motion. The subject can locate a local maximum in the rate of change of magnification, but this does not provide a useful cue in all environments. (From D. Regan & K. I. Beverley. How do we avoid confounding the direction we are looking with the direction we are moving?, *Science, 215*. Copyright 1982 by American Association for the Advancement of Science. Reprinted with permission.)

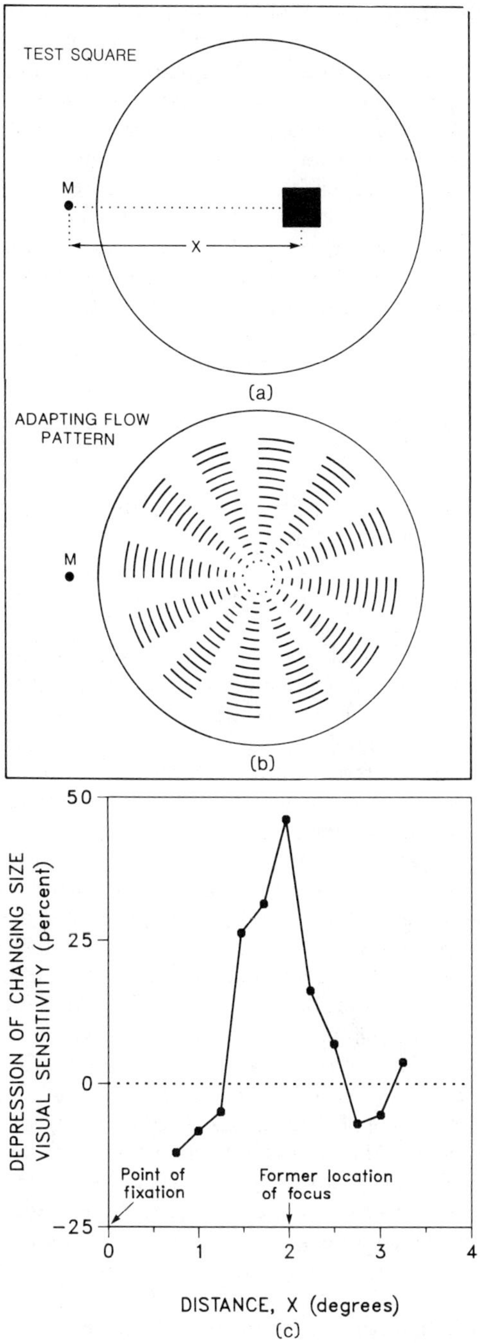

Figure 19.34. Reduction of looming sensitivity after adaptation to a radially expanding and contracting flow pattern. Panel (a) shows the test stimulus. Subjects fixated point M while viewing a square that oscillated in size at a distance *X* from the point of fixation. The smallest detectable oscillation in size was measured as a function of *X*. The adapting pattern is shown in (b). Subjects fixated on point M while the pattern alternately expanded and contracted for 5 sec each. After subjects viewed the flow pattern for 10 min, sensitivity to changing size was measured using the test pattern in (a). Graph (c) illustrates the effect of this adaptation on the threshold amplitude of size change as a function of the square's distance *X* from the fixation point. Sensitivity to oscillating size was sharply depressed when the square was in a region within about 0.5° of the focus of the radially expanding and contracting flow pattern. No such decline was found in a control study where the test square oscillated from side to side rather than oscillating in size. Thus the center of this expansion pattern can be located by means of sensitivity to changing size. (From D. Regan, K. I. Beverley, & M. Cynader, The visual perception of motion in depth, *Scientific American*, 1979, *241*. Reprinted with permission.)

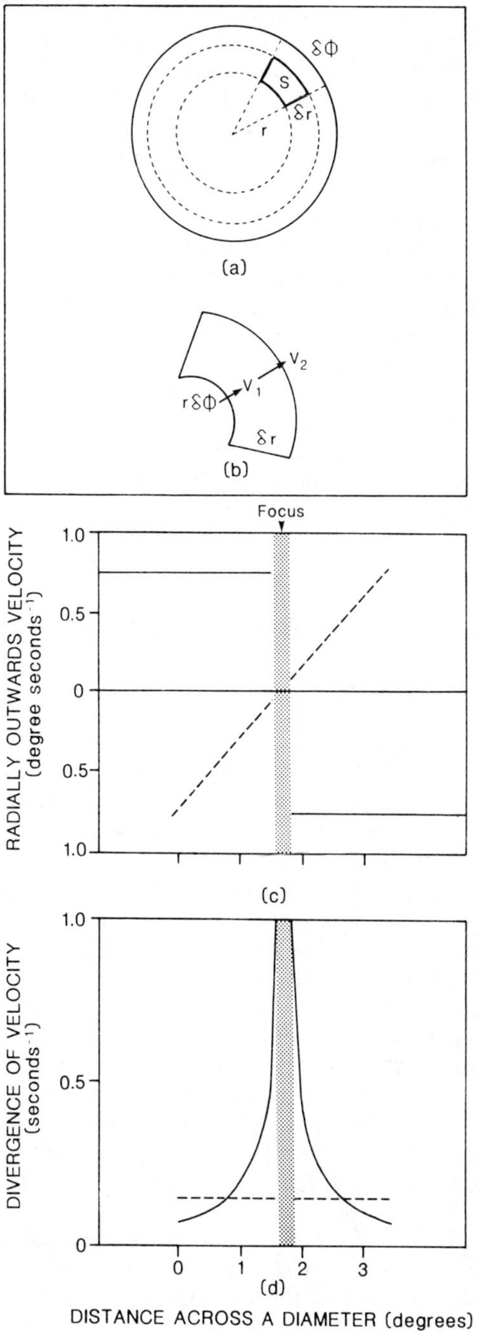

Figure 19.35. Velocity characteristics of radially expanding flow pattern. Panel (a): arbitrary small area *S* on the surface of a radially expanding flow pattern such as that in Figure 19.34(b). Panel (b): enlarged view of area *S*. Radial velocities at the inner and outer boundaries are V_1 and V_2, respectively. The inner boundary is of length $r\delta\phi$. Panel (c): the continuous line plots radial velocity across a diameter of the flow pattern used in the experiment of Figure 19.34. In the actual experiment, a black disk occluded the center of the pattern and is represented by the dotted area. The dashed line plots radial velocity for the kind of flow pattern that would be produced by a zooming lens. Panel (d): the continuous line shows the distribution of div **V** across a diameter of the flow pattern in Figure 19.34(b) and corresponds to the continuous line in (c). The dashed line represents the distribution of div **V** for the zooming-type flow pattern shown by the dashed line in (c). The experimental data presented in Figure 19.33 indicate that observers are able accurately to locate a local maximum of div **V** in a flow pattern.

imentally. One kind of hypothesis is framed in terms of local processes. The focus of expansion is a local property of the flow field; the direction of local motion reverses as the observer passes across the focus. Div **V** is also a local quantity. However, the recent studies described above have suggested that both the focus of expansion and div **V** are of limited value in guiding self-motion. An alternative to identifying a point in the flow pattern is a form of template matching over some large area of the visual field. A template might be the summed response of many small-field motion detectors, each of which responds best to motion directed radially outward from the focus. In some environments, exploratory eye movements could identify the direction of self-motion, because the summed activity of the motion detectors would be greatest when the eye was gazing directly at the destination, and the flow pattern would then best match the template. However, according to this model, judgments of self-motion would be systematically inaccurate in asymmetric environments, because flow patterns would be markedly asymmetric (Regan, in press).

4. CHANNEL THEORIES OF MOTION IN DEPTH

4.1. Background

One of the most pervasive theoretical concepts in current vision research is that of channels specialized to process different kinds of information. In fact, this same notion stimulated much of the research discussed in this chapter. Although the experimental results may be given other interpretations and have intrinsic value apart from their connection with the channel concept, it is important to be explicit about the theoretical ideas underlying the work that led to the results.

One common proposition is that early processing of visual information is accomplished in part by the activity of sets of parallel channels. Each set of channels is selectively sensitive to an abstract feature of the proximal visual stimulus. Also, each set of channels is presumed to operate independently of other sets, thus "decomposing" the visual input into a number of orthogonal units. The sensitivity of a given set of channels has no substantial overlap with the sensitivity of any other set of channels.

Interactions of the outputs of these hypothetical sets of channels may well occur at later stages of processing of visual information. Such interactions certainly occur among the outputs of individual channels.

It is important to distinguish between a set of channels, for example, the set of color channels, and the individual channels that constitute a set. It may not be possible to define an individual channel as strictly as a "set of channels," because the sensitivities of individual channels may overlap considerably. In addition, the interactions that occur between some individual channels affect their filtering properties. For example, spatial frequency channels may well inhibit each other (Braddick, Campbell, & Atkinson, 1978). The channel theory is discussed in detail elsewhere (Braddick et al., 1978; Graham, 1981; Regan, 1982; Westheimer, 1981). Parallels between the concept of the channel and the old idea of structuralist psychologists who treated sensations as independent elements of consciousness are described by Kaufman (1974, 1979).

Unfortunately, there is some lack of precision in the ways in which the term "channel" has been applied. Sometimes it is used to mean no more than "selective sensitivity." Other authors invoke the uniqueness of some sensation, such as that of "motion" or "pattern" in their usage of the term "channel," looking back to Hering, who inferred the "primacy" of yellow as well as red, green, and blue, partly because of their apparent "purity" (Hurvich & Jameson, 1957). The concept of a "set of channels" does not imply that every or even any unique or simple "sensation" has a corresponding set of channels (Regan, 1982).

Some authors have used the term "channel" to stand for a neural mechanism, a population of neurons, or even some independent structural element, a concept quite similar to the classic doctrine of specific nerve energies. In contrast, "set of channels" is defined here entirely in terms of psychophysics, and anatomical or cellular structures do not enter the definition at all, though interesting and suggestive correlations have indeed been found between channel properties and the properties of neurons and of aggregates of neurons.

4.2. Evidence for Independence of Motion-in-Depth Channels

Figure 19.10(d) shows evidence that the set of changing-size channels responds specifically to the line-of-sight component of a target's motion, and receives no input from the velocity component in the frontal plane; that is, they are "blind" to sideways motion. Contrast was also shown to be irrelevant to the set of changing-size channels, at least insofar as adaptation to changing size may be attributed to such a set of channels. Neither the percentage contrast nor the direction of contrast has any effect on threshold elevations for changing size, provided the stimulus is clearly visible (Petersik et al., 1981; Regan & Beverley, 1978b). Flicker is another attribute of visual stimulation that has no effect on threshold elevations for changing size. Of course, these results do not preclude the possibility that contrast or flicker sensitivity may be mediated by orthogonal channels.

The progenitor of channel theories is the Young-Helmholtz theory of color vision. The balance of activity among three "channels" defines the color sensation associated with any spectral hue or its metameric match. The absence of one such "channel" results in one of three kinds of "color blindness."

Similar specific "blindness" should occur if the channel concept is applicable to changing size and stereo motion, and indeed this is the case. For example, some individuals have a region of the visual field that is "blind" to changing disparity, but sensitive to static binocular disparity, whereas another region is sensitive to changing disparity but "blind" to static disparity. When stimuli are entirely stereoscopic, such individuals can be "blind" to motion in depth while retaining sensitivity to position in depth, and vice versa (Richards & Regan, 1973). A second example is that some patients lose visual sensitivity to intermediate spatial frequencies over a restricted range of orientations while retaining normal sensitivity to both low and high spatial frequencies (Regan, Silver, & Murray, 1977; Regan, Whitlock, Murray, & Beverley, 1980).

4.3. Some Practical Implications of the Channel Concept

Whether or not the channel concept proves to be theoretically sound, it may have heuristic value. Such value has already been displayed, in that the concept has led to many fruitful experimental studies of the visual process. This section considers the ways in which the channel notion may affect investigation in several areas of practical significance.

4.3.1. Transfer of Training. If a complicated skill, such as catching a ball, depends on learned computations carried out on the outputs of a few sets of channels, then, once learned, the skills should readily transfer to a wide variety of visual environments. This follows from the independence of the sets of channels from each other, because a given set is supposed to ignore all but one aspect or feature of a visual scene, regardless of the complexity or number of other features. By the same token, if there is considerable overlap or mutual interference among sets of channels in a particular individual, that individual would find it difficult to use learned eye-hand skills in a variety of complex visual environments. Section 5 describes a preliminary test of this prediction in which channel "cross talk" was evaluated in pilots, and this was compared with their performance in a number of flying tasks.

4.3.2. Visual Discrimination. Humans can discriminate among as many as 150 spectral colors even though the three kinds of receptors that mediate color vision are very coarsely tuned. Such observations suggest that stable outputs of coarsely tuned channels may be precisely compared at some secondary stage to mediate a high degree of visual discrimination. There is evidence that this process may take place in other sets of channels as well as the set of color channels. For example, the initial stage of analysis of motion in depth can be modeled by postulating binocular motion channels tuned to four different directions of motion in depth. The most sharply tuned of these channels accepts a range of directions of about 1.5°, as seen in Figure 19.17(b), implying that if a single channel signals the direction of motion in depth, discrimination of differences in direction of motion in depth could not be better than 1.5° (Beverley & Regan, 1973; Regan, Beverley, & Cynader, 1979). However, discrimination is an order of magnitude better, for subjects were able to discriminate among directions of motion in depth that differed by only 0.1–0.2°. [See Figure 19.17(a).] To explain this acute discrimination one might postulate a process in which the outputs of different channels are compared with each other. Evidence to support this conjecture includes the fact that discrimination of direction of motion in depth has submaxima along trajectories for which a small change in the direction of motion produces large changes in the balance between different channels. These submaxima are shown in Figure 19.17(a). The vertical dotted lines indicate their close correspondence with the crossover points of the channel sensitivities.

Similar arguments have been used to support a proposed opponent processing of the outputs of channels sensitive to different bands of spatial frequencies (Campbell et al., 1970; Spitzberg & Richards, 1975); and an analogous idea has been advanced to explain "hyperacuity" in orientation sensitivity (Westheimer, Shimamura, & McKee, 1976). Regan and Beverley (1983a, 1984a, 1984c) provide recent empirical evidence to support this notion in the spatial frequency domain and the orientation domain. Clearly this is an area suitable for further research.

4.3.3. Specific Visual Tests for Specific Flying Tasks. If different flying tasks depend on different sets of channels (Regan & Beverley, 1980a), it may be that specific tests of the appropriate sets of channels would predict flying performance in tasks that involve only a few sets of filters. Tests that fail to assess the relevant channels or confound several sets of channels would be less accurately predictive.

4.3.4. Prediction of Performance on Visual Tasks. As noted in Section 2.2.4.4, subtle forms of "blindness" might not be revealed by conventional tests, and would only be revealed behaviorally in tasks that involve the defective channels. Ginsburg, Evans, Sekuler, and Harp (1982) give another example where contrast sensitivity for intermediate spatial frequencies is better than visual acuity in predicting the detection of a target of substantial size. This is discussed in Chapter 34 by Ginsburg.

5. EXPERIMENTAL TESTS OF FLYING PERFORMANCE

Sections 2 and 3 described evidence that the human visual system has rather specific sensitivities to several abstract features of the visual environment including changing size, motion in depth, frontal-plane motion, and the vectors div **V** and curl **V** that can occur in the flow pattern produced by self-motion. The idea that different specific sensitivities are important in different flying tasks suggests that visual tests designed to measure individual variations in these specific sensitivities might prove more successful in predicting intersubject differences in flying performance than tests (such as the Snellen test or static stereoacuity test) that fail to test important special sensitivities or tests that confound several special sensitivities in one test result. It has been suggested that different specific tests might predict performance in different flying tasks (Regan & Beverley, 1980b).

In light of Gibson's work, an immediate candidate test is one of discriminating different rates of expansion of a flow pattern. Such a test was carried out, using the same stimulus illustrated in Figure 19.34(b), and subjects were required to judge which of two rates of expansion was the faster. Results of this laboratory test were compared with performance in flying tasks in real aircraft and in a flight simulator (Kruk & Regan, 1983; Kruk, Regan, Beverley, & Longridge, 1981, 1983). A second visual test used in these studies was also based on the "specific sensitivity" notion. In this test the subjects viewed a square whose size alternately expanded or contracted at a fixed rate, with the transition between expansion and contraction occurring at unpredictable moments. The subject's task was to turn a knob so as to maintain the square's size constant. This can be regarded as a changing-size or motion-in-depth tracking task as compared with the more conventional task of tracking frontal plane motion (Regan & Beverley, 1980a).

A second kind of visual test was generated by the basic research described above. Section 4 mentioned attempts to determine whether the degree of independence between a pilot's sets of channels affects performance in visually guided flying tasks. It was proposed that a lack of independence between sets of channels that are otherwise adequately sensitive may allow tasks to be carried out satisfactorily in a simple environment, but lead to degraded performance in a complicated visual environment. By the same token, extraordinarily accomplished pilots and athletes may well have highly independent sets of channels. In an attempt to test this hypothesis, groups of pilots with various degrees of experience in aviation were studied (Kruk & Regan, 1983; Kruk et al., 1981, 1983). The tests included many standard tests of visual sensitivity, such as Snellen acuity, contrast threshold, and motion threshold, as well as the expanding flow pattern test and a test designed to assess whether looming sensitivity was independent of frontal-plane motion. As in the tracking task described above, subjects were required to adjust the size of an oscillating test square so as to keep size constant but, in addition to the unpredictable changes in size, the test square was randomly moved in the frontal plane.

Flying tasks were carried out both in a flight simulator and in real aircraft whose locations, velocities, and other parameters were telemetered to a ground station. The simulator was the "Advanced Simulator for Pilot Training" (ASPT) at Williams Air Force Base, Arizona, using a simulated A-10 cockpit. The real aircraft were A-4 and F-14 jet fighters flown by U.S. Navy pilots over the U.S. Marine Corps Air Station Yuma Tactical Air Combat Training System (TACTS) range. Simulator flying tasks included bad visibility landing, formation flight, and a bombing task following a low-level approach under ground threat. Flying tasks in real aircraft included a low-level bombing task and air-to-air combat where success was assessed by the win/loss ratio, that is, the ratio between the number of times the pilot hit an adversary aircraft, and the number of times the pilot was hit by the adversary's missiles. In the low-level task in the simulator, pilots were likely to be shot down by surface-to-air missiles or antiaircraft artillery if they flew above 110 m for more than about 10 sec. The pilot's task was to make a 5000-m approach to the target at a designated altitude of about 36 m (from which altitude the target was not visible), visually judge the correct point to "pop up," pop up to about 760 m and identify the target, then dive and manually release a bomb. Visual factors, particularly judgments of flow patterns, were important for correctly placing the aircraft and hence correctly placing the bomb. The bombing task with real aircraft was similar except there was no ground threat. In both simulator and real aircraft, the low-level task was scored in terms of mean error in bomb impact point relative to the target.

Overall, visual thresholds for contrast sensitivity, motion, and acuity had little or no predictive value with regard to flying performance. Possible reasons include the following. (1) The pilots had nearly equal thresholds. (The Snellen may be too coarse to bring out any difference in acuity that there might be between individual pilots.) (2) The flying tasks largely involved suprathreshold motion and suprathreshold contrast.

The laboratory tests—the flow pattern test and the changing-size tracking test, with and without perturbing frontal-plane motion—did correlate reasonably well with several of the flying tasks. Table 19.2 shows correlations between performance on the flight simulator and visual test results for the flow pattern test, conventional frontal-plane motion tracking, and changing-size tracking with and without frontal-plane "jitter" motion. Subjects were instructor pilots, student pilots, and experienced fighter pilots. The strongest correlations were between flow pattern test results and low-visibility landing performance as measured by the number of crashes ($r = .82$ for the instructor group) and between flow pattern test results and low-level bombing accuracy ($r = .74$). These two correlations point to the importance for low-level maneuvers of accurately judging motion in depth on the basis of flow pattern cues. They emphasize the important role of motion and dynamic visual cues in low-level flight and draw attention to the importance of accurately representing *motion* as well as static spatial factors in flight simulator displays.

Table 19.3 shows correlations between visual test results and low-level bombing accuracy under "no-drop" and "real bomb" conditions. The strongest correlation of .71 was between flow pattern test results and accuracy with real bombs. These results

Table 19.2. Coefficients of Correlation (r) Between Simulator Performance and Performance on Visual Tests

	Fighter Pilots		Instructors		Student Pilots	
Simulator Task	r	p	r	p	r	p
Landing—correction to runway	Frontal-plane tracking −.65	.01	Frontal-plane tracking −.61	.03	Frontal-plane tracking −.66	.009
Landing—crashes on runway	Changing-size tracking .63	.02	Flow pattern test −.82	.01		
Formation flight—time in position for fingertip task	Flow pattern test .61	.03	—		Flow pattern ($n = 6$) .52	.15
					Perturbed changing-size tracking −.56	.03
Formation flight—time in position for trail task	—		Flow pattern test .55	.05	—	
			Changing-size tracking −.57	.03		
Bombing—hits on target	Flow pattern test .74	.008	—		—	

All correlations not included are of significance lower than .05. Visual tasks were flow pattern velocity discrimination, conventional frontal-plane motion tracking, changing-size tracking, and perturbed changing-size tracking (random frontal-plane motion added). Simulator flight tests included low-visibility landing, formation flying, and a bombing task with low-level approach under ground threat. (See text for fuller description.) Subjects were 12 instructor pilots and 12 student pilots from Williams Air Force Base and 12 experienced fighter pilots. Strong correlations of flow pattern test results with crashes during landing (instructor group) and with bombing accuracy (fighter pilot group) suggest the importance of suprathreshold motion discrimination and flow pattern cues for low-level flying. (From R. Kruk, D. Regan, K. I. Beverley, & T. Longridge, Flying performance on the Advanced Simulator for Pilot Training and laboratory tests of vision, *Human Factors*, 1983, *25*. Copyright 1983 by The Human Factors Society. Reprinted with permission.)

with real aircraft parallel the simulator findings. The low-level task was designed with the aim that guidance should strongly depend on visual cues, and on the assumption that guidance of the aircraft would be reflected in bombing accuracy. The correlations shown in Table 19.3 suggest that the visual abilities measured by discrimination of rate of change in expanding flow patterns and the ability to use changing-size stimulation in an eye-hand coordination task are important for accurate guidance in low-level flight. Furthermore, individual differences between these abilities correlate with individual differences in flying performance on this task. Section 3.2 provides evidence that specific sensitivity to changing size or looming may be common to both the tracking task and the flow pattern task.

In addition to laboratory tests and flying performance tasks, pilots were also required to carry out an airborne visual test (Kruk & Regan, 1983). In this test two A-4 aircraft were vectored toward each other from a range of about 40 km. One aircraft was designated as the target and the other as the attacker. The attacker gave a signal as soon as the target aircraft was detected. This "visual acquisition distance" was 5,500–10,600 m (mean 8,600 m) for nonsmoking aircraft. On hearing the attacker pilot's signal, the target aircraft immediately banked and turned sharply left or right. As soon as the attacker was able to judge the direction of turn, the attacker signaled leftward or rightward. Kruk and Regan (1983) measured the attacker's ability to detect the direction of turn in two ways—first, as the angular displacement of the target aircraft between the start of the target's turn and the attacker's correct signal and, second, as the distance between aircraft at the instant that this second signal was made. The rationale for these tests was that an advantage in air-to-air combat is held by the pilot who (1) sees his adversary before being seen, and/or (2) after combat is joined, responds early and correctly to a change in the adversary's heading.

Table 19.4 gives correlations between the results of both laboratory and airborne visual tests and measures of combat performance. Note that in Table 19.4 aircraft are divided into those whose engines smoked and those with nonsmoking engines. The correlations mentioned in the text are for aircraft that left no visible smoke trail. Success in combat, as measured by the win/loss ratio, correlated most strongly with the airborne visual test results (r = .74 for acquisition range, .79 for direction detection range, and .85 for angular deflection). Laboratory tests were comparatively unsuccessful in predicting performance, apart from the two changing-size tracking tests, which gave fair correlations with the number of missile shots fired per engagement. This latter finding seems reasonable because visual-motor tracking skills are involved in the ability to hold an aircraft in one's missile sights while the adversary maneuvers in an attempt to escape from a vulnerable position.

Among the visual cues that might have enabled the attacker pilot to discriminate between the target's leftward and rightward turns are (1) leftward or rightward frontal plane motion, and (2) the aspect or silhouette shape of the aircraft. Aspect might be important because, when turning, the target aircraft first briefly assumed the appropriate angle of bank (in less than 1 sec), and then altered heading. The aspect of the aircraft was quite different for the two angles of bank so that, as discussed by Kennedy et al. (1982), aspect provided a visual cue to heading. The two cues of aspect and frontal-plane motion could not be dissociated in the air, so Kruk and Regan (1983) carried out a subsidiary study using a model aircraft. Subjects were required to discriminate between the two angles of bank for the model aircraft at different viewing distances. Discriminations between left and right bank could be made from a distance at which the aircraft subtended only 3–4 min arc. One difficulty in comparing the detection and discrimination distances obtained in the laboratory using the model A-4 airplane with the distances obtained in the airborne visual tests using real A-4 aircraft is how to allow for the different atmospheric conditions and lighting levels. To deal with this problem, the two sets of data were normalized relative to visual acquisition distance. Kruk and Regan concluded that aspect alone could account for subjects' ability to judge direction of turn correctly at ranges of 1,700–8,800 m (mean 5,300 m) with real A-4 aircraft. On the other hand, this does not mean that the cue of frontal-plane motion was not used.

Table 19.3. Coefficients of Correlation (r) Between Visual Test Results and Performance in Low-Level Flying Tasks

Correlation	r	p
Between no-drop bombing accuracy and		
Flow pattern velocity discrimination	.67	.01
Perturbed changing-size tracking	.63	.02
Frontal-plane motion tracking	.52	.05
Between bombing accuracy (real bombs) and		
Flow pattern velocity discrimination	.71	.01
Perturbed changing-size tracking	.57	.04
Between no-drop bombing accuracy and bombing accuracy (real bombs)	.73	.01

Flight tests included accuracy of computer-scored "no-drop" bombing in the telemetered TACTS range at Yuma and bombing accuracy using real bombs. Subjects were 12 experienced fighter pilots who flew A-4 aircraft. (See text for fuller description of flying tasks and visual tests.) Results suggest that the flow pattern test and changing-size tracking measure visual abilities that are important to good performance on low-level flight tasks. (From R. Kruk & D. Regan, Visual test results compared with flying performance in telemetry-tracked aircraft, *Aviation, Space, and Environmental Medicine*, 1983, *54*. Reprinted with permission.)

The finding that flying performance correlates with the expanding flow pattern test results is consistent with the Gibsonian notion that information in the changing optic array can be used by the pilot. On the basis of research described in Section 3, we can add a suggestion that the information in the optic array actually used by the pilots may have included the location of the maximum div **V** as well as the location of the focus of the velocity flow pattern, noting that the flow pattern actually used had a sharp maximum of div **V** at the focus of expansion.

6. SUMMARY

The idea that the visual system has a specific response to dynamically changing size is supported by the finding that changing-size sensitivity is specifically reduced by adapting to chang-

Table 19.4. Coefficients of Correlation (r) Between Laboratory and Airborne Visual Test Results and Performance in Simulated Air-to-Air Combat Using Real Aircraft

	Nonsmoking Aircraft ($N=6$)		Smoking Aircraft ($N=8$)	
	r	p	r	p
Correlation between acquisition range and				
Kills/engagement	.80	.03	.69	.01
Died/engagement	−.85	.02	NS	—
Win/loss ratio	.74	.05	NS	—
Direction detect range	.79	.03	.96	.001
Flow pattern velocity discrimination	−.60	.10	−.61	.02
Correlation between detection range and				
Died/shot at	−.77	.04	NS	—
Died/engagement	−.88	.01	NS	—
Win/loss ratio	.79	.03	NS	—
Kills/shot	NS	—	.65	.04
Angular deflection	−.91	.006	NS	—
Correlation between angular deflection and				
Shots/engagement	−.83	.02	NS	—
Shot at/engagement	.78	.03	.77	.01
Died/engagement	.69	.06	.79	.009
Win/loss ratio	−.85	.02	NS	.08
Frontal-plane motion tracking	NS	—	−.71	.02
Changing-size tracking	.80	.03	NS	—
Flow pattern velocity discrimination	NS	—	−.66	.04

	All Aircraft	
	p	r
Correlation between shots/engagement and		
Changing-size tracking	−.67	.01
Perturbed changing-size tracking	−.67	.01

Correlations not reported were not statistically significant (NS). Subjects were 11 experienced fighter pilots. Airborne visual tests were conducted with subject (designated as attacker) engaged in maneuvers with a second aircraft (designated as target). Tests included (1) acquisition range—distance at which attacker first sighted target aircraft; (2) direction detection range—distance between attacking and target aircraft at time attacker first discriminated direction of an escape turn executed by target immediately upon detection by attacker; (3) angular deflection—angular displacement of target aircraft between beginning of escape turn and attacker's detection of direction of turn. Combat performance was measured during routine air combat training missions. Data collected included number of missiles fired, number of hits, times shot, and number of times shot down. (See text for more detailed description of both airborne and laboratory visual tests.) It was necessary to analyze individual aircraft whose engines emitted visible smoke separately from nonsmoking aircraft. For nonsmoking aircraft, visual acquisition difference ranged from 5,500 to 10,600 m and left/right discrimination distances ranged from 1,700 to 8,800 m. Airborne visual test results were more successful than laboratory visual tests in predicting pilots' performance during air-to-air combat. (From R. Kruk & D. Regan, Visual test results compared with flying performance in telemetry-tracked aircraft, *Aviation, Space, and Environmental Medicine*, 1983, *54*. Reprinted with permission.)

ing size and that this effect cannot be explained in terms of sensitivity to frontal plane motion. A changing-size stimulus can produce a sensation of motion in depth as well as a sensation of changing size, but these effects have different properties. Size oscillations can be perceived as such up to at least 10 Hz, but the associated sensations of motion in depth fail above about 3 Hz.

The human visual pathway seems to contain at least two stereoscopic systems, one for position in depth and the other for motion in depth. The first is the classic disparity-sensitive system for relative position in depth. The second involves sensitivity to the relative velocities of the left and right retinal images (V_L/V_R), and mediates the precise 0.1–0.2° stereoscopic judgments of the direction of motion in depth. The stereo motion system involves four pairs of channels, tuned to different values of the ratio V_L/V_R.

The sensation of motion in depth can be elicited both stereoscopically (by changing disparity) and monocularly (by changing size). Motion in depth is a unitary sensation in that it can be canceled to zero by pitting changing size against changing disparity. The relative effectiveness of the stereoscopic and monocular stimuli depend on object speed, width, and inspection time, but not on object distance.

The visual guidance of self-motion is understood in general terms, but the specific information processing and visual computations that underlie visual guidance are not known. When the magnification of a patterned target is increased so that the rate of change of magnification is uniform over its entire area, contours flow radially away from a focus where local velocity changes sign. This focus is a candidate cue for visual guidance, and subjects can locate this focus when no translational motion is impressed on the pattern. However, when the retinal image of the whole pattern translates across the retina as well as expanding, subjects can no longer locate the focus with precision, and this raises a problem for the general validity of this local cue. Subjects can locate a local maximum in the rate of expansion even when the pattern is translating, but the destination of self-motion often does not coincide with such a local maximum. Rather than explaining visual guidance in terms of sensitivity to local properties, a wide-field template-matching process could be suggested, but there is little pertinent experimental evidence.

Attempts have been made to correlate flying performance with the results of psychophysical tests of vision. Thresholds did not predict performance in other than detection tasks. For more complex flying tasks such as low-level flying performance and air-to-air combat, closer correlations were obtained with suprathreshold test results using an expanding flow pattern and motion-in-depth tracking.

APPENDIX: CALCULATION OF DIV V FOR A UNIDIRECTIONALLY EXPANDING PATTERN AND FOR A RADIALLY EXPANDING PATTERN

First we consider the unidirectionally expanding pattern as Figure 19.32. The dots outline an arbitrary small area S; x and y are Cartesian coordinates on the pattern. In the special case of a two-dimensional surface, such as that shown in Figure 19.32, we have

$$\operatorname{div} \mathbf{V} = \lim_{S\to 0} \frac{\oint \mathbf{V} \wedge \boldsymbol{dl}}{S}$$

where S is a small area and $\mathbf{V} \cdot \mathbf{dl}$ is the product of an element along the boundary of area S and the component of $\mathbf{V}$ perpendicular to the boundary. In Figure 19.32,

$$\text{div } \mathbf{V} = \frac{1}{S}(V_2\Delta y - V_1\Delta y) = \frac{\partial V}{\partial x}$$

where $\partial V/\partial x$ is the local rate of change of velocity with respect to distance across the pattern. Hence, in Experiment 1, div $\mathbf{V}$ was uniform across the pattern, because for $n = 1$, in Figure 19.33(a) the plot is a straight line so the magnitude of div $\mathbf{V} = \partial V/\partial x$ is the same at all points. On the other hand, in Experiment 3, with exponent $n = 0.5$, for example, the slope $(\partial V/\partial x)$ of the plot in Figure 19.33(a) is steeper at the center of the pattern than to either side; hence div $\mathbf{V}$ is larger at the center because the magnitude of div $\mathbf{V}$ is equal to $\partial V/\partial x$. Note that div $\mathbf{V}$ is formally defined in terms of the limiting case when area S becomes vanishingly small, but that any practical physiological mechanism would have a finite receptive field area, and so would be only a rough approximation to a div $\mathbf{V}$ detector.

Now we turn to the radially expanding pattern used in the experiment of Figure 19.34(b). The flow pattern is illustrated in Figure 19.35(a). First we calculate the area S of the small region outlined by the continuous line. The difference between the areas of the larger and smaller dotted circles is $\pi(r + \Delta r)^2 - \pi r^2$. Hence, approximately

$$S = \frac{\Delta\theta}{2\pi}(2\pi r\Delta r) = r\Delta r\Delta\theta \, . \qquad (1)$$

Div $\mathbf{V}$ is related to the stimulus parameters as follows:

In the two-dimensional case

$$\text{div } \mathbf{V} = \lim_{S \to 0} \frac{\oint \mathbf{V} \cdot \mathbf{dl}}{S} \, .$$

Therefore,

$$\text{div } \mathbf{V} = \lim_{S \to 0} \frac{[V_2(r + \Delta r)\Delta\theta - V_1 r\Delta\theta]}{S} \, . \qquad (2)$$

Substituting in Eq. (2) from Eq. (1)

$$\text{div } \mathbf{V} = \frac{\partial V}{\partial r} + \frac{V}{r} \qquad (3)$$

where V is the velocity at any point P on the surface and $\partial V/\partial r$ is the rate of change of velocity with respect to radial distance at point P. The continuous line in Figure 19.35(c) shows the radial distribution of velocity for the flow pattern used in the experiment of Figure 19.34. The distribution of div $\mathbf{V}$ over the surface can be calculated for Eq. (3), and is plotted as a continuous line in Figure 19.35(d). Div $\mathbf{V}$ was not uniform over the surface, but rather had a sharp maximum near the center.

For completeness we note the special case that velocity is directly proportional to radial distance. This special case [broken line in Fig. 19.35(c)] corresponds to the effect of a zoom lens; the rate of increase of magnification is the same over the whole scene. Because V is proportional to r, $\partial V/\partial r$ is uniform over the whole surface, so that at any point $V = \partial V/\partial r$. Equation (3) reduces to div $\mathbf{V} = 2(\partial V/\partial r)$, that is, div $\mathbf{V}$ is uniform over the whole surface. For comparison, div $\mathbf{V}$ for this special case is plotted as a broken line in Figure 19.35(d).

REFERENCES

Anstis, S. M. Phi movement as a subtraction process. *Vision Research*, 1970, *10*, 1411–1430.

Anstis, S. M., & Rogers, B. J. Illusory reversal of visual depth and movement during changes in contrast. *Vision Research*, 1975, *15*, 957–961.

Ball, W., & Tronick, E. Infant responses to impending collision. *Science*, 1971, *171*, 818–820.

Barlow, H. B., Blakemore, C. B., & Pettigrew, J. The neural mechanism of binocular depth discrimination. *Journal of Physiology* (London), 1967, *193*, 327–342.

Barlow, H. B., & Hill, R. M. Evidence for a physiological explanation of the waterfall phenomenon and figural aftereffects. *Nature* (London), 1963, *200*, 1345–1347. (a)

Barlow, H. B., & Hill, R. M. Selective sensitivity to direction of movement in ganglion cells of the rabbit retina. *Science*, 1963, *139*, 412–414. (b)

Barlow, H. B., Hill, R. M., & Levick, W. R. Retinal ganglion cells responding selectively to direction and speed of image motion in the rabbit. *Journal of Physiology*, 1964, *173*, 377–407.

Beverley, K. I., & Regan, D. Evidence for the existence of neural mechanisms selectively sensitive to the direction of movement in space. *Journal of Physiology*, 1973, *235*, 17–29. (a)

Beverley, K. I., & Regan, D. Evidence for the existence of neural mechanisms selectively sensitive to the direction of movement in space. *Journal of Physiology* (London), 1973, *249*, 387–398. (b)

Beverley, K. I., & Regan, D. Selective adaptation in stereoscopic depth perception. *Journal of Physiology* (London), 1973, *232*, 40–41. (c)

Beverley, K. I., & Regan, D. The relation between discrimination and sensitivity in the perception of motion in depth. *Journal of Physiology*, 1975, *249*, 387–398.

Beverley, K. I., & Regan, D. Separable aftereffects of changing-size and motion in depth: Different neural mechanisms? *Vision Research*, 1979, *19*, 727–732.

Beverley, K. I., & Regan, D. Device for measuring the precision of eye-hand coordination when tracking changing-size. *Aviation, Space, and Environmental Medicine*, 1980, *51*, 688–693. (a)

Beverley, K. I., & Regan, D. Temporal selectivity of changing-size channels. *Journal of the Optical Society of America*, 1980, *11*, 1375–1377. (b)

Beverley, K. I., & Regan, D. Adaptation to incomplete flow patterns: No evidence for "filling-in" the perception of flow patterns. *Perception*, 1982, *11*, 275–278.

Beverley, K. I., & Regan, D. Texture changes versus size changes as stimuli for motion in depth. *Vision Research*, 1983, *23*, 1387–1400.

Boff, K. The influence of rotary target motion on perceived vernier offset and vernier acuity (Doctoral dissertation, Columbia University, 1978). *Dissertation Abstracts International*, 1978, *39*, 1977B. (Order no. 7819300)

Boring, E. G. *A history of experimental psychology* (2nd ed.). New York: Appleton, 1950.

Bower, T. G. R., Broughton, J. M., & Moore, M. K. Infant responses to approaching objects: An indicator of response to distal variables. *Perception and Psychophysics*, 1970, *9*, 193–196.

Braddick, O. J. A short range process in apparent motion. *Vision Research*, 1974, *14*, 519–527.

Braddick, O. J., Campbell, F. W., & Atkinson, J. Channels in vision: Basic aspects. In R. Held, H. W. Leibowitz, & H.-L. Teuber (Eds.), *Handbook of sensory physiology* (Vol. 8). New York: Springer, 1978.

Brandt, T., Dichgans, J., & Koenig, E. Differential effects of central versus peripheral vision on egocentric and exocentric motion perception. *Experimental Brain Research*, 1973, *16*, 476–491.

Brown, J. F. The visual perception of velocity. *Psychologische Forschung*, 1931, *14*, 199–232.

Brown, R. H. Visual sensitivity to differences in velocity. *Psychological Bulletin*, 1961, *58*, 89–103.

Campbell, F. W., Nachmias, J., & Jukes, J. Spatial-frequency discrimination in human vision. *Journal of the Optical Society of America*,

1970, *60*, 555–559.

Cutting, J. E., & Proffitt, D. K. Gait perception as an example of how we may perceive events. In R. D. Walk & H. L. Pick, Jr. (Eds.), *Intersensory perception and sensory integration.* New York: Plenum, 1981.

Cynader, M., & Regan, D. Neurones in cat parastriate cortex sensitive to the direction of motion in three-dimensional space. *Journal of Physiology* (London), 1978, *274*, 549–569.

Cynader, M., & Regan, D. Neurons in cat visual cortex tuned to the direction of motion in depth: Effect of positional disparity. *Vision Research*, 1982, *22*, 967–982.

Dichgans, J., & Brandt, T. Visual-vestibular interactions: Effects on self-motion perception and postural control. In R. Held, H. W. Leibowitz, & H.-L. Teuber (Eds.), *Handbook of sensory physiology* (Vol. 8). New York: Springer, 1978.

Epstein, W. The influence of assumed size on apparent distance. *American Journal of Psychology*, 1963, *76*, 257–265.

Festinger, L., Sedgwick, H. A., & Holtzman, J. D. Visual perception during smooth eye movements. *Vision Research*, 1976, *16*, 1377–1386.

Fieandt, K. von, & Gibson, J. J. The sensitivity of the eye to two kinds of continuous transformations of a shadow pattern. *Journal of Experimental Psychology*, 1959, *57*, 344–347.

Filion, R. D. L. *On the visual detection of accelerated motion.* Unpublished doctoral dissertation, Princeton University, 1964.

Fishman, R., & Tallarico, R. B. Studies of visual perception: II. Avoidance reaction as an indicator response in chicks. *Perceptual and Motor Skills*, 1961, *12*, 251–257.

Foster, D. H. A model of the human visual system in its response to certain classes of moving stimuli. *Kybernetik*, 1971, *8*, 69–84.

Gibson, J. J. *The perception of the visual world.* Boston: Houghton-Mifflin, 1950.

Gibson, J. J. Optical motions and transformations as stimuli for visual perception. *Psychological Review*, 1957, *64*, 288–295.

Gibson, J. J. Visually controlled locomotion and visual orientation in animals. *British Journal of Psychology*, 1958, *49*, 182–194.

Gibson, J. J. *The senses considered as perceptual systems.* Boston: Houghton-Mifflin, 1966.

Gibson, J. J. *The ecological approach to visual perception.* Boston: Houghton-Mifflin, 1979.

Gibson, J. J., & Gibson, E. J. Continuous perspective transformations and the perception of rigid motion. *Journal of Experimental Psychology*, 1957, *54*, 129–138.

Gibson, J. J., Olum, P., & Rosenblatt, F. Parallax and perspective during aircraft landings. *American Journal of Psychology*, 1955, *68*, 372–375.

Gillam, B. False perspectives. *Perception*, 1981, *10*, 313–318.

Ginsburg, A. P., Evans, D. W., Sekuler, R., & Harp, S. A. Contrast sensitivity predicts pilots' performance in aircraft simulators. *American Journal of Optometry and Physiological Optics*, 1982, *59*, 105–109.

Gogel, W. C. The metric of visual space. In W. Epstein (Ed.), *Stability and constancy in visual space.* New York: Wiley, 1978.

Gogel, W. C., Hartman, B. O., & Harker, G. S. The retinal size of a familiar object as a determiner of apparent distance. *Psychological Monographs*, 1957, *71*, 1–16.

Gordon, D. A. Static and dynamic visual fields in human space perception. *Journal of the Optical Society of America*, 1965, *55*, 1296–1303.

Gottsdanker, R. M. The accuracy of predicted motion. *Journal of Experimental Psychology*, 1952, *43*, 26–36.

Gottsdanker, R. M. The ability of human operators to detect acceleration of target motion. *Psychological Bulletin*, 1956, *53*, 477–487.

Gottsdanker, R. M. How the identification of target acceleration is affected by modes of starting and ending. *British Journal of Psychology*, 1961, *52*, 155–160.

Gottsdanker, R. M. Assessment of motion as influenced by structure of background. *Scandinavian Journal of Psychology*, 1962, *3*, 122–128.

Gottsdanker, R. M., & Edwards, R. V. The prediction of collision. *American Journal of Psychology*, 1975, *70*, 110–113.

Gottsdanker, R. M., Frick, J. W., & Lockard, R. B. Identifying the acceleration of visual targets. *British Journal of Psychology*, 1961, *52*, 31–42.

Graham, N. Psychophysics and spatial frequency channels. In M. Kubovy & J. R. Pomerantz (Eds.), *Perceptual organization.* Hillsdale, N.J.: Erlbaum, 1981.

Graham, M., & Rogers, B. Interactions between monocular and binocular depth aftereffect. *Investigative Ophthalmology and Visual Science*, 1982, *22* (Suppl.), 272.

Gregory, R. L. *Eye and brain.* New York: McGraw-Hill, 1966.

Grosslight, J. H., Fletcher, H. J., Masterton, R. B., & Hagen, R. Monocular vision and landing performance in general aviation pilots: Cyclops revisited. *Human Factors*, 1978, *20*, 127–133.

Hayes, W. N., & Saiff, E. I. Visual alarm reactions in turtles. *Animal Behavior*, 1967, *15*, 102–108.

Held, R., Dichgans, J., & Bauer, J. Characteristics of moving visual scenes influencing spatial orientation. *Vision Research*, 1975, *15*, 357–365.

Hick, W. E. The threshold for sudden changes in the velocity of a seen object. *Quarterly Journal of Experimental Psychology*, 1950, *2*, 33–41.

Hochberg, C. B., & Hochberg, J. E. Familiar size and the perception of depth. *Journal of Psychology*, 1952, *34*, 107–114.

Hoyle, F. *The black cloud.* England: Heineman, 1957. (Penguin Edition, 1971.)

Hubel, D. H., & Wiesel, T. N. Receptive fields, binocular interaction and functional architecture in the cat's visual cortex. *Journal of Physiology*, 1962, *160*, 106–154.

Hubel, D. H., & Wiesel, T. N. Receptive fields and functional architecture of monkey striate cortex. *Journal of Physiology*, 1968, *195*, 215–243.

Hurvich, L. M., & Jameson, D. An opponent-process theory of colour vision. *Psychological Review*, 1957, *64*, 384–404.

Ittelson, W. H. Size as a cue to distance: Static localization. *American Journal of Psychology*, 1951, *64*, 54–67.

Ittelson, W. H. *Visual space perception.* New York: Springer, 1960.

Johansson, G. Configurations in the perception of velocity. *Acta Psychologica*, 1950, *7*, 25–79.

Johansson, G. Rigidity, stability, and motion in perceptual space. *Acta Psychologica*, 1958, *14*, 359–70.

Johansson, G. Projective transformations as determining visual space perception. In R. B. Macleod & H. L. Pick, Jr. (Eds.) *Perception: Essays in honor of James J. Gibson.* Ithaca: Cornell University Press, 1974.

Johansson, G., & Jansson, G. Perceived rotary motion from changes in a straight line. *Perception and Psychophysics*, 1968, *4*, 165–170.

Julesz, B. *Foundations of cyclopean perception.* Chicago: Chicago University Press, 1971.

Kaufman, L. *Research in visual perception for carrier landing: Supp. 2. Studies on the perception of the impact point based on shadowgraph techniques* (Report SDG-5265-0031). Great Neck, N.Y.: Sperry Rand Corp., 1964.

Kaufman, L. *Sight and mind.* New York: Oxford University Press, 1974.

Kaufman, L. *Perception: The world transformed.* New York: Oxford University Press, 1979.

Kaufman, L., Cyrulnick, I., Kaplowitz, J., Melnick, G., & Stoff, D. The complementarity of apparent and real motion. *Psychologische Forschung*, 1971, *34*, 343–348.

Kaufman, L., & Williamson, S. J. Visual sensitivity to changing speed. *Vision Research*, in press.

Kennedy, R. S., Collyer, S. C., May, J. G., & Dunlap, W. C. Visual simulation requirements for aircraft aspect recognition at real world distances. *Proceedings of the 26th Annual Meeting of the Human Factors Society*, 1982.

Koenderink, J. J., & van Doorn, A. J. Local structure of movement parallax of the plane. *Journal of the Optical Society of America*, 1976, *66*, 717–723.

Koenderink, J. J., & van Doorn, A. J. Exterospecific component of the motion parallax field. *Journal of the Optical Society of America*, 1981, *71*, 953–957.

Kruk, R., & Regan, D. Visual test results compared with flying performance in telemetry-tracked aircraft. *Aviation, Space, and Environmental Medicine*, 1983, *54*, 906–911.

Kruk, R., Regan, D., Beverley, K. I., & Longridge, T. Correlations between visual test results and flying performance on the Advanced Simulator for Pilot Training (ASPT). *Aviation, Space, and Environmental Medicine*, 1981, *52*, 455–460.

Kruk, R., Regan, D., Beverley, K. I., & Longridge, T. Flying performance on the Advanced Simulator for Pilot Training and laboratory tests of vision. *Human Factors*, 1983, *25*, 457–466.

Lee, D. N. *Visual information during locomotion*. In R. B. Macleod & H. L. Pick, Jr. (Eds.), *Perception: Essays in honor of James J. Gibson*. Ithaca: Cornell University Press, 1974.

Lee, D. N. A theory of visual control of braking based on information about time to collision. *Perception*, 1976, *15*, 437–459.

Lee, D. N., & Lishman, R. Visual control of locomotion. *Scandinavian Journal of Psychology*, 1977, *18*, 224–330.

Lee, D. N. The optic flow field: The foundation of vision. *Philosophical Transactions of the Royal Society* (Series B), 1980, *290*, 169–179.

Lewis, C. E., Jr., Blakeley, W. R., Swaroop, R., Masters, R. L., & McMurty, T. C. Landing performance by low time private pilots after the sudden loss of binocular vision—Cyclops II. *Aerospace Medicine*, 1973, *44*, 1241–1245.

Lewis, C. E., Jr., & Kriers, G. E. Flight research program: XIV. Landing performance in jet aircraft after the loss of binocular vision. *Aerospace Medicine*, 1969, *40*, 957–963.

Lisberger, S. G., & Fuchs, A. F. Role of the primate flocculus during rapid behavioral modification of vestibulo-ocular reflex. I. Purkinje cell activity during visually guided horizontal smooth-pursuit eye movements and passive head rotation. *Journal of Neurophysiology*, 1978, *41*, 733–763.

Llewellyn, K. R. Visual guidance of locomotion. *Journal of Experimental Psychology*, 1971, *91*, 245–261.

Longuet-Higgins, H. C., & Prazdny, K. F. The interpretation of a moving retinal image. *Proceedings of the Royal Society of London* (Series B), 1980, *208*, 385–397.

Mandriota, F. J., Mintz, D. E., & Notterman, J. M. Visual velocity discrimination: Effects of spatial and temporal cues. *Science*, 1962, *138*, 437–438.

Matin, L., Boff, K. R., & Pola, J. Vernier offset produced by rotary target motion. *Perception and Psychophysics*, 1976, *20*, 138–142.

Metzger, W. *Gesetze des Sehens*. Frankfurt: Waldemar-Kramer, 1953.

Michotte, A. *La perception de la causalité*. Louvain: Institut Superieur de Philosophe, 1946.

Michotte, A. *Causalité, permanence, et realité phenomenales*. Paris: Beatrice-Nauwelaerts, 1962.

Michotte, A. *The perception of causality*. London: Methuen, 1963.

Miles, F. A., & Fuller, J. H. Adaptive plasticity in the vestibulo-ocular responses of the Rhesus monkey. *Brain Research*, 1974, *80*, 512–516.

Miles, F. A., Fuller, J. H., Braitman, D. H., & Dow, B. M. Longterm adaptive changes in primate vestibulo-ocular reflex. III. Electrophysiological observations in flocculus of normal monkeys. *Journal of Neurophysiology*, 1980, *43*, 1437–1476.

Musatti, C. L. Sui fenomeni stereokinetici. *Archivo Italiano di Psicologia*, 1924, *3*, 105–120.

Nakayama, K., & Loomis, J. M. Optical velocity patterns, velocity sensitive neurons and perception: A hypothesis. *Perception*, 1974, *63*, 63–87.

Noda, H. Visual mossy fiber inputs to the flocculus of the monkey. In B. Cohen (Ed.), Vestibular and oculomotor physiology: International meeting of the Bárány Society. *Annals of the New York Academy of Sciences*, 1981, *374*, 465–475.

Noda, H., & Suzuki, D. A. Processing of eye movement signals in the flocculus of the monkey. *Journal of Physiology* (London), 1979, *194*, 317–334.

Notterman, J. M., Cicala, G. A., & Page, D. E. Demonstration of the influence of stimulus and response categories upon difference limens. *Science*, 1960, *131*, 83–84.

Notterman, J. M., & Page, D. E. Weber's law and the difference threshold for the velocity of a seen object. *Science*, 1957, *126*, 652.

Pellionisz, A., & Llinas, R. Brain modelling by tensor network theory and computer simulation. The cerebellum: Distributed processor for predictive coordination. *Neuroscience*, 1979, *4*, 323–348.

Petersik. J. T., Beverley, K. I., & Regan, D. Contrast sensitivity of the changing-size channel. *Vision Research*, 1981, *21*, 829–832.

Pfaffman, C. Aircraft landings without binocular cues: A study based upon observations made in flight. *American Journal of Psychology*, 1948, *61*, 323–335.

Poggio, T., Reichardt, W., & Hausen, K. Figure-ground discrimination by relative movement in the visual system of the fly. *Biological Cybernetics*, 1983, *46*, 1.

Poggio, G. R., & Talbot, W. H. Mechanisms of static and dynamic stereopsis in foveal cortex of the Rhesus monkey. *Journal of Physiology*, 1981, *315*, 469–492.

Prazdny, K. Egomotion and relative depth map from optical flow. *Biological Cybernetics*, 1980, *36*, 87–102.

Rashbass, C., & Westheimer, G. H. Independence of conjugate and disjunctive eye movements. *Journal of Physiology*, 1961, *159*, 361–364.

Regan, D. Visual information channeling in normal and disordered vision. *Psychological Review*, 1982, *89*, 407–444.

Regan, D. Masking of spatial frequency discrimination. *Journal of the Optical Society of America*, in press.

Regan, D., & Beverley, K. I. The dissociation of sideways movements from movements in depth: Psychophysics. *Vision Research*, 1973, *13*, 2403–2415.

Regan, D., & Beverley, K. I. Illusory motion in depth: Aftereffect of adaptation to changing size. *Vision Research*, 1978, *18*, 209–212. (a)

Regan, D., & Beverley, K. I. Looming detectors in the human visual pathway. *Vision Research*, 1978, *18*, 415–421. (b)

Regan, D., & Beverley, K. I. Binocular and monocular stimuli for motion-in-depth: Changing-disparity and changing-size inputs feed the same motion-in-depth stage. *Vision Research*, 1979, *19*, 1331–1342. (a)

Regan, D., & Beverley, K. I. Visually guided locomotion: Psychophysical evidence for a neural mechanism sensitive to flow patterns. *Science*, 1979, *205*, 311–313. (b)

Regan, D., & Beverley, K. I. Device for measuring the precision of eye-hand coordination while tracking changing size. *Aviation, Space, and Environmental Medicine*, 1980, *51*, 688–693. (a)

Regan, D., & Beverley, K. I. Visual responses to changing size and to sideways motion for different directions of motion in depth: Linearization of visual responses. *Journal of the Optical Society of America*, 1980, *70*, 1289–1296. (b)

Regan, D., & Beverley, K. I. Motion sensitivity measured by a psychophysical linearizing technique. *Journal of the Optical Society of America*, 1981, *71*, 958–965.

Regan, D., & Beverley, K. I. How do we avoid confounding the direction we are looking with the direction we are moving? *Science*, 1982, *215*, 194–196.

Regan, D., & Beverley, K. I. Spatial frequency discrimination and detection: Comparison of postadaptation thresholds. *Journal of the Optical Society of America*, 1983, *73*, 1684–1690. (a)

Regan, D., & Beverley, K. I. Visual fields for frontal plane motion and for changing size. *Vision Research*, 1983, *23*, 673–676. (b)

Regan, D., & Beverley, K. I. Figure-ground segregation by motion contrast and by luminance contrast. *Journal of the Optical Society of America*, 1984, *1*, 433–442. (a)

Regan, D., & Beverley, K. I. Postadaptation orientation discrimination. *Investigative Ophthalmology and Visual Science*, 1984, (Suppl.) *25*, 314. (b)

Regan, D., & Beverley, K. I. Postadaptation orientation discrimination. *Journal of the Optical Society of America*, 1984, in press. (c)

Regan, D., & Beverley, K. I. Visual responses to vorticity and the neural analysis of optic flow. *Journal of the Optical Society of America*, 1984. (d)

Regan, D., Beverley, K. I., & Cynader, M. Stereoscopic channels for position and for motion. In S. J. Cool & E. L. Smith (Eds.), *Frontiers in visual science*. New York: Springer, 1978.

Regan, D., Beverley, K. I., & Cynader, M. The visual perception of motion in depth. *Scientific American*, 1979, *241*, 136–151.

Regan, D., & Cynader, M. Neurons in area 18 of cat visual cortex selectively sensitive to changing size: Nonlinear interactions between responses to two edges. *Vision Research*, 1979, *19*, 699–711.

Regan, D., & Cynader, M. Neurons in cat visual cortex tuned to the direction of motion in depth: Effect of stimulus speed. *Investigative Ophthalmology and Visual Science*, 1982, *22*, 535–550.

Regan, D., Silver, R., & Murray, T. J. Visual acuity and contrast sensitivity in multiple sclerosis: Hidden visual loss. *Brain*, 1977, *100*, 563–579.

Regan, D., & Spekreijse, H. Electrophysiological correlate of binocular depth perception in man. *Nature*, 1970, *255*, 92–94.

Regan, D., Whitlock, J., Murray, T. J., & Beverley, K. I. Orientation-specific losses of contrast sensitivity in multiple sclerosis. *Investigative Ophthalmology and Visual Science*, 1980, *19*, 324–328.

Reichardt, W. Autocorrelation, a principle for the evaluation of sensory information by the central nervous system. In W. A. Rosenblith (Ed.), *Sensory communication*. New York: Wiley & M.I.T. Press, 1961.

Reichardt, W., & Poggio, T. Figure-ground discrimination by relative movement in the visual system of the fly. *Biological Cybernetics*, 1979, *35*, 81–100.

Restle, F. Coding theory of the perception of motion configurations. *Psychological Review*, 1979, *86*, 1–24.

Richards, W. Stereoperimetry: New techniques for analyzing visual function. *Journal of the Optical Society of America*, 1972, *62*, 715 (Abstract).

Richards, W. Visual space perception. In E. C. Carterette & M. P. Friedman (Ed.), *Handbook of perception* (Vol. 5). New York: Academic, 1975.

Richards, W. Selective stereoblindness. In H. Spekreijae & L. H. van der Tweel (Eds.), *Spatial contrast: Report of a workshop*. Amsterdam: North-Holland, 1977, 109–115.

Richards, W., & Regan, D. A stereo field map with implications for disparity processing. *Investigative Ophthalmology*, 1973, *12*, 904–909.

Rogers, B., & Graham, M. Horizontal-vertical anisotropies in the perception of 3-D depth surfaces. *Investigative Ophthalmology and Visual Science*, 1982, *22* (Suppl.), 273.

Rosenbaum, D. A perception and extrapolation of velocity and acceleration. *Journal of Experimental Psychology: Human perception and Performance*, 1975, *1*, 305–403.

Runeson, S. Constant velocity: Not perceived as such. *Psychological Review*, 1974, *37*, 3–23.

Runeson, S. Visual prediction of collision with natural and nonnatural motion functions. *Perception and Psychophysics*, 1975, *18*, 261–266.

Schey, H. M. *Div, grad, curl, and all that: An informal text on vector calculus*. New York: Norton, 1973.

Schiff, W. Perception of impending collision: A study of visually directed avoidant behavior. *Psychological Monographs*, 1965, *79* (Whole No. 604).

Schiff, W., Caviness, J. A., & Gibson, J. J. Persistent fear responses in rhesus monkeys to the optical stimulus of "looming." *Science*, 1962, *136*, 982–983.

Schiff, W., & Detwiler, M. L. Information used in judging impending collisions. *Perception*, 1979, *8*, 647–658.

Schmerler, J. The visual perception of accelerated motion. *Perception*, 1976, *5*, 167–185.

Spekreijse, H., & Reits, D. Sequential analysis of the visual evoked potential system in man: Nonlinear analysis of a sandwich system. *Annals of the New York Academy of Sciences*, 1982, *388*, 72–97.

Spitzberg, R., & Richards, W. Broad band spatial filters in the human visual system. *Vision Research*, 1975, *15*, 837–841.

Tauber, E. S., & Kaufman, L. Fixation and the stereokinetic phenomenon. *Perception and Psychophysics*, 1977, *22*, 241–244.

Ternus, J. The problem of phenomenal identity. In W. D. Ellis (Ed.), *A source book of Gestalt psychology*. London: Routledge & Kegan Paul, 1938.

Tronick, E. Approach responses of domestic chicks to an optical display. *Journal of Comparative and Physiological Psychology*, 1967, *64*, 529–531.

Ullman, S. The interpretation of structure from motion. *Proceedings of the Royal Society of London* (Series B), 1979, *203*, 405–426.

Van Essen, D. C. Visual areas of the mammalian cerebral cortex. *Annual Review of Neuroscience*, 1979, *2*, 227–263.

Wallach, H., & Frey, K. J. Adaptation in distance perception based on oculomotor cues. *Perception and Psychophysics*, 1972, *11*, 77–83.

Wallach, H., & Karsh, E. B. The modification of stereoscopic depth-perception and the kinetic depth effect. *American Journal of Psychology*, 1963, *76*, 429–435.

Wallach, H., & O'Connell, D. N. The kinetic depth effect. *Journal of Experimental Psychology*, 1953, *45*, 205–217.

Wallach, H., Weisz, A., & Adams, P. A. Circles and derived figures in rotation. *American Journal of Psychology*, 1956, *69*, 48–59.

Westheimer, G. Visual hyperacuity. In D. Ottoson et al. (Eds.), *Progress in sensory physiology* (Vol. 1). New York: Springer, 1981.

Westheimer, G. H., & Mitchell, A. M. Eye movement responses to convergence stimuli. *Archives of Ophthalmology*, 1956, *55*, 848–856.

Westheimer, G., Shimamura, K., & McKee, S. Interference with line-orientation sensitivity. *Journal of the Optical Society of America*, 1976, *66*, 332–338.

Wheatstone, C. Contributions to the physiology of vision. I. *Philosophical Transactions of the Royal Society*, 1838, *13*, 371–394.

Wheatstone, C. Contributions to the physiology of vision. II. *Philosophical Transactions of the Royal Society*, 1852, *142*, 1–18.

Zeki, S. Cells responding to changing image size and disparity in the cortex of Rhesus monkey. *Journal of Physiology*, 1974, *242*, 827–841.

CHAPTER 20

VISUAL LOCALIZATION AND EYE MOVEMENTS

LEONARD MATIN

Department of Psychology, Columbia University, New York, New York

CONTENTS

1. INTRODUCTION

1.1. The Fundamental Problem

Identical displacements of the retinal image at the back of the eye may be produced either by an eye movement that redirects gaze within the visual field [Figure 20.1(c)] or by a displacement of the stimulus that is imaged at the retina [Figure 20.1(b)]. Although displacements of visual stimuli normally appear to the observer to be displacements in the environment, stationary visual fields normally do not appear to change location in the presence of eye movements. This is only one feature of the remarkable flexibility of visual perception, but it distinguishes visual localization from a large number of other aspects of visual perception, such as the perception of color, intensity discrimination, and contour perception. For those latter aspects it has reasonably been assumed that eye position plays no independent role, and it has been possible to develop successful accounts based only on the processing of information available in the spatial pattern of light at the retina. On the other hand, although configurational factors deriving from retinal information (RI) alone within a structured visual field can account for some aspects of visual localization under some conditions, they are not sufficient by any means to provide a complete account of visual localization. Section 1.2 provides a proof that any account of the stability of visual localization in the presence of eye movements requires some channel of information regarding eye position and change in eye position (the term extraretinal eye position information [EEPI] is used to represent the information in such a channel) as well as a channel for conveying retinal information.

A substantial segment of the literature concerned with the relation of eye movements and visual localization has been directed toward dealing with the involvement of EEPI in visual localization, and the experiments have been conducted with the end in view of clarifying this involvement. Any intelligent presentation of this literature thus requires some introduction to the main approaches to dealing with the involvement of EEPI.

1.2. Visual Localization Uses Extraretinal Eye Position Information

The following is a simple proof that a channel for EEPI is involved in the mechanism that determines visual localization. In otherwise complete darkness with steady gaze at a fixation target employed to fix the horizontal angle of rotation of the eye in the orbit (gaze direction fixed) an observer is required to set the position of a second light to the location that appears to lie on an extension of the median plane of the body ("straight ahead") by positioning it within the horizontal plane containing the fixation target. The settings did not vary greatly with change of the direction of fixation as determined by the position of the fixation target over a 60° horizontal range. The use of EEPI is implied by the fact that the retinal location of the image of the target set to the median plane varied systematically with the direction of fixation [Figure 20.2(b)].

Figure 20.2(a) and (b) shows two useful representations of the results. If complete constancy of visual direction held when horizontal gaze direction was changed, the target set to appear straight ahead by the observer would be set to the same location for all gaze directions [horizontal line at ordinate 0, Figure 20.2(a)]. For this condition a given change in horizontal gaze direction would result in a change of identical magnitude in the horizontal position of the retinal image of the target [main diagonal, Fig. 20.2(b)]. If, on the other hand, the observers failed to take any account of the change in gaze direction when they made their settings, they would set the second target so that it struck the same retinal locus regardless of gaze direction [zero constancy, horizontal line at 0, Figure 20.2.(b)]. The target setting would then be shifted in the same direction as the fixation direction by an amount equal to the change in gaze direction [main diagonal, Figure 20.2(a)]. But any systematic departure of the setting from a fixed retinal locus that results from variation in gaze direction would imply some involvement of EEPI. In fact, the actual settings (Figure 20.2) do not deviate much from complete constancy; they are very far away from a constant retinal location when gaze direction is changed, implying that EEPI plays a significant role in the visual localization of the median plane in darkness.

An argument similar to the one above regarding the employment of EEPI for visual localization of the median plane holds for the situation in which the observer sets the height of a visual target to the direction perceived as eye-level horizontal. A similar approximation to constancy implies a major involvement of EEPI.

The above proof of an important role for EEPI in visual localization might appear to have a pro forma quality and the result in Figure 20.2 to be a simple extension of everyday observations. But, in fact, this is not so. As described below, in a normally rich environment EEPI's control of moderated visual localization is by the pattern of retinal stimulation. Egocentric as well as object relative visual localization is strongly influenced by relations within the pattern of retinal stimulation.

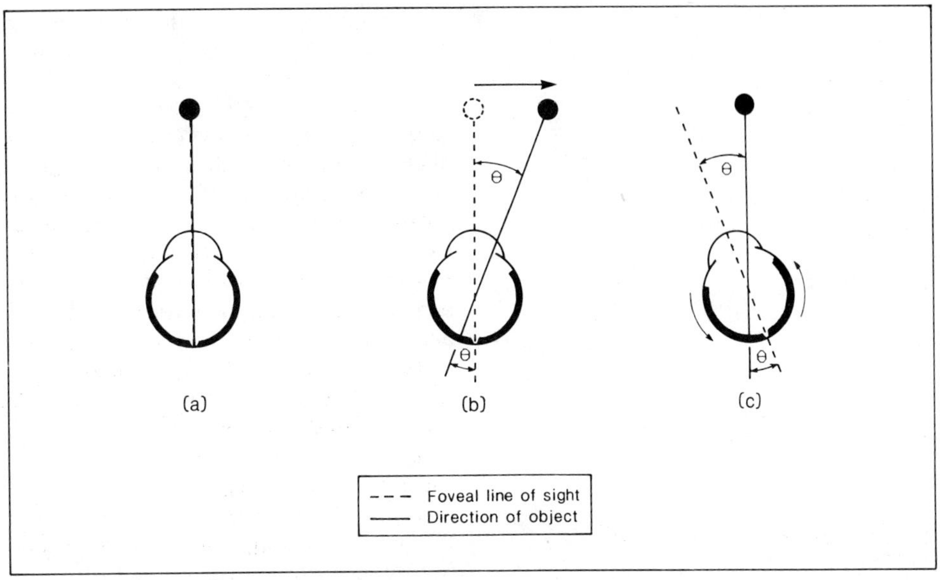

Figure 20.1. Identity of retinal image shift resulting from eye movement and stimulus movement. From an initial condition (a) in which the observer foveates the visual target (filled circle), identical shifts in retinal image location are produced by a displacement of the object through angle θ (b) and by an ocular rotation through angle θ (c).

The requirement of a channel of information in addition to the retinal input is common to a number of perceptual phenomena in space perception. In fact, most phenomena of spatial localization involve an integration of information from several sensory modalities. Most striking, perhaps, is the fact that, in complete darkness, when an observer's head and body are turned from an upright position to horizontal within a frontal plane, the direction within the frontal plane perceived as vertical deviates from the true physical vertical by no more than 10–15° (cf. Aubert, 1861; Bauermeister, 1964; Müller, 1916; Witkin & Asch, 1948; Figure 20.3). Allowing a liberal 10° for uncompensated ocular torsion (cf. Miller, 1962; Schöne, 1962; Woellner & Graybiel, 1958) leaves a rotation of as much as 65° between the orientation of a retinal stimulus and its perceived orientation in a frontal plane consequent to head and body turning. To account for this flexibility in the relation between retinal orientation of a visual stimulus and perceived orientation requires that information regarding head orientation within a frontal plane be dealt with by the mechanism determining the visually perceived orientation of the frontal plane (see Howard, Chapter 11). There are many other examples in which a channel of information is required in addition to the basic pattern of sensory stimulation in order for constancy of the perception of space to be maintained. I note two additional examples: (1) Not only is EEPI required to account for visual direction constancy, but very similar considerations hold for the use of extraretinal information regarding the position of the head on the neck for the perception of visual direction. (2) Judgments of the direction of a sound relative to the median plane shift only slightly with change in orientation of the head on the neck, a result that implies a contribution of nonauditory head position information to the mechanism controlling auditory localization (see Scharf & Houtsma, Chapter 15).

Questions about the influence of EEPI on visual localization are closely intertwined with questions regarding the influence of visual stimulation on nonvisual perceptions of the body. Problems pertaining to intermodal (or intersensory) discrimination (e.g., perception of the relative spatial locations of a visually presented target and an auditorily presented target), and the influence of visual stimulation on control of bodily movement (e.g., manually pointing to a visually presented target) provide additional connections (also see Welch and Warren, Chapter 25). This chapter pays some attention to these problems as well.

1.3. Defining and Measuring Visual Localization

The four procedures commonly used to measure visual localization and described below appear to include all of the important cases:

1. A seen object may be visually localized relative to another visual object simultaneously present. Such localizations are given by reports such as "A is to the left of B" or "A is above B." Either A or B (or both) may be an external object, or a view of the observer's own body or of part of the observer's own body.
2. A seen object may be visually localized relative to an "internal norm" such as "A is to the left of my median plane" or "A is above my eye-level horizontal."
3. Observers can be said to "identify absolutely" the location of a light if in darkness they are able to correctly name the light (e.g., "number 7") when it is illuminated alone from an array of lights that are identical except for location. Insofar as the observers' judgments depart from chance, some capacity for absolute identification is manifested. Such absolute identification could be treated under point 2 above as discrimination against a norm if observers carry out such identifications by judging a light to lie at a specific distance from a visual norm. But absolute identifications may be mediated by other means, and until the questions regarding their mediation are resolved empirically, absolute identification is best treated separately from matches to a norm.
4. One object may be visually localized relative to a second, although the two are visible only sequentially and not simultaneously. For example, such sequential visual localization characterizes the operation of observing the presence or absence

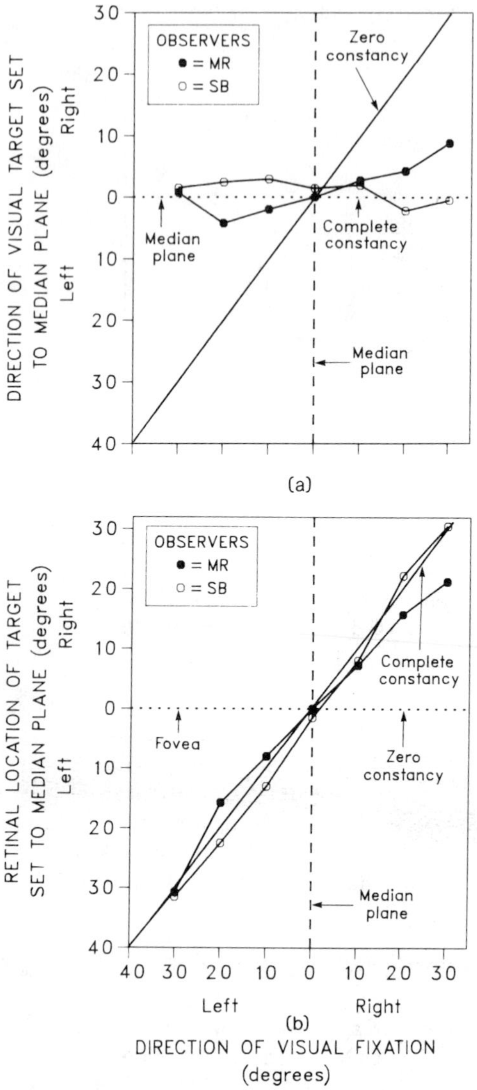

Figure 20.2. Visual localization of the median plane in darkness. In complete darkness each of two observers fixated a 7-min circular transilluminated visual target (whose horizontal displacement from the median plane determined the direction of visual fixation; abscissa) and set a second identical visual target to appear at the median plane. The setting was made at each of seven fixation directions. To bring out the relation to the retinal metric the data are plotted in two ways. In (a) the setting (ordinate) is plotted as a deviation from the true median plane. In (b) the same data are replotted with the ordinate representing the retinal location of the target set to the median plane. Change in gaze direction does not result in much change in the median plane setting (Matin & Rogan, unpublished data).

of visual stability when an eye movement occurs, with presaccadic and postsaccadic views being the items whose locations are compared.

Visual localization as defined in the fourfold classification above is not the only group of spatial localizations in which a stimulus item is visual. Intersensory localization and sensory/motor localization both may involve relating the location of a visual target to a nonvisual item. Thus an observer may match the locations of a sound and a light by reports such as "the light is to the left of the sound" on a series of trials in which the physical location of the sound source is varied from trial to trial ("visual/auditory matching"; a variety of intersensory localization), or an observer may point either finger or eye at a light or at a visual norm such as the eye-level horizontal (varieties of sensory/motor localization). In addition to providing ways of studying mechanisms underlying relations between different sense modalities and between sensory and motor behavior, intersensory or sensory/motor matching may be employed to learn about mechanisms subserving visual localization. Comparison of perceived location of a visual stimulus or of a visual norm with location perceived via another sense modality or with location of a limb is a particularly useful way for an experimenter to carry a subjective metric fixed relative to physical space across a set of different experimental conditions. If the variation across conditions involves an attempt at influencing visual localization by systematically modifying either stimulus conditions or the visual system itself (e.g., adaptation to optical displacement produced by viewing through a wedge prism, influence of drugs, changes in the pattern constituting a visual framework, rotating an observer), one has a means of determining whether an effect was obtained on visual localization by comparing visual localization to localization by another sense modality. Of course, it is important that the influence on visual localization of the experimental operation not be confounded with influences on localization of the "nonvisual pointer," and for this reason it is generally desirable that the experimental variable exert no influence on the pointer when the concern is with the study of visual localization alone and the intended use of the "pointer" is to "point" to a visually perceived location.

2. CANCELLATION THEORY

2.1. The Two Kernels of Helmholtz

Helmholtz (1866/1963) originally proposed that stationary visual fields appear stationary when we turn our eyes because the

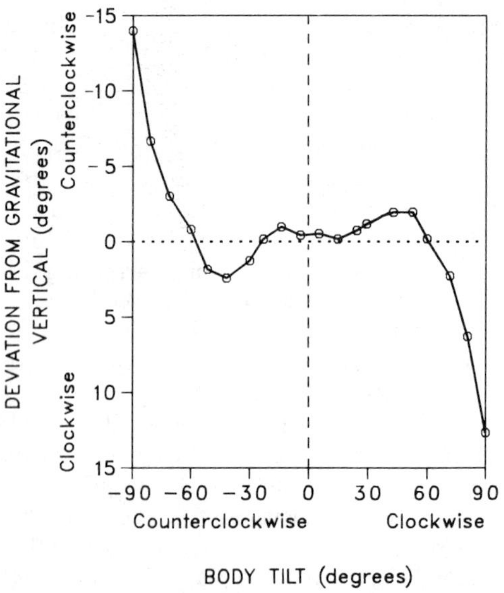

Figure 20.3. Visual vertical as a function of frontal-plane tilt of the observer. Setting of a visually perceived line in the frontal plane to appear vertical in complete darkness as a function of body tilt within the frontal plane of the observer. The setting at all body tilts is less than 15° from gravitational vertical although the retinal orientation of the image of the line set to vertical varies by at least 75° with the variation in body tilt. (From M. Bauermeister, Effect of body tilt on apparent verticality, apparent body position, and their relation, *Journal of Experimental Psychology*, *67*. Copyright 1964 by American Psychological Association. Reprinted with permission.)

"effort of will" in turning the eyes is taken into account. His proposal contains two kernel concepts, the first of which has provided the main basis for the predominant theoretical approach to the central problem regarding the involvement of eye movements and/or eye position change in visual localization. The two kernels are as follows:

1. Helmholtz's description suggests that the way in which the effort of will is taken into account by the process responsible for visual localization may be stated as follows:

$$\Delta VL = \Delta RI - \Delta EEPI$$

where VL is the perceptual response of visual localization, RI is retinal information, and EEPI designates extraretinal eye position information derived from the command to turn the eyes and/or point them in a specific direction. This algebraic relation is a statement of the cancellation theory (Figure 20.4). It defines a mechanism that performs algebraic subtraction between the two input variables to yield the perceptual output. As shown by the example in Figure 20.5, when the eye turns by 1° to the right, the retinal location stimulated by a given point in physical space is displaced by 1° to the right of the retinal point stimulated before the eye turn ($\Delta RI = +1$). If the map relating perceptual space to the retina remained rigid [Figure 20.5(b, left)] the perceived visual direction of each point in physical space would be displaced by 1° to the right ($\Delta VL = +1$; for this case EEPI = 0). For the case in which the cancellation mechanism is working as the theory predicts [compensatory mapping, Figure 20.5(b, right)], when $\Delta RI = +1$, then $\Delta EEPI = +1$ and $\Delta VL = 0$, leaving perceived visual directions stable.

2. The second kernel in Helmholtz's proposal is that the source of EEPI is directly derived from the command ("effort of will") to turn the eyes. Thus the proposal is that EEPI is conveyed to the mechanism processing visual localization by means of a signal that is fed forward from the mechanism initiating the movement rather than fed back as a signal derived from consequences of the movement itself. This theoretical fedforward signal has come to be referred to as an "outflowing signal."

Although linked historically, the two kernels of the theory have independent conceptual status. Cancellation theory does not require that EEPI be conveyed by a signal from an outflowing source. Nor is a subtractive cancellation mechanism the only mechanism by which an outflowing EEPI signal could be taken into account in determining visual localization.

2.2. Three Versions of Cancellation Theory: The Source of EEPI

Cancellation theory has been the basis for a number of influential treatments of the relation between visual localization and eye movements. The most frequent center of controversy has concerned the nature of the signal conveying EEPI to the mechanism responsible for determining visual localization. Other more recent versions of outflow theory include those by von Holst and Mittelstaedt (1950), von Holst (1954), Ludvigh (1952a, 1952b), and Merton (1964).

Although most workers have agreed that some second channel of information is required in addition to the pathway leading upstream from the retina, they have not all agreed that an outflowing channel serves that purpose. Alternative proposals for the second channel suggest that it contains signals from peripheral sense organs in the orbit that sense eye position either alone (inflow theory: James, 1890/1950; Sherrington, 1898, 1918) or modulated or combined with signals derived from commands to turn the eye (hybrid theory: Matin, 1972, 1976a; Shebilske, 1977). Thus three main sources for EEPI have been suggested: outflowing, inflowing, and hybrid (see Figure 20.6).

2.2.1. Helmholtz's Four Arguments for Outflow. Helmholtz's (1866/1963) basis for concluding that outflow was the source of EEPI consisted of four main points. Subsequent discussion and evidence (to be described below) have made them inconclusive and have reopened the question. Nevertheless, the four points remain as cogently reasoned focal points regarding the source of EEPI for visual localization and for some of our further discussion:

1. Helmholtz stated that individuals in whom a specific extraocular muscle is paralyzed see apparent motion when the attempt is made to turn the eye in the direction that would normally be controlled by the paralyzed muscle; the apparent motion is in the direction of the attempted eye turn. With no eye movement, no change in retinal spatial information is provided to the observer, and so Helmholtz reasoned that the appearance of visual movement must be due to the involvement of a second channel of information. Because there can be no

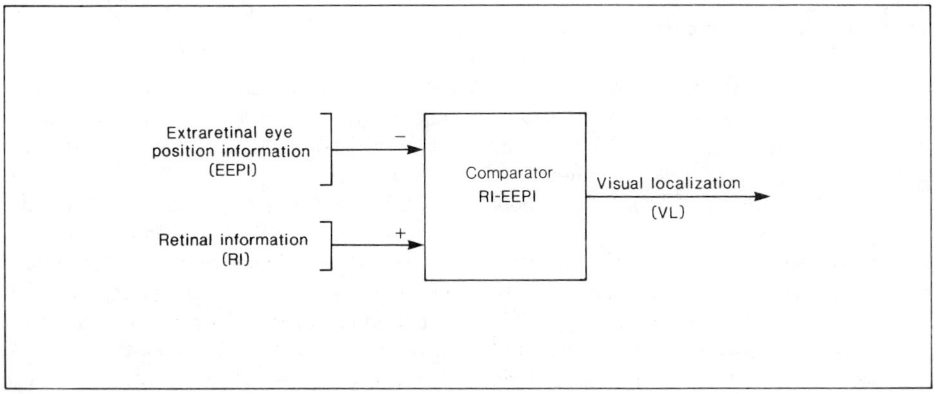

Figure 20.4. Cancellation theory for visual localization in the presence of eye movements. This is a representation of a class of theories that explain perceptual stability of visual direction in the presence of eye movements by assuming a neural mechanism that subtracts the magnitude of the registered eye movement (EEPI) from the magnitude of retinal image shift produced by the eye movement (RI).

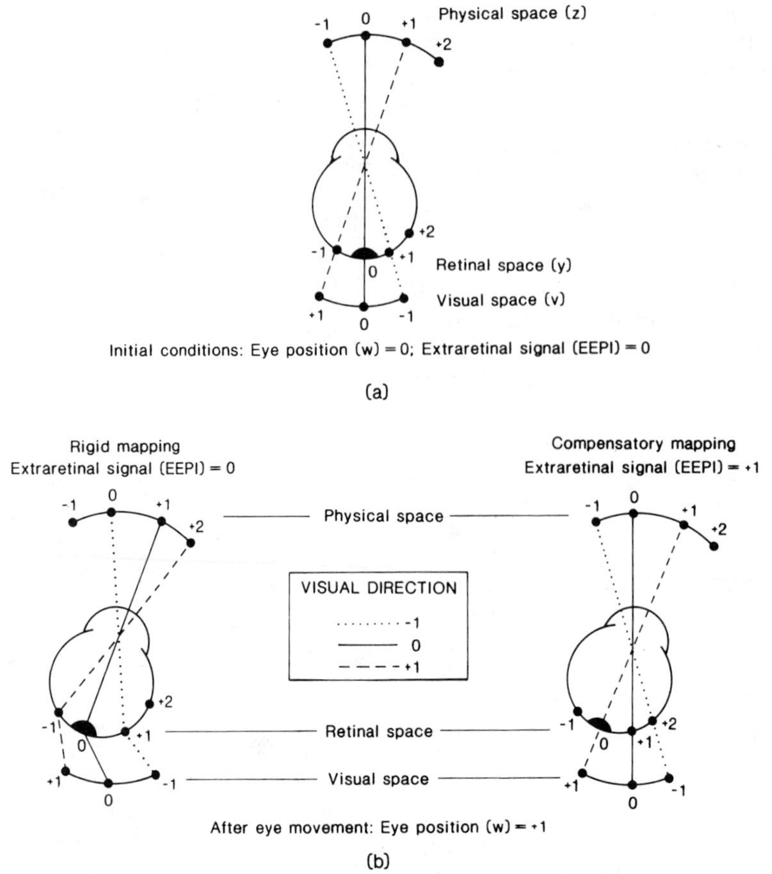

Figure 20.5. Relation between change in eye position, change of retinal location (retinal space) of a stationary target (physical space), and change in perceived location (visual space) of the target. View of an eye from above (a) while gaze is in some initial direction, and (b) following an eye movement that rotates the direction of gaze 1° to the right. The dark patch at the back of the eye represents the fovea. The figures show the relations between angular distances in the stimulus domain ("physical space"), at the retina ("retinal space"), and visually perceived directions psychophysically measured ("visual space") prior to the eye movement (a) and following the eye movement for two cases (b): left, no change has occurred in the relation between retinal locus stimulated and perceived visual direction ("rigid mapping"; cancellation theory is not operative), and right, the magnitude of change in the relation between retinal locus stimulated and perceived visual direction exactly compensates the magnitude of the eye movement ("compensatory mapping"; prediction from cancellation theory). This figure shows the consequences of cancellation theory in a quantitative-geometric format. (From L. Matin, Eye movements and perceived visual direction, in L. Hurvich & D. Jameson (Eds.), *Handbook of sensory physiology* (7/4), Springer-Verlag, Inc., 1972. Reprinted with permission.)

feedback from receptors sensing the consequences of eye movement if no eye movement occurs, the second channel of information must be due to an outflowing signal for EEPI: "... our judgment as to the direction of the visual axis is formed as if the will had produced its normal effects" (Helmholtz, 1866/1963, p. 245).

A command that results in no change in length of the extraocular musculature would produce no change in retinal information. The outflow model [Figure 20.6(a)] thus predicts that this combination of events would produce a change in visual localization, the inflow model [Figure 20.6(b)] predicts no change in visual localization, and the hybrid model [Figure 20.6(c)] predicts a change in visual localization only if the command to turn the eyes also changes the gamma motor input to the muscle spindles. [An alternative hybrid model that yields the same result was described by Matin, 1976a (completely alpha-dual-control system employing tendon organs or other retrobulbar sense organs), and it is recommended that the interested reader consider it.]

2. Referring to cases of incomplete clinical paralysis of an extraocular muscle, Helmholtz stated that the individual will pastpoint when reaching for an object with his arm; again he suggests that "... a wrong idea will be obtained of the direction of the visual axis and of the position of the object..." as a consequence of the fact that "... the impaired muscle requires a greater degree of innervation than would be needed under normal conditions..." (Helmholtz, 1866/1963, p. 245).

3. A push by an external object (e.g., a finger) that physically displaces the eye produces an appearance of movement of the visual field. Here, the push generates a change in retinal

image position. This is unaccompanied by the normal command to turn the eyes and so, Helmholtz reasoned, the outflowing source of EEPI is absent. The appearance of visual movement is thus to be regarded as a consequence of the cancellation mechanism receiving information regarding a retinal image shift unopposed by the normal outflowing EEPI that accompanies an eye-movement-produced retinal image shift. In addition, a mechanism that senses the mechanical consequences of an eye movement should sense the movement whether it was produced by a voluntary command to turn the eyes or by an external object pushing the eyes. Thus visual direction constancy in the face of eye movements can not be a consequence of an inflowing EEPI signal. If cancellation were mediated by an inflowing EEPI signal, no appearance of visual movement should result when the eye is pushed by an external object.

4. " . . . It is found that the positions of after-images in the closed eye, or as they are projected on a uniform screen of unlimited extent, appear to stay where they are while the eye is being pulled [Helmholtz indicates that the eye is moved by pulling on the skin near the eye], although, as a matter of fact, they do move with the eyes."

"On the other hand, while the eye is being pulled in this way, every movement of the eyes produced by the muscles leaves the apparent positions of external objects unchanged, whereas the after-images seem to move" (Helmholtz, 1866/1963, p. 244).

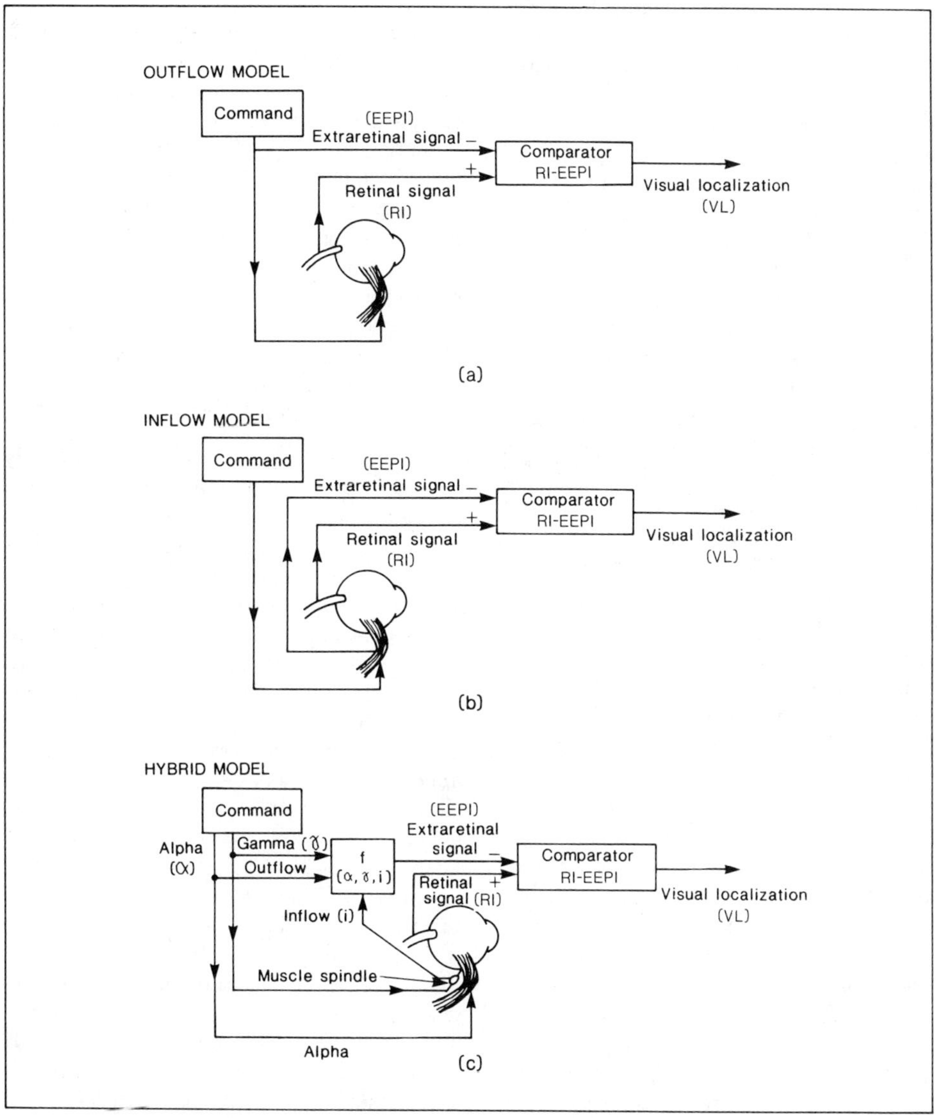

Figure 20.6. Three varieties of cancellation theory developed to explain stability of visual localization in the presence of eye movements. All three assume that extraretinal eye position information (EEPI) and information regarding shift of the image at the retina (RI) are added by a neural mechanism (comparator) whose output is "visual localization." The inflow theory proposes that EEPI is derived from retrobulbar receptors. The outflow theory proposes that EEPI is derived from a signal generated by the observer's motor command to turn the eye. The hybrid theory proposes that EEPI is an inflow signal derived from muscle spindle afferents but that outflow information contributes to the afferent consequences by modulating the stretch of the spindles via the gamma efferent motor fibers innervating the intrafusal muscles fibers of the spindles. (From L. Matin, Visual localization and eye movements, in A. Wertheim, W. A. Wagenaar, & H. Leibowitz (Eds.), *Tutorials on motion perception*, Plenum Publishing Corporation, 1982. Reprinted with permission.)

If an inflowing signal that corrects visual localization for the movements of the eye were present, the afterimage should appear to move in the direction in which the eye is turned (both active and passive eye turns); because no movement was observed by Helmholtz, he concluded that an inflowing signal was not present.

2.2.2. The Source of EEPI Has Not Yet Been Determined. Subsequent work has uncovered a number of difficulties with the Helmholtz argument. Some of these are noted here. In addition, several earlier reviews (Matin, 1972, 1976a) contain much neurophysiological material that remains relevant. A conclusion regarding the source of EEPI is not yet available. Although it is fairly clear that outflowing EEPI is involved in visual localization in darkness, it remains a judgment call rather than certainty; it also is not yet clear whether inflowing EEPI is involved at all. Some indication of the historical basis for the inconclusiveness is given here. Additional reasons are described below.

James (1890/1950) provided an explanation of the first three of Helmholtz's four main points in terms that employed an inflowing source of EEPI by assuming that afferent signals regarding eye position from the nonparalyzed eye were involved: (1) Because the nonparalyzed eye does move when an attempt to change gaze direction is made, inflowing signals from the unparalyzed eye would be provided that would not be canceled by the correct signals regarding changes of image location from the retina of the paralyzed eye. Such a disparity could yield unstable localizations of the kind to which Helmholtz referred. (2) Similarly, because pushing one eye produces no change in the inflowing signals from the eye that is not pushed, such inflowing signals could be a basis for the unstable localization when one eye is displaced. It is pertinent to this point that Ono and Nakamizo (1977) have reported that the posture of an occluded eye does influence visual localization of a target viewed with the other eye, a result that strongly suggests an inflow involvement in visual localization.

2.2.3. Other Evidence from Paralyzed-Eye Studies Opposing the Helmholtz Argument. Two other sets of observations discussed below provide difficulties for the argument as presented by Helmholtz. However, neither of them can be interpreted unequivocally at present.

2.2.3.1. No Perceived Displacement with the Completely Paralyzed Eye. Reports on a total of five observers from three different laboratories (Brindley, Goodwin, Kulikowski, & Leighton, 1976; Siebeck, 1954; Siebeck & Frey, 1953; Stevens, Emerson, Gerstein, Kallos, Neufeld, Nichols, & Rosenquist, 1976) have stated that when the extraocular muscles are completely paralyzed no visual movement or displacement of the visual field is visually perceived when the attempt is made (unsuccessfully) to turn the eye. Because the original argument for outflow theory and against inflow theory by Helmholtz relied heavily on the observation of movement when attempts were made to turn the paralyzed eye, the results appear to support the presence of an inflowing contribution to visual localization and against an outflowing contribution. However, there is a third possibility implied by more recent results (Matin, Picoult, Stevens, Edwards, Young, & MacArthur, 1980, 1982; Matin, Stevens, & Picoult, 1983): As far as can be determined from the published reports the observations by all the totally paralyzed observers were made under conditions in which no concern was given to the level of illumination or to the presence of visual structure normal to the carpentered environments in which the observations were made. But the observations with partially paralyzed observers (Matin, 1981; Matin et al., 1980, 1982; Matin et al., 1983) have shown that the use of cancellation for visual localization is strongly influenced by the presence of a normally illuminated and structured visual environment. Although it remains to be shown that this influence also holds for the totally paralyzed case, it is extremely likely that this is so, and that the previous observations of no visual movement or change in visual localization under total experimental paralysis during attempts to turn the totally paralyzed eye (noted above) have nothing to say about whether the source of EEPI is inflowing, outflowing, or hybrid because it is very likely that the observations were made in normally illuminated and structured visual environments.

2.2.3.2. Perceived "Jumping" Movement by the Partially Paralyzed Eye. Attempts to change the direction of gaze of a partially paralyzed eye result in an appearance of "jumping" at the time of the eye movement. Once the eye movement is completed, however, no appearance of visual displacement or other abnormal appearance linked to the eye movement is visible (Matin et al., 1982; Matin et al., 1983; Stevens et al., 1976). It is likely that this is the same phenomenon that Helmholtz reports for some patients with clinical paralysis of an extraocular muscle who try to turn the eye into the field of action of the paralyzed muscle. It is possible that "jumping" is a consequence of a mismatch between an outflowing EEPI signal and the shift of a target image's location on the retina in a cancellation mechanism. However, the following three observations raise the possibility that "jumping" has a different explanation:

1. The "jumping" observed by partially paralyzed observers is never observed during total paralysis (Stevens et al., 1976) as would be expected if it were a consequence of a mismatch between outflowing EEPI and the shift of retinal image location.

2. The jumping is accompanied by a failure of the first saccade to reach its goal. However, after subsequent saccades succeed in placing the central fovea on the original goal, the observer does not notice any further disturbance of visual localization; visual localization appears entirely normal during the subsequent steady fixation and as it was before the saccade. The "jumping" is a transient phenomenon. (The sequence of appearances is very close to, if not identical with, the sequence that accompanies a push or a pull of the normal observer's eyeball by an external object: a transient "jump" during the push, appearance of normality before and after the push). But if visual localization is undisturbed after the saccade either of two things must be true: (1) Under the conditions of observation in which "jumping" is alone observed (structured visual field), the cancellation mechanism deals only with the transients in visual localization related to saccades, and "jumping" is a manifestation of the mismatch of EEPI and RI for stimulation during the saccade; or (2) "jumping" is not a manifestation of a failure of cancellation but has some other basis. If the first is true, it must follow that some mechanism other than cancellation is responsible for visual localization during steady viewing in a normally illuminated and structured environment. [It is worth recalling here that an EEPI-based cancellation mechanism is responsible for constancy of visual localization during steady viewing in darkness (Section 1.2)]. If the second is true, and if "jumping" is the phenomenon of movement that was observed by the patients to whom Helmholtz refers, then it would also follow that the previously reported observations of movement with the paralyzed eye could not lead to a conclusion regarding

whether the source of EEPI is outflowing or inflowing. Further work will be required to clarify these matters. Thus regardless of whether (1) or (2) is true, the phenomenon of "jumping" with partially paralyzed eyes does not allow a ruling on whether the EEPI involved in visual localization is inflowing or outflowing.

3. The phenomenon of "jumping" appears sufficiently similar to a phenomenon observed during the production of parametric adjustment of saccade length that it is worth treating in the present context: Parametric adjustment was first described by McLaughlin (1966; also see Pola, 1976). Its description follows (Figure 20.7): An observer saccades from light A to light B in an otherwise dark visual field. During the saccade light B is extinguished by the experimenter and light C is simultaneously illuminated. On the first trial the observer's saccade carries the eye to the location where B had been; the eye immediately "corrects" by means of one or more following saccades and reaches C, where it remains fixated during the postsaccadic period. On subsequent trials the same stimulus sequence is followed and within 5–10 trials the length of the saccade is reduced to the distance A–C from its original length A–B. From the present point of view the interesting observations lie in the sequence of appearances that accompanies the adjustment in saccade length. On the first trial the observer notices a "jump" during the time period associated with the saccade. This "jump" is reduced and finally extinguished on subsequent trials in conjunction with the adjustment of saccade length. After parametric reduction in saccade length the observer reports that along with the disappearance of the jump, the appearance becomes one in which C as seen after the saccade appears to be identical with B before the saccade. There are three ways of interpreting the reduction in perception of the jump: (1) On the initial trial the saccade reaches its positional goal; EEPI is correct and the perception of the jump is a veridical perception of the occurrence in the stimulus world as signaled by the shift at the retinal image. (2) The jumping is a manifestation of the failure of the saccadic portion of the metacontrast-based suppression (see below) consequent on the abnormal saccadic stimulus. (3) The jumping is related to the failure of the saccade to reach its goal, a mismatch of expectation that is sensed by the observer noting that the target is not on the correct region of the retina. This observation would not require a cancellation mechanism for localization as such, but instead would be a manifestation of a cognitive mechanism (see MacKay, 1962, 1972, 1973). The fact that "jumping" is no longer visible when parametric adjustment of saccade length has taken place implies that the first explanation based on cancellation does not hold and increases the likelihood that the cognitive mismatch is responsible. Whatever the ultimate explanation of these instances of "jumping," the present evidence does not uniquely support an explanation based on mismatch of EEPI and RI in terms of cancellation theory.

2.3. Further Evaluation of Cancellation Theory

2.3.1. Steady Fixation and Partial Paralysis of Extraocular Muscle. Ever since Helmholtz's presentation (summarized in Section 2.2.1) the observations with paralysis have been viewed as providing the critical point of support for outflow as the source of EEPI involved in visual localization. Reviews of work relating observations on the paralyzed eye to the determination of the source of EEPI involved in spatial localization have been presented elsewhere (Matin, 1972, 1976a, 1982). The more recent results (Matin et. al., 1982) have uncovered a basis for the

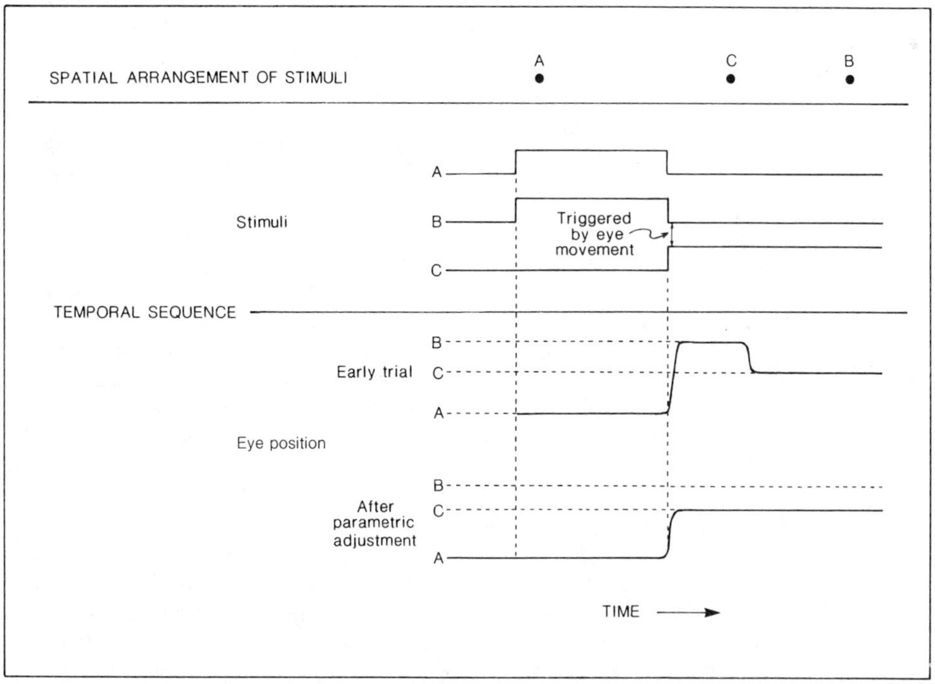

Figure 20.7. Stimulus arrangement for production of parametric adjustment of saccade length. A, B, and C represent three visual targets. The displacement of target B to location C is triggered by the saccade. During early trials the eye carries out a saccade to the location at which the target is seen before the saccade (to location B) and then corrects to the location at which the target appears after the saccade (to location C). On later trials, following parametric adjustment, the saccade takes the eye to location C directly.

conflicting reports but not yet disclosed the source of EEPI involved in localization; these results are described below.

2.3.1.1. ***Somatic Consequences of Paralysis.*** A brief comment on the somatic consequences of paralysis is worth making here by way of introducing those results. Chemical agents that induce paralysis do so by interfering with the mechanism of chemical transmission at the neuromuscular junction. Many of these paralytic agents do not cross the blood-brain barrier into the central nervous system; injection into the peripheral blood system produces paralysis of the somatic neuromuscular system without any diminution of cognitive abilities or confounding emotional effects. The interference with neuromuscular function can be complete or partial. In the case of partial paralysis, eye movements are possible but with reduced efficiency. A reduction in efficiency here means that a given neural bombardment arriving at the neuromuscular junction via the motor nerves will result in a weaker muscular contraction than in the untreated system. For the present case in which the reduction in efficiency is of an entire muscle group or of the entire somatic neuromuscular system of the individual, a number of poorly understood issues are involved in the microanalysis of reduced efficiency. But one thing is clear and it is this that provides the rationale for the employment of partial paralysis as the basis of a technique for analysis of the contribution of EEPI to visual localization: A given direction of gaze requires the same set of lengths in the six extraocular muscles of a normal (unparalyzed) individual as in those of the individual with reduced neuromuscular efficiency. But, in an actively contracting muscle operating with reduced junctional efficiency, an increase in the neural bombardment via the motor nerves is necessary to obtain the same length that will be obtained in the normal system. (Although a parallel paralytic reduction of the forces in antagonists may reduce this requirement of increased neural bombardment for a given muscle length in an active muscle, this may be expected to be a second-order effect.) Hence chemical production of partial paralysis of all six extraocular muscles controlling the position of an eye requires the observer to issue a different command to the neuromuscular system controlling the eye than the command required in the normal observer to attain the same position of ocular gaze.

2.3.1.2. ***Experimental Findings.*** The earlier observations with paralyzed extraocular muscles referred to above were carried out under the assumption that the cancellation mechanism is the exclusive agent for stabilization of visual localization. However, recent experiments in which the extraocular muscles were partially paralyzed with curare have shown that in normally illuminated and structured environments the physical location of the origin of egocentric coordinates is importantly influenced—and, under some conditions, can be completely determined—by features of the visual surroundings (Matin et al., 1982). The main results leading to that conclusion are displayed in Figures 20.8–20.10. Three main sorts of psychophysical discriminations were employed: (1) settings of a visual target to the observer's median plane (Figure 20.8); (2) setting of a visual target to the eye-level horizontal (Figure 20.9); (3) matching locations of a sound and light, both of whose locations were variable in the eye-level horizontal plane (Figure 20.10). With the room in normal illumination, median plane and eye-level horizontal settings (taken as in Figure 20.2) were made accurately by both the normal and the partially paralyzed observer regardless of gaze eccentricity. However, in darkness the curarized observer made large errors—systematic with gaze eccentricity—in both median plane and eye-level horizontal settings, although the settings of the normal observer in darkness were only slightly different from his settings in normal room illumination (Figures 20.8 and 20.9). These errors were a portion of those that together were labeled the "oculoparalytic illusion." If one were to look at only the settings made in normal room illumination one might conclude that the use of EEPI for visual localization was unaffected by the paralysis and the cancellation mechanism was still functioning entirely normally. However, the errors of the curarized individual in darkness—as large as 20°—leave no doubt that the curare did have a profound effect on the visual localization of both the median plane and the eye-level horizontal.

The results in Figures 20.8 and 20.9 raise two main questions: (1) What is the basis of the errors in localization of the curarized individual in darkness? (2) How was the influence of the curare negated by the presence of normal illumination?

(a) Basis for Localization Errors by the Curarized Observer. Four kinds of observations contribute to the answer to the first question. The first two sets of observations rule out some possible answers: (1) No large errors in gaze direction were involved in the errors of localization. That the observer was in fact foveating in the direction of the fixation target specified by the experimenter was ascertained by use of a fixation target that would have been unresolvable if it stimulated the retina at as little as 2° away from the fovea. (2) The errors of localization were a simple function of the angle of the eye in the orbit (as displayed in Figures 20.8 and 20.9) and unrelated to the angle of the head and/or body relative to gravity. This followed from the fact that the results in Figures 20.8 and 20.9 were unchanged when the measurements were repeated with the head and body tilted at different angles frontward and backward relative to the frontal plane of the observer.

Two additional aspects of the observations led to the conclusion that the errors of localization were a consequence of the cancellation mechanism treating the eye as if it were deviated further in the orbit than it actually was: (1) The localization errors increased linearly in each direction of gaze from a "no-illusion direction." For the eye-level-horizontal settings this increase was in the upward direction for downward directions of gaze and in the downward direction for upward directions of gaze; a similar result held around a no-illusion direction in the horizontal plane for the median plane settings. The no-illusion direction for the eye-level horizontal also was the direction for which the target appeared to move neither up nor down when room illumination was extinguished, although for all gaze directions above the no-illusion direction the fixation target appeared to move upward on extinction of room illumination and for all gaze directions below the no-illusion direction the fixation target appeared to move downward. This set of phenomena together indicates that for the eye of the curarized individual to reach a given direction of gaze the individual's effort had to increase by the same factor at all directions of gaze relative to the effort that the uncurarized observer exerted to reach the same direction of gaze. This conforms to the way in which a reduction in neuromuscular junctional efficiency would be expected to operate. Although only a segment of the set of curves in Figure 20.11 has so far been measured, it is clear that the main characteristics of the figure accurately represent the variation in visual localization with level of partial paralysis. (2) Figure 20.11 shows not only that increasing the level of paralysis brought about a change of the slope of the function relating localization error and gaze direction, but also that the range of

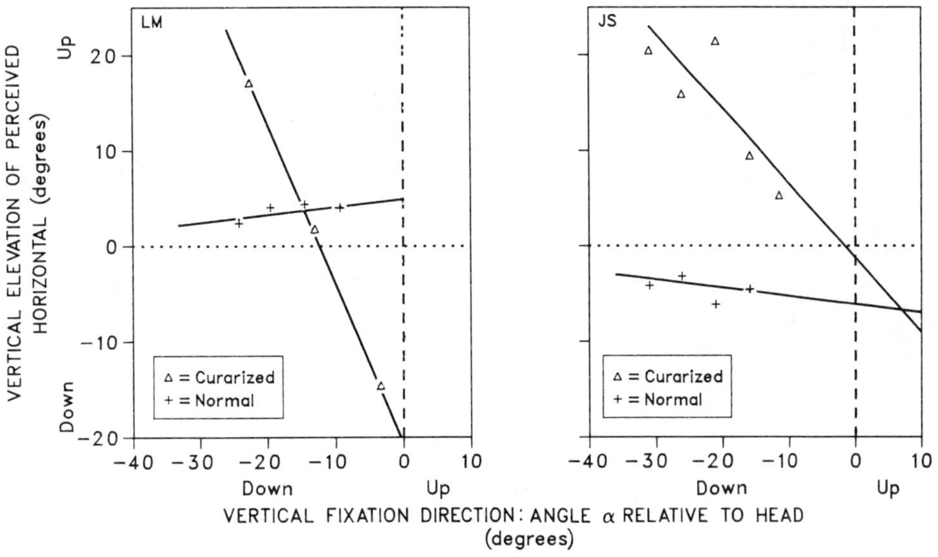

(a)

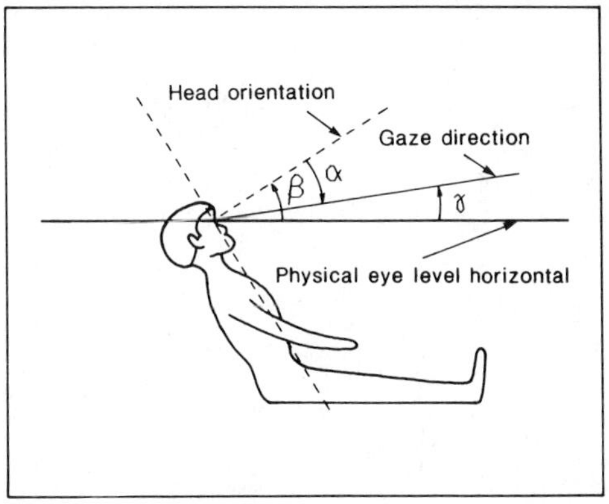

(b)

Figure 20.8. Errors in visually perceived eye-level horizontal resulting from curare-induced partial paralysis. (a) Setting of a visual target to eye-level horizontal (ordinate) as a function of the vertical position of the eye in the orbit (angle α; abscissa) by subjects LM and JS during partial paralysis of the extraocular muscles ("curare") and when normal (not paralyzed). Settings were made in total darkness. (b) Sketch of the observer indicating the direction of the head relative to the horizontal (angle β), the angle of fixation relative to the head (angle α), and the angle of gaze relative to the horizontal (angle γ). Curarized observers make large vertical errors in visually localizing eye-level horizontal; these errors are linearly related to vertical gaze eccentricity. (From L. Matin, E. Picoult, J. K. Stevens, M. W. Edwards, Jr., D. Young,. & R. MacArthur, Oculoparalytic illusion: Visual field dependent spatial mislocalizations by humans with experimentally paralyzed extraocular muscles, *Science, 216*. Copyright 1982 by Amrican Association for the Advancement of Science. Reprinted with permission.)

eye positions possible also decreased with increase in dose level. Along with this decrease in the maximum eccentricity of gaze was an increase in localization error at this limit whose amount appears to equal the reduction in maximum gaze eccentricity. The observers noted that at the gaze limit they seemed to be exerting the same maximum effort at all levels of paralysis. The results are thus in line with the conclusion that the errors in localization by the partially paralyzed eye are equal to the increase in effort above the effort required for the unparalyzed observer to place his eye in a given direction of gaze.

(b) Type B Suppression: Why Visual Localization Is Accurate in an Illuminated Environment Under Paralysis. The above account of the basis for the localization errors of the curarized observers is obviously not the whole story, however. It provides no explanation for the accuracy of median plane and eye-level-horizontal settings in illuminated environments. There are two parts to such an explanation, which build on the account given above. The first part demonstrates that EEPI is not itself suppressed in an illuminated environment as might have been concluded from the results in Figures 20.8 and 20.9. The second part is concerned with the way in which the EEPI-based cancellation mechanism is involved in visual localization in the illuminated environment.

The conclusion that EEPI is not suppressed in an illuminated environment is drawn from the results in Figure 20.10, where

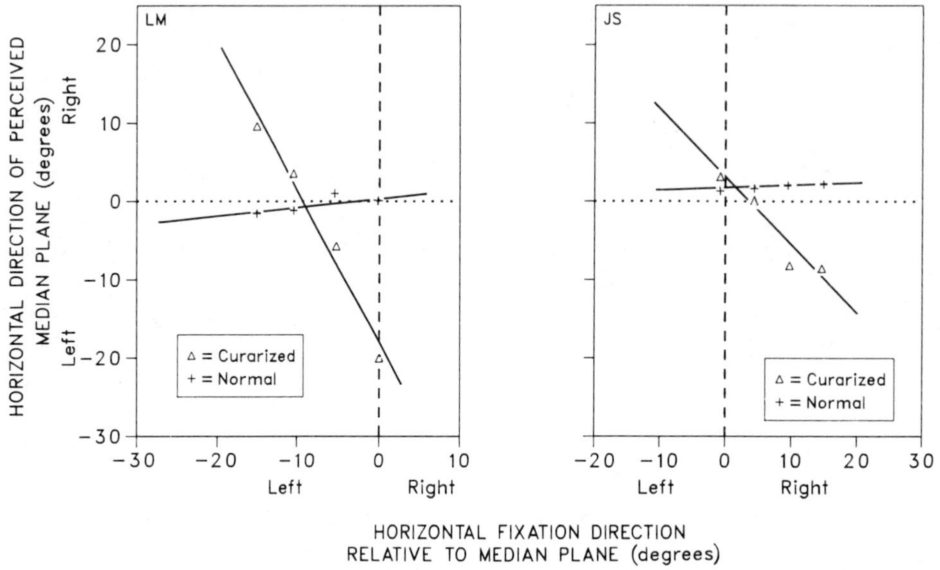

Figure 20.9. Errors in visually perceived median plane resulting from curare-induced partial paralysis. Settings of a single visual target to the median plane (ordinate) as a function of the horizontal position of the eye in the orbit (abscissa) by subjects LM and JS during partial paralysis of the extraocular muscles ("curare") and when normal (not paralyzed). Settings were made in total darkness. Curarized observers make large errors in visually localizing the horizontal direction of their median planes; these errors are linearly related to horizontal gaze eccentricity. (From Matin, E. Picoult, J. K. Stevens, M. W. Edwards, Jr., D. Young, & R. MacArthur, Oculoparalytic illusion: Visual field dependent spatial mislocalization by humans with experimentally paralyzed extraocular muscles, *Science, 216*. Copyright 1982 by American Association for the Advancement of Science. Reprinted with permission.)

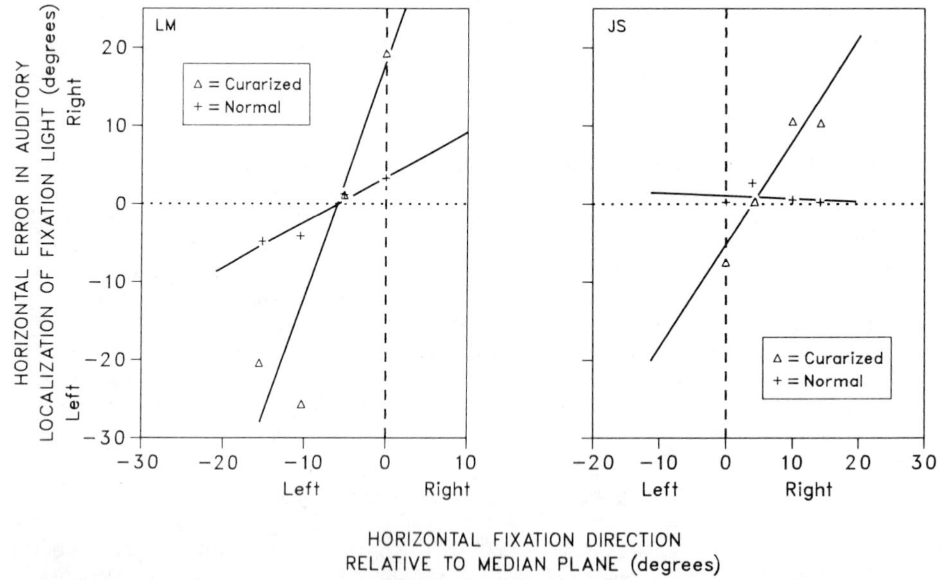

Figure 20.10. Visual/auditory localization matches as a function of horizontal gaze eccentricity. Error in selecting a loudspeaker from a horizontally distributed array of loudspeakers whose horizontal location appeared to match that of the fixated visual target is plotted as a function of the horizontal direction of fixation for observers LM and JS during partial paralysis of the extraocular muscles ("curare") and when normal (not paralyzed). Settings were made in total darkness. (From L. Matin, E. Picoult, J. K. Stevens, M. W. Edwards, Jr., D. Young, & R. MacArthur, Oculoparalytic illusion: Visual field dependent spatial mislocalization by humans with experimentally paralyzed extraocular muscles, *Science, 216*. Copyright 1982 by American Association for the Advancement of Science. Reprinted with permission.)

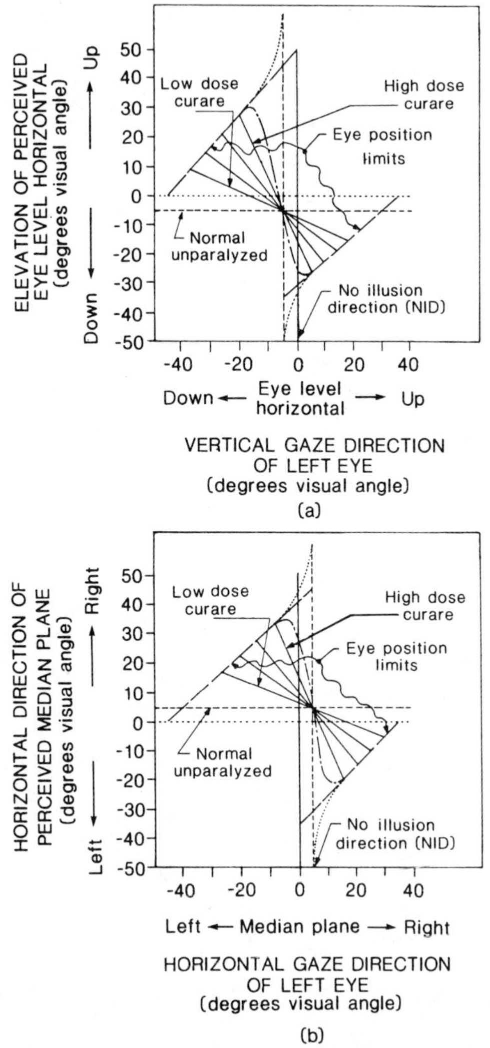

Figure 20.11. Functions relating error of visual localization to direction of gaze under various levels of paralysis. (a) Visually perceived direction of eye-level horizontal (ordinate) as a function of vertical gaze direction (abscissa). (b) Visually perceived direction of median plane (ordinate) as a function of horizontal gaze direction (abscissa). Illusion magnitude in (a) and (b) is equal to the negative of the ordinate value. Uncertainty regarding the outcome around total paralysis (0° range of possible eye movement) is indicated by the dotted lines (which suggests that the errors increase asymptotically), the dot-dash lines (which suggests a drop to zero of the localization errors), and the diagonal dashed lines (showing a simple intersection of the limit functions with the no-illusion direction). The figures show the linear relation between error of visual localization and gaze eccentricity as well as the increased error with increase in level of paralysis. It is also worth noting that the range of eye positions that can be spanned decreases with increase in dosage level (range of possible eye positions at a given dosage level is the horizontal distance between the two ends of the linear function for that dosage), and that the localization error at the limiting eye position is equal to the negative of the reduction in the range of eye positons from the range possible for the normal observer. In other words, whatever is lost in eye position range is "made up" in illusion magnitude. (From L. Matin, J. Stevens, & E. Picoult, Perceptual consequences of experimental extraocular muscle paralysis, in A. Hein & M. Jeannerod (Eds.), *Spatially oriented behavior*, Springer-Verlag, Inc., 1983. Reprinted with permission.)

it is shown that the errors of the curarized individual in making auditory-to-visual matches of location in the horizontal plane are no different in normal illumination from those in darkness, a result in marked contrast to the results in Figures 20.8 and 20.9, which show that the errors in median plane and eye-level-horizontal settings that occur in darkness are not present in the illuminated environment. The errors in the auditory-to-visual matches in both illumination and darkness followed the same function of gaze eccentricity as did the errors in median plane settings in darkness; and because the curare did not influence auditory localization per se it was clear that the auditory-to-visual matches displayed the presence of curare-caused errors in EEPI in the illuminated environment that were not observed in the median plane and eye-level-horizontal settings.

The errors in auditory-to-visual localization matches of the curarized observer were not present when, with eccentric gaze, the partially paralyzed observer viewed an individual talking (also see Picoult, MacArthur, Young, Edwards, Stevens, & Matin, 1980). That is, the voice did not appear to be displaced by 15°, for example, from the person's mouth when fixation of the person's mouth was with gaze 15° eccentric to primary position. The substantial errors in auditory-to-visual matches of the curarized observer when selecting one of 25 differently located loudspeakers to match the location of the fixated light were thus a consequence of the fact that the loudspeakers were freed from "visual capture"; that is, the observer had no visual information regarding which of the 25 differently located loudspeakers generated the sound, whereas in the case of an individual talking, the temporal correlation of sound and mouth movement provided the basis for overriding the auditory clues to auditory localization.

Mechanisms related to visual capture provide the basis for the accuracy of visual median plane settings. The observers were able to see their own bodies at the same time they viewed the target being set under the instruction to the median plane of their bodies. They were thus able to visually align the two visual items, an alignment that was done accurately. When this was done there was no impression of conflict on the part of the observer with another potential setting based on a cancellation mechanism; the basis for the median plane setting was thus entirely suppressed by the presence of a visual alignment.

Both visual capture of auditory localization and the capture of the visual median plane setting by the visual framework (with suppression of the basis for the setting by the cancellation mechanism) are cases in which an intermodal conflict has been resolved by suppressing one of the possible bases for localization. This has been labeled type B suppression to distinguish it from intramodal suppression (type A suppression; Matin, 1983).

2.3.2. Cancellation During Voluntary Saccades. The fact that the visual field does not appear to move or change location when we voluntarily turn our eyes from one gaze direction to another has often been presented as the prime example of the operation of an EEPI-based cancellation mechanism. In fact, the participation of the cancellation mechanism is important in relation to perceptual stability in the presence of voluntary saccades. However, the simple observation of perceptual stability belies a great deal of complexity in processing that involves considerably more than EEPI-based cancellation. The complexity involves mechanisms governing several processes in vision that have no unique connection to cancellation per se. These include visual persistence and the major (but not exclusive) factor in saccadic suppression (visual masking by metacontrast—as well as other factors related to eye movement). This is discussed in detail in several sections below. The concern in this section is only to make clear that an interpretation based simply on a cancellation mechanism yields predictions regarding localization for stimulation during voluntary saccades that are not in accord with experimental results, and thus to prove the point that mechanisms other than EEPI-based cancellation are central to the production of perceptual stability in the presence of voluntary saccades.

A prediction from cancellation theory of visual localization of a flash presented during a saccade is shown in Figure 20.12. This prediction derives from a strong form of the theory that assumes that cancellation between retinal information (RI) and EEPI (Figure 20.4) proceeds correctly at each moment before, during, and after a saccade, an assumption that is necessary if cancellation itself is to be the main basis for perceptual stability in the presence of voluntary saccades. Brief flashes were presented at specific known points in the saccade to specific retinal loci. The observer reported the direction at which the flash was seen relative to the previously viewed fixation target that was extinguished before the saccade began. Any failure of constancy of visual localization indicates a failure of the cancellation mechanism. In fact, such mislocalizations—failures of cancellation—are the norm in Figure 20.12. Other failures with brief flashes are described below. Those include (1) large influences of visual backgrounds on the magnitude of the mislocalizations; (2) no mislocalizations in some instances in which cancellation predicts that they should occur; and (3) trial-to-trial variability in visual localization of brief flashes that is very much larger (100–2,000 times) than the variability for similar localization judgments for the steadily fixating eye. If such large disparities were occurring during normal viewing of steadily presented visual fields as occur for the brief flashes presented in the temporal neighborhood of saccades they would be clearly visible as major breakdowns of perceptual stability of visual localization. But, although breakdowns of perceptual stability are readily produced with brief flashes, breakdowns of stability for steadily presented visual fields are extremely unusual; although they can be produced under certain conditions of extremely low illumination (Matin, Matin, & Pearce, 1969) they are not generally reported. It must be concluded, therefore, that perceptual stability in the presence of voluntary saccades normally involves more than simple moment-to-moment cancellation between RI and EEPI; further considerations regarding the relation between visual localization and voluntary saccades are discussed in the following sections.

2.3.3. Additional Considerations. Three other sets of results are pertinent to the inflow-outflow question:

1. Skavenski (1972) showed that inflowing EEPI was available for controlling eye position. Thus in darkness observers whose eyes were displaced from a fixation position by a maintained force were able to return the eye to near the original position. Whether this EEPI is available for visual localization as well as for the control of eye position is not yet clear. The fact that Skavenski's observers were also able to report on the direction of eye pull by the externally imposed force is in apparent disagreement with the earlier observations of Brindley and Merton (1960), whose observers could not report that their eye positions had been changed when externally forced eye turns of as much as 40° were imposed. Matin (1972, 1976a) suggested that the differences between Skavenski's and Brindley and Merton's results were due to the passivity of Brindley and Merton's observers, whereas Skavenski's were actively trying to do things with their eyes. Because the gamma motor system is under voluntary control, passivity would tend to release tonus in muscle spindles and reduce the possibility of useful inflowing signals whereas active attempts at doing things with the eyes would tend to maintain the presence of useful inflowing signals.

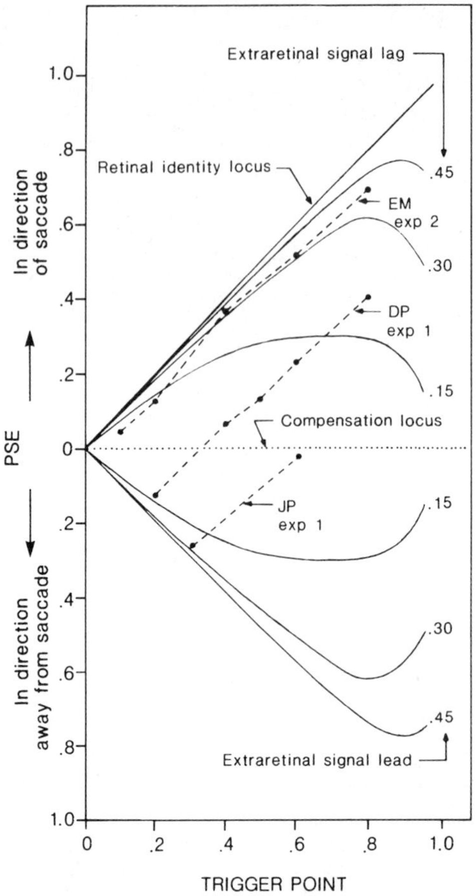

Figure 20.12. Comparison of data with a strong form of cancellation theory that predicts a moment-to-moment compensation of visual direction for changes in eye position. The observer compared the location of a 1-msec test flash presented at different points ("trigger point") during a 2° 11 min saccade (Experiment 1) or a 4° 22 min saccade (Experiment 2) to the location of a previously viewed fixation target; the saccade was carried out in complete darkness. Theoretical curves are shown for cases in which the cancellation process is exact or in which the extraretinal signal is assumed to lead or to lag the retinal signal by various proportions of the saccade duration. All the results are parallel to the retinal identify locus, indicating failure of the cancellation model. Thus either the cancellation process was not operative at all for stimulation during the saccade, or it was so slow that concellation had not yet begun until much after the saccade was complete. Displacement from the retinal identify locus was different for each observer, indicating some constant error related to the occurrence of a saccade, but such an error is not relatable to the cancellation model, which requires conformation to the compensation locus, nor is it relatable to the cancellation model with a latency mismatch, which requires conformation to one of the other theoretical curves. (From Matin, E. Matin, & D. G. Pearce, Visual perception of direction when voluntary saccades occur: In relation of visual direction of a fixation target extinguished before a saccade to a flash presented during the saccade, *Perception and Psychophysics*, 1969, *5*. Reprinted with permission.)

This interpretation attempts to resolve the disagreement by calling on a hybrid source of EEPI.

2. Stark and Bridgeman (1983) have reconsidered the effects of displacing the eye by use of finger pressure and conclude, in agreement with Helmholtz, that the results support an outflow source for EEPI within the cancellation mechanism responsible for controlling visual localization in the presence of eye movements. However, their analysis of the situation is very different from the analysis of Helmholtz.

They first note that an eye press produces ocular translation and not a rotation of the eye from a previous direction of gaze that lay at the basis of the Helmholtz argument. This conclusion was arrived at by measuring the magnitude of the perceived displacement of the projection of a viewed point on to a more distant screen; with the fixated point halfway distant to the screen the geometry of the sighting requires that the perceived displacement at the screen equal the ocular translation produced by the eye press, a distance they measure as ranging from 3 to 6 mm. This translation of the eye in the orbit must, of course result in a shift of the location of the retinal image of the point of fixation unless accompanied by a compensating ocular rotation. Because the observer is attempting to maintain fixation, he must issue a new command to keep the fovea centered on the point of fixation. Stark and Bridgeman demonstrate that the change in motor command does take place as expected by pressing the viewing eye in monocular viewing and measuring the yoked eye movements of the occluded eye; appropriate movements of the nonviewing eye did occur while the attempt to fixate was maintained but not when the eye press was carried out in darkness.

Stark and Bridgeman also obtained localization matches between pointing and vision and between audition and vision and report displacements of about 3° between matches made before and during the eye press. Because these displacements were obtained in both darkness and in structured visual fields they conclude, as did Matin et al. (1980, 1982) from the experiments with curare-induced partial paralysis, that the presence of a structured visual field suppresses the use of EEPI for visual localization.

Stark and Bridgeman attempt to go further and conclude that the perception of motion and displacement consequent on eye press is due to the outflow involved in maintaining fixation against the finger pressing on the eye, and not to inflow. However, Hershberger (1984) reports that eye press can be accompanied by apparent movement either with or against the direction of the eye press, and concludes that although one of these may reflect outflow involvement, the other must correspond to an involvement of inflow, an argument that Bridgeman and Delgado (unpublished ms) dispute.

3. Steinbach and Smith (1981) have measured the accuracy of pointing to a visual target by strabismic observers following extraocular muscle surgery and report that without any postoperative visual experience with the operated eye (although with up to 2 days experience with the nonoperated eye) the errors in pointing are only about 25% of the surgical realignment of the eyes. Because the operated eye requires a different motor command to acquire a given posture after the operation than before the operation, they conclude that visual localization of the target must involve inflowing EEPI. However, their result holds only for individuals who have undergone operation for the first time. Those who undergo second operations on the same muscles make postoperative errors in pointing that do not differ significantly from the magnitude of the strabismic correction.

The strabismic provides an interesting case for further analysis. Rogan, Eggers, and Matin (1983) have reported that strabismic observers are able to localize with considerable accuracy with each eye when matching against an auditory target as in Figure 20.10. But the monocular match with one eye was made with a different ocular posture of both eyes than when the match was made with the other eye, and the difference in match was close to (but not generally equal to the strabismic deviation). This result implies that when localization was with the left eye EEPI was more heavily related to signals regarding posture of the left eye, but when localization was with the right eye EEPI weighted signals from the right eye more heavily, a quasi-independence in the use of EEPI for the strabismic that is not unlike the independence of arm position information between the two arms of normal individuals.

The bottom line on the controversy regarding the source of EEPI for visual localization, then, has not yet been written. It must be either outflowing or hybrid, but cannot be inflowing alone. There is clearly more to be learned.

3. LOCAL SIGNS, REFERENCE DIRECTIONS, AND THE SPATIAL METRIC

3.1. The Approach via Local Signs

The most elementary fact of visual space perception is that the spatial order of stimulus points in the retinal image of the visual field is preserved correctly in perception. A number of classical writers [Helmholtz, 1866/1963; Hering, 1879/1942; James, 1890/1950; Lotze, 1886; Mach, 1885/1959; Wundt, 1863 (referred to in James, 1890/1950, p. 155)] have written about a theory of "local signs" with this fact at its center. The approach remains important today for a number of aspects of space perception including those concerned with visual localization. Although substantial differences have existed historically among classical writers and exist today among current workers regarding innateness and various other aspects of the arrangement, there was and is general agreement that visual perception of direction is mediated in the visual neurosensory pathway by a system of local signs that topographically maps locations of retinal stimuli into values of perceived direction. This viewpoint generally assumes that a foveally fixated point is perceived as lying in what may be called the principal visual direction. An object whose image strikes any other retinal point is then perceived at a distance to the left, right, above, or below this principal direction in accordance with the direction and distance values of the stimulated point relative to the fovea. Apart from any considerations regarding the neuroanatomical, genetic, or developmental basis of such a map or its modifiability, the perceived visual direction associated with stimulation of a particular retinal point is referred to as the local sign of that retinal point. An important concern of these approaches has been to deal with the main concern of this chapter—the question of how local signs are modified when gaze direction is changed.

Investigations of space perception do not always depend on the use of the principal visual direction as a reference direction. In fact, most of the matters considered in the context of local signs have been concerned with relations between visual directions without any reference to the principal direction and frequently without any explicit use of reference directions at all. Some considerations regarding the role of reference directions in localization follow.

3.2. Reference Directions and Observers' Reports

The term "perceived visual direction" refers to a subjective state of affairs and the term "subjective visual direction" is often used to emphasize this. The term "visual direction" employed alone has been used to refer either to this subjective state of affairs or to the physical direction of a line of sight. (The reader is generally left to infer which of the two very different meanings is intended by the context.) The observer may report the subjective state of affairs in a number of different ways. These reports are often described as belonging in one of two classes: "egocentric" or "object-centered."

Reports of the egocentric visual direction of an object reference it to some direction perceived by the observer as centered on his own body; the reference direction may be perceived visually, or proprioceptively, or auditorily, or via some combination of these modes, or, as is often the case, without clearly belonging to any one sensory modality. Object-centered reports make no explicit reference to the observer. Some examples of egocentric direction reports for the position of a visual stimulus are "to the left of my median plane," "to the left of where I am looking," "10° to the left of my median plane." Some examples of object-centered reports of perceived visual direction are "to the left of the reference stimulus," or "to the left of the visual target that was present a short time ago," or "to the left of the sound." Each of these designations is a verbal report that can be the basis of a valid measurement procedure for assessing the subjective state of affairs, that is, of objectively (psychophysically) measuring the perceived visual direction and ascertaining an aspect of the local sign of a given retinal point. Of course, both egocentric and object-centered reports may be given simultaneously for the same visual object.

Egocentric and object-centered visual directions refer to different aspects of the spatial relations among objects and the observer. Thus differences in objective spatial relations among observer and objects in the environment can yield (1) differences in the egocentric direction of an object with or without any difference in the object-centered visual direction of that object, (2) differences in the object-centered visual direction of an object with or without any difference in the egocentric direction of that object, or (3) differences in both egocentric and object-centered visual directions of the object (Figure 20.13). Whether differences in egocentric and/or object-centered visual directions give rise to differences in perceived visual directions is generally contingent on additional relations within the visual field and of the observer to it.

The division of reports of perceived visual direction into "egocentric" and "object-centered" is based solely on the phenomenology of the reports and does not pertain to specific differences in implied coordinate systems underlying the reports or to differences in objectivity or subjectivity of the reports. Thus an egocentric judgment of the location of an object by an observer is not any more independent of perceived spatial relations to other objects than is an object-centered judgment. Egocentric reports are as "object-relative" as are object-centered reports. But the object to which the judgment is relative in egocentric reports is either a part or a location within the observer's own body. For example, when the observer reports that the visual stimulus is "to the left of my median plane," he is referring the stimulus to his perception of the location of a portion of his own body. In the case of a norm such as the "median plane," the "reference object" of perception is a direction rather than a thing, but it generally (although not necessarily) has objective reference (i.e., the location of the true median plane is measurable by the experimenter) just as does the location of an object, and thus provides as good an example of the object-relative nature of egocentric judgments as would an egocentric judgment relative to an object (e.g., "to the left of my nose").

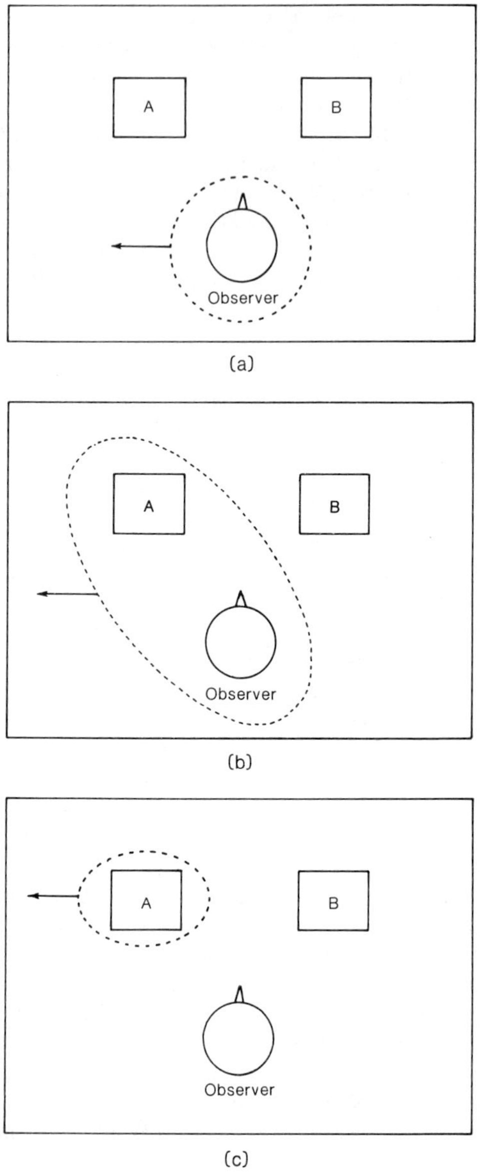

Figure 20.13. Egocentric and object-centered directions are differently determined. (a) Displacement of the observer to the left alone produces a difference in the egocentric visual direction of object A for the observer with no change in the object-centered visual direction of A relative to B; (b) displacement of object A and the observer with no change in their physical relation produces a difference in the object-centered visual direction of A relative to stationary object B but no difference in the egocentric visual direction of object A; (c) displacement of object A alone produces correlated differences in the egocentric direction of object A and the object-centered visual direction of object A relative to object B.

Frequently, however, the modality by means of which the norm is sensed is not readily stated, if statable at all, by the observer.

Thus egocentric judgments are no more nor less subjective than object-centered judgments, and object-centered visual directions depend as much on the relation of the observer to perceived objects as do egocentric visual directions. Still, in spite of their many commonalities, egocentric and object-centered judgments appear uniquely different in subjective quality to the observer; the phenomenological difference is normally of an "irreducible" nature not unlike the unbridgeable subjective difference between a sound and a sight.

Observers are extremely flexible in specifying the location of visual objects with respect to reference directions, whether the reference direction is visual or nonvisual. But certain directions are much more readily used by observers as reference direction in reporting visual directions than are others. For example, only two (egocentric) visual reference directions are generally employed in specifying the horizontal location of a visual target in darkness: "the direction in which I am looking," or "my median plane." The first is the principal egocentric direction whose physical correlate is centered on the central fovea (and is often referred to as "oculocentric"). The second is an egocentric direction centered on either the observer's head or body; it is often referred to as the "straight ahead." Similarly, only two (egocentric) visual reference directions are employed in specifying the vertical location of a visual target in darkness: "the direction in which I am looking," and "eye level" or "horizontal." [Each of the latter two terms is ambiguous alone. "Eye level" in the case of the head tilted back could refer to the direction perpendicular to the frontal plane of the head (the principal direction which, with head tilted, is not horizontal) or to the horizontal direction through the eyes. "Horizontal" could only refer to a direction perpendicular to gravity but by itself does not imply an origin and hence does not specify a unique direction line. Thus I employ the term "eye-level horizontal" to provide a visual direction with unambiguous origin.]

Not only is the "meaning" of these certain directions (median plane, eye-level horizontal, direction in which observer is looking) more readily communicated by language than are other egocentric directions, but they also appear to be directions against which other visual directions or locations are reported with greatest acuity. This is similar to the situation that holds for other kinds of acuity against other visual norms [e.g., resolution and detection acuity as well as vernier acuity is normally best within the frontoparallel plane for straight lines presented vertically or horizontally; these acuities are normally poorest at orientations intermediate within the frontoparallel plane ("oblique effect"; Appelle, 1972)]. Thus these reference directions do have some claim to centrality if not to uniqueness. The two main egocentric reference directions for horizontal and vertical visual direction differ in an important way: the eye-level horizontal is defined with respect to a stimulus arising from outside the body, the direction of the force of gravity, and a given direction in space retains the definition regardless of the orientation of the observer; the median plane is defined only with respect to body-centered coordinates and although (of course) it holds its relation to the body regardless of the orientation of the body in space, the relation of eye-level horizontal and median plane changes with the orientation of the body in space. Thus the two main egocentric reference directions in the frontal plane do not maintain an invariant relation to each other. Also, because there is no stimulus analogous to gravity that polarizes physical space in a horizontal plane, there is no unique direction in the horizontal plane outside the observer that serves to relate him to the environment as does gravity in the vertical plane. Any uniqueness of particular directions then arises only from either visual stimuli or directionally polarized stimuli in other sense modalities.

Egocentric reference directions for location become more difficult to specify for the observer whose head (and/or body) is tilted relative to gravity within his or her frontal plane while the frontal plane remains erect. But the "natural" reference frame for localization seems not to change from the one employed with body and head erect. Thus "above" and "below" eye-level horizontal seem to be the "natural" way of specifying the vertical egocentric visual direction. Similarly, "to the left" and "to the right" of a vertical that intersects both eye-level horizontal and the median plane seem to be the "natural" way of specifying the horizontal egocentric visual direction. It seems considerably less "natural" to specify "to the left" relative to the tilted median plane of the head. Although this suggests that the perceived median plane is only normally used as a primary reference for localization of visual targets when the head is symmetrically disposed relative to a vertical plane and not otherwise, when the body is tilted so that in addition to the median plane being tilted relative to vertical the frontal plane is also tilted relative to vertical, then the "natural" pair of reference directions becomes the median plane (relative to which "left" and "right" are specified) and a plane through the eyes perpendicular to the median plane (relative to which "above" and "below" are specified). Though agreement among individuals regarding "natural" reference directions for different body orientations is high, the basis for the change with body orientation and for "naturalness" remains to be determined.

3.3. Some Considerations Regarding Relations Among Behavior, Development, Neurophysiology, and Local Signs

There have been a number of experiments in which optic nerves have been cut and regenerated and in which the eyeballs and/or parts of eyeballs of lower vertebrates (frogs or fish) were rotated and interchanged during and after development (Gaze, 1970; Jacobson, 1970; Lund, 1978; Sperry, 1951). These have demonstrated that a basis for mapping of retinal locus onto higher brain centers exists in the chemotactic criteria for selectivity of connections at synapses in the visual system. They have also demonstrated that this provides the basis for their local sign map of visual space.

It is also clear that, at some level, the map in these animals is at least a relative one in the sense that if fiber groups A and B of the optic nerve normally innervate tectal regions A' and B', and if tectal region A' is made unavailable as a termination for the optic nerve, segments A and B both compress into an orderly arrangement in region B' of the tectum (Gaze & Sharma, 1970; Jacobson & Levine, 1975). This result establishes the existence of a "gradient" for connectivity (relative signing of connections) in which a given region of retina connects to a region of tectum whose location is determined by the region to which its neighbor connects. It would be highly desirable to know whether or how the animal's spatial behavior is distorted, but those observations have not yet been made. Some further experiments along these lines in higher organisms are described in the section below on localization in the presence of saccades.

Higher organisms (such as cats) require early experience in which they visually receive the consequences of their attempts at visually guided behavior if spatially oriented behavior is to develop normally. This has been demonstrated in experiments in which prevention of visual observation by a kitten of its own moving limbs during locomotion blocks normal sensorimotor development (Held & Hein, 1963). This finding has been carried further in work that has demonstrated that paralyzing the extraocular musculature prior to any visual exposure is sufficient to prevent the development of visually guided behavior even though the animal is visually exposed to the consequences of its own behavior at an age that would be early enough to result in normal development (Hein, Durand, Salinger, & Diamond, 1979). It is also clear that proprioceptive feedback regarding the consequences of the eye movements themselves is critically involved in the acquisition of visually guided behavior, for surgically severing a main route for this feedback (ophthalmic branch of the fifth cranial nerve) prior to any postnatal visual exposure is sufficient to prevent the development of the visually guided behavior (Hein and Diamond, 1983). This route for proprioceptive feedback is not necessary for the maintenance (as distinct from the original development) of the behavior because cranial nerve section carried out after visually guided behavior has developed does not interfere with the behavior. These results then demonstrate that in cats inflowing EEPI is involved in the development of spatial localization.

Although the usual cautions must be invoked in attempting to infer the basis of spatially oriented behavior in humans from the work with animals, the rough similarity in the broad architecture of the visual nervous system of humans and the animal species mentioned above makes it likely that the embryonic development of the mapping of the retina on to the visual cortex follows roughly similar rules, and that the basis for development and maintenance of visually guided behavior is at least similar in outline.

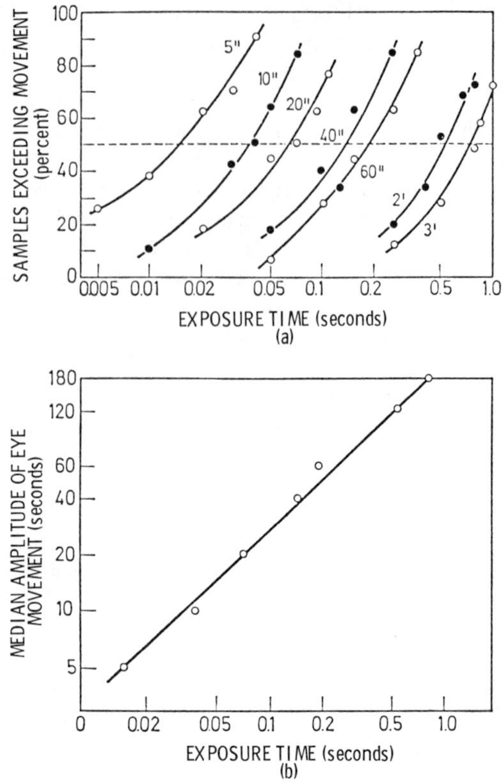

Figure 20.14. Quantitative characteristics of involuntary eye movements. (a) Percentage of eye movement records showing given amounts of motion as a function of the length of the record (exposure time) during attempts at steady fixation. Each experimental point is the result of measuring 50 eye-movement records having one particular duration. (b) The median extent of motion of the retinal image as a function of exposure time. Medians computed from data in (a). Because the diameter of a retinal photoreceptor subtends roughly 25 sec, the median involuntary eye movement in ½ sec (2 min) extends across only about 5 cones. (From L. A. Riggs, J. C. Armington, & F. Ratliff, Motion of the retinal image during fixation, *Journal of the Optical Society of America*, 1954, *44*. Reprinted with permission.)

3.4. Mean Retinal Local Sign and Spatial Discriminations

3.4.1. The Basic Approach. Early suggestions regarding local signs attached the spatial quality to the single photoreceptor (Hering, 1879/1942; Lotze, 1866). However, on this basis alone sensitivity to position could not be finer than a visual angle corresponding to the separation between two adjacent receptors. Because discrimination of vernier offset of two straight lines yields thresholds as small as 1–2 sec of arc in the central fovea—a dimension that is less than 1/10 the width of a single foveal cone—further theoretical developments were called for. It was thus suggested that the vernier discrimination is based on the ability of subjects to detect a difference in the mean retinal positional local sign between the two lines (Anderson & Weymouth, 1923; Averill & Weymouth, 1925; Hering, 1879/1942; Weymouth, Anderson, & Averill, 1923). This in effect suggests that the observer averages the local sign from each cone stimulated over the length of each line at a given moment, and further averages the signals over time from successively stimulated receptor arrays as a result of the continuous occurrence of involuntary fixation eye movements.

3.4.2. The Evidence Regarding Mean Retinal Local Signs. The view that local signs are averaged was supported by the facts that vernier acuity improves with increases in line length (Averill & Weymouth, 1925; Fender & Nye, 1962) and exposure duration (Averill & Weymouth, 1925; Baker, 1949; Keesey, 1960). Further, during attempts at steady fixation the median horizontal excursion of the eye grows linearly with interval duration up to at least 1 sec, at which point it is about 3 min arc (Riggs, Armington, & Ratliff, 1954; see Figure 20.14). This is roughly six cone diameters, and thus considerable opportunity for temporal averaging over different arrays is possible.

However, three kinds of evidence contradict the mean retinal local sign theory in conclusive fashion:

1. Ludvigh (1953) required observers to report on whether a point placed midway between two other vertically oriented points appeared to lie to the left or to the right of alignment with the two point. Precision in this task is as fine as in the vernier discrimination (thresholds reach as low as 2 sec). Because only three bundles of a few cones each are involved in this three-point discrimination as compared to the large number stimulated in the vernier task, averaging of positional local signs is clearly not a sufficient explanation, and some other mechanism is necessary for the discrimination to reach values below cone size.

2. Matin (1972) required observers to report on the alignment of two curved segments (Figure 20.15) and found that threshold acuities were as fine as those for the vernier discrimination with two straight lines. [Watt & Andrews (1982) report similar results.] Because averaging positional values separately over each of the two lines would not yield alignment for most of the configurations in Figure 20.15 some other mechanism than the one proposed by the mean retinal local sign theory must be responsible for the high acuity as well as accuracy in these discriminations. For some of the configurations in Figure 20.15 the first derivative of position is variable over the length of the segment and for others the second derivative is variable as well. Any simple variations of the mean retinal local sign approach in which derivative averaging replaces position averaging are also precluded, however, for predictions made on

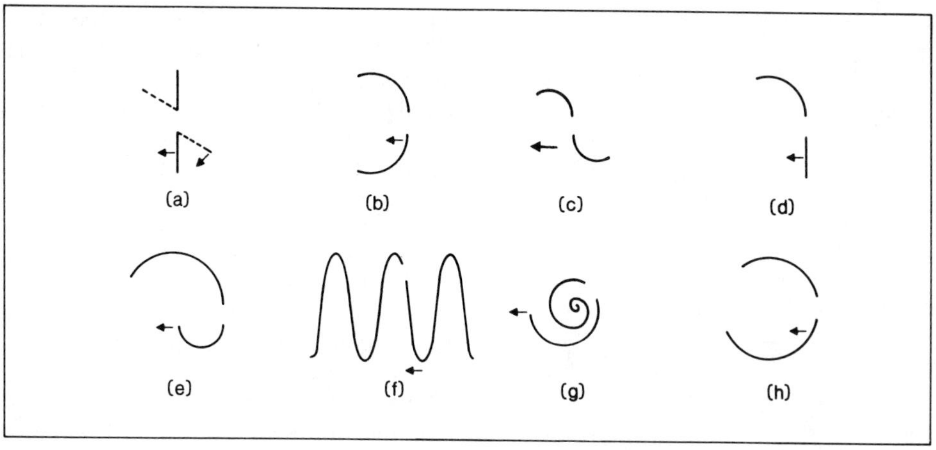

Figure 20.15. Target patterns for which the subject is required to report on alignment of two lines. The arrow in each pattern indicates the dimensions along which the experimenter varied the location of the test line during psychophysical experimentation. In (a) the solid line and dashed line are for two separate vernier target patterns. Only one is presented at a time in a given experimental trial; they have been superposed here for comparison by the reader only. In (a)–(e) a smooth continuous line can be formed by "filling the gap" with a straight line when the test line is located appropriately. In (h) only a curved line of uniform curvature in the gap yields a smooth continuous line: in (f) and (g) only a curved line with variable curvature does so. Alignments by the observer are made with the same precision in these cases, some of which involve variable first and/or second derivatives of position, indicating that simple averaging of local signs for position, direction, or change of direction does not provide a viable basis for a mechanism for alignment acuity. (From L. Matin, Eye movements and perceived visual direction, in L. Hurvich & D. Jameson (Eds.), *Handbook of sensory physiology* (7/4), Springer-Verlag, Inc., 1972. Reprinted with permission.)

these bases deviate widely from the measured values of thresholds and of constant errors.

3. Although vernier acuity improves with increased stimulus duration, no differences are obtained between acuities measured under normal and under stabilized conditions for durations up to at least 1.28 sec (Keesey, 1960; see Figure 20.16), indicating that the improvement consequent on increased exposure duration is not due to the fact that from moment to moment different receptor arrays look at the image. This result does not comment directly on the assumption of averaging over time or over space, for an average may still be taken, whether over the same spatial array from moment to moment (stabilized viewing) or over different arrays (normal viewing). Thus from this result one cannot conclude either that temporal factors are of lesser importance than spatial ones or that averaging of positional local signs is not involved in the vernier discrimination. The result does, however, establish that "scanning," which is a central feature of dynamic theories in which involuntary eye movements are implicated in the acuity process (Anderson & Weymouth, 1923; Averill & Weymouth, 1925; Marshall & Talbot, 1942; Weymouth et al., 1923), is not required for maximizing acuity in the interval from stimulus onset until stabilization-induced disappearance sets in.

Acuity for a large number of other spatial discriminations is as fine as those for vernier offset for straight and curved lines and for the three-dot alignment task (see Matin, 1972 for a review). These include (see Figure 20.17) the discrimination of parallelness, the angle of tilt between two lines, discrimination of rectangle width, orientation discrimination, the point-line measure of orientation discrimination, and stereoscopic acuity. In addition, a number of these also show minimum thresholds (about 2 sec) with target pattern length between 10 and 30 min (see Figure 20.18).

The commonalities in these results suggest that an overall theoretical approach to spatial discriminations that have this extremely high level of precision is necessary (Westheimer has labeled these "hyperacuities"). Although no satisfactory replacement for the mean retinal local sign theory has been developed, any such theory is likely to have to include the following: It will have to be part of a general theory for contour (and ultimately pattern) detection and discrimination rather than a theory of spatial localization alone. If an averaging principle is employed it will have to deal with averages of units of much higher order than photoreceptors. Each such higher-order unit would provide an output that would reflect the operation of considerable filtering by virtue of its selectivity for certain groupings of points (i.e., for certain shapes). Thus a principle of "mean cortical local sign" seems required. Finally, it is likely to make use of what seems to be a general principle for mechanisms of contour discrimination: perception of location corresponds to the location of a peak of a neural response distribution (see Matin, 1972, for review and references).

4. LOCALIZATION WITH STEADY GAZE

4.1. Visual Localization Relative to Visual Norms

With gaze steadily directed at a fixation target to fix eccentricity of the position of the eye in the orbit, observers are able to position a second light to perceived eye-level horizontal or to the median plane in otherwise total darkness (Fig. 20.2). The orderly change in retinal location of the visual stimuli set to the median plane with variation in gaze direction demonstrates the involvement in visual localization of an extraretinal channel providing EEPI and the operation of a mechanism whose basic configuration must be that of the cancellation mechanism of

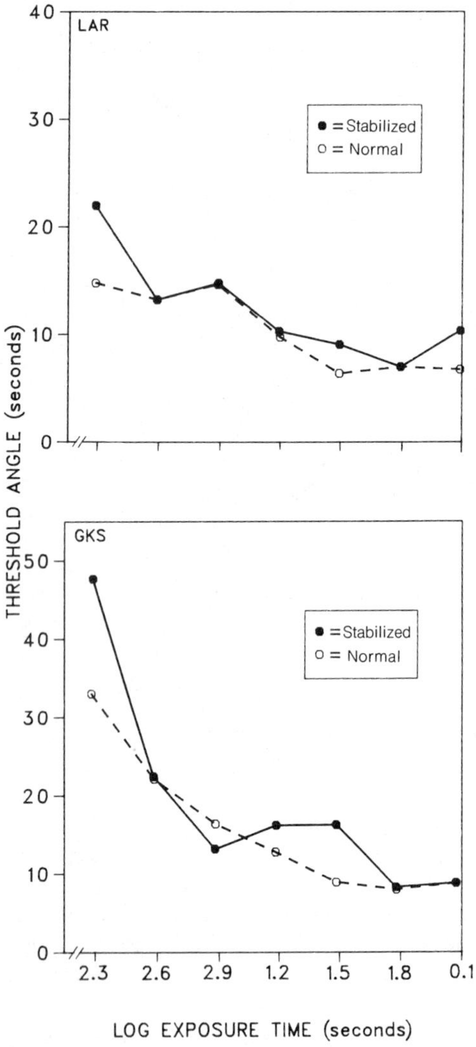

Figure 20.16. Vernier thresholds for normal and stabilized viewing. Threshold for vernier discrimination is plotted as a function of log exposure time under normal viewing and viewing with a stabilized image for two observers. Differences between normal and stabilized viewing are insubstantial. (From U. T. Keesey, Effects of involuntary eye movements on visual acuity, *Journal of the Optical Society of America*, 1960, *50*. Reprinted with permission.)

Figure 20.4. The reliability of repeated settings is about ±2°, a value that provides an indication of the reliability of the EEPI involved in visual localization. The variable errors in repeated settings are due to variation in EEPI and are not due to coarseness of the retinal information with increasing retinal eccentricity of the light set to the norm. This is shown by the fact that variability in setting is not noticeably increased by increasing eccentricity of gaze, although the retinal eccentricity is also increased, bringing with it an increase in coarseness of the retinally based acuity involved. A similar statement does not apply to the systematic errors of accuracy of the average settings; these errors may in part be related to distortions between retinal distances and perceived distances and in part to distortions between EEPI and actual eye position. Considerable evidence for the presence of distortions between retinal and perceptual distances is available (cf. Brown, 1953, 1955; Helmholtz., 1866/1963; Ogle, 1950; Pearce & Matin, 1969). The results in Figure 20.2 suggest no systematic influence of gaze eccentricity on accuracy of setting a visual target to the median plane in darkness. Under different conditions Hill (1972) and Morgan (1978) have reported a tendency to set the median plane in the direction of gaze eccentricity, an effect that Morgan reports to reach 6° at 42° of gaze eccentricity. Further work will be required to separate the influences of retinal and extraretinal distortions on the accuracy of setting visual targets to norms and to measure the extent of distortions in EEPI.

Holding the eye in an eccentric position of gaze for a period of time results in displacements of the apparent straight ahead (or median plane) in the direction of the eccentric gaze direction; increases in the displacement result from increasing gaze eccentricity and increasing duration for which the eccentric gaze position is held. The maximum effect reported is a displacement of about 8° following a 42° gaze eccentricity held for 120 sec (Paap & Ebenholtz, 1976). It is worth noting that sustained gaze at a single eccentrically placed point in darkness results in the appearance of a bias to autokinetic movement in the direction of the gaze eccentricity; the bias increases with gaze eccentricity (Adams, 1912; Carr, 1910; Gregory & Zangwill, 1963; Matin, Pearce, & MacKinnon, 1963; Levi, 1973). Whether these apparent movements (which become very substantial at

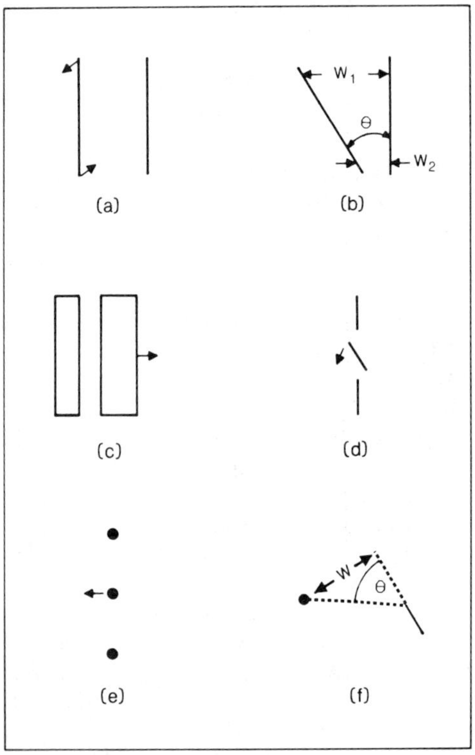

Figure 20.17. Some target patterns employed to measure spatial discrimination. (a) The discrimination of parallelness can be measured as shown in (b) by the angle of tilt between the two lines, **θ**, or by $W_1 - W_2$, the visual angle difference between horizontal offsets between the tops of the two lines and between the bottom of the two lines. (c) Discrimination of rectangle width. (d) A configuration sometimes employed for orientation discrimination. (e) The three-point task in which the subject is required to report on the offset of the center dot relative to the imaginary straight line connecting the two outer dots. Threshold can be given in terms of visual angle offset of the dot from this line or in terms of the tilt angle between the two lines formed by the three points; other measures are also possible. (f) The point/line measure of orientation discrimination. (From L. Matin, Eye movements and perceived visual direction, in L. Hurvich & D. Jameson (Eds.), *Handbook of sensory physiology* (7/4), Springer-Verlag, Inc., 1972. Reprinted with permission.)

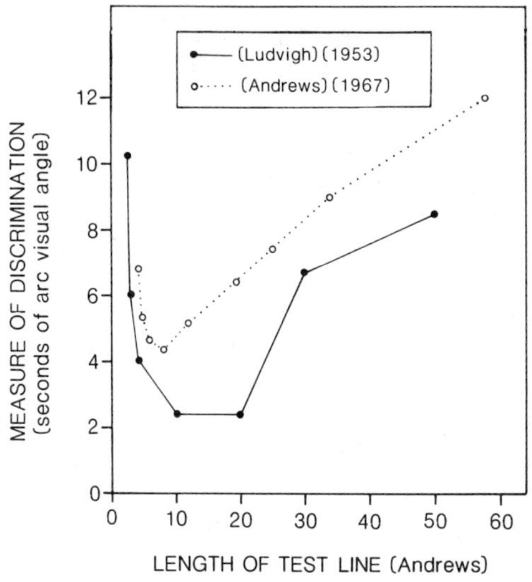

Figure 20.18. Three-point and parallelness discriminations compared. (a) Ludvigh's (1953) data for the three-point discrimination are plotted as offset of center dot for 75% correct detection of direction of displacement (ordinate) as a function of separation between the two vertically oriented reference points (abscissa). Andrews' (1967) data for discrimination of parallelness plotted as threshold differential retinal offset $W_1 - W_2$ as a function of line length; values of $W_1 - W_2$ calculated from Andrews' values of threshold angle by Matin. The two discriminations show similar U-shaped variations with target size. (From L. Matin, Eye movements and perceived visual direction, in L. Hurvich & D. Jameson (Eds.), *Handbook of sensory physiology* (7/4), Springer-Verlag, Inc., 1972. Reprinted with permission.)

extreme directions of gaze) are the basis for the bias of subjective visual direction reported by Paap and Ebenholtz has not yet been determined. The basis for an alternative explanation for the aftereffects of eccentric gaze on perceived visual direction lies in the adaptation of the extraocular muscles to asymmetric tonus in a fashion analogous to the upward movement of an arm hung passively at the side of an erect individual after pressing it outward from his body with the outer surface of his hand against a wall for a period of time while the arm is extended (Carr, 1910; Paap & Ebonholtz, 1976; see also Clark & Horch, Chapter 13).

For settings of the visual target to be made to eye-level horizontal it is necessary that EEPI regarding angle α (Fig. 20.8) be combined not only with information regarding retinal image location of the visual target, but with information regarding orientation of the head relative to gravity (angle β, Fig. 20.8) as well. In experiments where settings to the median plane of a single fixated light are made for different positions of the head around a vertical axis or settings of the eye-level horizontal for different positions of the head around a horizontal axis through the ears, there can be no influences of retinal distortions, and the results provide an indication of the accuracy of the combination of head position information and EEPI in visual localization. Different head positions yield either small or no systematic influences on the settings (Cohen, 1973, 1981: data at 1.00*g* in Figure 20.19 below; also Matin et al., 1982).

However, different values of downward acceleration produce a substantial influence on the perception of location of the eye-level horizontal. This influence, in which a target located at the physical eye-level horizontal appears displaced downward, is known as the elevator illusion (Cohen, 1973, 1981; Graybiel, 1952), [similar to the oculogravic illusion (Graybiel, 1952; also see Howard, Chapter 11) produced when gravitational-inertial forces are altered in both direction and magnitude instead of only magnitude, as is the case for the elevator illusion.] Cohen's results in Figure 20.19 show that the positioning of a target to appear at the eye-level horizontal is displaced upward by increasing amounts for increasing downward gravity when the head is erect, reaching values as large as 20° at 1.75*g*. The slope of the increase decreases with increasing forward head tilts, and no illusion is obtained when the forward tilt reaches 30° Cohen (1973, 1981) explains this influence of head tilt as due to changes in the shearing force directed backward along the macular surface of the utricle, and because the utricle is tilted at 30° to the horizontal, the shearing forces are eliminated at a head tilt of 30° when this surface is perpendicular to the action of the *g* forces. That the effect does depend on the labyrinth is in agreement with the finding that the elevator illusion is absent in individuals with damaged labyrinth (Niven, Whiteside, & Graybiel, 1963). Cohen also attributes a portion of the influence of head tilt on the production of target elevation to influences of the *g* forces on neck proprioception. It is also worth considering the alternative possibility that the portion of the influence of head tilt is due to the influence of *g* forces on the eyeball itself, requiring different commands to the extraocular muscles to obtain a different position of the eye in the orbit with the head in different positions, an effect that itself could be modulated by changes in gravity, as are the results in Figure 20.19.

4.2. Visual Direction During Fixation of a Visible Target and Involuntary Eye Movements

4.2.1. Characteristics and Control of Involuntary Eye Movements. Variation of the position of the eye during fixation of a visible target (see Figure 20.20) is extremely small. Standard deviations of eye position during steady fixation are 1–3 min arc visual angle (see Figure 20.14 from Riggs et al., 1954; also Ditchburn, 1973, for a substantial review and summary). This corresponds to between three and nine cone diameters.

Involuntary eye movements during an attempt at maintaining steady fixation are composed of three components: microsaccades, slow drift, and high frequency tremor (Figure 20.20; also see Hallett, Chapter 10).

The microsaccades are extremely brief and stereotyped with velocity increasing up to near the middle of the saccade and decreasing beyond while acceleration peaks near the end of the first quarter and deceleration peaks near the end of the third quarter of the saccade (Figure 20.21); duration increases with saccade length and reaches 20–30 msec for involuntary saccades as large as 40 min; peak velocity (middle of the saccade) reaches about $40°\cdot sec^{-1}$ for 40-min microsaccades.

The function relating peak velocity and saccade length fits on the main sequence relating saccade length to velocity for the larger voluntary saccades (Figure 20.22; Bahill & Stark, 1979; Zuber, Stark, & Cook, 1965). Microsaccades typically occur one to two times per second during attempts at steady fixation of a stationary target with a range of magnitudes from 1 to 10 min. The probability that an involuntary saccade will return the eye toward a mean or "optimum" position increases monotonically and approaches 1.0 as the deviation of the eye from this position approaches 7 min (Cornsweet, 1956). Involuntary

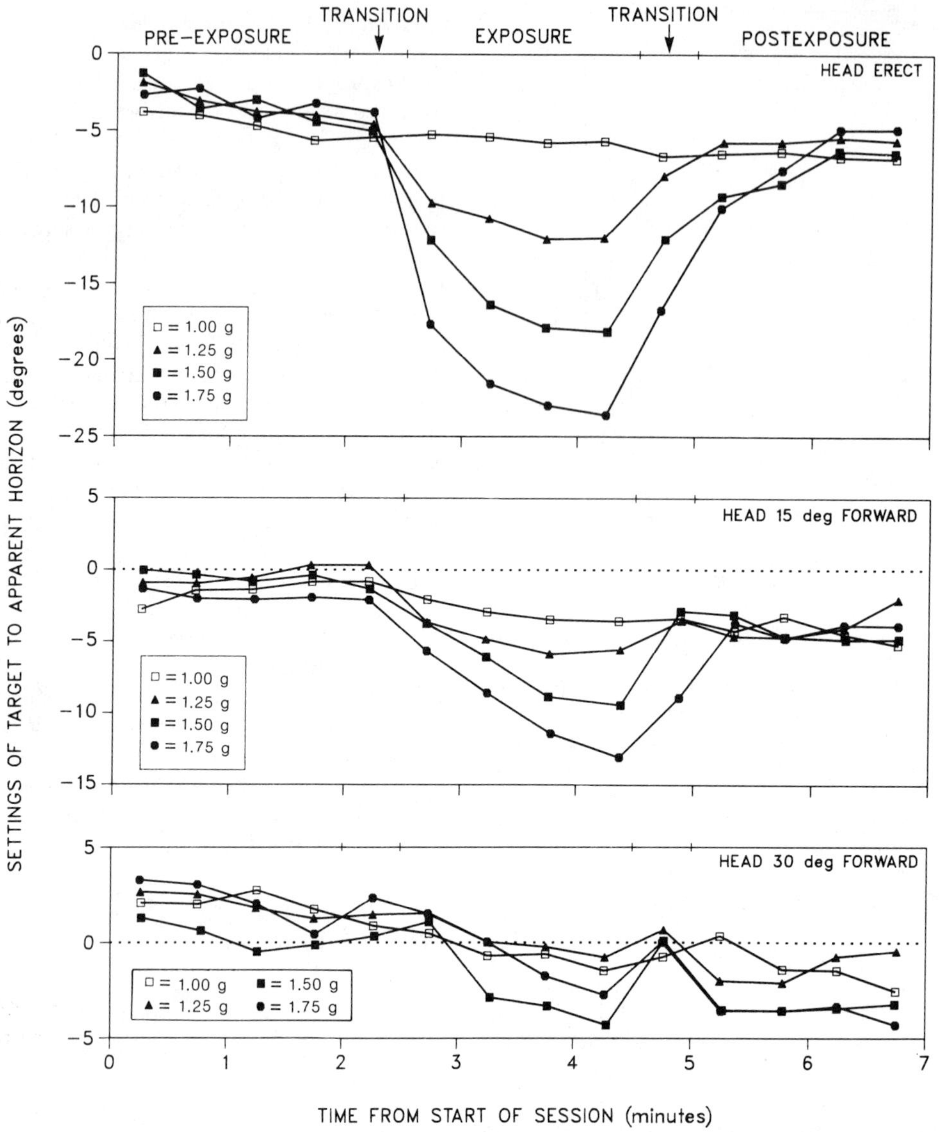

Figure 20.19. Elevator illusion: settings of a visual target to the apparent horizon during centrifugation, which produces an increase in magnitude of gravitational-inertial force (gaf) without change in direction of gaf. Values of gaf are indicated in each panel. The three panels show the time course of the illusion for different head tilts. During the period of increased gaf the eye-level horizontal is displaced downward by an amount that increases with increase in gaf. Tilting the head forward reduces the influence of the increased gaf on the eye-level horizontal. (From M. M. Cohen, Elevator illusion: Influence of otolith organ activity and neck proprioception, *Perception and Psychophysics*, 1973, *14*. Reprinted with permission.)

saccades are very much reduced in frequency in the dark during attempts at holding a prior position of fixation (Cornsweet, 1956; also see Figure 20.23). Fiorentini and Ercoles (1966) and Steinman, Cunitz, Timberlake, and Herman (1967) have also reported that observers can suppress the involuntary saccades without much loss of fixation stability.

The involuntary drifts during attempts at steady fixation have a median extent of 2.5 min (Ditchburn, 1973). They are not random (Nachmias, 1959, 1961; Steinman et. al., 1967), but, in addition to doing most of the work of carrying the eye away from an average fixation position, also bring the eye back toward the average fixation position. Nachmias (1959) found that for some meridians of ocular motion, the farther the eye was from mean position the greater the tendency for the eye to return toward mean position during saccade-free time periods (i.e., there was a negative correlation between eye position and direction of the subsequent drift) so that "... along those meridia where saccade compensation is poor, drift compensation becomes appreciable (Nachmias, 1959)." In addition, because observers who can adopt a "hold the eye steady" attitude instead of a "fixate the light" attitude maintain fixation with only infrequent involuntary saccades, it has been claimed (Steinman et al., 1967) that the main business of maintaining fixation is carried out by the involuntary slow drifts.

The extremely fine ability to maintain steady fixation clearly depends on processing of information derived from the displacement of the position of the visual image on the retina from some preferred position and not on EEPI regarding deviation of the eye itself from a preferred position. This point was first made most clearly by Cornsweet (1956), who showed that re-

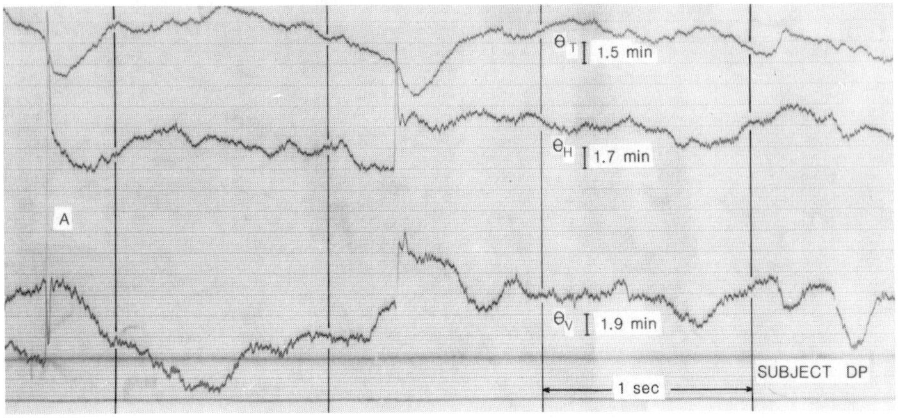

Figure 20.20. Recording of θ_H, θ_V, and θ_T during and immediately following a voluntary shift of fixation of 15 min in θ_H (at A). Upward deflection of the trace refers to an eye movement to the left in θ_H, upward in θ_V, and top of the eye turned temporally in θ_T. The very light time lines are 10 msec apart. (From L. Matin, Measurement of eye movements by contact lens techniques: Analysis of measuring systems and some methodology or three dimensional recording, *Journal of the Optical Society of America*, 1964, *54*. Reprinted with permission.)

moving the fixation target while requiring the observer to continue holding the same eye position yields an increase in positional variability of two to three orders of magnitude and substantial systematic errors which change with time as well. This has been supported by subsequent work (Allik, Rauk, & Luuk, 1981; Fiorentini & Ercoles, 1968; Matin, Matin, & Pearce, 1970; Matin, Pearce, Matin, & Kibler, 1966; Nachmias, 1961; Skavenski, 1971; Skavenski & Steinman, 1970; see Figure 20.23), who report increases in fixation errors at rates that range between 2 and 10 min·sec^{-1}. In darkness the mean (unsigned) deviation of the eye from a prior fixation position increases with time in the dark, reaching about 25 min in 3 sec and 2° in 2 min; mean position also changes irregularly. However, the eye may also reach distances as far as 10° in any direction from the desired position (standard deviation of 2 to 5°) during attempts at maintaining a fixed position extending over a minute of time [Figures 6–8 of Allik et al. (1981) are particularly instructive here]; departures from a random walk are measurable early in the dark interval and more substantial later. Furthermore, because subjects do not "perceive the retinal locus stimulated," but rather perceive targets in particular visual directions, the retinal displacement of the image of the fixation target can provide an effective signal regarding error in eye position only if the involuntary ocular displacement is not perfectly compensated by an EEPI signal involved in the stabilization of visual direction. A similar conclusion follows if it is assumed that the useful information in eye position correction is direction of retinal image travel rather than a specific retinal offset (or set of offsets). Further support for this conclusion may be found in Matin (1972, pp. 359–360).

4.2.2. The Vernier Discrimination and Involuntary Eye Movements. As described earlier, when two visual targets are presented simultaneously sensitivity for their relative localization is extremely good. Indeed, under conditions designed to maximize sensitivity, thresholds for spatial discriminations regarding alignment or offset as small as 2 sec of visual angle are obtained. This is an impressive manifestation of the complexity of neural processing of the visual system behind a photoreceptor layer whose grain size is about 25 sec. Because eye

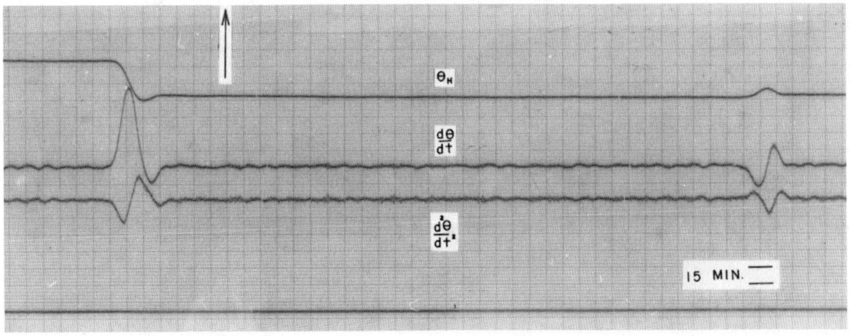

Figure 20.21. θ_H, $d\theta/dt$, and $d^2\theta/dt^2$ (position of the eye in the orbit, ocular velocity, and ocular acceleration, respectively) during a voluntary saccade (beginning of record) and an involuntary saccade (end of record). The time lines are separated by 10-msec intervals. The 15-min calibration applies to the θ_H trace. The oscillations (about one per time line) in the first and second derivative are due to the fine tremor of the eye, which is only barely visible here in the θ_H trace. (The small oscillation at about 1,200 Hz on the two lower traces is a parasite to the electronics of the differentiators only and is not represented in the upper trace.) (From L. Matin & D. G. Pearce, Three dimensional recording of rotational eye movements by a new contact lens technique, in W. E. Murry & P. F. Salisbury (Eds.), *Biomedical sciences instrumentation*, Plenum Publishing, 1964. Reprinted with permission.)

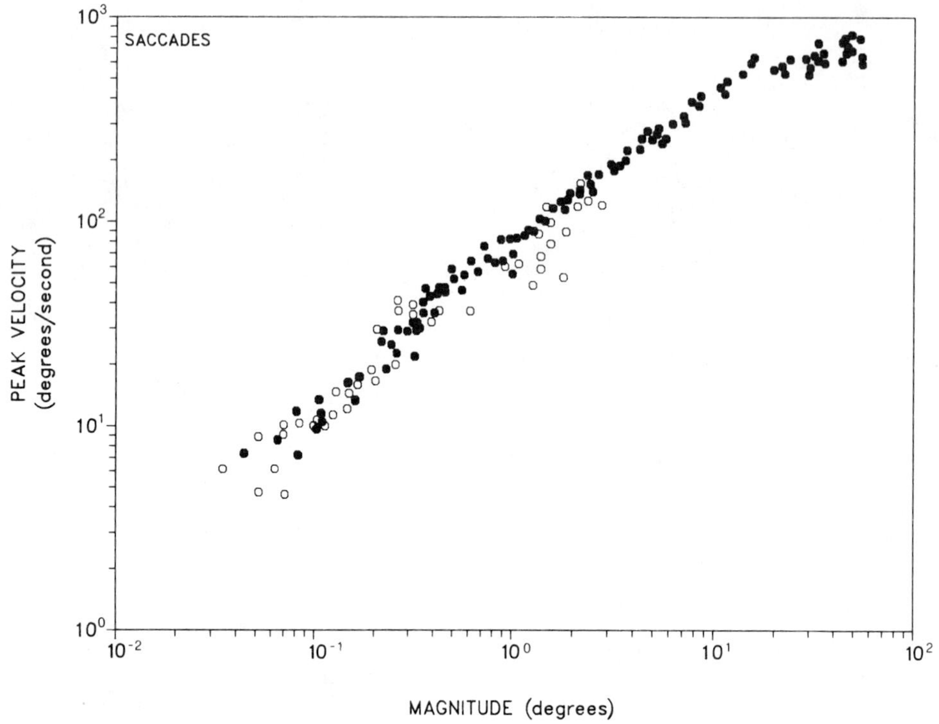

Figure 20.22. Main-sequence diagram for human saccadic eye movements. The figure plots the peak velocity during a saccade as a function of saccade length. Peak velocity increases nearly linearly with saccade length over the entire range of saccade lengths. (From A. T. Bahill & L. Stark, The trajectories of saccadic eye movements, *Scientific American, 240*. Copyright 1979 by Scientific American, Inc. Reprinted with permission.)

movements do not influence the relative retinal locations of two simultaneously viewed targets, any cancellation mechanism involving EEPI would not be expected to produce systematic distortions during attempts at steady fixation. We would not expect considerations regarding EEPI to be significant here at all. Along with the results showing that the use of EEPI for visual localization is modified by the presence of a visual field these considerations suggest an even more general statement: Whenever a discrimination can be made by means of mechanisms subserving pattern discrimination, EEPI will not be involved. Several experiments in which results could have shown effects of EEPI, if any were to be found, did not do so. As noted earlier, stabilized and normal viewing yield vernier acuities that are at most slightly different (Fender & Nye, 1962; Keesey, 1960). Krauskopf, Graf, and Gaarder (1966) report no change in vernier acuity for brief flashes measured in close temporal proximity

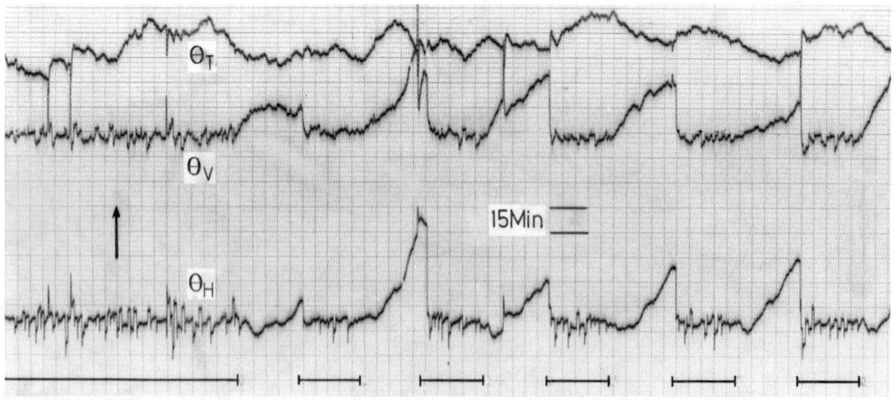

Figure 20.23. Three dimensions of ocular rotation during periods in which a single fixation target was alternately visible and extinguished in an otherwise dark environment. The straight lines at the bottom of the figure indicate periods during which the target was visible. The 15-min calibration applies to all three traces. The arrow indicates an ocular rotation to the right in θ_H, downward in θ_V, and top of the eye nasally in θ_T. The eye tends to drift off target in darkness and return to the target on reillumination, indicating that the retinal error signal exerts greater control over eye position than an error signal regarding eye position itself. (From L. Matin & D. G. Pearce, Three dimensional recording of rotational eye movements by a new contact lens technique, in W. E. Murry & P. F. Salisbury (Eds.), *Biomedical sciences instrumentation*, Plenum Publishing, 1964. Reprinted with permission.)

to an involuntary saccade. Rattle and Foley-Fisher (1968) report longer intersaccadic intervals are related to better vernier acuity, but this is most readily explained by the increased duration available for unimpeded temporal integration with longer intervals.

4.2.3. Visual Localization with Steady Gaze in Darkness. The increase in magnitude of involuntary eye movements that occurs in total darkness when an observer attempts to hold his eye in a given direction implies that accuracy of fixation of a visible target is controlled mainly, or perhaps wholly, by the displacement of the image on the retina from some preferred position. These movements typically contain very many fewer involuntary saccades than do movements in the presence of a visible target (see Figure 20.23 from Matin & Pearce, 1964).

The increase in variability of ocular position when an observer attempts to maintain eye position in the dark is accompanied by an increase in errors in the report of visual direction of a brief flash presented after fixation target removal relative to that of the previously viewed fixation target or of the relative visual direction of two sequentially presented flashes. When the discrimination is one of direction of horizontal offset these increases are obtained when both fixation target and flash are small circular targets (Findlay, 1974; Fiorentini & Ercoles, 1968; Foley, 1976, 1978; Matin, 1972; Matin & Kibler, 1966; Matin et al., 1966) or when they are two sequentially flashed lines of a vertical vernier target (Matin, Pola, Matin, & Picoult, 1981). Both constant (PSE) and variable errors of localization increase monotonically with the time interval between presentations of the two targets and are larger for eccentric directions of gaze than for viewing in primary position, with standard deviations (1/acuity) reaching values between 5 and 25 min at 1- to 3-sec intervals and standard deviations and PSEs both reaching 1° when the flash follows fixation target termination by 3 sec. PSEs shift opposite to gaze direction. Similar results were obtained for the discrimination of relative vertical visual direction (Figure 20.24).

The pattern of errors of the vernier discrimination with variable dark interval between the presentation of the two lines tells us that the discrimination does not make any systematic use of an EEPI-based cancellation mechanism. Thus the observer treats retinal image shifts produced by the eye movement as no different from the identical retinal image shifts produced by displacement in the stimulus array when no eye movement has occurred (Matin et al. 1966; Matin et al., 1981). For example, even when the second vernier line is flashed at a location substantially to the left of the first line at the stimulus array, the observer reports the second line to lie to the right of the first if the eye has moved sufficiently far to the left in the dark interval. The portion of the variance accounted for by these uncompensated eye movements rises monotonically from zero to about 50% for dark intervals of 800 msec (Matin et al., 1981) and reaches about 70% at 3 sec (Matin et al., 1966).

Three of the conclusions from these experiments are relevant here. EEPI related to the involuntary changes in eye position during the dark interval does not influence the sequential localization discrimination systematically. Although these changes in eye position may be as large as 3–4° or more in a 3-sec dark interval and influence the retinal offset between the images of the two targets as noted above, the perceptual mechanism responsible for the localization discrimination does not compensate for the eye-movement-produced retinal offset. This result is compatible with either the outflow or hybrid model (see Section

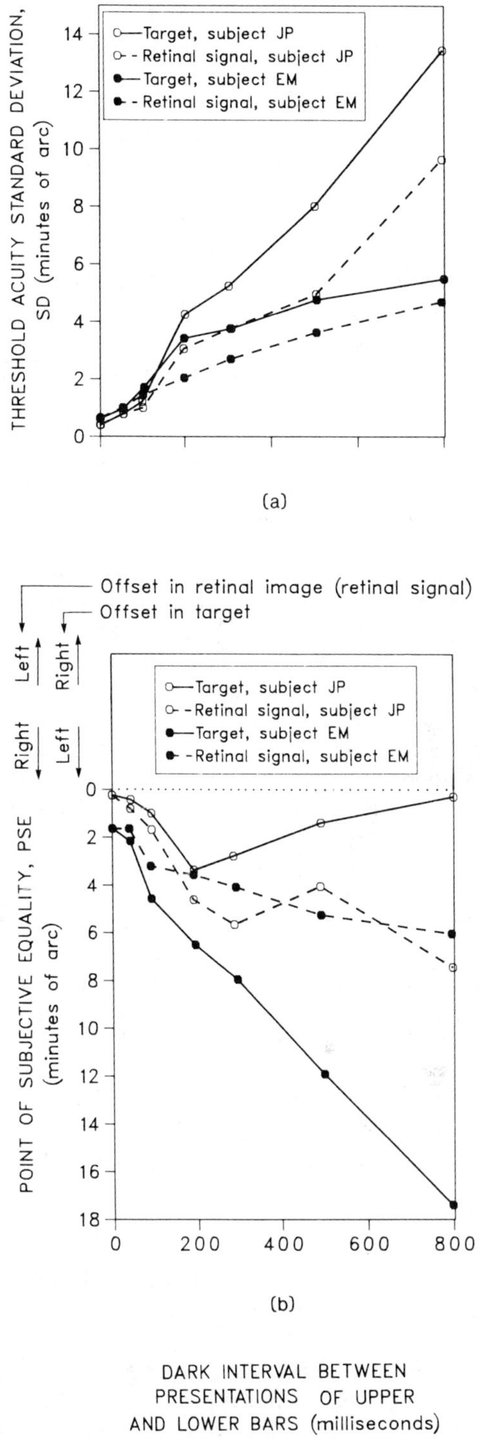

Figure 20.24. Vernier offset discrimination in total darkness with variable time between presentation of the two lines. The observer was presented with two sequentially flashed (2 msec) 34 min 20 sec vertical lines vertically separated by 2 min 20 sec. The time between onsets of the two lines is displayed on the abscissa. The ordinate plots threshold acuity (standard deviation of the offset judgments) (a) or point of subjective equality (b) calculated from measurements at the target display (solid lines) or, by taking into account measurements of the eye movements in the dark interval, from offsets at the retina (dashed lines). A large proportion of the variation of the discrimination is a consequence of the change in eye position without cancellation by EEPI. (From L. Matin, J. Pola, E. Matin, & E. Picoult, Vernier discrimination with sequentially flashed lines: Roles of eye movements, retinal offsets and short term memory, *Vision Research, 21*. Copyright 1981 by Pergamon Press, Ltd. Reprinted with permission.)

2.2 and Matin, 1972, 1976a) but not the inflow model (Figure 20.6). It is interesting that an eye-movement-produced change in retinal image location in as short an interval as 2 msec is sufficient to produce a change in discrimination of a vernier task with lines flashed sequentially (Matin et al., 1981).

A substantial error variance was unaccounted for by the change in retinal image location due to the uncompensated eye movements. This unaccounted-for error variance increases with the interstimulus interval and thus represents either (1) noise in EEPI (i.e., fluctuations in the correspondence between actual eye position and eye position as signaled to the mechanism determining visual localization, or (2) local sign noise in the visual system unrelated to EEPI but related to coarsening and distortion of the map between perceived space and the retina (Matin et al., 1966; Matin et al., 1981). Either would be a form of memory loss (also see Keller & Kinchla, 1968; Kinchla, 1976; Kinchla & Allan, 1969; and Kinchla & Smyzer, 1967, who developed a random-walk model of memory loss).

Whatever this variable error in the sequential localization task is due to, it is clearly smaller (by more than an order of magnitude) than the error in EEPI that is involved in maintaining fixation in darkness (Allik et al., 1981; Cornsweet, 1956; Matin et al., 1966; Matin et al., 1981; Matin, Matin, & Pearce, 1970; Skavenski, 1971; Skavenski & Steinman, 1970). In addition, fixation stability in darkness is 100 times better against a visible fixation target than without a fixation target, and localization errors with successive presentation are as much as 500 times greater than are obtained with simultaneous presentation. These provide evidence regarding the relative insensitivity of EEPI in comparison to the sensitivity of information derived from the retina.

As noted above, variability in the direction with which an observer points his eye when instructed to look in the direction of his median plane (or straight ahead) in darkness normally runs from 2 to 5°. The average direction is capable of some modification, however, as is demonstrated by its susceptibility to adaptation by wearing wedge prisms that laterally displace the visual field (Kalil & Freedman, 1966; McLaughlin & Webster, 1967; for a review dealing with questions related to such adaptation see Kornheiser, 1976; Welch, 1978; also see Welch, Chapter 24).

5. LOCALIZATION IN THE PRESENCE OF VOLUNTARY SACCADES

5.1. The Problem Presented for Perceptual Stability by Saccadic Eye Movements

A voluntary change of the direction of gaze in a normally illuminated and structured visual field is carried out by a saccadic eye movement (see Hallett, Chapter 10). It is an extremely rapid and stereotyped ocular rotation with a roughly fixed time versus position function for a given length (Figures 20.21, 20.22). When an individual attempts to turn his eye more slowly between two stationary points than would be the case for a saccade of the same length, the result is a series of short saccades each of which carries the eye a part of the distance between the two designated points until the goal is reached. An increase in time between the two points is indeed effected, but is almost entirely a consequence of an increase in the number of saccades (with a corresponding decrease in the length of the members of the saccadic series) and an increased duration between members of the series. (Individuals who are uninformed about the way in which their eyes are moving during these attempts at slower changes of gaze direction generally do not report that anything other than a single smooth transition has occurred.) An occasional individual is able to turn his eye slowly between two stationary points by carrying out relatively constant-velocity movements that appear identical to the pursuit eye movements that normally occur when an individual attempts to maintain fixation on a constant-velocity moving point (Figure 20.25), but this ability is rare. The main characteristics of the saccadic eye movements with their velocity peak near the center of the saccade, acceleration and deceleration peaks near the first and third quarter points, increase in duration with saccade length, and unusual shape stereotypy have been modeled with some success (Bahill & Stark, 1979; Robinson, 1964).

Our main concern here is with the normal maintenance of perceptual stability in the presence of voluntary saccades. This stability of localization occurs in the face of a great deal of variation of oculomotor behavior, of stimulus conditions, and of the conditions of visual adaptation: An individual saccade may take from 15 msec (for a saccade of 0.5° length) to 100 msec (for a 20° saccade). Velocity varies regularly during a given saccade, and the entire scale of velocities increases with increase in saccade length with peak velocity ranging from 10 $deg\cdot sec^{-1}$ for a 1° saccade to $950°\cdot sec^{-1}$ for a 20° saccade (Figure 20.22). The variety of stimulus conditions under which saccades are performed includes successive stimulations of a given retinal region by enormous differences in illumination between various parts of a saccade as well as differences in overall illumination. But stability of visual direction is generally maintained under nearly all combinations of saccade length and direction, stimulus complexity, and level of illumination.

5.2. Problems for the Cancellation Model: Requirements for Additional Mechanisms

Although a cancellation mechanism (see Section 2) is involved in maintaining perceptual stability in the presence of voluntary saccades, it is only part of the story. Under normal conditions when viewing structured illuminated visual fields, saccadic suppression—both of sensitivity (Matin, 1972; E. Matin 1974; E. Matin, Clymer, & Matin, 1972; Matin & E. Matin, 1972) and of displacement (Bridgeman, Hendry, & Stark, 1975; Bridgeman & Stark, 1979; Stark, Kong, Schwartz, Hendry, & Bridgeman, 1976)—is also important. Among other things both aspects of saccadic suppression contribute to the solution of several problems that arise for a cancellation mechanism in maintaining perceptual stability in the presence of saccades. These problems do not arise as such during steady fixation. The problems may be indicated by noting three aspects.

5.2.1. Visual Persistence. The moment of termination of a retinal stimulus does not coincide with the moment of termination of perception of that stimulus. Typically, perception of a stimulus outlasts the stimulus itself; such persistence may be as long as 200–300 msec (Bowen, Pola, & Matin, 1974; Efron, 1970a, 1970b; Matin & Bowen, 1976). If there were no mechanism reducing the duration of visual persistence, the presaccadic view of a visual field would continue to be perceived at the same time that the postsaccadic view was beginning to be perceived. But it has been shown (Figure 20.30) that simultaneity or temporal overlap of visual perception forces a retinotopic match between the presaccadic and postsaccadic views; such a match is the antithesis of perceptual stability.

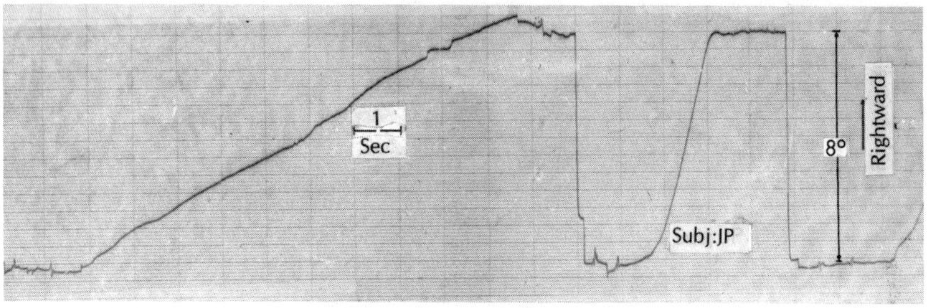

Figure 20.25. The ability to execute slow eye movements in the absence of a moving stimulus is rare. Most individuals produce a series of short saccades with increased pause durations between the saccades when requested to slow their eye movements between one point and another in a stationary visual field. This figure is a recording of slow horizontal eye movements in the absence of any moving stimulus by one of the rare individuals who does possess the ability to actually execute slow eye movements. Two stationary, continuously illuminated, circular 3.5-min targets horizontally separated by 8° were the only visual stimuli present. These were employed only to define for the subject the end points of the eye movements; essentially identical movements are made by this subject without any visible stimulus. The different velocities of the two slow movements in the figure are under voluntary control of the subject, who is able to produce velocities even slower than the one on the left of the figure, and can, in a graded series of such movements, produce velocities almost up to the speed of saccades. He can also produce these velocities with the eye moving in either direction, although only slow movement from left to right is shown in the figure with returns via saccades. (From L. Matin, Eye movements and perceived visual direction, in L. Hurvich & D. Jameson (Eds.), *Handbook of sensory physiology* (7/4), Springer-Verlag, Inc., 1972. Reprinted with permission.)

5.2.2. Retinal Blur. A saccade is accompanied by an extremely rapid shift of the image of each viewed stationary object across the retina. If the cancellation mechanism had to continuously produce perceptual stability for each of the points occupied by the retinal image during the saccade, the visual persistence problem noted above would be even more pronounced for successive stimulations during a saccade than it is for the relation between presaccadic and postsaccadic stimulation. But, in addition, spatiotemporal integration in the visual system would yield a perceptual blur (spatially extended appearance of successive stimulations by any given stimulus point) if visual persistence were not sufficiently reduced.

5.2.3. Visual Latency. Visual latency to onset of a visual stimulus varies with both level of light adaptation and stimulus intensity (Bowen et al., 1974; Lit, 1949; Matin & Bowen, 1976). Because different stimulus points in a complex field differ in intensity and different retinal points are simultaneously adapted to different levels, variations in visual response latency will result as different stimulus points strike different retinal points during a saccade. For a cancellation mechanism to maintain perceptual stability for stimulation during a saccade, it would be necessary for the latency of EEPI to be appropriately tuned to each of the combinations of stimulus and retinal points across all combinations simultaneously and to continuously vary this tuning as the saccade progressed. This would be a remarkable feat, made even more remarkable by the fact that such tuning requires prediction of the response latency to the visual stimulus at each of the points before appropriate cancellation could be affected. In effect, this implies that EEPI must be informed of the stimulus intensity at a given point before any response arises from that point, an inference that seems to pose a nearly impossible demand.

5.3. Measurements of EEPI in the Presence of Voluntary Saccades

5.3.1. A Basic Paradigm for Measurement. To extract directly the influence of an EEPI-based cancellation mechanism on visual localization in the presence of voluntary saccades an acceptable method must respond to two kinds of considerations. First, it must provide measures of perceptual stability. Because perceptual stability means, in this context, that a target will appear to be located in the same place before and after a saccade, measures of visual localization must be obtainable that will yield information on this point.

Second, stationary objects in a visual field themselves provide a possible basis for visual localization. Thus object A does remain in the same relation to object B after a saccade as it was before the saccade. In and of itself, this provides a basis for an observer's localizations and comparisons of localization before and after saccades. Although such relative localizations are normally stable when comparisons are made before and after saccades, the basis for stability need not involve any use of cancellation or other employment of EEPI; the stability of relative retinal distances could provide a sufficient basis for such perceptual stability alone. For a method to demonstrate that an EEPI-based cancellation mechanism was the means by which perceptual stability was attained, the possibility that stable retinal distances provide the basis for localization must be eliminated from the procedure.

A procedure developed by Matin and Pearce (1965) for determining the influence of EEPI on visual localization in the presence of saccades is diagramed in Figure 20.26. It meets the two requirements described above: on each trial the observer viewed three targets, but only one of the targets was presented at a time. The entire procedure was carried out in darkness with no other stimuli visible. The first target was foveally fixated for a long enough time to allow the observer to stabilize fixation, and to prepare for reception of subsequent stimuli, for making a saccade, and for making a localization judgment. The time period was also long enough so that a stable measure of average eye position could be obtained that did not include the initial adjustments an observer might make in beginning fixation. The second stimulus (first flash) was presented as a brief flash whose onset was several hundred milliseconds after extinction of the fixation target. The observer was required to attempt to

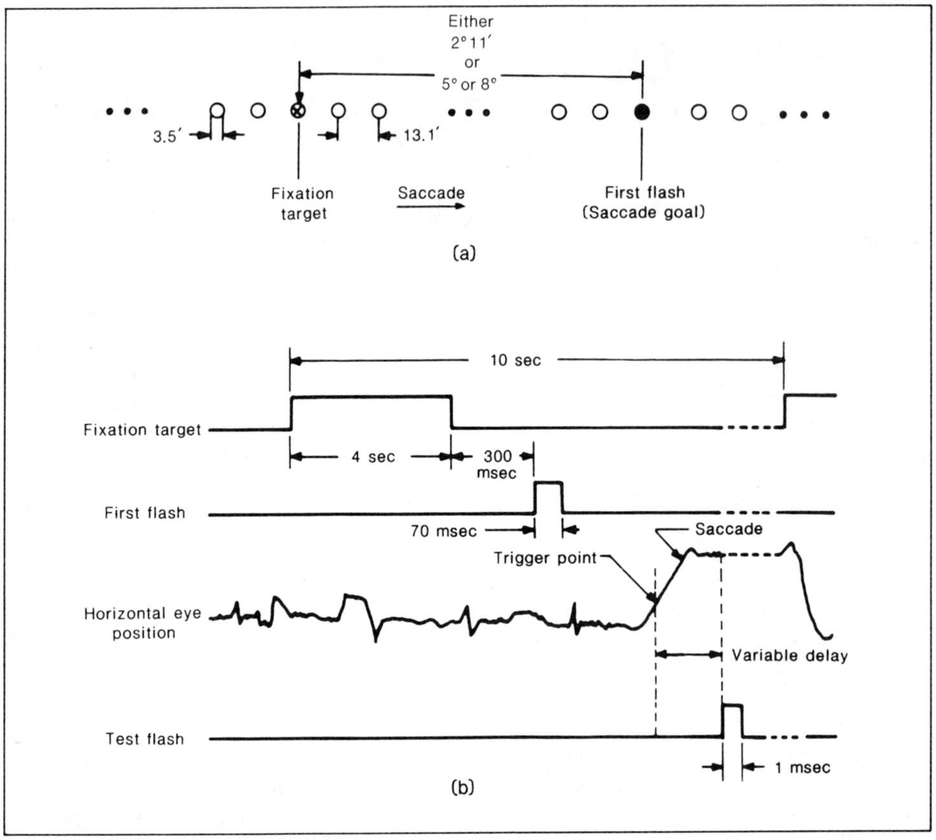

Figure 20.26. Conditions of stimulation for measuring the time course of visual direction in the presence of a voluntary saccade for which results are displayed in Figure 20.27 (2° 11 min saccade) and Figure 20.28 (5 and 8° saccades). (a) Spatial array of stimuli employed in measuring the relation of visual direction of a flash presented either before, during, or after a voluntary horizontal saccade to that of the previously viewed fixation target; any target in the array could be used as a test flash. (b) Temporal sequence of stimuli. For test flashes produced during the saccade the variable delay was zero; different trigger points within the saccade were employed. Test flashes before the saccade were initiated at a fixed duration following first flash onset.

maintain fixation on the fixation target during its presentation and to maintain this position even after the fixation target was extinguished and until the first flash was seen. On seeing the first flash the observer was to reposition his eye (saccade) to the site at which the flash occurred. However, the brevity of this flash in relation to the observer's reaction time to seeing guaranteed that it would be over before the saccade could begin, thereby ensuring that this first flash would be imaged exclusively at a retinal location whose visual angle separation from the retinal image of the fixation target was very close to the separation between the physical locations of the fixation target and the target generating the first flash. Subsequent to termination of the first flash the brief test flash was presented to the observer from some randomly chosen location at the stimulus array with different locations employed on different trials. The observer, whose eye position was monitored continuously, reported where the test flash appeared to lie relative to the previously viewed fixation target (left or right).

In one set of measurements the randomly located test flash was presented when the eye reached a predesignated distance into the saccade (Matin & Pearce, 1965; Matin et al., 1969; Pola, 1972, 1976). Psychophysical measurements were made at different distances into the saccade on different series of trials. In other sets of measurements the test flash was presented before the saccade began (Matin, Matin & Pola, 1970). Because the actual time interval at which the saccade followed the first flash varied from trial to trial, presentation of the test flash at a fixed time after termination of the first flash resulted in measurements with different time intervals between the first flash and the beginning of the saccade. In still other sets of measurements the test flash was presented at some particular time after the eye had reached a given distance into the saccade (Matin, Matin, & Pola, 1970; Pola, 1972, 1976); those time intervals included values that were long enough so that for some of them the test flash was presented following termination of the saccade.

5.3.2. Results with the Basic Paradigm. Figures 20.27 and 20.28 display results obtained with the method outlined above. The relevance of these results for considerations regarding the operation of a cancellation mechanism is summarized in the following.

When a saccade is performed there is a regular shift of retinal local signs (visual direction of a given retinal point) with time. This is measured by the value of the retinal point of subjective equality (retinal PSE or constant error) between fixation target and test flash, a value that is equal to the visual angle distance between the average retinal point stimulated by the fixation target during the fixation period and the retinal location of the test flash reported as lying to the left and to the

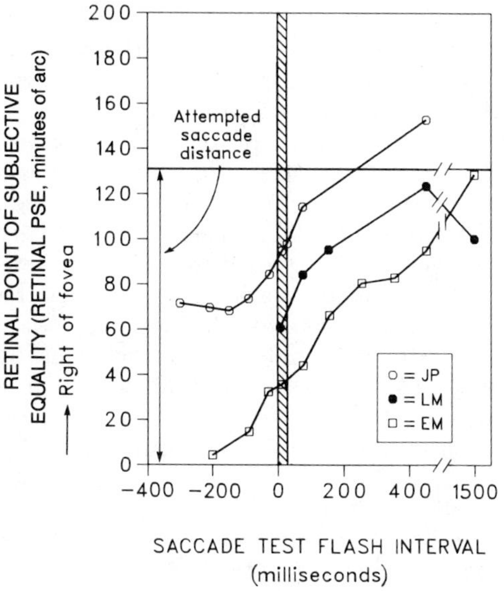

Figure 20.27. (*Above*) Change in visual direction in the presence of a 2° 11 min voluntary saccade. Point of subjective equality (PSE) in retinal coordinates for the fixation target as measured by the test flash plotted as a function of saccade test flash interval. The PSE plotted here is a distance at the retina between the location of the fixation target before the saccade and the retinal point that appears to lie in the same direction as the fixation target at the time plotted on the abscissa. The crosshatched region represents the period of the saccade. If EEPI were appropriate to maintain stability of visual direction the data would remain at zero until the saccade began, begin to climb from zero at the beginning of the saccade, and complete its climb to 131 min at the moment the saccade terminated. Instead the time course of visual direction change is much slower than the time course of the saccade itself. (From L. Matin, Saccades and extraretinal signal for visual direction, in R. A. Monty & J. W. Senders (Eds.), *Eye movement and psychological processes*, Lawrence Erlbaum Associates, 1976. Reprinted with permission.)

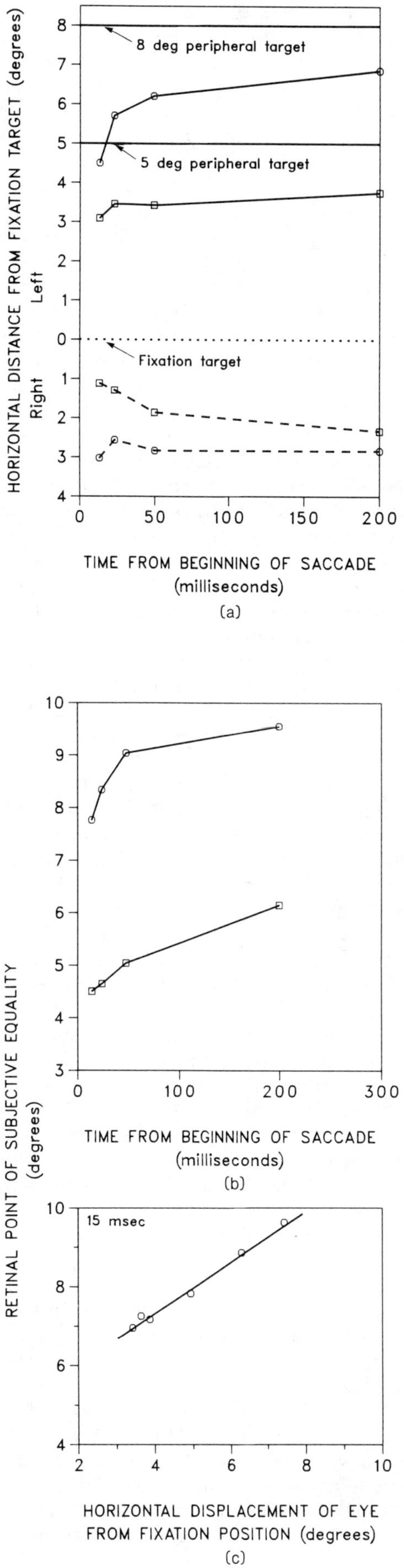

Figure 20.28. (*Opposite*) Change in visual direction in the presence of a 5 or 8° saccade for one observer. The temporal sequence of stimuli is as displayed in Figure 20.26. (a) Mean eye position at times during and after saccade when test flashes were presented (solid lines) and points of subjective equality at the stimulus array (dashed lines) for a 5° saccade (open circles) and 8° saccade (open squares) plotted as a function of time from the beginning of the saccade. (b) Point of subjective equality in retinal coordinates plotted as a function of time from the beginning of the saccade. (c) Point of subjective equality in retinal coordinates plotted as a function of the horizontal displacement of the eye 15 msec into the 8° saccade. As for the 2° 11 min saccade described in Figure 20.27, the time course of visual direction is slower than the time course of the saccade for 5° saccades and for 8° saccades. The slowing is less prominent here, however. In addition, the employment of EEPI is displayed in (c), which demonstrates that variation in EEPI employed for localization varies with actual eye position at a particular time into a 8° saccade. (From J. Pola, *The relation of visual direction to eye position during and following a voluntary saccade*, unpublished doctoral dissertation, Columbia University, 1972.)

right of the (previously seen) fixation target equally often ("50% point"). The shift with time is shown in Figure 20.27 for 2° 11 min saccades and in Figure 20.28 for 5 and 8° saccades. The shift began before the saccade and continued for some time after the saccade (the typical 2° 11 min saccade was completed in about 25 msec; the 8° saccade was completed in about 50 msec). Much of the shift of PSE was completed before the saccade was over, although this differed among individuals and apparently depended on how much of the shift occurred in the time period before the end of the saccade; a larger presaccadic shift left less for the later time period.

There was enough variability in saccade length, and in some cases there was also variability in the velocity/position characteristic for saccades of a given length, so that a further analysis was possible. [Although saccades executed in normally illuminated environments normally do exhibit inaccuracies that are corrected by one or more additional smaller saccades, the variability in the present case is also likely to have been increased by being carried out in total darkness with the saccade's target removed (Becker & Fuchs 1969).] A shorter saccade also resulted in the eye's having traveled a shorter distance at a particular time interval after the saccade had begun. Thus there was also trial-to-trial variation in the position of the eye at any particular time interval after the saccade had begun. Figure 20.28(c) displays the linear increase of retinal PSE with eye position (distance into the saccade) at a given time after the saccade's beginning. A similar effect of eye position at a given time holds at each duration (although not necessarily with the same slope). The intercept of the relation is not a 0,0; there is instead an offset of the shift of retinal local signs from the shift in eye position.

Although dependence of retinal PSE on both time and eye position is a manifestation of a mechanism related to the occurrence of the saccade it does not, in the present situation, produce the stability of localization that is normally present in viewing continuously visible structured visual fields. Thus, for example, in Figure 20.28 at about the end of the 8° saccade (50 msec), the observer sets the test flash to match the location of the fixation target at a position almost 2° away from the actual location of the fixation target. A shift of localization of this magnitude in a normally illuminated visual field would not only be noticeable as such by the observer, but also appear as a large and peculiar deviation from perceptual stability. The trial-to-trial standard deviations of the PSE values measured at the target array were also large, more than 1.5°.

The results outlined above cannot be accounted for exclusively on the basis of a cancellation mechanism. Other mechanisms are involved. These are described in the following section.

5.4. The Relation of Visual Persistence to Perceptual Stability

As noted earlier, extinction of a visual stimulus at a given retinal region does not imply that the visual perception will terminate simultaneously. The usual effect of stimulus extinction is a gradual fading of the visual response, a process that can take as long as 200–300 msec after stimulus extinction (Bowen et al., 1974; Efron, 1970a, 1970b; Matin & Bowen, 1976). Two experiments have demonstrated the way in which persistence can influence visual localization. The first of these experiments (Figs. 20.29 and 20.30) demonstrates that for a local sign shift to occur between two views, at least one of them must have receded from a persisting visual appearance into memory. If both are simultaneously seen their relative visual directions will be based on their retinotopic relation with no involvement of a cancellation mechanism. The solid-circle results in Figure 20.30 are from a set of measurements that employed the paradigm in Figure 20.29 (two flash); the open-circle measurements are from the previous paradigm represented in Figure 20.26 (in Figure 20.30 this is labeled one flash). The two-flash paradigm is the same as the one-flash paradigm with one major exception: in the two-flash paradigm the observer compared the relative locations of two 1-msec flashes. The first of the two (standard flash) was presented when the eye had reached 1° into the saccade and was presented to the same retinal location on all trials. That location was the one found to be the retinal PSE for the fixation target in the one-flash paradigm with the eye 1° into the saccade. The retinal PSE at this point in the saccade is at 340 min arc (Figure 20.30 at $t = 0$). In the two-flash paradigm the second flash was presented at a specific time after the first flash, and to a retinal position that was randomly varied from trial to trial. The retinal PSE for the first flash was thus measured with this second flash. Because the second flash in this experiment occurred at the same time relative to the saccade as the test flash in the first experiment, the variation of retinal PSE with time should be the same for both experiments if this variation was solely a function of the operation of a cancellation mechanism. However, there is a large divergence between the two sets of data at the early times (from 0 to 200 msec for the observer in Figure 20.30).

The importance of the divergence in Figure 20.30 and its basis in visual persistence can be understood by considering one portion of the results: At 100 msec after the 1° point into the saccade ($t = 0$ in the abscissa) the retinal PSE for the fixation target had already departed by about 110 min arc from its value at 0 msec (from 340 to 450 min—open circle ordinate values). Yet when the standard was presented as a flash at 0 msec, the retinal PSE for this standard as measured by flashes 100 msec later had barely moved from the retinal PSE at 0 msec (solid circles). Stated another way, when two flashes were presented on a given trial, one each at 0 and 100 msec, they had to be presented at almost the same retinal location to appear in the same location (retinotopic match), although the retinal PSEs for the previously viewed fixation target were very different at these same two times. Two important inferences follow from this result: (1) Transitivity has failed; that is, two retinal PSEs taken separately for the previously viewed fixation target (one at 0 and a second at 100 msec; open-circle results) are not equal to each other when directly compared (solid-circle results). (2) The transitivity failure took place in just the region of time over which we would expect persistence for the first flash to exist, suggesting that it was the simultaneity of visual perception of the two flashes in the closed-circle results that led to the retinal PSE holding at a nearly fixed value for the interflash intervals up to 100–200 msec.

A second experiment (Matin, 1976b) demonstrated the same point in a different way: neither the PSE nor the SD (standard deviation) of a vernier discrimination was affected by the relative intensities of the two vertical lines when the target was flashed for 1 msec to the central fovea at the midpoint of a voluntary 2° 11 min saccade. The results were indistinguishable between conditions in which the upper line was 100 times brighter, 100 times dimmer, or equal to the intensity of the lower line. But the eye was traveling at about 6 min·msec^{-1} at the time of

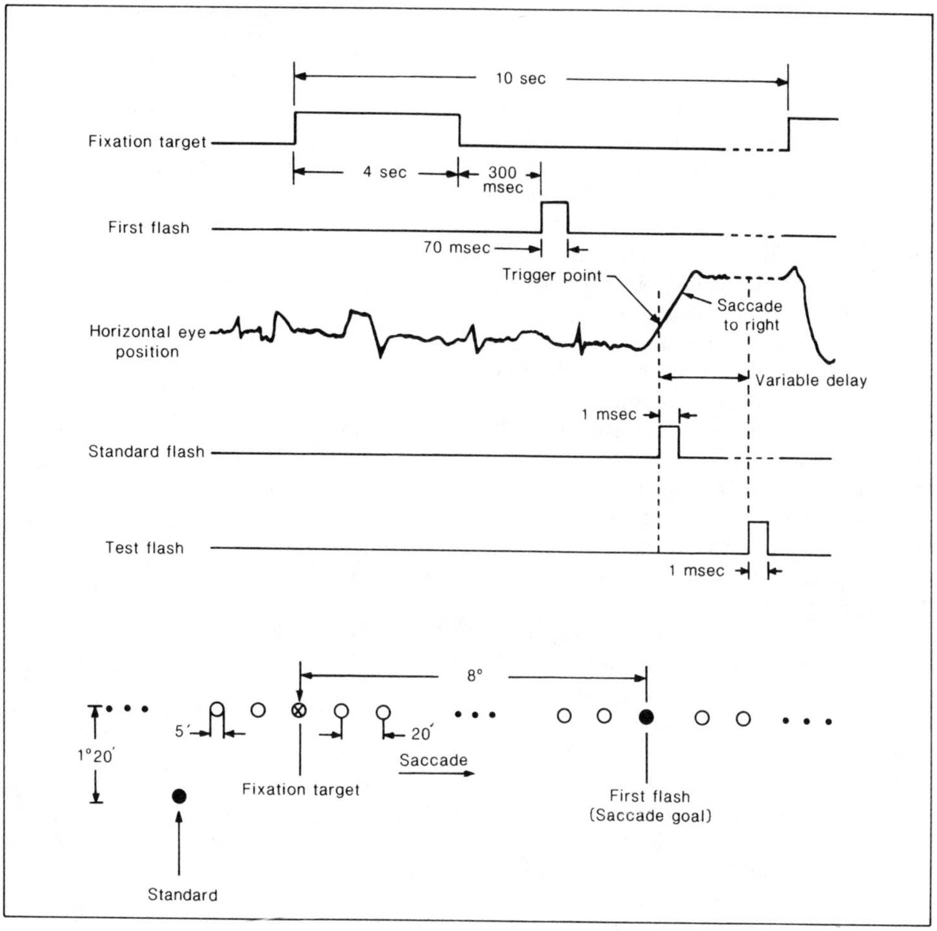

Figure 20.29. Stimulus paradigm used to evaluate effects of visual persistence on visual direction in the presence of voluntary saccades. The subject reported the location of the randomly located test flash relative to the location of the standard flash. The standard flash was set to a fixed location at that horizontal distance from the fixation target for which it appeared in the same visual direction as the fixation target as determined by the method described earlier. (From L. Matin, Saccades and extraretinal signal for visual direction, in R. A. Monty & J. W. Senders (Eds.), *Eye movements and psychological processes*, Lawrence Erlbaum Associates, 1976. Reprinted with permission.)

reception of the vernier target. Because a decrease in latency of the visual response is to be expected with the increased intensity, and because the only information regarding the presence of each of the lines in the flash must await the visual response from the optic nerve (where visual latency variations due to intensity variations are already manifested), one would predict a 6-min perceived offset for as little as a 1-msec difference in visual latency; that is, one would predict a failure of a cancellation mechanism here. The ineffectiveness of the intensity difference indicates either that the cancellation mechanism makes use of visual information that does not manifest an intensity-based latency difference (an extremely unlikely event) or that the cancellation mechanism was ineffective in shifting local signs between the two different-intensity flashed lines composing the vernier target. The latter interpretation fits exactly with the interpretation of the previous experiment, demonstrating that cancellation does not operate for two stimuli presented at different times as long as both can be seen simultaneously, a perception that is mediated by the visual persistence of the first stimulus continuing until the second stimulus becomes visible.

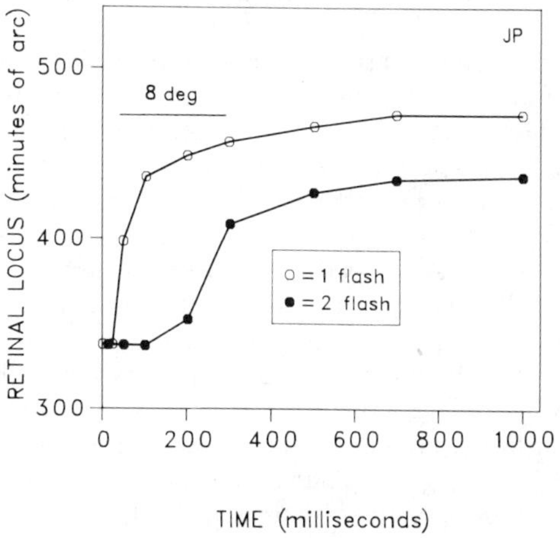

Figure 20.30. Data from experiment employing paradigm shown in Figure 20.29 (open points). Subject JP executed a 8° saccade. (From L. Matin, Saccades and extraretinal signal for visual direction, in R. A. Monty & J. W. Senders (Eds.), *Eye movements and psychological processes*, Lawrence Erlbaum Associates, 1976. Reprinted with permission.)

5.5. The Relation of Saccadic Suppression to Perceptual Stability

5.5.1. Metacontrast/Masking. The experiments in the preceding section show that when the perceptions of two stimuli overlap in time their relative localizations are based on a retinotopic match. Because visual persistence can extend for 200–300 msec beyond the termination of a visual stimulus (Bowen et al., 1974; Efron, 1970a, 1970b; Matin & Bowen, 1976) and because voluntary saccades rarely take as long as 100 msec for completion, the above results also imply that relative localizations of presaccadic and postsaccadic views would be carried out as a retinotopic match and thus perceptual instabilities should be the rule. However, perceptual instabilities rarely occur. Their absence implies that either visual persistence itself or the influence of visual persistence on localization has been eliminated. The fact that when a saccade is complete we normally do not see either a presaccadic view or the retinal "smear" (succession of stimulations present at the retina during the saccade) tells us as a minimum, without any further consideration or experimentation, that visual persistence of the presaccadic and during-saccade views has been curtailed. This saccadic suppression is essentially mediated by a mechanism based on metacontrast in which the spatiotemporal sequence of retinal stimulation produced by each target itself provides the interference for the persistence of the earlier stimulation. This conclusion is demonstrated (Matin, 1972; E. Matin et al., 1972; see also Holly, 1975; Mateeff, 1978, Figure 3) by the fact that a briefly flashed thin vertical line whose illumination onset is temporally coincident with a horizontal saccade's beginning will appear to have a horizontal extent whose length first increases with (and corresponds to) the extent of the retina across which the line's image is distributed by virtue of the eye movement (Figure 20.31). But this increase in perceived horizontal extent only holds for increases in flash duration up to the duration of the saccade. At moderate to high intensities (e.g., above 0.23 log mlam) if the flash duration extends into the postsaccadic period, the perceived horizontal extent of the smear appears shorter than on occasions when the flash duration equals the saccade duration; increases of flash duration within the postsaccadic period produce still further decreases in the perceived extent, until for a flash duration equal to 100 msec the line width appears no different from either an instantaneous presentation or a normal continuous presentation with no saccade. At lower intensities, although the perceived extent decreases when saccade duration is smaller than flash duration, the smear continues to have a perceived extent that is considerably longer than for continuous presentation even for flash durations of 300 msec. Because the increased duration of flash beyond the duration of the saccade only adds energy to the retinal locus of the postsaccadic image on an essentially stationary eye, the decrease in visually perceived length of the smear with increase in duration must be due to a metacontrast-type of inhibition produced by this buildup of energy; the larger and more prolonged the buildup, the greater the suppression of perception of the smear in adjacent regions. Thus each target in a visual field is a suppressor of presaccadic persistence and of the during-saccade retinal stimulation from itself. Although the "energy pileup" in one retinal location from a given target after the saccade provides the optimal condition for the operation of metacontrast in eliminating the visibility of the weaker during-saccade stimulation from the same target, further interference from other targets whose images cross on the retina during the saccade would only further increase the interference and so reduce the visibility of the earlier stimulation. Thus each target "carries its own suppressor" with it.

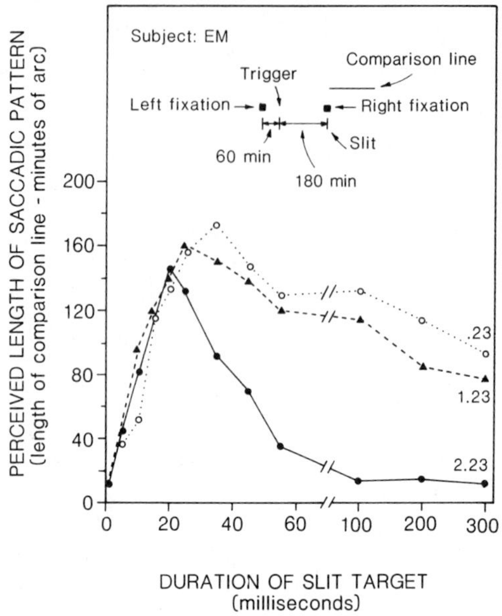

Figure 20.31. Perceived length of the saccadic pattern is shown as a function of the duration of illumination of a 2-min wide slit which was presented when the eye had traversed a distance of 1° in the course of a 4° saccade. The slit target's duration is shown on the abscissa. The three values of luminance are shown (log ml) at the right of the curves. The stimulus pattern is shown with all fields present, the comparison line at full length, and light and dark reversed relative to the experiment. (From E. Matin, B. Clymer, & L. Matin, Metacontrast and saccadic suppression, *Science*, 178. Copyright 1972 by American Association for the Advancement of Science. Reprinted with permission.)

The above description of saccadic suppression is further clarified by the experiments of Brooks and Fuchs (1975); Brooks, Impelman, and Lum (1980); MacKay (1970a, 1970b); Mitrani, Mateeff, & Yakimoff (1970a, 1970b). Thus MacKay (1970a) found that with a steadily fixating eye an instantaneous movement of a 10-min circular background produced an elevation in visual threshold for a test flash in the center of the background. The elevation follows the same time course as does the threshold elevation in the presence of a voluntary saccade. It begins 50–100 msec prior to the beginning of the saccade, rises to a maximum during the saccade, and decreases monotonically until 200–300 msec after the saccade, when it approximates the value of threshold temporally distant from the saccade. The magnitude of threshold elevation in the presence of saccadic eye movements is influenced by the temporal, spatial, and pattern relations between test flash and background (Brooks & Fuchs, 1975; Mitrani et al., 1970a, 1970b).

5.5.2. A Central Component of Saccadic Suppression. The component of saccadic suppression of visibility described above is capable of eliminating from perception smears that are many log units above threshold. But there is a component of saccadic suppression that has been observed in ways that make it clear that it lies in mechanisms other than metacontrast-type masking from moving or stationary backgrounds or fixation points, or to variations in retinal sensitivity across retinal regions (cf., Greenhouse, 1981; Greenhouse & Cohn, 1980; Greenhouse, Cohn, & Stark, 1980; Pearce & Porter, 1970; Riggs, Merton, & Moron, 1974; Volkmann, 1962; Volkmann, Schick, & Riggs, 1968; Zuber

& Stark, 1966). This component accounts for an increase of threshold to a value about 0.5 log units above the threshold for the stationary eye. It is clear that the increase is a central effect not due to visual masking. Although it is not clear that the increase has a unitary basis, some components of the mechanism have been separated out.

By a signal detection approach, Pearce and Porter (1970) established the existence of a criterion-free change in sensitivity as well as a criterion change whose time course paralleled the time course of the threshold change. Possibly connected to this is the observation that trial-to-trial variability exists for the perceived spatial location of flashes presented during saccades (Matin & Pearce, 1965; Matin et al., 1969); it was thus suggested (Matin, referred to in E. Matin, 1974) that the increase in visibility threshold for flashes in darkness during a saccade is a consequence of increased spatial uncertainty just as introducing spatial uncertainty for measurements of threshold with a fixated eye is also well known as a means of raising threshold (Blackwell, 1953). The actual existence of this component and its basis in spatial uncertainty have been demonstrated by showing that a clearly visible pedestal for a test flash which marks the spatial location also eliminates the suppression (Greenhouse, 1981; Greenhouse & Cohn, 1980; Greenhouse, Cohn & Stark, 1980). Although the proof of the existence of an influence of spatial uncertainty does not prove the nonexistence of other central effects as explanations for the 0.5 or so log units of suppression that can remain after factors related to the spatiotemporal pattern of retinal stimulation are eliminated, it does suggest that the existence of others is less likely. Thus, for example, if spatial uncertainty exists for phosphenes produced during saccades (as is extremely likely), it may be sufficient to explain the results of Riggs et al., Morton (1974), who measured a suppression equivalent to about 0.4 log units for electrical phosphenes.

5.6. Saccadic Suppression of Displacement

The spatial uncertainty of location in the presence of a voluntary saccade has itself been specifically separated out for study by several groups of workers (Bridgeman et al., 1975; Bridgeman & Stark, 1979; Li et al., 1985; Mack, 1970; Stark et al., 1976; Wallach & Lewis, 1966; Whipple & Wallach, 1978). Stark and Bridgeman and their co-workers have reported that when a complex target is displaced in the presence of a voluntary saccade an increase in threshold for the detection of the target displacement is obtained whose magnitude may reach one-third the length of the saccade and whose time course is locked to the saccade with the same relation observed for the change in visibility threshold (Figure 20.32). Most significant perhaps is the finding that increases in the threshold for displacements in the direction of the saccade are not only as large as for displacements against the direction of the saccade, but of the same size as the threshold rise for displacements orthogonal to the saccade. [A report of a larger threshold increase in the direction of the saccade than the increase orthogonal to the saccade (Whipple & Wallach, 1978) has been reinterpreted in terms of technical factors by Bridgeman & Stark (1979).] This identity of the

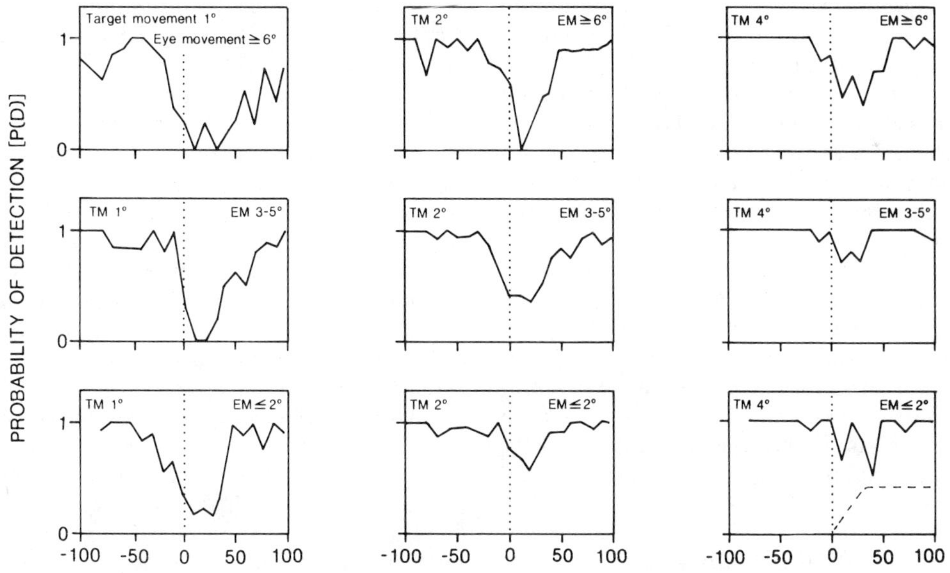

Figure 20.32. Saccadic suppression of displacement. The observer made saccades of various sizes from point to point in an array. The saccade triggered a displacement of the array by a randomly chosen magnitude, direction, and time from the saccade beginning. The observer reported whether or not a target displacement was detected. Each column of graphs displays results for one size of target displacement (1, 2, 4°). Each row represents data for eye movements greater than a given minimum. Each graph plots the probability of detection of a displacement against time relative to a zero that marks the beginning of the saccade. A 6° saccade is shown schematically in the lower right graph by the dashed line. A decrease in detectability of target displacement begins before the beginning of the saccade, detectability reaches a minimum for displacements during the saccade, detectability improves for displacements later in the saccade, and after the saccade is over detectability returns to the base line of near 100%. (From B. Bridgeman, D. Hendry, & L. Stark, Failure to detect displacement of the visual world during saccadic eye movements, *Vision Research, 15*. Copyright 1975 by Pergamon Press, Ltd. Reprinted with permission.)

threshold increase for same and orthogonal directions clearly does not fit with an interpretation simply in terms of the cancellation model. The basis for the increase in displacement threshold in the presence of saccades has not yet been uncovered and remains an important problem for future work to clarify.

5.7. Perceptual Stability in the Presence of a Visible Background

A number of experiments have been carried out in which flashes presented before, during, and after saccades are localized relative to objects on a steady background (Bischof & Kramer, 1968; Mateeff, 1978; Matin, 1976b; O'Regan, 1984). All observers manifest very substantial and frequent localization errors during and after the completion of the saccade, with the largest reported (but not at all untypical) being 15° during 16° saccades (Bischof & Kramer, 1968). A number of differences are observed in the pattern of errors relative to the paradigm of Figure 20.26 where the saccade is carried out in darkness and no further background stimulation is available. With the visible background the errors are reduced to very small values rapidly after the saccade, whereas in darkness they may remain high for some period. In effect, against the background the test flash presented shortly after the saccade must be presented at very nearly the same retinal location as the target with which its location is being compared for it to appear in the same visual direction. If the cancellation mechanism were involved in the control of visual localization with a continuously present visual background, the very different time courses of visual stimulation and masking for test flash and background would lead to the kinds of problems involving visual latency and persistence discussed above. However, O'Regan (1984) has shown that when the visible background is continuously present, the main, if not the exclusive, control of visual localization of test flashes is by means of two separately identifiable retinal factors (related to retinal eccentricity and to background smearing, respectively) and that in the presence of a visible steady background, the paradigm does not lend itself to extracting the influence of an EEPI-based cancellation mechanism.

Thus, as with steady fixation (above) and with pursuit eye movements (below) when a basis for localization is available in the retinal stimulus, this basis dominates the perception regardless of the potential availability of an EEPI-based cancellation mechanism. The cancellation mechanism remains simultaneously available for localization of other aspects of the visual stimulus where no basis in a retinal pattern can contribute and where such a basis is not in conflict.

6. LOCALIZATION DURING PURSUIT EYE MOVEMENTS

6.1. Two Bases for Visual Movement During Pursuit Eye Movements

When an observer visually tracks a fixed point on a slowly moving target that is undergoing uniform horizontal motion, the target appears to move. Such movement is observed whether the target is viewed in complete darkness or against a visible background. The appearance of movement of the tracked target in a normally illuminated and structured environment could be a consequence of changes in the spatial relations between the tracked target and stationary contours alone or in combination with a cancellation mechanism making use of EEPI. The appearance of correctly directed movement of the tracked target in complete darkness implies a basis in an extraretinally driven cancellation mechanism. In either situation the perception of movement determined by a cancellation mechanism would be correctly labeled as egocentric. The extent to which egocentric movement and object-centered movement combine, suppress, or support each other is an interesting question to which some attention is given below. However, the main concern, as throughout this chapter, is not with the perception of movement, but with spatial localization, with the extent to which the production of pursuit movements and related perceptions of movement influence spatial localization.

The separation of two bases for the perception of movement in the immediately preceding paragraph assumes that tracking is perfect. If tracking is not perfect the appearance of movement is likely to be a consequence, at least in part, of variations of retinal position or of retinal velocity of the tracked target. Such positional and velocity variation could, for example, generate the perception of movement by stimulating units in visual cortex selectively sensitive to particular directions of movement without either the participation of a cancellation mechanism or the participation of a mechanism concerned with background-to-target relations. Following the early suggestions that cortical units selectively sensitive to the direction of motion play a role in the perception of movement (Barlow & Hill, 1963; Matin & MacKinnon, 1964; Sekuler & Ganz, 1963), considerable attention has been given to their potential role in movement perception. However, the appearance of movement is readily generated in the absence of retinal movement. So, although such cortical units are likely to be implicated in some perceptions of movement, there are other perceptions of movement in which they are not likely to be involved.

The simple analysis of the basis for the perception of movement of a tracked target appears to be complicated further by the possibility that the tracking is done with a retinally eccentric location, with the perception of movement being a consequence of a continuously unsuccessful attempt at reducing the retinal eccentricity during the pursuit. It has been proposed on several occasions that when the observer intends to fixate a target, its presence as an eccentric stimulus is sufficient to generate the appearance of movement (Crone & Lunel, 1969; Heywood & Churcher, 1971; also see below). However, if the retinal location of the apparently moving tracked target is fixed, the perception of movement when viewing without a background remains correctly ascribed to a cancellation mechanism (although it is likely that the cancellation mechanism for the perception of motion is not congruent with the one controlling visual localization (see below, particularly regarding paradoxical movement). Thus the fact that tracking is not foveally centered does not destroy the simple analytic separation of the two bases for the generation of the perception of movement.

6.2. Control of Pursuit Eye Movements by Velocity and Position

Perfect tracking is impossible. By definition, "tracking" or "pursuit" implies that the eye follows the object tracked in time and in space. Without some "retinal error signal" there is no basis for tracking—the eyes cannot "know which way to move." Of course, by repeatedly presenting the same stimulus moving over the same path (i.e., presenting the observer with a predictable motion) correct anticipation becomes possible. Tracking

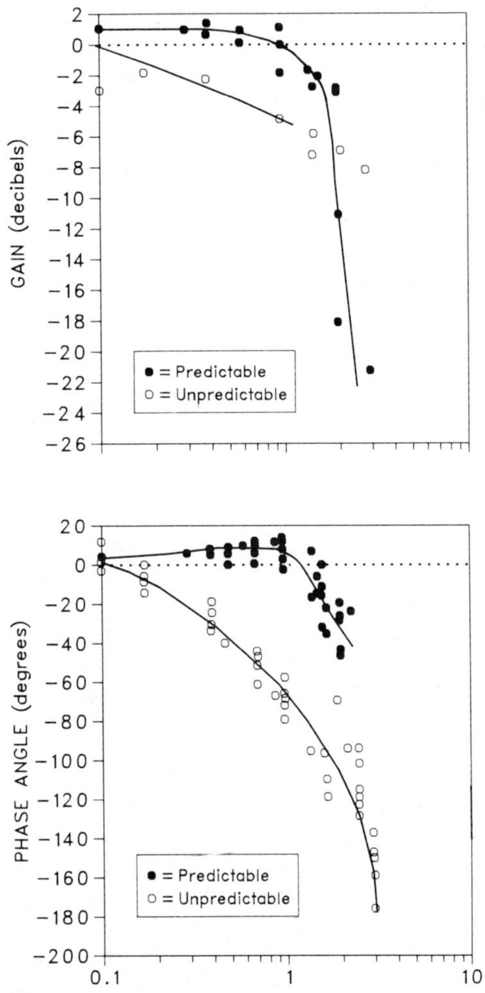

Figure 20.33. Gain and phase angle as a function of sinusoidal target frequency for continuous predictable and unpredictable target motion. The unpredictable stimulus was approximated by a sum of four to nine sinusoids of incommensurate frequencies. Following of the stimulus by the eye is better for the predictable target at all frequencies. (From L. Stark, G. Vossuis, & L. Young, Predictive control of eye tracking movements, *Transactions on Human Factor Electronics, HFE-3*. Copyright 1962 by the IRE (now IEEE). Reprinted with permission.)

is indeed better with a predictable target than with an unpredictable target (Fender & Nye, 1961; Stark, Vossius, & Young, 1962; Young & Stark, 1963; Figure 20.33). Reasonably accurate velocity matching of eye to target has been measured for velocities up to 20–40°·sec^{-1} (Dodge, Travis, & Fox, 1930; Rashbass, 1961; Robinson, 1965; Stark, et al., 1962; Westheimer, 1954), although with some lag even at very slow velocities (Fender & Nye, 1961; Puckett & Steinman, 1969; St-Cyr & Fender, 1969). Figure 20.33 shows results with periodic wave forms. Even at the lower sinusoidal frequencies for which the gain (amplitude of the eye movement/amplitude of the stimulus movement) approaches 1, phase lag and the standard deviation of eye position as a deviation from the tracked target can be substantial.

It is worth noting that the terms "pursuit" and "tracking" eye movements are misleading terms relative to what is being studied. The work still labeled "pursuit" or "tracking" includes the study of eye movements under conditions of retinal image stabilization. But the simple physical relations between retinal image location and eye movement under retinal image stabilization are the reverse of tracking or pursuit. Whereas in tracking the eye follows the target, under retinal image stabilization the target follows the eye (although with zero lag). What links the study of both is the class of eye movements that is generally of interest here: the "slow eye movements" produced in both cases.

The retinal error signal controlling the generation and maintenance of slow eye movements under the intention to fixate the tracked target could, in principle, either be one of velocity or one of position. Because both sorts of retinal errors normally tend to be correlated when one attempts to maintain fixation on a moving target, some experimental dissection is required. Observations with Rashbass's (1961) step-ramp stimulus have been most responsible for general acceptance of the conclusion that slow eye movements are under control of target velocity and not target position. Here the observer was required to maintain fixation on an initially stationary target. After a brief period the target was stepped to a new position in one direction from the original position and instantaneously began a uniform velocity return movement in the opposite direction (step to the left, ramp to the right; Figure 20.34b, c), thus returning the target toward the starting position and continuing through the starting position. For appropriate combinations of step distance and ramp velocity the observer's initial response to the step-ramp stimulus was a slow eye movement at roughly the velocity of the ramp (Figure 20.34). This eye movement was in the direction of the ramp (to the right) and began before the target crossed the starting position. Thus the eye initially made no movement to the left even though the eye started its motion from the starting position while the target was still to the left of the starting position. The eye thus preceded the target in the direction to which the target was moving during the

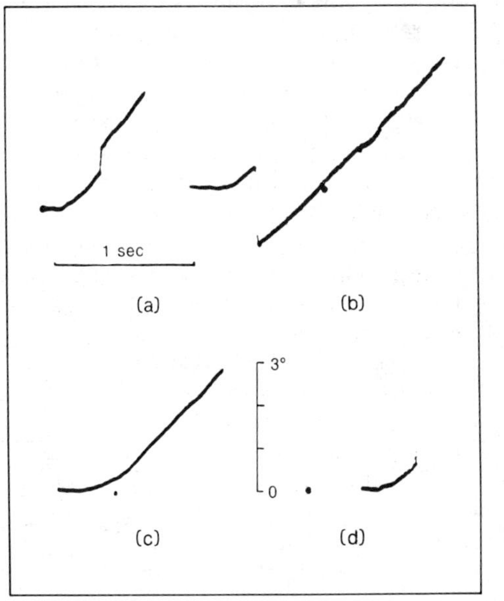

Figure 20.34. Tracking responses to a target moving with uniform velocity preceded by a variety of displacements. (a) No displacement; (b) 3° displacement in a direction opposite to the velocity; (c) 1° displacement in a direction opposite to the velocity; (d) 1° displacement in the same direction as the velocity. Note the similarity of the smooth pursuit in all cases. (From C. Rashbass, The relationship between saccadic and smooth tracking eye movements, *Journal of Physiology* (London), 1961, *159*. Reprinted with permission.)

ramp and initially moved away from the position of the target. A subsequent saccade corrected the position error. The view derived from this result is that the pursuit eye movement is responsive to target velocity and not target location, and further that location is dealt with by the saccadic system but not the pursuit system.

Further supporting the conclusion that the pursuit system is under the control of stimulus velocity is the fact that voluntary production of slow eye movements is normally impossible in a stationary visual field when an individual tries to change direction of gaze from one point to another. An occasional individual is able to make slow eye movements at will in a stationary visual field (Figure 20.25 is a recording from an individual who can produce slow eye movements of uniform velocity in which the velocity can be chosen to be any from a very slow value up to a velocity approximating those of saccades.)

6.2.1. Methods for Generating Slow, Smooth Eye Movements. However, most normal observers can generate slow, smooth eye movements in the absence of a slowly moving visual target by several different means: (1) Tracking one's own smoothly moving hand in complete darkness (Steinbach, 1976). (2) Attempting to fixate a retinally eccentric afterimage, if the eccentric placement is not too large (Heywood & Churcher, 1971; Kommerell & Taumer, 1972; Mack & Bachant, 1969; Steinbach & Pearce, 1972); within the range of eccentricities that yield slow eye movements (up to about 3°), increasing eccentricity was found to yield increased velocity by Komerall & Taumer (1972) but not by Steinbach & Pearce (1972). (3) Imagining smooth movement of an object (with eyes closed) can produce slow eye movements (Deckert, 1964; although Heywood & Churcher, 1971, could not reproduce this). (4) Rotating one's head while attempting to fixate a foveal afterimage (Yasui & Young, 1975). (5) Fixating a foveally stabilized target while a surrounding frame is oscillated, thus inducing perceived motion in the foveal target (Pola & Wyatt, 1980; Wyatt & Pola, 1979; although Mack, Fendrich, & Pleune, 1978, and Mack, Fendrich, & Wong, 1982, could not reproduce this). (6) Attempting to follow a target stepped back and forth between two eccentric retinal locations symmetrically placed on opposite sides of the fovea in open-loop (retinally stabilized) fashion yields oscillatory slow eye movements at the frequency of alternation of the stepped target (Pola & Wyatt, 1980). (7) Shifting attention from the left side of a foveal afterimage to the right side also results in a shift of the direction of the slow eye movement from left to right (Kommerell & Taumer, 1972); thus in effect voluntary control of the direction of motion of the slow eye movements is generated. Steinbach and Pearce (1972) report that slow eye movements could not be voluntarily generated in the direction opposite to the eccentricity of the afterimage (presumably then, the two sides of the afterimage employed by Kommerell & Taumer were on opposite sides of the central fovea). (8) Viewing the outline of an object (e.g., a tilted ellipse) slowly moving horizontally behind a vertical slit produces slow horizontal eye movements in the direction of the moving object even though the only retinal stimulus is the vertical movement of the two points forming the top and bottom of the outline as it passes the slit (Mack et al., 1982; Steinbach 1976). (9) In darkness, following the extinction of a foveally fixated target, the eye tends to drift further to the right if the prior autokinetic movement was leftward than if the prior autokinetic movement was rightward; if no autokinetic movement was present in the prior viewing period or if the autokinesis was orthogonal to the horizontal the extent of rightward movement fell between the amounts generated following leftward and rightward autokinesis (Picoult, Young, & Matin, 1979; Pola & Matin, 1977); this result was obtained with different horizontal gaze directions, but changing gaze direction rightward biased the entire eye movement distribution leftward and vice versa. (10) Slow involuntary eye movement is generated in the time interval between establishing the intention or expectation to execute a saccade and actual saccade execution. The ocular drift is in the direction of the anticipated saccade (Matin, Matin, & Pola, 1970; Kowler & Steinman (1981). (11) By appropriately vibrating the arm muscles with a hand-held vibrator the felt position of the arm can be made to change, to undergo felt motion. When a light is attached to the finger and viewed in otherwise total darkness, an apparent visual motion of the light is induced in a direction appropriate to the induced motion of the arm (Lackner & Levine, 1981).

6.2.2. Control of Pursuit Eye Movements. In 1972 Matin suggested that eccentricity of retinal image position is an important basis for control of pursuit eye movements and summarized some early evidence pointing to that conclusion. Since then considerable interest in the problem and support for this view have been forthcoming. Wyatt and Pola (1979) and Pola and Wyatt (1980a, 1980b) have carried out the most interesting work on this point and conclude that position is an even more important determinant than velocity. The problem of separating velocity and position is a peculiarly difficult one. One cannot change position without doing so at some velocity. The disentangling of the influence of position and of velocity from each other and from motion duration and extent has yielded important and interesting work on the absolute thresholds for motion and displacement where considerations regarding eye movements could be reasonably neglected (Henderson, 1971, 1973). Where eye movements are the focus, additional difficulties intrude. In the Pola and Wyatt experiments this intrusion appears in the fact that the slow eye movements of the size that they studied, whether generated by their "position-only" target or their "velocity-only" target, also generated perceived motion of the target. Such perceived motion (or change in perceived location) itself appears to be an important potential basis for the further generation of eye movements. Their solution to the chicken and egg problem—their separation of position and velocity—depends on a particular theoretical framework and is worth describing. Pola and Wyatt (1980b) employed a "pure" velocity target and a "pure" position target separately and in various combinations. The velocity-only target was an open-loop (foveally stabilized retinal position) fixation target made to appear to move in oscillatory fashion by surrounding it with a closed-loop (target location not controlled by eye movement or eye position) horizontally oscillating frame. The movement of the frame induced apparent motion (Duncker, 1929/1938) in the foveal target in a direction opposite to the motion of the frame. ("Velocity" in "velocity-only" refers to perceived velocity, not retinal velocity. The important characteristic of this stimulus is that by placing the target on the central fovea it could reasonably be assumed that there was no drive for pursuit eye movements to be derived from retinal position.) The position-only target was an open-loop target that alternated in square-wave fashion between two retinal points symmetrically placed on opposite sides of the fovea. (The important aspect of this target is that because retinal location was fixed except at the moments of alternation, any pursuit eye movements were generated without a retinal velocity stimulus. As the authors note, the initial "input" to the system generating eye movements is "pure" position but the substantial smooth eye movements that are generated do yield perceived movement.) Attempts at fixating the position-only target resulted in pursuit eye movements whose velocity increased linearly with retinal eccentricity of the target to reach velocities approximating $50°\cdot sec^{-1}$ at eccentricities of 3° for frequencies of target alternation at 0.5–1.0 Hz. [It is worth noting that 3° retinal eccentricity is about the outside value for which Steinbach and Pearce (1972) and Heywood and Churcher (1971) had previously reported open-loop targets to yield smooth pursuit motions.] In the velocity-only condition pursuit velocity increased with frame displacements of up to 40° to reach velocities as large as $8°\cdot sec^{-1}$ for frame oscillation frequencies at 0.5–1.0 Hz. Combinations of the position-only and velocity-only stimulus yielded appropriately larger eye movements than were obtained with only one of the components. Thus Pola and Wyatt conclude that position and velocity both control the generation of pursuit eye movements, a conclusion they support with several further experiments.

As noted above, Mack et al. (1979, 1982) have not found any influence of perceived movement on the production of slow eye movements. In addition to failing to find that the perception of induced motion of a foveally stabilized target surrounded by an oscillating frame resulted in pursuit movements in the direction of the perceived motion (the condition in which Wyatt and Pola find that slow, smooth eye movements are generated), they also report, in another condition, that the eye tracked the retinal motion of an actually moving nonstabilized target that was made to appear to move in the direction opposite to its actual motion by the inducing action of a surrounding oscillating frame. It is worth recalling some results of Steinman et al. (1967) that an observer can assume either of two modes of foveating a stationary fixation target. They labeled these the "fixate" and "hold" modes. When the observer chose the latter mode of foveating, the involuntary saccades that are normally observed [since their discovery by Ratliff and Riggs (1950) and by Ditchburn (1955)] during foveation do not occur; good foveation is maintained by the "slow" system alone. It is not unlikely that other "viewing modes," under voluntary control of the observer, are possible, particularly with the more complex stimuli employed by Pola and Wyatt and by Mack et al. Such differences in what the observer is trying to do can readily influence oculomotor behavior. In any given situation an observer can decide to track or not to track. Tracking is not an automatic reflex that is elicited regardless of the observer's intentions or attention. [Recall that even the characteristics of the tracking are influenced by the observer's voluntary shift (sic, "intended") shift of attention]. As noted above, shifting attention from the left side of an afterimage to the right converts a leftward pursuit movement to a rightward one (Kommerell & Taumer, 1972). In fact, although neither Mack et al. nor Wyatt and Pola account for the difference in their results, they agree that Mack et al.'s result is the reflection of the marked influence of retinal position in controlling the tracking under the intention to fixate. An important set of problems has just begun to be dealt with, then, and will require considerably more experimental attention in the future: how to delineate categories of intention and attention that yield distinguishable oculomotor patterns.

Although both attention and intention have been relatively opaque domains, "attention" has been the more readily accessed and controlled. This is simply because the experimenter can readily manipulate the external stimuli to which he generally wishes to direct attention, but the linkage between external stimulus and intention is more distant. The experimental study of the influence of intention on behavior will provide the more difficult challenges.

6.3. Relations Between Slow Eye Movements, Perceived Movement, and Visual Localization

Under normal viewing conditions in either an illuminated and structured visual field or in total darkness, objects that appear to move also appear to be undergoing a change in location by an amount that is at least in fair correspondence with the velocity and duration of the movement.

However, this correspondence between perceived movement and change in location undergoes severe breakdown in a number of situations in which apparent movement is generated without any corresponding movement of the physical object. The movement aftereffect is a case in point. For example, subsequent to viewing unidirectional movement of a periodic stimulus (e.g., a series of vertical bars moving in a horizontal direction), a stationary stimulus viewed with the same retinal area appears to move in the direction opposite to the previous real movement. This apparent movement can continue at velocities of several degrees per second but after a minute or more of viewing this aftermovement, the stationary stimulus does not appear to have changed location from the one at which it initially appeared.

As a second example of breakdown of the normal correspondence between change in apparent location and movement velocity, a very frequent report of observers viewing autokinetic movement—the apparent movement of a physically stationary visible target when viewed in complete darkness—is that the target appears to move for a considerable period of time in one direction yet does not appear to have gone any distance away from its starting point at the beginning of the motion. This distortion between the magnitudes of the apparent movement and apparent distance traveled—relative to relations that normally hold in physics between distance, velocity, and time—has been labeled "paradoxical movement." The discrepancies in paradoxical movement can be quite considerable. Apparent velocities of $15°\cdot sec^{-1}$ or more are observed with viewing in an extreme secondary position of gaze [where essentially unidirectional apparent movement can be obtained for long periods of time (Adams, 1912; Carr, 1910; Matin et al., 1963), values of apparent velocity being obtained either by magnitude estimation or matching to velocities of real movement against illuminated backgrounds]. This dissociation between apparent motion and apparent visual direction in darkness implies a corresponding difference in mechanisms for processing movement and visual direction. However, the basis of this dissociation is far from clear. Interestingly enough, the rapid apparent movements of a fixated stationary target are entirely nulled and the direction reversed by imposing physical movement on the target in the direction opposite that of the apparent movement at velocities as small as $15\ min\cdot sec^{-1}$ (Pearce & Matin, 1966), velocities near or at the absolute threshold for detecting movement in darkness (Henderson, 1971, 1973). Equally interesting is the fact that the observer does not discriminate the apparent movement from the real movement in this situation. When appropriately scaled, the two appear to add vectorially. But the scales required for the addition are of the order of 60/1 (using an estimate of $15°\cdot sec^{-1}$ for the apparent velocity that is nulled by a $15\text{-}min\cdot sec^{-1}$ real movement, the velocity of autokinetic movement must be scaled down by a factor of roughly 60 to enter the addition). This number is in line with what has been suggested as the open-loop low-velocity gain of the pursuit system as derived from measurements of eye movement dynamics (Pola & Wyatt, 1980a, 1980b)—a point that fits quite well with the fact that the observer whose high-velocity autokinetic movement is nulled by the low-velocity physical movement is in fact maintaining steady fixation on the visible (autokinetic + real) movement target. The difficulty with this, as well as with all the other derivations of "open-loop" gain (as has been noted above), is that although the loop is essentially "opened" with regard to the elimination of influences of the eye movement on the retinal stimulus, other consequences—specifically the influences of eye movements on perceived movement—have not necessarily been eliminated. Thus horizontally stabilizing a visible target on the central fovea markedly reduces autokinetic movement in the direction of stabilization (MacKinnon, 1964; Matin & MacKinnon, 1964) and, as discussed above, entirely stabilizing a target on an eccentric retinal location under instructions to "fixate the target" produces pursuit eye movements in the direction of the eccentricity with an accompanying appearance of apparent movement in the direction of the eye movement. To what extent the modified apparent movement influences the subsequent eye movement independently of the retinal stimulus is unclear; and so the extent to which the eye movement measured in the so-called open-loop tracking situation is truly open loop is also unclear.

That perceived movement is a causal agent for the production of slow eye movements has been proposed by several workers (Steinbach, 1976; Wyatt & Pola, 1979; Yasui & Young, 1975). This is of particular significance in the context of a general model (Figure 20.35) that incorporates the cancellation model in a framework that also deals with the generation of eye movements. Concern with a linkage between perceived movement and the generation of slow eye movements is thus of considerable interest in this chapter, where the focus is perception of spatial location, both because of the significance of the cancellation model in the treatment of the perception of location and because questions regarding perceived movement obviously have important ties to questions regarding perceived location. However, as indicated in the discussion of paradoxical autokinetic movement, exactly what those ties are remains a problem.

The model in Fig. 20.35 for the generation of pursuit eye movements attempts to bring together some of the ideas of Steinbach (1976), Yasui & Young (1975), and Wyatt & Pola (1979). These workers suggest that the production of slow eye movements is ultimately driven by perceived motion. Although the figure does a number of injustices to some of the other complexities of eye movement dynamics and relations to the vestibular-ocular linkage, the figure has been kept relatively uncomplicated in the interest of not straying too far afield. The model suggests that the EEPI generated by an eye movement is involved in the production of perceived motion via a positive feedback loop; the feedback is to the cancellation mechanism. The system's output is the pursuit eye movement. Such a system has large open-loop gain (eye movement/retinal motion), although the closed-loop gain is near to 1 {(closed-loop gain) = (open-loop gain)/[1 − (open-loop gain) × (EEPI/eye movement)]}. The gating of eye movement production by the intention to fixate the target is a critical point; as discussed earlier other intentions do not necessarily lead to the production of pursuit eye movements. The terms "retinal stimulus" and "target motion" do not only mean velocity, but are intended to refer to the function, as yet uncertain, involving stimulus position (location or visual direction) and stimulus velocity that controls the production of the eye pursuit movement.

6.4. Visual Localization During Slow Eye Movements

The relation between the pursuit eye movement and change in perceived visual direction is neither straightforward nor simple, particularly in visual environments that are relatively atten-

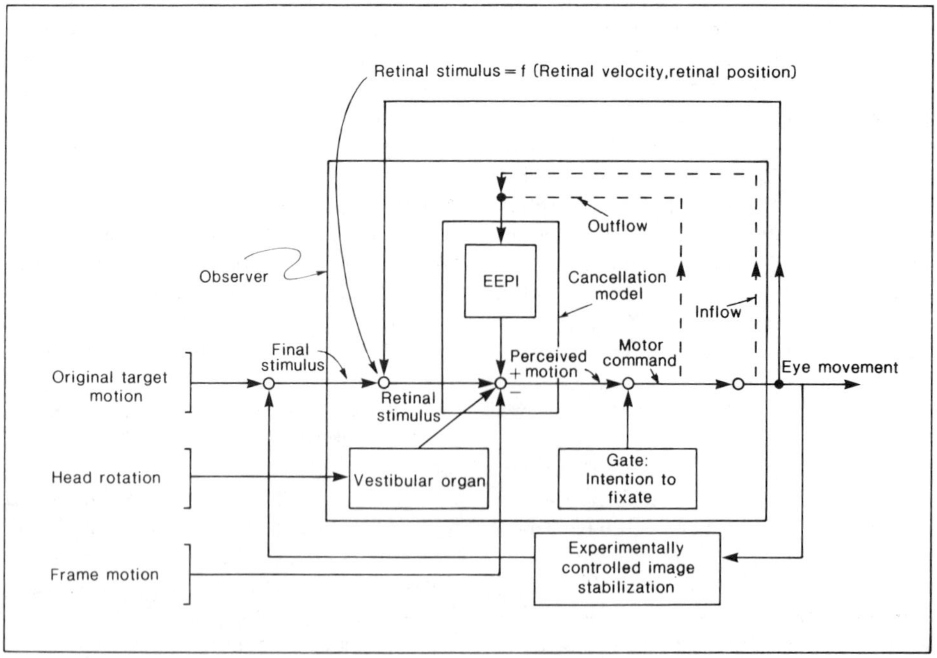

Figure 20.35. Model of system controlling pursuit eye movements. The model is derived from a number of studies that place perceived motion in a central position with regard to the generation of pursuit movement.

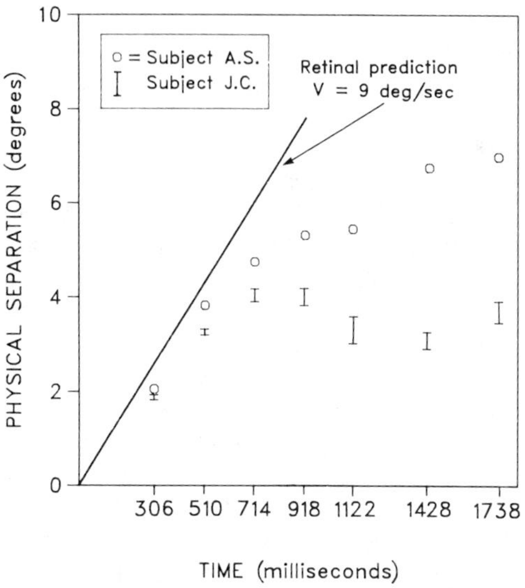

Figure 20.36. Visual direction during pursuit eye movement. Physical separation of two flashed lines reported to lie in the same visual direction whose presentations were separated by the time interval shown on the abscissa. The eye pursued a fixation target at the velocity indicated. The diagonal line in the figure is the locus of points for which the two lines would strike the same horizontal retinal location if ocular pursuit was accurate. Data would fall along the abscissa if the report was accurate with regard to physical location. Data for first experiment (not shown) lie close to the diagonal. (From A. E. Stoper, *Vision during pursuit movement: The role of oculomotor information*, unpublished doctoral dissertation, Brandeis University, 1968. Reprinted with permission.)

uated. Stoper (1973) has carried out psychophysical experiments that provide measures of relative visual direction during pursuit eye movements. Although direct determinations of eye position were not made, two types of controls were employed that gave some reasonable assurance that deviations of the eye from the moving fixation target were not greater than $\pm$ 2° and that ocular velocity did not deviate greatly from stimulus velocity. Stoper's observers tracked a small fixation target moving horizontally in darkness over a 27° distance at a constant velocity of either 0, 9, 13.5, or 27°·sec^{-1}. When this target reached the midpoint of its traverse, a vertical line was flashed at a predetermined distance from the moving fixation target's momentary location. At some time later a second vertical line was flashed at a location that varied from trial to trial. The observer reported whether the second target appeared to the left or the right of the first target. Results (PSEs) for one experimental condition are shown in Figure 20.36. It we assume accurate tracking by Stoper's observers, we can conclude that up to interflash intervals of 300–700 msec there is only a slight indication of involvement of EEPI in the discrimination. Up to this time range the settings depart only slightly from values that would result if the observer required that the two targets strike the same retinal meridian. Whatever deviation does occur could be due to the failure of the eye to keep up with the target. However, for interflash intervals beyond 700 msec deviations from a "retinal identity" basis cannot be attributed to such failure, and the departure of the data from a discrimination based on identity of horizontal retinal locus can only be attributed to a shift of local sign derived from an EEPI-driven cancellation mechanism. The error in localization appears to be approaching an asymptote of about 7° for observer AS and 4° for JC.

These results of Stoper's then have a great deal in common with the results shown earlier in Figures 20.27 and 20.28 for saccades. In both cases it is clear that for brief interflash intervals the change in eye position between the two flashes plays a minor role in judging the relative locations of the two flashes. At longer time intervals a substantial contribution of an EEPI-based cancellation mechanism is evident; the error remaining is independent of the eye movement.

Following on work of Mita, Hironaka, & Koika (1950), in which it was observed that a target flashed during a pursuit eye movement appeared to originate from a point further along the pursuit path than it actually did, Ward (1976) has carried out experiments that demonstrate the influence of stimulus intensity on the location at which a stimulus is localized during oculomotor pursuit, and interpreted the results as due to variations in visual latency with intensity, thus providing a basis for the original observations.

Ward's stimulus display is diagramed in Figure 20.37. His observer tracked a 6-min arc spot moving at a velocity of 12°·sec^{-1} from the left side of the 37° field to the right side. When the eye was in the region of the hatch marks that are close to the center of the field, a brief flash was presented from a variable location that itself was such that the observer always saw it superposed on the region of the hatch marks, and could thus report its location relative to the hatch marks. For all flash intensities the observer reported the flash as lying at a hatch mark to the right of the actual location from which it was generated. From his measurements of eye position, the observer's report of flash location, and knowledge of the actual position of the flashed target, Ward calculated a value of latency that represented the distance that the eye traveled from the moment at which the flash was generated to the moment when it was localized against the hatch marks. These calculated latency values decreased monotonically with flash intensity (Fig. 20.38) and were relatively unaffected by either ocular velocity or by the background illumination. An adequate interpretation in terms of visual latency requires only (1) that the latency of perception of the test flash be longer than the latency of perception of the continuously present hatch marks, (2) that latency decrease with increasing intensity, and (3) that the observer make his judgment of whether the flash lay to the right or the left of the hatch marks on the basis of their simultaneous appearance. It is well known from a variety of experiments including work on the Pulfrich phenomenon and on reaction time (cf. Lit, 1949) that intensity influences latency and thus visual

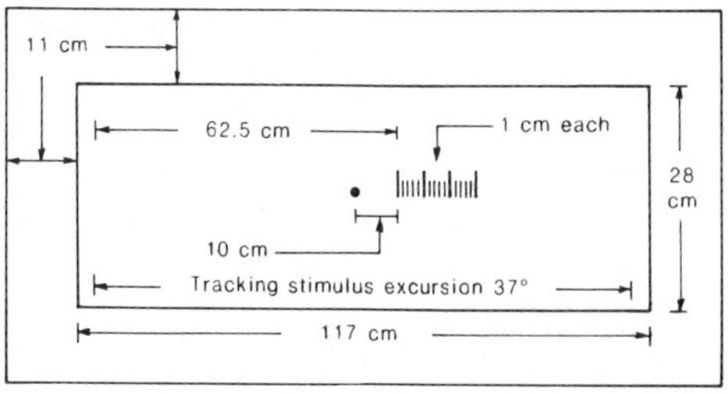

Figure 20.37. Stimulus display for measuring influence of stimulus intensity on latency and hence on visual localization during a pursuit eye movement. The observer tracked a 6-min target from the left of the screen to the right while eye movements were monitored. A test flash was presented when the eye was in the region of the hatch marks (shown enlarged here); the observer indicated localization by reporting the particular hatch mark against which the test flash was localized. (From F. Ward, Pursuit eye movements and visual localization, in R. A. Monty & J. W. Senders (Eds.), *Eye movements and psychological processes*, Lawrence Erlbaum Associates, 1976. Reprinted with permission.)

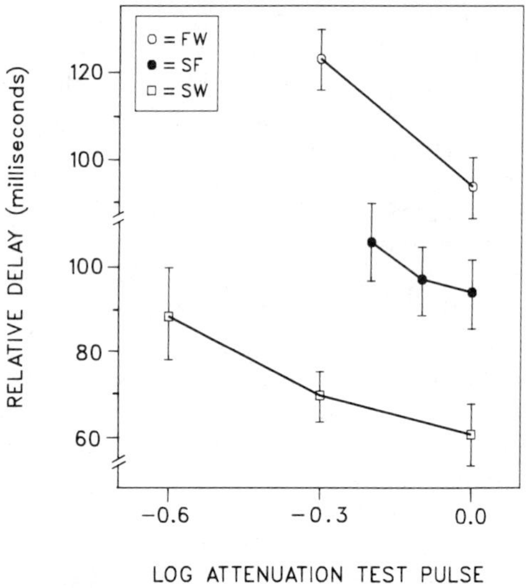

Figure 20.38. The influence of luminance of the test flash on relative visual latency as inferred from measurements of relative visual localization during pursuit eye movements. (From F. Ward, Pursuit eye movements and visual localization, in R. A. Monty & J. W. Senders (Eds.), *Eye movements and psychological processes*, Lawrence Erlbaum Associates, 1976. Reprinted with permission.)

localization in experiments where one stimulus is moved relative to a second under conditions in which no consideration need be taken of eye movements, EEPI, or cancellation. In Ward's experiments the observer is presented with a stimulus situation in which the two stimuli whose relative locations are being judged overlap considerably in time: the test flash is presented against the steady background of hatch marks. Thus Ward's results are entirely accounted for without any recourse to EEPI or cancellation. This is not to say that EEPI played no role, but only that no evidence for or against such a role can be inferred from Ward's experiment. This interpretation of Ward's results is consistent with Stoper's results described above and the other experiments involving pursuit eye movements to be described below. This is essentially the same interpretation that was described for the results of two-flash experiments in the presence of saccades and for the results with paralyzed eyes. Ward's results thus support the conclusion that only when sufficient time has elapsed for the visual persistence of the first of two stimuli to become negligible will an EEPI-based cancellation mechanism become involved in determining their perceived spatial relation, and then only when other visual context does not provide an alternate basis for the localization.

Sedgwick and Festinger (1976), Festinger, Sedgwick, and Holtzman (1976), and Holtzman, Sedgwick, and Festinger (1978) have measured the relative influence of retinal information and EEPI related to pursuit eye movements in several variations of the stimulus depicted in Figure 20.39 and found that both judgments of extent of position change and of the direction of moving spots of light depend relatively little on the use of EEPI in a cancellation mechanism that compensates for eye position change. Both position change and direction of moving spots are largely determined by the pattern of movement of the spots relative to each other and are little different from what would be perceived had the points undergone the same retinal pattern of movement while the eye was stationary instead of being a consequence of contributions by both pursuit eye movement and target movement that would be predicted by the cancellation mechanism.

The basic condition they employed required the observer to maintain fixation on point A while it oscillated horizontally with sinusoidally varying velocity. Point C started its movement from the tail of the arrow and moved in the direction of the arrow at the same time that point A began its movement; it also moved with sinusoidally varying velocity. The typical appearance involved two illusory aspects: point A appeared to move over a very much smaller horizontal distance than it actually did, and point C appeared to undergo motion whose direction was very near to the direction of C specified by its retinal path relative to A rather than its direction relative to a stationary set of spatial coordinates. The perceived extent of A's motion was measured by having the observer adjust the vertical distance of B (which traveled along with A on a horizontal path parallel to A's path) from A so that the vertical A–B distance appeared to match the perceived horizontal extent of A's motion. On a separate set of trials the perceived direction of C's motion was assessed by having the observer adjust the horizontal relation of B to A (by horizontally offsetting B) so

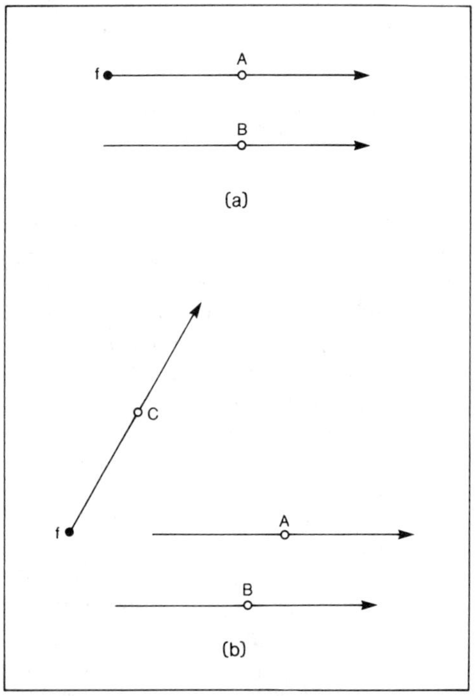

Figure 20.39. Visual displays employed for measuring visual localization during pursuit eye movements. (a) Visual display for trials in which the perceived extent of movement by spot A was measured. Spots A and B represent spots at the midpoints of their paths, always moving horizontally through equal extents. Spot B is the adjustment spot, its vertical offset adjustable to indicate the perceived horizontal extent of spot A. For control trials, spot f was also present to be fixated while the adjustment was made. Spots A and B remained aligned vertically throughout a trial. (b) Visual display for trials in which the perceived orientation of movement by spot C was measured. The linear orientation of direction of movement by spot C varied from trial to trial. Subjects tracked spot A and adjusted the horizontal offset of spot B so that the orientation of an imaginary line connecting spots A and B would be parallel to the perceived orientation of motion direction by spot C. For control trials, spot f was also presented to be fixated while the adjustment was made. (From L. Festinger, H. A. Sedgwick, & J. D. Holtzman, Visual perception during smooth pursuit eye movements, *Vision Research, 16*. Copyright 1976 by Pergamon Press, Ltd. Reprinted with permission.)

that the perceived orientation of the imaginary line between A and B appeared parallel to the direction of C's motion. Measurements of eye movements during tracking by the observer allowed calculation of retinal distances, directions, and velocities. For an extent of travel of 4° by A the observer set the A–B distance to about 1.3° for sinusoidal frequencies in the range between 0.125 and 1.0 Hz, a value that converted to a "perceptual" extent of eye travel of 0.3° at 1 Hz and increased to 1.8° at 0.125 Hz when calculations were made that "removed" the consequences of errors in tracking which themselves increased with increase in frequency of target oscillation. Increase in extent of the tracking distance produced an increase less than proportional in the perceived tracking distance in the range from 2 to 8°. From the settings of the B–A angle to match the perceived direction of travel of C, Festinger et al. also made calculations that indicated very little, if any, use of EEPI. When the observer saccaded to C under the instruction to follow C's path and the display was simultaneously "stabilized" (C remained locked to the fovea regardless of what the eye did), the eye followed a physical path that was very close to the (misperceived) direction that the observer indicated as the path he saw while tracking target A.

REFERENCES

Adams, H. F. Autokinetic sensations. *Psychological Monographs*, 1912, *14*, 1–45

Allik, J., Rauk, M., & Luuk, A. Control and sense of eye movement behind closed eyelids. *Perception*, 1981, *10*, 39–51.

Anderson, E. E., & Weymouth, F. W. Visual perception and the retinal mosaic. 1. Retinal mean local sign—an explanation of the fitness of binocular perception of distance. *American Journal of Physiology*, 1923, *64*, 591–594.

Andrews, D. Perception of contour orientation in the central fovea, part II. Spatial integration. *Vision Research*, 1967, *7*, 999–1013.

Appelle, S. Perception and discrimination as a function of stimulus orientation: The oblique effect in man and animals. *Psychological Bulletin*, 1972, *78*, 266–278.

Aubert, H. Eine scheinbare bedeutende Drehung von Objekten bei Neigung des Kopfes nach rechts oder links. *Archives of Pathological Anatomy*, 1861, *20*, 381–393.

Averill, H. L., & Weymouth, F. W. Visual perception and the retinal mosaic. II. The influence of eye-movements on the displacement threshold. *Journal of Comparative Psychology*, 1925, *5*, 147–176.

Bahill, A. T., & Stark, L. The trajectories of saccadic eye movements. *Scientific American*, 1979, *240*, 108–117.

Baker, K. E. Some variables influencing vernier acuity. 1. Illumination and exposure time. 2. Wave-length of illumination. *Journal of the Optical Society of America*, 1949, *39*, 567–575.

Barlow, H. B., & Hill, R. M. Selective sensitivity to direction of movement in ganglion cells of the rabbit retina. *Science*, 1963, *139*, 412–414.

Bauermeister, M. Effect of body tilt on apparent verticality, apparent body position, and their relation. *Journal of Experimental Psychology*, 1964, *67*, 142–147.

Becker, W., & Fuchs, A. G. Further properties of the human saccadic system: eye movements and correction sacades with and without visual fixation points. *Vision Research*, 1969, *9*, 1247–1257.

Bischof, N., & Kramer, E. Untersuchungen and Uverlegungen zur Richtungswahrnehmung bei willkulichen sakkadischen Augenbewegungen. *Psychologische Forschung*, 1968, *32*, 185–218.

Blackwell, H. R. Psychophysical thresholds: experimental studies of methods of measurement. *Bull. Dep. Eng. Res. Univ. lich*, 1953, No. 36.

Bowen, R. W., Pola, J., & Matin, L. Visual persistence: Effects of flash, luminance, duration and energy. *Vision Research*, 1974, *14*, 295–303.

Bridgeman, B., Hendry, D., & Stark, L. Failure to detect displacement of the visual world during saccadic eye movements. *Vision Research*, 1975, *15*, 719–722.

Bridgeman, B., & Stark, L. Omnidirectional increase in threshold for image shifts during saccadic eye movements. *Perception and Psychophysics*, 1979, *25(3)*, 241–243.

Brindley, G. S., Goodwin, G. M., Kulikowski, J. J., & Leighton, D. Stability of vision with a paralysed eye. *Journal of Physiology*, 1976, *258*, 65–66.

Brindley, G. A., & Merton, P. A. The absence of position sense in the human eye. *Journal of Physiology*, 1960, *153*, 127–130.

Brooks, B. A., & Fuchs, A. F. Influence of stimulus parameters on visual sensitivity during saccadic eye movements. *Vision Research*, 1975, *15*, 1389–1398.

Brooks, B. A., Impelman, D. M., & Lum, J. T. Influence of background luminance on visual sensitivity during saccadic eye movements. *Experimental Brain Research*, 1980, *40*, 322–329.

Brown, K. T. Factors affecting differences in apparent size between opposite halves of visual meridian. *Journal of the Optical Society of America*, 1953, *43*, 464–472.

Brown, K. T. An experiment demonstrating instability of retinal directional values. *Journal of the Optical Society of America*, 1955, *45*, 301–307.

Carr, H. A. The autokinetic sensation. *Psychological Review*, 1910, *17*, 42–75.

Cohen, M. M. Elevator illusion: influence of otolith organ activity and neck proprioception. *Perception and Psychophysics*, 1973, *14*, 401–406.

Cohen, M. M. Visual-proprioceptive interactions. In R. D. Walk & H. L. Pick Jr., (Eds.) *Intersensory perception and sensory interaction.* New York: Plenum Press, 1981.

Cornsweet, T. N. Determination of the stimuli for involuntary drifts and saccadic eye movements. *Journal of the Optical Society of America*, 1956, *46*, 987–993.

Crone, R., & Lunel, H. Autokinesis and the perception of movement: The physiology of eccentric fixation. *Vision Research*, 1969, *9*, 89–102.

Deckert, G. H. Pursuit eye movements in the absence of a moving stimulus. *Science*, 1964, *143*, 1192–1193.

Ditchburn, R. W. Eye-movements in relation to retinal action. *Optica Acta*, 1955, *1*, 171–176.

Ditchburn, R. W. Eye movements and visual perception. Oxford, England: Clarendon Press, 1973.

Dodge, R., Travis, R. C., & Fox, J. C. Optic nystagmus III. Characteristics of the slow phase. *Archives of Neurology*, 1930, *24*, 21–34.

Duncker, K. Über induzierte Bewegung (Ein Beitrag zur Theorie optisch wahrgenommener Bewegung). *Psychologische Forschung* 1929, *12*, 180–259. Translated and extracted in a *Source book of gestalt psychology* (prepared by W. D. Ellis, London: Routledge and Kegan Paul, 1938).

Efron, R. The minimum duration of a perception. *Neuropsychologica*, 1970, *8*, 56–63. (a)

Efron, R. The relationship between the duration of a stimulus and the duration of a perception. *Neuropsychologica*, 1970, *8*, 37–55. (b)

Evarts, E. V. Feedback and corollary discharge: A merging of the concepts. *Neurosciences Research Progress Bulletin*, 1971, *9*, 86–112.

Fender, D. H., & Nye, P. W. An investigation of the mechanisms of eye movement control. *Kyerbetik*, 1961, *1*, 81–88.

Fender, D. H., & Nye, P. W. The effects of retinal image motion in a simple pattern recognition task. *Kybernetik*, 1962, *1*, 192–199.

Festinger, L., Sedgwick, H. A., & Holtzman, J. D. Visual perception during smooth pursuit eye movements. *Vision Research*, 1976, *16*, 1377–1386.

Findlay, J. M. Direction percerption and human fixation eye movements. *Vision Research*, 1974, *14*, 703–711.

Fiorentini, A., & Ercoles, A. M. Involuntary eye movements during attempted monocular fixation. *Atti Della Fondazione Giorgio Ronchi*, 1966, *21*, 199–217

Fiorentini, A., & Ercoles, A. M. Visual direction of a point source in the dark. *Atti Della Fondazione Giogio Ronchi*, 1968, *23*, 405–428.

Foley, J. M. Successive stereo and vernier discrimination as a function of dark interval. *Vision Research*, 1976, *16*, 1269–1273.

Foley, J. M. Primary Distance Perception. In R. Held, H. W. Leibowitz, & H.-L. Teuber (Eds.), *Handbook of sensory physiology* (Vol. 8). New York: Springer, 1978.

Gaze, R. M. *The formation of nerve connections*. New York: Academic, 1970.

Gaze, R. M., & Sharma, S. C. Axial differences in the reinnvervation of the goldfish tectum by regenerating optic nerve fibers. *Experimental Brain Research*, 1970, *10*, 171–181.

Graybiel, A. Oculogravic illusion. *AMA Archives of Ophthalmology*, 1952, *48*, 605–615.

Greenhouse, D. S. *Saccadic suppression of flash detection: The uncertainty theory vs. alternative theories*. Unpublished doctoral dissertion, University of California, Berkeley, 1981.

Greenhouse, D. S., & Cohn, T. E. Saccadic suppression: uncertainty vs. alternative theories. April Supp., Investigative Opthalmology and Visual Science, 1980, 19 (April Suppl.), 164.

Greenhouse, D. S., Cohn, T. E., & Stark, L. Saccadic suppression may be due entirely to uncertainty of the frame of reference. April Suppl. Investigative Opthalmology and Visual Science, 1980, 17 (April Suppl.), 106.

Gregory, R. L. Eye movements and the stability of the visual world. *Nature* London, 1958, *182*, 1214–1216.

Gregory, R. L., & Zangwill, O. O. The origin of the autokinetic effect. *Quarterly Journal of Experimental Psychology*, 1963, *15*, 252–261.

Hein, A., & Diamond, R. Contribution of Eye Movement to the Representation of Space. In A. Hein & M. Jeannerod (Eds.), *Spatially oriented behavior*. New York: Springer, 1983.

Hein, A., Durand, F. V., Salinger, W., & Diamond, R. Eye movements initiate visual-motor developments in the cat. *Science*, 1979, *204*, 1321–1322.

Held, R., & Hein, A. Movement-produced stimulation in the development of visually guided behavior. *Journal of Comparative and Physiological Psychology*, 1963, *56*, 872–876.

Helmholtz, H., Von. Hanbuch der Phsyiologischen Optik. Leipzig: Voss, 1866. English translation from 3rd. ed., 1925. J. P. C. Southall (Ed); *A treatise on physiological optics* (Vol. 3). New York: Dover, 1963.

Henderson, D. Movement perception and the displacement threshold. *Perception and Psychophysics*, 1971, *10*, 313–320.

Henderson, D. Visual discrimination of motion: Stimulus relationships at threshold and the question of luminance-time reciprocity. *Perception and Psychophysics*, 1973, *13*, 121–130.

Hering, E. Der Raumsinn und die Bewegungen des Auges. In Hermann, L.: *Handbuch der physiologie* 3 (Part 1), 1879. English translation, C. A. Radde, (Ed.); *Spatial sense and movement of the eye*. American Journal of Optometry, 1942.

Hershberger, W. Impressions of visual direction from extraocular afference. *Perception and Psychophysics*, 1984, *35*, 400–401.

Heywood, S. & Churcher, J. Eye movements and the afterimage—I. Tracking the afterimage. *Vision Research*, 1971, *11*, 1163–1168.

Hill, A. L. Direction constancy. *Perception and Psychophysics*. 1972, *11*, 175–178.

Holly, F. Saccadic perception of a moving target. *Vision Research*, 1975, *15*, 331–335.

Holst, E. von. Relation between the central nervous system and the peripheral organs. *British Journal of Animal Behavior*, 1954, *2*, 89–94.

Holst, E. von, & Mittelstaedt, H. Das Reafferenzprinzip. *Naturwissenschaften*, 1950, *37*, 464–476.

Holtzman, J. D., Sedgwick, H. A., & Festinger, L. Interaction of perceptually monitored and unmonitored efferent commands for smooth pursuit eye movements. *Vision Research*, 1978, *18*, 1545–1555.

Jacobson, M. *Developmental neurobiology*. New York: Holt, 1970.

Jacobson, M., & Levine, R. L. Plasticity in the adult frog brain: Filling the visual scotoma after excision or translocation of parts of the optic tectum. *Brain Research*, 1975, *88*, 339–345.

James, W. *The principles of psychology* (vol. 2). New York: Dover, 1950. (Originally published, 1890.)

Kalil, R. E., & Freedman, S. J. Persistence of ocular rotation following compensation for displaced vision. *Perceptual and Motor Skills*, 1966, *22*, 135–139.

Keesey, U. T. Effects of involuntary eye movements on visual acuity. *Journal of the Optical Society of America*, 1960, *50*, 769–774.

Keller, W., & Kinchla, R. A. Visual movement discrimination. *Perception and Psychophysics*, 1968, *3*, 233–236.

Kinchla, R. A. A Psychophysical Model of Visual Movement Perception. In R. A. Monty & J. W. Senders (Eds.), *Eye movements and psychophysical processes*. Hillsdale, N.J.: Erlbaum, 1976.

Kinchla, R. A. & Allan, L. G. A theory of visual movement perception. *Psychological Review*, 1969, *76*, 537–558.

Kinchla, R. A. & Smyzer, F. A diffusion model of perceptual memory. *Perception and Psychophysics*, 1967, *2*, 219–229.

Kommerell, G., & Taumer, R. Investigations of the eye tracking system through stabilized retinal images. In J. Dichcans & E. Bizzi (Eds.), *Cerebral control of eye movements and motion perception*. Basel, Switzerland: Karger, 1972.

Kornheiser, A. S. Adaptation to laterally displaced vision: A review. *Psychological Bulletin*, 1976, *83*, 783–816.

Krauskopf, J., Graf, V., & Gaarder, K. Lack of inhibition during voluntary saccades. *American Journal of Psychology*, 1966, *79*, 73–81.

Kowler, E., & Steinman, R. The effect of expectations on slow ooculomotor control—Guessing unpredictable target displacements. *Vision Research*, 1981, *21*, 191–203.

Lackner, J. R., & Levine, M. S. The guidance of saccadic eye movements to perceptually visual and non-visual targets. *Aviation, Space, and Environmental Medicine*, 1981, *52*(8), 461–465.

Levi, J. Autokinesis direction during and after eye turn. *Perception and Psychophysics*, 1973, *13*, 337–343.

Li, W., Hayhoe, M., Davis, G., & Matin, L. Sensitivity to displacement during saccades. *Investigating Ophthmalogy & Visual Science* (Supp. 2) 1985, *26*, 48.

Lit, A. The magnitude of the Pulfrich stereophenomenon as a function of binocular differences of intensity at various levels of illumination. *American Journal of Psychology*, 1949, *62*, 159–181.

Lotze, G. *Outline of psychology* (G. T. Ladd, and trans.). Boston: Ginn, 1866.

Ludvigh, E. Control of ocular movements and visual interpretation of the environment. *Archives of Opthalmology*, 1952, *48*, 442–448. (a)

Ludvigh, E. Possible role of proprioception in the extraocular muscles. *Archives of Ophthalmology*, 1952, *48*, 442–441. (b)

Ludvigh, E. Direction sense of the eye. *American Journal of Ophthalmology*, 1953, *36*, 139–143.

Lund, R. D. *Development and plasticity of the brain*. New York: Oxford University Press, 1978.

Mach, E. *Analysis of sensations* (C. M. Williams, Ed. & trans.) New York: Dover, 1959. (Originally published, 1885.)

Mack, A. An investigation of the relationship between eye and retinal image movement in the perception of movement. *Perception and Psychophysics*, 1970, *8*, 291–298.

Mack, A. Perceived movement of the afterimage during eye movements. *Perception and Psychophysics*, 1969, *6*, 379–384.

Mack, A., Fendrich, R., & Pleune, J. Adaption to an altered relation between retinal image displacements and saccadic eye movements. *Vision Research*, 1978, *18*, 1321–1327.

Mack, A., Fendrich, R., & Wong, E. Is perceived motion a stimulus for smooth pursuit. *Vision Research*, 1982, *22*, 77–88.

MacKay, D. M. Theoretical models of space perception. In C. A. Muses (Ed.), *Aspects of the theory of artificial intelligence*. New York: Plenum, 1962.

MacKay, D. M. Elevation of the visual threshold by displacement of retinal image. *Nature* (London), 1970, *225*, 90–92. (a)

MacKay, D. M. Interocular transfer of suppression effect of retinal image displacement. *Nature*, 1970, *225*, 872–873. (b)

MacKay, D. M. Voluntary eye movements as questions. In J. Dichgans and E. Bizzi (Eds.), *Cerebral control of eye movements and motion perception*. Basel, Switzerland: Karger, 1972.

MacKay, D. M. Visual stability and voluntary eye movements. In R. Jung (ed.), *Handbook of sensory physiology*. Berlin: Springer, 1973.

MacKinnon, E. Unpublished doctoral dissertation, Johns Hopkins University, 1964.

Marshall, W. H., & Talbot, S. A. Recent evidence for neural mechanisms in vision leading to a general theory of sensory acuity. *Biological Symposium*, 1942, *7*, 117-164.

Mateeff, S. Saccadic eye movements and localization of visual stimuli. *Perception and Psychophysics*, 1978, *24*, 215–224.

Matin, E. Saccadic suppression: A review and analysis. *Psychological Bulletin*, 1974, *81*, 899–917.

Matin, E., Clymer, B., & Matin, L. Metocontrast and saccadic suppression. *Science*, 1972, *178*, 179–182.

Matin, L. Measurement of eye movements by contact-lens techniques: Analysis of measuring systems and some methodology or three dimensional recording. *Journal of the Optical Society of America.*, 1964, *54*, 1008–1018.

Matin, L. Eye movements and perceived visual direction. In D. Jameson & L. Hurvich (Eds). *Handbook of sensory physiology* (Vol. 7/4). Heidelberg: Springer, 1972.

Matin, L. A possible hybrid mechanism for modification of visual direction associated with eye movements—The paralyzed eye experiment reconsidered. *Perception*. 1976, *5*, 223–239. (a)

Matin, L. Saccades and extraretinal signal for visual direction. In R. A. Monty, & J. W. Senders (Eds.), *Eye movements and psychological processes*. Hillsdale, N.J.: Erlbaum, 1976. (b)

Matin, L. Suppression of the use of extraretinal eye position information (EEPI) for visual localization is normal in normally illuminated fields. *Investigative Opthalomology and Visual Science*, 1981, *20* (Suppl.), 55.

Matin, L. Visual localization and eye movements. In A. Wertheim, W. A. Wagenaar, & H. Leibowitz (Eds.), *Tutorials on motion perception*. New York: Plenum, 1982.

Matin, L. Interaction of EEPI and visual frameworks in the determination of visual and intersensory localization. *Investigative Ophthalmology and Visual Science*, 1983, *24* (Suppl.), 83. (Symposium at AVRO: Spatial Localization and the Oculomotor System, May 1983, Sarasota, Fl.)

Matin, L., & Bowen, R. W. Measuring the duration of perception. *Perception and Psychophysics*, 1976, *20*, 66–76.

Matin, L., & Kibler, G. Acuity of visual perception of direction in the dark for various positions of the eye in the orbit. *Perceptual and Motor Skills*. 1966, *22*, 407–420.

Matin, L., & MacKinnon, E. Autokinetic movement: Selective manipulation of directional components by image stabilization. *Science*, 1964, *143*, 147–148.

Matin, L., & Matin, E. Visual perception of direction and voluntary saccadic eye movements. In J. Dichgans, & H. Bizzi (Eds.), *Cerebral control of eye movements and motion perception*. Basel, Switzerland: Karger, 1972.

Matin, L., & Matin, E., & Pearce, D. G. Visual perception of direction when voluntary saccades occur: In relation of visual direction of a fixation target extinguished before a saccade to a flash presented during the saccade. *Perception and Psychophysics*, 1969, *5*, 65–80.

Matin, L., Matin, E., & Pearce, D. G. Eye movements in the dark during the attempts to maintain a prior fixation position. *Vision Research*, 1970, *10*, 837–857.

Matin, L., Matin E., & Pola, J. Visual perception of direction when voluntary saccades occur: II. Relation of visual direction of a fixation target extinguished before a saccade to a subsequant test flash presented before the saccade. *Perception and Psychophysics*, 1970, *8*, 9–14.

Matin, L., Matin, E., Pola, J., & Bowen, R. *Relative visual direction of two flashes presented at different times or intensities during a voluntary saccade—retinal constraints in the operation of extraretinal signals*. Paper presented at the meeting of the Eastern Psychological Association, 1971.

Matin, L., & Pearce, D. G. Three-dimensonal recording of rotational eye movements by a new contact-lens technique. In W. E. Murry, & P. F. Salisbury (Eds.) *Biomedical sciences instrumentation*. New York: Plenum 1964.

Matin, L., & Pearce, D. G. Visual perception of direction from stimuli flashed during voluntary saccadic eye movement. *Science*, 1965, *148*, 1485–1488.

Matin, L., Pearce, D. G., & MacKinnon, G. E., Variation in directional components of autokinetic movement as a function of the position of the eye in the orbit. *Journal of the Optical Society of America*, 1963, *53*, 521 (abstract).

Matin, L., Pearce, D. G. Matin, E., & Kibler, G. Visual perception of direction: Roles of local sign, eye movements and ocular proprioception. *Vision Research*, 1966, *6*, 453–469.

Matin, L., Picoult, E., Stevens, J. K., Edwards, M. W. Jr., Young, D., & MacArthur, R. Visual context dependent mislocalization under curare-induced partial paralysis of the extraocular muscles. *Investigating Ophthalmology and Visual Science*, 1980, *19* (Suppl.), 81.

Matin, L., Picoult, E., Stevens, J. K., Edwards, M. W. Jr., Young, D., & MacArthur, R. Oculoparalytic illusion: Visual field dependent spatial mislocalization by humans with experimentally paralyzed extraocular muscles. *Science*, 1982, *216*, 198–201.

Matin, L., Pola, J., & Matin, E. Changes of visual direction with voluntary saccadic eye movements: Influence of visual persistence. *Transactions of the American Acadamy of Optometry*, 1972, *49*, 897.

Matin, L., Pola, J., Matin, E., & Picoult, E. Vernier discrimination with sequentially-flashed lines: Roles of eye movements, retinal offsets and short-term memory. *Vision Research*, 1981, *21*, 647–656.

Matin, L., Stevens, J., & Picoult, E. Perceptual consequences of experimental extraocular muscle paralysis. In A. Hein & M. Jeannerod (Eds.) *Spatially oriented behavior*. New York: Springer, 1983.

McLaughlin, S. C. Parametric adjustment in saccodic eye movements. *Perception and Psychophysics*, 1966, *2*, 349–362.

McLaughlin, S. C., & Webster, R. G. Changes in straight-ahead eye position during adaption to wedge prisms. *Perception and Psychophysics*, 1967, *2*, 36–44.

Merton, P. Human position sense and sense of effort. *Symposium of the Society of Experimental Biology*, 1964, *18*, 387–400.

Miller, E. F., II. Counterrolling the human eyes produced by head tilt with respect to gravity. *Acta Otolaryngology*, 1962, *54*, 479–501.

Mita, T., Hironaka, K., & Koika, J. The influence of retinal adaption and location on the "Empfindungszeit." *Tohuku Journal of Experimental Medicine*, 1950, *52*, 397–405.

Mitrani, L., Mateef, St., & Yakimoff, N. Smearing of the retinal image during voluntary saccadic movements. *Vision Research*, 1970, *10*, 405–409. (a)

Mitrani, L., Mateef, St., & Yakimoff, N. Temporal and spatial characteristics of visual suppression during voluntary saccadic eye movment. *Vision Research*, 1970, *10*, 417–422. (b)

Morgan, C. T. Constancy of egocentric visual direction. *Perception and Psychophysics*, 1978, *23*, 61–68.

Müller, G. E. Über das Aubertsche Phanomen. *Zeitschrift Sinnesphysiologie*, 1916, *49*, 109–244.

Nachmias, J. Two-dimensional motion of the retinal image during monocular fixation. *Journal Optical Society of America*, 1959, *49*, 901–908.

Nachmias, J. Determiners of the drift of the eye during monocular fixation. *Journal of the Optical Socieity of America*, 1961, *51*, 761–766.

Niven, J., Whiteside, T., & Graybiel, A. *The elevator illusion: apparent motion of a visual target during vertical acceleration*. (Report # 89) Pensacola, FL: U.S. Naval Aviation Medical Center, Bureau of Medicine & Surgery, 1963.

Ogle, K. N. *Binocular vision*. New York: Hafner, 1950.

Ono, H., & Nakamizo, S. Saccidic eye movements during changes in fixation to stimuli at different distances. *Vision Research*, 1977, *17*, 223–238.

O'Regan, K. Retinal vs extraretinal influences in flash localization during saccadic eye movements in the presence of a visible background. *Perception and Psychophysics*, 1984 (in press).

Paap, K. R., & Ebenholtz, S. M. Perceptual consequences of potentiation in the extraocular muscles: an alternative explanation for adaptation to wedge prisms. *Journal of Experimental Psychology: Human Perception and Performance*, 1976, *2*, 457–468.

Pearce, D., Matin, L. The measurement of autokinetic speed. *Canadian Journal of Psychology*, 1966, *20*, 160–172.

Pearce, D., & Matin, L. Variation of the magnitude of the horizontal-vertical illusion with retinal eccentricity. *Perception and Psychophysics*, 1969, *6*, 241–243.

Pearce, D., & Porter, E. Changes in visual sensitivity associated with voluntary saccades. *Psychonomic Science*, 1970, *19*, 225–227.

Picoult, E., MacArthur, R., Young, D., Edwards, M. W. Jr., Stevens, J. K., & Matin, L. Relation between visual and auditory maps of space in room illumination and in darkness. *Investigative Ophthalmology and Visual Science*, 1980, *19*, (Suppl.), 164.

Picoult, E., Young, D., & Matin, L. Eye movement, gaze direction, and autokinesis. *Investigating Opthalmology and Visual Science*, 1979, *18*, (Suppl.), 102.

Pola, J. *The relation of visual direction to eye position during and following a voluntary saccade.* Unpublished doctoral dissertation, Columbia University, 1972.

Pola, J. Voluntary saccades, eye position, and perceived visual direction. In R. A. Monty & J. W. Senders (Eds.), *Eye movements and psychological processes*. Hillsdale, N.J.: Erlbaum, 1976.

Pola, J., & Matin, L. Eye movements following autokinesis. *Bulletin of the Psychonomic Society*, 1977, *10*, 397–398.

Pola, J., & Wyatt, H. J. Pursuit eye movements in response to stimulus velocity may be OKN. *Investigative Opthalmology and Visual Science*, 1980, *19* (Suppl.) 80–81 (a)

Pola, J., & Wyatt, H. J. Target position and velocity: the stimuli for smooth pusuit eye movements. *Vision Research*, 1980, *20*, 523–534. (b)

Puckett, J. D., & Steinman, R. M. Tracking eye movements with and without saccadic vision. *Vision Research*, 1969, *9*, 695–703.

Rashbass, C. The relationship between saccadic and smooth tracking eye movements. *Journal of Physiology* (London), 1961, *159*, 326–338.

Ratliff, F., & Riggs, L. A. Involuntary motions of the eye during monocular fixation. *Journal of Experimental Psychology*, 1950, *40*(6), 687–701.

Rattle, J. D., & Foley-Fisher, J. A. A relationship between vernier acuity and intersaccadic interval. *Optica Acta*, 1968, *15*, 617–620.

Riggs, L. A., Armington, J. C., & Ratliff, F. Motions of the retinal image during fixation. *Journal of the Optical Society of America*, 1954, *44*, 315–321.

Riggs, L. A., Merton, P. A., & Morton, H. B. Suppression of visual phosphenes during saccadic eye movements. *Vision Research*, 1974, *14*, 997–1011.

Riggs, L., Ratliff, F., Cornsweet, J., & Cornsweet, T. N. The disappearance of steadily fixated visual test objects. *Journal of the Optical Society of America*, 1953, *43*, 495–501.

Robinson, D. A. The mechanics of human saccadic eye movement. *Journal of Physiology*, 1964, *174*, 245–264.

Robinson, D. The mechanics of human smooth pursuit eye movement. *Journal of Physiology*, 1965, *180*, 569–591.

Rogan, M. Eggers, H., & Matin, L. Pre- and Postoperative visual localization by strabismic observers. *Investigative Ophthalmology and Visual Science*, 1983, *24* (Suppl.), 83.

Salapatek, P. Pattern perception in early infancy. In L. B. Cohen & P. Salapatek (Eds.), *Infant perception from sensation to cognition*. New York: Academic, 1975.

Schlodtman, W. Ein Beitrag zur Lehre von der optischen Lokalisation bei Blindgeborenen. *Archives fur Ophthalmologie*, 1902, *54*, 256–267.

Schone, H. Über den Einfluss der Schwerkraft auf die Augenrollung und die Wahrnehmung der Lage im Raum. *Zeitschrift für vergleichende Physiologie*, 1962, *46*, 57–87.

Sedgwick, H. A., & Festinger, L. Eye movements efference, and visual perception. In R. A. Monty & J. W. Senders (Eds.) *Eye movements and psychological processes*. Hillsdale NJ: Erlbaum, 1976.

Sekuler, R. W., & Ganz, L. Aftereffect of seen motion with a stabilized retinal image. *Science*, 1963, *139*, 419–420.

Shebilske, W. L. Extraretinal information in corrective saccades and inflow vs. outflow theories of visual direction constancy. *Vision Research*, 1976, *16*, 621–628.

Shebilske, W. L. Visuomotor coordination in visual direction and position constancies. In W. Epstein (Ed.) *Stability and constancy in visual perception*. New York: Wiley, 1977.

Sherrington, C. S. Further note on the sensory nerves of the eye muscles. *Proceedings of the Royal Society*, 1898, *64*, 120–121.

Sherrington, C. S. Observations on the sensual role ofthe proprioceptive nerve supply of the extrinsic ocular muscles. *Brain*, 1918, *41*, 332–343.

Siebeck, R. Wahrnehmungsstorung und Storungswahrnehmung bei Augenmuskellahmungen. *von Graufes Archiv fur Opthalmologie*, 1954, *155*, 26–34.

Siebeck, R., & Frey, R. Die Wirkungen muskeleschlaffender Mittel auf die Augenmuskein. *Anaesthesist*, 1953, *2*, 138–141.

Skavenski, A. A. Extraretinal correction and memory for target position. *Vision Research*, 1971, *11*, 743–746.

Skavenski, A. A. Inflow as a source of extraretinal eye position information. *Vision Research*, 1972, *12*, 221–230.

Skavenski, A. A., & Steinman, R. M. Control of eye position in the dark. *Vision Research*, 1970, *10*, 193–203.

Sperry, R. W. Mechanisms of neural maturation. In S. S. Stevens (Ed.), *Handbook of experimental psychology*. New York: Wiley, 1951.

Stark, L., & Bridgeman, B. Role of corollary discharge in space constancy. *Perception and Psychophysics*, 1983, *34*, 371–380.

Stark, L., Kong, R., Schwartz, S., Hendry, D., & Bridgeman, B. Saccadic suppression of image displacement. *Vision Research*, 1976, *16*, 1185–1187.

Stark, L., Vossius, G., Young, L. R. Predictive control of eye tracking movements. Institute of Radio Engineers. *Transactions of Human Factors Electronics*, 1962, *HFE-3*, 52–57.

St-Cyr, G. J., & Fender, D. H. Nonlinearities of the human oculomotor system: Time delays. *Vision Research*, 1969, *9*, 1491–1503.

Steinbach, M. J. Pursuing the perceptual rather than the retinal stimulus. *Vision Research*, 1976, *16*, 1371–1376.

Steinbach, M. J. & Pearce, D. G. Release of pursuit eye movements using after-images. *Vision Research*, 1972, *12*, 1307–1311.

Steinbach, M. J. & Smith, D. R. Spatial localization after strabismus surgery: Evidence for inflow. *Science*, 1981, *213*, 1407–1409.

Steinman, R. M., Cunitz, R. J., Timberlake, G.T., & Herman, M. The voluntary control of microsaccades during maintained monocular fixation. *Science*, 1967, *155*, 1579–1580.

Stevens, J. K., Emerson, R. C., Gerstein, G. L., Kallos, T., Neufeld, G. R., Nichols, C. W., & Rosenquist, A. C. Paralysis of the awake human: Visual perceptions. *Vision Research*, 1976, *16*, 93–98.

Stoper, A. E. *Vision during pursuit movement: The role of oculomotor information*. Unpublished doctoral dissertion, Brandeis University, 1968.

Stoper, A. E. Apparent motion of stimuli presented stroboscopically during pursuit eye movements. *Perception and Psychophysics*, 1973, *7*, 201–211.

Sumi, S. Temporary aspects of the loss of position contancy in visual smooth purst. *Japanese Psychological Research*, 1983, *25*, 156–163.

Volkmann, F. Vision during voluntary saccadic eye movements. *Journal of the Optical Society of America*, 1962, *52*, 571–578.

Volkmann, F., Schick, A. M. L., & Riggs, L. A. Time course of visual inhibition during voluntary saccades. *Journal of the Optical Society of America*, 1968, *58*, 562–569.

Wallach, H., & Lewis, C. The effect of abnormal displacement of the retinal image during eye movements. *Perception and Psychophysics*,

1966, *1*, 25–29.

Ward, F. Pursuit eye movements and visual localization. In R. A. Monty & J. W. Sanders (Eds.), *Eye movements and psychological processes*. Hillsdale, NJ: Erlbaum, 1976.

Watt, R. J. & Andrews, D. P. Contour curvature analysis: Hyperacuities in the discrimination of detailed shape. *Vision Research*, 1982, *22*, 449–460.

Welch, R. B. *Perceptual modification: adapting to altered sensory environments*. New York: Academic, 1978.

Westheimer, G. Eye movement responses to horizontally moving visual stimulus. *Archives of Ophthalmology*, 1954, *52*, 932–941.

Weymouth, F. W., Anderson, E. E., Averill, H. H. Retinal mean local sign: A new view of the relation of the retinal mosaic to visual perception. *American Journal of Physiology*, 1923, *63*, 410–411.

Whipple, W. R., & Wallach, H. Direction-specific motion thresholds for abnormal image shifts during saccadic eye movement. *Perception and Psychophysics*, 1978, *24*, 349–355.

Witkin, H. A., & Asch, S. E. Studies in space orientation. IV. Further experiments on perception of the upright with displaced visual fields. *Journal of Experimental Psychology*, 1948, *38*, 762–782.

Woellner, R. C. & Graybiel, A. *Reflex ocular torsion in healthy males*. (Rep. No. 47) Pensacola, Fl.: U.S. Naval School of Aviation Medicine, 1958.

Wyatt, H. J., & Pola, J. The role of perceived motion in smooth pursuit eye movement. *Vision Research*, 1979, *19*, 613–618.

Yasui, S., & Young, L. R. Perceived visual motion as effective stimulus to pursuit eye movement system. *Science*, 1975, *190*, 906–908.

Young, L. R., & Stark, L. Variable feedback experiments testing a sampled data model for eye tracking movements. *IEEE Transactions of Human Factors in Electronics*, 1963, *HFE-4*, 38–51.

Zuber, B. L., & Stark, L. Saccadic suppression: Elevation of visual threshold associated with saccadic eye movements. *Experimental Neurology*, 1966, *16*, 65–79.

Zuber, B. L., Stark, L., & Cook, G. Microsaccades and the velocity-amplitude relationship for saccadic eye movements. *Science*, 1965, *150*, 1459–1460.

CHAPTER 21

SPACE PERCEPTION

H. A. SEDGWICK

State University of New York, College of Optometry, New York, New York

CONTENTS

1. INTRODUCTION

1.1. What Is Space Perception?

Space perception is the ability to perceive the three-dimensional layout of our environment. Although some perception of space occurs through audition and through touch, it is generally acknowledged that the visual sensory modality has a range and precision in space perception that is unmatched by any of the other senses. This is so much the case that the very term "space perception" is often inferred to mean "visual space perception." This chapter is concerned almost exclusively with the visual perception of space.

If the environment is considered atomistically as being composed of an arrangement of a vast number of individual particles, each in a given location, then the three-dimensional layout of the environment can be fully specified simply by giving the location of each of those particles. One might, for instance, specify the location of each particle in terms of its direction and distance from the nodal point of an observing eye. How direction is perceived is the question of *visual localization*, considered by Matin in Chapter 20. How distance is perceived then becomes, in such a scheme, the central problem of space perception. Much of the work, both empirical and theoretical, done in the study of space perception has been directed toward this problem of distance perception.

There is little reason to believe, however, that any organism regards the environment so atomistically. If the environment is considered, more functionally, as being composed of a wide variety of substrata, each supporting or containing an even greater variety of objects, both animate and inanimate, then the problem of fully specifying the three-dimensional layout of the environment becomes considerably more complex. It is not obvious how best to describe an environment thought of as being so richly structured, nor is it obvious how to determine what description would be most appropriate to use in studying the space perception of some particular organism. Yet research on space perception is always grounded, either explicitly or implicitly, in some model of the environment to be perceived.

An alternative to the atomistic model is to think of the environment as a layout of visible textured surfaces (J. Gibson, 1950a). Although such a description of the environment is still far from complete, it does appear to encompass a far wider range of the three-dimensional environmental characteristics that can be perceived. Let us consider what some of these characteristics are and what problems they raise for the study of space perception.

Perhaps the most basic characteristic of a surface is simply its existence. What gives rise to the perception of a surface? In a uniformly illuminated visual field, or *Ganzfeld*, no surface is seen, only a sort of space-filling "fog" (J. Gibson & Waddell, 1952; Metzger, 1930, cited in Koffka, 1935, pp. 110–115). An atomistic view would say that the perception of a surface arises simply from the perception of the individual locations of each of the many elements (*texture elements*) that cover the surface, but this view is clearly inadequate. Although the perception of a surface can indeed arise from the perception of its "microtexture" (Metzger, 1930, cited in Koffka, 1935, pp. 110–115), it can also arise from a bounded patch of color that has no microtexture (as in the "surface color" of Katz, 1935; also see Beck, 1972; Wallach, 1948), or from an appropriate spacing of internal contours with no surface or microtexture between them (J. Gibson, Purdy, & Lawrence, 1955). Little work has yet been done to determine systematically the conditions governing when a surface will be perceived.

Visible surfaces can have many spatial characteristics. They can be continuous or have discontinuities. They can be flat or curved in an endless variety of ways. A bounded surface has shape and area and has an extent that is measurable in any direction along the surface. Surfaces have orientation that can be specified either relative to an observer or relative to other surfaces or frameworks in the environment. Surfaces may contact or intersect other surfaces, and these contiguities may help to specify the location of the surface in the environment. Location may also be specified by distances from an observer or from other surfaces. The perception of some of these spatial characteristics of surfaces, such as orientation, has been studied in detail whereas the perception of other characteristics, such as contiguity, has received little experimental attention.

The visible spatial characteristics of surfaces need not be constant. Surfaces may have many kinds of nonrigidity, and the way that the perception of surface rigidity is achieved has lately received considerable attention. Also, as an observer moves around in an environment, what is visible and what is not visible is continually changing as surfaces come into view or go out of sight. Here there is a gradual transition from the subject matter of space perception into the area of cognitive psychology whose subject matter is *cognitive maps*, but the problems lying in this transitional zone have been little explored.

1.2. Historical Overview of Space Perception

Concern with some of the problems related to the study of space perception is very ancient, but the focus of interest has shifted and evolved over the centuries. The emphasis in antiquity was on the geometric laws governing the visual angles subtended by objects at the eye, a study culminating in Euclid's laws of optics. This understanding was probably also applied to the production of pictorial representations of three-dimensional scenes, although the evidence here is fragmentary (White, 1967).

During the Renaissance there was a revival of interest in the methodology of making accurate pictorial representations of three-dimensional scenes. This led to a rediscovery of the laws of perspective and of other techniques for creating the appearance of depth on a flat surface (Alberti, 1436/1972; White, 1967). The emphasis here, however, was more on reproducing the structure of the light reaching the eye from a three-dimensional scene than on understanding how the visual system dealt with this light to extract the three-dimensional information. Thus the Renaissance study of techniques of painting was more closely allied in spirit to the modern study of computer graphics (see Chapter 3 by Freeman) than to the modern study of space perception (or of computer vision).

A brief but clear statement of the central problems of space perception emerged in the writings of Descartes (1637/1965), who observed that the perceived size and shape of an object do not vary with the size and shape of its image on the retina, but instead are much more in accord with its actual size and shape. Descartes suggested that actual sizes and shapes are perceived by taking into account our knowledge of the distances of objects and of the parts that compose them, and he offered a series of suggestions about how distances are perceived. Central to Descartes's proposed solution were the use of the relation between the distance of an object and the amount of accommodation necessary to bring it into focus and the use of the convergence of the lines of sight of the two eyes as a way of determining distance by triangulation. Descartes also proposed several other contributing factors, however, such as the degree to which the images of nonfixated objects are out of focus.

During the two centuries following Descartes emphasis was on clarifying the concept of perceived space and establishing its nature through philosophical argument and appeals to common knowledge rather than through experimentation. Although the details of space perception received relatively little attention, some of Descartes's specific suggestions about how distance is perceived were challenged. Notably, Berkeley (1709/1910) as part of the empiricist tradition challenged Descartes's conception of the visual system as a "natural geometer" that determined distance by trigonometry, arguing instead for an associationist view in which particular distances determined by experiences such as walking to an object or reaching out to touch it became associated with particular muscular sensations arising from the accommodation and convergence of the eyes.

Wheatstone's discoveries concerning stereopsis (1838) gave an important boost to the empirical investigation of space perception and strongly influenced the broad direction in which that investigation would go. By showing that the disparity between the views of a scene obtained by the two eyes produced a vivid and detailed perception of the depth relations within the scene, Wheatstone succeeded in establishing stereopsis as the primary source of depth perception and in evoking a great deal of interest in the details of its operation. The investigation of space perception for much of the next hundred years was thus largely identified with the investigation of binocular vision (see Chapter 23 by Arditi). That there were other contributing factors in space perception was generally recognized, but these other factors, such as motion and perspective, received relatively little attention. As an example of this predominant interest in binocular vision, Helmholtz's (1910/1962) monumental three-volume work on physiological optics devotes about 150 pages to the subject of binocular vision and stereopsis and about 17 pages to all other (monocular) aspects of space perception.

During the second quarter of this century, there was a significant shift toward giving greater recognition and attention to the role of nonbinocular factors in space perception. This shift was a progressive one in which several contributions may be noted. The first of these was the development of Gestalt psychology (Ellis, 1938; Koffka, 1935), which, by rejecting the view that perception was a mass of associations built up around a core of sensations, undercut the theoretical rationale for regarding stereopsis, convergence, and accommodation as the primary bases for space perception. A second contribution came from the work of Brunswik (1956; Brunswik & Kamiya, 1953), which drew attention to the wealth of nonbinocular "cues" for space perception that exist in normal environments and which attempted to measure probabalistically the validity of each of these cues. A third contribution was made by a series of ingenious demonstrations developed by Ames and his colleagues (Ittleson, 1952), which illustrated, often by producing dramatic illusions, the effectiveness of a variety of nonbinocular factors in space perception. The final contribution was that of J. Gibson (1950a), whose work with aircraft pilots during World War II led him to develop a theoretical approach that he referred to as a "ground theory" of space perception. This approach viewed the environment as a layout of textured, contiguous surfaces and argued for the importance in perceiving their layout of "higher-order" structures, such as gradients of texture and of motion, in the light reaching the eyes. Gibson gave to the nonbinocular information for space perception the kind of careful, extended, analytical attention previously given to binocular vision.

The analytical examination of the information for space perception has received further impetus in recent years from the field of computer vision (see Barrow & Tenenbaum, Chapter 38). Faced with the pragmatic problem of building computer-based machines that can extract information about three-dimensional scenes from images of them, some computer scientists have turned to the study of the human visual system for hints about how this task might be accomplished. In particular, Marr (1982), by emphasizing the utility of a preliminary processing stage that extracts the spatial layout of surfaces in the environment, has had an important influence on the development within computer vision of a field of study closely related to that of space perception.

1.3. Contemporary Approaches to Space Perception

The contemporary study of space perception possesses neither a generally accepted theoretical framework nor a set of clearly defined theoretical alternatives. Instead, research is guided by a variety of approaches, each differing in emphasis from the others, each having considerable common ground with at least some of the others, and none offering more than a partially worked out view of the processes of space perception. In what follows, some of these approaches are briefly described. It should be emphasized, however, that these different approaches are often as much complementary as opposed and that any given research effort may well weave together several lines of approach.

The *ecological* approach is now most closely associated with the work of J. Gibson (1950a, 1966, 1979) and his colleagues, although, as we have seen, the thematic emphasis on studying space perception in ecologically valid settings originated with Brunswik (1956). As developed by Gibson, this approach emphasizes the study of the ways in which normal environments complexly structure the light from them that reaches the eyes of an observer. The "higher-order" relations in such structured light are analyzed for the information that they can provide about the spatial layout of the environment. Empirical evidence is sought concerning the ability of observers to pick up and use this information.

Closely related to Gibson's approach is the *computational* approach of Marr (1982) and some other computer scientists (see Chapter 38 by Barrow & Tenenbaum). This approach emphasizes the study of the computational methods, or *algorithms*, that organisms or machines may use to extract the spatial layout of the environment from the structure of the light reaching the eye. The computational approach makes extensive use of computer models to simulate the implementation of these algorithms and the internal representations to which they would give rise.

In recent years the *information processing* approach has been widely applied in the study of human cognition and perception, and some efforts are being made to apply this approach to the study of space perception as well. In this approach, which has been applied by several researchers (e.g., Epstein & Hatfield, 1978; Epstein, Hatfield, & Muise, 1977; Massaro, 1973), techniques such as masking paradigms and the analysis of reaction times are used in an attempt to trace stages of processing within the visual system. The goals of this approach are thus similar to those of the computational approach although the methodology is somewhat different.

The perception of spatial layout in normal environments is usually quite close to being veridical and is almost always at least a plausible interpretation of the available information. The *cognitive* approach, which has been strongly advocated by Rock (1977, 1983), regards perception as an inference-like process that interprets all of the available information for spatial layout in a rational, syllogistic way. Research following this approach has stressed the importance of context and of relatively subtle stimulus variables in profoundly influencing the perceptual interpretation of scenes. This approach is closely related to what J. Hochberg (1981a, 1981b) has referred to as the *neo-Helmholtzian* approach, which hypothesizes that mental structures such as schemata are used to organize local sensory information into the perception of the most likely object or layout.

A more behavioristic stance characterizes the *psychophysical* approach (Baird, 1970a; Graham 1958, 1965). The term "psychophysics" refers to study of the mathematical functions relating physical stimuli to perceptual responses. Typical problems for this approach would be to determine the precise function relating projective convergence of parallel lines to perceived slant (Freeman, 1969) or to determine whether the function describing perceived depth intervals over the ground plane is invariant over size of the standard interval (Cook, 1978).

A final approach to space perception that requires mention is the *physiological* approach. This approach attempts to define the physiological mechanisms that underlie space perception. Although the physiological approach has had considerable success in some areas of perception, such as those concerned with form and motion, most of the basic processes of space perception continue to elude description at a physiological level. Some fragments of such a description can be seen, however, in investigations of neurons in the visual cortex that are sensitive to binocular disparity (Barlow, Blakemore, & Pettigrew, 1967) and of neurons that are sensitive to expansion ("looming") and contraction within the visual field (Regan & Cynader, 1979; also see Regan, Kaufman, & Lincoln, Chapter 19).

1.4. Key References

Among the important milestones in the development of thinking about space perception are the already mentioned works of Descartes (1637/1965), Berkeley (1709/1910), Helmholtz (1910/1962), Koffka (1935), Brunswik (1956), and J. Gibson (1950a).

More recent theoretical discussions and overviews of space perception are provided in volumes and chapters by Ittleson (1960), J. Hochberg (1971), Kaufman (1974), Richards (1975), Epstein (1977), Gogel (1978), Gibson (1979), and Marr (1982). Useful collections of conference papers have been edited by Baird (1970b) and by Leibowitz, Osaka, and Oyama (1979).

Key papers in particular areas are noted in the sections that follow. The basic characteristics of the perception of size, distance, shape, and slant of surfaces in the environment are discussed in the next section. Section 3 takes a close look at the information for spatial layout that is provided by surface texture and linear perspective. In the final section the ways in which motion of the observer provides information for the perception of spatial layout are considered.

It has not been possible to cover all aspects of space perception within the confines of this chapter. In particular, the roles of accommodation, convergence, and stereopsis in space perception are not given detailed consideration here. A review of the early literature in these areas is provided by Boring (1943), and more recent reviews are given by J. Hochberg (1971), Kaufman (1974), and Foley (1978). The mechanisms of accommodation and convergence are reviewed by Hallet in Chapter 10. For additional discussions of the role of stereopsis, the reader is also referred to Chapter 23 by Arditi in this section and to accounts by Ono and Comerford (1977) and Foley (1980).

2. VISUAL ANGLE RELATIONS

2.1. Basic Concepts

2.1.1. The Concept of Visual Angle. The structured array of light reaching a point of observation is referred to as the *optic array* (J. Gibson, 1961). The fundamental term for the description of extent in the optic array is *visual angle*, which now refers to angles subtended at the nodal point of the eye (although the concept of visual angle goes back at least to Euclid and thus long precedes any accurate understanding of the eye's optics). The term "visual angle," when left unqualified, usually refers to a one-dimensional visual angle subtended at the eye by a linear extent in space. Visual angles are measured either in degrees or in radians. A two-dimensional visual angle, sometimes referred to as a *solid visual angle*, is the two-dimensional patch of the optic array delineated by all of the angles, taken in every direction, that are subtended by a region of space. A solid visual angle thus covers an area in the optic array and is measured either in degrees squared or radians squared. A solid visual angle is not completely characterized by the measurement of its area, however, because solid visual angles having the same area can nevertheless have distinctive shapes.

It is sometimes convenient to discuss visual angles in terms of their projections onto a flat surface, or *projection plane*, located at some arbitrary or unit distance from the eye. In this case we may speak of the projective extent or projective shape that corresponds to a given physical extent or physical shape.

The angular extent, subtended along any dimension, of a surface that is perpendicular to the line of regard is determined jointly by the corresponding physical extent of the surface and by its distance from the eye of the observer. Thus angular extent, physical extent, and distance form a triadic relation in which fixing any two of these values determines the other. A similar triadic relation exists for the shapes of two-dimensional visual angles. Here, the shape of the solid visual angle subtended by a surface of a given size and distance is determined jointly by the physical shape of the surface and by the slant of the surface with respect to the line of regard. Questions about the dependence of the perceived layout of space on these two triadic visual angle relations are at the heart of the study of space perception and have proved to be a rich source of theorizing and experimentation over the years. The rest of Section 2 examines some of the issues and results arising from such work. Section 2.2 looks at the one-dimensional visual angle relation, and Section 2.3 considers the two-dimensional visual angle relation.

2.1.2. The Brunswik and Thouless Ratios. Much of the experimental work to be discussed in this section uses a matching paradigm to measure the perception of size-at-a-distance or shape-at-a-slant. For example, an observer may be asked to adjust the size of a comparison object, presented at a certain distance, to match the size of a standard object, presented at a different distance. To allow comparison between the results of experiments done with different variables or with different values of the same variable, it would be helpful to have some uniform way of assigning to data a value that in some way measures the accuracy of the match.

If S is the physical value of a standard object and S' is the chosen value of a comparison object, then the match between them could be measured simply by taking the difference, $S - S'$, between those values; the smaller the difference, the better the match. One obvious problem with such a difference measure is that it seems inappropriately dependent on the absolute values of the variables in question; another problem is that such a measure does not take any account of the difference in distance or slant between the standard and comparison object.

A widely used measure that attempts to avoid these problems is the *Brunswik ratio* (Brunswik, 1929).The Brunswik ratio is defined (using the terminology of J. Hochberg, 1971, p. 509; see also Woodworth, 1938, p. 605) as$(S' - s)/(S - s)$, where s is the value of the comparison object that would match the projective value of the standard object. The ratio varies from 1, when the comparison exactly matches the physical value of the standard object, to O, when the comparison exactly matches the projective value of the standard object.

Thouless (1931) offered an alternative measure that, as he noted, has several advantages over the Brunswik ratio. The *Thouless ratio* is defined as $(\log S' - \log s)/(\log S - \log s)$; this ratio thus has the same form as the Brunswik ratio but takes the logarithm of each of the values before forming the ratio. Like the Brunswik ratio, the Thouless ratio varies from 1, when the comparison matches the standard's physical value, to O, when the comparison matches the standard's projective value, but for other values of the comparison the Thouless ratio differs from the Brunswik ratio.

The most important advantage of the Thouless ratio over the Brunswik ratio is that the value of the Thouless ratio does not depend on which of the two objects in a matching task is designated as the standard, wheras this choice can drastically affect the value of the Brunswik ratio.

As an example of this difference between the Brunswik and Thouless ratios, consider the following hypothetical size-matching situation. Suppose that one object is 16 times farther from the observer than another object and that the observer says that the heights of the two objects are matched when the height of the far object is 64 and the height of the near object is 16. Now suppose that this match was obtained with the far object as the standard and the near object as the comparison; this means that $S = 64$, $S' = 16$, and we can calculate that $s = 4$. From these values we can calculate a Brunswik ratio of .20 and a Thouless ratio of .50. Next suppose that the same match was obtained with the near object as the standard and the far object as the comparison; this means that $S = 16$, $S' = 64$, and we can calculate that $s = 256$. From these values we calculate a Brunswik ratio of .80 and a Thouless ratio of .50. Thus exactly the same size match can be assigned a Brunswik ratio of either .20 or .80, depending on which object served as the standard, but the value of the Thouless ratio, .50, is independent of this choice.

This weakness of the Brunswik ratio, although mentioned by Thouless in a footnote (1931, p. 353) and analyzed in detail by Myers (1980), has generally escaped notice in discussions of the Brunswik ratio (Leibowitz, 1956; Smith & Smith, 1977). One reason for this may be that, in the case of size, the far object is almost always taken as the standard so that there has been little occasion for the effect of this choice on the Brunswik ratio to be noticed. The Brunswik ratio's dependence on details of the experimental paradigm clearly limits its usefulness as a measure of how much a match is in accord with objective as opposed to projective values (also see Section 2.2.2).

Myers (1980) notes that the Thouless ratio can also be written in the form

$$\frac{S'}{s} = \left(\frac{S}{s}\right)^n$$

where the exponent n is the value of the Thouless ratio. Myers then relates the Thouless ratio to the exponent in S. Stevens's (1975) power functions.

Both the Brunswik ratio and the Thouless ratio have been criticized by Koffka (1935, pp. 226–227) for not providing as uniform a basis for comparisons as they at first appear to. Both measures, Koffka argues, attempt to provide comparability across different situations by first establishing a well-defined range of possible results for each situation and then referring all results to that range; that is, for each situation the same procedure is used to scale the results so that they will lie between 0 and 1. This assumes, however, that the comparison object will always be adjusted to lie between the objective and the projective value of the standard object. As Koffka points out, it is not uncommon in actual experiments to find that the comparison object is set to a value that lies substantially outside of this range. Thus, Koffka argues, the appropriate range of values to consider in any experiment is itself a function of the particular experiment; the use of the Brunswik and Thouless ratios to make comparisons between varied experimental situations is not, in Koffka's words, fully justified. Carlson (1962) offers a similar criticism.

In spite of these criticisms, both these ratios, and particularly the Brunswik ratio, have continued in wide use; much of the data to be discussed below is reported in terms of them.

2.2. One-dimensional Visual Angles

2.2.1. Size, Distance, and Visual Angle. The size of an object is generally measured by its linear extent along some chosen dimension. The visual angle A subtended by a linear extent x is determined by its distance d from the point of observation and the angle B that it makes with the line of regard. For precise measurement, it is necessary to distinguish d_1 and d_2, the distances of the two end points of the linear extent, and to distinguish B_1 and B_2, the angles that it makes at its two end points with the line of regard (see Figure 21.1). From the law of sines it follows that

$$\frac{x}{\sin A} = \frac{d_1}{\sin B_2} = \frac{d_2}{\sin B_1} .$$

Thus

$$A = \sin^{-1}\left[\left(\frac{x}{d_1}\right)\sin B_2\right] = \sin^{-1}\left[\left(\frac{x}{d_2}\right)\sin B_1\right] . \quad (1)$$

In the commonly encountered special case where the linear extent is perpendicular to the line of regard, these equations can be simplified to

$$A = \sin^{-1}\left(\frac{x}{d_1}\right) \quad \text{when } B_2 = 90°$$

or (2)

$$A = \sin^{-1}\left(\frac{x}{d_2}\right) \quad \text{when } B_1 = 90° .$$

Simplifying approximations to these equations can be made when the linear extent x is small with respect to its distance

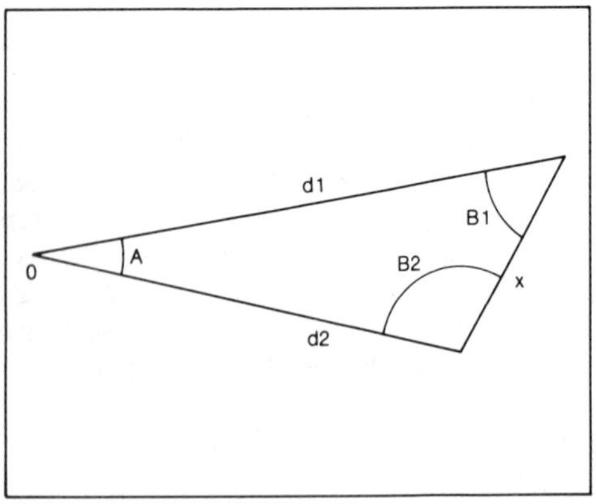

Figure 21.1. Linear extent, distance, and angular extent. The linear extent x subtends a visual angle A when viewed from O. The end points of x are at distances d_1 and d_2 from O and form the angles B_1 and B_2 with lines of regard from O. $x/\sin A = d_1/\sin B_2 = d_2/\sin B_1$.

from the point of observation. The differences between d_1 and d_2 and between B_1 and B_2 can be neglected, and the visual angle A (measured in radians) closely approximates sin A. Thus

$$A \approx \left(\frac{x}{d}\right)\sin B$$

and (3)

$$A \approx \frac{x}{d} \quad \text{when B} = 90° .$$

This last equation gives rise to the most commonly stated form of the *geometric size-distance relation*, which is that *the visual angle subtended by an object is directly proportional to its extent and inversely proportional to its distance from the eye.* As the above discussion makes clear, however, this relation is only an approximation of the more general relation described by Eq. (1).

2.2.2. The Perception of Visual Angle. Because the visual angles subtended by objects are immediately available in the optic array, it might be supposed that observers could readily give accurate perceptual reports of angular extents. No data appear to be available, however, in which observers attempt to estimate absolute angular extents in degrees or radians. Instead, estimates are usually of the relative angular extents of two objects. Here, two cases must be distinguished: in one case good information is available concerning the physical size and distance of the object; in the other case such information is systematically eliminated. In the first case, perceptual reports of the relative angular extents of objects are strongly affected by the relative physical extents of the objects. This effect is apparent when the angular extents of two objects at different distances from the observer are compared. Gilinsky (1955), for example, asked observers to match the angular extent of a comparison triangle to that of a standard triangle presented at various large distances across an open field. Her results (see Figure 21.2) show the observers' adjustments for relative angular extent to lie about halfway between the mathematically correct reports and the reports that would be obtained if observers were responding entirely on the basis of physical extents. Observers in other studies, mostly done over smaller distances, have generally been even less successful than those in Gilinsky's study in matching angular extents under conditions of good information for physical extent (Baird, 1965; Carlson, 1962; Carlson & Tassone, 1967, Epstein, 1963b; Ono, 1966).

The method chosen to describe the data in Gilinsky's and similar studies can affect the apparent accuracy of these judgments. The data discussed above are graphed using the Thouless ratio (see Section 2.1.2). If, on the other hand, the same data are graphed, and the same comparisons made, using the Brunswik ratio (see Section 2.1.2), then the observers' settings appear to be much closer to the true angular extents (see Figure 21.2). Hochberg, for example, has concluded on the basis of the same data that observers are able to make quite accurate judgments of relative angular extent when they attempt to do so (J. Hochberg, 1971, p. 509). The Thouless ratio would seem to be the preferable measure here, however, because its use of ratios rather than differences makes it inherently more robust in this type of experimental situation. If, for example, the observers in Gilinsky's experiment had been matching a distant object to a nearer one, rather than vice versa, and if in so doing they

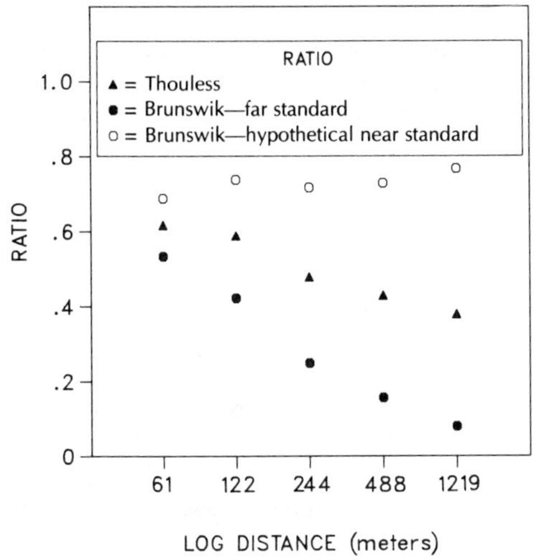

Figure 21.2. Perception of angular extent. Observers attempted to adjust a near (30.5 m) triangle to match the visual angle subtended by a more distant triangle seen resting on the ground in naturalistic, open-field conditions. Observers' results, measured in Thouless ratios (filled triangles), lie about midway between objective (1.0) and projective (0.0) matches. When Brunswik ratios (filled circles) are used, observers' results appear to be much closer to matching angular extent, but this is due to the nature of the Brunswik ratio. If, hypothetically, observers had made the identical matches using the near instead of the far object as the standard, their Brunswik ratios (open circles) would make their results appear to lie much closer to objective matches. (Data from Gilinsky, 1955.)

had arrived at a similar set of data, then the graph of the Thouless ratios would have remained invariant over this change in standard and comparison object. The graph of Brunswik ratios, however, would have been radically changed so that the perceptual reports would appear to be much closer to the relative physical extents of the objects than to their relative angular extents (see Figure 21.2 and Section 2.1.2).

For the case in which information for physical size and distance has been systematically eliminated, few experiments have explicitly asked observers to estimate relative angular extents. Over (1960), however, did find that observers were quite accurate in indicating which of two stimuli presented under reduced conditions had the larger angular extent. In addition, a number of experiments have asked observers to match the "size" or "apparent size" of two stimuli without specifying whether angular extent or physical extent was intended. Holway and Boring (1941) varied the physical size and distance of their standard stimulus from trial to trial so as to keep its visual angle constant. They found that the less information observers had about the physical size and distance of the standard, the more closely their adjustments of the comparison stimulus approached the angular extent of the standard. Lichten and Lurie (1950), achieving a further reduction in the available information for physical size and distance, found that observers' adjustments of the comparison object closely matched the angular extent of the standard.

It has been suggested,however, that observers in these experiments may not actually be matching perceived angular extents (Gogel, 1969c; Wallach & McKenna, 1960). As information for spatial layout is reduced, objects tend to be seen at the same distance (see Section 2.2.5.1), a situation in which perceived physical extent and perceived angular extent are not readily distinguishable experimentally. Rock and McDermott (1964) tested this alternative by asking observers to estimate the relative distance of two stimuli at different distances as well as to match their "size." The observers' matches were quite close to the relative angular extents of the stimuli, but their estimates of relative distance generally departed substantially from equidistance, leading Rock and McDermott to conclude that observers were making their matches on the basis of perceived angular extent rather than perceived physical extent. They also found that observers continued to match angular extents when one of the two stimuli was seen in binocular vision so that its physical size and distance were perceived with fair accuracy. Wallach and McKenna (1960), however, found that observers did not consistently make matches on the basis of angular extent when one of the two stimuli was seen in binocular vision with an illuminated surrounding. More research is needed in which observers are explicitly asked to estimate relative angular extents in reduced or partially reduced situations. Instructions to observers in which relative angular extents are explained in terms of relative proportions of the visual field rather than, as is often done, in terms of relative physical sizes under the assumption of equal distances might be helpful in clarifying for observers the distinction between physical and angular extents.

2.2.3. The Perception of Objective Size. It is generally accepted that in normal viewing situations perception of the objective, physical size of an object usually remains reasonably accurate despite changes in the distance of the object and, consequently, in the visual angle that it subtends. This phenomenon is referred to as *size constancy.* A precise account of the perception of objective size depends on a detailed consideration of the types of information for size that are present in the experimental situation; some of these types of information are considered in later sections. This section discusses some more general issues concerning size constancy.

As the available information for objective size and distance is reduced, size matches are increasingly controlled by the angular extent of the objects (Holway & Boring, 1941). When care is taken to completely eliminate such information, size matches are entirely controlled by angular extent (Lichten & Lurie, 1950), even when observers are explicitly asked to make their matches according to objective rather than projective size (Over, 1960). Also, Rogowitz (1984) has reported that the size constancy of moving observers deteriorates under certain frequencies of stroboscopic illumination.

Recently, the suggestion has been made, on the basis of anecdotal evidence, that even in normal viewing situations size constancy fails for objects subtending less than 0.50° of visual angle (J. Ross, Jenkins, & Johnstone, 1980). Subsequent attempts to test this suggestion, however, clearly show that it is incorrect; size constancy is just as much in evidence for very small visual angles (at least down to 0.125° of visual angle) as for larger ones (Day, Stuart, & Dickinson, 1980; Georgeson & Harris, 1981). The earlier literature also contains clear examples of size constancy at very small visual angles; size matches close to physical size are reported by J. Gibson (1950a, p. 186) for an object subtending about 0.15° of visual angle and by Gilinsky (1955) for objects subtending as little as about 0.05° of visual angle.

The principal deviation from size constancy found in information-rich viewing situations is in the direction of overestimating the size of distant objects, that is, making size matches that yield Thouless ratios of greater than 1. This finding has been common across a variety of experimental viewing situations. Gilinsky (1955) asked observers to adjust a triangle resting on the ground in an open field at a distance of 30.5 m to match the objective height of another triangle whose distance varied from 30.5 to 1219.2 m. The adjusted height of the comparison triangle increased regularly as the distance of the standard increased. For example, a 1.07-m standard at 30.5 m was matched by a 1.14-m comparison triangle, but at 1219.2 m was matched by a 1.43-m comparison. Some overestimation has been found in most other experiments asking for objective matches in outdoor settings (J. Gibson, 1950a, p. 186; Joynson, Newson, & May, 1965; W. Smith, 1953). Overestimation of the size of distant objects relative to near objects has also been found in a number of studies conducted indoors at a closer range of distances (Baird & Biersdorf, 1967; Carlson, 1960, 1962; Chalmers, 1952; Holway & Boring, 1941; Jenkin, 1957, 1959; Jenkin & Feallock, 1960).

When the amount of overestimation of an object's size increases with its distance, as it does in most but not all of the studies mentioned above, this result is referred to as *overconstancy*. M. Teghtsoonian (1974), in a review of the overconstancy literature, points out that the term overconstancy was originally used in this sense but has sometimes been applied indiscriminately to any case of overestimation of the size of the more distant object. Using the term overconstancy in its original sense, Teghtsoonian raises questions about the robustness of the phenomenon because it is not found in all studies, varies considerably in amount among different studies, and appears to depend on other stimulus factors such as the size of the standard.

Carlson (1960, 1962) has argued that overconstancy, used by him in the broader sense, is an artifact of "objective" instructions. The observer, Carlson suggests, sees the correct size of the distant object but, believing that perception underestimates distant objects, tries to compensate for this assumed underestimation by exaggerating the reported size of the more distant object. Carlson (1962) supports his argument by showing that "perspective" instructions, which ask for size matches that duplicate the effects of perspective, produce even greater overestimation of the distant object. The "perspective" instructions, however, impose a rather ill-defined and obscure task upon the subject, so that it is not at all clear what performance under these instructions tells us about performance under "objective" instructions. Although instructions may be partly responsible for overconstancy, it is also possible that it arises in part from the way that certain kinds of stimulus information for size are used by the observer; this possibility is discussed further in Section 3.3.2.

2.2.4. "Apparent Size" and the Effect of Instructions. Thouless (1931) argues that although we may be able to correctly judge a surface's objective size, the size that we actually see the surface as having is generally different, lying somewhere between the surface's objective size and its projective size. Thouless regards perceived size as a compromise between objective and projective size. In his research and in much of the research on size perception that follows him, observers are given instructions to respond to "apparent size," "phenomenal size," or simply "size," the intention of such instructions being to elicit the true perception of the observer rather than a cognitively based judgment of either objective or projective size (Hastorf & Way, 1952; Leibowitz & Dato, 1966; Taylor & Boring, 1942a; R. Teghtsoonian & Teghtsoonian, 1970a). (The term "projective size," or the term "perspective size" that is used by Thouless, refers in this context to the angular size of the surface, as discussed in Section 2.1.1.)

Whether such an attempt at neutrality in instructions is meaningful or merely ambiguous is open to question. Martin and Pickford (1938) report that when given "apparent size" instructions some observers interpret them as meaning objective size whereas others interpret them as meaning projective size. Joynson (1949, 1958a, 1958b; Joynson & Kirk, 1960) also finds this and shows that the experimental situation helps to determine which interpretation observers choose. Thus, for example, a high proportion of Joynson's observers spontaneously chose the objective size interpretation in matching the sizes of two widely separated objects, but as the angular separation between the two objects was made smaller the observers were increasingly likely to think of the projective interpretation.

These results, as well as the finding of Jenkin and Hyman (1959) that observers' responses when asked to make objective size matches are uncorrelated with their responses when asked to make projective size matches, suggest that objective and projective size matches should be thought of as two distinct and independent tasks, belonging on different psychological "dimensions," rather than as the end ponts of an apparent size continuum (Ono, 1970).

Carlson (1977), in reviewing the effect of instructions on size judgments, provides a detailed discussion of the complicated ways in which an observer's linguistic and theoretical preconceptions can interact with and distort the experimenter's instructions. Attempting, as Carlson advocates, to find "apparent size" instructions that exactly counterbalance these preconceptions seems like a precarious approach to solving this problem. A clear and unequivocal definition of the task, either objective or projective, along with appropriate explanations to defuse the observer's possible misconceptions, would seem to offer a somewhat sounder approach to obtaining interpretable results.

2.2.5. The Perception of Distance. An observer's ability to perceive distance varies with a number of circumstances, most prominent of which is the degree to which the experimental situation makes available information for distance. Three broad types of situation may be distinguished: (1) reduced information, (2) controlled information, and (3) full information. In the first situation, an isolated and unfamiliar object is viewed in total darkness with monocular vision, an artificial pupil, and a stationary head; the reduced situation provides a check on the experimenter's ability to eliminate extraneous information, establishes a base line against which the effects of adding information for distance can be measured, and provides conditions where endogenous variables are most free to express themselves. In the second situation, an object is viewed with limited information, such as binocular vision or linear perspective, in an effort to determine the effect that this particular type of information has on the perception of distance. In the third situation, an object is typically viewed in an illuminated, structured, and textured environment with binocular vision and at least some freedom of head movement; the full information situation aims to study distance perception under reasonably optimal, natural conditions. This section considers the reduced and full information situations, leaving the discussion of different types of controlled information for distance to the sections in which those types of information are discussed.

2.2.5.1. The Perception of Distance with Reduced Information. An object presented in a reduced information situation would logically seem to present no basis for the perception of its distance. Nevertheless, many experiments have obtained distance judgments under such circumstances, and in spite of the usually high variability of observers' responses, significant regularities have been observed. At least three factors have been reported to have an influence on distance judgments under such circumstances.

The first factor influencing perceived distance under reduced conditions is the angular extent of the object. When there are two objects in the field of view, the relative angular extent of the objects strongly affects their relative perceived distance, with the object having the smaller angular extent appearing to be farther away. This effect is more fully discussed in Section 2.2.8. What must be noted here is that the effect occurs for successive as well as simultaneous presentations; thus even when objects are presented one at a time in total isolation, if angular extent is allowed to vary across trials it will have a powerful influence on perceived distance (Gogel, 1969c; Over, 1963). Attempts to eliminate the effect of relative angular extent have either limited each observer to making only one judgment of a single object in isolation (Landauer & Epstein, 1969) or have separated out the data obtained on the first trial of a series of presentations (Gogel, 1969c). Here the results disagree. Landauer and Epstein (1969) found that even on a single trial the verbally estimated distance of an electroluminescent disk increased, across observers, as its angular extent decreased (see Figure 21.3). Gogel (1969c), however, found that on the first trial the verbally reported distance of a luminous rectangle did not vary across observers as its angular extent varied. The reason for this difference in findings is difficult to isolate because the experiments differed in a number of details.

Gogel's (1969c) results led him to postulate a second factor, which he refers to as the *specific distance tendency*, that would tend to furnish an endogenously supplied perceived distance when other information for distance was eliminated. Gogel suggests that the specific distance tendency might be related to the resting state of accommodation. Owens and Leibowitz (1976), following up on this suggestion, measured the resting states of convergence and accommodation, as well as perceived distance, under reduced conditions and found all three of these variables to be correlated. Estimates of the value of the specific distance tendency based on their results vary from about 0.5 to 2.0 m.

The third factor influencing an observer's judgments of distance under reduced conditions is the observer's knowledge of, or assumptions about, the viewing situation. Epstein (1967) suggests that even in total darkness observers imagine the extent of the space that they are in and that their perceptions, or at least their estimates, of distance are adjusted to fit this imagined space. Epstein found that, after 5 min of visual exploration of an illuminated viewing chamber that was 0.91, 1.83, or 2.74 m long, observers' verbal estimates of the distance of a fluorescent disk presented in total darkness were 0.65, 1.09, and 1.84 m, respectively (standard deviations were 0.29, 0.35, and 0.49 m). Gogel (1968) also found estimates of distance in total darkness to be strongly influenced by differences in observers' prior experience with the spatial layout of the testing environment.

The variability of observers' estimates of distance under reduced conditions is very high. Landauer and Epstein (1969), who prevented their observers from ever seeing the experimental room, had to reject three of their observers for reporting astronomical distances (e.g., "the distance of the moon"). It seems likely that as efforts to eliminate information for distance are made more and more thorough, observers become more and more responsive to subtle influences on their assumptions and criteria that may not be under the deliberate control of the experimenter.

2.2.5.2. The Perception of Distance with Full Information. The full information situation generally allows unrestricted viewing of an object resting on a horizontal surface that stretches between the observer and the object. In this situation, the perception of distance has generally been found to be quite good. As the physical distance of the object increases, its perceived distance increases also. A number of studies have

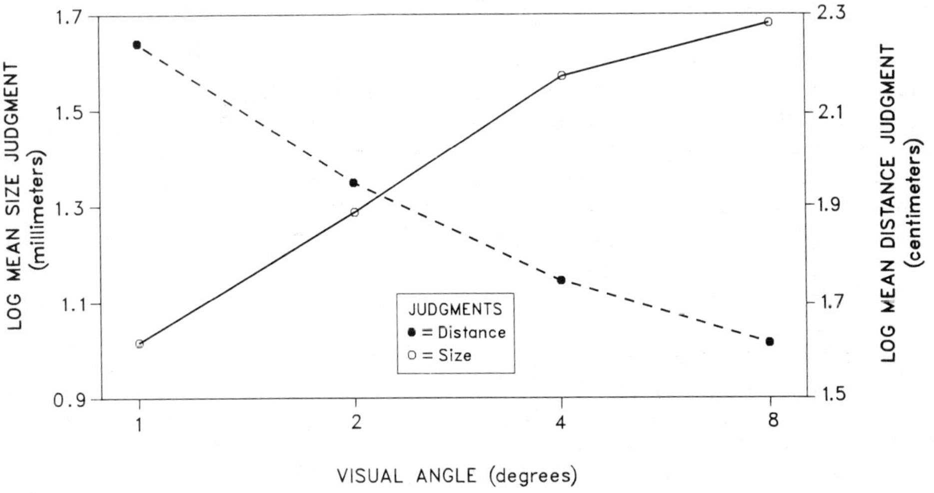

Figure 21.3. Perceived distance as a function of angular extent. Each observer made a single verbal estimate of the distance of an electroluminescent disk viewed monocularly in total darkness. For different observers, disks subtending different angular extents were displayed. Estimated distance decreased and estimated size increased as angular extent increased. (From A. A. Landauer & W. Epstein, Does retinal size have a unique correlate in perceived size?, *Perception and Psychophysics*, 1969, 6. Reprinted with permission.)

found relations between perceived distance and physical distance that are well described by a power function (see Section 2.1.2) whose exponent is fairly close to 1.0 (Baird & Biersdorf, 1967; Cook, 1978; J. Purdy & E. Gibson, 1955; M. Teghtsoonian & Teghtsoonian, 1969; for an exception see Gilinsky, 1951). The precise values found for this exponent do show substantial variability, however, ranging from lows of around 0.7 to highs of around 1.2. A number of factors have been suggested to help account for this variation.

Among the factors reported to influence full information distance judgments are the angular elevation of the target above the horizontal (Galanter & Galanter, 1973), whether the experiment is carried out indoors or outdoors (M. Teghtsoonian & Teghtsoonian, 1969; R. Teghtsoonian & Teghtsoonian, 1970b), what type of distance measuring task is used (Rogers & Gogel, 1975), and whether responses are made in "natural" units (such as arm length) or arbitrary units (such as a meter stick) (O. Smith & Smith, 1967).

Exponents greater than 1.0 in the power function relating physical and perceived distance indicate that perceived distance increases faster than physical distance, another example of overconstancy (see Section 2.2.3). As with size judgments, several researchers (Gogel, 1973; Rogers & Gogel, 1975; Wohlwill, 1964) have suggested that overconstancy in distance judgments may be produced by cognitive overcorrections on the part of observers who are trying to compensate for a tendency toward underconstancy. In an experiment comparing the effects of instruction emphasizing objectively correct distance with the effects of instructions emphasizing "apparent" distance, Rogers and Gogel (1975) obtained weak support for this suggestion. When observers were asked to reproduce a depth interval, there was no significant difference between the exponents obtained under the two types of instructions, but when the task was to bisect a depth interval, the exponent was slightly but significantly higher (1.13 vs. 1.04) in the objective instruction condition. Epstein (1963b), however, found that distance judgments did not vary systematically when the effects of "phenomenal" and "objective" instructions were compared, although the same instructions produced substantial differences in size judgments.

Cook (1978) examined the generality of the power functions obtained from asking observers to mark off a series of equal steps receding into distance on a horizontal plane. Cook obtained several different series using different step sizes, and found that all of the data were consistent with the same power function exponent (see Figure 21.4), suggesting that the power function does accurately characterize the underlying scale of perceived distance across the entire plane, not just across the particular points measured. Cook found large individual differences between his observers, whose distance functions had exponents ranging from 0.776 to 1.229. These individual differences proved to be quite reliable over a 3-week period.

Bradley and Vido (1984) found that the exponent of the power function for perceived distance was significantly larger than the exponent for remembered distance; when observers made magnitude estimations of the perceived distances of objects situated from about 6 m to about 23 km away in a natural landscape, the exponent of the power function of their grouped data was 0.811, but when other observers made their estimates from memory a day after viewing the same landscape, the exponent of their data's power function was only 0.596.

Observers' ability to make verbal estimates of absolute distances improves with corrected practice, both constant error and variability decreasing substantially; it appears that this improvement is due primarily to the more accurate learning of the metric scale (e.g., yards) in which the responses are made (E. Gibson & Bergman, 1954; E. Gibson, Bergman, & Purdy, 1955). Relative distance judgments, which do not depend on any particular metric scale, appear to be less susceptible to improvement through practice (Wohlwill, 1964).

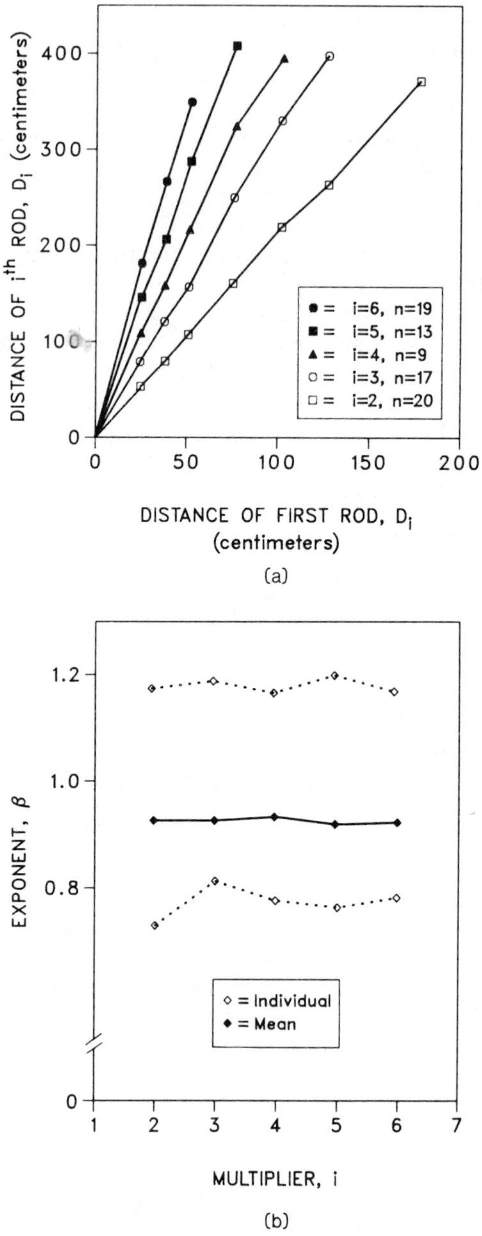

Figure 21.4. Perceived distance scales with full information. (a) Under the instructions of the observers, the experimenter adjusted binocularly viewed rods lying on a horizontal surface to mark off equal interval steps of distance away from the observer, with the size of the first step being fixed by the experimenter. (b) Average and extreme individual estimates of the exponent of the median distance scale for different multiplication functions. These exponents vary considerably from one individual to another but are constant across different multiplication functions, indicating that, for a given individual, a single exponent can give a good description of the perceived distance scale for the entire plane. (From M. Cook, The judgment of distance on a plane surface, *Perception and Psychophysics*, 1978, *23*. Reprinted with permission.)

2.2.6. The Size-Distance Invariance Hypothesis. As Eq. (1) shows, the size and distance of an object jointly determine the visual angle that it subtends. It follows that a given visual angle can be produced by infinitely many distinct combinations of size and distance, but that if either size or distance is specified the other quantity is also determined. The *size-distance invariance hypothesis* suggests that this geometric size-distance relation also holds true in perception, that is, that the ratio of perceived size to perceived distance is constant for a given visual angle. This hypothesis is made explicit by Kilpatrick and Ittleson (1953), who point out that its validity is often uncritically assumed in the earlier literature. Kilpatrick and Ittleson cite a variety of evidence that does not follow the predictions of the hypothesis. The large number of studies measuring the relation between perceived size and perceived distance that have been published since Kilpatrick and Ittleson's 1953 review have generally supported their critical assessment. More recent reviews are offered by Epstein, Park, and Casey (1961) and by J. Hochberg (1971).

Although perceived size and perceived distance are sometimes found to be related, at least loosely, to visual angle in the way that the hypothesis suggests (Epstein, 1965; Flock, 1965b; Gogel, 1971; Hartman, 1964; Rump, 1961; Ueno, 1962), this fact does not in itself demonstrate the existence of a functional connection between perceived size and perceived distance; it is also possible that perceived size and perceived distance are independently determined within the visual system but that the factors determining them are linked together in the environment in such a way as to tend to maintain this relation between them. For example, the geometric size-distance relation ensures that whenever perception is veridical, for whatever reasons, perceived size and perceived distance must conform to the size-distance invariance hypothesis.

Nevertheless, the empirically determined relation between perceived size, perceived distance, and visual angle is frequently not in accord with the size-distance invariance hypothesis. In a number of studies perceived distance actually changes in the direction opposite that which the hypothesis would predict (Alexander, 1974; Gruber, 1954; Higashiyama, 1977, 1979; Jenkin & Hyman, 1959; Rump, 1961; Ueno, 1962; see Kilpatrick & Ittleson, 1953 and Woodworth, 1938, p. 676, for references to some earlier observations of this phenomenon); thus, for example, of two objects subtending the same visual angle, one may appear to be both larger and closer than the other. Gruber (1954) has termed this effect the *size-distance paradox*.

Even when perceived size and perceived distance do change in the direction predicted by the invariance hypothesis, the amounts by which they change often deviate substantially from the amounts predicted by the geometric size-distance relation (Baird & Biersdorf, 1967; Epstein & Landauer, 1969; Vogel & Teghtsoonian, 1972).

If perceived size and perceived distance are linked in an invariant relation with visual angle, this linkage should be present not just in average group results but also in the individual results of each observer. Some studies have looked at the correlations across the data of their individual observers between measures of perceived size and measures of perceived distance. Results, however, generally show perceived size and perceived distance to be only weakly correlated, if at all (Epstein, 1963b, 1965; Gruber, 1954, 1956; Over, 1963).

Oyama (1977), adapting a method developed by Simon (1954; cited in Oyama, 1977) and Blalock (1962; cited in Oyama, 1977), examined the partial correlations within several sets of data from size-distance experiments and found that in most cases the pattern of results could best be explained by assuming that perceived size and perceived distance were independently determined by the stimulus situation. For a few subjects in some situations, however, Oyama found indications either that perceived distance exerted a causal influence on perceived size or that perceived size exerted a causal influence on perceived distance. These mixed conclusions, as well as other work discussed below, suggest that the size-distance invariance hypothesis should not be regarded as an overriding principle of size and distance perception. Rather, the geometric size-distance relation can be seen as one source of information among many and can be expected to exert an influence on perceptual judgments of size and distance that will depend both on the other information available and on the perceptual strategies of the subject.

The most common application of the size-distance invariance hypothesis in classical perceptual theory is to postulate that the perceived sizes of objects are derived from their perceived distances (it is assumed that accurate use can be made of the object's visual angle) (Epstein, 1973). The implicit assumption behind this postulate is often that perceived size can be arrived at only in this way, that is, by taking distance into account. Recent analyses, however, of the available visual information in the optic array have shown that the size of an object often can be specified independently of its distance, so that the theoretical need to explain size perception as being derived from distance perception has been correspondingly diminished (see, for example, Sections 3.1.2.2, 3.1.2.3, and 3.2.6).

If the visual angle of a stimulus is held constant, the size-distance invariance hypothesis predicts that changes in its perceived size will be proportional to changes in its perceived distance. One situation in which visual angle is held constant is provided by imprinting an afterimage on the retina. When the eye then fixates a surface, the afterimage is visually superposed on the surface and appears to be at the same distance as the surface. The perceived size of the afterimage is approximately proportional to the perceived distance of the surface on which it is projected. This relation is known as *Emmert's law*; the extensive literature concerning it is reviewed by Epstein et al. (1961). Emmert's law is sometimes used to support the size-distance hypothesis, but as J. Hochberg has pointed out (1971, p. 511), this situation is just as much open to the independent determination of perceived size and distance as are the more normal situations discussed above.

Two related approaches have been made to rescuing the size-distance hypothesis from its weak empirical support. One approach, developed by Carlson (1960, 1962, 1977), argues that the size responses obtained under objective size instructions do not accurately reflect true perceived size because observers distort their reports to compensate for their erroneous belief that things seen in the distance look smaller than they actually are. This hypothesis has been discussed in Section 2.2.3. A difficulty in applying this account to the size-distance invariance hypothesis is that it is not clear why it should not be applied equally to perceived distance as well as to perceived size (Baird & Biersdorf, 1967).

The second approach to shoring up the size-distance invariance hypothesis has been to suggest that information for distance can be registered by the perceptual system and used in the perception of size without itself becoming available to consciousness. This concept of *registered distance*, whose application to size perception is attributed by Koffka (1935, p. 229) to Holaday, has been widely used to account for the perception of size in situations where measurements of perceived distance are not in accord with the size-distance invariance hypothesis (Epstein, 1973; J. Hochberg, 1971, pp. 512–514; Higashiyama, 1977, 1979; Kaufman & Rock, 1962a; Rock & Kaufman, 1962; Woodworth and Schlosberg, 1954, p. 477). The chief difficulty with this approach is that, because registered distance is by definition not directly available for psychophysical measurement, it is not at all clear how its existence can be empirically established. The solution most often offered to this difficulty is to argue that if perceived size is affected by the traditional cues for distance, such as convergence, then the perception of size must be mediated by the registration of distance. This argument, however, lacks force because, as is noted above, convergence and the other traditional cues for distance can be shown to geometrically specify size just as directly as they specify distance.

The two approaches to saving the size-distance hypothesis are similar in that they both question the validity of observers' responses about size and distance as indicators of underlying perceptual activity. J. Hochberg (1971, p. 514), noting this similarity, suggests that it may be possible to develop indirect methods, such as suitable training procedures or the use of reaction time measures, to decide on appropriate values to use in evaluating the size-distance hypothesis.

A special case often discussed in connection with the size-distance invariance hypothesis is the *moon illusion*. As with an afterimage, the moon always subtends pretty much the same visual angle (about 0.5°). Nevertheless, when the moon is near the horizon it tends to appear much larger than when it is near the zenith. This size illusion has been known since antiquity and has been the subject of much theorizing and experimentation (Boring, 1943; Carter, 1977; Cobb, Cole, & Rainey, 1978; Dees, 1966; Gilinsky, 1980; Gruber, King, & Link, 1963; Holway & Boring, 1940; Kamman, 1967; Kaufman & Rock, 1962a, 1962b; W. King & Gruber, 1962; Leibowitz & Hartman, 1959; Restle, 1970; Rock & Kaufman, 1962; H. Ross & Ross, 1976; O. Smith, Smith, Geist, & Zimmermann, 1978; Taylor & Boring, 1942b; Van de Geer & Zwaan, 1964). Reviews of the moon illusion literature are also given in Reiman (1902, cited in Kaufman, 1974, p. 364), J. Hochberg (1971, pp. 511–512), and Kaufman (1974, pp. 362–366). A recurrent explanation, credited first to Ptolemy (Boring, 1943), accounts for the moon illusion within the context of the size-distance invariance hypothesis by asserting that the moon near the horizon is taken to be more distant than the moon near the zenith and is consequently seen to be larger.

Kaufman and Rock (1962a, 1962b; Rock & Kaufman, 1962), using an optical device that allowed a disk of light of variable size to be placed at optical infinity and superimposed against various portions of the sky, examined the moon illusion under a variety of conditions. Their results allowed them to reject several explanations of the illusion, including those that would attribute it to differences in angle of the regard or to differences in the color or brightness of the moon at the horizon and at the zenith. They did find that the illusion depended upon the existence of a visible terrain. The size of the illusion, measured as the ratio of the diameter of the moon near the horizon to the diameter of the moon near the zenith, varied from about 1.2 to about 1.6, depending on sky and terrain conditions. Kaufman and Rock adopt the hypothesis (R. Smith, 1738; cited in Kaufman & Rock, 1962a) that the perceived shape of the sky is that of a flattened bowl, with the horizon farther than the zenith, and that the moon is seen as being coplanar with the sky so that the moon is taken to be farther when at the horizon than when at the zenith.

A difficulty with this explanation of the moon illusion is, as Boring (1943) found, that the moon at the horizon generally appears to be both larger and closer than the moon at the zenith, thus giving rise to another instance of the size-distance paradox. Kaufman and Rock account for this result by suggesting that the moon is unconsciously registered as being farther at the horizon and is thus seen as being larger there, but that in consciously estimating its distance observers note that it looks larger and so conclude that it must be nearer.

Restle (1970), however, argues that neither registered nor perceived distance need enter into the moon illusion. He suggests instead that the illusion may be one of relative size (see Section 3.1.2.3), with the moon's apparent size being inversely related to a weighted average of adjacent extents in the visual field. Unfortunately, Restle's account lacks predictive power because he makes the weights in his weighting function depend on the selective attention of observers and gives positive weights to gaps in the field as well as to objects, thus apparently making it possible to give a post hoc account for virtually any conceivable result. Gilinsky (1980) attempts to reconcile the perceived flatness of the sky with the perceived closeness of the moon at the horizon by suggesting that the moon is not seen as being coplanar with the sky but rather appears to recede "into the depths of the sky" (Gilinsky, 1980, p. 280) as it rises.

As in the earlier discussion of the concept of registered distance, it is unclear what evidence might be used to show that the perceived size of the moon is mediated by its registered distance rather than being directly determined by the adjacent structures in the optic array; the latter class of explanation seems more parsimonious and deserves further examination. It may be that the moon illusion is best understood outside the framework of the size-distance invariance hypothesis.

2.2.7. Effects of Familiar or Suggested Size

2.2.7.1. Effects of Familiar Size on Perceived Distance. If the size of an object is already known, either because the object is familiar or because the observer is provided with this information by the experimenter, then the geometric size-distance relation makes it possible in principle to determine the object's distance as well. This reasoning thus leads to a variant of the size-distance invariance hypothesis in which perceived size determines perceived distance rather than vice versa (Epstein, 1967; J. Hochberg, 1971).

Although a number of experimental studies (Epstein, 1961; Gogel, Hartman, & Harker, 1957; C. Hochberg & J. Hochberg, 1952; J. Hochberg & McAlister, 1955) have failed to find evidence for the use of familiar size in the perception of distance, the preponderance of evidence (Epstein, 1963a, 1965; Eriksson & Zetterberg, 1975; Fitzpatrick, Pasnak, & Tyer, 1982; Gogel, 1969a, 1969b, 1976; Gogel & Mertens, 1967, 1968; Ittleson, 1951; Newman, 1972; Ono, 1969; Park & Michaelson, 1974; W. Smith, 1952) now favors the conclusion that familiar size can at least affect the judgment of distance. Epstein (1965), for example, used photographs of coins (dime, quarter, half-dollar) as his familiar objects. The photographs were enlarged or reduced to the same physical size (2.38 cm), and were presented one at a time at the same distance (135 cm) and in complete darkness except for a spot of light illuminating the photograph. Each observer viewed one photograph monocularly through a stationary aperture and reported its size and distance using a tactual response measure. Both reported size and reported distance varied directly with the actual size of the coin depicted in the photograph (see Table 21.1), the explanation of these results being that the familiar size of each coin influenced its perceived size and this, in combination with its visual angle, influenced its perceived distance.

Size information presented verbally or haptically can also influence the reported distance of a visible object (Baird, 1963; Coltheart, 1969, 1970; Gogel, 1981a; Park & Michaelson, 1974; Tyer, Allen, & Pasnak, 1983). Coltheart (1970), for example, asked observers to estimate the distance of a lighted triangle in a dark room; considerable care was taken to eliminate all visual information for the size (20.32 cm) and distance (4.27 m) of the triangle, but half of the observers were told that the size of the triangle was 4 in. (10.16 cm) and half were told that it was 8 in. (20.32 cm). The resulting average estimates of distance, 2.35 m and 4.18 m, respectively, reflect this verbally provided size information quite closely. Coltheart (1969) obtained similar results, although with distance somewhat underestimated, using the same stimulus display and task but providing size information haptically, by allowing observers to hold a triangle that they were told was the same size as the triangle at which they were looking. Not all studies have found such good results, however (see Park & Michaelson, 1974), so that the circumstances under which suggested size will influence reported distance remain to be clarified.

Group averages of reported distance in familiar or suggested size experiments can be fairly accurate, as the above results indicate, but individual performance tends to be highly variable, as is reflected in the large standard deviations of the group data. Coltheart's (1970) findings of standard deviations of 1.85 and 1.88 m for mean distance estimates of 2.35 and 4.18 m, respectively, are typical. That some of this variability can arise from variability in the perceived sizes of the stimulus objects has been shown by Gogel (1976) in a familiar size study that obtained verbal reports of size as well as distance. Variability can also be introduced in the link between perceived size and perceived distance; Epstein (1963a, 1965) found Spearman rank-correlation coefficients ranging from −.024 to .77 between his measures of perceived size and perceived distance. On the other hand, Park and Michaelson (1974), testing an hypothesis of Coltheart's (1970), concluded that individual differences in observers' use of verbal estimates to describe perceived distance did not contribute appreciably to the variability of their results.

Table 21.1. Influence of Familiar Size on Perceived Size and Distance

Standard	Apparent Distance (cm) Mean	Apparent Distance (cm) SD	Apparent Size (cm) Mean	Apparent Size (cm) SD
Dime	103.56	20.14	2.08	0.30
Quarter	128.10	27.65	2.26	0.31
Half-Dollar	151.30	31.62	2.60	0.43

Each observer made one tactual estimate of the size and distance of a monocularly viewed photograph of a coin seen in otherwise total darkness. Photographs of three different sizes of coins were used but were enlarged or reduced so that all had the same physical size (2.38 cm); each photograph was then displayed at the same distance (135 cm). Both the estimated size and distance of each coin increased with its real size, indicating that familiar size influences both perceived size and perceived distance. (From W. Epstein, Nonrelational judgments of size and distance, American Journal of Psychology, *78. Copyright 1965 by the University of Illinois Press. Reprinted with permission.)*

Although the effects of familiar size on perceived distance have most often been examined under conditions that attempt to eliminate all other information for size and distance, some studies have looked at the effect of familiar size in combination with other information. Fillenbaum, Schiffman, and Butcher (1965) failed to find an effect of familiar size on the distance of objects viewed with unrestricted vision, but Predebon (1979a) found that the judged absolute distance of a larger than normal chair, viewed at a distance of about 25 m with unrestricted vision, was somewhat less than the judged distance when a normally sized chair was presented at the same distance; this result is consistent with an effect of familiar size on perceived distance and was not found when unfamiliar stakes of the same sizes as the chairs were used instead. In addition, Predebon (1979a, 1979b) and Carlson and Tassone (1971) both found that the judged distance of a familiar object was somewhat greater than that of an equally sized unfamiliar object presented at the same distance. These investigators point out, however, that their familiar objects differed from their unfamiliar objects in other ways (Predebon, 1979b, mentions texture and Carlson & Tassone, 1971, mention color) that might have been responsible for the obtained differences in judged distance.

The question of whether the effect of familiar or suggested size on reported distance is truly a perceptual effect or merely reflects a cognitive judgment on the part of the observer has been raised repeatedly (J. Gibson, 1950a; Gogel, 1976, 1981a; C. Hochberg & Hochberg, 1952). Attempts to answer this question center around measures of distance perception that are thought to be free of cognitive influence, but to date the evidence is inconclusive. C. Hochberg and J. Hochberg (1952) found that familiar size was not able to bias the proportion of time that one organization of a reversible figure was seen. Ono (1969), however, repeated this experiment with modifications that called more attention to familiar size differences and did obtain a small but significant effect. O'Leary and Wallach (1980) have shown that familiar size can influence stereoscopic depth, presumably through its influence on perceived distance, and this effect seems unlikely to be cognitively based. Gogel (1976, 1981a), on the other hand, has developed a method for measuring perceived distance indirectly and has shown that although familiar size (1976) and suggested size (1981a) affect verbally reported distance, they do not affect perceived distance as measured by his indirect method. The validity of Gogel's indirect method, based on nulling the lateral motion perceived during small lateral head movements, is open to some question, however. The method assumes that lateral head movements and the compensatory eye movements associated with them are accurately taken into account in motion perception; the assumption concerning eye movements is probably incorrect for it has been shown that motion can be radically underestimated when its perception depends on taking eye movements into account (Festinger, Sedgwick, & Holtzman, 1976; Sedgwick & Festinger, 1976; and Chapter 17 by Mack). Although it seems clear that measurements obtained using Gogel's indirect method do reflect perceived distance, it seems unlikely that they do so with sufficient accuracy to be used as a valid measure of distance perception (see Shebilske & Proffitt, 1981, 1983; and Gogel, 1981b, 1983, for further discussion of the validity of this method). Higashiyama (1984) concludes from two experiments in which both instructions and available information were varied that both cognitive and perceptual effects of familiar size could be found.

2.2.7.2. Effects of Familiar Size on Perceived Size. When an object is familiar to the observer, the object's known or remembered size may influence the size that it is perceived to have. Bolles and Bailey (1956) established the basis for such an effect by showing that the accuracy with which observers were able to estimate the size of a familiar object such as a playing card was often as great when the object was merely named to them as when they were able to see it. More recently, however, Moyer, Bradley, Sorensen, Whiting, and Mansfield (1978) have compared magnitude estimates of the perceived and remembered sizes of familiar objects and have found that although both types of data can be fit by power functions, the exponents of these functions are about 20–30% smaller for remembered than for perceived size.

The question of whether size estimates are influenced by familiar size when good visual information for size is available has been approached by using "off-size objects," familiar objects such as chairs constructed to be either larger or smaller than their normal size, thus putting their familiar size into conflict with the size visually specified. These efforts have produced mixed results, with some studies finding a small effect of familiar size (McKennell, 1960; Predebon, 1979; Slack, 1956) whereas others find none at all (Fillenbaum et al., 1965). Schiffman (1967) and Predebon, Wenderoth, and Curthoys (1974) found no effect of familiar size at near distances but did find an effect at far distances, a result that may, as Schiffman suggests, reflect the reduction in sources of available visual information for size that occurs at large distances. The familiar size of one object has been found not to affect either the judged size of an adjacent object (Predebon, 1979) or the judged scale of a surrounding room (Mershon & Gogel, 1975).

Eriksson and Zetterberg (1975) found that estimates of the physical sizes of familiar objects in naturalistic settings were quite accurate even when the objects were viewed monocularly through an aperture that eliminated such visual information as location on the ground plane. Gogel and Newton (1969) have shown, however, that even under reduced conditions the perceived size of an object can differ considerably from its familiar size. Observers viewing transparencies of familiar objects under reduced conditions were asked whether the objects appeared to be their normal size or were "off-sized." For each off-sized object observers estimated the ratio between the perceived size and the normal size of the object. The mean obtained ratios for 16 familiar objects varied from 0.12 for the transparency of a guitar to 1.61 for the transparency of a key. Gogel and Newton attribute this effect to the tendency to localize objects at a specific distance (of about 2–3 m) under reduced conditions. The perceived size of a familiar object is taken to be a compromise between its familiar size and the size appropriate to its visual angle in conjunction with the specific distance tendency.

2.2.8. Relative Angular Extent as Information for Relative Distance. If the ratio k between the physical sizes s_1 and s_2 of two objects is known or assumed, then their relative distances d_1 and d_2 can in principle be found from the relative extents of the visual angles A_1 and A_2 that they subtend:

$$\left(\frac{d_1}{d_2}\right) \approx \frac{s_1/A_1}{s_2/A_2},$$

and so

$$\left(\frac{d_1}{d_2}\right) \approx k\,\frac{A_2}{A_1}. \qquad (4)$$

The hypothesis that such information is effective in distance perception is yet another application of the size-distance invariance hypothesis. The situation most commonly hypothesized is one in which the physical sizes of the two objects are unknown but are assumed to be equal, so that $k = 1$.

Historically, the potential use of relative angular extent information (often referred to as the "relative size cue") was first brought clearly into focus as a confounding variable in familiar size experiments. C. Hochberg and J. Hochberg (1952) pointed out that whenever the distances of two instances of the same type of familiar object, for example, two playing cards, are compared, the similar shapes of the two objects could lead to the assumption that they are the same physical size even though they subtend different visual angles; thus the comparison of their distances could be made entirely on the basis of their relative angular extents and without any reference to their familiar size. This observation holds in principle whether the two objects are presented simultaneously or successively. C. Hochberg and J. Hochberg (1952) showed that the proportion of time one panel of a reversible screen figure was seen to be in front of the other panel could be influenced by the relative angular sizes of the familiar figures shown on the two panels of the screen. A number of other studies have since confirmed the influence of relative angular extent on the reported distance of familiar objects (Adelson, 1963; Epstein & Baratz, 1964; Gogel, 1969a; Gogel et al., 1957; Gogle & Mertens, 1967, 1968; Newman, 1972; Ono, 1969). The interaction of familiar size and relative size in perceived distance is reviewed by Gogel (1964), who subsumes both types of information under the concept of perceived size per unit of retinal size.

An effect of relative angular extent on reported distance can also be shown using simple geometrical figures that do not have any particular familiar size associated with them. J. Hochberg and McAlister (1955), using two-dimensional line drawings of pairs of figures (circle-circle, square-square, or circle-square) in which one figure in each pair was four times wider than the other, found that pairs of similar figures were more likely to appear three-dimensional than were pairs of dissimilar figures and that only with the similar figures was the larger figure more likely to appear to be in front when the drawing was seen as three-dimensional. Epstein and Franklin (1965), however, found that relative angular extent was just as effective between pairs of dissimilar figures as between pairs of similar figures. They asked observers both to give verbal estimates and to make tactual settings to indicate the ratio between the apparent distances of two luminous geometric figures seen under reduced conditions. Their results, given in Table 21.2, show little difference between similar pairs (circle-circle and square-square) and dissimilar pairs (circle-square); for both types of pairs the reported distance ratios are strongly influenced by, but tend to be somewhat less than, the angular extent ratios. In the same paper Epstein and Franklin also determined that it is the ratio between two angular extents rather than the difference between them that determines their effect on reported relative distance. For the results shown in Table 21.2, angular difference was held constant while angular ratio was varied; here, reported relative distance is clearly affected. In a second experiment, angular ratio was held constant while angular difference was varied; in that experiment reported relative distance remained nearly constant. These results are what would be expected from Eq. (4). Burnham (1983) has also found that the relative angular sizes of dissimilar figures, as well as similar figures, affect judgments of apparent distance.

Table 21.2. Effect of Relative Angular Extent on Perceived Relative Distance

Angular Ratio	Estimated Relative Distance			
	Tactual		Verbal	
	Mean	SD	Mean	SD
	Shapes Identical			
2–1	2.07	0.28	1.95	0.15
3–1	2.84[a]	1.78	2.90	1.11
5–1	3.65	1.76	3.55	1.21
	Shapes Dissimilar			
2–1	2.43	0.81	2.30	0.78
3–1	2.63	0.85	2.63	0.92
5–1	3.50	1.29	3.15	1.26

Observers indicated the relative distance of two objects seen under reduced conditions by making either a tactual adjustment or a verbal estimate. The estimated relative distance of the two objects increased as the ratio of their angular extents increased, with the angularly smaller object being seen as farther away. Whether the two objects had identical or dissimilar shapes had little effect on the observers' estimates. (From W. Esptein & S. Franklin, Some conditions of the effect of relative size on perceived distance, American Journal of Psychology, 78. *Copyright 1965 by the University of Illinois Press. Reprinted with permission.)*

[a] *Two observers are excluded because of very high values.*

As mentioned above, in discussing the effects of relative angular extent on relative perceived distance, it is often assumed that the two objects are perceived to be equal in size. Epstein and Landauer (1969) tested this assumption by obtaining magnitude estimations of perceived size as well as perceived distance. Their display consisted of two luminous disks separated horizontally by 35° and seen under reduced conditions. The disk on the right was the standard. It was unchanged from trial to trial, and the observer was told to assign it a constant size and distance of 10. The disk on the left was variable, and on each trial the observer estimated its size and distance relative to those of the standard. Control conditions were included to ensure that observers' responses were not affected by the actual sizes and distances of the disks, but only by their relative angular extents. the results are shown in Figure 21.5. As can be seen there, the perceived relative distance of the variable disk increased as its angular extent decreased. Also, however, the perceived relative size of the variable disk decreased as its angular extent decreased. Neither the change in perceived relative distance nor the change in perceived relative size is as great as would have been predicted by the size-distance invariance hypothesis if the other term had remained constant, but the combined changes in both terms are greater than that hypothesis would predict. To explain these results Epstein and Landauer hypothesize that perceived relative size and perceived relative distance are each determined directly by relative angular extent. Similar results have been found by Higashiyama (1977).

Another factor influencing perceived relative distance is the tendency to see objects in the visual field as being at the same distance from the observer. Termed the *equidistance tendency* by Gogel, who was the first to study it systematically (Gogel, 1956a, 1956b, 1965), this effect is most pronounced under reduced conditions of viewing, where it is unopposed by other visual information for distance. Even when other information is present, however, the equidistance tendency may have some effect; it may, for instance, be responsible for the observation that differences in the perceived distances of objects tend not to be as great as the differences in their angular extents.

The strength of the equidistance tendency between two objects is inversely proportional to their angular separation (Gogel, 1965). For instance, Gogel reports that if two angularly separated objects are seen to be at different distances and a third object is presented adjacent to one object but with no information to specify its distance from either object, then the perceived distance of the third object will be similar to that of the object to which it is adjacent; if the third object has an angular direction midway between the two objects, its perceived distance will also be approximately midway between their perceived distances. Roelofs and Zeeman (1957) report a similar effect.

2.3. Two-dimensional Visual Angles

2.3.1. Shape, Slant, and Visual Angle. Every rigid object has a definite *shape*, by which is generally meant the set of spatial characteristics that would remain invariant over translations, rotations, or changes in scale of the object. Because the variety of shapes is infinite, there are many different schemes for describing and classifying shapes. Here we shall be no more specific than is necessary for describing the role of shape in layout perception.

Every surface of an object has its own shape, and if that surface is flat, then the shape of the surface can be completely specified by specifying the boundaries of the surface. If the surface is visible, then it subtends a two-dimensional, or solid, visual angle in the optic array. This section describes these solid visual angles in terms of their corresponding two-dimen-

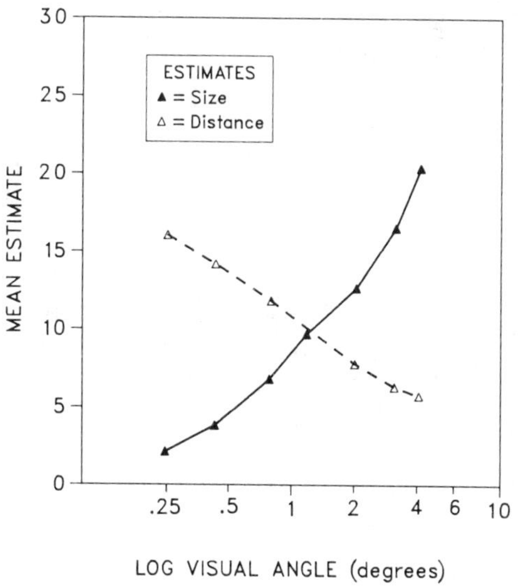

Figure 21.5. Relative angular extent affects both perceived size and perceived distance. Observers viewed two luminous disks separated by 35° under reduced conditions. One disk was the standard and was assigned a constant size and distance of 10. The other disk was the comparison whose angular extent varied from trial to trial. Observers made magnitude estimates of the size and distance of the comparison disk relative to the standard. As the angular extent of the comparison disk decreased, its estimated relative size decreased and its estimated relative distance increased. (From W. Epstein & A. A. Landauer, Size and distance judgments under reduced conditions of viewing, *Perception and Psychophysics*, 1969, 6. Reprinted with permission.)

sional projections on the local projection plane that is perpendicular to the line of regard.

The projection of a surface is not unique to that surface. A simple generalization of the one-dimensional geometric size-distance relation (see Section 2.2.1) indicates that the same projection could be produced by an infinite number of different surfaces, all having the same shape and the same orientation to the line of regard as the original surface, but whose sizes and distances have been increased or decreased proportionally. In addition, however, the same projection also could be produced by an infinite number of surfaces, all at the same distance, whose shape and orientation to the line of regard are varied concurrently so that their projections are identical. Thus, for example, the trapezoidal projection produced by a slanted square could also be produced by any number of other differently slanted and differently proportioned trapezoids (see Figure 21.6). The projection can thus be said to determine a whole family of shapes, each linked to a particular slant with respect to the line of regard. For a given projection of a flat surface, specifying the slant of the surface with respect to the line of regard also determines its shape and vice versa. This geometric interdependency between shape and slant for a given projection is referred to here as the *geometric shape-slant relation.*

2.3.2. The Perception of Projective Shape. A number of studies have been done in which observers were explicitly asked to indicate the projective shape of an object. The general finding has been that, when there is information available concerning the objective shape of a surface, observers are rather poor at judging its projective shape. Lappin and Preble (1975) asked observers to judge one of the projective angles of a briefly exposed random polygon (observers were told in advance that the angle would be 65, 75, 85, 95, 105, or 115°). On each trial the observer viewed a slide showing the polygon lying on a cluttered desk. Lappin and Preble report that in this visually complex and meaningful environment their observers were "profoundly inept" at judging projective shapes. Only 11% of the variance in their responses was determined by the actual projective shapes; observers' judgments were apparently heavily influenced by the objective shapes of the polygons, which determined 49% of the variance in their responses.

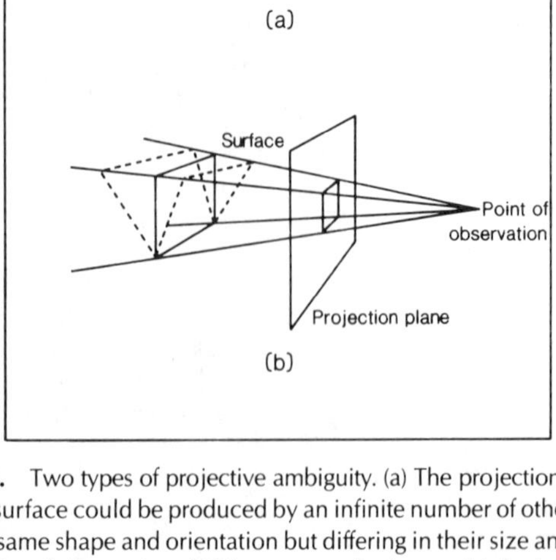

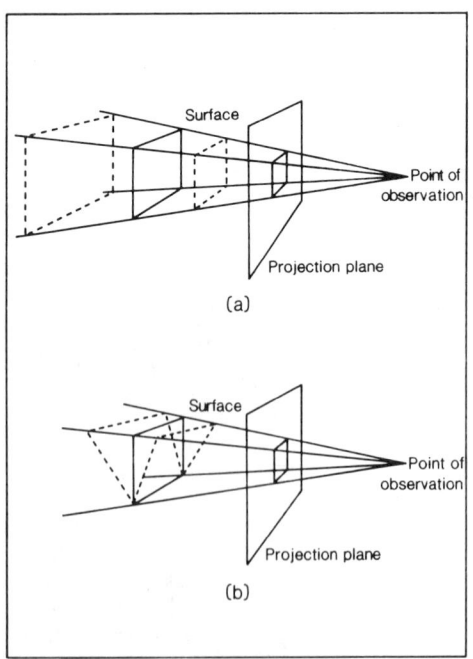

Figure 21.6. Two types of projective ambiguity. (a) The projection produced by a given surface could be produced by an infinite number of other surfaces having the same shape and orientation but differing in their size and distance from the point of observation. (b) The same projection could also be produced by an infinite number of other surfaces at the same location but having differing shapes and orientations.

Kaess (1978) also found an influence of objective shape on judgments of projective shape. Kaess asked observers to judge which of two binocularly viewed, slanted rectangles had the larger projective width. Clearly, as a rectangle is rotated around the vertical axis, the horizontal extent of its projection decreases as the angle of rotatation away from the frontal plane increases. A rectangle whose objective width is greater than that of another rectangle can be made to have a smaller projective width simply by giving the first rectangle a sufficiently large slant away from the frontal plane. Thus, by adjusting the amount that each rectangle was rotated around the vertical axis, Kaess was able to vary the relative projective widths of the two rectangles independently of their objective widths. Kaess found that when the projective width of one rectangle was much larger (more than twice as large) than that of the other, observers made the correct choice more than 90% of the time even when there was a large difference in the other direction between the objective widths of the two rectangles. When the projective width of one rectangle was only slightly larger (10% larger) than that of the other, observers were still able to choose the correct rectangle about 65% of the time if the objective widths of the two rectangles were the same or only slightly different. If, however, there was only a small difference (10% larger) in the projective widths of the two rectangles and there was a large difference (50% larger) in the other direction between the objective widths of the two rectangles, observers correctly chose the projectively wider rectangle only about 10% of the time.

Lichte and Borresen (1967), using complex and irregularly shaped slanted stimulus objects that were viewed binocularly from 1.2 m, asked observers to match their projective shapes by adjusting the width of a patch of light in the frontal plane until it matched the projective width of the stimulus object. Their observers' settings were about midway between the correct projective matches and the correct objective matches. Rather similar results have been found with binocular viewing of simple geometrical figures (Epstein, Bontrager, & Park, 1962; Landauer, 1969). In an apparent exception to this trend, Gottheil and Bitterman (1951) obtained good projective matches between two differently slanted triangles under conditions of free binocular viewing; their results may be accounted for, however, by noting that they set their two triangles side by side in such a way that accurate projective matches could be obtained simply by lining up the tops of the triangles.

When care is taken to eliminate extrinsic information concerning the objective shape of a slanted surface, observers are then able to match its projective shape with considerable accuracy (Epstein et al., 1962; Campione, 1977). Campione (1977) found that the projective shapes of a variety of figures (including a circle, a square, and a triangle) could be matched accurately when the slanted standard figure was viewed monocularly through a reduction screen while the comparison figures, which were a set of photographs of the standard figure at various slants, were viewed binocularly in the frontal plane and without a reduction screen. Although his results were quite variable, the average of the Brunswik ratios (see Section 2.1.2) that

Campione obtained was −.01. It is of course possible in such a matching procedure that neither the standard nor the comparison is seen in its correct projective proportions, but no attempts have been made to obtain absolute rather than relative measures of perceived projective proportions.

Hake and Myers (1969) examined the effect of familiarity on projective shape matches made under reduction conditions. Following a familiarization period, observers were shown a slide of an irregularly shaped figure at a standard slant and then a series of slides of the figure at various comparison slants. Their task was to indicate which slides in the comparison series were exact projective matches of the standard slide. Hake and Myers found that prior familiarity with the frontal view of the figure did not change the point of subjective equality but did broaden the range of projective shapes that were matched to the standard.

2.3.3. The Perception of Objective Shape. When observers view slanted surfaces binocularly and in normally complex environments, they are able, if asked clearly, to make quite accurate judgments about the objective shapes of the surfaces. Lichte and Borresen (1967) showed their observers unfamiliar, complex, slanted "nonsense" figures in an unrestricted binocular viewing situation and took considerable pains to ensure that the observers understood that they were being asked to make objective matches of the real widths (i.e., maximum horizontal extents) of the figures. From their observers' settings they computed an average Brunswik ratio of .90, indicating that their observers' settings were very close to the objective widths of the figures. In a very similar experiment, Landauer (1969) obtained results that actually showed "overconstancy"; that is, his observers' average setting was somewhat greater than the objective width of the slanted surface that they viewed.

Olson, Pearl, Mayfield, and Millar (1976) showed adult observers a cross lying on the slanted surface of a box [see Figure 21.7(a)] and asked the observers to judge which arm of the cross was longer. By varying the ratio of the actual lengths of the two arms over a series of trials, Olson et al. determined the ratio for which the two arms were judged as being equal in length. With binocular viewing of a real box, this ratio was quite close to 1.0 even when one arm was made projectively much shorter than the other by slanting the surface 80° away from the frontal plane [see Figure 21.7(b)].

Even without binocular viewing, the static perception of a complex natural scene can lead to fairly accurate judgments of objective shape. Olson et al. (1976) found that, when observers were shown slides of boxes with crosses on them, the ratios for which the two arms were judged as being equal lay about midway between the projectively equal and the objectively equal ratios [see Figure 21.7(b)]. Lappin and Preble (1975), in the experiment described above (see Section 2.3.2) asked observers to estimate the objective sizes of angles in projected slides of random polygons lying on a desk. Observers' errors were quite small, averaging only 8.2°, and the objective size of the angles accounted for 55.5% of the variance in their results.

As the available information for objective shape is increasingly restricted or degraded, judgments of shape become more variable and more divergent from objective shape, generally moving more toward the projective shape. Such changes can be seen in data from monocular viewing (Leibowitz, Bussey, & McGuire, 1957; Olson et al., 1976; Stavrianos, 1945, p. 68), from binocular viewing in minimally structured surroundings (Epstein et al., 1962), and from viewing under various degraded conditions such as increased distance (Gottheil & Bitterman, 1951; Meneghini & Leibowitz, 1967), reduced exposure duration or intensity (Epstein & Hatfield, 1978a, 1978b; Epstein, Hatfield, & Muise, 1977; Leibowitz & Bourne, 1956), and increased blur (Leibowitz, Wilcox, & Post, 1978). Some of these studies asked observers to judge "phenomenal" rather than objective shape (see Section 2.3.4), but it seems reasonable to assume that the trends that they found under varying conditions would also be found with objective shape instructions even though the overall level of the results would probably be different. These results

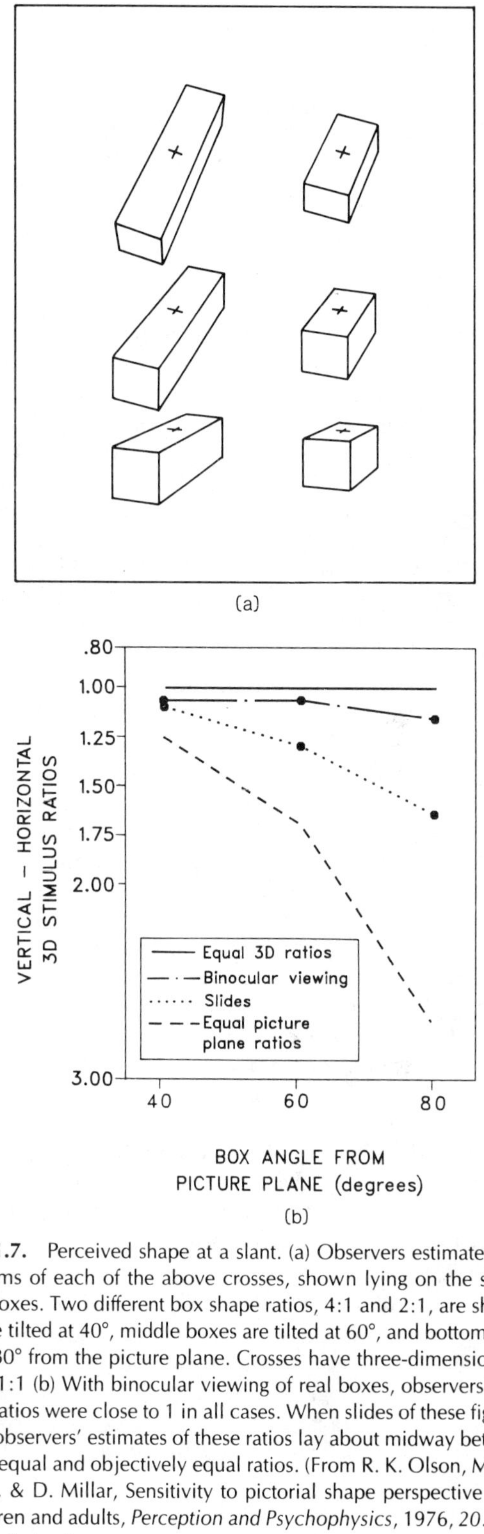

Figure 21.7. Perceived shape at a slant. (a) Observers estimated the ratio of the arms of each of the above crosses, shown lying on the surfaces of slanted boxes. Two different box shape ratios, 4:1 and 2:1, are shown. Top boxes are tilted at 40°, middle boxes are tilted at 60°, and bottom boxes are tilted at 80° from the picture plane. Crosses have three-dimensional length ratios of 1:1 (b) With binocular viewing of real boxes, observers' estimates of these ratios were close to 1 in all cases. When slides of these figures were viewed, observers' estimates of these ratios lay about midway between projectively equal and objectively equal ratios. (From R. K. Olson, M. Pearl, N. Mayfield, & D. Millar, Sensitivity to pictorial shape perspective in 5-year-old children and adults, *Perception and Psychophysics*, 1976, *20*. Reprinted with permission.)

parallel the results found for judgments of objective size under reduced viewing conditions (see Section 2.2.3).

Familiarity can also affect objective shape judgments. Borresen and Lichte (1962) found that binocular viewing of complex and irregularly slanted shapes produced average Brunswik ratios of .46 when the shapes were unfamiliar and of .66–.74 when the shapes had been seen from 4 to 16 times before at various other slants closer to but not including the frontal plane.

Objective shape judgments of figures seen with monocular static vision in total darkness tend to be close to the projective shape of the figure (Beck & J. Gibson, 1955; Nelson & Bartley, 1956), but even under these circumstances regular geometric figures may sometimes be judged as having objective shapes appreciably different from their projective shapes (Beck & J. Gibson, 1955; Campione, 1977). Tendencies toward seeing shapes as being circular (i.e., as having the most stable organization, in the Gestalt sense) (Koffka, 1935, p. 232), as being symmetrical (M. King, Meyer, Tangney, & Beiderman, 1976), or has having parallel edges (Thouless, 1931) have been postulated. Campione (1977) obtained an average Brunswik ratio of 0.34 for regular figures (a circle, triangle, square, cross, and diamond) viewed under total reduction conditions; for an "amoeboid pattern" the Brunswik ratio was only .09. Judgments of objective shape are highly variable when little visual information about objective shape is available; for example, the Brunswik ratios of Campione's observers ranged from −.12 to .99 for the regular figures and from −.52 to .80 for the amoeboid figure.

When a surface lies in the frontal plane, its objective and projective shapes are of course the same. As the surface is slanted increasingly far away from the frontal plane, its projective shape becomes increasingly different from its objective shape. Projective shape, as distinct from objective shape, becomes increasingly salient under these conditions (Joynson & Newson, 1962) and, when information for objective shape is somewhat limited, becomes more likely to interact with objective shape judgments (Kaess, 1978). Judgments of objective shape tend to show increasing constant and variable error when the slant of the surface is increased (Kaess, 1978; M. King et al., 1976; Massaro, 1973; Stavrianos, 1945, pp. 60, 68). A detailed review of the earlier literature on this subject is given by Epstein and Park (1963). Some of the variability and contradictions found in these early studies may be due to the inherent ambiguity of the "phenomenal shape" instructions (see the following section) that many of them used.

2.3.4. The Question of "Phenomenal Shape." Thouless (1931) asserted that the shape actually seen when an observer looks at a slanted surface is neither the objective shape, which the observer may be cognitively aware of, nor the projective shape, but is some "phenomenal" or "apparent" shape that lies somewhere in between. Thouless and many other investigators have found that such intermediate results indeed are obtained when observers are asked to respond to shape but are given instructions that either do not specify what to respond to or specify that the responses should be based on "a spontaneous impression," "the way it looks," "the appearance," etc. (Joynson & Newson, 1962; Langdon, 1951, 1953, 1955a, 1955b; Leibowitz & Bourne, 1956; Leibowitz et al., 1957; Leibowitz et al., 1978; Lichte, 1952; Meneghini & Leibowitz, 1967; Thouless, 1931). This result is not very informative, however, because as we have already seen (Sections 2.3.2 and 2.3.3) instructions to respond either to objective shape or to projective shape often also produce results that lie between the true objective and projective shapes. A stronger case for a distinct perceptual entity that could be referred to as phenomenal shape is made by investigations that have included all three types of instructions—objective, phenomenal, and projective—within the same study; such investigations have confirmed repeatedly that the average results obtained with phenomenal instructions lie between the average results obtained with the other two types of instructions (Epstein et al., 1962; Gottheil & Bitterman, 1951; Landauer, 1964a, 1964b, 1969; Lichte & Borresen, 1967).

Average results, however, may not adequately represent individual responses to the experimental situation. Joynson and Newson (1962) closely examined the various ways that different individuals responded when they were given deliberately nondirective phenomenal instructions to match the shape of a binocularly viewed slanted triangle. Taking care to avoid biasing their observers, Joynson and Newson questioned them about what they were doing when they made their judgments. They concluded that their observers showed a continuum of attitudes but could be broadly divided into two groups. One group (38%) was spontaneously aware that two distinct types of judgments were possible, one type being objective, the other nonobjective. (Joynson and Newson are cautious about characterizing this second type of judgment that their observers described, but from the protocols that they quote, it seems that their observers were thinking of projective shape and were also expressing the "educated layperson's" theory that our immediate impression of shape is projective.) The second group (62%) was spontaneously aware of only one way of responding—in terms of objective shape. Observers in the first group were asked first to make their preferred type of judgment, then their nonpreferred type; about 70% responded first in terms of objective shape. Observers were most likely to be aware of and to choose the nonobjective type of response when the slant of the triangle away from the frontal plane was greatest. The objective judgments of all of Joynson and Newson's observers were close to the true objective shape of the triangle [see Figure 21.8(a)]. The nonobjective judgments, for those who made them, were intermediate between projective and objective shape [see Figure 21.8(b)], which is typical of projective judgments made with similar viewing conditions (see Section 2.3.2). Joynson and Newson conclude that "it seems advisable to abandon the term 'apparent shape'."

A similar conclusion was reached by Lichte and Borresen (1967), who analyzed the individual responses of observers making shape judgments under objective, apparent, or projective shape instructions. They found that the responses, expressed in Brunswik ratios, of the objective shape group and the projective shape group had nonoverlapping distributions. The responses of the apparent shape group were bimodally distributed, with one lobe of the distribution being similar to the objective shape distribution and the other lobe being similar to the projective shape distribution (see Figure 21.9). In addition to concluding that the "apparent shape" instruction is ambiguous and should be avoided, Lichte and Borresen point to the importance of taking great care in formulating objective or projective shape instructions and to the need for questioning observers carefully to make sure that they have understood the instructions.

The arguments against apparent shape instructions have not been universally accepted. Landauer (1964b, 1969) argues that at least in some circumstances observers may make an apparent shape judgment that is truly distinct from either objective or projective shape judgments. Carlson (1977) gives a nuanced review of the effect of instructions on performance and

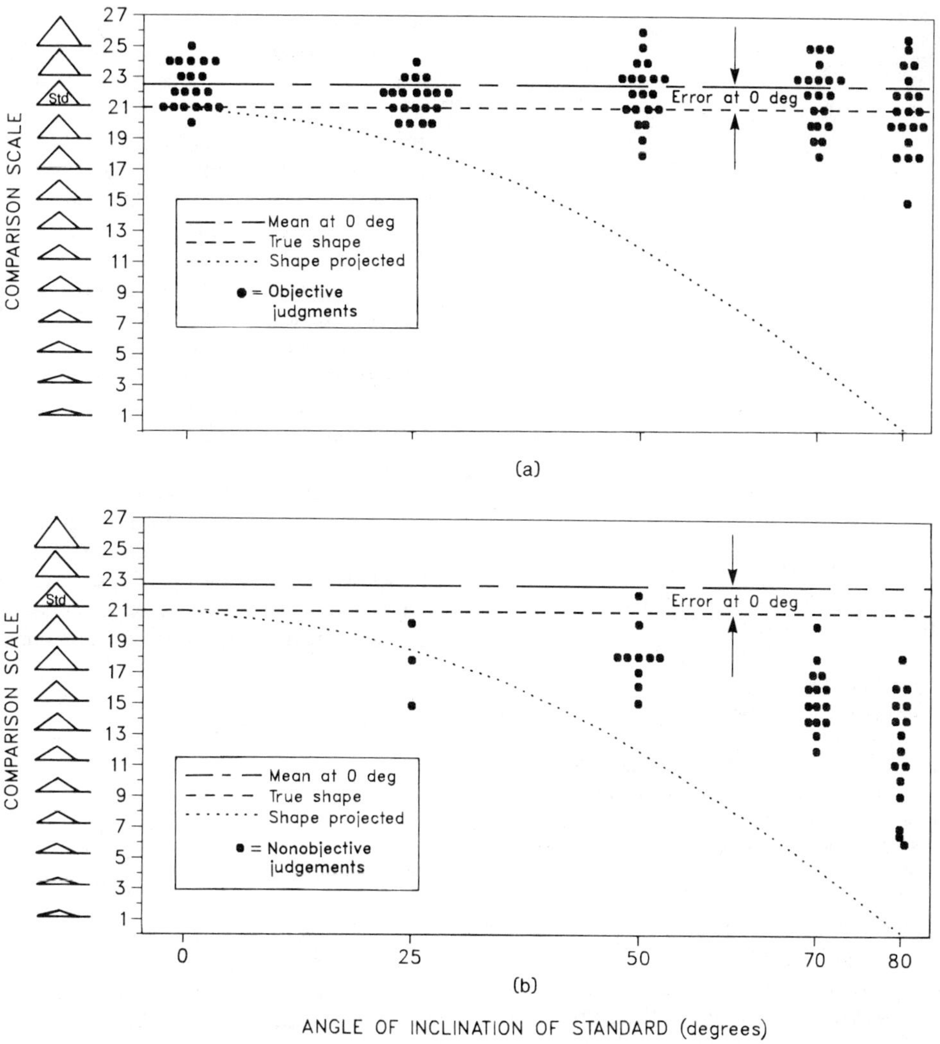

Figure 21.8. Perceived shape under nondirective instructions. Observers matched the shape of a binocularly viewed triangle under deliberately nondirective instructions and were then questioned about what they had done. (a) Observers whose comments indicated that they were matching objective shape made settings very close to true shape. (b) Observers whose comments were classified as "nonobjective," which appears to correspond to "projective," made settings that were intermediate between actual projective shape and objective shape. (From R. B. Joynson & L. J. Newson, The perception of shape as a function of inclination, *British Journal of Psychology*, 1962, *53*. Reprinted with permission.)

concludes, somewhat tentatively, that a "neutral-apparent-shape" instruction is most likely to elicit a response indicating perceived shape. Most recent studies of shape-at-a-slant, however, have abandoned apparent shape instructions in favor of either objective or projective shape instructions. As with studies of objective and projective size (see Section 2.2.4), this would seem to offer a more robust approach to obtaining unambiguous results.

2.3.5. The Specification of Slant. The perception of surface orientation, or slant, is most often considered either in connection with questions about possible linkages between shape and slant perception or in connection with questions about the roles of particular sources of visual information (texture, perspective, motion, etc.) in slant perception. The first set of questions, grouped under the heading of the shape-slant invariance hypothesis, is considered in the next section. Questions in the second group are considered in later sections where the different sources of visual information for layout perception are examined individually. Before considering either of these groups of questions, however, we must look at how surface slant is specified.

Three types of reference frames have commonly been used in specifying surface slant. First, the orientation of a local patch of surface can be specified in relation to the line of regard from a point of observation; slant specified in this way is referred to as *optical slant* (J. Gibson & Cornsweet, 1952). Second, the orientation of a surface can be specified in relation to some fixed environmental frame of reference, such as the horizontal plane of the ground; slant specified in this way is referred to as *geographical slant* (J. Gibson & Cornsweet, 1952). Finally, the orientation of a surface can be specified relative to the orientation of some other locally adjacent surface or surfaces; slant specified in this way is referred to as *relative slant.*

The orientation of a planar surface has three degrees of freedom. One degree of freedom can be identified with the surface's ability to rotate around an axis perpendicular to the surface, as a rotating phonograph record does; this transformation,

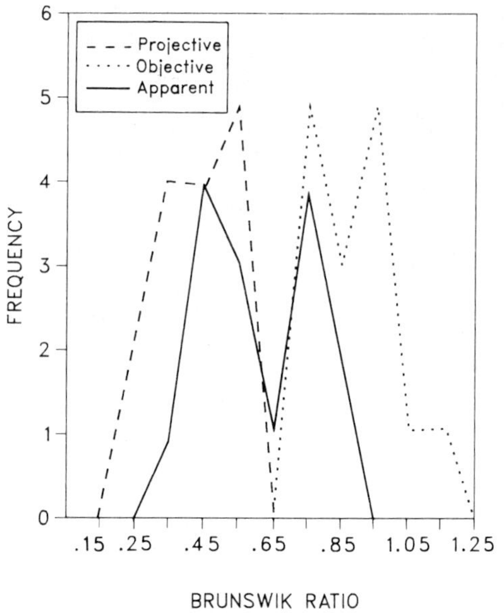

Figure 21.9. Perceived shape under three instructions. Observers matched the width of a binocularly viewed unfamiliar complex shape under three different instruction conditions: objective, projective, and "apparent." Brunswik ratios were calculated and their frequency distributions for each condition are shown here. Observers in the "apparent" instruction condition had a bimodal distribution of results, some apparently attempting to make objective matches, whereas others apparently attempted projective matches. (From W. H. Lichte & C. R. Borresen, Influence of instruction on degree of shape constancy, *Journal of Experimental Psychology, 74*. Copyright 1967 by the American Psychological Association. Reprinted with permission.)

which does not change the overall position of the surface in space but only the position of local landmarks on the surface, is not considered further here. Two additional degrees of freedom are needed to specify the *direction of slant* of the surface and the *amount of slant* of the surface. Taking optical slant as an example, consider a reference plane that is perpendicular to the line of regard at the point where it meets a surface having some arbitrary orientation. This reference plane is tangent to the sphere of the optic array, and the projection of the surface onto this reference plane is locally approximately equivalent to the surface's projection in the optic array. The surface can be described as having been rotated away from the reference plane around some axis that lies in the reference plane. The perpendicular in the reference plane to this axis of rotation gives the direction of slant of the surface. The angle between the surface and the reference plane gives the amount of slant of the surface.

2.3.6. The Shape-Slant Invariance Hypothesis. The geometric relation that exists between shape, slant, and solid visual angle (see Section 2.3.1) leads naturally to the hypothesis that a similar relation exists between perceived shape, perceived slant, and solid visual angle. Such a hypothesis was explicitly formulated by Koffka (1935, pp. 222–235) and was named the *shape-slant invariance hypothesis*, in analogy to the size-distance invariance hypothesis, by Beck and J. Gibson (1955). Their formulation of the hypothesis is "a retinal projection of a given form determines a unique relation of apparent shape to apparent slant" (p. 126). The considerable body of literature that has arisen around this hypothesis has been frequently reviewed (Epstein, 1973, 1977; Epstein & Park, 1963; Hake, 1966; J. Hochberg, 1971).

Before reviewing the experimental evidence concerning the shape-slant invariance hypothesis, a few conceptual points must be considered. First, it should be noted that in statements of the hypothesis, the invariant term is almost always taken to be the shape of the solid visual angle subtended by the surface; this term may be referred to as the "retinal shape," "retinal form," or "projective shape" (Beck & J. Gibson, 1955; Epstein, 1973; Epstein & Hatfield, 1978a, 1978b; Epstein et al., 1977; Epstein & Park, 1963; M. King et al., 1976; Koffka, 1935, p. 229; Massaro, 1973, 1975). This formulation is presumably based on the assumption that projective shape is the invariant term in the geometric shape-slant relation. Such an assumption is inaccurate, however, because it erroneously implies that projective shape alone is sufficient to determine a unique family of shapes-at-a-slant. Actually, both the shape and the size of the projection must be given; projections having the same shape but differing in size will each determine a different family of shapes-at-a-slant (see Figure 21.10).

Second, it should be observed that the shape term in the geometric shape-slant relation refers to objective shape, so that the most direct formulation of the shape-slant invariance hypothesis would be in terms of "perceived objective shape." Although some formulations of the hypothesis follow this approach, others substitute "apparent" or "phenomenal" shape. The dif-

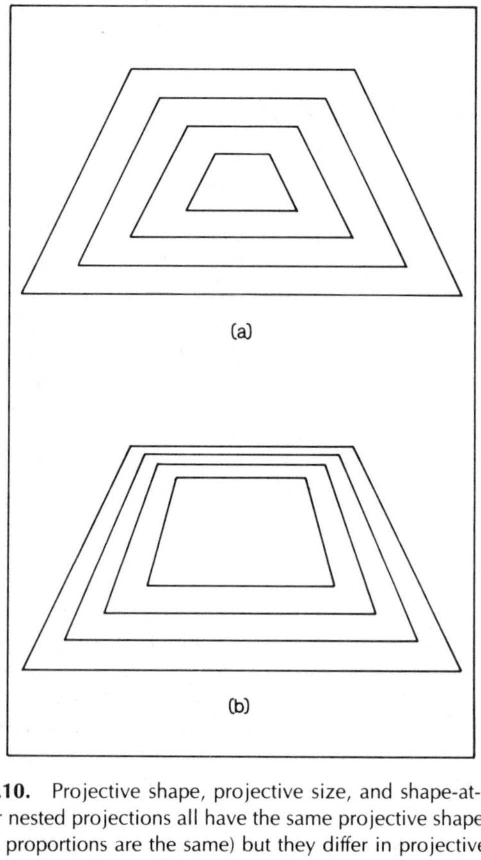

Figure 21.10. Projective shape, projective size, and shape-at-a-slant. (a) These four nested projections all have the same projective shape (i.e., their projective proportions are the same) but they differ in projective size. The rectangular surfaces that would give rise to these projections must necessarily differ in slant because they have different horizons, as indicated by the vanishing points of their converging sides. The rectangles would also have different proportions. (b) These four nested projections correspond to rectangular surfaces all having the same slant because their projections' converging sides all converge to the same horizon. Because the projections share the same diagonal, the rectangles that give rise to them must also all have the same proportions. These figures illustrate that projective shape alone is insufficient to determine a unique family of shapes-at-a-slant; projective size must also be given.

ficulties with such terms have already been discussed (see Section 2.3.4). What must be noted here is that it is by no means clear that "apparent slant" is a coordinate term with "apparent shape," although the two are generally paired. There is considerable evidence that some observers interpret "apparent shape" to mean "projective shape" (see Section 2.3.4) and respond accordingly; although the question has not been examined experimentally, it seems much less likely that observers would interpret "apparent slant" instructions to mean "projective slant" because projective slant is always simply zero slant, or absence of slant; thus asking for "apparent slant" would seem to carry a much stronger implication that "objective slant" is intended. A hypothesized linkage between apparent shape and apparent slant is thus more problematic than it might at first appear.

Third, it should be observed that the slant term in the geometric shape-slant relation is optical slant as distinct from geographical slant (see Section 2.3.5). Most statements of the shape-slant invariance hypothesis simply refer to perceived slant although they may implicitly intend perceived optical slant. Failure to attend to this distinction, however, can lead to faulty experimental designs in which geographical slant rather than optical slant is manipulated (Beck & Gibson, 1955; Epstein et al., 1962).

Finally, it should be noted that formulations of the shape-slant invariance hypothesis vary in the strictness of the relation that they postulate between perceived shape and perceived slant. In the most straightforward formulation of the hypothesis, the relation between perceived shape and perceived slant would be the one that was geometrically consistent with the invariant projection. This hypothesis yields precise quantitative predictions. Early informal reports contradicting these predictions, however, led Koffka (1935) to weaken his hypothesis by adding the qualification that "the invariant may depend upon total sets of conditions, and need not necessarily be the same under all circumstances" (p. 233). Beck and J. Gibson (1955) postulated that a perceptual linkage between shape and slant would appear, if at all, only under reduced stimulus conditions, when the higher-order variables, such as gradients of texture and motion, that normally geometrically specify both shape and slant had been eliminated. We consider some other variants of the hypothesis in Sections 2.3.7 and 2.3.8.

Although some earlier studies had investigated shape constancy as a function of variations in stimulus conditions that were assumed to influence slant perception, Stavrianos (1945) was the first to systematically measure both shape and slant perception under the same experimental conditions. Her detailed analysis of individual results clearly shows that, just as perceived size is not always coordinated with perceived distance (see Section 2.2.6), so perceived shape and perceived slant are not precisely related. Looking at averaged results, however, she concluded in several experiments that there are indications of a weak statistical link between perceived shape and perceived slant under reduced monocular conditions although not under binocular conditions. In one study she also found some indications of a weak statistical link under binocular conditions.

Beck and Gibson (1955) attempted to determine whether, under reduced conditions, observers' matches of shape-at-a-slant would belong to the family of shapes-at-a-slant specified by the projection. Although a small percentage of their results (13%) does not satisfy this constraint, it is not clear whether these exceptions are significant departures or only reflect failures to discriminate small differences between their stimuli. They also attempted to determine the effect of induced slant on perceived shape, but the results of this experiment, as well as those of a similar experiment by Epstein et al. (1962), are made difficult to interpret by a failure to measure the perceived slant of the inducing background, which contained the comparison figure, as well as by the manipulation of geographical rather than optical slant that was noted above.

Results obtained by Winnick and Rogoff (1965) give little support to the shape-slant invariance hypothesis; errors in judging the width of binocularly viewed, slanted rectangles were generally in the direction opposite to that predicted on the basis of errors, obtained in a separate study, in judging the slant of the rectangles. Winnick and Rosen (1966) obtained results that appear to be much more closely in correspondence with the invariance hypothesis, but the demand characteristics of their procedure make the validity of these results questionable (for example, one group of observers was asked to adjust the width of a binocularly viewed frontal rectangle until it appeared to be slanted at 20, 40, 60, and 80° to the frontal plane). Kraft and Winnick (1967) investigated the relation between slant and shape judgments under three sets of instructions, but their instructions are confusingly worded and appear, as Carlson (1977, p. 248) has noted, to have been misinterpreted by their observers, thus making their results difficult to interpret. A number of other studies have failed to find much support for the shape-slant invariance hypothesis (Flock, 1964c; Kaess, 1971; Langdon, 1953).

Some of the strongest data in support of a link between perceived slant and perceived shape come from a careful study by Kaiser (1967). Kaiser asked observers to judge both the shape and the slant of three slanted trapezoids under both monocular and binocular viewing conditions. To maximize comparability of shape and slant judgments he presented the standard, the slant comparison, and the shape comparison simultaneously within the same enclosure and asked his observers to look back and forth between their slant and shape settings until they were satisfied with both of them. Kaiser's analyses of his data show high and significant correlations between shape and slant for the monocular but not for the binocular condition.

The high correlations obtained for the monocular data, however, are to an appreciable extent an artifactual function of the analyses themselves. For example, in one analysis, rather than correlating shape and slant judgments directly, Kaiser correlates errors in shape judgments with errors in slant judgments; these errors are obtained by comparing the observers' settings with the objective shapes and slants of the three different trapezoids, all of which were chosen to have the same projection. Observers' monocular settings are, necessarily, not systematically different for the three trapezoids, because the trapezoids were monocularly indistinguishable. The calculated errors do differ systematically, however, as a function of the objective shapes and slants of the trapezoids; these systematic differences tend to produce a high positive correlation between shape and slant errors that is of no relevance to the interpretation of the perceptual data.

A simpler assessment of these data can be made by comparing the judged slant for each observer with the slant that would be compatible, according to the geometric shape-slant relation, with the judged shape. In Figure 21.11 the relevant monocular data have been replotted in this way for the two different types of shape setting that Kaiser obtained. The correlations obtained in this way are .664 and .616 for the two types of shape measure (see Oyama, 1977, p. 205). Thus Kaiser's

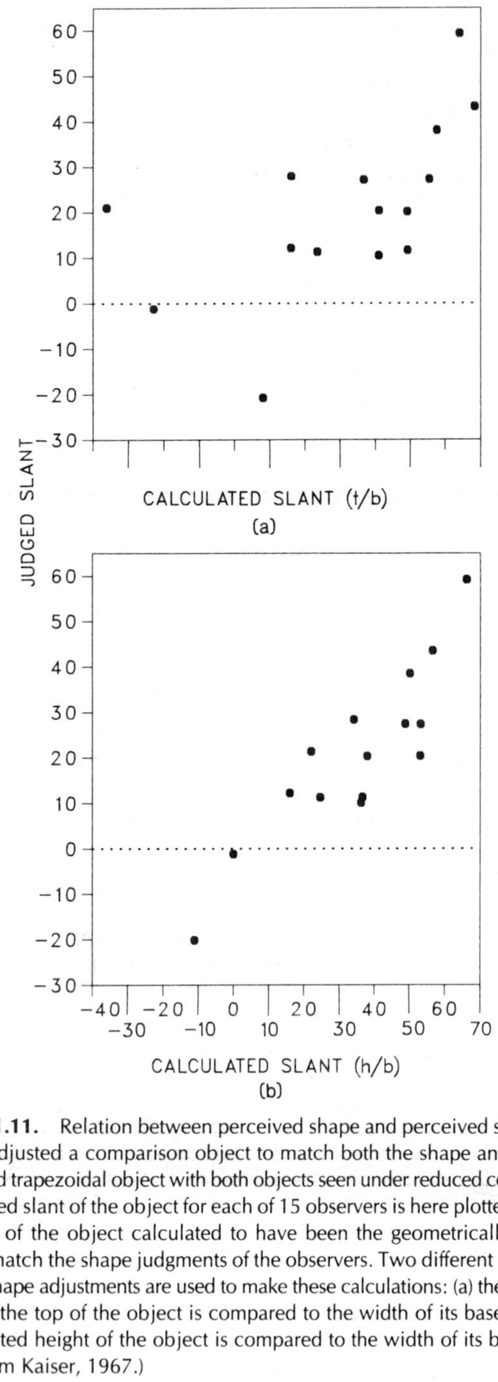

Figure 21.11. Relation between perceived shape and perceived slant. Observers adjusted a comparison object to match both the shape and slant of a standard trapezoidal object with both objects seen under reduced conditions. The judged slant of the object for each of 15 observers is here plotted against the slant of the object calculated to have been the geometrically correct slant to match the shape judgments of the observers. Two different measures of their shape adjustments are used to make these calculations: (a) the adjusted width of the top of the object is compared to the width of its base (*t/b*); (b) the adjusted height of the object is compared to the width of its base (*h/b*). (Data from Kaiser, 1967.)

data do suggest a linkage, under reduced conditions, between perceived shape and perceived slant, but the linkage appears to be considerably weaker than Kaiser concluded.

Oyama (1977) has calculated the partial correlations between physical slant, perceived slant, and perceived shape in Kaiser's data and has shown from these that there is a statistically significant linkage between perceived shape and perceived slant in the monocular data but not in the binocular data.

Gillam (1967) has reported an effect that could be referred to as the *shape-slant paradox*. When one eye's image is subjected to a small horizontal magnification, the resulting binocular disparities can, under certain conditions, lead to distortions of perceived shape that are in the geometrically predicted direction and distortions of perceived slant that are opposite to the geometrically predicted direction.

Overall, then, the strict formulation of the shape-slant invariance hypothesis can clearly be rejected. A weaker linkage between perceived shape and perceived slant does receive some support. In particular, the data of Stavrianos (1945) and Kaiser (1967) lend support to Beck and Gibson's (1955) hypothesis that a perceptual coupling between shape and slant is most likely to be observed under reduced stimulus conditions, when most of the normal visual information for shape and slant has been eliminated.

2.3.7. Taking Slant into Account in Perceiving Shape. A more restrictive version of the shape-slant invariance hypothesis than that considered above proposes that perceived shape is determined by an algorithm that combines projective shape with slant (Epstein, 1973; Massaro, 1973). This version appears to be what many investigators have in mind in referring to the shape-slant invariance hypothesis, although Koffka (1935, p. 232) explicitly postulates that the perceptual coupling between shape and slant works in both directions so that perceived shape may sometimes influence perceived slant (see also Eriksson, 1967).

Massaro (1973, 1975) developed the taking-slant-into-account hypothesis into a two-stage model of the process of shape perception. In the first stage of this model the sensory system processes the visual input to obtain values for the perceived projective shape and the perceived slant of the surface. In the second stage these values are inserted into an invariance algorithm that then calculates perceived shape. Massaro attempted to assess this model in a series of experiments in which he measured the reaction times and errors of observers who were asked, on each of a number of trials, to select the circle from a pair of binocularly viewed slanted figures, one a circle and the other an ellipse. Massaro concluded that the invariance model was inadequate to account for his results; he suggested instead that "the extension in depth of the figure is the critical variable that affects perceputal encoding time" (1973, p. 421).M. King et al. (1976), however, pointed out that Massaro had not controlled the similarity (measured by height-to-width ratios) of his figures across experiments. When M. King et al. did control figural similarity in three experiments, they found that extension in depth could not account for the time necessary to make comparative shape-at-a-slant judgments; they also concluded that neither their results nor Massaro's were inconsistent with the invariance model.

Epstein (1973) proposed a general information-processing model of the taking-into-account hypothesis that, for the case of shape and slant, is quite similar to Massaro's (1973). Epstein et al. (1977), using phenomenal shape and slant instructions (see Section 2.3.4), showed that for some carefully selected stimulus parameters the judged shape and slant of binocularly viewed ellipses were much closer to their projective values when the ellipses were followed after a very short interval by a masking stimulus. Epstein and Hatfield (1978a, 1978b) showed that adding a mask is functionally equivalent to switching from binocular to monocular vision and that the presence of a mask is also effective dichoptically in disrupting the effects of perspective information for shape and slant. They interpreted all these experiments as supporting the taking-slant-into-account hypothesis by showing that removing slant information also affects shape perception.

The implicit assumption motivating the taking-slant-into-account version of the invariance hypothesis is that the available optic array information that specifies the slant of surfaces does not also specify their shape; thus slant must be taken into account to disambiguate the projective shape of the surface. Some researchers have challenged this assumption in some areas while accepting it in others. For example, J. Hochberg (1971, p. 507) points out that the texture of a surface has the potential of specifying the surface's shape without any need for taking slant into account, but he does not see how binocularity could do so (1971, p. 516). Wallach and Moore (1962), on the other hand, assert that it is quite feasible that both shape and slant could result directly from binocular disparities, but believe that it is possible to arrange a perspective display that provides information for slant but not shape. Even Wallach and Moore's very carefully constructed display, however, can be considered to contain information for shape apart from slant (see Section 3.2.4). Gillam (1967) offers a clear demonstration of how shape is specified directly by binocular disparity.

As we shall see in the following sections, all of the broad sources of information for surface slant also provide information for surface shape. It is thus not warranted to conclude, as many studies have done, that manipulations of this information that affect shape perception must do so through their effect on slant. It may be possible eventually to devise a display containing potential information for slant that can be shown not to also contain potential information for shape, but this has not yet been done.

2.3.8. The Concept of Registered Slant. The observation that perceived shape is not closely coupled to perceived slant led Eissler and Klempfinger (cited in Koffka, 1935, p. 229) to postulate that slant information may be registered by the perceptual system and taken into account in determining perceived shape without necessarily influencing perceived slant. This concept of a *registered slant* that is distinct from perceived slant and that is not available to the observer for perceptual reports has been accepted by some investigators as a way of preserving the shape-slant invariance hypothesis (Epstein, 1973, 1977; J. Hochberg, 1971, p. 517); others, however, while not denying the logical possibility of such a concept, have been reluctant to adopt it (Koffka, 1935, p. 230; Stavrianos, 1945).

As with the concept of registered distance (see Section 2.2.6), the difficulty with the registered-slant-perceived-shape invariance hypothesis is that it postulates a relationship between three variables, only two of which can be measured. It is thus unclear how the hypothesis could ever be adequately tested. The usual approach has depended on the manipulation of aspects of the display, such as binocular viewing, that are assumed to influence available visual information for slant but not for shape. As has been mentioned above (see Section 2.3.7), however, this assumption is not supported when the available sources of information for shape and slant are analyzed.

Epstein (1973), speaking of the more general application of the registered-perceived distinction, suggests two constraints that should be observed in deciding that a variable such as slant may be registered but not perceived. First, there should be prior knowledge that the perceptual system has the capability to register the variable and, second, there should be convincing evidence that the relevant experimental manipulations can affect that variable. The variable of slant does satisfy these constraints, but this only establishes the possibility that slant might be registered without being perceived.

Acceptance of the registered-slant-perceived-shape invariance hypothesis thus appears to rest largely on the perceived lack of a more parsimonious alternative hypothesis to account for the data on perceived shape. The hypothesis that perceived shape is normally determined directly by the available visual information, without the intervention of perceived or registered slant, would seem to be more parsimonious, but this hypothesis depends on demonstrating that the various forms of visual information are potentially capable of specifying shape directly. Such demonstrations are considered in the following sections, where the various different sources of visual information for surface layout are analyzed individually, and the empirical evidence concerning their use in human perception is examined.

3. TEXTURE AND PERSPECTIVE

3.1. Texture

3.1.1. Definition and Measurement of Texture. The visible texture of a surface provides potential information for the relative sizes of objects touching the surface, for the relative distances of locations on the surface, and for the shape and slant of the surface itself. The potential importance of surface texture in the visual perception of layout was first pointed out and analyzed by J. Gibson (1950a).

Texture, in this context, refers to any visible features of a surface that are homogeneous in size and spacing across the extent of the surface. Thus the weave of a fabric, pebbles on a beach, or trees on a distant hillside may all be taken as elements of surface texture. A strand of thread, a pebble, or a tree each has textured surfaces of its own, however, so that the visible environment may be thought of as containing nested hierarchies of textured surfaces (J. Gibson, 1950a, p. 85; W. Purdy, 1960).

The textural homogeneity of a surface may be only statistical. That is, individual elements of texture may vary somewhat in size and spacing while still maintaining local averages of size and spacing that remain the same across the surface. Such local variation introduces noise into the underlying relations between surface layout and projected surface texture without systematically distorting them (Flock, 1964b; J. Gibson, 1950b; W. Purdy, 1960; K. Stevens, 1980, 1981). On the other hand, if the size and spacing of texture elements vary systematically across a surface, then these underlying relations can be systematically distorted (Gibson & Flock, 1962; K. Stevens, 1980, 1981).

A variety of texture measures have been proposed, including the angular width of individual texture elements (W. Purdy, 1960; K. Stevens, 1980, 1981), the angular width of a given number of texture elements along a specified line (Flock, 1964b), and the number of texture elements per unit of angular width (texture density). Almost all the mathematical formulations of texture information and most of the experimental work on perceiving spatial layout from surface texture have been done with artificially simplified textures, such as checkerboard grids, parallel lines, and randomly spaced points or circles, presumably because such textures can be analyzed and manipulated most readily. Bajesy and Lieberman (1976), however, have developed a computerized analysis of real photographic textures using the techniques of Fourier analysis. Other sophisticated analyses of visible texture have been developed in other contexts (see Zucker, 1976) but have not yet been applied to the use of texture in the perception of spatial layout.

3.1.2. Texture Scale

3.1.2.1. Texture Scale and Distance Perception. If a surface is homogeneously textured, then that texture establishes a uniform scale across the entire extent of the surface. This scale provides an intrinsic measure of the distance from any location on the surface to any other location on the surface in terms of the amount of surface texture along a straight line between the two locations. If we think of the texture as being composed of texture "elements," then the texture element is the intrinsic unit of measurement for the surface. For a distance specified in such units to be meaningful to a particular observer, the observer must be aware of the value of the unit of measurement or must be able to associate it with some functionally relevant value. Relative distances, however, are the ratios of pairs of distances and so are independent of the units in which the individual distances are measured.

These surface texture measures of distance are unaffected by the projective transformation that takes a visible surface into the optic array; the number of projected texture elements between any two projections of locations is the same as the number of actual texture elements between those two actual locations on the surface. Thus the visible texture of a surface in the optic array provides the surface with an intrinsic scale that specifies the relative distances between any two pairs of locations on the surface and that also specifies absolute distances in texture element units. This is true for any visible continuous surface, curved as well as flat, that is homogeneously textured.

Although texture scale information for distance is available across any homogeneously textured surface, it is most commonly discussed in connection with the surface of the ground. Distances between locations or objects on the ground are specified by this information if the relevant stretch of ground is homogeneously textured.

If an observer is standing on the ground, then the distance from the feet of the observer to any object or location on the ground is also specified by this texture scale information, as is the relative distance of any two such objects from the feet of the observer. The distance from an observer to a location is referred to as *egocentric distance*. Taking the egocentric distance of an object to be its distance along the ground from the feet of the observer rather than its distance from the observer's eyes is to treat the observer as just another object resting on the ground and might also be considered to be the most functionally relevant measure of distance when perception is being used to control locomotion.

Information concerning egocentric distance from an observer's eyes to an object or location on a surface is also provided by homogeneous surface texture. The geometric relation between angular extent, physical extent, and distance from the eye [see Eq. (1)] implies that the egocentric distance to a surface location is specified in texture element units by the angular extent of the texture elements at that location. Also, the relative egocentric distance of two surface locations is specified, independently of the particular size of the texture element units, by the relative angular extents of the texture elements at the two locations. This formulation of texture scale information for egocentric distance (K. Stevens, 1980, 1981) is simply an application of the more general formulation in which the absolute or relative distances of objects from the eye are specified whenever their absolute or relative physical sizes are known to the observer (see Section 2.2.8).

A number of studies have systematically investigated the influence of the texture of the ground surface on the perception of distance. All these studies have found that ground texture affects distance perception, although in some cases the effect has been slight.

Wohlwill (1963) found that when observers are asked to set a marker to bisect the distance between a nearer and a farther marker, they tend to be somewhat more accurate in their settings when the horizontal surface extending under the markers is regularly rather than irregularly textured; Wohlwill (1965), using a distance bisection task with photographs of textured surfaces, replicated this finding. Although the earlier study (Wohlwill, 1963) did not find an effect of texture density, the later study (Wohlwill, 1965) did find that accuracy increased somewhat with texture density. Wohlwill (1962) also found that, when observers tried to bisect a frontal plane distance whose background was a drawing of a receding textured surface, they made small errors, indicating that their judgments were being influenced by the background drawing. This effect, which Wohlwill refers to as the "perspective illusion," was greater when the depicted texture was denser or more regular.

Levine and Rosinski (1976) had observers monocularly view an irregular shaped object resting on a horizontal surface and then asked them to reproduce the object's egocentric distance in a similar, binocularly viewed display. Observers were more accurate when the monocularly viewed surface was textured with a series of stripes parallel to the frontal plane than when the surface was untextured. They were even more accurate when each stripe was broken up into black and white squares so that information for linear perspective as well as compression was made available (see Sections 3.2.3.1 and 3.2.5).

Newman (1971), noting that the texture in displays such as those used by Wohlwill, although varying in density or regularity, always specified the same distance scale and was always in accord with other information such as that arising from height in the field (see Section 3.3.1), generated a series of textured surfaces that were systematically nonhomogeneous. All the surfaces were textured with stripes parallel to the frontal plane, but for some surfaces the width and separation of the stripes increased with increasing distance, whereas for others the width and separation decreased or remained constant. Newman's observers, when asked to bisect the distance between two markers resting on nonhomogeneously textured surfaces, produced errors in the direction, and of approximately the magnitude, that would be expected if they were using the texture of the surface to make their judgments and were treating the texture as being homogeneously distributed.

Taken together, the above results show that surface texture may indeed be used in human distance perception, even when it is in conflict with other available information for distance, but that texture's effectiveness in distance perception may depend on parameters such as its density and regularity.

3.1.2.2. Texture Scale and Size Perception. The intrinsic scale provided by the texture of a surface also specifies the sizes of any objects resting on the surface. The length of an edge of such an object is specified by the number of texture elements that it covers (J. Gibson, 1950a, p. 174). Just as with distances, individual lengths are only meaningfully specified if the texture element unit is meaningful to the observer, but relative lengths are specified in any case. Only the lengths of edges that are in continuous contact with the surface are specified in this way, because only for such edges does the covering of a number of projected texture elements by the projection of the edge in the optic array correspond to the covering of the same number of actual texture elements by the actual edge (the rather common failure of authors to observe this restriction in their discussions of texture scale information has been noted by Gillam, 1981). In general, one end of an edge is farther from the observer than the other, and so the edge undergoes some perspective compression in the optic array. If the edge is lying on a surface, however, the intrinsic texture scale of the surface along the edge undergoes exactly the same perspective compression and so remains a valid measure of the edge's extent.

Although much of the experimental work on the perception of size in naturalistic settings (see Section 2.2.3) has been done with objects resting on textured surfaces and has shown, as has already been noted, that size perception tends to be quite good under such circumstances, very little work has been done that attempts to isolate the contribution of surface texture to size perception. In naturalistic settings, even viewed monocularly and with a stationary head, a variety of other sources of information for size are available (see Section 3.2.6) so that performance in size perception tasks cannot automatically be attributed to the use of texture information. What is needed is work like that of Newman (1976) on distance perception (see the preceding section) that deliberately manipulates texture information while leaving other forms of information unaltered.

3.1.2.3. The Contextual Determination of Perceived Size. The idea that the texture scale of a surface specifies the relative sizes of objects resting on the surface can be thought of as a special case of the more general idea that the sizes of objects can be specified by their relations to their surroundings (Rock & Ebenholtz, 1959). Another special case that has received considerable attention arises when surfaces or edges of objects lie in the same frontal plane. In this case every edge undergoes a uniform projective compression along its entire length so that proportional relations between edges (or within a single edge) remain invariant; that is, all extents within a given frontal plane have the same projective scale. This can be expressed by saying that, within a given frontal plane, the physical extent, s, of any edge divided by its angular extent, S, is constant:

$$\frac{s}{S} = k\,. \tag{5}$$

If the scale of a frontal plane is specified then the physical extents of all edges in the plane are specified. Even if the scale is not specified, the relation between any two extents in a frontal plane is specified by the relation between their angular extents:

$$\frac{s_1}{s_2} = \frac{S_1}{S_2}\,. \tag{6}$$

These relations form the basis for what Gogel (1971; Gogel & Mershon, 1968; Gogel & Sturm, 1972) has called the *context theory of perceived size*, which hypothesizes that objects perceived to be in the same locally frontal plane will have equal values of perceived size per unit of angular extent. Gogel and Mershon (1968), for example, use this hypothesis to explain the distortions of perceived size that occur in viewing objects through the windows of an Ames distorted room (see Figure 21.12).

If the relation between the scales, k_1 and k_2, of any two locally frontal planes at different distances can be established, then the relations between any two extents, one from each plane, are also specified:

$$\frac{s_1}{s_2} = \left(\frac{S_1}{S_2}\right)\left(\frac{k_1}{k_2}\right)\,. \tag{7}$$

When several locally frontal planes are intersected by a textured surface, as happens when there are a number of frontal planes

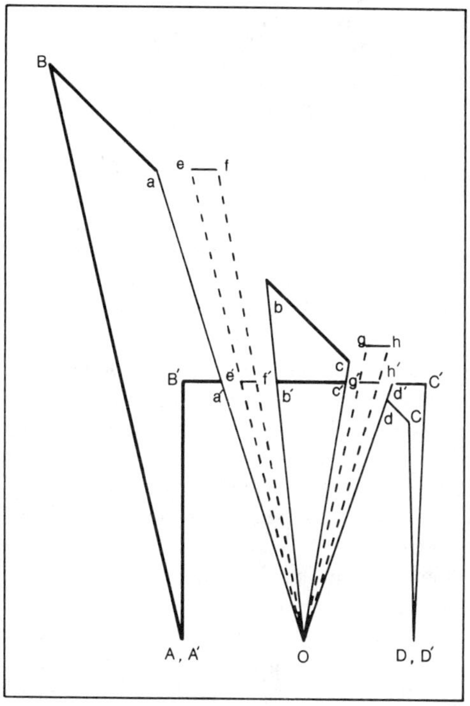

Figure 21.12. Ames's distorted room. This is a schematic top-view drawing of physical (unprimed letters) and apparent (primed letters) positions in an Ames's distorted room. The observer views the room monocularly from O. The monocular view of the distorted room is carefully arranged to be consistent with the view of a normal room, which is what the observer perceives. The perceived context of the room then affects the perceived size and distance of the objects seen through the windows. The objects are perceived to lie in the plane of the windows so that the actually equal-sized but unequally distant objects, *ef* and *gh*, appear to be unequal in size but equal in distance. (From W. C. Gogel & D. H. Mershon, The perception of size in a distorted room, *Perception and Psychophysics*, 1968, *4*. Reprinted with permission.)

resting on a continuous receding surface of support, then the supporting surface's texture, if it is homogeneous, specifies a uniform scale for every frontal plane that it intersects. Some such combination of texture scale and contextual information seems to be what J. Gibson (1950a, p. 6) had in mind in formulating his "ground theory" of space perception (see Section 1.2).

Rock and Ebenholtz (1959) showed in a series of experiments that the relative perceived size of two luminous vertical lines viewed in the dark was strongly influenced by the relative size of the luminous rectangular frameworks surrounding the lines. When the linear dimensions of the frameworks were in a ratio of 3:1 with each other, the vertical lines were reported to be equal when their heights were actually in a ratio of about 2:1 with each other. This result is particularly striking because, in some of the experiments, the frameworks were viewed binocularly, and, the evidence suggests, their own sizes and distances were perceived approximately correctly. Rock and Ebenholtz concluded that the relative angular extent ("retinal size") of the two frameworks was the relevant variable in what they referred to as the "relational determination of perceived size."

Wenderoth (1976), using somewhat different stimuli and instructions, found a substantially smaller effect; the ratio of line heights surrounded by frameworks having a size ratio of 3:1 was only 1.15–1.33 times greater than the ratio of line heights with no surrounding framework. Kunnapas (1955), with the frameworks side-by-side and clearly equidistant, found that the line in the larger framework was perceived to be only 10–15% larger than the line in the smaller framework.

Rock and Ebenholtz (1959) and Wenderoth (1976) both found large individual differences in their results, with some observers showing a much larger relational effect than others. Sigman and Oltman (1977) suggested that these differences could arise from differences in cognitive style among the observers, with observers who were more "field dependent" being more influenced by the relative angular extents of the frameworks. They found that the size of the relational effect was positively correlated with performance on accepted measures of field dependence.

The context theory of perceived size would predict no errors in the perceived sizes of the enclosed lines if the sizes of their equidistant frameworks were perceived correctly. The greater angular extent of the larger framework would be equaled by its greater perceived size, so that the perceived size per unit of angular extent would be the same for the two frameworks. Gogel and Sturm (1972), using a situation similar to that of Rock and Ebenholtz, found that the two frameworks were generally not perceived to be equal in size and that the scale determined by the perceived size of the framework per unit of angular extent better accounted for the perceived sizes of the enclosed lines than did the frameworks' actual relative angular extent. Rock's (1977, p. 339) more recent account of this work appears to accept this conclusion.

Other support for the influence of a frontal plane framework on the perceived size of an object comes from a study by Hake, Faust, McIntyre, and Murray (1967). On each trial their observers saw, in otherwise complete darkness, an inner square surrounded by an outer square. From trial to trial the sizes of both the inner and the outer square varied by small amounts, but the observers were instructed to report the size of the inner square only, ignoring the size of the outer square. Hake et al. found that their observers were unable to ignore the relation between the inner and outer squares; instead, their responses were based on a linear combination of inner and outer square sizes.

We can conclude then that the frontal plane context of an object can exert a considerable effect on its perceived size, although, as Wenderoth (1976) suggests, more work is needed to tease out all of the relevant variables influencing this effect. It also seems reasonable to conclude that relational effects will be most pronounced when they are not placed in conflict with other aspects of the stimulus situation

3.1.2.4. Texture Scale and Shape Perception. Surface shape may be specified by texture scale in two ways, either by the intrinsic scale provided by the texture of the surface itself [see Figure 21.13(a)], or by the scale provided by the texture of an extended supporting surface on which the surface is resting [see Figure 21.13(b)]. In both cases shape is specified by distances between locations on the boundary of the surface. The shape of a triangle is determined when the lengths of its three edges are specified. For other shapes some internal distances also must be specified. The shape of a polygon is determined when the lengths of enough of its diagonals, in addition to its sides, are specified so that the polygon is divided internally into triangles; a quadrilateral, for instance, must have one of its diagonals specified. A curved shape may need to have many internal distances between boundary locations determined before its shape is fully specified. In general, however, because the intrinsic scale provided by texture specifies the distance between any two boundary locations of the surface, texture scale may be thought of as providing highly redundant information for surface shape.

It should be noted here that the shape information provided by texture scale is potentially independent of information for slant; that is, it would be possible in principle to perceive accurately the shape of a surface without registering its slant at all. It is also possible that perceived shape and perceived slant could be linked together not through an internal perceptual coupling but through their mutual dependence on the same features of the optic array. For example, in J. Gibson's (1950a, pp. 169–174; Beck & Gibson, 1955) psychophysical hypothesis of surface perception, the perceived slant of a surface and its perceived uniform distribution of texture are simultaneous responses of the visual system to the surface's projected gradient of texture.

Although texture scale information for surface shape is described by J. Gibson (1950a, p. 174) and referred to by J. Hochberg (1971, p. 507), very little experimental work has been done to determine its effectiveness in human shape perception. Kraft and Winnick (1967) found, for three different instruction conditions, that monocular matches of slanted shapes were closer to the objective shape when the surface was regularly textured than when it was irregularly textured. Whether this resulted

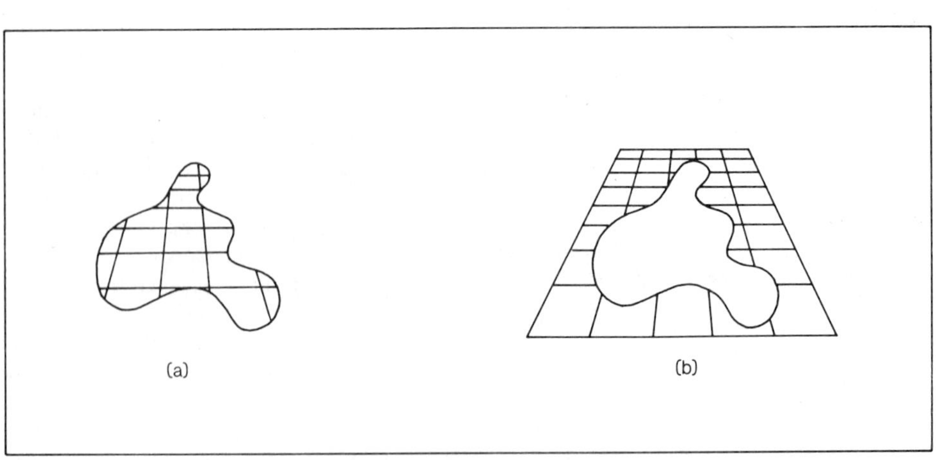

Figure 21.13. Shape specified by texture scale. The shape of a slanted object can be specified by either (a) the texture covering it or (b) the texture of the surface that it covers.

directly from having a more effective texture scale or was mediated by the effect of texture regularity on perceived slant, which also varied, was not determined; it is possible that Oyama's (1977) method of partial correlations could distinguish between these two potential mechanisms.

3.1.3. Texture Gradients

3.1.3.1. Definitions of Texture Gradients. A surface that recedes from an observer undergoes a graded perspective transformation in the optic array; there is a continuous change in the angular size, the density, and various other measures of the projected texture elements from progressively farther locations on the surface (J. Gibson, 1950a; Ogasawara, 1966). J. Gibson (1950a; 1950b) pointed out that such gradients of projected surface texture provide potential information about the orientation of surfaces. In particular, the gradients of texture at any particular location on a surface specify the orientation of the surface, with respect to the line of regard, at that location.

There has been some lack of clarity in the literature concerning the definition of the term "texture gradient." J. Gibson (1950a) gives many examples of texture gradients but uses the term gradient quite broadly to mean simply "an increase or decrease of something along a given axis or dimension" (p. 73). Texture gradients are defined more precisely by W. Purdy (1960). Purdy defines several different angular measures of projected texture, such as angular size, angular width, compression, and density, and then he defines a texture gradient corresponding to each of these measures. Consider, for example, the angular size A of texture elements. As an observer's line of regard is swept along a surface in the direction that the surface is receding, the angular size A of the texture elements encountered by the line of regard decreases continuously. Moreover, the rate of change, that is, the amount of decrease in angular size that occurs for each incremental change, dR, in line of regard, steadily decreases. W. Purdy (1960) defines the gradient of angular size, G_a, at a given location on the surface as the instantaneous rate of change in angular size at that location relative to the angular size at that location:

$$G_a = \frac{dA/dR}{A}. \tag{8}$$

Gradients for the other texture measures are defined analogously (W. Purdy, 1960; Sedgwick, 1983). This definition of texture gradients has the effect of making the texture gradient of a surface at a given location invariant with respect to the scale of the texture elements of the surface.

More recently, some researchers have defined texture gradients simply as instantaneous rates of change with respect to the line of regard (K. Stevens, 1981); by this definition, the gradient of angular size would be dA/dR. This latter definition is more in keeping with the general use of the term "gradient" in mathematics and so might be preferred for that reason, but will not be adopted here because it is at variance with the meaning of the term as it has been widely used in perceptual research over the past 30 years. Disagreements as to whether texture gradients actually do mathematically specify surface slant (K. Stevens, 1981) appear to stem, at least in part, from the use of different definitions. By the definition of W. Purdy (1960) they do, but by the definition of K. Stevens (1981) they do not.

3.1.3.2. Texture Gradients and Surface Slant. Every location on a continuous surface has some specifiable orientation in space. The orientation of any given location on a curved surface can be approximated by the orientation of a plane that is tangent to the surface at that point. We confine ourselves here to considering the orientations of planar surfaces and or curved surfaces that can be locally approximated by planar surfaces.

Specifying the orientation of a surface requires that some frame of reference be established. Optical slant (see Section 2.3.5) is the most natural frame of reference in discussing the relation between texture gradients and surface orientation because there is a one-to-one relation between the texture gradient of a surface at any given location and its amount of optical slant at that location. Direction of slant is also specified by the texture gradient.

Consider the reference plane perpendicular to the line of regard to some arbitrary location on a surface. If the surface is projected onto the reference plane, texture gradients can be measured along any reference plane line that intersects the line of regard. If the surface is perpendicular to the line of regard, that is, if it lies in the reference plane, the texture gradient is zero in every direction. Otherwise, there is exactly one line for which the texture gradient is zero; this is the axis in the reference plane around which the surface is rotated. For directions farther and farther from the zero texture gradient line, the texture gradient steadily increases, reaching a maximum along a line in the reference plane that is perpendicular to the zero texture gradient line. The direction of maximum texture gradient thus specifies the direction of slant of the surface. To assign a numerical value to a direction of slant, some scheme is needed for establishing a reference axis in the reference plane; then direction of slant can be measured as the angular difference between the reference axis and the maximum texture gradient line.

Although a number of authors have described the texture gradient information that specifies the direction of slant (Flock, 1964b; J.Gibson, 1950b; W. Purdy, 1960), there has been little research to determine how accurately people can make use of this information. This neglect appears to be due in part to the unstated belief that performance on such a task could be assumed to be quite good. Recently K. Stevens (1983) did systematically investigate observers' ability to indicate a surface's direction of slant, which he refers to as its *tilt*, and found that observers did in fact show considerable accuracy at this task.

J. Gibson (1950a, 1950b) and J. Gibson and Cornsweet (1952) asserted, and W. Purdy (1960) later demonstrated mathematically, that the amount of optical slant of a locally planar patch of homogeneously textured surface is specified by the maximum texture gradient of the surface at that location. For the texture gradient of angular size, G_a, the amount of optical slant, S, is given by

$$S = \frac{\text{arc cot } G_a}{3} \tag{9}$$

(the derivations of this equation and of similar equations for gradients based on texture measures other than angular size are given by W. Purdy, 1960; Sedgwick, 1980; and K. Stevens, 1980, 1981).

W. Purdy's derivations of one-to-one relations between optical slants and texture gradients are essentially existence proofs; that is, they are directed more at demonstrating that such one-to-one relations exist than at providing detailed computational models of how the visual system might process such information.

Flock (1964b) provides a more detailed computational model based on the angular extent subtended by a fixed number of texture elements lying along a zero-texture-gradient line. Flock's equation uses three such measures, taken at different distances from the observer. A simplified version of Flock's computation is given by Braunstein (1968). Phillips (1970) gives equations for seven alternative texture measures (including one based on Flock's). Five of these measures are essentially the same as Purdy's five measures, but Phillips' equations are based on geographical rather than optical slant and are incorporated in a computational scheme in which slant would be determined by solving the simultaneous equations whose terms are obtained by sampling the surface texture at two different locations.

J. Gibson's hypothesis that texture gradients provide a basis for perception of amount of slant has given rise to a considerable body of experimental work, which has been reviewed by a number of authors (Epstein & Park, 1963; Flock, 1964a; J. Hochberg, 1971). The broadly stated conclusion of this work is that although a gradient of texture does generally produce the perception of a receding surface, the perceived slant of the surface is generally less than its optically specified slant and is influenced both by the nature of the surface texture and by the angular extent of the surface.

J. Gibson (1950b) determined that the perceived slant of surfaces that were rotated around a horizontal axis increased as a monotonic function of optically specified slant for both a regular and an irregular texture pattern. The perceived slant was consistently closer to the vertical plane than was the optically specified slant, however, and this effect was stronger for the irregular than for the regular texture [see Figure 21.14(a)]. Subsequent research (Flock, 1964c; Flock & Moscatelli, 1964; Kraft & Winnick, 1967) has confirmed these results. J. Gibson also compared the perception of slant obtained when the surface was rotated backward (i.e., with its top away from the observer) with the perception obtained when the surface was rotated forward; the increases in backward slant were estimated more accurately than were increases in forward slant [see Figure 21.14(b)], a result also found by Rosinski, Degelman, and Mulholland (1978).

To avoid the possibility that perception might be influenced by the outline of the object, J. Gibson (1950b) used a rear projection screen and an aperture in such a way as to present the information for a textured surface without visible edges. Gibson (see also Epstein & Park, 1963) suggested that the underestimation of slant that he observed may have been due in part to a perceptual compromise between texture information for the slanted surface and some residual information for the frontal surface of the frontal projection screen.

Phillips (1970), using computer-generated textures having circular and elliptical elements, compared the perceived relative slants of pairs of surfaces for which the gradients of element size and compression and of element density were varied independently. His results showed that the gradient of element density contributed only weakly to perceived slant and was overridden by the gradient of element size and compression when the two gradients were in conflict. The gradient of element size and compression alone, however, produced highly reliable perceptions of the relative slants of two surfaces slanted at 45 and 70°. Other research, in which no gradients of element size and compression were present because dots were used to produce the texture gradients, confirms the conclusion that gradients of texture density alone are rather ineffectual in producing perceptions of slant. Braunstein (1968), for example, found that

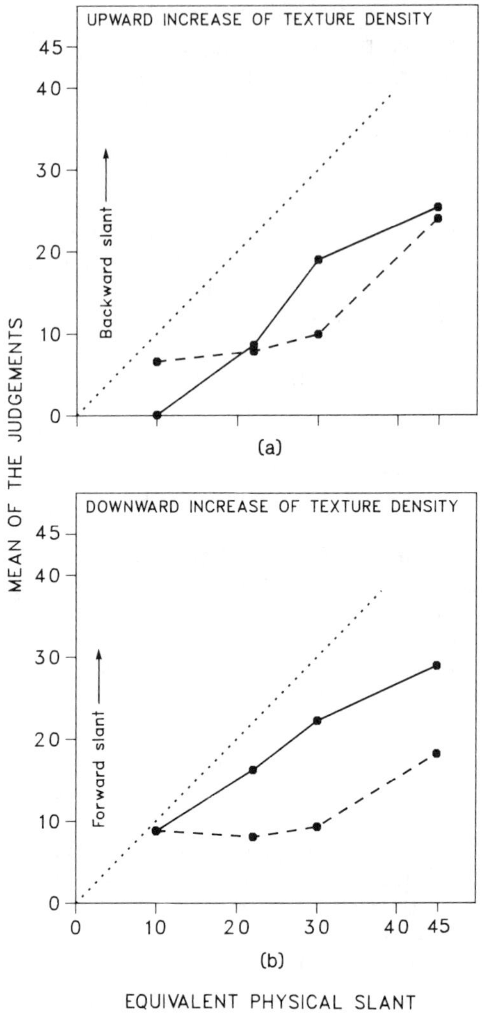

Figure 21.14. Texture gradients and perceived slant. Observers manually rotated a board to match the estimated slant of a projected texture, which was either regular (solid lines) or irregular (dotted lines) and whose density increased going either upward (a) or downward (b). In general estimated slant away from the frontal plane was less than the equivalent physical slant, and more slant was perceived for regular than for irregular textures. In both the backward slant (a) and the forward slant (b) conditions there is a constant error in the forward slant direction, but the slopes of the functions relating estimated to physical slant are greater for backward (a) than for forward (b) slant. Means are of 160 estimates from 10 observers. (From J. J. Gibson, The perception of visual surfaces, *American Journal of Psychology, 63*. Copyright 1950 by the University of Illinois Press. Reprinted with permission.)

a dot texture slanted at 60° from the frontoparallel plane was matched by a binocularly viewed square slanted at 11.6°, and Clark, Smith, and Rabe (1956) found that a dot texture slanted at 40° was perceived to be slanted at 9.07°.

The importance of texture element size was also demonstrated by Gruber and Clark (1956) and by Eriksson (1964), who showed that, up to a point, the perceived slant of a surface increased as the physical size of its texture elements was increased; when the circular texture elements became so large as to be almost touching, however, the perceived slant of the surface decreased somewhat (see Figure 21.15). Gruber and Clark (1956) showed a similar effect for element spacing: perceived slant was several degrees less for either a very dense or very sparse spacing of circular texture elements than for an intermediate spacing. Eriksson (1964) and Flock, Tenney, and

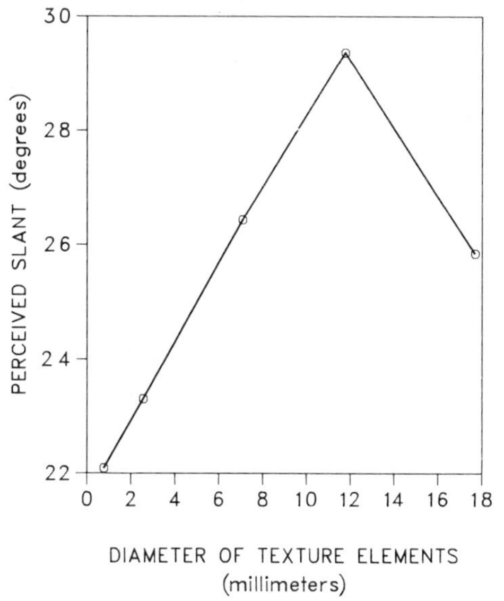

Figure 21.15. Perceived slant as a function of texture element size. Ten observers matched the slant of a monocularly viewed surface of circular texture elements slanted at 43° away from the frontal plane by adjusting the slant of a binocularly viewed checkerboard. The mean distance between the circular elements was 20 mm and their diameter was varied across trials. As the size of the elements increased the matched slant of the surface also increased until the elements almost completely covered the surface, at which point the matched slant decreased somewhat. (From E. Ericksson, Monocular slant perception and the texture gradient, *Scandinavian Journal of Psychology*, 1964, 5. Reprinted with permission.)

Graves (1966) have also shown that the perceived slant of a surface is affected by the angular extent of the aperture through which the surface is viewed, with the most common finding being that perceived slant increases somewhat as aperture size increases.

3.2. Linear Perspective

3.2.1. Definition of Linear Perspective. *Perspective* may be taken to refer generally to the effects of distance on objects' projections in the optic array. Subtypes of perspective can be distinguished according to the specific ways in which distance has its effect. Thus, for example, *aerial perspective* refers to the distance-dependent effects produced by the atmosphere as light from an object passes through it to reach the point of observation. The study of perspective has historically been of great interest to artists because it is possible from an understanding of perspective to derive rules about how to construct pictorial representations that convey accurate information about the three-dimensional layout of a scene. The term "perspective" is thus sometimes also used to refer to these artists' rules. For example, "aerial perspective" could refer to the set of techniques that artists have developed to represent the effects of increasing distance through the atmosphere. *Linear perspective* refers in common usage to the complex set of rules developed to allow artists to accurately create two-dimensional projections of the outline forms of three-dimensional objects (e.g., Ware, 1900). In the study of visual perception, however, the term "linear perspective" may be taken to refer to the optic array relations that underlie this complex set of rules and that may also partially underlie the human perception of spatial layout.

The best known of the artists' rules for linear perspective is that parallel lines in three-dimensional space are represented in two dimensions by lines converging toward a single point called the *vanishing point*. Probably for this reason the term "linear perspective" is most often used in the study of visual perception to refer to the projective convergence of parallel lines (J. Gibson, 1950a, p. 35). Figure 21.16(a) shows a rectangle in the frontoparallel plane; Figures 21.16(b)–(d) show the projection of the same rectangle slanted back at three different angles around a horizontal axis. Linear perspective is present in the sides of the projected slanted rectangles, which converge toward vanishing points located above the figures (the compression that occurs between the top and the bottom of the rectangles is discussed in Section 3.2.3.1). Figures 21.16(e)–(h) show the projection of a rectangle rotated around a vertical axis. As is evident from Figure 21.16, the direction and amount of projective convergence are related to the direction and amount of slant of the surface. The nature of this relation and the evidence concerning its use in human perception are discussed in this section.

3.2.2. The Geometry of Linear Perspective and Orientation

3.2.2.1. Vanishing Points and Edge Orientation. If the orientation of an edge is measured relative to the fixed framework of the environment, then all edges having the same orientation are parallel to each other. The projection of this set of parallel edges onto a projection plane is a set of lines converging toward a single vanishing point (ignoring for the moment the special case of edges parallel to the projection plane). The vanishing point of an edge may be thought of as the terminus of the edge's projection when the edge itself is extended infinitely into the distance. For every distinct edge orientation there is a corresponding distinct vanishing point, and conversely, every distinct point on the projection plane is the vanishing point of a set of parallel edges having a distinct orientation. There is thus a one-to-one correspondence between vanishing points and edge orientations, which implies that an edge's vanishing point is specific to, that is, provides information for, its orientation. The nature of this specificity is quite simple and direct: the line of regard from the point of view to a vanishing point has the same orientation as all the parallel edges whose projections converge toward that vanishing point (see Figure 21.17). It follows that the relative orientations of nonparallel edges are specified by the angles between the lines of regard to their vanishing points; for example, the lines of regard to the three vanishing points of the three edges that form the corner of a cube will necessarily be at right angles to each other.

The relation between vanishing points and edge orientation remains invariant with motion of the point of observation. When the point of observation moves, every vanishing point remains fixed in its position in the optic array, in correspondence to the fixed orientations of the edges in the environment.

Hay (1974) offers a detailed analysis of the relation between vanishing points and orientation and gives the name "ghost image" to the set of vanishing points in the optic array. Hay's analysis is somewhat limited, however, by its failure to distinguish clearly between edge and surface orientation and to include horizon information. Rosinski and Farber (1980) have used the vanishing point structure of the optic array to analyze the projective distortions that occur when pictures are viewed from different viewpoints.

3.2.2.2. Horizons and Surface Orientation. If a surface is extended infinitely in every direction, its projection on the projection plane will terminate in a single line, the *horizon* of the surface. If the orientation of a surface is measured relative to

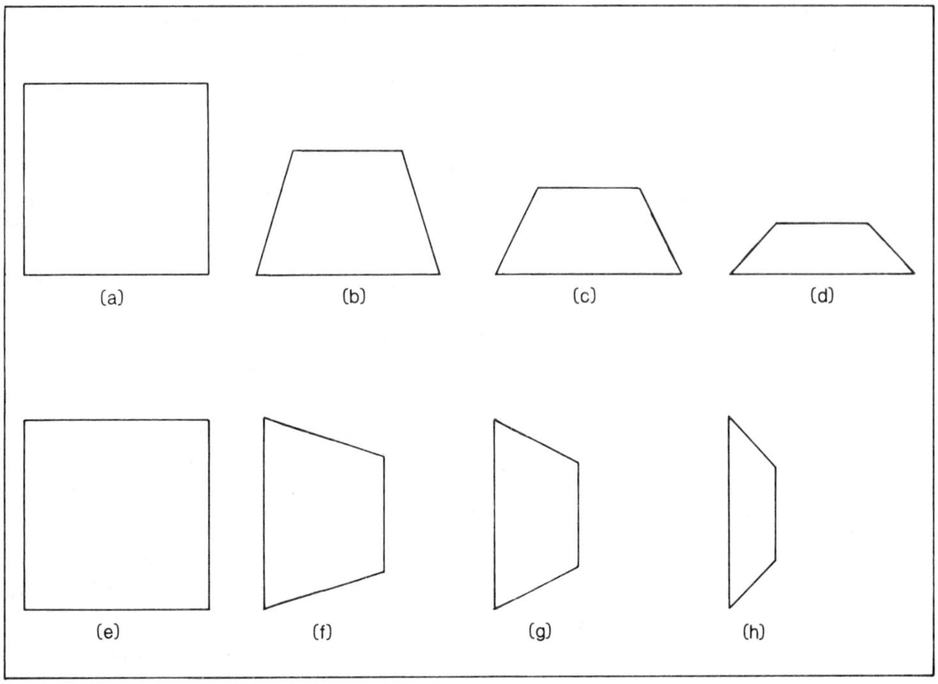

Figure 21.16. Linear perspective of an outline figure. (a) and (e) depict squares in the frontal plane. (b)–(d) depict a square at increasing slants around a horizontal axis, and (f)–(h) depict a square at increasing slants around a vertical axis. Taken together the figures illustrate that linear perspective is affected both by the direction and by the amount of slant.

the fixed framework of the environment, then all surfaces having the same orientation are parallel to each other. Analogously to the situation with vanishing points and edges, the projections of this set of parallel surfaces onto a projection plane all have the same horizon line (again ignoring the special case of surfaces parallel to the projection plane). For every distinct surface orientation there is a corresponding distinct horizon line, and conversely, every distinct line on the projection plane is the horizon of a set of parallel edges having a distinct orientation. There is thus a one-to-one correspondence between horizons and surface orientations, which implies that a surface's horizon provides information about its orientation. Once again, the relation is quite simple and direct: the plane passing through the point of view and containing the horizon of a surface has the same orientation as the surface itself, as seen in Figure 21.18. The relative orientations of nonparallel surfaces are the same as the relative orientations of the planes that contain the horizons of these surfaces and pass through the point of view.

Because the horizon of a surface, like the vanishing point of an edge, is the projection of something that is infinitely far away, every horizon in the optic array maintains a fixed, invariant position in the optic array when the point of view moves. Thus the relation between the horizon of a surface and the surface's orientation remains invariant with movement of the point of view.

3.2.2.3. The Implicit Perspective Structure of the Optic Array. Taken together, the vanishing points and horizons of all the edges and surfaces in the environment form what I have referred to (Sedgwick, 1983) as the *perspective structure of the optic array* (Gibson, 1979, pp. 73–75, uses this term in a different sense). This structure uniquely specifies the orientation of every edge and surface in the environment; there is thus an isomorphism between the perspective structure of the optic array and the orientation structure of the environment.

Because edges and surfaces are limited in extent, however, their vanishing points and horizons are not explicitly present as points and lines in the optic array. A vanishing point or a horizon may be said to be implicitly present in the optic array, however, if its location is specified by other structures in the optic array. The following are some ways in which such specification can occur:

1. A vanishing point is specified as the point toward which the projections from a set of parallel lines are converging.
2. A horizon line of a surface is specified as the line through two or more vanishing points of sets of parallel lines that lie in the surface.
3. The vanishing point of an edge that lies in a surface is specified as the point that lies at the intersection of the edge's projection, if extended, and the horizon of the surface. (Note that this form of specification might be functionally important not only for single edges but also for parallel edges whose projections are so slightly convergent as to make their point of intersection very difficult to detect accurately.)

All these structural specifications are in various ways contingent on other constraints within the scene; for example, in (1) and (2) the constraint is that these are sets of parallel lines, and in (2) and (3) there is the constraint that the lines lie in the surface. Nevertheless, these constraints may be met either through additional information within the scene or through default conditions set by the visual system. These structural specifications, discussed in more detail elsewhere (Sedgwick, 1983), make it possible to speak of the more or less completely specified *implicit perspective structure of the optic array*. This implicit perspective structure, like Hay's (1974) ghost image, which is a subset of it, is both a potentially useful tool for analyzing the optic array and a potential source of information that could be used by the visual system in the perception of the orientations of edges and surfaces.

*3.2.2.4. **Local Analyses of Linear Perspective***. The implicit perspective structure of the optic array that is described in the preceding paragraphs is not the only analysis that can be given of linear perspective. Other analyses, here termed "local," tend to be based on explicit local features of the perspective projection. Some of these analyses, such as those of W. Purdy (1960), of Flock (1964b), and of Phillips (1970), subsume linear perspective under a more general discussion of texture gradients; these analyses are treated in Section 3.1.3.

Most other local analyses are made under rather restrictive conditions. Freeman (1966b, 1966c) offers two alternative local measures of the linear perspective of a rectangle that is rotated around a horizontal axis. These are (1) the angle that the sides of the rectangle's projection make with its base and (2) the angular difference between the top and the bottom of the rectangle's projection. Neither of these measures is adequate to specify the veridical slant of the rectangle, but Freeman argues that they are adequate to specify the rectangle's perceived slant (see Section 3.2.3) and that it is on simpler "cues" of this sort rather than on the complex "higher-order variables" of J. Gibson and Flock that slant perception is based (Freeman, 1965, 1969).

Braunstein and Payne (1969) offer two formulas, in addition to that of Flock (1964b), that specify slant in terms of optic array variables. One of these, derived from Freeman's (1966b) analysis and based on the projective angle of a single line, is valid only for lines that lie in vertical planes perpendicular to the projection plane. Braunstein and Payne's second formula derives amount of slant from a local measure of the rate of perspective convergence. As they state it, their formula lacks generality, but the idea behind it can be generalized to give a general formula. Any measure that takes appropriate account of the rate of convergence of the sides of the projected rectangle, that is, the angular difference between its top and bottom as a function of the angular separation between them, can be equivalent to specifying the vanishing point of the sides.

3.2.3. Linear Perspective and Slant Perception. Numerous investigations have shown that the projective outline of a slanted rectangle having no surface texture produces a perception of slant. Slanted rectangles, like texture gradients, are generally perceived as being less slanted from the frontal plane than they actually are, although the amount of underestimation varies considerably from study to study. At one extreme of this range, Beck and Gibson (1955) found that most of their subjects matched a slanted rectangle with a frontal trapezoid. More typical of the studies showing large underestimation are those of Clark, Smith, and Rabe (1955, 1956), who found that a rectangle slanted at 40° away from the frontal plane was perceived to be slanted at 13.8° on the average. Other studies (Epstein, 1962; Epstein & Mountford, 1963; Kaess & Deregowski, 1980; Olson, 1974) have reported perceived slants that are much closer to being veridical. In a carefully controlled study in which monocularly seen rectangles slanted at from 50 to 80° from the frontal plane were matched by a binocularly seen stimulus, Olson (1974) found the average underestimation, compared to a "full-cue" situation, to be 13.1°; some of his results are shown in Figure 21.19. Although it is not clear how to account for these differences

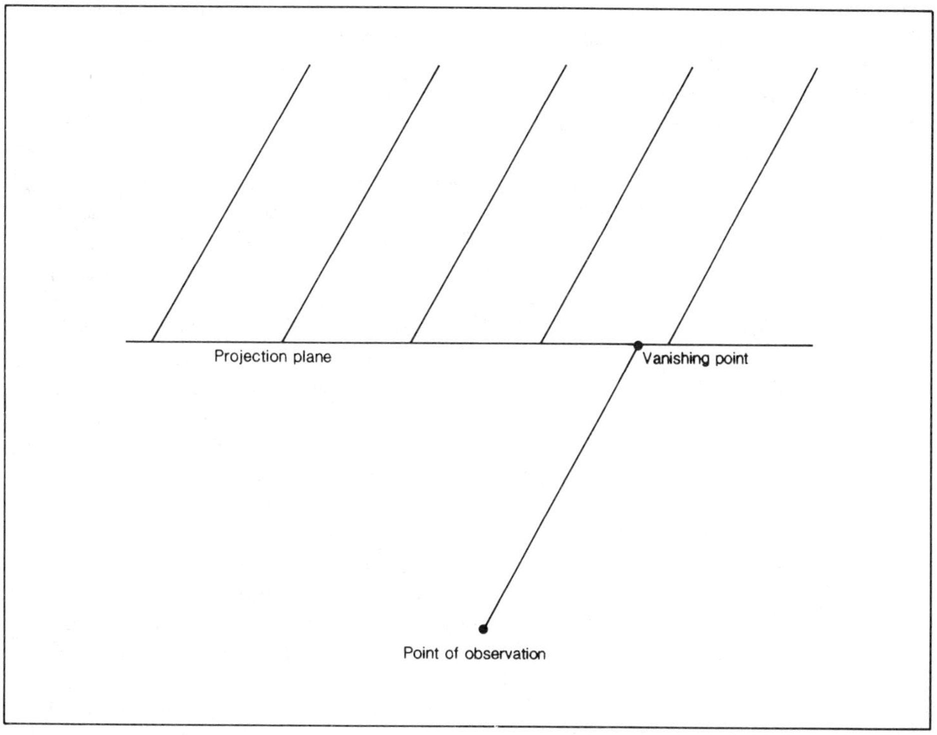

Figure 21.17. Line orientation specified by a vanishing point. The figure shows a set of five parallel lines, their vanishing point on the projection plane, and the line of regard from the point of observation to their vanishing point. The line of regard to the vanishing point of a set of parallel lines is the member of that set whose projection is a single point, and so the line of regard's orientation is the same as the orientation of all the other lines in the set. (From H. A. Sedgwick, The geometry of spatial layout in pictorial representation, in M. A. Hagen (Ed.), *The perception of pictures* (Vol. 1), Academic Press, Inc., 1980. Reprinted with permission.)

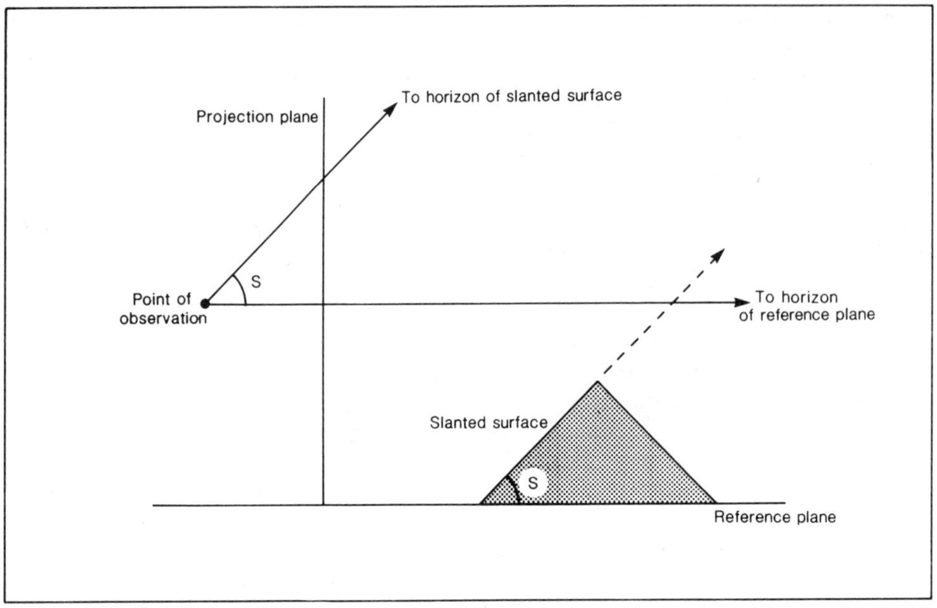

Figure 21.18. Surface orientation specified by an horizon. Side view showing that a line of regard to the horizon of a slanted surface is parallel to that surface and so has the same orientation relative to a reference plane such as the ground. (From H. A. Sedgwick, The geometry of spatial layout in pictorial representation, in M. A. Hagen (Ed.), *The perception of pictures* (Vol. 1), Academic Press, Inc., 1980. Reprinted with permission.)

between studies, it does appear that encouraging observers to take the attitude that they are looking at rectangles rather than trapezoids helps to produce more veridical slant matches, as does using response methods based on matching perceived slants as opposed to translating perceived slant into some other more abstractly related form of response, such as the adjustment of a dial.

The perceived slant of a rectangle may be influenced by the projective size of the rectangle as well as by its slant, with

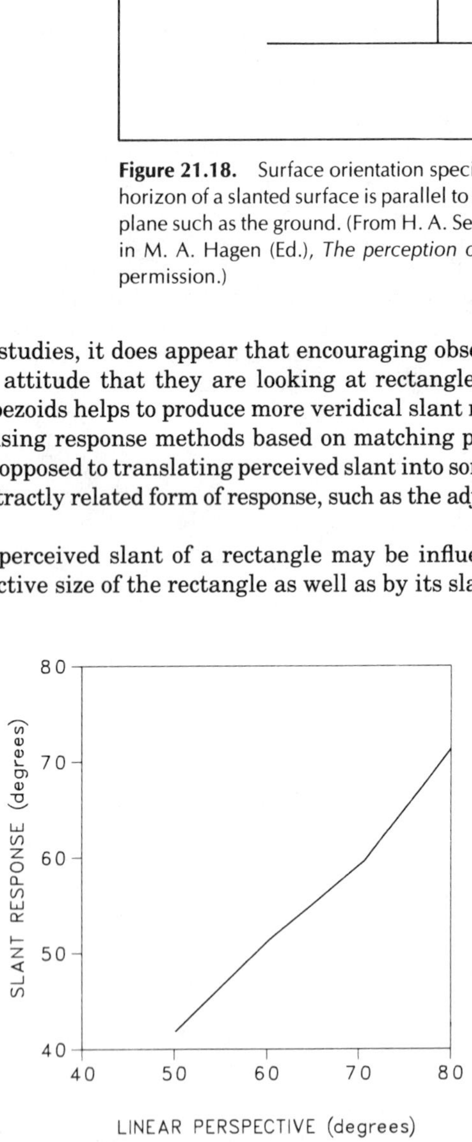

Figure 21.19. Perceived slant as a function of linear perspective. Nine observers monocularly viewed trapezoids that were perspective projections of rectangles slanted at from 50 to 80° from the frontal plane. They matched the perceived slant of these figures by adjusting the slant of a binocularly viewed rod. Increases in the slant responses closely followed increases in the slant specified by linear perspective, but with a fairly constant underestimation. (From R. K. Olson, Slant judgments from static and rotating trapezoids correspond to rules of perspective geometry, *Perception and Psychophysics*, 1974, *15*. Reprinted with permission.)

the larger rectangle appearing more slanted (Flock, Graves, Tenney, & Stephenson, 1967; Freeman, 1966c; Stavrianos, 1945). A. Smith (1967) concluded just the opposite, but did so on the basis of the mistaken assumption that scaling up the projective dimensions of his stimuli would not change the slant that they specified; when the correct slants specified by his stimuli are calculated, Smith's results also show that perceived slant increases with projective size. Flock (1965a) has criticized Freeman's finding on the grounds that observers may have been matching projective shape rather than perceived slant, and Olson (1974) found essentially no difference in perceived slant when he doubled the size of his stimuli. Olson also examined Freeman's claim that perceived slant is simply a function of the angle of convergence of the rectangles' sides and concluded that, for his own data, linear perspective defined in terms of projective geometry is the best predictor of slant responses.

Freeman (1966d) measured the threshold amount of slant necessary for detecting whether a rectangle was tilted forward or backward from the frontal plane and found that the threshold decreased as the angular size of the rectangle increased.

Some studies have examined slant perception using geometric outline forms other than rectangles. Flock et al. (1966) found that a single slanted triangle was perceived to be in the frontal plane, although a surface covered with triangles was perceived to be slanted. A. Smith (1956) compared the perception of slanted circles with that of slanted rectangles and found that the slant of the circles was perceived somewhat more accurately.

Although slanted outline rectangles have often been used to assess the use of linear perspective by human observers, these stimuli are arguably not best suited for this purpose because rectangles contain at least two other potential sources of information for slant besides linear perspective [these are compression (Section 3.2.3.1) and angle configuration] and because, having only two edges converging toward each vanishing point, rectangles are only minimal sources of linear perspective information. These two converging edges alone, however, have been found to yield the same slant perception as the entire rectangle (A. Smith, 1959). A richer stimulus for presenting linear perspective information is a set of parallel lines that lie on a slanted surface and are perpendicular to its axis of rotation (see Figure 21.20). Rosinski and Levine (1976) used such a stimulus to study the perception of slants around a horizontal axis. Fitting a regression line to data for slants ranging from 30 to 70° away from the frontal plane, they found a slope of 1.09 and an intercept of -20.4 in their adult observers. Thus over this range, change in perceived slant accurately reflected change in slant as specified by linear perspective, but with an average constant underestimation of about 20°. Gillam (1968), using horizontal lines rotated around a vertical axis to slants of 10, 14, and 18°, obtained slant matches that were accurate to within a few degrees. Attneave and Olson (1966) asked observers to judge the direction of slant of a grid of lines in which the direction of slant specified by linear perspective was in conflict with a gradient of increasing compression in the opposite direction. Their observers almost unanimously chose the direction of slant consistent with the linear perspective. It thus appears that linear perspective alone is a good source of information for slant perception.

3.2.3.1. Compression. As a surface is slanted away from the frontal plane, its projection becomes compressed along the direction of slant. This effect is also referred to as foreshortening. Individual forms or texture elements, as well as the spacing between forms or texture elements, are affected by compression. The effect of compression on a slanted square is shown in Figure 21.21, and its effect on evenly spaced lines parallel to the axis of rotation is shown in Figure 21.22.

Compression is primarily a function of optical slant. The angular extent subtended by a linear extent lying along the direction of slant is, however, a combined function of the linear extent, its distance from the point of observation, and compression. To isolate the effect of compression, the factors of linear extent and distance must be eliminated; two somewhat complementary approaches have been offered for doing this. One approach is to compare the angular extent of the linear extent lying in the direction of slant with the angular extent of an equal linear extent lying perpendicular to the direction of slant at the same location. This ratio, sometimes referred to as the *form ratio*, is approximately equal to sin r, where r is the optical slant at that location (Braunstein, 1968, gives cos r because he defines optical slant as the complement of the angle used to define it here). This measure of compression permits the determination of the slant of each of the squares in Figure 21.21 under the constraint that they are in fact square, but does not permit the determination of the optical slant of the parallel lines in Figure 21.22.

The second approach to isolating the effect of compression is to determine the relative rate of change of compression as the line of regard is swept along the direction of slant. Such a gradient of compression is approximately equal to 2 cot r, where r is again the optical slant at the surface location at which compression is determined (this approach is referred to by Rosinski & Levine, 1976, and is similar to, but not quite the same as, the gradient of texture compression defined by Purdy, 1960). This approach permits the determination of the optical slant of the parallel lines in Figure 21.22, under the constraint that they are densely and evenly spaced, but does not permit the determination of the optical slant of the single squares in Figure 21.21.

Few experimental studies have attempted to determine the effect on slant perception of compression information in isolation from other forms of information for slant perception. Gillam (1970) asked observers to match the slant of a monocularly seen surface of vertical lines, rotated around a vertical axis as in Figure 21.22(e)–(h), with a binocularly viewed comparison stimulus. She obtained measurements at four slants for three different widths of viewing apparatus; her results are given in Table 21.3. As can be seen there, slant settings varied with the slant of the surface but were quite variable and were always underestimates. Widening the viewing aperture improved the accuracy of the settings but does not appear to have decreased their variability. Some of Gillam's observers reported spontaneously that the surface did not look slanted to them but that they used its appearance as a cue to figure out its slant. Rosinski and Levine (1976) used parallel horizontal lines, like those in Figure 21.21(a)–(d), to determine the perceived slant produced by optical slants, around the horizontal axis, ranging

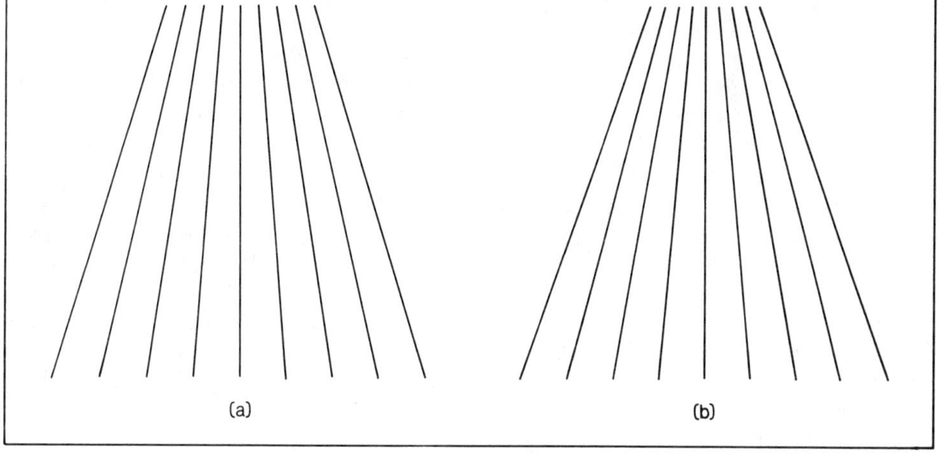

Figure 21.20. Linear perspective of parallel lines. A set of parallel lines on a receding surface is projected as a set of lines converging toward a vanishing point. (a) and (b) show two such projections, with (b) having a larger slant relative to the frontal plane than (a).

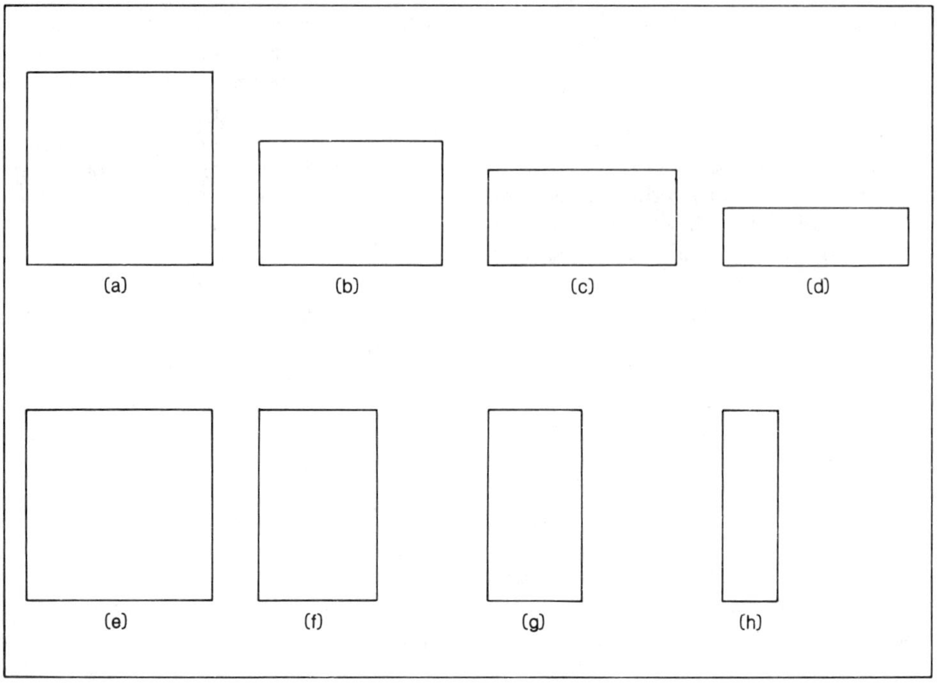

Figure 21.21. Compression of an outline figure. (a)–(d) show the compression of an outline square as it is slanted progressively around a horizontal axis. (e)–(h) show the compression of the outline square as it is slanted progressively around a vertical axis. The square is shown in parallel projection (as seen from a very great distance) to eliminate the convergence produced by linear perspective.

from 30 to 70°. The linear regression line for the data from their adult observers had a slope of 0.69 and an intercept of 25.11, implying that perceived slant did not change as rapidly as optical slant but that there was generally a constant error in the direction of overestimation. Kaess and Deregowski (1980) found that rectangles having the same compression as squares slanted at 36 and 65° but having linear perspective appropriate to being in the frontal plane were perceived as being only slightly slanted out of the frontal plane. The tentative conclusion from these limited data is that compression information can be used at least in the estimation, if not in the perception, of slant but is less effective than linear perspective information.

3.2.3.2. Relations between Texture and Linear Perspective in Slant Perception. J. Gibson's suggestion (1950a, 1950b) that texture gradients provide a basis for slant perception has given rise to an extended debate over the relative effectiveness of texture gradients versus linear perspective, which was the previously accepted "cue," in slant perception.

We have already seen that both surface texture and outline perspective can elicit a perception of surface slant but that for both types of display surface slant is almost always underestimated relative to the frontal plane. Most studies that have directly compared the two forms of display have found that outline perspective tends to produce somewhat more accurate slant perception than does surface texture. Studies that have looked at surface texture in combination with outline perspective have generally found that the combination is only slightly, if at all, better than outline perspective alone (Clark et al., 1956; Epstein, 1962; Epstein & Mountford, 1963). A. Smith (1964) found that slant perception with outline perspective was unaffected by texture gradients in the reverse direction.

The comparison between surface texture and outline perspective is not as clear as it might at first seem, however, because many of the artificial surface "textures" used in this research have distinct outline forms within them; for example, J. Gibson's (1950b) regular surface texture was a pattern of rectangles arranged in offset rows like brickwork and W. Purdy's (1960) surface texture consisted of a grid of squares. The comparison is further undercut because, on the one hand, the linear perspective of parallel lines can be analyzed as a form of texture gradient (J. Gibson; 1950a; W. Purdy, 1960), and on the other hand, linear perspective is implicit even in textures of random dots (Braunstein, 1968; Freeman, 1966a; Sedgwick, 1983).

What can be concluded from the available data is that the visual system is not very good at extracting information about slant from displays in which that information is implicit only statistically. It seems reasonable also to conclude here, as a number of authors have done, that the presence of strong linear perspective, whether in the outline of the surface or in clearly visible converging lines, line segments, or rows of elements on the surface, contributes substantially to accurate slant perception. Such a conclusion must be tempered, however, by the observation that most, although not all, of the displays that include strong linear perspective also include other types of information such as compression and angle configuration.

3.2.3.3. Optical Slant and Geographical Slant. J. Gibson and Cornsweet (1952) in defining and distinguishing optical and geographical slant (see Section 2.3.5), pointed out that the characteristics of these two forms of slant pose a problem for understanding slant perception. In J. Gibson's formulation (1950a), it is optical slant, which is the slant with respect to the line of regard to a given surface location, that is specified by the texture gradients at that location. In general, different locations on the same surface have different optical slants; as the line of regard sweeps away in the direction of slant, the optical slant changes continuously (see Figure 21.23). On the

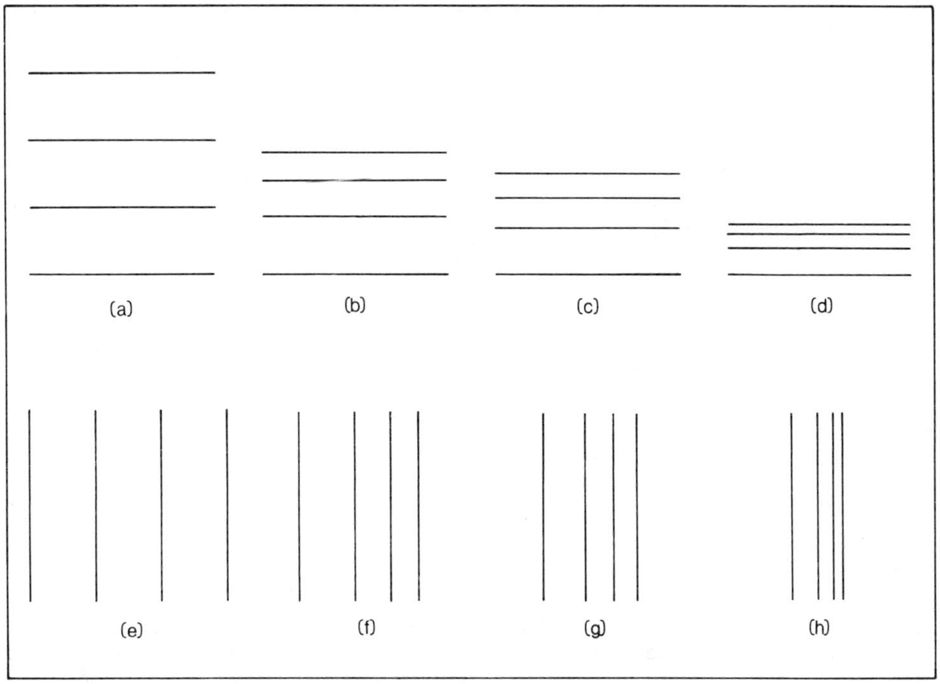

Figure 21.22. Compression of parallel lines. (a)–(d) show the compression of a set of evenly spaced parallel lines as the surface on which they are lying is slanted progressively around a horizontal axis. (e)–(h) show the same progressive slant around a vertical axis. The lines are shown in parallel projection (as if seen from a very great distance) to eliminate the convergence produced by linear perspective.

other hand, geographical slant, which is the slant of the surface with respect to some external frame of reference and which is constant over the extent of a flat surface, is the more functionally important type of slant, yet it is not specified by the optical information, as J. Gibson analyzed it. J. Gibson and Cornsweet (1952) suggested, somewhat tentatively, that geographical slant may be perceived by integrating optical slant, based on visual information, with postural-kinesthetic information about eye and head position as the line of regard is swept across the surface.

Purdy (1960) observed that there is a very simple relation between amount of optical slant and amount of geographical slant when they are both in the same direction. If S is the geographical slant of a surface with respect to some reference orientation such as the horizontal, R is the optical slant at a given location on that surface, and U is the visual angle between that location and the reference orientation (see Figure 21.24), then

$$S = R - U \quad . \tag{10}$$

W. Purdy pointed out that the horizontal reference plane may be specified either visually (by the ground or floor), vestibularly, or possibly in some other way. This relation between geographical and optical slant is also embodied in the relation between the surface and the implicit structure of the optic array outlined in Section 3.2.2.3. As can be seen in Figure 21.24, geographical

Table 21.3. Slant Estimates from Projective Compression

	Estimated Slant					
	14° Visual Angle		28° Visual Angle		44° Visual Angle	
True Slant	Mean	SD	Mean	SD	Mean	SD
5L	−3.5	12.3	−2.9	11.9	3.5	12.0
15R	10.9	11.5	12.6	11.9	17.0	10.2
30L	13.6	17.4	21.4	19.25	25.0	14.9
45R	20.9	13.7	32.2	11.6	36.0	11.0

Observers used an adjustment method to estimate the slant of surfaces of vertical lines slanted around a vertical axis. Surfaces were viewed monocularly subtending three different visual angles and at four different slants. Estimated slant increased regularly with physical slant although it was consistently underestimated. Increasing the visual angle subtended by the display increased the estimated slant. L indicates clockwise slant and R indicates counterclockwise slant from the frontal plane. A negative sign indicates that the mean slant setting was in the opposite direction from the actual slant. All values are in degrees. (From B. Gillam, Judgments of slant on the basis of foreshortening, Scandinavian Journal of Psychology, *1970, 11. Reprinted with permission.)*

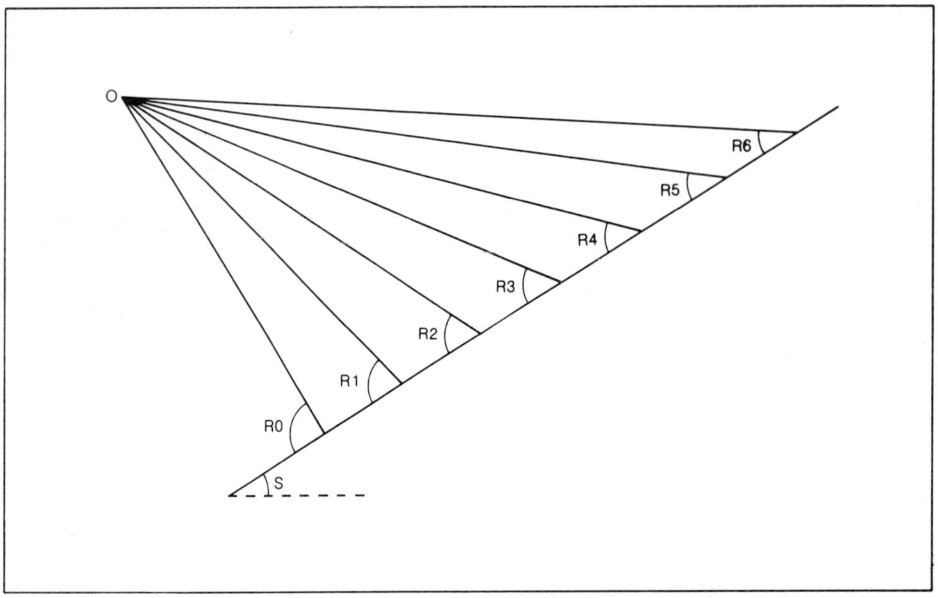

Figure 21.23. Variation in optical slant along a surface. As the line of regard from O sweeps along the surface, the optical slant of the surface changes progressively (from R_0 to R_6 in this illustration). The geographical slant *S* of the surface is constant along its entire length.

slant is specified by the visual angle between the horizon of the surface and the horizon of the reference plane, and optical slant at a given location is specified by the visual angle between the horizon of the surface and that particular location.

J. Gibson and Cornsweet noted that Gibson's original experiment on the perception of slant from texture gradients (J. Gibson, 1950b) confounded optical slant and geographical slant by keeping the line of regard in the horizontal plane. Thus matches made on the basis of geographical slant, assuming the horizontal to be the reference plane, would be identical to matches made on the basis of optical slant. Almost all subsequent research on slant perception has confounded optical and geographical slant in this or similar ways, so that there is very little data available that allows any comparison of optical slant perception with geographical slant perception. This is a comparison of considerable theoretical importance because of its bearing on the question of the type of information that observers are using in perceiving slant.

J. Gibson and Cornsweet (1952) asked observers to adjust a surface either so that it was perpendicular to the line of sight

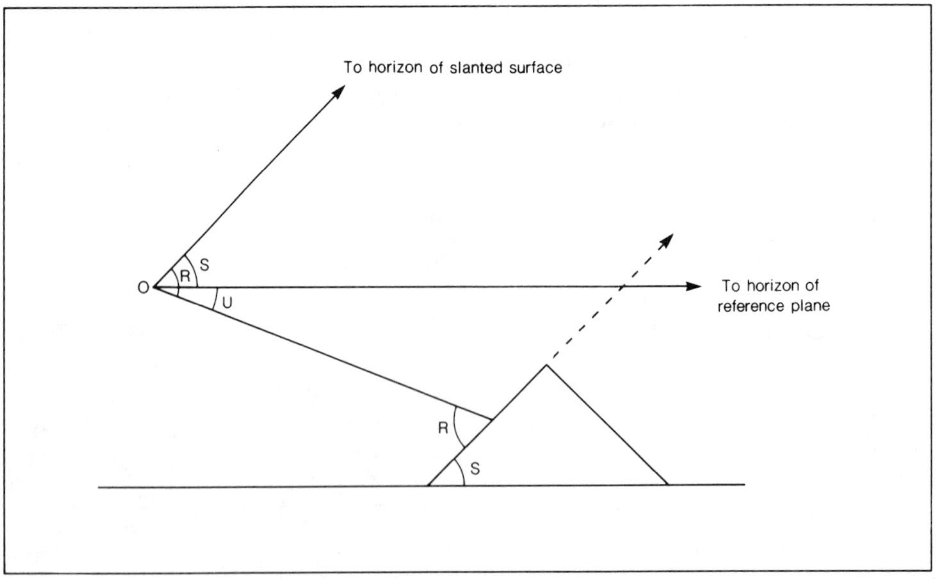

Figure 21.24. Optical slant and geographical slant. The geographical slant *S* of a surface relative to some reference plane is equal to the difference between its optical slant *R* at a given location and the visual angle *U* subtended at the point of observation *O* between that location and the horizon of the reference plane. (From H. A. Sedgwick, The geometry of spatial layout in pictorial representation, in M. A. Hagen (Ed.), *The perception of pictures* (Vol. 1), Academic Press, Inc., 1980. Reprinted with permission.)

(optical slant) or so that it was parallel to one wall of the experimental room (geographical slant); the surface was positioned so that these two settings were at a 45° angle to each other. They found that observers were able to make both kinds of judgment with considerable accuracy for either regularly or irregularly textured surfaces. Constant error was similar for the optical and geographical slant conditions, as was variable error with regular texture. Observers' variability in the irregular texture condition was somewhat higher for geographical than for optical slant, however, thus giving Gibson and Cornsweet some support for their contention that perceived geographical slant is derived from optical slant. The generality of their conclusion is questionable, however, because the only optical slant that they tested was perpendicular to the line of sight and so had a zero texture gradient in every direction.

Rosinski et al. (1978) tested the ability of children at several ages to perceive geographical slant when it was different from or the same as optical slant. They used linear perspective displays of parallel lines whose optical slant varied over a wide range and they arranged their displays so that they included no visual information for the reference plane. Their data show underestimation of geographical slant in all conditions, but the perception of geographical slant is approximately as good when geographical and optical slant differ by 45° as when they are the same. (Rosinski et al. conclude that geographical slant shows only about 50% compensation for deviation from optical slant, but this conclusion appears to overlook the underestimation that occurs in all conditions.)

On the basis of these limited data, it seems safe to conclude that observers can make estimates of either optical or geographical slant when requested to do so, but there is not yet sufficient evidence to indicate whether one kind of response is easier, more natural, or more accurate than the other.

Perrone (1980) has offered a model of slant underestimation based in part on the common experimental confounding of optical and geographical slant. Perrone proposes that observers choose one of two options for estimating slant depending on which one gives results closest to the plane of the aperture through which, or the screen on which, the surface is presented. In the first option they respond on the basis of optical slant, using the bottom of the aperture as their estimate of where their line of regard is perpendicular to the surface. In the second option they respond on the basis of geographical slant, using their line of regard to the bottom of the aperture as their estimate of the horizontal reference orientation. Unfortunately, Perrone's model is undercut by his analysis of optical slant, which leads him to conclude, incorrectly, that local texture or perspective information is not mathematically sufficient to specify optical slant so that the viewer is forced to use the edge of the aperture to estimate essential information otherwise unavailable. Because optical slant actually is specified locally, however, there is no need for the estimate on which Perrone's first option is based, and that section of his model is thus invalid.

Perrone's second option is analytically sound, making the point that if observers are trying to make judgments based on geographical slant, they are often doing so in circumstances in which visible information for the true location of the reference plane is lacking. Thus they might use some visible feature of the display, such as the edge of the viewing aperture, to estimate the direction of the horizontal. This section of the model by itself, however, does not provide a very good fit to the data that Perrone tests it on. It can account for the underestimation that occurs in the backward slant conditions of J. Gibson (1950b), but it predicts overestimation rather than underestimation in Gibson's forward slant condition. Thus it appears that mistaking the edge of the aperture for the direction of the horizontal reference plane is not the principal cause of slant underestimation, although such misjudgments may sometimes contribute to slant errors.

In a revised model of slant underestimation Perrone (1982) derives an equation for perceived slant based on Freeman's (1966b) linear perspective equation (see Section 3.2.2.4) but modified by a series of hypotheses about approximations and substitutions that observers might make in reduced information conditions. Although Perrone shows that his model provides a good match to some existing data on slant underestimation, the existing data do not adequately test the more striking predictions of his revised model, which is highly sensitive to shape and can predict either underestimation or overestimation depending on the proportions of the slanted figure.

3.2.4. Linear Perspective and Shape Perception. The shape of any arbitrarily chosen polygon is determined by linear perspective when the horizon of the surface in which the polygonal shape lies is specified in some way. If that horizon is specified, then the vanishing point of each of the polygon's edges is specified as the point where the edge's projection, if extended, intersects the horizon (see Figure 21.25). The angle between any two adjacent edges of the polygon then equals, as has already been indicated (see Section 3.2.2.1), the angle subtended at the point of observation between the vanishing points of the two edges. The angle so specified is either an internal angle of the polygon or its supplement depending on the orientation of the polygon. Specifying all the internal angles of a polygon, however, is not sufficient, except for the limiting case of the triangle, to determine the polygon's shape uniquely; it is also necessary to specify the relative proportions of the polygon's sides. The relative lengths of any two adjacent sides of a polygon are determined by the angular relations within the triangle formed by those two sides and the appropriate diagonal (see Figure 21.25). If a and b are the lengths of the two sides, and they are opposite to the two angles A and B, respectively, of the triangle, then by the law of sines,

$$\frac{a}{b} = \frac{\sin A}{\sin B} \quad . \tag{11}$$

Because the angles A and B of the triangle are specified similarly to the internal angles of the polygon, by optic array angles between vanishing points, the ratio a/b is also determined for every pair of adjacent sides. Thus the shape of the polygon is uniquely specified by linear perspective relations involving its horizon.

The horizon of a surface may itself be specified in a variety of ways, as has already been noted. In the particular case of textureless outline forms, which have been most often studied, two ways may be mentioned here. First, there is the special case of rectangles and other figures with pairs of parallel sides. Under the constraint, or assumption, that these pairs of sides are parallel, the vanishing points of the sides are determined by the intersection of their projections, when extended, and the horizon of the surface is then specified as the projective line passing through the vanishing points. Second, there is the more general case in which the sides of the polygon either are not parallel or at least cannot be assumed to be so. In this case the horizon of the polygon may still be specified if the polygon is constrained, or assumed, to be lying on a more extended surface

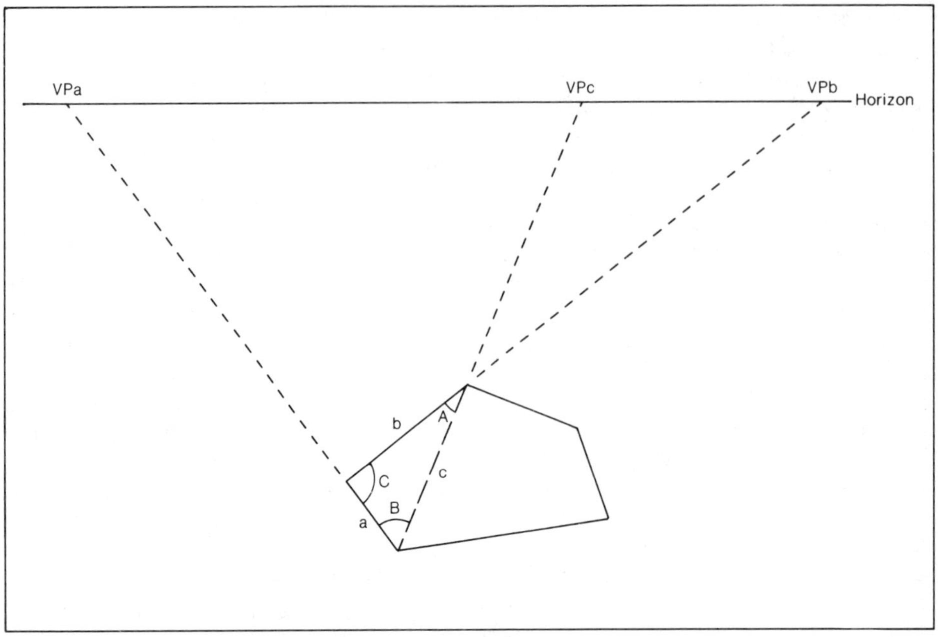

Figure 21.25. Shape specification from perspective structure. The shape of a polygon lying on a surface is geometrically determined when the horizon of the surface is specified. A polygon's shape is determined by the relative lengths of all its sides and by the angles between them. The angle *C* between any two adjacent sides *a* and *b* is equal to the visual angle (or its supplement) subtended at the point of observation between the vanishing points VP_a and VP_b of the two sides. Implicit diagonals, such as *c*, divide the polygon into traingles, and the ratio of any two adjacent sides *a* and *b* is then equal to sin *A*/sin*B*, where *A* and *B* are the angles formed between the sides and their diagonal.

whose horizon is determined in some way; an arbitrarily chosen polygon lying on the ground or on a rectangulary shaped table would be an example of this case (see, for instance, Lappin & Preble, 1975).

The specification of the shape of a surface by linear perspective does not depend upon the registration of the surface's slant. Nevertheless, the specification of shape by linear perspective is related to the specification of slant by linear perspective in the sense that each depends upon determining the horizon of the surface, so that constant error or variability in locating the horizon would produce coordinated errors in shape and slant.

There is considerable evidence that linear perspective influences human shape perception in both the special and the general cases discussed above. The special case of the outline form of an isolated, monocularly viewed rectangle offers only the minimum amount of perspective information necessary for specifying shape, yet some studies report that significant shape constancy can be obtained with this display (Campione, 1977; Epstein & Hatfield, 1978b). Nevertheless, shape responses in this situation can be highly variable, as has already been noted (see Section 2.3.3), and probably are highly susceptible to influence by nuances of the instructions and the experimental situation (Beck & Gibson, 1955).

A variety of evidence pertains to the more general case of an arbitrarily shaped figure lying on a more extended background. When a figure is viewed monocularly against a background there is a strong perceptual tendency to see the figure as lying on the background even when it is actually slanted away from the background (Beck & Gibson, 1955; Epstein et al., 1962). A number of studies have shown that, when there is perspective information available concerning the background of a figure but not concerning the figure per se, the objective shape of the figure can be responded to with fair accuracy (Lappin & Preble, 1975; Olson et al., 1976; Wallach & Moore, 1962; see Section 2.3.2 and Section 2.3.3 for discussions of these studies). Deregowski (1976a, 1976b) has referred to this effect as "implicit shape constancy." Kaess and Deregowski (1980) showed that the effect is not simply due to the relational perception of a figure embedded within a frame.

Although it is theoretically possible that the effects of linear perspective on perceived shape could be mediated by its effects on perceived slant, the weakness of the empirically demonstrated perceptual coupling between shape and slant (see Section 2.3.6) suggests that linear perspective affects perceived shape directly.

3.2.5. Linear Perspective and Distance Perception. If the horizon of a surface is specified in the optic array, the egocentric distance of any location on the surface is also specified, to within a scale factor. If d is the egocentric distance along the surface of a given location, and if A is the angular distance of that location from the horizon of the surface, then

$$d = h \operatorname{ctn} A \quad , \tag{12}$$

where h is the perpendicular distance from the eye to the surface. Relative egocentric distances are specified independently of the scale factor h. If d_1 and d_2 are two such distances and if A_1 and A_2 are their respective angular distances from the horizon (see Figure 21.26), then

$$\frac{d_1}{d_2} = \frac{\operatorname{ctn} A_1}{\operatorname{ctn} A_2} \quad . \tag{13}$$

Relations specifying range, that is, distance in a line from the eye to the location rather than along the ground, can be obtained simply by substituting the cosecant for the cotangent in the above relations. If the distances are fairly large relative to the scale factor, a close approximation to the relative distance relation is given by

$$\frac{d_1}{d_2} \approx \frac{A_2}{A_1} \quad . \tag{14}$$

As with texture, linear perspective can also specify relative distance by a simple generalization of the principle that the relative angular extents of physically identical objects are inversely related to their relative distances (see Section 2.2.8). Consider, for example, the converging projections of two edges that are actually parallel; the angular separations, S_1 and S_2, between the edges at two locations are inversely proportional to the ranges, r_1 and r_2, of the locations:

$$\frac{r_1}{r_2} \approx \frac{S_2}{S_1} \quad . \tag{15}$$

Angular separation is here taken in a direction parallel to the horizon of the surface in which the edges lie.

The use of linear perspective has long been recognized as an effective technique for representing depth in pictures. Efforts to empirically verify the influence of linear perspective on perceived distance have manipulated linear perspective in two ways: (1) by using photographic or pictorial stimuli and varying perspective by varying the distance of the point of observation, and (2) by building three-dimensional displays with nonparallel surfaces.

O. Smith, Smith, and Hubbard (1958) asked observers to estimate the relative length of two corridors whose images were shown on adjacent rear projection screens. Actually both images were of the same corridor, but whereas one of the images stayed the same fron trial to trial, five different projection distances were used for the other image, thus producing linear perspective specific to five different corridor lengths. Estimated length ratios varied in approximately the way that reliance on linear perspective would predict. Smith et al. also found that line drawings, either detailed or containing only the edges essential to the perspective view of the corridor, elicited estimates very similar to those elicited by a photograph of the corridor, thus supporting the conclusion that the linear perspective information in the images was primarily responsible for the perception of distance. Linear perspective is of course not the only source of information for depth in pictures, a point demonstrated by Topper and Simpson (1981), who showed that depth was still seen in a medieval Italian painting containing "inverse perspective," that is, depictions of receding parallel edges by lines that diverged somewhat rather than converging.

The approach of building displays with nonparallel surfaces was taken by Blessing, Landauer, and Coltheart (1967), who constructed two corridors, both 450 cm long, but one with surfaces that actually converged so as to present the same projection as a parallel-surface corridor 675 cm long and the other with surfaces that actually diverged so as to present the same projection as a parallel-surface corridor 225 cm long. Observers viewed each of these corridors monocularly through a small peephole at one end and matched the distance of a rectangle located at the end of each corridor by adjusting the distance of another rectangle in a binocularly viewed, parallel-surface corridor. The matched distances for the two corridors were, on the average, 459 and 332 cm. Thus distortions in linear perspective did pro-

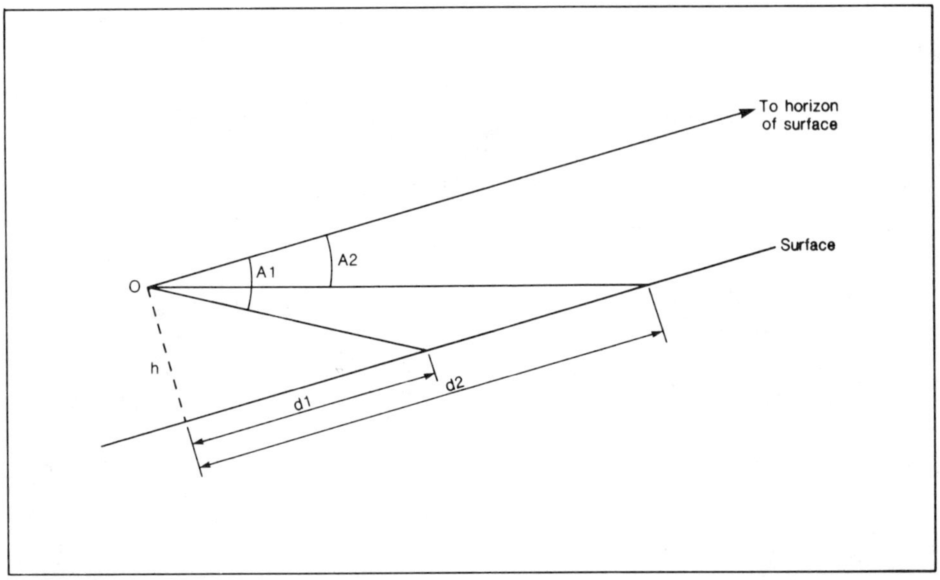

Figure 21.26. Distance specification from perspective structure. The egocentric distance d_1 of a location on a surface is equal to h ctn A, where h is the perpendicular distance from the point of observation O to the surface and A_1 is the visual angle subtended between that location and the horizon of the surface. The ratio of two distances d_1 and d_2 is equal to ctn A_1/ctn A_2, which in turn is closely approximated by A_2/A_1 when d_1 and d_2 are large relative to h. (From H. A. Sedgwick, *The visible horizon: A potential source of visual information for the perception of size and distance*, Unpublished doctoral dissertation, Cornell University, 1973. Reprinted with permission.)

duce changes in perceived distance, although the changes were not as great as would have been predicted from the perspective information. Other studies, using similar displays, have also found significant effects of linear perspective on distance judgments (Thompson, Valenti, & Schiffman, 1978; Vogel & Teghtsoonian, 1972).

3.2.6. Linear Perspective and Size Perception. As with distance, linear perspective specifies size in two different ways. If the horizon of a surface is specified in the optic array, then the frontal size of any object in contact with the surface is also specified, to within a scale factor. This scale factor is the perpendicular distance, h, from the eye to the surface. The line of sight from the eye to the surface's horizon is parallel to the surface and so is at a constant distance h from the surface. Thus the frontal plane of every object on the surface is projectively intersected by the horizon at a height h above the surface; this is true independently of the object's distance from the observer. The horizon of the surface thus provides a constant scale, whose unit is h, across the entire surface. From this observation we can derive the following ratio, as seen in Figure 21.27:

$$\frac{v}{h} = \left(\frac{\tan E + \tan F}{\tan F}\right), \qquad (16)$$

which I refer to as the *horizon-ratio relation* (Sedgwick, 1973, 1980, 1983). The ratio specifies the height, v, perpendicular to the surface, of every object in contact with the surface, relative to the scale unit, h. E and F are the optic array angles subtended between the horizon of the surface and the top and bottom, respectively, of the object. For objects that are small relative to their distance from the point of observation this ratio can be approximated by

$$\frac{v}{h} \approx \frac{V}{F}, \qquad (17)$$

where $V = E + F$.

The ratio of the heights, v_1 and v_2, perpendicular to the surface, of two objects in contact with the surface is specified independently of the scale factor h:

$$\frac{v_1}{v_2} \approx \frac{V_1/F_1}{V_2/F_2}. \qquad (18)$$

When parallel receding edges are present on the surface, linear perspective can also specify relative size in the same way that units of surface texture do, by providing an explicit constant scale factor. Here it is the angular separation between the edges' projections that provides this scale factor.

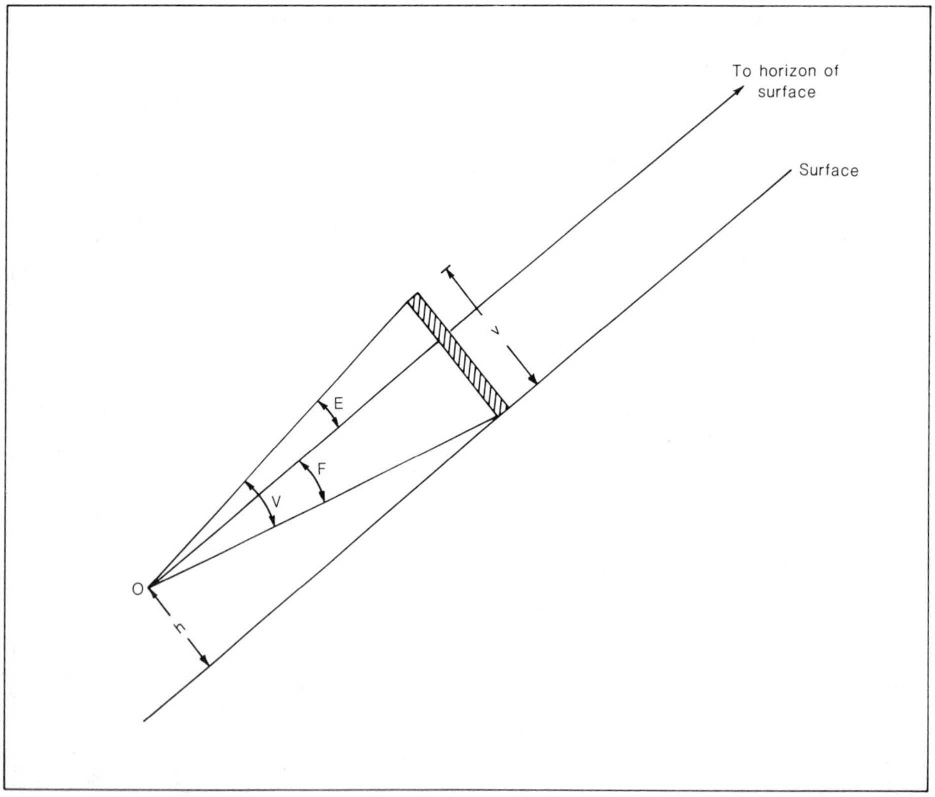

Figure 21.27. The horizon-ratio relation. The perpendicular height (v) of an object above a surface on which it is resting is geometrically specified, relative to the perpendicular height (h) of the point of observation (O) above the surface, by the trigonometric equation $v/h = (\tan E + \tan F)/\tan F$, where E and F are the angles in the optic array subtended between the horizon of the surface and the top and bottom, respectively, of the object. When E and F are fairly small, this relation is closely approximated by the simple horizon-ratio relation: $v/h \approx V/F$. (From H. A. Sedgwick, *The visible horizon: A potential source of visual information for the perception of size and distance*, Unpublished doctoral dissertation, Cornell University, 1973. Reprinted with permission.)

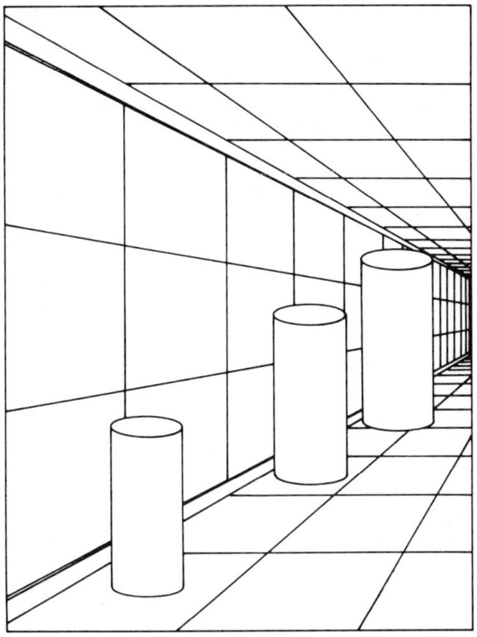

Figure 21.28. The corridor illusion. The cylinders in this perspective drawing of a corridor are depicted as being of increasing size and distance, but on the page they are all identical. Even when observers attempt to estimate the two-dimensional relative sizes of the cylinders, they tend to see the depicted larger cylinder as actually being larger. (From J. J. Gibson, *The perception of the visual world*, Copyright 1950, renewed 1977 by Houghton Mifflin Company. Reprinted with permission.)

An illustration of the effect of linear perspective on the perception of size is given by the "corridor illusion" (J. Gibson, 1950a, p. 182; see Figure 21.28). In this two-dimensional line drawing, linear perspective is used to depict two cylinders located at different distances in a long corridor; the more distant cylinder is drawn to be just enough larger than the nearer cylinder so that their projections on the paper are the same size. The perception of the more distant cylinder as being larger, however, is so compelling that it tends to persist even when observers attempt to judge the relative projective sizes of the cylinders rather than their relative depicted sizes. Richards and Miller (1971), after correcting for the constant errors that occured in comparing the sizes of two cylinders without the presence of the perspective drawing of the corridor, found that the size of the corridor illusion (measured by how much taller the near cylinder had to be in order to look equal in height to the far cylinder) was about 17% when the picture was presented for only 50 msec and was reduced in magnitude by about one-third when the picture was left on for a longer time and observers were allowed to scan it. Richards and Miller also found that the average size of the illusion was unaffected when the picture was turned upside-down. This study, as well as several other studies suggesting the influence on size perception of linear perspective in pictorial displays (Boring, 1964; Hayes & King, 1967; Wilcox & Teghtsoonian, 1971), uses only one linear perspective display and so does not examine the effect on size perception of varying the linear perspective.

In studies using corridors with nonparallel sides to create distorted linear perspective, several researchers (Blessing et al., 1967; Vogel & Teghtsoonian, 1972) have found corresponding distortions in perceived size. Thompson et al. (1978) failed in a similar study to find more than a minor effect of distorted linear perspective on perceived size. The results of this study are somewhat open to question, however, in that good size constancy was found in all conditions, suggesting that some uncontrolled information for veridical size perception was available to the observers. McDermott (1969) also failed to find an appreciable effect of linear perspective on perceived size in a study in which size matches were made of a luminous triangle viewed in the dark with linear perspective being provided by luminous lines that gave the appearance of a receding railroad track. The reason for this failure may be that the comparison triangle was presented binocularly in a separate viewing space that lacked any perspective information so that the observers, if they were unable to determine the magnitude of any scale factor in the perspective display, would have had no basis, in terms of perspective information, for matching the comparison triangle to the standard.

Overall, there is considerable evidence that linear perspective is used in the perception of size, but little work has been done to explore the relations between variables of linear perspective and their effects on perceived size.

3.3. Size and Distance over the Ground

The discussion of texture and perspective information for size and distance in this section has been couched in terms of the sizes and distances of objects in contact with surfaces of arbitrary extent and orientation. Thus the types of information discussed would be available, in principle, just as much for objects located on walls, ceilings, or inclines as for objects located on horizontal surfaces such a floor or an out-of-doors ground plane. Virtually all the experimental work done in this area, however, has been restricted to the perception of the size and distance of objects resting on a horizontal surface of support. This case deserves special attention both because of its ecological importance to terrestrial animals such as humans and because some forms of information for size and distance are available only in this case.

The preceding sections (3.2.5 and 3.2.6) have described perspective relations between the implicit horizon of a surface and the distance and size of objects touching the surface. There are two special ways that the location in the optic array of a surface's horizon can be specified when that surface is the ground plane. First, for any horizontal surface, such as the ground plane, the horizon of the surface is coincident with eye level, which can be registered nonvisually, at least approximately, by the vestibular system (see Howard, Chapter 11). Second, for a sufficiently extended ground plane, the projection of the far boundary of the plane provides a visible line in the optic array that can be taken as an approximation of the true horizon of the ground surface. These two possibilities are discussed in the following two sections.

3.3.1. Height in the Visual Field. For an observer positioned above a horzontal ground surface, the horizon of the ground is at eye level and all locations on the ground are projected into the lower half of the optic array, with their height in the array increasing as their distance from the observer increases. This geometric relation between distance and height in the optic array, also referred to as *height in the visual field* and as *slope of regard* (Wallach & O'Leary, 1982), is of course present even if the surface of the ground is not itself visible. This is the basis for the informal observation that when two objects are present in an empty visual field the higher object tends to appear farther away (J. Gibson, 1950a, p. 180). Strictly speaking, the geometry of the situation suggests that this effect should be observed only for locations below eye level. If objects above eye level are in contact with a horizontal surface, the surface would be a ceiling, or perhaps a cloudy sky, so that the higher object in the visual field would be closer to the observer.

Epstein (1966) investigated the effect on perceived distance of height in the visual field by asking observers to estimate the depth between two vertically separated points of light seen in darkness. The lights were positioned approximately at eye level and were viewed with three different backgrounds: a perspective drawing of a receding rectangular grid, a perspective drawing giving just the outline of the receding rectangular surface, and a blank field. For both the outline perspective and the grid perspective, the higher object was seen as significantly farther away, and this reported depth increased as the vertical interval between the lights increased; turning the drawings upside down in a subsequent experiment so that they represented a ceiling rather than a floor resulted in a reversal in the reported depth. For the blank field, however, the differences in depth, although consistently showing the higher object to be farther, were not statistically significant and did not increase as the vertical interval between the lights increased. Rather similar results were found by Dunn, Gray, and Thompson (1965) in several experiments, although the depth differences that they obtained with a blank background did reach significance under the conditions of one of their experiments. Dunn (1969) also found significant depth between vertically separated objects seen in a blank field, although he appears to have misinterpreted the direction of the depth shown in his results.

In the above studies, differences in perceived depth of vertically separated objects seen against a blank field were always in the direction of the higher object being seen as farther, even when the objects were located substantially above eye level. Bugelski (1967), however, reported that when one light was presented at eye level and a second light was presented 2° above it, the higher light was seen as closer; this effect dissipated as the vertical interval was made larger.

It seems that, as Epstein (1966) suggests, the effect on perceived depth of height in the field alone, that is, with a blank background, is variable and can be strongly influenced by the observer's assumptions about the layout of the unseen background. Even a minimal background, such as Epstein's (1966) trapezoidal outline of a receding surface, can make the effect of height in the field much stronger and more reliable.

The relative sizes of objects seen against a blank background are also specified by their heights in the field, if it can be assumed that they are resting on the same horizontal ground plane. Referring to the horizon-ratio relation (see Section 3.2.6) and using nonvisually registered eye level to specify the horizon of the ground plane, the scale factor for each object is given by the angular distance of the base of that object below eye level; the absolute size of each object is also specified if the height of the point of observation above the ground plane is available. Several studies have reported results suggesting that height in the field alone can influence the perception of both relative and absolute size (O. Smith, 1958; Wallach & O'Leary, 1982; Weinstein, 1957).

An inherent limitation in the specification of size and distance of objects by their height in the field is the accuracy with which eye level can be registered. When eye level must be registered nonvisually, evidence suggests that there is both a constant error of several degrees and a standard deviation of the same magnitude (Howard & Templeton, 1966, pp. 183–186; MacDougall, 1903). As these errors become large relative to the scale factor determined by the angular separation between the base of the object and the horizon, the specification of size and distance by height in the field would have to become highly unreliable. This would occur as the distance, d, of the object becomes large relative to the height, h, of the point of observation above the ground. For example, when the ratio d/h is 10, the scale factor is 5.7°, and when d/h is 100, the scale factor is 0.57°, which is quite small relative to the errors in the registration of eye level. These considerations suggest that size matches made in studies such as those of Weinstein (1957) and O. Smith (1958), in which the farther object is at a large distance from the observer, may be made on some basis other than height in the field (one possible artifact, common to the design of both experiments, is suggested by Weinstein).

3.3.2. The Terrestrial Horizon. An extended ground surface, such as an open field, has a visible horizon formed by the far boundary of the surface. The greater the distance of this "terrestrial horizon," the more closely it approximates the true horizon of the surface. For example, if d/h, the ratio of its distance d to the height h of the point of observation, is 1,000, then the angular separation between the true horizon and the terrestrial horizon is only 0.057°. In such a situation, the terrestrial horizon offers a much more accurate indication of the ground's horizon than does the nonvisually registered eye level. It seems plausible that the terrestrial horizon may be used in this way in judgments of size and distance at large distances over the ground; other potential sources of information, such as texture or height in the field, may be ineffectual at such distances (Sedgwick, 1973, 1983). Langwiesche-Brandt (1944, pp. 267–277, 295–302) offers a detailed discussion of how airplane pilots can use the terrestrial horizon in estimating the heights and positions of objects on the ground during approach and landing.

Because a line of sight to a terrestrial horizon converges toward the ground rather than running parallel to it, the scale factor in the horizon-ratio relation (see Section 3.2.6) would be increasingly underestimated with increasing distance if the terrestrial horizon were used in that relation as an approximation to the true horizon (see Figure 21.29 and Sedgwick, 1973). This in turn would lead to an increasing overestimation of size with increasing distance, a result that has been found with some consistency in research on the perception of size at large distances over an open ground (J. Gibson, 1950a, p. 186; Gilinsky, 1955a; Joynson et al., 1965; W. Smith, 1953). Sedgwick (1973), in a size comparison task using pictorial displays of rectangular objects resting on an extended ground plane, found that size overconstancy could be increased by lowering the visible horizon of the ground (i.e., by decreasing the depicted distance, b, in Figure 21.29, to the terrestrial horizon) while leaving information from surface texture and height in the field unchanged.

The effect of a visible terrestrial horizon on size perception in pictorial displays has also been noted by Rock, Shallo, and Schwartz (1978). Rock et al. also showed that in very simplified pictorial displays a horizontal line must be recognized as representing the terrestrial horizon if it is to have an effect on size perception.

4. MOTION-PRODUCED INFORMATION FOR SPATIAL LAYOUT

As has often been pointed out (e.g., J. Gibson, 1968; Chapter 17 by Mack in this Handbook), not all motion of images on the retina gives rise to the perception of motion. In particular, as an observer moves through the environment, the projection of the environment in the optic array undergoes a complex, con-

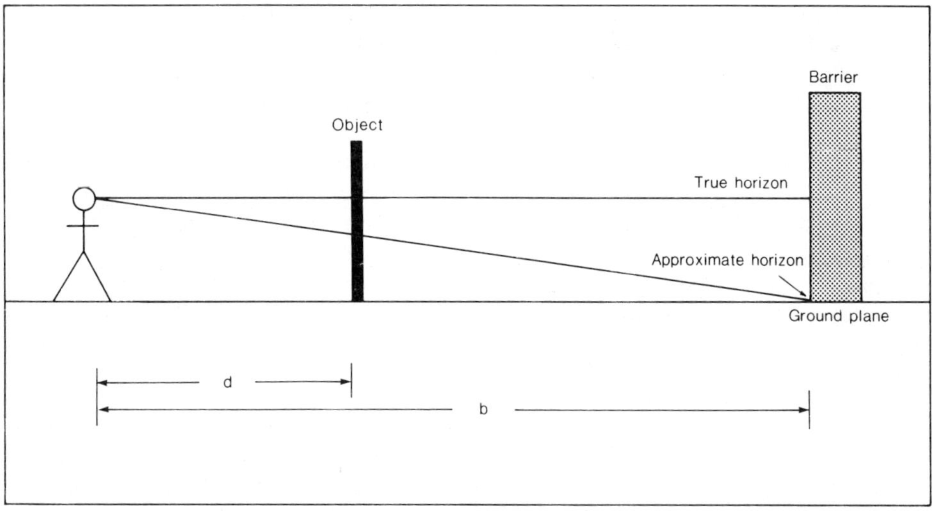

Figure 21.29. Reliance on a terrestrial horizon predicts overconstancy of size. A line of sight to the terrestrial horizon, which is a visible approximation to the true horizon, comes closer to the ground plane with increasing distance from the observer. Thus the horizon-ratio relation specifies sizes that are too large. This effect increases with distance, thus predicting overconstancy. If v' is the height specified by the horizon-ratio relation and v is the true height, then $v'/v = b/(b-d)$, where d is the distance to the object and b is the distance to the terrestrial horizon. (From H. A. Sedgwick, *The visible horizon: A potential source of visual information for the perception of size and distance*, Unpublished doctoral dissertation, Cornell University, 1973. Reprinted with permission.)

tinuing transformation arising from the continually shifting viewpoint from which it is being viewed. Projected surfaces and parts of surfaces move relative to one another; the projected shapes of surfaces and objects change; and some surfaces come into view while others go out of sight. All these changes in the optic array, as well as the movements of the eye in viewing them, produce motions on the retina, yet the observer's perception is ordinarily of a stationary, unchanging environment. Rather than giving rise to the perception of a shifting, distorting environment, these optic array transformations ordinarily contribute concomitantly to the perception of the observer's path of movement and to the perception of the fixed spatial layout of the environment (J. Gibson, 1950a, p. 118). The perception of self-motion is considered elsewhere in this Handbook (see Chapter 18 by Howard and Chapter 19 by Regan, Kaufman, & Lincoln). This chapter only addresses the question of how motion-produced changes in the optic array can contribute to the perception of spatial layout.

Helmholtz (1910/1962, pp. 295–297) appears to have been the first to discuss motion-produced contributions to the perception of spatial layout. He provides a vivid description of the efficacy of this source of information, but his empirical investigations in this area were limited to a few informal observations. Although a number of empirical investigations, to be discussed below, were carried out prior to the middle of this century, it was not until then that the contribution of motion to the perception of spatial layout came into prominence, being made a cornerstone in the theories of both J. Gibson (1950a, 1966, 1979) and Johansson (1964, 1978).

In the sections that follow, several different aspects of the motion-produced contribution to the perception of spatial layout will be considered (also see Hochberg, Chapter 22).

4.1. Motion Parallax

4.1.1. Absolute Motion Parallax. Motion parallax is usually taken to refer to the effects that movements of an observer have on the projective relations among objects in the visual field. It is helpful in approaching this subject, however, to first consider what happens to the projection of a single object when an observer is moving relative to it. This has been referred to as *absolute motion parallax* (Gogel & Tietz, 1973). In this situation, potential information for the absolute distance of the object from the observer would be available if the observer were able to register both the translatory component of the eye's movement relative to the object and the visual direction of the object. For a given translation, t, of the point of observation, the greater the distance of the object, the smaller the angular change in its visual direction will be. If D is the angular direction, relative to the direction of translation, and d is the distance of the object at the beginning of the observer's movement, and if D' and d' are its angular direction and distance at the end of the observer's movement, then

$$d = t\frac{\sin D'}{\sin (D' - D)}$$

and

$$d' = t\frac{\sin D}{\sin (D' - D)} \quad . \tag{19}$$

A special case of motion parallax often considered arises when the object is directly in front of the observer and the motion parallax is produced by lateral movements of the observer's head. Here, both D and D' are close to 90°, so that sin D and sin D' are both approximately equal to 1. Also, $(D' - D)$ is generally small in this situation unless the object is very close to the observer. Thus $\sin (D' - D)$ is closely approximated by $(D' - D)$, expressed in radians. Taking these approximations into account and letting C stand for $(D' - D)$, the change in angular direction, results in the simpler relation

$$d \approx \frac{t}{C} \, . \tag{20}$$

Equation (20) can be differentiated to derive an expression relating v, the linear velocity of the observer's translation, to w, the angular velocity of the object's change in angular direction:

$$d \approx \frac{v}{w}. \tag{21}$$

When only a single object is visible, information concerning v and w would have to come from nonvisual, proprioceptive sources. How accurately observers are actually able to perceive distance when only this information is available is still somewhat open to question. Eriksson (1972a) asked observers to estimate the distances of small luminous squares viewed monocularly in total darkness. Observers moved their heads back and forth through a distance of about 5.5 cm while making their judgments. The squares were presented one at a time, and their sizes varied with their distances so that they all subtended the same visual angle. As the actual distance of the squares was increased from 200 to 400 cm, their estimated distance increased from 631 to 810 cm, suggesting that observers were able to make some use of the absolute motion parallax information. There are several reasons, however, to question the contribution that the motion parallax of a single object makes to distance perception. First, variability of observers' judgments was quite high, ranging from standard deviations of 600 cm at the 200 cm distance to 820 cm at the 400 cm distance. Also, although some observers reported that they were basing their estimates on vague, immediate impressions of depth, others reported that they were cognitively estimating distance on the basis of the perceived side to side movement of the squares. Finally, because the squares were presented sequentially at different distances, it is quite likely that the observers' estimates were influenced by the relative movements of the squares, as perceived across trials, rather than being based entirely on the absolute motion of the single square visible on each trial.

A further indication that absolute parallax has at most a weak influence on perceived distance is provided in a study by Gogel and Tietz (1973). They found that the specific distance tendency (see Section 2.2.5.1), which they describe as a tendency to localize an object at a distance of about 2 m in the absence of information concerning the object's actual distance, occurs even in the presence of the absolute motion parallax produced by lateral head movements. They conclude that absolute motion parallax can have only a weak influence on perceived distance because it is not enough to overcome the specific distance tendency. In another study, however, Gogel and Tietz (1979) concluded that absolute motion parallax was almost as effective as oculomotor information in specifying distance.

Johansson (1973) reported more positive evidence concerning the use of motion parallax information to perceive absolute distance. His experimental apparatus allowed observers to switch back and forth between binocular viewing of a fully lit laboratory containing an adjustable distance indicator and monocular viewing of a dark tunnel containing only four lights forming a square that subtended 10° of visual angle and slanted back 60° from the frontal plane. A semitransparent mirror caused these two scenes, only one of which was visible at a time, to appear to occupy the same space. The observers' task was to move their heads back and forth while viewing the square in the dark and then to switch to the lighted environment and adjust the distance indicator to the perceived distance of the square. The head movements allowed during the monocular viewing were quite small, about 1 cm, and during the binocular viewing head movements were entirely prevented by a bite bar.

Observers were quite successful at Johansson's distance matching task. Their average settings ranged from 40 cm when the square was at 30 cm to 121 cm when the square was at 120 cm. The variability of their settings was also relatively low, ranging from standard deviations of 6.7 cm at the nearest distance to 35.2 cm at the farthest distance. Why Johansson obtained results so much better than those mentioned above is not entirely clear, but some differences from the other studies may be mentioned. Johansson's stimuli were presented at a nearer range of distances than Eriksson's, so that although Eriksson had a control condition that showed accommodation alone to be ineffectual in his study, accommodation may have contributed somewhat to Johansson's results. Secondly, observers' ability to quickly and repeatedly switch back and forth between the monocular and the binocular scenes and to match distances rather than verbally estimating them undoubtedly increased the sensitivity of Johansson's measures. Finally, the large slanted square that Johansson used as his stimulus underwent a perspective transformation when the observer's head moved. As Johansson suggests, this introduces additional potential information that may have enhanced the effect of the motion parallax (see Gogel & Tietz, 1980). Thus Johansson's results were not intended to be taken, and cannot be taken, to indicate the effectiveness of absolute motion parallax alone in influencing distance perception.

Positive evidence for an effect of absolute motion parallax on distance perception was found by Wallach and O'Leary (1979) using an adaptation paradigm. Their observers spent 20 min watching a television broadcast in otherwise total darkness while wearing spectacles that required their eyes to converge and accommodate to approximately half the actual distance (60 cm) of the screen. During this time the observers were turning their heads back and forth continuously through an angle of about 40°. Following this adaptation period, the observers made estimates of the sizes and distances of stimuli viewed under conditions such that only information from convergence and accommodation was available. Comparison with preadaptation measures showed a significant adaptive change, which Wallach and O'Leary attribute to the influence of the motion parallax information, available during the adaptation period, on the interpretation of the oculomotor information. Their paradigm, however, does not permit a quantitative estimate of the efficacy of the motion parallax information in specifying distance.

Overall, it appears that absolute motion parallax can exert some influence on distance perception, but it is most effective at very close distances (i.e., less than 1 m) and when combined with other information such as accommodation and perspective transformations.

There is potential information for the size of objects, as well as their distance, from absolute motion parallax. For the simple case of small movements in a direction perpendicular to the direction of the object, for which the specification of distance is given by Eq. (21), the physical extent, s, of the object is approximately equal to the angular extent, S, expressed in radians, multiplied by the distance, d. Substituting into this relation the expression for distance given in Eq. (21) gives

$$s \approx S\frac{v}{w}, \tag{22}$$

where v is the linear velocity of the observer and w is the angular velocity of the object. Although there is little empirical evidence concerning observers' ability to use this potential information, there is some evidence concerning the ability to perceive relative size on the basis of relative motion parallax, as will be discussed in the next section.

4.1.2. Relative Motion Parallax. When two or more objects are at different distances from the observer, their projections in the optic array move relative to each other when the observer moves. This projective relative motion is referred to as *relative motion parallax* (Gogel & Tietz, 1973) or simply as *motion parallax.* The existence of relative motion parallax follows from the description of absolute motion parallax given above (see Section 4.1.1). Because the change in an object's angular direction that occurs with movement of the observer decreases as the distance of the object increases, it follows that the angular directions of two objects at different distances change at different rates and so change relative to each other. Considering the simple case in which two objects are approximately straight ahead, at distances d_1 and d_2, and their projections are moving with angular velocities of w_1 and w_2, respectively, as the observer moves, it can be seen from Eq. (21) that

$$\frac{d_1}{d_2} \approx \frac{w_2}{w_1} \quad . \tag{23}$$

Thus if the relative angular velocities of two objects can be detected, motion parallax can specify their relative distances independently of the velocity of the observer's movement.

How good are observers at making use of this information? Eriksson (1972a) found that observers were quite accurate at judging which of two objects was nearer on the basis of motion parallax produced by head movements. When motion parallax was produced by walking 1–2 m back and forth, the correct order in depth of a series of objects could be perceived even when their sizes and locations were arranged so that both their relative angular extents (see Section 2.2.8) and their heights in the visual field (see Section 3.3.1) specified the reverse order in depth (Eriksson, 1974). The smaller amount of motion parallax produced by head movements alone, however, was not enough to overcome conflicting information from relative angular extent and height in the field (Eriksson, 1972b).

Ferris (1972) asked observers to make estimates of the distance from themselves to targets seen one at a time at distances ranging from 1.22 to 4.57 m. A wall was visible behind the targets at a distance of 5.92 m from the observers. Observers viewed the targets monocularly and produced motion parallax by rotating their heads back and forth. Ferris calculated that the power-function exponent relating judged distance to physical distance was 0.80 when the wall was strongly textured and was 0.85 when the wall was only lightly textured, an insignificant difference. Following ten trials on which feedback was given, these power-function exponents increased to 0.99 and 0.93, respectively, and this difference was statistically significant. Ferris points out, however, that questioning revealed the observers' improvements in performance following training to be based largely on conscious adjustments rather than on changes in perceived distance.

As with relative distances, the relative physical sizes, s_1 and s_2, of two objects are specified by motion parallax if their angular velocities, w_1 and w_2, can be detected. From Eq. (22) it can be seen that

$$\frac{s_1}{s_2} \approx \left(\frac{S_1}{S_2}\right)\left(\frac{w_2}{w_1}\right) , \tag{24}$$

where S_1 and S_2 are the angular extents of the two objects.

Hell (1978) asked observers to adjust the width of a comparison object to match the width of a standard object located at a closer distance. Both objects were viewed monocularly through a slot that hid their tops and bottoms; a textured background was visible behind them. When their heads were stationary, observers came quite close to making visual angle matches, but when they were moving their heads back and forth they made matches whose Brunswik ratios (see Section 2.1.2) were, at best, around 0.50. Hell found that for quite low velocities of head movement (e.g., 3 $\text{cm}\cdot\text{sec}^{-1}$) and for quite small back and forth head movements (e.g., 1.5 cm) observers were somewhat closer to matching visual angle, but as velocity and extent of head movements were increased the size matches quickly asymptoted about halfway between angular and physical extent. Hell and Freeman (1977) found that increasing the angular separation between the two objects decreased the effects of motion parallax somewhat. They also found that the presence of the background texture slightly interfered with the effects of relative motion parallax.

4.1.3. Simulated Motion Parallax. Much research that has addressed itself to questions concerning motion parallax has done so by creating situations in which the point of observation remains stationary but the entire display moves back and forth, thus simulating the optical effects of lateral head movements. This has been done partly for reasons of convenience—it is sometimes easier to simulate movement of the display than to allow the head to move—and partly to eliminate questions about the role of proprioceptive information concerning head movements.

C. Graham, Baker, Hecht, and Lloyd (1948) attempted to measure monocular motion parallax thresholds for depth with an apparatus in which two needles, one above the other and separated in depth, moved back and forth together. Their observers' task was to adjust one of the needles until both were at the same distance. The observers were able to perform this task with high accuracy and low variability, but because it could be done by simply nulling the relative motion between the two needles, the results give little information about the use of motion parallax in depth perception.

Dees (1966) found that training resulted in quite accurate estimates of the distance of individual objects seen with simulated motion parallax against a fixed background, but because his observers made many repetitions of the same set of distance estimates and were given the correct answer after each trial, these results could be due to the conscious estimation of the amount of relative motion rather than to the accurate perception of distance.

E. Gibson, Gibson, Smith, and Flock (1959) tested the effects of suprathreshold differential motion by projecting the shadows of two parallel, randomly textured panes of glass onto a rear projection screen. When the two panes of glass were stationary, observers saw a single textured surface. When the two panes were translated laterally, however, observers immediately saw the projection as the shadows of two surfaces separated in depth. The amount and direction of the depth separation were highly ambiguous, though. Experiments by Mace and Shaw (1974) and by McConkie and Farber (1979) using computer-generated displays have also shown that observers have a strong tendency to see a separation in depth between two textured fields that are superimposed and moving in different directions or with different speeds. As with the results obtained by E. Gibson et al. (1959), the amount and direction of the depth separation is ambiguous.

4.2. Motion Perspective

Movement of an observer relative to a textured surface produces gradients of motion in the optic array. J. Gibson (1950a, p. 124) suggested that such gradients of optical flow from a surface be given the name *motion perspective* to distinguish them from the relative optical motions of two isolated objects in space that the term motion parallax usually refers to.

A mathematical description of the flow field produced by linear motion relative to a flat surface was given by J. Gibson, Olum, and Rosenblatt (1955). The analysis was extended to include curved paths of motion by Gordon (1965, 1966). A more general analysis that included curved surfaces was given by Longuet-Higgins and Prazdny (1980, 1981), who also considered the visual system's problem of separating the flow field produced by motion of the point of observation from the retinal flow field produced by rotation of the eye (also see Clocksin, 1980; Koenderink & van Doorn, 1976; Prazdny, 1980). As Gibson (1950a, 1958) pointed out, and as these later analyses confirmed, motion perspective carries potential information for the path of motion of the observer as well as for the spatial layout of the stationary surfaces past which the observer is moving. As noted above, this potential information for self-motion and observers' ability to make use of it are discussed in Howard, Chapter 18, and in Regan, Kaufman, and Lincoln, Chapter 19. A hypothetical physiological mechanism for processing optical flow fields has been offered by Nakayama and Loomis (1974).

J. Gibson (1950a, p. 129) hypothesized that "an artificially produced gradient of point-motions on the retina, in isolation from other gradients, will yield an observer the impression of continuous distance on a surface" and that variations in the gradient will "produce variations in the slant of the surface." In a first attempt to produce such a gradient, J. Gibson and Carel (1952) used a rotating upright disk with luminous radial line segments that, when seen through a screen with narrow horizontal slits cut into it, created a triangular field with a gradient of moving points. This motion gradient was not the same, however, as that which would be produced by a slanted flat surface moving relative to the observer, and it failed to produce a reliable perception of a slanted surface. E. Gibson et al. (1959) used a point source of light to project onto a rear projection screen the shadow of a paint-splattered transparent surface slanted back 45° from the vertical. Observers viewing the projection of this surface when it was stationary did not report seeing a slanted surface, but when the surface was translated back and forth observers did reliably see a slanted moving surface. The median slant seen by observers who had not previously viewed the stationary surface was 40°, a small underestimation of the slant specified by the motion perspective. Observers' estimates of the surface's distance from them were highly variable and uncertain.

Flock (1964), using the same apparatus as E. Gibson et al. (1959), measured perceived slant of randomly textured, transparent surfaces moving back and forth at nine different slants, ranging from 40° forward from the vertical to 40° backward from the vertical. Flock found that the average of the linear regression coefficients relating each observer's settings to the actual slants was close to 1.0 and that this remained true over a range of movement velocities and for several different textures. On the other hand, when the surfaces were stationary the average regression coefficient was only 0.13, indicating that the stationary gradients of texture from these surfaces were not primarily responsible for the observers' settings in the motion conditions.

Computer-generated displays of moving spots were used by Braunstein (1968) to independently vary texture gradient information and motion perspective information for slant. When the texture gradient specified that the surface was in the frontal plane, motion perspective was nevertheless effective in producing judgments of some slant although it was considerably underestimated. Motion perspective specifying slants of 20, 40, and 60° from the frontal plane produced judgments of 11.6, 18.6, and 20.7°, respectively. Even when texture gradients and motion perspective were in agreement, however, there was still considerable underestimation. This is in accord with the observation made earlier concerning stationary surfaces (see Section 3.1.3.2) that textures made up of randomly placed dots are relatively ineffectual in producing the perception of slant.

Wiley and Gyr (1969) found that adding motion perspective to the linear perspective produced by slanted rectangles produced only a slight improvement in slant matches. In addition to using untextured rectangles rather than textured surfaces whose boundaries were occluded, however, their experiment differed from those referred to above in that their surfaces were slanted around a vertical rather than a horizontal axis. Hence the lateral head movements of their observers produced compression transformations rather than shear transformations in the optic array. Rogers and M. Graham (1983) have shown, as discussed below, that the compression transformation is less effective than the shear transformation.

Computer-generated random dot patterns were used by Farber and McConkie (1979) to assess observers' ability to use motion perspective in the perception of "internal depth," the dihedral angle formed by intersecting surfaces. The simulated projection of two oppositely slanted surfaces that met to form either a concave or convex wedge was viewed by observers as the surfaces translated back and forth parallel to the line of their intersection. The observers were unable to make consistent judgments of the direction of the slant of this internal angle; that is, they could not reliably say whether the wedge was concave or convex. Braunstein and Andersen (1981), however, repeated this experiment with variations in duration of exposure time, velocity of translation, shape of viewing window, and fixation instructions and found that their observers were able to correctly judge the direction of internal depth on 84% of the trials. Pradzny (1981) has criticized the theoretical analysis that Farber and McConkie use to argue that even the potential information for internal depth is ambiguous when the effects of eye movements on retinal flow fields are included in the analysis.

In an important series of experiments, Rogers and M. Graham (1979) have demonstrated the effectiveness of motion parallax alone in producing vivid perceptions of surface layout in depth. They suggest that previous failures to find such compelling effects have been due to limitations in the experimental displays used to simulate motion parallax rather than to limitations in the visual system's ability to make use of motion parallax information. Rogers and Graham modeled their display on random dot stereograms (see Chapter 23 by Arditi), but used motion disparity rather than binocular disparity to carry information about surface layout. They presented a random dot pattern on the screen of an oscilloscope. When the observer and the oscilloscope were stationary, the pattern contained no information for depth and looked completely flat. When the observer's head moved back and forth laterally, however, this movement was monitored and was used to generate gradients of horizontal motion in the random dot display. These motions corresponded to the projection of a surface that was modulated in depth, along the vertical axis, by either a square wave, a sine wave, a triangular wave, or a sawtooth wave. Observers were unanimous in reporting the perception of a rigid surface modulated in depth. Apart from an occasional confusion of the triangular wave for the sine wave, observers were always correct in describing the number, direction, and wave form of the modulations. The amount of depth seen in these motion parallax displays was measured by having observers make matches with the same surface layouts presented in binocular disparity. Perceived depth increased regularly with specified depth, but was somewhat underestimated at the greater depths.

Rogers and Graham (1979) found very similar results when the observer's head remained fixed and the oscilloscope was moved back and forth with internal depth in the display specified by motion gradients tied to the movement of the oscilloscope. Perceived depth was somewhat less compelling, however, than when motion parallax was produced by head movements of the observer.

In another study using similar displays, Rogers and Graham (1983) found that observers are much more sensitive to depth modulations when the direction of head movement is parallel, rather than perpendicular, to the axis along which the modulations occur. They interpret this result as indicating that the visual system is more sensitive to shear transformations produced by motion perspective than to expansion/contraction transformations.

4.3. Kinetic Depth Effect

As an object rotates in depth, its projection undergoes a continuous, cyclical transformation. For a flat surface this transformation includes repeated compression from the frontal shape of the surface into a single line coincident with the axis of rotation, followed by expansion back into the frontal shape. For a three-dimensional object the cycle of transformations depends in complex ways on the shape of the object and its orientation to the axis of rotation. The projected boundary of a sphere is invariant during rotation in depth, as is the projected boundary of any object that is completely symmetrical about its axis of rotation. If such an object is textured, however, there is a flow of projected texture as the object rotates. The projected boundaries of other objects deform in various ways as they rotate, and there is a flow of projected texture as well.

The same transformations occur in the optic array if the object remains stationary while the observer revolves around it. Even if the observer is moving past the object on a straight path, the orientation of the object relative to the observer continually changes, so that part of the transformation its projection undergoes is equivalent to that produced by a partial rotation.

When an observer views a transforming projection that either is or could be produced by an object rotating in depth, there is a very strong tendency for the observer to perceive such an object rather than a two-dimensional shape undergoing a nonrigid transformation. The research in this area has been carefully reviewed by Braunstein (1962a, 1976), Johansson (1978), and Ullman (1979b).

Weber (1930) and Philip and Fisichelli (1945) observed this tendency with Lissajou figures, which are transforming figures painted using wave form generators or tuning forks to create rapid harmonic oscillations of a point of light with slow progressive phase shifts between the horizontal and vertical components of the spot's movements. In the simplest of these figures, a circle transforming into a diagonal line is seen as a circle rotating in depth.

Even when a rigid two-dimensional interpretation of a transformation is possible, it may still give rise to the perception of an object in depth. Musatti (1924) observed that an ellipse rotating in the frontal plane tends to be seen as a revolving circular disk slanted out of the frontal plane and that rotation in the frontal plane of a circle containing a smaller, off-centered circle tends to lead to the perception of a truncated rotating cone standing out in depth. Mussati referred to these occurrences as *stereokinetic phenomena*, a term which he attributes to Benussi. The characteristics of stereokinetic phenomena have been extensively investigated by Mefferd (1968a, 1968b, 1968c, 1968d), who concluded that the stereokinetic effect arises in asymmetric figures, such as ellipses, that tend to be seen in depth even when they are stationary; rotation in the frontal plane merely enhances this tendency. Recently, some quite complex examples of the stereokinetic effect have been offered by Wilson, Robinson, and Piggins (1983) and by Braunstein and Andersen (1984).

The projective transformations of the boundaries of a real object rotating in depth can be isolated from other potential information about the object by using a point source of light to project the shadow of the rotating object onto a rear projection screen (Miles, 1931; Metzger, 1934, cited in Wallach & O'Connell, 1953). Wallach and O'Connell (1953) used this technique both with solid geometric objects and with open three-dimensional shapes formed of bent wire. Although the shadows of these objects gave no impression of depth when they were stationary, they gave rise to vivid perceptions of rigid three-dimensional objects when they were rotated. Wallach, O'Connell, and Neisser (1953) found that the shadows tended to retain some of their apparent three-dimensionality even after their rotation had ceased. Wallach and O'Connell introduced the term *kinetic depth effect*, which has been widely accepted as a general term for the perception of three-dimensional shape from the two-dimensional transformations produced by object rotation. They concluded from their observations that the kinetic depth effect requires that the transforming boundaries or lines must be simultaneously changing both in length and in orientation. Using this criterion, Wallach, Weisz, and Adams (1956) concluded that some of Musatti's stereokinetic phenomena could be considered to be examples of the kinetic depth effect.

Wallach and O'Connell (1953) attempted in their experiments to approximate the conditions of *parallel projection*, in which the point of projection is at a very large, effectively infinite, distance from the object. They did this to avoid confounding the effects of motion with the effects of perspective that arise in *polar projection*, in which the point of projection is at a finite distance from the object. In the parallel projection of a transparent object there is no information to distinguish the front from the back of the object or to indicate its direction of rotation. Nevertheless, although these characteristics of the situation are perceptually ambiguous, the internal depth organization of the object, apart from the possible front/back reversal, is clearly perceived.

Several experiments have tested the accuracy of the kinetic depth effect. Epstein (1964) found that observers were able to indicate both the internal depth and the angle of rotation of oscillating wire figures with considerably accuracy. White and Mueser (1960) used shadows of five vertical pegs on a rotating turntable to eliminate changes in contour length and orientation. Nevertheless, when the shadow of each peg had a distinctive shape observers generally saw them as having a rigid arrangment in depth and showed considerably accuracy in indicating their placement on the turntable.

J. Gibson and Gibson (1957), using the shadow-casting technique, asked observers to estimate the maximum slant of textured surfaces or solid shapes that oscillated back and forth between that maximum angle and the frontal plane. Their observers were highly accurate in judging rotations of from 15 to 70°. In a control condition, the slants of stationary surfaces were estimated and were found to be strongly underestimated, showing that the accurate judgments in their experimental conditions were due to the dynamic transformation of the projections.

Lappin and Fuqua (1983) used three collinear points on an oscilloscope screen to present the projection of a rigid line segment oscillating either in the frontal plane or in a plane slanted back in depth. Observers were asked to adjust the middle point so that it was at the midpoint of the rotating three-dimensional line segment. Observers' settings were just as accurate when the plane of oscillation was slanted back as when it was frontal, indicating to Lappin and Fuqua that the information carried by oscillation in depth leads to perception of distance in three dimensions that is as accurate as the perception of distance in the frontal plane.

The work of White and Mueser (1960) demonstrates that simulataneous changes in both length and orientation of contours are not essential for the kinetic depth effect. This has also been shown by a series of investigations in which the perception of a rigid rod rotating about its center is obtained from the projection of a one-dimensional rotating dotted line (Hershberger, 1967; Hershberger & Carpenter, 1972; Hershberger, Carpenter, Starzec, & Laughlin, 1974; Hershberger & Starzec, 1974; Hershberger & Urban, 1970a; Hershberger & Urban, 1970b). The use of a rotating dotted line introduces a minimal texture into this display, and it may be the relative motions of these texture elements rather than changing length and orientation of contours that produce the kinetic depth effect here.

Green (1961) used motion picture animation of static computer-generated frames displayed on an oscilloscope screen to generate movies of rotating objects. Green obtained ratings of the apparent rigidity and coherence of these objects as he varied their characteristics. He found that rated coherence increased with the number of texture elements, a finding confirmed by Braunstein (1962b), and that coherence was greater when the texture elements were line segments, which changed in length and orientation, rather then merely spots. Braunstein (1966) used Green's technique to produce the projection of a much more densely textured rotating transparent sphere, which was seen as a rotating three-dimensional object by a very high percentage of his observers. Lappin, Doner, & Kottas (1980), using a similar display, found that two successive frames were sufficient to produce an impression of a sphere rotating in depth. They also found that observers were quite accurate in discriminating a sphere in which dot positions were perfectly correlated between frames from one in which they were not. Their observers showed little sensitivity, however, to differences in the amount of decorrelation between dot positions. Petersik (1979) also found that the introduction of noise degraded but did not destroy the perception of depth in the projections of rotating transparent spheres. From a series of experiments in which they varied the number and duration of frames and the intervals and amount of decorrelation between them, Doner, Lappin, and Perfetto (1984) have concluded that perceiving the structure of a rotating sphere of dots involves a process that detects global properties of the set of dot motions rather than merely being sensitive to the local relations among the dots.

Rock and Smith (1981) developed a borderline instance of the kinetic depth effect in which a luminous line segment oscillating in the frontal plane was seen in darkness through a window that occluded the ends of the line. They found that whether the line appared to be oscillating in the frontal plane or rotating in depth depended on whether the border of the window was or was not made visible.

The necessary and sufficient conditions for obtaining the kinetic depth effect are not easy to specify. The tendency to see objects rotating in depth rather than shapes distorting in two dimensions is so strong that it appears even under rather minimal conditions and even when the displayed transformations only partially correspond to the actual projections of rotating objects. The effect, however, can be more or less vivid, can vary in its latency, and can be more or less spontaneous depending on the extent to which the projective information for rotation in depth has been reduced or degraded.

Attempts to produce mathematical analyses of the information that the visual system uses in perceiving the structure of an object from its projective changes during rotation have so far concentrated on rigid objects (Hay, 1966; Longuet-Higgins & Prazdny, 1980; Ullman, 1979a, 1979b; Todd, 1982). Although a number of algorithms have been produced that describe how rigid three-dimensional structures could be extracted from two-dimensional projective transformations, there is little evidence concerning whether any of them describes what the visual system actually does. Such algorithms can account for observers' ability to distinguish rigid from nonrigid motion (von Fieandt & J. Gibson, 1959; Todd, 1982), but they do not account for instances in which a nonrigid motion is seen even though a rigid motion exists that would be consistent with the projective transformations (e.g., the stereokinetic effect) nor can they account for the particular nonrigid motions that are seen (for reviews of the perception of nonrigid motion see Johansson, 1978, and Johansson, von Hofsten, & Jansson, 1980). Ullman (1984a), however, has suggested that the principle of searching for a rigid interpretation is not seriously challenged by the stereokinetic effect because that effect is based on misperceiving the two-dimensional motions of the figures' smooth contours as they slide along themselves; the rigidity principle, in Ullman's view, would then operate on the misperceived, rather than the true, motions of the figures' contours.

Johansson (1964, 1977, 1978) and his colleagues (Johansson & Janssen, 1968; Johansson et al., 1980) are developing a *vector analysis* model to describe how the visual system extracts both the motion of an object or dot configuration and its structure from its projective transformations. An advantage of this analysis is that is can accommodate itself to nonrigid as well as rigid objects under the general principle that the amount of perceived nonrigidity is minimized. The visual system accounts for as much as possible of the projective transformation in terms of motion of a rigid object and then ascribes whatever portion of the transformation is unaccounted for to nonrigid deformation of the object. Although this approach seems to offer an appropriate level of flexibility, its very generality has made its precise specification difficult.

Following this general approach, Ullman (1984b) has formulated an *incremental rigidity* model that recovers three-dimensional structure by minimizing the amount of change that occurs in the perceived structure of the object between temporally adjacent "frames" (time is quantized in the model). Using computer simulations, Ullman has shown that this approach is able eventually to arrive at something close to the correct shape of an object even when the initial perception is quite inaccurate. The incremental rigidity scheme also shows some ability to track the shape of an object that is slowly deforming while it rotates.

It is possible to theorize that the visual system possesses a separate mechanism for perceiving the structure of rigid objects, but as Todd (1984) has pointed out, such a theory would be parsimonious only if the structures of objects undergoing rigid movements were perceived more accurately or more readily than the structure of nonrigid objects. Todd (1984) tested this possibility by having observers estimate the curvature of cylinders oscillating around their axes. His displays were computer-generated projections of cylinders with a sparse texture of dots. The oscillating cylinders in one condition were rigid, but in a second condition they oscillated around their axes while simultaneously stretching and contracting along their axes. Observers were equally accurate in estimating the curvature of the cylinders in these two conditions. These results thus provide no evidence that the visual system has any special mechanism for perceiving the structure of rigid objects. Braunstein and Andersen (1984a, 1984b) have suggested that a single set of automatically applied heuristics may be able to account for the perception through rotary motion of the shapes of both rigid and nonrigid objects, and they have supplied evidence concerning the operation of several such heuristics that do not explicitly rely on any rigidity principle.

4.4. Occlusion and Disocclusion

In a normal, complex environment, many surfaces and parts of surfaces are hidden from view by other surfaces lying along the same lines of regard. When an observer moves through such an environment, some surfaces are progressively hidden, or occluded, and others are progressively revealed, or disoccluded. In the case of one surface lying behind another, this occlusion or disocclusion takes place at the edge separating the two surfaces and has differential effects on the visibility of the texture of the two surfaces. The texture of the surface lying in front remains unchanged, whereas there is a progressive deletion or accretion of visible texture of the surface that lies behind. This "kinetic disruption of optical texture," as Kaplan (1969) refers to it, thus provides potential information for both the existence and the direction of a depth difference at the edge. J. Gibson (1966, 1979) provides detailed discussions of the potential information for spatial layout that is specified by occlusion and disocclusion.

Kaplan (1969) used filmed animation sequences of pseudorandom textures to test two hypotheses about the perception of depth at an edge produced by the progressive accretion or deletion of projected texture. First, Kaplan found that when accretion/deletion occurs on only one side of a margin in the optic array that side is seen as being farther away on a very high percentage of trials (98%). The surface seen as farther away is also seen as moving behind the nearer surface. Second, generalizing from this situation, Kaplan found that when there is accretion or deletion of texture on both sides of a margin in the optic array, the surface undergoing the greater amount of accretion/deletion is seen as farther away on a high percentage of trials (87%). In such conditions, however, the surface seen as farther is not generally seen as moving behind the nearer surface. Instead, the two surfaces may be seen as two abutting rollers with one roller nearer than the other. Thus the perception that one surface is occluding another generally requires that there be no change in the texture of the occluding surface, but the perception of depth at an edge is responsive to the relative amount of accretion or deletion of texture occuring on the two sides of the edge.

When a rotating transparent sphere is viewed in parallel projection, there is no information available to indicate either the direction of rotation of the sphere or, concomitantly, which is the front and which the back of the sphere. When the sphere is opaque, however, no such ambiguity exists. Braunstein, Andersen, and Reifer (1982) examined whether the occlusion/disocclusion of opaque surface patches on a transparent sphere could specify direction of rotation of the sphere. Using computer-generated projections of transparent spheres with opaque pentagonal shapes on their surfaces, they found that as they increased the size of the shapes on the sphere, and hence increased the number of occlusion/disocclusion events that occurred during rotation, the tendency to see the correct direction of rotation also increased, exceeding 80% for the largest size. Andersen and Braunstein (1983) performed a similar experiment but replaced each pentagon with a number of dots randomly placed within its boundaries. The effect of this alteration was to remove the possibility that the effective occlusion information might be the essentially static interposition information provided by having the contours of some pentagons interrupting and hiding the contours of other pentagons. The dot pentagons produced essentially the same results as the contour pentagons, thus demonstrating that the dynamic information provided by the accretion/deletion of texture elements is effective in determining both which side of the sphere is seen in front and the direction in which the sphere is seen to rotate.

The progressive occlusion and disocclusion of surfaces as an observer moves through the environment is clearly an important source of information for spatial layout, as Gibson (1979) has emphasized. As yet, however, this area has received relatively little empirical or analytical investigation. The accretion/deletion of projected texture elements poses particular problems for mathematical analysis because the mathematical tools used for the analysis of flowing projected texture generally deal only with transformations in which the entire set of elements remains continuously visible. Much work remains to be done to integrate all the projective changes produced by observer movement into an analytical framework that is both detailed and comprehensive.

REFERENCES

Adelson, D. The relational influence of size on judgments of distance. *Journal of General Psychology*, 1963, *69*, 319–333.

Alberti, L. B. *On painting* and *On sculpture* (C. Grayson, Ed. and trans.). London: Phaidon, 1972. (Originally published in Latin, in 1436.)

Alexander, K. R. The foundations of the silo response. *Optometric Weekly*, 1974, *65*, 446–450.

Andersen, G. J., & Braunstein, M. L. Dynamic occlusion in the perception of rotation in depth. *Perception and Psychophysics*, 1983, *34*, 356–362.

Attneave, F., & Olson, R. Inferences about visual mechanisms from monocular depth effects. *Psychonomic Science*, 1966, *4*, 133–134.

Baird, J. C. Retinal and assumed size cues as determinants of size and distance perception. *Journal of Experimental Psychology*, 1963, *66*, 155–162.

Baird, J. C. Stimulus and response factors in size instruction effects. *Perceptual and Motor Skills*, 1965, *21*, 915–924.

Baird, J. C. *Psychophysical analysis of visual space.* New York: Pergamon Press, 1970. (a)

Baird, J. C. (Ed.) Human space perception: Proceedings of the Dartmouth conference. *Psychonomic Monograph Supplements*, 1970, *3*, (Whole No. 45). (b)

Baird, J. C., & Biersdorf, W. R. Quantitative functions for size and distance. *Perception and Psychophysics*, 1967, *2*, 161–166.

Bajesy, R., & Lieberman, L. Texture gradient as a depth cue. *Computer Graphics and Image Processing*, 1976, *5*, 52–67.

Barlow, H. B., Blakemore, C., & Pettigrew, J. D. The neural mechanism of binocular depth discrimination. *Journal of Physiology* (London), 1967, *193*, 327–342.

Beck, J. *Surface color perception.* Ithaca, NY: Cornell University Press, 1972.

Beck, J., & Gibson, J. J. The relation of apparent shape to apparent slant in the perception of objects. *Journal of Experimental Psychology*, 1955, *50*, 125–133.

Berkeley, G. *An essay towards a new theory of vision.* New York: Dutton, 1910. (Originally published, 1709.)

Blalock, H. M. Four-variable causal models and partial correlations. *American Journal of Sociology*, 1962, *68*, 182–194.

Blessing, W. W., Landauer, A. A., & Coltheart, M. The effect of false perspective cues on distance and size judgments: An examination of the invariance hypothesis. *American Journal of Psychology*, 1967, *80*, 250–256.

Bolles, R. C., & Bailey, D. E. Importance of object recognition in size constancy. *Journal of Experimental Psychology*, 1956, *51*, 222–225.

Boring, E. G. *Sensation and perception in the history of experimental psychology.* New York: Appleton-Century, 1942.

Boring, E. G., The moon illusion. *American Journal of Physics*, 1943, *11*, 55–60.

Boring, E. G. Size-constancy in a picture. *American Journal of Psychology*, 1964, *77*, 494–498.

Borresen, C. R., & Lichte, W. H. Shape constancy: Dependence upon stimulus familiarity. *Journal of Experimental Psychology*, 1962, *63*, 91–97.

Bradley, D. R., & Vido, D. Psychophysical functions for perceived and remembered distance. *Perception*, 1984, *13*, 315–320.

Braunstein, M. L. Depth perception in rotating dot patterns: Effects of numerosity and perspective. *Journal of Experimental Psychology*, 1962, *64*, 415–420. (a)

Braunstein, M. L. The perception of depth through motion. *Psychological Bulletin*, 1962, *59*, 422–433. (b)

Braunstein, M. L. Sensitivity of the observer to transformations of the visual field. *Journal of Experimental Psychology*, 1966, *72*, 683–689.

Braunstein, M. L. Motion and texture as sources of slant information. *Journal of Experimental Psychology*, 1968, *78*, 247–253.

Braunstein, M. L. *Depth perception through motion.* New York: Academic, 1976.

Braunstein, M. L. & Andersen, G. J. Velocity gradients and relative depth perception. *Perception and Psychophysics*, 1981, *29*, 145–155.

Braunstein, M. L., & Andersen, G. J. A counterexample to the rigidity assumption in the visual perception of structure from motion. *Perception*, 1984, *13*, 213–217. (a)

Braunstein, M. L., & Andersen, G. J. Shape and depth perception from parallel projections of three-dimensional motion. *Journal of Experimental Psychology: Human Perception and Performance*, 1984, *10*, 749–760. (b)

Braunstein, M. L., Andersen, G. J., & Riefer, D. M. The use of occlusion to resolve ambiguity in parallel projections. *Perception and Psychophysics*, 1982, *31*, 261–267.

Braunstein, M. L., & Payne, J. W. Perspective and form ratio as determinants of relative slant judgments. *Journal of Experimental Psychology*, 1969, *81*, 584–590.

Brunswik, E. Zur Entwicklung der Albedowahrnehmung. *Zeitschrift fur Psychologie*, 1929, *109*, 40–115.

Brunswik, E. *Perception and the representative design of psychological experiments* (2nd ed.). Berkeley: University of California Press, 1956.

Brunswik, E. & Kamiya, J. Ecological cue-validity of "proximity" and other Gestalt factors. *American Journal of Psychology*, 1953, *66*, 20–32.

Bugelski, B. R. Traffic signals and depth perception. *Science*, 1967, *157*, 1464–1465.

Burnham, D. K. Apparent relative size in the judgement of apparent distance. *Perception*, 1983, *12*, 683–700.

Campione, F. Shape constancy: a systematic approach. *Perception*, 1977, *6*, 97–105.

Carlson, V. R. Overestimation in size-constancy judgments. *American Journal of Psychology*, 1960, *73*, 199–213.

Carlson, V. R. Size-constancy judgments and perceptual compromise. *Journal of Experimental Psychology*, 1962, *63*, 68–73.

Carlson, V. R. Instructions and perceptual constancy judgments. In W. Epstein (Ed.), *Stability and constancy in visual perception.* New York: Wiley, 1977.

Carlson, V. R., & Tassone, E. P. Independent size judgments at different distances. *Journal of Experimental Psychology*, 1967, *73*, 491–497.

Carlson, V. R., & Tassone, E. P. Familiar versus unfamiliar size: A theoretical derivation and test. *Journal of Experimental Psychology*, 1971, *87*, 109–115.

Carter, D. S. The moon illusion: A test of the vestibular hypothesis under monocular viewing conditions. *Perceptual and Motor skills*, 1977, *45*, 1127–1130.

Chalmers, E. L. Monocular and binocular cues in the perception of size and distance. *American Journal of Psychology*, 1952, *65*, 415–423.

Clark, W. C., Smith, A. H., & Rabe, A. Retinal gradient of outline as a stimulus for slant. *Canadian Journal of Psychology*, 1955, *9*, 247–253.

Clark, W. C., Smith, A. H., & Rabe, A. The interaction of surface texture, outline gradient, and ground in the perception of slant. *Canadian Journal of Psychology*, 1956, *10*, 1–8.

Clocksin, W. F. Perception of surface slant and edge labels from optical flow: A computational approach. *Perception*, 1980, *9*, 253–269.

Cobb, S. R., Cole, C., & Rainey, M. T. The effect of exposure time upon perceived size. *British Journal of Physiological Optics*, 1978, *32*, 94–96.

Coltheart, M. The influence of haptic size information upon visual judgments of absolute distance. *Perception and Psychophysics*, 1969, *5*, 143–144.

Coltheart, M. The effect of verbal size information upon visual judgments of absolute distance. *Perception and Psychophysics*, 1970, *9*, 222–223.

Cook, M. The judgment of distance on a plane surface. *Perception and Psychophysics*, 1978, *23*, 85–90.

Day, R. H., Stuart, G. W., & Dickenson, R. G. Size constancy does not fail below half a degree. *Perception and Psychophysics*, 1980, *28*, 1263–1265.

Dees, J. W. Accuracy of absolute visual distance and size estimation in space as a function of stereopsis and motion parallax. *Journal of Experimental Psychology*, 1966, *72*, 466–476.

Dees, J. W. Moon illusion and size-distance invariance: An explanation based upon an experimental artifact. *Perceptual and Motor Skills*, 1966, *23*, 629–630.

Deregowski, J. B. Implicit-shape constancy: a cross-cultural comparison. *Perception*, 1976, *5*, 343–348. (a)

Deregowski, J. B. Implicit-shape constancy as a factor in pictorial perception. *British Journal of Psychology*, 1976, *67*, 23–29. (b)

Descartes, R. *Discourse on method, optics, geometry*, and *meterology* (P. Olscamp, Ed. and trans.). Indianapolis, Ind.: Bobbs-Merrill, 1965. (Originally published in French, in 1637.)

Doner, J., Lappin, J. S., & Perfetto, G. Detection of three-dimensional structure in moving optical patterns. *Journal of Experimental Psychology: Human Perception and Performance*, 1984, *10*, 1–11.

Dunn, B. E. Relative distance of lights: An extension of Bugelski's findings. *Perception and Psychophysics*, 1969, *6*, 414–415.

Dunn, B. E., Gray, G. C., & Thompson, D. Relative height on the picture plane and depth perception. *Perceptual and Motor Skills*, 1965, *21*, 227–236.

Ellis, W. D. (Ed.) *A source book of Gestalt psychology*. London: Routledge, 1938.

Epstein, W. The known-size-apparent-distance hypothesis. *American Journal of Psychology*, 1961, *74*, 333–347.

Epstein, W. Apparent shape of a meaningful representational form. *Perceptual and Motor Skills*, 1962, *15*, 239–246.

Epstein, W. The influence of assumed size on apparent distance. *American Journal of Psychology*, 1963, *76*, 257–265. (a)

Epstein, W. Attitudes of judgment and the size-distance invariance hypothesis. *Journal of Experimental Psychology*, 1963, *66*, 78–83. (b)

Epstein, W. Perceptual invariance in the kinetic depth-effect. *American Journal of Psychology*, 1964, *77*, 301–303.

Epstein, W. Nonrelational judgments of size and distance. *American Journal of Psychology*, 1965, *78*, 120–123.

Epstein, W. Perceived depth as a function of relative height under three background conditions. *Journal of Experimental Psychology*, 1966, *72*, 335–338.

Epstein, W. Perceived distance in imagined space. *Quarterly Journal of Experimental Psychology*, 1967, *19*, 341–343.

Epstein, W. The process of "taking-into-account" in visual perception. *Perception*, 1973, *2*, 267–285.

Epstein, W. (Ed.) *Stability and constancy in visual perception*. New York: Wiley, 1977.

Epstein, W. Historical introduction to the constancies. In W. Epstein (Ed.), *Stability and constancy in visual perception*. New York: Wiley, 1977.

Epstein, W., & Baratz, S. S. Relative size in isolation as a stimulus for relative perceived distance. *Journal of Experimental Psychology*, 1964, *67*, 507–513.

Epstein, W., Bontrager, H., & Park, J. N. The induction of non veridical slant and the perception of shape. *Journal of Experimental Psychology*, 1962, *63*, 472–479.

Epstein, W., & Franklin, S. Some conditions of the effect of relative size on perceived relative distance. *American Journal of Psychology*, 1965, *78*, 466–470.

Epstein, W., & Hatfield, G. Functional equivalence of masking and cue reduction in perception of shape at a slant. *Perception and Psychophysics*, 1978, *23*, 137–144. (a)

Epstein, W., & Hatfield, G. The locus of masking shape-at-a-slant. *Perception and Psychophysics*, 1978, *24*, 501–504. (b)

Epstein, W., Hatfield, G., & Muise, G. Perceived shape at a slant as a function of processing time and processing load. *Journal of Experimental Psychology: Human Perception and Performance*, 1977, *3*, 473–483.

Epstein, W., & Landauer, A. A. Size and distance judgments under reduced conditions of viewing. *Perception and Psychophysics*, 1969, *6*, 269–272.

Epstein, W., & Mountford, D. Judgment of slant in response to an isolated gradient of stimulation. *Perceptual and Motor Skills*, 1963, *16*, 733–737.

Epstein, W., & Park, J. N. Shape constancy: Functional relationships and theoretical formulations. *Psychological Bulletin*, 1963, *60*, 265–288.

Epstein, W., Park, J., & Casey, A. The current status of the size-distance hypothesis. *Psychological Bulletin*, 1961, *58*, 491–514.

Eriksson, E. S. Monocular slant perception and the texture gradient concept. *Scandinavian Journal of Psychology*, 1964, *5*, 123–128.

Eriksson, E. S. The shape slant invariance hypothesis in static perception. *Scandinavian Journal of Psychology*, 1967, *8*, 193–208.

Eriksson, E. S. *Movement parallax and distance perception*. (Report 117). Department of Psychology, University of Uppsala, Uppsala, Sweden, 1972. (a)

Eriksson, E. S. *Movement parallax, anisotropy, and relative size as determinants of space perception*. (Report 131). Department of Psychology, University of Uppsala, Uppsala, Sweden, 1972. (b)

Eriksson, E. S. Movement parallax during locomotion. *Perception and Psychophysics*, 1974, *16*, 197–200.

Eriksson, E. S., & Zetterberg, P. *Experience and veridical space perception*. (Report 169). Department of Psychology, University of Uppsala, Uppsala, Sweden, 1975.

Farber, J. M., & McConkie, A. B. Optical motions as information for unsigned depth. *Journal of Experimental Psychology: Human Perception and Performance*, 1979, *3*, 494–500.

Ferris, S. H. Motion parallax and absolute distance. *Journal of Experimental Psychology*, 1972, *95*, 258–263.

Festinger, L., Sedgwick, H. A., & Holtzman, J. D. Visual perception during smooth pursuit eye movement. *Vision Research*, 1976, *16*, 1377–1386.

Fillenbaum, S., Schiffman, H. R., & Butcher, J. Perception of off-size versions of a familiar object under conditions of rich information. *Journal of Experimental Psychology*, 1965, *69*, 298–303.

Fitzpatrick, V., Pasnak, R., & Tyer, Z. E. The effect of familiar size at familiar distance. *Perception*, 1982, *11*, 85–91.

Flock, H. R. Three theoretical views of slant perception. *Psychological Bulletin*, 1964, *62*, 110–121. (a)

Flock, H. R. A possible optical basis for monocular slant perception. *Psychological Review*, 1964, *71*, 380–391. (b)

Flock, H. R. Some conditions sufficient for accurate monocular perceptions of moving surface slants. *Journal of Experimental Psychology*, 1964, *67*, 560–572. (c)

Flock, H. R. Optical texture and linear perspective as stimuli for slant perception. *Psychological Review*, 1965, *72*, 505–514. (a)

Flock, H. R. Invariance of size-distance estimates. *American Journal of Psychology*, 1965, *78*, 144. (b)

Flock, H. R., Graves, D., Tenney, J., & Stephenson, B. Slant judgments of single rectangles at a slant. *Psychonomic Science*, 1967, *7*, 57–58.

Flock, H. R., & Moscatelli, A. Variables of surface texture and accuracy of space perceptions. *Perceptual and Motor Skills*, 1964, *19*, 327–334.

Flock, H. R., Tenney, J. H., & Graves, D. Depth information in single triangles and arrays of triangles. *Psychonomic Science*, 1966, *6*, 291–292.

Foley, J. M. Primary distance perception. In R. Held, H. Leibowitz, & L. Teuber (Eds.), *Handbook of sensory physiology* (Vol. 8). Berlin: Springer, 1978.

Foley, J. M. Binocular distance perception. *Psychological Review*, 1980, *87*, 411–434.

Freeman, R. B. Ecological optics and visual slant. *Psychological Review*, 1965, *72*, 501–504.

Freeman, R. B. Optical texture versus retinal perspective: A reply to Flock. *Psychological Review*, 1966, *73*, 365–371. (a)

Freeman, R. B. Function of cues in the perceptual learning of visual slant: An experimental and theoretical analysis. *Psychological Monographs*, 1966, *80* (2, Whole No. 610). (b)

Freeman, R. B. Effect of size on visual slant. *Journal of Experimental Psychology*, 1966, *71*, 96–103. (c)

Freeman, R. B. Absolute threshold for visual slant: The effect of stimulus size and retinal perspective. *Journal of Experimental Psychology*, 1966, *71*, 170–176. (d)

Freeman, R. B. A perspective metric for visual slant and shape. *Psychologische Forschung*, 1969, *32*, 296–323.

Galanter, E., & Galanter, P. Range estimates of distant visual stimuli. *Perception and Psychophysics*, 1973, *14*, 301–306.

Georgeson, M. A., & Harris, M. G. Size constancy does not fail below half a degree. *Nature*, 1981, *289*, 826.

Gibson, E. J., & Bergman, R. The effect of training on absolute estimation of distance over the ground. *Journal of Experimental Psychology*, 1954, *6*, 473–482.

Gibson, E. J., Bergman, R., & Purdy, J. The effect of prior training with a scale of distance on absolute and relative estimation of distance over the ground. *Journal of Experimental Psychology*, 1955, *50*, 97–105.

Gibson, E. J., Gibson, J. J., Smith, O. W., & Flock, H. R. Motion parallax as a determinant of perceived depth. *Journal of Experimental Psychology*, 1959, *58*, 40–51.

Gibson, J. J. *The Perception of the Visual World.* Boston: Houghton Mifflin, 1950. (a)

Gibson, J. J. The perception of visual surfaces. *American Journal of Psychology*, 1950, *63*, 367–384. (b)

Gibson, J. J. Visually controlled locomotion and visual orientation in animals. *British Journal of Psychology*, 1958, *49*, 182–194.

Gibson, J. J. Ecological Optics. *Vision Research*, 1961, *1*, 253–262.

Gibson, J. J. *The senses considered as perceptual systems.* Boston: Houghton Mifflin, 1966.

Gibson, J. J. What gives rise to the perception of motion? *Psychological Review*, 1968, *75*, 335–346.

Gibson, J. J. *The ecological approach to visual perception.* Boston: Houghton Mifflin, 1979.

Gibson, J. J., & Carel, W. Does motion perspective independently produce the impression of a receding surface? *Journal of Experimental Psychology*, 1952, *44*, 16–18.

Gibson, J. J. & Cornsweet, J. The perceived slant of visual surfaces—optical and geographical. *Journal of Experimental Psychology*, 1952, *44*, 11–15.

Gibson, J. J., & Flock, H. R. The apparent distance of mountains. *American Journal of Psychology*, 1962, *75*, 501–503.

Gibson, J. J., & Gibson, E. J. Continuous perspective transformations and the perception of rigid motion. *Journal of Experimental Psychology*, 1957, *54*, 129–138.

Gibson, J. J., Olum, P., & Rosenblatt, F. Parallax and perspective during aircraft landing. *American Journal of Psychology*, 1955, *68*, 372–385.

Gibson, J. J., Purdy, J., & Lawrence, L. A method of controlling stimulation for the study of space perception: The optical tunnel. *Journal of Experimental Psychology*, 1955, *50*, 1–14.

Gibson, J. J., & Waddell, D. Homogeneous retinal stimulation and visual perception. *American Journal of Psychology*, 1952, *65*, 263–270.

Gilinsky, A. S. Perceived size and distance in visual space. *Psychological Review*, 1951, *58*, 460–482.

Gilinsky, A. S. The effect of attitude upon the perception of size. *American Journal of Psychology*, 1955, *68*, 173–192.

Gilinsky, A. S. The paradoxical moon illusions. *Perceptual and Motor skills*, 1980, *50*, 271–283.

Gillam, B. Changes in the direction of induced aniseikonic slant as a function of distance. *Vision Research*, 1967, *7*, 777–783.

Gillam, B. Perception of slant when perspective and stereopsis conflict: Experiments with aniseikonic lenses. *Journal of Experimental Psychology*, 1968, *78*, 299–305.

Gillam, B. Judgments of slant on the basis of foreshortening. *Scandinavian Journal of Psychology*, 1970, *11*, 31–34.

Gillam, B. False perspectives. *Perception*, 1981, *10*, 313–318.

Gogel, W. C. The tendency to see objects as equidistant and its inverse relation to lateral separation. *Psychological Monographs*, 1956, *70* (4, Whole No. 411). (a)

Gogel, W. C. Relative visual direction as a factor in relative distance perceptions. *Psychological Monographs*, 1956, *70* (11, Whole No. 418). (b)

Gogel, W. C. Size cue to visually perceived distance. *Psychological Bulletin*, 1964, *62*, 217–235.

Gogel, W. C. Equidistance tendency and its consequences. *Psychological Bulletin*, 1965, *64*, 153–163.

Gogel, W. C. The effect of set on perceived egocentric distance. *Acta Psychologica*, 1968, *28*, 283–292.

Gogel, W. C. The absolute and relative size cues to distance. *American Journal of Psychology*, 1969, *82*, 228–234. (a)

Gogel, W. C. The effect of object familiarity on the perception of size and distance. *Journal of Experimental Psychology*, 1969, *21*, 239–247. (b)

Gogel, W. C. The sensing of retinal size. *Vision Research*, 1969, *9*, 1079–1094. (c)

Gogel, W. C. The validity of the size-distance invariance hypothesis with cue reduction. *Perception and Psychophysics*, 1971, *9*, 92–94.

Gogel, W. C. The organization of perceived space. *Psychologische Forschung*, 1973, *36*, 195–221.

Gogel, W. C. An indirect method of measuring perceived distance from familiar size. *Perception and Psychophysics*, 1976, *20*, 419–429.

Gogel, W. C. Size, distance, and depth perception. In E. C. Carterette & M. P. Friedman (Eds.), *Handbook of perception.* Vol. 9: *Perceptual processing.* New York: Academic Press, 1978.

Gogel, W. C. The role of suggested size in distance responses. *Perception and Psychophysics*, 1981, *30*, 149–155. (a)

Gogel, W. C. Perceived depth is a necessary factor in apparent motion concomitant with head motion: A reply to Shebilske and Proffitt. *Perception and Psychophysics*, 1981, *29*, 173–177. (b)

Gogel, W. C. An illusory movement of a stationary target during head motion is unaffected by paradoxical retinal motion: A reply to Shebilske and Proffitt (1983). *Perception and Psychophysics*, 1983, *34*, 482–487.

Gogel, W. C., Hartman, B. O., & Harker, G. S. The retinal size of a familiar object as a determiner of apparent distance. *Psychological Monographs*, 1957, *71* (Whole No. 13).

Gogel, W. C., & Mershon, D. H. The perception of size in a distorted room. *Perception and Psychophysics*, 1968, *4*, 26–28.

Gogel, W. C., & Mertens, H. W. Perceived size and distance of familiar objects. *Perceptual and Motor Skills*, 1967, *25*, 213–225.

Gogel, W. C., & Mertens, H. W. Perceived depth between familiar objects. *Journal of Experimental Psychology*, 1968, *77*, 206–211.

Gogel, W. C., & Newton, R. E. Perception of off-sized objects. *Perception and Psychophysics*, 1969, *5*, 7–9.

Gogel, W. C., & Sturm, R. D. A test of the relational hypothesis of perceived size. *American Journal of Psychology*, 1972, *85*, 201–216.

Gogel, W. C., & Tietz, J. D. Absolute motion parallax and the specific distance tendency. *Perception and Psychophysics*, 1973, *13*, 284–292.

Gogel, W. C., & Tietz, J. D. A comparison of oculomotor and motion parallax cues of egocentric distance. *Vision Research*, 1979, *19*, 1161–1170.

Gogel, W. C., & Tietz, J. D. Relative cues and absolute distance perception. *Perception and Psychophysics*, 1980, *28*, 321–328.

Gordon, D. A. Static and dynamic visual fields in human space perception. *Journal of the Optical Society of America*, 1965, *55*, 1296–1303.

Gordon, D. A. Perceptual basis of vehicular guidance. *Public Roads*, 1966, *34*, 53–68.

Gottheil, E., & Bitterman, M. E. The measurement of shape-constancy. *American Journal of Psychology*, 1951, *64*, 406–408.

Graham, C. H. Sensation and perception in an objective psychology. *Psychological Review*, 1958, *65*, 65–76.

Graham, C. H. Visual space perception. In C. H. Graham (Ed.), *Vision and visual perception.* New York: Wiley, 1965.

Graham, C. H., Baker, K. E., Hecht, M., & Lloyd, V. V. Factors influencing thresholds for monocular movement parallax. *Journal of Experimental Psychology*, 1948, *38*, 205–223.

Green, B. F. Figure coherence in the kinetic depth effect. *Journal of Experimental Psychology*, 1961, *62*, 272–282.

Gruber, H. E. The relation of perceived size to perceived distance. *American Journal of Psychology*, 1954, 411–426.

Gruber, H. E. The size-distance paradox: A reply to Gilinsky. *American Journal of Psychology*, 1956, 469–476.

Gruber, H. E., & Clark, W. C. Perception of slanted surfaces. *Perceptual and Motor Skills*, 1956, *6*, 97–106.

Gruber, H. E., King, W. L., & Link, S. Moon illusion: An event in imaginary space. *Science*, 1963, *139*, 750–751.

Hake, H. W. Form discrimination and the invariance of form. In L. Uhr (Ed.), *Pattern recognition.* New York: Wiley, 1966.

Hake, H. W., Faust, G. W., McIntyre, J. S., & Murray, H. G. Relational perception and modes of perceiver operation. *Perception and Psychophysics*, 1967, *2*, 469–478.

Hake, H. W., & Myers, A. E. Familiarity and shape constancy. *Journal of Experimental Psychology*, 1969, *80*, 205–214.

Hartman, A. M. Effect of reduction on the relationship between apparent size and distance. *American Journal of Psychology*, 1964, *77*, 353–366.

Hastorf, A. H., & Way, K. S. Apparent size with and without distance cues. *Journal of General Psychology*, 1952, *47*, 181–188.

Hay, J. C. Optical motions and space perception: An extension of Gibson's analysis. *Psychological Review*, 1966, *73*, 550–565.

Hay, J. C. The ghost image: A tool for the analysis of the visual stimulus. In R. B. MacLeod & H. L. Pick, Jr. (Eds.), *Perception: Essays in honor of James J. Gibson*. Ithaca, NY: Cornell University Press, 1974.

Hayes, C. J. A., & King, W. L. Two types of instructions for size and distance judgments of objects presented on a two dimensional plane. *Perception and Psychophysics*, 1967, *2*, 556–558.

Hell, W. Movement parallax: An asymptotic function of amplitude and velocity of head motion. *Vision Research*, 1978, *18*, 629–635.

Hell, W., & Freeman, R. B. Detectability of motion as a factor in depth perception by monocular movement parallax. *Perception and Psychophysics*, 1977, *22*, 526–530.

Helmholtz, H. von *Treatise on physiological optics* (Vol. 3) (J. P. C. Southall, Ed. and trans.). New York: Dover, 1962. (From the third German edition, 1910.)

Hershberger, W. A. Comment on apparent reversal (oscillation) of rotary motion in depth. *Psychological Review*, 1967, *74*, 235–238.

Hershberger, W. A., & Carpenter, D. L. Veridical rotation in depth in unidimensional, polar projections devoid of three motion-parallax cues. *Journal of Experimental Psychology*, 1972, *93*, 213–216.

Hershberger, W. A., Carpenter, D. L., Starzec, J., & Laughlin, N. K. Simulation of an object rotation in depth: Constant and reversed projection ratios. *Journal of Experimental Psychology*, 1974, *103*, 844–853.

Hershberger, W. A., & Starzec, J. J. Motion-parallax cues in one-dimensional polar and parallel projections: Differential velocity and acceleration/displacement change. *Journal of Experimental Psychology*, 1974, *103*, 717–723.

Hershberger, W. A., & Urban, D. Depth perception from motion parallax in one-dimensional polar projections: Projection versus viewing distance. *Journal of Experimental Psychology*, 1970, *86*, 133–136. (a)

Hershberger, W. A., & Urban, D. Three motion-parallax cues in one-dimensional polar projections of rotation in depth. *Journal of Experimental Psychology*, 1970, *86*, 380–383. (b)

Higashiyama, A. Perceived size and distance as a perceptual conflict between two processing modes. *Perception and Psychophysics*, 1977, *22*, 206–211.

Higashiyama, A. The perception of size and distance under monocular observation. *Perception and Psychophysics*, 1979, *26*, 230–234.

Higashiyama, A. The effects of familiar size on judgments of size and distance: An interaction of viewing attitude with spatial cues. *Perception and Psychophysics*, 1984, *35*, 305–312.

Hochberg, C. B., & Hochberg, J. E. Familiar size and the perception of depth. *Journal of Psychology*, 1952, *34*, 107–114.

Hochberg, J. Perception II: Shape and movement. In J. W. Kling & L. A. Riggs (Eds.), *Woodworth and Schlosberg's experimental psychology* (3rd ed.). New York: Holt, Rinehart & Winston, 1971.

Hochberg, J. Levels of perceptual organization. In M. Kubovy & J. Pomerantz (Eds.), *Perceptual organization*. Hillsdale, N.J.: Erlbaum, 1981. (a)

Hochberg, J. On cognition in perception: Perceptual coupling and unconscious inference. *Cognition*, 1981, *10*, 127–134. (b)

Hochberg, J. E., & McAlister, E. Relative size vs. familiar size in the perception of represented depth. *American Journal of Psychology*, 1955, *68*, 294–296.

Holway, A. H., & Boring, E. G. The moon illusion and the angle of regard. *American Journal of Psychology*, 1940, *53*, 109–116.

Holway, A. H., & Boring, E. G. Determinants of apparent visual size with distance variant. *American Journal of Psychology*, 1941, *54*, 21–37.

Howard, I. P., & Templeton, W. B. *Human spatial orientation*. New York: Wiley, 1966.

Ittleson, W. H. Size as a cue to distance: static localization. *American Journal of Psychology*, 1951, *64*, 54–67. (a)

Ittleson, W. H. *The Ames demonstrations in perception*. Princeton, N.J.: Princeton Unversity Press, 1952.

Ittleson, W. H. *Visual space perception*. New York: Springer, 1960.

Jenkin, N. Effects of varied distance on short-range size-judgments. *Journal of Experimental Psychology*, 1957, *54*, 327–331.

Jenkin, N. A relationship between increments of distance and estimates of objective size. *American Journal of Psychology*, 1959, *72*, 345–364.

Jenkin, N., & Feallock, S. M. Developmental and intellectual processes in size-distance judgment. *American Journal of Psychology*, 1960, *73*, 268–273.

Jenkin, N., & Hyman, R. Attitude and distance-estimation as variables in size-matching. *American Journal of Psychology*, 1959, *72*, 68–76.

Johansson, G. Perception of motion and changing form. *Scandinavian Journal of Psychology*, 1964, *5*, 181–208.

Johansson, G. Monocular movement parallax and near-space perception. *Perception*, 1973, *2*, 135–146.

Johansson, G. Spatial constancy and motion in visual perception. In W. Epstein (Ed.), *Stability and constancy in visual perception*. New York: Wiley, 1977.

Johansson, G. Visual event perception. In R. Held, H. W. Leibowitz, & H. L. Turner (Eds.), *Handbook of sensory physiology*. Vol. 8: *Perception*. New York: Springer, 1978.

Johansson, G., & Jansson, G. Perceived rotary motion from changes in a straight line. *Perception and Psychophysics*, 1968, *4*, 165–170.

Johansson, G., von Hofsten, C., & Jansson, G. Event perception. *Annual Review of Psychology*, 1980, *31*, 27–63.

Joynson, R. B. The problem of size and distance. *Quarterly Journal of Experimental Psychology*, 1949, *1*, 119–135.

Joynson, R. B. An experimental synthesis of the Associationist and Gestalt accounts of the perception of size. Part I. *Quarterly Journal of Experimental Psychology*, 1958, *10*, 65–76. (a)

Joynson, R. B. An experimental synthesis of the Associationist and Gestalt accounts of the perception of size. Part II. *Quarterly Journal of Experimental Psychology*, 1958, *10*, 142–154. (b)

Joynson, R. B., & Kirk, N. S. An experimental synthesis of the Associationist and Gestalt accounts of the perception of size. Part III. *Quarterly Journal of Experimental Psychology*, 1960, *12*, 221–230.

.Joynson, R. B., & Newson, L. J. The perception of shape as a function of inclination. *British Journal of Psychology*, 1962, *53*, 1–15.

Joynson, R. B., Newson, L. J., & May, D. S. The limits of over-constancy. *Quarterly Journal of Experimental Psychology*, 1965, *17*, 209–216.

Kaess, D. W. Methodological study of form constancy development. *Journal of Experimental Child Psychology*, 1971, *12*, 27–34.

Kaess, D. W. Importance of relative width differences and instructions on shape constancy performance. *Perception*, 1978, *7*, 179–186.

Kaess, D. W., & Deregowski, J. B. Depicted angle of forms and perception of line drawings. *Perception*, 1980, *9*, 23–29.

Kaiser, P. K. Perceived shape and its dependence on perceived slant. *Journal of Experimental Psychology*, 1967, *75*, 345–353.

Kammann, R. The overestimation of vertical distance and slope and its role in the moon illusion. *Perception and Psychophysics*, 1967, *2*, 585–589.

Kaplan, G. A. Kinetic disruption of optical texture: The perception of depth at an edge. *Perception and Psychophysics*, 1969, *6*, 193–198.

Katz, D. *The world of color* (R. B. MacLeod & C. W. Fox, Ed. and trans.) London: Kegan Paul, 1935. (Originally published, 1911.)

Kaufman, L. *Sight and mind*. New York: Oxford University Press, 1974.

Kaufman, L., & Rock, I. The moon illusion, I. *Science*, 1962, *136*, 953–961. (a)

Kaufman, L., & Rock, I. The moon illusion. *Scientific American*, 1962, *207*, 120–130. (b)

Kilpatrick, F. P., & Ittleson, W. H. The size-distance invariance hypothesis. *Psychological Review*, 1953, *60*, 223–231.

King, M., Meyer, G. E., Tangney, J., & Biederman, I. Shape constancy and a perceptual bias toward symmetry. *Perception and Psychophysics*, 1976, *19*, 129–136.

King, W. L., & Gruber, H. E. Moon illusion and Emmert's law. *Science*, 1962, *135*, 1125–1126.

Koenderink, J. J., & Van Doorn, A. J. Local structure of movement parallax of the plane. *Journal of the Optical Society of America*, 1976, *66*, 717–723.

Koffka, K. *Principles of Gestalt Psychology*. New York: Harcourt, Brace, & World, 1935.

Kraft, A. L., & Winnick, W. A. The effect of pattern and texture gradient on slant and shape judgments. *Perception and Psychophysics*, 1967, *2*, 141–147.

Kunnapas, T. M. Influence of frame size on apparent length of a line. *Journal of Experimental Psychology*, 1955, *50*, 168–170.

Landauer, A. A. The effect of viewing conditions and instructions on shape judgments. *British Journal of Psychology*, 1964, *55*, 49–57. (a)

Landauer, A. A. The nature of "apparent" shape judgments. *Australian Journal of Psychology*, 1964, *16*, 209–213. (b)

Landauer, A. A. Influence of instructions on judgments of unfamiliar shapes. *Journal of Experimental Psychology*, 1969, *79*, 129–132.

Landauer, A. A., & Epstein, W. Does retinal size have a unique correlate in perceived size? *Perception and Psychophysics*, 1969, *6*, 273–275.

Langdon, J. The perception of changing shape. *Quarterly Journal of Psychology*, 1951, *3*, 157–165.

Langdon, J. Further studies in the perception of a changing shape. *Quarterly Journal of Experimental Psychology*, 1953, *5*, 89–107.

Langdon, J. The role of spatial stimuli in the perception of shape. Part I. *Quarterly Journal of Experimental Psychology*, 1955, *7*, 19–27. (a)

Langdon, J. The role of spatial stimuli in the perception of shape. Part II. *Quarterly Journal of Experimental Psychology*, 1955, *7*, 28–36. (b)

Langwiesche-Brandt, E. W. *Stick and rudder*. New York: McGraw-Hill, 1944.

Lappin, J. S., Doner, J. F., & Kottas, B. L. Minimal conditions for the visual detection of structure and motion in three dimensions. *Science*, 1980, *209*, 717–719.

Lappin, J. S., & Fuqua, M. A. Accurate visual measurement of three-dimensional moving patterns. *Science*, 1983, *221*, 480–482.

Lappin, J. S., & Preble, L. D. A demonstration of shape constancy. *Perception and Psychophysics*, 1975, *17*, 439–444.

Leibowitz, H. W. Relation between the Brunswik and Thouless ratios and functional relations in experimental investigations of perceived shape, size and brightness. *Perceptual and Motor Skills*, 1956, *6*, 65–68.

Leibowitz, H., & Bourne, L. E. Time and intensity as determiners of perceived shape. *Journal of Experimental Psychology*, 1956, *51*, 277–281.

Leibowitz, H., Bussey, T., & McGuire, P. Shape and size constancy in photographic reproductions. *Journal of the Optical Society of America*, 1957, *47*, 658–661.

Leibowitz, H. W., & Dato, R. A. Visual size-constancy as a function of distance for temporarily and permanently monocular observers. *American Journal of Psychology*, 1966, *79*, 279–284.

Leibowitz, H., & Hartman, I. Magnitude of the moon illusion as a function of the age of the observer. *Science*, 1959, *130*, 569.

Leibowitz, H. W., Osaka, R., & Oyama, T. (Eds.). *Perception of space and motion*. Kyoto, Japan: Psychologia Society, Department of Educational Psychology, Kyoto University, 1979.

Leibowitz, H. W., Wilcox, S. B., & Post, P. B. The effect of refractive error on size constancy and shape constancy. *Perception*, 1978, *7*, 557–562.

Levine, N. P., & Rosinski, R. R. Distance perception under binocular and monocular viewing conditions. *Perception and Psychophysics*, 1976, *19*, 460–465.

Lichte, W. H. Shape constancy: Dependence upon angle of rotation; individual differences. *Journal of Experimental Psychology*, 1952, *43*, 49–57.

Lichte, W. H., & Borresen, C. R. Influence of instructions on degree of shape constancy. *Journal of Experimental Psychology*, 1967, *74*, 538–542.

Lichten, W., & Lurie, S. A new technique for the study of perceived size. *American Journal of Psychology*, 1950, *63*, 280–282.

Longuet-Higgins, H. C., & Prazdny, K. The interpretation of a moving retinal image. *Proceedings of the Royal Society of London*, 1980, *208 B*, 385–397.

MacDougal, R. The subjective horizon. *Psychological Review Monographs Supplement*, 1966, *4*, 145–166.

Mace, W. M., & Shaw, R. Simple kinetic information for transparent depth. *Perception and Psychophyics*, 1974, *15*, 201–209.

Marr, D. *Vision: A computational investigation into the human representation and processing of visual information*. San Francisco: Freeman, 1982.

Martin, T. M., & Pickford, R. W. The effect of veiling glare on apparent size relations. *British Journal of Psychology*, 1938, *29*, 91–103.

Massaro, D. W. The perception of rotated shapes: A process analysis of shape constancy. *Perception and Psychophysics*, 1973, *13*, 413–422.

Massaro, D. W. *Experimental Psychology and Information Processing*. Chicago: Rand McNally, 1975.

McConkie, A. B., & Farber, J. M. Relation between perceived depth and perceived motion in uniform flow-fields. *Journal of Experimental Psychology: Human Perception and Performance*, 1979, *5*, 501–508.

McDermott, W. P. Linear perspective and perceived size. *Perception and Psychophysics*, 1969, *5*, 33–36.

McKennell, A. C. Visual size and familiar size: Individual differences. *British Journal of Psychology*, 1960, *51*, 27–35.

Mefferd, R. B. Perception of depth in rotating objects: 4. Fluctuating stereokinetic perceptual variants. *Perceptual and Motor Skills*, 1968, *27*, 255–276. (a)

Mefferd, R. B. Perception of depth in rotating objects: 5. Phenomenal motion in stereokinesis. *Perceptual and Motor Skills*, 1968, *27*, 903–926. (b)

Mefferd, R. B. Perception of depth in rotating objects: 6. Effects of fixation and pursuit on the phenomenal motion of stereokinesis. *Perceptual and Motor Skills*, 1968, *27*, 1135–1139. (c)

Mefferd, R. D. Perception of depth in rotating objects: 7. Influence of attributes of depth on stereokinetic percepts. *Perceptual and Motor Skills*, 1968, *27*, 1179–1193. (d)

Meneghini, K., & Leibowitz, H. W., Effect of stimulus distance and age on shape constancy. *Journal of Experimental Psychology*, 1967, *74*, 241–248.

Mershon, D. H., & Gogel, W. C. Failure of familiar size to determine a metric for visually perceived distance. *Perception and Psychophysics*, 1975, *17*, 101–106.

Metzger, W. Optische Untersuchungen am Gansfeld: II. Zur Phanomenologie des homogenen Ganzfelds. *Psychologische Forschung*, 1930, *13*, 6–29.

Metzger, W. Tiefenerscheinungun in optischen Bewegungsfeldern. *Psychologische Forschung*, 1934, *20*, 195–260.

Miles, W. R. Movement interpretation of the silhouette of a revolving fan. *American Journal of Psychology*, 1931, *43*, 392–405.

Moyer, R. S., Bradley, D. R., Sorensen, M. H., Whiting, J. C., & Mansfield, D. P. Psychophysical functions for perceived and remembered size. *Science*, 1978, *200*, 330–332.

Musatti, C. L. Sui fenomeni stereokinetici. *Archivio Italiano di Psicologia*, 1924, *3*, 105–120.

Myers, A. K. Quantitative indices of perceptual constancy. *Psychological Bulletin*, 1980, *88*, 451–457.

Nakayama, K., & Loomis, J. M. Optical velocity patterns, velocity-sensitive neurons, and space perception: A hypothesis. *Perception*, 1974, *3*, 63–80.

Nelson, T. M., & Bartley, S. H. The perception of form in an unstructured field. *Journal of General Psychology*, 1956, *54*, 57–63.

Newman, C. V. The influence of visual texture density gradients on relative distance judgements. *Quarterly Journal of Experimental*

Psychology, 1971, *23*, 225–233.

Newman, C. V. Familiar and relative size cues and surface texture as determinants of relative distance judgments. *Journal of Experimental Psychology*, 1972, *96*, 37–42.

Ogasawara, J. Three formulae for the density-gradient of stimuli in depth perception. *Perceptual and Motor Skills*, 1966, *23*, 1086.

O'Leary, A., & Wallach, H. Familiar size and linear perspective as distance cues in stereoscopic depth constancy. *Perception and Psychophysics*, 1980, *27*, 131–135.

Olson, R. K. Slant judgments from static and rotating trapezoids correspond to rules of perspective geometry. *Perception and Psychophysics*, 1974, *15*, 509–516.

Olson, R. K., Pearl, M., Mayfield, N., Millar, D. Sensitivity to pictorial shape perspective in 5-year-old children and adults. *Perception and Psychophysics*, 1976, *20*, 173–178.

Ono, H. Distal and proximal size under reduced and non-reduced viewing conditions. *American Journal of Psychology*, 1966, *79*, 234–241.

Ono, H. Apparent distance as a function of familiar size. *Journal of Experimental Psychology*, 1969, *79*, 109–115.

Ono, H. Some thoughts on different perceptual tasks related to size and distance. *Psychological Monographs Supplement*, 1970, *3*, No. 13 (Whole No. 45), 143–151.

Ono, H., & Comerford, H. Stereoscopic depth constancy. In W. Epstein (Ed.), *Stability and constancy in visual perception*. New York: Wiley, 1977.

Over, R. The effect of instructions on size-judgments under reduction conditions. *American Journal of Psychology*, 1960, *73*, 599–602.

Over, R. Size- and distance-estimates of a single stimulus under different viewing conditions. *American Journal of Psychology*, 1963, *76*, 452–457.

Owens & Leibowitz, H. W. Specific distance tendency. *Perception and Psychophysics*, 1976, *20*, 2–9.

Oyama, T. Analysis of causal relations in the perceptual constancies. In W. Epstein (Ed.), *Stability and constancy in visual perception*. New York: Wiley, 1977.

Park, J. N., & Michaelson, G. J. Distance judgments under different size-information conditions. *Perception and Psychophysics*, 1974, *15*, 57–60.

Perrone, J. A. Slant underestimation: a model based on the size of the viewing aperture. *Perception*, 1980, *9*, 285–302.

Perrone, J. A. Visual slant underestimation: A general model. *Perception*, 1982, *11*, 641–654.

Petersik, J. T. Three-dimensional object constancy: Coherence of a simulated rotating sphere in noise. *Perception and Psychophysics*, 1979, *25*, 328–335.

Philip, B. R., & Fisichelli, V. R. Effect of speed of rotation and complexity of pattern on the reversals of apparent movement in Lissajous figures. *American Journal of Psychology*, 1945, *58*, 530–539.

Phillips, R. J. Stationary visual texture and the estimation of slant angle. *Quarterly Journal of Experimental Psychology*, 1970, *22*, 389–397.

Prazdny, K. Egomotion and relative depth map from optical flow. *Biological Cybernetics*, 1980, *36*, 87–102.

Prazdny, S. A note on "Perception of surface slant and edge labels from optical flow." *Perception*, 1981, *10*, 579–582.

Prazdny, K. A note on "Optical motions as information for unsigned depth." *Journal of Experimental Psychology: Human Perception and Performance*, 1981, *7*, 286–289.

Predebon, J. Role of familiar size in spatial judgments under natural viewing conditions. *Perceptual and Motor Skills*, 1979, *48*, 171–176. (a)

Predebon, J. Effect of familiar size on judgments of relative size and distance. *Perceptual and Motor Skills*, 1979, *48*, 1211–1214. (b)

Predebon, J., Wenderoth, P. M., & Curthoys, I. S. The effects of instructions and distance on judgments of off-size familiar objects under natural viewing conditions. *American Journal of Psychology*, 1974, *87*, 425–439.

Purdy, J., & Gibson, E. J. Distance judgments by the method of fractionation. *Journal of experimental Psychology*, 1955, *50*, 374–380.

Purdy, W. C. *The hypothesis of psychophysical correspondence in space perception* (General Electric Technical Information Series No. R60ELC56). Ithaca, NY: General Electric Advanced Electronics Center, 1960.

Regan, D., & Cynader, M. Neurons in area 18 of cat visual cortex selectively sensitive to changing size: Nonlinear interactions between responses to two edges. *Vision Research*, 1979, *19*, 699–711.

Reimann, E. Die scheinbare Vergrosserung der Sonne und des Monde am Horizont. *Zeitschrift für Psychologie*, 1902, *30*, 1–38, 161–195.

Restle, F. Moon illusion explained on the basis of relative size. *Science*, 1970, *167*, 1092–1096.

Richards, W. Visual space perception. In E. C. Carterette & M. P. Friedman (Eds.), *Handbook of perception*. Vol. 5: *Seeing*. New York: Academic Press, 1975.

Richards, W., & Miller, J. F. The corridor illusion. *Perception and Psychophysics*, 1971, *9*, 421–423.

Rock, I. In defense of unconscious inference. In W. Epstein (Ed.), *Stability and constancy in visual perception*. New York: Wiley, 1977.

Rock, I. *The logic of perception*. Cambridge, MA: MIT Press, 1983.

Rock, I., & Ebenholtz, S. The relational determination of perceived size. *Psychological Review*, 1959, *66*, 387–401.

Rock, I., & Kaufman, L. The moon illusion: II. *Science*, 1962, *136*, 1023–1031.

Rock, I., & McDermott, W. The perception of visual angle. Acta Psychologica, 1964, *22*, 119–134.

Rock, I., Shallo, J., & Schwartz, F. Pictorial depth and related constancy effects as a function of recognition. *Perception*, 1978, *7*, 3–19.

Rock, I., & Smith, D. Alternative solutions to kinetic stimulus transformations. *Journal of Experimental Psychology: Human Perception and Performance*, 1981, *7*, 19–29.

Rock, I., Wheeler, D., Shallo, J., & Rotunda, J. The construction of a plane from pictorial information. *Perception*, 1982, *11*, 463–475.

Roelofs, C. O., & Zeeman, W. P. C. Apparent size and apparent distance in binocular and monocular distance. *Ophthalmologica*, 1957, *133*, 188–204.

Rogers, B., & Graham, M. Motion parallax as an independent cue for depth perception. *Perception*, 1979, *8*, 125–134.

Rogers, B., & Graham, M. Anisotropies in the perception of three-dimensional surfaces. *Science*, 1983, *221*, 1409–1411.

Rogers, S. P., & Gogel, W. C. Relations between judged and physical distance in multicue conditions as a function of instructions and tasks. *Perceptual and Motor Skills*, 1975, *41*, 171–178.

Rogowitz, B. E. The breakdown of size constancy under stroboscopic illumination. In L. Spillman & B. R. Wooten (Eds.), *Sensory experience, adaptation, and perception: Festschrift for Ivo Kohler*. Hillsdale, N.J.: Erlbaum, 1984.

Rosinski, R. R., Degelman, D., & Mulholland, T. Intermodel relationships in children's perception. *Child Development*, 1978, *49*, 1089–1095.

Rosinski, R. R., & Farber, J. M. Compensation for viewing point in the perception of pictured space. In M. A. Hagen (Ed.), *The perception of pictures*. Vol. 1: *Alberti's window*. New York: Academic, 1980.

Rosinski, R. R., & Levine, N. P. Texture gradient effectiveness in the perception of surface slant. *Journal of Experimental Child Psychology*, 1976, *22*, 261–271.

Ross, H. E., & Ross, G. M. Did Ptolemy understand the moon illusion? *Perception*, 1976, *5*, 377–385.

Ross, J., Jenkins, B., & Johnstone, J. R. Size constancy fails below half a degree. *Nature*, 1980, *283*, 473–474.

Rump, E. E. The relationship between perceived size and perceived distance. *British Journal of Psychology*, 1961, *52*, 111–124.

Schiffman, H. R. Size-estimation of familiar objects under informative and reduced conditions of viewing. *American Journal of Psychology*, 1967, *80*, 229–235.

Sedgwick, H. A. The visible horizon: A potential source of visual information for the perception of size and distance (Doctoral dissertation, Cornell University, 1973). *Dissertation Abstracts International*, 1973, *34*, 1301B–1302B. (University Microfilms No. 73-22,530).

Sedgwick, H. A. The geometry of spatial layout in pictorial representation. In M. A. Hagen (Ed.), *The perception of pictures*. Vol. 1: *Alberti's Window*. New York: Academic, 1980.

Sedgwick, H. A. Environment-centered representation of spatial layout: Available information from texture and perspective. In A. Rosenthal & J. Beck (Eds.), *Human and machine vision*. New York: Academic, 1983.

Sedgwick, H. A., & Festinger, L. Eye movements, efference, and visual perception. In R. A. Monty & J. W. Senders (Eds.), *Eye movements and psychological processes*. Hillsdale, N.J.: Erlbaum, 1976.

Shebilske, W. L., & Proffitt, D. R. The priority of perceived distance for perceiving motion has not been demonstrated: Critical comments on Gogel's "The sensing of retinal motion." *Perception and Psychophysics*, 1981, *29*, 170–172.

Shebilske, W. L., & Proffitt, D. R. Paradoxical retinal motions during head movements: Apparent motion without equivalent apparent displacement, *Perception and Psychophysics*, 1983, *34*, 476–481.

Sigman, E., & Oltman, P. K. Field dependence and the role of visual frameworks in the perception of size. *Perception*, 1977, *6*, 661–666.

Simon, H. A. Spurious correlation: A causal interpretation. *Journal of the American Statistical Association*, 1954, *49*, 467–479.

Slack, C. W. Familiar size as a cue to size in the presence of conflicting cues. *Journal of Experimental Psychology*, 1956, *52*, 194–198.

Smith, A. H. Gradients of outline convergence and distortion as stimuli for slant. *Canadian Journal of Psychology*, 1956, *10*, 211–218.

Smith, A. H. Outline convergence versus closure in the perception of slant. *Perceptual and Motor Skills*, 1959, *9*, 259–266.

Smith, A. H. Judgment of slant with constant outline convergence and variable surface texture gradient. *Perceptual and Motor Skills*, 1964, *18*, 869–875.

Smith, A. H. Perceived slant as a function of stimulus contour and vertical dimension. *Perceptual and Motor Skills*, 1967, *24*, 167–173.

Smith, O. W. Judgments of size and distance in photographs. *American Journal of Psychology*, 1958, *71*, 529–538.

Smith, O. W., & Smith, P. C. Response produced vs. non-response-produced visual stimuli for distance judgments in natural and unnatural units by children and adults. *Perceptual and Motor Skills*, 1967, *24*, 487–492.

Smith, O. W., & Smith, P. C. Brunswik ratios: A ratio scale for comparative analysis of size constancy from different experiments. *Perceptual and Motor Skills*, 1977, *45*, 1255–1258.

Smith, O. W., Smith, P. C., Geist, C. G., & Zimmermann, R. R. Apparent size contrasts of retinal images and size constancy as determinants of the moon illusion. *Perceptual and Motor Skills*, 1978, *46*, 803–808.

Smith, O. W., Smith, P. C., & Hubbard, D. Perceived distance as a function of the method of representing distance. *American Journal of Psychology*, 1958, *71*, 662–674.

Smith, R. *A compleat system of opticks* (Vol. 1). Cambridge, England: 1738.

Smith, W. M. Past experience and the perception of visual size. *American Journal of Psychology*, 1952, *65*, 389–403.

Smith, W. M. A methodological study of size-distance perception. *Journal of Psychology*, 1953, *35*, 143–153.

Stavrianos, B. K. The relation of shape-perception to explicit judgments of inclination. *Archives of Psychology*, 1945, No. 296.

Stevens, K. A. *Surface perception from local analysis of texture and contour* (Technical Report No. TR-512). Cambridge, MA: Massachusetts Institute of Technology Artificial Intelligence Laboratory, 1980.

Stevens, K. A. The information content of texture gradients. *Biological Cybernetics*, 1981, *42*, 95–105.

Stevens, K. A. Surface tilt (the direction of slant): A neglected psychophysical variable. *Perception and Psychophysics*, 1983, *33*, 241–250.

Stevens, S. S. *Psychophysics: Introduction to its perceptual, neural, and social prospects*. New York: Wiley, 1975.

Taylor, D. W., & Boring, E. G. Apparent visual size as a function of distance for monocular observers. *American Journal of Psychology*, 1942, *55*, 102–105. (a)

Taylor, D. W., & Boring, E. G. The moon illusion as a function of binocular regard. *American Journal of Psychology*, 1942, *55*, 180–201. (b)

Teghtsoonian, M. The doubtful phenomenon of over-constancy. In H. R. Moskowitz, B. Scharf, & J. C. Stevens (Eds.), *Sensation and measurement*. Dordrecht, Holland: Reidel, 1974.

Teghtsoonian, M., & Teghtsoonian, R. Scaling apparent distance in a natural indoor setting. *Psychonomic Science*, 1969, *16*, 281–283.

Teghtsoonian, R., & Teghtsoonian, M. The effects of size and distance on magnitude estimations of apparent size. *American Journal of Psychology*, 1970, *83*, 601–612. (a)

Teghtsoonian, R., & Teghtsoonian, M. Scaling apparent distance in a natural outdoor setting. *Psychonomic Science*, 1970, *21*, 215–216. (b)

Thompson, J. G., Valenti, C. A., & Schiffman, H. R. Effect of perspective and slant on perception of apparent size and distance. *Perceptual and Motor Skills*, 1978, *47*, 575–582.

Thouless, R.H. Phenomenal regression to the real object: I. *British Journal of Psychology*, 1931, *21*, 339–359.

Todd, J. T. Visual information about rigid and nonrigid motion: A geometric analysis. *Journal of Experimental Psychology: Human Perception and Performance*, 1982, *8*, 238–252.

Todd, J. T. The perception of three-dimensional structure from rigid and non-rigid motion. *Perception and Psychophysics*, 1984, *36*, 97–103.

Topper, D. R., & Simpson, W. A. Depth perception in linear and inverse perspective pictures. *Perception*, 1981, *10*, 305–312.

Tyer, Z. E., Allen, J. A., & Pasnak, R. Instruction effects on size and distance judgments. *Perception and Psychophysics*, 1983, *34*, 135–139.

Ueno, T. The size-distance invariance hypothesis and the psychophysical law. *Japanese Psychological Research*, 1962, *4*, 99–112.

Ullman, S. The interpretation of structure from motion. *Proceedings of the Royal Society of London*, 1979, *203 B*, 405–426. (a)

Ullman, S. *The interpretation of visual motion*. Cambridge, Mass.: MIT Press, 1979. (b)

Ullman, S. Rigidity and misperceived motion. *Perception*, 1984, *13*, 219–220. (a)

Ullman, S. Maximizing rigidity: The incremental recovery of 3-D structure from rigid and nonrigid motion. *Perception*, 1984, *13*, 255–274. (b)

Van de Geer, J. P., & Zwaan, E. J. Size-constancy as dependent upon angle of regard and spatial direction of the stimulus-object. *American Journal of Psychology*, 1964, *77*, 563–575.

Vogel, J. M., & Teghtsoonian, M. The effects of perspective alterations on apparent size and distance scales. *Perception and Psychophysics*, 1972, *11*, 294–298.

von Fieandt, K., & Gibson, J. J. The sensitivity of the eye to two kinds of continuous transformation of a shadow-pattern. *Journal of Experimental Psychology*, 1959, *57*, 344–347.

Wallach, H. Brightness constancy and the nature of achromatic colors. *Journal of Experimental Psychology*, 1948, *38*, 310–324.

Wallach, H., & O'Connell, D. N. The kinetic depth effect. *Journal of Experimental Psychology*, 1953, *45*, 205–217.

Wallach, H., O'Connell, D. N., & Neisser, U. The memory effect of visual perception of three-dimensional form. *Journal of Experimental Psychology*, 1953, *45*, 360–368.

Wallach, H., & O'Leary, A. Adaptation in distance perception with head-movement parallax serving as the veridical cue. *Perception and Psychophysics*, 1979, *25*, 42–46.

Wallach, H., & O'Leary, A. Slope of regard as a distance cue. *Perception and Psychophysics*, 1982, *31*, 145–148.

Wallach, H., & McKenna, V. V. On size-perception in the absence of cues for distance. *American Journal of Psychology*, 1960, *73*, 458–460.

Wallach, H., & Moore, M. E. The role of slant in the perception of shape. *American Journal of Psychology*, 1962, *75*, 285–293.

Wallach, H., Weisz, A., & Adams, P. A. Circles and derived figures in rotation. *American Journal of Psychology*, 1956, *69*, 48–59.

Ware, W. R. *Modern Perspective* (Rev. ed.). New York: Macmillan, 1900.

Weber, C. O. Apparent movement in Lissajous figures. *American Journal of Psychology*, 1930, *42*, 647–649.

Weinstein, S. The perception of depth in the absence of texture gradient. *American Journal of Psychology*, 1957, *70*, 611–615.

Wenderoth, P. The contribution of relational factors to line-length matches. *Perception*, 1976, *5*, 265–278.

Wheatstone, C. On some remarkable, and hitherto unresolved, phenomena of binocular vision. *Royal Society of London, Philosophical Transactions*, 1838, 371–394.

White, B. W., & Mueser, G. E. Accuracy in reconstructing the arrangement of elements generating kinetic depth displays. *Journal of Experimental Psychology*, 1960, *60*, 1–11.

White, J. *The birth and rebirth of pictorial space*. New York: Harper & Row, 1967.

Wilcox, B. L., & Teghtsoonian, M. The control of relative size by pictorial depth cues in children and adults. *Journal of Experimental Child Psychology*, 1971, *11*, 413–429.

Willey, R., & Gyr, J. W. Motion parallax and projective similarity as factors in slant perception. *Journal of Experimental Psychology*, 1969, *79*, 525–532.

Wilson, J. A., Robinson, J. O., & Piggins, D. J. Wobble cones and wobble holes: The stereokinetic effect revisited. *Perception*, 1983, *12*, 187–193.

Winnick, W. A., & Rogoff, I. Role of apparent slant in shape judgments. *Journal of Experimental Psychology*, 1965, *69*, 554–563.

Winnick, W. A., & Rosen, B. E. Shape-slant relations under reduction conditions. *Perception and Psychophysics*, 1966, *1*, 157–160.

Wohlwill, J. F. The perspective illusion: Perceived size and distance in fields varying in suggested depth, in children and adults. *Journal of Experimental Psychology*, 1962, *64*, 300–310.

Wohlwill, J. F. Overconstancy in distance perception as a function of the texture of the stimulus field and other variables. *Perceptual and Motor Skills*, 1963, *17*, 831–846.

Wohlwill, J. F. Changes in distance judgments as a function of corrected and noncorrected practice. *Perceptual and Motor Skills*, 1964, *19*, 403–413.

Wohlwill, J. F. Texture of the stimulus field and age as variables in the perception of relative distance in photographic slides. *Journal of Experimental Child Psychology*, 1965, *2*, 163–177.

Woodworth, R. S. *Experimental psychology*. New York: Holt, 1938.

Woodworth, R. S., & Schlosberg, H. *Experimental psychology*. New York: Holt, 1954.

Zucker, S. W. On the structure of texture. *Perception*, 1976, *5*, 419–436.

CHAPTER 22

REPRESENTATION OF MOTION AND SPACE IN VIDEO AND CINEMATIC DISPLAYS

JULIAN HOCHBERG

Columbia University, Department of Psychology, New York, New York

CONTENTS

This chapter is concerned with the representation of events by means of motion pictures, including video displays and film. Although decisions that should be grounded in perceptual fact and theory are being made continually by those who make motion pictures of all kinds, psychology is very far from being able to make any real contribution to the field. That state of affairs is neither necessary nor desirable.

Until relatively recently, this has not been a hardship. Most of the problems in making the motion picture could be solved by trial and error, and the uses to which films were put—mostly entertainment, education, and surveillance—could tolerate considerable gaps in the viewer's comprehension. For example, it usually matters little precisely how the actor leaves the house, and indeed, the editor will usually remove the sequence entirely and leave it to the viewer to fill in.

Furthermore, until recently the filmmaker generally worked within a wider margin than was needed. Given some simple precautions, the filmmaker usually need only point a camera toward an event and a comprehensible record is more likely than not to result. These wide margins for error, and tolerance of uncertainty, are being reduced, in part because of the demands of practice: visual simulation of the view from high-speed vehicles (e.g., low-altitude flight simulation); navigational displays; and instructional devices. All these make extreme demands on the motion-picture medium. Furthermore, the tasks for which the motion pictures are now being used are often intolerant of even minor incomprehensibilities in representation.

Finally, computer-generated or -enhanced moving pictures are intruding into all aspects of use. Some of these are "canned" (noninteractive and fixed in nature), for example television commercials, logos, special effects, and animated cartoons, in which an artist contributes a few "storyboard" sketches and models the three-dimensional layout to be animated and a computer fills in the intervening stretches (see Freeman, Chapter 3; Whitted, 1982; Youngblood, 1983). Some of them are interactive, or contingent upon the behavior of a viewer, for example, the display in a flight simulator, which is generated from some predetermined *virtual environment* in response to the manipulation of the aircraft controls; the visualizations in an architectural layout, which change in response to changes in viewpoint and in design; the view sequences and animations generated in an interactive training device, which are contingent on the particular query made by the user.

In the case of computer-generated graphics, the maker cannot count on the structure of correlated attributes in the physical world that provides the pictorial information that the viewer expects in a picture and that furnishes multiple cues about the event and the space in which it occurs. To take two obvious examples, the motion-picture cinematographer may (and often does) know little about the geometry of physical space that is expressed in the "laws of perspective" and usually needs to know even less about the "laws of apparent movement" that transform a succession of still frames on a stationary scene into a representation of a sweep through three-dimensional space in a moving vehicle. The structure of the physical world will ensure (within limits) that the appropriate information is present in the motion-picture image. The maker of computer graphics, in contrast, must make explicit provision for everything that may eventually be needed in the final image, which in turn includes both an adequate treatment of the *relevant* physical structures (e.g., the various expressions of perspective) and an adequate use of the relevant perceptual processes (e.g., apparent movement and its vicissitudes).

This issue is particularly important in the case of interactive graphics. In canned material (e.g., television commercials), a human editor normally catches and corrects incomprehensible or misleading displays. In interactive graphics, on the other hand, sequences may turn up that have never been generated or viewed before. Unless the program has correctly drawn on both physical structure and perceptual laws, the sequences may well be incomprehensible to the viewer.

Motion-picture makers, particularly in the case of *computer-generated images* (CGI), can no longer remain ignorant of the applicable perceptual laws, nor can they tolerate the present state of ignorance in this area of perceptual psychology. Applicable theory and specific data are needed now.

The gap problem is now important from the psychologist's side as well. The notion of fundamental motion-sensitive or event-sensitive analyzing mechanisms in the nervous system has had its enthusiasts since Exner (1875) and Wolhgemuth (1911). What has changed in recent years is not the exhortation but the demonstration that there are indeed neural structures that we can think of as "event detectors" (see Anstis, Chapter 16, and Mack, Chapter 17) and the availability of relatively cheap and convenient devices for producing moving stimuli of some complexity and of considerable precision.

1. FILM AND VIDEO AS MODES OF REPRESENTATION

Section 1 considers the major means of producing moving pictures and their characteristics, and surveys what we need to know for the formulation and testing of perceptual theory and for the application of that knowledge in practice.

1.1. The Characteristics of the Media

A few points can be presented in real motion on a cathode-ray tube (CRT) or some similar device. It becomes prohibitively difficult to present more complex events (e.g., moving objects) in this way, and all practical means of presenting pictures that appear to move depend on sequences of brief, static views, either on film or in a video display, that change by relatively small amounts from one display to the next.

Different parameters are used in different devices, depending on the purposes for which the motion picture is to be used and on the history of the device.

Two systems of producing motion pictures are by far the most widespread at present: film and video. These are described briefly in Sections 1.1.1 and 1.1.2.

1.1.1. The Nature of Motion Pictures on Film. Motion-picture films, as everyone knows, consist of a succession of still transparencies, illuminated from the rear and projected one at a time through a lens and shutter to a viewing screen (Figure 22.1).

1.1.1.1. The Succession of Still Pictures. In modern standard projection of film with a sound track, there are 24 still pictures per sec. In the most common procedure, the projection light is transmitted only while a short section of the film is kept stationary in the film gate for a period of some 30 msec; the film is then rapidly advanced by an intermittent mechanism (e.g., a downward-moving claw that briefly engages the sprocket-holes in the short film section), replacing the still frame that had already been projected with a fresh one. Loops of film before and after the film gate serve to provide the slack that is needed because the continuously moving film is periodically halted in the film gate.

A rotary shutter occludes the projection light during the change, to avoid a blur during each period (as brief as 8 msec) that the film moves through the gate. Because an interruption rate of 24 per sec is readily visible to most viewers as a detectable and unacceptable flicker, projectors are normally equipped with additional blades on the rotary shutter to interrupt the projection more frequently and bring the interruption rate above the average viewer's critical flicker frequency (CFF), the threshold beyond which the interruptions become undetectable. The greater the duration of the interruptions, the less the average light reaching the screen (see Chapter 6 by Watson). Most projectors use two or three blades, with flicker rates of 48 and 72 Hz, respectively; five blades are used only for transferring motion pictures from film to video (we return to this in Section 1.1.2).

There are other means, such as rotating prisms, of providing a sequence of stationary images from a continuously moving film strip, but the overwhelming majority of projectors, and cameras as well, use some variant of the intermittent, saltatory principle described in the preceding paragraph.

1.1.1.2. The Palette of Representation. The image on each successive frame of the film consists of a photographic transparency; information in the projected image therefore depends on the size of the film, the resolution of the film, the projection lens, and so on. Film sizes in common use range from 8–70 mm. The size of the image on the screen will depend, of course, on the focal length of the projector lens and the distance to the screen.

Most commonly, the image on each frame of the film was originally made by a motion-picture camera. The amount of detail that can be recorded on each frame of film has an upper limit, set by size of the frame and the resolution of the image. The resolution, in turn, depends on the camera lens, on its aperture while the picture was being taken, on the nature of the film, on how it was processed and stored, and so on.

In film the image is usually produced by *subtraction*, using small opaque silver grains, or regions of dye, to filter all but the desired wavelengths from the projection light. The ratio of transmittances determines the ratio of light intensities and the spectral distribution of the light projected to the screen. Although transmittances vary greatly with conditions of exposure and processing, the maximum ratio of adjacent areas is probably of the order of 40/1 (Millerson, 1982). This is a great deal better than the ratio of luminances that can be obtained in video (about 10/1 or 20/1 in adjacent areas; see Millerson, 1982) but less than a good transparency (about 80/1) and vastly less than the ratios of intensity that can be expected to occur in a natural optic array. A point in the optic array corresponding to a highlight of sunlight on a specular surface may have thousands of times the photic energy of a spot corresponding to deep shade. Painters and still photographers have learned to restrict their subject matter, on the one hand, and to exploit the phenomena of simultaneous constrast (Evans, 1948; Goldstein, 1980; Hochberg, 1971a; Kaufman, 1974; Wyszecki, Chapter 9), on the other, in the attempt to make up for this deficiency in the range of the pictorial palette. But the restricted ratios remain a major way

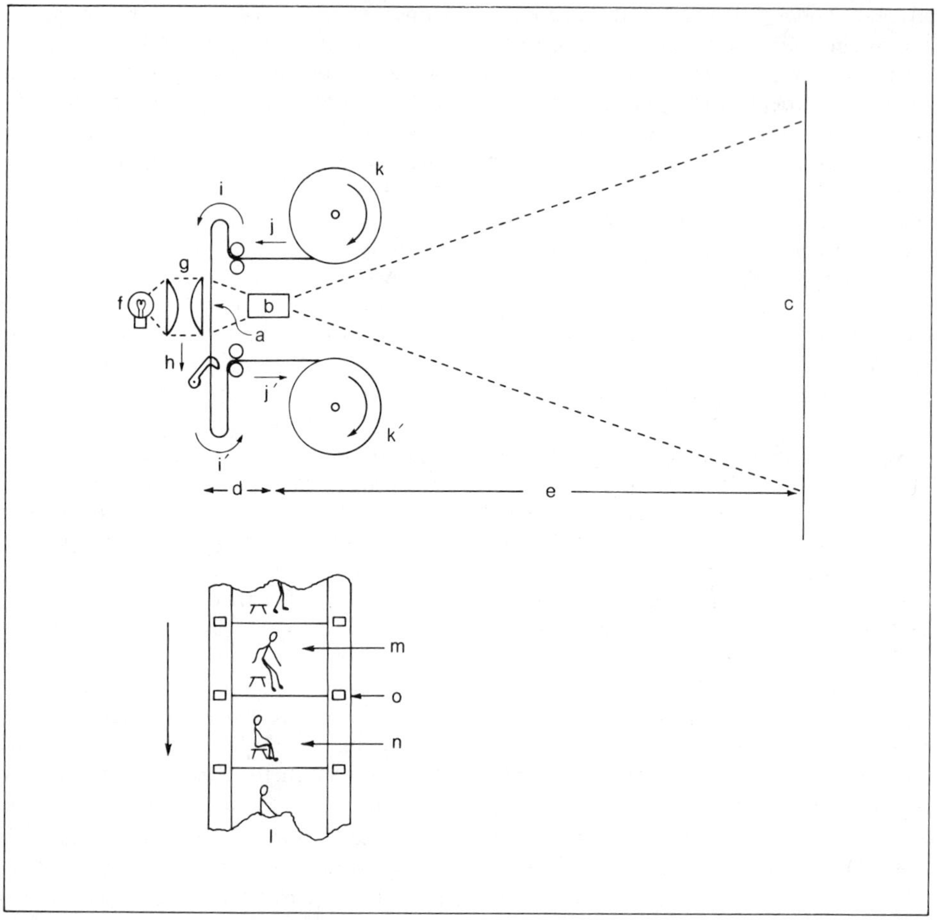

Figure 22.1. Moving pictures from film, in a typical projection system. A still-picture transparency *a*, transilluminated by a lamp *f* and a condenser system *g* is projected by a lens *b* to a screen *c*. The size of the focused image on *c* depends on the size of *a* and on the distances *d* and *e*, where *d* is the distance from the film plane to the nodal point of the lens and *e* is the distance from that point to the screen. The picture is replaced by another still picture through the action of a claw *h*, producing an intermittent movement of the film from loop *i* to loop *i'*. The film is moved continuously *j–j'* into and out of the region of intermittent movement by reels *k* and *k'*. The claw *h* replaces one frame *n* of the film strip with another *m* by engaging and pulling down through a sprocket hole *o* and then disengaging that hole and moving to engage the next one up. While the film is in motion, one of the blades of a rotating shutter (not shown) between the condenser *g* and the film *a* occludes the light. Thus while there is continuous movement at various points in the system, the parts involving the image are carefully engineered to provide only brief, stationary views.

in which the optic array provided by a film differs from that normally provided by the scene being represented, and the filmmaker must keep that in mind constantly.

The size and configuration of these opacities and semiopacities determine the resolution of the film. In moving pictures, however, the grain size is less of a limiting factor than in still pictures, because the details of the object being photographed may be constant across several frames, whereas the grain varies randomly and cancels out except as a level of "noise" that perturbs the details.

Various measures have been used with which to express the usable detail in film or other visual displays. (See Roufs & Bouma, 1980; Snyder, 1973.) We should note that a statement of the number of independently variable points in the two-dimensional array *must* suffice, in the sense that all other measures must be translatable into those terms. Other measures may be more convenient for a particular medium or may capture more of what is deemed important about the visual uses to which the display will be put. Modulation transfer functions, long used in the analysis of temporal properties of sound transmission systems, have been adopted to measure image quality. They are particularly suited to television (Schade, 1964) and, with the introduction of Fourier technique, have been widely used in the form of contrast-sensitivity functions (van Nes & Bouman, 1967). Some theories of vision, particularly those in which spatial-frequency channels play a significant part (Ginsburg, 1980, and Chapter 34), virtually mandate this measure. Other measures, such as point-spread functions and line-spread functions, have attractive features for some purposes, but there is no general measure that is the best summary of image quality regardless of perceptual function (Roufs & Bouma, 1980).

The number of picture elements, or *pixels*, indicates the number of separate regions that can be made to vary independently in spectral distribution and thereby construct the image. The number of different pictures that can be made, and the detail that can be represented, obviously depends on the number of pixels available. In principle, by making the pixels so small and close together that the viewer cannot distinguish them as discrete regions, and by breaking down the scene being pictured into corresponding small regions, each of which precisely matches the light coming from the scene, the still picture can in theory be made to present to the eye of the viewer (or to any physical measuring instrument) an optic array of light that is under certain strict conditions, discussed in Section 1.2.2, indistinguishable from that produced by the scene.

1.1.2. The Nature of Moving Pictures on Video. Electro-optical imaging techniques are discussed in Chapter 3 by Freeman and in Whitted (1982). Of these, by far the most prevalent are raster scan methods, essentially those of the familiar television display, in which an electron beam traces horizontal lines across a CRT. Mixture in a color set is additive, in that three separate phosphors are modulated, in essence independently. Usable adjacent contrast is (as noted above) drastically less than that for film.

The actual resolution of the image depends on the number of lines, the bandwidth of the modulation, the focus of the beam, the scatter and glow in the tube and phosphor, and so on. In commercial use, 30 frames per sec are displayed in a 512-line picture. To alleviate flicker, each frame is scanned in two interlaced half-rasters.

Given the coarse raster scan and the low resolution generally available, expansive stretches of small detail are impossible, and texture (which is important information about form [Stevens, 1981]) virtually drops out as an important pictoral feature (see Section 1.2.2). The "cartoonlike" nature of the resulting images has been noted, its likely effects on spatial representation deplored (Hochberg & Brooks, 1973; Stenger, Thomas, Braunstein, & Zimmerlin, 1979). In addition, the scanning pattern provides a source of interaction between the form being displayed and the fixed pixel structure of the display that provides for moiré patterns, scintillation, and "aliasing" (the jagged appearance of edges at an angle to the raster).

Each of these problems can be ameliorated but at some cost. Antialiasing can be approached by suitably modulating the edge's intensity (Crow, 1977); resolution can be concentrated in the region of interest, by suitable use of programmed closeups (Hochberg & Brooks, 1973) or perhaps by actually tracking the viewer's gaze direction (Stenger et al., 1979). There is no general solution at hand, so the specific needs of the representational task become paramount. In an admirably task-specific study, Sperling (1980) showed that a bandwidth of approximately 20 kHz is sufficient for the video communication of American Sign Language. We discuss in Section 1.2.2 the effects of video display limitations on the representation of space.

1.2. The Display as Picture

We noted in Section 1.1.1.2 that under certain conditions, to be discussed in Section 1.2.2, a display can substitute for some physical event by presenting an array of light to the eye (the *optic array* in Figure 22.2) that is physically indistinguishable from that produced by the event, and the picture is then a *surrogate* for that event. Although we will also see that a picture need not be a surrogate to be an effective representation, comparison of optic arrays to analyze the adequacy of any medium for representing any event would be a straightforward combination of engineering and psychophysics. It offers a seductive metaphor for a picture and has influenced a great many approaches to the psychology of picture perception and, indeed, approaches to the psychology of perception in general (cf. Gibson, 1954, 1971; Hochberg, 1962). Unfortunately, it is highly misleading, for reasons we consider next.

First, we should note that the optic array provided by a real set of surfaces in depth will not, in general, provide the eye with a set of points that can all be focused by the same *accommodation*, or adjustment of the eye's lens, or brought to corresponding points in the two eyes' views by the same angle of *convergence* of the two eyes. Only if both scene and picture are at a great distance, or if the light from both is collimated, can the optic array provide a true surrogate in this extremely important respect.

Second, if it really were necessary to match each point in the optic array in spectral energy distribution to the corresponding point in the scene, the engineering problems would prove insurmountable by any known technology. The fact is, of course, that a very small number of bands of wavelength and a small number of steps of photic energy will serve as a palette by which the surrogate can be psychophysically matched, point by point, to the scene it represents. A picture made up of a set of points that differ only in these relatively few ways can there-

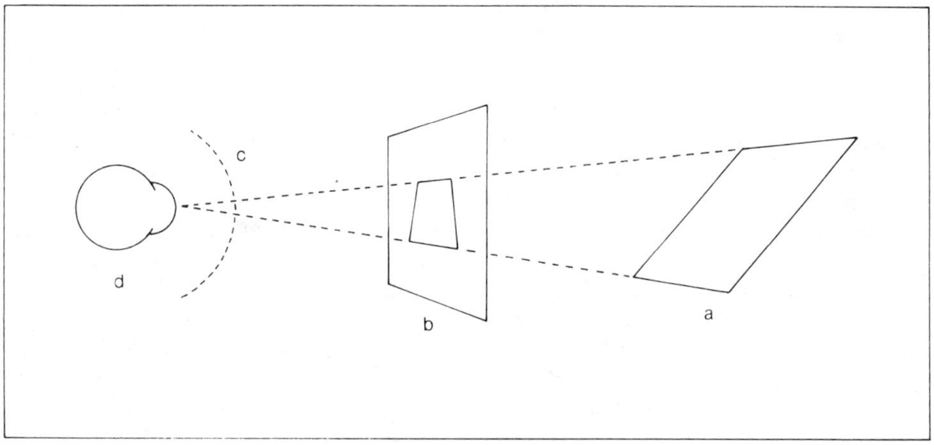

Figure 22.2. Optical surrogates. Any object *a* can in principle be replaced by another object *b* that provides the same array *c* of light rays to the eye *d* or other optical instrument. To the degree that *a* and *b* have the same effects in this regard, one can be used as a surrogate for the other.

fore substitute for objects and events in space that differ in many more ways. The picture is similar to the scene but only in its point-by-point appearance to a normal human observer. It is this set of purely subjective phenomena, by which we set up the matching procedure in the first place, not the physics of the match per se, that makes pictures possible at all.

Nor should it be inferred that by specifying the perceived lightnesses and colors at each point on the film, we will in any sense specify what the appearance of the whole image will be. Although the pixels of film are, unlike those of video, at least roughly independent of each other, how a particular spot appears to a normal human viewer depends very much on the configuration of surrounding stimulation and on the time course of stimulation (see *simultaneous contrast, successive contrast*, and *adaptation*). Indeed, it may depend, as well, on much more interpretive factors, such as what the apparent arrangement of surfaces in space is perceived to be (Hochberg & Beck, 1954; Kardos, 1934; Wyszecki, Chapter 9).

1.2.1. The Still Image: I. As a Record of Objects' Reflectances. Such interactions as simultaneous contrast probably work to help the viewer, who is looking at the real world, to recognize and respond to the permanent properties of the object—for example, to the object's constant reflectance, rather than to the particular and changing light that falls on the screen at any moment. This is the issue of the perceptual constancies, discussed in Chapter 33 by Rock and in Chapter 36 by Pomerantz and Kubovy; see also Hochberg, 1971a, 1971b; Kaufman, 1974). The constancy problem affects our present concerns as follows.

Reflectances help the viewer perceive where one surface in the world ends and another begins. If a set of objects all received the same illumination and their surfaces were all oriented toward the camera at the same angle [Figure 22.3(a)], then the luminances of the points they contribute to the optic array and to the photographic image are proportional to, and informative of, their reflectances. Pixels of the same lightness and color are then likely to be part of the image of the same object, and pixels that differ are then likely to belong to images of different objects. In a normally cluttered scene, this is extremely important; one of the virtues of color pictures, of course, is that pixels can be identified as belonging with each other in accordance with their hues and not only according to their lightnesses. We should note, however, that two adjacent regions that differ only in their hue do not segregate well in static displays (Bishop, 1966; Liebman, 1927); luminance difference is also needed, and that should be kept in mind when using diffuse illumination which tends to eliminate the shadows at objects' boundaries. See Figure 22.3(b) and (d).

In general, however, surfaces do not receive the same illumination, nor do they lie at the same angle to either the source of the illumination or the camera. Under these more natural conditions, pixels that correspond to surfaces of identical reflectance need not be identical in color, nor do pixels of the same color correspond in general to objects of the same reflectance [Figure 22.3(b)–(d)]. In the optic array offered by such a scene in the real world, there is a hierarchy of informative features that leads to the correct segregation of objects and the correct perception of their uniform reflectance. For example, even a slight movement of an object moves the shadow over its surface and informs the viewer that the terminator of the shadow [Fig. 22.3(b)iii] marks a change in illumination and not a difference in reflectance.

Many of these factors that cause (or allow) the viewer to separate reflectance from shadow and modeling are missing in the still picture, and artists and still photographers have had to learn to use the devices of contrast and chiaroscuro (adjacent contrast as controlled by steep or shallow gradients; Hochberg, 1979, 1981) to control the apparent colors of parts of the picture. Such devices are probably still appropriate to the motion picture produced when the camera is stationary with respect to the scene. But when the camera moves relative to the scene, many of the factors that lead to correct object segregation, when looking at the real world, are present, as well, in the film. Especially when a wide field of view is included within the single frame, as in Figure 22.4(a), and high resolution is provided, object segregation and the perception of reflectances are probably close to what they are in viewing real scenes. This is probably true as well of many medium shots [Fig. 22.4(b)]. (Although that is conjecture; for there is no work at all that I know of on reflectance perception in motion pictures.)

A small field of view, however, as in Figure 22.4(c), acts something like a "reduction screen" (Woodworth, 1938), removing contexts as in Figure 22.3(c) and leaving the viewer only the local color of the picture. And when in addition low resolution removes the diffraction pattern that characterizes the *penumbra* of a shadow [Fig. 22.3(c)iii] or the depth information about the object's orientation to the illumination [e.g., the right face of the block in Figure 22.3(b)], constancy should be similarly impaired. Most important, when the film is not being photographed from the real world but is constructed by animation (either manual or computer-generated), then the mechanisms that provide for reflectance perception must either be deliberately built in or they cannot be counted on.

Especially in such cases, therefore, the motion-picture maker must be aware of the sensory and perceptual interactions that change any region's appearance when its context is changed and that affect how regions are parsed into surfaces and how objects' reflectances are assigned (see Sedgwick, Chapter 21).

1.2.2. The Still Image: II. The Representation of Real and Virtual Space within the Frame. Consider a camera placed on a tripod of height H before the field of objects 1–9, as shown in Figure 22.5(a). If the aperture of the lens is small or if the distance D is large compared to the focal length of the lens, the *depth of field* will be large, and all the objects in the field will project reasonably sharp images to the film plane (f_p) at the same time. Given that the two boys are the same size, that the playing field is rectangular, that the markings on the field are equally spaced, and that the two billboards are rectangular, then the patterns in the resulting picture [Fig. 22.5(b), on page 22-10] are predictable consequences of the geometrical optics.

All stationary pictures are ambiguous, in that many different virtual spaces would provide the same optic array, a point about which much philosophy has been, and continues to be, written (Gibson, 1971; Goodman, 1968; Wartofsky, 1979), quite unjustifiably in my opinion (Hochberg, 1983). The characteristic patterns displayed in Figure 22.5(b) are what are traditionally known as the *pictorial depth cues*. They are discussed at greater length in Chapter 21 by Sedgwick, in Hochberg (1971b), and Kaufman (1974). Note that they can serve as information about spatial layout only if we assume the regularities in the environment cited above; that is, that lines are parallel, that texture is equally spaced, and so forth. A pictorial depth cue is therefore some specifiable feature in the picture plane that characteristically occurs because of the regularities of the normal three-dimensional world and because of the geometry of projection on a two-dimensional plane. If this feature of proximal stimulation contributes to the perception of the three-

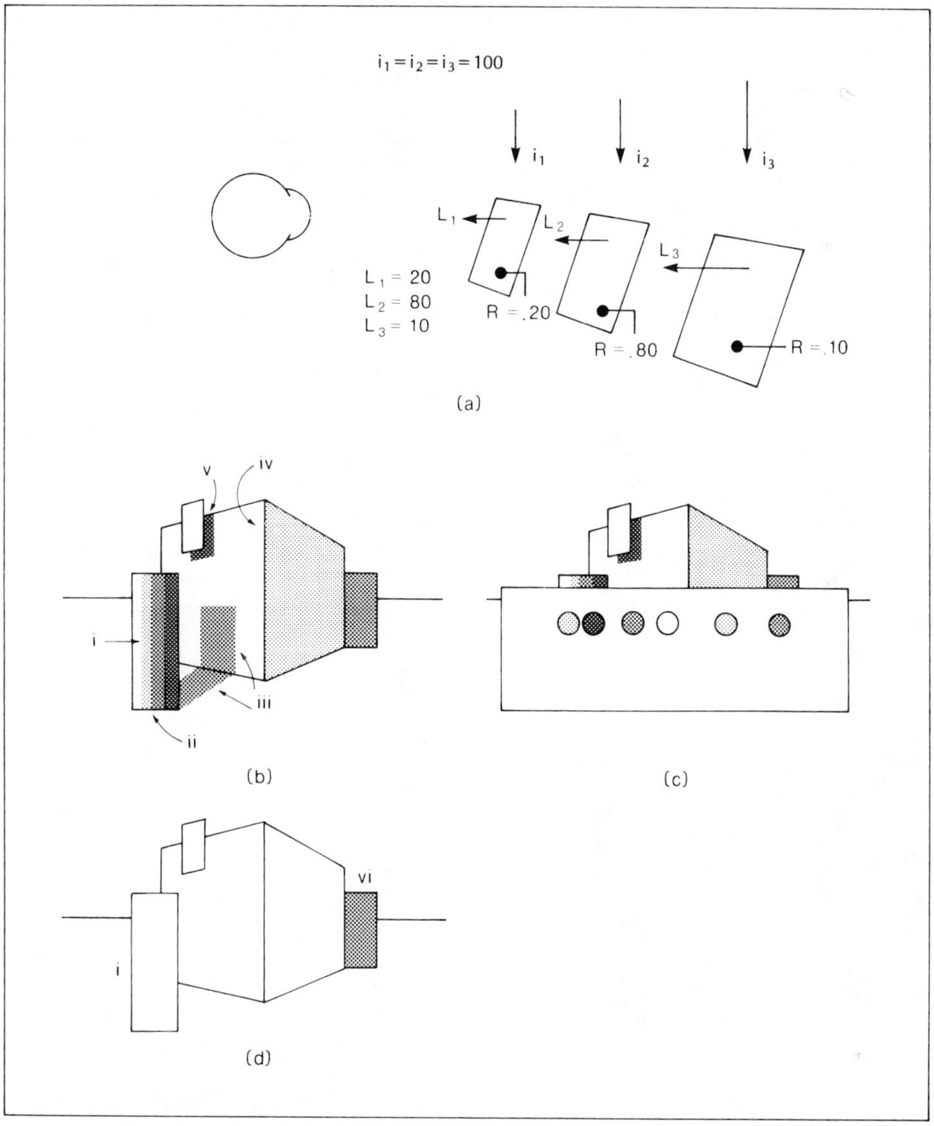

Figure 22.3. Reflectance and illumination. (a) If a set of surfaces receive equal illumination ($i_1 = i_2 = i_3$) and are set equal in reflectance angles to illumination and line of sight, luminances (L_1, L_2, L_3) are proportional to surfaces' reflectances. (b) A scene in which luminance changes are provided by changes in incidence and reflection angle (cylinder i, corner iv) and cast shadows at a distance iii and at objects' edges v. (c) The luminance changes therefore provide information about, or "cues to," spatial form and layout, as well as to reflectance. By using a "reduction screen" to remove the surrounding spatial context for any region, the luminance differences themselves are revealed. (d) By illuminating the layout at (b) by diffuse light, which distributes the effective reflectance angle for all the surfaces, important and sometimes essential information about layout is removed—for example the picture of the cylinder i can become indistinguishable from that of a rectangle—but local luminance then becomes a more reliable index of reflectance (e.g., the region at vi is seen to be darker than adjacent regions).

dimensional property of the world that would normally have provided it in the picture plane, it is a functioning or effective cue (Titchener, 1910; Woodworth, 1938).

Given the constraints on the distal layout for which a picture is a surrogate, the pictorial depth cues theoretically define a set of *virtual spaces* (Rosinski & Farber, 1980; Sedgwick, 1980)—that is, a set of layouts of surfaces distributed in three-dimensional space [Fig. 22.5(c)]. Given their respective constraints, the cues define sets of different sizes. The smallest set, and therefore the least ambiguous, is defined by *familiar size*: if a table is always 22 in high, then the angle subtended in Figure 22.5(b) defines an object at a distance of 100 ft in virtual space. Most of the cues—perspective, texture-density gradient, and so forth—define a set of virtual spaces to a *factor of scale*. For example, an indefinitely large set of layouts, all proportionally larger and more distant, will project the same optic array for these cues. Some cues are merely signed indications of depth. For example, *interposition* indicates that one surface is nearer than another but not how much so. Also, there are *unsigned depth cues*, which indicate that one place lies at a different distance than another but do not indicate which is nearer. *Modeling gradients* are such, and luminance contours and lines probably also serve that function (Hochberg, 1978, 1980).

In addition to the different constraints on set size of equivalent virtual spaces they provide, these cues differ in their *ecological validity*. Ecological validity is the measure of the degree

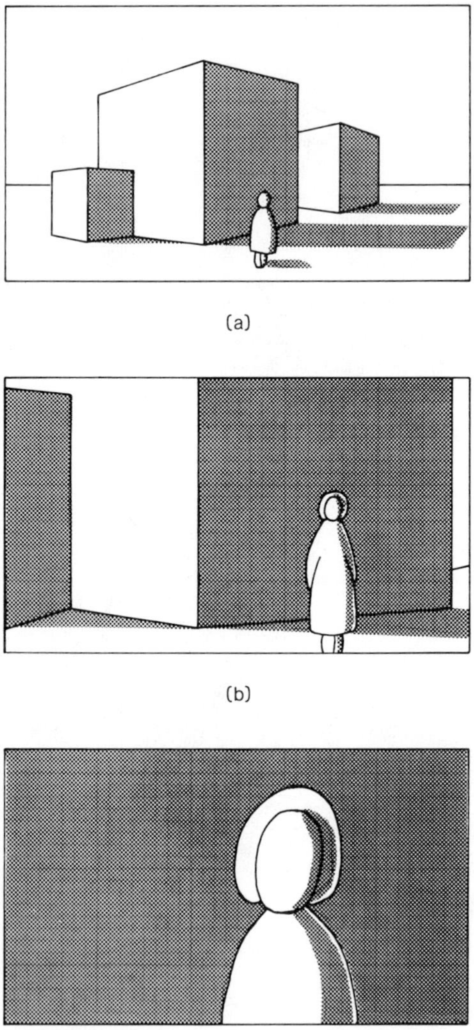

(a)

(b)

(c)

Figure 22.4. In a picture that covers a wide angle of view (a), the context establishes the spatial arrangement and, therefore, the relationship betwen luminance and reflectance. With a narrower angle (b), context is reduced. A still narrower angle (c), or close-up, is equivalent to the reduction screen in Figure 22.3(c), in that the viewer may have no spatial context by which to separate luminance from reflectance and to recognize that the background wall and foreground person are actually light (see (a)). Given adequate depth of field, however, the close-up may, by increasing the detail of the background, reveal the texture of the surface that remains undetectable at a greater distance (e.g., in (b)), and that texture may help separate luminance from reflectance in two ways: (1) by reflecting "highlights" from its small protuberances (Beck, 1972), and (2) by the relative slant of the surface through its texture-density gradient (see Figure 22.5) to the line of sight and to the apparent direction of illumination.

to which a given cue is in fact associated with a particular environmental attribute (Brunswik, 1956); that is, the ecological validity of a depth cue is the degree to which it covaries with distance. Brunswik believed that the relative strengths of the depth cues would match their ecological validities and hoped to measure ecological validities by determining how often the occurrence of a particular cue (e.g., converging edges, as in linear perspective) is the result of depth—that is, the projection of parallel lines in three dimensions—and how often it is merely a flat pattern. Extremely little has been done along this line, either to measure ecological validities (Brunswik & Kamiya, 1953) or to determine the relative strengths of the depth cues.

In connection with the study of motion pictures (and of the uses of motion pictures in simulator training), the question of how cues combine is obviously of the greatest importance. The viewer receives many cues to the flatness of the screen, cues that are therefore in conflict with the depth cues in the picture itself. There is some evidence that, at least in still pictures, perception of space is not all or none: that as the conflicting cues to flatness are removed or weakened, the pictured depth cues increase in their effectiveness both in providing a compelling spatial experience (Ames, 1925) and in terms of spatial performance (Attneave & Frost, 1969).

Analyses of the video displays used in flight simulation have emphasized the inadequacy of the medium as far as most of the depth cues are concerned (Buffett, 1980; Stenger et al, 1979), and in addition, it has been argued that the raster and the frame, by serving as cues to the flatness of the screen, thereby render the pictorial depth cues ineffectual (Stenger et al, 1979). The strengths of the individual cues, and the rules according to which their effects combine have, however, been tested only in one very primitive experiment with still pictures (Schriever, 1925), with equivocal results. More sophisticated research on the strength of the depth cues and on the appropriate combinatorial principles seems very much in order.

One reason why so little work has been done in this area may be the prevalent theoretical bias, shared by Gibson (1979), Johansson (1977a), and others, that only movement-produced information about distance is the normal and lawful basis of perception and that such information is not probabilistic but *certain*. To this view, the depth cues are inappropriate as a measure of stimulus information, and they are irrelevant to perceptual response in normal circumstances.

This approach places the entire burden of accounting for perception on the information available to the perceiver who is in motion relative to the environment.

We consider the movement-produced information to depth and distance in the next section.

1.3. Motion-Generated Depth Cues: Motion Parallax, Motion Perspective, and Kinetic Occlusion and Shear in the Optic Array

Relative motion between viewer and layout results in changes in the optic array [Fig. 22.5(e)]. Those changes are a function of the velocity V of the relative motion, the distance D of each point or surface in question, and the arrangement or disposition of the surfaces in space relative to the viewer. A variety of layouts and the flow patterns they provide the eye of a moving viewer are shown in Figure 22.6(a)–(e).

Given that the surfaces in the environment are rigid and not, in fact, under going the deformations indicated as flow patterns in Figure 22.6, the changes (and the rates of change) in the optic array define sets of virtual spaces, as did the static pictorial cues described in Section 1.2.2. For a given rigid surface, the velocity relative to the viewer imposes a definite transformation on all the discriminable points (including the edges of the surface); conversely, the transformation in the optic array specifies a set of loci in virtual spaces or of events in virtual space—a surface in motion relative to the viewer.

Like the pictorial depth cues, motion-produced cues to space and motion differ in the set size of virtual events they specify and in their ecological validities. They also differ greatly in the *magnitude* of the change in the optic array that is produced by a given velocity and distance. First, we consider the different classes of motion-produced depth cues, next we consider their set sizes and ecological validities, and finally we review what little is known directly and indirectly about their cue strengths.

Leonardo da Vinci knew that there were certain ways, some of them due to motion parallax, in which pictures could never fully masquerade as real scenes. If the viewer makes even a slight motion that changes his or her viewpoint, the changes in the optic array produced by the three-dimensional scene in Figure 22.5(e)ii and iii are very different from those produced by the flat picture.

In the optic array that results when a viewer or a camera approaches a flat surface, all distinguishable points on that surface (features, markings, texture, etc.) will expand out from a center that marks the destination of the motion, in the sense that all vectors in the field originate at that point. This geometrical fact was remarked by Helmholtz (1856/1962) and has been formally developed for different slants of surface to the line of motion by Gibson, Olum, and Rosenblatt (1955) and by successors for more general slants of motion toward the surface (Hay, 1966; Lee, 1974; Purdy, 1958). The general geometry is shown in Figure 22.6(c)–(e), adapted from Gibson and colleagues (1955). If we constrain the represented virtual space to be one of rigid surfaces, the optical expansion pattern produced by motion toward such space specifies a set of such spaces and relative velocities to a factor of scale (Purdy, 1958). That is, only those sets of rigid surfaces that preserve the slants of those in the original layout and that maintain an invariant ratio of surface sizes and distances, on the one hand, to relative motion, on the other, will fit the optic array.

The same facts of geometry apply to motion at right angles to the point of regard: near points in the field of view move more rapidly in the optic array and far points move more slowly, providing a gradient of *motion perspective* that specifies the distance of each point of the surface and, hence, the slant of the surface to the line of sight of the moving observer [Fig. 22.6(a) and (b)]. Again, distances and sizes are specified only to a factor of scale.

In both examples, therefore, it we set constraints of rigidity on the virtual space fitted to the optic array, that array will fit equally well to an infinite number of layouts of surfaces, as long as the surfaces have the same slants to the line of motion and their sizes and distances are all proportional to each other and are in a constant ratio to the relative velocity of the viewer. The optic array of a perfect model, 10 cm high and approaching at a velocity of 1 cm/sec, would be identical to the array of a mountain 10 km high approached at 1km/sec. In both cases, there is information in the optic array that specifies whether the present course will lead to a collision (i.e., if the center of the expansion pattern lies within the boundaries of the mountain) and even how long it will be before the collision occurs. The graph in Figure 22.6(f) shows relative size on the ordinate and distance from collision (with collision at the origin) on the abscissa.

As with the static pictorial cues, the motion-produced cues differ in their specificity; some specify a unique virtual event to a factor of scale (Fig. 22.6); some motion-produced cues are merely signed (i.e., do not imply any distance even to a factor of scale), such as kinetic occlusion in Figure 23.7(b); and others, such as kinetic shear in Figure 22.7(c), are not even that—are *unsigned* indications of depth-difference and relative motion, a point first explored by Farber and McConkie (1979).

The strongest constraints on virtual space are provided by a motion that has some well-known and *familiar speed* or *familiar excursion*; as an example of the former, a clock with a sweep second hand hanging on the wall and, as an example of the latter, a camera motion, into the scene, that simulates normal human locomotion. By such means (and indeed, by the inclusion of objects of familiar size), the optic array can specify a single virtual event—*if* that event is suitably constrained (i.e., if we stipulate that surfaces are rigid, that the relative motion that produced the optic array is indeed of the indicated speed or magnitude, etc.). Although I know of no research on familiar speeds, it is clear from any slow-motion or speeded-up sequence that we have a visual vocabulary of such events, and it would be of theoretical and practical importance to learn its limits.

In the film *One Million B.C.* (1940), live iguanas were introduced (by traveling mattes and miniature sets) as prehistoric lizards. Their movements were far too quick to be taken as the giants they were supposed to be, and they therefore disclosed the true scale (Fry & Fourzon, 1977). Of course, the viewer's assumptions may be wrong: the sweep second hand may well be rotating at 1/10th speed, and the familiar figure of a mouse or an elephant may be a model—or, more likely today, "matted," or inserted, into the picture by optical or electronic means.

This point applies, of course, to the motion picture itself. The optic array provided by film or video is not in fact produced by a set of rigid objects but by the nonrigid play of light and shade on a screen. To go further still, the transformations may not result from continuous motion in space at all but from the succession of discrete stationary flat pictures, perhaps drawn by hand or by computer; thus the virtual event for which the optic array is a convincing surrogate may never have existed.

The optical expansion pattern and motion perspective discussed in connection with Figures 22.6(a)–(e) are readily (if uncritically) conceived of as abstract transformations imposed on the constants of the three-dimensional layout, regardless of what those constraints may be. It is easy therefore to consider them abstractly, as being in some sense "direct" sources of information that can be dealt with regardless of the specific situation, that is, regardless of the specific distribution of points and surfaces on which they operate (Gibson, 1959, 1979; Johansson, 1977a, 1982).

As we shall see, that would be wrong for two reasons. Note first that the information that is carried by the gradients in Figure 22.6 depends on the presence of what has been called *carrier elements* (Hochberg, Green, & Virostek, 1978), for example, the texture elements that are being transformed by the effects of motion parallax, and so on. We now know that the detectability of the carrier elements is important in the usability of the information in the superordinate modulation (Hochberg, 1982). This is obviously practically important but theoretically trivial, in cases in which the surfaces in question lack texture or in which the representational medium fails to provide it. Video displays, because of raster limitations, tend to lose texture (Stenger et al., 1979), and computer-generated displays tend to lack texture from their inception, although something equivalent can be provided by the modeling of parallel lines on the virtual surface (Stevens, 1981). It is theoretically important to note that texture elements can be detectably present yet fail to provide depth information if they are too small in the array or too eccentric to foveal vision (Hochberg, 1982).

The second reason why we cannot simply expect that every real scene will provide motion-produced depth information is that the actual magnitude and availability of the information depend on the specifics of layout.

Consider first the effect of size and detectability of carrier elements. *Kinetic occlusion*, in which a near surface's edge moves to conceal or reveal discernible parts of further surfaces, is not inherent in all layouts: it clearly occurs only in particular ar-

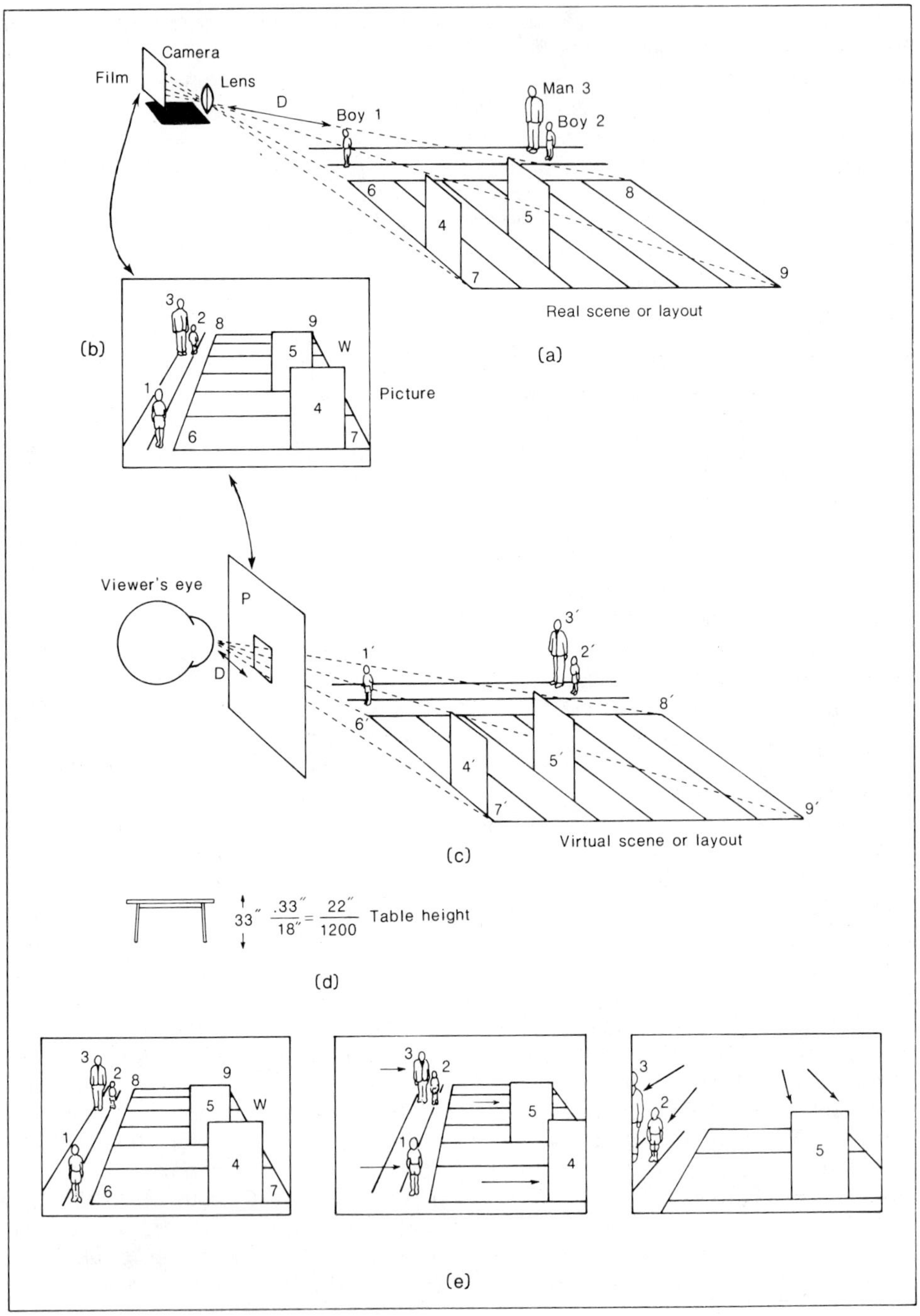

Figure 22.5. (*Legend opposite.*)

rangements of the world, from particular viewpoints, and is obtained only with particular movements [see Fig. 22.7(a)–(c)]. It is difficult to think of them as transformations upon a scene and easy to consider them as *cues*. Discussed over the years by Helmholtz (1856/1962), Michotte (1963), Gibson, Kaplan, Reynolds, & Wheeler (1969), Kaplan (1969), and Hochberg (1982), kinetic occlusion is only a *qualitative* depth cue. In Figure 22.7(b), the rectangle on the left is specified as being in front in Figure 22.7(b)3 and behind in Figure 22.7(b)2, but in neither is the amount of depth specified.

Indeed, even when one object is moving in front of another and the edge between them is visible, a relative movement parallel to that edge will produce a degenerate form of kinetic occlusion, that is *kinetic shear* (Figure 22.7(c).) This is an *unsigned motion-produced depth cue*, in that it only specifies that two surfaces lie at different depths, and not which one is nearer.

Whether kinetic occlusion, kinetic shear, or both will occur in the optic array does not depend only on the fact that relative motion occurs between layout and viewer. It depends on the specific arrangement in the layout as well. And that is just as true in a general sense for whatever motion parallax and motion perspective may be provided. For example, if there is no discernible texture or other markings on a plane past which the viewer or the camera moves, if the camera moves past a smooth and evenly lit or self-luminous sphere against a horizon or floor dihedral, or past a vertical cylinder, there will be no motion-produced information about depth or distance in the optic array. Similarly, if an object at a distance rotates around a vertical axis so that one edge approaches the viewer and one recedes [Fig. 22.8(b)], there is information in the expansion pattern that specifies which edge is moving away and which is moving toward the viewer. But the magnitude of the changes in the optic array that provides the information in question is itself a function of the size of the object and of its distance from the viewer, as well as of its angular velocity. The information may be present in the optic array but, depending on circumstances, may not be usable [Fig. 22.8(d)].

Similarly, as we noted previously, if the carrier elements of texture, and so forth, are too small to permit their separate registration by the film or by the eye, then even though every point on the surface is being transformed by the relative motion, no usable information will be carried by the optic arry.

We know that the detectability of the carrier elements is important in the usability of the information in the supraordinate modulation (see Fig. 22.29), but we do not know the precise relationship.

Figure 22.5. (*Opposite*) Pictorial depth cues. (a) Photographing a scene or layout. It contains two boys of equal height (1 and 2), a man of twice that height (3), two upright squares or walls (4 and 5), a pair of parallel receding lines, and a square playing field *W*, ruled by equidistant parallel lines perpendicular to the line of sight of the camera, within the rectangular field marked by corners (6, 7, 8, and 9). (b) The image on the film in the camera, projected by the straight dotted lines through the lens, in (a). The characteristic patterns produced by the layout of the scene in depth upon the flat surface of the film provide potential information about that layout and are traditionally known as the pictorial (or monocular) depth cues. Those shown here are:

1. Linear Perspective. The lines parallel to the line of sight converge in the picture plane as the angle that their separation projects to the lens diminishes.
2. Size Perspective, or Relative Size. The further of the two boys (1 and 2) projects a smaller image on the picture even though the two are really of equal height; the same is true of the two walls (4 and 5) and of the horizontal extents in the field (e.g., 6–7 and 8–9).
3. Interposition, or Occlusion. The nearer wall (4) interrupts, and occludes part of the view of, the further wall (5).
4. Texture-Density Gradient. In the image projected by a uniform spacing of markings or inhomogeneities on the ground plane, such as the parallel lines on the playing field, the size and spacing on the picture plane become progressively less as the distance increases. The relative rate of change, or gradient, of the density of the elements, or texture, is constant for a surface of a particular slant to the line of sight.
5. Blur, Illumination Direction, and Haze. Other important monocular or pictorial depth cues, not shown here, are blur, or focus (i.e., if one part of the image is in focus and another is not, the two do not normally lie at equal distances from the camara; in the eye itself, the focusing of the lens mechanism that resolves the blur is called the cue of accommodation); illumination direction, as seen in Figure 22.3(b); atmospheric perspective, or haze (with increasing distance, the particulates in the atmosphere provide a decrease in resolution and characteristic changes in wavelength, which provide information about the relative distance within the scene).
6. Familiar Size. Because of his greater distance, the man (3), who is twice the height of the boy (1) in the layout at (a), projects a pictorial image in (b) that is equal to that of the boy. In order to use the pictorial information given by the relative sizes of (b)1 and (b)3, the viewer must know the specific relative sizes of the man and the boy in the world.

(c) If the viewer's eye is placed at such a distance from the picture made in (a) that the markings on it provide the same pattern that would be provided by the original layout in (a), (b) can now function as a surrogate for the layout (and vice versa, of course). The original layout is then one of the family of virtual spaces, or layouts, that can be fitted to the light offered by the picture. (d) The cue of familiar size is potentially an absolute (as opposed to relative) indication of distance: if this page is held at a distance of 18 inches from the eye, the picture of the table (which 8 mm on the printed page) subtends the same visual angle and provides a surrogate for a table at a distance of 30 m from the viewer. (e) If the camera moves parallel to edge 6–7 in (a), toward 6, or into the layout along the line of sight (e.g., perpendicular to edge 6–7), the image provided on the film will change from that of i to ii or iii, respectively. The arrows indicate vectors of displacement of particular objects between the view in i and that in ii or iii, respectively.

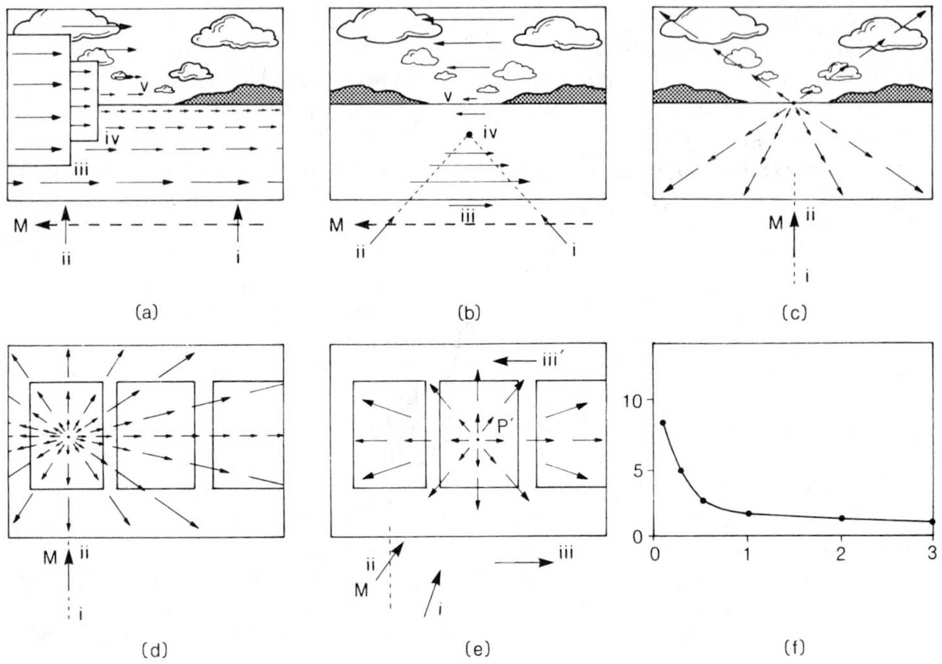

Figure 22.6. The components of motion perspective and the optical expansion pattern. As the viewer or camara moves in the world, each discernible point in the environment moves in the optic array provided to the eye's or camera's lens. The pattern of the resulting optic flow provides information of various kinds about the spatial layout and about the motion of the viewer relative to the layout. One class is derived from the same principles as those of linear perspective and is readily obtained by drawing vectors to connect corresponding points in successive views. In the scenes below, adapted from Gibson (1950), the change in viewpoints is from i to ii in each case. This familiy of potentially usable cues partitions into several distinct components comprising a vocabulary of layouts and camera movements. (a) Lateral translation, or viewpoint movement perpendicular to line of sight. Viewer moves as shown by arrow *M*, with gaze direction constant (i and ii). Note gradient of vectors to zero at infinity (approximated by horizon) for a surface at some slant to line of sight; with surfaces of zero slant (approximated by surfaces perpendicular to line of sight), the nearer iii moves uniformly faster than the further iv. (b) Lateral translation, with line of sight not perpendicular to viewpoint movement: gaze fixed on point iv. Note that there are two component movements here, the movement *M* of the viewer, which is responsible for the parallax, and the rotation of the eye or camera, which is needed to keep point iv stationary on the film or retina. If rotation is confined to the optic node, it introduces only a uniform translation of the image (vector at iii) which modulates but cannot cancel the motion perspective due to *M*. If we take the horizon to approximate infinite distance, the vector at v equals iii. (c) Forward (radial) motion along the line of sight, surface parallel to *M*, that is, ground or floor. (d) Forward motion along the line of sight, surface perpendicular to motion (wall). Notice that the point at which collision will occur if the movement is continued is itself the one stationary point in the field of view and is in addition the center of the optical expansion pattern. (e) Forward motion, line of sight changing to keep the center of the middle panel fixed on the film or retina, analogous to the situation shown in (b). The middle panel now contains the stationary point, which no longer coincides with the point of projected collision nor with the center of the optical expansion pattern. That point remains the same, inasmuch as the actual movements on the film or retina describe curved paths, which can be partitioned into the optical pattern of (d), itself unchanged but modulated by the lateral displacement iii provided by the rotation of the line of regard from i to ii; the latter superimposes a constant opposite and equal vector at iii′ on all points in the display. Note that sketches in (a), (c), and (d) refer both to the optic array and to the retinal image or film image; those in (b) and (e) refer only to the retinal or film images, inasmuch as the optic array refers to the pattern of light that confronts the eye or camera at a station point and precedes the effects of changing the direction of regard. There has recently been some needless confusion about this point (see Section 1.4.4). (f) Rate of optical expansion as an indication of time to collision. Solving equations for the optical expansion pattern of (d) shows that in addition to point of projected collision, time to collison is given by the rate of the expansion. This is independent of viewer distance and velocity, as this graph makes clear: The abscissa marks off unit distance from collision with an object of unit size, with motion progressing from right to left, and with the point of collision at $x = O$; the ordinate plots how much the image of the object has expanded at each distance in approaching from the previously plotted point, in unit time (i.e., divided by time elapsed). Retreat along the line of sight produces the reciprocal function.

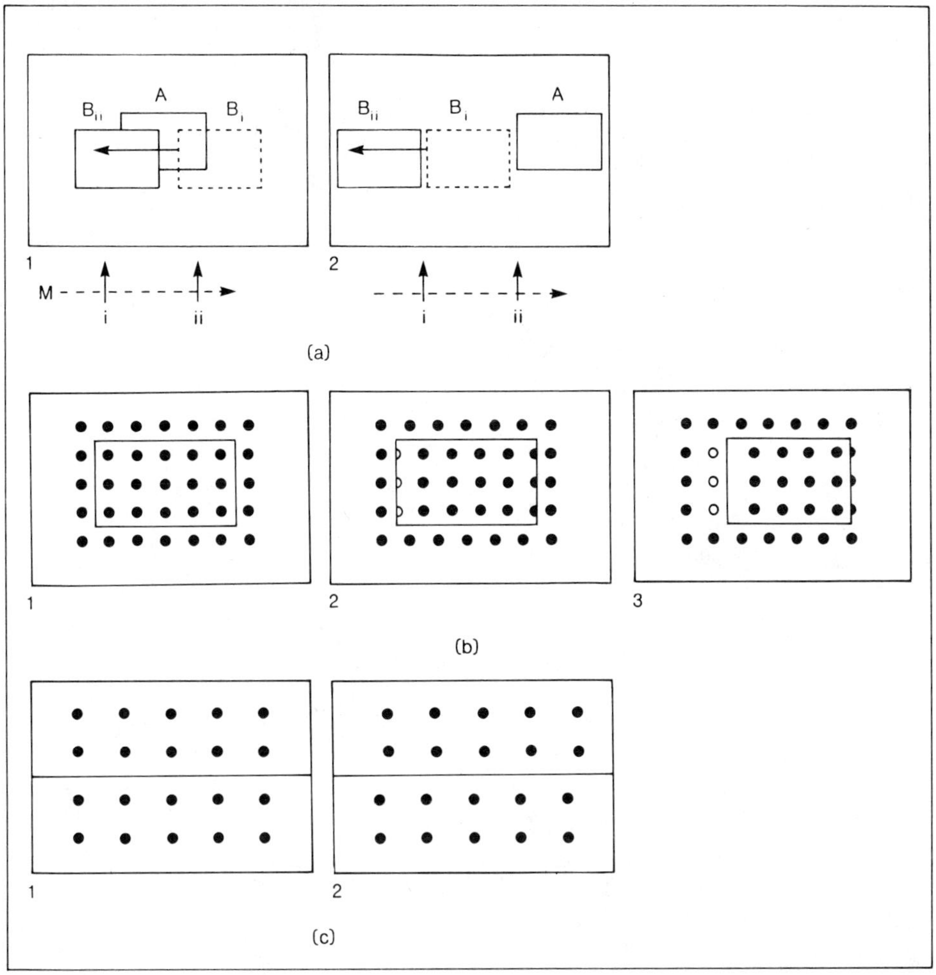

Figure 22.7. Occlusion through movement. (a) At (1), for a viewer or camera moving from i to ii, the resulting parallax will change the occlusion of *A* by *B* as shown by the vector between B_1 *and* B_{ii}. At (2), whether or not movement-produced occlusion occurs is a question of layout, viewpoint, and extent of movement—it is not an inevitable concomittant of movement. (b) Kinetic occlusion. Where surface texture or markings are pervasive, kinetic occlusion can usually be counted on to provide depth information. At (1), two textured regions; at (2), the occlusion of the column of elements at the right of the rectangle and the disocclusion of the column at the left (the empty half-circles) specify the surface within the rectangle to be to the rear and viewed through an aperture; at (3), the occlusion and disocclusion specify the rectangle as the nearer surface. The clipping that occurs at the edges of the screen on which the scene is being displayed specifies the screen as a visual aperture behind which a larger layout is being viewed, with its own important properties (see Figure 22.32). (c) Shear. The abrupt change in alignment of elements at the horizontal edge here, and in the corresponding horizontal edges in (b), is characteristic of separable surfaces and, often, of surfaces at different distances.

Thus far we have been talking only about the optic array that confronts a viewer (or a camera) with a fixed angle of regard with respect to the line of motion. That arrangement is by no means always the case, of course, and it has been subject of considerable recent misunderstandings. We consider that topic next.

1.4. The Variables of Shooting, Projecting, and Viewing: Eye, Camera, Projector, and Screen in Canonical Arrangement

In what follows, we have several separable levels of stimulus patterns to keep track of, going from distal layout to the most proximal (i.e., to the retinal image). These are sketched in Figure 22.9 (the drawing is not proportional).

In this section, whenever we discuss the viewer before a projection screen, we will assume that the essential elements—camera, projector, screen, and viewer—are in what will be considered the *canonical arrangement*, in which the eye receives the same sheaf of rays as did the camera. The viewer's eye will then be at the projection center of the perspective in the film. In Section 1.4.1, we consider what happens when we depart from the canonical arrangement, as we most generally do.

Suppose a viewer's eye or a motion-picture camera changes direction of regard from point 1 to point 2 by rotating around the optical nodal point (see Hallett, Chapter 10, and Westheimer, Chapter 4). [The eye does not in fact rotate precisely around its node, and motion-picture tripod heads generally pivot some distance to the rear of both optical node and film plane, so that there is inevitably some translatory motion, like that in Figure

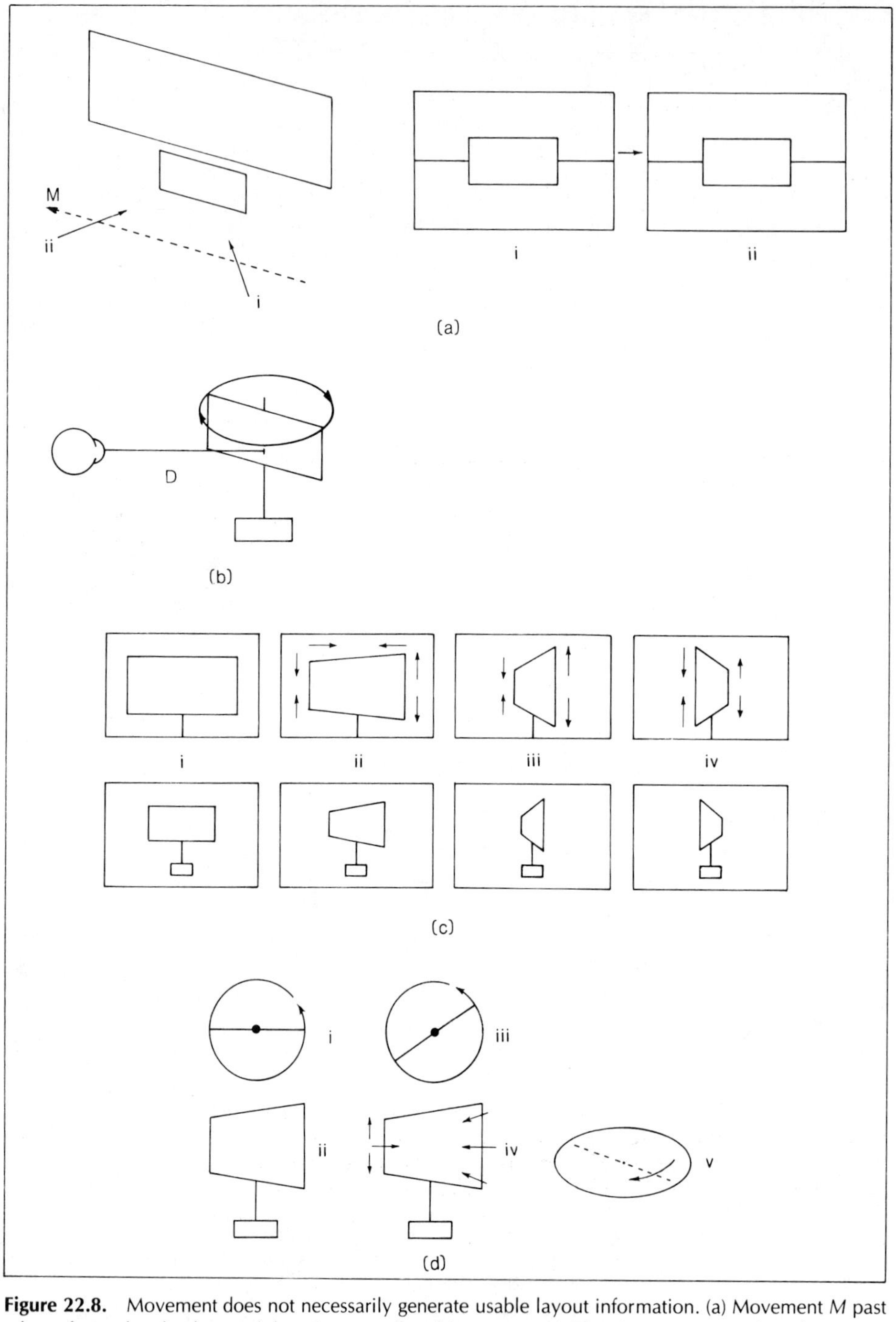

Figure 22.8. Movement does not necessarily generate usable layout information. (a) Movement *M* past a large featureless background, keeping a smaller object centered. The views are at i and ii. There is no occlusion information, and although there should be changes in the shape of the nearer object between views i and ii, they may be too small to detect (see (c)). (b) and (c) Approach and retreat, like lateral movement, may fail to provide usable depth information. (b) A rectangular surface rotating around its vertical axis relative to the viewer seen from distance *D* (the viewer may equally well be circling the object). (c) A succession of views out of the resulting sequence. In the upper row, the rectangle is heavily textured, and it is viewed from nearby, so that the expansion of the edge coming toward the viewer and the contraction of the edge retreating from the viewer are detectable and noticeable (i–iv); see Figure 22.6(e). In the lower row, the distance *D* between viewer and rectangle is large, and the changes with approach and retreat are small. As we see next, the differences between approach and retreat may be too small to detect and may be ineffectual even when they are detectable. (d) If the rotating object is a trapezoid, an important and robust illusion results. At i and ii, the shape is in its frontal position, viewed in plane and elevation i.e., from above and from in front), respectively. Ames demonstrated in 1951 that a rotating trapezoid, when viewed from some distance, appears to reverse periodically and, therefore, to oscillate instead, presumably because the large end of the trapezoid appears to be the nearer even when it is the further, as at iii and iv. In motion pictures on film and video, this illusion is extremely strong, and even when photographed from close range, oscillatory motion is seen instead of rotation: the object appears to be moving in a direction opposite to its true path (v) even though the shape then appears to undergo the rubbery deformations shown by the arrows at iv (Hochberg, 1984b; Hochberg, Amira, & Peterson, 1984).

22.6(a), involved in both cases; we disregard that component in this discussion, however, and it will usually be trivial except when objects lie close in space to the eye or to the camera.]

The optic array, of course, remains unchanged by the rotation of the eye, although which section of the array is in the field of view has been changed. In the retinal image and in the motion-picture image, the loci of all points in the field of view will undergo a transformation. There are two causes for transformation to be considered.

1.4.1. Homogeneous Translation: An Approximation. For the time being, we ignore the fact that the distances from the eye (or lens) to the screen are different at different directions of gaze; that difference occasionally becomes an important source of distortion in the pereived shapes of photographed objects (Pirenne, 1970; see Fig. 22.11), but it is often negligible. Thus if the distance D is large compared to the width W of the field of view and compared to the extent of the rotation X, then each point is translated by a vector T, as shown in Figure 22.10(a). That is, each discernible point and patch of color in the image undergoes a uniform transformation, namely, the translation in Figure 22.10(a), so that the relative spatial relationships of the contents of the field of view remain invariant under the transformation.

Most generally, the scene and optic array before the viewer are larger than the momentary field of view, and the translation will be accompanied by a deletion and an accretion at the opposite margins of the retinal image or the motion-picture screen (Figures 22.7(b) and 22.10(a)). The contents of the image are therefore only invariant in the central or overlapping part of the field o.

Objects at different distances are (to an approximation) translated by equal extents; that is, there is *no* motion parallax, motion perspective, or kinetic occlusion within the image. This

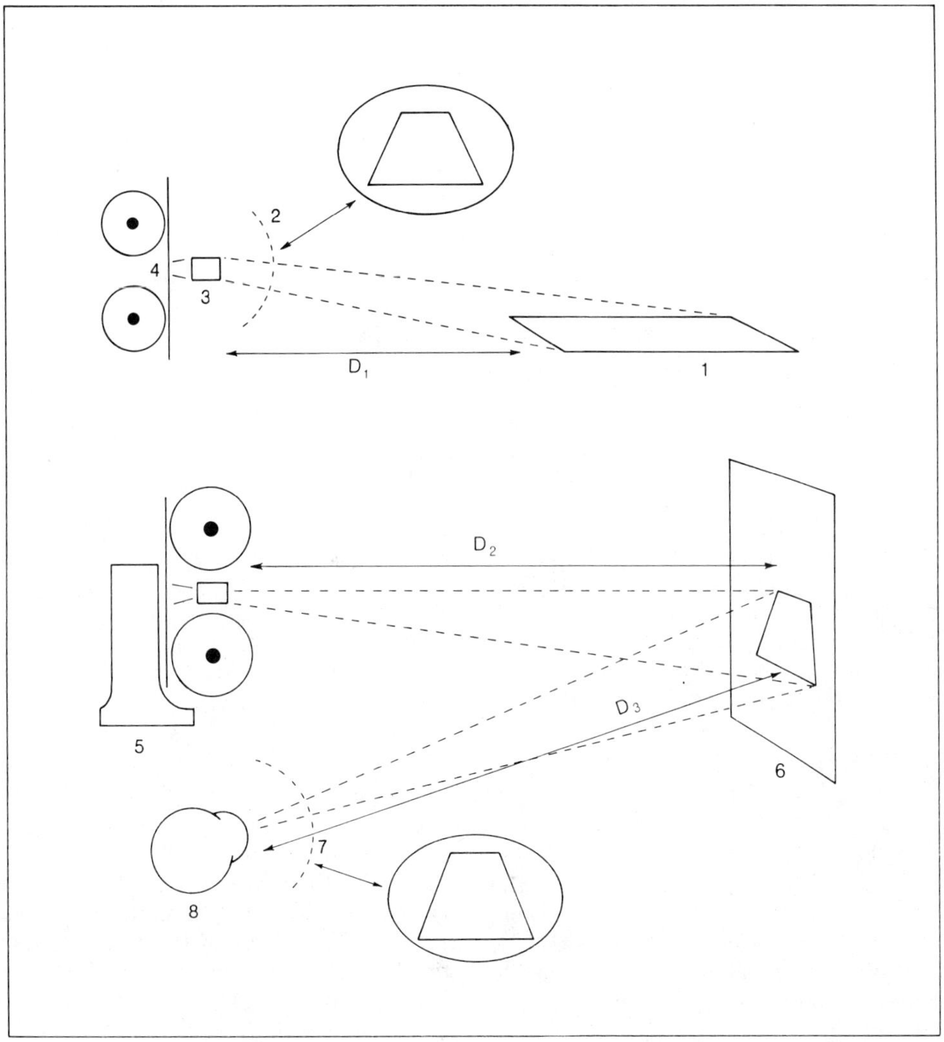

Figure 22.9. From layout to eye. Light from the scene (1) provides the optic array (2) confronting the projector lens (3), which focuses the image on the film plane (4). The projector (5) casts an enlarged image on the screen (6). The optic array (7), provided to the eye (8) by the light reflected from the screen, is the starting point for the perception of moving pictures. The optic array provided to the viewer thus depends not only on the object but on the lenses of the camera and the projector and on the recording distance D_1, the projection distance D_2, and the viewing distance D_3, as well. There are many different combinations of parameters that will provide effectively identical optic arrays for camera and for viewer's eye, that is, for which (7) can be superimposed on (2) with no detectable or effective difference. That condition will be referred to as the canonical arrangement. For considerations that limit typical installations, see McVey (1970), Meister (1966), and Miller and Strenge (1969).

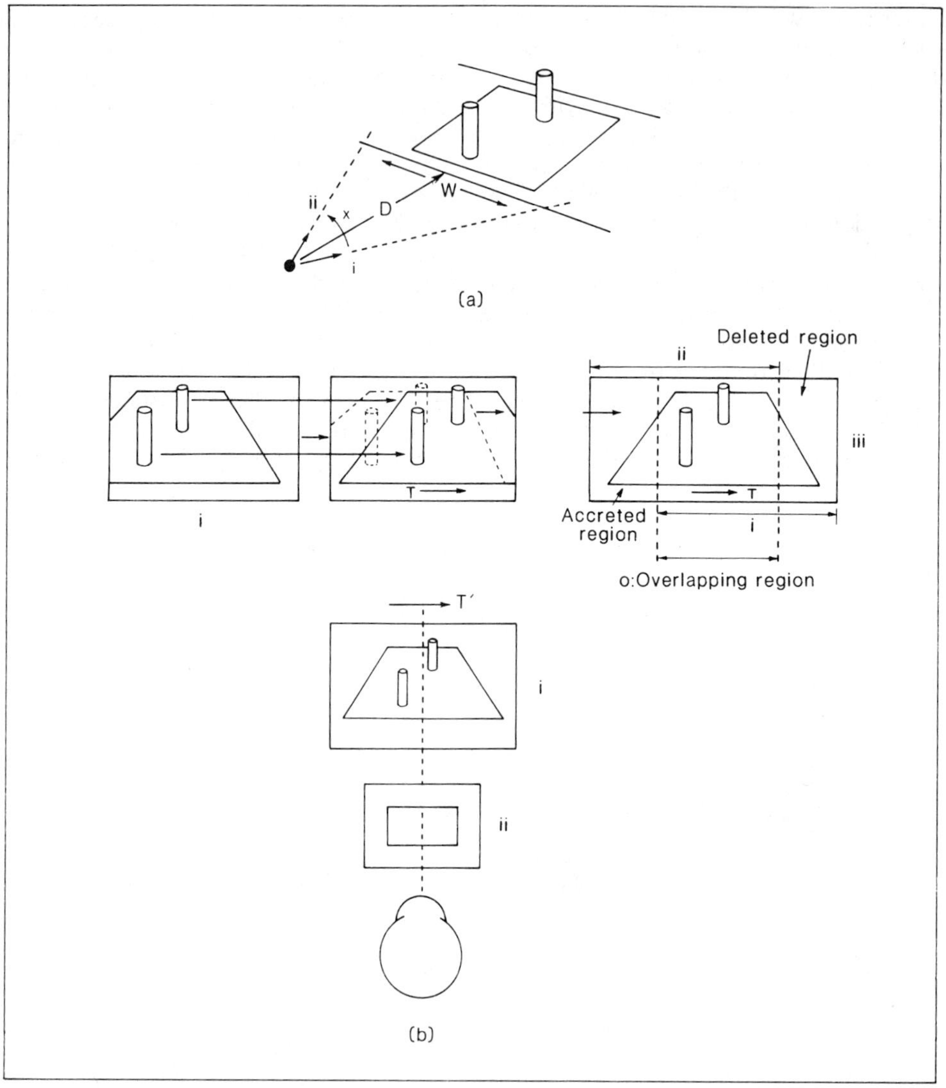

Figure 22.10. Movement around the optical node of the eye or camera. (a) Rotating the eye or camera from i to ii, through angle x, transforms each point in the scene by the translation **T**. As considered here, the distance D is large compared to x. Depending on the parameters, the last and first view may share an overlapping region, with perhaps an accreted and deleted region as shown. (b) The sequence in (a)i and ii can equally well be produced by a two-dimensional display (i) moving with the appropriate velocity T' behind an aperture (ii).

means that the transformation in Figure 22.10(a) is a surrogate equally well for all the following events

1. A three-dimensional display moves with the relative motion of vector **T**. This can either be due to a rotation x of the lens around its node, of the display itself in orbit around the node as a center T', or some combination of both. The set of three-dimensional layouts that will fit this surrogate is constrained no more than is any still picture.
2. A two-dimensional display translates across the field of view, all parts equally displaced by vector **T** [Figure 22.10(b)]. If the optic array is read by the viewer in this way, the uniformity of the translation vector specifies a flat surface, at some distance and velocity relative to the viewer that is specified to a factor of scale, that is, in virtual space D/x is fixed.

1.4.2. Inhomogeneous Translation: The General Case. Consider now the case in which the ratio of W/D is relatively large. Figure 22.11(b)iv represents a photograph of a slat fence [or it can represent a photograph of a flat picture of the pipe fence in Figure 22.11(a)i]. In the case of the slats (or the picture), both the target and the film plane are flat; so as far as the *geometry* is concerned, the decrease in visual angle with eccentricity that the target subtends is compensated for by the increasing obliqueness of the film plane with eccentricity (we consider how these appear later). The pipes, on the other hand, being circular in cross section, present the same tangent to the line of sight at all eccentricities, projecting film images that (paradoxically) increase in width with increasing eccentricity. These phenomena are well known in still pictures, and are discussed at length by Pirenne (1970). As long as each picture is viewed from the projection center, of course, they all present the eye with undistorted optic arrays of the layout [Fig. 22.1(b)i and iii]. One simple way to avoid the distortion is to keep the ratio of W/D low.

Now let us compare what happens when the eye or the camera rotates [Fig. 22.11(c) and (d)] in a pan shot, so as to change direction from one end of the fence to the other, with what happens when the eye or the camera moves, with parallel regard, from one end of the fence to the other [Fig. 22.11(e) and (f)] in a tracking shot. Note that the transformations provided by the flat fence and by the picture in fact present a uniform translation in Figure 22.11(f). In the other cases, however, there are real and systematic gradients of size and velocity, within the transformation, that are different for rotation and for translation.

Indeed, when *W/D* is large, the succession of images in the camera or the eye is very different for rotation and translation: compare the sequences of views in Figure 22.11(c) and (e). Although the layouts are the same—a straight colinear row of fence posts, in all cases—the sequences of both film image and retinal images are different.

These changes in shape and motion are often referred to as "distortions," particularly in the case of still pictures. We see that they are not, any more than perspective, texture-density

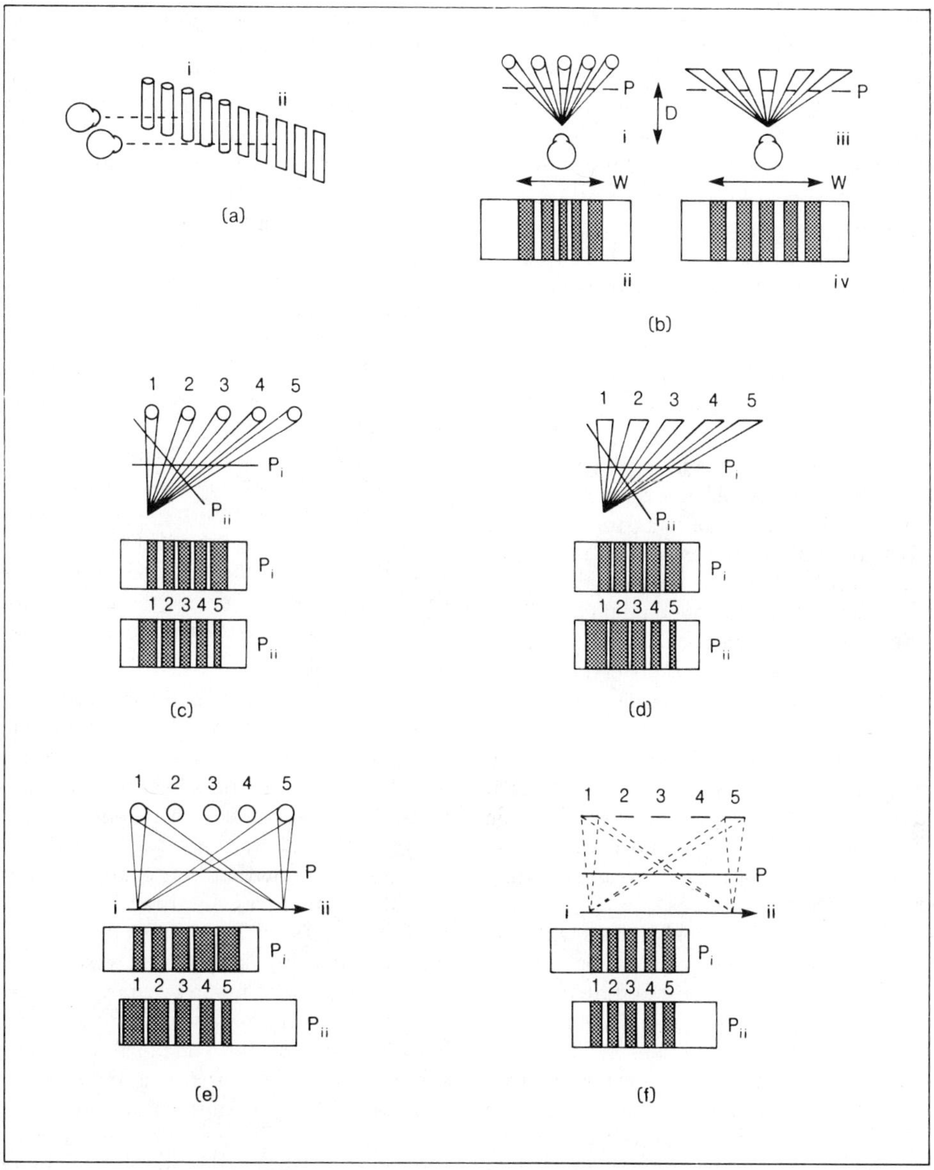

Figure 22.11. The projections of a pipe or slat fence. A fence made of pipes or cylinders, as at (a) i, or one made of slats or flat boards, as at (a) ii, provides very different picture projections, in ways that are important to the effects of different camera motions and departures from canonical arrangements. Given some distance *D*, the picture that produces the same optic array as does the uniform pipe fence (b) i is nonuniform (b) ii over the width *w* of the picture. The flat fence (b) iii, however, provides a uniform picture (b) iv. Pans: In the case of the pipe fence (c), if the viewer swivels his or her gaze from the nearest post (1) to the furthest (5), the picture that is perpendicular to the line of sight and that provides the same optic array as the fence itself changes from P_i to P_{ii}; in neither picture is the spacing of contours uniform. In the case of the slat fence (d), the spacing in the picture is uniform as long as the latter is parallel to the fence P_i, but it departs from uniformity as the gaze pans to center on slat 5, and the picture plane is then at some angle to the fence. Track Shots: In the case of the pipe fence, a lateral displacement of the camera from i to ii in (e) results in a change from one skewed picture P_i to another P_{ii}. In the case of the slat fence in (f), the pictures remain uniform and unskewed as the camera is displaced from i to ii.

gradient, or the optical-expansion pattern are distortions. They merely show what the pattern of light rays provided by the three-dimensional scene looks like on one particular plane surface that intersects those rays. In the case of the motion-picture screen or CRT face, the parallel sides of the road moving directly into the distance can be shown to converge, and the fence posts in Figure 22.11 can be shown to undergo the transformations described. But as long as the canonical arrangement is maintained and the viewer's eye (with monocular regard) is at the center of projection, the light available to the eye is the same from these still and moving pictures as it is from the scene itself (setting aside matters of binocularity and accommodation, i.e., orientation of wave front). There is no distortion.

Sections 1.4.3 and 1.4.4 consider what happens when we depart from the canonical arrangement and what happens when we take into account the fact that the viewer is not really moving when looking at a motion picture made by a moving camera.

1.4.3. Eye, Camera, and Screen in Noncanonical Arrangements. In the general case, the geometry of the eye, camera, and screen is not that of Figure 22.9. There are three reasons why this should be so. The first two are simply due to conditions of viewing.

1.4.3.1. Conditions of Viewing. The viewer does not in general sit perfectly motionless, looking at the screen with one eye closed and the other at the center of the projection. First, most viewing is binocular. At best, only one eye is at the projection center, and the other is at some eccentric viewing angle and, therefore, obtains a disparate view. At any viewing distance smaller than approximately 6 m, it is safe to assume that the normal viewer localizes the planar surface of the projection screen by means of this binocular disparity (and usually by the other cues as well, such as accommodation and motion parallax). The flatness of the surface, of course, then specifies that shapes and transformations on the screen are indeed "distortions"; that is that the lines converge, that the fence posts widen, and so on.

Moreover, the viewer's head is usually not perfectly stationary. This has two major consequences: The first, is that motion parallax should result, which will specify the location of the screen at even the longest viewing distance and should make perfectly evident to the viewer the distortions and nonrigid transformations occuring on the screen.

This point will be of theoretical importance to us when we consider explanations of motion-picture perception. Let us here note only that because of binocular disparity and head movements, the motion-picture display actually specifies only what is in fact there *before* the viewer—a flat planar surface with moving nonrigid patterns spread out on it. This is true in even the largest motion-picture theatre and is a fortiori true with small screens and video displays. (At a distance up to a few meters, which is appropriate viewing for small screens, accommodation also normally informs the viewer that the screen is flat.)

The second consequence of the fact that the head is not maintained stationary at the projection center is that the optic array provided by the image on the screen is different for each eccentricity. The virtual spaces and motions that can be fitted to the motion picture (given constraints of rigidity, colinearity, etc.) must therefore *change* with each such departure from the canonical arrangement.

Consider a layout in space as in Figure 22.12(a). That layout, the actual distal situation, is a member of the class of virtual spaces that can be fit to the optic array that is presented to the eye of a viewer at the projection center of the image on the screen as in Figure 22.12(b)iv and v. If the viewer moves eccentrically, as in Figure 22.12(c), so that the eye is no longer at the projection center, the same set of virtual spaces can no longer fit the optic array. In short, the picture can no longer represent the same spatial layout but must represent a different one.

Similarly, if the viewer changes his or her distance from the screen, so that the eye is further [Fig. 22.29(d)] or nearer [Fig. 22.12(e)] than the center of projection, the original layout will no longer fit the optic array offered on the motion-picture screen, and the latter will represent a changed set of virtual spaces [Fig. 22.12(d) and (e)].

The ways in which represented or virtual space changes with each departure from the canonical arrangement have been well explored (Rosinski & Farber, 1980). These changes in virtual space will necessarily be accompanied by changes in virtual motions as well, and in Figure 22.12, the relative vectors in the represented space show the effects on the unit velocities in the original layout.

Both space and motion, therefore, are affected by where the viewer sits relative to the screen and by each head movement. These are conditions of viewing, and to some extent they are adventitious. They can be overcome in principle by setting and enforcing the viewing locations. Even where there are large discrepancies in viewing position, viewers tend simply to tolerate or ignore the resulting deformations. (More important than the fact that the distortions are ignored is the fact that we perceive the actors and layouts being represented, even though they cannot possibly be called rigid solutions to the problem of fitting virtual spaces to the optic array.) As we see next, however, there are violations of the canonical arrangement that are *built into* most motion pictures (although they need not be in computer-generated representations of space and motion).

1.4.3.2. Changes in Focal Length and Their Consequences. With a lens of fixed focal length, the camera must be placed at some specific distance in order to fill the screen with an object of a given size. If the screen is viewed from the appropriate distance, the canonical arrangement is preserved and the optic array can be fit by the set of virtual events that include the real space and motion that confront the camera.

Motion pictures simply are not made with cameras at fixed positions in space. Transitions from *long shot* [Fig. 22.13(a)] to *medium shot* [Fig. 22.13(b)] to *close-up* [Fig. 22.13(c)] are ubiquitous and may be made by changing camera position. Assume for the moment that the latter was true in this case. Thus a viewer seated at a fixed distance before the screen while viewing a motion picture, which was made while the camera moved from far off to a medium distance [Fig. 22.13(d)i and ii] or from medium to near [Fig. 22.13(d)ii and iii], receives motion-produced information about space appropriate to a decrease of his or her distance from the objects in the scene. If the transitions are abrupt cuts (Section 2.2.3), the viewer then receives the same optic array that would have been perceived if the relative distance between eye and layout had changed instantly. Such cuts from long shot to medium, or from medium to close-up [Fig. 22.13(d)ii and (e)] may still provide motion-produced information about space, and they will usually provide the stationary pictorial depth cues as well. Both kinds of information about space will now fit the actual layout only for a new viewing position.

That much is reasonably straightforward and obvious. Motion pictures are seldom made using a lens of one fixed focal length, however. By changing the focal length, the cinematog-

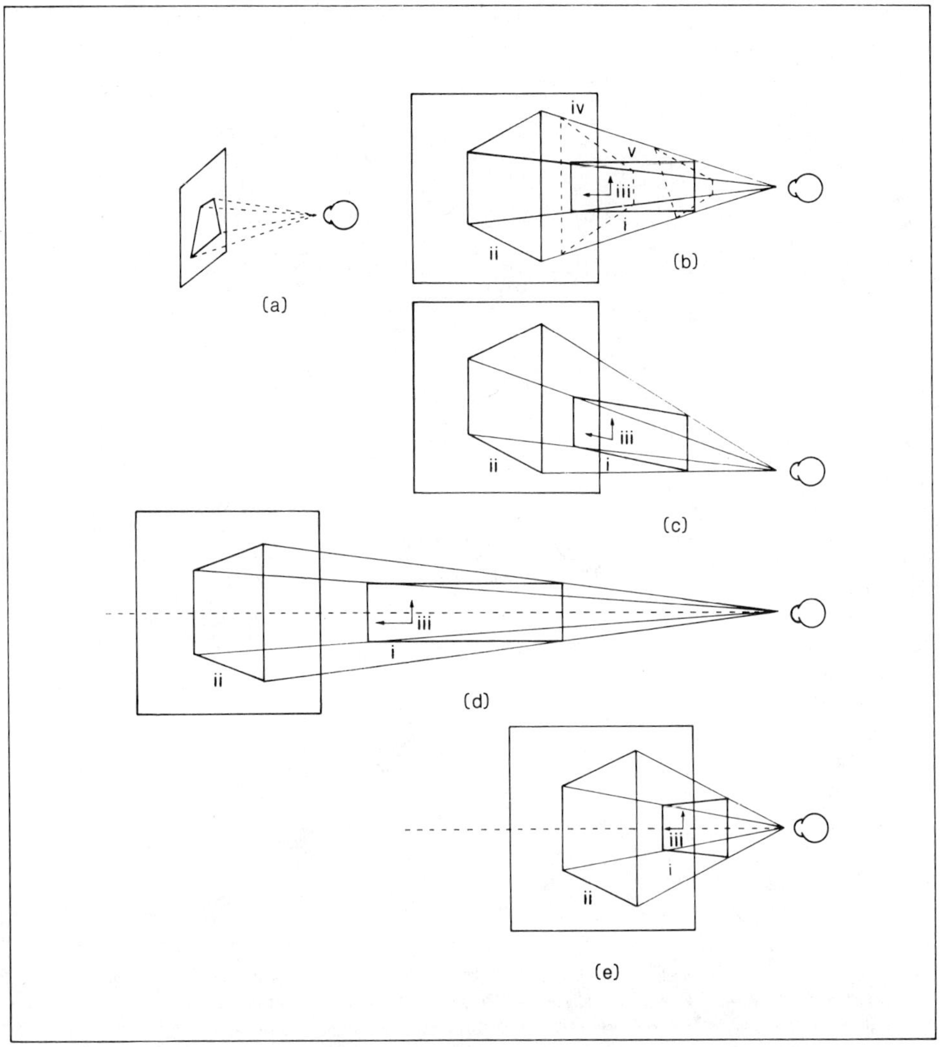

Figure 22.12. Departures from canonical arrangement result in distortions of space, form, and motion. The diagrams (b)–(e) represent the projections to the eye from a screen, as at (a). In those diagrams, both the screen and the projection lines to the eye are drawn as viewed from above, so the geometry is distorted in the interests of showing the consequences of different arrangements. These distortions do not affect the consequences described. (b) Canonical arrangement. The image of a rectangle that is viewed at a slant (i) is projected to the screen (ii) and presents to the eye an optic array that will fit the rectangle (i), the image on the screen (ii), and an indeterminately large number of alternative objects (e.g., iv and v). In the canonical viewing arrangement, two motion vectors (iii), parallel and perpendicular to the picture plane, respectively, remain equal in projection to the eye. (c) Viewed from a noncanonical position (i.e., off the projection center), the image on the screen (ii) no longer fits to the rectangle but to a trapezoid (i) and the angle between the projected images of the unit vectors (iii) is not 90°. (d) Viewed from further than the canonical position (i.e., from a distance greater than that at which the picture was taken, as when the screen is viewed from a normal distance and the picture was taken with a wide-angle or "short" lens), the screen image of the rectangle (ii) provides an optic array that is fit not by the original rectangle but by one that is much longer in depth (i); that is, depth is accentuated, and the projected image of the unit motion vector (iii) perpendicular to the screen is enlarged relative to the vector parallel to the screen. (e) Viewed from nearer than the canonical position (as in a picture taken with a telephoto or close-up lens), depth is compressed relative to width and height, and the image of the unit motion vector in depth is reduced relative to the vector parallel to the screen.

rapher can vary what is included in the field of view from a fixed camera position, achieving the same frame contents from different distances. Rather than move the camera, what is superficially the same end result can be achieved by using a fixed camera distance and using a long focal length for the close-up, a medium focal length for the medium shot, and a short focal length for the wide-angle or long shot.

For the viewer who remains at a fixed distance from the screen and an object or actor that maintains the same size on the screen, changes in focal length are equivalent to having moved away from the projection center, nearer or farther from the screen, and the real space and motions being photographed no longer fit the optic array.

If the image was achieved by using a long focal length (telephoto) lens and the viewer is seated at a distance appropriate for a shorter lens, depth in the virtual space is compressed relative to frontal extents [Fig. 22.12(e)], component movements toward or away from the camera are slowed down relative to

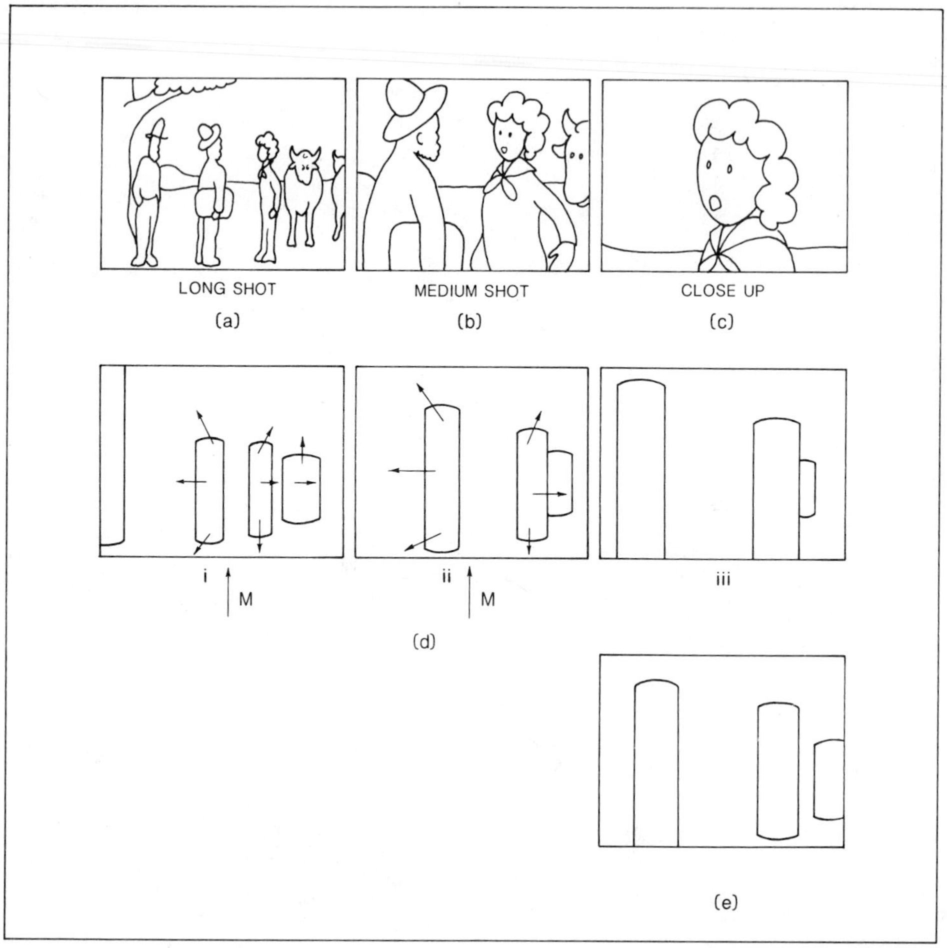

Figure 22.13. Long shot, medium shot and close-up: changes in station point and focal length. (a), (b), and (c) Long shot, medium shot and close-up. These comprise a substantial part of the tool kit of the filmmaker, for reasons discussed in the text. They can be arrived at in two quite different ways, that is, by changing the setup and photographing from far, middle distance, and nearby, respectively, or by changing the focal length of the lens from wide angle to medium to telephoto, or close-up, respectively. (d) A camera moving into the scene, producing the sequence in (a)–(c) by changing the camera distance (i, ii, and iii). Note how the different parts of the field of view move outward at unequal rates from the point at which the motion is directed, as noted in Figure 22.6(c) and (d). (e) By changing from a wide-angle to a telephoto lens, a change from long shot to medium shot can be achieved without moving the camera. The change results from a simple enlargement of the field of view and shows none of the differential expansion pattern that characterizes the dolly that provides the medium shot in (d).

movements in the frontal plane, and objects that rotate through the third dimension must change their lengths. That is, the rigidity of a moving rigid object is not in general preserved. If the long shot is achieved by using a short focal length (wide-angle) lens, the inverse occurs [Fig. 22.12(d)]: depth is accentuated relative to frontal extents, movements toward or away from the camera are speeded up relative to those in the frontal plane, and rigidity is not preserved.

These effects are often ignored by the filmmaker because it is so convenient to use changes in focal length to accomplish the desired framing. Indeed, some of these consequences of violating the canonical arrangements are themselves often desired by the motion-picture maker for aesthetic reasons: to produce an unreal flatness of field, or slowness of motion in depth, by using a long focal length lens (cf. the excruciating scene in *The Graudate* (1967), in which Dustin Hoffman races interminably toward the camera yet, because he is shot with an extremely long focal length lens, adjusted to maintain his size approximately constant upon the screen, makes no apparent progress). To produce "extreme perspective" and "loneliness" and to emphasize movement in depth, the short focal length is used (cf. the closing shot in *My Darling Clementine* (1946), in which Henry Fonda rides off toward the horizon, diminishing to half his size on the screen in approximately 1.5 sec).

To use changes in focal length in this manner and to depart from canonical arrangement in any way, the motion-picture maker must be confident that the viewer will ignore the departures from rigidity of shape and nonuniformities of motion in virtual space that these necessarily imply. This seems to be safe to do in many circumstances, perhaps because the moving objects are human and there is a wide range of acceptable deformations and limb movements. In filming dance, in which the relative sizes and velocities of the movements and gestures are themselves well defined and important, the deformations introduced by the changes in focal length seem to be noticeable and critical (cf. Brooks, 1984). And in moving the camera with respect to scale models, as well as in computer-generated events (in which image size and relationship to the vanishing point are independently variable), there is real danger of producing objects and scenes that appear to deform and change shape while moving. In general, the fact that the viewer will accept the sorts of nonrigidities and noninvariances that are routinely produced by changes in focal length will prove to be of considerable theoretical importance when we discuss the study of motion pictures from the standpoint of perceptual psychology.

Indeed, one method of changing focal length that is both very common and of great theoretical importance is the *zoom*, in which the focal length of the camera lens is changed continuously from short to long or from long to short. See Figure 22.14(f). The zoom is very widely used to pull into or out of a scene, mimicking in some regards the results of a dolly shot, crane shot, or helicopter shot. See Figure 22.6(b). It is a simple magnification of the field of view, with each point receiving a uniform radial vector **v**, as in Figure 22.14(f). As such, it must either be fit by a flat picture of the scene that is enlarging (perhaps by a nonuniform approach velocity) or by a three-dimensional scene which, since it is almost certainly viewed from a noncanonical position, must be undergoing a complex set of deformations. Nevertheless, zooms take their place as widely used component motions, filling out the quartet of track, dolly, pan, and zoom shots, down in Figure 22.14, that comprise the elementary visual screen changes.

We next consider briefly the consequences of combining these component motions and some recent misunderstandings of them that have been introduced into the scientific literature.

1.4.4. Composite, Nonlinear, and Complex Viewer–Camera Movements. The preceding discussion of information about space and observer motion inherent in the optical flow pattern and conceivably usable by the viewer has dealt with very simple situations. They have been simple in several quite different ways that must be separated before we consider more complex events.

If we subject each point in the optic array (or on the moving-picture screen) to analysis, as to whether it is light or dark at any moment, we obtain a matrix of changes that is bewildering, complex, and unpredictable in the general case. A single point of light that goes on and off in some predictable pattern over time is obviously simpler. This kind of punctiform analysis is often taken to provide the opposition viewpoint by proponents of more global analysis.

Such matrices of intensity change are normally redundant; that is, not every possible combination occurs with equal likelihood. A set of correlated but temporally offset intensity changes is the more usual case; the correlation and the offset both occur as a result of identifiable elements in the world that move in the optic array.

As an alternative to an intensity-change matrix, we can imagine a matrix of points in the array each of which signals a movement, with velocity $V(i)$ in the optic array. Such a matrix can still be regarded as being very complex, in that there are all the individual velocities to calculate and compare. In fact, such a matrix will also normally prove to be redundant, because many of the points that move in the optic array are elements of objects and surfaces—corners, patches of repeating texture, shadows, and so on. They often will either share the same vector [Fig. 22.15(a)] or the vectors will be organized into some simple and regular structure; for example, they might have some specific divergence or curl over some substantial region [Fig. 22.15(b)ii].

If the analysis of a field of such vectors must proceed point by point before the viewer can recognize the redundancies—recognize which parts go together and which are separate—the task of computation would still be an immense one, the display still very complex. It is precisely this analytic approach that the Gibsonians, or "direct realists," oppose. They propose that there is a direct response to the redundancies in the vector field (although they do not use those terms), so that a field, in which all the vectors are equal or in which a coherent relationship between them holds (e.g., a uniform divergence), is a simple stimulus pattern.

What is simple becomes a question of the level and units of analysis. A field full of points as in Figure 22.15(b)ii, moving with different velocities and accelerations, is simple if we have some means of detecting that the pattern of movements is generated by a revolving cylinder of dots through which a stationary background of dots is seen, without first measuring the individual element velocities and accelerations and then attempting to compute their relationship.

One of the strong points of the Gibsonian approaches (e.g., Gibson, 1959, 1979; Johansson, 1977a, 1977b, 1982) is that they seem to offer a simple specification of such globally simple but locally complex situations. Perhaps for this reason, they ignore questions of limits on the viewers to cope with complexity in the optic array; one looks through that literature in vain for a hint that such limits exist.

But they do. Complexity, we will see, is a limiting factor in the kinds of objects, movements, and layouts that we can perceive (Figure 22.20), in the cuts and transitions that can be made from one view to the next (Figure 22.28), and as we see next, in the kinds of relative motions between viewer and objects that will produce comprehensible motion-picture sequences.

We consider first the effects of complex viewer or camera motions. The simple classes of movement-produced stimulation described in Figures 22.6 and 22.14 can be combined. The viewer's eyes can move in one direction while the viewer moves in another direction. Similarly, the cinematographer can execute a pan or a zoom while moving in a dolly or tracking shot. A simple composite of two camera motions is shown in Figure 22.16(c) and (d). We show first the two components, provided by each of the two image transformations [Figure 22.16(a) and (b)]; then we show the field that is produced by the resolutions of those two components [Figure 22.16(c) and (d)].

There are several important points to be made about the fields of view provided by such composite motions of viewer or camera. First, note that Figure 22.16(c) and (d) must provide exactly the same information to the eye because *they* are the same motions, expressed in different vector sets.

Second, in each case, any change in the way the motions are combined will produce a different pattern in the composite vectors. In Figure 22.16(c) and (d), the viewer has changed the point in the field on which the gaze remains fixed during the body's movement, and (depending on the layout of surfaces in the scene) the flow pattern can be substantially changed when we consider the composed field of vectors [Figure 22.16(d)], whereas in the field decomposed as in Figure 22.16(c) with the components due to the eye movements being separated from those due to the body movements, each of the two patterns remains substantially unaltered and directly interpretable.

For this reason, it is tempting not only to keep the vectors decomposed but to assume that the viewer's perceptual system does the same. Several perceptual theorists concerned with the retrieval of motion-produced information about space assume

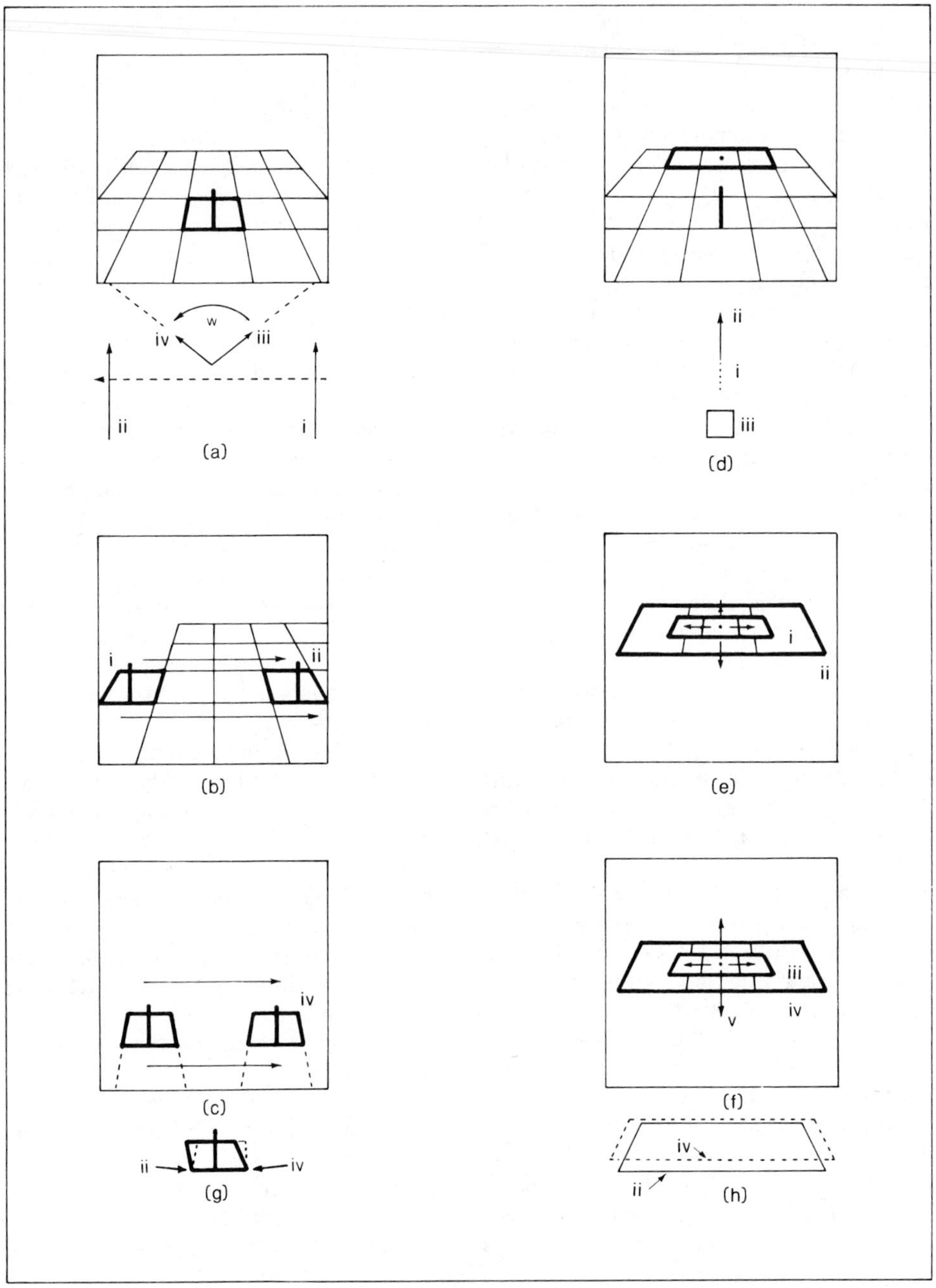

Figure 22.14. Pan and track, dolly and zoom: the elementary visual motions of the moving camera. (a) A layout in space that is scanned by a camera from right to left, so that the image moves from left to right on the screen. This can be done by tracking the camera parallel to the screen, from i to ii, or it can be done by panning the camera through angle *w*, from iii to iv. (b) The image that results from tracking, as in Figure 22.6(a). (c) The image that results from panning. Note that the displacements of the representations of the far and near parts of the field of view are equal, and that no motion parallax appears in the relationship between the vertical pole and the square element of the field on which it stands. (d) If the heavily outlined region in the depicted spatial layout is photographed by a camera approaching from i to ii (a dolly shot), it produces an enlargement in the image as shown at (e). The same region can be enlarged by changing the focal length of the lens (iii and iv), in a zoom shot (f). (e) The image of the outlined region in (d), as it expands on the screen because the camera approaches from i to ii in a track shot. Note that the expansion is asymmetrical (see Figure 22.6). (f) The expansion of the same region through simple magnification (zoom). Note the symmetry of the expansion. (g) and (h) Although pan and zoom are superficially similar to track and dolly, respectively, they differ significantly in the optical results. The results of pan (iv) and track (ii) are superimposed, for a small region, at (g); those for dolly and zoom, at (h). Note that each of these imparts a characteristic set of distortions of space, form, and motion as they must inherently depart from canonical arrangement (see Figures 22.12 and 22.13).

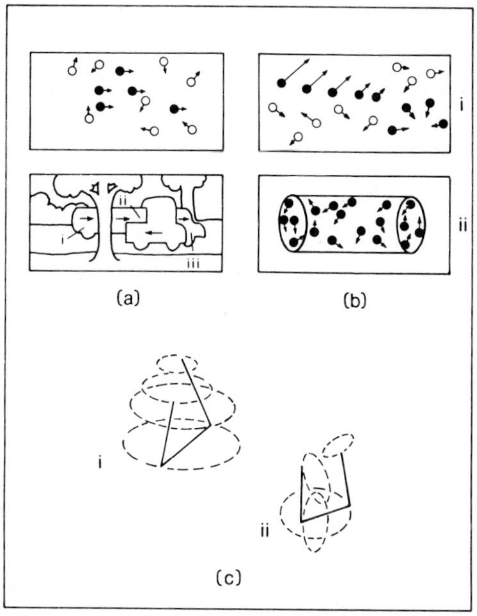

Figure 22.15. In one sense, a matrix made up of a large number of moving dots is necessarily complex if each dot must be specified (and is perceived) as a separate event. There is usually redundancy in such matrices, in that groups of points, whether adjacent or separate, move with the same or related velocities. In (a)i, the black dots stand out immediately because of their common motion. (Wertheimer, 1912). At ii, the separated regions of points i, ii, and iii all move with the same velocities because they belong to the same object and, treated as a single object, the complexity of the field is greatly reduced. (b) Even if no two dots move with exactly the same velocities, there is usually another specifiable order in the field of movements, that is, relationships that remain invariant despite the transformations of the array. Many of these can be expressed in the language of vector calculus, that is, as vector fields; this is especially true when the movements are produced by the flow of fluids or by the optical expansion pattern and motion perspective is produced by specified points on surfaces. Any continuous vector field can be resolved into an irrotational field (for which *curl* is zero) and a solenoidal field (for which *divergence* is zero)—for example, the upper-left set of black dots and the lower-right set of black dots, respectively—and in recent years an attempt has begun to express optical information in these terms (e.g., Gordon, 1965; Koenderink & Van Doorn, 1981). The set of motions shown in ii is exceedingly complex in the sense that every vector differs from every other vector; on the other hand, they all fit the function that would be generated by dots on a rotating, transparent cylinder. If our nervous systems constituted a kind of device that responds not by computing the path of each dot but by responding to the single function that comprises the rotating cylinder, the display would not be a complex one at all. This is essentially the point of the "direct theory" of J. J. Gibson (1979) and of Johansson (1982), and it is true that at least under some circumstances viewers can correctly identify such displays as rotating cylinders (Ullman, 1977) or (with the appropriate displays) rotating spheres, in some cases after only a single displacement of two frames (Lappin, et al., 1980). These findings should not be overinterpreted, however, to mean that such visual feats are quite general (for reasons that we consider in (c) and in connection with Figures 22.23 and 22.28). (c) Most formulations intended to apply to such multielement displays as in (b) are addressed to the motions of rigid objects and achieve their simplicity in that way. The conditions that lead to the perception of a rigid object or surface are only imperfectly known. Mathematically, a very small sample would in principle suffice (cf. Ullman, 1977), and Johansson (1982) and Lappin and colleagues (1980), as noted, report correct recognition of motion in a very few successive frames. Todd (1982) proposed that the judgments that viewers actually make are based on the coherence of the elipses that are provided in the optic array by distinguishable features on a rotating object (that is, on the coherence of their orientation, frequency, *x* intercept, and eccentricity). For example, i would be judged a rigid object, whereas because each path has a different orientation in ii, the latter would appear nonrigid. In fact, given a stationary axis of rotation and paths of 180° or better, judgments were mostly correct; with an 18° rotation, performance was barely above chance; and with a moving axis of rotation, judgments were poor, as they should be if they were in fact based on the trajectories of rotation. There are several important lessons to be drawn from these findings: information (or invariance under transformation) presented by a display does not assure that it will be used; a response obtained with a very small sample of one display does not imply a general ability; and—most important, I believe—complexity remains a fundamental limit on what can be perceived even in cases in which one can show invariance in the transformation. Those limits are what make the study of perception of practical importance and enable us to assign one, rather than another, formulation to account for the perceptual lawfulness we found.

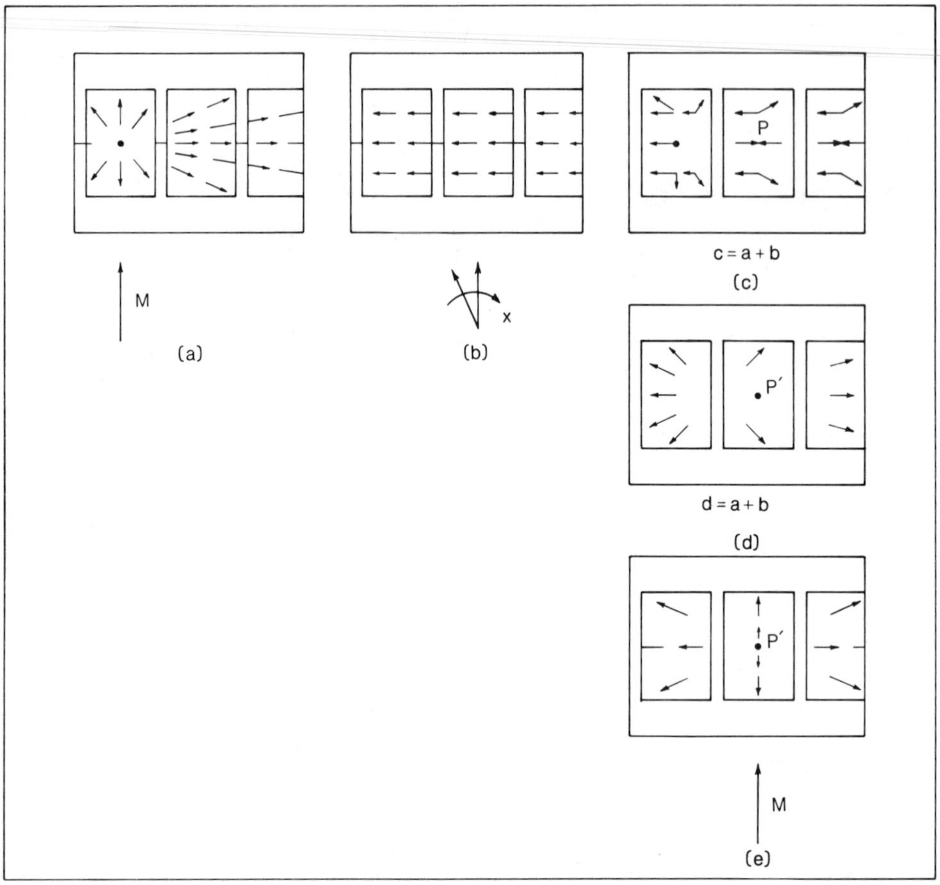

Figure 22.16. Compound motions. (a) The optical expansion pattern produced by a movement *M* toward the left-most wall (see Figure 22.6(d)). (b) The optical flow pattern produced by a pan through angle *x*. (c) If the camera (or viewer) pans through angle *x* while moving toward the left-most wall, so as to keep the center point of the middle wall fixed on the film (or retina), as in Figure 22.6(e), the two fields shown in (a) and (b) will act on the same points, as shown here. (d) If the two fields at (c) are summed, point by point, the opposed vectors cancel at *P′*. Note that although *P′* is then stationary, it is not the center of expansion; that is, the vectors in the display do not point back to *P′*. (e) Only if the camera or viewer both moves toward and sights on *P*, will the latter be both stationary and the center of the expansion pattern on the film. This analysis is both wrongly stated and pictured in recent papers, notably Regan and Beverly (1982). It is an empirical question, however, whether viewers can distinguish fields (c) or (d), on the one hand, from field (e), on the other, and there is evidence (Johnston, 1972; Regan & Beverly, 1982) that at least in the situations tested, they cannot do so.

(with varying degrees of explicitness; see Section 1.6) that that is just what the perceptual system does. It is not clear how that can be accomplished unless we adopt some sort of "simplicity" constraint on the perceptual system (see Section 1.6), because although it is easy to establish what the correct decomposition is when we start with the component motions as executed by viewer or camera, there is no unique solution in working back the other way.

Various formulations have been offered, none of them as yet successful, to solve this partitioning problem. As we will see, this issue is central to the perception of objects moving in space, as well as to the problem of using information generated by the motions of the viewer or camera. The viewer who is moving through the scene has knowledge, however, that the viewer of the motion picture does not share. There are various kinds of theories about how information about such movements might be utilized (or compensated for), and there is evidence that under certain circumstances such information can be used (see Goldstein, 1979; Matin, 1982; Wallach & Bacon, 1976). In fact, we simply do not at present know the range of conditions under which the viewer would be able to use such information to disambiguate the partitioning problem. It would be important to our understanding of space perception in general, therefore, if we could show how the visual system deals with this problem, drawing only on visual information, when the visual-motor system cannot serve to disambiguate the partitioning possibilities.

That is, of course, precisely what makes the representation of space by means of motion pictures and video so important to the psychologist. Gibson (1959, 1979) and Johansson (1977a, 1977b, 1982) propose that the uniform translation vector offers information about eye movement (in the case of a viewer before a scene). The proposal has the strength that it offers a direct extension to the perception of motion pictures. It faces the problem of providing a principle by which one can extract the appropriate uniform vector field from the complex patterns offered by a normally cluttered field of view.

Despite criticisms of Gibson's analysis (e.g., Regan & Beverly, 1982), Gibson does note (1950) that the eye movement provides a uniform translation on the field and, therefore, can be distinguished from otherwise similar flow patterns produced by locomotion. Johansson has proposed a principle, originally formulated in connection with the perception of object motion, that under certain constraints would work to partition out the effects of changing gaze or camera direction: that we extract the longest common vector and treat that as the "framework" within which other motions appear.

This sounds simple enough. Although I do not know of a rigorous mathematical proof, it will surely do to sort out the components of the flow patterns that are produced by composite movements like those in Figure 22.16. We will see, however, that it will not do as a general theoretical principle (Figures 22.19, 22.20, 22.27, and 22.28). And it does not tell us *how* the viewer extracts the common vectors (i.e., by what computational principle or receptor mechanism), nor does it address the myriad questions of *threshold* that such a formulation must confront. Two examples serve to illustrate these points and to introduce us to the next section on object motion.

With respect to the mechanisms or principles by which such separation might occur, since Helmholtz first proposed that motion parallax provides a sufficient basis for the perception of radial distance and motion in space (1856/1962), we have progressed slowly toward greater specificity about what is invariant under the transformation (a phrasing introduced by Cassirer, 1944) and about what aspects of motion-generated patterns are *potentially* informative. Gibson and his colleagues and followers have laid out the basic geometry, as we have seen (Section 1.3) and given us a set of rough ideas as to how the motion patterns might be decomposed to provide potentially useful information about the viewer's motion and about the layouts of the surfaces in the world. Subsequent analyses (Gordon, 1965; Koenderink & van Doorn, 1976, 1981; Prazdny, 1980) have progressively inclined to the coordinate-free terms of vector calculus, that is, in terms of the divergence, grad, and curl of the field of motion parallax vectors.

Whatever else it does, analysis in such terms should make it easier to study how to decompose the flow patterns provided by composite motions. For example, there is Helmholtz's theorem in vector calculus (McQuistan, 1965) that any vector field which (with its first derivatives) is continuous may be resolved into an irrotational and a solenoidal portion. (In an irrotational vector field, curl is zero; in a solenoidal field, divergence is zero.) In this vein, Koenderink and van Doorn (1981) split the parallax field into what they call a lamellar part and a solenoidal part. The lamellar flow, completely determined by the divergence of the parallax field, provides the information about the world; the solenoidal part gives no information about the environment inasmuch as it can be completely canceled by an eye movement.

The solenoidal field, free of any expansion or contraction, would therefore include the translatory effects of eye movement shifts or camera pans. That would put a premium on the viewer's ability to pick up expansion in the retinal image, a point to which we return below. Let us consider a concrete example, shown in Figures 22.6(e) and 22.16, to illustrate the issues involved here.

Imagine that a viewer's eye or a camera is so swiveled as to keep a point P' motionless in the eye or on film while the viewer approaches a wall on which point P is the projected point of impact. The focus of expansion on the retina or on the film is not fixed by the viewer's direction of motion but depends on eye movements as well. To take this as a critique (Regan & Beverley, 1982) of Gibson's assertion that the focus of expansion specifies the direction of motion is mistaken because Gibson was discussing the optic array, not the retinal image, but it also obscures the fact of geometry with which we must here be concerned: the focus of expansion is the point from which all vectors are directed outward (and not as the extremum of divergence, as Regan & Beverley are really using the term). It is simply *not* true, therefore, that the pursuit movement in Figure 22.16(b) has provided a new focus of expansion. If the viewer chooses to decompose the resultants in such a way that there is a single focus of expansion, as in Figure 22.16(c), then that would automatically separate the pattern due to the eye movements from the pattern due to locomotion in the world, and the focus of expansion would be detected in its proper place in the latter.

This raises a serious question that has come up before, the question of threshold. Regardless of the mathematics of stimulus analysis, would the viewer be adequately sensitive to the differences between the vector fields? As we see in the next section, we actually have very little data to this point or to other questions about the perceptual use of the spatial information potentially available in consequence of relative movement between viewer and scene, and what little we have is not encouraging.

1.5. The Multiple Ambiguity of Object Motions and Properties

Whatever else they are, moving pictures are a clear demonstration of the fact that the information in the light to the eye is ambiguous. The visual information for spaces and motions within them is being presented by means of a very different arrangement, one of colored lights on a flat surface.

But there are more specific sets of ambiguities remaining in motion pictures that are of practical and theoretical as distinct from philosophical importance. We consider the most salient of these next.

1.5.1. The Multiple Readings of Motions in Space. The first source of ambiguity is that the viewer has no grounds, on the basis of optical information alone, for partitioning the motion on the screen as being due to motion of the camera, motion of the object, or some combination of the two. In order to arrive at an unambiguous partitioning, constraints are needed as to the nature of the scene that produced the moving picture.

Thus a point (or an object) may be stationary on the screen because it was stationary before a stationary camera [Figure 22.17] or because the camera was tracking (moving or changing direction in phase with) a moving object [Figure 22.17(a)ii]. On occasion, a filmmaker may ignore this point and spend a great deal of money to keep up with a moving actor against what turns out to be an effectively blank background, to end up with a stationary-looking actor (or rocket or airplane); see Vorkapich (1972) for a sad example of this.

Alternatively, the object may be stationary, the camera moving, and the image moving on the screen (a device that is often used in "tabletop" simulations), as in Figure 22.17(b)i; the object may move while the camera is stationary [Figure 22.17(b)ii]; or both may move, with different velocities, and the vector difference will provide the motion on the screen [Figure 22.17(b)iii]. Nor need those vectors be restricted to the plane of the screen: the object may move in any direction in three-dimensional space, and so may the camera. Different situations can yield the same moving display [Figures 22.18(c,d)]. However, there appear to be perceptual preferences or assumptions to resolve the ambiguities inherent in the moving picture in one way rather than in another. For example, the viewer assumes

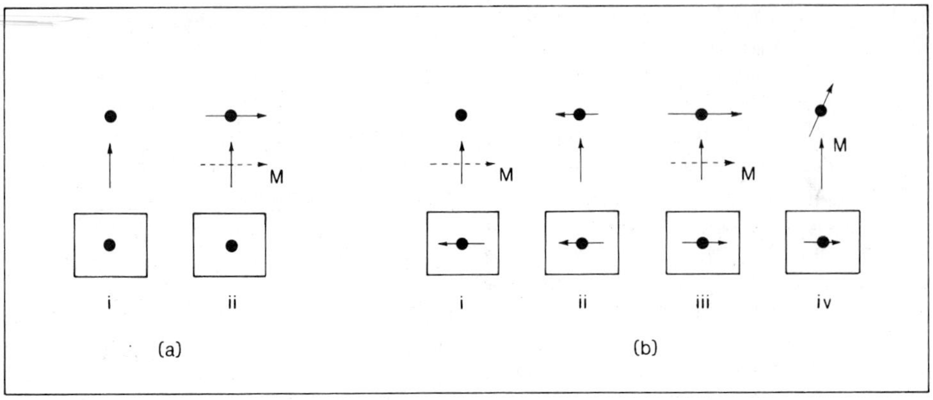

Figure 22.17. The components of viewer-relative motion. (a) The sources of a stationary image. (i) A stationary object and a stationary camera (or eye) yields a stationary image on film (or retina). (ii) A moving object, and a camera (or an eye) tracking it at the same velocity, yields a stationary image on film (or retina). (b) The sources of a moving image. (i) Stationary object, moving camera: moving image. (ii) Moving object, stationary camera: moving image. (iii) Moving object, camera moving with different velocity. (iv) Only those components of motion in i–iii that are perpendicular to the line of sight contribute to the image motion.

that the background is stationary, rather than the viewer, as shown in Figure 22.18(c) and (d).

Note that Figure 22.18(d) implies either that the actor must be moving off the screen in direction x, and moving relative to the viewer, or that the viewer and the actor are moving together. Under normal viewing conditions (as distinct from certain laboratory situations), the viewer remains completely aware of the fact that the actor has indeed not moved on the screen and at the same time that the viewer has not moved in space. (The phenomenon is reminiscent of the fact that we perceive both a flat picture and the three-dimensional space that it represents in static, as well as in moving, pictures.) This means that the

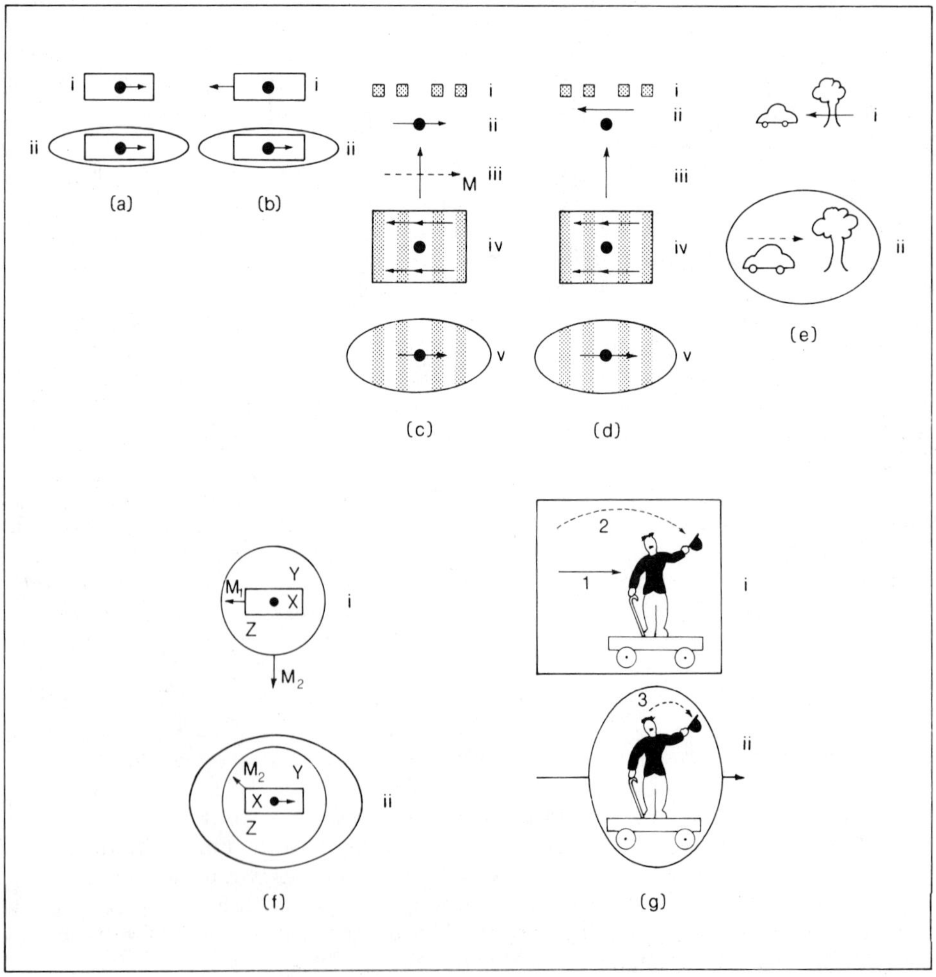

movement in the optic array is *not* conserved, is *not* parsed in a consistent and unitary fashion. The kinds of explanation that we survey next tend to assume that the resolution of ambiguity in one way or another follows perceptual principles that are obligatory and consistent, which is not obviously true in the movie-viewing situation.

Indeed, as we will see, it is generally not a justified assumption for the laboratory situation either.

1.5.2. The Partitioning of Represented Motions. We can separate classes of attempts to explain how we choose one reading or another of the possible events in represented motion. I believe that these are all demonstrably false as *general* theories but that elements of all will serve as rough explanations. We will not be able to use them even in a rough predictive and practical way, however, until we know their limits. That is, we know that all of them work on some occasions, but we cannot with any assurance say which of them, if any, will serve to predict what will be perceived on any specific occasion.

1.5.2.1. General Theories. I: Familiarity and Unconscious Inference. One sturdy and obvious explanation as to why we perceive a stationary background and a moving viewer in Figure 22.18(d) is that we are accustomed to that condition in our normal experience with the world. Indeed, with a few exceptions—and even those can be dealt with qualitatively (Hochberg, 1981a, 1982)—all the rules of perceptual organization can be interpreted as being the expression of our experiences with the regularities of the world. One example that cannot be explained in other terms is sketched in Figure 22.18(e). When the relative motion can be partitioned between an object normally stationary and one normally mobile, the latter is seen to move (Brosgole & Whalen, 1967). We must note, however, that the inference principle often fails to predict in advance and that there are unknown but important limits on its applicability across the gamut of perceptual phenomena (Hochberg, 1981a, 1981b; 1982).

1.5.2.2. Specific Organizational Principles. Practically all the observations that can be made about the partitioning of apparent movement, relevant to moving pictures, were made by Duncker in 1929 (1929/1937). The most important of these are exemplified in Figure 22.18(a)–(e).

Two principles that are important to moving pictures are due to Wallach (1959, 1982; see also Anstis, Chapter 16, and Mack, Chapter 17): *separation of systems* [Figure 22.18(f)] and *object-relative movement* [Figure 22.18(g)]. The first [Figure 22.18(f)] seems to summarize the kinds of paradoxes that appear when we try to add up or account for the movements that are perceived by stationary viewers in response to the moving pic-

Figure 22.18. (*Opposite*) Perceptual partitioning of the moving image: I. Induced movement. In (a)–(f), the ovals show what is perceived by the viewer; in (g), the oval encloses the most salient perceived movement. (a) A dot moving within a stationary frame (i) is perceived just that way, as shown in (ii). (b) A stationary dot moving within a frame (i) with a slow to moderate velocity is perceived as a moving dot within a stationary frame (ii). Were this not the case, moving objects tracked by a moving camera, as in Figure 22.6(b)iv, would appear stationary to the viewer. This is considered further in (c) and (d). (c) The stationary background (i) changes the situation of Figure 22.17(a)ii by providing the stationary dot with a moving frame, which encloses it, and the stationary dot then appears to move. (d) Indeed, the situation shown in Figure 22.17(a)i (i.e., stationary camera, stationary object, and stationary image) is the most common surrogate for an object or person moving through the world. As here, moving background (i) then provides the frame to induce perceived movement (v) of the stationary image. The moving frame is most often itself produced either by physically projecting a motion picture of the moving world on a background or by a "matting" or "keying" procedure that adds the background by optical or electronic means, respectively. (e) The factors that affect induced motion are discussed in detail in Chapter 18. To the degree that they can be defined entirely in terms of such stimulus variables as size, configuration (i.e., enclosedness), and such, they can be viewed as psychophysical variables and formulated in mathematical terms (see Figure 22.19 and the discussion of "direct theories") and incorporated into computer programs in quite general terms. But just as *familiar size* (see Figure 22.5(b)) is a critical depth cue because it depends on the history of the perceiver's experience with the partially "accidental" distribution of sizes within the world and resists incorporation within a direct theory of space perception, what might be called "familiar mobility" provides a similar challenge to a direct theory of motion perception and to general computer animation programs (if the latter are to provide for the way that human viewers indeed partition the motions presented to them). A study by Brosgole and Whalen (1967) demonstrates partitioning according to familiar mobility. Given relative motion between the car and the tree (i), it is the car that appears to move (ii). As with familiar size, the direct and indirect effectiveness of this factor and its limits remain to be explored. Theoretically, even a small effect is important; practically, it is important to know its strength. (f) Separation of systems, which is Wallach's term (1959) for the laboratory phenomenon illustrated here. (i) Spot X is stationary within frame Y, which itself moves M_1 within frame Z, which moves with velocity M_2. (ii) Perceptually, point X moves in the opposite direction from M_1, just as expected from Figure 22.18(b)ii, while frame Y moves with the vector resolution of M_1 and M_2 (the latter induced by the motion of enclosing frame Z). The point here is that the induced movement of X appears to be determined only by the actual movement of its immediate surround. This effect is important to motion-picture perception but is entangled with the phenomenon discussed next in (g). Further work is needed. (g) Object-relative motion. (i) An actor moves at velocity 1; he doffs his hat while transported across the screen, so that the hat describes path 2, which arcs from one end of the screen to the other. That arc is generally not the perceived movement. Instead, the actor, arm, and hat are perceived to move as a unit (ii), and the hat appears to move through a much smaller arc 3, with a motion that is relative to the actor, not to the overall screen. This aspect of the partitioning of depicted motion is clearly important in motion pictures, constructed by moving cameras aimed at moving objects, of which the parts are themselves engaged in relative motion. It would be valuable to be able to provide a general principle and definition for such partitioning; one such attempt is considered in Figure 22.19.

tures produced on the screen by a moving camera directed at moving objects. The second [Figure 22.18(g)] reflects our ability to partition the complex swirl of movements on the screen when we are confronted by a moving object's moving parts or a moving actor's moving members.

Although these latter principles appear relevant to things that we see on the screen and seem reasonably straightforward as laboratory demonstrations, their use is hampered by the absence of objective formulation, by the fact that we cannot presently state the range of conditions for their occurrence (see Anstis, Chapter 16, and Mack, Chapter 17), and by their theoretical status; at best, they are isolated "rules," in that they are not derivable from any more fundamental principles or theoretical framework.

Sections 1.5.2.3 and 1.5.2.4 consider briefly, from the standpoint of moving pictures, theories that have purported to include most or all of these principles. We will see that they are in fact actually less than convincing, despite their inclusive claims.

1.5.2.3. General Theories: II. Vector Extraction and Invariance Pickup. The "direct theory" in its various versions looks to stimulus information to determine perceptual organization. The general position is that we perceive what is specified by the invariant information in the transformation. This does not in general serve to distinguish between the alternative readings of moving pictures. Johansson, as we noted, has proposed that in any motion configuration [e.g., Figure 22.19(a)–(c)] we perform a vector decomposition on the moving elements in the field of view, extracting the longest common vector as the framework within which all residual movements are perceived. That seems intuitively plausible, and also seems objective enough, when we consider that in fact subjects often report seeing such cases as Figure 22.19(a)i and (b)i–iii as the motions shown in Figure 22.19(a)ii and (b)iv, respectively.

First, we should note that what the eyes are doing and the speed of the dots affect the degree to which the described organization is obtained (Wallach, 1982). Second, there are few quantitative or objective data. Although the magnitude of these effects can be measured psychophysically (Hochberg, Brooks, & Fallon, 1977; Hochberg & Fallon, 1976; see also Figure 22.31), that is almost never done in this research, which consists mostly of unquantified assertions about what subjects see. A third reservation is that this account will not work in any way that we can define solely in terms of stimulus measures. As formulated,

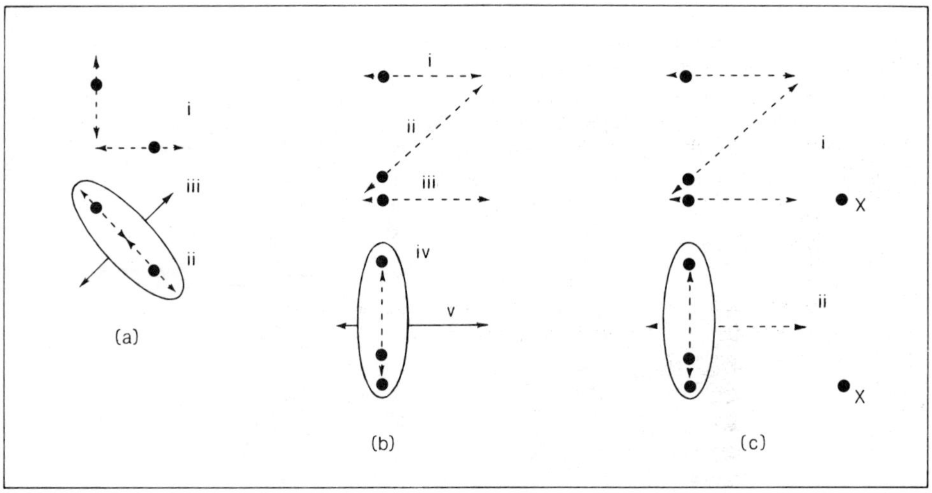

Figure 22.19. Perceptual partitioning of the moving image: II. Event perception as vector analysis or invariance extraction. Johansson has proposed (1950, 1982) that the perception of events, like those in Figures 22.15(c) and in this figure, can be viewed as the direct response to mathematical formulations of the stimulus event. As examples, consider his demonstrations at (a) and (b). In both cases, a set of simple objective movements (a)i and (b)i–iii are perceived in ways that are quite different from the real motions. In (a), a pair of colinear moving dots are seen, which approach and recede from each other ((a)ii), while the path of their movement itself moves (in a nonsalient and sometimes invisible fashion) as shown at iii. In (b), a single light appears to move along the vertical path iv, which is defined by the two dots on paths i and iii, and the diagonal path ii is simply not seen; the vertical path itself (iv) moves nonsaliently from left to right (v), in the residual movement. Johansson sees this phenomenon as closely related to Gibson's direct perception theory (see Section 1.5.2.3) and as a direct response to the results of a vector decomposition in which a common vector is extracted as the framework ((a)iii and (b)v) and the residual movements are seen against that framework. In fact, the phenomena are far more robust than the theory can allow. In (c), the same phenomenon is obtained when the viewer keeps his or her gaze fized on X, a stationary fixation point (Hochberg & Fallon, 1976), using the quantitative procedure described in Figure 22.31. The presence of the stationary fixation point means that the common vector that fits the display is of zero length, and in the vector-analytic formulation the consequent percept should be that of (c)i. Moreover, Johansson's early demonstrations (1950) used black dots against a light ground, and the edges of the screen were clearly visible. Were the effect not independent of context in this fashion, it would be of little or no practical importance in motion pictures and video displays. However, that makes Johansson's theory, and other similar attempts to base motion partitioning on the entire configuration (Restle, 1979), inapplicable as now put. Both as theories and for practical application, they must make some provision for delimiting the event over which the analysis is to proceed. Other difficulties with the vector-extraction approach are discussed in Figure 22.21 and 22.31.

a stationary point should make for a stationary framework, but the presence of stationary points does not constrain subjects to see only the true motion path. In Figure 22.19(c), a stationary fixation point lies near the moving configuration (Hochberg & Fallon, 1976), but the perceived paths are still those of Figure 22.19(b). The same results obtain, moreover, when the events in Figure 22.19(a) are surrounded by a strongly visible stationary framework (Hochberg, Brooks, & Fallon, 1977; Johansson, 1950). Evidently the visual system must make a prior decision as to *what* is being parsed, before any parsing is done, and we cannot apply vector analyses until that process is explicated. Essentially the same conclusion is reached from the work by Profitt, Cutting, and Stier (1979) and Profitt and Cutting (1980), who studied the apparent paths followed by lights mounted on rolling wheels (first studied by Duncker, 1929/1937).

I know of only one attempt to formulate a general principle for extracting configurations or events, that is, a "minimum," or a "simplicity," principle. Originally proposed to explain the perception of form, that proposal has recently been revived in connection with the parsing of events (e.g., Restle, 1979).

1.5.2.4. General Theories: III. Minimum Principle "Coding Theories." The notion that we perceive what is simplest to perceive is as old as modern psychology (e.g., Mach, 1886/1959). The Gestalt psychologists made this proposal central to their attempts to account for perceptual organization, and Koffka (1935) suggested that organization so occurs as to minimize the distribution of forces in a (quite imaginary) field of electrical activity in the brain. An attempt was made to make this more objective in terms of measures that could be applied to objects and pictures of objects (Attneave, 1954; Hochberg & MacAlister, 1953). Hochberg and MacAlister proposed that the likelihood that we perceive any given reading or alternative organization of an object or event is in inverse proportion to the complexity of that reading, compared to the complexities of the alternative readings (e.g., in terms of the numbers of different angles, lines, etc., needed to specify the particular reading; see Hochberg & Brooks, 1960, for specific terms for coding shapes in this way). This notion has recently been revived by Leeuwenberg and his colleagues (Buffart, Leeuwenberg, & Restle, 1981; Leeuwenberg, 1971, 1982) and been applied by Restle (1979) to moving dots. The patterns of movement are coded according to some formal scheme for the two major alternate readings of the entire event, and it is held that the perceptual reading with the lowest measure is the one that will be perceived.

Two reservations must be raised about this proposal. First, we should note that, again, quantitative psychophysical measures were not used, though available (Hochberg & Fallon, 1976). Second, it fails as a general theory; like the Johansson analysis, it fails to specify what will comprise the event being parsed and, therefore, is vulnerable to the criticism exemplified by Figure 22.19(c). More damaging, the coding theory necessarily rests on an assumption of consistency *within* an object. That assumption is clearly false and was raised as an objection to encoding approaches since 1962 (Hochberg, 1962). It is false with respect to static pictures (Hochberg, 1962, 1968, 1980), and it is false with respect to moving objects as well, as seen in Figure 22.20(a) and (b) (Gillam, 1972; Peterson & Hochberg, 1981). An object, like the partially skeletal cube in Figure 22.20(b), rotating in space, fixed in its orientation at one intersection *i*, is perceived as reversing at the relatively unfixed intersection *ii*, conclusively showing that we do not perceive the simplest overall reading of the object. We discuss this further in Section 1.5.2.5.

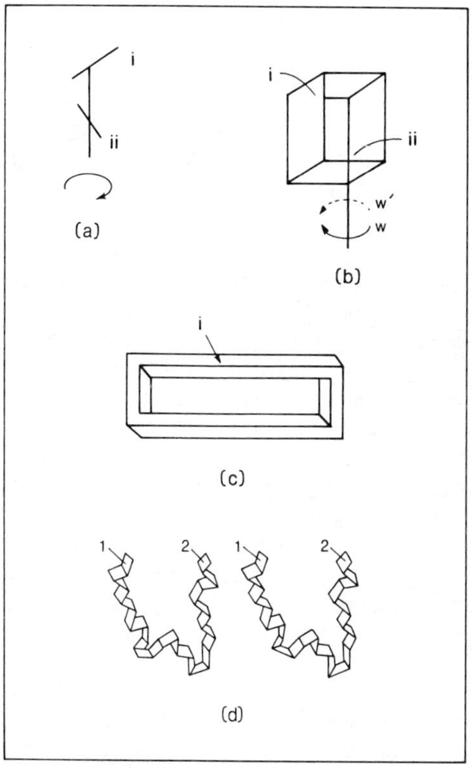

Figure 22.20. How much is included in an event? None of the attempts to predict the appearances of events in space has attended to the fundamental requirement of defining the span of the event to be taken into account. And that may not be a fixed variable—it may well depend on the perceptual inquiry the viewer elects to make. There is, in fact, ample reason to reject any holistic formulations. (a) Rotating wire objects spontaneously break up during viewing, and the parts may then appear to rotate in opposite directions (Gillam, 1972). (b) A three-dimensional cube, constructed of wire with one face filled in to form a surface, reverses in orientation when regarded at intersection ii, even though it is fixed by the depth cue of interposition at intersection i (Hochberg, 1980, 1981a) and even though its motion theoretically specifies its orientation (Peterson & Hochberg, 1982). When its apparent orientation reverses and the vertical wire appears nearer than the horizontal wire at intersection ii, its apparent direction of rotation changes as well, for example, from *W* to *W′* (Peterson & Hochberg, 1983). (c) The opposite sides of this drawing, adapted (Hochberg, 1968) from the famous "impossible" figure of Penrose and Penrose (1958), look perfectly three-dimensional and unaffected by their inconsistency; one has to elect to trace the three-dimensional dihedral represented by line i, from one end to the other, to detect the inconsistency (Hochberg, 1968). (d) In ribbon-shaped objects, of which this is a drawing, the relative orientation of each dihedral is completely specified by the information in the light to the eye as received by a free observer, yet the relationship between more distant parts must be separately searched out, and that occurs only if the viewer elects to do so. Information about the relationships between the parts of the object is present to the eye, but those relationships are neither directly nor automatically perceived (Hochberg, 1978; Klopfer, 1983).

It is hard to see how any coding theory that incorporates a minimum principle and that is to be applied to the whole object can be maintained in the face of such findings; in any case, no attempt to do so has as yet been made.

1.5.2.5. Rigidity. It is clear that if we allow each point in the display to take on an arbitrary distance, a moving picture remains infinitely ambiguous. Similarly, a perfectly legitimate solution to the motion perspective and parallax patterns in Figure 22.15(a) and (b) is that of a set of points independently moving in space (or a pattern being deformed on an elastic surface). Some form of minimum principle, if it could be made consistent, would solve this problem. A weaker form of the solution is to assume that the surfaces and objects that we fit to the moving points are rigid, if a rigid solution is possible. That assumption, in varying degrees of explicitness, has been made repeatedly in recent years (Gibson et al., 1955; Johansson, 1977a, 1977b; Rock, 1977; Todd, 1982; Ullman, 1979) and serves to fix the solution in many cases of ambiguity.

The most recent version of this proposal, by Ullman (1977, 1979), is discussed in some detail by Chase in Chapter 28. Based on local sets of noncoplanar points in motion, his model predicts a number of phenomena that do indeed emerge in psychophysical study of moving dots and wire forms. Most intriguing is the fact that because it is based on parallel (orthographic) projection, it only specifies each region to within a front–back reversal around the motion-picture screen, which in fact is what we often find in the perception of both real objects and motion pictures of them (Figure 22.20). This is true even when the effects of linear perspective are sufficiently above threshold that the parts of the object appear to undergo marked nonrigid deformations as the object moves [Figures 22.20(b) and 22.8(d)], which means that even an accurate display of a moving rigid object is potentially ambiguous.

There is no mystery about why the nonrigid deformation is perceived; for example, a part that is receding projects a decreasing retinal image, but if it is construed as approaching, it appears to be shrinking in physical size. Mach (1886/1959) had noted its occurrence long ago; the Ames trapezoid in Figure 22.8 provided a powerful example; and Schwartz and Sperling (1983) have shown that a skeletal cube rotating in perspective projection, computer generated with its rear face always the brighter, appears in reverse rotation and in continuous rubbery deformation. While rigidity may indeed operate as a constraint on admissible readings under some circumstances, it certainly does not do so in all. In Figure 22.20(b), although the object really is a rigid cube and there is no reason in the stimulus for it to be read as anything else, it nevertheless spontaneously reverses periodically, and when it does so, it naturally appears to deform in a rubbery fashion.

Some limits are needed before rigidity can be taken seriously as a constraint on perceptual structuring. This is most important in video and CGI, given their lack of texture and other dense depth cues (Section 1.1.1.2). In any case, a more general formulation is needed to predict response to moving patterns; perhaps something based on mere connectedness and the response to local depth cues will do.

1.5.3. Perceptual Tolerance of Ambiguity or Inconsistency. Any tangible physical object in the real world must have some specifiable location and velocity. In addition to a well-defined set of coordinates in phase space, objects and their surfaces have consistency constraints that are not applicable to the ways in which they are perceived. The inconsistent figure in Figure 22.20(c) is not immediately perceived as such. The viewer must trace the continuous line marked *i*, using a finger or fovea, to discover that somewhere between the two sides it must change the orientation of the dihedral that it represents. The viewer cannot tell merely by glancing at the ribbon figures in Figure 22.20(d) whether the two tabs, marked *i* and *ii*, are in each case the same or different sides of the object (i.e., whether they would be painted the same color if we painted only one side of the strip), but that fact does not impel the viewer to parse the figure panel by panel. We simply do not know the extent to which the perceptual system registers and is driven to resolve ambiguity and inconsistency. Large sections of the world, and of the virtual world presented through moving pictures, may remain perceptually indeterminate. As will be seen, that must certainly be so in the course of viewing moving pictures as they are normally produced and edited.

2. WHY DO THEY MOVE? PHYSICS AND PSYCHOLOGY

First, we outline the physics of the procedures by which moving pictures are recorded and displayed and the limits these procedures impose on the effective stimuli for apparent movement. Second, we review the psychological and physiological constraints on the perception of apparent movement and of moving pictures. Finally, we consider the theories advanced to explain the perception of moving pictures. In Section 4.2.2, we survey aspects of the perception and comprehension of moving pictures that cannot be dealt with by sensory theories, that take us out of the realm of sensory and perceptual explanations and into the domain in which cognitive factors interact in compelling and critical ways with "purely" sensory and perceptual factors to determine how moving pictures are attended and comprehended.

2.1. The Physics of Recording and Display

As discussed in Section 1.1, by far the most general method for making moving pictures at this time entails some form of stroboscopic sampling of the changing optic array. That is, a set of essentially static views of a changing scene is taken in rapid succession, either by simultaneous photography or by analytic raster scan, and displayed in rapid succession to a viewer.

Figure 22.21, following an analysis by Gibson in 1950, shows the major changes in view to be displayed. The nature of the time samples and the important parameters are schematized for recording and display in Figure 22.22. We consider recording and display constraints in Sections 2.1.1 and 2.1.2.

2.1.1. Recording by Successive Still Views. As every amateur photographer knows, if the target (the object one is photographing) moves while the shutter is open, a blur will result in the snapshot. Moving pictures are snapshots and, usually, not exceedingly fast ones, and in general, the target is in motion relative to the camera. One aspect of the temporal resolution obtained in moving pictures is given by the displacement that can be allowed to occur while the shutter is open.

There is another and considerably more important aspect of temporal resolution that is often ignored in the discussion of moving pictures. That is the amount that the target has moved during the interstimulus interval (ISI) (Figure 22.23); such motion provides for a displacement between contours provided by the same target in successive views, *S* in Figure 22.23(b) and (c). That displacement is, as we will see, of great importance to the theory and practice of moving pictures. One reason why this is important is that with rapidly moving targets, the displacement may be so great that no apparent movement (or misleading and inappropriate apparent movement) will occur between the successive views. For this reason, cinematographers must learn not to pan a camera too fast. We return to this point in connection with Figures 22.27 and 22.28. There is far more to the recording of moving pictures that is of perceptual importance: for example, the relationship between focal length of lens, aperture of lens, and depth of field; related to this, the perceptual consequence of "racking focus," in which a narrow plane in space is focused sharply and that focused plane is then moved in depth; and so forth.

Having outlined issues of greatest importance, we next consider the characteristics of the display by which the moving picture is presented.

2.1.2. Display Factors. Where the recorded image was obtained photographically in real space, the field of view (FOV) recorded from and the FOV provided by the display are identical only in the canonical configuration. Where the recorded image was obtained by photographing a tabletop or mockup or by CGI, the FOV is meaningful only in terms of the display. It is to this *virtual* FOV, that is, the field of view that would be represented by the display at canonical viewing distance if the record had been made in real space, that we will refer all our remarks.

It is tempting to talk about the information on the screen in terms of number of different displays that can be presented, which translates roughly into different combinations of discriminable pixels. But that is probably misleading for various reasons. Movement that is used to provide the viewer with information about "self" (or camera), as in Figures 22.6 and 22.20, probably depends heavily on the stimulation of peripheral vision (Johansson, 1977a; Leibowitz & Dichgans, 1980) or at least on large areas of the retinal field (Held, Dichgans, & Bauer, 1975), which comes to the same thing. Large screens should be better for self-movement and for some purposes may be essential. Large screens may be accomplished in several ways, all of which suffer characteristic disadvantages. But simply enlarging the display for a given film or video record runs into two other problems that are probably very important. The first is resolution; grain size and raster size increase with such enlargement, and while they probably have little effect on peripheral vision, the degradation for foveal vision may be substantial. (In video, it may be prohibitive.)

The second problem is that a large screen and an increased visual angle may provide displacements between contours in successive views that exceed the distances at which smooth apparent movement will result.

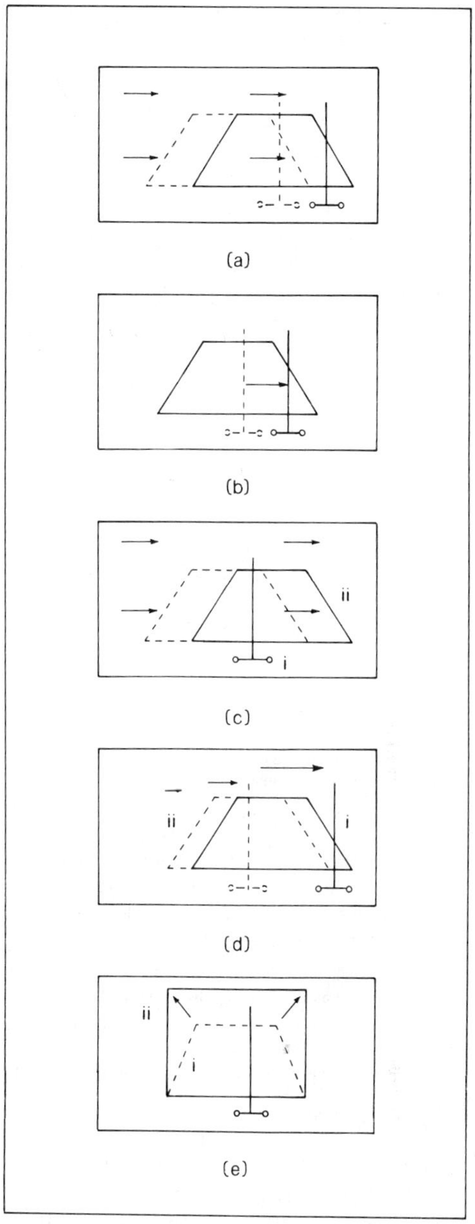

Figure 22.21. Types of image movement and their perceptual consequences, following Gibson's (1950) classification of retinal motion information. These are related to the effects of camera movement described in Figure 22.14. (a) Rigid displacement of the total image. This arises as a result of saccadic eye movements, and in the present context, it results (as an approximation) from a pan. The perceptual response is not one of object movement, but of a stable world. (b) Rigid motion of part of the image. This usually results from a stationary eye (or camera) and an object that is moving with a component perpendicular to the line of sight. The perceptual response is that of an object moving within a stable world. (c) Rigid motion of the entire image save for one part. This usually results from the pursuit by the eye (or tracking by the camera) of a frontally moving object (see Figure 22.18). The perceptual response is of a moving object in a stable world. (d) Relationships within the entire image are changed according to the transformations described in Figures 22.6 and 22.14(a) and (e). This usually results from a displacement of the viewer's (or camera's) station point. The perceptual response is of a moving viewer in a stationary world. (e) A limited part of the image changes its proportions. This situation usually arises with an object moving in depth, with respect to the eye or camera. The perception is of an object moving in depth in a stable world. Exceptions can be found to all these assertions, and they clearly must be refined in any case, but they do provide a partial taxonomy for informative shots and their perceptual effects that would be valuable to develop further for the analysis of motion-picture information.

2.2. The Perception of Moving Pictures: History, Conditions, and Constraints

Although moving pictures are often mentioned in psychology texts as though they were illustrations of psychological studies of apparent movement, it is true only in a trivial sense, and we have much to learn before we can claim to understand the phenomena that underlie the perception and comprehension of moving pictures. In this section, we first describe the origin of moving pictures and then consider what we know about the component phenomena from a psychophysical, sensory, and perceptual standpoint.

2.2.1. Origins and Early Explanations of Movies. Moving pictures were developed out of a set of empirical observations, going back at least as far as the *Thaumatrope*, invented in 1827 by J. Paris. This was a toy consisting of a paper disk, with a different picture on each face. The disk could be caused to rotate rapidly on a string held between the fingers and thumbs of both hands. This causes the two pictures to be superimposed by visual persistence. (It was derived from Roget's argument in 1824, cited in Cook, 1963, and Manchel, 1969, answering a question originally raised by Ptolemy, that the human retina retains an image for about 0.1 sec after the image has changed or gone.) By controlling the string in such devices, it is possible to flip

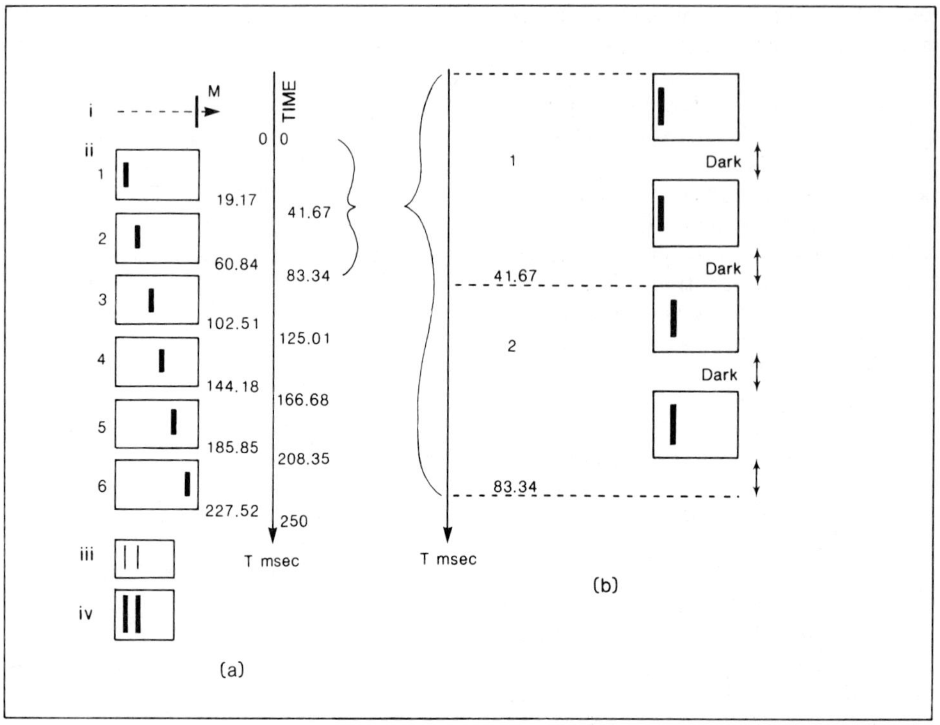

Figure 22.22. (a) Photography. (i) A thin rod moving in direction *M*. (ii) A succession of snapshots made by a camera, like that in Figure 22.1. Note that each image is somewhat spread out (iv) compared to what would be provided by instantaneous snapshots (iii), to remind us that discrete samples are being taken of a continuously moving object. Normal rate for film is 24 pictures per sec, exposed at about 20 msec. In this example, each picture represents a 22-msec sample, the intervals between pictures, allowing for transit, here is 19.17 msec. (b) Projection. Normal projection rate is also 24 pictures per sec, with a dark period imposed by a shutter during the time that the film is moving from one picture to the next. Shown here are the first two frames, from the sequence at (a). At 24 per sec, the alternation rate of dark and light is near the borderline of visibility of flicker. To bring the alternation of dark and light above the critical flicker fusion frequency (cff), projection shutters normally have at least one more blade, so that each frame is itself interrupted at least once by a dark interval, bringing the rate to at least 48 per sec and above the cff. Number of blades varies from two to five (the latter is used in film-chain projectors and help to bridge the discrepancy between the frame rate of 24 per sec in film and 30 per sec in video.

abruptly between the two views, and apparent motion then occurs between the two pictures. There is a continuous historical line to be drawn between such toys and the commercial development of the motion picture after Edison in the 1890s (for a review, see Cook, 1963, pp. 122–136). Perhaps because the effect of superimposition clearly is the result of visual persistence, the phenomenon of apparent movement has, since Roget in 1824, also been attributed to visual persistence and, in books on moving pictures, is still often "explained" in terms of persistence (cf. Cook, 1963, p. 121; Manchel, 1969, p. 3; Wilson, 1983).

"Persistence of vision" will explain the fact that the dark time between the successive frames is not perceived. It will also explain the fact that points or contours presented in rapid succession will often appear to be simultaneous, or superimposed. But that is not what happens in moving pictures. Under normal conditions, we do not see the man in Figure 22.18(g) as having many arms; we perceive one arm *moving*. By itself, therefore, persistence does not serve to explain moving pictures.

In psychology books, moving pictures are usually dealt with as though they are explained by *stroboscopic* movement, or movement between interrupted or flashing lights. These have been studied in the psychology laboratory since Exner in 1875. Moving pictures came to Germany in 1895 (Linke, 1907), and the relationships between stroboscopic movement, real motion, and moving pictures have been discussed repeatedly, with considerable recapitulation and rediscovery. Early examples of such discussions and study are Linke (1907), Munsterberg (1916/1970), and Wertheimer (1912). To Exner, the facts of stroboscopic movement had suggested that apparent movement is a direct sensory response to certain conditions of succession. Wertheimer used the phenomenon to make a far more sweeping set of points, providing the foundation of Gestalt theory.

What was important in apparent movement to Wertheimer were the following points:

1. One classical explanation of movement perception is that movement is a derived perception, elaborated from more fundamental sensory qualities of local sign (e.g., Wundt, 1902), a notion still current (e.g., Kinchla & Allan, 1969). Under the appropriate conditions, stepwise succession and continuous motion are indistinguishable even to a carefully trained observer (DeSilva, 1929). To Wertheimer, this showed that apparent motion could not be attributed to sensations of successive location and showed also that the classical theory was wrong. Against this point, we should notice that in its most comprehensive form (e.g., Helmholtz), the classical theory did not expect fundamental sensations to be consciously detectable; they were

only to be viewed as the first stage of the psychological processing that eventuates in experience (Hochberg, 1984a).

2. To much the same theoretical point, Wertheimer noted that under certain conditions ("pure phi"), viewers perceive movement, even though they see nothing moving, a phenomenon that Wertheimer used to explain the fundamental nature of the experience of apparent movement.

3. As an explanation of the phenomena of stroboscopic movement and of real movement, Wertheimer proposed that cortical processes, isomorphic to the movement that is perceived in these cases, actually occur as physical fields and current flows between the parts of the brain that are stimulated successively. Not only is this explanation immensely implausible in terms of known neurophysiology, but the explanation rests on, and is used as support for, a notion of localized brain processes that is implausible both from the Gestalt point of view and in terms of two classes of phenomena of apparent movement.

The first is that there is a body of literature showing that the determinants of apparent movement are not those of the retinal image—which is what would be needed if we are to give any credence to the current-flow explanation as it has been most explicitly developed (Köhler, 1920; Köhler & Wallach, 1944)—but the *perceived* separation of the objects between which apparent movement occurs (Attneave & Block, 1973; Corbin, 1942; Rock & Ebenholtz, 1962; Shepard & Judd, 1976). That is, in Figure 22.24(b) there are conditions under which it is the distal variable in the scene D, rather than the retinal projection (or displacement in the optic array) d, that determines the occurrence and direction of apparent movement. This point and its relationship to the perception of moving pictures will become clearer in Section 2.2.2. But we should note here that the issues discussed in connection with Figures 22.27, 22.39, and 22.40(d) show that although this point is enough to make the current-flow explanation inapplicable, we cannot ignore the variables that inhere in the picture plane and retinal image either.

Second, this kind of isomorphic explanation simply cannot account for the movements in depth that are easy to achieve in laboratory demonstrations [e.g., Figure 22.24(c)] and that common observation shows us are even more characteristic of moving pictures in their normal usage. In fact, Wertheimer's explanation (which, we should note, is the only explanation that the Gestalt theorists ever offered for apparent movement) does not even work to explain the many demonstrations of perceptual organization the Gestalt theorists themselves devised (Hochberg, 1982).

Of the two early explanations of apparent movement—persistence and isomorphic field actions, both of which are still invoked—neither will help us understand how we perceive moving pictures. One consequence of the Gestalt interest in apparent movement, however, was the laboratory study of its conditions, which we discuss next.

2.2.2. The Characteristics and Constraints of Apparent Movement

2.2.2.1. Korte's Laws and Their Limitations. The systematic study of the conditions under which stroboscopic movement is obtained was initiated by Korte in 1915, following Wertheimer's seminal article. Subsequent research by Neuhaus (1930) and Sgro (1963) has added to this attempt at psychophysical formulation. These inquiries used simple configurations of successive lights, as in Figure 22.24(a), in which the physical parameters of spatial separation (s), temporal separation (ISI), duration (d_1, d_2), and luminances of the lights were varied. Subjects' response has been essentially "phenomenological" in such research, that is, describing whether they perceived moving lights ("beta movement"); pure movement with no discernible

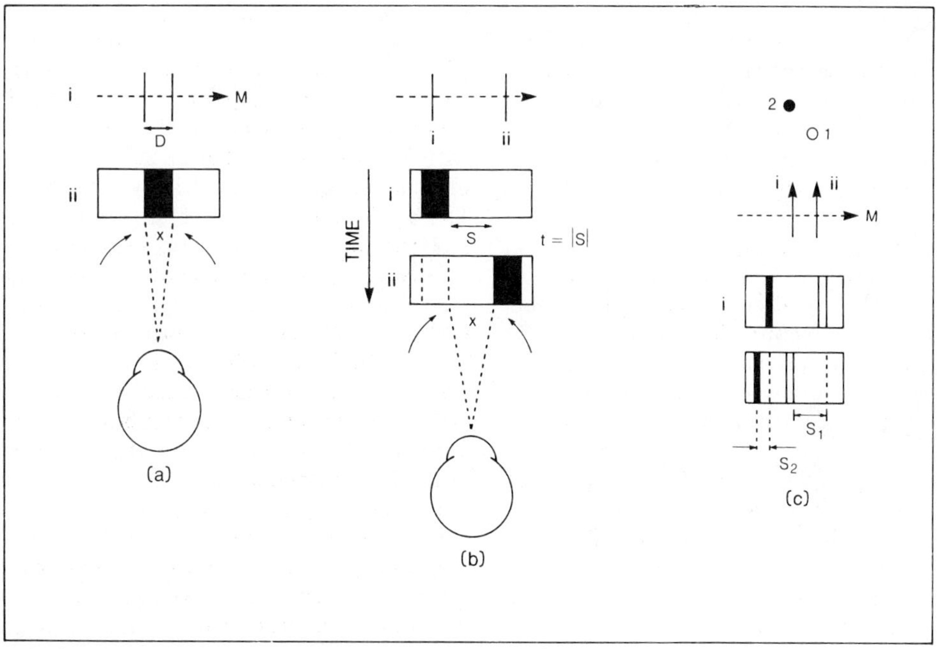

Figure 22.23. (a) A thin rod moves in direction M. Because the exposure is a finite duration, it contributes to the image on the film throughout the distance D and the width of the image subtends a finite visual angle x. (b) Given a velocity such that the rod moves from i to ii in 1/24 sec, a distance S will separate the rod's image on successive frames. (c) If two rods 1 and 2 lie at different distances from the camera moving from i to ii, the separation of their images will differ in successive frames.

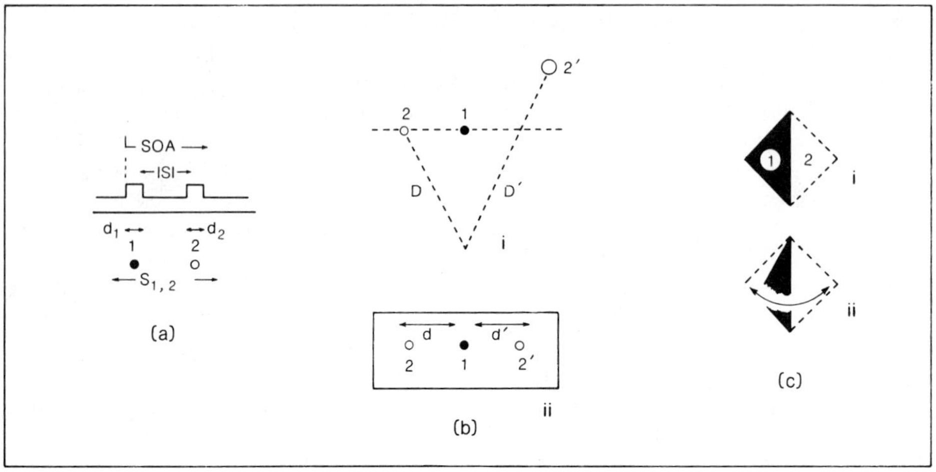

Figure 22.24. (a) The basic condition for cinematic (stroboscopic) movement. A region or contour at 1 presented at some displacement $S_{1,2}$ (measured in visual angle) from some other region or contour 2 and occurring at different times. These are measured by stimulus onset asynchrony (SOA) and interstimulus interval (ISI). (b) Objects 2 and 2′, at different distances from the viewer, may be equidistant from point 1 in the picture plane. There is some evidence (Attneave & Block, 1973; Corbin, 1942; Rock & Ebenholtz, 1962; Shepard & Judd, 1976) that the distances in depth (1–2, 1–2′), which are unequal, are the determinant values for apparent movement (see Shepard, 1981, p. 323), but we will see in connection with Figures 22.27, 22.28, 22.39, and 22.40 that distances within the picture plane (i.e., visual angle) can be ignored neither by the perceptual theorist nor by the filmmaker. (c) Apparent movement through the third dimension often occurs when that is needed to connect the end states. For example, if as in i a triangle is presented in position 1, alternating with another in position 2, a single triangle will appear to flip through the third dimension as shown in ii.

objects doing the moving ("phi movement"); simultaneity; or discrete succession.

The results are often called *Korte's laws* and are usually implied to be responsible for, or explanatory of, moving-picture perception. They cannot be used with much confidence, however, because of the severe limits that must be placed on their generality in almost every way.

Following are five major ways in which these "laws" are inadequate as predictors of apparent movement and as explanations of moving pictures or as guidelines for their production. The five factors considered here are important to a psychological understanding not only of stroboscopic movement perception but of the determinants of comprehensibility in the cutting and editing of moving pictures as well.

1. The subjective responses of phenomenal apparent movement bear no established relationship to other possible perceptual responses to moving pictures (i.e., to the detection of movement, to the recognition of some region that is defined only by its movement relative to some other region, to the judgment of distance or velocity based on the information in moving pictures).

2. As we noted in Figure 22.23(c), a moving picture taken in real space will, in general, contain a variety of different spatial separations ($s_1, s_2, \ldots$) between the corresponding contours in successive frames. The ISI or stimulus onset asynchrony (SOA, i.e., the interval between successive stimulus onsets) is constant in the presentation of any moving picture. Therefore, some contours should show simultaneity, some should show clear succession, and only a subset (the smallest displacements, s_1, considering the very short ISIs characteristic of moving pictures and video—see Sections 1.1.1 and 1.1.2) should yield strong apparent movement, which should occur some of the time between contours that do not originate with the same object. This point will concern us further (Figures 22.25, 22.27 and 22.28).

3. Indeed, when we step from a simple space-time configuration, like that of Figure 22.24(a), and turn to patterns even marginally more complex, the inapplicability of Korte's laws becomes evident. For example, the movements into three dimensions that we noted in connection with Figure 22.24(c) seem amenable to some formulation in terms of Gestalt simplicity; that is, we perceive movement into depth when it provides a simpler perceptual organization than the alternatives (which would be to perceive nonrigid motion). As we saw in connection with Figures 22.8(d) and 22.20(a) and (b), there is no way at present to make that intuitively plausible assertion less vague. There are many examples of the perceptual tolerance for nonrigid motions; and in any case, to introduce a simplicity principle into Korte's laws would totally change their psychophysical nature and make their applicability await the objective formulation of the simplicity principle.

4. As we noted in connection with Figure 22.24(b), in at least some cases the determinants of the strength and category of apparent movement are functions not of the retinal separations but of the distal parameters (Attneave & Block, 1973; Corbin, 1942; Rock & Ebenholtz, 1962; Shepard & Judd, 1976). It might be possible to rephrase Korte's laws in terms of distal separations and movements. To do that we would have to include provision either for predicting the precise layouts in three-dimensional space that would be perceived with any objectively measurable stimulus configuration or for including terms for subjective quantities—that is, for *perceived* distal separations—in the very psychophysical laws with which we are trying to predict those subjective appearances.

Not too much should be made of this point, because the predominance of the measures of the parameters in virtual space over those of the retinal image is not well established. In fact, the kinds of factors discussed later in connection with Figures 22.27, 22.28, and 22.40 are all much more connected with the parameters of the retinal image than they are with the distal layout of objects in the world.

5. A quite different kind of exception to Korte's laws arises in connection with what is often claimed to be the dependence of apparent movement on a prior perceptual decision as to *identity*. The classic example is the Ternus phenomenon (Ternus, 1938) in Figure 22.25. Three lights [*A*, *B*, and *C* in Figure 22.25(a)] are followed by three lights [*B*, *C*, and *D* in Figure 22.25(b)]. If a dark period intervenes between the first and second set of three (the ISI in Figure 22.25), *A* is perceived to move to *B*, *B* to *C*, and *C* to *D*. If, however, lights *B* and *C* remain illuminated continuously in the ISI between (a) and (e), *A* appears to move through the third dimension, to *D*.

It was presumed (cf. Koffka, 1935) that the movement which is perceived depends on whether *A*, *B*, and *C* are perceived as being identical to *B*, *C*, and *D*, respectively, or whether dots *B* and *C* are perceived as being the identical objects in both presentations, in which case *A* and *C* are identical. That is, perceived identity must precede perceived movement—or so it would seem.

We return to a discussion of this paradigm in the next section, because there is much less to this explanation than meets the eye. First, we must examine more closely the notion that apparent movement depends on "perceptual assumptions" about the identity of the objects between which the movement is perceived to occur.

2.2.2.2. Varieties and Domains of Apparent Movement. It is evident that there is more than one stimulus basis for the perception of movement. For example, an object moving relative to the viewer presents motion in the retinal image if the eye is stationary or it presents a static image if the eye tracks the object, but information that it is in motion is offered to the viewer in either case.

Given this fact, one can try to fit some single processing mechanism (or response rule) to the diverse means by which motion affects the organism, including unconscious inference (Hochberg, 1974, 1981a; Rock, 1977; see also Chapter 33 by Rock), notions of reafference (von Holst, 1954; Matin, 1982; see also Chapter 20 by Matin), first- or second-order isomorphisms (Wertheimer, 1923/1958, and Shepard, 1981, respectively), and so on. Alternatively, one can assert that there are multiple mechanisms and multiple modes of experience, elicited by different aspects of relative motion in the world, and that each mechanism may have quite different characteristics.

I believe strongly in this latter view. Several different kinds of movement perception have been known for a long time as having different characteristics, and these are important to separate in any attempt to understand the perception of moving pictures. I list the major divisions briefly, giving their characteristics and possible mechanisms.

(a) ABSOLUTE AND RELATIVE MOTION. In the case of "real" (continuous) motion, thresholds for the detection of a single moving object are much higher than for the detection of relative motion or displacement in space between two or more objects (Aubert, 1886; Bonnet, 1982). Although I know of no research to this point, the time scales are such that we should expect this fact to be true as well of the stroboscopic presentations of moving pictures. To Exner (1875), this fact suggested that there are two systems for responding to motion, one a sensory response, the other a more mediated or cognitive response. More recent writers subscribing to this view are reviewed in Chapter 16 by Anstis and Chapter 17 by Mack.

If the strength of the experience of movement is related to how far a particular response lies above its threshold, the slowest component in any motion configuration should (other things equal) be least noticeable so that a partitioning of movements would result which would be very similar to those described in connection with Johansson's research, Figure 22.19.

The notion of a direct sensory response to retinal motion automatically suggests something like a receptive field, or direction-sensitive analyzing mechanism, of a sort that is now widely believed to serve a functional role in movement perception (Sekuler, 1975; Regan, Kaufman, and Lincoln, Chapter 19). Inasmuch as these mechanisms should have relatively limited extents, we would expect that the detection of relative motion

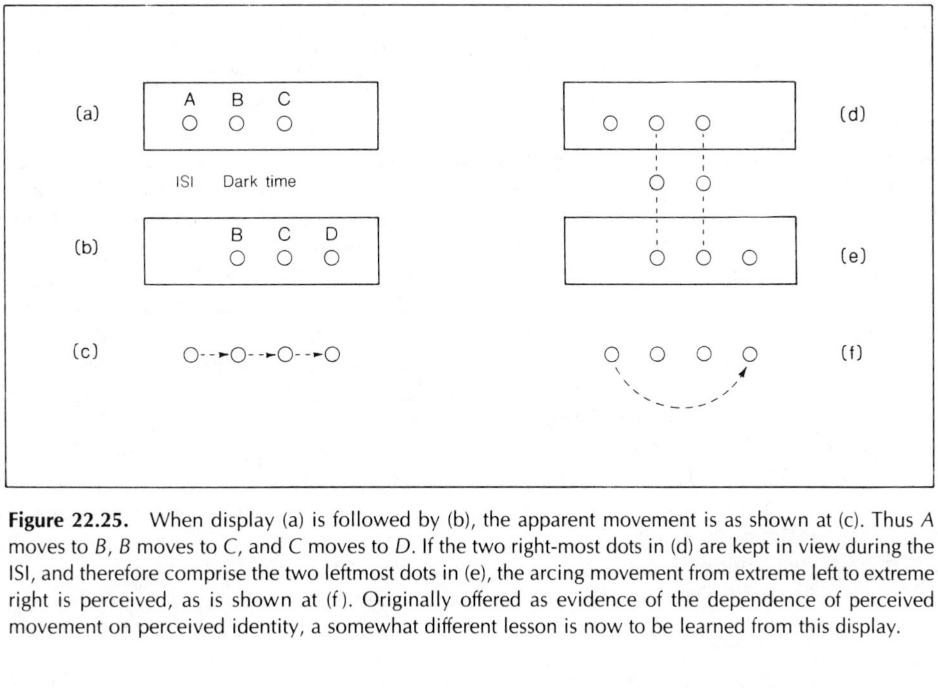

Figure 22.25. When display (a) is followed by (b), the apparent movement is as shown at (c). Thus *A* moves to *B*, *B* moves to *C*, and *C* moves to *D*. If the two right-most dots in (d) are kept in view during the ISI, and therefore comprise the two leftmost dots in (e), the arcing movement from extreme left to extreme right is perceived, as is shown at (f). Originally offered as evidence of the dependence of perceived movement on perceived identity, a somewhat different lesson is now to be learned from this display.

should not be as good at greater retinal separations as at smaller ones. There is evidence to that point in the direct measurement of motion-detection thresholds. Additional evidence of differences between short- and long-range displacements is discussed in Section (d).

(b) Only Some Movement Yields Aftereffects. It has been known for more than a century and a half that after one stares at a set of stripes moving in one direction, stationary targets appear to move in the opposite direction on subsequent inspection. Although the stationary targets appear to move in one sense of the word (and indeed their apparent motion can be canceled, and thereby measured, by giving the test target a movement opposite to the aftereffect), there are other ways in which they do not appear to move; for example, they do not change position or size in the world. Two different components of perceived movement have thus been separated, resulting in a paradox that becomes evident to viewers only when it is called to their attention. As we see later, a similar paradox is involved whenever a moving-picture viewer perceives the images provided by a moving camera, which is the rule, rather than the exception.

Wohlgemuth argued in 1911 that the retina becomes adjusted to the motion and takes time to overcome the effect. Sekuler and Ganz (1963), using a stabilized image technique, proved that the aftereffects could not be attributed to eye movements, and the adaptation-aftereffect technique is now widely used in the attempt to dissect the component mechanisms of movement perception. The interesting point about these aftereffects for our present discussion is that they appear to occur only in consequence of stimulus displacement on the retina (Anstis & Gregory, 1964) and, indeed, only in the case of relatively small retinal displacements (see Anstis, 1980). This picture is consistent with the proposal that it is largely or wholly the adaptation of direction-sensitive cells that underlies the motion aftereffects (Sutherland, 1959) and that the mechanisms that underlie the perception of short displacements in the retinal image have quite different characteristics from other motion-detection mechanisms.

(c) Fast Blobs and Slow Details. Saucer, in 1954, argued that there are two components in apparent movement: a fast but global process and a detailed but slower process. That is, at fast speeds the gross shapes of objects determine apparent movement, whereas only at slower speeds do the details of shape and form determine what apparent movement will be perceived.

A set of phenomena of central importance to the understanding of how we perceive moving pictures, which will be surveyed in Figures 22.27, 22.39, and 22.40(d), seems in a general way to fit this prescription. There is evidence of faster response to lower- than to higher-spatial-frequency patterns of stripes (which is equivalent to Saucer's proposal), using reaction time measures (Breitmeyer, Love, & Wepman, 1974) and electrical responses of the visual cortex (Williamson, Kaufman, & Brenner, 1977), and there is a widespread fashion in visual science today for identifying the fast and slow responses with two different classes of neurons (X and Y fibers).

Although in a general descriptive way this blob–detail distinction fits the phenomena in Figures 22.27 and 22.39, we cannot assume that those phenomena are thereby explained. A rigorous analysis in these terms has not been undertaken; neither the psychophysical nor the neurophysiological basis for attributing such distinctions to two different neuron classes seems well founded (Lennie, 1980); and there is another set of differences in classes of apparent movement, having to do with the range and duration of the displacement between views, which must contribute heavily to the phenomena of Figures 22.27 and 22.39 and to the perceptual characteristics of moving pictures.

(d) Short- and Long-Range Phenomena. Mathematically, we can reduce continuous motion to stepwise motion if we make the steps small enough. One approach to the problem of apparent movement was to assert that the two are identical because the stepwise motion falls below the ability of the perceptual system to resolve the differences between such small displacements and continuous motion (e.g., Gibson, 1950). It should be noted that the longest ISI for good stroboscopic movement is also the shortest at which real motion can be clearly seen (Kaufman, Cyrulnick, Kaplowitz, Melnick, & Stof, 1971).

A more elegant formulation in more modern terms was offered by Morgan (1980). We perceive smooth movement in response to successive static presentations or step displacements, as seen in Figure 22.26, because the latter can be decomposed into two components: a sawtooth component [Figure 22.26(b) iv] and a ramp component [Figure 22.26(b) iii]. With a sawtooth whose frequency is above 25 Hz, we perceive only the ramp component—that is, only smooth movement—because the visual system is too sluggish to respond to the higher frequencies.

This explanation will only do for small displacements, so that Morgan (1980) argues that only such small displacements produce real apparent movement. Within these limits much that appears to be the result of separate cognitive factors in movement perception may instead be the direct consequences of the mechanisms of response to small displacements. For example, in Figure 22.26(c), if one point moves leftward in stepwise displacement and a second point immediately below and spatially aligned with it is presented with a brief temporal lag, the two spots appear to be presented at different places in space as though the first point were actually in the course of *moving* between the steps when the second point is presented. Morgan argues that because of persistence of response in the motion analyzers involved, the response to a moving stimulus covers some spatial interval and the apparent position must lie at some midpoint. The same thing would happen in the case of stepwise movement, explaining the effects described. If this were true, the conditions that increase persistence (e.g., decreased luminance; see Watson, Chapter 6) should affect apparent position, and Morgan shows that this is indeed the case with stereo and vernier measures of position.

In a sense, then, we have returned to a version of Roget's explanation (Section 2.2.1), combined with two new features: an "averaging" assumption for position and the notion of local-motion analyzers in the visual system. It is very different from the naive persistence explanation and has specific consequences that remain to be explored. The phenomena of Figures 22.27, 22.39, and 22.40(d), which must be taken into account very seriously in the making of comprehensible moving pictures, are compatible with this explanation. But it should be noted that this explanation will only serve as an explanation for apparent movement over short displacements (ca. 0.2°) in space and short intervals in time (ISI in the 30-msec range).

What about apparent movement over larger distances and over longer periods of time? Inspection of Figure 22.23 shows that step displacements between frames will often exceed that amount. Morgan maintains that only small displacements provide for real apparent movement. Although problems do arise when the displacement is large between successive frames (see Section 2.1.1), we do have reports of apparent movement over

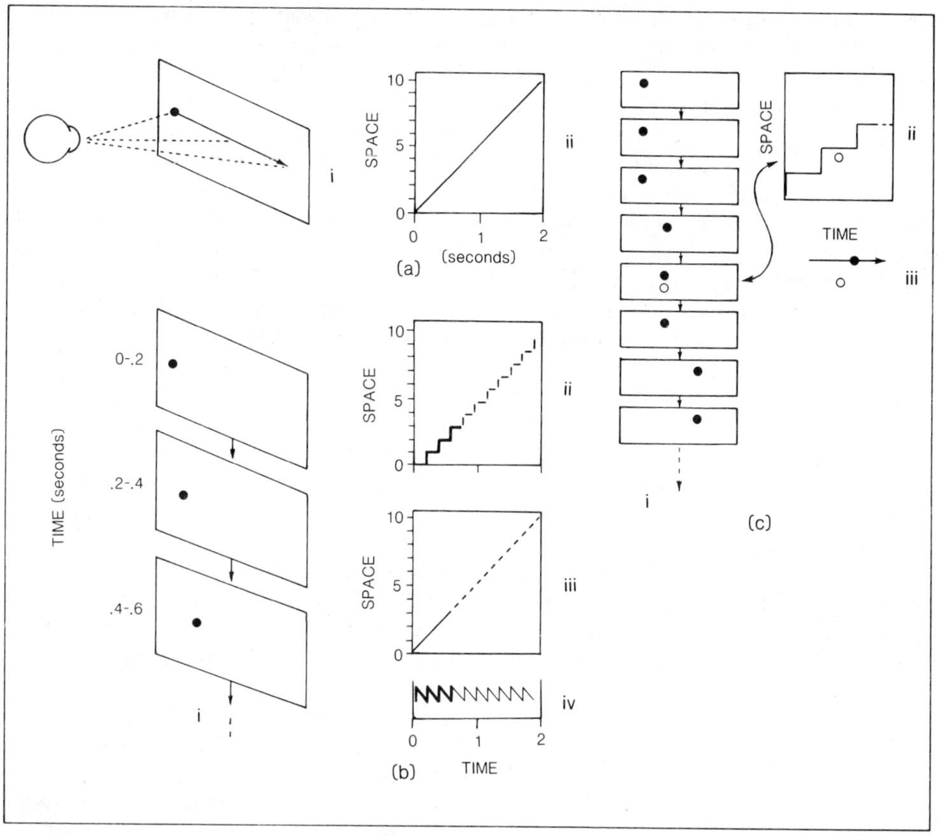

Figure 22.26. Components of stroboscopic motion. (a)(i) A dot moving continuously from left to right; (ii) its locus in space as a function of time. (b)(i) A dot moving in steps from left to right; (ii) its locus in space as a function of time; (iii, iv) the function at ii decomposed into the sum of a ramp iii and a sawtooth iv. If the sawtooth is at too high a frequency, only the ramp component should be detectable. This is one way, discussed by Morgan (1980), in which stroboscopic displays are equivalent to continuous motions. (Compare (a)(ii) and (b)(iii). (c)(i) A step function of a dot, moving from left to right. Dwell time is 3 units (indicated by three frames) at each step. If a second dot is spatially aligned with the first and momentarilly exposed, with a lag in its onset (ii), it will appear to be offset in space as well (iii) (Morgan, 1980). Many of the phenomena of stroboscopic movement are plausibly explained in terms of temporal and spatial frequency analysis (Adelson & Bergen, in press, Morgan, 1980; Watson & Ahumada, 1983).

much longer spans (Neuhaus, 1930; Rock & Ebenholtz, 1962; Zeeman & Roelofs, 1953), and the example of the Ternus case in Figure 22.25 is a good laboratory example of such large span movement.

Braddick (1974, 1980) uses that phenomenon to good advantage in arguing that there are two different kinds of apparent movement, long range and short range. He proposes the distinction because the constraints governing the apparent movement of a subset of dots within a random-dot array are different from those for obtaining smooth apparent movement for a single element or object. Most important is the fact that for random-dot arrays, spatial displacement must be 15 min or less and ISIs must be less than 80–100 msec. The short-range response is presumably identified with responses made to discontinuous stimulation by directionally sensitive neurons in the visual pathway. The other kind of apparent movement, spanning longer distances and longer durations, is more interpretive, and associated with higher-level processes. Anstis (1980) has identified a large number of examples of phenomena loaded differentially in the two processes and maintains that only the short-range process generates movement aftereffects.

The most interesting case is provided by Braddick's analysis of the Ternus phenomenon. In the case shown in Figure 22.25, the longer apparent movement appears to occur under just those conditions that favor the short-range phenomena (e.g., Pantle & Picciano, 1976). Braddick argues that the short-range process indeed prevails under such conditions, but inasmuch as its effect is to indicate that the two centerlines are *not* moving, this constrains the longer-range interpretive process to provide the alternative shown in Figure 22.25. This position seems to me well supported by data that Braddick reviews, and although the distinction between the short- and long-range processes and between their characteristics remains to be established, it is clearly consistent with the set of phenomena we discuss next.

(e) Identity as a Determinant in Apparent Movement: Apparent Movement between Dissimilar Forms and between Noncorresponding Elements. As long as we remain concerned with the stroboscopic movement that occurs between simple points of light, as in Figure 22.24(a), it is easy to phrase the phenomenon in relatively simple terms; for example, in cognitive terms, we perceive just that movement that would normally generate the successive display, or that movement occurs between corresponding objects within the constraints of Korte's laws. In the case of moving pictures, of course, we face a succession of views normally containing more than one object at a time and different shapes and colors. The casual assumption one would bring to such displays is that apparent movement will then occur between *corresponding* objects in the two successive views if they fall within some spatial limits. The question is, What comprises correspondence? That, as we will see, is very difficult to say at this time.

As Orlansky showed in 1940, stroboscopic movement will occur between successive views of quite different objects. Apparent movement will occur between objects of different shapes as readily as between objects of the same shape, as shown in Figure 22.27(a) (Kolers, 1972; Kolers & Pomerantz, 1971; Navon, 1976). The related phenomena, demonstrated in Figure 22.27(b) with simple geometrical shapes, occur as well in moving pictures and provide a source of apparent movement between noncorresponding objects in successive views. Examples of problems that arise when such unintentional movements occur in film are described by Vorkapich (1972). This problem is particularly important in the case of movie *cutting*, which we discuss in Section 4. I believe that many or even most of the rules of film editing reduce at base to this factor (Hochberg & Brooks, 1974, 1978b).

Laboratory demonstrations that this is a real phenomenon in moving pictures have been replicated in many versions, with different kinds of stimuli (see Section 4.2). In all cases, the

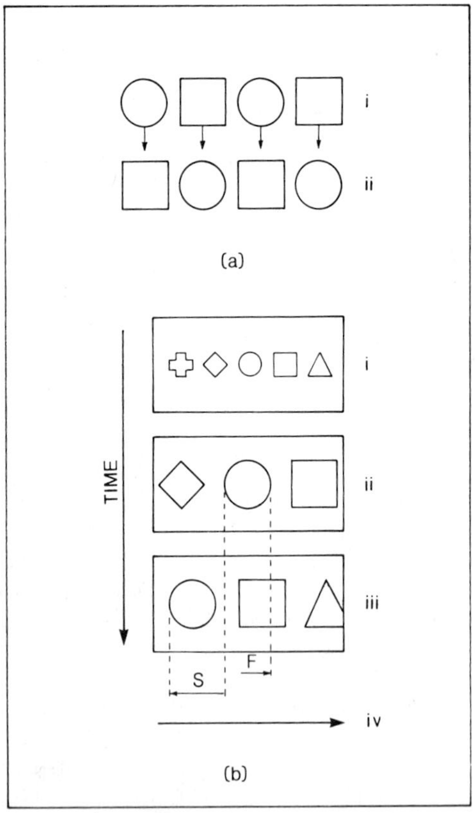

Figure 22.27. Apparent movement occurs between noncorresponding objects. (a) At (i) a row of circles and squares. When replaced after an ISI by the row at ii, the circles become squares and the squares become circles, instead of manifesting a diagonal apparent movement that will preserve shape (Kolers, 1972; Kolers & Pomerantz, 1971). (b)(i) A long shot of geometric forms; (ii–iv) a sequence of close-up views, the array of forms moving leftward in successive views *S* but displaced slightly with respect to the place occupied by the different form in the previous view *F*. At very slow rates (2–3 sec per view), the sequence is judged to move leftward; at faster rates, the sequence is seen to move rightward (Hochberg & Brooks, 1974, 1978b).

movement is seen in the direction of the small vector **F**. Only when the views are presented very slowly, with SOAs so great (1.5–3 sec) that the apparent movement produced at each displacement has time to dissipate and the viewer can identify some specific shape and its loci in successive views can the correct direction of motion be perceived.

One way of expressing such phenomena is in terms of spatial-frequency differences; for example, at higher velocities, the direction of apparent movement is determined by the lower spatial frequencies. Indeed, one might take the description as an explanation if we accept any of the proposals about the associations between spatial and temporal frequency in neural channels (see Lennie, 1980, however).

Another likely factor in the phenomena shown in Figure 22.27 is that movement will occur between local elements that are close together, regardless of overall configuration. This certainly seems to be true of random-dot patterns (Braddick, 1974), and if we consider it plausible that the same will hold for line segments and edges as well, then the phenomena in Figure 22.27 could also be viewed in these terms.

This latter explanation surely must be invoked in the following class of phenomena. Consider three successive views of the maze shown in Figure 22.28(a). In this example, each view is displaced to the right of the preceding view with 50% overlap between successive views. In an experiment by Hochberg, Brooks, and Roule (1977), the sequence of views was shown at 250 msec per view and the subject's task was to detect the direction of motion. The amount of overlap between successive views was one of two main independent variables, ranging 25–85% overlap [see the abscissa in Figure 22.28(c)]. When a full maze is used [e.g., Figure 22.28(a)] with the smallest amount of displacement between views (i.e., with 85% overlap), the direction of motion is correctly perceived. This surely is so because when such small displacements are made between views, corresponding contour elements fall near each other in successive views and apparent movement occurs between them. With larger steps between views and smaller amounts of overlap, the perception of direction of motion falls to chance. One might think that this is so because corresponding contours fall too far from each other, but that is not the way things appear to the viewer. Fragmentary motions do appear to occur between partial regions of the maze, but they are not consistent from one region to another or from one transition to the next. This must occur because contours in one view fall close to noncorresponding but locally similar features in the next view, and misleading *local apparent movements* therefore occur. Note that this occurs *even though* the sequences *mathematically specify the invariant maze and its transformation in all cases.*

The second independent variable consisted of a reduction in the clutter in the maze, obtained by removing all but a small and recognizable packet of the detail, as has been done in Figure 22.28(b). Using the same tasks and procedures, subjects perceive the correct direction of displacement at all degrees of overlap, as shown in curve *B* in Figure 22.28(c). Inasmuch as the ISIs were the same in both the cluttered and the uncluttered conditions, a comparison of curves *A* and *B* most plausibly implicates the short-range process discussed previously. It is also plausible that the low-spatial-frequency components of the envelope in Figures 22.28(b) contribute to the difference, but no attempts have yet been made to separate these factors.

2.2.2.3. Sensitivity Distributions and Apparent Movement. The parameters given previously for apparent movement were defined without regard for direction of gaze. We must now

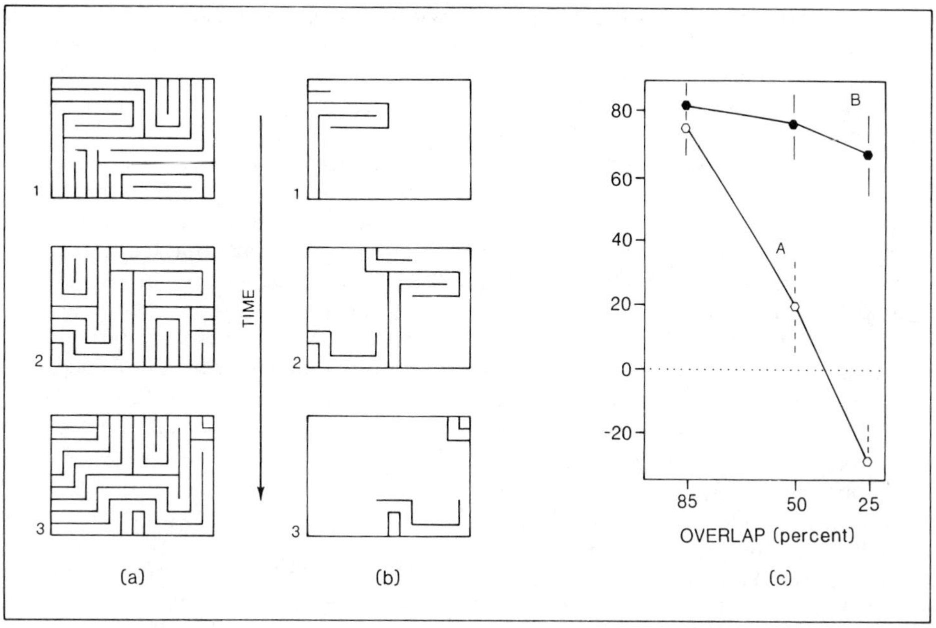

Figure 22.28. Invariance under transformation does not guarantee the correct perception of translatory movement. Three views from a sequence of views of a maze are shown here. One of the variables is degree of overlap between successive views (here, 50%). At (a), the full maze; at (b), views from a sequence in which only a small part of the maze is retained; and at (c), the ordinate shows the subjects' judgments of motion direction (right minus wrong x 100), and the abscissa shows percentage overlap between successive views (Hochberg, Brooks, & Roule, 1977).

consider the fact that where one looks affects both apparent movement and the spatial information it carries.

In the course of discussing the perception of depth through motion-based information and, particularly, the cue of kinetic occlusion (Figure 22.7), we noted that the elements of texture and so forth that serve as the carrier elements for the optical flow pattern and for kinetic occlusion must themselves exceed some threshold before the information that they carry can be picked up and used.

In moving pictures, kinetic occlusion of one region of a random-dot matrix by another can be used to define objects in space without any luminance-difference contours being used to bound the objects. Figure 22.29(a) and (b) shows a stationary field of dots enclosing a moving set of dots; the latter moves horizontally left (a) and right (b); it is arranged so that dots on either the stationary or the moving set are deleted and accreted, respectively, by only one of the vertical edges (here, the left edge). That is, in this situation, only one of the edges is informative as to whether the enclosed field is in front of the background or is being viewed through an aperture in the enclosing field. In experiments by Hochberg, Green, and Virostek (1978), it was shown that with the subject's gaze fixed at various places

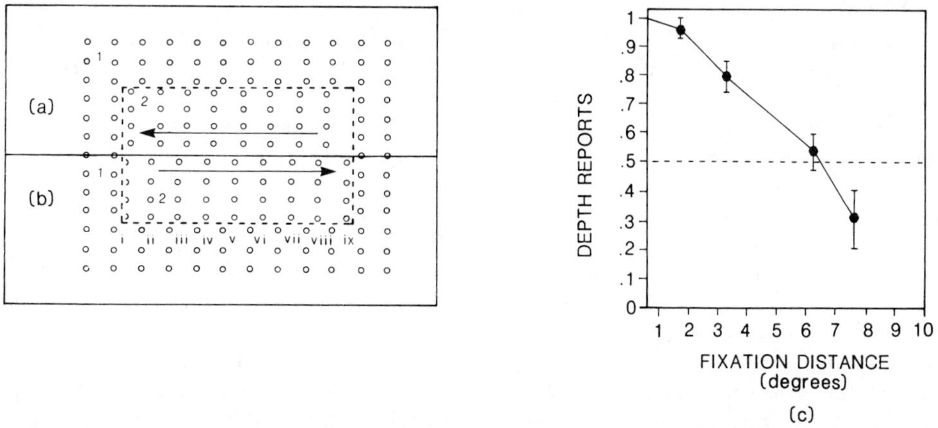

Figure 22.29. Dot-matrix surface (2) moving behind aperture in surrounding dot-matrix (1), so arranged as to give depth information at only one edge. The aperture is indicated here by the dotted rectangle that was not visible to subjects. (a) Surface 2 at left-most extreme. (b) Surface 2 at right-most extreme. Note that another column of dots has been partially disoccluded at the left edge of the aperture. Information that 2 lies behind 1 is given only by the disocclusion of dots at the left edge i in (b), when surface 2 is at its extreme right. In the alternative arrangement, not shown here, surface 2 moves leftward and rightward in front of surface 1. (c) Subjects' reports of relative depth, made at different fixation distances from edge i, corrected for chance (Hochberg, Green, & Verostek, 1978).

along the upper or lower edge (i–ix), the ability to detect whether the central region was nearer or further than the background fell off rapidly with distance from the single informative edge [Figure 22.29(c)]. Moreover, when the viewer is required to move his or her gaze back and forth between the right and left vertical edges, evidence of the same effect is found.

The pickup of kinetic occlusion information is different in foveal and peripheral vision when that information is carried by small elements like those of texture, even when the eye is engaged in active search. Regan and Beverly (1982) found that the ability to use the information in the expansion pattern [Figure 22.6(d)] also fell off with eccentric viewing.

2.2.3. Beyond Continuous Apparent Movement: Stop Action and Cuts. The conditions for obtaining continuous movement are often violated deliberately, both for reasons of economy and for reasons of aesthetics and comprehensibility. Indeed, the most extreme cases of discontinuity, or cuts, form the heart of moving pictures made for communication and entertainment. As long as we were discussing continuous movement, the participation of cognitive psychological processes in the construction of motion pictures could be ignored. When our sights are broadened to include cuts, we can no longer act as though the physics of the pattern of stimulation and the action of direction-sensitive cells and other pattern-analyzing devices in the visual nervous system will suffice to explain the phenomena at hand or to predict the efficacy of the motion-picture sequence. Such concepts as schematic maps, schematic events, and cognitive processing (and perhaps, even a "linguistics of film") become necessary to any intelligent discussion of the problem. I introduce these higher-level factors only when it becomes necessary to our discussion to do so, but this should not be taken to imply that they are not involved in the phenomena we have dealt with up to that point. It is simply that the major aspects of what was being discussed could be dealt with in other terms.

We can distinguish three classes of departures from continuous apparent motion:

1. *Stop Action.* Simulating a succession of still pictures taken at a sampling rate much slower than the standard 24 or 30 per sec is known as stop action. (This is to be distinguished from *time lapse* and *pixillation,* which we consider latter.) In stop action, each individual picture is noticeably a still picture, but an entire event is represented [Figure 22.30(b)]. This method is sometimes used for reasons of economy, especially where separate drawings or diagrams are involved, providing a kind of motion-picture record of a film-strip presentation. But it is also often used as a device with its own dramatic or communicative virtues.

Although the perception of continuous movement is not intended with such stop-action sequences, we must note that the conditions for short-range apparent movement still exist between frames. In Figure 22.30(b), the contours of the actor in frame 2 fall to the right of the corresponding contours in frame 1 [Figure 22.30(c)i]. If the event being filmed and the sampling rate of the stop action are such that the short-range movement and the actual motion being represented coincide in direction, as in Figure 22.30(c)i, the sequence will be readily apprehended as it should be. Aside from the presence of stationary views interspersed between very brief (one-frame) movements, the stop-action sequence will still be a moving picture (albeit a saltatory one). It is quite possible, as we have learned from the studies described in connection with Figure 22.27, to sample an event so that the short-range movement between successive frames will inadvertently occur in the opposite direction to that of the event being represented. That is the case illustrated between frames 3 and 2 in Figure 22.30(c)ii. Given enough time—say, 1–3 sec per view—we would expect the viewer to overcome the short-range movement and to identify the direction of displacement between views, so it would be advisable to keep stop-action sequences to rates no faster than this range. In addition, even if all the short-range movements fell in the right direction [as they do in views 1–2 in Figure 22.30(b)], the sequence looks like a jagged or rough attempt at continuous movement, so again it is probably desirable to keep stop-action movements at a relatively small number of changes per minute unless a rough or comedic effect is intended.

2. *Cuts.* Moving pictures of all kinds rely heavily on discontinuous transitions between continuous sequences. Discontinuous transitions are generally called *cuts*; the different continuous sequences separated by a cut are *shots.* Cuts are often made between shots of the same scene, taken from two different camera viewpoints. In such circumstances, the view in the two shots overlaps substantially, as in Figure 22.30(b). There is usually visual information in the two successive shots that in principle could serve to specify the relationship between the viewpoints from which they were taken and that in principle could be available to the viewer. Whether and how that information is used is of practical importance to the filmmaker and of theoretical importance to the perception psychologist, as discussed in Section 4.

3. *Nonoverlapping Cuts.* Many cuts are placed between shots that do not overlap at all, providing views that may differ widely in time and in place. Once again, we can expect to obtain some short-range apparent movement across the cuts, as in Figure 22.30(d). In terms solely of the visual stimulus relationships, that movement is not in principle informative about the station points from which the shots were taken, although such movement can be deliberately given a direction which could relate the successive views. (See Figures 22.40(b), 22.41(b), and 22.42(c).) It is the ready comprehension of such visually noninformative transitions, and the techniques movie makers use to that end, that provide a serious theoretical challenge and opportunity for the perceptual psychologist.

3. THE USES OF MOVEMENT: THE PRESENTATION OF SPACE, FORM, AND EVENTS

Moving pictures are needed if we are to present motions in a direct, rather than a symbolic, manner, for example, by dotted arrows and flow lines or by superimposed successive images (e.g., strobe light sequence or futurist painting or separated adjacent pictures of successive events). In addition, they are used to present the shapes and forms of objects, the layout of objects and surfaces in space, and the form and structure of events (i.e., the relationships between objects in space over time). We discuss each of these in turn, as they are provided by continuously moving pictures, after which we discuss the probable limits of the distinction between continuous and discontinuous successive pictures as devices for representing these attributes of objects and events.

3.1. The Shapes, Forms, and Structures of Objects

3.1.1. Shape. By *shape,* we mean the orthographic projection of the main surface or surfaces of an identifiable volume

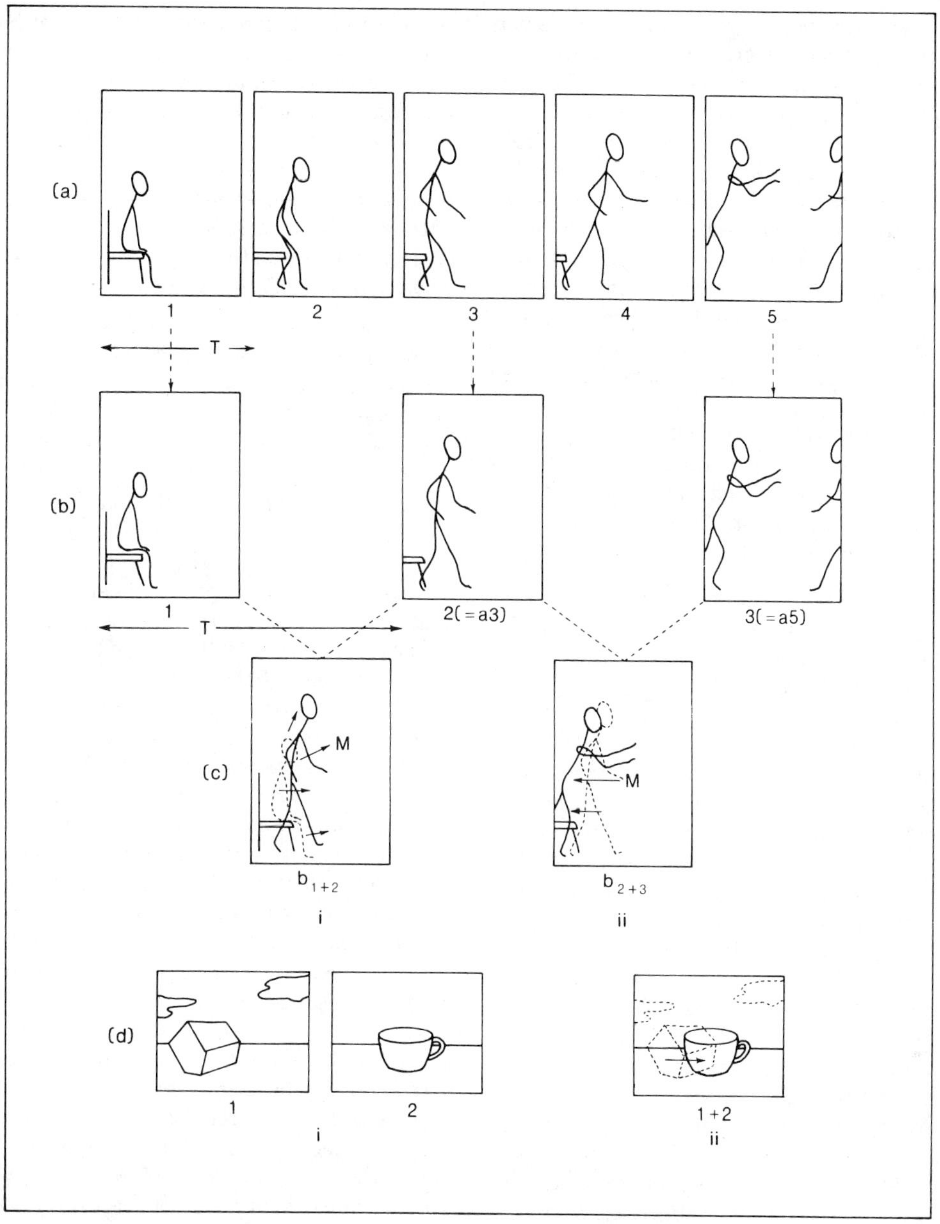

Figure 22.30. Departures from continuous motion. (a) Five frames from a motion picture. Run in real time, continuous movement is seen. (b) Three frames, taken from (a); dwell times increased to fill the same interval; "stop-action" sequence, in which the views are clearly static or momentarily "frozen". (c) Motions as seen between views. (i) Between b_1 and b_2, the motion between the contours in successive views is in the same direction *M* as the displacement of the actor. (ii) Between b_2 and b_3, the motion *M* between successive contours is opposite to that of the actor. (d)(i) Two successive unrelated views; (ii) views 1 and 2 superimposed, to show a source of apparent movement between them.

of space, whether of a single homogeneous object or of some bounded region of individual elements that bear some relationship to each other (specifically, that move as a unit). There are three ways in which shapes can be represented better by moving pictures than by still pictures:

1. In a still picture, the viewpoint may not permit the principal plane to be that of the picture. The distal shape of the object may therefore be difficult or impossible to recognize from the picture, depending on the efficacy of the static pictorial depth cues, whereas in a moving picture, relative motion between camera and object may offer information about the object's shape by indicating its slant to the line of sight. But as we see in connection with the Ames trapezoid in Figure 22.8, such information is not necessarily usable or used. The matter is very much one of degree and seems to depend on particular configurations and movements (Braunstein, 1983; Hershberger, Stewart, & Laughlin, 1976), so that the facts are clearly more consonant with a language of specific cues, features, and thresholds than with the "invariant information" of the Gibsonian and neo-Gibsonian "direct theory" approaches.

2. In a cluttered and variegated visual field, it is not ordinarily evident which elements in the field of view comprise part of a single surface. In a general way, we can say that

elements that share the same motion are grouped together as a single entity and define a single object or surface. This is not quite as straightforward as it sounds, inasmuch as common movement in three-dimensional space will not, in general, provide equal vectors in the flat projection on the screen. The random-dot pattern, as the extreme of this condition, offers a valuable research tool, inasmuch as it can be set up so that when it is static, no demarcated shape is detectable within a homogeneous frame of dots, but when the motion is provided, shapes are clearly visible as they are defined by the common motion of some subset of dots. For example, the limited range of displacement and ISI that distinguished short- from long-range bases of apparent motion (Braddick, 1974) is most readily studied with this tool.

3. A shape may be too large to include in a single still picture if both the overall configuration and the local details are to be clearly represented. Moving pictures use both continuous and discontinuous transitions for just this purpose, and these techniques, too, provide research tools of use to the perception psychologist (Figures 22.32 and 22.42).

3.1.2. Form. By *form*, we mean the configuration of a three-dimensional volume that is demarcated in three-dimensional space. In the case of an opaque object, by rotating the object relative to the camera, occluded portions can be brought into view. And as we have seen in connection with Figure 22.15(b) and (c), relative motion between camera and object provides such information even when that is wholly missing from the still picture and from the momentary glance (Lappin, Doneer, & Kottas, 1980; Metzger, 1934; Wallach & O'Connell, 1953).

As we discussed in connection with Figure 22.15, such stimulus situations are not always unequivocally or correctly perceived, and there is a growing body of data to show that strong limits must be placed on any assertions that relative motion between viewer and layout directly reveals the structure of the latter. The theoretical implications have been developed elsewhere in this chapter. The practical consequence is that the prudent filmmaker or graphics programmer should not assume that small amounts of motion perspective, as provided by central perspective, will suffice to remove the ambiguities of form that characterize parallel projection (or telephoto distances) and should maximize the static cues, as well, in the representation of form.

3.1.3. Structure. By *structure* is meant the perception of articulation, that is, of how a given object is composed of delimitable parts that move in relation to each other and to the overall center of the object. Most of the objects about which motion pictures are made are articulated: they bend at their joints, are flexible and elastic, or both. There is a very small body of work to the point of distinguishing rigidity from articulation and distinguishing either of these from flexibility and elasticity (Cutting, 1982; von Fieandt & Gibson, 1959; Jansson, 1977; Jansson & Johansson, 1973; Todd, 1982). With respect to the minimum needs for representing rigidity or nonrigidity, Ullman's (1979) computational scheme offers what seems to be a natural mathematical starting place. In principle, two different views of five identifiable points should distinguish rigid from nonrigid motion. Todd (1982) found, however, that observers could not distinguish rigid from nonrigid movements even with many more views if the center of rotation of the test object was itself in motion, and we have discussed the ample evidence that viewers often perceive nonrigidity when given full view of rigid objects (see Figure 22.8). Considering how important a rigidity constraint is for perceptual theory—yet how pervasive are the nonrigid motions in the world that we must be equipped to perceive—taxonomic and psychophysical studies of apparent rigidity and nonrigidities would appear to deserve high priority.

The practical purposes of such inquiry seem clear enough. These are properties with which computer animation will have to deal, and even human artists have had a terrible time in animating such resilient articulated objects as other humans. [It is worthwhile studying such films as *Fantasia*, 1940, and *Snow White*, 1937, with this in mind.]

3.1.4. The Form and Structure of Events. By *event*, we mean some demarcative set of changes in state and location that occurs over the course of time. A great deal of interest has been displayed, over the years, in the notion of a general study of event perception (Heider & Simmel, 1944), but the characteristic outlines and purpose of a coherent discipline have not yet emerged. In recent years, the claim has repeatedly been made that it is profitable (or even methodologically or philosophically necessary) to discover the invariant information that characterizes ecologically important events, or "affordances," and that underlies the direct perception of such events (cf. Gibson, 1979). A "new" physics of ecological optics is purported to be needed for this purpose (Gibson, 1974).

It is surely true, however, that all events can be completely specified in terms of any of the standard coordinate systems and in the fundamental units of physical measurement. Those are not always, or even generally, the most convenient, of course. Other variables may be more convenient and elegant for describing some sets of events, and by not knowing what those more convenient notational systems might be, we face greater difficulties in formulating and studying the event in question.

The fact is that the very definition of an event must proceed by isolating or demarcating that event. In a scene that is otherwise static, the ballistic trajectory of a thrown ball is easy to isolate, and it is easy to formulate its parabolic course. So, probably, is its reformulation in terms of the changing optic array provided by that event (Todd, 1981). But in the temporally and spatially cluttered manifold of a real scene, other things happen that overlap in time and space, and we must decide what constitutes an event before we can undertake its analysis. We first must separate those features of any changing environment that comprise *texture* from those that have some beginning, middle, and end, that is, those that have an *outcome structure* in the intentions of the person or persons who made the film or video sequence and that have some moment-by-moment *subjective* outcome structure (Hochberg, 1978; Virostek, 1983) in the expectations of the viewer.

Tools for analyzing the particular stimulus patterns that are characteristically provided by sets of motions [e.g., Figure 22.34(a)] do not by themselves define a field of perceptual research, that is event perception. Nor does the movement itself that comprises the event necessarily serve best to communicate the event (which is what seems to be the premise behind recent writing on the matter).

3.1.5. Continuous versus Discontinuous Successive Pictures. This last consideration raises a question as to when moving pictures are needed for representation, and how continuous such movement need be. We have seen that motion is sometimes needed to make shape and form visible and may be needed for the perception of certain classes of events. *How much* motion? If we consider the work of Braddick (1980) and of Morgan (1980) (see Section 2.2.2.2(b)),we can estimate that if the displacement between successive views does not exceed 0.2° of visual angle, patent apparent movement will occur sufficient to demarcate shapes, because in normal moving pictures, whether film or video, the duration between two frames will always be short enough to fall within the range of the short-range phenomenon. (The duration of the dwell time between one transition and the next is 33 and 42 msec for video and sound film, respectively.) If the motion pauses for some number of frames and the dwell time is too long, the viewer should in a sense forget the direction of the previous displacement. I don't know of any work directed to this point, but in the kind of experiment shown in Figure 22.27(b), the effects of the short-range displacement S are overcome when dwell time exceeds about 1500 msec.

According to this logic, the lower bounds of the sampling rate for successive views will depend on two factors: (1) a limit that should not exceed about 1500 msec in any case and (2) the velocity to be sampled (measured in degrees of visual angle per second).

I know of only one experiment (Hochberg, Brooks, & Fallon, 1977) testing whether a particular phenomenon known to occur with continuous motion will occur also at a rate of succession that fully appears discontinuous. The phenomenon concerned was one of Johansson's "vector resolution" demonstrations [see Fig. 22.19(b)]. As a measure, subjects were required to indicate the relative angle between the movement of the center dot *ii* while the entire configuration was in motion and the direction of movement of the dot *ii′* after the rest of the configuration disappeared from the screen (Figure 22.31). The changes were clearly saltatory, rather than a continuous movement; the magnitude of the effect was about as much as a similar measure produced using a similar configuration under conditions that provide for continuous apparent movement.

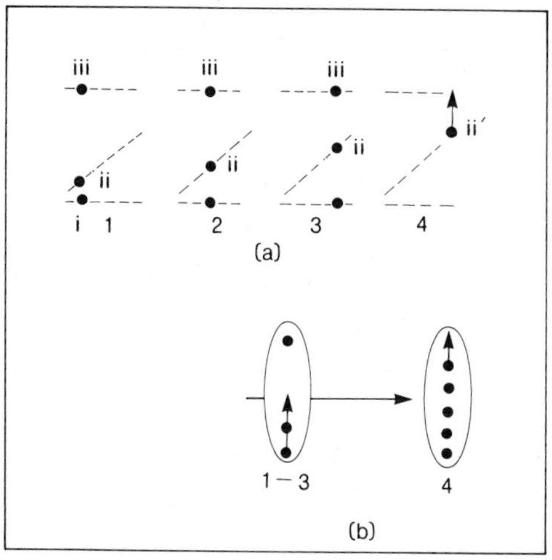

Figure 22.31. Partitioning of saltatory motions. (a) Lights moving in the configuration of Figure 22.19(b) and (c) but in a slow step function (see Figure 22.26 for discussion of step functions). Near the end of the projected trajectories, the three spots of light are extinguished and a new dot, moving at some adjustible angle to the vertical (ii′), is presented. When ii′ is vertical, it is perceived as continuing smoothly in the line previously traversed by ii, as in (b).

3.2. Space beyond the Screen: In the Mind's Eye

Consider a sequence in which the background or the entire layout moves in one direction across the screen, for example, from left to right, at some velocity on the screen of v°/sec. After some time t such that $v{\cdot}t = W$, where W is the width of the screen, none of what was present in the view at the beginning of the sequence is still present [Figure 22.32(a)]. The viewer will not normally perceive only a moving pattern in which new material accretes on the left-hand edge and is deleted on the right-hand edge; in most situations there is a compelling perception of space, in which an extent has been traversed and about which the viewer has a clear visual knowledge. That extent is larger than the screen [Figure 22.32(b)] and exists nowhere but in the mind of the viewer; that is, point X is clearly to the right of point Y, after such a viewing, but the two were never simultaneously present on the screen.

This is a central feature of all but the most static cinema: representing layouts in virtual space that are many times larger than can be accommodated (for a given scale) on the screen. Each pan or tracking shot (Figure 22.14), as taken by the cinematographer or as provided by computer animation, relies on the viewer's ability to build up space over time in the mind's eye. What should make this phenomenon of interest to the perception psychologist is that it is closely related to what happens when we move our gaze through the world, by movements of the eye, head, or body, and thereby move the projected image of the world past our retinas.

3.2.1. Some Aspects of the Space beyond the Screen.

What would it mean to say that the viewer has "perceived" a larger space than that provided at any moment on the screen? At one extreme, everything that one could say about the perception of objects and events, in normal simultaneously presented space, would be true, as well, about this special space. That cannot be true, in at least one respect: in real space, one can see out of the corner of one's eye objects that are not currently being looked at directly; in this constructed space, once a part of the scene has moved beyond the screen, clipped or deleted by the screen's margin, it is no longer available to peripheral vision and cannot be regained simply by shifting one's direction of gaze.

At the other extreme, there might be nothing one could say about the perception of objects and events that would draw on the spatial properties of the display. That is, the accretion–deletion relationship might simply act as a signal to the viewer that a space larger than the screen is being traversed, but the sequence might provide neither a medium for the perception of objects nor a metric for their relationships.

There has been little direct research addressed to the qualitative and quantitative nature of the space provided by motion on a screen or behind an aperture. (The latter is the situation closest to what the moving picture simulates in these situations.) I am about to describe the results of unpublished research, and although some of the findings have been replicated one or more times, all of them should be taken as suggestions for research that can and should be expanded and repeated, rather than as facts upon which one can presently base applications.

3.2.1.1. Shapes in Mind's Eye Space.

The question here is how shapes laid out in "mind's eye space" compare with shapes that are simultaneously available to the eye in real space.

In all the research that I describe here, real or pictured surfaces move behind apertures that are often quite small. This is equivalent to the projection of the results of a pan or a tracking shot on a small motion-picture screen or video display. Over a wide range of conditions, adult viewers can recognize the shape of a pattern that is presented by aperture viewing in this way.

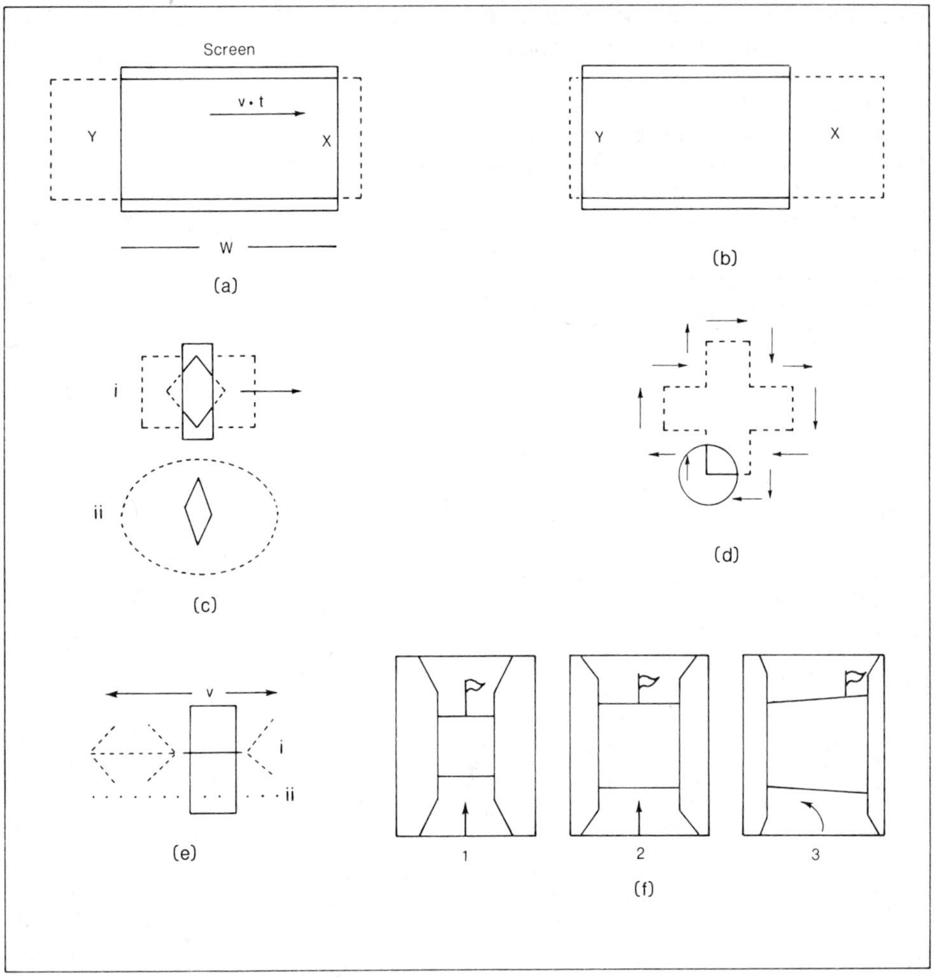

Figure 22.32. Space in the mind's eye. (a) A projection screen (or an aperture) of width *W* on which is displayed a layout, with *X* at the right, moving rightward with velocity *v*. (b) By the time *Y* appears on the screen, *X* has moved off to the right, so that they never are shown simultaneously. Their relative locations are usually clearly perceived nevertheless. (c) At i, a diamond is pulled past the aperture in an occluding screeen. It will generally be perceived as a complete figure (as in the ellipse at ii), compressed in the direction of motion. This phenomenon has a long history; it has often been attributed to constructive processes within the perceptual system, and to perseverance processes, coupled with tracking eye movements, in the peripheral visual system. Although the latter processes can clearly be demonstrated to occur, so can the former, as seen in (d). (d) Reasonably large figures can be displayed, moving them behind the aperture, and correctly identified (see also Figure 22.42). Retinal persistence, coupled with eye movements, cannot explain such phenomena, considering the relatively long periods elapsed, the irregular eye movements that would have to be made (see the arrows in the figure), and the distance from the aperture at which the fovea would have to end up (Hochberg, 1968). (e) Mueller-Lyer pattern i is moved horizontally, with velocity *v*, behind an aperture. The aperture size is such that the arrowheads are not simultaneously visible in the slit. As it does when seen normally, the right side appears significantly longer than the left (Hochberg, 1968, 1984a). The two sides can be brought to apparent equality by pausing during the period when only the left horizontal line is visible in the slit. This implies that some apparent movement is interpolated even when no stimulus movement is present. If information as to *v* is given by the row of dots at ii even when the pattern at i is at a position that reveals only a featureless horizontal line, the effect of the pause is lost and the illusion returns. (f) Successive views of a passage in space. Three-dimensional space can be built up in this way; there is almost no research thus far on the characteristics of such virtual layout in depth.

There is a peripheral component that contributes under certain conditions to this ability: if the width of the aperture is small relative to the extent of the pattern and if the pattern's excursion is rapid and brief, the shape will be recognizable, but it will appear to be compressed in the direction of motion [Figure 22.32(c)]. Under such conditions, the aperture-viewing phenomenon is known as *anorthoscopic perception* (Zöllner, 1862), and a peripheral explanation is plausible (Anstis & Atkinson, 1967; Haber & Nathanson, 1968; Helmholtz, 1856/1962): the eye tracks the motion of the shape and thus paints on the retina the entire pattern. The compression in apparent shape and actual reversals of shape that can occur (Anstis & Atkinson, 1967) would, in this case, be due to a mismatch between the velocity of the eye and that of the moving pattern.

The phenomenon has also been attributed to a process of postretinal storage (Parks, 1965) or mental (i.e., central) construction (Hecht, 1924; Hochberg, 1968; Rock, 1981). Inasmuch as some degree of pattern recognition occurs even when the eye is effectively stabilized, however (Fendrich, 1982; Fendrich & Mack, 1980), retinal painting cannot possibly be the whole story. Both processes must contribute to viewing in this situation (Fendrich, 1982; Hochberg, 1971a; Morgan, 1981), and to understand the characteristics of each it is important to isolate them.

In motion pictures and video pans and tracks, the screen sizes and excursion extents are much larger than those of the anorthoscopic situation, and the integration of successive views then cannot be explained in peripheral terms [Hochberg, 1968; Figure 22.32(d)]. The painted record (or afterimage) would have to extend into the far periphery, where seeing is too poor for many of the perceptual phenomena that can be demonstrated under those conditions. For example, it should then be impossible to perceive forms in this manner if they are presented as binocularly viewed Julesz (random-dot) stereograms, but in fact they can be (Hochberg, 1968). It is clear that with large shapes and large total displacement, more central mechanisms must be invoked.

In fact, adults are quite capable of recognizing such extended shapes in piecemeal presentation (Hochberg, 1968; Murphy, 1973). Recognition per se is only one indication that subjects perceive something and not a particularly powerful one (Hochberg, 1956). More convincing evidence is the fact that when subjects are shown portions of a regular figure, like the cross in Figure 22.42(a), drawn in succession behind an aperture, the subjects announce that a shortcut is taken from one arm to another if that has been done [as shown at 9 in Figure 22.42(a)] without advance notice (Hochberg, 1968).

Two other phenomena associated with particular shapes are the geometrical illusions and apparent depth, given the appropriate configurations for each. In fact, both phenomena are obtained with aperture viewing of the suitable patterns. In Figure 22.32(e), the familiar Mueller-Lyer pattern is moved back and forth behind an aperture cyclically at a rate of 0.5 Hz. Despite the fact that no two arrowheads are simultaneously visible within the slit, the left side is judged to be shorter when the two are in fact equal (Hochberg, 1968). We do not know whether the effects of variation in the arrowhead angles and lengths are the same in this illusion as in normal viewing, but the phenomenon may offer a tool with which to study the metric of space as constructed in the mind's eye. It would be particularly important to determine how motion proceeds offscreen or when no cues are given. My purely subjective impression is that after a brief (ca. 0.5 sec) period without any indication of v, the motion declines to zero.

As far as depth is concerned, reversible perspective figures appear three dimensional when presented piecemeal in the aperture-viewing situation and, indeed, continue to reverse (although no comparison has been made with the reversal rates that occur under normal viewing), lending plausibility to the assertion that depth has really been perceived in response to this piecemeal sequential presentation (Hochberg, 1968).

3.2.1.2. Locations in Mind's Eye Space. When I glance from X to Y and back again in Figure 22.32(a), as they lie on the page under normal viewing conditions, and X remains visible in peripheral vision while I look toward Y, the relative locations of X and Y remain perceptually fixed to some tolerance that is probably quite small.

Experience in commercial cinema suggests that the recognition of location and change in the space offscreen as a two-dimensional array is quite poor (see Sections 3.2.2 and 4.2.2.2). A similar question can be asked about three-dimensional location and change in location: How well does a viewer, when taken through a series of vistas by a moving camera [Figure 22.32(f)], know the shape of the space through which he or she was taken? In psychological theory, in general, that is the question of cognitive maps and imagery, an issue explored in the 1940s and early 1950s, mainly with animals, with the critical question being whether there is any knowledge that can be referred to a *cognitive map* as distinct from a chained stimulus–response series. It is still being explored today (Hein & Jeannerod, 1982). The related question of spatial imagery has recently undergone something of a reival (see Chapter 37 by Finke and Shepard), with the same emphasis. That is, can we show that something like mental space exists? or Can it be reduced to the operation of nonspatial ("propositional") processes? We will see in Section 4 that it is essentially impossible talk about motion-picture representation of events in space without drawing upon some conception of mental space. Desite that, the mechanisms underlying such mental space may be nonspatial and propositional. This particular question has not been dealt with in a really satisfactory way, with regard to real space, so there is no reason why we should expect more from film or video.

Regardless of whether the ability has any implications whatsoever with respect to the issue of analog versus propositional processes, it is clear that by making an effort, viewers can keep track of direction changes; that is particularly true in the case of regular shapes [see Figure 22.32(b)]. They seem to do less well with the distances traversed; I have no real evidence to this point except for a pilot study using vistas like those in Figure 22.32(f). Subjects did very poorly. The same thing seems to be true in those moving pictures in which any complexity of continuous camera movement is employed, and the problem seems to be aggravated beyond remedy if the camera follows curved paths in its movements through space (a film providing evidence to this point is *The Servant*, 1963).

3.2.1.3. Theories. There are basically two theories that can be brought to this phenomenon. First is the Helmholtzian "computational" theory, which is that we normally take into account the apparent movements of the surfaces moving across the field of view in arriving at a perception of the real world, a skill that we draw upon when viewing motion pictures. In short, it is another application of the notion that we perceive whatever would, under most normal viewing conditions, best fit the pattern of sensory responses provided by the stimulation at the eye.

Although the dictum is too general and unspecific to answer the kinds of questions that I have raised while surveying this issue, particularly those in connection with Figures 22.8, 22.20, 22.27, and 22.39, I know of nothing that actually contradicts it *in principle* (Hochberg, 1982). Many other writers in the general area of motion perception seem to agree with this cognitive formulation (e.g., Epstein, 1977; Gregory, 1970; Rock, 1977), but we should note that although it is not actually contradicted by the examples I have just mentioned (and particularly those of Figures 22.8 and 22.20), it remains vacuous unless it can deal with these concretely.

The second theory is that of Gibson and the "ecological realists," opposing the classical approach, who hold that our nervous systems respond directly to the invariants that are under transformation. In this case, the invariant is the spatial relationship between the parts of the surface, or layout, and the transformations are the translations that move the display behind the aperture or across the screen. I will not pursue this issue further at this point, because it seems to me to be seriously contradicted by the examples I noted previously and because we will see in Section 4 that the direct theory fails its original purpose, which was to eliminate the notions of mental structure and of intervening cognitive processes central to other conceptions of the perceptual process.

3.2.2. Space through Cuts, Deletions, and Insertions. Imagine that some object continues to move relative to the projector and viewer—the side of a railroad train, the landscape across which the camera is panning—and that the sequence is interrupted by a cut. After the cut, the new shot may be another sequence of the same direction of movement; for example, in *Grand Illusion* (1937), the train journey is a very long series of tracking shots of the landscape as viewed from the train, the camera tracking to the right at approximately the same velocity as the film cuts from one part of the countryside to the next [Figure 22.33(a)]. Or the camera starts to pan to one direction, say, upward [Figure 22.33(b)], and then cuts directly to the point at which it would have ended its traverse. In both of these cases, the relative directions in space of endpoint and origin are more or less strongly implied, but no particular distance can be assigned. We should note that with respect to extent, as with respect to structure, mental space may indeed be indeterminate. Unlike real space, our cognitive maps are not uniformly dense: they are *schematic* maps (Hochberg, 1968).

In addition to the elisions in Figure 22.33(a) and (b), the camera can cut away to some other event (usually occurring at the same time, in *parallel action*) and then return to the continuing movement [Figure 22.41(c)]. This is the classic use of parallel action (first used by Williamson in 1900 and systematically explored and developed by Griffith in his Biograph films, 1908–1913), the counterpart of the cliff-hangers popularized by Dickens long before the motion picture adapted the device. It is plausible (although I have no evidence to this point) that some rough account can be kept of the space traversed, $v \cdot t$ during the cutaway, and that the viewer would then be surprised if no progress in the pursuit had been made during the cut to the pursued. But it is clear that, at least in these conditions, there is a great deal of tolerance for deviations. We know that viewers do not keep account of $v \cdot t$ very carefully, because cutaways of this kind are routinely used to expand and compress time (Cheshire, 1979) by cutting back either too early or too late.

These elisions and cutaways are very easy to discuss in Helmholtzian terms, at least in a general way, and very difficult to discuss in Gibsonian terms of registering invariances under transformation. In Sections 3.3.2 and 4.4, we consider the results of elisions that demand the Helmholtzian language.

3.3. Events and Their Distinctive Features

We have precise and general physical coordinates for describing space, and it must be possible to use them to describe all events that can occur over time in space. As noted, some descriptive languages and coordinate systems may be much more usable than others, even though they must in the final analysis all be intertranslatable. Thus Johansson (1982) argues that the description of motions in terms of projective geometry provides the natural tool for the perception of movement. We should note, however, that such formulations do not even provide a good language for his best-known demonstrations: human figures, photographed on videotape with reflective patches at their joints and shown at high contrast and reduced brightness so that only the joints show, as represented in Figure 22.34(a), are readily recognized as human figures dancing, wrestling, bicycling, and so on, as the case may be (Johansson, 1973).

3.3.1. Events Reduced to Moving Dots. These films and reports should not be overinterpreted. First, we should note that they are not discrimination experiments, in that no distractor stimuli were used. Second, we do not know that continuous movement is needed for this phenomenon to occur (see Figure 22.31). Third, the variety of motions shown have far outstripped the actual analyses performed, and it remains to be demonstrated that a vector analysis will come up with the correct solution. Some additional or preliminary parsing into groups would seem needed.

Nevertheless, the general procedure and the line of research that it has opened up are extremely promising, particularly as a source of basic knowledge for computer-image generation. By reducing complex movements to a manageable set of dots, computer analysis of existing events and the synthesis of new events become possible and convenient. It has been shown that viewers can identify the gender (Koslowski & Cutting, 1977) of such patterns, a friend's identity (Cutting & Kozlowski, 1977), and the amount of force used when the "actor" lifts a weight (Runeson & Frykholm, 1982). In an ingenious application of the procedure,

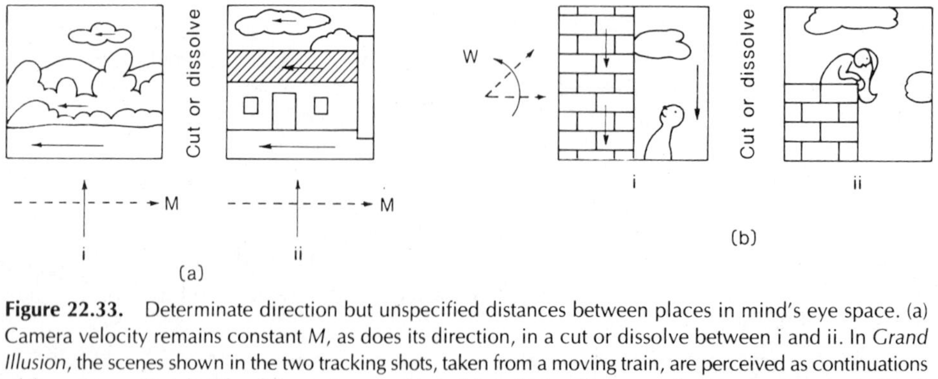

Figure 22.33. Determinate direction but unspecified distances between places in mind's eye space. (a) Camera velocity remains constant *M*, as does its direction, in a cut or dissolve between i and ii. In *Grand Illusion*, the scenes shown in the two tracking shots, taken from a moving train, are perceived as continuations of the same motion, but the distance traversed is indeterminate. (b) Camera begins a pan upward *W* in i, then cuts or dissolves to stationary nonoverlapping shot of ii. Shot ii is clearly perceived above shot i, but we know only that it is so by more than the length of the girl's hair. Other cuts that are indeterminate as to distance but that specify direction to a greater or lesser degree are shown in Figures 22.37(b) and 22.41(e).

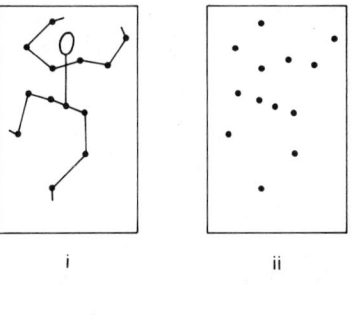

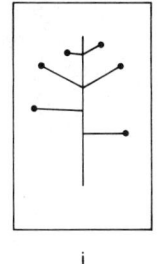

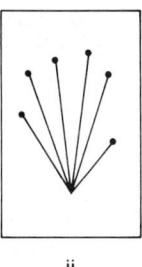

i ii i ii

(a) (b)

Figure 22.34. Coherent nonrigid motions. (a)(i) An important technique provided by Johansson (1973) reduces the actions of a rigid or nonrigid object or actor to configurations of moving dots. Reflecting tape on the joints of darkly dressed actors against dark backgrounds, recorded on videotape and played back with increased contrast and lowered brightness, leaves only the dots visible, as at ii. These provide a pattern that may be quite unrecognizable when stationary but that becomes recognizable (Johansson, 1973) both as to humanity and even gender (Cutting, 1978; Cutting & Kozlowski, 1977) and as to activity (i.e., dancing, boxing, walking) when in motion. (b) The phenomena of Figure 22.19, and of (a), are often referred to as *event perception*, and Johansson considers those of (a) to fit under the vector analysis described in Figure 22.19. The vector analysis, at most, might account for the perception of the rigid movements of the limbs; perceptions of the actions and actors themselves will require different kinds of explanations. Steps toward characterizing types of arrangements of movement are the extraction of gait variables that distinguish male from female movers and the introduction of the notion of "centers of moment" as the points around which movement pivot (Cutting, 1978). That is, sets of dots that move as though at the ends of limbs of imaginary swaying trees (i) are perceived as being more similar to each other than those (ii) on imaginary swaying bushes (Cutting, 1982), and the complexity of a structure of articulated motions may be characterizable in these terms.

Bassili (1978) showed that facial expressions can be conveyed by such moving dot patterns. Given that such events can be conveyed by experimentally tractable stimuli, analysis of their essential features comes next. Cutting and his colleagues have isolated features that specify the gender of synthetic moving figures (Cutting, 1978; Cutting, Proffitt, & Kozlowski, 1978), and study of the factors that determine the perceived gait of such reduced human figures has been very successful (Hoenkamp, 1978; Todd, 1983). Rules for generating such events can become almost as accessible for use in CIG as rules for presenting images of surfaces with some desired degree of specularity are now.

The parsing of such complex movement patterns demands its own level of analysis. Cutting (1982) proposes that viewers are sensitive to what he and his colleagues call *centers of moment.* A center of moment is the pivot point around which some reasonably rigid object or segment rotates. There is some evidence that viewers can identify the center of such rotation for simple dot-pattern movements like those in Figure 22.34(b), even when that center is not itself one of the dots. We do not know the precision with which such centers of moment can be located, nor whether higher-order centers can also be detected. (The notion of higher-order centers of moment reflects the fact that except with greatly simplified machines or laboratory experiments, we are normally faced with the motions of wheels within wheels; that is, limbs, or branches, that pivot around some joint themselves, usually have digits, or twigs, that pivot around them in turn.)

To describe some event involving human movement in a way that would be free of the coordinate system chosen requires something like an accounting of all the significant centers of moment, where they exist in a way that can be specified. Many important objects probably do not have well-defined centers of moment. For example, despite the fact that Cutting assigns a specific point between shoulders and hips as the center of moment for the human body, the location of which determines the perceived gender of the dot figures, the point around which the real torso pivots probably shifts with each degree of bending of the spine, as different vertebrae contribute differently to the movement. Two major systems of dance and human movement notation are in use: the Benesh system (Benesh & Benesh, 1956/1969) and the Levi-Eshkol method (Eshkol & Wachsman, 1958). The latter has proved useful not only for dance but for sports and for the description of animal behavior as well. The Levi-Eshkol method rests on what amounts to using centers of moment as reference points, so the center-of-moment conception probably captures something important about event description.

The fact that centers of moment are hierarchically nested raises three points about the representation of events by moving pictures.

1. It is unlikely that anything much less than continuous sampling (i.e., 24 frames per sec) will do justice to an event involving full human motion because different parts of a complex articulated moving structure, like the human body, will move at different velocities, and some of these will be in counterphase to others. Adjusting the sampling rate so as to bring the smallest displacement to the upper limit of what would be clarified by stop action (see Section 2.2.3) would place the larger displacements past those limits.

2. It is hard to see in Figure 22.34(a) how anything like vector analysis could provide a profitable mode of specification of what the humans are doing. Any mathematical specification of the stimulus for event perception will have to be more object centered (and therefore subject to some prior grouping analysis), like the centers-of-moment notion.

3. But even that will not do to describe events in any general sense. Consider the Heider-Simmel animated film rep-

resented by the sketches in Figure 22.35. It comprises an exceedingly simple set of motions (indicated by the dotted arrows in the frames that are sampled from the sequence). As physical stimulus motions to be specified, they are vastly simpler than any normal event, especially if that event involves moving humans. Nevertheless, when viewers attempt to remember and describe what they have seen in such objective or physical terms, memory becomes overloaded within a few seconds and they lapse into a very different descriptive mode, of motivated action and a schematic story. That is, the larger triangle, or father, attempts to keep the small circle, his daughter, from meeting the smaller triangle, her boyfriend, and so forth. This is not to say that all events are best described in a language of human behavior. But neither will centers of moment, nor vector analysis, nor the rubric of "invariants under transformation" serve as a universally useful descriptive system for the stimuli that serve in the perception of events.

As we will see next, the schematic events that the viewer has in mind and can bring to the moving picture are, in normal usage, at least as important as the stimulus information, regardless of how sophisticated the analysis of the latter.

3.3.2. Elisions, Event Structure, and Distinctive Features. In real life, an event runs its course in real time. We may divert our attention from those parts of it that are totally predictable and uninformative, but the event unrolls regardless of our attention. In the theater, a great deal of compression is possible, and much can take place offstage. Events that occur onstage must still, however, run their course in real time and be staged in real space. To make an exit, the seated actor must rise from the chair, cross the stage, grasp the doorknob, and open the door, before disappearing through the doorway. In moving pictures, the filmmaker can keep only the few parts of that long sequence that he or she desires; see Figures 22.30(b) and 22.36(c). There is probably a strong presupposition by the viewer that real time and screen time run in the same direction (Arnheim, 1960). Aside from that, the viewer is perfectly able to fill in many kinds of intervening visual events that have been elided in this way. Indeed, the viewer today is perfectly capable of recognizing flashbacks (which are temporal regressions) and parallel action.

This ability to accept or fill in elisions raises two questions:

1. How well does the offscreen event continue during a cutaway or flashback if it is indeed presented as continuing and not merely elided? This is the same question that we asked with respect to constructed space, and research addressed to one would seem to serve the other question as well.
2. What aspects of events can be elided, and what should or must be presented?

3.3.2.1. The Rate of Offscreen Events. There is a great deal of evidence that the time it takes subjects to decide whether two shapes are identical (or if one is a mirror image of the other) is a neatly linear function of the angle theta between them (Cooper & Shepard, 1973; Shepard & Cooper, 1982). If a "rate of mental rotation" w is calculated from that function for each subject and the second of the two shapes to be compared is presented after some time t, where t = (angle theta)/w, the time needed to decide whether the shapes are identical is then found to be independent of theta (Cooper, 1976). This is a very important demonstration and operational definition of mental structure. But one cannot assume from the fact that subjects perform a task defined as "rotating" the object that anything akin to an object is being subjected to anything akin to rotation. Whatever the underlying mechanisms ("analog," "propositional," or whatever), the normal viewer must in dealing with the world develop tracking and anticipating mechanisms. Inasmuch as these mechanisms must predict the real movement of a real physical object, their output must be consistent with that movement (Hochberg, 1982). Furthermore, one should not assume that the object is somehow grabbed and rotated as a unit; by making it difficult for the viewer to identify corresponding parts on the two objects being compared, reaction time is drastically increased (Hochberg & Gellman, 1977). That is, the viewer needs landmarks (see Figure 22.28).

Finally, the fact that viewers can do the mental rotation task does not mean that they automatically continue the rotation of such an object when it is occluded or when it is elided by a cutaway. Although it seems plausible that there is some brief period, at least within the range of the short-range movement phenomena, in which something like a low-level process runs its brief course, I know of no evidence to this point.

3.3.2.2. Which Event Features Can Be Elided? In the case of simple static shapes, it is possible to do a reasonably good job of communicating a shape by presenting the major points of inflection and eliding the rest (Attneave, 1954), as in Figure 22.36(a)i (Hochberg, 1980). In general, eliminating the sections of continuing lines that do not significantly change direction is safe, and it will probably work in eliding events as well. In Figure 22.36(b), we can eliminate the frames underscored by the dotted lines, yielding a compressed and more economical version of the event, as in Figure 22.36(c). And just as there are parts of a figure that do and do not define a shape [Figures 22.36(a)i and ii], there are clearly parts of an event that do define a reasonable summary of the event [Figure 22.36(c)] and those that do not [Figure 22.36(d)].

The redundant or (what is not the same thing) the nonrepresentative features in an event that involve a repetitive causal action are easier to mark. Thus in filming a person who

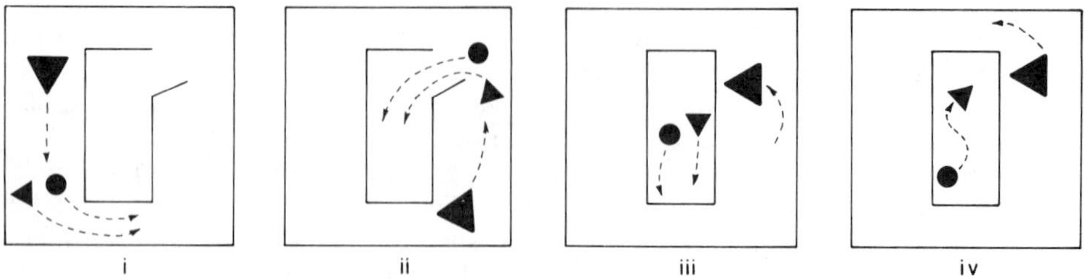

Figure 22.35. Events involving multiple objects. Short sequences from a smoothly animated film by Heider and Simmel (1944). Subjects asked to report the trajectories in geometrical terms find their memories quickly overloaded, whereas the sequences are readily remembered and reproduced in terms of human intentions and actions (a story).

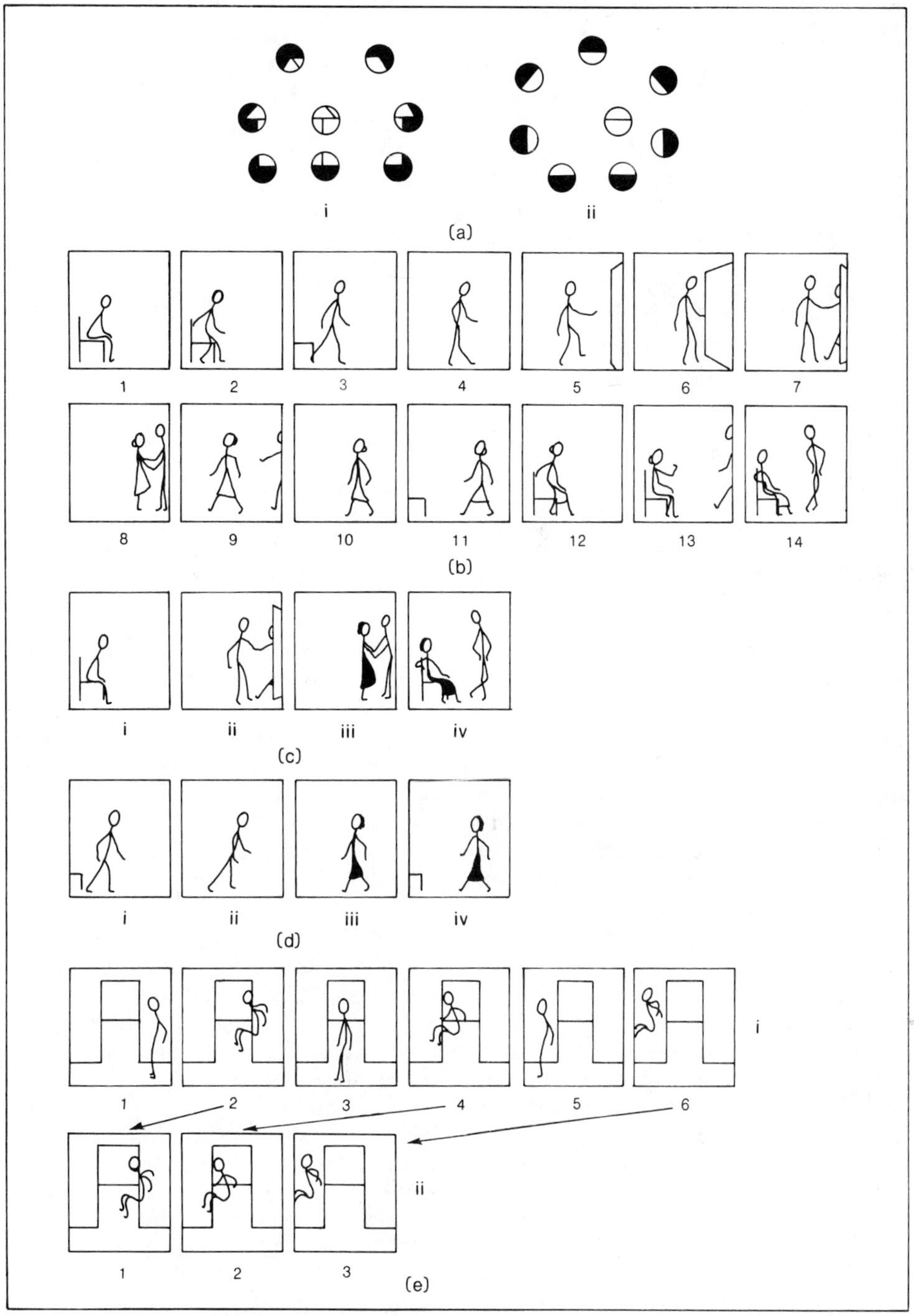

Figure 22.36. Effective elision of events. (a) Two views through judiciously placed apertures of the same house, selected to be (i) informative and (ii) less informative. (b) A short event. (c) and (d) Sequences of four views chosen from (b), so as to be informative and uninformative, respectively. (e)(i) Sequence of man hopping across room, repetitively; (ii) subset of i, chosen so that a man is perceived to float across room ("pixillation," a specialized form of strobing).

is hopping along, as in Figure 22.36(e)i, if we elided either all the contacts with the ground, as in Figure 22.36(e)ii, or retained only those frames, quite misleading versions of the events would result. What we have done in these sequences is what is known as *pixillation*, and it can produce some remarkable or ludicrous effects but does not suffice as a précis of the event.

When we consider anything less periodic and more unpredictable, the possibilities of finding general principles seem to recede rapidly. The cinematic events that are most generally packed with information are probably conversations. It is usually possible to provide a summary, or précis, of the verbal portion of a conversation, preserving only the gist. It seems possible to do that, too, with respect to the visual channel: judges reliably pick the same frames when asked to find the points at which expressions change in a conversation, and stills taken from the midpoints and end points of such agreed-on subsequences form stop-action units that other viewers find meaningful (Hochberg, 1964; Kahan, 1973; Newtson, 1976).

In the case of some social events, then (and perhaps especially in those involving *acting*), there appear to be particular

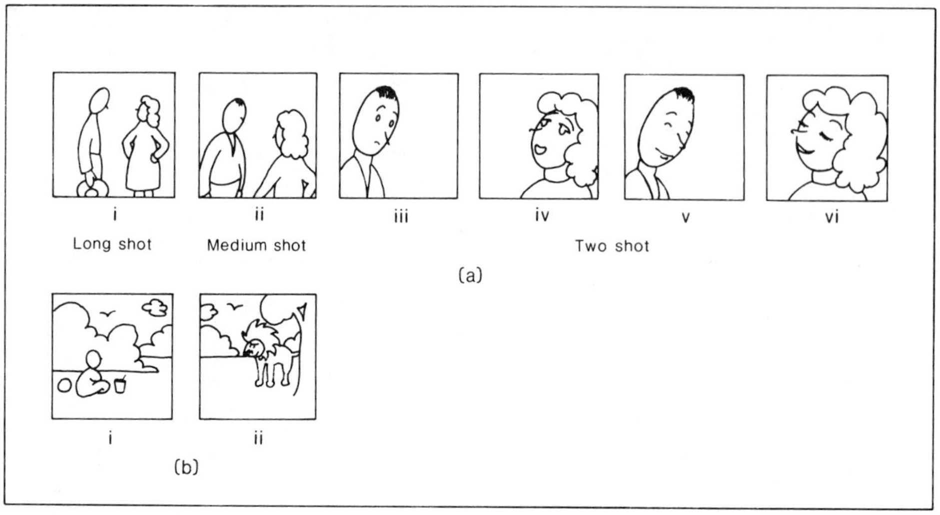

Figure 22.37. Frequently used sequence of cuts between nonoverlapping views. (a) Long shot (i); medium shot (ii); close-up sequence of nonoverlapping views ("two shot") (iii–vi). (b) Sequence of nonoverlapping shots intended to represent nearby parts of a scene.

stances with less important transitions interspersed between them. Most of the transitions are probably less standard and meaningful than the stances (although one would expect that the transition often serves as a meaningful modulator of the stances in at least some cases). If we must elide anything, it should be the transitions. As I watch a "two-shot" [the term for the most common form of parallel action; see Figure 22.37(a)], I expect that, in general, nothing particularly important will be expressed by the face of the actor who is offscreen at the moment and that I am being given only those transitions that are needed to tell me what the expression was while I was looking at the other actor.

There are of course larger and more complex events that we can identify, such as episodes and stories (see Figure 22.35). The rules for what can be left out of stories is a question for literary analysis, not for perceptual psychology, although work is being done in the field, and it seems likely that we can learn something from it as it progresses (Kintsch & van Dijk, 1978; Mandler & Johnson, 1977; Schmidt, 1976; Virostek, 1983).

4. CUTS: KINDS AND USES OF ABRUPT TRANSITIONS

In the course of this chapter, I have referred repeatedly to what I take to be the two current major approaches to visual perception and their different adequacies in explaining and summarizing the phenomena that make it possible for moving pictures to represent space, and events within time and space. The two general approaches were the multilevel approach (also known as the constructivist, schema-testing, computational, cognitive, or Helmholtzian approach) and the single-process, or "direct," approach (also known as the stimulus-information, ecological realist, Gibsonian, or neo-Gibsonian approach).

In the first approach, all the following must be taken into account in the explanation of any perceptual phenomenon: the stimulus information, neural sensitivity and encoding constraints, and relevant cognitive processes.

In the second approach, two aspects must be recognized:

1. An attempt to specify the information in the light to the eye which should normally be in direct correspondence with (in invariant relationship with) the distal properties of the world of space and movement. This is needed by every approach to perception that aspires to prediction and control; indeed, practically all the invariances to which this approach makes claim were already noted by Helmholtz at the time of the beginning of scientific perceptual theory (Hochberg, 1982). In this context, we should note that both Gibson and Helmholtz stress that it is important to view perception as an exploratory activity. To Helmholtz, that activity necessarily involved some set of expectations that the subject tests against the raw sensory response to stimulation, and specific exploratory actions to be taken into account in interpreting those tests. To Gibson, the role that exploration plays is to provide for the transformations that reveal the invariants, and neither expectations nor the exploratory actions themselves figure in the perception when stimulus information suffices.

2. Our visual systems pick up those invariances directly ("resonate to" them): This "argument" has gained supporters in recent years, and much of the small amount of research with moving pictures that we have is due to this school (Cutting, 1978; Johansson, 1982; Lee, 74; Mace & Shaw, 1974; Todd, 1981; Warren, 1976). This direct approach is appealing in that it drastically simplifies the theoretical structure of any explanation and decreases what one must know in order to offer predictions. Most important, it eliminates any need for speculations about, and research aimed at, unobservable mental processes, such as expectations or mental schemas. So there are real reasons to attend to this approach and to wish its proponents well.

Throughout this chapter, however, I have had occasion to point to inadequacies of the direct theory, mostly on the basis of two kinds of objection. The first is that the approach ignores questions of sensitivity and threshold and that those questions, when they are in fact entertained as they must be, make the distinction between the two approaches much harder to maintain.

The second objection is occasioned by the attempt to apply the direct theory to pictures and to moving pictures, that is, the attempt to apply the notion that we respond directly and veridically as an explanation of a set of perceptual phenomena that are inherently illusory and unveridical. That is, in the case of moving pictures (as with all pictures), viewers make the same or similar spatial responses to patterns of light and shade on a flat screen as they make to the movements of objects in three-dimensional space. Moving pictures are therefore a particularly interesting test of this confrontation between major perceptual approaches. Direct theorists have dealt with this problem by asserting that pictures and the real world provide the same information in the optic array (Gibson, 1971, 1979). In the course of this chapter, I have repeatedly had occasion to take note of ways in which the information in the optic array provided by moving pictures and by the real world simply do not agree.

The very strongest limitation on any application of direct theory to motion pictures rests on the fact that when all is said and done, motion pictures use cuts in ways that require the viewer to draw upon schemas of space and events, and these simply do not reside in the stimulus display itself.

It is this last point that makes the use of cuts in moving pictures, which are practically essential to film and absolutely essential to television, theoretically important to perceptual and cognitive psychology.

4.1. The Purposes and Varieties of Cuts

There is nothing in principle that prevents a moving picture from being made in one continuous sequence [Hitchcock's film *Rope*, 1948, comes close.] One could move back and forth to provide long shot, medium shot, and close-up, swivel (or pan) and track to change viewpoint, and follow each unfolding event from start to finish. If we approach the moving picture as a surrogate (Section 1) that provides in the optic array the same information as would be obtained by a viewer in the world, those are the procedures we would follow.

Instead, the great majority of commercially made moving pictures employ a very large number of cuts. Although no average can be given, 300 cuts in the course of a 90-min film would not be extraordinary. Such cuts should, in general, be very different from anything that happens in the course of perceiving the real world; they should (and often do) provide sources of incomprehension and place demands on the viewer that, one would think, are not provided by continuous films or continuous video presentations. Why are they used, and under what conditions?

We can distinguish six major purposes for which cuts are made: economics or convenience; practical possibilities; communicative efficiency and succinctness; dramatic or narrative structure; visual interest maintenance; and rhythmic structure. In general, any cut that is actually made should be done for a reason and should serve as many of these functions as possible. That is the premise of the craft, as well as the goal of the art of making moving pictures.

The six purposes for which cuts are made are discussed in the following. There are many different varieties of cuts, along several dimensions, and we describe them after outlining the purposes.

4.1.1. Cutting for Economy or Convenience. It used to be extremely expensive to move a camera smoothly from one place to the next. Tracks had to be laid, and special dollies built for the purpose. The zoom lens, power cranes, and gyroscopic stabilizers for handheld cameras make this factor somewhat less important, but it is still cheaper and more convenient to cut from inside to outside a room [Figure 22.40(g)] or from departure to arrival than it is to attempt a continuous record. Even if the viewer had the time to sit and watch during the entire event, the cost of production would far exceed the value of the message.

Cuts are also used to provide "joints" at which one performance or enactment of the same event can be replaced by another. For example, inasmuch as a dance is unlikely to be executed perfectly on any one performance, skilled planning of the cinematography will provide places at which cuts can be made (e.g., from one camera viewpoint to another), at which the final moving picture may switch from one performance to the corresponding point in another without interfering with the perception of the event.

Note that it is difficult, if not impossible, to match setups before a camera seamlessly, and failures to match may be jarring to the viewer. For that reason, the provision for the cut may include a switch to a different camera distance or angle [Figure 22.40(f), Figure 22.37(e)iii, iv] or to a cutaway interpolated between the two successive shots of the same event [Figure 22.41(c)].

This last point is both theoretically and practically important—practically, because the cutaway will cover a multitude of sins; theoretically, because it is a clear, everyday demonstration of perceptual memory as something different from the flow of stimulus information. Possible research tools that might be applicable to the study of the perceptual memory implicated in cuts are described in section 4.2.

4.1.2. Practical Possibilities. Depicting an event in real time is often so inconvenient and expensive as to be *practically* impossible. In many cases, what is to be represented is *literally* impossible, in the sense that the virtual space and virtual events do not exist. The special effects techniques that have developed so powerfully from Melies (*Le Voyage dans la Lune*, 1902) to Trumbull (*Star Wars*, 1977) and the development of graphics that exist nowhere outside of the computer are merely more noteworthy examples of the construction in moving pictures of nonexistent events.

4.1.3. Communicative Efficiency and Succinctness. Given a long event that is redundant over some appreciable period, or a layout in space that is uninformative or irrelevant to the message over part of its extent, the camera can cut from one time to the next, from one place to another. By this procedure, not only is monetary economy achieved but the viewer is not required to sit through periods during which attention is neither required nor rewarded.

Indeed, by an efficient use of cutting the maker of moving pictures can both direct the attention of the viewer and answer the perceptual questions that are thus raised (Reisz & Millar, 1968). Thus, the most prevalent traditional sequence, long shot–medium shot–close-up, sets the stage [Figure 22.37(a)i–iv], provides the players of concern (or defines the event), and answers the question of what the first element in the event is [Figure 22.37(a)iii]. This is then usually followed by a sequence of "two-shots," in which the camera cuts back and forth between the two characters in the dialog (Figure 22.37(a)iii–vi), without cutting back to the long shot, or "establishing" shot, to maintain the setting or mise-en-scène. Other devices for directing the gaze within and between successive shots are mentioned in Figure 22.42(e).

Note that the two-shot normally represents sequential time. Not all such cuts do: the filmmaker may cut to a place where parallel action is to be represented as occurring, to some earlier or later time (flashback and flashforward), or to some event that need not be anchored at all with respect to the time of the other events in the film.

Indeed, the pace of the informativeness is completely under the filmmaker's control, as noted in connection with cutting to elide redundancy (Section 3.3.2). In its extreme form, the elisions may not be discernible; *time lapse* (or "undercranking") and pixillation [Figure 22.36(e)] appear as continuous movement on the screen but are the result of eliding undesired sections of events as they occur in real time (*Slow motion*, or "overcranking," is the complement of time lapse and expands the time scale of the event being reproduced by taking more frames per second than the rate at which the film is projected.)

4.1.4. Dramatic or Narrative Structure: Film Language. Most moving pictures are made to tell a story, whether for entertainment or for edification, and the cuts are made with that story in mind—for example, to conceal something that the viewer should not yet know, to place two shots in contrast with each other, and so forth. As such, dramatic structure does not concern us in this chapter, except insofar as the techniques used to that end draw on more general rules of visual communication.

There have been a few ambitious attempts to describe or even prescribe an abstract structure for moving pictures. It is certainly true that during the years between Griffith's introduction and popularization of the major editing techniques and the 1950s, Hollywood perfected "invisible," or seamless, cuts. In these, the viewer simply is not aware that a cut has been made. Directors and editors had learned how to incorporate a cut into the viewer's expectations, avoiding the sources of obtrusiveness that we describe in Section 4.2.1. Some of the filmic devices developed during this period are purely conventions and are arbitrary. But some probably draw on innate characteristics of the nervous system, and some are learned but rest on a great deal of perceptual habit that must be established outside the cinema and have much greater strength and stability than would be expected with conventions that had been learned merely through experience with cinema. It should be important to the filmmaker to know in which category any technique belongs, inasmuch as it seems reasonable to expect different speeds and strengths for each. Such knowledge should be *essential* to anyone who aspires to be a theorist of film; unfortunately, few of the latter have had the expertise in visual science necessary to appreciate the distinctions, let alone undertake the research needed to draw them.

Perhaps the best known of those attempting a film language was Metz (1974), writing within the tradition of semiotics. Of what Metz has written, only his listing of directorial techniques is relevant to this chapter, and while that does provide a catalog of the palette that filmmakers can employ, it does not qualify as an analysis of a visual "film language."

Some of the devices that filmmakers employ merely reflect past or present specific constraints of the medium. Thus reel length once dictated film duration (for video, it is the program schedule to which modules must fit). Low-resolution lenses and grainy film often made the close-up essential to providing any detailed information; slow film meant little depth of field, and therefore the triad of shots in Figure 22.37(a)i–iii [or Figure 22.13(a)–(c)], followed by a flurry of nonoverlapping close-ups, was virtually mandated, and the techniques of making such cuts comprehensible were developed to a fine pitch.

Nevertheless, the techniques are not used with sufficient inviolability or uniformity to comprise a language. Thus Carroll (1980), in a recent attempt at providing a "phrase grammar" and a "transformational grammar" of film (cognate with those of Chomskian linguistics and similarly intended to offer a tool with which to study the universal structure of the mind), asserts that each properly filmic sequence must start with a long shot. This mark enables him to bound what he takes as a filmic unit, and without it he is left with no unit of analysis. In fact, however, sequences may just as well start with a close-up and pull back to a long shot, as in the "slow disclosure" (Sharff, 1982), and Bazin (1967), one of the most influential film critics of the past three decades, argued that such cutting to direct attention was itself uncinematic and false to the medium.

Bazin's argument is worth outlining. To realize the full potential of the medium (he holds), the viewers should be permitted to direct their attention as they wish, just as they do in the world. Indeed, the new lenses and fast, fine-grain films available since World War II do permit the filmmaker to present moving pictures that are at once inclusive (like a wide-angle shot), detailed, and with sufficient depth of field that viewers can elect to look at whatever in the film their inquiry suggests will be rewarding. As an example of what is desirable, if a child and a lion are to be represented as being nearby in the same space (as in the 1951 film, *Where No Vultures Fly*), they should be simultaneously present on the screen in a long shot or, at worst, the two shots should be connected by a continuous pan, and not presented by two discontinuous shots as in Figure 22.37(b). Only in the case of the inclusive shot (and perhaps in the case of the pan) should the viewer be convinced of the authentic, simultaneous presence of lion and child.

I find this argument weak. If the cutting is expertly done, unless extremely vigilant to detect such cutting, the viewers can be led to come away convinced that they saw lion and child simultaneously present even in the case of Figure 22.37(b). Indeed, given the expertise in special effects available today, the simultaneous presence of lion and child upon the screen would probably serve only to lower the overall sense of veridicality of the film by suggesting to the viewers that tricks are being played with what they see. In any case, the *resolution limits* characteristic of video displays (and therefore characteristic of television presentations of even the most modern films) have brought us back to the situation of the early days in films. Close-ups are more essential in video than they ever were in films, and the techniques of cutting not only must be maintained but must be adapted to the special needs of the small screen (Hochberg & Brooks, 1973; see Section 1.1.2).

Cutting has also been used in a more directly semantic sense: Eisenstein's brilliant use of *montage* (rapid, rhythmic sequence of cuts) included at least one cognitive conception which is surely of dubious validity. He used the visual apposition of conflicting ideas as a dialectic from which a conceptual synthesis would emerge, for example, a cutaway to a peacock while tracking a man ascending stairs or to a flock of sheep while panning a crowd, when neither cutaway could logically be taken to imply the actual presence of the bird or sheep. These presumably induce the ideas that the man is proud as a peacock and the crowd is led like sheep, respectively. I know of no reason to believe that there is any special pathway through visual imagery to such literary conceits, although perhaps for some purposes (as in the attempts at subliminal influence through inserts of a dripping knife or the word "blood") access to emotional tone might be well achieved by brief inserts (Erdelyi, 1974). Surely if the viewer is not to be totally confused, he or she must be informed (either during the course of the film or by exposure to earlier films using the same methods) that the inserted peacock or flock of sheep is not to be taken as physically present. One of the many things that the student of cognition and perception can learn from the astonishing rapidity and ease with which

Griffith's innovations were received (see Jesionowski, 1981) is that watching a film is a *communicative act*, in which the viewer expects that the filmmaker has undertaken to present something in an intelligible fashion and will not provide indecipherable strings of shots.

4.1.5. Visual Interest: A Potential Measure of Comprehension Time? Unless it is trivial, a cut provides a discontinuous and abrupt change in the field of view. It has been maintained by Spottiswoode (1933/1962), on the basis of his introspections alone, that cuts provide an affective effect. That effect is a function of the cut itself, of the time that it takes to assimilate the new scene, and of the complexity and expectedness (or familiarity) of the shot shown after the cut. With a single cut to a simple or expected shot, the effect would rise rapidly and fall off somewhat less rapidly; in a single cut to a complex and unexpected shot, the effect would fall off less rapidly, and if a cut is repeated before the effect of the previous one has had time to fall off substantially, the rate of interest should be maintained for a longer period [Figure 22.38(a) and (b)].

In fact, using various measures of visual interest (e.g., glance rate) in laboratory studies of animated story sequences (and abstract shot sequences), more or less the expected curves are obtained [Figure 22.38(c); Hochberg & Brooks, 1978a]. There is reason to doubt that these findings represent any automatic mechanism, however; the viewer must start with some intent to look before these relationships become manifest (Hochberg & Brooks, 1978a). A great deal more in the way of research is necessary on the motivation for looking—a field with immense commercial and practical possibilities, as well as considerable theoretical importance for the understanding of perception as a psychological activity.

What makes such research of interest in this present chapter is that the relationship between simplicity (or expectedness) and the rate of decline in interest strongly suggests that it should be possible to titrate cutting rate against measures of interest maintenance (e.g., eye-movement rate) to obtain a measure of comprehension time and of simplicity-complexity (Hochberg & Brooks, 1978a). This has not yet been sufficiently explored, but the measurement of simplicity, comprehensibility, or expectedness is of great importance, and any such functional measure is worth investigating.

4.1.6. Rhythmic Structure and Pacing. A moving picture must inevitably have periods that are more emphatic or demanding than others; that is, it has some structure of density of interest, or of viewer's arousal. The filmmaker is necessarily concerned with rhythm and with maintaining pacing. Eisenstein (1942, 1949) and Pudovkin (1958) both believed that the cutting rhythm directly engages physiological responses in the viewers, and it does seem plausible (to take a simple and extreme case) that frenzied rhythmic cutting will not suit a pastoral, nor will slow and seamless cuts suit a scene of great excitement.

Because our concerns here are not artistic, we have no reason to discuss at any length the use of cuts for rhythmic purposes. There are some circumstances, however, in which rhythm is itself part of what is made to be recorded. In documentary recording of dance for staging purposes, for example, injudicious cuts may, by introducing spurious beats, alter the apparent relationship between movement and music (Brooks, 1981, 1984). Furthermore, because the apparent duration of an interval of time may well be a function of the complexity or familiarity of the events with which it is filled (Kowal, 1983; Ornstein, 1960), rhythm may be indirectly affected by complexity or rapidity of comprehension. It may be possible, therefore, to develop rhythm as another indirect measure of complexity or expectedness.

Complexity and cutting rate bear another relationship to pacing, which was implied in our previous discussion in Section 4.1.5. If the filmmaker wishes both to maintain interest at some level and to use a slow and sedate cutting rate, the shots must be relatively complex or unfamiliar; if a rapid rate is desired, maintaining the same level of interest, then the cuts must be rapidly comprehended and the shots must be simple and familiar. The ease of comprehension of cuts is important, therefore, for reasons of pacing; it is important for achieving ready communication; and as we will see in Section 4.2, it is important for a theoretical understanding of the perceptual process. We discuss the comprehensibility of cuts in the next section.

4.2. The Comprehensibility of Cuts

For both theoretical and practical reasons, we must distinguish two general classes of cuts and discuss them separately. Over-

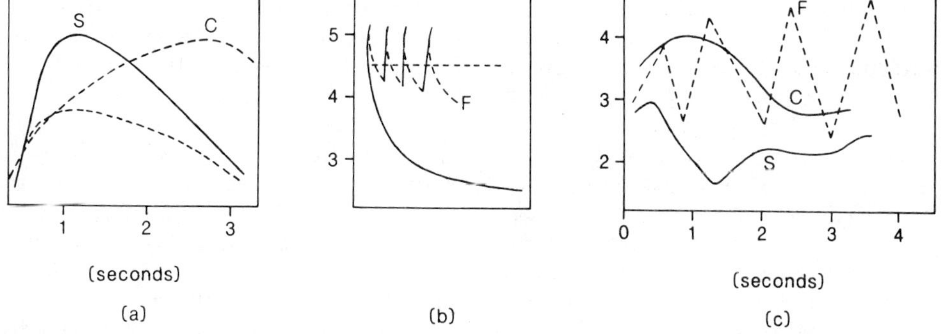

Figure 22.38. The effect of cuts on visual interest. (a) Subjective judgment of the time course of viewer's arousal after a cut to *S*, a simple or familiar and expected shot, and *C*, a complex or unfamiliar shot (after Spottiswoode, 1962). (b) The solid curve shows how the frequency of glances at a picture declines after the picture is first presented (after Antes, 1974). The graph at *F* shows the expected effect on glance rate that would be obtained by changing pictures before the glance rate has fallen far (Hochberg & Brooks, 1978a). (c) Time course of frequency of glances made after cuts to *S* simple shots lasting 4 sec each, *C* complex shots lasting 4 sec each, and *F* simple shots lasting 1 sec each (Brooks & Hochberg, 1976; Hochberg & Brooks, 1978a).

lapping cuts are discontinuous transitions between two shots that include some of the same objects and regions of space. Nonoverlapping cuts occur between shots that have no content in common.

4.2.1. Overlapping Cuts. A variety of overlapping cuts has been shown in Figures 22.27, 22.28, and 22.29. In each case, the two shots that straddle the cut contain information within them that specifies their spatial relationship (or the movement of the viewer).

As such, they provide an opportunity to apply the Gibsonian notion that we perceive the invariant under transformation: In these figures and in others (Figures 22.4, 22.5(e), 22.6(a)–(e), 22.7, 22.10, 22.13, and 22.14), the structure of a layout remains invariant under a translation in viewpoint. Indeed, Gibson has applied this explanation both to moving pictures (1979) and to eye movements (1950). From the Helmholtzian standpoint, additional (cognitive) processes must also be posited: at some level of the nervous system, each shot must be identified, the contents of the successive shots compared, and something like a cognitive or computational process must be used to compute the relationship between the two.

It is clear from what we have already considered in the course of this chapter that both these approaches are wrong in some respects and both are right in some ways but that Helmholtz's (though vague) is the more general case and includes whatever aspects of the direct theory (no less vague) we can retain. To spell that out, let us separate two kinds of overlapping cuts, those with small displacements and those with large displacements between the successive shots.

4.2.1.1. Laboratory Research. If one subregion of an array of random dots is displaced between two successive views, apparent movement results and the shape of the subregion is readily seen (Green, 1961; White & Mueser, 1960). Braddick (1974), as we saw previously, found that the displacement must be less than about 6 min arc in extent and the interstimulus interval (ISI) must be less than 80–100 msec, or the apparent movement of the subset of dots and the shape of the subregion will not be perceived. As Julesz (1964) had shown in using random-dot-matrix stereograms, this phenomenon proves that the perception of the displaced shape cannot be based on recognition of the two separate views, with subsequent cognitive combination of their content (which is what Helmholtz would have maintained), inasmuch as each of the two views, considered separately, is an unmemorable and unrecognizable random field of dots. What Braddick showed is that within the constraints of the short-range effect, apparent movement is a *noncognitive* process; beyond those constraints, this low-level process is ineffectual.

Helmholtz thus is clearly wrong in this case. There *is* a basis for relating the two successive views to each other which is sensory, or "direct," and noncognitive in character. But Gibson's proposal does not fit the facts either, in that the invariant (the patterns of dots common to the two subregions of the random-dot matrices) is not "picked up" in any general sense; the shape and motion are perceived only within a very narrow range of distances and times.

Figure 22.28 (Hochberg, Brooks, & Roule, 1977) makes that point clear. Overlap between successive views of a maze was varied as shown on the abscissa in Figure 22.28(c). Whereas in condition *B* the direction of movement was detected at all degrees of overlap, in condition *A* the correct direction of motion was detected better than chance only with small displacements. These results by themselves might be explained in two other ways.

Note that the envelope of the maze remaining in *B* provides a recognizable shape. This shape might act as a *landmark* (Hochberg & Gellman, 1977) that permits the viewer to recognize the direction of motion at the larger displacements. Alternatively, the envelope might provide low-spatial-frequency components that bridge the larger displacements at these particular speeds (see Morgan, 1980). We cannot separate these theoretical possibilities on the basis of these experiments, but we can constrain them somewhat when we consider the following research.

There is a very considerable body of laboratory research demonstrating apparent movement between noncorresponding elements (Hochberg & Brooks, 1974; Kolers, 1972; Kolers & Pomerantz, 1971; Navon, 1976; Orlansky, 1940). To demonstrate the importance of that fact in the present context, consider Figure 22.39(a)–(e), which summarizes a set of studies by Hochberg and Brooks (1974), described in connection with Figure 22.27(b). In each of these, the subject views a sequence of views, presented at various dwell times per view, and is asked to report the apparent direction of movement between views. So long as the dwell time per view is less than 1 sec, what subjects report seeing, unequivocally and reliably, is movement in the direction of the **F** vector (in this case, movement to the right). This is so even though the actual displacement is that of the **S** vector (in this case, movement to the left). These results obtain with the geometrical shapes of Figure 22.27; for words, as in Figure 22.39(c); and even for people in a scene, as in Figure 22.39(d). Only at much slower speeds is the correct movement reported.

As far as the explanation of the phenomena in Figure 22.39 is concerned, there seems clearly to be two effects: a fast factor, determined by local conditions, and a slower one that is clearly cognitive in nature. The fast factor may depend largely or entirely on the nearness of parts of the successive figures, obeying the constraints of the short-range components of apparent movement [Section 2.2.2.2(d)], with no account taken of the overall configuration of the objects. That cognition plays a very small role under these conditions is shown by the fact that presenting a long shot [i, in Figure 22.27(b)] before presenting the medium shots in each sequence has no detectable effect, although we will see that it has a substantial effect on what is clearly cognitive processing of sequential visual information [Figure 22.42(d)].

I think that these results are consistent with the proposal that something like "blob" processing occurs before detail processing, as Saucer first suggested in 1954, but that a fully appropriate way of characterizing this in the terms of visual science has not yet been found.

As far as perceptual theory is concerned, however, we can certainly rule out a Gibsonian explanation of these results: Where the perception is direct (at the higher rates) it is not in accord with anything like the invariant under transformation. It accords instead with the short-range local displacements and does so even when to do so is to oppose completely the relevant stimulus information based on the invariant objects being transformed. We can also rule out any direct application of the Helmholtzian explanation, inasmuch as any recognition of the contents of the successive views should accord with the **S** vectors, and that should occur only at much slower speeds and with considerable effort (conscious effort, in the case of these laboratory studies).

Of the two classes of explanation, however, the Helmholtzian suffers the least, inasmuch as this body of results shows merely

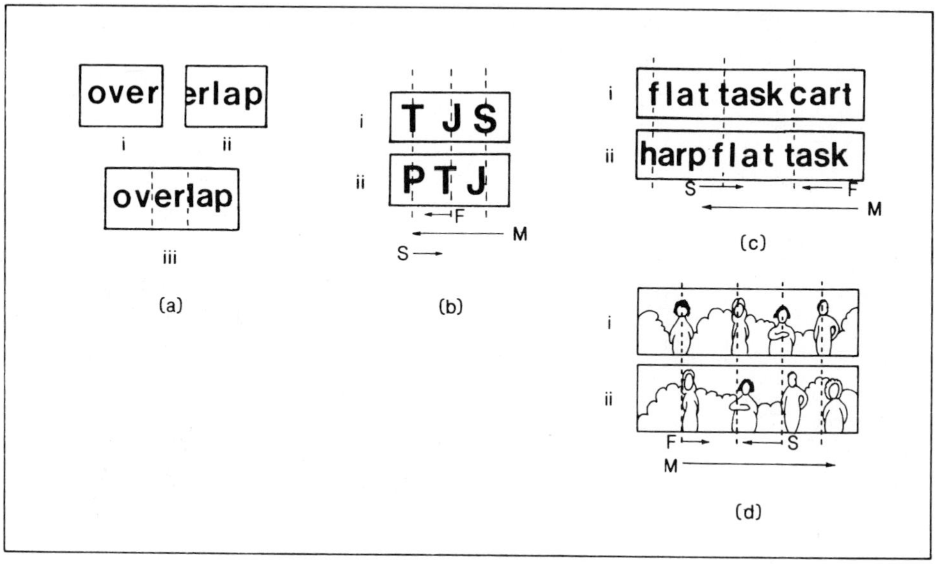

Figure 22.39. The problem of the comprehensibility of cuts. (a) Two successive views (i and ii) that contain a common area of overlap, specifying the relative directions and distances of the two views (i.e., their relative locations and the direction and extent of translation from one to the other viewpoint). This is Gibson's (1950) proposal as to how the space sampled by saccades and by discontinuous shots is perceived. (b), (c), and (d) The phenomena in Figures 22.27 and 22.28 show that the specification described in (a) does not ensure the correct perception of the spatial relationship and motion between successive views. It might be argued, however, that the shapes used in those examples are not sufficiently distinctive to be informative, but the same phenomena occur with strings of letters (b), of words (c), and even of pictures of various people differently dressed (d). In all such cases, unless very long dwell times are used (of 2–3 sec per view), apparent movement *M* is always determined by vector **F** (see Figure 22.27) and not by the actual translation vector **S**.

that the sensory determinants are somewhat more complicated than those that Helmholtz envisioned over 100 years ago, and that cognitive factors, if and when they contribute to these perceptual situations, are not as automatic. The Gibsonian explanation accommodates neither aspect of the findings (cf. Hochberg, 1982).

As far as practical application is concerned, how can the filmmaker avoid or harness this phenomenon? One method is to avoid the **F** vector, that is, to ensure that the major object (or person) in the field of view in the first few frames of a new shot falls on precisely the same place on the *screen* as the major object (or person) in the last few frames of the preceding shot [Figure 22.40(a)]. Alternatively, have the **F** and the **S** vectors agree in direction, as in Figure 22.30(a)1–3, (c)i. Finally, arrange sufficiently large displacements so that contours will not fall near any *noncorresponding* contours in a systematic fashion, that is, so that whatever local apparent movements do occur will cancel out over the field. We will see that all these methods can be readily recognized in exemplary filmmakers' practice.

4.2.1.2. Practical Experience with Moving Pictures. A considerable lore exists about the assemblage of shots into a moving picture, and there are a few books that offer rules and principles on editing (Cheshire, 1979; Giannetti, 1976; Mascelli, 1965; Monaco, 1977; Reisz & Millar, 1968), a remarkable set of lecture notes and a few papers by Vorkapich (1972), and a great many films to study.

It was during the 1950s that Hollywood developed the art of invisible, or seamless, cutting to its highest pitch, a technique that is at least as important for video and computer-generated images as it was for film. The aim was to conceal from the viewer that a cut had been made. The viewer was to be prepared for the cut by asking the visual question to which the next shot was an answer (Reisz & Millar, 1968), and any visual shock or jarring discontinuity was to be avoided in making the transition between shots. Among the causes for such visual shock are *jump cuts* [Figure 22.40(b)], in which the actor or object is displaced more than could be expected to occur within a single frame but not so much that no apparent movement results. (The term is sometimes used to denote any disorienting cut, as in Giannetti, 1976, but more generally it refers to any cut within a scene which may or may not be obtrusive, as in Monaco, 1977.) Also to be avoided are *reverse angle shots*, in which the camera crosses the axis, as in Figure 22.40(d), showing the subjects from their other side. [A reverse angle shot also is used to refer to the shot of the second participant in a two-shot Figure 22.37(a)iv]. Finally, when changing focal length, as in the familiar long-shot–medium shot–close-up sequence, small changes like those in Figure 22.40(e) should be avoided in favor of substantial ones like those in Figure 22.37(a)i–iii and 22.40(f) (Cheshire, 1979; Reisz & Millar, 1968).

What do these injunctions have in common? Vorkapich (1972) pointed out that the problem in many cuts is that apparent movement occurs, a movement that does not reflect any real motion in the world. In the case of crossing the axis, it provides in addition a momentary disorientation as each of the two speakers turns momentarily into the other (Hochberg & Brooks, 1978b). An inadvertent jumping movement is probably also the basis of the injunction to avoid small changes in focal length (Cheshire, 1979, Hochberg & Brooks, 1978b): with small changes the actor appears to jump in size from shot to shot [Figure

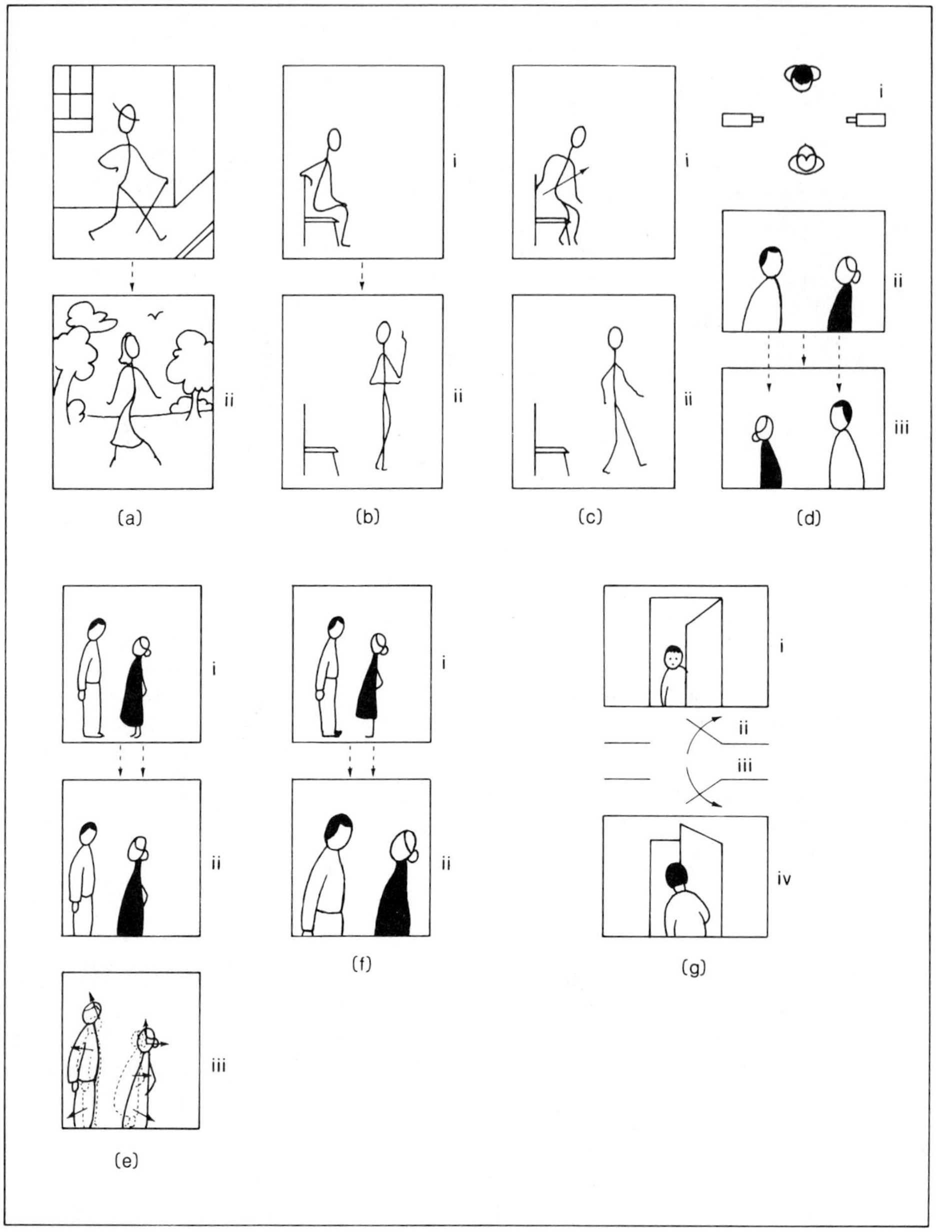

Figure 22.40. Cutting practice in film and video. (a) An abrupt cut between different views, smoothed by placing the focal chatacters in the same place on the screen. No jump or obtrusive apparent movement, then, occurs between them. (b) A jump cut. The distance between focal figures in successive views is too great for smooth movement but too small for no movement at all to occur. (c) Making the cut during the action makes the jump less obtrusive. (d) If the camera "crosses the axis" as at i, confusion will occur in the sequence of views ii and iii, as the man on the left turns into the woman on the left and the woman on the right turns into the man on the right (see Figure 22.39(d)). (e) and (f) In cutting from long shot to medium shot or from medium shot to close-up, a common injunction is to make the change substantial rather than minor. One reason why this should be so is that with small changes, as from i to ii, the figures will appear to expand or to jump forward, rather than be viewed from a close position, as in (f). (g) Door rehung between shots i and iv, as shown in ii and iii, to avoid a jarring cut.

22.40(e)iii), whereas with larger changes [Figure 22.40(f)] the successive contours fall past the limits of the short-range conditions for apparent movement.

The solution then is to avoid small but noticeable displacements. (It is impossible at present to specify what this means more precisely.) We might add that only those noticeable changes or displacements should occur as are attributable to the event depicted, to the filmmaker's intentions, or to the noise level of the medium.

One way to avoid small displacements between corresponding (or noncorresponding but similar) contours is to keep focal objects away from each other in successive views [see Figure 22.37(a)iii and iv]. If the circumstances do not permit this, cutaways to different views [Figure 22.41(c)] should prevent the occurrence of undesired apparent movement.

The case of reverse angle shots is more difficult. In general, they arise from crossing the axis. What this means is shown in Figure 22.40(d). One way to avoid confusing apparent movement is by *not* cutting, that is, by completing the event, as in Figure 22.41(a) and (b). Another is to insert a cutaway, as in Figure 22.41(c), our all-purpose cure. There are some cases in which although neither device is used, no confusion appears to result. One instance that is particularly instructive for what we will discuss next is a series of reverse angle shots in a courtroom scene in the film *Boomtown* (1940). For reasons described in the caption of Figure 22.41(d), there is no jump or disorientation that I can discern.

The counterpart of the solution in Figure 22.41(d) occurs in a class of overlapping cuts in which only the focal object is shared between successive views. In the film *On Borrowed Time* (1939), the main actors, centered on the screen, are pictured as moving through the layout in the first shot in a sequence [Figure 22.41(e)i]; after the cut, they remain in exactly the same place on the screen, but the background has changed to a new locale [Figure 22.41(e)ii]. The transitions appear to be smooth and unobtrusive, even though the transformation in which they are embedded has been exceedingly abrupt. It is hard to see how these results could be reconciled with any interpretation that places predominant weight on the pickup of invariance under transformation. The situation is reminiscent of Braddicks's explanation of the Pantle and Picciano (1976) finding described in Section 2.2.2.2(d): no movement signal has occurred for those contours that are shared between the two views, so no displacement is registered, even though the entire environment has been replaced.

This procedure is particularly useful in making cuts seamless, especially the nonoverlapping cuts that we discuss next.

4.2.2. Nonoverlapping Cuts. If the Gibsonian direct theory is hard put to explain the actual results of laboratory research and the facts of film usage in regard to overlapping cuts, it is completely mute on the subject of interpreting nonoverlapping cuts. These are therefore of considerable theoretical importance. They are also very widely used in motion pictures in three ways.

First, they provide the basis of *montage*. This term refers to a sequence of views (usually rhythmic in structure) that are not, in general, related to each other either by overlap or by common background, although they are related by the theme that is being built up. Montage is regarded by many film theorists as the heart of cinema (Colpi, 1966; Eisenstein, 1942; Godard, 1966; Pudovkin, 1958).

Second, cuts that are made between scenes do not in general overlap: cutaways, parallel action, flash forwards, flashbacks, and changes of scene to a new locale do not in general provide transformational information about the relative location of the two shots that span the cut.

Third, even when cuts are made within a single depicted locale, there is often very little or no overlap between the successive shots. This is particularly true in close-up sequences [e.g., the two-shots in Figure 22.37(a)iii and vi]. Furthermore, by avoiding small displacements across cuts we often minimize what they have in common (unless they have some common feature in the far background or pivot around some nearer landmark).

In all these cases, the viewer must be given some information as to how the successive views relate to each other, or they remain indeterminate. That information must be entered and stored by the viewer in a mental structure, inasmuch as it is not given in the stimulus structure. First, we will demonstrate in terms of laboratory research and practical use that such structure exists in more than a poetic or metaphorical sense.

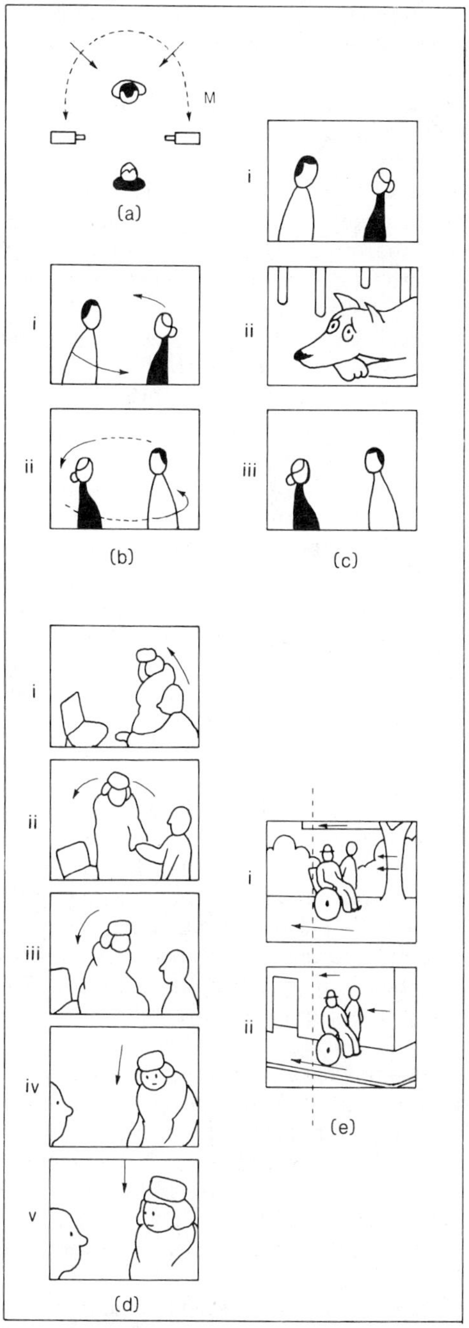

Figure 22.41. Making seamless cuts. (a) and (b) If the scene is filmed continuously while crossing the axis or if a cut is made preserving enough of the action, the opportunity for confusion will not arise. (c) In theory, a cutaway to another shot will break the apparent motion between unlike objects, which makes crossing the axis confusing and objectionable. (d) In this sequence from *Boomtown* (1940), the axis is crossed between iii and iv, but the crossing appears virtually unnoticeable and completely unjarring to my eye. Although no actual research has been done to this point, possible reasons why the crossing is unnoticeable include the following: Only one of the actors is in motion at the time of the cut; the motion is primarily downward, so that no substantial change in motion direction occurs; the action is at the end of a sweep that anticipates the turn, as in (b) above; and the gaze of the one character who is in clear view (the actress) establishes the location of the other character, a very potent cue to the relationship between shots. (e) There is always a danger that jump cuts will occur when action is deleted within a scene (Figure 22.40(b)). These can be avoided, and space and time can be smoothly elided, by keeping the same characters in virtually the same position on the screen when cutting to a new background. The procedure used in Figure 22.40(a) runs the risk of causing confusion by being mistaken for this situation.

Second, we will discuss the nature of that structure: that it is abstract or schematic to a greater or lesser extent and that it cannot be equated either with the layout, the physical world, or any concrete neural process, and often exists only in the mind's eye of the filmmaker and of the viewer (i.e., it is cognitive or mental in nature).

Finally, we will list some of the major procedures followed by film and video editors in making such nonoverlapping sequences comprehensible, trying to indicate which of these are arbitrary and probably slow and prone to error and which probably rest on less arbitrary and faster mechanisms and should, therefore, be less prone to error when properly employed. Throughout, we will try to take note of theoretical as well as practical implications wherever these arise.

4.2.2.1. Maps That Integrate Nonoverlapping View Sequences. Consider the sequence of right angles in Figure 22.42(a), shown one after the other on the same place on the screen. Accompanied by no additional information, they specify no spatial extent beyond the screen or location within that extent. If the viewer is told, either verbally or by a prliminary sequence of long shot–medium shot–close-up [Figure 22.42(b)], that the first view is the upper-left corner of a cross and if the presentation rate is not too fast (i.e., if it is slower than about 2 views per sec), the viewer can then recognize that the sequence of views represents the circumnavigation of the cross and that one arm of the cross has been skipped (at views 8–10) (Hochberg, 1968).

Alternatively, instead of being given a long shot, the viewer can simply be told that the views are corners presented in counterclockwise order. The latter is easy to do by including within each shot a few frames of motion, as indicated by the arrows in Figure 22.42(c) (Hochberg, 1978). With such purely visual information about the relationship between successive shots, the viewer can build up quite complicated shapes. These must involve memory or storage on the part of the viewer, from which information can be retrieved. What I mean by the latter is that the subject can say where each corner lies within the overall layout and can recognize that an arm has been skipped. Note that whether a view functions as an inside angle of 270° or an outside angle of 90° depends entirely on the mental structure of the sequence in which it is embedded. The form in which the individual views are stored therefore has structure, and that structure can take on various shapes and layouts (Hochberg, 1968, 1978).

We can make this notion of structure much more operational and quantitative. A sequence of static right angles, as in Figure 22.42(a), if not organized into some readily memorizable form (e.g., right, left, right, left, etc.) can readily be made to exceed the viewer's memory span. For example, if 2 sequences of 16 views are identical at their beginnings and ends and differ only in the middle, subjects shown such sequences cannot tell whether they are the same or different better than chance. If they were first shown a long and a medium shot [Figure 22.42(b)i and ii] that indicated the underlying shape and the starting point, however, and enough time (ca. 350–500 msec) to compare the flow of sensory information to the structure provided by their memory of the long shot, subjects could readily detect that the two sequences are different, in that one fit the stored shape and one did not [Figure 22.42(d), Hochberg & Brooks, 1974].

4.2.2.2. Schematic Maps versus Sensory Integration. If the sequence of views in Figure 22.42(a) is presented at too rapid a rate (e.g., 10/sec), with or without preliminary long shots, the views simply summate, and what is seen is the cross at Figure 22.42(a)iii. That is, of course, the most straightforward kind of sensory integration. If the sequence is shown at a somewhat slower rate (e.g., 4/sec), subjects report seeing something like a square jumping back and forth behind the aperture or hands of a clock rotating and jumping (Hochberg, 1968). I don't know of any systematic work to this point, but direction-sensitive pattern-analyzing mechanisms would seem to offer a plausible explanation for this level of sensory integration. These are also plausible mechanisms for the response to the **F** vector in Figures 22.27, 22.28, and 22.39.

The phenomena of Figures 22.42(a)i and 22.42(d), however, seem to implicate stored information, or *maps*—maps that are not physically spread out in front of the viewer, but that are nevertheless available to the viewer when it comes to interpreting successive sensory input as spatial layout.

We do not have much evidence about the nature of these maps as opposed to the sensory integration with which they are often confounded. It is tempting to assume that the summation processes [Figure 22.42(a)iii] and those of the short-range, two-dimensional apparent movement phenomena of Figures 22.31 and 22.35 are more rapid and take precedence over more cognitive or constructive processes (Hochberg & Brooks, 1978b). Where the different processes all agree in direction, there is no issue. Where they do not, there should be at least some momentary disorientation and initial resolution in terms of the fast factors.

This analysis gives priority to those readings of displacement that assign the movement to the picture plane or, at any rate, that favor movements between local contours even when these are contradicted by the larger tridimensional picture. I know of no conclusive research specifically to this point, but film practice suggests that filmmakers tend to share these expectations. As an extreme example, I have been told that in the heyday of seamless cuts, doors would be rehung between shots in which they would be viewed from opposite sides [Figure 22.40(g)] to avoid the jarring effects of having the door's axis of rotation shift across the screen. I have not found this anywhere in print or in motion pictures, but it does appear to be extremely common to keep the vertical line around which the door hinges close to the same place across the cuts.

The maps in which we store the information from nonoverlapping cuts are not then merely sensory responses. Neither are they simple reflections of the physical world, nor are their constraints those of real objects and layouts in space. The impossible figures in Figure 22.30(c) and the indeterminacy of the ribbon figures in Figure 22.20(d) assure us there is much in the world that simply goes unnoticed and unrepresented in the structure that we use to store and to assimilate new views. For example, in the 1957 film *Nights of Cabiria*, an approaching truck, visible over the shoulder of one of two actors in a two-shot series of close-ups, disappears from one close-up to the next, an absence that is simply unnoticed even though there is nowhere for the truck to have gone to. It is precisely this sketchiness of visual memory that makes it possible to use cutaways to avoid jump cuts.

We don't know as much as we should about the differences between remembered space on the one hand and physical space on the other, but we do know that they differ, and that is enough to make the next point important.

4.2.2.3. Deep Structure, Physical Space, and Mental Structure. In linguistics, "surface structure" (the actual string of spoken or printed words) must be distinguished from another level of structure, called "deep structure," because it is possible

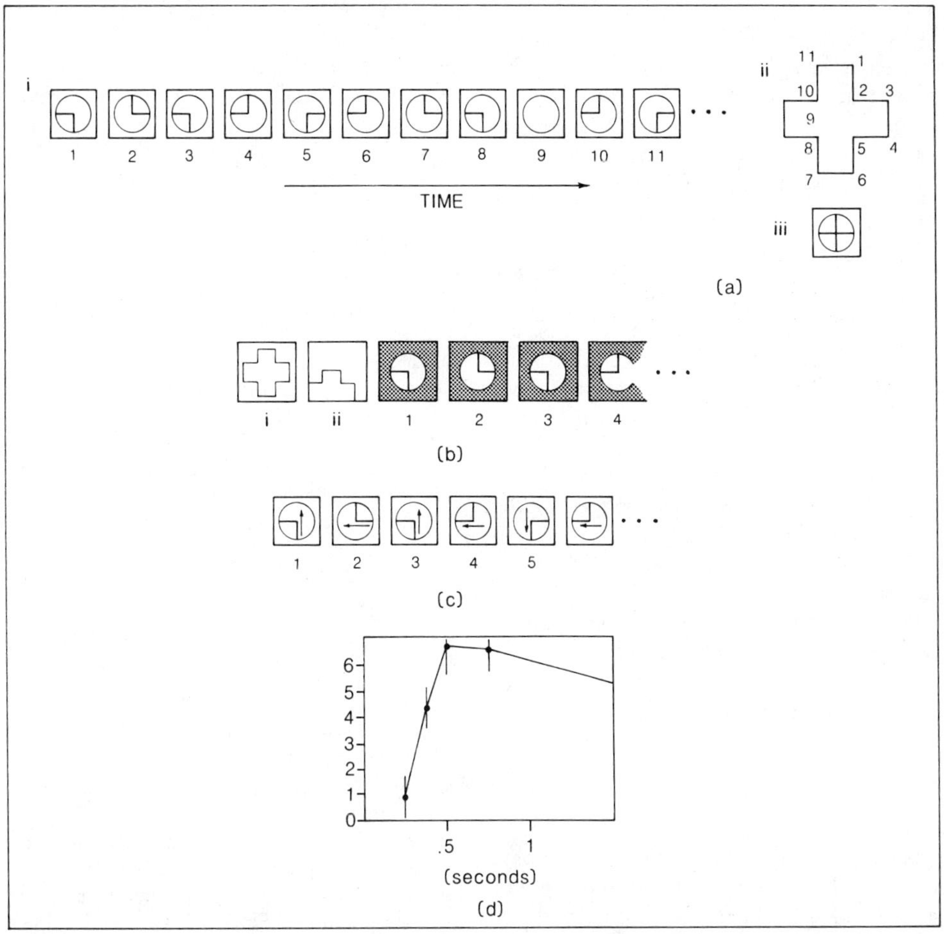

Figure 22.42. Combining discrete nonoverlapping shots of a scene. (a) At i, a sequence of static shots of the corners of the outline cross shown at ii. At short dwell times ($<$250 msec), superposition of the successive images occurs, as at iii. At longer dwell times, a right angle appears to swivel erratically or a square appears to jump around behind the aperture showing one corner at a time. (b) If the sequence of static shots is shown at moderate dwell times ($>$250 msec) and a long shot (i) and a medium shot (ii) show the viewer the cross and the location of the first shot within it, the adult viewer perceives that there is a cross moving behind the aperture and can detect that one arm has been skipped from shot 8 to shot 10. (Hochberg, 1968). (c) If a few frames of movement are placed within each shot, the cross is readily constructed from the successive views without any introductory long shots (e.g., 2 frames of small displacement in the direction of the arrow in each view, out of a total dwell time of 12 frames per view at 24 frames per sec). The incomplete motions in this case serve as cues that indicate to the subject the relative directions of successive views, functioning in this abstract situation as the partial movements functioned in figures 22.33(b) and 22.40(c). (d) In shots of an abstract layout, like this one, factors that contribute to the comprehensible combination of successive views can be measured by the following method. After being shown a rapid sequence of unrelated but meaningful shots, recognition tests show that the viewer has picked up and stored a remarkable amount of the content of those shots (Potter, 1976; Potter & Levy, 1969). But if two abstract sequences, like that in (a), differ in a shot or two in their middle portions, subjects cannot tell one sequence from another unless they can fit the pieces correctly in some underlying schematic map. That map can be provided in various ways, as by the long shots in (b). The time needed to mobilize and use such a map can be studied by varying the dwell time and measuring the viewer's ability to tell whether two such sequences are the same or different. Here the abscissa represents the dwell time, and the ordinate shows subjects' detection (0 = chance) of whether two sequences are same or different (Hochberg, 1978).

to recognize that two very different surface structures are essentially identical, that is, are paraphrases of each other. In assembling shots of spaces and events, we can surely represent the identical spatial structure by very different strings of shots, so we can distinguish deep and surface structure from each other in construction of moving pictures as well. Indeed, in our normal perceptions of the world, very different strings of glances and what we see from different viewpoints can elicit almost indistinguishable equivalent perceptions; that is the massive fact usually dealt with as "the perceptual constancies."

In making films, there often is no physical layout being shot from different positions. The mark of moving pictures since Porter first assembled *Life of an American Fireman* (1902) from fragments is that the space and events being represented usually exist nowhere but in the mind's eye of the filmmaker and of the viewer.

The structure that bridges nonoverlapping cuts (and probably all shots, but that is not as evident elsewhere) is not the physical structure of space; it is not the stimulus information about the invariant under transformation; it is not the responses of specifiable (or even imaginable) mechanisms of sensory integration. It does not exist in real space, and it does not inhere in known physiological processes. It does affect perception and behavior in measurable ways. We can only call such structure "mental structure."

The philosophical arguments that spilled over from the mind–body problem into the methodological and metatheoretical restrictions of behaviorist psychology are not worth rehashing here. There are a few areas, however, in which the nature of the phenomena actually forces us to introduce mentalistic conceptions. The structure of the events and layouts portrayed in film and video provides one of those areas that force mentalistic conceptions on us and in which those mentalistic conceptions have practical value. The structure that bridges nonoverlapping cuts is perhaps the strongest example of such mentalistic conceptions, and its quantitative study would have real value beyond that of potential application.

Such study has yet to be undertaken in any systematic fashion. All we really have is the body of technique, most of it developed in the period between Porter and Griffith, used by filmmakers in assembling their montages and scenes.

5. CONCLUSION

In my first draft of this chapter, I included titles for 27 tables which, in my opinion, would have been valuable to designers of moving pictures in film, video, and computer-generated images. Those tables have not been given here because their data, although obtainable and desirable, are as yet imaginary. That must be regretted, especially because those data would also, in many cases, be important to theories of perceptual psychology.

It is not that nothing of substance connects the disciplines of perception and moving pictures: The principles presented in connection with Figures 22.25–27 and 22.39, for example, consolidate many otherwise unconnected rules of thumb for making cuts comprehensible that filmmakers learn only by trial and error [see Figures 22.40(d) and 22.41]. Because the relatively small and coarse screens available in video and computer-generated images require close-ups, and therefore require cutting at least as much as film does, and because what filmmakers have learned is not automatically transferable to the small screen, the underlying principles rather than the rules of thumb must be discovered and used. Moreover, Figures 22.8(d) and 22.20 show that more than physical fidelity is needed if computer-generated images are to be correctly perceived by human viewers.

Conversely, many aspects of motion-picture perception, such as Figures 22.12 and 22.37, have received less attention by students of perceptual theory than they should and will receive. There appears to be a fortunate historical confluence. Just after World War II, there was a felt need for psychologists to direct their research interests to the real world, a call for "global psychophysics." Fruitful substantive theory and appropriate means of generating stimuli, however, were both lacking. In the 1960s and 1970s, J. J. Gibson and Gunnar Johansson inspired an impressive number of young scientists with the necessity and possibilities of studying "events," that is, changing patterns of stimuli. The theory of *invariants* that was then proposed is, as I have argued, either vacuous or wrong, but by this time moving pictures (especially those generated by computer) have become tractable and economically feasible tools, and the field of computer-image generation has urgent and growing needs for a broad base of perceptual knowledge. That need, the scientists, and the tools are now all in place, and we may expect rapid progress in this field of inquiry.

REFERENCES

Adelson, E., & Bergen, J. Spatio-temporal energy models for the perception of motion. *Journal of the Optical Society of America*, in press.

Ames, A., Jr. Illusion of depth from single pictures. *Journal of the Optical Society of America*, 1925, *10*, 137–148.

Ames, A., Jr. Visual perception and the rotating trapezoidal window. *Psychological Monographs*, 1951, *65* (Whole No. 324).

Anstis, S. M. The perception of apparent movement. In H. C. Longuet-Higgins & N. S. Sutherland (Eds.), *The psychology of vision*. London: Royal Society, 1980.

Anstis, S. M., & Atkinson, J. Distortions in moving figures viewed through a stationary slit. *American Journal of Psychology*, 1967, *80*, 572–585.

Anstis, S. M., & Gregory, R. The after-effect of seen motion: The role of retinal stimulation and of eye movements. *Quarterly Journal of Experimental Psychology*, 1964, *17*, 173–174.

Antes, J. R. The time course of picture viewing. *Journal of Experimental Psychology*, 1974, *103*, 62–70.

Arnheim, R. *Film as art*. Berkeley: University of California Press, 1960.

Attneave, F. Some informational aspects of visual perception. *Psychological Review*, 1954, *61*, 183–193.

Attneave, F., & Block, G. Apparent movement in tridimensional space. *Perception and Psychophysics*, 1973, *13*, 301–307.

Attneave, F., & Frost, R. The discrimination of perceived tridimensional orientation by minimum criteria. *Perception and Psychophysics*, 1969, *6*, 391–396.

Aubert, H. Die Bewegungempfindung. *Archiv für die Gesamte Physiologie*, 1886, *39*, 347–370.

Bassili, J. N. Facial motion in the perception of faces and emotional expression. *Journal of Experimental Psychology: Human Perception and Performance*, 1978, *4*, 373–379.

Bazin, A. The virtues and limitations of montage. In H. Gray (Ed.), *What is cinema?* Berkeley: University of California Press, 1967.

Beck, J. *Surface color perception*. Ithaca, N.Y.: Cornell University Press 1972.

Benesh, R., & Benesh, J. *An introduction to Benesh movement-notation: Dance*. New York: Dance Horizons, 1969. (Originally published, 1956.)

Bishop, H. P. Separation thresholds for bar targets presented with color contrast only. *Psychonomic Science*, 1966, *6*, 293–294.

Bonnet, C. Thresholds of motion perception. In A. H. Wertheim, W. A. Wagenaar, & H. W. Leibowitz (Eds.), *Tutorials on motion perception*. New York: Plenum, 1982.

Braddick, O. J. A short-range process in apparent motion. *Vision Research*, 1974, *14*, 519–527.

Braddick, O. J. Low-level and high-level processes in apparent motion. In H. C. Longuet-Higgins & N. S. Sutherland (Eds.), *The psychology of vision*. London: Royal Society, 1980.

Braunstein, M. L. Perception of rotation in depth: The psychophysical evidence. In *Motion: Representation and perception*. Baltimore, Md.: Association for Computing Machinery, 1983.

Breitmeyer, B., Love, R., & Wepman, B. Contour suppression during stroboscopic motion and metacontrast. *Vision Research*, 1974, *14*, 1451–1455.

Brooks, V. *The art and craft of filming dance*. Unpublished doctoral dissertation, Columbia University, 1981.

Brooks, V. Why dance films do not look right: A study in the nature of the documentary of movement as visual communication. *Journal of Visual Communication*, 1984, *10*, 44–67.

Brooks, V., & Hochberg, J. Control of active looking by motion picture cutting rate. *Proceedings of the Eastern Psychological Association*, 1976, *49*. (Abstract)

Brosgole, L., & Whalen, P. M. The effect of meaning on the allocation of visually induced movement. *Perception and Psychophysics*, 1967, *2*, 275–277.

Brunswik, E. *Perception and the representative design of psychological experiments*. Berkeley: University of California Press, 1956.

Brunswik, E., & Kamiya, J. Ecological cue-validity of "proximity" and other Gestalt factors. *American Journal of Psychology*, 1953, *66*, 20–32.

Buffart, H., Leeuwenberg, E., & Restle, F. Coding theory of visual pattern completion. *Journal of Experimental Psychology: Human Perception and Performance*, 1981, *7*, 241–274.

Buffett, A. R. The visual perception of depth using electro-optical display systems. *Displays*, 1980, *2*, 39–45.

Burch, N. *Theory of film practice* (H. R. Lane, Trans.). New York: Praeger, 1973. (Originally published, 1969.)

Carroll, J. M. *Toward a structural psychology of cinema*. The Hague: Mouton, 1980.

Cassirer, E. The concept of group and the theory of perception. *Psychologia*, 1944, *5*, 1–35.

Cheshire, D. *The book of movie photography*. New York: Knopf, 1979.

Colpi, H. Debasement of the art of montage. *Cahiers du Cinema in English*, 1966, *3*, 44–45.

Cook, O. *Movement in two dimensions*. London: Hutchinson, 1963.

Cooper, L. A. Demonstration of a mental analog of an external rotation. *Perception and Psychophysics*, 1976, *19*, 296–302.

Cooper, L. A., & Shepard, R. N. Chronometric studies of the rotation of mental images. In W. G. Chase (Ed.), *Visual information processing*. New York: Academic, 1973.

Corbin, H. H. The perception of grouping and apparent movement in visual depth. *Archives of Psychology*, 1942, *27*(3).

Crow, F. C. The aliasing problem in computer-generated shaded images. *Communications of the Association for Computing Machines*, 1977, *20*, 794–805.

Cutting, J. E. Generation of synthetic male and female walkers through manipulation of a biomechanical invariant. *Perception*, 1978, *7*, 393–405.

Cutting, J. E. Blowing in the wind: Perceiving structure in trees and bushes. *Cognition*, 1982, *12*, 25–44.

Cutting, J. E., & Kozlowski, L. T. Recognizing friends by their walk: Gait perception without familiarity cues. *Bulletin of the Psychonomic Society*, 1977, *9*, 353–356.

Cutting, J. E., Proffitt, D. R., & Kozlowski, L. T. A biomechanical invariant for gait perception. *Journal of Experimental Psychology: Human Perception and Performance*, 1978, *4*, 357–372.

DeSilva, H. R. An analysis of the visual perception of movement. *British Journal of Psychology*, 1929, *19*, 268–305.

Duncker, K. Uber induzierte Bewegung. *Psychologische Forschung*, 1929, *12*, 180–259. (Translated and reprinted in W. D. Ellis (Ed.)), *A sourcebook of Gestalt psychology*. London: Routledge and Kegan Paul, 1937.)

Eisenstein, S. M. *Film sense*. New York: Harcourt, 1942.

Eisenstein, S. M. *Film form*. New York: Harcourt, 1949.

Epstein, W. (Ed.). *Stability and constancy in visual perception*. New York: Wiley, 1977.

Erdelyi, M. H. A new look at the new look: Perceptual defense and vigilance. *Psychological Review*, 1974, *81*, 1–25.

Eshkol, N., & Wachsman, A. *Movement notation*. London: Weidenfeld and Nicholson, 1958.

Evans, R. M. *An introduction to color*. New York: Wiley, 1948.

Exner, S. Über das Sehen von Bewegungen und die Theories des zusammengesetzen Auges. *Sitzungsberichte der Akademie der Wissenschaften*, 1875, *72*, 156–190.

Farber, J. M., & McConkie, A. B. Optical motions as information for unsigned depth. *Journal of Experimental Psychology: Human Perception and Performance*, 1979, *5*, 494–500.

Fendrich, R. *Anorthoscopic figure perception: The role of retinal painting produced by observer eye motions*. Unpublished doctoral dissertation, New School, 1982.

Fendrich, R., & Mack, A. Anorthoscopic perception occurs with a retinally stabilized image. *Supplement to Investigative Ophthalmology and Visual Science*, 1980, *19*, 166. (Abstract)

Fry, R., & Fourzon, P. *The saga of special effects*. Englewood Cliffs, N.J.: Prentice-Hall, 1977.

Giannetti, L. D. *Understanding movies*. Englewood Cliffs, N.J.: Prentice-Hall, 1976.

Gibson, J. J. *The perception of the visual world*. Boston: Houghton Mifflin, 1950.

Gibson, J. J. A theory of pictorial perception. *Audio-Visual Communications Review*, 1954, *1*, 3–23.

Gibson, J. J. Perception as a function of stimulation. In S. Koch (Ed.), *Psychology: A study of a science* (Vol. 1). New York: McGraw-Hill, 1959.

Gibson, J. J. The information available in pictures. *Leonardo*, 1971, *4*, 27–35.

Gibson, J. J. A note on ecological optics. In E. C. Carterette & M. P. Friedman (Eds.), *Handbook of perception* (Vol. 1). New York: Academic, 1974.

Gibson, J. J. *The ecological approach to visual perception*. Boston: Houghton Mifflin, 1979.

Gibson, J. J., Kaplan, G. A., Reynolds, H. N., & Wheeler, K. The change from visible to invisible: A study of optical transitions. *Perception and Psychophysics*, 1969, *5*, 113–116.

Gibson, J., Olum, P., & Rosenblatt, F. Parallax and perspective during aircraft landings. *American Journal of Psychology*, 1955, *68*, 372–385.

Gillam, B. Perceived common rotary motion of ambiguous stimuli as a criterion for perceptual grouping. *Perception and Psychophysics*, 1972, *11*, 99–101.

Ginsburg, A. Specifying relevant spatial information for image evaluation and display design: An explanation of how we see objects. *Proceedings of the Society for Information Display*, 1980, *21*, 219–118.

Godard, J. L. Montage, mon beau souci. *Cahiers du Cinema in English*, 1966, *3*, 45–46.

Goldstein, E. B. Rotation of objects in pictures viewed at an angle: Evidence for different properties of two types of pictorial space. *Journal of Experimental Psychology: Human Perception and Performance*, 1979, *5*, 78–87.

Goldstein, E. B. *Sensation and perception*. Belmont, Calif.: Wadsworth, 1980.

Goodman, N. *Languages of art: An approach to a theory of symbols*. Indianapolis: Bobbs-Merrill, 1968.

Gordon, D. Static and dynamic visual fields in human space perception. *Journal of the Optical Society of America*, 1965, *55*, 1296–1303.

Green, B. F. Figure coherence in the kinetic depth effect. *Journal of Experimental Psychology*, 1961, *62*, 272–282.

Gregory, R. L. *The intelligent eye*. London: Wiedenfeld, 1970.

Haber, R. N., & Nathanson, L. S. Post-retinal storage? Some further observations on Park's camel as seen through the eye of a needle. *Perception and Psychophysics*, 1969, *3*, 349–355.

Hay, J. C. Optical motions and space perception: An extension of Gibson's analysis. *Psychological Review*, 1966, *73*, 550–565.

Hecht, H. Die simultane Erfassung der Figuren. *Zeitschrift für Psychologie*, 1924, *94*, 153–194.

Heider, F., & Simmel, M. An experimental study of apparent behavior. *American Journal of Psychology*, 1944, *57*, 243–259.

Hein, A., & Jeannerod, M. (Eds.). *Spatially oriented behavior*. New York: Springer-Verlag, 1982.

Held, R., Dichgans, J., & Bauer, J. Characteristics of moving visual scenes influencing spatial orientation. *Vision Research*, 1975, *15*, 357–365.

Helmholtz, H. L. F. von. (*Treatise on physiological optics* (Vols. II and III). Trans. from the 3rd German ed., 1909–1911, J. P. C. Southall,

Ed. and Trans. Rochester, N.Y.: Optical Society of America, 1856/1962, 1924–1925.)

Hershberger, W. A., Stewart, M. R., & Laughlin, N. K. Conflicting motion perspective simulating simultaneous clockwise and counterclockwise rotation in depth. *Journal of Experimental Psychology: Human Perception and Performance*, 1976, *2*, 174–178.

Hochberg, J. Perception: Toward the recovery of a definition. *Psychological Review*, 1956, *63*, 400–405.

Hochberg, J. The psychophysics of pictorial perception. *Audio-Visual Communication Review*, 1962, *10*, 22–54.

Hochberg, J. *Perception*. Englewood Cliffs, N.J.: Prentice-Hall, 1964.

Hochberg, J. In the mind's eye. In R. N. Haber (Ed.), *Contemporary theory and research in visual perception*. New York: Appleton-Century-Crofts, 1968.

Hochberg, J. Perception: Color and shape. In J. A. Kling & L. A. Riggs (Eds.), *Woodworth and Schlosberg's experimental psychology*. New York: Holt, 1971. (a)

Hochberg, J. Perception: Space and movement. In J. A. Kling & L. A. Riggs (Eds.), *Woodworth and Schlosberg's experimental psychology*, New York: Holt, 1971. (b)

Hochberg, J. Higher-order stimuli and interresponse coupling in the perception of the visual world. In R. B. MacLeod & H. L. Pick (Eds.), *Perception: Essays in honor of James J. Gibson*. Ithaca, N.Y.: Cornell University Press, 1974.

Hochberg, J. *Motion pictures of mental structures*. Presidential address of the Eastern Psychological Association, 1978.

Hochberg, J. Sensation and perception. In E. Hearst (Ed.), *The first century of experimental psychology*. Hillsdale, N.J.: Erlbaum, 1979.

Hochberg, J. Pictorial functions and perceptual structures. In M. A. Hagen (Ed.), *The perception of pictures* (Vol. 2). New York: Academic, 1980.

Hochberg, J. Levels of perceptual organization. In M. Kubovy & J. Pomerantz (Eds.), *Perceptual organization*. Hillsdale, N.J.: Erlbaum, 1981. (a)

Hochberg, J. On cognition and perception: Perceptual coupling and unconscious inference. *Cognition*, 1981, *10*, 127–134. (b)

Hochberg, J. How big is a stimulus? In J. Beck (Ed.), *Organization and representation in perception*. Hillsdale, N.J.: Erlbaum, 1982.

Hochberg, J. Problems of picture perception. *Visual Arts Research*, 1983, *9*, 7–24.

Hochberg, J. Form perception: Experience and explanation. In P. Dodwell & T. Caelli (Eds.), *Figural synthesis*. Hillsdale, N.J.: Erlbaum, 1984. (a)

Hochberg, J. *Visual worlds in collision: Invariants and premises, theories vs. facts*. Presidential address, Div. 3, presented at the American Psychological Association Convention, Toronto, 1984. (b)

Hochberg, J., Amira, L., & Peterson, M. Extensions of the Schwartz/Sperling phenomenon: Invariance under transformation fails in the perception of objects' moving pictures. *Proceedings of the Eastern Psychological Association*, April 1984, p. 44. (Abstract)

Hochberg, J., & Beck, J. Apparent spatial arrangement and perceived brightness. *Journal of Experimental Psychology*, 1954, *47*, 263–266.

Hochberg, J., & Brooks, V. The psychophysics of form: Reversible perspective drawings of spatial objects. *American Journal of Psychology*, 1960, *73*, 337–354.

Hochberg, J., & Brooks, V. *The perception of television displays*. New York: Experimental Television Laboratory of the Education Broadcasting System, 1973.

Hochberg, J., & Brooks, V. The integration of successive cinematic views of simple scenes. *Bulletin of the Psychonomic Society*, 1974, *4*, 263. (Abstract)

Hochberg, J., & Brooks, V. Film cutting and visual momentum. In J. W. Senders, D. F. Fisher, & R. A. Monty (Eds.), *Eye movements and the higher psychological functions*. Hillsdale, N.J.: Erlbaum, 1978. (a)

Hochberg, J., & Brooks, V. The perception of motion pictures. In E. C. Carterette & M. Friedman (Eds.), *Handbook of perception* (Vol. 10). New York: Academic, 1978. (b)

Hochberg, J., Brooks, V., & Fallon, P. Motion organization in "stop action" sequences. *Scandinavian Journal of Psychology*, 1977, *18*, 187–191.

Hochberg, J., Brooks, V., & Roule, P. Movies of mazes and wallpaper. *Proceedings of the Eastern Psychological Association*, April 1977, p. 179. (Abstract)

Hochberg, J., & Fallon, P. Perceptual analysis of moving patterns. *Science*, 1976, *194*, 1081–1083.

Hochberg, J., & Gellman, L. The effect of landmark features on mental rotation times. *Memory and Cognition*, 1977, *5*, 23–26.

Hochberg, J., Green, J., & Virostek, S. *Texture occlusion requires central viewing: Demonstrations, data and theoretical implications*. Paper delivered at the APA Convention, 1978.

Hochberg, J., & McAlister, E. A quantitative approach to figural "goodness." *Journal of Experimental Psychology*, 1953, *46*, 361–364.

Hoenkamp, E. Perceptual cues that determine the labeling of human gait. *Journal of Human Movement Studies*, 1978, *4*, 59–69.

Holzt, E. von. Relations between the central nervous system and the peripheral organs. *British Journal of Animal Behavior*, 1954, *2*, 89–94.

Jansson, G. Perceived bending and stretching motions from a line of points. *Scandinavian Journal of Psychology*, 1977, *18*, 209–215.

Jansson, G., & Johansson, G. Visual perception of bending motion. *Perception*, 1973, *2*, 321–326.

Jesionowski, J. A visual narrative: Structure in D. W. Griffith's biograph films (1908–1913). Unpublished doctoral dissertation, Columbia University, 1981.

Johansson, G. *Configurations in event perception*. Uppsala, Sweden: Almqvist and Wiksell, 1950.

Johansson, G. Visual perception of biological motion and a model for its analysis. *Perception and Psychophysics*, 1973, *14*, 201–211.

Johansson, G. Spatial constancy and motion in visual perception. In W. Epstein (Ed.), *Stability and constancy in visual perception*, New York: Wiley, 1977. (a)

Johansson, G. Studies on visual perception of locomotion. *Perception*, 1977, *6*, 365–376. (b)

Johansson, G. Visual space perception through motion. In A. H. Wertheim, W. A. Wagenaar, & H. W. Leibowitz (Eds.), *Tutorials on motion perception*. New York: Plenum, 1982.

Johnston, I. R. *Visual judgments in locomotion*. Unpublished doctoral dissertation, University of Melbourne, 1972.

Julesz, B., Binocular depth without familiarity cues. *Science*, 1964, *45*, 356–362.

Kahan, E. The perception of nonverbal behavior. Unpublished doctoral dissertation, Columbia University, 1973.

Kaplan, G. Kinetic disruption of optical texture: The perception of depth at an edge. *Perception and Psychophysics*, 1969, *6*, 193–198.

Kardos, L. Ding und Schatten. *Zeitschrift für Psychologische Ergebnisse*, 1934. (No. 23)

Kaufman, L. *Sight and mind*. New York: Oxford University Press, 1974.

Kaufman, L., Cyrulnick, I., Kaplowitz, J., Melnick, G., & Stof, D. The complementarity of apparent and real motion. *Psychologische Forschung*, 1971, *34*, 343–348.

Kinchla, R., & Allan, L. G. A theory of visual movement perception. *Psychological Review*, 1969, *76*, 537–558.

Kintsch, W., & van Dijk, T. A. Toward a model of text comprehension and production. *Psychological Review*, 1978, *85* (5), 363–394.

Klopfer, D., Perception of unfamiliar objects and their drawings. Unpublished doctoral disseration, Columbia University, 1983.

Koenderink, J. J., & van Doorn, A. J. Local structure of movement parallax of the plane. Journal of the Optical Society of America, 1976, *66*, 717–723.

Koenderink, J. J., & van Doorn, A. J. Exterospecific component of the motion parallax field. *Journal of the Optical Society of America*, 1981, *71*, 953–957.

Koffka, K. *Principles of Gestalt psychology*. New York: Harcourt, Brace & World, 1935.

Köhler, W. *Die physischen Gestalten in Ruher und im stationaren Zu-*

stand. Braunschweig: Vieweg, 1920.

Köhler, W., & Wallach, H. Figural after-effects: An investigation of visual processes. *Proceedings of the American Philosophical Society*, 1944, *88*, 269–357.

Kolers, P. A. *Aspects of motion perception*. Oxford: Pergamon, 1972.

Kolers, P. A., & Pomerantz, J. R. Figural change in apparent motion. *Journal of Experimental Psychology*, 1971, *87*, 99–108.

Korte, A. Kinematoskopsiche Untersuchungen. *Zeitschrift für Psychologie*, 1915, *72*, 193–296.

Kowal, K. *Familiar melodies seem shorter, not longer when played backwards: Data and theory*. Paper presented at Conference on Timing and Time Perception, The New York Academy of Sciences, 1983. (Abstract)

Kozlowski, L. T., & Cutting, J. E. Recognizing the sex of the walker from a dynamic point-light display. *Perception and Psychophysics*, 1977, *21*, 575–580.

Lappin, J. S., Doneer, J. F., & Kottas, B. Minimal conditions for the visual detection of structure and motion in three dimensions. *Science*, 1980, *209*, 717–719.

Lee, D. N. Visual information during locomotion. In R. B. MacLeod & H. Pick (Eds.), *Perception: Essays in honor of James Gibson*. Ithaca, N.Y.: Cornell University Press, 1974.

Leeuwenberg, E. A perceptual coding language for visual and auditory patterns. *American Journal of Psychology*, 1971, *84*, 307–349.

Leeuwenberg, E. Metrical aspects of patterns and structural information theory. In J. Beck (Ed.), *Organization and representation in perception*. Hillsdale, N.J.: Erlbaum, 1982.

Leibowitz, H. W., & Dichgans, J. The ambient visual system and spatial organization. *Proceedings of the AGARD Conference on Spatial Disorientation in Flight*. Bodø, Norway, 1980.

Lennie, P. Perceptual signs of parallel pathways. In H. C. Longuet-Higgins & N. S. Sutherland (Eds.), *The psychology of vision*. London: Royal Society, 1980.

Liebman, S. Uber das Verhalten farbiger Formen bei Heligkeitsgleichheit von Figur und Grund. *Psychologische Forschung*, 1927, *9*, 300–353.

Linke, P. Die stroboskopische Tauschungen und das Problem des Sehens von Bewegungen. *Psychologische Studien*, 1907, *3*, 393–545.

Mace, W. M., & Shaw, R. E. Simple kinetic information for transparent depth. *Perception and Psychophysics*, 1974, *15*, 201–209.

Mach, E. *The analysis of sensations and the relation of the physical to the psychical* (Trans. by S. Waterlow from the 5th German Ed., 1886.) New York: Dover, 1959.

Manchel, F. *When pictures began to move*. Englewood Cliffs, N.J.: Prentice-Hall, 1969.

Mandler, J. M., & Johnson, N. S. Remembrance of things parsed: Story structure and recall. *Cognitive Psychology*, 1977, *9*, 111–151.

Mascelli, J. *The five Cs of cinematography*. Hollywood: Cine:Graphic, 1965.

Matin, L. Visual location and eye movements. In A. H. Wertheim, W. A. Wagenaar, & H. W. Leibowitz (Eds.), *Tutorials on motion perception*. New York: Plenum, 1982.

McQuistan, R. B. *Scalar and vector fields: A physical interpretation*. New York: Wiley, 1965.

McVey, G. F. Television: Some viewer-display considerations. *Audio-Visual Communications Review*, 1970, *18*, 277–290.

Meister, R. The iso-deformation of images and the criterion for delineation of the usable areas in cine-auditoriums. *Journal of the Society of Motion Picture and Television Engineers*, 1966, *75*, 179–182.

Metz, C. *Film language: A semiotics of the cinema*. New York: Oxford University Press, 1974.

Metzger, W. Tiefenerscheinungen in optischen Bewegungsfeldern. *Psychologische Forschung*, 1934, *20*.

Michotte, A. *The perception of causality* (T. and E. Miles, Trans.). London: Methuen, 1963. (Originally published, 1946.)

Miller, A. C., & Strenge, W. *American cinematographer manual* (3rd ed.). Hollywood: American Society of Cinematographers, 1969.

Millerson, G. *The technique of lighting for television and motion pictures*. Boston: Focal, 1982.

Monaco, J. *How to read a film*. New York: Oxford University Press, 1977.

Morgan, M. J. Analogue models of motion perception. In H. C. Longuet-Higgins & N. S. Sutherland (Eds.), *The psychology of vision*. London: Royal Society, 1980.

Morgan, M. J. How pursuit eye motions can convert temporal into spatial information. In D. F. Fisher, R. A. Monty, & J. W. Senders (Eds.), *Eye movements: Cognition and visual perception*. Hillsdale, N.J.: Erlbaum, 1981.

Munsterberg, H. *The film: A psychological study*. New York: Dover, 1970. (Originally published, 1916.)

Murphy, R. Recognition memory for sequentially presented pictorial and verbal spatial information. *Journal of Experimental Psychology*, 1973, *100*, 327–334.

Navon, D. Irrelevance of figural identity for resolving ambiguities in apparent motion. *Journal of Experimental Psychology: Human Perception and Performance*, 1976, *2*, 130–138.

Neuhaus, W. Experimentelle Untersuchung der Scheinbewegung. *Archiv für gesamte Psychologie*, 1930, *75*, 315–458.

Newtson, D. Foundations of attribution: The perception of ongoing behavior. In J. Harvey, W. Ickes, & R. Kidd (Eds.), *New directions in attribution research* (Vol. 1). Hillsdale, N.J.: Erlbaum, 1976.

Orlansky, J. The effect of similarity and difference in form on apparent visual movement. *Archives of Psychology*, 1940, *246*, 85.

Ornstein, R. *On the experience of time*. New York: Penguin, 1960.

Pantle, A. J., & Picciano, L. A multistable movement display: Evidence of two separate systems in human vision. *Science*, 1976, *193*, 500–502.

Parks, T. E. Post-retinal storage. *American Journal of Psychology*, 1965, *246*, 85.

Penrose, L., & Penrose, R. Impossible objects: A special type of visual illusion. *British Journal of Psychology*, 1958, *49*, 31–33.

Peterson, M. A., & Hochberg, J. Attention and local depth cues affect the perception of (and not merely the reports about) real objects. *Proceedings of the Eastern Psychological Association*, 1981, *97*. (Abstract)

Peterson, M. A., & Hochberg, J. The opposed-set measurement procedure: The role of local cues and intention in form perception. *Journal of Experimental Psychology: Human Perception and Performance*, 1983.

Pirenne, M. *Optics, painting and photography*. London: Cambridge University Press, 1970.

Potter, M. C. Short-term conceptual memory for pictures. *Journal of Experimental Psychology: Human Learning and Memory*, 1976, *2*, 509–522.

Potter, M. C., & Levy, E. I. Recognition memory for a rapid sequence of pictures. *Journal of Experimental Psychology*, 1969, *81*, 10–15.

Prazdny, K. Egomotion and relative depth from optical flow. *Biological Cybernetics*, 1980, *36*, 87–102.

Proffitt, D. R., & Cutting, J. E. Perceiving the centroid of curvilinearly bounded rolling shapes. *Perception and Psychophysics*, 1980, *28*, 484–487.

Proffitt, D. R., Cutting, J. E, & Stier, D. M. Perception of wheel-generated motions. *Journal of Experimental Psychology: Human Perception and Performance*, 1979, *5*, 289–302.

Pudovkin, V. I. *Film technique and film acting*. London: Vision Press, 1958.

Purdy, W. C. The hypothesis of psychophysical correspondence in space perception. Unpublished doctoral dissertation, Cornell University, 1958. (University microfilms, No. 58–5594)

Regan, D., & Beverley, K. I. How do we avoid confounding the direction we are looking and the direction we are moving? *Science*, 1982, *215*, 194–196.

Reisz, K., & Millar, G. *The technique of film editing*. New York: Hastings House, 1968.

Restle, F. Coding theory and the perception of motion configuration. *Psychological Review*, 1979, *86*, 1–24.

Rock, I. In defense of unconscious inference. In W. Epstein (Ed.), *Stability and constancy in visual perception*. New York: Wiley, 1977.

Rock, I. Anorthoscopic perception. *Scientific American*, 1981, *244*, 145–153.

Rock, I., & Ebenholtz, S. Stroboscopic movement based on change of phenomenal rather than retinal location. *American Journal of Psychology*, 1962, *75*, 193–207.

Roget, P. M. The persistence of vision with regard to moving objects, 1824.

Rosinski, R. R., & Farber, J. Compensation for viewing point in the perception of pictured space. In M. A. Hagen (Ed.), *The perception of pictures* (Vol. I). New York: Academic, 1980.

Roufs, J. A. J., & Bouma, H. Toward linking perception research and image quality. *Proceedings of the Society for Information Displays*, 1980, *21* (3), 247–270.

Runeson, S. & Frykholm, G. Kinematic specification of dynamics as an informational basis for person and action perception: Expectation, gender recognition, and deceptive intention. *Uppsala Psychological Reports*, 1982, *324*, 1–80.

Saucer, R. T. Processes of motion perception. *Science*, 1954, *120*, 806–807.

Schade, O. Modern image evaluation and television (the influence of electronic television on the method of image evaluation). *Applied Optics*, 1964, *3*, 17–21.

Schiff, W. Perception of impending collision. *Psychological Monographs*, 1965, *79* (11, Whole No. 604).

Schmidt, C. Understanding human actions: Recognizing the plans and motives of other persons. In J. S. Carroll & J. W. Payne (Eds.), *Cognition and social behavior*. Hillsdale, N.J.: Erlbaum, 1976.

Schriever, W. Experimentelle Studien über das stereoskopische Sehen. *Zeitschrfit für Psychologie*, 1925, *96*, 113–170.

Schwartz, B. J., & Sperling, G. Non-rigid 3 D percepts from 2 D representations of rigid objects. *Investigative Opthalmology and Visual Science*, ARVO supplement, 1983, *24*, 239. (Abstract)

Sedgwick, H. A. The geometry of spatial layout in pictorial representation. In M. A. Hagen (Ed.), *The perception of pictures* (Vol. I). New York: Academic, 1980.

Sekuler, R. Visual motion perception. In E. C. Carterette & M. P. Friedman (Eds.), *Handbook of perception* (Vol. 5). New York: Academic, 1975.

Sekuler, R., & Ganz, L. Aftereffect of seen motion with a stabilized retinal image. *Science*, 1963, *139*, 419–420.

Sgro, R. J. Beta motion thresholds. *Journal of Experimental Psychology*, 1963, *66*, 281–285.

Sharff, S. *The elements of cinema*. New York: Columbia University Press, 1982.

Shepard, R. Psychophysical complementarity. In M. Kubovy & J. Pomerantz (Eds.), *Perceptual organization*. Hillsdale, N.J.: Erlbaum, 1981.

Shepard, R. N., & Cooper, L. A. *Mental images and their transformations*. Cambridge, Mass.: M.I.T., Press 1982.

Shepard, R. N., & Judd, S. A. Perceptual illusion of rotation of three-dimensional objects. *Science*, 1976, *191*, 952–954.

Snyder, H. L. Image quality and observer performance. In L. M. Biberman (Ed.), *Perception of displayed information*. New York: Plenum, 1973.

Sperling, G. Bandwidth requirements for video transmission of American Sign Language and finger spelling. *Science*, 1980, *210*, 797–799.

Spottiswoode, R. *A grammar of the film*. Berkeley: University of California Press, 1962. (Originally published, 1933.)

Stenger, A. J., Thomas, J. P., Braunstein, M., & Zimmerlin, T. A. *Advanced CIG techniques exploiting perceptual characteristics*. Santa Monica, Calif.: Technology Service Corporation, 1979. (Report AFHRL-TSC-PD-A208-15.)

Stevens, K. A. The information content of texture gradients. *Biological Cybernetics*, 1981, *42*, 95–105.

Sutherland, N. S. Stimulus analyzing mechanisms. In *Proceedings of a symposium on the mechanization of thought processes*. London: Her Majesty's Stationery Office, 1959.

Ternus, J. The problem of phenomenal identity. In W. D. Ellis (Ed. and Trans.), *A source-book of Gestalt psychology*. London: Routledge and Kegan Paul, 1938.

Titchener, E. B. *A text-book of psychology*. New York: Macmillan, 1910.

Todd, J. T. Visual information about moving objects. *Journal of Experimental Psychology: Human Perception and Performance*, 1981, *7*, 795–810.

Todd, J. T. Visual information about rigid and nonrigid objects. *Journal of Experimental Psychology: Human Perception and Performance*, 1982, *8*, 238–252.

Todd, J. T. Perception of gait. *Journal of Experimental Psychology: Human Perception and Performance*, 1983, *9*, 31–42.

Ullman, S. The interpretation of visual motion. Unpublished doctoral dissertation, Massachusetts Institute of Technology, 1977.

Ullman, S. *The interpretation of visual motion*. Cambridge, Mass.: M.I.T., Press, 1979.

Van Nes, F. L., & Bouman, M. A. Spatial modulation transfer in the human eye. *Journal of the Optical Society of America*, 1967, *57*, 401–406.

Virostek, S. Storyline, texture and the reader of short fiction. Unpublished doctoral dissertation, Columbia University, 1983.

von Fieandt, K., & Gibson, J. J. The sensitivity of the eye to two kinds of continuous transformation of a shadow-pattern. *Journal of Experimental Psychology*, 1959, *57*, 344–347.

Vorkapich, S. A fresh look at the dynamics of film-making. *American Cinematographer*, 1972, *53*, 182–195.

Wallach, H. The perception of motion. *Scientific American*, 1959, *201*, 56–60.

Wallach, H. Eye movement and motion perception. In A. H. Wertheim, W. A. Wagenaar, & H. W. Leibowitz (Eds.), *Tutorials on motion perception*. New York: Plenum, 1982.

Wallach, H., & Bacon, J. The constancy of the orientation of the visual field. *Perception and Psychophysics*, 1976, *19*, 492–498.

Wallach, H., & O'Connell, D. N. The kinetic depth effect. *Journal of Experimental Psychology*, 1953, *45*, 205–217.

Warren, R. The perception of egomotion. *Journal of Experimental Psychology: Human Perception and Performance*, 1976, *2*, 448–456.

Wartofsky, M. Picturing and representing. In C. F. Nodine & D. F. Fisher (Eds.), *Perception and pictorial representation*. New York: Praeger, 1979.

Watson, A. B., & Ahumada, A. J. A look at motion in the frequency domain. In *Motion: Representation and perception*. Baltimore, Md.: Association for Computing Machinery, 1983.

Wertheimer, M. Experimentelle Studien Über das Sehen von Bewegung. *Zeitschrift für Psychologie*, 1912, *61*, 161–265.

Wertheimer, M. Principles of perceptual organization. In D. C. Beardslee & M. Wertheimer (Eds.), *Readings in perception*. Princeton, N.J.: Van Nostrand Reinhold, 1958. (Originally published in German, 1923.)

White, B., & Mueser, G. Accuracy of reconstructing the arrangement of elements generating kinetic depth displays. *Journal of Experimental Psychology*, 1960, *60*, 1–11.

Whitted, T. Some recent advances in computer graphics. *Science*, 1982, *215*, 767–774.

Williamson, S. J., Kaufman, L., & Brenner, D. Biomagneticism. In B. B. Schwartz & S. Foner (Eds.), *Superconductor applications: SQUIDS and machines*. New York: Plenum, 1977.

Wilson, A. *Anton Wilson's cinema workshop*. Hollywood, Calif.: A.S.C. Holding Corp., 1983.

Wohlgemuth, A. On the aftereffect of seen movement. *British Journal of Psychology Monographs*, 1911, *1*, 1–117.

Woodworth, R. S. *Experimental psychology*. New York: Holt, 1938.

Wundt, W. *Outlines of psychology* (4th German ed., trans. by C. H. Judd). Leipzig: Englemann, 1902.

Youngblood, G. Next . . . total scene simulation. *Video Systems*, 1983, *9*, 18–27.

Zeeman, W. P. C., & Roelofs, C. O. Some aspects of apparent motion. *Acta Psychologika*, 1953, *9*, 159–181.

Zöllner, F. Über eine neue art anorthoskopischer zerrbilder. *Annalen der Physik und Chemie*, 1862, *117*, 477–484.

CHAPTER 23

BINOCULAR VISION

ARIES ARDITI
Department of Research, The New York Association for the Blind, New York, New York
and
Department of Psychology, New York University, New York, New York

CONTENTS

In humans and other higher mammals, a large portion of the visual field is shared by both eyes. Binocular vision is here defined as the neural and psychological interaction of the two eyes pertaining to this region of overlap.

Although a single eye can function well alone, human vision is fundamentally binocular. Indeed, electrophysiological recordings from the brains of animals with visual abilities similar to those of humans show that many neurons in the earliest stages of cortical visual processing are responsive to binocular stimulation. The organ of vision is thus best viewed as having an array of receptors distributed on the retinal surfaces of two distinct *optical* systems in the same way that the tactile senses have receptors distributed within the extensive surface of the skin. The two eyes, then, function neurophysiologically as a single sensory system.

The predominant feature of binocular vision is that of *stereopsis*, a function that transforms those differences between the monocular images, which are due to differences in angle of regard, into a vivid impression of solid three-dimensional space. When these image disparities are large, an observer may experience *diplopia*, or double vision, which may or may not accompany the stereoscopic depth sensation. The two monocular images of a single object or contour are often referred to as *half-images*, whereas each monocular image as a whole is called a *half-field*.

The fact that the eyes can be stimulated separately allows us to re-create the geometry of three-dimensional space with two-dimensional stereoscopic displays. By presenting each eye with a different visual pattern (half-field) through a stereoscope or other suitable means of image separation, one can study the phenomena of binocular vision with a high degree of control and precision.

Due to the geometry of visual space, points arising from only a single surface in space can be imaged in nondisparate (i.e., corresponding) retinal locations when the eyes are stationary. This surface, at sufficient distance and close to the point of fixation, is roughly planar and is referred to as the *plane of fixation*. Since objects in space are often located at some distance from this surface, half-images of different objects often fall on corresponding retinal locations. If these objects are very different in their color or contour information, one of the monocular images may appear to be *suppressed*. The mechanisms underlying binocular suppression may be one reason for the apparent singleness of the visual world despite the preponderance of geometrically double images.

Stereopsis and singleness of vision are the traditional topics of study in binocular vision. Perhaps this is because these are representative of more general mental functions: (1) stereopsis as a *discrimination* of differences between two patterns of stimulation resulting in the synthesis of a new percept (depth) and (2) singleness of vision as an *integration* of different patterns of stimulation into a unitary (single) percept.

These functions are uniquely binocular in that they cannot, by definition, be performed monocularly. But there are quantitative differences between monocular and binocular visual performance as well. The folk wisdom that "two eyes are better than one" is in fact true within a single individual, for a wide variety of common visual functions. These are taken up in Section 1.

1. BINOCULAR VERSUS MONOCULAR SENSITIVITIES

The use of two eyes provides an advantage in performing many tasks that are possible to perform with only one eye. These include traditional threshold measures, such as detection of very dim lights, increments of light flashed on lit backgrounds (increment thresholds), contrast, and flicker. Form recognition accuracy, acuity, and reaction time experiments show that this quantitative binocular advantage also extends to suprathreshold levels of stimulation. However, differences between binocular and monocular sensitivities are nearly always small, and individual differences between subjects in such experiments tend to be large; a long-standing debate was required to firmly establish the existence of such advantages. Blake and Fox (1973) have provided a clear and comprehensive history and review of this literature. Blake, Sloane, and Fox (1981) have also published an update to the earlier review.

There are two possible sources of binocular advantage. One results from the probabilistic nature of the detection process. Suppose for a moment that the two eyes are completely independent and are able, each alone, to assess the presence or absence of a stimulus signal. Suppose, also, that if either eye detects the signal, the observer as a whole detects it. These assumptions are tantamount to supposing that when the two eyes try to detect the stimulus, they will do as well as a single eye that has two independent opportunities (assuming equal sensitivity for the two eyes). This type of binocular advantage is an instance of what is called *probability summation*, since it arises from probabilistic considerations. The magnitude of the advantage to be expected on probabilistic grounds, as we shall see, is highly dependent on the specific decision and sensory models chosen to represent the detection process. Section 1.1 discusses several models of binocular probability summation.

A second possible source of enhanced detectability with binocular viewing is peripheral interaction between monocular signals. If monocular neural pathways converge to common binocular pathways in the brain prior to the decision process, then one might expect binocular responses to be greater than monocular responses since both monocular signals contribute to the binocular response. Such convergence has been called *neural summation* (Blake & Fox, 1973) even though strict algebraic addition of signals is not implied. Obviously, evidence for the existence of neural summation entails demonstrating binocular versus monocular differences, which significantly exceed those predicted by a plausible model of probability summation. Sections 1.2 through 1.5 discuss the various types of binocular advantage attributed to neural summation.

Although it is now well accepted that binocular is often better than monocular performance, it is a difficult problem to assess the precise magnitude of those advantages. Many paradigms described here seek to compare monocular with binocular performance probabilities. Such experiments may give statistical information valuable in deciding whether the advantage is due to probability or neural summation. But determining, for example, how much less light is required to detect a stimulus binocularly than monocularly requires either knowledge of the psychometric function from which the performance probabilities arise or direct measurement of monocular and binocular thresholds. The latter usually gives little insight on the nature of the advantage but may provide more practical information.

1.1. Probability Summation

Pirenne (1943) is usually credited with the first application of the independence theorem of probability theory to binocular summation. He noted that if the eyes were considered to make independent decisions about the presence or absence of a threshold signal, then the probability of a correct binocular detection P_b, given left-eye and right-eye detection probabilities P_l and P_r is predicted by the equation

$$P_b = 1 - (1 - P_l)(1 - P_r) \ . \tag{1}$$

Thus the binocular probability is 1 (the certain event) minus the probability that neither eye detected the signal.

Suppose that we empirically estimate left-eye, right-eye, and binocular detection probabilities by measuring performance independently for each eye and for the two eyes together. According to Pirenne, substituting these monocular performance estimates into the right side of Eq. (1) should provide an estimate of the binocular detection probability that is expected on purely statistical grounds. We can now compare this probability summation estimate with the empirically determined estimate of binocular detectability in order to test for a significant departure from independence. If the empirically determined estimate significantly exceeds the probability summation estimate, then we have evidence for neural summation.

Let us examine the plausibility of this simple model of probability summation. The model assumes that each eye alone is capable of carrying on the detection task and that the observer then combines each eye's decision with a logical *OR* operation. Thus if the left eye detects and the right eye fails to detect the stimulus, then the observer as a whole will detect the stimulus. This analysis, however, assumes that monocular decision processes are similar to the decision processes of whole observers. Specifically, it assumes that a monocular channel is capable of making a "guess" when there is incomplete information in that channel.

As Eriksen (1966) has pointed out, Eq. (1) provides an inappropriate estimate of probability summation for experiments in which guessing is a factor, for, as in the hypothetical experiment described, each empirically determined monocular probability reflects the guessing factor associated with each monocular experiment, as well as those factors associated with detection. It seems implausible that each monocular pathway can make guesses prior to the combination of decisions. It is more reasonable to assume that the observer's guessing behavior takes place after information from both eyes is available. Since Eq. (1) implicitly assumes that each eye can guess, it overestimates the level of performance to be expected on statistical grounds.

Eriksen (1966) applied the independence theorem in a way which includes the guessing factor only once, by making a few additional assumptions. Blake and Fox (1973) applied and extended this analysis to binocular summation. For simplicity, they first assumed a two-state model of the threshold; that is, that on any given trial, a monocular channel can be in only one of two states: a correct-detection state, in which the stimulus has exceeded a strict monocular threshold, or a guessing state. Assuming that C represents the probability of being in the correct-detection state after a single observation (one eye's view), and $1/n$ is the a priori probability of a correct guess (where n equals the number of response alternatives), the probability of responding correctly after a single binocular trial is given by:

$$P_c = 2C(1 - C) + C^2 + \frac{(1 - C)^2}{n} \ . \tag{2}$$

The first factor is the probability of being in the correct-detection state due to exactly one of the two observations (i.e., one but not both eyes correctly detected the signal). The second factor is the probability that both observations resulted in the correct-detection state (both eyes correctly detected the signal). The third factor is the probability of being in the correct-detection state after neither of the observations but guessing correctly.

Equation (2) assumes that the two eyes behave identically; that is, that the two observations on a given trial are like two independent "looks" by the same eye. Since P_l and P_r may differ considerably in such experiments, this equation is of less practical value. For this reason, Blake and Fox also provide an equation for estimating binocular performance from corrected monocular probabilities. The estimated proportions of guess trials in each monocular experiment are G_l and G_r, and they are given by $(1 - 1/n)^{-1}(1 - P_l)$ and $(1 - 1/n)^{-1}(1 - P_r)$ respectively (Eriksen & Greenspon, 1968). Then $1 - G_lG_r$ estimates the proportion of trials in which the observer was in the correct-detection state for one or both observations (eyes). This expression, plus the proportion of trials in which the observer correctly guesses (G_lG_r/n), is the expected binocular performance under this two-state, high-threshold model. That is,

$$P_b = 1 - G_lG_r + \frac{G_lG_r}{n} \ . \tag{3}$$

Equation (3) is appropriate for calculating probabilistic baselines in n-alternative forced-choice detection experiments when it is reasonable to assume that on any single trial the observer is in either a correct perception state or a guessing state. Decision models based on more than two perceptual states will predict even lower performance levels due to probability summation than will either the Pirenne or the two-state high-threshold models (Eriksen, 1966).

While much contemporary psychophysical work suggests that thresholds are better represented by several distinct states or by a continuously varying sensitivity function, the two-state model is the one most often employed as the probabilistic baseline in binocular summation experiments. The best reason for this is that this model provides higher estimates of binocular performance than multistate and continuous models. As the baseline against which to assess evidence for neural summation, its use provides the most conservative test.

However, Watson, Thompson, Murphy, and Nachmias (1980) have developed a general model of probability summation that is based on a continuous threshold function. Anderson (Note 1) has extended this model to binocular detection of contrast. Suppose that the probability of detecting the stimulus with the left- or right-eye mechanisms is given by the analytic form of the psychometric function suggested by Brindley (1960) and Quick (1974):

$$P_l = 1 - \exp\left[-\left(\frac{I_l}{\alpha_l}\right)^{\beta}\right], \tag{4}$$

$$P_r = 1 - \exp\left[-\left(\frac{I_r}{\alpha_r}\right)^{\beta}\right], \tag{5}$$

where I_l, I_r are the intensities of the left and right eye stimuli, α_l, α_r are thresholds defined as the intensity at which 0.63 $(1 - 1/e)$ of the stimuli are detected, and β is a parameter equal to the slope of the psychometric function at $P = 0.50$ and is assumed to be equal for the two eyes. Now, assume that the left- and right-eye mechanisms are stochastically independent. Then the probability of responding correctly to a binocular stimulus is

$$P_b = 1 - (1-\gamma)(1-p_l)(1-p_r) , \tag{6}$$

where γ is the probability of a correct guess (i.e., when I_l and I_r are zero). Combining Eq. (4) and (5) with (6) yields

$$P_b = 1 - (1 - \gamma) \exp\left[-R^{\beta}\right] , \tag{7}$$

where

$$R = \left[\left(\frac{I_l}{\alpha_l}\right)^{\beta} + \left(\frac{I_r}{\alpha_r}\right)^{\beta}\right]^{1/\beta} . \tag{8}$$

The stimulus is a threshold when $R = 1$, so that

$$1 = \left(\frac{\alpha_b}{\alpha_l}\right)^{\beta} + \left(\frac{\alpha_b}{\alpha_r}\right)^{\beta}, \tag{9}$$

where α_b is the threshold intensity of a binocular stimulus.

If the additional assumption is made that the monocular thresholds α_l and α_r are equal, then substituting and simplifying Eq. (9) gives

$$\left(\frac{1}{2}\right)^{1/\beta} = \frac{\alpha_b}{\alpha_l} . \tag{10}$$

For some applications, it may be more convenient to express this relationship in amplitude decibels. Hence

$$\mathrm{dB}(\alpha_l) - \mathrm{dB}(\alpha_b) = \frac{6}{\beta} . \tag{11}$$

Thus the rather general model of Watson and colleagues makes the strong prediction that provided thresholds and the slope parameter are equal for the two eyes, a binocular stimulus at threshold should be less intense by a factor of $(1/2)^{1/\beta}$ than a monocular stimulus at threshold. If $\beta = 1$, binocular sensitivity should thus be 6 dB, or roughly twice monocular sensitivity from probability summation alone.

Thus far, probability summation and neural summation have been described as completely distinct. Yet there is an important sense in which probability summation must be neural as well. For even if monocular pathways are treated as independent, the decisions they generate must combine somewhere in the brain prior to the observer's response. The distinction is, in essence, according to the order of combinatorial and decision processes. Probability summation implies that some sort of monocular detection decisions are made and *then* combined, whereas neural summation implies that monocular pathways combine *before* the decision process begins.

The signal detection and integration models of binocular summation (Campbell & Green, 1965; Green & Swets, 1966) are cases in which this distinction is not so easy to draw. The Green and Swets model, based on the theory of signal detection (see Chapter 1 by Falmagne), uses the ratio of signal strength to the standard deviation of the noise in the channel as the measure of sensitivity (d'). The model states that binocular responses are obtained by sampling from independent noisy monocular channels. Since the signal is correlated in the two eyes, the resultant sampling distribution will have the summed signal strength of the monocular channels. The standard deviation of the uncorrelated noise, on the other hand, will grow only as the square root of the sum of its squares. Thus if the signal and the noise are equal in the two eyes, then the predicted binocular d' is $\sqrt{2}$ greater than the monocular d'. Additionally assuming, as did Campbell and Green, that d' is proportional to stimulus contrast, it follows that binocular thresholds should be $\sqrt{2}$ lower than monocular thresholds. Such models are like probability summation models in that two independent statistical processes are combined prior to the response but are also like neural summation models in that monocular channels are combined prior to the decision process.

1.2. Binocular versus Monocular Threshold Sensitivities

The preceding section revealed a few of the central problems in determining the proper baseline for measuring the amount of neural binocular interaction in binocular detection experiments. Such issues have long been in dispute. A number of recent studies have attempted to circumvent these theoretical problems by using empirically determined baselines, rather than model-bound estimates of probability summation. Such studies show with little doubt the existence of genuine neural summation between monocular channels.

The alternative baselines are performance measures under circumstances in which it is reasonable to assume independence of the eyes. The two methods that have been used either present the stimuli to very disparate retinal locations (Crozier & Holway, 1938; Shaad, 1935; Thorn & Boynton, 1974) or present the stimuli under conditions of nonsimultaneous stimulation (Matin, 1962; Thorn & Boynton, 1974; Westendorf & Fox, 1974, 1975, 1977). All these studies demonstrate that binocular performance is better than monocular only under conditions of synchronous and retinally correspondent stimulation.

As an example, the latter technique was used by Matin (1962), who measured the probability of detecting a flashed circular patch of light presented to corresponding peripheral areas of one or both eyes under scotopic conditions. In the binocular condition, he also varied the interstimulus interval (ISI) separating the flashes to the two eyes. For ISIs less than 100 msec, binocular performance significantly exceeded that predicted by Pirenne's equation (Eq. (1)). But for ISIs greater than 100 msec, the two eyes behaved as independent detectors [as predicted by Eq. (1)]. Even with the smallest ISIs, however, binocular probabilities were less than they were when the two flashes were presented to the same eye. Matin concluded that there was significant neural interaction between the eyes prior to the decision process, even though that interaction was not strictly additive. It is worth noting that Matin's finding would seem to validate Pirenne's equation as the proper baseline for measuring neural summation, since that equation predicts the performance at long ISIs, where the flashes might reasonably be assumed to be independent. Thorn and Boynton (1974), however, found Pirenne's equation to be a poor predictor of their empirical measures of probability summation, although they, too, found strong evidence for neural summation of signals in simple detection of lights.

Westendorf and Fox (1974) and Cohn and Lasley (1976) have studied binocular interactions in detecting combinations of flashed light increments and decrements. The former authors found that binocular combinations of the same polarity generate response probabilities consistent with neural summation but that stimuli of opposite polarity are detected as if the eyes were independent detectors. They, however, used only one luminance increment and one luminance decrement in their study. Cohn and Lasley (1976) measured isosensitivity for several combinations of increments and decrements. Their data, taken as a whole (see Figure 23.1), are inconsistent with both probability summation models, and energy integration models, that is, models that postulate that the responses to increments and decrements are added prior to binocular combination. Note that the latter type of model predicts that flashes of equal energy but opposite polarity will never be detected since their effects will cancel. This clearly does not occur; their findings suggest that equal but opposite flashes are somewhat less detectable than either monocular flash. Instead of either an energy summation or a probability summation model, the authors propose a two-process model, in which the sums and differences of signals from the two eyes are independently computed and are then combined at a central decision center by summing logarithmically transformed likelihood ratios from each channel. This model has the advantage of describing all their data with a single rule. But as it involves two independent binocular interactions (sums and differences), it is not clear what further theoretical advantage it has over the more general hypothesis that similar inputs summate while dissimilar inputs are treated as independent or inhibitory events.

Many recent experiments have also demonstrated a binocular advantage in the detection of contrast in grating stimuli (Arditi, Anderson, & Movshon, 1981; Bacon, 1976; Blake & Levinson, 1977; Blake & Rush, 1980; Blakemore & Hague, 1972; Campbell & Green, 1965; Lema & Blake, 1977; Levi, Harwerth, & Smith, 1979; Rose, 1978). Most of these studies have found a binocular–monocular sensitivity ratio of about 1.4 or $\sqrt{2}$ for gratings of the same spatial frequency and contrast and when the eyes are of equal sensitivity. Typical data, taken from Campbell and Green (1965), are shown in Figure 23.2. The 1.4 value is consistent with both integration and signal detection models discussed in Section 1.1. The binocular improvement disappears, however, when the spatial frequencies of the gratings differ in the two eyes by more than about ½ octave, suggesting

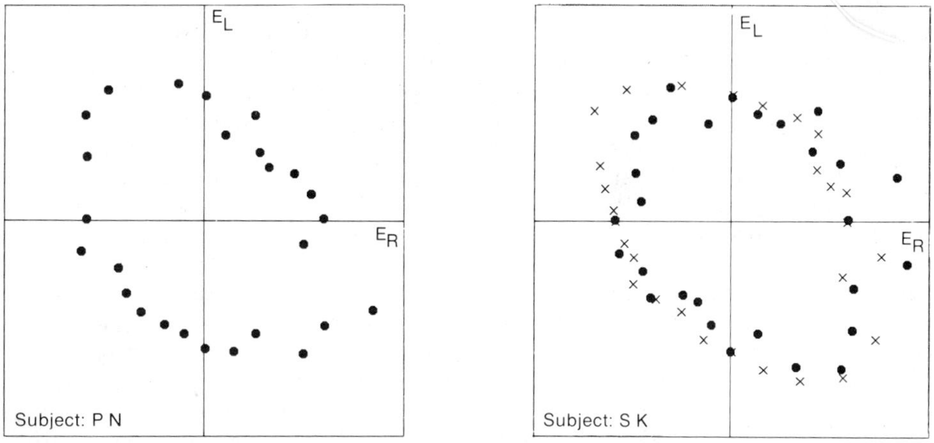

Figure 23.1. Isosensitivity for flashed binocular light increments and decrements. Note, E_L and E_R are luminance change energy, with positive coordinates indicating increments and negative coordinates decrements. Each closed circle represents two observer-controlled adjustments of pulse amplitude maintaining constant-amplitude ratio and polarity. Each cross in the data of *SK* is the median of seven adjustments. Flashes of the same polarity exhibit binocular summation, whereas those of opposite polarity do not and perhaps are even less detachable than when presented alone. (Adapted from T. E. Cohn & D. J. Lásley, Binocular vision: Two possible central interactions between signals from the two eyes, *Science, 192*. Copyright 1976 by the American Association for the Advancement of Science. Reprinted with permission.)

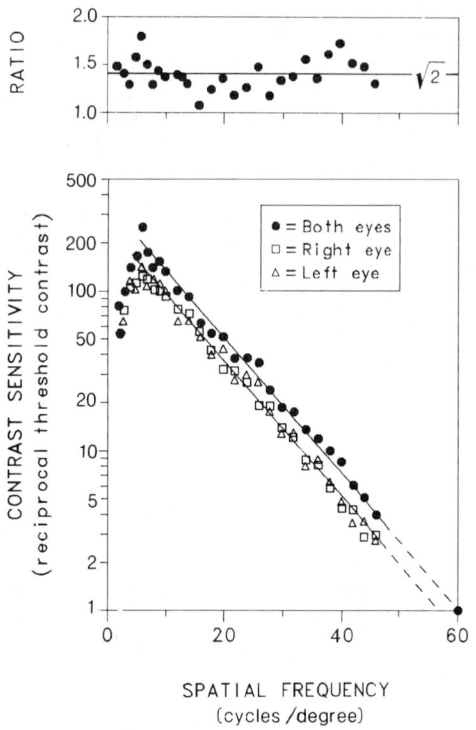

Figure 23.2 Comparison of monocular and binocular contrast sensitivity. The observer adjusted the contrast $(I_{max} - I_{min})/(I_{max} + I_{min})$, where I is luminance) of a sinusoidal grating until it was just resolvable. The straight lines are fit to the data by eye and are $\sqrt{2}$ apart in contrast. The upper panel plots the ratio of binocular sensitivity to mean monocular sensitivity at each spatial frequency. (From F. W. Campbell & D. G. Green, Monocular versus binocular visual acuity, *Nature, 208*. Copyright 1965 by Macmillan Journals, Ltd. Reprinted with permission.)

that binocular summation operates on or subsequent to the outputs of size-tuned mechanisms.

1.3. Similarity Requirements for Neural Binocular Summation

The experiments discussed thus far suggest several requirements for demonstrating the superiority of binocular over monocular stimuli in the two retinas, at least at threshold. The stimuli must be presented in spatial correspondence in the two retinas, in temporal correspondence within about 100 msec, and must have similar size or spatial frequency. Recent experiments have revealed other interesting similarity requirements.

Westendorf and Fox (1975), for example, found that binocular probabilities for the detection of flashed rectangles were at the level of probability summation (two-state model) when the rectangles were oriented orthogonally in the two eyes but were significantly better than that when the rectangles were presented at the same orientation. Similarly, Blake and Levinson (1977) found significantly lower binocular thresholds for detecting contrast only when the orientations of the grating patterns in the two eyes differed by less than 15°. These results show that binocular summation is orientation selective and are consistent with the idea that signals that add binocularly are selective for, or have previously been filtered with respect to, orientation.

Several investigators have studied binocular summation with stimuli that vary over time. As discussed in Section 1.2, a flashed luminance increment to one eye is independent of, or slightly inhibits detection of a flashed luminance decrement to, the other eye, at least at the level of threshold detection.

Cavonious (1979), dealing more explicitly with the temporal resolution of binocular summation, presented continuously varying increments and decrements and measured binocular sensitivity to full-field flicker, with the fields flickering in phase or 180° out of phase in the two eyes. While in-phase flicker produced higher sensitivity than out-of-phase flicker, this phase dependence was most critical at low rates of flicker. This result explains why Sherrington (1904) failed to find evidence for binocular interaction: Sherrington's variable of interest was the critical fusion frequency, a measure which reflects only the high flicker frequency response. Rose (1978) and Blake and Rush (1980) found that binocular summation of contrast-modulated counterphase flickering gratings is greatest when the flicker frequency is the same in the two eyes. The latter investigators found this temporal frequency selectivity to be greatly diminished when high spatial frequencies were used; that is, a greater range of temporal frequency disparities between the eyes exhibited binocular summation with high spatial frequencies than with low spatial frequencies. Furthermore, they found that binocular summation with flickering low spatial frequency gratings required presenting the two flickering monocular patterns in the same temporal phase.

Arditi, Anderson, and Movshon (1981), using moving stimuli, found a marked enhancement of binocular sensitivity to low spatial frequency gratings that drift in the same direction in the two eyes. When the gratings drifted in opposite directions in the two eyes *or* were of high spatial frequency, binocular summation was greatly reduced or absent. Thus it seems that the binocular advantage also requires similarity of temporal properties (temporal frequency and temporal phase) and direction of motion in the two eyes, especially for low spatial frequency patterns.

There is some evidence that threshold binocular summation may not be uniform across the retina. Wolf and Zigler (1963) compared monocular and binocular thresholds obtained with the method of limits, for a 1° square test field positioned at 24 locations on a 10° circle centered on the fovea, under both scotopic and photopic conditions. Binocular thresholds were lower than monocular thresholds everywhere on the circle except along the vertical meridian, where binocular summation was found to be absent. Binocular summation could be obtained again either by slight displacement of one eye's target into the periphery or by using larger horizontally oriented rectangular targets that extended into regions peripheral to the vertical meridian. The authors offer a complicated hypothesis concerning the partial decussation of nasal and temporal retinal fibers along the vertical meridian, which has been criticized by Blake and Fox (1973) on logical grounds. Nevertheless, the effect is a puzzling one and deserves further study.

As discussed, stimulation of widely disparate retinal locations appears to produce only probability summation and, indeed, has been employed as an empirical measure of the effects of probability. This measure has intuitive appeal because large disparities produce diplopic images, which must in some sense be independent. However, if neural binocular summation occurs only with stimulation of corresponding retinal areas, it is of interest to know how close that spatial correspondence must be. Of particular interest is the relation between the region within which singleness of vision occurs and the region within which summation occurs. If single vision is mediated by peripheral binocular mechanisms that integrate activity from the two eyes, one might expect summation to occur only within that region.

Unfortunately, there are serious technical problems in conducting such experiments. First, the measured size of the region of single vision varies widely according to the method of measurement (see Section 5.2). Second, it is extremely difficult to control the vergence of the observer sufficiently to stimulate defined regions of the retinas with good precision. This is due both to fixation disparity (see Section 3.2.1.3) and to involuntary vergence eye movements. Nevertheless, Westendorf and Fox (1977), who measured the detectability of small light flashes, found evidence for neural summation with 6 min of arc disparity. While this value is within the range of some measurements of the region of single vision, they did not find evidence for neural summation at somewhat larger disparities (20 to 25 min). Blake, Martens, and DiGianfillipo (1980) and Harwerth, Smith, and Levi (1980) have obtained similar results using reaction time measures of binocular summation. On the other hand, Bacon (1976), measuring detection of sinusoidal grating patterns, which were either in phase or 180° out of phase in the two eyes, found that the gratings must be in phase for neural summation to occur. Bacon used 5 cycles/degree gratings that when 180° out of phase, produce 6 min of disparity. Since this is the same amount of disparity at which Westendorf and Fox (1977) found evidence for neural summation, these two observations would seem to conflict.

1.4. Binocular versus Monocular Suprathreshold Sensitivities

Although many years in the history of binocular summation were spent establishing the existence of genuine neural interaction between the eyes on the basis of threshold stimulation, the existence of binocular interactions above threshold has been largely undisputed since the time of Fechner (1861). Most attention has been directed to binocular brightness phenomena. Often in the literature, the collective phenomena are referred to as "binocular brightness summation," even though what is described is often more of an average of monocular brightnesses, rather than an increment in brightness resulting from binocular viewing. Recently, some investigators have begun studying binocular contrast interactions as well.

In this section, *summation* is used as it was in the previous section, to describe binocular responses that are more intense than the more intense of the two monocular responses. *Averaging* describes binocular responses whose intensity falls between those of the two monocular stimuli.

1.4.1. Suprathreshold Brightness Interactions. Fechner (1861) noticed that the brightness of the visual world is greater when only one eye is open than it is when both eyes are open and one eye's view is attenuated in brightness; this paradox accordingly bears Fechner's name. Thus even though in the latter case the visual system receives more light than it does in the former, the binocular view is somewhat dimmer.

The bulk of subsequent suprathreshold binocular brightness studies have focused not on this phenomenon but on how the brain combines brightness signals that are *not* extremely disparate. Specific issues are (1) the type of interaction (e.g., summation or averaging) and (2) the relevant stimulus dimensions on which that interaction occurs (e.g., luminance, brightness, discriminal responses).

The first of these issues concerns the question of whether binocular brightness can ever exhibit summation or whether it always falls between monocular brightnesses. For a broad range of binocular brightness combinations, the binocular percept is conveniently described as an average of monocular brightnesses. Indeed, even under conditions of extreme brightness disparity, as seen in *Fechner's paradox*, the binocular brightness is a compromise between monocular brightnesses. On the other hand, when monocular brightnesses are nearly equal, some investigators find that binocular brightness is slightly greater than the brighter monocular stimulus (Curtis & Rule, 1978; De Silva & Bartley, 1930; Engel, 1967, 1969, 1970; Fry & Bartley, 1933), while other investigators do not find this binocular brightness summation effect (Levelt, 1968) or find it to depend on experimental method (Engel, 1967).

Figure 23.3, taken from Levelt (1968), exhibits some of the basic binocular brightness phenomena. The stimuli used in this experiment were 3° circular patches presented against a black background. The observer viewed a comparison stimulus with patches of equal luminance in the two eyes and a test stimulus with unequal luminances in the two eyes. The luminance of one half-field of the test stimulus was fixed at some value, and the observer's task was to adjust the luminance of the other half-field until a match was found between the test and comparison stimuli.

The typical features of this "equibrightness contour" are evident in these data. First, throughout most of the curve, that is, when the difference between the luminance of the fixed component of the test pattern and the comparison stimulus luminance is not great, the data fit a straight line with a slope of about −1. This means that the binocular luminance that matches a pair of unequal luminances presented to the two eyes can be expressed as the average of those luminances. If those data fell on a straight line with a negative slope other than −1, as they often will because of individual differences, the binocular luminance can still be expressed as an average, but

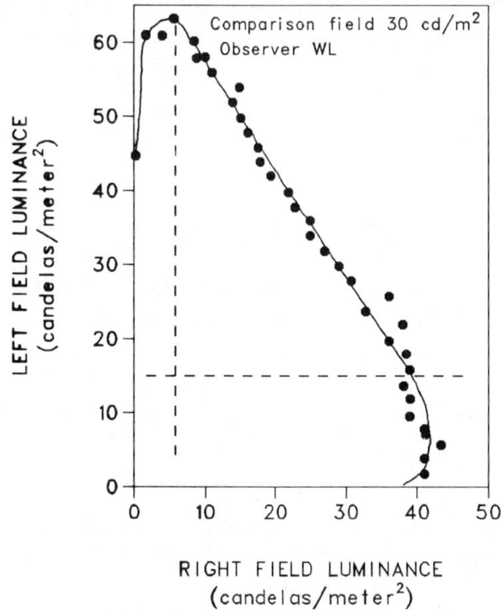

Figure 23.3. Binocular equal brightness contours. The observer adjusted the luminance of either the left (x's) or the right (o's) half-image of a 3° circular patch so that it appeared equal in brightness to a binocular 30 cd/m^2 comparison patch. The departure from −1 of the slope of the linear portion (often found in such curves) reflects unequal contributions of the two eyes in the binocular brightness percept. (From W. J. M. Levelt, *On binocular rivalry*, Mouton Publishing, 1968. Reprinted with permission.)

an average in which the monocular luminances are given different weights. According to Levelt (1968), such differences in slope reflect the effects of eye dominance.

Another important feature, referred to previously as Fechner's paradox, is evident at the nonlinear tails of the curves, where the two eyes receive very different luminances. Under such conditions, as one increases the ratio of luminances presented to the two eyes beyond some value (the points of inflection on the equibrightness contour), the binocular percept increases in brightness, so that the total of the two monocular test luminances, which match the comparison stimulus, is smaller than elsewhere along the curve.

Many models have attempted to account for such data. Among them are models that as in Levelt's earlier work, describe binocular brightness summation as a simple average of weighted monocular luminances. This model, while an attractive description of data obtained in such experiments, is implausible in that it is likely that binocular interaction involves quantities that vary nonlinearly with luminance. In addition, this model fails entirely to account for Fechner's paradox. Other models attempt to describe such data in terms of a vector sum of monocular brightnesses as estimated by Stevens' power law (Curtis & Rule, 1978, 1980; Engel, 1967, 1969, 1970). Such models describe binocular brightness as the length of a vector that is the sum of two monocular brightness vectors. In Engel's models, the monocular vectors are separated by 90°, where there is no interaction term between monocular brightnesses added. These models also weight each monocular brightness with coefficients reflecting the amount of contour in each monocular image, whose squares must sum to unity. Engel's models are thus actually averaging models, since binocular brightness can never exceed the greater of the monocular brightnesses.

Curtis and Rule (1978) have proposed a vector-sum model in which the angle separating the vectors is a free parameter falling between 90 and 120°. Since the vector sum does in this case contain an interaction term, they are able to predict both the small summation effects, which they and other investigators have found when the monocular luminances are nearly equal, and Fechner's paradox. In their model,

$$\Psi_{ij} = (\Psi_{Li}^2 + \Psi_{Rj}^2 + 2\Psi_{Li}\Psi_{Rj}\cos\alpha)^{1/2} , \qquad (12)$$

where Ψ_{Li} and Ψ_{Rj} are the monocular brightnesses and $2\cos\alpha$ is a weight representing the interaction component. When $2\cos\alpha$ falls between 0 and -1, the vector sum will be greater than either monocular vector when the two monocular vectors are near equal (predicting some binocular summation for equal monocular brightnesses) but will fall between the monocular vectors when they are disparate in brightness (predicting "averaging"). When one eye alone is stimulated, the binocular brightness will be equal to that of the stimulated eye, thus predicting Fechner's paradox as well.

Finally, several models describe binocular brightness as a centroid average of unspecified "monocular effects" (Schrodinger, 1926), of logarithmically transformed luminances (MacLeod, 1972), or of discriminal responses obtained by adding the stimulus luminance to a background luminance and raising this quantity to a parametrically estimated power (De Weert & Levelt, 1974). If Ψ_l and Ψ_r are the monocular terms that result from application of the appropriate transformation of each of these models and eye dominance is not taken into account, then

$$B = \frac{\Psi_l^2 + \Psi_r^2}{\Psi_l + \Psi_r} , \qquad (13)$$

where B is the binocular response. If Ψ is unspecified (Schrodinger, 1926), then this equation describes a circle or an ellipse. Both the MacLeod and the De Weert and Levelt models provide good qualitative fits to data such as those in Figure 23.3, although as Curtis and Rule (1978) point out, they predict unrealistically small binocular brightness summation effects found in other studies. Finally, when only one eye receives the patch and the other the black background, the binocular percept is predicted to be less bright than if both eyes receive the patch, since that eye's luminance must be increased to a value greater than that of the comparison stimulus (see Figure 23.3).

1.4.2. Suprathreshold Contrast Interactions. Since contrast is an intensive dimension underlying the performance of most visual tasks, it would certainly be useful to predict apparent binocular contrast from monocular contrasts and to know the rule governing binocular contrast combination. Do binocular contrast interactions parallel those of brightness? Is there an analogue to Fechner's paradox when grossly different contrasts are presented to the two eyes?

Such questions have been addressed in recent studies by Legge and Rubin (1981), Iverson, Movshon, Arditi, and Westendorf (1981), and Birch (1979). Figure 23.4, from Legge and Rubin, shows two sets of equal apparent contrast contours for gratings of 1 and 8 cycles/degree sinusoidal gratings, at several standard contrasts. The observer's task was to adjust the contrast of a pair of different binocular contrasts (test) to the same apparent contrast of a single contrast (standard) presented to both eyes. The contrast ratio of the test stimulus was held constant, and thus the adjustments correspond to movements along radii from the origins of the graphs. Now, if apparent binocular contrast was the simple average of monocular contrasts ($2C_b = C_l + C_r$), all the points would fall on the negative diagonal of the graph. Similarly, if apparent binocular contrast was determined solely by the greater of the monocular contrasts ($C_b = \max(C_l, C_r)$), the data would fall on horizontal and vertical lines at 100% of the standard contrast. From the data, one can see that an intermediate case holds: binocular contrast is more strongly but not wholly determined by the greater of the monocular contrasts. Similar results have been obtained by Birch (1979) and Iverson and colleagues (1981).

In the Rubin and Legge study, there is some evidence, for one subject (GR), for a contrast version of Fechner's paradox. This is exemplified by the connected points indicated in Figure 23.4, which shows that when left-eye contrast is low, an increase in contrast in either eye requires an *increase* in contrast in the other eye to retain the match to the standard. Iverson and colleagues (1981), using a somewhat different procedure, were unable to find evidence for Fechner's paradox in any of their subjects.

1.5. Other Types of Binocular Interaction

The preceding sections have described the concerns of vision scientists that have received the most attention in the binocular versus monocular literature. This section describes some of the other important areas of interest that have received less attention.

1.5.1. Acuity. Although there have been many comparative studies of monocular and binocular intensity thresholds,

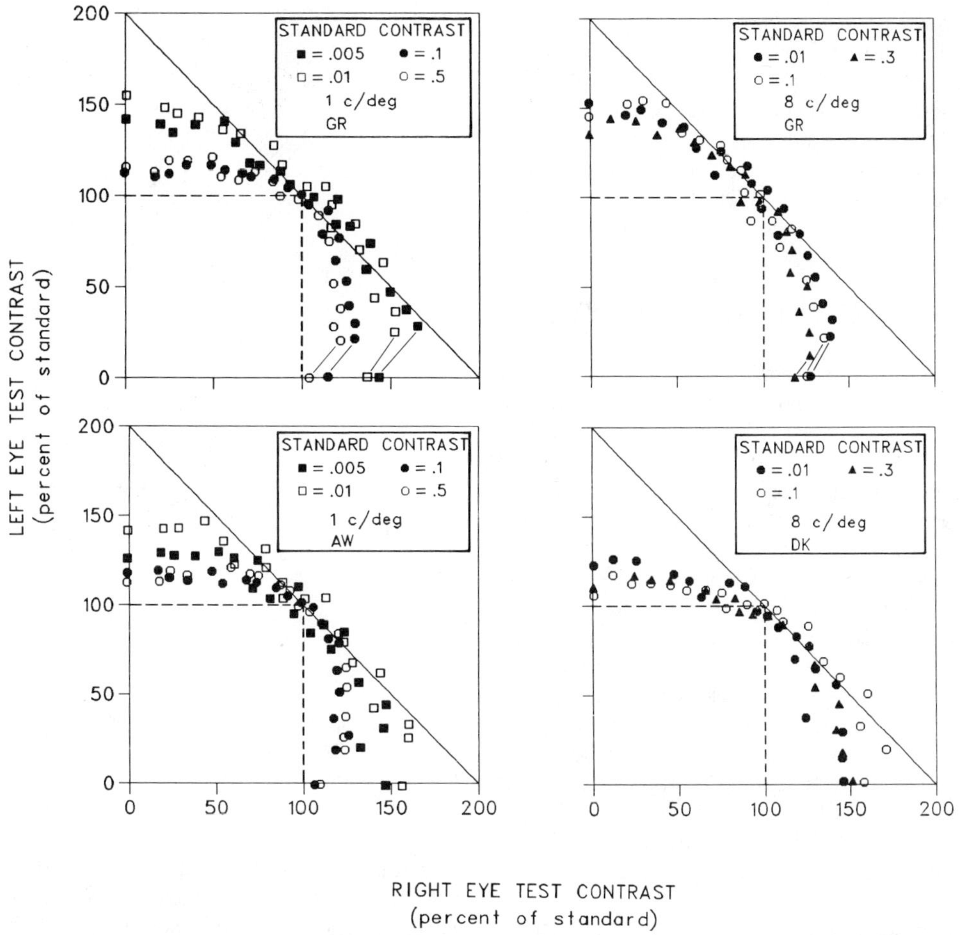

Figure 23.4. Binocular equal contrast contours. The observer was presented with sinusoidal gratings of equal contrast (standard) in the two eyes and a pair of gratings of unequal contrast in the two eyes (variable). The observer adjusted the contrasts of the variable pair so that the standard and variable grating pairs appeared equal in contrast. The contrast ratio was held constant so that adjustments correspond to movements along radii from the origins of the graphs. The data are plotted as percentages of the standard contrast to permit shape comparisons between the curves. The sets of connected points lying near the horizontal axis for observer GR suggest the possibility of a weak version of Fechner's paradox for contrast. (From G. E. Legge & G. S. Rubin, Binocular interactions in suprathreshold contrast perception, *Perception and Psychophysics*, 1981, *30*. Reprinted with permission.)

surprisingly little work has been done comparing binocular and monocular visual acuity. Although several studies (Cobb 1922; Ferree, Rand, & Buckley 1920; Kahneman, Norman, & Kubovy, 1967) have demonstrated binocular superiority in most individuals, Horowitz (1949) showed that some of this superiority may be accounted for by factors that may have artifactually reduced the measured monocular acuity. Specifically, he found that when artificial pupils are used and a homogeneous field is present in the untested eye of the same luminance as that of the tested eye, the binocular–monocular difference is greatly reduced. Nevertheless, he found that even under optimal conditions for monocular viewing, binocular acuity is slightly better than monocular acuity.

1.5.2. Form Recognition. Form recognition has been studied in the context of binocular summation by a few investigators. Eriksen, Greenspon, Lappin, and Carlson (1966) and Eriksen and Greenspon (1968) measured three-alternative forced-choice accuracy in identifying letters briefly flashed under monocular and binocular conditions.

For interocular flash intervals of 50 msec or more, binocular performance was at the level of probability summation (two-state model), while for smaller intervals, binocular performance was significantly higher. Townsend (1968), using a more complex display composed of four-by-four matrix of letters containing one of two target letters, found no binocular advantage. Blake, Fox, and MacIntyre (unpublished observations described in Blake & Fox, 1973) have replicated both the Eriksen and colleagues and the Townsend results. They conclude that binocular superiority in form recognition tasks is confined to simple displays.

1.5.3. Reaction Time. Reaction time to onset of light flashes (Ueno, 1977) and sinusoidal gratings (Blake, Martens, & DiGianfillipo, 1980; Harwerth, Smith, & Levi, 1980) is consistently smaller under binocular viewing conditions than under monocular ones. The Blake and colleagues study found that a roughly 10% difference holds regardless of grating contrast, spatial frequency, or orientation and exceeds the probability level measured with empirical control conditions. The Harwerth and colleagues study, however, found large individual differences in suprathreshold contrast levels and found that horizontal gratings yield less binocular summation than vertical gratings. Given the results described in Section 1.2, the near-threshold results are not surprising. However, since reaction time may be a more relevant performance measure for many applications, further research into the possible dependence of suprathreshold summation on contrast, orientation, and individual differences would be most useful.

2. BINOCULAR SUPPRESSION AND RIVALRY

When very different half-images are presented to corresponding regions of the two retinas, the visual system usually reduces the visibility of one image. Usually the dominant image alternates from eye to eye over time, a phenomenon which is called *binocular rivalry*. *Binocular suppression* and rivalry usually go unnoticed under natural viewing conditions. But they demonstrate the existence of important underlying processes that may be operating constantly, for there is almost always a correspondence of grossly dissimilar half-images somewhere on the retinas, and yet we neither mix nor confuse half-images.

By definition, all objects in space not falling on corresponding points cast disparate images in the two eyes. When the disparity is large, objects may appear double (see Section 5.2); this is a geometric consequence of viewing a scene whose objects are widely distributed in depth. An equally important effect is that very different objects, with conflicting attributes, often fall on corresponding locations in the two eyes. Although we rarely notice this conflict, its presence is virtually ubiquitous in binocular viewing.

The geometry of binocular space thus presents the visual system with an enormous amount of conflicting visual information. There must be some means of resolving such conflicts. The mechanism underlying suppression is an obvious candidate, but it has most often been viewed within the theoretical context of single vision, as one designed to cope with very small disparities. Since with small disparities only a single image is noticed, it seems possible that only one eye's view of an object is visible at any one time. This is an alternative to the more popular view that the disparate images "fuse" into a single image. Regardless of its possible role of producing single vision with small disparities, suppressive mechanisms must certainly be important in resolving the gross conflicts of monocular visual information arising from objects well off the plane of fixation.

The most comprehensive single work on suppression, from both a scholarly and an experimental point of view, is that of Levelt (1968).

What, then are the important observable properties of binocular rivalry and suppression? Figure 23.5 shows the classic orthogonal grid stereogram with which rivalry may be demonstrated. When stereoscopically combined, the pattern, at any given instant, may appear to be composed of only one of the half-images, the other being suppressed. Over time, the two half-images alternate in phases of dominance or suppression, whose periods are on the order of 1–4 sec. This alternation, or rivalry, may occur in a piecemeal fashion throughout the pattern. In other words, suppression may occur locally, with parts of both half-images dominant in different parts of the binocular visual field (Hochberg, 1964). Piecemeal suppression tends to occur with larger patterns, while patterns subtending about 1° of visual angle or less tend to rival more or less as a unit. Hollins (1980) has found that high spatial frequencies rival in

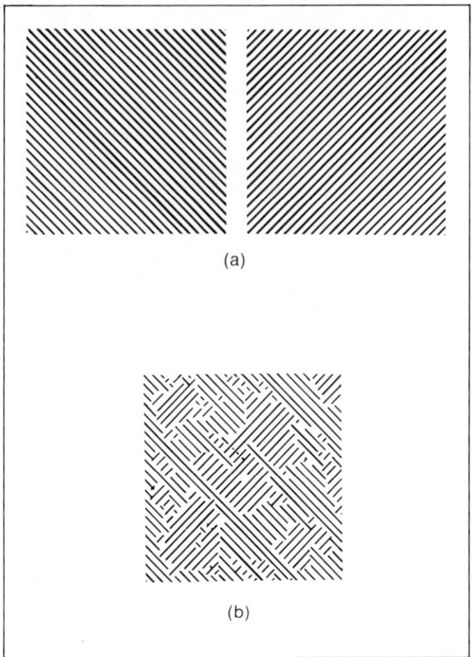

Figure 23.5. Binocular rivalry is the result of grossly dissimilar patterns of stimulation on corresponding regions of the two eyes. (a) Stereogram consisting of lines orthogonally oriented in the two eyes. Binocular viewing produces a percept similar to that in (b).

a unitary fashion less than low spatial frequencies and, also, that high-contrast patterns rival as a unit more than low-contrast patterns. Low contrasts and low spatial frequencies can make patterns more susceptible to the spontaneous fading of images that is thought *not* to be dependent on binocular stimulation (e.g., Blakemore, Muncey, & Ridley, 1973). Such fading may be responsible for some instances of what has been called "spurious rivalry" (Levelt, 1968). On the other hand, Rozhkova, Nickolayev, and Shchadrin (1982) have recently argued that monocularly observed spontaneous fading is itself the result of rivalry between the stimulated and unstimulated eyes.

In addition to contour orientation differences, differences in contour length, size, brightness, or hue may lead to suppression and rivalry. Even stimuli of equal luminance, if made to appear very different in intensity or hue through simultaneous contrast, may rival (Wallach & Adams, 1954). The phenomenal quality of rivalry induced with patterns identically contoured (i.e., with differences only of hue, brightness, or lightness) is that the binocular image takes on a lustrous appearance, with the luster randomly changing as one views the pattern. It is not surprising that large differences in nearly every dimension along which visual stimuli vary can induce suppression, since such large differences exist in the natural environment only when different points in space are imaged on corresponding retinal areas.

2.1. Methods of Studying Suppression and Rivalry

One of the problems encountered in studying suppression phenomena is the fact that large variations in the stimulus patterns used often have relatively small effects on the response dimensions associated with suppression. One does not, for example, produce total predominance of one eye's view if one eye is presented with a high-contrast patterned field and the other eye a field at contrast threshold (Blake, 1977). While various factors described in the following may influence the time course of rivalry and the relative sensitivity of the eyes, rivalry often seems not to be completely determined by conflicts in stimulation of the eyes; it seems to be at least partially driven by a random process that is independent of visual information altogether.

2.1.1. Time Course Methods. The pioneering efforts of Breese (1899, 1909) showed that stimulus factors can influence both the prevalence of one eye over the other (the duration of one eye's predominance relative to the other) and the average rate of alternation (the number of cycles of eye predominance per unit time). These variables are represented schematically in Figure 23.6. To use such measures, one typically presents the stimuli to the two eyes for a period on the order of a minute or two. The observer's task is to track, throughout the observation period, which of the two stimuli is visible. Responses may be given by button presses, and the entire time course of suppression thus recorded.

Breese (1899) found that alternation rate varied directly with field luminance and field area and inversely with blur of the pattern and retinal eccentricity. Thus factors that increase the amount of visual information available to the observer produce more frequent alternation. He also found that field luminance, the presence of contour, and contour motion all increase prevalence of one eye over the other.

Increased stimulus contrast also increases prevalence of an eye (Blake, 1977; Kakizaki, 1960; Levelt, 1968; Roelofs & Zeeman, 1919). This factor covaried with field luminance in the Breese study, and both Roelofs and Zeeman (1919) and Levelt (1968) found that luminance independent of contrast is of negligible importance in prevalence.

Some data from Blake (1977) are shown in Figure 23.7. The two panels are graphs of the same data. Blake points out an interesting property of rivalry also noted by Levelt (1968) and Fox and Rasche (1969): increasing stimulus "strength" (in this case, contrast) may have far more dramatic effects on the duration of suppression than on prevalence, with no fixed rivalry cycle time within which only the proportions of time each eye's view is visible vary. Rather, the amounts of time each eye is predominant seem to be independent of one another and depend only on the contrast in the suppressed eye. Fox and Rasche (1969) have tested this using statistical methods and have shown how this observation makes untenable any model of binocular rivalry that relies on reciprocal inhibition between the eyes. In addition, Fox and Herrmann (1967) have found that rivalry phases are sequentially independent as well.

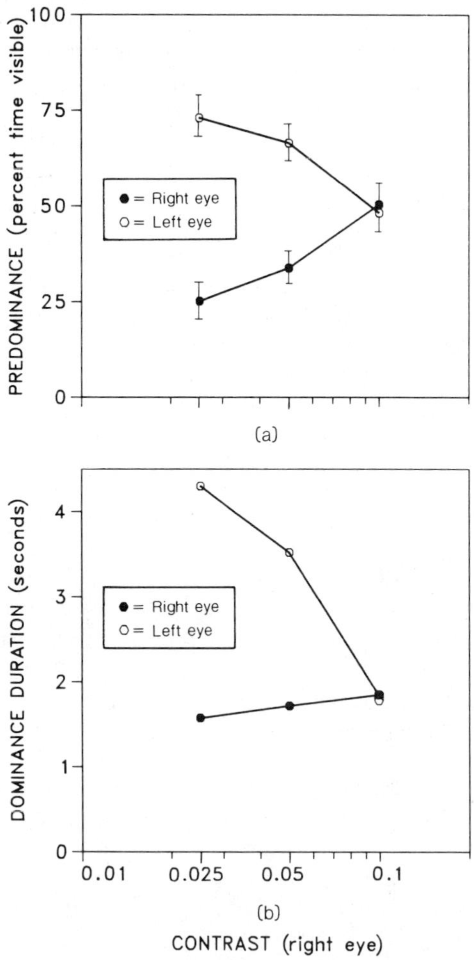

Figure 23.7. Prevalence of orthogonally oriented sinusoidal gratings presented to the two eyes, as a function of contrast. The right eye viewed a vertical grating of variable contrast (filled circles), while the left eye (open circles) viewed a horizontal grating of 0.10 contrast. (a) Plots the percentage of time each eye's view was visible (prevalence) during ten 70-sec observation periods, averaged over four observers; (b) shows average duration of predominance within rivalry alternation cycles, from the same experiment. In contrast to (a), (b) shows that predominance duration of the more predominant eye depended primarily on the contrast of the pattern in the suppressed eye. Contrast of the pattern in the less predominating eye did not affect that eye's predominance durations. (From R. Blake, Threshold conditions for binocular rivalry, *Journal of Experimental Psychology: Human Perception and Performance, 3*. Copyright 1977 by the American Psychological Association. Reprinted with permission.)

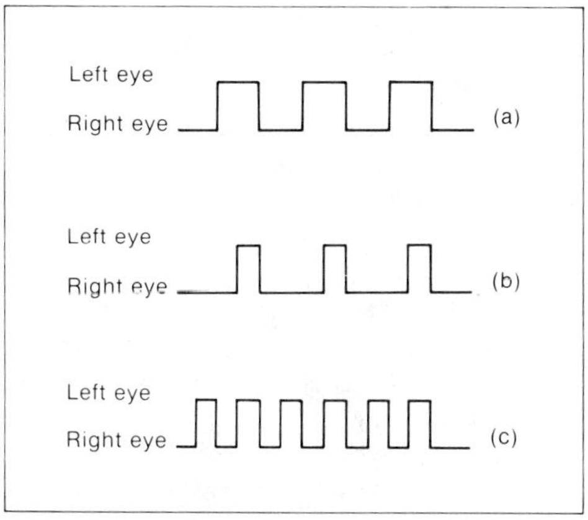

Figure 23.6. Hypothetical binocular rivalry alternation time courses. (a) Shows a regular pattern of alternation which, in practice, is rarely observed; (b) demonstrates higher prevalence of the right eye (percentage of time an eye's view is predominant), without any change in alternation rate (number of transitions per unit time). In (c) the rate of alternation is increased relative to that shown in (a), while prevalence is unaffected.

Several investigators (Alexander, 1951; Alexander & Bricker, 1952; Breese, 1899; Levelt, 1968) have found that prevalence varies directly with the amount of contour in the monocular patterns. While "amount of contour" is rather loosely defined in terms of Gestalt "figure strength" in Alexander's study and in terms of the number of lines in the patterns in the Breese and Levelt studies, this result may point to an important functional aspect of binocular suppression.

Assume, for a moment, that the amount of contour in a pattern corresponds to the amount of visible "detail" or, in analytic terms, to the amount of visible high spatial frequency content in the pattern. Thus the finding described above may be due to a general tendency for patterns with more high spatial frequency content to suppress those with less.

To see the functional value of this for the binocular system, consider the fact that images of objects located well *off* the plane of fixation have attenuated high spatial frequency content due to the eye's focus at the fixation plane, rather than the plane of the object. Binocular suppression of retinal images of such objects located off the fixation plane would be advantageous since such objects would presumably be located away from the locus of attention as well.

Thus far, the time course measures described have sought to describe the "steady state" of binocular rivalry. But when does rivalry begin? Anderson, Bechtoldt, and Dunlap (1978) varied the presentation time of rivalrous orthogonally oriented line stereograms and found that for presentations shorter than about 200 msec, both half-images were simultaneously visible, that is, observers reported a pattern of crossed lines. Although there was no distinct latency at which rivalry occurred, the authors estimate that the onset of rivalry takes between 200 and 400 msec. Similar results have been reported by Wolfe (1982).

2.1.2. Visual Sensitivity Measures. Another way to measure suppression, which has become popular in recent years, is to compare the threshold for a stimulus when the eye is in a dominant phase (and/or under nonrivalrous monocular conditions) with the threshold when the same eye is in a suppression phase. Such experiments often require the observer to monitor concurrently which visual pattern (eye) is visible (dominant) and perform another psychophysical task from which thresholds are derived. Alternatively, trials may be initiated by the observer's signal of a clear instance of suppression (or nonsuppression).

Wales and Fox (1970), for example, compared the threshold for test flashes superimposed on one eye's view of a rivalrous stereo display when that eye's view was suppressed with the threshold for nonrivalrous monocular viewing of that same half-field. They found that the difference in thresholds measured this way is on the order of 0.5 log unit, a rather modest effect when compared to the complete phenomenal disappearance of patently suppressed stimuli. Similar results have been obtained by Makous and Sanders (1978) and Blake and Camisa (1979). However, it should be noted that this amount of threshold elevation may not accurately reflect the amount of suppressive activity, for "monocular" stimulus control conditions do not preclude the possibility of significant interaction between a closed or uniformly illuminated eye and the nominally "stimulated" eye. Thus the choice of the appropriate baseline condition in such experiments is not yet resolved.

Other kinds of thresholds have been found to be higher in suppression phase than in dominance phase or under "nonrivalrous" monocular conditions, including recognition of letter forms (Collyer & Bevan, 1970; Fox & Check, 1966, 1972) and latencies for detection of motion onset (Fox & Check, 1968), sudden spatial frequency, and sudden orientation changes (Blake & Fox, 1974; and see Section 2.2).

2.2. The Nature of the Suppressed Stimulus

An experiment by Blake, Westendorf, and Overton (1980) has shown that when rivalrous orthogonal grating patterns are abruptly interchanged between the eyes, it is the initially dominant *eye* that remains dominant throughout the transition and *not* the dominant pattern. Furthermore, as reviewed in Section 2.1, binocular rivalry suppression seems to depress sensitivity to a wide range of stimuli. Taken together, these and other observations suggest that suppression acts upon a retinal area as a whole, rather than upon any specific set of stimulus dimensions to which that area is sensitive. But there is also some evidence favoring the idea that suppression can depress sensitivity somewhat selectively to certain aspects of the stimulus pattern.

For example, there are reports (Breese, 1909; Makous & Pulos, 1981) that orthogonally oriented red and green grating patterns presented to the two eyes may simultaneously produce a binocular mixture of colors and a rivalry of contours. In such cases, it seems that contour information alone was suppressed while monocular color sensitivity was unimpaired to the extent that it contributed to the binocular color mixture. However, binocular color mixture, when studied alone, seems to be subject to rather specific stimulus requirements, including long exposure time, uniform surround, small stimulus fields, equal luminances of the components (Thomas, Dimmick, & Luria, 1961), and the minimization of contour differences (Hering, 1861). Such specificities are probably in part responsible for Makous and Pulos's reported departures of colorimetric matches from phenomenal appearances of the binocular mixtures and for the large individual differences they observed.

Blake and Fox (1974) measured reaction times for detection of large changes in the spatial frequency or orientation of gratings made at the onset of suppression or dominance phases. They found, in support of the nonselective hypothesis, that when an eye is suppressed, the changes are detected only after the gratings return to dominance phase 2–4 sec later. When the changes occured in the newly dominant eye, reaction times were on the order of milliseconds. They also measured reaction times for detection of contrast increments and decrements under similar circumstances. In this case, they found that contrast decrements presented at the onset of suppression were not detected until dominance was reestablished, whereas contrast increments were detected almost immediately (and perhaps caused the termination of the suppression phase). This latter result supports the idea that suppression constitutes a reduction in sensitivity, since only an energic increment could disturb the suppression.

However, Walker and Powell (1979) performed a similar experiment and obtained results in quite direct contradiction to those of Blake and Fox. Rather than measuring detection latencies, they chose to measure the duration of the suppression phase. Phase reversal, spatial frequency change (1 octave), and contrast increments *and* decrements (0.065–0.7 and vice versa) all produced suppression phases with, on average, ⅓ the duration of suppression phases in which no stimulus change occurred. Thus the changes seemed to cause the termination of the suppression phase. This conclusion was buttressed by a second experiment, in which the authors found that phase reversals are not detected when they occur during the suppression phase but are easily detected when repeated 20 msec after the first stimulus change. Since the first reversal terminated the suppression phase but was not itself detected and the second reversal was detected, the authors conclude that the initially suppressed eye must have become nonsuppressed within 20 msec after the initial stimulus change. Further experiments are needed to resolve the differences between the observations of Walker and Powell and those of Blake and Fox.

Other experiments relevant to this issue are those that deal with informational cooperativity of rivalrous processes. For example, Whittle, Bloor, and Pocock (1968) found, in one of a series of experiments, that when vertical and horizontal contours rival, only one orientation tends to dominate at a time, even when both eyes contain both orientations. They hypothesize that contour elements that form a line, even if distributed across the two eyes, will tend to dominate synchronously. Such synchronies would be evidence that the rivalry process in one part of the binocular field "cooperates," or is dependent on both the orientation of contours and state of rivalry of a neighboring region. Whittle and colleagues, however, found no evidence that proximity of contours within an eye is by itself sufficient to produce synchronous rivalry.

Wade (1973) used similar stimuli but presented them as rivalrous afterimages. Under these stabilized retinal image conditions, contours in the same eye do tend to dominate synchronously regardless of their orientation, suggesting that the information content in the monocular images plays no role in suppression. Wade suggests that the Whittle and colleagues result is an artifact due to differences in relative frequency of vertical and horizontal disjunctive eye movements and the fact that only vertical and horizontal contours were used in the study. It would be useful to repeat the Whittle and colleagues study using oblique contours. But Wade's results were not unequivocal; he also found that lines of the same orientation did tend to rival synchronously, provided they were presented to the same eye.

A particularly puzzling aspect of suppression is it affects only monocular sensitivities, leaving the purely binocular stereoscopic function unimpaired (Kaufman, 1963). As shown in Figure 23.8, depth is apparent despite the fact that all contours in the stereogram are rivalrous. Thus even though at any one time each region of the stereogram contains visible areas from only one half-field, both half-fields contribute to stereoscopic depth.

In summary, it seems clear that suppression and rivalry involve the alternating modulation of sensitivity of the monocular images. It is not yet clear, however, whether suppressive mechanisms can operate selectively on any particular aspects of the stimulus, or whether they must act on all monocular sensitivities equally. Whatever the case, however, the observable modulation of sensitivity during the suppression process is very slight compared to the phenomenal disappearance and reappearance of portions of the visual world during rivalry.

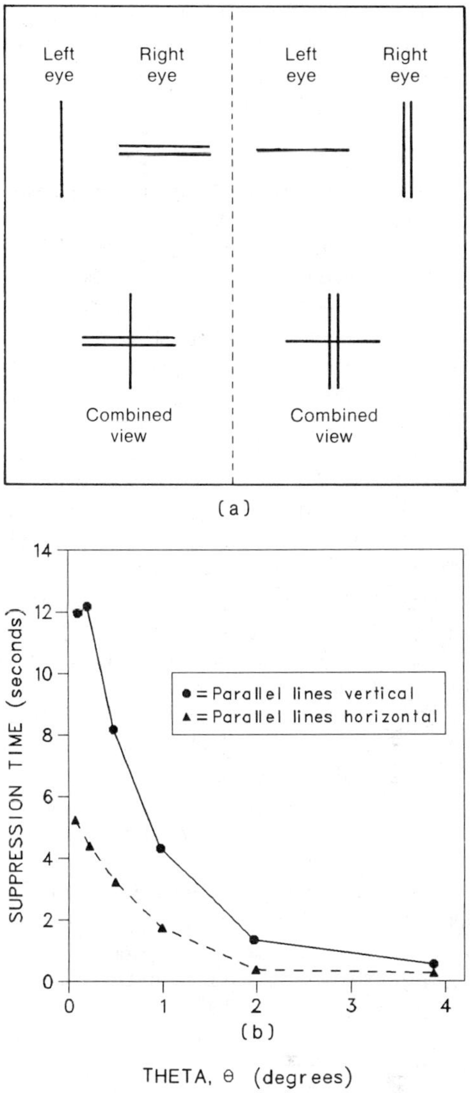

Figure 23.9. The spatial extent of suppression. The observer viewed two lines (vertical or horizontal) in one eye and a single line (of orthogonal orientation) in the other eye, as shown in (a). (b) Plots the average time in which the segment of the single line that fell in the gap between the two lines in the other eye was completely suppressed, as a function of the gap size (θ). The data are averaged over the eye containing the suppression lines and over 10 observers. Each point represents data from twenty-four 30-sec observation periods for each observer. These data indicate that the zone of influence of binocular suppression is about 1°. (From L. Kaufman, On the spread of suppression and binocular rivalry, *Vision Research*, *3*. Copyright 1963 by Pergamon Press, Ltd. Reprinted with permission.)

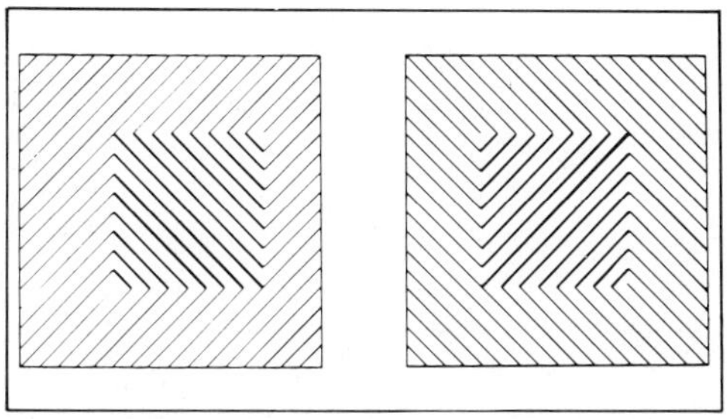

Figure 23.8. Rivalry does not destroy stereopsis. All the contours in this stereogram are rivalrous, yet stereoscopic depth is preserved. (From L. Kaufman, On the nature of binocular disparity, *American Journal of Psychology*, *77*. Copyright 1964 by University of Illinois Press. Reprinted with permission.)

2.3. The Spatial Extent of Suppression

As can be observed in the stereogram of Figure 23.5, suppression can occur in piecemeal fashion. At any one time the binocular image may appear as a continuously changing mosaic, a composite in which local patches from both eyes contribute. It is reasonable to ask how small such local patches may be. Or, as Helmholtz (1925) asked, given a suppressed point, how far does the suppression spread? Kaufman (1963) attempted to measure this spatial extent of suppression by presenting a pair of parallel vertical or horizontal lines in one eye and an orthogonally oriented signal line to the other eye, as depicted in Figure 23.9(a).

Observers were asked to press a key when the portion of the single line that fell between the parallel lines of the other eye was suppressed in its entirety. The results of this experiment, averaged over observers and 30-sec trials, are shown in Figure 23.9(b). Assuming that each of the parallel lines carries into the binocular view a zone of suppression around it, suppression measured this way seems to have appreciable spread of about 1° (corresponding to a gap size of 2°).

Another interesting result of this experiment is the finding that the measured spread of suppression is far greater in the horizontal dimension (parallel lines vertical) than in the vertical dimension (parellel lines horizontal). Kaufman's explanation for this, which requires assumptions about the temporal response of suppression mechanisms, is as follows: When a dominant contour slides over a suppressed contour, as is the case when the eyes move disjunctively, the effective spread of suppression is greater than if the eyes were stationary because of the sluggishness of the suppression mechanism relative to the velocity of the eye movements. The fact that horizontal disjunctive movements (vergence) are more extensive than vertical movements causes the measured spread of suppression to be greater horizontally than vertically. This hypothesis was partially supported by other experiments and demonstrations by Kaufman in the same study. One experiment demonstrated greater magnitude and frequency of horizontal than vertical disjunctive eye drifts with stimuli similar to those used in the first experiment, as measured by a modified nonius technique (see Section 3.2.1.3). However, the difference between vertical and horizontal disjunctive movements was not sufficient to account fully for the differences in suppression.

For now, questions concerning the minimum spatial extent of, and effects of eye movements on, suppression remain unanswered. It is not surprising that predictive theories of suppression and rivalry are also rare in the vision literature (but see Levelt, 1968; Sperling, 1970).

3. STEREOSCOPIC SPACE

Perhaps the most exquisite capability of the binocular visual system is its ability to evaluate depth relations among objects and surfaces in the world. This capability, called *stereopsis*, amounts to a detailed comparison of the two retinal images on the basis of parallax geometry; it yields a vivid and highly accurate perception of three-dimensional space. But, contrary to common belief, stereopsis is not necessary for valid depth perception. The world appears very much the same with one or with both eyes open, and those with good stereopsis are only marginally better at coping with the physical environment than those with only one functioning eye or with deficient stereopsis.

3.1. The Physical Geometry of Space as Viewed by the Two Eyes

This section examines the relations between the images projected onto the two retinas and the objects to which they refer in the physical world; these geometric relations provide the inputs from which the binocular system must extract depth information. This topic is complex and only a simplified analysis is offered; for a more detailed examination of binocular geometry, see Graham (1965), Ogle (1950), or Luneburg (1947).

3.1.1. Classical Definition of Disparity. Consider the relation between distance D from the interocular axis to a fixated point in space and the angle formed by the lines of sight of the two eyes, that is, the angle of convergence α, as diagrammed in Figure 23.10(a). It is obvious that for this case of *symmetric convergence*,

$$\alpha = 2\tan^{-1}(i/2D)\ , \tag{14}$$

where i is the interocular distance. For the case of *asymmetric convergence* shown in Figure 23.10(b),

$$\alpha = 2\tan^{-1}(i/2R)\ , \tag{15}$$

where R is the distance along the midsagittal plane to the fixated point, provides a reasonably good approximation for moderate deviations from the midsagittal plane. Graham (1965) describes a method for calculating the percentage error in this equation.

Figure 23.11 shows that with increasing distance to a point in space, less and less change in convergence angle is required to fixate that point. Because of this, the judgment of distance on the basis of convergence angle is of little value at and beyond the distance at which the observer can accurately resolve changes in that angle. Many investigations have found that, even at

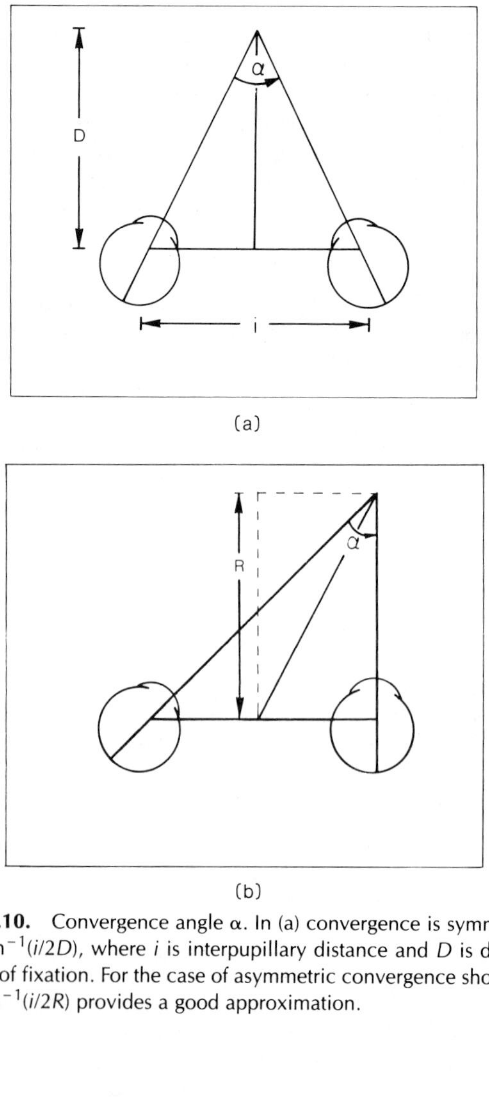

Figure 23.10. Convergence angle α. In (a) convergence is symmetric and $\alpha = 2\tan^{-1}(i/2D)$, where i is interpupillary distance and D is distance to the plane of fixation. For the case of asymmetric convergence shown in (b), $\alpha = 2\tan^{-1}(i/2R)$ provides a good approximation.

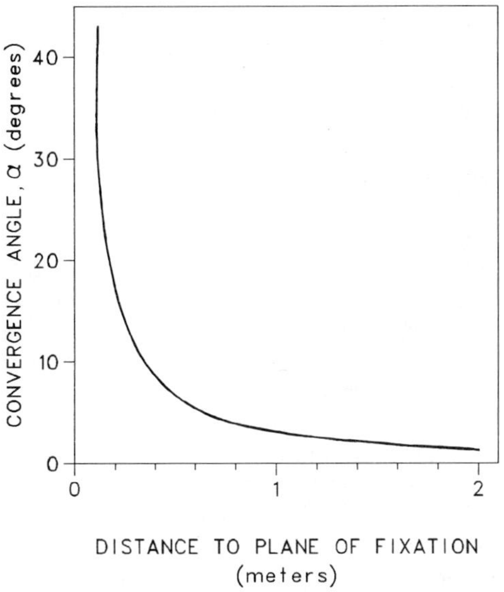

Figure 23.11. Convergence angle α as a function of distance to the plane of fixation, assuming an interpupillary distance *i* of 6.4 cm. As distance increases beyond about 1 m, convergence angle changes are minimal.

close distances, vergence information is a rather weak cue to the distance of an object (e.g., Foley & Richards, 1972; Gogel, 1961; Heineman, Tulving, & Nachmias, 1959).

Figure 23.12(a) shows the eyes fixating a point *f* at distance D_f. Also shown is point *g* at distance D_g from the observer. The difference in distance *d*, or depth between the points, is in a one-to-one correspondence with the difference in vergence angles $(\alpha - \beta)$ required to fixate the two points. This difference in vergence angles is called *retinal disparity*, since it is equivalent to the differences in retinal location between g_l and g_r on the two retinas, in units of visual angle. The difference of visual angles is usually the more convenient computation for most applications. Figure 23.12(b) is a stereogram that mimics the difference between the retinal images of the top view shown in 23.12(a), and if viewed in a stereoscope or by other suitable means, they will appear to have the same depth relations. Figure 23.12(c) shows the half-images of the stereogram physically superimposed.

Since relative depth *d* depends on a difference of vergence angles and since vergence angle itself is nonlinearly related to fixation distance, the function relating linear depth to disparity must contain terms corresponding to the vergence angles α, β required to fixate the two points in space. Thus

$$d = \frac{i}{2[1/\tan(\beta/2) - 1/\tan(\alpha/2)]}. \tag{16}$$

A more convenient formula for disparity in terms of linear depth and distance is given by

$$\delta = \frac{id}{D^2 + dD}, \tag{17}$$

where δ is in radians. This approximation is based on the fact that for small α, α in radians is roughly equal to tan α. Figure 23.13 graphs *d* against disparity δ for several observation distances.

Because the eyes are separated horizontally in the head, retinal disparities arising from depth in the visual world will, under most circumstances, be horizontal disparities. This means that stereoscopic mechanisms need compare only the horizontal coordinates of a point in space in order to compute its depth. It also means that disparities of objects may be reduced or eliminated with purely horizontal vergence rotation. Thus fixation of point *g* in Figure 23.12 may be accomplished by a simple convergence of the eyes through angle $\alpha - \beta$. Once point *g* is fixated, it is now point *f* which is disparate and by the same amount. One can see from this that the total retinal disparity in a visual scene remains constant regardless of eye movements. Vergence eye movements merely redistribute that disparity throughout the binocular "image." Vertical disparities also may exist due to slight vertical or torsional misalignment of the eyes, or more commonly, to the naturally occurring aniseikonia

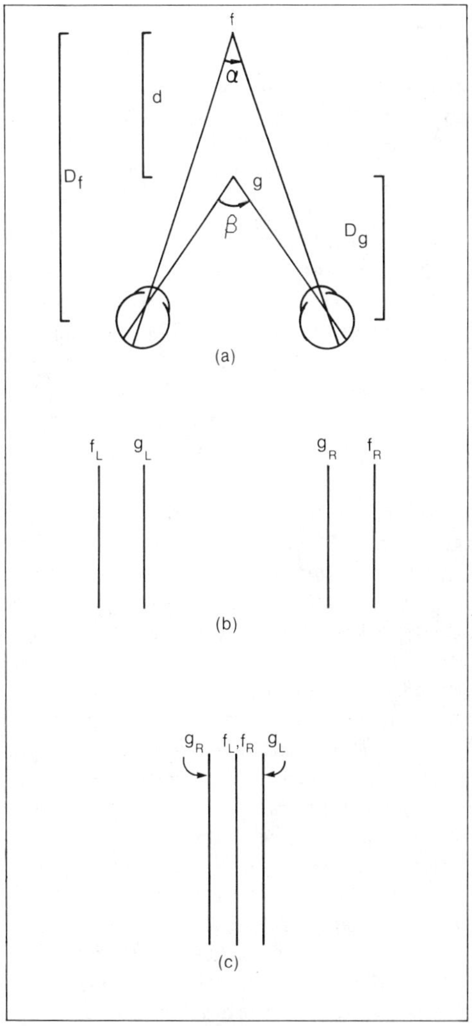

Figure 23.12. Computation of point-for-point retinal disparity. (a) Shows the observer fixating point *f* at distance D_f with linear depth *d* between *f* and *g*; (b) is a stereogram portraying similar depth relations; (c) shows the half-images of (b) superimposed. Disparity δ of point *g* is equal to the difference in convergence angles required to fixate the two points $(\alpha - \beta)$ shown in (b) or, equivalently, to the difference, in units of visual angle, between the half-images of *g* in the two eyes $(g_l - g_r)$ shown in (c).

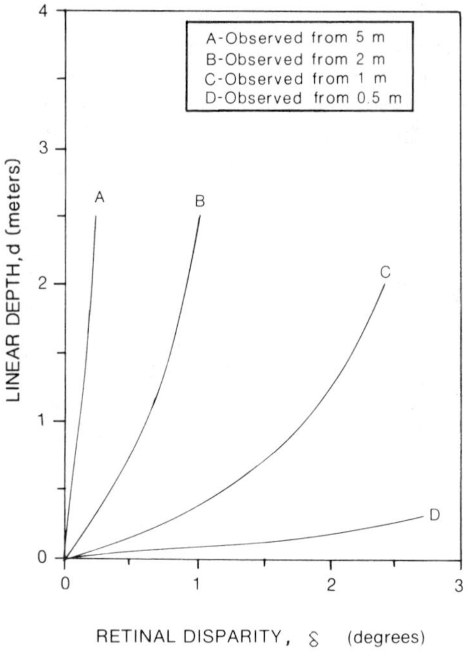

Figure 23.13. Graph showing how linear depth d is related to retinal disparity δ for several observation distances. A constant linear depth produces drastically different retinal disparities depending on the absolute distance to the object or objects in space.

in images of objects lying off the median plane (see Section 3.2.3). These are simply the vertical disparity component of overall magnification differences between the monocular images resulting from the object being closer to one eye than the other.

When an object is nearer than the fixation plane, the disparity is said to be *crossed* (in order to fixate the object, the eyes must cross), whereas an object more distant than the fixation point has *uncrossed* disparity (the eyes must uncross).

3.1.2. Alternate Definitions of Disparity. Consider the famous Wheatstone (1838) stereogram depicted in Figure 23.14(a) and (b). In (a), with points f_l and f_r fixated in the two eyes, lines g_l and g_r are disparate by amount $g_l - g_r$. In the binocular view, g appears farther from the observer than f. Figure 23.14(b) shows the half-images superimposed.

Although the classical definition of disparity is in terms of point-for-point horizontal differences between the monocular images, there are other useful ways to define disparity. One is in terms of the difference in separation between the lines in each eye (Wallach & Lindauer, 1961). This definition ($s_l - s_r$ in the figure) emphasizes the analysis of each monocular image prior to binocular comparison, in that separation between the lines is measured prior to the comparison and in that these separations are compared, rather than coordinates on the retinas. Another way to define this disparity is as the ratio of separations between the lines in each eye. What makes one definition of disparity better than another is how well the definition describes the actual coding of disparity by the visual system.

For example, one may consider the idea that monocular images undergo analysis through a set of size-tuned spatial filters prior to binocular comparison and that it is the outputs of such filters applied to each monocular image that are compared in stereopsis. Neurons well suited to perform such filtering are known to exist as early in the visual pathway as the striate cortex (Hubel & Wiesel, 1962). But since these neurons have receptive fields that are tuned not only to size but also to orientation, it may be more useful to consider both orientation and size comparisons of the monocular images.

Consider Figure 23.15(a), a stereogram consisting of two obliquely related dots, horizontally disparate in the two half-images. Figure 23.15(b) is a schematic representation of the physical superposition of those half-images. Fourier analysis of the patterns would reveal a prominent spatial component with spatial frequency $1/\tau$ in the left image and with $1/(\tau + \Delta\tau)$ in the right image. In fact, the spatial frequency spectra at all orientations except the horizontal are different in the two half-images; the right half-image spectra have energy at slightly lower spatial frequencies than the left half-image spectra. This disparity of spatial frequency, or pattern width, may in fact be a depth cue independent of the classical point-for-point disparity. In a similar way, the orientation spectra of the patterns are different in the two eyes for all fixed spatial frequencies (e.g., Ω). There is increasing evidence that disparities of spatial frequency and/or orientation may play a role in stereopsis independently of the classic point-for-point disparities (Arditi, Kaufman, & Movshon, 1981; Blakemore, 1970; Blakemore, Fiorentini, & Maffei, 1972; Braddick, 1979; Fiorentini & Maffei, 1971; Levinson & Blake, 1979; Tyler & Sutter, 1979).

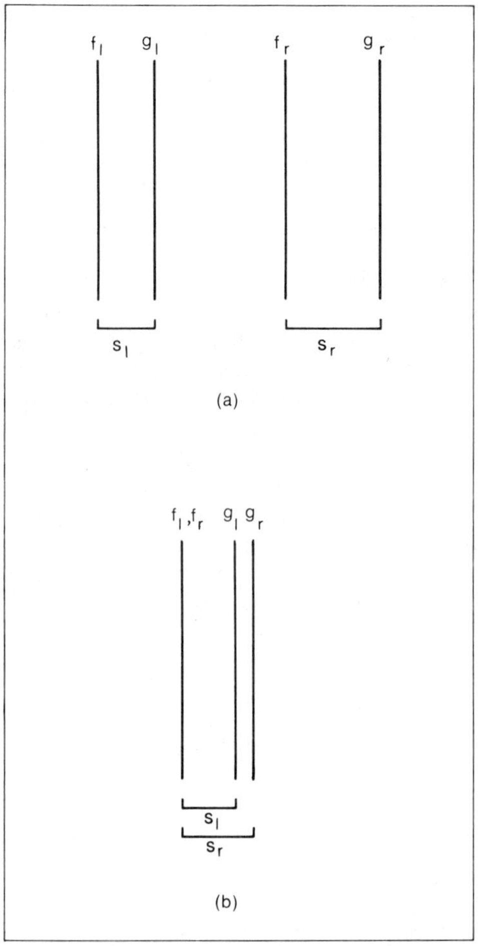

Figure 23.14. Point-for-point and some alternative definitions of disparity in Wheatstone stereograms. (a) Contains point-for-point disparity ($g_1 - g_r$). It may also be relevant to describe the disparity as $s_1 - s_r$ or s_1/s_r. (b) Shows the half-images of (a) superimposed.

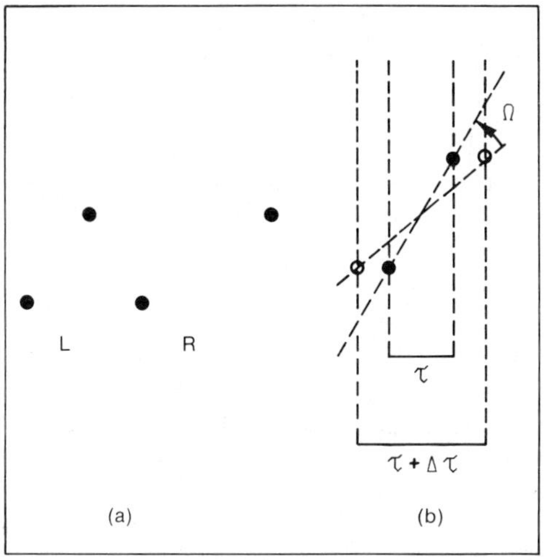

Figure 23.15. Harmonic spatial-analysis definitions of disparity. (a) A Stereogram consisting of two slightly disparate dots; (b) shows the half-images superimposed and illustrates disparity of spatial frequency $(\tau + \Delta\tau)/\tau$ at one orientation, and disparity of orientation Ω at one spatial frequency.

A disadvantage of modeling disparity coding this way is the fact that the relationship of these disparities to geometrically predicted depth is complex. For example, if the stimulus represented in Figure 23.15 were simply oriented differently, a different orientation disparity spectrum would be required to produce the same amount of geometrically predicted depth. A similar problem exists for disparities of spatial frequency. While such coding may not be economical, it is possible that such disparities give qualitative information about the direction but not the magnitude of relative depth.

3.1.3. The Theoretical Horopter. An issue receiving attention and promoting debate since the time of Aguilonius (1613) is the question of how to determine the locus of points in space having zero retinal disparity. This locus, called the *horopter*, has geometric, anatomical, and functional significance in that it attempts to link specific retinal distances with perceived distances in space. Assuming that the eyes are perfect spheres, and the optics perfectly spherical, and that the eyes rotate about axes passing only through their optical nodes, the horopter through the horizontal plane through the eyes, which contains the foveas, is a circle known as the *Vieth-Muller circle* (see Figure 23.16). It is the consequence of a theorem in geometry that states that all triangles erected upon a chord (the interocular axis) to points on the periphery of the circle have equal angles at the periphery of the circle (vergence angles). If the assumptions stated previously were accurate, the Vieth-Muller circle would demarcate the set of corresponding retinal points along the major horizontal meridian. In other words, taking the fovea as the origin of a Cartesian retinal coordinate system, the circle would define the locus of points along the x axis with equal effective values of x, in visual angle units. Unfortunately the ophthalmic optics of corresponding points are far more complex than the Vieth-Muller treatment would imply. Good historical accounts of horopter theory are given by Shipley and Rawlings (1970a) and Gulick and Lawson (1976).

The important point is simply that the theory of the horopter assumes that there exists some set of points in space which fall on points in the two eyes that share the same oculocentric (monocular) visual direction. Empirical studies of the horopter have shown that the Vieth-Muller circle is an inaccurate description of correspondence. Some of the inaccuracy may be accounted for by ophthalmic considerations: the location of the optical nodes relative to the rotation of the eyes and the displacement of the nodes with eye rotation (Fry & Hill, 1962). There are many refinements of the Vieth-Muller circle that attempt to account for the discrepancies without discarding the idea of a horopter reflecting fixed correspondence. A critical question is whether such errors can successfully be accounted for, or whether they point to a fundamental plasticity of correspondence. Another issue, seldom treated, is the shape of the horopter in horizontal planes through the eye other than that passing through the fovea, although there has been some study of the vertical horopter (see Section 3.2.2).

3.2. Perceived Space

One of the central tasks of a theory of binocular vision is to provide a rational and unified description of retinal correspondence. There are, in general, two approaches to this problem. First, one may assume that the binocular system has its own fixed geometry, which may or may not correspond to the ordinary geometry of the physical world, and then attempt to describe that geometry more fully. For example, basing his theory on lawful deviations of apparent space from the space of the physical world, Luneburg (1947, 1950) proposed that visual space is essentially non-Euclidean. The problem for him and later proponents of his theory (e.g., Blank, 1959; Foley, 1964; Hardy, Rand, Rittler, Blank, & Boeder, 1953) was to identify what were the geometrical characteristics of binocular space.

The opposite approach is to assume that the visual system constructs a space which is isomorphic with physical space. The problem for such theories is to provide an account of the mapping between ophthalmic binocular optics (i.e., the behavior of light impinging on the two retinas), on the one hand, and visual-physical space, on the other. But binocular ophthalmics are complex, and psychophysically measured binocular space may

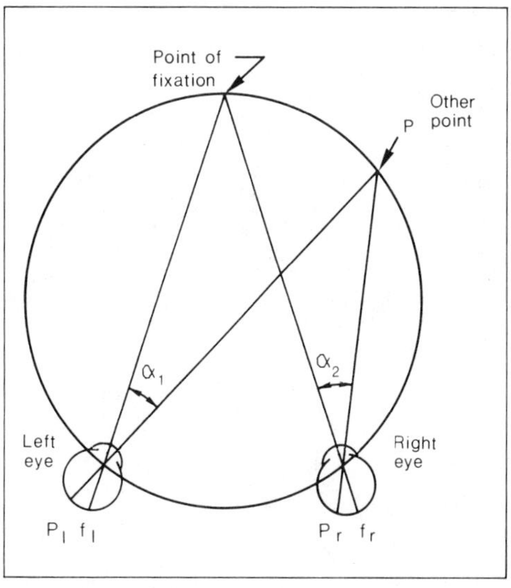

Figure 23.16. The Vieth-Muller circle. If the eyes are assumed to be perfect spheres that rotate about axes passing through their optical nodes and have perfectly spherical optics, all points in space with zero disparity will fall on this circle. This analysis applies only to the horizontal plane through the eyes.

differ from both physical space (see Section 3.2.1) and from more richly defined visual space. Thus most theories of correspondence fall into neither of the extreme categories. Rather, the task is usually to make empirical measurements of binocular space (i.e., the empirical horopter) and to account for those measurements with a theory of correspondence. It is not surprising that the history of the theoretical horopter is one of constant redefinition, from Aguilonius's (1613) original conception of it as the locus of points seen singly to Muller's (1826) geometrical conception, to the modern anatomical-physiological formulation as the locus of points having equal monocular visual directions.

3.2.1. The Empirical Horopter. Many methods for empirical determination of this horopter have been developed. These differ in difficulty of measurement and in theoretical emphasis. A more extensive treatment of this is given in Ogle (1950).

3.2.1.1. The Apparent Frontoparallel Plane. This criterion for mapping the horopter was first suggested by Hering (1861). The observer is presented with an array of vertical rods, each independently adjustable in depth. While fixating a central rod, the observer arranges the other rods so that they appear to lie on a frontoparallel plane. This method is simple and accurate, since it depends on stereoscopic localization. But, as Ogle (1950) pointed out, there is a fundamental ambiguity in the use of the apparent frontoparallel criterion, since the observer may unwittingly choose to adjust the rods to be equidistant from his subjective ego center, rather than as parallel to a coronal plane. Even worse, there seems to be more reason to expect that the locus of zero-disparity points *should* be perceived as equidistant from the ego center (i.e., circular) than as lying on a frontoparallel plane. It is not clear why Hering and other early theorists viewed this as a true horopter at all.

Typical measurements are shown in Figure 23.17. One can see that this empirically determined "horopter" differs considerably from the Vieth-Muller circle by varying amounts depending on the observation distance. This difference has come to be known as the *Hering-Hillebrand deviation.* Hillebrand (1929) showed that with an asymmetry in the dioptrics of the eyes or in the effective horizontal positions of corresponding elements in the eyes, the deviation should vary as a function of observation distance in the way that is observed (i.e., becoming flatter at intermediate distances and often becoming convex at greater distances). If Hillebrand's theory were to be both correct and complete, however, it would have to provide some explanation for why the apparent frontoparallel approaches the Vieth-Muller circle at close distances to begin with.

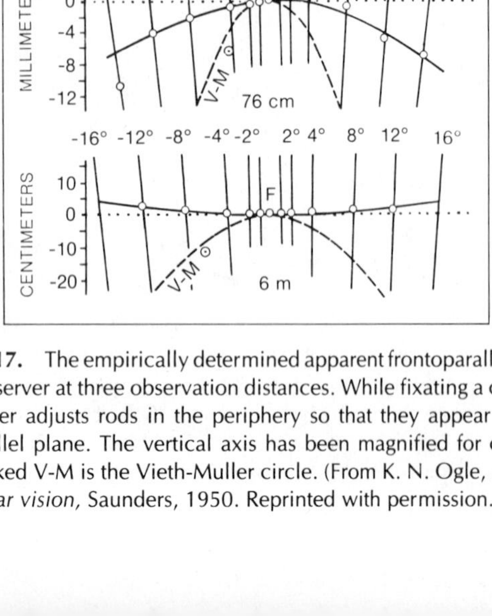

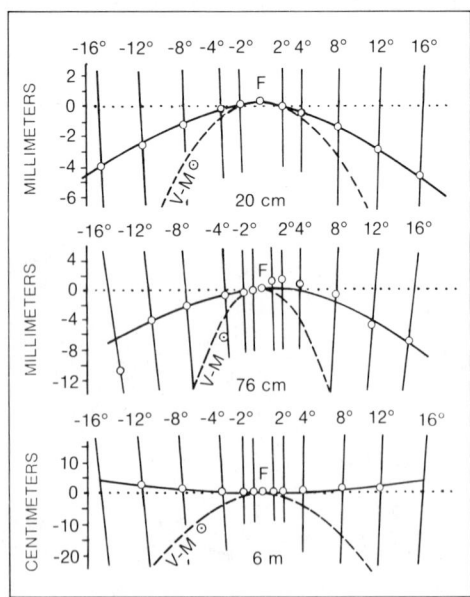

Figure 23.17. The empirically determined apparent frontoparallel horopter for one observer at three observation distances. While fixating a central rod, the observer adjusts rods in the periphery so that they appear to lie in a frontoparallel plane. The vertical axis has been magnified for clarity. The curve marked V-M is the Vieth-Muller circle. (From K. N. Ogle, *Researches in binocular vision,* Saunders, 1950. Reprinted with permission.)

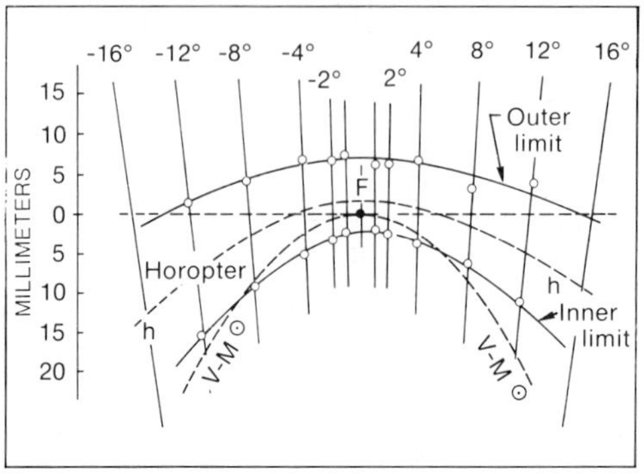

Figure 23.18. The empirically determined single-vision horopter for one observer. While fixating a central rod, the observer adjusts rods in the periphery to determine near and far limits of single vision. The horopter surface indicated is the mean of the curves fit to the near and far limits. The vertical axis is magnified by a factor of 2. (From K. N. Ogle, *Researches in binocular vision,* Saunders, 1950. Reprinted with permission.)

3.2.1.2. The Singleness of Vision Criterion. This determination is made by measuring the region of single vision as a function of retinal eccentricity and then using the mean values at each eccentricity to describe the horopter. Representative data are shown in Figure 23.18. This method has several weaknesses. First, many measurements must be taken to derive accurate estimates of each horopter locus. Second, the region of single vision increases and also becomes more difficult for the observer to judge, with increasing retinal eccentricity. Finally, it is best suited to highly practiced observers since the region of single vision diminishes greatly with practice (Arditi & Kaufman, 1978; Duwaer & van den Brink, 1981; Ogle, 1950).

3.2.1.3. The Nonius Criterion. This method, a variant of which was first suggested by Tschermak (1900), attempts to equate the oculocentric visual directions of points in the two eyes directly, that is, without the influences of stereoscopic depth or of single vision. Ames's "grid-nonius" apparatus for determining the horopter is shown in Figure 23.19. A fixation rod is visible to the two eyes.

In a nearby portion of the field, one eye views the lower portion of a test rod, while a gridlike mask allows only interrupted areas of the upper portion of the test rod to be visible to the other eye (the grid is used only for convenience to clearly distinguish the two eyes' views but is not a necessary part of the measurements). The test rod is adjusted in depth until the upper and lower portions appear aligned; at this position, the horizontal monocular visual directions are equated. Figure 23.20 shows horopter measurements determined this way. It can be seen in the figure that the Hering-Hillebrand deviation in the horopter determined this way is similar to that found with the apparent frontoparallel horopter criterion, although it is con-

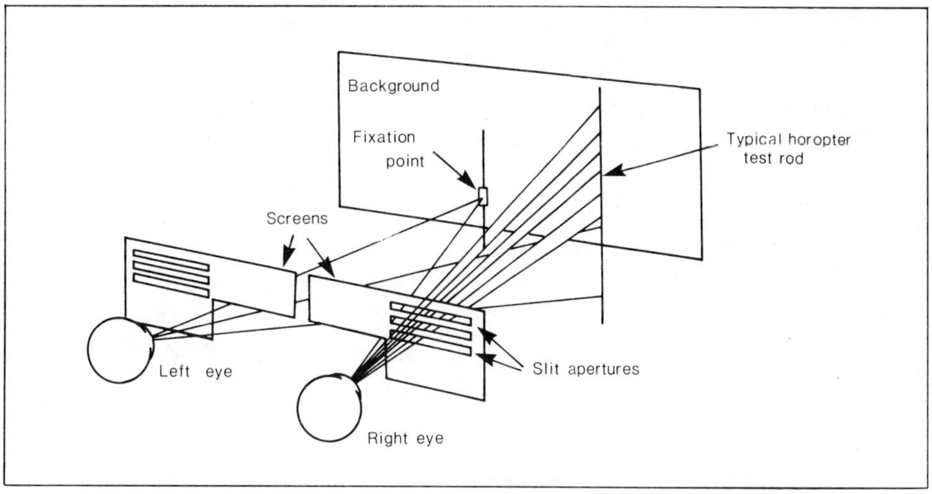

Figure 23.19. The grid-nonius apparatus for determining the nonius horopter. The lower potion of the test rod is visible to the left eye, while interrupted areas of the upper portion of the rod are visible to the right eye. Movement of the test rod in depth causes its "dashed" (right eye) and continuous (left eye) portions to become vertically misaligned. The nonius horopter is the locus of apparently aligned test rods. (From K. N. Ogle, *Researches in binocular vision,* Saunders, 1950. Reprinted with permission.)

siderably less, especially at close distances. A limitation of the nonius method is that reduced acuity in the periphery allows only the central 24° of the field to be plotted.

The nonius method is often used to determine what is called *fixation disparity* or *vergence disparity*. This is a slight overconvergence or underconvergence to the plane of fixation. It is usually determined by presenting two vertically aligned and vertically separated lines to both eyes to establish the normal plane of fixation. Then the vertical lines are presented one to each eye. If there is a fixation disparity, the lines will now be misaligned. The amount of fixation disparity is measured as the angular separation required to restore vernier alignment. Some degree of fixation disparity is normal; often it is the result of *heterophoria*, a latent tendency for one eye or the other to deviate. Ogle himself had discernible esophoria (tendency to overconverge); this, however, is not apparent in Figure 23.20 because of the scale of the drawing.

3.2.1.4. The Stereoacuity Criterion. This criterion defines the horopter as the locus of points in which stereoacuity is maximal. Implicit in this definition is the assumption that sensitivity to small depth displacements is maximal in the vicinity of zero disparity. To determine the horopter in this way is a lengthy and tedious task, and such stereoacuity horopters are not available. However Tschermak and Kiribuchi (cited in Tschermak, 1900) made some measurements and reported that the locus of maximal stereoacuity was coincident with the apparent frontoparallel horopter (see also Section 5.1.1).

3.2.2. Significance of the Horopter. As the locus of points in the binocular image with zero disparity, the horopter is a sort of reference contour, defining the locations in the third dimension where objects must lie in order to be (1) in the region of maximal stereoacuity and (2) not elicit fusional disjunctive eye movements. As such, it is a useful concept. On the other hand, most work on the horopter has been confined to a handful of highly specific cases. Almost all the experimental work has dealt with symmetric convergence in the horizontal plane with stationary fixation. Following are a few exceptions.

Ames, Ogle, and Gliddon (1932) made measurements of the nonius horopter with asymmetric convergence in the horizontal plane and found a smaller Hering-Hillebrand deviation than they found with symmetric convergence. But some years later, Herzau and Ogle (1937) found that the nonius horopter was invariant with symmetry of convergence.

Nakayama, Tyler, and Appelman (1977) made measurements of the vertical horopter, that is, the locus of points centered

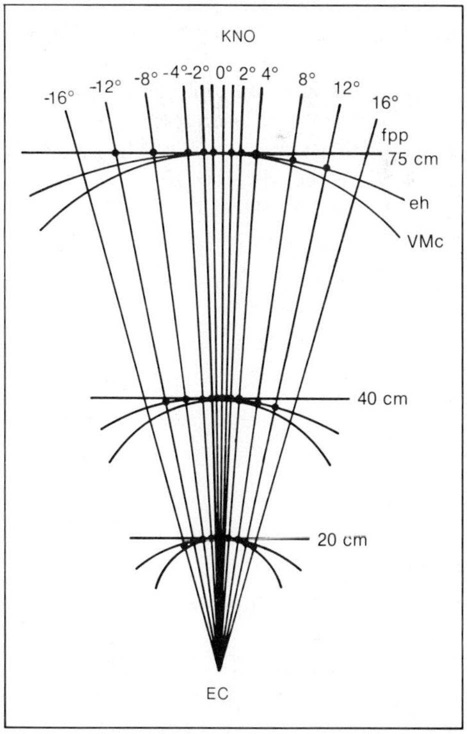

Figure 23.20. The empirically determined nonius horopter *eh*, obtained with the apparatus described in Figure 23.19, for one observer (K. N. Ogle) at three observation distances. Note, *EC* denotes the ego center, midway between the eyes of the observer, while *fpp* and *VMc* denote the frontoparallel plane and the Vieth-Muller circle, respectively. (From T. Shipley & S. C. Rawlings, The nonius horopter—I. History and theory, *Vision Research, 10*. Copyright 1970 by Pergamon Press, Ltd. Reprinted with permission.)

along the vertical meridians of the eyes with zero disparity. They used a method similar to the nonius technique, with the nulling of apparent motion between flashing lights presented one to each eye, as the psychophysical judgment. Their results, which are presented in greater detail in Nakayama (1977), showed that the vertical horopter is a straight line tilted in depth, passing through the point of fixation and a point on the ground directly below the eyes (see Figure 23.21). In other words, lines which are oppositely tilted off the vertical in the two retinal images are nondisparate. The authors, in addition, demonstrated that their results could not be accounted for by cyclorotational disjunctive eye movements. Their findings agree with the conjectures of Helmholtz (1925), who made only informal observations about the vertical horopter.

Shipley and Rawlings (1970b) compared nonius horopters with fixed and moving eyes and found that the Hering-Hillebrand deviation was less with moving eyes than with stationary eyes. They interpret this finding as an indication of a compensatory mechanism that interprets disparity for moving eyes in terms of muscle innervation (and, therefore, in terms of angles of rotation about the center of the eye). When the eyes are stationary, the disparity calculated is with reference to the optical center of the eye, which lies several millimeters anterior to the rotational center.

While the horopter has proved to be a useful theoretical and empirical concept, it has been applied with rather limited scope. As stated, rather little work has focused on determining the horopter for fixations off the horizontal plane and/or for asymmetric convergence. Furthermore, the horopter has never been described for nonzero disparities. What is the locus of, say, +10 min of arc disparity values? Is this "horopter" the same shape as the null horopter, and if not, what is the relation between the two? Horopter theory has been limited to the determination of a single correspondence at each retinal location. Rather, the traditional horopter could be viewed more generally as one in a family of contours, each corresponding to a different disparity. These isodisparity contours would more richly describe the structure of binocular visual space.

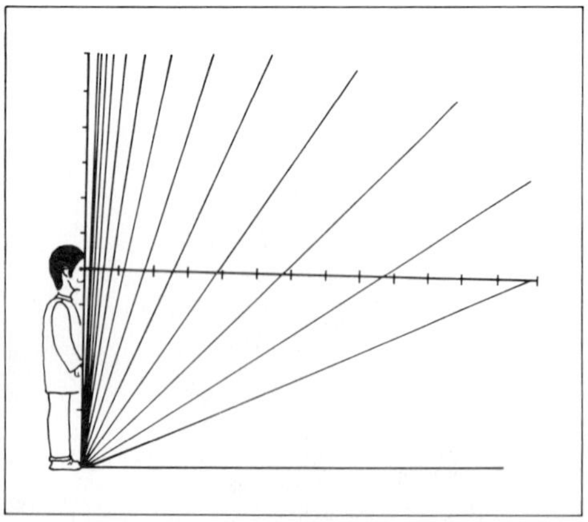

Figure 23.21. The vertical horopter is a straight line passing through the point of fixation and a point on the ground directly below the eyes. A line which falls on the horopter will cast images on the retinas which are oriented obliquely at opposite orientations about the vertical and which have increasingly crossed disparity in the inferior visual field. (From K. Nakayama, Geometrical and physiological aspects of depth perception, in S. Benton (Ed.), *Three dimensional imaging. Proceedings of the Society of Photo-Optical Instrumentation Engineers*, 1977, *SPIE 120*. Reprinted with permission.)

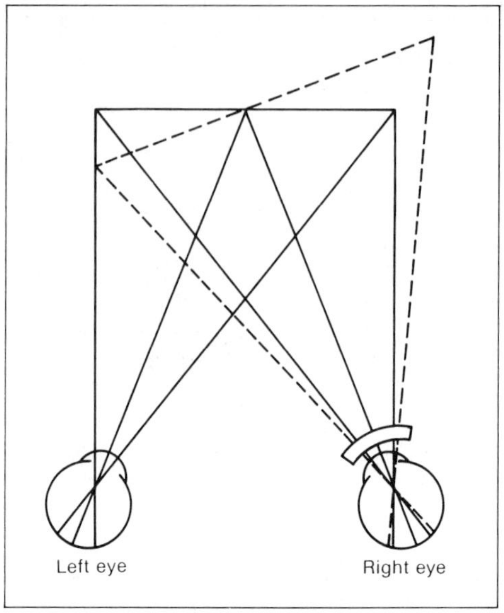

Figure 23.22. Horizontal expansion of one eye's image causes a frontoparallel plane to appear tilted because it produces the same disparities as would arise from a truly tilted plane.

3.2.3. Aniseikonic Effects. *Aniseikonia* is a clinical condition in which the eyes' images differ in size or shape. A normal and naturally occurring situation in which such differences exist is when an object is situated at close distance and off the median plane. Under such circumstances, the overall magnification of the image of the object is greater in the closer eye. Significant aniseikonia may arise in a variety of clinical conditions, but smaller amounts also occur in the "normal" population. Overall magnification differences in the monocular images may be found clinically as an artifact in the clinical correction of *anisometropia*, the condition in which the eyes differ in refractive power, or *aphakia*, the absence of a lens (usually resulting from surgical removal due to cataract). Severe conditions may of course impede the development of normal stereoscopic vision. But when stereoscopic function is intact, whatever aniseikonia is present may affect the horopter.

This is especially true when there are differences in magnification in the horizontal meridian. This may be appreciated by examining the consequences of magnification of one eye's image along the horizontal meridian with a meridional lens, such as a cylinder, as depicted in Figure 23.22. The lens horizontally expands contours in the right eye arising from a frontoparallel plane, mimicking the image that a truly tilted plane would present. Thus if this type of lens is worn over one eye, the apparent frontoparallel, and indeed any horopter, will be skewed. Ogle (1938) termed this the "geometric effect" since it follows from the fundamental geometric principles of binocular disparity. In fact, though, this artificial aniseikonia is geometrically no different from the basic stereoscopic phenomenon Wheatstone (1838) described, for the endpoints of the surface depicted in Figure 23.22 form precisely the same horizontally disparate configuration as that in the stereogram of Figure 23.14(b).

In fact, meridional magnification need not be in the horizontal meridian for this effect to occur. Any meridian of magnification except for the vertical will produce some residual horizontal expansion, even though less than the maximum. Thus it is only vertical magnification that produces no horizontal expansion and, therefore, does not produce horizontal disparities of this type. (Vertical magnification may produce other kinds of horizontal disparity, however. See Section 3.3.)

Overall magnification of one eye's image with lenses may also result in a horopter shift, although for small magnifications it is a smaller shift than that produced by horizontal magnification alone (Ogle, 1950). Ogle felt that overall magnification should result in no horopter shift for small magnifications; his reasons why this should be the case are based on his theory of the induced size effect described in Section 3.3.3. But it should be noted that overall image expansion produces both vertical and horizontal disparities. If the non-depth-producing vertical disparities are assumed to have no effect or only a small inhibitory effect on stereoscopic mechanisms, then horopter shifts resulting from overall magnification of one half-field are also predictable from the classical principles of stereopsis. It is evident, for example, that the stereograms depicted in Figure 23.23 produce the same magnitude of perceived depth, even though (a) is constructed with horizontal magnification and (b) with overall magnification.

3.3. Anomalous Instances in Which Stereopsis Occurs

Nearly all instances of stereoscopic depth may be accounted for by the single principle that, given normal stereopsis, horizontal disparities of similar object contours give rise to apparent depth. This section discusses a few exceptions to this rule and other anomalous examples of stereopsis. Undoubtedly, an understanding of these phenomena will shed light on the underlying mechanisms of binocular vision.

3.3.1. Panum's Limiting Case. Consider Figure 23.24(a), a stereogram consisting of a fixation line in both eyes and a single additional line viewed by the right eye alone. Analogous top views are shown in (b). Only the right half-field contains the image of line g because the fixation line occludes it. This stereogram was described by Panum (1858) as a limiting case because it contains the minimum number of lines that can cause stereoscopic depth. Other observations about the phe-

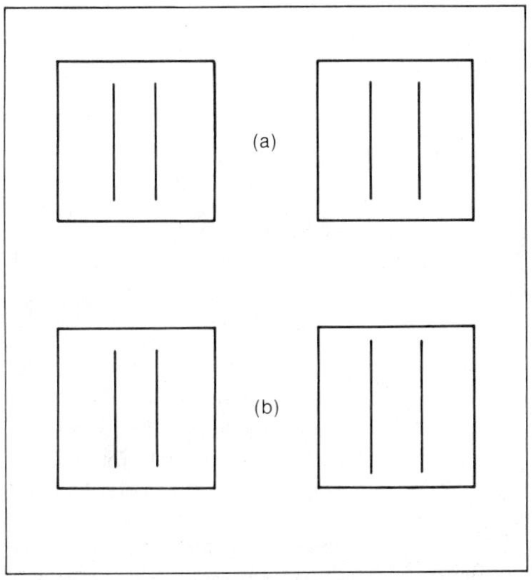

Figure 23.23. Wheatstone stereograms in which the right half-image has been expanded 10% horizontally (a) and overall (b). Apparent depth magnitude is the same for both stereograms, indicating that the vertical disparities have little or no influence on apparent depth.

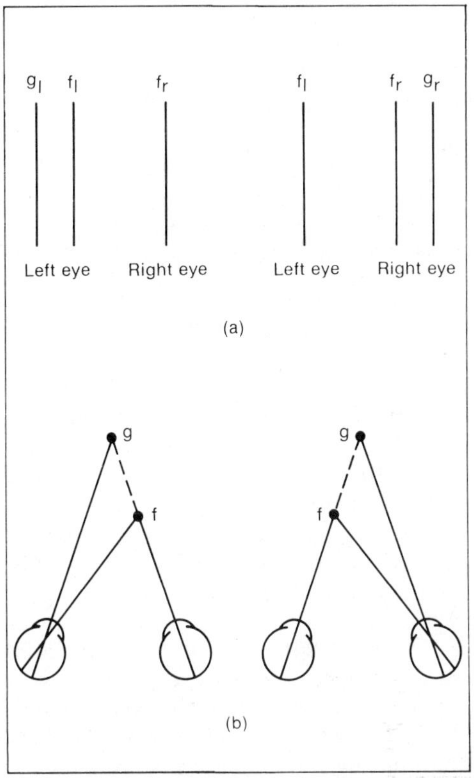

Figure 23.24. Panum's limiting case stereograms and their real-space counterparts. One eye views a fixation line and another line, the other eye only a fixation line. Apparent depth in stereograms of (a) is consistent with the situations depicted in top view in (b), in which the fixation line occludes the view of the other line in the eye whose view contains only the single line.

nomenon, as well as a study of apparent depth magnitude in the limiting case, are provided by Gettys and Harker (1967).

The limiting case is anomalous for two reasons. First, if it is a normal instance of stereopsis, in which lines in the two eyes are associated prior to disparity computations, then the uniocular line either has no counterpart in the other eye or *both* lines in the right half-field must associate with the single line in the left half-image. The possibility of multiple associations is a general problem for theories of stereopsis because if they are allowed to occur, then several depth values may be assigned to a single point at the same time, corresponding to all the points in the other eye with which it might associate. Additional mechanisms must then be invoked to eliminate these "ghosts."

A second reason why it is anomalous is the fact that the contour corresponding to the near object need not be one that could plausibly occlude the far object. Figure 23.25, for example, yields quite vivid depth, yet it is an impossible situation geometrically, since the fixation dots could not possibly occlude the entire line in the left half-image.

Kaufman (Note 2) has proposed a theory of Panum's limiting case, diagrammed in Figure 23.26, which requires two assumptions. First, he proposes that a uniocular element (i.e., one which has no counterpart in the fellow eye) will always be apparently located on the plane of fixation. A second assumption is that the presence of an adjacent element will tend to cause slight over- or underconvergence (fixation disparity), due to the eyes' attempt to bring both elements into foveal registration. Now, using the figure as an example, line g_r tends to cause a partial underconvergence because the right eye turns out to an

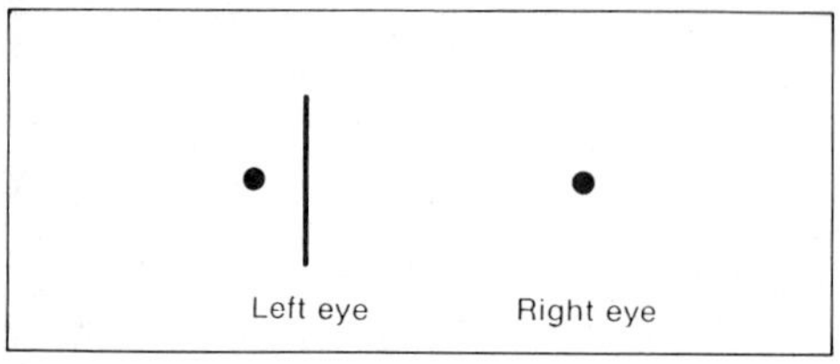

Figure 23.25. Panum's limiting case stereogram that has no plausible interpretation in terms of physical space, since the fixation dot cannot occlude the entire line (cf. Fig. 23.24.).

intermediate position between f_r and g_r. The depth of line f relative to the true fixation plane is determined by the retinal disparity of its half-images (a crossed disparity), and by the first assumption, line g will be apparently located at the true fixation plane. Kaufman's theory successfully accounts for the qualitative facts about the Panum's limiting case phenomenon, even the occasional reversals of depth observed by Gettys and Harker (1967) since the direction of depth perceived depends on the direction of the fixation disparity. Kaufman's theory predicts (see Figure 23.26) that g will be seen in front of f if the presence of g_r causes the left eye to turn inward, rather than causing the right eye to turn outward. An untested prediction of the theory is that perceived depth should be slightly less with the limiting case than is predicted on the basis of plausible visual space geometry. The theory predicts apparent depth magnitude to be determined by the amount of fixation disparity, whereas the only plausible geometric interpretation of the depth in stereograms such as figure 23.26(a) is that determined by the separation between f_r and g_r or, equivalently, the depth between the filled circle and the X in Figure 23.26(b).

3.3.2. The Pulfrich and Related Effects. If an object (e.g., a pendulum) moving in harmonic motion in a frontoparallel plane is observed with both eyes, but with a luminance-attenuating filter over one eye, the apparent path of the object will roughly describe an ellipse in depth, rather than the simple lateral path it actually follows. Within limits, the higher the density of the filter, the greater the apparent excursion of the object in depth. Fertsch and Pulfrich's (Pulfrich, 1922) explanation for the effect, diagrammed in Figure 23.27, was that the action of the filter is to introduce a constant time lag of a few milliseconds in the neural processing of the filtered eye. Since the object is moving, this time lag locates the object at a recent point in its path for that eye's view, rather than at its true location (without the filter). This spatial translation produces the same effect as a geometric disparity in the neural representation of the object and, hence, apparent depth. Recently, Morgan (1977) has suggested a mechanism for the delay of filtered images in the Pulfrich effect that is based on visual persistence.

A related phenomenon, referred to as the Mach-Dvorak phenomenon and studied by Harker (1967, 1973) and Lee (1970a), is the perception of depth arising from actually delaying the presentation of a moving object to one eye in binocular view. Since the object is moving, the delayed presentation causes a true retinal disparity between the monocular images. If the delay is short enough, however, the object is perceived as being simultaneously viewed by the two eyes but in stereoscopic depth by an amount predicted by the retinal disparity.

Most studies of the Pulfrich phenomenon have corroborated Fertsch and Pulfrich's explanation. Support is provided by the fact that an actual delay introduced between the half-images of this kind of moving display produces a similar effect, as in the Mach-Dvorak phenomenon. Moreover, the effects of actual time delay and attenuation of one eye's image are additive, in that the effects of attenuation of one eye's image can be canceled by introducing an actual time delay in the other eye (Julesz & White, 1969). Lit (1949) estimated time delays as a function of stimulus intensity from judgments of apparent depth excursion. More recently, Rogers and Anstis (1972) measured the interocular delay times required to null the effect as a function of stimulus intensity and adaptation over a 6 log unit range and have fit the Fuortes and Hodgkin (1964) exponential delay model of visual response to their intensity data. They also found a paradoxical reversal of the effect at extremely high intensities.

Lee (1970b) and Morgan and Thompson (1975) have demonstrated the Pulfrich effect with stroboscopic motion. The effect occurs even when the equivalent time delay is smaller than the interframe interval of the motion, which suggests that disparity may be computed using extrapolated portions of the apparent motion path.

Effects similar to the Pulfrich effect but using dynamic visual noise (such as the "snow" on a detuned television receiver) have also been reported. Tyler (1974, 1977) has shown that the

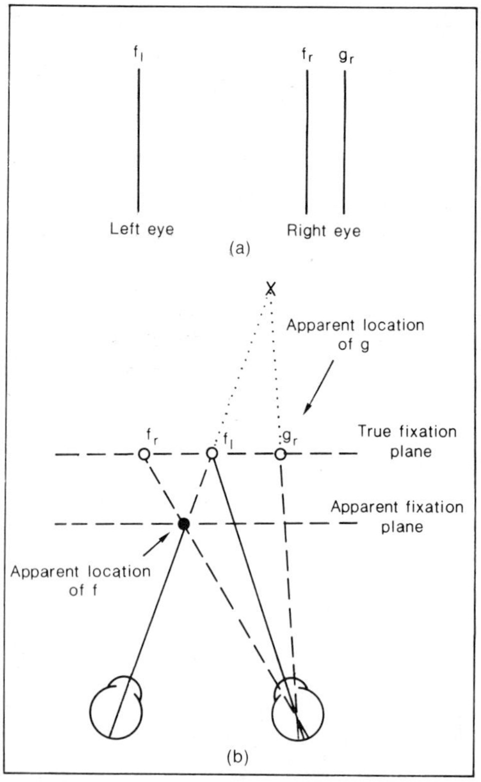

Figure 23.26. Kaufman's (Note 2) explanation of Panum's limiting case. (a) A typical Panum's limiting case stereogram; (b) a top view illustrating how fixation disparity can explain the apparent depth. The solid lines represent the lines of sight. Point f is a point which is observed with some fixation disparity induced by the tendency to try to fixate f in the left eye and g, the uniocular line, in the right eye (the right eye turns outward slightly). The line g, according to the theory, is apparently located at the true convergence distance. The filled circle and the x indicate the plausible locations of f and g in space that would cause this pattern of retinal stimulation. Note that the magnitude of apparent depth predicted by the theory is less than that predicted on the basis of plausible three-dimensional interpretation.

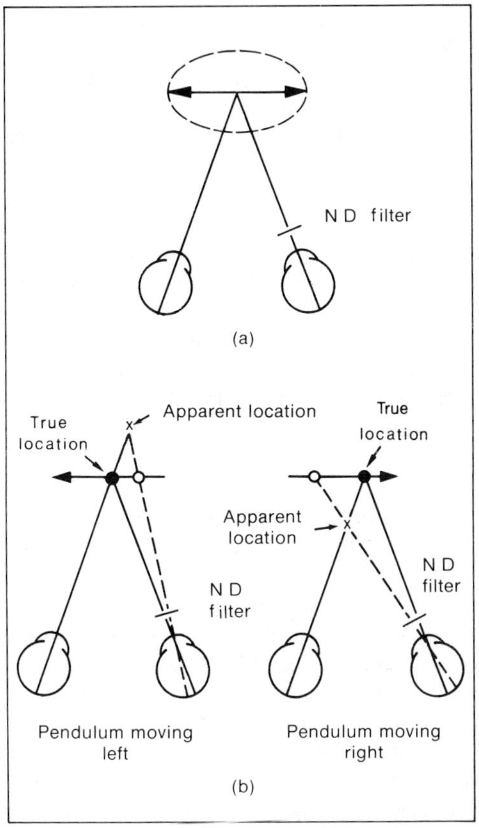

Figure 23.27. The Pulfrich phenomenon. (a) A neutral density filter placed over one eye while viewing a pendulum oscillating in harmonic motion in the frontal plane produces an apparently elliptical trajectory of the pendulum. (b) Pulfrich's explanation for the effect. The arrows indicate the direction of motion of the pendulum. When it is moving, the temporal lag produced by the filter causes the right eye's image (open circles) to appear behind its actual location and its location as seen by the left eye (filled circles). Thus the temporal lag produces a spatial lag, which, in turn, is interpreted by the visual system as retinal disparity.

random motion of such noise takes on a coherent motion in depth when viewed with a filter over one eye. Tyler's "random spatial disparity hypothesis" is similar to the Fertsch-Pulfrich explanation but includes statistical averaging of disparity computations.

Ross (1974) reported that a square region within a field of dynamic visual noise stands out in depth if the square is presented with an interocular delay. This effect occurs only with interocular delays of 70 msec or more and, thus, argues against a direct comparison with the Pulfrich effect.

3.3.3. The Induced Size Effect. Section 3.2.3 described the skewness of the horopter when a horizontal meridional magnifying lens is placed over one eye. If the lens is rotated 90°, so that its magnification is vertical, surprisingly, the horopter appears skewed in the opposite direction, as if a horizontally magnifying lens were instead placed over the *other* eye. This effect, termed the *induced size effect* (Ogle, 1938) has long been an enigma in the binocular literature, since it seems as if vertical disparities in the eyes' images give rise to stereoscopic depth. Ogle (1938, 1939a, 1939b) proposed that the geometric effect (horizontal magnification) and the induced effect (vertical magnification) were complementary and that the induced effect reflects the action of a mechanism opposing the distortions of space that would otherwise occur as the result of overall (vertical and horizontal) magnification differences in the two eyes.

There are many theories that account for the effect by invoking the idea that the vertical expansion of one eye's image *induces* horizontal or overall size changes in the neural representations of one or both monocular images (Julesz, 1971; Lippincott, 1917; Nelson, 1977; Ogle, 1938, 1939a, 1939b). It is these transformed neural representations, with induced horizontal disparities, that cause the apparent depth. Such theories require elaborate feedback circuitry and/or the addition of an entire stage of binocular comparison to explain the effect.

The more recent theory of Arditi, Kaufman, and Movshon (1981, 1983) requires no induced size changes whatsoever and suggests that the effect is misnamed. This theory attributes the apparent depth with vertical magnification to genuine horizontal disparities that exist between nonhomologous points on oblique lines and their vertically magnified counterparts. Such disparities are shown in Figure 23.28(a). Figure 23.28(b) shows the result of overall magnification of the oblique line. The point-for-point disparities disappear, but there are still both vertical and horizontal disparities associated with the different line

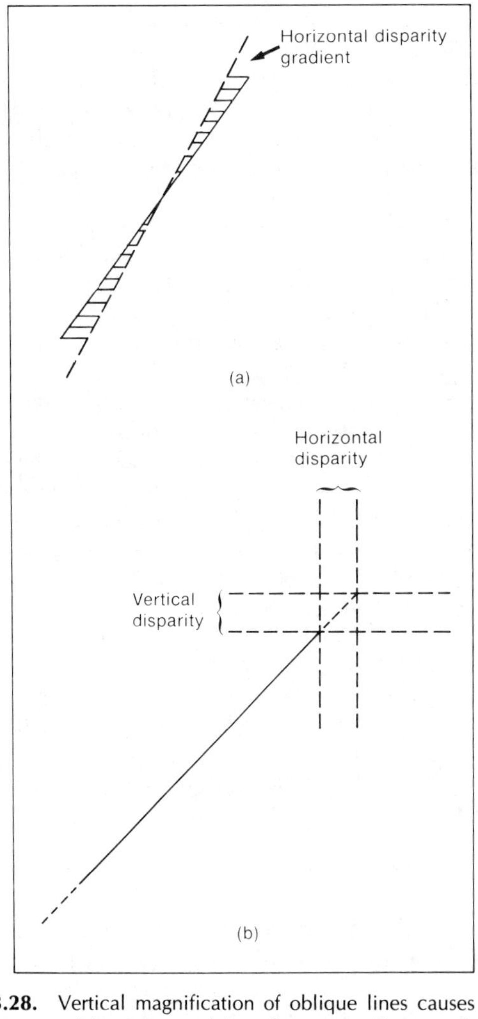

Figure 23.28. Vertical magnification of oblique lines causes horizontal disparity. (a) An oblique line (solid) and its vertically magnified (dashed) counterpart superimposed. There is a gradient of horizontal disparity along the length of the unmagnified line. (b) How overall magnification removes the point-for-point disparity along most of the length of the lines. There is still some horizontal and vertical disparity of the endpoints.

lengths. That horizontal disparity might account for the somewhat weaker tilt observed by Ogle (1950) with overall magnification of one half-image. As noted in Mayhew and Frisby (1982) and Arditi and colleagues (1983), this theory can account for the induced effect observed with random textures only with additional assumptions.

Other theories of the induced effect proposed that vertical image size differences are used as a cue in locating the midsaggital plane (Householder, 1943) or posit the existence of mechanisms that use the naturally occurring increase of vertical disparity along a frontoparallel plane with increasing eccentricity to compute absolute distance and the angle of gaze (Mayhew, 1982; Gillam & Lawergren, 1983). The induced effect, according to such theories, is a nonveridical response of these mechanisms to vertical magnification. Further study is required, of course, to ascertain whether vertical disparity information actually has an effect on apparent distance and/or apparent angle of gaze.

4. METHODS OF STEREOSCOPIC DISPLAY

There are many methods for displaying a visual scene in three apparent dimensions, but the most vivid exploit stereoscopic, as well as pictorial, depth cues. All stereoscopic methods share the feature that different two-dimensional images are viewed separately by the two eyes. These images contain disparities the same as those that might arise from horizontal parallax.

Any method of presenting a separate image to each eye, then, is a potential stereoscopic method. Indeed, since Wheatstone's time, hundreds of methods have been described. An excellent survey of these is given in Valyus (1966). The possibilities range from free stereoscopy methods requiring no instruments whatsoever to the more sophisticated *autostereoscopic* methods, such as holography, in which the visible pattern of light varies continuously with the angle of regard in the same way as it does with a truly three-dimensional scene, to volumetric displays, which are images actually projected into three-dimensional display spaces. Because of space limitations, only the simplest popular methods and concepts of binocular image segregation are considered here. Okoshi (1976), however, provides an excellent discussion of the newer optical and electronic techniques for generating autostereoscopic images. A more readable but less complete source is Benton (1977).

The history of stereo displays is a fascinating one. Although Wheatstone (1838) is usually credited with the invention of the first stereoscopic instrument, Gregory (1980, 1981) has recently uncovered evidence that a stereomicroscope was built as early as 1677 by a French Capuchin friar named Cherubin d'Orleans. The history of these devices is beyond the scope of this chapter; the reader is referred to Gregory's discussions.

4.1. Free Stereoscopy

The simplest kind of stereoscopic presentation requires no special viewing equipment. The half-fields of a stereogram can be binocularly combined by increasing or decreasing the convergence angle of the eyes, as shown in Figure 23.29. This method, of course, requires an extra measure of voluntary control over vergence eye movements, but with some practice most observers can learn the technique and can view the stereogram demonstrations in this chapter.

To learn the "crossed eyes" method (see Figure 23.29(a)) start by placing a pencil or other suitable thin object on the page between the half-fields of a stereogram. While fixating the pencil, move it slowly in a straight line towards the bridge of your nose. As you do this, try to *attend* to the images on the page, even though you are maintaining fixation on the pencil. As your eyes increase convergence to fixate the approaching pencil, the blurred half-images of the stereogram will approach each other in the binocular view. When the half-images are in proper registration, you should see three squares. The flanking squares will be greatly disparate in the two eyes. The central square will be the one of interest; it is the binocular combination of the two half-images of the stereogram. At this point, the binocular image will probably appear blurred, since your eyes are accommodated for the distance of the pencil and not the page.

Note that the left-hand half-image will be imaged in the right eye, and the right half-image in the left. For this reason, the depth relations will be reversed in relation to their depth using the uncrossed method or a conventional stereoscope. That is, in terms of their disparities, near objects should appear far, and far objects near. The crossed eyes method is easiest to learn, especially for young people, whose accommodation can more effectively focus the images.

The uncrossed eyes method, as shown in Figure 23.29(b), is identical to the crossed eyes method except that the eyes must be converged to a distance more distant than the page containing the stereogram. It is perhaps more difficult to learn since the page occludes the "fixation pencil." This may be overcome by the use of a simple hand-drawn stereogram drawn on a transparent surface.

The uncrossed eyes method is perhaps preferable, since most published stereograms are printed with the intention that the left half-image will be viewed by the left eye and the right half-image by the right. Thus this method avoids the reversal of disparity that occurs with the crossed eyes method. But it may be more difficult to master, especially for the youthful eye whose accommodation tends more to focus at the convergence distance.

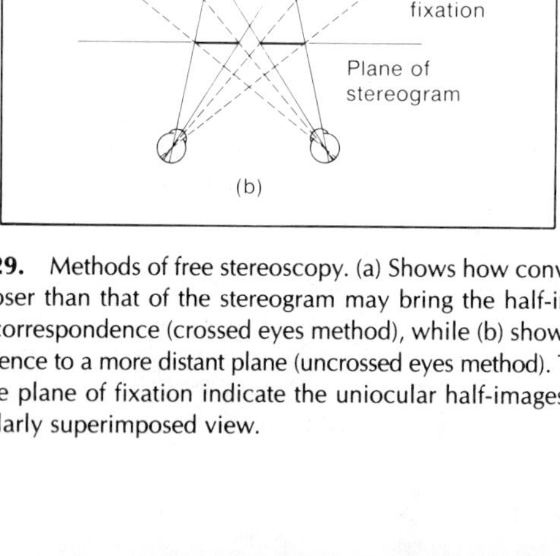

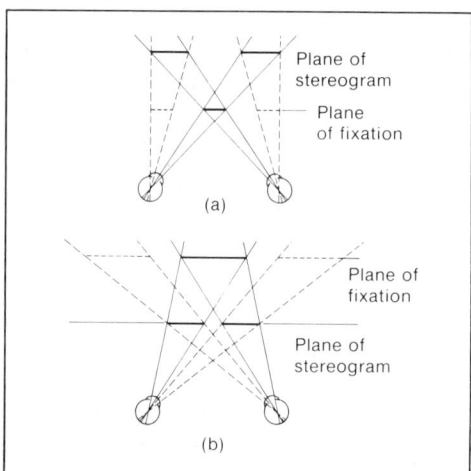

Figure 23.29. Methods of free stereoscopy. (a) Shows how convergence at a plane closer than that of the stereogram may bring the half-images into binocular correspondence (crossed eyes method), while (b) shows the same for convergence to a more distant plane (uncrossed eyes method). The dashed lines on the plane of fixation indicate the uniocular half-images that flank the binocularly superimposed view.

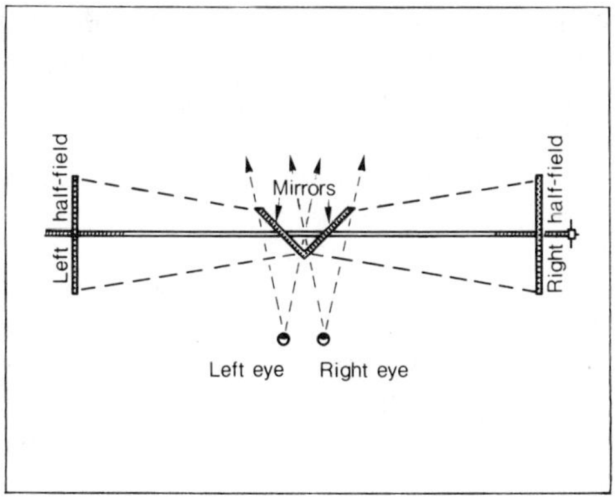

Figure 23.30. The Wheatstone stereoscope. Each half-field is viewed through a single mirror. Note that the images must be presented left-right reversed in order to depict true left-right order.

Note that with both free stereoscopic methods, there is a conflict between convergence angle and accommodative cues to distance, on the one hand, and disparity cues, on the other. This makes little difference in ordinal judgments of distance, but the most accurate renditions of three-dimensional scenes must use methods in which these cues are in accord as well.

Reversing the half-images of a stereogram that depicts a natural scene, by this or any other method, incidentally, gives what is called a *pseudoscopic* view of that scene, and a device that exchanges the left and right eye's normal views of the world is called a *pseudoscope*. In such viewing situations, the "monocular" cues to depth and distance are in conflict with the stereoscopic cues. Studies of pseudoscopic viewing have, in general, shown that simply reversing the eyes' views is not sufficient to reverse the apparent depth in natural scenes (Fineman, 1971; Schreiver, 1925), although there is some recent evidence that long-term pseudoscopic adaptation can reverse the relationship between disparity and apparent depth (Shimojo & Nakajim, 1981).

4.2. Stereoscopes

A stereoscope is a device that makes binocular registration easier than it is with free stereoscopy, through the use of mirrors, lenses, prisms, slits, or other means. Many different designs have been implemented; most incorporate combinations of the basic features described in the following sections.

4.2.1. Mirror Stereoscopes. Wheatstone's (1838) original stereoscope used a design similar to that depicted in Figure 23.30. Adjustment screws vary the stimulus to accommodation and the angular subtense of the half-images. Note that since only one mirror is used for each half-field, the image will be left–right reversed. Thus alphabetic material must be printed in reverse to be easily readable.

The addition of a second mirror for each eye remedies this problem, as shown in Figure 23.31. This kind of mirror arrangement is convenient to implement by arranging mirrors (preferably front surface to reduce light loss) on mountings that are adjustable in rotation and tilt. This makes calibration easier and allows small adjustments of horizontal and vertical vergence settings to suit each individual observer. This arrangement, in which cathode-ray tube (CRT) or other displays are used for the two eyes' views, is common in visual psychophysics laboratories. Even though it differs slightly from the original design, this kind of stereoscope is usually classified as the Wheatstone type.

4.2.2. Lenticular Stereoscopes. The principle of the simple lenticular stereoscope is depicted in Figure 23.32. The use of plus lenses supports parallel convergence, because the images of the half-images are formed at optical infinity. The sizes of the half-fields, however, are limited because their nasal extents can be no larger than half the interocular distance. Again, the accommodative stimulus can be varied by varying the distance of the half-images.

The Brewster stereoscope (Figure 23.33) overcomes the size limitation significantly by decentering the lenses. This effectively provides a base-out prismatic deviation, so that the half-images can be made larger. This prismatic effect, however, introduces considerable distortion of the images.

4.2.3. The Haploscope. The haploscope, schematized in Figure 23.34, is a special kind of Wheatstone stereoscope originally designed by Hering, who used it as a laboratory instrument. Its mirrors and stereo targets are mounted on arms that pivot about vertical axes, which pass through the centers of rotation of the two eyes. This design allows a great deal of flexibility in settings of symmetric or asymmetric convergence and a wide range of accommodation (through target distance). There are many specialized clinical varieties of the haploscope. Modern improvements have increased the adjustability of interpupillary distance.

4.3. Filter Separation Techniques

Among the simplest methods of generating stereoscopic displays are the filter separation methods. These techniques, commonly used in presenting stereoscopic information to audiences (e.g., three-dimensional movie and video presentations), are best described by example.

In the *anaglyph* method, the two half-images are printed in roughly complementary hues and then physically superimposed. The placement of filters of the same complementary hues over the two eyes is used to separate the images. Note that a contour printed in green will appear white through a green filter and black through a red filter. Similarly a target printed in red will appear white through a red filter and black through a green filter. Thus to present a dark contour exclusively to one eye, one covers that eye with a filter complementary to the hue the contour is printed in. To present a stereoscopic view,

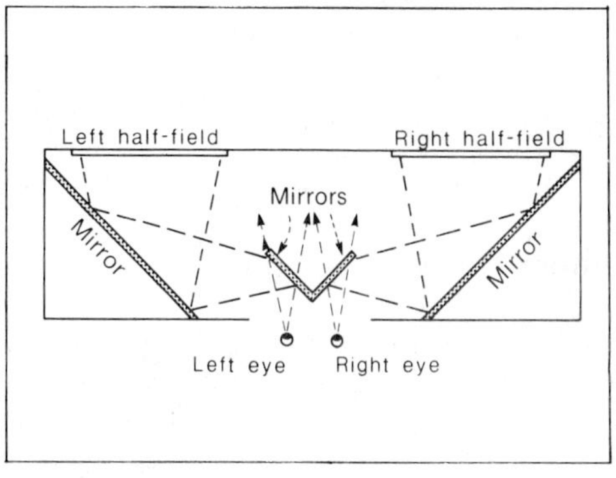

Figure 23.31. Modified Wheatstone stereoscope. The two-mirror arrangement requires no left-right reversal of half-fields, as is required in the simple Wheatstone stereoscope.

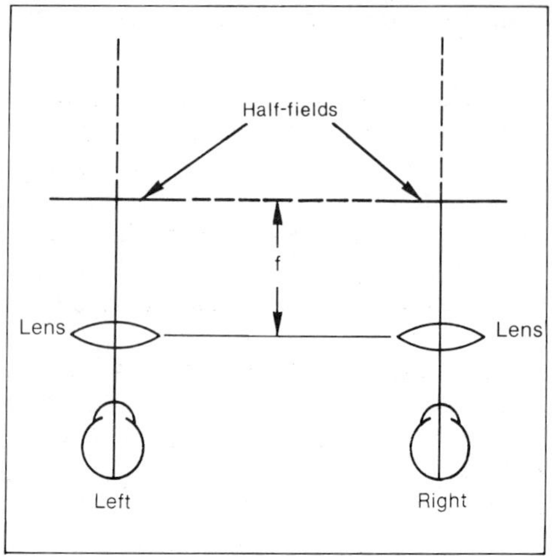

Figure 23.32. A simple lenticular stereoscope. Placing the half-fields at the focal length *f* of the lenses supports parallel convergence, the horizontal extent of the half-fields is limited to the interocular distance.

one covers the eyes with filters complementary to the print colors of the original half-images.

The anaglyph method provides a simple and relatively inexpensive method for viewing stereograms in print (Julesz's 1971 book, for example, contains a wide variety of interesting stereo demonstrations). Its chief disadvantage is that only achromatic images can be effectively portrayed.

Another inexpensive method uses polarizing filters oriented 90° with respect to one another over the stereo targets and the eyes, to achieve image separation. This method does pass chromatic information but is impractical for use in printed material. Furthermore, the targets must be illuminated from behind or projected as slides onto an aluminized screen that retains the polarization of light reflected on it. The vectograph technique is a method of printing the two half-images of a stereo pair, with appropriate polarization, on a single slide.

An interesting research tool is the stereoscopic shadowcaster, described by Gregory (1964) and Lee (1969). This simple device uses the polarizing filter method of image separation in conjunction with a rear-projection screen and two small horizontally separated light sources. The virtual images of shadows cast by three-dimensional objects from behind the screen contain disparity information, which may be magnified or minified by varying the separation between the light sources. Furthermore, motion parallax is eliminated, and thus the device provides an opportunity to study the kinetic properties of stereoscopic depth under controlled circumstances.

Finally, mention should be made of the fact that filter methods usually suffer from imperfect image separation due to "crosstalk" between the half-images. This is of little consequence in viewing ordinary scenes but limits their usefulness in laboratory situations when bright displays are needed.

4.4. Random-Dot Stereograms

The random-dot stereogram, first described by Julesz (1960), is not a method of stereoscopic display in the same way as described in Sections 4.2 and 4.3, but it is discussed here because it has become an important technique in vision research for portraying stimuli that are visible to neither eye alone but are visible in the binocular view.

Consider Figure 23.35(a), a stereogram with half-images consisting of *nearly* identical random textures. The critical difference between the half-images is schematized in Figure 23.35(b). In both the square area enclosed by the dashed lines and in the peripheral areas outside the squares, but excluding the shaded strips, the dots are perfectly correlated. But these correlated regions are displaced horizontally with respect to one another. In this way, a horizontal disparity is produced between the identically dotted square regions relative to the surrounding region. Two different convergence angles are required to perfectly register the square and its surrounding area, and thus a depth cue exists. The shaded strips are filled in with dots uncorrelated in the two eyes.

When this stereogram is viewed stereoscopically, the square region appears to float above the plane of the page, even though the half-images monocularly viewed provide no hint that there is a square or any other embedded form in the pattern. This property is extremely useful, for it allows one to present an embedded stimulus directly to a central level of visual processing, which by logical necessity is beyond the level of monocular peripheral processing. Sometimes this property is erroneously interpreted as meaning that random-dot stereograms are devoid of monocular form information. It is more accurate to regard such patterns as containing binocular forms that do not exist monocularly, for there is certainly a good deal of both coarse and fine luminance variation across space in such patterns, even though that variation may have been generated with pseudorandom methods.

There are many variants of the basic random-dot stereogram method, many of which are discussed and demonstrated in Julesz's (1971) book. They may, for example, be made to vary in the type of pixel element used to generate the patterns, the statistical properties of the correlation, and the form portrayed. One important variant is the dynamic random-dot stereogram in which the patterns vary randomly in time, as well as space, but preserve the correlation defining the binocular form. It is not surprising that random-dot stereograms have stimulated an enormous interest in binocular vision since their invention in 1960.

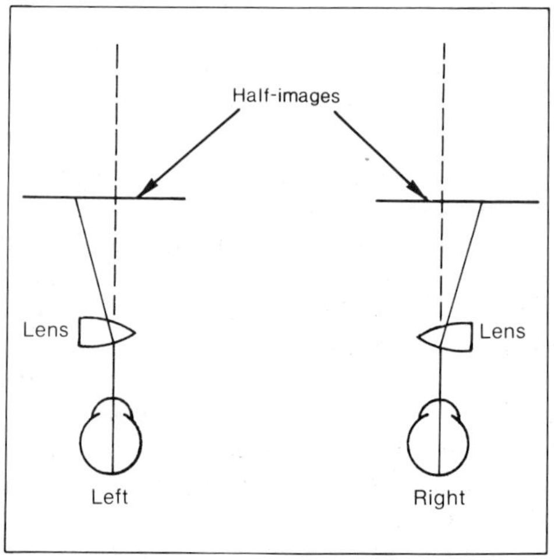

Figure 23.33. Brewster's prismatic lenticular stereoscope. This allows the use of larger half-images than does the ordinary lenticular stereoscope, since the prism power in the lense shifts the half-images nasally.

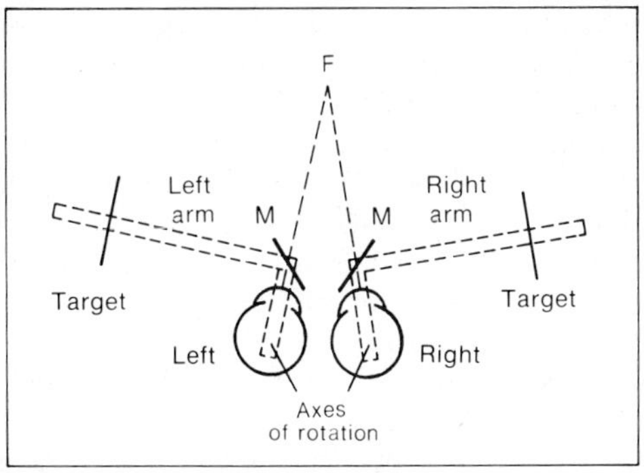

Figure 23.34. The haploscope is a stereoscope whose arms can be rotated to a wide range of symmetric and asymmetric convergence angles. Mirrors at *M* cause the virtual image of the fixated object to be formed at *F*. The arms rotate about the centers of rotation of the eyes.

5. RESOLUTION AND DYNAMICS OF BINOCULAR VISION

The binocular visual system maintains simultaneously two processes that are conceptually opposite. One is the stereoscopic process that allows extraordinarily precise localization of objects in depth. To perform this function, the system must resolve minute differences between the monocular images. At the same time, however, the processes underlying single vision necessitate, at a different level, a failure of resolution of the same differences giving rise to apparent depth. The coexistence of these opposing processes allows the veridical interpretation of the visual world as both single and extended in space. The purpose of this section is to outline the boundaries of both stereopsis and single vision.

Throughout the modern history of vision science, stereopsis and single vision have widely been considered as two aspects of a single hypothetical process called *fusion*. Disparate images are said to fuse into a single percept localized in depth. Indeed, most contemporary theories of binocular vision employ this kind of construct. Empirically, however, apparent depth and single vision do not covary strictly enough to consider them as two aspects of a single process. Disparate images can appear single without apparent depth, and apparent stereoscopic depth often occurs in the presence of diplopia. For this reason, this section will treat stereopsis and single vision as independent processes with different characteristics and dynamic ranges.

5.1. Functional Parameters of Stereoscopic Vision

It is natural to ask what is the range of disparities over which stereoscopic depth perception occurs. The smallest disparity yielding valid apparent depth is the *threshold for stereopsis*. This threshold determines *stereoacuity* in a way similar to that in which the smallest detectable spatial differences are a measure of visual acuity. There are abundant data about stereoacuity, summarized in Section 5.1.1.

The upper boundaries of stereoscopic function, on the other hand, are more difficult to determine, for the detection and discrimination of depth from image disparities may be accomplished by other means than those ordinarily associated with stereoscopic mechanisms. For example, when attention is directed to an object that is very distant from the plane of fixation, the direction and magnitude of the vergence eye movements required to fixate that object constitute the same information that traditional stereoscopic mechanisms would provide. Thus when large disparities produce apparent depth, it is not clear whether the depth is mediated by vergence eye movements, efferent vergence signals, or by mechanisms that can operate without eye movement information altogether. Mitchell (1969, 1970) has demonstrated that stimuli in the two eyes yielding qualitative depth localization need not even be similar.

Ogle (1952a, 1952b) has suggested that stereoscopic depth may be mediated by two distinct mechanisms. For small disparities stereopsis is said to be *obligatory*, or *patent*. Patent stereopsis yields a percept with both direction and magnitude of depth. For larger disparities, on the other hand, stereopsis may be *qualitative*, yielding an impression only of the direction of depth. Westheimer and Tanzman (1956) showed that reliable qualitative depth localization occurs with up to 6° of convergent disparity and up to 10° of divergent disparity. According to Ogle, the range of patent stereopsis overlaps both the region of single vision and some of the region in which double images are seen. This is schematized in Figure 23.36.

Ogle's distinction between patent and qualitative stereopsis is one that describes two separate mechanisms, each processing a different band of disparities. However, this should be clearly distinguished from the independent idea that there exist distinct

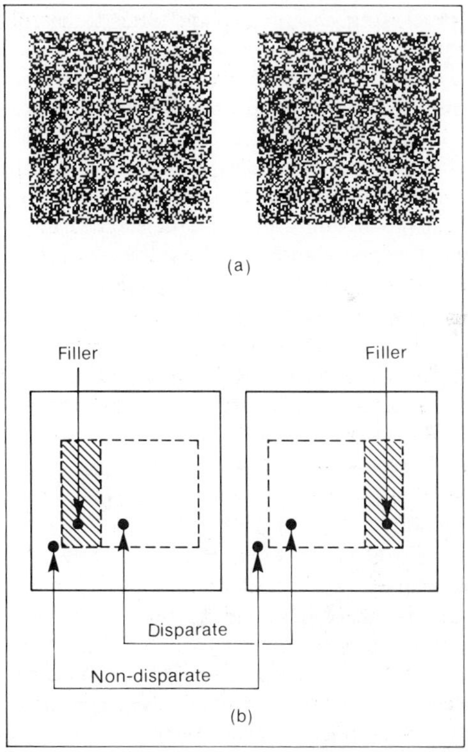

Figure 23.35. A random-dot stereogram and its structure. (b) Schematizes the construction of the stereogram (from Julesz, 1977) in (a). The areas enclosed by the dashes contain dots perfectly correlated in the two eyes but displaced inward relative to one another, introducing a crossed horizontal disparity. The dots in the area surrounding the squares are also perfectly correlated in the two eyes, but these dots are nondisparate. The shaded areas contain uncorrelated "filler" dots, which fill in the gaps in each half-image brought about by the introduction of horizontal disparity. ((a) From B. Julesz, Recent results with dynamic random dot stereograms, in S.Benton, (Ed.), *Three dimensional imaging. Proceedings of the Society of Photo-Optical Instrumentation Engineers*, 1977, *SPIE 120*. Reprinted with permission.)

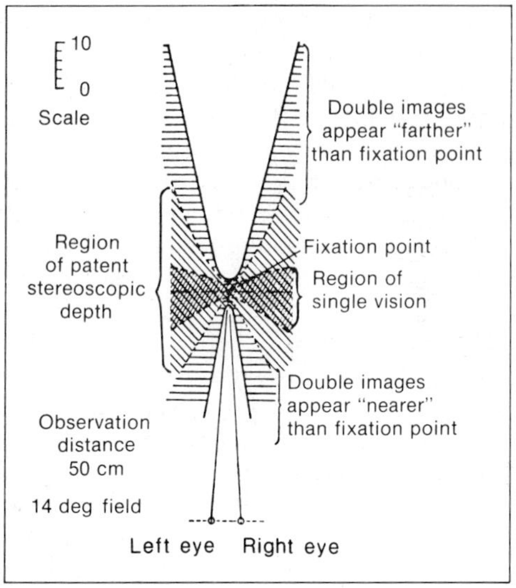

Figure 23.36. Ogle's regions of patent and qualitative stereopsis. The patent stereopsis region is indicated by coarse oblique crosshatching, while the qualitative region is indicated by horizontal cross-hatching. Also shown is the region of single vision (fine, oblique cross-hatching). All points outside this region will produce diplopia. The region of patent stereopsis extends well into the region of diplopia (from Ogle, 1952b).

disparity processing channels responding to coarse and fine spatial luminance changes in the monocular images (Kaufman & Pitblado, 1965). This latter idea, expressed in terms of monocular spatial frequency content, has been the basis for a number of recent theories of disparity processing (Felton, Richards, & Smith, 1972; Frisby & Mayhew, 1976; Julesz & Miller, 1975; Marr & Poggio, 1979). Note that the processing of disparity subsequent to monocular spatial frequency filtering or analysis requires no assumptions in and of itself about the sizes of disparities to which a channel might respond.

5.1.1. Stereoacuity. This section briefly describes some of the methods for determining stereoacuity, the basic data, and some of the factors which influence stereoacuity. Other surveys of the existent stereoacuity literature can be found in Graham (1965) and Ogle (1950).

5.1.1.1. Measures and Tests of Stereoacuity. Typical three-dimensional tests of stereoacuity are the Howard-Dolman apparatus (Howard, 1919) and the Verhoeff stereopter. The former consists of two thin rods situated 6 m from the observer, viewed through an aperture that masks all but the central part of the rods. One rod is placed nearer or farther from the second rod, and the distance is determined at which the observer correctly identifies the depth in 75% of the trials. In Howard's original study, stereoacuity varied enormously between subjects: of 106 tested, the 14 best had thresholds between 1.8 and 2.07 sec of arc, while the 24 worst had thresholds values ranging between 10.6 and 135.2 sec. There are many variants of this test, employing other stimulus configurations (e.g., a central rod adjustable in depth relative to two flanking rods), and other psychophysical scoring procedures. It is most widely used for screening purposes. The commercially available Verhoeff apparatus, used mostly in clinical application, consists of a small box containing several standing wires placed at different distances and of different thicknesses (to remove size cues). Normal observers can accurately locate the relative depths of the wires at 100 cm away. Von Noorden (1980) recommends that stereoacuity measured this way be recorded in a manner similar to Snellen acuity. That is, an observer who performs the task successfully at 50 cm would have 50/100 stereoacuity.

Stereoscopic stereoacuity measures are numerous, both in mode of presentation (e.g., stereoscope, anaglyph, vectograph) and in the content of the forms whose depth must be judged. Commercially available tests (e.g., Titmus Stereo Test, A-O Project-O-Chart System), in general, measure stereothresholds with only moderate precision and are usually not suitable for laboratory experimentation.

A recent advance in stereo testing is to embed the test object in a random-dot stereogram (see Section 4.4). This mode of presentation has the advantage that the form to be located in depth is unrecognizable monocularly and can be recognized only with binocular viewing. Correct identification of the form and relative depth provide certain evidence of stereoscopic function. However, an observer's first experience with such stereograms may require prolonged viewing, even up to several minutes (Julesz, 1971), and the test may thus be difficult to administer. Furthermore, the time required to perceive a form in depth with random-dot stereograms decreases with trials (Frisby & Clatworthy, 1975; Julesz, 1971; Ramachandran, 1976; Ramachandran & Braddick, 1973; Saye & Frisby, 1975). Although this learning phenomenon is probably not due to cognitive factors (Staller, Lappin, & Fox, 1980), it makes these stimuli difficult to use in repeated measures of stereoscopic function.

In comparing stereoacuity measured in the stereoscope with that obtained with stimuli presented in real three-dimensional space, Berry (1948) concluded that the two measures yield essentially equivalent results. He also compared vernier acuity with stereoacuity and found that for small vertical separations of small vertical line segments, vernier acuity is superior to stereoacuity, but as the separation exceeds about 2 min of arc, stereoscopic depth thresholds are smaller than vernier and grow at a smaller rate than do vernier thresholds with increasing separations.

5.1.1.2. Factors That Influence Stereoacuity. Although their role is usually described as that of "fixation" stimuli, the presence of adjacent stimuli near disparate contours is one of the most powerful factors determining stereoacuity. As described in Section 3.1.1, convergence alone provides only a crude form of depth signal. Furthermore, as Westheimer (1979) has shown, a step disparity displacement of a single line with no comparison stimulus requires 10 times the disparity for detection of one detected with flanking comparison stimuli. Thus it is not the mere presence of a comparison disparity which is important. Rather, maximal stereoacuity requires in addition that the comparison stimulus be presented synchronously with the test stimulus and with appropriate placement (e.g., flanking lines aid discrimination better than do vertically separated vertical lines).

It is not surprising that an important variable affecting stereoacuity is the separation between the so-called fixation point and the stereo target. Figure 23.37 shows the variation of stereoscopic threshold with eccentricity of the target.

As Rawlings and Shipley (1969) have pointed out, such data tell us something about peripheral stereoacuity referenced to a foveal or otherwise distant fixation point but do not show how discrimination of depth between two targets in the same peripheral area varies. Those investigators used the mean deviation of equidistance settings for two points centered about a variable eccentricity, as a measure of stereoacuity. Their data are shown in Figure 23.38. They attribute the discontinuity in the graph to a change in rod–cone optic nerve ratio. Although

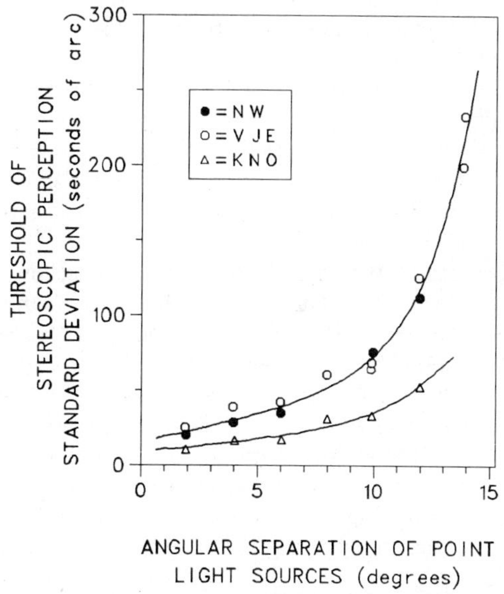

Figure 23.37. The variation of stereoscopic threshold with retinal eccentricity, for three observers with visual acuity of 20/15 in both eyes. The observers viewed a central fixation light and two laterally displaced flanking lights, which were disparate relative to one another. The threshold is taken as the standard deviation of the relative depths correctly identified. (From K. N. Ogle, *Researches in binocular vision,* Saunders, 1950. Reprinted with permission.)

such data better represent stereoacuity confined to the region of eccentricity, they are not fundamentally different from those found with the more widely used foveal–peripheral comparison. That is, stereoacuity is maximal at the fovea and falls off more rapidly as eccentricity increases beyond about 6°.

The Westheimer (1979) study alluded to previously also provides some data on differential stereoscopic thresholds. The graph in Figure 23.39 shows the thresholds for discrimination of a step disparity displacement of a central vertical line with two flanking lines as a function of a standing disparity (pedestal) on which the test disparity is superimposed. It is not surprising that thresholds are smallest at the plane of fixation and grow with increasing crossed or uncrossed disparity. It is also evident that a 1 min of arc standing disparity more than doubles the threshold. Schumer and Julesz (1984) obtained similarly steep decrements in stereoacuity using random-dot stereograms, with disparity pedestals up to 50 min of arc. In addition, they found that as pedestal size grows, peak stereoscopic sensitivity occurs with coarser and coarser disparity changes over space (lower spatial disparity modulation frequency). Thus maximum stereoscopic discriminability occurs when the comparison stimulus has zero disparity. For stationary stimuli, this may be of little consequence, since eye movements may always register the half-images of one of two objects on the foveas in order to provide a zero or near-zero disparity comparison.

Another important factor that can determine stereoacuity is the intensity of illumination of the stimulus (Berry, Riggs, & Duncan, 1950; Mueller & Lloyd, 1948). Figure 23.40 demonstrates that the stereoscopic threshold is maximal and is constant over high levels of illuminance but increases with decreasing luminance to what is presumably the cone threshold. These data also show that reasonably good stereoacuity is maintained by scotopic mechanisms, albeit worse than with photopic levels of illumination.

A rather surprising finding is the fact that stereoacuity varies with orientation of the stimulus lines. Consider Figure 23.41(a), which shows, physically superimposed, the half-fields that would result from viewing a binocular fixation rod and a disparate (in-depth) target rod. As the stimulus is rotated in space as in (b) and (c), the horizontal disparity between the half-images of the target rod remains constant. If horizontal disparity measured across horizontal meridians (the distance between the squares and filled circles in Figure 23.41) were the only determinant of stereoacuity in such patterns, one would expect no effect of orientation. However, Ebenholtz and Walchli (1965) found that stereoscopic thresholds were proportional to the cosine of the angle of elevation (θ in the figure) of such lines. Ogle (1955) and Blake, Camisa, and Antoinetti (1976) also fit the cosine function to the dependence of stereoscopic thresholds on orientation.

There is a simple explanation for this cosine dependence (Arditi, 1982). Suppose that in this situation, the binocular system computes horizontal disparities from matches not between horizontally correspondent points but between *nearest* points on the lines. In other words, horizontal disparity is what is measured, but it is the horizontal component of the disparity between nearest points on the two lines which is relevant. This hypothesis predicts both the cosine dependence of stereoacuity on orientation and the orientation dependence of the induced size effect as measured with line stimuli as well.

Finally, mention should be made of the fact that, contrary to intuition, lateral retinal image motion of up to 2°/sec does *not* seem to appreciably affect stereoacuity (Westheimer & McKee, 1978). Motion in depth (opposite directions of motion for each half-image) also has little effect on stereo thresholds provided the stimulus remains within a central 5 min of arc region (the region of maximal stereoacuity). When the motion is not confined to this area, stereoacuity does deteriorate.

5.1.2. Mechanism-Specific Disparity Limits. Stereoacuity is an important measure of stereoscopic resolution, but there

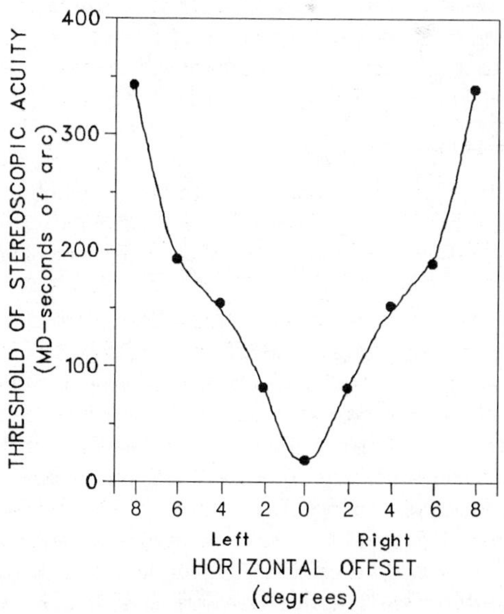

Figure 23.38. The variation of stereoscopic threshold with retinal eccentricity with the threshold defined as the mean deviation of equidistance settings for two point-sources centered about the test region of eccentricity (1° apart in one eye). Each point is the average of 24 settings for each observer, averaged over three observers. The falloff in sensitivity is similar to that observed when the comparison stimulus is always foveal. (From S. C. Rawlings & T. Shipley, Stereoscopic acuity and horizontal angular distance from fixation, *Journal of the Optical Society of America*, 1969, *59*. Reprinted with permission.)

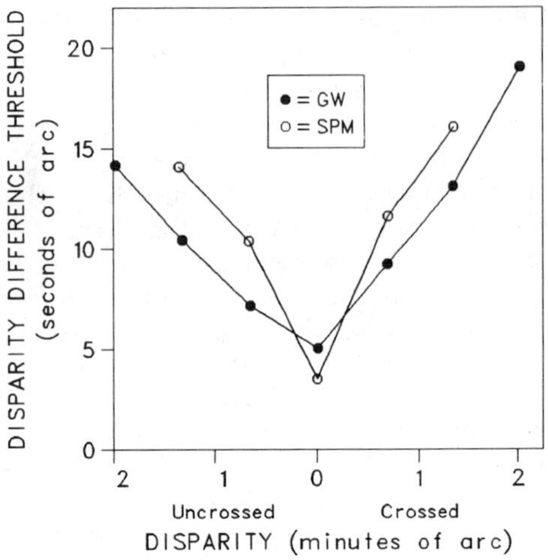

Figure 23.39. Difference thresholds for disparity as a function of standing disparity using a three-line stereo target. The observer judged whether a step-disparity displacement of the central line appeared nearer or farther than its initial position in depth. Lines were 15 min of arc long and laterally separated by 14 min of arc. Even a 1 min of arc standing disparity severely degrades the threshold. (From G. Westheimer, Cooperative neural process involved in stereoscopic acuity, *Experimental Brain Research*, 1979, *36*. Reprinted with permission.)

are other functional parameters of interest to the theorist. For example, given the possible roles of independent spatial frequency–tuned channels in binocular vision or of separate coarsely and finely disparity-tuned stereopsis mechanisms, one may ask what are the dynamic ranges of such mechanisms. If there is a stereoscopic channel that processes disparities only for gross features of the pattern, one might suspect that this mechanism would respond only to large disparities. This, of course, is not necessarily the case, but if such mechanisms exist, one would like to know their individual functional characteristics. Currently, these questions have broad implications for theories of stereopsis that incorporate independent spatial frequency–tuned disparity processing (Felton, Richards, & Smith, 1972; Julesz & Miller, 1975; Marr & Poggio, 1979; Mayhew & Frisby, 1980a). The Marr and Poggio (1979) theory explicitly relates the spatial frequency tuning of its mechanisms to the range of disparities processed by those mechanisms with small disparities processed by high spatial frequencies, and large disparities by low spatial frequencies.

There is mounting evidence that fails to provide support for this relationship, however. Mayhew and Frisby (1979) showed that the spectral content of filtered random-dot stereograms has little effect on apparent depth, and that small convergent disparity (0–8 min) discriminations are possible with filtered stereograms containing only medium and low spatial frequencies. Furthermore, Frisby and Mayhew (1980) and Mowforth, Mayhew, and Frisby (1981) have shown that large vergence eye movements can be elicited by narrow-band, high spatial frequency, filtered random-dot stereograms, although low spatial frequency stereograms can elicit somewhat larger movements. Thus although there seems to be some relationship between the size of the disparity and the spectrum of the stimulus for coarse disparity discriminations made on the basis of vergence movements, that relationship does not seem strong enough to support the idea (e.g., Marr & Poggio, 1979) that vergence control is mediated through spatial frequency–selective channels. This alone would not rule out spatial frequency–selective disparity processing for those stereoscopic mechanisms that do not rely on vergence.

But Schumer and Julesz (1982) recently measured the lower (stereoacuity) and upper disparity limits of depth discrimination using stereograms composed of one-dimensional noise whose spatial spectrum was limited to 1-octave bands. They found that both limits were roughly constant, regardless of the center frequencies of the noise.

While spatial filtering seems to have little effect on difference in disparity limits for random patterns, it does seem to reduce stereoacuity for line patterns. Westheimer and McKee (1980), who studied the effects of several sorts of image degradation on stereoacuity, found that low-pass and high-pass horizontal filtering and optical blur all had detrimental effects on stereoacuity. It is surprising that the high-pass filtering was more deleterious to depth discrimination with three-line patterns than was low-pass, suggesting that fine disparity discriminations are not mediated solely by mechanisms tuned to high spatial frequencies.

5.1.3. Contrast Threshold for Stereopsis. Another variable of interest is the contrast required for stereoscopic mechanisms to operate. There has been very little direct study of this question, yet it is important from both a theoretical and a human factors point of view. The important theoretical issue is whether stereopsis requires stimulus energy above and beyond that required for simple detection of a pattern. If so, it might be argued that simple detection mechanisms exist logically, and perhaps physiologically, prior to stereopsis mechanisms.

This was indirectly studied by Frisby and Mayhew (1978), who compared contrast sensitivity functions for detection with those for obtaining valid stereopsis using narrow-band, spatially filtered, two-dimensional noise patterns. While they found that 0.3–0.4 log units more contrast was required for stereopsis than for simple detection, the patterns they used were of different

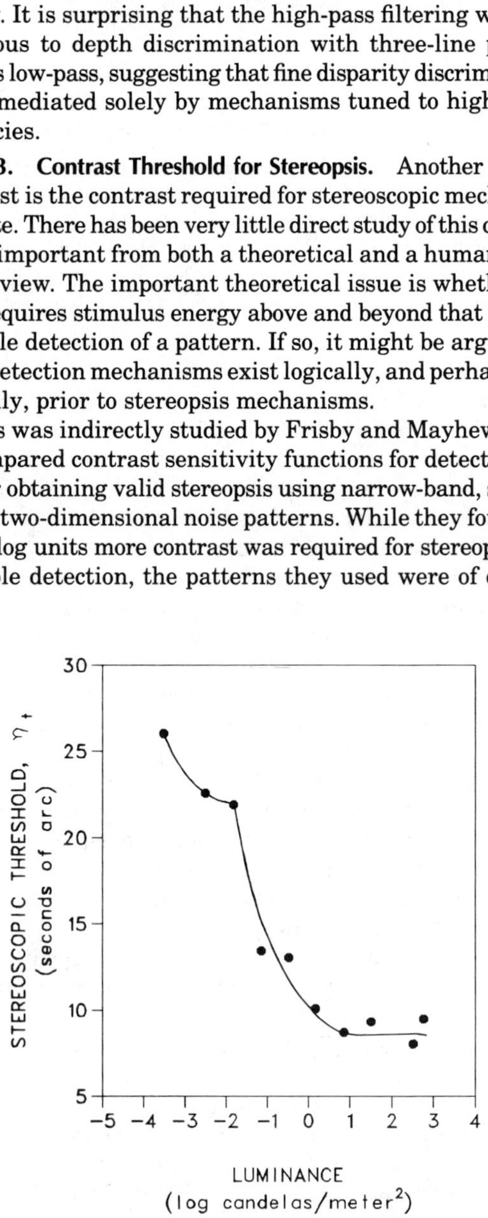

Figure 23.40. Stereoscopic threshold as a function of intensity of illumination following dark adaptation. The observer made equidistance settings of a stereoscopic vertical line to three fixed binocular comparison lines. Each point is the average of 60 settings made by each of two observers, averaged over observers. The threshold shows the usual discontinuity of rod and cone functions. (From C. G. Mueller & V. V. Lloyd, Stereoscopic acuity for various levels of illumination, *Proceedings of the National Academy of Science*, 1948, *34*. Reprinted with permission.)

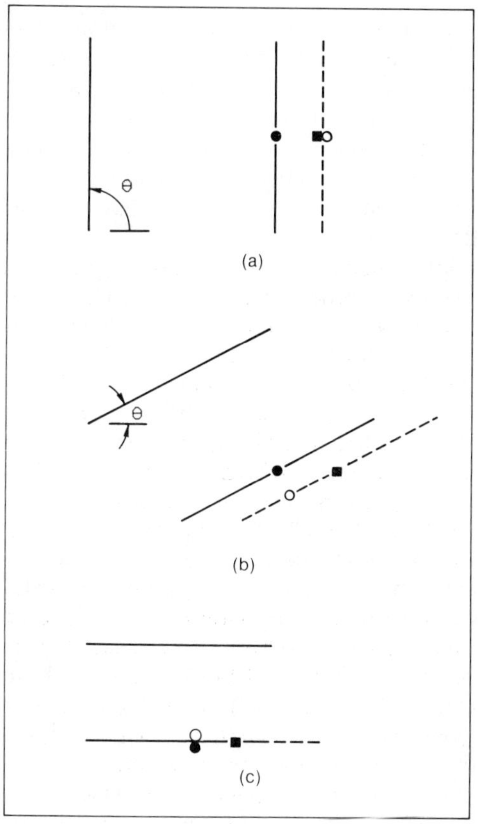

Figure 23.41. Superimposed half-fields of a binocular fixation rod and another rod at some relative depth at three angles of elevation θ. As the entire dispaly is rotated (θ = 45° in (b) and 0° in (c)), the purely horizontal disparity (the difference between the filled circles and squares) remains constant, while the horizontal disparity between nearest points on the lines in the two eyes (the difference between the filled and open circles) decreases as the cosine of θ. If horizontal disparity between nearest points on the lines determines stereoacuity, then thresholds should be proportional to the cosine of θ. (From A. Arditi, The dependence of the induced effect on orientation and a hypothesis concerning disparity computations in general, *Vision Research, 22*. Copyright 1982 by Pergamon Press, Ltd. Reprinted with permission.)

size in the stereopsis and simple detection conditions, and as the authors point out, the thresholds are not directly comparable. The central theme of their study was that the *shape* of the contrast sensitivity function is the same for stereopsis and for detection, suggesting that whatever spatial filter mechanisms are involved in stereopsis, they have the same overall tuning as those used in detection.

Wilson (1977) also reported a gap between monocular contrast detection threshold and the threshold for perceiving tilt in gratings of slightly different spatial frequency. Again, however, this was not the central motive of his experiment, and the small difference is reported for only one subject, with no statistical tests. Thus while the existing evidence suggests that higher stimulus contrasts are required for stereopsis than for simple detection, the area clearly warrants further study.

5.1.4. Hysteresis in Binocular Mechanisms. Another important recent development in the stereopsis literature is the reporting of three different kinds of *hysteresis* in binocular vision. This refers to the dependence of a system's reaction to change upon the history of its prior reactions to change. The first report of such an effect is due to Helmholtz (1925), who described it for the vergence eye movement system. By gradually increasing the separation between the half-images of a stereogram, he was able to diverge his eyes to as much as 8°, whereas if he began with widely separated half-images and gradually diminished the separation between them, he could bring them into binocular registration only at a much smaller separation. In this case the path, or history of fusional eye movements (i.e., increasing or decreasing vergence), influenced the amount of divergence that could be maintained.

A second kind of hysteresis was reported by Fender and Julesz (1967), who performed a similar experiment to Helmholtz's but used a contact lens technique to retinally stabilize the half-images of stereograms to remove the effects of eye vergence. They found a similar hysteresis effect in stereopsis. That is, the maximum disparity limit for stereopsis depended on whether the prior history was of increasing or decreasing disparity. They found that maximum increasing disparity (with stereopsis) of static random-dot stereograms was 114 min of arc more than the maximum found when disparity is decreased from diplopic values. With vertical-line stimuli, the path-dependent effect was 23 min of arc. Their experiment is often cited as evidence for the plasticity of retinal correspondence.

However, Burt and Julesz (1978) measured the same effect using a different paradigm with no retinal image stabilization and with dynamic, rather than static, random-dot stereograms. They found a hysteresis effect of only 17 min of arc. Diner (Note 3), who repeated the Fender and Julesz experiment with a modified version of their original apparatus, but used only line stimuli, also found much smaller path dependence, about 6 min of arc. These reasons for the much larger effects found by Fender and Julesz are unclear, but Diner's contact lenses were held to the sclera by suction, whereas Fender and Julesz's were not, suggesting that slippage may have played some role. More research is needed in this area to accurately assess the magnitude of this phenomenon.

Wilson (1977) reported a third kind of hysteresis in stereoscopic vision. Using grating patterns of slightly different spatial frequency, he found that by gradually increasing the contrast of one half-field from zero to some suprathreshold value, the contrast at which tilt became apparent was greater than it was for the gradual decrease of contrast. Wilson interprets this result as a reflection of the dynamic cooperative nature of stereopsis in which zero disparity reflects a default stable state. It is possible, however, that this result reflects some kind of hysteresis of suppression mechanisms, rather than stereopsis mechanisms. It may be that the visibility of the grating in the eye receiving the changing contrast is path dependent and that this, in turn, determines the point at which stereoscopic depth occurs.

5.1.5. Utrocular Discrimination. Logically, patent stereopsis requires both an absolute disparity measurement and a sign indicating the direction of depth (crossed or uncrossed). The latter requirement may be studied in isolation, since, logically, determining the sign of a disparity is equivalent to determining which eye receives which stimulus. This is sometimes referred to as the problem of *eye signature*, and the task of discriminating which eye receives a stimulus is called *utrocular*, or *eye-of-origin*, discrimination.

Despite the logical necessity of eye-of-origin information for stereoscopic vision, utrocular discrimination is a difficult task for most observers. The meager utrocular discrimination literature prior to this decade, in fact, shows disagreement as to whether observers can successfully perform such tasks above chance levels (for a review of the early utrocular discrimination literature, see Templeton & Green, 1968). Paradoxically, Blake and Cormack (1979a) found that stereoblind observers can discriminate which eye receives a grating (when paired with a blank field in the other eye) quite easily, whereas normal observers have difficulty making this discrimination unless the spatial frequency of the gratings is lower than about 4 cycles/degree. These results, however, have recently been challenged by Ono and Barbeito (1985) and by Barbeito and colleagues (1985).

Even within those with normal stereopsis, there is large individual variability. Blake and Cormack (1979b) found that for normal observers who can successfully discriminate eye of origin at low spatial frequencies, neither retinal location, grating orientation, contrast stimulus duration, feedback, nor practice influenced performance on this task.

5.2. Singleness of Vision

As described previously, while stereopsis represents the ability of the visual system to resolve small horizontal differences between the images of the two eyes, singleness of vision represents the ability to discount such differences in the interests of veridical perception. Although geometrically double images abound in our visual worlds, we seldom notice them, even when the disparity between them is enormous. With adequate attention, however, we can detect them, as we may demonstrate to ourselves by *attending* to a raised finger while fixating a far point in space. In artificial laboratory situations, of course, diplopic images often seem more prominent.

With large disparities, diplopia is easily discerned with adequate attention, and our failure to be confused by this conflicting information can be explained by the same mechanisms that underly binocular suppression and rivalry and by our bias to judge the world as single. Indeed, the conspicuous lack of research explicitly dealing with the apparent singleness of widely (retinally) disparate objects would indicate that this is the accepted view.

Single vision with small disparities, however, has been a vigorously pursued line of research since Wheatstone's (1838) demonstrations. With small disparities, single vision has special theoretical interest because of its possible linkage with stereopsis. Indeed the combination of disparate images into a "fused" image has proved to be a useful construct in theories of stereopsis. The term "fusion" will be avoided here, since there is little consensus on its usage and since that usage is in many cases bound to a particular class of binocular vision theories (Kaufman, 1974; Kaufman & Arditi, 1976b). But in the context of single vision, the term refers to the process in which the effective monocular visual directions of disparate points become altered and assume a new, intermediate, and *single* visual direction in the combined or "cyclopean" view.

The limits of fusion, specified in units of visual angle, delimit what are often referred to as *Panum's areas*. Panum's area, for a specific retinal locus, defines a region of retina in the other eye that, when stimulated with a similar pattern or contour, will produce single vision. The concept carries with it the idea that correspondence is plastic. Thus when measurements of Panum's area are reported, they are often interpreted as reflecting the spatial extent of this plasticity, when in fact, as will be shown in Section 5.2.1., a much simpler interpretation is possible. This is one reason to refer to diplopia thresholds, rather than fusion thresholds or to Panum's area. Another is that *diplopia threshold* is less confusing: there are fewer definitions in use in the literature (Mitchell, 1966b). Note that there may be an ambiguity in the units reported, because sometimes the horizontal extent of Panum's area is considered to be twice the diplopia threshold, in order to encompass both crossed and uncrossed single-appearing disparities.

5.2.1. Direct Judgments of Single Vision. This section describes measurements of single vision based on the direct judgment or detection of diplopia, or single vision. Mitchell's (1966b) coverage of this topic is excellent.

One method, using stimuli presented in three-dimensional space, is described in Section 3.2.1.2 and gives measurements similar to those shown in Figure 23.18. It simply involves adjustment of the horopter rods to the near and far limits of single vision. Indeed, this is one method of determining the empirical horopter. Note that the magnification of the ordinate of the graph in Figure 23.18 makes it difficult to see the increase of the region of single vision with peripheral angle. Figure 23.42 shows the diplopia threshold, that is, one-half the difference between the "inner" and "outer" settings of the horopter rods, as a function of retinal eccentricity, for four observers.

An important variable affecting diplopia threshold measurements is the extent to which free eye movements are allowed to occur. This is demonstrated in Figure 23.43, which is identical to the stereogram in Figure 23.14(a), except for the addition of the nonius lines. If one carefully aligns the nonius lines in the binocular view, one can see distinct diplopic images. Without these lines, only single lines are apparent.

A better way of controlling for the effects of eye movements, of course, is to flash the stimulus for a time shorter than that required to initiate vergence eye movements, that is, less than about 160 msec (Rashbass & Westheimer, 1961). Mitchell (1966a) has made careful measurements of this sort, and his estimates, based on observers' responses of "single" or "double" to flashed lines or spots, ranged 4.45–11.5 min of arc, for the foveal diplopia threshold (one-half of Panum's area), with little intrasubject variability.

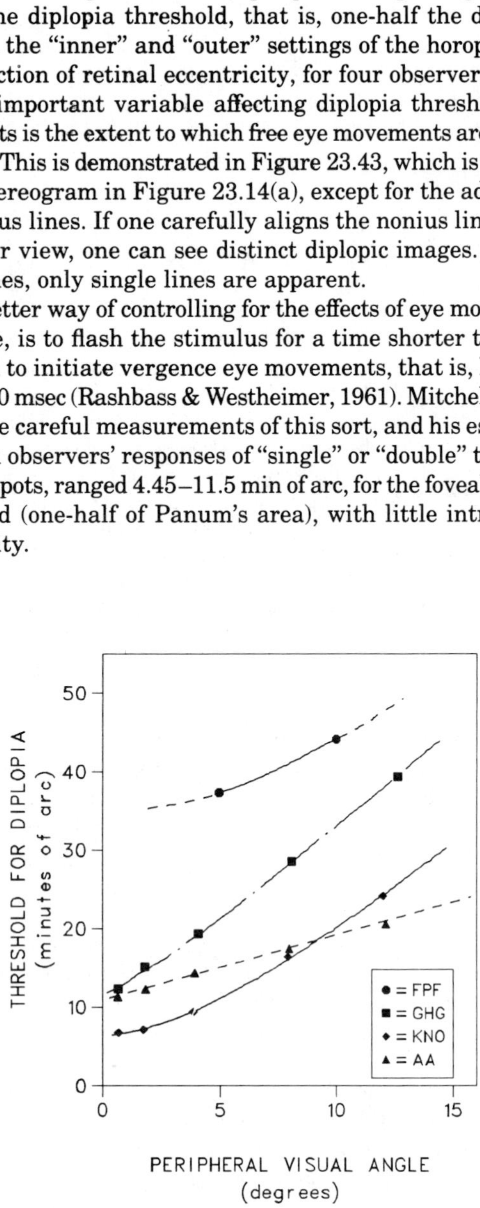

Figure 23.42. The threshold for diplopia as a function of retinal eccentricity, extracted from horopter measurements using the singleness-of-vision criterion (see Section 3.2.1.2. for method). Data for four observers is shown. There are large individual differences between observers in this kind of measurement. (From K. N. Ogle, *Researches in binocular vision*, Saunders, 1950. Reprinted with permission.)

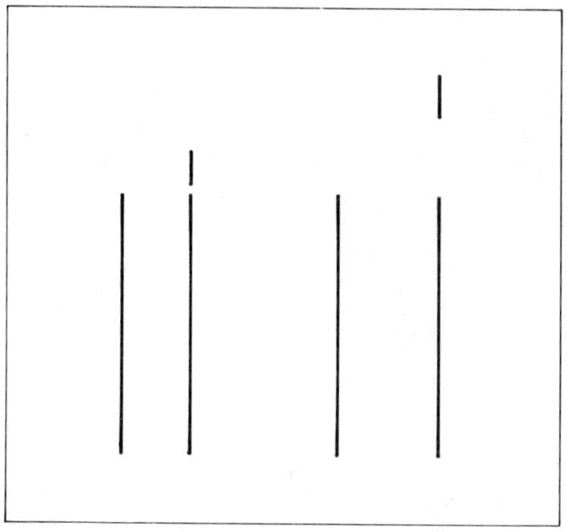

Figure 23.43. Stereogram identical to that of Figure 23.14a but with nonius lines added. When nonius lines are carefully aligned in binocular view, distinct diplopic images of the left-hand line are apparent.

Mitchell also found no difference between the vertical and horizontal diplopia thresholds, a result contrary to that found in some earlier studies (Lyding, 1939; Rosch, 1943; Volkmann, 1859). Mitchell attributes the earlier finding to the free eye movements allowed in those studies, insofar as horizontal vergence eye movements were more abundant than vertical.

A final result reported in Mitchell's paper, and reported earlier by Burchadt (1861) and Bourdon (1902), is that color differences between the eyes' views can make diplopia more salient and decrease the measured threshold. He found that luminance differences between the images of the test object had a similar effect. This suggests the possibility that binocular suppression and rivalry are always present under normal viewing conditions and are not inhibited when small disparities are being viewed.

5.2.2. Discrimination of Nondepth-Producing Disparities. It is important to recognize that while our stereoscopic ability amounts to a *discrimination* between the two eyes' views, single vision amounts mainly to a *judgment* about such disparities. This is not a trivial distinction. In nearly all studies of single vision, the observer is required either to judge the presence of a single image or, at best, to detect when an image appears diplopic (see Section 3.2.1.2). In measuring stereoacuity, on the other hand, observers are usually required to discriminate disparities. Discrimination experiments, of course, are designed to measure the maximum resolution of a system. Thus in order to compare stereoscopic resolution with the failure of resolution in single vision, discrimination of depth should be compared with discrimination of diplopia. Key references for this approach to single vision are Kaufman and Arditi (1976a, 1976b) and Duwaer and van den Brink (1981).

There is one methodological problem deserving mention in measuring the discriminability of disparate from nondisparate stimuli. If horizontal disparities are used, the discrimination can always be made on the basis of apparent depth, and thus one would be measuring stereoacuity and not necessarily the diplopia threshold. This is not an insurmountable problem, however, since nondepth-producing vertically disparate stimuli appear single, and there is little reason to believe that the mechanisms underlying single vision are fundamentally different for vertical and horizontal disparities. This, in fact, is what makes the discrimination experiment interpretable.

If one measures the diplopia threshold with a sensitive, criterion-free method, such as that provided by the methods of signal detection theory, one finds that the diplopia threshold is commensurate, or nearly so, with stereoscopic resolution.

As an example, Kaufman and Arditi (1976b) used torsionally disparate stimuli, such as those shown in Figure 23.44, in a signal detection paradigm. Previous studies of single vision with torsionally disparate stimuli had used judgments of apparent fusion and found torsional diplopia thresholds (θ in Figure 23.44) to range between 4° (Kertesz & Jones, 1970) and 13° (Kertesz, 1972). Eye movements were found to be absent in these studies, and the authors attributed these large tolerances to a central fusional mechanism.

When Kaufman and Arditi measured *discriminability* of such binocularly crossed lines from a single horizontal binocular line, they found the torsional diplopia threshold to be only about 1½°. This corresponded to a maximum disparity at the ends of the tilted lines (d in Figure 23.44) of about 1½ min of arc, at 1° eccentricity. Even smaller thresholds were obtained when a nearby comparison line was available. Furthermore, with long-term practice, thresholds decrease even more. Arditi and Kaufman (1978), for example, report a torsional diplopia threshold of 0.57° with d equal to 36 sec of arc for a highly practiced observer (see also Duwaer & van den Brink, 1981). Such small values, of course, are commensurate with resolution as measured in stereoacuity experiments at that eccentricity. Duwaer and van den Brink (1981, 1982) have performed similar experiments using pure vertical disparities and have provided an extensive signal detection model of vertical disparity detection.

This kind of experiment indicates that the failure of disparity resolution observed in experiments measuring judgments of single vision is due to observers' adoption of lenient criteria in making such judgments. And, indeed, the singleness of the world provides adequate reason for this bias to be operative. An important theoretical consequence of this is that apparent singleness of vision can be explained without recourse to plasticity of monocular visual directions.

6. THEORETICAL ISSUES IN BINOCULAR VISION

This chapter has thus far attempted to summarize the enormous body of empirical data that has been amassed about binocular vision. This section considers some recent thematic attempts to organize these observations into theory. It is not surprising that there is no theory at present that can satisfactorily account for all the data. Each emphasizes one particular subset of facts. The large number of theories, however, prohibits individual

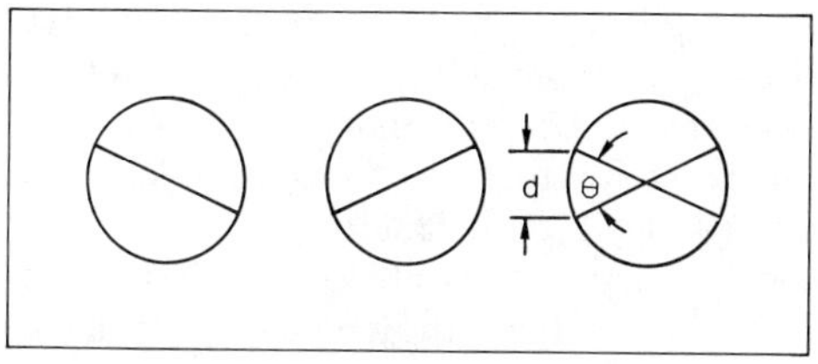

Figure 23.44. Torsionally disparate stimulus used by Kaufman and Arditi (1976b). Observers successfully discriminate such stimuli from those with zero torsional (θ in the figure) disparity, when d, the maximum vertical disparity at the ends of the lines (1° eccentricity), is about 1.5. min of arc. (From L. Kaufman & A. Arditi, The fusion illusion, *Vision Research, 16.* Copyright 1976 by Pergamon Press, Ltd. Reprinted with permission.)

description of each. Instead, theoretical issues and classes of solutions proposed will be emphasized. A more extensive historical account of binocular vision theories and a review of some recent individual theories can be found in Chapter 8 of Kaufman (1974).

6.1. The Computation of Depth: The Projection Field

Given associated elements in the two eyes, how might the binocular visual system go about transforming horizontal disparities between them into a direction and magnitude of perceived depth? Many theories adopt the scheme depicted in Figure 23.45, whose structure is traceable to Johannes Kepler (Boring, 1933). Kepler thought that mental rays project outward from the eyes to objects in space. The intersection of those mental rays is, of course, at the locus of the object toward which they are directed. Many modern theories make use of an analogous scheme to model the computation of depth, except that the projections from the retina now project inward to a central neural *projection field* (Boring, 1933; Charnwood, 1951; Dev, 1975; Dodwell & Engel, 1963; Julesz, 1971; Linksz, 1952; Nelson, 1975; Sperling, 1970; Sugie & Suwa, 1977). This provides a simple and convenient method for computation of disparity. A major assumption of this kind of model is that the firing of a neuron at one particular level of the neural projection field will be associated with the appropriate direction and magnitude of disparity. For veridical depth perception, this computation must subsequently be scaled by the absolute distance to the object.

Recent electrophysiological evidence lends credence to the existence of a projection field in the visual cortex. This possible neural substrate consists of cells responding to binocular stimulation and whose receptive fields are centered on disparate loci in the two eyes (Barlow, Blakemore, & Pettigrew, 1967; Bishop, Henry, & Smith, 1971; Joshua & Bishop, 1970; Nikara, Bishop, & Pettigrew, 1968; Poggio & Fischer, 1977). Although the discovery of such cells is not proof that depth is actually computed this way, their existence makes such neural networks plausible candidates for at least this computational aspect of binocular processing.

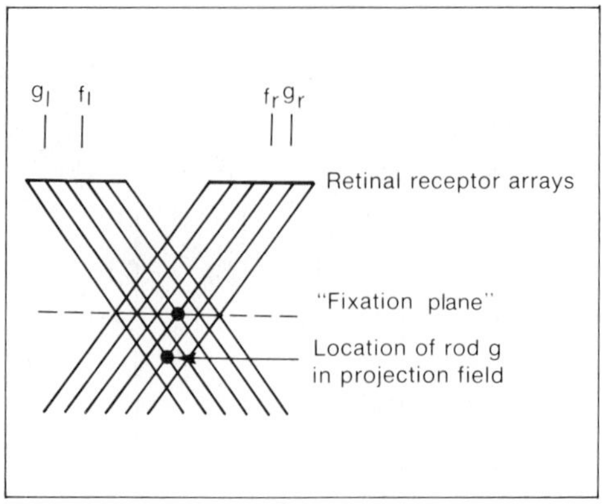

Figure 23.45. The projection-field neural network as a model of binocular depth computation. Fibers from the retinas of each eye transmit the retinal locations of half-images and intersect at a location that is isomorphic to their locations in three dimensions.

6.2. The Problem of Binocular Visual Direction

One issue that divides many of the early theories is the question of whether visual directions of points on the retinas are fixed or plastic with regards to binocular processing (for a review of this general issue, see Walls, 1951). One school, associated with Hering, asserts that each point on the monocular retina is innately associated not only with the two-dimensional visual directions (the horizontal and vertical coordinates on the retinas) but also with a depth value (this is the signed horizontal distance from the fovea). These depth values summate in the binocular view to give the overall depth value of an object in space, while the monocular visual direction values are unchanged by stereoscopic viewing (see Figure 23.46).

The school of thought opposite to that of Hering (and sometimes incorrectly associated with Helmholtz) held that monocular visual directions become modified by the stereoscopic depth process. In other words, the disparate visual directions associated with an object or contour "fuse." This so-called sensory fusion results in a modification of the monocular visual directions to a single intermediate locus and, at the same time, imparts a depth value to the fused object, as shown in Figure 23.47. There are many theories of binocular vision, both old and new, which make use of this notion (Charnwood, 1951; Dodwell, 1970; Koffka, 1935; Linschoten, 1956; Nelson, 1975; Sperling, 1970; von Tschermak-Seysenegg, 1952; Werner, 1937). Many early instances of such theories modeled fusion as an attractive force that drew similar monocular contours together in binocular view.

A problem with this notion of fusion is that it requires that monocular visual direction information be lost in the binocular percept. This is inconsistent with the fact that observers can easily discriminate disparate images from nondisparate intermediate images (see section 5.2.2) within the accepted disparity range of fusion. Furthermore, the concept has limited explanatory power in that stereopsis clearly occurs when such fusion does not, that is, with diplopic and rivalrous images.

6.3. The Classic Theory of Ogle

Hering's "local signs" theory has its closest modern counterpart in the theory of Ogle (1959). While Ogle did not believe that monocular retinal points were associated with depth values, he felt that binocular correspondence was innately structured and immutable. Much of his supporting evidence came from

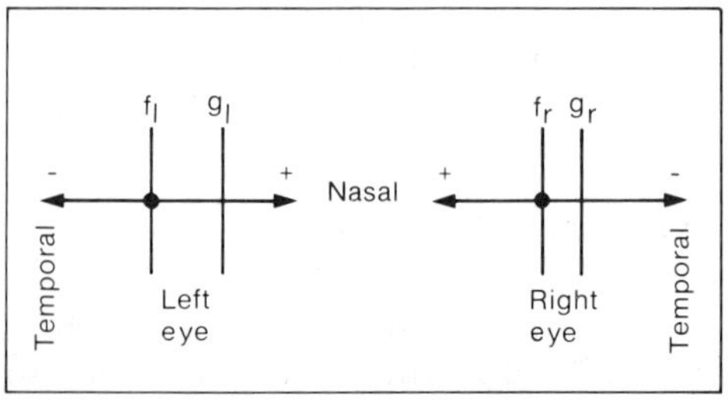

Figure 23.46. Schematic representation of Hering's local signs theory of stereopsis. The dots represent the fovea and have local sign values of zero. Nasal retinal locations are given positive values, temporal locations negative values. The direction and magnitude of depth are given by the sum of the values from the two eyes, with positive values indicating "in front" and negative values "behind" the fixation plane. In the figure, the sum of the values for line g is positive. Therefore, the line should appear in front of the fixation plane.

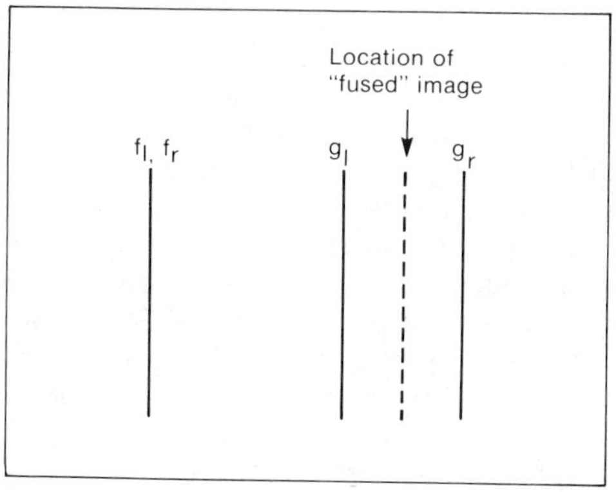

Figure 23.47. Sensory fusion is a model of binocular combination that predicts that the visual directions of objects become altered in binocular view. The figure shows the superimposed half-images of a Wheatstone stereogram. The sensory fusion model predicts that the visual directions of g_l and g_r will shift as the result of fusion and be apparently located in an intermediate visual direction.

studies showing both highly predictable stereoscopic distortions due to aniseikonia and the unchanged character of these distortions over many years.

Another central feature of Ogle's theory was his demarcation of the regions of patent and qualitative stereopsis and his demonstration that these regions do not exactly correspond to the regions of single and diplopic vision (see Figure 23.36). The dual character of stereopsis, which he described, seems to have been the precursor of later descriptions of coarse versus fine and local versus global stereoscopic mechanisms.

A weakness of Ogle's theory is the ambiguity of his description of the necessary stimulus conditions for achieving stereopsis. He stated that stereopsis required disparity of "identifiable contours," yet he never explicitly defined what he meant either by "contour" or by "identifiable." Hence it is not clear whether his theory would predict stereopsis with, say, subjective contours. Neither does he make predictions about random-dot stereograms, in which contours abound but in which they cannot be "identified" as the same ones that appear binocularly.

Ogle's theory is a conservative one that seeks more to adhere to established facts than to generate new predictions. But it is an example of a modern "classical" theory at the time when the random-dot stereogram was being developed by Julesz (1960). This new stimulus caused most workers in the field to restructure the way they thought about stereopsis and generated new interest in modeling the binocular visual system.

6.4. Binocular Point Matching: False Correspondences

Given the stereogram of Figure 23.45 and reproduced in Figure 23.48, why is it that the line labeled f_l interacts only with f_r and line g_l with g_r? This is the problem of *false correspondences*, or *ghosts*. Although the problem is conveniently represented in a projection field, it is a problem all models of stereopsis must contend with. It is one aspect of the more general question of what kind of representation of the retinal image is the input (to, say, a projection field) on which depth is computed.

For example, the Gestalt psychologists thought that *similarity* of contours was a requirement for fusion (e.g., Koffka, 1935). This hypothesis implies that the inputs used in stereoscopic computations are to a considerable extent monocularly analyzed forms, rather than simply points of light on the retina.

The advent of the random-dot stereogram (Julesz, 1960) focused attention away from similarity of contours as a prerequisite for stereopsis, since these contain no monocular cues as to the form contained in the binocular percept. This stimulus proves that there need not be a simple comparison of the attributes and features of the depicted object, prior to stereopsis. For this reason, there are many contemporary models of stereopsis which make no assumptions about form analysis prior to stereopsis. Such theories assume that the elements of stereoscopic combination are simply points on the two retinal images with similar luminance values.

For such theories, random-dot stereograms and depth in textured surfaces pose the central problem. Indeed, the number of false correspondences with such stimuli grows geometrically with the number of dots that comprise the random-dot pattern. A single dot in one half-image, conceived this way, could in principle match with any dot in the other half-image. How then does the binocular visual system match the points in the half-images to produce the coherent, uniformly textured surfaces we see when we view such stereograms? Each of the contemporary theories answers this question in a way that characterizes it as either a cooperative-competitive or a filter theory.

6.4.1. Cooperative-Competitive Theories. Julesz (1978) uses the term *local* stereopsis to describe the depth that arises when there is no ambiguity in matching, that is, no false correspondence problem. *Globality*, on the other hand, conveys the idea that unambiguous uniform depth arises in spite of the many point-for-point ambiguities in the stimulus. A global stereoscopic perception, then, is one which exists as one of many possible perceptions but which is preferred because it produces a unitary, global percept. Models of global stereopsis need a method for seeking this preferred solution. With random-dot stereograms, the preferred solution is the one in which correlation between large areas of the half-images is maximal.

The way in which many theorists have implemented the process of seeking the preferred solution involves the concepts of *cooperativity* and *competition* (Dev, 1975; Julesz, 1971; Julesz & Chang, 1976; Nelson, 1975; Sperling, 1970; Sugie & Suwa, 1977). A term borrowed from physics, which describes the molecular behavior of ferromagnets, cooperativity in this context refers to the idea that the computed disparity at one location facilitates the computation of an equal disparity nearby. Com-

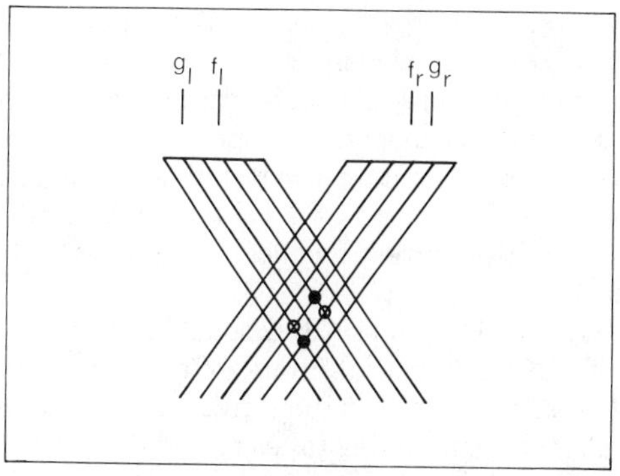

Figure 23.48. Illustration of the false-correspondence problem. Without additional assumptions, a projection-field model of binocular space predicts false localizations of lines f and g at loci indicated by the open circles, as well as the veridical localizations (filled circles).

petition refers to the similar idea that a computed disparity can suppress the computation of unequal disparities nearby. The difference between cooperativity and competition is not important in this context since both concepts serve to explain the same phenomena; both may produce waves of influence used to explain the global percept, and both may have the effect of sharpening depth borders.

The various cooperative-competitive models differ widely in scope and in detail. The models of Julesz, for example, confine themselves for the most part to the perception of depth in random-dot stereograms, whereas Sperling's (1970) model attempts to encompass vergence and accommodation phenomena and to encompass depth with diplopic and rivalrous stimuli, in addition to the perception of random-dot stereograms.

Sperling (1981) has provided a very readable introduction to mathematical descriptions of binocular cooperative and multistable phenomena; Nelson's (1975) paper provides both his own model and a wealth of explanatory material on a wide range of binocular phenomena that may be handled by such theories.

6.4.2. Filter Theories. Recently, another approach to the false correspondence problem has received attention. To understand the basis for this approach, reconsider for a moment the appearance of the monocular half-images of a random-dot stereogram. While the form depicted in binocular view is not present in these half-images, it would be false to claim that such half-images contain no monocular contour information. Although the patterns are generated randomly and with uniform dot probability across space, the patterns are far from uniform textures. The reader may appreciate this fact by squinting the eyes to remove detail information from the retinal images and observing the coarse, low spatial frequency features within the patterns.

Kaufman (1964, 1965) and Kaufman and Pitblado (1965) showed that coarse differences in luminance added to letter matrix stereograms are sufficient to produce stereopsis. They proposed the existence of "blob" detectors on which disparity may be processed in addition to the "element" disparities that exist in such stimuli. The notion of disparity detectors tuned to coarse and fine luminance changes across space is one of the basic ideas of the filter theories of stereopsis.

There is a good deal of additional support for spatial frequency–selective stereopsis, which is reviewed in Mayhew and Frisby (1980b). As an example, Julesz and Miller (1975) found that masking noise affects stereopsis only when the spectral content of that noise lies within 2 octaves of the center frequency of bandpass-filtered stereograms. Now, given the existence of filter channels as inputs to the stereopsis computational mechanism, how is the false correspondence problem handled? At first glance it might seem that there are even more "ghosts" to contend with, since each disparity-computing, spatial frequency–selective channel must contain something like a projection field of its own. In fact, filter theories may, with additional assumptions, solve the false correspondence without resorting to the notion of cooperativity.

The Marr and Poggio (1979) model, for example, applies four sizes of bar-mask spatial filters (of the kind proposed by Wilson & Giese, 1977) to each monocular image and at 12 orientations. Disparity matching takes place only within filtered representations of the same filter size and orientation. The depth computations are assumed to be made on signed zero crossings (i.e., where light–dark gradients pass through the average luminance) in the filtered images and only within a specified disparity range related to the filter size.

This range is chosen on the basis of the statistical distribution of zero crossings in a limited band of noise; it is this choice that forms the basis of their noncooperative algorithm. Because the filtered images only contain locative information within a specific range related to the spatial period corresponding to the center frequency and bandwidth of the filters, ghosts outside this range are eliminated. Since fine disparities may fall outside the region of computation for the coarser bar masks, coarse computations are made first. Those computations guide vergence eye movements to bring smaller and smaller disparities within the range of the finer-filtered images. The model also includes a buffer memory in which successful disparity matches are stored. Although there is considerable evidence mounting (see section 5.1.2) that contradicts the role ascribed by Marr and Poggio to low spatial frequencies in guiding vergence, their theory represents an innovative noncooperative method for solving the false correspondence problem.

There are several variants of this model, one of which gives greater disparity latitude to each image comparison, at the expense of invoking a small degree of cooperativity to disambiguate remaining ghosts, and one which uses circularly symmetric, rather than oriented, masks (Grimson, 1981).

Mayhew and Frisby (1980b) have also proposed a similar filter model that uses circularly symmetric filtering. Their model differs structurally from Marr and Poggio's in several ways, the most important being that (1) the tuned filter channels are assumed not to be independent of one another—thus there can be cooperativity between channels—and (2) rather than invoking eye movements to compare successively finer and finer images, they use figural continuities (e.g., lines, edges) in the patterns and in the disparity domain to remove ghosts. Thus their model makes limited use of cooperativity, to the extent that figural continuity is used to disambiguate ghosts in neighboring disparity computations.

REFERENCE NOTES

1. Anderson, P. *The psychophysics of binocular summation.* Unpublished doctoral dissertation, New York University, 1982.
2. Kaufman L. *An explanation of Panum's limiting case.* Unpublished manuscript, New York University, 1978.
3. Diner, D. *Hysteresis in human binocular fusion: A second look.* Unpublished doctoral dissertation, California Institute of Technology, 1978.

REFERENCES

Aguilonius, F. *Opticorum Libri Sex.* Plantin: Antwerp, 1613.

Alexander, L. T. The influence of figure–ground relationships in binocular rivalry. *Journal of Experimental Psychology*, 1951, *41*, 376–381.

Alexander, L. T., & Bricker, P. D. Figure–ground contrast and binocular rivalry. *Journal of Experimental Psychology*, 1952, *44*, 452–454.

Ames, Jr., A., Ogle, K. N., & Gliddon, G. H. Corresponding retinal points, the horopter and the size and shape of ocular images. *Journal of the Optical Society of America*, 1932, *22*, 538–631.

Anderson, J. D., Bechtoldt, H. P., & Dunlap, G. L. Binocular integration in line rivalry. *Bulletin of the Psychonomic Society*, 1978, *11*, 399–402.

Arditi, A. The dependence of the induced effect on orientation and a hypothesis concerning disparity computations in general. *Vision Research*, 1982, *22*, 247–256.

Arditi, A., Anderson, P., & Movshon, J. A. Monocular and binocular detection of moving sinusoidal gratings. *Vision Research*, 1981, *21*, 329–336.

Arditi, A., & Kaufman, L. Singleness of vision and the initial appearance of binocular disparity. *Vision Research*, 1978, *18*, 117–120.

Arditi, A., Kaufman, L., & Movshon, J. A. A simple explanation of the induced size effect. *Vision Research*, 1981, *21*, 755–764.

Arditi, A., Kaufman, L., & Movshon, J. A. The induced effect: A reply to Mayhew and Frisby. *Vision Research*, 1983, *23*, 665–668.

Bacon, J. H. The interaction of dichoptically presented spatial gratings. *Vision Research*, 1976, *16*, 337–344.

Barbeito, R., Levi, D., Klein, S., Loshin, D., & Ono, H. Stereo-deficients and stereoblinds cannot make utrocular discriminations. *Vision Research*, 1985, *25*, 1345–1348.

Barlow, H. B., Blakemore, C., & Pettigrew, J. D. The neural mechanisms of binocular depth discrimination. *Journal of Physiology* (London), 1967, *193*, 327–342.

Benton, S. (Ed.). Three-dimensional imaging. *Proceedings of the Society of Photo-Optical Instrumentation Engineers*, *120*, Bellingham: SPIE, 1977.

Berry, R. N. Quantitative relations among vernier, real depth and stereoscopic depth acuities. *Journal of Experimental Psychology*, 1948, *38*, 708–721.

Berry, R. N., Riggs, L. A., & Duncan, C. P. The relation of vernier and depth discrimination to field brightness. *Journal of Experimental Psychology*, 1950, *40*, 349–354.

Birch, E. E. Binocular processing of contrast: a vector sum model. *Investigative Ophthalmology and Visual Science*, supplement, 1979, *18*, 246.

Bishop, P. O., Henry, G. H., & Smith, C. J. Binocular interaction fields of single units in the cat striate cortex. *Journal of Physiology*, 1971, *216*, 39–68.

Blake, R. Threshold conditions for binocular rivalry. *Journal of Experimental Psychology: Human Perception and Performance*, 1977, *3*, 251–257.

Blake, R., & Camisa, J. On the inhibitory nature of binocular rivalry suppression. *Journal of Experimental Psychology: Human Perception and Performance*, 1979, *5*, 315–323.

Blake, R., Camisa, J., & Antoinetti, D. N. Binocular depth discrimination depends on orientation. *Perception and Psychophysics*, 1976, *20*, 113–118.

Blake, R., & Cormack, R. H. On utrocular discrimination. *Perception and Psychophysics*, 1979, *26*, 53–68. (a)

Blake, R., & Cormack, R. H. Psychophysical evidence for a monocular visual cortex in stereoblind humans. *Science*, 1979, *203*, 274–275. (b)

Blake, R., & Fox, R. The psychophysical inquiry into binocular summation. *Perception and Psychophysics*, 1973, *14*, 161–185.

Blake, R., & Fox, R. Binocular rivalry suppression: Insensitive to spatial frequency and orientation change. *Vision Research*, 1974, *14*, 687–692.

Blake, R., & Levinson, E. Spatial properties of binocular neurones in the human visual system. *Experimental Brain Research*, 1977, *27*, 221–232.

Blake, R., Martens, W., & DiGianfillipo, A. Reaction time as a measure of binocular interaction in human vision. *Investigative Ophthalmology and Visual Science*, 1980, *19*, 930–941.

Blake, R., & Rush, C. Temporal properties of binocular mechanisms in the human visual system. *Experimental Brain Research*, 1980, *38*, 333–340.

Blake, R., Sloane, M., & Fox, R. Further developments in binocular summation. *Perception and Psychophysics*, 1981, *30*, 266–276.

Blake, R., Westendorf, D. H., & Overton, R. What is suppressed during binocular rivalry? *Perception*, 1980, *9*, 223–231.

Blakemore, C. Binocular depth discrimination and the nasotemporal division. *Journal of Physiology*, 1969, *205*, 471–497.

Blakemore, C. A new kind of stereoscopic vision. *Vision Research*, 1970, *10*, 1181–1199.

Blakemore, C., Fiorentini, A., & Maffei, L. A second neural mechanism of binocular depth discrimination. *Journal of Physiology* (London), 1972, *226*, 725–740.

Blakemore, C., & Hague, B. Evidence for disparity detecting neurones in the human visual system. *Journal of Physiology*, 1972, *255*, 437–455.

Blakemore, C., Muncey, J. P. J., & Ridley, R. M. Stimulus specificity in the human visual system. *Vision Research*, 1973, *13*, 1915–1931.

Blank, A. The Luneburg theory of binocular space perception. In S. Koch (Ed.), *Psychology, a study of a science* (Study I, Vol. 1). New York: McGraw-Hill, 1959.

Boring, E. G. *The physical dimensions of consciousness*. New York: Century, 1933.

Bourdon, B. *La perception visualle de l'espace*. Paris: Libraire C. Reinwald, 1902.

Braddick, O. J. Binocular single vision and percentual processing. *Processings of the Royal Society of London* Series *B*, 1979, *204*, 503–512.

Breese, B. B. On inhibition. *Psychological Monographs*, 1899, *3* (1, Whole No. 11).

Breese, B. B. Binocular rivalry. *Psychological Review*, 1909, *16*, 410–415.

Brindley, G. S. *Physiology of the retina and visual pathway*. London: Edward Arnold, 1960.

Burchadt, F. Die Empfindlichkeit des Augenpaars fur Doppelbilder. *Annln Phys*, 1861, *112*, 596–606.

Burt, P., & Julesz, B. Extended Panum's area for dynamic random-dot stereograms. *Investigative Ophthalmology and Visual Science Supplement*, 1978, *18*, 287.

Campbell, F. W., & Green, D. G. Monocular versus binocular visual acuity. *Nature*, 1965, *208*, 191–192.

Cavonious, C. R. Binocular interactions in flicker. *Quarterly Journal of Experimental Psychology*, 1979, *1*, 273–280.

Charnwood, J. R. B. *Essay on binocular vision*. London: Halton, 1951.

Cobb, P. W. Individual variations in retinal sensitivity and their correlation with ophthalmological findings. *Journal of Experimental Psychology*, 1922, *5*, 227–246.

Cohn, T. E., & Lasley, D. J. Binocular vision: Two possible central interactions between signals from the two eyes. *Science*, 1976, *192*, 561–562.

Collyer, G., & Bevan, W. Objective measurement of dominance control in binocular rivalry. *Perception and Psychophysics*, 1970, *8*, 437–438.

Crozier, W. J., & Holway, A. H. Theory and measurement of visual mechanisms I. A visual discriminometer II. Threshold stimulus intensity and retinal position. *Journal of General Physiology*, 1938, *22*, 341–364.

Curtis, D. W., & Rule, S. J. Binocular processing of brightness information: A vector-sum model. *Journal of Experimental Psychology*, 1978, *4*, 132–143.

Curtis, D. W., & Rule, S. J. Fechner's paradox reflects a nonmonotone relation between binocular brightness and luminance. *Perception and Psychophysics*, 1980, *27*, 263–266.

De Silva, H. R., & Bartley, S. H. Summation and subtraction of brightness in binocular perception. *British Journal of Psychology*, 1930, *20*, 242–252.

Dev, P. Perception of depth surfaces in random-dot stereograms: A neural model. *International Journal of Man-Machine Studies*, 1975, *7*, 511–528.

De Weert, M. M., & Levelt, W. J. M. Binocular brightness combinations: Additive and nonadditive aspects. *Perception and Psychophysics*, 1974, *15*, 551–562.

Dodwell, P. C. *Visual pattern recognition*. New York: Holt, 1970.

Dodwell, P. C. & Engel, G. R. A theory of binocular fusion. *Nature*, 1963, *198*, 39–40.

Duwaer, A. L., & van den Brink, G. What is the diplopia threshold? *Perception and Psychophysics*, 1981, *29*, 295–309.

Duwaer, A. L., & van den Brink, G. The effect of presentation time on detection and diplopia thresholds for vertical disparities. *Vision Research*, 1982, *22*, 183–189.

Ebenholtz, S., & Walchli, R. Stereoscopic thresholds as a function of head- and object-orientation. *Vision Research*, 1965, *5*, 455–461.

Engel, G. R. The visual process underlying binocular brightness summation. *Vision Research*, 1967, *7*, 753–767.

Engel, G. R. The autocorrelation function and binocular brightness mixing. *Vision Research*, 1969, *9*, 1111–1130.

Engel, G. R. Tests of a model of binocular brightness. *Canadian Journal of Psychology*, 1970, *24*, 335–352.

Eriksen, C. W. Independence of successive inputs and uncorrelated error in visual form perception. *Journal of Experimental Psychology*, 1966, *72*, 26–35.

Eriksen, C. W., & Greenspon, T. S. Binocular summation over time in the perception of form at brief durations. *Journal of Experimental Psychology*, 1968, *76*, 331–336.

Eriksen, C. W., Greenspon, T. S., Lappin, J. S., & Carlson, W. A. Binocular summation in the perception of form at brief durations. *Perception and Psychophysics*, 1966, *1*, 415–419.

Fechner, G. T. Ueber einige Verhaltnisse des binocularen Sehens. *Abhandlungen der koniglichen sachsischen Gesellschaft fur Wissenschaften*, 1861, *5*, 336–564.

Felton, T. B., Richards, W., & Smith, Jr., R. A. Disparity processing of spatial frequencies in man. *Journal of Physiology* (London), 1972, *25*, 349–362.

Fender, D., & Julesz, B. Extension of Panum's fusional area in binocularly stabilized vision. *Journal of the Optical Society of America*, 1967, *57*, 819–830.

Ferree, C. W., Rand, G., & Buckley, D. Study of ocular functions with special reference to the lookout and signal service of the navy. *Journal of Experimental Psychology*, 1920, *3*, 347–356.

Fineman, M. B. Facilitation of stereoscopic depth perception by a relative-size cue in ambiguous disparity stereograms. *Journal of Experimental Psychology*, 1971, *90*, 215–221.

Fiorentini, A., & Maffei, L. Binocular depth perception without geometrical cues. *Vision Research*, 1971, *11*, 1299–1362.

Foley, J. M. Desarguesian property in visual space. *Journal of the Optical Society of America*, 1964, *54*, 684–692.

Foley, J. M., & Richards, W. Effects of voluntary eye movement and convergence on the binocular appreciation of depth. *Perception and Psychophysics*, 1972, *11*, 423–427.

Fox, R., & Check, R. Forced-choice form recognition during binocular rivalry. *Psychonomic Science*, 1966, *6*, 471–472.

Fox, R., & Check, R. Detection of motion during binocular rivalry suppression. *Journal of Experimental Psychology*, 1968, *78*, 388–395.

Fox, R., & Check, R. Independence between binocular rivalry suppression, duration, and magnitude of suppression. *Journal of Experimental Psychology*, 1972, *93*, 283–289.

Fox, R., & Herrmann, J. Stochastic properties of binocular rivalry alternations. *Perception and Psychophysics*, 1967, *2*, 432–436.

Fox, R., & Rasche, F. Binocular rivalry and reciprocal inhibition. *Perception and Psychophysics*, 1969, *5*, 215–217.

Frisby, J. P., & Clatworthy, J. L. Learning to see complex random-dot stereograms. *Perception*, 1975, *4*, 173–178.

Frisby, J. P., & Mayhew, J. E. W. Global processes in stereopsis: Some comments on Ramachandran and Nelson (1976). *Perception*, 1976, *6*, 195–206.

Frisby, J. P., & Mayhew, J. E. W. Contrast sensitivity function for stereopsis. *Perception*, 1978, *7*, 423–429.

Frisby, J. P., & Mayhew, J. E. W. The role of spatial frequency tuned channels in vergence control. *Vision Research*, 1980, *20*, 727–732.

Fry, G. A., & Bartley, S. H. The brilliance of an object seen binocularly. *American Journal of Ophthalmology*, 1933, *16*, 687–693.

Fry, G. A., & Hill, W. W. The center of rotation of the eye. *American Journal of Optometry*, 1962, *39*, 581–595.

Fuortes, M., & Hodgkin, A. Changes in time scale and intensity in the ommatidia of Limulus. *Journal of Physiology* (London), 1964, *172*, 239–263.

Gettys, C. F., & Harker, G. S. Some observations and measurements of the Panum phenomenon. *Perception and Psychophyics*, 1967, *2*, 387–395.

Gillam, B., & Lawergren, B. The induced effect, vertical disparity and stereoscopic theory. *Perception and Psychophysics*, 1983, *34*, 121–130.

Gogel, W. C. Convergence as a cue to absolute distance. *Journal of Psychology*, 1961, *51*, 287–301.

Graham, C. H. Visual space perception. In C. H. Graham (Ed.), *Vision and visual perception*. New York: Wiley, 1965.

Green, D. M., & Swets, J. A. *Signal detection theory and psychophysics*. New York: Wiley, 1966.

Gregory, R. L. Stereoscopic shadow-images. *Nature*, 1964, *203*, 1407.

Gregory, R. L. The 4th dimension of 3-D (1). *Perception*, 1980, *9*, 613–616.

Gregory, R. L. The 4th dimension of 3-D (2). *Perception*, 1981, *10*, 1–4.

Grimson, W. E. L. *From images to surfaces: A computational study of the human early visual system*. Cambridge, Mass.: M.I.T., 1981.

Gulick, W. L., & Lawson, R. B. *Human stereopsis*. New York: Oxford University Press, 1976.

Hardy, L. H., Rand, G., Rittler, M. C., Blank, A. A., & Boeder, P. *The geometry of binocular space perception*. Knapp Memorial Laboratories, Institute of Ophthalmology, Columbia University College of Physicians and Surgeons, 1953.

Harker, G. S. A saccadic suppression explanation of the Pulfrich phenomenon. *Perception and Psychophysics*, 1967, *2*, 387–395.

Harker, G. S. The Mach-Dvorak phenomenon and binocular fusion of moving stimuli. *Vision Research*, 1973, *13*, 1041–1058.

Harwerth, R. S., Smith, E. L., & Levi, D. M. Suprathreshold binocular interactions for grating patterns. *Perception and Psychophysics*, 1980, *27*, 43–50.

Heineman, E. G., Tulving, E., & Nachmias, J. The effect of oculomotor adjustments on apparent size. *American Journal of Psychology*, 1959, *72*, 32–45.

Helmholtz, H. von. *Treatise on physiological optics*, (Trans. from 3rd German ed., J. P. C. Southall, Ed., Opt. Soc. Amer., 1925.)

Hering, E. *Beitrage zur Physiologie*. Leipzig: Engelmann, 1861.

Herzau, W., & Ogle, K. N. Uber den GoBenunterscheid der Bilder beider Augen bei asymmetrischer Konvergenz und seine Bedeutung fur das Zweiaugige Sehen. *Albrecht v. Graefes Arch. Ophthal.*, 1937, *137*, 327–363.

Hillebrand, F. *Lehre von den Gesichtsempfindungen*. Wien: Springer, 1929.

Hochberg, J. E. A theory of the binocular cyclopean field: On the possibility of stimulating stereopsis. *Perceptual and Motor Skills*, 1964, *19*, 685.

Hollins, M. The effect of contrast on the completeness of binocular rivalry suppression. *Perception and Psychophysics*, 1980, *27*, 550–556.

Horowitz, M. W. An analysis of the superiority of binocular over monocular visual acuity. *Journal of Experimental Psychology*, 1949, *39*, 581–596.

Householder, A. E. A theory of the induced effect. *Bulletin of Mathematical Biophysics*, 1943, *5*, 155–161.

Howard, H. J. A test for the judgment of distance. *American Journal of Ophthalmology*, 1919, *2*, 656–675.

Hubel, D. H., & Wiesel, T. N. Receptive fields, binocular interaction, and functional architecture in the cat's visual cortex. *Journal of Physiology*, 1962, *160*, 106–154.

Iverson, G., Movshon, J. A., Arditi, A., & Westendorf, D. Binocular additivity of monocular contrasts. *Investigative Ophthalmology and Visual Science Supplement*, 1981, *20*, 224.

Joshua, D. E., & Bishop, P. O. Binocular single vision and depth discrimination: Receptive field disparities for central and peripheral vision and binocular interaction on peripheral single units in cat striate cortex. *Experimental Brain Research*, 1970, *10*, 389–416.

Julesz, B. Binocular depth perception of computer-generated patterns. *Bell System Technical Journal*, 1960, *39*, 1125–1162.

Julesz, B. *Foundations of cyclopean perception*. Chicago: University of Chicago Press, 1971.

Julesz, B. Recent results with dynamic random-dot stereograms. In S. Benton (Ed.), *Three dimensional imaging. Proceedings of the Society of Photo-Optical Instrument Engineers*, 1977, *120*, 30–35.

Julesz, B. Global stereopsis: Cooperative phenomena in stereoscopic depth perception. In R. Held, H. Leibowitz, H.-L. Teuber (Eds.), *Handbook of sensory physiology* (Vol. 8): *Perception*. Berlin: Springer, 1978.

Julesz, B., & Chang, J. J. Interaction between pools of binocular disparity detectors tuned to different disparities. *Biological Cybernetics*, 1976, *22*, 107–119.

Julesz, B., & Miller, J. E. Independent spatial-frequency-tuned channels in binocular fusion and rivalry. *Perception*, 1975, *4*, 125–143.

Julesz, B., & White, B. W. Short term visual memory and the Pulfrich phenomenon. *Nature*, 1969, *22*, 639–641.

Kahneman, D., Norman, J., & Kubovy, M. Critical duration for the resolution of form: Centrally or peripherally determined? *Journal of Experimental Psychology*, 1967, *73*, 323–327.

Kakizaki, S. Binocular rivalry and stimulus intensity. *Japanese Psychological Research*, 1960, *2*, 94–105.

Kaufman, L. On the spread of suppression and binocular rivalry. *Vision Research*, 1963, *3*, 401–415.

Kaufman, L. On the nature of binocular disparity. *American Journal of Psychology*, 1964, *77*, 398–401.

Kaufman, L. Some new stereoscopic phenomena and their implications for theories of stereopsis. *American Journal of Psychology*, 1965, *78*, 1–20.

Kaufman, L. *Sight and mind*. New York: Oxford University Press, 1974.

Kaufman, L., & Arditi, A. Confusion prevails! A reply to Kertesz and Sullivan. *Vision Research*, 1976, *16*, 551–552. (a)

Kaufman, L., & Arditi, A. The fusion illusion. *Vision Research*, 1976, *16*, 535–543. (b)

Kaufman, L., & Pitblado, C. B. Further observations on the nature of effective binocular disparities. *American Journal of Psychology*, 1965, *78*, 379–391.

Kertesz, A. E. The effect of stimulus complexity on human cyclofusional response. *Vision Research*, 1972, *12*, 699–704.

Kertesz, A. E., & Jones, R. W. Human cyclofusional response. *Vision Research*, 1970, *10*, 891–896.

Koffka, K. *Principles of Gestalt psychology*. New York: Harcourt, Brace, 1935.

Lee D. N. Theory of the stereoscopic shadow-caster: An instrument for the study of binocular kinetic space perception. *Vision Research*, 1969, *9*, 145–156.

Lee, D. N. Spatio-temporal integration in binocular-kinetic space perception. *Vision Research*, 1970, *10*, 65–78. (a)

Lee, D. N. A stroboscopic stereophenomenon. *Vision Research*, 1970, 587–593. (b)

Legge, G. E., & Rubin, G. S. Binocular interactions in suprathreshold contrast perception. *Perception and Psychophysics*, 1981, *30*, 49–61.

Lema, S. A., & Blake, R. Binocular summation in normal and stereoblind humans. *Vision Research*, 1977, *17*, 69.

Levelt, W. J. M. *On binocular rivalry*. The Hague: Mouton, 1968.

Levi, D., Harwerth, R., & Smith, E. L. Humans deprived of normal binocular vision have binocular interactions tuned to size and orientation. *Science*, 1979, *206*, 852–853.

Levinson, E., & Blake, R. Stereopsis by harmonic analysis. *Vision Research*, 1979, *19*, 73–78.

Linksz, A. *Physiology of the eye* (Vol. 2): *Vision*. New York: Grune & Stratton, 1952.

Linschoten, J. *Stucturanalyse der binocularen Tiefenwahrenehmung*. New York: Gregory Lounz, 1956.

Lippincott, J. A. On the binocular metamorphopsia produced by optical means. *Archives of Ophthalmology*, 1917, *18*, 18–30.

Lit, A. The magnitude of the Pulfrich stereo-phenomenon as a function of binocular differences of intensity at various levels of illumination. *American Journal of Psychology*, 1949, *62*, 159–181.

Luneburg, R. K. *Mathematical analysis of binocular vision*. Princeton, N.J.: Princeton, 1947.

Luneburg, R. K. The metric of visual space. *Journal of the Optical Society of America*, 1950, *40*, 627–647.

Lyding, Uber die Netzhutdeckstellen. *Klin. Mbl. AugenReilk*, 1939, *102*, 874.

MacLeod, D. I. A. The Schrodinger equation in binocular brightness combination. *Perception*, 1972, *1*, 321–324.

Makous, W., & Pulos, E. Grating colors mix while their contours rival. *Investigative Ophthalmology and Visual Science Supplement*, 1981, *20*, 225.

Makous, W., & Sanders, K. Suppressive interactions between fused patterns. In J. C. Armington, J. Krauskopf, & B. R. Wooten (Eds.), *Visual psychophysics and physiology. A volume dedicated to Lorrin Riggs*. New York: Academic, 1978.

Marr, D., & Poggio, T. A computational theory of human stereo vision. *Proceedings of the Royal Society of London*, 1979, *204*, 301–328.

Matin, L. Binocular summation at the absolute threshold for peripheral vision. *Journal of the Optical Society of America*, 1962, *52*, 1276–1286.

Mayhew, J. E. W. The interpretation of stereo-disparity information: The computation of surface orientation and depth. *Perception*, 1982, *11*, 387–404.

Mayhew, J. E. W., & Frisby, J. P. Convergent disparity discriminations in narrow-band-filtered random-dot stereograms. *Vision Research*, 1979, *19*, 63–71.

Mayhew, J. E. W., & Frisby, J. P. The computation of binocular edges. *Perception*, 1980, *9*, 69–86. (a)

Mayhew, J. E. W., & Frisby, J. P. Spatial frequency tuned channels: Implications for structure and function from psychophysical and computational studies of stereopsis. *Philosophical Transactions of the Royal Society of London*, Series B, 1980, *290*, 95–116. (b)

Mayhew, J. E. W., & Frisby, J. P. The induced effect: Arguments against the theory of Arditi, Kaufman and Movshon (1981). *Vision Research*, 1982, *22*, 1225–1228.

Mitchell, D. Retinal disparity and diplopia. *Vision Research*, 1966, *6*, 441–451. (a)

Mitchell, D. A review of the concept of "Panum's fusional areas," *American Journal of Optometry*, 1966, *43*, 387–401. (b)

Mitchell, D. E. Qualitative depth localization with diplopic images of dissimilar shape. *Vision Research*, 1969, *9*, 991–994.

Mitchell, D. E. Properties of stimuli eliciting vergence eye movements and stereopsis. *Vision Research*, 1970, *10*, 145–162.

Morgan, M. J. Differential visual persistence between the two eyes: A model of the Fertsch-Pulfrich effect. *Journal of Experimental Psychology: Human Perception and Performance*, 1977, *3*, 484–495.

Morgan, M. J., & Thompson, P. Apparent motion and the Pulfrich effect. *Perception*, 1975, *5*, 187–195.

Mowforth, P., Mayhew, J. E. W., & Frisby, J. P. Vergence eye movements made in response to spatial-frequency-filtered random-dot stereograms. *Perception*, 1981, *10*, 299–304.

Mueller, C. G., & Lloyd, V. V. Stereoscopic acuity for various levels of illumination. *Proceedings of the National Academy of Science*, 1948, *34*, 223–227.

Muller, J. *Beitrage zur vergleichenden Physiologie des Gesichtsinnes*. Leipzig: Cnoblock, 1826.

Nakayama, K. Geometrical and physiological aspects of depth perception. In S. Benton (Ed.), *Three dimensional imaging. Proceedings of the Society of Photo-Optical Instrumentation Engineers*, 1977, *120*, 2–9.

Nakayama, K., Tyler, C., & Appelman, J. A new angle on the vertical horopter. *Investigative Ophthalmology Supplement*, 1977, *16*, 82.

Nelson, J. I. Globality and stereoscopic fusion in binocular vision. *Journal of Theoretical Biology*, 1975, *49*, 1–88.

Nelson, J. I. The plasticity of correspondence: Aftereffects, illusions and horopter shifts in depth perception. *Journal of Theoretical Biology*, 1977, *66*, 203–266.

Nikara, T., Bishop, P. O., & Pettigrew, J. D. Analysis of retinal correspondence by studying receptive fields of binocular single units in cat striate cortex. *Experimental Brain Research*, 1968, *6*, 353–372.

Ogle, K. N. Induced size effect. I. A new phenomenon in binocular space perception associated with the relative sizes of the images of the two eyes. *Archives of Ophthalmology*, 1938, *20*, 604–623.

Ogle, K. N. Induced size effect. II. An experimental study of the phenomenon using restricted fusion stimuli. *Archives of Ophthalmology*, 1939, *21*, 604–625. (a)

Ogle, K. N. Induced size effect. III. A study of the phenomenon as influenced by horizontal disparity of the fusion contours. *Archives of Ophthalmology*, 1939, *22*, 613–635. (b)

Ogle, K. N. *Researches in binocular vision*. Philadelphia: Saunders, 1950.

Ogle, K. N. Disparity limits of stereopsis. *Archives of Ophthalmology*, 1952, *48*, 50–60. (a)

Ogle, K. N. On the limits of stereoscopic vision. *Journal of Experimental Psychology*, 1952, *44*, 253–259. (b)

Ogle, K. N. Stereopsis and vertical disparity. *Archives of Opthalmology*, 1955, *53*, 495–504.

Ogle, K. N. Theory of stereoscopic vision. In S. Koch (Ed.), *Psychology: A study of a science* (Vol. 1). New York: McGraw-Hill, 1959.

Okoshi, T. *Three-dimensional imaging techniques*. New York: Academic Press, 1976.

Ono, H. & Barbeito, R. Utrocolar discrimination is not sufficient for utrocular identification. *Vision Research*, 1985, *25*, 289–299.

Panum, P. L. *Physiologische Untersuchungen uber das Sehen mit zwei Augen*. Kiel: Schwers, 1858.

Pirenne, M. H. Binocular and uniocular thresholds in vision. *Nature*, 1943, *152*, 698–699.

Poggio, G. F., & Fischer, B. Binocular interaction and depth sensitivity in striate and prestriate cortex of behaving rhesus monkey. *Journal of Neurophysiology*, 1977, *40*, 1392–1405.

Pulfrich, C. Die stereoskopie im Dienste der isochromen und heterochromen Photometric. *Naturwissenschaften*, 1922, *10*, 533–564; 569–601; 714–722; 735–743; 751–761.

Quick, R. F. A vector magnitude model of contrast detection. *Kybernetic*, 1974, *16*, 65–67.

Ramachandran, V. S. Learning-like phenomena in stereopsis. *Nature*, 1976, *262*, 382–383.

Ramachandran, V. S., & Braddick, O. Orientation-specific learning in stereopsis. *Perception*, 1973, *2*, 371–376.

Rashbass, C., & Westheimer, G. Disjunctive eye movements. *Journal of Physiology* (London), 1961, *159*, 339–360.

Rawlings, S. C., & Shipley, T. Stereoscopic acuity and horizontal angular distance from fixation. *Journal of the Optical Society of America*, 1969, *59*, 991–993.

Roelofs, C. O., & Zeeman, W. C. P. Uber den Wettstreit der Kontouren. *v. Graefes Arch. Ophthal.*, 1919, *99*, 79–104.

Rogers, B. J., & Anstis, S. M. Intensity versus adaptation and the Pulfrich stereophenomenon. *Vision Research*, 1972, *12*, 909–928.

Rosch, J. Measures stereoscopiques appliquees a l'astronomie et recherches connexes d'optique Physiologique. Part I. Physiologie et geometrie de la vision binoculaire et des mesures stereoscopiques. *Actual. scient. ind.*, 1943, 954.

Rose, D. Monocular vs. binocular contrast thresholds for movement and pattern. *Perception*, 1978, *7*, 195–200.

Ross, J. Stereopsis by binocular delay. *Nature*, 1974, *248*, 363–364.

Rozhkova, G. I., Nickolayev, P. P., & Shchadrin, V. E. Perception of stabilized retinal stimuli in dichoptic viewing conditions. *Vision Research*, 1982, *22*, 293–302.

Saye, A., and Frisby, J. P. The role of monocularly conspicuous features in facilitating stereopsis from random-dot stereograms. *Perception*, 1975, *4*, 159–171.

Schreiver, W. Experimentelle Studien uber stereoskopisches Sehen. *Zeit. f. Psychol.*, 1925, *96*, 113–170.

Schrodinger, E. Die Gesichtsempfindungen. In *Mueller-Pouillet's Lehrbuch der Physik* (11th ed.). Braunschweig: Vieweg, 1926.

Schumer, R., & Julesz, B. Disparity limits in bandpass random grating stereograms. *Investigative Ophthalmology and Visual Science Supplement*, 1982, *22*, 272.

Schumer, R., & Julesz, B. Binocular disparity modulation sensitivity to disparities offset from the plane of fixation. *Vision Research*, 1984, *24*, 533–542.

Shaad, D. Binocular summation in scotopic vision. *Journal of Experimental Psychology*, 1935, *4*, 391–413.

Sherrington, C. S. On binocular flicker and the correlation of activity of "corresponding retinal points." *British Journal of Psychology*, 1904, *1*, 26–60.

Shimojo, S., & Nakajima, Y. Adaptation to the reversal of binocular depth cues: Effects of wearing left-right reversing spectacles on stereoscopic depth perception. *Perception*, 1981, *10*, 391–402.

Shipley, T., & Rawlings, S. C. The nonius horopter—I. History and theory. *Vision Research*, 1970, *10*, 1225–1262. (a)

Shipley, T., & Rawlings, S. C. The nonius horopter—II. An experimental report. *Vision Research*, 1970, *10*, 1263–1299. (b)

Sperling, G. Binocular vision: A physical and a neural model. *American Journal of Psychology*, 1970, *83*, 461–534.

Sperling, G. Mathematical models of binocular vision. In S. Grossberg (Ed.), *Mathematical psychology and psychophysiology*. Providence, R.I.: SIAM-AMS Proceedings, 1981, *13*, 281–300.

Staller, J. D., Lappin, J. S., & Fox, R. Stimulus uncertainty does not impair stereopsis. *Perception and Psychophysics*, 1980, *27*, 361–367.

Sugie, N., & Suwa, M. A scheme for binocular depth perception suggested by neurophysiological evidence. *Biological Cybernetics*, 1977, *26*, 1–15.

Templeton, W. B., & Green, F. A. Chance results in utrocular discrimination. *Quarterly Journal of Experimental Psychology*, 1968, *20*, 200–203.

Thomas, F. H., Dimmick, F. L., & Luria, S. M. A study of binocular color mixture. *Vision Research*, 1961, *1*, 108–120.

Thorn, F., & Boynton, R. M. Human binocular summation at absolute threshold. *Vision Research*, 1974, *14*, 445–458.

Townsend, J. T. Binocular information summation and the serial processing model. *Perception and Psychophysics*, 1968, *4*, 125–128.

Tschermak, A. Beitrage zur Lehre vom Langshoropter. (Ueber die Tiefenlokalisation bei Dauer- und bei Momentreizen nach Beobachtungen von Dr. Kiribuchi, Tokio). *Pflugers, Arch. Physiol.*, 1900, *81*, 328–348.

Tschermak-Seysenegg, A. von. *Introduction to physiological optics* (P. Boeder, Trans.). Springfield, Ill.: Thomas, 1952.

Tyler, C. Stereopsis in dynamic visual noise. *Nature*, 1974, *250*, 781–782.

Tyler, C. Stereomovement from interocular delay in dynamic visual noise: A random spatial disparity hypothesis. *American Journal of Physiological Optics*, 1977, *54*, 374–386.

Tyler, C., & Sutter, E. Depth from spatial frequency difference: An old kind of stereopsis? *Vision Research*, 1979, *19*, 859–865.

Ueno, T. Reaction time as a measure of temporal summation at suprathreshold levels. *Vision Research*, 1977, *17*, 227.

Valyus, N. A. *Stereoscopy*. London: Focal, 1966.

Volkmann, A. W. Kie stereoskopischen Erscheinurgen in ihrer Beziehung zu der Lehre von den identischen Netzhautpunkter. *Albrecht. v. Graefes Arch. Ophthal.*, 1859, *5*(2), 1–100.

Von Noorden, G. K. *Binocular vision and ocular motility*. St. Louis: Mosby, 1980.

Wade, N. J. Contour synchrony in binocular rivalry. *Perception and Psychophysics*, 1973, *13*, 423–425.

Wales, R., & Fox, R. Increment detection thresholds during binocular rivalry suppression. *Perception and Psychophysics*, 1970, *8*, 90–94.

Walker, P., & Powell, D. J. The sensitivity of binocular rivalry to changes in the nondominant stimulus. *Vision Research*, 1979, *19*, 247–249.

Wallach, H., & Adams, P. A. Binocular rivalry of achromatic colors. *American Journal of Psychology*, 1954, *67*, 513–516.

Wallach, H., & Lindauer, J. On the definition of binocular disparity.

Psychologische Beitrage, 1961, *6*, 521–530.
Walls, G. The problem of visual direction. *Journal of Optometry*, 1951, *28*, 55–83; 115–146; 173–212.
Watson, A. B., Thompson, P. G., Murphy, B. J., & Nachmias, J. Summation and discrimination of gratings moving in opposite directions. *Vision Research*, 1980, *20*, 341–347.
Werner, H. Dynamics in binocular depth perception. *Psychological Monographs*, 1937 (Whole No. 218).
Westendorf, D., & Fox, R. Binocular detection of positive and negative flashes. *Perception and Psychophysics*, 1974, *15*, 61–65.
Westendorf, D., & Fox, R. Binocular detection of vertical and horizontal line segments. *Vision Research*, 1975, *15*, 471–476.
Westendorf, D., & Fox, R. Binocular detection of disparate light flashes. *Vision Research*, 1977, *17*, 697–702.
Westheimer, G. Cooperative neural process involved in stereoscopic acuity. *Experimental Brain Research*, 1979, *36*, 585–597.
Westheimer, G., & McKee, S. P. Stereoscopic acuity for moving retinal images. *Journal of the Optical Society of America*, 1978, *68*, 450–455.
Westheimer, G., & McKee, S. P. Stereoscopic acuity with defocused and spatially filtered retinal images. *Journal of the Optical Society of America*, 1980, *70*, 772–778.
Westheimer, G., & Tanzman, I. J. Qualitative depth localization with diplopic images. *Journal of the Optical Society of America*. 1956, *46*, 116–117.
Wheatstone, C. Contributions to the physiology of vision. Part the first, on some remarkable and hitherto unobserved phenomena of binocular vision. *Philosophical Transactions of the Royal Society*, 1838, *148*, 371–394.
Whittle, P., Bloor, D. C., & Pocock, S. Some experiments on figural effects in binocular rivalry. *Perception and Psychophysics*, 1968, *4*, 183–188.
Wilson, H. R. Hysteresis in binocular grating perception: Contrast effects. *Vision Research*, 1977, *17*, 843–851.
Wilson, H. R., & Giese, S. C. Threshold visibility of frequency gradient patterns. *Vision Research*, 1977, *17*, 1177–1190.
Wolf, E., & Zigler, M. J. Effects of uniocular and binocular excitation of the peripheral retina with test fields of various shapes on binocular summation. *Journal of the Optical Society of America*, 1963, *53*, 1199–1205.
Wolfe, J. M. When rivalry fails: the false fusion phenomenon and the temporal course of suppression. *Perception*, 1982, *11*, A17.

CHAPTER 24

ADAPTATION OF SPACE PERCEPTION

ROBERT B. WELCH

Department of Psychology, University of Kansas, Lawrence, Kansas

CONTENTS

1. OVERVIEW

1.1. Background

Human beings are remarkably adaptable organisms. The aim of this chapter is to describe and to evaluate critically the evidence for one general example of this capacity, namely, the ability to modify one's perception and perceptual-motor coordination when confronted with a significant discrepancy between or within the spatial modalities.

The simplest example of adaptation to perceptual rearrangement involves viewing the actively moving hand through a wedge prism that displaces the visual field to one side by about 11°. When this is done, as Helmholtz (1925) noted in the late 19th century, the observer's initial prism-induced errors in reaching for objects are quickly overcome. More revealing, however, is that if the prism is removed and the subject then requested to reach *quickly* for an object, the target is missed, the error being in the direction opposite the previous prismatic displacement. This phenomenon may be referred to as the "visuomotor negative aftereffect."

This demonstration reveals that human beings are capable of rapidly resolving a discrepancy between visual and proprioceptive-kinesthetic information concerning the position of the limb, and that this modification persists for some time after the distorting device is removed. Thus we may define "adaptation" (when used to refer to the *end product* of an adaptive process) as a *semipermanent change of perception or perceptual-motor coordination that serves to reduce or eliminate a registered discrepancy between or within sensory modalities or the errors in behavior induced by this discrepancy.* Excluded by this definition are such perceptual changes as (1) sensory habituation, (2) figural aftereffects (e.g., Köhler & Wallach, 1944), and the perceptual "normalization" resulting from passive exposure to tilted or curved lines (e.g., J. J. Gibson, 1933; J. J. Gibson & Radner, 1937a, 1937b). These phenomena do not qualify as adaptation as it is defined here because they do not entail a *discrepancy* between sensory modalities and they are typically quite short-lived. In addition, these excluded effects tend to be highly localized (e.g., limited to the stimulated retinal region), whereas adaptation, as we shall see, is a more generalizable, higher-order event. One final note about this definition is that it does not specify the *direction* in which the intersensory discrepancy will be resolved. Indeed, as will be seen later, it is frequently the initially accurate body position sense that undergoes modification from exposure to visual rearrangement.

A long line of research has demonstrated that adult human beings are capable of adapting, at least partially, to almost any conceivable form of stable rearrangement of spatial information as produced by a variety of optical and acoustical devices. (See Kornheiser, 1976; Rock, 1966; and Welch, 1974a, 1978, for reviews of this literature.) Some lower organisms have also proved capable of such adaptation; these studies were reviewed by Taub (1968) and Welch (1978, Chapter 11).

As will become clear in later sections, the specific perceptual modifications that underlie the perceptual-motor changes that occur, either during exposure to the intersensory discrepancy (the "reduction of effect") or afterward (the "negative aftereffect"), vary with the form of rearrangement and type of exposure. The distinction between these two general indexes of adaptation, as exemplified in eye-hand corrections for prismatic displacement, is depicted in Figure 24.1.

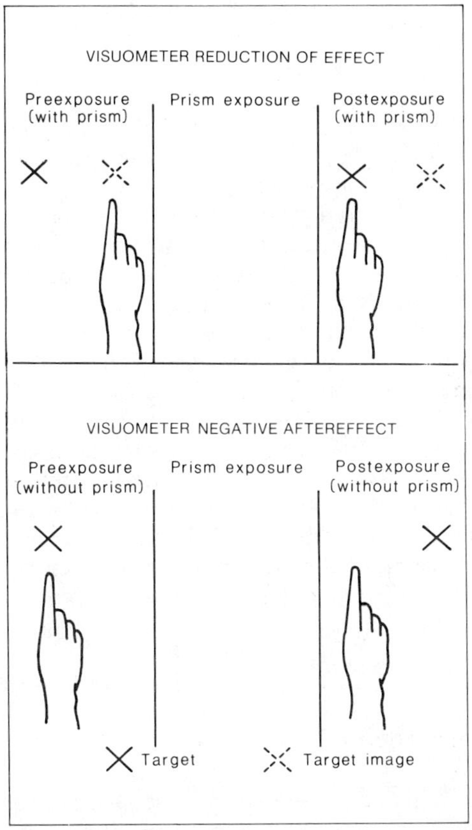

Figure 24.1. A schematic representation of the distinction between the visuomotor reduction of effect and the visuomotor negative aftereffect. In the case of the reduction of effect, the subject, while wearing rightward-displacing prisms, initially points at where the target appears to be located, missing it by approximately the amount of the prismatic displacement. After a period of exposure to the prism, during which the hand is viewed, the subject comes to point accurately at the target despite the fact that the latter is still prismatically displaced. With respect to the negative aftereffect, the subject, with normal vision, initially points at the target with approximate accuracy. After a period of prism exposure, the prism is removed and the subject errs to the left of the target (i.e., in the direction opposite the prismatic displacement), thereby revealing the adaptation acquired during prism ex posure. (From R. B. Welch, *Perceptual modification: Adapting to altered sensory environments*, Academic Press, Inc., 1978. Reprinted with permission.)

The experimental paradigm used by Helmholtz has served as the model for nearly all the subsequent research in this area. It involves (1) preexposure measures of perception or perceptual-motor performance, (2) a period of exposure to the rearrangement, and (3) postexposure measures. Adaptation is revealed by a compensatory shift between the pre- and postexposure measures, both usually obtained in the absence of accuracy feedback to the subject and with the distorting medium removed. During the exposure period the subject is confronted with the effects of the sensory rearrangement, typically by means of visuomotor behavior, such as moving the hand, reaching for objects, or actively locomoting in the environment.

Studies of adaptation to perceptual rearrangement were reported only sporadically after Helmholtz's pioneering observation. The most frequently cited investigation was by Stratton (1896, 1897a, 1897b) who, for as long as 8 days, wore monocular goggles that rotated his visual field by 180°. In these studies Stratton proved capable of overcoming completely the initial visuomotor and locomotory difficulties he encountered in his everyday activities inside his house and in his garden. Furthermore, he revealed apparently complete adaptation to the nausea-inducing illusory motion of the visual field that occurred whenever he moved his head. However, the crucial question of whether the optically inverted world could ever come to look right side up while wearing the inverting goggles was never satisfactorily answered. At best, the world looked "normal" when Stratton was engrossed in some activity and not critically comparing his visual experience to his memory of the preexperimental appearance of things. More telling, perhaps, is that (contrary to the situation with his eye-hand coordination and apparent visual motion with head movements) the apparent orientation of the visual field did not undergo a negative aftereffect when the goggles were removed.

Beginning in the late 1950s and continuing throughout the 1960s, interest in the question of adaptation to perceptual rearrangement increased dramatically, especially among American psychologists, resulting in a tremendous accumulation of research findings. This interest was inspired by the publication in English of the extensive investigations by Erismann (1947) and Kohler (1955, 1962, 1964) and by the research and theorizing of Held (e.g., 1961).

1.2. The Aims of Adaptation Research and of This Chapter

Three major aims have motivated research on perceptual adaptation. These are (1) to understand better the origin and development of spatial perception, (2) to reveal aspects of perception and perceptual-motor coordination in adult observers that might otherwise be obscured when examining "normal" perception, and (3) to assess the adaptability of the perceptual and perceptual-motor systems to spatial distortions encountered in the laboratory or in "real-life" situations.

The degree to which these aims have been realized is assessed in the final section of this chapter. Prior to this conclusion, the research findings are summarized for each of the many varieties of perceptual rearrangement that have been investigated. These include prismatic displacement, visual transposition, tilt, loss of visual stability when moving head or eyes, size-depth distortion, distortion of form, auditory right-left reversal and displacement, and distortions in underwater perception. An additional section deals with the important issue of individual differences in adaptation.

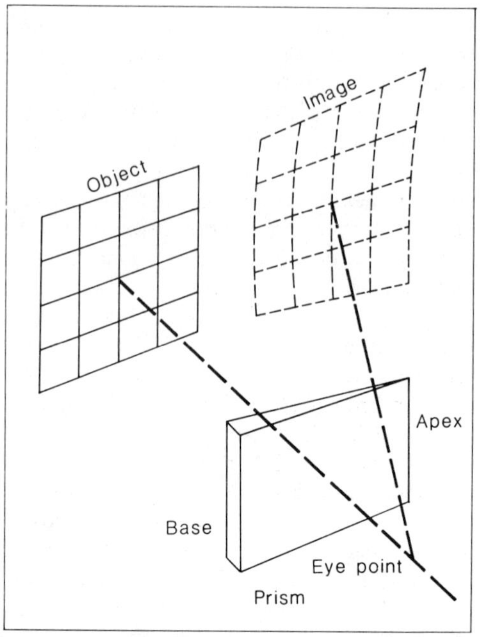

Figure 24.2. A 20-diopter base-left wedge prism and its optical properties. The prism produces a rightward lateral rotation of the visual field of approximately 11°. In addition, the visual field appears compressed on the base side and expanded on the apex side, as a result of the varying thickness of the prism and angle of incidence of the light rays. For the same reasons, vertical contours appear curved, particularly toward the apex side. Not depicted is the prism-induced chromatic aberration—a fringe of red and blue that appears to be attached to vertical brightness contours. Finally, up-down head movements while wearing prism goggles cause an apparent see-saw motion of the field, whereas left-right head movements induce an alternating expansion and compression of the visual field. (From K. N. Ogle, *Optics: An introduction for ophthalmologists* (2nd ed.), Charles C Thomas, Publishers, 1968. Reprinted with permission.)

2. ADAPTATION TO PRISMATIC DISPLACEMENT

2.1. Background

Although Helmholtz was the first to use wedge prisms to study adaptation to perceptual rearrangement, it was Held and his colleagues (Held & Hein, 1958) who popularized this particular form of optical distortion. This section examines the results of the many studies of prism adaptation that have appeared over the last two decades.

As a form of perceptual rearrangement to investigate, prismatic displacement has at least two major advantages over inversion or right-left reversal. First, prism adaptation can be observed after exposure periods of as little as 1 min. Second, it is possible to measure *partial* adaptation to prismatic displacement, whereas only "all-or-none" modifications would appear likely with visual transposition.

The effects of a wedge prism are not limited to displacement, as may be seen in Figure 24.2. Not depicted in this figure are the chromatic aberration that occurs for vertical brightness contours and the "rubbery" appearance of the visual field that is experienced if the head is moved about. Mirrors may be used to produce visual displacement without these side effects (e.g., Warren & Cleaves, 1971).

Subjects may be exposed to the effects of a wedge prism in either an *unconstrained* or *constrained* manner. In the former the prism-wearing subject is allowed to move about freely in a natural indoor or outdoor environment. In the latter, the subject typically sits at a table with head held steady, viewing the hand and perhaps part of the arm through the distorting device (usually a wedge prism). An example of such an arrangement is depicted in Figure 24.3. The majority of studies of prism adaptation have used the constrained procedure, apparently to avoid many of the "extraneous" effects of prismatic displacement described previously.

Two popular varieties of the constrained procedure are referred to as "concurrent" and "terminal." In the concurrent exposure condition (e.g., Held & Gottlieb, 1958), the subject is provided with a continuous view of the hand while moving it about, usually from side to side, and observing it against a homogeneous background (see Figure 24.4). With terminal exposure (e.g., Welch, 1969), the subject reaches out in front of the body and, owing to the presence of an occluding shelf, can view the hand or finger only after each limb movement has reached its terminus. Frequently, the responses are directed toward a target located at the far edge of the occluding shelf.

2.2. Experimental Results

2.2.1. General Characteristics and Parameters

2.2.1.1. Acquisition Functions. Prism adaptation, as measured by the visuomotor negative aftereffect or the reduction of effect, increases in magnitude as a negatively accelerated function of exposure time or trials (Dewar, 1970b; Efstathiou, 1969; Redding, 1975a). This curve is particularly steep and reaches a relatively high asymptote when prism exposure includes error-corrective feedback (e.g., Welch, 1971a; Wertheimer & Arena, 1959). Acquisition functions for the study by Welch (1971a) are depicted in Figure 24.5, with adaptation reaching asymptote at 85% of the maximum for the target-pointing condition and 53% for the no-target condition. Prism adaptation very rarely (Hay & Pick, 1966a; Hein, 1972) reaches 100% of the theoretical maximum, even when error-corrective feedback and other salient forms of information are provided.

It is not surprising that the various components of the adaptive shifts in eye-hand coordination (components discussed in Section 2.2.3), when measured separately, also reveal

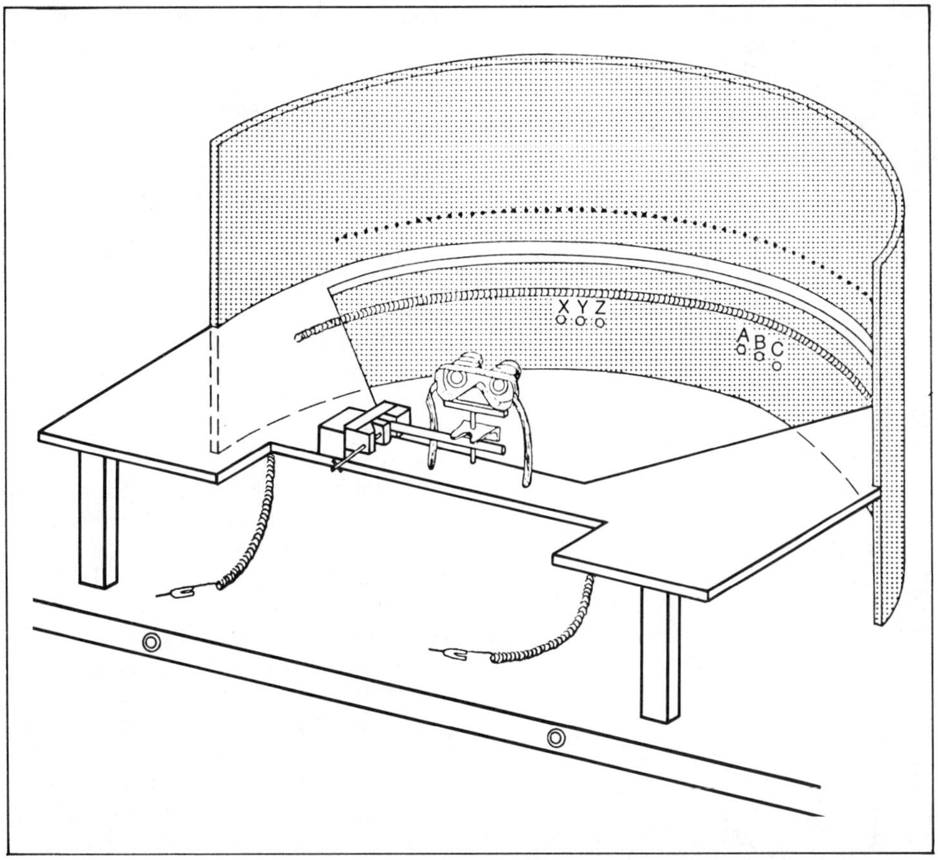

Figure 24.3. An example of an apparatus used for inducing and measuring prism adaptation. The subject sits at the apparatus with face pressed against the mounted prism goggles. Target-pointing responses are made by reaching beneath the horizontal panel at targets located directly above the far edge. When the panel is covered, the visuomotor reduction of effect (with prismatic displacement still present) or visuomotor negative aftereffect (normal vision) can be assessed. Target-pointing accuracy is measured by having the subject touch a curved position transducer (located beneath the horizontal panel, directly below the targets) by means of a metal stylus worn on the left or right index finger. The transducer is attached to a digital voltmeter which provides readings accurate to the nearest 0.13°. (From J. J. Uhlarik, A device for presenting targets and recorded positioning responses in one dimension, *Behavior Research Methods and Instrumentation*, 1972, *4*. Reprinted with permission.)

asymptotic acquisition curves (Hay & Pick, 1966a; McLaughlin & Webster, 1967; Redding, 1973b, 1975b; Rekosh & Freedman, 1967).

2.2.1.2. Postacquisition Functions. There are three possible fates of prism adaptation after the exposure period has been concluded. First, the adaptation may spontaneously *decay* as the subject remains relatively immobile and with eyes shut. Second, it may be replaced by the normal state of affairs by allowing the subject to interact with the undistorted visual environment. This may be referred to as "*unlearning*." Finally, one may confront the subject with a new perceptual rearrangement, such as a prismatic displacement in the direction opposite that to which the subject has just adapted. This may be referred to as "*relearning*."

Both the negative aftereffect and the reduction of effect for prism-induced eye-hand shifts undergo spontaneous decay as a negatively accelerated function of postexposure time in the dark (Fishkin, 1969; Hamilton & Bossom, 1964; Taub & Goldberg, 1973). This function is typically less steep than the acquisition curve (e.g., Dewar, 1971) and reaches completion if the postexposure period is sufficiently long (e.g., Goldberg, Taub, & Berman, 1967; Redding, 1975b; Taub & Goldberg, 1973). Rate of decay of this form of adaptation is apparently more rapid if prism exposure has been concurrent than if it has been terminal (Dewar, 1970b; Goldberg et al., 1967; Welch, 1971a); the presence or absence of error-corrective feedback, however, has no effect, at least over a 15-min postexposure period (Welch, 1971a). There is some evidence to suggest that decay of the proprioceptive component of the visuomotor negative aftereffect is more rapid than the decay of the visual component (Choe & Welch, 1974; Redding, 1973b; Templeton, Howard, & Wilkinson, 1974). It may be speculated that the relative resistance to decay of the visuomotor negative aftereffect in the terminal prism exposure condition (Dewar, 1970b; Goldberg et al., 1967; Welch, 1971a) is due to the long-lasting visual component of this adaptation, a component that has been shown to be facilitated by this form of exposure (see Section 2.2.4.3).

It has been proposed by several investigators (Day & Singer, 1967; Devane, 1968; Wallach & Floor, 1970; Wallach & Frey, 1972a) that the decay of prism and other forms of adaptation results from a process similar or identical to *proactive inhibition*. That is, during the postexposure period, memory traces for the normal (i.e., nondisplaced) visual arrangement override the more recently acquired changes induced by the prism. Direct support for this claim was provided by Devane (1968). The results of his study are depicted in Figure 24.6.

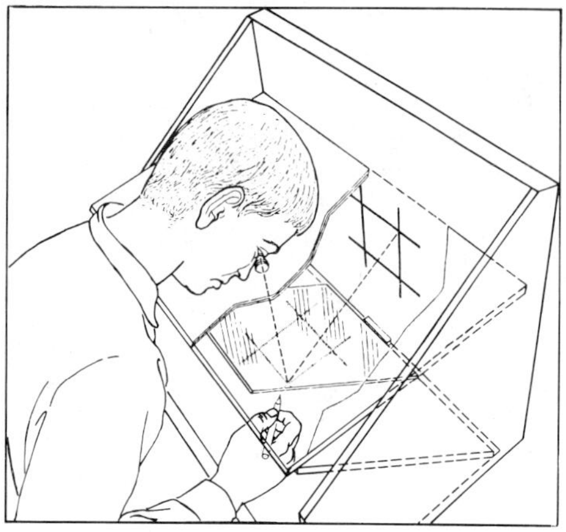

(a) MIRROR APPARATUS

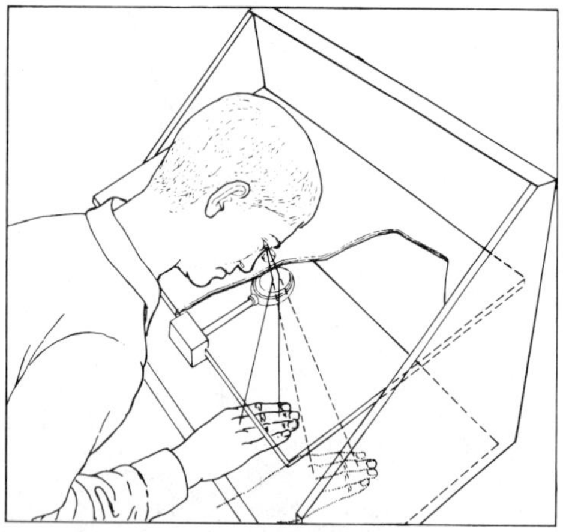

(b) VIEW THROUGH PRISM

Figure 24.4. Apparatus used by Held and his colleagues for inducing and measuring prism adaptation. (a) During the preexposure period, the subject points at the apparent location of each of the corners of a square seen in a mirror. The hand is beneath the mirror and thus cannot be seen during these measures of target-pointing accuracy. (b) Then the mirror is replaced by a prism, allowing the subject to see the displaced image of the hand as the latter is moved (actively or passively) from side to side against a homogeneous background. This prism exposure period is followed by the postexposure measures, which are taken with the apparatus returned to the configuration depicted in (a). (From R. Held, Plasticity in sensory-motor systems, *Scientific American*, 1965, *213*. Reprinted with permission.)

With one exception (Beckett & Melamed, 1980), studies in which the postexposure decline of prism adaptation as a result of normal visual experience (i.e., unlearning) has been compared to spontaneous decay (Hamilton & Bossom, 1964; Melamed, Moore, & Beckett, 1979; Welch, Bleam, & Needham, 1970) have all obtained data indicating that the former is more rapid and/or complete than the latter.

The unpublished study by Welch et al. (1970) represents the only attempt to examine the relearning of prism adaptation. These investigators compared the acquisition rate of prism adaptation to the rate at which subjects readapted to the opposite displacement. As expected, strong negative transfer was found. That is, asymptotic adaptation to the second displacement required substantially longer exposure than did adaptation to the first displacement. It is interesting that Ebenholtz (1967), who carried out the same experiment on adaptation to optically induced *tilt* (see Section 3.2.2), failed to obtain any negative transfer. This latter result suggests that there is a qualitative difference between the processes of visual and visuomotor adaptation and/or between displacement and tilt adaptation.

2.2.1.3. ***Stimulus and Response Generalization.*** Prism adaptation acquired under one set of stimulus conditions is manifested under somewhat different stimulus conditions, although usually to a lesser extent, and thus, in learning terminology, demonstrates *stimulus generalization* with decrement.

Kohler (1964, p. 85) was the first to report stimulus generalization decrement of prism adaptation. He made the serendipitous discovery that visual negative aftereffect to 10° prismatic displacement involving only the upper half of the visual field ("split-half" prism spectacles) was greater when the postexposure measures were obtained while the subject wore empty spectacle frames with a horizontal dividing wire than when wearing no spectacles.

Stimulus generalization (and decrement) of adaptation may be distinguished from a similar phenomenon referred to as the *situational effect* (see Section 2.2.1.7). In the latter, certain initially "neutral" stimuli, such as the feel of the goggles, become associated with adaptation and, on a later occasion, elicit a partial adaptive response in a subject *before* exposure to the perceptual rearrangement occurs. Thus adaptation is subject to discriminative conditioning. In contrast, a test of stimulus generalization involves the situation in which an *already adapted* subject is measured for adaptation in one or more conditions varying in their stimulus characteristics. The distinction between the two phenomena is not clear-cut, however, because a certain amount of conditioned adaptation is undoubtedly manifested in tests of stimulus generalization.

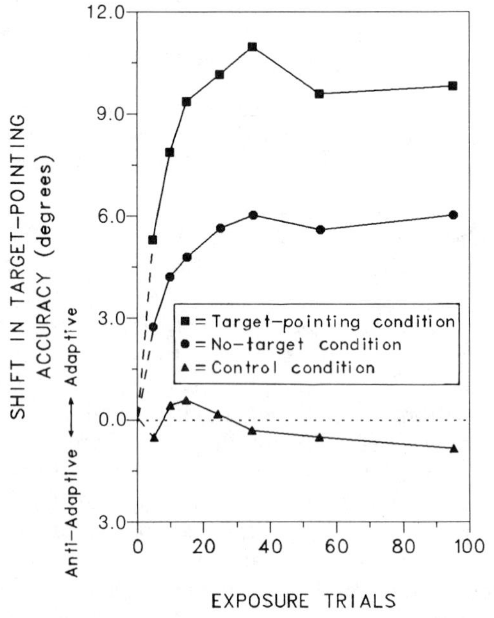

Figure 24.5. Visuomotor negative aftereffect (degrees) as a function of 20-diopter prism exposure trials (brief terminal exposure) for target-pointing, no-target, and control (no prism) conditions. From the first test on, adaptation was significantly greater for the target-pointing than for the no-target condition, both curves reaching their respective asymptotes after about 35 exposure trials (approximately 86% of maximum for the target-pointing condition and 53% for the no-target condition). No change in pointing occurred for the no-prism condition. (From R. B. Welch, Prism adaptation: The "target-pointing effect" as a function of exposure trials, *Perception and Psychophysics*, 1971, 9. Reprinted with permission.)

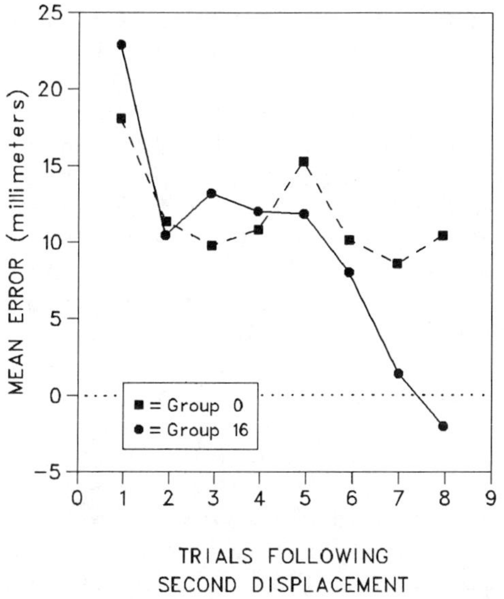

Figure 24.6. Postexposure decay curves of the visuomotor negative aftereffect for proactive inhibition condition (Group 16) and control condition (Group 0). Prior to the decay period depicted here, subjects in Group 16 adapted by pointing 30 times at targets that were optically displaced (left or right) by 16-diopter prisms. This adaptation period was followed by a second set of target-pointing trials while exposed to the effects of 16-diopter prismatic displacement in the direction opposite that of the first adaptation period. Subjects in Group 0 pointed at 16-diopter prismatically displaced targets until reaching the same criterion of accuracy imposed on Group 16 subjects in their second adaptation period. The finding of more complete decay of adaptation for Group 16 than for Group 0 (as seen in the figure) was interpreted as support for the proactive inhibition hypothesis, because the preceding adaptation of Group 16 to displacement in one direction appeared to be accelerating the decay of adaptation to displacement in the opposite direction. (From J. R. Devane, Proaction in the recovery from practice under visual displacement, *Perceptual and Motor Skills*, 1968, *27*. Reprinted with permission.)

In a study specifically designed to examine generalization decrement, Uhlarik and Canon (1970) demonstrated that when the visuomotor negative aftereffect to 30-diopter prismatic displacement was obtained without goggles its magnitude was less than when it was measured with the (prismless) goggles. Tietz and Gogel (1974) found that prism adaptation acquired at one distance generalized to another distance with a decrement (or increment) that was greater when the observer was provided with a visual field during prism exposure than when only the hand could be seen.

In an unpublished study, Hillyard and Hamilton (1971) reviewed a variety of studies in which prism adaptation was measured by means of both a visual target (quite similar to the prism exposure situation) and a nonvisual target (e.g., a sound source). They reported that for the 20 studies they reviewed the ratio of nonvisual target adaptation to visual target adaptation was 0.83, revealing a small but statistically significant generalization decrement.

To the extent that prism adaptation is revealed in a variety of different responses, it may be said to manifest what is referred to in the traditional learning literature as *response generalization*. Several studies (Bailey, 1972a, 1972b; Harris, 1965; Yachzel & Lackner, 1977) reported that adaptation obtained by means of pointing in one direction was fully manifested when different arm movements were required. Using a different paradigm, Freedman, Hall, and Rekosh (1965) found that prism adaptation acquired by means of a sagittal limb movement during the exposure period resulted in equal postexposure effects for sagittal and transverse arm movements. In contrast, adaptation acquired via transverse arm movements revealed a large response generalization decrement when tested with the sagittal motion. Another example of "asymmetric" response generalization was obtained by Baily (1972a). In this study subjects who adapted by means of ballistic target-pointing responses revealed equally large visuomotor negative aftereffect for ballistic and slow ("zeroing in") target-pointing motions during the postexposure tests. However, if the exposure period entailed the slow response, postexposure measures using this limb movement revealed much more adaptation than if the ballistic motions were required.

Finally, in several studies (Kinney, McKay, Luria, & Gratto, 1970; Mikaelian, 1967, 1970a) the magnitude of prism adaptation obtained was shown to be greatest for a postexposure task identical to that practiced during the exposure period and less for tasks that differed.

2.2.1.4. Intermanual Transfer. Prism adaptation obtained for one hand has been found under some conditions to transfer in part (frequently about 50%) to the nonexposed hand. Terminal exposure appears to be especially conducive to this intermanual transfer (e.g., M. M. Cohen, 1967; Melamed, Beckett, & Hill, 1976; Wallace, 1978). Transfer also appears to be facilitated by unconstrained (versus constrained) head position during prism exposure (Hamilton, 1964b; Wallace, 1978). Typically, such transfer has been attributed to a prism-induced shift in apparent visual direction which, in turn, may be based on a shift in the felt direction of gaze (e.g., Kalil & Freedman, 1966a) or of head position (e.g., M.M. Cohen, 1974; Hamilton, 1964b). With concurrent exposure, intermanual transfer is minimal or nonexistent (H.B. Cohen, 1966; M.M. Cohen, 1967; Greene, 1967; Hamilton, 1964a; Mikaelian, 1963, 1966; Mikaelian & Malatesta, 1974).

2.2.1.5. Interocular Transfer. There are several reasons why one should expect adaptation acquired when one eye is exposed to the prism to transfer *completely* to the other eye. First, if prism exposure has resulted in a shift in the felt position of the visible limb, it should make no difference to adaptation which eye is used during the measure of this adaptation. Second, if the adaptation is based, at least in part, on a change in the felt direction of gaze (and hence of apparent visual direction), one would expect complete interocular transfer because normally it is not possible to innervate the muscles of one eye independently of the other (Hering's law of equal innervation; Hering, 1868).

In line with the second point, Crawshaw and Craske (1976a) and Foley and Miyanshi (1969) have obtained 100% interocular transfer of a prism-induced shift in visual direction. It should be noted that because prism adaptation may undergo some spontaneous decay over even a relatively short period of time, a valid test of the magnitude of interocular transfer must entail counterbalancing of the order in which the two eyes are tested during the postexposure period.

Some recent research by Mann, Hein, and Diamond (1979, Experiment 1) represents an apparent contradiction to the preceding line of reasoning. These investigators demonstrated that whereas subjects with normal vision do indeed reveal complete interocular transfer of prism adaptation, as measured by eye-hand coordination, individuals suffering from strabismus (who either constantly suppress vision in one eye or reveal alternating suppression) do not. More specifically, strabismic alternating suppressors could adapt with either eye but showed no transfer of this adaptation to the nonexposed eye, whereas strabismic constant suppressors were capable of adapting only when the dominant eye was exposed, but did reveal transfer to the normally suppressed eye. Because the adaptation period used involved continuous exposure to the hand, one would expect a shift in felt limb position as a major component of adaptation. Consequently, using this logic, it is difficult to understand why no interocular transfer was obtained for the alternating suppressors.

2.2.1.6. Learning Sets. Only two investigations have examined the possibility that repeated experience with prismatic displacement will result in an increase in the rate and/or extent of adaptation, a phenomenon that may be referred to as a "learning set." Lazar and Van Laer (1968) confronted each of three groups with three successive 10-min prism exposure periods involving, respectively, displacements of (1) 10, 20, and 30 diopters, (2) 20, 20, and 30 diopters, or (3) 30, 30, and 30 diopters. The investigators hypothesized that adaptation to the earlier (lesser) displacements in the "10-20-30" and "20-20-30" groups would lead to an increased rate of adaptation in the final (30-diopter displacement) period relative to that achieved in the final exposure period in the "30-30-30" group. However, no such change was observed.

In a more recent study by Flock and McGonigle (1977) evidence for a learning set in prism adaptation was obtained. With both human subjects and squirrel monkeys the investigators found that repeated alternation between leftward and rightward 30-diopter prismatic displacement led to a gradual decline in errors (with prisms still on) primarily when the two prism situations were spatially separated and thus easily distinguished. Despite their arguments to the contrary, it is not completely clear that the progressively more efficient responding to each switch from one prism to the other was not merely reflective of deliberate corrective responses, rather than genuine adaptation.

2.2.1.7. Situation-Specific Effects. As mentioned in Section 2.2.1.3, it has been demonstrated in a wide variety of studies that prism adaptation can be conditioned to the specific situational context in which it occurs. The most common observation of this phenomenon comes from within-subjects studies in which subjects are adapted on two (or more) occasions, separated by a relatively long period of normal visual experience (as much as 2 weeks in some experiments). Typically, such studies reveal, as a subsidiary finding, a partial adaptive response during the *preexposure* measures of the experimental conditions occurring subsequent to the first.

Some investigators (e.g., Held, 1968; Klapp, Nordell, Hoekenga, & Patton, 1974; Yachzel & Lackner, 1977) have assumed that this effect represents incomplete decay of the previously acquired adaptation. However, it seems quite unlikely that subjects would remain partially adapted in the face of the extended "unlearning" period provided during the intertest interval. It is much more reasonable to assume that some or all of the cues associated with the initial adaptation, cues that may include the feel of the goggles, the reduced visual field, the apparatus at which the subject sits, and the testing room, have acquired the ability to induce partial adaptation when the subject is once again exposed to them. This so-called *"situational effect"* has been obtained with a variety of prism adaptation measures, including the visuomotor negative aftereffect and reduction of effect (Hein, 1972; Klapp et al., 1974; Lackner & Lobovits, 1977; Welch, Choe, & Heinrich, 1974; Wooster, 1923; Yachzel & Lackner, 1977), shift in apparent visual direction (Welch et al., 1974), and shift in felt direction of gaze (McLaughlin & Webster, 1967). Furthermore, Welch et al. (1974) and Lackner and Lobovits (1977) noted that the situational effect appears to limit the magnitude of the adaptation obtained in the second (and subsequent) adaptation periods, owing, it seems likely, to the partial adaptation already present in the preexposure measures.

More systematic tests of conditioned prism adaptation (Foley, 1967; Foley & Abel, 1967; Kravitz, 1972; Kravitz & Yaffe, 1972; Welch, 1971b) have met with mixed results. Of those that have succeeded, the conditional stimuli included the feel of the prism goggles (Kravitz, 1972; Welch, 1971b), an auditory tone (Kravitz & Yaffe, 1972), and the felt direction of gaze (Hay & Pick, 1966a). Another experiment that obtained evidence of conditioned adaptation was by Kohler (1951), who found that many days of continuous exposure to split-half prism spectacles led to a state where eye movements in the upward direction produced immediate, partial visual adaptation while the goggles were being worn and an aftereffect when they were not. In neither condition did downward eye movements have an effect. Thus it would appear that in this situation the presence of particular eye movements served as the conditional stimulus.

2.2.1.8. Massed versus Distributed Practice. Although a number of studies of prism adaptation have examined the potential effect of distribution of exposure trials, no firm conclusion can be drawn. Some studies reported that when the exposure period is interspersed with no-vision rest periods, prism adaptation is facilitated over that resulting from massed exposure (Choe & Welch, 1974; Goldberg, Gordon, & Taub, cited by Taub & Goldberg, 1974; Hein, 1972; Taub & Goldberg, 1973). Figure 24.7 depicts the effect of this variable on adaptation, intermanual transfer of adaptation, and spontaneous decay. Others, however, have obtained no difference between massed and distributed exposure (M. M. Cohen, 1973; Dewar, 1970a; Van Laer, 1968). Because the various studies of this variable have differed on a number of procedural details, it is unclear how the apparent contradiction in results is to be interpreted. It seems likely, however, that the crucial parameter concerns the way "spaced" and "massed" exposures are operationally defined; this distinction has rarely been the same from one experiment to another. Related is the fact, as noted by Taub and Goldberg (1973), that terminal display can be viewed as a form of spaced practice, even if prism exposure trials are presented one after the other without respite. Hence it may be argued that only with the use of concurrent exposure is it possible to have a truly massed-trials condition of prism adaptation.

2.2.1.9. Delayed Feedback. The degree to which a delay in visual feedback during prism exposure has an effect on adaptation depends on whether exposure is concurrent or terminal. In a study using the former condition, Held, Efstathiou, & Greene (1966) exposed subjects to a prismatically displaced luminous oscilloscope trace that substituted for the unseen hand. Delays of 0, 0.3, 0.5, 0.9, 1.7, or 3.3 sec were imposed between the hand's motion and movement of the oscilloscope trace. Only in the no-delay condition was adaptation (visuomotor negative aftereffect) obtained (see Figure 24.8). Adaptation to a loss of visual stability contingent on head movements (see Section 4) has also been shown to be severely disrupted when continuous exposure is coupled with a delay of feedback (Hay, 1974; Hay & Goldsmith, 1973).

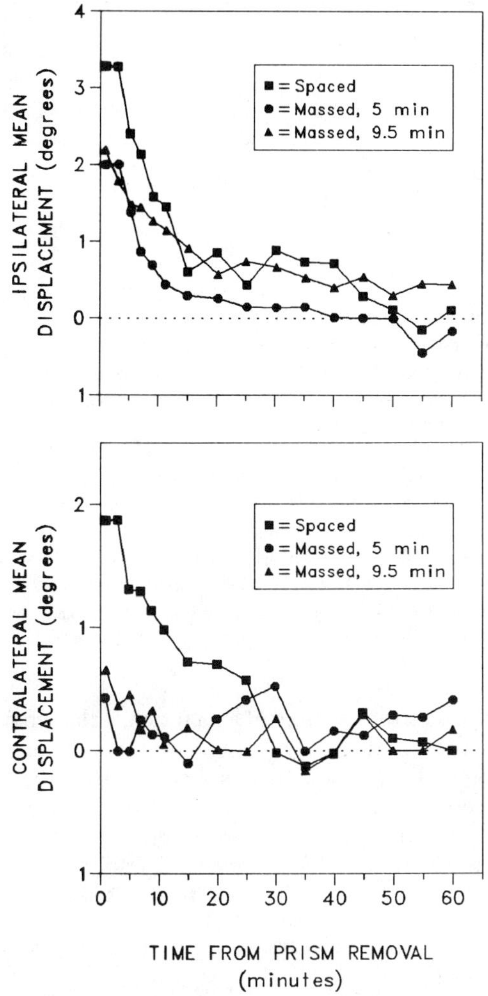

Figure 24.7. Decay of visuomotor negative afterffect to prismatic displacement for ipsilateral and contralateral (transfer) testing following spaced and massed practice during prism exposure. Testing was always with the right arm. During prism exposure either the right arm (ipsilateral group) or left arm (contralateral group) was viewed. Each data point is the mean for ten trials each for 16 subjects. Magnitude of aftereffect was measured 2, 3, 5, 7, 9, and 15 min after prism exposure, and every fifth minute thereafter through minute 60. Both ipsilateral and contralateral postexposure measures revealed significantly greater adaptation and slower decay for spaced trials than for either of the massed practice conditions. (From E. Taub & I. A. Goldberg, Prism adaptation: Control of intermanual transfer by distribution of practice, *Science, 180*, Copyright 1973 by American Association for the Advancement of Science. Reprinted with permission.)

Although no published studies of the effect of delayed feedback in a terminal (separate-trials) exposure condition have been reported, a number of investigators have been forced, for procedural reasons, to institute a short delay between response and feedback and in all cases obtained substantial adaptation (Bailey, 1972a; Dewar, 1970a; Gyr, Willey, & Gordon, 1972; Templeton, Howard, & Lowman, 1966; Templeton, Howard & Wilkinson, 1974; Welch, 1972). Rhoades (1968), in an unpublished study, systematically examined delayed feedback (0, 4, and 8 sec) in a terminal exposure condition. He obtained significant adaptation in all three delay conditions, although there was a significant decline as a function of the length of delay.

It may be concluded, on the basis of admittedly sparse data, that delays of feedback are devastating for adaptation when prism exposure is concurrent but only moderately disruptive when discrete exposure trials are used.

2.2.2. Necessary and Sufficient Conditions for Prism Adaptation

2.2.2.1. The Need for a Stable Rearrangement. In brief, it appears clear that the two necessary conditions for the production of prism adaptation (and other forms of adaptation, for that matter) are that the rearrangement be *stable* and that the observer be provided with salient information concerning its presence and nature.

If the observer is confronted by prismatic displacement that is constantly changing (independently of the subject's bodily movements), adaptation fails to occur (Abplanalp & Held, 1965; M.M. Cohen & Held, 1960; Efstathiou, 1963). This, of course, should not be surprising, for in such a situation the rearrangement never "stands still" long enough to be dealt with by the adaptive mechanism. On the other hand, it was demonstrated by M.M. Cohen and Held (1960) that when a subject *actively* moved the hand back and forth while viewing it through prisms whose strength varied continuously from 22° leftward displacement to 22° rightward displacement and back again, there was an increase in the within-subject *variability* of subsequent target-reaching accuracy. Thus exposure to what has come to be referred to as "disarrangement" leads to a decrease in the precision of one's eye-hand coordination, although the *average* response remains accurate. Whether this decrease in precision of visuomotor behavior is, in turn, based on an increase in variability of perception (vision and/or proprioception) has not yet been determined.

2.2.2.2. Prism Awareness and the "Assumption of Unity." It does not appear to be necessary for the occurrence of prism

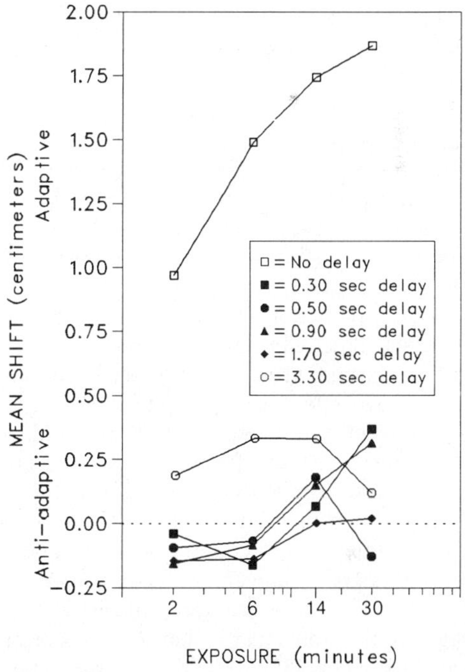

Figure 24.8. Visuomotor negative aftereffect to 20-diopter prismatic displacement as a function of delays of feedback (0, 0.30, 0.50, 0.90, 1.70, or 3.30 sec) and minutes of exposure. Prism exposure involved side-to-side arm movements and no target. Statistically significant adaptation was obtained only in the no-delay condition. (From R. Held, A. Efstathiou, & M. Greene, Adaptation to displaced and delayed visual feedback from the hand, *Journal of Experimental Psychology*, 1966, *72*. Reprinted with permission.)

adaptation that subjects be *aware* that their vision is being distorted. This fact is seen most clearly in the concurrent exposure condition. Although subjects in this situation typically reveal significant adaptation after 20–30 min of prism exposure, it is rare that they spontaneously report that anything seemed to be wrong with their vision. (Systematic post-experiment interrogation on this matter, however, is not commonly performed.) This apparent lack of prism awareness with concurrent exposure is undoubtedly due to the use of a relatively small prismatic displacement and the absence of a target and resulting initial errors in pointing.

Whether awareness of the presence and the nature of the prismatic distortion influences (augments or degrades) the adaptation that appears to occur without it is not entirely clear. As will be seen shortly, it is certain that the presence of target-pointing errors leads to a substantial increase in the magnitude of adaptation. It is difficult, however, to assess the degree to which this facilitating effect is due to heightened awareness of the prismatic displacement or the clear-cut information about the rearrangement provided by the error feedback. Similarly, it is unclear if there is any effect of revealing to the subjects the nature of the distortion *before* (or after) they are exposed to it. Uhlarik (1973) examined this variable, but the apparent decrease in visuomotor negative aftereffect that was associated with pretest awareness may have been an artifact (Welch, 1978, pp. 20–21).

Another cognitive variable that, although perhaps not necessary for prism adaptation, appears to influence its magnitude, is the degree to which the subject is under the impression that vision and proprioception are providing information about a single distal object, a factor that may be referred to as the "assumption of unity." Welch (1972) demonstrated that adaptation was reduced, but not eliminated, when the subject believed that the apparently prismatically displaced luminous finger seen at the far edge of the occluding board actually belonged to the *experimenter*.

2.2.2.3. Active versus Passive Movement. An issue of great theoretical importance (and controversy) is the claim by Held and his colleagues (e.g., Held & Gottlieb, 1958) that *active* bodily movement on the part of the subject is a necessary condition for prism adaptation. Held's influential model, which was inspired by von Holst (1954), is depicted in Figure 24.9. According to this notion, simultaneous with the initiation of a particular motor act is the production of a neural copy of the efferent signal for this act. This "efference copy" resides temporarily in the "correlation storage" area. With repeated experience, a correlation between the efference copy and the resulting "reafference" (e.g., view of the moving hand) is established and strengthened. The placement of a prism before the eye disrupts the efferent-reafferent correlation, causing it to be replaced by a new one. Thus according to this model, in the absence of other forms of usable information, adaptation should be limited to situations of active bodily movement for only then can efferent copies be supplied for the recorrelation process.

Although studies from Held's laboratory (e.g., Held & Gottlieb, 1958; Held & Hein, 1958; Held & Schlank, 1959) found no adaptation when subjects' limbs were moved passively under concurrent display, a variety of subsequent experiments by other investigators (Baily, 1972b; Fishkin, 1969; Foley & Maynes, 1969; Mather & Lackner, 1980; Melamed, Halay, & Gidlow, 1973; Melamed, Wallace, & Seyfried, 1979; Pick & Hay, 1965; Singer & Day, 1966; Wallace, 1975; Weinstein, Sersen, & Weinstein, 1964) have generally reported that passive bodily motion

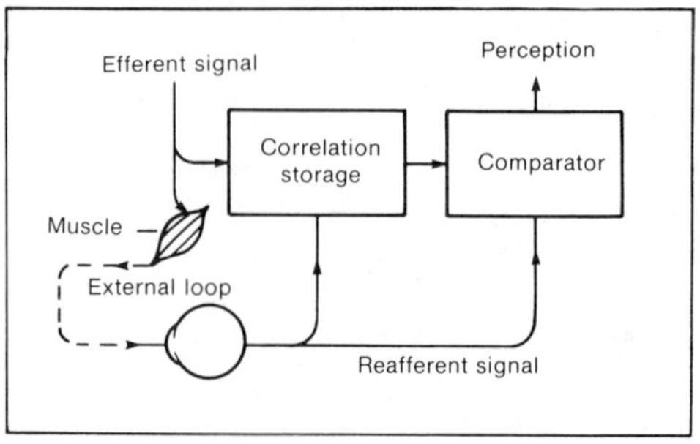

Figure 24.9. Schematic representation of the Held reafference hypothesis model. An efferent command to the muscles (e.g., the arm muscles) is simultaneously "copied" neurologically. This efference copy for a particular motor act is sent to the correlation storage where it becomes combined (by association) with the visual "reafference" signal caused by the movement. When future instances of the same movement occur, the reafferent memory trace that has become associated with the current efferent signal is sent to the comparator where it is compared to the current reafference. A match signifies that visuomotor coordination is normal. A mismatch indicates the presence of visual rearrangement and serves to activate the adaptive process. (From A. Hein & R. Held, A neural model for labile sensorimotor coordinations, in E. E. Bernard & M. R. Kare (Eds.), *Biological prototypes and synthetic systems*, Plenum Press, 1962. Reprinted with permission.)

does lead to a certain amount of adaptation, although frequently less than that produced by active movement. Thus the safest conclusion to draw at this time is that active bodily movement is not necessary for prism adaptation, but does facilitate it.

It seems most unlikely, as several investigators (e.g., Freedman, 1968; Rock, 1966; Uhlarik & Canon, 1971; Wallach, 1968; Welch, 1978; Wohlwill, 1966) have argued, that a *variety* of information sources are sufficient to produce adaptation, a notion that may be referred to as the "information hypothesis." Thus it has been proposed (e.g., Howard & Templeton, 1966) that the facilitation of adaptation resulting from active visuomotor behavior may be attributed to the many salient forms of information about the perceptual rearrangement that are provided by the activity.

2.2.2.4. Enhanced Visual-Proprioceptive Discrepancy as the Critical Aspect of Active Movement. One important form of information that may result from active movement concerns the discrepancy between visual and proprioceptive information. Thus it may be argued that when the arm is moved actively its felt position is more intense, precise, and salient than during passive movement (e.g., Paillard & Brouchon, 1968). This, as Lackner (1977, 1981) and others have argued, should increase the salience of the visual-proprioceptive discordance, leading to a more vigorous activation of the adaptive mechanism. Support for this alternative interpretation of the active-passive difference in prism adaptation comes from an ingenious study by Moulden (1971). In one condition the subject on each back-and-forth swing of the hand was provided with one extremely brief glimpse of the limb through 20-diopter prisms. Because the view of the hand was so short as to preclude visual *motion* (i.e., no visual reafference), no adaptation should have occurred according to Held's model. Alternatively, the information hypothesis would suggest that such a form of exposure, although devoid of visually perceived limb movement, should present the subject with a marked discrepancy between seen and felt limb position and that this form of information ought to be sufficient to produce adaptation. This, indeed, was what occurred; after 3 min of prism exposure, adaptation (visuomotor negative aftereffect) was just as great for "stopped" viewing as for full viewing, the latter replicating Held's active exposure condition. Moulden concluded that active limb movement serves to enhance proprioceptive afference (and thus the discrepancy between proprioception and vision) which, in turn, strongly activates the adaptive mechanism.

Congruent with this conclusion is the report by Mather and Lackner (1975, 1977) of a very substantial visuomotor negative aftereffect for subjects whose prismatically displaced arm was moved *involuntarily* by means of 100-Hz vibration of the skeletal muscles. Clearly, this result is not predicted from Held's reafference hypothesis, for only when limb movement is active can the necessary efference copies be emitted. Also inconsistent with the Held model is the report by Kravitz and Wallach (1966) of adaptation as a result of vibrating the stationary hand. Again, an enhanced discrepancy between felt and seen limb position would appear to be the most likely source of the resulting prism adaptation. [It should be noted, however, that Welch & Warren (1984) were unable to replicate this result.]

Wallace and his associates (Garrett & Wallace, 1975; Wallace, 1980; Wallace & Fisher, 1979; Wallace & Garrett,, 1973, 1975; Wallace & Hoyenga, 1980) demonstrated that prism adaptation, as measured by the visuomotor negative aftereffect, was completely absent if subjects were given the hypnotic suggestion that they had lost the sense of position of the arm and hand. (However, a recent study by Spanos, Gorassini, and Petrusic, 1981, failed to replicate this finding.)

Finally, in a study by Mather and Lackner (described by Lackner, 1981) prism adaptation occurred in situations in which the hand was either stationary or passively moved, as long as the conditions of visual fixation (attention) favored a registered discrepancy between felt and seen limb position.

Thus there appears to be a compelling empirical basis for questioning the validity of the reafference hypothesis as an explanation of prism adaptation. Furthermore, some writers (Howard, 1970, 1971; Lackner, 1974, 1981; Rock, 1966, pp. 116–119; Welch, 1978, pp. 28–29) have argued on logical grounds that the reafference hypothesis should never have been applied to prism adaptation in the first place. Howard (1971), for example, noted that efferent outflow is known to determine amplitude, direction, and speed of limb movement, but not limb *position*. Thus, because the effect of prismatic displacement is to create a discrepancy between felt and seen limb position, Held's model in which efference is the crucial component is inappropriate as an explanation of prism adaptation.

2.2.2.5. The Role of Error-Corrective Feedback. According to the information hypothesis, a variety of types of information concerning the prismatic displacement should be sufficient to produce or facilitate adaptation. Support for this claim comes from the demonstration that, along with the visual-proprioceptive discrepancy, the presence of error-corrective feedback from target-pointing facilitates adaptation. Furthermore, this contribution to adaptation can occur whether the feedback is provided by means of vision (Baily, 1972a; Coren, 1966; Templeton et. al., 1966; Weinstein, Sersen, Fisher, & Weisinger, 1964; Welch 1969, 1971a; Welch & Rhoades, 1969), verbal feedback (Dewer, 1970; Uhlarik, 1973), touch (Howard, Craske, & Templeton, 1965; Lackner, 1974a; Wooster, 1923), or even *imagery* (Finke, 1979). An example of this so-called "target-pointing effect" was depicted in Figure 24.5 (Section 2.2.1.1).

It must be noted that the presence of error-corrective feedback is nearly always confounded with practice of the correct target-pointing response. Thus, as Foley and Maynes (1969) have claimed, it is possible that a portion or all of the facilitating effect that such errors have on adaptation is attributable to the fact that the subject is learning and practicing the very response that is required during the measure of the postexposure negative aftereffect. Indeed, Howard (1968) was able to produce very substantial adaptation in subjects by means of a procedure known as *prismatic shaping*, in which the prismatic displacement is incremented by such small steps that the subject never makes a large enough target-pointing error to suspect the presence of visual displacement.

However, evidence to support the importance of target-pointing error per se as a facilitator of adaptation comes from a study by Welch and Abel (1970). These investigators found that the enhancing effect of target-pointing errors (and practice of the correct response) remained quite substantial even when the motor response used to measure the visuomotor negative aftereffect was markedly different (transverse) from that used during prism exposure (sagittal).

In a recent study by Paillard, Jordan, and Brouchon (1981), it was found that the target-pointing effect does *not* occur when only peripheral vision is allowed. They proposed that this (and other observations) are congruent with the notion that there are two separate channels ("displacement analyzing system" and "movingness analyzing system") used for the visual guidance of pointing movements (Bonnet, 1975; Paillard, 1980).

2.2.2.6. The Relative Impact of Different Forms of Information. A compilation of the many different forms of information that can produce or enhance adaptation is only a first step. The next is to ascertain their relative importance. The tentative conclusion that may be drawn from the few studies relevant to this issue is that visual information (regarding the discrepancy and/or target-pointing errors) has by far the most impact, followed by tactual and verbal feedback, the latter two being rather poor (and equally so) sources of adaptation (Uhlarik, 1973; Welch, 1978, pp. 36–42; Wooster, 1923).

2.2.3. Immediate Responses to the Prismatic Displacement

2.2.3.1. Intersensory Bias. Although only prolonged exposure to the consequences of the prism-induced visual-proprioceptive discrepancy can produce the semipermanent modification known as prism adaptation, immediate attempts of the perceptual system to resolve the discrepancy also occur. The best known of these is "visual capture" (e.g., Hay, Pick, & Ikeda, 1965), in which the stationary hand viewed through a wedge prism is immediately felt to be located quite close to where it is seen. There is also a corresponding "proprioceptive capture" of vision, but it is quite small. With prism strengths of about 20 diopters (11°), the sum of these two forms of intersensory bias frequently serves to resolve completely the visual-proprioceptive discrepancy. If the limb is actively moved, however, intersensory bias decreases while true adaptation is produced (Welch, Widawski, Harrington, & Warren, 1979). Other studies have demonstrated the existence of intersensory bias for situations of visual-auditory spatial discrepancy (e.g., Jackson, 1953; Radeau & Bertelson, 1974; Weerts & Thurlow, 1971), proprioceptive-auditory discrepancy (Pick, Warren, & Hay, 1969), and for conflicts between visual and felt size (e.g., E. A. Miller, 1972; Rock & Victor, 1964), visual and felt shape (Rock & Victor, 1964), and vision and touch (Over, 1966). These and other studies of intersensory bias have been reviewed recently by Welch and Warren (1980; and Chapter 25 of this *Handbook*).

Thus when a human observer is confronted with a prismatically displaced view of the hand, there are at least two major processes by which the perceptual system attempts to resolve the discrepancy—adaptation and intersensory bias. Correction for the prism effects, if measured while the subject is still viewing the hand through the prism, is likely to be complete, adaptation resolving a portion of the discrepancy and bias handling the remainder. That the prism-induced negative aftereffect typically falls far short of the maximum defined by the prism strength (as seen in Section 2.2.1.1) is certainly due largely to the dissipation of the intersensory bias in a matter of seconds after view of the hand is eliminated (Hay et al., 1965), leaving only the adaptive shift (e.g., the visuomotor negative aftereffect).

2.2.3.2. "Immediate Correction Effect" and "Straight-Ahead Shift." There are other immediate responses to prismatic displacement that serve to reduce the discrepancy. One of these is the "immediate correction effect" (Melamed, Beckett, & Wallace, 1978; Melamed & Wallace, 1971; Rock, Goldberg, & Mack, 1966; Wallace, Melamed, & Cohen, 1973; Wallace, Melamed, & Kaplan, 1973; Wilkinson, 1971, Experiment 1), in which an object located in a well-structured field and viewed through a prism immediately appears to be shifted perhaps only 40% as much as it ought to be, given the prismatic displacement.

Harris (1974) and Harris and Gilchrist (1976) convincingly argued and demonstrated that the immediate correction effect is the result of the subjects' *interpretation* of the concept of "straight ahead," which can be significantly biased by the apparent orientation of the major axes of the visual framework. The straight-ahead shift, then, is limited to tasks that involve judgments of straight ahead and, even then, may be avoided by the use of an exposure condition in which no visual framework is present.

2.2.3.3. Deliberate Corrective Responses. A final immediate response to prismatic displacement is the deliberate correction of one's prism-induced target-pointing errors. Indeed, if instructed to point to the true location of the target after the first error has revealed the displacing properties of the prism goggles, most subjects will point quite accurately on the second trial. Because removal of the prism after this first accurate response would undoubtedly fail to reveal a negative aftereffect of commensurate size, it is clear that conscious correction of one's errors during exposure to the distortion does not qualify as true adaptation.

2.2.4. Long-Term Responses to the Prismatic Displacement

2.2.4.1. The Logical Possibilities. Just as there are many potential sources of prism adaptation, so are there many possible adaptive end states. Logically, there would seem to be three major alternatives: (1) changes in proprioception, (2) changes in vision, and (3) changes in visuomotor coordination that are independent of (1) and (2). Furthermore, there are many potential sites for alterations in proprioception. Thus recalibration could theoretically occur at the wrist, elbow, shoulder, neck, or the eye muscles. It should be noted that shifts in felt eye (and/or felt head) position would directly affect vision, thereby blurring the distinction between the two types of perceptual recalibration. A more purely visual change that might result from prism exposure is an alteration of the egocentric significance of retinal loci. Finally, with respect to (3), it is possible that when an observer is allowed to reach for objects in the prism-displaced field, a new eye-hand coordination may be acquired, one that becomes so ingrained as to qualify as adaptation and yet does not signify an underlying change in either vision or proprioception. This then would represent pure motor learning. All these possible sites of recalibration (and two potential "complex" sites) are presented in Table 24.1, along with procedures for their detection.

2.2.4.2. Changes in Felt Position Sense. The evidence clearly indicates that prism exposure leads to recalibrations at a variety of sites, although the type of adaptive end state that predominates is greatly influenced by the type of prism exposure provided.

As first demonstrated by Hamilton (1964a, 1964b) and Harris (1963, 1965), and important component of prism adaptation is a recalibration of the limb position sense, as manifested, for example, by placing the unseen, adapted hand so that it feels straight ahead of the nose (see Table 24.1). Thus, despite the fact that in this situation the nonveridical sensory modality is vision, the ensuing resolution of the prism-induced intersensory discrepancy frequently entails the alteration of the initially accurate felt body position sense. This is an example of what Wallach (Wallach & Frey, 1972c; Wallach & Huntington, 1973) has referred to as "counteradaptation," a term actually first coined by Franklin, Ross, and Weltman (1970) in their research on adaptation to underwater distortions of distance and size (Section 8.2.2.2).

It would appear that the optimal condition for producing this form of adaptive end product is concurrent exposure to the prism-displaced limb. Harris (1963), for instance, found that after a continuous view of the target-pointing arm, which the subject moved ballistically in the sagittal plane, the magnitudes of the visuomotor negative aftereffect and shift in pointing straight ahead with eyes shut were nearly equal, implying that the recalibration was limited entirely to the felt position of the prism-exposed arm. This result was replicated independently by Pick, Hay, & Pabst (1963). Further evidence that concurrent exposure is especially conducive to proprioceptive adaptation is the observation in numerous studies (H. B. Cohen, 1966; M. M. Cohen, 1967; Greene, 1967; Hamilton, 1964a; Mikaelian, 1963, 1966; Mikaelian & Malatesta, 1974; Prablanc, Tzavaras, & Jeannerod, 1975) that in this condition (in contrast to some others) little or no intermanual transfer of the negative aftereffect occurs. This observation rules out a visual or other "central" basis for the adaptation and implies that the adaptive shift was limited to the felt position of the exposed limb.

Concurrent prism exposure provided by active locomotion in the environment appears to lead to a shift in the felt relation of head to trunk (e.g., Kohler, 1964, p. 38; Teixeira & Lackner, 1976), which in turn leads to an adaptive shift in visual direction and a concomitant shift in auditory direction (Lackner, 1973a).

The few studies that have attempted to measure or isolate position sense change within specific points of articulation such as wrist, elbow, shoulder, and neck have either been indirect or obtained equivocal results (Bossom & Held, 1959; M. M. Cohen, 1974; Craske, 1966a; Hamilton, 1964b; Kohler, 1964, p. 38; Putterman, Robert, & Bregman, 1969). Further research is clearly needed here.

Several recent studies by Craske and his colleagues (Craske, Kenny, & Keith, 1984; Kenny & Craske, 1981) have found changes in the felt length of the arm as a result of discordant *tactile* stimuli. In this novel procedure, the subject (in the dark) pressed with the index finger of the right hand a pushbutton located directly adjacent to the palm of the left hand but was actually stimulated on the write of that limb (Craske et al., 1984). Thus by this means a discrepancy was created between the expected location of the tactile stimulus (as specified by the

Table 24.1. Potential End States of Adaptation to Prismatic Displacement: Some Direct Tests and Other Manifestations (See Text for Details)[a]

Recalibration Site	Test[b]	Evidence of Recalibration	Other Manifestations[c]
Simple sites			
Wrist	Align hand with forearm	Misalignment—hand turned to side opposite the displacement	Misreaching, with the hand only, at targets in any sensory modality, as well as to the straight-ahead position
Elbow	Align forearm with upper arm	Misalignment—forearm turned (if possible) to side opposite the displacement	Same as above, for the forearm
Shoulder	Point straight ahead of the nose. Point at unadapted part of body (e.g., big toe)	Misalignment—arm placed off to side opposite of the displacement	Same as above, for the entire arm
Neck	Align head with trunk	Misalignment—head turned to the same side as the displacement	Misreaching, with any limb, at either visual or auditory targets and possibly the straight-ahead position. Shift in apparent visual and auditory straight ahead in the direction opposite the displacement (All effects assume that the trunk is used as the standard of reference)
Eyes	Place eyes in felt straight-ahead position. Direct eyes to unadapted part of body (e.g., big toe)	Misalignment—eyes turned to same side as the displacement	Misreaching, with any limb, at visual targets. Shift in apparent visual straight ahead in the direction opposite the displacement
Retina	Indicate when a visual target appears straight ahead. Place eyes in felt straight-ahead position	A shift in apparent visual straight ahead in the absence of a shift in the felt position of the eyes	Misreaching, with any limb, at visual targets
Complex sites			
Assimilated corrective response	Point at visual target, together with separate measures of recalibration for arm, head, eyes, head-arm, and eye-arm sites	Error in pointing—in the direction opposite the displacement. Either no other shifts or algebraic sum of shifts is less than target-pointing error	No other manifestations
Head-arm	Point head toward hand, together with separate measures of felt arm and head position	Misalignment—head turned in the same direction as displacement. No shift in the felt arm or head position	Misreaching for visual or auditory targets in the direction opposite the displacement
Eye-arm	Direct eyes toward hand, together with separate measures of felt arm position and of the felt direction of gaze	Misalignment—eyes turned in the same direction as the displacement. No shift in felt arm position or direction of gaze	Misreaching for visual targets in the direction opposite the displacement

[a] From R. B. Welch, *Perceptual modification: Adapting to altered sensory environments*, Academic Press, Inc., 1978. Reprinted with permission.
[b] Unless otherwise indicated, test occurs in the absence of vision.
[c] Assumes that the prism has been removed.

location of the pointing right index finger) and the actual tactile stimulus location.

Research from Held's laboratory (Efstathiou, Bauer, Greene, & Held, 1967; Greene, 1967; Hardt, Held, & Steinbach, 1971) has provided some evidence for prism-induced changes at "complex" sites such as the neural centers that serve the articulation of head and arm or eye and arm (see Table 24.1). Specifically, these investigators found that prism exposure failed to result in a shift in the placement of the unseen hand in *remembered* positions, despite the fact that a significant visuomotor negative aftereffect could be measured. One interpretation of this finding is that the recalibration involved the relations between *non-adjacent* body parts such as the head and arm. Unfortunately, it is unclear what conditions are necessary and sufficient to produce adaptation of this sort. This situation is particularly perplexing because several later studies (Hamilton, Sullivan, & Hillyard, 1971; Kennedy, 1969) have failed to replicate the remembered hand position findings of the Held group.

2.2.4.3. Changes in Vision. As indicated above, there are two general ways in which prism exposure could potentially lead to changes in apparent visual direction. First, a modification might occur in the egocentric significance of retinal loci. The evidence for this possibility, which may be referred to as "oculocentric adaptation," is, however, both sparse and conflicting (H. B. Cohen, 1966; Crawshaw & Craske, 1974; Howard, 1970) and thus it remains uncertain if such an adaptive response to prismatic displacement actually takes place. To be sure, retinocentric space is not completely unmodifiable, as seen in the occurrence of figural aftereffects (e.g., Köhler & Wallach, 1944) or visual normalization of tilted or curved lines (e.g., Gibson, 1933). However, as indicated at the beginning of this chapter (Section 1.1), these minor visual effects do not qualify as adaptation.

The second way in which apparent visual direction could be altered by prism exposure would be as a result of a change in the felt direction of eyes to head (referred to as "oculomotor adaptation") and/or head to shoulders. Prism-adaptive shifts in visual direction have been obtained in a number of experiments (e.g., Foley & Maynes, 1969; Mikaelian, 1970a; Uhlarik & Canon, 1971; Welch et al., 1974; Wilkinson, 1971) and do indeed appear to be based on a shift in the felt direction of gaze (e.g., Craske, 1967; Craske & Templeton, 1968; Kalil & Freedman, 1966b; McLaughlin & Webster, 1967; Pick, Hay, & Martin, 1969; Webster, 1969), or of felt head position (Kornheiser, 1976; Lackner, 1973b, 1981). Further, albeit less direct, evidence for prism-adaptive shifts in apparent visual direction comes from a variety of studies that have obtained intermanual transfer of the visuomotor negative aftereffect (Baily, 1972b, M. M. Cohen, 1967, 1973, 1974; Howard, Anstis, & Lucia, 1974; Taub & Goldberg, 1973).

The prism exposure conditions conducive to visual shift are quite varied, ranging from walking about in everyday surroundings (e.g., Hay & Pick, 1966a; Held & Mikaelian, 1964; Redding & Wallace, 1978; Wallach & Huntington, 1973) to viewing one's stationary feet (e.g., Craske & Templeton, 1968; Mikaelian, 1970a; Wallach, Kravitz, & Lindauer, 1963). One hypothesis that has gained a certain amount of support is that adaptation will be manifested primarily in the *non*-attended modality (Canon, 1970, 1971). Thus if conditions favor close attention to the visual information, adaptation takes the form of a large shift in felt limb position and vice versa. Uhlarik and Canon (1971), for example, demonstrated that concurrent prism display resulted in a substantial proprioceptive shift, but little visual shift. The reverse was the case for a condition of terminal display, in which the observer saw the hand only at the terminus of each reaching response. The authors argued convincingly that with concurrent display, one's limb movements are continuously monitored by vision which therefore is the attended modality, whereas with terminal display, one must use (and attend) proprioceptive information throughout most of each arm movement. An analogous observation for the visual and proprioceptive components of optical tilt adaptation (see Section 3.2.2) has been reported by Redding (1981).

The fact that intermanual transfer of the negative aftereffect is favored by terminal display (e.g., M. M. Cohen, 1967, 1973, 1974; Howard et al., 1974) represents indirect corroboration of the Uhlarik and Canon finding. Further support for the "directed attention" hypothesis of the locus of prism adaptation comes from Kelso, Cook, Olson, and Epstein (1975) and Redding (1979).

2.2.4.4. The "Additivity" Hypothesis. It seems likely that in many prism adaptation experiments there occur shifts in both vision and felt limb position, their relative proportions varying with the nature of the exposure conditions (e.g., relative attention to the two modalities). It follows, then, that the algebraic sum of these two types of adaptation ought to approximate the magnitude of the adaptive shift in eye-hand coordination that we refer to as the visuomotor negative aftereffect. This "additivity" hypothesis, which was first proposed by Hamilton (1964b) and Harris (1965), has found support in a number of studies. Wilkinson (1971), for example, in an experiment involving target-pointing exposure to 12 ° prismatic displacement, found that the sum of adaptive visual and proprioceptive shifts equaled (and was highly correlated with) the visuomotor negative aftereffect. Other evidence supporting the additivity hypothesis comes from studies by Beckett, Melamed, and Halay (1975), Hay and Pick (1966a), McLaughlin, Rifkin, and Webster (1966), McLaughlin and Webster (1967), Templeton et al. (1974), Wallace (1977), and Wallace and Redding (1979). Additivity has also been demonstrated for adaptation to optical tilt (see Section 3.2.2) by Redding (1978).

Under certain circumstances, a *third*, although perhaps relatively minor, component of prism adaptation has been detected, a change in eye-hand coordination that is relatively independent of any perceptual changes that might also have occurred. Welch and his associates (Welch, 1974b; Welch et al., 1974) proposed that when the prism-exposure period entails pointing at targets, particularly with spaced trials and terminal display, the subject quickly acquires a "rule" for correct pointing, which, after some practice, becomes quite automatic. This automaticity causes it to persist for a while after the prism is removed, despite the observer's awareness that a corrective response is no longer necessary. This, then, is a form of motor learning. Other studies (Beckett, 1980; Beckett et al., 1975; Choe & Welch, 1974; Melamed et al., 1979; Templeton et al., 1974; Wallace, 1977; Wallace & Redding, 1979) have supported this three-component model of prism adaptation. Although this component, when it is observed, accounts for only a small portion of the visuomotor negative aftereffect obtained from prism exposure, it may contribute quite substantially to the adaptive response to the more dramatic distortions such as inversion and right-left reversal, as discussed in Section 3.2.1.

Finally, "overadditivity" (where the sum of the visual and proprioceptive modifications is greater than the visuomotor negative aftereffect) has been reported (Redding & Wallace, 1976, 1978). Redding (1981) also observed this anomalous result for optical tilt adaptation (see Section 3.2.2).

2.2.4.5. "Eye Muscle Potentiation" as an Alternative to Visual Recalibration. Ebenholtz (e.g., 1974) has provided evidence for the rather radical suggestion that, contrary to the traditional view, oculomotor shifts as a result of prism exposure do not represent a perceptual *recalibration*. Instead, he argues, prism-adaptive changes in felt eye position and the concomitant shift in apparent visual direction are actually artifacts arising from the fact that the subject is typically forced to maintain an asymmetric eye position during prism exposure. Prolonged deviation of the eyes from their normal position of rest leads to a reflexive tendency to maintain this ocular position even after attempting to relax the eye, a phenomenon that may be referred to as "eye muscle potentiation" (EMP).

The phenomenon of EMP has predictable visual effects. For example, if (for whatever reason) the eyes have been directed off to the right for a time and then relaxed, the observer will feel as if they are now pointing straight ahead when, in fact, they are still aimed off to the right. If a point of light is then placed directly in line with the eyes, the observer will incorrectly perceive the stimulus to be straight ahead of the nose because that is where the eyes are felt to be directed. Likewise, if the subject is requested to fixate a visual target that has been placed directly in front of the nose, the efference necessary to rotate they eyes from their EMP-induced rightward deviation to the straight ahead should be such as to produce the experience that the eyes have been turned off to the left and, consequently, that is where the subject will perceive the object to be located. It should be noted that the EMP interpretation of adaptation requires neither eye movement toward nor fixation on the target. That is, whether or not the object is foveated, the potentiation-induced misperception of felt eye position should cause a misperception of the object's location.

Ebenholtz and his colleagues (Ebenholtz, 1974, 1976; Ebenholtz & Wolfson, 1975; Paap & Ebenholtz, 1976) have provided convincing evidence in support of these notions. For example, Paap and Ebenholtz (1976) pitted the EMP and recalibration hypotheses against each other by examining the impact of various kinds of postexposure activity upon prism-induced shifts in apparent visual straight ahead. Of the five conditions examined by the investigators, two are of particular interest. In the Exercise Group, subjects spent their time after the prisms had been removed moving their eye back and forth between two visual targets in an otherwise dark room. In the Induction Group, they held their eyes off in the same direction and by the same amount as the previous prismatic displacement. Because in neither case were the subjects provided with any visual feedback during their postexposure activities, the recalibration hypothesis would predict equal adaptation decay rates. According to the EMP hypothesis, however, a very significant difference should appear, for in the first condition the EMP is presumably being eradicated by the vigorous eye movements, whereas in the second the deviated position of the eyes is maintained. The results clearly confirmed the EMP prediction. The prism-induced shift in apparent visual direction had completely disappeared for the Exercise Group by the 3-min post-test measure, whereas there was no evidence of decay for the Induction Group, even by the end of the 15-min postexposure period. A third condition entailing active exposure to the visual environment with the prisms removed did not lead to as rapid dissipation of the visual effect as had occurred for the Exercise Group. This result contradicts the recalibration hypothesis, for here the subjects were provided with informational feedback about their now-normal vision and therefore, according to this hypothesis, should have "readapted" most rapidly of all.

The point of all this is that because prism exposure is typically "confounded" by prolonged asymmetric positioning of the eyes, the visual and oculomotor shifts that have been reported and that do, indeed, serve to compensate for the prismatic displacement, may not actually be the outcome of a process of adaptation to the cue discrepancy induced by the sensory rearrangement.

An investigator of prism adaptation wishing to avoid EMP-induced shifts of apparent visual direction may include a control condition in which subjects with *undistorted* vision must hold their eyes off to one side by the same amount as subjects in the prism-wearing condition(s). Alternatively, the situation may be designed in such a fashion that subjects' eyes are maintained in a straight-ahead position throughout the prism exposure period. Both these control conditions were implemented by Willey, Gyr, and Henry (1978), who found (prism-adaptive) changes in visual straight ahead only in the first situation, where potentiation was the only possibility. Craske and Crawshaw (1978), on the other hand, found that 5 min of exposure to the prismatically displaced right foot, which was placed off in the direction opposite the visual displacement, thereby necessitating a straight-ahead eye (and head) position, produced a 2° prism-adaptive shift in visual direction. Thus it may be concluded that some portion of the prism-induced visual shifts reported in many previous studies may almost certainly be accounted for by EMP effects. Whether *all* of it may be so interpreted, however, remains unclear, for in nearly all instances the necessary controls for or independent measures of these confounding effects have not been implemented.

2.3. Conclusions

Like learning in general, prism adaptation (1) reveals negatively accelerated acquisition, decay, and unlearning functions, (2) transfers intermanually (under some conditions), (3) is subject to stimulus and response generalization (frequently with decrements), (4) is conditionable, (5) is (sometimes) affected by distribution of "practice," and (6) is inhibited by delays of feedback. It is unclear how far one can take this similarity to traditional learning phenomena or whether it signifies a similarity or identity in underlying process, although this view has been championed by some, most notably Taub (1968).

We have seen that a wide variety of conditions are sufficient to produce prism adaptation, a view referred to here as the "information hypothesis." Contrary to earlier notions, active visuomotor behavior is not a *necessary* condition for adaptation, although it does appear to facilitate it, probably by making the discrepancy between the felt and seen positions of the limb more salient or by generally increasing the amount of information available concerning the presence and nature of the perceptual rearrangement.

Some or all of a variety of end products—proprioceptive, visual, motor learning—are produced by prism exposure. It appears that the modality most susceptible to adaptive recalibration is the one being essentially *ignored*; frequently this is proprioception. Even when visual direction undergoes the primary modification, the basis is probably not an alteration of the egocentric significance of retinal loci but rather a change in the felt direction of gaze and/or felt relation of head to shoulder. Thus even here one might say that it is proprioception—with visual consequences—that has been modified.

Although genuine adaptation (as assessed by the negative aftereffect) is rarely, if ever, complete, subjects are capable of consciously redirecting their responses (when a target is available) while wearing the prism such that completely accurate visuomotor behavior is possible within one or two trials. Furthermore, some immediate perceptual responses to the prismatic displacement—intersensory bias and the "straight-ahead shift"—significantly reduce the registered visual-proprioceptive discrepancy before the adaptive mechanism even has a chance to operate.

Finally, it is important to acknowledge Ebenholtz's serious challenge to the generally accepted interpretation of prism-induced visual change. His arguments and support for the notion that such a change is an artifact of eye-muscle potentiation, (EMP), rather than evidence for visual recalibration, are quite persuasive. It is, however, still far from clear whether the phenomenon of EMP accounts for the entirety of prism-induced visual effects in all situations.

2.4. Key References

Ebenholtz, S. M. (1974). This is a clear presentation of the argument for a reinterpretation of prism-induced visual effects as artifacts of "eye-muscle potentiation" (EMP).

Harris, C. S. (1965). This is a well-written review of much of the "early" adaptation literature, coupled with compelling arguments (and supporting data) that a wide variety of adaptive responses can be interpreted in terms of recalibration of the felt position of body parts (including the eyes).

Hay, J. C., & Pick, H. L., Jr. (1966a). This commonly cited article describes the results of a 42-day prism adaptation study which, among other things, demonstrated the existence of both visual and proprioceptive components of prism adaptation and how these sum to produce the visuomotor negative aftereffect (the "additivity" hypothesis).

Held, R., & Freedman, S. J. (1963). In this article the authors present Held's "reafference model" and a wide variety of supporting data. Naturally this paper is rather out of date concerning the more recent findings relevant to this issue.

3. ADAPTATION TO DISTORTION OF VISUAL ORIENTATION

3.1. Background

Motivated by the question of whether the inverted retinal image is necessary for the world to appear upright, Stratton (1896, 1897a, 1897b) carried out his now-famous studies of adaptation to a 180° rotated visual field. He proposed that if an observer whose retinal image is made upright by means of spectacles is ultimately able to see the world as right side up, the normally inverted retinal image must not be a necessary condition for the perception of visual orientation. In addition, it has been claimed by some writers that such a finding would imply that for the *newborn infant* the orientation of the retinal image is arbitrary; the infant would come to see the world as upright regardless of the orientation of the retinal image. Only many years after the completion of Stratton's experiment did it become apparent to investigators (e.g., Rock, 1966, Chapter 2) that the question concerning the necessity of a specific (inverted) retinal image for normal visual orientation could be answered just as well (and perhaps better) by exposing an observer to the relatively mild perceptual rearrangement of optical tilt.

3.2. Experimental Findings

3.2.1. Transposed Vision: Inversion and Right-Left Reversal. As indicated in (Section 1.1), despite the occurrence of visuomotor adaptation and reacquisition of a stable visual field during head movements (and subsequent aftereffects) in Stratton's (1896, 1897a, 1897b) studies, there is little or no reason to believe that the world ever came to look upright to him. At best, he occasionally found himself *disregarding* the orientation of the field. The clearest evidence that Stratton had failed to undergo adaptation of visual orientation was the absence of an aftereffect in this regard. He reported, immediately after removing his goggles, that although things appeared strange in comparison to his memory of the preceding days of optical rotation, there was no doubt in his mind that the world looked upright.

Most of the subsequent studies of adaptation to visual transposition (Ewert, 1930, 1936, 1937; Peterson & Peterson, 1938; Snyder & Pronko, 1952; Snyder & Snyder, 1957) found little to modify Stratton's conclusions. One possible exception to the general failure to induce adaptive changes in visual orientation comes from the studies of Erismann and Kohler at the University of Innsbruck in Austria (Erismann, 1947; Kohler, 1951, 1955, 1962, 1964). Distinguishing this extensive research program are the many vigorous and potentially dangerous activities required of the subjects. These tasks included fencing, mountain climbing, skiing, and bicycle riding in heavy traffic! In one study (Kohler, 1964, p. 32) a subject wore inverting goggles for 9 days and reported seeing progressively more and more objects to be right side up. More dramatically, when the goggles were removed, he reported a clear experience of an upside-down world. In an experiment involving exposure of a subject to right-left reversal (but not simultaneous inversion) for a period of 37 days (Kohler, 1964, pp. 140–161), objects came eventually to look normally oriented and led to a visual aftereffect when the goggles were removed. A particularly surprising observation was made by Taylor (1962), who spent some time at the Innsbruck laboratory. He reported that vigorous training of his subject, who was wearing right-left reversing spectacles for half of each day, eventually resulted in complete adaptation to the transposed field but no disruption (aftereffect) when shifted to normal vision.

Characteristic of the reports from the Innsbruck laboratory are rather bizarre experiences of partial or paradoxical adaptive effects. For example, one subject, while wearing right-left reversing goggles, reported seeing an automobile as being located on the correct side of the road while, at the same time, the license plate numbers looked right-left reversed. Another example of this so-called "piecemeal adaptation" (e.g., Harris, 1965) was a report by a subject wearing inverting goggles that when confronted with a drawing of two faces, inverted relative to one another, they *both* appeared to be upright! Harris (1965, 1980) has shown quite convincingly how such strange effects can be understood as the result of changes in the felt relationship among various body parts.

Smith and Smith (1962) have reported the results of an extensive series of experiments in which subjects engaged in various visuomotor tasks while viewing their hands by means of video feedback. In some of the experiments this feedback was 180° rotated, up-down reversed, or right-left reversed. Although these studies clearly involved visual rearrangement, they are probably not relevant to the present topic. That is, because the rearranging device was never attached to the observer's head, a number of the visual effects produced by distorting spectacles were absent. Thus it is unlikely that adaptation, as defined here, actually occurred in these experiments.

The most recent study of adaptation to prolonged exposure to visual transposition is by Dolezal (1982). In this engaging book, the author demonstrates, among other things, that some of the visual and visuomotor effects previously attributed to the transposition (up-down reversal) are actually due to the restricted visual field that typically accompanies this form of visual rearrangement.

In a recent study, Gonshor and Melvill Jones (1980) found that subjects who wore right-left reversing goggles during their waking hours for periods ranging from 6 to 27 days revealed both postural adaptation (e.g., rail walking performance) and reacquisition of visual stability with lateral head movements. The aftereffects persisted for as long as 2 weeks after the goggles were removed. It is interesting that the visual motion-induced nausea typically experienced by subjects during the early stages of the exposure period (and immediately after removing the goggles) does not occur in *stroboscopic* light (Melvill Jones & Mandl, 1979), even though a certain amount of adaptation results.

There are at least three likely reasons why the studies of adaptation to visual transposition have found so little evidence of consistent visual adaptation with respect to perceived orientation. First, human beings may be incapable of such adaptation, perhaps indicative of an innate and unmodifiable connection between the orientation of the retinal image and perceived orientation. Second, it may be that the exposure periods used have simply not been long enough to overcome a lifetime of experience with normal visual orientation. This may be particularly important with visual transposition because *partial* adaptation is not a viable outcome (e.g., an object should look either upside down or right side up, but not somewhere in between). Finally, it may be that if visual adaptation is to occur to transposed vision, it is necessary for the subject to interact with the environment much more vigorously than has typically been the case. As we have seen, Kohler (1964) and Taylor (1962), in contrast to previous investigators, had subjects perform very demanding activities. It may be argued plausibly that the visual adaptation apparently obtained in the Innsbruck studies was due to the high degree of subject motivation and the necessity of rapid and automatic visuomotor responding, the latter providing unambiguous and salient information about the nature of the rearrangement.

It has been suggested by Rock (1966, Chapter 2) that in attempting to answer Stratton's original question it is unnecessary to transpose the visual field. Instead, a sufficient test of the issue should be possible by merely *tilting* it. Thus if visual adaptation to this form of optical distortion can be demonstrated, one could validly conclude that visual spatial orientation is not an inevitable consequence of a particular orientation of the retinal image.

3.2.2. Optically Induced Tilt

3.2.2.1. The Paradigm. The first study of adaptation to optically induced tilt was by Brown (1928), who viewed the world through a pair of Dove prisms placed in tandem within a brass tube and rotated so as to produce a 75° tilt from the visual vertical (see Figure 24.10). Brown, like Stratton, wore the distorting goggles himself while moving about in an everyday environment for a number of days. Brown reported that after the second day of a week-long continuous wearing period the field had come to appear much less tilted. Unfortunately, he took no quantitative measures of the presumed adaptation, either during or after the exposure period. Subsequent studies of adaptation to optical tilt have used smaller tilts (from 10 to 32°) and shorter exposure periods (from 15 min to 4 hr), and objective measures instead of introspective reports.

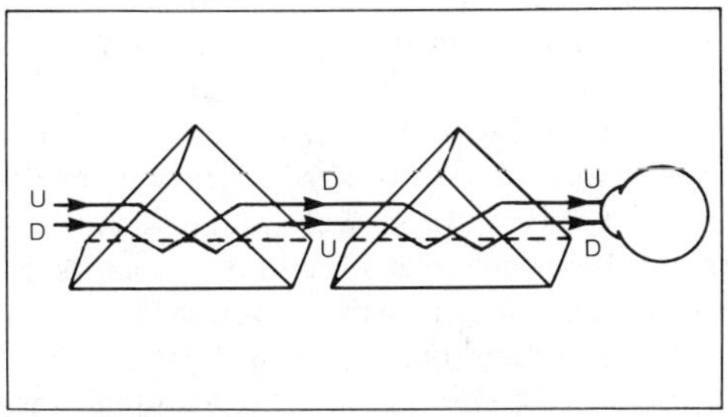

Figure 24.10. Two Dove prisms in tandem arrangement. Each prism entails a mirrored base which inverts the visual image and two refracting surfaces which prevent it from being displaced. Light rays U and D are up-down reversed by the first prism and normalized by the second before entering the eye. In order to produce optical tilt, one of the prisms is rotated by the desired amount. (From R. B. Welch, *Perceptual modification. Adapting to altered sensory environments*, Academic Press, 1978. Reprinted with permission.)

A representative study of tilt adaptation was done by Ebenholtz (1966). Subjects each wore a monocoluar Dove prism that tilted the visual field clockwise or counterclockwise by 10, 20, or 32° while engaging for 4 hr in a variety of activities (e.g., walking through corridors, throwing darts). Prior to and at hourly intervals during the exposure period, the prism was removed and the subject was asked to set to apparent vertical a luminous line in an otherwise dark room. Tilt adaptation (in terms of negative aftereffect) increased rapidly during the exposure period, reaching asymptote after 1–2 hr at approximately 30% of the imposed optical tilt (see Figure 24.11).

3.2.2.2. General Characteristics and Parameters. Numerous studies have demonstrated that tilt adaptation increases as a negatively accelerated function of exposure time and reaches asymptote at only 20–30% of the theoretical maximum (e.g., Ebenholtz, 1966; Rierdan & Wapner, 1967). The magnitude of adaptation is a linear function of the size of the imposed tilt, at least for tilts up to about 30° (Ebenholtz, 1966; Redding, 1973b) and reveals substantial or complete interocular transfer (e.g., Ebenholtz, 1966; Mack & Chitayat, 1970; Quinlan, 1970; Redding, 1973b).

Redding (1973a, 1973b, 1975a, 1975b) demonstrated that the visual shift in prism adaptation is acquired more gradually but reaches a higher asymptote than is the case for visual tilt adaptation. Furthermore, the decay curve for the visual shift is more gradual and reaches zero, whereas the curve for tilt adaptation levels off *above* the preexposure base line. Acquisition and decay curves for adaptation to two magnitudes of optical tilt are depicted in Figure 24.12. These findings, together with the observation by Redding (1973a, 1973b, 1975a) that tilt and prism adaptation can be acquired simultaneously without mutual interference, suggest that the two types of adaptation are not based on the same process.

3.2.2.3. Necessary and Sufficient Conditions for Tilt Adaptation. There is some controversy about whether active bodily movement is a necessary condition for tilt adaptation. Although both Mikaelian and Held (1964) and Quinlan (1970) failed to find adaptation to a 20° tilt for conditions of passive whole-body movement, Mack (1967) reported equal adaptation for active and passive conditions. Quinlan (1970) has suggested that this contradiction in results may, in some way, be due to the fact that the head was free to move in the passive conditions of his and Mikaelian and Held's (1964) studies, whereas it was immobilized in Mack's (1967) experiment.

Merely viewing a familiar scene leads to a small amount of tilt adaptation (Mack, 1967; Mack & Chitayat, 1970; Morant & Beller, 1965), although Harris (1974) has suggested that this corrective shift is due to the subject's interpretation of "vertical," an analogue of the prism-induced "straight-ahead shift" (Section 2.2.3.2).

Viewing part or all of the body through the tilt goggles leads to little or no adaptation (Mack & Rock, 1968; Mikaelian, 1967) unless the entire body is viewed during active movement (Quinlan, 1970; Rierdan & Wapner, 1966).

The optimal condition for tilt adaptation appears to be walking in a natural indoor environment (e.g., corridors, stairs). Redding (1978, 1981) has compared this form of exposure to that of viewing the actively moving hand. The former condition (referred to as "hall" exposure) produced a great deal of visual tilt adaptation, but very little change in proprioception (i.e.,

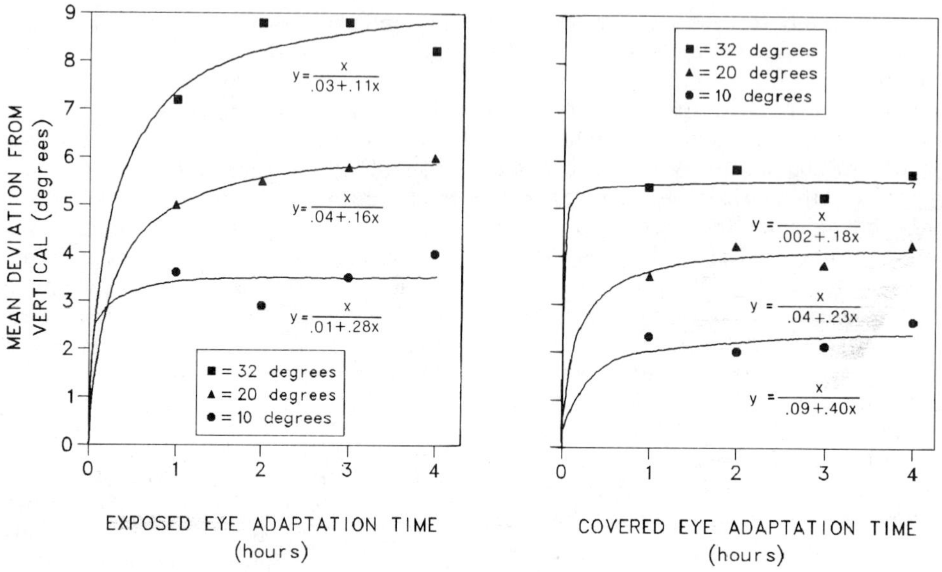

Figure 24.11. Adaptation to optical tilt for exposed (right) and covered (left) eye as a function of magnitude of tilt (10, 20, or 32°) and adaptation time (1–4 hr). Subjects wore a pair of Dove prisms, mounted in tandem, before the right eye while walking through long corridors and up and down steps, and engaging in various eye-hand activities (e.g., dart throwing). Subjects were measured (with prism removed) on their setting of an electroluminescent rod to apparent vertical in an otherwise dark room before and at 1-hr intervals for 4 hr. Magnitude of adaptation was a linear function of optical tilt and a negatively accelerated function of adaptation time. Adaptation for the unexposed eye was approximately 62% of the adaptation for the exposed eye (which was measured first). (From S. M. Ebenholtz, Adaptation to a rotated visual field as a function of degree of optical tilt and exposure time, *Journal of Experimental Psychology, 72*. Copyright 1966 by American Psychological Association. Reprinted with permission.)

attempting, in the absence of vision, to point to locations aligned with the vertical axis of the head). In contrast, the hand exposure condition produced very little visual adaptation but a great deal of proprioceptive adaptation. These results do not necessarily indicate that "hall" exposure is incapable of producing any proprioceptive adaptation. If, for example, measures of the felt position of the *legs* had been obtained, proprioceptive shift might have been obtained.

Ebenholtz (e.g., 1967, 1968a) has argued that with "hall" exposure the crucial information for the adaptive process is the "retinal flow pattern" (the flow of retinal images that occurs during head or entire body movement and which, it has been argued, serves as an unambiguous cue for the direction of one's bodily motion). Thus, for example, with normal vision, a lateral head movement causes the field to move in the opposite direction along the same axis. When optical tilt goggles are worn, however, the same head movement leads to a diagonal flow pattern (i.e., perpendicular to the tilt). According to Ebenholtz, the discrepancy between long- and short-term memory of the flow pattern contingent upon a particular movement of the head or body is the stimulus for the adaptive process. This *comparator model* is presented in schematic form in Figure 24.13. Although quite similar to the mechanism by Held (e.g., 1961) for prism adaptation (see Figure 24.9), it does not demand that body movement be self-initiated.

According to Ebenholtz's model, tilt adaptation is independent of how the visual field *appears* to the subject and whether (or to what extent) the subject has adapted to the optical tilt. This hypothesis attributes the negatively accelerated acquisition curve to the weakening of the long-term memory for the preexposure optical situation with time. As a consequence, the proposed comparator becomes increasingly less sensitive to the discrepancy between the current effect of a given bodily movement and the remembered preexposure optical/retinal state of affairs from the same movement. When this memory reaches a critical degree of "deterioration," adaptation will have reached asymptote.

In a study by Ebenholtz and Mayer (1968) it was demonstrated that if optical tilt was *increased* in steps of 5° at 5-min intervals (compared to a condition in which the tilt was left at a constant 30° for the entire exposure period), the acquisition curve increased linearly rather than asymptotically (see Figure 24.14). It was argued that the increments in tilt served periodically to "rejuvenate" the adaptive process by counteracting the normal tendency of the comparator to become less sensitive to the discrepancy between "old" and "new" retinal events. More convincing support for this conclusion would come from a study that allowed adaptation in the incremental condition to reach its maximum at each prism strength before moving to the next level. In this way, it would be clear if the final level of adaptation would exceed that of the 30° group, a finding that should occur if the authors' interpretation is correct. Similar results to those of Ebenholtz and Mayer (1968) were found with 8° increments (Ebenholtz, 1969) but not with 10 or 12° increments (Ebenholtz, 1973). As an aside, it is interesting to note that adaptation to the visual effects of head movement during vestibular stimulation (as a result of bodily rotation) is also facilitated by the use of incremental exposure (Graybiel & Wood, 1969). Likewise, Lackner and Lobovits (1977, 1978) demonstrated that exposure to prismatic displacement that was incremented periodically facilitated adaptation and its retention. It would thus appear that Ebenholtz's notion of a comparator that is maximally responsive to a *change* in the magnitude of the sensory distortion may be applicable to a wide range of perceptual rearrangements.

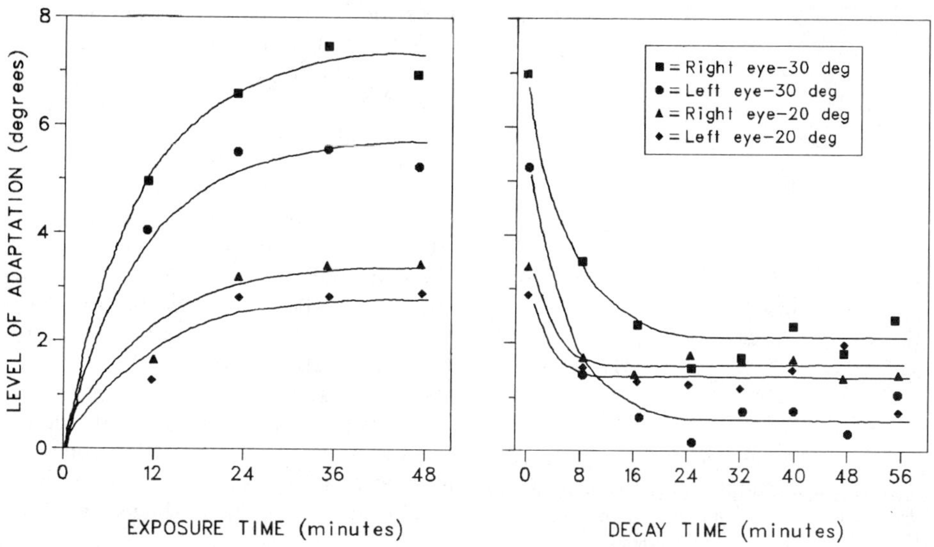

Figure 24.12. Mean level of adaptation to 30 and 20° of optical tilt in the exposed (right) and unexposed (left) eye as a function of exposure time in acquisition and decay time in the dark. Subjects wore a pair of Dove prisms, mounted in tandem, before the right eye while walking through hallways for 48 min. Before and at 12-min intervals during this adaptation period subjects were measured (with prisms removed) on their setting of an electroluminescent rod to apparent vertical in an otherwise dark room. These measurements were also obtained at the termination of the exposure period and at 8-min intervals during a 56-min decay period during which subjects sat quietly in the dark. Adaptation was significantly greater for 30° tilt than for 20° tilt and greater for exposed (right) eye than for unexposed (left) eye. Neither of these factors, however, was significant for the decay rates. Adaptation reached asymptote at 24 min of exposure time and decay reached asymptote at from 8 to 16 min, but remained significantly above zero (base line), even by the 56-min test. (From G. M. Redding, Decay of visual adaptation to tilt and displacement, *Perception and Psychophysics*, 1975, *17*. Reprinted with permission.)

Ebenholtz and Callan (1980) recently examined the optical tilt adaptation process in the context of a control system (e.g., Toates, 1975). In brief, they manipulated the rate of input of optical tilt by incrementing it by varying amounts and time intervals. They found that the maximum ratio of input to output (i.e., level of adaptation) was obtained when tilt was increased by 1.4° for tilts up to about 35°.

Ebenholtz proposed that exposure to the undistorted environment is not qualitatively different from exposure to other optical tilts. Support for this claim was provided in two experiments (Ebenholtz, 1968b) in which it was demonstrated that the rate of "unlearning" of adaptation to 15–30° tilt was no more rapid than the rate of its acquisition. Potentially embarrassing to this view is the fact that tilt adaptation reveals very rapid (although incomplete) spontaneous decay toward base line (i.e., "zero" tilt) when vision is precluded. Ebenholtz (1969) argued that perhaps when vision is occluded, random "noise" generated by the comparator may cause a regression toward the mean preexposure value.

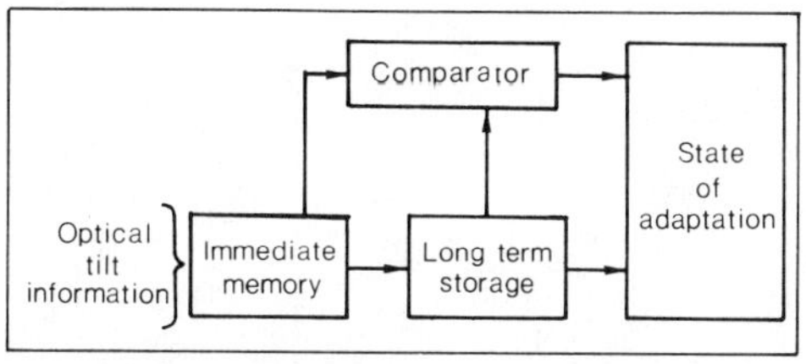

Figure 24.13. The flow of information in a memory-comparator model of optical tilt adaptation. Information about the optical tilt (presumed to be the atypical "retinal flow pattern" contingent on locomotion through space) is compared (in the "comparator") with the long-term memory of the normal retinal state of affairs. A discrepancy between these two neural events leads to adaptation. (From S. M. Ebenholtz, Transfer and decay functions in adaptation to optical tilt, *Journal of Experimental Psychology, 81*. Copyright 1969 by American Psychological Association. Reprinted with permission.)

*3.2.2.4. **The End Products of Tilt Adaptation.*** Exposure to optical tilt has been shown to result in changes in orientation-specific contrast thresholds and visually evoked potentials (Fiorentini, Ghez, & Maffei, 1972), a shift in the retinal orientation required for optimal McCollough effects (Mikaelian, 1976), and changes in apparent vertical. It is, however, the last mentioned that has been the subject of nearly all studies in this area.

Tilt adaptation, in terms of apparent vertical, does not appear to be based on an unnoticed rotation of the eyes, for no such eye torsion has been observed in tilt-adapted subjects (Howard & Templeton, 1964; Mack & Chitayat, 1970; Russotti, 1968). Nor is it likely that a change in felt eye movements is responsible because, according to this hypothesis, whenever adapted subjects stopped moving their eyes the field would have to once again appear tilted. (Although Callan & Ebenholtz, 1982, found an adaptive change in the vestibulo-ocular reflex with head movements as a result of exposure to 30° optical tilt, it is not clear if this end product is a cause or merely a correlate of the adaptive shift in apparent vertical.) Two possibilities that remain are a shift in the felt rotation of head to trunk and a change in the egocentric significance of retinal loci (oculocentric adaptation).

In only a few studies of tilt adaptation has an unambiguous measure of felt head orientation been obtained. Lotto, Kern, and Morant (1967) found that 30 min of unrestricted exposure to a 40° optical tilt resulted in feeling that the upright head

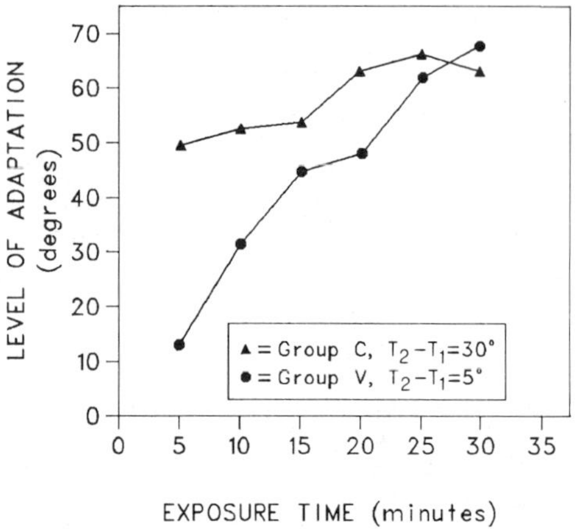

Figure 24.14. Magnitude of adaptation as a function of exposure time for constant (30°) tilt condition (Group C) and 5° tilt increment condition (Group V). Subjects wore a pair of Dove prisms, mounted in tandem, before the right eye (left eye remained occluded) while walking through a hallway. For one group the tilt was a constant 30°; for the other group the tilt increased (every 5 min) from an initial setting of 5° to a final setting of 30 °. Adaptation was measured by having the subject set to vertical an electroluminescent rod in an otherwise dark room. Although both adaptation curves were essentially linear, the slope for Group V was significantly steeper. These results provided support for Ebenholtz' comparator model. (From S. M. Ebenholtz & D. Mayer, Rate of adaptation under constant and varied optical tilt, *Perceptual and Motor Skills*, 1968, *26*. Reprinted with permission.)

was tilted. When the subject felt that the head was aligned with the trunk, it was actually turned in the same direction as the optical tilt. However, the extent of visual tilt adaptation exceeded the observed change in felt head orientation. Thus in the absence of any other possibility, the unaccounted-for tilt adaptation most likely represented oculocentric adaptation.

In support of the latter component of tilt adaptation, Mack and Rock (1968) measured optical tilt adaptation in a situation designed to rule out a change in the felt relation of head to shoulders as a viable basis for the adaptive shift. It was concluded from this outcome that tilt adaptation can occur as a result of a change in the egocentric significance of the tilted retinal image.

Unfortunately, even when prism-adaptive shifts in apparent vertical can be shown to be retinally based, the investigator must be concerned with a confounding phenomenon known, generically, as "configurational adaptation." Thus Gibson and Radner (1973a, 1973b) demonstrated that when one views edges that are *physically* tilted, there occurs a small, but reliable, decrease in perceived tilt and a subsequent aftereffect when viewing objectively vertical lines, a sequence of events depicted in Figure 24.15. This phenomenon, which has come to be referred to as the "Gibson effect," after its discoverer, is strongest for a 20° tilt, with no effect at all for a 45° tilt. Furthermore, it occurs whether the eyes are stationary or moving. Obviously, because configurational adaptation does not represent a response to the visual distortion per se (for it can occur when one views edges that are actually tilted), it does not qualify as adaptation to perceptual rearrangement.

The investigator wishing to isolate tilt adaptation from configurational effects may prevent the latter from occurring either by eliminating all vertical contours from the exposure environment (e.g., Mikaelian & Held, 1964) or by obtaining the preexposure measures of visual vertical only after configurational adaptation has reached completion (Rock, 1966, pp. 75–76). Very few studies of tilt adaptation have taken these precautions. However, those that have done so have obtained evidence of genuine tilt adaptation (e.g., Mikaelian & Held, 1964). In the many studies in which this problem has been ignored, the magnitude of the shift in apparent vertical (5–7°), indicating that tilt adaptation has indeed occurred.

One of the few studies in which the conditions and measures were appropriately designed to obtain evidence for "pure" tilt adaptation was by Mack and Chitayat (1970). In this study the subject's left eye was exposed to a 5° optical tilt in one direction while the right eye was exposed to the *opposite* tilt. Adaptive shifts in apparent tilt were obtained for each eye (in opposite directions). A stationary viewing condition led to no shift in the visual vertical, thereby ruling out the possibility of configurational adaptation. Furthermore, because no evidence of eye torsion was obtained and potential adaptive changes in head orientation were irrelevant in this situation, the results represent good support for the conclusion that an important basis of tilt adaptation is a change in the values of retinal loci.

3.3. Conclusions

It would appear that the answer to Stratton's original question about whether the inverted retinal image is necessary for the normal experience of egocentric orientation is a qualified "No." The answer would be less equivocal if tilt adaptation were found to be complete. In fact, as we have seen, it rarely exceeds one-third of the theoretical maximum. Such a poor showing suggests that egocentric adaptation to inverted or reversed vision would never occur, regardless of the length of the exposure period.

3.4. Key References

Kohler, I. (1964). This monograph covers a variety of adaptation studies, many of visual transposition, carried out by Kohler and his colleagues at the University of Innsbruck. It gives a good account of how complex and occasionally bizarre adaptation to visual inversion and right-left reversal can be and describes the various, rather dramatic, situations with which subjects in these studies were forced to interact.

Rock, I. (1966, Chapter 2). In this chapter of Rock's book the entire issue of visual orientation, its relation to the

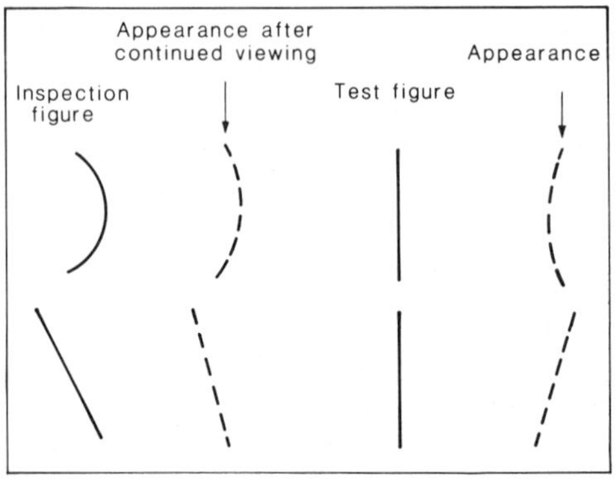

Figure 24.15. Perceptual effects and aftereffects from viewing a physically curved or tilted line. These so-called "Gibson effects" reach their maximum in 1–2 min of viewing. It is not necessary for these effects that the eyes remain stationary. (From R. B. Welch, *Perceptual modification: Adapting to altered sensory environments*, Academic Press, Inc., 1978. Reprinted with permission.)

orientation of the retinal image, and the results of relevant studies are optically induced transposition and of tilt are presented. Also included is a discussion of several visual changes (e.g., the "Wertheimer effect") that involve the perceptual righting of a visually tilted object but do not qualify as genuine adaptation.

Stratton, G. M. (1896, 1897a, 1897b). These are a fascinating account of Stratton's adventures while wearing monocular 180° rotating goggles for periods of up to 8 days.

4. ADAPTATION TO THE LOSS OF VISUAL POSITION CONSTANCY (VPC)

4.1. Background

Nearly all the optical devices used in research on adaptation to perceptual rearrangement have as one of their effects the disruption of visual stability with head movements. In Stratton's experiment, for example, perhaps the most disturbing of all the initial effects was the experience of the normally stationary visual field appearing to turn in the same direction as the head was moving and by twice the angle of rotation. Human observers have proved capable of adapting relatively rapidly, and sometimes completely, to this disruption of the capacity known as *visual position constancy* (VPC). This disruption has been produced by means of either optical or nonoptical devices.

4.2. Adaptation to the Loss of VPC Induced by Optical Devices

When a subject is wearing wedge prisms, the loss of VPC takes the form of an expansion and contraction of the visual field with lateral head movements and a "seesaw" effect with up-down head movements. Partial adaptation to this "rubbery" appearance of the visual field has been measured in several studies (Pick & Hay, 1964, 1966a; Wallach & Flaherty, 1976).

In one experiment (Wallach & Flaherty, 1976), exposure to a prismatically displaced field while nodding the head for 10 min led to a compensatory shift of VPC amounting to 9% of the theoretical maximum. Interestingly, this value is comparable to that reported by Pick and Hay (1964) for subjects who were allowed to engage in unsupervised, everyday activities for many days. Wallach and Flaherty (1976) demonstrated that adaptation to wedge prism-altered VPC fails to occur when the deformations of the visual field are viewed with a stationary head, indicating that this form of adaptation requires for its occurrence a linkage between atypical visual motion and the bodily movements that cause it.

Other studies of VPC adaptation have involved optical right-left reversal as a result of mirrors (Gonshor & Melvill Jones, 1973, 1976a, 1976b; Melvill Jones & Gonshor, 1975) or Dove prisms (Oman, Bock, & Huang, 1980). These studies have demonstrated that prolonged exposure (entailing a great deal of head turning) to this form of rearrangement leads to a decline and sometimes a reversal of the vestibulo-ocular reflex (Gonshor & Melvill Jones, 1973, 1976a, 1976b; Melvill Jones & Gonshor, 1975) and a reversal of the "circular-vection" phenomenon (Oman et al., 1980). The latter is the situation in which a pattern of stripes revolving around a stationary observer elicits an extremely compelling sensation of self-rotation in the opposite direction.

4.3. Adaptation to the Loss of VPC Induced by Nonoptical Devices

4.3.1. Apparatus, Procedure, and General Findings. Adaptation to a loss of VPC was first *specifically* examined by Wallach and Kravitz (1965a, 1965b) and Posin and Rock (described by Rock, 1966, pp. 87–91). Later studies were carried out by Hay (1968, 1971, 1974, 1981), Hay and Goldsmith (1973), and Wallach and his collaborators (e.g., Wallach, 1976).

In the pioneering studies by Wallach and Kravitz a single luminous spot was projected onto a curved screen via headgear worn by the subject. By means of this device, the position of the visual stimulus could be displaced in any ratio to the subject's head rotation and in either direction. Thus, for example, if a 15° leftward head turn were coupled with a 15° rightward rotation of the spot (a "displacement ratio" of 100%), the result would be a physically stationary spot that, because of VPC, the observer correctly perceives as such. This apparatus allows for a precise measurement of both the normal capacity of VPC and the degree to which it may be prone to adaptation. (Wallach & Bacon, 1976, used a similar device to measure the constancy of visual *orientation* with side-to-side head tilting as well as adaptation to a disruption of this capacity.)

In one experiment (Wallach & Kravitz, 1965a), subjects engaged in everyday outdoor activities for 6 hr while wearing reducing goggles (×0.66), which initially cause the visual field to appear to move in the same direction as the head, although more slowly (displacement ratio = 34%). At the end of the 6-hr exposure period, adaptation had reached 50% of the theoretical maximum. That is, the displacement ratio required to experience no motion was reduced from the initial 34 to 17.5%. Merely turning the head back and forth for 10 min while viewing a large patterned field moving in the opposite direction at a greater rate (displacement ratio = 150%) was found in a second study (Wallach & Kravitz, 1965b) to produce substantial adaptation, even when head rotation was *passively* induced. The latter result was replicated independently by Posin (see Rock, 1966, pp. 87–91).

In an extensive series of studies by Wallach and his associates (e.g., Wallach, 1976) it was demonstrated that adaptation to altered VPC increases in magnitude as a negatively accelerated function of exposure time (e.g., Wallach & Floor, 1970) and as a direct function of the extent of distortion (e.g., Wallach & Frey, 1969). In other studies it was revealed that:

1. VPC adaptation is subject to rapid spontaneous decay (Wallach & Frey, 1969, 1972a).
2. Concentrated prior exposure to the normal relationship between head movements and optical motion inhibits subsequent adaptation (Wallach & Floor, 1970).
3. Exposure to optical motion in the same direction as the head's rotation produces greater, more decay-resistant adaptation than does exposure involving optical motion against head rotation, the latter, of course, being the normal state of affairs (Wallach, Frey, & Romney, 1969).
4. Adaptation to altered VPC when the optical motion is in the same direction as the head movement is subject to much greater decay than adaptation to optical motion in the orthogonal direction (Wallach & Frey, 1972a).

One conclusion suggested by these results is that normal visual experience establishes and/or maintains a "long-term memory" for the normal relationship between head movement and the resulting optical motion and that this memory interferes proactively with adaptation to altered VPC.

4.3.2. Necessary/Sufficient Conditions for and End Products of VPC Adaptation. It may be concluded from the preceding discussion that adaptation of the present sort requires for its occurrence exposure to a new relationship between head movement and optical motion; head movements or optical motions alone are insufficient (Hay, 1968; Posin, described by Rock, 1966, pp. 87–91; Wallach & Flaherty, 1974, 1976). Because adaptation occurs equally well for active or passive head turning (Posin, 1966; Wallach & Kravitz, 1965b), it is clear that neural outflow is not a necessary condition for this form of adaptation.

Of the three logically possible end products of adaptation to altered VPC—(1) a change in visual motion perception, (2) a change in felt head rotation, and (3) a change in the *relationship* between these two elements—only the third appears viable. Ruling out the first is Hay's (1971) finding that VPC adaptation does not lead to a change in the apparent motion of a moving spot of light when viewed with head stationary. One form of evidence that contradicts the second possibility is Wallach and Kravitz's (1968) failure to obtain a concomitant change in *auditory* position constancy, a change that would be expected to occur if the felt rotation of the head had undergone modification. Direction evidence that VPC adaptation results in a change in the relationship between head turn and visual motion perceptions comes from the studies mentioned earlier in which prolonged wearing of right-left reversing spectacles was found to alter dramatically the gain in the vestibulo-ocular reflex (Gonshor & Melvill Jones, 1973, 1976a, 1976b; Melvill Jones & Gonshor, 1975).

4.3.3. A Model. Hay (1974) has proposed a model (see Figure 24.16) of the process of VPC adaptation, a model bearing a striking resemblance to that used by Held and his associates to explain adaptation to prismatic displacement (see Figure 24.9). According to Hay, an observer will perceive a stable visual field so long as the visual motion experienced is just that which is "expected" (in terms of both the space vector and time lag), given the particular head movement that has been made. If a mismatch occurs (due, perhaps, to some experimental intervention), an initial illusory experience of external visual motion (i.e., a loss of VPC) occurs and adaptation is activated by means of a "cross-correlator" that "searches" for the best correlation between head movement and the new visual motion to which it leads. Significantly, this adaptive process has been shown by Hay (1968, 1971, 1981) to be unaffected by the simultaneous presence of random visual *exafference* ("real" visual motion).

4.4. Loss of Visual Stability as a Result of Eye Movement

Although head movements while wearing distorting devices lead to visual instability, eye movements do not. Thus, for example, when wearing right-left reversing goggles a turn of the eyes to the left to fixate a target seen there results in accurate foveation and thus no illusory experience of motion. Only if the distorting medium is attached to or controlled by the eyes would visual instability result from eye movements, and a variety of procedures have been devised to do this (Henson, 1978; Mack, 1970; Mack & Bachant, 1969; McLaughlin, 1967; Pola, 1976; Wallach & Lewis, 1965; Yarbus, 1967).

Visual and/or oculomotor adaptation to this loss of visual stability has been observed in several studies (Henson, 1978; Mack, Fendrich & Pleune, 1978; McLaughlin, 1967; McLaughlin, Kelly, Anderson, & Wenz, 1968; Miller, Anstis, & Templeton, 1981). In the Mack et al., study, for example, it was shown that repeated coupling of a rightward saccadic eye movement with an upward (or downward) movement of a spot of light in an otherwise dark room led to a change in thresholds for upward and downward visual motion with eye movements. These threshold changes were precisely what would be expected if a (partial) reacquisition of visual stability had occurred.

Related to this topic are several studies from Wallach's laboratory in which cues for visual motion perception were placed

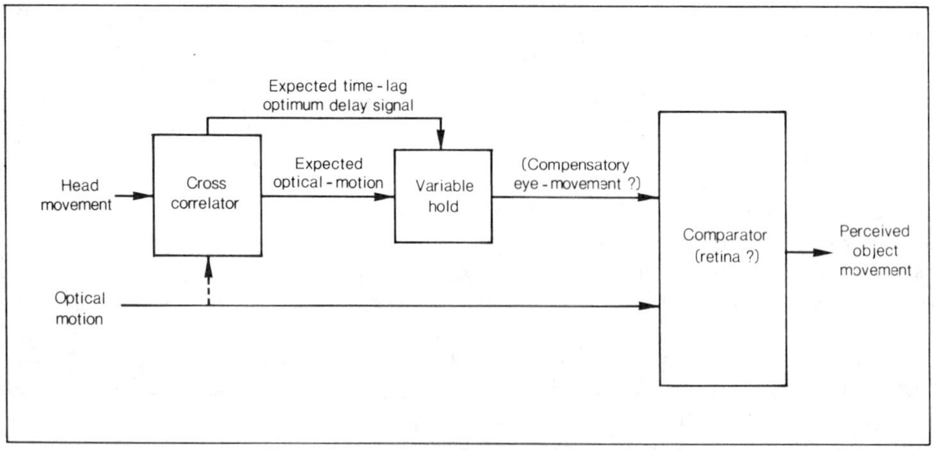

Figure 24.16. A cross-correlator model of adaptation to the loss of visual position constancy. Head movement leads to optical motion and, simultaneously, an expectancy for the optical motion normally contingent on this head movement. These two neural events are compared in the "comparator" (which may be the retina). A match results in the perception of a stable visual field (i.e., visual position constancy); a mismatch results in the experience of a loss in visual position constancy and activates a process of adaptation to this perceived disruption. During exposure to such a discrepancy the "cross-correlator" measures both the time lag and the space vector of the optical motion and, after a period of exposure, produces an expected time lag and an expected optical motion for a given head movement. (From J. C. Hay & W. M. Goldsmith, Space-time adaptation of visual position constancy, *Journal of Experimental Psychology, 99*. Copyright 1973 by American Psychological Association. Reprinted with permission.)

in mutual conflict. Wallach, Bacon, and Schulman (1978) provided subjects with prolonged (10 min) exposure to induced motion—a situation in which a stationary spot appeared to move to one side owing to a vertical line pattern physically moving in the opposite direction. A cue discrepancy existed because information concerning angular displacement indicated no motion of the spot whereas the moving pattern signified motion. As predicted, the magnitude of induced motion was significantly reduced by the exposure period.

Similarly, Bacon and Wallach (1982) found that the experience of motion in a visually tracked object could be altered by exposure to a situation in which the initial direction of a moving spot was changed at about the time that retinal image displacement was replaced by visual pursuit. Exposure to this cue discrepancy for 10 min caused the tracked spot to appear to be moving in the direction that the spot had been moving during the initial image displacement phase.

4.5. Conclusions

It is reasonable to propose that the mechanism of adaptation to illusory visual motion caused by head and/or eye movements serves the purpose of maintaining visual stability for the human infant as the head undergoes its rapid spurt of growth, causing a continuous change in the relationship between head movements and the resulting optical motion.

Of all the forms of adaptation that have been examined, adaptation to altered VPC would seem to be the most nearly complete. It appears from Stratton's (1896, 1897a, 1897b) reports that by the end of the exposure period he was no longer experiencing any illusory motion at all. Similarly, Melvill Jones and Gonshor (1975) obtained complete reversal of the vestibuloocular reflex in a subject who wore right-left reversing spectacles for 14 days. Perhaps the explanation for why this particular variety of adaptation is so extensive lies in the fact that adaptation to the loss of VPC requires only that a concomitance (Rock, 1966, pp. 85–87) or covariance (Wallach & Flaherty, 1974) exist between bodily motion and retinal image displacement. For adaptation to other forms of perceptual rearrangement, some kind of information about *actual* object location, orientation, and so forth is required.

4.6. Key References

Hay, J. C. (1974). This is a review of a number of the studies carried out by Hay and his colleagues on adaptation to disruptions of VPC. Included is a brief exposition on the Hay and Goldsmith (1973) model of the capacity of VPC and of adaptation to its temporary loss.

Shebilske, W. L. (1977). This is a chapter in a book edited by Epstein (1977) which discusses the issue of visual stability (and instability) for the observer with *normal* vision.

Wallach, H. (1976). This book reprints and organizes many of the studies by Wallach and his colleagues described in this section.

5. ADAPTATION TO DISTORTIONS OF DEPTH, DISTANCE, AND SIZE

5.1. Background

Goggles that transpose or tilt the visual field for *both* eyes may have the additional effect of transposing depth. Thus, for example, when wearing binocular right-left reversing spectacles, the reversal of the very important depth cue of *binocular disparity* tends to make the near side of an object look farther away than the far side and vice versa. This misperception, however, will be countered by veridical depth cues that may also be present. Because the studies on adaptation to inverted and right-left reversed vision by Ewert (1930, 1936, 1937) and Peterson and Peterson (1938) and to 75° tilt by Brown (1928) involved binocular viewing, the opportunity for adaptation to depth transposition was provided. In none of these studies, however, were adaptive changes in perceived depth obtained. Thus it is not surprising that studies designed specifically to examine this form of visual rearrangement have used only relatively minor depth distortions.

Human beings are capable of perceiving not only the *relative* distance of visual objects by means of the various depth cues (e.g., binocular disparity, interposition), but also the *absolute* distance of objects. Cues that can potentially indicate the distance of a visual object are accommodation of the lens, convergence of the eyes, and head movement parallax.

Distortions of perceived distance automatically include distortions in perceived size as part of the so-called size-distance invariance hypothesis, although, as will be seen it is possible to magnify or minify objects without altering their perceived distance.

5.2. Experimental Results

5.2.1. Distortions of Depth. Wallach, Moore, and Davidson (1963) had subjects view a rotating three-dimensional wire form through a *telestereoscope*. This device, which is depicted schematically in Figure 24.17, involved an arrangement of mirrors that functionally increases the distance between the eyes, thereby altering the magnitude of the binocular disparity cue while leaving the other depth cues (e.g., interpostition, linear perspective) unaffected. Thus if a solid object is viewed with this apparatus, the aberrant binocular disparity cue will cause the in-out dimension of the object to appear greater (or less) than it actually is. In one of the experiments by Wallach et al.

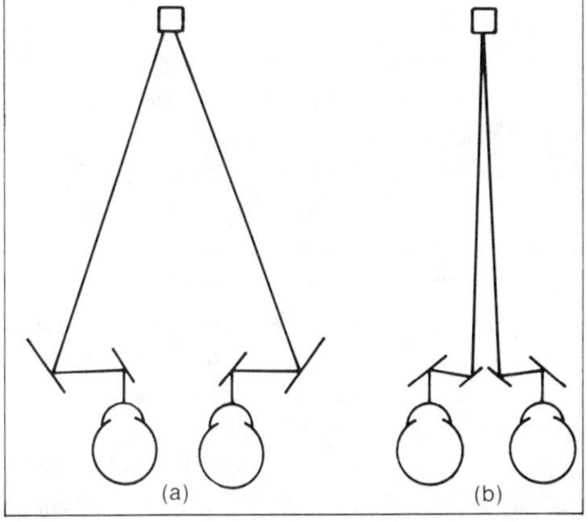

Figure 24.17. Schematic representation of the light paths from the target (cube) through the telestereoscope set to produce enhancement (a) and reduction (b) of binocular disparity. (From H. Wallach, M. E. Moore, & L. Davidson, Modification of stereoscopic depth perception, *American Journal of Psychology, 76*. Copyright 1963 by University of Illinois Press. Reprinted with permission.)

(1963) the telestereoscope was arranged to add 7.6 cm to the subject's normal interocular distance (thereby increasing it more than twofold). After 1, 4, or 10 min of passively viewing a rotating wire form, the subjects experienced an adaptive shift (reduction) in its apparent depth, as measured with the form stationary. Adaptation increased as a negatively accelerated function of the length of exposure to a level equal to 20% of the theoretical maximum and declined either quite rapidly when subsequently viewing the rotating form with normal vision or less rapidly when the eyes were closed. When, in a second experiment, the telestereoscope was set to produce abnormally *small* disparity, the same results were obtained, except that adaptation involved an *increase* in perceived depth. A later experiment by Epstein (1968) confirmed the Wallach et al. findings.

Wallach and Karsh (1963a) demonstrated that this form of adaptation is attenuated if exposure to the altered binocular disparity is preceded by a period of normal visual experience (i.e., observing the rotating wire form for 10 min with undistorted vision).

In a study by Mack and Chitayat (1970), which was introduced in Section 3.2.2.4, right-angle prisms were used to rotate the retinal image of each of the subject's eyes 5° in opposite directions. Such an arrangement causes an objectively upright line, viewed binocularly, to appear tilted either away from or toward the observer, depending on the direction of the rotation. Unconstrained exposure to an indoor environment for at least 20 min led to measurable adaptation assessed in terms of a compensatory shift in the apparent inclination of a vertical line. The investigators concluded that a recalibration between the binocular disparity cue and apparent depth had occurred.

The same conclusion was reached by Epstein and his colleagues (Epstein, 1971, 1972a, 1972b; Epstein & Daviess, 1972; Epstein & Morgan, 1970; Epstein & Morgan-Paap, 1974) in studies of optically induced rotation of the frontoparallel place produced by monocular exposure to a 4–8° "meridional-size lens" (MSL) while the other eye remained uncovered. An MSL magnifies the visual image along the meridian perpendicular to its axis. With the lens in a vertical orientation and the other eye uncovered, the magnification of the horizontal dimension alters the disparities between the images of the two eyes. This in turn causes the visual frontoparallel plane to appear slanted, the side in front of the lens-covered eye appearing farther away.

Epstein and his associates obtained substantial MSL-induced adaptive shifts (up to 63% of the theoretical maximum) in depth discrimination as a result of 1 hr of unrestricted activity in an indoor environment (Epstein & Morgan, 1970; Epstein & Morgan-Paap, 1974). In further experiments they demonstrated that this shift was based on neither a change in registered gaze (Epstein, 1972b; Epstein & Daviess, 1972, Experiment 1) nor a change in apparent *distance* (Epstein & Daviess, 1972, Experiment 2). The investigators concluded that MSL adaptation represents a recalibration of the relationship between binocular disparity and perceived depth, based on the many veridical monocular cues (e.g., interposition, texture gradient) available. Direct support for this conclusion came from studies showing that (1) the adaptive shift is greatly enhanced by the provision of a preadaptation period during which binocular disparity cues are precluded (Epstein, 1971) and (2) the decline of this form of adaptation is more rapid when the postexposure period provides experience with the normal relationship between binocular disparity and monocular depth cues than when it does not (Epstein, 1972a).

5.2.2. Distortions of Distance

5.2.2.1 General Findings. In a series of studies of adaptation to distortion in perceived distance, Wallach and his colleagues (Wallach & Frey, 1972b; Wallach, Frey, & Bode, 1972; Wallach & Smith, 1972) placed before their subjects' eyes a combination of a 1.5-diopter spherical lens (affecting accommodation) and a 5-diopter wedge prism (affecting convergence). The use of negative lenses and base-out prisms causes a foreshortening of perceived distance, whereas positive lenses and base-in prisms lead to an increase in perceived distance. With these devices, significant adaptation was obtained for subjects after as little as 15 min of visuomotor exposure (Wallach & Frey, 1972b), an effect shown not to be based on a change in stereoscopic depth perception (Wallach et al., 1972). If, in contrast to the preceding experiment, the subject was allowed during the exposure period to use the (unseen) hand to move a stimulus object toward and away from the body, the adaptive change was limited almost entirely to the eye-hand coordination (Wallach & Smith, 1972). If in this same situation the subject could see the hand, adaptation was found in both eye-hand coordination and visual distance perception.

Wallach and Frey (1972c) carried out an interesting study of adaptation to a discrepancy between distance cues that was created *without* the use of distorting goggles. In their experiment they caused a luminous figure *physically* to expand as it moved toward the observer and contract as it receded. Thus whereas accommodation and convergence were accurately signaling the relative distance of the object, the fluctuation of retinal image size indicated a longer path of motion than was actually the case. Twenty minutes of exposure to this arrangement led to adaptive changes in apparent distance.

Types of exposure activity sufficient to produce adaptation to distance distortion include walking about in a naturalistic environment (e.g., Wallach & Frey, 1972b), eye-hand tasks (e.g., Von Hofsten, 1979), and repeated head turning (Wallach & O'Leary, 1979).

5.2.2.2. An Interpretation in Terms of "Eye Muscle Potentiation" (EMP). Ebenholtz (1970, 1974, 1981) has proposed that here, as in prism adaptation, the effects that have been labeled visual adaptation may, instead, be manifestations of eye muscle potentiation, or EMP (see Section 2.2.4.5). Thus, according to Ebenholtz, because the exposure conditions used by Wallach's group entailed a maintained convergence of the eyes at a "near" or a "far" point, the result is a tendency to maintain this convergence (the "slow" fusional component of the vergence system) after voluntary relaxation. The presence of this potentiation effect should force the observer to emit an abnormal amount of voluntary neural outflow when attempting to fixate an object at some other distance. The result of this atypical efference, argues Ebenholtz, is a misperception of distance in the direction that mimics true adaptation.

In one study (Ebenholtz & Wolfson, 1975) favoring this reinterpretation, subjects who were required to fixate a target at a specified distance for 6–8 min subsequently underestimated the distance of a target that was placed closer than the previous fixation target and overestimated the distance of the test target when it was placed farther away than the fixation target. Thus these results raise the serious possibility that the induced changes in apparent distance obtained in the studies by Wallach and his colleagues were merely the visual effects of maintained convergence rather than the recalibration of the relationship between initially conflicting distance cues.

The EMP hypothesis has received further confirmation by Ebenholtz (1981), Ebenholtz and Fisher (1982), and Paap and Ebenholtz (1977), but was contradicted by Wallach and Halperin (1977). Thus the preponderance of evidence favors the EMP position, although it is still possible that *both* EMP and recalibration are viable mechanisms for dealing with distance distortions, depending upon the specific nature of the distance distortion and of the prevailing exposure conditions.

5.2.3. Distortions of Size. It is interesting to note that of the very few studies of adaptation to optically induced changes in apparent size, the majority have occurred *underwater*, where objects seen through a diving mask look larger than they actually are. Briefly, it has been demonstrated that many subjects eventually come to see underwater objects as more nearly their true size. A detailed discussion of these experiments is presented in Section 8.2.2.2.

Unfortunately, several of the studies of size distortions in the air have made use of magnifying lens systems that produce a change in both apparent distance and retinal size, resulting in an appearance of *normal* size, due, presumably, to size-distance invariance. Foley (1965; cited by Rock, 1966, pp. 158–159; and by E. J. Gibson, 1969, p. 205) apparently found only marginal adaptation to magnification or reduction for observers who wore binoculars for 6 hr a day over a 3-week period. Moreover, these minor effects were primarily in terms of apparent distance, because the subjects generally failed to experience a distortion of size. Rock (1966, pp. 164–165) reported essentially the same outcome in a study of potential adaptation to reduction as produced by a reverse Gallilean telescope.

By using a *convex mirror*, Rock (1965, 1966, pp. 164–175) was able to create a situation in which apparent size but not distance was altered. In a series of experiments subjects looked through a large cardboard tube at a 12-in mirror that reduced by a factor of two the apparent size of an array of familiar objects and various parts of the observer's body that could be seen in it. It was found that 10–30 min of exposure to this optical reduction produced adaptation of as much as 23% of the theoretical maximum, as seen in a pre-post shift of the apparent size of a luminous line with respect to a remembered length. Adaptation was obtained even when the stationary subject was not allowed to see any part of the body. Rock demonstrated by means of control experiments that the altered perception of size was not the result of a change in apparent distance or of successive contrast. Rock proposed that the crucial determinant of this form of adaptation is the observer's experience that the *relationship* among objects, with respect to their apparent size, is unchanged during exposure to the distortion from the relationship that exists with normal vision.

5.3. Conclusions

The ability of human subjects to undergo a recalibration of the relationship between binocular disparity and other monocular depth cues as a result of exposure to distortions of depth indicates that there exists no immutable relation between the physical correspondence or noncorrespondence of retinal points and stereoscopic depth.

Optical distortions of distance can also be overcome, the adaptive end state here being a recalibration of accommodation, convergence, or both. However, it is clear that, at least under some conditions, this so-called adaptation may actually represent the visual effects of EMP.

It seems likely that the capacity to adapt to distortions in the in-out dimension serves to counteract in the rapidly growing child the changes in perceived depth that would otherwise occur with the developmental increase in interocular distance. Furthermore, the basis of this presumed process would seem to be the monocular depth cues, for they are relatively unaffected by head growth.

5.4. Key Reference

Rock, I. (1966, Chapter 5). In this chapter Rock discusses the issue of how an observer (with normal or size-altered vision) can perceive *absolute* size. This is followed by a detailed description of some of the very few experiments on adaptation to a magnified or minified visual field.

6. ADAPTATION TO DISTORTIONS OF FORM

6.1. Background

Among the many perceptual effects of viewing the world through a wedge prism is the apparent curvature of objectively straight edges perpendicular to the direction of displacement (See Figure 24.2). Adaptation to this type of distortion, which represents an alteration of form perception, was apparently first reported by Wundt (1898; cited by Rock, 1966). After wearing prism goggles for several days, he observed that the apparent curvature of straight contours had diminished significantly and that upon removing the prism, objectively straight lines appeared curved in the direction opposite the prism-induced curvature (i.e., the negative aftereffect). This sequence of perceptual events is presented in Figure 24.18.

Prismatic curvature adaptation and the subsequent negative aftereffect were investigated by J. J. Gibson (1933) in a study in which a subject engaged in everyday activities for four consecutive days (45 waking hours) while wearing 14–15° prism

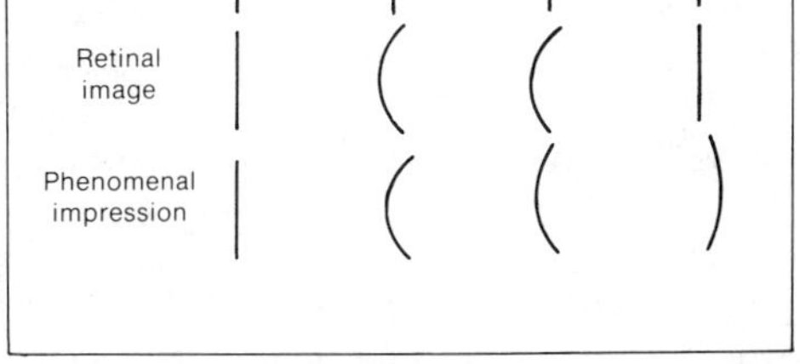

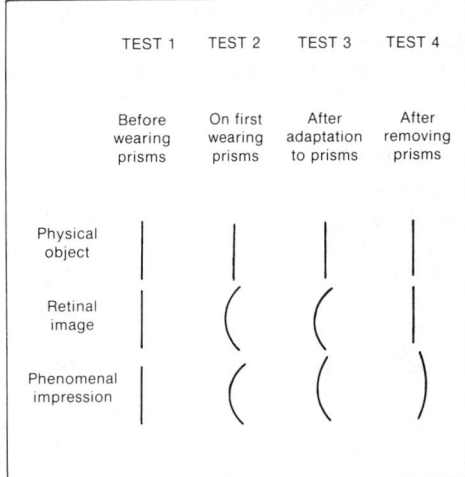

Figure 24.18. Sequence of perceptual events indicative of adaptation (the slight reduction in the phenomenal impression of curvature from Test 2 to Test 3) and aftereffect (difference in phenomenal impression curvature between Test 1 and Test 4) to a base-left prism. Thus after the prism is worn for a period of time, an objectively vertical line appears somewhat less curved than it did when the prism was first placed before the eye. When the prism is removed the line appears slightly curved in the opposite direct.

goggles. In other experiments by Gibson it was demonstrated that as little as 1 hr of active exposure was sufficient to produce measurable effects. One of Gibson's tests for adaptation, a test used in virtually all the subsequent experiments in this area, required that the subject cause a visual contour to appear straight. This measure was obtained before and after the exposure period and, as usual, the difference between the two tests served as the measure of adaptation.

6.2. Experimental Results

6.2.1. Adaptation to Prismatic Curvature

6.2.1.1. The Problem of Configurational Effects. It is now clear that, just as with tilt adaptation (see Section 3.2.2), adaptation to prismatic curvature is likely to be confounded by configurational effects. Thus, as J. J. Gibson (1933) showed, prolonged examination of *objectively* curved contours leads to a lessening of perceived curvature and a negative aftereffect when subsequently looking at straight contours. There are at least three ways in which the problem of configurational effects in prismatic curvature adaptation can be eliminated: (1) use an exposure condition devoid of straight contours (e.g., Held & Rekosh, 1963), (2) use an exposure condition involving contours objectively curved in the direction opposite the prismatic curvature, which therefore appear through the prism to be straight (M. M. Cohen, 1965), and (3) take the preexposure measures for adaptation only after an initial period in which configurational adaptation is allowed to reach completion (suggested by Rock, 1966, pp. 75–76).

Unfortunately, only a few studies (e.g., M. M. Cohen, 1965) have take steps to disentangle (or preclude) configurational effects from genuine curvature adaptation. However, the changes in apparent curvature and aftereffect obtained in many studies (Hajos & Ritter, 1965; Hay & Pick, 1966a; Kohler, 1964, pp. 34–42; Pick, Hay, & Willoughby, 1966) have greatly exceeded the rather small effects expected for configurational adaptation, and thus it seems legitimate to conclude that genuine prismatic curvature adaptation occurred in these studies. In one marathon (42-day) study of prism adaptation by Hay and Pick (1966a), for example, adaptation represented an approximately 30% reduction of the prism effect. Not only is this substantially larger than the effect expected from configurational adaptation alone, but its acquisition was very gradual, requiring days to reach asymptote, rather than occurring almost immediately, as is the case with the Gibson effect.

6.2.1.2. Necessary/Sufficient Conditions for and End Products of Optical Curvature Adaptation. Bodily movement of some form is probably necessary for the production of genuine curvature adaptation. Wallach and Barton (1975) demonstrated this point in a study of adaptation to curvature of the frontoparallel plane in the outward direction as a result of wearing binocular base-in wedge prisms. The investigators found that stationary viewing led to no adaptive shift whatsoever, whereas vertical head nodding during exposure was quite effective, even when the *test* for adaptation involved a stationary head. Wallach and Flaherty (1974) reported the same results for adaptation to prism-induced expansion and contraction effects.

As with other forms of adaptation, active movement is frequently found to be more conducive to curvature adaptation than passive movement. The probable reason for this advantage is that activity is very likely to lead to unambiguous, salient information about the nature of the distortion (i.e., that apparently curved lines are actually straight and vice versa). Thus, for example, although Held and Rekosh (1963) obtained no curvature adaptation for prism-wearing subjects who were pulled about in a cart in a room devoid of straight contours, Victor (1968) demonstrated that if such passive movement occurred in the presence of good information about the prismatic curvature (in the form of appropriately oriented straight contours), active and passive movement led to *equal* amounts of adaptation. Indeed, there is now some doubt that adaptation to curvature can occur when there are no visible contours present, as seen in the failure of Gyr, Willey, and Henry (1979) to replicate the oft-cited study by Held and Rekosh (1963) in which only random shapes were visible.

Other studies (Burnham, 1968, 1979; Festinger, Burnham, Ono, & Bamber, 1967; Gyr & Willey, 1970) have demonstrated that some forms of active body movements are more conducive to curvature adaptation than others. Thus, for example, Festinger et al. (1967, Experiment 2) found significantly more adaptation for subjects who were forced by the task to learn a new "efferent command" with respect to the prismatic curvature than for subjects who were not. Specifically, in the efferent command-learning condition the subject made a rapid downward swing of a hand-held stylus between two parallel rods that appeared curved but were straight or vice versa, attempting to avoid touching either rod. In the "nonlearning" condition the subject was merely required to slide the stylus *along* one of the rods. As predicted, curvature adaptation was greater in the first of these conditions and, as it seems likely now, the reason is that in that condition the nature of the prismatic distortion was more accurately conveyed.

As noted previously (Section 4.4), only if the distorting device is actually attached to or controlled by the eyes are the subject's initial eye movements in conflict with the visual rearrangement. Such a situation has been arranged in several studies of prismatic curvature adaptation (Festinger et al., 1967; Miller & Festinger, 1977; Taylor, 1962, pp. 221–231; Slotnick, 1969) and the outcome is a surprisingly large percentage of adaptation. Festinger et al. (1967), for example, obtained 44% adaptation (the Gibson effect included) after relatively short periods of exposure to the effects of a rather small curvature (4–8 diopters) produced by means of a prism attached to a contact lens. This can be compared to the 30% adaptation that Pick and Hay (1964) found after their subjects had worn 20-diopter prism goggles for 42 days. Two possible reasons for the significant enhancement of curvature adaptation with eye involvement are that (1) the information from visuomotor errors is more heavily weighted when it results from eye movements than from other forms of bodily motion and/or (2) when wearing prism goggles (as opposed to prism contact lenses) the presence of nonconflicted eye movements *counteracts* to some extent the adaptation that results from those bodily interactions (hand, head, etc.) that *are* in conflict with the distortion. A third possibility is simply that the very small prismatic displacements used with contact lenses are subject to a greater percentage of adaptation than are the large displacements associated with goggles.

With respect to the end product(s) of prismatic curvature adaptation it is clear that because such adaptation can be measured (and produced) in the absence of eye movements (i.e., when prism *goggles* are worn) its basis cannot be a change in the felt direction of gaze or of eye scanning. (Miller & Festinger, 1977, directly confirmed this argument). Thus, in contrast to adaptation to prismatic displacement, curvature adaptation may be based on a genuine recalibration of retinal values.

6.2.2. Adaptation to Distortions of Closed Figures. A prismatically curved straight edge may be considered an "open" figure. When a "closed" figure, such as a square, is viewed through a prism, it too is distorted. As was seen in Figure 24.2, an objectively square figure is caused by a prism to look like a trapezoid (with curved vertical edges). Furthermore, head movements will cause the form to expand and contract (with lateral movements) or to rock in a seesaw fashion (with up and down movements)—a loss of VPC that is at least partially overcome after a period of head or entire body movement (see Section 4.3).

In a study by Pick and Hay (1966a) subjects revealed, after about 6 days of prism exposure, an average of 51% adaptation to the distortion of an apparent square comprised of four dots. It may be argued that by constructing the form out of dots rather than straight edges, one facilitates potential adaptation by avoiding the constraints of the internal geometry of the form. That is, it seems likely that the "object-relative" aspects (internal geometry) of a form will be more resistant to adaptive changes than the "subject-relative" aspects (egocentric location of the points of the form relative to the observer). Other studies obtaining adaptation to distortion of closed forms were reported by Mack and Quartin (1974), Malatesta and Mikaelian (1975), and Wallach and Bacon (1977).

6.3. Conclusions

Briefly, it may be concluded that human observers are capable of a limited amount of adaptation to prism-induced changes in the perception of forms of both the "open" (e.g., a curve) and "closed" (e.g., a square) variety. An important basis of this adaptation is almost certainly the modification of the egocentric significance of retinal points.

It is possible that the reason curvature adaptation rarely exceeds 30% of the theoretical maximum, even after very extended exposure periods, is that the eye movements of the subject wearing prism goggles remain accurate in their localization of apparent positions in space. Thus perhaps more substantial adaptation would occur if observers were required to wear prism contact lenses, as well as to move about and reach for objects, for under these circumstances *all* their initial interactions with the environment would result in error-corrective information concerning the nature of the perceptual rearrangement. Adaptation of this sort might be enhanced still further if the observer were tested for curvature adaptation by means of, say, a column of widely separated points of light (in an otherwise dark room), rather than a straight line, because in the former situation the presumably more modifiable "subject-relative" aspects of form perception would be maximized.

6.4. Key References

Festinger, L., Burnham, C. A., Ono, H., & Bamber, D. (1967). In this monograph the authors present a series of experiments the aim of which was to evaluate the hypothesis that the conscious perception of visual form (specifically, curvature) and adaptation to prismatically induced alterations of form result from the acquisition and/or presence of a *readiness* to make the appropriate motor responses with respect to the visual sensations. The data are interesting and congruent with the "efferent readinesss" theory. However, subsequent research (most notably, Miller & Festinger, 1977) has not confirmed this notion. It now appears that the results of Festinger et al. (1967) can more satisfactorily be explained in terms of the "information hypothesis" discussed in this chapter.

Gibson, J. J. (1933). This is the classic study of adaptation to prismatically induced curvature. It introduces a paradigm used in nearly all subsequent studies. In addition, it clarifies the distinction between (1) "genuine" adaptation to this distortion and (2) a passive "normalization" process evoked by exposure to curved contours (real or illusory). The latter is one example of what we have referred to as the "Gibson effect" or, more generally, configurational adaptation.

Rock, I. (1966, Chapter 6). In this chapter of Rock's (1966) influential book various studies of adaptation to optically induced distortions of form are described, together with Rock's theoretical viewpoint concerning the nature of this type of adaptation. The important distinction is made between *object-relative* and *subject-relative* aspects of form perception, the latter, according to Rock, being much more susceptible to adaptation than the former.

7. ADAPTATION TO AUDITORY REARRANGEMENT

7.1. Background

When the world is viewed through distorting goggles it is not only proprioception that is placed in conflict with vision, but the auditory modality as well. Thus a visible sound source viewed through right-left-reversing spectacles initially is seen in one place but heard on the opposite side. Whether genuine adaptation to induced visual-auditory discrepancy is possible depends on the type of auditory rearrangement being considered. With auditory transposition, such as is encountered when wearing inverting and right-left reversing goggles, the best that can be said in this regard is that, for some observers, a sound may eventually come to be heard to emanate from its visible source, as long as attention is being concentrated on the visual stimulus (Ewert, 1930; Stratton, 1897b). This resolution of the visual-auditory discrepancy appears, however, to be an instance of intersensory bias (Section 2.2.3.1 and Welch & Warren, Chapter 25) known as the "ventriloquism effect" (Howard & Templeton, 1966, p. 361) because it disappears as soon as the source is no longer visible. Later studies designed specifically as tests of adaptation to auditory rearrangement made use of "pseudophones," which functionally reverse the right-left position of the two ears by placing a sound-collecting device on each side of the head and connecting it to the ear on the opposite side (Willey, Inglis, & Pearce, 1937; Young, 1928). They, too, failed to obtain the aftereffects of auditory localization required to demonstrate the occurrence of true visual-auditory adaptation.

Thus, as with vision, the human auditory localization system may not be able to overcome an induced *reversal* of auditory space. On the other hand, it might be possible to adapt, at least partially, to auditory *displacement.* Studies of this sort of rearrangement, beginning with Held (1955), have demonstrated that indeed a substantial adaptive shift occurs as a result of exposure to a rotation of auditory space in the range of 20–30°.

These studies have used a pseudophone whose interaural axis is turned such that one "ear" (e.g., an electronic hearing aid) may be rotated forward and the other "ear" backward by an equal amount. When the output of these receivers is fed into the subject's ears the experience is of a clockwise or counterclockwise rotation of the auditory field.

7.2. Experimental Results

7.2.1. Necessary Conditions for Adaptation to Auditory Rearrangement. In the first of two experiments, Held's (1955) three subjects revealed an average adaptive shift in the apparent auditory midline of 10° after 7 hr of everyday activities while wearing the pseudophone set for 22° displacement. In his second experiment it was demonstrated that the occurrence of auditory adaptation required that the subject move toward or away from the sound source. Lateral body movements were insufficient for adaptation, but whether the sound source was visible or not proved to be irrelevant.

Other studies also obtained adaptation to pseudophonic displacement, using the activities of walking (Freedman & Stampfer, 1964) or of listening to a hand-held sound source as the subject moved it from side to side in the dark (Freedman & Gardos, 1965; Freedman, Wilson, & Rekosh, 1967; Mikaelian, 1969). In a more naturalistic setting, Wells and Ross (1980) demonstrated the occurrence of adaptation to auditory displacements experienced by underwater divers partly as a result of the increased speed of sound transmission (and thus reduced difference in interaural arrival time).

It is surprising that a direct comparison between passive and active exposure to auditory displacement had yet to be made, although there are some experimental observations that bear indirectly on this issue. Specifically, several experiments (Canon, 1970, 1971; Radeau, 1973; Radeau & Bertelson, 1974) have obtained auditory adaptation in situations in which no bodily motion occurred at all, indicating that active movement is not necessary for such adaptation. Nevertheless, it seems likely, based on the examples of a variety of forms of adaptation to visual rearrangement, that active movement would *facilitate* auditory adaptation. However, the only relevant experiments in which active and passive movement have been compared dealt with *dis*arrangement, a procedure introduced in Section 2.2.2.1. In a series of experiments by Freedman and his colleagues (Freedman & Pfaff, 1961, cited by Held & Freedman, 1963; Freedman & Pfaff, 1962a, 1962b; Freedman & Secunda, cited by Held & Freedman, 1963; Freedman & Zacks, 1964), each of the subjects' ears was exposed separately to white noise, the two inputs being made slightly asynchronous. Thus the experience was one of a series of fused sounds whose apparent location along the right-left dimension varied randomly. As a consequence, a given movement of the head or entire body would, over a period of exposure, be paired with a variety of interaural arrival-time differences, in contrast to the normally occurring one-to-one relationship.

Congruent with the results of the previously described studies of visual disarrangement (Section 2.2.2.1) and with the predictions of the reafference hypothesis, exposure to the dichotic noise led to an increase in variability in localizing an unseen sound source as a result of active behavior (walking or rotation of the head or of the entire body). No change in the precision of localization occurred when the subject was recumbent, passively rotated, or moved about in a wheelchair.

It is unclear how to interpret these results. Specifically, it is difficult to understand how, in the absence of any information to indicate the presence of a *fixed* sound source, the localizing mechanism (whatever it is) can "know" if the randomly changing interaural arrival-time difference is indicative of a fixed sound source whose apparent auditory locus is changing unpredictably or is merely a number of different fixed sources located at various positions along the right left dimension. If the latter is the case, there would seem to be no "reason" for the auditory localizing mechanism to undergo modification. Investigators who wish to continue this line of research are encouraged to arrange a situation comparable to those in the area of visual disarrangement. As an example, one might require subjects to walk about in the presence of visible sound sources while wearing an *oscillating* pseudophone. Here, vision would indicate that a given sound source is fixed, even though its apparent auditory location is fluctuating.

7.2.2. The End Products of Adaptation to Auditory Rearrangement. Although a logically possible basis for auditory adaptation to pseudophonic displacement is a change in the felt relation of head to trunk, no evidence has been provided, one way or another, for this adaptive end state. The possibility that at least one product of adaptation is a recalibration of the interaural cues of localization is indicated by Freedman and Stampfer's (1964) finding of adaptive auditory shifts when the subject attempted to align visual and (unseen) auditory targets.

Several studies of auditory rearrangement have involved exposing subjects to the auditory source by having them hold the sound-emitting object in the hand which they swing back and forth in the manner of the concurrent display/no-target condition of prism adaptation popularized by Held and his colleagues (e.g., Held & Gottlieb, 1958). By finding no evidence of intermanual transfer of adaptive ear-hand shifts to 30° pseudophonic displacement, Mikaelian (1970b, 1972) supported the hypothesis that it is possible to limit adaptation of this sort to the exposed hand. Clearly, this finding rules out the possibility of changes in either the ear-head or head-torso relationship. Mikaelian (1974) also demonstrated that the basis of this adaptation was not a recalibration of felt limb position, for he obtained no systematic error when pseudophonically adapted subjects pointed at visual targets. Thus it would appear possible to produce adaptation to auditory rearrangement that is limited specifically to the coordination between ear and hand, presumably a form of motor learning.

7.2.3. The Relationship Between Visual and Auditory Adaptation. Auditory rearrangement can have visual effects and vice versa. A number of studies have obtained adaptation of visual perception or eye-hand coordination (Craske, 1966b; Freedman & Gardos, 1965) as a result of exposure to auditory rearrangement. Furthermore, to the extent that prism exposure produces a change in the felt position of the arm, ear-hand coordination will automatically be affected. Direct evidence for this form of "generalization" was provided by Harris (1965), Freedman and Gardos (1965), and Mikaelian (1974, Experiment 2), all of whom showed that prismatic exposure leads to a change in ear-hand (as well as eye-hand) coordination. Furthermore, if exposure to visual rearrangement leads to a change in the felt relation of head to torso, both auditory and visual localization relative to the trunk as well as auditory and visual target-reaching responses should be influenced (M. M. Cohen, 1974; Lackner, 1974b, 1976). In the study by Cohen (1974), terminal exposure to prismatic displacement produced pre-post shifts in

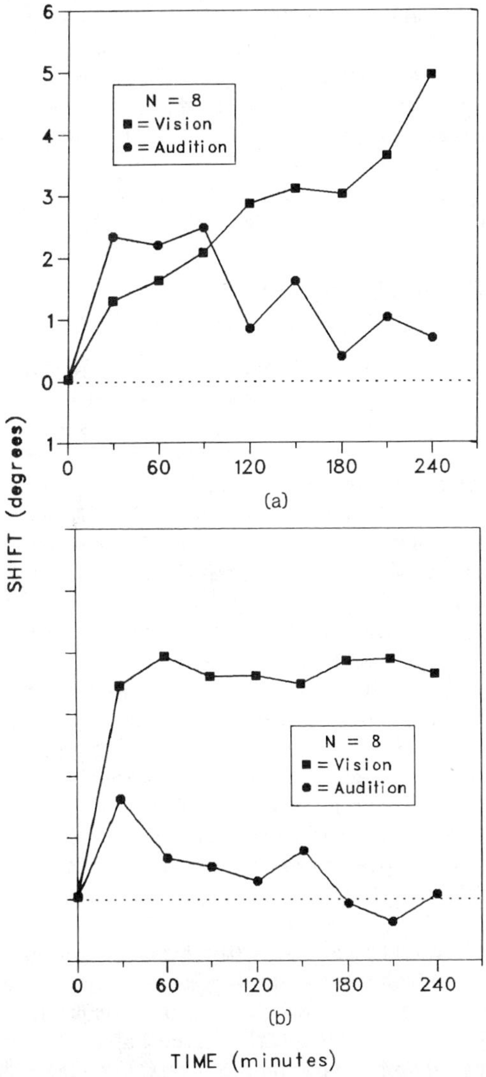

Figure 24.19. (a) Mean shifts in visual and auditory straight-ahead judgments during prolonged exposure to displaced vision: attentuated auditory stimulation. Subjects in this condition wore 30-diopter prisms and walked about outdoors for 4 hr while wearing sound-attentuating ear muffs. The initial adaptive shifts in both auditory and visual straight ahead were followed by a decline in the auditory shift whereas the visual shift continued to increase. (b) Mean shifts in visual and auditory straight-ahead judgments during exposure to displaced vision: normal auditory stimulation. Subjects in this condition had unimpaired hearing during the 4-hr exposure period. Auditory adaptation was obtained only at the 30-min test and, even then, was significantly less than the very substantial visual shift found on this test (as well as on all the remaining tests). (From J. H. Rekosh & S. J. Freedman, Errors in auditory direction-finding after compensation for visual rearrangement. *Perception and Psychophysics*, 1967, *2*. Reprinted with permission.)

pointing at both auditory and visual targets. The fact that both types of adaptation were subject to intermanual transfer suggests that a change in felt head position might have occurred, causing a shift in both auditory and visual judgments of egocentric direction relative to the torso.

In a study by Rekosh and Freedman (1967) subjects who wore 30-diopter prisms and walked about outdoors for 4 hr were measured on both visual and auditory straight ahead. In one of two experiments, half the subjects wore sound-attenuating earmuffs and half did not. During the initial part of the adaptation period shifts in both visual and auditory straight ahead were obtained. Further exposure, however, led to the gradual elimination of the auditory shift, whereas visual adaptation continued to increase. It is possible that these interesting results, which are depicted in Figure 24.19, are due to an initial prism-induced change in the felt relation of head to torso, affecting both visual and auditory straight ahead, followed by a decline in this head-torso recalibration but the maintenance of a shift in the felt eye-head relationship. The latter would, of course, affect only the visual straight ahead.

Finally, in an unpublished study by Lackner (briefly described by Lackner, 1981), exposure to abnormal auditory motion during head movements (loss of auditory position constancy) led to a change in visual position constancy, presumably due to an induced change in the felt relation of head to torso.

7.3. Conclusions

It may be concluded that a certain amount of genuine adaptation to auditory rearrangement is possible, at least with the relatively minor distortions of 20–30° lateral displacement. This adaptation may comprise up to three components: (1) a recalibration of interaural difference cues (e.g., time of arrival), (2) a shift in the felt position of the head relative to the torso, and (3) an alteration specific to ear-hand coordination.

It seems likely that the capacity of auditory adaptation comes into play for the human being during the period of rapid head growth in infancy. Because the increase in the distance between the ears must inevitably lead to changes in the egocentric significance of specific interaural differences in auditory input (see Figure 24.20), it is clearly imperative that the infant be capable of recalibrating these cues.

7.4. Key References

Held, R. (1955). This paper describes two studies that constitute the first unequivocal demonstration of adaptation

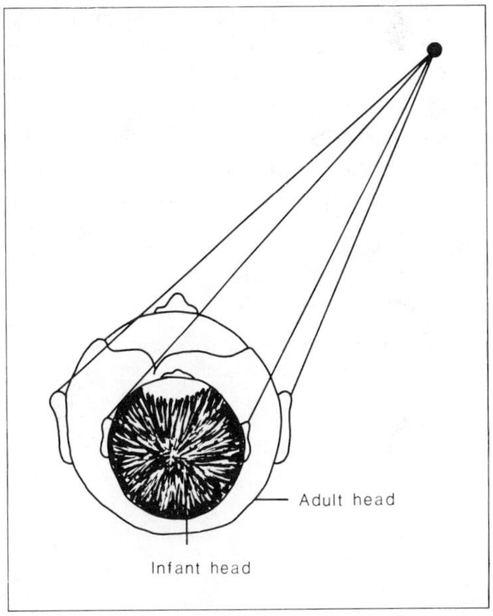

Figure 24.20. A schematic representation of the increase in head size from infancy to adulthood. The change causes the difference in arrival time at the two ears for a given auditory source to be less for the infant than for the adult. (From T. G. R. Bower, *Development in infancy*. Copyright 1974 by W. H. Freeman and Company. Reprinted with permission.)

to auditory rearrangement. Using prolonged exposure to 22° pseudophonic displacement and testing procedures emulated by many of the subsequent researchers in this area, Held discriminated between some exposure activities that lead to auditory adaptation and some activities that fail.

Young, P. T. (1928). This is a detailed presentation (à la Stratton) of the pioneering study of adaptation to auditory rearrangement. Young's awkward and uncomfortable right-left-reversing pseudophones that entailed ear trumpets have subsequently been replaced by lightweight devices, using miniature microphones.

8. ADAPTATION TO UNDERWATER OPTICAL DISTORTIONS

8.1. Background

Nearly all research on adaptation to perceptual rearrangement involves the deliberate introduction of an artificial distortion to the subject's perception. There is, however, at least one "natural" environment where perceptual distortions abound—the world of the underwater diver. It is probably safe to say that every one of the underwater observer's sensory modalities is altered in some way (Adolfson & Berghage, 1974; Ross, 1971; Woods & Lythgoe, 1971). Sounds reach the ears much more quickly than in air, whereas their localizability is somewhat displaced and attenuated (e.g., Feinstein, 1966). Also substantially influenced are gravitational and kinesthetic-proprioceptive cues (Ross, Crickmar, Sills, & Owen, 1969; Ross & Rejman, 1972). Indeed, Ross and her colleagues (Ross, 1981; Ross, Rejman, & Lennie, 1972) have found adaptation to the decreased apparent weight of objects lifted under water, with corresponding negative aftereffects upon emergence. It is vision, however, that is most frequently the source of difficulty for the diver and it is this modality that has been the subject of the majority of experiments on underwater perception.

Viewing the underwater environment through a face mask incurs a wide variety of complex visual effects, the magnitudes of which are influenced by a number of variables, including the type of diving equipment worn, relative clarity of the water, and direction of view. Briefly, these effects include, for close objects, an increase in apparent size and a decrease in apparent distance (see Figure 24.21) and, for distant objects, an increase in both perceived size and distance. In addition, there is color attenuation and distortion, illusory visual motion (i.e., loss of VPC), and an expansion and distortion of perceived contours. The last mentioned phenomenon is referred to as the "pincushion effect" (e.g., Ross, 1970) and is most apparent when viewing head-on a large square through the face mask. In this situation the square appears enlarged, with sides bowed inward and the center displaced away from the observer, much like an inverted pincushion.

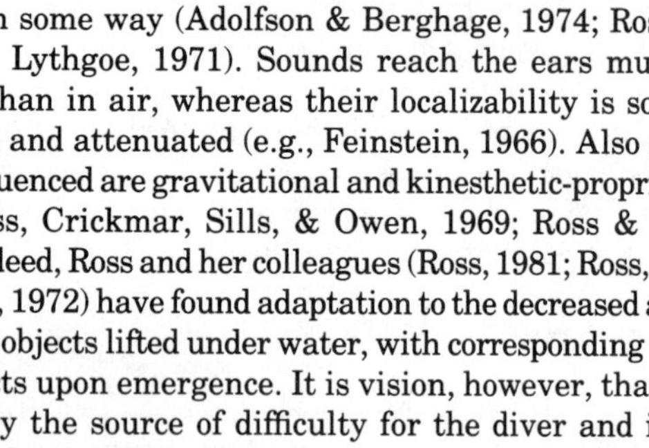

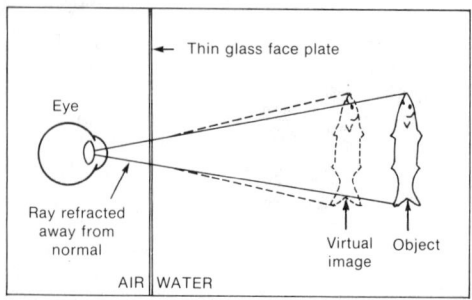

Figure 24.21. The optical effect of viewing an object under water through a face mask. For an eye located about 2 in. behind the glass faceplate, and assuming the latter to be quite thin, the optical size of near objects increases by 27%, with a corresponding decrease in optical distance. (From H. E. Ross, Water, fog, and the size-distance invariance hypothesis, *British Journal of Psychology*, 1967, *58*. Reprinted with permission.)

8.2. Experimental Results

8.2.1. "Immediate" Adaptation. As with other forms of perceptual rearrangement, exposure to underwater distortion induces both immediate and long-term compensatory responses. Concerning the former, a number of observations, both casual and experimental, have indicated that, especially for experienced divers, there is an "immediate," partial correction for the underwater distortion as soon as the observer submerges (e.g., Kinney, Luria, Weitzman, & Markowitz, 1970; Luria & Kinney, 1970). Luria and Kinney (1970), for example, found in a comparison of a number of studies that the magnitude of the initial error (underreaching) for subjects attempting to grasp a nearby object in clear water declined regularly as a function of the amount of prior underwater experience (see Table 24.2). They also reported a correlation of .85 between degree of immediate adaptation and diving proficiency for a group of Navy divers. Similar observations have been reported with respect to far distance (over) estimates (Luria, Kinney, & Weissman, 1967; Nichols, 1967), apparent size-distance distortion (Ross, 1967; Ross, Franklin, Weltman, & Lennie, 1970), and curvature (Ross, 1970).

Thus, it would seem that, with repeated experience, various cues (e.g., the feel of the water, pressure of the diving gear, or perhaps merely the acknowledge that one is looking into water) come to elicit partial adaptation or perhaps a "cognitive correction" based on the experienced diver's knowledge of the underwater distortions.

8.2.2. "Long-Term" Adaptation

8.2.2.1. The Paradigm. Much more is known about the long-term acquistion of adaptation to distortions during underwater exposure than about so-called "immediate" adaptation. The typical paradigm followed in these studies is patterned after that used in the traditional adaptation studies. Specifically, it entails (1) preexposure measures in air and then underwater, (2) an underwater adaptation period, and (3) postexposure measures underwater and then in air. The difference between the pre- and postexposure measures in the air represent the negative aftereffect, whereas the difference between the pre-and postexposure measures underwater represent the reduction of effect.

8.2.2.2. Adaptation to Distance and Size Distortions. Many different activities have been used in experiments designed to induce and measure long-term adaptation to underwater distortions of distance and size (see also Section 5.2.2). Kinney, McKay, Luria, and Gratto (1970) examined the adaptation of eye-hand coordination to the optical foreshortening of near objects in clear water. They found that substantially greater adaptation occurred as a result of playing underwater games (e.g., checkers) than for free swimming or a lecture plus specific underwater target-pointing practice. Distributed practice was more beneficial than massed practice; indeed, distributed underwater game playing for only 15 min was found to produce

Table 24.2. A Comparison of a Number of Studies, Each of Which Included Measures of Eye-Hand Coordination Taken in Air and in Clear Water

Subjects	N	Amount of Distortion Experienced[a] (cm)
Never used snorkel, mask	42	5.59
Occasionally used snorkel, mask	69	5.00
Frequently used snorkel, mask	20	3.30
Scuba class		
No scuba experience	14	3.23
Some scuba experience	12	2.64
Navy divers	8	2.03

The dependent variable is the air-water difference in target-reaching accuracy for subjects in that experiment. It may be seen that this number declines as a direct function of amount of diving experience. (From S. M. Luria and J. A. S. Kinney, Underwater vision, Science, 167. Copyright 1970 by the American Association for the Advancement of Science. Reprinted with permission.)

[a] The theoretical optical displacement in the test situation was calculated to be 5.60 cm.

more adaptation (70% of the theoretical maximum) than did 4 weeks of scuba-diving lessons.

Examining the same type of distortion, Ono and O'Reilly (1971) found that terminal exposure produced substantially more adaptation than a condition of concurrent display or one that required a certain amount of visually predirected movement. O'Reilly (1975a, 1975b) provided evidence that for expert divers (40–1,200 hr of previous diving experience) this form of adaptation was based more on a change of vision than on recalibrated limb position sense, whereas for novices (0–10 hr experience) the reverse was true.

Ross, Franklin, Weltman, and Lennie (1970) obtained adaptation to the perceived enlargement of near objects for both novice and expert divers after 20–40-min periods of relatively unrestricted underwater activity. The aftereffects of this adaptation decayed quite rapidly, especially for the expert divers. The particularly rapid rate at which experienced divers can return to normal vision is probably to be expected from the fact that they also show large initial adaptation. Thus it would appear that their extensive diving experience serves to provide the existing situational cues with the power to induce both immediate adaptation underwater and equally rapid recovery out of water.

Several investigators (Luria, McKay, & Ferris, 1973; Ross et al., 1970; Ross & Lennie, 1972) in this area have reported an interesting phenomenon which they refer to as "counter-adaptation." For example, Franklin et al. (1970), using experienced divers, found that adaptation to underwater size distortions was negatively correlated ($r = -.71$) with adaptation to the perceived foreshortening of distance.

8.2.2.3. Adaptation to Apparent Curvature. Adaptation to the apparent curvature (in all three dimensions) known as the "pincushion effect" has been the subject of investigation. Ross (1970) obtained adaptation (25% of maximum) to the apparent outward bowing of the frontoparallel plane after 30 min of free swimming in the ocean. In addition, a certain amount of "instantaneous" adaptation occurred for practiced divers but not for novices. In a more recent study, Vernoy and Luria (1977) demonstrated that it is possible for the underwater observer to adapt to the apparent curvature in all three dimensions simultaneously, even when the diver remains stationary during the entire (15-min) adaptation period.

8.2.2.4. Adaptation to Illusory Visual Motion. Head movements by the diver wearing a face mask cause illusory visual motion, a loss of VPC. Ferris (1972b) obtained only marginally significant adaptation to this effect in a study in which his subjects spent 15 min under water, either rotating the head back and forth or making eye-hand responses.

Another variety of illusory motion effect for the underwater observer occurs because objects moving across the line of sight appear to move faster than they do in air and an object moving along the line of sight appears to move more slowly (if it is nearby and/or the water is clear) or more quickly (if far away and/or the water is turbid). Adaptation to all these effects was produced in a study by Ross and Rejman (1972) in which submerged subjects swam around and played a pegboard game for 10 min.

8.3. Conclusions

Although much is left to do by way of cataloging and understanding the various forms of adaptation to underwater distortions, it is most unlikely that this undertaking will reveal many conclusions qualitatively different from those already derived from the study of comparable forms of adaptation induced by prisms and lenses.

One interesting and reliable outcome from the study of underwater perceptions has been the observation that experienced divers are capable of an apparently instantaneous, albeit partial, adaptation to many of the face mask-induced distortions. Because these effects disappear almost as soon as the diver emerges from the water, they are probably most accurately interpreted as examples of "conditioned adaptation" (see Section 2.2.1.7). That is, by repeatedly switching from one perceptual environment to another, various cues (feel of the water, pressure of the diving gear, etc.) come to be associated with and discriminative of the two situations, thereby serving as stimuli for instantaneous adaptation at the outset of the dive and perhaps equally rapid recovery upon leaving the water.

One of the most important outcomes of the extensive research by Ross and her associates (e.g., Ross, 1967; Ross, King, & Snowden, 1970) was the conclusion that the size-distance distortion produced when viewing *distant* objects underwater is the result of the exaggerated aerial perspective cue produced by turbidity and diffusion of light. Thus because the edges of distant objects appear rather blurred, they are seen as farther away than they actually are and, as a consequence of this, they also appear unusually large. Generalizing from these observations, Ross (1967, 1975b) has demonstrated the same sort of distortion in fog or mist that, she speculates, is likely to lead to potentially dangerous misperceptions of the speed of moving vehicles.

Adaptation occurring underwater, like that in the air with optical devices, is far less than complete, rarely exceeding 50% of the theoretical maximum. It would appear that in order to deal effectively with the remaining distortion the diver must use some sort of deliberate, intellectual correction strategy. Ferris (1972a, 1973a, 1973b) attempted such a procedure and demonstrated that, by means of verbal accuracy feedback, even relative novices can be taught to reduce quite substantially their initial errors in underwater distance judgments. In sum, the most efficient procedure for equipping the diver to overcome the underwater distortions would seem to be a combination of (1) activities conducive to genuine visual and visuomotor adaptation and (2) intellectual correction strategies to handle that portion of the distortion remaining after adaptation has reached its limit.

8.4. Key References

Ross, H. E. (1967). In this article Ross makes the case that both the underwater size-distance distortions and comparable illusions in fog or mist are due to exaggerated aerial perspective. She also notes that these illusions cause, in turn, misperceptions of one's own locomotion and the motion of other objects.

Ross, H. E. (1975a). This short book deals with the perceptual responses of human beings who find themselves in unusual physical environments. Of particular interest here are the descriptions of the very extensive investigations by Ross and her colleagues of perception and adaptation in the underwater observer.

Ross, H. E., Franklin, S.S., Weltman, G., & Lennie, P. (1970). This article describes an investigation of adaptation to the visual enlargement of near underwater objects, using the paradigm that has become the standard in underwater adaptation research. Evidence is provided for the distinction between "immediate" and more gradually acquired adaptation and for the difference between expert and novice divers with respect to both the immediate adaptation and dissipation of aftereffects.

Woods, J. P., & Lythgoe, J. N. (1971). This edited book presents a variety of studies on both the underwater perceptual effects and adaptation to them.

9. INDIVIDUAL DIFFERENCES

9.1. Background

The differences between conditions or groups in experiments on adaptation to perceptual rearrangement are inevitably partially obscured by a certain amount of within-group variability. Representative examples of this variation are seen in the results of the long-term prism adaptation study by Hay and Pick (1966a). As seen in Figure 24.22, the 95% confidence intervals for the various kinds of adaptation obtained in this 6-day experiment were quite large. For example, the lower and upper limits of the confidence interval for the eye-hand measure of adaptation (i.e., the negative aftereffect) were 2.9 and 9.1° , respectively, which represents approximately 26 and 81% of the maximum possible adaptation to the 20-diopter prisms. To the extent that this variability is the result of stable within-subject "traits" of adaptability (as opposed to measurement error, temporary fluctuations, etc.) it may be of both practical and theoretical importance. Nevertheless, most investigators have considered this within-group variance to be a nuisance and have often attempted to minimize it by means of various screening and/or training procedures. Thus potential subjects have been eliminated from the final sample for demonstrating excessive variability or inaccuracy on the preexposure measures (e.g., Kennedy, 1969; Wallach & Floor, 1970; Wallach & Karsh, 1963b), failing to experience the distortion (e.g., Epstein, 1968), or undergoing little or no adaptation (e.g., Redding, 1975b).

9.2. Experimental Results

9.2.1. Evidence for Intrasubject Reliability in Adaptation. Evidence directly relevant to the existence of stable individual differences in adaptability is sparse and not entirely consistent. Redding (1973b) found no correlation between subjects' visual adaptation to prismatic displacement and their visual adaptation to optical tilt, a result that argues against any *general* trait of adaptability. On the other hand, test-retest reliability for the *same* type of adaptation was relatively high: rank-order correlations of −.74 for visual shift and .76 for optical tilt adaptation (Redding, 1973a). Likewise, in a within-subjects study of tilt adaptation by Mack (1967) in which passive- and active-movement conditions occurred two days apart, the intrasubject correlation for the magnitude of adaptation was .78. Welch et al. (1974) reported test-retest (1-week interval) correlations for prism-induced visuomotor negative aftereffect, proprioceptive shift, and visual shift of .68, .77, and .75, respectively. Finally, in a study by Kottenhoff (1957) of adaptation to the loss of VPC during head movement with right/left reversal, the split-half reliability coefficient was found to be .83.

Contradicting the preceding results are those of a study by Crawshaw and Craske (1976b) in which the test-retest reliability coefficients (intervals between tests not reported) for prism-induced shifts in the felt direction of gaze were found to be essentially zero. By and large, however, it does appear that, within a specific type of perceptual rearrangement, a subject's degree of adaptability is relatively stable over time. Assuming that this is true, it is legitimate to ask if the magnitude of a person's adaptation is correlated with other subject characteristics.

9.2.2. Personality Traits and Adaptation. The search for correlations between personality traits and adaptation to perceptual rearrangement has met with mixed results. In the study by Kottenhoff (1957) introduced in the preceding section, a highly significant correlation (.72) was obtained for the relationship between magnitude of adaptation to loss of VPC and introversion/extroversion. Introverted subjects experienced an increase in the illusory motion of the visual field, whereas the more extroverted subjects showed either no change or a decrease.

Field dependence/independence, according to the rod-and-frame test, was shown by Melamed, Wallace, Cohen, and Oakes (1972) to be negatively correlated (−.70) with the magnitude of the "immediate correction effect" (see Section 2.2.3.2). This correlation indicated that the greater the field dependence, the less the correction effect.

In a study briefly described by Welch et al. (1974), subjects were adapted to prismatic displacement as measured by the visuomotor negative aftereffect, proprioceptive shift, visual shift, and reduction of effect, and were given a battery of personality tests. The latter included the California Psychological Inventory (CPI; Gough, 1957), the Trait Anxiety Scale (Spielberger, Gorsuch, & Lushene, 1968), the Achievement Anxiety Test (Alpert & Haber, 1960), the Tennessee Self-Concept Scale (Fitts, 1965), the Internal-External Locus of Control of Reinforcement Test (I-E Scale; Rotter, 1966), and the Extroversion Scale (Eysenck, 1965). In brief, very few of the personality measures correlated with any of the measures of prism adaptation and those rare correlations that were statistically significant were quite weak.

Another failure to obtain a relationship between prism effects and personality was reported by Wallace, Melamed, Cohen, and Oakes (Note 1). They failed to find a correlation between prism adaptation (as measured by the immediate cor-

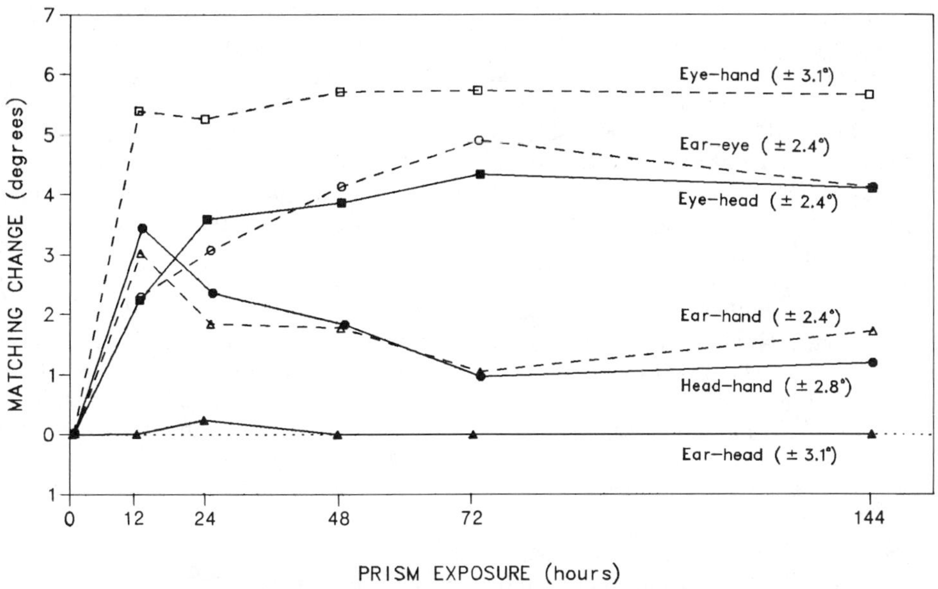

Figure 24.22. Changes in six adaptive measures as a result of prolonged (144-hr) prism exposure. For 6 days, subjects wore base-right or base-left (20-diopter) prism goggles while engaging in everyday activities. A battery of six perceptual and perceptual-motor measures was administered before the exposure period and after 12, 24, 48, 72, and 144 hr of exposure. The measures were (1) eye-hand (reaching for a visual target), (2) ear-eye (identifying the visual direction of a concealed sound source), (3) eye-head (turning the head until directly facing a visual target), (4) ear-hand (reaching for an unseen sound source), (5) head-hand (pointing straight ahead of the nose with the unseen hand), and (6) ear-head (turning the head until directly facing an unseen auditory source). Adaptation was manifested for all but the ear-head measure. The pattern of results indicates the occurrence of a small shift in felt limb position (ear-hand and head-hand measures) and a large shift in visual direction (ear-eye and eye-head measures). Furthermore, the sum of the shifts in felt position sense and vision equaled the eye-hand shift, a finding that supports a two-component model of prism adaptation. (From J. C. Hay & H. L. Pick, Jr. Visual and proprioceptive adaptation to optical displacement of the visual stimulus, *Journal of Experimental Psychology, 71*. Copyright 1966 by American Psychological Association. Reprinted with permission.)

rection effect and visuomotor negative aftereffect) and either internal-external locus of control (Rotter, 1966) or ambiguity tolerance (McDonald, 1970). Finally, Welch (unpublished study reported by Welch, 1978) found no relation between field dependence/independence (rod-and-frame test) and prism-induced visuomotor negative aftereffect, proprioceptive shift, or reduction of effect.

It may be concluded that, with a few exceptions (e.g., Kottenhoff, 1957), there does not appear to be a relationship between adaptation and personality traits. On the other hand, the Melamed et al. (1972) finding of a high correlation between rod-and-frame test performance and the immediate correction effect suggests that it is one's "perceptual traits," rather than broad personality characteristics, that are most likely to prove useful predictors of adaptability.

9.2.3. "Perceptual Traits" and Adaptation. In two rather extensive experiments by Warren and Platt (1974, 1975), it was found that the magnitude of adaptation (i.e., reduction of effect) for the exposed (right) hand was negatively correlated with the subjects' accuracy and smoothness in positioning the unseen limb, as measured during pretests without the prism, and positively correlated with the subjects' accuracy and smoothness in pretest measures of eye placement and tracking. For intermanual transfer of adaptation (about 50%), just the opposite relations were obtained. It was argued that the terminal prism display condition used had led to both proprioceptive and visual shifts (the latter inferred from the intermanual transfer) and that good control over the hand should inhibit the former and favor the latter, whereas good control over the eyes should have the reverse effects.

Warren and Platt's "microanalysis" of the component behaviors of prism adaptation would appear to be a useful strategy for the better understanding not only of adaptation to perceptual rearrangement but of other perceptual capacities as well.

9.2.4. Other Subject Characteristics

9.2.4.1. Sex and Age. A variety of other studies have used basic subject characteristics as one of the factors of their designs. Sex of subject has not been found to be related to adaptability (Hay, 1971; Lotto et al., 1967). As seen below, age may be correlated with adaptation to some forms of perceptual rearrangement but not for prism adaptation.

Several studies of video-induced visual rotations (Smith & Greene, 1963; Smothergill, Martin, & Pick, 1971) have obtained evidence for age trends in responses to these distortions. However, because it is unlikely that video feedback experiments result in genuine adaptation as it has been defined here (see Section 1.1), these studies are probably not directly relevant to the present issue.

Giannitrapani (1958) reported a decline with increasing age (6–21 years) in adaptation to size distortions for both males and females and a decline in adaptation to optical tilt for males only.

Adaptability to prism-displaced vision seems to be unrelated to age. Although it appears that some of the prism effects (i.e., displaced visual straight ahead, rotated apparent frontoparallel plane) are initially of lesser magnitude for 5- to 7-year-olds than for adults (Ishii & Wapner, 1977), no age trends in adaptation have been detected. Pick and Hay (1966b), for example, found no difference in proprioceptive or visual prism adaptation for 9-, 13-, and 16-year-olds and Wallace and Anstadt (1974) failed to obtain an age trend for 6-, 11-, and 18-year-olds. Even infants as young as 6 months reveal adult levels of prism adaptation (McDonnell & Abraham, 1979, 1981).

9.2.4.2. Athletic and Artistic Skill. Samuel (1981) found that "above-average" athletic subjects (according to self-report) revealed less prism adaptation (negative aftereffect) than did "below-average" athletes, whereas artistic subjects adapted more than nonartists. The adaptation was assumed to be primarily based on a shift in proprioception. Hence the investigator concluded that the reason why the athletes showed little adaptation is that they are particularly proficient at proprioceptive tasks. Because artists, on the other hand, are presumed to be visually skillful (compared to nonartists), proprioception should be more easily modified by prism exposure.

9.2.4.3. Mental Illness. Different categories of mental health appear to be associated with differential adaptation to perceptual rearrangement. Both Jaensch and Mandowsky (1932) and Eysenck, Granger, and Brengelmann (1957) obtained greater adaptation to prism-induced curvature (Section 6.2.1) for "normal" than for neurotic or psychotic subjects. Similarly, Kranz (cited by Eysenck et al., 1957) obtained a positive correlation between compensation for prism-induced errors in eye-hand coordination and degree of "personality integration." Eysenck et al., however, were unable to replicate this finding.

Finally, Ebner, Broekema, and Ritzler (1971) compared a group of nonorganic schizophrenics to a group of nonschizophrenics and found prism adaptation (after 2 min of terminal display) only for the latter group.

It appears safe to conclude from the data presented in this section that the mentally ill are less capable of adaptation to perceptual rearrangement than are the mentally healthy. One might speculate that this result is due to some basic differences between these populations with respect to flexibility or adaptability in the general sense of the word.

9.2.4.4. Brain Damage. Only two studies of the potential relationship between brain damage and adaptability have been reported. Meier and French (1966) found that the presence (versus the absence) of extratemporal spike foci in temporally lobectomized patients was associated with (1) poorer initial performance on a drawing task carried out during various degrees of visual rotation and (2) weaker subsequent adaptation to some of the rotations.

Welch and Goldstein (1972) found less prism-induced negative aftereffect for a group of heterogeneous brain-damaged subjects than for a non-brain-damaged psychiatric group or a group of normals. No differences, however, were found for purely proprioceptive adaptation. It was also demonstrated that frontally damaged subjects adapted just as much (on both measures) as did non-brain-damaged subjects, a finding that raises doubts about Teuber's (1961, 1964) suggestion that the frontal lobes are involved in adaptation.

9.3. Conclusions

Because adaptation to perceptual rearrangement does not appear to be related to sex, age, or various measures of personality, it would seem that attempts to control for these (and perhaps other) "general" subject characteristics are unnecessary. This fact also suggests that the adaptive process is a relatively noncognitive event. On the other hand, the subjects' so-called "perceptual traits," such as general level of proficiency in eye-hand coordination, do appear to be lawfully related to level of adaptation. Thus future attempts to discern correlates of adaptability should concentrate on measurement of subjects' capabilities on tasks that tap the basic perceptual and perceptual-motor components upon which this adaptation is based.

9.4. Key Reference

Warren, D. H., & Platt, B. B. (1974). In this article the authors introduce the strategy of "microanalysis" of the various perceptual and perceptual-motor components of the responses involved in prism adaptation. They demonstrate lawful relations between level of adaptation and degree of proficiency on each of several component groupings.

10. CONCLUSIONS

10.1. The Aims

The three motives underlying the vast array of studies on adaptation to perceptual rearrangement have been (1) to examine the nature-nurture issue as it pertains to perception, (2) to acquire a better understanding of perception and perceptual-motor coordination, and (3) to elucidate the capacities of perceptual and perceptual-motor plasticity. The fulfillment of these aims has met with varying success.

10.2. The Nature-Nurture Issue

It may be concluded that although adult human beings have proved capable of substantially adjusting their perception and perceptual-motor behavior when confronted by visual or auditory rearrangement, this is no guarantee that the capacities involved in these modifications were acquired from experience by the newborn and developing infant. It is now clear to most psychologists that only by directly examining the neonatal organism can the nature-nurture issue be unambiguously evaluated. Thus, for example, the demonstration that an adult (or, for that matter, an infant) is able to adapt to perceptual rearrangement does not preclude the possibility that the perceptual capacity involved was "wired in" at birth. Likewise, the observation of a *failure* of adaptation in an adult does not represent unequivocal evidence that the capacity in question is innate.

At best, then, the findings from the adaptation research with adults may be used to suggest *possible* neonatal events, which must then be tested with newborn or neonatal subjects. Hein and his colleagues (Hein, 1970; Hein & Diamond, 1971a, 1971b, 1972; Hein, Gower, & Diamond, 1970; Hein & Held, 1967; Hein, Held, & Gower, 1970; Held, 1964; Held & Bauer, 1967; Held & Hein, 1963), using kittens and neonatal monkeys, have been the most heavily involved in this venture. Held and Hein (1963), for example, carried out a now-classic study inspired by their conclusion (Held & Hein, 1958) that active bodily movement is a necessary condition for prism adaptation (see Figure 24.23). In short, they found that only when the first visual experience of very young kittens involved *active* visuomotor behavior were such responses as avoidance of the "visual cliff" and the appropriate reaction to an oncoming visual object

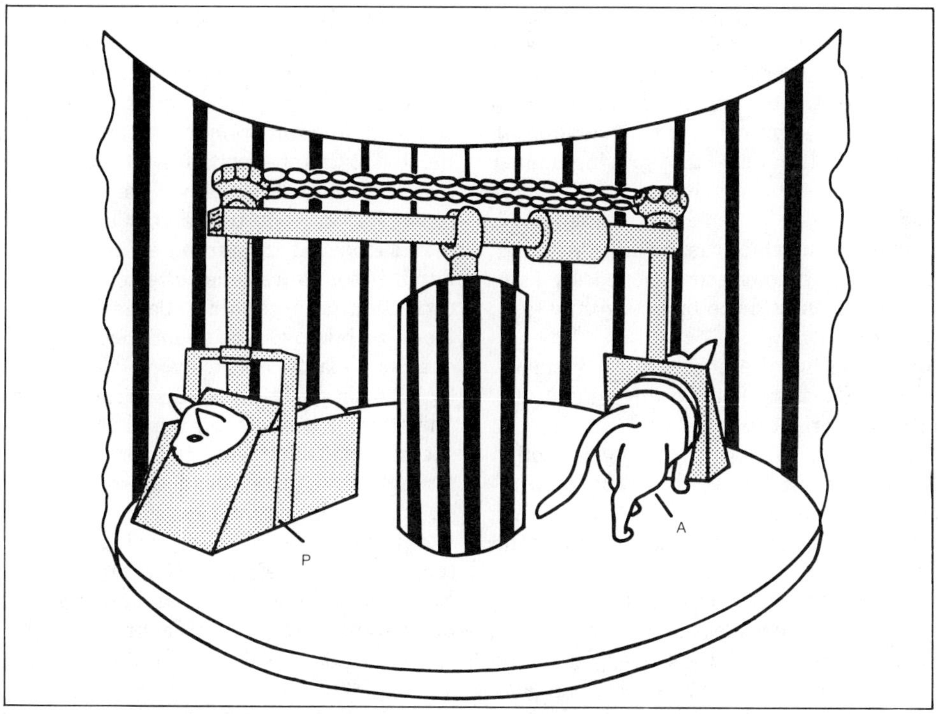

Figure 24.23. Apparatus for equating motion and consequent visual feedback for an actively moving (A) and a passively moved (P) kitten. (From R. Held & A. Hein, Movement-produced stimulation in the development of visually guided behavior, *Journal of Comparative and Physiological Psychology, 56*. Copyright 1963 by American Psychological Association. Reprinted with permission.)

or surface acquired. Although these and later results from Hein's laboratory have generally supported conclusions drawn from some adult prism studies, rather convincing alternative interpretations have been offered (e.g., Welch, 1978, pp. 286–292). For example, it may be argued from other evidence that, contrary to Hein's position, visual localization is an innate capacity in kittens (and monkeys), but that the neonatal dark-rearing procedures used by Hein and his associates prior to the institution of active or passive visual experience causes a *suppression* of this capacity, a suppression that may, perhaps, be released subsequently only by means of active visuomotor behavior (Ganz, 1975).

Even if a perceptual capacity proves to be innate, it is extremely likely that, as a result of experience, it will be subject to modification in the form of refinement and increased precision. Furthermore, the very existence of the adult ability to adapt to perceptual rearrangement suggests that certain naturally occurring situations must arise that require the use of this capacity. Likely candidates for such a situation are the changes in visual and auditory localization that must result from the increases in interocular and interaural distance concomitant with head growth in the infant and young child, as well as the changes in the size and proportion of the body in general.

10.3. Implications for "Normal" Perception and Perceptual-Motor Coordination

By the use of artificially induced perceptual rearrangements a number of important insights about perception have emerged. These studies have, for example, made it even more certain that when it comes to spatial localization the visual modality is far superior to the other spatial senses. The best support for this conclusion comes from the relative unmodifiability of vision (at least in terms of changes in retinal values) when placed in conflict with proprioception or audition, coupled with its substantial influence over the latter modalities.

The adaptation research has also pointed out that the weighting of the various modalities involved in an instance of multimodal perception is significantly affected by the distribution of the observer's attention. Thus it would appear that at least one reason why vision typically carries more weight in spatial localization than do proprioception and audition (when one or both of these are also available) is that vision is the most heavily attended.

Within the visual modality, in particular in depth and distance perception, the relative weighting of various cues has also been suggested by the adaptation research. It has been demonstrated (primarily by Wallach and his colleagues) that (1) the "kinetic depth effect" (retinal deformations resulting from viewing a rotating three-dimensional object) is a more powerful cue than is binocular disparity (Wallach et al., 1963) and (2) changes in retinal size contingent on an approaching or receding object are more heavily weighted than is the accommodation/convergence cue (Wallach & Frey, 1972c; Wallach et al., 1972), whereas the latter is dominant over the body position sense (Wallach & Smith, 1972).

The adaptation paradigm has also revealed that normal perception may be *conditioned* to situational cues. This discovery has led to a plethora of studies of the so-called "contingent aftereffects." The prime example is the "McCollough effect," a phenomenon whose discovery appears to have been inspired by some of Ivo Kohler's research. The effect involves an initial induction period in which a grating of vertical red and black bars is viewed for about 5 sec, alternating with a horizontal grating of green and black bars which is also viewed for about 5 sec. After repeated alternation between these two patterns for several minutes, the white bars of a vertical black and white grating test pattern appear distinctly tinged with green (complementary to the induction hue seen with this bar orientation), whereas those of a horizontal black and white grating appear pink. This discovery, which was initially attributed to "color-coded" edge detectors, now appears to be best explained as an example of associative learning in which the initially "neutral" vertical (or horizontal) grating becomes conditioned, by association, to the *adaptation* response to the induction hue (e.g., Harris, 1980; Murch, 1976).

Other varieties of contingent aftereffects are movement-contingent color aftereffects (Hepler, 1968; Stromeyer & Mansfield, 1970), color-contingent orientation aftereffects (Held & Shattuck, 1971; Shattuck, & Held, 1975), color-contingent motion aftereffects (Favreau, Emerson, & Corballis, 1972), texture-contingent visual motion aftereffects (Mayhew & Anstis, 1972; Walker, 1972), and tactual size aftereffects contingent on hand position (Walker & Shea, 1974).

Another phenomenon of normal perception that has become apparent as a result of adaptation to perceptual rearrangement concerns the visual effects of sustained eye convergence. The research of Ebenholtz and his colleagues (e.g., Paap & Ebenholtz, 1976) has shown quite convincingly that the prolonged maintenance of a specific convergence of the eyes leads to a significant change in visual localization.

Another conclusion that has been drawn from the adaptation area is that efference is a more important contributor to the body position sense and eye-hand coordination than had previously been believed.

Studies of optically induced tilt, loss of VPC, and distortions of depth/distance have revealed that the normal perceptual capacities involved require continued, everyday visual experience for their maintenance.

The research on underwater distortions has made evident the importance of the aerial perspective cue for depth and distance and its potential role in illusions both underwater and in fog or mist.

Finally, Redding's (1973a, 1973b, 1975a, 1975b) discovery that optical tilt adaptation and prismatic displacement adaptation (1) have different acquisition and decay functions, (2) are not correlated with one another, and (3) can occur simultaneously without mutual interference indicates that the two visual capacities (egocentric orientation and egocentric localization) are independent of one another.

10.4. The Nature of Perceptual and Perceptual-Motor Plasticity

It is not surprising that the third aim—to measure the modifiability of human perception and perceptual-motor coordination—has been the one most satisfactorily met by the adaptation research. The major conclusions regarding the nature of human adaptability to perceptual rearrangement are summarized here.

It is clear from the contents of this chapter that human beings are capable of adjusting their perception and/or behavior in response to every stable rearrangement of spatial perception to which they have been exposed. These adjustments can take any or all of a variety of forms, only some of which, however, are the gradually acquired, semi-permanent changes that qualify as adaptation according to the present definition.

If one examines only the level of "genuine" adaptation resulting from a given exposure period, it is almost always found to be significantly less than the maximum set by the strength of the rearranging medium, a result that argues against the empiricistic assumption of total modifiability of human behavior. Related to this observation is the fact that in all but one instance (Kohler, 1964), it has proved impossible to induce genuine perceptual adaptation to the very large and dramatic rearrangements of visual or auditory spatial transposition. On the other hand, if configurational effects, intersensory bias, deliberate correction, and genuine adaptation are all allowed to occur, along with knowledge about the nature of the rearrangement, observers may be able to overcome *entirely* the problems induced by even the most severe distortion. In addition to this overall adjustment, it has been found that repeated experience with the distortion hastens its initial resolution and reduces the strength and duration of subsequent aftereffects (e.g., Ross, 1970). Finally, it has been demonstrated that incremented (stepwise) exposure to increasingly greater magnitudes of distortion facilitates adaptation to optical tilt (Ebenholtz, 1969; Ebenholtz & Mayer, 1968) and prismatic displacement (Lackner & Lobovitz, 1977; 1978; Yachzel & Lackner, 1977), as well as adaptation to vestibularly induced visual effects (Graybiel & Wood, 1969).

The general plasticity of human perception and perceptual-motor coordination revealed by the laboratory studies described in this chapter has clear implications for a number of "real-life" situations. As we have seen, this adaptability allows the underwater diver to overcome, at least partially, a wide variety of visual distortions induced by the face mask. Likewise, it is reasonable to presume that the distortions confronted by a pilot viewing the world through the cockpit windscreen are subject to a certain amount of adaptation, although to date no research on this topic has appeared in the literature. Thus it may be predicted that, to the extent that visual distortions caused by airplane transparencies remain stable over time (or in relation to specific movements of head, eye, or plane), a certain amount of adaptation will occur. The prevalence of optical distortions for pilots may be increasing because, generally, the faster airplanes are designed to travel, the thicker the transparent windscreens must be made to withstand such events as high-speed bird impact, and this increased thickness exacerbates certain optical problems and introduces new ones (Eggleston & Genco, 1980). These optical effects include distortion, multiple imaging, chromatic aberration, haze, internal reflections, and transmission loss. Relating these effects to those examined in the many laboratory studies described in this chapter, one may speculate on the extent of adaptation that the pilot may expect to achieve. The distortion, which is due to differential refraction of light as a function of its angle of incidence to the windscreen, would cause the visual field to appear somewhat "rubbery" with head movements and/or when the plane is in motion. Because a certain amount of adaptation to this form of distortion occurs for prism-wearing subjects who move their heads about (e.g., Pick & Hay, 1964), the same should be true for pilots, given good information about head movements and bodily motion. Chromatic aberration (although probably not a hazard to the pilot) should also decrease, based on the results of several studies described previously (e.g., Hay & Pick, 1966b). There is no good evidence that double imaging can be perceptually resolved and therefore this could represent a serious problem for the pilot. Finally, as with underwater divers, it seems likely that pilots could be taught the nature of the optical distortions they will encounter and how to compensate "intellectually" for that portion of these distortions not resolved by the adaptive process.

Vision, as we have noted, is much less modifiable than the other senses, except to the extent that proprioceptive changes have visual implications (e.g., changes in felt direction of gaze) or when the adaptation involves a recalibration of the relationship between expected and actual visual motion with head or bodily movement. With regard to *oculocentric* changes (altered retinal values), effects are usually quite small, as seen in the very modest amounts of adaptation to prismatic curvature and optical tilt. There is, however, a hint that these visual changes would be substantially larger if *eye movements* were involved in the distortion (as with a prism-contact lens).

It appears that the modality that reveals the primary modification when confronted with perceptual rearrangement is generally the one *not* being attended. Thus when vision and proprioception are placed in conflict, it is typically vision that is attended and thus proprioception that undergoes the major alteration. It seems likely that the modality to which the observer typically pays more attention is the one assumed (not necessarily consciously) to be the more veridical or trustworthy. That this modality is frequently vision may be due, at least in part, to its high degree of precision and general adeptness at spatial tasks. However, both instructions and task demands can alter and even reverse this normal deployment of attention, leading to an increase in visual adaptation and a decrease in proprioceptive (or auditory) adaptation (Canon, 1970, 1971; Kelso et al., 1975; Uhlarik & Canon, 1971).

As we have seen, not only are the end products of adaptation varied by so too are the sources of this adaptation. It now seems clear that although active perceptual-motor behavior is an ideal condition for the production of adaptation to perceptual rearrangement, it is not a necessary one. Rather, a variety of forms of information (e.g., error-corrective feedback, passive exposure to a sharply defined visual-proprioceptive discrepancy) will suffice. Thus Held's "reafference hypothesis" may be replaced by the more encompassing "information hypothesis."

10.5. Key Reference

Held, R. (1980). This chapter in a book edited by Harris (1980) deals with contingent aftereffects, specifically those involving color vision. Held makes the argument that investigators may have been mistaken to assume that such effects imply or are the manifestation of specific neural feature detectors.

REFERENCE NOTE

Wallace, B., Melamed, L. E., Cohen, R. R., & Oakes, S. *The relation of various field factors to prism adaptation.* Unpublished manuscript. Kent State University.

REFERENCES

* References preceded by an asterisk are "key references."

Abplanalp, P., & Held, R. Effects of de-correlated visual feedback on adaptation to wedge prisms. Paper presented at meetings of Eastern Psychological Association, Atlantic City, April 1965.

Adolfson, J., & Berghage, T. *Perception and performance under water.* New York: Wiley, 1974.

Alpert, R., & Haber, R. N. Anxiety in academic achievement situations. *Journal of Abnormal and Social Psychology*, 1960, *61*, 207–215.

Bacon, J., & Wallach, H. Adaptation in motion perception: Alteration of motion evoked by ocular pursuit. *Perception and Psychophysics*, 1982, *31*, 251–255.

Baily, J. S. Adaptation to prisms: Do proprioceptive changes mediate adapted behavior with ballistic arm movements? *Quarterly Journal of Experimental Psychology*, 1972, *24*, 8–20. (a)

Baily, J. S. Arm-body adaptation with passive arm movements. *Perception and Psychophysics*, 1972, *12*, 39–44 (b)

Beckett, P. A. Development of the third component in prism adaptation: Effects of active and passive movement. *Journal of Experimental Psychology: Human Perception and Performance*, 1980, *6*, 433–444.

Beckett, P. A. & Melamed, L. E. Further evidence for dissociating decay and readaptation in prism adaptation. *Bulletin of the Psychonomic Society*, 1980, *16*, 73–75.

Beckett, P. A., Melamed, L. E., & Halay, M. Prism awareness, exposure duration, and the linear model in prism adaptation. Paper presented at meetings of Midwestern Psychological Association, Chicago, May 1975.

Bonnet, C. A tentative model for visual motion detection. *Psychologia*, 1975, *18*, 35–50.

Bossom, J., & Held, R. Transfer of error-correction in adaptation to prisms. *American Psychologist*, 1959, *14*, 436.

Bower, T. G. R. *Development in infancy.* San Francisco: Freeman, 1974.

Brown, G. G. Perception of depth with disoriented vision. *British Journal of Psychology*, 1928, *19*, 117–146.

Burnham, C. A. Adaptation to prismatically induced curvature with nonvisible arm movements. *Psychonomic Science*, 1968, *10*, 273–274.

Burnham, C. A. Adaptation to curvature in the absence of contour. *The Behavioral and Brain Sciences*, 1979, *2*, 65–66.

Callan, J. W., & Ebenholtz, S. M. Directional changes in the vestibular ocular responses as a result of adaptation to optical tilt. *Vision Research*, 1982, *22*, 37–42.

Canon, L. K. Intermodality inconsistency of input and directed attention as determinants of the nature of adaptation. *Journal of Experimental Psychology*, 1970, *84*, 141–147.

Canon, L. K. Directed attention and maladaptive "adaptation" to displacement of the visual field. *Journal of Experimental Psychology, 1971, 88*, 403–408.

Choe, C. S., & Welch, R. B. Variables affecting the intermanual transfer and decay of prism adaptation. *Journal of Experimental Psychology*, 1974, *102*, 1076–1084.

Cohen, H. B. Some critical factors in prism adaptation. *American Journal of Psychology*, 1966, *79*, 285–290.

Cohen, M. M. *Curvature after-effects following exposure under prismatic viewing conditions.* Unpublished doctoral dissertation, University of Pennsylvania, 1965.

Cohen, M. M. Continuous versus terminal visual feedback in prism aftereffects. *Perceptual and Motor Skills*, 1967, *24*, 1295–1302.

Cohen, M. M. Visual feedback, distribution of practice, and intermanual transfer of prism aftereffects. *Perceptual and Motor Skills*, 1973, *37*, 599–609.

Cohen, M. M. Changes in auditory localization following prismatic exposure under continuous and terminal visual feedback. *Perceptual and Motor Skills*, 1974, *38*, 1202.

Cohen, M. M., & Held, R. Degrading visual-motor coordination by exposure to disordered re-afferent stimulation. Paper presented at meetings of Eastern Psychological Association, New York City, April 1960.

Coren, S. Adaptation to prismatic displacement as a function of the amount of available information. *Psychonomic Science*, 1966, *4*, 407–408.

Craske, B. Change in transfer function of joint receptor output. *Nature*, 1966, *210*, 764–765. (a)

Craske, B. Intermodal transfer of adaptation to displacement. *Nature*, 1966, *210*, 765. (b)

Craske, B. Adaptation to prisms: Change in internally registered eye-position. *British Journal of Psychology,* 1967, *58*, 329–335.

Craske, B., & Crawshaw, M. Spatial discordance is a sufficient condition for oculomotor adaptation to prisms: Eye muscle potentiation need not be a factor. *Perception and Psychophysics*, 1978, *23*, 75–79.

Craske, B., Kenny, F. T., & Keith, D. Modifying an underlying component of perceived arm length: Adaptation of tactile location induced by spatial discordance. *Journal of Experimental Psychology: Human Perception and Performance*, 1984, *10*, 307–317.

Craske, B., & Templeton, W. B. Prolonged oscillation of the eyes induced by conflicting position output. *Journal of Experimental Psychology*, 1968, *76*, 387–393.

Crawshaw, M., & Craske, B. No retinal component in prism adaptation. *Acta Psychologica*, 1974, *38*, 421–423.

Crawshaw, M., & Craske, B. Correlation of prism adaptation with other measures: A cautionary note. *Perceptual and Motor Skills*, 1976, *42*, 1150. (a)

Crawshaw, M., & Craske, B. Oculomotor adaptation to prisms: Complete transfer between eyes. *British Journal of Psychology*, 1976, *67*, 475–478. (b)

Day, R. H., & Singer, G. Sensory adaptation and behavioral compensation with spatially transformed vision and hearing. *Psychological Bulletin*, 1967, *67*, 307–322.

Devane, J. R. Proaction in the recovery from practice under visual displacement. *Perceptual and Motor Skills*, 1968, *27*, 411–416.

Dewar, R. Adaptation to displaced vision: Amount of optical displacement and practice. *Perception and Psychophysics*, 1970, *8*, 313–316. (a)

Dewar, R. Adaptation to displaced vision: The influence of distribution of practice on retention. *Perception and Psychophysics*, 1970, *8*, 33–34. (b)

Dewar, R. Adaptation to displaced vision—type of information feedback. Paper presented at meetings of Canadian Psychological Association, Winnipeg, May, 1970. (c)

Dewar, R. Adaptation to displaced vision: Variations on the "prismatic shaping" technique. *Perception and Psychophysics*, 1971, *9*, 155–157.

Dolezal, H. *Living in a world transformed: Perceptual and performatory adaptation to visual distortion*. New York: Academic Press, 1982.

Ebenholtz, S. M. Adaptation to a rotated visual field as a function of degree of optical tilt and exposure time. *Journal of Experimental Psychology*, 1966 *72*, 629–634.

Ebenholtz, S. M. Transfer of adaptation as a function of interpolated optical tilt to the ipsilateral and contralateral eye. *Journal of Experimental Psychology*, 1967, *73*, 263–267.

Ebenholtz., S. M. Readaptation and decay after exposure to optical tilt. *Journal of Experimental Psychology*, 1968, *78*, 350–351. (a)

Ebenholtz, S. M. Some evidence for a comparator in adaptation to optical tilt. *Journal of Experimental Psychology*, 1968, *77*, 94–100. (b)

Ebenholtz, S. M. Transfer and decay functions in adaptation to optical tilt. *Journal of Experimental Psychology*, 1969, *81*, 170–173.

Ebenholtz, S. M. On the relation between interocular transfer of adaptation and Hering's law of equal innervation. *Psychological Review*, 1970, *77*, 343–347.

Ebenholtz, S. M. Optimal input rates for tilt adaptation. *American Journal of Psychology*, 1973, *86*, 193–200.

*Ebenholtz, S. M. The possible role of eye-muscle potentiation in several forms of prism adaptation. *Perception*, 1974, *3*, 477–485.

Ebenholtz, S. M. Additivity of aftereffects of maintained head and eye rotations: An alternative to recalibration. *Perception and Psychophysics*, 1976, *19*, 113–116.

Ebenholtz, S. M. Hysteresis effects in the vergence system: Perceptual implications. In D. F. Fisher, R. A. Monty, and J. W. Senders (Eds.), *Eye movements: Visual perception and cognition*. Hillsdale, NJ: Erlbaum, 1981.

Ebenholtz, S. M., & Callan, J. W. Tilt adaptation as a feedback control process. *Journal of Experimental Psychology: Human Perception and Performance*, 1980, *6*, 413–432.

Ebenholtz, S. M., & Fisher, S. K. Distance adaptation depends upon plasticity in the oculomotor system. *Perception and Psychophyics*, 1982, *31*, 551–560.

Ebenholtz, S. M., & Mayer, D. Rate of adaptation under constant and varied optical tilt. *Perceptual and Motor Skills*, 1968, *26*, 507–509.

Ebenholtz, S. M., & Wolfson, D. M. Perceptual aftereffects of sustained convergence. *Perception and Psychophysics*, 1975, *17*, 485–491.

Ebner, E., Broekema, V., & Ritzler, B. Adaptation to altered visual-proprioceptive input in normals and schizophrenics. *Archives of General Psychiatry*, 1971, *24*, 367–371.

Efstathiou, A. Correlated and de-correlated visual feedback in modifying eye-hand coordination. Paper presented at meetings of Eastern Psychological Association, New York, April 1963.

Efstathiou, A. Effects of exposure time and magnitude of prism transform on eye-hand coordination. *Journal of Experimental Psychology*, 1969, *81*, 235–240.

Efstathiou, A., Bauer, J., Greene, M., & Held, R. Altered reaching following adaptation to optical displacement of the hand. *Journal of Experimental Psychology*, 1967, *73*, 113–120.

Eggleston, R. G., & Genco, L. V. Transparency design decisions: Assessing their impact on visual performance. Unpublished manuscript, 1980.

Epstein, W. Modification of the disparity-depth relationship as a result of exposure to conflicting cues. *American Journal of Psychology*, 1968, *81*, 189–197.

Epstein, W. Adaptation to uniocular image magnification after varying preadaptation activities. *American Journal of Psychology*, 1971, *84*, 66–74.

Epstein, W. Adaptation to uniocular image magnification: Is the underlying shift proprioceptive? *Perception and Psychophysics*, 1972, *11*, 89–91. (a)

Epstein, W. Retention of adaptation to uniocular image magnification: Effect of interpolated activity. *Journal of Experimental Psychology*, 1972, *92*, 319–324. (b)

Epstein, W., & Daviess, N. Modification of depth judgment following exposures to magnification of uniocular image: Are changes in perceived absolute distance and registered direction of gaze involved? *Perception and Psychophysics*, 1972, *12*, 315–317.

Epstein, W., & Morgan, C. L. Adaptation to uniocular image magnification: Modification of the disparity-depth relationship. *American Journal of Psychology*, 1970, *83*, 322–329.

Epstein, W., & Morgan-Paap, C. L. The effect of level of depth processing and degree of informational discrepancy on adaptation to uniocular image magnification. *Journal of Experimental Psychology*, 1974, *102*, 585–594.

Erismann, T. Das Werden der Wahrnehmung. *Tagungsbericht d. Berufsverbandes Deutscher Psychologen*, Bonn, 1947, 54–56.

Ewert, P. H. A study of the effect of inverted retinal stimulation upon spatially coordinated behavior. *Genetic Psychology Monographs*, 1930, *7*, 177–363.

Ewert, P. H. Factors in space localization during inverted vision: I. Interference. *Psychological Review*, 1936, *43*, 522–546.

Ewert, P. H. Factors in space localization during inverted vision: II. An explanation of interference and adaptation. *Psychological Review*, 1937, *44*, 105–116.

Eysenck, H. J. The questionnaire measurement of neuroticism and extraversion. *Revista di Psicologia*, 1965, *50*, 113–140.

Eysenck, H. J., Granger, G.W., & Brengelmann, J. C. *Perceptual processes and mental illness*. New York: Basic Books, 1957.

Favreau, O. E., Emerson, V. F., & Corballis, M. C. Motion perception: A color-contingent aftereffect. *Science*, 1972, *176*, 78–79.

Feinstein, S. H. Human hearing under water: Are things as bad as they seem? *The Journal of the Acoustical Society of America*, 1966, *40*, 1561–1562.

Ferris, S. H. Improvement of absolute distance estimation underwater. *Perceptual and Motor Skills*, 1972. *35*, 299–305. (a)

Ferris, S. H. Loss of position constancy underwater. *Psychonomic Science*, 1972, *27*, 337–338. (b)

Ferris, S. H. Improving absolute distance estimation in clear and in turbid water. *Perceptual and Motor Skills*, 1973, *36*, 771–776. (a)

Ferris, S. H. Improving distance estimation underwater: Long-term effectiveness of training. *Perceptual and Motor Skills*, 1973, *36*, 1089–1090. (b)

*Festinger, L., Burnham, C. A., Ono, H., & Bamber, D. Efference and the conscious experience of perception. *Journal of Experimental Psychology Monograph*, 1967, *74* (4, Whole No. 637).

Finke, R. The functional equivalence of mental images and errors of movement. *Cognitive Psychology*, 1979, *11*, 235–264.

Fiorentini, A., Ghez, C., & Maffei, L. Physiological correlates of adaptation to a rotated visual field. *Journal of Physiology*, 1972, *227*, 313–322.

Fishkin, S. M. Passive vs. active exposure and other variables related to the occurrence of hand adaptation to lateral displacement. *Perceptual and Motor Skills*, 1969, *29*, 291–297.

Fitts, W. H. Tennessee self-concept scale. Nashville, TN: Counselor Recordings and Tests, 1965.

Flock, J. P., & McGonigle, B. O. Serial adaptation to conflicting prismatic rearrangement effects in monkey and man. *Perception*, 1977, *6*, 15–29.

Foley, J. E. Adaptation to magnifying and minifying spectacles. Unpublished manuscript, University of Toronto, 1965.

Foley, J. E. A further study of alternation of normal and distorted vision. *Psychonomic Science*, 1967, *9*, 483–484.

Foley, J. E., & Abel, S. M. A study of alternation of normal and distorted vision. *Canadian Journal of Psychology*, 1967, *21*, 220–230.

Foley, J. E., & Maynes, F. J. Comparison of training methods in the production of prism adaptation. *Journal of Experimental Psychology*, 1969, *81*, 151–155.

Foley, J. E., & Miyanshi, K. Interocular effects in prism adaptation. *Science*, 1969, *165*, 311–312.

Franklin, S. S., Ross, H. E., & Weltman, G. Size-distance invariance in perceptual adaptation. *Psychonomic Science*, 1970, *21*, 229–231.

Freedman, S. J. On the mechanisms of perceptual compensation. In S.J. Freedman (Ed.), *The neuropsychology of spatially oriented behavior*. Homewood, IL: Dorsey, 1968.

Freedman, S. J., & Gardos, G. Compensation for auditory re-arrangement and transfer to hand-eye coordination. Paper presented at MIT Conference on Adaptation, Cambridge, Mass., June, 1965.

Freedman, S. J., Hall, S. B., & Rekosh, J. H. Effects on hand-eye coordination of two different arm motions during adaptation to displaced vision. *Perceptual and Motor Skills*, 1965, *20*, 1054–1056.

Freedman, S. J., & Pfaff, D. W. The effect of dichotic noise on auditory localization. *Journal of Auditory Research*, 1962, *2*, 305–310. (a)

Freedman, S. J., & Pfaff, D. W. Trading relations between dichotic time and intensity differences in auditory localization. *Journal of Auditory Research*, 1962, *2*, 311–318 (b)

Freedman, S. J., & Stampfer, K. Changes in auditory localization with displaced ears. Paper presented at meetings of Psychonomic Society, Niagara Falls, Ontario, October 1964.

Freedman, S. J., Wilson, L., & Rekosh, J. H. Compensation for auditory rearrangement in hand-ear coordination. *Perceptual and Motor Skills*, 1967, *24*, 1207–1210.

Freedman, S. J., & Zacks, J. L. Effects of active and passive movement upon auditory function during prolonged atypical stimulation. *Perceptual and Motor Skills*, 1964, *18*, 361–366.

Ganz, L. Orientation in visual space by neonates and its modification by visual deprivation. In A. H. Riesen (Ed.), *The developmental neuropsychology of sensory deprivation*. New York: Academic Press, 1975.

Garrett, J. B., & Wallace, B. A novel test of hypnotic anesthesia. *International Journal of Clinical and Experimental Hypnosis*, 1975, *23*, 139–147.

Giannitrapani, D. *Changes in adaptation to prolonged perceptual distortion: A developmental study*. Unpublished doctoral dissertation, Clark University, 1958.

Gibson, E. J. *Principles of perceptual learning and development*. New York: Appleton-Century-Crofts, 1969,

*Gibson, J. J. Adaptation, after-effect, and contrast in the perception of curved lines. *Journal of Experimental Psychology*, 1933, *16*, 1–31.

Gibson, J. J., & Radner, M. Adaptation, after-effect, and contrast in the perception of tilted lines. I. Quantitative studies. *Journal of Experimental Psychology*, 1937, *20*, 453–467. (a)

Gibson, J. J., & Radner, M. Adaptation, after-effect, and contrast in the perception of tilted lines. II. Simultaneous contrast and the areal restriction of the after-effect. *Journal of Experimental Psychology*, 1937, *20*, 553–569. (b)

Goldberg, I. A., Taub, E., & Berman, A. J. Decay of prism after-effect and interlimb transfer of adaptation. Paper presented at meetings of Eastern Psychological Association, Boston, April 1967.

Gonshor, A., & Melvill Jones, G. Changes of human vestibulo-ocular response induced by vision-reversal during head rotation. *Journal of Physiology* (London), 1973, *234*, 102P–103P.

Gonshor, A., & Melvill Jones, G. Extreme vestibulo-ocular adaptation induced by prolonged optical reversal of vision. *Journal of Physiology*, 1976, *256*, 381–414. (a)

Gonshor, A., & Melvill Jones, G. Short-term adaptive changes in the human vestibulo-ocular reflex arc. *Journal of Physiology*, 1976, *256*, 361–379. (b)

Gonshor, A., & Melvill Jones, G. Postural adaptation to prolonged optical reversal of vision in man. *Brain Research*, 1980, *192*, 239–248.

Gough, G. H. *California psychological inventory*. Palo Alto, CA: Consulting Psychological Press, 1957.

Graybiel, A., & Wood, C. Rapid vestibular adaptation in a rotating environment by means of controlled head movements. *Aerospace medicine*, 1969, *40*, 638–643.

Greene, M. E. A further study of the proprioceptive change hypothesis of prism adaptation. Paper presented at meetings of Eastern Psychological Association, Boston, April 1967.

Gyr, J. W., & Wiley, R. The effect of efference to the arm on visual adaptation to curvature: A replication. *Psychonomic Science*, 1970, *21*, 89–91.

Gyr, J. W., Willey, R., & Gordon, D. G. Correlations between motor learning and visual and arm adaptation under conditions of computer-simulated visual distortion. *Perceptual and Motor Skills*, 1972, *35*, 551–561.

Gyr, J. W., Willey, R., & Henry, A. Motor-sensory feedback and geometry of visual space: An attempted replication. *The Behavioral and Brain Sciences*, 1979, *2*, 59–94.

Hajos, A., & Ritter, M. Experiments to the problem of interocular transfer. *Acta Psychologica*, 1965, *24*, 81–90.

Hamilton, C. R. Intermanual transfer of adaptation to prisms. *American Journal of Psychology*, 1964, *77*, 457–462. (a)

Hamilton, C. R. *Studies on adaptation to deflection of the visual field in split-brain monkeys and man*. Unpublished doctoral dissertation, California Institute of Technology, 1964. (b)

Hamilton, C. R., & Bossom, J. Decay of prism aftereffects. *Journal of Experimental Psychology*, 1964, *67*, 148–150.

Hamilton, C. R., Sullivan, M. V., & Hillyard, S. A. Effects of adaptation to displaced vision on reaching to remembered positions. Unpublished manuscript, Stanford University, 1971.

Hardt, M. E., Held, R., & Steinbach, M. J. Adaptation to displaced vision: A change in the central control of sensorimotor coordination. *Journal of Experimental Psychology*, 1971, *89*, 229–239.

Harris, C. S. Adaptation to displaced vision: Visual, motor, or proprioceptive change? *Science*, 1963, *140*, 812–813.

*Harris, C. S. Perceptual adaptation to inverted, reversed, and displaced vision. *Psychological Review*, 1965, *72*, 419–444.

Harris, C. S. Beware of the straight-ahead shift—a nonperceptual change in experiments on adaptation to displaced vision. *Perception*, 1974, *3*, 461–476.

Harris, C. S. Insight or out of sight? Two examples of perceptual plasticity in the human adult. In C. S. Harris (Ed.), *Visual coding and adaptability*. Hillsdale, N.J.: Erlbaum, 1980.

Harris, C. S., & Gilchrist, A. Prism adaptation without prisms: A nonvisual change with implications about plasticity in the human visual system. Paper presented at Association for Research in Vision and Ophthalmology, Sarasota, Fl., April 1976.

Hay, J. C. Visual adaptation to an altered correlation between eye movements and head movement. *Science*, 1968, *160*, 429–430.

Hay, J. C. Does head-movement feedback calibrate the perceived direction of optical motions? *Perception and Psychophysics*, 1971, *10*, 286–288.

*Hay, J. C. Motor transformation learning. *Perception*, 1974, *3*, 487–496.

Hay, J. C. Reafference learning in the presence of exafference. *Perception and Psychophysics*, 1981, *30*, 277–282.

Hay, J. C., & Goldsmith, W. M. Space-time adaptation of visual position constancy. *Journal of Experimental Psychology*, 1973, *99*, 1–9.

Hay, J. C., & Pick, H. L., Jr. Gaze-contingent prism adaptation: Optical and motor factors. *Journal of Experimental Psychology*, 1966, *72*, 640–648. (a)

*Hay, J. C., & Pick, H. L., Jr. Visual and proprioceptive adaptation to optical displacement of the visual stimulus. *Journal of Experimental Psychology*, 1966, *71*, 150–158. (b)

Hay, J. C., Pick, H. L., Jr., & Ikeda, K. Visual capture produced by prism spectacles. *Psychonomic Science*, 1965, *2*, 215–216.

Hein, A. Visual-motor development of the kitten. *Optometric Weekly*, 1970, *61*, 890–892.

Hein, A. Acquiring components of visually guided behavior. In A. D. Pick (Ed.), *Minnesota symposia on child psychology*. Minneapolis: University of Minneapolis Press, 1972.

Hein, A., & Diamond, R. M. Contrasting development of visually triggered and guided movements in kittens with respect to interocular and interlimb equivalence. *Journal of Comparative and Physiological Psychology*, 1971, *76*, 219–224. (a)

Hein, A., & Diamond, R. M. Independence of the cat's scotopic and photopic systems in acquiring control of visually guided behavior. *Journal of Comparative and Physiological Psychology*, 1971, *76*, 31–38. (b)

Hein, A., & Diamond, R. M. Locomotory space as a prerequisite for acquiring visually guided reaching in kittens. *Journal of Comparative and Physiological Psychology*, 1972, *81*, 394–398.

Hein, A., Gower, E. C., & Diamond, R. M. Exposure requirements for developing the triggered component of the visual-placing response. *Journal of Comparative and Physiological Psychology*, 1970, *73*, 188–192.

Hein, A., & Held, R. A neural model for labile sensorimotor coordinations. In E. E. Bernard and M. R. Kare (Eds.), *Biological prototypes and synthetic systems* (Vol. 1). New York: Plenum, 1962.

Hein, A., & Held, R. Dissociation of the visual placing response into elicited and guided components. *Science*, 1967, *158*, 390–392.

Hein, A., Held, R., & Gower, E. C. Development and segmentation of visually controlled movement by selective exposure during rearing. *Journal of Comparative and Physiological Psychology*, 1970, *73*, 181–187.

*Held, R. Shifts in binaural localization after prolonged exposure to atypical combinations of stimuli. *American Journal of Psychology*, 1955, *68*, 526–548.

Held, R. Exposure-history as a factor in maintaining stability of perception and co-ordination. *Journal of Nervous and Mental Disease*, 1961, *132*, 26–32.

Held, R. The role of movement in the origin and maintenance of visual perception. *Acta Psychologica*, 1964, *23*, 308–309.

Held, R. Plasticity in sensory-motor systems. *Scientific American*, 1965, *213* (No. 5), 84–94.

Held, R. Action contingent development of vision in neonatal animals. In D. P. Kimble (Ed.), *Experience and capacity*. New York: New York Academy of Sciences, 1968.

*Held, R. The rediscovery of adaptability in the visual system: Effects of intrinsic and extrinsic dispersion. In C. S. Harris (Ed.), *Visual coding and adaptability*. Hillsdale, NJ: Erlbaum, 1980.

Held, R., & Bauer, J. A., Jr. Visually guided reaching in infant monkeys after restricted rearing. *Science*, 1967, *155*, 718–720.

Held, R., Efstathiou, A., & Greene, M. Adaptation to displaced and delayed visual feedback from the hand. *Journal of Experimental Psychology*, 1966, *72*, 887–891.

*Held, R., & Freedman, S. J. Plasticity in human sensorimotor control. *Science*, 1963, *142*, 455–462.

Held, R., & Gottlieb, N. Technique for studying adaptation to disarranged hand-eye coordination. *Perceptual and Motor Skills*, 1958, *8*, 83–86.

Held, R., & Hein, A. Adaptation to disarranged hand-eye coordination contingent upon reafferent stimulation. *Perceptual and Motor Skills*, 1958, *8*, 87–90.

Held, R., & Hein, A. Movement-produced stimulation in the development of visually guided behavior. *Journal of Comparative and Physiological Psychology*, 1963, *56*, 872–876.

Held, R., & Mikaelian, H. Motor-sensory feedback versus need in adaptation to rearrangement. *Perceptual and Motor Skills*, 1964, *18*, 685–688.

Held, R., & Rekosh, J. Motor-sensory feedback and the geometry of space. *Science*, 1963, *141*, 722–723.

Held, R., & Schlank, M. Adaptation to disarranged eye-hand coordination in the distance-dimension. *American Journal of Psychology*, 1959. *72*, 603–605.

Held, R., & Shattuck, S. Color- and edge-sensitive channels in the human visual system: Tuning for orientation. *Science*, 1971, *174*, 314–316.

Helmholtz, H. V. *Treatise on physiological optics* (Vol. 3). Rochester, NY: Optical Society of America, 1925.

Henson, D. B. Corrective saccades: Effects of altering visual feedback. *Vision Research*, 1978, *18*, 63–67.

Hepler, N. Color: A motion-contingent aftereffect. *Science*, 1968, *162*, 376–377.

Hering, E. *Die Lehre vom Binocularen Sehen*. Leipzig: Engelman, 1868.

Hillyard, S. A., & Hamilton, C. R. *Mislocalization of the arm following adaptation to displaced vision*. Unpublished manuscript, University of California, San Diego, 1971.

Holst, E., von. Relations between the central nervous system and the peripheral organs. *British Journal of Animal Behavior*, 1954, *2*, 89–94.

Howard, I. P. Displacing the optical array. In S. J. Freedman (Ed.), *The neuropsychology of spatially oriented behavior*. Homewood, Ill.: Dorsey, 1968.

Howard, I. P. The adaptability of the visual-motor system. In K. J. Connolly (Ed.), *Mechanisms of motor skill development*. London: Academic Press, 1970.

Howard, I. P. Perceptual learning and adaptation. *British Medical Bulletin*, 1971, *27*, 248–252.

Howard, I. P., Anstis, T., & Lucia, H. C. The relative lability of mobile and stationary components in a visual-motor adaptation task. *Quarterly Journal of Experimental Psychology*, 1974, *26*, 293–300.

Howard, I. P., Craske, B., & Templeton, W. B. Visuomotor adaptation to discordant exafferent stimulation. *Journal of Experimental Psychology*, 1965, *70*, 189–191.

Howard, I. P., & Templeton, W. B. Visually induced eye torsion and tilt adaptation. *Vision Research*, 1964, *4*, 433–437.

Howard, I. P., & Templeton, W. B. *Human spatial orientation*. New York: Wiley, 1966.

Ishii, S., & Wapner, S. Age differences in the effect of lateral displacing prisms (base left/20 diopter) on perception and walking. *Bulletin of the Psychonomic Society*, 1977, *9*, 423–426.

Jackson, C. V. Visual factors in auditory localization. *Quarterly Journal of Experimental Psychology*, 1953, *5*, 52–65.

Jaensch, W., & Mandowsky, C. Die klinische Bedeutung psychischer Labilitat bei optischen Wahrnehmungsvorgangen, *Medizinische Welt*, 1932, *6*, 1162.

Kalil, R. E., & Freedman, S. J. Intermanual transfer of compensation for displaced vision. *Perceptual and Motor Skills*, 1966, *22*, 123–126. (a)

Kalil, R. E., & Freedman, S. J. Persistence of ocular rotation following compensation for displaced vision. *Perceptual and Motor Skills*, *1966, 22*, 135–139. (b)

Kelso, J. A. S., Cook, E., Olson, M. E., & Epstein, W. Allocation of attention and the locus of adaptation to displaced vision. *Journal of Experimental Psychology: Human Perception and Performance*, 1975, *1*, 237–245.

Kennedy, J. M. Prismatic displacement and the remembered location of targets. *Perception and Psychophysics*, 1969, *5*, 218–220.

Kenny, F. T., & Craske, B. The kinesthetic fusion effect: Perceptual elimination of spatial discordance in the kinesthetic modality. *Perception and Psychophysics*, 1981, *30*, 211–216.

Kinney, J. A. S., Luria, S. M., Weitzman, D. O., & Markowitz, H. *Effects of diving experience on visual perception under water* (NSMRL Report No. 612). U.S. Naval Submarine Medical Center, Groton, CT, Feb. 1970.

Kinney, J. A. S., McKay, C. L., Luria, S. M., & Gratto, C. L. *The improvement of divers' compensation for underwater distortions* (NSMRL Report No. 633). U.S. Naval Submarine Medical Center, Groton, CT, June 1970.

Klapp, S. T., Nordell, S. A., Hoekenga, K. C., & Patton, C. B. Long-lasting aftereffect of brief prism exposure. *Perception and Psychophysics*, 1974, *15*, 399–400.

Kohler, I. Warum sehen wer aufrecht? *Die Pyramide*, 1951, *2*, 30–33.

Kohler, I. Experiments with prolonged optical distortions. *Acta Psychologica*, 1955, *11*, 176–178.

Kohler, I. Experiments with goggles. *Scientific American*, 1962, *206*, 62–86.

*Köhler, I. The formation and transformation of the perceptual world (Trans. by H. Fiss). *Psychological Issues*, 1964, *3*(4), 1–173.

Köhler, W., & Wallach, H. Figural after-effects: An investigation of visual processes. *Proceedings of the American Philosophical Society*, 1944, *88*, 269–357.

Kornheiser, A. S. Adaptation to laterally displaced vision: A review. *Psychological Bulletin*, 1976, *83*, 783–816.

Kottenhoff, H. Situational and personal influences on space perception with experimental spectacles. *Acta Psychologica*, 1957, *13*, 79–97; 151–161.

Kravitz, J. H. Conditioned adaptation to prismatic displacement. *Perception and Psychophysics*, 1972, *11*, 38–42.

Kravitz, J. H., & Wallach, H. Adaptation to displaced vision contingent upon vibrating stimulation. *Psychonomic Science*, 1966, *6*, 465–466.

Kravitz, J. H., & Yaffe, F. Conditioned adaptation to prismatic displacement with a tone as the conditional stimulus. *Perception and Psychophysics*, 1972, *12*, 305–308.

Lackner, J. R. The role of posture in adaptation to visual rearrangement. *Neuropsychologia*, 1973, *11*, 33–44. (a)

Lackner, J. R. Visual rearrangement affects auditory localization. *Neuropsychologia*, 1973, *11*, 29–32. (b)

Lackner, J. R. Adaptation to displaced vision: Role of proprioception. *Perceptual and Motor Skills*, 1974, *38*, 1251–1256. (a)

Lackner, J. R. Influence of visual rearrangement and visual motion on sound localization. *Neuropsychologia*, 1974, *12*, 291–293. (b)

Lackner, J. R. Influence of abnormal postural and sensory conditions on human sensorimotor localization. *Environmental Biology and Medicine*, *2*(3), 1976, 136–177.

Lackner, J. R. Adaptation to visual and proprioceptive rearrangement: Origin of the differential effectiveness of active and passive movements. *Perception and Psychophysics*, 1977, *21*, 55–59.

Lackner, J. R. Some aspects of sensory-motor control and adaptation in man. In R. D. Walk and H. L. Pick, Jr. (Eds.), *Intersensory perception and sensory integration*. New York: Plenum, 1981.

Lackner, J. R., & Lobovits, D. Adaptation to displaced vision: Evidence for prolonged aftereffects. *Quarterly Journal of Experimental Psychology*, 1977, *29*, 65–69.

Lackner, J. R., & Lobovits, D. Incremental exposure facilitates adaptation to sensory rearrangement. *Aviation, Space, and Environmental Medicine*, 1978, *49*, 362–364.

Lazar, G., & Van Laer, J. Adaptation to displaced vision after experience with lesser displacements. *Perceptual and Motor Skills*, 1968, *26*, 579–582.

Lotto, D., Kern, A., & Morant, R. B. Prism induced tilt after-effects and changed felt head position. Paper presented at meetings of Eastern Psychological Association, Boston, April 1967.

Luria, S. M., & Kinney, J. A. S. Underwater vision. *Science*, 1970, *167*, 1454–1461.

Luria, S. M., Kinney, J. A. S., & Weissman, S. Estimates of size and distance underwater. *American Journal of Psychology*, 1967, *80*, 282–286.

Luria, S. M., McKay, C. L., & Ferris, S. H. Handedness and adaptation to visual distortions of size and distance. *Journal of Experimental Psychology*, 1973, *100*, 263–269.

Mack, A. The role of movement in perceptual adaptation to a tilted retinal image. *Perception and Psychophysics*, 1967, *2*, 65–68.

Mack, A. An investigation of the relationship between eye and retinal image movement in the perception of movement. *Perception and Psychophysics*, 1970, *8*, 291–298.

Mack, A., & Bachant, J. Perceived movement of the afterimage during eye movements. *Perception and Psychophysics*, 1969, *6*, 379–384.

Mack, A., & Chitayat, D. Eye-dependent and disparity adaptation to opposite visual-field rotations. *American Journal of Psychology*, 1970, *83*, 352–371.

Mack, A., Fendrich, R., & Pleune, J. Adaptation to an altered relation between retinal image displacements and saccadic eye movements. *Vision Research*, 1978, *18*, 1321–1327.

Mack, A., & Quartin, T. A new kind of form adaptation: Adaptation to a unidimensional distortion of the image. Paper presented at meetings of Eastern Psychological Association, Philadelphia, April 1974.

Mack, A., & Rock, I. A re-examination of the Stratton effect: Egocentric adaptation to a rotated visual image. *Perception and Psychophysics*, 1968, *4*, 57–62.

Malatesta, V., & Mikaelian, H. H. Dissociation of two modes of visually controlled behavior by prism adaptation. Paper presented at meetings of Eastern Psychological Association, New York, April 1975.

Mann, V. A., Hein, A., & Diamond, R. Patterns of interocular transfer of visuomotor coordination reveal differences in the representation of visual space. *Perception and Psychophysics*, 1979, *25*, 35–41.

Mather, J. A., & Lackner, J. R. Adaptation to visual rearrangement elicited by tonic vibration reflexes. *Experimental Brain Research*, 1975, *24*, 103–105.

Mather, J. A., & Lackner, J. R. Adaptation to visual rearrangement: Role of sensory discordance. *Quarterly Journal of Experimental Psychology*, 1977, *29*, 237–244.

Mather, J. A., & Lackner, J. R. Adaptation to visual displacement with active and passive limb movements: Effect of movement frequency and predictability of movement. *Quarterly Journal of Psychology*, 1980, *32*, 317–323.

Mayhew, J. E. W., & Anstis, S. M. Movement aftereffects contingent on color, intensity and pattern. *Perception and Psychophysics*, 1972, *12*, 77–85.

McDonald, A. P. Revised scale for ambiguity tolerance: Reliability and validity. *Psychological Reports*, 1970, *26*, 791–798.

McDonnell, P. M., & Abraham, W. C. Adaptation to displacing prisms in human infants. *Perception*, 1979, *8*, 175–185.

McDonnell, P. M., & Abraham, W. C. A longitudinal study of prism adaptation in infants from six to nine months of age. *Child Development*, 1981, *52*, 463–469.

McLaughlin, S. C. Parametric adjustment in saccadic eye movements. *Perception and Psychophysics*, 1967, *2*, 359–362.

McLaughlin, S. C., Kelly, M. J., Anderson, R. E., & Wenz, T. G. Localization of a peripheral target during parametric adjustment of saccadic eye movements. *Perception and Psychophysics*, 1968, *4*, 45–48.

McLaughlin, S. C., Rifkin, K. I., & Webster, R. G. Oculomotor adaptation to wedge prisms with no part of the body seen. *Perception and Psychophysics*, 1966, *1*, 452–458.

McLaughlin, S. C., & Webster, R. G. Changes in straight-ahead eye position during adaptation to wedge prisms. *Perception and Psychophysics*, 1967, *2*, 37–44.

Meier, M. J., & French, L. A. Readaptation to prismatic rotations of visual space as a function of lesion laterality and extratemporal

EEG spike activity after temporal lobectomy. *Neuropsychologia*, 1966, *4*, 151–157.

Melamed, L. E., Beckett, P. A., & Halay, M. Individual differences in the visual component of prism adaptation. *Perception*, 1979, *8*, 699–706.

Melamed, L. E., Beckett, P. A., & Hill, G. Individual differences in components of prism adaptation derived from the terminal exposure, distributed practice paradigm. Paper presented at meetings of Midwestern Psychological Association, Chicago, May 1976.

Melamed, L. E., Beckett, P. A., & Wallace, B. The effect of prism strength and response mode on the magnitude of the correction effect in prism viewing. *Perception and Psychophysics*, 1978, *23*, 176–180.

Melamed, L. E., Haley, M., & Gildow, J. W. Effect of external target presence on visual adaptation with active and passive movement. *Journal of Experimental Psychology*, 1973, *98*, 125–130.

Melamed, L. E., Moore, L. A., & Beckett, P. A. Readaptation and decay after prism viewing: An exploration of task variables from the viewpoint of the information discordance hypothesis. *Perception and Psychophysics*, 1979, *26*, 215–220.

Melamed, L. E., & Wallace, B. An analysis of the role of the correction effect in visual adaptation. Paper presented at meetings of Eastern Psychological Association, New York, April 1971.

Melamed, L. E., Wallace, B., Cohen, R. R., & Oakes, S. Correction effect in visual adaptation as measure of field independence-dependence. *Perceptual and Motor Skills*, 1972, *34*, 554.

Melamed, L. E., Wallace, B., & Seyfried, B. Acceleration information for prism adaptation need not be reafferent: A comment on McCarter and Mikaelian (1978). *Perception and Psychophysics*, 1979, *25*, 70–72.

Melvill Jones, G., & Gonshor, A. Goal-directed flexibility in the vestibulo-ocular reflex arc. In G. Lennerstrand and P. Bach-y-Rita (Eds.), *Basic mechanisms of ocular motility and their clinical implications*. New York: Pergamon, 1975.

Melvill Jones, G., & Mandl, G. Effects of strobe light on adaptation of vestibulo-ocular reflex (VOR) to vision reversal. *Brain Research*, 1979, *164*, 300–303.

Mikaelian, H. H. Failure of bilateral transfer in modified eye-hand coordination. Paper presented at meetings of Eastern Psychological Association, New York, April 1963.

Mikaelian, H. H. Adaptation to rearranged eye-foot coordination. Paper presented at meetings of Eastern Psychological Association, New York, April 1966.

Mikaelian, H. H. Relation between adaptation to rearrangement and the source of motor-sensory feedback. *Psychonomic Science*, 1967, *9*, 485–486.

Mikaelian, H. H. Adaptation to rearranged ear-hand coordination. *Perceptual and Motor Skills*, 1969, *29*, 147–150.

Mikaelian, H. H. Adaptation to rearranged eye-foot coordination. *Perception and Psychophysics*, 1970, *8*, 222–224. (a)

Mikaelian, H. H. Failure of intermanual transfer of adaptation to rearranged ear-hand coordination. Paper presented at meetings of Eastern Psychological Association, Atlantic City, April 1970. (b)

Mikaelian, H. H. Lack of bilateral generalization of adaptation to auditory rearrangement. *Perception and Psychophysics*, 1972, *11*, 222–224.

Mikaelian, H. H. Adaptation to displaced hearing: A nonproprioceptive change. *Journal of Experimental Psychology*, 1974, *103*, 326–330.

Mikaelian, H. H. Plasticity of orientation specific chromatic aftereffects. *Vision Research*, 1976, *16*, 459–462.

Mikaelian, H. H., & Held, R. Two types of adaptation to an optically-rotated field. *American Journal of Psychology*, 1964, *77*, 257–263.

Mikaelian, H. H., & Malatesta, V. Specialized adaptation to displaced vision. *Perception*, 1974, *3*, 135–139.

Miller, E. A. Interaction of vision and touch in conflict and non-conflict form perception tasks. *Journal of Experimental Psychology*, 1972, *96*, 114–123.

Miller, J., & Festinger, L. Impact of oculomotor retraining on the visual perception of curvature. *Journal of Experimental Psychology: Human Perception and Performance*, 1977, *3*, 187–200.

Miller, J. M., Anstis, T., & Templeton, W. B. Saccadic plasticity: Parametric adaptive control by retinal feedback. *Journal of Experimental Psychology: Human Perception and Performance*, 1981, *7*, 356–366.

Morant, R. B., & Beller, H. K. Adaptation to prismatically rotated visual fields. *Science*, 1965, *148*, 530–531.

Moulden, B. Adaptation to displaced vision: Reafference is a special case of the cue-discrepancy hypothesis. *Quarterly Journal of Experimental Psychology*, 1971, *23*, 113–117.

Murch, G. M. Classical conditioning of the McCollough effect: Temporal parameters. *Vision Research*, 1976, *16*, 615–619.

Nichols, A. K. *A study of some aspects of perception in the underwater situation*. Unpublished dissertation, University of Leeds. 1967.

Ogle, K. N. *Optics: An introduction for opthalmologists* (2nd ed.). Springfield, IL: Thomas, 1968.

Oman, C. M., Bock, O. L., & Huang, J.-K. Visually induced self-motion sensation adapts rapidly to left-right visual reversal. *Science*, 1980, *209*, 706–708.

Ono, H., & O'Reilly, J. P. Adaptation to underwater distance distortion as a function of different sensory-motor tasks. *Human Factors*, 1971, *13*, 133–140.

O'Reilly, J. P. Adaptation to underwater distance distortion. *Studies on human performance in the sea* (Vol. 1). University of Hawaii, 1975. (a)

O'Reilly, J. P. Shifting adaptive systems with visually distorted input. *Studies on human performance in the sea* (Vol. 1). University of Hawaii, 1975. (b)

Over, R. An experimentally induced conflict between vision and proprioception. *British Journal of Psychology*, 1966, *57*, 335–341.

Paap, K. R., & Ebenholtz, S. M. Perceptual consequences of potentiation in the extraocular muscles: An alternative explanation for adaptation to wedge prisms. *Journal of Experimental Psychology: Human Perception and Performance*, 1976, *2*, 457–468.

Paap, K. R., & Ebenholtz, S. M. Concomitant direction and distance aftereffects of sustained convergence: A muscle potentiation explanation for eye-specific adaptation. *Perception and Psychophysics*, 1977, *21*, 307–314.

Paillard, J. Multichannelling of visual cues and the organization of visually guided responses. In G. E. Stelmach and J. Reguin (Eds.), *Tutorials in motor behavior*. Amsterdam: North-Holland, 1980.

Paillard, J., & Brouchon, M. Active and passive movements in the calibration of position sense. In S. J. Freedman (Ed.), *The neuropsychology of spatially oriented behaviors*. Homewood, IL: Dorsey, 1968.

Paillard, J., Jordan, P., & Brouchon, M. Visual motion cues in prismatic adaptation: Evidence of two separate and additive processes. *Acta Psychologica*, 1981, *48*, 253–270.

Peterson, J., & Peterson, J. K. Does practice with inverting lenses make vision normal? *Psychological Monograph*, 1938, *50* (5, Serial No. 225).

Pick, H. L., Jr., & Hay, J. C. Adaptation to prismatic distortion. *Psychonomic Science*, 1964, *1*, 199–200.

Pick, H. L., Jr., & Hay, J. C. A passive test of the Held reafference hypothesis. *Perceptual and Motor Skills*, 1965, *20*, 1070–1072.

Pick, H. L., Jr., & Hay, J. C. *The distortion experiment as a tool for studying the development of perceptual-motor coordination*. In N. Jenkins & R. H. Pollack (Eds.), *Perceptual development: Its relation to theories of intelligence and cognition*. Chicago: Institute for Juvenile Research, Research Programs in Child Development, 1966. (a)

Pick, H. L., Jr., & Hay, J. C. Gaze-contingent adaptation to prismatic spectacles. *American Journal of Psychology*, 1966, *79*, 443–450. (b)

Pick, H. L., Jr., Hay, J. C., & Martin, R. Adaptation to split-field wedge prism spectacles. *Journal of Experimental Psychology*, 1969, *80*, 125–132.

Pick, H. L., Jr., Hay, J. C., & Pabst, J. Kinesthetic adaptation to visual distortion. Paper presented at meetings of Midwestern Psychological Association, Chicago, May 1963.

Pick, H. L., Jr., Hay, J. C., & Willoughby, R. H. Interocular transfer of adaptation to prismatic distortion. *Perceptual and Motor Skills*, 1966, *23*, 131–135.

Pick, H. L., Jr., Warren, D. H., & Hay, J. C. Sensory conflict in judgments of spatial direction. *Perception and Psychophysics*, 1969, *6*, 203–205.

Pola, J. Voluntary saccades, eye position, and perceived visual direction. In R. A. Monty and J. W. Senders (Eds.), *Eye movements and psychological processes*. Hillsdale, NJ: Erlbaum, 1976.

Posin, R. L. *Perceptual adaptation to contingent visual-field movement: An experimental investigation of position constancy*. Unpublished doctoral dissertation, Yeshiva University, 1966.

Prablanc, C., Tzavaras, A., & Jeannerod, M. Adaptation of the two arms to opposite prism displacements. *Quarterly Journal of Experimental Psychology*, 1975, *27*, 667–671.

Putterman, A. H., Robert, A. L., & Bregman, A. S. Adaptation of the wrist to displacing prisms. *Psychonomic Science*, 1969, *16*, 79–80.

Quinlan, D. Effects of sight of the body and active locomotion in perceptual adaptation. *Journal of Experimental Psychology*, 1970, *86*, 91–96.

Radeau, M. The locus of adaptation to auditory-visual conflict. *Perception*, 1973, *2*, 327–332.

Radeau, M., & Bertelson, P. The aftereffects of ventriloquism. *Quarterly Journal of Experimental Psychology*, 1974, *25*, 63–71.

Redding, G. M. Simultaneous visual adaptation to tilt and displacement: A test of independent processes. *Bulletin of Psychonomic Society*, 1973, *2*, 41–42. (a)

Redding, G. M. Visual adaptation to tilt and displacement: Same or different processes? *Perception and Psychophysics*, 1973, *14*, 193–200. (b)

Redding, G. M. Decay of visual adaptation to tilt and displacement. *Perception and Psychophysics*, 1975, *17*, 203–208. (a)

Redding, G. M. Simultaneous visuomotor adaptation to optical tilt and displacement. *Perception and Psychophysics*, 1975, *17*, 97–100. (b)

Redding, G. M. Additivity in adaptation to optical tilt. *Journal of Experimental Psychology: Human Perception and Performance*, 1978, *4*, 178–190.

Redding, G. M. Modality of task control and the locus of prism adaptation. Paper presented at meetings of Psychonomic Society, Phoenix, November 1979.

Redding, G. M. Effects of homogeneous and variable exposure on magnitude of adaptation to optical tilt. *Journal of Experimental Psychology: Human Perception and Performance*, 1981, *7*, 130–140.

Redding, G. M., & Wallace, B. Components of displacement adaptation in acquisition and decay as a function of hand and hall exposure. *Perception and Psychophysics*, 1976, *20*, 453–459.

Redding, G. M., & Wallace, B. Sources of "overadditivity" in prism adaptation. *Perception and Psychophysics*, 1978, *24*, 58–62.

Rekosh, J. H., & Freedman, S. J. Errors in auditory direction-finding after compensation for visual re-arrangement. *Perception and Psychophysics*, 1967, *2*, 466–468.

Rhoades, R. W. *The effect of a visual feedback delay on adaptation to distorted vision*. Unpublished manuscript, University of California, Riverside, 1968.

Rierdan, J. E., & Wapner, S. Experimental study of adaptation to visual rearrangement deriving from an organismic-developmental approach to cognition. *Perceptual and Motor Skills*, 1966, *23*, 903–916.

Rierdan, J., & Wapner, S. Adaptive changes in the relationship between visual and tactual-kinesthetic perception. *Psychonomic Science*, 1967, *7*, 61–62.

Rock, I. Adaptation to a minified image. *Psychonomic Science*, 1965, *2*, 105–106.

*Rock, I. *The nature of perceptual adaptation*. New York: Basic Books, 1966.

Rock, I., Goldberg, J., & Mack, A. Immediate correction and adaptation based on viewing a prismatically displaced scene. *Perception and Psychophysics*, 1966, *1*, 351–354.

Rock, I., & Victor, J. Vision and touch: An experimentally created conflict between the two senses. *Science*, 1964, *143*, 594–596.

*Ross, H. E. Water, fog and the size-distance invariance hypothesis. *British Journal of Psychology*, 1967, *58*, 301–313.

Ross, H. E. Adaptation of divers to curvature distortion underwater. *Ergonomics*, 1970, *13*, 489–499.

Ross, H. E. Spatial perception underwater. In J. D. Woods and J. N. Lythgoe (Eds.), *Underwater science*, London: Oxford University Press, 1971.

*Ross, H. E. *Behavior and perception in strange environments*. New York: Basic Books, 1975. (a)

Ross, H. E. Mist, murk and visual perception. *New Scientist*, 1975, *19*, 658–660. (b)

Ross, H. E. How important are changes in body weight for mass perception. *Acta Astronautica*, 1981, *8*, 1051–1058.

Ross, H. E., Crickmar, S. D., Sills, N. V., & Owen, E. P. Orientation to the vertical in free divers. *Aerospace Medicine*, 1969, *40*, 728–732.

*Ross, H. E., Franklin, S. S., Weltman, G., & Lennie, P. Adaptation of divers to size distortion under water. *British Journal of Psychology*, 1970, *61*, 365–373.

Ross, H. E., King, S. R., & Snowden, H. Size and distance judgments in the vertical plane under water. *Psychologische Forschung*, 1970, *33*, 155–164.

Ross, H. E., & Lennie, P. Adaptation and counteradaptation to complex optical distortion. *Perception and Psychophysics*, 1972, *12*, 273–277.

Ross, H. E., & Rejman, M. H. Adaptation to speed distortions under water. *British Journal of Psychology*, 1972, *63*, 257–264.

Ross, H. E., Rejman, M. H., & Lennie, P. Adaptation to weight transformation in water. *Ergonomics*, 1972, *15*, 387–397.

Rotter, J. B. Generalized expectancies for internal versus external control of reinforcement. *Psychological Monographs*, 1966, *80*(1, Whole No. 287).

Russotti, J. The measurement of eye torsion during adaptation to a tilted visual field. Unpublished master's thesis. Connecticut College, New London, CT, 1968.

Samuel, J. M. F. Individual differences in the interaction of vision and proprioception. In R. D. Walk and H. L. Pick, Jr. (Eds.), *Intersensory perception and sensory integration*. New York: Plenum, 1981.

Shattuck, S., & Held, R. Color and edge sensitive channels converge on stereo-depth analyzers. *Vision Research*, 1975, *15*, 309–311.

*Shebilske, W. L. Visuo-motor coordination in visual direction and position constancies. In W. Epstein (Ed.), *Perceptual stability and constancy: Mechanisms and processes*. New York: Wiley, 1977.

Singer, G., & Day, R. H. Spatial adaptation and aftereffect with optically transformed vision: Effects of active and passive responding and the relationship between test and exposure responses. *Journal of Experimental Psychology*, 1966, *71*, 725–731.

Slotnick, R. S. Adaptation to curvature distortion. *Journal of Experimental Psychology*, 1969, *81*, 441–448.

Smith, K. U., & Greene, P. A critical period in maturation of performance with space-displaced vision. *Perceptual and Motor Skills*, 1963, *17*, 627–639.

Smith, K. U., & Smith, W. K. *Perception and motion*. Philadelphia: Saunders, 1962.

Smothergill, D. W., Martin, R., & Pick, H. L., Jr. Perceptual-motor performance under rotation of the central field. *Journal of Experimental Psychology*, 1971, *87*, 64–70.

Snyder, F. W., & Pronko, N. H. *Vision with spatial inversion*. Wichita: University of Wichita Press, 1952.

Snyder, F. W., & Snyder, C. W. Vision with spatial inversion: A follow-up study. *Psychological Record*, 1957, *7*, 20–30.

Spanos, N. P., Gorassini, D. R., & Petrusic, W. Hypnotically induced limb anesthesia and adaptation to displacing prisms: A failure to confirm. *Journal of Abnormal Psychology*, 1981, *90*, 329–333.

Spielberger, C. D., Gorsuch, R. L., & Lushene, R. E. *The state-trait anxiety inventory*. Palo Alto, CA; Consulting Psychological Press, 1968.

*Stratton, G. M. Some preliminary experiments on vision without inversion of the retinal image. *Psychological Review*, 1896, *3*, 611–617.

*Stratton, G. M. Upright vision and the retinal image. *Psychological Review*, 1897, *4*, 182–187. (a)

*Stratton, G. M. Vision without inversion of the retinal image. *Psychological Review*, 1897, *4*, 341–360; 463–481. (b)

Stromeyer, C. F., III, & Mansfield, R. J. W. Colored aftereffects produced with moving edges. *Perception and Psychophysics*, 1970, *7*, 108–114.

Taub, E. Prism compensation as a learning phenomenon: A phylogenetic perspective. In S. J. Freedman (Ed.), *The neuropsychology of spatially oriented behavior*, Homewood, Ill.: Dorsey, 1968.

Taub, E., & Goldberg, I. A. Prism adaptation: Control of intermanual transfer by distribution of practice. *Science*, 1973, *180*, 755–757.

Taub, E., & Goldberg, I. A. Use of sensory recombination and somatosensory deafferentation techniques in the investigation of sensory-motor integration. *Perception*, 1974, *3*, 393–408.

Taylor, J. G. *The behavioral basis of perception*. New Haven: Yale University Press, 1962.

Teixeira, R., & Lackner, J. Influence of apparent head position on optokinetic nystagmus and eye posture. *Experimental Brain Research*, 1976, *24*, 435–440.

Templeton, W. B., Howard, I. P., & Lowman, A. E. Passively generated adaptation to prismatic distortion. *Perceptual and Motor Skills*, 1966, *22*, 140–142.

Templeton, W. B., Howard, I. P., & Wilkinson, D. A. Additivity of components of prismatic adaptation. *Perception and Psychophysics*, 1974, *15*, 249–257.

Teuber, H. L. Sensory deprivation, sensory suppression and agnosia: Notes for a neurologic theory. *Journal of Nervous and Mental Disease*, 1961, *132*, 32–40.

Teuber, H. L. The riddle of frontal-lobe function in man. In J. M. Warren and G. Akert (Eds), *The frontal granular cortex and behavior*. New York: McGraw-Hill, 1964.

Tietz, J. D., & Gogel, W. C. Depth generalization of prismatic aftereffects. *American Journal of Psychology*, 1974, *87*, 223–235.

Toates, F. *Control theory in biology and experimental psychology*. London: Hutchinson Educational, 1975.

Uhlarik, J. J. A device for presenting targets and recording positioning responses in one dimension. *Behavior Research Methods and Instrumentation*, 1972, *4*, 15–16.

Uhlarik, J. J. Role of cognitive factors on adaptation to prismatic displacement. *Journal of Experimental Psychology*, 1973, *98*, 223–232.

Uhlarik, J. J., & Canon, L. K. Effects of situational cues on prism-induced aftereffects. *Perception and Psychophysics*, 1970, *7*, 348–350.

Uhlarik, J. J., & Canon, L. K. Influence of concurrent and terminal exposure conditions on the nature of perceptual adaptation. *Journal of Experimental Psychology*, 1971, *91*, 233–239.

Van Laer, E. Transfer effects in adaptation to prismatic displacement. *Psychonomic Science*, 1968, *13*, 85–86.

Vernoy, M. W., & Luria, S. M. Perception of, and adaptation to, a three-dimensional curvature distortion. *Perception and Psychophysics*, 1977, *22*, 245–248.

Victor, J. *The role of movement in perceptual adaptation to curvature*. Unpublished doctoral dissertation, Yeshiva University, 1968.

Von Hofsten, C. Recalibration of the convergence system. *Perception*, 1979, *8*, 37–42.

Walker, J. T. A texture-contingent visual motion aftereffect. *Psychonomic Science*, 1972, *28*, 333–335.

Walker, J. T., & Shea, K. S. A tactual size aftereffect contingent on hand position. *Journal of Experimental Psychology*, 1974, *103*, 668–694.

Wallace, B. Prism adaptation to moving and stationary target exposures. *Perception*, 1975, *4*, 341–347.

Wallace, B. Stability of Wilkinson's linear model of prism adaptation over time for various targets. *Perception*, 1977, *6*, 145–151.

Wallace, B. Visuomotor coordination and intermanual transfer for a proprioceptive reaching task. *Journal of Motor Behavior*, 1978, *10*, 139–147.

Wallace, B. Factors affecting proprioceptive adaptation to prismatic displacement. *Perception and Psychophysics*, 1980, *28*, 550–554.

Wallace, B., & Anstadt, S. P. Target location aftereffects for various age groups. *Journal of Experimental Psychology*, 1974, *103*, 175–177.

Wallace, B., & Fisher, L. E. Proprioception and the production of adaptation and intermanual transfer to prismatic displacement. *Perception and Psychophysics*, 1979, *26*, 113–117.

Wallace, B., & Garrett, J. B. Reduced felt arm sensation effect on visual adaptation. *Perception and Psychophysics*, 1973, *14*, 597–600.

Wallace, B., & Garrett, J. B. Perceptual adaptation with selective reductions of felt sensation. *Perception*, 1975, *4*, 437–445.

Wallace, B., & Hoyenge, K. B. Production of proprioceptive errors with induced hypnotic anesthesia. *International Journal of Clinical and Experimental Hypnosis*, 1980, *28*, 140–147.

Wallace, B., Melamed, L. E., & Cohen, R. R. An analysis of aftereffects in the measurement of the correction effect. *Perception and Psychophysics*, 1973, *14*, 21–23.

Wallace, B., Melamed, L. E., & Kaplan, C. Movement and illumination factors in adaptation to prismatic viewing. *Perception and Psychophysics*, 1973, *13*, 164–168.

Wallace, B., & Redding, G. M. Additivity in prism adaptation as manifested in intermanual and interocular transfer. *Perception and Psychophysics*, 1979, *25*, 133–136.

Wallach, H. Informational discrepancy as a basis of perceptual adaptation. In S. J. Freedman (Ed.), *The neuropsychology of spatially oriented behavior*. Homewood, ILL.: Dorsey, 1968.

*Wallach, H. *On perception*. New York: Quadrangle, 1976.

Wallach, H., & Bacon, J. The constancy of the orientation of the visual field. *Perception and Psychophysics*, 1976, *19*, 492–498.

Wallach, H., & Bacon, J. Two kinds of adaptation in the constancy of visual direction and their different effects on the perception of shape and visual direction. *Perception and Psychophysics*, 1977, *21*, 227–242.

Wallach, H., Bacon, J., & Schulman, P. Adaptation in motion perception: Alteration of induced motion. *Perception and Psychophysics*, 1978, *24*, 509–514.

Wallach, H., & Barton, W. Adaptation to optically produced curvature of frontal planes. *Perception and Psychophysics*, 1975, *18*, 21–25.

Wallach, H., & Flaherty, E. W. Covariance as a principle in perceptual adaptation. *Psychologia*, 1974, *17*, 159–165.

Wallach, H., & Flaherty, E. W. Rapid adaptation to a prismatic distortion. *Perception and Psychophysics*, 1976, *19*, 261–266.

Wallach, H., & Floor, L. On the relation of adaptation to field displacement during head movements to the constancy of visual direction. *Perception and Psychophysics*, 1970, *8*, 95–98.

Wallach, H., & Frey, K. J. Adaptation in the constancy of visual direction measured by a one-trial method. *Perception and Psychophysics*, 1969, *5*, 249–252.

Wallach, H., & Frey, K. J. Adaptation in distance perception based on oculomotor cues. *Perception and Psychophysics*, 1972, *11*, 77–83. (a)

Wallach, H., & Frey, K. J. Differences in the dissipation of the effect of adaptation to two kinds of field displacement during head movements. *Perception and Psychophysics*, 1972, *11*, 31–34. (b)

Wallach, H., & Frey, K. J. On counteradaptation. *Perception and Psychophysics*, 1972, *11*, 161–165. (c)

Wallach, H., Frey, K. J., & Bode, K. A. The nature of adaptation in distance perception based on oculomotor cues. *Perception and Psychophysics*, 1972, *11*, 110–116.

Wallach, H., & Frey, K. J., & Romney, G. Adaptation to field displacement during head movement unrelated to the constancy of visual direction. *Perception and Psychophysics*, 1969, *5*, 253–256.

Wallach, H., & Halperin, P. Eye muscle potentiation does not account for adaptation in distance perception based oculomotor cues. *Perception and Psychophysics*, 1977, *22*, 427–430.

Wallach, H., & Huntington, D. Counteradaptation after exposure to displaced visual direction. *Perception and Psychophysics*, 1973, *13*,

519–524.

Wallach, H., & Karsh, E. B. The modification of stereoscopic depth perception and the kinetic depth effect. *American Journal of Psychology*, 1963, *76*, 429–435. (a)

Wallach, H., & Karsh, E. B. Why the modification of stereoscopic depth-perception is so rapid. *American Journal of Psychology*, 1963, *76*, 413–420. (b)

Wallach, H., & Kravitz, J. H. The measurement of the constancy of visual direction and of its adaptation. *Psychonomic Science*, 1965, *2*, 217–218. (a)

Wallach, H., & Kravitz, J. H. Rapid adaptation in the constancy of visual direction with active and passive rotation. *Psychonomic Science*, 1965, *3*, 165–166. (b)

Wallach, H., & Kravitz, J. H. Adaptation in the constancy of visual direction tested by measuring the constancy of auditory direction. *Perception and Psychophysics*, 1968, *4*, 299–303.

Wallach, H., Kravitz, J. H., & Lindauer, J. A passive condition for rapid adaptation to displaced visual direction. *American Journal of Psychology*, 1963, *76*, 568–578.

Wallach, H., & Lewis, C. The effect of abnormal displacement of the retinal image during eye movements. *Perception and Psychophysics*, 1965, *1*, 25–29.

Wallach, H., Moore, M. E., & Davidson, L. Modification of stereoscopic depth perception. *American Journal of Psychology*, 1963, *76*, 191–204.

Wallach, H., & O'Leary, A. Adaptation in distance perception with head-movement parallex serving as the veridical cue. *Perception and Psychophysics*, 1979, *25*, 42–46.

Wallach, H., & Smith, A. Visual and proprioceptive adaptation to altered oculomotor adjustments. *Perception and Psychophysics*, 1972, *11*, 413–416.

Warren, D. H., & Cleaves, W. T. Visual-proprioceptive interaction under large amounts of conflict. *Journal of Experimental Psychology*, 1971, *90*, 206–214.

*Warren, D. H., & Platt, B. B. The subject: A neglected factor in recombination research. *Perception*, 1974, *3*, 421–438.

Warren, D. H., & Platt, B. B. Understanding prism adaptation: An individual differences approach. *Perception and Psychophysics*, 1975, *17*, 337–345.

Webster, R. G. The relationship between cognitive, motor-kinesthetic, and oculomotor adaptation. *Perception and Psychophysics*, 1969, *6*, 33–38.

Weerts, T. C., & Thurlow, W. R. The effects of eye position and expectation on sound localization. *Perception and Psychophysics*, 1971, *9*, 35–39.

Weinstein, S., Sersen, E. A., Fisher, L., & Weisinger, M. Is reafference necessary for visual adaptation? *Perceptual and Motor Skills*, 1964, *18*, 641–648.

Weinstein, S. Sersen, E. A., & Weinstein, D. S. An attempt to replicate a study of disarranged eye-hand coordination. *Perceptual and Motor Skills*, 1964, *18*, 629–632.

Welch, R. B. Adaptation to prism-displaced vision: The importance of target pointing. *Perception and Psychophysics*, 1969, *5*, 305–309.

Welch, R. B. Discriminative conditioning of prism adaptation. *Perception and Psychophysics*, 1971, *10*, 90–92. (a)

Welch, R. B. Prism adaptation: The "target-pointing effect" as a function of exposure trials. *Perception and Psychophysics*, 1971, *9*, 102–104. (b)

Welch, R. B. The effect of experienced limb identity upon adaptation to simulated displacement of the visual field. *Perception and Psychophysics*, 1972, *12*, 453–456.

Welch, R. B. Research on adaptation to rearranged vision: 1966–1974. *Perception*, 1974, *3*, 367–392. (a)

Welch, R. B. Speculations on a model of prism adaptation. *Perception*, 1974, *3*, 451–460. (b)

*Welch, R. B. *Perceptual modification: Adapting to altered sensory environments*. New York: Academic Press, 1978.

Welch, R. B., & Abel, M. R. The generality of the "target-pointing effect" in prism adaptation. *Psychonomic Science*, 1970, *20*, 226–227.

Welch, R. B., Bleam, R., & Needham, S. A. *Variables affecting the postexposure decline of prism adaptation*. Unpublished manuscript, University of Kansas, 1970.

Welch, R. B., Choe, C. S., & Heinrich, D. R. Evidence for a three-component model of prism adaptation. *Journal of Experimental Psychology*, 1974, *103*, 700–705.

Welch, R. B., & Goldstein, G. Prism adaptation and brain damage. *Neuropsychologia*, 1972, *10*, 387–394.

Welch, R. B., & Rhoades, R. W. The manipulation of informational feedback and its effects upon prism adaptation. *Canadian Journal of Psychology*, 1969, *23*, 415–428.

Welch, R. B., & Warren, D. H. Immediate perceptual response to intersensory discrepancy. *Psychological Bulletin*, 1980, *88*(3), 638–667.

Welch, R. B., & Warren, D. H. A comparison of intersensory bias and prism adaptation. In L. Spillman and B. R. Wooten (Eds.), *Sensory experience, adaptation and perception*. New York: Erlbaum, 1984.

Welch, R. B., Widawski, W. H., Harrington, J., & Warren, D. H. An examination of the relationship between visual capture and prism adaptation. *Perception and Psychophysics*, 1979, *25*, 126–132.

Wells, M. J., & Ross, H. E. Distortion in underwater sound localization. *Aviation, Space, and Environmental Medicine*, 1980, *51*, 767–774.

Wertheimer, M., & Arena, A. J. Effect of exposure time on adaptation to disarranged hand-eye coordination. *Perceptual and Motor Skills*, 1959, *9*, 159–164.

Wilkinson, D. A. Visual-motor control loop: A linear system? *Journal of Experimental Psychology*, 1971, *89*, 250–257.

Willey, C. F., Inglis, E., & Pearce, C. H. Reversal of auditory localization. *Journal of Experimental Psychology*, 1937, *20*, 114–130.

Willey, R., Gyr, J. W., & Henry, A. Changes in the perception of spatial location: A test of potentiation vs. recalibration theory. *Perception and Psychophysics*, 1978, *24*, 356–360.

Wohlwill, J. F. Perceptual learning. *Annual Review of Psychology*, 1966, *17*, 201–232.

*Woods, J. D., & Lythgoe, J. N. (Eds), *Underwater science*. London: Oxford University Press, 1971.

Wooster, M. Certain factors in the development of a new spatial coordination. *Psychological Monographs*, 1923, *32*(4, Whole No. 146).

Wundt, W. Zur Theorie der raumlichen. Gesichtswohrnehmungen. *Philosophische Studien*, 1898, *14*, 1–118.

Yachzel, B., & Lackner, J. Adaptation to displaced vision: Evidence for transfer of adaptation and long-lasting aftereffects. *Perception and Psychophysics*, 1977, *22*, 147–151.

Yarbus, A. L. *Eye movements and vision*. New York: Plenum, 1967.

*Young, P. T. Auditory localization with acoustical transposition of the ears. *Journal of Experimental Psychology*, 1928, *11*, 399–429.

CHAPTER 25

INTERSENSORY INTERACTIONS

ROBERT B. WELCH

Department of Psychology, University of Kansas, Lawrence, Kansas

DAVID H. WARREN

Department of Psychology, University of California, Riverside, California

CONTENTS

Traditionally, the sensory modalities have been studied in isolation from one another. This strategy, however, flies in the face of the anatomical, physiological, and behavioral facts of human perception. Sherrington (1920), for example, noted that "All parts of the nervous system are connected together and no part of it is probably ever capable of reaction without affecting and being affected by various other parts . . . "(p.8). It should be clear, then, that the procedure of examining each of the senses as if it were independent of the others can lead, at best, to only partial understanding of everyday perceptual experience. Certainly, one is rarely if ever confronted in the everyday world with only a single form of sensory stimulation. For example, a person might be looking at an object while simultaneously feeling it and hearing someone's voice off to one side. In this instance, then, the visual and haptic senses are both conveying information about the shape of the object, and the auditory modality happens to be stimulated at the same time. Thus sometimes two (or more) modalities may be providing the same sort of information about an object (e.g., its shape) whereas at other times several sensory modalities may be simultaneously active but signaling very different events. The question in either case is whether and to what extent perception of an event by means of one modality is influenced by concurrent activity in other sensory modalities. This, then, is the question of *intersensory interaction*, the area to which this chapter is addressed.

It is important at the outset to explicate as clearly and operationally as possible what we mean by "intersensory interaction." We define it as the situation in which *the perception of an event as measured in terms of one sensory modality is changed in some way by the concurrent stimulation of one or more other sensory modalities*. In operational terms, the necessary conditions for the evaluation of intersensory interaction are (1) the measurement of the nature of the perception of an event via one modality and (2) the measurement of the perception of the event through this modality while another modality is simultaneously being stimulated. If perception by means of the primary modality differs as a function of the presence or absence of the second modality, then intersensory interaction may be said to have occurred. It will be noted that the current definition of intersensory interaction presupposes neither some specific underlying physiological mechanism(s) nor a single theoretical account common to all the various forms of interaction observed. Although for some forms of intersensory interaction possible physiological explanations are apparent and will be discussed, for other effects the potential physiological mechanisms are not obvious and we have not felt the need to speculate about them. Indeed it is, we believe, quite possible to provide perfectly satisfactory explanations for some forms of intersensory interaction without reference to physiological processes. It will become clear that a variety of mechanisms are necessary to account for the great diversity of the intersensory interaction effects described in this chapter. It will also be apparent that many of the findings in this area are mutually contradictory and that a number of important variables have not been adequately controlled or parameters explored. The literature on nonspecific accessory effects on sensory thresholds (Section 1.2) is a prime example of confusing, contradictory, and occasionally nonreplicable intersensory interactions. The aim of this chapter is to organize systematically the various types of intersensory interaction and to clarify some of the methodological and theoretical issues in this area. This, then, represents the logical initial step toward a better understanding of this crucial aspect of perceptual functioning.

Our view of intersensory interaction assumes that the sensory modalities are functionally differentiated in important ways that extend well beyond the physiological distinctness of the anatomically separate receptors and neural pathways. The various senses are not simply equivalent ways of perceiving important classes of events; they differ in both the precision and rapidity of their action. In short, they differ in their *appropriateness* for the perception of various events. As an example, for human beings vision is more precise and accurate than any other modality for the perception of spatial events, whereas audition is best suited for the perception of temporal events. In these respects, at least, the modalities differ and must be separately assessed.

The interaction between sensory modalities represents one aspect of the larger issue concerning how the various senses are related to each other—the area of intersensory organization. It was noted as long ago as the time of Aristotle that sensory modalities have both unique and common characteristics. Thus whereas hue can be perceived only by vision and pitch by audition, information about spatial location can be conveyed by both modalities. Research has documented and analyzed the many commonalities among the sensory modalities (e.g., Marks, 1978). At issue in this chapter, however, is not whether the sensory modalities share common capacities or are wholly or partially interchangeable, but rather if the presence of one modality affects perception through another modality. As a consequence of this aim, this chapter is *not* concerned with the voluminous literature demonstrating that many sensory modalities are interchangeable. Thus we omit the research on cross-modality matching and transfer (e.g., Jones, 1981), sensory substitution (e.g., Bach-y-Rita, Collins, Saunders, White, & Scadden, 1969), and synesthesia (e.g., Marks, 1975). Also generally absent from the chapter is research in which the primary aim was the evaluation of special populations, such as children, the blind, the retarded, and poor readers. Finally, we are not concerned with intermodality relations as they bear on the areas of language, speech, or memory.

The chapter has been organized according to the major perceptual capacities. First to be discussed are intersensory interactions that affect detection thresholds and response speed. These are followed by sections on spatial events (spatial acuity, orientation, egocentric localization, and shape/size/texture), and, finally, temporal events (rate, duration, pattern).

Within most of the major sections the material is organized into four topics. First, each relevant modality is compared with respect to the characteristic manner in which it provides information about the class of events (e.g., spatial perception) under consideration. This section, then, provides the basic information about each modality that may prove useful in understanding the interaction between or among these modalities. Second, it will be asked if experience via a specific sensory modality is affected by the mere presence of other sensory stimulation when the two (or more) sensory inputs are unrelated meaningfully to each other. This may be referred to as the effect of *nonspecific accessory stimulation.* A third issue concerns the extent to which one form of sensory information serves as a *context* that is either necessary for or facilitative of perception in another modality. An example is the finding by Warren (1970) and others that the localization of an unseen sound source is more precise when presented in the context of a textured visual background than when heard in the dark. Finally, each major section concludes by assessing the degree to which two (or more) sensory modalities interact when they are providing information about the same characteristic of an object or event (e.g., its shape, location, temporal pattern). It may be asked, for example, whether the perception of spatial location of an object as signaled by vision is changed when auditory information about its location is added. Thus it may be seen that our discussion of intersensory interactions, within a particular perceptual task, moves from nonspecific to specific effects. We examine first intersensory interactions with respect to detection thresholds and response speed.

1. DETECTION THRESHOLDS AND RESPONSE SPEED

1.1. Comparisons of the Various Modalities

It is nonsensical to attempt to compare the various sensory modalities with respect to their detection thresholds if there is no common unit of measurement available. Thus the fact that, under optimal conditions, the lowest perceptible skin pressure (applied to the tip of the tongue) is about 2 $g{\cdot}mm^{-2}$, whereas the least intense light that can be seen is about 0.000003 $cd{\cdot}m^{-2}$, tells us nothing about the relative sensitivity of touch and vision. In short, we have no direct way of comparing $g{\cdot}mm^{-2}$ to $cd{\cdot}m^{-2}$. On the other hand, it does make some sense to compare modalities with respect to observers' reaction time (RT) to each because this represents a common unit of measure (i.e., latency between stimulus and response, in seconds).

It has been found in a variety of studies that, for human observers, RT is faster to a sound or to a tactual stimulus than to a light. Thus Riggs (1971) noted that for practiced observers and high stimulus intensities (units of measurement not specified), RTs for visual stimuli are about 150 msec, whereas RTs for strong auditory or tactual stimuli are about 110–120 msec. The values for these RTs are inversely related to intensity (e.g., Kohfeld, 1971; Raab, Fehrer, & Hershenson, 1961; Woodrow, 1915) and duration (e.g., Froeberg, 1907) and, in the case of vision and touch, to spatial extensity (e.g., Froeberg, 1907) and locus on the receptor surface (e.g., Poffenberger, 1912).

Evidence from neurophysiological studies suggests that the basis of the relatively long RT to respond to light is the time required for processing signals in the retina (e.g., Bartley & Bishop, 1933; Malis & Kruger, 1956). This extra time is required because of the relatively slow photochemical processes in the rods and cones and the spatial analysis that the eye performs so much better than the other "spatial" senses.

In a relatively recent study, Kohfeld (1971) argued that the traditionally reported difference between visual and auditory RT is merely the result of a failure to match the two stimuli for subjective intensity. Indeed, when Kohfeld used a common scale of measurement (i.e., decibels, as proposed by S. S. Stevens, 1955) he found no difference between auditory and visual RT when the two stimuli were both set at 60 or 90 dB, but did obtain the traditional difference at 30 dB. He argued that the difference in visual and auditory RTs in the latter case was due to the relatively slow response of vision under scotopic conditions. On the other hand, Goldstone (1968b), using psychophysically matched auditory and visual intensities (84 dB sound pressure level (SPL) and 18.8 $cd{\cdot}m^{-2}$, respectively) obtained the typical 40-msec RT difference in favor of audition.

For other sensory modalities (e.g., warmth, cold, pain, smell, taste) it is difficult to get "pure" measures of RT because touch receptors are frequently also stimulated. Nevertheless, attempts have been made to measure reaction latencies to these stimuli; the outcomes of these studies were reviewed by Woodworth and Schlosberg (1960, Chapter 2).

Finally, the RT to the onset of bodily rotation (vestibular stimulation) appears to be quite variable, with a median value of about 400 msec (Baxter & Travis, 1938).

1.2. Effects of Nonspecific Accessory Stimulation on Detection Thresholds

Numerous studies have demonstrated that detection thresholds measured for one sensory modality (the "primary stimulus") are influenced by concomitant or temporally proximal stimulation of a second modality (the "accessory stimulus"). For reviews of this literature, see Gilbert (1941), Loveless, Brebner, and Hamilton (1970), London (1954), and Ryan (1940). These experiments are characterized by the absence of any meaningful or structural relationship (other than temporal proximity) between the two stimuli. An example of such a study would be one in which the auditory absolute threshold obtained with the lights on is compared to that found in the dark. The majority of studies on the effects of nonspecific accessory stimulation on sensory thresholds have been carried out by Russian investigators whose published reports, unfortunately, have rarely been translated into English. For the Western world, the primary source of information about the vast Soviet literature on this subject is a relatively old review by London (1954). Unhappily, London concludes that these investigations were frequently problematical. To quote London, " . . . even a casual survey of the Soviet literature yields ready evidence of inadequate instrumentation and methodology, scanty detail, and a primitiveness in the statistical treatment of data which makes anything beyond an arithmetic mean a rare encounter" (London, 1954, p. 531). Perhaps the most serious drawback to all this research has been the systematic failure to use criterion-free methods (e.g., the signal-detection paradigm) by which to examine these phenomena. As a consequence of these problems and the fact that most of the reported effects are small and fragile, we only cursorily review the literature in this area. We hope that such a review will serve to point out topics and methodological considerations for further research in this potentially important area.

Although it seems that nearly every possible combination of the human senses has been the subject of at least one investigation, the great majority of the studies on nonspecific interactions involve vision and audition.

1.2.1. Visual Sensitivity. Although some investigators (e.g., Maruyama, 1959; Newhall, 1923; Watkins, 1964) have reported a lowered visual absolute threshold as a result of accessory auditory stimulation, others have obtained either an increased threshold (e.g., Davis, 1966) or both effects, depending on the experimental condition (e.g., Ince, 1968; Thorne, 1934). Variables affecting the direction and magnitude of the effects are the intensity, frequency, and time of onset of the auditory accessory stimulation (e.g., Maruyama, 1959), predominant wavelength and retinal locus of the visual primary stimulus (e.g., London, 1954), and the relationship between ear stimulated and the half of the visual field tested (Allen & Schwartz, 1940; Maruyama, 1961).

London (1954) has described Russian studies purporting to have obtained effects on visual thresholds from an extremely diverse set of accessory stimuli, including stimulation of the cold (versus warm) receptors, sitting in a comfortable position (versus standing), the taste of sweet, salt, acid, and quinine solutions, light-to-moderate (versus heavy) exercise, bodily rotation, uteral expansion, and bladder distention.

The Russians (as cited by London, 1954) have also claimed that the time required for dark adaptation is substantially reduced by such accessory events as stimulation of the cold receptors, physical exercise, and a variety of taste objects. Other investigators have either failed to replicate these observations (Chapanis, Rouse, & Schacter, 1949; H.W. Rose & Schmidt, 1947) or found only minor effects (Matthews & Luczak, 1944). Chapanis et al., for example, were unable to obtain any change in the rate of dark adaptation as a result of exposure to an olfactory stimulus (oil of wintergreen), loud and soft tones, light muscular exercise, or pressure to the back of the hand.

1.2.2. Auditory Sensitivity. Perhaps the earliest observation of intersensory interaction was that of Bartholmus (1669, cited by Knox, 1945b), who noted that partially deaf people seem to be able to hear better in the light than in the dark. This report was corroborated by Freund and Hoffmann (1929), who found that, indeed, light improved the auditory acuity of the hard-of-hearing. As usual, subsequent research has shown the situation to be complicated by a variety of factors. These include the predominant hue of the accessory visual stimulus (London, 1954; O'Hare, 1956), the predominant pitch of the primary auditory stimulus (O'Hare, 1956; Sheridan, Cimbalo, Sills, & Alluisi, 1966), the relative onsets of the two stimuli (Kuroki, 1937), and the relationship between the side of the visual field stimulated and the ear tested (Maruyama, 1961, Experiment 1).

The interval between the accessory and primary stimuli has been shown to bear on the effect. Child and Wendt (1938) obtained the greatest facilitation of auditory sensitivity when the light preceded the tone by 0.5 sec (see Figures 25.1 and 25.2). Other types of accessory stimulation shown by the Russians (as cited by London, 1954) to influence auditory detection thresholds include exposure to cold, certain tastes, and head tilt. Heymans (1904) also reported effects from the application of electrical shock to the fingers.

1.2.3. Tactual Sensitivity. Thresholds for touch and pressure are lowered by exposure to weak sounds but raised when the accessory auditory stimulation is intensified (Jacobson, 1911; Urbantschitsch, 1888). Johnson (1920) found that tactual discrimination is slightly better (2%) in the light than in the dark, whereas von Schiller (1932b, cited by Ryan, 1940) facilitated his subjects' tactual impressions of vibration and roughness by providing them with concomitant exposure to a "rough" auditory stimulus.

1.2.4. Important Factors. A number of factors appear to be importantly involved in the diverse results described in this section. One of these is stimulus intensity. The preponderance of evidence indicates that when the accessory stimulus is of low-to-moderate intensity the effect on the primary stimulus is one of facilitation, whereas highly intense accessory stimuli are inhibitory (Jacobson, 1911); T. Shigehisa & Symons, 1973a, 1973b; P.M.J. Shigehisa, Shigehisa, & Symons, 1973).

ec Naturally, it is uncertain how, in absolute terms, one is to judge the intensity of an accessory stimulus. Nevertheless, it seems likely that some of the apparent contradictions in this literature can be explained by inter-investigator differences in the choice of stimulus intensities. It would seem, furthermore, that what is crucial here is the *relationship* between the apparent intensity (loudness) of the accessory stimulus to that of the primary stimulus. Little or no research has involved the systematic manipulation of the intensities of both the accessory and the primary stimulus. Another important variable that must be taken into consideration in evaluating and comparing the myriad studies of nonspecific accessory effects is the timing and duration of the accessory and primary stimuli. It appears safe to conclude that the initial effects of the accessory stimulus are different from the later effects. For example, several studies (Child & Wendt, 1938; Kuroki, 1937) found that the greatest increase in auditory sensitivity as a result of visual stimulation occurred when the light preceded the sound by 0.3–0.5 sec. Continued presentation of the accessory stimulus appears to

Figure 25.1. (*Opposite*) Proportion of reported occurrence of a tone as a function of delay between the onset of a light flash (the accessory stimulus) and a tone (the primary stimulus) for each of 11 subjects. (The dashed horizontal line represents the frequency of reports of a tone in the absence of light.) The accessory visual stimulation entailed a foveally presented 2° circular patch whose intensity was increased to 150 cd · mm^{-2} for 0.1 sec at varying intervals relative to a 1,000-Hz tone which was presented for 165 msec at each of five intensitites, chosen so as to bracket the subject's absolute threshold. The intervals used were light 2, 1, and 0.5 sec before tone, light and tone simultaneous, and light following tone by 0.5 sec. The accessory visual stimulus facilitated auditory sensitivity for all subjects, the optimal delay differing for various subjects, but generally falling around 0.5 sec (light before tone), with essentially no facilitation with the 2-sec interval. (From I. L. Child & G. R. Wendt, The temporal course of the influence of visual stimulation upon the auditory threshold, *Journal of Experimental Psychology, 23*. Copyright 1938 by American Psychological Association. Reprinted with permission.)

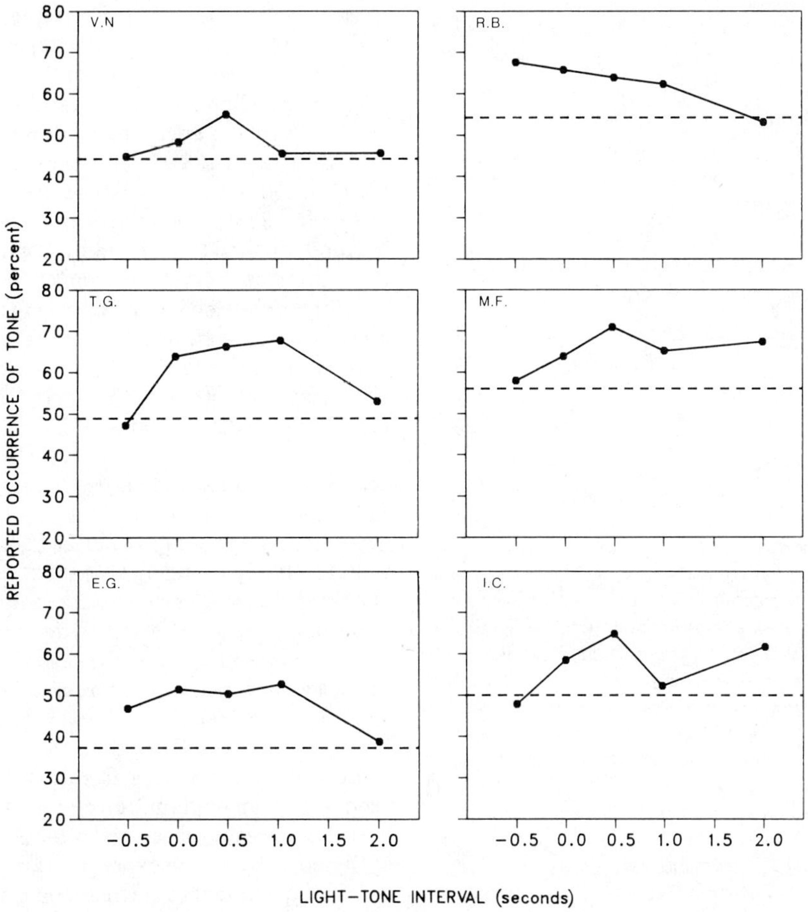
V.N
R.B.
T.G.
M.F.
E.G.
I.C.
REPORTED OCCURRENCE OF TONE (percent)
LIGHT–TONE INTERVAL (seconds)
-0.5 0.0 0.5 1.0 1.5 2.0
20 30 40 50 60 70 80

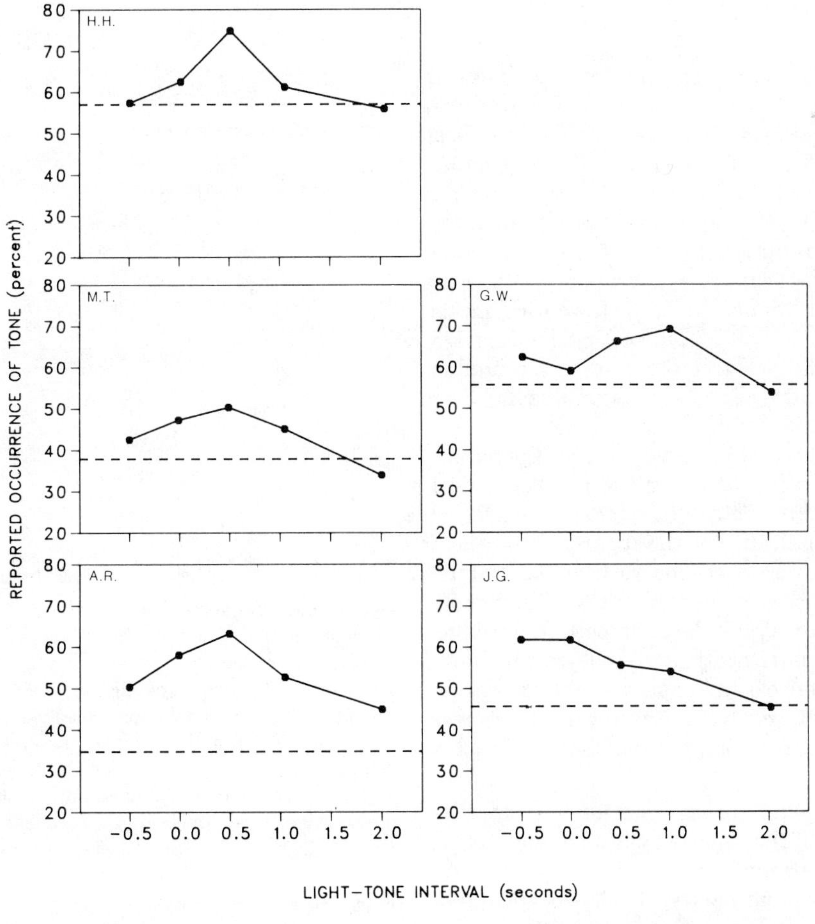
H.H.
M.T.
G.W.
A.R.
J.G.
REPORTED OCCURRENCE OF TONE (percent)
LIGHT–TONE INTERVAL (seconds)
-0.5 0.0 0.5 1.0 1.5 2.0
20 30 40 50 60 70 80

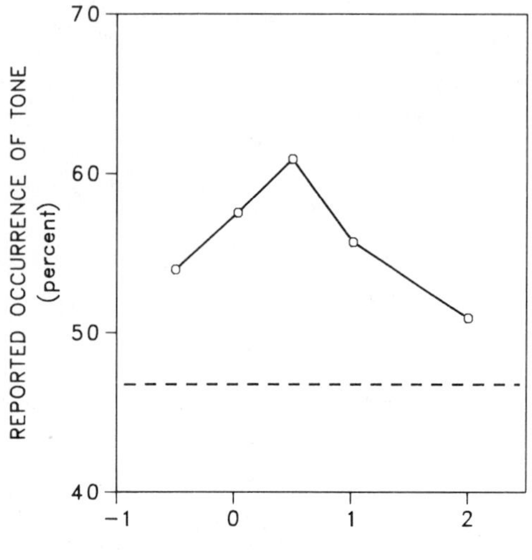

Figure 25.2. Proportion of reported occurrence of tone as a function of delay between the onset of a light flash (the accessory stimulus) and a tone (the primary stimulus) for 11 subjects combined. (The dashed horizontal line represents the frequency of reports of a tone in the absence of light.) The accessory visual stimulation entailed a foveally presented 2° circular patch whose intensity was increased to 150 cd · mm^{-2} for 0.1 sec at varying intervals relative to a 1,000-Hz tone which was presented for 165 msec at each of five intensities, chosen so as to bracket the subject's absolute threshold. The intervals used were light 2, 1, and 0.5 sec before tone, light and tone simultaneous, and light following tone by 0.5 sec. The maximal visual facilitation of audition occurred with a 0.5-sec light-tone interval. (From I. L. Child & G. R. Wendt, The temporal course of the influence of visual stimulation upon the auditory threshold, *Journal of Experimental Psychology, 23*. Copyright 1938 by American Psychological Association. Reprinted with permission.)

reduce its effectiveness (facilitatory or inhibitory), probably as a result of habituation (Davis, 1966; London, 1954; Watkins, 1964; Watkins & Feehrer, 1964, 1965). An example of this effect is presented in Figure 25.3. As with the parameter of stimulus intensity, a consideration of the timing and duration of the accessory and primary stimuli may help to clarify apparent contradictions in the literature. Ogilvie (1956), for example, explained his failure to replicate Kravkov's (e.g., 1935, cited by London, 1954) effect of continuous sound on the critical flicker fusion (CFF) threshold (see Section 3.3.1) by noting that Kravkov examined the effect at the onset of the accessory stimulus, whereas Ogilvie waited until the accessory stimulus had been present for 3 min.

A final potentially important variable concerns the nature of the primary stimulus task, including the psychophysical method used. Von Schiller and Wolff (1933), for example, found that changes in auditory pitch affected the apparent brightness of a visual field if the latter were in the form of *film color* (labile) but not if it were in *surface color* (see Wyszecki, Chapter 9). The complexity of the task may also be an important variable. T. Shigehisa (1974) found that, for introverted subjects, auditory stimuli inhibited performance on a simple visual task, but facilitated complex task performance; for extroverts there was some facilitation of the simple task, but none of the complex task.

1.2.5. Theoretical Implications and Conclusions. Despite the tenuousness of many of the reported effects of nonspecific accessory stimulation, a variety of explanations have been offered. These include, most prominently, (1) physiological processes, (2) attention deployment and distraction, (3) suggestion, and (4) changes in response criteria.

The most common interpretation proposed involves physiological mechanisms, peripheral or central. At a peripheral level, some of the effects may be due to changes in muscle tonus (e.g., Börnstein, 1931, 1936; Johnson, 1920), pupil dilation, (e.g., London, 1954), changes in the tension of the ossicles (e.g., Child & Wendt, 1938), ionic balance in the eyeball (e.g., Semenovskaia & Kondorskaia, 1950, cited by London, 1954), or activation of the autonomic nervous system (ANS).

Interpretations in terms of central physiological processes have focused on stimulation of the reticular activating system (RAS) and "cross talk" between sensory nerves that happen to pass near each other in the brain (Davis, 1966; London, 1954; H.L. Miller, 1969; Symons, 1954).

A possible basis of at least some of the intersensory effects described in this section is the observers' attention deployment. Thus, for example, if the accessory stimulus attracts attention away from the primary stimulus task, performance on the latter would be likely to suffer. This effect would be expected primarily at the onset (and perhaps shortly thereafter) of the accessory stimulus. In cases where the effects are observable much later, the distraction hypothesis is less viable. If, on the other hand, the accessory stimulus increases observers' attention to the primary stimulus, perhaps via a general arousal effect due to stimulation of the RAS, then the effect should be one of facilitation. Of course, before attentional processes can be seriously proposed as an explanation of a given intersensory effect some basis for assessing observers' attention deployment, independent of the outcome of the experiment, must be provided.

In experiments in which one sensory modality appears to affect another in terms of a dimension that they share (e.g.,

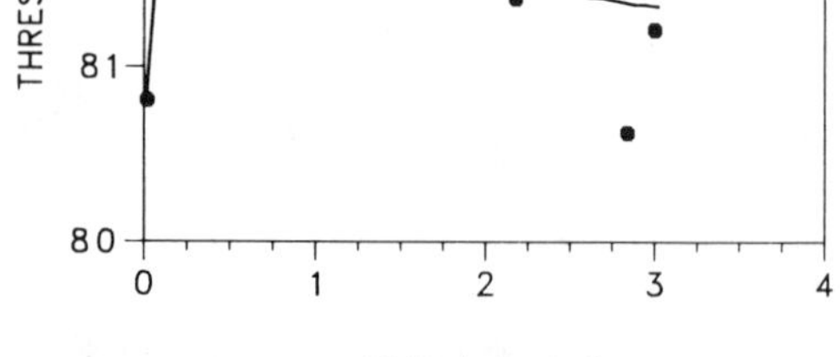

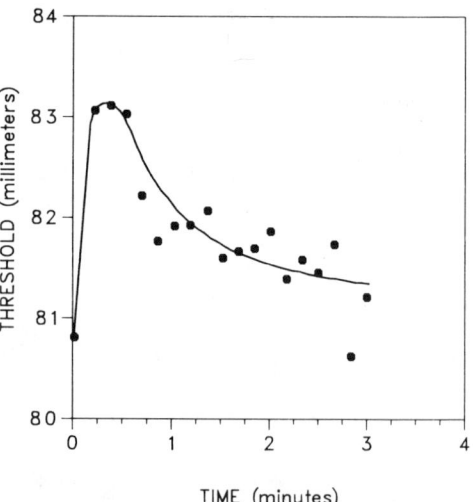

Figure 25.3. Visual threshold as a function of duration of accessory auditory stimulation. Dark-adapted subjects viewed a circular visual target with a 0.5-in. diameter, located 2° below the fovea; absolute thresholds were obtained by means of the method of adjustment. Simultaneous with the light, a 70-dB SPL, 1,550-Hz tone was presented via earphones for 3.5 min, followed by a 4–5 min rest and two more 6-min presentations with an intervening rest period. The figure, which depicts the results for the first 3 min, reveals an initial increase in visual threshold, followed by a rapid decrease toward the baseline. A neurophysiological explanation was offered for this effect. (From E. T. Davis, Heteromodal effects upon visual thresholds, *Psychological Monographs, 80*. Copyright 1966 by American Psychological Association. Reprinted with permission.)

intermittency, intensity) the results may merely reveal the effects of *suggestion*. Thus, for example, if a light is reported as brighter when a loud sound is present, one must be concerned with the possibility that the observers' awareness of the common psychological dimension (intensity) may be biasing their *report* and that the effect is therefore not actually one of perception.

Finally, related to the preceding point, it is very important to note that some of the reported intersensory effects may be interpreted merely as changes in response criteria. Thus, for example, if a sound and a light are presented simultaneously or in close temporal proximity and this situation is compared to one of sound alone, a lowering of the absolute threshold for the light in the presence of the sound might be due simply to the observers' invocation of a more liberal response decision rule, rather than a facilitation of visual sensitivity. The use of a signal detection procedure would clarify this situation (see Falmagne, Chapter 1). To be sure, there are a number of situations in which this interpretation would not be reasonable. For example, studies demonstrating an effect of an auditory accessory stimulus that is different for visual sensitivity in the retinal periphery than in the fovea cannot be reasonably explained by a criterion change. More will be said about this potential explanation of the effects of nonspecific accessory stimulation in the next section.

Whether the effects of nonspecific accessory stimulation on sensory thresholds are of any practical or theoretical significance remains to be seen. Because the effects are generally small,. they probably do not have much practical importance. And because the results have so far not been amenable to any unifying theory (or even convincing mini-theories), it is difficult to assess their theoretical significance.

1.3. The Effects of Discrete Signals in One Modality on Detection RT in a Second Modality—A Context Effect

Another measure of perceptual sensitivity is the speed with which the observer is able to react to the presence of a suprathreshold stimulus. As seen in Section 1.1, there are intermodality differences in stimulus detection RTs. This section deals with the literature demonstrating a facilitatory effect (i.e., shortened RT) for the detection of a stimulus in one modality when it is preceded by or coincident with a stimulus in another modality. According to the classification system discussed in the introduction, this phenomenon, which we refer to as *intersensory RT effects*, represents an example of sensory *context*.

The literature on intersensory RT effects falls roughly into three categories. The first involves studies of *bisensory effects*: two (or theoretically more) signals in different modalities are presented at once, or closely in time, and the subject responds to the entire multisensory event. In the second category are studies in which the two stimuli are separated by a fairly long temporal interval such as 0.5 sec or more, and consequently the first stimulus may be considered to be a warning signal for the upcoming stimulus in the sensory modality to which the subject is to respond (e.g., Kohfeld, 1969). Thus this group of studies demonstrates the occurrence of *warning signal effects*. The third type of RT experiment examines *accessory signal effects*. Here an accessory stimulus is presented and is then followed after a *very brief* interval by the executive stimulus, the stimulus to which a response is to be made (e.g., Morrell, 1967). In some instances, the accessory stimulus actually occurs *after* the executive. The use of a short interstimulus interval (ISI) is one important distinction between this design and that used to study warning signal effects. The fact that the subject is asked, or perhaps required by the design, to respond specifically to the executive stimulus distinguishes this design from that used to study bisensory effects.

1.3.1. Bisensory Effects. Although there are classical reports (e.g., Todd, 1912) of intersensory effects on RTs, the recent interest in this phenomenon was stimulated by a report by Hershenson (1962).

Hershenson (1962) measured RT in three conditions. In one, only auditory signals were used, and in a second, only visual signals occurred. In the third, both an auditory and a visual signal were presented and the subject was instructed to respond as soon as one of them occurred. Of these paired-stimulus trials, the visual signal either occurred simultaneously with the auditory or preceded the auditory by as much as 85 msec. Hershenson reasoned that when the signals were simultaneous or when there was a relatively brief precedence of the visual signal, the RT should be the same as the RT to auditory-alone signals because of the typically shorter auditory RT. When the visual signal preceded the auditory by considerably more than the difference between visual and auditory RTs, the resulting RT should be like that of the visual-alone RT. In the range of precedence near the difference between visual-alone and auditory-alone RT, Hershenson hypothesized that intersensory facilitation should occur. That is, the RT would be faster than that predicted by either the visual or the auditory function. Evidence for such facilitation was indeed found. With both high and low values of visual signal precedence, RT was not different from the visual-alone (with very long precedence) or the auditory-alone (with very short precedence or simultaneity) RT. However, in the range of 30–50 msec precedence, RT values were significantly lower than either single-modality RT would predict (by as much as 10 msec). As predicted by Hershenson, the greatest effect was typically, although not uniformly, found for a precedence value very close to the subject's mean difference between visual-alone and auditory-alone RTs.

Hershenson also used two intensities of the light signal and two of the auditory signal. The magnitude of the facilitation decreased only slightly with lesser auditory signal intensity, but decreased more substantially with lesser visual signal intensity.

Hershenson argued that, because of the relation of the RT facilitation effect to the onset asynchrony parameter, the effect is truly an intersensory one, where both modalities are contributing to produce a faster RT than either modality alone would be capable of producing. Alternatively, if one signal served an alerting function (to "prime" the subsequent reaction to the other signal), the facilitation function would not have so closely corresponded to the onset asynchrony function that was in turn based on the difference between simple visual and auditory RTs.

There is some question whether such results can be attributed to true intersensory reaction, for the notion of *probability summation* predicts similar results without true interaction, A recent study by Gielen, Schmidt, and van den Heuvel (1983), however, offers evidence that a true intersensory interaction effect operates in situations such as that used by Hershenson (1962), in addition to any probability summation effect. This issue is discussed in a later section (1.3.4).

1.3.2. Warning Signal Effects. A warning signal occurs some time before the executive stimulus to which the observer is to respond and serves in some way to alert the subject to the upcoming event. It does not, therefore, serve as part of the perceptual act of responding to the executive stimulus, but rather establishes a contextual setting within which the response to the executive stimulus occurs. The contextual/perceptual distinction helps to differentiate the warning signal effect from accessory signal effects, to be discussed below (Section 1.3.3). The other distinction is quantitative rather than qualitative: A warning signal typically is considered to be an alerting event that occurs well before the executive stimulus, typically by 0.5 sec or more, whereas an accessory signal occurs in close temporal proximity with the executive stimulus, either right before it or in some cases immediately afterward.

A study by Kohfeld (1969) serves to illustrate intersensory effects with the warning signal paradigm. The executive signal in this work was consistently auditory, and Kohfeld compared the effectiveness of an auditory with that of a visual warning signal. The primary purpose of the study was to examine the effect of the intensity of the warning signal on RT; the study was only secondarily concerned with the intersensory issue. However, because subjectively similar values of visual and auditory warning signal intensity were used, the warning signal manipulation provided a useful way of examining whether the intrasensory and intersensory effects follow the same function.

The initial experiment examined potential *within*-modality interactions. The executive signal was a 30-, 60-, or 90-dB SPL, 1,000-Hz tone, and the subject responded by pressing a telegraph key. The warning signal was also auditory: a 0.5-sec, 1,000-Hz signal of 30, 60, or 90 dB SPL, given 1, 2, or 3 sec before the executive signal. In each of the first three of five daily sessions, the warning signal was consistently set at a single intensity. In the fourth session, the three warning signal intensities were intermixed at random, whereas in the fifth session the 30-dB SPL warning signal was used, and after each response the subject was informed of the RT over a loudspeaker. As seen in Figure 25.4, RT decreased with increasing executive signal intensity. The warning signal intensity effect was also found: Mean RT decreased from 304 msec at 90 dB SPL to 284 msec at 60 dB SPL to 267 msec at 30 dB SPL; when feedback was presented with the 30-dB SPL signal, mean RT was 324 msec. When warning signals were intermixed at random (Session 4), there was no differential effect of signal intensity, the mean RT being 289 msec. Kohfeld interpreted these results as supporting a "decision theory" model, in contrast to a simpler adaptation-level theory. According to the decision model, the subject does not respond to an executive signal until it reaches a critical level of "cumulative impulse count." The intensity of the warning signal sets a criterion level: When it is more intense, the subject sets a higher criterion level, and thus the executive signal has to last longer before a response is made than if the criterion level is lower, as with a less intense warning signal. In the randomly intermixed warning signal intensity condition, the subject takes some intermediate level as a criterion level.

In a second experiment, a visual warning signal was used, consisting of a briefly illuminated 15-in square Plexiglas window, with the signal intensity set at 100, 0.10, or 0.003 $cd \cdot m^{-2}$. These intensity levels were chosen on the basis of results of J.C. Stevens, Mack, and Stevens (1960) of subjective intensity matching with the auditory warning signals used in Experiment 1. The same design was used except for the omission of Session 5 with feedback. As in the preceding experiment, RT to the auditory executive signal was faster for the weakest warning signal, intermediate for the intermediate (and randomly intermixed) warning signal, and slowest for the most intense

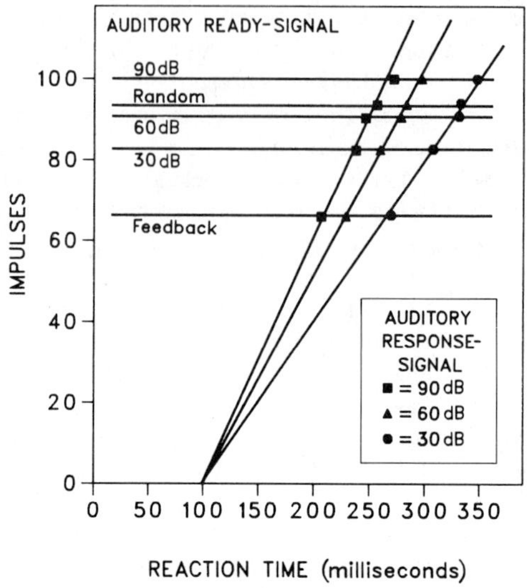

Figure 25.4. Effects of intensity of auditory ready signal on RT to several response signal intensities, based on 16 subjects. The five conditions of ready-signal intensity are represented by the horizontal lines. The overall mean RT for each condition was calculated, and then 100 msec was subtracted from each in order to remove an assumed irreducible minimum RT. The resulting 90-dB SPL condition value was assigned an arbitrary value of 100 "impulse units," and the vertical positions of the remaining condition lines were determined by taking the mean RTs of these conditions as proportions of the 90-dB SPL mean. (The conversion to impulse units rests on an assumption of the decision theory model that response is initiated when the effective signal reaches a critical level of impulse units.) The 15 data points, then, represent the mean RTs for each of the five RT conditions, plotted along the appropriate horizontal line for that condition. Then linear fit lines were constructed with each function originating at 100 msec (the irreducible minimum), to provide a least squares fit for each response signal condition. It is evident that the data points do not deviate substantially from the least squares functions. The data indicate that as warning signal intensity increases, RT to the response signal increases. Thus the decision theory model is supported as a reasonable account of the effects of ready signal intensity on RT. It may be noted that the RTs shown here are longer than are typically reported to auditory stimuli (normally in the 100–150-msec range). It may be that the RTs were lengthened by the presence of the warning signal. This would occur if the warning signal was serving to set an "impulse criterion," as predicted by the decision model advanced by Kohfeld (1969). Unfortunately, no condition was conducted in which no warning signal was used, and so this possible explanation remains speculative. (From D. L. Kohfeld, Effects of the intensity of auditory and visual ready signals on simple reaction time, *Journal of Experimental Psychology, 82*. Copyright 1969 by American Psychological Association. Reprinted with permission.)

warning signal (see Figure 25.5). In essence the results paralleled those from the first experiment, and clearly demonstrated a warning signal effect that is the same whether the warning signal is intra- or intersensory, particularly in its common variation with warning signal intensity. Kohfeld argued from these results that the warning signal effect must be central (i.e., integrative) rather than peripheral (i.e., modality specific).

1.3.3. Accessory Signal Effects. An early study by Morrell (1967) serves to illustrate the basic paradigm (as well as a major methodological issue) in this area. Morrell required an RT response (closing a small switch) to a visual executive stimulus (a 10-msec flash). The auditory accessory signal was a click that occurred from 20 to 120 msec *after* the onset of the visual stimulus. On some trials the visual stimulus occurred without any auditory accessory stimulus. As seen in Figure

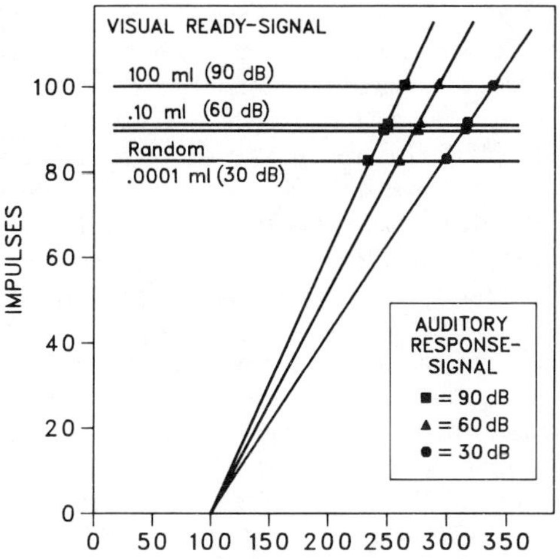

Figure 25.5. Effects of intensity of visual ready signal on RT to several auditory response signal intensities, based on 16 subjects. The four conditions are identical to those represented in Figure 25.4, except that here the feedback condition was omitted. Data were reduced as described in Figure 25.4, and least squares functions were constructed. The data points fell uniformly on or very near the least squares lines, again supporting the ability of the decision theory model to account for RT with warning signal data. In this experiment, though, the warning signal was in a different modality from the response signal, and therefore the demonstration is of a cross-modality ready-signal effect and the ability of the decision theory model to account for such an effect as well as intrasensory effects. (From D. L. Kohfeld, Effects of the intensity of auditory and visual ready signals on simple reaction time, *Journal of Experimental Psychology, 82*. Copyright 1969 by American Psychological Association. Reprinted with permission.)

25.6, the presence of the accessory stimulus generally quickened ("facilitated") RT to the visual executive signal: the effect was greatest when the ISI was only 20 msec, but a significant effect still occurred with as much as an 80-msec flash-click interval. A logical problem arises with the paradigm used by Morrell (1967), in that there is no way to be sure that the response was in fact made to the visual stimulus rather than to the auditory signal. A means of circumventing this problem was reported by Morrell in two studies (1968a, 1968b). Morrell (1968b) presented an auditory accessory signal at intervals varying from 20 to 120 msec *after* a visual executive signal. On six of every eight trials, both signals occurred as described, whereas on the remaining two, either the auditory or the visual signal was omitted. The trial on which the visual (executive) signal was omitted was thus a catch trial, to which no response should occur if the subject, as instructed, is responding to the visual signal as the executive. Reliable intersensory RT facilitation was found. In a related study, Morrell (1968a) examined the effect of a visual accessory signal on auditory and visual RT. In the auditory RT condition, a following visual accessory signal decreased RT only if the ISI was 40 msec or less. By contrast, RT to a visual executive signal was decreased by a following auditory accessory over the entire ISI range of 20–120 msec.

Posner, Nissen, and Klein (1976) reported a set of experiments in which an accessory signal in either the visual or the auditory modality preceded or followed the executive signal, which could also occur in either modality. The subject was forced to distinguish between the accessory and executive stimuli by the use of a disjunctive task. In one study, the subject, while fixating a central location, was to decide whether an X appeared to the right or left of the fixation point and to respond by depressing the appropriate (right or left) telegraph key as quickly as possible. On 80% of the trials an accessory auditory stimulus (a burst of white noise) was presented 25, 50, 75, or 100 msec prior to the executive stimulus, 25, 50, 75, or 100 msec afterward, or coincident with the executive. In another experiment an X could appear to the right or left of the fixation point or a tone could be presented to the right or left ear. The subject's task was to press the right key when either the X or the tone was on the right, and the left key when these visual or auditory accessory stimuli (a square flash of light at the fixation point) was presented up to 100 msec before or after the executive stimulus.

Partial results of these two studies are depicted in Figure 25.7. Looking at the point at which the accessory and executive stimuli occur at the same time, it may be seen that an auditory accessory stimulus facilitates the visual executive RT substantially (a 50-msec reduction in comparison to the vision-alone control value on the left side of the figure), whereas a visual accessory stimulus has little or no effect on either the visual or auditory executive stimulus. Posner et al. (1976) argued from this asymmetric result that auditory signals generally have a more effective alerting function than do visual signals. The visual accessory, however, did have a facilitating effect if it preceded the visual or auditory executive stimulus, perhaps because it then served as a warning signal (see Section 1.3.2).

Posner et al. (1976) obtained replications of these results, using high and low tones and high and low digits for the auditory and visual executive signals, respectively. They found the same pattern of results, indicating that it was not the use specifically of the localization task that accounted for the asymmetry of the results.

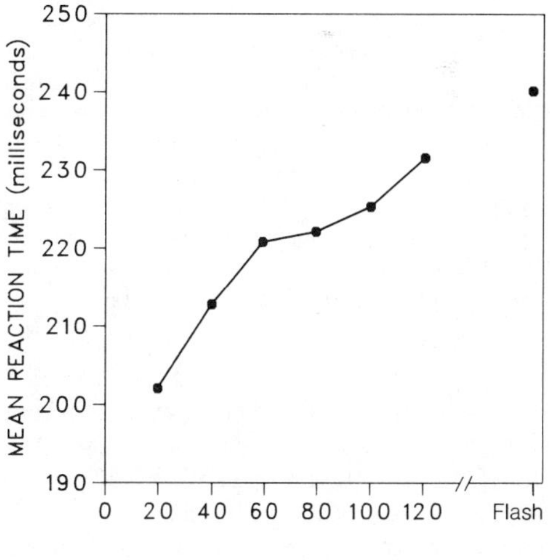

Figure 25.6. Mean RT to visual flash as a function of flash-click interval. RT was assessed to a visual flash, in a darkened room, under seven conditions: visual flash alone (data point on the far right of the figure) and visual flash *followed by* an audible (70-dB SPL) click with a flash-click delay of 20, 40, 60, 80, 100, or 120 msec. The ordinate shows the mean of the six subjects' mean RTs for each of these seven conditions. Compared to the flash-alone condition, all but the 100- and 120-msec means revealed a reliably faster RT. Thus even a click occurring physically after a flash can be facilitatory of visual RT, as long as the time period by which the click follows the flash does not exceed about 80 msec. (From L. K. Morrell, Intersensory facilitation of reaction time, *Psychonomic Science*, 1967, *8*. Reprinted with permission.)

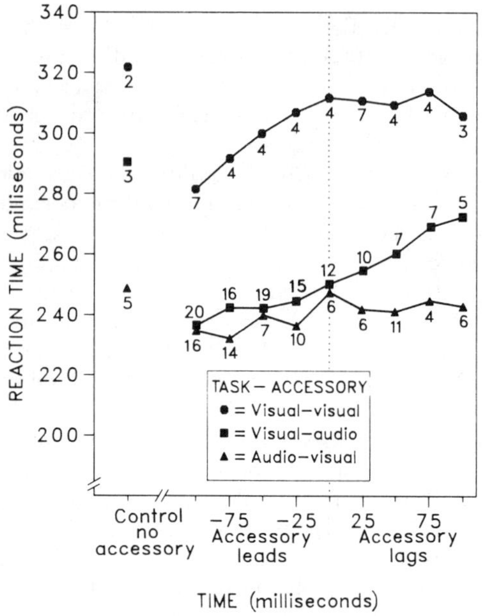

Figure 25.7. A comparison of the effectiveness of visual and auditory accessory signals at varying timing relationships to the response signal. A discriminative response rather than a simple response was involved. The accessory signal could coincide with the response signal, or precede or follow the response signal by up to 100 msec. These values are shown on the abscissa. Mean RT is shown on the ordinate for three conditions: Visual accessory/visual response signal, visual accessory/auditory response signal, and auditory accessory/visual response signal. The data points on the far left represent no-accessory control values. If the accessory signal has no effect on RT, the results should approximate these control values for the various conditions. Consider the data points on the vertical line through the zero time lag value, in which the accessory and response signals were temporally coincident. The visual accessory had no effect on either the visual response signal or the auditory response signal. However, the auditory accessory signal significantly reduced RT to the visual response signal, by about 40 msec. At other values of accessory lead or lag as well, the auditory accessory facilitated visual RT. In addition, an increase in errors on the visual task occurred with increased RT facilitation. By constrast, the visual accessory signal had no consistent effect on the auditory response task, though the visual accessory signal did facilitate the visual response signal task when the accessory signal preceded the response signal by 75–100 msec. In general, these results are taken to support the notion that human subjects are less alerted by visual signals than by auditory signals. (From M. I. Posner, M. J. Nissen, & R. M. Klein, Visual dominance: An information-processing account of its origins and significance, *Psychological Review, 83*. Copyright 1976 by American Psychological Association. Reprinted with permission.)

1.3.4. Explanations. A criticism that was brought to bear on the earlier work in the intersensory RT facilitation area (e.g., Hershenson, 1962; Morrell, 1967) by Nickerson (1973) and others is that the results may reflect a probability summation phenomenon, rather than a true intersensory effect. The reductions in RT, it is argued, may be due simply to the existence of two signals, each with its probability distribution of RTs, with the combination of the two distributions producing the probability of a faster RT than either taken alone. There need be no intersensory interaction whatever for such a result to occur, although, of course, a lowered RT may be a joint function of an intersensory interaction and the probability summation effect. Using a situation similar to that of Hershenson (1962), Gielen et al. (1983) compared the RT to the presentation of visual stimuli alone to that when the visual stimulus was followed by an auditory or kinesthetic event 50 or 65 msec later. The RT to the combined stimuli was faster than that to the visual signal alone by 20–40 msec. Gielen et al. (1983) argued that this degree of lowered RT cannot be accounted for by probability summation alone, based on their revision of Raab's (1962) formulation, and that therefore a true intersensory interaction effect of about 12 msec must have occurred. Furthermore, research using a disjunctive response task (as in Morrell, 1968a, 1968b; Posner et al., 1976) would seem to defeat the use of the probability summation formulation as an account for all of the intersensory interaction effects.

Although it is not an example of intersensory interaction as we are using the term, an "energy summation" notion has been advanced to account for some of the intersensory RT effects. It is well documented that increasing the intensity of a signal serves to decrease RT to that signal. The energy summation hypothesis suggests, with respect to accessory stimuli, that the energy contained in the accessory signal combines with that in the executive signal to produce more energy than is contained in the executive signal alone. Just as increasing the intensity of an individual signal reduces RT, so too does the combination of energies of accessory and executive signals. In effect, the separate signal energies combine to decrease RT, as would a more intense executive signal.

This formulation does explain many of the intersensory RT effects, such as those of Hershenson (1962), Morrell (1967, 1968a, 1968b), Taylor and Campbell (1976), and Bernstein (1970). Results by Kohfeld (1969), discussed earlier, are counter to the energy summation hypothesis, however. Bernstein, Chu, Briggs, and Schurman (1973) also report results that are not easily explained by energy summation. They reasoned that if the subject is only responding to cumulative intensity rather than to modality-specific energy, then an accessory signal of increased intensity should be effectively equivalent to the sum of a less intense accessory and an executive signal, and the subject should make a false positive response to a higher energy accessory signal. In these conditions, however, the subject did not make an inappropriate response to the increased intensity accessory without the executive signal. Something more than effective overall intensity level was apparently affecting the RT.

Similarly difficult for the energy summation model to handle are various findings reported by Simon and Craft (1970), Bernstein, Rose, and Ashe (1970a, 1970b), Bernstein, Clark, and Edelstein (1969a, 1969b), and Bernstein and Edelstein (1971). The last-mentioned will serve to illustrate the problem. The paradigm was similar to that used by Posner et al. (1976), in that the subject had to make a disjunctive reaction to the executive signal, that is, reporting left or right rather than just occurrence. An auditory accessory signal was used. A tone was presented monaurally either to the ear ipsilateral to the visual signal or to the contralateral ear. An auditory accessory in the ipsilateral ear facilitated RT, whereas one in the contralateral ear eliminated any facilitatory effect. Clearly there was specific information content in the accessory signal that affected performance, rather than simply energy. Thus the energy summation model does not easily handle this result. The model similarly has difficulty with the Posner et al. (1976) results, in which visual accessory signals do not have as effective an alerting influence as auditory signals. Apparently, more than just total energy is involved. The energy summation hypothesis thus falls short in that it fails to account for many results in the literature.

Nickerson (1973) and others have proposed an alternative *preparation enhancement* model to account for RT facilitation effects. According to this account, an accessory signal has the effect of preparing the subject to respond, not in a specific way but as an alerting function. Nickerson makes the distinction between preparedness to process a stimulus and preparedness to respond, and emphasizes the latter, although he does not rule out the possibility of the former. Nor is this distinction critical to our treatment, although we would place perhaps more emphasis on processing preparedness than on response preparedness.

1.4. Multimodal Event Detection

One of the first studies to measure RT to two or more sensory modalities presented both singly and together (the "bisensory trials") was by Todd (1912). His results indicated some facilitation of RT when sound and shock were combined, relative to when they occurred alone.

A more recent series of studies, beginning with Colavita (1974), has compared the detectability of visual and auditory stimuli presented unimodally and bimodally. In Colavita's (1974) experiment subjects first matched for apparent intensity a 4,000-Hz, 65-dB SPL tone and a 30-cm square light panel. Next, RT was assessed to auditory or visual signals presented singly or in bisensory combinations. The subject pressed a telegraph key with one hand in response to the auditory signal and another key with the other hand for the visual signal. In a condition where the subject was forewarned to modality, comparison of auditory-only and visual-only RTs produced the typical advantage to audition, whose mean RT was 179 msec, as compared with a mean RT of 197 msec for vision. When auditory and visual signals were presented in interspersed fashion without prior identification of the signal for each trial, RT did not differ significantly between modalities: mean RT for audition was 297 msec and that for vision was 299 msec. These mean RTs are longer than those for the single-modality conditions presumably because in the "unannounced" condition the subject had to attend to two channels simultaneously. Interspersed within this set of trials were occasional trials on which both signals occurred (the bisensory trials), again without prior identification. The mean RT for these latter trials was 303 msec, not different from that for either modality alone. There were 50 such bisensory trials across the 10 subjects: on 49 of the 50, the subject's reaction was made on the visual key! This finding is particularly striking in view of the routinely observed superiority of auditory RT reported in the literature, and in view of the equality of visual and auditory RT in the Colavita (1974) study for choice RT signals. On only 33 of these 49 trials, in fact, did the subject appear to recognize that an auditory signal had occurred. (On the lone trial in which the auditory key was pressed, the subject reported that the response had been an error, that the visual key should have been pressed.)

As noted earlier, intensities of visual and auditory signals were matched before the session. Nevertheless, the relative intensities are a crucial issue in this design. Accordingly, in a second experiment, Colavita (1974) had each subject match the 4,000-Hz tone to equal twice the intensity of the 150 $cd \cdot mm^{-2}$ light. In other respects, the second experiment was a replication of the first. Mean RT for identified visual signals was 203 msec, whereas that for auditory signals was 191 msec. Mean RTs for choice condition visual and auditory signals were, respectively, 284 and 297 msec. On the 110 dual or bisensory trials, light responses occurred 97 times (mean RT 296 msec) and tone responses 13 times (mean RT 200 msec). Awareness of the tone occurred on 86 trials and of the light on all 110 trials. A third experiment, with several procedural changes, resulted in essentially the same pattern of results.

In a fourth experiment, the procedures were basically the same, except that subjects were instructed to press the auditory key when both signals occurred on a trial. Three of ten subjects were unaware of any of the 60 such trials. Overall, light responses occurred on 36 and tone responses on 24 of the dual or bisensory trials, and the mean RTs for light and tone response trials were, respectively, 330 and 389 msec; the difference was highly significant.

Thus across the four experiments there was a distinct prepotency of the visual signal when visual and auditory signals occurred together, despite the fact that RT was generally faster to auditory than to visual signals when the subject knew which signal would occur. Colavita (1974) discussed his results in the context of an attentional model in which only one channel can be attended at a time. Furthermore, he suggested that the visual channel tends to be sampled first. Posner et al. (1976) suggested, similarly, that visual stimuli are allocated relatively more attention than auditory signals. Their reasoning is that vision is inherently less alerting because the eyes are directional sense organs, whereas the ears do not depend on orientation to the signal. Therefore, the visual channel must be allocated more of the observer's attentional capacity or, in Colavita's (1974) terms, be sampled first. Although this formulation seems reasonable enough, it would appear, at this time, to have more post hoc explanatory capability than predictive power.

Colavita, Tomko, and Weisberg (1976) determined that the visual prepotency phenomenon does not depend on fixation of the visual stimulus. The design was identical to that used in the original Colavita (1974) work, except that the loci of the auditory and visual signals were separated by 25 cm. The visual prepotency effect occurred whether the subject was instructed to fixate a point midway between them (42 visual responses out of 50 bisensory trials) or fixated the speaker, thus placing the visual signal even farther in the retinal periphery (38 visual responses in 40 bisensory trials).

A study by Egeth and Sager (1977) was concerned with whether the visual dominance effect demonstrated by Colavita (1974) was at the level of sensory function (such as masking of one stimulus by the other), which would be demonstrated by its involuntary nature, or at a higher, voluntary level, in which case it would be susceptible to attention or response effects. The subject was to respond with a tone key whenever an auditory signal occurred, but not to respond at all to a visual signal. The majority of the trials were either tone-only or light-only, but among these were several trials on which both light and tone were presented. Egeth and Sager (1977) reasoned that if visual prepotency occurred at a sensory level, such as a masking effect, then response to the tone on these bisensory trials should be slower than that to the tone-alone trials. No such difference was obtained, and it was concluded that voluntary attention, rather than an involuntary sensory process, was involved.

Colavita and Weisberg (1979) also concluded that a higher-level process was operating. They had subjects respond to stimulus offset rather than onset. This requirement should maintain the visual prepotency if it is based on relative attention to the two signals, but not if it is based on blocking of the signal at the sensory level. The visual prepotency effect was still found.

Collectively, these findings show a clear intersensory interaction effect: whereas responsiveness to an auditory signal is normally extremely quick, it is slower if a visual signal is present and the subject is instructed to attend to the visual signal. The attention manipulations show the intersensory effect to be at a level beyond the sensory pathways. The importance of attention in many situations of intersensory interaction is thus underscored.

1.5. Key References

Colavita, F. B. (1974). This study demonstrates the primacy of visual over auditory signals when both are presented together, despite the fact that reaction time is faster to auditory signals than to visual.

Hershenson, M. (1962). This study was an early example of the use of the paradigm where signals are presented to two modalities at once, demonstrating that with appropriate timing relationships, RT is faster to the pair than it would be to either modality taken alone.

Kohfeld, D. L. (1969). This study shows the basic paradigm of the facilitatory effect of a warning signal on RT to a subsequent signal. Both intra- and intermodality warning signal effects were shown.

London, I. D. (1954). This is a review of the huge number of early experiments on the effects of nonspecific accessory stimuli carried out by the Russian investigators. For the non-Russian-speaking reader it represents virtually the only source of information about this extensive research program.

Morrell, L. K. (1968a). This study illustrates the paradigm of the accessory signal. RT is measured to an executive signal in one modality, and the facilitatory effects of a signal given to another modality (the accessory signal) are demonstrable.

2. SPATIAL EVENTS

This section presents what is known about intersensory interactions involving the perception of spatial events (see also Sections 2.5 and 2.6). Human spatial capacities include (1) spatial acuity, (2) orientation, (3) egocentric localization, and (4) the perception of shape, size, and texture. For each of these topics we begin by comparing the sensory modalities with respect to their appropriateness for the task. We then deal, in turn, with the effects of nonspecific accessory stimulation and the perceptual context. Finally, we examine the ways in which the two senses interact in the multimodal perception of the event.

2.1. Spatial Acuity

2.1.1. Comparisons Among the Modalities. There are at least four sensory modalities capable of providing spatial information to the human perceiver. These are vision, audition, touch, and proprioception. A comparison among these modalities with respect to spatial acuity can be made on the basis of either of two behavioral measures. One of these is the minimum amount by which two stimulus objects, within a given modality, must be separated in order that they be reliably perceived as spatially disparate events. The other is the extent of observers' trial-to-trial variability, or the absolute error, in the perception of a particular spatial locus—the less the variability or the smaller the absolute error, the greater the spatial acuity.

Under optimal conditions, vision has proved to be by far the most spatially acute of the so-called "spatial modalities." Thus for vision the resolution acuity (i.e., the ability to detect that two visual stimuli are spatially distinct) is about 1 min of arc for foveally viewed targets (e.g., Howard, 1982). In contrast, measures of the spatial localization of a 1,000-Hz tone placed at varying angular distances from the median plane of the head reveal a minimum audible angle of about 1° (e.g., Mills, 1958). The analogous measure of tactual acuity is the two-point threshold and, as is well known, the outcome varies greatly with the part of the body being stimulated. The most sensitive area is the tip of the tongue, where the two-point threshold is 1 mm. Because angular units of measurement are not appropriate for a proximal sense such as touch, it is difficult to compare this level of acuity with that of vision and audition.

Fisher (1960) directly compared the spatial acuity of vision, audition, and touch/kinesthesia by having subjects repeatedly manually locate, without feedback, targets within each of these modalities. The absolute size of the within-subject variabilities for each modality is undoubtedly exaggerated by the inherent variability of the reaching response itself. Nevertheless, it is not unreasonable to compare the modalities in terms of the relative size of these measures of acuity. Fisher found that the order of decreasing relative acuity as measured in this fashion was vision, touch/kinesthesia, and audition.

2.1.2. The Effects of Nonspecific Accessory Stimulation. All the various types of nonspecific accessory stimuli that have been presented concomitant with a test of visual spatial acuity have revealed a facilitating effect. Most of this research has involved auditory accessory stimuli (Gotoh, 1931; Hartmann, 1933; Jakovlev, 1938; Kravkov, 1934; London, 1954; Loveless, et al., 1970; Urbantschitsch, 1888). Urbantschitsch (1883) found that mild tactual stimulation to the ears and facial areas facilitated visual acuity. Hartmann (1933) reported that tactual stimulation (and pain) increased visual acuity, although Burnham (1941) demonstrated that Hartmann's results were probably unreliable.

2.2. Orientation

2.2.1. Comparisons Among the Modalities. There appear to be four sensory modalities for which the perception of orientation is possible—vision, touch, proprioception, and the vestibular sense. Visual objects can appear to be in line with or tilted from (1) one's body (or part of the body), (2) gravity, or (3) a visual framework. Likewise, tactual objects (placed on the skin) can be felt to be in line with or tilted from the body or parts of the body. In terms of the proprioceptive sense, the orientation of one part of the body (e.g., the forearm) can be perceived relative to another part of the body (e.g., the upper arm). Finally, one can assess the orientation of the entire body relative to gravity. Although numerous studies have examined these modalities individually as they provide information about spatial orientation (e.g., Howard & Templeton, 1966), few, if any, have directly compared them in the same experiment.

Comparisons suggest that vision and the vestibular sense are equally accurate and precise at indicating gravitational orientation. Thus subjects make errors (unsigned) of about 1° whether setting a luminous line (in an otherwise dark room) to apparent gravitational vertical (e.g., Neal, 1926; Witkin & Asch, 1948) or setting the body to gravitational vertical without vision (e.g., Gemelli, Tessier, & Galli, 1920). That these two measures would produce essentially the same results is perhaps not surprising, for both involve the use of the vestibular sense (which is then translated into a visual response in the second measure). If, on the other hand, the observer is measured on the ability to discriminate departures from *oculocentric* vertical of a luminous line, errors as small as 25 sec of arc are found (Westheimer, Shimamura, & McKee, 1976). The task of setting a rod (with the hand) to gravitational horizontal without vision appears to be somewhat more difficult than the ability to set the rod to the visual horizontal. Thus Over (1966) found an average within-subject standard deviation of 1.6 ° for the former but only 0.9 ° for the latter, the difference being statistically significant.

2.2.2. The Effects of Nonspecific Accessory Stimulation. The only research concerning the effect of nonspecific accessory stimuli on perceptual orientation appears to have been that performed as tests of Werner and Wapner's (e.g., 1949) "sensory-tonic" theory. Wapner, Werner, and Chandler (1951) demonstrated that asymmetric electrical stimulation of the neck muscles causes a shift in the gravitational orientation of a luminous rod in an otherwise dark room. Similarly, an auditory stimulus presented more intensely in one ear than the other causes a shift in apparent visual vertical (Chandler, 1961), as do counterweights applied to the head in such a way that it is forced to work against resistance when tilted (Kleint, 1937; Schneider & Bartley, 1962). In all cases it was argued that the increased body tonus on one side of the body caused the apparent visual vertical to tilt to the opposite side. The results for auditory and muscular stimuli, however, were not replicated by Naylor (1963). Also complicating matters is the finding by Aarons and Goldenberg (1964) that the effects of electrical stimulation on visual orientation differ as a function of the location and polarity of the electrodes.

2.2.3. Context Effects—Interactions Between Vestibular Stimulation and Vision, Audition, and Touch. Stimulation of the vestibular organs, most commonly by means of bodily rotation or tilt, produces a variety of perceptual effects (besides felt bodily tilt or motion), involving vision, audition, and touch. Because Howard (Chapter 18) provides an extensive discussion of the mutual interactions of the vestibular sense and vision, these effects are described only briefly here. The most prominent of the visual-vestibular interactions are the "oculogyral" and "oculogravic" illusions and a phenomenon referred to as "vection."

The oculogyral illusion (e.g., Graybiel & Hupp, 1946) is the result of semicircular canal stimulation (e.g., from bodily rotation) and is the experience that the visual field is spinning around. In contrast, the oculogravic illusion represents a change in the perceived orientation of visual objects as a result of centripetal acceleration (as occurs for an observer in a rotating human centrifuge). A phenomenon similar to the oculogravic illusion has been reported in which prolonged body or head tilt causes an underestimation of the degree of tilt, with a resulting underestimation of the degree to which a luminous line is tilted. Returning the subject to the physically upright position causes postural and visual negative aftereffects of perceived tilt (Day & Wade, 1966; McFarland & Clarkson, 1966; Wade, 1968; Wade & Day, 1968a, 1968b). Finally, vection (cf. Dichgans & Brandt, 1978) represents the experience of bodily rotation or sway as a result of exposure to a moving textured visual field.

As might be expected, there are auditory analogues to the vestibularly induced visual illusions. Thus an "audiogyral illusion" has been reported (e.g., Arnoult, 1950; Clark & Graybiel, 1949; Lester & Morant, 1970), in which bodily rotation causes subjects to experience a sound source located directly ahead of the body as moving during the post-rotary period in a direction predictable from the subject's perceived bodily rotation. A similar finding was reported by Welch and Krausert (Note 1) for galvanic stimulation of the vestibular organs.

Likewise, misperception of the relationship between the body and the direction of gravity causes a change in the localization of a sound source, a phenomenon termed the "audiogravic illusion" (Graybiel & Niven, 1951). In the study by Graybiel and Niven, the observer, when facing the center of rotation in a centrifuge and with head turned 90 ° , perceived an auditory stimulus to move in the same direction as his sense of gravitational direction had been altered.

Finally, underestimation of the degree to which the body is misaligned with gravity as a result of prolonged body tilt produces errors in auditory localization which, for an external sound source, are in the *opposite* direction to those found in setting a luminous line to apparent vertical under the same postural conditions (Lackner, 1974a; Teuber & Liebert, 1956). Thus, for example, Lackner (1974a) found that sitting in a chair tilted to one side caused subjects to set an ambient sound source off to the same side when attempting to align it with the body midline. The investigator proposed that the reason why this effect is opposite that found in the visual situation is that in the latter the subject's task was to set the luminous line to gravitational vertical, whereas in the auditory studies the frame of reference was the subject's head. However, it is unclear to us why there should be any misperception of the alignment of a stimulus object *with respect to the body*, regardless of one's perception of the body's orientation to gravity. That is, logically speaking, it would seem that setting a stimulus in line with the body should be just as accurate if the observer feels tilted as if he or she feels upright. In agreement with other vestibularly induced illusions, the effects of misperceived body tilt on auditory localization does not occur when visual information about true body orientation is provided (Lackner, 1974a).

Several recent studies have demonstrated that (in the absence of vision) touch and pressure will have a strong effect on apparent orientation of the body. Specifically, Lackner and Graybiel (1978a, 1978b) found that the feeling and direction of rotation experienced by horizontal subjects who were being rotated about the z-axis at 30 rpm were dramatically affected by pressure applied to various parts of the body. For example, a reclining subject pressing the soles of the feet against the centrifuge walls may feel upright, whereas pressure on the top of the head causes a tendency to feel upside down. Similarly, Graybiel and Kellogg (1967) found that subjects in zero-G (parabolic flight) feel that "down" is wherever their feet are in contact with a surface.

2.2.4. Multimodal Perception of Orientation. It appears that the only study to compare two sensory modalities with respect to their individual contributions in the multimodal perception of orientation was by Over (1966). In this study, the subjects' task was to set a bar so that it was felt to be horizontal. Subjects could (1) see, (2) feel, or (3) both see and feel the bar. In the conditions in which vision was allowed the subjects peered through Dove prisms that optically rotated the visual field by amounts that ranged (for different groups) from 15 to 90 ° and viewed the rod against a white, textureless background. One control group (V_0) was provided with undistorted vision and another (P) was allowed only to feel the bar.

The results for the first trial of the bisensory measures are depicted in Figure 25.8. It may be seen that with small amounts of tilt (15 and 30°) the bar was felt by most subjects to be horizontal when in fact it was tilted by approximately the amount of the optical rotation. Thus very substantial visual bias occurred

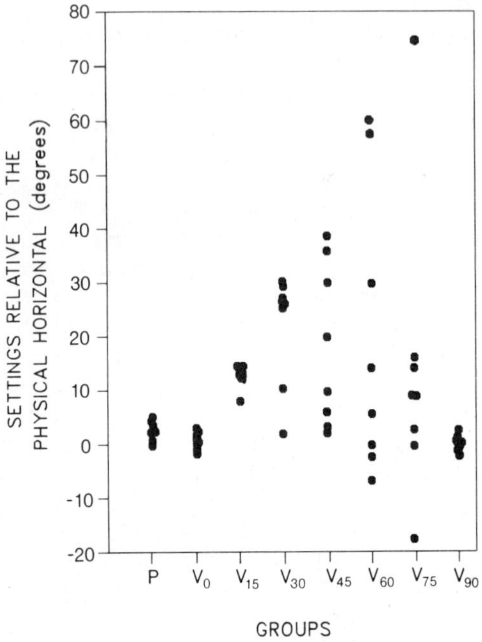

Figure 25.8. Settings of a bar to the felt horizontal for each of eight subjects as a function of amount of optical tilt. Group P (proprioception) made settings without vision; a pair of Dove prisms rotated the visual field by 0, 15, 30, 45, 60, 75, and 90° for groups V_0 to V_{90}, respectively. The values of extremely discrepant settings made by two subjects in group V_0 and by one subject in group V_{90} are given. These results indicated that with tilts up to 30° the felt horizontal was almost entirely determined by the seen horizontal. With increasing optical tilt the dominance of vision declined. (From R. Over, An experimentally induced conflict between vision and proprioception. *British Journal of Psychology*, 1966, *57*. Reprinted with permission.)

for these groups. With larger tilts, the intersensory bias declined markedly until, for the 90 ° group, settings were uniformly unaffected by the visual rearrangement. Thus it may be concluded that under everyday conditions of nondiscrepant visual-haptic perception of orientation it is the visual modality that is most heavily weighted in the multimodal experience. This is consistent with data on "visual capture" (e.g., Hay, Pick, & Ikeda, 1965, as discussed in Section 2.3.3.).

2.3. Egocentric Localization

2.3.1. Comparisons Among the Modalities. Egocentric localization refers to the capacity to perceive the direction and distance of objects *relative to the observer*. This task can be performed by at least four different sensory modalities—vision, audition, proprioception, and touch. Frequently, several of these modalities operate simultaneously to provide information about spatial location. Thus, for example, if one looks at the hand while audibly snapping the fingers, the first three of these spatial modalities redundantly inform the observer of the fingers' location.

This is not to say that the various modalities are equally adept at the task of spatial localization. Vision, for humans at least, is clearly the superior spatial modality. Thus it has been shown that vision is more precise (i.e., reveals less trial-to-trial variability in localizing targets) than either proprioception or audition (Fisher, 1960). Furthermore, the latency for perceiving the location of a visual object is shorter than for an auditory object, although the reverse is true when the task is that of detection (e.g., Simpson, 1972). Another difference is that whereas vision is capable of very exact localization in all three dimensions, audition provides reasonably good localization only in the lateral dimension; up-down and in-out localizations are relatively poor. Finally, in contrast to vision and audition, proprioceptive localization is limited by the length of the observer's reach.

2.3.2. Context Effects

2.3.2.1. The Role of Felt Eye and Head Position in Visual Egocentric Localization. The ability to locate visual objects in the frontal plane relative to the body depends crucially on the simultaneous registration of eye and/or head position. Thus the stimulation of a particular point on the retina can unambiguously and accurately signal egocentric direction only if the felt positions of the eyes relative to the head and of the head relative to the torso are accurately perceived.

Although it is clear that head position can be sensed by means of both proprioceptive and vestibular inflow, there is some controversy about whether this is true for eye position. The long-running debate has been between those (e.g., Sherrington, 1918) who have argued in favor of neural inflow and those (e.g., Helmholtz, 1866/1963) who have maintained that ocular position is sensed solely on the basis of neural outflow (the "effort of will"). More recently, a "hybrid" theory has gained favor. According to this notion, the evidence for which has been reviewed by Shebilske (1977), neural inflow is used to assess ocular position, but these afferent impulses depend on or are facilitated by neural outflow. More specifically, it is proposed that motor commands to the eye muscles, via the gamma efferents, induce neural inflow from the intrafusal muscle spindles, even before the eye muscles have had a chance to contract or perhaps in the complete absence of muscular movement. The entire issue of the neural basis for felt eye position and oculomotor control is addressed by Matin, Chapter 20.

Experimental manipulations of felt eye position (whatever its neural basis may be) should lead to predictable changes in apparent visual direction. Several forms of evidence confirm this expectation. Studies of adaptation to prismatically displaced vision (see Welch, Chapter 24) have found evidence of several adaptive end products. One of these is a change in apparent visual direction, most commonly measured by having the observer set a small visual target to apparent straight ahead in an otherwise dark room (e.g., Hay & Pick, 1966). Of the two logically possible bases for this prism-induced shift in visual direction—a change in the egocentric significance of retinal loci and a change in the felt position of the eyes relative to the head—the evidence is strongly in favor of the second. Kalil and Freedman (1966), for example, found that after 4 min of active exposure to prismatically displaced vision, subjects, when asked to point their eyes straight ahead of the nose (in a totally dark room), pointed them in the direction of the previous prismatic displacement. Prism-induced shifts in felt eye position have also been reported by Craske (1967), McLaughlin and Webster (1967), and Webster (1969). Thus it appears that if an observer is exposed to, say, rightward prismatic displacement, and is provided with certain kinds of feedback regarding the visual rearrangement, rightward-turned eyes will come to feel as if they are straight ahead. Consequently, a visual target placed off to the right by the same amount as the eyes are turned will be interpreted by the observer as straight ahead. Likewise, a target fixated directly ahead of the subject's nose will be seen as located off to the left because the eyes in this position will feel as if they are off to the left.

A second line of research demonstrating the effects of felt eye position on visual direction is concerned with the fact that when a muscle system is subject to sustained innervation it will continue to contract reflexively for some time after the voluntary signal to relax (Kohnstamm, 1915; Matthaei, 1924). A common example involves forcefully pressing the back of one's hand against a wall for a minute or so and then moving away with arm relaxed. As if by magic, the arm will lift away from the body.

Assuming that all muscle systems are susceptible to the so-called "muscle potentiation" effect, a sustained turning of the eyes to one side should lead to some interesting visual-spatial effects. Thus, for example, if the eyes are held off to the left for a period of time and then relaxed, they, like the arm in the initial example, should involuntarily persist in their leftward turn. Because the observer would be unaware of this turn, the eyes should feel as if they are straight ahead (the *position of rest*) when, in fact, they are still turned to the left. Such a misperception of eye position should, in turn, result in a misperception of visual direction such that a visual target off to the left appears to be straight ahead. Confirmation of these predicted effects of *eye muscle potentiation* (EMP) comes from a variety of studies. Park (1969), for example, found a small change in apparent straight ahead as the result of a 30-sec period of lateral eye turn. Much earlier, MacDougall (1903) had reported an analogous shift in the level of the visual horizon in the direction in which the observer had previously held the eyes. More recently, Paap and Ebenholtz (1976) demonstrated

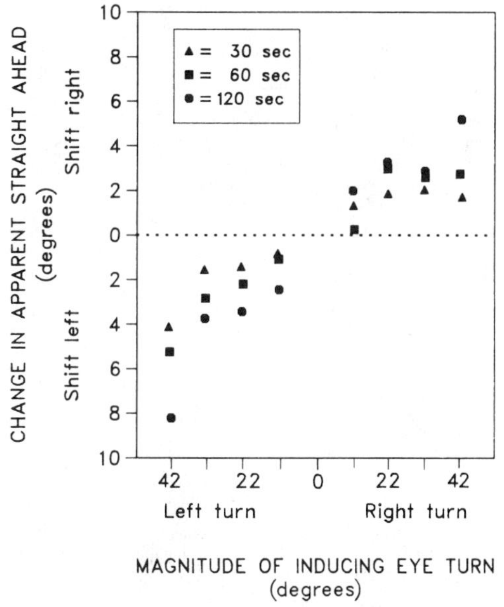

Figure 25.9. Apparent visual straight ahead as a function of magnitude and duration of preceding left or right eye turn. Subjects fixated a visual target placed 12, 22, 32, or 42° to the left or right of straight ahead for 30, 60, or 120 sec. Before and after this induction period, subjects indicated when a point of light in the otherwise dark testing room appeared to be straight ahead. The dependent variable was the pre-post shift in the judgment. The results indicated that prolonged eye turn leads to a shift in apparent visual straight ahead in the same direction as the eyes had been deviated. Additionally, the magnitude of the shift increased as a positive function of amount of eye turn and duration. (From K. R. Paap & S. M. Ebenholtz, Perceptual consequences of potentiation in the extra-ocular muscles, *Journal of Experimental Psychology: Human Perception and Performance, 2*. Copyright 1976 by American Psychological Association. Reprinted with permission.)

that the shift in apparent straight-ahead position of a visual target increased as a monotonic function of both eye turn duration (30, 60, or 120 sec) and magnitude (12, 22, 32, or 42° for 2 min). These results are depicted in Figure 25.9.

It has been argued by Ebenholtz and his associates (e.g., Ebenholtz, 1974) that it is EMP, rather than the traditionally assumed *recalibrative* process, that serves as the basis of prism-induced visual shifts. That is, because prism exposure nearly always results in the observer holding the eyes off in the direction of the prismatic displacement, perhaps the resulting shift in visual straight ahead is due merely to the prolonged eye turn rather than to a response to the visual rearrangement per se. A variety of studies have supported this contention (Ebenholtz, 1974; Ebenholtz & Fisher, 1982; Ebenholtz & Wolfson, 1975; Paap & Ebenholtz, 1976), although at least one study (Craske & Crawshaw, 1978) obtained a prism-induced visual shift under conditions that appeared to have precluded EMP.

What is the role of felt head position or motion in egocentric visual localization? An observer's head may be stationary or moving. The first condition is signaled by proprioception, the second by both proprioception and the vestibular sense. (If the entire body, including the head, is turning, only the vestibular sense would be operative.) With a stationary head, proprioception allows for the accurate perception of visual direction relative to the trunk. With head motion, one is able in addition to perceive more accurately in the in-out dimension, via the motion parallax cue of depth, although it is also possible to receive this cue without head or body motion. Similarly, the vestibular sensations of movement of the entire body through space may serve as one source of the motion parallax cue. Because Howard (Chapter 18) discusses this visual depth cue (and others), we concentrate here on the role of the felt position of the static head in the perception of visual direction.

Logically, it is clear that knowledge of the position of the head relative to the trunk is necessary if the observer is to point accurately at a visual object. Of course, if the observer's standard of egocentric reference is the *head* (a rather unnatural state of affairs, because the arms are attached to the trunk), then the perception of the head-trunk relation is irrelevant to apparent visual direction.

Several studies of prism adaptation have found some evidence (usually indirect) of changes in the felt position of the head. Cohen (1974), for example, obtained a large postexposure error in pointing at *auditory* targets, an error found for both prism-exposed and nonexposed hand. It seems likely that these effects were the result of a change in the felt relation of head to trunk, for such a change would influence auditory (as well as visual) direction and the effects would not be limited to the prism-exposed hand. Direct evidence for a shift in felt head position was reported by Kohler (1964, p. 38), who observed that prism-wearing subjects eventually became unaware of the fact that they were walking around with their heads turned in the direction of the displacement.

As with changes in felt eye position, prism-induced modifications of felt head position may be the result merely of the muscle potentiation induced by prolonged head turn. Hein (Note 2) has demonstrated, for example, that a shift in eye-hand coordination resulted from merely having the subject (with eyes shut) hold the head to one side for 10 min. Ebenholtz (1976) more directly confirmed the existence of neck muscle potentiation and the predicted visual effects by finding shifts in apparent visual direction as the result of 10-min maintenance of a leftward or rightward head turn.

Thus it is clear that the perception of visual direction requires the presence of information regarding felt ocular and head position and that if this information is incorrect, the perception is also incorrect.

*2.3.2.2. **The Role of Felt Head Position in Auditory Egocentric Localization.*** As we have seen, audition is not nearly as good a modality as vision at providing information about spatial location. The primary cues for auditory localization in the lateral dimension are the interaural differences in sound intensity and arrival time. (See Scharf & Houtsma, Chapter 15). However, although these cues are sufficient for accurate perception of auditory direction relative to the head, they are useless for the perception of auditory direction relative to the trunk unless information about head position is included in the equation. It follows, then, that changes in felt relation of head to trunk will be correlated with changes in auditory localization relative to the trunk. Unfortunately, the data relevant to this prediction are sparse indeed. As indicated earlier, Cohen (1974) noted prism-induced changes in pointing at auditory targets that *might* have been the result of a change in the felt position of the head; however, he failed to obtain independent measures of felt head orientation. Even in studies of adaptation to auditory rearrangement (e.g., Held, 1955), such measures have been lacking.

As with vision, auditory localization of auditory targets is greatly influenced by head movements (Wallach, 1940). The ability to perceive the front-back locus of a nonvisible sound source, for example, usually demands head movements. Thus, if a turn of the head to the right (whether actively initiated or from an external force) should cause a sound to favor the left ear, the auditory object must be in front of the observer; if the same movement favors the right ear, the sound must be in back. The up-down locus of a sound is also potentially disambiguated by head movements. Thus the higher the auditory target, the less the angle of aural displacement with a given head movement. In a classic paper, Wallach (1940) found empirical support for both these effects of head motion on auditory localization. A final effect that should be mentioned is the potential motion parallax cue for auditory depth/distance afforded by head movements. Thus the interaural shift in intensity and time-of-arrival should be greater for near objects than for more distant ones.

Further evidence of the role of static head position in auditory localization comes from Lackner (1973a, 1973c, 1974b), who found that prism-induced errors in localizing auditory objects were precisely correlated with adaptive shifts in felt relation of head to trunk. In another study, Lackner (1973b) found that when subjects held the head in a turned position for 3 min, it came to feel less turned than it actually was. When the head was returned to objective straight ahead it was felt to be off to the opposite side of the previous head turn. As expected, the errors in felt relation of head to trunk were highly correlated with errors in auditory localization. These results are depicted in Figures 25.10 and 25.11. However, as noted with respect to perceived orientation (Section 2.2.3), it is difficult to understand why a change in the felt position of a body part should lead to a change in spatial location with respect to that same body part.

*2.3.2.3. **Role of Visual Context and Eye Movements in Auditory Egocentric Localization.*** A number of studies (e.g., Warren, 1970) have demonstrated that localization of auditory targets is performed more precisely (i.e., less variably) when a textured visual field is seen than in the dark, even though the sound

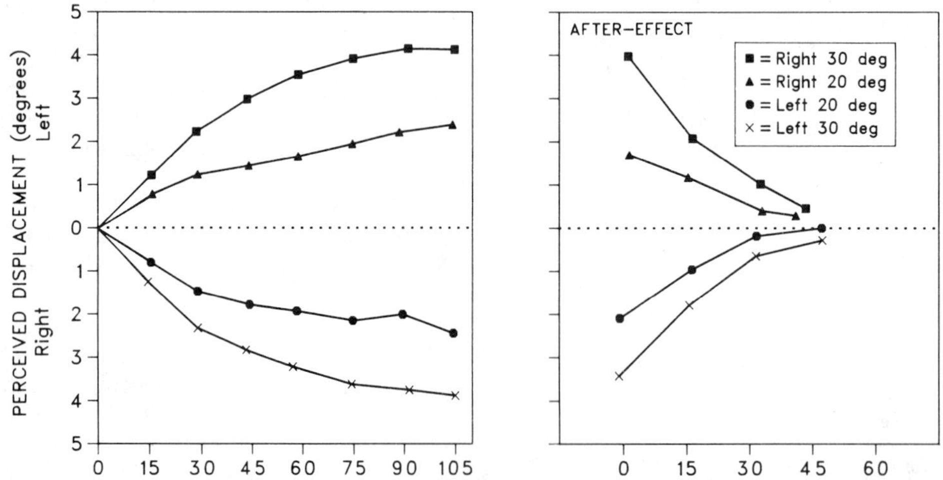

Figure 25.10. Changes in the localizations of ambient sounds as a function of time elapsed after deviation of the head in relation to the trunk and aftereffects upon return of the head to the straight ahead. The ordinate specifies the angle of the head to the torso upon return of the head to the perceived straight ahead. Blindfolded subjects held their heads off to one side, right or left, by 20 to 30° angles from the body midline for 3 min. Measures of the apparent straight ahead of a click sound source were obtained before, during, and after this period of head turn. The results indicated that the apparent auditory straight ahead (1) shifted in the direction of the head turn, (2) was greater for the 30° than for the 20° turn, and (3) increased in magnitude over about the first 2 min of head turn. Aftereffects also occurred, but dissipated rapidly. It was argued that the basis of this shift in apparent auditory direction is a concomitant shift in the felt orientation of head to trunk, an effect depicted in Figure 25.11. (From J. R. Lackner, The role of posture in sound localization, *Quarterly Journal of Experimental Psychology*, 1973, 26. Reprinted with permission.)

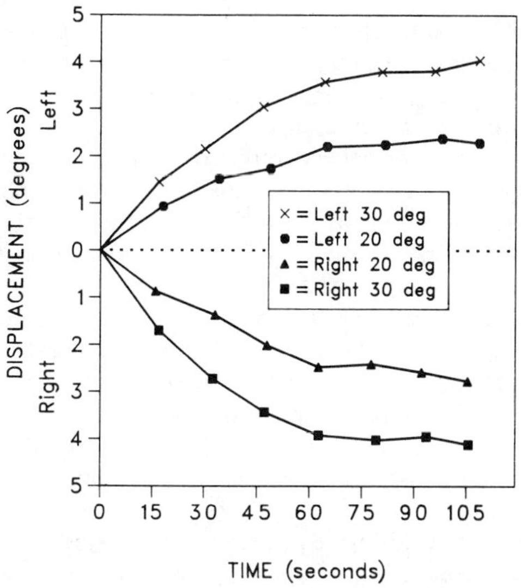

Figure 25.11. Development of postural adaptation as a function of head deviation and elapsed time. The ordinate specifies the angle of the head to the torso upon return of the head to the perceived straight ahead. Blindfolded subjects held their heads off to one side, right or left, by 20 to 30° angles from the body midline for 3 min. Measures of the apparent straight ahead of a click sound source were obtained before, during, and after this period of head turn. It may be seen that as duration of head turn increased, the felt straight-ahead position of the head changed such that it was perceived to be straight-ahead when it was actually rotated in the same direction as the preceding head turn. A comparison of Figures 25.10 and 25.11 indicates the close correlation between the changes in felt head position and changes in auditory localization. (From J. R. Lackner, The role of posture in sound localization, *Quarterly Journal of Experimental Psychology*, 1973, *26*. Reprinted with permission.)

source itself is not visible in either condition. This improvement has generally been referred to as visual facilitation of auditory localization.

Interest in this area was stimulated by a report by Fisher (1964) that blindfolded sighted adults make better use of auditory (and proprioceptive) location information than the blind, presumably because the sighted subjects have access to a visual frame of reference that serves as a localization context. Warren (1970) studied the phenomenon in more detail, attempting to delineate the conditions under which visual facilitation does and does not occur. Sighted adult subjects pointed beneath a shelf at an unseen auditory target. They could see neither their responses nor the sound source, which was behind a cloth screen. No error-corrective feedback was given. The target was a repetitive click with a frequency of 2 clicks per second. In an initial experiment, subjects localized auditory clicks with their eyes open and with them shut in separate tasks. Subjects kept the head fixed but were told that they could move the eyes at will. When the eyes were open, localization was significantly less variable than when they were closed. In fact, performance with eyes open was about midway between that found with eyes closed and that found when a visual target was localized (Figure 25.12). In a second experiment, three auditory localization conditions were used: eyes closed, as in the previous experiment, eyes open but in a dark apparatus with only a small light for reference at the straight-ahead point, and eyes closed but with the forefinger of the left hand at the straight-ahead reference point. The last condition produced localization identical to the eyes-closed condition (no facilitation), whereas the light reference point produced a significant improvement (see Figure 25.13). Clearly the facilitation effect on auditory localization is specifically a visual one, because a proprioceptive reference point had no effect. A subsequent experiment identified this effect as taking place in the listening part of the localization task rather than in the response part.

Platt and Warren (1972) explored further the role of a textured visual environment and of target-directed eye movements, using the electro-oculogram (Beckman Dynograph system) to monitor eye position and movements. Straight-ahead fixation in a lighted environment did not improve localization over the eyes-closed condition, whereas target-directed eye movements produced significant improvement in precision. In a subsequent condition, target-directed eye movements in a dark environment did not produce significant facilitation. From these results it is clear that eye movements are necessary for visual facilitation of auditory localization, but that they must occur in a visibly textured environment.

Warren (1970) and Platt and Warren (1972) argued that these results show the involvement of visual space in auditory localization as well as an oculomotor component. The visual environment provides a frame of reference to which auditory signals are referred by eye movements. It may be that the more precise monitoring of eye position and movements, allowed by the textured visual field, is a mediating state in the facilitation.

Simpson (1972) used a localization RT paradigm to study a similar issue. Simpson replicated the well-known observation that RT for detection of a simple auditory signal is faster than that of a simple visual signal. However, when a location discrimination was introduced, so that subjects had to report whether the visual or auditory targets were to the right or left

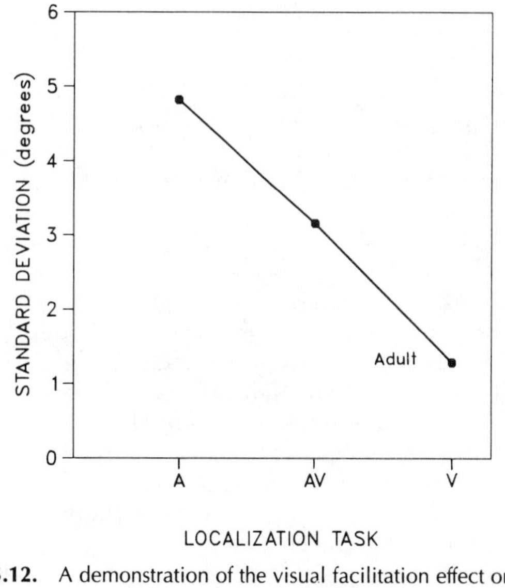

Figure 25.12. A demonstration of the visual facilitation effect on auditory localization. Task A involved localization (by pointing) of a clicking sound with the eyes closed; Task V involved pointing under an opaque shelf to a light point target; Task AV involved pointing to the click, but with the eyes open in a dark apparatus with a light reference point at the straight-ahead position. Mean SD scores for 12 subjects in the localization conditions are plotted, in degrees. Having the eyes open in the dark, with a light reference point, significantly improved click localization (Task AV compared to Task A), despite the invisibility of the click source, suggesting that auditory targets are localized with respect to a visual frame of reference that becomes effective with only minimal visual structure. (From D. H. Warren, Intermodality interactions in spatial localization, *Cognitive Psychology*, 1970, *1*. Reprinted with permission.)

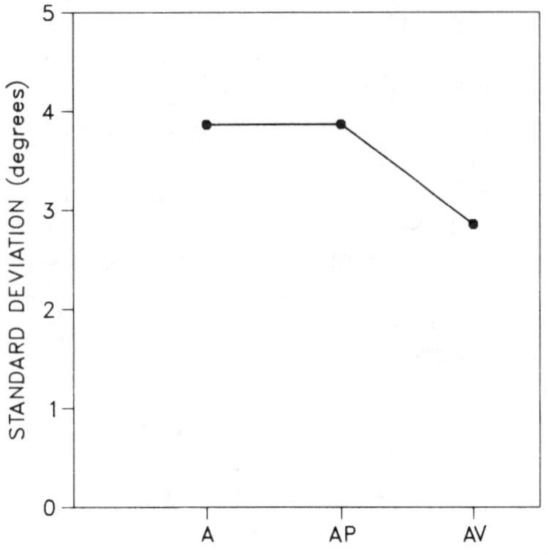

Figure 25.13. Visual versus proprioceptive facilitation of auditory localization. Refer to Figure 25.12 for the basic experiment on visual facilitation. From that experiment, the two tasks involving auditory localization of clicks (with the eyes closed, A, and with the eyes open in a darkened apparatus with a light reference point at the straight ahead, AV) were repeated, and a third task, AP, was added in which clicks were localized with the eyes closed, but with the subject's arm and forefinger extended out to a straight-ahead point, to serve as a proprioceptive reference point. Twelve subjects were tested and mean SD scores for the three tasks appear in degrees. The AV task was significantly better than the A task, replicating the basic visual facilitation effect shown Figure 25.12. The AP task did not differ from the A task, demonstrating that proprioception cannot serve the same facilitating role that vision does. This result strengthens the hypothesis that the context for auditory localization is specifically visual, rather than simply a generalized intermodality effect. (From D. H. Warren, Intermodality interactions in spatial localization, *Cognitive Psychology*, 1970, *1*. Reprinted with permission.)

of the midline, auditory RT was slower than visual RT. Simpson argued that the auditory localization target was referred or translated to a visual frame of reference, and that it was this added processing step that lengthened the auditory localization RT.

In contrast to the visual frame of reference hypothesis, Jones and Kabanoff (1975) suggested an eye-movement mediation hypothesis, according to which eye movements serve to update and stabilize auditory memory for location. Their experimental arrangement was somewhat different from that in the Warren work. Jones and Kabanoff placed the auditory target 3 ° right or left of the subject's straight ahead and required a verbal right or left judgment, whereas Warren used an array of auditory target locations ranging over 60 ° and required a pointing localization response rather than a directional report. In addition, whereas the subject's responses were made to a continuing auditory signal in Warren's work, Jones and Kabanoff used a single 0.01-sec auditory signal, thus introducing a memory component into the task. Despite the procedural differences, Jones and Kabanoff found that better localization occurred when eye movements were allowed than when fixation was required. [One point of contrast, however, occurs in their Experiment 3, where facilitation was found with target-directed eye movements in the dark. Mastroianni (1982), on the other hand, found no facilitation in this condition.] Where the subject moved the eyes in the direction opposite that of the auditory signal (either because of prior instruction or because of the occurrence of a visual signal on the opposite side), auditory performance was degraded. Based on these results, Jones and Kabanoff argued that "visual information may do no more than enable subjects to control their eye movements and hence more efficiently stabilize auditory position memory" (p. 243).

These results do not contradict the hypothesis that a visual frame of reference is involved and that eye movements serve to locate the auditory target within this frame. If the eyes are kept from moving or made to move in the opposite direction, then they cannot perform their function of placing the auditory target in the visual frame. Jones and Kabanoff's results certainly show that target-directed eye movements *are* important (a point clearly demonstrated by Platt & Warren, 1972), but not that a visual frame of reference is not also involved.

Shelton and Searle (1980) also suggested that the improvement of auditory spatial memory by eye movements and the visual frame of reference hypotheses may be complementary rather than contraditory. Targets located behind the head were better localized with eyes open, a phenomenon that could not be mediated by eye movements (Experiment 1). In a second experiment, Shelton and Searle (1980) presented a visual signal for 1,000 msec. In one condition the onset of the LED was coincident with the onset of the 200-msec auditory signal and in another condition the offsets were coincident. Improved auditory localization (facilitation) was found for both these conditions. The investigators suggested that facilitation in the simultaneous onset condition was produced by spatial memory, whereas facilitation in the simultaneous offset condition must have been produced by a visual frame of reference. Thus they argued that both factors may be involved and are not mutually exclusive.

A study by Thurlow and Kerr (1970) is informative on this point as well. Subjects judged the direction of the subjective straight ahead, as well as the position of an unseen auditory signal, while in a revolving striped drum. Both judgments were shifted in the direction of rotation of the drum. The shift in the judgment of the auditory target, however, was greater than that of the subjective straight ahead. Thurlow and Kerr concluded that two components must be involved in these bias effects: the shift in the straight ahead was produced by the repeated nystagmic movements of the eyes in following the visual stripes and thus represents a general shift in the visual frame of reference, whereas the further shift in the localization of auditory targets is due to "an additional, direct biasing effect of eye position on the sound-localization system" (p. 118).

Two points of interest may be noted in relation to the Thurlow and Kerr (1970) study. The auditory shift was apparently mediated by the nystagmic movements of the eyes in following the moving stripes. When subjects were required to fixate a stationary rod, the auditory shift effect was seriously reduced, thus further implicating eye movements in auditory localization. Second, Wallach (1940) reported a *vertical* shift in perceived auditory location under conditions of rotation of the visual field. Thurlow and Kerr (1970) failed to report whether such a phenomenon occurred. It may be noted, though, that their experimental situation may not have been conducive to reporting perceived vertical shifts, because the alignment rod used for response extended vertically and therefore could have been matched to auditory signals even if these were perceived as elevated.

The congenitally blind are, typically, worse than blindfolded sighted subjects in localizing auditory targets and in comparing two auditory locations (Warren, Anooshian, & Bollinger, 1973). This phenomenon is consonant with both the eye-movement mediated memory and the visual frame of reference hypotheses.

For those blind from birth, there is no visual experience and thus no visual frame of reference, and there can be no effective target-directed eye movements. However, people who have had several years of vision before becoming blind are significantly better at auditory localization than those blind from birth. Warren et al. (1973) argued that early visual experience establishes a visual frame of reference, a framework that may continue to be effective in mediating auditory localization performance even after the loss of vision. The later blind cannot make use of effective target-directed eye movements, and thus it must be that a residual visual framework mediates their better performance. Target-directed eye movements may further improve performance, but a visual frame of reference is clearly an important component of the auditory localization process, whether or not eye movements occur.

Another theoretical approach is represented by Auerbach and Sperling (1974), who posited two alternatives. One is that there is a "common space" to which both auditory and visual signals are referred, so that visual and auditory targets are compared directly within this common space. The other is that there are separate representations of visual and auditory direction, and that comparison of visual and auditory locations requires a translation from one representation to the other. Their experimental procedure involved the 0.5-sec presentation of an auditory or a visual target in one of two locations separated by about 6°, then an interstimulus interval of 1.5 sec, then the presentation of a second signal in either of the two locations, in either of the two modalities. The subject made a verbal judgment about whether the two signals were in the same or in different locations. The visual-visual trials were performed perfectly. The mixed-modality and auditory-auditory results were of interest, however. If the signals are referred to a common space, their distributions should not differ. In fact, the distributions had roughly 96% overlapping variance. Thus it was concluded that the common space hypothesis was valid.

The Auerbach and Sperling results do contradict the argument that there are separate visual and auditory frameworks for target localization, and support the notion that a single frame of reference is involved. However, the results do not seem to rule out the possibility that the "common space" involved is in fact a visual space, as Warren (1970) and Platt and Warren (1972) have suggested, or that its usefulness in mediating localization may be enhanced by visual referents.

2.3.3. Multimodal Perception of Egocentric Location and Studies of "Intersensory Bias." In the everyday world, instances abound in which two or more spatial modalities simultaneously inform the observer of the location of an object. In these situations the several modalities contribute to the percept, with one of the modalities perhaps providing more than the other. However, the nature of the relative contribution is obscured by the very redundancy of the information. To disambiguate the situation, investigators have placed normally congruent spatial modalities into conflict with one another. An example is viewing the hand through an image-displacing wedge prism, thereby creating a discrepancy between the visually and proprioceptively perceived locations of the limb [or, more properly, a discrepancy between (1) the "expected" position sense information, given the altered visual input, and (2) the actual position sense infromation]. The rationale for this procedure is that by creating a discrepancy between the two modalities it is possible to keep track of each of their respective inputs, because they are differentially "tagged" by having different apparent locations. By means of this procedure, then, judgments can be made about the relative contribution of each modality to the multimodal percept.

Thus a voluminous literature has accumulated in which human subjects are exposed for various lengths of time to a variety of perceptual rearrangements, including displacement, inversion, right-left reversal, tilt, and curvature of visual space, and displacement and right-left reversal of auditory space. Subjects confronted with these distortions reveal both an immediate response and long-term adaptation to the imposed intersensory discrepancy. Of the two phenomena, more is known about adaptation. It has been shown in a multitude of experiments that extended exposure (particularly if it involves active perceptual-motor behavior) to any stable visual or auditory rearrangement will produce at least some adaptation, frequently measurable for many minutes after the exposure period has been terminated (e.g., Choe & Welch, 1974). The basis for this adaptation is usually a change in the felt position of various body part such as the limbs, head, or eyes, although with some forms of rearrangement (e.g., prismatically induced curvature of physically straight contours) a small amount of purely visual (i.e., oculocentric) adaptation has been noted (e.g., Hay & Pick, 1966). (See Welch, 1978, and Chapter 24 for comprehensive reviews of this literature).

It may be argued that the observer's *immediate* response to intersensory discrepancy reveals more about normal intermodality organization than do the long-term adaptive effects, because the latter often involve learning, conscious strategies, and other processes not generally found in nondiscrepant (i.e., normal) perceptual situations. The typical immediate response to a discrepancy between two sensory modalities is for one or both of the modalities to influence the other in a manner referred to as "intersensory bias." In an oft-cited study, Hay et al. (1965) demonstrated that upon initially viewing the stationary hand through a light-displacing wedge prism, the limb feels as if it is located rather near its seen (prismatically displaced) position, as indicated by the subject's attempts to point to it with the other (unseen) hand. Hay et al. (1965) referred to this dramatic intersensory interaction between vision and felt limb position as "visual capture," a term borrowed from Tastevin (1937).

Bias effects have been examined for three combinations of spatial modalities—vision and proprioception, vision and audition, and proprioception and audition. The finding by Hay et al. (1965) of very substantial visual bias of proprioception, typically symbolized $V(P)$, was confirmed in a number of later studies (e.g., Klein, 1966; Pick, Warren, & Hay, 1969; Smothergill, 1968; Warren & Pick, 1970), with $V(P)$ ranging from about 60 to 75% of the total visual-proprioceptive discrepancy. Also obtained in many of these studies was small, but statistically reliable, proprioceptive bias of vision, $P(V)$, ranging from around 16 to 40%. The latter result contradicts the conclusion of Hay et al. (1965) that the proprioceptive information has no influence in the visual-proprioceptive discrepancy situation.

It has been noted in nearly all these studies that the *sum* of $V(P)$ and $P(V)$ equals or is not statistically different from 100% It is not surprising, therefore, that subjects in these experiments generally fail to report any visual-proprioceptive discrepancy.

When vision and audition are caused to provide discrepant information about spatial location, observers tend to hear the sound to be near or at its seen location (Bermant & Welch, 1976; Choe, Welch, Guilford, & Juola, 1975; Fisher, 1968; Jack & Thurlow, 1973; Jackson, 1953; Pick et al., 1969; Stratton, 1897; Thomas, 1941; Thurlow & Jack, 1973; Warren & Pick,

1970; Willey, Inglis, & Pearce, 1937; Witkin, Wapner, & Leventhal, 1952; Young, 1928). This strong bias of audition by vision, symbolized *V(A)*, is frequently referred to as the "ventrioloquism effect" (Howard & Templeton, 1966, p. 361) because it is an important basis of the ventriloquist's ability to "throw the voice." It amounts to 40 to 80% of the discrepancy. Attempts to obtain auditory bias of vision, *A(V)*, have found little or none (Pick et al., 1969; Warren & Pick, 1970).

In the few studies to examine auditory-proprioceptive discrepancies, the mean proprioceptive bias of audition, symbolized *P(A)*, has ranged from about 50 to 80%, whereas auditory bias of proprioception, *A(P)*, of from 1 to 18% has been obtained (Fisher, 1968; Pick et al., 1969; Warren & Pick, 1970).

2.4. Shape, Size, and Texture

2.4.1. Comparisons Among the Modalities. The perception of size, shape, and texture comes to us primarily through two senses—vision and touch (the latter including the active grasping and manipulating of objects, a sense that may be referred to as "haptic touch"). A number of studies have compared these (and occasionally other) senses in terms of their relative performance on these spatial tasks.

2.4.1.1. Perception of Size in One or Two Dimensions. Connolly and Jones (1970) and others (using a variety of measures, such as magnitude estimation, and cross-modality matching) found little difference between visual length and distance of arm movements, which is contrary to the results of an old study of Jastrow (1886). This is, however, consistent with the findings by Ronco (1963), S. S. Stevens and Guirao (1963), M. Teghtsoonian and Teghtsoonian (1965), and R. Teghtsoonian and Teghtsoonian (1970) that visual and kinesthetic distance are directly proportional to physical length. Finally, Abravanel (1971b) demonstrated that judgments of length are about as accurate when vision and active touch are combined as when either modality is used alone. Thus the general conclusion appears to be that linear extent is perceived about equally accurately by all of the spatial senses.

In contrast to linear extents, two-dimensional objects do not appear to be equally well perceived by vision and touch. Anstis and Loizos (1967), for example, found that holes appear about the same to tongue and eye but smaller to the fingers. Waterman (1917) reported that holes appeared larger to the eye than to the tongue or palm of the hand.

2.4.1.2. Perception of Shape Although people are able to make rough matches of seen and felt shapes, careful analysis indicates that haptic touch is inferior to vision in this respect, in terms of both accuracy and precision (Abravanel, 1971a; Bryant & Raz, 1975; Cashdan, 1968; Milner & Bryant, 1970; Rudel & Teuber, 1964). It is interesting that Owen and Brown (1970) found for both vision and haptic touch that the relationship between number of sides (i.e., complexity) of a shape and its discriminability is nonlinear. That is, for both modalities, eight-sided shapes are more readily distinguished from one another than are shapes with either fewer or more sides.

2.4.1.3. Texture Perception. The data are mixed concerning the relative efficacy of vision and touch in the perception of surface texture. Some studies have shown visual judgments to be either more accurate (S. A. Rose, Blank, & Bridger, 1972), less variable (Bjorkman, 1967), or more rapid (I. D. Brown, 1960) than tactual judgments. On the other hand, some more recent studies (Heller, 1982; Lederman & Abbott, 1981) have found visual and tactual texture perception to be equally accurate and precise. It is possible that this contradiction is due to experimenters' choices of texture densities.

2.4.2. Multimodal Perception of Size, Shape, and Texture. Several studies have investigated the relative contributions of vision and the haptic sense in the perception of shape by means of the conflict-induced sensory modality tagging procedure. An example is a study by Rock and Victor (1964). Subjects grasped a square with the unseen hand while looking at it through a distorting optical device that made it appear rectangular. The subject's perception was typically determined entirely by the visual information. That is, the viewed square was felt to be rectangular. A variety of studies have replicated this form of visual capture (Fishkin, Pishkin, & Stahl, 1975; Kinney & Luria, 1970; Klein, 1966; McDonnell & Duffett, 1972; E. A. Miller, 1972; Power & Graham, 1976; Rock, Mack, Adams, & Hill, 1965; Singer & Day, 1969). Similarly, it has been shown that a straight edge viewed through a wedge prism, and thereby caused to look curved, feels curved (Easton, 1976; Easton & Falzett, 1978; Easton & Moran, 1978; Festinger, Burnham, Ono, & Bamber, 1967, Gibson, 1933). Thus it seems reasonable to conclude that under normal (i.e., nondiscrepant) circumstances of visual-haptic redundancy the perception of shape is determined primarily by vision.

The investigation by Lederman and Abbott (1981), referred to in the preceding section, included an experiment in which vision and touch were placed into conflict with respect to the perception of texture. The investigators found equally substantial visual bias of touch and tactual bias of vision, a finding congruent with their demonstration that the two sensory modalities, when measured alone, were equally proficient at detecting texture.

2.5. Important Variables in Intersensory Bias Involving Spatial Events

The variables influencing the magnitude of intersensory bias in the situations of intersensory discrepancy involving spatial perception may be grouped into two classes: (1) stimulus variables (i.e., the nature of the stimuli and their mode of presentation) and (2) response variables (i.e., the response demands made of subjects).

2.5.1. Stimulus Variables. Stimulus variables may be further subdivided into structural and cognitive, the former entailing the manner in which the discrepant spatial information is administered and the latter the observers' assumptions concerning the origin and cause of the discrepancy.

2.5.1.1. Structural Factors. There are two major structural factors that have been shown to affect intersensory bias: (1) the magnitude of the discrepancy and (2) active versus passive placement of the limb. Not surprisingly, increasing intersensory discrepancies are associated with decreasing magnitudes of intersensory bias, at least if measured as a percentage of the total discrepancy (Bermant & Welch, 1976; Thurlow & Jack, 1973; Warren & Cleaves, 1971). The results of the Warren and Cleaves (1971) study are seen in Figures 25.14 and 25.15. The second major structural variable concerns the degree of activity of the limb being viewed. Welch, Widawski, Harrington, and Warren (1979) compared the passive placement of the subject's target hand (the traditional precedure) to its active placement and found *V(P)* of 89 and 66%, respectively. This outcome confirmed the authors' hypothesis that the greater salience of actively generated proprioceptive information allows this modality to

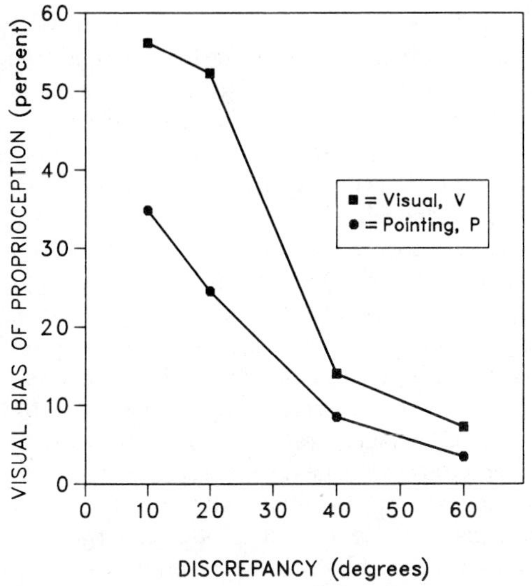

Figure 25.14. Effects of magnitude of intersensory discrepancy on visual bias of proprioception. The experimental situation involves giving the adult subject discrepant information about the visual and felt locations of the forefinger, using a mirror system, and asking for either a pointing (P) or a visual (V) judgment about the *felt* location of the finger. The dependent variable is the location response, taken as a percentage of the distance between the felt (i.e., real) location of the finger and its optically displaced seen location. Thus, for example, 60% bias in the 10° discrepancy condition means that the subject responded slightly closer to the optical location than to the real (felt) location, in fact 6° from the real location and only 4° from the optical location. The results show that the percent magnitude of intersensory bias decreases dramatically as the amount of intersensory discrepancy increases. The extent of intersensory bias is not, therefore, a simple characteristic of the two modalities involved, but depends on physical parameters such as the magnitude of the imposed discrepancy. (From D. H. Warren & W. T. Cleaves, Visual-proprioceptive interaction under large amounts of conflict, *Journal of Experimental Psychology, 90*. Copyright 1971 by American Psychological Association. Reprinted with permission.)

withstand better the biasing influence of vision. It should be noted that the effect of the active/passive manipulation on intersensory bias is exactly opposite the effect traditionally (e.g., Held & Hein, 1958) obtained when prism *adaptation* is measured. Consequently, Welch et al. (1979) concluded that "visual capture of felt limb position and proprioceptively based prism adaptation are qualitatively different phenomena or the outcome of different processes" (p. 656). Radeau and Bertelson (1977) came to the same general conlusion with regard to the ventriloquism effect.

2.5.1.2. Cognitive Factors. The two major cognitive factors in intersensory bias are the subject's (1) degree of awareness of the intersensory discrepancy and (2) assumptions concerning the unitariness of the distal object from which the discrepant inputs are emanating. Informing subjects that the seen and felt positions of the prism-exposed limb may not, or indeed will not, be the same appears to have no effect on $V(P)$ or $P(V)$, or on the subjects' ability to detect the presence of the prismatic displacement, at least when this visual-proprioceptive discrepancy is in the range of 10–16 ° (e.g., Pick et al., 1969). Even a concrete demonstration of the optical effects of the prism has no effect on visual or proprioceptive bias (Warren, 1979, Experiment 1). Interestingly, Warren (1979) found that such a demonstration *did* affect the visual bias of audition, reducing it substantially.

The notion of intersensory discrepancy would seem to have no functional psychological significance unless the observer assumes (not necessarily consciously) that the information being provided by the two sensory modalities concerns one and the same distal event. Several investigators (Radeau & Bertelson, 1977; Welch & Warren, 1980) have argued that such an "assumption of unity" is necessary if intersensory bias or adaptation is to occur, a conclusion first supported by Welch (1972), with respect to prism adaptation. In the latter experiment, the subject in a darkened room viewed a luminous finger (the experimenter's) that was consistently placed a fixed distance to one side of the subject's (nonvisible) finger, a situation that mimicked the effects of prismatic displacement. It was found that if the subject were told that the finger being viewed was his/her own, "adaptation" was about twice that occurring for a subject informed that the visible finger was the experimenter's. Welch concluded that the presence of a certain amount of adaptation even when the subject was aware that vision and proprioception were not discrepant indicates the difficulty in attempting to destroy by instructions alone the observer's assumption of unity between felt and seen limb position.

Welch and Warren (1980) have proposed that the term "compelling" be used to describe intersensory relationships about which the subject's assumption of unity is likely to be strong. (Radeau & Bertelson, 1977, refer to this as the degree of "realism.") A view of the hand, for example, represents a highly compelling visual-proprioceptive situation.

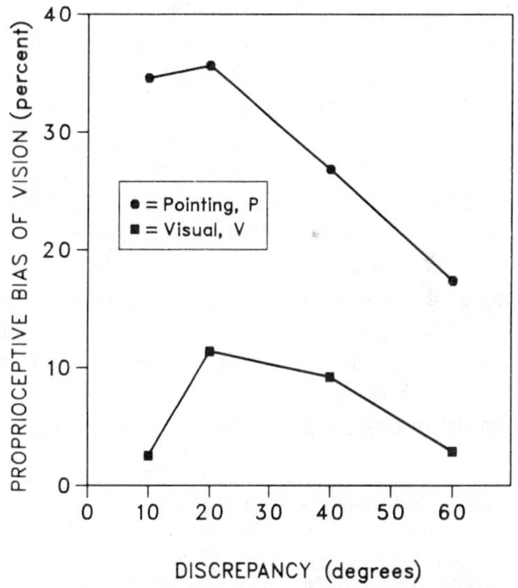

Figure 25.15. Effects of magnitude of intersensory discrepancy on proprioceptive bias of vision. The experiential situation is as described in the legend for Figure 25.14, except that here the subject is asked to indicate the *seen* (rather than the felt) location of the finger, in order to investigate the amount of bias of vision by proprioception. Combining the two response types, the percent bias decreased with increases in discrepancy from 20 to 60°; the difference between the 10 and 20° discrepancy conditions was not statistically significant. Taking Figures 25.14 and 25.15 together, it is evident that visual bias of proprioception, *V(P)*, is greater than proprioceptive bias of vision, *P(V)*, at least at moderate amounts of imposed discrepancy. It should also be noted that there is an effect of response type: When a visual response is used, *V(P)* is greater and *P(V)* smaller than when a pointing (proprioceptive) response is used. (From D. H. Warren & W. T. Cleaves, Visual-proprioceptive interaction under large amounts of conflict, *Journal of Experimental Psychology, 90*. Copyright 1971 by American Psychological Association. Reprinted with permission.)

Several studies (Jack & Thurlow, 1973; Jackson, 1953; Radeau & Bertelson, 1977; Warren, Welch, & McCarthy, 1981) reported that increased compellingness is associated with stronger intersensory bias. Radeau and Bertelson (1977, Experiment 3), for example, showed that physically separated visual and auditory sources appeared to be fused about 78% of the time when they consisted of a moving mouth synchronized with a voice, but only 49% of the time when the visual stimulus was a light whose intensity was synchronously modulated by the sound of the voice.

2.5.2. Response Variables. The second major category of variables affecting the magnitude of intersensory bias is the nature of the indicator response and its timing. Warren (1980) compared the traditional pointing indicator response (using the nontarget hand) to one in which vision was used (i.e., a numbered scale that could be viewed immediately after exposure to the prism-displaced index finger). The results were clear: $V(P)$ for the pointing group was 71%, as compared to 91% for the vision group. $P(V)$ was 35 and -3%, respectively.

Thus when a given sensory modality is being used for the response indicator, it plays the greater role in determining the resolution of an intersensory discrepancy, both in biasing the other modality more and in being biased less. One possible explanation for this outcome is that using an indicator involving a particular sensory modality forces subjects to *attend* closely to that modality, thereby making it a more powerful biasing agent and more resistant to bias by other modalities. The potential role of attention in intersensory bias is addressed in Section 2.6. In any event, it is clear that if one wishes to obtain a "pure" measure of bias, it is necessary to use some sort of "amodal" indicator response such as magnitude estimation. Indeed, a recent study by Warren, McCarthy, and Welch (1983) has successfully used the latter measure.

With respect to the timing of the response measure, it appears, in studies of visual capture, that if the localizing responses are delayed until after vision is precluded, $V(P)$ declines in strength and $P(V)$ is enhanced. Warren, Widawski, and Schmitt (Note #3), for example, compared delays of 0, 10, 20, 40, and 60 sec between subjects' retraction of the target finger and pointing to its (remembered) felt or seen position. They found a decline of $V(P)$ from 62% in the 0-sec delay condition to 33% for 40- and 60-sec delays, whereas $P(V)$ increased from 25% in the 0-sec condition to 61% in the 60-sec condition.

2.6. Theories of Intersensory Bias

The three major contenders as an explanation of intersensory bias in situations of conflict between spatial localizing modalities are (1) modality precision, (2) directed attention, and (3) modality appropriateness. As we shall see shortly, these theories may be complementary to one another rather than mutually exclusive.

According to the modality precision hypothesis, the resolution of an intersensory discrepancy will always be in favor of the more precise of the two modalities (e.g., Choe et al., 1975; Fisher, 1968; Howard & Templeton, 1966, p. 361; Kaufman, 1974, p. 437). The origin of this notion is the observation that the order of "dominance" among the spatial modalities is congruent with their relative precision—vision, proprioception, audition (e.g., Pick et al., 1969; Warren et al., 1981; Welch et al., 1979). Thus, as demonstrated by Pick et al. (1969), vision (the most precise spatial modality) dominates both proprioception and audition (the second and third in precision) and proprioception dominates audition. Likewise, vision dominates audition more than it dominates proprioception, although only if precautions are taken to control for the relative compellingness of the respective intersensory relationships (Warren et al., 1981). Further support for the modality precision hypothesis comes from two observations by Welch et al. (1979). First, it was noted that, across all experimental conditions, the less the subjects' proprioceptive localization precision relative to their visual precision, the greater the $V(P)$, the correlation being .70. Second, the active/passive manipulation examined in this experiment created a difference in proprioceptive precision (lower precision with passive limb placement), which, in turn, was associated with the difference in intersensory bias predicted by the modality precision hypothesis [i.e., greater $V(P)$ for the passive condition].

Contradictory to the modality precision hypothesis was the failure of Radeau and Bertelson (1976) to find a difference in the magnitude of $V(A)$ when the precision of the auditory stimulus was manipulated by a comparison between presenting a sound in a textured visual field and presenting it in the dark, the latter producing a relatively large intrasubject variance in localization.

Thus the evidence as it relates to intersensory bias in situations of spatial localization is, for the most part, favorable to the modality precision hypothesis. It should be mentioned, however, that the evidence for this hypothesis in situations of visual-haptic discrepancies of shape and size is quite contradictory or equivocal (Becker-Carus, 1973; Derrick & Dewar, 1970; Power & Graham, 1976).

According to the directed-attention hypothesis, the degree to which two sensory modalities bias one another is determined by the observer's distribution of attention to each of them. Thus if a great deal of attention is paid to one modality relative to the other, the former will strongly bias the latter but will not be biased very much itself. Support for this notion comes from studies of both prism adaptation (Canon, 1970, 1971; Kelso, Cook, Olson, & Epstein, 1975; Uhlarik & Canon, 1971) and visual capture (Warren & Schmitt, 1978), in which task demands forced subjects to devote attention primarily to one of the sensory modalities over the other. It has not, however, proved effective merely to *instruct* the subject to pay attention to one or the other of the modalities. For example, during the prism-exposure phase of some intersensory bias studies (e.g., Pick et al., 1969) subjects are instructed either to ignore the felt position of the finger and respond to its seen position or vice versa. The resulting localization is essentially the same in both cases, indicating that instructions to redirect attention have no effect on the extent of $V(P)$ or $P(V)$ in this situation.

In the study by Warren and Schmitt (1978) the subject's attention was drawn to either the visual or proprioceptive modality by including either a large number of visual localization trials (Visual Attention Condition) during the prism-exposure phase of the experiment or a large number of proprioceptive localization trials (Proprioceptive Attention Condition). Interspersed among these many "context" trials were a few trials on which the subject's hand was both seen (through the prism) and felt; the measures of intersensory bias were obtained on these bisensory trials. In the Visual Attention Condition, $V(P)$ greatly exceeded $P(V)$, whereas in the proprioceptive context, $P(V)$ exceeded $V(P)$, results that support the directed-attention hypothesis. A number of studies of the perception of visual-auditory temporal duration (e.g., Lhamon & Goldstone, 1974) have also supported this hypothesis (see Section 3.2.2).

The modality appropriateness hypothesis stems from the observation that each sensory modality is capable of a variety of functions but has one or more functions that it performs very well and even better than do the other modalities (e.g., Freides, 1974; O'Connor & Hermelin, 1972). Relating this fact to intersensory bias, it is claimed that, of the two sensory modalities involved in an instance of intersensory discrepancy, the one that is more appropriate *for the task in question* will be the more influential in terms of intersensory bias. Thus, for example, if vision is pitted against audition with respect to a spatial localization task, vision will have the stronger biasing effect (and be biased less) because, according to the present hypothesis, it is more appropriately designed for spatial judgments than is audition.

Although, for human beings, vision represents the spatial modality par excellence, audition is the superior modality for *temporal* judgments. According to the modality appropriateness hypothesis, then, temporal discrepancies between vision and audition should reveal dominance of audition over vision. As will be seen in Sections 3.2.2 and 3.3.2, precisely this result has been obtained for the judgment of both temporal duration (J. T. Walker & Scott, 1981) and rate (e.g., Myers, Cotton, & Hilp, 1981; Welch, DuttonHurt, & Warren, in press).

2.7. A Synthesis

It seems likely that all three theories of intersensory bias are at least partially correct. Thus Welch and Warren (1980) have argued that the relative bias between two sensory modalities is determined by the distribution of the observer's attention to these modalities (directed-attention hypothesis) which, in turn, stems (innately and/or ontogenetically) from their relative appropriateness for the task at hand (modality appropriateness hypothesis) and that an obvious manifestation of the relative appropriateness of a modality is its precision (modality precision hypothesis).

This integrative model of intersensory bias is depicted in Figure 25.16. In brief, the model proposes that the mediator of the effect of differential modality appropriateness is the observers' deployment of attention (see "Observer Processes" in Figure 25.16). It is likely, however, that situational constraints (e.g., experimental instructions, task demands) can modify, and perhaps even reverse, the normal distribution of attention. Finally, the greater the number of redundant stimulus properties (see "Stimulus Properties" in Figure 25.16), such as shape, motion, and texture, that are present and/or the greater the familiarity of the intersensory relationship ("Historical Factors"), the more *unified* the intersensory percept will be and the greater the contribution of the more appropriate modality to this unified experience. As noted earlier, these factors are known, collectively, as the "compellingness" of the intersensory relationship. Thus, for example, the sight and feel of the moving hand represents a more compelling visual-proprioceptive relationship than does the sight of a luminous dot attached to the unseen and stationary hand. Recent studies by Welch and his colleagues (Welch, Note 4; Welch, Warren, With & Wait, Note 5) have confirmed this prediction.

2.8. Key References

Auerbach, C., & Sperling, P. (1974). The results of this study contradict the hypothesis that there are separate visual and auditory frameworks for localization, and support the hypothesis that a single frame of reference is involved, a "common space" to which both visual and auditory signals are referred.

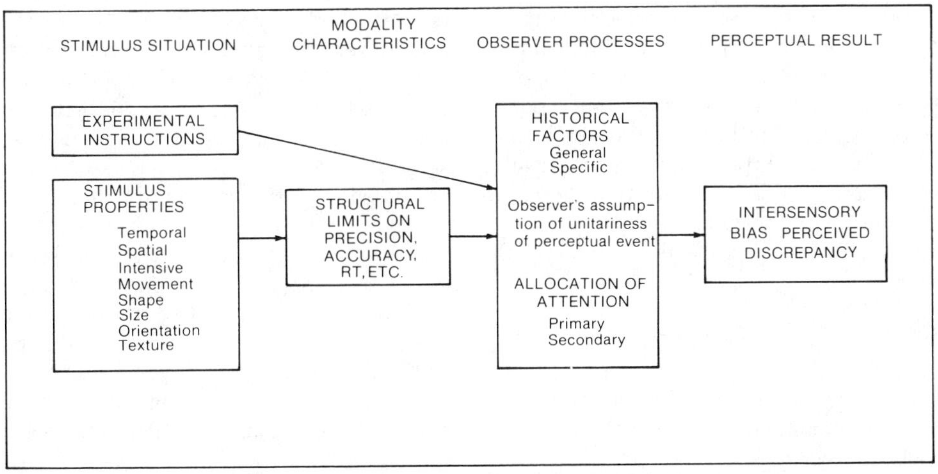

Figure 25.16. A model of intersensory bias in situations of imposed discrepancy between two (or more) sensory modalities. The *stimulus situation* includes, most importantly, the various event characteristics (e.g., size, spatial location) that are presented to the observer by the modalities. The manner in which this information is acquired by the observer is dictated by the physical characteristics of the modalities (e.g., the "fine grainness" of the receptor surface). Crucial to the model are the *observer processes*, which include the observer's (1) specific and general experience with the bisensory event in question, (2) assumption that the two (or more) sensory inputs are emanating from a single distal object, and (3) allocation of attention to the two (or more) modalities (as determined by the relative "appropriateness" of each of the modalities for the event in question). Finally, the *perceptual result* is the partial or complete perceptual resolution of the imposed intersensory discrepancy in the form of the bias of each modality by the other. (From R. B. Welch & D. H. Warren, Immediate perceptual response to intersensory discrepancy, *Psychological Bulletin, 88*. Copyright 1980 by American Psychological Association. Reprinted with permission.)

Ebenholtz, S. M. (1974). This is a clear, documented presentation of the argument that visual effects of prism adaptation that have traditionally been considered evidence of adaptive recalibration may actually be artifacts of a change in felt ocular position due to "eye muscle potentiation."

Platt, B., & Warren, D. H. (1972). This study was important in clarifying that the visual context effect, wherein auditory localization is better with a visual field present than not present, depends on both a textured visual environment and target-directed eye movements.

Wallach, H. (1940). This article describes a classic series of studies that clearly revealed the role of head movements in the spatial localization of auditory objects.

Welch, R.B., & Warren, D.H. (1980). This is an extensive review of research on the immediate perceptual response to imposed discrepancies between sensory modalities, a form of intersensory interaction referred to as "intersensory bias."

3. TEMPORAL EVENTS

There are numerous situations in which human observers perceive temporal events, either unimodally or multimodally. By temporal events, we refer to events whose defining structure is distributed over time, in contrast, for example, to spatial events, whose defining structure is distributed over space. The principal categories of temporal events that have been studied with a multimodality orientation are the perception of temporal duration, rate, and pattern. In each of these areas, the relative capability of each modality taken individually is assessed, followed by an examination of the various nonspecific and specific influences that a signal occurring to one modality may have on the perception of a signal occurring to another modality. Finally, we may examine the instances in which the joint contributions of two or more modalities have been studied in the formation of a single, multimodal percept of a temporal event.

Briefly, the distinction among these categories of temporal perception is as follows. Studies of temporal duration examine the veridicality of the relative judgments of individual signals of varying durations. Temporal rate refers to a train of pulses delivered repetitively over time, with the subject asked to make some judgment of their rapidity. Temporal pattern may involve both duration and rate, signals of varying durations being interspersed at varying rates, with the subject asked to make an evaluation of the relationship of the various elements of the pattern to one another.

3.1. Comparisons Among the Modalities

Although in principal nearly all the sensory modalities can provide information about temporal events, it is vision and audition that have been studied most.

Several studies have shown that audition, in comparison to vision, is a fundamentally more accurate modality for the judgment of short durations. Goodfellow (1933) studied the ability of subjects to judge an empty 1-sec interval by visual, tactual, or auditory markers. Performance was best for auditory judgments, followed by touch (34% higher than audition) and vision (65% higher). Although the magnitude of the differences is impressive and the direction would undoubtedly be sustained in any case, it should be noted that no attempt was made to equate the intensities of the signals in the various modalities, a factor that in subsequent research (e.g., Goldstone, Boardman, & Lhamon, 1959) has been found to affect duration judgments.

Tanner, Patton, and Atkinson (1965) evaluated subjects' ability to judge which of two successively presented signals, differing by 0.1 sec in duration, was longer. Judgment of successive auditory signals was more accurate than that of successive visual signals over the 0.5- to 1.5-sec range studied.

Goldstone et al. (1959) reported an interesting intersensory difference between audition and vision that has received a great deal of subsequent attention, Briefly, the observation is that an auditory signal of a given duration is judged as lasting longer than a visual signal of the same physical duration. The approach taken by Goldstone et al. (1959) was to present an ascending or descending series of signals in one modality, with the successive signals differing in duration by 0.1 sec, and to ask the subject to report when the duration was one second. The average auditory signal judged to equal 1 sec was 0.65 sec, whereas the visual signal was 1.1 sec. This basic difference, also noted by Behar and Bevan (1961), has been replicated many times under different conditions, and is thus a robust and reliable phenomenon. It occurs, for example, when the physical size of the visual target is varied (Goldstone et al., 1959), with filled as well as unfilled intervals (Goldstone & Goldfarb, 1963), with direct comparison of auditory and visual durations, as opposed to comparison of each to an internal standard (Goldstone & Goldfarb, 1964b), and with a reproduction method (Goldstone, 1968a). Intensity of the signals is also a relevant factor, with durations of more intense signals usually judged longer, regardless of modality. However, the auditory-visual difference is generally sustained even in the face of at least moderate differences in intensity between the two modalities.

Along with these various positive reports, there are also instances where investigators have not found the phenomenon. Tanner et al. (1965) found a visual signal to be judged longer than an auditory signal at 0.5 sec. They used many more trials than the studies cited above, and it is possible that the difference is attributable to this factor, or it may be that the normal direction of difference tends to change at shorter durations, a finding reported by J.T. Walker and Scott (1981). D.R. Brown and Hitchcock (1965) used time intervals of up to 17 sec and found, using a reproduction method, no differences between auditory and visual duration judgments. The possibility that subjects used a counting mediator was not controlled for or discussed, and the results are therefore in question. Finally, Furukawa (1978) found no difference between auditory and visual judgments using a repetitive cycling method, where subjects experienced the two signals in alternating cadence and made continuous adjustments until they were satisfied with the match. Under such conditions, it is perhaps not surprising that judgments approach veridicality. [It should also be noted that Ehrensing and Lhamon (1966) also reported no differences between auditory and tactual durations, using a similar stimulus cycling method.]

With respect to the perception of temporal rate, vision has been shown to be less acute than audition. That is, the visual critical flicker fusion rate is substantially lower than the auditory flutter fusion rate. With subfusion temporal rates (e.g., 2–10 Hz), several studies (e.g., Myers et al., 1981; Welch, DuttonHurt, & Warren, in press) have demonstrated that an auditory rate will be perceived as slower than a physically identical visual rate.

Studies of the perception of temporal pattern have revealed differences among the various sensory modalities that are very

Table 25.1. Results of Pattern Recognition and Reproduction Tests in Several Modalities

	% Correct Responses			
	Initial Test		Post Practice	
Modality	Recognition	Reproduction	Recognition	Reproduction
A	85	67	87	77
V	75	32	78	70
T	70	47	74	76

Patterns of various elements were created and presented to the ear (A), the eye (V), or the fingertips (T). In the discrimination test, two patterns were presented successively to a modality, and the subject judged whether they were the same or different. In the reproduction test, the subject experienced a pattern in one of the three modalities, and then attempted to reproduce the pattern by tapping with a baton. The results of the discrimination and reproduction tests appear in the table as percentage of correct responses under "Initial Test." Subjects were then given ten 0.5-hr periods of practice on the task and then were retested. The results of the post-practice retest are shown under "Post Practice." Some effect of training clearly occurred, although it is also apparent that training was more effective in those situations in which initial performance was rather poor. Audition is clearly the best of these three modalities for the perception of patterns. (From R. H. Gault & L. D. Goodfellow, An empirical comparison of audition, vision, and touch in the discrimination of temporal patterns and ability to reproduce them, Journal of General Psychology, 18. Copyright 1938 by American Psychological Association. Reprinted with permission.)

similar to the differences found with respect to duration and rate judgments. Gault and Goodfellow (1938) presented temporal patterns to audition via a loudspeaker, to vision via a neon flash tube, and to touch via a device that presented vibratory signals to the fingertip. In a recognition task, the subject judged whether two successively presented patterns were the same or different. As seen in Table 25.1, both recognition and reproduction of patterns was best for audition, both initially and after 30 min of practice. Vision was better than touch for recognition measures, whereas the reverse was true for reproduction.

J. R. Nazzaro and Nazzaro (1970) found faster learning of Morse code signals by audition than by vision. Rubinstein and Gruenberg (1971) used temporal patterns consisting of sequences of long and short time intervals, separated by either visual or auditory signals (see Figure 25.17). Discrimination involved subjects' ability to determine at which position in the sequence the single "long" interval occurred. The task required subjects to judge whether two successively presented stimuli were the same or different in their temporal pattern. The two patterns could be both auditory (AA), both visual (VV), or mixed (AV, VA). In Experiment 1, the intersignal intervals were shorter than in Experiment 2. In Experiment 1, with faster patterns, the VV performance was worse than AA, with the mixed-modality performances worse yet. In Experiment 2, there were no notable differences among the conditions. The timing differences were not large. However, it seems reasonable to conclude that although with easier (i.e., slower) patterns the VV and AA comparisons were comparably difficult, as the patterns became more difficult (i.e., faster), the superiority of auditory pattern perception emerged. The mixed-modality performance was clearly limited by the visual modality.

Handel and Yoder (1975) demonstrated a comparable effect. The key discrimination in the auditory pattern was pitch, and that for the visual pattern was color. At relatively slow pattern rates (one element per second) the modalities were comparable in accuracy, whereas with more difficult stimuli (five elements per second), auditory performance was better. Similarly, Garner and Gottwald (1968) and Handel and Buffardi (1969) found auditory pattern performance superior to visual performance as element rate increased. All these studies thus demonstrated auditory superiority in pattern perception, but it is a superiority that emerges only with more difficult patterns. Rosenbusch and Gardner (1968), looking at the auditory/visual difference over age, found auditory discrimination to be consistently better over ages 5–13. The performance of both modalities improved with age, but the auditory superiority was consistent regardless of age.

Hill (1971) made comparisons of vision and touch, finding interesting modality differences that parallel the "discrimination difficulty" results cited above for audition-vision. Thus with relatively simple spatial-temporal patterns, visual and tactual error functions were comparable, whereas as the complexity of the patterns increased, tactual errors increased at a faster rate.

3.2. Interactions Involving Temporal Duration

There is a long history of study of the human ability to judge temporal duration, and a good deal of it has involved a comparison of the various sensory modalities. Much of this work did not, however, originate with the question of the relative quality of the sensory modalities, but with the issue of how duration is judged. Specifically, it is reasoned that if duration judgments by various sensory modalities tend to behave in the same ways with variations in certain parameters (e.g., signal intensity), then this provides support for a central, as opposed to a peripheral (modality-specific), mechanism. This question is not germane to this chapter, but it is worth mentioning because it serves as the impetus for much of the research that is, for other reasons, relevant to this section.

A great deal of the temporal duration literature does not address questions of true intersensory interaction. There are,

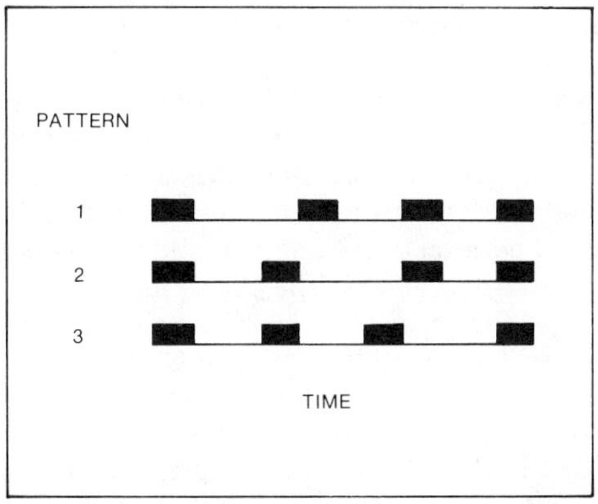

Figure 25.17. Representation of the temporal patterns used by Rubinstein and Gruenberg (1971) to investigate intra- and cross-modal pattern matching abilities. The black segments represent either 1-msec square pulses, presented binaurally, or 3-msec light flashes, and the spaces between segments represent short and long (0.222 and 0.487 sec, respectively) time gaps between stimulus pulses. The critical difference between the patterns shown lies, therefore, not in any difference between the duration of stimulus segments, but rather in the location of a single *long* gap among several *short* gaps. (From L. Rubinstein & E. M. Gruenberg, Intramodal and crossmodal sensory transfer of visual and auditory temporal patterns, *Perception and Psychophysics*, 1971, 9. Reprinted with permission.)

however, two phenomena of clear interest to this chapter. One is the phenomenon of "intersensory anchors," where a prior stimulus of a certain duration delivered to one modality may have an effect on the judged duration of a signal presented to another modality. The other intersensory effect has to do with bisensory duration judgments in which a signal is presented simultaneously to two modalities and the resulting judgment is evaluated to determine the relative contributions of the two modalities.

3.2.1. Sensory Context—Intersensory Anchor Effects. Generally, an anchor effect occurs when one signal given prior to another affects the judgments of a quality of the second signal, as for example when an object of moderate weight seems lighter if lifted directly after a heavy object, or heavier if lifted directly after a light object. Goldstone et al. (1959, Experiment 2) demonstrated such anchor effects for duration judgments within each of the auditory and visual modalities. The long and short anchors were, respectively, 2.0 and 0.1 sec. A short anchor series began with the presentation of a 0.1-sec signal, then successively longer (by 0.1 sec each time) signals, until the subject judged the duration to be equal to a standard interval of 1 sec. Briefly, the expected anchor effects were found within each of the visual and auditory modalities, although there was some indication that the visual judgments were more susceptible to anchor effects than were the auditory judgments. Behar and Bevan (1961) also examined intramodal anchor effects, but with longer anchors (up to 9 sec), and found results similar to those of Goldstone et al. (1959).

Given that such intramodal anchor effects on duration judgments exist, the question arises whether an anchor in one modality can affect duration judgments in another modality. Goldstone et al. (1959) demonstrated such an effect. Two groups received visual and auditory sequence series interspersed with one another; the data indicated, although not reliably, that an initial visual series raised the point at which a subsequent auditory series was judged to equal 1 sec, and that an initial auditory series lowered the subsequent visual 1-sec judgment point. Behar and Bevan (1961, Experiment 4) addressed the intersensory anchor issue more directly, using long (10- and 20-sec) anchors and signal durations of 1–5 sec, with instructions to use an 11-point scale (very-very-very-short to very-very-very long) to rate each signal. The anchor was interspersed on every fourth trial. Auditory anchors within the visual judgment series had a very significant effect, as did visual anchors within the auditory judgments. Furthermore, the two intersensory effects were roughly parallel to one another, and to the corresponding intrasensory anchor effects. The effects for the 10-sec anchors were stronger than those for the 20-sec anchors, although the latter were still statistically significant.

Goldstone and Goldfarb (1964a) used an interesting variation on this basic approach to intersensory anchors. The rationale was as follows: If physically equal durations are judged longer for auditory than for visual signals, then a visual signal should serve as a short anchor for an auditory test signal of the same *physical* duration, making it seem longer than it would be without the visual signal. Likewise, an auditory stimulus should serve as a long anchor for a visual test signal of the same *physical* duration. These effects were indeed found, showing an intersensory influence that resulted from a naturally occurring difference in stimulus characteristics between the two modalities.

3.2.2. Multimodal Perception of Duration. In this intersensory situation a paired presentation of visual and auditory stimuli is used. The question is whether the paired stimulus acts like a single stimulus in one modality or in the other (or some combination). There is much interesting work yet to be done using this paradigm, but several initial and provocative results are available. In their early study, Goldstone et al. (1959) examined one such condition, varying the intensity of the visual and auditory signals. The intensity values for each modality were, 13.7 and 10.6 $cd \cdot m^{-2}$ for vision and 53 and 78 dB SPL for audition. A preliminary study had shown that the more intense light was judged to be more intense than the less intense sound, and vice versa, although no formal procedures for comparison were implemented. Two groups were used, one receiving the weak auditory and the strong visual stimulus and the other the reverse combination. Ascending and descending series with 0.1-sec steps were used, with the subject required to judge when the paired signal was equal to 1 sec. After this procedure, a 1-sec rest occurred. Then half of each group was instructed to focus attention on the visual stimulus and the other half to attend to the auditory stimulus. In the initial test, a low-intensity visual stimulus paired with a high-intensity auditory stimulus produced duration judgments like those of auditory stimuli presented alone. The higher intensity auditory signal controlled the bisensory percept. A high-intensity visual signal paired with a low-intensity signal of equal duration was judged in favor of vision. In both cases, then, the higher-intensity stimulus controlled the nature of the percept. The subsequent attempt to influence judgments by attentional instruction failed; regardless of instruction, the percept was controlled by the modality whose signal was of higher intensity.

In a later study, Lhamon and Goldstone (1974) used a paired comparison approach, in which they presented either an auditory or a visual signal as the standard stimulus, followed by a paired visual and auditory signal as the comparison stimulus. They compared the relative duration functions with earlier results in which visual-alone and auditory-alone signals were used in a similar paired comparison method. Alternatively, the paired stimulus as the standard was followed by a single modality stimulus as comparison. In general, the results followed the rule that the bisensory stimulus, whether serving as standard or comparison, acted like an auditory stimulus. Apparently, subjects' natural tendency was to attend the auditory signal of the bisensory pair. In a second experiment, the subject's attention was directed to either the visual or the auditory component of the bisensory stimulus. Here the attentional manipulation was effective. When subjects were instructed to attend to the auditory component, the bisensory stimulus acted as an auditory-alone stimulus (as, indeed, it had when no attentional instructions were given) and with instructed attention to the visual component, the bisensory stimulus acted as a visual-alone stimulus, countering the apparently spontaneous tendency to attend to the auditory component. It can be seen that these results are congruent with the directed-attention hypothesis of intersensory bias introduced in Section 2.6.

Finally, J. T. Walker and Scott (1981) report a provocative series of studies, the results of which are seen in Table 25.2. In this investigation the naturally occurring difference in visual and auditory duration functions was used in place of an experimental manipulation (note the similarity to Goldstone & Goldfarb, 1964a). That is, auditory and visual durations of equal physical magnitude are judged differently, the auditory being judged longer. When auditory and visual signals of physically equal duration were presented simultaneously, they were judged to be similar to an auditory-alone stimulus of the same duration.

Table 25.2. Mean Response Time for Light, Tone, and Light plus Tone Conditions in Three Experiments by Walker and Scott (1981)

	Light			Tone			Both		
Modality and Duration	500	1,000	1,500	500	1,000	1,500	500	1,000	1,500
Experiment 1— filled intervals (75 dBA)	588 (104)	1,029 (148)	1,405 (205)	581 (103)	1,128 (122)	1,542 (220)	579 (108)	1,110 (163)	1,553 (151)
Experiment 2— gaps (50 dBA)	483 (107)	930 (151)	1,335 (160)	525 (94)	1,030 (156)	1,440 (173)	539 (95)	1,059 (141)	1,438 (184)
Experiment 3— filled intervals (50 dBA)	575 (89)	992 (117)	1,387 (185)	509 (71)	1,041 (130)	1,468 (147)	557 (74)	1,061 (139)	1,444 (169)

After experiencing a signal, the subject reproduced it by depressing a key. The mean response times shown in the light and tone columns demonstrate the difference in perceived duration for visual and auditory signals of physically equal duration. The mean response times when both light and tone signals were presented are more similar to those of the tone alone than the light alone, indicating that when both signals are present, the subject tends to process the temporal information of the auditory rather than the visual stimulus. Mean response times are in milliseconds; means of within-subjects standard deviations are in parentheses. (From J. T. Walker & K. J. Scott, Auditory-visual conflicts in the perceived duration of lights, tones, and gaps, Journal of Experimental Psychology: Human Perception and Performance, *7. Copyright 1981 by American Psychological Association. Reprinted with permission.)*

The subject, as in the Lhamon and Goldstone (1974) study, apparently used the auditory signal rather than the visual signal of the bisensory pair as the determining stimulus. In a subsequent experiment, Walker and Scott asked the subject to make separate judgments of the visual and the auditory members of a simultaneously presented pair. In effect, this is an attentional manipulation which should operate in a fashion similar to that used by Lhamon and Goldstone (1974). With stimuli of 500 msec, there was no difference between visual and auditory signals presented alone, nor between these and the bisensory stimuli. At 1,000 and 1,500 msec, however, subjects treated the bisensory pair as if it were an auditory-alone signal, whether they were asked to respond to the visual or to the auditory component. The tendency to attend spontaneously to the auditory component was, in this situation, strong enough to overcome the instructions to respond to the visual component.

In other paradigms of intersensory interaction (such as the more completely studied perception of spatial location, as discussed in Section 2), the effects of attentional and other "cognitive" factors have been more extensively studied than in the temporal duration paradigm. The latter would seem a rich arena in which to test the generality of the findings from other perceptual capacities, and concentrated efforts in this area are likely to prove fruitful.

3.3. Interactions Involving Temporal Rate

Considerable research has been devoted to the perception of temporal rate by the various sensory modalities, particularly vision and audition, and a number of studies have examined intersensory phenomena in which stimulation of one modality affects the perception of rate in another. Generally, this work may be divided into two types. In one, intersensory effects in the "fusion" range are studied, including visual factors that affect the rate at which auditory flutter ceases and fusion occurs, and auditory factors that affect visual critical flicker fusion (CFF). The other type consists of phenomena that occur at subfusion rates, where the perception of the rate of clearly discontinuous signals is affected by concomitant stimulation of other sensory modalities. We discuss the fusion phenomena first.

3.3.1. Fusion Range Stimuli. Two types of effect may be noted, one in which a continuous (i.e., nonintermittent) signal in one modality affects the fusion rate in another modality, and the other in which a discontinuous signal in one modality affects the fusion rate in another modality.

The instance in which a continuous signal in one modality affects the flicker or fusion rate in another is an example of nonspecific intersensory influence. The available research centers about the reciprocal influences of vision and audition. Continuous auditory stimulation facilitates temporal visual acuity (i.e., raises the CFF) at low intensities (e.g., Levine, 1958), but either has no effect or inhibits it at higher intensities (Gorrell, 1953; Knox, 1945b; Levine, 1958; Ogilvie, 1956). The basis of this biphasic effect of auditory stimuli on the CFF may be an analogous effect on perceived intensity of the visual stimulus, because CFF is greater for bright lights than for dim ones (e.g., Hecht & Smith, 1936). Maier, Bevan, and Behar (1961) evaluated monocular foveal CFF, using an ascending and descending method of limits, under varying conditions of auditory intensity and frequency. The effects on CFF were small and complex. With long-wavelength visual stimuli, CFF decreased with an increase in auditory intensity (i.e., the sensitivity of the visual system decreased with increasing auditory intensity), whereas with short-wavelength visual stimuli, CFF increased with increasing auditory intensity. Auditory pitch affected visual CFF only as part of a three-way interaction involving pitch, visual wavelength, and auditory intensity. In any case, these effects seem trivial in view of the fact that CFF changes ranged only in the area of 2–4%.

H. L. Miller (1969), using a much simpler design, examined the variation in visual CFF at six values of auditory intensity, ranging from 70 to 109 dB SPL. The CFF thresholds were determined using the ascending and descending method of limits. A significant effect was found, with CFF increasing (i.e., the visual system becoming more sensitive) with increasing auditory intensity up to a point (90 dB), and then decreasing. The maximal rise of CFF over that with only ambient auditory stimulation was, however, only about 3%. Thus, although there are statistically significant effects of continuous stimulation, they are generally quite small and probably of little importance.

There have been reported several studies of the effects of an intermittent stimulus in one modality on the fusion rate in another, beginning with the experiments of von Schiller (1932a, 1932b; cited by Ryan, 1940). Von Schiller (1932a, cited by Ryan, 1940) examined the effects on visual CFF rate of a flickering auditory signal, in comparison with a steady auditory signal and no signal. The visual signal was maintained at a rate just below the CFF rate, so that with no auditory signal a "very fine flicker" was present. When the steady auditory signal was present, the visual flicker was barely evident, whereas when the intermittent auditory signal was present, visual flicker was most pronounced. That is, the visual system was most sensitive to discontinuity of stimulation when auditory flicker occurred.

Further results reported by von Schiller (1932; cited by Ryan, 1940) were that dissonant auditory stimulation increased the pronoucedness of visual flicker, whereas consonant auditory stimulation decreased perceived flicker. Tactual stimulation similarly increased or decreased apparent visual flicker, depending on its degree of "roughness" or "smoothness." In a subsequent report, von Schiller (1932b; cited by Ryan 1940) reported parallel auditory effects on tactual judgments, visual effects on tactual judgments, and visual effects on auditory judgments. In each case, greater discontinuity in one modality produced the perception of the greater discontinuity in the other.

Knox (1945a) addressed a similar question—whether visual flicker could be created by the addition of auditory stimulation—using a visual presentation rate that would ordinarily produce fusion. (Knox thus worked with fusion, whereas von Schiller had used flicker.) The auditory conditions were (1) silence, (2) continuous tone, (3) fine flicker (30 Hz), and (4) coarse flicker (15 Hz). The auditory signal was at 50 dB (referent unspecified). In each of these conditions, subjects adjusted a variable flash to the CFF, using the method of limits. In addition, Knox instructed two subjects to attend to the visual stimulus and two other subjects to attend to the auditory stimulus; one received no such instructions. None of the auditory conditions or the instructions had a differential effect on the visual CFF. It should be noted that a 50-dB tone is a moderately weak sound and it may be that more intense auditory stimulation would have produced some effect.

Ogilvie (1956) used auditory white noise signals of 80 and 90 dB SPL in a similar experiment. Visual CFF rate was not affected by a continuous auditory signal, a result that conforms to the generally small effects reported above for continuous stimulation (e.g., Maier et al., 1961). Ogilvie used two conditions of interrupted auditory signal, one where the auditory burst was synchronous (in phase) with the visual signal and the other where the auditory burst occurred between successive visual signals (out of phase). The out-of-phase condition produced no difference in visual CFF from the no-noise condition, whereas the in-phase condition produced a significant increase in CFF (heightened sensitivity of the visual system). Although the increase was statistically significant, it was small, averaging only about 1.3%. E. L. Walker and Sawyer (1961) attempted to replicate Ogilvie's (1956) findings under monocular conditions, but failed to find an effect. The E. L. Walker and Sawyer study is weakened, however, by the absence of an attempt to replicate the Ogilvie (1956) binocular findings and is thus of questionable validity.

In summary, a variety of studies have found auditory stimulation to influence visual CFF. In no case, however, are these effects large. Indeed, they are generally so small as to be regarded as trivial.

3.3.2. Subfusion Range Stimuli. There is considerably more interesting material in this area. Knox (1945b), following his work in the fusion range, used visual flicker rates of 16 (coarse flicker) and 24 (fine flicker) Hz, with a visual signal whose CFF rate was 48 Hz. The general approach involved presenting subjects with a base visual signal (e.g., 16 Hz) and then giving the visual signal again in the presence of an auditory signal and asking the subject to set the visual frequency to match the remembered base signal (of 16 Hz). The auditory signal was intermittent, with frequencies ranging from 15 to 30 Hz. Three subjects were used, one instructed to attend to the visual signal, another to the auditory signal, and the third with no attentional instructions. The data in general supported the conclusion that there is an effect of auditory flutter on visual frequency judgments; auditory flutter caused a decrease in apparent visual frequency. That is, with auditory flutter present, the visual flicker was seen as coarser. To compensate, the subject would have to increase the visual flicker rate to match the vision-alone base signal. It is interesting that instructions to attend to the auditory signal produced the greatest adjustment of the visual signal, and the instructions to attend to the visual signal produced the least adjustment. The no-instruction subject resembled the auditory attention subject. These results suggest that in this task the subject naturally attends to the auditory signal more than to the visual. The magnitudes of the increases in visual frequency setting were considerable, ranging from about 5% for the 30-Hz auditory signal to about 30% for the 10-Hz signal. This very substantial intersensory interaction has been referred to as the auditory "driving" of the perceived visual signal frequency.

Gebhard and Mowbray (1959) began with the intention of studying the apparently simple matching task whereby subjects would equate rates of auditory flutter and visual flicker. In the course of this procedure they encountered procedural difficulties that turned out to be more interesting than their initial pursuit. The procedure was quite simple. The experimenter set a rate of visual flicker or auditory flutter, set the comparison signal at either a higher or lower rate, and had subjects adjust the comparison rate to match the standard. It is important that subjects were not allowed to pass the standard and return (bracketing procedure), but instead repeated the trial if they judged that they had gone past the standard value. The standard values ranged from 5 to 40 Hz and were thus subfusion for both modalities. The initial finding was that the DL for matching intermodally was far greater than that for either intramodal match, and various attempts to increase the accuracy of intermodality matches failed. It was noted that when the subject was adjusting the auditory signal to match the visual, with both signals occurring at once, the former appeared to "drive" the latter. As the subject adjusted the flutter, the flicker was perceived to shift as well, although in fact it remained physically constant within a trial. The reverse phenomenon did not occur; flicker did not "drive" flutter. Apparently the auditory signal has a prepotent characteristic in this kind of temporal-perceptual task, and this is a theme that recurs in subsequent research. In several variations on the matching task used by Gebhard and Mowbray, the condition in which the subject adjusted the flicker to match the flutter was routinely more accurate (smaller DL) than the opposite, which is to say again that the auditory signal drove the visual, but not vice versa. Perception of the visual signal was less stable than that of the auditory signal.

Shipley (1964) explored the "driving" phenomenon further, inquiring in particular whether the phenomenon might effectively be quantified. The frequency range studied was in the low end of that used by Gebhard and Mowbray (1959), varying from 2 to 10 Hz. The signals were presented only to the right eye and right ear. The auditory and visual rates were set at the same value and then subjects adjusted the auditory signal either upward or downward until inequality became apparent. Phenomenally, the visual rate seemed to move together with the changing auditory rate until a point beyond which the asynchrony suddenly became apparent. This point of perceived asynchrony was the dependent variable of interest. Generally, perceived synchrony was maintained longer when the flutter rate was increased than when it was decreased, no doubt because of the low range of rates used in the experiment. Evidently, the most extreme result was obtained for a flicker (and initial flutter) rate of 10 Hz, where the flutter rate could be decreased to 7 Hz or increased to about 22 Hz before asynchrony became apparent. The magnitude of this effect is considerable, and clearly far greater than was obtained in any of the studies using fusion-range stimuli.

Regan and Sperkreijse (1977) worked with frequencies in the 5–20-Hz range, using a method similar to that of Shipley (1964). The auditory and visual frequencies were initially set to the same values and then the auditory frequency was increased or decreased until asynchrony was detected. Several interesting variations on the basic driving phenomenon were observed. When the flutter rate was raised, and then still before the point of perceived asynchrony the auditory signal was turned off, the visual rate continued to be perceived (incorrectly) at the higher rate. However, if the subject looked away, then back again, the visual rate was (correctly) perceived at its lower rate. The effect was somewhat more effective with the visual stimulus in the periphery than in the fovea. Finally, the effect occurred even with the auditory signal emanating from a speaker spatially removed from the visual signal by as much as 50° azimuth. (The latter result was confirmed recently by Welch et al., Note 6.)

In a study by Myers et al. (1981), the method was similar to that used by Gebhard and Mowbray (1959), but with the important change that subjects were allowed to bracket the standard with the comparison stimulus. This procedure was undoubtedly what allowed Myers et al. to have subjects successfully produce a stable match of one rate to the other, in contrast to the inability of previous researchers to obtain a consistent auditory-to-visual match. Standard rates were 4, 7, and 10 Hz. A major goal of the study was to examine the effects of the visual surround on intersensory matching, but it is the results on rate mismatching that are of interest in this section. In the first experiment, flutter was matched to flicker. The auditory rate was uniformly set at a higher rate than the visual, and more so the higher the visual base rate. (With a dark visual surround, this overmatching increased as well.) The greatest effect was a setting of the auditory signal at a frequency 72% greater than that of the visual standard. Of all the subjects, 80% reported that they experienced change in the visual rate as they adjusted the auditory signal; this is the auditory driving phenomenon. In Experiment 2, the subjects varied the visual rate to match a standard auditory rate. Only 2 of 16 subjects reported any driving effect. The mismatching phenomenon was not as clear as in Experiment 1, however. When the visual surround was not illuminated, the auditory rate was set higher than the visual rate to produce a match, but when the surround was illuminated, the auditory rate was set at a lower rate than the visual standard. A third experiment further complicated the picture. Here the visual signal was a green-yellow LED, in contrast to the red LED used in the previous experiments, and the visual comparison was adjusted to match the auditory standard. Equality of rate was again produced by a lower auditory than visual rate.

The initial results of Myers et al. (1981) were straightforward in demonstrating both auditory driving of visual rate and perceived equality of rate with a higher auditory than visual setting. Beyond this point their results become more difficult to interpret. The conflicting results with visual-to-auditory matching and with different colored visual signals obviously show that there is much research to be done in this area before the phenomena are fully understood.

One problem in the interpretation of auditory driving effects is that the typical procedure involves matching the rate in one sensory modality with that in the other. Thus, because each modality is interacting with the other, it is likely that the subject's means of indicating perceived rate will itself be affected. In order to obtain a "pure" measure of the degree of visual and auditory interaction in this situation it will be necessary to use a measurement procedure that is unaffected by this interaction. Direct magnitude estimation or the use of a third, uninvolved, sensory modality would solve this problem. The former procedure was used successfully by Welch et al., in press).

In summary, the subfusion research on temporal rate perception shows three main outcomes, with qualification necessary. First, there are clear intersensory interaction effects. Second, faster auditory rates tend to be perceived equal to slower visual rates (note, however, the complications introduced by the later experiments of Myers et al., 1981). Third, and perhaps most interesting, is that there appears to be auditory prepotency, especially obvious in the cross-modality rate-matching studies, such that auditory rates are perceived to drive visual rates (but not vice versa).

3.4. Interactions Involving Temporal Pattern

In the area of temporal pattern perception there is little research concerning situations in which specific information given to one modality affects the perception of comparable information given to another modality. Handel and Buffardi (1969) examined the combined use of the auditory, visual, and tactual modalities in judging patterns that were constructed of sequences of spatially separated left or right signals. The results are seen in Table 25.3. As we noted earlier, the modalities were about equally effective at slower (1 and 2 elements per second) presentation rates, but audition and touch were more effective than vision at a faster (4 elements per second) rate. When a pattern was presented to two modalities at once, the A-V combination was best, and in fact better than either audition or vision alone. Performance with the A-T combination was next best, and that with V-T was worst. In both these latter two combinations performance was intermediate to that of the components. In another experiment, incompatible patterns were presented to two modalities: the left-right character of the elements was reversed for one modality in relation to the other. This change did not produce a deterioration of performance, and the relative ordering of modality pairs was the same as that cited above for compatible patterns.

Dixon and Spitz (1980) demonstrated a clear instance of intersensory interaction in their study of the detection of auditory-visual asynchrony in temporally patterned stimuli, as presented by motion pictures (see Hochberg, Chapter 22). The film of a hammer hitting a peg, complete with its sound track, was begun with the visual and auditory stimuli in temporal synchrony. Subjects then pressed a key that gradually took the two signals out of synchrony in an unspecified direction, and were instructed to release the key as soon as asynchrony was detected. The results are presented in Table 25.4. There was an interesting imbalance, depending on whether the auditory

Table 25.3. Individual Modality and Combined Modality Judgments of Temporal Patterns

	Rate of Presentation (elements per second)			
Modality or Combination	1	2	4	Combined Rates
A	25	36	131	75
T	26	40	133	94
V	24	38	255	116
A-T	27	41	135	82
A-V	24	32	91	58
T-V	23	44	145	94
A-T-V	23	31	128	74

Each of several patterns, consisting of eight elements, was continuously cycled until the subject could identify it. Each pattern element could have either of two values: 1,200 or 3,000 Hz for sound (A), right or left hand for touch (T), and right or left position for light (V). The lights were further distinguished by being red or green. The entries in the table represent the number of elements that had to be presented before successful identification occurred. Eighty-four subjects were tested. Three rates of presentation were used: 1, 2, or 4 elements per second. Performance deteriorated as the rate of presentation increased. At the slowest rate there were no notable differences between modalities or among modality combinations. As rate increased, though, the auditory and tactual modalities proved better than vision, and the auditory-visual (A-V) combination proved to be the best. Indeed, the A-V combination at the fastest rate proved better than the combination of all three modalities, suggesting that the information load in the latter condition was too high. (From S. Handel & L. Buffardi, Using several modalities to perceive one temporal pattern, Quarterly Journal of Experimental Psychology, *1969, 21. Reprinted with permission.)*

signal was caused to precede the visual signal or to follow it. When the auditory signal preceded the visual, there was less tolerance for asynchrony. Dixon and Spitz argued that there is an ecological basis for this difference. In the everyday world, observers more often encounter situations in which the auditory signal follows the visual, because of the differential propagation rates of visual and auditory signals, and they thus have a higher tolerance for asynchrony in this situation. The direction of tolerance was consistent for verbal and nonverbal (a hammer hitting a peg) material, but the degree of tolerance was greater for verbal than for nonverbal material. From this difference, Dixon and Spitz argued that the phenomenon is the result of ontological development rather than being innate, for people hear speech and see mouths producing it much more frequently than they see and hear hammers hitting pegs. Although this argument is interesting, it may be questioned on the basis of the probably differential "compellingness" of the two stimulus situations (cf. Welch & Warren, 1980). That is, it seems likely that the correspondence between the visual and the auditory material was more believable in the verbal case than in the hammer case, thus producing the greater tolerance for asynchrony in the former situation. Alternatively, it may be that the synchrony of auditory and visual signals is simply more difficult to detect when a voice is involved, because of the greater complexity of the stimuli as compared to the hammer situation.

Table 25.4. Mean Threshold for Perceived Visual-Auditory Asynchrony

	Mean Detected Asynchrony (msec)
Voice	
Auditory delay	257.9
Auditory advance	131.1
Hammer	
Auditory delay	187.5
Auditory advance	74.8

A film, with its sound track, was begun with the visual and auditory signals in synchrony and then the voice track was made gradually to precede or follow the video track. The subject responded as soon as the asynchrony was detected. Asynchrony was detected sooner with the hammer than with the voice and earlier detection occurred when the auditory signal preceded the visual signal than when the auditory signal followed the visual signal. (From N. F. Dixon & L. Spitz, The detection of auditory visual desynchrony, Perception, *1980, 9. Reprinted with permission.)*

3.5. Key References

Behar, I., & Bevan, W. (1961). This study demonstrates the existence of anchor effects for judgment of temporal duration of signals, and furthermore shows that anchor effects can operate across, as well as within, sensory modalities.

Dixon, N. F., & Spitz, L. (1980). This study explores the extent to which the auditory and visual signals in a moving picture can be moved out of synchrony while retaining a unified perception. There was less tolerance for asynchrony when the auditory signal preceded the visual than when the visual preceded the auditory.

Gebhard, J. W., & Mowbray, G. H. (1959). This study was the initial demonstration of the auditory driving effect. When auditory and visual signals are presented repetitively, at slightly different rates, the visual signal is perceived to be occurring at the rate of the auditory signal.

Goldstone, S., Boardman, W. K., & Lhamon, W. T. (1959). This study contained an early demonstration that auditory and visual signals of physically equal duration are perceived as having different durations: the auditory signal is judged as being of longer duration than the visual signal.

Miller, H. L. (1969). This study demonstrates that the visual CFF is subject to influences from auditory stimulation, in particular the intensity of the auditory signal. Visual sensitivity increases with increasing auditory intensity up to a point, beyond which a decrease is seen.

Ogilvie, J. C. (1956). This study demonstrates the temporal sensitization of the visual system (as measured by the CFF) by an auditory signal whose frequency is in phase with the visual signal. An out-of-phase auditory signal does not have the same influence.

4. SUMMARY

In this chapter we have presented a survey of research on intersensory interactions with respect to each of the major multimodal perceptual tasks—detection, spatial perception, and temporal perception. For each of these tasks, perception in one sensory modality may be affected by nonspecific accessory stimulation, by the sensory context, and by the presence of information coming to other sensory modalities that are concurrently specifying the same event.

Both detection of and RT to stimuli in one sensory modality are affected by concomitant stimulation in other (accessory) modalities, even if the information available to the other modalities has no meaningful relation to the primary event being perceived. Most of the work on sensory detection thresholds has, unfortunately, come to us secondhand. The vast majority of this research was carried out in the Soviet Union and has only been summarized for the Western psychologist (London, 1954). Further, the effects of nonspecific accessory stimulation reported by the Russian investigators have proved to be small, fragile, and not always replicable. It would seem wise, therefore, to take these reports as very tentative. On the other hand, the fact that so many positive results have been reported argues against simply ignoring these findings.

Somewhat more substantial and better documented is the work in intersensory facilitation of *RT* in which an accessory stimulus facilitates response to the "executive" signal (e.g., Kohfeld, 1969), although some of these results can be attributed to probability summation.

A series of studies has involved assessing the observer's RT to a signal in only one modality, to a signal in only a second modality, and finally, to signals presented simultaneously to both modalities. The traditional advantage of audition over vision in RT may be negated by failing to forewarn the observer which modality is going to be presented (Colavita, 1974), even when the two stimuli have been subjectively matched for intensity. Furthermore, on visual-auditory trials the subject, when given a choice, almost always responds to the visual stimulus. The best explanation for this "prepotency" effect is a chronic tendency for observers to direct their attention to visual information.

Much of the work on intersensory interaction has centered on spatial perception. In general, visual spatial acuity appears to be facilitated by a variety of nonspecific accessory stimuli, as is the perception of orientation. Vestibular perception of orientation also interacts intimately with visual, auditory, proprioceptive, and tactual information; this evidence is congruent with the notion that these modalities are redundant systems for many perceptual events. With regard to the relative contributions of these modalities to perceived spatial orientation, vision appears to take priority, as manifested most clearly when it is pitted against another modality that is also specifying orientation (e.g., Over, 1966).

Egocentric localization is also subject to significant intersensory interaction, as seen in the role of felt eye and head position in visual and auditory localization, the effects of a visual context in auditory localization, and the intersensory bias that results from prism-induced conflicts among the spatial modalities.

As with egocentric localization, shape and size perception are dominated by vision, as demonstrated, for example, by the strong visual bias of haptic perception when the two modalities are placed into conflict (e.g., Rock & Victor, 1964).

Whereas spatially structured events can be perceived more readily and precisely via the visual than the auditory modality, the reverse is true for events that are temporally structured. This difference is one basis for the claim that although different sensory modalities may be capable of signaling the same event, some are better (e.g., faster, more precise, more accurate) at this than others. Further evidence for this "modality appropriateness" hypothesis from the area of temporal perception is seen in research in which vision and audition are placed in conflict with respect to duration (e.g., J.T. Walker & Scott, 1981) or temporal rate (e.g., Myers et al., 1981). Here, in contrast to the visual dominance situation that is normally found for spatial events, audition contributes substantially more to the percept than does vision.

Nonspecific accessory stimulation of other modalities has a small effect on the CFF. On the other hand, the perception of both visual and auditory rate at frequencies below the fusion point is subject to significant interaction. In particular, auditory rate has been found consistently to "drive" perceived visual rate.

In has been hypothesized (e.g., Welch & Warren, 1980) that the underlying basis for the superiority of one sensory modality over another is the observer's distribution of attention between the two modalities. The natural tendency to attend to one modality instead of another when both are providing information about the same environmental characteristic is probably due, in turn, to the relative appropriateness of the modality for the task. How the perceiver "knows" which modality is the more appropriate for a given perceptual task is unclear. It seems likely, however, that both innate and experiential factors are involved.

REFERENCE NOTES

1. Welch, R. B., & Krausert, D. D. *Control of autokinetic movement by means of electrical stimulation.* Paper presented at the meeting of the Western Psychological Association, San Francisco, April, 1973.
2. Hein, A. *Postural after-effects and visual-motor adaptation to prisms.* Paper presented at meetings of Eastern Psychological Association. Atlantic City, April, 1965.
3. Warren, D. H., Widawaski, M. H., & Schmitt, T. L. *Visual-proprioceptive conflict: An information processing approach.* Paper presented at the meeting of the Psychonomic Society, Denver, November 1975.
4. Welch, R. B. *The effect of visual-proprioceptive "compellingness" and limb vibration on visual capture and prism adaptation.* Paper presented at the meeting of the Psychonomic Society, Phoenix, Nov., 1979.
5. Welch, R. B., Warren, D. H., With, R., & Wait, J. S. *Visual Capture: The effects of "compellingness" and the assumption of unity.* Paper presented at the meeting of the Psychonomic Society, St. Louis, Nov. 1980.

REFERENCES

* References preceded by an asterisk are "key references."

Aarons, L., & Goldenberg, L. Galvanic stimulation of the vestibular system and perception of the vertical. *Perceptual and Motor Skills*, 1964, *19*, 59–66.

Abravanel, E. Active detection of solid-shape information by touch and vision. *Perception and Psychophysics*, 1971, *10*, 358–360. (a)

Abravanel, E. The synthesis of length within and between perceptual systems. *Perception and Psychophysics*, 1971, *9*, 327–328. (b)

Allen, F., & Schwartz, M. The effect of stimulation of the senses of vision, hearing, taste, and smell upon the sensibility of the organs of vision. *Journal of General Physiology*, 1940, *24*, 105–121.

Anstis, S. M., & Loizos, C. M. Cross-model judgments of small holes. *American Journal of Psychology*, 1967, *80*, 51–58.

Arnoult, M. D. Post-rotatory localization of sound. *American Journal of Psychology*, 1950, *63*, 229–236.

*Auerbach, C., & Sperling, P. A common auditory-visual space: Evidence for its reality. *Perception and Psychophysics*, 1974, *16*, 129–135.

Bach-y-Rita, P., Collins, C. C., Saunders, F., White, B., & Scadden, L. Visual substitution by tactile image projection. *Nature*, 1969, *221*, 963–964.

Bartley, S. H., & Bishop, G. H. The cortical response to stimulation of the optic nerve in the rabbit. *American Journal of Physiology*, 1933, *103*, 159–172.

Baxter, B., & Travis, E. The reaction time to vestibular stimuli. *Journal of Experimental Psychology*, 1938, *22*, 277–282.

Becker-Carus, C. Verandert die Wahrnehmungsschwelle die dominanz schen und tasten? *Zeitschrift für Experimentelle und Angewandte Psychologie*, 1973, *20*, 347–365.

*Behar, I., & Bevan, W. The perceived duration of auditory and visual intervals: Cross-model comparison and interaction. *American Journal of Psychology*, 1961, *74*, 17–26.

Bermant, R. I., & Welch, R. B. The effect of degree of visual-auditory stimulus separation and eye position upon the spatial interaction of vision and audition. *Perceptual and Motor Skills*, 1976, *43*, 487–493.

Bernstein, I. H. Can we see and hear at the same time? *Acta Psychologica*, 1970, *33*, 21–35.

Bernstein, I. H., Chu, P. K., Briggs, P., & Schurman, D. L. Stimulus intensity and foreperiod effects in intersensory facilitation. *Quarterly Journal of Experimental Psychology*, 1973, *25*, 171–181.

Bernstein, I. H., Clark, M. H., & Edelstein, B. A. Effects of an auditory signal on visual reaction time. *Journal of Experimental Psychology*, 1969, *80*, 567–569. (a)

Bernstein, I. H., Clark, M. H., & Edelstein, B. A. Intermodal effects in choice reaction time. *Journal of Experimental Psychology*, 1969, *81*, 405–407. (b)

Bernstein, I. H., & Edelstein, B. A. Effects of some variations in auditory input upon visual choice reaction time. *Journal of Experimental Psychology*, 1971, *87*, 241–247.

Bernstein, I. H., Rose, R., & Ashe, V. Energy integration in intersensory facilitation. *Journal of Experimental Psychology*, 1970, *86*, 196-203. (a)

Bernstein, I. H., Rose, R., & Ashe, V. Preparatory state effects in intersensory facilitation. *Psychonomic Science*, 1970, *19*, 113–114. (b)

Björkman, M. Relations between intra-modal and cross-modal matching. *Scandinavian Journal of Psychology*, 1967, *8*, 65–80.

Börnstein, W. Über die hormonale Steuerung der Korrelation zwischen den Sinnesleistungen und dem Tonus. *Klinische Wochschrifte*, 1931, *10*, 1331.

Börnstein, W. On the functional relations of the sense organs to one another and to the organism as a whole. *Journal of General Psychology*, 1936, *15*, 117–131.

Brown, I. D. Visual and tactual judgments of surface roughness. *Ergonomics*, 1960, *3*, 51–61.

Brown, D. R., & Hitchcock, L., Jr. Time estimation: Dependence and independence of modality-specific effects. *Perceptual and Motor Skills*, 1965, *21*, 727–734.

Bryant, P. E., & Raz, I. Visual and tactual perception of shape by young children. *Developmental Psychology*, 1975, *11*, 525–526.

Burnham, R. W. A note concerning Hartmann's studies of intersensory effects. *Journal of Experimental Psychology*, 1941, *29*, 81–84.

Canon, L. K. Intermodality inconsistency of input and directed attention as determinants of the nature of adaptation. *Journal of Experimental Psychology*, 1970, *84*, 141–147.

Canon, L. K. Directed attention and maladaptive "adaptation" to displacement of the visual field. *Journal of Experimental Psychology*, 1971, *88*, 403–408.

Cashdan, S. Visual and haptic form discrimination under conditions of successive stimulation. *Journal of Experimental Psychology*, 1968, *76*, 215–218.

Chandler, K. A. The effect of monaural and binaural tones of different intensities on the visual perception of verticality. *American Journal of Psychology*, 1961, *74*, 260–265.

Chapanis, A., Rouse, R. O., & Schachter, S. The effect of inter-sensory stimulation on dark adaptation and night vision. *Journal of Experimental Psychology*, 1949, *39*, 425–437.

Child, I. L., & Wendt, G. R. The temporal course of the influence of visual stimulation upon the auditory threshold. *Journal of Experimental Psychology*, 1938, *23*, 109–127.

Choe, C. S., & Welch, R. B. Variables affecting the intermanual transfer and decay of prism adaptation. *Journal of Experimental Psychology*, 1974, *102*, 1076–1084.

Choe, C. S., Welch, R. B., Guilford, R. M., & Juola, J. F. The "ventriloquist effect": Visual dominance or response bias? *Perception and Psychophysics*, 1975, *18*, 55–60.

Clark, B., & Graybiel, A. The effect of angular acceleration on sound localization: The audiogyral illusion. *Journal of Psychology*, 1949, *28*, 235-244.

Cohen, M. M. Changes in auditory localization following prismatic exposure under continuous and terminal visual feedback. *Perceptual and Motor Skills*, 1974, *38*, 1202.

*Colavita, F. B. Human sensory dominance. *Perception and Psychophysics*, 1974, *16*, 409–412.

Colavita, F. B., Tomko, R., & Weisberg, D. Visual prepotency and eye orientation. *Bulletin of the Psychonomic Society*, 1976, *8*, 25–26.

Colavita, F. B., & Weisberg, D. A further investigation of visual dominance. *Perception and Psychophysics*, 1979, *25*, 345–347.

Connolly, K., & Jones, B. A developmental study of afferent-reafferent integration. *British Journal of Psychology*, 1970, *61*, 259–266.

Craske, B. Adaptation to prisms: Change in internally registered eye-position. *British Journal of Psychology*, 1967, *58*, 329–335.

Craske, B., & Crawshaw, M. Spatial discordance is a sufficient condition for oculomotor adaptation to prisms: Eye muscle potentiation need not be a factor. *Perception and Psychophysics*, 1978, *23*, 75–79.

Davis, E. T. Heteromodal effects upon visual thresholds. *Psychological Monographs*, 1966, *80* (633).

Day, R. H., & Wade, N. J. Visual spatial aftereffect from prolonged head-tilt. *Science*, 1966, *154*, 1201–1202.

Derrick, E., & Dewar, R. Visual-tactual dominance relationship as a function of accuracy of tactual judgments. *Perceptual and Motor Skills*, 1970, *31*, 935–939.

Dichgans, J., & Brandt, T. Visual-vestibular interaction: Effects on self-motion perception and postural control. In *Handbook of sensory psychology* (Vol 8). New York: Springer, 1978.

*Dixon, N. F., & Spitz, L. The detection of auditory visual desynchrony. *Perception*, 1980, *9*, 719–721.

Easton, R. D. Prismatically induced curvature and finger-tracking pressure changes in a visual capture phenomenon. *Perception and Psychophysics*, 1976, *19*, 201–205.

Easton, R. D., & Falzett, M. Finger pressure during tracking of curved contours: Implications for a visual dominance phenomenon. *Perception and Psychophysics*, 1978, *24*, 145–153.

Easton, R. D., & Moran, P. W. A quantitative confirmation of visual capture of curvature. *Journal of General Psychology*, 1978, *98*, 105–112.

*Ebenholtz, S. M. The possible role of eye-muscle potentiation in several forms of prism adaptation. *Perception*, 1974, *3*, 477–485.

Ebenholtz, S. M. Additivity of aftereffects of maintained head and eye rotations: An alternative to recalibration. *Perception and Psychophysics*, 1976 *19*, 113–116.

Ebenholtz, S. M., & Fisher, S. K. Distance adaptation depends upon plasticity in the oculomotor system. *Perception and Psychophysics*, 1982, *31*, 551–560.

Ebenholtz, S. M., & Wolfson, D. M. Perceptual aftereffects of sustained convergence. *Perception and Psychophysics*, 1975, *17*, 485–491.

Egeth, H. E., & Sager, L. C. On the locus of visual dominance. *Perception and Psychophysics*, 1977, *22*, 77–86.

Ehrensing, R. H., & Lhamon, W. T. Comparison of tactile and auditory time judgments. *Perceptual and Motor Skills*, 1966, *23*, 929–930.

Festinger, L., Burnham, C. A., Ono, H., & Bamber, D. Efference and the conscious experience of perception. *Journal of Experimental Psychology Monograph*, 1967, *74*(4, Whole No. 637).

Fisher, G. H. Intersensory localisation in three modalities. *Bulletin of the British Psychological Society*, 1960, *41*, 24–25A.

Fisher, G. H. Spatial localisation by the blind. *American Journal of Psychology*, 1964, *77*, 2–14.

Fisher, G. H. Agreement between the spatial senses. *Perceptual and Motor Skills*, 1968, *126*, 849–850.

Fishkin, S. M., Pishkin, V., & Stahl, M. L. Factors involved in visual capture. *Perceptual and Motor Skills*, 1975, *40*, 427–434.

Freides, D. Human information processing and sensory modality: Cross-modal functions, information complexity, memory, and deficit. *Psychological Bulletin*, 1974, *81*, 284–310.

Fruend, L., & Hoffman, L. Licht und Hörren. *Med. Klin.*, 1929, *25*, 226–228.

Froeberg, S. The relation between the magnitude of stimulus and the time of reaction. *Archives of Psychology*, NY, 1907, *16*, 1–38.

Furukawa, M. A study on the difference in visual and auditory temporal judgment. *Tohoku Psychologica Folia*, 1978, 37, 87–93.

Garner, W. R., & Gottwald, R. L. The perception and learning of temporal patterns. *Quarterly Journal of Experimental Psychology*, 1968, *20*, 97–109.

Gault, R. H., & Goodfellow, L. D. An empirical comparison of audition, vision, and touch in the discrimination of temporal patterns and ability to reproduce them. *Journal of General Psychology*, 1938, *18*, 41–47.

*Gebhard, J. W., & Mowbray, G. H. On discriminating the rate of visual flicker and auditory flutter. *American Journal of Psychology*, 1959, *72*, 521–528.

Gemelli, A., Tessier, G., & Galli, A. La percezione della posizioni del nostro corpo e dei suoi spostamenti. *Arch. ital. psichol.*, 1920, *1*, 107–182.

Gibson, J. J. Adaptation, after-effect and contrast in the perception of curved lines. *Journal of Experimental Psychology*, 1933, *16*, 1–31.

Gielen, S. C. A. M., Schmidt, R. A., & van den Heuvel, P. J. M. On the nature of intersensory facilitation of reaction time. *Perception and Psychophysics*, 1983, *34*, 161–168.

Gilbert, G. M. Inter-sensory facilitation and inhibition. *Journal of General Psychology*, 1941, *24*, 381–407.

Goldstone, S. Production and reproduction of duration: Intersensory comparisons. *Perceptual and Motor Skills*, 1968, *26*, 755–760. (a)

Goldstone, S. Reaction time to onset and termination of lights and sounds. *Perceptual and Motor Skills*, 1968, *27*, 1023–1029. (b)

*Goldstone, S., Boardman, W. K., & Lhamon, W. T. Intersensory comparisons of temporal judgments. *Journal of Experimental Psychology*, 1959, *57*, 243–248.

Goldstone, S., & Goldfarb, J. L. Judgment of filled and unfilled durations: Intersensory factors. *Perceptual and Motor Skills*, 1963, *17*, 763–774.

Goldstone, S., & Goldfarb, J. L. Auditory and visual time judgment. *Journal of General Psychology*, 1964, *70*, 369–387. (a)

Goldstone, S., & Goldfarb, J. L. Direct comparison of auditory and visual durations. *Journal of Experimental Psychology*, 1964, *5*, 483–485. (b)

Goodfellow, L. D. An empirical comparison of audition, vision, and touch in the discrimination of short intervals of time. *American Journal of Psychology*, 1933, *45*, 243–258.

Gorrell, R. B. The effect of extraneous auditory stimulation on critical flicker frequency. *Dissertation Abstracts*, 1953, *13*, 883–884.

Gotoh, C. Über die Zentrale Beeinflussung der Sehschärfe. *Acta Soc. opthlal. jap.*, 1931, *35*, 887.

Graybiel, A., & Hupp, D. I. The oculo-gyral illusion, a form of apparent motion which may be observed following stimulation of the semicircular canals. *Journal of Aviation Medicine*, 1946, *17*, 3–27.

Graybiel, A., & Kellogg, R. S. The inversion illusion in parabolic flight: Its probable dependence on otolith function. *Aerospace Medicine*, 1967, *38*, 1099–1102.

Graybiel, A., & Niven, J. I. The effect of a change in direction of resultant force on sound localization: The audiogravic illusion. *Journal of Experimental Psychology*, 1951, *42*, 227–230.

Handel, S., & Buffardi, L. Using several modalities to perceive one temporal pattern. *Quarterly Journal of Experimental Psychology*, 1969, *21*, 256–266.

Handel, S., & Yoder, D. The effects of intensity and interval rhythms on the perception of auditory and visual temporal patterns. *Quarterly Journal of Experimental Psychology*, 1975, *27*, 111–122.

Hartmann, G. W. Changes in visual acuity through simultaneous stimulation of other sense organs. *Journal of Experimental Psychology*, 1933, *16*, 393–407.

Hay, J. C., & Pick, H. L., Jr. Visual and proprioceptive adaptation to optical displacement of the visual stimulus. *Journal of Experimental Psychology*, 1966, *71*, 150–158.

Hay, J. C., Pick, H. L., Jr., & Ikeda, K. Visual capture produced by prism spectacles. *Psychonomic Science*, 1965, *2*, 215–216.

Hecht, S., & Smith, E. L. Intermittent stimulation by light: VI. Area and the relation between critical frequency and intensity. *Journal of General Physiology*, 1936, *19*, 979–989.

Held, R. Shifts in binaural localization after prolonged exposure to atypical combinations of stimuli. *American Journal of Psychology*, 1955, *68*, 526–548.

Held, R., & Hein, A. Adaptation to disarranged hand-eye coordination contingent upon reafferent stimulation. *Perceptual and Motor Skills*, 1958, *8*, 87–90.

Heller, M. A. Visual and tactual texture perception: Intersensory cooperation. *Perception and Psychophysics*, 1982, *31*, 339–344.

Helmholtz, H., von. A treatise on physiological optics (Vol. 3) (J. P. C. Southall, Ed. and Trans.). New York: Dover, 1963. (Originally published, 1866.)

*Hershenson, M. Reaction time as a measure of intersensory facilitation. *Journal of Experimental Psychology*, 1962, *63*, 289–293.

Heymans, G. Untersuchungen über psychische Hemmung: V. Die Verdrängung von Schallempfindungen durch elektrische Hautemfindungen. *Zeitschrift für Psychologie*, 1904, *34*, 15–28.

Hill, J. W. Processing of tactual and visual point stimuli sequentially presented at high rates. *Journal of Experimental Psychology*, 1971, *88*, 340–348.

Howard, I. P. *Human visual orientation*. New York: Wiley, 1982.

Howard, I. P., & Templeton, W. B. *Human spatial orientation*. New York: Wiley, 1966.

Ince, L. P. Effects of low-intensity acoustical stimulation on visual thresholds. *Perceptual and Motor Skills*, 1968, *26*, 115–121.

Jack, C. E., & Thurlow, W. R. Effects of degree of visual association and angle of displacement on the "ventriloquism" effect. *Perceptual and Motor Skills*, 1973, *37*, 967–979.

Jackson, C. V. Visual factors in auditory localization. *Quarterly Journal of Experimental Psychology*, 1953, *5*, 52–65.

Jacobson, E. Experiments on the inhibition of sensations. *Psychological Review*, 1911, *18*, 24–53.

Jakovlev, P. A. The influence of acoustic stimuli upon the limits of visual fields for different colors. *Journal of the Optical Society of America*, 1938, *28*, 286–289.

Jastrow, J. The perception of space by disparate senses. *Mind*, 1886, *11*, 539–554.

Johnson, H. M. The dynamogenic influence of light on tactile discrimination. *Psychobiology*, 1920, *2*, 351–374.

Jones, B. The developmental significance of cross-modal matching. In R. D. Walk and H. L. Pick, Jr. (Eds.), *Intersensory perception and sensory integration*, New York: Plenum, 1981.

Jones, B., & Kabanoff, B. Eye movements in auditory space perception. *Perception and Psychophysics*, 1975, *17*, 241–245.

Kalil, R. E., & Freedman, S. J. Persistence of ocular rotation following compensation for displaced vision. *Perceptual and Motor Skills*, 1966, *22*, 135–139.

Kaufman, L. *Sight and mind*. New York: Oxford University Press, 1974.

Kelso, J. A. S., Cook, E., Olson, M. E., & Epstein, W. Allocation of attention and the locus of adaptation to displaced vision. *Journal of Experimental Psychology: Human Perception and Performance*, 1975, *1*, 237–245.

Kinney, J. A. S., & Luria, S. M. Conflicting visual and tactual-kinesthetic stimulation. *Perception and Psychophysics*, 1970, *8*, 189–192.

Klein, R. E. A developmental study of perception under conditions of conflicting sensory cues (Doctoral dissertation, University of Minnesota [Minneapolis], 1966). *Dissertation Abstracts*, 1966, *27*, 2162B–2163B. (University Microfilms No. 66-12, 213).

Kleint, H. Versuche über die Wahrnehmung. *Zeitschrift für Psychologie*,

1937, *140*, 109–138.

Knox, G. W. Investigations of flicker and fusion: III. The effect of auditory stimulation on the visual CFF. *Journal of General Psychology*, 1945, *33*, 139–143. (a)

Knox, G. W. Investigations of flicker and fusion: IV. The effect of auditory flicker on the pronouncedness of visual flicker. *Journal of General Psychology*, 1945, *33*, 145–154. (b)

*Kohfeld, D. L. Effects of the intensity of auditory and visual ready signals on simple reaction time. *Journal of Experimental Psychology*, 1969, 82, 88–95.

Kohfeld, D. L. Simple reaction time as a function of stimulus intensity in decibels of light and sound. *Journal of Experimental Psychology*, 1971, *88*, 251–257.

Kohler, I. The formation and transformation of the perceptual world. (Trans. by H. Fiss), *Psychological Issues*, 1964, *3* (4), 1–173.

Kohnstamm, D. Demonstration einer katatonieartigen Erscheinung beim Gesunden. *Neurologie Zentralblatt*, 1915, *34*, 290–291.

Kravkov, S. V. Changes of visual acuity in one eye under the influence of the illumination of the other or of acoustic stimuli. *Journal of Experimental Psychology*, 1934, *17*, 805–812.

Kuroki, S. The influence of a light stimulus upon hearing. *Japanese Journal of Psychology*, 1937, *12*, 253–269.

Lackner, J. R. The role of posture in adaptation to visual rearrangement. *Neuropsychologia*, 1973, *11*, 33–44. (a)

Lackner, J. R. The role of posture in sound localization. *Quarterly Journal of Experimental Psychology*, 1973, *26*, 235–251. (b)

Lackner, J. R. Visual rearrangement affects auditory localization. *Neuropsychologia*, 1973, *11*, 29–32. (c)

Lackner, J. R. Changes in auditory localization during body tilt. *Acta Otolaryngology*. (Stockholm) 1974, 19–28. (a)

Lackner, J. R. Influence of visual rearrangement and visual motion on sound localization. *Neuropsychologia*, 1974, *12*, 291–293. (b)

Lackner, J. R., & Graybiel, A. Postural illusions experienced during Z-axis recumbent rotation and their dependence on somatosensory stimulation of the body surface. *Aviation, Space, and Environmental Medicine*, 1978, *49*, 484–488. (a)

Lackner, J. R., & Graybiel, A. Some influences of touch pressure cues on human spatial organization. *Aviation, Space, and Environmental Medicine*, 1978, *49*, 798–804. (b)

Lederman, S. J., & Abbott, S. G. Texture perception: Studies on intersensory organization using a discrepancy paradigm and visual versus tactual psychophysics. *Journal of Experimental Psychology: Human Perception and Performance*, 1981, *7*, 902–915.

Lester, G., & Morant, R. B. Apparent sound displacement during vestibular stimulation. *American Journal of Psychology*, 1970, *83*, 554–566.

Levine, B. *Sensory interaction: The joint effects of visual and auditory stimulation on critical flicker fusion frequency*. Unpublished doctoral dissertation, Columbia University, 1958.

Lhamon, W. T., & Goldstone, S. Studies of auditory-visual differences in human time judgment: 2. More transmitted information with sounds than lights. *Perceptual and Motor Skills*, 1974, *39*, 95–307.

*London, I. D. Research on sensory interaction in the Soviet Union. *Psychological Bulletin*, 1954, *51*, 531–568.

Loveless, N. E., Brebner, J., & Hamilton, P. Bisensory presentation of information. *Psychological Bulletin*, 1970, *73*, 161–199.

MacDougall, R. The subjective horizon. *Psychological Review Monographs*, 1903, *4*, 145–166.

Maier, B., Bevan, W., & Behar, I. The effect of auditory stimulation upon the critical flicker frequency for different regions of the visible spectrum. *American Journal of Psychology*, 1961, *77*, 67–73.

Malis, L. C., & Kruger, L. Multiple response and excitability of cat's visual cortex. *Journal of Neurophysiology*, 1956, *19*, 172–186.

Marks, L. E. On colored-hearing synesthesia: Cross-modal translations of sensory dimensions. *Psychological Bulletin*, 1975, *82*, 303–331.

Marks, L. E. *The unity of the senses*. New York: Academic Press, 1978.

Maruyama, K. The effect of intersensory tone stimulation on absolute light threshold. *Tohoku Psychologica Folia*, 1959, *17*, 51–81.

Maruyama, K. "Contralateral relationship" between the ears and the halves of the visual field in sensory interaction. *Tohoku Psychologica Folia*, 1961, *19*, 81–92.

Mastroianni, G. R. The influence of eye movements and illumination on auditory localization. *Perception and Psychophysics*, 1982, *31*, 581–584.

Matthaei, R. Nachbewegungen beim Menschen. (Untersuchungen über das sog. Kohnstammishche Phänomen). *Pflugers Archiv für die Gesamte Physiologie des Menschen und der Tiere*, 1924, *202*, 88–111, 587–600.

Matthews, B. H. C., & Luczak, A. K. *Some factors influencing dark adaptation*. (Flying Personnel Research Committee Report No. 577), RAF Physiological Laboratory, Farnborough, June, 1944.

McDonnell, P. M., & Duffett, J. Vision and touch: A reconsideration of conflict between the two senses. *Canadian Journal of Psychology*, 1972, *26*, 171–180.

McFarland, J. H., & Clarkson, F. Perception of orientation: Adaptation to lateral body tilt. *American Journal of Psychology*, 1966, *79*, 265–271.

McLaughlin, S. C., & Webster, R. G. Changes in straight-ahead eye position during adaptation to wedge prisms. *Perception and Psychophysics*, 1967, *2*, 37–44.

Miller, E. A. Interaction of vision and touch in conflict and nonconflict form perception tasks. *Journal of Experimental Psychology*, 1972, *96*, 114–123.

*Miller, H. L. Effect of auditory stimulation on critical flicker fusion frequency. *Journal of Experimental Psychology*, 1969, *81*, 365–369.

Mills, A. W. On the minimum audible angle. *Journal of Acoustical Society of America*, 1958, *30*, 237–246.

Milner, A. D., & Bryant, P. E. Cross-modal matching by young children. *Journal of Comparative and Physiological Psychology*, 1970, *71*, 453–458.

Morrell, L. K. Intersensory facilitation of reaction time. *Psychonomic Science*, 1967, *8*, 77–78.

*Morrell, L. K. Cross-modality effects upon choice reaction time. *Psychonomic Science, 1968, 11*, 129–130. (a)

Morrell, L. K. Temporal characteristics of sensory interaction in choice reaction times. *Journal of Experimental Psychology*, 1968, *77*, 14–18. (b)

Myers, A. K., Cotton, B., & Hilp, H. A. Matching the rate of concurrent tone bursts and light flashes as a function of flash surround luminance. *Perception and Psychophysics*, 1981, *30*, 33–38.

Naylor, G. F. K. Effects of stress on the perception of direction. *Australian Journal of Psychology*, 1963, *15*, 17–28.

Nazzaro, J. R., & Nazzaro, J. N. Auditory versus visual learning of temporal patterns. *Journal of Experimental Psychology*, 1970, *84*, 477–478.

Neal, E. Visual localization of the vertical. *American Journal of Psychology*, 1926, *37*, 287–291.

Newhall, S. M. Effects of attention on the intensity of cutaneous pressure and on visual brightness. *Archives of Psychology*, 1923, 9(61), 5–75.

Nickerson, R. S. Intersensory facilitation of reaction time: Energy summation or preparation enhancement? *Psychological Review*, 1973, *80*, 489–509.

O'Connor, N., & Hermelin, B. Seeing and hearing in space and time. *Perception and Psychophysics*, 1972, *11*, 46–48.

*Ogilvie, J. C. Effect of auditory flutter on the visual critical flicker frequency. *Canadian Journal of Psychology*, 1956, *10*, 61–68.

O'Hare, J. J. Intersensory effects of visual stimuli on the minimum audible threshold. *Journal of General Psychology*, 1956, *54*, 167–170.

Over, R. An experimentally induced conflict between vision and proprioception. *British Journal of Psychology*, 1966, *57*, 335–341.

Owen, D. H., & Brown, D. R. Visual and tactual form discrimination: Psychophysical comparison within and between modalities. *Perception and Psychophysics*, 1970, *7*, 302–306.

Paap, K. R., & Ebenholtz, S. M. Perceptual consequences of potentiation in the extraocular muscles: An alternative explanation for adaptation to wedge prisms. *Journal of Experimental Psychology: Human Perception and Performance*, 1976, *2*, 457–468.

Park, J. N. Displacement of apparent straight ahead as an aftereffect of deviation of the eyes from normal position. *Perceptual and Motor Skills*, 1969, *28*, 591–597.

Pick, H. L., Jr., Warren, D. H., & Hay, J. C. Sensory conflict in judgments of spatial direction. *Perception and Psychophysics*, 1969, *6*, 203–205.

*Platt, B. B., & Warren, D. H., Auditory localization: The importance of eye movements and a textured visual environment. *Perception and Psychophysics*, 1972, *12*, 245–248.

Poffenberger, A. T. Reaction time in retinal stimulation with special reference to the time lost in conduction through nerve centers. *Archives of Psychology, N. Y.*, 1912 (No. 23).

Posner, M. I., Nissen, M. J., & Klein, R. M. Visual dominance: An information-processing account of its origins and significance. *Psychological Review*, 1976, *83*, 157–171.

Power, R. P., & Graham, A. Dominance of touch by vision: Generalization of the hypothesis to a tactually experienced population. *Perception*, 1976, *5*, 161–166.

Raab, D. H. Statistical facilitation of simple reaction time. *Transactions of the New York Academy of Sciences*, 1962, *24*, 574–590.

Raab, D. H., Fehrer, E., & Hershenson, M. Visual reaction time and the Broca-Sulzer phenomenon. *Journal of Experimental Psychology*, 1961, *61*, 193–199.

Radeau, M., & Bertelson, P. The effect of a textured visual field on modality dominance in a ventriloquism situation. *Perception and Psychophysics*, 1976, *20*, 227–235.

Radeau, M., & Bertelson, P. Adaptation to auditory-visual discordance and ventriloquism in semirealistic situations. *Perception and Psychophysics*, 1977, *22*, 137–146.

Regan, D., & Spekreijse, H. Auditory-visual interactions and the correspondence between perceived auditory space and perceived visual space. *Perception*, 1977, *6*, 133–138.

Riggs, L. A. Vision. In J. W. Kling and L. A. Riggs (Eds.), *Woodworth & Schlosberg's experimental psychology* (3rd ed.). New York: Holt, Rinehart and Winston, 1971.

Rock, I., Mack, A., Adams, L., & Hill, A. L. Adaptation to contradictory information from vision and touch. *Psychonomic Science*, 1965, *3*, 435–436.

Rock, I., & Victor, J. Vision and touch: An experimentally created conflict between the two senses. *Science*, 1964, *143*, 594–596.

Ronco, P. G. An experimental quantification of kinesthetic sensation: Extent of arm movement. *Journal of Psychology*, 1963, *55*, 227–238.

Rose, H. W., & Schmidt, I. Factors affecting dark adaptation. *Journal of Aviation Medicine*, 1947, *18*, 218–230.

Rose, S. A., Blank, M. S., & Bridger, W. H. Intermodal and intramodal retention of visual and tactual information in young children. *Developmental Psychology*, 1972, *6*, 482–486.

Rosenbusch, M. H., & Gardner, D. B. Reproduction of visual and auditory rhythm patterns by children. *Perceptual and Motor Skills*, 1968, *26*, 1271–1276.

Rubinstein, L., & Gruenberg, E. M. Intramodal and crossmodal sensory transfer of visual and auditory temporal patterns. *Perception and Psychophysics*, 1971, *9*, 385–390.

Rudel, R. G., & Teuber, H.-L. Cross-modal transfer of shape discrimination by children. *Neuropsychologia*, 1964, *2*, 1–8.

Ryan, T. A. Interrelations of the sensory systems in perception. *Psychological Bulletin*, 1940, *37*, 659–698.

Schiller, P., von, & Wolff, W. Gegenseitige Beeinflussung der optischen und der akustischen Helligkeit. *Zeitschrift für Psychologie*, 1933, *129*, 135–148.

Schneider, C. W., & Bartley, S. H. A study of the effects of mechanically induced tension of the neck muscles on the perception of verticality. *Journal of Psychology*, 1962, *54*, 245–248.

Shebilske, W. L. Visuomotor coordination in visual direction and position constancies. In W. Epstein (Ed.), *Stability and constancy in visual perception: Mechanisms and processes.* New York: Wiley, 1977.

Shelton, B. R., & Searle, C. L. The influence of vision on the absolute identification of sound-source position. *Perception and Psychophysics*, 1980, *28*, 589–596.

Sheridan, J. A., Cimbalo, R. A., Sills, J. A., & Alluisi, E. A. Effects of darkness, constant illumination and synchronized photic stimulation on auditory sensitivity to pulsed tones. *Psychonomic Science*, 1966, *5*, 311–312.

Sherrington, C. S. Observations on the sensual role of the proprioceptive nerve-supply of the extrinsic ocular muscles. *Brain*, 1918, *41*, 332–343.

Sherrington, C. S. *Integrative action of the nervous system.* New Haven: Yale University Press, 1920.

Shigehisa, T. Effect of auditory stimulation on visual tracking as functions of stimulus intensity, task complexity and personality. *Japanese Psychological Research*, 1974, *16*, 186–196.

Shigehisa, T., & Symons, J. R. Effect of intensity of visual stimulation on auditory sensitivity in relation to personality. *British Journal of Psychology*, 1973, *64*, 205–213. (a)

Shigehisa, T., & Symons, J. R. Reliability of auditory responses under increasing intensity of visual stimulation in relation to personality. *British Journal of Psychology*, 1973, *64*, 375–381. (b)

Shigehisa, P. M. J., Shigehisa, T., & Symons, J. R. Effects of intensity of auditory stimulation on photopic visual sensitivity in relation to personality. *Japanese Psychological Research*, 1973, *15*, 164–172.

Shipley, T. Auditory flutter-driving of visual flicker. *Science*, 1964, *145*, 1328–1330.

Simon, J. R., & Craft, J. L. Effects of an irrelevant auditory stimulus on visual choice reaction time. *Journal of Experimental Psychology*, 1970, *86*, 272–274.

Simpson, W. E. Latency of locating lights and sounds. *Journal of Experimental Psychology*, 1972, *93*, 169–175.

Singer, G., & Day, R. H. Visual capture of haptically judged depth. *Perception and Psychophysics*, 1969, *5*, 315–316.

Smothergill, D. W. A developmental study of the influence of memory for proprioceptive and visual cues on the visual capture phenomenon (Doctoral dissertation, University of Minnesota [Minneapolis], 1968). *Dissertation Abstracts*, 1968, *29*, 2225B. (University Microfilms No. 68–17, 720)

Stevens, J. C., Mack, J. D., & Stevens, S. S. Growth of sensation on seven continua as measured by force of handgrip. *Journal of Experimental Psychology*, 1960, *59*, 60–67.

Stevens, S. S. Decibels of light and sound. *Physics Today*, 1955, *8*, 12–17.

Stevens, S. S., & Guirao, M. Subjective scaling of length and area and the matching of length to loudness and brightness. *Journal of Experimental Psychology*, 1963, *66*, 177–186.

Stratton, G. M. Vision without inversion of the retinal image. *Psychological Review*, 1897, *4*, 341–360, 463–481.

Symons, J. R. *An investigation of intersensory relationships.* Unpublished doctoral dissertation, Reading University, 1954.

Tanner, T. A., Jr., Patton, R. M., & Atkinson, R. C. Intermodality judgments of signal duration. *Psychonomic Science*, 1965, *2*, 271–272.

Tastevin, J. En partant de l'experience d'Aristote. *L'Encephale*, 1937, *1*, 57–84, 140–158.

Taylor, R. L., & Campbell, G. T. Sensory interaction: Vision is modulated by hearing. *Perception*, 1976, *5*, 467–477.

Teghtsoonian, M., & Teghtsoonian, R. Seen and felt length. *Psychonomic Science*, 1965, *3*, 465–466.

Teghtsoonian, R., & Teghtsoonian, M. Two varieties of perceived length. *Perception and Psychophysics*, 1970, *8*, 389–392.

Teuber, H.-L., & Liebert, R. Effects of body tilts on auditory localization. *American Psychologist*, 1956, *11*, 430A.

Thomas, G. J. Experimental study of the influence of vision on sound localization. *Journal of Experimental Psychology*, 1941, *28*, 167–177.

Thorne, F. C. The psychological measurement of the temporal course of visual sensitivity. *Archives of Psychology*, 1934, *25* (170), 66.

Thurlow, W. R., & Jack, C. E. Certain determinants of the "ventriloquism effect." *Perceptual and Motor Skills*, 1973, *36*, 1171–1181.

Thurlow, W. R., & Kerr, T. P. Effect of a moving visual environment on localization of sound. *American Journal of Psychology*, 1970, *83*, 112–118.

Todd, J. W. Reaction to multiple stimuli. *Archives of Psychology, N. Y.*, 1912, *3* (25).

Uhlarik, J. J., & Canon, L. K. Influence of concurrent and terminal exposure conditions on the nature of perceptual adaptation. *Journal of Experimental Psychology*, 1971, *91*, 233–239.

Urbantschitsch, V. Über den Einfluss von Trigeminus-Reizen auf die Sinnesempfindungen, insbesondere auf den Gesichtsinn. *Archives von Gesamte Physiologie*. 1883, *30*, 129–175.

Urbantschitsch, V. Über den Einfluss einer Sinneserregung auf die übrigen Sinnesempfindungen. *Pflugers Archiv für die Gesamte Physiologie*, 1888, *42*, 154–182.

Wade, N. J. Visual orientation during and after lateral head, body, and trunk tilt. *Perception and Psychophysics*, 1968, *3*, 215–219.

Wade, N. J., & Day, R. H. Apparent head position as a basis for a visual aftereffect of prolonged head tilt. *Perception and Psychophysics*, 1968, *3*, 324–326. (a)

Wade, N. J., & Day, R. H. Development and dissipation of a visual spatial aftereffect from prolonged head tilt. *Journal of Experimental Psychology*, 1968, *76*, 439–443. (b)

Walker, E. L., & Sawyer, T. M., Jr. The interaction between critical flicker frequency and acoustic stimulation. *Psychological Record*, 1961, *11*, 187–193.

Walker, J. T., & Scott, K. J. Auditory-visual conflicts in the perceived duration of lights, tones, and gaps. *Journal of Experimental Psychology: Human Perception and Performance*, 1981, *7*, 1327–1339.

*Wallach, H. The role of head movements and vestibular and visual cues in sound localization. *Journal of Experimental Psychology*, 1940, *27*, 339–368.

Wapner, S., Werner, H., & Chandler, K. A. Experiments on sensory-tonic field theory of perception: I. Effect of extraneous stimulation on the visual perception of verticality. *Journal of Experimental Psychology*, 1951, *42*, 341–343.

Warren, D. H. Intermodality interactions in spatial localization. *Cognitive Psychology*, 1970, *1*, 114–133.

Warren, D. H. Spatial localization under conflict conditions: Is there a single explanation? *Perception*, 1979, *8*, 323–337.

Warren, D. H. Response factors in intermodality localization under conflict conditions. *Perception and Psychophysics*, 1980, *27*, 28–32.

Warren, D. H., Anooshian, L. J., & Bollinger, J. C. Early versus late blindness: The role of early vision in spatial behavior. *Research Bulletin: American Foundation for the Blind*, 1973, *26*, 151–170.

Warren, D. H., & Cleaves, W. T. Visual-proprioceptive interaction under large amounts of conflict. *Journal of Experimental Psychology*, 1971, *90*, 206–214.

Warren, D. H., McCarthy, T., & Welch, R. B. Discrepancy and nondiscrepancy methods of assessing visual-auditory interaction. *Perception and Psychophysics*, 1983, *33*, 413–419.

Warren, D. H., & Pick, H. L., Jr. Intermodality relations in blind and sighted people. *Perception and Psychophysics*, 1970, *8*, 430–432.

Warren, D. H., & Schmitt, T. L. On the plasticity of visual-proprioceptive bias effects. *Journal of Experimental Psychology: Human Perception and Performance*, 1978, *4*, 302–310.

Warren, D. H., Welch, R. B., & McCarthy, T. J. The role of visual-auditory "compellingness" in the ventriloquism effect: Implications for transitivity among the spatial senses. *Perception and Psychophysics*, 1981, *30*, 557–564.

Waterman, C. N. Jr. Hand-tongue space perception. *Journal of Experimental Psychology*, 1917, *2*, 289–294.

Watkins, W. Effect of certain noises upon detection of visual signals. *Journal of Experimental Psychology*, 1964, *67*, 72–75.

Watkins, W. H., & Feehrer, C. E. *Investigations of acoustic effects upon visual signal detection. (Tech. Rep. No. 64–577)*. Bedford, Mass.: United States Air Force Electronic Systems Division, 1964.

Watkins, W. H., & Feehrer, C. E. Acoustic facilitation of visual detection. *Journal of Experimental Psychology*, 1965, *70*, 332–333.

Webster, R. G. The relationship between cognitive, motor-kinesthetic, and oculomotor adaptation. *Perception and Psychophysics*, 1969, *6*, 33–38.

Welch, R. B. The effect of experienced limb identity upon adaptation to simulated displacement of the visual field. *Perception and Psychophysics*, 1972, *12*, 453–456.

Welch, R. B. *Perceptual modification: Adapting to altered sensory environments*. New York: Academic Press, 1978.

Welch, R. B., DuttonHurt, L. D., & Warren, D. H. Contributions of audition and vision to temporal rate perception. *Perception and Psychophysics*, in press.

*Welch, R. B., & Warren, D. H. Immediate perceptual response to intersensory discrepancy. *Psychological Bulletin*, 1980, *88*, 638–667.

Welch, R. B., Widawski, M. H., Harrington, J., & Warren, D. H. An examination of the relationship between visual capture and prism adaptation. *Perception and Psychophysics*, 1979, *25*, 126–132.

Werner, H., & Wapner, S. Sensory-tonic field theory of perception. *Journal of Personality*, 1949, *18*, 88–107.

Westheimer, G., Shimamura, K., & McKee, S. P. Interference with line-orientation sensitivity. *Journal of the Optical Society of America*, 1976, *66*, 332–338.

Willey, C. F., Inglis, E., & Pearce, C. H. Reversal of auditory localization. *Journal of Experimental Psychology*, 1937, *20*, 114–130.

Witkin, H. A., & Asch, S. E. Studies in space orientation: III. Perception of the upright in the absence of a visual field. *Journal of Experimental Psychology*, 1948, *38*, 603–614.

Witkin, H. A., Wapner, S., & Leventhal, T. Sound localization with conflicting visual and auditory cues. *Journal of Experimental Psychology*, 1952, *43*, 58–65.

Woodrow, H. Reactions to the cessation of stimuli and their nervous mechanism. *Psychological Review*, 1915, *22*, 423–452.

Woodworth, R. S., & Schlosberg, H. *Experimental psychology* (revised). New York: Holt, 1960.

Young, P. T. Auditory localization with acoustical transposition of the ears. *Journal of Experimental Psychology*, 1928, *11*, 399–429.

AUTHOR INDEX

Note: Numbers in *italics* indicate pages on which full references appear.

SUBJECT INDEX